Subject Guide

to

Children's Books in Print®

1995

A Subject Index to Books for Children
and Young Adults

This edition of
SUBJECT GUIDE
TO
CHILDREN'S BOOKS IN PRINT 1995
was prepared by the R.R. Bowker Bibliographic Group
in collaboration with the Publication Systems Department

Database Publishing Group
Leigh Yuster-Freeman, Vice President, Production - Bibliographies

Editorial
Judy Salk, Executive Editor
Beverley Lamar, Senior Managing Editor
Doret Dixon, Senior Editor
Kathleen A. Keiderling, Associate Editor, Enhancements
Dorothy Perry-Gilchrist, Associate Editor
Margaret Allen, Edward Han, Ila Joseph, George Krubski, Assistant Editors

Subject Guide
Michael Olenick, Managing Editor
Angela Barrett and Kate Magrath, Senior Associate Editors
Marilyn Fay, Mark D. MacDonald, Joseph V. Tondi, Assistant Editors

Quality Control
Raymond Padilla, Senior Editor
Daniel Dickholtz, Senior Associate Editor

Production
Doreen Gravesande, Production Director
Myriam Nunez, Managing Editor
Barbara Holton, Frank McDermott, Senior Editors
Megan Roxberry, Senior Associate Editor
Clarice D. Isaacs, Assistant Editor

Electronic Data Transfer Group
Frank Accurso, Senior Managing Editor
Mary Craig Daley, Managing Editor
William Zavorskas, Senior Associate Editor

Publishers Authority Database
&
International Standard Book Number Agency
Albert Simmonds, Director, Standards/Development
Don Riseborough, Senior Managing Editor
Lynn DeVita, William D. McCahery, Senior Editors
Diana Fumando, Coordinator
Janet Weiss, Assistant Editor

Data Collection & Processing Group
Bonnie Walton, Manager
Cheryl Patrick, Rhonda McKendrick, Coordinators
Leslie Fisher, Cynthia Werry, Assistant Coordinators

Computer Operations Group
Nick Wikowski, Director, Network/Computer Operations
Max Kobrinsky, Manager
Jack Murphy, Supervisor

Subject Guide
to
Children's Books in Print®
1995

A Subject Index to Books for Children
and Young Adults

R. R. Bowker
A Reed Reference Publishing Company
New Providence, New Jersey

Published by R.R. Bowker
A Reed Reference Publishing Company
121 Chanlon Rd., New Providence, NJ 07974

International Standard Book Number 0-8352-3596-3

International Standard Serial Number 0000-0167

Library of Congress Catalog Number 70-101705

Printed and bound in the United States of America

ISBN 0-8352-3596-3

9 780835 235969

CONTENTS

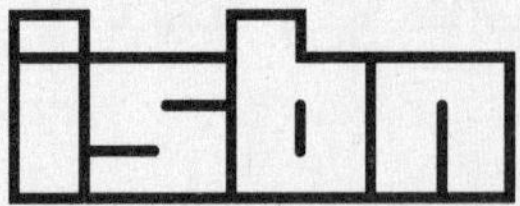

INTERNATIONAL STANDARD BOOK NUMBER

The 1995 SUBJECT GUIDE TO CHILDREN'S BOOKS IN PRINT lists each title or edition of a title in the book indexes with an ISBN. All publishers were notified and requested to submit a valid ISBN for their titles.

During the past decade, the majority of the publishers complied with requirements of the standard and implemented the ISBN. At present, approximately 97% of all new titles and all new editions are submitted for listing with a valid ISBN.

To fulfill the responsibility of accomplishing total book numbering, the ISBN Agency allocated the ISBN prefixes 0-317, 0-318, 0-685 and 0-686 to number the titles in the BOOKS IN PRINT database without an ISBN. Titles not having an ISBN at the closing date of this publication were assigned an ISBN with one of these prefixes by the International Standard Book Numbering Agency.

Titles numbered within the prefixes 0-317, 0-318, 0-685 and 0-686 are:

—Publishers who did not assign ISBNs to their titles.

—Distributors with titles published and imported from countries not in the ISBN system, or not receiving the ISBN from the originating publisher.

—Errors from transposition and transcription which occurred in transmitting the ISBN to the BOOKS IN PRINT database.

All the ISBNs listed in BOOKS IN PRINT are validated by using the check digit control, and only valid ISBNs are listed in the database.

All publishers participating in the ISBN system having titles numbered within the prefixes 0-317, 0-318, 0-685 and 0-686 will receive a computer printout, requesting them to submit the correct ISBN.

Publishers not participating in the ISBN system may request from the ISBN Agency the assignment of an ISBN Publisher Prefix, and start numbering their titles.

The Book Industry System Advisory Committee (BISAC) has developed a standard format for data transmission, and many companies are already accepting orders transmitted on magnetic tape using the ISBN.

BISAC has also developed several other formats, also using the ISBN, including the title status format from which it is possible to update bibliographic information by magnetic tape exchange. Books in Print has been participating in such an exchange with many publishers, and welcomes inquiries from prospective participants.

The ISBN Agency and the Database Publishing Group of R. R. Bowker wish to express their appreciation to all publishers who collaborated in making the ISBN system the standard of the publishing industry.

SAN, an acronym of Standard Address Number, is a unique identification code for each address of each organization in or served by the book industry.

SANs are assigned to publishers, distributors, wholesalers, associations, software producers and manufacturers in the U.S.

The SAN itself merely defines an address. It becomes functional only in its application to activities such as purchasing, invoicing, billing, shipping, receiving, paying, crediting and refunding.

For additional information related to the ISBN total numbering, please refer to Emery Koltay, Director of the ISBN/SAN Agency c/o R.R. Bowker.

FOREWORD

STARTING FROM THE SUBJECT

Patrons in bookstores and libraries serving children often begin their request by referring to the subject of the book they seek rather than its title or author, optimistic that the staff can supply from the subject clue the finding or ordering essentials. But knowledgeable staff with a children's book specialty have always been in far shorter supply than the demand, and such requests have produced more quandaries than complete patron satisfaction. Booksellers could rely only on highly trained memories and self-made lists; librarians could turn only to what was listed in their catalogs, part of their own selective collections. *Subject Guide to Children's Books in Print* is now the starting point for answers to such stumping requests as, "How many books are there on bionics for kids?" or "Can I get a children's book on the care and training of elephants?"

Subject Guide to Children's Books in Print is a cross-referenced subject arrangement of the 94,330 children's books listed in the 1995 edition of its companion volumes, the author, title, illustrator index *Children's Books in Print*. Both of these bibliographies are scheduled for annual correction, expansion and general revision and both are part of R.R. Bowker's continuing effort to expand its essential ***In Print*** services, *Books in Print* and *Subject Guide to Books in Print*.

Children's Books in Print and its separate *Subject Guide* are the result of planning that began in the Spring of 1965, when The Children's Book Council, Inc., through its joint committee with the American Library Association, formally proposed that R.R. Bowker undertake to publish a subject guide to the available children's books. R.R. Bowker promised to publish this bibliography as soon as data could be collected that would allow us to produce as nearly complete *In Print* bibliography as possible. At that time, Bowker was in the first stages of planning the transfer to computer storage of all of its bibliographic data, so it was 1969 before the first step in fulfilling the promise was achieved. The first step was the first edition of *Children's Books in Print* because, logically, its *Subject Guide* could not be produced until we had obtained the necessary information on as many of the available children's books as possible for subject classification.

Subject Guide to Children's Books in Print is compiled by Bowker's Database Publishing Group based upon information supplied by the juvenile book publishers. Our subject headings are those normally employed for library catalogs, drawn from the fourteenth edition of *Sears List of Subject Headings* and the fifteenth edition of *Library of Congress Subject Headings*. Because fiction and picture books make up a major part of the books published for children, their main subject headings presented a major problem. It was finally decided that formal library subject headings, as many as reasonable for each title, would be employed, rather than attempt full thematic groupings of books.

Subject Guide to Children's Books in Print is designed as an aid, not a replacement, for the children's book specialists who can read any number of thematic overtones into the fiction and picture books published for children. It is intended as the bibliography from which to start, but only knowledgeable, well-read personnel can follow through on the sensitivity, always challenging, task of finding the right books at the right time for the children who want them.

Lillian N. Gerhardt
Editor-in-Chief
SCHOOL LIBRARY JOURNAL

How to Use
SUBJECT GUIDE TO CHILDREN'S BOOKS IN PRINT 1995

This twenty-fifth edition of *Subject Guide to Children's Books in Print* was produced from records stored on magnetic tape, edited by computer programs, and set in type by computer-controlled photo-composition. This volume includes the titles listed in *Children's Books in Print*. In *Subject Guide* some 94,330 titles appear 101,103 times under 7,232 subject categories. These titles are available from 5,844 United States publishers and distributors. A Key to Publishers' and Distributors' Abbreviations appears at the end of the book.

NEW FEATURE: PUBLISHER PROVIDED ANNOTATIONS

Appearing for the second time this year are annotated entries, using information provided by participating publishers. This feature allows publishers to purchase space to highlight and describe their titles, and provide the reader with extra book information which he or she will find valuable for reference and acquisition decisions. If you wish to participate in this program, please contact Bowker at 908-464-6800.

HOW THE SUBJECT HEADINGS WERE ASSIGNED

Subject Guide to Children's Books in Print 1995 is based primarily on the fifteenth edition of *Sears List of Subject Headings*. When appropriate subject headings were unavailable in the Sears List, subject headings were chosen from the fifteenth edition of *Library of Congress Subject Headings*. The Sears listing does not include headings for persons and places. These headings were derived from the official LC cataloging information, where available, or from official bibliographic tools. Many heading were consolidated where they seemed too cumbersome for the needs of this *Subject Guide*. Wherever cataloging information was unavailable headings were assigned from the Sears or LC listings by a trained cataloger. Some books have been assigned to a single category, while other books have been assigned two, three or more headings.

ALPHABETICAL ARRANGEMENT OF SUBJECT CATEGORIES

Headings are filed alphabetically with the following conditions and variations. First, punctuation is not considered:

ART, ANCIENT
ART—FICTION
ART, GREEK

Second, proper nouns precede improper nouns and names of people precede geographical names:

CLAY, HENRY
CLAY MISSOURI
CLAY

Third, when personal names appear as headings, those without surnames appear first and religious titles precede royal titles:

JOHN, POPE
JOHN, ST.
JOHN 2ND, KING OF ENGLAND
JOHN, ROBERT

ALPHABETICAL ARRANGEMENT OF TITLES WITHIN THE SUBJECT CATEGORIES

Under each subject heading entries are filed *alphabetically by word*, with the following exceptions:

Initial articles of titles in English, French, German, Italian and Spanish are deleted from both author and title entries.

M', *Mc* and *Mac* are filed as if they were written Mac and are interfiled with other names beginning with *Mac*; for example, Macan, McAnally, Macardle, McAree, McArthur, Macarthur, Macartney, M'Aulay, Macaulay, McAuley. Within a specific name grouping *Mc* and *Mac* are interfiled according to the given name of the author; for example, Macdonald, Agnes; MacDonald, Alexander; McDonald, Annie L.; MacDonald, Austin F.;

MacDonald, Betty. Compound names are listed under the first part of the name, and cross-references appear under the last part of the name.

Entries beginning with initial letters (whether authors' given names, or titles) are filed first, e.g., Smith, H.C., comes before Smith, Harold A.; B is for Betsy comes before Baba, Babar, etc.

Numerals, including year dates, are written out in most cases and are filed alphabetically.

U.S., UN, Dr., Mr., and St. are filed as though they were spelled out.

SPECIAL NOTE ON HOW TO FIND AN AUTHOR'S COMPLETE LISTING

When sorting author listings by computer it is not possible to group the entire listing for an individual together under one heading unless a standard spelling and format for each name is used. The information in *Subject Guide to Children's Books in Print 1995* comes from data received from the publishers. If a name appears in various forms in this data, the listing in the index may be divided into several groups.

INFORMATION INCLUDED IN ENTRIES AND TITLE ENTRIES

Entries include the following bibliographic information, when available: author, co-author, editor, co-editor, translator, co-translator, illustrator, co-illustrator, photographer, co-photographer, title, number of volumes, edition, Library of Congress number, series information, language if other than English, whether or not illustrated, grade range, year of publication, type of binding if other than cloth over boards, price, International Standard Book Number, publisher's order number, imprint, and publisher abbreviation. When an entry includes the prices for both the hardcover and paperback editions, the publication date within the entry refers to the hardcover binding; however, when the paperback binding is the only one included in the entry, the publication date is the paperback publication date. (Information on the International Standard Book Numbering System is available from R.R. Bowker.)

The prices cited are those provided by the publishers and generally refer to either the trade edition or the Publisher's Library Bound edition (PLB). The abbreviation PLB is used whenever the price cited is for a publisher's library bound edition.

Since some trade editions are bound to the same standards as some library editions, the symbol "g" is used *after* a price to indicate that the edition is guaranteed by the publisher to give satisfaction in normal library use.

If the price is merely tentatively suggested, a lower case "t" follows the anticipated price, e.g., 5.87t; "x" indicates a short discount—20%, or less. Short discount (20% or less) information is generally supplied by publishers to Bowker for each publication. However, all publishers do not uniformly supply this information, and Bowker can only make its best efforts to transmit this information when it is provided. PLB indicates a publishers' library binding.

The symbol "a" after a price indicates that a library binding is available at a special price.

An "i" following the price indicates an invoice price. Specific policies for such titles should be obtained from individual publishers.

KEY TO PUBLISHERS' AND DISTRIBUTORS' ABBREVIATIONS

Publishers' and distributors' names are abbreviated in the listings of *Subject Guide to Children's Books in Print*. A Key to these abbreviations will be found in *Key to Publishers' & Distributors' Abbreviations* at the end of this volume. Entries in this "Key" are arranged alphabetically by the abbreviations used in the bibliographic entries. The full name, ISBN prefix, editorial address, telephone number, ordering address (if different from the editorial address), and imprints follow the abbreviation. SAN (Standard Address Number) is a unique identification code for each address of each organization in or served by the book industry.

For example:

Bowker, *(Bowker, R.R.; 0-8352)*, A Reed Reference Publishing Company, 121 Chanlon Rd., New Providence, NJ 07974 (SAN 214-1191) Tel 908-464-6800; Toll free: 800-521-8110,800-537-8416 (in Canada).

If an entry contains a "Pub. by" note after the price, the title should be ordered from the distributor whose abbreviation appears at the end of the entry. Entries which include the note "Dist. by" should also be ordered from the distributor, not the publisher.

The information in this bibliography has been obtained from publishers' catalogs and from other information submitted by publishers for *Books in Print 1994-95*.

LIST OF ABBREVIATIONS

a	after price, specially priced library edition available
abr.	abridged
adpt.	adapted
Amer.	American
annot.	annotation(s), annotated
ans.	answer(s)
app.	appendix
approx.	approximately
assn.	association
auth.	author
bd.	bound
bdg.	binding
bds.	boards
bibl(s).	bibliography(ies)
bk(s).	book(s)
bklet(s)	booklet(s)
Bro.	Brother
coll.	college
comm.	commission, committee
co.	company
cond.	condensed
comp(s).	compiler(s)
corp.	corporation
dept.	department
diag(s).	diagram(s)
dir.	director
disk	software disk or diskette
dist.	distributed
Div.	Division
doz.	dozen
ea.	each
ed.	editor, edited, edition
eds.	editors, editions
educ.	education
elem.	elementary
ency.	encyclopedia
ENG	English
enl.	enlarged
exp.	expurgated
fac.	facsimile
fasc.	fascicule
fict.	fiction
fig(s)	figure(s)
for.	foreign
FRE	French
frwd.	foreward
g	after price, guaranteed juvenile binding
gen.	general
GER	German
GRE	Greek
gr.	grade, grades
hdbk.	handbook
HEB	Hebrew
i	invoice price — see publisher for specific pricing policies
ISBN	International Standard Book Number
i.t.a.	initial teaching alphabet
Illus.	illustrated, illustration(s), illustrator(s)
in prep.	in preparation
incl.	includes, including
inst.	institute
intro.	introduction
ITA	Italian
Jr.	Junior
jt. auth.	joint author
jt. ed.	joint editor
k	kindergarten audience level
l.p.	long playing
ltd. ed.	limited edition
lab.	laboratory
lang(s)	language(s)
LAT	Latin
lea.	leather
lib.	library
lit.	literature, literary
math.	mathematics
mod.	modern
MOR	Morocco
MS, MSS	manuscript, manuscripts
natl.	national
no., nos.	number, numbers
o.p.	out of print
orig.	original text, not a reprint
o.s.i.	out of stock indefinitely
pap.	paper
photos	photographs, photographer
PLB	publisher's library binding
POL	Polish
pop. ed.	popular edition
POR	Portuguese
prep.	preparation
probs.	problems
prog. bk.	programmed book
ps	preschool audience level
pseud.	pseudonym
pt(s).	part(s)
pub.	published, publishing, publisher
pubn.	publication
ref(s).	reference(s)
repr.	reprint
reprod(s).	reproduction(s)
rev.	revised
rpm.	revolution per minute (phono records)
RUS	Russian
SAN	Standard Address Number
S&L	Signed and Limited
s.p.	school price
scp	single copy Directed to the Consumer Price
sec.	section
sel.	selected
ser.	series
Soc.	Society
sols.	solutions
SPA	Spanish
Sr. (after given name)	Senior
Sr. (before given name)	Sister
St.	Saint
subs.	subsidiary
subsc.	subscription
suppl.	supplement
t	after price, tentative price
tech.	technical
text ed.	text edition
tr.	translator, translated, translation
univ.	university
vol(s).	volume, volumes
wkbk.	workbook
x	after price, short discount (20% or less)
YA	young adult audience level
yrbk.	yearbook

SUBJECT GUIDE

A

A B C BOOKS
see Alphabet Books
A. D. C.
see Child Welfare
AARON, HENRY, 1934-
Margolies, Jacob. Hank Aaron: Home Run King. Mathews, V., ed. LC 91-29776. (Illus.). 64p. (gr. 3-6). 1992. PLB 12.90 (*0-531-20075-2*) Watts.
Tackach, James. Hank Aaron. Murray, Jim, intro. by. (Illus.). 64p. (gr. 3 up). 1991. PLB 14.95 (*0-7910-1165-8*) Chelsea Hse.
Zennert, Richard. Hank Aaron. King, Coretta Scott, intro. by. (Illus.). 112p. (gr. 5 up). 1993. PLB 17.95 (*0-7910-1859-8*); pap. write for info. (*0-7910-1888-1*) Chelsea Hse.
ABACUS
Cotter, Joan A. Worksheets for the Abacus, Vol. 2. (Illus.). 122p. (gr. 3-4). 1988. 16.95 (*0-9609636-5-0*) Activities Learning.
ABANDONED TOWNS
see Cities and Towns, Ruined, Extinct, etc.
ABDUL-JABBAR, KAREEM, 1947-
Borrello, Helen A. Kareem Abdul Jabbar. LC 94-5774. 1994. 14.95 (*0-7910-2426-1*) Chelsea Hse.
Margolies, Jacob. Kareem Abdul-Jabbar: Basketball Great. LC 91-31662. (Illus.). 64p. (gr. 3-6). 1992. PLB 12.90 (*0-531-20076-0*) Watts.
ABNORMAL PSYCHOLOGY
see Psychology, Pathological
ABOLITION OF SLAVERY
see Abolitionists
ABOLITIONISTS
Coil, Suzanne M. Slavery & Abolitionists. (Illus.). 64p. (gr. 5-8). 1995. bds. 15.95 (*0-8050-2984-2*) TFC Bks NY.
Ferris, Jeri. Walking the Road to Freedom: A Story about Sojourner Truth. Hanson, Peter E., illus. 64p. (gr. 3-6). 1989. pap. 5.95 (*0-87614-505-5*, First Ave Edns) Lerner Pubns.
Fritz, Jean. Harriet Beecher Stowe & the Beecher Preachers. LC 93-6408. (Illus.). 144p. (gr. 6-9). 1994. 16.95 (*0-399-22666-4*, Putnam) Putnam Pub Group.
Jackson, Garnet N. Frederick Douglass, Freedom Fighter. Holliday, Keaf, illus. LC 92-28777. 1992. 56.40 (*0-8136-5229-4*); pap. 28.50 (*0-8136-5702-4*) Modern Curr.
Kerby, Mona. Frederick Douglass. LC 94-15. (gr. 4 up). 1994. write for info. (*0-531-20173-2*) Watts.
McKissack, Patricia & McKissack, Fredrick. Frederick Douglass: The Black Lion. LC 86-32695. (Illus.). 136p. (gr. 4 up). 1987. PLB 14.40 (*0-516-03221-6*); pap. 5.95 (*0-516-43221-4*) Childrens.
Taylor-Boyd, Susan. Sojourner Truth: The Courageous Former Slave Whose Eloquence Helped Promote Human Equality. LC 89-4345. (Illus.). 68p. (gr. 5-6). 1990. PLB 19.93 (*0-8368-0101-6*) Gareth Stevens Inc.
ABOLITIONISTS–FICTION
Rosen, Michael J. A School for Pompey Walker. Robinson, Aminah B., illus. LC 94-6240. 1995. write for info. (*0-15-200114-X*, HB Juv Bks) Harbrace.
Weinberg, Larry. Ghost Hotel. LC 94-2970. (Illus.). 160p. (gr. 3-6). 1994. pap. 2.95 (*0-8167-3420-8*) Troll Assocs.
ABORTION
Brownlow, Bette H. Tyler's Descent. (Illus.). 32p. (Orig.). 1993. pap. 5.25 (*1-883516-00-5*) Peregrine & Hayes.
Caruana, Claudia M. The Abortion Debate. LC 92-22417. (Illus.). 64p. (gr. 5-8). 1992. PLB 15.90 (*1-56294-311-1*) Millbrook Pr.
Center for Learning Network. Abortion: Beyond Personal Choice: Looking at Life. 12p. (gr. 9-12). 1992. pap. text ed. 0.80 (*1-56077-222-0*) Ctr Learning.
Cozic, Charles P. & Tipp, Stacey, eds. Abortion: Opposing Viewpoints. LC 91-21279. (Illus.). 216p. (gr. 10 up). 1991. lib. bdg. 17.95 (*0-89908-181-9*); pap. 9.95 (*0-89908-156-8*) Greenhaven.
Emmens, Carol A. The Abortion Controversy. rev. ed. LC 86-28532. 144p. (gr. 7 up). 1991. lib. bdg. 13.98 (*0-671-74539-5*, J Messner); pap. 6.95 (*0-671-74967-6*, J Messner) S&S Trade.
Flanders, Carl N. Abortion. 256p. (gr. 9-12). 1990. 22.95x (*0-8160-1908-8*) Facts on File.
Gold, Susan D. Roe vs. Wade (1973) Abortion. LC 93-40627. 1994. text ed. 14.95 (*0-02-736273-6*, New Discovery Bks) Macmillan Child Grp.
Herda, D. J. Roe v. Wade: The Abortion Question. LC 93-22403. (Illus.). 104p. (gr. 6 up). 1994. lib. bdg. 17.95 (*0-89490-459-0*) Enslow Pubs.
Kelly, Francis D., pref. by. Choose Life! Unborn Children & the Right to Life. (Illus.). 72p. (Orig.). (gr. 11-12). 1991. pap. 12.95 (*1-55833-106-9*) Natl Cath Educ.
Nelson, Joan. Abortion. LC 91-15566. (Illus.). 112p. (gr. 5-8). 1992. PLB 14.95 (*1-56006-128-6*) Lucent Bks.
ABORTION–FICTION
Beckman, Gunnel. Mia Alone. Tate, Joan, tr. 112p. (gr. 7 up). 1978. pap. 1.25 (*0-440-95586-6*, LFL) Dell.
Minshull, Evelyn W. But I Thought You Really Loved Me. LC 76-14992. 150p. (gr. 7 up). 1976. 8.00 (*0-664-32600-5*, Westminster) Westminster John Knox.
ABRAHAM, THE PATRIARCH
Barrett, Ethel. Abraham: God's Faithful Pilgrim. LC 82-12330. 128p. (Orig.). (gr. 3 up). 1982. pap. 3.99 (*0-8307-0769-7*, 5810906) Regal.
Frank, Penny. Abraham, Friend of God. (ps-3). 1984. 3.99 (*0-85648-729-5*) Lion USA.
Zlotowitz, Bernard M. & Maiben, Dina. Abraham's Great Discovery. Sweeny, Raquel, illus. 32p. 1991. 12.95t (*0-911389-04-0*) NightinGale Res.
ABSENCE FROM SCHOOL
see School Attendance
ACADIANS
Amoss, Berthe. The Loup Garou. Amoss, Berthe, illus. LC 79-20536. 48p. (ps-4). 1979. 9.95 (*0-88289-189-8*) Pelican.
Goodrum, Don. Lettres Acadiennes. LC 92-5124. (Illus.). 32p. (gr. k-3). 1992. 14.95 (*0-88289-899-X*) Pelican.
Longfellow, Henry Wadsworth. Evangeline & Other Poems. Bennet, C. L., intro. by. (gr. 7 up). pap. 1.50 (*0-8049-0094-9*, CL-94) Airmont.
Reneaux, J. J. Cajun Folktales. 176p. (gr. 5 up). 1992. 19.95 (*0-87483-283-7*); pap. 9.95 (*0-87483-282-9*) August Hse.
Trosclair. Cajun Night Before Christmas: Full-Color Edition. Jacobs, Howard, ed. Rice, James, illus. LC 92-8375. 48p. (gr. k-3). 1992. 14.95 (*0-88289-940-6*); boxed ed. 25.00 (*0-88289-947-3*); audio 9.95 (*0-88289-914-7*) Pelican.
ACCIDENTS–FICTION
see also Aeronautics–Accidents; Disasters; Fires; First Aid; Traffic Accidents–Fiction
Bodkin, Odds. The Banshee Train. Rose, Ted, illus. LC 93-39635. Date not set. write for info. (*0-395-69426-4*, Clarion Bks) HM.
Byars, Betsy C. The Eighteenth Emergency. Grossman, Robert, illus. (gr. 4-6). 1981. pap. 3.99 (*0-14-031451-2*, Puffin) Puffin Bks.
Carrick, Carol. The Accident. Carrick, Donald, illus. LC 76-3532. 32p. (ps-3). 1981. (Clarion Bks); pap. 5.95 (*0-89919-041-3*) HM.
Fromm, Pete. Monkey Tag. LC 93-34593. (gr. 4-7). 1994. 14.95 (*0-590-46525-2*) Scholastic Inc.

Good, Janis. Summer of the Lost Limb. Cates, Elizabeth, illus. 110p. (Orig.). 1994. pap. 7.95 (*0-9640365-5-X*) Christ Recollect.
Readers will step back 90 years in time to horse & buggy days. Young Mary & her people are of a religious sect similar to the Amish who live yet today as years ago. A tragic farm accident changes Mary's life, dashing her dreams of walking the half mile to her community school with other children. Readers follow Mary through a country operation on her own kitchen table, a trip to Washington, D.C., for an artificial limb, adjustments & struggles. They will feel with the limitations of the handicapped & even learn some valuable lessons & bits of history. Who believes teddy bears always existed? This book tells two stories behind the beginning of teddy bears. Then there are two strangers on horseback who meet Mary. Will she allow horses to cross the narrow swinging bridge that spans the river? Will she be able to perform a difficult duty on her wooden leg? Her faith makes all the difference. Christian Recollections, Rt. 1, Box 351, Mt. Solon, VA 22821.
Publisher Provided Annotation.

Lester, Helen. It Wasn't My Fault. Munsinger, Lynn, illus. LC 84-19212. 32p. (gr. k-3). 1985. 14.45 (*0-395-35629-6*) HM.
Steel, Danielle. Freddie's Accident. Rogers, Jacqueline, illus. 32p. (Orig.). (gr. 1-3). 1992. pap. 2.99 (*0-440-40576-9*, YB) Dell.
Strasser, Todd. The Accident. (gr. k up). 1990. pap. 3.50 (*0-440-20635-9*, LFL) Dell.
Tricker, Andy. Accidents Will Happen. 196p. (gr. 7-9). 1989. pap. 9.95 (*0-233-98095-4*, Pub. by A Deutsch England) Trafalgar.

Uchida, Yoshiko. The Terrible Leak. (gr. 4-12). 1989. 13. 95 (*0-88682-357-9*, 97223-098) Creative Ed.

ACCIDENTS–PREVENTION

see also Safety Education

Lampton, Christopher. Chemical Accident. (Illus.). 48p. (gr. 4-6). 1994. 13.90 (*1-56294-316-2*) Millbrook Pr.

Safety. (Illus.). 48p. (gr. 6-12). 1986. pap. 1.85 (*0-8395-3347-0*, 33347) BSA.

ACCLIMATIZATION

see Adaptation (Biology); Man–Influence of Environment

ACCOUNTING

Halbur, Donna K. Accountants Visit School. Kearney, Paul, illus. 24p. (gr. 3-5). 1979. pap. 3.00 (*0-686-25249-7*) Halbur.

Rosenthal, Lawrence. Exploring Careers in Accounting. rev. ed. (Illus.). 148p. (gr. 7-12). 1993. PLB 14.95 (*0-8239-1501-8*); pap. 9.95 (*0-8239-1721-5*) Rosen Group.

ACCOUNTING MACHINES

see Calculating Machines

ACID RAIN

Acid Rain Foundation, Inc. Staff, compiled by. Acid Rain Curriculum: Grades 6-12. (Illus.). (gr. 6-12). 1986. 59. 95 (*0-935577-03-3*) Acid Rain Found.

The Acid Rain Hazard. LC 91-50340. (Illus.). 32p. (gr. 3-8). 1993. PLB 17.27 (*0-8368-0697-2*); PLB 17.27 s.p. (*0-685-61491-3*) Gareth Stevens Inc.

Asimov, Isaac. What Is Acid Rain? LC 91-50362. (Illus.). 24p. (gr. 2-3). 1992. PLB 15.93 (*0-8368-0741-3*) Gareth Stevens Inc.

Bright, Michael. Acid Rain. LC 90-44679. (Illus.). 32p. (gr. 2-4). 1991. PLB 11.90 (*0-531-17303-8*, Gloucester Pr) Watts.

Gutnik, Martin J. Experiments That Explore Acid Rain. LC 91-19958. (Illus.). 72p. (gr. 5-8). 1992. PLB 14.40 (*1-56294-115-1*) Millbrook Pr.

Hessler, Edward W. & Stubbs, Harriett. Acid Rain Science Projects. 20p. (Orig.). (gr. 5-12). 1987. pap. 9.95 (*0-935577-09-2*) Acid Rain Found.

Hocking, Colin, et al. Acid Rain. Bergman, Lincoln & Fairwell, Kay, eds. Bavilacqua, Carol & Craig, Rose, illus. Hoyt, Richard & Bergman, Lincoln, photos by. 168p. (gr. 6-10). 1990. pap. 15.00 (*0-912511-74-5*) Lawrence Science.

Lucas, Eileen. Acid Rain. LC 91-3879. 128p. (gr. 4-8). 1991. PLB 20.55 (*0-516-05503-8*) Childrens.

McCormick, John. Acid Rain. LC 91-3876. (Illus.). 32p. (gr. 5-8). 1991. PLB 12.40 (*0-531-17358-5*, Gloucester Pr) Watts.

Neal, Philip. Acid Rain. (Illus.). 48p. (gr. 7-12). 1986. 19. 95 (*0-85219-784-5*, Pub. by Batsford UK) Trafalgar.

Snodgrass, M. E. Environmental Awareness: Acid Rain. James, Jody, ed. Vista Three Design Staff, illus. LC 90-26255. 48p. (gr. 4 up). 1991. lib. bdg. 14.95 (*0-944280-30-7*) Bancroft-Sage.

Stubbs, Harriett, et al. Acid Rain Curriculum. Flor, Dick, illus. (Orig.). (gr. 4-8). 1985. tchrs' ed. 19.95 (*0-935577-00-9*) Acid Rain Found.

Stubbs, Harriett S., et al. Acid Rain Reader. Eclov, Homer, illus. 20p. (Orig.). (gr. 4-8). 1989. pap. 5.95 (*0-935577-12-2*); pap. 2.50 (*0-685-17881-1*) Acid Rain Found.

Turck, Mary. Acid Rain. LC 90-35495. (Illus.). 48p. (gr. 6). 1990. text ed. 12.95 RSBE (*0-89686-547-9*, Crestwood Hse) Macmillan Child Grp.

Tyson, Peter. Acid Rain. (Illus.). 128p. (gr. 5 up). 1992. lib. bdg. 19.95 (*0-7910-1577-7*) Chelsea Hse.

ACOUSTICS

see Hearing; Music–Acoustics and Physics; Sound

ACQUIRED IMMUNE DEFICIENCY SYNDROME

see Aids (Disease)

ACTING

see also Actors and Actresses; Pageants; Pantomimes; Theater

Custer, Jim, et al. The Best of the Jeremiah People: Humorous Sketches & Performance Tips by America's Leading Christian Repertory Group. LC 91-34195. 192p. (Orig.). (gr. 9 up). 1991. pap. 14.95 (*0-916260-81-X*, B117) Meriwether Pub.

Foley, Kathryn, et al. The Good Apple Guide to Creative Drama. 128p. (gr. 2-6). 1981. 11.95 (*0-86653-030-4*, GA 258) Good Apple.

Roddy, Ruth M. Monologues for Kids. 64p. (Orig.). (gr. 1-3). 1987. pap. 6.95 (*0-940669-02-1*) Dramaline Pubns.

—Scenes for Kids. 64p. (Orig.). (gr. 2-6). 1990. pap. 7.95 (*0-940669-14-5*) Dramaline Pubns.

Sackett, Pamela. Two Minutes to Shine, Bk. 3. 48p. (Orig.). 1993. pap. text ed. 8.95 (*0-573-69384-6*) French.

Slaight, Craig & Sharrar, Jack, eds. Great Scenes & Monologues for Children. 192p. (gr. 2-9). 1993. pap. 11.95 (*1-880399-15-6*) Smith & Kraus.

Sternberg, Patricia. On Stage: How to Put on a Play. LC 82-60651. (Illus.). 160p. (gr. 7 up). 1983. (J Messner) S&S Trade.

ACTING–FICTION

Anderson, Mary. Tune in Tomorrow. 192p. (gr. 7 up). 1985. pap. 2.50 (*0-380-69870-6*, Flare) Avon.

Cain, Joy D. The Team on & off the Set. (gr. 1-3). 1993. pap. 3.50 (*0-553-48090-1*) Bantam.

Cruise, Beth. Exit, Stage Right. LC 94-16981. (gr. 5 up). 1994. pap. 3.95 (*0-02-042792-1*, Collier) Macmillan.

DeGroat, Diane. Annie Pitts, Swamp Monster. LC 93-2474. 1994. pap. 13.00 (*0-671-87004-1*, S&S BFYR) S&S Trade.

Dreiser, Theodore. Sister Carrie. Simpson, Claude, ed. LC 59-1819. (gr. 9 up). 1972. pap. 9.96 (*0-395-05134-7*, RivEd) HM.

Greydanus, Rose. Let's Pretend. Winborn, Marsha, illus. LC 81-2357. 32p. (gr. k-2). 1981. PLB 11.59 (*0-89375-545-1*); pap. text ed. 2.95 (*0-89375-546-X*) Troll Assocs.

Herman, Charlotte. Max Malone, Superstar. Smith, Cat B., illus. LC 91-25191. 64p. (gr. 2-4). 1992. 14.95 (*0-8050-1375-X*, Redfeather BYR) H Holt & Co.

Hill, Elizabeth S. Broadway Chances. 160p. (gr. 5 up). 1994. pap. 3.99 (*0-14-034929-4*) Puffin Bks.

Howe, James. Stage Fright. 1987. pap. 3.50 (*0-380-70173-1*) Avon.

Hughes, Dean. Nutty, the Movie Star. LC 91-15517. 144p. (gr. 3-7). 1991. pap. 3.95 (*0-689-71524-2*, Aladdin) Macmillan Child Grp.

Kaplan, Marcia P. & Kaplan, David E. Happiness. Mendez, Phil, et al, illus. 96p. (Orig.). (gr. 1 up). 1986. 6.95 (*0-9617744-3-6*) Cheers.

Koehler-Pentacoff, Elizabeth. Curtain Call. (Illus.). 80p. (gr. k-6). 1989. pap. text ed. 7.95 (*0-86530-065-8*, IP 166-4) Incentive Pubns.

Korman, Gordon. Macdonald Hall Goes Hollywood. (gr. 4-7). 1994. pap. 3.25 (*0-590-43941-3*) Scholastic Inc.

Kroll, Steven. I'm George Washington & You're Not! LC 93-7536. (Illus.). 64p. (gr. 2-5). 1994. 11.95 (*1-56282-579-8*); PLB 11.89 (*1-56282-580-1*) Hyprn Child.

Nixon, Joan L. Caught in the Act. (gr. 7 up). 1989. pap. 3.99 (*0-553-27912-2*, Starfire) Bantam.

Peet, Bill. Encore for Eleanor Pa. (ps-3). 1985. pap. 5.95 (*0-395-38367-6*) HM.

Pevsner, Stella. I'm Emma, I'm a Quint. LC 92-36952. 1993. 13.95 (*0-395-64166-7*, Clarion Bks) HM.

Pfeffer, Susan B. Starring Peter & Leigh. LC 78-72855. 1978. 7.95 (*0-440-08226-9*) Delacorte.

Philpot, Graham. The Fabulous Fairy Tale Follies. LC 93-30479. (Illus.). 32p. (gr. k up). 1994. 12.00 (*0-679-85316-2*) Random Bks Yng Read.

Rosofsky, Iris. My Aunt Ruth. LC 90-4940. 224p. (gr. 7 up). 1991. HarpC Child Bks.

Stephens, Michael. Matinee. (Orig.). (gr. 6 up). 1993. pap. 10.95 (*0-04-442194-X*, Pub. by Allen & Unwin Aust Pty AT) IPG Chicago.

Streatfield, Noel. Ballet Shoes. Goode, Diane, illus. LC 89-24390. 288p. (gr. 4-9). 1991. gift ed. 15.00 (*0-679-80105-7*) Random Bks Yng Read.

Tanner, Suzy-Jane. Starring Fred & Ursulina. (Illus.). 32p. (ps-1). 1994. 17.95 (*0-09-176436-X*, Pub. by Hutchinson UK) Trafalgar.

Walker, Paul R. Method. 200p. (gr. 7 up). 1990. 14.95 (*0-15-200528-5*) HarBrace.

Weyn, Suzanne. Ashley's Big Mistake. LC 93-43505. (Illus.). 128p. (gr. 4-8). 1994. PLB 9.89 (*0-8167-3231-0*); pap. text ed. 2.95 (*0-8167-3232-9*) Troll Assocs.

Zindel, Paul. David & Della. LC 93-12719. 176p. (gr. 7 up). 1993. 14.00 (*0-06-023353-2*); PLB 13.89 (*0-06-023354-0*) HarpC Child Bks.

ACTING–VOCATIONAL GUIDANCE

Rawson, Ruth. Acting. Matthau, W., intro. by. LC 68-21664. (Illus.). (gr. 7 up). 1970. PLB 14.95 (*0-8239-0151-3*) Rosen Group.

Williamson, Walter. Early Stages: The Professional Theater & the Young Actor. LC 85-26467. (Illus.). 128p. (gr. 6 up). 1986. 12.95 (*0-8027-6624-2*); lib. bdg. 12.85 (*0-8027-6630-7*) Walker & Co.

ACTORS AND ACTRESSES

see also Acting; Acting–Vocational Guidance; Black Actors; Motion Pictures–Biography; Theater

Adams, Mary A. Whoopi Goldberg: From Street to Stardom. LC 92-23766. (Illus.). 64p. (gr. 3 up). 1993. text ed. 13.95 RSBE (*0-87518-562-2*, Dillon) Macmillan Child Grp.

Anthony Quinn. (Illus.). 112p. (gr. 6-12). 1993. PLB 17. 95 (*0-7910-1251-4*); pap. write for info. (*0-7910-1278-6*) Chelsea Hse.

Axiom Information Resources Staff. Celebrity Birthday Guide: Names & Birthdays of Major Movie-TV Stars & Other Famous People. rev. ed. 32p. (Orig.). 1993. pap. 5.95 (*0-943213-09-6*) Axiom Info Res.

—Star Guide, 1994-1995: Where to Contact over 3200 Movie Stars, TV Stars, Rock Stars, Sports Stars, & Other Famous Celebrities. rev. ed. Robinson, Terry, ed. (Illus.). 208p. 1994. pap. 12.95 (*0-943213-12-6*) Axiom Info Res.

Beaton, Margaret. Oprah Winfrey: TV Talk Show Host. LC 90-2150. (Illus.). (gr. 4 up). 1990. PLB 14.40 (*0-516-03270-4*) Childrens.

Bergman, Carol. Mae West. Horner, Matina. (Illus.). 112p. (gr. 5 up). 1988. lib. bdg. 17.95 (*1-55546-681-8*) Chelsea Hse.

Brandt, Keith. Pearl Bailey: With a Song in Her Heart. Griffith, Gershom, illus. LC 92-20190. 48p. (gr. 4-6). 1992. PLB 10.79 (*0-8167-2921-2*); pap. text ed. 3.50 (*0-8167-2922-0*) Troll Assocs.

Brown, Gene. Bette Davis: Film Star. (Illus.). 64p. (gr. 3-7). PLB 14.95 (*1-56711-028-2*) Blackbirch.

Buffalo, Audreen. Meet Oprah Winfrey. (Illus.). 112p. (gr. 3-5). 1993. pap. 2.99 (*0-679-85425-8*, Bullseye Bks) Random Bks Yng Read.

Burke, Bronwen. Christian Slater. (Illus.). 48p. 1992. 1.49 (*0-440-21425-4*) Dell.

—Jason Priestley: Who's Hot! 48p. (gr. 4-7). 1992. pap. 1.49 (*0-440-21378-9*) Dell.

—Who's Hot! Grant Show. (gr. 4-7). 1993. pap. 1.49 (*0-440-21477-7*) Dell.

Catalano, Grace. Alyssa Milano: She's the Boss. (gr. 7 up). 1989. pap. 2.95 (*0-318-41642-5*, Starfire) Bantam.

—Alyssa Milano: She's the Boss. (gr. 6-9). 1989. pap. 2.75 (*0-553-28158-5*) Bantam.

—River Phoenix: Hero & Heartthrob. (gr. 7 up). 1988. pap. 2.75 (*0-553-27728-6*, Starfire) Bantam.

Coleman, Kate. Who's Hot -- Blossom. (gr. 4-7). 1993. pap. 1.49 (*0-440-21602-8*) Dell.

Conklin, Thomas. Meet Arnold Schwarzenegger. LC 94-5180. (Illus.). 112p. (gr. 2-7). 1994. pap. 3.50 (*0-679-86748-1*, Bullseye Bks) Random Bks Yng Read.

Cruise, Beth. Saved by the Bell Mario Lopez: High-Voltage Star. LC 91-27462. (Illus.). 120p. (Orig.). (gr. 5 up). 1992. pap. 2.95 (*0-02-041851-5*, Collier Young Ad) Macmillan Child Grp.

—Saved by the Bell Mark-Paul Gosselaar: Ultimate Gold. LC 91-27456. (Illus.). 120p. (Orig.). (gr. 5 up). 1992. pap. 2.95 (*0-02-041841-8*, Collier Young Ad) Macmillan Child Grp.

Doherty, Craig & Doherty, Catherine. Arnold Schwarzenegger: Larger Than Life. 128p. (gr. 5 up). 1993. 14.95 (*0-8027-8236-1*); PLB 15.85 (*0-8027-8238-8*) Walker & Co.

Fox, Fiona. How to Reach Your Favorite Star. LC 92-17291. (Illus.). 64p. (gr. 4-8). 1992. pap. 3.95 (*1-56288-330-5*) Checkerboard.

Gabrielle Carteris. 1992. 1.25 (*0-590-46211-3*, 076) Scholastic Inc.

Geraghty, Helen M. Chris Burke: Actor. (Illus.). 1994. 18.95 (*0-7910-2081-9*, Am Art Analog); pap. write for info. (*0-7910-2094-0*, Am Art Analog) Chelsea Hse.

Greenberg, Keith E. Michael J. Fox. (Illus.). 32p. (gr. 4-9). 1986. PLB 13.50 (*0-8225-1611-X*) Lerner Pubns.

Greene, Constance C. Star Shine. (gr. k-6). 1987. pap. 2.75 (*0-440-47920-7*, YB) Dell.

Hamilton, Sue. Arnold Schwarzenegger. LC 92-16035. 1992. 12.94 (*1-56239-144-5*) Abdo & Dghtrs.

Hargrove, Jim. Martin Sheen: Actor & Activist. LC 91-7793. (Illus.). 152p. (gr. 4 up). 1991. PLB 14.40 (*0-516-03274-7*); pap. 5.95 (*0-516-43274-5*) Childrens.

Haskins, James S. Shirley Temple Black: Actress to Ambassador. Ruff, Donna, illus. 64p. (gr. 2-5). 1989. pap. 3.95 (*0-14-032491-7*, Puffin) Puffin Bks.

Haskins, Jim. Bill Cosby: America's Most Famous Father. 128p. (gr. 7-9). 1988. 13.95 (*0-8027-6785-0*); PLB 14. 85 (*0-8027-6786-9*) Walker & Co.

Hunter, Higel. Twenty Names in the Movies. LC 89-23912. (Illus.). 48p. (gr. 3-8). 1990. PLB 12.95 (*1-85435-254-7*) Marshall Cavendish.

Italia, Bob. Chris Burke. LC 92-16037. 1992. 12.94 (*1-56239-143-7*) Abdo & Dghtrs.

Italia, Robert. Roseanne Barr. Wallner, Rosemary, ed. LC 91-73035. 1991. 12.94 (*1-56239-058-9*) Abdo & Dghtrs.

James, Robert. Twenty Names in Theater. LC 89-23949. (Illus.). 48p. (gr. 3-8). 1990. PLB 12.95 (*1-85435-257-1*) Marshall Cavendish.

Jason Priestley. 1992. 1.25 (*0-590-46208-3*, 073) Scholastic Inc.

Jennie Garth. 1992. 1.25 (*0-590-46210-5*, 075) Scholastic Inc.

Jerome, Jerome K. On the Stage - & Off: The Brief Career of a Would-Be Actor. (Illus.). 192p. (gr. 6-9). 1991. text ed. 30.00 (*0-86299-886-7*) A Sutton Pub.

Jerome, Leah. Schwarzenegger. (Illus.). 48p. 1992. 1.49 (*0-440-21430-0*) Dell.

Keith, Evan. The Girls of Beverly Hills, 90210. (Illus.). 48p. 1993. 1.49 (*0-440-21426-2*) Dell.

—Luke Perry: Who's Hot! 48p. (gr. 4-7). 1992. pap. 1.49 (*0-440-21375-4*) Dell.

—Who's Hot! Denzel Washington. (gr. 4-7). 1993. pap. 1.49 (*0-440-21476-9*) Dell.

—Winona Ryder. (Illus.). 48p. 1992. 1.49 (*0-440-21432-7*) Dell.

Krohn, Katherine E. Lucille Ball: Pioneer of Comedy. (Illus.). 64p. (gr. 4-7). 1992. PLB 13.50 (*0-8225-0543-6*); pap. 4.95 (*0-8225-9603-2*) Lerner Pubns.

—Roseanne Arnold: Comedy's Queen Bee. LC 92-42653. 1993. 13.50 (*0-8225-0520-7*) Lerner Pubns.

—Roseanne Arnold: Comedy's Queen Bee. (gr. 4-7). 1993. pap. 4.95 (*0-8225-9644-X*) Lerner Pubns.

Latham, Caroline. Katherine Hepburn. Horner, Matina, intro. by. (Illus.). 112p. (gr. 5 up). 1988. 17.95 (*1-55546-658-3*); pap. 9.95 (*0-7910-0416-3*) Chelsea Hse.

Lee, Gregory. Chris Burke: He Overcame Down Syndrome. LC 93-18213. 1993. 14.60 (*0-86593-263-8*); 10.95s.p. (*0-685-66611-5*) Rourke Corp.

Lipsyte, Robert. Arnold Schwarzenegger: Hercules in America. LC 92-46901. (Illus.). 96p. (gr. 5-9). 1993. 14.00 (*0-06-023002-9*); PLB 13.89 (*0-06-023003-7*) HarpC Child Bks.

Luke Perry. 1992. 1.25 (*0-590-46207-5*, 072) Scholastic Inc.

Martinez, Elizabeth C. Edward James Olmos: Committed Actor. LC 93-37659. 32p. (gr. 2-4). 1994. PLB 12.90 (*1-56294-410-X*) Millbrook Pr.

Meeks, Christopher. Arnold Schwarzenegger: Hard Work Brought Success. LC 92-42288. 1993. 14.60 (*0-86593-260-3*); 10.95s.p. (*0-685-66328-0*) Rourke Corp.

Micklos, John, Jr. Leonard Nimoy: A Stars Trek. LC 87-32457. (Illus.). 64p. (gr. 3 up). 1988. text ed. 13.95 RSBE (*0-87518-376-X*, Dillon) Macmillan Child Grp.

North, Jack. Arnold Schwarzenegger. LC 93-40891. 1994. text ed. 14.95 (*0-87518-638-6*, Dillon) Macmillan Child Grp.
Perl, Lila. Molly Picon: A Gift of Laughter. Ruff, Donna, illus. 64p. (gr. 4-7). 1990. 12.95 (*0-8276-0336-3*) JPS Phila.
Petrucelli. Cher, Reading Level 2. (Illus.). 24p. (gr. 1-4). 1989. PLB 14.60 (*0-86592-432-5*) Rourke Corp.
Regan, William. Keanu Reeves: What's Hot! 48p. (gr. 4-7). 1992. pap. 1.49 (*0-440-21376-2*) Dell.
Scordato, Mark & Scordato, Ellen. The Three Stooges. LC 94-19343. (gr. 3 up). 1995. write for info. (*0-7910-2344-3*); pap. write for info. (*0-7910-2369-9*) Chelsea Hse.
Shannen Doherty. 1992. 1.25 (*0-590-46209-1*, 074) Scholastic Inc.
Shea, Regan. Brad Pitt. (gr. 4-7). 1992. pap. 1.49 (*0-440-21474-2*) Dell.
Shorto, Russell. Jane Fonda: Political Activism. (Illus.). 104p. (gr. 7 up). 1991. PLB 15.40 (*1-56294-045-7*); pap. 5.95 (*1-56294-831-8*) Millbrook Pr.
—Jane Fonda: Political Activist. 1992. pap. 5.95 (*0-395-63564-0*) HM.
Smith, Betsy C. A Day in the Life of an Actress. Buckley, F. Reid, Jr., illus. LC 84-8678. 32p. (gr. 4-8). 1985. PLB 11.79 (*0-8167-0105-9*); pap. text ed. 2.95 (*0-8167-0106-7*); cassettes avail. Troll Assocs.
Surcouf, Elizabeth G. Grace Kelly, American Princess. LC 92-9626. 1992. 17.50 (*0-8225-0548-7*) Lerner Pubns.
Tager, Miriam. Macaulay Culkin. (Illus.). 48p. 1992. 1.49 (*0-440-21427-0*) Dell.
Teitelbaum, Michael. Family Matters: Behind the Scenes. LC 92-33899. 1992. pap. 2.95 (*0-8167-3038-5*) Troll Assocs.
Tori Spelling. 1992. 1.25 (*0-590-46212-1*, 077) Scholastic Inc.
Wallner, Rosemary. Beverly Hills 90210. LC 92-16789. 1992. 12.94 (*1-56239-139-9*) Abdo & Dghtrs.
—Blossom. LC 92-14779. 1992. 12.94 (*1-56239-141-0*) Abdo & Dghtrs.
—Family Matters. LC 92-16788. 1992. 12.94 (*1-56239-142-9*) Abdo & Dghtrs.
—Fresh Prince of Bel Air. LC 92-16790. 1992. 12.94 (*1-56239-140-2*) Abdo & Dghtrs.
—Julia Roberts. LC 91-73038. 1991. 12.94 (*1-56239-055-4*) Abdo & Dghtrs.
—Luke Perry. LC 92-16036. 1992. 12.94 (*1-56239-146-1*) Abdo & Dghtrs.
—Macaulay Culkin. LC 93-19061. (Illus.). 1993. 12.94 (*1-56239-227-1*) Abdo & Dghtrs.
Watson, B. S. Arnold Schwarzenegger: Unauthorized Biography. (Illus.). 64p. (Orig.). 1991. pap. 2.95 (*1-56156-063-4*) Kidsbks.
Wheeler, Jill. Michael Landon. Wallner, Rosemary, ed. LC 92-16571. (gr. 4). 1992. PLB 13.99 (*1-56239-113-5*) Abdo & Dghtrs.
Zwocker, Ray. Who's Hot: Wesley Snipes. (gr. 4-7). 1993. pap. 1.49 (*0-440-21589-7*, YB) Dell.

ADAGES
see Proverbs

ADAM (BIBLICAL CHARACTER)
Adam & Eve. (ps-2). 1989. text ed. 3.95 cased (*0-7214-5259-0*) Ladybird Bks.
Blair, Grandpa. The Gospel Rag: Adam & Eve Straight Up. 2nd ed. 16p. (gr. 11 up). 1992. 5.95 (*0-930366-71-9*) Northcountry Pub.
Frank, Penny. Adam & Eve. (ps-3). 1988. 3.99 (*0-85648-727-9*) Lion USA.
—Adam & Eve. Haysom, John & Morris, Tony, illus. Burow, Daniel, contrib. by. LC 92-29470. 1992. 6.95 (*0-7459-2609-6*) Lion USA.
Storr, Catherine, retold by. Adam & Eve. Russell, Jim, illus. LC 82-23060. 32p. (gr. k-4). 1983. 14.65 (*0-8172-1981-1*) Raintree Steck-V.

ADAMS, ABIGAIL (SMITH) 1744-1818
Bober, Natalie S. Abigail Adams: A Life of Letters, Loyalties & Love. LC 94-19259. 1995. 16.00 (*0-689-31760-3*, Atheneum Child Bk) Macmillan Child Grp.
Fradin, Dennis B. Abigail Adams: Adviser to a President. LC 88-31331. (Illus.). 48p. (gr. 3-6). 1989. lib. bdg. 14.95 (*0-89490-228-8*) Enslow Pubs.
Osborne, Angela. Abigail Adams. Horner, Matina S., intro. by. (Illus.). 112p. (gr. 5 up). 1989. 17.95 (*1-55546-635-4*); pap. 9.95 (*0-7910-0405-8*) Chelsea Hse.
Quackenbush, Robert. John Adams & Abigail Adams & Their Times. Quackenbush, Robert, illus. 40p. (gr. 2-5). 1994. 14.95 (*0-945912-24-2*) Pippin Pr.
Sabin, Francene. Young Abigail Adams. Miyake, Yoshi, illus. LC 91-17112. 48p. (gr. 4-6). 1992. PLB 10.79 (*0-8167-2503-9*); pap. text ed. 3.50 (*0-8167-2504-7*) Troll Assocs.
Sandak, Cass R. John Adamses. LC 92-9262. (Illus.). 48p. (gr. 5). 1992. text ed. 12.95 RSBE (*0-89686-640-8*, Crestwood Hse) Macmillan Child Grp.
Stone-Peterson, Helen. Abigail Adams: Dear Partner. Fraser, Betty, illus. 80p. (gr. 2-6). 1991. Repr. of 1967 ed. lib. bdg. 12.95 (*0-7910-1402-9*) Chelsea Hse.
Wagoner, Jean B. Abigail Adams: Girl of Colonial Days. LC 92-345. (Illus.). 192p. (gr. 7 up). 1992. pap. 3.95 (*0-689-71657-5*, Aladdin) Macmillan Child Grp.
Waldrop, Ruth. Abigail Adams. LC 88-6137. (Illus.). 109p. (gr. 3 up). 1988. PLB 10.95 (*0-9616894-2-0*); pap. 6.95 (*0-9616894-1-2*) Rusk Inc.
Witter, Evelyn. Abigail Adams: First Lady of Faith & Courage. Hanzel, Linda & Hanzel, Linda, illus. LC 76-2416. (gr. 3-6). 1976. pap. 6.95 (*0-915134-94-2*) Mott Media.

ADAMS, JOHN, PRESIDENT U. S. 1735-1826
Brill, Marlene T. John Adams. (Illus.). 100p. (gr. 3 up). 1986. PLB 14.40 (*0-516-01384-X*); pap. 6.95 (*0-516-41384-8*) Childrens.
Dwyer, Frank. John Adams. (Illus.). (gr. 5 up). 1989. 17.95 (*1-55546-801-2*) Chelsea Hse.
Quackenbush, Robert. John Adams & Abigail Adams & Their Times. Quackenbush, Robert, illus. 40p. (gr. 2-5). 1994. 14.95 (*0-945912-24-2*) Pippin Pr.
Sandak, Cass R. John Adamses. LC 92-9262. (Illus.). 48p. (gr. 5). 1992. text ed. 12.95 RSBE (*0-89686-640-8*, Crestwood Hse) Macmillan Child Grp.
Santrey, Laurence. John Adams, Brave Patriot. Smolinski, Dick, illus. LC 85-1095. 48p. (gr. 4-6). 1986. lib. bdg. 10.79 (*0-8167-0559-3*); pap. text ed. 3.50 (*0-8167-0560-7*) Troll Assocs.
Stefoff, Rebecca. John Adams: 2nd President of the United States. Young, Richard G., ed. LC 87-32752. (Illus.). (gr. 5-9). 1988. PLB 17.26 (*0-944483-10-0*) Garrett Ed Corp.

ADAMS, JOHN QUINCY, PRESIDENT U. S. 1767-1848
Favors, John & Favors, Kathryne. John Quincy Adams & the Amistad: A President Who Fought for the Rights of Africans. Dellums, Ronald, intro. by. (Illus.). 28p. (Orig.). (gr. 12). 1974. write for info. (*1-878794-02-7*) Jonka Enter.
Greenblatt, Miriam. John Quincy Adams: Sixth President of the United States. Young, Richard G., ed. LC 89-39950. (Illus.). 128p. (gr. 5-9). 1990. PLB 17.26 (*0-944483-21-6*) Garrett Ed Corp.
Harness, Cheryl. Young John Quincy. Harness, Cheryl, illus. LC 92-37266. 48p. (gr. k-5). 1994. RSBE 15.95 (*0-02-742644-0*, Bradbury Pr) Macmillan Child Grp.
Kent, Zachary. John Quincy Adams. LC 86-31022. (Illus.). 100p. (gr. 3 up). 1987. PLB 14.40 (*0-516-01386-6*); pap. 6.95 (*0-516-41386-4*) Childrens.
Sandak, Cass R. John Adamses. LC 92-9262. (Illus.). 48p. (gr. 5). 1992. text ed. 12.95 RSBE (*0-89686-640-8*, Crestwood Hse) Macmillan Child Grp.

ADAMS, SAMUEL, 1722-1803
Farley, Karin C. Samuel Adams--Grandfather of His Country. Shenton, James P., intro. by. LC 94-12646. 1994. write for info. (*0-8114-2379-4*) Raintree Steck-V.
Fritz, Jean. Why Don't You Get a Horse, Sam Adams? Hyman, Trina S., illus. 48p. (gr. 2-6). 1982. 13.95 (*0-698-20292-9*, Coward); pap. 6.95 (*0-698-20545-6*, Coward) Putnam Pub Group.

ADAPTATION (BIOLOGY)
see also Man–Influence of Environment
Capon, Brian. Plant Survival: Adapting to a Hostile World. Capon, Brian, illus. LC 93-43342. 144p. 1994. 24.95 (*0-88192-283-8*); pap. 15.95 (*0-88192-287-0*) Timber.
Cochrane, Jennifer. Nature. LC 91-9194. (Illus.). 48p. (gr. 5-8). 1991. PLB 13.90 (*0-531-19143-5*, Warwick) Watts.
Evans, Lisa G. An Elephant Never Forgets Its Snorkel: How Animals Survive Without Tools & Gadgets. De Groat, Diane, illus. LC 91-31828. 40p. (gr. 1-5). 1992. 10.00 (*0-517-58401-8*); PLB 10.99 (*0-517-58404-2*) Crown Bks Yng Read.
Markham-David, Sally. It Takes All Kinds. Ruth, Trevor, illus. LC 93-21246. 1994. 4.25 (*0-383-03753-0*) SRA Schl Grp.
Morrison, Rob & Morrison, James. Monsters! Just Imagine. Crossett, Warren, illus. LC 93-26927. 1994. 4.25 (*0-383-03763-8*) SRA Schl Grp.
Natural History Museum, London, England Staff, compiled by. Creepy Crawlies: Ladybugs, Lobsters, & Other Amazing Arthropods. LC 90-27531. (Illus.). 108p. 1991. 14.95 (*0-8069-8336-1*) Sterling.

ADDAMS, JANE, 1860-1935
Gleiter, Jan & Thompson, Kathleen. Jane Addams. (Illus.). 32p. (Orig.). (gr. 2-5). 1987. PLB 19.97 (*0-8172-2662-1*) Raintree Steck-V.
Kent, Deborah. Jane Addams & Hull House. LC 91-37882. (Illus.). 32p. (gr. 3-6). PLB 12.30, Apr. 1992 (*0-516-04852-X*); pap. 3.95, Jul. 1992 (*0-516-44852-8*) Childrens.
Klingel, Cynthia & Zadra, Dan. Jane Addams. (Illus.). 32p. 1987. PLB 14.95 (*0-88682-165-7*) Creative Ed.
Wheeler, Leslie A. Jane Addams. Gallin, Richard, ed. (Illus.). 144p. (gr. 5-9). 1990. PLB 10.95 (*0-382-09962-1*); pap. 6.95 (*0-382-09968-0*) Silver Burdett Pr.

ADDING MACHINES
see Calculating Machines

ADENAUER, KONRAD, 1876-1967
Finke, Blythe F. Konrad Adenauer: Architect of the New Germany. Rahmas, D. Steve, ed. LC 79-190241. 32p. (Orig.). (gr. 7-12). 1972. lib. bdg. 4.95 incl. catalog cards (*0-87157-523-X*) SamHar Pr.

ADIRONDACK MOUNTAINS

Steinberg, Michael. Our Wilderness: How the People of New York Found, Changed, & Preserved the Adirondacks. Burdick, Neal S., ed. LC 91-16550. (Illus.). 112p. (gr. 5 up). 1994. 18.95 (*0-935272-56-9*); pap. 9.95 (*0-935272-57-7*) ADK Mtn Club. A history of the 6-million-acre Adirondack Park of New York State, which includes towns & farms, businesses & timberlands as well as 1.2 million acres of wilderness. Written for ages 10 & up (Gr. 4 plus). Described by KIRKUS REVIEWS as "a cultural history full of charming, quirky people, plus both funny & sobering anecdotes... Gracefully written with lessons that go far beyond regional interest." APPALACHIA noted that "there is probably no other book available that can provide as thorough an introduction to Adirondack history, particularly with anything close to the brevity & efficiency of this book." Author received award from Adirondack Park Centennial Committee for his contribution to education via OUR WILDERNESS. Historic photographs by Stoddard & Apperson. Publication coincided with the 1992 Centennial of the Adirondack Park. Book carries conservationist message. "The entertaining & informative 'young people's history'... contains plenty of interest the mature mind."--New York's Rochester DEMOCRAT & CHRONICLE. *Publisher Provided Annotation.*

Vesty, John. Adirontreks: Places & People in the Adirondacks. LC 90-82523. (Illus.). 268p. (Orig.). (gr. 8). 1991. pap. 19.95 (*0-9626876-0-X*) J Vesty Co.

ADIRONDACK MOUNTAINS–FICTION
Pearce, J. C. Tug of War. LC 93-15037. 144p. (gr. 3-7). 1993. pap. 2.99 (*0-14-036663-6*, Puffin) Puffin Bks.

ADJUSTMENT, SOCIAL
see Social Adjustment

ADMINISTRATION
see Political Science
see names of countries, cities, etc. with the subdivision Politics and Government, e.g. U. S.–Politics and Government; etc.

ADMINISTRATION OF JUSTICE
see Justice, Administration of

ADOLESCENCE
Bourgeois & Wolfish. Changes in You & Me: A Book about Puberty, Mostly for Boys. LC 94-1162. (gr. 7-12). 1994. 14.95 (*0-8362-2814-6*) Andrews & McMeel.
Bourgeois, Paulette & Wolfish, Martin. Changes in You & Me: A Book about Puberty, Mostly for Girls. Phillips, Louise & Yu, Kam, illus. LC 94-1161. (gr. 7-12). 1994. 14.95 (*0-8362-2815-4*) Andrews & McMeel.
Callister, Joann I. Teenagers in Crisis: Not Alone. LC 90-23970. 128p. (Orig.). 1991. pap. 8.95 (*0-931832-80-2*) Fithian Pr.
Childre, Doc L. The How-to Book of Teen Self Discovery: Helping Teens Find Balance, Security & Esteem. 2nd ed. Cryer, Bruce & Rozman, Deborah, eds. Putman, Brian, illus. (SPA.). 128p. (ps-12). 1992. pap. 8.95 (*1-879052-36-9*) Planetary Pubns.
Cohen, Daniel & Cohen, Susan. Teenage Stress. 176p. (gr. 7 up). 1992. pap. 3.99 (*0-440-21391-6*, LFL) Dell.
Coombs, H. Samm. Teenage Survival Manual: How to Reach '20' in One Piece (& Enjoy Every Step of the Journey) 4th, rev. ed. Lipney, Stephanie & Moore, Dick, illus. 235p. (gr. 9-12). 1993. pap. 9.95 (*0-925258-08-3*) DB Inc CA.
D, Lisa, ed. Stepping Stones to Recovery for Young People. LC 91-8676. 240p. (Orig.). (gr. 9-12). 1991. pap. 6.95 (*0-934125-19-8*) Glen Abbey Bks.
Darling, Benjamin. Tips for Teens: Telephone Tactics, Petting Practices, & Other Milestones on the Road to Popularity. LC 93-35815. 60p. (gr. 7-12). 1994. 9.95 (*0-8118-0520-4*) Chronicle Bks.
Dockrey, Karen. What's Your Problem? 96p. (gr. 7 up). 1987. pap. 12.99 (*0-89693-381-4*, Victor Books); pap. 2.99 student bk. (*0-317-60085-0*) SP Pubns.
Espeland, Pamela & Wallner, Rosemary. Making the Most of Today: Daily Readings for Young People on Self-Awareness, Creativity & Self-Esteem. LC 91-14494. 392p. (Orig.). (gr. 5 up). 1991. pap. 8.95 (*0-915793-33-4*) Free Spirit Pub.
Feller, Robyn M. Everything You Need to Know about Peer Pressure. Rosen, Ruth, ed. (gr. 7-12). 1993. PLB 14.95 (*0-8239-1528-X*) Rosen Group.
Go Ask Alice. 192p. (gr. 7 up). 1976. pap. 3.99 (*0-380-00523-9*, Flare) Avon.
Hartley, Fred. Growing Pains: First Aid for Teenagers. LC 81-11952. 160p. (Orig.). (gr. 7-12). 1981. pap. 6.99 (*0-8007-5067-5*) Revell.

Johnson, Eric W. How to Live with Parents & Teachers. LC 86-9273. 156p. (gr. 5-10). 1986. 15.00 (*0-664-21273-5*, Westminster) Westminster John Knox.

Keltner, Nancy, compiled by. If You Print This, Please Don't Use My Name: Questions from Teens & Their Parents about Things That Matter. Coffman, Gina, illus. Keltner, Nancy, intro. by. LC 91-36306. (Illus.). 256p. (Orig.). (gr. 7-12). 1992. pap. 8.95 (*0-944176-03-8*) Terra Nova.

McCoy, Kathy & Wibbelsman, Charles. The New Teenage Body Book. rev. ed. (Illus.). 288p. (Orig.). (gr. 9-12). 1992. pap. 15.00 (*0-399-51725-1*, Body Pr-Perigee) Berkley Pub.

McDowell, Josh & Hostetler, Bob. Don't Check Your Brains at the Door. (gr. 7 up). 1992. pap. write for info. (*0-8499-3234-3*) Word Inc.

Mayle, Peter. What's Happening to Me? Walter, Paul & Robins, Arthur, illus. LC 75-14410. 56p. (gr. 3 up). 1975. 12.00 (*0-8184-0221-0*); pap. 6.95 (*0-8184-0312-8*) Carol Pub Group.

Miller, Alice. Young Girl's Diary. 1991. pap. 10.95 (*0-385-41596-6*, Anchor NY) Doubleday.

Packer, Alex J. Bringing up Parents, the Teenager's Handbook. 264p. 1994. 12.95 (*0-685-71613-9*, 752) W Gladden Found.

Packer, Kenneth L. Puberty: The Story of Growth & Change. Green, Anne C., illus. LC 89-5665. 109p. (gr. 6-9). 1989. PLB 13.40 (*0-531-10810-4*) Watts.

Parramon, J. M., et al. Teenagers. 32p. (gr. 3-5). 1987. Eng. ed. pap. 3.95 (*0-8120-3851-7*); Span. ed.: Los Jovenes. pap. 6.95 (*0-8120-3855-X*) Barron.

Powledge, Fred. You'll Survive: Late Blooming, Early Blooming, Loneliness, Klutziness, & Other Problems of Adolescence, & How to Live Through Them. LC 85-43351. 144p. (gr. 6-8). 1986. SBE 13.95 (*0-684-18632-2*, Scribners Young Read) Macmillan Child Grp.

Roberts, Gail C. & Guttormson, Lorraine. You & School: A Survival Guide for Adolescence. Wallner, Rosemary, ed. 120p. (Orig.). (gr. 4-8). 1990. pap. 8.95 (*0-915793-25-3*) Free Spirit Pub.

—You & Stress: A Survival Guide for Adolescence. Wallner, Rosemary, ed. 128p. (Orig.). (gr. 4-8). 1990. pap. 8.95 (*0-915793-26-1*) Free Spirit Pub Co.

—You & Your Family: A Survival Guide for Adolescence. Espeland, Pamela, ed. 112p. (Orig.). (gr. 4-8). 1990. pap. 8.95 (*0-915793-24-5*) Free Spirit Pub.

Rosenberg, Ellen. Growing up Feeling Good: A Growing up Handbook Especially for Kids. 1989. pap. 11.99 (*0-14-034264-8*, Puffin) Puffin Bks.

Sheperd, Scott. What Do You Think of You? A Teen's Guide to Finding Self-Esteem. Hesse, Bonnie, ed. (Illus.). 100p. (Orig.). 1990. 6.95 (*0-89638-220-6*) Hazelden.

Smith, Lucinda I. Growing up Female: New Challenges, New Choices. LC 86-31261. 160p. (gr. 7 up). 1987. lib. bdg. 12.98 (*0-671-63445-3*, J Messner) S&S Trade.

Smith, Michael W. & Ridenour, Fritz. Old Enough to Know. large type ed. 111p. (gr. 7 up). 1989. pap. 12. 99 (*0-8499-3163-0*) Word Inc.

Snyder, Linda. Guys & Girls: Understanding Each Other. (Illus.). 48p. (gr. 6-8). 1991. pap. 8.99 (*1-55945-110-6*) Group Pub.

Stephens, Andrea. Stressed-Out but Hangin' Tough. LC 89-10676. 160p. (Orig.). (gr. 8-12). 1989. pap. 7.99 (*0-8007-5326-7*) Revell.

Stewart, Gail. Peer Pressure. LC 89-31258. (Illus.). 48p. (gr. 5-6). 1989. text ed. 12.95 RSBE (*0-89686-444-8*, Crestwood Hse) Macmillan Child Grp.

Tucker, Nicholas. Adolescence. LC 90-21868. (Illus.). 64p. (gr. 5-9). 1991. PLB 11.95 (*0-8114-7805-X*) Raintree Steck-V.

Wallace, Carol M. Should You Shut Your Eyes When You Kiss? Or, How to Survive "The Best Years of Your Life" Weston, Martha, illus. LC 83-5458. 112p. (gr. 7 up). 1983. 13.45i (*0-316-91998-5*) Little.

Wingerd, William N. Understanding & Enjoying Adolescence. 1988. pap. text ed. 13.05 (*0-8013-0215-3*, 75873) Longman.

ADOLESCENCE–FICTION

Allen, Richard E. Ozzy. 1989. pap. 13.95 (*0-440-50146-6*) Dell.

Baer, Judy. Broken Promises. 128p. (Orig.). (gr. 7 up). 1989. pap. 3.99 (*1-55661-087-4*) Bethany Hse.

—Cedar River Daydreams, Bks. 11-15. (Orig., Set incls. Something Old, Something New, Vanishing Star, No Turning Back, Second Chance & Lost & Found). (gr. 7-10). 1992. Giftset. pap. 19.99 (*1-55661-765-8*) Bethany Hse.

Bawden, Nina. Henry. Powzyk, Joyce, illus. LC 87-29339. (gr. 3 up). 1988. PLB 14.00 (*0-688-07894-X*) Lothrop.

Bennett, Cherie. Surviving Sixteen, No. 3: Did You Hear about Amber? 224p. (gr. 7 up). 1993. pap. 3.50 (*0-14-036318-1*, Puffin) Puffin Bks.

Blume, Judy. La Ballena "Blubber" Ada, Alma F., tr. LC 83-2731. (SPA.). 160p. (gr. 4-6). 1983. SBE 14.95 (*0-02-710940-2*, Bradbury Pr) Macmillan Child Grp.

—Estas Ahi Dios? Soy Yo, Margaret. Ada, Alma F., tr. LC 83-2730. (SPA.). 160p. (gr. 4-6). 1983. 14.95 (*0-02-710950-X*, Bradbury Pr) Macmillan Child Grp.

—It's Not the End of the World. 1979. pap. 1.95 (*0-553-13628-3*) Bantam.

Brooks, Robert F. Children's Stories for Teenage Adults. rev. ed. (Illus.). 32p. (Orig.). (gr. 5-9). pap. 3.00 (*0-936868-05-8*) Freeland Pubns.

Bunting, Eve. Fifteen. (Illus.). (gr. 3-8). 1992. PLB 8.95 (*0-685-62602-4*) Childs World.

Byars, Betsy C. Bingo Brown & the Language of Love. 160p. (gr. 3-7). 1989. 12.95 (*0-670-82791-6*) Viking Child Bks.

Callan, Jamie. Over the Hill at Fourteen. 176p. (gr. 7 up). pap. 1.95 (*0-451-13090-1*, Sig Vista) NAL-Dutton.

Campbell, Barbara. Bob II. 224p. (gr. 6-9). Date not set. write for info. (*1-56282-346-9*); PLB write for info. (*1-56282-347-7*) Hyprn Child.

Cavanna, Betty. Going on Sixteen. 188p. (gr. 6-9). 1992. pap. 2.50 (*0-8167-1266-2*) Troll Assocs.

Cleary, Beverly. Fifteen. Krush, Joe & Krush, Beth, illus. LC 56-7509. 256p. (gr. 6-9). 1956. 12.95 (*0-688-21285-9*); PLB 12.88 (*0-688-31285-3*, Morrow Jr Bks) Morrow Jr Bks.

—Fifteen. 192p. 1991. pap. 3.99 (*0-380-70920-1*, Flare) Avon.

Collier, James L. The Winchesters. 176p. (gr. 4). 1989. pap. 2.95 (*0-380-70808-6*, Flare) Avon.

Cooney, Linda A. Breaking Away. 224p. 1991. pap. 2.95 (*0-590-44561-8*) Scholastic Inc.

—Playing Games. 1992. pap. 2.95 (*0-590-44565-0*, Point) Scholastic Inc.

Cooney, Linda A. & Cooney, Kevin. Making Changes. 176p. 1992. pap. 2.95 (*0-590-44563-4*) Scholastic Inc.

—Standing Alone. 176p. 1991. pap. 2.95 (*0-590-44562-6*) Scholastic Inc.

Cooper, Ilene. Hollywood Wars, No. 4: Trouble in Paradise. 144p. (gr. 3-7). 1993. pap. 3.25 (*0-14-036158-8*, Puffin) Puffin Bks.

—Seeing Red. LC 92-42426. 144p. (gr. 3-7). 1993. pap. 3.25 (*0-14-036157-X*, Puffin) Puffin Bks.

Cormier, Robert. Fade. 1991. pap. 4.50 (*0-440-21091-7*, YB) Dell.

Crew, Linda. Someday I'll Laugh about This. 176p. (gr. 5-9). 1992. pap. 3.25 (*0-440-40679-X*, YB) Dell.

Danziger, Paula. Earth to Matthew. 160p. (gr. 4-7). 1992. pap. 3.99 (*0-440-40733-8*, YB) Dell.

—The Pistachio Prescription. LC 77-86330. 168p. (gr. 7 up). 1978. pap. 12.95 (*0-385-28784-4*) Delacorte.

Deans, Sis B. Blazing Bear. Comyns, Nantz, illus. LC 92-60478. 40p. (gr. 3-7). 1992. pap. 9.95 (*0-932433-94-4*) Windswept Hse.

Edwards, Archibald C. Charlotte. Musser, Rebecca F., illus. LC 90-63680. 112p. (Orig.). (gr. 7 up). 1990. pap. 11.95 (*0-9626413-0-8*) Rosedale Pr.

Ellis, Jana. Hometown Hero. LC 89-34374. 160p. (gr. 7 up). 1989. pap. text ed. 2.50 (*0-8167-1609-9*) Troll Assocs.

—Slave for a Day. LC 89-34375. 160p. (gr. 7 up). 1989. pap. text ed. 2.50 (*0-8167-1610-2*) Troll Assocs.

Family of the America's Staff & Sincro Communications Staff. If You Love Me...Show Me! CCC of America Staff, illus. 41p. (Orig.). (gr. 5-7). 1992. incl. video 21. 95 (*1-56814-400-8*); pap. text ed. 6.95 book (*0-685-62406-4*) CCC of America.

Fitzpatrick, Regina D. It Wasn't the Truth They Told. Graves, Helen, ed. LC 88-50112. 80p. (gr. 4-8). 1988. 6.95 (*1-55523-142-X*) Winston-Derek.

Foley, June. Susanna Siegelbaum Gives up Guys. 1992. pap. 3.25 (*0-590-43700-3*) Scholastic Inc.

Gold, Robert S. Point of Departure. (gr. 7-12). 1981. pap. 2.75 (*0-685-01409-6*, LE) Dell.

Greene, Constance C. Just Plain Al. LC 86-5516. 144p. (gr. 5-9). 1986. pap. 12.95 (*0-670-81250-1*) Viking Child Bks.

—Your Old Pal, Al. LC 79-12350. (gr. 5-9). 1979. pap. 13.95 (*0-670-79575-5*) Viking Child Bks.

Griffith, Helen V. Journal of a Teenage Genius. (gr. 3-7). 1987. 11.75 (*0-688-07226-7*) Greenwillow.

—Journal of a Teenage Genius. 128p. (gr. 7 up). 1988. pap. 2.50 (*0-8167-1325-1*) Troll Assocs.

Hall, Lynn. Flying Changes. LC 90-45516. (gr. 9-12). 1993. pap. 4.95 (*0-15-228791-4*) HarBrace.

Halverson, Marilyn. Dare. 1992. pap. 3.25 (*0-590-43545-0*) Scholastic Inc.

Hamilton, Morse. Effie's House. LC 89-11918. 224p. (gr. 7 up). 1990. 13.95 (*0-688-09307-8*) Greenwillow.

Hautzig, Deborah. Hey, Dollface. LC 78-54685. 160p. (gr. 7-9). 1978. PLB 11.88 (*0-688-84170-8*) Greenwillow.

Holman, Felice. Slake's Limbo. LC 74-11675. 126p. (gr. 4-8). 1974. RSBE 14.95 (*0-684-13926-X*, Scribners Young Read) Macmillan Child Grp.

Howard, Jean G. Bound by the Sea: A Summer Diary. LC 86-50255. (Illus.). 96p. (gr. 6-12). 1986. text ed. 15.00 (*0-930954-25-4*); pap. 10.00 (*0-930954-26-2*) Tidal Pr.

It's Just a Stage. 1993. 3.99 (*0-553-48045-6*) Bantam.

Judy Blume. Incl. Are You There, God? It's Me, Margaret; Blubber; Otherwise Known As Sheila the Great; Superfudge; Tales of a Fourth Grade Nothing. 1983. pap. 13.00 boxed set (*0-440-44348-2*) Dell.

Kaplow, Robert. Alessandra in Between. LC 91-45343. 208p. (gr. 7 up). 1992. 14.00 (*0-06-023297-8*); PLB 13.89 (*0-06-023298-6*) HarpC Child Bks.

—Alessandra in Love. LC 88-23141. 160p. (gr. 7 up). 1989. (Lipp Jr Bks); (Lipp Jr Bks) HarpC Child Bks.

Keats. Song about Myself. (ps-1). 1994. 15.95 (*0-8050-1746-1*) H Holt & Co.

Kerr, M. E. Dinky Hocker Shoots Smack! LC 72-80366. 204p. (gr. 7 up). 1972. PLB 15.89 (*0-06-023151-3*) HarpC Child Bks.

—I'll Love You When You're More Like Me. LC 76-58709. 192p. (gr. 7 up). 1989. pap. 3.95 (*0-06-447004-0*, Trophy) HarpC Child Bks.

Kidd, Ronald. Sammy Carducci's Guide to Women. 112p. (gr. 3-7). 1991. 14.95 (*0-525-67363-6*, Lodestar Bks) Dutton Child Bks.

Knowles, John. Separate Peace. (gr. 7 up). 1985. pap. 4.99 (*0-553-28041-4*) Bantam.

Koertge, Ron. Mariposa Blues. 176p. 1993. pap. 3.50 (*0-380-71761-1*, Flare) Avon.

—Where the Kissing Never Stops. 224p. 1993. pap. 3.50 (*0-380-71796-4*, Flare) Avon.

Koff, Richard M. Christopher. Kelly, Orly, ed. Reinertson, Barbara, illus. LC 81-65885. 128p. (gr. 7 up). 1981. 8.95 (*0-89742-050-0*) Celestial Arts.

Koller, Jackie F. Nothing to Fear. LC 90-39444. 1993. pap. 4.95 (*0-15-257582-0*, HB Juv Bks) HarBrace.

Konigsburg, E. L. Throwing Shadows. 168p. (gr. 7 up). 1988. pap. 3.95 (*0-02-044140-1*, Collier Young Ad) Macmillan Child Grp.

Krieger, Michael T. Melvin Howard's Fireside Chats. Mills, Tiffany, illus. 149p. (Orig.). (gr. 7 up). 1992. pap. 9.00 (*0-9634329-0-7*) M T Krieger.

Larimer, Tamela. Buck. LC 86-90774. 176p. (Orig.). (gr. 7 up). 1986. pap. 2.50 (*0-380-75172-0*, Flare) Avon.

Lee, Joanna. I Want to Keep My Baby! 176p. (Orig.). (gr. 9-12). 1977. pap. 3.50 (*0-451-15733-8*, Sig) NAL-Dutton.

Le Guin, Ursula K. Very Far Away from Anywhere Else. LC 76-4472. 96p. (gr. 5-9). 1976. SBE 13.95 (*0-689-30525-7*, Atheneum Child Bk) Macmillan Child Grp.

L'Engle, Madeleine. A Wind in the Door. LC 73-75176. 224p. (gr. 7 up). 1973. 17.00 (*0-374-38443-6*) FS&G.

McCullers, Carson. Heart Is a Lonely Hunter. LC 83-61845. (gr. 10-12). 1970. pap. 3.95 (*0-553-25481-2*) Bantam.

McDaniel, Lurlene. Someone Dies, Someone Lives. 1992. pap. 3.50 (*0-553-29842-9*) Bantam.

McDonnell, Christine. Friends First. 176p. (gr. 4 up). 1990. pap. 11.95 (*0-670-81923-9*) Viking Child Bks.

—Friends First. LC 92-20290. 176p. (gr. 5 up). 1992. pap. 3.99 (*0-14-032477-1*) Puffin Bks.

McManus, Dorothy. Song of Sirius. Myhre, M., ed. McManus, Michael, illus. 155p. (Orig.). 1990. pap. 8.00 (*0-929686-01-2*) Temple Golden Pubns.

Maguire, Jesse. Breaking the Rules, No. 6: Nowhere High. (Orig.). 1992. pap. 3.99 (*0-8041-0849-8*) Ivy Books.

Major, Kevin. Far from Shore: A Novel. LC 81-65495. 192p. (gr. 7 up). 1981. 12.95 (*0-385-28266-4*) Delacorte.

Matas, Carol. Kris's War. 176p. 1992. pap. 3.25 (*0-590-45034-4*, Point) Scholastic Inc.

Mazer, Norma F. Babyface. 176p. 1991. pap. 3.99 (*0-380-75720-6*, Flare) Avon.

Miller, Frances A. Aren't You the One Who...? 187p. 1987. pap. 3.99 (*0-449-70286-3*, Juniper) Fawcett.

Naughton, Jim. My Brother Stealing Second. LC 88-22035. 224p. (gr. 7 up). 1989. HarpC Child Bks.

Nelson, Peter. Six Deadly Lies. 1993. pap. 3.50 (*0-06-106110-7*, Harp PBks) HarpC.

Neufeld, John. Lisa, Bright & Dark. (gr. 7 up). 1969. 21. 95 (*0-87599-153-X*) S G Phillips.

Neville, Emily C. It's Like This, Cat. Weiss, Emil, illus. LC 62-21292. 192p. (gr. 5-9). 1975. pap. 3.95 (*0-06-440073-5*, Trophy) HarpC Child Bks.

Norton, Ann. Brooke's Little Lies. 112p. (gr. 4-9). 1992. pap. 2.95 (*0-448-40491-5*, G&D) Putnam Pub Group.

Oneal, Zibby. Language of Goldfish. 1990. pap. 3.99 (*0-14-034540-X*, Puffin) Puffin Bks.

Otherwise Known As... 1984. pap. 2.50 (*0-440-76701-6*) Dell.

Peck, Richard. Don't Look & It Won't Hurt. 1992. pap. 3.50 (*0-440-21213-8*) Dell.

Pfeffer, Susan B. Future Forward. (gr. 4-7). 1991. pap. 3.25 (*0-440-40475-4*) Dell.

—Rewind to Yesterday. (gr. 4-7). 1991. pap. 3.25 (*0-440-40474-6*) Dell.

—Turning Thirteen. LC 88-11347. 144p. (gr. 6-8). 1988. pap. 12.95 (*0-590-40764-3*, Scholastic Hardcover) Scholastic Inc.

Pike, Christopher. Gimme a Kiss. 160p. (gr. 8 up). 1991. pap. 3.99 (*0-671-73682-5*, Archway) PB.

Pines, Tonya, ed. Thirteen. 304p. 1991. pap. 3.50 (*0-590-45256-8*, Point) Scholastic Inc.

Posner, Richard. Goodnight, Cinderella. LC 89-17091. 242p. 1989. 13.95 (*0-87131-587-4*) M Evans.

Powell, Randy. My Underrated Year. 184p. (gr. 6 up). 1991. pap. 3.95 (*0-374-45453-1*, Sunburst) FS&G.

Reiss, Johanna. The Journey Back. LC 76-12615. 224p. (gr. 7 up). 1992. PLB 17.89 (*0-06-021457-0*) HarpC Child Bks.

Rockwell, Thomas. Hey, Lover Boy. LC 80-68739. 160p. (gr. 8-12). 1981. 8.95 (*0-440-03583-X*) Delacorte.

Roos, Stephen. Thirteenth Summer. 112p. (gr. 4-7). 1992. pap. 2.95 (*0-8167-1840-7*) Troll Assocs.

Ruckman, Ivy. No Way Out. LC 87-47817. 224p. (gr. 7 up). 1989. pap. 3.95 (*0-06-447003-2*, Trophy) HarpC Child Bks.

Sachs, Marilyn. Thirteen Going on Seven. LC 92-44427. 112p. (gr. 5-9). 1993. 14.95 (*0-525-45096-3*, DCB) Dutton Child Bks.

Schwartz, Joel L. The Diary of a Teenage Health Freak. (gr. k-12). 1990. pap. text ed. 3.50 (*0-440-20636-7*, LFL) Dell.

Service, Pamela F. Weirdos of the Universe, Unite! 1993. pap. 3.99 (*0-449-70429-7*) Fawcett.

Shannon, Jacqueline. Faking It. 176p. (Orig.). 1989. pap. 2.95 (*0-380-75601-3*, Flare) Avon.

Shaw, G. I. Watermelon in a Cucumber Patch. LC 93-81154. 96p. (Orig.). (gr. 8-11). 1994. pap. 5.00 (*0-9639450-0-9*, Joy Bks) Joy Ent.
On the first day of school, fifteen year-old Stevi is taunted by her classmates because she's overweight. Her best friend offers to help her lose weight, but also gets her involved with a boy that she has a crush on. Stevi overcomes obstacles at home, at work, & in dating as she wades through the confusing world of diets, pills, & exercise. She faces the everyday temptations of teenagers living in the 1990s: shoplifting, sex, & drugs. Finally introduced to a new concept for weight control, she learns how to respect & accept herself, & how to get control of her life. Ms. Shaw lives near Baltimore, Maryland, with her husband, six cats, two dogs & four plus goats. All her life she has struggled to keep her weight under control. "I've always liked doing the opposite of what I'm supposed to do. When I tried to diet I always gained weight. Finding a new idea about successful weight control changed everything. Finally, here was a way of life I could live with." Joy Enterprises, 332 S. Queen Street, Littletown, PA 17340 (717-359-7529).
Publisher Provided Annotation.

Shles, Larry. Aliens in My Nest: Squib Meets the Teen Creature. Winch, Bradley L., ed. Shles, Larry, illus. LC 88-80770. 80p. (Orig.). (gr. k up). 1988. pap. 7.95 (*0-915190-49-4*, JP9049-4) Jalmar Pr.
Smith, Doris B. Last Was Lloyd. 144p. (gr. 3-7). 1981. pap. 12.95 (*0-670-41921-4*) Viking Child Bks.
Stewart, A. C. Dark Dove. LC 74-14814. 192p. (gr. 6-9). 1974. 21.95 (*0-87599-203-X*) S G Phillips.
Thrash, Jacquelyn R. Big Precious Patty Pride. 1992. pap. 12.95 (*0-9635247-6-3*) Three Pines.
—Brody Bates' Choice. 298p. 1992. 21.95 (*0-9635247-0-4*); pap. write for info. (*0-9635247-1-2*) Three Pines.
—The Chubby Cheek Dilemma. 1992. pap. 14.95 (*0-9635247-5-5*) Three Pines.
—Echoes in Detention. 1992. write for info. (*0-9635247-8-X*) Three Pines.
—Final Battleground. 1992. 22.95 (*0-9635247-9-8*) Three Pines.
—For Better, for Worse. 1992. 22.95 (*0-9635247-3-9*) Three Pines.
Van Leeuwen, Jean. Dear Mom, You're Ruining My Life. LC 88-3705. (Illus.). 160p. (gr. 4-7). 1989. 13.95 (*0-8037-0572-7*); PLB 13.89 (*0-8037-0573-5*) Dial Bks Young.
Wardlaw, Lee. Corey's Fire. 160p. (gr. 5). 1990. pap. 2.95 (*0-380-75791-5*, Flare) Avon.
Wersba, Barbara. Just Be Gorgeous. LC 87-45858. 160p. (gr. 7 up). 1988. HarpC Child Bks.
—Wonderful Me. LC 88-21166. 160p. (gr. 7 up). 1989. HarpC Child Bks.
Wheeler, Ron. Help! I'm Late for School & I Can't Get Up! (Illus.). 100p. (Orig.). (gr. 7-12). 1993. pap. 4.95 (*0-8341-1495-X*) Beacon Hill.
—Love & Dating & Other Natural Disasters! Wheeler, Ron, illus. 86p. (Orig.). (gr. 7-12). 1993. pap. 4.95 (*0-8341-1505-0*) Beacon Hill.
Wilder, Laura Ingalls. The First Four Years. Williams, Garth, illus. Macbride, R. L., intro. by. LC 76-135774. (Illus.). 160p. (gr. 3-7). 1971. 15.95 (*0-06-026426-8*); PLB 15.89 (*0-06-026427-6*) HarpC Child Bks.
Willey, Margaret. If Not for You. LC 88-3343. 160p. (gr. 7 up). 1988. HarpC Child Bks.
Wilson, Budge. Thirteen Never Changes. 160p. 1991. pap. 2.95 (*0-590-43488-8*, Apple Paperbacks) Scholastic Inc.
Windsor, Patricia. The Hero. (gr. k-12). 1990. pap. 3.25 (*0-440-20638-3*, LFL) Dell.
Wolff, Virginia E. Make Lemonade. large type ed. LC 93-21003. (gr. 9-12). 1993. 15.95 (*0-7862-0056-1*) Thorndike Pr.
Wyss, Thelma H. Here at the Scenic-Vu Motel. LC 87-45308. 160p. (gr. 7 up). 1989. pap. 3.95 (*0-06-447001-6*, Trophy) HarpC Child Bks.
Zindel, Paul. I Never Loved Your Mind. LC 73-105476. 192p. (gr. 7 up). 1970. PLB 13.89 (*0-06-026822-0*) HarpC Child Bks.
—Pardon Me, You're Stepping on My Eyeball. LC 75-25410. 272p. (gr. 7 up). 1976. PLB 19.89 (*0-06-026838-7*) HarpC Child Bks.

ADOPTION

Banish, Roslyn. A Forever Family: A Book About Adoption. Banish, Roslyn, illus. LC 90-28725. 48p. (gr. k-3). 1992. 14.00 (*0-06-021673-5*); PLB 13.89 (*0-06-021674-3*) HarpC Child Bks.
—A Forever Family: A Book About Adoption. Banish, Roslyn, illus. LC 90-28726. 48p. (gr. k-3). 1992. pap. 5.95 (*0-06-446116-5*, Trophy) HarpC Child Bks.
Barris, Sara L. & Seltzer, Doryle P. Together Forever: An Adoption Story Coloring Book. Mazer, Susan, illus. 32p. 1992. pap. 3.95 (*0-9632023-0-8*) Shoot Star Pr.
Bunin, Catherine & Bunin, Sherry. Is That Your Sister? A True Story of Adoption. Welch, Sheila K., illus. 32p. (gr. 2-6). 1992. Repr. of 1976 ed. 14.95 (*0-9611872-6-3*) Our Child Pr.
Cohen, Shari. Coping with Being Adopted. Rosen, Ruth, ed. 132p. (gr. 7 up). 1988. PLB 14.95 (*0-8239-0770-8*) Rosen Group.
Crook, Marion. Teenagers Talk about Adoption. 116p. (Orig.). (gr. 6 up). 1990. pap. 10.95 (*1-55021-047-5*, Pub. by NC Press CN) U of Toronto Pr.
Dellinger, Annetta E. Adopted & Loved Forever. (Illus.). (ps-2). 1987. 5.99 (*0-570-04167-8*, 56-1624) Concordia.
DuPrau, Jeanne. Adoption: The Facts, Feelings & Issues of a Double Heritage. rev. ed. Steltenpohl, Jane, ed. 128p. (gr. 7 up). 1990. lib. bdg. 12.98 (*0-671-69328-X*, J Messner); lib. bdg. 5.95 (*0-671-69329-8*) S&S Trade.
Fairbank, Anna. Lucky Me! An Adoption Story. Weston, Martha, illus. LC 88-60649. 32p. (Orig.). (ps-1). 1988. pap. 8.95 (*0-945436-01-7*) Mariah Pr.
Fisher, Iris L. Katie-Bo: An Adoption Story. Schaer, Miriam, illus. (ps-3). 1988. 12.95 (*0-915361-91-4*) Modan-Adama Bks.
Gabel, Susan. Filling in the Blanks: A Guided Look at Growing up Adopted. Seregny, Julie, illus. 160p. (gr. 5-10). 1988. pap. 15.00 (*0-9609504-8-6*) Perspect Indiana.
Gay, Kathlyn. Adoption & Foster Care. LC 89-36476. (Illus.). 128p. (gr. 6 up). 1990. lib. bdg. 17.95 (*0-89490-239-3*) Enslow Pubs.
Girard, Linda W. Adoption Is for Always. Levine, Abby, ed. LC 86-15843. (Illus.). 32p. (gr. 1-5). 1986. PLB 11. 95 (*0-8075-0185-9*); pap. 4.95 (*0-8075-0187-5*) A Whitman.
Glotzbach, Gerri. Adoption. (Illus.). 64p. (gr. 7 up). 1990. lib. bdg. 17.27 (*0-86593-078-3*); lib. bdg. 12.95s.p. (*0-685-36294-9*) Rourke Corp.
Gravelle, Karen & Fischer, Susan. Where Are My Birth Parents? A Guide for Teenage Adoptees. LC 92-34586. 112p. (gr. 5 up). 1993. 14.95 (*0-8027-8257-4*); PLB 15.85 (*0-8027-8258-2*) Walker & Co.
Herbert, Stephanie. Being Adopted. (Illus.). 24p. 1991. 12.95 (*0-87868-478-6*, 4786) Child Welfare.
Koch, Janice. Our Baby: A Birth & Adoption Story. Goldberg, Pat, illus. LC 85-6392. 27p. (ps-2). 1985. 10.95 (*0-9609504-3-5*) Perspect Indiana.
LaCure, Jeffrey R. Adopted Like Me. 24p. (ps-2). 1993. pap. 9.95 (*0-9635717-0-2*) Adoption Advocate.
Lindsay, Jeanne W. Pregnant Too Soon: Adoption Is an Option. rev. ed. Morford, Pam P., illus. Monserrat, Catherine, frwd. by. LC 87-22042. (Illus.). 224p. (gr. 7-12). 1987. pap. 9.95 (*0-930934-25-3*); tchr's. guide 2.50 (*0-930934-27-X*) Morning Glory.
Livingston, Carole. Why Was I Adopted? Robins, Arthur, illus. (gr. 1 up). 1978. text ed. 12.00 (*0-8184-0257-1*) Carol Pub Group.
Lowe, Darla. Story of Adoption: Why Do I Look Different? Carney, Christina S., illus. LC 87-46273. (Orig.). (gr. 3-6). 1987. pap. 4.95 (*0-9606090-2-4*) EastWest Pr.
Miller, Kathryn M. Did My First Mother Love Me? A Story for an Adopted Child. Moffett, Jami, illus. 48p. (Orig.). (ps-3). 1994. 12.95 (*0-930934-85-7*); pap. 5.95 (*0-930934-84-9*) Morning Glory.
Nickman, Steven L. The Adoption Experiences. LC 85-8957. 192p. (gr. 7 up). 1985. lib. bdg. 14.98 (*0-671-50817-2*, J Messner) S&S Trade.
Peebles, Catherine & Edge, Denzil. A Natural Curiosity: Taffy's Search for Self. LC 87-36882. (Illus., Orig.). 1988. pap. 6.95 (*0-939991-01-2*) Learning KY.
Powledge, Fred. So You're Adopted. LC 81-23278. 112p. (gr. 5 up). 1982. SBE 13.95 (*0-684-17347-6*, Scribners Young Read) Macmillan Child Grp.
Rosenberg, Maxine B. Being Adopted. Ancona, George, photos by. LC 83-17522. (Illus.). 48p. (gr. 1-4). 1984. 13.95 (*0-688-02672-9*); lib. bdg. 13.88 (*0-688-02673-7*) Lothrop.
—Growing up Adopted. LC 89-9899. 128p. (gr. 4 up). 1989. SBE 14.95 (*0-02-777912-2*, Bradbury Pr) Macmillan Child Grp.
—Talking about Stepfamilies. Visher, Emily, afterword by. LC 90-33540. (Illus.). 160p. (gr. 4-7). 1990. SBE 14.95 (*0-02-777913-0*, Bradbury Pr) Macmillan Child Grp.
Silber, Kathleen & Parelskin, Debra M. My Special Family: A Children's Book about Open Adoption. Denman, Andrew, illus. 28p. (Orig.). (ps-4). 1994. pap. 12.95 (*0-9640009-1-1*); 12.95 (*0-9640009-4-6*) Open Adoption.
Stein, Sara B. The Adopted One. Stone, Erika, illus. (gr. k-6). 1979. 12.95 (*0-8027-6346-4*); pap. 7.95 (*0-8027-7224-2*) Walker & Co.
Stewart, Gail B. Adoption. LC 89-1525. (Illus.). 48p. (gr. 5-6). 1989. text ed. 12.95 RSBE (*0-89686-443-X*, Crestwood Hse) Macmillan Child Grp.

ADOPTION–FICTION

see also Foster Home Care–Fiction

Angel, Ann. Real for Sure Sister. LC 87-29217. (Illus.). 72p. (gr. 3-6). 1988. 10.95 (*0-9609504-7-8*) Perspect Indiana.
Auch, Mary J. A Sudden Change of Family. LC 90-55100. 112p. (gr. 3-7). 1990. 13.95 (*0-8234-0842-6*) Holiday.
Baer, Judy. Special Kind of Love. 1993. pap. 3.99 (*1-55661-367-9*) Bethany Hse.
Blomquist, Geraldine M. & Blomquist, Paul B. Zachary's New Home: A Story for Foster & Adopted Children. Lemieux, Margo, illus. LC 90-41914. 32p. (ps-2). 1990. 16.95 (*0-945354-28-2*); pap. 6.95 (*0-945354-27-4*) Magination Pr.
—Zachary's New Home: A Story for Foster & Adopted Children. Lemieux, Margo, illus. LC 92-56876. 1993. PLB 17.27 (*0-8368-0937-8*) Gareth Stevens Inc.
Bloom, Suzanne. A Family for Jamie: An Adoption Story. Bloom, Suzanne, illus. LC 90-42589. 24p. (ps-1). 1991. 13.00 (*0-517-57492-6*, Clarkson Potter); PLB 13.99 (*0-517-57493-4*, C N Potter Bks) Crown Bks Yng Read.
Blume, Judy. Are You There, God? It's Me, Margaret. (gr. 4-7). 1991. pap. 3.99 (*0-440-90419-6*, YB) Dell.
Boyd, Lizi. The Not-So-Wicked Stepmother. (Illus.). 32p. (ps-3). 1989. pap. 3.95 (*0-14-050720-5*, Puffin) Puffin Bks.
Braff Brodzinsky, Anne. The Mulberry Bird: Story of an Adoption. LC 86-2460. (Illus.). 48p. (gr. k-5). 1986. 10.95 (*0-9609504-5-1*) Perspect Indiana.
Corcoran, Barbara. Family Secrets. LC 91-13104. 176p. (gr. 3-7). 1992. SBE 13.95 (*0-689-31744-1*, Atheneum Child Bk) Macmillan Child Grp.
Dillon, Barbara. My Stepfather Shrank! Casale, Paul, illus. LC 91-23901. 128p. (gr. 3-6). 1994. pap. 3.95 (*0-06-440459-5*, Trophy) HarpC Child Bks.
Freudberg, Judy & Geiss, Tony. Susan & Gordon Adopt a Baby. Mathieu, Joe, illus. LC 86-2951. 24p. (ps-2). 1986. 8.99 (*0-394-88341-1*) Random Bks Yng Read.
Gabel, Susan L. Where the Sun Kisses the Sea. Bowring, Joanne, illus. LC 89-16296. 32p. (ps-5). 1989. 12.95 (*0-944934-00-5*) Perspect Indiana.
George, Jean C. Shark Beneath the Reef. LC 88-25194. 192p. (gr. 7 up). 1991. pap. 3.95 (*0-06-440308-4*, Trophy) HarpC Child Bks.
Haywood, Carolyn. Penny & Peter. rev. ed. Haywood, Carolyn & Yakovetic, Joe, illus. LC 46-21128. 160p. (gr. 1-5). 1986. pap. 4.95 (*0-15-260467-7*, Voyager Bks) HarBrace.
Holland, Isabelle. House in the Woods. 1991. 15.95 (*0-316-37178-5*) Little.
Horn, Tryntje. Nana's Adoption Farm: The Story of Little Rachell. Lacroix, Dana, illus. 40p. (gr. k-6). 1992. 16.95 (*0-9617426-8-2*) J N Townsend.
Howard, Ellen. Her Own Song. LC 88-3393. 176p. (gr. 3-7). 1988. SBE 14.95 (*0-689-31444-2*, Atheneum Child Bk) Macmillan Child Grp.
Keller, Holly. Horace. LC 90-30750. (Illus.). 32p. (ps up). 1991. 15.00 (*0-688-09831-2*); PLB 14.93 (*0-688-09832-0*) Greenwillow.
Koehler, Phoebe. The Day We Met You. LC 89-35344. 32p. (ps-k). 1990. SBE 14.00 (*0-02-750901-X*, Bradbury Pr) Macmillan Child Grp.
Lifton, Betty J. Tell Me a Real Adoption Story. LC 90-26506. (ps-3). 1994. 13.00 (*0-679-80629-6*); PLB 13. 99 (*0-679-90629-0*) Knopf Bks Yng Read.
London, Jonathan. A Koala for Katie. Jabar, Cynthia, illus. LC 93-16085. 1993. write for info. (*0-8075-4209-1*) A Whitman.
McCully, Emily A. My Real Family. LC 92-46290. 1994. 13.95 (*0-15-277698-2*, Browndeer Pr) HarBrace.
Magorian, Michelle. Good Night, Mr. Tom. LC 80-8444. 336p. (gr. 7 up). 1982. PLB 15.89 (*0-06-024079-2*) HarpC Child Bks.
Maguire, Gregory. Missing Sisters. LC 93-8300. 160p. (gr. 5-9). 1994. SBE 14.95 (*0-689-50590-6*, M K McElderry) Macmillan Child Grp.
Mills, Claudia. Boardwalk with Hotel. 144p. (gr. 7-12). 1986. pap. 2.50 (*0-553-15397-8*, Skylark) Bantam.
Myers, Walter D. Mop, Moondance, & the Nagasaki Knights. LC 91-36824. 160p. (gr. 3-7). 1992. 14.00 (*0-385-30687-3*) Delacorte.
Neufeld, John. Edgar Allan. Dunlap, Loren, illus. LC 68-31175. (gr. 5-8). 1968. 21.95 (*0-87599-149-1*) S G Phillips.
Nichols, Kathie. Sarah: A Story of Love & Adoption. Nichols, Fran, illus. 32p. (Orig.). (gr. 2-4). 1992. pap. 6.95 (*0-943861-21-7*) Lone Tree.
Pellegrini, Nina. Families Are Different. Pellegrini, Nina, illus. LC 90-22876. 32p. (ps-3). 1991. reinforced bdg. 15.95 (*0-8234-0887-6*) Holiday.
Rosen, Michael J. Bonesy & Isabel. Ransome, James E., illus. LC 93-7892. 1995. write for info. (*0-15-209813-5*) HarBrace.
Sachs, Marilyn. What My Sister Remembered. LC 91-32263. 120p. (gr. 5-9). 1992. 15.00 (*0-525-44953-1*, DCB) Dutton Child Bks.
Schnitter, Jane. William Is My Brother. LC 90-21364. (Illus.). 32p. (ps-3). 1991. 10.95 (*0-944934-03-X*) Perspect Indiana.
Shope, Kimberly A. A Bear Named Song: The Gift of a Lifetime. (Illus.). 32p. 1992. 11.99 (*0-87403-865-0*, 24-03565) Standard Pub.
Simon, Sherry & Fischman, Debra. Where Gardens Grow: An Adoption Story for Children. 1994. 7.95 (*0-533-10829-2*) Vantage.
Stahl, Hilda. Kayla O'Brian: Trouble at Bitter Creek Ranch. 128p. (Orig.). (gr. 4-7). 1991. pap. 4.95 (*0-89107-611-5*) Crossway Bks.

Stein, Stephanie. Lucy's Feet. Imler, Kathryn A., illus. LC 92-4602. 32p. (ps-3). 1992. 12.95 (*0-944934-05-6*) Perspect Indiana.

Stinson, Kathy. Steven's Baseball Mitt: A Book about Being Adopted. Lewis, Robin B., illus. 32p. (ps-4). 1992. PLB 14.95 (*1-55037-233-5*, Pub. by Annick CN); pap. 4.95 (*1-55037-232-7*, Pub. by Annick CN) Firefly Bks Ltd.

Swartley, David W. My Friend, My Brother. Converse, James, illus. LC 79-26273. 104p. (gr. 6 up). 1980. pap. 3.95 (*0-8361-1916-9*) Herald Pr.

Turner, Ann. Through Moon & Stars & Night Skies. Hale, James G., illus. LC 87-35044. 32p. (ps-3). 1990. 13.00 (*0-06-026189-7*); PLB 12.89 (*0-06-026190-0*) HarpC Child Bks.

Viglucci, Pat C. Cassandra Robbins, Esq. 176p. (Orig.). (gr. 8-12). 1987. pap. 4.95 (*0-938961-01-2*, Stamp Out Sheep Pr) Sq One Pubs.

Wasson, Valentina P. The Chosen Baby. 3rd ed. LC 76-41391. (gr. k-3). 1977. 15.00 (*0-397-31738-7*, Lipp Jr Bks) HarpC Child Bks.

Wright, Betty R. The Scariest Night. LC 91-55030. 166p. (gr. 3-7). 1991. 14.95 (*0-8234-0904-X*) Holiday.

ADULTHOOD

Doolittle, Hilda. The Hedgehog. Schaffner, Perdita, intro. by. Plank, George, illus. LC 88-3927. 96p. 1988. 12.95 (*0-8112-1069-3*) New Directions.

Liptak, Karen. Coming-of-Age: Traditions & Rituals Around the World. LC 93-1414. (Illus.). 128p. (gr. 7 up). 1994. PLB 15.90 (*1-56294-243-3*) Millbrook Pr.

Sinclair-House, Elizabeth & Muir, Alison. Adulthood. LC 90-28921. (Illus.). 64p. (gr. 5-9). 1991. PLB 11.95 (*0-8114-7806-8*) Raintree Steck-V.

ADVENTURE AND ADVENTURERS

see also Discoveries (In Geography); Escapes; Explorers; Frontier and Pioneer Life; Heroes; Sea Stories; Seafaring Life; Shipwrecks; Underwater Exploration; Voyages and Travels

Alwin-Hill, Raymond. Treasure Island. LC 91-52607. (Orig.). 1991. pap. 6.00 (*0-88734-412-7*) Players Pr.

Anderson, Peter. Into the Unknown: Major Powells River Journey. (Illus.). 32p. (Orig.). (gr. 4-7). 1992. pap. 5.95 (*1-56044-133-X*) Falcon Pr MT.

Armstrong, Beverly. Pirates, Explorers, Tailblazers. 112p. (gr. 4-6). 1987. 9.95 (*0-88160-152-7*, LW 908) Learning Wks.

Birenbaum, Barbara. The Gooblins Night. Birenbaum, Barbara, illus. LC 85-62585. 44p. (gr. 2-5). 1985. 10.95 (*0-935343-32-6*); pap. 5.95 (*0-935343-31-8*) Peartree.

Boga, Steve. On Their Own: Adventure Athletes in Solo Sports, 3 bks. Kratoville, B. L., ed. (Illus.). (gr. 3-9). 1992. Set, 64p. ea. bk. pap. text ed. 11.00 (*0-87879-928-1*); wkbk. 12.50 (*0-87879-929-X*) High Noon Bks.

Boy Scouts of America Staff. Venture Discovering Adventure. (Illus.). 20p. 1990. pap. 3.15 (*0-8395-3472-8*, 33472) BSA.

Clifford, Eth. Harvey's Wacky Parrot Adventure. MacDonald, Patricia, ed. 128p. 1991. pap. 2.95 (*0-671-72908-X*, Minstrel Bks) PB.

Cole, Joanna. Riding the Magic School Bus with Joanna Cole & Bruce Degen. 1993. pap. 39.95 (*0-590-45904-X*) Scholastic Inc.

Danielson, Peter. The Golden Pharoah. 416p. (Orig.). 1986. pap. 4.95 (*0-553-26885-6*) Bantam.

Dixon, Franklin W. Panic on Gull Island. 160p. (Orig.). 1991. pap. 3.99 (*0-671-69276-3*, Minstrel Bks) PB.

Donev, Stef. Amazing Adventures. Hughes, Mark, illus. 48p. (gr. 5-9). 1985. pap. 5.95 (*0-88625-093-5*) Durkin Hayes Pub.

Duggleby, John. Doomed Expeditions. LC 89-25459. (Illus.). 48p. (gr. 5-6). 1990. text ed. 11.95 RSBE (*0-89686-506-1*, Crestwood Hse) Macmillan Child Grp.

—Impossible Quests. LC 89-28988. (Illus.). 48p. (gr. 5-6). 1990. text ed. 11.95 RSBE (*0-89686-509-6*, Crestwood Hse) Macmillan Child Grp.

Dumas, Alexandre. The Three Musketeers. unabridged ed. Bair, Lowell, tr. from FRE. 560p. 1984. pap. 5.95 (*0-553-21337-7*, Bantam Classics) Bantam.

Eager, George B. Explorers. (Illus.). 128p. (gr. 8-10). 1993. pap. 4.95 (*1-879224-16-X*) Mailbox.

Estes, James L. Alabama's Youngest Admirals. Krauel, Mary E., ed. Christian, Releta, illus. 132p. (Orig.). (gr. 4-12). 1991. pap. 8.95 (*0-9628634-0-8*) J L Estes.

Field, Rachel. Calico Bush. (gr. 4-8). 1988. pap. 3.50 (*0-440-40100-3*, YB) Dell.

Foster, Janet. A Cabin Full of Mice. (Illus.). 36p. (gr. 2 up). 1992. pap. 4.95 (*0-919872-66-2*, Pub. by Greey de Pencier CN) Firefly Bks Ltd.

Goold, I. The Rutan Voyager. (Illus.). 32p. (gr. 4 up). 1988. PLB 17.27 (*0-86592-869-X*); lib. bdg. 12.95 (*0-685-58288-4*) Rourke Corp.

Guillot, Rene. Wind of Chance. Dale, Norman, tr. Collot, Pierre, illus. (gr. 6-9). 1958. 21.95 (*0-87599-048-7*) S G Phillips.

Johnson, Annabel & Johnson, Edgar. The Grizzly. Riswold, Gilbert, illus. LC 64-11831. 194p. (gr. 5-9). 1973. pap. 3.95 (*0-06-440036-0*, Trophy) HarpC Child Bks.

Kehret, Peg. Nightmare Mountain. MacDonald, Patricia, ed. 176p. (Orig.). 1991. pap. 3.99 (*0-671-72864-4*, Minstrel Bks) PB.

Kelly, Terry, et al. Daring Deeds. Gagne, Dennis, illus. 48p. (gr. 5-9). 1985. pap. 5.95 (*0-88625-092-7*) Durkin Hayes Pub.

Kramer, Emmanuel M. Start Exploring Places of Mystery. Driggs, Helen I., illus. 128p. (Orig.). (gr. 3 up). 1994. pap. text ed. 8.95 (*1-56138-193-4*) Running Pr.

McCaughren, Tom. Run to Earth. (Illus.). 144p. (ps-8). 1988. pap. 8.95 (*0-86327-116-2*, Pub. by Wolfhound Press Eire) Dufour.

McClung, Robert M. The True Adventures of Grizzly Adams. LC 85-8886. (Illus.). 208p. (gr. 5 up). 1985. 11.95 (*0-688-05794-2*) Morrow Jr Bks.

Masters, Anthony, compiled by. Heroic Stories. Molan, Chris, illus. LC 93-45413. 256p. (gr. 5-10). 1994. 6.95 (*1-85697-983-0*, Kingfisher LKC) LKC.

Melanos, Jack. Sinbad & the Evil Genii. (Orig.). (gr. k up). 1985. pap. 4.50 (*0-87602-251-4*) Anchorage.

Monro, Louise. Forest of Fear. Packard, Edward, created by. 128p. (Orig.). (gr. 4). 1986. pap. 2.25 (*0-553-25490-1*) Bantam.

Morey, Walt. Angry Waters. Spillman, Fredicka, illus. (Orig.). (gr. 5-9). 1990. Repr. 7.95 (*0-936085-10-X*) Blue Heron OR.

Morris, Deborah. Real Kids, Real Adventures. LC 94-11741. 112p. (gr. 3-10). 1994. 5.99 (*0-8054-4051-8*, 4240-51) Broadman.

Nottridge, Rhoda. Adventure Films. LC 91-25839. (Illus.). 32p. (gr. 5). 1992. text ed. 13.95 RSBE (*0-89686-718-8*, Crestwood Hse) Macmillan Child Grp.

O'Hare, Jeff. Globe Probe: Exciting Geographical Adventures All Around the World. 32p. (gr. 4-7). 1993. 10.95 (*1-56397-037-6*) Boyds Mills Pr.

Paulsen, Gary. Sentries. LC 85-26978. 160p. (gr. 7 up). 1986. SBE 14.95 (*0-02-770100-X*, Bradbury Pr) Macmillan Child Grp.

Rappaport, Doreen. Living Dangerously: American Women Who Risked Their Lives for Adventure. LC 90-28915. (Illus.). 128p. (gr. 4-7). 1991. 14.00 (*0-06-025108-5*); PLB 13.89 (*0-06-025109-3*) HarpC Child Bks.

Rathert, Donna. Advent Is for Waiting. (Illus.). 24p. (ps). 1987. pap. 2.99 (*0-570-04140-6*, 56-1569) Concordia.

Rawlinson, J. Space to Seabed. (Illus.). 32p. (gr. 4 up). 1988. PLB 17.27 (*0-86592-872-X*); s.p. 12.95 (*0-685-58292-2*) Rourke Corp.

Razzi, Jim, adapted by. The Jungle Book. 48p. (Orig.). (gr. 4). 1986. pap. 4.95 (*0-553-05409-0*) Bantam.

Ripley, Robert L. Incredible Journeys. Stott, Carol, illus. 48p. (gr. 3-6). Date not set. PLB 12.95 (*1-56065-129-6*) Capstone Pr.

Roddy, Lee. Secret of the Shark Pit. 136p. (Orig.). (gr. 3-6). 1989. pap. 4.99 (*0-929608-14-3*) Focus Family.

Rudig, Doug. Big Bend Adventure Guide. Pearson, John R. & Deckert, Frank J., eds. (Illus.). 32p. (Orig.). (gr. k-6). 1983. pap. 2.00 (*0-912001-10-0*) Big Bend.

Sharp, Margery. The Rescuers. (gr. 3-6). 17.00 (*0-8446-6412-X*) Peter Smith.

Sonnleitner, A. T. Cave Children. Bell, Anthea, tr. from GER. LC 70-120785. (Illus.). (gr. 8 up). 1971. 21.95 (*0-87599-169-6*) S G Phillips.

Sweetgall, Robert & Peleg, Dorith E. Road Scholars: The Story of Twenty-Eight Kids Who Decided to Take a Hike for Their Health. (Illus.). 64p. (Orig.). 1989. pap. 20.00 (*0-939041-07-3*) Creative Walking.

Thompson, Jonathon J., Jr. Air Raiders. (Illus.). 75p. (gr. 6-12). 1992. 4.50 (*0-933479-02-6*) Thompson.

—Superflyer: Captain John Champion Flyer. 40p. (gr. 3-6). 1992. 3.95 (*0-933479-08-5*) Thompson.

Ware, Derek. Stunt Performers. Stefoff, Rebecca, ed. LC 91-41209. (Illus.). 32p. (gr. 5-9). 1992. PLB 17.26 (*1-56074-045-0*) Garrett Ed Corp.

ADVENTURE AND ADVENTURERS–FICTION

Abbott, Tony. Danger Guys. Scribner, Joanne, illus. LC 93-29799. 80p. (gr. 2-5). 1994. pap. 3.95 (*0-06-440519-2*, Trophy) HarpC Child Bks.

Aber, Linda W. Lost Girls Adrift. 176p. (gr. 3-7). 1991. pap. 2.75 (*0-590-43536-1*, Apple Paperbacks) Scholastic Inc.

Ackerman, Karen. The Night Crossing. Sayles, Elizabeth, illus. 64p. (gr. 2-5). 1994. 14.00 (*0-679-83169-X*) Knopf Bks Yng Read.

Adair, Dennis & Rosenstock, Janet. The Journey Begins, No. 1. (gr. 3-7). 1992. pap. 3.99 (*0-553-48027-8*, Skylark) Bantam.

Adler, C. S. The Silver Coach. 112p. (gr. 3-7). 1988. pap. 2.50 (*0-380-75498-3*, Camelot) Avon.

Adler, David A. Cam Jansen & the Mystery of the Gold Coins. Natti, Susanna, illus. 64p. (gr. k-6). 1984. pap. 2.75 (*0-440-40996-9*, YB) Dell.

Adventure Classics: Robin Hood. 1991. 4.99 (*0-517-06523-1*) Random Hse Value.

Adventure with Crom. (Illus.). (ps-2). 1991. PLB 6.95 (*0-8136-5162-X*, TK3829); pap. 3.50 (*0-8136-5662-1*, TK3830) Modern Curr.

Adventures, No. 2. 1987. pap. 1.25 (*0-440-82087-1*) Dell.

The Adventures of Jason Ashley. (gr. 4-6). 1990. 1.55 (*0-89636-119-5*) Accent CO.

Adventures of Tom Sawyer. 1993. pap. text ed. 6.50 (*0-582-09677-4*, 79814) Longman.

Ahern, Jerry & Ahern, Sharon. The Defender, No. 3. (Orig.). 1988. pap. 3.50 (*0-318-33285-X*) Dell.

Aiken, Joan. Bridle the Wind. LC 83-5355. 224p. (gr. 7 up). 1983. 14.95 (*0-385-29301-1*) Delacorte.

—Is Underground. LC 92-27423. 1993. 15.00 (*0-385-30898-1*) Delacorte.

Albertson, Jon. Falklands Fiasco. Hooper, Anne, ed. Pheris, William E., IV, illus. 284p. (gr. 12). 1989. 16.95 (*0-9621448-1-9*) Aeolus Bks.

—Valley of the Condor. Hooper, Anne, ed. 300p. (gr. 12). 1990. write for info. (*0-9621448-3-5*) Aeolus Bks.

Alcock, Vivien. Singer to the Sea God. LC 92-9832. 1993. 15.00 (*0-385-30866-3*) Delacorte.

Alexander, Lloyd. Book of Three. Date not set. write for info. H Holt & Co.

—The Drackenberg Adventure. (gr. k-6). 1990. pap. 3.50 (*0-440-40296-4*, Pub. by Yearling Classics) Dell.

—The Drackenburg Adventure. LC 87-36881. 160p. (gr. 5-9). 1988. 12.95 (*0-525-44389-4*, 01258-370, DCB) Dutton Child Bks.

—The El Dorado Adventure. LC 86-29157. 176p. (gr. 5-9). 1987. 13.95 (*0-525-44313-4*, DCB) Dutton Child Bks.

—The Illyrian Adventure. LC 85-30762. (Illus.). 160p. (gr. 5-9). 1986. 13.95 (*0-525-44250-2*, DCB) Dutton Child Bks.

—The Illyrian Adventure. (gr. k-12). 1987. pap. 3.50 (*0-440-94018-4*, LFL) Dell.

—The Jedera Adventure. LC 88-38865. 160p. (gr. 5-9). 1989. 13.95 (*0-525-44481-5*, DCB) Dutton Child Bks.

—The Jedera Adventure. 1990. pap. 3.99 (*0-440-40295-6*, YB) Dell.

—Marvelous Misadventures of Sebastian. LC 70-166879. (gr. 4 up). 1973. 14.95 (*0-525-34739-9*, DCB); (DCB) Dutton Child Bks.

—The Philadelphia Adventure. LC 89-34990. 160p. (gr. 5-9). 1990. 13.95 (*0-525-44564-1*, DCB) Dutton Child Bks.

—The Remarkable Journey of Prince Jen. LC 91-13720. 288p. (gr. 5 up). 1991. 15.00 (*0-525-44826-8*, DCB) Dutton Child Bks.

Allard, Harry. Bumps in the Night. Marshall, James, illus. 48p. (gr. 1-4). 1984. pap. 2.25 (*0-553-15284-X*, Skylark) Bantam.

Allston, Aaron. Mythic Greece: Age of Heroes. Charlton, Coleman, ed. Loubet, Dennis, illus. 160p. (Orig.). (gr. 10-12). 1988. pap. 12.00 (*1-55806-002-2*, 1020) Iron Crown Ent Inc.

Altsheler, Joseph A. After the Battle. rev. ed. (gr. 9-12). 1989. Repr. of 1905 ed. multi-media kit 35.00 (*0-685-31125-2*) Balance Pub.

—The Forest Runners. 300p. 1990. 13.95 (*0-929146-04-2*) Voyageur Pub.

Amthor, Terry K. Action on Akaisha Outstation. 32p. (gr. 10-12). 1985. 6.00 (*0-915795-46-9*, 9101) Iron Crown Ent Inc.

Anderson, C. W. Blaze & the Mountain Lion: Billy & Blaze to the Rescue. Anderson, C. W., illus. LC 92-27148. 48p. (gr. k-3). 1993. pap. 3.95 (*0-689-71711-3*, Aladdin) Macmillan Child Grp.

Ansell, Rod & Percy, Rachel. To Fight the Wild. LC 85-22023. (Illus.). 156p. (gr. 7 up). 1986. 12.95 (*0-15-289068-8*, HB Juv Bks) HarBrace.

Apple, Victor, II. Tom Swift: The Astral Fortress. (gr. 5-6). 18.95 (*0-88411-461-9*, Pub. by Aeonian Pr) Amereon Ltd.

Appleton, Victor. The Black Dragon. Greenberg, Anne, ed. 176p. (Orig.). 1991. pap. 2.95 (*0-671-67823-X*, Archway) PB.

—The Invisible Force. Barish, Wendy, ed. 192p. (Orig.). (gr. 3-8). 1983. 8.50 (*0-671-43958-8*) S&S Trade.

—Monster Machine. Greenberg, Anne, ed. 160p. (Orig.). 1991. pap. 2.99 (*0-671-67827-2*, Archway) PB.

—Moonstalker. Greenberg, Ann, ed. 160p. (Orig.). 1992. pap. 2.99 (*0-671-75645-1*) PB.

—The Negative Zone. Greenberg, Anne, ed. 176p. (Orig.). 1991. pap. 2.95 (*0-671-67824-8*, Archway) PB.

—The Tom Swift Gift Set, 3 vols. Boxed Set. pap. 7.95 (*0-317-12430-7*) S&S Trade.

Appleton, Victor, II. Tom Swift & His Electronic Electroscope. (gr. 5-6). 18.95 (*0-88411-462-7*, Pub. by Aeonian Pr) Amereon Ltd.

—Tom Swift & His Space Solatron. (gr. 5-6). 18.95 (*0-88411-457-0*, Pub. by Aeonian Pr) Amereon Ltd.

—Tom Swift & His Triphibian Atomicar. (gr. 5-6). 17.95 (*0-88411-459-7*, Pub. by Aeonian Pr) Amereon Ltd.

—Tom Swift: Terror on the Moons of Jupiter. (gr. 5-6). 18.95 (*0-88411-460-0*, Pub. by Aeonian Pr) Amereon Ltd.

—Tom Swift: The Alien Probe. (gr. 5-6). 18.95 (*0-88411-464-3*, Pub. by Aeonian Pr) Amereon Ltd.

—Tom Swift: The City in the Stars. (gr. 5-6). 18.95 (*0-88411-463-5*, Pub. by Aeonian Pr) Amereon Ltd.

—Tom Swift: The Rescue Mission. (gr. 5-6). 18.95 (*0-88411-458-9*, Pub. by Aeonian Pr) Amereon Ltd.

—Tom Swift: The Water in Outer Space. (gr. 5-6). 17.95 (*0-88411-465-1*, Pub. by Aeonian Pr) Amereon Ltd.

Aragones, Sergio & Zone, Ray. Aragones 3-D. Aragones, Sergio, illus. 64p. (Orig.). (gr. 9-12). 1989. pap. 4.95 (*0-317-93126-1*) Three-D Zone.

Ardizzone, Edward. The Little Tim & Brave Sea Captain. (Illus.). 48p. (ps-3). 1983. pap. 3.99 (*0-14-050175-4*, Puffin) Puffin Bks.

Argaman, Shmuel. The Captivity of Mahram. Henlicky, Gregg, illus. LC 90-83947. 120p. (gr. 3-5). 1990. 11.95 (*1-56062-045-5*); pap. 8.95 (*0-685-46904-2*) CIS Comm.

Arnold, Eugene. Big Water: Flight to Okeechobee. Siegrist, Wes, illus. LC 92-61845. 201p. (gr. 12). 1993. pap. 12.95 (*0-9628828-2-8*) Prospector Pr.

Arrick, Fran. God's Radar. 224p. (gr. 6-12). 1986. pap. 2.95 (*0-440-92960-1*, LFL) Dell.

Asch, Frank. Skyfire. Asch, Frank, illus. LC 88-3193. 32p. (ps-2). 1988. (Little Simon); pap. 4.95 (*0-671-66861-7*, Little Simon) S&S Trade.

Ashby, Ruth, ed. Nintendo Book, No. 4: Koopa Kapers. 128p. (Orig.). 1991. pap. 3.50 (*0-671-74202-7*, Archway) PB.
Ashwill, Beverley. The Blue-Eyed Ninja Warrior. Ashwill, Betty J., illus. LC 90-83313. 43p. (gr. 3-9). 1990. pap. 5.98 (*0-941381-05-6*) BJO Enterprises.
Auch, Mary J. Kidnapping Kevin Kowalski. 1992. pap. 2.95 (*0-590-44335-6*, Apple Paperbacks) Scholastic Inc.
Avi. Shadrach's Crossing. LC 82-19008. 192p. (gr. 5 up). 1983. 10.95 (*0-394-85816-6*) Pantheon.
—Windcatcher. 128p. 1992. pap. 3.99 (*0-380-71805-7*, Camelot) Avon.
Ayme, Marcel. Mauvais Jars. Sabatier, C. & Sabatier, R., illus. (FRE.). 72p. (gr. 1-5). 1990. pap. 10.95 (*2-07-031236-4*) Schoenhof.
Babbitt, Natalie. Cuentos del Pobre Diablo. (gr. 4-7). 1994. 13.00 (*0-374-31769-0*, Mirasol); pap. 4.95 (*0-374-41624-9*, Mirasol) FS&G.
—The Eyes of the Amaryllis. 128p. (gr. 3 up). 1986. pap. 3.95 (*0-374-42238-9*, Sunburst) FS&G.
Bach, Jennifer & Brost, Amy. The Great Zopper Toothpaste Treasure. 64p. (Orig.). (gr. 5 up). 1988. pap. 2.50 (*0-553-15583-0*, Skylark) Bantam.
Bader, Bonnie. Big Strike at Spindletop. 80p. (gr. 4-6). 1994. PLB 12.95 (*1-881889-60-2*) Silver Moon.
Bagdon, Paul. Scrapper John: Rendezvous at Skull Mountain. 128p. (Orig.). 1992. pap. 3.50 (*0-380-76418-0*, Camelot) Avon.
Baker, Carin G. To Catch a Thief! LC 92-39517. 144p. (gr. 3-7). 1993. pap. 3.50 (*0-14-036291-6*) Puffin Bks.
Baker, Michael K. The Sword. LC 84-90678. 303p. (gr. 5up). 1985. text ed. 8.00 (*0-932543-01-4*); pap. 8.00 (*0-932543-00-6*) M B Pub.
Baldry, Cherith. Cradoc's Quest. Reck, Sue, ed. 160p. (gr. 8-12). Date not set. pap. 4.99 (*0-7814-0093-7*, Chariot Bks) Chariot Family.
—Storm Wind. Reck, Sue, ed. 160p. (gr. 8-12). Date not set. pap. 4.99 (*0-7814-0095-3*, Chariot Bks) Chariot Family.
Ball, Duncan. Emily Eyefinger & the Lost Treasure. Ulrich, George, illus. LC 93-39648. (gr. 2-5). 1994. 13. 00 (*0-671-86535-8*, S&S BFYR) S&S Trade.
Ball, Karen. Choice Adventures: Hazardous Homestead. 160p. (gr. 4-8). 1992. pap. text ed. 4.99 (*0-8423-5032-2*) Tyndale.
—The Overnight Ordeal. LC 93-40182. 1994. 4.99 (*0-8423-5134-5*) Tyndale.
Balmer, Helen. Jungle Adventure. (ps-6). 1993. pap. 14. 00 (*0-671-86768-7*, S&S BFYR) S&S Trade.
Bang, Molly. Yellow Ball. Bang, Molly, illus. LC 90-46077. 24p. (ps up). 1991. 55.99 (*0-688-06314-4*); PLB 12.88 (*0-688-06315-2*, Morrow Jr Bks) Morrow Jr Bks.
Bannister, Ned. Code Name: North Star. (gr. 4 up). 1989. pap. 2.95 (*0-345-35921-6*) Ballantine.
Bannon, Troy. Air Walk. (gr. 4-7). 1991. pap. 2.99 (*0-440-40532-7*, YB) Dell.
—Power Grind. (gr. 4-7). 1992. pap. 2.99 (*0-440-40559-9*) Dell.
Barchas. I Was Walking down the Road. 1993. pap. 28.67 (*0-590-71883-5*) Scholastic Inc.
Baroness Orczy. The Scarlet Pimpernel. (gr. k-6). 1989. pap. 3.50 (*0-440-40220-4*, YB) Dell.
Bashful Bard. Search for Rainbow's End. Bashful Bard, illus. LC 89-84962. 28p. (Orig.). (ps-1). 1989. pap. 3.99 (*1-877906-01-8*) Kenney Pubns.
Batman. (Illus.). 24p. (ps up). 1992. deluxe ed. write for info. incl. long-life batteries (*0-307-74023-4*, 64023, Golden Pr) Western Pub.
Baum, L. Frank. Sky Island. Neill, John R., illus. 288p. (gr. 3 up). 1988. 19.95 (*0-929605-02-0*); pap. 11.95 (*0-929605-01-2*) Books Wonder.
Bawden, Nina. The Finding. (gr. k-6). 1988. pap. 2.95 (*0-440-40004-X*) Dell.
—White Horse Gang. Bawden, Nina, illus. 176p. (gr. 4-7). 1992. 13.95 (*0-395-58709-3*, Clarion Bks) HM.
Beasley, Sterling. Captain Miraculous & the Bound for Glory Kid. (Illus.). 32p. (Orig.). 1993. pap. 4.95 (*0-8059-3421-9*) Dorrance.
Beckett, Jim. Incan Gold. 176p. (Orig.). 1988. pap. 2.50 (*0-553-27415-5*) Bantam.
Bell, Clare. Ratha's Creature. (gr. k-12). 1987. pap. 2.95 (*0-440-97298-1*, LFL) Dell.
—Tomorrow's Sphinx. (gr. k-12). 1988. pap. 3.25 (*0-440-20124-1*, LFL) Dell.
Bell, Sally. The Young Indiana Jones Chronicles: Safari in Africa. Vincente, Gonzalez, illus. 48p. (gr. 2-4). 1992. pap. write for info. (*0-307-11470-8*, 11470, Golden Pr) Western Pub.
Bell, William. Forbidden City. (gr. 7 up). 1990. 14.95 (*0-553-07131-9*, Starfire); pap. 3.99 (*0-553-28864-4*, Starfire) Bantam.
Bellairs, John. The Lamp from the Warlock's Tomb. LC 87-21404. 176p. (gr. 5 up). 1988. 12.95 (*0-8037-0512-3*) Dial Bks Young.
Benedict, Rex. Run for Your Sweet Life. Christiana, David, illus. LC 86-45507. 128p. (gr. 5 up). 1986. 14. 00 (*0-374-36359-5*) FS&G.
Bennett, Cherie. Sunset Stranger: It's a Strange World. 224p. (Orig.). 1994. pap. text ed. 3.99 (*0-425-14129-2*) Berkley Pub.
Ben-Vri, Galilia. Hijacked. 190p. 1993. 12.95 (*0-685-66698-0*) CIS Comm.
Bibee, John. The Spirit Flyers Series, 4 bks, Set A. Turnbaugh, Paul, illus. (Orig.). 1992. Boxed Set. pap. 24.99 (*0-8308-1208-3*, 1208) InterVarsity.
—The Spirit Flyers Series, 4 bks, Set B. Turnbaugh, Paul, illus. (Orig.). 1993. Set. pap. 24.99 boxed (*0-8308-1289-X*, 1289) InterVarsity.
Bicknell, Arthur. Scavenger's Hunt. (Orig.). (gr. k-12). 1987. pap. 2.95 (*0-440-97672-3*, LFL) Dell.
Biggar, Joan R. Shipwreck on the Lights. 160p. (Orig.). (gr. 5-8). 1992. pap. 3.99 (*0-570-04710-2*) Concordia.
Billac, Pete. The Annihilator: All Must Die. Davis, Sharon K., ed. LC 80-85318. 176p. (Orig.). (gr. 12 up). 1987. pap. 1.95 (*0-317-67266-5*) Swan Pub.
Bischof, Larry & Lowry, William B. Amazon Adventure. LC 92-12844. (gr. 2). 1992. 13.99 (*1-56239-150-X*) Abdo & Dghtrs.
The Black Cauldron. 96p. 1990. 6.98 (*1-57082-035-X*) Mouse Works.

Blake, Doron W. The Adventure of George the Dinosaur (La Adventura de Jorge il Dinosaurio) Lucas, Winafred B., ed. Gremard, Anna, tr. Gremard, David, illus. 32p. (gr. k-3). 1994. English ed. 11.95 (*1-882530-04-7*); Spanish ed. 11.95 (*1-882530-05-5*) Deep Forest Pr.
This book relates the delightful adventure of a small dinosaur named George who wanted to know if spooks were real. When his mother & grandmother would not tell him, he went out into the forest to find out for himself. His journey took him into unusual situations & won him interesting friends. The story suggests the rewards to a child when he reaches out in expanded states of awareness. Doron Blake, now eleven, typed out the original draft of this story when he was six years old. At ten, he edited it & put it on computer. As the first boy born from the Nobel Prize Sperm Bank, he gives frequent magazine & TV interviews. David Gremard was named one of the top artists in the 1993 high school graduation class in California & drew the illustrations for the book when he was 17. Together, the boys worked on many details of the adventure, each suggesting to the other small embellishments of the original story so that the result is a sparkling fusion of painting & narrative. Available from Deep Forest Press, P.O. Drawer 4, Crest Park, CA 92326 (909-337-1179) or from Bookpeople.
Publisher Provided Annotation.

Blanchette, Rick. Choice Adventure: Class Project Showdown. LC 92-30501. 1993. 4.99 (*0-8423-5047-0*) Tyndale.
Blyton, Enid. Five Fall Into Adventure. large type ed. (gr. 1-8). 1994. sewn 16.95 (*0-7451-2089-X*, Galaxy Child Lrg Print) Chivers N Amer.
Board, Sherri L. Ambrosia & the Coral Sun. Board, Timothy A., ed. Barnes-Million, Kathy, illus. LC 93-61236. 256p. (Orig.). 1994. pap. 8.95 (*0-9634767-7-7*) Tug Pr CA.
Bodie, Idella. The Mystery of the Pirate's Treasure. Yancey, Louise, illus. LC 72-94930. 136p. (gr. 4-6). 1984. pap. 6.95 (*0-87844-059-3*) Sandlapper Pub Co.
—Stranded! Sookikian, Charles J., illus. LC 84-14098. 132p. (Orig.). (gr. 4-6). 1984. pap. 6.95 (*0-87844-060-7*) Sandlapper Pub Co.
Bohl, Al. Zaanan: The Dream of Delasor. (Illus.). 224p. (gr. 3 up). 1990. pap. 2.50 (*1-55748-124-5*) Barbour & Co.
Bond, Nancy. A String on the Harp. (gr. 5-9). 1987. pap. 5.99 (*0-14-032376-7*, Puffin) Puffin Bks.
Bond, Ruskin. The Hidden Pool. Das, Arup, illus. 64p. (Orig.). (gr. k-3). 1980. pap. 2.75 (*0-89744-211-3*, Pub. by Childrens Bk Trust IA) Auromere.
Bosco, Clyde. Pipe Down. Ashby, Ruth, ed. 128p. (Orig.). 1991. pap. 3.50 (*0-671-74203-5*, Archway) PB.
Bosse, Malcolm. Captives of Time. LC 86-32943. 256p. (gr. 7 up). 1987. pap. 14.95 (*0-385-29583-9*) Delacorte.
—Captives of Time. (gr. k-12). 1989. pap. 3.50 (*0-440-20311-2*, LFL) Dell.
Bowkett, Stephen. Dualists. (gr. 5-8). 1990. pap. 17.95 (*0-575-04106-4*, Pub. by Gollancz UK) Trafalgar.
Boyd, John R. & Boyd, Mary A. Input - Output. (Illus.). 272p. (Orig.). (gr. 7-12). 1989. pap. 8.95 (*0-933759-14-2*); 4.95 (*0-933759-15-0*); cassette tape set 29.95 (*0-933759-16-9*) Abaca Bks.
Bradman, Tony. The Bluebeards: Adventure on Skull Island. Murphy, Rowan B., illus. 64p. (gr. 3-6). 1990. pap. 2.95 (*0-8120-4421-5*) Barron.
Bradshaw, Gillian. The Dragon & the Thief. LC 90-48259. (Illus.). (gr. 5 up). 1991. 13.95 (*0-688-10575-0*) Greenwillow.
Brandenberg, Franz. Leo & Emily's Big Idea. (gr. k-6). 1990. pap. 2.95 (*0-440-40302-2*, Pub. by Yearling Classics) Dell.
Breathed, Berkeley. The Last Basselope: One Ferocious Story. LC 92-14467. (Illus.). 1992. 14.95 (*0-316-10761-1*) Little.
Brennan, J. H. The Gateway of Doom. (Orig.). (gr. k-12). 1987. pap. 2.50 (*0-440-92800-1*, LFL) Dell.
—Realm of Chaos. (Orig.). (gr. k-12). 1987. pap. 2.50 (*0-440-97325-2*, LFL) Dell.
—Shiva Accused: An Adventure of the Ice Age. LC 90-25888. 288p. (gr. 5 up). 1993. pap. 4.95 (*0-06-440431-5*, Trophy) HarpC Child Bks.
Brightfield, Richard. African Safari. (gr. 4-7). 1993. pap. 3.25 (*0-553-29953-0*) Bantam.
—Behind the Great Wall. (gr. 4-7). 1993. pap. 3.25 (*0-553-56103-0*) Bantam.
—Curse of Batterslea. 1984. pap. 1.95 (*0-553-23937-6*) Bantam.
—The Curse of Batterslea Hall, No. 30. 128p. (gr. 4 up). 1984. pap. 2.25 (*0-553-26374-9*) Bantam.
—The Deadly Shadow. 128p. (Orig.). (gr. 4 up). 1985. pap. 2.25 (*0-553-25498-7*) Bantam.
—The Dragon's Den. (Illus.). 128p. (gr. 5-9). 1984. pap. 2.25 (*0-553-25918-0*) Bantam.
—Escape. (ps-7). 1987. pap. 1.95 (*0-553-23294-0*) Bantam.
—Escape from the Kingdom of Frome, No. 3: The Caverns of Mornas. 144p. (Orig.). (gr. 7-12). 1987. pap. 2.50 (*0-553-26200-9*) Bantam.
—Hijacked. (gr. 9-12). 1990. pap. 3.25 (*0-553-28635-8*) Bantam.
—Hurricane! 176p. (Orig.). (gr. 4 up). 1988. pap. 2.50 (*0-553-27356-6*) Bantam.
—Hyperspace. (ps-7). 1987. pap. 2.25 (*0-553-26371-4*) Bantam.
—Invaders of the Planet Earth. 128p. (Orig.). (gr. 4 up). 1987. pap. 2.50 (*0-553-26669-1*) Bantam.
—Master of Kung Fu. 128p. 1989. pap. 2.99 (*0-553-27718-9*) Bantam.
—Master of Tae Kwon Do. 1990. pap. 3.50 (*0-553-28516-5*) Bantam.
—Masters of the Louvre. (gr. 4-7). 1993. pap. 3.25 (*0-553-29969-7*) Bantam.
—Planet of the Dragons. (gr. 5 up). 1988. pap. 2.50 (*0-553-26887-2*) Bantam.
—Revolution in Russia. 1992. pap. 3.25 (*0-553-29784-8*) Bantam.
—The Roaring Twenties. (gr. 4-7). 1993. pap. 3.25 (*0-553-56348-3*) Bantam.
—Secret of the Pyramids. (ps-7). 1987. pap. 2.25 (*0-553-25761-7*) Bantam.
—The Secret Treasure of Tibet. 128p. (Orig.). (gr. 4). 1984. pap. 2.25 (*0-553-25501-0*) Bantam.
—South of the Border. (gr. 4-7). 1992. pap. 3.25 (*0-553-29757-0*, Starfire) Bantam.
—The Valley of the Kings. (gr. 4-7). 1992. pap. 3.50 (*0-553-29756-2*, Starfire) Bantam.
Brin, Susannah. The Seal Killers. Parker, Liz, ed. Taylor, Marjorie, illus. 45p. (Orig.). (gr. 6-12). 1992. pap. text ed. 2.95 (*1-56254-051-3*) Saddleback Pubns.
Brown. Where Have You Been? 1993. pap. 28.67 (*0-590-71408-2*) Scholastic Inc.
Brown, Margaret W. Where Have You Been? (Illus.). 32p. (ps). 1990. Repr. of 1952 ed. 8.95 (*0-8038-8018-9*) Hastings.
—Willie's Adventures. LC 84-43141. 72p. (ps-3). 1988. PLB 11.89 (*0-06-020769-8*) HarpC Child Bks.
Brown, Rose M. The PMS Zone. Skeeter, illus. 80p. (Orig.). 1988. pap. 7.95 (*0-9622109-0-0*) Skeetoonies.
Brown, Ryan & Clarrian, Dean. The Collected Teenage Mutant Ninja Turtles Adventures, Vol. 1. Gaydos, Michael, et al, illus. 96p. 1991. pap. 5.95 (*1-879450-03-8*) Tundra MA.
—The Collected Teenage Mutant Ninja Turtles Adventures, Vol. 2. Mitchroney, Ken, et al, illus. 88p. 1991. pap. 5.95 (*1-879450-04-6*) Tundra MA.
Bryant, Gary. The True-Life Adventures of Nicky Ridge. 78p. (gr. 4-8). 1992. pap. 6.95 (*1-881442-02-0*) New Legends Pub.
Buchanan, Joan. The Nana Rescue. Cooper-Brown, Jean, illus. LC 93-20803. 1994. 4.25 (*0-383-03740-9*) SRA Schl Grp.
Buckley, Joe. Run Donny Run. 140p. (gr. 6-10). 1991. pap. 7.95 (*0-86327-297-5*, Pub. by Wolfhound Pr EIRE) Dufour.
Budbill, David. Bones on Black Spruce Mountain. 128p. (gr. 5 up). 1994. pap. 3.99 (*0-14-036854-X*) Puffin Bks.
—Snowshoe Trek to Otter River. (Illus.). 96p. (gr. 4-6). 1984. pap. 2.75 (*0-553-15469-9*, Skylark) Bantam.
Bunting, Eve. Hideout. (gr. 4-7). 1993. pap. 4.95 (*0-15-233991-4*) HarBrace.
—Jumping the Nail. LC 94-11090. (gr. 9-12). 1993. pap. 4.95 (*0-15-241358-8*) HarBrace.
—Wall. (ps-3). 1992. pap. 5.70 (*0-395-62977-2*, Clarion Bks) HM.
Burnford, Sheila. The Incredible Journey. 1985. pap. 3.99 (*0-553-15616-0*) Bantam.
—The Incredible Journey. 1984. pap. 3.99 (*0-553-27442-2*) Bantam.

Burningham, John. Would You Rather... Burningham, John, illus. LC 78-7088. 32p. (ps-3). 1978. 17.00 (*0-690-03917-4*, Crowell Jr Bks); PLB 16.89 (*0-690-03918-2*, Crowell Jr Bks) HarpC Child Bks.

Burt, William F. The Adventures of Herby. 1993. 7.95 (*0-8062-4782-7*) Carlton.

Bush, Timothy. Three at Sea. LC 93-3677. (Illus.). 32p. (ps-2). 1994. 14.00 (*0-517-59299-1*) Crown Bks Yng Read.

Byars, Betsy C. Cracker Jackson. LC 84-24684. 168p. (gr. 5-7). 1985. pap. 12.95 (*0-670-80546-7*) Viking Child Bks.

Cairis, Nicholas T. Island of the Titans. Mather, Pamela, ed. (Illus.). 90p. (Orig.). 1989. pap. 4.95 (*0-929624-02-5*) Pegasus Bks.

Call of the Jungle. (Illus.). 48p. (Orig.). (gr. k-3). 1989. pap. 2.95 (*0-8431-2705-8*) Price Stern.

Calmenson, Stephanie, adapted by. Race to Danger. LC 92-56396. 136p. (Orig.). (gr. 4-8). 1993. pap. 3.50 (*0-679-84388-4*) Random Bks Yng Read.

Campbell, Joanna. Battlecry Forever. (gr. 7 up). 1992. pap. 3.50 (*0-06-106771-7*, Harp PBks) HarpC.

Cannon, A. E. Cal Cameron by Day, Spider-Man by Night. LC 87-24655. 160p. (gr. 7 up). 1988. pap. 13. 95 (*0-385-29635-5*) Delacorte.

—Cal Cameron by Day, Spiderman by Night. (gr. k-12). 1989. pap. 3.25 (*0-440-20313-9*, LFL) Dell.

Captives of Time. 1987. pap. 14.95 (*0-440-50227-6*) Dell.

Caribbean Adventure Package. 1990. pap. 2.95 (*0-553-61198-4*) Bantam.

Carlson, Natalie S. The Happy Orpheline. (gr. k-6). 1987. pap. 2.75 (*0-440-43455-6*, YB) Dell.

Carpenter, Humphrey. The Captain Hook Affair. write for info. HM.

Carrie, Christopher. Quest for the Jungle City. (Illus.). 40p. (gr. k up). 1990. 1.59 (*0-86696-245-X*) Binney & Smith.

Carter, Alden R. The Shoshoni. (Illus.). 64p. (gr. 3 up). 1991. pap. 5.95 (*0-531-15605-2*) Watts.

—Up Country. 224p. (gr. 7 up). 1989. 15.95 (*0-399-21583-2*, Putnam) Putnam Pub Group.

Cartwright, Pauline. Arthur & the Dragon. LC 90-10091. (Illus.). 32p. (gr. 1-4). 1990. PLB 17.28 (*0-8114-2689-0*) Raintree Steck-V.

Cassabois, Jacques. Port Englouti. Boucher, Michel, illus. (FRE.). 79p. (gr. 3-7). 1989. pap. 8.95 (*2-07-031204-6*) Schoenhof.

Cate, Dick. Twisters. Binch, Caroline, illus. 160p. (gr. 5-8). 1989. 17.95 (*0-575-04099-8*, Pub. by Gollancz England) Trafalgar.

Cech, John. The Southernmost Cat. Osborn, Kathy, illus. LC 93-40671. 1995. 14.00 (*0-02-717885-4*) Macmillan Child Grp.

Celestri, John. The Christian Crusader: The Quest Begins. rev. ed. Celestri, John, illus. 80p. 1992. pap. 3.99 (*0-9634183-1-9*) CC Comics.

Chant, Barry. Spindles & the Giant Eagle Rescue. 1991. PLB 3.99 (*0-8423-6214-2*) Tyndale.

Charnas, Suzy M. The Silver Glove. 1988. 13.95 (*0-553-05470-8*) Bantam.

Chartier, Normand. Over the River & Thro' the Woods. (Illus.). 24p. (ps-3). 1990. 5.95 (*0-671-64150-6*, Little Simon); pap. 2.25 (*0-671-72337-5*) S&S Trade.

Cheatham, Ann. Black Harvest. (Orig.). (gr. k-12). 1987. pap. 2.50 (*0-440-91039-0*, LFL) Dell.

Chevat, Richie. Amazement Park Adventure. (gr. 1-3). 1994. pap. 1.99 (*0-553-48091-X*) Bantam.

Children's Story. 1981. 7.95 (*0-685-53208-9*) Delacorte.

Choose Your Own Adventure, 5 vols, No. 2. (gr. 4). Boxed Set. pap. 9.75 (*0-553-30308-2*, Skylark) Bantam.

Choose Your Own Adventure, 5 vols, No. 3. Boxed Set. pap. 9.75 (*0-553-30310-4*, Skylark) Bantam.

Choose Your Own Adventure, 5 vols, No. 4. (gr. 4). Boxed Set. pap. 9.75 (*0-553-30434-8*) Bantam.

Christopher, John. Beyond the Burning Lands. (gr. 5-9). 1991. 17.50 (*0-8446-6447-2*) Peter Smith.

Christopher, Matt. Skateboard Tough. (gr. 4-7). 1991. 15. 95 (*0-316-14247-6*) Little.

—Too Hot to Handle. (gr. 4-7). 1991. pap. 3.95 (*0-316-14074-0*) Little.

Clarke, Elizabeth L. The Big Mistake. LC 94-60126. (gr. k-3). 1994. pap. 5.95 (*1-55523-673-1*) Winston-Derek.

Clarrain, Dean & Brown, Ryan. Collected Teenage Mutant Ninja Turtles Adventures, Vol. 3. Mutchroney, Ken, et al, illus. 88p. 1991. pap. 5.95 (*1-879450-05-4*) Tundra MA.

—The Collected Teenage Mutant Ninja Turtles Adventures, Vol. 4. Mitchroney, Ken, et al, illus. 88p. 1991. pap. 5.95 (*1-879450-06-2*) Tundra MA.

Cleary, Beverly. Ramona the Brave. Tiegreen, Alan, illus. 192p. (gr. k-6). 1984. pap. 3.99 (*0-440-47351-9*, YB) Dell.

—The Real Hole. (gr. k-6). 1987. pap. 3.95 (*0-440-47521-X*, YB) Dell.

Cleaver, Vera & Cleaver, Bill. Delpha Green & Company. LC 79-172141. 144p. (gr. 6 up). 1972. (Junior Bks); pap. 2.95 (*0-397-31344-6*, LSC-8) HarpC.

Clifford, Eth. Just Tell Me When We're Dead! Hughes, George, illus. LC 83-10865. 144p. (gr. 2-5). 1983. 13. 95 (*0-395-33071-8*) HM.

Cohen, Miriam. See You in Second Grade. (gr. k-6). 1990. pap. 2.95 (*0-440-40303-0*, Pub. by Yearling Classics) Dell.

Cohen, Peter Z. Deadly Game at Stony Creek. Deas, Michael J., illus. LC 93-9364. 96p. (gr. 5 up). 1993. pap. 3.99 (*0-14-036476-5*, Puffin) Puffin Bks.

Coleman, Clay. Attack. (gr. 9-12). 1990. pap. 2.95 (*0-06-106022-4*, PL) HarpC.

—Discovered! (gr. 9-12). 1991. pap. 2.95 (*0-06-106044-5*, PL) HarpC.

—Mutiny. (gr. 4-7). 1991. pap. 2.95 (*0-06-106039-9*, PL) HarpC.

—Stranded. 1990. pap. 2.95 (*0-06-106021-6*, PL) HarpC.

Collier, James L. & Collier, Christopher. Jump Ship to Freedom. (gr. k-6). 1987. pap. 3.99 (*0-440-44323-7*, Yearling) Dell.

Compton, Sara. Stranded. 1989. pap. 2.99 (*0-553-15762-0*) Bantam.

Conaway, Judith, adapted by. Twenty-Thousand Leagues under the Sea. D'Achille, Gino, illus. 96p. (gr. 2-5). 1983. lib. bdg. 4.99 (*0-394-95333-9*) Random Bks Yng Read.

Cone, Molly. Mishmash & The Big Fat Problem. Shortall, Leonard, illus. (gr. 2-5). 1982. 13.45 (*0-395-32078-X*) HM.

Conford, Ellen. Luck of Pokey Bloom. (gr. 4-7). 1991. pap. 4.95 (*0-316-15365-6*) Little.

Conkie, Heather. The Materializing of Duncan McTavish, No. 4. (gr. 3-7). 1992. pap. 3.99 (*0-553-48030-8*, Skylark) Bantam.

Conley, Pauline C. The Code Breaker. (Orig.). (gr. 4 up). 1983. pap. 4.50 (*0-87602-241-7*) Anchorage.

Cool, Joyce. The Kidnapping of Courtney Van Allen & What's-Her-Name. 176p. 1988. pap. 2.75 (*0-553-15597-0*, Starfire) Bantam.

Cooney, Caroline B. The Fire. 1990. pap. 3.25 (*0-590-41641-3*) Scholastic Inc.

Cooper, Kay. Discover It Yourself: Who Put the Canon in the Courthouse Square? 96p. 1993. pap. 3.50 (*0-380-71298-9*, Camelot) Avon.

Cooper, Marva. Livingston's Vision. (Illus.). (gr. 1-7). 3.95 (*1-882185-08-0*) Crnrstone Pub.

Cooper, Susan. Over Sea, under Stone. 256p. (gr. 5 up). 1989. pap. 3.95 (*0-02-042785-9*, Collier Young Ad) Macmillan Child Grp.

Corby, Ellen. The Pebble of Gibraltar. 1988. 13.95 (*0-533-07623-4*) Vantage.

Cossi, Olga. The Great Getaway. LC 89-42637. 32p. (gr. 1-2). 1991. PLB 18.60 (*0-8368-0107-5*) Gareth Stevens Inc.

Cottonwood, Joe. The Adventures of Boone Barnaby. 1992. pap. 2.95 (*0-590-43547-7*, Apple Paperbacks) Scholastic Inc.

Coursen, H. R. The Search for Archerland. (Illus.). 245p. (Orig.). (gr. 8 up). 1993. pap. 12.50 (*1-880664-02-X*) E M Pr.

Cresswell, Helen. Bagthorpes Abroad: Being the Fifth Part of The Bagthorpe Saga. LC 84-7125. 180p. (gr. 5-9). 1984. SBE 14.95 (*0-02-725390-2*, Macmillan Child Bk) Macmillan Child Grp.

Cross, Gillian. Born of the Sun. (gr. k-12). 1987. pap. 2.95 (*0-440-90710-1*, LFL) Dell.

—A Map of Nowhere. LC 88-24559. 160p. (gr. 4-7). 1989. 13.95 (*0-8234-0741-1*) Holiday.

Cruise, Beth. Silver Spurs. 144p. (Orig.). (gr. 5 up). 1994. pap. 2.95 (*0-02-042788-3*, Collier Young Ad) Macmillan Child Grp.

Crutcher, Chris. Running Loose. (gr. 7 up). 1986. pap. 3.50 (*0-440-97570-0*, LFL) Dell.

—Stonan! (gr. k-12). 1988. pap. 3.99 (*0-440-20080-6*, LFL) Dell.

Crutchfield, Charles. Brigands of Mirkwood. Fenlon, Peter C., Jr., ed. McBride, Angus, illus. 32p. (Orig.). (gr. 10-12). 1987. pap. 7.00 (*0-915795-85-X*, 8090) Iron Crown Ent Inc.

—Far Harad, the Scorched Land. Charlton, Coleman, ed. McBride, Angus, illus. 64p. (gr. 10-12). 1988. pap. 12. 00 (*1-55806-007-3*, 3800) Iron Crown Ent Inc.

Curry, Jane L. The Daybreakers. Robinson, Charles, illus. (gr. 3-7). 1991. 20.50 (*0-8446-6474-X*) Peter Smith.

Dahl, Roald. Charlie & the Chocolate Factory: (Charlie y la Fabrica de Chocolate) (SPA.). 8.95 (*968-6026-71-1*) Santillana.

—Going Solo. (Illus.). 208p. (gr. 8 up). 1986. 14.95 (*0-374-16503-3*) FS&G.

Dale, Penny. Bet You Can't. Dale, Penny, illus. LC 87-3780. 32p. (ps-1). 1988. (Lipp Jr Bks) HarpC Child Bks.

Daniells, Trenna. Don't Blame Others: Timothy Chicken Learns to Lead. Braille International, Inc. Staff & Henry, James, illus. (Orig.). (gr. 2). 1992. pap. 10.95 (*1-56956-016-1*) W A T Braille.

—It's Okay to Be Different: Oliver's Adventures on Monkey Island. Braille International, Inc. Staff & Henry, James, illus. (Orig.). (gr. 1). 1992. pap. 10.95 (*1-56956-008-0*) W A T Braille.

—It's Okay to Be Different: Oliver's Adventures on Monkey Island. Braille International, Inc. Staff & Henry, James, illus. (Orig.). (gr. 2). 1992. pap. 10.95 (*1-56956-017-X*) W A T Braille.

Darkwing Duck: Just Us Justice Duck. (Illus.). 48p. (gr. 3-7). 1992. pap. 2.95 (*1-56115-268-4*, 21809, Golden Pr) Western Pub.

Davoll, Barbara. A Load of Trouble. Hockerman, David, illus. 24p. 1988. pap. 6.99 (*0-89693-407-1*, Victor Books); cassette 9.99 (*0-89693-618-X*) SP Pubns.

—Rainy Day Rescue. Hockerman, Dennis, illus. 24p. 1988. 6.99 (*0-89693-408-X*, Victor Books); cassete 9.99 (*0-89693-619-8*) SP Pubns.

—Saved by the Bell. Hockerman, Dennis, illus. 24p. 1988. text ed. 6.99 (*0-89693-403-9*, Victor Books); cassette 9.99 (*0-89693-614-7*) SP Pubns.

Dawnay, Romayne. The Champions of Appledore. Dawnay-Timms, Romayne, illus. 160p. (gr. 3-7). 1994. SBE 14.95 (*0-02-789355-3*, Four Winds) Macmillan Child Grp.

DC Comics Staff. I, Werewolf. (gr. 4-7). 1992. pap. 3.95 (*0-316-17769-5*) Little.

De Brunhoff, Jean & De Brunhoff, Laurent. Babar's Anniversary Album. De Brunhoff, Jean & De Brunhoff, Laurent, illus. Sendak, Maurice, intro. by. LC 81-5182. 144p. (ps-3). 1993. 18.00 (*0-394-84813-6*); lib. bdg. 16.99 (*0-394-94813-0*) Random Bks Yng Read.

Dee, M. M. Adventures of Dusty. LC 84-81557. (Illus.). 48p. (gr. k-4). 1985. 9.95 (*0-937460-14-1*) Hendrick-Long.

DeFelice, Cynthia. Devil's Bridge. LC 92-7497. 96p. (gr. 5 up). 1992. SBE 13.95 (*0-02-726465-3*, Macmillan Child Bk) Macmillan Child Grp.

—Lostman's River. LC 93-40857. 160p. (gr. 5 up). 1994. SBE 13.95 (*0-02-726466-1*, Macmillan Child Bk) Macmillan Child Grp.

Defoe, Daniel. Robinson Crusoe. Larsen, Dan, adapted by. (gr. 3 up). 1992. 9.95 (*1-55748-277-2*) Barbour & Co.

—Robinson Crusoe. Wyeth, N. C., illus. LC 90-84707. 370p. (gr. 7 up). 1993. Repr. of 1990 ed. 16.95 (*1-56138-263-9*) Running Pr.

Defoe, Daniel, et al. Robinson Crusoe. (Illus.). 52p. Date not set. pap. 4.95 (*1-57209-021-9*) Classics Int Ent.

DeFord, Deborah H. & Stout, Harry S. An Enemy among Them. 208p. (gr. 5-9). 1987. 13.45 (*0-395-44239-7*) HM.

De Goscinny, Rene. Asterix Chez les Helvetes. (FRE., Illus.). (gr. 7-9). 1990. 19.95 (*0-8288-5110-7*, FC889) Fr & Eur.

—Asterix en Hispanie. (FRE., Illus.). (gr. 7-9). 1990. 19. 95 (*0-8288-5111-5*, FC887) Fr & Eur.

—Asterix et la Serpe d'or. (FRE., Illus.). (gr. 3-8). 1990. 19.95 (*0-8288-4939-0*) Fr & Eur.

—Asterix et le Chaudron. (FRE., Illus.). (gr. 7-9). 1990. 19.95 (*0-8288-5113-1*, FC885) Fr & Eur.

—Asterix la Zizanie. (FRE., Illus.). (gr. 7-9). 1990. 19.95 (*0-8288-5117-4*, FC888) Fr & Eur.

De Goscinny, Rene & Uderzo, M. Asterix & Operation Getafix. 1990. 19.95 (*0-8288-8570-2*) Fr & Eur.

—Asterix & Son. 1990. 19.95 (*0-8288-8568-0*) Fr & Eur.

—Asterix & the Banquet. 1990. 19.95 (*0-8288-8590-7*) Fr & Eur.

—Asterix & the Black Gold. 1990. 19.95 (*0-8288-8592-3*) Fr & Eur.

—Asterix & the Great Divide. 1990. 19.95 (*0-8288-8567-2*) Fr & Eur.

—Asterix & the Magic Carpet. 1990. 19.95 (*0-8288-8569-9*) Fr & Eur.

—Asterix Chez Rahazade. (FRE.). 1990. 19.95 (*0-8288-8572-9*) Fr & Eur.

—Asterix: Comment Obelix est Tombe dans la Marmite du Druide Quand Il Etait Petit. (FRE.). 1990. 19.95 (*0-8288-8597-4*) Fr & Eur.

—Asterix et la Rose et le Glaive. (FRE.). 1990. 19.95 (*0-8288-8573-7*) Fr & Eur.

—Asterix: How Obelix Fell into the Magic Cauldron When He Was a Little Boy. 1990. 19.95 (*0-8288-8594-X*) Fr & Eur.

—Asterix in Belgium. 1990. 19.95 (*0-8288-8591-5*) Fr & Eur.

—Asterix in Corsica. 1990. 19.95 (*0-8288-8566-4*) Fr & Eur.

—Asterix, Obelix & Company. 1990. 19.95 (*0-8288-8565-6*) Fr & Eur.

—Asterix vs Caesar. 1990. 19.95 (*0-8288-8593-1*) Fr & Eur.

—Domaine des Dieux. (FRE., Illus.). (gr. 7-9). 1990. 19. 95 (*0-8288-5123-9*, FC886) Fr & Eur.

—Fils d'Asterix. (FRE.). 1990. 19.95 (*0-8288-8571-0*) Fr & Eur.

—Grand Fosse. (FRE.). 1990. 19.95 (*0-8288-8595-8*) Fr & Eur.

—Odyssee d'Asterix. (FRE.). 1990. 19.95 (*0-8288-8596-6*) Fr & Eur.

Delporte, pseud. Romeo & Smurfette & Twelve Other Smurfy Stories. Peyo, illus. LC 82-60258. 48p. (gr. 4-7). 1983. 2.95 (*0-394-85618-X*) Random Bks Yng Read.

Delton, Judy. Back Yard Angel. Morrill, Leslie, illus. 112p. (gr. k up). 1990. pap. 3.25 (*0-440-40445-2*, YB) Dell.

—Sky Babies. (ps-3). 1991. pap. 3.25 (*0-440-40530-0*, YB) Dell.

DePaola, Tomie. Legend of the Bluebonnet. (SPA., Illus.). 32p. (ps-3). 1993. pap. 5.95 (*0-399-22441-6*, Putnam) Putnam Pub Group.

De Pauw, Linda G. Seafaring Women. (gr. 7 up). 1982. 13.45 (*0-395-32434-3*) HM.

Derwent, Lavinia. Return to Sula. 128p. (gr. 5-8). 1989. pap. 6.95 (*0-86241-073-8*, Pub. by Cnngt Pub Ltd) Trafalgar.

De Segur. General Dourakine. Bayard, Emile, illus. (FRE.). 220p. (gr. 5-10). 1979. pap. 8.95 (*2-07-033092-3*) Schoenhof.

—Nouveaux Contes de Fees Pour les Petits. Dore, G. & Didier, J., illus. (FRE.). 216p. (gr. 5-10). 1980. pap. 9.95 (*2-07-033149-0*) Schoenhof.

De Trevino, Elizabeth B. El Guero. (Illus.). 112p. (gr. 3 up). 1991. pap. 3.95 (*0-374-42028-9*) FS&G.

Dewey, Ariane. Gib Morgan, Oilman. Dewey, Ariane, illus. LC 86-284. 48p. (gr. 1-3). 1987. 11.75 (*0-688-06566-X*); PLB 11.88 (*0-688-06567-8*) Greenwillow.
—Pecos Bill. LC 82-9229. (Illus.). 56p. (gr. k-3). 1983. 14.95 (*0-688-01410-0*) Greenwillow.
Dicks, Terrance. Goliath at the Dog Show. Littlewood, Valerie, illus. 64p. (gr. k-4). 1987. 7.95 (*0-8120-5821-6*); pap. 3.50 (*0-8120-3818-5*) Barron.
—Goliath on Vacation. Littlewood, Valerie, illus. 64p. (gr. k-4). 1987. 7.95 (*0-8120-5824-0*); pap. 3.50 (*0-8120-3821-5*) Barron.
DiGirolamo, Vincent. Whispers under the Wharf. LC 90-331073. 144p. (Orig.). 1990. pap. 8.95 (*0-931832-52-7*) Fithian Pr.
Dillon, Eilis. The Cruise of the Santa Maria. (Illus.). (gr. 3-7). 1991. pap. 9.95 (*0-86278-263-5*, Pub. by OBrien Pr IE) Dufour.
—The Five Hundred. (Illus.). 87p. (gr. 2-6). 1991. pap. 8.95 (*0-86278-262-7*, Pub. by OBrien Pr IE) Dufour.
—The Singing Cave. 259p. (gr. 6 up). 1992. pap. 7.95 (*1-85371-153-5*, Pub. by Poolbeg Pr ER) Dufour.
Disney, Walt. Aladdin Junior Graphic Novel. (gr. 4-7). 1993. pap. 3.95 (*0-8167-3062-8*) Troll Assocs.
—Goof Troop Graphic Novel. (gr. 4-7). 1993. pap. 3.95 (*0-8167-3063-6*) Troll Assocs.
Dixon. Ice Age Explorer. (ps-7). 1987. pap. 2.50 (*0-553-27049-4*) Bantam.
Dodson, Susan. The Eye of the Storm. (gr. 7 up). pap. 2.25 (*0-317-62893-3*) S&S Trade.
Dolb, K. Danger at Demon's Cove. (Illus.). 48p. (gr. 4-9). 1988. PLB 11.96 (*0-88110-333-0*); pap. 4.95 (*0-7460-0179-7*) EDC.
Dolphin's Cave. (Illus.). 48p. (Orig.). (gr. k-3). 1989. pap. 2.95 (*0-8431-2707-4*) Price Stern.
Dopey Loses the Diamonds. 24p. 1994. 7.98 (*1-57082-150-X*) Mouse Works.
Doty, Randall. Ents of Fangorn. Fenlon, Peter C., Jr., ed. McBride, Angus, illus. 60p. (Orig.). (gr. 10-12). 1987. pap. 12.00 (*0-915795-84-1*, 3500) Iron Crown Ent Inc.
Doyle, Arthur Conan. The Lost World. (Illus.). 272p. (gr. 5 up). 1991. pap. 2.95 (*0-14-035013-6*, Puffin) Puffin Bks.
Dragonwagon, Crescent & Zindel, Paul. To Take a Dare. 240p. (gr. 7-12). 1984. pap. 2.95 (*0-553-26601-2*) Bantam.
Dumas, Alexandre. The Three Musketeers. 1994. pap. 4.99 (*0-8125-3602-9*) Tor Bks.
—The Three Musketeers. Felder, Deborah, adapted by. LC 93-42782. 108p. (gr. 2-6). 1994. pap. 3.50 (*0-679-86017-7*, Bullseye Bks) Random Bks Yng Read.
Dumas, Alexandre, et al. The Count of Monte Cristo. (Illus.). 52p. Date not set. pap. 4.95 (*1-57209-005-7*) Classics Int Ent.
Duncan, Lois. Locked in Time. 240p. (gr. 7 up). 1985. 15.95 (*0-316-19555-3*) Little.
Dunrea, Olivier. Fergus & Bridey. Dunrea, Olivier, illus. 32p. (ps-3). 1992. pap. 3.99 (*0-440-40691-9*, YB) Dell.
Dygard, Thomas J. The Rookie Arrives. 176p. (gr. 5-9). 1989. pap. 3.95 (*0-14-034112-9*, Puffin) Puffin Bks.
Edler, Timothy J. T-Boy & the Trial for Life. (Illus.). 36p. (gr. k-8). 1978. pap. 6.00 (*0-931108-02-0*) Little Cajun Bks.
Edmonds, Walter. Matchlock Gun. 50p. (gr. 3-6). 1991. pap. 4.95 (*0-8167-2367-2*) Troll Assocs.
Edwards, Michelle. Misha the Minstrel. LC 84-62336. (Illus.). 32p. (gr. 3-7). 1985. 8.95 (*0-930100-19-0*) Holy Cow.
Elbl, Martin. Tales of the Amazon. Neubacher, Gerda, illus. 32p. (gr. k-3). 1985. 10.95 (*0-88625-127-3*) Durkin Hayes Pub.
Elford, George R. Recall to Inferno: Devil's Guard Two. (Orig.). 1988. pap. 3.95 (*0-440-20199-3*) Dell.
Elliott, Dan. The Adventures of Ernie & Bert in Twiddlebug Land. LC 83-61719. (Illus.). 32p. (ps-3). 1984. pap. 1.50 (*0-394-85925-1*) Random Bks Yng Read.
Ellis, Terry. The Invasion of Willow Wood Springs. LC 85-63826. (Illus.). 168p. (Orig.). (gr. 4 up). 1989. pap. 4.75 (*0-915677-32-6*) Roundtable Pub.
Ellis, Veronica F. Land of the Four Winds. Walker, Sylvia, illus. LC 92-72001. 32p. (gr. 1-4). 1993. 14.95 (*0-940975-38-6*); pap. 6.95 (*0-940975-39-4*) Just Us Bks.
Elwood, Roger. Forbidden River. (gr. 3-7). 1991. pap. 4.99 (*0-8499-3304-8*) Word Inc.
Emberley, Rebecca. Taking a Walk Caminando. (ps-3). 1990. 15.95 (*0-316-23640-3*) Little.
Evans, Shirlee. Tree Tall & the Whiteskins. LC 85-13952. (Illus.). 112p. (gr. 9 up). 1985. pap. 3.95 (*0-8361-3402-8*) Herald Pr.
Evslin, Bernard. The Adventures of Ulysses. 1989. pap. 3.25 (*0-590-42599-4*) Scholastic Inc.
Fannoun, Kathy. Jamal's Prayer Rug. Abdullah, Fadel, ed. Fannoun, Kathy, illus. 20p. Date not set. text ed. write for info. (*1-56316-316-0*) Iqra Intl Ed Fdtn.
The Fantastic Four in the Island of Danger. 32p. 1988. pap. 1.50 (*0-517-55633-2*) Crown Bks Yng Read.
Fasco, Rudolph. In Quest of the Zohar. Frades, Ernesto, ed. Pereira, Ernesto, illus. 275p. (Orig.). 1990. pap. write for info. (*0-9624929-0-6*) Little Great Whale.
Ferguson, Alane. Overkill. LC 92-11426. 176p. (gr. 7 up). 1992. SBE 14.95 (*0-02-734523-8*, Bradbury Pr) Macmillan Child Grp.
Ferris, Jean. Across the Grain. (ps-3). 1993. pap. 3.95 (*0-374-40057-1*) FS&G.
Fidler, Kathleen. The Desperate Journey. (Illus.). 158p. (gr. 5-8). 1989. pap. 6.95 (*0-86241-056-8*, Pub. by Cnngt Pub Ltd) Trafalgar.
Field, Arthur W. Cisco & the Twin Foals. Cosgrove, Colleen B., illus. LC 83-61713. 160p. (gr. 8 up). 1983. 12.00 (*0-935356-06-1*) Mills Pub Co.
Field, Eugene. Wynken, Blynken & Nod. 1989. pap. 2.95 (*0-590-42422-X*) Scholastic Inc.
—Wynken, Blynken & Nod. Looney, Barbara, illus. 32p. 1991. Repr. of 1964 ed. 9.95 (*0-8038-9333-7*) Hastings.
Finlay, Winifred. Danger at Black Dyke. (Illus.). (gr. 7-12). 1968. 21.95 (*0-87599-150-5*) S G Phillips.
Fleischman, Sid. The Whipping Boy. Sis, Peter, illus. LC 85-17555. 96p. (gr. 2-6). 1986. PLB 15.00 (*0-688-06216-4*) Greenwillow.
Fleming, Ian. Chitty Chitty Bang Bang. reissued ed. Burningham, John, illus. 112p. (gr. 3-7). 1993. pap. 2.99 (*0-679-81948-7*, Bullseye Bks) Random Bks Yng Read.
Fleming, Red. Recollections of a Mountain Boy Plus Stories of Sudden Death. Rose, Jennifer, ed. Rose, Krystal, illus. 112p. (Orig.). 1992. pap. 9.95 (*0-930401-55-7*) Artex Pub.
Flory, Jane. The Great Bamboozlement. Flory, Jane, illus. 160p. (gr. 5-9). 1982. 13.45 (*0-395-31859-9*) HM.
Foley, Louise M. The Cobra Connection. 1990. pap. 3.25 (*0-553-28574-2*) Bantam.
—Danger at Anchor Mine. 128p. (gr. 4). 1985. pap. 2.25 (*0-553-25496-0*) Bantam.
—Ghost Train. (gr. 4-7). 1992. pap. 3.50 (*0-553-29358-3*) Bantam.
—The Lost Tribe, No. 23. (Illus.). 128p. 1984. pap. 2.25 (*0-553-26182-7*) Bantam.
Foley, Tod. Beyond the Core: Frontier Zone 5. Amthor, Terry K., ed. 64p. (Orig.). (gr. 10-12). 1987. pap. 12.00 (*0-915795-83-3*, 9600, Dist. by Berkley Pub Group) Iron Crown Ent Inc.
—Tales from Deep Space. Amthor, Terry K., ed. McKie, Angus, illus. 32p. (Orig.). (gr. 10-12). 1988. pap. 6.00 (*1-55806-006-5*, 9103) Iron Crown Ent Inc.
Follow the Drinking Gourd. LC 88-9661. 48p. (gr. 1-4). 1988. 17.00 (*0-394-89694-7*); PLB 17.99 (*0-394-99694-1*) Knopf Bks Yng Read.
Fontes, Ron, adapted by. Rocketeer. (gr. 4-7). 1991. pap. 2.95 (*1-56282-065-6*) Disney Pr.
Forsse, Ken. The Airship. High, David, et al, illus. 26p. (ps). 1985. incl. audio-cassette 9.95 (*0-934323-00-3*) Alchemy Comms.
—Teddy Ruxpin's Lullabies. High, David, et al, illus. 26p. (ps). 1985. incl. audio-cassette 9.95 (*0-934323-01-1*) Alchemy Comms.
Foster, Janet. Journey to the Top of the World. Foster, Janet, photos by. (Illus.). (gr. 3-7). 1988. 14.95 (*0-13-511445-4*) P-H.
Fox, J. N. Young Indiana Jones & the Pirates' Loot. LC 93-46831. 132p. (Orig.). (gr. 3-7). 1994. pap. 3.99 (*0-679-86433-4*, Bullseye Bks) Random Bks Yng Read.
Fox, Paula. Monkey Island. 1993. pap. 3.99 (*0-440-40770-2*) Dell.
Fradon, Dana. Sir Dana - A Knight: As Told by His Trusty Armor. Fradon, Dana, illus. LC 88-3968. 32p. (gr. 3-7). 1988. 13.95 (*0-525-44424-6*, DCB) Dutton Child Bks.
Francis, Neil. Super Flyers. LC 88-19336. 1988. pap. 6.68 (*0-201-14933-8*) Addison-Wesley.
French, Allen. The Story of Rolf: And the Viking Bow. Reynolds, Lydia, intro. by. 256p. (gr. 6-12). 1994. pap. 12.95 (*1-883937-01-9*) Bethlehem WA.
French, Michael. Circle of Revenge. LC 88-19340. 160p. (gr. 6 up). 1988. 13.95 (*0-553-05495-3*, Starfire) Bantam.
—Pursuit. 192p. (gr. 9 up). 1983. pap. 2.95 (*0-440-96665-5*, LFL) Dell.
Frick, Dumas F. The Adventures of Phineous. Shauck, Chuck, illus. 96p. (gr. 1-3). 1993. 21.95 (*1-56167-112-6*) Noble Hse MD.
Friedman, Judith & Sonnenblick, Carol. Attack Pack. 128p. (gr. 4-12). 1982. write for info. (*0-9609616-0-7*) New Dir Pr.
Fritz, Jean. Stonewall. Gammell, Stephen, illus. 160p. (gr. 5-9). 1989. pap. 4.99 (*0-14-032937-4*, Puffin) Puffin Bks.
Frost, Erica. Jonathan's Amazing Adventure. Hall, Susan, illus. LC 85-14129. 48p. (Orig.). (gr. 1-3). 1986. PLB 10.59 (*0-8167-0662-X*); pap. text ed. 3.50 (*0-8167-0663-8*) Troll Assocs.
Furman, Abraham L., ed. Everygirls Adventure Stories. (Illus.). (gr. 6-10). PLB 7.19 (*0-8313-0053-1*) Lantern.
Fusonie, Donna J. Wicca, Flicka & JJ: The Night of the Poachers Moon. LC 92-72679. 144p. (gr. 7-9). 1993. 14.95 (*1-880851-05-9*) Greene Bark Pr.
Gallagher, Matthew P., Jr. Hans & the Gold Nugget. 16p. (gr. 3). 1993. pap. 6.95 (*0-9636119-0-9*) Gallagher & Assocs.
Garcia, Vince. Quest of the Ancients. Cabuco, et al, illus. 224p. (Orig.). (gr. 9-12). 1990. pap. 23.00 (*0-9628003-0-9*) Unicorn Game Pubns.
Gardiner, John R. Top Secret. Simont, Marc, illus. 129p. (gr. 3-7). 1985. 15.95 (*0-316-30368-2*) Little.
Garfield, Leon. The Saracen Maid. O'Brien, John, illus. LC 93-6612. (gr. 1-4). 1994. pap. 14.00 (*0-671-86646-X*, S&S BFYR) S&S Trade.
Garner, Alan. The Stone Book Quartet. (gr. k-12). 1988. pap. 4.95 (*0-440-40049-X*, Pub by Yearning Classics) Dell.
Gaspar, Tomas R. La Aventura de Yolanda; Yolanda's Hike. (ENG & SPA., Illus.). (ps-3). 1974. 5.95 (*0-938678-03-5*) New Seed.
Gasperini, Jim. Secrets of the Knights. (ps-7). 1984. pap. 2.50 (*0-553-26960-7*) Bantam.
Gates, Doris. A Fair Wind for Troy. Mikolayack, Charles, illus. 96p. (gr. 4-6). 1984. pap. 4.95 (*0-14-031718-X*, Puffin) Puffin Bks.
Geller, Norman. Unto Dust You Shall Return. Grant, Larry & Jalbert, Marc, illus. 16p. (gr. 6-10). 1986. pap. 4.95 (*0-915753-11-1*) N Geller Pub.
Gibbons, Dave. War Machine. Burton, Richard, ed. Simpson, Will, illus. 80p. 1993. text ed. 14.95 (*1-56862-018-7*) Tundra MA.
Gibson, Andrew. The Abradizil. Riddell, Chris, illus. 164p. (gr. 3-7). 1992. pap. 4.95 (*0-571-16508-7*) Faber & Faber.
Gilbert, Lela. The Journey with the Golden Book. (Illus.). 1992. pap. 6.99 (*1-56121-070-6*) Wolgemuth & Hyatt.
—Quest for the Silver Castle, Bk. 1: Tales of the King. 1991. pap. 6.99 (*1-56121-069-2*) Wolgemuth & Hyatt.
Gilbert, Ray. We Think the World Is Round. (Illus.). 24p. (Orig.). (ps-7). 1992. pap. 6.95 incl. cassette (*0-943351-56-1*, XE 2001) Astor Bks.
Gilliam, Terry & McKeown, Charles. The Adventures of Baron Munchausen: The Novel. Gilliam, Terry, illus. 192p. (Orig.). 1989. pap. 12.95 (*1-55783-039-8*) Applause Theatre Bk Pubs.
Gilligan, Alison. The Treasure of the Onyx. 1990. pap. 3.25 (*0-553-28610-2*) Bantam.
Gilligan, Shannon. The Case of the Silk King. large type ed. Bolle, Frank, illus. 114p. (gr. 3-7). 1987. Repr. of 1986 ed. 8.95 (*0-942545-14-1*); PLB 9.95 (*0-942545-19-2*, Dist. by Grolier) Grey Castle.
—Case of the Silk King. (gr. 5-12). 1986. pap. 3.25 (*0-553-25489-8*) Bantam.
—The Fairy Kidnap. 64p. (Orig.). (gr. 2 up). 1985. pap. 2.25 (*0-553-15488-5*) Bantam.
—Showdown. 1992. pap. 3.50 (*0-553-29297-8*) Bantam.
Gilligan, Shannon, pseud. Terror in Australia. 128p. (Orig.). 1988. pap. 2.50 (*0-553-27277-2*) Bantam.
Gilligan, Shannon. The Three Wishes. 64p. (Orig.). (gr. 1-3). 1984. pap. text ed. 2.25 (*0-553-15444-3*, Skylark) Bantam.
Gire, Ken. Adventures in the Big Thicket. (Illus.). 112p. (gr. k-5). 1990. 14.99 (*0-929608-72-0*) Focus Family.
Gjelfriend, George E. High Island Treasure. Little, Carl, ed. LC 91-58093. (Illus.). 120p. (gr. 4-8). 1992. pap. 9.95 (*0-932433-84-7*) Windswept Hse.
Glassman, Judy. Morning Glory War. (gr. 4-7). 1993. pap. 3.50 (*0-440-40765-6*) Dell.
Gold, Avner. The Dream. Reinman, Y. Y., ed. Hinlicky, G., illus. 112p. (gr. 7-11). 1983. pap. 7.95 (*0-935063-01-3*) CIS Comm.
—The Promised Child. Reinman, Y. Y., ed. Hinlicky, G., illus. LC 85-72493. 128p. (gr. 7-11). 1985. 9.95 (*0-935063-10-2*); pap. 7.95 (*0-935063-00-5*) CIS Comm.
—Twilight. Reinman, Y. Y., ed. Hinklicky, G., illus. LC 85-72404. 128p. (gr. 7-11). 1985. 9.95 (*0-935063-11-0*); pap. 7.95 (*0-935063-03-X*) CIS Comm.
—The Year of the Sword. Reinman, Y. Y., ed. Hinlicky, G., illus. 112p. (gr. 5 up). 1984. pap. 7.95 (*0-935063-02-1*) CIS Comm.
Goodall, John S. The Story of a Castle. Goodall, John S., illus. LC 86-70130. 60p. 1986. SBE 14.95 (*0-689-50405-5*, M K McElderry) Macmillan Child Grp.
Goodman, Deborah L. The Throne of Zeus. 128p. 1985. pap. 2.25 (*0-553-26265-3*) Bantam.
—The Trumpet of Terror. 128p. (Orig.). (gr. 4). 1986. pap. 2.25 (*0-553-25491-X*) Bantam.
—Vanished! 128p. (Orig.). (gr. 4). 1986. pap. 2.25 (*0-553-25941-5*) Bantam.
Goodman, Julius. The Magic Path. 64p. (Orig.). (gr. 2). 1985. pap. 2.25 (*0-553-15482-6*) Bantam.
—Space Patrol, No. 22. (Illus.). 128p. 1983. pap. 2.50 (*0-553-27520-8*) Bantam.
Gorman, S. S. Survive! Clancy, Lisa, ed. 128p. 1992. pap. 2.99 (*0-671-74503-4*, Minstrel Bks) PB.
Gould, Toni. The Adventures of Mel & Tess. (Illus.). (gr. 1-3). 1984. pap. text ed. 12.95x (*0-8027-9189-1*) Walker & Co.
Grant, Myrna. Ivan & the Daring Escape. LC 89-80820. (Illus.). 167p. (gr. 1-8). 1989. pap. 4.99 (*0-88419-257-1*, Creation Hse) Strang Comms Co.
—Ivan & the Informer. LC 89-80819. (Illus.). 108p. (gr. 1-8). 1989. pap. 4.99 (*0-88419-256-3*, Creation Hse) Strang Comms Co.
Graver, Fred. The Journey to Stonehenge. (gr. 4 up). 1984. pap. 2.25 (*0-553-25961-X*) Bantam.
Green, Michelle Y. Willie Pearl: Under the Mountain. McCracken, Steve, illus. Green, Oliver W., contrib. by. (Illus., Orig.). (gr. 4-6). 1992. pap. 9.95 (*0-9627697-1-1*) W Ruth Co.
Greenwald, Sheila. Mat Pit & the Tunnel Tenants. Greenwald, Sheila, illus. 128p. (gr. k-6). 1989. pap. 2.75 (*0-440-40155-0*, YB) Dell.
Greer, Gery & Ruddick, Robert. Jason & the Aliens down the Street. Sims, Blanche L., illus. LC 90-47386. 96p. (gr. 2-5). 1991. 12.95 (*0-06-021761-8*); PLB 12.89 (*0-06-021762-6*) HarpC Child Bks.
—Jason & the Escape from Bat Planet. Sims, Blanche L., illus. LC 92-41169. 96p. (gr. 2-5). 1993. 14.00 (*0-06-021221-7*); PLB 13.89 (*0-06-021222-5*) HarpC Child Bks.

Griffin, Judith B. Phoebe the Spy. (gr. 4-6). 1979. pap. 1.50 (*0-590-05758-8*) Scholastic Inc.
Gripari, Pierre. Sorciere de la Rue Mouffetard et Autre Contes de la Rue Broca. Rosado, Puig, illus. (FRE.). 153p. (gr. 5-10). 1987. pap. 8.95 (*2-07-033440-6*) Schoenhof.
Grubbs, J. The Survival Kit. rev. ed. Abell, ed. & illus. (gr. 7-8). Date not set. PLB 25.00 (*1-56611-011-4*); pap. 15.00 (*1-56611-039-4*) Jonas.
Gutman, Bill. Across the Wild River. (gr. 4-7). 1993. pap. 3.50 (*0-06-106159-X*, Harp PBks) HarpC.
Haggard, H. Rider. Allan Quartermain. (Illus.). 288p. (gr. 5 up). 1991. pap. 2.95 (*0-14-035117-5*, Puffin) Puffin Bks.
—King Solomon's Mines. 256p. (gr. 3-7). 1983. pap. 2.95 (*0-14-035014-4*, Puffin) Puffin Bks.
Hahn, Mary D. The Spanish Kidnapping Disaster. 144p. 1993. pap. 3.50 (*0-380-71712-3*, Camelot) Avon.
Halecroft, David. Blindside Blitz. (gr. 4-7). 1991. pap. 2.95 (*0-14-034906-5*, Puffin) Puffin Bks.
Haley, Patrick. Wildflower & the Big Voice in the Sky. Kool, Jonna, illus. LC 82-82990. 44p. (gr. 3-4). 1982. 9.00 (*0-9605738-1-X*) East Eagle.
Hamerstrom, Frances. Adventure of the Stone Man. (gr. 4-7). 1990. pap. 10.95 (*1-55821-084-9*) Lyons & Burford.
Hamilton, Gail. The Story Girl Earns Her Name, No. 2. (gr. 3-7). 1992. pap. 3.99 (*0-553-48028-6*, Skylark) Bantam.
Hamilton, Virginia. The Magical Adventures of Pretty Pearl. LC 84-48344. 320p. (gr. 6 up). 1986. pap. 5.95 (*0-06-440178-2*, Trophy) HarpC Child Bks.
Hampton, Bill. Captive. 1989. pap. 2.50 (*0-553-28009-0*) Bantam.
Hanna, J. Steven. The New American Storybook. 1993. 7.95 (*0-533-10553-6*) Vantage.
Harris, Geraldine. The Seventh Gate, No. 4. (gr. k-12). 1987. pap. 2.95 (*0-440-97747-9*, LFL) Dell.
Haseley, Dennis. Shadows. (gr. 4-7). 1993. pap. 3.95 (*0-374-46611-4*, Sunburst) FS&G.
Haskell, Bess C. The Hunky Dory. Poole, Ann, illus. 41p. (Orig.). (gr. 4 up). 1991. pap. 10.95 (*0-9626857-2-0*) Coastwise Pr.
—Sailing to Pint Pot. Poole, Ann M., illus. 72p. (Orig.). (gr. 4 up). 1993. pap. 10.95 (*0-9626857-4-7*) Coastwise Pr.
Hastings. Rufus & Christopher in the Land of Lies. LC 70-190271. (Illus.). 32p. (gr. 2-4). 1972. PLB 9.95 (*0-87783-061-4*); pap. 3.94 deluxe ed. (*0-87783-107-6*); cassette 7.94x (*0-87783-198-X*) Oddo.
Hayes, Frederick & Hayes, Jean. The Adventures of Pinto Bean & Chapulin. Kiefer, Jill, illus. 20p. (Orig.). (gr. 1-8). 1988. pap. text ed. 6.95 (*0-317-93098-2*) Pinto Pub.
Hayes, Geoffrey. The Treasure of the Lost Lagoon. Hayes, Geoffrey, illus. LC 90-40118. 48p. (Orig.). (gr. 2-3). 1991. lib. bdg. 7.99 (*0-679-91484-6*); pap. 3.50 (*0-679-81484-1*) Random Bks Yng Read.
Haynes, Betsy. In Trouble. (gr. 3-6). 1990. pap. 2.95 (*0-553-15814-7*) Bantam.
—Taffy Sinclair Strikes Again. 128p. (gr. 4-6). 1991. pap. 2.99 (*0-553-15645-4*, Skylark) Bantam.
—Teen Taxi. (gr. 4-7). 1990. pap. 2.75 (*0-553-15794-9*) Bantam.
Heide, Florence P. The Adventures of Treehorn. Gorey, Edward, illus. 128p. (gr. k-3). 1983. pap. 1.95 (*0-440-40045-7*, YB) Dell.
—Treehorn Times Three. (gr. 4-7). 1992. pap. 3.50 (*0-440-40553-X*) Dell.
Heine, Helme. The Marvelous Journey Through the Night. Manheim, Ralph, tr. (Illus.). 26p. (ps-3). 1992. pap. 5.95 (*0-374-44741-1*, Sunburst) FS&G.
Heisch, Glan & Heisch, Elisabeth. The Cinnamon Bear: The Missing Star. Bishop, Kathryn, ed. Jackson, Jett & Arnoff, Julie, illus. Bishop, Kathryn, intro. by. 32p. 1992. PLB 13.95 (*1-880623-01-3*); pap. 8.95 (*1-880623-02-1*) Stiles-Bishop.
Helfer, Andrew. Batman: The Purrfect Crime. (Illus.). (ps-3). 1991. pap. write for info. (*0-307-12621-8*, Golden Pr) Western Pub.
Heller, Nicholas. An Adventure at Sea. LC 87-25525. (Illus.). 24p. (ps-3). 1988. 11.95 (*0-688-07846-X*); PLB 11.88 (*0-688-07847-8*) Greenwillow.
Henney, Carolee W. Calbert & His Adventures. Macneil, Melanie F., illus. LC 90-83140. 104p. (Orig.). (gr. 2-5). 1990. collector's first ed., numbered, signed by author, with dust jacket, sim. gold imprint title-author on spine 24.95 (*0-9626580-1-4*); pap. 9.95 (*0-9626580-0-6*) Aton Pr.
Herge. Der Arumbaya-Fetisch. (GER., Illus.). 62p. pap. 19.95 (*0-8288-5008-9*) Fr & Eur.
—El Asunto Tornasol. (SPA., Illus.). 62p. 19.95 (*0-8288-5009-7*) Fr & Eur.
—Aterrizaje en la Luna. (SPA., Illus.). 62p. 19.95 (*0-8288-5010-0*) Fr & Eur.
—The Black Island. (Illus.). 62p. 19.95 (*0-8288-5012-7*) Fr & Eur.
—The Black Island. LC 74-21624. (gr. k up). 1975. pap. 7.95 (*0-316-35835-5*, Joy St Bks) Little.
—Der Blaue Lotos. (GER., Illus.). 62p. pap. 19.95 (*0-8288-5013-5*) Fr & Eur.
—The Blue Lotus. (Illus.). 64p. 1992. 12.95 (*0-316-35891-6*, Joy St Bks) Little.
—The Calculus Affair. (Illus.). 62p. 19.95 (*0-8288-5014-3*) Fr & Eur.
—El Cangrejo Pinzas Oro. (SPA., Illus.). 62p. 19.95 (*0-8288-5015-1*) Fr & Eur.
—The Castafiore Emerald. (Illus.). 62p. (Also avail. in FR. & Span.). 19.95 (*0-8288-5016-X*) Fr & Eur.
—El Cetro de Ottokar. (SPA., Illus.). 62p. 19.95 (*0-8288-5017-8*) Fr & Eur.
—Les Cigares du Pharaon. (FRE.). 64p. (gr. 7-9). 1992. Repr. write for info. (*0-7859-4560-1*) Fr & Eur.
—Los Cigarros del Faraon. (SPA., Illus.). 62p. 19.95 (*0-8288-5019-4*) Fr & Eur.
—Les Cigars du Pharon. (FRE., Illus.). 62p. 19.95 (*0-8288-5020-8*) Fr & Eur.
—Cigars of the Pharaoh. (Illus.). 62p. 19.95 (*0-8288-5021-6*) Fr & Eur.
—Cigars of the Pharoah. LC 74-21620. (gr. k up). 1975. pap. 7.95 (*0-316-35836-3*, Joy St Bks) Little.
—Coke en Stock. (FRE., Illus.). 64p. (gr. 7-9). 1992. Repr. write for info. (*0-7859-4563-6*) Fr & Eur.
—The Crab with the Golden Claws. (Illus.). 62p. (gr. 3-8). 19.95 (*0-8288-5023-2*) Fr & Eur.
—Crabe aux Pinces d'or. (FRE., Illus.). (gr. 7-9). looseleaf bdg. 19.95 (*0-8288-5025-9*) Fr & Eur.
—Crabe aux Pinces d'Or. (FRE., Illus.). 64p. 1992. Repr. 19.95 (*0-7859-4561-X*) Fr & Eur.
—Destination Moon. (gr. 3-8). looseleaf bdg. 19.95 (*0-8288-5026-7*) Fr & Eur.
—Destination Moon. (Illus.). 62p. 19.95 (*0-8288-5027-5*) Fr & Eur.
—Il Drago Blu. (ITA., Illus.). 62p. pap. 19.95 (*0-8288-5028-3*) Fr & Eur.
—La Estrella Misteriosa. (SPA., Illus.). 62p. 19.95 (*0-8288-5029-1*) Fr & Eur.
—Etoile Mysterieuse. (FRE., Illus.). 64p. (gr. 7-9). 1992. Repr. write for info. (*0-7859-4562-8*) Fr & Eur.
—Explorers of the Moon. (Illus.). 62p. 19.95 (*0-8288-5031-3*) Fr & Eur.
—Der Fall Bienlein. (GER., Illus.). 62p. pap. 19.95 (*0-8288-5033-X*) Fr & Eur.
—Flight Seven-Fourteen. (Illus.). 62p. 19.95 (*0-8288-5034-8*) Fr & Eur.
—Flight Seven-Fourteen. LC 74-21623. (gr. k up). 1975. pap. 7.95 (*0-316-35837-1*, Joy St Bks) Little.
—Flug 714 nach Sydney. (GER., Illus.). 62p. pap. 19.95 (*0-8288-5035-6*) Fr & Eur.
—Das Geheimnis der "Einhorn" (GER., Illus.). 62p. pap. 19.95 (*0-8288-5036-4*) Fr & Eur.
—Der Geheimnisvolle Stern. (GER., Illus.). 62p. pap. 19.95 (*0-8288-5037-2*) Fr & Eur.
—Il Granchio d'Oro. (ITA., Illus.). 62p. pap. 19.95 (*0-8288-5038-0*) Fr & Eur.
—Im Reiche des Schwarzen Goldes. (GER., Illus.). 62p. pap. 19.95 (*0-8288-5040-2*) Fr & Eur.
—La Isla Negra. (SPA., Illus.). 62p. 19.95 (*0-8288-5041-0*) Fr & Eur.
—Las Joyas de la Castafiore. (SPA., Illus.). 62p. 19.95 (*0-8288-5042-9*) Fr & Eur.
—Die Juwelen der Sangerin. (GER., Illus.). 62p. pap. 19.95 (*0-8288-5043-7*) Fr & Eur.
—King Ottokar's Sceptre. (Illus.). 62p. 19.95 (*0-8288-5044-5*) Fr & Eur.
—Kohle an Bord. (GER., Illus.). 62p. pap. 19.95 (*0-8288-5045-3*) Fr & Eur.
—Konig Ottokars Zepter. (GER., Illus.). 62p. pap. 19.95 (*0-8288-5046-1*) Fr & Eur.
—Die Krabbe mit den Goldenen Scheren. (GER., Illus.). 62p. pap. 19.95 (*0-8288-5047-X*) Fr & Eur.
—Land of Black Gold. (Illus.). 62p. 19.95 (*0-8288-5048-8*) Fr & Eur.
—Lo Scettro di Ottokar. (ITA., Illus.). 62p. pap. 19.95 (*0-8288-5061-5*) Fr & Eur.
—El Loto Azul. (SPA., Illus.). 62p. 19.95 (*0-8288-5049-6*) Fr & Eur.
—Le Lotus Bleu. (FRE.). (gr. 2-9). 19.95 (*0-8288-5050-X*) Fr & Eur.
—Objetivo: la Luna. (SPA., Illus.). 62p. 19.95 (*0-8288-5052-6*) Fr & Eur.
—L' Oreille Cassee. (FRE., Illus.). 62p. 19.95 (*0-8288-5054-2*) Fr & Eur.
—La Oreja Rota. (SPA., Illus.). 62p. 19.95 (*0-8288-5055-0*) Fr & Eur.
—Prisoners of the Sun. (Illus.). 62p. 19.95 (*0-8288-5056-9*) Fr & Eur.
—Red Rackham's Treasure. (Illus.). 62p. 19.95 (*0-8288-5057-7*) Fr & Eur.
—The Red Sea Sharks. (Illus., J). (gr. 3-8). 19.95 (*0-8288-5058-5*) Fr & Eur.
—Reiseziel Mond. (GER., Illus.). 62p. pap. 19.95 (*0-8288-5059-3*) Fr & Eur.
—Sceptre D'ottokar. (FRE., Illus.). (gr. 7-9). looseleaf bdg. 19.95 (*0-8288-5060-7*) Fr & Eur.
—Der Schatz Rackhams des Roten. (GER., Illus.). 62p. pap. 19.95 (*0-8288-5062-3*) Fr & Eur.
—Schritte auf dem Mond. (GER., Illus.). 62p. pap. 19.95 (*0-8288-5063-1*) Fr & Eur.
—Die Schwarze Insel. (GER., Illus.). 62p. pap. 19.95 (*0-8288-5064-X*) Fr & Eur.
—Secret de la Licorne. (FRE., Illus.). (gr. 7-9). 19.95 (*0-8288-5065-8*) Fr & Eur.
—The Secret of the Unicorn. (Illus.). 62p. 19.95 (*0-8288-5066-6*) Fr & Eur.
—El Secreto del Unicornio. (SPA., Illus.). 62p. 19.95 (*0-8288-5067-4*) Fr & Eur.
—Il Segreto del Liocorno. (ITA., Illus.). 62p. pap. 19.95 (*0-8288-5068-2*) Fr & Eur.
—Le Sette Sfere di Cristallo. (ITA., Illus.). 62p. pap. 19.95 (*0-8288-5070-4*) Fr & Eur.
—The Seven Crystal Balls. (Illus.). 62p. (gr. 3-8). 19.95 (*0-8288-5071-2*) Fr & Eur.
—Shooting Star. (Illus.). (gr. 3-8). looseleaf bdg. 19.95 (*0-8288-5073-9*) Fr & Eur.
—Die Sieben Kristallkugeln. (GER., Illus.). 62p. pap. 19.95 (*0-8288-5072-0*) Fr & Eur.
—Las Siete Bolas de Cristal. (SPA., Illus.). 62p. 19.95 (*0-8288-5074-7*) Fr & Eur.
—I Sigari del Faraone. (ITA., Illus.). 62p. pap. 19.95 (*0-8288-5075-5*) Fr & Eur.
—Der Sonnentempel. (GER., Illus.). 62p. pap. 19.95 (*0-8288-5076-3*) Fr & Eur.
—Stock de Coque. (SPA., Illus.). 62p. 19.95 (*0-8288-5077-1*) Fr & Eur.
—Temple du Soleil. (FRE., Illus.). (gr. 7-9). 19.95 (*0-8288-5078-X*) Fr & Eur.
—El Templo del Sol. (SPA., Illus.). 62p. 19.95 (*0-8288-5079-8*) Fr & Eur.
—Il Templo del Sol. (ITA., Illus.). 62p. pap. 19.95 (*0-8288-5080-1*) Fr & Eur.
—El Tesoro de Rackham. (SPA., Illus.). 62p. 19.95 (*0-8288-5081-X*) Fr & Eur.
—Il Tesoro di Rakam. (ITA., Illus.). 62p. pap. 19.95 (*0-8288-5082-8*) Fr & Eur.
—Tim in Tibet. (GER., Illus.). 62p. pap. 19.95 (*0-8288-5083-6*) Fr & Eur.
—Tim und der Haifschsee. (GER., Illus.). 62p. pap. 19.95 (*0-8288-5084-4*) Fr & Eur.
—Tim und die Picaros. (GER., Illus.). 62p. pap. 19.95 (*0-8288-5085-2*) Fr & Eur.
—Tintin & the Broken Ear. (Illus.). 62p. 19.95 (*0-8288-5086-0*) Fr & Eur.
—Tintin & the Golden Fleece. (gr. 3-8). 19.95 (*0-8288-5087-9*) Fr & Eur.
—Tintin & the Lake of Sharks. (Illus.). 62p. 19.95 (*0-416-78950-1*) Fr & Eur.
—Tintin & the Picaros. (Illus.). 62p. 19.95 (*0-8288-5089-5*) Fr & Eur.
—Tintin au Congo. (FRE., Illus.). (gr. 7-9). 19.95 (*0-8288-5090-9*) Fr & Eur.
—Tintin au Pays de L'or Noir. (FRE.). (gr. 7-9). 19.95 (*0-8288-5091-7*) Fr & Eur.
—Tintin Au Tibet. (gr. 7-9). looseleaf bdg. 19.95 (*0-8288-5092-5*) Fr & Eur.
—Tintin en America. (SPA., Illus.). 62p. 19.95 (*0-8288-5094-1*) Fr & Eur.
—Tintin en Amerique. (FRE., Illus.). 62p. 19.95 (*0-8288-5093-3*) Fr & Eur.
—Tintin en el Congo. (SPA., Illus.). 62p. 19.95 (*0-8288-5095-X*) Fr & Eur.
—Tintin en el Pais del Oro Negro. (SPA., Illus.). 62p. 19.95 (*0-8288-4995-1*) Fr & Eur.
—Tintin en el Tibet. (SPA., Illus.). 62p. 19.95 (*0-8288-4996-X*) Fr & Eur.
—Tintin et les Picaros. (FRE., Illus.). 62p. 19.95 (*0-8288-4997-8*) Fr & Eur.
—Tintin im Amerika. (GER., Illus.). 62p. pap. 19.95 (*0-8288-4999-4*) Fr & Eur.
—Tintin im Kongo. (GER., Illus.). 62p. pap. 19.95 (*0-8288-4998-6*) Fr & Eur.
—Tintin in America. (Illus.). 62p. 19.95 (*0-8288-5000-3*) Fr & Eur.
—Tintin in Tibet. (Illus.). 62p. 19.95 (*0-8288-5001-1*) Fr & Eur.
—Tintin in Tibet. LC 74-21621. (gr. k up). 1975. pap. 7.95 (*0-316-35839-8*, Joy St Bks) Little.
—Tintin y los Picaros. (SPA., Illus.). 62p. 19.95 (*0-8288-5002-X*) Fr & Eur.
—Tresor De Rackham le Rouge. (FRE., Illus.). 62p. (gr. 7-9). 19.95 (*0-8288-5003-8*) Fr & Eur.
—Vuelo 714 para Sidney. (SPA., Illus.). 62p. 19.95 (*0-8288-5004-6*) Fr & Eur.
—Y las Naranjas Azules. (SPA., Illus.). 62p. 19.95 (*0-8288-5005-4*) Fr & Eur.
—Die Zigarren des Pharaos. (GER., Illus.). 62p. pap. 19.95 (*0-8288-5006-2*) Fr & Eur.
Herman, Charlotte. Millie Cooper, 3B. Cogancherry, Helen, illus. LC 84-25951. 112p. (gr. 2-6). 1985. 11.95 (*0-525-44157-3*, DCB) Dutton Child Bks.
Herndon, Ernest. The Secret of Lizard Island. LC 93-5011. 144p. 1994. pap. 4.99 (*0-310-38251-3*) Zondervan.
Herzig, Alison C. Boonsville Bombers. (gr. 4-7). 1991. 11.95 (*0-670-83595-1*) Viking Child Bks.
Hezlep, William. Cayman Duppy. (gr. 5 up). 1984. pap. 5.00 play script (*0-88734-403-8*) Players Pr.
The Hides It. (Illus.). (ps-2). 1991. PLB 6.95 (*0-8136-5123-9*, TK2612); pap. 3.50 (*0-8136-5623-0*, TK2611) Modern Curr.
Higbie, William F. Circle of Power. Knight, Denise E., ed. LC 90-82883. (Illus.). 96p. (gr. 3 up). 1990. 13.95 (*0-943604-29-X*); pap. 7.95 perfect bdg. (*0-943604-27-3*) Eagles View.
Higgins, Betty. The Knight Riders. Sun Star Publications Staff, ed. (Illus.). 32p. (gr. 3-8). 1986. pap. 2.95 (*0-937787-17-5*) Sun Star Pubns.
—Passing Through. Sun Star Publications Staff, ed. (Illus.). 26p. (gr. 3-8). 1986. pap. 2.95 (*0-937787-03-5*) Sun Star Pubns.
Highlights for Children Staff. In the Shadow of an Eagle: And Other Adventure Stories. LC 91-77001. (Illus.). 96p. (gr. 3-7). 1992. pap. 2.95 (*1-56397-078-3*) Boyds Mills Pr.
Hildick, E. W. The Ghost Squad & the Halloween Conspiracy. 176p. 1986. pap. 1.95 (*0-8125-6852-4*) Tor Bks.
Hill, Douglas. Day of the Starwind. (Orig.). (gr. k-12). 1987. pap. 2.50 (*0-440-91762-X*, LFL) Dell.
—Deathwing over Veynaa. (Orig.). (gr. k-12). 1987. pap. 2.50 (*0-440-91743-3*, LFL) Dell.
—Planet of the Warlord. (gr. 7 up). 1987. pap. 2.50 (*0-440-97126-8*) Dell.

—Young Legionary. (gr. k-12). 1987. pap. 2.50 (*0-440-99910-3*, LFL) Dell.
Hiller, B. B. The Sacred Scroll of Death. (gr. 4-7). 1993. pap. 3.99 (*0-440-40800-8*) Dell.
Hilts, Len. Quanah Parker: Warrior for Freedom, Ambassador for Peace. LC 87-8488. 148p. (gr. 3-7). 1987. 12.95 (*0-15-200565-X*, Gulliver Bks) HarBrace.
Ho, Minfong. Clay Marble. (gr. 4-7). 1993. pap. 4.50 (*0-374-41229-4*) FS&G.
Hobbs, Will. Downriver. (gr. 7 up). 1992. pap. 3.99 (*0-553-29717-1*, Starfire) Bantam.
Hodgman, Ann. The Missing Mermaid. 128p. (Orig.). 1987. pap. 2.25 (*0-553-26471-0*) Bantam.
Hol, Coby. Der Sonnenhof. Hol, Coby, illus. (GER.). 32p. (gr. k-3). 1992. 13.95 (*3-85825-315-4*) North-South Bks NYC.
Holl, Kristi. Danger at Hanging Rock. LC 89-460. (gr. 7-9). 1989. pap. 3.99 (*1-55513-067-4*, Chariot Bks) Chariot Family.
Holyer, Erna M. Reservoir Road Adventure. (Orig.). (gr. 5-8). 1982. pap. 3.99 (*0-8010-4261-5*) Baker Bk.
Hooks, William J. Pioneer Cat. Robinson, Charles, illus. LC 88-4708. 64p. (Orig.). (gr. 2-4). 1988. 2.99 (*0-394-82038-X*); lib. bdg. 6.99 (*0-394-92038-4*) Random Bks Yng Read.
Hope, Anthony. Prisoner of Zenda. Teitel, N. R., intro. by. (Illus.). (gr. 8 up). 1967. pap. 1.25 (*0-8049-0139-2*, CL-139) Airmont.
—Prisoner of Zenda. 176p. (gr. 4-6). 1984. pap. 2.95 (*0-14-035032-2*, Puffin) Puffin Bks.
Horie, Michiaki & Horie, Hildegard. Lost Identity. Huff, Dawn, tr. from GER. 96p. (Orig.). (gr. 7 up). 1987. pap. 5.95 (*0-939925-09-5*) R C Law & Co.
The Horror of High Ridge. (gr. 4). 1983. pap. 2.25 (*0-553-26309-9*) Bantam.
Houston, James R. Drifting Snow: An Arctic Search. 160p. 1994. pap. 3.99 (*0-14-036530-3*) Puffin Bks.
—River Runners: A Tale of Hardship & Bravery. 160p. (gr. 5 up). 1992. pap. 4.50 (*0-14-036093-X*, Puffin) Puffin Bks.
Howard, Milly. Brave the Wild Trail. (Illus.). 129p. (Orig.). (gr. 4-6). 1987. pap. 4.95 (*0-89084-384-8*) Bob Jones Univ Pr.
Hunter, Mollie. A Pistol in Greenyards. 192p. (gr. 5-8). 1990. pap. 6.95 (*0-86241-175-0*, Pub. by Cnngt UK) Trafalgar.
—A Sound of Chariots. LC 72-76523. 256p. (gr. 5-9). 1988. pap. 3.95 (*0-06-440235-5*, Trophy) HarpC Child Bks.
—A Stranger Came Ashore. 128p. (gr. 4 up). 1994. pap. 7.95 (*0-85241-465-X*, Pub. by Cnngt UK) Trafalgar.
Hurwitz, Johanna. The Adventures of Ali Baba Bernstein. LC 84-27387. (Illus.). 96p. (gr. 2-5). 1985. 12.95 (*0-688-04161-2*); PLB 12.88 (*0-688-04345-3*, Morrow Jr Bks) Morrow Jr Bks.
Hutchens, Paul. The Killer Bear. rev. ed. (gr. 2-7). 1989. pap. 4.99 (*0-8024-6957-4*) Moody.
—The Lost Campers. rev. ed. (gr. 2-7). 1989. pap. 4.99 (*0-8024-6959-0*) Moody.
—Lost in the Blizzard. (gr. 2-7). 1970. pap. 4.99 (*0-8024-4817-8*) Moody.
—The Mystery Cave. rev. ed. (gr. 2-7). 1989. pap. 4.99 (*0-8024-4807-0*) Moody.
—The Secret Hideout. rev. ed. 1989. pap. 4.99 (*0-8024-6960-4*) Moody.
—The Sugar Creek Gang & Blue Cow. (Illus.). 128p. (gr. 3-7). 1971. pap. 4.99 (*0-8024-4822-4*) Moody.
—Sugar Creek Gang & Screams in the Night. (gr. 3-7). 1967. pap. 4.99 (*0-8024-4812-7*) Moody.
—Sugar Creek Gang & the Chicago Adventure & One Stormy Day. (gr. 3-7). 1968. pap. 6.99 (*0-8024-1237-8*) Moody.
—Sugar Creek Gang & the Colorado Kidnapping. (gr. 3-7). 1970. pap. 4.99 (*0-8024-4827-5*) Moody.
—Sugar Creek Gang & the Ghost Dog. (gr. 3-7). 1968. pap. 4.99 (*0-8024-4832-1*) Moody.
—Sugar Creek Gang & the Indian Cemetary. (gr. 3-7). 1970. pap. 4.99 (*0-8024-4813-5*) Moody.
—The Sugar Creek Gang & the Killer Bear. (gr. 3-7). pap. 4.99 (*0-8024-4802-X*) Moody.
—Sugar Creek Gang & the Killer Cat. (gr. 3-7). 1966. pap. 4.99 (*0-8024-4825-9*) Moody.
—Sugar Creek Gang & the Lost Campers. (gr. 3-7). 1968. pap. 4.99 (*0-8024-4804-6*) Moody.
—Sugar Creek Gang & the Palm Tree Manhunt. (gr. 3-7). 1969. pap. 4.99 (*0-8024-4808-9*) Moody.
—Sugar Creek Gang & the Secret Hideout. (gr. 3-7). 1968. pap. 4.99 (*0-8024-4806-2*) Moody.
—The Swamp Robber. (gr. 2-7). 1966. pap. 4.99 (*0-8024-4801-1*) Moody.
—The Teacher Trouble. (gr. 2-7). 1970. pap. 4.99 (*0-8024-4811-9*) Moody.
—The Thousand Dollar Fish. (gr. 2-7). 1966. pap. 4.99 (*0-8024-4815-1*) Moody.
—The Treasure Hunt. (gr. 2-7). 1967. pap. 4.99 (*0-8024-4814-3*) Moody.
—The Watermelon Mystery. (Illus.). 128p. (gr. 2-7). 1971. pap. 4.99 (*0-8024-4826-7*) Moody.
—The Western Adventure. (gr. 2-7). 1966. pap. 4.99 (*0-8024-4824-0*) Moody.
—The White Boat Rescue. (gr. 3-7). 1970. pap. 4.99 (*0-8024-4833-X*) Moody.
—The Winter Rescue. rev. ed. 1989. pap. 0.00 cancelled (*0-8024-6958-2*) Moody.
Hutchinson, Haji U. Invincible Abdullah, Vol. 1: The Deadly Mountain Revenge. Siddiqui, Zeba, ed. Al-Amin, Abd A., illus. 222p. (Orig.). (gr. 6-12). 1992. pap. 5.95 (*0-89259-121-8*) Am Trust Pubns.
Hutton, John. Guale. 201p. (gr. 8). 1993. pap. 4.80 (*1-882534-01-8*) Am Efficiency.
—Gulla Island: An Island Kids' Adventure. LC 92-97148. 160p. (gr. 8). 1992. pap. 4.80 (*1-882534-00-X*) Am Efficiency.
Hwa-I Publishing Co., Staff. Chinese Children's Stories, Vol. 51: Moginlin Saves His Mother, Hwang Shun & His Father. Ching, Emily, et al, eds. Wonder Kids Publications Staff, tr. from CHI. (Illus.). 28p. (gr. 3-6). 1991. Repr. of 1988 ed. 7.95 (*1-56162-051-3*) Wonder Kids.
—Chinese Children's Stories, Vol. 56: Catching a Thief, The Plum Tree by the Road. Ching, Emily, et al, eds. Wonder Kids Publications Staff, tr. from CHI. (Illus.). 28p. (gr. 3-6). 1991. Repr. of 1988 ed. 7.95 (*1-56162-056-4*) Wonder Kids.
Ingle, Annie, adapted by. Robin Hood. reissued ed. D'Andrea, Domenick, illus. LC 90-23078. 96p. (Orig.). (gr. 2-6). 1993. pap. 2.99 (*0-679-81045-5*) Random Bks Yng Read.
It's Your Adventure, Unit 11. (gr. 3). 1991. 5-pack 21.25 (*0-88106-791-1*) Charlesbridge Pub.
Jackson, Bobby L. & Carter, Michael C. Martin "The Hero" Merriweather. Fultz, Jim, illus. Reuter, Janet R., frwd. by. LC 93-77056. (Illus.). 48p. (Orig.). (gr. 4-8). 1993. 12.95g (*0-9634932-2-1*); pap. 7.95g (*0-9634932-3-X*) Multicult Pubns.
Jackson, Dave. Attack in the Rye Grass. (gr. 4-7). 1994. pap. 4.99 (*1-55661-273-7*) Bethany Hse.
—Listen for the Whippoorwill. (gr. 4-7). 1993. pap. 4.99 (*1-55661-272-9*) Bethany Hse.
Jackson, Dave & Jackson, Neta. Escape from the Slave Traders. LC 92-11170. 128p. (Orig.). (gr. 3-7). 1992. pap. 4.99 (*1-55661-263-X*) Bethany Hse.
Jackson, Steve & Livingstone, Ian. Seas of Blood. (Orig.). (gr. 5 up). 1986. pap. 2.50 (*0-440-97708-8*, LFL) Dell.
Jacques, Brian. Redwall. LC 86-25467. (gr. k up). 1987. 16.95 (*0-399-21424-0*, Philomel Bks) Putnam Pub Group.
James L. & Collier, Christopher. War Comes to Willy Freeman. (gr. k-6). 1987. pap. 3.99 (*0-440-49504-0*, YB) Dell.
Joachim, Mary J. Captain & Joey & the Tumbled down Cabin. Decker, Tim, illus. LC 89-81198. 47p. (Orig.). 1990. pap. 4.95 (*0-916383-99-7*) Aegina Pr.
Johnson, Crockett. Harold's Circus. LC 59-5318. (ps-3). 1959. PLB 11.89 (*0-06-022966-7*) HarpC Child Bks.
Johnson, Lois W. The Disappearing Stranger. 144p. (Orig.). (gr. 3-5). 1990. pap. 5.99 (*1-55661-100-5*) Bethany Hse.
—Grandpa's Stolen Treasure. LC 92-30093. 144p. (Orig.). (gr. 3-8). 1992. pap. 5.99 (*1-55661-239-7*) Bethany Hse.
—The Hidden Message. LC 89-78390. 144p. (Orig.). (gr. 3-8). 1990. pap. 5.99 (*1-55661-101-3*) Bethany Hse.
—Mysterious Hideaway: Adventures of the Northwoods. (gr. 4-7). 1992. pap. 5.99 (*1-55661-238-9*) Bethany Hse.
—Trouble at Wild River. 144p. (Orig.). (gr. 3-8). 1991. pap. 5.99 (*1-55661-144-7*) Bethany Hse.
—Vanishing Footprints. 144p. (Orig.). (ps-8). 1991. pap. 5.99 (*1-55661-103-X*) Bethany Hse.
Johnson, Neil. Born to Run. (ps-4). 1989. pap. 3.95 (*0-590-42836-5*) Scholastic Inc.
Johnson, Paul H. Samurai in Valhalla - Past the Future. 367p. (Orig.). (gr. 9 up). 1993. pap. 5.95 (*0-9636833-1-4*) Piros Pr.
Johnson, Seddon. Alien, Go Home. 1990. pap. 3.25 (*0-553-28482-7*) Bantam.
—South Pole Sabotage. 1989. pap. 2.50 (*0-553-27770-7*) Bantam.
Johnson, Stacie. Sky Man. 1993. pap. 3.50 (*0-553-29723-6*) Bantam.
Johnson, Tara. Huckleberry Fun. LC 89-51090. 44p. (gr. k-3). 1990. 5.95 (*1-55523-248-5*) Winston-Derek.
Johnston, Tony. The Adventures of Mole & Troll. (gr. k-6). 1989. pap. 2.95 (*0-440-40218-2*, YB) Dell.
Jonas, Ann. El Trayecto: The Trek. Mlawer, Teresa, tr. from ENG. (Illus.). 32p. (gr. 5-7). 1991. PLB 13.95 (*0-9625162-3-6*) Lectorum Pubns.
—The Trek. Jonas, Ann, illus. LC 84-25962. 32p. (gr. k-3). 1985. 14.95 (*0-688-04799-8*); lib. bdg. 14.88 (*0-688-04800-5*) Greenwillow.
Jones, Amy. Abracadabra. Thatch, Nancy R., ed. Jones, Amy, illus. Melton, David, intro. by. LC 93-13421. (Illus.). 29p. (gr. 3-5). 1993. PLB 14.95 (*0-933849-46-X*) Landmark Edns.
Jones, J. David. The Adventures of Little Red. Krull, Kathleen, ed. Sieck, Judythe, illus. 64p. 1993. write for info. (*1-883088-01-1*) Source CA.
Jones, Rebecca C. Germy Blew the Bugle. 128p. (gr. 2-5). 1990. 14.95 (*1-55970-088-2*) Arcade Pub Inc.
Jones, Terry. The Saga of Erik the Viking. Foreman, Michael, illus. 192p. (gr. 3-7). 1993. pap. 3.99 (*0-14-032261-2*, Puffin) Puffin Bks.
Joval, Nomi. Salon de Espejos. Kubinyi, Laszlo, illus. (SPA.). 16p. (gr. k-4). 1992. PLB 13.95 (*1-879567-07-5*, Valeria Bks) Wonder Well.
Joyce, James. The Boarding House. (Illus.). 1982. PLB 13.95 (*0-87191-895-1*) Creative Ed.
Karate Kid. 1986. pap. 1.25 (*0-440-82199-1*) Dell.
Karlin, Bernie & Karlin, Mati. Night Ride. Karlin, Bernie, illus. (ps-2). 1988. pap. 12.95 jacketed (*0-671-66733-5*, S&S BFYR) S&S Trade.
Kassem, Lou. The Treasures of Witch Hat Mountain. 112p. (Orig.). 1992. pap. 2.99 (*0-380-76519-5*, Camelot) Avon.
Kaufman, Gershen. Journey to a Magic Castle. Jeffery, Megan E., illus. LC 91-78278. 30p. (gr. 5-8). 1993. pap. write for info. incl. worksheets (*0-916634-14-0*) Double M Pr.
Keefer, Mikal. Ready for Something New. Yacoba, illus. 48p. (Orig.). (gr. 1-3). 1993. pap. text ed. 3.99 (*0-7847-0097-4*, 24-03947) Standard Pub.
Keene, Carolyn. Junior Class Trip. Greenberg, Ann, ed. 224p. (Orig.). 1991. pap. 2.95 (*0-671-73124-6*, Archway) PB.
Keller, Kent. The Mayan Mystery. LC 93-48838. (Illus.). 1994. 4.99 (*0-8423-5132-9*) Tyndale.
Kelley, Shirley. The Rainy Day Blues. Herbst, Eric & Genee, Gloria, eds. Claridy, Jimmy, illus. King, B. B., intro. by. (Illus.). 32p. (ps-4). 1993. Incl. audio cass. 9.95 (*1-882436-01-6*) Better Pl Pub.
Kellogg, Steven. Ralph's Secret Weapon. Kellogg, Steven, illus. LC 82-22115. (ps-3). 1983. 13.95 (*0-8037-7086-3*); PLB 13.89 (*0-8037-7087-1*); pap. 3.95 (*0-8037-0307-4*) Dial Bks Young.

Kempton, Kate. The World Beyond the Waves. Salk, Larry, illus. Trehearn, Carol, created by. (Illus.). 96p. (gr. 4-8). 1995. 19.95 (*0-9641330-1-6*) Portunus Pubng.
Like Dorothy in THE WIZARD OF OZ, Sam, the young heroine of THE WORLD BEYOND THE WAVES, is carried away by the tremendous force of a storm only to wake up in a strange & magical world beneath the sea, a refuge for animals escaping from mankind's abuse of the world's oceans. Helped to recover by these marine creatures & led on a series of adventures, Sam develops a deep awareness of the consequences of mankind's collective behavior towards the oceans from the use of drift nets for fishing to the pollution of the sea by industrial waste, oil & garbage. After her return to the surface, where her aunt & uncle have been leading the search for her, Sam succeeds in preventing an oil-test drilling ship from destroying the magical world which had saved her life, affirming in the process that with love & determination, one person can make a difference. With its skillful combination of a message of environmental awareness with a moving story of initiation into responsibility, THE WORLD BEYOND THE WAVES should prove a favorite for parents, children & teachers alike. *Publisher Provided Annotation.*

Kendall, Sarita. The Bell Reef. Hudson, Mark, illus. 144p. (gr. 5-9). 1990. 13.45 (*0-395-53354-6*) HM.
Kennaway, James. Tunes of Glory. 192p. 1989. pap. 9.95 (*0-86241-223-4*, Pub. by Cnngt Pub Ltd) Trafalgar.
Kennedy, Richard. Amy's Eyes. Egielski, Richard, illus. LC 82-48841. 448p. (ps up). 1985. 15.00 (*0-06-023219-6*) HarpC Child Bks.
Kessler, Leonard. The Big Mile Race. Kessler, Leonard, illus. LC 82-9274. 48p. (gr. 1-3). 1983. 9.00 (*0-688-01420-8*) Greenwillow.
Kherdian, David. Bridger: The Story of Mountain Man. LC 86-7558. 160p. (gr. 7 up). 1987. 11.75 (*0-688-06510-4*) Greenwillow.
Kidd, Ronald. Sizzle & Splat. (gr. 5-8). 1986. pap. 2.95 (*0-440-47970-3*, YB) Dell.
Kidd, Ronald, adapted by. Robin Hood. 20p. (ps up). 1992. write for info. (*0-307-74703-4*, 64703) Western Pub.
Kindell, Roy. Night Sky Star Lore. (Illus.). 52p. (Orig.). (gr. 7 up). 1989. pap. 5.95 (*0-9625388-0-9*) Ursa Major Corp.
King, Clive, ed. Adventure Stories. Walker, Brian, illus. LC 92-26452. 1993. pap. 6.95 (*1-85697-882-6*, Kingfisher LKC) LKC.
King, Vivienne, et al. Let's Go on Safari. O'Halloran, Tim, illus. 32p. (ps-3). 1985. pap. 3.95 (*0-88625-107-9*) Durkin Hayes Pub.
King-Smith, Dick. The Toby Man. Hemmant, Lynette, illus. LC 90-28443. 128p. (gr. 2-7). 1991. lib. bdg. 14.99 (*0-517-58135-3*) Crown Bks Yng Read.
Kipling, Rudyard. Gunga Din. Parker, Robert A., illus. LC 86-19388. 28p. (gr. 1 up). 1987. 12.95 (*0-15-200456-4*, Gulliver Bks) HarBrace.
—The Jungle Book: A Young Reader's Edition of the Classic Story. Barrett, G. C., retold by. Dally, Don, illus. 56p. 1994. 9.98 (*1-56138-475-5*) Running Pr.

—Just So Stories. Salter, Safaya, illus. LC 86-46271. 96p. (gr. 2-4). 1987. 17.95 (*0-8050-0439-4*, Bks Young Read) H Holt & Co.

—Kim. (gr. 8 up). 1965. pap. 1.95 (*0-8049-0075-2*) Airmont.

—Livre de la Jungle. Pilorget, Bruno, illus. (FRE.). 254p. (gr. 5-10). 1987. pap. 10.95 (*2-07-033456-2*) Schoenhof.

—Puck of Pook's Hill. 1987. pap. 2.25 (*0-14-035077-2*, Puffin) Puffin Bks.

—Stalky & Co. (gr. 4-7). 1991. pap. 3.50 (*0-440-40519-X*, Pub. by Yearling Classics) Dell.

Kirchoff, Mary L. Kendermore. LC 88-51719. (Illus.). 352p. (Orig.). 1989. pap. 4.95 (*0-88038-754-8*) TSR Inc.

Kjelgaard, Jim. Wild Trek. 1984. pap. 3.99 (*0-553-15687-X*) Bantam.

—Wild Trek. (gr. 4-7). 1992. 16.75 (*0-8446-6594-0*) Peter Smith.

Kline, Suzy. Orp. 96p. (gr. 3-7). 1989. 13.95 (*0-399-21639-1*, Putnam) Putnam Pub Group.

Knight, Sarah K. The Journal of Madam Knight. LC 91-46984. 88p. 1992. pap. 7.95 (*1-55709-115-3*) Applewood.

Knox, Bob. Dave & Jane's Adventures with Lewis & Clark. LC 94-14446. (Illus.). 32p. (gr. 2-7). 1994. 15.95 (*0-8478-1834-9*) Rizzoli Intl.

Knudson, R. R. Sanboomer. 192p. (gr. 6 up). 1980. pap. 1.95 (*0-440-99908-1*, LFL) Dell.

Koike, Kazuo. Crying Freeman, Vol. 1. Horibuchi, Seiji, ed. Fujii, Satoru, et al, trs. from JPN. Ikegami, Ryoichi, illus. 64p. (Orig.). (gr. 12 up). 1989. pap. text ed. 3.50 (*0-929279-50-6*) Viz Commns Inc.

—Crying Freeman, Vol. 2. Horibuchi, Seiji, ed. Fujii, Satoru, et al, trs. from JPN. Ikegami, Ryoichi, illus. 64p. (Orig.). (gr. 12 up). 1989. pap. text ed. 3.50 (*0-929279-51-4*) Viz Commns Inc.

—Crying Freeman, Vol. 3. Horibuchi, Seiji, ed. Fujii, Satoru, et al, trs. from JPN. Ikegami, Ryoichi, illus. 64p. (Orig.). (gr. 12 up). 1989. pap. text ed. 3.50 (*0-929279-52-2*) Viz Commns Inc.

—Crying Freeman, Vol. 4. Horibuchi, Seiji, ed. Fujii, Satoru, et al, trs. from JPN. Ikegami, Ryoichi, illus. 64p. (Orig.). (gr. 12 up). 1990. pap. text ed. 3.50 (*0-929279-53-0*) Viz Commns Inc.

—Crying Freeman, Vol. 5. Horibuchi, Seiji, ed. Fujii, Satoru, et al, trs. from JPN. Ikegami, Ryoichi, illus. 64p. (Orig.). (gr. 12 up). 1990. pap. text ed. 3.50 (*0-929279-54-9*) Viz Commns Inc.

—Crying Freeman, Vol. 6. Horibuchi, Seiji, ed. Fujii, Satoru, et al, trs. from JPN. Ikegami, Ryoichi, illus. 64p. (Orig.). (gr. 12 up). 1990. pap. text ed. 3.50 (*0-929279-55-7*) Viz Commns Inc.

—Crying Freeman, Vol. 7. Horibuchi, Seiji, ed. Fujii, Satoru, et al, trs. from JPN. Ikegami, Ryoichi, illus. 64p. (Orig.). (gr. 12 up). 1990. pap. text ed. 3.50 (*0-929279-56-5*) Viz Commns Inc.

—Crying Freeman, Vol. 8. Horibuchi, Seiji, ed. Fugii, Satoru, et al, trs. from JPN. Ikegami, Ryoichi, illus. 64p. (Orig.). (gr. 12 up). 1990. pap. text ed. 3.50 (*0-929279-57-3*) Viz Commns Inc.

Koltz, Tony. Terror Island. 128p. (gr. 4). 1986. pap. 2.25 (*0-553-25885-0*) Bantam.

Kontoyiannaki, Elizabeth. The Adventures of Millie. Kontoyiannaki, Elizabeth, illus. 15p. (gr. 1-3). 1992. pap. 10.95 (*1-56606-012-5*) Bradley Mann.

Kool Kat. (Illus.). 1986. pap. 0.95 (*0-440-82098-7*) Dell.

Korman, Justine & Fontes, Ron. Batman Returns: The Movie Storybook. (Illus.). 48p. (ps-3). 1992. write for info. (*0-307-15954-X*, 15954, Golden Pr) Western Pub.

Kramer, Stephen. Lightning. (ps-3). 1993. pap. 7.95 (*0-87614-617-5*) Carolrhoda Bks.

Kreuger, Cynthia M. & Kreuger, Kirsten M. Adventure to Orbital. LC 92-61367. 45p. (gr. k-4). 1993. pap. 5.95 (*1-55523-558-1*) Winston-Derek.

Kushner, Ellen. The Camelot Caper. 176p. (Orig.). (gr. 4 up). 1988. pap. 2.50 (*0-553-27595-X*) Bantam.

—Enchanted Kindom. (ps-7). 1986. pap. 2.25 (*0-553-25861-3*) Bantam.

—The Knights of the Round Table. 128p. (gr. 4). 1988. pap. 2.50 (*0-318-37113-8*) Bantam.

—Mystery of the Secret Room. (gr. 5-12). 1987. pap. 2.25 (*0-553-26270-X*) Bantam.

—Outlaws of Sherwood Forest. 128p. (Orig.). (gr. 5 up). 1985. pap. 2.25 (*0-553-26388-9*) Bantam.

—Statue of Liberty Adventure. (ps-7). 1986. pap. 2.25 (*0-553-25813-3*) Bantam.

Kyte, Dennis. Zackary Raffles. 1989. pap. 13.95 (*0-385-24652-8*) Doubleday.

Lagerlof, Selma. The Further Adventures of Nils. rev. ed. Johnson, Nancy, rev. by. Howard, Velma S., tr. from SWE. Baumhauer, Hans, illus. Johnson, Nancy, intro. by. (Illus.). 262p. (gr. 4-12). 1992. pap. 12.95x (*0-9615394-4-5*) Skandisk.

—The Wonderful Adventures of Nils, Bk. 1. rev. ed. Johnson, Nancy, intro. by. Howard, Velma S., tr. from SWE. Baumhauer, Hans, illus. Johnson, Nancy, rev. by. (Illus.). 254p. (gr. 4-12). 1991. pap. 12.95 (*0-9615394-3-7*) Skandisk.

Lake, Simon. Death Cycle. 1993. pap. 3.50 (*0-553-56102-2*) Bantam.

Lam, Roger. The Cuckoo Clock Adventure. Gibb, George, ed. Sweetman, Daniel, illus. LC 82-99848. (Orig.). (gr. 5-12). 1983. pap. 2.25 (*0-943310-01-6*) Six Pr.

Lamb, F. Bruce & Rios, Manual C. Kidnapped in the Amazon Jungle. Cotts, Claire, illus. 120p. (Orig.). 1994. pap. 14.95 (*1-55643-173-2*) North Atlantic.

Lanagan, Margo. Tankermen. 1993. pap. 6.95 (*1-86373-253-5*, Pub. by Allen & Unwin Aust Pty AT) IPG Chicago.

Landis, Mary M. Trouble at Windy Acres. (gr. 5-10). 1976. 7.15 (*0-686-15486-X*) Rod & Staff.

LaPiana, Maxine F. Westward Ho! 1994. 7.95 (*0-8062-4925-0*) Carlton.

Larrick, Nancy, intro. by. Piping Down the Valleys Wild. Raskin, Ellen, illus. LC 68-27742. 256p. (ps-3). 1985. 14.95 (*0-385-29429-8*) Delacorte.

Larsen, Anita. Lost & Never Found. (gr. 4-7). 1991. pap. 2.75 (*0-590-44447-6*) Scholastic Inc.

—Lost & Never Found Two. (gr. 4-7). 1991. pap. 2.75 (*0-590-43878-6*) Scholastic Inc.

Lasky, Kathryn. Beyond the Divide. (gr. 7 up). 1986. pap. 3.25 (*0-440-91021-8*, LFL) Dell.

—The Bone Wars. LC 88-13426. 378p. (gr. 7 up). 1988. 12.95 (*0-688-07433-2*) Morrow Jr Bks.

Laughlin, Rosemary M. Trouble on the Shoshone. LC 88-50762. 94p. (gr. 5-8). 1989. pap. 5.95 (*1-55523-154-3*) Winston-Derek.

Laury, Jean R. No Dragons On My Quilt. (gr. k up). 1990. 12.95 (*0-89145-967-7*) Collector Bks.

Lavender, David. The Trail to Santa Fe. rev. ed. Eggenhoffer, Nicholas, illus. LC 58-9634. 112p. (gr. 4-8). 1988. pap. 8.95 (*0-939729-15-6*) Trails West Pub.

Lawrence, Edith. The Wayfaring Princes: A Tale of Questing & Adventure. Keltz, Martha, illus. 136p. (Orig.). (gr. 4-7). 1987. pap. 8.00 (*0-936132-86-8*) Merc Pr NY.

Lawson, Robert. The Fabulous Flight. (Illus.). 152p. (gr. 4-8). 1984. pap. 5.95 (*0-316-51731-3*) Little.

Learngis. Amazing Ben Franklin. 80p. (Orig.). 1987. pap. 2.50 (*0-553-15504-0*) Bantam.

Le Clezio, J. M. Voyage au Pays des Arbres. Galero, Henri, illus. (FRE.). 48p. (gr. 3-7). 1990. pap. 8.95 (*2-07-031187-2*) Schoenhof.

Lee, Chas. Totally Trusting. Ritner, Wanda, illus. 222p. (gr. 4-10). 1992. 19.95 (*1-878044-09-5*) Mayhaven Pub.

Lee, Jeanne M. Ba-Nam. Lee, Jeanne M., illus. LC 86-27127. 32p. (ps-2). 1987. 13.95 (*0-8050-0169-7*, Bks Young Read) H Holt & Co.

Leedy, Loreen. A Dragon Christmas: Things to Make & Do. Leedy, Loreen, illus. LC 88-4635. 32p. (ps-3). 1988. reinforced bdg. 13.95 (*0-8234-0716-0*) Holiday.

Leeson, Muriel. The Bedford Adventure. Ponter, James, illus. LC 87-11943. 136p. (Orig.). (gr. 4-9). 1987. pap. 4.50 (*0-8361-3448-6*) Herald Pr.

Le Guin, Ursula K. The Farthest Shore. rev. ed. Garraty, Gail, illus. LC 72-75273. 240p. (gr. 6 up). 1990. SBE 16.95 (*0-689-31683-6*, Atheneum Child Bk) Macmillan Child Grp.

Lehmann, G. D. The Curse of the Amulet. 164p. (gr. 4-8). 1992. pap. 4.95 (*0-87508-443-5*) Chr Lit.

—Saved by Fire. (Illus.). 125p. (gr. 4-8). 1992. pap. 4.95 (*0-87508-441-9*) Chr Lit.

Lehner, Devony. Tinker's Journey Home. Maloney, P. Dennis, ed. Adamson, Charlotte, illus. 34p. (ps-6). 12.95 (*0-940305-00-3*) P D Maloney.

Leibold, Jay. Beyond the Great Wall. (gr. 5 up). 1987. pap. 2.50 (*0-553-26725-6*) Bantam.

—Fight for Freedom. 1990. pap. 3.25 (*0-553-28766-4*) Bantam.

—Grand Canyon Odyssey. 128p. (Orig.). (gr. 5). 1985. pap. 2.25 (*0-553-26522-9*) Bantam.

—The Lost Ninja. 1991. pap. 3.50 (*0-553-28960-8*) Bantam.

—Return of the Ninja. 1989. pap. 3.25 (*0-553-27968-8*) Bantam.

—Revenge of the Russian Ghost. 1990. pap. 2.75 (*0-553-28381-2*) Bantam.

L'Engle, Madeleine. Many Waters. (gr. 4-7). 1987. pap. 4.50 (*0-440-40548-3*) Dell.

Leonard, Larry. Far Walker. Gustavson, Susan, illus. LC 88-12290. 120p. (gr. 1 up). 1988. 12.95 (*0-932576-60-5*) Breitenbush Bks.

Leonard, Laura. Finding Papa. LC 90-23742. 192p. (gr. 3-7). 1991. SBE 14.95 (*0-689-31526-0*, Atheneum Child Bk) Macmillan Child Grp.

Leonard, Marcia. Your First Adventure: Little Goat's Big Brother, No. 12. Santoro, Christopher, illus. 24p. (Orig.). 1987. pap. 2.50 (*0-553-15503-2*) Bantam.

Leppard, Lois G. Mandie & the Dangerous Imposter. (gr. 4-7). 1994. pap. 3.99 (*1-55661-459-4*) Bethany Hse.

Lerangis, Peter, adapted by. Safari Sleuth. LC 91-53168. (Illus.). 136p. (Orig.). (gr. 4-8). 1992. PLB cancelled (*0-679-92776-X*); pap. 3.50 (*0-679-82776-5*) Random Bks Yng Read.

Lessac, Frane. My Little Island. Lessac, Frane, illus. LC 84-48355. 48p. (gr. 1-4). 1985. (Lipp Jr Bks); PLB 13.89 (*0-397-32115-5*) HarpC Child Bks.

Levitin, Sonia. Incident at Loring Groves. LC 87-24591. 192p. (gr. 7 up). 1988. 14.95 (*0-8037-0455-0*) Dial Bks Young.

—The Mark of Conte. 240p. (gr. 7 up). 1987. pap. 3.95 (*0-02-044191-6*, Collier Young Ad) Macmillan Child Grp.

Lewis, Jennifer. The Adventures of Bugsy McDougal. rev. ed. 1994. 6.95 (*0-8062-4915-3*) Carlton.

Lewis, Thomas P. Clipper Ship. Sandin, Joan, illus. LC 77-11858. 64p. (gr. k-3). 1992. pap. 3.50 (*0-06-444160-1*, Trophy) HarpC Child Bks.

Lindgren, Astrid. Pippi Goes on Board. 172p. 1980. PLB 12.95x (*0-89967-014-8*) Harmony Raine.

—Pippi Longstocking. 175p. 1980. Repr. PLB 12.95x (*0-89967-013-X*) Harmony Raine.

—The Runaway Sleigh Ride. Wikland, Ilon, illus. LC 83-23347. 32p. (ps-3). 1984. pap. 11.95 (*0-670-40454-3*) Viking Child Bks.

Lionni, Leo. Tico & the Golden Wings. LC 64-18321. (Illus.). 32p. (ps-6). 1975. 4.99 (*0-394-83078-4*) Knopf Bks Yng Read.

Lipsyte, Robert. The Contender. LC 67-19623. 190p. (gr. 7-9). 1967. PLB 14.89 (*0-06-023920-4*) HarpC Child Bks.

Little Brown Staff. George Balanchine's the Nutcracker, Vol. 1: A Keepsake Edition. (gr. 4-7). 1993. 8.95 (*0-316-23154-1*) Little.

Little, Jean & De Vries, Maggie. Once upon a Golden Apple. Gilman, Phoebe, illus. 32p. (ps-3). 1991. 12.95 (*0-670-82963-3*) Viking Child Bks.

Littleton, Mark R. Trouble Down the Creek. Norton, LoraBeth, ed. 208p. (gr. 4-6). Date not set. pap. 5.99 (*0-7814-0082-1*, Chariot Bks) Chariot Family.

London, Jack. Call of the Wild. (gr. 9-12). 1987. pap. 2.95 (*0-590-44001-2*, NAL) Scholastic Inc.

—Call of the Wild. 128p. (gr. 9-12). 1990. pap. 2.50 (*0-8125-0432-1*) Tor Bks.

—Call of the Wild. (Illus.). 1991. pap. 2.95 (*1-56156-094-4*) Kidsbks.

—The Call of the Wild. (gr. 8). 1991. pap. write for info. (*0-663-56265-1*) Silver Burdett Pr.

—Jack London's Stories of the North. 256p. (gr. 4 up). 1989. pap. 2.95 (*0-590-44229-5*) Scholastic Inc.

—White Fang: Illustrated Classics. Arneson, D. J., ed. Walker, Karen, illus. 128p. (Orig.). 1990. pap. 2.95 (*0-942025-84-9*) Kidsbks.

London, Jack & Conrad, Joseph. Reader's Digest Best Loved Books for Young Readers: The Call of the Wild & Typhoon. Ogburn, Jackie, ed. Schoenherr, John & Mullins, Frank, illus. 136p. (gr. 4-12). 1989. 3.99 (*0-945260-28-8*) Choice Pub NY.

London, Jack, et al. The Call of the Wild. (Illus.). 52p. Date not set. pap. 4.95 (*1-57209-010-3*) Classics Int Ent.

Lost in the Cave. (Illus.). 40p. (gr. k-5). 1994. pap. 4.95 (*0-685-71587-6*, 523) W Gladden Found.

Lost on the Amazon. (Illus.). (gr. 4). 1983. pap. 2.25 (*0-553-25795-1*) Bantam.

Lowry, Lois. Anastasia at Your Service. 160p. (gr. 3-6). 1984. pap. 3.50 (*0-440-40290-5*, YB) Dell.

Luceno, James. The Mata Hari Affair. (gr. 4-6). 1992. pap. 4.99 (*0-345-38009-6*) Ballantine.

Lum, Ray J. The Rebus Escape. LC 91-76970. 64p. (Orig.). (gr. 3-5). 1992. pap. 5.95x (*0-943864-63-1*) Davenport.

Lynn, Claire. A Cave Is a Deep Dark Hole. 48p. (gr. 1-4). 1978. pap. 1.00 (*0-89323-012-X*, 100) Bible Memory.

Macaulay, David. Unbuilding. Macaulay, David, illus. LC 80-15491. 128p. (gr. 5 up). 1987. pap. 6.95 (*0-395-45360-7*) HM.

McCarthy, M. Dianne. The Maple Leaf. LC 92-91176. 168p. (gr. 3 up). 1994. pap. 9.00 (*1-56002-280-9*, Univ Edtns) Aegina Pr.

McCay, William. Young Indiana Jones & the Circle of Death, Bk. 3. LC 89-43390. 112p. (Orig.). (gr. 3-7). 1990. PLB 6.99 (*0-679-90578-2*); pap. 2.95 (*0-679-80578-8*) Random Bks Yng Read.

—Young Indiana Jones & the Curse of the Ruby Cross, Bk. 8. LC 90-53242. 128p. (Orig.). (gr. 3-7). 1991. pap. 2.95 (*0-679-81181-8*) Random Bks Yng Read.

—Young Indiana Jones & the Face of the Dragon. 132p. (gr. 3-7). 1994. pap. 3.50 (*0-679-85092-9*) Random Bks Yng Read.

—Young Indiana Jones & the Ghostly Riders, Bk. 7. LC 90-53241. 128p. (Orig.). (gr. 3-7). 1991. pap. 2.95 (*0-679-81180-X*) Random Bks Yng Read.

—Young Indiana Jones & the Mountain of Fire. LC 93-46118. 132p. (Orig.). (gr. 3-7). 1994. pap. 3.99 (*0-679-86384-2*, Bullseye Bks) Random Bks Yng Read.

—Young Indiana Jones & the Plantation Treasure, Bk. 1. LC 89-43388. 112p. (Orig.). (gr. 3-7). 1990. pap. 3.50 (*0-679-80579-6*) Random Bks Yng Read.

McCay, William & Martin, Les. Young Indiana Jones, 4 vols. (gr. 3-7). 1992. Boxed set incls. Young Indiana Jones & The Plantation Treasure, The Gypsy Revenge, The Tomb of Terror & The Ghostly Riders, 128p. ea. 11.80 (*0-679-83866-X*) Random Bks Yng Read.

McCay, William, adapted by. The Secret Peace. LC 91-58100. (Illus.). 136p. (Orig.). (gr. 4-8). 1992. PLB cancelled (*0-679-92777-8*); pap. 3.50 (*0-679-82777-3*) Random Bks Yng Read.

McCay, Winsor. The Complete Little Nemo in Slumberland: In the Land of Wonderful Dreams, Part 2 - 1913-1914, Vol. VI. Marschall, Richard, ed. McCay, Winsor, illus. 96p. (gr. 6 up). 1992. 34.95 (*0-924359-36-6*) Remco Wrldserv Bks.

McClung, Jean. Mischief & Mercy: Tales of the Saints. (Illus.). 228p. (gr. 9 up). 1993. pap. 10.95 (*1-883672-02-3*) Tricycle Pr.

McCorkle, Beth. The Kramurg. Stewart, Alan, illus. 32p. (Orig.). (gr. 1-8). 1991. pap. write for info. (*0-9626729-1-2*) Work Study Assn.

McDaniel, Lurlene. Somewhere Between Life & Death. (gr. 5 up). 1991. pap. 3.50 (*0-553-28349-9*, Starfire) Bantam.

McDonald, Julie. Nils Discovers America Adventures with Eric. 96p. (gr. 2-6). 7.95 (*0-941016-74-9*) Penfield.

McDonald, Stuart. The Adventures of Endill Swift. 180p. (gr. 5-8). 1994. pap. 6.95 (0-86241-352-4, Pub. by Cnngt UK) Trafalgar.

McDonough, Barbara. Meet Me at the Fair: A "Choose Your Own Adventure" that lets You Explore the Exciting Treasures of the 1904 St. Louis World's Fair. Wissmann, Joyce, illus. 64p. (Orig.). (gr. 4-6). 1988. pap. 4.50 (0-931821-43-6) Info Res Cons.

McGovern, Ann. Shark Lady. (Illus.). 96p. (gr. k-3). 1991. pap. 2.50 (0-590-44771-8) Scholastic Inc.

McHugh, Fiona. Song of the Night, No. 3. (gr. 3-7). 1992. pap. 3.99 (0-553-48029-4, Skylark) Bantam.

Mack, Jacqueline. Tales about Tails. Halloway, Jan, illus. 24p. (ps-k). 1985. 10.95 (0-88625-089-7) Durkin Hayes Pub.

McKeage, Jeff. Raiders of Cardolan. Charlton, Coleman, ed. Horne, Daniel, illus. 32p. (Orig.). (gr. 10-12). 1988. pap. 6.00 (1-55806-005-7, 8108) Iron Crown Ent Inc.

Macken, Walter. Island of the Great Yellow Ox. LC 90-22515. 192p. (gr. 5-9). 1991. pap. 14.00 jacketed, 3-pc. bdg. (0-671-73800-3, S&S BFYR) S&S Trade.

—Island of the Great Yellow Ox. LC 90-22515. 192p. (gr. 5-9). 1993. pap. 2.95 (0-671-86689-3, Half Moon Bks) S&S Trade.

McKinley, Robin. Outlaws of Sherwood. LC 88-45227. 256p. (gr. 7 up). 1988. 12.95 (0-688-07178-3) Greenwillow.

McKinney, Jack. Death Dance. (gr. 10 up). 1988. pap. 4.95 (0-345-35302-1, Del Rey) Ballantine.

McKinstry, Anne P. Can You Come with Me? McKinstry-Peterson, Laurel, illus. 44p. (gr. 4-8). 1986. 5.95 (1-55523-034-2) Winston-Derek.

MacLachlan, Patricia. Unclaimed Treasures. LC 83-47714. 128p. (gr. 5-7). 1984. 14.00 (0-06-024093-8); PLB 13.89 (0-06-024094-6) HarpC Child Bks.

McMahon, Sean. The Three Seals. 181p. (Orig.). (gr. 7-9). 1992. pap. 7.95 (1-85371-148-9, Pub. by Poolbeg Pr ER) Dufour.

McPhail, David. Lost! (gr. 4-8). 1993. pap. 5.95 (0-316-56336-6, Joy St Bks) Little.

MacRaois, Cormac. Lightning over Giltspur. Dunne, Jeannette, illus. 139p. (gr. 4-6). 1991. 14.95 (0-86327-308-4, Pub. by Wolfhound Pr EIRE) Dufour.

McSwigan, Marie. Snow Treasure. 160p. (gr. 3-7). 1986. pap. 2.95 (0-590-42537-4) Scholastic Inc.

Madinaveitia, Horacio. La Gran Aventura de Don Roberto. Madinaveitia, Horacio, illus. (SPA.). 32p. (gr. k-4). 1992. PLB 13.95 (1-879567-02-4, Valeria Bks) Wonder Well.

Mahy, Margaret. The Blood-&-Thunder Adventure on Hurricane Peak. Smith, Wendy, illus. LC 89-8098. 144p. (gr. 4-7). 1989. SBE 13.95 (0-689-50488-8, M K McElderry) Macmillan Child Grp.

—The Blood-&-Thunder Adventure on Hurricane Peak. (gr. 4-7). 1991. pap. 3.25 (0-440-40422-3) Dell.

—Dangerous Spaces. 1991. 12.95 (0-670-83734-2) Viking Child Bks.

Malam, John. Indiana Jones Explores Egypt. (Illus.). 48p. (gr. 3-7). 1992. 13.95 (1-55970-183-8) Arcade Pub Inc.

—Indiana Jones Explores the Incas. (Illus.). 48p. (gr. 3-7). 1993. 14.95 (1-55970-199-4) Arcade Pub Inc.

Malcolm, Jahnna N. The House of Fear. 1991. pap. 2.99 (0-553-28392-8) Bantam.

—Run for Your Life. 1991. pap. 2.99 (0-553-28794-X) Bantam.

Malone, P. M. Into the High Branches. Lewison, Terry, illus. 196p. (Orig.). (gr. 1-8). 1992. pap. text ed. 11.95 (0-9631957-1-9) Raspberry Hill.

Maloney, Ray. Impact Zone. LC 85-16156. 256p. (gr. 7 up). 1986. 14.95 (0-385-29447-6) Delacorte.

Mandrell, Louise & Collins, Ace. Sunrise over the Harbor: A Story About the Meaning. Gale, Mark, illus. LC 93-310. 1993. 12.95 (1-56530-040-8) Summit TX.

Maney, Carla. The Maze. 1993. 7.95 (0-533-10152-2) Vantage.

Mann, Roland. Cat & Mouse Collection. Ulm, Chris, ed. Byrd, Mitch & Butler, Steven, illus. 139p. 1990. pap. 9.95 (0-944735-70-3) Malibu Graphics.

Mantell, Paul & Hart, Avery, eds. Experiment on Muir Island. (Illus.). 32p. (Orig.). (ps-3). 1994. pap. 2.50 (0-679-86201-3) Random Bks Yng Read.

—Second Genesis. Ruiz, Aristides, illus. 108p. (Orig.). (gr. 2 up). 1994. pap. 3.50 (0-679-86012-6) Random Bks Yng Read.

Marrone, Russell. The Wizard's Quest. Marrone, Russell, illus. LC 87-50268. 102p. (gr. 3-5). 1987. 7.95 (1-55523-078-4) Winston-Derek.

Marsano, Daniel T. Sir Day the Knight. Stroschin, Jane H., illus. 48p. (gr. k-6). 1993. 15.00 (1-883960-11-8) Henry Quill.

Marshall, Anthony. George's Story. LC 89-50143. (gr. 6-12). 1989. 9.95 (0-932433-58-8) Windswept Hse.

Marshall, James. Taking Care of Carruthers. (Illus.). (gr. 4-6). 1981. 14.45 (0-395-28593-3) HM.

—Yummers! (Illus.). (gr. 4-8). 1986. pap. 5.95 (0-395-39590-9, Sandpiper) HM.

Martin, Bill, Jr. & Archambault, John. White Dynamite & Curly Kidd. Rand, Ted, illus. LC 85-27214. 48p. (ps-2). 1986. 12.95 (0-8050-0658-3, Bks Young Read) H Holt & Co.

Martin, Les. Prisoner of War. LC 92-56395. 136p. (Orig.). (gr. 4-8). 1993. pap. 3.50 (0-679-84389-2) Random Bks Yng Read.

—Young Indiana Jones & the Gypsy Revenge, Bk. 6. LC 90-52818. 128p. (Orig.). (gr. 3-7). 1991. pap. 2.95 (0-679-81179-6) Random Bks Yng Read.

—Young Indiana Jones & the Princess of Peril, Bk. 5. LC 90-52817. 128p. (Orig.). (gr. 3-7). 1991. pap. 2.95 (0-679-81178-8) Random Bks Yng Read.

—Young Indiana Jones & the Secret City, Bk. 4. LC 89-43391. 112p. (Orig.). (gr. 3-7). 1990. PLB 6.99 (0-679-90580-4); pap. 2.95 (0-679-80580-X) Random Bks Yng Read.

—Young Indiana Jones & the Titanic Adventure. 132p. (Orig.). (gr. 3-7). 1993. pap. 3.50 (0-679-84925-4, Bullseye Bks) Random Bks Yng Read.

—Young Indiana Jones & the Tomb of Terror, Bk. 2. LC 89-43389. 112p. (Orig.). (gr. 3-7). 1990. pap. 3.50 (0-679-80581-8) Random Bks Yng Read.

Martin, Les, adapted by. Field of Death. LC 91-53164. (Illus.). 136p. (Orig.). (gr. 4-8). 1992. PLB cancelled (0-679-92775-1); pap. 3.50 (0-679-82775-7) Random Bks Yng Read.

—Trek of Doom. (Illus.). 136p. (Orig.). (gr. 4-8). 1992. pap. 3.50 (0-679-83237-8) Random Bks Yng Read.

Masefield, John. The Midnight Folk. (gr. k-6). 1985. pap. 4.95 (0-440-45631-2, Pub. by Yearling Classics) Dell.

Master of the World. (gr. 4-7). 1993. pap. 2.95 (0-8167-0459-7) Troll Assocs.

Masuda, Akiko. The Adventures of Kalakoa: A Hawaiian Rainbow Fantasy. Van Loon, Roland, illus. 32p. (gr. k-7). 1991. 7.95 (0-9629842-1-3) Stew & Rice.

Matalon, David. Target: Hero. Bell, Robert, ed. Lyle, Tom, illus. 32p. (Orig.). (gr. 10-12). 1988. pap. 6.00 (1-55806-004-9, 34) Iron Crown Ent Inc.

Matas, Carol. Safari Adventure in Legoland. (gr. 4-7). 1993. pap. 2.75 (0-590-45876-0) Scholastic Inc.

Matthews, Morgan. Brave Sir Laughalot. Baer, Mary A., illus. LC 85-14010. 48p. (Orig.). (gr. 1-3). 1986. PLB 10.59 (0-8167-0594-1); pap. text ed. 3.50 (0-8167-0595-X) Troll Assocs.

Maxwell, Arthur. Uncle Arthur's Storytime: Children's True Adventures, 3 vols. (Illus.). 1989. Set. 29.95 (0-685-37412-2); Vol. 1. 12.95 (0-943497-71-X); Vol. 2. 12.95 (0-943497-72-8); Vol. 3. 12.95 (0-943497-73-6) Wolgemuth & Hyatt.

Mayer-Skumanz, Lene. The Tower. (gr. 2-5). 1993. 12.95 (0-685-68827-5) Yllw Brick Rd.

Mayper. Come & See. Date not set. 15.00 (0-06-023526-8); PLB 14.89 (0-06-023527-6) HarpC Child Bks.

Merino, Jose M. Gold of Dreams. 1994. pap. 4.95 (0-374-42584-1, Sunburst) FS&G.

Meyer, Rich. Thieves of Tharbad. (Illus.). 36p. (gr. 10-12). 1985. 7.00 (0-915795-35-3, 8050) Iron Crown Ent Inc.

Miklowitz, Gloria. The Killing Boy. 1993. pap. 3.50 (0-553-56037-9) Bantam.

Miller, Timothy B. Just in the Nick of Time. LC 87-72303. 90p. (Orig.). (gr. 5 up). 1989. pap. 6.00 (0-916383-48-2) Aegina Pr.

Miner, Sharon. The Delmarva Conspiracy. LC 92-72680. 136p. (gr. 7-9). 1993. 14.95 (1-880851-06-7) Greene Bark Pr.

Miyazaki, Hayao. Tokuma's Magical Adventure Series. Zimmerman, Maureen, ed. Saburi, Eugene, tr. from JPN. Miyazaki, Hayao, illus. 112p. (gr. 3-6). 1992. PLB 44.85 (4-19-086974-0) Tokuma Pub.

Monson, A. M. The Secret of Sanctuary Island. ALC Staff, ed. LC 90-6479. 176p. (gr. 5 up). 1992. pap. 3.95 (0-688-11693-0, Pub. by Beech Tree Bks) Morrow.

Montgomery. Help! You're Shrinking. (gr. 2-4). 1987. pap. 2.25 (0-553-15532-6, Skylark) Dell.

—Indian Trail. (gr. 2-4). 1987. pap. 2.25 (0-553-15496-6, Skylark) Dell.

Montgomery, Lucy M. Golden Road. 1976. 21.95 (0-8488-0720-0) Amereon Ltd.

—Road to Yesterday. 1993. pap. 3.99 (0-553-56068-9) Bantam.

Montgomery, Ramsey. Grave Robbers. 1990. pap. 2.95 (0-553-28554-8) Bantam.

—Outlaw Gulch. (gr. 4-7). 1992. pap. 3.50 (0-553-29295-1) Bantam.

Montgomery, Raymond A. The Abominable Snowman. large type ed. Granger, Paul, illus. 116p. (gr. 2-7). 1987. 8.95 (0-942545-02-8); PLB 9.95 (0-942545-08-7, Dist. by Grolier) Grey Castle.

—Abominable Snowman. (ps-7). 1987. pap. 2.25 (0-553-25965-2) Bantam.

—Beyond Escape. 128p. (gr. 4). 1986. pap. 2.25 (0-553-26169-X) Bantam.

—Blood on the Handle. 1989. pap. 2.75 (0-553-28076-7) Bantam.

—Caravan. 64p. (Orig.). (gr. 4). 1987. pap. 2.25 (0-553-15477-X, Skylark) Bantam.

—Chinese Dragons. (gr. 9-12). 1991. pap. 2.95 (0-553-28828-8) Bantam.

—Danger Zones. 176p. (Orig.). (gr. 4). 1987. pap. 2.95 (0-553-26791-4) Bantam.

—Dream Trips. (gr. 2-4). 1987. pap. 2.25 (0-553-15506-7, Skylark) Bantam.

—Exiled to Earth. 176p. (Orig.). 1989. pap. 2.50 (0-553-27651-4) Bantam.

—Fire. 64p. (Orig.). (gr. 2 up). 1985. pap. 2.25 (0-553-15462-1) Bantam.

—Genie in the Bottle. (gr. 2-4). 1987. pap. 2.25 (0-553-15495-8, Skylark) Bantam.

—Home in Time for Christmas. 64p. (gr. 1-4). 1987. pap. 2.25 (0-553-15553-9, Skylark) Bantam.

—House of Danger. 128p. (gr. 1-8). 1982. pap. 2.25 (0-553-26181-9) Bantam.

—Inside UFO 54-40. (ps-7). 1987. pap. 2.25 (0-553-25987-3) Bantam.

—The Island of Time. 1991. pap. 3.50 (0-553-29057-6) Bantam.

—Journey to the Sea. 1982. pap. 3.50 (0-553-27393-0) Bantam.

—Lost Dog! 64p. (Orig.). 1985. pap. 2.25 (0-553-15508-3) Bantam.

—The Owl Tree. 64p. (Orig.). (gr. 4). 1986. pap. 2.25 (0-553-15449-4) Bantam.

—Prisoner of the Ant People. Reese, Ralph, illus. 115p. (gr. 4). 1983. pap. 2.25 (0-553-25763-3) Bantam.

—The Race Forever. large type ed. 116p. (gr. 3-7). 1987. Repr. of 1983 ed. 8.95 (0-942545-12-5); PLB 9.95 (0-942545-17-6, Dist. by Grolier) Grey Castle.

—The Race Forever. (ps-7). 1987. pap. 2.25 (0-553-25988-1) Bantam.

—Race of the Year. 1989. pap. 2.99 (0-553-15696-9) Bantam.

—Return to Atlantis, No. 78. 176p. (Orig.). (gr. 5 up). 1988. pap. 2.75 (0-553-27123-7) Bantam.

—Sand Castle. 64p. (Orig.). (gr. 4). 1986. pap. 2.25 (0-553-15458-3) Bantam.

—Secret of the Ninja. (ps-7). 1987. pap. 2.25 (0-553-26484-2) Bantam.

—Smoke Jumper. 1991. pap. 2.95 (0-553-28861-X) Bantam.

—Space & Beyond. (ps-7). 1982. pap. 3.25 (0-553-27453-8) Bantam.

—Spooky Thanksgiving. 64p. (gr. 2). 1988. pap. 2.75 (0-553-15672-1, Skylark) Bantam.

—Stock Car Champion. 1989. pap. 3.25 (0-553-28294-8) Bantam.

—Survival at Sea. (ps-7). 1987. pap. 2.25 (0-553-26560-1) Bantam.

—Track of the Bear. 64p. (gr. 2). 1988. pap. 2.50 (0-553-27533-X) Bantam.

—Trouble on Planet Earth. Reese, Ralph, illus. (Orig.). (gr. 4). 1984. pap. text ed. 2.25 (0-553-26308-0) Bantam.

—War with the Evil Power Master. 128p. (Orig.). (gr. 4). 1984. pap. 2.25 (0-553-25778-1) Bantam.

Moon, Sheila. Hunt down the Prize. Renfrew, Susan, illus. LC 86-19576. 245p. (gr. 8-12). 1986. pap. 8.95 (0-917479-09-2) Guild Psy.

Morey, Walt. Canyon Winter. 208p. (gr. 5 up). 1994. pap. 3.99 (0-14-036856-6) Puffin Bks.

—Death Walk. Spillman, Fredrika, illus. (gr. 5-12). 1991. 13.95 (0-936085-18-5) Blue Heron OR.

—Deep Trouble. Spillman, Fredrika, contrib. by. (gr. 5-9). 1989. pap. 7.95 (0-936085-15-0) Blue Heron OR.

—Home Is the North. Spillman, Fredrika, contrib. by. (gr. 4-9). 1989. pap. 7.95 (0-936085-11-8) Blue Heron OR.

—Run Far, Run Fast. Spillman, Fredrika, contrib. by. (gr. 4-9). 1989. pap. 6.95 (0-936085-16-9) Blue Heron OR.

Morgan, Jeff. The Rescue. Cocozza, Chris, illus. 160p. (gr. 3-7). 1994. pap. 3.50 (0-448-40436-2, G&D) Putnam Pub Group.

Morpurgo, Michael. King of the Cloud Forests. (gr. 10 up). 1988. pap. 12.95 (0-670-82069-5) Viking Child Bks.

Morris, Gilbert. Captain Chip & the March to Victory. (gr. 4-7). 1994. pap. 5.99 (0-8024-1584-9) Moody.

—Corporal Chip & the Call to Battle. (gr. 4-7). 1994. pap. 5.99 (0-8024-1585-7) Moody.

—Flight of the Eagles. 1994. pap. 5.99 (0-8024-3681-1) Moody.

—The Saintly Buccaneer. LC 88-33337. 288p. (Orig.). (gr. 11 up). 1989. pap. 8.99 (1-55661-048-3) Bethany Hse.

Moulton, Dwayne. The Mystery of the Pink Waterfall. Headley, Adriane M., illus. LC 80-84116. 192p. (gr. 3-8). 1980. 14.95 (0-9605236-0-X) Pandoras Treasures.

Mullin, Penn. High-Five Series: Whale Summer, Spirits of the Canyon & Trail to Danger, 3 bks. (Orig.). (gr. 6-11). 1991. Set. pap. text ed. 12.50 ea. (0-87879-913-3); wkbk. 9.00 (0-87879-924-9) High Noon Bks.

Munsch, Robert. I Have to Go! Martchenko, Michael, illus. 24p. (gr. k-2). 1987. PLB 14.95 (0-920303-77-3, Pub. by Annick CN); pap. 4.95 (0-920303-74-9, Pub. by Annick CN) Firefly Bks Ltd.

—I Have to Go! (CHI., Illus.). 32p. 1993. pap. 5.95 (1-55037-299-8, Pub. by Annick CN) Firefly Bks Ltd.

Murakami, Haruki. A Wild Sheep Chase: A Novel. Birnbaum, Alfred, tr. 272p. 1989. 18.95 (0-87011-905-2) Kodansha.

Murray, Cleitus O. Stories of the Southern Mountains & Swamps. Murray, Cleitus O., illus. 192p. (Orig.). 1992. pap. 9.95 (0-9632132-0-2) Murray Pubns.

Murrow, Liza K. West Against the Wind. 240p. (gr. 7 up). 1988. pap. 2.50 (0-8167-1324-3) Troll Assocs.

Myers, Walter D. The Legend of Tarik. 180p. (gr. 7 up). 1991. pap. 2.95 (0-590-44426-3) Scholastic Inc.

—Mop, Moondance, & the Nagasaki Knights. (gr. 4-7). 1994. pap. 3.50 (0-440-40914-4) Dell.

—Won't Know Till I Get There. LC 87-7340. (gr. 3 up). 1988. pap. 3.99 (0-14-032612-X, Puffin) Puffin Bks.

Napoli, Donna J. Hero of Barletta. (ps-3). 1992. pap. 2.99 (0-440-40562-9) Dell.

Naylor, Phyllis R. The Grand Escape. Daniel, Alan, illus. LC 91-40816. 160p. (gr. 3-7). 1993. SBE 14.00 (0-689-31722-0, Atheneum Child Bk) Macmillan Child Grp.

—To Walk the Skypath. (gr. 4-7). 1992. 3.50 (0-440-40636-6, YB) Dell.

Nelson, Peter. First to Die. (gr. 7 up). 1992. pap. 3.50 (*0-06-106100-X*, Harp PBks) HarpC.
Nelson, Ray, Jr. Incredible Adventures of Donovan Willoughby. LC 90-42652. (Illus.). (ps-7). 1990. 12.95 (*0-89802-551-6*) Beautiful Am.
Nelson, Theresa. Devil Storm. (gr. 4-7). 1991. pap. 3.25 (*0-440-40409-6*) Dell.
—The Twenty-Five Cent Miracle. LC 85-17061. 224p. (gr. 7 up). 1986. SBE 14.95 (*0-02-724370-2*, Bradbury Pr) Macmillan Child Grp.
Nesbit, Edith. New Treasure Seekers. (gr. 5-8). 1988. 15.50 (*0-8446-6348-4*) Peter Smith.
—The Railway Children. 240p. (gr. 3-7). 1983. pap. 2.95 (*0-14-035005-5*, Puffin) Puffin Bks.
—Story of the Amulet. 1986. pap. 2.95 (*0-14-035063-2*, Puffin) Puffin Bks.
Neubacher, Gerda. Tales from the Beechy Woods: Fluff's Birthday. Neubacher, Gerda, illus. 32p. (ps-k). 1983. 10.95 (*0-88625-044-7*) Durkin Hayes Pub.
Newman, Marc. Longhorn Territory. 128p. (Orig.). (gr. 4). 1987. pap. 2.50 (*0-553-26904-6*) Bantam.
Newth, Mette. The Abduction. Nunnally, Tiina & Murray, Steve, trs. (gr. 7 up). 1989. 15.00 (*0-374-30008-9*) FS&G.
—Abduction. 1993. pap. 3.95 (*0-374-40009-1*) FS&G.
Ngugi wa Thiong'o. Njamba Nene & the Flying Bus. Wangui wa Goro, tr. Kariuki, Emmanuel, illus. LC 88-70433. 34p. (gr. 2-7). 1995. 12.95 (*0-86543-079-9*); pap. 5.95 (*0-86543-080-2*) Africa World.
—Njamba Nene's Pistol. Wangui wa Goro, tr. Kariuki, Emmanuel, illus. LC 88-70432. 32p. (gr. 2-7). 1995. 12.95 (*0-86543-081-0*); pap. 5.95 (*0-86543-082-9*) Africa World.
Nicholson, Michael. Across the Limpopo: A Family's Hazardous Journey Through Africa. 196p. 1991. pap. 6.95 (*0-86051-369-6*, Robson-Parkwest) Parkwest Pubns.
Nicieza, Mariano. Space: 34-24-34: The Exciting Adventures of the Nova Girls. O'Connor, Thom, et al, illus. 64p. (Orig.). (gr. 9). 1989. write for info. MN DPPD Inc.
Nintendo Adventure Book, No. 6: Doors to Doom. 128p. (Orig.). (gr. 4 up). 1991. pap. 3.50 (*0-671-74204-3*, Archway) PB.
Nintendo Staff. Super Mario Bros. Adventures. Nintendo Staff, illus. 32p. (Orig.). (gr. 1-7). 1991. pap. 6.95 incl. cassette (*0-679-81822-7*) Random Bks Yng Read.
Nixon, Joan L. High Trail to Danger. (gr. 4-7). 1992. pap. 3.50 (*0-553-29602-7*) Bantam.
—The Stalker. (gr. 7 up). 1987. pap. 3.99 (*0-440-97753-3*, LFL) Dell.
Noll, Sally. Off & Counting. LC 84-17943. (Illus.). 32p. (ps). 1985. pap. 3.95 (*0-14-050502-4*, Puffin) Puffin Bks.
Norman, Jane & Beazley, Frank. Maxi's Big Adventure. 24p. (ps-3). 1993. pap. write for info. (*1-883585-04-X*) Pixanne Ent.
Northern Lights. PLB 15.95 (*1-55037-339-0*, Pub. by Annick CN); pap. 5.95 (*1-55037-338-2*, Pub. by Annick CN) Firefly Bks Ltd.
Norton, Mary. The Borrowers Avenged. (gr. 3-6). 1988. 17.50 (*0-8446-6358-1*) Peter Smith.
Notaro, Diane & Notaro, Joe. From the Dragon's Tale, Bk. I: A Door to Watch. LC 93-92776. (Illus.). 96p. (gr. 4 up). 1994. pap. 8.00 (*1-56002-381-3*, Univ Edtns) Aegina Pr.
Noyes, Alfred. Highwayman. Waldman, Neil, illus. 28p. (ps-3). 1990. 14.95 (*0-15-234340-7*) HarBrace.
O'Brien, Robert C. Secret of Nimh. 1988. pap. 2.75 (*0-590-41708-8*) Scholastic Inc.
O'Byrne-Pelham, Fran & Balcer, Bernadette. The Search for the Atocha Treasure. LC 88-20201. (Illus.). 128p. (gr. 4 up). 1988. text ed. 14.95 RSBE (*0-87518-399-9*, Dillon) Macmillan Child Grp.
Ochs, Carol P. When I'm Alone. (ps-3). 1993. pap. 6.95 (*0-87614-620-5*) Carolrhoda Bks.
O'Connor, Jane. Sir Small & the Dragonfly. O'Brien, John, illus. LC 87-35309. 32p. (Orig.). (ps-1). 1988. pap. 3.50 (*0-394-89625-4*, Random Juv) Random Bks Yng Read.
O'Connor, Jim. The Blizzard. Cocozza, Chris, illus. 160p. (gr. 3-7). 1994. pap. 3.50 (*0-448-40435-4*, G&D) Putnam Pub Group.
O'Dell, Scott. Sing Down the Moon. LC 71-98513. (gr. 5 up). 1970. 13.45 (*0-395-10919-1*) HM.
—Zia. Lewin, Ted, illus. LC 75-44156. 224p. (gr. 4-8). 1976. 14.95 (*0-395-24393-9*) HM.
O'Donohoe, Nick. Too, Too Solid Flesh. LC 88-51731. 352p. (Orig.). 1989. pap. 3.95 (*0-88038-767-X*) TSR Inc.
Oestreicher, James. Choice Adventures: Monumental Discovery. 160p. 1992. pap. 4.99 (*0-8423-5030-6*) Tyndale.
Ofosu-Appiah, L. H. People in Bondage. (gr. 4-7). 1992. 15.95 (*0-8225-3150-X*) Lerner Pubns.
O'Hara, Mary. Thunderhead. LC 87-45653. 320p. (gr. 7 up). 1988. pap. 7.00 (*0-06-080903-5*, P-903, PL) HarpC.
Oliver, M. Agent Arthur's Arctic Adventure. (Illus.). 48p. 1990. PLB 11.96 (*0-88110-408-6*); pap. 4.95 (*0-7460-0145-2*) EDC.
—Agent Arthur's Desert Challenge. (Illus.). 48p. (gr. 2-7). 1994. PLB 11.96 (*0-88110-696-8*, Usborne); pap. 4.95 (*0-7460-1406-6*, Usborne) EDC.
Ollivant, Alfred. Bob, Son of Battle. Hinkle, Don, ed. Riccio, Frank, illus. LC 87-15477. 48p. (gr. 3-6). 1988. PLB 12.89 (*0-8167-1211-5*); pap. text ed. 3.95 (*0-8167-1212-3*) Troll Assocs.
Olsen, Tillie. Yonnondio: From the Thirties. 144p. (gr. 9 up). 1975. pap. 1.95 (*0-440-39881-9*, LE) Dell.
One Hundred & One Dalmatians. (Illus.). 48p. (gr. 3-7). 1992. pap. 2.95 (*1-56115-271-4*, 21812, Golden Pr) Western Pub.
Orczy, Emmuska. The Scarlet Pimpernel. 256p. (gr. 5 up). 1989. pap. 4.99 (*0-14-035056-X*, Puffin) Puffin Bks.
Osborne, Mary P. Run, Run, As Fast As You Can. LC 81-68781. 156p. (gr. 3-7). 1993. pap. 3.99 (*0-679-84649-2*, Bullseye Bks) Random Bks Yng Read.
Osborne, Thelma. The Adventures of Speedy. Caroland, Mary, ed. LC 90-71229. (Illus.). 44p. (gr. k-3). 1991. 5.95 (*1-55523-383-X*) Winston-Derek.
O'Toole, Sharon S. Brave Dog Blizzard. 1992. pap. 2.75 (*0-590-44409-3*) Scholastic Inc.
Packard, Andrea. The Evil Wizard. 64p. 1984. pap. 2.25 (*0-553-15418-4*) Bantam.
Packard, Edward. The Castle of Frome. 144p. (Orig.). (gr. 7-12). 1986. pap. 2.50 (*0-553-26089-8*) Bantam.
—The Cave of Time. (gr. 4-8). 1982. pap. 3.50 (*0-553-26965-8*) Bantam.
—The Cave of Time. large type ed. (Illus.). 115p. (gr. 3-7). 1987. 8.95 (*0-942545-01-X*); PLB 9.95 (*0-942545-07-9*, Dist. by Grolier) Grey Castle.
—Ghost Hunter. 128p. (Orig.). (gr. 4). 1986. pap. 3.25 (*0-553-26983-6*) Bantam.
—The Great Easter Bunny Adventure. 64p. (Orig.). (gr. 4). 1987. pap. 2.50 (*0-553-15492-3*, Skylark) Bantam.
—Journey to the Year Three Thousand: Cyoa Superadventure. (Orig.). (gr. 4). 1987. pap. 3.50 (*0-553-26157-6*) Bantam.
—Kidnapped. 1991. pap. 3.50 (*0-553-29143-2*) Bantam.
—The Luckiest Day of Your Life. (gr. 4-7). 1993. pap. 3.25 (*0-553-29304-4*) Bantam.
—Magic Master. 1992. pap. 3.50 (*0-553-29606-X*) Bantam.
—Mountain Survival. 128p. (gr. 4-6). pap. text ed. 2.25 (*0-553-26252-1*) Bantam.
—Mutiny. 1989. pap. 2.75 (*0-553-27854-1*) Bantam.
—The Polar Bear Express. 64p. (Orig.). 1984. pap. 2.25 (*0-553-15409-5*) Bantam.
—The Power Dome. (gr. 9-12). 1991. pap. 3.25 (*0-553-28837-7*) Bantam.
—Reality Machine. 1993. pap. 3.50 (*0-553-56401-3*) Bantam.
—Roller Star. (gr. 4-7). 1993. pap. 3.25 (*0-553-56006-9*) Bantam.
—Secret of the Sun God. (ps-7). 1987. pap. 2.25 (*0-553-26529-6*) Bantam.
—Skateboard Champion. 1991. pap. 3.50 (*0-553-28898-9*) Bantam.
—Spy Trap (Your Code Name Is Jonah, Vol. 1. 1989. pap. 2.50 (*0-553-23182-0*) Bantam.
—Sugarcane Island. 128p. (gr. 4). 1986. pap. 2.25 (*0-553-26040-5*) Bantam.
—Supercomputer. 128p. (Orig.). (gr. 4). 1984. pap. 2.25 (*0-553-25818-4*) Bantam.
—Through the Black Hole. 1990. pap. 3.50 (*0-553-28440-1*) Bantam.
—Underground Kingdom. (ps-7). 1983. pap. 2.25 (*0-553-25989-X*) Bantam.
—Who Killed Harlowe Thrombey, Vol. 1. 1989. pap. 2.50 (*0-553-23181-2*) Bantam.
—Worst Day of Your Life. 1990. pap. 3.50 (*0-553-28316-2*) Bantam.
—You Are a Genius. 1989. pap. 3.25 (*0-553-28155-0*) Bantam.
—You Are a Shark. (gr. 5-12). 1985. pap. 2.25 (*0-553-26386-2*) Bantam.
—You Are Microscopic. (gr. 4-7). 1992. pap. 3.50 (*0-553-29298-6*) Bantam.
—Your Code Name Is Jonah. large type ed. Granger, Paul, illus. 114p. (gr. 3-7). 1987. Repr. of 1979 ed. 8.95 (*0-942545-15-X*); PLB 9.95 (*0-942545-20-6*, Dist. by Grolier) Grey Castle.
Padoan, Gianni. Danger Kid. LC 90-48381. 1989. 11.95 (*0-85953-312-3*) Childs Play.

Papagapitos, Karen. Gemini Code II. Kleinman, Estelle, ed. Middleton, Curt, illus. Nicholson, David, ed. (Illus.). 96p. (Orig.). (gr. 5-9). 1994. pap. 7.95 (*0-9637328-2-X*); pap. 4.95 (*0-9637328-3-8*) Kapa Hse Pr.
THE GEMINI CODE II, the third book in the "JB Series" (JB=Jose's Basket), takes place in the 1990s. Jose & his wife Alicia, a banking executive, have twin ten-year-old sons, Hector & Luis. A favorite hobby of theirs is to play computer games, each trying to outsmart the other with new codes for different games. Alicia & Jose, who are now successful authors, are delighted with this shared interest. When Hector, the first-born twin, lost his hearing at the age of two because of a severe ear infection, the ability to communicate by computer, in addition to sign language, contributed to the closeness of the brothers & their parents. Little does anyone realize just how important this computer knowledge will be. Luis gets trapped on the other side of an arroyo filled with rushing water during a flash flood. Hector, Jose & Alicia are running out of time in their search for him when suddenly a code of Luis' is transmitted on the computer screen. Without waiting to figure out who could have sent the message, Hector breaks the code & Luis is found before it's too late. Distributed by: Baker & Taylor Books, 652 E. Main St., P.O. Box 6920, Bridgewater, NJ 08807-0920; 908-218-0400.
Publisher Provided Annotation.

Parish, Peggy. Pirate Island Adventure. (gr. 3-6). 1991. 17.00 (*0-8446-6453-7*) Peter Smith.
Pascal, Francine. Hostage! 1986. pap. 3.25 (*0-553-27670-0*) Bantam.
—Last Chance. 1987. pap. 3.50 (*0-553-27662-X*) Bantam.
—Out of Control. 1987. pap. 3.50 (*0-553-27666-2*) Bantam.
—Who's Who. 1990. pap. 3.25 (*0-553-28352-9*) Bantam.
Paterson, Katherine. Bridge to Terabithia. 182p. 1992. text ed. 14.56 (*1-56956-199-0*) W A T Braille.
—The Sign of the Chrysanthemum. Landa, Peter, illus. LC 72-7553. 128p. (gr. 6 up). 1988. pap. 3.95 (*0-06-440232-0*, Trophy) HarpC Child Bks.
Patience, John. Adventures in Fern Hollow. (Illus.). 64p. (ps-1). 1985. 2.98 (*0-517-45856-X*) Random Hse Value.
Paton-Walsh, Jill. Fireweed. LC 73-109554. 144p. (gr. 6 up). 1970. 14.95 (*0-374-32310-0*) FS&G.
Paul Bunyan. 48p. 1994. 5.98 (*1-57082-205-0*) Mouse Works.
Paulsen, Gary. Amos Gets Famous. (gr. 4-7). 1993. pap. 3.25 (*0-440-40749-4*) Dell.
—Amos's Last Stand. (gr. 4-7). 1993. pap. 3.25 (*0-440-40775-3*) Dell.
—The Case of the Dirty Bird. 96p. (gr. 4-7). 1992. pap. 3.50 (*0-440-40598-X*, YB) Dell.
—The Crossing. LC 87-7738. 128p. (gr. 6-8). 1987. 11.95 (*0-531-05709-7*); PLB 11.99 (*0-531-08309-8*) Orchard Bks Watts.
—The Crossing. (gr. k up). 1990. pap. 3.99 (*0-440-20582-4*, LFL) Dell.
—Dunc & Amos & the Red Tatoos, No. 12. (gr. 4-7). 1993. pap. 3.50 (*0-440-40790-7*) Dell.
—Dunc & the Haunted House. 1993. pap. 3.50 (*0-440-40893-8*) Dell.
—Dunc Breaks the Record. 96p. (Orig.). (gr. 3-7). 1992. pap. 3.25 (*0-440-40678-1*, YB) Dell.
—Dunc Gets Tweaked. 96p. (Orig.). (gr. 3-5). 1992. pap. 3.25 (*0-440-40642-0*, YB) Dell.
—Dunc's Doll. 80p. (gr. 4-7). 1992. pap. 3.50 (*0-440-40601-3*, YB) Dell.
—Dunc's Dump. (gr. 4-7). 1993. pap. 3.25 (*0-440-40762-1*) Dell.
—The Foxman. 128p. (gr. 4 up). 1990. pap. 11.95 (*0-670-83360-6*) Viking Child Bks.
—Hatchet. LC 87-6416. 208p. (gr. 6-8). 1987. SBE 14.95 (*0-02-770130-1*, Bradbury Pr) Macmillan Child Grp.
—Prince Amos. (gr. 4-7). 1994. pap. 3.50 (*0-440-40928-4*) Dell.
—Sentries. (gr. 5-9). pap. 3.95 (*0-317-62279-X*, Puffin) Puffin Bks.
—Tracker. (gr. 5-9). pap. 3.95 (*0-317-62280-3*, Puffin) Puffin Bks.
Payne, Bernal C., Jr. Experiment in Terror. 224p. (gr. 5-9). 1987. 13.45 (*0-395-44260-5*) HM.
Peck, Robert N. Soup on Fire. 1987. pap. 13.95 (*0-440-50226-8*) Dell.
Pecos Bill. 48p. 1994. 5.98 (*1-57082-206-9*) Mouse Works.
Pepper Bird Staff. Frozen Fury: Adventures of Matthew Henson. Rose, Ann C., illus. 48p. (Orig.). (gr. 4-7). 1993. pap. 4.95 (*1-56817-001-7*) Pepper Bird.
Peretti, Frank E. The Tombs of Anak. LC 86-73183. 144p. (gr. 4-7). 1990. pap. 4.99 (*0-89107-593-3*) Crossway Bks.
Perkins, Al. Hugh Lofting's Travels of Doctor Dolittle. reissued ed. LC 67-25853. (Illus.). 64p. (ps-2). 1967. 6.95 (*0-394-80048-6*); PLB 7.99 (*0-394-90048-0*) Random Bks Yng Read.
Perrin, Steve. Voice of Doom. 32p. (Orig.). (gr. 10-12). 1987. pap. 6.00 (*0-915795-80-9*, 38) Iron Crown Ent Inc.
Petersen, Ken. Choice Adventures: Quarterback Sneak. 160p. (gr. 4-8). 1992. pap. 4.99 (*0-8423-5029-2*) Tyndale.
Petersen, Randy. The Appalachian Ambush. LC 93-40183. 1994. 4.99 (*0-8423-5133-7*) Tyndale.
Peterson, Beth. Myrna Never Sleeps. LC 93-8301. 1995. 12.00 (*0-689-31893-6*, Atheneum Child Bk) Macmillan Child Grp.
Peterson, John. The Littles Go Exploring. (gr. 4-7). 1993. pap. 2.75 (*0-590-46596-1*) Scholastic Inc.

—The Littles Take a Trip. (gr. 2-5). 1988. 14.50 (*0-8446-6351-4*) Peter Smith.

Pfeffer, Susan B. Courage, Dana. 160p. (gr. k-6). 1984. pap. 2.75 (*0-440-41541-1*, YB) Dell.

Phillips, Tony. Turbo Cowboys: Jump Start, No. 1. (gr. 3 up). 1988. pap. 2.95 (*0-345-35121-5*) Ballantine.

Piequet, Miriam. The Flying Mule Car. Anyone Can Read Staff, ed. Blanton, Betty, illus. 149p. (Orig.). (gr. 4-6). 1988. pap. 15.00 (*0-914275-11-9*) Anyone Can Read Bks.

Pierce, Tamora. Alanna: The First Adventure Song of the Lioness, Bk. One. LC 83-2595. 252p. (gr. 6 up). 1983. SBE 16.95 (*0-689-30994-5*, Atheneum Child Bk) Macmillan Child Grp.

Pingry, Patricia. Story of Joshua & the Bugles of Jericho. Spence, James, illus. 24p. (Orig.). (ps-3). 1988. pap. 3.95 (*0-8249-8178-2*, Ideals Child) Hambleton-Hill.

Pini, Wendy & Pini, Richard. Elfquest: Fire & Flight. rev. ed. (Illus.). 192p. (gr. 4 up). 1993. 19.95 (*0-936861-16-9*, Father Tree Pr) Warp Graphics.

Piumini, Roberto. Knot in the Tracks. LC 93-203043. (ps-3). 1994. 14.00 (*0-688-11166-1*, Tambourine Bks); PLB 13.93 (*0-688-11167-X*) Morrow.

Ploetz, Craig T. Milo's Friends in the Dark. Koslowski, Richard K., illus. 32p. (ps-4). 1992. PLB 11.95 (*1-882172-00-0*) Milo Prods.

Popkin, Michael H. Free the Horses: Storybook & Songbook. Greathead, Susan D. & Sardinas-Wyssling, Karen, eds. Bork, Beatrice, illus. 80p. (gr. 1-3). 1991. pap. 6.95 (*0-9618020-7-3*) Active Parenting.

Poulin, Stephane. Travels for Two: Stories & Lies from My Childhood. Poulin, Stephane, illus. 32p. (ps-2). 1991. PLB 15.95 (*1-55037-205-X*, Pub. by Annick CN); pap. 5.95 (*1-55037-204-1*, Pub. by Annick CN) Firefly Bks Ltd.

Preiss, Byron. Time Traveler. 80p. 1987. pap. 2.50 (*0-553-15483-4*, Skylark) Bantam.

Press, Skip. Cliffhanger. Parker, Liz, ed. Taylor, Marjorie, illus. 45p. (Orig.). (gr. 6-12). 1992. pap. text ed. 2.95 (*1-56254-055-6*) Saddleback Pubns.

Prince, Michael. The Totems of Seldovia. 144p. (gr. 5-6). 1994. pap. 8.95 (*0-9642662-1-0*) Sundog Pubng. Michael Prince writes adventure stories for children aged approximately 9 to 13. His stories take place in Alaska locales. He features children in positive working relationships with adults while still showing them with a precocious wisdom that endears readers to the characters. Even though his stories are fiction, he provides substantial information on human nature, wildlife & the natural sciences. His topics are well researched & he's achieved local success within schools in his hometown of Anchorage, Alaska. Instructors have used his books as classroom educational material. Sundog Publishing's books display the "Made in Alaska" emblem. This denotes that all facets of production were done within Alaska. We proudly use children as artists & provide short biographies of them as well as the author. All books are printed & assembled by Alaska Specialized Education & Training Services (ASETS), a training & employment program for Alaskans with substantial disabilities. THE TOTEMS OF SELDOVIA is a fast paced adventure tale of three children who go on a trail of adventure seeking an elusive treasure from an old mariner's map. The clues lie in the uniquely painted fire hydrants & landmarks located in their hometown of Seldovia, Alaska.
Publisher Provided Annotation.

Prior, Natalie J. Amabel Abroad: More Amazing Adventures. Nicholson, John, illus. (Orig.). (gr. 6 up). 1993. pap. 7.95 (*1-86373-130-X*, Pub. by Allen & Unwin Aust Pty AT) IPG Chicago.

—The Amazing Adventures of Amabel. Nicholson, John, illus. 112p. (Orig.). (gr. 6 up). 1993. pap. 7.95 (*0-04-442163-X*, Pub. by Allen & Unwin Aust Pty AT) IPG Chicago.

Prisoner of Zenda. 1993. pap. text ed. 6.50 (*0-582-09680-4*, 79824) Longman.

Proctor, R. P. Motor Bike Mayhem. LC 93-38898. 1994. 4.99 (*0-8423-5131-0*) Tyndale.

Profilet, Cynthia. Kamal's Quest. Livingston, Francis, illus. 40p. (gr. 5-6). 1993. 15.95 (*0-9637735-0-X*) Sterling Pr MS.

Pullman, Philip. The Ruby in the Smoke. Greenstein, Mina, designed by. LC 86-20983. 208p. (gr. 7 up). 1987. lib. bdg. 11.99 (*0-394-98826-4*) Knopf Bks Yng Read.

—Shadow in the North. LC 87-29846. 320p. (gr. 7 up). 1988. PLB 13.99 (*0-394-99453-1*) Knopf Bks Yng Read.

—The Tin Princess. LC 93-38305. 304p. (gr. 9-12). 1994. 16.00 (*0-679-84757-X*) Knopf Bks Yng Read.

Pyle, Howard. Otto of the Silver Hand. Pyle, Howard, illus. xv, 173p. (gr. 5-9). 1967. pap. 5.95 (*0-486-21784-1*) Dover.

—Reader's Digest Best Loved Books for Young Readers: The Merry Adventures of Robin Hood. Ogburn, Jackie, ed. Huens, Jean L., illus. 136p. (gr. 4-12). 1989. 3.99 (*0-945260-20-2*) Choice Pub NY.

Radin, Ruth Y. Tac's Island. 80p. (gr. 2-9). 1989. pap. 2.95 (*0-8167-1320-0*) Troll Assocs.

—Tac's Turn. 80p. (gr. 2-9). 1989. pap. 2.95 (*0-8167-1319-7*) Troll Assocs.

Raney, Ken. Stick Horse. (Illus.). 32p. (ps-1). 1991. 9.95 (*0-9625261-4-2*, Green Tiger) S&S Trade.

Raven, James. The Best Enemy. 1993. pap. 3.25 (*0-553-29930-1*) Bantam.

—Entering the Way. 1993. pap. 3.25 (*0-553-29929-8*) Bantam.

—Sword of the Sensei. 1993. pap. 3.25 (*0-553-56300-9*) Bantam.

—Test of Wills. 1993. pap. 3.25 (*0-553-56243-6*) Bantam.

—The Ultimate Opponent. 1993. pap. 3.25 (*0-553-56133-2*) Bantam.

Razzi, Jim. Disney. 1987. 4.95 (*0-553-05420-1*) Bantam.

—Disney. 1987. 4.95 (*0-553-05422-8*) Bantam.

—The Flying Carpet. 64p. (Orig.). (gr. 2). 1985. pap. 1.95 (*0-553-15306-4*) Bantam.

Razzi, Jim, adapted by. Disney CYOA. 48p. (Orig.). 1986. pap. 4.95 (*0-553-05419-8*) Bantam.

Reese, Bob. The Critter Race. LC 81-3874. (Illus.). 24p. (ps-2). 1981. pap. 2.95 (*0-516-42302-9*) Childrens.

—Huzzard Buzzard. LC 81-6118. (Illus.). 24p. (ps-2). 1981. pap. 2.95 (*0-516-42303-7*) Childrens.

—Tweedle-De-Dee Tumbleweed. LC 81-6155. (Illus.). 24p. (ps-2). 1981. pap. 2.95 (*0-516-42307-X*) Childrens.

Reeves, Adrienne E. Willie & the Number Three Door & Other Adventures. Hosack, Leona H., illus. 120p. (Orig.). (gr. 1-3). 1991. pap. 8.95 (*0-87743-703-3*) Bahai.

Regan, Peter. Touchstone. Leonard, Pamela, illus. 208p. (gr. 4-7). 1989. 13.95 (*0-947962-44-1*, Pub. by Childrens Pr) Irish Bks Media.

Reinhard, Lisa A. The Nutmeg Adventure. (Illus.). 40p. (ps-2). 1994. 9.95 (*0-87935-099-7*) Williamsburg.

Rescue of Sir Clyde the Clumsy. 1991. pap. 1.97 (*1-56297-114-X*) Lee Pubns KY.

Richardson, Dawn. Smoke. 112p. (gr. 9-12). 1985. 7.95 (*0-920806-73-2*, Pub. by Penumbra Pr CN) U of Toronto Pr.

Robbins, Neal. The Island of the Three Sapphires. Mayfield, Helen, illus. 98p. (gr. 6 up). Date not set. pap. 4.00 (*1-884993-04-4*) Koldarana.

Roberts, Rachel S. Crisis at Pemberton Dike. Converse, James, illus. LC 83-18664. 152p. (gr. 7-10). 1984. pap. 4.95 (*0-8361-3350-1*) Herald Pr.

Roberts, Willo D. Caught! LC 93-14422. 160p. (gr. 3-7). 1994. SBE 14.95 (*0-689-31903-7*, Atheneum Child Bk) Macmillan Child Grp.

Robinson, Andrew. Wrath of the Seven Horsemen. MacDonald, George & Charlton, S. Coleman, eds. 32p. (Orig.). (gr. 10-12). 1987. pap. 6.00 (*0-915795-86-8*, 31) Iron Crown Ent Inc.

Robinson Crusoe. (Illus.). 224p. (gr. 3 up). 1990. pap. 2.50 (*1-55748-118-0*) Barbour & Co.

Robinson Crusoe. 352p. 1989. pap. 2.50 (*0-8125-0482-8*) Tor Bks.

Roche, P. K. Webster & Arnold & the Giant Box. Roche, P. K., illus. LC 80-11595. 56p. (ps-3). 1980. Dial Bks Young.

Roddy, Lee. The City Bear's Adventures. 144p. (gr. 3-7). 1985. pap. 4.99 (*0-88207-496-2*, Victor Books) SP Pubns.

—Danger on Thunder Mountain. 176p. (Orig.). (gr. 3 up). 1989. pap. 5.99 (*1-55661-028-9*) Bethany Hse.

—Dooger, the Grasshopper Hound. 144p. (gr. 3-7). 1985. pap. 4.99 (*0-88207-497-0*, Victor Books) SP Pubns.

—The Flaming Trap. 176p. (Orig.). (gr. 4-8). 1990. pap. 5.99 (*1-55661-095-5*) Bethany Hse.

—The Ghost Dog of Stoney Ridge. 144p. (gr. 3-7). 1985. pap. 4.99 (*0-88207-498-9*, Victor Books) SP Pubns.

—The Hair-Pulling Bear Dog. 144p. (gr. 3-7). 1985. pap. 4.99 (*0-88207-499-7*, Victor Books) SP Pubns.

—High Country Ambush. 176p. (Orig.). (gr. 3-8). 1992. pap. 5.99 (*1-55661-287-7*) Bethany Hse.

—The Overland Escape. LC 88-63471. 160p. (gr. 2-6). 1989. pap. text ed. 5.99 (*1-55661-026-2*) Bethany Hse.

—The Secret of the Howling Cave. 192p. (Orig.). (gr. 4-10). 1990. pap. 5.99 (*1-55661-094-7*) Bethany Hse.

Rogers, Barbara. God Rescues His People Activity Book. 72p. (Orig.). (ps-1). 1983. pap. 3.00 (*0-8361-3338-2*) Herald Pr.

Romain, Trevor. Under the Big Sky. Romain, Trevor, illus. 64p. (gr. 5-12). 1994. 13.95 (*1-880092-13-1*) Bright Bks TX.

Root, Phyllis. The Old Red Rocking Chair. Sandford, John, illus. 32p. (ps-3). 1992. Arcade Pub Inc.

Rose, John R. The Donkey Hide. 272p. 1994. pap. 10.00 (*1-881170-04-7*) Rose Pub OR. "Donkey Hide, what in the world is that?"..."It's the leather strap they whip us with!" This is the first in a series of adventure books, all fiction, featuring Jape & Tubbs, two nine-year-old boys. The setting is 1938, "Crossroads," USA. Two mischievous farm boys, in their quest for adventure, end up in deep trouble. Their imagination & childish wit got them into trouble & with those same tools they attempt to wiggle out. The author is a new "Mark Twain" & if you liked TOM SAWYER, you'll love JAPE & TUBBS. Order from Rose Publishing, 3303 Ward Drive N.E., Salem, OR 97305. 800-842-7421.
Publisher Provided Annotation.

Rosen, Sidney & Rosen, Dorothy. The Baghdad Mission. LC 93-36965. 1994. 19.95 (*0-87614-828-3*) Carolrhoda Bks.

Ross, Tony. Treasure of Cozy Cove. (ps-3). 1990. 14.00 (*0-374-37744-8*) FS&G.

Roth, Arthur. Iceberg Hermit. 1989. pap. 2.95 (*0-590-44112-4*) Scholastic Inc.

Rotsler, William. Plot-It-Yourself Adventure: Goonies Cavern of Horror. Arico, Diane, ed. 128p. (Orig.). (gr. 3-7). 1985. pap. 3.95 (*0-671-60135-0*) S&S Trade.

Rovetch, Lissa. Trigwater Did It. Rovetch, Lissa, illus. LC 88-31791. 32p. (ps up). 1989. 12.95 (*0-688-08057-X*); PLB 12.88 (*0-688-08058-8*, Morrow Jr Bks) Morrow Jr Bks.

—Trigwater Did It. (Illus.). 32p. (ps-3). 1991. pap. 3.95 (*0-14-054238-8*, Puffin) Puffin Bks.

Ruckman, Ivy. Night of the Twisters. LC 83-46168. 160p. (gr. 3-6). 1986. pap. 3.95 (*0-06-440176-6*, Trophy) HarpC Child Bks.

Rushford, Patricia H. Pursued. 1994. pap. 3.99 (*1-55661-333-4*) Bethany Hse.

Russell, David A. The Majked Driver. Askew, Stella, ed. 240p. (Orig.). 1994. pap. 4.95 (*1-884559-01-8*) Allen Pubng.

—Superbike. 180p. (gr. 4-7). 1993. 3.95 (*1-883174-00-7*) High Octane.

Rylant, Cynthia. A Fine White Dust. (gr. k-6). 1987. pap. 3.50 (*0-440-42499-2*, YB) Dell.

—Henry & Mudge in Puddle Trouble: The Second Book of Their Adventures. LC 89-39810. (Illus.). 48p. (gr. 1-3). 1990. pap. 3.95 (*0-689-71400-9*, Aladdin) Macmillan Child Grp.

—Henry & Mudge: The First Book of Their Adventures. Stevenson, Sucie, illus. LC 89-39809. 48p. (gr. 1-3). 1990. pap. 3.95 (*0-689-71399-1*, Aladdin) Macmillan Child Grp.

Saban, Vera. Johnny Egan of the Paintrock. Saban, Sonja, illus. LC 85-30958. 130p. (Orig.). (gr. 4-8). 1986. pap. 6.95 (*0-914565-13-3*, Timbertrails) Capstan Pubns.

—Test of the Tenderfoot. Elliott, Tony, illus. LC 89-9729. 147p. (gr. 5-8). 1989. 6.95 (*0-914565-35-4*, Timbertrails) Capstan Pubns.

Salassi, Otto. On the Ropes. LC 80-20399. 256p. (gr. 6 up). 1992. pap. 4.95 (*0-688-11500-4*, Pub. by Beech Tree Bks) Morrow.

Samuelson, Rita. Super Speech Adventures. (Illus.). 96p. (gr. k-4). 1991. pap. 10.00 (*0-930599-70-5*) Thinking Pubns.

Sandberg, Inger. Dusty Wants to Help. Mauver, Judy A., tr. from SWE. Sandberg, Lasse, illus. 32p. (ps up). 1987. 6.95 (*91-29-58336-5*, Pub. by R & S Bks) FS&G.

Sanders, Franklin. Heiland. 276p. (Orig.). 1989. pap. text ed. 6.00 (*0-685-26841-1*) Footstool Pubns.

Sandling, R. Harris. What Do You Do with a Cardboard Box on a Day When the Rain's Pourin' Down? Carter, Mary C., ed. Venema, Jon R., illus. 50p. (gr. 3 up). 1993. write for info. (*1-883194-00-8*) Emerald Hummngbrd.

Sanfield, Steve. Adventures of High John the Conqueror. (gr. 4-7). 1992. pap. 3.50 (*0-440-40556-4*) Dell.

Sargent, Dave. Raw Courage. 204p. 1992. pap. write for info. (*1-56763-003-0*) Ozark Pub.

Saunders, Susan. Blizzard at Black Swan Inn. 64p. (Orig.). (gr. 4). 1986. pap. 2.25 (*0-553-15379-X*) Bantam.

—Haunted Halloween Party. 64p. (Orig.). (gr. 4). 1986. pap. 2.99 (*0-553-15453-2*) Bantam.

—Light on Burro Mountain. 64p. (Orig.). (gr. 4 up). 1987. pap. 2.25 (*0-553-15517-2*, Skylark) Bantam.

—Miss Liberty Caper. (gr. 2-4). 1986. pap. 2.25 (*0-553-15416-8*, Skylark) Bantam.

—The Movie Mystery. (gr. 2-4). 1987. pap. 2.25 (*0-553-15509-1*, Skylark) Bantam.

—You Are Invisible. 1989. pap. 2.99 (*0-553-15685-3*) Bantam.

Saunders, Susan & Packard, Edward. Ice Cave. (gr. 2-4). 1987. pap. 2.25 (*0-553-15467-2*, Skylark) Bantam.

Savin, Marcia. Will Lithuania Comstock Please Come to the Courtesy Phone? LC 93-28441. (Illus.). 160p. (gr. 5-9). 1993. PLB 13.95 (*0-8167-3324-4*); pap. 3.95 (*0-8167-3325-2*) BrdgeWater.

Say, Allen. Lost Lake. Say, Allen, illus. (gr. 1-4). 1989. 14.45 (*0-395-50933-5*) HM.

Schneider, Rex. That's Not All! Gregorich, Barbara, ed. (Illus.). 32p. (gr. k-2). 1992. pap. 3.95 (*0-88743-417-7*, 06069) Sch Zone Pub Co.

Schott, Carolyn J. & Smith, Phillipa A. The Cracker Crumb Rescue. 40p. (gr. 3-6). 1992. PLB 16.95 (*0-9632461-0-0*) Harbour Duck.

Schraff, Anne. Swamp Furies. Parker, Liz, ed. Taylor, Marjorie, illus. 45p. (Orig.). (gr. 6-12). 1992. pap. text ed. 2.95 (*1-56254-056-4*) Saddleback Pubns.

Schultz, Irene. The Woodland Gang & the Missing Will. (Illus.). 128p. (gr. 3 up). 1984. pap. 4.95 (*0-201-50073-6*) Addison-Wesley.

—The Woodland Gang & the Old Gold Coins. (Illus.). 128p. (gr. 3 up). 1984. pap. 4.95 (*0-201-50075-2*) Addison-Wesley.

—The Woodland Gang & the Stolen Animals. (Illus.). 128p. (gr. 3 up). 1984. pap. 4.95 (*0-201-50074-4*) Addison-Wesley.

—The Woodland Gang & the Two Lost Boys. (Illus.). 128p. (gr. 3 up). 1984. pap. 4.95 (*0-201-50072-8*) Addison-Wesley.

Schurch, Maylan. The Sword of Denis Anwyck. LC 92-22127. 1992. pap. 7.95 (*0-8280-0658-X*) Review & Herald.

Scieszka, Jon. The Not-So-Jolly-Roger. Smith, Lane, illus. 64p. (gr. 3-7). 1991. 11.00 (*0-670-83754-7*) Viking Child Bks.

Scott, Gavin, adapted by. Revolution! LC 91-51201. (Illus.). 136p. (Orig.). (gr. 4-8). 1992. pap. 3.50 (*0-679-83238-6*) Random Bks Yng Read.

Scott, Michael. The Seven Treasures: The Quest of the Sons of Tuireann. (Illus.). 158p. (gr. 3-7). 1993. pap. 9.95 (*0-86278-309-7*, Pub. by OBrien Pr IE) Dufour.

Scullard, Sue. Miss Fanshawe & the Great Dragon Adventure. Scullard, Sue, illus. 32p. (ps-4). 1987. 9.95 (*0-312-00510-5*) St Martin.

Seabrooke, Brenda. The Boy Who Saved the Town. Burns, Howard M., illus. LC 89-52027. 30p. (gr. 2-5). 1990. 7.95 (*0-87033-405-0*) Tidewater.

Seale, Jan E. The Ballad of the Men at Mier: The Black Bean Expedition. Coleman, Bernice, illus. 46p. (gr. 4-8). 1986. lib. bdg. 10.95 (*0-936927-14-3*); pap. 7.95 (*0-936927-15-1*) Knowing Pr.

Sealey, Patricia. Caught in the Act. (ps-3). 1992. pap. 2.95 (*0-7910-2901-8*) Chelsea Hse.

The Second Conquest. 96p. (gr. 6-9). 1985. pap. 6.50 (*0-521-31705-3*) Cambridge U Pr.

Secret of Ghost Mountain. (Illus.). 48p. (Orig.). (gr. 1-4). 1989. pap. 2.95 (*0-8431-2706-6*) Price Stern.

Serenne, Jean-Pierre. Crazy Sunday. (Illus.). 48p. (gr. 3-8). 1990. 8.95 (*0-89565-811-9*) Childs World.

Serraillier, Ian. Escape from Warsaw. 1990. pap. 2.95 (*0-590-43715-1*) Scholastic Inc.

Severance, Charles L. Tales of the Thumb. 2nd ed. LC 72-86863. (Illus.). (gr. 3-6). 1972. pap. 4.75 (*0-932411-00-2*) Pub Div JCS.

Sharmat, Marjorie W. Nate the Great & the Snowy Trail. Simont, Marc, illus. 48p. (gr. k-6). 1984. pap. 3.50 (*0-440-46276-2*, YB) Dell.

—Nate the Great Stalks Stupidweed. Simont, Marc, illus. 48p. (gr. 9-12). 1989. pap. 3.50 (*0-440-40150-X*, YB) Dell.

Shepard, Aaron. The Legend of Lightning Larry. Goffe, Toni, illus. LC 91-43779. 32p. (gr. 1-3). 1993. SBE 14.95 (*0-684-19433-3*, Scribners Young Read) Macmillan Child Grp.

Shepard, Steven. Fogbound. Thatch, Nancy R., ed. Shepard, Steven, illus. Melton, David, intro. by. LC 93-13422. (Illus.). 29p. (gr. 5-8). 1993. PLB 14.95 (*0-933849-43-5*) Landmark Edns.

Shulevitz, Uri. The Strange & Exciting Adventures of Jeramiah Hush. (Illus.). 96p. (gr. 2-5). 1986. 14.00 (*0-374-33656-3*) FS&G.

Shusterman, Neal. Piggyback Ninja. Boddy, Joe, illus. 32p. (ps up). 1994. 12.95 (*1-56565-105-7*) Lowell Hse Juvenile.

—Speeding Bullet. 1992. 3.25 (*0-590-45424-2*, Point) Scholastic Inc.

Siegman, Meryl. Volcano. 128p. (Orig.). (gr. 4). 1987. pap. 2.25 (*0-553-26197-5*) Bantam.

Simmons, Herbert R. & Boyice, Lester L. Star Patrol: The Adventures Begin. Peck, Bill, illus. 56p. (ps-7). 1987. lib. bdg. 8.95 (*0-930355-05-9*) ELRAMCO Enter.

Simons-Ailes, Sandra. Roundup. (Illus.). 34p. (Orig.). (ps-7). 1981. pap. 3.75 (*0-915347-04-0*) Pueblo Acoma Pr.

Singer, A. L. Home Alone Two: Lost in New York Mass Market Novelization. 1992. 3.25 (*0-590-45718-7*) Scholastic Inc.

—Surf Warriors. (gr. 4-7). 1993. pap. 3.50 (*0-440-40799-0*) Dell.

Skifton, Chrys. God's Country Kids: The Adventure Begins. White, James W., ed. Barber, Jeannie, illus. LC 94-71146. 57p. (gr. k-6). 1994. 22.00 (*0-9640794-7-X*) Celebration Pr. "This book is a breath of fresh air. We share the innocence of children as they show us the world about them through their eyes in a time travel adventure. It is a subtle testament to the way the world should be family oriented, moral, ethical. Give yourself a treat & step out of the adult world into that of the child. This children's book is for all ages." - James Wm. White, Director of the LaCrosse Public Library & The Winding Rivers Library System. This is the first book of a beautifully illustrated series. It introduces two brothers & their sister. This is a fantasy adventure. Each chapter has a different adventure that is educational as well as magical. To order contact: Celebration Press, P.O. Box 693, Onalaska, WI 54650 or call 608-783-3561 or (800) HY-CHRYS. Also available from Baker & Taylor & The Bookmen.
Publisher Provided Annotation.

Sliva, Carolyn J. The Adventures of Lucky. 1995. 7.95 (*0-8062-4982-X*) Carlton.

Slote, Alfred. The Trouble on Janus. Watts, James, illus. LC 85-40099. 192p. (gr. 3-6). 1985. PLB 13.89 (*0-397-32159-7*, Lipp Jr Bks) HarpC Child Bks.

—The Trouble on Janus. Watts, James, illus. LC 85-40099. 192p. (gr. 3-6). 1988. pap. 3.95 (*0-06-440216-9*, Trophy) HarpC Child Bks.

Smith, Doris B. Return to Bitter Creek. 176p. (gr. 3-7). 1988. pap. 4.99 (*0-14-032223-X*, Puffin) Puffin Bks.

Smith, Duane. Heritage Revealed Series for Younger Readers, 3 Bks. 1994. Set. pap. 13.95 (*1-886218-00-5*); The Legend of the Golden Hawk. pap. 4.95 (*0-9632074-1-5*); Journey to Clay Mountain. pap. 4.95 (*0-9632074-2-3*); Lost on Victoria Lake. pap. 4.95 (*0-9632074-3-1*) Azimuth Ga. Introducing THE HERITAGE REVEALED SERIES FOR YOUNGER READERS! These three stories of cultural understanding & identity from the author of the critically acclaimed novel, THE NUBIAN, are designed for children ages 7 through 14. THE LEGEND OF THE GOLDEN HAWK: A wild hawk becomes trapped in a game preserve. During his capture he loses his memory, & struggles with the despair of his captivity until he is miraculously rescued by the faithfulness of his brother. JOURNEY TO CLAY MOUNTAIN: A small village at the base of a mountain range is dominated by the shadows from the largest of these, the Clay Mountain. The villagers toil in frustration until a young boy discovers the wonderful secret of the Clay Mountain, a secret which has been hidden for centuries. LOST...ON VICTORIA LAKE: Two children are cast adrift in their father's fishing boat during a storm. They are rescued by the guidance & provision of their royal ancestors, who appear to the children in a series of magnificent visions. For order information, call 1-800-373-5000 or write to the Azimuth Press, 3002 Dayna Dr, College Park, GA 30349.
Publisher Provided Annotation.

Smith, L. J. Night of the Solstice. 1993. pap. 3.99 (*0-06-106172-7*, Harp PBks) HarpC.

Smith, Parker. The Young Indiana Jones Chronicles: The Mummy's Curse. Mones, illus. 24p. (ps-3). 1992. pap. write for info. (*0-307-12689-7*, 12689, Golden Pr) Western Pub.

Smith, Sherwood. Wren to the Rescue. (gr. 4-7). 1993. pap. 3.50 (*0-440-40773-7*) Dell.

Smothers, Ethel F. Down in the Piney Woods. 156p. (gr. 3-7). 1994. pap. 3.99 (*0-679-84714-6*, Bullseye Bks) Random Bks Yng Read.

Sobel, Barbara. Papa, Molly & the Great Prairie. LC 87-81236. (gr. 3-6). 1987. 7.59 (*0-87386-045-4*); bk. & cassette 16.99 (*0-317-55334-8*); pap. 1.95 (*0-87386-044-6*) Jan Prods.

Sochard, Ruth. Pirates of Pelargir. Fenlon, Peter, ed. McBride, Angus, illus. 32p. (Orig.). (gr. 10-12). 1987. pap. 6.00 (*0-915795-44-2*, 8104) Iron Crown Ent Inc.

Somper, J. Pyramid Plot. (Illus.). 48p. (gr. 3-8). 1993. PLB 11.96 (*0-88110-403-5*); pap. 4.95 (*0-7460-0506-7*) EDC.

Souter, John. Choice Adventures: Abandoned Gold Mine. 160p. (gr. 4-8). 1992. pap. 4.99 (*0-8423-5031-4*) Tyndale.

South, Sheri C. The Terrorist Group. (gr. 4-7). 1991. pap. 3.25 (*0-553-29289-7*) Bantam.

Southey, Robert. Cataract of Lodore. (ps-3). 1991. 13.95 (*0-8037-1025-9*); PLB 13.89 (*0-8037-1026-7*) Dial Bks Young.

Springstubb, Tricia. Which Way to the Nearest Wilderness? (gr. k-12). 1987. pap. 2.75 (*0-440-99554-X*, LFL) Dell.

Stahl, Hilda. Kayla O'Brian & the Dangerous Journey. LC 90-80618. 128p. (Orig.). (gr. 4-7). 1990. pap. 4.95 (*0-89107-577-1*) Crossway Bks.

Standish, Burt L. Frank Merriwell's Chums. Rudman, Jack, ed. (gr. 9 up). 1970. 9.95 (*0-8373-9302-7*); pap. 3.95 (*0-8373-9002-8*) F Merriwell.

—Frank Merriwell's Foes. Rudman, Jack, ed. (gr. 9 up). 1970. 9.95 (*0-8373-9303-5*); pap. 3.95 (*0-8373-9003-6*) F Merriwell.

—Frank Merriwell's Trip West. Rudman, Jack, ed. (gr. 9 up). Date not set. 9.95 (*0-8373-9304-3*); pap. 3.95 (*0-8373-9004-4*) F Merriwell.

Staplehurst, Graham. Gates of Mordor. Fenlon, Peter C., Jr., ed. McBride, Angus, illus. 32p. (Orig.). (gr. 10-12). 1987. pap. 6.00 (*0-915795-81-7*, 8105, Dist. by Berkley Pub Group) Iron Crown Ent Inc.

—Robin Hood. Fenlon, Peter & Charlton, S. Coleman, eds. McBride, Angus, illus. 160p. (Orig.). (gr. 10-12). 1987. pap. 15.00 (*0-915795-28-0*, 1010) Iron Crown Ent Inc.

Steele, Mary Q. Journey Outside. Negri, Rocco, illus. (gr. 3-7). 1979. pap. 3.95 (*0-14-030588-2*, Puffin) Puffin Bks.

Steele, Philip. The Samurai Warriors. LC 93-43401. (Illus.). 24p. (gr. 2-5). 1994. 8.95 (*0-317-05938-6*, Kingfisher LKC) LKC.

Steig, William. Spinky Sulks. LC 88-81292. (Illus.). 32p. (ps up). 1988. 15.00 (*0-374-38321-9*) FS&G.

—The Zabajaba Jungle. Steig, William, illus. LC 87-17690. (ps-4). 1987. 15.00 (*0-374-38790-7*) FS&G.

—The Zabajaba Jungle. LC 87-17690. (Illus.). (ps-4). 1991. pap. 4.95 (*0-374-49594-7*) FS&G.

Stein, Kevin. Brothers Majere. LC 88-51720. (Illus.). 352p. (Orig.). 1990. pap. 4.95 (*0-88038-776-9*) TSR Inc.

Steiner, Barbara. Dreamstalker. 160p. (Orig.). (gr. 4 up). 1992. pap. 3.50 (*0-380-76611-6*, Flare) Avon.

—Ghost Cave. Ashby, Ruth, ed. 144p. (gr. 3-6). 1993. pap. 2.99 (*0-671-74785-1*, Minstrel Bks) PB.

Stevenson. Sword of Caesar. (ps-7). 1987. pap. 2.50 (*0-553-26531-8*) Bantam.

Stevenson, James. All Aboard! LC 94-5825. (Illus.). 32p. 1995. write for info. (*0-688-12438-0*); PLB write for info. (*0-688-12439-9*) Greenwillow.

—Higher on the Door. LC 86-14925. (Illus.). 32p. (gr. k-3). 1987. 11.75 (*0-688-06636-4*); PLB 11.88 (*0-688-06637-2*) Greenwillow.

Stevenson, Laura C. Happily after All. 256p. (gr. 5-9). 1990. 14.95 (*0-395-50216-0*) HM.

Stevenson, Robert Louis. Black Arrow. (gr. 4 up). 1990. pap. 3.50 (*0-440-40359-6*) Dell.

—Ile au Tresor. (FRE.). 284p. (gr. 5-10). 1987. pap. 9.95 (*2-07-033441-4*) Schoenhof.

—Kidnapped. (gr. 8 up). 1964. pap. 1.95 (*0-8049-0010-8*, CL-10) Airmont.

—Kidnapped. Wyeth, N. C., illus. 304p. 1989. 12.99 (*0-517-68783-6*) Random Hse Value.

—Kidnapped. Mattern, Joanne, retold by. Parton, Steve, illus. LC 92-5803. 48p. (gr. 3-6). 1992. PLB 12.89 (*0-8167-2862-3*); pap. text ed. 3.95 (*0-8167-2863-1*) Troll Assocs.

—Kidnapped. Wyeth, N. C., illus. LC 89-43033. 290p. (gr. 6 up). 1993. Repr. of 1989 ed. 16.95 (*1-56138-262-0*) Running Pr.

—Kidnapped. (gr. 4-7). 1993. pap. 3.50 (*0-440-40836-9*) Dell.

—Kidnapped. Norby, Lisa, adapted by. LC 93-4609. 1994. pap. 2.99 (*0-679-85091-0*, Bullseye Bks) Random Bks Yng Read.

—Kidnapped. LC 94-5859. 1994. 13.95 (*0-679-43638-3*, Evrymans Lib Childs) Knopf.

—Kidnapped: Being Memoirs of the Adventures of David Balfour in the Year 1751. (Illus.). 326p. 1992. Repr. PLB 29.95 (*0-685-59599-4*) Regal Pubns.

—Treasure Island. (Illus.). (gr. 1-9). 1947. deluxe ed. 13.95 (*0-448-06025-6*, G&D) Putnam Pub Group.

—Treasure Island. Letley, Emma, ed. (gr. 7-12). 1985. pap. 3.95 (*0-19-281681-0*) OUP.

—Treasure Island. (gr. 7 up). 1965. pap. 1.75 (*0-451-51917-5*, Sig Classics) NAL-Dutton.

—Treasure Island. Hitchner, Earle, ed. De John, Marie, illus. LC 89-20561. 48p. (gr. 3-6). 1990. lib. bdg. 12.89 (*0-8167-1877-6*); pap. text ed. 3.95 (*0-8167-1878-4*) Troll Assocs.

—Treasure Island. reissued ed. Norby, Lisa, adapted by. Fernandez, Fernando, illus. LC 89-70039. 96p. (Orig.). (gr. 2-6). 1990. PLB 5.99 (*0-679-90402-6*, Bullseye Bks); pap. 2.99 (*0-679-80402-1*, Bullseye Bks) Random Bks Yng Read.
—Treasure Island. 272p. 1990. pap. 2.50 (*0-8125-0508-5*) Tor Bks.
—Treasure Island. 304p. 1992. 9.49 (*0-8167-2560-8*); pap. 2.95 (*0-8167-2561-6*) Troll Assocs.
—Treasure Island. Ingpen, Robert, illus. 176p. 1992. 20.00 (*0-670-84685-6*) Viking Child Bks.
—Treasure Island. Peake, Mervyn, illus. LC 92-53174. 240p. 1992. 12.95 (*0-679-41800-8*, Evrymans Lib Childs Class) Knopf.
—Treasure Island. LC 92-29791. 160p. 1993. pap. 1.00 (*0-486-27559-0*) Dover.
—Treasure Island. McNaughton, Colin, illus. LC 93-18941. 272p. (gr. 4-8). 1993. 15.95 (*0-8050-2773-4*, Bks Young Read) H Holt & Co.
—Treasure Island. Price, Norman, illus. LC 93-50905. 1994. write for info. (*0-448-40562-8*, G&D) Putnam Pub Group.
Stevenson, Robert Louis & Boyette, Pat. Treasure Island. (Illus.). 52p. Date not set. pap. 4.95 (*1-57209-015-4*) Classics Int Ent.
Stine, Bob. The Amazing Adventures of Me, Myself, & I. (gr. 2-5). 1991. pap. 2.75 (*0-553-15834-1*, Skylark) Bantam.
Stine, Megan & Stine, H. William. Young Indiana Jones & the Journey to the Underworld. LC 93-36821. 132p. (Orig.). (gr. 3-7). 1994. pap. 3.50 (*0-679-85458-4*) Random Bks Yng Read.
—Young Indiana Jones & the Lost Gold of Durango. 132p. (Orig.). (gr. 3-7). 1993. pap. 3.50 (*0-679-84926-2*, Bullseye Bks) Random Bks Yng Read.
Stine, R. L. Twisted. 1987. pap. 3.50 (*0-590-43139-0*) Scholastic Inc.
Stockton, Frank R. The Griffin & the Minor Canon. Sendak, Maurice, illus. LC 85-45827. 56p. (ps up). 1986. Repr. of 1964 ed. 13.95 (*0-06-025816-0*); PLB 13.89 (*0-06-025817-9*) HarpC Child Bks.
Storr, Catherine, ed. Odysseus & the Enchanters. (Illus.). 32p. (gr. k-5). 1985. PLB 19.97 (*0-8172-2502-1*) Raintree Steck-V.
Strasser, Todd. Beyond the Reef. 1991. pap. 3.50 (*0-440-20881-5*) Dell.
—Super Mario Brothers Junior Novelization. LC 92-55045. (Illus.). 128p. (Orig.). (gr. 2-6). 1993. 3.95 (*1-56282-471-6*) Hyprn Child.
—Wildlife. (gr. k-12). 1988. pap. 2.95 (*0-440-20151-9*, LE) Dell.
Stroh, R. W. Adventure in the Lost World. Mulkey, Kim, illus. LC 85-2530. 96p. (gr. 3-6). 1985. lib. bdg. 9.49 (*0-8167-0535-6*); pap. text ed. 2.95 (*0-8167-0536-4*) Troll Assocs.
Strommen, Judith B. Johnson Falls Story. 1995. write for info. (*0-8050-2415-8*) H Holt & Co.
Sutton, Larry. Taildraggers High. LC 85-47592. 161p. (gr. 5 up). 1985. 14.00 (*0-374-37372-8*) FS&G.
Sweeney. Disaster. 1980. 8.95 (*0-679-20954-9*) McKay.
Sweeny, Joyce. Center Line. 256p. (gr. k-12). 1985. pap. 2.95 (*0-440-91127-3*, LFL) Dell.
Swift, Jonathan. Gulliver's Stories. 1989. pap. 2.95 (*0-590-41842-4*) Scholastic Inc.
—Gulliver's Travels. Riordan, James, ed. Ambrus, Victor G., illus. 96p. 1992. 20.00 (*0-19-279897-9*) OUP.
Swoboda, Dana. Mr. Man in the Skies. LC 88-35619. (Orig.). (gr. 5-9). 1991. pap. 4.00 (*0-915541-89-0*) Star Bks Inc.
Tada, Joni T. & Jensen, Steve. Darcy's Great Expectations. Norton, LoraBeth, ed. 128p. (gr. 4-8). Date not set. pap. 4.99 (*0-7814-0168-2*, Chariot Bks) Chariot Family.
Tafuri, Nancy. Junglewalk. LC 87-8558. (Illus.). 32p. (ps-3). 1988. 14.95 (*0-688-07182-1*); lib. bdg. 14.88 (*0-688-07183-X*) Greenwillow.
Talespin: Surprise in the Skies. (Illus.). 48p. (gr. 3-7). 1992. pap. 2.95 (*1-56115-269-2*, 21810, Golden Pr) Western Pub.
Tankersley-Cusick, Richie. The Drifter. Clancy, Lisa, ed. 240p. (Orig.). 1994. pap. 3.99 (*0-671-88741-6*, Archway) PB.
Taylor, Lisa. Beryl's Box. Dann, Penny, illus. LC 92-44990. 32p. (ps-2). 1993. 12.95 (*0-8120-6355-4*); pap. 5.95 (*0-8120-1673-4*) Barron.
Taylor, Mildred D. Let the Circle Be Unbroken. (gr. 4-7). 1991. pap. 4.50 (*0-14-034892-1*, Puffin) Puffin Bks.
—Roll of Thunder, Hear My Cry. 276p. (gr. 5-9). 1991. pap. 4.50 (*0-14-034893-X*) Puffin Bks.
Teichman, Avigail. The Captive Sultan. Reinman, Y. Y., ed. Hinklicky, G., illus. LC 85-72403. 128p. (gr. 7-11). 1985. 7.95 (*0-935063-12-9*); pap. 5.95 (*0-935063-04-8*) CIS Comm.
Teitelbaum, Michael. Batman Returns. (Illus.). 24p. (ps-3). 1992. pap. write for info. (*0-307-12687-0*, 12687, Golden Pr) Western Pub.
Terman, Douglas. By Balloon to the Sahara. (gr. 4). 1989. pap. 2.99 (*0-553-26593-8*) Bantam.
Thesman, Jean. When the Road Ends. 192p. 1993. pap. 3.50 (*0-380-72011-6*, Camelot) Avon.
Thoene, Brock & Thoene, Bodie. Cannons of the Comstock. 224p. 1992. pap. 7.99 (*1-55661-166-8*) Bethany Hse.
Thomas, Janis & Thomas, Lenerd. Sir Lacksalot & the Two Headed Dragon Meet the Savage Sea Serpent. Yakovetic, illus. LC 91-61114. 48p. (gr. k-5). 1991. 16.95 (*1-879480-01-8*) L T Pub.
Thomas, Joyce C. Journey. (gr. 7 up). 1988. pap. 12.95 (*0-590-40627-2*, Scholastic Hardcover) Scholastic Inc.
Thompson, Jonathon J., Jr. Air Raiders Five. 50p. (gr. 7-12). 1992. 5.00 (*0-933479-09-3*) Thompson.
—Air Raiders Four. (Illus.). 65p. (gr. 7-12). 1992. 4.35 (*0-933479-07-7*) Thompson.
—Air Raiders Six. (Illus.). (gr. 7-12). 1992. write for info. (*0-933479-17-4*) Thompson.
—Air Raiders Three. (Illus.). 85p. (gr. 7-12). 1992. 5.25 (*0-933479-06-9*) Thompson.
—Air Raiders Two. (Illus.). 70p. (gr. 7-12). 1987. 4.60 (*0-933479-10-7*) Thompson.
—Semantography. (Illus.). 60p. (gr. 7-12). 1992. write for info. (*0-933479-13-1*) Thompson.
Thompson, Julian F. The Taking of Mariasburg. (gr. 8 up). 1989. pap. 2.95 (*0-590-41246-9*) Scholastic Inc.
Thompson, Paul B. & Carter, Tonya R. Darkness & Light. LC 88-51718. (Illus.). 352p. (Orig.). 1989. pap. 4.95 (*0-88038-722-X*) TSR Inc.
Thompson, Richard. Jill & the Jogero. Durham-Moulin, Francoise, illus. 24p. (ps-2). 1992. PLB 14.95 (*1-55037-245-9*, Pub. by Annick Pr); pap. 4.95 (*1-55037-246-7*, Pub. by Annick Pr) Firefly Bks Ltd.
Thomsen, Paul. Mountain of Fire. 64p. (ps-7). 1990. pap. 6.95 (*1-56121-025-0*) Wolgemuth & Hyatt.
—Operation Rawhide. 64p. (gr. 4-7). 1990. pap. 6.95 (*1-56121-015-3*) Wolgemuth & Hyatt.
Thomson, Pat. One of Those Days. (gr. k-6). 1987. pap. 2.50 (*0-440-46646-6*, YB) Dell.
Tjepkema, Edith R. Alaskan Paradise. 115p. (Orig.). (gr. 8 up). 1989. pap. 4.50 (*0-9620280-1-0*) Northland Pr.
—North to Paradise. 103p. (Orig.). (gr. 8-12). 1987. pap. 4.50 (*0-9620280-0-2*) Northland Pr.
Tournier, Michel. Vendredi ou la Vie Sauvage. Lemoine, Georges, illus. (FRE.). 191p. (gr. 5-10). 1987. pap. 8.95 (*2-07-033445-7*) Schoenhof.
Treasure Island. (Illus.). 24p. (Orig.). (gr. k up). 1993. pap. 2.50 (*1-56144-103-1*, Honey Bear Bks) Modern Pub NYC.
Treasure Island: Adventure Classics. 1992. 4.99 (*0-517-06524-X*) Random Hse Value.
Troll. Legend of Sleepy Hollow Activity Book. 64p. (gr. 3-6). 1991. pap. 1.95 (*0-8167-2284-6*) Troll Assocs.
Truus. What Kouka Knows. LC 92-54428. (Illus.). 32p. (ps-3). 1993. 13.00 (*0-688-12381-3*) Lothrop.
Turner, Ann. Dakota Dugout. Himler, Ronald, illus. LC 85-3084. 32p. (gr. k-3). 1985. RSBE 13.95 (*0-02-789700-1*, Macmillan Child Bk) Macmillan Child Grp.
Twain, Mark. Adventures of Huckleberry Finn. LC 85-9576. 187p. (gr. 4-6). 1983. Repr. PLB 17.95 (*0-89966-468-7*) Buccaneer Bks.
—Adventures of Tom Sawyer. LC 62-19420. 167p. (gr. 4-6). 1983. Repr. PLB 15.95x (*0-89966-467-9*) Buccaneer Bks.
—The Adventures of Tom Sawyer. Moser, Barry, illus. Glassman, Peter, afterword by. LC 89-60838. (Illus.). 272p. (ps up). 1989. 21.95 (*0-688-07510-X*) Morrow Jr Bks.
—Adventures of Tom Sawyer. 1993. pap. 2.95 (*0-590-43352-0*) Scholastic Inc.
Twain, Mark, pseud. Aventures de Tom Sawyer. Lapointe, Claude, illus. (FRE.). 296p. (gr. 5-10). 1987. pap. 9.95 (*2-07-033449-X*) Schoenhof.
—Huckleberry Finn. Vogel, Nathaele, illus. (FRE.). 380p. (gr. 5-10). 1990. pap. 10.95 (*2-07-033230-6*) Schoenhof.
—Huckleberry Finn. (gr. 4-7). 1993. pap. 4.95 (*0-8114-6826-7*) Raintree Steck-V.
Twain, Mark. The Man That Corrupted Hadleyburg: A Classic Story of Honesty. (Illus.). 72p. (gr. 6 up). 1986. PLB 13.95 (*0-88682-006-5*) Creative Ed.
—The Prince & the Pauper. 256p. 1992. pap. 2.50 (*0-8125-0477-1*) Tor Bks.
—Tom Sawyer. Edwards, June, adapted by. Naprstek, Joel, illus. LC 80-22095. 48p. (gr. 4 up). 1983. PLB 20.70 (*0-8172-1665-0*) Raintree Steck-V.
Twain, Mark, pseud. Tom Sawyer. (gr. 4-7). 1993. pap. 4.95 (*0-8114-6843-7*) Raintree Steck-V.
Twain, Mark & Ploog, Michael. Tom Sawyer. (Illus.). 52p. Date not set. pap. 4.95 (*1-57209-007-3*) Classics Int Ent.
Tyler, Jenny & Round, Graham. Escape from Blood Castle. (Illus.). 48p. (gr. 4-9). 1986. PLB 11.96 (*0-88110-388-8*); pap. 4.95 (*0-86020-950-4*) EDC.
Uncle Scrooge: Blast to the Past. (Illus.). 48p. (gr. 3-7). 1992. pap. 2.95 (*1-56115-270-6*, 21811, Golden Pr) Western Pub.
Ungerer, Tomi. Emile. Ungerer, Tomi, illus. 32p. (ps-2). 1992. pap. 3.99 (*0-440-40593-9*, YB) Dell.
—Mellops Go Diving for Treasure. (ps-3). 1993. pap. 3.99 (*0-440-40522-X*) Dell.
—Mellops Strike Oil. (ps-3). 1993. pap. 3.99 (*0-440-40523-8*) Dell.
Urbide, Fernando & Engler, Dan. Ben-Hur, A Race to Glory. CCC of America Staff, illus. 35p. (Orig.). (ps-8). 1992. incl. video 21.95 (*1-56814-006-1*); pap. text ed. 4.95 book (*0-685-62399-8*) CCC of America.
Vallet, Roxanne. How Tall Is Too Tall? Vallet, Roxanne, illus. 12p. (gr. 1-3). 1992. pap. 10.95 (*1-56606-007-9*) Bradley Mann.
Valloglise, P. Luc. The Search for the Rabbit. 138p. (gr. 7 up). 1988. pap. 10.00 (*0-934852-55-3*) Lorien Hse.
Van Allsburg, Chris. The Wreck of the Zephyr. Van Allsburg, Chris, illus. LC 82-23371. 32p. (ps up). 1983. 16.45 (*0-395-33075-0*) HM.
Van Eeden, Maria. Robbers Five...or Is It Six? Homan, Anneke, illus. 24p. (Orig.). (ps-1). 1994. pap. 4.95 (*1-55037-363-3*, Pub. by Annick CN) Firefly Bks Ltd.
Vardeman, Robert E. Road to the Stars. LC 87-45307. 224p. (gr. 7 up). 1988. HarpC Child Bks.
Vera, Rene, Jr. The Ninth Street Bridge. 1992. 7.95 (*0-533-09612-X*) Vantage.
Verne, Jules. Around the World in Eighty Days. 253p. (gr. 5 up). 1964. pap. 2.95 (*0-440-90285-1*, LFL) Dell.
—Around the World in Eighty Days. Moser, Barry, illus. LC 87-62829. 256p. (gr. 5 up). 1988. 19.95 (*0-688-07508-8*); signed ltd. ed. 175.00 (*0-688-08257-2*, Morrow Jr Bks) Morrow Jr Bks.
—Around the World in Eighty Days. 224p. (gr. 9-12). 1990. pap. 2.50 (*0-8125-0430-5*) Tor Bks.
—Around the World in Eighty Days. 1990. pap. 2.25 (*0-14-035114-0*, Puffin) Puffin Bks.
—The Mysterious Island. reissued ed. Wyeth, N. C., illus. LC 88-3167. 512p. 1988. (Scribners Young Read); SBE 25.95 (*0-684-18957-7*, Scribner) Macmillan Child Grp.
—Tour du Monde en Quatre-Vingts Jours. De Neuville, C. & Benett, L., illus. (FRE.). 333p. (gr. 5-10). 1988. pap. 10.95 (*2-07-033521-6*) Schoenhof.
—Twenty-Thousand Leagues under the Sea. reissued, adpt. ed. Conaway, Judith, adapted by. D'Achille, Gino, illus. 96p. (gr. 2-6). 1994. pap. 2.99 (*0-679-85363-4*, Bullseye Bks) Random Bks Yng Read.
Vickery, Eugene L. Enchanted Hike: Children's Adventure Story in Verse. Meet Magical Rabbit in California. St. George, Adrianne B., illus. 20p. (Orig.). (gr. 1-8). 1987. pap. 3.95 (*0-937775-04-5*) Stonehaven Pubs.
Vincent, John. The Eiffel Target. (Illus.). 128p. (gr. 3-7). 1992. pap. 2.99 (*0-14-036012-3*) Puffin Bks.
—Live & Let's Dance. (Illus.). 128p. (gr. 3-7). 1992. pap. 2.99 (*0-14-036013-1*) Puffin Bks.
—Sandblast! (Illus.). 128p. (gr. 3-7). 1992. pap. 2.99 (*0-14-036014-X*) Puffin Bks.
—The Sword of Death. (Illus.). 128p. (gr. 3-7). 1992. pap. 2.99 (*0-14-036049-2*, Puffin) Puffin Bks.
—A View to a Thrill. (Illus.). 128p. (gr. 3-7). 1992. pap. 2.99 (*0-14-036011-5*) Puffin Bks.
Voight, Cynthia. The Wings of a Falcon. LC 92-41946. (gr. 5 up). 1993. 14.95 (*0-590-46712-3*) Scholastic Inc.
Voigt, Cynthia. On Fortune's Wheel. LC 89-39010. 288p. (gr. 6 up). 1990. SBE 15.95 (*0-689-31636-4*, Atheneum Child Bk) Macmillan Child Grp.
—On Fortune's Wheel. 304p. 1991. pap. 3.95 (*0-449-70391-6*, Juniper) Fawcett.
Wald, Ann. Choice Adventure: Counterfeit Collection. LC 92-36279. 1993. 4.99 (*0-8423-5049-7*) Tyndale.
Wall, Dorothy. Complete Adventures of Blinky Bill. (gr. 4-7). 1993. pap. 7.00 (*0-207-16732-X*, Pub. by Angus & Robertson AT) HarpC.
Wallace. Rock & Roll Mystery, No. 69. 1987. pap. 2.25 (*0-553-26653-5*) Bantam.
Wallace, Bill. Danger in Quicksand Swamp. LC 89-83485. 196p. (gr. 3-7). 1989. 14.95 (*0-8234-0786-1*) Holiday.
—Shadow on the Snow. LC 84-48743. 160p. (gr. 4-7). 1985. 14.95 (*0-8234-0557-5*) Holiday.
Wallach, Susan. Operation Isolation. (gr. 4-7). 1993. pap. 3.50 (*0-553-48068-5*) Bantam.
Walt Disney Choose Your Own Adventure. (ps-1). 1985. write for info Bantam.
Walt Disney Staff. Jungle Book. 1987. 6.98 (*0-8317-5291-2*) Viking Child Bks.
—The Rescuers. (gr. 5-8). 1989. 6.98 (*0-8317-7388-X*) Viking Child Bks.
Walt Disney's Feature Animation Dept. Animators Staff. Walt Disney's Mickey Mouse in "The Little Whirlwind" An Animated Flip Book. (Illus.). 96p. 1993. pap. 3.95 (*1-56282-837-1*) Hyperion.
Watts, Bernadette. Tattercoats. Watts, Bernadette, illus. LC 87-30198. 32p. (gr. k-3). 1989. 13.95 (*1-55858-002-6*) North-South Bks NYC.
Wayne, Matt. The Crystal Trap. Ashby, Ruth, ed. 128p. (Orig.). 1992. pap. 3.50 (*0-671-74207-8*, Archway) PB.
Weil, Ann. Red Sails to Capri. 160p. (gr. 5-9). 1988. pap. 3.95 (*0-14-032858-0*, Puffin) Puffin Bks.
Weinberg, Larry. The Hostage. Cocozza, Chris, illus. 160p. (gr. 3-7). 1994. pap. 1.99 (*0-448-40433-8*, G&D) Putnam Pub Group.
Weingardt, Richard. Sound the Charge. Mayabb, Darrell, illus. LC 78-59321. 184p. (gr. 6-12). 9.95 (*0-932446-00-0*); pap. 4.95 (*0-932446-01-9*) Jacqueline Enter.
Welch, Catherine A. Danger at the Breaker. (ps-3). 1992. pap. 5.95 (*0-87614-564-0*) Carolrhoda Bks.
Werlin, Marvin & Werlin, Mark. The Savior. 480p. (gr. 9 up). 1979. pap. 2.75 (*0-440-17748-0*, LFL) Dell.
Westall, Robert. Gulf. large type ed. 1993. 16.95 (*0-7451-2034-2*, Galaxy Child Lrg Print) Chivers N Amer.
—Kingdom by the Sea. (ps-3). 1993. pap. 3.95 (*0-374-44060-3*) FS&G.
—Stones of Muncaster Cathedral. (gr. 4-7). 1993. 11.00 (*0-374-37263-2*) FS&G.
Westcott, C. T. Silver Wings & Leather Jackets. (Orig.). 1989. pap. 3.50 (*0-440-20239-6*) Dell.
White, Ellen E. Long Live the Queen. (gr. 7 up). 1989. pap. 13.95 (*0-590-40850-X*) Scholastic Inc.
White, Theodore H. The Sword in the Stone. 288p. (gr. 7 up). 1978. pap. 3.99 (*0-440-98445-9*, LE) Dell.
Wicke, Ed. The Muselings. LC 91-13346. 160p. (gr. 3-7). 1991. pap. 5.99 (*0-8308-1351-9*, 1351) InterVarsity.

Wiesner, David. Hurricane. (ps-3). 1992. pap. 5.70 (*0-395-62974-8*, Clarion Bks) HM.
Willard, Nancy. Firebrat. Willard, Nancy, illus. 1992. pap. 3.50 (*0-553-15985-2*) Bantam.
Williams, Barbara. Mitzi & Frederick the Great. (gr. k-6). 1987. pap. 2.50 (*0-440-45867-6*, YB) Dell.
Williams, Geoffrey T. Saber Tooth: A Dinosaur World Adventure. Cremins, Robert, illus. 32p. (gr. k-6). 1988. pap. 9.95 incl. cass. (*0-8431-2319-2*) Price Stern.
Williams, Marcia. Sinbad the Sailor. Williams, Marcia, illus. LC 93-3531. (gr. 2 up). 1994. 17.95 (*1-56402-310-9*) Candlewick Pr.
Williams, Michael J. Cousins in Wonderland. 1993. 7.95 (*0-533-10273-1*) Vantage.
Williams, Sue. I Went Walking. LC 89-7847. (ps-3). 1992. pap. 5.95 (*0-15-238011-6*, HB Juv Bks) HarBrace.
Willner, Carl. Havens of Gondor, Land of Belfalas. Fenlon, Peter, ed. McBride, Angus, illus. 64p. (Orig.). (gr. 10-12). 1987. pap. 12.00 (*0-915795-25-6*, 3300) Iron Crown Ent Inc.
Wilson, Neil S. Choice Adventures, No. 9: The Tall Ship Shakedown. LC 92-30500. 1993. 4.99 (*0-8423-5046-2*) Tyndale.
Wofford, Roberta A. Sidney & Sally: The Danger of Strangers. Wofford, Roberta A., illus. 38p. (gr. k-4). 1987. pap. text ed. 1.85 (*0-9616198-0-5*) Pt Orchard Spec.
Wolkstein, Diane. The Banza. Brown, Mark, illus. LC 81-65845. 32p. (gr. k-2). 1984. pap. 4.95 (*0-8037-0058-X*) Dial Bks Young.
Wolverton, Linda. Running Before the Wind. (gr. 6 up). 1987. 13.95 (*0-395-42116-0*) HM.
World's Great Adventure Stories. facsimile ed. LC 79-163049. (gr. 7 up). Repr. of 1929 ed. 38.50 (*0-8369-3963-8*) Ayer.
Worley, Daryl. Billy & the Attic Adventure. Daab, John, illus. (ps). 1989. 9.95 (*0-924067-00-4*) Tyke Corp.
Wren, Percival C. Reader's Digest Best Loved Books for Young Readers: Beau Geste. Ogburn, Jackie, ed. Galli, Stan, illus. 160p. (gr. 4-12). 1989. 3.99 (*0-945260-33-4*) Choice Pub NY.
Wright, Betty R. The Pike River Phantom. LC 88-45276. 160p. (gr. 3-7). 1988. 14.95 (*0-8234-0721-7*) Holiday.
Wright, David, tr. Beowulf. (Orig.). (gr. 9 up). 1957. pap. 5.95 (*0-14-044070-4*) Viking Child Bks.
Wyss, Johann D. The Swiss Family Robinson. 1990. pap. 2.95 (*0-451-52481-0*, Sig Classics) NAL-Dutton.
—Swiss Family Robinson. (gr. 4-7). 1991. pap. 3.25 (*0-590-44014-4*) Scholastic Inc.
—Swiss Family Robinson. (gr. 4-7). 1991. pap. 3.50 (*0-440-40430-4*, Pub. by Yearling Classics) Dell.
Yogi Big Jungle Adventure. (Illus.). 32p. (gr. 6-9). 1993. 12.95 (*1-878685-66-X*, Bedrock Press) Turner Pub GA.
Yolen, Jane. Sky Dogs. Moser, Barry, illus. LC 89-26960. 32p. (ps-3). 1990. 15.95 (*0-15-275480-6*); limited ed., numbered & s 100.00 (*0-15-275481-4*) HarBrace.
Yorinks, Arthur. It Happened in Pinsk. (Illus.). (ps up). 1987. pap. 3.95 (*0-374-43649-5*, Sunburst) FS&G.
Young, Alida E. Dead Wrong. 128p. (gr. 5-8). 1992. pap. 2.99 (*0-87406-602-6*) Willowisp Pr.
Yue, David & Yue, Charlotte. The Pueblo. (Illus.). (gr. 8-11). 1986. 13.45 (*0-395-38350-1*) HM.
Zaanan: Conflict on Cada Maylon. (gr. 3 up). pap. 2.50 perfect bdg. (*1-55748-190-3*) Barbour & Co.
Zeder, Suzan. Wiley & the Hairy-Man. (gr. k up). 1978. 4.50 (*0-87602-219-0*) Anchorage.
Zindel, Paul. The Amazing & Death-Defying Diary of Eugene Dingman. (gr. 7 up). 1989. pap. 3.99 (*0-553-27768-5*, Starfire) Bantam.

ADVERTISING
see also Posters; Salesmen and Salesmanship; Signs and Signboards
Bernards, Neal. Advertising: Distinguishing Between Fact & Opinion. LC 91-28266. (Illus.). 32p. (gr. 4-7). 1991. PLB 10.95 (*0-89908-614-4*) Greenhaven.
Frisch, C. Advertising. (Illus.). 48p. (gr. 4-8). 1989. lib. bdg. 17.27 (*0-86592-078-8*); lib. bdg. 12.95s.p. (*0-685-58626-X*) Rourke Corp.
Frisch, Carlienne. Hearing the Pitch: Evaluating All Kinds of Advertising. LC 93-46200. 1994. write for info. (*0-8239-1694-4*) Rosen Pub.
Gay, Kathlyn. Caution: This May Be an Advertisement: A Teen Guide to Advertising. LC 91-38159. (Illus.). 160p. (gr. 9-12). 1992. PLB 14.90 (*0-531-11039-7*) Watts.
McGlothlin, Bruce. Search & Succeed: A Guide to Using the Classifieds. LC 93-47545. 1994. 13.95 (*0-8239-1695-2*) Rosen Group.
Wake, Susan. Advertising. Stefoff, Rebecca, ed. LC 90-3895. (Illus.). 32p. (gr. 4-8). 1991. PLB 17.26 (*0-944483-95-X*) Garrett Ed Corp.

ADVERTISING, PICTORIAL
see Posters

AENEAS
Virgil. Virgil's Aeneid. Dryden, John, tr. Andrews, C. A., intro. by. (gr. 11 up). 1968. pap. 1.95 (*0-8049-0177-5*, CL-177) Airmont.

AERIAL ROCKETS
see Rockets (Aeronautics)

AERODYNAMICS
see also Aeronautics

AERONAUTICAL INSTRUMENTS
see also names of specific instruments, e.g. Gyroscope, etc.

AERONAUTICAL SPORTS
see also names of specific sports, e.g. Airplane Racing; Skydiving; etc.

AERONAUTICS
see also Airplanes; Airships; Astronautics; Balloons; Flight; Flying Saucers; Gliders (Aeronautics); Helicopters; High Speed Aeronautics; Kites; Rocketry; Rockets (Aeronautics)
Aviation. (Illus.). 72p. (gr. 6-12). 1968. pap. 1.85 (*0-8395-3293-8*, 33293) BSA.
Bellville, Cheryl W. Airplane Book. (ps-3). 1993. pap. 5.95 (*0-87614-618-3*) Carolrhoda Bks.
Berliner, Don. Distance Flights. (Illus.). 72p. (gr. 5 up). 1990. 21.50 (*0-8225-1589-X*) Lerner Pubns.
Carter, Sharon. Careers in Aviation. Rosen, Ruth, ed. (gr. 7-12). 1989. PLB 14.95 (*0-8239-0965-4*) Rosen Group.
Cohen, Lynn. Air & Space. 64p. (ps-2). 1988. 6.95 (*0-912107-80-4*, MM984) Monday Morning Bks.
Crisfield, Deborah. An Air Show Adventure. Emmerich, Donald, illus. LC 89-34372. 32p. (gr. 3-6). 1990. PLB 10.79 (*0-8167-1735-4*); pap. text ed. 2.95 (*0-8167-1736-2*) Troll Assocs.
Croome, Angela. Hovercraft. Wilkinson, Gerald, illus. (gr. 5 up). 1962. 14.95 (*0-8392-3008-7*) Astor-Honor.
Grant, Donald, illus. Airplanes & Flying Machines. (ps). 1992. bds. 10.95 (*0-590-45267-3*, 037, Cartwheel) Scholastic Inc.
Hawkes, Nigel. Space & Aircraft. (Illus.). 32p. (gr. 5-8). 1994. bds. 13.95 (*0-8050-3416-1*) TFC Bks NY.
Hines, Gary. Flying Firefighters. Hines, Anna G., illus. LC 92-35500. 1993. 14.95 (*0-395-61197-0*, Clarion Bks) HM.
Hodges-Caballero, Jane. Air & Space Activities. rev. ed. LC 85-81658. 152p. (ps-3). 1993. pap. text ed. 17.95 (*0-685-65254-8*) Humanics Ltd.
Ingoglia, Gina. Airplanes & Things That Fly. (Illus.). 24p. (ps-k). 1989. pap. write for info. (*0-307-11807-X*, Pub. by Golden Bks) Western Pub.
Jennings, Terry. Planes, Gliders, Helicopters, & Other Flying Machines. LC 92-28422. (Illus.). 40p. (gr. 3-8). 1993. 10.95 (*1-85697-870-2*, Kingfisher LKC); pap. 5.95 (*1-85697-869-9*) LKC.
Kerrod, Robin. The Story of Flight. Smith, Guy & Jobson, Ron, illus. 11p. 1994. 14.95 (*0-525-67402-0*, Lodestar Bks) Dutton Child Bks.
Mackie, Dan. Flight. Shulist, Steve, illus. 32p. (gr. 5-9). 1985. pap. 5.95 (*0-88625-112-5*) Durkin Hayes Pub.
Martin, John. Jet Watercraft. 48p. (gr. 3-10). 1994. PLB 17.27 (*1-56065-201-2*) Capstone Pr.
Millspaugh, Ben. Aviation & Space Science Projects. 1991. 16.95 (*0-8306-2157-1*); pap. 9.95 (*0-8306-2156-3*) TAB Bks.
Moore, Kathryn C. My First Flight. rev. ed. Hutson, Ronald, ed. Grant, Leslie, illus. (ps-4). 1991. PLB 3.95 (*0-9633295-0-2*) K Cs Bks N Stuff.
Sabin, Louis. Wilbur & Orville Wright: The Flight to Adventure. Lawn, John, illus. LC 82-15879. 48p. (gr. 4-6). 1983. PLB 10.79 (*0-89375-851-5*); pap. text ed. 3.50 (*0-89375-852-3*) Troll Assocs.
Seller, Mick. Air, Wind, & Flight. LC 92-374. 1992. 12.40 (*0-531-17375-5*, Gloucester Pr) Watts.
Seymour, Peter. Pilots. Ingersoll, Norm, illus. 12p. (gr. k-3). 1992. 13.00 (*0-525-67372-5*, Lodestar Bks) Dutton Child Bks.
Tunney, Christopher. Aircraft Carriers. LC 79-64384. (Illus.). 36p. (gr. 3-6). 1980. PLB 13.50 (*0-8225-1176-2*) Lerner Pubns.
Williams, Brian. Pioneers of Flight. LC 90-9470. (Illus.). 48p. (gr. 4-8). 1990. PLB 11.95 (*0-8114-2755-2*) Raintree Steck-V.
Wood, Tim. Air Travel. LC 92-43977. (Illus.). 32p. (gr. 5-9). 1993. 14.95 (*1-56847-036-3*) Thomson Lrning.

AERONAUTICS–ACCIDENTS
see also Survival (After Airplane Accidents, Shipwrecks, Etc.)
Barrett, Norman S. Picture World of Airport Rescue. LC 90-31221. (Illus.). 32p. (gr. k-4). 1991. PLB 12.40 (*0-531-14088-1*) Watts.
Coote, Roger. Air Disasters. LC 93-6831. 48p. (gr. 4-6). 1993. 15.95 (*1-56847-083-5*) Thomson Lrning.
Horton, Madelyn. The Lockerbie Airline Crash. LC 91-25741. (Illus.). 96p. (gr. 5-8). 1991. PLB 11.95 (*1-56006-017-4*) Lucent Bks.
Lightner, Robert. Triumph Through Tragedy. 70p. (Orig.). (gr. 7 up). 1980. pap. 1.00 (*0-89323-008-1*, 330) Bible Memory.
Stein, R. Conrad. Hindenburg Disaster. LC 92-34520. (Illus.). 32p. (gr. 3-6). 1993. PLB 12.30 (*0-516-06663-3*); pap. 3.95 (*0-516-46663-1*) Childrens.
Tanaka, Shelley. The Disaster of the Hindenburg: The Last Flight of the Greatest Airship Ever Built. LC 92-39434. 64p. 1993. 16.95 (*0-590-45750-0*) Scholastic Inc.
Terror in the Skies: The Inside Story of the World's Worst Air Crashes. (Illus.). 256p. 1988. 16.95 (*0-8065-1091-9*, Citadel Pr) Carol Pub Group.

AERONAUTICS–BIOGRAPHY
see also Air Pilots; Women in Aeronautics
Hook, Jason. Twenty Names in Aviation. LC 89-23912. (Illus.). 48p. (gr. 3-8). 1990. PLB 12.95 (*1-85435-253-9*) Marshall Cavendish.

AERONAUTICS, COMMERCIAL
Gunning, Thomas G. Dream Planes. LC 92-8397. (Illus.). 72p. (gr. 3 up). 1992. text ed. 14.95 RSBE (*0-87518-556-8*, Dillon) Macmillan Child Grp.
Parramon, J. M. Mi Primera Vista al Aviario. 1990. pap. 5.95 (*0-8120-4403-7*) Barron.

AERONAUTICS–FICTION
Benjamin, Cynthia. I Am a Pilot. Sagasti, Miriam, illus. 24p. (ps-k). 1994. 6.95 (*0-8120-6407-0*) Barron.
—Somos Pilotos. Sagasti, Miriam, illus. 24p. (ps-k). 1994. 6.95 (*0-8120-6417-8*) Barron.
Cooney, Caroline B. Flight Number 116 Is Down. 176p. 1992. 13.95 (*0-590-44465-4*, Scholastic Hardcover) Scholastic Inc.
—Flight Number 116 is Down. 1993. pap. 3.25 (*0-590-44479-4*) Scholastic Inc.
Felix, Monique. The Plane. Felix, Monique, illus. LC 92-44058. 1993. PLB 10.95 (*0-88682-604-7*) Creative Ed.
Fisher, Cyrus. The Avion My Uncle Flew. Floethe, Richard, illus. 254p. (gr. 5 up). 1993. pap. 4.99 (*0-14-036487-0*, Puffin) Puffin Bks.
Hall, Lynn. Flying Changes. D'Andrade, Diane, ed. 148p. (gr. 9 up). 1991. 13.95 (*0-15-228790-6*) HarBrace.
—Flying Changes. 1992. write for info. HarBrace.
Hallam, Leslie T. Andy's Headache. 1990. 6.95 (*0-533-08821-6*) Vantage.
Horgan, Dorothy. Then the Zeppelins Came. 112p. (gr. 6 up). 1990. jacketed 15.00 (*0-19-271598-4*) OUP.
Lindgren, Barbro. Shorty Takes Off. Fisher, Richard E., tr. Landstrom, Olof, illus. 28p. (ps-3). 1990. 13.95 (*91-29-59770-6*, Pub. by R & S Bks) FS&G.
Meyer, Linda. John Meyer Pants-on-Fire: Pilot Adventures. James-Curry, Jo, illus. LC 94-65977. 15p. (gr. k-2). 1994. pap. 14.95 (*0-9640577-0-0*) Sunshine Advent.
Montgomery, Raymond A. Silver Wings. 1992. pap. 3.25 (*0-553-29293-5*) Bantam.
Pilgrim, Millie W. Jason's Adventures with the Tuskegee Airmen. rev. ed. Pilgrim, Millie W., illus. 54p. (gr. 3 up). 1992. pap. text ed. 8.00 (*0-685-60294-X*, 133-720); tchr's. guide 2.00 (*0-685-60295-8*) H&M Ent.
Vallet, Muriel. Take the Plane. Vallet, Muriel, illus. 10p. (gr. k-3). 1993. pap. 10.95 (*1-895583-59-4*) MAYA Pubs.
Zoom the Airplane. 1994. 3.99 (*0-517-10275-7*) Random Hse Value.

AERONAUTICS–FLIGHTS
see also Space Flight
Taylor, Richard L. The First Nonstop, Unrefueled Flight Around the World: The Story of Dick Rutan & Jeana Yeager & Their Airplane, Voyager. LC 94-2596. 1994. write for info. (*0-531-20176-7*) Watts.

AERONAUTICS–HISTORY
Berliner, Don. Before the Wright Brothers. (Illus.). 72p. (gr. 5 up). 1990. 19.95 (*0-8225-1588-1*) Lerner Pubns.
Blackman, Steven. Planes & Flight. LC 93-17392. (Illus.). 32p. (gr. 5-7). 1993. PLB 11.90 (*0-531-14277-9*) Watts.
Carlisle, Robert L. Tower, This Is Andy & Other Flying Stories from Northeast Nebraska. Plimpton, George, frwd. by. LC 91-18416. (Illus.). 178p. (Orig.). 1991. pap. 8.95 (*0-934988-24-2*, CIP) Foun Bks.
Dale, Henry. Early Flying Machines. LC 92-21664. 1992. 16.00 (*0-19-520966-4*) OUP.
Gibbons, Gail. Flying. Gibbons, Gail, illus. LC 85-22027. 32p. (ps-3). 1986. reinforced bdg. 15.95 (*0-8234-0599-0*); pap. 5.95 (*0-8234-0977-5*) Holiday.
Guttmacher, Peter. The China Clipper. LC 93-46204. 1994. text ed. 13.95 (*0-89686-826-5*, Crestwood Hse) Macmillan Child Grp.
Parker, Steve. Flight & Flying Machines. Corbella, Luciano, illus. LC 92-54316. 64p. (gr. 3-7). 1993. 12.95 (*1-56458-236-1*) Dorling Kindersley.
Pearl, Lizzy. The Story of Flight. Bergin, Mark, illus. LC 91-33412. 32p. (gr. 1-4). 1993. PLB 11.89 (*0-8167-2709-0*); pap. text ed. 3.95 (*0-8167-2710-4*) Troll Assocs.
Prunier, James. Livre des As et des Heros: Histoire de l'Aviation, No. 2. (FRE.). 77p. (gr. 4-9). 1988. 13.95 (*2-07-039548-0*) Schoenhof.
Spangenburg, Ray & Moser, Diane. The Story of Air Transport in America. (Illus.). 96p. (gr. 6-12). 1992. bds. 18.95x (*0-8160-2260-7*) Facts on File.
Stoff, Joshua. From Airship to Spaceship: Long Island Aviation & Spaceflight. LC 90-47647. (Illus.). 96p. (gr. 4-10). 1991. 15.00 (*1-55787-074-8*, NY71060, Empire State Bks); pap. 7.95 (*1-55787-075-6*, NY71059, Empire State Bks) Heart of the Lakes.
Teitelbaum, Michael. First Facts about Flying Machines. Persico, F. S., illus. 24p. 1991. 2.98 (*1-56156-086-3*) Kidsbks.

AERONAUTICS, HIGH SPEED
see High Speed Aeronautics

AERONAUTICS, MILITARY
see also Aircraft Carriers; Airplanes, Military
also names of wars with the subdivision Aerial Operations
Baker, David. Airborne Early Warning. (Illus.). 48p. (gr. 3-8). 1989. lib. bdg. 18.60 (*0-86592-533-X*) Rourke Corp.
—Airlift. (Illus.). 48p. (gr. 3-8). 1989. lib. bdg. 18.60 (*0-86592-531-3*) Rourke Corp.
—Anti-Submarine Warfare. 48p. (gr. 3-8). 1989. lib. bdg. 18.60 (*0-86592-532-1*) Rourke Corp.
—Future Fighters. (Illus.). 48p. (gr. 3-8). 1989. lib. bdg. 18.60 (*0-86592-535-6*); 13.95s.p. (*0-685-58601-4*) Rourke Corp.
—Ground Attack Planes. 48p. (gr. 3-8). 1989. lib. bdg. 18.60 (*0-86592-536-4*); 13.95s.p. (*0-685-58603-0*) Rourke Corp.
—Navy Strike Planes. (Illus.). 48p. (gr. 3-8). 1989. lib. bdg. 18.60 (*0-86592-534-8*); 13.95s.p. (*0-685-58602-2*) Rourke Corp.
Nicholaus, J. Air Defence Weapons. (Illus.). 48p. (gr. 3-8). 1989. lib. bdg. 18.60 (*0-86592-423-6*); lib. bdg. 13.95s.p. (*0-685-58578-6*) Rourke Corp.
—Army Air Support. (Illus.). 48p. (gr. 3-8). 1989. lib. bdg. 18.60 (*0-86592-421-X*) Rourke Corp.

Watry, Charles A. & Hall, Duane L. Aerial Gunners: The Unknown Aces of World War II. LC 85-91368. (Illus.). 256p. (Orig.). 1986. pap. 12.95 (*0-914379-01-1*) C Watry.

AERONAUTICS, NAVAL

see Aeronautics, Military

AERONAUTICS–PILOTING

see Airplanes–Piloting

AERONAUTICS–SAFETY MEASURES

Hawkes, Nigel. Safety in the Sky. 1990. PLB 12.40 (*0-531-17207-4*) Watts.

AERONAUTICS–VOCATIONAL GUIDANCE

Ayres, Carter M. Pilots & Aviation. (Illus.). 72p. (gr. 5 up). 1990. PLB 21.50 (*0-8225-1590-3*) Lerner Pubns.

Zink, Richard M. Airline Industry Jobs: The New Job Manual. 4th ed. (Illus.). 50p. (gr. 9 up). 1992. pap. 14. 95x (*0-939469-27-8*) Zinks Career Guide.

AERONAUTICS–VOYAGES

see Aeronautics–Flights

AEROSPACE MEDICINE

see Space Medicine

AFFECTION

see Friendship; Love

AFGHANISTAN

Ansary, Mir T. Afghanistan: Fighting for Freedom. LC 91-15648. (Illus.). 128p. (gr. 4-6). 1991. text ed. 14.95 RSBE (*0-87518-482-0*, Dillon) Macmillan Child Grp.

Clifford, Mary L. The Land & People of Afghanistan. LC 88-21419. (Illus.). 240p. (gr. 6 up). 1989. (Lipp Jr Bks); PLB 14.89 (*0-397-32339-5*, Lipp Jr Bks) HarpC Child Bks.

Griffiths, J. Conflict in Afghanistan. (Illus.). 80p. (gr. 7 up). 1988. PLB 18.60 (*0-86592-039-7*) Rourke Corp.

Herda, D. J. Afghan Rebels. LC 89-22603. (ps-3). 1990. PLB 13.90 (*0-531-10897-X*) Watts.

Knowledge Unlimited Staff. Afghanistan: The Long Fight for Freedom. (Illus.). 22p. (gr. 4-12). 1983. incl. filmstrip, cass., guide 28.00 (*0-915291-00-2*) Know Unltd.

Lerner Publications, Department of Geography Staff, ed. Afghanistan in Pictures. (Illus.). 64p. (gr. 5 up). 1989. 17.50 (*0-8225-1849-X*) Lerner Pubns.

AFRICA

Barnes-Svarney, Patricia. Zimbabwe. (Illus.). 128p. (gr. 5 up). 1989. 14.95 (*1-55546-799-7*) Chelsea Hse.

Benoit, Marie. Mauritius. (Illus.). 96p. (gr. 5 up). 1989. 14.95 (*0-7910-0126-1*) Chelsea Hse.

Browder, Atlantis T. & Browder, Anthony T. My First Trip to Africa. Browder, Anne, ed. Aaron, Malcolm, illus. LC 91-70328. 38p. (Orig.). 1991. 16.95 (*0-924944-02-1*); pap. 8.95 (*0-924944-01-3*) Inst Karmic.

Burch, Joann J. Kenya: Africa's Tamed Wilderness. LC 91-43104. (Illus.). 128p. (gr. 4 up). 1992. text ed. 14. 95 RSBE (*0-87518-512-6*, Dillon) Macmillan Child Grp.

Byrnes, Ron. Exploring the Developing World: Life in Africa & Latin America. (Illus.). (gr. 7-12). 1993. pap. 26.95 (*0-943804-78-7*) U of Denver Teach.

Carpenter, Allan. Benin (Dahomey) Owen, Wilfred, Jr., ed. LC 77-20877. (gr. 6-12). pap. 26.00 (*0-8357-3475-7*, 2039762) Bks Demand.

Carpenter, Allan & Balow, Tom. Botswana. Cohen, Ronald, ed. LC 72-10379. (gr. 6-12). pap. 25.40 (*0-8357-3476-5*, 2039763) Bks Demand.

Carpenter, Allan & Maginnis, Matthew. Burundi. Rowe, John, ed. LC 73-4971. (gr. 6-12). pap. 25.20 (*0-8357-2700-9*, 2039764) Bks Demand.

Carrick, Noel. New Guinea. (Illus.). 96p. (gr. 5 up). 1989. 14.95 (*0-222-00916-0*) Chelsea Hse.

Chad. (Illus.). (gr. 5 up). 1989. 14.95 (*0-7910-0147-4*) Chelsea Hse.

Cheney, Patricia. The Land & People of Zimbabwe. LC 89-36244. (Illus.). 256p. (gr. 6 up). 1990. (Lipp Jr Bks); PLB 15.89 (*0-397-32393-X*, Lipp Jr Bks) HarpC Child Bks.

Chiasson, John. African Journey. Chiasson, John, photos by. LC 86-8233. (Illus.). 64p. (gr. 3-6). 1987. SBE 17. 95 (*0-02-718530-3*, Bradbury Pr) Macmillan Child Grp.

Chijioke, F. A. Ancient Africa. LC 75-80850. (Illus.). 48p. (gr. 5-8). 1969. pap. 5.50 (*0-8419-0013-2*, Africana) Holmes & Meier.

Clark, Leon E. Through African Eyes, Vol. 2: The Present: Tradition & Change. (Illus.). 292p. (Orig.). (gr. 9-12). 1994. pap. text ed. 19.95x (*0-938960-28-8*) CITE.

Dahl, Roald. Going Solo. 224p. (gr. 7 up). 1993. pap. 4.99 (*0-14-032528-X*, Puffin) Puffin Bks.

De Bruycker, Daniel & Dauber, Maximilien. Africa. (Illus.). 76p. (gr. 5 up). 1994. 13.95 (*0-8120-6425-9*); pap. 7.95 (*0-8120-1864-8*) Barron.

Department of Geography, Lerner Publications. Zimbabwe in Pictures. (Illus.). 64p. (gr. 5 up). 1988. 17.50 (*0-8225-1825-2*) Lerner Pubns.

Eko, Paul M. Cry Cry My Beloved People. Scalist, Paula, ed. 286p. 1990. 18.95x (*0-685-28130-2*) Backwards & Backwards.

—Water Finds Its Own Level. Scalist, Paula, ed. 105p. 1990. pap. 8.95 (*0-685-28132-9*) Backwards & Backwards.

Ellis, Veronica F. Afro-Bets Activity & Enrichment Guide: First Book about Africa. (gr. 1-4). 1989. pap. 7.95 (*0-940975-07-6*) Just Us Bks.

—Afro-Bets First Book about Africa. Ford, George, illus. LC 89-85157. 32p. (Orig.). (gr. 1-4). 1990. PLB 13.95 (*0-940975-12-2*); pap. 6.95 (*0-940975-03-3*) Just Us Bks.

Equatorial Guinea. (Illus.). (gr. 5 up). 1989. 13.95 (*0-7910-0121-0*) Chelsea Hse.

Feelings, Muriel & Feelings, Tom. Jambo Means Hello: Swahili Alphabet Book. (Illus.). 56p. (gr. k-3). 1985. pap. 4.99 (*0-8037-4428-5*, Puff Pied Piper) Puffin Bks.

Georges, D. V. Africa. LC 86-9586. (Illus.). 48p. (gr. k-4). 1986. PLB 12.85 (*0-516-01287-8*); pap. 4.95 (*0-516-41287-6*) Childrens.

Gess, Denise. Togo. (Illus.). 96p. (gr. 5 up). 1988. lib. bdg. 14.95x (*1-55546-190-5*) Chelsea Hse.

Green, Ernest L. Uncle Ernie's African Stories. Ellens, Don, illus. 81p. (gr. 1-4). 1982. 4.50 (*0-89814-057-9*) Grace Publns.

Greenfield, Eloise. Africa Dream. Byard, Carole, illus. LC 77-5080. 32p. (ps-3). 1989. PLB 13.89 (*0-690-04776-2*, Crowell Jr Bks) HarpC Child Bks.

Halliburton, Warren J. African Wildlife. LC 91-43514. (Illus.). 48p. (gr. 6). 1992. text ed. 13.95 RSBE (*0-89686-674-2*, Crestwood Hse) Macmillan Child Grp.

—Celebrations of African Heritage. LC 92-7989. (Illus.). 48p. (gr. 6). 1992. text ed. 13.95 RSBE (*0-89686-676-9*, Crestwood Hse) Macmillan Child Grp.

Haskins, Jim. Count Your Way Through Africa. Knutson, Barbara, illus. 24p. (gr. 1-4). 1989. 17.50 (*0-87614-347-8*); pap. 5.95 (*0-87614-514-4*) Carolrhoda Bks.

Head, Bessie. When Rain Clouds Gather. 188p. (Orig.). 1987. pap. 8.95 (*0-435-90726-3*, 90726) Heinemann.

Henry-Biabaud, Chantal. Living in the Heart of Africa. Bogard, Vicki, tr. from FRE. Poissenot, Jean-Marie, illus. LC 90-50774. 38p. (gr. k-5). 1991. 5.95 (*0-944589-29-4*, 294) Young Discovery Lib.

Ibazemo, Isimeme. Exploration into Africa. LC 94-43720. (gr. 5 up). 1994. text ed. 15.95 (*0-02-718081-6*, New Discovery Bks) MacMillan Child Grp.

Jacobsen, Karen. Zimbabwe. LC 90-2202. (Illus.). 48p. (gr. k-4). 1990. PLB 12.85 (*0-516-01110-3*); pap. 4.95 (*0-516-41110-1*) Childrens.

James, R. S. Mozambique. (Illus.). 104p. (gr. 5 up). 1988. lib. bdg. 14.95 (*1-55546-194-8*) Chelsea Hse.

Kamba, Polo. Why Do Africans Hate Cats. Scalist, Paula, ed. (Illus.). 98p. 1990. pap. 7.95x (*0-685-28131-0*) Backwards & Backwards.

Kerina, Jane. African Crafts. Feelings, Tom, illus. LC 69-18916. (gr. 2-6). 1970. PLB 13.95 (*0-87460-084-7*) Lion Bks.

Kreikemeier, Gregory S. Come with Me to Africa. (gr. 4-7). 1993. 11.95 (*0-307-15660-5*, Golden Pr) Western Pub.

Larson, Russell J. Africa by Four: Coloring Book. (Illus.). 14p. (Orig.). (gr. k-6). 1992. pap. text ed. 1.85 (*1-881087-01-8*) Storm Moutain.

Laure, Jason. Angola. LC 90-2143. (Illus.). 128p. (gr. 5-9). 1990. PLB 20.55 (*0-516-02721-2*) Childrens.

—Botswana. LC 93-753. (Illus.). 128p. (gr. 5-9). 1993. PLB 20.55 (*0-516-02616-X*) Childrens.

Lerner Publications, Department of Geography Staff. Botswana in Pictures. (Illus.). 64p. (gr. 5 up). 1990. PLB 17.50 (*0-8225-1856-2*) Lerner Pubns.

Levine, Bobbie & Lichter, Carolyn. A Child's Walk Through Africa. (Illus.). 38p. (gr. 3-6). 1987. spiral bdg. 1.50 (*0-912303-38-7*) Michigan Mus.

Middleton, Nick. Southern Africa. LC 94-18330. 1995. write for info. (*0-8114-2785-4*) Raintree Steck-V.

Murray, Jocelyn. Africa. 96p. 1990. 17.95 (*0-8160-2209-7*) Facts on File.

Musgrove, Margaret W. Ashanti to Zulu: African Traditions. Dillon, Leo D. & Dillon, Diane, illus. LC 76-6610. 32p. (gr. k up). 1980. pap. 4.95 (*0-8037-0308-2*, Puff Pied Piper) Puffin Bks.

Nii-owoo, Ife. A Is for Africa: Looking at Africa Through the Alphabet. Nii-owoo, Ife, illus. LC 90-81575. 32p. (ps-k). 1992. 12.95 (*0-86543-182-5*); pap. 5.95 (*0-86543-183-3*) Africa World.

Onyefulu, Ifeoma. A Is for Africa. Onyefulu, Ifeoma, photos by. LC 92-39964. (Illus.). 32p. (ps-3). 1993. 14. 99 (*0-525-65147-0*, Cobblehill Bks) Dutton Child Bks.

Sabin, Francene. Africa. Eitzen, Allan, illus. LC 84-10560. 32p. (gr. 3-6). 1985. PLB 9.49 (*0-8167-0236-5*); pap. text ed. 2.95 (*0-8167-0237-3*) Troll Assocs.

Schwartz, Linda. The African Question Collection. 120p. (gr. 4-8). 1994. 6.95 (*0-88160-264-7*, LW228) Learning Wks.

Stark, Al. Zimbabwe: A Treasure of Africa. LC 85-6944. (Illus.). 160p. (gr. 5 up). 1986. text ed. 14.95 RSBE (*0-87518-308-5*, Dillon) Macmillan Child Grp.

Steyn. The Bushman of the Kalahari, Reading Level 5. (Illus.). 48p. (gr. 4-8). 1989. PLB 16.67 (*0-86625-267-3*); 12.50 (*0-685-58810-6*) Rourke Corp.

Wekesser, Carol, ed. Africa: Opposing Viewpoints. LC 91-42292. (Illus.). 264p. (gr. 10 up). 1992. PLB 17.95 (*0-89908-186-X*); pap. text ed. 9.95 (*0-89908-161-4*) Greenhaven.

Zareef, Linda. Africa: A Glance at an Amazing Continent. (Illus.). (ps-6). 1989. write for info. (*0-9625787-0-3*) An Awareness.

Zimmerman, Robert. The Bambia. LC 94-7008. (Illus.). 128p. (gr. 5-9). 1994. PLB 27.40 (*0-516-02625-9*) Childrens.

AFRICA–BIOGRAPHY

AESOP Enterprises, Inc. Staff & Crenshaw, Gwendolyn J. Nzinga: Developing Determination & Persistence. 16p. (gr. 3-12). 1991. pap. write for info. incl. cassette (*1-880771-14-4*) AESOP Enter.

Freetland, Julianna, ed. African Healer: I Want to Say Another Story. Wechsler, Howell, tr. Breen, Carole, illus. Prance, Ghillean T., intro. by. (Illus., Orig.). (gr. k-4). Date not set. pap. text ed. 5.00 (*0-9605700-7-1*); tchr's. ed. 10.00 (*0-9605700-9-8*) Lifeline Res.

Greene, Carol. Desmond Tutu: Bishop of Peace. LC 86-9582. (Illus.). 32p. (gr. 2-5). 1986. PLB 11.80 (*0-516-03634-3*); pap. 3.95 (*0-516-43634-1*) Childrens.

Griffin, Michael. A Family in Kenya. (Illus.). 32p. (gr. 2-5). 1988. lib. bdg. 13.50 (*0-8225-1680-2*) Lerner Pubns.

Hoobler, Dorothy & Hoobler, Thomas. African Portraits. Gampert, John, illus. LC 92-17284. 96p. (gr. 7-8). 1992. PLB 22.80 (*0-8114-6378-8*) Raintree Steck-V.

Lee, George L. Worldwide Interesting People: One Hundred Sixty-Two History Makers of African Descent. LC 91-50939. (Illus.). 144p. 1992. lib. bdg. 19.95 (*0-89950-670-4*) McFarland & Co.

Meltzer, Milton. Winnie Mandela: The Soul of South Africa. Marchesi, Stephen, illus. (gr. 2-6). 1987. pap. 3.99 (*0-14-032181-0*, Puffin) Puffin Bks.

Wisniewski, David. Sundiata: Lion King of Mali. Wisniewski, David, illus. 32p. (gr. k-4). 1992. 15.95 (*0-395-61302-7*, Clarion Bks) HM.

AFRICA, CENTRAL

Central African Republic. (Illus.). (gr. 5 up). 1989. 14.95 (*0-7910-0146-6*) Chelsea Hse.

Lerner Geography Department Staff, ed. Zaire in Pictures. (Illus.). 64p. (gr. 5-12). 1992. PLB 17.50 (*0-8225-1899-6*) Lerner Pubns.

Lerner Publications, Department of Geography Staff, ed. Cameroon in Pictures. (Illus.). 64p. (gr. 5 up). 1989. PLB 17.50 (*0-8225-1857-0*) Lerner Pubns.

—Central African Republic in Pictures. (Illus.). 64p. (gr. 5 up). 1989. 17.50 (*0-8225-1858-9*) Lerner Pubns.

AFRICA, EAST

Dichmann, Kurt. Operations East Africa. Brown, Bill, ed. (Illus.). 96p. (Orig.). (gr. 9-12). 1989. pap. write for info. Ceise Corp.

Hallett, Bill & Hallett, Jane. Look up Look down Look All Around East African Safari. Jackson, Lori, illus. 32p. (Orig.). (gr. 3-8). 1990. pap. 2.95 activity bk. (*1-877827-01-0*) Look & See.

Kaufmann, Herbert. Lost Freedom. (Illus.). (gr. 7 up). 1969. 12.95 (*0-8392-3083-4*) Astor-Honor.

McKinzie, Harry & Tindimwebwa, Issy. Names from East Africa. Campbell, Elisabeth, ed. 42p. (Orig.). 1980. pap. 4.95 (*0-86626-007-2*) McKinzie Pub.

Ricciuti, Edward R. Somalia: A Crisis of Famine & War. LC 93-15094. (Illus.). 64p. (gr. 5-8). 1993. PLB 15.90 (*1-56294-376-6*); pap. 6.95 (*1-56294-751-6*) Millbrook Pr.

Stelson, Caren B. Safari. Stelson, Kim A., illus. 40p. (gr. k-4). 1989. pap. 5.95 (*0-87614-512-8*, First Ave Edns) Lerner Pubns.

AFRICA, EAST–FICTION

Chase, Alyssa. Jomo & Mata. Chase, Andra, illus. LC 93-25206. 32p. (gr. 1-4). 1993. 16.95 (*1-55942-051-0*, 7656); video, tchr's. guide & storybook 79.95 (*1-55942-054-5*, 9375) Marshfilm.

Gehman, Mary W. Abdi & the Elephants. 104p. (Orig.). (gr. 6-8). 1995. pap. 5.95 (*0-8361-3699-3*) Herald Pr.

AFRICA–FICTION

Aardema, Verna. Bringing the Rain to Kapiti Plain. Vidal, Beatriz, illus. LC 80-25886. 32p. (ps). 1981. 14.95 (*0-8037-0809-2*); PLB 13.89 (*0-8037-0807-6*) Dial Bks Young.

Bandele, Ramla. Nzinga. 1992. pap. 6.95 (*0-88378-023-2*) Third World.

Bell, Sally. The Young Indiana Jones Chronicles: Safari in Africa. Vincente, Gonzalez, illus. 48p. (gr. 2-4). 1992. pap. write for info. (*0-307-11470-8*, 11470, Golden Pr) Western Pub.

Bess, Clayton. Story for a Black Night. LC 81-13396. (gr. 7 up). 1982. 13.45 (*0-395-31857-2*) HM.

Bianchi, J. Bushmen Brouhaha. (Illus.). 24p. (ps-8). 1987. 12.95 (*0-921285-10-8*, Pub. by Bungalo Bks CN); pap. 4.95 (*0-921285-08-6*, Pub. by Bungalo Bks CN) Firefly Bks Ltd.

Campbell, E. Year of the Leopard Song. 1992. write for info. (*0-15-299806-3*, HB Juv Bks) HarBrace.

Cheney-Coker, Syl. The Last Harmattan of Alusine Dunbar. 398p. (Orig.). (gr. 9-12). 1990. pap. 9.95 (*0-435-90572-4*, 90572) Heinemann.

Fabian, Stella. Is Your Heart Happy? Is Your Body Strong? (Orig.). (gr. 6). 1992. pap. 3.75 (*0-685-52888-X*) Brighton & Lloyd.

Ferguson, Dwayne J. Captain Africa: The Battle for Egyptica. Ferguson, Dwayne J., illus. LC 92-78316. 156p. (gr. 7-10). 1992. 24.95 (*0-86543-335-6*); pap. 9.95 (*0-86543-336-4*) Africa World.

Fourie, Corlia. Ganekwane & the Green Dragon: Four Stories from Africa. Grant, Christy, ed. Epanya, Christian A., illus. LC 93-45922. 40p. (gr. 3-6). 1994. PLB 14.95 (*0-8075-2744-0*) A Whitman.

Frost, T. Olly on Safari. (Illus.). 32p. (ps-3). 1987. PLB 14.65 (*0-88625-189-3*); pap. 4.95 (*0-88625-187-7*) Durkin Hayes Pub.

Geraghty, Paul. The Hunter. LC 93-22730. (Illus.). 32p. (ps-3). 1994. 15.00 (*0-517-59692-X*); PLB 15.99 (*0-517-59693-8*) Crown Bks Yng Read.

Greenfield, Eloise. Africa Dream. Byard, Carole, illus. LC 77-5080. 32p. (ps-3). 1992. pap. 4.95 (*0-06-443277-7*, Trophy) HarpC Child Bks.

Grifalcon, Ann. Flyaway Girl. (ps-3). 1992. 15.95 (*0-316-32866-9*) Little.

Grimsdell, Jeremy. Kalinzu. LC 92-45573. (Illus.). 32p. (ps-3). 1993. 14.95 (*1-85697-886-9*, Kingfisher LKC) LKC.

Guthrie, Donna. Nobiah's Well: A Modern African Folk Tale. Roth, Robert, illus. LC 93-586. 32p. (ps-2). 1993. PLB 15.00 (*0-8249-8631-8*, Ideals Child); 14.95 (*0-8249-8622-9*) Hambleton-Hill.

Guy, Rosa. Mother Crocodile: An Uncle Amadou Tale from Senegal. Steptoe, John L., illus. LC 80-393. 32p. (ps-3). 1982. 8.89 (*0-385-28455-1*); pap. 8.95 (*0-385-28454-3*) Delacorte.

Hadithi, Mwenye. Baby Baboon. Kennaway, Adrienne, illus. LC 92-56397. 1993. 15.95 (*0-316-33729-3*) Little.

Hampton, Janie. Come Home Soon, Baba. Brent, Jenny, illus. 32p. (gr. 4 up). 1993. 12.95 (*0-87226-511-0*, Bedrick Blackie) P Bedrick Bks.

Jacobs, Shannon K. Song of the Giraffe. Johnson, Pamela, illus. (gr. 2-4). 1991. 11.95 (*0-316-45555-5*) Little.

Kelleher, Victor. Rescue! LC 91-30490. 224p. (gr. 5 up). 1992. 15.00 (*0-8037-0900-5*) Dial Bks Young.

Kennaway, Adrienne. Little Elephant's Walk. Kennaway, Adrienne, illus. LC 91-19727. 32p. (ps-2). 1992. 13.95 (*0-06-020377-3*) HarpC Child Bks.

Lewin, Hugh. Jafta & the Wedding. Kopper, Lisa, illus. LC 82-12836. 24p. (ps-3). 1983. pap. 4.95 (*0-87614-497-0*) Carolrhoda Bks.

Lichtveld, Noni. I Lost My Arrow in a Kan Kan Tree. LC 92-56102. 1993. 14.00 (*0-688-12748-7*) Lothrop.

Lindblad, Lisa & Lindlbad, Sven-Olof. Serengeti Migration. LC 93-26338. (Illus.). 40p. (gr. 3-7). 1994. 15.95 (*1-56282-668-9*); PLB 15.89 (*1-56282-669-7*) Hyprn Child.

McAllister, Angela. The Honey Festival. Fitzgerald, Gerald, photos by. LC 92-46079. (gr. 1-8). 1994. 13. 99 (*0-8037-1240-5*) Dial Bks Young.

McDowell, Robert E. & Lavitt, Edward, eds. Third World Voices for Children. Isaac, Barbara K., illus. LC 71-169091. 156p. (gr. 5-9). 1981. 7.95 (*0-89388-020-5*, Odarkai) Okpaku Communications.

Mbengue, Demba, illus. Aesop: Tales of Aethiop the African, Vol. 1. 64p. (gr. 2-9). 1991. 6.95 (*1-877610-03-8*); cass. 6.95 (*0-685-50185-X*) Sea Island.

Mollel, Tololwa M. Big Boy. Lewis, E. B., illus. LC 93-21176. 1995. write for info (Clarion Bks) HM.

—A Promise to the Sun: A Story of Africa. Vidal, Beatriz, illus. 32p. (ps-3). 1992. 15.95 (*0-316-57813-4*, Joy St Bks) Little.

Muchene, Barbara S. & Muchene, Munene. Suzanne's African Adventure: A Visit to Cucu's Land. Wagner, Shirley L., ed. Jarvis, David, illus. LC 92-75821. 90p. (Orig.). (gr. 3-6). 1993. pap. 9.95 (*1-878398-18-0*) Blue Note Pubns.

Mugo, Phoebe, ed. Lodu's Escape: And Other Stories from Africa. (Illus.). 64p. (Orig.). (gr. 3-5). 1994. pap. 6.95 (*0-377-00269-0*) Friendship Pr.

Njoku, Scholastica I. Dog What? Fergurson, Meg, illus. 49p. (gr. k up). 1989. perfect bdg. 6.95x (*0-9617833-1-1*) S I NJOKU.

Noble, Kate. Bubble Gum. Bass, Rachel, illus. 32p. (ps-3). 1992. 14.95 (*0-9631798-0-2*) Silver Seahorse.

—Oh Look, It's a Nosserus. Bass, Rachel, illus. 32p. (ps-4). 1993. 14.95 (*0-9631798-2-9*) Silver Seahorse. Robbi is a young rhino who lives in a game park in Africa. He can't wait to have a horn as beautiful as his Mama's; he gets teased for being clumsy, & he sets out to save his friends from terrible danger. Children who loved & laughed with Kimbi in BUBBLE GUM will be delighted to meet Robbi & his zebra & giraffe friends. Once again, Rachel Bass creates the beauty of Africa & the charm of its animals in her vivid paintings. BUBBLE GUM. Kate Noble (Africa Stories Ser.) (Illus. by Rachel Bass). 32p. 1992. pre K-4th gr. 14.95 (0-9631798-0-2) Kimbi is a young baboon who lives in a park in Africa. He wishes tourists didn't pay so much attention to the lions. He loves sweets, & he stumbles into an amazing adventure. The illustrations for this delightful story capture the magic of the African landscape. There's also a learning plus: the details of animal behavior are correct, & the pictures show both black & white children & adults. Silver Seahorse Press, 2568 N. Clark St., Suite 320, Chicago, IL 60614; 312-871-1772; FAX: 312-327-8978. Distributed by Lifetime Books, Inc., 2131 Hollywood Blvd., Hollywood, FL 33020-6750; 1-800-771-3355; FAX: 1-800-931-7411.
Publisher Provided Annotation.

Oliver, Vickie. Kalyn's Life Adventures: Not Even in a Book. 32p. (gr. 4-10). 1991. 4.95 (*1-877610-07-0*) Sea Island.

Paton, Alan. Cry, the Beloved Country. abr. ed. 115p. 1991. pap. text ed. 5.95 (*0-582-53009-1*, 79129) Longman.

Poland, Marguerite. The Wood-Ash Stars. Altshuler, Shanne, illus. 64p. 1990. pap. 5.95 (*0-86486-089-7*, Pub. by D Philip South Africa) Interlink Pub.

Sackett, Elisabeth. Danger on the African Grassland. (ps-3). 1991. 12.95 (*0-316-76596-1*) Little.

Shepard, Eva & Lehman, Celia. Nzuzi & the Spell. Hofstetter, Virginia, illus. LC 92-60935. 160p. (gr. 2-8). 1992. pap. 6.95 (*1-878893-22-X*) Telcraft Bks.

Silver, Norman. No Tigers in Africa. LC 91-29121. (Illus.). 100p. (gr. 7 up). 1992. 15.00 (*0-525-44733-4*, DCB) Dutton Child Bks.

Steig, William. Doctor De Soto Goes to Africa. Steig, William, illus. LC 91-76414. 32p. (ps up). 1992. 15.00 (*0-06-205002-8*); PLB 14.89 (*0-06-205003-6*) HarpC Child Bks.

Walter, Mildred P. Brother to the Wind. Dillon, Diane & Dillon, Leo, illus. LC 83-26800. 32p. (ps-2). 1985. PLB 14.88 (*0-688-03812-3*) Lothrop.

Watson, Pete. The Market Lady & the Mango Tree. Watson, Mary, illus. LC 93-7725. 32p. 1994. 14.00 (*0-688-12970-6*, Tambourine Bks); PLB 13.93 (*0-688-12971-4*, Tambourine Bks) Morrow.

Weerusinghe, Christabel. Happy New Year in Sri Lanka. Deepa, illus. 52p. (Orig.). (gr. 2 up). 1986. pap. 6.50 (*0-941402-05-3*) Devon Pub.

Weir, Bob & Weir, Wendy. Panther Dream: A Story of the African Rainforest. Weir, Wendy, illus. LC 91-71385. 40p. (gr. k-5). 1993. pap. 4.95 (*1-56282-525-9*); incl. cassette 8.95 (*1-56282-591-7*); Incl. tchr's. guide, 12 bks. & 1 cassette. classroom pkg. 32.95 (*1-56282-548-8*) Hyprn Ppbks.

Williams, Karen L. When Africa Was Home. Cooper, Floyd, illus. LC 90-7684. 32p. (ps-1). 1991. 14.95 (*0-531-05925-1*); PLB 14.99 (*0-531-08525-2*) Orchard Bks Watts.

—When Africa Was Home. Cooper, Floyd, illus. LC 90-7684. 32p. (ps-2). 1994. pap. 5.95 (*0-531-07043-3*) Orchard Bks Watts.

Zimelman, Nathan. Treed by a Pride of Irate Lions. Goffe, Toni, illus. LC 89-30344. (gr. k-3). 1990. Little.

AFRICA–HISTORY

Across Africa & Arabia. (Illus.). 128p. 1990. 17.95x (*0-8160-1878-2*) Facts on File.

Africa & the Origin of Humans. (Illus.). 80p. (gr. 4 up). 1988. PLB 25.67 (*0-8172-3301-6*) Raintree Steck-V.

Chu, Daniel & Skinner, Eliott. A Glorious Age in Africa: The Story of Three Great African Empires. Barnett, Moneta, illus. LC 90-80150. 124p. (gr. 6-12). 1990. 19.95 (*0-86543-166-3*); pap. 7.95 (*0-86543-167-1*) Africa World.

Cosgrove, Stephen. Bangalee. 32p. (gr. 1-4). 1976. pap. 2.95 (*0-8431-0550-X*) Price Stern.

Frazee, Charles & Yopp, Hallie K. The Ancient World. Frazee, Kathleen & Lumba, Eric, illus. (gr. 6). 1990. text ed. 21.08 (*1-878473-51-4*); tchr's. ed. 27.08 (*1-878473-54-9*); wkbk. 3.00 (*1-878473-55-7*) Delos Pubns.

—Medieval & Early Modern Times. Frazee, Kathleen & Lumba, Eric, illus. (gr. 7). 1990. pap. text ed. 24.77 (*1-878473-56-5*); tchr's. ed. 30.77 (*1-878473-58-1*); wkbk. 3.00 (*0-685-58493-3*) Delos Pubns.

Galloway-Blake, Jacqueline. My African Roots: A Child's Create Your Own Keepsake Book of Family History & African-Awareness. 32p. (ps-7). 1992. Wkbk. 5.95 (*0-9637243-6-3*) Brwn Sug & Spice.

Halliburton, Warren J. African Industries. LC 92-27325. (Illus.). 48p. (gr. 6). 1993. text ed. 13.95 RSBE (*0-89686-672-6*, Crestwood Hse) Macmillan Child Grp.

—African Landscapes. (Illus.). 48p. (gr. 6). 1993. text ed. 13.95 RSBE (*0-89686-673-4*, Crestwood Hse) Macmillan Child Grp.

—Africa's Struggle for Independence. LC 92-3755. (Illus.). 48p. (gr. 6). 1992. text ed. 13.95 RSBE (*0-89686-679-3*, Crestwood Hse) Macmillan Child Grp.

—Africa's Struggle to Survive. LC 92-7501. (Illus.). 48p. (gr. 6). 1993. text ed. 13.95 RSBE (*0-89686-675-0*, Crestwood Hse) Macmillan Child Grp.

—City & Village Life. (Illus.). 48p. (gr. 6). 1993. text ed. 13.95 RSBE (*0-89686-677-7*, Crestwood Hse) Macmillan Child Grp.

Jones, Constance. A Short History of Africa, 1500-1900. LC 92-22677. 144p. (gr. 6-9). 1993. 16.95 (*0-8160-2774-9*) Facts on File.

Neve, Herbert, ed. Homeward Journey: Readings in African Studies. LC 93-28433. 340p. 1994. 45.95 (*0-86543-407-7*); pap. 14.95 (*0-86543-408-5*) Africa World.

Rowell, Trevor. The Scramble for Africa. (Illus.). 72p. (gr. 7-12). 1987. 19.95 (*0-7134-5200-5*, Pub. by Batsford UK) Trafalgar.

AFRICA–NATIVE RACES

African Islamic Mission Staff. One Hundred Amazing Facts about the Nubian Man & Woman. Obaba, Al I., ed. (Illus.). 124p. (Orig.). 1991. pap. text ed. 8.95 (*0-916157-87-3*) African Islam Miss Pubns.

Stevens, Rita. Venda. (Illus.). 96p. (gr. 5 up). 1989. lib. bdg. 14.95 (*1-55546-788-1*) Chelsea Hse.

AFRICA, NORTH

Ayoub, Abderrahaman, et al. Umm el Madayan: An Islamic City Through the Ages. Corni, Francesco, illus. LC 93-757. (ENG.). (gr. 5 up). 1994. 16.95 (*0-395-65967-1*) HM.

AFRICA–SOCIAL LIFE AND CUSTOMS

Jefferson, Margo & Skinner, Elliott P. Roots of Time: A Portrait of African Life & Culture. LC 90-80149. 1990. pap. 7.95 (*0-86543-169-8*) Africa World.

Musgrove, Margaret W. Ashanti to Zulu: African Traditions. Dillon, Diane, illus. Dillon, Leo D., ed. LC 76-6610. (Illus.). (gr. k-4). 1976. 17.00 (*0-8037-0357-0*); PLB 15.89 (*0-8037-0358-9*) Dial Bks Young.

Osei, G. K. The African Concept of Life & Death. Obaba, Al I., ed. (Illus.). 49p. (Orig.). 1991. pap. text ed. 3.00 (*0-916157-64-4*) African Islam Miss Pubns.

Westbrook, Henry S. Burned at the Stake. Obaba, Al I., ed. 124p. (Orig.). 1991. pap. text ed. 9.95 (*0-916157-88-1*) African Islam Miss Pubns.

AFRICA, SOUTH

Bigelow, William. Strangers in Their Own Country: A Curriculum Guide on South Africa. Brutus, Dennis, frwd. by. LC 85-71369. (Illus.). 104p. (Orig.). (gr. 8 up). 1987. pap. 12.95 (*0-86543-010-1*) Africa World.

Brandenburg, Jim. Sand & Fog: Adventures in Southern Africa. Guernsey, JoAnn B., ed. LC 93-30425. (Illus.). 48p. 1994. 16.95 (*0-8027-8232-9*); PLB 17.85 (*0-8027-8233-7*) Walker & Co.

Brickhill, Joan. South Africa: The End of Apartheid? (Illus.). 40p. (gr. 6-8). 1991. PLB 12.90 (*0-531-17283-X*, Gloucester Pr) Watts.

Department of Geography, Lerner Publications. South Africa in Pictures. (Illus.). 64p. (gr. 5 up). 1988. PLB 17.50 (*0-8225-1835-X*) Lerner Pubns.

Gould, Dennis E. Botswana. (Illus.). 96p. (gr. 5 up). 1988. 14.95 (*0-222-01101-7*) Chelsea Hse.

Harris, Sarah. Timeline: South Africa. (Illus.). 64p. (gr. 7-9). 1988. 19.95 (*0-85219-724-1*, Pub. by Batsford UK) Trafalgar.

Rogers, Barbara R. South Africa. Rogers, Stillman, illus. LC 89-43188. 64p. (gr. 5-6). 1991. PLB 21.26 (*0-8368-0247-0*) Gareth Stevens Inc.

Sheehan, Sean. Zimbabwe. LC 92-38751. 1993. 21.95 (*1-85435-577-5*) Marshall Cavendish.

Stein, R. Conrad. South Africa. LC 86-9651. (Illus.). 128p. (gr. 5-9). 1986. PLB 20.55 (*0-516-02784-0*) Childrens.

Tonsing-Carter, Betty. Lesotho. (Illus.). 96p. (gr. 5 up). 1988. 14.95 (*0-7910-0097-4*) Chelsea Hse.

AFRICA, SOUTH–BIOGRAPHY

Bentley, Judith. Archbishop Tutu of South Africa. LC 88-410. (Illus.). 96p. (gr. 6 up). 1988. lib. bdg. 16.95 (*0-89490-180-X*) Enslow Pubs.

Denenberg, Barry. Nelson Mandela. (gr. 4-7). 1991. pap. 2.95 (*0-590-44154-X*) Scholastic Inc.

—Nelson Mandela: "No Easy Walk to Freedom" 160p. (gr. 3-9). 1991. 12.95 (*0-590-44163-9*, Scholastic Hardcover) Scholastic Inc.

Feinberg, Brian. Nelson Mandela. (Illus.). 72p. (gr. 3-5). 1991. lib. bdg. 12.95 (*0-7910-1569-6*) Chelsea Hse.

First, Ruth. One Hundred Seventeen Days. Sachs, Albie & Lodge, Tomfrwd. by. 192p. (gr. 11-12). 1989. 24.00 (*0-85345-789-1*); pap. 9.00 (*0-85345-790-5*) Monthly Rev.

Hargrove, J. Nelson Mandela: South Africa's Silent Voice of Protest. (Illus.). (gr. 4 up). 1989. 14.40 (*0-516-03266-6*); pap. 5.95 (*0-516-43266-4*) Childrens.

Kumalo, Alf. Mandela Echoes of Era. Es'Kia Mphahlele & Sisulu, Waltertext by. 176p. (ps-3). 1990. pap. 16.95 (*0-14-014316-5*) Viking Child Bks.

Meyer, Carolyn. Voices of South Africa: Growing up in a Troubled Land. LC 86-45059. 244p. (gr. 7 up). 1986. 16.95 (*0-15-200637-0*) HarBrace.

Otfinoski, Steven. Nelson Mandela: The Fight Against Apartheid. LC 91-35031. (Illus.). 128p. (gr. 7 up). 1992. PLB 15.90 (*1-56294-067-8*) Millbrook Pr.

Pogrund, Benjamin. Nelson Mandela: Strength & Spirit of a Free South Africa. LC 90-24026. (Illus.). 68p. (gr. 5-6). 1992. PLB 19.93 (*0-8368-0357-4*) Gareth Stevens Inc.

Sansevere-Dreher, Diane. Stephen Biko. (gr. 4-7). 1991. pap. 3.50 (*0-553-15931-3*) Bantam.

Vail, John. Nelson & Winnie Mandela. Schlesinger, Arthur M. (Illus.). 112p. (gr. 5 up). 1989. lib. bdg. 17. 95 (*1-55546-841-1*) Chelsea Hse.

Wimer, David. Desmond Tutu: Religious Leader Devoted to Freedom. Lantier, Patricia, adapted by. LC 90-10044. (Illus.). 64p. (gr. 3-4). 1991. PLB 19.93 (*0-8368-0459-7*) Gareth Stevens Inc.

Winner, David. Desmond Tutu: The Courageous & Eloquent Archbishop Struggling Against Apartheid in South Africa. Sherwood, Rhoda, ed. LC 88-4883. (Illus.). 68p. (gr. 5-6). 1989. PLB 19.93 (*1-55532-822-9*) Gareth Stevens Inc.

AFRICA, SOUTH–FICTION

Haggard, H. Rider. King Solomon's Mines. 256p. (gr. 3-7). 1983. pap. 2.95 (*0-14-035014-4*, Puffin) Puffin Bks.

Naidoo, Beverley. Journey to Jo'burg: A South African Story. reissued ed. Velasquez, Eric, illus. LC 85-45508. 96p. (gr. 4-7). 1986. 14.00 (*0-397-32168-6*, Lipp Jr Bks); PLB 13.89 (*0-397-32169-4*) HarpC Child Bks.

—Journey to Jo'burg: A South African Story. Velasquez, Eric, illus. LC 85-45508. 96p. (gr. 4-7). 1988. pap. 3.95 (*0-06-440237-1*, Trophy) HarpC Child Bks.

AFRICA, SOUTH–HISTORY

Stewart, Gail B. South Africa. LC 90-36292. (Illus.). 48p. (gr. 6-7). 1990. text ed. 4.95 RSBE (*0-89686-539-8*, Crestwood Hse) Macmillan Child Grp.

AFRICA, SOUTH–RACE RELATIONS

Bower, Paula R. Apartheid Is Wrong: A Curriculum for Young People. (Illus.). 280p. (gr. 1-12). 1989. 3-ring hard cover notebook 15.00 (*1-878537-00-8*) Educ Racism & Apart.

Hughes, Libby. Nelson Mandela: Voice of Freedom. LC 91-31543. (Illus.). 144p. (gr. 5 up). 1992. text ed. 13.95 RSBE (*0-87518-484-7*, Dillon) Macmillan Child Grp.

Smith, Chris. Conflict in Southern Africa. LC 92-23331. (Illus.). 48p. (gr. 6 up). 1993. text ed. 13.95 RSBE (*0-02-785956-8*, New Discovery) Macmillan Child Grp.

AFRICA, SOUTHWEST

Laure, Jason. Namibia. LC 92-39137. (Illus.). 128p. (gr. 5-9). 1993. PLB 20.55 (*0-516-02615-1*) Childrens.

AFRICA, SUB-SAHARAN

Roddis, Ingrid. Sudan. (Illus.). 96p. (gr. 5 up). 1988. 14.95 (*0-222-00964-0*) Chelsea Hse.

Twist, Clint. Stanley & Livingstone: Expeditions Through Africa. LC 94-21642. 1995. write for info. (*0-8114-3976-3*) Raintree Steck-V.

AFRICA, WEST

Cote D'Ivoire (Ivory Coast) in Pictures. (Illus.). 64p. (gr. 5 up). 1988. 17.50 (*0-8225-1828-7*) Lerner Pubns.

Koslow, Philip. Centuries of Greatness, 750-1900: The West African Kingdoms. LC 93-40667. 1994. write for info. (*0-7910-2266-8*); pap. write for info. (*0-7910-2692-2*) Chelsea Hse.

—Mali: The Land of Gold. LC 94-26193. (gr. 10 up). 1995. write for info. (*0-7910-3127-6*); pap. write for info. (*0-7910-2942-5*) Chelsea Hse.

Laure, Jason. Zambia. LC 89-34281. 128p. (gr. 5-9). 1989. PLB 20.55 (*0-516-02716-6*) Childrens.

Lerner Publications, Department of Geography Staff, ed. Mali in Pictures. (Illus.). 64p. (gr. 5 up). 1990. PLB 17.50 (*0-8225-1869-4*) Lerner Pubns.

Naylor, Kim. Mali. (Illus.). 96p. (gr. 5 up). 1988. 14.95 (*1-55546-181-6*) Chelsea Hse.

Perryman, Andrew. Gabon. (Illus.). 96p. (gr. 5 up). 1988. 14.95 (*0-7910-0122-9*) Chelsea Hse.

Preston, Edna M. Squawk to the Moon, Little Goose. Cooney, Barbara, illus. LC 84-22296. 32p. (ps-1). 1985. pap. 3.95 (*0-14-050546-6*, Puffin) Puffin Bks.

Schwartz, L. Ride & Seek. (gr. 3 up). 1987. 5.95 (*0-88160-159-4*, LW 103) Learning Wks.

Wilkins, Frances. Gambia. (Illus.). 96p. (gr. 5 up). 1988. 14.95 (*0-222-01129-7*) Chelsea Hse.

AFRICA, WEST–FICTION

Ellis, Veronica F. Land of the Four Winds. Walker, Sylvia, illus. LC 92-72001. 32p. (gr. 1-4). 1993. 14.95 (*0-940975-38-6*); pap. 6.95 (*0-940975-39-4*) Just Us Bks.

Herge. Tintin au Congo. (FRE., Illus.). (gr. 7-9). 19.95 (*0-8288-5090-9*) Fr & Eur.

Mokosso, Henry E. My First Pair of Shoes & the Little Altar Boy: Two Childhood Memories. LC 91-33536. 90p. (gr. 6-12). 1992. 7.95 (*0-944957-08-0*) Rivercross Pub.

AFRICAN-AMERICANS

see Blacks

AFRICAN LANGUAGES

Feelings, Muriel. Jambo Means Hello: Swahili Alphabet Book. Feelings, Tom, illus. LC 73-15441. 56p. (gr. k-3). 1985. Repr. of 1974 ed. 15.00 (*0-8037-4346-7*); PLB 13.89 (*0-8037-4350-5*) Dial Bks Young.

AFRO-AMERICANS

see Blacks

AGE

Edelson, Edward. Aging. (Illus.). 112p. (gr. 6-12). 1991. 18.95 (*0-7910-0035-4*) Chelsea Hse.

AGED

Adams, Pam. Elderly People. LC 90-45702. (gr. 4 up). 1990. 7.95 (*0-85953-362-X*); pap. 3.95 (*0-85953-352-2*) Childs Play.

Langone, John J. Growing Older. (gr. 9-12). 1991. 15.95 (*0-316-51459-4*) Little.

Sinclair-House, Elizabeth & Muir, Alison. Advanced Years. LC 90-28922. (Illus.). 64p. (gr. 5-9). 1991. PLB 11.95 (*0-8114-7807-6*) Raintree Steck-V.

Swisher, Karin & Deal, Tara, eds. The Elderly: Opposing Viewpoints. LC 89-25950. (Illus.). 264p. (gr. 10 up). 1990. lib. bdg. 17.95 (*0-89908-475-3*); pap. text ed. 9.95 (*0-89908-450-8*) Greenhaven.

Van Zwanenberg, Fiona. Caring for the Aged. LC 89-31783. (Illus.). 64p. (gr. 7-10). 1989. PLB 12.40 (*0-531-17190-6*, Gloucester Pr) Watts.

Whitelaw, Nancy. A Beautiful Pearl. Tucker, Kathleen, ed. Friedman, Judith, illus. LC 90-28761. 32p. (gr. 2-5). 1991. 13.95 (*0-8075-0599-4*) A Whitman.

Wilkinson, Beth. Coping When a Grandparent Has Alzheimer's Disease. rev. ed. Rosen, Ruth, ed. (gr. 7-12). 1994. PLB 14.95 (*0-8239-1947-1*) Rosen Group.

AGED–FICTION

Adams, Pam. This is the House that Jack Built. LC 90-46922. 1972. 11.95 (*0-85953-076-0*) Childs Play.

Albright, Nancy T., illus. I Know an Old Lady Who Swallowed a Fly. (Orig.). (ps-6). 1985. pap. 3.50 (*0-913545-10-4*) Moonlight FL.

Butterworth, W. E. Leroy & the Old Man. 168p. (gr. 7 up). 1989. pap. 3.25 (*0-590-42711-3*) Scholastic Inc.

Conford, Ellen. Loving Someone Else. 160p. 1991. 15.00 (*0-553-07353-2*) Bantam.

Dugan, Barbara. Loop the Loop. Stevenson, James, illus. LC 90-21727. 32p. (gr. k up). 1992. 15.00 (*0-688-09647-6*); PLB 14.93 (*0-688-09648-4*) Greenwillow.

Goudge, Eileen. Old Enough: Super Seniors, No. 1. (gr. 6 up). 1986. pap. 2.95 (*0-440-96118-1*, LFL) Dell.

Greene, Carol. The Old Ladies Who Liked Cats. Krupinski, Loretta, illus. LC 90-4443. 32p. (gr. k-3). 1991. 15.00 (*0-06-022104-6*); PLB 14.89 (*0-06-022105-4*) HarpC Child Bks.

Hughes, Shirley. The Snow Lady. (Illus.). 32p. 1990. 13.95 (*0-688-09874-6*); PLB 13.88 (*0-688-09875-4*) Lothrop.

Johnson, Angela. When I Am Old with You. Soman, David, illus. LC 89-70928. 32p. (ps-2). 1990. 14.95 (*0-531-05884-0*); PLB 14.99 (*0-531-08484-1*) Orchard Bks Watts.

Palmer, Michele. Zoup Soup. Gugler, Janine, illus. LC 78-66342. (ps-1). 1978. pap. 1.95 (*0-932306-00-4*) Rocking Horse.

Waggoner, Karen. Lemonade Babysitter. (ps-3). 1992. 14.95 (*0-316-91711-7*, Joy St Bks) Little.

Wakeman, Cheryl A. Johnnie Ollie Carri III & His Friend. Womack, Fred, illus. 32p. (ps-3). 1985. 5.95 (*0-9614819-0-0*) R E Moen.

AGENTS

see Salesmen and Salesmanship

AGGREGATES (MATHEMATICS)

see Set Theory

AGNEW, SPIRO T., 1918-

Kurland, Gerald. Spiro Agnew: Controversial Vice-President of the Nixon Administration. Rahmas, D. Steve, ed. LC 72-190234. 32p. (Orig.). (gr. 7-12). 1972. PLB 4.95 incl. catalog cards (*0-87157-516-7*) SamHar Pr.

AGRICULTURAL BANKS

see Banks and Banking

AGRICULTURAL CHEMISTRY

see also Soils

AGRICULTURAL LABORERS

see also Migrant Labor

Altman, Linda J. Migrant Farm Workers: The Temporary People. LC 93-11921. 1994. 13.40 (*0-531-13033-9*) Watts.

Atkin, S. Beth. Voices from the Fields: America's Migrant Children. LC 92-32248. 96p. 1993. 16.95 (*0-316-05633-2*) Little.

Brimner, Larry D. A Migrant Family. (Illus.). 40p. (gr. 4-8). 1992. PLB 17.50 (*0-8225-2554-2*) Lerner Pubns.

AGRICULTURAL MACHINERY

Boy Scouts of America. Farm Mechanics. (Illus.). 64p. (gr. 6-12). 1984. pap. 1.85 (*0-8395-3346-2*, 33346) BSA.

Bushey, Jerry. Farming the Land: Modern Farmers & Their Machines. (Illus.). (gr. k-4). 1987. pap. 4.95 (*0-87614-493-8*, First Ave Edns) Lerner Pubns.

Kalman, Bobbie. The Gristmill. (Illus.). 32p. (gr. 3-4). 1991. PLB 15.95 (*0-86505-486-X*); pap. 7.95 (*0-86505-506-8*) Crabtree Pub Co.

Olney, Ross R. The Farm Combine. LC 84-5288. (Illus.). 64p. (gr. 4 up). 1984. PLB 10.85 (*0-8027-6568-8*) Walker & Co.

AGRICULTURAL PRODUCTS

see Farm Produce

AGRICULTURAL TOOLS

see Agricultural Machinery

AGRICULTURE

see also Dairying; Domestic Animals; Farms; Forests and Forestry; Fruit Culture; Gardening; Land; Livestock; Organiculture; Soils

also names of agricultural products e.g. Corn; etc.; and headings beginning with the words Agricultural and Farm

Becklake, John & Becklake, Sue. Food & Farming. LC 90-45655. (Illus.). 40p. (gr. 6-9). 1991. PLB 12.90 (*0-531-17288-0*, Gloucester Pr) Watts.

Bellville, Cheryl W. Farming Today Yesterday's Way. LC 84-3215. (Illus.). 32p. (gr. k-4). 1984. PLB 13.50 (*0-87614-220-X*) Carolrhoda Bks.

Boy Scouts of America. Agribusiness. (Illus.). 72p. (Orig.). (gr. 6-12). 1987. pap. 1.85 (*0-8395-3272-5*, 3272) BSA.

Condon, Judith. Farming. LC 92-32910. Date not set. write for info. (*0-531-14251-5*) Watts.

Fun to Make Farm. 1989. pap. 3.99 (*0-517-68794-1*) Random Hse Value.

Gibbons, Gail. Farming. Gibbons, Gail, illus. LC 87-21254. 32p. (ps-3). 1988. reinforced bdg. 15.95 (*0-8234-0682-2*); pap. 5.95 (*0-8234-0797-7*) Holiday.

Huggett, Frank. Farming in Great Britain. (Illus.). 64p. (gr. 7 up). 1970. 14.95 (*0-7136-1527-3*) Dufour.

Imershein, Betsy. Farmer. Steltenpohl, Jane, ed. (Illus.). 32p. (gr. k-3). 1990. PLB 9.98 (*0-671-68185-0*, J Messner) S&S Trade.

Kerr, James L. Egyptian Farmers. LC 90-35696. (Illus.). 24p. (gr. 2-5). 1991. PLB 10.90 (*0-531-18374-2*, Pub. by Bookwright Pr) Watts.

Lambert, Mark. Farming & the Environment. LC 90-45614. (Illus.). 48p. (gr. 4-9). 1990. PLB 21.34 (*0-8114-2392-1*); pap. 5.95 (*0-8114-3453-2*) Raintree Steck-V.

McConnell, Em. The Great Farm Adventure. Moser, Jeanie W., illus. (gr. k-3). Bk. & cassette 4.95 (*0-932715-07-9*) Evans FL.

Manci, William E. Farming & the Environment. LC 93-13046. 1993. 17.27 (*0-8368-0731-6*) Gareth Stevens Inc.

Morris, Scott, ed. Agriculture & Vegetation of the World. De Blij, Harm J., intro. by. LC 92-22290. (Illus.). 1993. 15.95 (*0-7910-1804-0*, Am Art Analog); pap. write for info. (*0-7910-1817-2*, Am Art Analog) Chelsea Hse.

National Dairy Council Staff. Growth Record. (Illus.). 8p. (gr. 3-4). 1988. pap. text ed. write for info. (*1-55647-003-7*) Natl Dairy Coun.

Patent, Dorothy H. The Vanishing Feast. LC 94-2227. (gr. 7 up). 1994. write for info. (*0-15-292867-7*) HarBrace.

Reed-King, Susan. Food & Farming. LC 93-3719. (Illus.). 32p. (gr. 4-6). 1993. 14.95 (*1-56847-054-1*) Thomson Lrning.

Sabin, Louis. Agriculture. Veno, Joseph, illus. LC 84-2710. 32p. (gr. 3-6). 1985. PLB 9.49 (*0-8167-0204-7*); pap. text ed. 2.95 (*0-8167-0205-5*) Troll Assocs.

Steele, Philip. Farm Through the Ages. Howett, Andrew & Davidson, Gordon, illus. LC 91-37819. 32p. (gr. 3-6). 1993. PLB 11.89 (*0-8167-2731-7*); pap. text ed. 3.95 (*0-8167-2732-5*) Troll Assocs.

Sully, Nina. Looking at Food. (Illus.). 72p. (gr. 7-12). 1984. 18.95 (*0-7134-3536-4*, Pub. by Batsford UK) Trafalgar.

Swallow, Su. Food for the World. LC 90-44954. (Illus.). 48p. (gr. 5-8). 1991. PLB 22.80 (*0-8114-2800-1*) Raintree Steck-V.

Taylor, Belinda. Joseph & the Cottonseed. Taylor, John, illus. 12p. (Orig.). (gr. 2). 1994. pap. 6.95 (*0-87844-124-7*) Sandlapper Pub Co. JOSEPH & THE COTTONSEED, the result of a unique father-daughter collaboration, provides an entertaining history lesson on how the cotton crop made its way to America. Using information derived from old family letters, Miss Taylor has written a narrative that traces the efforts made by her ancestor Joseph Leitner to introduce this crop to his new homeland. Miss Taylor effectively relates the importance of this historical event in American's agricultural & economic development by offering examples of the common uses of cotton in our current everyday lives. John Taylor's colorful illustrations of a time past are a great addition to the story. Although it was written for children, parents & teachers will also enjoy this book. To order copies or receive additional information, call 1-800-849-7263.

Publisher Provided Annotation.

Watt, F. World Farming. (Illus.). 48p. (gr. 5-8). 1994. PLB 13.96 (*0-88110-705-0*, Usborne); pap. 7.95 (*0-7460-0737-X*, Usborne) EDC.

Williams, Brian. Farming. Green, Gwen, illus. LC 92-29905. 48p. (gr. 5-8). 1993. PLB 21.34 (*0-8114-4786-3*) Raintree Steck-V.

Winckler, Suzanne & Rodgers, Mary M. Our Engandered Planet: Soil. LC 92-39902. 1993. PLB 21.50 (*0-8225-2508-9*) Lerner Pubns.

Woolfitt, Gabrielle. Sow & Grow. LC 94-7927. (Illus.). 32p. (gr. 2-4). 1994. 14.95 (*1-56847-195-5*) Thomson Lrning.

AGRICULTURE–BIOGRAPHY

Johnson, LaVerne C. George Washington Carver: Writer. Perry, Craig R., illus. LC 92-35254. (gr. 6-9). 1992. pap. 3.95 (*0-922162-91-3*) Empak Pub.

AGRICULTURE–FICTION

Farm. (Illus.). 16p. (ps-1). 1994. pap. 6.95 (*1-56458-522-0*) Dorling Kindersley.

Harding, Jacqueline. Farm: First Readers. Sliwinska, Sara, illus. 28p. (gr. k-1). 1992. 3.50 (*0-7214-1482-6*, 929-1) Ladybird Bks.

Hawksley, Gerald. Farm Window. (Illus.). 10p. (ps). 1988. 3.95 (*0-681-40467-1*) Longmeadow Pr.

Hines, Anna G. Come to the Meadow. Hines, Anna G., illus. LC 83-14408. 32p. (ps-3). 1984. 12.95 (*0-89919-227-0*, Clarion Bks) Hm.

Kamstra, Angela. Old MacDonald's Farm. Kamstra, Angela, illus. 20p. (Orig.). (ps-3). 1994. pap. 7.95 (*0-8249-8658-X*, Ideals Child) Hambleton-Hill.

Pryor, Bonnie. Greenbrook Farm. Graham, Mark, illus. LC 89-11573. 40p. (ps-2). 1993. pap. 4.95 (*0-671-79606-2*, S&S BFYR) S&S Trade.

Scheidl, Gerda M. Pickle & Patch: A Story. Lanning, Rosemary, tr. Corderoc'h, Jean-Pierre, illus. LC 93-39755. 32p. (gr. k-3). 1994. 14.95 (*1-55858-269-X*); PLB 14.88 (*1-55858-270-3*) North-South Bks NYC.

Selden, George. The Old Meadow. Williams, Garth, illus. 192p. (gr. 3-7). 1987. 15.00 (*0-374-35616-5*) FS&G.

Shufflebotham, Anne. Old Macdonald's Tub. (gr. 3 up). 1990. 5.95 (*0-85953-444-8*) Childs Play.

Turner, Gewnda. Over on the Farm. (Illus.). 32p. (ps-1). 1994. 10.99 (*0-670-85437-9*) Viking Child Bks.

AGRICULTURE–VOCATIONAL GUIDANCE

Smith, Marcella, et al. Careers in Agribusiness & Industry. 4th ed. LC 76-106341. (Illus.). 395p. (gr. 9-12). 1991. 34.60 (*0-8134-2898-X*); text ed. 25.95 (*0-685-54235-1*); tchr's. manual 6.95 (*0-8134-2899-8*) Interstate.

AGRONOMY

see Agriculture

AIDS (DISEASE)

AIDS: Answers for Everyone. 96p. (Orig.). (gr. 6-12). 1989. pap. text ed. 9.95 (*0-929496-01-9*) Treehaus Comns.

Arehart, Lynda L. & Torrie, Margaret. Understanding HIV-AIDS: A Workbook Suitable for Mainstreamed Students. (Illus.). 48p. (gr. 9-12). 1990. tchrs. ed. 8.95 (*0-8138-1619-X*); wkbk. 4.95x (*0-8138-1618-1*) Iowa St U Pr.

Arrick, Fran. What You Don't Know Can Kill You. LC 91-26617. 160p. (gr. 7-10). 1992. 15.00 (*0-685-53824-9*) Bantam.

Baker. You & HIV: A Day at a Time. (Illus.). 272p. 1991. pap. text ed. 19.95 (*0-7216-3606-3*) Saunders.

Bartel, Nettie R., et al. SIDA: Lo Que Todos Debemos Saber: Cuaderno del Estudiante. Rojas, Miriam M., tr. from ENG. (SPA., Illus.). (gr. 7-12). 1989. Level I, 96 p. wkbk. 8.00 (*0-929853-00-8*); Level II, 112 p. wkbk. 9.00 (*0-929853-01-6*); parents hdbk. 3.00 (*0-929853-02-4*) Condor Pubns Inc.

Beshara, Raymond, et al. What You Should Know about AIDS. (Illus.). 72p. (gr. 6-10). 1989. pap. text ed. 9.85 (*0-9623161-2-1*); tchr's. ed. 3.00 (*0-9623161-3-X*) ERN Inc.

Bosworth, et al. AIDS. (gr. 7-12). Date not set. incl. software 120.00 (*0-912899-53-0*) Lrning Multi-Systs.

Boulden, Jim. Uncle Jerry Has AIDS. Winter, Peter, illus. 32p. (Orig.). (gr. 3-7). 1992. pap. 3.95 (*1-878076-18-3*) Boulden Pub.

Check, William A. AIDS. (Illus.). 128p. (gr. 6-12). 1988. lib. bdg. 18.95 (*0-7910-0054-0*); pap. 9.95 (*0-7910-0481-3*) Chelsea Hse.

Consumer Reports Books Editors, et al. AIDS: Trading Fears for Facts: A Guide for Young People. rev. ed. (Illus.). 176p. (gr. 8 up). 1992. pap. 4.95 (*0-89043-481-6*) Consumer Reports.

Cozic, Charles & Swisher, Karin, eds. The AIDS Crisis. LC 91-30034. 200p. (gr. 10 up). 1991. PLB 16.95 (*0-89908-578-4*); pap. text ed. 9.95 (*0-89908-584-9*) Greenhaven.

Cummings, Margaret A. Touched by AIDS. Butler, Cathy, ed. 22p. (Orig.). (gr. 7-12). 1992. pap. text ed. 1.95 (*1-56309-024-4*, Wrld Changers Res) Womans Mission Union.

Dounuts, Kevin. Doomed to Die: A Lonely Walk. Anderson, Mignon, ed. 70p. (Orig.). 1993. pap. 9.95 (*0-9636006-3-X*) Old Ctry Bks.

Draimin, Barbara H. Coping When a Parent Has AIDS. LC 93-5070. 1993. 14.95 (*0-8239-1664-2*) Rosen Group.

—Drugs & AIDS. LC 94-2331. 1994. 14.95 (*0-8239-1702-9*) Rosen Group.

Enns, Peter. Putting the Brakes on AIDS: The Story of Macho McKar. Wolverton, Lock, illus. 40p. (Orig.). (ps-6). 1992. pap. 5.98 incl. cassette (*0-943593-97-2*) Kids Intl Inc.

Fassler, David & McQueen, Kelly. Que Es Un Virus? Un Libro Para Ninos Sobre el SIDA. Quinones, Wanda M., tr. from ENG. LC 90-24631. (Illus.). 70p. (Orig.). (ps-5). 1991. pap. 8.95 (*0-914525-17-4*); pap. 12.95 plastic comb. (*0-685-47790-8*) (*0-914525-16-6*) Waterfront Bks.

—What's a Virus, Anyway? The Kids' Book about AIDS. LC 89-40719. (Illus.). 85p. (Orig.). (ps-6). 1990. plastic comb spiral 10.95 (*0-914525-14-X*); pap. 8.95 (*0-914525-15-8*) Waterfront Bks.

Flanders, Stephen A. & Flanders, Carl N. AIDS. 240p. (gr. 9-12). 1990. 22.95x (*0-8160-1910-X*) Facts on File.

Flynn, Tom & Lound, Karen. AIDS: Examining the Crisis. LC 94-13326. 1994. 21.50 (*0-8225-2625-5*) Lerner Pubns.

Ford, Michael. One Hundred Questions & Answers about AIDS: What You Need to Know Now. 208p. (gr. 7 up). 1993. pap. 4.95 (*0-688-12697-9*, Pub. by Beech Tree Bks) Morrow.

Ford, Michael T. One Hundred Questions & Answers about AIDS: A Guide for Young People. LC 92-15072. (Illus.). 208p. (gr. 6 up). 1992. text ed. 14.95 RSBE (*0-02-735424-5*, New Discovery Bks) Macmillan Child Grp.

Fox, Cecil H. AIDS & HIV Diseases. Head, J. J., ed. Botzis, Ka, illus. 16p. (Orig.). (gr. 10 up). 1991. pap. text ed. 2.75 (*0-89278-120-3*, 45-9620) Carolina Biological.

Gage, Rodney. Let's Talk about AIDS & Sex. LC 92-30853. 1992. 5.99 (*0-8054-6073-X*) Broadman.

Girard, Linda W. Alex, the Kid with AIDS. Levine, Abby, ed. Sims, Blanche, illus. LC 89-77592. 32p. (gr. 2-5). 1991. PLB 13.95 (*0-8075-0245-6*); pap. 5.95 (*0-8075-0247-2*) A Whitman.

Hausherr, Rosmarie. Children & the AIDS Virus: A Book for Children, Parents, & Teachers. Hausherr, Rosmarie, illus. (ps up). 1989. 15.45 (*0-89919-834-1*, Clarion Bks); pap. 5.95 (*0-395-51167-4*, Clarion Bks) HM.

Hein, Karen. Aids: Trading Fear for Facts; A Guide for Young People. 3rd ed. 1994. pap. 5.95 (*0-89043-721-1*) Consumers Union.

Hyde, Margaret O. AIDS: What Does It Mean to You? rev. ed. 128p. (gr. 7 up). 1987. 12.95 (*0-8027-6699-4*); lib. bdg. 13.85 (*0-8027-6705-2*); pap. 6.95 (*0-8027-6747-8*) Walker & Co.

Hyde, Margaret O. & Forsyth, Elizabeth. AIDS: What Does It Mean to You? 3rd, rev. ed. 124p. (gr. 7 up). 1990. 13.95 (*0-8027-6897-0*); lib. bdg. 14.85 (*0-8027-6898-9*) Walker & Co.

—AIDS: What Does It Mean to You? 4th, rev. ed. LC 92-14670. 128p. 1992. 13.95 (*0-8027-8202-7*); lib. bdg. 14.85 (*0-8027-8203-5*) Walker & Co.

—Know about AIDS. rev. ed. Weber, Deborah, illus. 102p. (gr. 3-7). 1990. 12.95 (*0-8027-6920-9*); lib. bdg. 13.85 (*0-8027-6921-7*) Walker & Co.

Jackson, Tim. AIDS: Just the Facts Jack. Jackson, Tim, illus. (Orig.). (gr. 5 up). 1988. pap. 1.95 (*0-942675-06-1*, 6) Creative License.

—What Are Friends For? HIV Safe Coloring Book. Jackson, Tim, illus. 32p. (Orig.). (gr. 3-6). 1990. pap. write for info. (*0-942675-08-8*, 0942675088) Creative License.

Kellogg, Nancy R. AIDS: Elementary-Intermediate Curriculum. (gr. 5-7). 1990. tchr's. ed. 8.95 (*0-944584-11-X*) Sopris.

Kerrins, Joseph & Jacobs, George W. The AIDS File. 2nd ed. Doohan, Julie, ed. (Illus.). 160p. (gr. 8 up). 1989. cloth 14.95 (*0-9618059-2-7*) Cromlech Bks.

Kittredge, Mary. Teens with AIDS Speak Out. (gr. 7 up). 1992. lib. bdg. 8.95 (*0-671-74543-3*, J Messner); lib. bdg. 13.98 (*0-671-74542-5*, J Messner) S&S Trade.

—Teens with AIDS Speak Out. large type ed. Garell, Dale C., intro. by. LC 93-6878. 161p. 1993. Alk. paper. lib. bdg. 15.95 (*1-56054-691-3*) Thorndike Pr.

Koop, C. Everett. Safe Sex in the Age of AIDS. 1992. pap. 3.99 (*0-8129-2063-5*, Times Bks) Random.

Kuklin, Susan. Fighting Back: What Some People Are Doing about AIDS. (Illus.). 144p. (gr. 8 up). 1989. 14. 95 (*0-399-21621-9*, Putnam) Putnam Pub Group.

Kurland, Morton L. Coping with AIDS: Facts & Fears. rev. & updated ed. (gr. 7-12). 1990. PLB 14.95 (*0-8239-1148-9*) Rosen Group.

Landau, Elaine. We Have AIDS. LC 89-24801. 126p. (gr. 7 up). 1990. PLB 13.40 (*0-531-10898-8*) Watts.

Lerner, Ethan A. Comprendiendo el SIDA. Wilken, Mark, illus. (SPA.). 64p. (gr. 3-6). 1988. 15.95 (*0-8225-2000-1*) Lerner Pubns.

Lets Learn about AIDS. 16p. 1994. 0.95 (*0-685-71604-X*, 729) W Gladden Found.

LeVert, Suzanne. AIDS: In Search of a Killer. LC 86-33218. (Illus.). 128p. (gr. 6 up). 1987. lib. bdg. 12.98 (*0-671-62840-2*, J Messner); lib. bdg. 5.95 (*0-671-65662-7*) S&S Trade.

Lord, John. Infection, the Immune System, & AIDS. (Illus.). 56p. (Orig.). (gr. 11-12). 1989. pap. 4.95x (*0-934653-18-6*) Enterprise Educ.

McDonough, Jerome. Carriers. 34p. (Orig.). (gr. 7-12). 1992. pap. 3.00 (*0-88680-370-5*); royalty on application 35.00 (*0-685-62706-3*) I E Clark.

Madaras, Lynda. Lynda Madaras Talks to Teens about AIDS: An Essential Guide for Parents, Teachers & Young People. rev. ed. Levin, Linda, frwd. by. (Illus.). 128p. (gr. 9-12). 1993. 16.95 (*1-55704-188-1*); pap. 7.95 (*1-55704-180-6*) Newmarket.

Moutoussamy-Ashe, Jeanne. Daddy & Me. Moutoussamy-Ashe, Jeanne, photos by. LC 93-11513. (Illus.). 40p. (ps-3). 1993. 13.00 (*0-679-85096-1*); PLB 14.99 (*0-679-95096-6*) Knopf Bks Yng Read.

Mozeleski, Peter A. The Rubber Bros AIDS Educational Publications. Mozeleski, Paul M. & Pinatti, Gloria J, eds. (Illus.). (gr. 6-12). 1992. Set of Vol. 1, Nos. 1-4 in English or Spanish. pap. 5.00 (*1-880058-00-6*) Rubbers Bros Comics.

—The Rubbers Bros. Comics, Vol. 1, No. 2. Mozeleski, Paul M. & Pinatti, Gloria J., eds. Pagan, Margarita, tr. (Illus.). 16p. (gr. 6-12). 1991. English. pap. 0.85 (*0-685-74371-3*) Spanish. pap. 0.85 (*1-880058-14-6*) Rubbers Bros Comics.

—The Rubbers Bros. Comics, Vol. 1, No. 1: Purpose: AIDS Prevention, Condom Awareness, AIDS Education. Mozelski, Paul M. & Pinatti, Gloria J., eds. Pagan, Margarita, tr. (Illus.). 16p. (gr. 6-12). 1990. pap. text ed. English. 0.85 (*0-685-72498-0*); Spanish. 0.85 (*0-685-72499-9*) Rubbers Bros Comics.

Mozeleski, Peter A. & Mozelski, Paul M. When AIDS Strikes, Vol. 1, No. 2. Pinatti, Gloria J., ed. (Illus.). 8p. 1992. Set of Vol. 1, No. 1 & Vol. 1, No. 2 avail. pap. 0.55 (*0-685-60121-8*) Rubbers Bros Comics.

Newton, David E. AIDS Issues: A Handbook. LC 92-10071. 144p. (gr. 6 up). 1992. lib. bdg. 18.95 (*0-89490-338-1*) Enslow Pubs.

Nourse, Alan E. Teen Guide to AIDS Prevention. LC 90-12750. (Illus.). 64p. (gr. 9-12). 1990. PLB 13.40 (*0-531-10966-6*) Watts.

Opheim, Teresa. AIDS: Distinguishing Between Fact & Opinion. LC 89-12006. (Illus.). 32p. (gr. 3-6). 1990. PLB 10.95 (*0-89908-633-0*) Greenhaven.

Quackenbush, Marcia & Villarreal, Sylvia. Does AIDS Hurt? Educating Young Children about AIDS. Nelson, Mary, ed. 148p. (Orig.). (ps-6). 1988. pap. 14.95 (*0-941816-52-4*) ETR Assocs.

Redfield, Robert & Franz, Wanda K. AIDS & Young People. 32p. (gr. 9-12). 1987. pap. 4.00 (*0-89526-774-8*) Regnery Pub.

Rico, Armando B. Later with the Latex: AIDS. 44p. (Orig.). 1992. pap. 2.95 (*1-879219-06-9*) Veracruz Pubs.

Roper, Gayle. The Puzzle of the Poison Pen. LC 94-6755. 1994. write for info. (*0-7814-1507-1*, Chariot Bks) Chariot Family.

Sanford, Doris. David Has AIDS. Evans, Graci, illus. LC 89-3162. 28p. (gr. k-4). 1989. 6.99 (*0-88070-299-0*, Gold & Honey) Questar Pubs.

Schwabacher, Martin. Magic Johnson: Basketball Wizard. LC 93-16556. (Illus.). 1993. 13.95 (*0-7910-2037-1*, Am Art Analog); pap. write for info. (*0-7910-2038-X*, Am Art Analog) Chelsea Hse.

Schwartz, Linda. AIDS Answers for Teens. rev. ed. (Illus.). 32p. (Orig.). (gr. 7-12). 1993. pap. 4.95 (*0-88160-155-1*, LW273) Learning Wks.

—AIDS Questions & Answers for Kids. rev. ed. (Illus.). 24p. (gr. 4-6). 1993. 3.95 (*0-88160-154-3*, LW272) Learning Wks.

Silverstein, Alvin & Silverstein, Virginia B. AIDS: Deadly Threat. rev. & expanded ed. LC 89-33145. (Illus.). 160p. (gr. 6 up). 1991. lib. bdg. 18.95 (*0-89490-175-3*) Enslow Pubs.

Sirimarco, Elizabeth. AIDS. LC 93-24967. (gr. 4 up). 1993. write for info. (*1-85435-609-7*, Cavendish Schl LIb UK); 14.95 (*1-85435-610-0*) Marshall Cavendish.

Sroka, Stephen R. Guia Para Educadores Sobre el SIDA y Otras ETS. Urizar, Hugo, tr. from ENG. (SPA., Illus.). 105p. (gr. 5-12). 1991. tchr's. ed. 25.00 (*0-9622034-1-6*) Hlth Educ Consults.

Taylor, Barbara. Everything You Need to Know about AIDS. rev. ed. Rosen, Ruth, ed. (Illus.). 64p. (gr. 7 up). 1992. PLB 14.95 (*0-8239-1401-1*) Rosen Group.

Toussant, Eliza. The Cootie Dragons. Douglas, Cal, illus. 120p. (gr. 4 up). 1993. pap. text ed. write for info. (*0-9630583-2-0*) E Toussant.

Turck, Mary. AIDS. LC 88-20259. (Illus.). 48p. (gr. 5-6). 1988. text ed. 12.95 RSBE (*0-89686-412-X*, Crestwood Hse) Macmillan Child Grp.

Westman, Randall P. Trust, AIDS & Your Dentist: Key Questions to Ask Your Dentist about Infection Control, HIV & Sterilization. (Illus.). 114p. (Orig.). 1993. pap. text ed. 11.95 (*0-9637088-0-5*) Sweettooth.

White, Ryan & Cunningham, Ann M. Ryan White: My Own Story. (Illus.). 144p. (gr. 5 up). 1991. 16.95 (*0-8037-0977-3*) Dial Bks Young.

Wilson, Jonnie. AIDS. LC 89-12619. (Illus.). 96p. (gr. 5 up). 1989. PLB 14.95 (*1-56006-105-7*) Lucent Bks.

Yarber, William L. STD & HIV: A Guide for Today's Young Adults. (Illus.). 106p. (Orig.). 1992. pap. text ed. 6.95 (*0-88314-533-2*) AAHPERD.

AIR

Here are entered works treating of air as an element and of its chemical and physical properties. Works treating of the body of air surrounding the earth are entered under Atmosphere.

see also Atmosphere

Allen, David. Air: All about Cyclones, Rainbows, Clouds, Ozone & More. Bain, Gordon, illus. 32p. 1993. pap. 5.95 (*1-895688-08-6*, Pub. by Greey dePencier CN) Firefly Bks Ltd.

Ardley, Neil. Science Book of Air. 29p. (gr. 2-5). 1991. 9.95 (*0-15-200578-1*) HarBrace.

Benedict, Kitty. Air: My First Nature Books. Felix, Monique, illus. 32p. (gr. k-2). 1993. pap. 2.95 (*1-56189-167-3*) Amer Educ Pub.

Brandt, Keith. Air. Burns, Raymond, illus. LC 84-2608. 32p. (gr. 3-6). 1985. PLB 9.49 (*0-8167-0130-X*); pap. text ed. 2.95 (*0-8167-0131-8*) Troll Assocs.

Branley, Franklyn M. Air Is All Around You. Rev. ed. Keller, Holly, illus. LC 85-47884. 32p. (gr. k-3). 1986. (Crowell Jr Bks); PLB 14.89 (*0-690-04503-4*) HarpC Child Bks.

Charman, Andrew. Air. LC 93-31748. 1994. PLB 18.99 (*0-8114-5509-2*) Raintree Steck-V.

Devonshire, Hilary. Air. LC 91-34421. (Illus.). 32p. (gr. 3-5). 1992. PLB 12.40 (*0-531-14134-9*) Watts.

Glover, David. Flying & Floating. LC 92-40212. 32p. (gr. 1-4). 1993. 10.95 (*1-85697-843-5*, Kingfisher LKC); pap. 5.95 (*1-85697-937-7*) LKC.

Heslewood, Juliet. Earth, Air, Fire & Water. Lydbury, Jane, et al, illus. 182p. (gr. 4-8). 1989. jacketed 15.95 (*0-19-278107-3*) OUP.

Jefferies, Lawrence. Air, Air, Air. Johnson, Lewis, illus. LC 82-15808. 32p. (gr. 3-6). 1983. PLB 10.59 (*0-89375-880-9*); pap. text ed. 2.95 (*0-89375-881-7*) Troll Assocs.

Johnston, Tom. Air, Air Everywhere. Pooley, Sarah, illus. LC 87-42752. 32p. (gr. 4-6). 1988. PLB 17.27 (*1-55532-406-1*) Gareth Stevens Inc.

Kalman, Bobbie & Schaub, Janine. The Air I Breathe. DeBiasi, Antoinette, illus. 32p. (Orig.). (gr. k-8). 1993. PLB 15.95 (*0-86505-556-4*); pap. 7.95 (*0-86505-582-3*) Crabtree Pub Co.

Larson, Wendy. Air. Curti, Anna, illus. 14p. (ps-1). 1994. bds. 4.95 (*0-448-40569-5*, G&D) Putnam Pub Group.

Llewellyn, Claire. First Look in the Air. (Illus.). 32p. (gr. 1-2). 1991. PLB 17.27 (*0-8368-0701-4*) Gareth Stevens Inc.

Mebane, Robert & Rybolt, Thomas. Air & Gasses. (Illus.). 64p. (gr. 5-8). 1995. bds. 15.95 (*0-8050-2839-0*) TFC Bks NY.

Murphy, Bryan. Experiment with Air. 32p. (gr. 2-5). 1991. PLB 17.50 (*0-8225-2452-X*) Lerner Pubns.

Nielsen, Shelly. I Love Air. LC 93-7597. 1993. 14.96 (*1-56239-189-5*) Abdo & Dghtrs.

Oxlade, Chris. Air. Thompson, Ian, illus. LC 94-5547. 30p. (gr. 2-5). 1994. 12.95 (*0-8120-6444-5*); pap. 4.95 (*0-8120-1983-0*) Barron.
Parramon, J. M., et al. Air. 32p. (ps). 1985. pap. 6.95 (*0-8120-3597-6*) Barron.
—El Aire. (SPA.). 32p. (ps). 1985. pap. 5.95 (*0-8120-3620-4*) Barron.
Pluckrose, Henry A. In the Air. LC 93-45662. (Illus.). 32p. (ps-3). 1994. PLB 11.95 (*0-516-08118-7*) Childrens.
Robbins. Air. 1994. write for info. (*0-8050-2292-9*) H Holt & Co.
Sauvain, Philip. Air. LC 91-27905. (Illus.). 48p. (gr. 6 up). 1992. text ed. 13.95 RSBE (*0-02-781076-3*, New Discovery) Macmillan Child Grp.
Science with Air. 24p. 1992. PLB 12.96 (*0-88110-581-3*); pap. 4.95 (*0-7460-0972-0*) EDC.
Searle-Barnes, Bonita. Air. (Illus.). 32p. (gr. k-3). 1993. 6.99 (*0-7459-2694-0*) Lion USA.
—The Wonder of God's World: Air. Smithson, Colin, illus. LC 92-44575. 1993. 6.99 (*0-7459-2021-7*) Lion USA.
Smith, Henry. Amazing Air. Firth, Barbara, et al, illus. LC 82-80991. 48p. (gr. 3-6). 1983. PLB 11.88 (*0-688-00973-5*) Lothrop.
Spangler, Steven D. All about Air. Myers, Elaine M., ed. Myers, Tom, illus. 16p. (gr. k-6). 1994. pap. 25.85 (*0-944943-46-2*, 92225-6) Current Inc.
Stafford, Kim R. We Got Here Together. Frasier, Debra, illus. LC 93-9814. (gr. 5 up). 1994. 13.95 (*0-15-294891-0*) HarBrace.
Swallow, Su. Air. LC 90-31033. (Illus.). 32p. (gr. k-4). 1991. PLB 11.90 (*0-531-14097-0*) Watts.
Taylor, Barbara. Air & Flight. (Illus.). 40p. (gr. k-4). 1991. PLB 12.90 (*0-531-19129-X*, Warwick) Watts.
—Air & Flying. LC 90-46261. (Illus.). 32p. (gr. 4-6). 1991. PLB 12.40 (*0-531-14183-7*) Watts.
—Up, Up & Away! The Science of Flight. Bull, Peter, et al, illus. LC 91-4292. 40p. (Orig.). (gr. 2-5). 1992. pap. 4.95 (*0-679-82039-6*) Random Bks Yng Read.
Wheeler, Jill. For the Birds: A Book about Air. LC 93-7751. 1993. 14.96 (*1-56239-196-8*) Abdo & Dghtrs.
Wilkins, Mary-Jane. Air, Light & Water. Bull, Peter, illus. LC 90-42620. 40p. (Orig.). (gr. 2-5). 1991. pap. 3.95 (*0-679-80859-0*) Random Bks Yng Read.
Williams, John. Simple Science Projects with Air. LC 91-50543. (Illus.). 32p. (gr. 2-4). 1992. PLB 17.27 (*0-8368-0765-0*) Gareth Stevens Inc.

AIR–POLLUTION

The Acid Rain Hazard. LC 91-50340. (Illus.). 32p. (gr. 3-8). 1993. PLB 17.27 (*0-8368-0697-2*); PLB 17.27 s.p. (*0-685-61491-3*) Gareth Stevens Inc.
Amos, Janine. Pollution. LC 92-16338. (Illus.). 32p. (gr. 2-3). 1992. PLB 18.99 (*0-8114-3405-2*) Raintree Steck-V.
Anderson, Robert. Pollution: Examining Cause & Effect Relationships. LC 92-25958. (Illus.). 32p. (gr. 4-7). 1992. PLB 10.95 (*0-89908-574-1*) Greenhaven.
Asimov, Isaac. Is Our Planet Warming Up? LC 91-50359. (Illus.). 24p. (gr. 2-3). 1992. PLB 15.93 (*0-8368-0744-8*) Gareth Stevens Inc.
—What Is Acid Rain? LC 91-50362. (Illus.). 24p. (gr. 2-3). 1992. PLB 15.93 (*0-8368-0741-3*) Gareth Stevens Inc.
—What's Happening to the Ozone Layer? LC 92-5347. (Illus.). 24p. (gr. 1-8). 1993. PLB 15.93 (*0-8368-0795-2*) Gareth Stevens Inc.
—Why Is the Air Dirty? (Illus.). 24p. (gr. 2-3). 1992. PLB 15.93 (*0-8368-0743-X*) Gareth Stevens Inc.
Bailey, Donna. What We Can Do about Noise & Fumes. (Illus.). 32p. (gr. k-4). 1992. PLB 11.40 (*0-531-11018-4*) Watts.
Black, Wallace B. & Willis, Terri. Cars: An Environmental Challenge. LC 92-9797. (Illus.). 128p. (gr. 4-8). 1992. PLB 20.55 (*0-516-05504-6*) Childrens.
Boyd, Susan, et al. Global Warming & Energy Choices: A Community Action Guide. (Illus.). 38p. (Orig.). (gr. 5-12). 1991. 4.00 (*0-^37345-07-5*) Concern.
Breiter, Herta S. Pollution. LC 87-23233. (Illus.). 48p. (Orig.). (gr. 2-6). 1987. PLB 10.95 (*0-8172-3259-1*); pap. 4.95 (*0-8114-8216-2*) Raintree Steck-V.
Bright, Michael. The Ozone Layer. LC 90-45648. 32p. (gr. 2-4). 1991. PLB 11.90 (*0-531-17302-X*, Gloucester Pr) Watts.
—Traffic Pollution. LC 91-11577. (Illus.). 32p. (gr. k-4). 1991. PLB 11.90 (*0-531-17349-6*, Gloucester Pr) Watts.
Cast, C. Vance. Where Does Pollution Come From? Wilkinson, Sue, illus. 40p. (ps-2). 1994. pap. 4.95 (*0-8120-1571-1*) Barron.
Collinson, Alan. Pollution. LC 91-24081. (Illus.). 48p. (gr. 4-6). 1992. text ed. 13.95 RSBE (*0-02-722995-5*, New Discovery) Macmillan Child Grp.
Dolan, Edward F. Our Poisoned Sky. LC 90-14031. (Illus.). 144p. (gr. 7 up). 1991. 15.00 (*0-525-65056-3*, Cobblehill Bks) Dutton Child Bks.
Edelson, Ed. Clean Air. (Illus.). (gr. 5 up). 1992. lib. bdg. 19.95 (*0-7910-1582-3*) Chelsea Hse.
Gay, Kathlyn. Air Pollution. LC 91-17780. (Illus.). 144p. (gr. 9-12). 1991. PLB 13.90 (*0-531-13002-9*) Watts.
Gold, Susan D. Toxic Waste. LC 90-36295. (Illus.). 48p. (gr. 6). 1990. text ed. 12.95 RSBE (*0-89686-542-8*, Crestwood Hse) Macmillan Child Grp.
Greene, Carol. Caring for Our Air. LC 91-9236. (Illus.). 32p. (gr. k-3). 1991. lib. bdg. 12.95 (*0-89490-351-9*) Enslow Pubs.
The Greenhouse Effect. (gr. 7-12). 1992. 24.95 (*0-7134-6500-X*, Pub. by Batsford UK) Trafalgar.
Gutnik, Martin J. The Challenge of Clean Air. LC 89-39422. (Illus.). 64p. (gr. 6 up). 1990. lib. bdg. 15.95 (*0-89490-272-5*) Enslow Pubs.
—Experiments That Explore the Greenhouse Effect. (Illus.). 72p. (gr. 5-8). 1991. PLB 14.40 (*1-56294-012-0*) Millbrook Pr.
Hare, Tony. Polluting the Air. LC 91-34101. (Illus.). 32p. (gr. 4-8). 1992. PLB 12.40 (*0-531-17346-1*, Gloucester Pr) Watts.
Jennings, Terry. Air. LC 89-453. (Illus.). 32p. (gr. 3-6). 1989. pap. 4.95 (*0-516-48435-4*) Childrens.
Jezek, Alisandra. Miloli's Orchids. (ps-3). 1993. pap. 4.95 (*0-8114-5209-3*) Raintree Steck-V.
Johnson, Rebecca L. Investigating the Ozone Hole. LC 93-15225. 1993. 23.95 (*0-8225-1574-1*) Lerner Pubns.
Kiefer, Irene. Poisoned Land: The Problems of Hazardous Waste. LC 80-22120. (Illus.). 96p. (gr. 6-9). 1981. SBE 13.95 (*0-689-30837-X*, Atheneum Child Bk) Macmillan Child Grp.
Lee, Sally. The Throwaway Society. LC 90-33027. (Illus.). 128p. (gr. 9-12). 1990. PLB 13.40 (*0-531-10947-X*) Watts.
Leggett, Jeremy. Air Scare. LC 90-46420. (Illus.). 48p. (gr. 5-9). 1991. PLB 12.95 (*1-85435-274-1*) Marshall Cavendish.
Lopez, Gary. Air Pollution. (gr. 4-7). 1993. 15.95 (*1-56846-050-3*) Creat Editions.
Lo Pinto, Richard W. Pollution. Head, J. J., ed. Steffen, Ann T., illus. LC 86-72203. 16p. (Orig.). (gr. 10 up). 1987. pap. text ed. 2.75 (*0-89278-392-3*, 45-9792) Carolina Biological.
Lucas, Eileen. Acid Rain. LC 91-3879. 128p. (gr. 4-8). 1991. PLB 20.55 (*0-516-05503-8*) Childrens.
Markle, Sandra. The Kids' Earth Handbook. Markle, Sandra, illus. LC 90-27478. 48p. (gr. 3-7). 1991. SBE 13.95 (*0-689-31707-7*, Atheneum Child Bk) Macmillan Child Grp.
Miller, Christina G. & Berry, Louise A. Acid Rain. LC 86-8605. (Illus.). 128p. (gr. 7 up). 1986. lib. bdg. 12.98 (*0-671-60177-6*, J Messner) S&S Trade.
National Wildlife Federation Staff. Pollution: Problems & Solutions. (gr. k-8). 1991. pap. 7.95 (*0-945051-40-9*, 75045) Natl Wildlife.
O'Neill, Mary. Air Scare. Bindon, John, illus. LC 89-49626. 32p. (gr. 3-6). 1991. lib. bdg. 12.89 (*0-8167-2082-7*); pap. text ed. 3.95 (*0-8167-2083-5*) Troll Assocs.
Pringle, Laurence. Vanishing Ozone. LC 94-25928. 1995. write for info. (*0-688-04157-4*); PLB write for info. (*0-688-04158-2*) Morrow Jr Bks.
Rybolt, Thomas R. & Mebane, Robert C. Environmental Experiments about Air. LC 92-26297. (Illus.). 96p. (gr. 4-9). 1993. lib. bdg. 16.95 (*0-89490-409-4*) Enslow Pubs.
Sandak, Cass R. A Reference Guide to Clean Air. LC 89-25601. 128p. (gr. 6 up). 1990. lib. bdg. 17.95 (*0-89490-261-X*) Enslow Pubs.
Shelby, Anne. What to Do about Pollution. Trivas, Irene, illus. LC 92-24173. 32p. (ps-1). 1993. 14.95 (*0-531-05471-3*); PLB 14.99 (*0-531-08621-6*) Orchard Bks Watts.
Snodgrass, M. E. Environmental Awareness: Air Pollution. James, Jody, ed. Vista Three Design Staff, illus. LC 90-25726. 48p. (gr. 4 up). 1991. lib. bdg. 14.95 (*0-944280-31-5*) Bancroft-Sage.
Snow, Ted. Global Change. LC 90-37680. (Illus.). 48p. (gr. k-4). 1990. PLB 12.85 (*0-516-01105-7*); pap. 4.95 (*0-516-41105-5*) Childrens.
Stille, Darlene. Air Pollution. LC 89-25348. (Illus.). 48p. (gr. k-4). 1990. PLB 12.85 (*0-516-01181-2*); pap. 4.95 (*0-516-41181-0*) Childrens.
—The Greenhouse Effect. LC 90-2147. (Illus.). 48p. (gr. k-4). 1990. PLB 12.85 (*0-516-01106-5*); pap. 4.95 (*0-516-41106-3*) Childrens.
—The Ozone Hole. LC 90-20843. (Illus.). 48p. (gr. k-4). 1991. PLB 12.85 (*0-516-01117-0*); pap. 4.95 (*0-516-41117-9*) Childrens.
Thompson, Sharon E. The Greenhouse Effect. LC 92-27848. (Illus.). 112p. (gr. 5-8). 1992. PLB 14.95 (*1-56006-133-2*) Lucent Bks.
The Threat of Global Warming. LC 91-50341. (Illus.). 32p. (gr. 3-8). 1993. PLB 17.27 (*0-8368-0698-0*) Gareth Stevens Inc.

AIR CARGO

see Aeronautics, Commercial

AIR CRASHES

see Aeronautics–Accidents

AIR FREIGHT

see Aeronautics, Commercial

AIR HOSTESSES

see Air Lines–Hostesses

AIR LINES–HOSTESSES

Kirkwood, Tim. The Flight Attendant Career Guide. Gibbons Plummer, Jeanne, ed. LC 93-85322. (Illus.). 96p. (Orig.). (gr. 9-12). 1993. pap. 14.95 (*0-9637301-4-2*) T K Enterprises.

AIR PILOTS

see also Astronauts; Women in Aeronautics

Bauer, Judith. What's It Like to Be an Airline Pilot. Iosa, Ann W., illus. LC 89-34397. 32p. (gr. k-3). 1990. PLB 10.89 (*0-8167-1791-5*); pap. text ed. 2.95 (*0-8167-1792-3*) Troll Assocs.
Brown, Don, text by. & illus. Ruth Law Thrills a Nation. LC 92-45701. 32p. (ps-2). 1993. PLB 13.95 (*0-395-66404-7*) Ticknor & Flds Bks Yng Read.
Burleigh, Bob. Flight: The Journey of Charles Lindbergh. Wimmer, Mike, illus. 32p. (ps-3). 1991. 14.95 (*0-399-22272-3*, Philomel) Putnam Pub Group.
Dahl, Roald. Going Solo. 224p. (gr. 7 up). 1993. pap. 4.99 (*0-14-032528-X*, Puffin) Puffin Bks.
Davies, Kath. Amelia Earhart Flies Around the World. LC 93-29954. (Illus.). 32p. (gr. 4 up). 1994. text ed. 13.95 RSBE (*0-87518-531-2*, Dillon) Macmillan Child Grp.
Gaffney, Timothy R. Chuck Yeager: First Man to Fly Faster than Sound. LC 86-9555. (Illus.). 128p. (gr. 4 up). 1986. PLB 14.40 (*0-516-03223-2*) Childrens.
Harris, Jack. Test Pilots. LC 89-31126. (Illus.). 48p. (gr. 5-6). 1989. text ed. 11.95 RSBE (*0-89686-429-4*, Crestwood Hse) Macmillan Child Grp.
Hart, Philip S. Flying Free: America's First Black Aviators. Lindbergh, Reeve, frwd. by. (Illus.). 72p. (gr. 5 up). 1992. 19.95 (*0-8225-1598-9*) Lerner Pubns.
Jaspersohn, William. A Week in the Life of an Airline Pilot. (gr. 4-7). 1991. 14.95 (*0-316-45822-8*) Little.
Kerby, Mona. Amelia Earhart: Courage in the Sky. McKeating, Eileen, illus. LC 92-19520. 64p. (gr. 3-5). 1992. pap. 3.99 (*0-14-034263-X*) Puffin Bks.
Larsen, Anita. Amelia Earhart: Missing, Declared Dead. LC 91-19246. (Illus.). 48p. (gr. 5-6). 1992. text ed. 11.95 RSBE (*0-89686-613-0*, Crestwood Hse) Macmillan Child Grp.
Levinson, Nancy S. Chuck Yeager the Man Who Broke the Sound Barrier. LC 87-25431. 133p. (gr. 5 up). 1988. 13.95 (*0-8027-6781-8*); PLB 14.85 (*0-8027-6799-0*) Walker & Co.
Peacock, Lindsay. Pilots. Stefoff, Rebecca, ed. LC 91-39097. (Illus.). 32p. (gr. 5-9). 1992. PLB 17.26 (*1-56074-040-X*) Garrett Ed Corp.
Rosenbaum, Robert. Aviators. (Illus.). 128p. (gr. 6-12). 1992. lib. bdg. 16.95x (*0-8160-2539-8*) Facts on File.
Russell, William. Pilots. LC 93-45009. 1994. write for info. (*1-57103-059-X*) Rourke Pr.
Seymour, Peter. Pilots. Ingersoll, Norm, illus. 12p. (gr. k-3). 1992. 13.00 (*0-525-67372-5*, Lodestar Bks) Dutton Child Bks.
Smith, Elizabeth S. Coming Out Right: The Story of Jackie Cochran, the First Woman Aviator to Break the Sound Barrier. (Illus.). 128p. (gr. 5 up). 1991. 14.95 (*0-8027-6988-8*); PLB 15.85 (*0-8027-6989-6*) Walker & Co.
Taylor, Richard L. The First Flight Across the United States: The Story of Calbraith Perry Rodgers & His Airplane, the Vin Fiz. LC 93-6881. (Illus.). 64p. (gr. 4-6). 1993. PLB 12.90 (*0-531-20159-7*) Watts.
—The First Solo Flight Around the World: The Story of Wiley Post & His Airplane, the Winnie Mae. LC 93-6880. (Illus.). 64p. (gr. 4-6). 1993. PLB 12.90 (*0-531-20160-0*) Watts.
Worthington, George. In Search of World Records. LC 80-82032. (gr. 10-12). 1980. 18.95 (*0-938282-01-8*) Hang Gliding.

AIR POLLUTION

see Air–Pollution

AIR RAIDS–PROTECTIVE MEASURES

see Aeronautics, Military

AIR STEWARDESSES

see Air Lines–Hostesses

AIR TRANSPORT

see Aeronautics, Commercial

AIR WARFARE

see Aeronautics, Military; Airplanes, Military;
see names of wars with the subdivision Aerial Operations, e.g. World War, 1939-1945–Aerial Operations; etc.

AIRCRAFT

see Airplanes; Airships; Gliders (Aeronautics); Helicopters

Coombs, Charles I. Ultralights: The Flying Featherweights. LC 83-17411. (Illus.). 160p. (gr. 5 up). 1984. 12.95 (*0-688-02775-X*) Morrow Jr Bks.

AIRCRAFT CARRIERS

Black, Wallace B. & Blashfield, Jean F. Flattops at War. LC 91-7916. (Illus.). 48p. (gr. 5-6). 1991. text ed. 12.95 RSBE (*0-89686-559-2*, Crestwood Hse) Macmillan Child Grp.
Budgie Goes to Sea. 40p. (ps-1). 1991. pap. 12.00 jacketed (*0-671-73474-1*, S&S BFYR) S&S Trade.
Norman, C. J. Aircraft Carriers. LC 85-51452. (Illus.). 32p. (gr. 3-6). 1989. pap. 4.95 (*0-531-15136-0*) Watts.
Preston, Anthony. Aircraft Carriers. Gibbons, Tony, et al, illus. LC 84-9669. 48p. (gr. 5 up). 1985. PLB 13.50 (*0-8225-1377-3*, First Ave Edns); pap. 4.95 (*0-8225-9504-4*, First Ave Edns) Lerner Pubns.
Rawlinson, J. Nuclear Carriers. (Illus.). 48p. (gr. 3-8). 1989. lib. bdg. 18.60 (*0-86625-084-0*); 13.95s.p. (*0-685-58646-4*) Rourke Corp.
Stephen, R. J. Picture World of Aircraft Carriers. (Illus.). 1990. PLB 12.40 (*0-531-14008-3*) Watts.

AIRPLANE ACCIDENTS

see Aeronautics–Accidents

AIRPLANE CARRIERS

see Aircraft Carriers

AIRPLANE HOSTESSES

see Air Lines–Hostesses

AIRPLANES

see also Aeronautics; Gliders (Aeronautics);
also types of airplanes, e.g. Bombers; Vertically Rising Airplanes; etc.

Aircraft. (Illus.). 32p. (ps-6). 1983. Set of 10. pap. 29.50 (*0-87474-825-9*, AICBP) Smithsonian.
The Aircraft Encyclopedia. 192p. (gr. 3 up). 1985. pap. 8.95 (*0-671-55337-2*, S&S BFYR) S&S Trade.
Aircraft: Superfacts. 1992. pap. 4.99 (*0-517-07324-2*) Random Hse Value.

Asimov, Isaac. How Do Airplanes Fly? (Illus.). 24p. (gr. 1-8). 1992. PLB 15.93 (*0-8368-0800-2*); PLB 15.93 s.p. (*0-685-61486-7*) Gareth Stevens Inc.
Barrett, Norman. Flying Machines. LC 93-33238. (Illus.). 48p. (gr. 5-7). 1994. PLB 13.95 (*0-531-14301-5*) Watts.
Barton, Byron. Airplanes. LC 85-47899. (Illus.). 32p. (ps-k). 1986. 6.95 (*0-694-00060-4*, Crowell Jr Bks); PLB 12.89 (*0-690-04532-8*) HarpC Child Bks.
Baxter, Leon. Famous Flying Machines. (Illus.). 48p. (gr. 1-5). 1992. pap. 7.95 (*0-8249-8532-X*, Ideals Child) Hambleton-Hill.
Bendick, Jeanne. Eureka! It's an Airplane! Murdocca, Sal, illus. LC 91-34791. 48p. (gr. 2-6). 1992. PLB 15.40 (*1-56294-058-9*); pap. 5.95 (*1-56294-701-X*) Millbrook Pr.
Bowden, Joan. Planes of the Aces: A Three-Dimensional Collection of the Most Famous Aircraft in the World. 1993. pap. 14.95 (*0-385-30910-4*) Doubleday.
Browne, Gerard, illus. The Aircraft Lift-the-Flap Book. 18p. (gr. 2-5). 1992. 13.00 (*0-525-67351-2*, Lodestar Bks) Dutton Child Bks.
Cooper, J. Airplanes. 1991. 8.95s.p. (*0-86592-493-7*) Rourke Enter.
—Aviones (Airplanes) 1991. 8.95s.p. (*0-86592-507-0*) Rourke Enter.
Dale, Henry. Early Flying Machines. LC 92-21664. 1992. 16.00 (*0-19-520966-4*) OUP.
Emert, Phyllis R. Mysteries of Ships & Planes. 128p. 1990. pap. 2.50 (*0-8125-9427-4*) Tor Bks.
—Special Task Aircraft. (Illus.). 64p. (gr. 5-9). 1990. lib. bdg. 12.98 (*0-671-68963-0*, J Messner) S&S Trade.
—Transports & Bombers. (Illus.). 64p. (gr. 5-9). 1990. lib. bdg. 12.98 (*0-671-68961-4*, J Messner) S&S Trade.
Evans, Frank. All Aboard Airplanes. Guzzi, George, illus. LC 93-39845. 32p. (ps-3). 1994. pap. 2.25 (*0-448-40214-9*, G&D) Putnam Pub Group.
Gifford, C. Planes. (Illus.). 12p. (ps). 1994. bds. 4.50 (*0-7460-1978-5*, Usborne) EDC.
Grant, Donald, illus. Airplanes & Flying Machines. (ps). 1992. bds. 10.95 (*0-590-45267-3*, 037, Cartwheel) Scholastic Inc.
Grimm, Rosemary. Stunt Planes. LC 87-29020. (Illus.). 48p. (gr. 5-6). 1988. text ed. 11.95 RSBE (*0-89686-363-8*, Crestwood Hse) Macmillan Child Grp.
Gunning, Thomas G. Dream Planes. LC 92-8397. (Illus.). 72p. (gr. 3 up). 1992. text ed. 14.95 RSBE (*0-87518-556-8*, Dillon) Macmillan Child Grp.
Guttmacher, Peter. The China Clipper. LC 93-46204. 1994. text ed. 13.95 (*0-89686-826-5*, Crestwood Hse) Macmillan Child Grp.
Hewish, Mark. Jets. (gr. 5-9). 1976. pap. 6.95 (*0-86020-051-5*, Usborne-Hayes) EDC.
Incredible Flying Machines. (Illus.). 32p. (Orig.). (gr. 2-5). 1994. pap. 4.95 (*1-56458-552-2*) Dorling Kindersley.
Jennings, Terry. Planes, Gliders, Helicopters, & Other Flying Machines. LC 92-28422. (Illus.). 40p. (gr. 3-8). 1993. 10.95 (*1-85697-870-2*, Kingfisher LKC); pap. 5.95 (*1-85697-869-9*) LKC.
Kerrod, Robin. Amazing Flying Machines. Dunning, Mike, photos by. LC 91-53137. (Illus.). 32p. (Orig.). (gr. 1-5). 1992. PLB 9.99 (*0-679-92765-4*); pap. 6.95 (*0-679-82765-X*) Knopf Bks Yng Read.
Lantier-Sampon, Patricia. Airplanes. LC 91-50344. (Illus.). 24p. (ps-2). 1991. PLB 15.93 (*0-8368-0539-9*) Gareth Stevens Inc.
Lenga. Amazing Fact Book of Planes. (Illus.). 32p. (gr. 4-8). 1987. PLB 14.95 (*0-87191-848-X*) Creative Ed.
Lenski, Lois. Little Airplane. Lenski, Lois, illus. LC 59-12487. (gr. k-3). 1980. 5.25 (*0-8098-1004-2*) McKay.
Little, Karen E. & Thomas, A. Things That Fly. (Illus.). 24p. (gr. 2-4). 1987. pap. 3.95 (*0-7460-0104-5*) EDC.
McPhail, David. First Flight. (Illus.). (ps-3). 1991. Repr. 4.95 (*0-316-56332-3*, Joy St Bks) Little.
Magee, Doug & Newman, Robert. Let's Fly from A to Z. LC 91-39774. (Illus.). 48p. (ps-3). 1992. 14.00 (*0-525-65105-5*, Cobblehill Bks) Dutton Child Bks.
Malfatti, Patrizia, tr. Look Inside an Airplane. Michelini, Carlo A., illus. 16p. (ps-3). 1994. bds. 11.95 (*0-448-40543-1*, G&D) Putnam Pub Group.
Maynard, Christopher. Airplanes. LC 92-32843. 32p. (gr. 1-4). 1993. 3.95 (*1-85697-895-8*, Kingfisher LKC) LKC.
Moore, Kathryn C. My First Flight. rev. ed. Hutson, Ronald, ed. Grant, Leslie, illus. (ps-4). 1991. PLB 3.95 (*0-9633295-0-2*) K Cs Bks N Stuff.
Moxon, Julian. How Jet Engines Are Made. LC 85-21049. (Illus.). 32p. (gr. 7 up). 12.95x (*0-8160-0037-9*) Facts on File.
Munro, Bob. Aircraft. Moores, Ian, illus. LC 93-19868. 32p. (gr. 4-6). 1993. PLB 19.97 (*0-8114-6161-0*) Raintree Steck-V.
Murray, Peter. World's Greatest Paper Airplanes. (Illus.). (gr. 2-6). 1992. PLB 14.95 (*0-89565-963-8*) Childs World.
Nahum, Andrew. Flying Machine. King, Dave, et al, photos by. LC 90-4007. (Illus.). 64p. (gr. 5 up). 1990. 16.00 (*0-679-80744-6*); PLB 16.99 (*0-679-90744-0*) Knopf Bks Yng Read.
Pearl, Lizzy. The Story of Flight. Bergin, Mark, illus. LC 91-33412. 32p. (gr. 1-4). 1993. PLB 11.89 (*0-8167-2709-0*); pap. text ed. 3.95 (*0-8167-2710-4*) Troll Assocs.
Peterson, David. Airplanes. LC 81-7671. (Illus.). 48p. (gr. k-4). 1981. PLB 12.85 (*0-516-01606-7*); pap. 4.95 (*0-516-41606-5*) Childrens.
Planes. LC 91-25688. (Illus.). 24p. (ps-k). 1992. pap. 7.95 POB (*0-689-71564-1*, Aladdin) Macmillan Child Grp.
Planes. LC 92-52831. 24p. (ps-3). 1993. 8.95 (*1-56458-135-7*) Dorling Kindersley.
Planes. (Illus.). 32p. (gr. 1-4). 1994. pap. 5.95 (*1-56458-520-4*) Dorling Kindersley.
Potter, Tony. See How It Works: Planes. Lawrie, Robin, illus. 28p. (ps-3). 1989. pap. 7.95 POB (*0-689-71304-5*, Aladdin) Macmillan Child Grp.
Richardson, Joy. Airplanes. LC 93-42184. (Illus.). 1994. write for info. (*0-531-14324-4*) Watts.
Rockwell, Anne. Planes. Rockwell, Anne, illus. LC 84-13732. 24p. (ps-1). 1985. 12.95 (*0-525-44159-X*, DCB) Dutton Child Bks.
—Planes. 1994. pap. 4.99 (*0-14-054782-7*, Puff Unicorn) Puffin Bks.
Rowe, Frank. The Famous Airplanes of Kansas. Lickei, Elizabeth, ed. Rowe, Frank, illus. 64p. (Orig.). 1992. pap. 3.95 (*1-880652-12-9*) Wichita Eagle.
Royston, Angela. My Lift-the-Flap Plane Book. King, Colin, illus. LC 92-38631. 18p. (ps-1). 1993. 14.95 (*0-399-22533-1*, Putnam) Putnam Pub Group.
Schultz, Charles, ed. Earth, Water, & Air. LC 94-15102. (Illus.). 1994. 9.99 (*0-517-11897-1*, Pub. by Derrydale Bks) Random Hse Value.
Siebert, Diane. Plane Song. Nasta, Vincent, illus. LC 92-17359. 32p. (ps-3). 1993. 15.00 (*0-06-021464-3*); PLB 14.89 (*0-06-021467-8*) HarpC Child Bks.
Space, Peggy. A Trip on a Jet Plane: Photos & Fun for Boys & Girls. Space, Peggy & Scarpace, Frank, illus. 32p. (gr. 3-7). 1981. pap. 2.50 (*0-942772-00-8*) Image Pubns.
Spizzirri Publishing Co. Staff. Aircraft: An Educational Coloring Book. Spizzirri, Linda, ed. Fuller, Glenn & Spizzirri, Peter M., illus. 32p. (gr. 1-8). 1981. pap. 1.75 (*0-86545-033-1*) Spizzirri.
Stacey, Tom. Airplanes: The Lure of Flight. LC 90-6471. (Illus.). 96p. (gr. 5-8). 1990. PLB 15.95 (*1-56006-203-7*) Lucent Bks.
Steele, Philip. Planes. LC 90-41181. (Illus.). 32p. (gr. 5-6). 1991. text ed. 3.95 RSBE (*0-89686-524-X*, Crestwood Hse) Macmillan Child Grp.
Stephen, R. J. The Picture World of Airliners. (Illus.). 32p. (gr. k-4). 1989. PLB 12.40 (*0-531-10724-8*) Watts.
Tunney, Christopher. Aircraft Carriers. LC 79-64384. (Illus.). 36p. (gr. 3-6). 1980. PLB 13.50 (*0-8225-1176-2*) Lerner Pubns.

AIRPLANES–ACCIDENTS
see Aeronautics–Accidents

AIRPLANES–FICTION
The Airplane Ride. 28p. (ps-2). 1992. 3.95 (*0-7214-5311-2*, S915-4 SER.) Ladybird Bks.
Airport. 1993. pap. text ed. 6.50 (*0-582-08479-2*, 79815) Longman.
Bursik, Rose. Amelia's Fantastic Flight. Bursik, Rose, illus. LC 91-28809. 32p. (ps-2). 1992. 14.95 (*0-8050-1872-7*, Bks Young Read) H Holt & Co.
Cotler, Joanna. Sky above Earth Below. Cotler, Joanna, illus. LC 89-26743. 32p. (ps-k). 1990. 14.95 (*0-06-021365-5*) HarpC Child Bks.
Damashek, Sandy. Teeny-Tiny Train & Planes, 6 bks. Filippo, Margaret S., illus. (ps-k). 1992. bds. 14.95 (*1-56293-241-1*, Set, mini-board bks. in a tray) McClanahan Bk.
Falken, Linda C. Kitty's First Airplane Trip. Adams, Lynn, illus. 32p. (ps-2). 1993. pap. 2.50 (*0-590-45788-8*) Scholastic Inc.
Hasan, Khurshid. Manzur Goes to the Airport. (Illus.). 25p. (gr. 2-4). 1991. 15.95 (*0-237-60159-1*, Pub. by Evans Bros Ltd) Trafalgar.
Holland, Alex N. The Children's Big Airplane. Holland, Alex N., illus. 12p. (gr. 1-4). 1992. pap. 10.95 (*1-56606-000-1*) Bradley Mann.
Hoobler, Dorothy & Hoobler, Thomas. And Now a Word from Our Sponsor. Leer, Rebecca, illus. 64p. (gr. 4-6). 1992. 5.95 (*0-382-24153-3*); PLB 7.95 (*0-382-24146-0*); pap. 3.95 (*0-382-24350-1*) Silver Burdett Pr.
Jukes, Mavis. I'll See You in My Dreams. Schuett, Stacey, illus. LC 91-47605. 40p. (gr. k-5). 1993. 15.00 (*0-679-82690-4*); PLB 15.99 (*0-679-92690-9*) Knopf Bks Yng Read.
Lindbergh, Reeve. View from the Air: Charles Lindbergh's Earth & Sky. Brown, Richard, photos by. (Illus.). 32p. 1992. 15.00 (*0-670-84660-0*) Viking Child Bks.
The Lunettes. rev. ed. 50p. 1992. PLB 25.00 (*1-56611-005-X*); pap. 15.00 (*1-56611-849-2*) Jonas.
Munsch, Robert. Angela's Airplane. Martchenko, Michael, illus. 24p. (gr. k-3). 1988. PLB 14.95 (*1-550370-27-8*, Pub. by Annick CN); pap. 4.95 (*1-550370-26-X*, Pub. by Annick CN) Firefly Bks Ltd.
—Angela's Airplane. Martchenko, Michael, illus. 24p. (ps-1). 1986. pap. 0.99 (*0-920236-75-8*, Pub. by Annick CN) Firefly Bks Ltd.
—Angela's Airplane. (CHI., Illus.). 32p. 1993. pap. 5.95 (*1-55037-295-5*, Pub. by Annick CN) Firefly Bks Ltd.
Scarry, Richard. Richard Scarry's Planes. (Illus.). 24p. (ps-k). 1992. pap. write for info. (*0-307-11535-6*, 11535, Golden Pr) Western Pub.
Spier, Peter. Bored, Nothing to Do. Spier, Peter, illus. LC 77-20726. 48p. (gr. 1-3). 1978. 11.95 (*0-385-13177-1*) Doubleday.
Testa, Fulvio. The Paper Airplane. LC 81-8358. (Illus.). 32p. (gr. k-3). 1988. 14.95 (*1-55858-060-3*) North-South Bks NYC.
Tubby, I. M. I'm a Little Airplane. Kraus, Robert, ed. (Illus.). 10p. (ps). 1982. pap. 3.95 vinyl (*0-671-45565-6*, Little Simon) S&S Trade.
Tucker, Sian. The Little Plane. (Illus.). 10p. (ps-k). 1993. pap. 2.95 (*0-671-79735-2*, Little Simon) S&S Trade.
Wehr, Fred. Amelia. LC 93-46451. 1994. 14.95 (*1-87785-333-X*) Nautical & Aviation.
Yep, Laurence. Dragonwings. LC 74-2625. 256p. (gr. 6 up). 1977. pap. 4.95 (*0-06-440085-9*, Trophy) HarpC Child Bks.

AIRPLANES–FLIGHT TESTING
see Airplanes–Testing

AIRPLANES, MILITARY
see also types of military airplanes, e.g. Bombers
Baker, David. Bombers. (Illus.). 48p. (gr. 3-8). 1987. PLB 18.60 (*0-86592-355-8*) Rourke Corp.
—Land-Based Fighters. (Illus.). 48p. (gr. 3-8). 1987. PLB 18.60 (*0-86592-351-5*); 13.95s.p. (*0-685-67591-2*) Rourke Corp.
—Military Aircraft Library, 6 bks, Set II, Reading Level 5. (Illus.). 288p. (gr. 3-8). 1989. Set. PLB 111.60 (*0-86592-530-5*); 83.70s.p. (*0-685-58763-0*) Rourke Corp.
—Navy Fighters. (Illus.). 48p. (gr. 3-8). 1987. PLB 18.60 (*0-86592-352-3*); 13.95s.p. (*0-685-67594-7*) Rourke Corp.
—Research Planes. (Illus.). 48p. (gr. 3-8). 1987. PLB 18.60 (*0-86592-354-X*); 13.95s.p. (*0-685-67595-5*) Rourke Corp.
—Spy Planes. (Illus.). 48p. (gr. 3-8). 1987. PLB 18.60 (*0-86592-353-1*); PLB 13.95s.p. (*0-685-67592-0*) Rourke Corp.
Begarnie, Luke. Fighters, Choppers & Bombers. (Illus.). 32p. 1987. pap. 3.95 (*0-590-40738-4*) Scholastic Inc.
Sullivan, George. Modern Bombers & Attack Planes. (Illus.). 128p. (gr. 7 up). 1992. PLB 17.95x (*0-8160-2354-9*) Facts on File.

AIRPLANES–MODELS
Arceneaux, Marc. Paper Airplanes. (Illus.). 32p. 1974. pap. 4.50 (*0-8431-1703-6*, Troubador) Price Stern.
Churchill, E. Richard. Fantastic Paper Flying Machines. Michaels, James, illus. LC 93-44604. 128p. 1994. 14.95 (*0-8069-0435-6*) Sterling.
Lord, Suzanne. Radio-Controlled Model Airplanes. LC 88-7109. (Illus.). 48p. (gr. 5-6). 1988. text ed. 11.95 RSBE (*0-89686-378-6*, Crestwood Hse) Macmillan Child Grp.
McNeil, M. J. Flying Models. (Illus.). 32p. (gr. 3-6). 1977. pap. 6.95 (*0-86020-007-8*) EDC.
Smith, Bob. Stunt Flying with Paper Airplanes. (Illus.). 32p. (gr. 3 up). 1992. pap. 2.50 (*0-87406-625-5*) Willowisp Pr.
Somerville, L. How to Make Superplanes. (Illus.). 32p. (gr. 3-7). 1992. PLB 12.96 (*0-88110-542-2*, Usborne); pap. 5.95 (*0-7460-0667-5*, Usborne) EDC.
Ward, Brian. Flying Models. LC 92-9908. 1993. 12.40 (*0-531-14241-8*) Watts.
Watermill Press Staff. Make It & Fly It. (gr. 4-7). 1992. pap. 5.95 (*0-8167-2848-8*, Pub. by Watermill Pr) Troll Assocs.

AIRPLANES, NAVAL
see Airplanes, Military

AIRPLANES–OPERATION
see Airplanes–Piloting

AIRPLANES–PILOTING
Behrens, June. I Can Be a Pilot. LC 85-10961. 32p. (gr. k-3). 1985. PLB 11.80 (*0-516-01888-4*); pap. 3.95 (*0-516-41888-2*) Childrens.
Paulson, Tim. How to Fly a 747. Keating, Edward, illus. 48p. (Orig.). (gr. 3 up). 1992. pap. 9.95 (*1-56261-061-9*) John Muir.

AIRPLANES–PILOTS
see Air Pilots

AIRPLANES–TESTING
Berliner, Don. Research Airplanes: Testing the Boundaries of Flight. (Illus.). 64p. (gr. 5 up). 1988. PLB 21.50 (*0-8225-1582-2*) Lerner Pubns.

AIRPORTS
Barton, Byron. Airport. Barton, Byron, illus. LC 79-7816. 32p. (ps-k). 1982. 15.00 (*0-690-04168-3*, Crowell Jr Bks); PLB 14.89 (*0-690-04169-1*) HarpC Child Bks.
—Airport. Barton, Byron, illus. LC 79-7816. 32p. (ps-1). 1987. pap. 4.95 (*0-06-443145-2*, Trophy) HarpC Child Bks.
Butler, Daphne. First Look at the Airports. LC 90-10266. (Illus.). 32p. (gr. 1-2). 1991. PLB 17.27 (*0-8368-0501-1*) Gareth Stevens Inc.
Richardson, Joy. Airports. (Illus.). 32p. (gr. 2-4). 1994. PLB 11.40 (*0-531-14292-2*) Watts.
Stamper, Judith B. Save the Everglades! Davis, Allen, illus. LC 92-18085. 56p. (gr. 2-5). 1992. PLB 19.97 (*0-8114-7219-1*) Raintree Steck-V.
Sullivan, George. How an Airport Really Works. LC 92-20154. 128p. (gr. 5-9). 1993. 15.99 (*0-525-67378-4*, Lodestar Bks) Dutton Child Bks.
Ziegler, Sandra. A Visit to the Airport. LC 87-35470. 32p. (ps-3). 1988. PLB 11.45 (*0-516-01488-9*); pap. 3.95 (*0-516-41488-7*) Childrens.

AIRSHIPS
see also Aeronautics; Balloons
Stein, R. Conrad. Hindenburg Disaster. LC 92-34520. (Illus.). 32p. (gr. 3-6). 1993. PLB 12.30 (*0-516-06663-3*); pap. 3.95 (*0-516-46663-1*) Childrens.
Tanaka, Shelley. The Disaster of the Hindenburg: The Last Flight of the Greatest Airship Ever Built. LC 92-39434. 64p. 1993. 16.95 (*0-590-45750-0*) Scholastic Inc.

ALABAMA

Brown, Dottie. Alabama. LC 93-37796. (Illus.). (gr. 3-6). 1994. PLB 17.50 (*0-8225-2741-3*) Lerner Pubns.

Carole Marsh Alabama Books, 44 bks. 1994. Set. lib. bdg. 1027.80 (*0-7933-1274-4*); pap. 587.80 (*0-7933-5122-7*) Gallopade Pub Group.

Carroll, Merle T. This Is Alabama. 3rd, rev. & updated ed. (Illus.). 336p. (gr. 4). 1993. Repr. of 1975 ed. text ed. 14.50 (*0-9632262-0-7*) J Y Carroll.

Estes, James L. Alabama's Youngest Admirals. Krauel, Mary E., ed. Christian, Releta, illus. 132p. (Orig.). (gr. 4-12). 1991. pap. 8.95 (*0-9628634-0-8*) J L Estes.

Fradin, Dennis. Alabama: In Words & Pictures. Wahl, Richard, illus. LC 80-15135. 48p. (gr. 2-5). 1980. PLB 12.95 (*0-516-03901-6*) Childrens.

Fradin, Dennis B. Alabama. LC 92-37047. (Illus.). 64p. (gr. 3-5). 1993. PLB 16.45 (*0-516-03801-X*) Childrens.

McNair, Sylvia. Alabama. LC 88-11744. (Illus.). 144p. (gr. 4 up). 1988. PLB 20.55 (*0-516-00447-6*) Childrens.

—Alabama. 178p. 1993. text ed. 15.40 (*1-56956-159-1*) W A T Braille.

Marsh, Carole. Alabama & Other State Greats (Biographies) (Illus.). (gr. 3-12). 1994. PLB 24.95 (*1-55609-469-8*); pap. 14.95 (*1-55609-468-X*); computer disk 29.95 (*0-7933-1338-4*) Gallopade Pub Group.

—Alabama Bandits, Bushwackers, Outlaws, Crooks, Devils, Ghosts, Desperadoes & Other Assorted & Sundry Characters! (Illus.). (gr. 3-12). 1994. PLB 24.95 (*0-7933-0041-X*); pap. 14.95 (*0-7933-0040-1*); computer disk 29.95 (*0-7933-0042-8*) Gallopade Pub Group.

—Alabama Classic Christmas Trivia: Stories, Recipes, Activities, Legends, Lore & More! (Illus.). (gr. 3-12). 1994. PLB 24.95 (*0-7933-0044-4*); pap. 14.95 (*0-7933-0043-6*); computer disk 29.95 (*0-7933-0045-2*) Gallopade Pub Group.

—Alabama Coastales! (Illus.). (gr. 3-12). 1994. PLB 24.95 (*1-55609-465-5*); pap. 14.95 (*1-55609-120-6*); computer disk 29.95 (*0-7933-1334-1*) Gallopade Pub Group.

—Alabama Coastales! 1994. lib. bdg. 24.95 (*0-7933-6938-X*) Gallopade Pub Group.

—Alabama "Crinkum-Crankum" A Funny Word Book about Our State. (Illus.). 1994. lib. bdg. 24.95 (*0-7933-4810-2*); pap. 14.95 (*0-7933-4811-0*); disk 29.95 (*0-7933-4812-9*) Gallopade Pub Group.

—Alabama Dingbats! Bk. 1: A Fun Book of Games, Stories, Activities & More about Our State That's All in Code! for You to Decipher. (Illus.). (gr. 3-12). 1994. PLB 24.95 (*0-7933-3773-9*); pap. 14.95 (*0-7933-3774-7*); computer disk 29.95 (*0-7933-3775-5*) Gallopade Pub Group.

—Alabama Festival Fun for Kids! (Illus.). (gr. 3-12). 1994. lib. bdg. 24.95 (*0-7933-3926-X*); pap. 14.95 (*0-7933-3927-8*); disk 29.95 (*0-7933-3928-6*) Gallopade Pub Group.

—The Alabama Hot Air Balloon Mystery. (Illus.). (gr. 2-9). 1994. 24.95 (*0-7933-2318-5*); pap. 14.95 (*0-7933-2319-3*); computer disk 29.95 (*0-7933-2320-7*) Gallopade Pub Group.

—Alabama Jeopardy! Answers & Questions about Our State! (Illus.). (gr. 3-12). 1994. PLB 24.95 (*0-7933-4079-9*); pap. 14.95 (*0-7933-4080-2*); computer disk 29.95 (*0-7933-4081-0*) Gallopade Pub Group.

—Alabama "Jography" A Fun Run Thru Our State! (Illus.). (gr. 3-12). 1994. PLB 24.95 (*1-55609-461-2*); pap. 14.95 (*1-55609-092-7*); computer disk 29.95 (*0-7933-1327-9*) Gallopade Pub Group.

—Alabama Kid's Cookbook: Recipes, How-to, History, Lore & More! (Illus.). (gr. 3-12). 1994. PLB 24.95 (*0-7933-0082-7*); pap. 14.95 (*0-7933-0081-9*); computer disk 29.95 (*0-7933-0083-5*) Gallopade Pub Group.

—The Alabama Mystery Van Takes Off! Book 1: Handicapped Alabama Kids Sneak Off on a Big Adventure. (Illus.). (gr. 3-12). 1994. 24.95 (*0-7933-4964-8*); pap. 14.95 (*0-7933-4965-6*); computer disk 29.95 (*0-7933-4966-4*) Gallopade Pub Group.

—Alabama Quiz Bowl Crash Course! (Illus.). (gr. 3-12). 1994. PLB 24.95 (*1-55609-467-1*); pap. 14.95 (*1-55609-466-3*); computer disk 29.95 (*0-7933-1333-3*) Gallopade Pub Group.

—Alabama Rollercoasters! (Illus.). (gr. 3-12). 1994. PLB 24.95 (*0-7933-5224-X*); pap. 14.95 (*0-7933-5225-8*); computer disk 29.95 (*0-7933-5226-6*) Gallopade Pub Group.

—Alabama School Trivia: An Amazing & Fascinating Look at Our State's Teachers, Schools & Students! (Illus.). (gr. 3-12). 1994. PLB 24.95 (*0-7933-0079-7*); pap. 14.95 (*0-7933-0049-5*); computer disk 29.95 (*0-7933-0080-0*) Gallopade Pub Group.

—Alabama Silly Basketball Sportsmysteries, Vol. I. (Illus.). (gr. 3-12). 1994. PLB 24.95 (*0-7933-0047-9*); pap. 14.95 (*0-7933-0046-0*); computer disk 29.95 (*0-7933-0048-7*) Gallopade Pub Group.

—Alabama Silly Basketball Sportsmysteries, Vol. II. (Illus.). (gr. 3-12). 1994. PLB 24.95 (*0-7933-1562-X*); pap. 14.95 (*0-7933-1563-8*); computer disk 29.95 (*0-7933-1564-6*) Gallopade Pub Group.

—Alabama Silly Football Sportsmysteries, Vol. I. (Illus.). (gr. 3-12). 1994. PLB 24.95 (*1-55609-464-7*); pap. 14.95 (*1-55609-463-9*); computer disk 29.95 (*0-7933-1329-5*) Gallopade Pub Group.

—Alabama Silly Football Sportsmysteries, Vol. II. (Illus.). (gr. 3-12). 1994. PLB 24.95 (*0-7933-1339-2*); pap. 14.95 (*0-7933-1340-6*); computer disk 29.95 (*0-7933-1341-4*) Gallopade Pub Group.

—Alabama Silly Trivia! (Illus.). (gr. 3-12). 1994. PLB 24.95 (*1-55609-460-4*); pap. 14.95 (*1-55609-038-2*); computer disk 29.95 (*0-7933-1326-0*) Gallopade Pub Group.

—Alabama Timeline: A Chronology of Alabama History, Mystery, Trivia, Legend, Lore & More. (Illus.). (gr. 3-12). 1994. PLB 24.95 (*0-7933-5875-2*); pap. 14.95 (*0-7933-5876-0*); computer disk 29.95 (*0-7933-5877-9*) Gallopade Pub Group.

—Alabama's (Most Devastating!) Disasters & (Most Calamitous!) Catastrophies! (Illus.). (gr. 3-12). 1994. PLB 24.95 (*0-7933-0038-X*); pap. 14.95 (*0-7933-0037-1*); computer disk 29.95 (*0-7933-0039-8*) Gallopade Pub Group.

—Alabama's Unsolved Mysteries (& Their "Solutions") Includes Scientific Information & Other Activities for Students. (Illus.). (gr. 3-12). 1994. PLB 24.95 (*0-7933-5722-5*); pap. 14.95 (*0-7933-5723-3*); computer disk 29.95 (*0-7933-5724-1*) Gallopade Pub Group.

—Avast, Ye Slobs! Alabama Pirate Trivia. (Illus.). (gr. 3-12). 1994. PLB 24.95 (*0-7933-0088-6*); pap. 14.95 (*0-7933-0087-8*); computer disk 29.95 (*0-7933-0089-4*) Gallopade Pub Group.

—The Beast of the Alabama Bed & Breakfast. (Illus.). (gr. 3-12). 1994. PLB 24.95 (*0-7933-1332-5*); pap. 14.95 (*0-7933-1331-7*); computer disk 29.95 (*0-7933-1330-9*) Gallopade Pub Group.

—Bow Wow! Alabama Dogs in History, Mystery, Legend, Lore, Humor & More! (Illus.). (gr. 3-12). 1994. PLB 24.95 (*0-7933-3467-5*); pap. 14.95 (*0-7933-3468-3*); computer disk 29.95 (*0-7933-3469-1*) Gallopade Pub Group.

—Chill Out: Scary Alabama Tales Based on Frightening Alabama Truths. (Illus.). 1994. lib. bdg. 24.95 (*0-7933-4657-6*); pap. 14.95 (*0-7933-4658-4*); disk 29.95 (*0-7933-4659-2*) Gallopade Pub Group.

—Christopher Columbus Comes to Alabama! Includes Reproducible Activities for Kids! (Illus.). (gr. 3-12). 1994. PLB 24.95 (*0-7933-3620-1*); pap. 14.95 (*0-7933-3621-X*); computer disk 29.95 (*0-7933-3622-8*) Gallopade Pub Group.

—The Hard-to-Believe-But-True! Book of Alabama History, Mystery, Trivia, Legend, Lore, Humor & More. (Illus.). (gr. 3-12). 1994. PLB 24.95 (*0-7933-0085-1*); pap. 14.95 (*0-7933-0084-3*); computer disk 29.95 (*0-7933-0086-X*) Gallopade Pub Group.

—If My Alabama Mama Ran the World! (Illus.). (gr. 3-12). 1994. PLB 24.95 (*0-7933-1335-X*); pap. 14.95 (*0-7933-1336-8*); computer disk 29.95 (*0-7933-1337-6*) Gallopade Pub Group.

—Jurassic Ark! Alabama Dinosaurs & Other Prehistoric Creatures. (gr. k-12). 1994. PLB 24.95 (*0-7933-7428-6*); pap. 14.95 (*0-7933-7429-4*); computer disk 29.95 (*0-7933-7430-8*) Gallopade Pub Group.

—Let's Quilt Alabama & Stuff It Topographically! (Illus.). (gr. 3-12). 1994. PLB 24.95 (*1-55609-462-0*); pap. 14.95 (*1-55609-073-0*); computer disk 29.95 (*0-7933-1328-7*) Gallopade Pub Group.

—Let's Quilt Our Alabama County. 1994. lib. bdg. 24.95 (*0-7933-6936-3*); pap. text ed. 14.95 (*0-7933-6935-5*); disk 29.95 (*0-7933-6937-1*) Gallopade Pub Group.

—Let's Quilt Our Alabama Town. 1994. lib. bdg. 24.95 (*0-7933-6933-9*); pap. text ed. 14.95 (*0-7933-6932-0*); disk 29.95 (*0-7933-6934-7*) Gallopade Pub Group.

—Meow! Alabama Cats in History, Mystery, Legend, Lore, Humor & More! (Illus.). (gr. 3-12). 1994. PLB 24.95 (*0-7933-3314-8*); pap. 14.95 (*0-7933-3315-6*); computer disk 29.95 (*0-7933-3316-4*) Gallopade Pub Group.

—My First Book about Alabama. (gr. k-4). 1994. PLB 24.95 (*0-7933-5569-9*); pap. 14.95 (*0-7933-5570-2*); computer disk 29.95 (*0-7933-5571-0*) Gallopade Pub Group.

—Uncle Rebus: Alabama Picture Stories for Computer Kids. (Illus.). (gr. k-3). 1994. PLB 24.95 (*0-7933-4504-9*); pap. 14.95 (*0-7933-4505-7*); disk 29.95 (*0-7933-4506-5*) Gallopade Pub Group.

Thompson, Kathleen. Alabama. LC 87-26486. 48p. (gr. 3 up). 1988. 19.97 (*0-8174-4613-3*) Raintree Steck-V.

Tompkins, Susie P. Cotton-Patch Schoolhouse. LC 91-23331. 224p. (Orig.). 1992. pap. 19.95t (*0-8173-0563-7*) U of Ala Pr.

Townsend, Sandra S. The Old Jail Remembers Tuscaloosa. (Illus.). 44p. (Orig.). (gr. 5-12). 1987. pap. 4.50 (*0-943487-03-X*) Sevgo Pr.

Walter, Eugene. Mobile Mardi Gras Annual 1948, Vol. 1, No. 2. Plummer, Cameron, ed. Walter, Eugene, illus. 32p. (gr. 7 up). 1948. pap. 10.00 (*0-940882-05-1*) HB Pubns.

ALABAMA–FICTION

Blackshear, Helen F. The Creek Captives: And Other Alabama Stories. Raymond, Thomas, illus. 112p. (Orig.). (gr. 4-9). 1990. pap. 9.95 (*0-9622815-2-2*) Black Belt Pr.

Brown, Faye. Chinch Bugs, Chinky Pins, & Chinie-Berry Beads. Brown, Trillie, illus. 191p. (Orig.). 1990. pap. 9.95 (*0-943487-24-2*) Sevgo Pr.

Hager, Betty. Marcie & the Monster of the Bayou. LC 93-44490. 112p. (gr. 3-7). 1994. pap. 4.99 (*0-310-38431-1*) Zondervan.

—Miss Tilly & the Haunted Mansion. 112p. (gr. 3-7). 1994. pap. 4.99 (*0-310-38411-7*) Zondervan.

—Old Jake & the Pirate's Treasure. Dawkins, Ron, illus. LC 93-44489. 112p. (gr. 3-7). 1994. pap. 4.99 (*0-310-38401-X*) Zondervan.

Johnson, Allen, Jr. Picker McClikker. Hanson, Stephen, illus. (gr. k-3). 1993. 16.95 (*1-878561-20-0*) Seacoast AL.

ALAMO–SEIGE, 1836

Carter, Alden R. Last Stand at the Alamo. LC 89-22688. (ps-3). 1990. PLB 12.90 (*0-531-10888-0*) Watts.

Fisher, Leonard E. The Alamo. Fisher, Leonard E., illus. LC 86-46204. 64p. (gr. 3-7). 1987. reinforced bdg. 14.95 (*0-8234-0646-6*) Holiday.

Ragsdale, Crystal S. The Women & Children of the Alamo. LC 93-41998. 1994. 21.95 (*1-880510-11-1*); signed ltd. ed. 60.00 (*1-880510-13-8*); pap. 14.95 (*1-880510-12-X*) State House Pr.

Richards, Norman. The Story of the Alamo. LC 70-100698. (Illus.). 32p. (gr. 3-6). 1970. 12.30 (*0-516-04601-2*); pap. 3.95 (*0-516-44601-0*) Childrens.

Silverstein, Herma. The Alamo. LC 91-42461. (Illus.). 72p. (gr. 4 up). 1992. text ed. 14.95 RSBE (*0-87518-502-9*, Dillon) Macmillan Child Grp.

Sorensen, Lynda. The Alamo. LC 94-7054. 1994. write for info. (*1-55916-049-7*) Rourke Bk Co.

Wade, L. Alamo: Battle of Honor & Freedom. 1991. 11.95s.p. (*0-86592-470-8*) Rourke Enter.

ALAMO–SEIGE, 1836–FICTION

Cousins, Margaret. The Boy in the Alamo. Eggenhofer, Nicholas, illus. LC 83-72585. 180p. (gr. 5-7). 1983. pap. 5.95 (*0-931722-26-8*) Corona Pub.

Hoobler, Dorothy & Hoobler, Thomas. A Promise at the Alamo. Hewitson, Jennifer, illus. 64p. (gr. 4-6). 1992. 5.95 (*0-382-24154-1*); lib. bdg. 7.95 (*0-382-24147-9*); pap. 3.95 (*0-382-24352-8*) Silver Burdett Pr.

Jakes, John. Susanna of the Alamo: A True Story. Bacon, Paul, illus. LC 85-27143. 32p. (gr. 1-5). 1986. 13.95 (*0-15-200592-7*, Gulliver Bks) HarBrace.

Rice, James. Texas Jack at the Alamo. Rice, James, illus. LC 88-31691. 40p. 1989. 12.95 (*0-88289-725-X*) Pelican.

Wheatly, Mark. Build the Alamo. Eakin, Ed, ed. (Illus.). 32p. (gr. 4-5). 1989. 10.95 (*0-89015-721-9*) Sunbelt Media.

ALASKA

Carole Marsh Alaska Books, 44 bks. 1994. lib. bdg. 1027.80 set (*0-7933-1275-2*); pap. 587.80 set (*0-7933-5124-3*) Gallopade Pub Group.

Carpenter, Allan. Alaska. LC 78-12419. (Illus.). 96p. (gr. 4 up). 1979. PLB 16.95 (*0-516-04102-9*) Childrens.

Cobb, Vicki. This Place Is Cold. Lavallee, Barbara, illus. (gr. 2-4). 1989. 14.95 (*0-8027-6852-0*); PLB 13.85 (*0-8027-6853-9*) Walker & Co.

—This Place Is Cold. Lavallee, Barbara, illus. 32p. (gr. 2-5). 1990. pap. 7.95 (*0-8027-7340-0*) Walker & Co.

Crisman, Ruth. Racing the Iditarod Trail. LC 92-25870. (Illus.). 72p. (gr. 5 up). 1993. text ed. 14.95 RSBE (*0-87518-523-1*, Dillon) Macmillan Child Grp.

Dunmire, Marj. National Parks of Alaska. (Illus.). 48p. (gr. 2-8). 1991. pap. 4.95 (*0-942559-07-X*) Pegasus Graphics.

Fradin, Dennis. Alaska: In Words & Pictures. Ulm, Robert, illus. LC 77-4353. 48p. (gr. 2-5). 1977. PLB 12.95 (*0-516-03902-4*) Childrens.

Fradin, Dennis B. Alaska - From Sea to Shining Sea. (Illus.). 64p. (gr. 3-5). 1993. PLB 21.27 (*0-516-03802-8*) Childrens.

Gill, Shelley R. Thunderfeet, Alaska's Dinosaurs & Other Prehistoric Critters. (Illus.). 36p. (Orig.). (gr. k-4). 1988. pap. 11.95 incl. cass. (*0-934007-03-9*) Paws Four Pub.

Heinrichs, Ann. Alaska. LC 90-33847. (Illus.). 144p. (gr. 4 up). 1990. PLB 20.55 (*0-516-00448-4*) Childrens.

—Alaska. 201p. 1993. text ed. 15.40 (*1-56956-127-3*) W A T Braille.

Hiscock, Bruce. Tundra: The Arctic Land. Hiscock, Bruce, illus. LC 85-28769. 144p. (gr. 3 up). 1986. SBE 14.95 (*0-689-31219-9*, Atheneum Child Bk) Macmillan Child Grp.

Holen, Susan D. Alaska Wildlife: A Coloring Book. Holen, Anne M., ed. Holen, Betsy L., illus. 48p. (gr. 3-8). 1988. pap. 4.95 (*0-922127-00-X*) Paisley Pub.

—Alaska's Wild Coast. Holen, Anne M., ed. Holen, Betsy L., illus. 48p. (Orig.). (gr. 3-8). 1995. pap. 4.95 (*0-922127-02-6*) Paisley Pub.

Johnston, Joyce. Alaska. LC 93-25401. (gr. 5 up). 1994. lib. bdg. write for info. (*0-8225-2735-9*) Lerner Pubns.

Kramer, S. A. Adventure in Alaska. 80p. (Orig.). (gr. 2-7). 1993. PLB 9.99 (*0-679-94511-3*, Bullseye Bks); pap. 2.99 (*0-679-84511-9*, Bullseye Bks) Random Bks Yng Read.

Madison, Kathy. Fun Guide to Anchorage. Lauzen, Elizabeth, ed. Burrus, Sue, illus. 32p. (Orig.). (gr. 1-6). 1987. pap. 3.50 incl. wkbk. (*0-942553-00-4*) Madison Aves.

Marsh, Carole. Alaska & Other State Greats (Biographies) (Illus.). (gr. 3-12). 1994. PLB 24.95 (*1-55609-483-3*); pap. 14.95 (*1-55609-482-5*); computer disk 29.95 (*0-7933-1354-6*) Gallopade Pub Group.

—Alaska Bandits, Bushwackers, Outlaws, Crooks, Devils, Ghosts, Desperadoes & Other Assorted & Sundry Characters! (Illus.). (gr. 3-12). 1994. PLB 24.95 (*0-7933-0094-0*); pap. 14.95 (*0-7933-0093-2*); computer disk 29.95 (*0-7933-0095-9*) Gallopade Pub Group.

—Alaska Classic Christmas Trivia: Stories, Recipes, Activities, Legends, Lore & More! (Illus.). (gr. 3-12). 1994. PLB 24.95 (*0-7933-0097-5*); pap. 14.95 (*0-7933-0096-7*); computer disk 29.95 (*0-7933-0098-3*) Gallopade Pub Group.
—Alaska Coastales. (Illus.). (gr. 3-12). 1994. PLB 24.95 (*1-55609-479-5*); pap. 14.95 (*1-55609-478-7*); computer disk 29.95 (*0-7933-1353-8*) Gallopade Pub Group.
—Alaska Coastales. 1994. lib. bdg. 24.95 (*0-7933-7266-6*) Gallopade Pub Group.
—Alaska "Crinkum-Crankum" A Funny Word Book about Our State. (Illus.). 1994. lib. bdg. 24.95 (*0-7933-4813-7*); pap. 14.95 (*0-7933-4814-5*); disk 29.95 (*0-7933-4815-3*) Gallopade Pub Group.
—Alaska Dingbats! Bk. 1: A Fun Book of Games, Stories, Activities & More about Our State That's All in Code! for You to Decipher. (Illus.). (gr. 3-12). 1994. PLB 24.95 (*0-7933-3776-3*); pap. 14.95 (*0-7933-3777-1*); computer disk 29.95 (*0-7933-3778-X*) Gallopade Pub Group.
—Alaska Festival Fun for Kids! (Illus.). (gr. 3-12). 1994. lib. bdg. 24.95 (*0-7933-3929-4*); pap. 14.95 (*0-7933-3930-8*); disk 29.95 (*0-7933-3931-6*) Gallopade Pub Group.
—The Alaska Hot Air Balloon Mystery. (Illus.). (gr. 2-9). 1994. 24.95 (*0-7933-2327-4*); pap. 14.95 (*0-7933-2328-2*); computer disk 29.95 (*0-7933-2329-0*) Gallopade Pub Group.
—Alaska Jeopardy! Answers & Questions about Our State! (Illus.). (gr. 3-12). 1994. PLB 24.95 (*0-7933-4082-9*); pap. 14.95 (*0-7933-4083-7*); computer disk 29.95 (*0-7933-4084-5*) Gallopade Pub Group.
—Alaska "Jography" A Fun Run Thru Our State! (Illus.). (gr. 3-12). 1994. PLB 24.95 (*1-55609-473-6*); pap. 14.95 (*1-55609-472-8*); computer disk 29.95 (*0-7933-1343-0*) Gallopade Pub Group.
—Alaska Kid's Cookbook: Recipes, How-to, History, Lore & More! (Illus.). (gr. 3-12). 1994. PLB 24.95 (*0-7933-0106-8*); pap. 14.95 (*0-7933-0105-X*); computer disk 29.95 (*0-7933-0107-6*) Gallopade Pub Group.
—Alaska Quiz Bowl Crash Course! (Illus.). (gr. 3-12). 1994. PLB 24.95 (*1-55609-481-7*); pap. 14.95 (*1-55609-480-9*); computer disk 29.95 (*0-7933-1352-X*) Gallopade Pub Group.
—Alaska Rollercoasters! (Illus.). (gr. 3-12). 1994. PLB 24.95 (*0-7933-5227-4*); pap. 14.95 (*0-7933-5228-2*); computer disk 29.95 (*0-7933-5229-0*) Gallopade Pub Group.
—Alaska School Trivia: An Amazing & Fascinating Look at Our State's Teachers, Schools & Students! (Illus.). (gr. 3-12). 1994. PLB 24.95 (*0-7933-0103-3*); pap. 14.95 (*0-7933-0102-5*); computer disk 29.95 (*0-7933-0104-1*) Gallopade Pub Group.
—Alaska Silly Basketball Sportsmysteries, Vol. I. (Illus.). (gr. 3-12). 1994. PLB 24.95 (*0-7933-0100-9*); pap. 14.95 (*0-7933-0099-1*); computer disk 29.95 (*0-7933-0101-7*) Gallopade Pub Group.
—Alaska Silly Basketball Sportsmysteries, Vol. II. (Illus.). (gr. 3-12). 1994. PLB 24.95 (*0-7933-1565-4*); pap. 14.95 (*0-7933-1566-2*); computer disk 29.95 (*0-7933-1567-0*) Gallopade Pub Group.
—Alaska Silly Football Sportsmysteries, Vol. I. (Illus.). (gr. 3-12). 1994. PLB 24.95 (*1-55609-477-9*); pap. 14.95 (*1-55609-476-0*); computer disk 29.95 (*0-7933-1345-7*) Gallopade Pub Group.
—Alaska Silly Football Sportsmysteries, Vol. II. (Illus.). (gr. 3-12). 1994. PLB 24.95 (*0-7933-1346-5*); pap. 14.95 (*0-7933-1347-3*); computer disk 29.95 (*0-7933-1348-1*) Gallopade Pub Group.
—Alaska Silly Trivia! (Illus.). (gr. 3-12). 1994. PLB 24.95 (*1-55609-471-X*); pap. 14.95 (*1-55609-470-1*); computer disk 29.95 (*0-7933-1342-2*) Gallopade Pub Group.
—Alaska Timeline: A Chronology of Alaska History, Mystery, Trivia, Legend, Lore & More. (Illus.). (gr. 3-12). 1994. PLB 24.95 (*0-7933-5878-7*); pap. 14.95 (*0-7933-5879-5*); computer disk 29.95 (*0-7933-5880-9*) Gallopade Pub Group.
—Alaska's (Most Devastating!) Disasters & (Most Calamitous!) Catastrophies! (Illus.). (gr. 3-12). 1994. PLB 24.95 (*0-7933-0091-6*); pap. 14.95 (*0-7933-0090-8*); computer disk 29.95 (*0-7933-0092-4*) Gallopade Pub Group.
—Alaska's Unsolved Mysteries (& Their "Solutions") Includes Scientific Information & Other Activities for Students. (Illus.). (gr. 3-12). 1994. PLB 24.95 (*0-7933-5725-X*); pap. 14.95 (*0-7933-5726-8*); computer disk 29.95 (*0-7933-5727-6*) Gallopade Pub Group.
—Avast, Ye Slobs! Alaska Pirate Trivia. (Illus.). (gr. 3-12). 1994. PLB 24.95 (*0-7933-0112-2*); pap. 14.95 (*0-7933-0111-4*); computer disk 29.95 (*0-7933-0113-0*) Gallopade Pub Group.
—The Best of the Alaska Bed & Breakfast. (Illus.). (gr. 3-12). 1994. PLB 24.95 (*0-7933-1349-X*); pap. 14.95 (*0-7933-1350-3*); computer disk 29.95 (*0-7933-1351-1*) Gallopade Pub Group.
—Bow Wow! Alaska Dogs in History, Mystery, Legend, Lore, Humor & More! (Illus.). (gr. 3-12). 1994. PLB 24.95 (*0-7933-3470-5*); pap. 14.95 (*0-7933-3471-3*); computer disk 29.95 (*0-7933-3472-1*) Gallopade Pub Group.
—Christopher Columbus Comes to Alaska! Includes Reproducible Activities for Kids! (Illus.). (gr. 3-12). 1994. PLB 24.95 (*0-7933-3623-6*); pap. 14.95 (*0-7933-3624-4*); computer disk 29.95 (*0-7933-3625-2*) Gallopade Pub Group.
—The Hard-to-Believe-But-True! Book of Alaska History, Mystery, Trivia, Legend, Lore, Humor & More. (Illus.). (gr. 3-12). 1994. PLB 24.95 (*0-7933-0109-2*); pap. 14.95 (*0-7933-0108-4*); computer disk 29.95 (*0-7933-0110-6*) Gallopade Pub Group.
—If My Alaska Mama Ran the World! (Illus.). (gr. 3-12). 1994. PLB 24.95 (*0-7933-1355-4*); pap. 14.95 (*0-7933-1356-2*); computer disk 29.95 (*0-7933-1357-0*) Gallopade Pub Group.
—Jurassic Ark! Alaska Dinosaurs & Other Prehistoric Creatures. (gr. k-12). 1994. PLB 24.95 (*0-7933-7431-6*); pap. 14.95 (*0-7933-7432-4*); computer disk 29.95 (*0-7933-7433-2*) Gallopade Pub Group.
—Let's Quilt Alaska & Stuff It Topographically! (Illus.). (gr. 3-12). 1994. PLB 24.95 (*1-55609-475-2*); pap. 14.95 (*1-55609-094-3*); computer disk 29.95 (*0-7933-1344-9*) Gallopade Pub Group.
—Let's Quilt Our Alaska County. 1994. lib. bdg. 24.95 (*0-7933-7116-3*); pap. text ed. 14.95 (*0-7933-7117-1*); disk 29.95 (*0-7933-7118-X*) Gallopade Pub Group.
—Let's Quilt Our Alaska Town. 1994. lib. bdg. 24.95 (*0-685-60854-9*); pap. text ed. 14.95 (*0-7933-6967-3*); disk 29.95 (*0-7933-6968-1*) Gallopade Pub Group.
—Meow! Alaska Cats in History, Mystery, Legend, Lore, Humor & More! (Illus.). (gr. 3-12). 1994. PLB 24.95 (*0-7933-3317-2*); pap. 14.95 (*0-7933-3318-0*); computer disk 29.95 (*0-7933-3319-9*) Gallopade Pub Group.
—My First Book about Alaska. (gr. k-4). 1994. PLB 24.95 (*0-7933-5572-9*); pap. 14.95 (*0-7933-5573-7*); computer disk 29.95 (*0-7933-5574-5*) Gallopade Pub Group.
—Uncle Rebus: Alaska Picture Stories for Computer Kids. (Illus.). (gr. k-3). 1994. PLB 24.95 (*0-7933-4507-3*); pap. 14.95 (*0-7933-4508-1*); disk 29.95 (*0-7933-4509-X*) Gallopade Pub Group.
Murphy, Claire R. A Child's Alaska. Mason, Charles, photos by. LC 93-48164. (Illus.). 48p. (gr. 4-10). 1994. 14.95 (*0-88240-457-1*) Alaska Northwest.
Nault, Andy. Staying Alive in Alaska's Wild. Loftin, Tee, ed. (Illus.). 224p. (Orig.). (gr. 5 up). 1980. pap. 8.95 (*0-934812-01-2*) Tee Loftin.
Oberle, Joseph G. Anchorage. LC 89-26068. (Illus.). 60p. (gr. 3 up). 1990. text ed. 13.95 RSBE (*0-87518-420-0*, Dillon) Macmillan Child Grp.
O'Meara, Jan. Kids' Guide to Common Alaska Critters. O'Meara, Michael, illus. 32p. (Orig.). 1994. pap. text ed. 7.95 (*0-9621543-3-4*) Wizard Works.
Postell, Alice E. Where Did the Reindeer Come From? Alaska Experience the First Fifty Years. York, Susan P., ed. DeArmond, Robert N., frwd. by. LC 90-146. (Illus.). 144p. (gr. 9 up). 1990. write for info. (*0-9626090-0-5*) Amaknak Pr.
Puhalo, Lazar. Innokenty of Alaska. Novakshonoff, V., illus. 86p. (Orig.). (gr. 8 up). 1986. pap. 5.00 (*0-913026-86-7*) Synaxis Pr.
Seibert, Patricia. Mush! Across Alaska in the World's Longest Sled-Dog Race. Ellis, Jan D., illus. LC 91-38883. 32p. (gr. 2-4). 1992. PLB 15.40 (*1-56294-053-8*); pap. 5.95 (*1-56294-705-2*) Millbrook Pr.
Shields, Mary. Can Dogs Talk, Vol. 1. Gates, Donna, illus. 32p. (Orig.). (ps-3). 1991. pap. 10.00 (*0-9618348-1-1*); incl. tape 13.00 (*0-9618348-4-6*); write for info. Pyrola Pub.
Standiford, Natalie. The Bravest Dog Ever: The True Story of Balto. Cook, Donald, tr. LC 89-3465. (Illus.). 47p. (Orig.). (gr. 1-3). 1989. pap. 3.50 (*0-394-89695-5*) Random Bks Yng Read.
Stone, Lynn M. Alaska, the Great Land. LC 93-42650. 1994. write for info. (*1-55916-025-X*) Rourke Bk Co.
—Alaska's National Lands. LC 93-43982. 1994. write for info. (*1-55916-024-1*) Rourke Bk Co.
—People of Alaska. LC 93-43981. 1994. write for info. (*1-55916-029-2*) Rourke Bk Co.
—Products of Alaska. LC 93-40429. 1994. write for info. (*1-55916-027-6*) Rourke Bk Co.
—Wildlife of Alaska. LC 93-42649. 1994. write for info. (*1-55916-026-8*) Rourke Bk Co.
—Wonders of Alaska. LC 93-42648. 1994. write for info. (*1-55916-028-4*) Rourke Bk Co.
Thompson, Kathleen. Alaska. LC 87-26487. 48p. (gr. 3 up). 1988. 19.97 (*0-8174-4710-5*) Raintree Steck-V.
Warbelow, Willy L. Empire on Ice. Clark, Marvin, ed. (Illus.). 256p. (Orig.). (gr. 9 up). 1990. pap. 19.95 (*0-937708-21-6*) Great Northwest.
Yarber, Yvonne & Choy, Carol E. The Athabaskans: People of the Boreal Forest. Dickey, Terry P. & Smetzer, Mary B., eds. 39p. (Orig.). (gr. 7-12). 1983. tchr's. guide 4.00 (*0-931163-10-2*); pap. 9.95 (*0-931163-09-9*) U Alaska Museum.

ALASKA–FICTION

Arnold, Marti. Alaska, Uncle Jim & Me. Lesko, Marian, ed. Dessereau, April & Present, David, illus. 146p. (Orig.). (gr. 6 up). 1983. pap. 5.95 (*0-912683-00-7*) Fireweed.
Carey, Mary. Texas Brat in Alaska: The Cat Train Kid. (Illus.). 96p. (gr. 5-7). 1991. 10.95 (*0-89015-831-2*) Sunbelt Media.
DeClements, Barthe. The Bite of the Gold Bug: A Story of the Alaskan Gold Rush. Andreasen, Dan, illus. 64p. (gr. 2-6). 1992. 13.00 (*0-670-84495-0*) Viking Child Bks.
Dixon, Ann. The Sleeping Lady. Smith, Carolyn, ed. Johns, Elizabeth, illus. 32p. (ps-5). 1994. 14.95 (*0-88240-444-X*) Alaska Northwest.
Herndon, Ernest. Smugglers on Grizzly Mountain. 144p. 1994. pap. 4.99 (*0-310-38281-5*) Zondervan.
London, Jack. Call of the Wild. (gr. 6 up). 1964. pap. 2.25 (*0-8049-0030-2*, CL-30) Airmont.
—Call of the Wild. 128p. (gr. 9-12). 1990. pap. 2.50 (*0-8125-0432-1*) Tor Bks.
—The Call of the Wild. (gr. 8). 1991. pap. write for info. (*0-663-56265-1*) Silver Burdett Pr.
—Jack London's Stories of the North. 256p. (gr. 4 up). 1989. pap. 2.95 (*0-590-44229-5*) Scholastic Inc.
—White Fang. (gr. 6 up). 1964. pap. 2.50 (*0-8049-0036-1*, CL-36) Airmont.
—White Fang: Illustrated Classics. Arneson, D. J., ed. Walker, Karen, illus. 128p. (Orig.). 1990. pap. 2.95 (*0-942025-84-9*) Kidsbks.
London, Jack, et al. The Call of the Wild. (Illus.). 52p. Date not set. pap. 4.95 (*1-57209-010-3*) Classics Int Ent.
Morey, Walt. Gentle Ben. Schoenherr, John, illus. LC 65-21290. 192p. (gr. 4 up). 1965. 12.95 (*0-525-30429-0*, DCB) Dutton Child Bks.
—Kavik, the Wolf Dog. Parnall, Peter, illus. LC 68-24727. (gr. 5-9). 1977. 14.95 (*0-525-33093-3*, DCB); (DCB) Dutton Child Bks.
Murphy, Claire R. To the Summit. 160p. (gr. 7 up). 1992. 15.00 (*0-525-67383-0*, Lodestar Bks) Dutton Child Bks.

Prince, Michael. The Totems of Seldovia. 144p. (gr. 5-6). 1994. pap. 8.95 (*0-9642662-1-0*) Sundog Pubng. Michael Prince writes adventure stories for children aged approximately 9 to 13. His stories take place in Alaska locales. He features children in positive working relationships with adults while still showing them with a precocious wisdom that endears readers to the characters. Even though his stories are fiction, he provides substantial information on human nature, wildlife & the natural sciences. His topics are well researched & he's achieved local success within schools in his hometown of Anchorage, Alaska. Instructors have used his books as classroom educational material. Sundog Publishing's books display the "Made in Alaska" emblem. This denotes that all facets of production were done within Alaska. We proudly use children as artists & provide short biographies of them as well as the author. All books are printed & assembled by Alaska Specialized Education & Training Services (ASETS), a training & employment program for Alaskans with substantial disabilities. THE TOTEMS OF SELDOVIA is a fast paced adventure tale of three children who go on a trail of adventure seeking an elusive treasure from an old mariner's map. The clues lie in the uniquely painted fire hydrants & landmarks located in their hometown of Seldovia, Alaska.
Publisher Provided Annotation.

Rand, Gloria. Prince William. Rand, Ted, illus. LC 91-25180. 32p. (gr. 1-3). 1992. 14.95 (*0-8050-1841-7*, Bks Young Read) H Holt & Co.
—Salty Takes Off. Rand, Ted, illus. LC 90-46371. 32p. (ps-2). 1991. 14.95 (*0-8050-1159-5*, Bks Young Read) H Holt & Co.
Ritchie, Jo-An. Jonie in Alaska. Wheeler, Gerald, ed. 128p. (Orig.). (gr. 8 up). 1985. pap. 5.50 (*0-8280-0250-9*) Review & Herald.
Roe, JoAnn. Marco the Manx Series, 3 bks. Runestrand, Meredith & Mayo, Steve, illus. (gr. k-5). Set. write for info. (*0-931551-06-4*); Fisherman Cat, 1988. PLB 10.95 (*0-931551-02-1*); Alaska Cat. PLB 10.95 (*0-931551-05-6*); Castaway Cat. pap. 5.95 (*0-931551-03-X*); Fisherman Cat, 1988. pap. 6.95 (*0-931551-01-3*); Alaska Cat. pap. 6.95 (*0-931551-04-8*) Montevista Pr.
Schurfranz, Vivian. Megan, No. 16. 224p. (Orig.). (gr. 7 up). 1986. pap. 2.75 (*0-590-41468-2*) Scholastic Inc.

Shields, Mary. The Alaskan Happy Dog Trilogy: Can Dogs Talk?, Loving a Happy Dog, Secret Messages--Training a Happy Dog, 3 vols. Gates, Donna, illus. 32p. (ps-3). 1993. Set. pap. 30.00 (*0-9618348-2-X*) Pyrola Pub. THE ALASKAN HAPPY DOG TRILOGY, $30.00, ISBN 0-9618348-2-X, CAN DOGS TALK?, $10.00, ISBN 0-9618348-1-1, with audio tape, $13.00, ISBN 0-9618348-4-6, LOVING A HAPPY DOG, $12.00, ISBN 0-9618348-3-8, SECRET MESSAGES--TRAINING A HAPPY DOG, $12.00, ISBN 0-9618348-6-2. In the first volume, CAN DOGS TALK? Rita & Ryan answer their own question with the help of an Alaskan dog musher, a book, a team of friendly huskies & a lost puppy. In volume two, LOVING A HAPPY DOG, the kids learn the responsibilities of loving & caring for a Dog, including the understanding of a dog's life span. A pull-out puzzle is included. The final volume, SECRET MESSAGES--TRAINING A HAPPY DOG, unfolds as Rita, Ryan & Happy discover messages along the trail while hiking to Mary's cabin. The kids learn how to train their dog, & another important lesson--it's okay to ask for help. Each volume stands alone, but the complete trilogy gives the young reader a well-rounded introduction into enjoying the companionship of a dog. The author, Mary Shields, lives in Fairbanks, Alaska, where she raises sled dogs for companions & wilderness travelers. Mary was the first woman to finish the Iditarod. Donna Gates creates her fine art images of sled dogs & interior Alaskan wildlife at her home near Denali Park, Alaska. Pyrola Publishing, P.O. Box 80961, Fairbanks, AK 99708. 907-455-6469 (Alaskan time please). *Publisher Provided Annotation.*

TallMountain, Mary. Green March Moons. Senungetuk, Joseph E., illus. LC 87-6018. 32p. (Orig.). (gr. 6 up). 1987. pap. 7.95 (*0-938678-10-8*) New Seed.
Tjepkema, Edith R. Alaskan Paradise. 115p. (Orig.). (gr. 8 up). 1989. pap. 4.50 (*0-9620280-1-0*) Northland Pr.
Van Gorden, Charles L. Olive, Char, Lizzie & Izzie: A Sea Otter Story. Moler, Kathy, illus. 24p. (Orig.). (gr. 1-4). 1991. pap. 4.95 saddle-stitched (*1-56167-050-2*) Am Literary Pr.
Wakeland, Marcia A. The Big Fish: An Alaskan Fairy Tale. Sagan, Alexander, illus. 32p. (ps-4). 1993. 14.95 (*0-9635083-1-8*) Misty Mtn.
Wittanen, Etolin. Auke Lake Tales. Alenov, Nick & Alenov, Lydia, illus. 53p. (Orig.). (gr. 3-6). 1986. pap. 5.00 (*0-911523-05-7*) Synaxis Pr.

ALASKA–HISTORY

Barry, Mary J. Seward, Alaska: A History of the Gateway City, Vol. II: 1914-1923. Barry, Richard E., illus. 225p. (gr. 8 up). 1993. pap. 25.00 (*0-9617009-2-0*) M J P Barry.
Bowkett, Gerald E. Reaching for a Star: The Final Campaign for Alaska Statehood. Matson, Sue, ed. Stevens, Ted, intro. by. LC 89-1563. (Illus.). 162p. (Orig.). (gr. 9-12). 1989. 22.95 (*0-945397-04-6*); pap. 14.95 (*0-945397-05-4*) Epicenter Pr.
Calvin, Margaret. An Alaskan A B C Coloring Book. Griffith, Sandy, illus. 32p. (Orig.). (ps-4). 1986. pap. 3.95 (*0-9615529-3-X*) Old Harbor Pr.
Hedrick, Basil & Savage, Susan. Steamboats on the Chena: The Founding & Development of Fairbanks, Alaska. LC 87-83742. (Orig.). (gr. 9-12). 1988. pap. 9.95 (*0-945397-00-3*) Epicenter Pr.
Herda, D. J. Historical America: The Northwestern States. LC 92-16312. (Illus.). 64p. (gr. 5-8). 1993. PLB 15.40 (*1-56294-122-4*) Millbrook Pr.
Madison, Curt & Yarber, Yvonne Y. Edgar Kallands-A Biography: Kaltag. 64p. (Orig.). 1983. pap. 6.95 (*0-910871-00-0*) Spirit Mount Pr.
Marsh, Carole. The Alaska Mystery Van Takes Off! Book 1: Handicapped Alaska Kids Sneak Off on a Big Adventure. (Illus.). (gr. 3-12). 1994. 24.95 (*0-7933-4967-2*); pap. 14.95 (*0-7933-4968-0*); computer disk 29.95 (*0-7933-4969-9*) Gallopade Pub Group.
—Chill Out: Scary Alaska Tales Based on Frightening Alaska Truths. (Illus.). 1994. lib. bdg. 24.95 (*0-7933-4660-6*); pap. 14.95 (*0-7933-4661-4*); disk 29.95 (*0-7933-4662-2*) Gallopade Pub Group.
Miller, Luree & Miller, Scott. Alaska: Pioneer Stories of a Twentieth-Century Frontier. LC 91-10744. (Illus.). 144p. (gr. 6 up). 1991. 14.95 (*0-525-65050-4*, Cobblehill Bks) Dutton Child Bks.
Puckett, Christine S. & Barnes, Joe. A Panorama of Northeast Alabama & Etowah County: Lookout Mountain Meets the Coosa. 2nd ed. (Illus.). 136p. (Orig.). (gr. 4 up). 1992. pap. 8.95 (*0-9633116-0-3*) Starr Pub AL.

ALBERTA–FICTION

London, Jack. The Call of the Wild. new ed. Platt, Kin, ed. Carrillo, Fred, illus. LC 73-75461. 64p. (Orig.). (gr. 5-10). 1973. pap. 2.95 (*0-88301-095-X*) Pendulum Pr.
—The Call of the Wild. Nordlicht, Lillian, adapted by. & adapted by. LC 79-24464. (Illus.). 48p. (gr. 4 up). Pub. 1980. PLB 20.70 (*0-8172-1656-1*) Raintree Steck-V.
Sohl, Marcia & Dackerman, Gerald. The Call of the Wild Student Activity Book. (Illus.). 16p. (gr. 4-10). 1976. pap. 1.25 (*0-88301-182-4*) Pendulum Pr.

ALCINDOR, LEW, 1947-

see Abdul-Jabbar, Kareem, 1947-

ALCOHOLICS

see Alcoholism

ALCOHOLISM

Abbey, Nancy & Wagman, Ellen. Saying No to Alcohol. Nelson, Mary, ed. (Illus.). 72p. 1987. tchrs. ed. 11.95 (*0-941816-37-0*) ETR Assocs.
Anderson, Peggy K. Coming Home: Children's Stories for Adult Children of Alcoholics. Detterbeck, Nancy, illus. LC 87-73388. 136p. (Orig.). (gr. 5-10). 1988. pap. 7.95 (*0-934125-06-6*) Glen Abbey Bks.
Babor, Thomas. Alcohol: Customs & Rituals. updated ed. (Illus.). (gr. 5 up). 1992. lib. bdg. 19.95 (*0-685-52235-0*) Chelsea Hse.
Benton, John W. New Hope Series, 10 bks. 2004p. (gr. 3-12). Date not set. Set. ten pack 35.00 (*0-9635411-1-0*) J Benton Bks.
Berger, Gilda. Alcoholism & the Family. LC 93-10898. (Illus.). 128p. (gr. 7-12). 1993. PLB 13.40 (*0-531-12548-3*) Watts.
Bollendorf, Robert. Sober Spring. LC 91-17474. 176p. 1991. pap. 5.99 (*0-8066-2539-2*, 9-2539) Augsburg Fortress.
Bosworth, et al. Alcohol & Other Drugs. (gr. 7-12). Date not set. incl. software 120.00 (*0-912899-59-X*) Lrning Multi-Systs.
Brooks, Cathleen. The Secret Everyone Knows. 40p. (gr. 5-10). 1989. pap. 3.00 (*0-89486-483-1*, 5165B) Hazelden.
Campbell, Chris. No Guarantees. large type ed. LC 93-42933. 1994. pap. 15.95 (*0-7862-0146-0*) Thorndike Pr.
—No Guarantees: A Young Woman's Fight to Overcome Drug & Alcohol Addiction. LC 92-25183. (Illus.). 192p. (gr. 6 up). 1993. text ed. 14.95 RSBE (*0-02-716445-4*, New Discovery) Macmillan Child Grp.
Claypool, Jane. Alcohol & You. rev. ed. Greenberg, Lorna, ed. LC 88-10258. (Illus.). 112p. 1988. PLB 13.40 (*0-531-10566-0*) Watts.
Coffey, Wayne. Straight Talk about Drinking: Teenagers Speak Out about Alcohol. LC 87-32446. 256p. (gr. 7 up). 1988. pap. 9.00 (*0-452-26061-2*, Plume) NAL-Dutton.
Cohen, Daniel & Cohen, Susan. A Six-Pack & a Fake I.D. Teens Look at the Drinking Question. LC 85-25337. 156p. (gr. 7 up). 1985. 13.95 (*0-87131-459-2*) M Evans.
Cohen, Susan & Cohen, Daniel. A Six Pack & a Fake I. D. Teens Look at the Drinking Question. 176p. (gr. 7 up). 1992. pap. 3.99 (*0-440-21297-9*, LFL) Dell.
Coleman, William L. What You Should Know about a Parent Who Drinks Too Much. LC 92-18313. 96p. (Orig.). (gr. 3-8). 1992. pap. 5.99 (*0-8066-2610-0*, 9-2610, Augsburg) Augsburg Fortress.
Diamond, Arthur. Alcoholism. LC 92-23601. (Illus.). 112p. (gr. 5-8). 1992. PLB 14.95 (*1-56006-136-7*) Lucent Bks.
Drugs & Drinking. 48p. (gr. 6-8). 1990. pap. 8.99 (*1-55945-118-1*) Group Pub.
Duggan, Maureen H. Mommy Doesn't Live Here Anymore. Liberman, Jane, illus. 48p. (Orig.). (ps-7). 1987. pap. 8.95 (*0-944453-01-5*) B Brae.
Englebardt, Stanley L. Kids & Alcohol, the Deadliest Drug. LC 75-20327. 64p. (gr. 5 up). 1975. PLB 12.93 (*0-688-51717-X*) Lothrop.
Fishman, Ross. Alcohol & Alcoholism. updated ed. (Illus.). (gr. 5 up). 1992. lib. bdg. 19.95 (*0-685-52234-2*) Chelsea Hse.
Fitzmahan, Don. The Roller Coaster: A Story of Alcoholism & the Family. Cocklin-Ray, Christine, illus. Black, Claudia, intro. by. LC 88-63798. (Illus.). 36p. (Orig.). (gr. 6). 1986. pap. 8.00 (*0-935529-11-X*) Comprehen Health Educ.
Focus on Alcohol. (Illus.). 64p. (gr. 3-7). 1990. PLB 15.40 (*0-516-07351-6*) Childrens.
Graeber, Laurel. Are You Dying for a Drink? Teenagers & Alcohol Abuse. LC 85-8880. (Illus.). 128p. (gr. 7 up). 1985. lib. bdg. 12.98 (*0-671-50818-0*, J Messner); lib. bdg. 5.95 (*0-671-63180-2*) S&S Trade.
Grosshandler, Janet. Coping with Drinking & Driving. rev. ed. Rosen, Ruth, ed. (gr. 7-12). 1994. PLB 14.95 (*0-8239-1603-0*) Rosen Group.
Gunn, Jeffrey. Pen Pals, Vol. 11: Facts about Alcohol. Wolfe, Debra, illus. (Orig.). (gr. 3). 1990. pap. write for info. (*1-879146-11-8*) Knowldg Pub.
Hall, Lindsey & Cohn, Leigh. Dear Kids of Alcoholics. Lingenfelter, Rosemary E., illus. 96p. (gr. 3-10). 1988. pap. 6.95 (*0-936077-18-2*) Gurze Bks.
Hamilton, Dorothy. Mari's Mountain. Graber, Esther R., illus. LC 78-10620. 120p. (gr. 7-10). 1978. pap. 3.95 (*0-8361-1869-3*) Herald Pr.
Hastings, Jill M. & Typpo, Marion H. Elephant in the Living Room: The Children's Book. Noland, Mimi, illus. LC 84-70189. 88p. (Orig.). (gr. 3-8). 1984. wkbk. 9.95 (*0-89638-071-8*) Hazelden.
Heegaard, Marge. When a Family Is in Trouble: Children Can Cope with Grief from Drug & Alcohol Addictions. (gr. 4-7). 1993. pap. 6.95 (*0-9620502-7-X*) Woodland Pr.
Hipp, Earl. The First Step - Humility. Yencho, Mike, illus. 30p. (gr. 9-12). 1992. pap. 2.50 (*0-89486-624-9*, 5248B) Hazelden.
Hjelmeland, Andy. Drinking & Driving. LC 89-25406. (Illus.). 48p. (gr. 5-6). 1990. text ed. 12.95 RSBE (*0-89686-496-0*, Crestwood Hse) Macmillan Child Grp.
Holmes, Pamela. Alcohol. LC 91-30344. (Illus.). 64p. (gr. 6-12). 1991. PLB 22.80 (*0-8114-3203-3*); pap. text ed. write for info. (*0-8114-3206-8*) Raintree Steck-V.
Hyde, Margaret O. Alcohol: Uses & Abuses. LC 87-12161. (Illus.). 96p. (gr. 6 up). 1988. lib. bdg. 16.95 (*0-89490-155-9*) Enslow Pubs.
Jones, Michael P., ed. What Getting Drunk Doesn't Make You. (Illus.). 20p. 1984. text ed. 5.00 (*0-89904-027-6*); pap. text ed. 2.00 (*0-89904-197-3*) Crumb Elbow Pub.
Jones, Ralph E. Straight Talk: Answers to Questions Young People Ask about Alcohol. Joiner, Lee M., ed. 64p. (Orig.). (gr. 10 up). 1988. pap. 4.95 (*0-943519-08-X*, B1908) Sulzburger & Graham Pub.
—Straight Talk: Answers to Questions Young People Ask about Alcohol. 1989. No. 70005. pap. 4.95 (*0-8306-9005-0*) TAB Bks.
Laik, Judy. Under Whose Influence? Strecker, Rebekah, illus. LC 93-86233. 64p. 1994. lib. bdg. 16.95 (*0-943990-98-X*); pap. 5.95 (*0-943990-97-1*) Parenting Pr.
Landau, Elaine. Teenage Drinking. (Illus.). 104p. (gr. 6 up). 1994. lib. bdg. 17.95 (*0-89490-575-9*) Enslow Pubs.
Lang, Alan R. Alcohol: Teenage Drinking. updated ed. (Illus.). (gr. 5 up). 1992. lib. bdg. 19.95 (*0-685-52236-9*) Chelsea Hse.
Miner, Jane C. Alcohol & Teens. LC 84-658. (Illus.). 64p. (gr. 7-11). 1984. lib. bdg. 9.29 (*0-671-44890-0*, J Messner) S&S Trade.
Monroe, Judy. Alcohol. LC 93-28607. (Illus.). 128p. (gr. 6 up). 1994. lib. bdg. 17.95 (*0-89490-470-1*) Enslow Pubs.
Morreim, Dennis C. Changed Lives: The Story of Alcoholics Anonymous. (ps-3). 1991. pap. 8.99 (*0-8066-2548-1*) Augsburg Fortress.
Nielsen, Nancy. Teen Alcoholism. LC 90-66. (Illus.). 96p. (gr. 5-8). 1990. PLB 14.95 (*1-56006-121-9*) Lucent Bks.
No Drugs! No Alcohol! 16p. 1994. 0.95 (*0-685-71607-4*, 732) W Gladden Found.
O'Neill, Catherine. Focus on Alcohol. Neuahaus, David, illus. 56p. (gr. 2-4). 1990. PLB 14.95 (*0-941477-96-7*) TFC Bks NY.
O'Sullivan, Carol. Alcohol: Understanding Words in Context. LC 89-11712. (Illus.). 32p. (gr. 3-6). 1990. PLB 10.95 (*0-89908-634-9*) Greenhaven.
Porterfield, Kay M. Coping with an Alcoholic Parent. rev. ed. (gr. 7-12). 1990. 14.95 (*0-8239-1143-8*) Rosen Group.
Read, Edward M. & Daley, Dennis C. You've Got the Power: A Recovery Guide for Young People with Drug & Alcohol Problems. Butler, Ralph, illus. Gondles, James A., Jr., frwd. by. (Illus.). 98p. (Orig.). 1993. pap. 10.00 (*0-929310-87-X*, 349) Am Correctional.
Rosenberg, Maxine B. Not My Family: Sharing the Truth about Alcoholism. LC 88-10468. 112p. (gr. 4-7). 1988. SBE 14.95 (*0-02-777911-4*, Bradbury Pr) Macmillan Child Grp.
Ryan, Alizabeth A. Straight Talk about Drugs & Alcohol. 144p. (gr. 7 up). 1992. pap. 3.99 (*0-440-21392-4*, LFL) Dell.
Ryan, Elizabeth. Hablemos Francamente de las Drogas y el Alcohol. Terrana, Alma, tr. from ENG. (SPA.). 160p. 1990. 16.95x (*0-8160-2496-0*) Facts on File.
Ryan, Elizabeth A. Straight Talk about Drugs & Alcohol. 160p. 1989. 16.95x (*0-8160-1525-2*) Facts on File.
Schenkerman, Rona D. Growing up with an Alcoholic Parent. 16p. (gr. 3-8). 1993. 1.95 (*1-56688-114-5*) Bur For At-Risk.
Seixas, Judith S. Alcohol: What It Is, What It Does. LC 76-43344. (Illus.). 56p. (gr. k up). 1977. pap. 6.95 (*0-688-00462-8*, Mulberry) Morrow.
—Living with a Parent Who Drinks Too Much. LC 78-11108. 128p. (gr. 3-6). 1979. 12.95 (*0-688-80196-X*); PLB 11.88 (*0-688-84196-1*) Greenwillow.
Shuker, Nancy. Everything You Need to Know about an Alcoholic Parent. Rosen, Ruth, ed. (gr. 7-12). 1989. PLB 14.95 (*0-8239-1614-6*) Rosen Group.
Silverstein, Alvin, et al. The Addictions Handbook. LC 90-14093. 192p. (gr. 6 up). 1991. lib. bdg. 18.95 (*0-89490-205-9*) Enslow Pubs.

Silverstein, Herma. Alcoholism. LC 90-12578. (Illus.). 96p. (gr. 9-12). 1990. PLB 13.40 (*0-531-10879-1*) Watts.

Smith, Sandra L. Drugs & Your Parents. rev. ed. (Illus.). 64p. (gr. 7-12). 1993. lib. bdg. 14.95 (*0-8239-1684-7*) Rosen Group.

Starbuck, Marnie. The Gladden Book about Alcohol. (gr. 1-4). 1994. 0.75 (*0-685-71636-8*, 657) W Gladden Found.

Stronck, David. Alcohol-The Real Story. Nelson, Mary & Clark, Kay, eds. Ransom, Robert D., illus. 30p. (gr. 5-8). 1987. pap. text ed. 2.95 (*0-941816-35-4*) ETR Assocs.

Tate, Albert J., III. Dad: Are People Using Alcohol & Drugs As an Alternative to Problem Solving? Design in Demand Staff, illus. 68p. (Orig.). (gr. 10). 1992. pap. 12.95 (*0-9622996-9-3*) Unique Memphis.

Taylor, Barbara. Everything You Need to Know about Alcohol. rev. ed. Glassman, Richard, photos by. (Illus.). 64p. (gr. 7-12). 1993. 14.95 (*0-8239-1613-8*) Rosen Group.

Turck, Mary. Alcohol & Tobacco. LC 88-20253. (Illus.). 48p. (gr. 5-6). 1988. text ed. 12.95 RSBE (*0-89686-411-1*, Crestwood Hse) Macmillan Child Grp.

Varley, Chris. Alcoholism. LC 93-23961. 1993. 14.95 (*1-85435-612-7*) Marshall Cavendish.

Vigna, Judith. I Wish Daddy Didn't Drink So Much. Fay, Ann, ed. LC 88-108. (Illus.). 32p. (ps-3). 1988. PLB 13.95 (*0-8075-3523-0*); pap. 5.95 (*0-8075-3526-5*) A Whitman.

Wekesser, Carol, ed. Alcoholism. LC 93-22396. 1994. lib. bdg. 16.95 (*1-56510-074-3*); pap. 9.95 (*1-56510-073-5*) Greenhaven.

What's "Drunk," Mama? (Illus.). 30p. (ps-5). 1977. 1.25 (*0-910034-64-8*); cass. 4.00 (*0-910034-65-6*); booklet & cassette pkg. 5.00 (*0-685-46152-1*) Al-Anon.

Wijnberg, Ellen. Alcohol. LC 93-25156. (Illus.). (gr. 6-9). 1993. PLB 21.34 (*0-8114-3528-8*) Raintree Steck-V.

ALCOHOLISM–FICTION

Anderson, Peggy K. Safe at Home! LC 90-19133. 128p. (gr. 3-7). 1992. SBE 13.95 (*0-689-31686-0*, Atheneum Child Bk) Macmillan Child Grp.

Bauer, Marion D. Shelter from the Wind. LC 75-28184. 112p. (gr. 6 up). 1979. 13.95 (*0-395-28890-8*, Clarion Bks) HM.

Black, Claudia. My Dad Loves Me, My Dad Has a Disease. LC 59-776. (Illus.). 88p. (Orig.). (gr. k-9). 1982. pap. 9.95 (*0-9607940-2-6*) MAC Pub.

Brooks, Bruce. No Kidding. LC 88-22057. 224p. (gr. 7 up). 1989. 14.00 (*0-06-020722-1*); PLB 13.89 (*0-06-020723-X*) HarpC Child Bks.

Carbone, Elisa L. My Dad's Definitely Not a Drunk! Weber, Susan B., ed. Neuhaus, Roy, illus. LC 92-53883. 116p. (Orig.). (gr. 4-9). 1992. text ed. 11.95 (*0-914525-21-2*); pap. text ed. 7.95 (*0-914525-22-0*) Waterfront Bks.

Carrick, Carol. Banana Beer. Apple, Margot, illus. LC 94-256. 1994. write for info. (*0-8075-0568-4*) A Whitman.

Conly, Jane L. Crazy Lady! LC 92-18348. 192p. (gr. 5 up). 1993. 13.00 (*0-06-021357-4*); PLB 12.89 (*0-06-021360-4*) HarpC Child Bks.

Ferry, Charles. Binge. LC 92-93408. 94p. (Orig.). (gr. 7 up). 1992. pap. 8.95 (*0-9632799-0-4*) DaisyHill Pr.
AN ALA BEST BOOK FOR YOUNG ADULTS. "A vitally important book... an incredibly powerful, mesmerizing, tragic, read-in-one-sitting little book with an authenticity & understanding rare in adolescent literature...It pulls no punches, offers no pat endings, just describes a kid mired in his own alcohol denial...an absolutely superb book, highly readable, & relentlessly constructed to make its point without being a tract...We have needed a book like this for a very long time."--VOYA. Recommended by The National Council of Teachers of English & The H. W. Wilson Company.
Publisher Provided Annotation.

Frye, Tom. Scratchin' on the Eight Ball. 240p. (gr. 6 up). 1993. pap. 9.95 (*1-881663-16-7*) Advent Mean Pr.

Hughes, Dean. The Trophy. LC 93-42234. 128p. (gr. 3-7). 1994. 13.00 (*0-679-84368-X*); lib. bdg. cancelled (*0-679-94368-4*) Knopf Bks Yng Read.

Kenny, Kevin. Sometimes My Mom Drinks Too Much. (ps-3). 1993. pap. 3.95 (*0-8114-7159-4*) Raintree Steck-V.

Kenny, Kevin & Krull, Helen. Sometimes My Mom Drinks Too Much. Cogancherry, Helen, illus. Neidengard, Ted, intro. by. LC 80-14515. (Illus.). 32p. (gr. k-6). 1980. PLB 19.97 (*0-8172-1366-X*) Raintree Steck-V.

Knoedler, Michael. Callie's Way Home. 160p. (gr. 6-12). 1991. pap. 3.95 perfect bdg. (*0-89486-729-6*, 5116A) Hazelden.

Lindquist, Marie. In a Perfect World. 160p. (gr. 6-12). 1991. pap. 3.95 perfect bdg. (*0-89486-775-X*, T5127) Hazelden.

Nickerson, Sara. Peter Parrot, Private Eye. Bagley, Michael, illus. Counts, Sandra J., frwd. by. LC 88-63800. (Illus.). 43p. (Orig.). (gr. 2-6). 1988. pap. 8.00 (*0-935529-07-1*) Comprehen Health Educ.

Rodowsky, Colby. Hannah in Between. (gr. 5 up). 1994. 15.00 (*0-374-32837-4*) FS&G.

Starkman, Neal. The Apple. Yasuki, Meredith, illus. LC 91-16800. 44p. (Orig.). (gr. 7-9). 1991. pap. 7.00 (*0-935529-29-2*) Comprehen Health Educ.

—The Forever Secret. Karas, G. Brian, illus. LC 91-16799. 50p. (Orig.). (gr. 5). 1991. pap. 9.00 (*0-935529-28-4*) Comprehen Health Educ.

Tapp, Kathy K. Smoke from the Chimney. LC 89-6816. 176p. (gr. 4-7). 1989. pap. 3.95 (*0-689-71323-1*, Aladdin) Macmillan Child Grp.

Wallace, Bill. Never Say Quit. LC 92-54420. 160p. (gr. 3-7). 1993. 14.95 (*0-8234-1013-7*) Holiday.

Wood, June R. A Share of Freedom. LC 94-6578. 256p. 1994. 15.95 (*0-399-22767-9*, Putnam) Putnam Pub Group.

Zindel, Paul. David & Della. LC 93-12719. 176p. (gr. 7 up). 1993. 14.00 (*0-06-023353-2*); PLB 13.89 (*0-06-023354-0*) HarpC Child Bks.

ALCOTT, LOUISA MAY, 1832-1888

Alcott, Louisa May. Louisa's Wonder Book: An Unknown Alcott Juvenile. Stern, Madeline B., ed. LC 76-358119. (Illus.). 1975. Repr. of 1870 ed. 7.50 (*0-916699-08-0*) CMU Clarke Hist Lib.

Burke, Kathleen. Louisa May Alcott. Horner, Matina, intro. by. (Illus.). 112p. (gr. 5 up). 1988. lib. bdg. 17.95 (*1-55546-637-0*) Chelsea Hse.

Greene, Carol. Louisa May Alcott: Author, Nurse, Suffragette. LC 84-5902. (Illus.). 112p. (gr. 4 up). 1984. PLB 14.40 (*0-516-03208-9*) Childrens.

Johnston, Norma. Louisa May: The World & Works of Louisa May Alcott. LC 91-7896. (Illus.). 224p. (gr. 6 up). 1991. SBE 15.95 (*0-02-747705-3*, Four Winds) Macmillan Child Grp.

—Louisa May: The World & Works of Louisa May Alcott. Cohn, Amy, ed. 256p. 1995. pap. 4.95 (*0-688-12696-0*, Beech Tree Bks) Morrow.

Mcgill, Marcy. Louisa May Alcott. (Orig.). (gr. k-6). 1988. pap. 2.95 (*0-440-40022-8*, YB) Dell.

Meigs, Cornelia. Invincible Louisa. LC 68-21174. (Illus.). (gr. 7 up). 1968. 17.95 (*0-316-56590-3*) Little.

Ryan, Cary, ed. Louisa May Alcott: Her Girlhood Diary. Graham, Mark, illus. LC 93-22343. 56p. (gr. 5 up). 1993. PLB 14.95 (*0-8167-3139-X*); pap. write for info. (*0-8167-3150-0*) BrdgeWater.

Santrey, Laurence. Louisa May Alcott, Young Writer. Speidel, Sandra, illus. LC 85-1086. 48p. (gr. 4-6). 1986. lib. bdg. 10.79 (*0-8167-0563-1*); pap. text ed. 3.50 (*0-8167-0564-X*) Troll Assocs.

ALEUTIAN ISLANDS–FICTION

Taylor, John. Volcano in Our Yard. (Illus.). (gr. 2-5). 1975. 4.95 (*0-686-11663-1*) Thompson's.

ALEXANDER THE GREAT, 356-323 B.C.

Ash, Maureen. Alexander the Great: Ancient Empire Builder. LC 91-1386. 128p. (gr. 3 up). 1991. PLB 20.55 (*0-516-03063-9*) Childrens.

Lasker, Joe. The Great Alexander the Great. (ps-3). 1990. pap. 3.95 (*0-14-054318-X*, Puffin) Puffin Bks.

Stewart, Gail B. Alexander the Great. LC 93-39983. (gr. 5-8). 1994. 14.95 (*1-5600-6047-6*) Lucent Bks.

ALEXANDER THE GREAT, 356-323 B.C.–FICTION

Johnson, Vargie, ed. Alexander the Great, the Conqueror: King of Macedonia, Pharaoh of Egypt, & Emperor of Persia, the Story of a Young Leader, Legend in His Time. 1994. 12.95 (*0-533-10697-4*) Vantage.

ALGAE

Greenaway, Theresa. First Plants. LC 90-10003. (Illus.). 48p. (gr. 5-9). 1990. PLB 21.34 (*0-8114-2734-X*) Raintree Steck-V.

ALGEBRA

see also Numbers Theory; Probabilities

Burchard, Elizabeth & Bernstock, Peter. Algebra I: In a Flash. 436p. (gr. 7-12). 1994. pap. 9.95 (*1-881374-13-0*) Flash Blasters.

Burchard, Elizabeth & Soroka, Matthew. Algebra Two - Trigonometry: In a Flash. 450p. (gr. 7-12). 1994. pap. 9.95 (*1-881374-14-9*) Flash Blasters.

Bureloff, Morris. Algebra Acrobatic Puzzles. (Illus.). (gr. 7-12). 1988. pap. 7.95 (*0-918932-93-9*) Activity Resources.

Churchill, Eric R. Algebra Flipper, No. 1. 49p. (gr. 5 up). 1989. Repr. of 1987 ed. trade edition 5.95 (*1-878383-03-5*) C Lee Pubns.

CMSP Projects. Prealgebra. rev. ed. (Illus.). 101p. pap. text ed. write for info. (*0-942851-00-5*) CMSP Projects.

Edmondson, Amy. Success Through Algebra. (gr. 8-12). 1989. 24.95 (*0-945525-12-5*) Supercamp.

Gray, Virginia. The Write Tool to Teach Algebra. 104p. (gr. 9-12). 1993. pap. 16.95 (*1-55953-064-2*) Key Curr Pr.

Isdell, Wendy. A Gebra Named Al. LC 93-15294. 128p. (Orig.). (gr. 5 up). 1993. pap. 4.95 (*0-915793-58-X*) Free Spirit Pub.

Laycock, Mary & Schadler, Reuben. Algebra in Concrete. (gr. 6-10). 1973. pap. 7.95 (*0-918932-00-9*) Activity Resources.

McCabe, J. L. Everyday Algebra. 133p. (Orig.). 1987. pap. text ed. 13.95 (*0-942465-07-5*, 2 212 939) Summertree Bks.

Radvany, Ruth, et al. Intermediate Algebra Study Aid. 1974. pap. 2.50 (*0-87738-038-4*) Youth Ed.

Stallings, Pat. Puzzling Your Way into Algebra. new ed. Stallings, Pat, illus. (gr. 7-10). 1978. pap. text ed. 7.95 (*0-918932-58-0*) Activity Resources.

Thompson, Frances M. More Five Minute Challenges: Mini-Problem Solving Activities. (Illus.). 64p. (Orig.). (gr. 8-12). 1992. pap. text ed. 7.95 (*0-918932-98-X*, A-2224) Activity Resources.

Wohlberg, Myrna F., et al. Elementary Algebra Study Aid. 1980. pap. 2.50 (*0-87738-037-6*) Youth Ed.

ALGERIA

Brill, Marlene T. Algeria. LC 89-25436. (Illus.). 128p. (gr. 5-9). 1990. PLB 20.55 (*0-516-02717-4*) Childrens.

Carpenter, Allan & Balow, Tom. Algeria. LC 77-20876. (gr. 6-12). pap. 26.00 (*0-8357-3474-9*, 2039761) Bks Demand.

Lerner Geography Department Staff, ed. Algeria in Pictures. (Illus.). 64p. (gr. 5-12). 1992. PLB 17.50 (*0-8225-1901-1*) Lerner Pubns.

ALGERIA–FICTION

Camus, Albert. The Guest. (gr. 4-9). 1982. 13.95 (*0-88682-356-0*, 97217-098) Creative Ed.

ALIENS

see also Citizenship

Barbour, William, ed. Illegal Immigration. LC 93-1808. 1994. lib. bdg. 16.95 (*1-56510-072-7*); pap. 9.95 (*1-56510-071-9*) Greenhaven.

Crosby, Nina E. & Marten, Elizabeth H. Don't Teach Let Me Learn about Presidents, of the U. S. People, Genealogy, Immigrants. (Illus.). 80p. (Orig.). (gr. 3-9). 1979. pap. 8.95 tchr's. enrichment manual (*0-914634-67-4*, 7912) DOK Pubs.

Freedman, Russell. Immigrant Kids. LC 79-20060. 64p. (gr. 3-7). 1980. 16.95 (*0-525-32538-7*, DCB) Dutton Child Bks.

Kurelek, William & Engelhart, Margaret S. They Sought a New World: The Story of European Immigration to North America. (Illus.). 48p. (gr. 4 up). 1985. 14.95 (*0-88776-172-0*, Dist. by U of Toronto Pr); pap. 7.95 (*0-88776-213-1*) Tundra Bks.

Perrin, Linda. Immigrants from the Far East. LC 80-65840. 192p. 1980. 12.95 (*0-385-28115-3*) Delacorte.

Robbins, Albert. Immigrants from Northern Europe. LC 80-68741. 224p. 1982. 9.95 (*0-385-28138-2*) Delacorte.

ALIENS–FICTION

Buss, Fran L. Journey of the Sparrows. 160p. (gr. 5-9). 1991. 15.00 (*0-525-67362-8*, Lodestar Bks) Dutton Child Bks.

Coville, Bruce. Bruce Coville's Book of Aliens: Tales to Warp Your Mind. (gr. 4-7). 1994. pap. 2.95 (*0-590-46162-1*) Scholastic Inc.

Garehime, Ed. Mr. Jelly Bean, No. 1. 2nd ed. American Red Cross Staff, tr. Garehime, Marianne, illus. LC 77-82261. 64p. (ps-4). 1979. 9.95 (*0-918822-01-7*) Deem Corp.

Paulsen, Gary. Amos & the Alien. (gr. 4-7). 1994. 3.50 (*0-440-40990-X*) Dell.

Rowe, Alan. Aliens on Earth. (Illus.). 32p. (ps-3). 1994. pap. 2.99 (*1-56402-407-5*) Candlewick Pr.

Temple, Frances. Grab Hands & Run. LC 92-34063. 176p. (gr. 5 up). 1993. 14.95 (*0-531-05480-2*); PLB 14.99 (*0-531-08630-5*) Orchard Bks Watts.

ALL FOOLS' DAY

see April Fools' Day

ALL HALLOWS' EVE

see Halloween

ALLEGORIES

see also Fables; Parables

Bunting, Eve. Terrible Things: An Allegory of the Holocaust. rev. ed. Gammell, Stephen, illus. 24p. (gr. 1-4). 1989. 11.95 (*0-8276-0325-8*); pap. 7.95 (*0-8276-0507-2*) JPS Phila.

Bunyan, John. Pilgrim's Progress. (gr. 9 up). 1968. pap. 1.95 (*0-8049-0183-X*, CL-183) Airmont.

—The Pilgrim's Progress. Larsen, Dan, adapted by. (gr. 3 up). 1992. 9.95 (*1-55748-276-4*) Barbour & Co.

Butler, Samuel. Erewhon. Threapleton, M. M., intro. by. (gr. 11 up). 1967. pap. 1.25 (*0-8049-0130-9*, CL-130) Airmont.

Haseley, Dennis. Ghost Catcher. Bloom, Lloyd, illus. LC 91-4426. 40p. (gr. 1-5). 1991. HarpC Child Bks.

Le Guin, Ursula K. Fish Soup. Wynne, Patrick, illus. LC 91-29740. 40p. (gr. 2-4). 1992. SBE 13.95 (*0-689-31733-6*, Atheneum Child Bk) Macmillan Child Grp.

Orwell, George. Animal Farm. 122p. (Orig.). 1945. pap. text ed. 5.95 (*0-582-53008-3*) Longman.

ALLERGY

Bergman, Thomas. Determined to Win: Children Living with Allergies & Asthma, 9 titles. LC 93-37273. (Illus.). 48p. 1994. PLB 167.40 Set (*0-8368-1075-9*) Gareth Stevens Inc.

Dees, Susan C. Allergy. Head, J. J., ed. Imrick, Ann T., illus. LC 86-72199. 16p. (Orig.). (gr. 10 up). 1988. pap. text ed. 2.75 (*0-89278-169-6*, 45-9769) Carolina Biological.

Don't Turn Away Series, 9 vols. (gr. 4 up). PLB 167.40 Set (*0-8368-1097-X*) Gareth Stevens Inc.

Edelson, Edward. Allergies. Koop, C. Everett, intro. by. (Illus.). 96p. (gr. 6-12). 1989. 18.95 (*0-7910-0055-9*); pap. 9.95 (*0-7910-0482-1*) Chelsea Hse.

Landau, Elaine. Allergies. (Illus.). 64p. (gr. 5-8). 1994. bds. 15.95 (*0-8050-2989-3*) TFC Bks NY.

Lerner, Carol. Plants That Make You Sniffle & Sneeze. Lerner, Carol, illus. LC 92-21561. 32p. 1993. 15.00 (*0-688-11489-X*); PLB 14.93 (*0-688-11490-3*) Morrow Jr Bks.

Newman, Gerald & Layfield, Eleanor N. Allergies. LC 91-33862. (Illus.). 112p. (gr. 7-12). 1992. PLB 13.40 (*0-531-12516-5*) Watts.

Seixas, Judith. Allergies--What They Are, What They Do. Huffman, Tom, illus. LC 90-30753. 56p. (gr. 1 up). 1991. 12.95 (*0-688-09638-7*); PLB 12.88 (*0-688-08877-5*) Greenwillow.

Terkel, Susan N. All about Allergies. Harvey, Paul, illus. LC 92-17770. 64p. (gr. 2-5). 1993. 13.99 (*0-525-67410-1*, Lodestar Bks) Dutton Child Bks.

ALLIGATORS

Aliki. Use Your Head, Dear. Aliki, illus. LC 82-11911. 48p. (gr. k-3). 1983. 13.95 (*0-688-01811-4*); PLB 13. 88 (*0-688-01812-2*) Greenwillow.

Arnosky, Jim. All about Alligators. LC 93-41045. (ps-3). 1994. 14.95 (*0-590-46788-3*) Scholastic Inc.

Barrett, Norman S. Cocodrilos y Caimanes. LC 90-71415. (SPA., Illus.). 32p. (gr. k-4). 1991. PLB 11.90 (*0-531-07919-8*) Watts.

—Crocodiles & Alligators. LC 88-51517. (Illus.). 32p. (gr. k-6). 1990. 11.90 (*0-531-10705-1*) Watts.

Bright, Michael. Alligators & Crocodiles. LC 90-3225. (Illus.). 32p. (gr. 5-8). 1990. PLB 12.40 (*0-531-17245-7*, Gloucester Pr) Watts.

Butterworth, Christine. Alligators. LC 90-9927. (Illus.). 32p. (gr. 1-4). 1990. PLB 18.99 (*0-8114-2639-4*); pap. 3.95 (*0-8114-4608-5*) Raintree Steck-V.

Crozat, Francois. I Am a Little Alligator. 28p. (ps-k). 1993. 8.95 (*0-8120-6342-2*); Miniature. 3.50 (*0-8120-6343-0*) Barron.

Dow, Lesley. Alligators & Crocodiles. 72p. 1990. 17.95 (*0-8160-2273-9*) Facts on File.

Farre, Marie. Crocodiles & Alligators. Matthews, Sarah, tr. from FRE. Wallis, Diz, illus. LC 87-31804. 38p. (gr. k-5). 1988. 5.95 (*0-944589-01-4*, 014) Young Discovery Lib.

George, Jean C. The Moon of the Alligators. new ed. Rothman, Michael, illus. LC 90-38169. 48p. (gr. 3-7). 1991. 15.00 (*0-06-022427-4*); PLB 14.89 (*0-06-022428-2*) HarpC Child Bks.

George, Michael. Alligators & Crocodiles. 32p. 1991. 15. 95 (*0-89565-720-1*) Childs World.

Guiberson, Brenda Z. Spoonbill Swamp. Lloyd, Megan, illus. LC 91-8555. 32p. (ps-3). 1992. 14.95 (*0-8050-1583-3*, Bks Young Read) H Holt & Co.

Knight, David. I Can Read About Alligators & Crocodiles. LC 78-73733. (Illus.). (gr. 2-4). 1979. pap. 2.50 (*0-89375-200-2*) Troll Assocs.

Lauber, Patricia. Alligators: A Success Story. Silva, Lou, illus. LC 93-3302. 64p. (gr. 2-4). 1994. 14.95 (*0-8050-1909-X*, Bks Young Read) H Holt & Co.

Love, Hallie. A Is for Alligator. Kennedy, Maureen, illus. 64p. (gr. 1 up). 1993. 15.95 (*1-879244-02-0*) Windom Bks.

Martin, L. Alligators. (Illus.). 24p. (gr. k-5). 1989. lib. bdg. 11.94 (*0-86592-579-8*) Rourke Corp.

Patent, Dorothy H. The American Alligator. Munoz, William, photos by. LC 93-37704. 1994. 15.95 (*0-395-63392-3*, Clarion Bks) HM.

Petty, Kate. Crocodiles & Alligators. Johnson, Karen, illus. 1990. pap. 3.95 (*0-531-15153-0*) Watts.

Robinson, Fay. Real Bears & Alligators. Iosa, Ann W., illus. LC 92-10755. 32p. (ps-2). 1992. PLB 11.60 (*0-516-02374-8*) Childrens.

—Real Bears & Alligators. Iosa, Ann, illus. LC 92-10755. 32p. (ps-2). 1993. pap. 3.95 (*0-516-42374-6*) Childrens.

Rothaus, Jim. Alligators & Crocodiles. 24p. (gr. 3). 1988. PLB 14.95 (*0-88682-220-3*) Creative Ed.

Serventy, Vincent. Crocodile & Alligator. LC 84-15890. (Illus.). 24p. (gr. k-5). 1985. PLB 9.95 (*0-8172-2404-1*); pap. 3.95 (*0-8114-6873-9*) Raintree Steck-V.

—Crocodile & Alligator. Serventy, Vincent, et al, illus. 24p. (gr. k-3). 1986. pap. 2.50 (*0-590-44722-X*) Scholastic Inc.

Stone, Lynn M. Alligators & Crocodiles. LC 89-9985. 48p. (gr. k-4). 1989. PLB 12.85 (*0-516-01170-7*); pap. 4.95 (*0-516-41170-5*) Childrens.

Stoops, Erik D. & Stone, Debbie L. Alligators & Crocodiles. LC 94-15691. (Illus.). 80p. 1994. 14.95 (*0-8069-0422-4*) Sterling.

Taylor, Dave. The Alligator & the Everglades. (Illus.). 32p. (gr. 3-4). 1990. PLB 15.95 (*0-86505-367-7*); pap. 7.95 (*0-86505-397-9*) Crabtree Pub Co.

Wildlife Education, Ltd. Staff. Alligators & Crocodiles. Hoopes, Barbara, illus. 20p. (Orig.). (gr. 5 up). 1984. pap. 2.75 (*0-937934-25-9*) Wildlife Educ.

ALLIGATORS–FICTION

Alligators Trail. 1979. pap. 9.95 (*0-385-28041-6*) Doubleday.

Bare, Colleen S. Never Kiss an Alligator! (Illus.). 32p. (ps-3). 1994. pap. 3.99 (*0-14-055257-X*, Puff Unicorn) Puffin Bks.

Camp, Martin. Why Alligators Don't Have Wings. Archer, RIck, illus. 32p. (ps-5). 1994. 13.95 (*1-880092-06-9*) Bright Bks TX.

Childress, Mark. Joshua & Bigtooth. Meyerowitz, Rick, illus. 32p. (ps-3). 1992. 14.95 (*0-316-14011-2*) Little.

Dorros, Arthur. Alligator Shoes. Dorros, Arthur, illus. LC 82-2409. (ps-k). 1982. 3.95 (*0-525-44001-1*, Dutton) NAL-Dutton.

George, Jean C. The Missing 'Gator of Gumbo Limbo: An Ecological Mystery. LC 91-20779. 176p. (gr. 3-7). 1992. 14.00 (*0-06-020396-X*); PLB 13.89 (*0-06-020397-8*) HarpC Child Bks.

Grambling, Lois. An Alligator Named...Alligator. Cushman, Doug, illus. 32p. (ps-1). 1991. lib. bdg. 12. 95 (*0-8120-6224-8*); pap. 5.95 (*0-8120-4756-7*) Barron.

Hall, N. & Packard, Mary. Spike & Mike. McCue, Lisa, illus. 40p. (ps-2). 1994. 12.00 (*0-679-85830-X*) Random Bks Yng Read.

Hall, Nancy & Packard, Mary. Spike & Mike. McCue, Lisa, illus. LC 93-13684. 40p. (ps-4). 1993. PLB 11.80 (*0-516-00830-7*) Childrens.

Hayes, Geoffrey. The Curse of the Cobweb Queen. LC 92-37272. 48p. (gr. 1-3). 1994. 7.99 (*0-679-93878-8*); pap. 3.50 (*0-679-83878-3*) Random Bks Yng Read.

Herndon, Ernest. Double-Crossed in Gator Country. 144p. 1994. pap. 4.99 (*0-310-38261-0*) Zondervan.

Johnson, Nancy L. The Best Teacher "Stuff" from Nancy L. Johnson. (Illus.). 96p. (gr. k-8). 1993. pap. 10.95 (*1-880505-06-1*) Pieces of Lrning.

Kennedy, Barbara. The Boy Who Loved Alligators. LC 93-15982. 144p. (gr. 3-7). 1994. SBE 14.95 (*0-689-31876-6*, Atheneum Child Bk) Macmillan Child Grp.

Kinnell, Galway. How the Alligator Missed Breakfast. Munsinger, Lynn, illus. 32p. (gr. k-3). 1982. 8.95 (*0-395-32436-X*) HM.

Kraus, Robert. Miss Gator's School House, 6 bks. Kraus, Robert, illus. (gr. k-3). 1989. Set, 48p. ea. lib. bdg. 53. 88 (*0-671-94105-4*, J Messner); Set, 48p. ea. pap. 21. 00 (*0-671-94106-2*) S&S Trade.

Lionni, Leo. An Extraordinary Egg. LC 93-28565. (Illus.). 40p. (ps-2). 1994. 15.00 (*0-679-85840-7*); PLB 15.99 (*0-679-95840-1*) Knopf Bks Yng Read.

McClung, Robert M. Black Jack: Last of the Big Alligators. Sanford, Lloyd, illus. LC 91-14387. 64p. (gr. 3-7). 1991. Repr. of 1967 ed. PLB 15.00 (*0-208-02326-7*, Linnet) Shoe String.

McMahon, James. Forty-Seven Alligators. Little, Carl, ed. Martin, Shawna, illus. 48p. (Orig.). (ps-3). 1993. pap. 10.95 (*0-932433-95-2*) Windswept Hse.

McNutt, Timothy E., Sr. Alley Alligator's Awesome Smile. (Illus.). (ps). 1994. pap. text ed. 3.95 (*0-9642475-0-X*) T E McNutt.
Colorfully illustrated, ALLEY ALLIGATOR'S AWESOME SMILE was written to present pediatric preventive oral care in a positive manner. Alfred & Abbey Alligator take little Alley Alligator to visit Dr. Smiley, Pleasant View Pond's favorite dentist. Dr. Smiley explains with non-threatening language the names of his dental instruments, & Alley completes her first dental visit with an awesome smile. This book is ideal for introducing young children to dentistry. Dr. McNutt's specialization in pediatric dentistry caused him to write this book to introduce parents & children to the following concepts: *not all baby teeth must be present to go to the dentist *children can "like" dental visits *the doctor intends to help the child *pain is not required to seek dental care, & *that a healthy oral environment should be promoted to the child at an early age. This book can be a useful educational tool for parents, children & dental care professionals. Dr. McNutt is a member of the American Dental Association & the American Academy of Pediatric Dentistry.
Publisher Provided Annotation.

Mayer, Mercer. There's an Alligator under My Bed. LC 86-19944. (Illus.). 32p. (ps-3). 1987. 14.00 (*0-8037-0374-0*); PLB 13.89 (*0-8037-0375-9*) Dial Bks Young.

Minarik, Else H. No Fighting, No Biting! Sendak, Maurice, illus. LC 58-5293. 64p. (gr. k-3). 1958. 13.00 (*0-06-024290-6*); PLB 13.89 (*0-06-024291-4*) HarpC Child Bks.

Mozelle, Shirley. Zack's Alligator. Watts, James, illus. LC 88-32069. 64p. (gr. k-3). 1989. 14.00 (*0-06-024309-0*); PLB 13.89 (*0-06-024310-4*) HarpC Child Bks.

—Zack's Alligator Goes to School. Watts, James, illus. LC 92-29871. 64p. (gr. k-3). 1994. 14.00 (*0-06-022887-3*); PLB 13.89 (*0-06-022888-1*) HarpC Child Bks.

Nickl, Peter. Crocodile, Crocodile. Schroeder, Binnette, illus. Cutler, Ebbitt, tr. (Illus.). 32p. 1989. 11.95 (*0-940793-33-4*, Pub. by Crocodile Bks); pap. 7.95 (*0-940793-32-6*, Pub. by Crocodile Bks) Interlink Pub.

Nobisso, Josephine & Krajnc, Anton C. For the Sake of a Cake. LC 92-38391. (Illus.). 28p. 1993. 9.95 (*0-8478-1685-0*) Rizzoli Intl.
Here's a multi-species cautionary tale for people who know how to share the work - or those who SHOULD know! Written in droll verse & illustrated with subtle drawings of sophisticated wit & whimsical zaniness, FOR THE SAKE OF A CAKE tells the tale of a Koala & an Alligator, already in bed, who argue whose turn it is to get up to check the cake baking in the oven. No holds are barred & no punches pulled as each lays claim to having already done too much work. Who's right? As in life, the reader is never sure. But one thing is certain: unless they find a way to cooperate, they're putting their very lives in danger! Written by the author of GRANDPA LOVED, GRANDMA'S SCRAPBOOK, & SSH! THE WHALE IS SMILING, FOR THE SAKE OF A CAKE crosses over from the children's fiction section to adult gift books to food & specialty shops, setting a delicious example & offering a rare Viennese cake recipe at the end. Order from Rizzoli International, 300 Park Ave., New York, NY 10010-5399, 1-800-462-2357.
Publisher Provided Annotation.

Olson, Margaret J. Aloysious Alligator. 2nd ed. Olson, Margaret J., illus. (gr. k-2). 1980. pap. 3.00 (*0-934876-14-2*) Creative Storytime.

Packard, Mary. Fairest of All. McCue, Lisa, illus. LC 93-11056. 40p. (ps-4). 1993. PLB 11.80 (*0-516-00826-9*) Childrens.

—Playing by the Rules. McCue, Lisa, illus. LC 93-4423. 40p. (ps-4). 1993. PLB 11.80 (*0-516-00827-7*) Childrens.

—Safe & Sound. McCue, Lisa, illus. LC 93-11058. 40p. (ps-4). 1993. PLB 11.80 (*0-516-00828-5*) Childrens.

—Save the Swamp. McCue, Lisa, illus. LC 93-11059. 40p. (ps-4). 1993. PLB 11.80 (*0-516-00829-3*) Childrens.

—Spike & Mike & the Treasure Hunt. McCue, Lisa, illus. LC 92-50295. 1993. write for info. (*0-679-93936-9*); lib. bdg. write for info. (*0-679-83936-4*) Random Bks Yng Read.

—Starting Over. McCue, Lisa & Scribner, Toni, illus. LC 93-11060. 40p. (ps-4). 1993. PLB 11.80 (*0-516-00831-5*) Childrens.

Rice, James. Gaston Goes to Nashville. Rice, James, illus. LC 85-6605. 32p. (gr. 1-6). 1985. 12.95 (*0-88289-477-3*) Pelican.

—Gaston Goes to Texas. Rice, James, illus. LC 78-12490. 32p. (gr. 1-6). 1978. 12.95 (*0-88289-204-5*) Pelican.

—Gaston Lays an Offshore Pipeline. LC 79-20335. (Illus.). (gr. 1-6). 1979. 12.95 (*0-88289-177-4*) Pelican.

—Gaston the Green-Nosed Alligator. (Illus.). 40p. (gr. 1-6). 1974. 12.95 (*0-88289-049-2*) Pelican.

Roberts, Jo-Anna. Alligator & the Toothfairy. Kinnell, Shannon, illus. 56p. (ps-2). 1991. 11.50g (*1-879212-00-5*) Desert Star Intl.

Robinson, Fay. When Nicki Went Away. Iosa, Ann, illus. LC 92-13835. 32p. (ps-2). 1993. pap. 3.95 (*0-516-42376-2*) Childrens.

Rubel, Nicole. It Came from the Swamp. LC 87-24653. (Illus.). 32p. (ps-3). 1992. pap. 3.99 (*0-14-054541-7*, Puff Pied Piper) Puffin Bks.

Searcy, Margaret Z. Alli Gator Gets a Bump on His Nose. Wise, Lu Celia, illus. LC 78-61369. (gr. 2-4). 1978. 7.50 (*0-916620-20-4*) Portals Pr.

Smath, Jerry. A Hat So Simple. LC 93-22205. (Illus.). 32p. (ps-3). 1993. PLB 13.95 (*0-8167-3016-4*); pap. write for info. (*0-8167-3017-2*) BrdgeWater.

Stevenson, James. Monty. LC 91-20657. 32p. (ps up). 1992. 14.00 (*0-688-11241-2*) Greenwillow.

Stone, Kazuko. Aligay Saves the Stars. 32p. 1991. 13.95 (*0-590-44382-8*, Scholastic Hardcover) Scholastic Inc.

Stover, Jill. Alamo Across Texas. LC 91-47572. (Illus.). 32p. (ps up). 1993. 13.00 (*0-688-11712-0*); 12.95 (*0-688-11713-9*) Lothrop.

Thomassie, Tynia. Feliciana Feydra LeRoux. Smith, Cat B., illus. LC 93-30347. 1995. 14.95 (*0-316-84125-0*) Little.

Updike, John. The Alligators. (gr. 4-12). 1989. 13.95 (*0-88682-358-7*, 97211-098) Creative Ed.

Vesey, Amanda. Hector's New Sneakers. Vesey, Amanda, illus. 32p. (ps-3). 1993. 13.50 (*0-670-84882-4*) Viking Child Bks.

Waber, Bernard. Lyle & the Birthday Party. (Illus.). 48p. (gr. k-3). 1973. pap. 5.70 (*0-395-17451-1*, 4-97508, Sandpiper) HM.

Warren, Sandra & Pfleger, Deborah B. Arlie the Alligator. Thomas, Deborah, illus. LC 91-73758. 48p. (ps-3). 1992. PLB 13.95 casebound (*1-880175-13-4*); bk. & cass. 19.90 (*1-880175-11-8*); audiocassette 5.95 (*1-880175-12-6*) Arlie Enter.
Arlie is a very curious alligator who longs to make friends with the strange creatures at the beach. Find out who the strange creatures are & what happens when he attempts to talk to them. The 10-minute audio cassette is fully produced with actors & actresses in mini-musical style. Four catchy tunes have children singing along the first time they listen. In beautiful color, this casebound, open-ended story book also includes a page about real alligators & sheet music. A creative use of fonts signals the change from song lyrics to dialogue. Non-readers enjoy the audio tape & pictures, while young readers & middle readers love to follow along, singing & reading, word-for-word, as the delightful story unfolds. Creative thinking is enhanced as children are encouraged to help Arlie find a way to communicate with the creatures. Unique in children's literature, ARLIE THE ALLIGATOR makes a great addition to the children's books-on-tape section of the library, elementary music libraries, elementary classrooms, in homes or for that long trip in the car. Activity guide also available, making that important classroom connection.
Publisher Provided Annotation.

Wiles, Mary J. The Alligator with a Toothache. (ps-3). 1978. pap. 1.75 (*0-8198-0355-3*) St Paul Bks.

ALLOYS

see also Metallurgy

ALMANACS

see also Calendars; Yearbooks

Anthony, Susan C. Facts Plus: An Almanac of Essential Information. 3rd ed. (Illus.). 256p. (gr. 3-9). 1995. pap. 15.95 (*1-879478-03-X*) Instr Res Co.

Aylesworth, Thomas G. Kids' World Almanac of the United States. 288p. (gr. 3-7). 1990. 14.95 (*0-88687-479-3*); pap. 7.95 (*0-88687-478-5*) Wrld Almnc.

Duden, Jane. Nineteen Ninety. LC 92-72890. (Illus.). 48p. (gr. 5). 1992. text ed. 12.95 RSBE (*0-89686-769-2*, Crestwood Hse) Macmillan Child Grp.

Elfman, Eric. Almanac of the Gross, Disgusting & Totally Repulsive: Odious Information for Oddball Bibliophiles. Pruitt, Ginny, illus. LC 93-48678. 80p. (gr. 4-7). 1994. pap. 4.99 (*0-679-85805-9*) Random Bks Yng Read.

Elwood, Ann & Madigan, Carol O. The Macmillan Book of Fascinating Facts: An Almanac for Kids. Martin, Dick, illus. LC 88-22844. 448p. (gr. 4 up). 1989. pap. 16.95 SBE (*0-02-733461-9*, Macmillan Child Bk) Macmillan Child Grp.

Elwood, Ann, et al. Macmillan Illustrated Almanac for Kids. Barrett, Lindsey, illus. LC 83-26296. 448p. (gr. 4 up). 1986. pap. 10.95 (*0-02-043100-7*, Aladdin) Macmillan Child Grp.

Franklin, Benjamin. Poor Richard's Almanack. (gr. 7 up). 1952. dust jacket 9.95 (*0-88088-918-7*) Peter Pauper.

Ganeri, A. Nature Facts & Lists. (Illus.). 144p. (gr. 3-7). 1993. pap. 10.95 (*0-7460-0645-4*, Usborne) EDC.

Lipkind, William. Days to Remember. Snyder, Jerome, illus. (gr. 3 up). 1961. 10.95 (*0-8392-3006-0*) Astor-Honor.

McLoone-Basta, Margo & Siegel, Alice. The Second Kids' World Almanac of Records & Facts. World Almanac Staff, ed. 288p. (gr. 3-9). 1987. 14.95 (*0-88687-397-5*); pap. 7.95 (*0-88687-317-7*) Wrld Almnc.

Martinet, Jeanne. The Year You Were Born, 1984. Lanfredi, Judy & Lanfredi, Judy, illus. LC 91-34577. 56p. 1992. PLB 13.93 (*0-688-11080-0*, Tambourine Bks); pap. 7.95 (*0-688-11079-7*, Tambourine Bks) Morrow.

—The Year You Were Born, 1985. Lanfredi, Judy, illus. LC 91-37439. 56p. 1992. PLB 13.93 (*0-688-11082-7*, Tambourine Bks); pap. 7.95 (*0-688-11081-9*, Tambourine Bks) Morrow.

The New York Public Library Student's Desk Reference. LC 93-22842. (gr. 6 up). 1993. 20.00 (*0-671-85013-X*) P-H Gen Ref & Trav.

Pinkney, Andrea D. Dear Benjamin Banneker. Pinkney, Brian, illus. LC 93-31162. (gr. 1-5). 1994. 14.95 (*0-15-200417-3*, Gulliver Bks) HarBrace.

Siegel, Alice & Basta, Margo M. The Information Please Kids' Almanac. (Illus.). 400p. (gr. 3-9). 1992. pap. 7.95 (*0-395-58801-4*) HM.

Siegel, Alice & McLoone, Margo. Kids' World Almanac of Records & Facts. (gr. 3-7). 1986. pap. 7.95 (*0-88687-319-3*) Wrld Almnc.

ALPHABET

see also Writing

ABC. (Illus.). 24p. (ps). 1994. bds. 2.95 (*1-56458-533-6*) Dorling Kindersley.

Alphabet Connections. (Illus.). 24p. 1991. write for info. picture cards (RR-001) Wonder Well.

Amery. Alphabet Book. (gr. k-2). 1979. (Usborne-Hayes); PLB 11.96 (*0-88110-065-X*) EDC.

Angel, Marie. Marie Angel's Exotic Alphabet: An Alphabet to Unfold in Words & Pictures. LC 92-8850. (Illus.). 1992. 12.95 (*0-8037-1247-2*) Dial Bks Young.

Aylesworth, Jim. The Folks in the Valley: A Pennsylvania Dutch ABC. Vitale, Stefano, illus. LC 91-12451. 32p. (ps-3). 1992. 15.00 (*0-06-021672-7*); PLB 14.89 (*0-06-021929-7*) HarpC Child Bks.

Blankholm, Robert F. Twenty-Six Friends: The Shape of the Alphabet Letters. 2nd ed. LC 90-71355. (Illus.). 64p. 1990. pap. 7.95 (*0-933499-02-7*) Stagecoach Rd Pr.

Borba, Michele & Ungaro, Dan. The Complete Letter Book. 112p. (ps-3). 1980. 11.95 (*0-916456-80-3*, GA 182) Good Apple.

Bridwell, Norman. Clifford's ABC. LC 94-9787. 1994. 10.95 (*0-590-48694-2*) Scholastic Inc.

Burningham, John. First Steps: Letters, Numbers, Colors, Opposites. Burningham, John, illus. LC 93-18844. 48p. (ps up). 1994. lib. bdg. 14.95 (*1-56402-205-6*) Candlewick Pr.

Cerf, C. B. Pop-up Animal Alphabet Book. Shirakawa, Akihito, illus. 20p. (ps). 1994. 8.99 (*0-394-81866-0*) Random Bks Yng Read.

Clarkson, Virginia C. The Alphabet of Civility. Vehslage, Cynthia, illus. LC 93-16585. 1993. write for info. (*0-913515-86-8*, Starrhill) Elliott & Clark.

Cox, Lynn. Crazy Alphabet. McRae, Rodney, illus. LC 91-3734. 32p. (ps-1). 1992. 13.95 (*0-531-05966-9*); lib. bdg. 13.99 (*0-531-08566-X*) Orchard Bks Watts.

Domanska, Janina. A Was an Angler. LC 88-35589. (Illus.). 32p. (ps up). 1991. 13.95 (*0-688-06990-8*); PLB 13.88 (*0-688-06991-6*) Greenwillow.

Dowdell, D. Secrets of the ABCs. LC 65-22301. (Illus.). 64p. (gr. 2 up). 1968. PLB 10.95 (*0-87783-035-5*) Oddo.

Edens, Cooper, compiled by. The Glorious ABC. LC 90-30566. (Illus.). 40p. 1990. SBE 15.95 (*0-689-31605-4*, Atheneum Child Bk) Macmillan Child Grp.

Fain, Kathleen. Handsigns: An Animal Alphabet. LC 92-32103. 1993. 13.95 (*0-8118-0310-4*) Chronicle Bks.

Feldman, Judy. The Alphabet in Nature. LC 90-22315. (Illus.). 32p. (ps-2). 1991. PLB 13.35 (*0-516-05101-6*) Childrens.

Feraro, Bonita. Letters & Sounds. Robison, Don, illus. 32p. (Orig.). (ps). 1993. wkbk. 1.99 (*1-56189-059-6*) Amer Educ Pub.

Fisher, Leonard E. Alphabet Art: Thirteen ABCs from Around the World. LC 84-28752. (Illus.). 64p. (gr. 3-7). 1984. Repr. of 1978 ed. SBE 16.95 (*0-02-735230-7*, Four Winds) Macmillan Child Grp.

Fitzgerald, Phyllis. Alphabets. LC 87-51494. (Illus.). 30p. (gr. k-2). 1988. 6.95 (*1-55523-130-6*) Winston-Derek.

Gaudrat, Marie-Agnes & Courtin, Thierry. My First ABC. Herbst, Judith, adapted by. LC 94-562. (Illus.). 60p. (ps-k). 1994. 12.95 (*0-8120-6313-9*) Barron.

Geringer, Laura. The Cow Is Mooing Anyhow. Zimmer, Dirk, illus. LC 85-45251. 40p. (ps-4). 1991. HarpC Child Bks.

Gregorich, Barbara. Capital Letters. Pape, Richard, illus. 24p. (gr. 3-4). 1980. wkbk. 2.95 (*0-89403-604-1*) EDC.

Hausman, Gerald. Turtle Island ABC: A Gathering of Native American Symbols. Moser, Barry & Moser, Cara, illus. LC 92-14982. 32p. (gr. 1 up). 1994. 15.00 (*0-06-021307-8*); PLB 14.89 (*0-06-021308-6*) HarpC Child Bks.

Huelsberg, Enid L. Alphabet Mastery Manuscript, Level 1: Reusable Edition. 32p. (ps-3). 1977. 6.50 (*0-87879-785-8*, Ann Arbor Div) Acad Therapy.

Hunt, Jonathan. Illuminations. Hunt, Jonathan, illus. LC 92-23542. 40p. (ps-12). 1993. pap. 5.95 (*0-689-71700-8*, Aladdin) Macmillan Child Grp.

Isadora, Rachel. City Seen from A to Z. Isadora, Rachel, illus. LC 82-11966. 32p. (gr. k-3). 1983. PLB 11.88 (*0-688-01803-3*) Greenwillow.

Jensen, Steve. Great Alphabet Fight. (ps-3). 1993. 8.99 (*0-88070-612-0*, Gold & Honey) Questar Pubs.

Johnson, Jean. Sanitation Workers: A to Z. (Illus.). (gr. k-3). 1988. 11.95 (*0-8027-6772-9*); PLB 12.85 (*0-8027-6773-7*) Walker & Co.

Johnson, Laura R. The Teddy Bear ABC. Sanford, Margaret L., illus. LC 91-18207. 64p. (ps-2). 1992. 12.00 (*0-671-74979-X*, Green Tiger); pap. 7.95 (*0-671-75949-3*, Green Tiger) S&S Trade.

Lear, Edward. An Edward Lear Alphabet. Newsom, Carol, illus. LC 82-10037. 32p. (ps up). 1986. 4.95 (*0-688-06523-6*, Mulberry) Morrow.

Lecourt, Nancy. Abracadabra to Zigzag. (Illus.). (ps-3). 1991. 13.95 (*0-688-09481-3*); PLB 13.88 (*0-688-09482-1*) Lothrop.

Lessac, Frane. Caribbean Alphabet. Lessac, Frane, illus. LC 93-15833. 32p. 1994. 15.00 (*0-688-12952-8*, Tambourine Bks); PLB 14.93 (*0-688-12953-6*, Tambourine Bks) Morrow.

Letters. (Illus.). 24p. (ps-3). 1992. pap. 3.50 (*0-7460-1036-2*) EDC.

Lippman, Sidney, et al. A You're Adorable. Alexander, Martha, illus. LC 93-931. 32p. (ps up). 1994. 9.95 (*1-56402-237-4*) Candlewick Pr.

Lobel, Arnold. On Market Street. Lobel, Anita, illus. LC 80-21418. 40p. (gr. k-3). 1981. 14.00 (*0-688-80309-1*); PLB 13.93 (*0-688-84309-3*); Greenwillow.

Mahiri, Jabari. The Day They Stole the Letter J. Carter, Dorothy, illus. (Orig.). (gr. 3-5). 1981. pap. 3.95 (*0-88378-084-4*) Third World.

Mecklenberg, Jan. Alphabet Animals. Mecklenberg, Jan, illus. LC 93-35479. 1994. 4.99 (*0-7852-8218-1*) Nelson.

Pallotta, Jerry. The Extinct Alphabet Book. Masiello, Ralph, illus. LC 93-1512. 1993. 14.95 (*0-88106-471-8*); PLB 15.88 (*0-88106-686-9*); pap. 6.95 (*0-88106-470-X*) Charlesbridge Pub.

—The Great Tasting Alphabet Book. LC 94-5178. (gr. k up). 1994. 14.95 (*0-685-72620-7*); PLB 15.00 (*0-685-72621-5*); pap. 6.95 (*0-685-72622-3*) Charlesbridge Pub.

Patton, Sally J. Alphabetics: A History of Our Alphabet. rev. ed. 92p. (gr. 2-8). 1989. pap. text ed. 14.95 (*0-913705-40-3*) Zephyr Pr AZ.

Rice, James. Texas Alphabet. Rice, James, illus. LC 87-31159. 132p. (gr. k-5). 1988. 12.95 (*0-88289-692-X*) Pelican.

Simpson, Gretchen D. Gretchen's Abc. Simpson, Gretchen D., illus. LC 90-19332. 32p. (ps up). 1991. 16.95 (*0-06-025645-1*) HarpC Child Bks.

Taulbee, Annette. Alphabet. (Illus.). 24p. (ps-k). 1986. 3.98 (*0-86734-059-2*, FS-3051) Schaffer Pubns.

—Alphabet Dot-to-Dot. (Illus.). 24p. (ps-k). 1986. 3.98 (*0-86734-062-2*, FS-3054) Schaffer Pubns.

Thompson, Kim M. & Hilderbrand, Karen M. A Little Rhythm, Rhyme & Read: Letters & Numbers. Kozjak, Goran, illus. 28p. (ps-1). 1993. Wkbk., incl. audio cass. 9.98 (*1-882331-15-X*) Twin Sisters.

Time-Life Books Editors. The Great ABC Treasure Hunt: A Hidden Picture Alphabet Book. (Illus.). 56p. (ps-2). 1991. write for info. (*0-8094-9254-7*); lib. bdg. write for info. (*0-8094-9255-5*) Time-Life.

Walton, Rick. One Was Named Abel, He Slept on the Table. LC 94-14594. 1995. write for info. (*0-688-13656-7*); PLB write for info. (*0-688-13657-5*) Lothrop.

Warren, Vic & Reasoner, Charles. Alpha Books. Woodman, Nancy, illus. (ps-1). 1991. miniature board books in a tray 14.95 (*1-878624-66-0*) McClanahan Bk.

—Alpha-Books & Count with Us. Woodman, Nancy, illus. (ps-1). 1991. miniature board books in a tray 19.95 (*1-878624-83-0*) McClanahan Bk.

Weiss, Monica. Pop! ABC Letter & Sounds: Learning the Alphabet. Berlin, Rosemary, illus. LC 91-18704. 24p. (gr. k-2). 1992. PLB 10.59 (*0-8167-2492-X*); pap. text ed. 2.95 (*0-8167-2493-8*) Troll Assocs.

Wise, Beth A. Letters & Sounds. Nayer, Judith E., ed. Regan, Dana & DeMarco, Susanne, illus. 32p. (gr. k-1). 1991. wkbk. 1.95 (*1-878624-60-1*) McClanahan Bk.

ALPHABET BOOKS

Here are entered A B C books.

ABC & You. (ps-k). 1990. text ed. 3.95 cased (*0-7214-5274-4*) Ladybird Bks.

ABC Colouring Book. (Illus.). (ps-6). pap. 2.95 (*0-565-00834-X*, Pub. by Natural Hist Mus) Parkwest Pubns.

ABCs. (Illus.). 32p. (ps-1). 1992. pap. 2.95 (*1-56144-104-X*, Honey Bear Bks) Modern Pub NYC.

ABCs in Arabic. (Illus.). (ps-3). 1987. 3.95x (*0-86685-180-1*) Intl Bk Ctr.

Abranson, Lillian. Hanukkah ABC. (Illus.). (gr. 3-7). 1968. pap. 5.00 (*0-914080-60-1*) Shulsinger Sales.

Agard, John. The Calypso Alphabet. Bent, Jennifer, illus. LC 89-945617. 32p. (ps-2). 1989. 13.95 (*0-8050-1177-3*, Bks Young Read) H Holt & Co.

Alda, Arlene. Arlene Alda's ABC. LC 93-24999. (Illus.). 32p. (gr. 3 up). 1993. Repr. of 1981 ed. 13.95 (*1-883672-01-5*) Tricycle Pr.

Alden, L. Cat's Adventure in Alphabet Town. McCallum, J., illus. LC 91-3605. 32p. (ps-2). 1992. PLB 11.80 (*0-516-05403-1*) Childrens.

—Elfin's Adventure in Alphabet Town. Hohag, L., illus. LC 91-20545. 32p. (ps-2). 1992. PLB 11.80 (*0-516-05405-8*) Childrens.

Alden, Laura. Nightingale's Adventure in Alphabet Town. McCallum, Jodie, illus. LC 92-1069. 32p. (ps-2). 1992. PLB 11.80 (*0-516-05414-7*) Childrens.

—Owl's Adventure in Alphabet Town. McCallum, Jodie, illus. LC 92-4091. 32p. (ps-2). 1992. PLB 11.80 (*0-516-05415-5*) Childrens.

—Penguin's Adventure in Alphabet Town. Williams, Jenny, illus. LC 92-1068. 32p. (ps-2). 1992. PLB 11.80 (*0-516-05416-3*) Childrens.

—Squirrel's Adventure in Alphabet Town. Collins, Judi, illus. LC 92-1314. 32p. (ps-2). 1992. PLB 11.80 (*0-516-05419-8*) Childrens.

Alpers, Jody. T Is for Tortilla: A Southwestern Alphabet Book. Johnson, Celeste, illus. 30p. (gr. k-6). 1993. pap. 5.95 (*0-9640533-0-6*) Libros de Ninos.

Alphabet. (Illus.). 12p. (gr. k-2). 1982. bds. 3.95 (*0-87449-175-4*) Modern Pub NYC.

Alphabet Action. (Illus.). (gr. 2 up). 1991. 5.95 (*0-87449-576-8*) Modern Pub NYC.

The Alphabet House. (Illus.). 24p. (ps up). 1992. write for info. incl. long-life batteries (*0-307-74811-1*, 64811, Golden Pr) Western Pub.

Alvarez, Juan. Jose Rabbit's Southwest Adventures: An ABC Coloring Book with Spanish Words. Alvarez, Juan, illus. 32p. (Orig.). (gr. 1-3). 1990. pap. 3.95 (*1-878610-00-7*) Red Crane Bks.

An Amazing Alphabet. 1993. 3.99 (*0-517-08759-6*) Random Hse Value.

Andersen, Karen B. An Alphabet in Five Acts. Born, Flint, illus. LC 92-26947. 32p. 1993. 13.99 (*0-8037-1440-8*); PLB 13.89 (*0-8037-1441-6*) Dial Bks Young.

Anglund, Joan W. In a Pumpkin Shell. Anglund, Joan W., illus. LC 60-10243. 32p. (ps-2). 1977. pap. 3.95 (*0-15-644425-9*, Voyager Bks) HarBrace.

—In a Pumpkin Shell: A Mother Goose ABC. Anglund, Joan W., illus. LC 60-10243. (ps-2). 1960. 10.95 (*0-15-238269-0*, HB Juv Bks) HarBrace.

Animal Alphabet Book. (gr. k-3). 3.95 (*0-7214-9532-X*) Ladybird Bks.

Anno, Mitsumasa. Anno's Alphabet: An Adventure in Imagination. Anno, Mitsumasa, illus. LC 73-21652. 64p. (gr. k up). 1975. 16.00 (*0-690-00540-7*, Crowell Jr Bks); PLB 15.89 (*0-690-00541-5*) HarpC Child Bks.

Aronoff, Daisy P. ABC Bible & Holiday Stories. Danciger, Leila N., illus. 58p. (ps-7). 1992. pap. 15.95 (*1-878612-28-X*) Sunflower Co.

Ashton, Elizabeth A. An Old-Fashioned ABC Book. Smith, Jessie W., illus. 32p. (ps-3). 1992. pap. 3.99 (*0-14-054189-6*) Puffin Bks.

Aylesworth, Jim. Old Black Fly. Gammell, Stephen, illus. LC 91-26825. 32p. (ps-2). 1992. 15.95 (*0-8050-1401-2*, Bks Young Read) H Holt & Co.

Azarian, Mary. A Farmer's Alphabet. LC 80-84938. 56p. (ps-2). 1981. 16.95 (*0-87923-394-X*); pap. 12.95 (*0-87923-397-4*) Godine.

—Farmers Alphabet Junior. LC 80-84938. 64p. 1985. pap. 7.95 (*0-87923-589-6*) Godine.

Babson, Jane F. Babson's Bestiary. Babson, Jane F., illus. LC 90-71155. 32p. (ps-4). 1991. casebound 10.95 (*0-940787-02-4*) Winstead Pr.
Second in a learning to read series for children & adults. Illustrated with original art, writing designed to stimulate interest, curiosity & intellectual skills. Thought-provoking. Acid-free paper. Special discounts to libraries, literacy programs. "The art book offers a superior presentation... includes some fun animal rhymes within the alphabet form...intriguing, unusual art."--THE MIDWEST BOOK REVIEW. "Attractive alphabet primer with its well-executed illustrations, a fun & funny book about animals."--THE BLOOMSBURY REVIEW.
Publisher Provided Annotation.

Baby's First ABC. 12p. (ps). 1978. 3.95 (*0-448-40864-3*, G&D) Putnam Pub Group.

Bannatyne-Cugnet, Jo. A Prairie Alphabet. Moore, Yvette, illus. LC 92-80414. 32p. (gr. k up). 1992. 19.95 (*0-88776-292-1*) Tundra Bks.

Banner, Angela. Ant & Bee & Kind Dog. Ward, Bryan, illus. 96p. (ps-1). 1992. 6.95 (*0-434-92960-3*, Pub. by W Heinemann Ltd) Trafalgar.

Bassett, Lisa. The Bunny's Alphabet Eggs. Bassett, Jeni, illus. LC 92-37987. (gr. 2 up). 1993. 3.99 (*0-517-08153-9*) Random Hse Value.

Bassett, Scott & Bassett, Tammy. Artemus & the Alphabet. Bassett, Scott, illus. 32p. (ps-k). 1980. 6.95x (*0-9605548-0-7*); PLB 6.95x (*0-9605548-1-5*) Bassett & Brush.

Bayer, Jane. A My Name Is Alice. Kellogg, Steven, illus. 32p. (ps-2). 1994. pap. 18.99 (*0-14-050429-X*, Puff Pied Piper); Set incl. 1 Giant copy, 6 regular paperbacks, Giant-sized bookmark & full-color mobile. pap. 48.69 (*0-14-774196-3*, Puff Pied Piper) Puffin Bks.

Benji's Book of ABC. (ps). 1976. bds. 5.50 (*0-904494-12-8*, Brimax Bks) Borden.

Berenstain, Stan & Berenstain, Janice. The B Book. (Illus.). (ps-1). 1971. lib. bdg. 7.99 (*0-394-92324-3*) Random Bks Yng Read.

—C Is for Clown. (Illus.). (ps-1). 1972. lib. bdg. 7.99 (*0-394-92492-4*) Random Bks Yng Read.

Berger, Terry. Ben's ABC Day. Kandell, Alice, illus. LC 81-13754. 32p. (gr. k-3). 1982. 14.93 (*0-688-00881-X*); PLB 14.93 (*0-688-00882-8*) Lothrop.

Bernhard, Durga. Alphabeasts. LC 92-24980. (Illus.). 32p. (ps-3). 1993. reinforced bdg. 14.95 (*0-8234-0993-7*) Holiday.

Bernthal, Mark. Baby Bop's ABC's. Hartley, Linda, ed. Daste, Larry, illus. LC 93-77869. 32p. (ps-k). 1993. pap. 2.25 (*1-57064-008-4*) Barney Pub.

Bliss, Richard B., ed. Dinosaur ABC's Activity Book. rev. ed. Schmitt, Doug, illus. 32p. (gr. k-3). 1986. pap. 3.95 (*0-89051-113-6*) Master Bks.

BMA Staff. The Bible ABCs: A Memory Book for Boys & Girls ages 3-5. Lautermilch, John, illus. 54p. (ps). 1980. pap. text ed. 4.95 (*0-89323-051-0*) Bible Memory.

Boddy, Marlys. ABC Book of Feelings. (Illus.). 32p. (ps-3). 1991. 8.99 (*0-570-04190-2*, 56-1649) Concordia.

Bond, Michael. Paddington Book & Bear Box. (Illus.). 32p. (ps-1). 1993. incl. plush toy 16.95 (*0-670-84683-X*) Viking Child Bks.

Bond, Susan. Ride with Me Through ABC. Lemke, Horst, illus. LC 67-19376. 32p. (ps-k). 6.95 (*0-87592-043-8*) Scroll Pr.

Borlenghi, Patricia. From Albatross to Zoo. (Illus.). (ps up). 1992. 14.95 (*0-590-45483-8*, 018, Scholastic Hardcover) Scholastic Inc.

Boynton, Sandra. Moo Baa La La La. Klimo, Kate, ed. Boynton, Sandra, illus. 14p. 1982. 3.95 (*0-671-44901-X*, Little Simon) S&S Trade.

Bragg, Ruth G. Alphabet Out Loud. LC 91-14546. (Illus.). 32p. (gr. k up). 1991. pap. 14.95 (*0-88708-172-X*) Picture Bk Studio.

Brent, Isabelle, illus. An Alphabet of Animals. LC 92-54652. 1993. 12.95 (*0-316-10852-9*) Little.

Bridwell, Norman. Clifford's ABC. (ps-3). 1986. pap. 2.25 (*0-590-44286-4*) Scholastic Inc.

—Clifford's ABC. LC 94-9787. 1994. 10.95 (*0-590-48694-2*) Scholastic Inc.

Brown, Margaret W. Sleepy ABC. Slobodkina, Esphyr, illus. LC 93-36398. 40p. (ps-2). 1994. 12.95 (*0-06-024284-1*); PLB 12.89 (*0-06-024285-X*) HarpC Child Bks.

Brown, Ruth. Alphabet Times Four: An International ABC. LC 91-3162. (Illus.). 32p. (ps up). 1991. 13.95 (*0-525-44831-4*, DCB) Dutton Child Bks.

Bruce, Lisa. Oliver's Alphabets. Gliori, Debi, illus. LC 92-39471. 24p. (ps-1). 1993. SBE 13.95 (*0-02-735996-4*, Bradbury Pr) Macmillan Child Grp.

Buckman, Mary. The Alphagator. (Illus.). 32p. (ps). 1992. pap. 8.95 (*1-879414-10-4*) Mary Bee Creat.

Burningham, John. John Burningham's ABC. Burningham, John, illus. LC 92-42765. 64p. (ps-2). 1993. 13.00 (*0-517-59503-6*); PLB 13.99 (*0-517-59504-4*) Crown Bks Yng Read.

Bustard, Anne. T Is for Texas. LC 89-35633. (Illus.). 32p. (ps-2). 1989. 12.95 (*0-89658-113-6*) Voyageur Pr.

Calmenson, Stephanie. It Begins with an A. Russo, Marisabina, illus. LC 92-72016. 32p. (ps-2). 1993. 12.95 (*1-56282-122-9*); PLB 12.89 (*1-56282-123-7*) Hyprn Child.

—It Begins with an A. LC 92-72016. (Illus.). 32p. (ps-2). 1994. pap. 4.95 (*1-56282-689-1*) Hyprn Ppbks.

Cerf, C. B. Pop-up Animal Alphabet Book. Shirakawa, Akihito, illus. 20p. (ps). 1994. 8.99 (*0-394-81866-0*) Random Bks Yng Read.

Chesely, Mary. Miss Purdy's Problem. Weinberger, Jane, ed. (Illus.). 48p. (gr. 1-5). 1994. pap. 9.95 (*0-932433-75-8*) Windswept Hse.

Christensen, Bonnie. An Edible Alphabet. LC 93-7799. 1994. write for info. (*0-8037-1404-1*); lib. bdg. write for info. (*0-8037-1406-8*) Dial Bks Young.

Coats, Laura J. Alphabet Garden. Coats, Laura J., illus. LC 92-6235. 32p. (ps-1). 1993. RSBE 13.95 (*0-02-719042-0*, Macmillan Child Bk) Macmillan Child Grp.

Cohan, Leo M. The Hebrew Alphabet: From Generation to Generation. (Illus.). 21p. (Orig.). (gr. 4). 1989. pap. 5.95 (*0-9636415-0-6*) Kol Yisrael Pub.

Cohen, Nora. From Apple to Zipper. Kern, Donna, illus. LC 92-43691. 32p. (ps-1). 1993. pap. 8.95 POB (*0-689-71708-3*, Aladdin) Macmillan Child Grp.

Conran, Sebastian. My First ABC Book. Conran, Sebastian, illus. LC 87-14562. 64p. (ps-1). 1988. pap. 6.95 POB (*0-689-71198-0*, Aladdin) Macmillan Child Grp.

Cook, D. Dinosaur's Adventure in Alphabet Town. Rigo, R., illus. LC 91-20544. 32p. (ps-2). 1992. PLB 11.80 (*0-516-05404-X*) Childrens.

Cook, Lynn. A Canadian ABC: An Alphabet Book for Kids. MacDonald, Thoreau, illus. 60p. 1990. pap. 8.95 (*0-921254-24-5*, Pub. by Penumbra Pr CN) U of Toronto Pr.

Coon, Alma S. Amy, Ben, & Catalpa the Cat: A Fanciful Story of This & That. Owens, Gail, illus. 40p. (ps-2). 1990. 8.95 (*0-87935-079-2*) Williamsburg.

Cory, Fanny Y. The Fairy Alphabet of F. Y. Cory. Cory, Fanny Y., illus. 32p. 1991. 14.95 (*1-56037-006-8*) Am Wrld Geog.

Coudron, Jill M. Alphabet Activities. (ps-3). 1982. pap. 11.95 (*0-8224-0297-1*) Fearon Teach Aids.

—Alphabet Stories. (ps-3). 1982. pap. 11.95 (*0-8224-0299-8*) Fearon Teach Aids.

Crews, Donald. We Read: A to Z. Crews, Donald, illus. LC 83-25453. 64p. (ps-1). 1984. 15.95 (*0-688-03843-3*); PLB 15.88 (*0-688-03844-1*) Greenwillow.

Crowther, Robert. The Most Amazing Hide-&-Seek Alphabet Book. LC 77-79334. (Illus.). (ps-1). 1978. pap. 13.95 (*0-670-48996-4*) Viking Child Bks.

Cushman, Doug. ABC Mystery. Cushman, Doug, illus. LC 92-9621. 32p. (ps-2). 1993. 14.00 (*0-06-021226-8*); PLB 13.89 (*0-06-021227-6*) HarpC Child Bks.

Daniel, Becky. Animals Love Their Alphabet. 32p. (ps-k). 1991. 8.95 (*0-86653-579-9*, GA1307) Good Apple.

De Bruhoff, Jean, illus. A.B.C. de Babar. LC 94-5913. (gr. 3 up). 1994. write for info. (*0-679-86842-9*) Random Bks Yng Read.

De Brunhoff, Laurent. Babar's ABC. LC 83-2987. (Illus.). 36p. (gr. k-1). 1983. pap. 13.00 (*0-394-85920-0*) Random Bks Yng Read.

De Mejo, Oscar. Oscar de Mejo's ABC. De Mejo, Oscar, illus. LC 91-28768. 32p. (ps up). 1992. PLB 16.89 (*0-06-020517-2*) HarpC Child Bks.

Dodd, Lynley. The Minister's Cat, ABC. LC 93-36139. 1994. 17.27 (*0-8368-1073-2*) Gareth Stevens Inc.

Dodson, Peter. An Alphabet of Dinosaurs. Barlowe, Wayne, illus. LC 94-15522. 1995. 15.95 (*0-590-46486-8*) Scholastic Inc.

Downie, Jill. Alphabet Puzzle. Downie, Jill, illus. LC 88-80278. 64p. (ps-1). 1988. 16.00 (*0-688-08044-8*) Lothrop.

Dragonwagon, Crescent. Alligator Arrived with Apples: A Potluck Alphabet Feast. Aruego, Jose & Dewey, Ariane, illus. LC 91-38490. 40p. (gr. k-3). 1992. pap. 4.95 (*0-689-71613-3*, Aladdin) Macmillan Child Grp.

Dr. Seuss. Dr. Seuss's ABC. Dr. Seuss, illus. LC 63-9810. 72p. (gr. k-3). 1963. 6.95 (*0-394-80030-3*); lib. bdg. 7.99 (*0-394-90030-8*) Random Bks Yng Read.

—Dr. Seuss's ABC. (Illus.). 64p. (ps-1). 1988. pap. 7.95 bk. & cassette pkg. (*0-394-89784-6*) Random Bks Yng Read.

Drucker, M. A Jewish Holiday ABC. Pocock, Rita, illus. 1992. 13.95 (*0-15-200482-3*, HB Juv Bks) HarBrace.

Duke, Kate. The Guinea Pig ABC. Duke, Kate, illus. LC 83-1410. 32p. (ps-1). 1983. 12.95 (*0-525-44058-5*, DCB) Dutton Child Bks.

Dulac, Glen. The Color Coded Alphabet: The Best Coloring Book Ever. Fischer, Robert, et al, illus. (gr. k-3). 1991. pap. 5.00 (*0-9628227-4-4*) Desert Bks.

Dulac, Glen J. The Color Coded Alphabet, an Alphabet for Easy Reading: The Alphabet as It Has Never Been Seen Before. Dulac, Glen J. & Dulac, John J., illus. (ps-2). 1990. 49.50 (*0-9628227-2-8*) Desert Bks.

Eastman, Philip D. The Alphabet Book. Eastman, Philip D., illus. LC 73-16859. 32p. (ps-3). 1974. pap. 2.25 (*0-394-82818-6*) Random Bks Yng Read.

Edades, Jean. An Animal ABC. Garibay, U. N., illus. (gr. 3-5). 1979. pap. 3.50 (*0-686-25221-7*, Pub. by New Day Pub Pl) Cellar.

Edwards, Michelle. Alef-Bet: A Hebrew Alphabet Book. Edwards, Michelle, illus. LC 91-31011. 32p. (ps-3). 1992. 15.00 (*0-688-09724-3*); PLB 14.93 (*0-688-09725-1*) Lothrop.

Egermeier, Elsie E. Picture Story Bible ABC Book. rev. ed. (Illus.). (ps-1). 1963. 9.95 (*0-87162-262-9*, D1703) Warner Pr.

Ehlert, Lois. Eating the Alphabet. LC 88-10906. (gr. 2 up). 1993. pap. 4.95 (*0-15-224436-0*, HB Juv Bks) HarBrace.

—Eating the Alphabet. LC 88-10906. (ps-3). 1994. pap. 19.95 (*0-15-200902-7*, HB Juv Bks) HarBrace.

Ehrlich, Doris. Animal Alphabet. 2nd ed. O'Rourke, Dawn M., illus. 36p. (ps-k). 1988. pap. text ed. 80.00 classroom pack (*0-932957-90-0*); tchr's. ed. 4.50 (*0-932957-91-9*); wkbk. 3.90 (*0-932957-89-7*); wall posters 17.50 (*0-932957-96-X*) Natl School.

Eichenberg, Fritz. Ape in a Cape: An Alphabet of Odd Animals. Eichenberg, Fritz, illus. LC 52-6908. 26p. (ps-3). 1952. 15.95 (*0-15-203722-5*, HB Juv Bks) HarBrace.

Ellison, Virginia. Pooh's Alphabet Book. 1991. pap. 3.50 (*0-440-40630-7*) Dell.

Emberley, Ed E. Ed Emberley's A. B. C. (Illus.). 56p. (gr. k-2). 1978. lib. bdg. 15.95 (*0-316-23408-7*) Little.

Emerson, Sally, selected by. ABCs & Other Learning Rhymes. Maclean, Moira & Maclean, Colin, illus. LC 92-32576. 1993. pap. 4.95 (*1-85697-899-0*, Kingfisher LKC) LKC.

Epstin, Vivian S. The ABCs of What a Girl Can Be. (Illus.). 32p. (ps-3). 1980. 5.95 (*0-9601002-2-9*) V S Epstein.

Feelings, Muriel & Feelings, Tom. Jambo Means Hello: Swahili Alphabet Book. (Illus.). 56p. (gr. k-3). 1985. pap. 4.99 (*0-8037-4428-5*, Puff Pied Piper) Puffin Bks.

Felix, Monique. Alphabet: Mouse Books. (Illus.). 32p. (ps). 1993. pap. 2.95 (*1-56189-094-4*) Amer Educ Pub.

Ferguson, Don. Disney's Winnie the Pooh's A to Zzzz: Miniature Edition. Langley, Bill & Wakeman, Diana, illus. 32p. (ps-k). 1994. 5.95 (*0-7868-3009-3*) Disney Pr.

Ferguson, Dwayne. Afro-Bets A B C Coloring & Activity Book. (ps-3). 1989. pap. 3.95 (*0-940975-13-0*) Just Us Bks.

Fisher, Leonard E. The ABC Exhibit. LC 90-6639. (Illus.). 32p. (ps up). 1991. SBE 15.95 (*0-02-735251-X*, Macmillan Child Bk) Macmillan Child Grp.

Fletcher, Cynthia H. My Jesus Pocketbook of ABC's. Sherman, Erin, illus. LC 81-80218. 32p. (Orig.). (ps-3). 1981. pap. 0.69 (*0-937420-01-8*) Stirrup Assoc.

Foltzer, Monica. Alphabet Picture Key Word Cards. Hoffman, Jo-Ann, illus. 38p. 1987. 38 cards 4.60 (*0-9607918-5-X*, A 505419) St Ursula.

Fortey, Richard. Dinosaur's Alphabet. (gr. 4-8). 1990. 14.95 (*0-8120-6202-7*) Barron.

Funtime ABC & 123. (Illus.). 24p. (gr. k-2). 1988. 3.95 (*0-87449-498-2*) Modern Pub NYC.

Gabriele. ABCs. 1985. pap. 1.95 (*0-911211-65-9*) Penny Lane Pubns.

Gag, Wanda. ABC Bunny. Gag, Wanda, illus. LC 33-27359. (gr. k-2). 1978. 14.95 (*0-698-20000-4*, Sandcastle Bks); (Sandcastle Bks); pap. 6.95 (*0-698-20683-5*, Coward) Putnam Pub Group.

Gamec, Hazel S. The Disappearing ABC Game Book. Gamec, Hazel S., illus. 12p. write for info. (*0-938042-02-5*) Printek.

Garcia, Mary H. & Gonzalez-Mena, Janet. English All Around Us. Ragan, Lise B., ed. LC 75-27579. (Prog. Bk.). 1985. 21.25 (*0-8325-0464-5*, Natl Textbk); (Natl Textbk) NTC Pub Grp.

Geisert, Arthur. Alphabet Book. (ps-1). 1985. write for info. HM.

Goldberg, Eric & Goldberg, Susan, illus. Disney's Genie ABC. 32p. (ps-k). 1994. 11.95 (*0-7868-3010-7*) Disney Pr.

Goodrum, Don. Lettres Acadiennes. LC 92-5124. (Illus.). 32p. (gr. k-3). 1992. 14.95 (*0-88289-899-X*) Pelican.

Gorham, Zoe. ABC I Can Be. (ps-3). 1993. pap. 3.95 (*0-85953-129-5*) Childs Play.

Gould, Ellen. The Red Letter Alphabet Book. Kelley, Cathy, illus. 29p. (gr. k up). 1983. pap. 7.00 (*0-938017-00-4*) Learn Tools.

Gravatt, Andrea. The Asheville Alphabet Book. Hall, Kathryn, ed. Grandy, Melody, illus. (Orig.). (ps-9). 1993. pap. 12.95 (*1-56664-058-X*) WorldComm.

Greenaway, Kate. A Apple Pie. 1993. 4.99 (*0-517-09302-2*) Random Hse Value.

Greenfield, Eloise. Aaron & Gayla's Alphabet Book. Gilchrist, Jan S., illus. 20p. 1992. 9.95 (*0-86316-208-8*) Writers & Readers.

—Aaron & Gayla's Alphabet Book. (ps). 1994. pap. 6.95 (*0-86316-213-4*) Writers & Readers.

Gregorich, Barbara. El Alfabeto: Mayusculas: Alphabet: Uppercase. Hoffman, Joan, ed. Shepherd-Bartram, tr. from ENG. Pape, Richard, illus. (SPA.). 32p. (Orig.). (ps). 1987. wkbk. 1.99 (*0-938256-75-0*) Sch Zone Pub Co.

—El Alfabeto: Minusculas: Alphabet: Lowercase. Hoffman, Joan, ed. Shepherd-Bartram, tr. from ENG. Pape, Richard, illus. (SPA.). 32p. (Orig.). (ps). 1987. wkbk. 1.99 (*0-938256-76-9*) Sch Zone Pub Co.

—Alphabet Avalanche. Hoffman, Joan, ed. Alexander, Barbara, et al, illus. 32p. (Orig.). (ps-1). wkbk. 1.99 (*0-88743-128-3*) Sch Zone Pub Co.

—Alphabet Skills: Kindergarten. Hoffman, Joan, ed. Koontz, Robin M., illus. 32p. (gr. k). 1990. wkbk. 2.29 (*0-88743-177-1*) Sch Zone Pub Co.

Gregory, Elizabeth. Alfred's Alphabet Antics. (Illus.). 1981. 6.95 (*0-933184-07-7*); pap. 4.95 (*0-933184-08-5*) Flame Intl.

Groening, Matt & Groening, Maggie. Maggie Simpson's Alphabet Book. LC 91-2867. (Illus.). 32p. (ps-1). 1991. HarpC Child Bks.

Grover, Max. The Accidental Zucchini: An Unexpected Alphabet. LC 93-2488. 1993. write for info. (*0-15-277695-8*, Browndeer Pr) HarBrace.

Hague, Kathleen. Alphabears. Hague, Michael, illus. (ps-2). 1985. PLB incl. cassette 19.95 (*0-941078-99-X*) Live Oak Media.

—Alphabears: An ABC Book. Hague, Michael, illus. LC 83-26476. 32p. (ps-2). 1991. pap. 4.95 (*0-8050-1637-6*, Bks Young Read) H Holt & Co.

—Numbears: Alphabears. Hague, Michael, illus. LC 85-27006. 32p. (ps-2). 1991. pap. 4.95 (*0-8050-1679-1*, Bks Young Read) H Holt & Co.

Hall, Mahji. T Is for "Terrific", Mahji's ABC's. Hall, Mahji, illus. LC 88-62371. 32p. (Orig.). (ps-3). 1989. PLB 9.95 (*0-940880-21-0*); pap. text ed. 4.95 (*0-940880-22-9*) Open Hand.

Hammond, Arissa, et al. My Friends ABC Book. LC 88-70949. (Illus.). 32p. (gr. 2 up). 1988. 10.00 (*0-9605968-4-4*) Bright Bks.

Harada, Joyce. It's the A B C Book. (ENG & VIE., Illus.). 32p. (Orig.). (gr. k-2). 1992. pap. 8.95 (*0-89346-344-2*) Heian Intl.

—It's the A B C Book. (ENG & CAM., Illus.). 32p. (Orig.). (gr. k-2). 1992. pap. 8.95 (*0-89346-345-0*) Heian Intl.

Harada, Joyce, illus. It's the A.B.C. Book. 32p. (ps). 1982. limp 7.95 (*0-89346-157-1*) Heian Intl.

Harrison, Ted. A Northern Alphabet. Harrison, Ted, illus. LC 82-50244. 32p. (ps-1). 1989. 14.95 (*0-88776-209-3*); pap. 6.95 (*0-88776-233-6*) Tundra Bks.

Hatay, Nona. Charlie's ABC. Hatay, Nona, illus. LC 92-72030. 32p. (ps-k). 1993. 10.95 (*1-56282-352-3*); PLB 10.89 (*1-56282-353-1*) Hyprn Child.

Healy, Therese. A to Z with Quincy. Martin, Joan S., illus. 50p. (Orig.). (ps-1). 1986. pap. text ed. 8.95 spiral bdg. (*0-9617581-0-4*) T Healy.

Heath, Dixie. My Alphabet Animals Draw Along Book: Alpahbet Animals Drawing Book. Wexler, Terry, ed. Heath, Dixie, illus. 70p. (gr. k-5). 1994. 12.95 (*0-9637484-0-8*) Knight Pub WA. MY ALPHABET ANIMALS DRAW ALONG BOOK is unique because of the variety of things it does for children. This book teaches children our alphabet via big, beautiful & colorful illustrations. Writing the letters & then drawing them into animals helps you to visually remember the letters. The reading of the basic sentence also stimulates the memory of the alphabet in young minds. For example: A-Airedale-Amanda's Airedale Abode. B-Bunny-Blue Bonnie Bunny Bites, etc. The children also have draw along friends to help them through the book. Anni Alphadraw, Pencil Dude & Paper Pals Pad take them on a learning & drawing safari. This helps the children feel it's a personal book, with friends helping which is more fun & adventurous. From beginning to end the children are involved with each step. MY ALPHABET ANIMALS DRAW ALONG BOOK also teaches awareness of our endangered animal friends. Seventeen of the animals in this book are endangered--either their lives or their habitat. There's also a glossary of words new to young minds & their meaning. I have taught this book in three different schools & the teachers & children love it - even the 6th graders. The expressions on the illustrations will leave a lasting impression for young & old to keep them coming back for more. Poster available for $6.00.
Publisher Provided Annotation.

Hepworth, Cathi. Antics! An Alphabetical Anthology. Hepworth, Cathi, illus. 32p. (ps-6). 1992. PLB 14.95 (*0-399-21862-9*, Putnam) Putnam Pub Group.

Hirsch, Lynn A., illus. Have You Met the Alphabet? 32p. (ps-k). 1992. 4.99 (*0-517-07393-5*, Pub. by Derrydale Bks) Random Hse Value.

Ho, Jane. ABC Alphabet Book, No. 1. 29p. (ps). Date not set. 20.00 (*0-9619126-0-X*) J H Childs Bks.

Hoban, Tana. A, B, See! LC 81-6890. (Illus.). 32p. (gr. k-3). 1982. PLB 14.93 (*0-688-00833-X*) Greenwillow.

—Twenty-Six Letters & Ninety-Nine Cents. LC 86-11993. (Illus.). 32p. (ps-3). 1987. 15.00 (*0-688-06361-6*); PLB 14.93 (*0-688-06362-4*) Greenwillow.

Hofbauer, Michele P. All the Letters. LC 93-77607. (Illus.). 56p. (ps-2). 1993. 15.95 (*1-880851-08-3*) Greene Bark Pr.

Hoffman, Joan. Alphabet. rev. ed. Cook, Chris, illus. 32p. (ps-1). 1987. wkbk. 1.99 (*0-938256-03-3*) Sch Zone Pub Co.

Holland, Alex N. Time to Learn Our ABC's. Holland, Alex N., illus. 10p. (gr. k-3). 1992. pap. 8.95 (*1-895583-14-4*) MAYA Pubs.

Holmes, Stephen. Alphabet Zoo: A Rhyming Menagerie. 1994. 5.98 (*0-8317-0454-3*) Smithmark.

Holt, Virginia. A, My Name Is Alice: A Sesame Street Alphabet Book. Mathieu, Joe, illus. LC 88-18520. 32p. (Orig.). (ps). 1989. lib. bdg. 5.99 (*0-394-92241-7*); pap. 2.25 (*0-394-82241-2*) Random Bks Yng Read.

Honey Bear ABC & Counting Book. (gr. 2-4). 1991. 6.95 (*0-87449-782-5*) Modern Pub NYC.

Houts, Amy. An A-B-C Christmas. Munger, Nancy, illus. 28p. (ps-k). 1993. 4.99 (*0-7847-0063-X*, 24-03843) Standard Pub.

Howland, Naomi. ABCDrive! A Car Trip Alphabet. LC 93-11530. (ps-1). 1994. 13.95 (*0-395-66414-4*, Clarion Bks) HM.

Hubbard, Woodleigh. C Is for Curious: An ABC of Feelings. Hubbard, Woodleigh, illus. 40p. (ps-1). 1990. 12.95 (*0-87701-679-8*) Chronicle Bks.

Hyman, Trina S. A Little Alphabet. Hyman, Trina S., illus. LC 92-29692. 40p. 1993. Repr. of 1980 ed. 5.95 (*0-688-12034-2*); PLB 14.93 (*0-688-12035-0*) Morrow Jr Bks.

Isadora, Rachel. City Seen from A to Z. ALC Staff, ed. LC 82-11966. (Illus.). 32p. (gr. k up). 1992. pap. 3.95 (*0-688-12032-6*, Mulberry) Morrow.

Jacobs, Leland. Alphabet of Girls. rev. ed. Ohlsson, Ib, illus. LC 93-8328. 1994. 14.95 (*0-8050-3018-2*) H Holt & Co.

Jeffares, Jeanne. An Around-the-World Alphabet. Jeffares, Jeanne, illus. LC 89-32135. 36p. 1989. 14.95 (*0-87226-324-X*) P Bedrick Bks.

Jensen, Steven & Tada, Joni E. The Great Alphabet Fight. Tada, Joni E., illus. (ps-3). 1993. 12.99 (*0-88070-572-8*, Gold & Honey) Questar Pubs.

Johannson, Anna T. The Great ABC Search. Lowe, Dave, illus. 48p. (ps-k). 1993. pap. 5.95 (*1-56565-059-X*) Lowell Hse.

Johnson, Audean, illus. A to Z: Look & See. 32p. (Orig.). 1989. pap. 2.25 (*0-394-86127-2*) Random Bks Yng Read.

Johnson, Crockett. Harold's ABC. Johnson, Crockett, illus. LC 63-14444. 64p. (ps-3). 1981. pap. 3.95 (*0-06-443023-5*, Trophy) HarpC Child Bks.

Johnson, Florence. Santa's ABC. (ps-3). 1993. pap. 4.95 (*0-307-10360-9*, Golden Pr) Western Pub.

Jonas, Ann. Aardvarks, Disembark! (Illus.). 40p. (ps-3). 1994. pap. 4.99 (*0-14-055309-6*) Puffin Bks.

Jones, Lily. Baby Kermit's Playtime ABC. Prebenna, David, illus. 24p. (ps-k). 1992. pap. 1.79 laminated covers (*0-307-10024-3*, 10024, Golden Pr) Western Pub.

Kahn, Peggy. The Care Bears' Book of ABC's. Bracken, Carolyn, illus. LC 82-18538. 40p. (ps-2). 1983. lib. bdg. 4.99 (*0-394-95808-X*) Random Bks Yng Read.

King-Smith, Dick. Alphabeasts. Blake, Quentin, illus. LC 91-38435. 64p. (gr. 1 up). 1992. SBE 14.95 (*0-02-750720-3*, Macmillan Child Bk) Macmillan Child Grp.

Kishta, Leila. ABC Rhymes for Young Muslims. Quinlan, Hamid, ed. Ali, Abdullah, illus. LC 83-70183. 32p. (gr. 1-6). 1983. pap. 2.50 (*0-89259-044-0*) Am Trust Pubns.

Kitamura, Satoshi. From Acorn to Zoo & Everything in Between in Alphabetical Order. (Illus.). 32p. (ps-3). 1992. bds. 15.00 (*0-374-32470-0*) FS&G.

—What's Inside: The Alphabet Book. Kitamura, Satoshi, illus. LC 84-73117. 32p. (ps up). 1985. 14.00 (*0-374-38306-5*) FS&G.

Kitchen, Bert. Animal Alphabet. Kitchen, Bert, illus. LC 83-23929. 32p. (ps up). 1984. 13.95 (*0-8037-0117-9*) Dial Bks Young.

—Animal Alphabet. Kitchen, Bert, illus. LC 83-23929. 32p. (Orig.). (ps up). 1988. pap. 4.95 (*0-8037-0431-3*, Puff Pied Piper) Puffin Bks.

—Animal Alphabet. 1992. pap. 5.99 (*0-14-054601-4*) Viking Child Bks.

Kreeger, Charlene. The Alaska ABC Book. (Illus.). 36p. (Orig.). (gr. k-1). 1978. pap. 8.95 (*0-933914-01-6*) Paws Four Pub.

The Kuekumber Kids Meet the Alphabet Alien. 12.95x (*0-9617199-0-7*) Sutton Pubns.

Kunin, Claudia. My Christmas Alphabet. (ps-3). 1993. 6.95 (*0-307-13720-1*, Golden Pr) Western Pub.

—My Hanukkah Alphabet. (ps-3). 1993. 6.95 (*0-307-13719-8*, Golden Pr) Western Pub.

Kunstadter, Maria. Women Working A-Z. (Illus.). 32p. (ps-3). 1994. PLB 15.00 (*0-917846-25-7*, 95564) Highsmith Pr.

Laird. The Alphabet Zoo. LC 74-190264. (Illus.). 32p. (ps-2). 1972. PLB 9.95 (*0-87783-053-3*); pap. 3.94 deluxe ed. o.s.i (*0-87783-079-7*) Oddo.

Larsen, Rayola C. Alphabet Talk: Gospel Rhymes for Each Letter of the Alphabet. Perry, Lucille R., illus. LC 89-83429. 32p. (Orig.). (gr. k-3). 1989. pap. 4.98 (*0-88290-147-8*) Horizon Utah.

Lear, Edward. An Edward Lear Alphabet. Newsom, Carol, illus. LC 82-10037. 32p. (gr. k-3). 1983. PLB 11.88 (*0-688-00965-4*) Lothrop.

Lecourt, Nancy. Abracadabra to Zigzag: An Alphabet Book. Lehman, Barbara, illus. LC 92-12503. 32p. (ps-3). 1992. pap. 4.99 (*0-14-054470-4*) Puffin Bks.

Leman, Martin. The Little Cats ABC Book. LC 93-26272. 1994. 13.00 (*0-671-88612-6*) S&S Trade.

Lencek, Lena. The Antic Alphabet. LC 93-31010. (Illus.). 36p. 1994. 11.95 (*0-8118-0480-1*) Chronicle Bks.

Leonard, Marcia. Alphabet Bandits: An ABC Book. Cocca-Leffler, Maryann, illus. LC 89-4933. 24p. (gr. k-2). 1990. PLB 9.59 (*0-8167-1718-4*); pap. text ed. 2.50 (*0-8167-1719-2*) Troll Assocs.

Lichtner, Schomer. Alphabet Drawings. Lichtner, Schomer, illus. 88p. (Orig.). (gr. k up). 1973. pap. 4.50 (*0-686-97176-0*) Lichtner.

Lieberman, Lillian. ABC Consonants. 64p. (gr. k-2). 1985. 6.95 (*0-912107-29-4*) Monday Morning Bks.

—ABC Letters. 64p. (gr. k-2). 1984. 6.95 (*0-912107-10-3*) Monday Morning Bks.

—ABC Order. 64p. (gr. k-3). 1984. 6.95 (*0-912107-12-X*) Monday Morning Bks.

—ABC Rhymes. 64p. (gr. k-3). 1985. 6.95 (*0-912107-28-6*) Monday Morning Bks.

—ABC Vowels. 64p. (gr. k-2). 1985. 6.95 (*0-912107-30-8*) Monday Morning Bks.

Linn's ABC Book. (Illus.). 28p. (Orig.). (ps-k). 1993. 9.95 (*0-940403-57-9*) Linns Stamp News.

A Little ABC Book. 16p. (ps-k). 1980. pap. 3.50 (*0-671-41342-2*, Little) S&S Trade.

Lobel, Anita. Away from Home. LC 93-36521. (Illus.). 32p. 1994. 16.00 (*0-688-10354-5*); PLB 15.93 (*0-688-10355-3*) Greenwillow.

—Pierrot's ABC Garden. (Illus.). 24p. (ps-k). 1992. write for info. (*0-307-00139-3*, 312-04, Golden Pr) Western Pub.

—Pierrot's ABC Garden. (ps-3). 1993. 12.95 (*0-307-17551-0*, Artsts Writrs) Western Pub.

Lucero, Faustina H. Little Indians' ABC. LC 73-87800. (Illus.). 32p. (gr. k-2). 1974. PLB 9.95 (*0-87783-129-7*); pap. 3.94 deluxe ed. (*0-87783-130-0*) Oddo.

Lundell, Margo. Disney Babies A to Z. (Illus.). 14p. (ps-k). 1989. write for info. (*0-307-12317-0*, Pub. by Golden Bks) Western Pub.

McCloskey-Padgett, Patty. The Real Mother Goose ABC's. McCloskey-Padgett, Patty, illus. 32p. 1993. pap. 5.95 (*1-56565-090-5*) Lowell Hse.
McConnell, Keith. The SeAlphabet Encyclopedia. McConnell, Keith, illus. 48p. (gr. 4 up). 1982. pap. 5.95 (*0-88045-016-9*) Stemmer Hse.
McCord, Cindy & Ross, Shirley. Animal Rhythms Alphabet. 64p. (ps-2). 1988. 6.95 (*0-912107-69-3*, MM976) Monday Morning Bks.
—Animal Rhythms Consonants. 64p. (ps-2). 1988. 6.95 (*0-912107-70-7*, MM977) Monday Morning Bks.
—Animal Rhythms Vowels. 64p. (ps-2). 1988. 6.95 (*0-912107-71-5*, MM978) Monday Morning Bks.
MacDonald, Suse. Alphabatics. MacDonald, Suse, illus. LC 91-38497. 56p. (ps-1). 1992. pap. 6.95 (*0-689-71625-7*, Aladdin) Macmillan Child Grp.
McDonnell, Janet. Ape's Adventure in Alphabet Town. Hohag, L., illus. LC 91-20539. 32p. (ps-2). 1992. 11.80 (*0-516-05401-5*) Childrens.
—Bear's Adventure in Alphabet Town. Hohag, L., illus. LC 91-20543. 32p. (ps-2). 1992. PLB 11.80 (*0-516-05402-3*) Childrens.
—Fox's Adventure in Alphabet Town. McCallum, J., illus. LC 91-20546. 32p. (ps-2). 1992. PLB 11.80 (*0-516-05406-6*) Childrens.
—Goat's Adventure in Alphabet Town. Dunnington, T., illus. LC 91-20548. 32p. (ps-2). 1992. PLB 11.80 (*0-516-05407-4*) Childrens.
—Hippo's Adventure in Alphabet Town. McDonnell, J., illus. LC 91-20549. 32p. (ps-2). 1992. PLB 11.80 (*0-516-05408-2*) Childrens.
—Ichabod's Adventure in Alphabet Town. Peltier, P., illus. LC 91-20547. 32p. (ps-2). 1992. PLB 11.80 (*0-516-05409-0*) Childrens.
—Kangaroo's Adventure in Alphabet Town. McCallum, J., illus. LC 91-20540. 32p. (ps-2). 1992. PLB 11.80 (*0-516-05411-2*) Childrens.
—Mouse's Adventure in Alphabet Town. Williams, Jenny, illus. LC 91-47717. 32p. (ps-2). 1992. PLB 11.80 (*0-516-05413-9*) Childrens.
—Quarterback's Adventure in Alphabet Town. McCallum, Jodie, illus. LC 92-1067. 32p. (ps-2). 1992. PLB 11.80 (*0-516-05417-1*) Childrens.
—Raccoon's Adventure in Alphabet Town. Endres, Helen, illus. LC 92-1066. 32p. (ps-2). 1992. PLB 11.80 (*0-516-05418-X*) Childrens.
—Turtle's Adventure in Alphabet Town. McDonnell, Janet, illus. LC 92-2984. 32p. (ps-2). 1992. PLB 11.80 (*0-516-05420-1*) Childrens.
—Victor's Adventure in Alphabet Town. Peltier, Pam, illus. LC 92-4036. 32p. (ps-2). 1992. PLB 11.80 (*0-516-05422-8*) Childrens.
—An XYZ Adventure in Alphabet Town. Hohag, Linda, illus. LC 92-2985. 32p. (ps-2). 1992. PLB 11.80 (*0-516-05424-4*) Childrens.
McGee, Marni. The Alphabet Between. Dennis, Lynne, illus. LC 91-25489. 32p. (ps-1). 1995. SBE 14.95 (*0-689-31753-0*, Atheneum Child Bk) Macmillan Child Grp.
Mack, Stan. The King's Cat Is Coming. Mack, Stan, illus. (ps-1). 1976. lib. bdg. 4.99 (*0-394-93302-8*) Pantheon.
Mackenzie, Ellen K. ABC House. Lloyd, Megan, illus. (gr. k-3). 1994. 14.95 (*0-8050-1946-4*) H Holt & Co.
McKenzie, Marni S. Alphabet of Bible Creatures. Patterson, Karen T., illus. 56p. (ps-8). 1993. 14.95 (*1-882630-00-9*) Mercy Pr.
MacKinnon, Debbie. My First ABC. Sieveking, Anthea, photos by. LC 92-11500. (Illus.). (ps). 1992. 11.95 (*0-8120-6331-7*) Barron.
McKissack, Patricia & McKissack, Fredrick. Big Bug Book of the Alphabet. Bartholomew, illus. LC 87-61653. 24p. (Orig.). (gr. k-1). 1987. spiral bdg. 14.95 (*0-88335-764-X*); pap. text ed. 4.95 (*0-88335-774-7*) Milliken Pub Co.
McMillan, Mary. God's ABC Zoo. Grossman, Dan, illus. 48p. (ps-1). 1987. pap. 7.95 (*0-86653-405-9*, SS1802, Shining Star Pubns) Good Apple.
McPhail, David. David McPhail's Animals A to Z. (Illus.). 32p. (ps-1). 1993. 2.50 (*0-590-46462-0*, Cartwheel) Scholastic Inc.
Magee, Doug & Newman, Robert. All Aboard ABC. LC 89-29852. (Illus.). (ps). 1990. 13.95 (*0-525-65036-9*, Cobblehill Bks) Dutton Child Bks.
—Let's Fly from A to Z. LC 91-39774. (Illus.). 48p. (ps-3). 1992. 14.00 (*0-525-65105-5*, Cobblehill Bks) Dutton Child Bks.
Marie, Jeanne. Moving Through Your ABC's. Drum, Stacy, illus. LC 92-9944. 32p. (ps-2). Date not set. 11.95 (*1-56065-166-0*) Capstone Pr.
Marshall, Janet. Look Once, Look Twice. LC 94-27259. 1995. 14.95 (*0-395-71644-6*) Ticknor & Flds Bks Yng Read.
Martin, Bill, Jr. Chicka Chicka ABC. (ps-6). 1993. 4.95 (*0-671-87893-X*, Little Simon) S&S Trade.
Maurer, Donna. Annie, Bea, & Chi Chi Dolores: A School Day Alphabet. Cazet, Denys, illus. LC 92-25104. 32p. (ps-k). 1993. 14.95 (*0-531-05467-5*); PLB 14.99 (*0-531-08617-8*) Orchard Bks Watts.
Mayer, Marianna. The Unicorn Alphabet. Hague, Michael, illus. 32p. (gr. 1 up). 1989. 14.95 (*0-8037-0372-4*); PLB 14.89 (*0-8037-0373-2*) Dial Bks Young.
—The Unicorn Alphabet. Hague, Michael, illus. 32p. 1993. pap. 5.99 (*0-14-054922-6*, Puff Pied Piper) Puffin Bks.
Mayer, Marianna & McDermott, Gerald. The Brambleberrys Animal Alphabet. LC 91-70420. (Illus.). 32p. (ps up). 1991. 3.95 (*1-878093-78-9*) Boyds Mills Pr.
Mayers, Florence C. Baseball ABC. LC 94-1167. 1994. 12.95 (*0-8109-1938-9*) Abrams.
Mazzarella, Mimi. Alphabatty Animals & Funny Foods. Mazzarella, Mimi & Mazzarella, James, illus. LC 83-81449. 96p. (Orig.). (gr. k-3). 1984. pap. 5.95 (*0-89709-045-4*) Liberty Pub.
Merriam, Eve. Goodnight to Annie: An Alphabet Lullaby. Schwartz, Carol, illus. 32p. (ps-2). 1994. pap. 4.95 (*0-7868-1005-X*) Hyprn Ppbks.
Metaxes, Eric. The Birthday ABC. Raglin, Tim, illus. LC 93-46896. 1995. 14.00 (*0-671-88306-2*, S&S BFYR) S&S Trade.
Micklethwait, Lucy, selected by. I Spy: An Alphabet in Art. LC 91-42212. (Illus.). 64p. 1992. 19.00 (*0-688-11679-5*) Greenwillow.
Mike, Jan. New Mexico, Land of Enchantment Alphabet Book. Lowmiller, Cathie, illus. 32p. (Orig.). (gr. k-5). 1993. pap. 7.95 (*0-918080-55-X*) Treasure Chest.
Miller, Edna. Mousekin's ABCs. LC 72-176159. (Illus.). 32p. (gr. k-4). 1974. pap. 5.95 (*0-671-66473-5*, S&S BFYR) S&S Trade.
Miller, Jane. The Farm Alphabet Book. Miller, Jane, illus. 32p. (ps-2). 1987. pap. 2.50 (*0-590-31991-4*) Scholastic Inc.
Mr. Lion's I-Spy ABC. LC 90-48945. 16p. (Orig.). (ps-2). 1975. pap. 5.95 (*0-85953-065-5*, Pub. by Child's Play England) Childs Play.
Mister Tom. Queen Fussy. Spivey, Elvera, illus. 48p. (gr. 2-4). 1973. Cassette. write for info. Oddo.
Moak, Allen. A Big City ABC. (Illus.). 32p. (ps up). 1989. text ed. 14.95 (*0-88776-161-5*, Dist. by U of Toronto Pr); pap. 6.95 (*0-88776-238-7*) Tundra Bks.
Modesitt, Jeanne. The Story of Z. Johnson, Lonnie S., illus. LC 92-6626. 28p. 1992. pap. 4.95 (*0-88708-278-5*) Picture Bk Studio.
Moncure, Jane B. Magic Monsters Act the Alphabet. Endres, Helen, illus. LC 79-23841. (ps-3). 1980. PLB 14.95 (*0-89565-116-5*) Childs World.
—My "b" Sound Box. Sommers, Linda, illus. LC 77-23588. (ps-2). 1977. PLB 14.95 (*0-913778-92-3*) Childs World.
—My "d" Sound Box. Sommers, Linda, illus. LC 78-8450. (ps-2). 1978. PLB 21.35 (*0-89565-044-4*) Childs World.
—My "f" Sound Box. Sommers, Linda, illus. LC 77-9377. (ps-2). 1977. PLB 14.95 (*0-913778-93-1*) pap. 6.96 (*0-685-57684-1*) Childs World.
—My "h" Sound Box. Sommers, Linda, illus. LC 77-8977. (ps-2). 1977. PLB 14.95 (*0-913778-94-X*) Childs World.
—My "l" Sound Box. Sommers, Linda, illus. LC 78-8373. (ps-2). 1978. PLB 14.95 (*0-89565-045-2*) Childs World.
—My "p" Sound Box. Sommers, Linda, illus. LC 78-7841. (ps-2). 1978. PLB 14.95 (*0-89565-047-9*) Childs World.
—My "r" Sound Box. Sommers, Linda, illus. LC 78-7842. (ps-2). 1978. PLB 14.95 (*0-89565-048-7*) Childs World.
—My "s" Sound Box. Sommers, Linda, illus. LC 77-8970. (ps-2). 1977. PLB 14.95 (*0-913778-95-8*) Childs World.
—My "t" Sound Box. Sommers, Linda, illus. LC 77-23587. (ps-2). 1977. PLB 14.95 (*0-913778-96-6*) Childs World.
—My "w" Sound Box. Sommers, Linda, illus. LC 78-8614. (ps-2). 1978. PLB 14.95 (*0-89565-046-0*) Childs World.
Monteith, Jay. ABCs African Art Coloring Book. Monteith, Jay, illus. 32p. (ps-3). 1992. pap. text ed. 6.95 (*0-9627366-3-5*) Arts & Comns NY.
Montresor, Beni. The Dragon Drummer: A Story ABC. LC 92-27684. 1993. Repr. of 1969 ed. write for info. (*0-385-30845-0*) Doubleday.
Mullins, Patricia. V for Vanishing: An Alphabet of Endangered Animals. Mullins, Patricia, illus. LC 93-8181. 32p. (ps-2). 1994. 15.00 (*0-06-023556-X*); PLB 14.89 (*0-06-023557-8*) HarpC Child Bks.
The Muppet Babies' ABC. LC 83-62170. 28p. (ps). 1984. bds. 3.25 (*0-394-86363-1*) Random Bks Yng Read.
Murphy, Chuck. My First Book of the Alphabet. (Illus.). 12p. 1993. 6.95 (*0-590-46304-7*) Scholastic Inc.
Murray, Patricia A. Let's Learn the Hawaiian Alphabet. Tanaka, Cliff, illus. 24p. (ps-k). 1987. 7.95 (*0-89610-075-8*) Island Heritage.
—Let's Learn the Hawaiian Alphabet. Tanaka, Cliff, illus. 24p. (ps-k). 1988. incls. cass. 11.95 (*0-89610-079-0*) Island Heritage.
Name Game Staff. Hanukkah Alphabet. (Illus.). (ps-5). 1977. pap. 2.50 (*0-914080-63-6*) Shulsinger Sales.

Nedobeck, Don. Nedobeck's Alphabet Book. (Illus.). 16p. (gr. 1-8). 1993. Repr. of 1981 ed. 9.95 (*0-944314-00-7*) New Wrinkle.
Where would you find an Alligator In An Armchair Eating An Apple? Or a Zebra Named Zola Who Snores Zig-Zagging Zs? In DON NEDOBECK'S ALPHABET BOOK, of course, along with their delightful friends that enchant & teach children of all ages. Through colorful repetition of silliness, sounds & vividly imaginative artwork (such as JEREMIAH JACKRABBIT WEARS HIS JADE GREEN JACKET & EATS A JAM SANDWICH), Don Nedobeck makes learning the alphabet a magical experience. Each page you turn is a "feast for the child" - The Book Reader, & NEDOBECK'S ALPHABET BOOK brings the A to Zs to life before their very eyes! - Carmen A. Murguia.
Publisher Provided Annotation.

Nelson, Lynn A. Learning to Print Animal Alphabet Book. 1990. 9.95 (*0-88047-221-9*, D9007) DOK Pubs.
Neumeier, Marty & Glaser, Byron. Action Alphabet. Neumeier, Marty & Glaser, Byron, illus. LC 84-25322. 56p. (ps-1). 1985. 14.00 (*0-688-05703-9*); lib. bdg. 13.93 (*0-688-05704-7*) Greenwillow.
Newberry, Clare T. Kittens ABC. reissue ed. Date not set. 14.95 (*0-06-024450-X*); PLB 14.89 (*0-06-024451-8*) HarpC Child Bks.
Nii-owoo, Ife. A Is for Africa: Looking at Africa Through the Alphabet. Nii-owoo, Ife, illus. LC 90-81575. 32p. (ps-k). 1992. 12.95 (*0-86543-182-5*); pap. 5.95 (*0-86543-183-3*) Africa World.
Novit, Renee Z. Alphabet Aa to Zz. R. Z. Novit Graphic Design Staff, illus. 16p. (ps-k). Date not set. pap. 7.95 (*1-883371-00-7*) Kidz & Katz.
Ong, Cristina, illus. The Little Engine That Could ABC. 20p. (ps-3). 1994. bds. 2.95 (*0-448-40262-9*, Platt & Munk Pubs) Putnam Pub Group.
—The Little Engine That Could: Let's Sing ABC. 24p. (ps). 1993. 9.95 (*0-448-40509-1*, Platt & Munk Pubs) Putnam Pub Group.
—The Little Engine That Could: Little Library, 3 bks. (Set incls. Colors, ABC & Numbers, 20 pgs. ea. bk.). (ps). 1992. Set. bds. 7.95 slipcased (*0-448-40261-0*, Platt & Munk Pubs) Putnam Pub Group.
Onyefulu, Ifeoma. A Is for Africa. Onyefulu, Ifeoma, photos by. LC 92-39964. (Illus.). 32p. (ps-3). 1993. 14.99 (*0-525-65147-0*, Cobblehill Bks) Dutton Child Bks.
Owens, Mary B. A Caribou Alphabet. McCollough, Mark, contrib. by. (Illus.). 40p. (gr. k-6). 1988. 16.95 (*0-937966-25-8*) Tilbury Hse.
—A Caribou Alphabet. McCollough, Mark, contrib. by. (Illus.). 40p. (ps-3). 1990. pap. 4.95 (*0-374-41043-7*, Sunburst) FS&G.
Oxenbury, Helen. Helen Oxenbury's ABC of Things. Oxenbury, Helen, illus. 28p. (ps). 1993. pap. 3.95 (*0-689-71761-X*, Aladdin) Macmillan Child Grp.
Pajot-Smith, Jean. Li'l Tuffy & His ABC's. Smith, Jean P., illus. 64p. (ps-4). pap. 5.00 (*0-87485-063-0*) Johnson Chi.
Pallotta, Jerry. The Desert Alphabet Book. Astrella, Mark, illus. LC 93-42651. 32p. (Orig.). (ps-4). 1994. 14.95 (*0-88106-473-4*); PLB 15.88 (*0-88106-687-7*); pap. 6.95 (*0-88106-472-6*) Charlesbridge Pub.
—The Dinosaur Alphabet Book. (Illus.). 32p. (Orig.). (ps-4). 1990. 14.95 (*0-88106-467-X*); PLB 15.88 (*0-88106-683-4*); pap. 6.95 (*0-88106-466-1*) Charlesbridge Pub.
—The Extinct Alphabet Book. Masiello, Ralph, illus. LC 93-1512. 1993. 14.95 (*0-88106-471-8*); PLB 15.88 (*0-88106-686-9*); pap. 6.95 (*0-88106-470-X*) Charlesbridge Pub.
—The Flower Alphabet Book. Evans, Leslie, illus. 32p. (ps-3). 1989. 14.95 (*0-88106-459-9*); pap. 6.95 (*0-88106-453-X*) Charlesbridge Pub.
—The Frog Alphabet Book. Masiello, Ralph, illus. 32p. (Orig.). (ps-4). 1990. 14.95 (*0-88106-463-7*); PLB 15.88 (*0-88106-681-8*); pap. 6.95 (*0-88106-462-9*) Charlesbridge Pub.
—The Furry Alphabet Book. Stuart, Edgar, illus. 32p. (Orig.). (ps-4). 1990. 14.95 (*0-88106-465-3*); PLB 15.88 (*0-88106-682-6*); pap. 6.95 (*0-88106-464-5*) Charlesbridge Pub.
—Going Lobstering. Bolster, Rob, illus. 32p. (Orig.). (ps-4). 1990. 15.95 (*0-88106-475-0*); pap. 7.95 (*0-88106-474-2*) Charlesbridge Pub.
—The Ocean Alphabet Book. Mazzola, Frank, Jr., illus. 32p. (ps-3). 1989. 14.95 (*0-88106-458-0*); PLB 15.88 (*0-88106-678-8*); pap. 6.95 (*0-88106-452-1*) Charlesbridge Pub.
—The Spice Alphabet Book: Herbs, Spices, & Other Natural Flavors. Evans, Leslie, illus. 32p. (Orig.). (ps-4). 1994. 14.95 (*0-88106-898-5*); PLB 15.00 (*0-88106-899-3*); pap. 6.95 (*0-88106-897-7*) Charlesbridge Pub.
—The Underwater Alphabet Book. (Illus.). 32p. (ps-8). 1991. 14.95 (*0-88106-461-0*); PLB 15.88 (*0-88106-684-2*); pap. 6.95 (*0-88106-455-6*) Charlesbridge Pub.
—The Victory Garden Vegetable alphabet Book. (Illus.). 32p. (gr. 3-8). 1992. 14.95 (*0-88106-469-6*); PLB 15.88 (*0-88106-685-0*); pap. 6.95 (*0-88106-468-8*) Charlesbridge Pub.
—Yucky Reptile Alphabet Book. (ps-3). 1990. 14.95 (*0-88106-460-2*); PLB 15.88 (*0-685-71869-7*); pap. 6.95 (*0-88106-454-8*) Charlesbridge Pub.

Palmer, Glenda. P Is for Pink Polliwogs: God's Wonderful World of Letters. LC 92-34715. (Illus.). 1993. pap. 4.99 (*0-7814-0708-7*, Chariot Bks) Chariot Family.

Palotta, Jerry. The Icky Bug Alphabet Book. Masiello, Ralph, illus. 32p. (ps-3). 1989. 14.95 (*0-88106-456-4*); PLB 15.88 (*0-88106-676-1*); pap. 6.95 (*0-88106-450-5*) Charlesbridge Pub.

Pare, Roger. L' Alphabet: A Child's Introduction to the Letters & Sounds of French. Pare, Roger, illus. 32p. 1991. 7.95 (*0-8442-1395-0*, Natl Textbk) NTC Pub Grp.

—The Annick ABC. Pare, Roger, illus. 24p. (ps-2). 1989. pap. 0.99 (*0-920303-78-1*, Pub. by Annick CN) Firefly Bks Ltd.

Parker. The Norfin Trolls from A to Z. 1993. pap. 2.50 (*0-590-46957-6*) Scholastic Inc.

Paterson, Bettina, illus. Merry ABC. 24p. (ps). 1993. bds. 2.95 (*0-448-40553-9*, G&D) Putnam Pub Group.

Paul, Ann W. Eight Hands Round: A Patchwork Alphabet. Winter, Jeanette, illus. LC 88-745. 32p. (gr. 3 up). 1991. 15.00 (*0-06-024689-8*); PLB 14.89 (*0-06-024704-5*) HarpC Child Bks.

Pavao, John. Understanding Book. Perle, Ruth L., ed. Abisch, Roz & Kaplan, Boche, illus. (gr. 1). 1977. pap. text ed. 3.25 (*0-89796-863-8*) New Dimens Educ.

Pearson, C. E. Above & Below the ABSeas. Pearson, S. E., illus. 56p. (Orig.). (gr. k-5). 1994. pap. 9.95 (*0-9640585-0-2*) Mt Hope Pubng. "Come, come along. Come sail with me. And see the sights from A to Z. We'll find what we can both above & below, so hop on the ship & away we'll go!" So begins a highly imaginative & delightful voyage on the little ship the ABC as we travel both above & below the ocean to learn the letters of the alphabet & experience life in & out of the sea. Rhythmic prose & superb imagery create an alphabet adventure for children that they will enjoy reading time & time again. With great attention to detail, the artist has created an original & fascinating book filled with thousands of child-friendly creatures & characters, including pirates, swordfish, whales, kelp, & more fish than you can shake a fin at. Although its primary target is children K-5, it has been equally well received by older children & adults. As an example, the L page would read, "L is for Lots of Long Lovely eels, Lurking in Lairs, waiting for meals." The Z page is a visual feast which reads, "Z is for zillions & zillions of fish zipping & zooming wherever they wish." A delight to read & experience, this book is for those who desire something different & truly fun. To order contact: Mt. Hope Publishing Co., E. 6106 Spangle Waverly Rd., Spangle, WA 99031. 509-245-3545.
Publisher Provided Annotation.

Peek-a-Boo ABC. LC 82-60108. (ps). 1982. bds. 5.95 (*0-394-85418-7*) Random Bks Yng Read.

Pelham, David. A Is for Animals. (ps). 1991. pap. 15.95 casebound, pop-up (*0-671-72495-9*, S&S BFYR) S&S Trade.

Pessin, Deborah. Aleph-Bet Story Book. (Illus.). (gr. 1-3). 1989. pap. 6.95 (*0-8276-0337-1*) JPS Phila.

Pienkowski, Jan. ABC. Pienkowski, Jan, illus. (ps). 1989. 2.95 (*0-671-68133-8*, Little Simon) S&S Trade.

Pienkowski, Jan, illus. ABC Dinosaurs: And Other Prehistoric Creatures. 10p. (ps-k). 1993. 18.99 (*0-525-67468-3*, Lodestar Bks) Dutton Child Bks.

Piers, Helen. Puppy's ABC. (Illus.). 32p. (ps-k). 1987. 9.95 (*0-19-520606-1*) OUP.

Piette, Nadine, illus. Mi Primer ABC. (SPA.). 60p. (ps). 1993. Repr. of 1991 ed. 3.95 (*970-607-186-5*, Larousse LKC) LKC.

Polette, Nancy. Apple Trees to Zinnias. (Illus.). 48p. 1992. pap. 5.95 (*1-879287-14-5*) Bk Lures.

Poltarnees, Welleran, et al, eds. A. B. C. of Fashionable Animals. Neilson, Harry B., et al, illus. 64p. 1991. 12.95 (*0-88138-122-5*, Green Tiger) S&S Trade.

Portugal, Jan. ABC Sillies. Portugal, Jan, illus. LC 83-10291. 56p. (Orig.). (ps-1). 1983. pap. 3.00 (*0-937148-13-X*) Wild Horses.

Potter, Beatrix. Peter Rabbit's ABC. Potter, Beatrix, illus. 48p. (ps-2). 1987. 6.95 (*0-7232-3423-X*) Warne.

—Peter Rabbit's ABC Frieze. 1987. 5.00 (*0-7232-5637-3*) Warne.

Pragoff, Fiona. Alphabet. LC 87-635. (Illus.). (ps-k). 1987. pap. 6.95 (*0-385-24171-2*) Doubleday.

Qazi, M. A. Arabic Alphabet Coloring Book. 20p. (ps). 1984. pap. 3.50 (*1-56744-220-X*) Kazi Pubns.

Rasburry, Kaitlin. Hillary's Book of ABC's. Rasburry, Kaitlin, illus. 28p. (gr. k-2). 1994. 14.95 (*1-884825-00-1*) Raspberry Pubns.

Reasoner, Chuck. A Big Alphabet Book. Reasoner, Chuck, illus. (ps). 1993. bds. 9.95 (*0-8431-3552-2*) Price Stern.

Red Hawk, Richard. ABCs the American Indian Way. (Illus.). 55p. (Orig.). (ps-8). 1988. pap. 6.95 (*0-940113-15-5*) Sierra Oaks Pub.

Reid, Elizabeth. Bilingual ABC: Spanish & English. (SPA & ENG., Illus.). 64p. (gr. k-3). 1995. pap. text ed. 2.50 (*0-9627080-6-2*) In One EAR.

Reit, Seymour V. Things That Go: A Traveling Alphabet. 1990. 9.99 (*0-553-05856-8*) Bantam.

Ressmeyer, Roger. Astronaut to Zodiac: A Young Stargazer's Alphabet. LC 92-9615. (Illus.). 32p. (gr. k-6). 1992. 15.00 (*0-517-58805-6*); PLB 15.99 (*0-517-58806-4*) Crown Bks Yng Read.

Rey, H. A. Curious George Learns the Alphabet. (Illus.). 72p. (gr. k-3). 1963. 12.70 (*0-395-16031-6*) HM.

Rice, James. Cajun Alphabet: Full-Color Edition. LC 90-39342. (Illus.). 64p. (ps-8). 1991. 16.95 (*0-88289-822-1*) Pelican.

Rice, James, illus. Cowboy Alphabet. 40p. (gr. k-4). 1983. 11.95 (*0-88289-427-7*) Pelican.

Rich, Beatrice. ABCDEFGHIJKLMNOPQRSTUVWXYZ in English & French. LC 81-20838. (Illus.). 64p. (gr. k-2). 1983. PLB 15.95 (*0-87460-353-6*) Lion Bks.

Ricklen, Neil. First Word Books: ABC. (ps). 1994. pap. 5.95 (*0-671-86725-3*, Little Simon) S&S Trade.

Riehecky, J. Jack & Jill's Adventure in Alphabet Town. Hohag, L., illus. LC 91-20541. 32p. (ps-2). 1992. PLB 11.80 (*0-516-05410-4*) Childrens.

—Little Lady's Adventure in Alphabet Town. McCallum, J., illus. LC 91-20542. 32p. (ps-2). 1992. PLB 11.80 (*0-516-05412-0*) Childrens.

Riehecky, Janet. Walrus' Adventure in Alphabet Town. Magnuson, Diana, illus. LC 92-1330. 32p. (ps-2). 1992. PLB 11.80 (*0-516-05423-6*) Childrens.

Robinson, Lafayette. Rite Easy from A to Z. Gonzalez, Inez, tr. Wigglesworth, Sheila, illus. (SPA & ENG.). 48p. (gr. 1-3). 1993. lib. bdg. write for info. (*0-9621081-0-3*) Educ Graphics.

Rosario, Idalia. Idalia's Project ABC-Proyecto ABC: An Urban Alphabet Book in English & Spanish. Idalia, Rosario, illus. LC 80-21013. (ps-2). 1988. (Bks Young Read); pap. 5.95 (*0-8050-0296-0*) H Holt & Co.

Ross, Anna. Little Ernie's ABC's. Gorbaty, Norman, illus. LC 91-27823. 24p. (ps). 1992. 3.99 (*0-679-82240-2*) Random Bks Yng Read.

Ross, Shirley. ABCs Beginning Sounds. 80p. (Orig.). (ps). 1985. pap. 2.95 (*0-8431-2506-3*) Price Stern.

Rosser, J. K. Teenage Mutant Ninja Turtles ABC's for a Better Planet. GEE Studio Staff, illus. LC 90-53247. 32p. (Orig.). (ps-3). 1991. PLB 5.99 (*0-679-91383-1*) Random Bks Yng Read.

Roziere, Gael. Artist's Alphabet: A Child's Activity Book for Language, Movement & Painting. 28p. (ps-4). 1988. pap. 5.95 wkbk. (*0-9619004-2-3*) M Press NM.

Rubin, Cynthia E., selected by. ABC Americana from the National Gallery of Art. (Illus.). 26p. (ps up). 1989. 11.95 (*0-15-200660-5*, Gulliver Bks) HarBrace.

RuDenski, Kathy. Amazing Alphabet Animals. Brady, Steve, illus. LC 91-65792. 44p. (gr. k-3). 1992. 8.95 (*1-55523-447-X*) Winston-Derek.

Salinas-Norman, Bobbi. Salinas-Norman's ABC's. Rodriguez-Nieto, Catherine & Rodriguez-Nieto, Alcides, eds. (Illus.). 80p. (ps-6). 1986. wkbk. 7.95 (*0-934925-02-X*); tchr's guide, 150 p. 13.95 (*0-934925-01-1*) Pinata Pubns.

Sardegna, Jill. K Is for Kiss Good Night. Hayes, Michael, illus. LC 92-34404. 1994. 13.95 (*0-385-31044-7*) Doubleday.

Scarry, Richard. Mein Allerschonstes A B C. (Illus.). 19.95 (*0-317-05632-8*) Intl Lang.

—Richard Scarry's ABC Word Book. (Illus.). (ps-2). 1971. 11.00 (*0-394-82339-7*); lib. bdg. 5.99 (*0-394-92339-1*) Random Bks Yng Read.

—Richard Scarry's ABCs. Scarry, Richard, illus. (ps-k). 1991. pap. 1.25 (*0-307-11515-1*, Golden Pr) Western Pub.

—Richard Scarry's Find Your ABC's. (Illus.). (ps-1). 1973. pap. 2.25 (*0-394-82683-3*) Random Bks Yng Read.

Schaffer, Frank, Publications Staff. The Alphabet. (Illus.). 24p. (ps-2). 1978. wkbk. 3.98 (*0-86734-001-0*, FS-3002) Schaffer Pubns.

—Beginning Activities with the Alphabet. (Illus.). 24p. (ps-k). 1980. 3.98 (*0-86734-015-0*, FS-3028) Schaffer Pubns.

—Printing with Peter Possum. (Illus.). 24p. (gr. k-2). 1978. wkbk. 3.98 (*0-86734-006-1*, FS-3007) Schaffer Pubns.

Schmid-Belk, Donna D. The Arizona Alphabet Book. Belk, Gordon G., ed. Ives, Michael, illus. 32p. (Orig.). (ps-8). 1989. pap. text ed. 7.95 (*0-685-28841-2*) Donna Dee Bks.

Sendak, Maurice. Alligators All Around. Sendak, Maurice, illus. 32p. (ps-3). 1962. PLB 13.89 (*0-06-025530-7*) HarpC Child Bks.

—Alligators All Around: An Alphabet. Sendak, Maurice, illus. LC 62-13315. 32p. (ps-3). 1991. pap. 3.95 (*0-06-443254-8*, Trophy) HarpC Child Bks.

Sesame Street Editors. The Sesame Street ABC Book of Words. McNaught, Harry, illus. LC 86-62405. 48p. (ps-k). 1988. pap. 11.00 (*0-394-88880-4*) Random Bks Yng Read.

Shaine, Frances. A Walk in the Alphabet Zoo. Bingham, Edith, illus. 30p. (Orig.). (ps-2). 1993. pap. 4.95 (*1-884217-00-1*) Wellford.

—A Walk Through the Alphabet Garden. Bingham, Edith, illus. 30p. (Orig.). (ps-3). 1993. pap. 4.95 (*1-884217-01-X*) Wellford.

Shannon, George. Tomorrow's Alphabet. Crews, Donald, illus. LC 94-19484. 1995. write for info. (*0-688-13504-8*); PLB write for info. (*0-688-13505-6*) Greenwillow.

Shepherd, Sarah & Shepherd, Thomas. AlphaBuddies Coloring & Reading Book, No. 1. 56p. (gr. 1-2). 1992. wkbk. 4.95 (*0-9634846-0-5*) AlphaBuddies.

Shirley, Gayle. A Is for Animals. Bergum, Connie, illus. 56p. (ps-3). 1991. pap. 8.95 (*1-56044-025-2*) Falcon Pr MT.

Shroyer, Susan P. & Kimmel, Joan G. ABC - Sign with Me. Kimmel, Joan G., illus. 32p. (Orig.). (ps-2). 1987. pap. 4.95 (*0-939849-00-3*) Sugar Sign Pr.

Shumsky, Adaia & Shumsky, Abraham. The Alef-Bet Primer Reading Practice Book. Bass, Marilyn, illus. 80p. (gr. k-3). 1984. pap. text ed. 5.00 (*0-8074-0257-5*, 405315) UAHC.

Siede, George & Preis, Donna, photos by. Alphabet: Active Minds. Schwager, Istar, contrib. by. (Illus.). 24p. (ps-3). 1992. PLB 9.95 (*1-56674-000-2*) Forest Hse.

Silbert, Linda P. & Silbert, Alvin J. Make My Own Book Kit Alphabet. (ps-2). 1984. wkbk. 4.98 (*0-89544-319-8*) Silbert Bress.

Silverman, Maida. Baby's Book of ABC. Gleeson, Kate, illus. 12p. (ps). 1993. pap. 1.95 (*0-307-06037-3*, 6037, Golden Pr) Western Pub.

Sloane, Eric. ABC Book of Early Americana. LC 89-24603. (Illus.). 64p. 1990. 16.95 (*0-8050-1294-X*) H Holt & Co.

Smalley, Guy, illus. My Very Own Book of ABCs. 32p. (ps-2). 1989. 9.95 (*0-929793-02-1*) Camex Bks Inc.

Smalls-Hector, Irene. The Alphabet Witch. LC 94-6196. (Illus.). 1994. 7.95 (*0-681-00542-4*) Longmeadow Pr.

Smee, Nicola. A B C. (gr. k up). 1993. 7.00 (*0-00-195465-2*) Collins SF.

Smiles & Frowns - Ups & Downs with the Alphabet Pals: Rainy Days & Rainbows. LC 89-51291. 20p. (ps). 1989. lib. bdg. write for info. (*0-7166-1903-2*) World Bk.

Snow, Alan. The Monster Book of ABC Sounds. Snow, Alan, illus. LC 90-39384. 32p. (ps-2). 1991. 12.95 (*0-8037-0935-8*) Dial Bks Young.

Spizman, Robyn. Bulletin Boards: For Reading, Spelling & Language Skills. Pesiri, Evelyn, illus. 64p. (gr. k-6). 1984. wkbk. 7.95 (*0-86653-210-2*, GA 574) Good Apple.

Steig, Jeanne. Alpha Beta Chowder. Steig, William, illus. LC 92-52641. 48p. (gr. k up). 1992. 15.00 (*0-06-205006-0*); PLB 14.89 (*0-06-205007-9*) HarpC Child Bks.

Stockham, Leslie C. Divirtamonos Con el Abecedario. Stockham, Leslie C., illus. 96p. (gr. k-2). 1993. wkbk. 8.95 (*0-9624096-2-6*) Bilingual Lang Mat.

Stockham, Peter, ed. The Mother's Picture Alphabet. Anelay, Henry, illus. 64p. (ps-3). 1975. pap. 4.50 (*0-486-23089-9*) Dover.

Stutson, Caroline. On the River ABC. Crum, Anna M., illus. LC 92-61907. 32p. (gr. k-3). 1993. lib. bdg. 12.95 (*1-879373-46-7*) R Rinehart.

Suarez, Maribel. La Letras: The Letters. (Illus.). 14p. (ps-1). 1990. 10.75 (*970-05-0094-2*) Hispanic Bk Dist.

Sullivan, Charles. Alphabet Animals. 1991. 15.95 (*0-8478-1377-0*) Rizzoli Intl.

Szekeres, Cyndy. ABC. Szekeres, Cyndy, illus. LC 82-839989. 22p. (ps up). 1983. write for info. (*0-307-12120-8*, 12120, Pub. by Golden Bks) Western Pub.

Tabor, Nancy. Albertina Anda Arriba: El Abecedario: Albertina Goes Up: An Alphabet Book. (Illus.). 32p. (ps-3). 1993. PLB 15.88 (*0-88106-638-9*); pap. 6.95 (*0-88106-418-1*) Charlesbridge Pub.

Tallarico, Tony. Preschool Can You Find ABC Picture Book. (Illus.). 12p. (ps). 1992. 3.95 (*0-448-40426-5*, G&D) Putnam Pub Group.

Tallarico, Tony, illus. A B C. 28p. (ps-1). 1988. bds. 2.95 (*0-448-48817-5*, Tuffy) Putnam Pub Group.

Tarlow, Nora. An Easter Alphabet. (Illus.). 32p. 1991. 15.95 (*0-399-22194-8*, Putnam) Putnam Pub Group.

Taylor, Kenneth N. Big Thoughts for Little People. (ps-3). 1983. 10.99 (*0-8423-0164-X*) Tyndale.

Thompson, Carol. Alphaboo! A Hidden Letter ABC Book. Hartelius, Margaret A., illus. LC 93-26925. 32p. (ps-3). 1994. pap. 2.25 (*0-448-40213-0*, G&D) Putnam Pub Group.

Thornhill, Jan. Wild Life ABC: A Natural Alphabet Book. LC 89-19711. (ps-3). 1994. pap. 5.95 (*0-671-88614-2*, Half Moon Bks) S&S Trade.

—Wildlife ABC: A Nature Alphabet Book. LC 89-19711. (ps-3). 1990. pap. 14.95 (*0-671-67925-2*, S&S BFYR) S&S Trade.

Timmons, Dayle M. A Is for Amazing. (ps-1). 1991. pap. 25.95 (*0-8224-0253-X*) Fearon Teach Aids.

Tinies ABC Pop-Up Book. (Illus.). (ps-1). 1.49 (*0-517-43893-3*) Random Hse Value.

Torrence, Susan. The California Alphabet Book. Torrence, Charles, ed. Torrence, Susan, illus. LC 86-51505. 32p. (gr. k-3). 1987. pap. 6.95 (*0-914281-48-8*) Torrence Pubns.
Torrence, Susan & Polansky, Leslie. The Oregon Alphabet Book. 2nd ed. Torrence, Susan, illus. 32p. (ps-6). 1983. 5.95 (*0-914281-00-3*) Torrence Pubns.
Travers, Pamela L. Mary Poppins from A to Z. Shepard, Mary, illus. LC 62-15629. (gr. 1-4). 1962. 10.95 (*0-15-252590-4*, HB Juv Bks) HarBrace.
—Mary Poppins from A to Z. (gr. 4-7). 1991. pap. 3.50 (*0-440-40526-2*, YB) Dell.
Tryon, Leslie. Albert's Alphabet. 1st ed. LC 93-48408. (ps-2). 1994. pap. 4.95 (*0-689-71799-7*, Aladdin) Macmillan Child Grp.
Tubbs, Beth. Z Is for Zebra. Schmacker, Pam, illus. 32p. (ps). 1992. 9.95 (*0-9632993-3-6*) Storytime Pub.
Tudor, Tasha. A Is for Annabelle. Tudor, Tasha, illus. LC 60-15911. 64p. (ps-1). 1988. pap. 5.95 (*0-02-688534-4*, Aladdin) Macmillan Child Grp.
Twinem, Neecy. Aye-Ayes, Bears, & Condors: An ABC of Endangered Animals & Their Babies. LC 93-37698. 1993. text ed. write for info. (*0-7167-6525-X*, Sci Am Yng Rdrs) W H Freeman.
Tyler, J. & Cartwright, S. Stephen Cartwright's ABC. (Illus.). 32p. (ps). 1990. 8.95 (*0-7460-0434-6*, Usborne); lib. bdg. 13.96 (*0-88110-446-9*, Usborne) EDC.
University of Mexico City Staff, tr. El Alfabeto: Mentes Activas. Siede, George & Preis, Donna, photos by. Schwager, Istar, contrib. by. (SPA., Illus.). 24p. (ps-8). 1992. PLB 11.95 (*1-56674-036-3*) Forest Hse.
Updike, John. A Helpful Alphabet of Friendly Objects. Updike, David, photos by. LC 93-29922. (Illus.). Date not set. 14.00 (*0-679-84324-8*); PLB 14.99 (*0-679-94324-2*) Knopf.
Velk, Suzanne. The Animal Kingdom ABC. Velk, Suzanne, illus. 30p. (ps-3). 1994. 11.95 (*0-85572-220-7*, Pub. by Hill Content Pubng AT) Seven Hills Bk Dists.
Viorst, Judith. The Alphabet from Z to A: With Much Confusion on the Way. Hull, Richard, illus. LC 91-39338. 32p. (gr. 2-5). 1994. SBE 14.95 (*0-689-31768-9*, Atheneum Child Bk) Macmillan Child Grp.
Wagenman, Mark A. Aloha Bear ABC: Coloring & Activity Book. Wagenman, Mark A., illus. 24p. (ps-k). 1989. pap. 2.95 (*0-89610-146-0*) Island Heritage.
Walker. Alphabox. 1993. 28.95 (*0-8050-1581-7*) H Holt & Co.
Wall, Dorothy. Blinky Bill's ABC. (ps-3). 1993. 7.00 (*0-207-17713-9*, Pub. by Angus & Robertson AT) HarpC.
Walsh, Abigail M. The A to Z Book. Stearns, Helen M., ed. Urbahn, Clara, illus. 32p. (ps-5). 1988. 10.95 (*0-9614281-4-7*, Cricketfld Pr) Picton Pr.
Warren, Jean. Alphabet & Number Rhymes. Bittinger, Gayle, ed. Walker-Carleson, Cora, illus. 160p. (Orig.). (ps-1). 1989. pap. text ed. 14.95 (*0-911019-27-8*) Warren Pub Hse.
Warren, Jean, et al, eds. Alphabet Theme-a-Saurus: The Great Big Book of Letter Recognition. Mohrmann, Gary, illus. LC 90-71272. 280p. (ps-1). 1991. pap. text ed. 19.95 (*0-911019-38-3*) Warren Pub Hse.
Watson, Clyde. Applebet: An ABC. Watson, Wendy, illus. 32p. (ps up). 1987. pap. 3.95 (*0-374-40427-5*) FS&G.
Weeks, Sarah. Hurricane City. Warhola, James, illus. LC 92-23389. 32p. (ps-1). 1993. 15.00 (*0-06-021572-0*); PLB 14.89 (*0-06-021573-9*) HarpC Child Bks.
Wegman, William. ABC. (Illus.). 64p. (ps-2). 1994. 17.95 (*1-56282-696-4*); PLB 17.89 (*1-56282-699-9*) Hyprn Child.
Weiss, Ellen. Muppet Babies: A to Z. (ps). 1993. 3.95 (*0-307-12538-6*, Golden Pr) Western Pub.
Welsh, Patricia A. It's My Alphabet Book. 78p. (gr. k-1). 1979. wkbk. 4.95 (*1-884620-01-9*) PAW Prods.
Whitehead, Patricia. Arnold Plays Baseball. Karas, Brian, illus. LC 84-8827. 32p. (gr. k-2). 1985. PLB 11.59 (*0-8167-0367-1*); pap. text ed. 2.95 (*0-8167-0368-X*) Troll Assocs.
—Best Halloween Book. Britt, Stephanie, illus. LC 84-8828. 32p. (gr. k-2). 1985. PLB 11.59 (*0-8167-0373-6*); pap. text ed. 2.95 (*0-8167-0374-4*) Troll Assocs.
—Best Thanksgiving Book. Hall, Susan T., illus. LC 84-8831. 32p. (gr. k-2). 1985. PLB 11.59 (*0-8167-0371-X*); pap. text ed. 2.95 (*0-8167-0372-8*) Troll Assocs.
—Best Valentine Book. Harvy, Paul, illus. LC 84-8829. 32p. (gr. k-2). 1985. PLB 11.59 (*0-8167-0369-8*); pap. text ed. 2.95 (*0-8167-0370-1*) Troll Assocs.
—Dinosaur Alphabet Book. Snyder, Joel, illus. LC 84-8839. 32p. (gr. k-2). 1985. PLB 11.59 (*0-8167-0363-9*); pap. text ed. 2.95 (*0-8167-0364-7*) Troll Assocs.
Willard, Nancy. The Alphabet of Angels. LC 93-48836. (ps up). 1994. 16.95 (*0-590-48480-X*, Blue Sky Press) Scholastic Inc.
Williams, Jennifer. Everyday ABC. LC 91-9161. (Illus.). 32p. (ps-1). 1992. 10.95 (*0-8037-1079-8*) Dial Bks Young.
Wilner, Isabel. A Garden Alphabet. Wolff, Ashley, illus. LC 90-19619. 32p. (ps-2). 1991. 12.95 (*0-525-44731-8*, DCB) Dutton Child Bks.
Winslow, Phillips. The Alfalfabet. 26p. (gr. k). 1992. pap. text ed. 23.00 big bk. (*1-56843-015-9*); pap. text ed. 4.50 (*1-56843-065-5*) BGR Pub.
Wise, Beth A. My ABCs: Lowercase. Dorr, Mary A., illus. 32p. (ps). 1992. wkbk. 1.95 (*1-56293-167-9*) McClanahan Bk.
Wiskur, Darrell. Silver Dollar City's ABC Words & Rhymes. Silver Dollar City, Inc. Staff, ed. Wiskur, Darrell, illus. (ps-1). 1977. 1.99g (*0-686-19127-7*) Silver Dollar.
Wood, Jakki. Animal Parade. Wood, Jakki, illus. LC 92-22826. 32p. (ps-k). 1993. SBE 14.95 (*0-02-793394-6*, Bradbury Pr) Macmillan Child Grp.
World Book Staff, ed. Look at You, Zak! Feeling Good about Me with the Alphabet Pals. LC 90-70419. (Illus.). 22p. (ps). 1990. bds. write for info. (*0-7166-1904-0*) World Bk.
—Why Do We Have To? Learning Why We Have to with the Alphabet Pals. LC 90-71689. (Illus.). 24p. (ps). 1991. bds. write for info. (*0-7166-1905-9*) World Bk.
Wormell, Christopher. Alphabet of Animals. LC 90-2774. 64p. 1990. 17.95 (*0-8037-0876-9*) Dial Bks Young.
Wren & Maile. Pi'a'pa: Alphabet. Wren, illus. (ENG & HAW.). 10p. (ps). 1992. bds. 3.95 (*1-880188-30-9*) Bess Pr.
Wrenn, Romel. Super ABC's of the Human Body. Tripp, Charles, illus. 56p. (gr. k-4). 1993. Wkbk. write for info. (*0-9637869-0-3*) Chldrns Med.
Wynne, Patricia, illus. The Animal ABC. LC 77-74470. 14p. (ps-k). 1977. bds. 3.95 (*0-394-83589-1*) Random Bks Yng Read.
Zerner, Amy, illus. Zen ABC. LC 92-22940. 1993. 14.95 (*0-8048-1806-1*) C E Tuttle.

ALPS–FICTION

Bishop, Claire H. All Alone. Rojanovsky, Feodor, illus. 96p. (gr. 2-5). 1953. 15.00 (*0-670-11336-0*) Viking Child Bks.
Spyri, Johanna. Heidi. LC 85-13292. (gr. 5 up). 1964. pap. 1.95 (*0-8049-0018-3*, CL-18) Airmont.
—Heidi. LC 85-13292. (Illus.). (gr. 4-6). 1988. pap. 3.25 (*0-590-42046-1*) Scholastic Inc.
Ullman, James R. Banner in the Sky. LC 54-7296. 256p. (gr. 7 up). 1988. (Lipp Jr Bks); (Lipp Jr Bks) HarpC Child Bks.

ALTITUDE, INFLUENCE OF

see Man–Influence of Environment

AMATEUR THEATRICALS

see also Acting; Make-Up, Theatrical; One-Act Plays; Pantomimes; Shadow Pantomimes and Plays; Theater–Production and Direction

AMATEUR THEATRICALS–FICTION

Ryan, Mary C. Who Says I Can't? 160p. (gr. 12 up). 1988. 12.95 (*0-316-76374-8*) Little.

AMAZON RIVER

Murray, Peter. The Amazon. LC 93-7617. (ENG & SPA.). (gr. 2-6). 1993. 15.95 (*1-56766-021-5*) Childs World.
Reynolds, Jan. Amazon: Vanishing Cultures. LC 92-21089. (Illus.). 1993. 16.95 (*0-15-202831-5*, HB Juv Bks); pap. 8.95 (*0-15-202832-3*, HB Juv Bks) HarBrace.
Waterlow, Julia. The Amazon. Waterlow, Julia, photos by. LC 92-25446. (Illus.). 48p. (gr. 5-6). 1993. PLB 22.80 (*0-8114-3101-0*) Raintree Steck-V.

AMAZON RIVER–FICTION

Bischof, Larry & Lowry, William B. Amazon Adventure. LC 92-12844. (gr. 2). 1992. 13.99 (*1-56239-150-X*) Abdo & Dghtrs.
Kendall, Sarita. Ransom for a River Dolphin. LC 93-19929. 1993. 18.95 (*0-8225-0735-8*) Lerner Pubns.
Lewin, Ted. Amazon Boy. Lewin, Ted, illus. LC 92-15798. 32p. (gr. k-3). 1993. RSBE 14.95 (*0-02-757383-4*, Macmillan Child Bk) Macmillan Child Grp.

AMAZON VALLEY

Cobb, Vicki. This Place Is Wet. Lavallee, Barbara, illus. 32p. (gr. 2-4). 1989. 12.95 (*0-8027-6880-6*); PLB 13.85 (*0-8027-6881-4*) Walker & Co.
Cousteau Society Staff. An Adventure in the Amazon. LC 91-34167. (Illus.). 48p. (gr. 3-7). 1992. pap. 14.00 jacketed (*0-671-77071-3*, S&S BFYR) S&S Trade.
Lourie, Peter. Amazon: A Young Reader's Look at the Last Frontier. Santilli, Marcos, photos by. LC 90-85720. (Illus.). 48p. (gr. 3-7). 1991. 17.95 (*1-878093-00-2*) Boyds Mills Pr.
Reynolds, Jan. Amazon: Vanishing Cultures. LC 92-21089. (Illus.). 1993. 16.95 (*0-15-202831-5*, HB Juv Bks); pap. 8.95 (*0-15-202832-3*, HB Juv Bks) HarBrace.
Siy, Alexandra. The Amazon Rainforest. LC 91-37640. (Illus.). 80p. (gr. 5 up). 1992. text ed. 14.95 RSBE (*0-87518-470-7*, Dillon) Macmillan Child Grp.

AMBASSADORS

see Diplomats

AMERICA

see also Central America; Latin America; North America; South America

Aten, Jerry. Americans, Too! 80p. (gr. 4 up). 1982. 9.95 (*0-86653-099-1*, GA 444) Good Apple.
Dambrosio, Monica & Barbieri, Roberto. The Americas in the Colonial Era. Ianni, Mary D., tr. from ITA. Berselli, Remo, illus. LC 92-19154. 72p. (gr. 5-6). 1992. PLB 25.67 (*0-8114-3326-9*) Raintree Steck-V.
Frazee, Charles & Yopp, Hallie K. Medieval & Early Modern Times. Frazee, Kathleen & Lumba, Eric, illus. (gr. 7). 1990. pap. text ed. 24.77 (*1-878473-56-5*); tchr's. ed. 30.77 (*1-878473-58-1*); wkbk. 3.00 (*0-685-58493-3*) Delos Pubns.
The Southern World. (Illus.). 128p. 1990. 17.95x (*0-8160-1881-2*) Facts on File.

AMERICA–ANTIQUITIES

Bendick, Jeanne. Tombs of the Ancient Americas. LC 92-24546. (Illus.). 64p. (gr. 5-8). 1993. PLB 12.40 (*0-531-20148-1*) Watts.
Civilizations of the Americas. (Illus.). 80p. (gr. 4 up). 1988. PLB 25.67 (*0-8172-3306-7*) Raintree Steck-V.
Sattler, Helen R. The Earliest Americans. Zallinger, Jean D., illus. 128p. (gr. 4-7). 1993. 16.95 (*0-395-54996-5*, Clarion Bks) HM.

AMERICA–DISCOVERY AND EXPLORATION

see also Explorers; Northwest Passage

Barden, Renardo. The Discovery of America: Opposing Viewpoints. LC 89-11709. (Illus.). 112p. (gr. 5-8). 1989. PLB 14.95 (*0-89908-071-5*) Greenhaven.
Brenner, Barbara. If You Were There in 1492. LC 90-24099. (Illus.). 112p. (gr. 3-7). 1991. SBE 13.95 (*0-02-712321-9*, Bradbury Pr) Macmillan Child Grp.
Brown, Gene. Discovery & Settlement: Europe Meets the New World (1490-1700) LC 93-8537. (Illus.). 64p. (gr. 5-8). 1993. PLB 15.95 (*0-8050-2574-X*) TFC Bks NY.
Carson, Robert. Hernando de Soto: Expedition to the Mississippi River. LC 91-12665. 128p. (gr. 3 up). 1991. PLB 20.55 (*0-516-03065-5*) Childrens.
Chrisp, Peter. Search for a Northern Route. LC 93-30920. (Illus.). 48p. (gr. 4-6). 1993. 14.95 (*1-56847-122-X*) Thomson Lrning.
—The Spanish Conquests in the New World. LC 93-24396. (Illus.). 48p. (gr. 4-6). 1993. 14.95 (*1-56847-123-8*) Thomson Lrning.
—Voyages to the New World. LC 93-9473. 48p. (gr. 4-6). 1993. 14.95 (*1-56847-121-1*) Thomson Lrning.
Clare, John D., ed. Voyages of Christopher Columbus. (gr. 4-7). 1992. 16.95 (*0-15-200507-2*, Gulliver Bks) HarBrace.
Crouch, Robin. The Americas: A Sticker Atlas of Exploration & Discovery. McRae, Patrick, illus. 16p. (Orig.). (gr. 1-3). 1993. pap. 5.95 (*0-8249-8556-7*, Ideals Child) Hambleton-Hill.
Eckhart, Mary L. Columbus' Dictionary. 100p. (Orig.). (gr. 5-10). 1992. pap. 11.95 (*0-8283-1993-6*) Branden Pub Co.
Faber, Harold. The Discoverers of America. LC 91-17001. (Illus.). 304p. (gr. 9 up). 1992. SBE 17.95 (*0-684-19217-9*, Scribners Young Read) Macmillan Child Grp.
Fritz, Jean. Where Do You Think You're Going, Christopher Columbus? Tomes, Margot, illus. 80p. (gr. 3-7). 1981. (Putnam); pap. 7.95 (*0-399-20734-1*, Putnam) Putnam Pub Group.
Gaffron, Norma. El Dorado, Land of Gold: Opposing Viewpoints. LC 90-3838. (Illus.). 112p. (gr. 5-8). 1990. PLB 14.95 (*0-89908-086-3*) Greenhaven.
Jacobs, Francine. The Tainos: The People Who Welcomed Columbus. Collins, Patrick, illus. 112p. (gr. 5-9). 1992. 15.95 (*0-399-22116-6*, Putnam) Putnam Pub Group.
Jacobs, William J. Champlain: A Life of Courage. LC 93-31176. (Illus.). 64p. (gr. 5-8). 1994. PLB 12.90 (*0-531-20112-0*) Watts.
—La Salle: A Life of Boundless Adventure. LC 93-29699. (Illus.). 64p. (gr. 5-8). 1994. PLB 12.90 (*0-531-20141-4*) Watts.
Jaeger, Gerard. Vespucci. 1992. PLB 14.95 (*0-88682-485-0*) Creative Ed.
Kent, Zachary. Christopher Columbus: Expeditions to the New World. LC 91-13863. 128p. (gr. 3 up). 1991. PLB 20.55 (*0-516-03064-7*); pap. 9.95 (*0-516-43064-5*) Childrens.
Krensky, Stephen. Who Really Discovered America? Sullivan, Steve, illus. 64p. (Orig.). (gr. 4-6). 1987. pap. 2.50 (*0-590-40854-2*) Scholastic Inc.
—Who Really Discovered America? Donnelly, Judy, ed. Sullivan, Steve, illus. 64p. (gr. 3-7). 1991. Repr. of 1987 ed. 12.95 (*0-8038-9306-X*) Hastings.
Las Casas, Bartholomew. The Log of Christopher Columbus' First Voyage to America: In the Year 1492, As Copied Out in Brief by Bartholomew Las Casas. LC 88-32567. (Illus.). 84p. (gr. 3 up). 1989. Repr. of 1938 ed. lib. bdg. 17.00 (*0-208-02247-3*, Pub. by Linnet) Shoe String.
Lauber, Patricia. Who Discovered America? Mysteries & Puzzles of the New World. new ed. Eagle, Mike, illus. LC 90-43604. 80p. (gr. 2-6). 1992. 16.00 (*0-06-023728-7*); PLB 15.89 (*0-06-023729-5*) HarpC Child Bks.
Leon, George D. Explorers of the Americas Before Columbus. LC 88-38064. (Illus.). 64p. (gr. 7-9). 1990. 12.90 (*0-531-10667-5*) Watts.
McCall, Barbara. The European Invasion. LC 94-5530. (gr. 5 up). 1994. write for info. (*0-86625-535-4*) Rourke Pubns.
Maestro, Betsy. The Discovery of the Americas Activities Book. Maestro, Guilio, illus. 92p. (gr. 1-6). 1992. pap. 7.95 (*0-688-08590-3*) Lothrop.
Maestro, Betsy & Maestro, Giulio. Discovery of the Americas. (gr. 4-7). 1991. 14.95 (*0-688-06837-5*); PLB 14.88 (*0-688-06838-3*) Lothrop.
—Discovery of the Americas. LC 89-32375. (Illus.). 48p. (gr. k up). 1992. pap. 5.95 (*0-688-11512-8*, Mulberry) Morrow.
—Exploration & Conquest: The Americas After Columbus, 1500-1620. LC 93-48618. 1994. 16.00 (*0-688-09267-5*); lib. bdg. 15.93 (*0-688-09268-3*) Lothrop.
Martini, Teri. Christopher Columbus: The Man Who Unlocked the Secrets of the World. LC 91-44755. 96p. (gr. 4-7). 1992. pap. 4.95 (*0-8091-6604-6*) Paulist Pr.

Marx, Robert F. Following Columbus: The Voyage of the Nina II. (Illus.). 80p. 1991. 17.95 (*0-88415-004-6*, 5004) Gulf Pub.

Marzollo, Jean. In Fourteen Ninety-Two. Bjorkman, Steven, illus. 40p. 1991. 14.95 (*0-590-44413-1*, Scholastic Hardcover) Scholastic Inc.

Marzollo, Jean & Bjorkman, Steven. In 1492. 1993. pap. 19.95 (*0-590-72737-0*) Scholastic Inc.

Morison, Samuel E. Christopher Columbus, Mariner. (Illus.). 192p. (gr. 9-12). 1983. pap. 9.00 (*0-452-00992-8*, Mer) NAL-Dutton.

Pelta, Kathy. Discovering Christopher Columbus: How History Is Invented. 112p. (gr. 4-6). 1991. PLB 19.95 (*0-8225-4899-2*) Lerner Pubns.

Roop, Peter & Roop, Connie, eds. I, Columbus: My Journal - 1492. Hanson, Peter, illus. 57p. (gr. 4-7). 1990. 13.95 (*0-8027-6977-2*); lib. bdg. 14.85 (*0-8027-6978-0*) Walker & Co.

Sauvain, Philip. Over Four Hundred & Fifty Years Ago: In the New World. Rowe, Eric, illus. LC 93-2649. 32p. (gr. 6 up). 1993. text ed. 13.95 RSBE (*0-02-726327-4*, New Discovery Bks) Macmillan Child Grp.

Smith, Carter, ed. Explorers & Settlers: A Sourcebook on Colonial America. (Illus.). 96p. (gr. 5-8). 1991. PLB 18.90 (*1-56294-035-X*); pap. 5.95 (*1-878841-64-5*) Millbrook Pr.

Spencer, Eve. Three Ships for Columbus. Sperling, Tom, illus. LC 92-14401. 32p. (gr. 2-5). 1992. PLB 18.51 (*0-8114-7212-4*) Raintree Steck-V.

Stein, R. Conrad. Francisco de Coronado: Explorer of the American Southwest. LC 91-32207. 128p. (gr. 3 up). 1992. PLB 20.55 (*0-516-03068-X*) Childrens.

Stopsky, Fred. Bartolome De las Casas: Champion of Indian Rights. 64p. (Orig.). (gr. 5-9). 1992. pap. 4.95 (*1-878668-12-9*) Disc Enter Ltd.

Twist, Clint. Christopher Columbus: The Discovery of the Americas. LC 93-19017. 1994. PLB 22.80 (*0-8114-7253-1*) Raintree Steck-V.

Weisberg, Barbara. Coronado's Golden Quest. Eagle, Mike, illus. LC 92-18078. 79p. (gr. 2-5). 1992. PLB 21.34 (*0-8114-7232-9*); pap. 4.95 (*0-8114-8072-0*) Raintree Steck-V.

West, Delno C. & West, Jean M. Christopher Columbus: The Great Adventure & How We Know about It. LC 90-936. (Illus.). 144p. (gr. 5-9). 1991. SBE 15.95 (*0-689-31433-7*, Atheneum Child Bk) Macmillan Child Grp.

Yue, Charlotte & Yue, David. Christopher Columbus: How He Did It. Yue, David, illus. 144p. (gr. 3-6). 1992. 14.95 (*0-395-52100-9*) HM.

AMERICA–DISCOVERY AND EXPLORATION–FICTION

Bresnick-Perry, Roslyn. Leaving for America. Reisberg, Mira, illus. LC 92-8450. 32p. (ps-7). 1992. PLB 13.95 (*0-89239-105-7*) Childrens Book Pr.

Cecil, Terry & Cecil, Barbara. Chrisgopher Columbus in Stowaway on the Santa Maria. Smallwood, Steve, illus. 32p. (Orig.). (gr. k-6). 1992. PLB 4.00 (*0-9633016-0-8*) Infiniti.

Dorris, Michael. Morning Girl. LC 92-52989. 80p. (gr. 3 up). 1994. 3.50 (*1-56282-661-1*) Hyprn Ppbks.

Martin, Susan. I Sailed with Columbus: The Adventures of a Ship's Boy. La Padulla, Tom, illus. 154p. (gr. 5 up). 1991. 17.95 (*0-87951-431-0*) Overlook Pr.

Merino, Jose M. The Gold of Dreams. Lane, Helen, tr. 224p. (gr. 7 up). 1992. 15.00 (*0-374-32692-4*) FS&G.

Merino, Jose Maria. Beyond the Ancient Cities. Lane, Helen, tr. from SPA. LC 93-35482. 1994. 16.00 (*0-374-34307-1*) FS&G.

O'Dell, Scott. King's Fifth. Bryant, Samuel, illus. (gr. 7-10). 1966. 14.45 (*0-395-06963-7*) HM.

Piercy, Patricia A. The Great Encounter: A Special Meeting Before Columbus. Wilkerson, Napoleon, illus. 47p. (gr. 1-7). 1991. pap. 5.95 (*0-913543-26-8*) African Am Imag.

AMERICAN ABORIGINES

see Indians of North America; Indians of South America

AMERICAN ARTISTS

see Artists, American

AMERICAN AUTHORS

see Authors, American

AMERICAN BISON

see Bison

AMERICAN CIVIL WAR

see U. S.–History–Civil War

AMERICAN CIVILIZATION

see U. S.–Civilization

AMERICAN COLONIES

see U. S.–History–Colonial Period

AMERICAN ESSAYS

Musical Lynn. Musical Lynn Essays, Vol. I: A Baker's Dozen. 13p. (Orig.). (gr. 12). 1991. pap. 8.95 (*1-880718-02-2*); pap. text ed. 8.95 (*1-880718-03-0*) Genius New.

Paget, Stephen. I Wonder: Essays for the Young People. facs. ed. LC 68-54365. (gr. 7 up). 1968. Repr. of 1911 ed. 14.00 (*0-8369-0765-5*) Ayer.

AMERICAN FEDERATION OF LABOR

The Founding of the AFL & the Rise of Organized Labor. (Illus.). 64p. (gr. 5 up). 1991. PLB 12.95 (*0-382-24123-1*); pap. 7.95 (*0-382-24118-5*) Silver Burdett Pr.

AMERICAN INDIANS

see Indians; Indians of North America; Indians of South America

AMERICAN LITERATURE

Bachelder, Marvin. Snow Treasure: A Study Guide. Friedland, Joyce & Kessler, Rikki, eds. (gr. 5-7). 1991. pap. text ed. 14.95 (*0-88122-582-7*) LRN Links.

Center for Learning Network Staff. A Farewell to Arms by Ernest Hemingway: Curriculum Unit. 64p. (gr. 9-12). 1993. tchr's. ed. 18.95 (*1-56077-274-3*) Ctr Learning.

—The Old Man & the Sea by Ernest Hemingway - Ethan Frome by Edith Wharton: Curriculum Unit. 83p. (gr. 9-12). 1993. tchr's. ed. 18.95 (*1-56077-279-4*) Ctr Learning.

—A Tree Grows in Brooklyn by Betty Smith: Curriculum Unit. 88p. (gr. 9-12). 1993. tchr's. ed. 18.95 (*1-56077-277-8*) Ctr Learning.

Christopher, Garrett. Annie & the Old One: A Study Guide. Friedland, Joyce & Kessler, Rikki, eds. (gr. 1-4). 1991. pap. text ed. 14.95 (*0-88122-564-9*) LRN Links.

—Caps for Sale: A Study Guide. Friedland, Joyce & Kessler, Rikki, eds. (gr. k-3). 1991. pap. text ed. 14.95 (*0-88122-587-8*) LRN Links.

—Corduroy: A Study Guide. Friedland, Joyce & Kessler, Rikki, eds. (gr. k-3). 1991. pap. text ed. 14.95 (*0-88122-588-6*) LRN Links.

—Gregory the Terrible Eater: A Study Guide. Friedland, Joyce & Kessler, Rikki, eds. (gr. k-3). 1991. pap. text ed. 14.95 (*0-88122-589-4*) LRN Links.

—Leo the Late Bloomer: A Study Guide. Friedland, Joyce & Kessler, Rikki, eds. (gr. k-3). 1991. pap. text ed. 14.95 (*0-88122-591-6*) LRN Links.

—The Little Island: A Study Guide. Friedland, Joyce & Kessler, Rikki, eds. (gr. k-3). 1991. pap. text ed. 14.95 (*0-88122-592-4*) LRN Links.

—Make Way for Ducklings: A Study Guide. Friedland, Joyce & Kessler, Rikki, eds. (gr. k-3). 1991. pap. text ed. 14.95 (*0-88122-593-2*) LRN Links.

—Sylvester & the Magic Pebble: A Study Guide. Friedland, Joyce & Kessler, Rikki, eds. (gr. k-3). 1991. pap. text ed. 14.95 (*0-88122-595-9*) LRN Links.

—Whistle for Willie: A Study Guide. Friedland, Joyce & Kessler, Rikki, eds. (gr. k-3). 1991. pap. text ed. 14.95 (*0-88122-596-7*) LRN Links.

Claydon, Dina. The Cabin Faced West: A Study Guide. Friedland, Joyce & Kessler, Rikki, eds. 21p. (gr. 9-12). 1990. pap. text ed. 14.95 (*0-88122-409-X*) Lrn Links.

—Maurice's Room: A Study Guide. Friedland, Joyce & Kessler, Rikki, eds. (gr. 2-4). 1991. pap. text ed. 14.95 (*0-88122-569-X*) LRN Links.

—Shoeshine Girl: A Study Guide. Friedland, Joyce & Kessler, Rikki, eds. 20p. (gr. 9-12). 1990. pap. text ed. 14.95 (*0-88122-396-4*) Lrn Links.

—Stone Fox: A Study Guide. Friedland, Joyce & Kessler, Rikki, eds. 21p. (gr. 9-12). 1990. pap. text ed. 14.95 (*0-88122-407-3*) Lrn Links.

Cooper, James Fenimore. The Two Admirals: A Tale. LC 88-12190. 511p. (Orig.). (gr. 9-12). 1990. 49.50x (*0-88706-905-3*); pap. 18.95x (*0-88706-907-X*) State U NY Pr.

Croil, Marianne. Superfudge: A Study Guide. Friedland, Joyce & Kessler, Rikki, eds. (gr. 2-5). 1991. pap. text ed. 14.95 (*0-88122-574-6*) LRN Links.

Diamond, Laurie. Anastasia Krupnik: A Study Guide. Friedland, Joyce & Kessler, Rikki, eds. 26p. (gr. 9-12). 1990. pap. text ed. 14.95 (*0-88122-402-2*) Lrn Links.

—The Chalk Box Kid: A Study Guide. Friedland, Joyce & Kessler, Rikki, eds. 23p. (gr. 9-12). 1990. pap. text ed. 14.95 (*0-88122-398-0*) Lrn Links.

—The Hundred Dresses: A Study Guide. Friedland, Joyce & Kessler, Rikki, eds. 21p. (gr. 9-12). 1990. pap. text ed. 14.95 (*0-88122-404-9*) Lrn Links.

—Jacob Two-Two Meets the Hooded Fang: A Study Guide. Friedland, Joyce & Kessler, Rikki, eds. (gr. 2-5). 1991. pap. text ed. 14.95 (*0-88122-568-1*) LRN Links.

—The One in the Middle Is the Green Kangaroo: A Study Guide. Friedland, Joyce & Kessler, Rikki, eds. 16p. (gr. 9-12). 1990. pap. text ed. 14.95 (*0-88122-408-1*) Lrn Links.

—Rip-Roaring Russell: A Study Guide. Friedland, Joyce & Kessler, Rikki, eds. 20p. (gr. 9-12). 1990. pap. text ed. 14.95 (*0-88122-405-7*) Lrn Links.

Faulkner, William. Portable Faulkner. rev. ed. Cowley, Malcolm, ed. (gr. 10 up). 1977. pap. 9.95 (*0-14-015018-8*, Penguin Bks) Viking Penguin.

Forsten, Charlene. The Indian in the Cupboard: A Study Guide. Friedland, Joyce & Kessler, Rikki, eds. 23p. (gr. 9-12). 1990. pap. text ed. 14.95 (*0-88122-406-5*) Lrn Links.

—The Littles: A Study Guide. Friedland, Joyce & Kessler, Rikki, eds. 21p. (gr. 9-12). 1990. pap. text ed. 14.95 (*0-88122-412-X*) Lrn Links.

—The Wish Giver: A Study Guide. Friedland, Joyce & Kessler, Rikki, eds. 24p. (gr. 9-12). 1990. pap. text ed. 14.95 (*0-88122-401-4*) Lrn Links.

Gifford, Scott. The Call of the Wild: A Study Guide. (gr. 9-12). 1990. pap. text ed. 14.95 (*0-88122-411-1*) Lrn Links.

Golden, Michael. Interstellar Pig: A Study Guide. Friedland, Joyce & Kessler, Rikki, eds. (gr. 6-9). 1991. pap. text ed. 14.95 (*0-88122-584-3*) LRN Links.

Goldish, Meish. Journey to Jo'burg: A Study Guide. Friedland, Joyce & Kessler, Rikki, eds. (gr. 3-6). 1991. pap. text ed. 14.95 (*0-88122-573-8*) LRN Links.

Holmes, Oliver W. Autocrat of the Breakfast-Table. Andrews, C. A., intro. by. (gr. 11 up). 1968. pap. 1.95 (*0-8049-0159-7*, CL-159) Airmont.

McGee, Brenda H. Old Yeller: A Study Guide. Friedland, Joyce & Kessler, Rikki, eds. 21p. (gr. 9-12). 1990. pap. text ed. 14.95 (*0-88122-415-4*) Lrn Links.

—Rascal: A Study Guide. Friedland, Joyce & Kessler, Rikki, eds. 26p. (gr. 9-12). 1990. pap. text ed. 14.95 (*0-88122-416-2*) Lrn Links.

Marsh, Norma. Follow My Leader: A Study Guide. Friedland, Joyce & Kessler, Rikki, eds. 18p. (gr. 9-12). 1990. pap. text ed. 14.95 (*0-88122-403-0*) Lrn Links.

—Park's Quest: A Study Guide. Friedland, Joyce & Kessler, Rikki, eds. (gr. 5-8). 1991. pap. text ed. 14.95 (*0-88122-581-9*) LRN Links.

Medland, Mary. The Red Badge of Courage: A Study Guide. (gr. 9-12). 1990. pap. text ed. 14.95 (*0-88122-414-6*) Lrn Links.

—Where the Lilies Bloom: A Study Guide. Friedland, Joyce & Kessler, Rikki, eds. 30p. (gr. 9-12). 1990. pap. text ed. 14.95 (*0-88122-399-9*) Lrn Links.

Pelphrey, Jo Ann. Into the Think Tank with Literature. Keeling, Jan, ed. (Illus.). 160p. (Orig.). (gr. k-3). 1992. pap. text ed. 14.95 (*0-86530-192-1*, IP193-6) Incentive Pubns.

Reeves, Barbara. Bunnicula: A Study Guide. Friedland, Joyce & Kessler, Rikki, eds. (gr. 2-5). 1991. pap. text ed. 14.95 (*0-88122-572-X*) LRN Links.

—Farewell to Manzanar: A Study Guide. Friedland, Joyce & Kessler, Rikki, eds. (gr. 7-10). 1991. pap. text ed. 14.95 (*0-88122-583-5*) LRN Links.

—The Lillies of the Field: A Study Guide. Friedland, Joyce & Kessler, Rikki, eds. (gr. 8-12). 1991. pap. text ed. 14.95 (*0-88122-585-1*) LRN Links.

—The War Between the Classes: A Study Guide. Friedland, Joyce & Kessler, Rikki, eds. (gr. 7-10). 1991. pap. text ed. 14.95 (*0-88122-586-X*) LRN Links.

Snodgrass, Mary E. Silver: A Study Guide. Friedland, Joyce & Kessler, Rikki, eds. (gr. 2-5). 1991. pap. text ed. 14.95 (*0-88122-571-1*) LRN Links.

Stewart & Champanier. The Door in the Wall: A Study Guide. (gr. 9-12). 1990. pap. text ed. 14.95 (*0-88122-410-3*) Lrn Links.

Thoreau, Henry David. Walden. Langmack, F., intro. by. Bd. with On Civil Disobedience. (gr. 10 up). pap. 1.50 (*0-8049-0083-3*, CL-83) Airmont.

—Walden. Sherman, Paul, ed. Bd. with Civil Disobedience. LC 60-16148. (gr. 9 up). 1960. pap. 9.96 (*0-395-05113-4*, RivEd) HM.

Tretler, Marcia. Hatchet: A Study Guide. Friedland, Joyce & Kessler, Rikki, eds. (gr. 9-12). 1990. pap. text ed. 14.95 (*0-88122-413-8*) Lrn Links.

—The Lottery Rose: A Study Guide. 22p. (gr. 9-12). 1990. pap. text ed. 14.95 (*0-88122-395-6*) Lrn Links.

—Luke Was There: A Study Guide. Friedland, Joyce & Kessler, Rikki, eds. 19p. (gr. 9-12). 1990. pap. text ed. 14.95 (*0-88122-400-6*) Lrn Links.

Witt, Sandi. Across Five Aprils: A Study Guide. (gr. 9-12). 1990. pap. text ed. 14.95 (*0-88122-394-8*) Lrn Links.

Witt, Sandi & Petrovich, Janice. Daphne's Book: A Study Guide. Friedland, Joyce & Kessler, Rikki, eds. 20p. (gr. 9-12). 1990. pap. text ed. 14.95 (*0-88122-397-2*) Lrn Links.

AMERICAN LITERATURE–BIOGRAPHY

see Authors, American

AMERICAN LITERATURE–COLLECTIONS

Aparicio, Frances R., ed. Latino Voices. LC 93-42893. (Illus.). 144p. (gr. 7 up). 1994. PLB 15.90 (*1-56294-388-X*) Millbrook Pr.

Fung, Urania, ed. Tapestry, Vol. III. Reid, Bernice, intro. by. (Illus.). 230p. (Orig.). (gr. 9-12). 1994. write for info. (*0-9636974-2-0*) Lamar HS.

Hirschfelder, Arlene B. & Singer, Beverly R., eds. Rising Voices: Writings of Young Native Americans. LC 91-32083. 128p. (gr. 7 up). 1992. SBE 13.95 (*0-684-19207-1*, Scribners Young Read) Macmillan Child Grp.

Larrick, Nancy. To Ride a Butterfly: Original Pictures, Stories, Poems, & Songs for Children. (ps-3). 1991. 17.00 (*0-440-50402-3*) Dell.

Minnesota Humanities Commission Staff, ed. Braided Lives: An Anthology of Multicultural American Writing. 288p. (gr. 9-12). 1991. pap. text ed. 12.95 (*0-9629298-0-8*) MN Humanities.

Sullivan, Charles, ed. Children of Promise: African-American Literature & Art for Young People. Campbell, Mary S., frwd. by. (Illus.). 128p. 1991. 24.95 (*0-8109-3170-2*) Abrams.

Trelease, Jim, ed. Read All About It! Great Stories, Poems, & Newspaper Pieces for Reading Aloud for Preteens & Teens. LC 93-21781. 416p. (Orig.). 1993. pap. 11.00 (*0-14-014655-5*, Penguin Bks) Viking Penguin.

Wolfe, Thomas, et al. A Southern Appalachian Reader. McNeil, Nellie, et al, eds. LC 87-19589. (Illus.). 500p. (gr. 10-12). 1988. pap. text ed. 14.95 (*0-913239-50-X*) Appalach Consortium.

Writers' League of Washington Staff. A Diamond Anthology of Prose & Poetry: Seventy-Fifth Year. Ricketts, Marijane, et al, eds. Archambauer, Alan H., illus. Leighton, Frances S., intros. by. (Illus.). 112p. (gr. 8-12). 1992. pap. write for info. (*0-9618223-2-5*) M G Ricketts.

Yep, Laurence. American Dragons: Twenty-Five Asian American Voices. LC 92-28489. 256p. (gr. 7 up). 1993. 16.00 (*0-06-021494-5*); PLB 15.89 (*0-06-021495-3*) HarpC Child Bks.

AMERICAN LITERATURE–HISTORY AND CRITICISM

Faber, Doris & Faber, Harold. Great Lives: American Literature. LC 94-10866. 1995. 22.95 (*0-684-19448-1*, Scribner) Macmillan.

Lyon, Sue, ed. Great Writers of the English Language, 14 vols. LC 88-21077. (Illus.). 1450p. 1991. PLB 449.95 (*1-85435-000-5*) Marshall Cavendish.

Magill, Frank N., ed. Masterplots II, 3 vols. 1530p. (gr. 9-12). 1994. Set. PLB 275.00 (*0-89356-594-6*, Magill Bks) Salem Pr.

AMERICAN MUSIC

see Music, American

AMERICAN MUSICIANS

see Musicians, American

AMERICAN PAINTERS

see Painters, American

AMERICAN POETRY

see also Black Poetry

Adoff, Arnold. Eats: Poems. Russo, Susan, illus. LC 79-11300. (gr. 4 up). 1979. 13.95 (*0-688-41901-1*); PLB 12.88 (*0-688-51901-6*) Lothrop.

Angelou, Maya. Life Doesn't Frighten Me. Boyers, Sara J., ed. Basquiat, Jean-Michel, illus. LC 92-40409. (gr. 7 up). 1993. write for info. (Dist. by Workman Pub.) Stewart Tabori & Chang.

Anglund, Joan W. Love Is a Baby. LC 91-1224. 1992. write for info. (*0-15-200517-X*, HB Juv Bks) HarBrace.

—Peace Is a Circle of Love. LC 92-28855. 1993. 8.95 (*0-15-259922-3*) HarBrace.

Aylesworth, Jim. The Cat & the Fiddle & More. Hull, Richard, illus. LC 91-30956. 32p. (ps-1). 1992. SBE 13.95 (*0-689-31715-8*, Atheneum Child Bk) Macmillan Child Grp.

Bates, Katharine L. America the Beautiful. Waldman, Neil, illus. LC 92-46199. 32p. 1993. SBE 14.95 (*0-689-31861-8*, Atheneum Child Bk) Macmillan Child Grp.

—O Beautiful for Spacious Skies. Thiebaud, Wayne, illus. Boyers, Sara J., ed. LC 94-6599. 1994. 13.95 (*0-8118-0832-7*) Chronicle Bks.

Behn, Harry. Trees. Endicott, James, illus. LC 91-25179. 32p. (ps-2). 1992. 14.95 (*0-8050-1926-X*, B Martin BYR) H Holt & Co.

Benjamin, Alan. A Nickel Buys a Rhyme. Schmidt, Karen L., illus. LC 92-6475. 40p. (ps up). 1993. 15.00 (*0-688-06698-4*); PLB 14.93 (*0-688-06699-2*) Morrow Jr Bks.

Bitker, Marian. Thanks for Giving & Other Poems. LC 90-93454. 63p. (Orig.). 1991. 15.00x (*0-9628150-0-4*); pap. 10.00x (*0-9628150-1-2*) M Bitker.

Blos, Joan W. A Seed, a Flower, a Minute, an Hour. Poppel, Hans, illus. LC 91-4992. 40p. (ps-2). 1992. pap. 14.00 jacketed, 3-pc. bdg. (*0-671-73214-5*, S&S BFYR) S&S Trade.

—A Seed, Flower a Minute, an Hour. LC 91-4992. (ps-3). 1994. pap. 4.95 (*0-671-88632-0*, Half Moon Bks) S&S Trade.

Bodecker, N. M. Water Pennies & Other Poems. Blegvad, Erik, illus. LC 90-6477. 64p. 1991. SBE 12.95 (*0-689-50517-5*, M K McElderry) Macmillan Child Grp.

Bolin, Frances S., ed. Emily Dickinson: Poetry for Young People. Chung, Chi, illus. LC 94-13809. 48p. 1994. 14.95 (*0-8069-0635-9*) Sterling.

Brown, Margaret W. The Diggers. Kirk, Daniel, illus. LC 94-7995. (gr. 2-5). 1995. write for info. (*0-7868-0006-2*); lib. bdg. write for info. (*0-7868-2001-2*) Hyprn Child.

—Four Fur Feet. Hubbard, Woodleigh, illus. LC 93-31523. 24p. (ps-1). 1994. 12.95 (*0-7868-0002-X*); PLB 12.89 (*0-7868-2000-4*) Hyprn Child.

—Under the Sun & the Moon & Other Poems. Leonard, Tom, illus. LC 92-72031. 40p. (ps-2). 1993. 14.95 (*1-56282-354-X*); PLB 14.89 (*1-56282-355-8*) Hyprn Child.

Buchanan, Ken & Buchanan, Debby. Lizards on the Wall. Schweitzer-Johnson, Betty, illus. LC 92-13664. (gr. 1-4). 1992. 12.95 (*0-943173-77-9*) Harbinger AZ.

Callahan, John. The King of Things & the Cranberry Clown. LC 94-12781. 1995. write for info. (*0-688-13975-2*) Morrow.

Carlstrom, Nancy. Northern Lullaby. Dillon, Leo & Dillon, Diane, illus. 32p. (ps-3). 1992. PLB 15.95 (*0-399-21806-8*, Philomel Bks) Putnam Pub Group.

Carryl, Charles E. The Walloping Window-Blind. LaMarche, Jim, illus. LC 92-40338. (gr. k-5). 1993. 15.00 (*0-688-12517-4*); lib. bdg. 14.93 (*0-688-12518-2*) Lothrop.

Cassedy, Sylvia. Zoomrimes: Poems About Things That Go. Chessare, Michele, illus. LC 90-1463. 64p. (gr. 3-7). 1993. 14.00 (*0-06-022632-3*); PLB 13.89 (*0-06-022633-1*) HarpC Child Bks.

Chan, Jennifer L. Why Does a B Look Like a D. LC 93-45793. 1994. 12.95 (*1-879965-06-2*) Polychrome Pub.

Chandra, Deborah. Rich Lizard: And Other Poems. (gr. 4-7). 1993. 14.00 (*0-374-36274-2*) FS&G.

Ciardi, John. Doodle Soup. (gr. 4-7). 1992. pap. 3.80 (*0-395-61617-4*) HM.

Cohen, F. Fred's First Book of Poetry. (Orig.). (gr. 9-12). 1990. pap. 15.00 (*1-878109-10-3*) ASP PA.

Collman, Marthamarie C. Ballads & Other Island Things. Collman, Martha R., illus. 104p. (Orig.). (gr. 9 up). 1992. pap. 8.95 (*0-9631903-0-X*) M R Collman.

Cumpian, Carlos. Latino Rainbow: Poems about Latino Americans. Leonard, Richard, illus. LC 94-5069. 48p. (gr. 3-6). 1994. PLB 20.60 (*0-516-05153-9*); pap. 6.95 (*0-516-45153-7*) Childrens.

Dahlen, Beverly. A Reading. 101p. (Orig.). (gr. 6-12). 1989. pap. 8.50 (*0-937013-33-1*) Potes Poets.

Dakos, Kalli. Don't Read This Book Whatever You Do! More Poems about School. Karas, G. Brian, illus. LC 92-23236. 64p. (gr. 2-6). 1993. RSBE 13.95 (*0-02-725582-4*, Four Winds) Macmillan Child Grp.

—Mrs. Cole on an Onion Roll, & Other Poems about School. Adinolfi, JoAnn, illus. LC 94-8018. 1995. 14.00 (*0-02-725583-2*, Four Winds) Macmillan Child Grp.

Davis, Charles E. Creatures at My Feet. Neidigh, Sherry, illus. LC 92-81235. 32p. (ps). 1993. 12.95 (*0-87358-560-7*) Northland AZ.

Dickinson, Emily. I'm Nobody! Who Are You? Poems of Emily Dickinson for Children. Schneider, Rex, illus. Sewall, Richard, intro. by. LC 78-6828. (Illus.). 96p. (gr. 1 up). 1978. 21.95 (*0-916144-21-6*); pap. 14.95 (*0-916144-22-4*) Stemmer Hse.

Elias, Joyce. Whose Toes Are Those? Sturm, Cathy, illus. LC 92-8603. (ps). 1992. 11.95 (*0-8120-6215-9*) Barron.

Esbensen, Barbara J. Echoes for the Eye. Davie, Helen K., illus. LC 94-623. 1995. 15.00 (*0-06-024398-8*, HarpT); PLB 14.89 (*0-06-024399-6*) HarpC.

—Who Shrank My Grandmother's House? Poems of Discovery. Beddows, Eric, illus. LC 90-39631. 48p. (gr. 3-7). 1992. 15.00 (*0-06-021827-4*); PLB 14.89 (*0-06-021828-2*) HarpC Child Bks.

Evans, Dilys. Monster Soup. (Illus.). (ps). 1992. 14.95 (*0-590-45208-8*, 001, Scholastic Hardcover) Scholastic Inc.

Evans, Lezlie. Rain Song. Jabar, Cynthia, illus. LC 94-17368. Date not set. write for info. (*0-395-69865-0*) HM.

Feelings, Tom. Soul Looks Back in Wonder. Angelou, Maya, et al. LC 93-824. (Illus.). 40p. 1994. 15.99 (*0-8037-1001-1*, Dial Pr) Doubleday.

Field, Eugene. Wynken, Blynken, & Nod. 1993. pap. 28.67 (*0-590-71588-7*) Scholastic Inc.

Field, Rachel. If Once You Have Slept on an Island. Cohn, Amy, ed. Van Rynbach, Iris, illus. LC 94-25758. 32p. (ps up). 1995. pap. 4.95 (*0-688-13207-3*, Mulberry) Morrow.

Fletcher, Ralph. I Am Wings: Poems about Love. Baker, Joe, illus. 48p. (gr. 5-9). 1994. SBE 12.95 (*0-02-735395-8*, Bradbury Pr) Macmillan Child Grp.

—Water Planet. 2nd ed. 34p. (Orig.). (gr. 2-10). 1991. pap. 8.00x (*0-9628238-5-6*) Arrowhead Bks.

A poetry collection about water arranged in two parts. The poems in Part One (Water Songs) are humorous & rhythmic as in "H2O": "The recipe /for water is/ the same as/ it's always been/ two parts/ hydrogen/ one part/ oxygen." These playful poems will encourage young readers to wade into Part Two (Deeper Water) which includes "A Writing Kind of Day": "Each word hits the page/ like a drop in a puddle/ and starts off a tiny circle/ of trembling feeling/ that expands from the source/ & slowly fades away..." Essential collection for teachers doing theme units on water or the water cycle. "Ralph Fletcher's WATER PLANET, like water itself, refreshes & laves the reader into new ways of feeling & looking. These poems rescue the young from drowning in the sea of mediocre verse, the false metaphors & tired cliches which threaten to become the standard of our time. This is an important collection with its variety of forms & felicitous images." (Myra Cohn Livingston). To order, write to: Arrowhead Books, 3 Gerrish Drive, Durham, NH 03824. Or call 603-868-7145.

Publisher Provided Annotation.

Florian, Douglas. Beast Feast. LC 93-10720. (gr. 5 up). 1994. write for info. (*0-15-295178-4*) HarBrace.

—Bing Bang Boing: Poems & Drawings. LC 94-3894. (gr. 1 up). 1994. write for info. (*0-15-233770-9*) HarBrace.

—Monster Motel. LC 92-7309. (ps-3). 1993. 13.99 (*0-15-255320-7*) HarBrace.

Frost, Robert. Stopping by Woods on a Snowy Evening. Jeffers, Susan, illus. LC 78-8134. (ps up). 1978. 13.00 (*0-525-40115-6*, 01063-320, DCB) Dutton Child Bks.

Gautier, Dick. A Child's Garden of Weirdness: Illustrations, Verse, & Worse. LC 92-43033. 1993. 14.95 (*0-8048-1825-8*) C E Tuttle.

Ghigna, Charles. Tickle Day: Poems from Father Goose. Moore, Cyd, illus. LC 93-40847. 40p. (ps-2). 1994. 14.95 (*0-7868-0015-1*); PLB 14.89 (*0-7868-2010-1*) Hyprn Child.

Gillespie, Bill. Butterflies' Wings & Beautiful Things. Poe, Janice, illus. 24p. 1986. pap. 3.50 (*0-940859-02-5*) Snd Dollar Pub.

Giovanni, Nikki. Ego-Tripping & Other Poems for Young People. 2nd, rev. ed. Ford, George, illus. LC 93-29578. 72p. (gr. 5-12). 1993. 14.95 (*1-55652-188-X*); pap. 9.95 (*1-55652-189-8*) L Hill Bks.

—Knoxville, Tennessee. Johnson, Larry, illus. LC 93-8877. 32p. 1994. 14.95 (*0-590-47074-4*) Scholastic Inc.

Graham, Joan B. Splish Splash. Scott, Steven M., illus. LC 94-1237. 40p. (gr. k-3). 1994. 13.95 (*0-395-70128-7*, Ticknor & Flds Bks Yng Read) HM.

Green, Barbara-Marie, et al. More Poetic Thoughts: By Love Pain Hope Poet, Barbara-Marie Green & Others. 70p. (Orig.). 1993. pap. 5.50 (*1-883414-01-6*) Bar JaMae.

Greenfield, Eloise. Night on Neighborhood Street. (ps-3). 1991. 14.00 (*0-8037-0777-0*); PLB 13.89 (*0-8037-0778-9*) Dial Bks Young.

Griffith, Neysa & Duarte, Steven. The Magic of Green. Morse, Deborah, illus. LC 93-34811. 1994. 4.95 (*1-56844-028-6*) Enchante Pub.

—The Magic of Orange. Morse, Deborah, illus. LC 93-35439. 1994. 4.95 (*1-56844-026-X*) Enchante Pub.

—The Magic of Red. Morse, Deborah, illus. LC 93-34813. 1994. 4.95 (*1-56844-025-1*) Enchante Pub.

—The Magic of Yellow. Morse, Deborah, illus. LC 93-34812. 1994. 4.95 (*1-56844-027-8*) Enchante Pub.

Grimes, Nikki. Meet Danitra Brown. Cooper, Floyd, illus. LC 92-43707. (gr. 4 up). 1995. 15.00 (*0-688-12073-3*); PLB 14.93 (*0-688-12074-1*) Lothrop.

Hackett, Iris. Touch Your Dream. 90p. (Orig.). (gr. 8 up). 1994. pap. 13.95 (*0-9643422-0-0*) H to H Pubs.

Hale, Robert B. Song Full of Children. Ewing, Carolyn S., illus. LC 94-11979. 1994. write for info. (*0-688-12218-3*); lib. bdg. write for info. (*0-688-12219-1*) Lothrop.

Hale, Sarah J., retold by. Mary Had a Little Lamb. Mavor, Salley, illus. LC 94-24847. (gr. 1-8). 1995. write for info. (*0-531-06875-7*); PLB write for info. (*0-531-08725-5*) Orchard Bks Watts.

Hall, Donald, ed. The Oxford Book of Children's Verse in America. 368p. (gr. 3 up). 1990. pap. 13.95 (*0-19-506761-4*) OUP.

Hearne, Betsy. Polaroid: And Other Poems of View. LC 90-45577. (Illus.). 80p. (gr. 7 up). 1991. SBE 13.95 (*0-689-50530-2*, M K McElderry) Macmillan Child Grp.

Hennedy, Hugh. Halcyon Time. Chu, Charles, illus. 160p. (Orig.). 1993. pap. 12.95 (*1-552291-54-5*) Oyster River Pr.

Herford, Oliver. The Most Timid in the Land: A Bunny Romance. Long, Sylvia, illus. 32p. (ps-1). 1992. 12.95 (*0-87701-862-6*) Chronicle Bks.

Herskowitz, Joel & Herskowitz, Ira. Double Talking Helix Blues. Cuddihy, Judy, illus. LC 93-36775. 32p. (gr. k-8). 1994. 20.00 (*0-87969-431-9*) Cold Spring Harbor.

Hoberman, Mary A. Fathers, Mothers, Sisters, Brothers: A Collection of Family Poems. Hafner, Marylin, illus. LC 92-26587. 1993. pap. 4.99 (*0-14-054849-1*, Puffin) Puffin Bks.

—A Fine Fat Pig: And Other Animal Poems. Zeldis, Malcah, illus. LC 90-37403. 32p. (ps-2). 1991. HarpC Child Bks.

Holkner, Jean. The Wind. Greenstein, Susan, illus. LC 92-21450. 1993. 3.75 (*0-383-03668-2*) SRA Schl Grp.

Hopkins, Lee B. Through Our Eyes: Poems & Pictures about Growing Up. (ps-3). 1992. 15.95 (*0-316-19654-1*) Little.

Hughes, Langston. The Dream Keeper: And Other Poems. Pinkney, Brian, illus. 96p. 1994. 12.00 (*0-679-84421-X*); PLB 12.99 (*0-679-94421-4*) Knopf Bks Yng Read.

—The Sweet & Sour Animal Book. Students of the Harlem School for the Arts Staff, illus. Vereen, Ben & Cunningham, Georgeintro. by. (Illus.). 48p. 1994. 15.95 (*0-19-509185-X*) OUP.

Hurst, Ida Olivia. My Kaleidoscope of Poetry & Stories. Meyer, Monty Dale, illus. LC 91-92380. 96p. (Orig.). 1992. pap. 11.95 (*0-9632521-0-0*) Gemstone OR.

Izuki, Steve. Believers in America: Poems about Americans of Asian & Pacific Island Descent. McCoy, Bill, illus. LC 94-5081. 48p. (gr. 3-6). 1994. PLB 20.60 (*0-516-05152-0*); pap. 6.95 (*0-516-45152-9*) Childrens.

Jacobs. Just Around the Corner. 1993. write for info. (*0-8050-3024-7*) H Holt & Co.

Jacobs, Leland B. Is Somewhere Always Far Away? Poems about Places. Kaufman, Jeff, illus. 32p. (gr. k-3). 1993. 14.95 (*0-8050-2677-0*, Bks Young Read) H Holt & Co.

—Just Around the Corner: Poems about the Seasons. Kaufman, Jeff, illus. LC 93-18342. 32p. (gr. k-3). 1993. 14.95 (*0-8050-2676-2*, Bks Young Read) H Holt & Co.

Janeczko, Paul B. Stardust Otel. Leech, Dorothy, illus. LC 92-44514. 64p. (gr. 7 up). 1993. 14.95 (*0-531-05498-5*); lib. bdg. 14.99 (*0-531-08648-8*) Orchard Bks Watts.

Johnson, James Weldon. The Creation. Ransome, James, illus. LC 93-3207. 32p. (ps-3). 1994. reinforced bdg. 15.95 (*0-8234-1069-2*) Holiday.
—The Creation: A Poem. Golembe, Carla, photos by. LC 92-24304. (Illus.). 1993. 15.95 (*0-316-46744-8*) Little.
Joseph, Lynn. Coconut Kind of Day: Island Poems. 1992. pap. 4.99 (*0-14-054867-X*, Puffin) Puffin Bks.
—Coconut Kind of Day: Island Poems. (gr. 4 up). 1992. pap. 4.99 (*0-14-054527-1*) Puffin Bks.
Katz, Bobbi. Ghosts & Goose Bumps: Poems to Chill Your Bones. Ray, Deborah K., illus. LC 89-37134. 32p. (Orig.). (ps-3). 1991. pap. 2.25 (*0-679-80372-6*) Random Bks Yng Read.
Kearney, Jill. A Fishmas Carol. LC 94-6198. 1994. write for info. (*0-681-00582-3*) Longmeadow Pr.
Kennedy, X. J. The Beasts of Bethlehem. McCurdy, Michael, illus. LC 91-38417. 48p. (gr. 1 up). 1992. SBE 13.95 (*0-689-50561-2*, M K McElderry) Macmillan Child Grp.
—Drat These Brats! Watts, James, illus. LC 92-33686. 48p. (gr. 3 up). 1993. SBE 12.95 (*0-689-50589-2*, M K McElderry) Macmillan Child Grp.
Krupinski, Loretta. New England Scrapbook: A Journey through Poems, Prose, & Pictures. Krupinski, Loretta, illus. LC 92-37705. 40p. (gr. 1 up). 1994. 15.00 (*0-06-022950-0*); PLB 14.89 (*0-06-022951-9*) HarpC Child Bks.
Kulkarni, Shyamkant. The Sun Dance & Other Poems. Andrews, Duane, illus. LC 91-90016. iv, 32p. (Orig.). (gr. 5 up). 1991. pap. 5.50 (*0-9627083-1-3*) S Kulkarni.
Langstaff, John. Over in the Meadow. Rojankovsky, Feodor, illus. (ps-1). 1992. pap. 19.95 (*0-15-258853-1*) HarBrace.
Lansky, Bruce, compiled by. Kids Pick the Funniest Poems. LC 91-31072. (Illus.). 120p. 1991. 14.00 (*0-88166-149-X*) Meadowbrook.
Lawrence, Valerie. What's Yr Hair Like after U Wash It? Natural Poems by Valerie Lawrence. LC 90-6188. 100p. (gr. 6 up). 1990. 10.95 (*0-929917-01-4*) Magnolia PA.

Lesser, Carolyn. Flamingo Knees. 4th ed. Shles, Larry, illus. 52p. (gr. k-12). 1993. pap. 10.00 (*0-9630604-2-2*) Oakwood MO.
FLAMINGO KNEES, a delightful book of poems by Carolyn Lesser, leads the reader through a variety of short verses featuring Pearl the flamingo & her many 'twists & bends.' Sprinkled throughout the book are poems such as "A Rainbow Named Igor," an iguana; "Low Spots, High Spots," spotted animals; "Lawanda Jean," the girl who hated to brush her teeth; & "Great Crystal Bear," the cold & lonely life of a polar bear, a poem which will soon become a children's picture book published by Harcourt Brace & Co. FLAMINGO KNEES, ISBN 0-9630604-2-2. Paperback retails at $10. THE KNEES KNOCK AGAIN, a second book of Ms. Lesser's poems, adds Ringo Flamingo to the family, along with the adventures of Humperdink the penguin & his problems in learning to swim. Dooley the dog, Miss Gertrude, Mary Margaret, five shaggy llamas & box turtles are some of the fascinating creatures you'll meet in this second book loved by children of all ages. THE KNEES KNOCK AGAIN, ISBN 0-9630604-3-0. Paperback retails at $10. Published by Oakwood Press at new address, Carolyn Lesser Creative, 301 Oak St., Quincy, IL 62301; 217-222-5742.
Publisher Provided Annotation.

Levy, Constance. A Tree Place: And Other Poems. Sabuda, Robert, illus. LC 93-20586. 48p. (gr. k-5). 1994. SBE 12.95 (*0-689-50599-X*, M K McElderry) Macmillan Child Grp.
Lewis, J. Patrick. Earth Verses & Water Rhymes. Sabuda, Robert, illus. LC 90-40709. 32p. (gr. 2-5). 1991. SBE 13.95 (*0-689-31693-3*, Atheneum Child Bk) Macmillan Child Grp.
—July Is a Mad Mosquito. Hall, Melanie W., illus. LC 93-19743. 32p. (gr. 2-5). 1994. SBE 14.95 (*0-689-31813-8*, Atheneum Child Bk) Macmillan Child Grp.
—Riddle-Icious. Roberts, Victoria, illus. LC 93-43759. 1995. 15.00 (*0-679-84011-7*); PLB write for info. (*0-679-94011-1*) Knopf.
—Two Legged, Four-Legged, No-Legged Rhymes. Paparone, Pamela, illus. LC 90-20651. 40p. (ps-3). 1991. 13.00 (*0-679-80771-3*); lib. bdg. 13.99 (*0-679-90771-8*) Knopf Bks Yng Read.
Lillegard, Dee. Do Not Feed the Table. (gr. 5 up). 1993. pap. 14.95 (*0-385-30516-8*) Doubleday.
Lindbergh, Reeve. Grandfather's Lovesong. Isadora, Rachel, illus. LC 92-22212. 32p. 1993. 14.99 (*0-670-84842-5*) Viking Child Bks.
Livingston, Myra C. Animal, Vegetable, Mineral: Poems about Small Things. Nasta, Vincent, illus. LC 93-43712. 80p. (gr. 3-7). 1994. 14.00 (*0-06-023008-8*); PLB 13.89 (*0-06-023009-6*) HarpC Child Bks.
—Flights of Fancy & Other Poems. LC 94-14476. (gr. 3-7). 1994. 13.95 (*0-689-50613-9*) Macmillan Child Grp.
—I Never Told: And Other Poems. Pinkney, Brian, contrib. by. LC 91-20475. 48p. (gr. 3-7). 1992. SBE 12.95 (*0-689-50544-2*, M K McElderry) Macmillan Child Grp.
—Keep on Singing: A Ballad of Marian Anderson. Byrd, Samuel, illus. LC 93-46909. 32p. 1994. reinforced bdg. 15.95 (*0-8234-1098-6*) Holiday.
—Light & Shadow. Rogasky, Barbara, photos by. LC 91-22355. (Illus.). 32p. (ps-3). 1992. reinforced bdg. 14.95 (*0-8234-0931-7*) Holiday.
Loewen, Nancy & Berry, S. L. Robert Frost. (Illus.). 48p. (gr. 5-12). 1994. lib. bdg. 18.95 RLB smythe-sewn (*0-88682-613-6*, 97866-098) Creative Ed.
Longfellow, Henry Wadsworth. Children's Own Longfellow. (Illus.). 109p. (gr. 4-6). 1908. 19.95 (*0-395-06889-4*) HM.
—Hiawatha's Childhood. (ps-3). 1994. pap. 5.95 (*0-374-42997-9*, Sunburst) FS&G.
—Paul Revere's Ride. Rand, Ted, illus. LC 89-25630. 40p. (gr. k-4). 1990. 14.95 (*0-525-44610-9*, DCB) Dutton Child Bks.
—Paul Revere's Ride. Parker, Nancy W., illus. LC 92-23319. 48p. (gr. 1 up). 1993. pap. 4.95 (*0-688-12387-2*, Mulberry) Morrow.
Lyons, Mark E. Selected Poems. 1992. 7.95 (*0-533-09578-6*) Vantage.
McCord, David. For Me to Say. Kane, Henry B., illus. (gr. 5 up). 1970. 12.95 (*0-316-55511-8*) Little.
McMillan, Bruce. Play Day: A Book of Terse Verse. McMillan, Bruce, illus. LC 90-29077. 32p. (ps-3). 1991. reinforced 14.95 (*0-8234-0894-9*) Holiday.
McNaughton, Colin. Making Friends with Frankenstein: A Book of Monstrous Poems & Pictures. McNaughton, Colin, illus. LC 93-20027. (ps up). 1994. 19.95 (*1-56402-308-7*) Candlewick Pr.

Markels, Bobby. How to Be a Human Bean. Leek, Kenny, illus. 24p. (gr. 3 up). 1975. pap. 4.50 (*1-880991-01-2*) Stone Pub.
"...delightful, whimsical poems for children of all ages...exuberant presentation part of its charm..." - S.F. Chronicle. Parents will applaud the reasoning used for why you should take a bath (dirt makes you sticky & someone will think you're a postage stamp & stick you on a letter, then you'll be stuck), why you should comb your hair (if you walk around looking like an old mop someone might turn you upside down & dust the floor with your head), why you should brush your teeth (so you don't have a space in your mouth where your teeth should go & you could only eat slop), why you should wash your ears (so grass won't grow in them & you'd have to lie down on your side & mow the grass in your ears everyday), "Markels writes as if she's been a parent for 200 years." - S.R. Press Democrat; "...useful material...from daily living with appealing, quirky illustrations...written in a delightful & graphic way..." - Mendocino Beacon. Order from Stone Press, Box 711, Mendocino, CA 95460; 707-937-0239.
Publisher Provided Annotation.

Merriam, Eve. Bam, Bam, Bam. Yaccarino, Dan, illus. LC 94-20300. 1995. write for info. (*0-8050-3527-3*) H Holt & Co.
—Higgle Wiggle: Happy Rhymes. Wilhelm, Hans, illus. LC 92-29795. 40p. (ps up). 1994. 15.00g (*0-688-11948-4*); PLB 14.93 (*0-688-11949-2*) Morrow Jr Bks.
—The Inner City Mother Goose. LC 93-19735. (Illus.). 1996. pap. 15.00 (*0-671-88033-0*, S&S BFYR) S&S Trade.
Metaxes, Eric. The Birthday ABC. Raglin, Tim, illus. LC 93-46896. 1995. 14.00 (*0-671-88306-2*, S&S BFYR) S&S Trade.
Moore, Clement C. The Night Before Christmas. Hirashima, Jean, illus. LC 92-27138. 32p. (ps-3). 1993. pap. 2.25 (*0-448-40482-6*, G&D) Putnam Pub Group.
—The Night Before Christmas. (ps-3). 1993. pap. 5.95 (*0-395-66508-6*, Clarion Bks) HM.
—Twas the Night Before Christmas. Downing, Julie, illus. LC 93-40243. (ps up). 1994. 14.95 (*0-02-767646-3*, Bradbury Pr) Macmillan Child Grp.
—A Visit from St. Nicholas. Hader, Berta & Hader, Elmer, illus. LC 93-33703. (gr. 2 up). 1994. pap. write for info. (*0-486-27978-2*) Dover.
Moore, Lilian. Adam Mouse's Book of Poems. McCord, Kathleen G., illus. LC 91-42223. 64p. (ps-5). 1992. SBE 12.95 (*0-689-31765-4*, Atheneum Child Bk) Macmillan Child Grp.
Mora, Pat. Listen to the Desert - Que Dice el Desierto? Mora, Francisco X., illus. LC 93-31463. (ENG & SPA.). (ps-2). 1994. 14.95 (*0-395-67292-9*, Clarion Bks) HM.
Morrison, Lillian, compiled by. Slam Dunk: Poems about Basketball. James, Bill, illus. LC 94-14620. (ps-3). Date not set. write for info. (*0-7868-0058-5*); PLB write for info. (*0-7868-2046-2*) Hyprn Child.
Moss, Jeff. The Sesame Street Book of Poetry. McNally, Bruce, illus. LC 90-8994. 48p. (ps-3). 1992. 10.00 (*0-679-80774-8*); PLB 10.99 (*0-679-90774-2*) Random Bks Yng Read.
Munsterberg, Peggy. Beastly Feasts: Tasty Treats for Animal Appetites. Gallup, Tracy, photos by. LC 94-2951. (Illus.). Date not set. write for info. (*0-8037-1481-5*); pap. write for info. (*0-8037-1482-3*) Dial Bks Young.
Musical Lynn. The Early Poems. 5p. (Orig.). (gr. 12). 1990. pap. 7.95 (*1-880718-05-7*) Genius New.
Nash, Ogden. The Adventures of Isabel. Marshall, James, illus. (ps-3). 1991. 14.95 (*0-316-59874-7*) Little.
Nielsen, Shelly. Telling the Truth. Wallner, Rosemary, ed. LC 91-73046. 1992. 13.99 (*1-56239-062-7*) Abdo & Dghtrs.
Nikola-Lisa, W. Bein' with You This Way. Bryant, Michael, illus. LC 93-5164. 32p. 1994. 14.95 (*1-880000-05-9*) Lee & Low Bks.
Numeroff, Laura J. Dogs Don't Wear Sneakers. Mathieu, Joe, illus. LC 92-27007. 1993. pap. 14.00 (*0-671-79525-2*, S&S BFYR) S&S Trade.
O'Donnell, Elizabeth L. The Twelve Days of Summer. Schmidt, Karen L., illus. LC 89-35161. 32p. (ps up). 1991. 13.95 (*0-688-08202-5*); PLB 13.88 (*0-688-08203-3*, Morrow Jr Bks) Morrow Jr Bks.
Panzer, Nora, ed. Celebrate America: In Poetry & Art. LC 93-32336. (Illus.). 96p. (gr. 3 up). 1994. 18.95 (*1-56282-664-6*); PLB 18.89 (*1-56282-665-4*) Hyprn Child.
Paraskevas, Betty. Junior Kroll & Company. Paraskevas, Michael, illus. LC 93-9138. (ps-6). 1994. 13.95 (*0-15-292855-3*) HarBrace.
—A Very Kroll Christmas. Paraskevas, Michael, illus. LC 93-41624. (ps up). 1994. 14.95 (*0-15-292883-9*) HarBrace.
Petrochilos, Elizabeth A. Stone the Poet. 110p. (Orig.). 1991. pap. write for info. (*0-9629730-0-9*) E Petrochilos.
Poe, Edgar Allan. Edgar Allan Poe, Stories & Poems. (gr. 9 up). 1962. pap. 3.25 (*0-8049-0008-6*, CL-8) Airmont.
—The Raven & Other Poems. 80p. (gr. 7 up). 1992. pap. 2.95 (*0-590-45260-6*, Apple Classics) Scholastic Inc.
Poe, Edgar Allen & Wilson, Gahan. The Raven & Other Poems. (Illus.). 52p. Date not set. pap. 4.95 (*1-57209-000-6*) Classics Int Ent.
Pomerantz, Charlotte. Halfway to Your House. Vincent, Gabrielle, illus. LC 92-30083. 32p. (ps up). 1993. 14.00 (*0-688-11804-6*); PLB 13.93 (*0-688-11805-4*) Greenwillow.
—If I Had a Paka. reissued ed. LC 81-6624. (Illus.). 32p. (ps). 1993. 14.00 (*0-688-11900-X*); PLB 13.93 (*0-688-11901-8*) Greenwillow.
—If I Had a Paka: Poems in Eleven Languages. Tafuri, Nancy & Rice, Eve, illus. LC 92-33088. 32p. (ps up). 1993. pap. 4.95 (*0-688-12510-7*, Mulberry) Morrow.
—The Tamarindo Puppy. reissued ed. Barton, Byron, illus. LC 79-16584. 32p. (ps up). 1993. 14.00 (*0-688-11902-6*); PLB 13.93 (*0-688-11903-4*) Greenwillow.
—The Tamarindo Puppy & Other Poems. Barton, Byron, illus. LC 79-16584. 32p. (ps up). 1993. pap. 4.95 (*0-688-11514-4*, Mulberry) Morrow.
Prelutsky, Jack. The Baby Uggs Are Hatching! Stevenson, James, illus. LC 81-7266. 32p. (gr. k-3). 1982. 15.00 (*0-688-00922-0*); PLB 14.93 (*0-688-00923-9*) Greenwillow.
—The Headless Horseman Rides Tonight. ALC Staff, ed. Lobel, Arnold, illus. LC 80-10372. 40p. (gr. 1 up). 1992. pap. 4.95 (*0-688-11705-8*, Mulberry) Morrow.
—It's Snowing! It's Snowing! Titherington, Jeanne, illus. LC 83-16583. 48p. (gr. 1-3). 1984. 12.95 (*0-688-01512-3*); PLB 14.93 (*0-688-01513-1*) Greenwillow.
—It's Thanksgiving. Hafner, Marylin, illus. LC 81-1929. 48p. (gr. 1-3). 1982. 14.00 (*0-688-00441-5*); lib. bdg. 13.93 (*0-688-00442-3*) Greenwillow.
—Nightmares: Poems to Trouble Your Sleep. Lobel, Arnold, illus. LC 92-43780. 40p. 1993. pap. 4.95 (*0-688-04589-8*, Mulberry) Morrow.

—Rolling Harvey Down the Hill. Chess, Victoria, illus. LC 92-24606. 40p. (gr. 2 up). 1993. pap. 4.95 (*0-688-12270-1*, Mulberry) Morrow.

—Sweet & Silly Muppet Poems. 24p. (ps). 1992. 1.09 (*0-307-10249-1*, Golden Pr) Western Pub.

—Tyrannosaurus Was a Beast: Big Book Edition. Lobel, Arnold, illus. 32p. (ps up). 1993. pap. 18.95 (*0-688-12613-8*, Mulberry) Morrow.

Rosenberg, Jane. Play Me a Story. LC 93-33490. (gr. 3 up). 1994. 25.00 (*0-679-84391-4*) Knopf Bks Yng Read.

Ross, Anna. Little Ernie's ABC's. Gorbaty, Norman, illus. LC 91-27823. 24p. (ps). 1992. 3.99 (*0-679-82240-2*) Random Bks Yng Read.

Rouss, Sylvia A. Fun with Jewish Holiday Rhymes. Steinberg, Lisa, illus. LC 91-40931. (ps). 1992. 10.95 (*0-8074-0463-2*, 101981) UAHC.

St. John, Eric M., II & St. John, Millie L. The Rainbow Kids. LC 94-92279. 20p. (ps up). 1994. pap. 10.95 (*0-9643453-0-7*) RKUP Pubng. In THE RAINBOW KIDS, Jeninne, a nine-year old multi-ethnic child, discusses the positive self-image instilled in her by her parents & grandmother. It is a self-image that transcends the racial make-up of her family, projecting itself across both ethnic & global boundaries & seeing unlimited possibilities that reach beyond our earth. In fact, the racial make-up of the family (which lives in Washington, D.C.) has very little to do with the message of the book. However, the racial make-up of the family is important because there are so few books that depict families of mixed heritage with the realism & honesty that this one does. Comfortably conversational poetry & vividly beautiful water color illustrations depict a family at work, at play & at odds with each other: a family that shares love like any other family. The illustrations also show that the world is what we make of it & that it is to be shared: a world that realizes that there is no need to fear difference. "Every parent will be interested." (Washington's Hill Rag). Order from: RKUP Publishing, 254 15th St., SE, Washington, DC 20003, 202-546-9026. *Publisher Provided Annotation.*

Sandburg, Carl. Arithmetic. LC 32-5291. (gr. 4-7). 1993. 15.95 (*0-15-203865-5*) HarBrace.

Schmidt, Gary D., ed. Robert Frost: Poetry for Young People. Sorenson, Henri, illus. LC 94-11161. 48p. 1994. 14.95 (*0-8069-0633-2*) Sterling.

Schwartz, Alvin. And the Green Grass Grew All Around: Folk Poetry from Everyone. Truesdell, Sue, illus. LC 89-26722. 208p. (gr. 1-7). 1992. 15.00 (*0-06-022757-5*); PLB 14.89 (*0-06-022758-3*) HarpC Child Bks.

Sendak, Maurice. Chicken Soup with Rice: A Book of Months. Sendak, Maurice, illus. LC 62-13315. 32p. (ps-3). 1991. pap. 3.95 (*0-06-443253-X*, Trophy) HarpC Child Bks,

Sheehan, William. Nature's Wonderful World in Rhyme. Maeno, Itoko, illus. LC 93-15247. 1993. 14.95 (*0-911655-47-6*) Advocacy Pr.

Sierra, Judy. Good Night, Dinosaurs. Chess, Victoria, illus. LC 93-8855. Date not set. write for info. (*0-395-65016-X*, Clarion Bks) HM.

Silverstein, Shel. Where the Sidewalk Ends. (Illus.). 1986. pap. 7.95 (*0-440-85056-8*) Dell.

Singer, Marilyn. Family Reunion. Alley, R. W., illus. LC 92-40336. 32p. (ps up). 1994. RSBE 14.95 (*0-02-782883-2*, Macmillan Child Bk) Macmillan Child Grp.

—In My Tent. McCully, Emily A., illus. LC 91-16115. 32p. (gr. k-3). 1992. RSBE 14.95 (*0-02-782701-1*, Macmillan Child Bk) Macmillan Child Grp.

—It's Hard to Read a Map with a Beagle on Your Lap. Oubrerie, Clement, photos by. LC 92-26166. (Illus.). 32p. (gr. 1-4). 1993. 15.95 (*0-8050-2201-5*, Bks Young Read) H Holt & Co.

—Turtle in July. Pinkey, Jerry, illus. LC 93-14430. 32p. (gr. 3-7). 1994. pap. 4.95 (*0-689-71805-5*, Aladdin) Macmillan Child Grp.

Soto, Gary. Neighborhood Odes. Diaz, D., illus. 1992. 15.95 (*0-15-256879-4*, HB Juv Bks) HarBrace.

Spires, Elizabeth, ed. One White Wing: Puzzles in Poems & Pictures. Blegvad, Erik, illus. LC 94-12927. 1995. 16.00 (*0-689-50622-8*, M K McElderry) Macmillan Child Grp.

Stafford, William. Learning to Live in the World: Earth Poems. Watson, Jerry & Apol, Laura, eds. LC 94-9900. (gr. 7 up). 1994. 15.95 (*0-15-200208-1*) HarBrace.

Steptoe, Lamont B. Crimson River. 3rd ed. 24p. (gr. 11 up). 1991. pap. text ed. 7.00 (*0-922827-07-9*) Whirlwind Pr.

Stevenson, James. Sweet Corn: Poems. Date not set. write for info. RTE (*0-688-12647-2*) Greenwillow.

Sullivan, Charles. Cowboys. LC 92-42980. (Illus.). 48p. 1993. 17.95 (*0-8478-1680-X*) Rizzoli Intl.

Swenson, May. The Complete Poems to Solve. Hale, Christy, illus. LC 92-26183. 128p. (gr. 3 up). 1993. SBE 13.95 (*0-02-788725-1*, Macmillan Child Bk) Macmillan Child Grp.

Teasdale, Sara. Christmas Carol. Gottlieb, Dale, illus. 32p. (ps-2). 1993. 14.95 (*0-8050-2695-9*, Bks Young Read) H Holt & Co.

Teichman, Mary, illus. Merry Christmas: A Victorian Verse. LC 92-29870. 32p. (ps up). 1993. 10.00 (*0-06-022889-X*); PLB 9.89 (*0-06-022892-X*) HarpC Child Bks.

Thomas, Joyce C. Brown Honey in Broomwheat Tea. Cooper, Floyd, illus. LC 91-46043. 32p. (gr. k up). 1993. 15.00 (*0-06-021087-7*); PLB 14.89 (*0-06-021088-5*) HarpC Child Bks.

Trapani, Iza. Twinkle Twinkle Little Star. LC 93-33635. (gr. 2 up). 1994. 14.95 (*1-879085-87-9*) Whsprng Coyote Pr.

Trosclair. Cajun Night Before Christmas: Full-Color Edition. Jacobs, Howard, ed. Rice, James, illus. LC 92-8375. 48p. (gr. k-3). 1992. 14.95 (*0-88289-940-6*); boxed ed. 25.00 (*0-88289-947-3*); audio 9.95 (*0-88289-914-7*) Pelican.

Turner, Ann. The Christmas House. Calder, Nancy E., illus. LC 93-12740. 32p. (gr. k-3). 1994. 15.00 (*0-06-023429-6*); PLB 14.89 (*0-06-023432-6*) HarpC Child Bks.

—A Moon for Seasons. Norieka, Robert, illus. LC 92-36857. 40p. (gr. 1-5). 1994. RSBE 14.95 (*0-02-789513-0*, Macmillan Child Bk) Macmillan Child Grp.

Updike, John. A Helpful Alphabet of Friendly Objects. Updike, David, photos by. LC 93-29922. (Illus.). Date not set. 14.00 (*0-679-84324-8*); PLB 14.99 (*0-679-94324-2*) Knopf.

Viorst, Judith. Sad Underwear & Other Complications. Hull, Richard, illus. LC 94-3357. 1995. 15.00 (*0-689-31929-0*, Atheneum) Macmillan.

Whales, Bostune. Cherish Life. 25p. 1991. write for info. (*0-9629599-1-X*) Rainbow IA.

Whipple, Laura, compiled by. Celebrating America: A Collection of Poems & Images of the American Spirit. LC 92-26197. (Illus.). 80p. (gr. 2 up). 1994. PLB 19.95 (*0-399-22036-4*, Philomel Bks) Putnam Pub Group.

Whitman, Walt. Leaves of Grass. Gemme, F. R., intro. by. (gr. 11 up). 1965. pap. 1.95 (*0-8049-0091-4*, CL-91) Airmont.

Wilbur, Richard. Opposites. Drescher, Henrik, illus. LC 92-39472. 1994. 15.95 (*0-15-230563-7*) HarBrace.

—Runaway Opposites. Drescher, Henrik, illus. LC 94-13188. 1995. write for info. (*0-15-258722-5*) HarBrace.

Willard, Nancy. The Alphabet of Angels. LC 93-48836. (ps up). 1994. 16.95 (*0-590-48480-X*, Blue Sky Press) Scholastic Inc.

Wilson, Jean A. Caz & His Cat: Now We Like the Night. Wilson, Richard C., illus. 32p. 1994. 14.95 (*1-884739-00-8*) Wahr.

Wilson, Sarah. June Is a Tune That Jumps on a Stair. LC 91-4053. (Illus.). 40p. (ps-2). 1992. pap. 14.00 jacketed (*0-671-73919-0*, S&S BFYR) S&S Trade.

Wong, Janet S. Good Luck Gold & Other Poems. LC 94-20743. (gr. 5 up). 1994. 14.95 (*0-689-50617-1*, M K McElderry) Macmillan Child Grp.

Wood, Nancy. Spirit Walker: Poems. Howell, Frank, illus. LC 92-29376. 80p. 1993. pap. 19.95 (*0-385-30927-9*) Doubleday.

Yanes, Audrey. Shaking Loose: Poetry. 2nd ed. 24p. 1991. pap. 6.95 (*0-938911-06-6*) Indiv Educ Syst.

Yolen, Jane. Animal Fare: Zoological Nonsense Poems. Street, Janet, illus. LC 92-44931. (gr. 4 up). 1994. 14. 95 (*0-15-203550-8*) Harbrace.

—Here There Be Dragons. Wilgus, David, illus. LC 92-23194. 1993. 16.95 (*0-15-209888-7*) HarBrace.

—Here There Be Unicorns. Wilgus, David, illus. LC 94-1790. (gr. 5 up). 1994. write for info. (*0-15-209902-6*) HarBrace.

—Raining Cats & Dogs. LC 91-24295. (ps-3). 1993. 14.95 (*0-15-265488-7*, HB Juv Bks) HarBrace.

—Sacred Places. Shannon, David A., illus. LC 92-30323. 1994. write for info. (*0-15-269953-8*) HarBrace.

—What Rhymes with Moon? Councell, Ruth T., illus. LC 92-7439. 40p. (ps). 1993. 15.95 (*0-399-22501-3*, Philomel Bks) Putnam Pub Group.

Zolotow, Charlotte. Snippets: A Gathering of Poems, Pictures, & Possibilities... Sweet, Melissa, illus. LC 91-37751. 48p. (ps-3). 1993. 16.00 (*0-06-020818-X*); PLB 15.89 (*0-06-020819-8*) HarpC Child Bks.

AMERICAN POETRY–COLLECTIONS

Bruchac, Joseph & London, Jonathan, eds. Thirteen Moons on Turtle's Back: A Native American Year of Moons. Locker, Thomas, illus. 32p. (ps-8). 1992. PLB 15.95 (*0-399-22141-7*, Philomel Bks) Putnam Pub Group.

Cole, Joanna, et al. Yours 'Till Banana Splits: 201 Autograph Rhymes. Tiegreen, Alan, illus. LC 94-10654. (gr. 1 up). 1995. write for info. (*0-688-13185-9*); text ed. write for info. (*0-688-13186-7*) Morrow.

Cowden, Frances B. & Hatchett, Eve B. Of Butterflies & Unicorns: And Other Wonders of the Earth. Grove, Eric, illus. 52p. (gr. 7-12). 1993. pap. 7.95 (*1-884289-02-9*) Grandmother Erth.

Daniel, Mark, compiled by. A Child's Treasury of Seaside Verse. LC 90-2819. (Illus.). 144p. (ps up). 1991. 16.95 (*0-8037-0889-0*) Dial Bks Young.

Eccleshare, Julia, compiled by. First Poems. Young, Selina, illus. LC 93-40894. 64p. 1994. 14.95 (*0-87226-373-8*) P Bedrick Bks.

Elledge, Scott, ed. Wider Than the Sky: Poems to Grow up With. LC 90-4135. 368p. (gr. 5 up). 1990. 20.00 (*0-06-021786-3*); PLB 19.89 (*0-06-021787-1*) HarpC Child Bks.

Family Treasury of One Thousand Poems. LC 93-18994. 1993. 9.99 (*0-517-09333-2*, Pub. by Wings Bks) Random Hse Value.

Field, Eugene. Wynken, Blynken & Nod. Jeffers, Susan, illus. LC 82-2434. 32p. (ps-1). 1982. 13.50 (*0-525-44022-4*, DCB) Dutton Child Bks.

Goldstein, Bobbye S., compiled by. What's on the Menu? Demarest, Chris L., illus. 32p. (ps-3). 1992. PLB 12.50 (*0-670-83031-3*) Viking Child Bks.

Harter, Penny. Shadow Play, Night Haiku. Greene, Jeffrey, illus. LC 93-39887. (gr. 1-6). 1994. 15.00 (*0-671-88396-8*, S&S BFYR) S&S Trade.

Hoberman, Mary A. Fathers, Mothers, Sisters, Brothers: A Collection of Family Poems. Hafner, Marylin, illus. (ps-3). 1991. 14.95 (*0-316-36736-2*) Little.

Hopkins, Lee B., compiled by. Flit, Flutter, Fly! Poems about Bugs & Other Crawly Creatures. Palagonia, Peter, illus. LC 91-12441. 32p. (gr. k-4). 1992. pap. 14.00 (*0-385-41468-4*) Doubleday.

Hopkins, Lee B., ed. Stop! A Book of Small Poems. Gaber, Susan, illus. LC 94-7601. 1995. write for info. (*0-15-276577-8*) HarBrace.

Hopkins, Lee B., compiled by. Weather. Hall, Melanie, photos by. LC 92-14913. (Illus.). 64p. (gr. k-3). 1994. 14.00 (*0-06-021463-5*); PLB 13.89 (*0-06-021462-7*) HarpC Child Bks.

Huck, Charlotte, selected by. Secret Places. George, Lindsay B., illus. LC 92-29014. 32p. (ps up). 1993. 15. 00 (*0-688-11669-8*); PLB 14.93 (*0-688-11670-1*) Greenwillow.

Hudson, Wade, compiled by. Pass It On: African-American Poetry for Children. Cooper, Floyd, illus. LC 92-16034. 32p. (gr. k-4). 1993. 14.95 (*0-590-45770-5*) Scholastic Inc.

Janeczko, Paul B., selected by. Looking for Your Name: A Collection of Contemporary Poems. LC 92-25648. 160p. (gr. 7-12). 1993. 14.95 (*0-531-05475-6*); PLB 14.99 (*0-531-08625-9*) Orchard Bks Watts.

Janeczko, Paul B., compiled by. Poetry from A to Z: A Guide for Young Writers. Bobak, Cathy, illus. LC 94-10528. (gr. 4-8). 1994. 15.95 (*0-02-747672-3*, Bradbury Pr) Macmillan Child Grp.

Josefowitz, Natasha. A Hundred Scoops of Ice Cream. 60p. 1989. pap. 3.95 (*0-88166-157-0*) Prestwick Pub.

Livingston, Myra C., ed. Roll Along: Poems on Wheels. LC 92-32714. 80p. (gr. 4 up). 1993. SBE 11.95 (*0-689-50585-X*, M K McElderry) Macmillan Child Grp.

Marcus, Leonard S., selected by. Lifelines: A Poetry Anthology Patterned on the Stages of Life. LC 93-26413. 112p. (gr. 6 up). 1994. 16.99 (*0-525-45164-1*, DCB) Dutton Child Bks.

Moore, Lilian, selected by. Sunflakes: Poems for Children. Ormerod, Jan, illus. 96p. (ps-3). 1992. 18.45 (*0-395-58833-2*, Clarion Bks) HM.

Paladino, Catherine. Land, Sea, & Sky: Poems to Celebrate the Earth. (ps-3). 1993. 15.95 (*0-316-68892-4*, AMP) Little.

Prelutsky, Jack. A. Nonny Mouse Writes Again! Priceman, Marjorie, illus. LC 92-5214. 40p. (ps-5). 1993. 13.00 (*0-679-83715-9*); PLB 13.99 (*0-679-93715-3*) Knopf Bks Yng Read.

Radley, Gail, selected by. Rainy Day Rhymes. Kandoian, Ellen, illus. 48p. (gr. 2-5). 1992. 13.45 (*0-395-59967-9*) HM.

Richardson, Polly. Animal Poems. (ps-3). 1992. 12.95 (*0-8120-6283-3*) Barron.

Rogasky, Barbara, selected by. Winter Poems. Hyman, Trina S., illus. 40p. (gr. 2 up). 1994. 15.95 (*0-590-42872-1*, Scholastic Hardcover) Scholastic Inc.

Ross, H. K., ed. Great Story Poems: Collection. 160p. (gr. 5-12). 1993. pap. 9.95 (*0-87460-385-4*) Lion Bks.

Time-Life Inc. Editors. On Top of Spaghetti: A Lift-the-Flap Poetry Book. (Illus.). 20p. (ps-2). 1992. write for info. (*0-8094-9291-1*); PLB write for info. (*0-8094-9292-X*) Time-Life.

Westcott, Nadine B., ed. & illus. Never Take a Pig to Lunch: And Other Poems about the Fun of Eating. LC 93-11801. 64p. 1994. 16.95 (*0-531-06834-X*); lib. bdg. 16.99 RLB (*0-531-08684-4*) Orchard Bks Watts.

AMERICAN WIT AND HUMOR

Bierce, Ambrose & Wilson, Gahan. The Devil's Dictionary & Other Works. (Illus.). 52p. Date not set. pap. 4.95 (*1-57209-018-9*) Classics Int Ent.

Bonham, Tal D. The Treasury of Clean Teenage Jokes. LC 85-4134. (gr. 7 up). 1985. pap. 3.99 (*0-8054-5713-5*, 4257-13) Broadman.

Corbett, Scott. Jokes to Read in the Dark. Gusman, Annie, illus. LC 79-23129. 80p. (gr. 5-9). 1980. 12.95 (*0-525-32796-7*, 01063-320, DCB); (DCB) Dutton Child Bks.

Fleischman, Sid. McBroom's Almanac. Lorraine, Walter H., illus. (gr. 3-7). 1984. 14.95 (*0-316-26009-6*, Joy St Bks) Little.

Hartman, Victoria G. Westward Ho Ho! Jokes from the Wild West. Karas, G. Brian, illus. 48p. (gr. 2-6). 1992. PLB 11.00 (*0-670-84040-8*) Viking Child Bks.

Innis, Pauline. Ernestine or the Pig in the Potting Shed. Weinberger, Jane, ed. Evans, Timothy, illus. 128p. 1992. pap. 9.95 (*0-932433-97-9*) Windswept Hse.

Keane, Bill. Wanna Be Smiled At? (Illus.). 128p. (gr. 4 up). 1985. pap. 3.50 (*0-449-12816-4*, GM) Fawcett.

Keller, Charles. King Henry the Ape: Animal Jokes. Frascino, Edward, illus. 40p. (gr. 2-5). 1990. PLB 13. 95 (*0-945912-08-0*) Pippin Pr.

Longo, Linda. Troll Jokes & Riddles. LC 92-22571. (Illus.). 48p. (gr. 1-7). 1992. pap. 1.95 (*0-8167-2940-9*) Troll Assocs.

McKie, Roy. The Joke Book. McKie, Roy, illus. LC 78-62699. (ps-2). 1979. pap. 2.25 (*0-394-84077-1*) Random Bks Yng Read.

Masin, Herman L. The Funniest Moments in Sports. Callahan, Kevin, illus. LC 73-86219. 128p. (gr. 4 up). 1973. 5.95 (*0-87131-133-X*) M Evans.

Michaels, Ski. One Hundred Two Haunted House Jokes. LC 91-21891. (Illus.). 64p. (gr. 2-6). 1991. pap. 2.95 (*0-8167-2578-0*) Troll Assocs.

Phillips, Bob. Best of the Good Clean Jokes. LC 89-32386. 192p. (gr. 5 up). 1993. spiral bdg. 10.99 (*1-56507-115-8*) Harvest Hse.

—Wacky Good Clean Jokes for Kids. 1993. pap. 4.99 (*1-56507-141-7*) Harvest Hse.

Rosenblum, Joseph. Fun Two: Daffy Definitions. 1992. 3.99 (*0-517-07776-0*) Random Hse Value.

Schwartz, Alvin. Witcracks: Jokes & Jests from American Folklore. (Illus.). 128p. (gr. 4 up). 1973. PLB 13.89 (*0-397-31475-2*, Lipp Jr Bks) HarpC Child Bks.

—Witcracks: Jokes & Jests from American Folklore. Rounds, Glen & Truesdell, Sue, illus. LC 73-7630. 128p. (gr. 5 up). 1993. 4.95 (*0-06-446146-7*, Trophy) HarpC Child Bks.

Woodworth, Viki. Jokes to Tell Your Dad. LC 93-15443. (gr. 1-4). 1995. 13.95 (*1-56766-098-3*) Childs World.

—Jokes to Tell Your Mom. LC 93-15444. (gr. 1-4). 1995. 13.95 (*1-56766-097-5*) Childs World.

AMERICAN WIT AND HUMOR, PICTORIAL

Ketcham, Hank. Dennis the Menace: The Short Swinger. (Illus.). 1981. pap. 1.50 (*0-449-13641-8*, GM) Fawcett.

Loveland, Nicole. Boogins' Rainy Day. Stebbins, Pat, illus. (ps-3). 1985. PLB 5.95 (*0-917107-02-0*) Cat-Tales Pr.

Roop, Peter. Go Hog Wild! (ps-3). 1990. pap. 2.95 (*0-8225-9555-9*) Lerner Pubns.

Roop, Peter & Roop, Connie. Out to Lunch: Jokes about Food. Hanson, Joan, illus. LC 84-4416. 32p. (gr. 1-4). 1984. PLB 11.95 (*0-8225-0983-0*, First Ave Edns); pap. 2.95 (*0-8225-9552-4*, First Ave Edns) Lerner Pubns.

Roop, Peter, et al. Go Hog Wild: Jokes from down on the Farm. Hanson, Joan, illus. LC 84-5662. 32p. (gr. 1-4). 1984. PLB 11.95 (*0-8225-0982-2*) Lerner Pubns.

—Space Out: Jokes about Outer Space. Hanson, Joan, illus. LC 84-5650. 32p. (gr. 1-4). 1984. PLB 11.95 (*0-8225-0984-9*) Lerner Pubns.

Williams, C. Fred. Adventure Tales of Arkansas: A Cartoon History of a Spirited People. Lisenby, Foy & Poole, Jerry D., illus. Clinton, Bill & Jonsson, Phillip R.intro. by. x, 38p. (Orig.). (gr. 5-7). 1986. pap. 5.95 (*0-9616677-0-2*); tchr's. ed. 3.50 (*0-9616677-1-0*) Signal Media.

AMERICANISMS

Thomas, Robert. How to Talk Midwestern. Carlson, Bruce, ed. Thomas, Tony & Carlson, Bruce, illus. 109p. (Orig.). (gr. 9 up). 1990. pap. 7.95 (*1-878488-21-X*) Quixote Pr IA.

AMERICANS IN EUROPE–FICTION

Chapin, Kim. The Road to Wembley. LC 93-50815. (gr. 4-7). 1994. 15.00 (*0-374-34849-9*) FS&G.

AMPHIBIANS

see also names of amphibians, e.g. Frogs; Salamanders; etc.

Berkowitz, Henry. Amphibians & Reptiles. Berkowitz, Henry, illus. 32p. (Orig.). (gr. 1-9). 1985. pap. 2.50 (*0-317-66182-5*) Banyan Bks.

Caitlin, Stephen. Discovering Reptiles & Amphibians. Johnson, Pamela, illus. LC 89-4972. 32p. (gr. 2-4). 1990. PLB 11.59 (*0-8167-1753-2*); pap. text ed. 2.95 (*0-8167-1754-0*) Troll Assocs.

Clarke, Barry, et al. Amphibian. LC 92-1589. 64p. (gr. 5 up). 1993. 16.00 (*0-679-83879-1*); PLB 16.99 (*0-679-93879-6*) Knopf Bks Yng Read.

Conant, Roger, et al. Peterson First Guide to Reptiles & Amphibians. Conant, Roger, et al, illus. 128p. (gr. 5 up). 1992. pap. 4.80 (*0-395-62232-8*) HM.

Howell, Catherine H. Reptiles & Amphibians; Mammals, 2 vols. (gr. 1-3). 1993. Set 24.95 (*0-87044-891-9*); incl. Mammals 24.95 (*0-685-70128-X*) Natl Geog.

Illustrated Encyclopedia of Wildlife, Vol. 9: Reptiles & Amphibians. 304p. (gr. 7 up). 1990. lib. bdg. write for info. (*1-55905-045-4*) Grey Castle.

Johnston, Ginny & Cutchins, Judy. Slippery Babies: Young Frogs, Toads, & Salamanders. LC 90-49665. (Illus.). 48p. (gr. 2 up). 1991. 13.95 (*0-688-09605-0*); PLB 13.88 (*0-688-09606-9*) Morrow Jr Bks.

Losito, Linda, et al. Reptiles & Amphibians. (Illus.). 96p. 1989. 17.95x (*0-8160-1965-7*) Facts on File.

Maruska, Edward J. Amphibians: Creatures of the Land & Water. LC 93-29843. (Illus.). 56p. (gr. 5-7). 1994. PLB 15.90 (*0-531-11158-X*); pap. 9.95 (*0-531-15714-8*) Watts.

Mattern, Joanne. Reptiles & Amphibians. Stone, Lynn M., illus. LC 92-20189. 24p. (gr. 4-7). 1992. pap. 1.95 (*0-8167-2954-9*, Pub. by Watermill Pr) Troll Assocs.

Parker, Nancy W. Frogs, Toads, Lizards & Salamanders. Wright, Joan R., illus. (gr. 1 up). 1990. 15.00 (*0-688-08680-2*); PLB 14.93 (*0-688-08681-0*) Greenwillow.

Parker, Steve. Awesome Amphibians. Savage, Ann, illus. LC 92-43196. 38p. (gr. 3-6). 1993. PLB 19.97 (*0-8114-0661-X*) Raintree Steck-V.

Ricciuti, Edward. Amphibians. (Illus.). 64p. (gr. 4-8). 1993. PLB 16.95 (*1-56711-045-2*) Blackbirch.

Sabin, Louis. Reptiles & Amphibians. Zink-White, Nancy, illus. LC 84-8445. 32p. (gr. 3-6). 1985. PLB 9.49 (*0-8167-0294-2*); pap. text ed. 2.95 (*0-8167-0295-0*) Troll Assocs.

Scott, Mary. A Picture Book of Reptiles & Amphibians. Kinnelay, Janice, illus. LC 92-19054. 24p. (gr. 1-4). 1992. lib. bdg. 9.59 (*0-8167-2838-0*); pap. text ed. 2.50 (*0-8167-2839-9*) Troll Assocs.

Snedden, Robert. What Is an Amphibian? Lascom, Adrian, illus. Oxford Scientific Films Staff, photos by. LC 93-11619. (Illus.). 32p. (gr. 2-5). 1994. 14.95 (*0-87156-469-6*) Sierra.

Steele, Philip. Extinct Amphibians: And Those in Danger of Extinction. Kline, Marjory, ed. LC 91-9886. (Illus.). 32p. (gr. 4-7). 1992. PLB 11.90 (*0-531-11031-1*) Watts.

—Reptiles & Amphibians. (gr. 4-7). 1991. lib. bdg. 4.95 (*0-671-72238-7*, J Messner) S&S Trade.

—Reptiles & Amphibians. (gr. 4-7). 1991. lib. bdg. 9.98 (*0-671-72237-9*, J Messner) S&S Trade.

Zappler, George & Zappler, Lisbeth. Amphibians As Pets. LC 72-92252. 160p. (gr. 3-9). 1973. pap. 5.95 (*0-385-08581-8*) Doubleday.

AMUNDSEN, ROALD ENGELBREGHT GRAVNING, 1872-1928

Flaherty, Leo & Goetzmann, William H. Roald Amundsen & the Quest for the South Pole. Collins, Michael, intro. by. (Illus.). 112p. (gr. 6-12). 1993. PLB 18.95 (*0-7910-1308-1*) Chelsea Hse.

AMUNDSEN-SCOTT SOUTH POLE STATION

Sipiera, Paul. Roald Amundsen & Robert Scott: Race for the South Pole. LC 90-2178. (Illus.). 128p. (gr. 3 up). 1990. PLB 20.55 (*0-516-03056-6*) Childrens.

AMUSEMENTS

see also Circus; Dancing; Entertaining; Fortune Telling; Games; Hobbies; Magic; Mathematical Recreations; Play; Puzzles; Recreation; Riddles; Scientific Recreations; Sports; Theater; Toys; Ventriloquism

Aladdin Flip 'N' Fun Activity Pads, Bks. 1 & 2. (Illus., 80 pgs. ea. bk.). (gr. k-3). 1992. Bk. 1. pap. 2.95 (*1-56144-159-7*, Honey Bear Bks) Bk. 2. pap. 2.95 (*1-56144-160-0*) Modern Pub NYC.

All Year Round Magic Pen Book. (gr. 2 up). 1991. pap. 1.97 (*1-56297-133-6*) Lee Pubns KY.

Anastasio, Dina. My Own Book. 48p. (Orig.). (gr. 2 up). 1992. pap. 2.95 incl. chipboard (*0-8431-0367-1*) Price Stern.

—My Secret Book. 48p. (Orig.). (gr. 2 up). 1992. pap. 2.95 incl. chipboard (*0-8431-3373-2*) Price Stern.

Armstrong, Bev. Have Fun Following Directions. Armstrong, Bev, illus. 32p. (gr. 1-3). 1979. wkbk. 3.95 (*0-88160-077-6*, LW 810) Learning Wks.

Around the World Magic Pen Book. (gr. 3 up). 1991. pap. 1.97 (*1-56297-134-4*) Lee Pubns KY.

Bauer, Martha J. Hey, This Is Fun! Dresselhaus, Richard, frwd. by. LC 90-80992. (Illus.). 128p. (gr. 6-12). 1990. pap. 6.95 (*0-9624398-1-9*) Abel II Pub.

Beard, Daniel C. American Boys Handy Book: What to Do & How to Do It. facs. ed. LC 66-15858. (Illus.). 392p. (gr. 4 up). 1966. 14.95 (*0-8048-0006-5*) C E Tuttle.

Bell, Alison. Fifty Frightening Things to Do & Make. Suckow, Will, illus. 64p. 1993. pap. 4.95 (*1-56565-067-0*) Lowell Hse.

Berry Magic. 80p. (gr. k-2). 1992. pap. 2.95 (*1-56144-133-3*, Honey Bear Bks) Modern Pub NYC.

Berry Special Fun. 80p. (gr. k-2). 1992. pap. 2.95 (*1-56144-132-5*, Honey Bear Bks) Modern Pub NYC.

Betts, Keith & McCollam, Dan. Junior High Game Nights: Wild & Crazy Outreach Events for Junior High Ministry. 96p. 1991. pap. 9.99 (*0-310-53811-4*, Pub. by Youth Spec) Zondervan.

Bony Skeleton's Cut-Out Fun Book. 24p. (Orig.). (ps-k). 1991. pap. 3.95 (*0-8249-8347-5*, Ideals Child) Hambleton-Hill.

Boynton, Alice. Halloween KidDoodles, No. 3. Silver, Pattie, illus. 64p. (ps-2). 1992. pap. 0.99 (*1-56293-261-6*) McClanahan Bk.

Bree, Loris T. & Bree, Marlin. Kid's Squish Book: Slimy, Pasty, Sticky Things to Do That Should Only Be Done When Wearing Your Oldest Clothes. (Illus.). 96p. 1993. pap. 8.95 (*0-943400-76-7*) Marlor Pr.

Bryant-Mole, Karen. Dot-to-Dot at the Seaside. (Illus.). 24p. (gr. k-1). 1993. pap. 3.50 (*0-7460-1376-0*, Usborne) EDC.

Burns, Marilyn. The Book of Think: Or How to Solve Problems Twice Your Size. Weston, Martha, illus. (gr. 5 up). 1976. 15.95 (*0-316-11742-0*); pap. 10.95 (*0-316-11743-9*) Little.

Butterfield, S. Borders & Beyond. (gr. 1-6). 1985. 5.95 (*0-88160-118-7*, LW250) Learning Wks.

Caney, Steven. Steve Caney's Toybook. LC 75-8814. (Illus.). 176p. (ps-5). 1972. pap. 7.95 (*0-911104-17-8*, 023) Workman Pub.

—Steven Caney's Play Book. LC 75-9816. (Illus.). 240p. (ps-5). 1975. pap. 9.95 (*0-911104-38-0*, 050) Workman Pub.

Carle, Eric. The Mixed-up Chameleon Sticker Book. Carle, Eric, illus. LC 75-5505. 32p. (ps-2). 1993. 8.95 (*0-694-00448-0*, Festival) HarpC Child Bks.

Carlson, Nancy. Harriet & the Roller Coaster. Carlson, Nancy, illus. (gr. k-3). 1985. bk. & cassette 19.95 (*0-941078-56-6*); pap. 12.95 bk. & cassette (*0-941078-54-X*); cassette, 4 paperbacks & guide 27.95 (*0-941078-55-8*) Live Oak Media.

Carroll, Jeri & Kear, Dennis. Writing Fun with Phonics. (Illus.). 160p. (ps-2). 1992. wkbk. 12.95 (*0-86653-686-8*, 1420) Good Apple.

Carter, Margaret. The Young Child's Busy Book: Of Playing, Learning, Stories & Rhymes. Maclean, Colin & Maclean, Moira, illus. LC 92-53094. 96p. (ps-k). 1992. 14.95 (*1-85697-822-2*, Kingfisher LKC) LKC.

Chapin, Laurie & Flagenheimer-Riggle, Ellen. Looking into Literature & Seeing Myself. (Illus.). 128p. (gr. k-3). 1992. wkbk. 11.95 (*0-86653-706-6*, 1427) Good Apple.

Chickadee Magazine Editors. The Chickadee Book of Puzzles & Fun. Perna, Debi, ed. & illus. 32p. (ps up). 1992. pap. 4.95 (*0-920775-82-9*, Pub. by Greey de Pencier CN) Firefly Bks Ltd.

Christie, Tom. Global Alert! (Illus.). 112p. (gr. 5-8). 1992. wkbk. 12.95 (*0-86653-692-2*, 1426) Good Apple.

Colby, Sas & Shirkus, Lorraine. The Pocket Book: A Child's Activity Book. Shirkus, Lorraine, illus. 10p. (ps-k). 1988. 39.95 (*0-922656-00-2*) Design Matters Inc.

Colligan, Louise. One Thousand & One Things to Do When There's Nothing to Do. (gr. 4-7). 1994. pap. 2.50 (*0-590-46359-4*) Scholastic Inc.

Colors & Opposites. (Illus.). 32p. (ps-1). 1992. pap. 2.95 (*1-56144-107-4*, Honey Bear Bks) Modern Pub NYC.

Conaway, Judith. Happy Day! Things to Make & Do. Barto, Renzo, illus. LC 86-7131. 48p. (gr. 1-5). 1987. PLB 11.89 (*0-8167-0842-8*); pap. text ed. 3.50 (*0-8167-0843-6*) Troll Assocs.

—Springtime Surprises: Things to Make & Do. Barto, Renzo, illus. LC 85-16497. 48p. (gr. 1-5). 1986. PLB 11.89 (*0-8167-0670-0*); pap. text ed. 3.50 (*0-8167-0671-9*) Troll Assocs.

—Things That Go! How to Make Toy Boats, Cars, & Planes. Barto, Renzo, illus. LC 86-7130. 48p. (gr. 1-5). 1987. PLB 11.89 (*0-8167-0838-X*); pap. text ed. 3.50 (*0-8167-0839-8*) Troll Assocs.

Crawford, Jean B., ed. Pterodactyl Tunnel: Amusement Park Math. (Illus.). 64p. (gr. k-2). 1993. write for info. (*0-8094-9990-8*) Time-Life.

Dale, Rodney & Weaver, Rebecca. Home Entertainment. (Illus.). 64p. 1994. PLB 16.00 (*0-19-521001-8*) OUP.

Dandola, John. Rogers' Rangers. Dandola, John, illus. 24p. (Orig.). (gr. k-6). 1992. pap. 3.95 (*1-878452-08-8*) Tory Corner Editions.

Davies, Kate. Play Mask Book - Wizard of Oz. 12p. (ps-3). 1991. pap. 5.95 (*0-8167-2373-7*) Troll Assocs.

Davies, Leah G. Kelly Bear Activities. Hallett, Joy D., illus. LC 92-70013. 40p. (ps-3). 1992. pap. 10.95 (*0-9621054-4-9*) Kelly Bear Pr.

Davis, Duane. Listen & Play with My Friends & Me Activity Manual. rev. ed. (ps-k). 1988. wkbk. 29.95 (*0-88671-331-5*, 4631) Am Guidance.

Drutman, Ava D. Land (Primary) (Illus.). 48p. (gr. 1-3). 1992. wkbk. 7.95 (*0-86653-599-3*, 1406) Good Apple.

—Water (Primary) (Illus.). 48p. (gr. 1-3). 1992. wkbk. 7.95 (*0-86653-604-3*, 1407) Good Apple.

Dunlavy, Kathy. Learn & Grow from A to Z: Learning Centers & Activities for Young Children. Terrill, Veronica, illus. 160p. (ps-2). 1992. Wkbk. wkbk. 13.95 (*0-86653-682-5*, GA1416) Good Apple.

Dwyer, Liz. Playtime Crafts & Activities: Fun Things to Make & Do. LeHew, Ron, illus. 32p. (gr. 2-7). 1994. pap. 4.95 (*1-56397-348-0*) Boyds Mills Pr.

Eccles, Anne M. United States Activity & Coloring Book. Eccles, Anne M., illus. 36p. (ps-8). 1992. activity/ coloring bk. 3.95 (*0-9618555-2-5*) Anne M Eccles.

Euretig, Mary & Kreisberg, Darlene. Rainbow Writing: A Journal with Activities for Budding Young Writers. Bacchini, Lisa, illus. (Orig.). (gr. 1-3). 1990. pap. 11.95 (*0-9628216-0-8*) Dream Tree Pr.

Everybody Once Was A Kid: Gemini-Fun Songs & Activites for Kids. (Illus.). 32p. 1993. Book & cassette pkg. pap. 9.95 (*0-7935-2875-5*); Book & CD pkg. pap. 9.95 (*0-7935-2874-7*) H Leonard.

The Fantastic Funny Finger Book. 24p. (ps-1). 1981. 5.95 (*0-8431-0630-1*) Price Stern.

Ferguson-Florissant Early Education Teachers Staff. Home Activities for Fours. Wilson, Marion M., ed. (Illus.). 110p. (Orig.). (ps). 1990. pap. text ed. 15.00 (*0-939418-60-6*) Ferguson-Florissant.

Filkins, Vanessa. Early Learning Bulletin Boards. 144p. (ps-2). 1990. 12.95 (*0-86653-529-2*, GA1141) Good Apple.
Find a Way Back Activity Book. (gr. 2). 1991. 3.90 (*0-88106-748-2*) Charlesbridge Pub.
Find a Way Back Activity Book (EV) (gr. 2). 1991. 3.90 (*0-88106-747-4*) Charlesbridge Pub.
First Words. (Illus.). 32p. (ps-1). 1992. pap. 2.95 (*1-56144-105-8*, Honey Bear Bks) Modern Pub NYC.
Fisher, Ann. Perplexing Puzzlers. (Illus.). 80p. (gr. 4-8). 1992. wkbk. 9.95 (*0-86653-677-9*, 1411) Good Apple.
Fun & Games. (Illus.). (ps-5). 3.50 (*0-7214-0543-6*) Ladybird Bks.
Fun Forms, Set 8. 1991. pap. 1.97 (*1-56297-148-4*, FF-74) Lee Pubns KY.
Games We Like. (Illus.). (ps-5). 3.50 (*0-7214-0555-X*); o.p. (*0-317-03994-6*) Ladybird Bks.
Gamiello, Elvira. Monster Activity & Game Book. (Illus., Orig.). (gr. 4-6). 1988. pap. 1.95 (*0-942025-28-8*) Kidsbks.
Gastman, Joseph W. Creatrivia. 112p. (gr. 4-8). 1989. 10.95 (*0-86653-482-2*, GA1087) Good Apple.
Gillis, Jennifer S. An Apple a Day! Over Twenty Apple Projects for Kids. Delmonte, Patti, illus. 64p. (Orig.). (gr. k-4). 1993. pap. 8.95 (*0-88266-849-8*, Garden Way Pub) Storey Comm Inc.
Gleason, Karan. Factivities. 144p. (gr. k-5). 1991. 12.95 (*0-86653-601-9*, GA1320) Good Apple.
Glover, Susanne & Grewe, Georgeann. Bulletin Board Smorgasbord. (gr. 2-6). 1982. 9.95 (*0-88160-091-1*, LW 233) Learning Wks.
Goldberg, Larry. Dear Mr. Rainbows, 1994. Wolf, Barbara & Waldron, Shirley, illus. LC 93-72611. 112p. (Orig.). (gr. 2-6). 1993. pap. 9.95 (*0-9638457-0-5*) Blue-Black.
Goodman, Beth. Fun with the Norfin Trolls: A Coloring & Activity Book. (ps-8). 1992. pap. 1.95 (*0-590-45926-0*) Scholastic Inc.
Greene, Leia A. I Am Special Too: Circle of Angels Workbook. Green, Leia A., illus. 99p. (gr. k-9). 1991. 18.95 (*1-880737-00-0*) Crystal Jrns.
—When the Earth Was New: An Experience in Healing Our Planet. Green, Leia A., illus. 20p. (gr. k-9). 1991. wkbk. 4.95 (*1-880737-02-7*) Crystal Jrns.
Hamilton, Leslie. Child's Play Six-Twelve: One Hundred Sixty Instant Activities, Crafts & Science Projects. 1992. 10.00 (*0-517-58354-2*, Crown) Crown Pub Group.
Hanging Out. (Illus.). 80p. (gr. 4-8). 1992. pap. 2.95 (*1-56144-095-7*, Honey Bear Bks) Modern Pub NYC.
Hart, Marj. Discovery Units for Young Children. (gr. k-3). 1991. pap. 11.95 (*0-8224-2323-5*) Fearon Teach Aids.
Heller, Ruth. Merry Go-Round. (Illus.). 48p. (ps-3). 1992. pap. 6.95 (*0-448-40315-3*, G&D) Putnam Pub Group.
Herman, Emmi. Christmas KidDoodles, No. 5. Radtke, Becky, illus. 64p. (ps-2). 1992. pap. 0.99 (*1-56293-270-5*) McClanahan Bk.
—Christmas KidDoodles, No. 6. Loh, Carolyn, illus. 64p. (ps-2). 1992. pap. 0.99 (*1-56293-271-3*) McClanahan Bk.
—Christmas KidDoodles, No. 7. Radtke, Becky, illus. 64p. (ps-2). 1992. pap. 0.99 (*1-56293-269-1*) McClanahan Bk.
—Christmas KidDoodles, No. 8. Loh, Carolyn, illus. 64p. (ps-2). 1992. pap. 0.99 (*1-56293-272-1*) McClanahan Bk.
Highlights for Children Editors. Let's Pretend: Costumes, Props, Projects. (Illus.). 48p. (Orig.). (ps-5). 1993. pap. 5.95 (*1-56397-060-0*) Boyds Mills Pr.
Highlights for Children Staff. Activity Books. Highlights for Children Staff, illus. 32p. (gr. 1-6). 1989. pap. 2.95 (*0-87534-381-3*) Highlights.
—Activity Books. Highlights for Children Staff, illus. 32p. (gr. 1-6). 1989. pap. 2.95 (*0-87534-382-1*) Highlights.
—Activity Books. Highlights for Children Staff, illus. 32p. (gr. 1-6). 1989. pap. 2.95 (*0-87534-383-X*) Highlights.
—Activity Books. Highlights for Children Staff, illus. 32p. (gr. 1-6). 1989. pap. 2.95 (*0-87534-384-8*) Highlights.
—Activity Books. Highlights for Children Staff, illus. 32p. (gr. 1-6). 1989. pap. 2.95 (*0-87534-385-6*) Highlights.
—Activity Books. Highlights for Children Staff, illus. 32p. (gr. 1-6). 1989. pap. 2.95 (*0-87534-386-4*) Highlights.
—Activity Books. Highlights for Children Staff, illus. 32p. (gr. 1-6). 1989. pap. 2.95 (*0-87534-387-2*) Highlights.
—Activity Books. Highlights for Children Staff, illus. 32p. (gr. 1-6). 1989. pap. 2.95 (*0-87534-388-0*) Highlights.
—Activity Books. Highlights for Children Staff, illus. 32p. (gr. 1-6). 1989. pap. 2.95 (*0-87534-389-9*) Highlights.
—Activity Books. Highlights for Children Staff, illus. 32p. (gr. 1-6). 1989. pap. 2.95 (*0-87534-390-2*) Highlights.
—Skills Fun: Critters. Highlights for Children Staff, illus. (ps-3). 1991. pap. text ed. 2.95 (*0-87534-192-6*) Highlights.
—Skills Fun: Free Time. Highlights for Children Staff, illus. (ps-3). 1991. pap. text ed. 2.95 (*0-87534-193-4*) Highlights.
—Skills Fun: Mystery. Highlights for Children Staff, illus. (ps-3). 1991. pap. text ed. 2.95 (*0-87534-194-2*) Highlights.
—Skills Fun: Outdoors. Highlights for Children Staff, illus. (ps-3). 1991. pap. text ed. 2.95 (*0-87534-198-5*) Highlights.
—Skills Fun: Space. Highlights for Children Staff, illus. (ps-3). 1991. pap. text ed. 2.95 (*0-87534-199-3*) Highlights.
—Skills Fun: Trips. Highlights for Children Staff, illus. (ps-3). 1991. pap. text ed. 2.95 (*0-87534-200-0*) Highlights.
—What's Wrong & Other Mixed-up Fun. Highlights for Children Staff, illus. 32p. (gr. k-6). 1990. pap. 2.95 (*0-87534-464-X*) Highlights.
—What's Wrong & Other Mixed-up Fun. Highlights for Children Staff, illus. 32p. (gr. k-6). 1990. pap. 2.95 (*0-87534-444-5*) Highlights.
—What's Wrong & Other Mixed-up Fun. Highlights for Children Staff, illus. 32p. (gr. k-6). 1990. pap. 2.95 (*0-87534-449-6*) Highlights.
—What's Wrong & Other Mixed-up Fun. Highlights for Children Staff, illus. 32p. (gr. k-6). 1990. pap. 2.95 (*0-87534-455-0*) Highlights.
—What's Wrong & Other Mixed-up Fun. Highlights for Children Staff, illus. 32p. (gr. k-6). 1990. pap. 2.95 (*0-87534-463-1*) Highlights.
—What's Wrong & Other Mixed-up Fun. Highlights for Children Staff, illus. 32p. (gr. k-6). 1990. pap. 2.95 (*0-87534-466-6*) Highlights.
—Winter Sports. Highlights for Children Staff, illus. 48p. (gr. 3-7). 1990. pap. 2.95 (*0-87534-351-1*) Highlights.
Hogrogian, Nonny. Handmade Secret Hiding Places. LC 75-4379. (Illus.). 48p. (ps-5). 1990. pap. 7.95 (*0-87951-033-1*); deluxe ed. 4.95 (*0-87951-376-4*) Overlook Pr.
Home Alone Two - Lost in New York. (80 pgs. ea. bk.). (gr. k-3). 1992. Bk. 1. pap. 2.95 (*1-56144-223-2*, Honey Bear Bks) Bk. 2. pap. 2.95 (*1-56144-224-0*) Modern Pub NYC.
Horowitz, Janet & Faggella, Kathy. My Trip to Walt Disney World Resort: A Photolog Book. Disney Staff, illus. 48p. 1991. 9.95 (*1-55670-141-1*) Stewart Tabori & Chang.
Hunt, Jeffrey. The Treasure Hunt Activity Book. (Orig.). 1994. pap. 2.99 (*0-8125-9440-1*) Tor Bks.
Hyndman, Kathryn. Hidden Picture Fun. 112p. (ps-2). 1991. 10.95 (*0-86653-614-0*, GA1333) Good Apple.
James, Robin, illus. Raz Ma Taz' Dazzling Dot-to-Dot. (gr. 2-6). 1983. wkbk. 2.95 (*0-8431-1404-5*) Price Stern.
Jenkins, Sheila, et al. Polka Dotted Pals, Pt. 1. 100p. (gr. k-1). 1980. pap. 8.95 (*0-932970-13-3*) Prinit Pr.
John, Anthony. School Fun Activity Book. (Illus.). 64p. (Orig.). 1991. pap. 1.95 (*1-56156-036-7*) Kidsbks.
Joy, Flora. Creative Writing. (Illus.). 64p. (gr. 1-6). 1992. wkbk. 7.95 (*0-86653-679-5*, 1413) Good Apple.
—Whole Language Celebrations. (Illus.). 176p. (gr. k-4). 1992. wkbk. 12.95 (*0-86653-690-6*, 1424) Good Apple.
—Whole Language for the Holidays. (Illus.). 144p. (gr. k-4). 1992. wkbk. 12.95 (*0-86653-689-2*, 1423) Good Apple.
Jumbo's Great Big Activity Book. 190p. 1991. 3.98 (*0-681-41042-6*) Longmeadow Pr.
Kaiser Syndicated Features Staff. Four Seasons Activity Book. (Illus.). 190p. (gr. k-5). 1992. pap. 3.75 (*0-9634746-0-X*) Kaiser Syndicated.
Kallen, Stuart A. Awesome Entertainment Records. LC 91-73054. 32p. 1991. 12.94 (*1-56239-047-3*) Abdo & Dghtrs.
Kalman, Bobbie. All about Me Activity Guide. (Illus.). 96p. (gr. k-2). 1985. pap. 15.95 (*0-86505-066-X*) Crabtree Pub Co.
Kaplan, Carol & Lyss, Ester. We're Moving, We're Moving. Gellman, Sim, illus. 32p. (ps-5). 1993. pap. 3.95 (*0-8431-3498-4*) Price Stern.
Kaplan, Carol & Lyss, Esther. Don't Flip, It's Only a Trip. Gellman, Sim, illus. 32p. (gr. 1-4). 1993. pap. 3.95 (*0-8431-3497-6*) Price Stern.
Karabatsos, Lewis T., ed. Bricks & Brackets: A Lowell Activity Book. 19p. (Orig.). (gr. 1-6). 1981. pap. 0.95 (*0-942472-04-7*) Lowell Museum.
Kicking Back. (Illus.). 80p. (gr. 4-8). 1992. pap. 2.95 (*1-56144-094-9*, Honey Bear Bks) Modern Pub NYC.
Kostic, Diane. The Biography of Me. (Illus.). 160p. (gr. 5-9). 1992. wkbk. 12.95 (*0-86653-687-6*, 1421) Good Apple.
Lerner, Andy. Halloween KidDoodles, No. 4. Silver, Pattie, illus. 64p. (ps-2). 1992. pap. 0.99 (*1-56293-262-4*) McClanahan Bk.
Levy, Nathan. Stories with Holes, Vol. VIII. 20p. (gr. 3 up). 1992. pap. 6.00 (*1-878347-11-X*) NL Assocs.
—Stories with Holes, Vol. I. (gr. 3 up). 1987. 6.00 (*0-685-63374-8*) NL Assocs.
—Stories with Holes, Vol. II. (gr. 3 up). 1990. pap. 6.00 (*1-878347-00-4*) NL Assocs.
—Stories with Holes, Vol. III. (gr. 3 up). 1990. pap. 6.00 (*1-878347-01-2*) NL Assocs.
—Stories with Holes, Vol. IV. (gr. 3 up). 1990. pap. 6.00 (*1-878347-02-0*) NL Assocs.
—Stories with Holes, Vol. V. (gr. 3 up). 1990. pap. 6.00 (*1-878347-03-9*) NL Assocs.
—Stories with Holes, Vol. VI. (gr. 3 up). 1991. pap. 6.00 (*1-878347-09-8*) NL Assocs.
—Stories with Holes, Vol. VII. (gr. 3 up). 1992. pap. 6.00 (*1-878347-10-1*) NL Assocs.
—Stories with Holes, Vol. IX. (gr. 3 up). 1992. pap. 6.00 (*1-878347-17-9*) NL Assocs.
—Stories with Holes, Vol. X. (gr. 3 up). 1992. pap. 6.00 (*1-878347-21-7*) NL Assocs.
—Stories with Holes, Vol. XI. (gr. 3 up). 1992. pap. 6.00 (*1-878347-22-5*) NL Assocs.
—Stories with Holes, Vol. XII. (gr. 3 up). 1993. pap. 6.00 (*1-878347-26-8*) NL Assocs.
—Stories with Holes, Vols. I-XII. (gr. 3 up). 1993. Set. 70.00 (*0-685-63375-6*, NL1970) NL Assocs.
—Stories with Holes, Vol. XIV. (gr. 3 up). 1993. write for info. (*1-878347-28-4*) NL Assocs.
—Stories with Holes, Vol. XV. (gr. 3 up). 1993. write for info. (*1-878347-29-2*) NL Assocs.
—Stories with Holes, Vol. XVI. (gr. 3 up). 1993. write for info. (*1-878347-30-6*) NL Assocs.
—Stories with Holes, Vol. XVII. (gr. 3 up). 1993. write for info. (*1-878347-31-4*) NL Assocs.
—Stories with Holes, Vol. XVIII. (gr. 3 up). 1993. write for info. (*1-878347-32-2*) NL Assocs.
Lewis, Shari. Shari Lewis Presents One Hundred & One Things for Kids to Do. Buller, Jon, illus. LC 86-43065. 96p. (gr. 1-5). 1987. lib. bdg. 9.99 (*0-394-98966-X*); pap. 8.00 (*0-394-88966-5*) Random Bks Yng Read.
Lipson, Greta B. Audacious Poetry. (Illus.). 128p. (gr. 6-12). 1992. wkbk. 11.95 (*0-86653-683-3*, 1417) Good Apple.
Lizon, Karen H. Colonial American Holidays & Entertainment. LC 92-40262. 1993. 12.90 (*0-531-12546-7*) Watts.
Longe, Bob. Nutty Challenges & Zany Dares. Longe, Bob, illus. LC 93-32391. 128p. 1994. pap. 4.95 (*0-8069-0454-2*) Sterling.
McClure, Nancee. Clip & Copy Art: Creative Curriculum Cutouts. (Illus.). (gr. k-8). 1989. 12.95 (*0-86653-487-3*, GA1086) Good Apple.
—Clip & Copy Art: Holidays, Seasons & Events. (Illus.). (gr. k-8). 1989. 12.95 (*0-86653-486-5*, GA1085) Good Apple.
McCully, Emily A. Picnic. LC 83-47913. (Illus.). 32p. (ps-1). 1984. PLB 14.89 (*0-06-024100-4*) HarpC Child Bks.
McKissack, Patricia & McKissack, Fredrick. Big Bug Book of Things to Do. Bartholomew, illus. LC 87-61651. 24p. (Orig.). (gr. k-1). 1987. spiral bdg. 14.95 (*0-88335-766-6*); pap. text ed. 4.95 (*0-88335-776-3*) Milliken Pub co.
McMillan, Mary. Christian Parties for Autumn & Winter. 96p. (ps-3). 1989. 10.95 (*0-86653-497-0*, SS1815, Shining Star Pubns) Good Apple.
Magic Pen Five. 1991. pap. 1.97 (*1-56297-109-3*, MP-5) Lee Pubns KY.
Magic Pen Four. 1991. pap. 1.97 (*1-56297-108-5*, MP-4) Lee Pubns KY.
Magic Pen One. (gr. 3 up). 1991. pap. 1.97 (*1-56297-105-0*, MP-1) Lee Pubns KY.
Magic Pen Three. 1991. pap. 1.97 (*1-56297-107-7*, MP-3) Lee Pubns KY.
Magic Pen Two. 1991. pap. 1.97 (*1-56297-106-9*, MP-2) Lee Pubns KY.
Manthey, Cynthia M. With Respect, Vol. 1P: Successful Primary Theme Activities. 100p. (ps-1). 1992. pap. text ed. 11.95 (*0-9634651-0-4*); audio music cass. 9.95 (*0-9634651-1-2*) Qual Instruct.
Markle, Sandra. Exploring Autumn: A Season of Science Activities, Puzzlers, & Games. Markle, Sandra, illus. LC 90-24209. 160p. (gr. 3-7). 1991. SBE 14.95 (*0-689-31620-8*, Atheneum Child Bk) Macmillan Child Grp.
Marsh, Carole. The Blood & Guts Dingbats Book. (Illus.). (gr. 3-12). 1994. PLB 24.95 (*0-7933-5398-X*); pap. 14.95 (*0-7933-5399-8*); computer disk 29.95 (*0-7933-5400-5*) Gallopade Pub Group.
—The Dragons & Dungeons Dingbats Book. (Illus.). (gr. 3-12). 1994. PLB 24.95 (*0-7933-5395-5*); pap. 14.95 (*0-7933-5396-3*); computer disk 29.95 (*0-7933-5397-1*) Gallopade Pub Group.
—For Your Eyes Only: Silly, Secret & Scary Code & Spy Trivia for Kids. (Illus.). (gr. 3-12). 1994. PLB 24.95 (*0-7933-5413-7*); pap. 14.95 (*0-7933-5414-5*); computer disk 29.95 (*0-7933-5415-3*) Gallopade Pub Group.
—The Ghost & Graveyards Dingbats Book. (Illus.). (gr. 3-12). 1994. PLB 24.95 (*0-7933-5386-6*); pap. 14.95 (*0-7933-5387-4*); computer disk 29.95 (*0-7933-5388-2*) Gallopade Pub Group.
—The Hairy Horrors Dingbats Book. (Illus.). (gr. 3-12). 1994. PLB 24.95 (*0-7933-5404-8*); pap. 14.95 (*0-7933-5405-6*); computer disk 29.95 (*0-7933-5406-4*) Gallopade Pub Group.
—The Magic & Sorcery Dingbats Book. (Illus.). (gr. 3-12). 1994. PLB 24.95 (*0-7933-5377-7*); pap. 14.95 (*0-7933-5378-5*); computer disk 29.95 (*0-7933-5379-3*) Gallopade Pub Group.
—The Monsters, Vampires & Werewolves Dingbats Book. (Illus.). (gr. 3-12). 1994. PLB 24.95 (*0-7933-5392-0*); pap. 14.95 (*0-7933-5393-9*); computer disk 29.95 (*0-7933-5394-7*) Gallopade Pub Group.
—The Pirate & Treasure Dingbats Book. (Illus.). (gr. 3-12). 1994. PLB 24.95 (*0-7933-5407-2*); pap. 14.95 (*0-7933-5408-0*); computer disk 29.95 (*0-7933-5409-9*) Gallopade Pub Group.
—The Secret Mysteries Dingbats Book. (Illus.). (gr. 3-12). 1994. PLB 24.95 (*0-7933-5383-1*); pap. 14.95 (*0-7933-5384-X*); computer disk 29.95 (*0-7933-5385-8*) Gallopade Pub Group.
—The Sinister Spies Dingbats Book. (Illus.). (gr. 3-12). 1994. PLB 24.95 (*0-7933-5389-0*); pap. 14.95 (*0-7933-5390-4*); computer disk 29.95 (*0-7933-5391-2*) Gallopade Pub Group.
—The Super Silly Riddles Dingbats Book. (Illus.). (gr. 3-12). 1994. PLB 24.95 (*0-7933-5410-2*); pap. 14.95 (*0-7933-5411-0*); computer disk 29.95 (*0-7933-5412-9*) Gallopade Pub Group.
—The Super Silly Sports Trivia Dingbats Book. (Illus.). (gr. 3-12). 1994. PLB 24.95 (*0-7933-5380-7*); pap. 14.95 (*0-7933-5381-5*); computer disk 29.95 (*0-7933-5382-3*) Gallopade Pub Group.

—The Terror & Tombstones Dingbats Book. (Illus.). (gr. 3-12). 1994. PLB 24.95 (*0-7933-5401-3*); pap. 14.95 (*0-7933-5402-1*); computer disk 29.95 (*0-7933-5403-X*) Gallopade Pub Group.

—Thirty Days Has September: Calendar Trivia & Activities for Kids. (gr. 3-9). 1994. 24.95 (*0-7933-0015-0*); pap. 14.95 (*0-7933-0016-9*); computer disk 29.95 (*0-7933-0017-7*) Gallopade Pub Group.

—Worlds Fair Kit S. P. A. R. K. (Illus., Orig.). (gr. 3-12). 1994. pap. 24.95 (*0-935326-85-5*) Gallopade Pub Group.

Nichols, V. Funny Faces Sticker Pad. M. J. Studios Staff, illus. 32p. (gr. k-6). 1993. pap. 2.95 (*1-879424-31-2*) Nickel Pr.

Numbers & Shapes. (Illus.). 32p. (ps-1). 1992. pap. 2.95 (*1-56144-106-6*, Honey Bear Bks) Modern Pub NYC.

Outdoor Fun. 32p. (ps-1). 1989. pap. 3.50 (*0-517-68797-6*, Chatham River Pr) Random Hse Value.

Owl Magazine Staff. Winter Fun: A Book Full of Things to Do in Cold Weather. (Illus.). 128p. (gr. 3 up). 1992. pap. 9.95 (*0-919872-86-7*, Pub. by Greey de Pencier CN) Firefly Bks Ltd.

Palumbo, Thomas J. Tuesday Timely Teasers. Hyndman, Kathryn, illus. 64p. (gr. 3-8). 1985. wkbk. 8.95 (*0-86653-309-5*, GA 648) Good Apple.

Patrick, Sally, et al. The Month by Month Treasure Box. LC 86-82599. (Illus.). 80p. (Orig.). (ps-1). 1988. 7.95 (*0-86530-124-7*, IP 130-1) Incentive Pubns.

Pendergast, Kathleen. Say Another One about Playing. LC 83-62129. (Illus.). 54p. (gr. k-6). 1983. pap. 6.95 (*0-942178-02-5*) Madison Park Pr.

Pincus, Debbie. Manners Matter. (Illus.). 112p. (gr. 3-7). 1992. wkbk. 10.95 (*0-86653-688-4*, 1422) Good Apple.

Preschool Activities. 24p. (ps-k). 1986. 3.98 (*0-86734-064-9*, FS-3056) Schaffer Pubns.

Preschool Color & Learn: I Can Do It Myself. 1992. pap. 1.95 (*0-590-45036-0*) Scholastic Inc.

Preschool Color & Learn: Kindergarten Skills. (ps). 1992. pap. 1.95 (*0-590-45038-7*) Scholastic Inc.

Preschool Color & Learn: Making Friends & Sharing. (ps). 1992. pap. 1.95 (*0-590-45059-X*) Scholastic Inc.

Preschool Color & Learn: Sounds All Around. (ps). 1992. pap. 1.95 (*0-590-45037-9*) Scholastic Inc.

Rice, Melanie. The Complete Book of Children's Activities. LC 92-30859. 1993. pap. 9.95 (*1-85697-907-5*, Kingfisher LKC) LKC.

Rieck, Sondra & Stippel, Lori. Learn Basic Concepts with Cuddles Clown. 24p. (ps-k). 1990. 9.95 (*0-9634082-0-8*) Woodville Pr.

Rosenberg, Mona. Stick-tivity. (gr. k-1). 1991. write for info., incl. stickers (*1-880056-07-0*) Play-Media.

—Stick-tivity, Bk. 1: The Talking Drum & Trumpet. 16p. (gr. k-1). 1991. write for info., incl. stickers (*1-880056-08-9*) Play-Media.

—Stick-tivity, Bk. 2: Bob's Zoo. 16p. (gr. k-1). 1991. write for info., incl. stickers (*1-880056-09-7*) Play-Media.

—Stick-tivity, Bk. 3: On a Wet Day in Botswana. 16p. (gr. k-1). 1991. write for info., incl. stickers (*1-880056-10-0*) Play-Media.

—Stick-tivity, Bk. 4: Magical Thoughts on a Hot Day. 16p. (gr. k-1). 1991. write for info., incl. stickers (*1-880056-11-9*) Play-Media.

—Stick-tivity, Bk. 5: Planning to See the Whole World. 16p. (gr. k-1). 1991. write for info., incl. stickers (*1-880056-12-7*) Play-Media.

—Stick-tivity, Bk. 6: Mainly Math. 16p. (gr. k-1). 1991. write for info., incl. stickers (*1-880056-13-5*) Play-Media.

Ryan, Mary C. Ghosts, Gadgets & Great Ideas. 96p. (Orig.). (gr. 3). 1993. pap. 3.50 (*0-380-76537-3*, Camelot Young) Avon.

Scary, Spooky Hunt Activity Book. 48p. (Orig.). 1994. pap. 2.99 (*0-8125-9436-3*) Tor Bks.

Schaffer, Frank, Publications Staff. Beginning Activities with Numbers. (Illus.). 24p. (ps-k). 1980. 3.98 (*0-86734-014-2*, FS-3027) Schaffer Pubns.

—Beginning Activities with Pencil & Paper. (Illus.). 24p. (ps-k). 1980. 3.98 (*0-86734-017-7*, FS-3030) Schaffer Pubns.

—Beginning Activities with Shapes. (Illus.). 24p. (ps-k). 1980. 3.98 (*0-86734-013-4*, FS-3026) Schaffer Pubns.

—Beginning Activities with the Alphabet. (Illus.). 24p. (ps-k). 1980. 3.98 (*0-86734-015-0*, FS-3028) Schaffer Pubns.

—Following Directions. (Illus.). 24p. (gr. 2-4). 1978. wkbk. 3.98 (*0-86734-008-8*, FS-3009) Schaffer Pubns.

—Getting Ready for Kindergarten. (Illus.). 24p. (ps-k). 1978. wkbk. 3.98 (*0-86734-000-2*, FS-3001) Schaffer Pubns.

Schwartz, L. Creative Capers. (gr. 4-6). 1985. 5.95 (*0-88160-117-9*, LW 251) Learning Wks.

—Flip Kit. (gr. 1-6). 1989. 4.95 (*0-88160-183-7*, LW 146) Learning Wks.

Schwartz, Linda. My Polly & Paul Activity Book. 16p. (ps). 1991. wkbk. 3.95 (*0-9631987-0-X*) Put-Together Dev Toys.

Silverstein, Herma. Scream Machines: Roller Coasters Past, Present & Future. (Illus.). 128p. (gr. 3 up). 1986. 13.95 (*0-8027-6618-8*); lib. bdg. 13.85 (*0-8027-6619-6*) Walker & Co.

Sohl, Marcia & Dackerman, Gerald. Me-Time Machine: Student Activity Book. (Illus.). 16p. (gr. 4-10). 1976. pap. 1.25 (*0-88301-186-7*) Pendulum Pr.

Spizman, Robyn. Bulletin Boards Plus. 112p. (gr. k-6). 1989. 9.95 (*0-86653-510-1*, GA1080) Good Apple.

Spizman, Robyn F. & Garber, Marianne D. Air (Intermediate) (Illus.). 48p. (gr. 4-7). 1992. wkbk. 7.95 (*0-86653-632-9*, 1408) Good Apple.

—Land (Intermediate) (Illus.). 48p. (gr. 4-7). 1992. wkbk. 7.95 (*0-86653-675-2*, 1409) Good Apple.

—Water (Intermediate) (Illus.). 48p. (gr. 4-7). 1992. wkbk. 7.95 (*0-86653-676-0*, 1410) Good Apple.

Staheli, Julie. Kachinas: A Color & Cut-out Collection. Staheli, Julie, illus. 32p. (gr. 1 up). 1984. pap. 4.50 (*0-8431-1722-2*, Troubador) Price Stern.

Stanish, Bob. The Ambidextrous Mind Book. 144p. (gr. 2-8). 1989. 12.95 (*0-86653-502-0*, GA1092) Good Apple.

—Creative Activity Cards. 96p. (gr. 3-8). 1991. 11.95 (*0-86653-613-2*, GA1332) Good Apple.

Stevenson, Peter. Play Mask Book - Goldilocks & the Three Bears. 12p. (ps-3). 1991. pap. 5.95 (*0-8167-2372-9*) Troll Assocs.

Stewart, Margaret A. The Best Book a Mother Ever Had. Imholte, Max, illus. 146p. (ps-3). 1985. pap. 12.95 spiral bdg. (*0-931047-00-5*) KinderPr.

Striker, Susan. Third Anti-Coloring Book. 96p. (gr. 2 up). 1980. pap. 6.95 (*0-8050-1447-0*, Owl) H Holt & Co.

Sugimura, et al. American-Japanese Coloring & Talking Books, Bks. 6-10. (gr. k-4). pap. Bk. 6, Customs. pap. 1.95 (*0-8048-0012-X*); Bk. 7, Dressing. pap. 1.95 (*0-8048-0013-8*); Bk. 8, Riding. pap. 1.95 (*0-8048-0017-0*) Vk. 9, Houses. pap. 1.95 (*0-8048-0016-2*); Bk. 10, Story Book Heroes. pap. 1.95 (*0-8048-0019-7*) C E Tuttle.

Tallarico, Anthony. Detect Donald. (Illus.). 24p. (Orig.). 1991. pap. 2.95 (*0-942025-79-2*) Kidsbks.

—Detect Donald. (Illus.). 24p. 1990. 9.95 (*0-942025-99-7*) Kidsbks.

—Find Frankie. (Illus., Orig.). 1991. pap. 2.95 (*0-942025-76-8*) Kidsbks.

—Find Frankie. (Illus.). 24p. 1990. 9.95 (*0-942025-82-2*) Kidsbks.

—Find Freddie. (Illus.). 24p. 1990. 9.95 (*0-942025-13-X*) Kidsbks.

—Hunt for Hector. (Illus.). 24p. 1990. 9.95 (*0-942025-27-X*) Kidsbks.

—Look for Laura. (Illus.). 24p. (Orig.). 1991. pap. 2.95 (*0-942025-77-6*) Kidsbks.

—Look for Laura. (Illus.). 24p. 1990. 9.95 (*0-942025-89-X*) Kidsbks.

—Look for Lisa. (Illus.). 24p. 1990. 9.95 (*0-942025-61-X*) Kidsbks.

—Search for Sam. (Illus.). 24p. 1990. 9.95 (*0-942025-58-X*) Kidsbks.

—Search for Santa. (Illus.). 32p. (Orig.). 1990. 10.95 (*0-942025-71-7*); pap. 3.95 (*0-942025-72-5*) Kidsbks.

—Search for Susie. (Illus.). 24p. (Orig.). 1991. pap. 2.95 (*0-942025-78-4*) Kidsbks.

—Search for Susie. (Illus.). 24p. 1990. 9.95 (*0-942025-97-0*) Kidsbks.

—What's Wrong Here, No. 2. (Illus.). 64p. (Orig.). 1990. pap. 1.95 (*0-942025-92-X*) Kidsbks.

Teacher Planning Guide, Units 1 & 2. (gr. 1). 1991. 27.50 (*0-88106-702-4*) Charlesbridge Pub.

Teacher Planning Guide, Units 3 & 4. (gr. 1). 1991. 27.50 (*0-88106-719-9*) Charlesbridge Pub.

Teacher Planning Guide, Units 5 & 6. (gr. 2). 1991. 27.50 (*0-88106-740-7*) Charlesbridge Pub.

Teacher Planning Guide, Units 7 & 8. (gr. 2). 1991. 27.50 (*0-88106-754-7*) Charlesbridge Pub.

Teacher Planning Guide, Units 9 & 10. (gr. 3). 1991. 27. 50 (*0-88106-771-7*) Charlesbridge Pub.

Terrell, Sandy & White, Frank. Teacher's Choice. (Illus.). 192p. (gr. 4-9). 1992. wkbk. 13.95 (*0-86653-691-4*, 1425) Good Apple.

Three-D Summertime Fun Book. (Illus.). 1992. pap. 2.95 (*1-56156-107-X*) Kidsbks.

Troll Books Staff. Last Action Hero Activity Book. (ps-3). 1993. pap. 2.50 (*0-8167-3146-2*) Troll Assocs.

Trolls Flip 'N' Fun Activity Pads, Bks. 1-2. (Illus.). 1992. Bk. 1. pap. 2.95 (*1-56144-153-8*, Honey Bear Bks) Bk. 2. pap. 2.95 (*1-56144-154-6*) Modern Pub NYC.

Tuchman, Gail. Halloween KidDoodles, No. 1. Solovic, Linda, illus. 64p. (ps-2). 1992. pap. 0.99 (*1-56293-259-4*) McClanahan Bk.

—Halloween KidDoodles, No. 2. Radtke, Becky, illus. 64p. (ps-2). 1992. pap. 0.99 (*1-56293-260-8*) McClanahan Bk.

Tynes, Rick & Whittemore, Diane. Monster Dots: Connect the Dots & Color. (Illus.). 80p. (gr. 1-6). 1993. pap. 4.95 (*0-8069-8642-5*) Sterling.

Wagenman, Mark A. Atlantis the Submarine: Coloring & Activity Book. Wagenman, Mark A., illus. 24p. (ps-k). 1990. pap. 2.95 (*0-89610-168-1*) Island Heritage.

—Maui the Whale: Coloring & Activity Book. (Illus.). 24p. (ps-k). 1989. pap. 2.95 (*0-89610-147-9*) Island Heritage.

Warner, Laverne & Craycraft, Ken. Themetivities. (Illus.). 144p. (ps-2). 1992. wkbk. 11.95 (*0-86653-680-9*, 1414) Good Apple.

Wayman & Plum. Secrets & Surprises. 96p. (gr. k-8). 1977. 9.95 (*0-916456-13-7*, GA70) Good Apple.

Windsor, Natalie. How to Fly - for Kids! Your Fun-in-the-Sky Airplane Companion. Azar, Joe, illus. 144p. (gr. 3-7). 1994. pap. 8.95 (*0-944042-33-3*) Globe Pequot.

Woofenden, Louise. Rainbow Colors in the Word: An Activity Book with Puzzles & Pictures to Color. Hill, Betty, ed. Woofenden, Louise, illus. 32p. (Orig.). 1992. pap. text ed. 2.50 (*0-917426-08-8*) Am New Church Sunday.

Yolen, Jane, compiled by. The Lap-Time Song & Play Book. Tomes, Margot, illus. Stemple, Adam, contrib. by. (Illus.). 28p. (ps up). 1989. 15.95 (*0-15-243588-3*) HarBrace.

Zubrowski, Bernie. A Children's Museum Activity Book: Bubbles. Drescher, Joan, illus. LC 78-27497. (gr. 5-7). 1979. pap. 8.95 (*0-316-98881-2*) Little.

ANALYSIS, MICROSCOPIC

see Microscope and Microscopy

ANATOMY

Here are entered general treatises and works on human anatomy. General works on animal anatomy are entered under Anatomy, Comparative.

see also Anatomy, Comparative; Bones; Nervous System; Physiology;

also subjects with the subdivision Anatomy, e.g. Birds–Anatomy; Botany–Anatomy; etc.; and names of organs and regions of the body, e.g. Heart

AIT Staff. Our Human Body from Science Source. Grewar, Mindy, ed. 32p. (Orig.). (gr. 7-12). 1992. text ed. 7.95 (*0-7842-0604-X*) Agency Instr Tech.

Allison, Linda. Blood & Guts. (Illus.). (gr. 5-12). 1976. pap. 11.95 (*0-316-03443-6*) Little.

The Amazing Body. LC 93-85989. 32p. (gr. 3 up). 1994. 5.95 (*1-56138-196-9*) Running Pr.

Arneson, D. J. The Human Body. (Illus.). 32p. 1991. pap. 2.50 (*1-56156-024-3*) Kidsbks.

Ask about the Human Body. (Illus.). 64p. (gr. 4-5). 1987. PLB 11.95 (*0-8172-2884-5*) Raintree Steck-V.

Avison, Brigid. I Wonder Why I Blink: And Other Questions about My Body. Green, Ruby & Kenyon, Tony, illus. LC 92-45599. 32p. (gr. k-3). 1993. 8.95 (*1-85697-875-3*, Kingfisher LKC) LKC.

Avraham, Regina. The Circulatory System. Koop, C. Everett, intro. by. (Illus.). 112p. (gr. 6-12). 1989. 18.95 (*0-7910-0013-3*) Chelsea Hse.

—The Reproductive System. (Illus.). 128p. (gr. 6-12). 1991. 18.95 (*0-7910-0025-7*) Chelsea Hse.

Bassett, Kerry. My Very Own Special Body Book. 4th ed. McDaniel, Diane, illus. Wooley, Marilyn J., intro. by. (Illus.). 18p. (ps-2). 1987. pap. 3.25 (*0-9620154-0-7*) Hawthorne Pr.

Bender, Lionel. The Body. LC 89-31786. (Illus.). 32p. (gr. 5-6). 1989. PLB 12.40 (*0-531-17183-3*) Watts.

Berger, Melvin. Why I Cough, Sneeze, Shiver, Hiccup, & Yawn. Keller, Holly, illus. LC 82-45587. 40p. (gr. k-3). 1983. PLB 13.89 (*0-690-04254-X*, Crowell Jr Bks) HarpC Child Bks.

Berry, Joy W. Teach Me about My Body. Dickey, Kate, ed. LC 85-45092. (Illus.). 36p. (ps). 1986. 4.98 (*0-685-10730-2*) Grolier Inc.

Blythe, William B. The Human Kidney. Head, J. J., ed. Imrick, Ann T., illus. LC 86-72196. 16p. (Orig.). (gr. 10 up). 1991. pap. text ed. 2.75 (*0-89278-167-X*, 45-9767) Carolina Biological.

The Body. 112p. (gr. 4-9). 1989. 18.95x (*1-85435-071-4*) Marshall Cavendish.

Bogot, Howard & Syme, Daniel. My Body Is Something Special. (Illus.). (ps). 1982. pap. 4.00 (*0-8074-0152-8*, 101715) UAHC.

Bosworth, et al. Body Management. (gr. 7-12). Date not set. incl. software 120.00 (*0-912899-58-1*) Lrning Multi-Systs.

Boynton, Sandra. The Going to Bed Book. Klimo, Kate, ed. Boynton, Sandra, illus. 14p. (ps-k). 1982. 3.95 (*0-671-44902-8*, Little Simon) S&S Trade.

Brady, Janeen. My Body Machine. 29p. (ps-6). 1990. Dialogue Bk. 1.50 (*0-944803-73-3*) Brite Music.

Brenner, Barbara A. Bodies. Ancona, George, illus. (ps-3). 1973. 13.95 (*0-525-26770-0*, DCB) Dutton Child Bks.

Bruun, Ruth D. & Bruun, Bertel. The Human Body. Wynne, Patricia, illus. LC 82-5210. 96p. (gr. 5 up). 1982. lib. bdg. 12.99 (*0-394-94424-0*); pap. 11.95 smythe-sewn (*0-394-84424-6*) Random Bks Yng Read.

Bryan, Jenny. Movement: The Muscular & Skeletal System. LC 92-35092. (Illus.). 48p. (gr. 5 up). 1993. text ed. 13.95 RSBE (*0-87518-565-7*, Dillon) Macmillan Child Grp.

Carratello, Patty. Body Basics. Wright, Theresa, illus. 48p. (gr. 1-5). 1987. wkbk. 6.95 (*1-55734-220-2*) Tchr Create Mat.

Cassin, Sue. Fascinating Facts about Your Body. 1990. 9.95 (*1-55782-328-6*, Pub. by Warner Juvenile Bks) Little.

Catherall, Ed. Exploring the Human Body. (Illus.). 48p. (gr. 4-8). 1992. PLB 22.80 (*0-8114-2599-1*) Raintree Steck-V.

Cobb, Vicki. For Your Own Protection: Stories Science Photos Tell. LC 89-2342. (Illus.). 32p. (gr. 3-6). 1989. 14.95 (*0-688-08787-6*); PLB 14.88 (*0-688-08788-4*) Lothrop.

Cole, Joanna. El Autubus Magico en el Cuerpo Humano-Spanish. (ps-3). 1994. pap. 5.95 (*0-590-46428-0*) Scholastic Inc.

—The Human Body: How We Evolved. Gaffney-Kessell, Walter, illus. LC 86-23679. 64p. (ps-3). 1987. 12.95 (*0-688-06719-0*); lib. bdg. 12.88 (*0-688-06720-4*, Morrow Jr Bks) Morrow Jr Bks.

—The Magic School Bus Inside the Human Body. Deger, Bruce, illus. (ps-3). 1990. pap. 3.95 (*0-590-41427-5*, Scholastic Hardcover) Scholastic Inc.

—The Magic School Bus Inside the Human Body. Degen, Bruce, illus. 1992. pap. 3.95 (*0-685-53602-5*) Scholastic Inc.

—Your Insides. Meisel, Paul, illus. 40p. (ps-1). 1992. 14. 95 (*0-399-22123-9*, Putnam) Putnam Pub Group.

Cole, Joanna & Degen, Bruce. The Magic School Bus Inside the Human Body. 1989. 14.95 (*0-590-41426-7*, Scholastic Hardcover) Scholastic Inc.
Conkle, Nancy E. Terrific Bee on Terrific Me. Blackard, Sandy, illus. 32p. (Orig.). (ps-1). 1993. pap. 9.50 (*0-9639061-0-0*) N Conkle.
Conway, Lorraine. Body Systems. Atkins, Linda, illus. 64p. (gr. 5 up). 1984. wkbk. 7.95 (*0-86653-153-X*, GA 552) Good Apple.
—The Human Body. 64p. (gr. 5 up). 1980. 7.95 (*0-916456-67-6*, GA 178) Good Apple.
Corps Humain - The Human Body. (ENG & FRE.). 63p. 1991. 24.95 (*2-07-057511-X*) Schoenhof.
Crelinsten, J. To the Limit. 1992. write for info. (*0-15-200616-8*, Gulliver Bks) HarBrace.
Cummings, Phil. Goodness Gracious! Smith, Craig, illus. LC 91-17473. 32p. (ps-1). 1992. 13.95 (*0-531-05967-7*); lib. bdg. 13.99 (*0-531-08567-8*) Orchard Bks Watts.
Davies, Nick. How Our Bodies Work: Fact Finders. (gr. 4-7). 1994. pap. 6.95 (*0-563-34602-7*, Pub. by BBC UK) Parkwest Pubns.
Demuth, Patricia. Inside Your Busy Body. Billin-Frye, Paige, illus. LC 92-44173. 32p. (ps-3). 1993. pap. 2.25 (*0-448-40189-4*, G&D) Putnam Pub Group.
Eastman, David. I Can Read About My Own Body. LC 72-96958. (Illus.). (gr. 2-4). 1973. pap. 2.50 (*0-89375-057-3*) Troll Assocs.
Edelson, Edward. The Immune System. (Illus.). 104p. (gr. 6-12). 1990. 18.95 (*0-7910-0021-4*) Chelsea Hse.
—Nervous System. (Illus.). 112p. (gr. 6-12). 1989. 18.95 (*0-7910-0023-0*) Chelsea Hse.
Elting, Mary. The Macmillan Book of the Human Body. Moldoff, Kirk, illus. LC 85-24204. 80p. (gr. 3-7). 1986. pap. 9.95 (*0-02-043080-9*, Aladdin) Macmillan Child Grp.
Evans, David & Williams, Claudette. Me & My Body. LC 92-52817. (Illus.). 32p. (gr. k-3). 1992. 9.95 (*1-56458-121-7*) Dorling Kindersley.
Fabricant, Norman. Fun with Tattoo Art. (gr. 4-7). 1994. pap. 4.95 (*0-8167-3378-3*) Troll Assocs.
Faulkner, Keith. This Is Me. Lambert, Jonathan, illus. 10p. (ps-k). 1987. 5.95 (*0-312-00967-4*) St Martin.
Feinberg, Brian. The Musculoskeletal System. Garell, Dale C. & Snyder, Solomon H., eds. (Illus.). 112p. (gr. 7-12). 1994. 19.95 (*0-7910-0028-1*, Am Art Analog) Chelsea Hse.
Freeman, Lory. Mi Cuerpo Es Mio. Dunn, Lois, tr. from ENG. Deach, Carol, illus. LC 85-62435. (SPA.). 32p. (Orig.). (ps). 1985. pap. 4.95 (*0-943990-19-X*) Parenting Pr.
FS Staff & Gamlin, Linda. The Human Body. Hayward, Ron, illus. LC 88-50507. 40p. (gr. 6-8). 1988. PLB 12. 40 (*0-531-17117-5*, Gloucester Pr) Watts.
Gabb, Michael. The Human Body. LC 92-53092. (Illus.). 48p. (Orig.). (gr. 3-8). 1992. pap. 5.95 (*1-85697-812-5*, Kingfisher LKC) LKC.
Gakken Co. Ltd., Staff, ed. Our Bodies. Time-Life Books Inc., Staff, tr. (Illus.). 90p. (gr. k-3). 1991. write for info. (*0-8094-9450-7*); lib. bdg. write for info. (*0-8094-9451-5*); text ed. write for info. (*0-8094-9452-3*); pap. write for info. (*0-8094-9453-1*) Time-Life.
Ganeri, A. Body Facts. (Illus.). 48p. (gr. 3-7). 1993. PLB 12.96 (*0-88110-599-6*); pap. 5.95 (*0-7460-0948-8*) EDC.
Ganeri, Anita. Body Science. LC 92-22722. (Illus.). 48p. (gr. 5 up). 1993. text ed. 13.95 RSBE (*0-87518-576-2*, Dillon) Macmillan Child Grp.
—What's Inside Us? LC 94-19406. (gr. 1 up). 1995. write for info. (*0-8114-3885-6*) Raintree Steck V.
Goldman, Meredith & Lissauer, T. Human Body. Ashman, Iain, illus. 32p. (gr. 6 up). 1983. lib. bdg. 13. 96 (*0-88110-150-8*); pap. 6.95 (*0-86020-747-1*) EDC.
Goldsmith, Ilse. Human Anatomy for Children. Krause, William, illus. (gr. 5-8). 1969. pap. 2.95 (*0-486-22355-8*) Dover.
Hanson. Your Amazing Body. (Illus.). 96p. 1994. text ed. write for info. (*0-7167-6533-0*); pap. text ed. write for info. (*0-7167-6552-7*) W H Freeman.
Hindley & Rawson. How Your Body Works. (gr. 2-5). 1975. (Usborne-Hayes); PLB 13.96 (*0-88110-113-3*); pap. 6.95 (*0-86020-198-8*) EDC.
The Human Body. 48p. (gr. 5-6). 1991. PLB 11.95 (*1-56065-060-5*) Capstone Pr.
The Human Body. LC 91-60899. (Illus.). 64p. (gr. 6 up). 1991. 14.95 (*1-879431-18-1*); PLB 15.99 (*1-879431-33-5*) Dorling Kindersley.
Human Body. 1992. 18.95 (*0-8094-9654-2*) Time-Life.
The Human Body: A Complete Guide. LC 93-85524. (Illus.). 256p. (Orig.). 1994. pap. 5.95 (*1-56138-385-6*) Running Pr.
Human Body: A Prentice Hall Illustrated Dictionary. LC 92-22213. (Illus.). 160p. 1993. 19.00 (*0-671-84693-0*) P-H Gen Ref & Trav.
Human Development, 4 bks. (gr. 5-6). 1992. Set. write for info. (*0-8114-7799-1*) Raintree Steck-V.
Intrater, Robert G. Two Eyes, a Nose & a Mouth: A Book of Many Faces, Many Races. LC 94-18390. (gr. 3 up). Date not set. 12.95 (*0-590-48247-5*, Cartwheel) Scholastic Inc.
Jefferies, David. The Human Body: A Thematic Unit. Bruce, Kathy, illus. 80p. (gr. 3-5). 1993. wkbk. 8.95 (*1-55734-235-0*) Tchr Create Mat.
Jennings, Terry. The Human Body. LC 88-22859. (Illus.). 32p. (gr. 3-6). 1989. pap. 4.95 (*0-516-48404-4*) Childrens.
Johnson, John E. The Me Book. Johnson, John E., illus. LC 79-62042. (ps). 1979. 3.50 (*0-394-84243-X*) Random Bks Yng Read.
Kalman, Bobbie. My Busy Body. (Illus.). 32p. (gr. k-2). 1985. 15.95 (*0-86505-065-1*); pap. 7.95 (*0-86505-089-9*) Crabtree Pub Co.
Kile, Marilyn & Baird, Kristin. My Body Belongs to Me. (gr. k-2). 1986. text ed. 17.50 (*0-88671-173-8*, 7202) Am Guidance.
—What Would You Do If...? 1986. pap. text ed. 17.25 (*0-88671-172-X*, 7205) Am Guidance.
Kingston, Arlene. I'm Small That's All. (Illus.). (ps up). 1989. pap. write for info. (*0-929934-02-4*) Child Time Pubs.
Kittredge, Mary. The Human Body: An Overview. (Illus.). 144p. (gr. 6-12). 1990. 18.95 (*0-7910-0019-2*) Chelsea Hse.
Lambourne, Mike. Inside Story: The Latest News about Your Body. LC 91-22960. (Illus.). 40p. (gr. 2-6). 1992. PLB 13.40 (*1-56294-148-8*) Millbrook Pr.
Lauber, Patricia. Your Body & How It Works. (Illus.). (gr. 3-5). 1966. PLB 12.99 (*0-394-90125-8*) Random Bks Yng Read.
Lee, Celeste. Understanding the Body Organs: And the Eight Laws of Health. 128p. 1994. pap. 7.95 (*0-945383-44-4*) Teach Servs.
Llewellyn, Claire. First Look at Keeping Warm. LC 91-9423. (Illus.). 32p. (gr. 1-2). 1991. PLB 17.27 (*0-8368-0704-9*) Gareth Stevens Inc.
Machotka, Hana. Breathtaking Noses. Machotka, Hana, photos by. LC 91-12252. (Illus.). 32p. (gr. k up). 1992. 15.00 (*0-688-09526-7*); PLB 14.93 (*0-688-09527-5*) Morrow Jr Bks.
MacKinnon, Debbie & Sieveking, Anthea. All about Me. LC 93-23143. (Illus.). 32p. (ps). 1994. 11.95 (*0-8120-6348-1*) Barron.
Markham-David, Sally. It Takes All Kinds. Ruth, Trevor, illus. LC 93-21246. 1994. 4.25 (*0-383-03753-0*) SRA Schl Grp.
Markle, Sandra. Outside & Inside You. Kuklin, Susan, illus. LC 90-37791. 40p. (ps-3). 1991. RSBE 15.95 (*0-02-762311-4*, Bradbury Pr) Macmillan Child Grp.
Mayes, S. What's Inside You? (Illus.). 24p. (gr. 1 up). 1991. PLB 11.96 (*0-88110-550-3*, Usborne); pap. 3.95 (*0-7460-0602-0*, Usborne) EDC.
Meredith, Sue. Why Are People Different? (Illus.). 24p. (gr. 1-5). 1993. lib. bdg. 11.96 (*0-88110-642-9*, Usborne); pap. 3.95 (*0-7460-1014-1*, Usborne) EDC.
My Body. LC 91-60535. (Illus.). 24p. (ps-3). 1991. 8.95 (*1-879431-07-6*) Dorling Kindersley.
Olivier, Pierre & Wessels, Florence. My Body. (Illus.). 128p. (ps-3). 1993. 7.00 (*0-679-84160-1*); PLB 11.99 (*0-679-94160-6*) Random Bks Yng Read.
Parker, Steve. The Body & How It Works. LC 91-58203. (Illus.). 64p. (gr. 3 up). 1992. 11.95 (*1-879431-95-5*); PLB 12.99 (*1-879431-96-3*) Dorling Kindersley.
—The Body Atlas. Fornari, Giuliano, illus. LC 92-54307. 64p. (gr. 3 up). 1993. 19.95 (*1-56458-224-8*) Dorling Kindersley.
—Human Body. LC 93-31076. (Illus.). 64p. (gr. k-5). 1994. 9.95 (*1-56458-322-8*) Dorling Kindersley.
Payne, Fiona, ed. The Human Body. LC 92-54481. (Illus.). (gr. k-3). 1993. 12.95 (*1-56458-249-3*) Dorling Kindersley.
Peacock, Graham & Hudson, Terry. The Super Science Book of Our Bodies. LC 93-7519. (Illus.). 32p. (gr. 4-8). 1993. 14.95 (*1-56847-023-1*) Thomson Lrning.
Pollard, Neil & McDonald, Mary. How Do You Measure Up? Wilkin, Mike, illus. LC 93-20060. 1994. pap. write for info. (*0-383-03697-6*) SRA Schl Grp.
Puncel, Maria & Basquez, Juan J., eds. Cuerpo Humano - The Human Body. Secanell, Jose M., tr. (SPA., Illus.). 63p. (gr. 5-12). 1992. write for info. (*84-372-4528-1*) Santillana.
Quinn, Kaye. The Human Body. (Illus.). 40p. (Orig.). (gr. k-5). 1988. pap. 2.95 (*0-8431-2378-8*) Price Stern.
Rauzon, Mark J. Feet, Flippers, Hooves, & Hands. (ps-3). 1994. 13.00 (*0-688-10234-4*); 12.93 (*0-688-10235-2*) Lothrop.
Reed, Helen R. All about You: A Religious Physiology & Hygiene for Parents to Read to Their Children. 1992. 7.95 (*0-533-10079-8*) Vantage.
Richardson, James. Science Dictionary of the Human Body. Hung, Gil, illus. LC 91-19162. 48p. (gr. 3-7). 1992. lib. bdg. 11.59 (*0-8167-2523-3*); pap. 3.95 (*0-8167-2442-3*) Troll Assocs.
Rowan, Pete. Some Body! A Life-Size Guide. LC 94-20402. (Illus.). Date not set. 20.00 (*0-679-87043-1*) Knopf.
Royston, Angela. The Human Body & How It Works. Shone, Rob, illus. LC 90-12977. 40p. (gr. 4-5). 1991. PLB 12.40 (*0-531-19102-8*, Warwick) Watts.
—The Human Body & How It Works. Stone, Rob, illus. LC 90-42978. 40p. (Orig.). (gr. 2-5). 1991. pap. 4.99 (*0-679-80860-4*) Random Bks Yng Read.
Sabin, Francene. Human Body. Sibley, Don, illus. LC 84-2591. 32p. (gr. 3-6). 1985. PLB 9.49 (*0-8167-0170-9*); pap. text ed. 2.95 (*0-8167-0171-7*) Troll Assocs.
Schlossberg, Leon. The Johns Hopkins Human Anatomy Series. (Illus.). (gr. 8 up). 1986. markable ed. 36.95 (*0-9603730-2-0*) Anatomical Chart.
Schoen, Mark. Bellybuttons Are Navels. Quay, M. J., illus. Calderone, Mary, intro. by. (Illus.). 48p. (ps-3). 1990. Repr. 17.95 (*0-87975-585-7*) Prometheus Bks.
Schoenberg, Jane. My Bodyworks. Fritz, Ronald, illus. 32p. (ps-3). 1993. pap. 2.50 (*0-590-47231-3*, Cartwheel) Scholastic Inc.
Schwartz, Linda. Your Body. (Illus.). 48p. (gr. 2-5). 1990. 5.95 (*0-88160-191-8*, LW 150) Learning Wks.
Senior, Kathryn. Your Body. Salariya, David & Salariya, Davidcreated by. LC 93-40314. 1994. write for info. (*0-531-14336-8*) Watts.
The Simon & Schuster Pocket Book of the Human Body. 188p. (gr. 3 up). 1987. pap. 6.95 (*0-671-62973-5*) S&S Trade.
Sproule, Anna. Body Watch: Know Your Insides. (Illus.). 48p. (gr. 1-4). 1987. 12.95x (*0-8160-1782-4*) Facts on File.
Stark, Fred. Start Exploring Gray's Anatomy: A Fact-Filled Coloring Book. (Illus.). 128p. (Orig.). (gr. 2 up). 1991. pap. 8.95 (*0-89471-863-0*) Running Pr.
Stein, Sara. The Body Book. LC 91-50957. (Illus.). (gr. 4-7). 1992. 19.95 (*1-56305-298-9*, 3298); pap. 11.95 (*0-89480-805-2*, 1805) Workman Pub.
Thomson, Arthur. Handbook of Anatomy for Art Students. 5th ed. (Illus.). (gr. 9-12). 1929. pap. text ed. 9.95 (*0-486-21163-0*) Dover.
Time-Life Books Editors. The Human Body. 128p. (gr. 7 up). 1989. 14.99 (*0-8094-6062-9*); lib. bdg. 23.93 (*0-8094-6063-7*) Time-Life.
Time Life Inc. Editors. From Head to Toe: Body Math. Crawford, Jean B. & Daniels, Patricia, eds. LC 92-34974. (Illus.). 64p. (gr. k-2). 1993. write for info. (*0-8094-9966-5*); PLB write for info. (*0-8094-9967-3*) Time-Life.
Townsend, Anne. Marvelous Me: All about the Human Body. (Illus.). 48p. (ps-1). 1985. 13.95 (*0-85648-577-2*) Lion USA.
Walker, Richard. The Children's Atlas of the Human Body. LC 93-41527. (Illus.). 64p. (gr. 2-6). 1994. PLB 18.90 (*1-56294-503-3*); pap. 12.95 (*1-56294-732-X*) Millbrook Pr.
Wells, Donna K. Your Body: Treasures Inside. Endres, Helen, illus. LC 90-30632. 32p. (ps-2). 1990. PLB 13. 95 (*0-89565-576-4*) Childs World.
Western, Joan & Wilson, Ron. The Human Body. Atkinson, Mike, illus. LC 90-38929. 96p. (gr. 3-6). 1991. PLB 14.89 (*0-8167-2234-X*); pap. text ed. 6.95 (*0-8167-2235-8*) Troll Assocs.
Wong, Ovid. Your Body & How It Works. Donahoe, Lindaanne, illus. LC 86-9686. 128p. (gr. 5 up). 1986. PLB 13.95 (*0-516-00534-0*) Childrens.
Wrenn, Romel. Super ABC's of the Human Body. Tripp, Charles, illus. 56p. (gr. k-4). 1993. Wkbk. write for info. (*0-9637869-0-3*) Chldrns Med.

ANATOMY, ARTISTIC

Brenner, Barbara A. Faces. Ancona, George, illus. LC 70-102737. 48p. (ps-2). 1970. 14.95 (*0-525-29518-6*, DCB) Dutton Child Bks.

ANATOMY, COMPARATIVE

see also Man–Origin and Antiquity

Burnie, David. Animals: How They Work. LC 93-43404. (Illus.). 48p. 1994. 14.95 (*0-8069-0742-8*) Sterling.
Davenport, Zoe. Animals. LC 94-20821. 1995. 4.95 (*0-395-71537-7*) Ticknor & Flds Bks Yng Read.
Goor, Ron & Goor, Nancy. Heads. Goor, Ron, illus. LC 87-30262. 64p. (gr. 2-6). 1988. SBE 14.95 (*0-689-31400-0*, Atheneum Child Bk) Macmillan Child Grp.
Kates, Bobbi J. We're Different, We're the Same. Mathieu, Joe, illus. LC 91-38545. 32p. (Orig.). (ps-3). 1992. pap. 2.25 (*0-679-83227-0*) Random Bks Yng Read.
Legg, Gerald. Amazing Animals. Salariya, David, created by. LC 93-36703. (Illus.). 48p. (gr. 5-8). 1994. 13.95 (*0-531-14285-X*); pap. 8.95 (*0-531-15708-3*) Watts.
Markham-David, Sally. Mouths & Noses. Ruth, Trevor, illus. LC 93-29008. 1994. 4.25 (*0-383-03764-6*) SRA Schl Grp.
Patent, Dorothy H. What Good Is a Tail? Munoz, William, photos by. LC 92-45639. (Illus.). 32p. (gr. 1-5). 1994. 13.99 (*0-525-65148-9*, Cobblehill Bks) Dutton Child Bks.
Perkins, Al. Nose Book. McKie, Roy, illus. LC 71-117540. (ps-1). 1970. 6.95 (*0-394-80623-9*); lib. bdg. 7.99 (*0-394-90623-3*) Random Bks Yng Read.
Santa Fe Writers Group. Bizarre & Beautiful Noses. (Illus.). 48p. (gr. 3 up). 1993. 14.95 (*1-56261-124-0*) John Muir.

ANATOMY, DENTAL

see Teeth

ANATOMY, VEGETABLE

see Botany–Anatomy

ANATOMY OF PLANTS

see Botany–Anatomy

ANCIENT ART

see Art, Ancient

ANCIENT CIVILIZATION

see Civilization, Ancient

ANCIENT HISTORY

see History, Ancient

ANDERSEN, HANS CHRISTIAN, 1805-1875

Brust, Beth W. The Amazing Paper Cuttings of Hans Christian Andersen. LC 93-24532. 80p. (gr. 2-4). 1994. 15.95 (*0-395-66787-9*) Ticknor & Flds Bks Yng Read.
Burch, Joann J. A Fairy-Tale Life: A Story about Hans Christian Andersen. Monson, Liz, illus. LC 93-48463. 1994. 14.95 (*0-87614-829-1*) Carolrhoda Bks.
Cote. Hans Christian Andersen, Reading Level 2. (Illus.). 24p. (gr. 1-4). 1989. PLB 14.60 (*0-86592-430-9*); 10. 95 (*0-685-58798-3*) Rourke Corp.

Greene, Carol. Hans Christian Andersen: Prince of Storytellers. Dobson, Steven, illus. LC 90-19998. 48p. (gr. k-3). 1991. PLB 12.85 (*0-516-04219-X*); pap. 4.95 (*0-516-44219-8*) Childrens.
—Hans Christian Andersen: Teller of Tales. LC 85-27991. (Illus.). 128p. (gr. 4-7). 1986. PLB 14.40 (*0-516-03216-X*) Childrens.
Moore, Eva. The Fairy Tale Life of Hans Christian Andersen. Hyman, Trina S., illus. 80p. 1992. pap. 2.75 (*0-590-45225-8*, Apple Paperbacks) Scholastic Inc.

ANDERSON, MARIAN, 1902-

Ferris, Jeri. What I Had Was Singing: The Story of Marian Anderson. LC 93-28502. (gr. 4 up). Date not set. 17.50 (*0-87614-818-6*) Carolrhoda Bks.
McKissack, Patricia & McKissack, Fredrick. Marian Anderson: A Great Singer. Ostendorf, Ned, illus. LC 90-19163. 32p. (gr. 1-4). 1991. lib. bdg. 12.95 (*0-89490-303-9*) Enslow Pubs.
Rutter, Jared. Marion Anderson: Opera Singer. (Illus.). 192p. 1994. pap. 3.95 (*0-87067-589-3*, Melrose Sq) Holloway.
Tedards, Anne. Marian Anderson. Horner, Matina, intro. by. (Illus.). 112p. (Orig.). (gr. 5 up). 1988. 17.95 (*1-55546-638-9*); pap. 9.95 (*0-7910-0216-0*) Chelsea Hse.

ANDES MOUNTAINS

Blue, Rose & Naden, Corinne. Andes Mountains. LC 94-3028. (Illus.). 64p. (gr. 5-8). 1994. PLB write for info. (*0-8114-6363-X*) Raintree Steck-V.
Cobb, Vicki. This Place Is High. Lavallee, Barbara, illus. 32p. (gr. 2-4). 1989. 12.95 (*0-8027-6882-2*); PLB 13.85 (*0-8027-6883-0*) Walker & Co.
Morrison, Marion. Ecuador, Peru, Bolivia. (Illus.). 96p. (gr. 6-12). 1992. PLB 22.80 (*0-8114-2453-7*) Raintree Steck-V.

ANESTHETICS–HISTORY

Galas, Judith. Anesthetics: Surgery Without Pain. LC 92-27852. (Illus.). 96p. (gr. 5-8). 1992. PLB 15.95 (*1-56006-224-X*) Lucent Bks.

ANGELS–FICTION

Bartone, Elisa. The Angel Who Forgot. Cline, Paul, illus. LC 91-34233. 48p. (Orig.). (ps up). 1992. 10.00 (*0-671-76037-8*, Green Tiger) S&S Trade.
Barwick, Mary. The Alabama Angels in Anywhere, L. A. (Lower Alabama) Barwick, Mary, illus. 32p. (Orig.). 1991. pap. 8.95 (*0-9622815-6-5*) Black Belt Pr.
Birch, David. Wrestle the Angel. LC 93-60917. (Illus.). 44p. (gr. k-3). 1994. 7.95 (*1-55523-652-9*) Winston-Derek.
Boone, Debby. The Snow Angel. Ferrer, Gabri, illus. 32p. (ps-1). 1991. text ed. 12.99 (*0-89081-871-1*) Harvest Hse.
Burgess. Angel for May. Date not set. 15.00 (*0-06-023513-6*); PLB 14.89 (*0-06-023514-4*) HarpC Child Bks.
Burgess, Melvyn. An Angel for May. large type ed. (gr. 1-8). 1994. sewn 16.95 (*0-7451-2086-5*, Galaxy Child Lrg Print) Chivers N Amer.
Carney, Mary L. Too Tough to Hurt. 128p. 1991. pap. 6.99 (*0-310-28621-2*, Youth Bks) Zondervan.
—Wrestling with an Angel: A Devotional Novel for Junior Highers. rev. ed. 160p. (gr. 6-9). 1993. pap. 6.99 (*0-685-63320-9*, Pub. by Youth Spec) Zondervan.
Ching Yee, Janice. God's Meekest Angels. (Illus.). (gr. k-6). 1981. pap. 3.00 (*0-931420-10-5*) Pi Pr.
Crump, Fred, Jr. The Other Little Angel. Crump, Fred, Jr., illus. LC 93-60369. 44p. (gr. k-3). 1993. pap. 6.95 (*1-55523-624-3*) Winston-Derek.
Cummings, Pat. C.L.O.U.D.S. LC 85-9719. (Illus.). 32p. (ps-3). 1986. 12.95 (*0-688-04682-7*); PLB 12.88 (*0-688-04683-5*) Lothrop.
Dellinger, Annetta E. Angels Are My Friends. LC 85-7858. 32p. (gr. 5-9). 1985. 5.99 (*0-570-04120-1*, 56-1531) Concordia.
Delton, Judy. Back Yard Angel. Morrill, Leslie, illus. 112p. (gr. 2-5). 1983. 14.45 (*0-395-33883-2*) HM.
Dubowski, Cathy E. The Littlest Angel. Pollard, Nan, illus. 24p. (ps-2). 1991. pap. 0.99 (*1-56293-116-4*) McClanahan Bk.
Ekberg, Susan. Pink Stars & Angel Wings. Neavill, Michelle, illus. LC 91-91216. 32p. (ps up). 1992. 16.95 (*0-9630419-0-8*) Spiritseeker.
Eliason, Peter. The Comeuppance of Dipsey Dolan. 162p. (Orig.). (gr. 2-10). 1984. pap. 5.95 (*0-916777-34-0*) W P Allen.
Elwood, Roger. Angelwalk. LC 87-70456. 192p. (Orig.). 1988. pap. 8.99 (*0-89107-440-6*) Crossway Bks.
Fontenot, Mary A. Star Seed. Cregan, Nannette, illus. LC 86-12171. 32p. (gr. k-4). 1986. Repr. 7.95 (*0-88289-628-8*) Pelican.
Greene, Leia A. The Angel Told Me to Tell You Good-Bye. Greene, Leia A., illus. 24p. (gr. k-12). 1991. pap. text ed. 4.95 (*1-880737-06-X*) Crystal Jrns.
Hamilton, Jamar W. Julie's Angel. (gr. 4-7). 1990. pap. 5.95 (*0-925928-06-2*) Tiny Thought.
Leppard, Lois G. Mandie & the Angel's Secret. (gr. 4-7). 1993. pap. 3.99 (*1-55661-370-9*) Bethany Hse.
McAllister, Angela. The Snow Angel. Fletcher, Claire, illus. LC 92-44155. 1993. 14.00 (*0-688-04569-3*) Lothrop.
Messmer, Barbara A. The Starshiners & the Gloomies. 1991. 7.95 (*0-533-08634-5*) Vantage.

Peckinpah, Sandra L. Chester... the Imperfect All-Star. Moore, Trisha, illus. LC 92-74057. (gr. 1-5). 1993. PLB 15.95 (*0-9627806-1-8*); pap. text ed. 8.95 (*0-9627806-2-6*) Dasan Prodns. In classic fairy tale tradition, CHESTER...THE IMPERFECT ALL STAR tells the tale of a special angel in the Land Called Above whose passion is to play baseball with the angels' "Windrunner" team. Chester looks & feels different than the other angels because he has one leg shorter than the other. With the loving guidance of Coach Angel, he becomes the all star & is rewarded with his own unique place in the Land Called Below. A book for all the world's different & special children, for any child who has ever felt different, for their parents, siblings, & classmates. Addresses the problems such children experience, & foretells a happy ending. Fully illustrated in color, vocabulary included. To order call Cimino Publishing Group (516) 997-3721. *Publisher Provided Annotation.*

—Rosey...the Imperfect Angel. Moore, Trisha, illus. LC 90-63058. 32p. (ps-4). 1991. 15.95 (*0-9627806-0-X*) Dasan Prodns. First in a series about the beauties hidden beneath defects. A classic fairy tale, Rosey is a little angel taunted by her angel peers & her poor self-image. Rosey triumphs & assumes her unique place in The Land Called Below. Addresses the problems children with birth defects experience; foretells happy ending. Vocabulary. "Rosey...is a delightful, whimsical allegory, with a profound theme - the greater sensitivity & acceptance of human difference...a wonderful book to share with a child or just enjoy."--Janet Salomonson, M.D. "Rosey...shows us how in our hearts & in our dreams we are all perfect. Her story is an inspiration to both adults & children."--Marlee Matlin, Actress. *Publisher Provided Annotation.*

Quisenberry, Stacey H. The Little Angel Who Lost Faith. Gress, Jonna, ed. Browning, Suzi, illus. LC 93-74773. 24p. (ps-1). 1994. pap. 4.95 (*0-944943-51-9*, CODE 24178-6) Current Inc.
Rodriguez, Anita. Jamal & the Angel. Rodriguez, Anita, illus. LC 91-11636. 32p. (ps-2). 1992. 14.00 (*0-517-58601-0*); PLB 15.99 (*0-517-59115-4*) Crown Bks Yng Read.
Skocz, Anita J. Crystal Star Angel. Christy, Cynthia, illus. 48p. 1994. pap. 5.95t (*0-8091-6617-8*) Paulist Pr.
Tazewell. Littlest Angel. new ed. 32p. 1991. 15.95 (*0-516-09218-9*) Childrens.
Tazewell, Charles. The Littlest Angel. Micich, Paul, illus. LC 91-2442. 32p. (gr. k-4). 1991. 14.95 (*0-8249-8516-8*, Ideals Child) Hambleton-Hill.
Thomas, Kathy. The Angel's Quest. Seitz, Jacqueline, illus. 32p. (gr. 2-6). 1983. casebound 9.95 (*0-914544-99-3*) Living Flame Pr.
Yolen, Jane. Good Griselle. Christiana, David, illus. LC 93-11691. (gr. 2 up). 1994. write for info. (*0-15-231701-5*) HarBrace.

ANGINA PECTORIS

see Heart–Diseases

ANGLING

see Fishing

ANGLO-SAXONS

Coote, Roger. The Anglo-Saxons. LC 93-34486. (Illus.). 32p. (gr. 4-6). 1994. 14.95 (*1-56847-062-2*) Thomson Lrning.
Loverance, Rowena. The Anglo-Saxons. (Illus.). 48p. (Orig.). (gr. 7 up). 1992. pap. 6.95 (*0-563-35001-6*, BBC-Parkwest) Parkwest Pubns.
Reeve, John & Chattington, Jenny. The Anglo-Saxons Activity Book. (Illus.). 16p. 1994. pap. 5.95 (*0-500-27762-1*) Thames Hudson.
Reeve, John, et al. The Anglo-Saxons. (Illus.). (gr. 2-6). pap. 3.95 (*0-7141-0537-6*, Pub. by Brit Mus UK) Parkwest Pubns.

ANIMAL BABIES

see Animals–Infancy

ANIMAL BEHAVIOR

see Animals–Habits and Behavior

ANIMAL COLORATION

see Color of Animals

ANIMAL COMMUNICATION

Bailey, Vanessa. Animal Sounds. Stillwell, Stella, illus. 16p. (ps). 1991. 5.95 (*0-8120-6243-4*) Barron.
Battaglia, Aurelius, illus. Animal Sounds. 22p. (ps). 1981. write for info. (*0-307-12122-4*, Golden Bks) Western Pub.
Burnie, David A. Communication. LC 91-31946. (Illus.). 32p. (gr. 4-7). 1992. PLB 12.40 (*0-531-17312-7*, Gloucester Pr) Watts.
Cole, Jacci. Animal Communication: Opposing Viewpoints. LC 88-24401. (Illus.). 112p. (gr. 5-8). 1989. PLB 14.95 (*0-89908-062-6*) Greenhaven.
Facklam, Margery. Bees Dance & Whales Sing: The Mysteries of Animal Communication. Johnson, Pamela, illus. 48p. (gr. 3-6). 1992. 14.95 (*0-87156-573-0*) Sierra.
Flegg, Jim. Animal Communication. (Illus.). 32p. (gr. 4-6). 1991. PLB 12.40 (*1-878137-23-9*) Newington.
Goodenough, J. E. Animal Communication. Head, John J., ed. LC 83-70598. (Illus.). 16p. (gr. 10 up). 1984. pap. 2.75 (*0-89278-343-5*, 45-9743) Carolina Biological.
Johnson, Rebecca L. The Secret Language: Pheromones in the Animal World. (Illus.). 64p. (gr. 5 up). 1989. 21.50 (*0-8225-1586-5*) Lerner Pubns.
McDonnell, Janet. Animal Communication. LC 88-36643. (Illus.). 48p. (gr. 2-6). 1989. PLB 14.95 (*0-89565-513-6*) Childs World.
—Animal Talk: Barks, Growls, Hisses, Howls. Ching, illus. LC 89-23990. 32p. (ps-2). 1990. PLB 14.95 (*0-89565-558-6*) Childs World.
Mcnulty, Faith. With Love from Koko. (gr. k up). 1990. pap. 12.95 (*0-590-42774-1*) Scholastic Inc.
Making Contact. (Illus.). 48p. (gr. 3-4). 1992. PLB 22.80 (*0-8114-3155-X*) Raintree Steck-V.
Mayes, S. How Do Animals Talk? (Illus.). 24p. (gr. 1 up). 1991. PLB 11.96 (*0-88110-549-X*, Usborne); pap. 3.95 (*0-7460-0600-4*, Usborne) EDC.
Payne, Katharine. Elephants Calling. Payne, Katharine, photos by. LC 91-34547. (Illus.). 36p. (gr. 2-6). 1992. 14.00 (*0-517-58175-2*); PLB 14.99 (*0-517-58176-0*) Crown Bks Yng Read.

ANIMAL DRAWING

see Animal Painting and Illustration

ANIMAL HOMES

see Animals–Habitations

ANIMAL INDUSTRY

see Domestic Animals; Livestock

ANIMAL INTELLIGENCE

see also Animals–Habits and Behavior

Boone, J. Allen & Leonard, Paul H. Adventures in Kinship with All Life. Leonardo, Bianca, ed. 128p. (gr. 9-12). 1990. pap. 9.95 (*0-930852-08-7*) Tree Life Pubns.
Facklam, Margery. What Does the Crow Know? The Mysteries of Animal Intelligence. Johnson, Pamela, illus. LC 93-17811. 48p. (gr. 3-6). 1993. 15.95 (*0-87156-544-7*) Sierra.
Hinde, R. A. & Hinde, J. S. Instinct & Intelligence. 3rd ed. Head, J. J., ed. LC 87-70404. (Illus.). 16p. (gr. 10 up). 1987. pap. 2.75 (*0-89278-063-0*, 45-9663) Carolina Biological.
Sattler, Helen R. Fish Facts & Bird Brains: Animal Intelligence. Maestro, Giulio, illus. LC 83-20805. 128p. (gr. 5-9). 1984. 13.95 (*0-525-66915-9*, Lodestar Bks) Dutton Child Bks.
Steiger, Brad & Steiger, Sherry H. The Mystery of Animal Intelligence. (Orig.). 1994. pap. 3.99 (*0-8125-3367-4*) Tor Bks.

ANIMAL KINGDOM

see Zoology

ANIMAL LANGUAGE

see Animal Communication

ANIMAL LIGHT

see Bioluminescence

ANIMAL LORE

see Animals, Mythical; Natural History

ANIMAL MAGNETISM

see Hypnotism

ANIMAL MIGRATION

see Animals–Migration

ANIMAL PAINTING AND ILLUSTRATION

see also Animals in Art; Photography of Animals

Arnosky, Jim. Near the Sea. (Illus.). 32p. 1990. 13.95 (*0-688-08164-9*); PLB 13.88 (*0-688-09327-2*) Lothrop.
DuBosque, Doug. Draw! Dinosaurs. (Illus.). 80p. (ps-4). 1993. pap. 8.95 (*0-939217-20-1*) Peel Prod.
Hart, Tony. Animals & Figures. (Illus.). 32p. (gr. 1-4). 1984. 5.95 (*0-7182-2950-9*, Pub. by W Heinemann Ltd) Trafalgar.
Laidman, Hugh. Animals: How to Draw Them. LC 75-11930. (Illus.). 160p. (gr. 7 up). 1979. pap. 12.95 (*0-685-46950-6*, Dutton) NAL-Dutton.
McHugh, Christopher. Animals. LC 93-43265. (Illus.). 32p. (gr. 4-6). 1993. 14.95g (*1-56847-025-8*) Thomson Lrning.
Plant, Andrew. Drawing Is Easy. Plant, Andrew, illus. LC 93-16116. 1994. pap. write for info. (*0-383-03692-5*) SRA Schl Grp.
Robertson, Bruce & Pinkus, Sue. Let's All Draw Dinosaurs, Pterodactyls & Other Prehistoric Creatures. (Illus.). 144p. (gr. 3-7). 1991. pap. 9.95 (*0-8230-2706-6*, Watson-Guptill Bks) Watson-Guptill.
Robertson, Jane & Pinkus, Sue. Let's All Draw Cats, Dogs & Other Animals. (Illus.). 144p. (gr. 3-7). 1991. pap. 9.95 (*0-8230-2705-8*, Watson-Guptill Bks) Watson-Guptill.

Savitt, Sam. Draw Horses with Sam Savitt. (Illus.). 96p. 1991. Repr. of 1981 ed. 20.95 (*0-939481-23-5*) Half Halt Pr.
Shackelford, Bud. Draw Animals: Learn From Former Disney Artist Bud Shackelford. Shackelford, Bud, illus. LC 92-96937. 64p. (Orig.). (gr. k-6). 1993. pap. 9.50 (*0-9634693-0-4*) B Shackelford.
Sperling, Anita. Funny Animals Tracing Fun. 1989. pap. 1.95 (*0-590-42197-2*) Scholastic Inc.
Wildsmith, Brian. Animal Shapes. Wildsmith, Brian, illus. (ps-3). 1981. 9.95 (*0-19-279733-6*) OUP.

ANIMAL PHOTOGRAPHY
see Photography of Animals

ANIMAL PHYSIOLOGY
see Zoology

ANIMAL PRODUCTS
see Dairy Products;
see names of special products, e.g. Hides and Skins; Ivory; etc

ANIMAL PSYCHOLOGY
see Animal Intelligence

ANIMALS
see also Color of Animals; Desert Animals; Domestic Animals; Fresh-Water Animals; Geographical Distribution of Animals and Plants; Marine Animals; Natural History; Pets; Zoological Gardens; Zoology also names of orders and classes of the animal kingdom (e.g. Birds; Insects; etc.); and names of animals, e.g. Dogs; Bears; etc.

Aaseng, Nathan. Prey Animals. Dornisch, Alcuin, illus. 48p. (gr. k-3). 1987. PLB 10.95 (*0-8225-1121-5*) Lerner Pubns.
Alborough, Jez. Beaky. Alborough, Jez, illus. 32p. (ps-3). 1990. 13.45 (*0-395-53348-1*) HM.
Alexander, R. McNeill. Animal Movement. Head, J. J., ed. Botzis, Ka, illus. LC 84-45834. 16p. (Orig.). (gr. 10 up). 1985. pap. text ed. 2.75 (*0-89278-364-8*, 45-9764) Carolina Biological.
All about Animals. (Illus.). (ps-7). 1987. 5.95 (*0-553-05413-9*) Bantam.
Altman, Joyce & Goldberg, Sue. Dear Bronx Zoo. Falk, Douglas, frwd. by. LC 89-28226. (Illus.). 144p. (gr. 3 up). 1990. SBE 14.95 (*0-02-700640-9*, Macmillan Child Bk) Macmillan Child Grp.
Anderson, Robert. Endangered Species: Understanding Words in Context. LC 91-29890. (Illus.). 32p. (gr. 4-7). 1991. PLB 10.95 (*0-89908-608-X*) Greenhaven.
Angel, Marie. Marie Angel's Exotic Alphabet: An Alphabet to Unfold in Words & Pictures. LC 92-8850. (Illus.). 1992. 12.95 (*0-8037-1247-2*) Dial Bks Young.
Animal. (Illus.). 20p. (gr. k-6). 1994. pap. 6.95 (*1-56458-481-X*) Dorling Kindersley.
Animal Antics. (Illus.). 32p. (Orig.). (gr. 1-3). 1994. pap. 4.95 (*1-56458-547-6*) Dorling Kindersley.
Animal Champions. 1991. PLB 14.95s.p. (*0-88682-409-5*) Creative Ed.
Animal Families, 4 vols. (Illus.). 32p. (gr. 4-6). 1991. Set. PLB 74.40 (*0-8368-0683-2*) Gareth Stevens Inc.
Animal Families, 12 vols. 48p. (gr. 4 up). PLB 223.20 (*0-8368-1095-3*) Gareth Stevens Inc.
Animal: Find the Difference. 1992. pap. 4.99 (*0-517-06726-9*) Random Hse Value.
Animal Wonders. 1991. PLB 14.95s.p. (*0-88682-407-9*) Creative Ed.
Animals. (Illus.). 10p. (ps-1). 1984. vinyl 4.95 (*0-8431-0993-9*) Price Stern.
Animals. 96p. (gr. 3-8). 1987. PLB 240.00 set (*0-685-18918-X*) Raintree Steck-V.
Animals. (gr. k-3). 1989. 3.95 (*0-7214-5215-9*) Ladybird Bks.
Animals. (Illus.). (ps). 3.50 (*0-7214-1096-0*) Ladybird Bks.
Animals. (gr. 1-4). 1991. pap. 3.95 (*0-7214-5323-6*) Ladybird Bks.
Animals & Where They Live. LC 91-58202. (Illus.). 64p. (gr. 3 up). 1992. 11.95 (*1-879431-99-8*); PLB 12.99 (*1-56458-000-8*) Dorling Kindersley.
Animals, Animals: Search & Color. 1989. 0.49 (*0-394-82449-0*) Random Bks Yng Read.
Animals, Birds & Fish. (Illus.). (ps-5). 3.50 (*0-7214-8003-9*); Ser. S50. wkbk. B 1.95 (*0-317-04633-0*) Ladybird Bks.
Animals, Birds, Bees, & Flowers. 24p. 1989. 5.99 (*0-517-68230-3*) Random Hse Value.
Animals in Action. 88p. (ps-3). 1989. 15.93 (*0-8094-4869-6*); lib. bdg. 21.27 (*0-8094-4870-X*) Time-Life.
Animals in Africa. (ps-k). 1992. 8.50 (*1-56021-112-1*) W J Fantasy.
Animals in North America. (ps-k). 1992. 8.50 (*1-56021-111-3*) W J Fantasy.
Animals of the World: A Guide to More Than 300 Mammals. LC 93-85517. (Illus.). 240p. 1994. pap. 5.95 (*1-56138-378-3*) Running Pr.
Arma, Tom, illus. Animal Time! 18p. (ps). 1994. bds. 4.95 (*0-448-40437-0*, G&D) Putnam Pub Group.
Armstrong, B. Animal Ecograms. (Illus.). (gr. 1 up). 1991. 20 picture postcards 7.95 (*0-88160-202-7*, LW296) Learning Wks.
Arnosky, Jim. Crinkleroot's Twenty-Five More Animals Every Child Should Know. Arnosky, Jim, illus. LC 93-7584. 32p. (ps-3). 1994. RSBE 12.95 (*0-02-705846-8*, Bradbury Pr) Macmillan Child Grp.
—Deer at the Brook. LC 84-12239. (Illus.). 32p. (ps-3). 1986. 13.95 (*0-688-04099-3*); PLB 13.88 (*0-688-04100-0*) Lothrop.
—I See Animals Hiding. LC 94-10422. 1995. write for info. (*0-590-46790-5*) Scholastic Inc.
Ask about Wild Animals. 64p. (gr. 4-5). 1987. PLB 11.95 (*0-8172-2880-2*) Raintree Steck-V.
Baby's First Book. 12p. (ps). 1978. 3.95 (*0-448-40861-9*, G&D) Putnam Pub Group.
Bailey, Jill & Seddon, Tony. Animal Movement. (Illus.). 64p. 1988. 15.95x (*0-8160-1656-9*) Facts on File.
—Animal Vision. (Illus.). 64p. 1988. 15.95x (*0-8160-1652-6*) Facts on File.
Bailey, Vanessa. Animal Colors. Stillwell, Stella, illus. 16p. (ps). 1991. 5.95 (*0-8120-6245-0*) Barron.
—Animal Opposites. (ps). 1991. 5.95 (*0-8120-6244-2*) Barron.
Bank Street College of Education Editors. Animals, Animals, Animals: At Home - In the Circus - At the Zoo. (Illus.). 64p. (ps-k). 1985. pap. 2.95 (*0-8120-3610-7*) Barron.
Bare, Colleen S. Who Comes to the Water Hole? Bare, Colleen S., photos by. LC 91-7915. (Illus.). 32p. (ps-3). 1991. 13.95 (*0-525-65073-3*, Cobblehill Bks) Dutton Child Bks.
Barr, Marilyn. Fearon's Animal Theme Activity Sheets. (ps-1). 1989. pap. 6.95 (*0-8224-0501-6*) Fearon Teach Aids.
Barrett, N. S. Polar Animals. FS Staff, ed. LC 87-50851. (Illus.). 32p. (gr. 1-6). 1988. PLB 11.90 (*0-531-10531-8*) Watts.
Barrett, Norman S. Animales Polares. LC 90-70882. (SPA., Illus.). 32p. (gr. k-4). 1990. PLB 11.90 (*0-531-07900-7*) Watts.
Baskin, Leonard. Leonard Baskin's Miniature Natural History. Baskin, Leonard, illus. 28p. (gr. k up). 1993. Repr. 14.95 (*0-88708-265-3*) Picture Bk Studio.
Beach, Stewart. Good Morning-Sun's Up. Sugita, Yataka, illus. LC 79-108178. 32p. (ps-3). 8.95 (*0-87592-021-7*) Scroll Pr.
Beattie, Laura C. Discover African Wildlife: Activity Book. Creative Company Staff, illus. 24p. (Orig.). (gr. 3-7). 1993. wkbk. 2.95 (*0-911239-38-3*) Carnegie Mus.
Bender, Lionel. Animals of the Night. 1990. pap. 4.95 (*0-531-17257-0*) Watts.
Benton, Michael. Dinosaur & Other Prehistoric Animal Factfinder. Channell, Jim & Maddison, Kevin, illus. LC 92-53119. 256p. (Orig.). (gr. 4-8). 1992. pap. 12.95 (*1-85697-802-8*, Kingfisher LKC) LKC.
Berger, Melvin. Animals & Their Babies: Student Edition. (Illus.). 16p. (ps-2). 1993. pap. text ed. 14.95 (*1-56784-030-2*) Newbridge Comms.
—Animals in Hiding: Student Edition. (Illus.). 16p. (ps-2). 1994. pap. text ed. 14.95 (*1-56784-035-3*) Newbridge Comms.
—Where Do Animals Live? (Illus.). 16p. (ps-2). 1994. pap. text ed. 14.95 (*1-56784-019-1*) Newbridge Comms.
Bernhard, Durga. Alphabeasts. LC 92-24980. (Illus.). 32p. (ps-3). 1993. reinforced bdg. 14.95 (*0-8234-0993-7*) Holiday.
Bishop, Dorothy S. The Lion & the Mouse. (FRE & ENG., Illus.). 72p. 1989. pap. 4.95 (*0-8442-1084-6*, Natl Textbk) NTC Pub Grp.
Bishop, Roma. Animals. (Illus.). 14p. (ps-k). 1991. pap. 2.95 casebound pop-up (*0-671-74833-5*, Little Simon) S&S Trade.
Blackmore, Michael. Your Book of Watching Wildlife. (gr. 7 up). 1972. 7.95 (*0-571-08347-1*) Transatl Arts.
Boney, Lesley, illus. Wild Animals. 48p. (gr. k-5). 1988. pap. 2.95 (*0-8431-2246-3*) Price Stern.
Borlenghi, Patricia. From Albatross to Zoo. (Illus.). (ps up). 1992. 14.95 (*0-590-45483-8*, 018, Scholastic Hardcover) Scholastic Inc.
Bowden, Joan. The Amazing Rhino. Cremins, Bob, illus. Moseley, Keith, contrib. by. LC 92-18891. (Illus.). (ps-3). 1993. 7.99 (*0-8037-1383-5*) Dial Bks Young.
Brent, Isabelle, illus. An Alphabet of Animals. LC 92-54652. 1993. 12.95 (*0-316-10852-9*) Little.
Bridwell, Norman. Clifford's Animal Sounds. (ps). 1991. 3.95 (*0-590-44734-3*) Scholastic Inc.
Brimner, Larry D. Unusual Friendships: Symbiosis in the Animal World. (Illus.). 64p. (gr. 5-8). 1993. pap. 6.95 (*0-531-15675-3*) Watts.
Broekel, Ray. Animal Observations. LC 89-25363. (Illus.). 48p. (gr. k-4). 1990. PLB 12.85 (*0-516-01182-0*); pap. 4.95 (*0-516-41182-9*) Childrens.
Brooks, Bruce. Making Sense: Animal Perception & Communication. LC 93-10474. 1993. 17.00 (*0-374-34742-5*) FS&G.
Brooks, F. Protecting Endangered Species. (Illus.). 24p. (gr. 2-5). 1991. lib. bdg. 11.96 (*0-88110-500-7*, Usborne); pap. 4.50 (*0-7460-0608-X*, Usborne) EDC.
Brown, Richard, illus. Muchas Palabras Sobre Animals. (SPA.). 32p. (ps-1). 1989. pap. 3.95 (*0-15-200531-5*) HarBrace.
—One Hundred Words about Animals. (ps-1). 1989. pap. 4.95 (*0-15-200554-4*, Voy B) HarBrace.
Bruce, Jill B. Austranimals. Wade, Jan, illus. 32p. (Orig.). (gr. k-4). 1994. 12.95 (*0-86417-569-8*, Pub. by Kangaroo Pr AT) Seven Hills Bk Dists.
Buck, Nola. Creepy Crawly Critters & Other Halloween Tongue Twisters. Truesdell, Sue, illus. LC 94-15405. 1995. 14.00 (*0-06-024808-4*); PLB 13.89 (*0-06-024809-2*) HarpC.
Buckman, Mary. Leap Frog. LC 89-63379. (Illus., Orig.). (gr. k-2). 1989. pap. text ed. 12.95 (*1-879414-05-8*) Mary Bee Creat.
Burgel, Paul H. Gorillas. (gr. 4-7). 1993. pap. 6.95 (*0-87614-612-4*) Carolrhoda Bks.
Burgess, Thornton W. Burgess Animal Book for Children. 28.95 (*0-8488-0716-2*) Amereon Ltd.
Burnie, David. Animals: How They Work. LC 93-43404. (Illus.). 48p. 1994. 14.95 (*0-8069-0742-8*) Sterling.
Burton, Jane. Animal Activities, 4 vols. Burton, Jane & Taylor, Kim, illus. 128p. (gr. 2-3). 1989. Set. PLB 69. 07 (*0-8368-0184-9*) Gareth Stevens Inc.
—Animals Keeping Clean. LC 88-43144. (Illus.). 24p. (Orig.). (ps-3). 1989. lib. bdg. 5.99 (*0-394-92261-1*) Random Bks Yng Read.
—Keeping Safe. Burton, Jane & Taylor, Kim, photos by. LC 89-11416. (Illus.). 32p. (gr. 2-3). 1989. PLB 17.27 (*0-8368-0186-5*) Gareth Stevens INc.
Burton, Jane, ed. & photos by Keeping Warm. LC 89-11411. (Illus.). 32p. (gr. 2-3). 1989. PLB 17.27 (*0-8368-0185-7*) Gareth Stevens Inc.
Burton, Maurice. Warm-Blooded Animals. (Illus.). 64p. (gr. 4-7). 1985. 15.95x (*0-8160-1059-5*) Facts on File.
Burton, Robert. Arctic. (Illus.). 24p. (gr. k-4). 1991. PLB 10.40 (*1-878137-16-6*) Newington.
—Desert. (Illus.). 24p. (gr. k-4). 1991. PLB 10.40 (*1-878137-17-4*) Newington.
Butterfield, Moira. Wild Animals. LC 92-53114. (Illus.). 48p. (Orig.). (gr. 3-8). 1992. pap. 5.95 (*1-85697-809-5*, Kingfisher LKC) LKC.
Caras, Roger. A World Full of Animals: The Roger Caras Story. LC 93-31009. 1994. 12.95 (*0-8118-0654-5*); pap. 6.95 (*0-8118-0682-0*) Chronicle Bks.
Carratello, John & Carratello, Patty. Hands on Science: Animals. Wright, Terry, illus. 32p. (gr. 2-5). 1988. wkbk. 5.95 (*1-55734-225-3*) Tchr Create Mat.
Carrie, Christopher. Playful Jungle Friends. (Illus.). 32p. (Orig.). (ps-k). 1990. 1.99 (*0-86696-238-7*) Binney & Smith.
Cartwright, Pauline. All Creatures. LC 90-10021. (Illus.). 16p. (gr. 1-4). 1990. PLB 14.64 (*0-8114-2695-5*) Raintree Steck-V.
Cassin, Sue. Fascinating Facts about Animals. 1990. 9.95 (*1-55782-329-4*, Pub. by Warner Juvenile Bks) Little.
Cavendish, Marshall. Wildlife of the World. LC 93-3581. (gr. 5 up). 1993. Set. 249.95 (*1-85435-592-9*); Vol. 1. write for info. (*1-85435-593-7*) Marshall Cavendish.
Cecotti, Loralie. Washington Wildlife. Hamer, Bonnie, illus. 24p. (Orig.). (gr. k-5). 1984. pap. text ed. 2.75 (*0-318-04105-7*) Coffee Break.
Chesney, Sandy. The Zapped Tadpole & More. 93p. (gr. 4 up). 1991. pap. 4.99 (*0-8163-1029-7*) Pacific Pr Pub Assn.
Chinery, Michael. All Kinds of Animals. LC 92-21677. (Illus.). 128p. (ps-3). 1993. 7.00 (*0-679-83697-7*); PLB 11.99 (*0-679-93697-1*) Random Bks Yng Read.
—Grassland Animals. Butler, John & McIntyre, Brian, illus. LC 91-53145. 40p. (Orig.). (gr. 2-5). 1992. pap. 4.99 (*0-679-82045-0*) Random Bks Yng Read.
—Rainforest Animals. Holmes, David & Robinson, Bernard, illus. LC 91-53143. 40p. (Orig.). (gr. 2-5). 1992. PLB 8.99 (*0-679-92047-1*); pap. 4.99 (*0-679-82047-7*) Random Bks Yng Read.
Civardi & Kilpatrick. How Animals Live. (gr. 4-6). 1981. (Usborne-Hayes); PLB 13.96 (*0-88110-081-1*); pap. 6.95 (*0-86020-196-1*) EDC.
Claridge, M. & Downswell, P. Animal Quizbook. (Illus.). 32p. (gr. 4 up). 1993. PLB 13.96 (*0-88110-536-8*, Usborne); pap. 6.95 (*0-7460-0720-5*, Usborne) EDC.
Coffen, Ron. K-Zoo News. 128p. 1992. pap. 8.95 (*0-8163-1086-6*) Pacific Pr Pub Assn.
Cold-Blooded Animals. LC 80-24150. (Illus.). 80p. (gr. k-6). 1986. pap. 199.00 per set (*0-8172-2603-6*); pap. 14.95 ea. Raintree Steck-V.
Collard, Sneed. Smart Survivors. LC 93-19650. (gr. 1-5). 1994. 9.95 (*1-55971-224-4*) NorthWord.
—Tough Terminators. LC 93-19627. (gr. 1-5). 1994. 9.95 (*1-55971-223-6*) NorthWord.
Collard, Sneed, III. Do They Scare You? Creepy Creatures. (Illus.). 32p. (ps-4). 1993. 14.95 (*0-88106-491-2*); PLB 15.88 (*0-88106-492-0*); pap. 6.95 (*0-88106-490-4*) Charlesbridge Pub.
Colonial Williamsburg Foundation Staff. Animals at Colonial Williamsburg. (Illus.). 8p. (ps). 1993. bds. 3.95 (*0-87935-092-X*) Williamsburg.
Colors, Shapes, Words, & Numbers. 24p. 1989. 5.99 (*0-517-68231-1*) Random Hse Value.
Compass Productions Staff. Awesome Animal Actions. Mirocha, Paul, illus. 10p. (gr. k-4). 1992. 5.95 (*0-694-00409-X*, Festival) HarpC Child Bks.
Conforth, Kellie. A Picture Book of Arctic Animals. Conforth, Kellie, illus. LC 90-44896. 24p. (gr. 1-4). 1991. lib. bdg. 9.59 (*0-8167-2144-0*); pap. text ed. 2.50 (*0-8167-2145-9*) Troll Assocs.
—A Picture Book of Australian Animals. Conforth, Kellie, illus. LC 91-18706. 24p. (gr. 1-4). 1992. PLB 9.59 (*0-8167-2470-9*); pap. 2.50 (*0-8167-2471-7*) Troll Assocs.
Conway, Lorraine. Animals. 64p. (gr. 5 up). 1980. 7.95 (*0-916456-68-4*, GA 177) Good Apple.
—Plants & Animals in Nature. Akins, Linda, illus. 64p. (gr. 5 up). 1986. wkbk. 7.95 (*0-86653-356-7*, GA 797) Good Apple.
Cook, David. Land Animals. Cook, David, illus. LC 84-12072. 32p. (gr. 3-7). 1985. bds. 5.95 (*0-517-55430-5*) Crown Bks Yng Read.
Cork. Wild Animals. (gr. 2-5). 1982. (Usborne-Hayes); PLB 11.96 (*0-88110-077-3*); pap. 3.95 (*0-86020-628-9*) EDC.
Cortright, Sandy. Zoo Animals. Carroll, Marilee, illus. 80p. (ps). 1990. pap. 6.95 (*0-8120-4436-3*) Barron.
Costa De Beauregard, Diane. Animals in Jeopardy. Bogard, Vicki, tr. from FRE. De Hugo, Pierre, illus. LC 90-50779. 38p. (gr. k-5). 1991. 5.95 (*0-944589-37-5*, 375) Young Discovery Lib.

Cousins, Lucy. Country Animals. Cousins, Lucy, illus. LC 90-35894. (ps). 1991. bds. 3.95 (*0-688-10070-8*, Tambourine Bks) Morrow.
—Garden Animals. Cousins, Lucy, illus. LC 90-36259. (ps). 1991. bds. 3.95 (*0-688-10072-4*, Tambourine Bks) Morrow.
Cresswall, Helen. The Weather Cat. rev. ed. Walker, Barbara, illus. 32p. (gr. k-2). 1990. Repr. of 1989 ed. PLB 10.95 (*1-878363-06-9*) Forest Hse.
Cunningham, Antonia. Rainforest Wildlife. (Illus.). 32p. (gr. 3-8). 1993. lib. bdg. 13.96 (*0-88110-640-2*, Usborne); pap. text ed. 6.95 (*0-7460-0940-2*, Usborne) EDC.
Cutts, David. I Can Read About Creatures of the Night. LC 78-68468. (Illus.). (gr. 2-5). 1979. pap. 2.50 (*0-89375-202-9*) Troll Assocs.
Dal Sasso, Cristiano. Animals: Origin & Evolution. Serini, Rocco, tr. from ITA. LC 94-2541. (Illus.). 48p. (gr. 6-8). 1994. PLB write for info. (*0-8114-3333-1*) Raintree Steck-V.
Davenport, Zoe. Animals. Davenport, Zoe, illus. 16p. (ps). 1995. 4.95 (*0-685-72232-5*) Ticknor & Flds Bks Yng Read.
—Animals. LC 94-20821. 1995. 4.95 (*0-395-71537-7*) Ticknor & Flds Bks Yng Read.
Davies, Gillian. Why Worms? rev. ed. Kramer, Robin, illus. 32p. (gr. k-2). 1990. Repr. of 1989 ed. PLB 10.95 (*1-878363-07-7*) Forest Hse.
De La Sota, Ann. Amazing Animals. (Illus.). 32p. (gr. 3 up). 1986. incl. hand held Decoder 5.95 (*0-88679-457-9*) Educ Insights.
Dennard, Deborah. Do Cats Have Nine Lives? The Strange Things People Say about Animals Around the House. Urbanovic, Jackie, illus. LC 92-10353. 1992. 19.95 (*0-87614-773-2*) Carolrhoda Bks.
—How Wise Is an Owl? The Strange Things People Say about Animals in the Woods. Neavill, Michelle, illus. LC 92-10354. 1992. 19.95 (*0-87614-721-X*) Carolrhoda Bks.
De Paola, Tomie. Fin M'Coul, the Giant of Knockmany Hill. LC 80-2254. (Illus.). 32p. (ps-3). 1981. reinforced bdg. 15.95 (*0-8234-0384-X*); pap. 5.95 (*0-8234-0385-8*) Holiday.
De Sairigne, Catherine. Animals in Winter. Matthews, Sarah, tr. from FRE. Mathieu, Agnes, illus. LC 87-34086. 38p. (gr. k-5). 1988. 5.95 (*0-944589-05-7*, 057) Young Discovery Lib.
Dikis, Eloise. The Twelve Powers of Animals. Wortman, Mary, ed. Ford, Phyllis, illus. 44p. (ps-5). 1989. comb bdg. 7.95 (*0-939339-06-4*) AFCOM Pub.
Donati, Annabelle. I Wonder If Sea Cows Give Milk & Other Neat Facts about Unusual Animals. (ps-3). 1993. pap. 4.95 (*0-307-11327-2*, Golden Pr) Western Pub.
—Wonder Which Snake Is the Longest & Other Neat Facts about Animal Records. (ps-3). 1993. pap. 4.95 (*0-307-11326-4*, Golden Pr) Western Pub.
Dorros, Arthur. Animal Tracks. 40p. 1991. 13.95 (*0-590-43367-9*, Scholastic Hardcover) Scholastic Inc.
Drew, David. Does a Duck Eat Honey? Fleming, Leanne, illus. LC 92-31917. 1993. 4.25 (*0-383-03563-5*) SRA Schl Grp.
—How Many Legs? Stewart, Chantal, illus. LC 92-34268. 1993. 4.25 (*0-383-03631-3*) SRA Schl Grp.
—Toenails. Fleming, Leanne, illus. LC 92-31135. 1993. 2.50 (*0-383-03661-5*) SRA Schl Grp.
Dreyer, Ellen. Wild Animals. Hall, Douglas & Dennison, Graham, illus. LC 90-11163. 96p. (gr. 2-5). 1991. PLB 14.89 (*0-8167-2242-0*); pap. text ed. 6.95 (*0-8167-2243-9*) Troll Assocs.
Dudley, Lynn. Farm Animals. 12p. (gr. 4-7). 1990. pap. 5.95 (*0-8167-2087-8*) Troll Assocs.
—Forest Animals. 12p. (gr. 4-7). 1990. pap. 5.95 (*0-8167-2084-3*) Troll Assocs.
Dunmire, Marj. Mountain Wildlife. Dunmire, Marj, illus. 48p. (Orig.). (gr. 2 up). 1986. pap. 3.95 (*0-942559-03-7*) Pegasus Graphics.
D'yley, Enid F. Animal Fables & Other Tales Retold: Africa in the New World. LC 87-73226. 40p. (Orig.). (gr. 1-7). 1989. 12.95 (*0-86543-075-6*); pap. 5.95 (*0-86543-076-4*) Africa World.
Earthbooks, Inc. Staff. National Wildlife Federation's Book of Endangered Species. Maestis, Ken, illus. 64p. (Orig.). (gr. 4-6). 1991. pap. 5.95 (*1-877731-17-X*) Earthbooks Inc.
Elliott, Tony. High Country Wildlife. Elliott, Tony, illus. LC 86-2218. 64p. (Orig.). (gr. 1-6). 1988. pap. 2.50 (*0-914565-20-6*, 20-6) Capstan Pubns.
Endangered Animals. 20p. (gr. k up). 1992. laminated, wipe clean surface 9.95 (*0-88679-906-6*) Educ Insights.
Endangered Young'uns. (ps-3). 1991. pap. 2.50 (*0-89954-505-X*) Antioch Pub Co.
Exotic Animals. (Illus.). 20p. (gr. k up). 1990. laminated, wipe clean surface 3.95 (*0-88679-588-5*) Educ Insights.
Explore the World of Amazing Animals. (gr. 3-6). 1991. write for info. (*0-307-15599-4*, Golden Pr) Western Pub.
Fagan, Elizabeth G. Rand McNally Children's Atlas of World Wildlife. Wills, Jan, illus. LC 93-503. 1993. write for info. (*0-528-83581-5*) Rand McNally.
Fain, Kathleen. Handsigns: An Animal Alphabet. LC 92-32103. 1993. 13.95 (*0-8118-0310-4*) Chronicle Bks.
Felder, Deborah G. The Kids' World Almanac of Animals & Pets. Lane, John, illus. 1990. 14.95 (*0-88687-556-0*); pap. 6.95 (*0-88687-555-2*) Wrld Almnc.
Feldman, Judy. The Alphabet in Nature. LC 90-22315. (Illus.). 32p. (ps-2). 1991. PLB 13.35 (*0-516-05101-6*) Childrens.
Few, Roger. Macmillan Animal Encyclopedia for Children. LC 91-3982. (Illus.). 120p. (gr. 2 up). 1991. 16.95 (*0-02-762425-0*, Macmillan Child Bks) Macmillan Child Grp.
Fichter, George S. Poisonous Animals. LC 91-3794. (Illus.). 64p. (gr. 5-8). 1991. PLB 12.90 (*0-531-20050-7*) Watts.
Field, Nancy & Machlas, Sally. Discovering Endangered Species. (Illus.). 40p. (Orig.). (gr. 3-6). 1990. pap. 4.95 (*0-941042-09-X*) Dog Eared Pubns.
Field, Nancy, et al. Nature Discovery Library. Machlis, Sally & Torvik, Sharon, illus. (gr. 3-6). 1990. Set. pap. text ed. 42.50 (*0-941042-15-4*) Dog Eared Pubns.
Fields, Sadie. Whose Coat? Hawcock, David, illus. 10p. (ps). 1993. pap. 4.95 (*0-671-79163-X*, Little Simon) S&S Trade.
—Whose Nose? Hawcock, David, illus. 10p. (ps). 1993. pap. 4.95 (*0-671-79162-1*, Little Simon) S&S Trade.
Fischer, Alexandra E. A to Z Animals Around the World. Paterosn, Bettina, illus. 32p. (ps-3). 1994. pap. 7.95 (*0-448-40474-5*, G&D) Putnam Pub Group.
Flegg, Jim. Animal Builders. (Illus.). 32p. (gr. 4-6). 1991. PLB 12.40 (*1-878137-05-0*) Newington.
—Animal Helpers. (Illus.). 32p. (gr. 4-6). 1991. PLB 12. 40 (*1-878137-06-9*) Newington.
—Animal Hunters. (Illus.). 32p. (gr. 4-6). 1991. PLB 12. 40 (*1-878137-04-2*) Newington.
—Animal Senses. (Illus.). 32p. (gr. 4-6). 1991. PLB 12.40 (*1-878137-21-2*) Newington.
Fleming, Denise. Count! Fleming, Denise, illus. LC 91-25686. 32p. (ps-1). 1992. 14.95 (*0-8050-1595-7*, Bks Young Read) H Holt & Co.
Florian, Douglas. At the Zoo. LC 89-77727. 32p. (ps up). 1992. 14.00 (*0-688-09628-X*); PLB 13.93 (*0-688-09629-8*) Greenwillow.
Forsyth, Adrian. Architecture of Animals. 72p. (gr. 8 up). 1989. 15.95 (*0-920656-16-1*, Pub. by Camden Hse CN); pap. 9.95 (*0-920656-08-0*, Pub. by Camden Hse CN) Firefly Bks Ltd.
Fortson, Walter. Amazing Animal Facts. Starver, Randy, et al, illus. LC 89-80109. 128p. (Orig.). (gr. 5). 1989. pap. 6.95 (*0-685-29400-5*) Fortson Pubs.
Fowler, Allan. The Biggest Animal Ever. LC 92-9410. (Illus.). 32p. (ps-2). 1993. pap. 3.95 (*0-516-46001-3*) Childrens.
Funny Faces. (Illus.). 32p. (Orig.). (gr. 1-3). 1994. pap. 4.95 (*1-56458-548-4*) Dorling Kindersley.
Gabb, Michael. Creatures Great & Small. LC 79-64386. (Illus.). 36p. (gr. 3-6). 1980. PLB 13.50 (*0-8225-1178-9*, First Ave Edns); pap. 4.95 (*0-8225-9540-0*, First Ave Edns) Lerner Pubns.
Gabriele. Wild Animals. 1986. pap. 1.95 (*0-911211-60-8*) Penny Lane Pubns.
Ganeri, A. Animal Facts. (Illus.). 48p. (gr. 3-7). 1988. PLB 12.96 (*0-88110-317-9*); pap. 5.95 (*0-86020-971-7*) EDC.
Ganeri, Anita. Animal Camouflage. Taylor, Kate, illus. 32p. (ps-1). 1991. 6.95 (*0-8120-6236-1*) Barron.
—Animal Movements. Taylor, Kate, illus. 32p. (ps-1). 1991. 6.95 (*0-8120-6238-8*) Barron.
—Animal Science. LC 92-25342. (Illus.). 48p. (gr. 5 up). 1993. text ed. 13.95 RSBE (*0-87518-575-4*, Dillon) Macmillan Child Grp.
—Animal Talk. Taylor, Kate, illus. 32p. (ps-1). 1991. 6.95 (*0-8120-6239-6*) Barron.
—Giant Book of Animal Worlds. Butler, John, illus. 14p. (gr. 2-5). 1992. 19.95 (*0-525-67369-5*, Lodestar Bks) Dutton Child Bks.
—I Wonder Why Camels Have Humps & Other Questions about Animals: And Other Questions about Animals. Holmes, Stephen & Kenyon, Tony, illus. LC 92-44260. 32p. (gr. k-3). 1993. 8.95 (*1-85697-873-7*, Kingfisher LKC) LKC.
George, Jean C. Animals Who Have Won Our Hearts. Merrill, Christine H., illus. LC 92-28326. 64p. (gr. 3-7). 1994. 15.00 (*0-06-021543-7*); PLB 14.89 (*0-06-021544-5*) HarpC Child Bks.
George, Michael. Rhinoceroses. (gr. 2-6). 1992. PLB 15. 95 (*0-89565-838-0*) Childs World.
Gerber, Carole. Weird, Wacky, & Totally True: Strange Tales about Animals. (Illus.). 32p. (gr. 2 up). 1992. pap. 2.99 (*0-87406-632-8*) Willowisp Pr.
Gise, Joanne. A Picture Book of Desert Animals. Pistolesi, Roseanna, illus. LC 90-40436. 24p. (gr. 1-4). 1991. lib. bdg. 9.59 (*0-8167-2148-3*); pap. text ed. 2.50 (*0-8167-2149-1*) Troll Assocs.
—A Picture Book of Wild Animals. Pistolesi, Roseanna, illus. LC 89-37334. 24p. (gr. 1-4). 1990. lib. bdg. 9.59 (*0-8167-1908-X*); pap. text ed. 2.50 (*0-8167-1909-8*) Troll Assocs.
Goin, Kenn, et al. Bugs to Bunnies: Hands-on Animal Science Activities for Young Children. (Illus.). 192p. (Orig.). (gr. k-2). 1989. pap. text ed. 14.95 (*0-943129-03-6*) Chatterbox Pr.
Gomboli, Marlo. Amazing Animals: The Fastest, Heaviest, Smallest, Largest, Fiercest, & Funniest. (Illus.). 48p. 1994. 9.98 (*1-56138-489-5*) Running Pr.
Goode, Diane, illus. The Little Books of Nursery Animals: The Little Book of Cats; The Little Book of Farm Friends; The Little Book of Mice; The Little Book of Pigs. (ps). 1993. Boxed set, 24p. ea. 11.99 (*0-525-45122-6*, DCB) Dutton Child Bks.
Greeley, Valerie, illus. Field Animals. LC 83-22507. 12p. (gr. k-2). 1984. bds. 3.95 (*0-911745-23-8*, Bedrick Blackie) P Bedrick Bks.
Greenaway, Theresa. Tongues & Tails. Savage, Ann, et al, illus. LC 94-16739. 1995. write for info. (*0-8114-8271-5*) Raintree Steck-V.
Greene, Carol. Caring for Our Animals. LC 91-9237. (Illus.). 32p. (gr. k-3). 1991. lib. bdg. 12.95 (*0-89490-352-7*) Enslow Pubs.
Greenway, Shirley. Can You See Me? LC 92-5215. (Illus.). 32p. (ps-2). 1992. PLB 11.00 (*0-8249-8575-3*, Ideals Child); pap. 3.95 (*0-8249-8560-5*) Hambleton-Hill.
—How Big Am I? Oxford Scientific Films, photos by. LC 93-18593. (Illus.). 32p. (ps-1). 1993. PLB 11.00 (*0-8249-8625-3*, Ideals Child); pap. 3.95 (*0-8249-8601-6*) Hambleton-Hill.
Groening, Matt & Groening, Maggie. Maggie Simpson's Book of Animals. LC 91-2866. (Illus.). 32p. (ps-1). 1991. PLB 11.89 (*0-06-020237-8*) HarpC Child Bks.
Gutfreund, Geraldine M. Vanishing Animal Neighbors. (Illus.). 64p. (gr. 5-8). 1993. pap. 6.95 (*0-531-15674-5*) Watts.
Hambly, Wilfrid D. Talking Animals. Porter, James A., illus. 1990. 7.95 (*0-87498-025-9*) Assoc Pubs DC.
Hanak, Mirko, illus. Animals We Love, Bks. 1 & 2. LC 72-89571. 32p. (gr. k-4). 1973. Bk. 1. 9.95 (*0-87592-005-5*) Bk. 2. 9.95 (*0-87592-006-3*) Scroll Pr.
Hanna, Jack. Petting Zoo. (ps). 1992. 10.00 (*0-385-41694-6*) Doubleday.
Harrison, Susan. AlphaZoo Christmas. Harrison, Susan, illus. LC 93-20351. 40p. (ps-2). 1993. 13.95 (*0-8249-8623-7*, Ideals Child); PLB 14.00 (*0-8249-8632-6*) Hambleton-Hill.
Harrison, Virginia & Losito, Linda. The World of Ants. LC 89-4466. (Illus.). 32p. (gr. 2-3). 1989. PLB 17.27 (*0-8368-0136-9*) Gareth Stevens Inc.
Hart, Trish. There Are No Polar Bears down There. Hart, Trish, illus. LC 92-31949. 1993. 3.75 (*0-383-03597-X*) SRA Schl Grp.
Hegeman, Kathryn T. The Animal Kingdom. Hegeman, Mark, et al, illus. (gr. k-3). 1982. tchr's. manual 10.00 (*0-89824-031-X*); wkbk. 4.99 (*0-89824-030-1*) Trillium Pr.
Herriot, James. James Herriot's Treasury for Children. 260p. 1992. 18.95 (*0-312-08512-5*) St Martin.
Hindley, Judy. Funny Walks. Ayliffe, Alex, illus. LC 93-28446. 32p. (ps-2). 1993. PLB 13.95 (*0-8167-3313-9*); pap. 3.95t (*0-8167-3314-7*) BrdgeWater.
Hirschi, Ron. Loon Lake. Cox, Daniel J., photos by. LC 90-34396. (Illus.). 32p. (ps-3). 1991. 13.95 (*0-525-65046-6*, Cobblehill Bks) Dutton Child Bks.
—Summer. Mangelsen, Thomas D., photos by. LC 90-19596. (Illus.). 32p. (ps-3). 1991. 13.95 (*0-525-65054-7*, Cobblehill Bks) Dutton Child Bks.
Hoffman, Mary. Wild Cat. LC 86-10007. (Illus.). 24p. (gr. k-5). 1986. PLB 9.95 (*0-8172-2399-1*); pap. 3.95 (*0-8114-6893-3*) Raintree Steck-V.
Hunt, Jonathan & Hunt, Lisa. One is a Mouse: A Counting Book. LC 94-25618. 1995. 13.00 (*0-02-745781-8*) Macmillan Child Grp.
Invisible Animals. LC 92-50790. (Illus.). 32p. (gr. 3 up). 1993. 5.95 (*1-56138-227-2*) Running Pr.
Irvine, Georgeanne. Protecting Endangered Species. (ps-6). 1993. pap. 5.95 (*0-671-79616-X*, S&S BFYR) S&S Trade.
Jacka, Martin. Waiting for Billy. LC 90-7957. (Illus.). 32p. (ps-2). 1991. 13.95 (*0-531-05933-2*); PLB 13.99 (*0-531-08533-3*) Orchard Bks Watts.
Jarrell, Randall. The Animal Family: (Familia Animal) (SPA.). 6.95 (*84-204-4105-8*) Santillana.
Jefferies, Lawrence. Amazing World of Animals. D'Adamo, Anthony, illus. LC 82-20061. 32p. (gr. 3-6). 1983. PLB 10.59 (*0-89375-898-1*); pap. text ed. 2.95 (*0-89375-899-X*) Troll Assocs.
Jennings, Terry. Small Garden Animals. LC 88-36216. (Illus.). 32p. (gr. 3-6). 1989. pap. 4.95 (*0-516-48442-7*) Childrens.
Johnson, Jinny. Poles & Tundra Wildlife. (Illus.). 24p. (gr. 4-7). 1993. 9.95 (*0-89577-538-7*, Dist. by Random) RD Assn.
—Rain Forest Wildlife. (Illus.). (gr. 2-7). 1993. 9.95 (*0-89577-537-9*, Dist. by Random) RD Assn.
Johnston, Ginny & Cutchins, Judy. Windows on Wildlife. LC 89-34487. (Illus.). 48p. (gr. 2 up). 1990. 13.95 (*0-688-07872-9*); PLB 13.88 (*0-688-07873-7*, Morrow Jr Bks) Morrow Jr Bks.
Jones, Frances. Nature's Deadly Creatures: A Pop-up Exploration. (Illus.). 16p. (gr. 1-5). 1992. 15.00 (*0-8037-1342-8*) Dial Bks Young.
Jones, Teri C. Little Book of Questions & Answers: Animals. Marsh, T. F., illus. 32p. (gr. k-3). 1992. PLB 10.95 (*1-56674-012-6*, HTS Bks) Forest Hse.
Jungle Animals. LC 91-16120. (Illus.). 24p. (ps-k). 1991. pap. 6.95 POB (*0-689-71519-6*, Aladdin) Macmillan Child Grp.
Jungle Animals. (Illus.). 96p. (ps-4). 1994. write for info. (*1-56458-794-0*) Dorling Kindersley.
Kalish, Muriel & Kalish, Lionel. Who Says Moo? A Beginner's Book of Rhymes. LC 92-10145. (Illus.). 12p. (ps-1). 1993. 7.95 (*0-590-44917-6*) Scholastic Inc.
Kallen, Stuart A. Amazing Animal Records. Wallner, Rosemary, ed. LC 91-73055. 1991. 12.94 (*1-56239-046-5*) Abdo & Dghtrs.
—If Animals Could Talk. Berg, Julie, ed. LC 93-18958. 1993. 14.96 (*1-56239-187-9*) Abdo & Dghtrs.
—Precious Creatures A-Z. Berg, Julie, ed. LC 93-19060. 1993. 14.96 (*1-56239-202-6*) Abdo & Dghtrs.
Kalman, Bobbie. Animal Worlds. (Illus.). 32p. (gr. 2-3). 1986. 15.95 (*0-86505-071-6*); pap. 7.95 (*0-86505-093-7*) Crabtree Pub Co.

—Arctic Animals. (Illus.). 56p. (gr. 3-4). 1988. 15.95 (*0-86505-145-3*); pap. 7.95 (*0-86505-155-0*) Crabtree Pub Co.

Kerrod, Robin. Animal Life. LC 93-4483. (Illus.). 64p. (gr. 5 up). 1993. PLB 15.95 (*1-85435-623-2*) Marshall Cavendish.

Kindersley, Dorling. Zoo Animals. LC 90-48751. (Illus.). 24p. (ps-k). 1991. pap. 7.95 POB (*0-689-71406-8*, Aladdin) Macmillan Child Grp.

Kitchen, Bert. Animal Alphabet. Kitchen, Bert, illus. LC 83-23929. 32p. (ps up). 1984. 13.95 (*0-8037-0117-9*) Dial Bks Young.

Koebner, Linda. For Kids Who Love Animals. 160p. (Orig.). 1993. pap. 4.50 (*0-425-13632-9*) Berkley Pub.

LaBonte, Gail. Leeches, Lampreys, & Other Cold-Blooded Bloodsuckers. LC 91-12620. (Illus.). 64p. (gr. 5-8). 1991. PLB 12.90 (*0-531-20027-2*) Watts.

Lacey, Elizabeth A. What's the Difference? A Guide to Some Familiar Animal Look-Alikes. Shetterly, Robert, illus. 80p. (gr. 4-7). 1993. 14.95 (*0-395-56182-5*, Clarion Bks) HM.

Lambert, David. Children's Animal Atlas. (gr. 4-7). 1993. pap. 10.95 (*1-56294-720-6*) Millbrook Pr.

Lantier-Sampon, Patricia. Flying Animals. LC 91-50346. (Illus.). 24p. (ps-2). 1991. PLB 15.93 (*0-8368-0540-2*) Gareth Stevens Inc.

Lauber, Patricia. What Big Teeth You Have! Weston, Martha, illus. LC 85-47902. 64p. (gr. 2-6). 1986. (Crowell Jr Bks); PLB 13.89 (*0-690-04507-7*, Crowell Jr Bks) HarpC Child Bks.

Lavies, Bianca. Tree Trunk Traffic. Lavies, Bianca, photos by. LC 88-30001. (Illus.). 32p. (ps-2). 1989. 14.95 (*0-525-44495-5*, DCB) Dutton Child Bks.

Legg, Gerald. Amazing Animals. Salariya, David, created by. LC 93-36703. (Illus.). 48p. (gr. 5-8). 1994. 13.95 (*0-531-14285-X*); pap. 8.95 (*0-531-15708-3*) Watts.

Litteral, Linda L. Bobos, Iguanas y Otros Animalejos - Boobies, Iguanas & Other Critters: Historia de la Naturaleza en los Galapagos - Nature's Story in the Galapagos. (SPA.). 72p. (gr. 4-9). 1993. 23.00 (*1-883966-02-7*) Am Kestrel Pr.

Little, Jocelyn. World's Strangest Animal Facts. Twinem, Nancy, illus. LC 93-47248. 96p. 1994. 12.95 (*0-8069-8520-8*) Sterling.

Little People Big Book about Animal Kingdom. 64p. (ps-1). 1990. write for info. (*0-8094-7487-5*); PLB write for info. (*0-8094-7488-3*) Time-Life.

Little People Big Book About Animals. 64p. (ps-1). 1989. write for info. (*0-8094-7450-6*); PLB write for info. (*0-8094-7451-4*) Time-Life.

Loveland Comm. Staff. Discover Animals. 1992. 4.49 (*1-55513-910-8*, Chariot Bks) Chariot Family.

Lovett, Sarah. Extremely Weird Endangered Species. (Illus.). 48p. (Orig.). (gr. 3 up). 1992. pap. 9.95 (*1-56261-042-2*) John Muir.

Mabie, Grace. A Picture Book of Animal Opposites. Kinnealy, Janice, illus. LC 91-33596. 24p. (gr. 1-4). 1992. text ed. 9.59 (*0-8167-2438-5*); 2.50 (*0-8167-2439-3*) Troll Assocs.

—A Picture Book of Night-Time Animals. Kinnealy, Janice, illus. LC 91-33597. 24p. (gr. 1-4). 1992. PLB 9.59 (*0-8167-2432-6*); pap. text ed. 2.50 (*0-8167-2433-4*) Troll Assocs.

MacCarthy, Patricia. Animals Galore. 1989. 11.95 (*0-8037-0721-5*) Dial Bks Young.

McCay, William. Animals in Danger: A Pop-up Book. Mosley, Keith, illus. 12p. (gr. 1-7). 1990. pap. 12.95 (*0-689-71408-4*, Aladdin) Macmillan Child Grp.

McClung, Robert M. Gorilla. Brady, Irene, illus. LC 84-718. 96p. (gr. 3-7). 1984. 11.00 (*0-688-03875-1*) Morrow Jr Bks.

McDonnell, Janet. Animal Builders. LC 88-36641. (Illus.). 48p. (gr. 2-6). 1989. PLB 14.95 (*0-89565-511-X*) Childs World.

Machines, Cars, Boats, & Airplanes. 224p. (ps-1). 1989. 5.99 (*0-517-68232-X*) Random Hse Value.

Machotka, Hana. Breathtaking Noses. Machotka, Hana, photos by. LC 91-12252. (Illus.). 32p. (gr. k up). 1992. 15.00 (*0-688-09526-7*); PLB 14.93 (*0-688-09527-5*) Morrow Jr Bks.

—Outstanding Outsides. LC 92-19517. (Illus.). 32p. (gr. k up). 1993. 15.00 (*0-688-11752-X*); PLB 14.96 (*0-688-11753-8*) Morrow Jr Bks.

McKean, Barb. Wild Animals. Rowden, Rick & Winik, J. T., illus. 32p. (gr. 3-7). 1985. pap. 3.50 (*0-88625-117-6*) Durkin Hayes Pub.

McKowen, K. D. Wildlife Activity & Coloring Book. rev. ed. McKowen, K. D., illus. 32p. (gr. 2-6). 1987. workbook 1.50 (*0-913635-02-2*) Aspen Prods.

McMillan, Bruce. The Baby Zoo. 32p. 1992. 13.95 (*0-590-44634-7*, Scholastic Hardcover) Scholastic Inc.

Mcphail, David. David Mcphail's Animals A to Z. 1989. pap. 2.50 (*0-590-40347-8*) Scholastic Inc.

Mangelsen, Thomas D. A Time for Singing. LC 93-36772. (Illus.). 32p. (ps-3). 1994. 13.99 (*0-525-65096-2*, Cobblehill Bks) Dutton Child Bks.

Markham-David, Sally. It Takes All Kinds. Ruth, Trevor, illus. LC 93-21246. 1994. 4.25 (*0-383-03753-0*) SRA Schl Grp.

—Mouths & Noses. Ruth, Trevor, illus. LC 93-29008. 1994. 4.25 (*0-383-03764-6*) SRA Schl Grp.

—The Secrets of a Garden. Russell-Arnot, Elizabeth, illus. LC 93-29003. 1994. 4.25 (*0-383-03773-5*) SRA Schl Grp.

Marshall, James. What's the Matter with Carruthers? Marshall, James, illus. LC 72-75607. 32p. (gr. k-3). 1972. 16.95 (*0-395-13895-7*) HM.

Mason, George F. Animal Tracks. LC 87-31124. (Illus.). 95p. (gr. 4-11). 1988. Repr. of 1943 ed. lib. bdg. 14.50 (*0-208-02213-9*, Linnet) Shoe String.

Maynard, Christopher. Amazing Animal Facts. (Illus.). (gr. 1-5). 1993. 18.00 (*0-679-85085-6*) Knopf Bks Yng Read.

—Jungle Animals. LC 92-32845. 32p. (gr. 1-4). 1993. 3.95 (*1-85697-896-6*, Kingfisher LKC) LKC.

Maynard, Thane. Animal Olympians. LC 93-30769. (Illus.). (gr. 5-7). 1994. PLB 15.90 (*0-531-11159-8*); pap. 9.95 (*0-531-15715-6*) Watts.

—A Rhino Comes to America. (Illus.). 40p. (gr. 4-8). 1993. 15.95 (*0-531-15258-8*); PLB 15.90 (*0-531-11173-3*) Watts.

Mecklenberg, Jan. Alphabet Animals. Mecklenberg, Jan, illus. LC 93-35479. 1994. 4.99 (*0-7852-8218-1*) Nelson.

—Counting God's Creatures. Mecklenberg, Jan, illus. LC 93-36019. 1994. 4.99 (*0-7852-8217-3*) Nelson.

Merriam, Eve. Where Is Everybody? DeGroat, Diane, illus. LC 88-19800. (ps-1). 1992. pap. 14.95 jacketed (*0-671-64964-7*, S&S BFYR); pap. 4.95 (*0-671-77821-8*, S&S BFYR) S&S Trade.

Miller, J. P., illus. The Cow Says Moo. (ps). 1979. 3.50 (*0-394-84131-X*) Random Bks Yng Read.

Miller, Jane. Farm Noises. (Illus.). 24p. (ps-4). 1992. pap. 5.00 (*0-671-75976-0*, S&S BFYR) S&S Trade.

Mollel, Tololwa M. Rhinos for Lunch & Elephants for Supper! Spurll, Barbara, illus. 32p. (ps-3). 1992. 15.95 (*0-395-60734-5*, Clarion Bks) HM.

Moncure, Jane B. Kinds of Animals: Flyers, Leapers, Crawlers, Creepers. Hohag, Linda, illus. LC 89-71172. 32p. (ps-2). 1990. PLB 14.95 (*0-89565-567-5*) Childs World.

Moore, Jo E. Endangered Species. (Illus.). 48p. 1992. pap. 5.95 (*1-55799-217-7*) Evan-Moor Corp.

Morris, Dean. Animals That Burrow. rev. ed. LC 87-16694. (Illus.). 48p. (gr. 2-6). 1987. PLB 10.95 (*0-8172-3201-X*) Raintree Steck-V.

—Animals That Live in Shells. rev. ed. LC 87-20556. (Illus.). 48p. (gr. 2-6). 1987. PLB 10.95 (*0-8172-3202-8*) Raintree Steck-V.

—Endangered Animals. (ps-3). 1990. pap. 4.95 (*0-8114-8220-0*) Raintree Steck-V.

Morris, Desmond. The World of Animals. Barrett, Peter, illus. 128p. 1993. 22.50 (*0-670-85184-1*) Viking Child Bks.

Morris, Neil. Do Animals Take Baths? Questions Kids Ask about Animals. Goffe, Toni, illus. LC 94-14119. 1994. write for info. (*0-89577-610-3*, Readers Digest Kids) RD Assn.

Morris, Ting & Morris, Neil. Animals. LC 93-20415. (Illus.). 32p. (gr. 2-4). 1993. PLB 12.40 (*0-531-14268-X*) Watts.

Morrison, Rob & Morrison, James. Monsters! Just Imagine. Crossett, Warren, illus. LC 93-26927. 1994. 4.25 (*0-383-03763-8*) SRA Schl Grp.

Most, Bernard. Catbirds & Dogfish. LC 94-17839. 1995. write for info. (*0-15-292844-8*) HarBrace.

Mullins, Patricia. Dinosaur Encore. Mullins, Patricia, illus. LC 92-19848. 32p. (ps-2). 1993. 15.00 (*0-06-021069-9*) HarpC Child Bks.

—V for Vanishing: An Alphabet of Endangered Animals. Mullins, Patricia, illus. LC 93-8181. 32p. (ps-2). 1994. 15.00 (*0-06-023556-X*); PLB 14.89 (*0-06-023557-8*) HarpC Child Bks.

Murray, Francis. World's Wildest Animal Jokes. LC 91-47701. (Illus.). 96p. (gr. 3-8). 1992. 12.95 (*0-8069-8538-0*) Sterling.

Myers, Jack. Can Birds Get Lost? And Other Questions about Animals. LC 90-85911. (Illus.). 64p. (gr. 1-5). 1991. 12.95 (*1-878093-32-0*) Boyds Mills Pr.

—Can Birds Get Lost? And Other Questions about Animals. (Illus.). 64p. (gr. 1-7). 1994. 7.95 (*1-56397-401-0*) Boyds Mills Pr.

Nash, Bartleby. Mother Nature's Greatest Hits: The Top 40 Wonders of the Animal World. (Illus.). 144p. (Orig.). 1991. pap. 5.95 (*0-9626072-7-4*) Living Planet Pr.

National Geographic Staff. At the Zoo. (ps-3). 1993. 16.00 (*0-87044-872-2*) Natl Geog.

National Wildlife Federation Staff. Endangered Species. (gr. k-8). 1991. pap. 7.95 (*0-945051-37-9*, 75033) Natl Wildlife.

Nayer, Judy. Jungle Life. Goldberg, Grace, illus. 10p. (ps-2). 1992. bds. 6.95 (*1-56293-221-7*) McClanahan Bk.

—Night Animals. Goldberg, Grace, illus. 10p. (ps-2). 1992. bds. 6.95 (*1-56293-223-3*) McClanahan Bk.

Neilsen, Shelly. I Love Animals. Berg, Julie, ed. LC 93-18955. 1993. 14.96 (*1-56239-191-7*) Abdo & Dghtrs.

Now You Know About: Animals, 5 bks. (ps-3). incl. cassettes 99.00 (*0-87827-090-6*) Ency Brit Ed.

On the Farm, a Book about Animals. (gr. 3 up). 1992. pap. 2.99 (*0-517-03595-2*) Random Hse Value.

On the Move. (Illus.). 48p. (gr. 3-4). 1992. PLB 22.80 (*0-8114-3156-8*) Raintree Steck-V.

Orangutans. 1991. PLB 14.95 (*0-88682-412-5*) Creative Ed.

Palazzo, Tony. The Biggest & the Littlest Animals. Palazzo, Tony, illus. LC 77-112374. 40p. (gr. k-3). 1973. PLB 13.95 (*0-87460-225-4*) Lion Bks.

Pallotta, Jerry. The Extinct Alphabet Book. Masiello, Ralph, illus. LC 93-1512. 1993. 14.95 (*0-88106-471-8*); PLB 15.88 (*0-88106-686-9*); pap. 6.95 (*0-88106-470-X*) Charlesbridge Pub.

Palmer, Glenda. Two Enormous Elephants: God's Wonderful World of Numbers. LC 92-34714. (Illus.). 1993. pap. 4.99 (*0-7814-0709-5*, Chariot Bks) Chariot Family.

Parker, Marjorie H. Jellyfish Can't Swim, & Other Secrets from the Animal World. LC 91-3236. (gr. 4-7). 1991. pap. 4.99 (*1-55513-393-2*, Chariot Bks) Chariot Family.

Parker, Steve. Alarming Animals. Savage, Ann, illus. LC 93-6651. 38p. (gr. 3-6). 1993. PLB 19.97 (*0-8114-0658-X*) Raintree Steck-V.

—Animals Can Think? LC 94-19405. (gr. k up). 1995. write for info. (*0-8114-3882-1*) Raintree Steck V.

—Cunning Carnivores. Savage, Ann, illus. LC 93-27256. 1993. 19.97 (*0-8114-2347-6*) Raintree Steck-V.

Parr, John. Baby Animals. Parr, John, illus. LC 79-62943. (ps). 1979. 3.50 (*0-394-84244-8*) Random Bks Yng Read.

Parsons, Alexandra. Amazing Poisonous Animals. Young, Jerry, photos by. LC 90-31883. 32p. (Orig.). (gr. 1-5). 1990. lib. bdg. 9.99 (*0-679-90699-1*); pap. 7.99 (*0-679-80699-7*) Knopf Bks Yng Read.

Patent, Dorothy H. How Smart Are Animals? 189p. (gr. 7 up). 1990. 17.95 (*0-15-236770-5*) HarBrace.

—What Good Is a Tail? Munoz, William, photos by. LC 92-45639. (Illus.). 32p. (gr. 1-5). 1994. 13.99 (*0-525-65148-9*, Cobblehill Bks) Dutton Child Bks.

Paterson, Bettina. My First Animals. Paterson, Bettina, illus. LC 89-17275. 32p. (ps-k). 1990. (Crowell Jr Bks); (Crowell Jr Bks) HarpC Child Bks.

—My First Wild Animals. Paterson, Bettina, illus. LC 89-17305. 32p. (ps-k). 1991. (Crowell Jr Bks); (Crowell Jr Bks) HarpC Child Bks.

Pearce, Q. L. Armadillos & Other Unusual Animals. Steltenpohl, Jane, ed. Fraser, Mary A., illus. 64p. (gr. 4-6). 1989. lib. bdg. 12.98 (*0-671-68528-7*, J Messner); pap. 5.95 (*0-671-68645-3*) S&S Trade.

—Giants of the Land. Bonforte, Lisa, illus. 48p. (gr. 3-7). 1993. pap. 5.95 (*1-56565-041-7*) Lowell Hse.

Peet, Bill. The Ant & the Elephant. Peet, Bill, illus. LC 74-179918. 48p. (gr. k-3). 1980. 13.95 (*0-395-16963-1*); pap. 5.95 (*0-395-29205-0*) HM.

Pelham, David. A Is for Animals. (ps). 1991. pap. 15.95 casebound, pop-up (*0-671-72495-9*, S&S BFYR) S&S Trade.

Penguins. 32p. (ps-1). 1986. pap. 1.25 (*0-8431-1524-6*) Price Stern.

Penny, Malcolm. Rhinos. LC 90-21968. (Illus.). 32p. (gr. k-4). 1991. 12.40 (*0-531-18396-3*, Pub. by Bookwright Pr) Watts.

Perenyi, Constance. Growing Wild: Inviting Wildlife into Your Yard. Perenyi, Constance, illus. 40p. (gr. 1-3). 1991. 14.95 (*0-941831-60-4*); pap. 9.95 (*0-941831-63-9*) Beyond Words Pub.

Peters, David. Giants of Land, Sea & Air - Past & Present: A Sierra Club Book Series. Peters, David, illus. LC 86-2719. 64p. (gr. 3 up). 1986. PLB 15.99 (*0-394-97805-6*) Knopf Bks Yng Read.

Petersen-Fleming, Judy & Fleming, Bill. Kitten Care & Critters, Too! Reingold-Reiss, Debra, photos by. LC 93-24200. (Illus.). 40p. 1994. 15.00 (*0-688-12563-8*, Tambourine Bks); PLB 14.93 (*0-688-12564-6*, Tambourine Bks) Morrow.

—Puppy Care & Critters, Too! Ringold-Reiss, Debra, photos by. LC 93-23129. (Illus.). 40p. 1993. 15.00 (*0-688-12565-4*, Tambourine Bks); PLB 14.93 (*0-688-12566-2*, Tambourine Bks) Morrow.

Phillips, Gina. First Facts about Wild Animals. Persico, F. S., illus. 24p. (Orig.). 1991. pap. 2.50 (*1-56156-038-3*) Kidsbks.

—First Facts about Wild Animals. Persico, F. S., illus. 24p. 1991. write for info. (*1-56156-061-8*) Kidsbks.

The Picture-Perfect Planet. LC 92-20831. 1992. write for info. (*0-8094-9319-5*); PLB write for info. (*0-8094-9320-9*) Time-Life.

Poisonous Creatures. (Illus.). 32p. 1994. incl. chart 5.95 (*1-56138-469-0*) Running Pr.

Pollock, Steve. Wildlife Safari. (Illus.). 48p. (gr. 7-9). 1992. 13.95 (*0-563-34354-0*, BBC-Parkwest); pap. 6.95 (*0-563-34162-9*, BBC-Parkwest) Parkwest Pubns.

Porter, Keith. Looking at Animals. (Illus.). 48p. (gr. 1-4). 1987. 12.95x (*0-8160-1784-0*) Facts on File.

Powzyk, Joyce. Madagascar Journey. LC 94-21053. (gr. 9-12). 1995. write for info. (*0-688-09487-2*); pap. write for info. (*0-688-13964-7*) Lothrop.

Presnall, Judith J. Animals That Glow. (Illus.). 64p. (gr. 5-8). 1993. pap. 5.95 (*0-531-15672-9*) Watts.

Propper, et al. World Animal Library, 17 bks, Reading Level 3-4. (Illus.). 476p. (gr. 2-5). 1983. Set. PLB 283.39 (*0-86592-850-9*); PLB 212.50s.p. (*0-685-58814-9*) Rourke Corp.

Purcell, John W. African Animals. LC 82-9541. (Illus.). 48p. (gr. k-4). 1982. 12.85 (*0-516-01665-2*); pap. 4.95 (*0-516-41665-0*) Childrens.

Quinn, Kaye. Zoo Animals. (Illus.). 40p. (Orig.). (gr. k-4). 1991. pap. 2.95 (*0-8431-2720-1*) Price Stern.

Raintree Publishers Staff. Animals. LC 87-28712. (Illus.). 64p. (Orig.). (gr. 5-9). 1988. PLB 11.95 (*0-8172-3083-1*) Raintree Steck-V.

—Animals at the Water's Edge. LC 87-20687. (Illus.). 48p. (gr. k-6). 1987. PLB 10.95 (*0-8172-3115-3*) Raintree Steck-V.

—Animals in Cities & Parks. LC 87-20684. (gr. k-6). 1987. 10.95 (*0-8172-3116-1*) Raintree Steck-V.

—Animals in Houses & Gardens. LC 87-20775. (Illus.). (gr. k-6). 1987. PLB 10.95 (*0-8172-3114-5*) Raintree Steck-V.

—Animals in Rivers & Ponds. LC 87-20685. (Illus.). 48p. (gr. k-6). 1987. PLB 10.95 (*0-8172-3113-7*) Raintree Steck-V.

—Animals in the Forest. LC 87-20689. (Illus.). 48p. (gr. k-6). 1987. PLB 10.95 (*0-8172-3111-0*) Raintree Steck-V.

—Animals in the Mountains. LC 87-20688. (Illus.). 48p. (gr. k-6). 1987. PLB 10.95 (*0-8172-3112-9*) Raintree Steck-V.

Rauzon, Mark. Horns, Antlers, Fangs, & Tusks. LC 90-49726. (ps-3). 1993. 13.00 (*0-688-10230-1*); PLB 12.93 (*0-688-10231-X*) Lothrop.

—Skin, Scales, Feathers, & Fur. LC 90-409858. (ps-3). 1993. 13.00 (*0-688-10232-8*); PLB 12.93 (*0-688-10233-6*) Lothrop.

Reilly, Pauline. Emu That Walks Toward Rain. 2nd ed. Rolland, Will, illus. 32p. (gr. 2-6). 1994. pap. 6.95 (*0-86417-571-X*, Pub. by Kangaroo Pr AT) Seven Hills Bk Dists.

—Kookaburra. 2nd ed. Rolland, Will, illus. 32p. (gr. 2-6). 1994. pap. 6.95 (*0-86417-528-0*, Pub. by Kangaroo Pr AT) Seven Hills Bk Dists.

—Sugar Glider. Russell, Gayle, illus. 32p. (gr. 2-6). 1994. pap. 6.95 (*0-86417-590-6*, Pub. by Kangaroo Pr AT) Seven Hills Bk Dists.

Rhinos. 1991. PLB 14.95 (*0-88682-333-1*) Creative Ed.

Riha, Susanne. Animals in Winter. (Illus.). 32p. (gr. 1-5). 1989. PLB 19.95 (*0-87614-355-9*) Carolrhoda Bks.

River, Chatham. Animal Fun: A-Z Activity Books. 32p. 1989. 3.50 (*0-517-68796-8*) Random Hse Value.

Roe, Richard. Baby Animals. Roe, Richard, illus. LC 85-2223. 24p. (ps-1). 1985. 3.95 (*0-394-86956-7*) Random Bks Yng Read.

Rosenbaum, Cindy, et al. For the Love of Animals: Six Delightful Songs & a Story about How the Children Save the Animals. Feiza, Anne, illus. 24p. (Orig.). (ps-4). 1992. pap. text ed. 12.95 incl. audio tape (*1-881567-00-1*) Happy Kids Prods.

Ruffault, Charlotte. Animals Underground. Matthews, Sarah, tr. from FRE. Underhill, Graham, illus. LC 87-34616. 38p. (gr. k-5). 1988. 5.95 (*0-944589-03-0*, 030) Young Discovery Lib.

Ryden, Hope. The Bobcat. (Illus.). 64p. 1992. pap. 9.95 (*1-55821-143-8*) Lyons & Burford.

—Wild Animals of Africa ABC. LC 89-2529. (Illus.). 32p. (ps-3). 1989. 12.95 (*0-525-67290-7*, Lodestar Bks) Dutton Child Bks.

Samuelson, Mary L. & Schlaepfer, Gloria. The African Rhinoceros. LC 91-40953. (Illus.). 60p. (gr. 4 up). 1992. text ed. 13.95 RSBE (*0-87518-505-3*, Dillon) Macmillan Child Grp.

Sanger, David. North America's ENDANGERED Species. Lynch, Don, ed. Mathewson, Mel, illus. 97p. (Orig.). (ps-8). 1992. pap. text ed. 4.00 (*0-913205-17-6*); special price 2.40 (*0-685-69239-6*) Grace Dangberg.

Sargent, William. Night Reef: Dusk to Dawn on a Coral Reef. (Illus.). 40p. (gr. 5-8). 1991. 14.95 (*0-531-15219-7*); PLB 14.90 (*0-531-11073-7*) Watts.

Schwartz, L. Trivia Trackdown - Animals & Science. (gr. 4-6). 1985. 3.95 (*0-88160-119-5*, LW 252) Learning Wks.

Selsam, Millicent E. & Hunt, Joyce. A First Look at Animals That Eat Other Animals. Springer, Harriet, illus. 64p. (gr. 5 up). 1990. 11.95 (*0-8027-6895-4*); PLB 12.85 (*0-8027-6896-2*) Walker & Co.

Serventy, Vincent. Kookaburra. LC 84-17969. (Illus.). 24p. (gr. k-5). 1985. PLB 9.95 (*0-8172-2417-3*); pap. 3.95 (*0-8114-6880-1*) Raintree Steck-V.

Settel, Joanne & Baggett, Nancy. Why Do Cats' Eyes Glow in the Dark? (And Other Questions Kids Ask about Animals) Tunney, Linda, illus. LC 87-13708. 112p. (gr. 3-7). 1988. SBE 13.95 (*0-689-31267-9*, Atheneum Child Bk) Macmillan Child Grp.

Sherrow, Victoria. Endangered Mammals. 1995. PLB write for info. (*0-8050-3253-3*); pap. write for info. (*0-8050-3252-5*) H Holt & Co.

Shirley, Gayle C. Montana Wildlife: A Children's Field Guide to the State's Most Remarkable Animals. Allnock, Sandy, illus. 48p. (Orig.). 1993. pap. 6.95 (*1-56044-154-2*) Falcon Pr MT.

Simon, Seymour. Animal Fact: Animal Fable. De Groat, Diane, illus. LC 78-14866. (gr. k-3). 1986. pap. 7.00 (*0-517-53794-X*) Crown Bks Yng Read.

—Little Giants. Carroll, Pamela, illus. LC 82-14139. 48p. (gr. k-5). 1983. PLB 14.88 (*0-688-01731-2*) Morrow Jr Bks.

—One Hundred & One Questions & Answers about Dangerous Animals. Friedman, Ellen, illus. LC 84-42975. 96p. (gr. 3-7). 1985. SBE 14.95 (*0-02-782710-0*, Macmillan Child Bk) Macmillan Child Grp.

Sinclair, Sandra. Extraordinary Eyes: How Animals See the World. LC 89-39618. (Illus.). 48p. (gr. 4-7). 1992. 15.00 (*0-8037-0803-3*); PLB 14.89 (*0-8037-0806-8*) Dial Bks Young.

Slier, Debby. Little Animals. 12p. (ps). 1989. 2.95 (*1-56288-147-7*) Checkerboard.

Small Animals. LC 91-60533. (Illus.). 24p. (ps-3). 1991. 8.95 (*1-879431-09-2*) Dorling Kindersley.

Smalley, Guy, illus. My Very Own Book of Mother Goose Animals. 24p. (ps-2). 1989. 9.95 (*0-929793-01-3*) Camex Bks Inc.

Smith, William J. Birds & Beasts. Hnizdovsky, Jacques, illus. (gr. k up). 1990. 18.95 (*0-87923-865-8*) Godine.

Sowler, Sandie. Amazing Animal Disguises. Young, Jerry, photos by. LC 91-53141. (Illus.). 32p. (Orig.). (gr. 1-5). 1992. PLB 9.99 (*0-679-92768-9*); pap. 6.95 (*0-679-82768-4*) Knopf Bks Yng Read.

—Amazing Armored Animals. Young, Jerry, photos by. LC 91-53140. (Illus.). 32p. (Orig.). (gr. 1-5). 1992. PLB 9.99 (*0-679-92767-0*); pap. 6.95 (*0-679-82767-6*) Knopf Bks Yng Read.

Spectacular Animals & Fascinating Animals. (Illus.). (gr. 1-7). 1990. 15.95 (*0-87449-817-1*) Fascinating Animals. 15.95 (*0-87449-818-X*) Modern Pub NYC.

Spencer, Eve. Animal Babies One Two Three. David, Susan, illus. 24p. (ps-2). 1990. PLB 17.10 (*0-8172-3581-7*); pap. 4.95 (*0-8114-6738-4*) Raintree Steck-V.

Spinelli, Eileen. Zoo Animals. (Illus.). 64p. (gr. k-4). 1992. PLB 13.75 (*1-878363-91-3*, HTS Bks) Forest Hse.

Spizzirri Publishing Co. Staff & Spizzirri, Linda. Animal Family Calendar: An Educational Coloring Book. (Illus.). 32p. (gr. k-5). 1983. pap. 2.25 (*0-86545-048-X*) Spizzirri.

—Animal Giants: An Educational Coloring Book. (Illus.). 32p. (gr. k-5). 1985. pap. 1.75 (*0-86545-066-8*) Spizzirri.

Stacy, Tom. The World of Animals. Robson, Eric, illus. LC 90-12978. 40p. (gr. 4-6). 1991. PLB 12.40 (*0-531-19103-6*) Watts.

—The World of Animals. Robson, Eric, illus. LC 90-42619. 40p. (Orig.). (gr. 2-5). 1991. pap. 4.99 (*0-679-80864-7*) Random Bks Yng Read.

Staple, Michele & Gamlin, Linda. The Random House Book of One Thousand One Questions & Answers about Animals. LC 90-30716. (Illus.). 160p. (Orig.). (gr. 3-7). 1990. lib. bdg. 13.00 (*0-679-80731-4*); pap. 12.99 (*0-679-90731-9*) Random Bks Yng Read.

Starbuck, Marnie. Meet the Gladimals a New Crew of Critters. (Illus.). 16p. 1990. 0.75 (*1-56456-200-X*, 470) W Gladden Found.

Stern, Charles. My Big Book of Animals. 1991. 5.99 (*0-517-05182-6*) Random Hse Value.

Stodart, Eleanor. Australian Echidna. LC 90-33538. (Illus.). 40p. (gr. 3-7). 1991. 14.45 (*0-395-55992-8*) HM.

Stone, L. Spanish Language Books, Set 2: Animales Norteamericanos (North American Animals, 6 bks. 1991. 53.70s.p. (*0-86592-786-3*) Rourke Enter.

Stone, Lynn. African Animals Discovery Library, 6 bks. (Illus.). 144p. (gr. k-5). 1990. Set. lib. bdg. 71.64 (*0-86593-047-3*); Set. lib. bdg. 53.70s.p. (*0-685-36343-0*) Rourke Corp.

—Australian Animals Discovery Library, 6 bks. (Illus.). 144p. (gr. k-5). 1990. Set. lib. bdg. 71.64 (*0-86593-054-6*); Set. lib. bdg. 53.70s.p. (*0-685-36368-6*) Rourke Corp.

—North American Animal Discovery Library, 6 bks. (Illus.). 144p. (gr. k-5). 1990. Set. lib. bdg. 71.64 (*0-86593-040-6*); Set. lib. bdg. 53.70s.p. (*0-685-36336-8*) Rourke Corp.

Strange Nature. (Illus.). 48p. (gr. 3-4). 1992. PLB 22.80 (*0-8114-3157-6*) Raintree Steck-V.

Stuart, Gene S. Animal Families. (Illus.). (gr. k-4). 1990. Set. 13.95 (*0-87044-819-6*) Natl Geog.

Suid, Annalisa. Save the Animals. (Illus.). 48p. (gr. 1-3). 1993. pap. 9.95 (*1-878279-46-7*) Monday Morning Bks.

Sussman, Susan & James, Robert. Lies (People Believe) about Animals. Tucker, Kathleen, ed. Leavitt, Fred, illus. LC 86-15949. 48p. (gr. 2-7). 1987. PLB 11.95 (*0-8075-4530-9*) A Whitman.

Swartzentruber. God Made the Animals. (gr. 1 up). 1976. 2.50 (*0-686-18185-9*) Rod & Staff.

Tabor, Nancy M. Fifty on the Zebra (Cincuenta en la Cebra) Counting with Animals (Contando Con los Animales) Tabor, Nancy M., illus. 32p. (Orig.). (ps-4). 1994. PLB 15.00 (*0-88106-858-6*); pap. 6.95 (*0-88106-856-X*) Charlesbridge Pub.

Talkabout Animals. (ARA., Illus.). (gr. 1-3). 1987. 3.95x (*0-86685-231-X*) Intl Bk Ctr.

Tallarico, Anthony. Endangered Animals Activity Book. (Illus.). 64p. (Orig.). 1990. pap. 1.95 (*0-942025-12-1*) Kidsbks.

Taylor, Dave. Endangered Forest Animals. (Illus.). (gr. 3-8). 1992. PLB 15.95 (*0-86505-529-7*); pap. 7.95 (*0-86505-539-4*) Crabtree Pub Co.

—Endangered Mountain Animals. (Illus.). 32p. (gr. 3-8). 1992. PLB 15.95 (*0-86505-531-9*); pap. 7.95 (*0-86505-541-6*) Crabtree Pub Co.

—Endangered Wetland Animals. (Illus.). 32p. (gr. 3-8). 1992. PLB 15.95 (*0-86505-530-0*); pap. 7.95 (*0-86505-540-8*) Crabtree Pub Co.

Taylor, David. Endangered Grassland Animals. (Illus.). 32p. (gr. 3-8). 1992. PLB 15.95 (*0-86505-528-9*); pap. 7.95 (*0-86505-538-6*) Crabtree Pub Co.

Taylor, Kim. Hidden by Darkness. (gr. 4-7). 1990. 9.95 (*0-385-30178-2*) Delacorte.

—Hidden Inside. (gr. 4-7). 1990. 9.95 (*0-385-30182-0*) Delacorte.

Tibbitts, Alison & Roocroft, Alan. Rhinoceros. (Illus.). 24p. (ps-2). 1992. PLB 12.95 (*1-56065-101-6*) Capstone Pr.

Time Life Inc. Editors. Do Bears Give Bear Hugs? First Questions & Answers about Animals. Fallow, Allan, ed. (Illus.). 48p. (gr. 2-5). 1994. write for info. (*0-7835-0870-0*); PLB write for info. (*0-7835-0871-9*) Time-Life.

Tomkins, Jasper. The Catalog. (Illus.). 56p. (gr. k up). 1991. pap. 5.95 (*0-671-74972-2*, Green Tiger) S&S Trade.

Trapani, Iza. What Am I? An Animal Guessing Game. Trapani, Iza, illus. LC 92-15029. 32p. (ps-3). 1992. smythe sewn reinforced 13.95 (*1-879085-76-3*) Whsprng Coyote Pr.

Triggs, Tracy. Exploring Virginia's Endangered Species: An Activity Book. (Illus.). 32p. (gr. 4 up). 1994. pap. 2.95 (*0-9625801-5-5*) VA Mus Natl Hist.

Tubbs, Beth. Z Is for Zebra. Schmacker, Pam, illus. 32p. (ps). 1992. 9.95 (*0-9632993-3-6*) Storytime Pub.

Tunney, Christopher. Midnight Animals. Atkinson, Mike & Francis, John, illus. LC 87-4792. 24p. (gr. 2-5). 1987. pap. 2.95 (*0-394-89213-5*, Random Juv) Random Bks Yng Read.

Turbak, Gary. Mountain Animals in Danger. Ormsby, Lawrence, illus. 32p. (gr. 1 up). 1994. 14.95 (*0-87358-573-9*) Northland AZ.

Turner, F. Bernadette. Faith of Little Creatures. (gr. 1-3). pap. 2.50 (*0-8315-0138-3*) Speller.

VanCleave, Janice. Janice VanCleave's Animals. 96p. (gr. 3 up). 1992. pap. text ed. 9.95 (*0-471-55052-3*) Wiley.

Van Der Meer, Ron. Amazing Animal Senses. (gr. 9-12). 1990. 10.95 (*0-316-89624-1*, Joy St Bks) Little.

Walker, Jane. Vanishing Habitats & Species. (Illus.). 32p. (gr. 5-7). 1993. PLB 12.40 (*0-531-17426-3*, Gloucester Pr) Watts.

Wallin, Carol A. Disappearing Faces: Florida's Animals in Danger. Mydske, Valerie, illus. 64p. (Orig.). (gr. 2 up). 1993. Saddlestitch bdg. pap. 9.95 (*0-9639432-0-0*) Cardinal FL. DISAPPEARING FACES, recent winner of the NAIP's Interior Design Award for a Softcover Title, is an excellent, creative learning & activity book offering information about many of Florida's animals being threatened or facing extinction. Interesting facts, word & picture puzzles, mini-art projects, & mazes provide areas of fun for children while they discover how & why they should protect Florida's wildlife. Many pages challenge children's imaginations by encouragining them to create their own illustrations or finish activities in their own special way. DISAPPEARING FACES includes lists of conservation groups to whom the children are encouraged to write & learn about the groups' goals as well as ways in which young citizens can help. In the process, children learn how to compose a proper, courteous business letter. All of DISAPPEARING FACES' activities are designed to captivate, stimulate & educate as well as reinforce children's skills in several curriculum areas. And, although the activites have been developed for elementary school-age children, older children & adults may learn something as well. To write or FAX for information on ordering DISAPPEARING FACES, contact: Carol A. Wallin, Publisher, 18721 S. Dixie Hwy. #106, Miami, FL 33157. FAX: 305-253-0110.
Publisher Provided Annotation.

Walter, Martin. S & S Young Readers Book of Animals. (gr. 4-7). 1991. pap. 7.95 (*0-671-73129-7*, S&S BFYR) S&S Trade.

Walton, Richard K. & Morrison, Gordon. A Field Guide to Endangered Wildlife Coloring Book. Walton, Richard K. & Morrison, Gordon, illus. 64p. 1991. pap. 4.80 (*0-395-57324-6*) HM.

Waters, Sarah A. Hidden Animals. (ps-3). 1992. 9.95 (*0-89577-462-3*, Dist. by Random) RD Assn.

Wexo, John B. Endangered Animals. 24p. (gr. 4). 1989. PLB 14.95 (*0-88682-269-6*) Creative Ed.

Wheeler, Jill C. Beastly Neighbors. Berg, Julie, ed. LC 93-19058. 32p. 1993. 14.96 (*1-56239-197-6*) Abdo & Dghtrs.

Who Goes Moo? 12p. (ps). 1994. 4.95 (*1-56458-737-1*) Dorling Kindersley.

Who's Who at the Zoo? 12p. (ps). 1994. 4.95 (*1-56458-738-X*) Dorling Kindersley.

Whyte, Malcolm. Zoo Animals. (Illus.). 32p. (Orig.). (gr. 1-4). pap. 3.95 (*0-8431-1961-6*, Troubador) Price Stern.

Wild Animals. 88p. (ps-3). 1989. 15.93 (*0-8094-4877-7*); lib. bdg. 21.27 (*0-8094-4878-5*) Time-Life.
Wild Animals. (Illus.). 20p. (gr. k up). 1990. laminated, wipe clean surface 3.95 (*0-88679-822-1*) Educ Insights.
Wild Animals. (Illus.). 16p. (gr. k up). 1990. 9.95 (*0-88679-660-1*) Educ Insights.
Wild Animals. (Illus.). 64p. 1991. 4.99 (*0-517-05156-7*) Random Hse Value.
Wildlife Education, Ltd. Staff. Animal Wonders. Stuart, Walter, illus. 20p. 1992. 13.95 (*0-937934-74-7*) Wildlife Educ.
—Gorillas. Orr, Richard, et al, illus. 20p. (Orig.). (gr. 1-8). 1984. pap. 2.75 (*0-937934-28-3*) WildLife Educ.
—Rhinos. Woods, Michael, et al, illus. 20p. (Orig.). (gr. 1-8). 1985. pap. 2.75 (*0-937934-29-1*) Wildlife Educ.
Wildlife Education, Ltd. Staff, ed. Animal Champions, Vol. 1. (Illus.). 20p. 1992. 13.95 (*0-937934-73-9*) Wildlife Educ.
Wildsmith, Brian. Animal Games. Wildsmith, Brian, illus. (ps-3). 1980. 9.95 (*0-19-279731-X*) OUP.
—Animal Homes. Wildsmith, Brian, illus. (ps-3). 1980. 9.95 (*0-19-279732-8*) OUP.
—Animal Homes. (Illus.). 32p. (ps up). 1991. pap. 5.95 (*0-19-272176-3*, 12407) OUP.
—Animal Tricks. (Illus.). 32p. (ps up). 1991. pap. 5.95 (*0-19-272173-9*, 12408) OUP.
Wilkes, Angela. Colorful Animals. Lilly, Kenneth, illus. LC 92-52799. 24p. (ps-1). 1992. 3.95 (*1-56458-103-9*) Dorling Kindersley.
—Feathery Animals. Lilly, Kenneth, illus. LC 92-52800. 24p. (ps-1). 1992. 3.95 (*1-56458-104-7*) Dorling Kindersley.
—Furry Animals. Lilly, Kenneth, illus. LC 92-52801. 24p. (ps-1). 1992. 3.95 (*1-56458-105-5*) Dorling Kindersley.
—Prickly Animals. Lilly, Kenneth, illus. LC 92-52802. 24p. (ps-1). 1992. 3.95 (*1-56458-106-3*) Dorling Kindersley.
—Scaly Animals. Lilly, Kenneth, illus. LC 92-52803. 24p. (ps-1). 1992. 3.95 (*1-56458-107-1*) Dorling Kindersley.
—Spotty Animals. Lilly, Kenneth, illus. LC 92-52804. 24p. (ps-1). 1992. 3.95 (*1-56458-108-X*) Dorling Kindersley.
—Stripey Animals. Lilly, Kenneth, illus. LC 92-52805. 24p. (ps-1). 1992. 3.95 (*1-56458-109-8*) Dorling Kindersley.
—Wrinkly Animals. Lilly, Kenneth, illus. LC 92-52806. 24p. (ps-1). 1992. 3.95 (*1-56458-110-1*) Dorling Kindersley.
Willis, Terri. Serengeti Plain. LC 94-3022. 1994. write for info. (*0-8114-6368-0*) Raintree Steck-V.
Woelflein, Luise. Forest Animals. Gibson, Barbara, illus. 24p. 1993. 7.95 (*0-590-46005-6*) Scholastic Inc.
Wolff, Robert. Animals of Europe. Dallet, Robert, illus. LC 77-78379. 160p. (gr. 3-9). 1969. PLB 29.95 (*0-87460-092-8*) Lion Bks.
Wolfstein, Luise. Desert Animals. Gibson, Barbara, illus. 24p. 1993. 7.95 (*0-590-46006-4*) Scholastic Inc.
Wood, A. J. Amazing Animals. Ward, Helen, illus. LC 90-85906. 24p. (ps-1). 1991. 8.95 (*1-878093-46-0*) Boyds Mills Pr.
Wood, John N. Nature Hide & Seek: Woods & Forests. Silver, Maggie, illus. LC 93-22506. 22p. (gr. k-4). 1993. 13.00 (*0-679-83691-8*) Knopf Bks Yng Read.
Wood, Robert W. Thirty-Nine Easy Animal Biology Experiments. (Illus.). 160p. (gr. 3-8). 1991. 9.70 (*0-8306-6594-3*, 3594); pap. 9.95 (*0-8306-3594-7*) TAB Bks.
Woodland Animals. (Illus.). 48p. (ps-3). 1994. 2.95 (*0-8431-3727-4*) Price Stern.
World Book Editors. Pets & Other Animals: Childcraft Annual, 1992. LC 65-25105. (Illus.). 256p. (gr. 1-7). 1992. lib. bdg. write for info. (*0-7166-0692-5*) World Bk.
World of the Mountain Gorillas, 3 vols. (Illus.). (gr. 2-3). 1994. Set. PLB 51.80 (*0-8368-0441-4*) Gareth Stevens Inc.
Wormell, Christopher. Alphabet of Animals. LC 90-2774. 64p. 1990. 17.95 (*0-8037-0876-9*) Dial Bks Young.
Wren & Maile. Na Holoholona Maoli: Native Animals. Wren, illus. (ENG & HAW.). 10p. (ps). 1992. bds. 3.95 (*1-880188-27-9*) Bess Pr.
Wright, Alexandra. Los Echaremo de Menos? Especies en Peligro de Extincion (Will We Miss Them? Endangered Species) (Illus.). 32p. (ps-3). 1993. PLB 15.88 (*0-88106-640-0*); pap. 6.95 (*0-88106-420-3*) Charlesbridge Pub.
Zadrzynska, Ewa. Peaceable Kingdom. (ps-3). 1994. 14. 95 (*0-9638904-0-9*) M M Art Bks.
Zeff. Animal Picture-English. (Illus.). (gr. 1-9). 1980. (Usborne); French ed. 11.95 (*0-86020-556-8*); English ed. pap. 8.95 (*0-7460-0395-1*) EDC.
Ziefert, Harriet. Animals of the Bible. Galli, Letizia, illus. LC 93-38568. 1995. write for info. (*0-385-32084-1*) Doubleday.
Zokeisha. A Little Book of Baby Animals. Klimo, Kate, ed. Zokeisha, illus. 16p. 1982. pap. 2.95 (*0-671-44840-4*, Little Simon) S&S Trade.

ANIMALS–ANATOMY
see Anatomy, Comparative

ANIMALS–COLOR
see Color of Animals

ANIMALS–DICTIONARIES

Animals. LC 91-60901. (Illus.). 64p. (gr. 6 up). 1991. 14. 95 (*1-879431-19-X*); PLB 15.99 (*1-879431-34-3*) Dorling Kindersley.
Arnold, Tim. Natural History from A to Z: A Terrestrial Sampler. Arnold, Tim, illus. LC 88-26879. 64p. (gr. 5-9). 1991. SBE 15.95 (*0-689-50467-5*, M K McElderry) Macmillan Child Grp.
Brown, Richard. One Hundred Words about Animals. Brown, Richard, illus. (gr. k-2). 1990. incl. cass. 19.95 (*0-87488-183-8*); pap. 12.95 incl. cass. (*0-87499-182-X*); Set; incl. 4 bks., cass., & guide. pap. 27.95 (*0-87499-184-6*) Live Oak Media.
Burnie, David & Gamlin, Linda. The Kingfisher First Encyclopedia of Animals. LC 93-46611. 144p. (gr. 3-7). 1994. 15.95 (*1-85697-994-6*, Kingfisher LKC) LKC.
Lambert, David. The Children's Animal Atlas. LC 91-30147. (Illus.). 96p. (gr. 2-6). 1992. 16.95 (*1-56294-101-1*); PLB 18.90 (*1-56294-167-4*) Millbrook Pr.
Puncel, Maria, ed. Animales - Animals. Del Carmen Blazquez, Maria, tr. (SPA., Illus.). 64p. (gr. 5-12). 1992. write for info. (*84-372-4525-7*) Santillana.
Richardson, James. Science Dictionary of Animals. Quinn, Kaye, illus. LC 91-18826. 48p. (gr. 3-7). 1992. lib. bdg. 11.59 (*0-8167-2521-7*); pap. 3.95 (*0-8167-2440-7*) Troll Assocs.
Scarry, Richard. Dictionnaire des Animaux. (FRE.). 96p. (gr. 3-8). 1992. 39.95 (*0-7859-1543-5*, 2719203341) Fr & Eur.
Tous les Animaux - All the Animals. (ENG & FRE.). 63p. 1991. 19.95 (*2-07-057512-8*) Schoenhof.

ANIMALS–DISEASES
see Veterinary Medicine

ANIMALS–FICTION
see also Animals–Habits and Behavior; Fables

Aardema, Verna. Princess Gorilla & a New Kind of Water. Chase, Victoria, illus. LC 86-32888. 32p. (ps-3). 1988. 10.95 (*0-8037-0412-7*); PLB 10.89 (*0-8037-0413-5*) Dial Bks Young.
Ackerman, Karen. This Old House. Wickstrom, Sylvie, illus. LC 91-20449. 40p. (ps-1). 1992. SBE 14.95 (*0-689-31741-7*, Atheneum Child Bk) Macmillan Child Grp.
Ada, Alam F. In the Cow's Backyard - La Hamaca de la Vaca. Escriva, Vivi, illus. (SPA & ENG.). 23p. (gr. k-2). 1991. English ed. 6.95 (*1-56014-275-8*); Spanish ed. 6.95 (*1-56014-219-7*) Santillana.
—A Strange Visitor - Una Extrana Visita. Escriva, Vivi, illus. (SPA & ENG.). 26p. (Orig.). (gr. k-2). 1989. English ed. 3.95 (*0-88272-802-4*); Spanish Ed. 3.95 (*0-88272-793-1*) Santillana.
Ada, Alma F. The Unicorn of the West: El Unicornio del Oeste. Zubizarreta, Rosa, tr. Pizer, Abigail, illus. LC 92-7425. (ENG & SPA.). 40p. (gr. 1-3). 1994. English ed. SBE 14.95 (*0-689-31778-6*, Atheneum Child Bk); Spanish ed. SBE 14.95 (*0-689-31916-9*, Atheneum Child Bk) Macmillan Child Grp.
—Who's Hatching Here? - Quien Nacera Aqui? Escriva, Vivi, illus. (SPA & ENG.). 24p. (gr. k-2). 1989. English ed. 3.95 (*0-88272-811-3*); Spanish ed. 3.95 (*0-88272-800-8*) Santillana.
Aesop. Aesop for Children. Winter, Milo, illus. LC 86-73175. 96p. (gr. 2 up). 1984. Repr. of 1919 ed. 12.95 (*1-56288-039-X*) Checkerboard.
—The Hare & the Tortoise. Friedman, Arthur, illus. LC 80-28162. 32p. (gr. k-3). 1981. PLB 9.79 (*0-89375-468-4*); pap. text ed. 1.95 (*0-89375-469-2*) Troll Assocs.
—The Lion & the Mouse. Dole, Bob, illus. LC 80-28154. 32p. (gr. k-3). 1981. PLB 9.79 (*0-89375-466-8*); pap. text ed. 1.95 (*0-89375-467-6*) Troll Assocs.
Agell, Charlotte. I Swam with a Seal. LC 94-5652. Date not set. write for info. (*0-15-200176-X*) HarBrace.
Ahlberg, Allan. The Pet Shop. Amstutz, Andre, illus. LC 92-45657. 32p. (gr. k up). 1993. pap. 4.95 (*0-688-12680-4*, Mulberry) Morrow.
Albert, Richard E. Alejandro's Gift. Long, Sylvia, illus. LC 93-30199. 1994. 13.95 (*0-8118-0436-4*) Chronicle Bks.
Alborough, Jez. Hide & Seek. LC 93-28542. (Illus.). 32p. (ps up). 1994. 5.99 (*1-56402-369-9*) Candlewick Pr.
Alda, Arlene. Sheep, Sheep, Sheep: Help Me Fall Asleep. Alda, Arlene, photos by. LC 91-43006. (Illus.). 32p. (ps-2). 1992. pap. 13.50 (*0-385-30791-8*) Doubleday.
Alexander, Liza. Babysitting with Big Bird. Leigh, Tom, illus. 24p. (ps-4). 1993. 20.00 (*0-307-74029-3*, 64029, Golden Pr) Western Pub.
Alexander, Martha. Even That Moose Won't Listen to Me. Alexander, Martha, illus. 32p. (ps-k). 1988. PLB 11.89 (*0-8037-0188-8*) Dial Bks Young.
Allan, Ted. Willie the Squowse. Blake, Quentin, illus. (gr. 2 up). 1991. Repr. of 1978 ed. 9.95 (*0-8038-9341-8*) Hastings.
Allen, Constance. Elmo's Guessing Game. (ps). 1993. 4.95 (*0-307-12398-7*, Golden Pr) Western Pub.
Allen, Julia. My First Animal Ride. Reese, Bob, illus. (gr. k-3). 1987. 7.95 (*0-89868-179-0*); pap. 2.95 (*0-89868-180-4*) ARO Pub.
Andersen, Hans Christian. Mary Engelbreit's The Snow Queen. Englebreit, Mary, illus. 48p. (gr. k up). 1993. 15.95 (*1-56305-438-8*, 3438) Workman Pub.
Anderson, Honey & Reinholdt, Bill. Don't Cut down This Tree. Ruth, Trevor, illus. LC 92-21446. 1993. 3.75 (*0-383-03621-6*) SRA Schl Grp.
Animal Stories. 1991. 8.99 (*0-517-03761-0*) Random Hse Value.
Argent, Kerry & Trinca, Rod. One Woolly Wombat. Argent, Kerry, illus. 32p. (ps-1). 1987. pap. 6.95 (*0-916291-10-3*) Kane-Miller Bk.
Ariev, Lauren. Who Are Baby's Friends? Morgan, Mary, illus. 24p. (ps). 1992. bds. write for info. (*0-307-06142-6*, 6142, Golden Pr) Western Pub.
Armstrong, Beverly. Endangered Animals - Superdoodles. LC 93-80434. 32p. (gr. 1-6). 1994. 4.95 (*0-88160-228-0*, LW323) Learning Wks.
—Reptiles - Superdoodles. LC 93-80433. 32p. (gr. 1-6). 1994. 4.95 (*0-88160-229-9*, LW324) Learning Wks.
Artell, Mike. Big Long Animal Song. 8p. (ps-k). 1994. text ed. 3.95 (*0-673-36190-X*) GdYrBks.
Aruego, Jose & Dewey, Ariane. We Hide, You Seek. LC 78-13638. (Illus.). 32p. (gr. k-3). 1979. 14.95 (*0-688-80201-X*); PLB 14.88 (*0-688-84201-1*) Greenwillow.
Asuka, Ken. Toto Visits Mystic Mountain. Young, Richard Y., ed. Kaisei-sha, tr. Asuka, Ken, illus. LC 89-11754. 32p. (gr. 1-3). 1989. PLB 14.60 (*0-944483-46-1*) Garrett Ed Corp.
Auch, Mary J. A Sudden Change of Family. MacDonald, Pat, ed. 160p. 1993. pap. 2.99 (*0-671-74892-0*, Minstrel Bks) PB.
Awdry, W. Thomas & the Hide-&-Seek Animals: A Thomas the Tank Engine Flap Book. Bell, Owain, illus. LC 90-62114. 24p. (ps-1). 1991. 7.95 (*0-679-81316-0*) Random Bks Yng Read.
Aych, Mary J. Pick of the Litter. (gr. 4-7). 1990. pap. 2.95 (*0-553-15808-2*) Bantam.
Baby Animals. (ARA., Illus.). (gr. 1-3). 1987. 3.95x (*0-86685-186-0*) Intl Bk Ctr.
Baby's Book of Animals. LC 92-54921. (ps). 1993. 9.95 (*1-56458-278-7*) Dorling Kindersley.
Backovsky, Jan. Trouble in Paradise. LC 91-47930. (Illus.). 32p. (ps up). 1992. 14.00 (*0-688-11857-7*, Tambourine Bks); PLB 13.93 (*0-688-11858-5*, Tambourine Bks) Morrow.
Bagley. Suppose the Wolf Were an Octopus: Grades 3-4. 1992. 9.99 (*0-89824-096-4*) Trillium Pr.
—Suppose the Wolf Were an Octopus: Grades 5-6. 1992. 9.99 (*0-89824-097-2*) Trillium Pr.
Bagley & Foley. Suppose the Wolf Were an Octopus: Grades K-2. 1992. 9.99 (*0-89824-087-5*) Trillium Pr.
Bailey, Jill. Save the Macaw. Baum, Ann, illus. LC 91-19871. 48p. (gr. 3-7). 1992. PLB 21.34 (*0-8114-2712-9*); pap. 4.95 (*0-8114-6549-7*) Raintree Steck-V.
Bains, Rae. Hiccups, Hiccups. Coontz, Otto, illus. LC 81-4638. 32p. (gr. k-2). 1981. PLB 11.59 (*0-89375-537-0*); pap. text ed. 2.95 (*0-89375-538-9*) Troll Assocs.
Baker, Alan. Two Tiny Mice. Baker, Alan, illus. LC 90-13939. 32p. (ps-1). 1991. 12.95 (*0-8037-0973-0*) Dial Bks Young.
—Where's Mouse? Baker, Alan, illus. LC 92-53117. 16p. (ps-k). 1992. 12.95 (*1-85697-821-4*, Kingfisher LKC) LKC.
Baker, Tanya & Holm, Carlton. Harvey the Hiccupping Hippopotamus. Wilkinson, Sue, illus. 32p. (ps-k). 1992. lib. bdg. 10.95 with dust jacket (*0-8120-6248-5*); pap. 5.95 (*0-8120-4927-6*) Barron.
Balian, Lorna. The Aminal. Balian, Lorna, illus. 32p. (ps-3). 1987. Repr. of 1972 ed. 7.50 (*0-687-37101-5*) Humbug Bks.
Banchek, Linda. Snake In, Snake Out. Arnold, Elaine, illus. 32p. (ps-1). 1992. pap. 2.99 (*0-440-40738-9*, YB) Dell.
Bandes, Hanna. Sleepy River. Winter, Jeanette, illus. LC 92-26198. 32p. (ps). 1993. 14.95 (*0-399-22349-5*, Philomel Bks) Putnam Pub Group.
Barasch, Marc I. No Plain Pets! Drescher, Henrik, illus. LC 90-22518. 40p. (ps-3). 1991. PLB 14.89 (*0-06-022473-8*) HarpC Child Bks.
Barberis, France. Would You Like a Parrot? Barberis, Franco, illus. LC 67-28671. 32p. (ps-k). 8.95 (*0-87592-060-8*) Scroll Pr.
Barnes, Jill & Asuka, Ken. Smile for Toto. Rubin, Caroline, ed. Japan Foreign Rights Centre Staff, tr. from JPN. Asuka, Ken, illus. LC 90-37747. 32p. (gr. k-4). 1990. PLB 14.60 (*0-944483-87-9*) Garrett Ed Corp.
—Toto in Trouble. Rubin, Caroline, ed. Japan Foreign Rights Centre Staff, tr. from JPN. Asuka, Ken, illus. LC 90-37749. 32p. (gr. k-4). 1990. PLB 14.60 (*0-944483-86-0*) Garrett Ed Corp.
Barnes, Jill & Ishinabe, Fusako. Spring Snowman. Rubin, Caroline, ed. Japan Foreign Rights Centre Staff, tr. from JPN. Ishinabe, Fusako, illus. LC 90-37748. 32p. (gr. k-3). 1990. PLB 14.60 (*0-944483-83-6*) Garrett Ed Corp.
Barnes, Joyce B. Patches, the Blessed Beast of Burden. Ramirez-Walker, Linda J., illus. 36p. 1990. 15.00 (*0-9628493-0-8*) J B Barnes.
Barnett, Ada & Wurfer, Nicole. Eddycat Brings Soccer to Mannersville. Hoffmann, Mark, illus. LC 92-56879. Date not set. PLB 17.27 (*0-8368-0941-6*) Gareth Stevens Inc.
Barnett, Ada, et al. Eddycat & Buddy Entertain a Guest. Hoffmann, Mark, illus. LC 92-56883. 32p. (gr. 1 up). 1993. Repr. of 1991 ed. PLB 17.27 incl. tchr's. guide (*0-8368-0946-7*) Gareth Stevens Inc.
—Eddycat Attends Sunshine's Birthday Party. Hoffmann, Mark, illus. LC 92-56881. 1993. PLB 17.27 (*0-8368-0943-2*) Gareth Stevens Inc.
—Eddycat Helps Sunshine Plan Her Party. Hoffmann, Mark, illus. LC 92-56880. 1993. PLB 17.27 (*0-8368-0942-4*) Gareth Stevens Inc.
—Eddycat Introduces Mannersville. Hoffmann, Mark, illus. LC 92-56877. 1993. PLB 17.27 (*0-8368-0939-4*) Gareth Stevens Inc.

—Eddycat Teaches Telephone Skills. Hoffmann, Mark, illus. LC 92-56882. 1993. PLB 17.27 (*0-8368-0944-0*) Gareth Stevens Inc.

Barrett, John. The Littlest Mule. Silver Dollar City, Inc. Staff, ed. Baer, Jane & Baer, Dale, illus. (ps-5). 1977. 2.99g (*0-686-19125-0*) Silver Dollar.

Barrett, Judi. Animals Should Definitely Not Act Like People. Barrett, Ron, illus. LC 80-13364. 32p. (ps-2). 1980. SBE 13.95 (*0-689-30768-3*, Atheneum Child Bk) Macmillan Child Grp.

—Animals Should Definitely Not Wear Clothing. Barrett, Ron, illus. LC 70-115078. 32p. (ps-2). 1970. SBE 13. 95 (*0-689-20592-9*, Atheneum Child Bk) Macmillan Child Grp.

Barton, Byron. Buzz, Buzz, Buzz. 1st ed. LC 93-46931. 1995. pap. 4.95 (*0-689-71873-X*, Aladdin) Macmillan Child Grp.

Base, Graeme. Animalia. (Illus.). 32p. 1993. 11.95 (*0-8109-1939-7*) Abrams.

Baylor, Byrd. Desert Voices. Parnell, Peter, illus. LC 92-24475. 32p. (gr. 1-5). 1993. pap. 3.95 (*0-689-71691-5*, Aladdin) Macmillan Child Grp.

Beatty, Patricia. Eight Mules from Monterey. LC 81-22284. 224p. (gr. 4-6). 1982. 13.95 (*0-688-01047-4*) Morrow Jr Bks.

Bell, Anthea. Animal Antics. Janosch, illus. 128p. (gr. k-2). 1987. 17.95 (*0-86264-033-4*, Pub. by Anderson Pr UK) Trafalgar.

Bemelmans, Ludwig. Rosebud. Bemelmans, Ludwig, illus. LC 92-47046. 40p. (ps-2). 1993. 8.99 (*0-679-84913-0*); PLB 9.99 (*0-679-94913-5*) Knopf Bks Yng Read.

Bender, Robert. A Most Unusual Lunch. LC 93-34068. (gr. 3 up). 1994. pap. 14.99 (*0-8037-1710-5*); PLB 14. 89 (*0-8037-1711-3*) Dial Bks Young.

—The Preposterous Rhinoceros, or, Alvin's Beastly Birthday. LC 93-14200. 1994. 14.95 (*0-8050-2806-4*) H Holt & Co.

Benjamin, Cynthia. Footprints in the Snow. Rogers, Jacqueline, illus. 48p. (ps-1). 1994. pap. 2.95 (*0-590-46663-1*, Cartwheel) Scholastic Inc.

Bennett, David. One Cow Moo Moo. Cooke, Andy, illus. LC 90-32065. 32p. (ps-2). 1990. 11.95 (*0-8050-1416-0*, Bks Young Read) H Holt & Co.

Bennett, Jill. Animal Fair. (ps-3). 1990. 12.95 (*0-670-82691-X*) Viking Child Bks.

Berenstain, Stan & Berenstain, Janice. After the Dinosaurs. Berenstain, Stan & Berenstain, Janice, illus. LC 88-42588. 32p. (Orig.). (gr. k-3). 1988. lib. bdg. 5.99 (*0-394-90518-0*); (Random Juv) Random Bks Yng Read.

Birney, Betty. Walt Disney's Winnie the Pooh Helping Hands: Oh, Bother! Someone Won't Share. Stevenson, Nancy, illus. 24p. (ps-3). 1993. pap. 1.95 (*0-307-12766-4*, 12766, Golden Pr) Western Pub.

—Winnie the Pooh & the Little Lost Bird: A Big Golden Book. (ps-3). 1993. 3.95 (*0-307-12369-3*, Golden Pr) Western Pub.

—Winnie the Pooh: The Merry Christmas Mystery. (ps-3). 1993. pap. 2.25 (*0-307-12774-5*, Golden Pr) Western Pub.

Biser, Len. Meet Mrs. Wiggywaggle: Mrs. Wiggywaggle Goes to Town. Bach, Katharina, illus. 32p. (ps-1). 1991. write for info. (*1-880015-29-3*) Petra Pub Co.

Blathwayt, Benedict. Stories from Firefly Island. LC 92-40786. 128p. (ps up). 1993. 16.00 (*0-688-12487-9*) Greenwillow.

Blocksma, Mary. Yoo Hoo, Moon! 1991. pap. 9.99 (*0-553-07094-0*) Bantam.

—Yoo Hoo, Moon! 1992. pap. 3.99 (*0-553-35212-1*) Bantam.

Bodsworth, Nan. A Nice Walk in the Jungle. (Illus.). 32p. (ps-3). 1992. pap. 4.99 (*0-14-054573-5*, Puffin) Puffin Bks.

Boland, Janice. Annabel. Halsey, Megan, illus. LC 91-46490. 32p. (ps-2). 1993. 12.99 (*0-8037-1254-5*); PLB 12.89 (*0-8037-1255-3*) Dial Bks Young.

—Annabel Again. Halsey, Megan, photos by. LC 94-189. (gr. 2 up). 1995. write for info. (*0-8037-1756-3*); pap. write for info. (*0-8037-1757-1*) Dial Bks Young.

Bonsall, Crosby N. Who's a Pest? Bonsall, Crosby N., illus. LC 62-13310. 64p. (gr. k-3). 1962. PLB 13.89 (*0-06-020621-7*) HarpC Child Bks.

Boyd, Patricia R. The Furry Wind. Spring, Grace J., illus. 28p. (gr. 2-3). 1982. pap. 2.25 (*0-9603840-4-9*) Andrew Mtn Pr.

Boyle, Doe & Thomas, Peter, eds. Big Town Trees: From an Original Article which Appeared in Ranger Rick Magazine, Copyright National Wildlife Federation. Beylon, Cathy, illus. LC 92-34778. 20p. (gr. k-3). 1993. 6.95 (*0-924483-83-0*); incl. audio tape 9.95 (*0-924483-84-9*); incl. audio tape & 13 inch plush toy 35.95 (*0-924483-87-3*); incl. 9 inch plush toy 21.95 (*0-924483-89-X*) Soundprints.

—Caribou Country: From an Original Article Which Appeared in Ranger Rick Magazine, Copyright National Wildlife Federation. Langford, Alton, illus. Luther, Sallie, contrib. by. LC 92-7732. (Illus.). 20p. (gr. k-3). 1992. 6.95 (*0-924483-53-9*); incl. audiocass. tape & 13" toy 35.95 (*0-924483-50-4*); incl. 9" toy 21. 95 (*0-924483-51-2*); incl. audiocass. tape 9.95 (*0-924483-52-0*); write for info. audiocass. tape (*0-924483-80-6*) Soundprints.

—Earth Day Every Day: From an Original Article which Appeared in Ranger Rick Magazine, Copyright National Wildlife Federation. Beylon, Cathy, illus. LC 92-27292. 20p. (gr. k-3). 1993. 6.95 (*0-924483-82-2*); incl. audio tape 9.95 (*0-924483-85-7*); incl. audio tape & 13 inch plush toy 35.95 (*0-924483-86-5*); incl. 9 inch plush toy 21.95 (*0-924483-88-1*) Soundprints.

Boynton, Sandra. A to Z. Boynton, Sandra, illus. 14p. (ps). 1984. 3.95 (*0-671-49317-5*, Little Simon) S&S Trade.

—Boynton on Board: Barnyard Dance! Boynton, Sandra, illus. 24p. (ps). 1993. bds. 6.95 (*1-56305-442-6*, 3442) Workman Pub.

—Boynton on Board: One, Two, Three! Boynton, Sandra, illus. 24p. (ps). 1993. bds. 6.95 (*1-56305-444-2*, 3444) Workman Pub.

Bread & Honey. (Illus.). 42p. (ps-3). 1992. PLB 13.26 (*0-8368-0880-0*); PLB 13.27 s.p. (*0-685-61512-X*) Gareth Stevens Inc.

Breathed, Berkeley. The Last Basselope: One Ferocious Story. LC 92-14467. (Illus.). 1992. 14.95 (*0-316-10761-1*) Little.

Brennan, J. H. The Den of Dragons. 192p. (gr. 6 up). 1986. pap. 2.50 (*0-440-91873-1*, LFL) Dell.

Brenner, Barbara A. Lion & Lamb Step Out. 1990. 9.99 (*0-553-05860-6*) Bantam.

Brett, Jan. Annie & the Wild Animals. Brett, Jan, illus. LC 84-19818. 32p. (gr. k-3). 1990. 14.95 (*0-395-37800-1*); pap. 7.95 (*0-395-53962-5*) HM.

—Annie & the Wild Animals. Brett, Jan, illus. (ps-3). 1989. pap. 4.95 (*0-395-51006-6*, Sandpiper) HM.

—Berlioz the Bear. LC 90-37634. (Illus.). 32p. 1991. 14. 95 (*0-399-22248-0*, Putnam) Putnam Pub Group.

Brooks, Bruce. Predator! 80p. (gr. 10 up). 1994. pap. 8.95 (*0-374-36112-6*) FS&G.

Brown, Bob. The Turtle's Darshan for All the Animals. (Illus.). 32p. (gr. 2 up). 1973. pap. 5.00 (*0-913078-17-4*) Sheriar Pr.

Brown, Craig. My Barn. LC 90-41758. (Illus.). 24p. (ps up). 1991. 13.95 (*0-688-08785-X*); PLB 13.88 (*0-688-08786-8*) Greenwillow.

Brown, Hayden & Dickins, Roberts. The Sombrero. Dickins, Robert, illus. LC 93-6633. 1994. write for info. (*0-383-03714-X*) SRA Schl Grp.

Brown, Ken. Nellie's Knot. LC 92-27910. (Illus.). 32p. (ps-1). 1993. SBE 13.95 (*0-02-714930-7*, Four Winds) Macmillan Child Grp.

Brown, Marc. Arthur's First Sleepover. LC 93-46113. (ps-3). 1994. 14.95 (*0-316-11445-6*) Little.

Brown, Marc T. Arthur Babysits. (Illus.). 32p. (ps-3). 1992. 14.95 (*0-316-11293-3*, Joy St Bks) Little.

—Arthur Goes to Camp. Brown, Marc T., illus. LC 81-15588. 32p. (ps-3). 1984. 14.95 (*0-316-11218-6*, Joy St Bks); pap. 4.95 (*0-316-11058-2*, Joy St Bks) Little.

—Arthur's Family Vacation. LC 92-26650. 1993. 15.95 (*0-316-11312-3*) Little.

—Arthur's Nose. Brown, Marc T., illus. 32p. (ps-3). 1986. lib. bdg. 14.95 (*0-316-11193-7*, Joy St Bks); pap. 4.95 (*0-316-11070-1*, Joy St Bks) Little.

—Arthur's Puppy. LC 92-46342. (gr. 1-8). 1993. 14.95 (*0-316-11355-7*, Joy St Bks) Little.

—Arthur's Teacher Trouble. Brown, Marc T., illus. 32p. (ps-3). 1989. 15.95 (*0-316-11244-5*, Joy St Bks); pap. 4.95 (*0-316-11186-4*, Joy St Bks) Little.

—Arthur's Tooth. Brown, Marc T., illus. 32p. (ps-3). 1985. 15.95 (*0-316-11245-3*, Joy St Bks) Little.

—D. W. All Wet. Brown, Marc T., illus. (ps-3). 1988. 10. 95 (*0-316-11077-9*, Joy St Bks) Little.

Brown, Marcia. Once a Mouse. Brown, Marcia, illus. LC 61-14769. 32p. (ps-3). 1972. SBE 14.95 (*0-684-12662-1*, Scribners Young Read) Macmillan Child Grp.

Brown, Margaret W. Animals in the Snow. Schwartz, Carol, illus. LC 94-8470. 1995. write for info. (*0-7868-0039-9*); pap. write for info. (*0-7868-2032-2*) Hyprn Child.

—A Child's Good Morning Book. Charlot, Jean, illus. LC 94-719. 1995. 10.00 (*0-06-024538-7*) HarpC.

—Four Fur Feet. Charlip, Remy, illus. 48p. (gr. 1-3). 1989. Repr. of 1961 ed. 13.95 (*0-929077-03-2*, Hopscotch Bks); PLB 12.95 (*0-317-92548-2*, Hopscotch Bks) Watermark Inc.

—Four Fur Feet. (ps-3). 1993. pap. 3.99 (*0-440-40684-6*) Dell.

—Little Fur Family. special rel. ed. Williams, Garth, illus. LC 51-11657. 32p. (ps-3). 1951. 14.00 (*0-06-020745-0*); PLB 13.89 (*0-06-020746-9*) HarpC Child Bks.

Brown, Margeret W. Little Donkey Close Your Eyes. Wolff, Ashley, illus. LC 94-16523. (gr. 2-5). 1995. 15. 00 (*0-06-024482-8*); PLB 14.89 (*0-06-024483-6*) HarpC.

Brown, Ruth. One Stormy Night. Brown, Ruth, illus. LC 92-27004. 32p. (ps-1). 1993. 13.99 (*0-525-45091-2*, DCB) Dutton Child Bks.

—The Picnic. LC 92-5718. (ps-2). 1993. 14.00 (*0-525-45012-2*, DCB) Dutton Child Bks.

Browne, Eileen. No Problem. Parkins, David, illus. LC 92-53134. 40p. (ps up). 1993. bk. ed. 14.95 (*1-56402-176-9*); bk. & kit ed. 14.99 (*1-56402-200-5*) Candlewick Pr.

—Where's That Bus? Browne, Eileen, illus. LC 90-20885. 32p. (ps-1). 1991. pap. 13.95 jacketed (*0-671-73810-0*, S&S BFYR) S&S Trade.

Buller, Jon & Schade, Susan. Toad on the Road. Buller, Jon, illus. LC 91-4246. 32p. (Orig.). (ps-1). 1992. PLB 7.99 (*0-679-92689-5*); pap. 3.50 (*0-679-82689-0*) Random Bks Yng Read.

Bullock, Kathleen. It Chanced to Rain. Bullock, Kathleen, illus. LC 87-32070. (ps-1). 1989. (S&S BFYR); pap. 3.95 (*0-671-77820-X*, S&S BFYR) S&S Trade.

Bunting, Eve. Summer Wheels. 1992. 14.95 (*0-15-207000-1*, HB Juv Bks) HarBrace.

Burgess, Thonrton W. The Adventures of Johnny Chuck. (gr. 5-6). 18.95 (*0-88411-787-1*, Pub. by Aeonian Pr) Amereon Ltd.

Burgess, Thornton. Mother West Wind's Neighbors. (Illus.). 160p. 1992. Repr. PLB 14.95x (*0-89966-901-8*) Buccaneer Bks.

—Old Mother West Wind. Hague, Michael, illus. LC 89-20088. 90p. (gr. 2-4). 1990. 18.95 (*0-8050-1005-X*, Bks Young Read) H Holt & Co.

—Old Mother West Wind. (Illus.). 160p. 1992. Repr. PLB 14.95x (*0-89966-900-X*) Buccaneer Bks.

Burgess, Thornton W. The Adventures of Buster Bear. Kliros, Thea, adapted by. Cady, Harrison, illus. LC 92-36949. 96p. 1993. pap. 1.00 (*0-486-27564-7*) Dover.

—The Adventures of Chatterer the Red Squirrel. unabr. ed. Kliros, Thea, adapted by. Cady, Harrison, illus. LC 92-14627. 96p. 1992. pap. 1.00 (*0-486-27399-7*) Dover.

—The Adventures of Danny Meadow Mouse. Cady, Harrison & Kliros, Thea, illus. LC 92-36950. 96p. 1993. pap. 1.00 (*0-486-27565-5*) Dover.

—The Adventures of Grandfather Frog. (gr. 5-6). 18.95 (*0-88411-777-4*, Pub. by Aeonian Pr) Amereon Ltd.

—The Adventures of Grandfather Frog. unabr. ed. Kliros, Thea, adapted by. Cady, Harrison, illus. LC 92-13146. 96p. 1992. pap. text ed. 1.00 (*0-486-27400-4*) Dover.

—The Adventures of Jerry Muskrat. (gr. 5-6). 18.95 (*0-88411-782-0*, Pub. by Aeonian Pr) Amereon Ltd.

—The Adventures of Jerry Muskrat. (Illus.). 96p. 1993. pap. text ed. 1.00t (*0-486-27817-4*) Dover.

—The Adventures of Jimmy Skunk. (Illus.). 96p. 1994. pap. 1.00 (*0-486-28023-3*) Dover.

—Adventures of Mister Mocker. 18.95 (*0-8488-0378-7*) Amereon Ltd.

—The Adventures of Ol' Mistah Buzzard. (gr. 5-6). 18.95 (*0-88411-784-7*, Pub. by Aeonian Pr) Amereon Ltd.

—The Adventures of Old Man Coyote. (gr. 5-6). 18.95 (*0-88411-781-2*, Pub. by Aeonian Pr) Amereon Ltd.

—The Adventures of Old Mr. Toad. (gr. 5-6). 18.95 (*0-88411-785-5*, Pub. by Aeonian Pr) Amereon Ltd.

—The Adventures of Peter Cottontail. large type ed. 96p. 1992. pap. 1.00 (*0-486-26929-9*) Dover.

—The Adventures of Poor Mrs. Quack. (gr. 5-6). 18.95 (*0-88411-775-8*, Pub. by Aeonian Pr) Amereon Ltd.

—The Adventures of Poor Mrs. Quack. (Illus.). 96p. 1993. pap. text ed. 1.00t (*0-486-27818-2*) Dover.

—The Adventures of Prickly Porky. (gr. 5-6). 18.95 (*0-88411-783-9*, Pub. by Aeonian Pr) Amereon Ltd.

—The Adventures of Reddy Fox. large type ed. 96p. 1992. pap. 1.00 (*0-486-26930-2*) Dover.

—Dear Old Briar Patch. 18.95 (*0-8488-0402-3*) Amereon Ltd.

—Happy Jack. 19.95 (*0-8488-0389-2*) Amereon Ltd.

—Longlegs the Heron. 19.95 (*0-8488-0400-7*) Amereon Ltd.

—Mother West Wind's Neighbors. Cady, Harrison, illus. LC 68-21862. (gr. 1 up). 1985. pap. 8.95 (*0-316-11656-4*) Little.

—Old Mother West Wind. golden anniversary ed. Cady, Harrison, illus. (gr. 1 up). 1985. 16.95 (*0-316-11648-3*); pap. 8.95 (*0-316-11655-6*) Little.

Burnford, Sheila. The Incredible Journey. (gr. 6-8). 1977. pap. 2.95 (*0-553-26218-1*) Bantam.

—The Incredible Journey. (gr. 6-8). 16.95 (*0-88411-099-0*) Amereon Ltd.

—The Incredible Journey. Burger, Carl, illus. (gr. 4-8). 1990. 16.00 (*0-553-05874-6*, Skylark) Bantam.

Burningham, John. Mr. Gumpy's Outing. LC 77-159507. (Illus.). 32p. (ps-2). 1971. 14.95 (*0-8050-0708-3*, Bks Young Read) H Holt & Co.

Buskohl, Esther E. Honey: Story of a Little Brown Mule. Buskohl, Esther E., illus. LC 85-80216. 80p. (Orig.). (gr. 3-5). 1985. 9.95 (*0-9614991-0-9*); pap. 4.95 (*0-9614991-1-7*) EEBART.

Butler, M. Christina. Picnic Pandemonium. Rutherford, Meg, illus. LC 90-10148. 28p. (gr. 1-2). 1991. PLB 17. 27 (*0-8368-0433-3*) Gareth Stevens Inc.

Byars, Betsy C. The Animal, the Vegetable, & John D. Jones. Sanderson, Ruth, illus. 160p. (gr. 5 up). 1983. pap. 3.50 (*0-440-40356-1*, YB) Dell.

—The House of Wings. Schwartz, Daniel, illus. 160p. (gr. 4-6). 1972. pap. 14.95 (*0-670-38025-3*) Viking Child Bks.

Calmenson, Stephanie, adapted by. Walt Disney's Winnie the Pooh & Tigger Too. LC 93-73813. (Illus.). 48p. (gr. 4-9). 1994. 12.95 (*1-56282-630-1*) Disney Pr.

Campbell, Rod. My Pop-up Garden Friends. LC 92-4382. (Illus.). 14p. (ps). 1993. pap. 4.95 POB (*0-689-71643-5*, Aladdin) Macmillan Child Grp.

Caraher, Kim. There's a Bat on the Balcony. Sofilas, Mark, illus. LC 92-34260. 1993. 4.25 (*0-383-03660-7*) SRA Schl Grp.

Carbone, Terry. Happy As a Tapir. DuQuette, Keith, illus. 32p. 1992. 13.00 (*0-670-84227-3*) Viking Child Bks.

Carlstrom, Nancy W. What Would You Do If You Lived at the Zoo? Boyd, Lizi, illus. LC 93-7036. 1994. 13.95 (*0-316-12867-8*) Little.

Carney, Charles. Twenty Thousand Leaks under the Sea. Kong, Emilie, illus. 24p. (ps-4). 1993. 20.00 (*0-307-74030-7*, 64030, Golden Pr) Western Pub.

Carpenter, Humphrey. The Wind in the Willows. write for info. HM.

Carratello, Patty. Duke the Blue Mule. Spivak, Darlene, ed. Smythe, Linda, illus. 16p. (gr. k-2). 1988. wkbk. 1.95 (*1-55734-384-5*) Tchr Create Mat.

Carrick, Carol. Banana Beer. Apple, Margot, illus. LC 94-256. 1994. write for info. (*0-8075-0568-4*) A Whitman.

—Big Old Bones: A Dinosaur Tale. Carrick, Donald, illus. 32p. (gr. k-2). 1989. 14.95 (*0-89919-734-5*, Clarion Bks) HM.

Carrier, Lark. A Christmas Promise. LC 91-14556. (Illus.). 28p. (gr. k up). 1991. pap. 4.95 (*0-88708-180-0*) Picture Bk Studio.

Carris, Joan. Hedgehogs in the Closet. Newsom, Carol, illus. LC 87-45309. 160p. (gr. 5 up). 1988. (Lipp Jr Bks); (Lipp Jr Bks) HarpC Child Bks.

Caruso, Carol. Harry the Hedgehog Goes Hunting. Caruso, Carol, illus. 20p. 1994. 11.95 (*0-9640429-1-6*) MinneApplePress.

Casad, Mary B. Bluebonnet at Dinosaur Valley State Park. Vinvent, Benjamin, illus. LC 90-7338. 32p. (gr. k-3). 1990. 13.95 (*0-88289-776-4*) Pelican.

Cazet, Denys. Mother Night. LC 88-36439. (Illus.). 32p. (ps-1). 1989. 14.95 (*0-531-05830-1*); PLB 14.99 (*0-531-08430-2*) Orchard Bks Watts.

Cecil, Laura. Preposterous Pets. Clark, Emma C., photos by. LC 94-6527. (Illus.). 80p. 1995. write for info. RTE (*0-688-13581-1*) Greenwillow.

Cecil, Terry & Cecil, Barbara. Chrisgopher Columbus in Stowaway on the Santa Maria. Smallwood, Steve, illus. 32p. (Orig.). (gr. k-6). 1992. PLB 4.00 (*0-9633016-0-8*) Infiniti.

Chapman, Cheryl. Pass the Fritters, Critters. Roth, Susan L., illus. LC 91-45055. 40p. (ps-k). 1993. RSBE 14.95 (*0-02-717975-3*, Four Winds) Macmillan Child Grp.

Chapman, William G. Green-Timber Trails: Wild Animal Stories of the North Country. Berle, Peter A., frwd. by. (Illus.). 304p. 1992. pap. 13.00 (*0-88150-240-5*) Countryman.

Chestney, P. L. When the Animals Left. Chestney, P. L., illus. 52p. (gr. 1-6). 1994. pap. 12.95 (*1-883533-00-7*) PL&R Chestney.

Chipperfield, Jean. A Fortnight of Bedtime Animal Tales. 1994. 7.95 (*0-533-10378-9*) Vantage.

Christiana, David. White Nineteens. (Illus.). 32p. (ps-3). 1992. 15.00 (*0-374-38390-1*) FS&G.

Clark, Judith. Too Many Animals Sleep in My Bed. Haughom, Lisa, illus. (ps-k). 1993. write for info. (*1-56156-264-5*) Kidsbks.

Clement, Claude. Be Careful, Little Antelope. Jensen, Patricia, adapted by. Pio, illus. LC 93-2950. 22p. (ps-3). 1993. 5.98 (*0-89577-504-2*, Readers Digest Kids) RD Assn.

—Be Patient, Little Chick. Jensen, Patricia, adapted by. Erost, illus. LC 93-2951. 22p. (ps-3). 1993. 5.98 (*0-89577-503-4*, Readers Digest Kids) RD Assn.

—Little Donkey Learns to Help. Jensen, Patricia, adapted by. Pascal, Robin, illus. LC 93-2952. 22p. (ps-3). 1993. 5.98 (*0-89577-502-6*, Readers Digest Kids) RD Assn.

—Little Squirrel's Special Nest. Jensen, Patricia, adapted by. LC 93-4243. (Illus.). 22p. (ps-3). 1993. 5.98 (*0-89577-542-5*, Reader's Digest Kids) RD Assn.

Clifford, Eth. Flatfoot Fox & the Case of the Bashful Beaver. Lies, Brian, illus. LC 94-14761. 1995. write for info. (*0-395-70560-6*) HM.

—Flatfoot Fox & the Case of the Missing Whoooo. Lies, Brian, illus. LC 92-21903. 1993. 13.95 (*0-395-65364-9*) HM.

—Flatfoot Fox & the Case of the Nosy Otter. Lies, Brian, illus. LC 91-26930. 48p. (gr. 2-5). 1992. 13.45 (*0-395-60289-0*) HM.

Coats, Laura J. Ten Little Animals. Coats, Laura J., illus. LC 89-36778. 32p. (ps-1). 1990. RSBE 12.95 (*0-02-719054-4*, Macmillan Child Bk) Macmillan Child Grp.

Cohen, Daniel. Phantom Animals. Ashby, Ruth, ed. 112p. 1993. pap. 2.99 (*0-671-75930-2*, Minstrel Bks) PB.

Cole, Michael. Head in the Sand. Clifford, Rowan, illus. LC 90-30086. 24p. (ps-3). 1990. PLB 13.50 (*0-87614-435-0*) Carolrhoda Bks.

Cole, William E. Arkful of Animals. (gr. 4-7). 1992. pap. 3.80 (*0-395-61618-2*) HM.

Coleman, William L. If Animals Could Talk. LC 87-7141. (Illus.). 144p. (Orig.). (gr. 2-6). 1987. pap. 6.99 (*0-87123-961-2*) Bethany Hse.

Collicott, Sharleen. Seeing Stars. Collicott, Sharleen, illus. LC 93-49846. 1994. 14.99 (*0-8037-1522-6*); write for info. (*0-8037-1523-4*) Dial Bks Young.

Collins, David R. Ceb's Amazing Tail. (Illus.). (ps-2). 1987. PLB 6.95 (*0-8136-5185-9*, TK7273); pap. 3.50 (*0-8136-5685-0*, TK7274) Modern Curr.

—Hali's Amazing Wings. (Illus.). (ps-2). 1987. PLB 6.95 (*0-8136-5183-2*, TK7271); pap. 3.50 (*0-8136-5683-4*, TK7272) Modern Curr.

Collins, Pat L. Tomorrow, up & Away. Munsinger, Lynn, illus. 32p. (gr. k-3). 1990. 13.45 (*0-395-51524-6*) HM.

Cooke, Tom, illus. Big Bird's Animal Game. 14p. (ps). 1993. bds. 3.95 (*0-307-12395-2*, 12395, Golden Pr) Western Pub.

Cooper, Susan. Matthew's Dragon. Smith, Jos. A., illus. LC 90-31532. 32p. (ps-3). 1991. SBE 14.95 (*0-689-50512-4*, M K McElderry) Macmillan Child Grp.

Corddry, Thomas. Kibby & the Red Elephant. Kock, Carl, illus. LC 72-13771. (gr. 3-6). 1973. 6.95 (*0-87955-106-2*) O'Hara.

Corey, Donna. Where is Manatee: A First Book. rev. ed. Corey, Donna, illus. Strykowski, Joe, photos by. LC 92-60557. (Illus.). 48p. (ps-6). 1992. pap. 4.95 (*1-879488-00-0*) Sundiver.

Cosgrove, Stephen. Catundra. James, Robin, illus. 32p. (Orig.). (gr. 1-4). 1978. pap. 2.95 (*0-8431-0571-2*) Price Stern.

—Kiyomi. James, Robin, illus. 32p. (Orig.). (gr. 1-4). 1984. pap. 2.95 (*0-8431-1164-X*) Price Stern.

—Minikin. James, Robin, illus. 32p. (Orig.). (gr. 1-4). 1984. pap. 2.95 (*0-8431-1163-1*) Price Stern.

Craig, Janet A. The Boo-Hoo Witch. Schories, Patricia L., illus. LC 93-2216. 32p. (gr. k-2). 1993. PLB 11.59 (*0-8167-3186-1*); pap. text ed. 2.95 (*0-8167-3187-X*) Troll Assocs.

Craig, Judi. Wally Whale: Wally's Wonderful Wish. Pamiel, illus. 32p. (gr. 1-3). 1994. 14.95 (*0-87604-322-8*) ARE Pr.

Croser, Nigel. Help! Alder, George, illus. LC 89-35648. 28p. (gr. 1-2). 1989. PLB 17.27 (*0-8368-0223-3*) Gareth Stevens Inc.

Crowe, Robert L. Tyler Toad & the Thunder. Chorao, Kay, illus. LC 80-347. 32p. (ps-1). 1980. 9.95 (*0-525-41795-8*, DCB) Dutton Child Bks.

Crowther, Robert. Who Lives in the Country? Crowther, Robert, illus. LC 91-58766. 10p. (ps). 1992. 6.95 (*1-56402-090-8*) Candlewick Pr.

—Who Lives in the Garden? Crowther, Robert, illus. LC 91-58767. 10p. (ps). 1992. 6.95 (*1-56402-091-6*) Candlewick Pr.

Crutcher, Chris. Running Loose. (gr. 7 up). 1986. pap. 3.50 (*0-440-97570-0*, LFL) Dell.

Culton, Wilma. Down at the Billabong. Crossett, Warren, illus. LC 92-31951. 1993. 3.75 (*0-383-03565-1*) SRA Schl Grp.

Cummings, Pat. Carousel. Cummings, Pat, illus. LC 93-8708. 32p. (ps-3). 1994. RSBE 14.95 (*0-02-725512-3*, Bradbury Pr) Macmillan Child Grp.

Cushman, Doug. Aunt Eater Loves a Mystery. 15p. 1991. text ed. 1.20 (*1-56956-189-3*) W A T Braille.

—Mouse & Mole & the Year - Round Garden. LC 93-37202. (gr. 4 up). 1993. text ed. write for info. (*0-7167-6524-1*, Sci Am Yng Rdrs) W H Freeman.

Cuyler, Margery. That's Good! That's Bad! Catrow, David, illus. LC 90-49353. 32p. (ps-2). 1991. 15.95 (*0-8050-1535-3*, Bks Young Read) H Holt & Co.

Dahl, Roald. The Wonderful Story of Henry Sugar & Six More. LC 77-5354. 32p. (gr. 5 up). 1977. 17.00 (*0-394-83604-9*) Knopf Bks Yng Read.

Dahlquist, Kathleen C. The Little Brown Donkey. Hoffman, Beverly, illus. 64p. (Orig.). (gr. 3). 1994. pap. write for info. (*0-9634122-8-0*) Feather Fables.

Dalgliesh, Alice. Fourth of July Story. Nonnast, Marie, illus. LC 56-6138. 32p. (ps-3). 1972. RSBE 13.95 (*0-684-13164-1*, Scribners Young Read); (Scribner) Macmillan Child Grp.

Daniel, Jennifer. Animal Shapes. Stinga, Frank, illus. 12p. (ps). Date not set. 2.95 (*1-56828-059-9*) Red Jacket Pr.

Daniel, Rebecca. Goldilocks & the Three Bears. (Illus.). 16p. (ps-2). 1992. 16.95 (*0-86653-667-1*, GA1399) Good Apple.

—The Three Little Pigs. (Illus.). 16p. (ps-2). 1992. 16.95 (*0-86653-668-X*, GA1397) Good Apple.

Danziger, Paula. It's an Aardvark-Eat-Turtle World. (gr. 5 up). 1986. pap. 3.50 (*0-440-94028-1*, LFL) Dell.

Davis, Lee. Big Or Little: The Lifesize Animal Opposites Book. (Illus.). 32p. (ps). 1994. 12.95 (*1-56458-720-7*) Dorling Kindersley.

Day, Alexandra. Frank & Ernest. Day, Alexandra, illus. 40p. (gr. k-3). 1988. 13.95 (*0-590-41557-3*, Pub. by Scholastic Hardcover) Scholastic Inc.

Day, David. The King of the Woods. Brown, Ken, illus. LC 93-9410. 32p. (ps-2). 1993. RSBE 13.95 (*0-02-726361-4*, Four Winds) Macmillan Child Grp.

De Beer, Hans. Kleiner Eisbar, Wohin Fahrst Du? De Beer, Hans, illus. (GER.). 32p. (gr. k-3). 1992. 13.95 (*3-85825-290-5*) North-South Bks NYC.

—Plume S'Echappe. De Beer, Hans, illus. (FRE.). 32p. (gr. k-3). 1992. 13.95 (*3-314-20719-0*) North-South Bks NYC.

—Le Voyage de Plume. De Beer, Hans, illus. (FRE.). 32p. (gr. k-3). 1992. 13.95 (*3-314-20619-4*) North-South Bks NYC.

De Brunhoff, Laurent. The Rescue of Babar. De Brunhoff, Laurent, illus. LC 92-50958. 36p. (ps-3). 1993. 20.00 (*0-679-83897-X*) Random Bks Yng Read.

DeGroat, Florence. Animal Stories. Wilson, Patricia, illus. 88p. (gr. 2-6). 1983. pap. 2.95 (*0-87516-509-5*) DeVorss.

Delton, Judy. Greedy Groundhogs. (ps-3). 1994. pap. 3.25 (*0-440-40931-4*) Dell.

—The Perfect Christmas Gift. McCue, Lisa, illus. LC 91-6549. 32p. (gr. k-3). 1992. RSBE 13.95 (*0-02-728471-9*, Macmillan Child Bk) Macmillan Child Grp.

DeLuca, June M. The Lily Pad Four & Friends. Faycheux, Wallace P., Jr., illus. 32p. (gr. k-2). 1992. pap. 2.95 (*0-8198-4431-4*) St Paul Bks.

Demers, Paul. Oliver & Ophelia: A Tale of Opossums. Delaney, Jacqueline K., illus. LC 85-6020. 20p. (Orig.). (gr. 1-6). 1986. pap. 2.95 (*0-916897-04-4*) Andrew Mtn Pr.

Demuth, Patricia B. Ornery Morning. Brown, Craig M., illus. LC 90-40188. 24p. (ps-1). 1991. 13.95 (*0-525-44688-5*, DCB) Dutton Child Bks.

Dennison, George. And Then a Harvest Feast. (gr. 4-7). 1992. pap. 4.50 (*0-374-40377-5*) FS&G.

Denzel, Justin. Land of the Thundering Herds. Watkinson, Brent, illus. LC 92-26222. 176p. (gr. 5 up). 1993. 14.95 (*0-399-21894-7*, Philomel Bks) Putnam Pub Group.

De Paola, Tomie. Jingle the Christmas Clown. (Illus.). 40p. (ps-3). 1992. 15.95 (*0-399-22338-X*, Putnam) Putnam Pub Group.

DePaola, Tomie. Little Grunt & the Big Egg. DePaola, Tomie, illus. (ps-3). 1993. pap. 5.95 (*0-8234-1027-7*) Holiday.

De Regniers, Beatrice S. Going for a Walk. newly illus ed. Knox, Robert, illus. LC 91-43177. 32p. (ps-1). 1993. 15.00 (*0-06-022954-3*); PLB 14.89 (*0-06-022957-8*) HarpC Child Bks.

Desputeaux, Helene. Lollypop's Animals. (Illus.). 8p. (ps). 1993. bath bk. 4.95 (*2-921198-41-X*, Pub. by Les Edits Herit CN) Adams Inc MA.

Devilleres, David L. The Rescuers. (gr. 3 up). 1993. 7.95 (*0-8062-4724-X*) Carlton.

Devlin, Wende & Devlin, Harry. Cranberry Summer. Devlin, Harry, illus. LC 90-24560. 40p. (gr. k-3). 1992. RSBE 13.95 (*0-02-729181-2*, Four Winds) Macmillan Child Grp.

Dewan, Ted. Inside the Whale & Other Animals. (ps). 1992. pap. 16.00 (*0-385-30651-2*) Doubleday.

De Wijs, Ivo. Where Is Springer? Van Den Hurk, Nicolle, illus. 32p. (ps-2). 1993. 12.95 (*0-8120-6360-0*); pap. 4.95 (*0-8120-1728-5*) Barron.

Diestel-Feddersen, Mary. Try Again, Sally Jane. Ashley, Yvonne, illus. LC 86-42810. 30p. (gr. 2-3). 1987. PLB 18.60 (*1-55532-150-X*) Gareth Stevens Inc.

Dijs, Carla. Who Sees You? In the Jungle. (Illus.). 12p. (ps-k). 1992. 5.95 (*0-448-40310-2*, G&D) Putnam Pub Group.

Dijs, Carla, illus. Who Sees You? Underground. 12p. (ps). 1993. 5.95 (*0-448-40080-4*, G&D) Putnam Pub Group.

Diop, Birago. Mother Crocodile: "Maman-Caiman" LC 80-393. (ps-3). 1993. 15.00 (*0-385-30803-5*) Doubleday.

Disney Babies del a al 10. (SPA.). (ps-3). 1993. pap. 4.95 (*0-307-72324-0*, Golden Pr) Western Pub.

Disney Little Libraries: White. 5p. (Incls. Minnie at the Beach, Mickey on the Farm, Donald in the Mountains & Goofy on Vacation). (ps). 1992. bds. 5.98 (*0-8317-2376-9*) Viking Child Bks.

Disney Little Libraries: Yellow. 5p. (Incls. Alice in Wonderland, Dumbo at the Airport, Winnie the Pooh is Hungry & Lady at the Pond). 1992. bds. 5.98 (*0-8317-2377-7*) Viking Child Bks.

Disney, Walt, Productions Staff. Walt Disney Productions Presents Tod & Copper from The Fox & the Hound. LC 81-2619. (Illus.). 48p. (ps-3). 1981. 4.95 (*0-394-84819-5*) Random Bks Yng Read.

—Walt Disney Productions Presents Tod & Vixey from The Fox & the Hound. LC 81-5209. (Illus.). 48p. (ps-3). 1981. 4.95 (*0-394-84904-3*) Random Bks Yng Read.

—Walt Disney's the Adventures of Mr. Toad Adapted from the Wind in the Willows. LC 81-2783. (Illus.). 48p. (ps-3). 1981. 4.95 (*0-394-84818-7*) Random Bks Yng Read.

Dobson, Danae. Forest Friends Help Each Other. Morales, Cuitlahuac, illus. 32p. (ps-k). 1993. 7.99 (*0-8499-0986-4*) Word Inc.

—Forest Friends Learn to Be Kind. Morales, Cuitlahuac, illus. 32p. 1993. 7.99 (*0-8499-1016-1*) Word Inc.

—Forest Friends Learn to Share. Morales, Cuitlahuac, illus. 32p. (ps-k). 1993. 7.99 (*0-8499-0985-6*) Word Inc.

—Forest Friends Play Fair. Morales, Cuitlahuac, illus. 32p. (ps-k). 1993. 7.99 (*0-8499-0987-2*) Word Inc.

Dockery, Della. Cami & Other Familiar Friends. Dockery, Della, illus. 20p. (ps). 1987. pap. 2.95 (*0-943487-05-6*) Sevgo Pr.

Dodd, Lynley. Find Me a Tiger. LC 91-50553. (Illus.). 32p. (gr. 1-2). 1992. PLB 17.27 (*0-8368-0762-6*) Gareth Stevens Inc.

Dodds, Dayle A. On Our Way to Market. Gurney, John, illus. LC 91-6436. 40p. (ps-k). 1991. pap. 13.95 jacketed (*0-671-73567-5*, S&S BFYR) S&S Trade.

Dodds, Dayle Ann. Someone Is Hiding. 1994. PLB 8.95 (*0-671-75542-0*, Little Simon) S&S Trade.

Doherty, Berlie. Willa & Old Miss Annie. Lewis, Kim, illus. LC 93-970. 96p. (gr. 3-6). 1994. 14.95 (*1-56402-331-1*) Candlewick Pr.

Doney, Meryl. The Ninety-Ninth Sheep. (Illus.). 1991. 8.99 (*0-8423-4740-2*) Tyndale.

Donovan, Mary L. Papa's Bedtime Story. Root, Kimberly B., illus. LC 91-27792. 40p. (ps-3). 1993. 15.00 (*0-679-81790-5*); PLB 15.99 (*0-679-91790-X*) Knopf Bks Yng Read.

Dorros, Arthur. Las Huellas de los Animales: Animal Tracks. Dorros, Sandra M., tr. from ENG. (SPA., Illus.). (ps-2). 1993. pap. 4.95 (*0-590-46847-2*) Scholastic Inc.

Dowling, Pat. The Hungry Anteater. (Illus.). 32p. (ps-2). 1992. 15.95 (*0-86264-345-7*, Pub. by Andersen Pr UK) Trafalgar.

Dowling, Paul. Where Are You Going, Jimmy? LC 92-27206. (Illus.). 24p. (ps-3). 1993. 12.95 (*1-56566-026-9*) Thomasson-Grant.

Downing, Julie. White Snow - Blue Feather. Downing, Julie, illus. LC 89-815. 32p. (ps-1). 1989. RSBE 14.95 (*0-02-732530-X*, Bradbury Pr) Macmillan Child Grp.

Dragonwagon, Crescent. Alligator Arrived with Apples: A Potluck Alphabet Feast. Aruego, Jose & Dewey, Ariane, illus. LC 91-38490. 40p. (gr. k-3). 1992. pap. 4.95 (*0-689-71613-3*, Aladdin) Macmillan Child Grp.

Drew, David. The Python Caught the Eagle. Reynolds, Pat, illus. LC 92-31134. 1993. 2.50 (*0-383-03648-8*) SRA Schl Grp.
—The Seesaw. Forss, Ian, illus. LC 92-21394. (gr. 2 up). 1993. 2.50 (*0-685-69191-8*) SRA Schl Grp.
—Two More. Jacobs, Elizabeth, illus. LC 92-31957. 1993. 3.75 (*0-383-03600-3*) SRA Schl Grp.
Druce, Arden. Witch, Witch. LC 91-29763. 1991. 11.95 (*0-85953-780-3*); pap. 5.95 (*0-685-52311-X*) Childs Play.
Duffey, Betsy. The Wild Things. Natti, Susanna, illus. LC 92-25938. 80p. (gr. 2-6). 1993. 12.99 (*0-670-84347-4*) Viking Child Bks.
Duke, Kate. Aunt Isabel Tells a Good One. Duke, Kate, illus. LC 91-14598. 32p. (ps-2). 1992. 14.00 (*0-525-44835-7*, DCB) Dutton Child Bks.
—If You Walk Down This Road. Duke, Kate, illus. LC 92-27685. 32p. (ps-k). 1993. 13.99 (*0-525-45072-6*, DCB) Dutton Child Bks.
Dummer, H. Boylston. Adventures of the Animal Town Aviators, Bk. I. Dummer, H. Boylston, illus. 118p. (ps-3). 1989. 17.95 (*0-87510-198-4*) Christian Sci.
—Adventures of the Animal Town Aviators, Bk. II. Dummer, H. Boylston, illus. 118p. (ps-3). 1989. 17.95 (*0-87510-199-2*) Christian Sci.
Duncan, Riana. A Nutcracker in a Tree: A Book of Riddles. Duncan, Riana, illus. LC 80-67492. 32p. (gr. k-3). 1981. PLB 8.95 (*0-385-28733-X*); pap. 8.95 (*0-385-28732-1*) Delacorte.
Dunrea, Olivier. Deep down Underground. Dunrea, Olivier, illus. LC 92-45273. 32p. (gr. k-3). 1993. pap. 4.95 (*0-689-71756-3*, Aladdin) Macmillan Child Grp.
DuQuette, Keith. Hotel Animal. DuQuette, Keith, illus. LC 93-14531. 32p. (ps-3). 1994. PLB 13.99 (*0-670-85056-X*) Viking Child Bks.
Dyer, Ruth. Starlights. LC 89-51255. 50p. (gr. k-3). 1992. pap. 5.95 (*1-55523-258-2*) Winston-Derek.
Economos, Chris. Let's Take the Bus. (Illus.). 32p. (gr. 1-4). 1989. PLB 18.99 (*0-8172-3500-0*); pap. 3.95 (*0-8114-6702-3*) Raintree Steck-V.
Edens, Cooper. Shawnee Bill's Enchanted Five-Ride Carousel. 1994. 15.00 (*0-671-75952-3*, Green Tiger) S&S Trade.
Edge, Nellie, compiled by. Make Friends with Mother Goose, Vol. II. Saylor, Melissa, illus. (ps-2). 1991. pap. text ed. 15.00 (*0-922053-24-3*) N Edge Res.
—Make Friends with Mother Goose Big Book, Vol. I. Saylor, Melissa, illus. (ps-2). 1988. pap. text ed. 15.00 (*0-922053-11-1*) N Edge Res.
Edmiston, Jim. Mizzy & the Tigers. (ps-3). 1992. pap. 5.95 (*0-8120-4828-8*) Barron.
Edwards, Richard. Moles Can Dance. Anstey, Caroline, illus. LC 93-2462. 32p. (ps up). 1994. 13.95 (*1-56402-361-3*) Candlewick Pr.
Elliott, Dan. Una Visita a la Estacion de Bomberos de Sesame Street. Miro, Norma S. & Saunders, Paola B., trs. from ENG. Mathieu, Joe, illus. LC 92-3814. (SPA.). 32p. (ps-3). 1992. pap. 2.25 (*0-679-83499-0*) Random Bks Yng Read.
Elliott, Joey. Beezle's Bravery. Chapin, Tom, narrated by. Buzzanco, Eileen M., illus. 32p. (gr. 2-5). 1989. 11.95 (*0-924483-17-2*); incl. audiocassette 16.95 (*0-924483-15-6*); incl. audiocassette & toy combination 39.95 (*0-924483-13-X*); incl. audiocassette & small toy combination 25.95 (*0-924483-35-0*); write for info. audiocassette (*0-924483-19-9*) Soundprints.
—Scamp's New Home. Chapin, Tom, narrated by. Buzzanco, Eileen M., illus. 32p. (gr. 2-5). 1989. 11.95 (*0-924483-16-4*); incl. audiocassette 16.95 (*0-924483-14-8*); incl. audiocassette & toy combination 39.95 (*0-924483-12-1*); incl. audiocassette & small toy combination 25.95 (*0-924483-39-3*); write for info. audiocassette (*0-924483-18-0*) Soundprints.
Enns, Peter & Forsberg, Glen. Six Stories of Jesus. Friesen, John H., illus. 24p. (ps-5). 1985. 4.95 (*0-936215-05-4*); cassette incl. STL Intl.
Erickson, Gina C. & Foster, Kelli C. Find Nat. Russell, Kerri G., illus. 24p. (ps-2). 1991. pap. 3.50 (*0-8120-4678-1*) Barron.
—The Tan Can. Gifford-Russell, Kerri, illus. 24p. 1992. pap. 3.50 (*0-8120-4856-3*) Barron.
Erickson, Gina C. & Goster, Kelli C. Tall & Small. Gifford, Kerri, illus. 24p. (ps-3). 1994. pap. 3.50 (*0-685-71901-4*) Barron.
Erickson, Russell. A Toad for Tuesday. Di Fiori, Lawrence, illus. LC 73-19900. 64p. (gr. k-4). 1974. PLB 12.93 (*0-688-51569-X*) Lothrop.
ETR Associates Staff. Messages from the Zoo. Paley, Nina, illus. LC 93-16477. 1993. write for info. ETR Assocs.
Ets, Marie H. Play with Me. Ets, Marie H., illus. (ps-1). 1955. pap. 13.95 (*0-670-55977-6*) Viking Child Bks.
Ewart, Claire. One Cold Night. (Illus.). 32p. (ps-1). 1992. 14.95 (*0-399-22341-X*, Putnam) Putnam Pub Group.
Farmer, Tony. How Small Is an Ant? (ps-3). pap. 3.95 (*0-85953-518-5*) Childs Play.
Farmer, Tony & Farmer, Lynne. How BIG Is an Elephant? LC 91-285. (gr. 3 up). 1991. 3.95 (*0-85953-516-9*) Childs Play.
Faulkner, Keith. Animal Tales. Lambert, Jonathan, illus. 24p. (ps-1). 1994. pap. 7.95 (*0-8431-3719-3*) Price Stern.
Feldman, Eve. Get Set & Go! (Illus.). 32p. (gr. 1-4). 1989. PLB 18.99 (*0-8172-3501-9*); pap. 3.95 (*0-8114-6701-5*) Raintree Steck-V.
Finzel, Julia. Large As Life. LC 90-49816. (Illus.). 32p. (ps up). 1991. PLB 14.88 (*0-688-10653-6*) Lothrop.
Fisher, Barbara. Big Harold & Tiny Enid. (Illus.). 26p. (Orig.). (gr. 1-3). 1975. pap. 2.00 (*0-934830-01-0*) Ten Penny.
FitzSimmons, Joy. Hide & Seek. FitzSimmons, Joy, illus. LC 91-38246. 32p. (ps). 1992. PLB 9.95 (*0-87226-467-X*, Bedrick Blackie) P Bedrick Bks.
Flack, Marjorie. Ask Mr. Bear. Flack, Marjorie, illus. LC 58-8370. 32p. (ps-1). 1971. pap. 4.95 (*0-02-043090-6*, Aladdin) Macmillan Child Grp.
Fleming, Denise. In the Small, Small Pond. Fleming, Denise, illus. LC 92-25770. 32p. (ps-1). 1993. 15.95 (*0-8050-2264-3*, Bks Young Read) H Holt & Co.
—In the Tall, Tall Grass. Fleming, Denise, illus. LC 90-26444. 32p. (ps-1). 1991. 15.95 (*0-8050-1635-X*, Bks Young Read) H Holt & Co.
Fontenot, Mary A. Clovis Crawfish & Batiste Bete Puante. Blazek, Scott R., illus. LC 93-1249. 32p. (gr. k-3). 1993. 14.95 (*0-88289-952-X*) Pelican.
—Clovis Crawfish & Bertile's Bon Voyage. Blazek, Scott R., illus. LC 90-22160. 32p. (ps-3). 1991. 12.95 (*0-88289-825-6*) Pelican.
—Clovis Crawfish & Bidon Box Turtle. Blazek, Scott R., illus. LC 93-44340. 1996. write for info. (*1-56554-057-3*) Pelican.
—Clovis Crawfish & Etienne Escargot. Blazek, Scott R., illus. LC 91-26896. 32p. (ps-3). 1992. 12.95 (*0-88289-826-4*) Pelican.
—Clovis Crawfish & His Friends: French Edition. Graves, Keith, illus. (FRE.). 32p. (ps-3). 1995. write for info. Pelican.
—Clovis Crawfish & Michelle Mantis. Blazek, Scott R., illus. LC 88-30305. 32p. (ps-3). 1989. 12.95 (*0-88289-730-6*) Pelican.
—Clovis Crawfish & Petit Papillon. Graves, Keith, illus. LC 83-27325. 32p. (ps-3). 1985. Repr. 12.95 (*0-88289-448-X*) Pelican.
—Clovis Crawfish & the Orphan Zo Zo. Vincent, Eric, illus. LC 81-17740. 32p. (ps-3). 1983. 12.95 (*0-88289-312-2*) Pelican.
—Clovis Crawfish & the Singing Cigales. Vincent, Eric, illus. LC 81-5608. 32p. (ps-3). 1981. 12.95 (*0-88289-270-3*) Pelican.
Fowler, Richard. Honeybee's Busy Day. LC 93-31152. 1994. 12.95 (*0-15-200055-0*, Gulliver Bks) HarBrace.
Fox, Mem. Time for Bed. Dyer, Jane, illus. LC 92-19771. 1993. 13.95 (*0-15-288183-2*) HarBrace.
The Fox with Cold Feet. 42p. (ps-3). 1993. PLB 13.26 (*0-8368-0890-8*); PLB 13.27 s.p. (*0-685-61522-7*) Gareth Stevens Inc.
Frederick, Ruth. A Surprise for Miss Van. O'Connell, Ruth A., illus. 32p. (gr. 1-2). 1991. pap. 3.99 (*0-87403-805-7*, 24-03895) Standard Pub.
Freeman, Chester D. & McGuire, John E. Runaway Bear. Kuper, Rachel, illus. LC 93-16893. 32p. (gr. k-3). 1993. 14.95 (*0-88289-956-2*); ltd. boxed signed ed. 29. 95 (*1-56554-016-6*) Pelican.
Galdone, Paul. The Little Red Hen. LC 72-97770. (Illus.). 32p. (ps-2). 1979. 13.45 (*0-395-28803-7*, Clarion Bks) HM.
Galdone, Paul, retold by. & illus. The Three Billy Goats Gruff. LC 72-85338. 32p. (ps-3). 1979. 14.95 (*0-395-28812-6*, Clarion Bks) HM.
Gambill, Henrietta D. Little Christmas Animals. LC 94-10000. 1994. 1.89 (*0-7847-0274-8*) Standard Pub.
Gantos, Jack. Rotten Ralph's Show & Tell. Rubel, Nicole, illus. 32p. (gr. k-3). 1991. pap. 4.80 (*0-395-60285-8*, Sandpiper) HM.
Garis, Howard R. Uncle Wiggily's Storybook. (Illus.). 260p. (ps-4). 1987. 10.95 (*0-448-40090-1*, G&D) Putnam Pub Group.
Garside, Alice H. The Man, the Fox & the Skunk. Meeks, Catherine F., illus. 24p. (Orig.). (gr. k-2). 1989. pap. text ed. 2.10 (*1-882063-06-6*) Cottage Pr MA.
Gee, John. Timbertoes. (Illus.). 32p. (gr. k-2). 1967. pap. 2.95 (*0-87534-133-0*) Highlights.
George, William T. & George, Lindsay B. Fishing at Long Pond. LC 89-77514. (Illus.). 24p. (ps up). 1991. 13.95 (*0-688-09401-5*); PLB 13.88 (*0-688-09402-3*) Greenwillow.
Geraghty, Paul. Stop That Noise! Geraghty, Paul, illus. LC 92-6608. 32p. (ps-2). 1992. 13.00 (*0-517-59158-8*); PLB 13.99 (*0-517-59159-6*) Crown Bks Yng Read.
Geringer, Laura. The Cow Is Mooing Anyhow. Zimmer, Dirk, illus. LC 85-45251. 40p. (ps-4). 1991. HarpC Child Bks.
Gerstein, Mordecai. Daisy's Garden. Date not set. 15.00 (*0-06-021141-5*, HarpT); PLB 14.89 (*0-06-021142-3*, HarpT) HarpC.
Gerstein, Mordicai & Harris, Susan Y. Daisy's Garden. LC 94-22123. (gr. 1-8). 1995. write for info. (*0-7868-0096-8*); write for info. (*0-7868-2080-2*) Hyprn Child.
Gibbons, Gail. Prehistoric Animals. Gibbons, Gail, illus. LC 88-4661. 32p. (ps-3). 1988. reinforced bdg. 15.95 (*0-8234-0707-1*) Holiday.
Giff, Patricia R. Lazy Lions, Lucky Lambs. Sims, Blanche, illus. 80p. (gr. k-6). 1985. pap. 3.50 (*0-440-44640-6*, YB) Dell.
Gifford, Griselda. Revenge of the Wildcat. (Illus.). 106p. (gr. 3-6). 1991. pap. 6.95 (*0-86241-334-6*, Pub. by Cnngt Pub Ltd) Trafalgar.
Ginsburg, Mirra. Across the Stream. Tafuri, Nancy, illus. LC 81-20306. 24p. (ps-1). 1982. 15.95 (*0-688-01204-3*); PLB 15.88 (*0-688-01206-X*) Greenwillow.
—Merry-Go-Round: Four Stories. Aruego, Jose & Dewey, Ariane, illus. LC 90-30439. 48p. 1992. 15.00 (*0-688-09256-X*); PLB 14.93 (*0-688-09257-8*) Greenwillow.
—Mushroom in the Rain. Aruego, Jose & Dewey, Ariane, illus. LC 72-92438. 32p. (ps-1). 1987. RSBE 13.95 (*0-02-736241-8*, Macmillan Child Bk) Macmillan Child Grp.
—Mushroom in the Rain. Ginsburg, Mirra, illus. LC 90-31814. 32p. (ps-1). 1990. pap. 3.95 (*0-689-71441-6*, Aladdin) Macmillan Child Grp.
Gipson, Morrell & Mangold, Paul. Whose Tracks Are These? Stefoff, Rebecca, ed. LC 90-13798. (Illus.). 24p. (gr. k-3). 1990. PLB 14.60 (*0-944483-93-3*) Garrett Ed Corp.
Glaser, Michael. Does Anyone Know Where a Hermit Crab Goes? Glaser, Michael, illus. LC 82-84341. 32p. (Orig.). (ps-3). 1983. pap. 3.95 (*0-911635-00-9*) Knickerbocker.
Gleeson, Kate. Kate Gleeson's Mary Had a Little Lamb. (ps). 1994. 2.25 (*0-307-06071-3*, Golden Pr) Western Pub.
Goldsborough, June. What's in the Woods? LC 76-10271. (Illus.). 32p. 1981. P-H.
Gomi, Taro. Everyone Poops. Stinchecum, Amanda M., tr. from JPN. 32p. (ps). 1993. 11.95 (*0-916291-45-6*) Kane-Miller Bk.
—My Friends. LC 89-23940. (Illus.). 40p. (ps-1). 1990. 9.95 (*0-87701-688-7*) Chronicle Bks.
Goodrich, Beatrice. Happy Hollow Stories, Bk. 1. LC 86-51204. (Illus.). 54p. (gr. k-6). 1987. pap. 5.95 (*0-932433-20-0*) Windswept Hse.
Goofy Gets Goofy. 20p. 1994. 7.98 (*1-57082-146-1*) Mouse Works.
Graham. Wind in the Willows. 1988. pap. 2.99 (*0-14-035087-X*, Puffin) Puffin Bks.
Graham, John. I Love You, Mouse. De Paola, Tomie, illus. LC 76-8022. (ps-2). 1976. 12.95 (*0-15-238005-1*, HB Juv Bks) HarBrace.
Graham, Kenneth W., Jr. Wind in the Willows. 224p. 1989. pap. 2.50 (*0-8125-0510-7*) Tor Bks.
Grahame, Kenneth. The Wind in the Willlows. LC 80-12509. 224p. (gr. 4-6). 1980. 19.95 (*0-8050-0213-8*, Bks Young Read) H Holt & Co.
—Wind in the Willows. (gr. 4 up). 1966. pap. 2.75 (*0-8049-0105-8*, CL-105) Airmont.
—The Wind in the Willows. 253p. (gr. 5-6). Repr. of 1908 ed. lib. bdg. 20.95x (*0-88411-877-0*, Pub. by Aeonian Pr) Amereon Ltd.
—Wind in the Willows. 234p. 1981. Repr. lib. bdg. 17.95 (*0-89966-305-2*) Buccaneer Bks.
—The Wind in the Willows. Morrill, Les, illus. Sale, Roger, intro. by. (Illus.). 256p. (gr. 4-12). 1983. pap. 1.95 (*0-553-21129-3*, Bantam Classics) Bantam.
—The Wind in the Willows. Burningham, John, illus. 240p. (gr. 1 up). 1983. 15.75 (*0-670-77120-1*) Viking Child Bks.
—The Wind in the Willows. Green, Peter, ed. (gr. 5 up). 1983. pap. 2.95 (*0-19-281640-3*) OUP.
—The Wind in the Willows. 75th Anniversary ed. Shepard, Ernest H., illus. Hodges, Margaret, pref. by. LC 83-11573. (Illus.). 256p. (gr. 3 up). 1983. SBE 18. 95 (*0-684-17957-1*, Scribners Young Read) Macmillan Child Grp.
—The Wind in the Willows. Burningham, John, illus. 240p. (gr. 4-6). 1984. pap. 2.95 (*0-14-031544-6*) Viking Child Bks.
—The Wind in the Willows. Flax, Zena, illus. LC 85-13538. 224p. (gr. 2 up). 1985. 12.95 (*0-915361-32-9*, Dist. by Watts) Modan-Adama Bks.
—The Wind in the Willows. Lee, Robert J., illus. 256p. (gr. 1 up). 1969. pap. 3.25 (*0-440-49555-5*, YB) Dell.
—The Wind in the Willows. Shepard, Ernest H., illus. LC 88-8046. 272p. (ps up). 1989. pap. 4.95 (*0-689-71310-X*, Aladdin) Macmillan Child Grp.
—Wind in the Willows. LC 87-15818. 1988. 12.99 (*0-517-63230-6*) Random Hse Value.
—The Wind in the Willows. Morrill, Les, illus. Sale, Roger, intro. by. (Illus.). 256p. 1983. pap. 2.95 (*0-553-21368-7*, Bantam Classics Spectra) Bantam.
—Wind in the Willows. 1988. 7.99 (*0-517-49284-9*) Random Hse Value.
—Wind in the Willows. 1987. 3.98 (*0-671-08895-5*) S&S Trade.
—Wind in the Willows. 256p. 1992. 9.49 (*0-8167-2562-4*); pap. 2.95 (*0-8167-2563-2*) Troll Assocs.
—Wind in the Willows. 1990. pap. 3.50 (*0-440-40385-5*, Pub. by Yearling Classics) Dell.
—The Wind in the Willows. Ashachik, Diane M., retold by. Lydecker, Laura, illus. LC 92-13203. 48p. (gr. 3-6). 1992. PLB 12.89 (*0-8167-2870-4*); pap. text ed. 3.95 (*0-8167-2871-2*) Troll Assocs.
—The Wind in the Willows. Daily, Don, illus. LC 93-70550. 56p. (gr. 2 up). 1993. 9.98 (*1-56138-276-0*) Courage Bks.
—The Wind in the Willows. (gr. 5 up). 1993. 13.95 (*0-679-41802-4*, Everymans Lib Childs) Knopf.
—Wind in the Willows. 1993. pap. 3.25 (*0-590-44774-2*) Scholastic Inc.
—Wind in the Willows. 1991. 19.95 (*0-8050-1664-3*) H Holt & Co.
—The Wind in the Willows. 176p. 1994. 5.98 (*0-685-72755-6*) Running Pr.
—Wind in the Willows, Vol. 1. 272p. (gr. 8 up). 1972. RSBE 13.95 (*0-684-12819-5*, Scribners Young Read) Macmillan Child Grp.

—Wind in the Willows: (El Viento en los Sauces I, II) (SPA.). Vol. I. 9.50 (*84-372-1882-9*) Vol. II. 9.50 (*84-372-1883-7*) Santillana.

Greaves, Margaret. The Naming. Baynes, Pauline, illus. 32p. (ps-3). 1993. 14.95 (*0-15-200534-X*) HarBrace.

Greeley, Valerie. Animals at Home. 12p. (gr. k-2). 1992. 5.95 (*0-87226-473-4*, Bedrick Blackie) P Bedrick Bks.

—White Is the Moon. Greeley, Valerie, illus. LC 90-40522. 32p. (ps-1). 1991. 13.95 (*0-02-736915-3*, Macmillan Child Bk) Macmillan Child Grp.

Green, Carl R. & Sanford, William R. The Porcupine. LC 85-7899. (Illus.). 48p. (gr. 5). 1985. RSBE 12.95 (*0-89686-280-1*, Crestwood Hse) Macmillan Child Grp.

Greenfield, Karen R. Sister Yessa's Story. Ewart, Claire, illus. LC 91-15634. 32p. (gr. k-4). 1992. 15.00 (*0-06-020278-5*); PLB 14.89 (*0-06-020279-3*) HarpC Child Bks.

Greer, Gery & Ruddick, Robert. Jason & the Aliens Down the Street. LC 90-47386. (Illus.). 96p. (gr. 2-5). 1992. pap. 3.95 (*0-06-440446-3*, Trophy) HarpC Child Bks.

Gregorich, Barbara. Nine Men Chase a Hen. Hoffman, Joan, ed. Sandford, John, illus. 16p. (Orig.). (gr. k-2). 1984. pap. 2.25 (*0-88743-009-0*, 06009) Sch Zone Pub Co.

Gretz, Susanna. Frog, Duck & Rabbit. Gretz, Susanna, illus. LC 91-16364. 32p. (ps-1). 1992. SBE 12.95 (*0-02-737327-4*, Four Winds) Macmillan Child Grp.

—Rabbit Rambles On. Gretz, Susanna, illus. LC 91-17069. 32p. (ps-1). 1992. SBE 12.95 (*0-02-737325-8*, Four Winds) Macmillan Child Grp.

Grey, J. The Turtle Who Wanted to Run. LC 68-56813. (Illus.). 32p. (gr. 1-3). 1968. PLB 9.95 (*0-87783-045-2*) Oddo.

Grindley, Sally, selected by. Animal Stories for the Very Young. LC 93-41503. (Illus.). 80p. (ps-2). 1994. 15.95 (*1-85697-944-X*, Kingfisher LKC) LKC.

Gross, Ruth B. The Bremen-Town Musicians. Kent, Jack, illus. 32p. (Orig.). (ps-2). 1985. pap. 2.50 (*0-590-42364-9*) Scholastic Inc.

Grosset & Dunlap Staff. Who Says Quack? (Illus.). 18p. (ps). 1991. bds. 2.95 (*0-448-40123-1*, G&D) Putnam Pub Group.

Grossman, Bill. Donna O'Neeshuck Was Chased by Some Cows. Truesdell, Sue, illus. LC 85-45823. 40p. (gr. k-3). 1988. PLB 12.89 (*0-06-022159-3*) HarpC Child Bks.

Grove, Vicki. Junglerama. (gr. 4-7). 1991. pap. 2.75 (*0-590-43163-3*, Apple Paperbacks) Scholastic Inc.

Gumbo Goes Downtown. (gr. 1-4). 1993. incl. video & tchr's. guide 79.95 (*1-55942-045-6*, 9373) Marshfilm.

Gurney, Nancy & Gurney, Eric. King, the Mice & the Cheese. Vallier, Jean, illus. LC 89-8463. 72p. (gr. k-3). 1965. 6.95 (*0-394-80039-7*); lib. bdg. 7.99 (*0-394-90039-1*) Random Bks Yng Read.

Guthrie, Donna. Nobiah's Well: A Modern African Folk Tale. Roth, Robert, illus. LC 93-586. 32p. (ps-2). 1993. PLB 15.00 (*0-8249-8631-8*, Ideals Child); 14.95 (*0-8249-8622-9*) Hambleton-Hill.

Haas, Jessie. The Sixth Sense & Other Stories. LC 88-45226. 192p. (gr. 1-5). 1988. 11.95 (*0-688-08129-0*) Greenwillow.

Hader, Berta & Hader, Elmer. The Big Snow. 3rd ed. Hader, Berta & Hader, Elmer, illus. LC 92-46365. 48p. (gr. k-4). 1993. pap. 4.95 (*0-689-71757-1*, Aladdin) Macmillan Child Grp.

Hadithi, Mwenye. Hungry Hyene. (ps-3). 1994. 15.95 (*0-316-33715-3*) Little.

—Lazy Lion. (ps-4). 1990. 15.95 (*0-316-33725-0*) Little.

Hague & Grahame. Wind in the Willows. 1991. 19.95 (*0-8050-1422-5*) H Holt & Co.

Hale, Hanna. Zelda Orangutan. Hale, Hanna, illus. 64p. (gr. 4-6). 1994. Perfect bdg. pap. 12.95 (*0-9638724-0-0*) Cando Pubng.

Haley, Gail E. A Story, A Story. Haley, Gail E., illus. LC 69-18961. 36p. (ps-3). 1970. SBE 15.95 (*0-689-20511-2*, Atheneum Child Bk) Macmillan Child Grp.

Hall, N. & Packard, Mary. Spike & Mike. McCue, Lisa, illus. 40p. (ps-2). 1994. 12.00 (*0-679-85830-X*) Random Bks Yng Read.

Hall, Nancy & Packard, Mary. Spike & Mike. McCue, Lisa, illus. LC 93-13684. 40p. (ps-4). 1993. PLB 11.80 (*0-516-00830-7*) Childrens.

Hall, Willis. The Return of the Antelope. large type ed. 256p. (gr. 3-7). 1990. 16.95 (*0-7451-1103-3*, Galaxy Child Lrg Print) Chivers N Amer.

Halpern, Shari. My River. Halpern, Shari, illus. LC 91-33582. 32p. (ps-2). 1992. RSBE 13.95 (*0-02-741980-0*, Macmillan Child Bk) Macmillan Child Grp.

Halverson, Lydia, illus. The Animals' Ballgame. LC 92-9416. 24p. (ps-3). 1992. PLB 13.85 (*0-516-05139-3*); pap. 5.95 (*0-516-45139-1*) Childrens.

Hamilton, Virginia. Jaguarundi. Cooper, Floyd, illus. LC 93-45384. (gr. k-7). 1995. 14.95 (*0-590-47366-2*) Scholastic Inc.

Hamlyn, J. Sheba Learns the Great Outdoors. 65p. (gr. 1-4). 1990. pap. 5.25 (*1-878950-00-2*) Sheba Bks Intl.

Hammer, Charles. Me, the Beef, & the Bum. LC 83-25521. 181p. (gr. 5 up). 1984. 15.00 (*0-374-34903-7*) FS&G.

Hanson, Fred. Down a Magic Stream. Hanson, Ann R., illus. 65p. (Orig.). (gr. 2-5). 1992. pap. 9.95 (*0-9624292-2-8*) Black Willow Pr.

Harris, Joel C. Complete Tales of Uncle Remus. Chase, Richard, ed. (Illus.). 832p. (gr. 7 up). 1955. 35.00 (*0-395-06799-5*) HM.

—Favorite Uncle Remus. Van Santvoord, George & Coolidge, Archibald C., eds. Van Santvoord, George & Coolidge, Archibald C., illus. 320p. (gr. 4-8). 1973. 17.45 (*0-395-06800-2*) HM.

—Walt Disney's Uncle Remus Stories. Palmer, Marion, ed. Dempster, Al & Justice, Bill, illus. (gr. 3-5). 1964. write for info. (*0-307-15551-X*, Golden Bks) Western Pub.

Harris, Joel C. & Metaxas, Eric, eds. Brer Rabbit & the Wonderful Tar Baby. Drescher, Henrik, illus. LC 90-7166. 32p. (gr. k up). 1991. pap. 14.95 (*0-88708-144-4*, Rabbit Ears); pap. 19.95 incl. cass. (*0-88708-145-2*, Rabbit Ears) Picture Bk Studio.

Harris, Rosemary. The Shadow on the Sun. 192p. (gr. 2-6). 1991. pap. 4.95 (*0-571-14185-4*) Faber & Faber.

Hartman, Gail. As the Crow Flies: A First Book of Maps. Stevenson, Harvey, illus. LC 90-33982. 32p. (ps-1). 1991. RSBE 13.95 (*0-02-743005-7*, Bradbury Pr) Macmillan Child Grp.

—As the Crow Flies: A First Book of Maps. Stevenson, Harvey, illus. LC 93-22101. 32p. (ps-1). 1993. pap. 4.95 (*0-689-71762-8*, Aladdin) Macmillan Child Grp.

Harwell, Helen B. Candy the Zoo Truck. Dollar, Diane, illus. 32p. 1987. 3.95 (*0-938991-37-X*) Colonial Pr AL.

Hawcock, David. Making Tracks. Lewis, Jan, illus. 16p. (ps-3). 1994. 12.95 (*0-7868-0000-3*) Hyprn Child.

Hayes, Joe. No Way, Jose! De Ninguna Manera, Jose! Jelinek, Lucy, illus. 32p. (Orig.). (ps-3). 1986. pap. 3.95 (*0-939729-00-8*); cassette & bk. pkg. 7.95 (*0-939729-01-6*) Trails West Pub.

Hayes, Sarah. The Grumpalump. Firth, Barbara, illus. 32p. (ps-2). 1991. 15.45 (*0-89919-871-6*, Clarion Bks) HM.

Hayward, Linda. All Stuck Up. Chartier, Normand, illus. LC 89-34675. 32p. (Orig.). (ps-1). 1990. PLB 7.99 (*0-679-90216-3*); pap. 3.50 (*0-679-80216-9*) Random Bks Yng Read.

Hearn, Diana D. Who Lives in the Field? (ps). 1992. 4.95 (*0-87483-244-6*) August Hse.

—Who Lives in the Forest? (ps). 1992. 4.95 (*0-87483-245-4*) August Hse.

—Who Lives in the Garden? (ps). 1992. 4.95 (*0-87483-246-2*) August Hse.

Heine, Helme. Friends. Heine, Helme, illus. LC 82-49350. 32p. (ps-2). 1982. SBE 14.95 (*0-689-50256-7*, M K McElderry) Macmillan Child Grp.

—Friends. Heine, Helme, illus. LC 86-3379. 32p. (ps-3). 1986. pap. 4.95 (*0-689-71083-6*, Aladdin) Macmillan Child Grp.

—Mollywoop. Manheim, Ralph, tr. (Illus.). 32p. (ps-3). 1991. bds. 14.95 bds. (*0-374-35001-9*) FS&G.

Heller, Ruth. Animals Born Alive & Well. Heller, Ruth, illus. LC 82-80872. 48p. (gr. k-2). 1982. 10.95 (*0-448-01822-5*, G&D) Putnam Pub Group.

Helmrath, M. O. & Bartlett, J. L. Bobby Bear in the Spring. LC 68-56810. (Illus.). 32p. (ps-1). 1968. PLB 12.35 prebound (*0-87783-007-X*); cassette 7.94x (*0-87783-180-7*) Oddo.

Hendrick, Mary J. If Anything Ever Goes Wrong at the Zoo. LC 91-25566. (ps-3). 1993. 13.95 (*0-15-238007-8*) HarBrace.

Hendry, Diana. Camel Called April. (ps-3). 1991. 10.95 (*0-688-10193-3*) Lothrop.

Hennessy, B. G. Eeney Meeney Miney Mo. LC 90-31535. (ps-3). 1990. 13.95 (*0-670-82864-5*) Viking Child Bks.

—Eeney, Meeney, Miney, Mo. Galli, Letizia, photos by. LC 92-23527. (Illus.). 1993. 3.99 (*0-14-054090-3*) Puffin Bks.

Henney, Carolee W. Calbert & His Adventures. Macneil, Melanie F., illus. LC 90-83140. 104p. (Orig.). (gr. 2-5). 1990. collector's first ed., numbered, signed by author, with dust jacket, sim. gold imprint title-author on spine 24.95 (*0-9626580-1-4*); pap. 9.95 (*0-9626580-0-6*) Aton Pr.

Henry, Marguerite. Brighty: Of the Grand Canyon. Dennis, Wesley, illus. LC 53-7233. 224p. (gr. 3-7). 1991. SBE 13.95 (*0-02-743664-0*, Macmillan Child Bk) Macmillan Child Grp.

Hiccups for Elephant. LC 94-15585. 2.95 (*0-590-48588-1*) Scholastic Inc.

Hicks, Grace R. The Critters of Gazink. Hicks, Bruce & Ashcraft, Karen H., illus. 64p. (gr. 4-7). 1992. 11.95 (*0-89015-816-9*) Sunbelt Media.

Highlights for Children Staff. No Pets Allowed! And Other Animal Stories. LC 91-77000. (Illus.). 96p. (gr. 3-7). 1992. pap. 2.95 (*1-56397-102-X*) Boyds Mills Pr.

Hill, Eric. Spot's Birthday Party. (Illus.). (ps-k). 1982. 11.95 (*0-399-20903-4*, Putnam) Putnam Pub Group.

Hills, Peter B. Inspector Hare & the Locked Room. Hills, Stephen, illus. LC 93-11734. 1994. 4.25 (*0-383-03752-2*) SRA Schl Grp.

Himmelman, John. Simpson Snail Sings. (Illus.). 48p. (gr. k-2). 1992. 11.00 (*0-525-44978-7*, DCB) Dutton Child Bks.

Hindley, Judy. Into the Jungle. Epps, Melanie, illus. 32p. (ps up). 1994. 14.95 (*1-56402-423-7*) Candlewick Pr.

Hiscock, Bruce. When Will It Snow? LC 94-9385. (Illus.). 1996. 15.95 (*0-689-31937-1*, Atheneum) Macmillan.

Hiser, Constance. Critter Sitters. MacDonald, Patricia, ed. 96p. 1993. pap. 2.99 (*0-671-86521-8*, Minstrel Bks) PB.

Hissey, Jane. Jolly Snow: An Old Bear Story. (Illus.). (ps-1). 1991. 14.95 (*0-399-22131-X*, Philomel Bks) Putnam Pub Group.

Hoban, Lillian. Silly Tilly's Thanksgiving Dinner. Hoban, Lillian, illus. LC 89-29287. 64p. (gr. k-3). 1990. 14.00 (*0-06-022422-3*); PLB 13.89 (*0-06-022423-1*) HarpC Child Bks.

Hoff, Syd. Albert the Albatross. Hoff, Syd, illus. LC 61-5767. 32p. (gr. k-3). 1961. PLB 13.89 (*0-06-022446-0*) HarpC Child Bks.

—Bernard on His Own. Hoff, Syd, illus. LC 92-21770. 32p. (gr. k-3). 1993. 14.95 (*0-395-65226-X*, Clarion Bks) HM.

Hogg, Gary. Friendship in the Forest. Anderson, Gary, illus. (gr. k-6). 1991. 11.95 (*0-89868-204-5*); pap. 4.95 (*0-89868-205-3*) ARO Pub.

—I Heard of a Nerd Bird. Anderson, Gary, illus. (gr. k-6). 1991. 11.95 (*0-89868-200-2*); pap. 4.95 (*0-89868-201-0*) ARO Pub.

—Lizzie Learns About Lying. Anderson, Gary, illus. (gr. k-6). 1991. 11.95 (*0-89868-202-9*); pap. 4.95 (*0-89868-203-7*) ARO Pub.

—Sir William the Worm. Anderson, Gary, illus. (gr. k-6). 1991. 11.95 (*0-89868-208-8*); pap. 4.95 (*0-89868-209-6*) ARO Pub.

Hol, Coby. Henrietta Saves the Show. Hol, Coby, illus. Graves, Helen, tr. from GER. LC 90-47063. (Illus.). 32p. (ps-k). 1991. 14.95 (*1-55858-102-2*) North-South Bks NYC.

—Niki's Little Donkey. James, J. Alison, tr. from GER. Hol, Coby, illus. LC 92-31332. 32p. (gr. k-3). 1993. 14.95 (*1-55858-183-9*); PLB 14.88 (*1-55858-184-7*) North-South Bks NYC.

Holl, Adelaide. Rain Puddle. Duvoisin, Roger, illus. LC 65-22026. 32p. (gr. k-3). 1965. PLB 15.93 (*0-688-51096-5*) Lothrop.

Hood, Thomas. Before I Go to Sleep. Begin-Callanan, Maryjane, illus. 32p. (ps-3). 1990. 14.95 (*0-399-21638-3*, Putnam) Putnam Pub Group.

Hooper, Patricia. A Bundle of Beasts. Steele, Mark, illus. LC 86-34413. 64p. (gr. 3-7). 1987. 12.70 (*0-395-44259-1*) HM.

—Bundle of Beasts. (gr. 4-7). 1992. pap. 3.80 (*0-395-61620-4*) HM.

Hopkins, Lee B., ed. Creatures. Ormai, Stella, illus. LC 84-15698. 32p. (ps-3). 1985. 14.95 (*0-15-220875-5*, HB Juv Bks) HarBrace.

Howard, Jane. When I'm Hungry. (Illus.). 24p. (ps-k). 1992. 12.50 (*0-525-44983-3*, DCB) Dutton Child Bks.

Howe, James. Hot Fudge. 48p. 1991. pap. 4.95 (*0-380-70610-5*, Camelot) Avon.

—Morgan's Zoo. (Illus.). 192p. (gr. 3-7). 1986. pap. 3.99 (*0-380-69994-X*, Camelot) Avon.

Howker, Janni. The Nature of the Beast. LC 84-25328. 137p. (gr. 7-9). 1985. reinforced bdg. 10.25 (*0-688-04233-3*) Greenwillow.

Hubbard, Woodleigh. Two Is for Dancing: A One, Two, Three of Actions. Hubbard, Woodleigh, illus. 32p. (ps-1). 1991. 13.95 (*0-87701-895-2*) Chronicle Bks.

Hubner, Carol K. The Whispering Mezuzah. Kramer, Devorah, illus. (gr. 3-9). 1979. 6.95 (*0-910818-18-5*) Judaica Pr.

Hurd, Edith T. Come & Have Fun. Hurd, Clement, illus. LC 62-13324. 32p. (gr. k-3). 1962. PLB 13.89 (*0-06-022681-1*) HarpC Child Bks.

—Day the Sun Danced. Hurd, Clement, illus. LC 64-16641. 32p. (gr. k-3). 1966. PLB 13.89 (*0-06-022692-7*) HarpC Child Bks.

—Last One Home Is a Green Pig. Hurd, Clement, illus. LC 59-8972. 64p. (gr. k-3). 1959. PLB 11.89 (*0-06-022716-8*) HarpC Child Bks.

Hurwitz, Johanna. Hurray for Ali Baba Bernstein. (gr. 4-7). 1990. pap. 2.75 (*0-590-43169-2*) Scholastic Inc.

Hutchins, Pat. Good-Night, Owl! Hutchins, Pat, illus. LC 91-8172. 36p. (gr. k-3). 1991. pap. 16.95 big book ed. (*0-689-71541-2*, Aladdin) Macmillan Child Grp.

—The Surprise Party. Hutchins, Pat, illus. LC 91-10599. 32p. (gr. k-3). 1991. pap. 16.95 big bk. (*0-689-71542-0*, Aladdin); pap. 3.95 (*0-689-71543-9*, Aladdin) Macmillan Child Grp.

Hutchison, Wick. The Adventures of Inquisitive Englebert. Davisson, Vanessa, illus. 64p. (gr. k-3). 1991. pap. 7.95 (*0-929690-11-7*) Herit Pubs AZ.

Hwa-I Publishing Co., Staff. Chinese Children's Stories, Vol. 11: Ker-Plunk is Coming!, Baby Chicks' Revenge. Ching, Emily, et al, eds. Wonder Kids Publications Staff, tr. from CHI. (Illus.). 28p. (gr. 3-6). 1991. Repr. of 1988 ed. 7.95 (*1-56162-011-4*) Wonder Kids.

—Chinese Children's Stories, Vol. 41: Brother Cat & Brother Rat, The Rooster's Antlers. Ching, Emily, et al, eds. Wonder Kids Publications Staff, tr. from CHI. (Illus.). 28p. (gr. 3-6). 1991. Repr. of 1988 ed. 7.95 (*1-56162-041-6*) Wonder Kids.

Ingle, Annie. The Rabbits' Carnival. Bratun, Katy, illus. LC 92-29930. 24p. (Orig.). (ps-3). 1995. pap. 2.50 (*0-679-85337-5*) Random Bks Yng Read.

Inkpen, Mick. Billy's Beetle. (ps-3). 1992. 13.95 (*0-15-200427-0*, HB Juv Bks) HarBrace.

—Kipper. (ps-3). 1992. 14.95 (*0-316-41883-8*) Little.

Jackson, Bobby L. Boon the Raccoon & Easel the Weasel: A Fable by Bobby L. Jackson. King, Kevin, illus. Reuter, Janet R., frwd. by. LC 92-62211. (Illus.). 32p. (ps-4). 1993. 9.95 (*0-9634932-0-5*); pap. 5.95 (*0-9634932-1-3*) Multicult Pubns.

Jacques, Brian. Mariel of Redwall. 400p. (gr. 5-9). 1992. 17.95 (*0-399-22144-1*, Philomel Bks) Putnam Pub Group.

—Salamandastron: A Tale from Red Wall. Chalk, Gary, illus. 400p. (gr. 5 up). 1993. 17.95 (*0-399-21992-7*, Philomel Bks) Putnam Pub Group.

James, Christopher. Bump & the Bucket. (Illus.). 24p. (ps-3). 1990. 6.95 (*0-88625-279-2*) Durkin Hayes Pub.
—Bump the Builder. (Illus.). 24p. (ps-3). 1990. pap. 6.95 (*0-88625-278-4*) Durkin Hayes Pub.
James, D. H. Sheba Consumes Whatever She Can. 98p. 1990. 19.95 (*1-878950-01-0*) Sheba Bks Intl.
Janice. Little Bear's Thanksgiving. Mariana, illus. LC 67-22593. 32p. (gr. k-3). 1967. PLB 12.93 (*0-688-51078-7*) Lothrop.
Janosch. I'll Make You Well, Tiger, Said the Bear. Janosch, illus. LC 86-11274. 48p. (ps up). 1987. 9.95 (*0-915361-42-6*) Modan-Adama Bks.
Jarrell, Randall. The Animal Family. 93p. 1992. text ed. 7.44 (*1-56956-107-9*) W A T Braille.
Jefferies, Richard. Wood Magic. LC 74-82725. 1974. 20. 00 (*0-89388-177-5*) Okpaku Communications.
Jensen, Patricia & Clement, Claude. Go to Sleep, Little Groundhog. Nouvelle, Catherine, illus. LC 91-46234. 24p. (ps-3). 1993. 6.99 (*0-89577-487-9*, Dist. by Random) RD Assn.
Jewell, Nancy. Christmas Lullaby. Vitale, Stefano, illus. LC 93-38786. 1994. 14.95 (*0-395-66586-8*, Clarion Bks) HM.
Johnson, Annabel. I Am Leaper. (gr. 4-7). 1990. 11.95 (*0-590-43400-4*) Scholastic Inc.
Johnson, Debra A. I Dreamed I Was--a Kitten. LC 94-5655. (gr. k up). 1994. write for info. (*1-56239-302-2*) Abdo & Dghtrs.
—I Dreamed I Was--a Panda. LC 94-5654. (gr. k up). 1994. write for info. (*1-56239-301-4*) Abdo & Dghtrs.
—I Dreamed I Was a Koala Bear. LC 94-6623. (gr. k up). 1994. write for info. (*1-56239-300-6*) Abdo & Dghtrs.
Johnston, Deborah. Mathew Michael's Beastly Day. LC 91-3084. (ps-3). 1992. write for info. (*0-15-200521-8*, HB Juv Bks) HarBrace.
Johnston, Tony. Yonder. Bloom, Lloyd, illus. LC 86-11549. 32p. (ps-3). 1988. 12.95 (*0-8037-0277-9*); PLB 12.89 (*0-8037-0278-7*) Dial Bks Young.
Jonas, Ann. Splash! LC 94-4110. 1995. write for info. (*0-688-11051-7*); lib. bdg. write for info. (*0-688-11052-5*) Greenwillow.
Jordan, Tanis. Journey of the Red-Eyed Tree Frog. Jordan, Martin, illus. LC 91-29526. 40p. (ps-3). 1992. 16.00 (*0-671-76903-0*, Green Tiger) S&S Trade.
Jorgensen, Gail. Crocodile Beat. Mullins, Patricia, illus. LC 94-7135. (ps-1). 1994. pap. 4.95 (*0-689-71881-0*, Aladdin) Macmillan.
Jwing-Ming Yang. The Fox Borrows the Tiger's Awe. Dougall, Alan, ed. Xieu-Lin, Li, illus. 54p. (gr. 4 up). 1990. 4.95 (*0-940871-12-2*) Yangs Martial Arts.
Kaghan, Joan. The Billy Goat Show. 32p. 1993. 14.00 (*0-374-30711-3*) FS&G.
Kalan, Robert. Stop, Thief! Abolafia, Yossi, illus. LC 92-30081. 24p. (ps up). 1993. 14.00 (*0-688-11876-3*); PLB 13.93 (*0-688-11877-1*) Greenwillow.
Kaplan, Carol B. Animal Tales Big Book Package, 6 bks. Bolinske, Janet L., ed. Quenell, Midge, illus. 144p. (ps-k). 1988. Set of 6 bks., 24 pgs. ea. bk. 100.00 (*0-88335-759-3*) Milliken Pub Co.
—Wicker's Wishes. Bolinske, Janet L., ed. Quenell, Midge, illus. LC 87-63001. 24p. (Orig.). (ps-k). 1988. 17.95 (*0-88335-757-7*); pap. 4.95 (*0-88335-075-0*) Milliken Pub Co.
Keats, Ezra J. Kitten for a Day. Keats, Ezra J., illus. LC 81-69518. 32p. (ps-3). 1984. RSBE 14.95 (*0-02-749630-9*, Four Winds) Macmillan Child Grp.
Kehret, Peg. Cages. LC 90-21230. 160p. (gr. 5 up). 1991. 14.99 (*0-525-65062-8*, Cobblehill Bks) Dutton Child Bks.
Kelleher, Victor. Rescue! LC 91-30490. 224p. (gr. 5 up). 1992. 15.00 (*0-8037-0900-5*) Dial Bks Young.
Keller, Beverly. Fowl Play, Desdemona. LC 88-9481. 176p. (gr. 4-7). 1989. 11.95 (*0-688-06920-7*) Lothrop.
—No Beasts! No Children! LC 87-45288. 128p. (gr. 3-7). 1988. pap. 3.95 (*0-06-440225-8*, Trophy) HarpC Child Bks.
Kellogg, Steven. The Mysterious Tadpole. (Illus.). 32p. (ps-3). 1992. pap. 17.99 (*0-14-054569-7*, Puff Pied Piper) Puffin Bks.
Kemp, Gene. Just Ferret. large type ed. (gr. 1-8). 1991. 16.95 (*0-7451-1427-X*, Galaxy Child Lrg Print) Chivers N Amer.
—The Mink War. Davidson, Andrew, illus. 48p. (Orig.). (gr. 5 up). 1992. pap. 8.95 (*0-571-16312-2*) Faber & Faber.
Kennaway, Mwalimu & Kennaway, Adrienne. Awful Aardvark. Kennaway, Mwalimu & Kennaway, Adrienne, illus. LC 89-80028. (ps-2). 1989. 14.95 (*0-316-59218-8*) Little.
Kennedy, Fiona & Noakes, Polly. The Last Little Duckling. LC 92-21695. (Illus.). 28p. (ps-1). 1993. 12. 95 (*0-8120-6326-0*); pap. 4.95 (*0-8120-1355-7*) Barron.
Kerven, Rosalind. King Leopard's Gift: And Other Legends of the Animal World. Waldman, Bryna, illus. 32p. 1990. 15.95 (*0-521-36180-X*) Cambridge U Pr.
—Legends of the Animal World. (Illus.). 32p. (gr. 3-7). 1986. 14.95 (*0-521-30576-4*) Cambridge U Pr.
Kesey, Ken. Little Trickster the Squirrel Meets Big Double the Bear. Moser, Barry, illus. LC 92-10605. (gr. 4 up). 1992. 4.99 (*0-14-050623-3*) Puffin Bks.
Kessler, Leonard. Old Turtle's Baseball Stories. Kessler, Leonard, illus. LC 81-6390. 56p. (gr. 1-3). 1982. 13.95 (*0-688-00723-6*); PLB 13.88 (*0-688-00724-4*) Greenwillow.
Key Concepts in Personal Development Series. (gr. 1-4). 1992. 16.95 (*1-55942-050-2*) Marshfilm.
Kidd, Ronald, adapted by. The Jungle Book. Kurtz, John, illus. 24p. (ps-4). 1993. 20.00 (*0-307-74028-5*, 64028, Golden Pr) Western Pub.
King, Loretta M. The Purple Sea Horse & Other Stories. LC 79-56712. (Illus., Orig.). (gr. k-3). 1979. pap. 4.95 (*0-934104-02-6*) Woodland.
King, Virginia. Breakfast. Fleming, Leanne, illus. LC 92-21391. 1993. 2.50 (*0-383-03556-2*) SRA Schl Grp.
Kingsley, Charles. The Water Babies. Smith, Jessie W., illus. 256p. (gr. k-6). 1986. 10.99 (*0-517-61817-6*) Random Hse Value.
King-Smith, Dick. The Animal Parade. Wild, Jocelyn, illus. LC 91-30332. 96p. (gr. 1-8). 1992. 16.00 (*0-688-11375-3*, Tambourine Bks) Morrow.
—The Toby Man. Hemmant, Lynette, illus. LC 90-28443. 128p. (gr. 2-7). 1991. lib. bdg. 14.99 (*0-517-58135-3*) Crown Bks Yng Read.
Kipling, Rudyard. The Beginning of the Armadillos. Cauley, Lorinda B., illus. LC 85-5444. 43p. (ps-3). 1985. 14.95 (*0-15-206380-3*, Pub. by HJ) HarBrace.
—Beginning of the Armadillos. 48p. (ps-3). 1990. pap. 3.95 (*0-15-206381-1*, Voyager Bks) HarBrace.
—Elephants Child. LC 90-46609. 1989. 14.95 (*0-85953-275-5*) Childs Play.
—The Elephant's Child & Other Just So Stories. (Illus.). 96p. 1993. pap. text ed. 1.00t (*0-486-27821-2*) Dover.
—How the Leopard Got His Spots. Lohstoeter, Lori, illus. 64p. 1993. Repr. of 1989 ed. incl. cass. 9.95 (*0-88708-301-3*, Rabbit Ears) Picture Bk Studio.
—How the Leopard Got His Spots & Other Just So Stories. Kliros, Thea, illus. LC 92-20780. 96p. 1992. pap. text ed. 1.00 (*0-486-27297-4*) Dover.
—How the Leopard Got His Spots: And Other Just So Stories. Kipling, Rudyard & Gleeson, Joseph, illus. LC 93-540. 184p. 1993. 6.00 (*1-56957-902-4*) Shambhala Pubns.
—The Jungle Book. 336p. (gr. 4). pap. 3.95 (*0-451-51716-4*, CE1716, Sig Classics) NAL-Dutton.
—The Jungle Book. 1987. pap. 2.95 (*0-14-035074-8*, Puffin) Puffin Bks.
—The Jungle Book. Detmold, Maurice, et al, illus. 320p. 1989. 12.99 (*0-517-67902-7*) Random Hse Value.
—The Jungle Book. Foreman, Michael, illus. (gr. 5-9). 1987. 19.99 (*0-670-80241-7*) Viking Child Bks.
—The Jungle Book. Bergh, Jerald E. & Donovan, Michael, eds. LC 90-64201. (gr. 3-4). 1991. pap. 5.95 incls. cassette (*1-879551-51-9*); cassette 2.95 (*1-879551-52-7*) Saban Pub.
—The Jungle Book. Alexander, Gregory, illus. 120p. (gr. 1 up). 1991. 17.95 (*1-55970-127-7*) Arcade Pub Inc.
—The Jungle Book. (Illus.). 1991. pap. text ed. 6.50 (*0-582-03587-2*) Longman.
—The Jungle Book. Robson, W. W., intro. by. 432p. 1992. pap. 4.95 (*0-19-282901-7*) OUP.
—Jungle Book. 240p. 1992. 9.49 (*0-8167-2552-7*); pap. 2.95 (*0-8167-2553-5*) Troll Assocs.
—The Jungle Book. Ashachik, Diane M., ed. Hannon, Holly, illus. LC 92-5806. 48p. (gr. 3-6). 1992. PLB 12. 89 (*0-8167-2868-2*); pap. text ed. 3.95 (*0-8167-2869-0*) Troll Assocs.
—The Jungle Book. Weise, Kurt, illus. LC 94-5860. 1994. 13.95 (*0-679-43637-5*) Knopf.
—The Jungle Book: Based on the Mowgli Tales from "The Jungle Book" by Rudyard Kipling. Oliver, Tony, ed. Animation Cottage Staff, illus. LC 90-64201. 36p. (Orig.). (gr. 3-4). 1990. pap. 2.95 (*1-879551-50-0*) Saban Pub.
—Jungle Books. (gr. 5 up). 1966. pap. 1.95 (*0-8049-0109-0*, CL-109) Airmont.
—Just So Stories. (gr. 3 up). 1966. pap. 1.75 (*0-8049-0123-6*, CL-123) Airmont.
—Just So Stories. (Illus.). 224p. (gr. 2-9). 1979. 5.99 (*0-517-26655-5*) Random Hse Value.
—Just So Stories. Gleeson, Joseph M. & Kipling, Rudyard, illus. 244p. (gr. 2-9). 1988. 12.99 (*0-517-63177-6*) Random Hse Value.
—Just So Stories. 1987. pap. 2.95 (*0-14-035075-6*, Puffin) Puffin Bks.
—Just So Stories. Frampton, David, illus. LC 90-19429. 128p. (gr. 3-7). 1991. PLB 19.89 (*0-06-023296-X*) HarpC Child Bks.
—Just So Stories. Kipling, Rudyard, illus. LC 92-53177. 192p. 1992. 12.95 (*0-679-41797-4*, Evrymans Lib Childs Class) Knopf.
—Mowgli Stories from "The Jungle Book" LC 94-467. (Illus.). 128p. (Orig.). 1994. pap. 1.00 (*0-486-28030-6*) Dover.
—New Illustrated Just So Stories. Nicholas, illus. (gr. 1-7). 1952. PLB o.p. (*0-385-02180-1*) Doubleday.
—Reader's Digest Best Loved Books for Young Readers: The Jungle Books. Ogburn, Jackie, ed. Jouve, Paul, illus. 160p. (gr. 4-12). 1989. 3.99 (*0-945260-26-1*) Choice Pub NY.
—The Second Jungle Book. 1987. pap. 2.95 (*0-14-035079-9*, Puffin) Puffin Bks.
Kipling, Rudyard & Busch, Jeffrey. The Jungle Books. (Illus.). 52p. Date not set. pap. 4.95 (*1-57209-022-7*) Classics Int Ent.
Kiser, SuAnn. Hazel Saves the Day. Day, Betsy, illus. LC 92-34782. 1994. write for info. (*0-8037-1488-2*); PLB write for info. (*0-8037-1489-0*) Dial Bks Young.
Kitchen, Bert. Somewhere Today. Kitchen, Bert, illus. LC 91-58754. 32p. (ps up). 1992. 15.95 (*1-56402-074-6*) Candlewick Pr.
Kneen, Maggie. Who's Getting Ready for Christmas? Kneen, Maggie, illus. LC 93-11061. (gr. 4-7). 1993. 13.95 (*0-8118-0470-4*) Chronicle Bks.
Kneen, Maggie, illus. The Great Egg Hunt. LC 93-27272. 1993. 13.95 (*0-8118-0552-2*) Chronicle Bks.
Knox, Montye S. My Day in the Country. 1991. 6.95 (*0-533-09308-2*) Vantage.
Koch, Michelle. Hoot, Howl, Hiss. LC 90-38484. (Illus.). 24p. (ps up). 1991. 13.95 (*0-688-09651-4*); PLB 13.88 (*0-688-09652-2*) Greenwillow.
Kohen, Clarita. El Rabo de Gato. Sanchez, Jose R., illus. (SPA.). 16p. (gr. k-3). 1993. PLB 7.50x (*1-56492-102-6*) Laredo.
Koller, Jackie F. Mole & Shrew Step Out. Ormai, Stella, illus. LC 91-20531. 32p. (ps-3). 1992. SBE 13.95 (*0-689-31713-1*, Atheneum Child Bk) Macmillan Child Grp.
Koopmans, Loek. The Woodcutter's Mitten: An Old Tale. Koopmans, Loek, illus. LC 90-2545. 32p. (ps-2). 1990. 13.95 (*0-940793-67-9*, Crocodile Bks) Interlink Pub.
Kovacs, Deborah. Brewster's Courage. Mathieu, Joe, illus. LC 91-21481. 112p. (gr. 2-6). 1992. pap. 14.00 jacketed, 3-pc. bdg. (*0-671-74016-4*, S&S BFYR) S&S Trade.
Kraus, Robert. The Adventures of Wise Old Owl. Kraus, Robert, illus. LC 92-20436. 32p. (ps-3). 1992. PLB 10. 89 (*0-8167-2943-3*); pap. text ed. 2.95 (*0-8167-2944-1*) Troll Assocs.
—Wise Old Owl's Christmas Adventure. LC 93-25544. (Illus.). 32p. (ps-3). 1993. PLB 10.89 (*0-8167-2945-X*); pap. text ed. 2.95 (*0-8167-2946-8*) Troll Assocs.
—Wise Old Owl's Halloween Adventure. LC 93-18686. (Illus.). 32p. (gr. k-3). 1993. PLB 10.89 (*0-8167-2949-2*); pap. text ed. 2.95 (*0-8167-2950-6*) Troll Assocs.
Kraus, Robert & Brook, Bonnie. Squirmy's Big Secret. Kraus, Robert, illus. 48p. (ps-3). 1990. lib. bdg. 5.95 (*0-671-70851-1*); pap. 3.95 (*0-671-70852-X*) Silver Pr.
Krauss, Ruth. The Happy Day. Simont, Marc, illus. LC 49-10568. 30p. (ps-3). 1949. PLB 14.89 (*0-06-023396-6*) HarpC Child Bks.
Kriegman, Mitchell. The Adventures of Puppycat. Barrett, Deborah, illus. (ps-3). 1990. PLB 8.95 (*0-553-05888-6*, Little Rooster) Bantam.
Krings, Antoon. Oliver's Bicycle. Krings, Antoon, illus. LC 91-25030. 32p. (ps-k). 1992. 6.95 (*1-56282-164-4*); PLB 6.89 (*1-56282-165-2*) Hyprn Child.
—Oliver's Pool. Krings, Antoon, illus. LC 91-24589. 32p. (ps-k). 1992. 6.95 (*1-56282-160-1*); PLB 6.89 (*1-56282-161-X*) Hyprn Child.
—Oliver's Strawberry Patch. Krings, Antoon, illus. LC 91-27022. 32p. (ps-k). 1992. 6.95 (*1-56282-162-8*); PLB 6.89 (*1-56282-163-6*) Hyprn Child.
Kuhn, Dwight R., photos by. Hungry Little Frog. Hirschi, Ron, text by. (Illus.). 32p. (ps-2). 1992. 9.95 (*0-525-65109-8*, Cobblehill Bks) Dutton Child Bks.
Kulling, Monica. Waiting for Amos. Lowe, Vicky, illus. LC 92-19550. 32p. (ps-2). 1993. SBE 13.95 (*0-02-751245-2*, Bradbury Pr) Macmillan Child Grp.
Kuskin, Karla. James & the Rain. Cartwright, Reg, illus. LC 93-49345. 1995. 15.00 (*0-671-88808-0*, S&S BFYR) S&S Trade.
—Roar & More. rev. ed. Kuskin, Karla, illus. LC 89-15650. 48p. (ps-1). 1990. PLB 13.89 (*0-06-023619-1*) HarpC Child Bks.
Laird, Donivee M. Will Wai Kula & the Three Mongooses. Jossem, Carol, illus. LC 83-8805. 44p. (gr. k-3). 1983. 7.95x (*0-940350-13-0*) Barnaby Bks.
Langerman, Jean. No Carrots for Harry! Remkiewicz, Frank, illus. LC 89-3373. (ps-3). 1989. 5.95 (*0-8193-1190-1*) Parents.
Latimer, Jim. James Bear & the Goose Gathering. Franco-Feeney, Betsy, illus. LC 92-26190. 32p. (gr. k-2). 1994. SBE 14.95 (*0-684-19526-7*, Scribners Young Read) Macmillan Child Grp.
—James Bear's Pie. Franco-Feeney, Betsy, illus. LC 90-36193. 32p. (ps-2). 1992. SBE 13.95 (*0-684-19226-8*, Scribners Young Read) Macmillan Child Grp.
—Moose & Friends. Ewing, Carolyn, illus. LC 91-14047. 32p. (gr. 1-3). 1993. SBE 14.95 (*0-684-19335-3*, Scribners Young Read) Macmillan Child Grp.
Lavies, Bianca. It's an Armadillo! (Illus.). 32p. (ps-2). 1994. pap. 4.99 (*0-14-050312-9*, Puff Unicorn) Puffin Bks.
Lawhead, Stephen R. Riverbank Stories: The Tale of Jeremy Vole. 112p. (gr. 4). 1993. pap. 3.50 (*0-380-72198-8*, Camelot) Avon.
Lawson, Robert. Rabbit Hill. Lawson, Robert, illus. (gr. 4-6). 1944. pap. 14.00 (*0-670-58675-7*) Viking Child Bks.
Leaf, Munro. El Cuento de Ferdinando. Belpre, Pura, tr. Lawson, Robert, illus. (SPA.). 72p. (ps-3). 1962. pap. 13.00 (*0-670-25065-1*) Viking Child Bks.
—El Cuento de Ferdinando: The Story of Ferdinand. Lawson, Robert, illus. Belpre, Pura, tr. (SPA., Illus.). 72p. (ps-3). 1990. pap. 4.50 (*0-14-054253-1*, Puffin) Puffin Bks.
Learner, Vickie M., illus. Willoughby Wallaby. 1987. pap. 6.99 incl. audiocassette (*0-553-45903-1*) Bantam.
Leedy, Loreen. The Great Trash Bash. Leedy, Loreen, illus. LC 90-46554. 32p. (ps-3). 1991. reinforced 14.95 (*0-8234-0869-8*) Holiday.
Lehan, Daniel. Wipe Your Feet! Lehan, Daniel, illus. LC 91-44145. 32p. (gr. k-3). 1993. 14.00 (*0-525-44992-2*, DCB) Dutton Child Bks.
Lehn, Cornelia. The Sun & the Wind. Regier, Robert, illus. 32p. (gr. k-5). 1983. 7.95 (*0-87303-072-9*) Faith & Life.

Lemaitre, Pascal. Zelda's Secret. Lemaitre, Pascal, illus. LC 93-28448. (ps-3). 1993. PLB 13.95 (*0-8167-3309-0*); pap. 3.95t (*0-8167-3310-4*) BrdgeWater.

L'Engle, Madeleine. Dance in the Desert. Shimin, Symeon, illus. LC 68-29465. 64p. (ps up). 1969. 14.95 (*0-374-31684-8*) FS&G.

Leonard, Alain. Barnaby & the Big Gorilla. LC 91-25414. (Illus.). 32p. (ps-3). 1992. 15.00 (*0-688-11291-9*, Tambourine Bks); PLB 14.93 (*0-688-11292-7*, Tambourine Bks) Morrow.

Leslie-Melville, Betty. Walter Warthog: The Warthog That Moved In. (Illus.). 48p. (ps-3). 1989. 12.95 (*0-385-26378-3*, Zephyr-BFYR); (Zephyr-BFYR) Doubleday.

—Walter Warthog: The Warthog That Moved In. (gr. 4-7). 1992. pap. 4.99 (*0-440-40672-2*) Dell.

—Walter Warthog: The Warthog Who Moved In. (gr. 2-6). 1992. 4.99 (*0-685-57132-7*, YB) Dell.

Lester, Alison. Imagine. Lester, Alison, illus. 32p. (gr. k-3). 1990. 13.45 (*0-395-53753-3*) HM.

Lester, Helen. It Wasn't My Fault. Munsinger, Lynn, illus. (ps-3). 1989. pap. 5.70 (*0-395-51007-4*, Sandpiper) HM.

Lester, Julius, as told by. More Tales of Uncle Remus: Further Adventures of Brer Rabbit, His Friends, Enemies & Others. Pinkney, Jerry, illus. LC 86-32890. 160p. (ps up). 1988. 15.95 (*0-8037-0419-4*); PLB 15. 89 (*0-8037-0420-8*) Dial Bks Young.

Lester, Julius & Fogelman, Phyllis J., eds. Further Tales of Uncle Remus: The Misadventures of Brer Rabbit, Brer Fox, Brer Wolf, the Doodang, & All the Other Creatures. Pinkney, Jerry, illus. LC 88-20223. 160p. (ps up). 1990. 15.00 (*0-8037-0610-3*); PLB 14.89 (*0-8037-0611-1*) Dial Bks Young.

Lewis, Naomi. Cry Wolf & Other Aesop Fables. Castle, Barry, illus. 32p. (ps up). 1988. 18.00 (*0-19-520710-6*) OUP.

—Hare & Badger Go to Town. Ross, Tony, illus. 32p. (ps-1). 1987. 9.95 (*0-905478-94-0*, Pub. by Century UK) Trafalgar.

Lewis, R. Aunt Armadillo. (Illus.). 24p. (ps-8). 1985. 12. 95 (*0-920303-38-2*, Pub. by Annick CN); pap. 4.95 (*0-920303-39-0*, Pub. by Annick CN) Firefly Bks Ltd.

Lewison, Wendy C. Buzz Said the Bee. Wilhelm, Hans, illus. 32p. 1992. pap. 2.95 (*0-590-44185-X*, Cartwheel) Scholastic Inc.

Lillegard, Dee. My Yellow Ball. Chamberlain, Sarah, illus. LC 92-27003. (gr. k-3). 1993. 12.99 (*0-525-45078-5*, DCB) Dutton Child Bks.

—Sitting in My Box. Agee, Jon, illus. 32p. (ps-2). 1993. pap. 17.99 (*0-14-054886-6*, Puff Unicorn) Puffin Bks.

Lippman, Peter. Mini House Books: Old Macdonald's Barn. (Illus.). 20p. (ps-1). 1993. bds. 9.95 (*1-56305-500-7*, 3500) Workman Pub.

Lively, Penelope. The Cat, the Crow, & the Banyan Tree. Milne, Terry, illus. LC 93-22355. (ps up). 1994. 14.95 (*1-56402-325-7*) Candlewick Pr.

Lobel, Arnold. Fables. Lobel, Arnold, illus. LC 79-2004. 48p. (gr. 1-4). 1980. 15.00 (*0-06-023973-5*); PLB 14. 89 (*0-06-023974-3*) HarpC Child Bks.

—Grasshopper on the Road. Lobel, Arnold, illus. LC 77-25653. 64p. (gr. k-3). 1978. PLB 13.89 (*0-06-023962-X*) HarpC Child Bks.

—Mouse Tales. Lobel, Arnold, illus. LC 66-18654. 64p. (gr. k-3). 1972. 14.00 (*0-06-023941-7*); PLB 13.89 (*0-06-023942-5*) HarpC Child Bks.

Lockwood, Barbara & McAuley, Marilyn. God Keeps Them Safe. LC 87-62019. (ps). 1988. bds. 4.99 (*1-55513-518-8*, Chariot Bks) Chariot Family.

—God Made Little & Big. LC 87-62019. (ps). 1988. bds. 4.99 (*1-55513-517-X*, Chariot Bks) Chariot Family.

Lofting, Hugh. Doctor Dolittle: A Treasury. 1990. Repr. lib. bdg. 25.95x (*0-89966-674-4*) Buccaneer Bks.

—Dr. Dolittle & the Green Canary. (gr. k-6). 1988. pap. 3.50 (*0-440-40079-1*, YB) Dell.

—Doctor Dolittle's Bag of Books. (gr. 4-7). 1988. pap. 13. 45 (*0-440-36000-5*) Dell.

—Gub-Gub's Book. LC 91-4672. (gr. 4-7). 1992. pap. 15. 00 (*0-671-78355-6*, S&S BFYR) S&S Trade.

—The Story of Doctor Dolittle. (gr. k-6). 1988. pap. 2.95 (*0-685-18953-8*) Dell.

—The Story of Doctor Dolittle. Lofting, Christopher, afterword by. (Illus.). 144p. (gr. 4-6). 1988. pap. 13.95 (*0-385-29662-2*) Delacorte.

—Story of Dr. Dolittle. (gr. 4-7). 1969. pap. 3.99 (*0-440-48307-7*) Dell.

—The Voyage of Doctor Dolittle. (gr. 4-7). 1988. pap. 4.50 (*0-440-40002-3*, YB) Dell.

London, Jonathan. The Owl Who Became the Moon. Rand, Ted, illus. LC 92-14699. (ps-2). 1993. 13.99 (*0-525-45054-8*, DCB) Dutton Child Bks.

—Voices of the Wild. McLoughlin, Wayne, illus. LC 92-27651. 32p. (ps up). 1993. 15.00 (*0-517-59217-7*); PLB 15.99 (*0-517-59218-5*) Crown Bks Yng Read.

Loomis, Christine. One Cow Coughs: A Counting Book for the Sick & Miserable. Dypold, Pat, illus. LC 93-1836. 32p. (ps-2). 1994. 14.95g (*0-395-67899-4*) Ticknor & Flds Bks Yng Read.

Lopshire, Robert. I Want to Be Somebody New. Lopshire, Robert, illus. LC 85-43098. 48p. (gr. k-3). 1986. 6.95 (*0-394-87616-4*); lib. bdg. 7.99 (*0-394-97616-9*) Beginner.

Loves, June. I Know That. Smith, Craig, illus. LC 92-34262. 1993. 4.25 (*0-383-03633-X*) SRA Schl Grp.

Lund, Jillian. Way Out West Lives a Coyote Named Frank. LC 91-46011. (Illus.). 32p. (ps-2). 1993. 13.95 (*0-525-44982-5*, DCB) Dutton Child Bks.

Lunn, Carolyn. Bobby's Zoo. Dunnington, Tom, illus. LC 88-36865. 32p. (ps-2). 1989. PLB 10.25 (*0-516-02089-7*); pap. 2.95 (*0-516-42089-5*) Childrens.

Lupsewicz, Veronica A. Misty the Manatee. Weinberger, Jane, ed. (Illus.). 46p. (gr. 1-5). 1993. pap. 9.95 (*0-932433-96-0*) Windswept Hse.

Luttrell, Ida. The Star Counters. Pretro, Korinna, illus. LC 93-20342. 32p. 1994. 15.00 (*0-688-12149-7*, Tambourine Bks); PLB 14.93 (*0-688-12150-0*, Tambourine Bks) Morrow.

—Three Good Blankets. McDermott, Michael, illus. LC 89-36353. 32p. (ps-2). 1990. SBE 13.95 (*0-689-31586-4*, Atheneum Child Bk) Macmillan Child Grp.

—Tillie & Mert. Cushman, Doug, illus. LC 85-42641. 64p. (gr. k-3). 1992. pap. 3.50 (*0-06-444159-8*, Trophy) HarpC Child Bks.

Lyon, George E. A Regular Rolling Noah. Gammell, Stephen, illus. LC 90-39984. 32p. (gr. k-3). 1991. pap. 4.95 (*0-689-71449-1*, Aladdin) Macmillan Child Grp.

McBarnet, Gill. The Pink Parrot. McBarnett, Gill, illus. 40p. (gr. k-2). 1986. 7.95 (*0-9615102-1-8*) Ruwanga Trad.

Maccarone, Grace. Oink! Moo! How Do You Do? Wilhelm, Hans, illus. LC 93-45962. (ps). 1994. 6.95 (*0-590-48161-4*) Scholastic Inc.

McCarthy, Eugene J. Mr. Raccoon & His Friends. Anderson-Miller, Julia, illus. 112p. 1992. 16.00 (*0-89733-377-2*); pap. 6.95 (*0-89733-374-8*) Academy Chi Pubs.

McConnell, Nancy P. Please Touch the Animals! Gress, Jonna, ed. Ruge, Don, Jr., illus. 12p. (ps-k). 1992. pap. text ed. 16.20 (*0-944943-16-0*, CODE 20017-9) Current Inc.

McDonnell, Janet. Fall: A Tale of What's to Come. Hohag, Linda, illus. LC 93-20171. 32p. (gr. 2 up). 1993. PLB 12.30 (*0-516-00676-2*) Childrens.

—Mouse's Adventure in Alphabet Town. Williams, Jenny, illus. LC 91-47717. 32p. (ps-2). 1992. PLB 11. 80 (*0-516-05413-9*) Childrens.

—Spring: New Life Everywhere. Hohag, Linda, illus. LC 93-10309. 32p. (gr. 2 up). 1993. PLB 12.30 (*0-516-00677-0*) Childrens.

—Summer, a Growing Time. Hohag, Linda, illus. LC 93-1182. 32p. (gr. 2 up). 1993. PLB 12.30 (*0-516-00678-9*) Childrens.

—Victor's Adventure in Alphabet Town. Peltier, Pam, illus. LC 92-4036. 32p. (ps-2). 1992. PLB 11.80 (*0-516-05422-8*) Childrens.

—Winter: Tracks in the Snow. Hohag, Linda, illus. LC 93-20172. 32p. (gr. 2 up). 1993. PLB 12.30 (*0-516-00679-7*) Childrens.

McDowell, Mildred. The Squirrel & the Frog. Brennan, Nancy, illus. Harman, Sandra L., intro. by. LC 76-133256. (Illus.). 44p. (gr. 1-2). 1971. 2.50 (*0-87884-007-9*) Unicorn Ent.

McFall, Gardner. Naming the Animals. Guarnaccia, Steven, illus. LC 93-14532. (ps-3). 1994. PLB 13.99 (*0-670-84814-X*) Viking Child Bks.

McManus, Patrick F. Real Ponies Don't Go Oink! large type ed. 242p. 1992. text ed. 18.95x (*0-8161-5343-4*, Large Print Bks) Hall.

McMullen, Shawn. That's What Friends Are For. Haley, Amanda, illus. LC 91-43656. (gr. 4-8). 1992. saddle-stitched 5.99 (*0-87403-975-4*, 24-03865) Standard Pub.

McNally, Darcie, adapted by. In a Cabin in a Wood. Koontz, Robin M., illus. LC 89-25192. 32p. (ps-3). 1991. 12.95 (*0-525-65035-0*, Cobblehill Bks) Dutton Child Bks.

McOmber, Rachel B., ed. McOmber Phonics Storybooks: Bags... Bags (Animals) rev. ed. (Illus.). write for info. (*0-944991-97-1*) Swift Lrn Res.

McPhail, David. The Bear's Toothache. McPhail, David, illus. (ps-3). 1988. pap. 5.95 (*0-316-56325-0*, Joy St Bks) Little.

—The Party. (ps-4). 1990. 14.95 (*0-316-56330-7*, Joy St Bks) Little.

—Those Terrible Toy-Breakers. McPhail, David, illus. LC 80-10450. 48p. (ps-3). 1980. 5.95 (*0-8193-1019-0*); PLB 5.95 (*0-8193-1020-4*) Parents.

McPhail, David M. The Glerp. LC 94-20298. (Illus.). 1994. 14.95 (*0-382-24669-1*); PLB 16.95 (*0-382-24668-3*); pap. 6.95 (*0-382-24670-5*) Silver Burdett Pr.

Madsen, Ross M. Stewart Stork. Halsey, Megan, illus. LC 92-30730. 40p. (ps-3). 1993. 11.99 (*0-8037-1325-8*); PLB 11.89 (*0-8037-1326-6*) Dial Bks Young.

Maguire, Gregory. The Peace-&-Quiet Diner. Perry, David, illus. LC 93-7770. 1994. PLB 13.27 (*0-8368-0971-8*) Gareth Stevens Inc.

Mariotti, Mario & Marchiori, Roberto, illus. Hanimals. 40p. (Orig.). (gr. 4 up). 1991. pap. 8.95 (*0-671-75232-4*, Green Tiger) S&S Trade.

Maris, Ron. Bernard's Boring Day. 1990. 12.95 (*0-385-29948-6*) Doubleday.

—Frogs Jump. Maris, Ron, illus. LC 91-58730. 14p. (ps). 1992. 4.95 (*1-56402-081-9*) Candlewick Pr.

Marks, Burton. Animals. Harvey, Paul, illus. LC 91-3656. 24p. (gr. k-2). 1992. PLB 9.89 (*0-8167-2415-6*); pap. text ed. 2.50 (*0-8167-2416-4*) Troll Assocs.

Marshall, James. Rats on the Range & Other Stories. LC 92-28918. (gr. 1-5). 1993. 12.99 (*0-8037-1384-3*); PLB 12.89 (*0-8037-1385-1*) Dial Bks Young.

—Rats on the Roof: And Other Stories. Marshall, James, illus. LC 90-44084. 80p. (gr. 1-5). 1991. 13.00 (*0-8037-0834-3*); lib. bdg. 12.89 (*0-8037-0835-1*) Dial Bks Young.

—Willis. Marshall, James, illus. (ps-3). 1989. pap. 4.95 (*0-395-51008-2*, Sandpiper) HM.

Martin, Bill, Jr. Brown Bear, Brown Bear, What Do You See? 25th Anniversary Edition. Carle, Eric, illus. LC 91-29115. 32p. (ps-k). 1992. 14.95 (*0-8050-1744-5*, Bks Young Read) H Holt & Co.

Martin, Francesca, retold by. The Honey Hunters. LC 91-58736. (Illus.). 32p. (ps up). 1992. 14.95 (*1-56402-086-X*) Candlewick Pr.

Marzollo, Jean. Pretend You're a Cat. Fogelman, Phyllis J., ed. Pinkney, Jerry, illus. LC 89-34546. 32p. (ps-3). 1990. PLB 12.89 (*0-8037-0774-6*) Dial Bks Young.

—Ten Cats Have Hats. McPhail, David, illus. LC 93-20136. (ps). 1994. 6.95 (*0-590-46968-1*) Scholastic Inc.

Mason, Judy S. Mr. Farmer & His Animals. Scoggan, Nita, ed. Wilson, Krista, illus. Shaw, Gwen, intro. by. (Illus.). 52p. (Orig.). (gr. 3 up). 1987. pap. 3.95 (*0-910487-11-1*) Royalty Pub.

Mathews, Nancy. Friends of Jesus: The Animals Tell Their Stories. (Illus.). 24p. (gr. 2-3). 1991. 9.99 (*0-8407-9609-9*) Nelson.

Mathiesen, Egon. Jungle in the Wheat Field. (Illus.). (gr. k-3). 1960. 9.95 (*0-8392-3014-1*) Astor-Honor.

Matthews, Morgan. The Big Race. Schindler, S. D., illus. LC 88-1287. 48p. (Orig.). (gr. 1-4). 1989. PLB 10.59 (*0-8167-1329-4*); pap. text ed. 3.50 (*0-8167-1330-8*) Troll Assocs.

Maurer, Donna. Annie, Bea, & Chi Chi Dolores: A School Day Alphabet. Cazet, Denys, illus. LC 92-25104. 32p. (ps-k). 1993. 14.95 (*0-531-05467-5*); PLB 14.99 (*0-531-08617-8*) Orchard Bks Watts.

Mayer, Gina & Mayer, Mercer. A Very Special Critter. (Illus.). 24p. (ps-3). 1993. pap. 1.95 (*0-307-12763-X*, 12763, Golden Pr) Western Pub.

Mayer, Mercer. Eight Favorite Little Critter Books Just for You. (Illus.). (ps-3). 1993. Incls. Just for You, Just Me & My Dad, Just Grandma & Me, When I Get Bigger, Just Go to Bed, I Was So Mad, The New Baby, & Me Too! 24p. ea. bk. pap. 15.95 shrink-wrapped slipcase (*0-307-16205-2*, 16205-0, Golden Pr) Western Pub.

—Little Critter's Read-It-Yourself Storybook: Six Funny Easy-to-Read Stories. (Illus.). 196p. (gr. k-2). 1993. 11.95 (*0-307-16840-9*, 16840, Golden Pr) Western Pub.

—Little Critter's: This Is My School. (ps-3). 1990. write for info. (*0-307-11589-5*) Western Pub.

—Little Critter's This Is My School. (Illus.). 32p. (ps-2). 1992. pap. write for info. (*0-307-15963-9*, 15963) Western Pub.

Mazer, Anne. The Salamander Room. Johnson, Steve, illus. LC 90-33301. 32p. (ps-3). 1991. 14.00 (*0-394-82945-X*); PLB 14.99 (*0-394-92945-4*) Knopf Bks Yng Read.

Mazzola, Toni & Guten, Mimi. Wally Koala & Friends. Cohen, Keri, ed. McCoy, William M., illus. LC 93-94001. 22p. (ps-3). 1993. saddlestitch bdg. incl. cassette 9.95 (*1-883747-00-7*) WK Prods.

—Wally Koala & the Little Green Peach. Cohen, Keri, ed. McCoy, William M., illus. LC 93-94002. 22p. (ps-3). 1993. saddlestitch bdg. incl. cassette 9.95 (*1-883747-01-5*) WK Prods. WALLY KOALA'S SLOGAN: "I'M WONDERFUL & SO ARE YOU." Books lovingly narrated by CHARLOTTE RAE (TV'S FACTS OF LIFE) who also sings original songs. IN WALLY KOALA & THE LITTLE GREEN PEACH, Farmer Jim picks all other peaches, leaving lonely little green peach at the top of the tree. Through the story of Mr. Big Peach Tree, Wally comforts Little Green Peach & previews all the changes he can expect during metamorphosis from green peach to glorious blossoming tree. (Vernon Woolf) "Magical journey into patience, trust in self, nature & process of life. A must for those who feel they're not blossoming as fast as their peers or their expectations." IN WALLY KOALA & FRIENDS, Wally travels from Australia to America with friends Sadie Kangaroo & Timmy Kookaburra. This book introduces the loveable characters. Self-esteem subtly emphasized. WALLY helps to make children aware that we all make mistakes, as he & Sadie did by sneaking Timmy on the plane. Mistakes are OK. We learn from them. (Vernon Woolf) "WALLY & FRIENDS teaches trust in the world

of adult authority in an easy-going, delightful style." (BUSINESS STARTUPS mag) "Loveable koala from 'down under,' winning the hearts of North American children..." To order contact: W.K. Productions, P.O. Box 801504, Dallas, TX 75380-1504. Distributors: Baker & Taylor, Brodart Co., 717-326-2461, Hervey's Booklink, 214-480-9987, Ingram.
Publisher Provided Annotation.

Melmed, Laura K. I Love You As Much... Sorensen, Henri, illus. LC 92-27677. 1993. write for info. (*0-688-11718-X*); PLB write for info. (*0-688-11719-8*) Lothrop.

Miles, John C., ed. Treasury of Animal Stories. Oak-Rhind, Mary & Dennison, Graham, illus. LC 90-11158. 96p. (gr. 2-5). 1991. lib. bdg. 14.89 (*0-8167-2240-4*); pap. text ed. 6.95 (*0-8167-2241-2*) Troll Assocs.

Millais, Raoul. Elijah & Pin-Pin. LC 91-20032. (Illus.). 48p. (ps-1). 1992. pap. 14.00 jacketed (*0-671-75543-9*, S&S BFYR) S&S Trade.

Milne, A. A. Christopher Robin Gives Pooh a Party. Shepard, Ernest H., illus. 32p. 1993. 4.99 (*0-525-45144-7*, DCB) Dutton Child Bks.

—Christopher Robin Leads an Expotition. Shepard, Ernest H., illus. 32p. 1993. 4.99 (*0-525-45142-0*, DCB) Dutton Child Bks.

—Eyeore Has a Birthday. Shepard, Ernest H., illus. 32p. 1993. 4.99 (*0-525-45043-2*, DCB) Dutton Child Bks.

—The House at Pooh Corner. Shepard, Ernest H., illus. 192p. 1992. pap. 3.99 (*0-14-036122-7*, Puffin) Puffin Bks.

—The House at Pooh Corner. 1923. pap. 1.75 (*0-440-73795-8*) Dell.

—Kanga & Baby Roo Come to the Forest. Shepard, Ernest H., illus. 32p. 1993. 4.99 (*0-525-45141-2*, DCB) Dutton Child Bks.

—Piglet Is Entirely Surrounded by Water. Shepard, Ernest H., illus. 32p. 1993. 4.99 (*0-525-45143-9*, DCB) Dutton Child Bks.

—Piglet Meets a Heffalump. Shepard, Ernest H., illus. 32p. 1993. 4.99 (*0-525-45042-4*, DCB) Dutton Child Bks.

—Pooh's Birthday Book. Shepard, Ernest H., illus. 160p. (gr. 1-3). 1991. pap. 3.50 (*0-440-46934-1*, YB) Dell.

—Pooh's Library, 4 bks. Shepard, Ernest H., illus. 1992. Set. pap. 16.00 slipcased (*0-14-095560-7*, Puffin) Puffin Bks.

—Winnie-the-Pooh. Shepard, Ernest H., illus. 176p. 1992. pap. 3.99 (*0-14-036121-9*, Puffin) Puffin Bks.

—Winnie the Pooh, 4 vols. 1992. Set. slipcased 75.00 (*0-525-45004-1*, DCB) Dutton Child Bks.

—Winnie-the-Pooh's Friendship Book. Shepard, Ernest H., illus. 48p. (gr. 4-7). 1994. 8.99 (*0-525-45204-4*, DCB) Dutton Child Bks.

—Winnie-the-Pooh's Story Box, 10 bks. Shepard, Ernest H., illus. 1993. Set. 49.90 (*0-525-45168-4*, DCB) Dutton Child Bks.

Milne, A. A. & Shepard. Pooh's Bedtime Book. LC 80-65523. (Illus.). 48p. (ps-3). 1980. 9.95 (*0-525-44895-0*, DCB) Dutton Child Bks.

Minarik, Else H. Am I Beautiful? Abolafia, Yossi, illus. LC 91-32562. 24p. (ps-4). 1992. 14.00 (*0-688-09911-4*); PLB 13.93 (*0-688-09912-2*) Greenwillow.

—Cat & Dog. Siebel, Fritz, illus. LC 60-14998. 32p. (gr. k-2). 1960. PLB 13.89 (*0-06-024221-3*) HarpC Child Bks.

—Kiss for Little Bear. Sendak, Maurice, illus. LC 57-9263. 32p. (gr. k-3). 1968. 14.00 (*0-06-024298-1*); PLB 13.89 (*0-06-024299-X*) HarpC Child Bks.

—The Little Girl & the Dragon. Gourlault, Martine, illus. LC 90-38495. 24p. (ps up). 1991. 13.95 (*0-688-09913-0*); PLB 13.88 (*0-688-09914-9*) Greenwillow.

Miranda, Altina. Love on an Animal Farm. (Illus.). 32p. (Orig.). 1993. pap. 8.95 (*0-86534-202-4*) Sunstone Pr.

Mishica, Clare. Max's Answer. Stortz, Diane, ed. LC 94-2100. (Illus.). 48p. (Orig.). (ps-3). 1994. pap. 4.49 (*0-7847-0177-6*) Standard Pub.

Modesitt, Jeanne. Lunch with Milly. Spowart, Robin, illus. LC 93-33808. 32p. (gr. k-3). 1995. PLB 14.95 (*0-8167-3388-0*); pap. text ed. 4.95 (*0-8167-3389-9*) BrdgeWater.

Moerbeek, Kees. Penguins Slide. LC 91-42040. 1992. 9.95 (*0-85953-544-4*) Childs Play.

Moers, Hermann. Little Ben. Corderoc'h, Jean-Pierre, illus. Lanning, Rosemary, tr. from GER. LC 90-47030. (Illus.). 32p. (gr. k-3). 1991. 14.95 (*1-55858-105-7*) North-South Bks NYC.

Mogensen, Jan. The Tiger's Breakfast. LC 91-3606. (Illus.). 32p. (ps-3). 1991. 14.95 (*0-940793-83-0*, Crocodile Bks) Interlink Pub.

Moncure, Jane B. How Many Ways Can You Cut a Pie? Hohag, Linda, illus. LC 87-15807. (SPA & ENG.). 32p. (ps-2). 1987. PLB 14.95 (*0-89565-408-3*) Childs World.

—Nanny Goat's Boat. Friedman, Joy, illus. LC 87-12839. (SPA & ENG.). 32p. (ps-2). 1987. PLB 14.95 (*0-89565-404-0*) Childs World.

Monsell, Mary E. Armadillo. Wickstrom, Sylvie, illus. LC 90-19135. 32p. (ps-1). 1991. SBE 13.95 (*0-689-31676-3*, Atheneum Child Bk) Macmillan Child Grp.

Montgomery, Rutherford G. Carcajou. Cram, L. D., illus. LC 36-6665. (gr. 6-8). 1936. 4.95 (*0-87004-105-3*) Caxton.

—Rufus. Nenninger, J. D., illus. LC 78-150819. (Orig.). (gr. 4-8). 1973. 4.95 (*0-87004-227-0*) Caxton.

Moon, Nicola. At the Beginning of a Pig. Ellis, Andy, illus. LC 93-41504. 24p. (ps-k). 1994. 8.95 (*1-85697-977-6*, Kingfisher LKC) LKC.

Mooney, Ann J. The Sock Animals: Tiger's New Friends. Mooney, Ann J., photos by. LC 91-76359. (Illus.). 32p. (Orig.). (ps-2). 1992. pap. 7.95 (*0-9631035-0-4*) Jamondas Pr.

Mora, Jo. Budgee Budgee Cottontail. Mitchell, Steve, ed. Mora, Jo, illus. (gr. 3). 1994. 24.95 (*0-922029-23-7*) D Stoecklein Photo.
A wonderful story written in verse & gorgeously illustrated by famous artist, sculptor, & writer, Jo Mora. Written in 1936, eleven years before his death, the book contains a multitude of animal sketches & color illustrations by Mora. He was known as a cowboy & author of classic books on the American West, but Mora began as a Boston cartoonist & children's book author at the turn of the century. After sculpting the Will Rogers Memorial, the Father Serra Sarcophagus at the Carmel, California, mission, & the Don Quixote statue in San Francisco's Golden Gate Park, Mora returned to complete the children's book he always wanted to write - BUDGEE BUDGEE COTTONTAIL!
Publisher Provided Annotation.

Morris, Johnny. Animal-Go-Round. LC 93-12376. (Illus.). 18p. (gr. 3 up). 1993. 12.95 (*1-56458-329-5*) Dorling Kindersley.

Moser, Erwin. The Crow in the Snow & Other Bedtime Stories. Agee, Joel, tr. from GER. Moser, Erwin, illus. LC 86-10740. 48p. (ps up). 1986. 10.95 (*0-915361-49-3*) Modan-Adama Bks.

Most, Bernard. Zoodles. LC 91-33490. (ps-3). 1994. pap. 19.95 (*0-15-200071-2*, HB Juv Bks) HarBrace.

Muller, Robin. Hickory, Dickory, Dock. Duranceau, Suzanne, illus. LC 92-37588. 32p. (ps-6). 1994. 15.95 (*0-590-47278-X*) Scholastic Inc.

Myers. The Story of the Three Kingdoms. 1995. 15.00 (*0-06-024286-8*); PLB 14.89 (*0-06-024287-6*) HarpC Child Bks.

Myers, Bernice. The Flying Shoes. LC 91-335. (ps up). 1992. 15.00 (*0-688-10695-1*); PLB 14.93 (*0-688-10696-X*) Lothrop.

Nadler, Ellis. The Bee's Sneeze. LC 92-32470. (Illus.). 32p. (ps-1). 1993. pap. 12.00 POB (*0-671-86575-7*, S&S BFYR) S&S Trade.

Nagel, Karen. Two Crazy Pigs. Schatell, Brian, illus. 32p. 1992. pap. 2.95 (*0-590-44972-9*, Cartwheel) Scholastic Inc.

Napoli, Donna J. Prince of the Pond. LC 91-40340. (Illus.). 112p. (gr. 2-5). 1992. 13.00 (*0-525-44976-0*, DCB) Dutton Child Bks.

Nash, Corey. Little Treasury of Beatrix Potter, 6 vols. in 1. 1988. boxed 5.99 (*0-517-46667-8*) Random Hse Value.

Nash, Ogden. The Animal Garden. Knight, Hilary, illus. LC 65-21772. 48p. (gr. 10 up). 1988. pap. 5.95 (*0-87131-568-8*) M Evans.

Naylor, Phyllis R. Shiloh. LC 90-603. 144p. (gr. 3-7). 1991. SBE 13.95 (*0-689-31614-3*, Atheneum Child Bk) Macmillan Child Grp.

Ned the Lonely Donkey. (ARA., Illus.). (gr. 3-5). 1987. 3.95x (*0-86685-211-5*) Intl Bk Ctr.

Nelson, Drew. Wild Voices. Schoenherr, John, illus. 96p. (gr. 3 up). 1991. 15.95 (*0-399-21798-3*, Philomel) Putnam Pub Group.

Newton, Jill. Polar Scare. (Illus.). (ps-3). 1992. 15.00 (*0-688-11232-3*); PLB 14.93 (*0-685-75779-X*) Lothrop.

Nister, Ernest. Farmyard Friends. Intervisual Staff, illus. 10p. (ps up). 1991. 4.95 (*0-399-22110-7*, Philomel) Putnam Pub Group.

Noble, Kate. Bubble Gum. Bass, Rachel, illus. 32p. (ps-3). 1992. 14.95 (*0-9631798-0-2*) Silver Seahorse.

—Oh Look, It's a Nosserus. Bass, Rachel, illus. 32p. (ps-4). 1993. 14.95 (*0-9631798-2-9*) Silver Seahorse.
Robbi is a young rhino who lives in a game park in Africa. He can't wait to have a horn as beautiful as his Mama's; he gets teased for being clumsy, & he sets out to save his friends from terrible danger. Children who loved & laughed with Kimbi in BUBBLE GUM will be delighted to meet Robbi & his zebra & giraffe friends. Once again, Rachel Bass creates the beauty of Africa & the charm of its animals in her vivid paintings. BUBBLE GUM. Kate Noble (Africa Stories Ser.) (Illus. by Rachel Bass). 32p. 1992. pre K-4th gr. 14.95 (0-9631798-0-2) Kimbi is a young baboon who lives in a park in Africa. He wishes tourists didn't pay so much attention to the lions. He loves sweets, & he stumbles into an amazing adventure. The illustrations for this delightful story capture the magic of the African landscape. There's also a learning plus: the details of animal behavior are correct, & the pictures show both black & white children & adults. Silver Seahorse Press, 2568 N. Clark St., Suite 320, Chicago, IL 60614; 312-871-1772; FAX: 312-327-8978. Distributed by Lifetime Books, Inc., 2131 Hollywood Blvd., Hollywood, FL 33020-6750; 1-800-771-3355; FAX: 1-800-931-7411.
Publisher Provided Annotation.

Nodset, Joan L. Who Took the Farmer's Hat? Siebel, Fritz, illus. LC 62-17964. 32p. (gr. k-3). 1963. PLB 14.89 (*0-06-024566-2*) HarpC Child Bks.

Noll, Sally. Watch Where You Go. LC 92-25333. 1993. pap. 3.99 (*0-14-054884-X*) Puffin Bks.

Norman, Jane & Beazley, Frank. Big Purr to the Rescue. 24p. (ps-3). 1993. pap. write for info. (*1-883585-11-2*) Pixanne Ent.

North, Carol. Jungle Book: Mowgli's Noisy Jungle. (ps). 1993. 9.95 (*0-307-06076-4*, Golden Pr) Western Pub.

—Walt Disney's Winnie the Pooh: Pooh Can... Can You? Baker, Darrell, illus. 12p. (ps). 1993. bds. 1.95 (*0-307-06081-0*, 6081, Golden Pr) Western Pub.

Novak, Matt. Elmer Blunt's Open House. LC 91-38424. (Illus.). 24p. (ps-1). 1992. 14.95 (*0-531-05998-7*); PLB 14.99 (*0-531-08598-8*) Orchard Bks Watts.

Nwabugwu, Frank. Antalo the Antelope, B-era the Bear, C-esto the Cheetah, D-opicooko the Deer. 18p. 1992. write for info. (*1-881687-04-X*); lib. bdg. write for info. (*1-881687-05-8*); pap. write for info. (*1-881687-06-6*); write for info. tchr's. ed. (*1-881687-07-4*) F Nwabugwu.

Oden, Fay G. Where Is Calvin? (Illus.). 48p. (Orig.). (gr. 2-6). 1994. pap. text ed. 6.95 (*0-9638946-0-9*) Tennedo Pubs.
Fay Giles Oden is a retired elementary school teacher, fiction writer, editor, illustrator & poet. Her recently published short fiction (child's book) is WHERE IS CALVIN? (Tennedo, $6.95). Mrs. Oden received motivation for the story WHERE IS CALVIN? after visiting the zoo. (Summer 1993). The story deals with respect for family life & a child's infatuation with animals. It is a simple story of friendship & entrancement with the animals that somehow caused the boys to become separated. The suspense of the boys' day at the zoo overwhelms you as the animals have been intentionally personified to talk to the boys. They become boys with a mission to find their friend Calvin. The plot is simple. The characters are believable. The narrative techniques of the story skillfully blends literature with poetry. The suspenseful, vivid & colorful story will delight young readers. In short, WHERE IS CALVIN? is a charming story with sympathetic characters. Children will love the humor of it all. You'll be surprised to find out what really happened to Calvin. The book

lends itself to a READ-ME-A-STORY book. Child care centers have expressed an interest in the book. WHERE IS CALVIN? can be ordered from the following distributors: Baker & Taylor, 501 South Gladiolus Street, Momence, IL 60954-1799; Tennedo Publishers, 6315 Elwynne Drive, Cincinnati, OH 45236, 1-513-791-3277. Fay Oden is also the author of: CALVIN & HIS VIDEO CAMERA. *Publisher Provided Annotation.*

Odgers, Sally F. Up the Stairs. Hunnam, Lucinda, illus. LC 92-21395. 1993. 4.25 (*0-383-03601-1*) SRA Schl Grp.

Oetting, Rae. Timmy Tiger to the Rescue. LC 70-108733. (Illus.). 32p. (ps-4). 1970. PLB 9.95x (*0-87783-043-6*); pap. 3.94x deluxe ed (*0-87783-112-2*); cassette 7.94x (*0-87783-229-3*) Oddo.

—Timmy Tiger's New Coat. LC 74-108734. (Illus.). 32p. (ps-2). 1970. PLB 9.95 (*0-87783-044-4*); pap. 3.94 deluxe ed (*0-87783-113-0*); cassette 7.94x (*0-87783-230-7*) Oddo.

—Timmy Tiger's New Friend. LC 77-108732. (Illus.). (ps-2). 1970. PLB 9.95 (*0-87783-042-8*); pap. 3.94 deluxe ed (*0-87783-114-9*); cassette 7.94x (*0-87783-231-5*) Oddo.

Offen, Hilda. As Quiet As a Mouse. (Illus.). 32p. (ps-2). 1994. 12.99 (*0-525-45309-1*, DCB) Dutton Child Bks.

—A Fox Got My Socks. LC 92-7380. (ps-2). 1993. 10.00 (*0-525-44991-4*, DCB) Dutton Child Bks.

—The Sheep Made a Leap. Offen, Hilda, illus. 32p. (ps-2). 1994. 10.99 (*0-525-45174-9*, DCB) Dutton Child Bks.

Ogawa & Katayama, eds. Animal Fables. (Illus.). 32p. 1994. pap. 7.00 (*4-7700-1794-4*) Kodansha.

Ogun, Funmi. Bobo & the Greedy Tito. (Illus.). 16p. (Orig.). (gr. 2 up). 1994. pap. 14.95 (*1-882188-09-8*) Magnolia Mktg.

Oke, Janette. Trouble in a Fur Coat. Mann, Brenda, illus. 152p. (Orig.). (gr. 1-6). 1990. pap. 4.99 (*0-934998-38-8*) Bethel Pub.

Old MacDonald's Farm. 24p. (ps-3). 1991. write for info. (*0-307-14161-6*, 14161) Western Pub.

O'Mara, Lesley, ed. Classic Animal Stories. Dominguez, Angel, illus. 160p. (gr. 1 up). 1991. 18.95 (*1-55970-143-9*) Arcade Pub Inc.

Ormerod, Jan. Our Ollie. LC 85-17133. (Illus.). 24p. (ps). 1986. 4.95 (*0-688-04208-2*) Lothrop.

—Young Joe. LC 85-17128. (Illus.). 24p. (ps). 1985. 4.95 (*0-688-04210-4*) Lothrop.

Osborne, Mary P. Spider Kane & the Mystery under the May-Apple. Chess, Victoria, illus. LC 90-33524. 128p. (gr. 1-7). 1992. 13.00 (*0-679-80855-8*); PLB 13.99 (*0-679-90855-2*) Knopf Bks Yng Read.

O'Toole, Donna. Aarvy Aardvark Finds Hope: A Read-Aloud Story for People of All Ages. McWhirter, Mary Lou, illus. 80p. (Orig.). (ps up). 1989. pap. 9.95 (*1-878321-25-0*, Mntn Rainbow); tchr's. guide 6.95 (*1-878321-26-9*, Mntn Rainbow); audio tape 9.95 (*0-685-20985-7*, Mntn Rainbow) Rainbow NC.

Oxenbury, Helen. It's My Birthday. LC 93-39667. (Illus.). 24p. (ps up). 1994. 9.95 (*1-56402-412-1*) Candlewick Pr.

Packard, Edward. Jungle Safari. Tomei, Lorna, illus. 51p. (gr. 4). 1983. pap. 2.25 (*0-553-15403-6*) Bantam.

Packard, Mary. Fairest of All. McCue, Lisa, illus. LC 93-11056. 40p. (ps-4). 1993. PLB 11.80 (*0-516-00826-9*) Childrens.

—Playing by the Rules. McCue, Lisa, illus. LC 93-4423. 40p. (ps-4). 1993. PLB 11.80 (*0-516-00827-7*) Childrens.

—Safe & Sound. McCue, Lisa, illus. LC 93-11058. 40p. (ps-4). 1993. PLB 11.80 (*0-516-00828-5*) Childrens.

—Save the Swamp. McCue, Lisa, illus. LC 93-11059. 40p. (ps-4). 1993. PLB 11.80 (*0-516-00829-3*) Childrens.

—Spike & Mike & the Treasure Hunt. McCue, Lisa, illus. LC 92-50295. 1993. write for info. (*0-679-93936-9*); lib. bdg. write for info. (*0-679-83936-4*) Random Bks Yng Read.

—Starting Over. McCue, Lisa & Scribner, Toni, illus. LC 93-11060. 40p. (ps-4). 1993. PLB 11.80 (*0-516-00831-5*) Childrens.

Pagnucci, Franco & Susan. Story Start Animals. (gr. 2-5). 1990. pap. 8.95 (*0-8224-6398-9*) Fearon Teach Aids.

Paraskevas, Betty. Shamlanders. Paraskevas, Michael, illus. LC 92-32980. 1993. 13.95 (*0-15-292854-5*) HarBrace.

Pare, Roger. Animal Capers. Pare, Roger, illus. 24p. 1992. PLB 14.95 (*1-55037-243-2*, Pub. by Annick Pr); pap. 4.95 (*1-55037-244-0*, Pub. by Annick Pr) Firefly Bks Ltd.

Parkes, Brenda. One Foggy Night. Cullo, Ned, illus. LC 92-32514. 1993. 4.25 (*0-383-03588-0*) SRA Schl Grp.

Parrish, Rhett. Puppy Dogs Polka at the Kitty Cat Carnival: A Music Gift Set with a Fun Approach to Learning. 48p. (ps-2). 1991. incl. 2 cass. 14.95 (*0-9632433-0-6*) RPM Record.

Parsons, Mary P. Farmer Brown's Friends. Geurts, Kelly, illus. LC 90-71980. 65p. (Orig.). 1992. pap. 8.00 (*1-56002-040-7*) Aegina Pr.

Paschkis. Wide Awake So Sleepy. (ps-1). 1994. 12.95 (*0-8050-3174-X*) H Holt & Co.

Paterson, Cynthia & Paterson, Brian. Robbery at Foxwood. (Illus.). 32p. (ps-3). 1985. 6.95 (*0-8120-5665-5*) Barron.

Patrick, Denise L. Walt Disney's the Jungle Book. (ps). 1994. 3.95 (*0-307-12548-3*, Golden Pr) Western Pub.

Paxton, Tom. Belling the Cat: And Other Aesop's Fables. Rayevsky, Robert, illus. LC 89-39851. 40p. (ps up). 1990. 13.95 (*0-688-08158-4*); PLB 13.88 (*0-688-08159-2*, Morrow Jr Bks) Morrow Jr Bks.

Peabody, Paul. Blackberry Hollow. Peabody, Paul, illus. LC 92-8968. 160p. (gr. 3-7). 1993. 15.95 (*0-399-22500-5*, Philomel Bks) Putnam Pub Group.

Peek, Merle. Mary Wore Her Red Dress, & Henry Wore His Green Sneakers. Peek, Merle, illus. LC 84-12733. 32p. (ps-2). 1985. 14.95 (*0-89919-324-2*, Clarion Bks) HM.

Peet, Bill. Farewell to Shady Glade. Peet, Bill, illus. 48p. (gr. k-3). 1991. 14.95 (*0-395-18975-6*); pap. 7.95 incl. cassette (*0-395-60166-5*) HM.

—Jethro & Joel Were a Troll. LC 86-20879. (Illus.). 32p. (gr. k-3). 1990. 12.95 (*0-395-43081-X*); pap. 5.95 (*0-395-53968-4*) HM.

—No Such Things. Peet, Bill, illus. LC 82-23234. 32p. (gr. k-3). 1983. 13.95 (*0-395-33888-3*); pap. 4.80 (*0-395-39594-1*) HM.

—Smokey. Peet, Bill, illus. 48p. (gr. k-3). 1983. pap. 5.95 (*0-395-34924-9*) HM.

Percy, Graham. Cock, the Mouse, & the Little Red Hen. Percy, Graham, illus. LC 91-71857. 32p. (ps up). 1994. pap. 5.99 (*1-56402-268-4*) Candlewick Pr.

Perkins, Al. Hugh Lofting's Travels of Doctor Dolittle. reissued ed. LC 67-25853. (Illus.). 64p. (ps-2). 1967. 6.95 (*0-394-80048-6*); PLB 7.99 (*0-394-90048-0*) Random Bks Yng Read.

Perkins, Anne T. What Is It? Lomax, James, illus. 8p. 1993. 12.00 (*1-884204-03-1*) Teach Nxt Door.

Peterson, Esther. A New Home for Chip. (Illus.). 16p. 1994. saddlestitched 5.95 (*0-8059-3568-1*) Dorrance.

Pfister, Marcus. Hopper. Pfister, Marcus, illus. LC 90-47065. 32p. (ps-k). 1991. 14.95 (*1-55858-106-5*) North-South Bks NYC.

—Hopper Hunts for Spring. Pfister, Marcus, illus. Lanning, Rosemary, tr. from GER. LC 91-29671. (Illus.). 32p. (gr. k-3). 1992. 14.95 (*1-55858-139-1*); lib. bdg. 14.88 (*1-55858-147-2*) North-South Bks NYC.

—Les Nouveaux Amis De Pit. Pfister, Marcus, illus. (FRE.). 32p. (gr. k-3). 1992. 13.95 (*3-85539-632-9*) North-South Bks NYC.

—Pinguin Pit. Pfister, Marcus, illus. (GER.). 32p. (gr. k-3). 1992. 13.95 (*3-314-00297-1*) North-South Bks NYC.

—Pit et Pat. Pfister, Marcus, illus. (FRE.). 32p. (gr. k-3). 1992. 13.95 (*3-85539-657-4*) North-South Bks NYC.

—Pit, le Petit Pingouin. Pfister, Marcus, illus. (FRE.). 32p. (gr. k-3). 1992. 13.95 (*3-314-20627-5*) North-South Bks NYC.

—Pit und Pat. Pfister, Marcus, illus. (GER.). 32p. (gr. k-3). 1992. 13.95 (*3-314-00327-7*) North-South Bks NYC.

—Pit's Neue Freunde. Pfister, Marcus, illus. (GER.). 32p. (gr. k-3). 1992. 13.95 (*3-85825-301-4*) North-South Bks NYC.

Pilling, Ann. Donkey's Day Out. (ps-3). 1990. 11.95 (*0-7459-1618-X*) Lion USA.

Platt, Kin. Darwin & the Great Beasts. LC 90-39674. 64p. (gr. 2 up). 1992. 14.00 (*0-688-10030-9*) Greenwillow.

Plumb, Sally. A Pika's Tail: A Children's Story about Mountain Wildlife. Milligan, Sharlene, ed. Ormsby, Lawrence, illus. 40p. (Orig.). 1994. 14. 95 (*0-931895-26-X*); pap. 9.95 (*0-931895-25-1*) Grand Teton NHA. Published by Grand Teton Natural History Association, A PIKA'S TAIL is a winsome children's story based on the life cycle of the pika. The pika, a small member of the rabbit family, lives in high mountain environments. The story features a pika, Beejer, & his relationship with other wildlife in his world. Without a tail, Beejer searches the mountains calling for the lost tails convinced he should have one at least as impressive as his friends'. Through many exciting adventures, the story ends happily with Beejer safe & content to be tailless. Rhythmic prose, full-color illustrations & the introduction of ideas to arouse understanding & appreciation of natural systems contribute to the special value of this book. A wonderful book for bedtime story hour. Author Sally Plumb wrote A PIKA'S TAIL while living in Grand Teton National Park, Wyoming where she learned to appreciate & "listen" to the little "rock rabbit." Lawrence Ormsby spent a summer in Grand Teton observing & gathering research materials before he began illustrations for the book. His realistic portrayals transport the reader to the mountain environment of the pika, weasel, & marmot. Order from Grand Teton Natural History Association, P.O. Box 170, Grand Teton National Park, Moose, Wyoming; 307-739-3406. *Publisher Provided Annotation.*

Poe, Edgar Allan. The Fall of the House of Usher. Cutts, David E., adapted by. Crowell, James, illus. LC 81-15958. 32p. (gr. 5-10). 1982. PLB 10.79 (*0-89375-624-5*); pap. text ed. 2.95 (*0-89375-625-3*) Troll Assocs.

Polette, Nancy. Favorite Novel Animals. (Illus.). 48p. (gr. 3-6). 1992. pap. 5.95 (*1-879287-15-3*) Bk Lures.

Polisar, Barry L. Peculiar Zoo. Clark, David, illus. 32p. (gr. k-6). 1993. 14.95 (*0-938663-14-3*) Rainbow Morn.

Potter, Beatrix. Animal Homes. 12p. 1991. bds. 3.50 (*0-7232-3782-4*) Warne.

—Beatrix Potter Collection, 3 vols. (ps-3). 1987. Set. write for info. (*0-317-52263-9*); Collection #1. 24.00 (*0-7232-5163-0*); Collection #2. 21.00 (*0-7232-5164-9*); Collection #3. 21.00 (*0-7232-5165-7*) Warne.

—Beatrix Potter Mask Book. (ps-3). 1990. pap. 9.95 (*0-7232-3619-4*) Warne.

—Beatrix Potter's Farmhouse Box. (Illus.). (ps-3). 1989. Set of 6. 28.95 (*0-7232-5169-X*) Warne.

—Dinner Time. 12p. 1991. bds. 3.50 (*0-7232-3781-6*) Warne.

—Further Tales from Beatrix Potter. (Illus.). 112p. (ps-3). 1987. 7.95 (*0-7232-3509-0*) Warne.

—Ginger & Pickles. LC 85-13641. (Illus.). 64p. (gr. 2 up). 1985. pap. 1.75 (*0-486-24969-7*) Dover.

—Happy Families. 12p. 1991. bds. 3.50 (*0-7232-3783-2*) Warne.

—Hill Top Tales. (Illus.). 128p. (ps up). 1989. 8.95 (*0-7232-3548-1*) Warne.

—Jeremie Peche-a-la-Ligne. (FRE., Illus.). 58p. 1990. 9.95 (*0-7859-3628-9*, 2070560740) Fr & Eur.

—Madame Piquedru. (FRE.). 58p. 1990. 10.95 (*2-07-056068-6*) Schoenhof.

—Madame Trotte-Menu. (FRE.). 59p. 1990. 10.95 (*2-07-056105-4*) Schoenhof.

—Mademoiselle Mitoufle. (FRE.). 37p. 1990. 10.95 (*2-07-056104-6*) Schoenhof.

—More Tales from Beatrix Potter. (ps-3). 1988. 8.95 (*0-7232-3366-7*) Warne.

—Mrs. Tiggy-Winkle. (Illus.). 10p. (ps). 1994. 3.99 (*0-7232-0019-X*) Warne.

—Peter Rabbit & Eleven Other Favorite Tales. Stewart, Pat, adapted by. Potter, Beatrix, illus. LC 93-14417. 96p. 1994. pap. 1.00t (*0-486-27845-X*) Dover.

—Peter Rabbit & His Friends. (Illus.). 24p. (ps). 1994. bds. 2.99 (*0-7232-4093-0*) Warne.

—Peter Rabbit & Other Stories. 1993. 4.98 (*0-89009-187-0*) Bk Sales Inc.

—The Pie & the Patty-Pan. (Illus.). 46p. 1976. pap. 1.75 (*0-486-23383-9*) Dover.

—The Stories of Beatrix Potter, Vol. 1. Potter, Beatrix, illus. 96p. (ps-2). 1991. 4 bks. & 2 audio cassettes 16. 98 (*1-55886-063-0*) Smarty Pants.

—The Stories of Beatrix Potter, Vol. 2. Potter, Beatrix, illus. 96p. (ps-2). 1992. 4 bks. & 2 audio cassettes 16. 98 (*1-55886-067-3*) Smarty Pants.

—The Tale of Mr. Jeremy Fisher. Horden, Michael, read by. (ps-3). 1989. pap. 6.95 bk. & tape (*0-7232-3669-0*) Warne.

—The Tale of Mrs. Tiggy-Winkle. Atkinson, Allen, illus. 1984. pap. 2.25 (*0-553-15204-1*) Bantam.

—The Tale of Peter Rabbit. (Illus.). 60p. (gr. 1-5). 1972. pap. 1.75 (*0-486-22827-4*) Dover.

—Tale of Peter Rabbit. new ed. Apple, Margot, illus. LC 78-18071. 32p. (gr. k-3). 1979. PLB 9.79 (*0-89375-124-3*); pap. 1.95 (*0-89375-102-2*) Troll Assocs.

—The Tale of Peter Rabbit. Atkinson, Allen, illus. 64p. (Orig.). 1984. pap. 2.50 (*0-553-15470-2*) Bantam.

—Tales from Beatrix Potter. Potter, Beatrix, illus. 228p. (ps-3). 1986. 8.95 (*0-7232-3971-1*) Warne.

Potter, Beatrix, created by. Ginger & Pickles. Thiewes, Sam & Nelson, Anita, illus. 24p. (gr. 2-4). 1992. PLB 10.95 (*1-56674-017-7*, HTS Bks) Forest Hse.

—Mrs. Tiggy-Winkle. Thiewes, Sam, et al, illus. 24p. (gr. 2-4). 1992. PLB 10.95 (*1-56674-007-X*, HTS Bks) Forest Hse.

Pratt, Davis. Magic Animals of Japan. Kula, Elsa, illus. LC 67-17483. (gr. 1-4). 1967. (Pub. by Parnassus); PLB 5.88 (*0-87466-020-3*) HM.

Preston, Edna M. & Bennett, Rainey. The Temper Tantrum Book. (Illus.). (ps-3). 1976. pap. 4.95 (*0-14-050181-9*, Puffin) Puffin Bks.

Pringle, Laurence. Octopus Hug. Palmer, Kate S., illus. 32p. (ps-3). 1993. 14.95 (*1-56397-034-1*) Boyds Mills Pr.

Provensen, Alice & Provensen, Martin. A Horse & a Hound, a Goat & a Gander. LC 80-13259. (Illus.). 32p. (ps-3). 1980. (Atheneum Child Bk) Macmillan Child Grp.

—An Owl & Three Pussycats. Provensen, Alice & Provensen, Martin, illus. LC 81-2855. 32p. (ps-2). 1981. (Atheneum Childrens Bks) Macmillan Child Grp.

Radley, Gail. Special Strengths. Boddy, Joe, illus. 64p. (gr. 2-6). 1984. pap. 6.50 (*0-87743-702-5*, Pub. by Bellwood Pr) Bahai.

Randall, Ronne P. Baby Forest Animals. Tourret, Gwen, illus. 24p. (ps-k). 1987. pap. 1.25 (*0-7214-9546-X*, S871-2) Ladybird Bks.

Rathmann, Peggy. Goodnight, Gorilla. Rathman, Peggy, tr. LC 92-29020. (Illus.). 40p. (ps-1). 1994. 12.95 (*0-399-22445-9*, Putnam) Putnam Pub Group.

Ray, Stephen & Murdoch, Kathleen. Just Right for the Night. Campbell, Caroline, illus. LC 92-21398. (gr. 4 up). 1993. 4.25 (*0-383-03580-5*) SRA Schl Grp.

Razzi, Jim, adapted by. Walt Disney's the Jungle Book. LC 91-58975. (Illus.). 64p. 1992. pap. 3.50 (*1-56282-243-8*) Disney Pr.

Reddix, Valerie. Millie & the Mud Hole. Wickstrom, Thor, illus. LC 90-21147. 32p. (ps-3). 1992. 14.00 (*0-688-10212-3*); PLB 13.93 (*0-688-10213-1*) Lothrop.

Reese, Bob. Abert & Kaibab. Reese, Bob, illus. (gr. k-6). 1987. 7.95 (*0-89868-226-6*); pap. 2.95 (*0-89868-227-4*) ARO Pub.

—Abert & Kaibab. Reese, Bob, illus. (gr. k-6). 1987. pap. 20.00 (*0-685-50872-2*) ARO Pub.

—Bugle Elk & Little Toot. Reese, Bob, illus. (gr. k-6). 1986. 7.95 (*0-89868-177-4*); pap. 2.95 (*0-89868-178-2*) ARO Pub.

—Camper Critters. Reese, Bob, illus. (gr. k-6). 1986. 7.95 (*0-89868-169-3*); pap. 2.95 (*0-89868-170-7*) ARO Pub.

—Jungle Train. Reese, Bob, illus. (gr. k-3). 1983. pap. 20. 00 (*0-685-50868-4*) ARO Pub.

—Pamba & the Bink. Reese, Bob, illus. (gr. k-6). 1984. 11.95 (*0-89868-152-9*) ARO Pub.

Reese, Bob, et al. Big Big Book Series, 7 bks. Reese, Bob, illus. (gr. k-6). 1987. pap. 140.00 (*0-89868-244-4*) ARO Pub.

Reeves, Mona R. I Had a Cat. Downing, Julie, illus. LC 93-45418. 1995. pap. 4.95 (*0-689-71759-8*, Aladdin) Macmillan Child Grp.

Reinsma, Carol. The Shimmering Stone. Cori, Nathan, illus. 48p. (Orig.). (gr. k-3). 1994. pap. 3.99 (*0-7847-0007-9*, 24-03957) Standard Pub.

Reiser, Lynn. Night Thunder & the Queen of the Wild Horses. LC 93-25734. 1994. write for info. (*0-688-11791-0*); PLB write for info. (*0-688-11792-9*) Greenwillow.

—Two Mice in Three Fables. LC 93-35935. 32p. 1995. write for info. (*0-688-13389-4*); PLB write for info. (*0-688-13390-8*) Greenwillow.

Relf, Pat & Hanavan, Louise. Barnyard Mystery. 24p. (ps up). 1992. write for info. (*0-307-74801-4*, 64801) Western Pub.

Rey, H. A. Feed the Animals. (Illus.). 24p. (gr. k-3). 1944. pap. 2.10 (*0-395-07063-5*, Sandpiper) HM.

—Where's My Baby? (Illus.). 24p. (ps-3). 1943. pap. 2.80 (*0-395-07069-4*, Sandpiper) HM.

Rice, Eve. Sam Who Never Forgets. LC 76-30370. 32p. (ps-3). 1977. PLB 13.88 (*0-688-84088-4*) Greenwillow.

Richardson, Judith B. Come to My Party. Mavor, Salley, illus. LC 91-16320. 32p. (ps-1). 1993. RSBE 13.95 (*0-02-776147-9*, Macmillan Child Bk) Macmillan Child Grp.

Robinson, Fay. A Ghost in the Toy Box. Iosa, Ann W., illus. LC 92-10758. 32p. (ps-2). 1993. PLB 11.50 (*0-516-02371-3*); pap. 3.95 (*0-516-42371-1*) Childrens.

—Old MacDonald Had a Farm. Iosa, Ann W., illus. LC 92-10757. 32p. (ps-2). 1993. PLB 11.60 (*0-516-02372-1*); pap. 3.95 (*0-516-42372-X*) Childrens.

—When Nicki Went Away. Iosa, Ann W., illus. LC 92-13835. 32p. (ps-2). 1992. PLB 11.80 (*0-516-02376-4*) Childrens.

Robinson, Marlene. What Good Is a Tail? (gr. 4-7). 1994. pap. 7.95 (*1-56171-086-5*) Shapolsky Pubs.

—Who Knows This Nose? (gr. 4-7). 1994. pap. 7.95 (*1-56171-085-7*) Shapolsky Pubs.

Robinson, Martha. The Zoo at Night. Fransconi, Antonio, illus. LC 94-12773. 1995. 16.00 (*0-689-50608-2*, M K McElderry) Macmillan Child Grp.

Roddie, Shen. Animal Stew. Gallagher, Patrick J., illus. 32p. (ps). 1992. 13.45 (*0-395-57582-6*) HM.

Rogers, Alan. Little Giants, 4 vols. Rogers, Alan, illus. 64p. (ps-1). 1990. Set. PLB 53.08 (*0-8368-0434-1*) Gareth Stevens Inc.

Rogers, Jacqueline. Best Friends Sleep Over. LC 92-56895. 1993. write for info. (*0-590-44793-9*) Scholastic Inc.

Rogers, Paul. Funimals. Fuge, Charles, illus. 32p. (ps-1). 1991. 12.95 (*0-8120-6216-7*) Barron.

Roloff, Nan & Flynn, Amy. The Bunnies' Easter Bonnet. Flynn, Amy, illus. LC 94-6728. 1994. 2.25 (*0-448-40739-6*, G&D) Putnam Pub Group.

Rose, Gerald. Trouble in the Ark. LC 89-37270. (ps-1). 1989. 10.95 (*0-8192-1511-2*) Morehouse Pub.

Rosenbaum, Eliza. Friends Afloat. Pidgeon, Jean, illus. LC 92-39029. 24p. (gr. 2-3). 1992. PLB 19.97 (*0-8114-3584-9*) Raintree Steck-V.

Ross, Katharine. Bunnies' Ball. Bratun, Katy, illus. LC 92-29930. 1994. 2.50 (*0-679-83503-2*); lib. bdg. cancelled (*0-679-93503-7*) Random Bks Yng Read.

Rotton, Wendy & Ossorio, Nelson A. Animal Fashions. (Illus.). 48p. (gr. 3-5). 1994. pap. 6.95 (*1-56721-069-4*) Twenty-Fifth Cent Pr.

Rounds, Glen, as told by. & illus. Washday on Noah's Ark: A Story of Noah's Ark. LC 91-4507. 32p. (ps-3). 1991. reinforced bdg. 14.95 (*0-8234-0555-9*); pap. 5.95 (*0-8234-0880-9*) Holiday.

Rubel, Nicole. Cyrano the Bear. 1st ed. LC 94-25902. 1995. write for info. (*0-8037-1444-0*); write for info. (*0-8037-1445-9*) Dial Bks Young.

Rudisill, Marie. Critter Cakes & Frog Tea: Tales & Treats from the Emerald River. McLendon, Robin, illus. LC 94-9086. (gr. 1). 1994. sprial bdg. 12.95 (*1-881548-09-0*) Crane Hill AL.

Ryden, Hope. Backyard Rescue. Rand, Ted, illus. LC 93-11683. 1994. write for info. (*0-688-12880-7*, Tambourine Bks) Morrow.

Ryder, Virginia P. Three Monkey Saves the Day. Kilgore, Julia, illus. 21p. (Orig.). (gr. k-12). 1991. pap. 8.95 (*0-935098-04-6*) Amigo Pr.

Rylant, Cynthia. Every Living Thing. Schindler, S. D., illus. LC 88-19359. 96p. (gr. 5 up). 1988. pap. 3.50 (*0-689-71263-4*, Aladdin) Macmillan Child Grp.

—Gooseberry Park. LC 94-11578. (Illus.). (gr. 1-8). 1995. write for info (*0-15-232242-6*) Harbrace.

Sadler, Marilyn. It's Not Easy Being a Bunny. Bollen, Roger, illus. LC 83-2680. 48p. (gr. k-3). 1983. 6.95 (*0-394-86102-7*); lib. bdg. 7.99 (*0-394-96102-1*) Beginner.

—P. J. Funnybunny Camps Out: A Step One Book. Bollen, Roger, illus. LC 92-6156. 32p. (Orig.). (ps-3). 1994. PLB 7.99 (*0-679-93269-0*); pap. 3.50 (*0-679-83269-6*) Random Bks Yng Read.

Sainz, Frances. El Toro y el Becerrito. 11p. (ps-1). 1992. pap. text ed. 23.00 big bk. (*1-56843-048-5*); pap. text ed. 4.50 (*1-56843-095-7*) BGR Pub.

Saller, Carol. Pug, Slug, & Doug the Thug. Redenbaugh, Vicki J., illus. LC 92-44340. 1993. 13.95 (*0-87614-803-8*) Carolrhoda Bks.

Samit & the Dragon. 36p. (ps-4). 1985. 8.95 (*0-88684-177-1*); cassette tape avail. Listen USA.

Sampton, Sheila. Frogs in Clogs. LC 94-16391. (Illus.). 1995. write for info. (*0-517-59874-4*); PLB write for info. (*0-517-59875-2*) Crown Pub Group.

Sans Souci, Daniel. Country Road. LC 92-8379. 1993. pap. 14.95 (*0-385-30867-1*) Doubleday.

Sargent, Dave & Sargent, Pat. Amy Armadillo. Sapaugh, Blaine, illus. 48p. (Orig.). (gr. k-8). 1993. text ed. 11. 95 (*1-56763-046-4*); pap. text ed. 5.95 (*1-56763-047-2*) Ozark Pub.

—The Animal Pride Series. Sapaugh, Blaine, illus. (gr. 1-5). 1992. Set 1, 10 bks. PLB 107.55 (*1-56763-153-3*); Set 2, 10 bks. PLB 107.55 (*1-56763-155-X*); Sets 1 & 2. PLB 199.95 (*1-56763-157-6*); Set 1, 10 bks. pap. 53. 55 (*1-56763-154-1*); Set 2, 10 bks. pap. 53.55 (*1-56763-156-8*); Sets 1 & 2. pap. 99.95 (*1-56763-158-4*) Ozark Pub. Emerging from a small farm in the beautiful Ozark Mountains comes Farmer John's high/low series of twenty very mischievous animals, stories with connecting story lines, making up Dave & Pat Sargent's ANIMAL PRIDE SERIES. (Accelerated Reader) Creatively written using whole language, this series contains twenty short chapter books with large 18 point type, a moral that all ages can relate to, & an animal facts section at the end of each book. Written with encyclopedia-quality information on a 2.2-3.0 vocabulary level with the use of pen & ink illustrations to insure the popularity through the seventh grade, this series is often used with child development, school counseling, ESL, Chapter & special-education classrooms. Other popular titles for animal lovers include Pat Sargent's THE GRIZZLY (Booklist) from the Barney the Bear Killer Series (illustrated in color) & Dave Sargent's SPIKE THE BLACK WOLF (illustrated). Both written on a fourth grade vocabulary level with high interest levels, these very popular titles explore animal loyalty & are sure to capture the hearts of any age reader.

THE GRIZZLY is the sequel to THE ANIMAL PRIDE SERIES (a must) & SPIKE THE BLACK WOLF has been nominated for various state awards. Ozark Publishing.
Publisher Provided Annotation.

—The Bandit. Sapaugh, Blaine, illus. 48p. (Orig.). (gr. k-8). 1993. text ed. 11.95 (*1-56763-048-0*); pap. text ed. 5.95 (*1-56763-049-9*) Ozark Pub.

—Big Jake. Sapaugh, Blaine, illus. 48p. (Orig.). (gr. k-8). 1993. text ed. 11.95 (*1-56763-030-8*); pap. text ed. 5.95 (*1-56763-031-6*) Ozark Pub.

—Mad Jack. Sapaugh, Blaine, illus. 48p. (Orig.). (gr. k-8). 1993. text ed. 11.95 (*1-56763-034-0*); pap. text ed. 5.95 (*1-56763-035-9*) Ozark Pub.

—Molly's Journey. Sapaugh, Blaine, illus. 48p. (Orig.). (gr. k-8). 1993. text ed. 11.95 (*1-56763-038-3*); pap. text ed. 5.95 (*1-56763-039-1*) Ozark Pub.

—White Thunder. 48p. (gr. 2-6). 1992. pap. write for info. (*1-56763-007-3*) Ozark Pub.

Say, Allen. The Bicycle Man. Say, Allen, illus. (ps-3). 1989. pap. 5.70 (*0-395-50652-2*, Sandpiper) HM.

Scamell, Ragnhild. Buster's Echo. Webster, Genevieve, illus. LC 92-29868. 32p. (ps-2). 1993. 14.00 (*0-06-022883-0*); PLB 13.89 (*0-06-022884-9*) HarpC Child Bks.

—Three Bags Full. Hobson, Sally, illus. LC 92-50882. 32p. (ps-1). 1993. 14.95 (*0-531-05486-1*) Orchard Bks Watts.

Scarry, Richard. Mr. Frumble's Worst Day Ever! Scarry, Richard, illus. LC 91-62215. 48p. (ps-k). 1992. 10.00 (*0-679-81616-X*) Random Bks Yng Read.

—Pie Rats Ahoy! LC 92-50998. 32p. (ps-1). 1994. PLB 7.99 (*0-679-94760-4*); pap. 3.50 (*0-679-84760-X*) Random Bks Yng Read.

—Richard Scarry's ABC Word Book. (Illus.). (ps-2). 1971. 11.00 (*0-394-82339-7*); lib. bdg. 5.99 (*0-394-92339-1*) Random Bks Yng Read.

—Richard Scarry's Animal Nursery Tales. (Illus.). (ps-1). 1975. write for info. (*0-307-16810-7*, Golden Bks) Western Pub.

Schaffer, Libor. Arthur Sets Sail. Mathieu, Agnes, illus. LC 87-1594. 32p. (gr. k-3). 1987. 14.95 (*1-55858-059-X*) North-South Bks NYC.

Scheidl, Gerda M. The Little Donkey. Watts, Bernadette, illus. LC 87-73271. 32p. (gr. k-3). 1988. 13.95 (*1-55858-026-3*) North-South Bks NYC.

Schick, Joel & Schick, Alice. Santaberry & the Snard. (gr. 4). 1976. 12.00 (*0-912846-23-2*) Bookstore Pr.

Schindel, John. What's for Lunch? O'Malley, Kevin, illus. LC 93-48621. 1993. 15.00 (*0-688-13598-6*); PLB 14. 93 (*0-688-13599-4*) Lothrop.

Schwartz, Alvin. Kickle Snifters & Other Fearsome Critters. Rounds, Glen, illus. LC 75-29048. 64p. (gr. 1-5). 1992. pap. 4.95 (*0-06-446129-7*, Trophy) HarpC Child Bks.

Sclavi, Tiziano. What Animal Is It? Michelini, Carlo A., illus. 10p. (ps). 1994. 4.95 (*1-56397-339-1*) Boyds Mills Pr.

Scott, Dixon. A Fresh Wind in the Willows. (gr. k-6). 1987. pap. 2.50 (*0-440-42741-X*, YB) Dell.

Sears, Jeanne. Danger-Watch Out! Cohen, Dorothy P., illus. 12p. (ps-3). 1988. pap. 1.95 (*0-9621086-0-X*) J Sears.

Selden, George. The Cricket in Times Square. Williams, Garth, illus. LC 60-12640. 160p. (gr. 4 up). 1960. 15. 00 (*0-374-31650-3*) FS&G.

—Tucker's Countryside. Williams, Garth, illus. LC 69-14975. 176p. (gr. 3 up). 1969. 16.00 (*0-374-37854-1*) FS&G.

Sendak, Maurice. Higglety Pigglety Pop: Or, There Must Be More to Life. Sendak, Maurice, illus. LC 67-18553. 80p. (gr. k-3). 1967. 15.00 (*0-06-025487-4*) HarpC Child Bks.

Sesame Street: Ernie Gets Lost. 24p. (ps-3). 1991. write for info. (*0-307-14156-X*, 14156) Western Pub.

Sesame Street: Oscar's Grouchy Day. 24p. (ps-3). 1991. write for info. (*0-307-14168-3*, 14168) Western Pub.

Sesame Street Staff. In & Out, Up & Down. Smollin, Michael J., illus. LC 81-83697. 28p. (ps). 1982. bds. 2.95 (*0-394-85151-X*) Random Bks Yng Read.

Sesame Street: What's up in the Attic? 24p. (ps-3). 1991. write for info. (*0-307-14171-3*, 14171) Western Pub.

Seton, Ernest T. Animal Heroes. rev. ed. Seton, Ernest T., illus. LC 87-71143. 368p. (gr. 5 up). 1987. pap. 9.95 (*0-88739-055-2*) Creative Arts Bk.

—The Pacing Mustang. rev. ed. Ryan, Donna, illus. 72p. (gr. 3-8). 1991. pap. 9.95 (*0-9623072-5-4*) S Ink WA.

—Wild Animals I Have Known. rev. ed. Seton, Ernest T., illus. LC 87-71147. 368p. (gr. 5 up). 1987. pap. 9.95 (*0-88739-053-6*) Creative Arts Bk.

Seymour, Tres. Pole Dog. Soman, David, photos by. LC 92-24174. (Illus.). 32p. (ps-1). 1993. 14.95 (*0-531-05470-5*); PLB 14.99 (*0-531-08620-8*) Orchard Bks Watts.

Shannon, George. Dance Away! Aruego, Jose & Dewey, Ariane, illus. LC 81-6391. 32p. (gr. k-3). 1982. 13.95 (*0-688-00838-0*); PLB 13.88 (*0-688-00839-9*) Greenwillow.

Shapiro, Arnold L. Who Says That? Wellington, Monica, illus. LC 90-3996. 32p. (ps). 1991. 13.95 (*0-525-44698-2*, DCB) Dutton Child Bks.

Sharmat, Marjorie W. Hooray for Father's Day. Wallner, John, illus. LC 86-15037. 32p. (ps-3). 1987. reinforced bdg. 14.95 (*0-8234-0637-7*) Holiday.

—I'm Terrific. Chorao, Kay, illus. LC 76-9094. 32p. (ps-3). 1977. reinforced bdg. 13.95 (*0-8234-0282-7*) Holiday.
Shasha, Mark. Hall of Beasts. LC 92-39520. 1994. pap. 15.00 (*0-671-79893-6*) S&S Trade.
Sheppard, Jeff. Splash, Splash. Panek, Dennis, illus. LC 92-26163. 40p. (ps-k). 1994. RSBE 14.95 (*0-02-782455-1*, Macmillan Child Bk) Macmillan Child Grp.
Sherman, Ori & Schwartz, Lynne S. The Four Questions. (Illus.). 32p. 1994. pap. 5.99 (*0-14-055269-3*, Puff Pied Piper) Puffin Bks.
Shivkumar. Stories from Panchatantra: Book I. Biswas, Pulak, illus. (gr. 1-9). 1979. 4.50 (*0-89744-162-1*); pap. 3.00 (*0-685-57661-2*) Auromere.
—Stories from Panchatantra: Book II. Bhusan, Reboti, illus. (gr. 1-9). 1979. 4.50 (*0-89744-163-X*); pap. 3.00 (*0-685-57662-0*) Auromere.
—Stories from Panchatantra: Book III. Mukerji, Debrabrata, illus. (gr. 1-9). 1979. 4.50 (*0-89744-164-8*); pap. 3.00 (*0-685-57663-9*) Auromere.
—Stories from Panchatantra: Book IV. Biswas, Pulak, illus. (gr. 1-9). 1979. 4.50 (*0-89744-165-6*); pap. 3.00 (*0-685-57664-7*) Auromere.
Sierra, Judy. The Elephant's Wrestling Match. Pinkney, Brian, illus. 32p. (gr. k-3). 1992. 14.00 (*0-525-67366-0*, Lodestar Bks) Dutton Child Bks.
Silverstein, Shel. Giraffe & a Half. Silverstein, Shel, illus. LC 64-19709. 48p. (gr. k-3). 1964. 15.00 (*0-06-025655-9*); PLB 14.89 (*0-06-025656-7*) HarpC Child Bks.
Simon, Francesca. But What Does the Hippopotamus Say? Floate, Helen, illus. LC 93-32297. (ps-1). 1994. 11.95 (*0-15-200029-1*, Gulliver Bks) HarBrace.
Singer, Bill. The Fox with Cold Feet. Kendrick, Dennis, illus. LC 80-10288. 48p. (ps-3). 1980. 5.95 (*0-8193-1021-2*); PLB 5.95 (*0-8193-1022-0*) Parents.
Siracusa, Catherine. No Mail for Mitchell: A Step 1 Book - Preschool-Gr. 1. Siracusa, Catherine, illus. LC 89-70010. 32p. (Orig.). (ps-1). 1990. lib. bdg. 7.99 (*0-679-90476-X*); pap. 3.50 (*0-679-80476-5*) Random Bks Yng Read.
Slater, Teddy. Looking for Lewis. Alley, Robert, illus. 24p. (ps-1). 1991. 4.95 (*0-671-72988-8*); PLB 6.95 (*0-671-72987-X*) Silver Pr.
Slater, Teddy, adapted by. Disney's Winnie the Pooh & a Day for Eeyore. Langley, Bill & Kurtz, John, illus. 48p. (ps-4). 1994. 12.95 (*1-56282-657-3*) Disney Pr.
Sly Fox & the Little Red Hen in Arabic. (Illus.). (gr. 4-6). 1987. 3.95x (*0-86685-224-7*) Intl Bk Ctr.
Smax, Willy. Big Pig's Hat. Ludlow, Keren, illus. LC 92-19442. (ps-3). 1993. 13.99 (*0-8037-1476-9*) Dial Bks Young.
Smith, Elizabeth S. A Dolphin Goes to School: The Story of Squirt, a Trained Dolphin. LC 85-28407. (Illus.). 96p. (gr. 2-5). 1986. 12.95 (*0-688-04815-3*); lib. bdg. 12.88 (*0-688-04816-1*, Morrow Jr Bks) Morrow Jr Bks.
Smith, Emma. Emily the Traveling Guinea Pig. (gr. 1-5). 1960. 10.95 (*0-8392-3007-9*) Astor-Honor.
Smith, Janice L. Wizard & Wart. Meisel, Paul, illus. LC 92-41170. 64p. (gr. k-3). 1994. 14.00 (*0-06-022960-8*); PLB 13.89 (*0-06-022961-6*) HarpC Child Bks.
—Wizard & Wart at Sea. LC 94-3200. 1995. 14.00 (*0-06-024754-1*); PLB 13.89 (*0-06-024755-X*) HarpC.
Smith, Lane. The Big Pets. LC 93-18608. (Illus.). 32p. (ps-3). 1993. pap. 4.99 (*0-14-054265-5*, Puffin) Puffin Bks.
Sneed, Brad. Lucky Russell. (Illus.). 32p. (ps-3). 1992. 14.95 (*0-399-22329-0*, Putnam) Putnam Pub Group.
Solotareff, Gregoire. Never Trust an Ogre! LC 87-30239. (Illus.). 32p. (ps-2). 1988. Repr. of 1986 ed. 11.95 (*0-688-07740-4*); lib. bdg. 11.88 (*0-688-07741-2*) Greenwillow.
Somerville, Sheila, illus. Over in the Meadow Big Book. (ps-2). 1988. pap. text ed. 14.00 (*0-922053-09-X*) N Edge Res.
Sonic & Hedgehog: Golden Mini Play Lights. (ps-3). 1993. 14.95 (*0-307-75401-4*, Pub. by Golden Bks) Western Pub.
Spier, Peter. Gobble, Growl, Grunt. Spier, Peter, illus. LC 79-14430. 24p. (ps-1). 1988. 8.95 (*0-385-24094-5*) Doubleday.
—Peter Spier's Little Animal Books, 4 bks. Spier, Peter, illus. (ps). 1987. Boxed Set. bds. 10.00 laminated (*0-385-19715-2*) Doubleday.
Stadler, John. Animal Cafe. LC 85-26789. (Illus.). 32p. (ps-2). 1986. pap. 3.95 (*0-689-71063-1*, Aladdin) Macmillan Child Grp.
—Cat is Back at Bat. Stadler, John, illus. LC 90-24831. 32p. (ps-2). 1991. 10.95 (*0-525-44762-8*, DCB) Dutton Child Bks.
Stafford, W. The Animal that Drank up Sound. Frasier, Debra, illus. 1992. 13.95 (*0-15-203563-X*, HB Juv Bks) HarBrace.
Staines, Bill. All God's Critters Got a Place in the Choir. Zemach, Margot, illus. 32p. (ps-2). 1993. pap. 4.99 (*0-14-054838-6*) Puffin Bks.
Stanish, Bob. Hippogriff Feathers. (gr. 3-12). 1981. 10.95 (*0-86653-009-6*, GA 237) Good Apple.
—I Believe in Unicorns. (gr. 3-8). 1979. 10.95 (*0-916456-51-X*, GA107) Good Apple.
Stapler, Sarah. Spruce the Moose Cuts Loose. (Illus.). 32p. (ps-3). 1992. 14.95 (*0-399-21861-0*, Putnam) Putnam Pub Group.
Starbuck, Marnie. The Gladimals Learn about Grief. 16p. (ps-3). 1991. pap. text ed. 0.75 (*1-56456-226-3*) W Gladden Found.
—The Gladimals Talk about Feelings. 16p. (ps-3). 1991. pap. text ed. 0.75 (*1-56456-225-5*) W Gladden Found.
Steig, William. The Amazing Bone. Steig, William, illus. 32p. (gr. 1-3). 1977. pap. 3.95 (*0-14-050247-5*, Puffin) Puffin Bks.
—The Real Thief. Steig, William, illus. LC 73-77910. 64p. (ps up). 1976. 12.95 (*0-374-36217-3*) FS&G.
—Sylvester & the Magic Pebble. LC 80-12314. (Illus.). 32p. (gr. k-4). 1988. pap. 14.00 (*0-671-66154-X*, S&S BFYR); pap. 5.95 (*0-671-66269-4*, S&S BFYR) S&S Trade.
Steiner, Jorge. The Animals' Rebellion. Muller, Jorg, illus. 32p. 1991. smythe sewn reinforced bdg. 15.95 (*1-56182-025-3*) Atomium Bks.
Stevenson, James. Monty. LC 91-20657. 32p. (ps up). 1992. 14.00 (*0-688-11241-2*) Greenwillow.
—The Mud Flat Olympics. LC 93-28118. 56p. 1994. 15.00 (*0-688-12923-4*); PLB 14.93 (*0-688-12924-2*) Greenwillow.
—Oh No, It's Waylon's Birthday! LC 88-4574. (Illus.). 48p. (gr. 1 up). 1989. 11.95 (*0-688-08235-1*); PLB 11.88 (*0-688-08236-X*) Greenwillow.
Stimson, Joan. Animals: Stories for under Fives. Maclean, Colin & Maclean, Moira, illus. 44p. (ps-k). 1992. 3.50 (*0-7214-1484-2*) Ladybird Bks.
Stock, Catherine. Where Are You Going, Manyoni? Stock, Catherine, illus. LC 92-29793. 48p. (ps up). 1993. 15.00 (*0-688-10352-9*); PLB 14.93 (*0-688-10353-7*) Morrow Jr Bks.
Stortz, Diane. Alexander's Praise Time Band. Garris, Norma, illus. LC 92-32817. 28p. (ps-k). 1993. 4.99 (*0-7847-0036-2*, 24-03826) Standard Pub.
Story Time Stories That Rhyme Staff. Story Habitat: Plant & Animal Stories. Story Time Stories That Rhyme Staff, illus. 40p. (Orig.). (gr. 4-7). 1992. GBC bdg. 19.95 (*1-56820-014-5*) Story Time.
Strommen, Judith B. Champ Hobarth. 160p. (gr. 4-6). 1993. 14.95 (*0-8050-2414-X*, Bks Young Read) H Holt & Co.
Strong, Stacie. Animal Families of the Forest. (Illus.). 6p. (gr. 1 up). 1993. pop-up 14.95 (*0-8431-3391-0*) Price Stern.
Suppertime for Frieda Fuzzypaws. (ps-k). 1991. write for info. (*0-307-12234-4*, Golden Pr) Western Pub.
Swan-Brown, Peter, illus. Stories from Toadstool Village. LC 94-13815. (gr. 1 up). 1994. 3.99 (*0-517-11866-1*) Random Bks Yng Read.
Tafuri, Nancy. Where We Sleep. LC 86-27115. (Illus.). (ps). 1987. pap. 3.95 (*0-688-07189-9*) Greenwillow.
Talkington, Bruce. Disney's Winnie the Pooh's Bedtime Stories. LC 93-74308. (Illus.). 96p. (ps-3). 1994. 14.95 (*1-56282-646-8*) Disney Pr.
Taylor, Linda L. The Lettuce Leaf Birthday Letter. Durrell, Julie, illus. LC 93-16906. 1994. 13.99 (*0-8037-1454-8*); PLB 13.89 (*0-8037-1455-6*) Dial Bks Young.
Tell, Paul. Adventures of Blaze. Wimer, Rodney, illus. LC 92-80452. 64p. (gr. 2-6). 1992. PLB 12.95 (*1-878893-19-X*); pap. 5.95 (*1-878893-18-1*) Telcraft Bks.
Thaler, Mike. Come & Play, Hippo. Chambliss, Maxie, illus. LC 87-33489. 64p. (gr. k-3). 1991. 14.00 (*0-06-026176-5*); PLB 13.89 (*0-06-026177-3*) HarpC Child Bks.
Those Terrible Toy Breakers. 42p. (ps-3). 1992. PLB 13.27 (*0-8368-0889-4*) Gareth Stevens Inc.
Three Best-Loved Tales: A Second Volume Featuring the Art of Gustaf Tenggren. (Illus.). 72p. (ps-1). 1993. 8.95 (*0-307-15636-2*, 15636, Golden Pr) Western Pub.
Tibo, Gilles. Simon & the Boxes. Tibo, Gilles, illus. LC 92-80416. 24p. (gr. k-4). 1992. PLB 10.95 (*0-88776-287-5*) Tundra Bks.
Tompert, Ann. Just a Little Bit. Munsinger, Lynn, illus. LC 92-31857. 1993. 14.95 (*0-395-51527-0*) HM.
Trent, John T. There's a Duck in My Closet. Love, Judy, illus. LC 93-15707. (gr. k-5). 1993. 12.99 (*0-8499-1037-4*) Word Pub.
Tresselt, Alvin. The Mitten. Mills, Yaroslava, illus. LC 64-14436. 30p. (ps up). 1989. pap. 4.95 (*0-688-09238-1*, Mulberry) Morrow.
—Wake up, Farm! Ewing, Carolyn, illus. LC 90-33646. 32p. (ps up). 1991. 14.95 (*0-688-08654-3*); PLB 14.88 (*0-688-08655-1*) Lothrop.
Tripp, Nathaniel. Thunderstorm! Wijngaard, Juan, illus. LC 93-4612. Date not set. write for info. (*0-8037-1365-7*); PLB write for info. (*0-8037-1366-5*) Dial Bks Young.
Tripp, Valerie. Happy, Happy Mother's Day! Martin, Sandra K., illus. LC 89-35757. 24p. (ps-2). 1989. pap. 3.95 (*0-516-41521-2*) Childrens.
Troughton, Joanna. Mouse-Deer's Market: A Folk Tale from Borneo. Troughton, Joanna, illus. LC 84-11049. 32p. (gr. k-3). 1984. PLB 14.95 (*0-911745-63-7*, Bedrick Blackie) P Bedrick Bks.
Troughton, Joanna, retold by. & illus. How the Seasons Came: A North American Indian Folk Tale. LC 91-40499. 32p. (gr. k-3). 1992. PLB 14.95 (*0-87226-464-5*, Bedrick Blackie) P Bedrick Bks.
Truelson, Thomas. Travels with Tiny Teddy: Cape Cod: The Great Escape. Burke, Kerry, illus. 40p. (Orig.). (gr. 1-3). 1988. pap. 3.95 (*0-685-19995-9*) Lighthse Bks MA.
Tryon, Leslie. Albert's Thanksgiving. LC 94-8025. (gr. k-3). 1994. 14.95 (*0-689-31865-0*, Atheneum) Macmillan Child Grp.
Tuer, Judy. Rocks. Vane, Mitch, illus. LC 92-30670. 1993. 2.50 (*0-383-03649-6*) SRA Schl Grp.
—Ten Crazy Caterpillars. Forss, Ian, illus. LC 92-30672. 1993. 2.50 (*0-383-03658-5*) SRA Schl Grp.
Turner, Edwin A. Adventures by the River Iki: Oscar Crow & Leapy Frog. (Illus.). 128p. 1992. 12.95 (*0-8059-3299-2*) Dorrance.
Twinn, Michael & Adams, Pam. Lady Who Loved Animals. LC 90-46603. (Illus.). 32p. (ps-2). 1981. 7.95 (*0-85953-121-X*, Pub. by Child's Play England) Childs Play.
Ungerer, Tomi. The Beast of Monsieur Racine. (Illus.). 32p. (ps up). 1986. pap. 5.95 (*0-374-40570-0*) FS&G.
Vaccaro Associates Staff & Durrell, Dennis, illus. Disney's Aladdin: Peek Abu. LC 92-53496. 18p. (ps-1). 1993. 9.95 (*1-56282-389-2*) Disney Pr.
Van der Meer, Ron & Van der Meer, Atie. Jumping Animals. (gr. 4 up). 1989. 4.95 (*0-85953-261-5*) Childs Play.
Vandine, JoAnn. Lunch for Three. Tulloch, Coral, illus. LC 92-31954. 1993. 4.25 (*0-383-03582-1*) SRA Schl Grp.
Van Fleet, Matthew. One Yellow Lion: Fold-Out Fun with Numbers, Colors, Animals. LC 91-11972. (Illus.). 24p. (ps up). 1992. 7.95 (*0-8037-1099-2*) Dial Bks Young.
Van Kampen, Vlasta. Orchestranimals. 1990. pap. 12.95 (*0-590-43149-8*) Scholastic Inc.
Van Laan, Nancy. Country Lullaby: All Around the World. Meade, Holly, illus. LC 93-44484. (gr. 1-4). 1995. 14.95 (*0-316-89732-9*) Little.
—This Is the Hat: A Story in Rhyme. (ps). 1992. 14.95 (*0-316-89727-2*, Joy St Bks) Little.
Van Lampen. Orchestranimals. 1993. pap. 28.67 (*0-590-73163-7*) Scholastic Inc.
Vargo, Vanessa. Tiger Talk. (ps-3). pap. 5.95 (*0-85953-397-2*) Childs Play.
Varley, Susan. Badger's Parting Gifts. LC 83-17500. (Illus.). 32p. (ps up). 1992. pap. 4.95 (*0-688-11518-7*, Mulberry) Morrow.
Vaughan, Marsha K. Whistling Dixie. Date not set. 15.00 (*0-06-021030-3*, HarpT); 14.89 (*0-06-021029-X*, HarpT) HarpC.
Vaughn, Marcia. Riddle by the River. Ruffins, Reynold, illus. LC 93-46890. (gr. 1 up). 1994. write for info. (*0-382-24603-9*); pap. write for info. (*0-382-24451-6*); PLB write for info. (*0-382-24602-0*) Silver Burdett Pr.
Vaughn, Marcia K. Tingo Tango Mango Tree. Saint James, Synthia, illus. LC 93-44867. 1994. write for info. (*0-382-24605-5*); pap. write for info. (*0-382-24454-0*) Silver.
Velk, Suzanne. The Animal Kingdom ABC. Velk, Suzanne, illus. 30p. (ps-3). 1994. 11.95 (*0-85572-220-7*, Pub. by Hill Content Pubng AT) Seven Hills Bk Dists.
Velthuijs, Max. Frog & the Birdsong. (ps-3). 1991. bds. 13.95 jacketed (*0-374-32467-0*) FS&G.
—Frog & the Stranger. Velthuijs, Max, illus. LC 93-26401. 32p. 1994. 14.00 (*0-688-13267-7*, Tambourine Bks); PLB 13.93 (*0-688-13268-5*, Tambourine Bks) Morrow.
—Frog in Winter. Velthuijs, Max, illus. LC 92-20545. 32p. (ps up). 1993. 14.00 (*0-688-12306-6*, Tambourine Bks); PLB 13.93 (*0-688-12307-4*, Tambourine Bks) Morrow.
Vermeylen, Terry J. I Am Juma, Manatee. 88p. (gr. 4 up). 1987. pap. 6.95 (*0-8059-3055-8*) Dorrance.
Vetterlein, Millicent. The Blessing of Animals. 24p. (gr. k-2). 1992. pap. 7.95 (*0-9635447-0-5*) St George ME.
El Viento En los Sauces. (SPA.). 1990. casebound 3.50 (*0-7214-1399-4*) Ladybird Bks.
Vigna, Judith. Zio Pasquale's Zoo. LC 93-19360. 1993. write for info. (*0-8075-9488-1*) A Whitman.
Vincent, Gabrielle. Ernest & Celestine's Picnic. Vincent, Gabrielle, illus. LC 82-2909. 24p. (gr. k-3). 1982. 15.95 (*0-688-01250-7*); PLB 15.88 (*0-688-01252-3*) Greenwillow.
Voce, Louise. Over in the Meadow: A Counting Rhyme. LC 93-21294. (Illus.). 32p. (ps up). 1994. 14.95 (*1-56402-428-8*) Candlewick Pr.
Vyner, Sue. The Stolen Egg. Vyner, Tim, illus. 32p. (ps-3). 1992. 14.00 (*0-670-84460-8*) Viking Child Bks.
Waber, Bernard. Anteater Named Arthur. Waber, Bernard, illus. LC 67-20374. 48p. (gr. k-3). 1977. 13.95 (*0-395-20336-8*); pap. 5.70 (*0-395-25936-3*) HM.
—Funny, Funny Lyle. Waber, Bernard, illus. 40p. (gr. k-3). 1991. pap. 4.80 (*0-395-60287-4*, Sandpiper) HM.
—Lyle Finds His Mother. Waber, Bernard, illus. (gr. k-3). 1978. pap. 5.95 (*0-395-27398-6*) HM.
—Nobody Is Perfick. Waber, Bernard, illus. 128p. (gr. k-3). 1994. pap. 3.95 (*0-395-60288-2*, Sandpiper) HM.
—You Look Ridiculous Said the Rhinoceros to the Hippopotamus. (Illus.). (gr. k-3). 1979. pap. 4.80 (*0-395-28007-9*) HM.
Waddell, Martin. Sam Vole & His Brothers. Firth, Barbara & Firth, Barbara, illus. LC 91-58755. 32p. (ps up). 1992. 14.95 (*1-56402-082-7*) Candlewick Pr.
Wadsworth, Olivia A. & Rae, Mary M. Over in the Meadow: A Counting-Out Rhyme. LC 84-19653. 32p. 1985. pap. 10.95 (*0-670-53276-2*) Viking Child Bks.
Wahl, Jan. Pleasant Fieldmouse. Sendak, Maurice, illus. LC 64-14684. 80p. (gr. k-3). 1964. PLB 14.89 (*0-06-026331-8*) HarpC Child Bks.
—The Sleepytime Book. Johnson, Arden, illus. LC 91-10176. 32p. (ps-3). 1992. 15.00 (*0-688-10275-1*, Tambourine Bks); PLB 14.93 (*0-688-10276-X*, Tambourine Bks) Morrow.
Wallner, S. J. Friendly Little Hobo. LC 68-56814. (Illus.). 48p. (gr. 2-4). 1968. PLB 10.95 (*0-87783-013-4*); pap. 3.94 deluxe ed. (*0-87783-092-4*) Oddo.

Walsh, Ellen S. Pip's Magic. (ps-3). 1994. 13.95 (*0-15-292850-2*) HarBrace.

Walsh, Jill P. Pepi & the Secret Names. French, Fiona, illus. LC 93-48620. 1994. 15.00 (*0-688-13428-9*) Lothrop.

Walt Disney Company Staff. Disney's Mickey Mouse Stories. (Illus.). (ps-1). 1989. Repr. of 1971 ed. Contains "Mickey Mouse Heads for the Sky," "Mickey Mouse & Goofy: the Big Bear Scare," & "Mickey Mouse: Those Were the Days" write for info. (*0-307-15751-2*, Golden Pr) Western Pub.

Walt Disney Staff. Jungle Book. 1987. 6.98 (*0-8317-5291-2*) Viking Child Bks.

—Winnie the Pooh. 1992. 6.98 (*0-453-03014-9*) Mouse Works.

Walt Disney's the Jungle Book. (ps-3). 1990. write for info. (*0-307-12107-0*) Western Pub.

Walton, Marilyn J. Chameleons' Rainbow. (ps-3). 1993. pap. 4.95 (*0-8114-8402-5*) Raintree Steck-V.

Warburg, Sandol S. Growing Time. Weisgard, Leonard, illus. (ps-3). 1989. pap. 4.80 (*0-395-51009-0*, Sandpiper) HM.

Watkins, Dawn L. A King for Brass Cobweb. Smith, Anne, ed. Hannon, Holly, illus. (Orig.). (gr. k-1). 1990. pap. write for info. (*0-89084-505-0*) Bob Jones Univ Pr.

Weiss, Nicki. Where Does the Brown Bear Go? (ps). 1990. pap. 3.95 (*0-14-054181-0*, Puffin) Puffin Bks.

Wellington, Monica. The Sheep Follow. Wellington, Monica, illus. LC 91-3420. 32p. (ps-k). 1992. 13.00 (*0-525-44837-3*, DCB) Dutton Child Bks.

Wells, Rosemary. Lucy Comes to Stay. Graham, Mark, illus. LC 91-15779. 32p. (gr. k-3). 1994. 14.99 (*0-8037-1213-8*); PLB 14.89 (*0-8037-1214-6*) Dial Bks Young.

—Morris's Disappearing Bag. Wells, Rosemary, illus. 1975. 9.95 (*0-8037-5441-8*) Dial Bks Young.

—Peabody. LC 83-7207. (Illus.). 32p. (ps-2). 1983. 13.95 (*0-8037-0004-0*) Dial Bks Young.

Werenko, Lisa V. It Zwibble & the Greatest Clean-up Ever. 1991. pap. 2.50 (*0-590-44840-4*) Scholastic Inc.

West, Mark I., ed. A Wondrous Menagerie: Animal Fantasy Stories from American Children's Literature. xvi, 139p. 1994. lib. bdg. 25.00 (*0-208-02383-6*, Pub. by Archon Bks) Shoe String.

What Was That? 24p. (ps-3). 1991. write for info. (*0-307-14175-6*, 14175) Western Pub.

Whayne, Susanne S. Watch the House. Morrill, Leslie, illus. LC 91-28071. 80p. (gr. k-3). 1992. pap. 12.00 jacketed (*0-671-75886-1*, S&S BFYR) S&S Trade.

White, E. B. Charlotte's Web. LC 52-9760. (Illus.). 1974. pap. 3.95 (*0-06-440055-7*, Trophy) HarpC Child Bks.

—E. B. White Boxed Set. Incl. Charlotte's Web; The Trumpet of the Swan; Stuart Little. (Illus.). (gr. 3 up). 1972. 39.00 (*0-06-026399-7*) HarpC Child Bks.

Whitney, Dorothy A. Creatures of an Exceptional Kind. LC 88-34736. (Illus.). 32p. (ps up). 1989. 12.95 (*0-89334-127-4*) Humanics Ltd.

Whitten, Wendy & McCullough, Herb. Someday...Someday, Bk. 1. Swerda, Mike, illus. 42p. (ps up). 1994. Incl. audio cass. 29.95 (*1-886184-00-3*) Ion Imagination.
Ion Imagination (tm) Entertainment, Inc. presents the first in a series of adventures with Flumpa (tm), a tree frog who introduces the children to the wonder of adventure as he meets new friends along the way. SOMEDAY... SOMEDAY has a twenty-one minute audiocassette incorporated into the outer hardcover. This cassette features a Sing Along Side: original "story" songs, sung by Wendy Whitten & recorded at Jack's Tracks-Nashville, TN, with lyrics in the back of the collectable book, & Read Along Side: narration with sound effects, from a powerful storm to the calming sounds of twilight, & page turn signals. This 9 3/4" x 12 3/4" full-color, perfect bound book has foil & metallic inks. SOMEDAY...SOMEDAY, mixed media only, $29.95, ISBN 1-886184-00-3. Published by Ion Imagination (tm) Entertainment, Inc. To order: call 1-800-3-FLUMPA or write P.O. Box 210943, Nashville, TN 37221-0943. *Publisher Provided Annotation.*

Whybrow, Ian. Quacky Quack-Quack! Ayto, Russell, illus. LC 91-8388. 32p. (gr. k up). 1991. SBE 13.95 (*0-02-792741-5*, Four Winds) Macmillan Child Grp.

Wickum, Mabel. The Egg. LC 88-51385. (Illus.). 44p. (gr. k-2). 1989. pap. 4.95 (*1-55523-199-3*) Winston-Derek.

Wild, Margaret. Thank You, Santa. (Illus.). 1992. 12.95 (*0-590-45805-1*, Scholastic Hardcover) Scholastic Inc.

Wilds, Kazumi I. Hajime in the North Woods. Wilds, Kazumi I., ed. LC 93-34689. (Illus.). 32p. (ps-2). 1994. 15.95 (*1-559702-40-0*) Arcade Pub Inc.

Wildsmith, Brian. The Miller, the Boy & the Donkey. Wildsmith, Brian, illus. 32p. (ps-1). 1987. 16.00 (*0-19-279652-6*); pap. 7.50 (*0-19-272114-3*) OUP.

—Professor Noah's Spaceship. Wildsmith, Brian, illus. 32p. (ps-3). 1980. 16.00 (*0-19-279741-7*); pap. 7.50 (*0-19-272149-6*) OUP.

—Seasons. Wildsmith, Brian, illus. (ps-3). 1980. 9.95 (*0-19-279730-1*) OUP.

—Wild Animals. (Illus.). (ps). 1976. pap. 7.50 (*0-19-272103-8*) OUP.

Wildsmith, Brian & Wildsmith, Rebecca. Jack & the Meanstalk. LC 93-30374. 1994. 15.00 (*0-679-85810-5*); pap. 15.99 (*0-679-95810-X*) Knopf Bks Yng Read.

—What Did I Find? LC 92-17666. 1993. 6.95 (*0-15-200688-5*); pap. write for info. (*0-15-200689-3*) HarBrace.

Willard, John A. Ember & His Friends in the Forest. Elliot, Stephen C., illus. 20p. (Orig.). (gr. 2-5). 1991. pap. 3.95 (*0-9612398-4-0*) J A Willard.
Ember, a cuddly but self-sufficient kitten who lives with a young couple deep in Montana's high mountain forest, tells all about his animal & bird friends who live among the firs, pines & larches. His friends include Soft Eyes, the white-tailed deer; Bugler, the huge bull elk from Yellowstone Park country; Jumpy, the Rocky Mountain mule deer; Harry, the snowshoe hare; Splash, the no-nonsense beaver; Ottie, the fun-loving otter; Ruffy, the ruffed grouse; & even Woody, the tiny white-footed wood mouse. Each animal & bird is pictured in a line drawing by Stephen C. Elliott, a Colorado artist who has shown in the prestigious Leigh Yawkey Woodson birds-in-art show & has published a naturalist history for Denver Natural History Museum. John Willard is a veteran western outdoor columnist & writer & is Montana's first & oldest member of the Outdoor Writers of America. Ember easily & quickly teaches children about their wild animal & bird friends. Text is simple & fully readable at first or second grade level. Adapts easily to classroom or home use to acquaint children with wildlife in their western mountains & forest - a striking combination of word & picture. Call or write for information or to order: John A. Willard, 3119 Country Club Circle, Billings, MT 59102; 406-259-1966. *Publisher Provided Annotation.*

Williams, H. Lickety Split, Adventure Through Time. (Illus.). 32p. (gr. 1-4). 1988. pap. 2.95 (*0-88625-173-7*) Durkin Hayes Pub.

—Lickety Split, Lost Your Marbles. (Illus.). 32p. (gr. 1-4). 1988. pap. 2.95 (*0-88625-178-8*) Durkin Hayes Pub.

—Lickety Split, Meets Fire Puffin. (Illus.). 32p. (gr. 1-4). 1988. pap. 2.95 (*0-88625-175-3*) Durkin Hayes Pub.

—Lickety Split, Who Are You? (Illus.). 32p. (gr. 1-4). 1988. pap. 2.95 (*0-88625-181-8*) Durkin Hayes Pub.

Williams, Karin. Swimming. Williams, Karin, illus. LC 93-83002. 12p. (ps-1). 1994. 4.99 (*0-679-85000-7*) Random Bks Yng Read.

Williams, Letty. Little Red Hen: La Pequena Gallina Roja. Williams, Herb, illus. LC 78-75684. (ENG & SPA.). (ps-3). 1972. (Pub. by Treehouse) P-H.

Williams, Sue. I Went Walking. Vivas, Julie, illus. 30p. (ps-2). 1990. 13.95 (*0-15-200471-8*, Gulliver Bks) HarBrace.

—I Went Walking. Vivas, Julie, illus. 32p. (ps-2). 1991. pap. 19.95 (*0-15-238010-8*) HarBrace.

Wilson, Sarah. Beware the Dragons! Wilson, Sarah, illus. LC 85-42614. 32p. (gr. k-3). 1985. HarpC Child Bks.

Wiltshire, Teri. The Tale of Gus the Grumbly Grizzly. Archer, Rebecca, illus. LC 92-46248. (ps). 1993. 8.95 (*1-85697-856-7*, Kingfisher LKC) LKC.

The Wind in the Willows. (gr. 4 up). 1988. pap. 6.50 (*0-318-32663-9*, 74252) Longman.

Winnie-the-Pooh. (Illus.). 24p. (ps-2). 1991. write for info. (*0-307-74019-6*, Golden Pr) Western Pub.

Wojciechowska, Maia. Shadow of a Bull. LC 64-12563. (Illus.). 176p. (gr. 5 up). 1972. SBE 14.95 (*0-689-30042-5*, Atheneum Child Bk) Macmillan Child Grp.

—Shadow of a Bull. 180p. 1991. text ed. 14.40 (*1-56956-316-0*) W A T Braille.

Wolkstein, Diane. Little Mouse's Painting. Begin, Maryjane, illus. LC 91-16017. 32p. (ps up). 1992. 15.00 (*0-688-07609-2*); PLB 14.93 (*0-688-07610-6*) Morrow Jr Bks.

Wonder Kids Publications Group Staff (USA) & Hwa-I Publishing Co., Staff. Animal Tales: Chinese Children's Stories, Vols. 11-15. Ching, Emily, et al, eds. Wonder Kids Publication Staff, tr. from CHI. Hwa-I Publishing Co., Staff, illus. LC 90-60793. 28p. (gr. 3-6). 1991. Repr. of 1988 ed. Five vol. set, 28p. ea. bk. 39.75 (*0-685-58702-9*) Wonder Kids.

Wood, Audrey. The Napping House. Wood, Don, illus. 32p. (ps-3). 1991. pap. 19.95 (*0-15-256711-9*) HarBrace.

Wood, Jakki. Animal Parade. Wood, Jakki, illus. LC 92-22826. 32p. (ps-k). 1993. SBE 14.95 (*0-02-793394-6*, Bradbury Pr) Macmillan Child Grp.

—Dads Are Such Fun. Bonner, Rog, illus. LC 91-21517. 32p. (ps). 1992. pap. 12.00 jacketed (*0-671-75342-8*, S&S BFYR) S&S Trade.

—One Tortoise, Ten Wallabies. LC 93-23534. (gr. 2 up). 1994. write for info. (Bradbury Pr) Macmillan Child Grp.

Wood, Jenny. My Baby Dinosaur. (ps). 1994. 12.95 (*0-316-10502-3*) Little.

—My First Book of Animals. (ps). 1992. 9.95 (*0-316-95199-4*) Little.

Wood, Leslie. Dig Dig. (Illus.). 16p. (ps up). 1988. pap. 2.95 (*0-19-272185-2*) OUP.

Woolf, Virginia. Nurse Lugton's Curtain. Van Doren, Liz, ed. Vivas, Julie, illus. 32p. (gr. 2 up). 1991. 14.95 (*0-15-200545-5*, Gulliver Bks) HarBrace.

The World of Peter Rabbit & Friends: Posters. (Illus.). 1993. Set. shrinkwrapped 7.95 (*0-7232-4129-5*) Warne.

Wrightson, Patricia. Moon-Dark. Young, Noela, illus. LC 87-3903. 176p. (gr. 4-7). 1988. SBE 14.95 (*0-689-50451-9*, M K McElderry) Macmillan Child Grp.

Wyllie, Stephen. The Red Dragon: A 3-D Picture Book. Allen, Jonathan, illus. LC 92-26670. 20p. (ps-2). 1993. 13.99 (*0-8037-1452-1*) Dial Bks Young.

Yee, Wong H. Eek! There's a Mouse in the House. LC 91-41823. (Illus.). 32p. (ps). 1992. 13.45 (*0-395-62303-0*) HM.

—Fireman Small. Yee, Wong H., illus. LC 93-31518. 1994. 13.95 (*0-395-68987-2*) HM.

Yolen, Jane. Baby Bear's Bedtime Book. LC 89-2161. 29p. (ps-3). 1990. 13.95 (*0-15-205120-1*) HarBrace.

—A Sending of Dragons. McKeveny, Tom, illus. LC 87-6689. 240p. (gr. 7 up). 1987. pap. 14.95 (*0-385-29587-1*) Delacorte.

Yoshi. Who's Hiding Here? Yoshi, illus. LC 92-6631. 32p. (ps up). 1992. pap. 4.95 minibk. (*0-88708-277-7*) Picture Bk Studio.

Zabar, Abbie. Fifty-Five Friends. LC 93-47366. (ps-2). 1994. 13.95 (*0-7868-0021-6*); pap. write for info. (*0-7868-2017-9*) Hyprn Child.

Zadra, Dan. Just Keep on Keepin' On. (Illus.). 32p. (gr. 6 up). 1986. PLB 12.95s.p. (*0-88682-020-0*) Creative Ed.

Zelver, Patricia. Don Octavio & the New Creature. Daste, Larry, illus. LC 93-29565. 1994. 15.00 (*0-688-13159-X*, Tambourine Bks); PLB 14.93 (*0-688-13160-3*, Tambourine Bks) Morrow.

Ziefert, Harriet. Animals for Baby. Baum, Susan, illus. 8p. (ps). 1993. 4.95 (*0-694-00508-8*, Festival) HarpC Child Bks.

Zimmerman. Henny Penny. 1993. pap. 28.67 (*0-590-71755-3*) Scholastic Inc.

Zimmerman, Andrea G. Riddle Zoo. 64p. (gr. 3-7). 1981. (Dutton) NAL-Dutton.

Zindel, Paul. The Pigman's Legacy. 128p. (gr. 12 up). 1984. pap. 3.99 (*0-553-26599-7*) Bantam.

ANIMALS–GEOGRAPHICAL DISTRIBUTION

see Geographical Distribution of Animals and Plants

ANIMALS–HABITATIONS

Ada, Alma F. El Patio de Mi Casa. Callen, Liz, illus. (SPA.). 16p. (Orig.). (gr. 1-3). 1991. pap. text ed. 29.95 big bk. (*1-56334-018-6*); pap. text ed. 36.00 small bk. (6 copies) (*1-56334-088-7*) Hampton-Brown.

Animal Habitats, 24 vols. 768p. (gr. 4-6). 1987. Set. PLB 414.40 (*0-8368-0262-4*) Gareth Stevens Inc.

Animal Homes. (gr. k-3). 1989. 3.95 (*0-7214-5216-7*) Ladybird Bks.

Animal Homes. LC 92-54271. 24p. (gr. k-3). 1993. 8.95 (*1-56458-218-3*) Dorling Kindersley.

Arvetis, Chris & Palmer, Carole. Forests. LC 93-500. (Illus.). 1993. write for info. (*0-528-83573-4*) Rand McNally.

Baby Animals in the Wild. (ps-k). 1989. bds. 3.50 (*0-7214-9535-4*) Ladybird Bks.

Bailey, Jill & Seddon, Tony. Animal Parenting. (Illus.). 64p. 1989. 15.95x (*0-8160-1654-2*) Facts on File.

—Anticipating the Seasons. (Illus.). 64p. 1988. 15.95x (*0-8160-1653-4*) Facts on File.

Black, Sonia. Animals & Their Homes Activity Book. (ps-3). 1994. pap. 1.95 (*0-590-47592-4*) Scholastic Inc.

Brooks, Bruce. Nature by Design. (Illus.). 80p. (gr. 5 up). 1991. bds. 13.95 bds. (*0-374-30334-7*) FS&G.

Brunke, Dawn B. Who Lives Here, Bk. 1. Shafer, Mary A., illus. (Orig.). (gr. k-6). 1993. pap. 6.95 (*1-55971-152-3*) NorthWord.

—Who Lives Here, Bk. 2. Shafer, Mary A., illus. (Orig.). (gr. k-6). 1993. pap. 6.95 (*1-55971-153-1*) NorthWord.
—Who Lives Here, Bk. 3. Shafer, Mary A., illus. (Orig.). (gr. k-6). 1993. pap. 6.95 (*1-55971-154-X*) NorthWord.
—Who Lives Here, Bk. 4. Shafer, Mary A., illus. (Orig.). (gr. k-6). 1993. pap. 6.95 (*1-55971-155-8*) NorthWord.
Burton, Robert. Towns. (Illus.). 24p. (gr. k-4). 1991. PLB 10.40 (*1-878137-18-2*) Newington.
Chastain, Frances. Animals of Ancient China. (Illus.). 34p. (ps-2). 1986. text ed. 5.95 (*0-8351-1790-1*) China Bks.
Coldrey, Jennifer. Chicken on the Farm. LC 86-5716. (Illus.). 32p. (gr. 4-6). 1986. PLB 17.27 (*1-55532-067-8*) Gareth Stevens Inc.
—The Crab on the Seashore. LC 85-30293. (Illus.). 32p. (gr. 4-6). 1987. PLB 17.27 (*1-55532-060-0*) Gareth Stevens Inc.
—Frog in the Pond. LC 85-30300. (Illus.). 32p. (gr. 4-6). 1987. 17.27 (*1-55532-059-7*) Gareth Stevens Inc.
—The Rabbit in the Fields. LC 85-30298. (Illus.). 32p. (gr. 4-6). 1987. 17.27 (*1-55532-061-9*) Gareth Stevens Inc.
—The Squirrel in the Trees. LC 85-30292. (Illus.). 32p. (gr. 4-6). 1986. 17.27 (*1-55532-062-7*) Gareth Stevens Inc.
—The Swan on the Lake. LC 86-5719. (Illus.). 32p. (gr. 4-6). 1987. 17.27 (*1-55532-066-X*) Gareth Stevens Inc.
—The World of Chickens. LC 86-5718. (Illus.). 32p. (gr. 2-3). 1986. 17.27 (*1-55532-071-6*) Gareth Stevens Inc.
—The World of Crabs. LC 85-30294. (Illus.). 32p. (gr. 2-3). 1986. 17.27 (*1-55532-063-5*) Gareth Stevens Inc.
—The World of Frogs. LC 85-30297. (Illus.). 32p. (gr. 2-3). 1987. 17.27 (*1-55532-024-4*) Gareth Stevens Inc.
—The World of Rabbits. LC 85-28988. (Illus.). 32p. (gr. 2-3). 1986. 17.27 (*1-55532-064-3*) Gareth Stevens Inc.
—The World of Squirrels. LC 85-30296. (Illus.). 32p. (gr. 2-3). 1987. PLB 17.27 (*1-55532-065-1*) Gareth Stevens Inc.
—The World of Swans. LC 86-5721. (Illus.). 32p. (gr. 2-3). 1987. PLB 17.27 (*1-55532-070-8*) Gareth Stevens Inc.
Compass Productions Staff. Grasslands & Deserts. (Illus.). 10p. (gr. k-4). 1993. 5.95 (*0-694-00444-8*, Festival) HarpC Child Bks.
—Jungles & Islands. (Illus.). 10p. (gr. k-4). 1993. 5.95 (*0-694-00443-X*) HarpC Child Bks.
—Oceans & Arctic. (Illus.). 10p. (gr. k-4). 1993. 5.95 (*0-694-00441-3*) HarpC Child Bks.
Cranfield, Ingrid. Animal World. (Illus.). 64p. (gr. 4-6). 1991. PLB 15.40 (*1-56294-008-2*) Millbrook Pr.
Crump, Donald J., ed. Animal Homes, No. 1. (Illus.). (ps-3). 1989. 21.95 (*0-87044-758-0*) Natl Geog.
Cumpiano, Ina. Homes Are for Living. (Illus.). 24p. (Orig.). (gr. 1-3). 1991. pap. text ed. 29.95 big bk. (*1-56334-047-X*); pap. text ed. 6.00 small bk. (*1-56334-053-4*) Hampton-Brown.
—Y Tu, Donde Vives? O'Neil, Sharron, illus. (SPA.). 24p. (Orig.). (gr. 1-3). 1992. pap. text ed. 29.95 big bk. (*1-56334-019-4*); pap. text ed. 6.00 small bk. (*1-56334-045-3*) Hampton-Brown.
Dewey, Jennifer O. Animal Architecture. LC 90-43010. (Illus.). 72p. (gr. 3-6). 1991. 14.95 (*0-531-05930-8*); PLB 14.99 (*0-531-08530-9*) Orchard Bks Watts.
Fields, Sadie. Whose Home? Hawcock, David, illus. 10p. (ps). 1993. pap. 4.95 (*0-671-79164-8*, Little Simon) S&S Trade.
Gamlin, Linda. The Deer in the Forest. Oxford Scientific Film Staff, illus. LC 87-9916. 32p. (gr. 4-6). 1987. PLB 17.27 (*1-55532-273-5*) Gareth Stevens Inc.
George, Jean C. One Day in the Prairie. Marstall, Bob, illus. LC 85-48254. 48p. (gr. 5-7). 1986. PLB 13.89 (*0-690-04566-2*, Crowell Jr Bks) HarpC Child Bks.
Goodman, Billy. Animal Homes & Societies. Goodman, Billy, illus. 96p. (gr. 3-7). 1992. 17.95 (*0-316-32018-8*) Little.
Grace, Theresa. A Picture Book of Swamp & Marsh Animals. Pistolesi, Roseanna, illus. LC 91-16034. 24p. (gr. 1-4). 1992. lib. bdg. 9.59 (*0-8167-2434-2*); pap. text ed. 2.50 (*0-8167-2435-0*) Troll Assocs.
Greenway, Shirley. Burrows. (Illus.). 24p. (gr. k-4). 1991. PLB 10.40 (*1-878137-11-5*) Newington.
—Water. (Illus.). 24p. (gr. k-4). 1991. PLB 10.40 (*1-878137-10-7*) Newington.
Guiberson, Brenda Z. Spoonbill Swamp. Lloyd, Megan, illus. LC 91-8555. 32p. (ps-3). 1992. 14.95 (*0-8050-1583-3*, Bks Young Read) H Holt & Co.
Hacker, Randi & Kaufman, Jackie. Habitats: Where the Wild Things Live. (Illus.). 48p. (Orig.). (gr. 3 up). Date not set. pap. 9.95 (*1-56261-060-0*) John Muir.
Harrison, Virginia & Banks, Martin. The World of Polar Bears. LC 89-4470. (Illus.). 32p. (gr. 2-3). 1989. PLB 17.27 (*0-8368-0139-3*) Gareth Stevens Inc.
Hickman, Pamela M. Habitats. English, Sarah J., illus. LC 93-12683. 1993. write for info. (*0-201-62651-9*); pap. 9.57 (*0-201-62618-7*) Addison-Wesley.
Kohl, Judith & Kohl, Herbert. Pack, Band & Colony: The World of Social Animals. La Farge, Margaret, illus. LC 82-20951. 114p. (gr. 6 up). 1983. 13.95 (*0-374-35694-7*) FS&G.
Madgwick, Wendy. Animaze! A Collection of Amazing Nature Mazes. Hussey, Lorna, illus. LC 91-46892. 40p. (ps-3). 1992. 13.00 (*0-679-82665-3*); PLB 13.99 (*0-679-92665-8*) Knopf Bks Yng Read.
Meyer, Nancy. Endangered Species Coloring-Learning Books Adventure Series. Meyer, George, illus. (ps-3). 1993. write for info. (*1-883408-05-9*) Meyer Pub FL.
Miranda, Anne M. Does a Mouse Have a House? LC 93-20587. (ps-1). 1994. 14.95 (*0-02-767251-4*, Bradbury Pr) Macmillan Child Grp.
Moncure, Jane B. What Does Word Bird See? Gohman, Vera, illus. LC 81-21594. (ps-2). 1982. PLB 14.95 (*0-89565-220-X*) Childs World.
Mora, Emma. Animals of the Forest. (Illus.). 30p. (ps-1). 1986. 3.95 (*0-8120-5722-8*) Barron.
Nussbaum, Hedda. Animals Build Amazing Homes. Santoro, Christopher, illus. LC 79-11326. (gr. 2-5). 1979. 7.95 (*0-394-83850-5*) Random Bks Yng Read.
Owl Magazine Editors. Bee Hives & Bat Caves: Amazing Animal Homes. Plewes, Andrew, illus. 48p. (gr. 1 up). 1992. pap. 6.95 (*0-920775-46-2*, Pub. by Greey dePencier CN) Firefly Bks Ltd.
Parramon, J. M. & Rius, Maria. Life in the Air. 32p. (gr. 3-5). 1987. Eng. ed. pap. 5.95 (*0-8120-3863-0*); Span. ed.: La Vida en el Aire. pap. 6.95 (*0-8120-3867-3*) Barron.
Peacock, Graham & Hudson, Terry. Exploring Habitats. Hughes, Jenny, illus. LC 92-29907. 48p. (gr. 4-8). 1992. PLB 22.80 (*0-8114-2608-4*) Raintree Steck-V.
Pemberton, Nancy. Animal Habitats: The Best Home of All. Dunnington, Tom, illus. LC 90-30633. 32p. (ps-2). 1990. PLB 14.95 (*0-89565-578-0*) Childs World.
Pezzoli, F. & Mora, E. Farm Animals. (Illus.). 30p. (ps-1). 1986. 3.95 (*0-8120-5723-6*) Barron.
Podendorf, Illa. Animal Homes. LC 82-4466. (Illus.). 48p. (gr. k-4). 1982. PLB 12.85 (*0-516-01666-0*) Childrens.
Pope, Joyce. Animal Homes. Field, James, illus. LC 91-45380. 32p. (gr. 3-6). 1993. PLB 11.59 (*0-8167-2775-9*); pap. text ed. 3.95 (*0-8167-2776-7*) Troll Assocs.
Reid, Struan. Bird World. (Illus.). 64p. (gr. 4-6). 1991. PLB 15.40 (*1-56294-009-0*) Millbrook Pr.
Robson, Denny. Animal Homes. (ps). 1991. 5.95 (*0-8120-6242-6*) Barron.
Saintsing, David. The World of Butterflies. LC 86-5706. (Illus.). 32p. (gr. 2-3). 1986. 17.27 (*1-55532-072-4*) Gareth Stevens Inc.
Shale, David & Coldrey, Jennifer. Man-of-War at Sea. LC 86-5703. (Illus.). 32p. (gr. 4-6). 1987. PLB 17.27 (*1-55532-069-4*) Gareth Stevens Inc.
—The World of a Jellyfish. LC 86-5704. (Illus.). 32p. (gr. 2-3). 1986. 17.27 (*1-55532-073-2*) Gareth Stevens Inc.
Taylor, Barbara. The Animal Atlas. Lilly, Kenneth, illus. LC 91-53142. 64p. (gr. 3-7). 1992. 20.00 (*0-679-80501-X*); PLB 21.99 (*0-679-90501-4*) Knopf Bks Yng Read.
Taylor, Kim. Hidden Underneath. (gr. 4-7). 1990. 9.95 (*0-385-30180-4*) Delacorte.
Tripp, Valerie. No Place Like Home. Callen, Liz, illus. 24p. (Orig.). (gr. 1-3). 1991. pap. text ed. 29.95 big bk. (*1-56334-046-1*); pap. text ed. 6.00 small bk. (*1-56334-052-6*) Hampton-Brown.
Waters, Sarah A. Animal Homes. LC 93-77341. (ps-3). 1993. 9.95 (*0-89577-512-3*, Dist. by Random) RD Assn.
Whalley, Mary & Whalley, Paul. Butterfly in the Garden. LC 86-5705. (Illus.). 32p. (gr. 4-6). 1986. PLB 15.93 (*1-55532-068-6*) Gareth Stevens Inc.
Where Animals Live, 24 vols. (Illus.). (gr. 2-3). 1988. Set. 414.40 (*0-8368-0263-2*) Gareth Stevens Inc.
Woodworth, Viki. Have You Seen an Elephant's Nest? Woodworth, Viki, illus. (ps-2). 1992. PLB 12.95 (*0-89565-824-0*) Childs World.

ANIMALS–HABITS AND BEHAVIOR

Here are entered factual books whose aim is to describe and instruct. Fictional or legendary tales about animals are entered under Animals–Stories.
see also Animal Intelligence; Animals–Fiction; Animals–Migration; Nature Study; Tracking and Trailing; also names of animals with the subdivision Habits and Behavior, e.g. Birds–Habits and Behavior; etc.

Aldis, Rodney. Towns & Cities. LC 91-35801. (Illus.). 48p. (gr. 5 up). 1992. text ed. 13.95 RSBE (*0-87518-496-0*, Dillon) Macmillan Child Grp.
Animal Science. (Illus.). 96p. (gr. 6-12). 1984. pap. 1.85 (*0-8395-3395-0*, 33395) BSA.
Animals & Their Homes Series. (Illus.). (gr. k-6). 1987. Set of 6 titles, 48 pp. PLB 95.94 (*0-8172-3110-2*); Set. 10.95 (*0-685-74138-9*) Raintree Steck-V.
Animals in the Wild. (Illus.). (gr. k-5). 1987. Set of 26 titles, 24 pp. PLB write for info. (*0-8172-2422-X*); 9.95 (*0-685-74137-0*) Raintree Steck-V.
Baby Animals in the Wild. (ps-k). 1989. bds. 3.50 (*0-7214-9535-4*) Ladybird Bks.
Bailey, Jill & Seddon, Tony. Animal Movement. (Illus.). 64p. 1988. 15.95x (*0-8160-1656-9*) Facts on File.
—Mimicry & Camouflage. 64p. (gr. 5 up). 1988. 15.95x (*0-8160-1657-7*) Facts on File.
Banks, Merry. Animals of the Night. Himler, Ronald, illus. LC 89-6194. 32p. (ps-k). 1990. SBE 13.95 (*0-684-19093-1*, Scribners Young Read) Macmillan Child Grp.
Barrett, Katharine. Animals in Action. Bergman, Lincoln & Fairwell, Kay, eds. Baker, Lisa H., illus. Barrett, Reginald & Craig, Rose, photos by. (Illus.). 44p. (Orig.). (gr. 6-9). 1986. pap. 10.00 (*0-912511-10-9*) Lawrence Science.
—Mapping Animal Movements. Bergman, Lincoln & Fairwell, Kay, eds. Baker, Lisa H. & Bevilacqua, Carol, illus. Barrett, Reginald, et al, photos by. 41p. (Orig.). (gr. 5-9). 1987. pap. 10.00 (*0-912511-60-5*) Lawrence Science.
Batten, Mary. Nature's Tricksters: Animals & Plants That Aren't What They Seem. Lovejoy, Lois, illus. (gr. 3-6). 1992. 14.95 (*0-316-08371-2*) Little.
Berger, Melvin. Animals in Danger. 16p. (gr. 2-4). 1993. pap. 14.95 (*1-56784-202-X*) Newbridge Comms.
Boone, J. Allen & Leonard, Paul H. Adventures in Kinship with All Life. Leonardo, Bianca, ed. 128p. (gr. 9-12). 1990. pap. 9.95 (*0-930852-08-7*) Tree Life Pubns.
Bowen, Betsy. Tracks in the Wild. LC 92-28691. 1993. 15.95 (*0-316-10377-2*) Little.
Brooks, Bruce. Predator! 80p. (gr. 5 up). 1991. bds. 13.95 bds. (*0-374-36111-8*) FS&G.
Browne, Anthony. Gorilla. Browne, Anthony, illus. LC 85-13. 32p. (ps-3). 1985. PLB 13.99 (*0-394-97525-1*) Knopf Bks Yng Read.
Burton, Jane. Animals at Home. (Illus.). 24p. (gr. k-4). 1991. PLB 10.40 (*1-878137-12-3*) Newington.
—Animals at Night. (Illus.). 24p. (gr. k-4). 1991. PLB 10.40 (*1-878137-13-1*) Newington.
—Animals at Work. (Illus.). 24p. (gr. k-4). 1991. PLB 10.40 (*1-878137-15-8*) Newington.
—Animals Eating. (Illus.). 24p. (gr. k-4). 1991. PLB 10.40 (*1-878137-00-X*) Newington.
—Animals Fighting. (Illus.). 24p. (gr. k-4). 1991. PLB 10.40 (*1-878137-03-4*) Newington.
—Animals Learning. (Illus.). 24p. (gr. k-4). 1991. PLB 10.40 (*1-878137-01-8*) Newington.
—Animals Talking. (Illus.). 24p. (gr. k-4). 1991. PLB 10.40 (*1-878137-02-6*) Newington.
—Keeping Clean. Burton, Jane & Taylor, Kim, photos by. LC 89-11557. (Illus.). 32p. (gr. 2-3). 1989. PLB 17.27 (*0-8368-0187-3*) Gareth Stevens Inc.
—Keeping Cool. Burton, Jane & Taylor, Kim, photos by. LC 89-11412. (Illus.). 32p. (gr. 2-3). 1989. PLB 17.27 (*0-8368-0188-1*) Gareth Stevens Inc.
Cain, Nancy W. Animal Behavior Science Projects. Date not set. pap. text ed. 12.95 (*0-471-02636-0*) Wiley.
Carwardine, Mark. Animals in the Cold. Young, Richard G., ed. Channell, Jim, illus. LC 89-32827. 45p. (gr. 3-5). 1989. PLB 14.60 (*0-944483-26-7*) Garrett Ed Corp.
—Animals on the Move. Young, Richard G., ed. Francis, John, illus. LC 89-32809. 45p. (gr. 3-5). 1989. PLB 14.60 (*0-944483-27-5*) Garrett Ed Corp.
—Nibblers & Gnawers. Young, Richard G., ed. Twinney, Dick, illus. LC 89-32807. 45p. (gr. 3-5). 1989. PLB 14.60 (*0-944483-29-1*) Garrett Ed Corp.
—Night Animals. Young, Richard G., ed. Camm, Martin, illus. LC 89-7880. 45p. (gr. 3-5). 1989. PLB 14.60 (*0-944483-30-5*) Garrett Ed Corp.
Chicago Zoological Society Staff, ed. Animal Families. (Orig.). (gr. k-2). 1986. pap. text ed. 30.00 (*0-913934-04-6*) Chicago Zoo.
—Creature Features. (Orig.). (gr. 2-3). 1986. pap. text ed. 30.00 (*0-913934-05-4*) Chicago Zoo.
Chlad, Dorothy. Animals Can be Special Friends. Halverson, Lydia, illus. LC 84-23300. 32p. (ps-2). 1985. pap. 3.95 (*0-516-41978-1*) Childrens.
Cleave, Andrew. Hunters. Lafford, Stuart, et al, illus. LC 94-6005. 1994. write for info. (*0-8114-6191-2*) Raintree Steck-V.
Coad, Penelope. Goodnight. Falla, Dominique, illus. LC 92-31960. 1993. 4.25 (*0-383-03569-4*) SRA Schl Grp.
Cole, Joanna. Daytime Animals. Lilly, Kenneth, illus. LC 85-4301. 32p. (ps-2). 1985. PLB 12.99 (*0-394-97188-4*) Knopf Bks Yng Read.
Craig, Janet. Amazing World of Night Creatures. Helmer, Jean, illus. LC 89-5002. 32p. (gr. 2-4). 1990. PLB 11.59 (*0-8167-1749-4*); pap. text ed. 2.95 (*0-8167-1750-8*) Troll Assocs.
Crump, Donald J., ed. Amazing Things Animals Do. (gr. 3-8). 1989. 8.95 (*0-87044-709-2*); PLB 12.50 (*0-87044-704-1*) Natl Geog.
—Animal Architects. LC 87-12198. (Illus.). 104p. (gr. 3-8). 1987. 8.95 (*0-87044-612-6*); PLB 12.50 (*0-87044-617-7*) Natl Geog.
—Animals at Play. (Illus.). (gr. k-4). 1988. Set. 13.95 (*0-87044-739-4*); Set. PLB 16.95 (*0-87044-744-0*) Natl Geog.
—Animals in Summer. (Illus.). (gr. k-4). 1988. Set. 13.95 (*0-87044-738-6*) Natl Geog.
—Books for Young Explorers, 4 vols, Set 13. Incl. Baby Bears & How They Grow. Buxton, Jane H; Saving Our Animal Friends. McGrath, Susan; Animals That Live in Trees. McCauley, Jane R; Animals & Their Hiding Places. McCauley, Jane R. 1986. Set. 13.95 (*0-87044-638-X*); Set. PLB 16.95 (*0-87044-643-6*) Natl Geog.
—How Animals Behave. LC 84-989. (Illus.). 104p. (gr. 3-8). 1984. 8.95 (*0-87044-500-6*); PLB 12.50 (*0-87044-505-7*) Natl Geog.
—Secrets of Animal Survival. LC 81-47895. (Illus.). 104p. (gr. 3 up). 1983. 8.95 (*0-87044-426-3*); PLB 12.50 (*0-87044-431-X*) Natl Geog.
Cutchins, Judy & Johnston, Ginny. Animal Fathers. LC 93-27014. 1994. write for info. (*0-688-12255-8*); lib. bdg. write for info. (*0-688-12256-6*) Morrow JR Bks.
Darling, David. Could You Ever Speak Chimpanzee? (Illus.). 60p. (gr. 5 up). 1991. text ed. 14.95 RSBE (*0-87518-448-0*, Dillon) Macmillan Child Grp.
Davis, Kay & Oldsfield, Wendy. Animals. LC 91-23413. (Illus.). 32p. (gr. 2-5). 1991. PLB 19.97 (*0-8114-3002-2*); pap. 4.95 (*0-8114-1528-7*) Raintree Steck-V.
De Zutter, Hank. Who Says a Dog Goes Bow-Wow? LC 92-4232. (ps-3). 1993. pap. 15.00 (*0-385-30659-8*) Doubleday.

Echols, Jean C. Animal Defenses. Bergman, Lincoln & Fairwell, Kay, eds. Bevilacqua, Carol, illus. Barrett, Reginald & Craig, Rose, photos by. (Illus.). 27p. (Orig.). (ps-2). 1987. pap. 8.50 (*0-912511-09-5*) Lawrence Science.

Emert, Phyllis R. Mysteries of Bizarre Animals & Freaks of Nature. 128p. (Orig.). 1994. pap. 2.99 (*0-8125-3630-4*) Tor Bks.

Eugene, Toni. Animal Acrobats; Secret Treasures, 2 vols. Cremins, Robert, illus. LC 93-9768. (Illus.). 1993. Set 27.50 (*0-87044-955-9*) Natl Geog.

Evans, Lisa G. An Elephant Never Forgets Its Snorkel: How Animals Survive Without Tools & Gadgets. De Groat, Diane, illus. LC 91-31828. 40p. (gr. 1-5). 1992. 10.00 (*0-517-58401-8*); PLB 10.99 (*0-517-58404-2*) Crown Bks Yng Read.

Feldman, Eve B. Animals Don't Wear Pajamas: A Book about Sleeping. Owens, Mary B., illus. LC 91-25192. 32p. (ps-3). 1992. 14.95 (*0-8050-1710-0*, Bks Young Read) H Holt & Co.

Flegg, Jim. Animal Movement. (Illus.). 32p. (gr. 4-6). 1991. PLB 12.40 (*1-878137-22-0*) Newington.

Fortman, Jan. Creatures of Mystery. LC 77-24705. (Illus.). 48p. (gr. 4 up). 1983. PLB 20.70 (*0-8172-1063-6*) Raintree Steck-V.

Foster, Susan Q. The Hummingbird among the Flowers. Oxford Scientific Films Ser., photos by. LC 89-31912. (Illus.). 32p. (gr. 4-6). 1989. PLB 17.27 (*0-8368-0115-6*) Gareth Stevens Inc.

Ganeri, Anita. Animal Behavior. Taylor, Kate, illus. 32p. (ps-1). 1992. 6.95 (*0-8120-6301-5*) Barron.

—Animal Families. Taylor, Kate, illus. 32p. (ps-1). 1992. 6.95 (*0-8120-6274-4*) Barron.

—Animal Food. Taylor, Kate, illus. 32p. (ps-1). 1992. 6.95 (*0-8120-6302-3*) Barron.

Gattis, L. S., III. Animal Tracking for Pathfinders: A Basic Youth Enrichment Skill Honor Packet. (Illus.). 26p. (Orig.). (gr. 5 up). 1989. pap. 5.00 tchr's. ed. (*0-936241-48-9*) Cheetah Pub.

George, Lindsay B. In the Woods: Who's Been Here? LC 93-16244. (Illus.). 40p. (ps up). 1994. write for info. (*0-688-12318-X*); PLB write for info. (*0-688-12319-8*) Greenwillow.

Gibbs, Bridget. Mommy & Baby on the Farm. Gatt, Elizabeth, illus. 12p. 1992. 4.95 (*0-681-41554-1*) Longmeadow Pr.

Goaman. Animal World. Quinn, David, illus. 32p. (gr. 6up). 1984. 13.96 (*0-88110-168-0*); PLB 5.95 (*0-86020-751-X*) EDC.

Goodman, Billy. Animal Homes & Societies. Goodman, Billy, illus. 96p. (gr. 3-7). 1992. 17.95 (*0-316-32018-8*) Little.

Gravelle, Karen. Animal Societies. LC 92-35877. (Illus.). 96p. (gr. 7-12). 1993. PLB 13.40 (*0-531-12530-0*) Watts.

Green, Carl R. & Sanford, William R. The Badger. LC 85-19486. (Illus.). 48p. (gr. 5). 1986. text ed. 12.95 RSBE (*0-89686-290-9*, Crestwood Hse) Macmillan Child Grp.

—The Hyena. LC 88-5876. (Illus.). 48p. (gr. 5). 1988. text ed. 12.95 RSBE (*0-89686-384-0*, Crestwood Hse) Macmillan Child Grp.

Greenway, Shirley. What Do I Eat? Oxford Scientific Films Staff, photos by. LC 93-18592. (Illus.). 32p. (ps). 1993. PLB 11.00 (*0-8249-8627-X*, Ideals Child); pap. 3.95 (*0-8249-8602-4*) Hambleton-Hill.

Hamsa, Bobbie. Animal Babies. Dunnington, Tom, illus. LC 84-27459. 32p. (ps-2). 1985. lib. bdg. 10.25 (*0-516-02066-8*); pap. 2.95 (*0-516-42066-6*) Childrens.

Harrar, George & Harrar, Linda. Signs of the Apes, Songs of the Whales. LC 89-30061. (Illus.). (gr. 3 up). 1989. (S&S BFYR); pap. 5.95 (*0-671-67767-5*, S&S BFYR) S&S Trade.

Harrison, Virginia. The World of Hummingbirds. Oxford Scientific Films Staff, photos by. LC 89-31913. (Illus.). 32p. (gr. 2-3). 1989. PLB 17.27 (*0-8368-0140-7*) Gareth Stevens Inc.

—The World of Snakes. Oxford Scientific Films Staff, photos by. LC 89-4634. (Illus.). 32p. (gr. 2-3). 1989. PLB 17.27 (*0-8368-0143-1*) Gareth Stevens Inc.

Heller, Ruth. Animals Born Alive & Well. (Illus.). 48p. (ps-3). 1993. pap. 6.95 (*0-448-40453-2*, G&D) Putnam Pub Group.

—Chickens Aren't the Only Ones. (Illus.). 48p. (ps-3). 1993. pap. 6.95 (*0-448-40454-0*, G&D) Putnam Pub Group.

Hemsley, William. Feeding to Digestion: Projects with Biology. LC 91-35075. (Illus.). 32p. (gr. 5-9). 1992. PLB 12.40 (*0-531-17327-5*, Gloucester Pr) Watts.

—Fins to Wings: Projects with Biology. LC 91-34410. (Illus.). 32p. (gr. 5-9). 1992. PLB 12.40 (*0-531-17271-6*, Gloucester Pr) Watts.

Herberman, Ethan. The City Kid's Field Guide. (gr. 3 up). 1989. (S&S BFYR); pap. 5.95 (*0-671-67746-2*, S&S BFYR) S&S Trade.

Hirschi, Ron. A Time for Playing. Mangelsen, Thomas D., photos by. LC 93-36773. (Illus.). (ps-3). 1994. 13.99 (*0-525-65159-4*, Cobblehill Bks) Dutton Child Bks.

—A Time for Sleeping. Mangelsen, Thomas D., photos by. LC 92-21408. (Illus.). 32p. (ps-3). 1993. 13.99 (*0-525-65128-4*, Cobblehill Bks) Dutton Child Bks.

Hirschland, Roger. How Animals Care for Their Babies. Crump, Donald J., ed. (Illus.). 32p. (ps-3). 1987. Set. 13.95 (*0-87044-678-9*); Set. lib. bdg. 16.95 (*0-87044-683-5*) Natl Geog.

Holley, Dennis. Animals Alive! An Ecological Guide to Animal Activities. Payne, Brian, illus. 300p. (gr. 5-12). 1993. pap. text ed. 29.95 (*1-879373-58-0*) R Rinehart.

Hornblow, Leonora & Hornblow, Arthur. Animals Do the Strangest Things. Kohler, Keith, illus. LC 88-37710. 64p. (gr. 2-4). 1990. lib. bdg. 6.99 (*0-394-94308-2*); pap. 4.95 (*0-394-84308-8*) Random Bks Yng Read.

Horton, et al. Amazing Fact Book of Animals. (Illus.). 32p. 1987. PLB 14.95s.p. (*0-87191-840-4*) Creative Ed.

Howard, Diane W. Jeremy Firefly: Oh to Glow. Kight, Joshua, illus. 48p. (Orig.). (gr. k-3). 1991. PLB 13.95 (*0-9623524-2-X*) Hunt Hse Pub.

Jansen, Curt, et al. Badger & Her Babies. (Orig.). (gr. k-4). pap. write for info. (*0-9614904-2-X*) Adventure Prods.

—Bobcat & Her Babies. (Orig.). (gr. k-4). pap. write for info. (*0-9614904-3-8*) Adventure Prods.

—Cougar & Her Babies. (Orig.). (gr. k-4). write for info.; pap. write for info. Adventure Prods.

Kerrod, Robin. Animal Life. LC 93-4483. (Illus.). 64p. (gr. 5 up). 1993. PLB 15.95 (*1-85435-623-2*) Marshall Cavendish.

Kipling, Rudyard. How the Leopard Got His Spots. Loestoeter, Lori, illus. LC 89-31374. (ps up). 1991. pap. 14.95 (*0-88708-111-8*, Rabbit Ears); book & cassette package 19.95 (*0-88708-112-6*, Rabbit Ears) Picture Bk Studio.

Kitchen, Bert. When Hunger Calls. LC 93-32360. (Illus.). 32p. (ps up). 1994. 15.95 (*1-56402-316-8*) Candlewick Pr.

Koebner, Linda. For Kids Who Love Animals: A Guide to Sharing the Planet. (Illus.). 150p. (Orig.). (gr. 2-7). 1991. pap. 6.95 (*1-879326-03-5*) Living Planet Pr.

Kohl, Judith & Kohl, Herbert. The View from the Oak. Bayless, Roger, illus. 112p. (gr. 5 up). 1988. 15.95 (*0-316-50137-9*) Little.

Kostyal, Karen. Raccoons. Crump, Donald J., ed. (Illus.). 32p. (ps-3). 1987. Set. 13.95 (*0-87044-677-0*); Set. lib. bdg. 16.95 (*0-87044-682-7*) Natl Geog.

Kramer, Michael. Funny Facts about Animals. 1991. 4.99 (*0-517-05663-1*) Random Hse Value.

Kudlinski, Kathleen V. Animal Tracks & Traces. Morgan, Mary, illus. 32p. (gr. 1 up). 1991. 12.95 (*0-531-15185-9*); PLB 12.90 (*0-531-10742-6*) Watts.

Kuskin, Karla. Roar & More. LC 56-8138. (Illus.). 32p. (ps-3). 1977. pap. 1.95 (*0-06-443019-7*, Trophy) HarpC Child Bks.

Lavies, Bianca. Lily Pad Pond. (Illus.). 32p. (ps-2). 1993. pap. 4.99 (*0-14-054836-X*) Puffin Bks.

—Tree Trunk Traffic. (Illus.). 32p. (ps-2). 1993. pap. 4.99 (*0-14-054837-8*) Puffin Bks.

Lesser, Carolyn. The Goodnight Circle. Cauley, Lorinda B., illus. LC 84-4501. 30p. (ps-3). 1984. 14.95 (*0-15-232158-6*, HB Juv Bks) HarBrace.

Linley, Mike. The Snake in the Grass. Oxford Scientific Films Staff, photos by. LC 89-4621. (Illus.). 32p. (gr. 4-6). 1989. PLB 17.27 (*0-8368-0118-0*) Gareth Stevens Inc.

M. J. Studios Staff, illus. Wacky Animals Sticker Pad. 32p. (gr. k-6). 1993. pap. 2.95 (*1-879424-30-4*) Nickel Pr.

McCauley, Jane. Africa's Animal Giants. Crump, Donald J., ed. (Illus.). 32p. (ps-3). 1987. 13.95 (*0-87044-680-0*); lib. bdg. 16.95 (*0-87044-685-1*) Natl Geog.

McGrath, Susan. How Animals Talk, 4 vols, No. 3. Crump, Donald J., ed. (Illus.). 32p. (ps-3). 1987. Set. 13.95 (*0-87044-679-7*); Set. lib. bdg. 16.95 (*0-87044-684-3*) Natl Geog.

Machotka, Hana. Terrific Tails. LC 93-17687. (Illus.). 32p. (gr. k up). 1994. 15.00g (*0-688-04562-6*); PLB 14.93 (*0-688-04563-4*) Morrow Jr Bks.

Markham-David, Sally. Tail Tales. Russell-Arnot, Elizabeth, illus. LC 93-6631. 1994. pap. write for info. (*0-383-03718-2*) SRA Schl Grp.

Martin, James. Hiding Out: Camouflage in the Wild. Wolfe, Art, illus. LC 92-38211. 32p. (gr. 2-6). 1993. 13.00 (*0-517-59392-0*); PLB 13.99 (*0-517-59393-9*) Crown Bks Yng Read.

Mirocha, Paul & Lauffer, Rhod. Back Off! Animal Defense Behavior. LC 94-4144. 1994. text ed. write for info. (*0-7167-6534-9*, Sci Am Yng Rdrs) W H Freeman.

—Look Again! Animal Camouflage & Disguise. LC 94-6224. 1994. text ed. write for info. (*0-7167-6535-7*, Sci Am Yng Rders) W H Freeman.

Moncure, Jane B. Night Animals: Wake-Up, Little Owl! Halverson, Lydia, illus. LC 89-71173. 32p. (ps-2). 1990. PLB 14.95 (*0-89565-568-3*) Childs World.

Morris, Dean. Dinosaurs & Other First Animals. LC 87-16670. (Illus.). 48p. (gr. 2-6). 1987. PLB 10.95 (*0-8172-3206-0*) Raintree Steck-V.

—Endangered Animals. rev. ed. LC 87-20459. (Illus.). 48p. (gr. 2-6). 1987. PLB 10.95 (*0-8172-3207-9*) Raintree Steck-V.

Nail, James T. Whose Tracks Are These? A Clue Book of Familiar Forest Animals. Skudder, Hyla, illus. LC 94-65087. 32p. (gr. k-4). 1994. PLB 13.95 (*1-879373-89-0*) R Rinehart.

National Wildlife Federation Staff. Amazing Mammals I. (gr. k-8). 1991. pap. 7.95 (*0-945051-29-8*, 75023) Natl Wildlife.

—Amazing Mammals II. (gr. k-8). 1991. pap. 7.95 (*0-945051-30-1*, 75024) Natl Wildlife.

Night Creatures. LC 93-85987. 32p. (gr. 2 up). 1994. 5.95 (*1-56138-197-7*) Running Pr.

North Country Night. 1990. pap. 14.95 (*0-385-41319-X*) Doubleday.

Otto. Camouflage. Date not set. 14.00 (*0-06-023342-7*, Festival); PLB 13.89 (*0-06-023343-5*, Festival) HarpC Child Bks.

Owl Magazine Editors. Singing Fish & Flying Rhinos: Amazing Animal Habits. Sisco, Sam, illus. 48p. (gr. 2 up). 1992. pap. 6.95 (*0-920775-45-4*, Pub. by Greey dePencier CN) Firefly Bks Ltd.

Parker, Steve. Camouflage. LC 91-10275. (Illus.). 32p. (gr. 5-8). 1991. PLB 12.40 (*0-531-17313-5*, Gloucester Pr) Watts.

Parker, Steve & Parker, Jane. Territories. LC 91-29820. (Illus.). 32p. (gr. 4-7). 1992. PLB 12.40 (*0-531-17310-0*, Gloucester Pr) Watts.

Pearce, Q. L. Animal Footnotes: A Nature's Footprints Guide. Bettoli, Delana, illus. 40p. (ps-3). 1990. PLB 10.95 (*0-671-69116-3*); pap. 7.95 (*0-671-69117-1*) Silver Pr.

Peissel, Michel & Allen, Missy. Dangerous Mammals. (Illus.). 112p. (gr. 5 up). 1993. PLB 19.95 (*0-7910-1790-7*, Am Art Analog) Chelsea Hse.

—Dangerous Water Creatures. (Illus.). 112p. (gr. 5 up). 1993. PLB 19.95 (*0-7910-1788-5*, Am Art Analog) Chelsea Hse.

Perez, Ed. A Look Around Endangered Animals. (Illus.). 32p. (gr. 1-3). 1992. pap. 2.50 (*0-87406-579-8*) Willowisp Pr.

Peters, Sharon. Animals at Night. Harvey, Paul, illus. LC 82-19226. 32p. (gr. k-2). 1983. lib. bdg. 11.59 (*0-89375-903-1*); pap. 2.95 (*0-8167-1477-0*) Troll Assocs.

Pope, Joyce. Do Animals Dream? Children's Questions about Animals Most Often Asked of the Natural History Museum. LC 86-40029. (Illus.). 96p. 1986. pap. 16.95 (*0-670-81233-1*) Viking Child Bks.

—Kenneth Lilly's Animals. Lilly, Kenneth, illus. LC 87-31147. 96p. (gr. 3 up). 1988. 17.00 (*0-688-07696-3*) Lothrop.

—Life in the Dark. LC 91-18646. (Illus.). 48p. (gr. 4-8). 1992. PLB 22.80 (*0-8114-3150-9*); pap. 4.95 (*0-8114-6252-8*) Raintree Steck-V.

—Mistaken Identity. LC 91-17136. (Illus.). 48p. (gr. 4-8). 1992. PLB 22.80 (*0-8114-3152-5*); pap. 4.95 (*0-8114-6253-6*) Raintree Steck-V.

—Night Creatures. Tamblin, Treave, illus. LC 91-45171. 32p. (gr. 3-6). 1993. PLB 11.59 (*0-8167-2783-X*); pap. text ed. 3.95 (*0-8167-2784-8*) Troll Assocs.

Powzyk, Joyce. Animal Camouflage: A Closer Look. Powzyk, Joyce, illus. LC 89-9848. 40p. (gr. 2-9). 1990. SBE 15.95 (*0-02-774980-0*, Bradbury Pr) Macmillan Child Grp.

Pragoff, Fiona. What Color? LC 87-645. (Illus.). 20p. (gr. k-3). 1987. pap. 6.95 (*0-385-24173-9*) Doubleday.

Quiri, Patricia R. Metamorphosis. LC 91-3104. (Illus.). 64p. (gr. 5-8). 1991. PLB 12.90 (*0-531-20042-6*) Watts.

Redmond, Ian. The Elephant in the Bush. Oxford Scientific Films Staff, photos by. LC 89-11297. (Illus.). 32p. (gr. 4-6). 1989. PLB 17.27 (*0-8368-0116-4*) Gareth Stevens Inc.

Rosenholtz, Stephen. Move Like the Animals. Yoshiko, Fujita, illus. LC 91-66970. 32p. (ps-3). 1992. incl. cassette 19.95 (*0-9630979-1-1*); pap. 14.95 incl. cassette (*0-9630979-0-3*) Rosewd Pubns.

Savage, Stephen. Animals Undercover. LC 92-30753. 1993. 12.95 (*0-525-67404-7*, Lodestar Bks) Dutton Child Bks.

—Making Tracks: A Slide-&-See Book. Savage, Stephen, illus. 10p. (gr. k-3). 1992. 10.00 (*0-525-67353-9*, Lodestar Bks) Dutton Child Bks.

Schmid, Eleonore. Farm Animals. Schmid, Eleonore, illus. LC 85-63302. 12p. (ps-k). 1986. 3.95 (*1-55858-045-X*) North-South Bks NYC.

Selsam, Millicent E. & Hunt, Joyce. A First Look at Seals, Sea Lions, & Walruses. Springer, Harriett, illus. LC 87-29491. 36p. (ps-3). 1988. pap. 10.95 (*0-8027-6787-7*); pap. text ed. 11.85 (*0-8027-6788-5*) Walker & Co.

Silver, Donald M. The Animal World: From Single-Cell Creatures to Giants of the Land & Sea. Wynne, Patricia, illus. LC 86-3894. 112p. (gr. 5 up). 1987. lib. bdg. 9.99 (*0-394-96650-3*); (BYR) Random Bks Yng Read.

Simon, Seymour. Animal Fact - Animal Fable. De Groat, Diane, illus. LC 78-14866. 48p. (gr. 1-5). 1992. PLB 12.99 (*0-517-58846-3*) Crown Bks Yng Read.

Stockley, C. Animal Behavior. (Illus.). 64p. (gr. 4-12). 1992. PLB 13.96 (*0-88110-513-9*, Usborne); pap. 7.95 (*0-7460-0639-X*, Usborne) EDC.

Taylor, Kim. Too Clever to See. (gr. 2-5). 1991. 9.95 (*0-385-30216-9*) Delacorte.

Tee-Van, Helen D. Small Mammals Are Where You Find Them. (Illus.). (gr. 3-7). 1967. lib. bdg. 5.99 (*0-394-91643-3*) Knopf Bks Yng Read.

Time-Life Books Staff, ed. Animal Behavior. 144p. 1992. write for info. (*0-8094-9658-5*); lib. bdg. write for info. (*0-8094-9659-3*) Time-Life.

Tomb, Howard. Living Monsters: The World's Most Dangerous Animals. Marchesi, Stephen, illus. 48p. (gr. 3-7). 1990. pap. 9.95 (*0-671-69017-5*, S&S BFYR) S&S Trade.

Walker, Dava J. Animal Behavior. Nolte, Larry, illus. 48p. (gr. 3-6). Date not set. PLB 12.95 (*1-56065-116-4*) Capstone Pr.

Wallace, Karen. Bears in the Forest. Frith, Barbara, illus. LC 93-39668. 32p. (ps up). 1994. 14.95 (*1-56402-336-2*) Candlewick Pr.

What Do Animals Eat Colouring Book. (Illus.). (ps-6). pap. 2.95 (*0-565-00808-0*, Pub. by Natural Hist Mus) Parkwest Pubns.

Wild Animals in the Park. (ps-3). 1991. pap. 2.50 (*0-89954-398-7*) Antioch Pub Co.

Wildlife Education, Ltd. Staff. Night Animals. Stuart, Walter, illus. 20p. (Orig.). (gr. 5 up). 1984. pap. 2.75 (*0-937934-26-7*) Wildlife Educ.

Wright, Alexander. Can We Be Friends? Nature's Partners. Peck, Marshall, III, illus. LC 93-42652. 1994. 14.95 (*0-88106-860-8*); PLB 15.00 (*0-88106-861-6*); pap. 6.95 (*0-88106-859-4*) Charlesbridge Pub.

Yolla Bolly Press Staff. Nightprowlers. Yolla Bolly Press Staff, illus. LC 93-27547. (gr. 3-7). 1994. 14.95 (*0-15-200694-X*, Gulliver Bks) HarBrace.

Ziefert, Harriet. Dark Night, Sleepy Night. Baruffi, Andrea, illus. LC 87-25759. 32p. (Orig.). (ps-3). 1988. pap. 3.50 (*0-14-050812-0*, Puffin) Puffin Bks.

ANIMALS–HIBERNATION

Arnosky, Jim. Every Autumn Comes the Bear. Arnosky, Jim, illus. LC 92-30515. 32p. (ps-1). 1993. 14.95 (*0-399-22508-0*, Putnam) Putnam Pub Group.

Bird, E. J. How Do Bears Sleep? Bird, E. J., illus. 32p. (ps-3). pap. 5.95 (*0-87614-522-5*) Carolrhoda Bks.

Brimner, Larry D. Animals That Hibernate. LC 90-13116. (Illus.). 64p. (gr. 3-6). 1991. PLB 12.90 (*0-531-20018-3*) Watts.

Facklam, Margery. Do Not Disturb: The Mysteries of Animal Hibernation & Sleep. Johnson, Pamela, illus. LC 88-10921. 48p. (gr. 3-6). 1989. 15.95 (*0-316-27379-1*) Little.

Stidworthy, John. Hibernation. LC 91-2674. (Illus.). 32p. (gr. 5-8). 1991. PLB 12.40 (*0-531-17309-7*, Gloucester Pr) Watts.

ANIMALS–INFANCY

Alderton, David. Baby Animals. (Illus.). 64p. 1991. 4.99 (*0-517-05155-9*) Random Hse Value.

Anderson, Honey & Reinholdt, Bill. What Are You Called? Bruere, Julian, illus. LC 92-31953. 1993. 3.75 (*0-383-03604-6*) SRA Schl Grp.

Aymerich, Angela F. The Three Pups. Billin-Frye, Paige, illus. 16p. (Orig.). (gr. 1-3). 1991. pap. text ed. 29.95 big bk. (*1-56334-049-6*); pap. text ed. 6.00 small bk. (*1-56334-055-0*) Hampton-Brown.

—Los Tres Perritos. Billin-Frye, Paige, illus. (SPA.). 16p. (Orig.). (gr. 1-3). 1991. pap. text ed. 29.95 big bk. (*1-56334-021-6*); pap. text ed. 6.00 small bk. (*1-56334-035-6*) Hampton-Brown.

Baby Animals. 32p. (Orig.). (ps-1). 1984. pap. 1.25 (*0-8431-1512-2*) Price Stern.

Baby Animals & Their Mothers. 1987. 1.95 (*0-8351-1707-3*) China Bks.

Baby Animals at Home. (ps-k). 1989. bds. 3.50 (*0-7214-9533-8*) Ladybird Bks.

Baby Animals Theme Pack: Level 1 English. (Orig.). (gr. 1-3). 1992. pap. 139.95 set incl. 2 big bks., 12 small bks. & tchr's. theme guide (*1-56334-075-5*) Hampton-Brown.

Baby Animals Two. 1991. PLB 14.95 (*0-88682-418-4*) Creative Ed.

Baby Farm Animals. (Illus.). (ps). pap. 1.25 (*0-7214-9548-6*) Ladybird Bks.

Baby Farm Animals. (Illus.). 18p. (ps). 1992. bds. 4.50 (*1-56288-305-4*) Checkerboard.

Baby Wild Animals. (Illus.). 18p. (ps). 1992. bds. 4.50 (*1-56288-306-2*) Checkerboard.

Baby Zoo Animals. (Illus.). 32p. (ps-1). 1986. pap. 1.25 (*0-8431-1521-1*) Price Stern.

Berger, Melvin. Animals & Their Babies. (Illus.). 16p. (ps-2). 1993. pap. text ed. 14.95 (*1-56784-005-1*) Newbridge Comms.

Binato, Leonardo. What Hatches from an Egg? Turn & Learn. 12p. (ps-3). 1992. 4.95 (*1-56566-007-2*) Thomasson-Grant.

Black, Sonia. All about Baby Animals Activity Book. (ps-3). 1993. pap. 1.95 (*0-590-46286-5*) Scholastic Inc.

Brown, Margaret W. Baby Animals. LC 88-18481. (Illus.). 32p. (ps-1). 1989. Repr. of 1941 ed. 15.00 (*0-394-82040-1*) Random Bks Yng Read.

Burton, Jane. Baby Animals Growing Up, 7 vols. Burton, Jane, illus. 384p. (gr. 2-3). 1989. Set. PLB 120.89 (*0-8368-1171-2*) Gareth Stevens Inc.

Burton, Jane, photos by. Chick. (Illus.). 24p. (gr. k-3). 1992. 6.95 (*0-525-67355-5*, Lodestar Bks) Dutton Child Bks.

—See How They Grow: Kitten. (Illus.). 24p. (gr. k-3). 1991. 6.95 (*0-525-67343-1*, Lodestar Bks) Dutton Child Bks.

—See How They Grow: Puppy. (Illus.). 24p. (gr. k-3). 1991. 6.95 (*0-525-67342-3*, Lodestar Bks) Dutton Child Bks.

Busy Baby Animals. (Illus.). 18p. (ps). 1992. bds. 4.50 (*1-56288-307-0*) Checkerboard.

Campbell, Janet B. Farm Babies. Lanza, Barbara, illus. 24p. (ps-3). 1994. 1.95 (*0-307-10059-6*, Pub. by Golden Bks) Western Pub.

Chinery, Michael. Baby Animals. LC 93-51048. (gr. k-2). 1994. 3.95 (*1-85697-501-0*, Kingfisher LKC) LKC.

Clayton, Gordon, photos by. Lamb. (Illus.). 24p. (gr. k-3) 1992. 6.95 (*0-525-67359-8*, Lodestar Bks) Dutton Child Bks.

Count Ten Baby Animals. (Illus.). 6p. (gr. k-2). 1988. bds. 6.95 (*0-87449-452-4*) Modern Pub NYC.

Crozat, Francois. I Am a Little Panda. LC 92-30962. 28p. (ps-k). 1993. 8.95 (*0-8120-6311-2*); Miniature. 3.50 (*0-8120-6312-0*) Barron.

Cutchins, Judy & Johnston, Ginny. Animal Fathers. LC 93-27014. 1994. write for info. (*0-688-12255-8*); lib. bdg. write for info. (*0-688-12256-6*) Morrow JR Bks.

Dickinson, Rebecca. Animal Babies. Bonforte, Lisa, illus. LC 87-81765. 22p. (ps). 1988. write for info. (*0-307-12116-X*, Pub. by Golden Bks) Western Pub.

Fowler, Allan. Cubs & Colts & Calves & Kittens. LC 91-3140. 32p. (ps-2). 1991. PLB 10.75 (*0-516-04913-5*); PLB 22.95 big bk. (*0-516-49473-2*); pap. 3.95 (*0-516-44913-3*) Childrens.

Fujikawa, Gyo, illus. Baby Animals. (ps). 1963. bds. 4.95 (*0-448-03083-7*, G&D) Putnam Pub Group.

Ganeri, Anita. Animal Babies. Taylor, Kate, illus. 32p. (ps-1). 1991. 6.95 (*0-8120-6241-8*) Barron.

Gibbs, Bridget. Mommy & Baby in the Wild. Gatt, Elizabeth, illus. 12p. 1992. 4.95 (*0-681-41553-3*) Longmeadow Pr.

Greenway, Shirley. Whose Baby Am I? LC 92-6133. 32p. (ps-2). 1992. 11.00 (*0-8249-8577-X*, Ideals Child); pap. 3.95 (*0-8249-8562-1*) Hambleton-Hill.

Hall, Derek. Baby Animals: Five Stories of Endangered Species. Butler, John, illus. LC 91-71861. 64p. (ps-3). 1994. pap. 7.99 (*1-56402-362-1*) Candlewick Pr.

Hewett, Joan. Tiger, Tiger, Growing Up. Hewett, Richard, photos by. LC 92-9741. (Illus.). 32p. (ps-2). 1993. 13.95 (*0-395-61583-6*, Clarion Bks) HM.

Hirschi, Ron. A Time for Babies. Mangelsen, Thomas D., photos by. LC 92-21409. (Illus.). 32p. (ps-3). 1993. 13. 99 (*0-525-65095-4*, Cobblehill Bks) Dutton Child Bks.

Hirschland, Roger. How Animals Care for Their Babies. Crump, Donald J., ed. (Illus.). 32p. (ps-3). 1987. Set. 13.95 (*0-87044-678-9*); Set. lib. bdg. 16.95 (*0-87044-683-5*) Natl Geog.

Hoban, Tana. Who Are They? LC 93-33644. (Illus.). 12p. (ps up). 1994. bds. 4.95 (*0-688-12921-8*) Greenwillow.

Holen-Roebuck, Susan D. Arctic Animal Babies. Arehart, Betsy L., illus. 40p. (Orig.). (ps-3). 1993. pap. 4.95 (*0-922127-04-2*) Paisley Pub.

Jansen, Curt, et al. Badger & Her Babies. (Orig.). (gr. k-4). pap. write for info. (*0-9614904-2-X*) Adventure Prods.

—Bobcat & Her Babies. (Orig.). (gr. k-4). pap. write for info. (*0-9614904-3-8*) Adventure Prods.

—Cougar & Her Babies. (Orig.). (gr. k-4). write for info.; pap. write for info. Adventure Prods.

Johnston, Ginny & Cutchins, Judy. Slippery Babies: Young Frogs, Toads, & Salamanders. LC 90-49665. (Illus.). 48p. (gr. 2 up). 1991. 13.95 (*0-688-09605-0*); PLB 13.88 (*0-688-09606-9*) Morrow Jr Bks.

Kalman, Bobbie. Animal Babies. (Illus.). 56p. (gr. 3-4). 1987. 15.95 (*0-86505-166-6*); pap. 7.95 (*0-86505-186-0*) Crabtree Pub Co.

Kindersley, Dorling. Baby Animals. LC 91-27723. (Illus.). 24p. (ps-k). 1992. pap. 7.95 POB (*0-689-71563-3*, Aladdin) Macmillan Child Grp.

Kratky, Lada J. Los Animales y Sus Crias. (SPA., Illus.). 24p. (Orig.). (gr. 1-3). 1991. pap. text ed. 29.95 big bk. (*1-56334-020-8*); pap. text ed. 6.00 small bk. (*1-56334-034-8*) Hampton-Brown.

—Animals & Their Young. (Illus.). 24p. (Orig.). (gr. 1-3). 1991. pap. text ed. 29.95 big.bk. (*1-56334-048-8*); pap. text ed. 6.00 small bk. (*1-56334-054-2*) Hampton-Brown.

Kuchalla, Susan. Baby Animals. Snyder, Joel, illus. LC 81-11434. 32p. (gr. k-2). 1982. lib. bdg. 11.59 (*0-89375-666-0*); pap. 2.95 (*0-89375-667-9*) Troll Assocs.

Mabie, Grace. A Picture Book of Baby Animals. Pistolesi, Roseanna, illus. LC 92-26264. 24p. (gr. 1-4). 1992. PLB 9.59 (*0-8167-2468-7*); pap. text ed. 2.50 (*0-8167-2469-5*) Troll Assocs.

McDonnell, Janet. Baby Animals: Safe & Sound. Hohag, Linda, illus. LC 89-23978. 32p. (ps-2). 1990. PLB 14. 95 (*0-89565-554-3*) Childs World.

McNaught, Harry. Baby Animals. McNaught, Harry, illus. LC 75-36462. 14p. (ps-1). 1976. Repr. of 1976 ed. bds. 3.95 (*0-394-83241-8*) Random Bks Yng Read.

McQueen, Lucinda. Pet the Baby Farm Animals: Their Fur Feels Real! (Illus.). 16p. (ps). 1994. 8.95 (*0-590-47687-4*, Cartwheel) Scholastic Inc.

Main, Katy. Baby Animals of the North. Main, Katy, illus. 36p. (ps-k). 1992. bds. 13.95 (*0-88240-395-8*) Alaska Northwest.

Martin, Chia. We Like to Nurse. Rainey, Shukyo L., illus. 36p. (Orig.). 1994. pap. 9.95 (*0-934252-45-9*) Hohm Pr. With vivid colors & captivating illustrations, WE LIKE TO NURSE presents both wild & domestic baby animals suckling their mothers. In simple, encouraging text, this book reminds young children of their deep feelings for the intimate bond created by nursing. A perfect book to gift the mother-to-be, or the nursing mother. "Any work of art that celebrates the profundity of the breastfeeding relationship is worthy of note... especially tender & vulnerable--open in the way that breastfeeding is...opens us up to the deeper feelings of this intimate relationship."--Peggy O'Mara, Editor & Publisher, MOTHERING MAGAZINE. To Order: Phone 1-800-729-6423.
Publisher Provided Annotation.

Mattern, Joanne. Baby Animals. Stone, Lynn M., illus. LC 91-40282. 24p. (gr. 4-7). 1993. pap. text ed. 1.95 (*0-8167-2958-1*) Troll Assocs.

Matthews, Downs. Polar Bear Cubs. (gr. 3). pap. 4.00 (*0-663-56236-8*) Silver Burdett Pr.

Maynard, Chris. Amazing Animal Babies. LC 92-23736. 32p. (Orig.). (gr. 1-5). 1993. PLB 10.99 (*0-679-93924-5*); pap. 7.99 (*0-679-83924-0*) Knopf Bks Yng Read.

My Book of Baby Forest Animals. (ps-2). 3.95 (*0-7214-5150-0*) Ladybird Bks.

My Book of Baby Zoo Animals. (ps-2). 3.95 (*0-7214-5149-7*) Ladybird Bks.

National Geographic Society Staff. Lion Cubs. (Illus.). Date not set. pap. 16.00 (*0-87044-871-4*) Natl Geog.

Patent, Dorothy H. Baby Horses. Munoz, William, photos by. 56p. (ps-1). 1991. PLB 17.50 (*0-87614-690-6*) Carolrhoda Bks.

Petty, Kate. Baby Animals: Bears. (Illus.). 24p. (ps-3). 1992. pap. 3.95 (*0-8120-4964-0*) Barron.

—Bears. LC 90-44447. (Illus.). 24p. (gr. k-3). 1991. PLB 10.90 (*0-531-17286-4*, Gloucester Pr) Watts.

Pfeffer, Wendy. From Tadpole to Frog. Keller, Holly, illus. LC 93-3135. 32p. (ps-1). 1994. 15.00 (*0-06-023044-4*); PLB 14.89 (*0-06-023117-3*) HarpC Child Bks.

Podendorf, Illa. Baby Animals. LC 81-9938. (Illus.). 48p. (gr. k-4). 1981. PLB 12.85 (*0-516-01605-9*); pap. 4.95 (*0-516-41605-7*) Childrens.

Pope, Joyce. Animal Babies. Aloof, Andrew, illus. LC 91-45381. 32p. (gr. 3-6). 1993. PLB 11.59 (*0-8167-2773-2*); pap. text ed. 3.95 (*0-8167-2774-0*) Troll Assocs.

Roe, Richard. Baby Animals. Roe, Richard, illus. LC 85-2223. 24p. (ps-1). 1985. 3.95 (*0-394-86956-7*) Random Bks Yng Read.

Ryden, Hope. Joey: The Story of a Baby Kangaroo. Ryden, Hope, photos by. LC 93-15419. (Illus.). 40p. 1994. 15.00 (*0-688-12744-4*, Tambourine Bks); PLB 14.93 (*0-688-12745-2*, Tambourine Bks) Morrow.

Smith, Roland. Inside the Zoo Nursery. Munoz, William, illus. LC 92-3344. 64p. (gr. 5 up). 1993. 15.00 (*0-525-65084-9*, Cobblehill Bks) Dutton Child Bks.

Spinelli, Eileen. Baby Animals. (Illus.). 64p. (gr. k-4). 1992. PLB 13.75 (*1-878363-80-8*, HTS Bks) Forest Hse.

Taylor, Kim & Burton, Jane, photos by. See How They Grow: Frog. (Illus.). 24p. (gr. k-3). 1991. 6.95 (*0-525-67345-8*, Lodestar Bks) Dutton Child Bks.

Twinem, Neecy. Aye-Ayes, Bears, & Condors: An ABC of Endangered Animals & Their Babies. LC 93-37698. 1993. text ed. write for info. (*0-7167-6525-X*, Sci Am Yng Rdrs) W H Freeman.

Wallace, Karen. Bears in the Forest. Frith, Barbara, illus. LC 93-39668. 32p. (ps up). 1994. 14.95 (*1-56402-336-2*) Candlewick Pr.

Warren, Elizabeth. I Can Read About Baby Animals. LC 74-24879. (Illus.). (gr. 1-2). 1975. pap. 2.50 (*0-89375-060-3*) Troll Assocs.

Watts, Barrie, photos by. Mouse. (Illus.). 24p. (gr. k-3). 1992. 6.95 (*0-525-67357-1*, Lodestar Bks) Dutton Child Bks.

—See How They Grow: Duck. (Illus.). 24p. (gr. k-3). 1991. 6.95 (*0-525-67346-6*, Lodestar Bks) Dutton Child Bks.

Wildlife Education, Ltd. Staff. Baby Animals. (Illus.). 20p. (Orig.). (gr. 5 up). 1981. pap. 2.75 (*0-937934-06-2*) Wildlife Educ.

Yee, Patrick. Baby Lion. (Illus.). 12p. (ps). 1994. bds. 3.99 (*0-670-85289-9*) Viking Child Bks.

ANIMALS–LANGUAGE

see Animal Communication

ANIMALS–LEGENDS

see Animals–Fiction

ANIMALS–MIGRATION

see also names of animals with the subdivision Migration, e.g. Birds–Migration

Flegg, Jim. Animal Travelers. (Illus.). 32p. (gr. 4-6). 1991. PLB 12.40 (*1-878137-07-7*) Newington.

McDonnell, Janet. Animal Migration. LC 88-36640. (Illus.). 48p. (gr. 2-6). 1989. PLB 14.95 (*0-89565-514-4*) Childs World.

Parker, Steve & Parker, Jane. Migration. LC 92-9831. 1992. 12.40 (*0-531-17311-9*, Gloucester Pr) Watts.

Pope, Joyce. Animal Journeys. Weare, Phil, illus. LC 91-45379. 32p. (gr. 3-6). 1993. PLB 11.59 (*0-8167-2777-5*); pap. text ed. 3.95 (*0-8167-2778-3*) Troll Assocs.

Sanders, John. All about Animal Migrations. Burns, Ray, illus. LC 83-6630. 32p. (gr. 3-6). 1984. PLB 10.59 (*0-89375-977-5*); pap. text ed. 2.95 (*0-89375-978-3*) Troll Assocs.

Stone, Lynn M. The Wildebeest's Great Migration. LC 90-38384. (Illus.). 48p. (gr. 4-6). 1991. PLB 16.67 (*0-86593-103-8*); lib. bdg. 12.50s.p. (*0-685-59354-1*) Rourke Corp.

ANIMALS–PHOTOGRAPHY

see Photography of Animals

ANIMALS–PICTURES, ILLUSTRATIONS, ETC.

Animal Babies. LC 90-80291. (ps-2). 1991. pap. 1.95 (*1-56288-076-4*) Checkerboard.

Babson, Jane F. Babson's Bestiary. Babson, Jane F., illus. LC 90-71155. 32p. (ps-4). 1991. casebound 10.95 (*0-940787-02-4*) Winstead Pr.
Second in a learning to read series for children & adults. Illustrated with original art, writing designed to stimulate interest, curiosity & intellectual skills. Thought-provoking. Acid-free paper. Special discounts to libraries, literacy programs. "The art book offers a superior presentation... includes some fun animal rhymes within the alphabet form...intriguing, unusual art."--THE MIDWEST BOOK REVIEW. "Attractive alphabet primer with its well-executed illustrations, a fun & funny book about animals."--THE BLOOMSBURY REVIEW.
Publisher Provided Annotation.

Baby Animals. (Illus.). 24p. (gr. k-2). 1988. 3.95 (*0-87449-500-8*) Modern Pub NYC.

Baby Animals at Home. (ps-k). 1989. bds. 3.50 (*0-7214-9533-8*) Ladybird Bks.

Ball, Sara. The Animal Show Mix & Match Book. (Illus.). (ps-1). 1992. 4.20 (*1-56021-141-5*) W J Fantasy.

Barr, Marilynn. Big Book of Animal Patterns. (Illus.). 64p. 1993. pap. text ed. 12.95 (*1-878279-67-X*) Evan-Moor Corp.

Barrett, Judi. Animals Should Definitely Not Wear Clothing. Barrett, Ron, illus. 32p. (gr. k-3). 1990. incl. cass. 19.95 (*0-87499-147-1*); pap. 12.95 incl. cass. (*0-87488-146-3*); Set; incl. 4 bks., cass., & guide. pap. 27.95 (*0-87499-148-X*) Live Oak Media.

Bloch, C. Endangered Animals Sticker Book. M. J. Studios Staff, illus. 32p. (Orig.). (gr. k-6). 1993. pap. 3.95 (*1-879424-62-2*) Nickel Pr.

Burton, Marilee R. Tail Toes Eyes Ears Nose. Burton, Marilee R., illus. LC 87-33276. 32p. (ps-1). 1988. PLB 14.89 (*0-06-020874-0*) HarpC Child Bks.

Campbell, Rod. Pop-up Pet Shop. 18p. (ps-1). 1990. pap. 4.95 (*0-689-71385-1*, Aladdin) Macmillan Child Grp.

Ching, Patrick. Exotic Animals in Hawaii. Ching, Patrick, illus. 32p. (Orig.). (ps-6). 1988. pap. 3.95 (*0-935848-56-8*) Bess Pr.

—Native Animals of Hawaii. Ching, Patrick, illus. 32p. (Orig.). (ps-6). 1988. pap. 3.95 (*0-935848-55-X*) Bess Pr.

Crump, Donald J., ed. Animals Showing Off. Chen, Tony, illus. (ps-5). 1988. Set. 21.95 (*0-87044-724-6*) Natl Geog.

Day, O. M. ABCs of Bugs & Beasts. Day, O. M., illus. 31p. (Orig.). (gr. 3-12). 1991. pap. 11.95 (*0-9629795-1-1*) Klar-Iden Pub.

Dragonwagon, Crescent. Alligators & Others All Year Long: A Book of Months. Aruego, Jose & Dewey, Ariane, illus. LC 91-2831. 32p. (gr. k-3). 1993. RSBE 14.95 (*0-02-733091-5*, Macmillan Child Bk) Macmillan Child Grp.

Eichenberg, Fritz. Ape in a Cape: An Alphabet of Odd Animals. Eichenberg, Fritz, illus. LC 52-6908. 26p. (ps-3). 1952. 15.95 (*0-15-203722-5*, HB Juv Bks) HarBrace.

Gardner, Beau. Guess What? LC 85-242. (Illus.). 48p. (ps-3). 1985. PLB 14.93 (*0-688-04983-4*) Lothrop.

Hayes, Kenn. I Know Rhino. (ps). 1993. 14.95 (*1-56729-024-8*) Newport Pubs.

Heath, Dixie. My Alphabet Animals Draw Along Book: Alpahbet Animals Drawing Book. Wexler, Terry, ed. Heath, Dixie, illus. 70p. (gr. k-5). 1994. 12.95 (*0-9637484-0-8*) Knight Pub WA.
MY ALPHABET ANIMALS DRAW ALONG BOOK is unique because of the variety of things it does for children. This book teaches children our alphabet via big, beautiful & colorful illustrations. Writing the letters & then drawing them into animals helps you to visually remember the letters. The reading of the basic sentence also stimulates the memory of the alphabet in young minds. For example: A-Airedale-Amanda's Airedale Abode. B-Bunny-Blue Bonnie Bunny Bites, etc. The children also have draw along friends to help them through the book. Anni Alphadraw, Pencil Dude & Paper Pals Pad take them on a learning & drawing safari. This helps the children feel it's a personal book, with friends helping which is more fun & adventurous. From beginning to end the children are involved with each step. MY ALPHABET ANIMALS DRAW ALONG BOOK also teaches awareness of our endangered animal friends. Seventeen of the animals in this book are endangered--either their lives or their habitat. There's also a glossary of words new to young minds & their meaning. I have taught this book in three different schools & the teachers & children love it - even the 6th graders. The expressions on the illustrations will leave a lasting impression for young & old to keep them coming back for more. Poster available for $6.00.
Publisher Provided Annotation.

Illustrated Encyclopedia of Wildlife, 15 vols. 3152p. (gr. 7 up). 1990. lib. bdg. 495.00 (*1-55905-052-7*) Grey Castle.

Jenkins, Steve. Biggest, Strongest, Fastest. Jenkins, Steve, illus. 32p. (ps-2). 1995. 14.95g (*0-395-69701-8*) Ticknor & Flds Bks Yng Read.

Kuzmier, Kerrie & McCann, Jennifer. Manatees & Dugongs: A Coloring Book in English & Spanish. Inchaustequi, Sixto, tr. Beath, Mary, illus. (ENG & SPA.). 28p. (Orig.). (gr. 3-6). 1991. pap. text ed. 4.00 (*0-685-39509-X*) Ctr Marine Cnsrv.

Lambert, Jonathan. Giant Jungle Pop-up Book: Animals of the Endangered Rain Forest. Lambert, Jonathan, illus. (ps-3). 1992. 28.00 (*1-56021-183-0*) W J Fantasy.

McCay, William. Animals in Danger: A Pop-up Book. Mosley, Keith, illus. 12p. (gr. 1-7). 1990. pap. 12.95 (*0-689-71408-4*, Aladdin) Macmillan Child Grp.

McMillan, Mary. God's ABC Zoo. Grossman, Dan, illus. 48p. (ps-1). 1987. pap. 7.95 (*0-86653-405-9*, SS1802, Shining Star Pubns) Good Apple.

Picture Book of Animals. (Illus.). (ps). 3.50 (*0-7214-0751-X*) Ladybird Bks.

Pienkowski, Jan. Pets. Pienkowski, Jan, illus. 24p. (ps). 1992. pap. 2.95 (*0-671-74518-2*, Little Simon) S&S Trade.

Prince, Pamela. The Best of Friends: Classic Illustrations of Children & Animals. (Illus.). 48p. 1991. 14.00 (*0-517-57620-1*, Harmony) Crown Pub Group.

Reilly, Pauline. Tasmanian Devil. Rolland, Will, illus. 32p. (Orig.). 1993. pap. 6.95 (*0-86417-207-9*, Pub. by Kangaroo Pr AT) Seven Hills Bk Dists.

—Wombat. Rolland, Will, illus. 32p. (Orig.). 1993. pap. 6.95 (*0-86417-148-X*, Pub. by Kangaroo Pr AT) Seven Hills Bk Dists.

Ringling Bros. & Barnum & Bailey Combined Shows, Inc. Staff. Animals of the Circus. Self, Kathy A., ed. LC 90-62395. (Orig.). 1990. pap. 3.50 (*1-878163-01-9*) Ringling Bros.

Sterne, Noelle. Tyrannosaurus Wrecks. Chess, Victoria, illus. LC 78-22499. 32p. (gr. 1-4). 1983. pap. 4.95 (*0-06-443043-X*, Trophy) HarpC Child Bks.

Sullivan, Charles. Alphabet Animals. 1991. 15.95 (*0-8478-1377-0*) Rizzoli Intl.

Troll. Photo Fun Book Baby Animals. 12p. (ps-3). 1991. pap. 5.95 (*0-8167-2085-1*) Troll Assocs.

Tucker, Sian. Nursery Board: Animals. (ps). 1994. pap. 2.95 (*0-671-88259-7*, Little Simon) S&S Trade.

Tyler, J. Dot to Dot on the Farm. (Illus.). 24p. (ps-2). 1991. pap. 3.50 (*0-7460-0595-4*, Usborne) EDC.

Watkins, Dawn L. Wait & See. Altizer, Suzanne R., photos by. (Illus.). 46p. (Orig.). (ps-1). 1991. pap. 4.95 (*0-89084-576-X*) Bob Jones Univ Pr.

Wildsmith, Brian. Animal Tricks. Wildsmith, Brian, illus. (ps-3). 1981. 9.95 (*0-19-279743-3*) OUP.

Woggon, Guillermo. Animales Que Dios Creo. Cranberry, Nola, tr. from ENG. (SPA., Illus.). 16p. (gr. 1-3). 1987. pap. 1.99 (*0-311-38560-5*) Casa Bautista.

Zoo Friends. LC 90-80289. 24p. (ps-2). 1991. pap. 1.95 (*1-56288-077-2*) Checkerboard.

ANIMALS–POETRY

Amery, H., compiled by. Animal Poems. (Illus.). 32p. (gr. 2-6). 1990. (Usborne); pap. 5.95 (*0-7460-0442-7*, Usborne) EDC.

Babson, Jane F. Babson's Bestiary. Babson, Jane F., illus. LC 90-71155. 32p. (ps-4). 1991. casebound 10.95 (*0-940787-02-4*) Winstead Pr.
Second in a learning to read series for children & adults. Illustrated with original art, writing designed to stimulate interest, curiosity & intellectual skills. Thought-provoking. Acid-free paper. Special discounts to libraries, literacy programs. "The art book offers a superior presentation... includes some fun animal rhymes within the alphabet form...intriguing, unusual art."--THE MIDWEST BOOK REVIEW. "Attractive alphabet primer with its well-executed illustrations, a fun & funny book about animals."--THE BLOOMSBURY REVIEW.
Publisher Provided Annotation.

Bernos De Gasztold, Carmen. Prayers from the Ark: Selected Poems. Godden, Rumer, tr. Moser, Barry, illus. 32p. 1992. 16.00 (*0-670-84496-9*) Viking Child Bks.

Bodecker, N. M. Water Pennies & Other Poems. Blegvad, Erik, illus. LC 90-6477. 64p. 1991. SBE 12.95 (*0-689-50517-5*, M K McElderry) Macmillan Child Grp.

Boden, Arthur & Woodside, John. Boden's Beasts. Boden, Art, illus. (gr. 1-5). 1964. 8.95 (*0-8392-3045-1*) Astor-Honor.

Brown, Margaret W. Four Fur Feet. Hubbard, Woodleigh, illus. LC 93-31523. 24p. (ps-1). 1994. 12.95 (*0-7868-0002-X*); PLB 12.89 (*0-7868-2000-4*) Hyprn Child.

Carle, Eric. Dragons Dragons & Other Creatures That Never Were. Carle, Eric, illus. 72p. (ps up). 1991. 18. 95 (*0-399-22105-0*, Philomel) Putnam Pub Group.

Carter, Ann, compiled by. Birds, Beasts, & Fishes: A Selection of Animal Poems. Cartwright, Reg, illus. Carter, Ann, intros. by. LC 90-21493. (Illus.). 64p. (ps up). 1991. SBE 16.95 (*0-02-717776-9*, Macmillan Child Bk) Macmillan Child Grp.

Cassedy, Sylvia & Suetake, Kunihiro. Red Dragonfly on My Shoulder: Haiku. Bang, Molly, illus. LC 91-18443. 32p. (gr. k-5). 1992. 15.00 (*0-06-022624-2*); PLB 14. 89 (*0-06-022625-0*) HarpC Child Bks.

Coats, Lucy. One Hungry Baby: A Bedtime Counting Rhyme. Hellard, Sue, illus. LC 93-42620. 32p. (ps-k). 1994. 9.99 (*0-517-59887-6*) Crown Bks Yng Read.

Cole, William E., ed. An Arkful of Animals: Poems for the Very Young. Munsinger, Lynn, illus. 128p. (gr. 3-7). 1978. 13.45 (*0-395-27205-X*) HM.

Cole, William E., selected by. A Zooful of Animals. Munsinger, Lynn, illus. 96p. (ps-8). 1992. 17.45 (*0-395-52278-1*) HM.

Davis, Charles E. Creatures at My Feet. Neidigh, Sherry, illus. LC 92-81235. 32p. (ps). 1993. 12.95 (*0-87358-560-7*) Northland AZ.

Dec, Myra & Dec, Sam. Wilderness Tails: A Book to Color, Poetry to Share. 32p. (ps-3). 1993. pap. 3.50 (*0-9638192-0-8*) Quinn Pubng.

Driver, Raymond. Animalimericks. 1994. pap. 5.95 (*0-671-87232-X*, Half Moon Bks) S&S Trade.

Edwards, Richard. Moon Frog. Fox-Davies, Sarah, illus. LC 92-53014. 48p. (ps up). 1993. 16.95 (*1-56402-116-5*) Candlewick Pr.

Elias, Joyce. Whose Toes Are Those? Sturm, Cathy, illus. LC 92-8603. (ps). 1992. 11.95 (*0-8120-6215-9*) Barron.

Farber, Norma. When It Snowed That Night. Mathers, Petra, illus. LC 92-27414. 40p. (gr. k up). 1993. 16.00 (*0-06-021707-3*); PLB 15.89 (*0-06-021708-1*) HarpC Child Bks.

Fisher, Robert, ed. Pet Poems. (Illus.). (gr. 1-6). 1989. bds. 12.95 laminated (*0-571-15248-1*) Faber & Faber.

—Pet Poems. Kindberg, Sally, illus. 96p. (gr. 1 up). 1993. pap. 4.95 (*0-571-16830-2*) Faber & Faber.

Florian, Douglas. Beast Feast. LC 93-10720. (gr. 5 up). 1994. write for info. (*0-15-295178-4*) HarBrace.

Gill, Shelley R. Alaska Mother Goose. Cartwright, Shannon, illus. 36p. (Orig.). (gr. k-6). 1987. 14.95 (*0-934007-05-5*); pap. 8.95 (*0-934007-02-0*) Charlesbridge Pub.

Harrison, Michael & Stuart-Clark, Christopher, eds. The Oxford Book of Animal Poems. (Illus.). 160p. 1992. 20.00 (*0-19-276105-6*) OUP.

Hoberman, Mary A. A Fine Fat Pig: And Other Animal Poems. Zeldis, Malcah, illus. LC 90-37403. 32p. (ps-2). 1991. HarpC Child Bks.

Hopkins, Lee B., ed. Creatures: Poems. (Illus.). 32p. (ps-3). 1990. pap. 3.95 (*0-15-220876-3*, Voyager Bks) HarBrace.

Hughes, Langston. The Sweet & Sour Animal Book. Students of the Harlem School for the Arts Staff, illus. Vereen, Ben & Cunningham, Georgeintro. by. (Illus.). 48p. 1994. 15.95 (*0-19-509185-X*) OUP.

Jones, Tim. Wild Critters. Sturgis, Kent, ed. Newman, Leslie, illus. Walker, Tom, photos by. LC 91-7308. (Illus.). 48p. (Orig.). 1992. 15.95x (*0-945397-10-0*); pap. 7.95 (*0-945397-25-9*) Epicenter Pr.

Kennedy, X. J. The Beasts of Bethlehem. McCurdy, Michael, illus. LC 91-38417. 48p. (gr. 1 up). 1992. SBE 13.95 (*0-689-50561-2*, M K McElderry) Macmillan Child Grp.

King-Smith, Dick. Alphabeasts. Blake, Quentin, illus. LC 91-38435. 64p. (gr. 1 up). 1992. SBE 14.95 (*0-02-750720-3*, Macmillan Child Bk) Macmillan Child Grp.

Kitchen, Bert. Gorilla-Chinchilla: And Other Animal Rhymes. Fogelman, Phyllis J., ed. Kitchen, Bert, illus. LC 89-16851. 32p. (ps up). 1990. 13.95 (*0-8037-0770-3*); PLB 13.89 (*0-8037-0771-1*) Dial Bks Young.

Kohen, Clarita. El Conejo y el Coyote. Menicucci, Gina, illus. (SPA.). 16p. (Orig.). (gr. k-5). 1993. PLB 7.50x (*1-56492-100-X*) Laredo.

Kohen, Gabriela. Circus Animals. Sanchez, Jose R., illus. 24p. (Orig.). (gr. k-5). 1993. PLB 9.95x (*1-56492-026-7*) Laredo.

Lacome, Julie. Walking Through the Jungle. Lacome, Julie, illus. LC 92-53018. 32p. (ps). 1993. 13.95 (*1-56402-137-8*) Candlewick Pr.

Larke, Joe. Dopie Dope Grin A Bit Poetry Series. Larke, Karol, illus. (gr. k-6). 1992. write for info. (*0-9620112-9-0*) Grin A Bit.

Lear, Edward. The Owl & the Pussy-Cat. Voce, Louise, illus. LC 90-39673. 32p. (ps up). 1991. 13.95 (*0-688-09536-4*); PLB 13.88 (*0-688-09537-2*) Lothrop.

Lesser, Carolyn. Flamingo Knees. 4th ed. Shles, Larry, illus. 52p. (gr. k-12). 1993. pap. 10.00 (*0-9630604-2-2*) Oakwood MO.
FLAMINGO KNEES, a delightful book of poems by Carolyn Lesser, leads the reader through a variety of short verses featuring Pearl the flamingo & her many 'twists & bends.' Sprinkled throughout the book are poems such as "A Rainbow Named Igor," an iguana; "Low Spots, High Spots," spotted animals; "Lawanda Jean," the girl who hated to brush her teeth; & "Great Crystal Bear," the cold & lonely life of a polar bear, a poem which will soon become a children's picture book published by Harcourt Brace & Co. FLAMINGO KNEES, ISBN 0-9630604-2-2. Paperback retails at $10. THE KNEES KNOCK AGAIN, a second book of Ms. Lesser's poems, adds Ringo Flamingo to the family, along with the adventures of Humperdink the penguin & his problems in learning to swim. Dooley the dog, Miss Gertrude, Mary Margaret, five shaggy llamas & box turtles are some of the fascinating creatures you'll meet in this second book loved by children of all ages. THE KNEES KNOCK AGAIN, ISBN 0-9630604-3-0. Paperback retails at $10. Published by Oakwood Press at new address, Carolyn Lesser Creative, 301 Oak St., Quincy, IL 62301; 217-222-5742.
Publisher Provided Annotation.

Lewis, J. Patrick. A Hippopotamusn't: And Other Animal Poems. Chess, Victoria, illus. 40p. (ps-3). 1994. pap. 4.99 (*0-14-055273-1*, Puff Pied Piper) Puffin Bks.

—Two Legged, Four-Legged, No-Legged Rhymes. Paparone, Pamela, illus. LC 90-20651. 40p. (ps-3). 1991. 13.00 (*0-679-80771-3*); lib. bdg. 13.99 (*0-679-90771-8*) Knopf Bks Yng Read.

Lewis, Patrick. A Hippopotamusn't: And Other Animal Verses. Fogelman, Phyllis J., ed. Chess, Victoria, illus. LC 87-24579. 40p. (ps-3). 1990. 12.95 (*0-8037-0518-2*); PLB 12.89 (*0-8037-0519-0*) Dial Bks Young.

McLoughland, Beverly. Hippo's a Heap: And Other Animal Poems. 32p. (ps-3). 1993. 14.95 (*1-56397-017-1*) Boyds Mills Pr.

Mado, Michio. The Animals: Selected Poems. HRM the Empress of Japan, tr. Mitsumasa Anno, illus. LC 92-10356. (ENG & JPN.). 48p. (ps up). 1992. SBE 16.95 (*0-689-50574-4*, M K McElderry) Macmillan Child Grp.

Marsh, James. Bizarre Birds & Beasts: Animal Verses. 1991. 12.95 (*0-8037-1046-1*) Dial Bks Young.

Metaxes, Eric. The Birthday ABC. Raglin, Tim, illus. LC 93-46896. 1995. 14.00 (*0-671-88306-2*, S&S BFYR) S&S Trade.

Mora, Pat. Listen to the Desert - Que Dice el Desierto? Mora, Francisco X., illus. LC 93-31463. (ENG & SPA.). (ps-2). 1994. 14.95 (*0-395-67292-9*, Clarion Bks) HM.

Munsterberg, Peggy. Beastly Feasts: Tasty Treats for Animal Appetites. Gallup, Tracy, photos by. LC 94-2951. (Illus.). Date not set. write for info. (*0-8037-1481-5*); pap. write for info. (*0-8037-1482-3*) Dial Bks Young.

Nister, Ernest. Animal Playmates. (Illus.). 10p. 1990. 5.95 (*0-399-21957-9*, Philomel Bks) Putnam Pub Group.

Numeroff, Laura J. Dogs Don't Wear Sneakers. Mathieu, Joe, illus. LC 92-27007. 1993. pap. 14.00 (*0-671-79525-2*, S&S BFYR) S&S Trade.

Polette, Nancy. Mother Goose's Animals. (Illus.). 128p. (gr. 1-4). 1992. pap. 12.95 (*1-879287-13-7*) Bk Lures.

Prelutsky, Jack. Zoo Doings: Animal Poems. Zelinsky, Paul O., illus. LC 82-11996. 80p. (gr. 1-3). 1983. 13.00 (*0-688-01782-7*); PLB 12.93 (*0-688-01784-3*) Greenwillow.

Richardson, Polly. Animal Poems. (ps-3). 1992. 12.95 (*0-8120-6283-3*) Barron.

Ryder, Joanne. Mockingbird Morning. Nolan, Dennis, illus. LC 88-21305. 32p. (gr. k-3). 1989. RSBE 14.95 (*0-02-777961-0*, Four Winds) Macmillan Child Grp.

Sheehan, William. Nature's Wonderful World in Rhyme. Maeno, Itoko, illus. LC 93-15247. 1993. 14.95 (*0-911655-47-6*) Advocacy Pr.

Singer, Marilyn. Turtle in July. Pinkey, Jerry, illus. LC 93-14430. 32p. (gr. 3-7). 1994. pap. 4.95 (*0-689-71805-5*, Aladdin) Macmillan Child Grp.

Taylor, Donald G. Story Picture Poem & Coloring Book for Children. (Illus.). 30p. (ps-3). 1993. pap. 6.95 (*0-9638002-0-5*) D G Taylor.
The book is in two sections. The first section consists of 10 animals in beautiful color, each accompanied by an original story poem. The second section consists of eight of the same animals in black & white that appear in the first section. The child then attempts to color the animals in the second section as close as possible to the animals in the first section. This makes it interesting & challenging. This book is unique in that the child learns by seeing & comparing while doing. The little story poems enhance the child's reading ability & create an urge to MEMORIZE these cute little stories. This is a very educational little book. The drawings are large & easily discernable & THE PRINT IS LARGE & EASY TO READ. To order, write or call Publisher, Donald G. Taylor, 3651 S. Arville St., Las Vegas, NV 89103. (702) 221-8380. Publisher's price $1.75. Suggested retail price to $6.95. Educational & fun. Great for little budding artists & poets.
Publisher Provided Annotation.

Waters, Fiona, ed. Whiskers & Paws. Julian-Ottie, Vanessa, illus. LC 89-77349. 32p. 1990. 9.95 (*0-940793-51-2*, Pub. by Crocodile Bks) Interlink Pub.

Wilkes, Angela, compiled by. Animal Nursery Rhymes. LC 92-52818. (Illus.). 32p. (ps-k). 1992. 13.95 (*1-56458-122-5*) Dorling Kindersley.

Yolen, Jane. Animal Fare: Zoological Nonsense Poems. Street, Janet, illus. LC 92-44931. (gr. 4 up). 1994. 14.95 (*0-15-203550-8*) Harbrace.

—Ring of Earth: A Child's Book of Seasons. Wallner, John, illus. LC 86-4800. 32p. (ps up). 1986. 14.95 (*0-15-267140-4*, HB Juv Bks) HarBrace.

ANIMALS–PROTECTION

see Animals–Treatment

ANIMALS–SONGS AND MUSIC

Craver, Mike. Beaver Ball at the Bug Club. Kaghan, Joan, illus. 32p. (ps-3). 1992. bds. 12.00 (*0-374-30662-1*) FS&G.

King, Bob. Sitting on the Farm. Slavin, Bill, illus. LC 91-17253. 32p. (ps-1). 1992. 13.95 (*0-531-05985-5*); lib. bdg. 13.99 (*0-531-08585-6*) Orchard Bks Watts.

Langstaff, John & Rojankovsky, Feodor. Frog Went A-Courtin' Rojankovsky, Feodor, illus. LC 55-5237. (ps-3). 1983. 14.95 (*0-15-230214-X*, HB Juv Bks) HarBrace.

—Over in the Meadow. Rojankovsky, Feodor, illus. LC 57-8587. (ps-3). 1957. 14.95 (*0-15-258854-X*, HB Juv Bks) HarBrace.

Manushkin, Fran. My Christmas Safari. Alley, R. W., illus. LC 92-28643. 32p. (ps-1). 1993. 13.99 (*0-8037-1294-4*); PLB 13.89 (*0-8037-1295-2*) Dial Bks Young.

Paxton, Tom. The Animals' Lullaby. Ingraham, Erick, illus. LC 92-18841. 40p. (ps up). 1993. 15.00 (*0-688-10468-1*); PLB 14.93 (*0-688-10469-X*) Morrow Jr Bks.

Simon, Paul. At the Zoo. (ps up). 1991. 15.00 (*0-385-41771-3*); PLB 15.99 (*0-385-41906-6*) Doubleday.

Young, Roger & Caggiano, Rosemary. The Safari. 48p. (gr. k-8). 1979. pap. 14.95 (*0-86704-006-8*) Clarus Music.

ANIMALS–TRAINING

see also names of animals with the subdivision Training, e.g., Dogs–Training; Horses–Training; etc.

Cebulash, Mel. Catnapper. (gr. 3-8). 1992. PLB 8.95 (*0-89565-878-X*) Childs World.

Duden, Jane. Animal Handlers & Trainers. LC 89-31125. (Illus.). 48p. (gr. 5-6). 1989. text ed. 11.95 RSBE (*0-89686-427-8*, Crestwood Hse) Macmillan Child Grp.

ANIMALS–TREATMENT

Catalano, Julie. Animal Welfare. Train, Russell E., intro. by. LC 93-26841. 1994. write for info. (*0-7910-1591-2*); pap. write for info. (*0-7910-1616-1*) Chelsea Hse.

Cohen, Daniel. Animal Rights: A Handbook for Young Adults. LC 92-40875. (Illus.). 128p. (gr. 7 up). 1993. PLB 15.90 (*1-56294-219-0*) Millbrook Pr.

Day, Nancy. Animal Experimentation: Cruelty or Science? (Illus.). 128p. (gr. 6 up). 1994. lib. bdg. 17.95 (*0-89490-578-3*) Enslow Pubs.

Field, Shelly. Careers As an Animal Rights Activist. Rosen, Ruth, ed. (gr. 7-12). 1993. PLB 14.95 (*0-8239-1465-8*); pap. 9.95 (*0-8239-1722-3*) Rosen Group.

Guernsey, JoAnn B. Animal Rights. LC 90-33664. (Illus.). 48p. (gr. 5-6). 1990. text ed. 12.95 RSBE (*0-89686-534-7*, Crestwood Hse) Macmillan Child Grp.

Kennedy, Teresa. Bringing Back the Animals. Williams, Sue, illus. 32p. (gr. 3 up). 1991. lib. bdg. 15.95 incl. dust jacket (*0-944256-06-6*) Amethyst Bks.

Kervin, Rosalind. Equal Rights for Animals. LC 92-6262. 1993. 11.90 (*0-531-14227-2*) Watts.

Lee. Animal Rights. 1991. 12.95s.p. (*0-86593-112-7*) Rourke Corp.

Loeper, John J. Crusade for Kindness: Henry Bergh & the ASPCA. LC 90-27682. (Illus.). 112p. (gr. 3-7). 1991. SBE 13.95 (*0-689-31560-0*, Atheneum Child Bk) Macmillan Child Grp.

McCoy, J. J. Animals in Research: Issues & Conflicts. LC 92-21117. (Illus.). 128p. (gr. 9-12). 1993. PLB 13.90 (*0-531-13023-1*) Watts.

Nierman, Lewis G. Lefty's Place. Nierman, Lewis G., illus. 32p. (gr. 1-4). 1994. 18.95g (*0-9636820-0-8*) Kindness Pubns.

Patterson, Charles. Animal Rights. LC 92-44286. (Illus.). 104p. (gr. 6 up). 1993. lib. bdg. 17.95 (*0-89490-468-X*) Enslow Pubs.

Rohr, Janelle, ed. Animal Rights: Opposing Viewpoints. LC 89-2227. (Illus.). 235p. (gr. 10 up). 1989. PLB 17.95 (*0-89908-440-0*); pap. 9.95 (*0-89908-415-X*) Greenhaven.

Scott, Elaine. Safe in the Spotlight: The Dawn Animal Agency & the Sanctuary for Animals. Miller, Margaret, photos by. LC 90-49677. (Illus.). 80p. (gr. 3 up). 1991. 12.95 (*0-688-08177-0*); PLB 12.88 (*0-688-08178-9*, Morrow Jr Bks) Morrow Jr Bks.

Steffens, Bradley. Animal Rights: Distinguishing Between Fact & Opinion. LC 89-2200. (Illus.). 32p. (gr. 3-6). 1990. PLB 10.95 (*0-89908-635-7*) Greenhaven.

Taylor, Dave. Endangered Desert Animals. Kalman, Bobbie, ed. (Illus.). 32p. (Orig.). (gr. 3-6). 1992. PLB 15.95 (*0-86505-534-3*); pap. 7.95 (*0-86505-544-0*) Crabtree Pub Co.

—Endangered Island Animals. Kalman, Bobbie, ed. (Illus.). 32p. (Orig.). (gr. 3-6). 1992. PLB 15.95 (*0-86505-532-7*); pap. 7.95 (*0-86505-542-4*) Crabtree Pub Co.

—Endangered Savannah Animals. Kalman, Bobbie, ed. (Illus.). 32p. (Orig.). (gr. 3-6). 1992. PLB 15.95 (*0-86505-535-1*); pap. 7.95 (*0-86505-545-9*) Crabtree Pub Co.

Twinn, M. Who Cares about Animal Rights? Lavie, Arlette, illus. LC 92-10852. 1992. 7.95 (*0-85953-358-1*, Pub. by Childs Play UK) Childs Play.

Watson, Mary G. Beds & Bedding. Vincer, Carole, illus. 24p. (Orig.). (gr. 3 up). 1988. pap. 10.00 (*0-901366-27-7*, Pub. by Threshold Bks) Half Halt Pr.

Wolkomir, Joyce & Wolkomir, Richard. Junkyard Bandicoots & Other Tales of the World's Endangered Species. LC 92-11114. 128p. (gr. 4-7). 1992. pap. text ed. 9.95 (*0-471-57261-6*) Wiley.

ANIMALS, AQUATIC

see Fresh-Water Animals; Marine Animals

ANIMALS, CRUELTY TO

see Animals–Treatment

ANIMALS, DOMESTIC

see Domestic Animals

ANIMALS, EXTINCT

see Extinct Animals

ANIMALS, FICTITIOUS

see Animals, Mythical

ANIMALS, FOSSIL

see Fossils

ANIMALS, FRESH-WATER

see Fresh-Water Animals

ANIMALS, IMAGINARY

see Animals, Mythical

ANIMALS, MARINE

see Marine Animals

ANIMALS, MYTHICAL

see also names of mythical animals, e.g. Unicorn, etc.

Anderson, Wayne. Dragon. LC 91-4790. (ps-3). 1992. 15.00 (*0-671-78397-1*, Green Tiger) S&S Trade.

Bertrand, Lynne. One Day, Two Dragons. Street, Janet, illus. LC 91-32743. 32p. (ps-2). 1992. 14.00 (*0-517-58411-5*); PLB 14.99 (*0-517-58413-1*) Crown Bks Yng Read.
Bradshaw, Gillian. The Land of Gold. LC 91-31810. 160p. (gr. 5 up). 1992. 14.00 (*0-688-10576-9*) Greenwillow.
Burgess, Thornton W. Old Mother West Wind's Neighbors. (gr. 5-6). 19.95 (*0-88411-786-3*, Pub. by Aeonian Pr) Amereon Ltd.
Cabat, Erni, illus. Erni Cabat's Magical World of Monsters. Cohen, Daniel, text by. (Illus.). 32p. (gr. 4 up). 1992. 14.00 (*0-525-65087-3*, Cobblehill Bks) Dutton Child Bks.
Carle, Eric. Dragons Dragons & Other Creatures That Never Were. Carle, Eric, illus. 72p. (ps up). 1991. 18. 95 (*0-399-22105-0*, Philomel) Putnam Pub Group.
Cosgrove, Stephen. Muffin Muncher. James, Robin, illus. 32p. (Orig.). (gr. 1-4). 1975. pap. 2.95 (*0-8431-0561-5*) Price Stern.
De Goscinny, Rene. La Serpe d'Or. (gr. 7-9). 1990. 19.95 (*0-8288-5126-3*, FC874) Fr & Eur.
Demi. Demi's Dragons & Fantastic Creatures. Demi, illus. 50p. (ps-2). 1993. 19.95 (*0-8050-2564-2*, Bks Young Read) H Holt & Co.
De Paola, Tomie. The Unicorn & the Moon. LC 94-20297. (Illus.). 1994. 12.95 (*0-382-24659-4*); PLB 14. 95 (*0-382-24658-6*); pap. 4.95 (*0-382-24660-8*) Silver Burdett Pr.
Discovering Dragons Activity Book. (Illus.). (ps-6). pap. 2.95 (*0-565-01005-0*, Pub. by Natural Hist Mus) Parkwest Pubns.
Fitch, Sheree. Sleeping Dragons All. 1991. PLB 14.99 (*0-385-42001-3*) Doubleday.
Fletcher, Susan. Dragon's Milk. LC 88-35059. 224p. (gr. 6 up). 1989. SBE 15.95 (*0-689-31579-1*, Atheneum Child Bk) Macmillan Child Grp.
—Dragon's Milk. LC 91-31358. 256p. (gr. 3-7). 1992. pap. 3.95 (*0-689-71623-0*, Aladdin) Macmillan Child Grp.
Gaffron, Norma. Unicorns: Opposing Viewpoints. LC 89-11660. (Illus.). 112p. (gr. 5-8). 1989. PLB 14.95 (*0-89908-063-4*) Greenhaven.
Gannett, Ruth S. My Father's Dragon. Gannett, Ruth S., illus. LC 48-6527. 88p. (gr. 2-5). 1948. 14.95 (*0-394-88460-4*) Random Bks Yng Read.
Grahame, Kenneth. Reluctant Dragon. Shepard, Ernest H., illus. LC 89-1658. 58p. (gr. 3-6). 1938. 12.95 (*0-8234-0093-X*); pap. 4.95 (*0-8234-0755-1*) Holiday.
—The Reluctant Dragon. Hague, Michael, illus. LC 83-209. 48p. (gr. 2-4). 1983. 16.95 (*0-8050-1112-9*, Bks Young Read) H Holt & Co.
—The Reluctant Dragon. Richardson, I. M., ed. Ekman, Marlene, illus. LC 87-10906. 32p. (gr. k-4). 1988. lib. bdg. 9.79 (*0-8167-1059-7*); pap. text ed. 1.95 (*0-8167-1060-0*) Troll Assocs.
Hillman, E. Min-Yo & the Moon Dragon. Wallner, J., illus. 1992. 14.95 (*0-15-254230-2*, HB Juv Bks) HarBrace.
Hjelm, J. Thaddeus Jones & the Dragon. LC 68-56830. (Illus.). 64p. (gr. 2-5). 1968. PLB 10.95 (*0-87783-039-8*); pap. 3.94 deluxe ed. (*0-87783-110-6*) Oddo.
Kelley, True. Buggly Bear's Hiccup Cure. LC 81-16903. (Illus.). 48p. (ps-3). 1982. 5.95 (*0-8193-1081-6*); PLB 5.95 (*0-8193-1082-4*) Parents.
King-Smith, Dick. The Swoose. (Illus.). 56p. (gr. 3-7). 1994. 12.95 (*1-56282-658-1*); PLB 12.89 (*1-56282-659-X*) Hyprn Child.
Lathrop, Dorothy B. Animals of the Bible. Fish, Helen D., selected by. Lathrop, Dorothy, illus. LC 86-46118. 68p. (ps up). 1937. 16.00 (*0-397-31536-8*, Lipp Jr Bks); PLB 15.89 (*0-397-30047-6*) HarpC Child Bks.
Leaf, Margaret. Eyes of the Dragon. Young, Ed, illus. LC 85-11670. 32p. (ps-2). 1987. 14.95 (*0-688-06155-9*); PLB 14.88 (*0-688-06156-7*) Lothrop.
Lear, Edward & Nash, Ogden. Scroobious Pip. Burkert, Nancy E., illus. LC 68-10373. (gr. 3 up). 1968. HarpC Child Bks.
Leedy, Loreen. A Number of Dragons. Leedy, Loreen, illus. LC 85-730. 32p. (ps-1). 1985. reinforced bdg. 14. 95 (*0-8234-0568-0*) Holiday.
Marx, Doug. Mythical Beasts. 48p. (gr. 3-4). 1991. PLB 11.95 (*1-56065-046-X*) Capstone Pr.
Moore, Jo E. Dragons. (Illus.). 48p. (gr. 2-5). 1989. pap. 5.95 (*1-55799-161-8*) Evan-Moor Corp.
Mountain, Lee. El Fuego del Dragon - Dragon Fire. (ENG & SPA., Illus.). 23p. (gr. k-1). 1992. pap. 23.75 (*0-89061-720-1*) Jamestown Pubs.
—Pelea con Dragon - Dragon Fight. (ENG & SPA., Illus.). 24p. (gr. k-1). 1992. pap. 23.75 (*0-89061-719-8*) Jamestown Pubs.
Nesbit, Edith. The Book of Dragons. (gr. 4-6). 1986. pap. 4.95 (*0-440-40696-X*, Pub. by Yearling Classics) Dell.
Peet, Bill. Cyrus the Unsinkable Sea Serpent. LC 74-20646. (Illus.). 48p. (gr. k-3). 1982. 13.45 (*0-395-20272-8*); pap. 4.80 (*0-395-31389-9*) HM.
—How Droofus the Dragon Lost His Head. Peet, Bill, illus. LC 75-135136. 48p. (gr. k-3). 1983. 13.45 (*0-395-15085-X*); pap. 4.80 (*0-395-34066-7*) HM.
Prelutsky, Jack. The Baby Uggs Are Hatching. LC 81-7266. (Illus.). 32p. (ps up). 1989. pap. 3.95 (*0-688-09239-X*, Mulberry) Morrow.
Ragache, Gilles. Dragons. LC 90-25902. (Illus.). 48p. (gr. 4-8). 1991. PLB 13.95 (*1-85435-265-2*) Marshall Cavendish.
Rice, James. Lyn & the Fuzzy. Rice, James, illus. LC 75-19096. 40p. (gr. 2-6). 1975. 12.95 (*0-88289-087-5*) Pelican.
Scavone, Daniel C. Vampires: Opposing Viewpoints. LC 90-40131. (Illus.). 112p. (gr. 5-8). 1990. PLB 14.95 (*0-89908-080-4*) Greenhaven.
Schotter, Richard & Schotter, Roni. There's a Dragon about: A Winter's Revel. Alley, R. W., illus. LC 93-46421. 32p. (ps-2). 1994. 14.95 (*0-531-06858-7*); lib. bdg. 14.99 (*0-531-08708-5*) Orchard Bks Watts.
Selsam, Millicent E. & Hunt, Joyce. A First Look at Animals with Horns. Springer, Harriett, illus. (gr. 1 up). 1989. 10.95 (*0-8027-6871-7*); PLB 11.85 (*0-8027-6872-5*) Walker & Co.
Sendak, Maurice. Where the Wild Things Are. 25th anniversary ed. Sendak, Maurice, illus. LC 63-21253. 48p. (ps up). 1988. 15.00 (*0-06-025492-0*); PLB 14.89 (*0-06-025493-9*) HarpC Child Bks.
Shute, Linda. Clever Tom & the Leprechaun. 1990. pap. 3.95 (*0-590-43170-6*) Scholastic Inc.
Snyder, Zilpha K. The Egypt Game. LC 67-2717. (gr. 4-6). 1986. pap. 4.50 (*0-440-42225-6*, YB) Dell.
Sobol, Donald J. Encyclopedia Brown's Book of Wacky Animals. Enik, Ted, illus. LC 84-22608. 128p. (gr. 3-7). 1985. 11.95 (*0-688-04152-3*) Morrow Jr Bks.
Sutcliff, Rosemary. Dragon Slayer. (gr. 4-6). 1976. pap. 3.99 (*0-14-030254-9*, Puffin) Puffin Bks.
—The Minstrel & the Dragon Pup. Clark, Emma C., illus. LC 92-53012. 48p. (ps up). 1993. 16.95 (*1-56402-098-3*) Candlewick Pr.
Thayer, Jane. Popcorn Dragon. McCue, Lisa, illus. LC 88-39855. 32p. (ps up). 1989. 12.95 (*0-688-08340-4*); PLB 12.88 (*0-688-08876-7*, Morrow Jr Bks) Morrow Jr Bks.
Voigt, Cynthia. Jackaroo. LC 85-7954. 320p. (gr. 8 up). 1985. SBE 18.95 (*0-689-31123-0*, Atheneum Child Bk) Macmillan Child Grp.
Walton, Robert. The Dragon & The Lemon Tree. Allen, Ginny, illus. LC 89-92122. 86p. (gr. 3-7). 1989. write for info. (*0-9623802-0-2*) Pisces Pr CA.
Yep, Laurence. Dragon War. LC 91-28921. 320p. (gr. 7 up). 1992. 15.00 (*0-06-020302-1*); PLB 14.89 (*0-06-020303-X*) HarpC Child Bks.

ANIMALS, PREHISTORIC
see Fossils

ANIMALS, SEA
see Marine Animals

ANIMALS AND CIVILIZATION
Arnosky, Jim. A Kettle of Hawks. Arnosky, Jim, illus. LC 89-12459. 32p. (gr. k-4). 1990. 13.95 (*0-688-09279-9*); lib. bdg. 13.88 (*0-688-09280-2*) Lothrop.
Burton, John A. Close to Extinction. LC 88-50523. (Illus.). 32p. (gr. 5-8). 1992. PLB 12.40 (*0-531-17383-6*, Gloucester Pr) Watts.
Lampton, Christopher & Kline, Marjory. Endangered Species. LC 87-25161. (Illus.). 128p. (gr. 7-12). 1988. PLB 13.40 (*0-531-10510-5*) Watts.

ANIMALS IN ART
see also Animal Painting and Illustration
Blizzard, Gladys S. Come Look with Me: Animals in Art. LC 92-5357. 32p. (gr. 1-8). 1992. 13.95 (*1-56566-013-7*) Thomasson-Grant.
Chwast, Seymour. Paper Pets: Make Your Own Three Dogs, 2 Cats, 1 Parrot, 1 Rabbit, 1 Monkey. LC 92-23609. (Illus.). 24p. 1993. pap. 19.95 (*0-8109-2531-1*) Abrams.
Green, Jen. Making Crazy Animals. LC 91-33868. (Illus.). 32p. (gr. 2-4). 1992. PLB 12.40 (*0-531-17324-0*, Gloucester Pr) Watts.
MacClintock, Dorcas. Animals Observed: A Look at Animals in Art. LC 91-36795. (Illus.). 64p. 1993. SBE 18.95 (*0-684-19323-X*, Scribners Young Read) Macmillan Child Grp.
Micklethwait, Lucy, selected by. I Spy a Lion: Animals in Art. LC 93-30017. 48p. 1994. 19.00 (*0-688-13230-8*); PLB 18.93 (*0-688-13231-6*) Greenwillow.
Richardson, Wendy & Richardson, Jack. Animals: Through the Eyes of Artists. LC 90-34276. (Illus.). 48p. (gr. 4 up). 1991. pap. 7.95 (*0-516-49281-0*) Childrens.
Roalf, Peggy. Dogs. LC 93-20585. (Illus.). 48p. (gr. 3-7). 1993. PLB 14.89 (*1-56282-530-5*); pap. 6.95 (*0-685-70878-0*) Hyprn Ppbks.
—Dogs. LC 93-10585. (Illus.). (gr. 3-7). 1993. PLB 14.89 (*1-56282-531-3*) Hyprn Child.
Rojas, Hector. Origami Animals. LC 92-18266. (Illus.). 160p. (gr. 3-9). 1992. 24.95 (*0-8069-8648-4*) Sterling.
Simpson, Anne. How to Draw Wild Animals. Botto, Lisa C., illus. LC 91-26928. 32p. (gr. 2-6). 1991. text ed. 10.65 (*0-8167-2481-4*); pap. text ed. 1.95 (*0-8167-2482-2*) Troll Assocs.
Wilson, Elizabeth. Bibles & Bestiaries: A Guide to Illuminated Manuscripts. LC 94-6687. 1994. write for info. (*0-374-30685-0*) FS&G.

ANNIVERSARIES
see Holidays;
see names of special days, e.g. Fourth of July; etc.

ANNULMENT OF MARRIAGE
see Divorce

ANSWERS TO QUESTIONS
see Questions and Answers

ANT
see Ants

ANTARCTIC EXPEDITIONS
see Antarctic Regions

ANTARCTIC REGIONS
see also Scientific Expeditions; South Pole
Asimov, Isaac. How Did We Find Out about Antarctica? Wool, David, illus. (gr. 5-8). 1979. PLB 11.85 (*0-8027-6371-5*) Walker & Co.
Billings, Henry. Antarctica. LC 94-9142. (Illus.). 128p. (gr. 5-9). 1994. PLB 27.40 (*0-516-02624-0*) Childrens.
Cowcher, Helen. Antarctica. Cowcher, Helen, illus. Grammer, Red, contrib. by. (Illus.). 32p. (gr. k-3). 1990. incl. audiocassette 19.95 (*0-924483-24-5*); incl. audio cass. tape & stuffed penguin toy 44.95 (*0-924483-65-2*) Soundprints.
—Antartida: Antarctica. (ps-3). 1993. 15.00 (*0-374-30370-3*) FS&G.
Davis, Lloyd S., photos by & text by. Penguin: A Season in the Life of the Adelie Penguin. LC 93-36407. (gr. 3 up). 1994. 18.95 (*0-15-200070-4*, HB Juv Bks) HarBrace.
Flaherty, Leo & Goetzmann, William H. Roald Amundsen & the Quest for the South Pole. Collins, Michael, intro. by. (Illus.). 112p. (gr. 6-12). 1993. PLB 18.95 (*0-7910-1308-1*) Chelsea Hse.
George, Michael. Antarctica. LC 93-18281. 1994. PLB 18.95 (*0-88682-600-4*) Creative Ed.
Hackwell, W. John. Desert of Ice: Life & Work in Antarctica. LC 89-35002. (Illus.). 48p. (gr. 5 up). 1991. SBE 14.95 (*0-684-19085-0*, Scribners Young Read) Macmillan Child Grp.
Hart, Trish. Antarctic Diary. Hart, Trish, illus. LC 93-110. 1994. pap. write for info. (*0-383-03675-5*) SRA Schl Grp.
—There Are No Polar Bears down There. Hart, Trish, illus. LC 92-31949. 1993. 3.75 (*0-383-03597-X*) SRA Schl Grp.
McMillan, Bruce. Summer Ice, Antarctic Life. McMillan, Bruce, illus. LC 93-38831. 1994. write for info. (*0-395-66561-2*) HM.
Naveen, Ron. Antarctica. (Illus.). 16p. (Orig.). (gr. 10 up). 1992. pap. text ed. 2.75 (*0-89278-124-6*, 45-9624) Carolina Biological.
Pollak, Richard A., ed. Explore Antarctica! (Illus.). 58p. (gr. 5-9). 1991. 3-ring binder/laserdisc 295.00 (*0-922649-14-6*) ETC MN.
—Explore Antarctica! Barcode Guide. 188p. (gr. 5-9). 1992. spiral bdg. 125.00 (*0-922649-15-4*) ETC MN.
Poncet, Sally. Destination South Georgia: An Antarctic Voyage. Osborne, Ben, photos by. LC 94-13376. (gr. 4 up). 1995. 17.00 (*0-02-774905-3*) Macmillan Child Grp.
Pringle, Laurence. Antarctica. 64p. 1992. pap. 15.00 jacketed (*0-671-73850-X*, S&S BFYR) S&S Trade.
Sabin, Francene. Arctic & Antarctic Regions. Eitzen, Allan, illus. LC 84-2730. 32p. (gr. 3-6). 1985. PLB 9.49 (*0-8167-0234-9*); pap. text ed. 2.95 (*0-8167-0235-7*) Troll Assocs.
Sauvain, Philip. Robert Scott in the Antarctic. LC 93-18209. (Illus.). 32p. (gr. 4-6). 1993. text ed. 13.95 RSBE (*0-87518-532-0*, Dillon) Macmillan Child Grp.
Stewart, Gail B. Antarctica. LC 91-8523. (Illus.). 48p. (gr. 6-7). 1991. text ed. 12.95 RSBE (*0-89686-656-4*, Crestwood Hse) Macmillan Child Grp.
Stone, Lynn M. Antarctica. 48p. (gr. k-4). 1985. PLB 12. 85 (*0-516-01265-7*) Childrens.
Swan, Robert. Destination: Antarctica. Mear, Roger & Ward, Rebecca, photos by. (Illus.). 48p. (gr. 2-7). 1989. pap. 5.95 (*0-590-41286-8*) Scholastic Inc.
Winckler, Suzanne & Rodgers, Mary M. Our Endangered Planet: Antarctica. 64p. (gr. 4-6). 1991. PLB 21.50 (*0-8225-2506-2*) Lerner Pubns.

ANTARCTIC REGIONS–FICTION
L'Engle, Madeleine. Troubling a Star. LC 93-50956. (gr. 7 up). 1994. 15.00 (*0-374-37783-9*) FS&G.

ANTELOPES
Ahlstrom, Mark. The Pronghorn. LC 85-28054. (Illus.). 48p. (gr. 5). 1986. text ed. 12.95 RSBE (*0-89686-292-5*, Crestwood Hse) Macmillan Child Grp.
Hoffman, Mary. Antelope. LC 86-17715. (Illus.). 24p. (gr. k-5). 1987. PLB 9.95 (*0-8172-2703-2*); pap. 3.95 (*0-8114-6870-4*) Raintree Steck-V.
Stone, Lynn. Antelopes. (Illus.). 24p. (gr. k-5). 1990. lib. bdg. 11.94 (*0-86593-053-8*); lib. bdg. 8.95s.p. (*0-685-36345-7*) Rourke Corp.

ANTHONY, SUSAN BROWNELL, 1820-1906
AESOP Enterprises, Inc. Staff & Crenshaw, Gwendolyn J. Susan B. Anthony: A Crusader for Womanhood. 14p. (gr. 3-12). 1991. pap. write for info. incl. cassette (*1-880771-09-8*) AESOP Enter.
Clinton, Susan. The Story of Susan B. Anthony. Canaday, Ralph, illus. LC 86-9613. 32p. (gr. 3-6). 1986. PLB 12. 30 (*0-516-04705-1*) Childrens.

Gehret, Jeanne. Susan B. Anthony: And Justice for All. (Illus.). 120p. (gr. 4 up). 1994. 14.95 (*0-9625136-9-5*); pap. 6.95 (*0-9625136-8-7*) Verbal Images Pr. Who WAS that woman whose image is on the one-dollar coin? Find out with this new book, which SCHOOL LIBRARY JOURNAL calls "a readable, lively biography of the women's suffrage advocate, abolitionist & temperance crusader." So important was Anthony that in 1995 the U.S. will celebrate her 175th birthday along with

the 75th anniversary of the women's suffrage (19th) amendment. This new biography, along with its extensive curriculum guide, provides everything teachers need to prepare Language Arts or Social Studies students for these anniversaries or for Women's History Month (March). It personalizes women's suffrage, abolition, temperance & the Civil War through the experiences of Susan B. Anthony & other noted reformers, including Elizabeth Cady Stanton, Frederick Douglass & Lucy Stone. "The book is well-written & well-researched," writes the Chicago STAR, "in a very understandable style. Gehret is a talented writer." American history students will appreciate the ample study helps, archival photographs & action-packed illustrations. The fully-reproducible teacher handbook (50pp., $19.95) contains complete chapter synopses, a 20-minute play, journal & essay exercises, role play, numerous discussion topics & quizzes. It activates all seven intelligences. Hardcover, softcover & workbook are all available through Quality Books, Follett, Baker & Taylor, & the publisher.
Publisher Provided Annotation.

Klingel, Cynthia & Zadra, Dan. Susan B. Anthony. (Illus.). 32p. 1987. PLB 14.95 (*0-88682-164-9*) Creative Ed.
Levin, Pamela. Susan B. Anthony: Fighter for Women's Rights. (Illus.). 80p. (gr. 3-5). 1993. PLB 13.95 (*0-7910-1762-1*, Am Art Analog); pap. write for info. (*0-7910-1965-9*, Am Art Analog) Chelsea Hse.
Monsell, Helen A. Susan B. Anthony: Champion of Women's Rights. Fiorentino, Al, illus. LC 86-10716. 192p. (gr. 2-6). 1986. pap. 3.95 (*0-02-041800-0*, Aladdin) Macmillan Child Grp.
Susan B. Anthony: Mini-Play. (gr. 5 up). 1974. 6.50 (*0-89550-365-4*) Stevens & Shea.
Weisberg, Barbara. Susan B. Anthony. Horner, Matina, intro. by. (Illus.). 112p. (gr. 5 up). 1988. lib. bdg. 17. 95x (*1-55546-639-7*); pap. 9.95 (*0-7910-0408-2*) Chelsea Hse.

ANTHONY OF PADUA, SAINT, 1195-1231
Windeatt, Mary F. St. Anthony of Padua. Harmon, Gedge, illus. 32p. (gr. 1-5). 1989. Repr. of 1954 ed. wkbk. 3.00 (*0-89555-369-4*) TAN Bks Pubs.

ANTHROPOGEOGRAPHY
see also Man–Influence of Environment
Stewart, G. In the Desert. (Illus.). 32p. (gr. 3-8). 1989. lib. bdg. 15.74 (*0-86592-106-7*); 11.95s.p. (*0-685-58594-8*) Rourke Corp.

ANTHROPOLOGY
see also Anthropogeography; Archeology; Civilization; Color of Man; Ethnology; Language and Languages; Man; Social Change
also names of races and tribes
Aliki. Dinosaur Bones. Aliki, illus. LC 85-48246. 32p. (ps-3). 1988. 11.00 (*0-690-04549-2*, Crowell Jr Bks); PLB 14.89 (*0-690-04550-6*) HarpC Child Bks.
Bell, Neill. Only Human: Why We Are the Way We Are. Clifford, Sandy, illus. LC 83-9826. 128p. (gr. 4 up). 1983. pap. 9.95 (*0-316-08818-8*) Little.
Bisel, Sara C. Secrets of Vesuvius: Exploring the Mysteries of an Ancient Buried City. (gr. 4-7). 1991. 15.95 (*0-590-43850-6*, Scholastic Hardcover) Scholastic Inc.
Diagram Group Staff & Lambert, David. The Field Guide to Early Man. (Illus.). 256p. (gr. 8-12). 1988. 25.95x (*0-8160-1517-1*) Facts on File.
FS Staff & Gamlin, Linda. The Human Race. Hayward, Ron, illus. LC 88-50506. 40p. (gr. 1-6). 1988. PLB 12. 40 (*0-531-17118-3*, Gloucester Pr) Watts.
Gallagher, I. J. The Case of the Ancient Astronauts. LC 77-10822. (Illus.). 48p. (gr. 4 up). 1977. PLB 20.70 (*0-8172-1059-8*) Raintree Steck-V.
Snedden, Genevra S. Mountain Cattle & Frontier People. 2nd ed. (Illus.). 160p. (gr. 6). 1989. pap. 16.00 (*0-685-32946-1*) Intervale Pub Co.
Tulling, Virginia. Threatened Cultures. (Illus.). 48p. (gr. 5 up). 1990. lib. bdg. 18.60 (*0-86592-096-6*); lib. bdg. 13. 95s.p. (*0-685-36381-3*) Rourke Corp.

ANTHROPOLOGY–BIOGRAPHY
Jerome, Leah. Dian Fossey. (gr. 4-7). 1991. pap. 3.50 (*0-553-15929-1*) Bantam.
Weitzman, David. Human Culture. LC 93-16791. (Illus.). 288p. (gr. 4-6). 1994. SBE 22.95 (*0-684-19438-4*, Scribners Young Read) Macmillan Child Grp.

ANTIBIOTICS
see also names of specific antibiotics, e.g. Penicillin; etc.

ANTIDOTES
see Poisons

ANTIPATHIES
see Prejudices and Antipathies

ANTIQUES
see also Collectors and Collecting
Dunnan, Nancy. Collectibles. Raston, Emily, ed. (Illus.). 128p. (gr. 7 up). 1990. PLB 9.95 (*0-382-09918-4*); PLB 11.24s.p. (*0-685-47044-X*); pap. 5.95 (*0-382-24029-4*); pap. 5.96s.p. (*0-685-47045-8*) Silver Burdett Pr.
Smith, Brad R. Country Antiques: A Child's Guide. Sagendorf, Kit, illus. 64p. (Orig.). (gr. 1-3). 1987. pap. 11.95 (*0-9618645-0-8*) Sanford Hse Pr.

ANTIQUITIES
see Archeology; Bible–Antiquities; Indians of North America–Antiquities; Man–Origin and Antiquity; Man, Prehistoric
see names of countries, cities, etc. with the subdivision Antiquities, e.g. U. S.–Antiquities; etc

ANTIQUITIES, BIBLICAL
see Bible–Antiquities

ANTI-REFORMATION
see Reformation

ANTISLAVERY
see Slavery in the U. S.

ANTS
Abell, J. The Ant. (Illus.). 50p. (ps-2). 1993. 25.00 (*1-56611-064-5*); pap. 15.00 (*1-56611-065-3*) Jonas.
Benedict, Kitty. The Ant: My First Nature Books. Felix, Monique, illus. 32p. (gr. k-2). 1993. pap. 2.95 (*1-56189-174-6*) Amer Educ Pub.
Berger, Melvin. The World of Ants. (Illus.). 16p. (ps-2). 1993. pap. text ed. 14.95 (*1-56784-008-6*) Newbridge Comms.
—The World of Ants: Student Edition. (Illus.). 16p. (ps-2). 1993. pap. text ed. 14.95 (*1-56784-033-7*) Newbridge Comms.
Costigan, Shirleyann. The Little Ant. Boyd, Patti, illus. 16p. (Orig.). (gr. 1-3). 1992. pap. text ed. 29.95 big. bk. (*1-56334-066-6*); pap. text ed. 6.00 small bk. (*1-56334-072-0*) Hampton-Brown.
Demuth, Patricia B. Ants. Schnidler, S. D., illus. LC 93-1769. (ps-3). 1994. 14.95 (*0-02-728467-0*, Macmillan Child Bk) Macmillan Child Grp.
Dorros, Arthur. Ant Cities. Dorros, Arthur, illus. LC 85-48244. 32p. (ps-3). 1987. (Crowell Jr Bks); PLB 14.89 (*0-690-04570-0*, Crowell Jr Bks) HarpC Child Bks.
—Ant Cities. Dorros, Arthur, illus. LC 85-48244. 32p. (gr. k-3). 1988. pap. 4.95 (*0-06-445079-1*, Trophy) HarpC Child Bks.
Fichter, George S. Bees, Wasps, & Ants. Kest, Kristin, illus. 36p. (gr. k-3). 1993. 4.95 (*0-307-11434-1*, 11434, Golden Pr) Western Pub.
Fischer-Nagel, Heiderose & Fischer-Nagel, Andreas. An Ant Colony. Fischer-Nagel, Andreas & Fischer-Nagel, Heiderose, illus. 48p. (gr. 2-5). 1989. PLB 19.95 (*0-87614-333-8*); pap. 6.95 (*0-87614-519-5*) Carolrhoda Bks.
Hawcock, David. Ant. Montgomery, Lee, illus. LC 93-85131. 12p. (ps-3). 1994. 5.99 (*0-679-85469-X*) Random Bks Yng Read.
Julivert, Maria A. The Fascinating World of Ants. Marcel Socias Studio Staff & Arridondo, F., illus. 32p. (gr. 3-7). 1991. 11.95 (*0-8120-6281-7*) Barron.
Lisker, Tom. Terror in the Tropics: The Army Ants. LC 77-10765. (Illus.). 48p. (gr. 4 up). 1983. PLB 20.70 (*0-8172-1060-1*) Raintree Steck-V.
Losito, Linda. The Ant on the Ground. Oxford Scientific Films Staff, photos by. LC 89-4460. (Illus.). 32p. (gr. 4-6). 1989. PLB 17.27 (*0-8368-0111-3*) Gareth Stevens Inc.
Moses, Amy. If I Were an Ant. Dunnington, Tom, illus. LC 92-12947. 32p. (ps-2). 1993. pap. 2.95 (*0-516-42011-9*) Childrens.
Nanao, Jun. Life of the Ant. Pohl, Kathy, ed. LC 85-28198. (Illus.). 32p. (gr. 3-7). 1986. PLB 10.95 (*0-8172-2539-0*) Raintree Steck-V.
Overbeck, Cynthia. Ants. LC 81-17216. (Illus.). 48p. (gr. 4 up). 1982. PLB 19.95 (*0-8225-1468-0*, First Ave Edns); pap. 5.95 (*0-8225-9525-7*, First Ave Edns) Lerner Pubns.
Parramon, J. M. The Fascinating World of Ants. (Illus.). 48p. (gr. 3-7). 1991. pap. 7.95 (*0-8120-4721-4*) Barron.
Patent, Dorothy H. Looking at Ants. Patent, Dorothy H., illus. LC 89-1943. 48p. (ps-4). 1989. reinforced 12.95 (*0-8234-0771-3*) Holiday.
Poole, Lynn & Poole, Gray. Weird & Wonderful Ants. Petersen, R. F., illus. (gr. 5 up). 1961. 8.95 (*0-8392-3041-9*) Astor-Honor.
Retan, Walter. Armies of Ants. Cassels, Jean, illus. LC 93-29782. 48p. (ps-4). 1994. pap. 3.50 (*0-590-47616-5*, Cartwheel) Scholastic Inc.
Ross, Edward S. Ants. LC 92-44257. (gr. 2-6). 1993. 15. 95 (*1-56766-056-8*) Childs World.
Sabin, Francene. Amazing World of Ants. Conner, Eulala, illus. LC 81-7492. 32p. (gr. 2-4). 1982. PLB 11.59 (*0-89375-558-3*); pap. text ed. 2.95 (*0-89375-559-1*) Troll Assocs.
Watts, Barrie. Ants. Watts, Barrie, photos by. LC 89-49721. (Illus.). 32p. (gr. k-4). 1991. PLB 11.40 (*0-531-14042-3*); pap. 4.95 (*0-531-15615-X*) Watts.

ANTS–FICTION
Allinson, Beverley. Effie. Reid, Barbara, illus. 32p. (ps-1). 1991. 11.95 (*0-590-44045-4*, Scholastic Hardcover) Scholastic Inc.
Clements, Jehan. Alfred the Ant, An Ant Who Lives & Has Fun in Central Park: The First Storytelling "Flip Over" Picture Book. Clements, Jehan, illus. LC 89-61138. 48p. (gr. k-3). 1991. 19.95 (*0-9622500-0-7*) Strytllr Co.
Davis, Rhonda K. Purnell the Curious Ant, Vol. I. (Illus.). 30p. (Orig.). (ps-1). 1992. pap. 3.00 (*1-881967-15-8*) Express In Writing.
—Purnell the Curious Ant. 16p. (ps-5). 1992. pap. 3.00 (*1-881967-01-8*) Express In Writing.
Farmer, Tony. How Small Is an Ant? (ps-3). pap. 3.95 (*0-85953-518-5*) Childs Play.
Kratky, Lada J. El Chivo en la Huerta (Small Book) Remkiewicz, Frank, illus. (SPA.). 16p. (Orig.). (gr. k-3). 1992. pap. text ed. 6.00 (*1-56334-080-1*) Hampton-Brown.
Lehman, James H. The Saga of Shakespeare Pintlewood & the Great Silver Fountain Pen. Raschka, Christopher, illus. LC 90-82303. 32p. (gr. k-3). 1990. PLB 13.95 (*1-878925-00-8*) Brotherstone Pubs.
Moses, Amy. If I Were an Ant. Dunnington, Tom, illus. LC 92-12947. 32p. (ps-2). 1992. PLB 10.25 (*0-516-02011-0*) Childrens.
—If I Were an Ant. Dunnington, Tom, illus. LC 92-12947. 32p. (ps-2). 1993. pap. 2.95 (*0-516-42011-9*) Childrens.
Pellowski, Michael J. Who Can't Follow an Ant? Swan, Susan, illus. LC 85-14009. 48p. (Orig.). (gr. 1-3). 1986. PLB 10.59 (*0-8167-0592-5*); pap. text ed. 3.50 (*0-8167-0593-3*) Troll Assocs.
Philpot, Lorna & Philpot, Graham. Amazing Anthony Ant. Philpot, Lorna & Philpot, Graham, illus. 24p. (gr. k-3). 1994. 13.00 (*0-679-85622-6*) Random Bks Yng Read.
Pinczes, Elinor J. One Hundred Hungry Ants. MacKain, Bonnie, illus. 32p. (gr. k-3). 1993. 13.95 (*0-395-63116-5*) HM.
Quackenbush, Robert M. Henry's Awful Mistake. LC 92-32870. (Illus.). 42p. (ps-3). 1992. PLB 13.27 (*0-8368-0882-7*); PLB 13.26 s.p. (*0-685-61513-8*) Gareth Stevens Inc.
Ray, Stephen & Murdoch, Kathleen. The Ant Nest. Stewart, Chantal, illus. LC 92-34254. 1993. 4.25 (*0-383-03614-3*) SRA Schl Grp.
Ross, Andrea. Chester's Coloring Book. Ross, Andrea, illus. 70p. (Orig.). (gr. k-2). 1992. 7.00 (*1-56002-016-4*, Univ Edtns) Aegina Pr.
Sushiela. The Ant & the Grasshopper: A Love Story. Sushiela, illus. LC 89-92067. 129p. (Orig.). (gr. 5 up). 1990. pap. 15.95 (*0-9623363-1-9*) Running Water.
Wolkstein, Diane. Step by Step. Smith, Joseph A., illus. LC 93-14667. 40p. (ps up). 1994. 15.00g (*0-688-10315-4*); PLB 14.93 (*0-688-10316-2*) Morrow Jr Bks.
Zippy the Ant Loses Her Way. LC 93-85481. 20p. (ps-1). 1994. 3.99 (*0-89577-569-7*) RD Assn.

ANXIETY
see Fear

APARTMENT HOUSES
see also Housing

APARTMENT HOUSES–FICTION
Alessandrini, Jean. Mystery & Chocolate. (Illus.). (gr. 3-8). 1992. PLB 8.95 (*0-89565-898-4*) Childs World.
Baker, Barbara. Oh, Emma. Stock, Catherine, illus. LC 93-7767. 144p. (gr. 2-5). 1993. pap. 3.99 (*0-14-036357-2*, Puffin) Puffin Bks.
Escudie, Rene. Little John's Fears. (Illus.). (gr. 3-8). 1992. PLB 8.95 (*0-89565-886-0*) Childs World.
Greenwald, Sheila. My Fabulous New Life. LC 92-44928. 160p. (gr. 3-7). 1993. 10.95 (*0-15-277693-1*, Browndeer Pr); pap. 3.95 (*0-15-276716-9*, Browndeer Pr) HarBrace.
Herman, Charlotte. Millie Cooper, Take a Chance. Cogancherry, Helen, illus. 112p. (gr. 3 up). 1990. pap. 3.95 (*0-14-034119-6*, Puffin) Puffin Bks.
Hest, Amy. Pete & Lily. LC 85-13992. 120p. (gr. 4-7). 1986. 11.95 (*0-89919-354-4*, Clarion Bks) HM.
—Pete & Lily. LC 92-42319. 128p. (gr. 6 up). 1993. pap. 4.95 (*0-688-12490-9*, Pub. by Beech Tree Bks) Morrow.
Hill, Elizabeth S. Evan's Corner. Speidel, Sandra, illus. LC 92-25334. 1993. pap. 4.99 (*0-14-054406-2*) Puffin Bks.
Hurwitz, Johanna. Busybody Nora. Hoban, Lillian, illus. 64p. (gr. 2-5). 1991. pap. 3.99 (*0-14-034592-2*, Puffin) Puffin Bks.
—Superduper Teddy. Hoban, Lillian, illus. 80p. (gr. 2-5). 1991. pap. 3.95 (*0-14-034593-0*, Puffin) Puffin Bks.
Koechlin, Lionel. Apartment for Rent. (Illus.). 32p. (gr. k-2). 1991. 12.95 (*0-89565-742-2*) Childs World.
Maxwell, William. Heavenly Tenants. (gr. 4-7). 1992. 13. 95 (*0-930407-25-3*) Parabola Bks.
Myers, Walter D. The Young Landlords. (gr. 6-10). 1992. 17.75 (*0-8446-6569-X*) Peter Smith.
Petersen, P. J. I Hate Company. James, Betsy, illus. LC 94-2801. 48p. (gr. 2-4). 1994. 12.99 (*0-525-45329-6*, DCB) Dutton Child Bks.
Roberts, Willo D. The Pet-Sitting Peril. LC 82-13757. 192p. (gr. 4-6). 1983. SBE 14.95 (*0-689-30963-5*, Atheneum Child Bk) Macmillan Child Grp.
Ross, Pat. M & M & the Halloween Monster. Hafner, Marylin, illus. LC 91-50294. 48p. (gr. 1-2). 1991. text ed. 10.95 (*0-670-83003-8*) Viking Child Bks.
—M & M & the Halloween Monster. Hafner, Marylin, illus. LC 93-15183. 64p. (gr. 2-5). 1993. pap. 3.99 (*0-14-034247-8*, Puffin) Puffin Bks.

Shapiro, Arnold L. The Neighbor Game: A Pop-up, Figure-It-Out Book. Billin-Frye, Paige, illus. LC 93-11199. 14p. (gr. 1-5). 1994. 12.99 (*0-8037-1239-1*) Dial Bks Young.

Thesman, Jean. Nothing Grows Here. LC 93-45739. 208p. (gr. 4 up). 1994. 14.00 (*0-06-024457-7*); PLB 13.89 (*0-06-024458-5*) HarpC Child Bks.

APES

see also Chimpanzees

Barrett, Norman S. Monos y Simios. LC 90-71420. (SPA., Illus.). 32p. (gr. k-4). 1991. PLB 11.90 (*0-531-07918-X*) Watts.

Carwardine, Mark. Monkeys & Apes. Young, Richard G., ed. Camm, Martin, illus. LC 89-32808. 45p. (gr. 3-5). 1989. PLB 14.60 (*0-944483-28-3*) Garrett Ed Corp.

Demuth, Patricia. Gorillas. Lopez, Paul, illus. LC 93-39844. 48p. (ps-1). 1994. 7.99 (*0-448-40218-1*, G&D); pap. 3.50 (*0-448-40217-3*, G&D) Putnam Pub Group.

Fitzpatrick, Michael. Apes. (Illus.). 32p. (gr. 4-6). 1991. 13.95 (*0-237-60176-1*, Pub. by Evans Bros Ltd) Trafalgar.

Fowler, Allan. Gentle Gorillas & Other Apes. LC 93-38590. (Illus.). 32p. (ps-2). 1994. PLB 12.85 (*0-516-06022-8*) Childrens.

Green, Carl R. & Sanford, William R. The Gorilla. LC 85-9991. (Illus.). 48p. (gr. 5). 1986. text ed. 12.95 RSBE (*0-89686-269-0*, Crestwood Hse) Macmillan Child Grp.

Hogan, Paula Z. The Gorilla. LC 79-13602. (Illus.). 32p. (gr. 1-4). 1979. PLB 19.97 (*0-8172-1501-8*) Raintree Steck-V.

Irvine, Georgeanne. Raising Gordy the Gorilla. (ps-6). 1993. pap. 5.95 (*0-671-79615-1*, S&S BFYR) S&S Trade.

Lemmon, Tess. Apes. Butler, John, illus. LC 92-37693. 32p. (gr. 2-4). 1993. 15.95 (*0-395-66901-4*) Ticknor & Flds Bks Yng Read.

Lumley, Kathryn W. Monkeys & Apes. LC 82-12779. (Illus.). (gr. k-4). 1982. PLB 12.85 (*0-516-01633-4*); pap. 4.95 (*0-516-41633-2*) Childrens.

Mattern, Joanne. Monkeys & Apes. LC 92-28080. (Illus.). 24p. (gr. 4-7). 1992. pap. text ed. 1.95 (*0-8167-2962-X*) Troll Assocs.

Maynard, Thane. Primates: Apes, Monkeys, Prosimians. (Illus.). 56p. (gr. 2 up). 1994. PLB 14.91 (*0-531-11169-5*) Watts.

Morris, Dean. Monkeys & Apes. rev. ed. LC 87-16688. (Illus.). 48p. (gr. 3). 1987. PLB 10.95 (*0-8172-3211-7*) Raintree Steck-V.

Redmond, Ian. Gorillas. LC 90-46477. (Illus.). 32p. (gr. k-4). 1991. 12.40 (*0-531-18395-5*, Pub. by Bookwright Pr) Watts.

Simon. Gorillas. (gr. 4 up). Date not set. 16.00 (*0-06-023033-9*); PLB 15.89 (*0-06-023034-7*) HarpC Child Bks.

Stone, Lynn. Gorillas. (Illus.). 24p. (gr. k-5). 1990. lib. bdg. 8.95s.p. (*0-86593-063-5*); 11.94 (*0-685-36318-X*) Rourke Corp.

Wexo, John B. Apes. 24p. (gr. 4). 1989. PLB 14.95 (*0-88682-265-3*) Creative Ed.

—Baby Animals. 24p. (gr. 4). 1989. PLB 14.95 (*0-88682-270-X*) Creative Ed.

Whitehead, Patricia. Monkeys. Dodson, Bert, illus. LC 81-11439. 32p. (gr. k-2). 1982. PLB 11.59 (*0-89375-670-9*); pap. text ed. 2.95 (*0-89375-671-7*) Troll Assocs.

Wildlife Education, Ltd. Staff. Apes. Hynes, Robert, et al, illus. 20p. (Orig.). (gr. 5 up). 1981. pap. 2.75 (*0-937934-03-8*) Wildlife Educ.

—Gorillas. Orr, Richard & Stuart, Walter, illus. 24p. 1992. 13.95 (*0-937934-78-X*) Wildlife Educ.

—Orangutans. Meltzer, Dave, illus. 20p. (Orig.). (gr. 5 up). 1980. pap. 2.75 (*0-937934-02-X*) Wildlife Educ.

—Orangutans. (Illus.). 24p. (gr. 5 up). 1992. 13.95 (*0-937934-83-6*) Wildlife Educ.

APES–FICTION

Buehner, Caralyn & Buehner, Mark. The Escape of Marvin the Ape. LC 91-10795. (Illus.). 32p. (ps-3). 1992. 14.00 (*0-8037-1123-9*); PLB 13.89 (*0-8037-1124-7*) Dial Bks Young.

Eichenberg, Fritz. Ape in a Cape: An Alphabet of Odd Animals. Eichenberg, Fritz, illus. LC 52-6908. 32p. (ps-3). 1988. pap. 4.95 (*0-15-607830-9*, Voyager Bks) HarBrace.

Knight, Hilary. Where's Wallace? Knight, Hilary, illus. LC 64-19717. (ps-3). 1964. 15.00 (*0-06-023170-X*); PLB 14.89 (*0-06-023171-8*) HarpC Child Bks.

Reese, Bob. Ape Escape. Reese, Bob, illus. 1983. 7.95 (*0-89868-147-2*); pap. 2.95 (*0-89868-146-4*) ARO Pub.

—The Ape Team. Reese, Bob, illus. 1983. 7.95 (*0-89868-145-6*); pap. 2.95 (*0-89868-144-8*) ARO Pub.

—Apricot Ape. Reese, Bob, illus. 1983. 7.95 (*0-89868-141-3*); pap. 2.95 (*0-89868-140-5*) ARO Pub.

—Going Bananas. Reese, Bob, illus. 1983. 7.95 (*0-89868-143-X*); pap. 2.95 (*0-89868-142-1*) ARO Pub.

—Honest Ape. Reese, Bob, illus. 1983. 7.95 (*0-89868-149-9*); pap. 2.95 (*0-89868-148-0*) ARO Pub.

—The Jungle Train. Reese, Bob, illus. 1983. 7.95 (*0-89868-151-0*); pap. 2.95 (*0-89868-150-2*) ARO Pub.

—Zero Word Going Ape Series, 6 bks. Reese, Bob, illus. 1983. Set. 47.70 (*0-89868-139-1*); Set. pap. 29.50 (*0-89868-138-3*) ARO Pub.

APICULTURE

see Bees

APOLLO PROJECT

see also headings beginning with Lunar and Moon

Charleston, Gordon. Armstrong Lands on the Moon. LC 93-32918. (Illus.). 32p. (gr. 4 up). 1994. text ed. 13.95 RSBE (*0-87518-530-4*, Dillon) Macmillan Child Grp.

Englehart, Steve. Countdown to the Moon. LC 94-5135. (Illus.). 96p. (Orig.). 1994. pap. 3.99 (*0-380-77538-7*, Camelot) Avon.

Fraser, Mary A. One Giant Leap. Fraser, Mary A., illus. LC 92-41044. 40p. (gr. 3-7). 1993. 15.95 (*0-8050-2295-3*) H Holt & Co.

Furniss, Tim. The First Men on the Moon. Bull, Peter, illus. LC 88-24166. 32p. (gr. 4-6). 1989. PLB 11.90 (*0-531-18240-1*, Pub. by Bookwright Pr) Watts.

Gold, Susan D. Countdown to the Moon. LC 91-30360. (Illus.). 48p. (gr. 5-6). 1992. text ed. 12.95 RSBE (*0-89686-689-0*, Crestwood Hse) Macmillan Child Grp.

Stein, R. Conrad. Apollo Eleven. 2nd ed. LC 91-33220. 32p. (gr. 3-6). 1992. PLB 12.30 (*0-516-06651-X*) Childrens.

Vogt, Gregory. Apollo & the Moon Landing. (Illus.). 112p. (gr. 4-6). 1991. PLB 15.90 (*1-878841-31-9*); pap. 4.95 (*1-878841-37-8*) Millbrook Pr.

APOSTLES

Hodges. Stephen, the First Martyr. 24p. (Orig.). (gr. k-4). 1985. pap. 1.99 (*0-570-06194-6*, 59-1295) Concordia.

Hutchinson, Joy. Twelve Friends Counting Book about Jesus's Disciples. LC 91-71037. 32p. (gr. 2 up). 1991. pap. 4.99 (*0-8066-2559-7*, 9-2559) Augsburg Fortress.

APPALACHIAN MOUNTAINS–FICTION

Bates, Artie A. Ragsale. Chapman-Crane, Jeff, illus. LC 94-17366. (gr. 1-8). 1995. write for info. (*0-395-70030-2*) HM.

Bradfield, Carl. Tecumseh's Trail: The Appalachian Trail, Then & Now. (Illus.). 137p. (Orig.). (gr. 8-12). Date not set. pap. write for info. (*0-9632319-3-6*) ASDA Pub.

Breeding, Robert L. From London to Appalachia. Moore, Erin C., illus. 200p. (gr. 4-7). 1991. pap. 9.95 (*1-880258-03-X*) Thriftecon.

Cleaver, Vera & Cleaver, Bill. Where the Lilies Bloom. LC 75-82402. (Illus.). 176p. (gr. 7 up). 1991. PLB 14.89 (*0-397-32500-2*, Lipp Jr Bks) HarpC Child Bks.

Cutlip, Ralph V. Mountain Massacres & Other Stories of Appalachia. Hallinan, Brenda C., illus. 167p. (Orig.). (gr. 8 up). 1986. pap. 6.50 (*0-317-47675-0*) B Cutlip.

Hamilton, Virginia. M. C. Higgins, the Great. LC 72-92439. 288p. (gr. 7 up). 1974. SBE 15.95 (*0-02-742480-4*, Macmillan Child Bk) Macmillan Child Grp.

Miller, Jim W. Newfound. LC 89-42540. 256p. (gr. 7 up). 1989. 14.95 (*0-531-05845-X*); PLB 14.99 (*0-531-08445-0*) Orchard Bks Watts.

Mills, Lauren. The Rag Coat. (Illus.). (ps-3). 1991. 15.95 (*0-316-57407-4*) Little.

Rawls, Wilson. Where the Red Fern Grows. (gr. 7 up). 1992. 16.95 (*0-553-08900-5*, Starfire) Bantam.

APPALACHIAN MOUNTAINS–SOCIAL LIFE AND CUSTOMS

Anderson, Joan W. Pioneer Children of Appalachia. (gr. 4-7). 1990. pap. 5.70 (*0-395-54792-X*, Clarion Bks) HM.

Jones, Loyal. Appalachian Values. Brunner, Warren E., photos by. (Illus.). 144p. (gr. 8 up). 1994. 19.95 (*0-945084-43-9*) J Stuart Found.

Logue, Frank. Appalachian Trail Fun Book. (ps-3). 1993. pap. 6.95 (*0-917953-60-6*) Appalachian Trail.

Rylant, Cynthia. Appalachia: The Voices of Sleeping Birds. (Illus.). 32p. (gr. k up). 1991. 14.95 (*0-15-201605-8*) HarBrace.

APPARATUS, SCIENTIFIC

see Scientific Apparatus and Instruments

APPARITIONS

see also Ghosts

Warner, John & Warner, Margaret. Apparitions. (Illus.). 160p. (gr. 6 up). 1987. pap. text ed. 7.75 (*0-89061-465-2*) Jamestown Pubs.

APPLE

Davies, Kay & Oldfield, Wendy. My Apple. Pragoff, Fiona, photos by. LC 94-7107. (Illus.). 32p. (gr. 1 up). 1994. PLB 17.27 (*0-8368-1114-3*) Gareth Stevens Inc.

Fowler, Allan. Apples of Your Eye. LC 94-10944. (Illus.). 32p. (ps-2). 1994. PLB 14.40 (*0-516-06026-0*); pap. text ed. 3.95 (*0-516-46026-9*) Childrens.

Jensen, Patricia A. Johnny Appleseed Goes a-Planting. Hogan, Patricia M., illus. LC 93-4811. 32p. (gr. k-2). 1993. PLB 11.59 (*0-8167-3159-4*); pap. text ed. 2.95 (*0-8167-3160-8*) Troll Assocs.

Johnson, Sylvia A. Apple Trees. Koike, Hiro, illus. LC 83-16230. 48p. (gr. 4 up). 1983. PLB 19.95 (*0-8225-1479-6*) Lerner Pubns.

McMillan, Bruce. Apples, How They Grow. (Illus.). 48p. (ps-3). 1979. 17.45 (*0-395-27806-6*) HM.

Maestro, Betsy. How Do Apples Grow? Maestro, Giulio, illus. LC 91-9468. 32p. (gr. k-4). 1992. 15.00 (*0-06-020055-3*); PLB 14.89 (*0-06-020056-1*) HarpC Child Bks.

—How Do Apples Grow? Maestro, Giulio, illus. LC 91-9468. 32p. (gr. k-3). 1993. pap. 4.95 (*0-06-445117-8*, Trophy) HarpC Child Bks.

Micucci, Charles. The Life & Times of the Apple. LC 90-22779. (Illus.). 32p. (ps-3). 1992. 14.95 (*0-531-05939-1*); lib. bdg. 14.99 (*0-531-08539-2*) Orchard Bks Watts.

Nottridge, Rhoda. Apples. (Illus.). 32p. (gr. 1-4). 1991. PLB 14.95 (*0-87614-655-8*) Carolrhoda Bks.

Patent, Dorothy H. An Apple a Day: From Orchard to You. Munoz, William, photos by. LC 89-33504. (Illus.). 64p. (gr. 3-7). 1990. 13.95 (*0-525-65020-2*, Cobblehill Bks) Dutton Child Bks.

Valat, Pierre-Marie, illus. Pomme. (FRE.). (ps-1). 1989. 13.95 (*2-07-035702-3*) Schoenhof.

Watts, Barrie. Apple Tree. (Illus.). 24p. (gr. k-4). 1991. PLB 7.95 (*0-382-09436-0*); pap. 3.95 (*0-382-24339-0*) Silver Burdett Pr.

Western Promotional Book Staff. Apple. (ps). 1994. 0.95 (*0-307-13460-1*) Western Pub.

APPLE II (COMPUTER)

Schiller, David. My First Computer Book: Apple II Series. LC 90-50367. 64p. (ps-2). 1991. pap. 17.95 (*0-89480-368-9*, 1368) Workman Pub.

Vernier, David L., ed. Chaos in the Laboratory & Thirteen Other Science Projects Using the Apple II. LC 91-90900. (Illus.). 288p. (Orig.). (gr. 9 up). 1991. pap. 25.95 (*0-918731-46-1*) Vernier Soft.

APPLE COMPUTERS

see also Macintosh (Computer)

Kemnitz, Thomas M. & Mass, Lynne. Kids Working with Computers: The Apple BASIC Manual. Schlendorf, Lori, illus. 42p. (gr. 4-7). 1983. pap. 4.99 (*0-89824-092-1*) Trillium Pr.

Luehrmann, Arthur & Peckham, Herbert. Appleworks Date Bases: A Hands-On Guide. (Illus.). 166p. (Orig.). (gr. 7-12). 1987. pap. text ed. 11.95 (*0-941681-03-3*); tchr's. ed. 24.95 (*0-941681-11-4*); 5.25 inch disk 19.95 (*0-941681-00-9*); tchr's. guide 14.95 (*0-941681-08-4*) Computer Lit Pr.

—Appleworks Spreadsheets: A Hands-On Guide. (Illus.). 160p. (Orig.). (gr. 7-12). 1987. pap. text ed. 11.95 (*0-941681-05-X*); tchr's. set 24.95 (*0-941681-12-2*); tchr's. guide 14.95 (*0-685-67549-1*); 5.25 inch disk 19.95 (*0-685-67550-5*) Computer Lit Pr.

—Hands-on Appleworks: A Guide to Word Processing, Data Bases & Spreadsheets, 3 bks. LC 87-836. (Illus.). 478p. (Orig.). (gr. 7-12). 1987. Set. pap. text ed. 21.95 (*0-941681-07-6*); Set. tchr's. ed. 34.95 (*0-941681-13-0*); tchr's. guide 14.95 (*0-685-58103-9*); 5.25 inch disk 19.95 (*0-685-67553-X*) Computer Lit Pr.

Rozakis, Laurie. Steven Jobs. LC 92-43268. (gr. 5 up). 1993. 15.93 (*0-86592-001-X*); 11.95s.p. (*0-685-66327-2*) Rourke Corp.

Taitt, Kathy. Apple, Vol. 1. 59p. (gr. 4-12). 1983. pap. text ed. 11.95 (*0-88193-001-6*) Create Learn.

—Apple, Vol. 2. 61p. (gr. 4-12). 1983. pap. text ed. 11.95 (*0-88193-002-4*) Create Learn.

—Apple, Vol. 3. 55p. (gr. 5-12). 1983. pap. text ed. 11.95 (*0-88193-003-2*) Create Learn.

—Apple, Vol. 4. 57p. (gr. 5-12). 1983. pap. text ed. 11.95 (*0-88193-004-0*) Create Learn.

—Apple, Vol. 5. 57p. (gr. 6-12). 1983. pap. text ed. 11.95 (*0-88193-005-9*) Create Learn.

—Apple, Vol. 6. 68p. (gr. 6-12). 1984. pap. text ed. 11.95 (*0-88193-006-7*) Create Learn.

APPLIED PSYCHOLOGY

see Psychology, Applied

APPLIED SCIENCE

see Technology

APPRAISAL OF BOOKS

see Books and Reading; Books and Reading–Best Books; Criticism; Literature–History and Criticism

APPRECIATION OF MUSIC

see Music–Analysis, Appreciation

APPRENTICES–FICTION

Cartwright, Pauline. The Bird Chain. Cooper-Brown, Jean, illus. LC 93-20805. 1994. 4.25 (*0-383-03736-0*) SRA Schl Grp.

Llorente, Pilar M. Apprentice. (gr. 4-7). 1993. 13.00 (*0-374-30389-4*) FS&G.

APRIL FOOLS' DAY

Kelley, Emily. April Fool's Day. Nobens, Cheryl A., illus. LC 82-23559. 48p. (gr. k-4). 1983. PLB 14.95 (*0-87614-218-8*); pap. 3.95 (*0-87614-481-4*) Carolrhoda Bks.

Kroll, Steven. It's April Fools' Day. (ps-3). 1991. pap. 2.50 (*0-590-44348-8*) Scholastic Inc.

AQUARIUMS

see also Fish Culture; Goldfish

Barrie, Anmarie. A Step-by-Step Book about Our First Aquarium. (Illus.). 64p. 1987. 3.95 (*0-86622-454-8*, SK003) TFH Pubns.

Boyd, Kevin W. The Complete Aquarium Problem Solver. (Illus.). 32p. (gr. 10). 1989. pap. write for info. Boylen.

Broekel, Ray. Aquariums & Terrariums. LC 82-4428. (gr. k-4). 1982. 12.85 (*0-516-01660-1*) Childrens.

—Tropical Fish. LC 82-19738. (Illus.). 48p. (gr. k-4). 1983. PLB 12.85 (*0-516-01687-3*) Childrens.

Curtis, Patricia. Aquatic Animals in the Wild & in Captivity. (Illus.). 64p. (gr. 3-8). 1992. 16.00 (*0-525-67384-9*, Lodestar Bks) Dutton Child Bks.

Dewhurst, William. Your First Aquarium Plants. (Illus.). 34p. (Orig.). (gr. 9-12). 1991. pap. 1.95 (*0-86622-112-3*, YF-101) TFH Pubns.

Evans, Mark. Fish. Caras, Roger, intro. by. LC 92-53476. (Illus.). 48p. (gr. 3-7). 1993. 9.95 (*1-56458-222-1*) Dorling Kindersley.

Field, Nancy & Machlis, Sally. Discovery Book for the Seattle Aquarium. rev. & abr. ed. Machlis, Sally, illus. 32p. (gr. 1-6). 1987. pap. 3.95 (*0-941042-07-3*) Dog Eared Pubns.

Gerstenfeld, Sheldon L. The Aquarium Take-along Book. Harvey, Paul, illus. 128p. (gr. 2-5). 1994. pap. 6.99 (*0-14-036019-0*) Puffin Bks.

Gilbert, Mariana. Your First Goldfish. (Illus.). 36p. (Orig.). 1991. pap. 1.95 (*0-86622-065-8*, YF-108) TFH Pubns.

Parramon, J. M. My First Visit to the Aquarium. Sales, G., illus. 32p. (ps). 1990. pap. 6.95 (*0-8120-4304-9*) Barron.

Quinn, John R. The Kid's Fish Book: How to Catch, Keep, & Observe Your Own Native Fish. LC 93-31691. 1994. pap. text ed. 10.95 (*0-471-58601-3*) Wiley.

Quinn, Kaye. Aquarium Creatures. 40p. (Orig.). 1991. pap. 2.95 (*0-8431-2719-8*) Price Stern.

Riley, Linda C. Aquarium: Bringing the Seas Inside. LC 93-16341. (Illus.). (ps-6). 1993. text ed. write for info. (*0-7167-6509-8*, Sci Am Yng Rdrs) W H Freeman.

Thomas, Charles B. Water Gardens for Plants & Fish. (Illus.). 189p. (gr. 7 up). 1988. PLB 19.95 (*0-86622-942-6*, TS-102) TFH Pubns.

AQUATIC ANIMALS

see Fresh-Water Animals; Marine Animals

AQUATIC PLANTS

see Fresh-Water Plants; Marine Plants

ARAB COUNTRIES

Department of Geography, Lerner Publications. Sudan in Pictures. (Illus.). 64p. (gr. 5 up). 1988. PLB 17.50 (*0-8225-1839-2*) Lerner Pubns.

Dutton, Roderic. An Arab Family. LC 85-10272. (Illus.). 32p. (gr. 2-5). 1985. PLB 13.50 (*0-8225-1660-8*) Lerner Pubns.

Haskins, Jim. Count Your Way Through the Arab World. (Illus.). 24p. (gr. 1-4). 1987. lib. bdg. 17.50 (*0-87614-304-4*); pap. 5.95 (*0-685-13264-1*) Carolrhoda Bks.

King, John. Bedouin. LC 92-16506. (Illus.). 48p. (gr. 5-6). 1992. PLB 22.80 (*0-8114-2304-2*) Raintree Steck-V.

ARAB-ISRAEL WAR, 1967

see Israel-Arab War, 1967-

ARAB-JEWISH RELATIONS

see Jewish-Arab Relations

ARABIA-FICTION

Abu Kir & Abu Sir. (gr. 2-5). 1989. 7.95x (*0-86685-480-0*) Intl Bk Ctr.

Dixey, Kay. Judar & His Two Brothers. (gr. 2-8). 1990. 7.95x (*0-86685-483-5*) Intl Bk Ctr.

Prince Jamil & Fair Leila. (gr. 1-6). 1990. 7.95x (*0-86685-490-8*) Intl Bk Ctr.

Riordan, James. Tales from the Arabian Nights. Ambrus, Victor G., illus. LC 84-62456. 128p. (gr. 4 up). 1985. 14.95 (*1-56288-258-9*) Checkerboard.

Singer, A. L., adapted by. Disney's Aladdin. LC 91-58972. (Illus.). 64p. (gr. 1-4). 1992. pap. 3.50 (*1-56282-241-1*) Disney Pr.

—Disney's Aladdin. LC 91-58973. (Illus.). 96p. 1992. 14.95 (*1-56282-240-3*); PLB 14.89 (*1-56282-275-6*) Disney Pr.

ARABIC LANGUAGE

First English & Arabic Picture Dictionary. (Illus.). (gr. 1-4). 1987. 3.95x (*0-86685-202-6*) Intl Bk Ctr.

Giblin, James C. The Riddle of the Rosetta Stone: Key to Ancient Egypt. LC 89-29289. (Illus.). 96p. (gr. 3-7). 1990. 15.00 (*0-690-04797-5*, Crowell Jr Bks); PLB 14.89 (*0-690-04799-1*, Crowell Jr Bks) HarpC Child Bks.

Girgis, Nazih. The Arabic Alphabet. Lowry-Elks, C., illus. (ENG & ARA.). 57p. (gr. k-12). 1983. pap. 15.00 incl. cass. (*0-86685-340-5*) Intl Bk Ctr.

Sheheen, Dennis, illus. A Child's Picture English-Arabic Dictionary. LC 85-15658. (gr. k-2). 1985. 9.95 (*0-915361-30-2*) Modan-Adama Bks.

ARBORICULTURE

see Forests and Forestry; Fruit Culture; Trees

ARABS

see also Bedouins

Ashabranner, Brent. An Ancient Heritage: The Arab-American Minority. Conklin, Paul, illus. LC 90-30641. 160p. (gr. 3-7). 1991. PLB 14.89 (*0-06-020049-9*) HarpC Child Bks.

Moktefi, Mokhtar. The Arabs: In the Golden Age. LaRose, Mary K., tr. Ageorges, Veronique, illus. LC 92-4989. 64p. (gr. 4-6). 1992. PLB 15.40 (*1-56294-201-8*) Millbrook Pr.

Naff, Alixa. The Arab Americans. Moynihan, Daniel P., intro. by. (Illus.). 112p. (gr. 5 up). 1988. lib. bdg. 17.95 (*0-87754-861-7*) Chelsea Hse.

ARABS-FICTION

Nye, Naomi S. Sitti's Secrets. Carpenter, Nancy, illus. LC 93-19742. 32p. (ps-3). 1994. RSBE 14.95 (*0-02-768460-1*, Four Winds) Macmillan Child Grp.

ARBOR DAY

Burns, Diane L. Arbor Day. Rogers, Kathy, illus. 48p. (gr. k-4). 1989. 14.95 (*0-87614-346-X*) Carolrhoda Bks.

ARCHEOLOGISTS

Scheller, William. Amazing Archaeologists & Their Finds. LC 93-46919. 160p. (gr. 5-12). 1994. 14.95 (*1-881508-17-X*) Oliver Pr MN.

Weitzman, David. Human Culture. LC 93-16791. (Illus.). 288p. (gr. 4-6). 1994. SBE 22.95 (*0-684-19438-4*, Scribners Young Read) Macmillan Child Grp.

Williams, Barbara. Breakthrough: Women in Archaeology. LC 80-7687. (Illus.). 174p. 1981. 9.95 (*0-8027-6406-1*) Walker & Co.

ARCHAEOLOGY

see Archeology

ARCHEOLOGY

see also Arms and Armor; Art, Primitive; Bible-Antiquities; Christian Art and Symbolism; Cities and Towns, Ruined, Extinct, etc.; Cliff Dwellers and Cliff Dwellings; Ethnology; Excavations (Archeology); Funeral Rites and Ceremonies; Gems; Heraldry; Indians of North America-Antiquities; Man, Prehistoric; Mounds and Mound Builders; Mummies; Numismatics; Pottery; Pyramids; Radiocarbon Dating; Stone Age

also names of countries, cities, etc. with the subdivision Antiquities, e.g. U. S.-Antiquities

Anderson, Joan. From Map to Museum: Uncovering Mysteries of the Past. Ancona, George, photos by. LC 87-31307. (Illus.). 64p. (gr. 3-7). 1988. 12.95 (*0-688-06914-2*); PLB 12.88 (*0-688-06915-0*, Morrow Jr Bks) Morrow Jr Bks.

Barrett, Katharine, et al. Investigating Artifacts. Bergman, Lincoln & Fairwell, Kay, eds. (Illus.). 120p. (gr. k-6). 1992. pap. 12.50 (*0-912511-83-4*) Lawrence Science.

Cork, Barbara. Archaeology. McEwan, Joe, illus. 32p. (gr. 5-8). 1985. PLB 13.96 (*0-88110-220-2*, Pub. by Usborne); pap. 6.95 (*0-86020-865-6*) EDC.

Fradin, Dennis B. Archaeology. LC 83-7309. 48p. (gr. k-4). 1983. PLB 12.85 (*0-516-01691-1*); pap. 4.95 (*0-516-41691-X*) Childrens.

Giblin, James C. The Riddle of the Rosetta Stone. Tobin, Patricia, illus. LC 89-29289. 96p. (gr. 3-7). 1993. pap. 5.95 (*0-06-446137-8*, Trophy) HarpC Child Bks.

Hackwell, W. John. Digging to the Past: Excavations in Ancient Lands. LC 86-13115. (Illus.). 64p. (gr. 3-7). 1986. SBE 14.95 (*0-684-18692-6*, Scribners Young Read) Macmillan Child Grp.

Hoobler, Dorothy & Hoobler, Tom. The Fact or Fiction Files: Lost Civilizations. 160p. (gr. 7-10). 1992. 14.95 (*0-8027-8152-7*); lib. bdg. 15.85 (*0-8027-8153-5*) Walker & Co.

Jessop, Joanne. Big Buildings of the Ancient World. Salariya, David, created by. LC 93-36704. (Illus.). 48p. (gr. 5-8). 1994. write for info. (*0-531-14286-8*); pap. 8.95 (*0-531-15709-1*) Watts.

Johnson, Eileen, ed. An Ancient Watering Hole: The Lubbock Lake Landmark Story. Dean, David & Cokendolpher, Jean, illus. LC 90-90258. 32p. (Orig.). (gr. 2-5). 1990. pap. 3.00 (*0-89672-218-X*) Tex Tech Univ Pr.

McIntosh, Jane. Archeology. LC 94-9378. 1994. 16.00 (*0-679-86572-1*); pap. 17.99 (*0-679-96572-6*) Knopf.

Marston, Elsa. Mysteries in American Archaeology. LC 85-20259. (Illus.). 115p. (gr. 7 up). 1986. 13.95 (*0-8027-6608-0*); lib. bdg. 13.85 (*0-8027-6627-7*) Walker & Co.

Prehistoric Sticker Book. (Illus.). 20p. (gr. k-6). 1994. pap. 6.95 (*1-56458-561-1*) Dorling Kindersley.

Pryor, Francis & Collison, David. Now Then: Digging up the Past. (Illus.). 48p. (gr. 7-10). 1994. 24.95 (*0-7134-7290-1*, Pub. by Batsford UK) Trafalgar.

Raintree Publishers Staff. Archaeology. LC 87-28634. (Illus.). 64p. (Orig.). (gr. 5-9). 1988. PLB 11.95 (*0-8172-3077-7*) Raintree Steck-V.

Rhodes, Frank H., et al. Fossils. Perlman, Raymond, illus. (gr. 6 up). 1962. PLB write for info. (*0-307-63515-5*); pap. write for info. (*0-307-24411-3*, Golden Pr) Western Pub.

Ronen, Avraham. Stones & Bones! How Archaeologists Trace Human Origins. LC 93-2480. (gr. 6 up). 1993. lib. bdg. write for info. (*0-8225-3207-7*, Runestone Pr) Lerner Pubns.

Scheller, William. Amazing Archaeologists & Their Finds. LC 93-46919. 160p. (gr. 5-12). 1994. 14.95 (*1-881508-17-X*) Oliver Pr MN.

Snyder, Thomas F. Archeology Search Book. O'Neill, Martha, ed. Cullinan, Dorothy K. & Podgorski, Mary E., illus. 32p. (gr. 4-12). 1982. pap. text ed. 8.08 (*0-07-059467-8*) McGraw.

Stuart, Gene S. Secrets from the Past. Crump, Donald J., ed. LC 79-1790. (Illus.). 104p. (gr. 3-8). 1979. PLB 12.50 (*0-87044-321-6*) Natl Geog.

Sylvester, Diane & Wiemann, Mary. Mythology, Archeology, Architecture. 112p. (gr. 4-6). 1982. 9.95 (*0-88160-081-4*, LW 901) Learning Wks.

Wilcox, Charlotte. Mummies & Their Mysteries. LC 92-32160. 64p. 1993. 22.95 (*0-87614-767-8*) Carolrhoda Bks.

ARCHEOLOGY, BIBLICAL

see Bible-Antiquities

ARCHEOLOGY-FICTION

Carris, Joan D. Stolen Bones: A Novel. LC 92-36479. 1993. 14.95 (*0-316-13018-4*) Little.

Clymer, Eleanor. The Spider, the Cave & the Pottery Bowl. (gr. k-6). 1992. 16.50 (*0-8446-6578-9*) Peter Smith.

James, Carollyn. Digging up the Past: The Story of an Archaeological Adventure. Schindler, Stephen D., illus. 64p. (gr. 5-8). 1990. PLB 11.90 (*0-531-10878-3*) Watts.

Kellogg, Steven. Prehistoric Pinkerton. (ps-3). 1991. pap. 4.99 (*0-14-054689-8*, Puff Pied Piper) Puffin Bks.

Starnes, Gigi. Grandma's Tales: Storm of Darkness. Mitchell, Mark, illus. LC 94-16080. 1995. 11.95 (*0-89015-979-3*) Sunbelt Media.

ARCHEOLOGY-HISTORY

Scheller, William. Amazing Archaeologists & Their Finds. LC 93-46919. 160p. (gr. 5-12). 1994. 14.95 (*1-881508-17-X*) Oliver Pr MN.

ARCHEOLOGY-VOCATIONAL GUIDANCE

Bryan, Betsy & Cohen, Judith. You Can Be a Woman Egyptologist. Katz, David, illus. LC 93-1267. 40p. (Orig.). (gr. 3-6). 1993. pap. 6.00 (*1-880599-10-4*) Cascade Pass.

ARCHERY

Boy Scouts of America. Archery. (Illus.). 56p. (gr. 6-12). 1986. pap. 1.85 (*0-8395-3381-0*, 33259) BSA.

ARCHIMEDES, 287-212 B.C.

Ipsen, D. C. Archimedes: Greatest Scientist of the Ancient World. LC 88-31006. (Illus.). 64p. (gr. 6 up). 1988. lib. bdg. 15.95 (*0-89490-161-3*) Enslow Pubs.

Taylor, Barbara. Sink or Swim! The Science of Water. Bull, Peter, et al, illus. LC 90-42618. 40p. (Orig.). (gr. 2-5). 1991. pap. 4.95 (*0-679-80815-9*) Random Bks Yng Read.

ARCHITECTS

Chong, Gordon H. Gordon H. Chong & Associates: An Architect's Success Story. (gr. 4-7). 1994. 14.95 (*0-8027-8307-4*); PLB 15.85 (*0-8027-8308-2*) Walker & Co.

Dell, Pamela. I. M. Pei, Designer of Dreams. LC 92-36903. (Illus.). 32p. (gr. 2-4). 1993. PLB 11.80 (*0-516-04186-X*); pap. 3.95 (*0-516-44186-8*) Childrens.

Kett-O'Connor, Pamela. The Arts - Julia Morgan. LC 92-46285. 1993. 19.93 (*0-86625-489-7*); 14.95s.p. (*0-685-66538-0*) Rourke Pubns.

Rubin, Susan G. Frank Lloyd Wright. LC 93-48523. 1994. 19.95 (*0-8109-3974-6*) Abrams.

Wadsworth, Ginger. Julia Morgan: Architect of Dreams. (Illus.). 128p. (gr. 5 up). 1990. PLB 21.50 (*0-8225-4903-4*) Lerner Pubns.

Williams, Paul R. & Hudson, Karen E. The Will & the Way. LC 93-39986. 64p. 1994. 14.95 (*0-8478-1780-6*) Rizzoli Intl.

ARCHITECTURAL ENGINEERING

see Building

ARCHITECTURE

see also Building; Castles; Cathedrals; Monuments; Skyscrapers; Synagogues; Theaters

also headings beginning with the word Architectural

Bellerophon Books Staff. Ancient Buildings. (gr. 4-7). 1992. pap. 3.95 (*0-88388-121-7*) Bellerophon Bks.

Boy Scouts of America. Architecture. (Illus.). 46p. (gr. 6-12). 1966. pap. 1.85 (*0-8395-3321-7*, 33321) BSA.

Brown, David. The Random House Book of How Things Were Built. LC 91-27638. (Illus.). 144p. (Orig.). (gr. 3-7). 1992. PLB 19.99 (*0-679-92044-7*); pap. 15.00 (*0-679-82044-2*) Random Bks Yng Read.

Cooper, J. Man-Made Wonders Series, 6 bks. 1991. Set. 53.70s.p. (*0-86592-626-3*) Rourke Enter.

—Maravillas de la Humanidad (Man-Made Wonders) Series, 6 bks, Set VI. (SPA.). 1991. 53.70s.p. (*0-685-53670-X*) Rourke Enter.

D'Alelio, Jane. I Know That Building! Discovering Architecture with Activities & Games. (Illus.). 88p. (gr. 3-6). 1989. pap. 14.95 (*0-89133-133-6*) Preservation Pr.

Diamonstein, Barbaralee. Landmarks: Eighteen Wonders of the New York World. Lorenz, Albert, illus. 160p. 1992. 35.00 (*0-8109-3565-1*) Abrams.

Dobrin, Peter. Start Exploring Architecture: A Fact-Filled Coloring Book. (Illus.). 128p. (Orig.). (gr. 3 up). 1993. pap. 8.95 (*1-56138-237-X*) Running Pr.

Eisen, David. Fun with Architecture: From the Metropolitan Museum of Art. (Illus.). 64p. 1992. shrink-wrapped incl. 32 r 22.50 (*0-670-84684-8*) Viking Child Bks.

Gardner, Robert. Architecture. (Illus.). 96p. (gr. 5-8). 1994. bds. 16.95 (*0-8050-2855-2*) TFC Bks NY.

Govier, Heather. Buildings. Young, Richard, ed. LC 91-19816. (Illus.). 32p. (gr. 3-5). 1991. PLB 15.93 (*1-56074-007-8*) Garrett Ed Corp.

Home. (Illus.). 16p. (ps-1). 1994. pap. 6.95 (*1-56458-525-5*) Dorling Kindersley.

Jann, Gayle. A Day in the Life of a Construction Foreman. Jann, Gayle, illus. LC 87-13761. 32p. (gr. 4-8). 1988. PLB 11.79 (*0-8167-1121-6*); pap. text ed. 2.95 (*0-8167-1122-4*) Troll Assocs.

Jessop, Joanne. Big Buildings of the Modern World. Salariya, David & Salariya, Davidcreated by. LC 93-40315. 1994. write for info. (*0-531-14307-4*) Watts.

Martin, Ana. Romanesque Art & Architecture. LC 93-3436. (Illus.). 36p. (gr. 3 up). 1993. PLB 14.95 (*0-516-08387-2*); pap. 6.95 (*0-516-48387-0*) Childrens.

Munro, Roxie, illus. Architects Make Zigzags: Looking at Architecture from A to Z. Maddex, Diane, contrib. by. LC 84-9679. (Illus.). 64p. (Orig.). (gr. 3 up). 1986. pap. 8.95 (*0-89133-121-2*) Preservation Pr.

Patton, Sally J. & Maxon, Dianne. Architexture: A Shelter Word. rev. ed. 56p. (gr. 2-6). 1989. pap. text ed. 14.95 (*0-913705-38-1*) Zephyr Pr AZ.

Platt, Richard. Incredible Cross Sections. Biesty, Stephen, illus. LC 91-27439. 48p. 1992. 20.00 (*0-679-81411-6*) Knopf Bks Yng Read.

Shemie, Bonnie. Houses of Snow, Skin & Bones: Native Dwellings: The Far North. LC 89-50778. (Illus.). 24p. (gr. 3-7). 1989. 13.95 (*0-88776-240-9*) Tundra Bks.

Singer, Donna. Structures That Changed the Way the World Looked. (Illus.). 48p. (gr. 4-8). 1994. PLB write for info. (*0-8114-4937-8*) Raintree Steck-V.

Stewart, G. In the Future. (Illus.). 32p. (gr. 3-8). 1989. lib. bdg. 15.74 (*0-86592-115-6*); 11.95s.p. (*0-685-58595-6*) Rourke Corp.

Sylvester, Diane & Wiemann, Mary. Mythology, Archeology, Architecture. 112p. (gr. 4-6). 1982. 9.95 (*0-88160-081-4*, LW 901) Learning Wks.

Wilkinson, Phil. Amazing Buildings. Donati, Paolo, illus. LC 92-54314. 48p. (gr. 3 up). 1993. 16.95 (*1-56458-234-5*) Dorling Kindersley.

Wilson, Forrest. What It Feels Like to Be a Building. rev. ed. Wilson, Forrest, illus. LC 88-22382. 80p. (gr. 2 up). 1988. pap. 10.95 (*0-89133-147-6*) Preservation Pr.

Wood, Richard. The Builder Through History. Smith, Tony, illus. LC 93-24398. 48p. (gr. 5-8). 1994. 15.95 (*1-56847-102-5*) Thomson Lrning.

Young, C. Castles, Pyramids & Palaces. (Illus.). 48p. (ps-8). 1990. lib. bdg. 13.96 (*0-88110-411-6*, Usborne); pap. 7.95 (*0-7460-0463-X*, Usborne) EDC.

ARCHITECTURE, DOMESTIC

see also Houses

Glenn, Particia B. Under Every Roof: A Kid's Study & Field Guide to the Architecture of American Houses. Stites, Joe, illus. 112p. (gr. 3-6). 1993. 16.95 (*0-89133-214-6*) Preservation Pr.

Marsh, Carole. The Boy-Is-This-Place-Big Biltmore House Spark Kit. (Illus., Orig.). (gr. 3-12). 1994. PLB 24.95 (*0-935326-22-7*) Gallopade Pub Group.

National Geographic Staff. My House. (ps). 1993. 4.50 (*0-7922-1835-3*) Natl Geog.

Stewart, Gail. Living Spaces, 6 bks, Reading Level 4. (Illus.). 192p. (gr. 3-8). 1990. Set. PLB 95.64 (*0-86592-105-9*); 71.70s.p. (*0-685-58770-3*) Rourke Corp.

Ventura, Piero. Houses: Structures, Methods, & Ways of Living. Casalini, Max, et al. LC 93-108. 1993. 16.95 (*0-395-66792-5*) HM.

ARCHITECTURE–FICTION

Crosbie, Michael J. & Rosenthal, Steve. Architecture Colors. (Illus.). 26p. (ps). 1993. 6.95 (*0-89133-212-X*) Preservation Pr.

—Architecture Counts. (Illus.). 26p. (ps). 1993. 6.95 (*0-89133-213-8*) Preservation Pr.

—Architecture Shapes. (Illus.). 26p. (ps). 1993. 6.95 (*0-89133-211-1*) Preservation Pr.

Gaughenbaugh, Michael & Camburn, Herbert. Old House, New House. Camburn, Herbert, illus. 56p. (gr. 4-6). 1993. 16.95 (*0-89133-236-7*) Preservation Pr.

Le Clezio, J. M. Villa Aurore. Lemoine, Georges, illus. (FRE.). 112p. (gr. 5-10). 1990. pap. 7.95 (*2-07-033603-4*) Schoenhof.

Rockwell, Anne. Pots & Pans. Rockwell, Lizzy, illus. LC 91-4976. 32p. (ps-1). 1993. RSBE 13.95 (*0-02-777631-X*, Macmillan Child Bk) Macmillan Child Grp.

Roy, Claude. Maison Qui S'Envole. Lemoine, Georges, illus. (FRE.). 90p. (gr. 5-10). 1977. pap. 7.95 (*2-07-033001-X*) Schoenhof.

Rylant, Cynthia. The Everyday Books: Everyday House. Rylant, Cynthia, illus. LC 92-40943. 14p. (ps-k). 1993. pap. 4.95 with rounded corners (*0-02-778024-4*, Bradbury Pr) Macmillan Child Grp.

Stern, Robert A. The House That Bob Built. LC 90-26901. (Illus.). 32p. 1991. 17.95 (*0-8478-1369-X*) Rizzoli Intl.

ARCHITECTURE–HISTORY

Giblin, James C. Let There Be Light: A Book about Windows. LC 87-35052. (Illus.). 176p. (gr. 3-7). 1988. (Crowell Jr Bks); PLB 15.89 (*0-690-04695-2*, Crowell Jr Bks) HarpC Child Bks.

ARCHITECTURE, RURAL

see Architecture, Domestic

ARCHITECTURE–VOCATIONAL GUIDANCE

Clinton, Susan. I Can Be an Architect. LC 85-28004. (Illus.). 32p. (gr. k-3). 1986. PLB 11.80 (*0-516-01890-6*); pap. 3.95 (*0-516-41890-4*) Childrens.

Cohen, Judith L. & Siegel, Margot. Tu Puedes Ser una Arquitecta. Yanez, Juan, tr. from ENG. Katz, David A., illus. (SPA.). 40p. (Orig.). (gr. 4-7). 1992. pap. 6.00 (*1-880599-05-8*) Cascade Pass.

—You Can Be a Woman Architect. Katz, David A., illus. 40p. (Orig.). 1992. pap. 6.00 (*1-880599-04-X*) Cascade Pass.

ARCTIC EXPEDITIONS

see Arctic Regions

ARCTIC REGIONS

see also North Pole; Northwest Passage; Scientific Expeditions

Barrett, N. S. Polar Animals. FS Staff, ed. LC 87-50851. (Illus.). 32p. (gr. 1-6). 1988. PLB 11.90 (*0-531-10531-8*) Watts.

Bullen, Susan. The Arctic & Its People. LC 93-27125. (Illus.). 48p. (gr. 5-8). 1994. 15.95 (*1-56847-153-X*) Thomson Lrning.

Burton, Robert. Arctic. (Illus.). 24p. (gr. k-4). 1991. PLB 10.40 (*1-878137-16-6*) Newington.

Dunphy, Madeleine. Here Is the Arctic Winter. Robinson, Alan J., illus. LC 92-72022. 32p. (ps-3). 1993. 14.95 (*1-56282-336-1*) Hyprn Child.

George, Michael. Tundra. LC 93-18275. 1994. PLB 18.95 (*0-88682-601-2*) Creative Ed.

Holen-Roebuck, Susan D. Arctic Animal Babies. Arehart, Betsy L., illus. 40p. (Orig.). (ps-3). 1993. pap. 4.95 (*0-922127-04-2*) Paisley Pub.

Hoyt-Goldsmith, Diane. Arctic Hunter. Migdale, Lawrence, photos by. 1994. pap. 6.95 (*0-8234-1124-9*) Holiday.

Johnson, LaVerne C. Matthew Henson. Perry, Craig Rex, illus. LC 92-35253. 1992. 3.95 (*0-922162-94-8*) Empak Pub.

Kalman, Bobbie. Arctic Animals. (Illus.). 56p. (gr. 3-4). 1988. 15.95 (*0-86505-145-3*); pap. 7.95 (*0-86505-155-0*) Crabtree Pub Co.

—The Arctic Land. (Illus.). 56p. (gr. 3-4). 1988. 15.95 (*0-86505-144-5*); pap. 7.95 (*0-86505-154-2*) Crabtree Pub Co.

Kalman, Bobbie & Belsey, William. An Arctic Community. (Illus.). 56p. (gr. 3-4). 1988. 15.95 (*0-86505-147-X*); pap. 7.95 (*0-86505-157-7*) Crabtree Pub Co.

Mateer, Charlotte F. Let's Go to the Arctic: A Story & Activities Book about Arctic People & Animals. Witt, Linda A., illus. 64p. (gr. 4-6). 1993. pap. text ed. 7.95 (*1-879373-24-6*) R Rinehart.

Pandell, Karen. Land of Dark, Land of Light: The Arctic National Wildlife Refuge. Bruemmer, Fred, photos by. LC 92-40405. (Illus.). 32p. (ps-3). 1993. 14.99 (*0-525-45094-7*, DCB) Dutton Child Bks.

Sabin, Francene. Arctic & Antarctic Regions. Eitzen, Allan, illus. LC 84-2730. 32p. (gr. 3-6). 1985. PLB 9.49 (*0-8167-0234-9*); pap. text ed. 2.95 (*0-8167-0235-7*) Troll Assocs.

Silver, Donald M. One Small Square: Arctic Tundra. Wynne, Patricia J., illus. LC 94-4143. (gr. 5 up). 1994. text ed. write for info. (*0-7167-6517-9*, Sci Am Yng Rdrs) W H Freeman.

Stone, Lynn M. The Arctic. LC 84-23248. (Illus.). 48p. (gr. k-4). 1985. PLB 12.85 (*0-516-01935-X*) Childrens.

Thomson, Ruth. Our Arctic Project. (Illus.). 25p. (gr. 2-4). 1991. 13.95 (*0-237-60150-8*, Pub. by Evans Bros Ltd) Trafalgar.

ARCTIC REGIONS–FICTION

Bjorke, Drew. The Arctic Trip. Bjorke, Drew, illus. 12p. (ps). 1993. 4.95 (*1-56828-035-1*) Red Jacket Pr.

Ekoomiak, Normee. Arctic Memories. LC 89-39194. (Illus.). 32p. (gr. 3 up). 1992. pap. 5.95 (*0-8050-2347-X*, Bks Young Read) H Holt & Co.

Fuge, Charles & Hayles, Karen. Whale Is Stuck. LC 92-34078. (ps-1). 1993. pap. 14.00 JRT (*0-671-86587-0*, S&S BFYR) S&S Trade.

Geiger, John & Beattie, Owen. Buried in Ice: The Mystery of a Lost Arctic Expedition. (gr. 8-12). 1993. pap. 6.95 (*0-590-43849-2*) Scholastic Inc.

Greaves, Margaret. The Ice Journey. Darke, Alison C., illus. 32p. (ps-1). 1994. 19.95 (*0-460-88133-7*, Pub. by J M Dent & Sons) Trafalgar.

Houston, James. Frozen Fire: A Tale of Courage. Houston, James, illus. LC 77-6366. 160p. (gr. 7 up). 1977. SBE 13.95 (*0-689-50083-1*, M K McElderry) Macmillan Child Grp.

—Frozen Fire: A Tale of Courage. 2nd ed. Houston, James, illus. LC 91-46062. 160p. (gr. 3-7). 1992. pap. 4.95 (*0-689-71612-5*, Aladdin) Macmillan Child Grp.

Joosse, Barbara M. Mama, Do You Love Me? Lavallee, Barbara, illus. 32p. (ps-1). 1991. 13.95 (*0-87701-759-X*) Chronicle Bks.

Miller, Sherry C. Snowharry Takes a Vacation (with Arctic Friends) Martinez, Jesse, illus. 32p. (gr. k-5). 1985. pap. write for info. saddle-stitched (*0-913379-03-4*) Double M Pub.

Munsch, Robert. Fifty Below Zero. Martchenko, Michael, illus. 24p. (gr. k-3). 1986. PLB 14.95 (*0-920236-86-3*, Pub. by Annick CN); pap. 4.95 (*0-920236-91-X*, Pub. by Annick CN) Firefly Bks Ltd.

—Fifty Below Zero. (CHI., Illus.). 32p. 1993. pap. 5.95 (*1-55037-298-X*, Pub. by Annick CN) Firefly Bks Ltd.

Sage, James. Where the Great Bear Watches. Flather, Lisa, illus. 32p. (ps-3). 1993. 13.99 (*0-670-84933-2*) Viking Child Bks.

Sis, Peter. A Small, Tall Tale from the Far, Far North. Sis, Peter, illus. LC 92-75906. 40p. (gr. k-5). 1993. 15. 00 (*0-679-84345-0*); PLB 15.99 (*0-679-94345-5*) Knopf Bks Yng Read.

Turner, Bonnie. Haunted Igloo. 160p. (gr. 3-7). 1991. 13. 45 (*0-395-57037-9*, Sandpiper) HM.

Vyner, Sue. Arctic Spring. Vyner, Tim, illus. LC 92-32280. (ps-3). 1993. 13.99 (*0-670-84934-0*) Viking Child Bks.

ARDENNES, BATTLE OF THE, 1944-1945

Black, Wallace B. & Blashfield, Jean F. Battle of the Bulge. LC 92-1722. (Illus.). 48p. (gr. 5-6). 1993. text ed. 12.95 RSBE (*0-89686-568-1*, Crestwood Hse) Macmillan Child Grp.

ARGENTINE REPUBLIC

Brusca, Maria C. My Mama's Little Ranch on the Pampas. LC 93-28113. 1994. 15.95 (*0-8050-2782-3*) H Holt & Co.

—On the Pampas. Brusca, Maria C., illus. LC 90-40938. 40p. (ps-2). 1991. 15.95 (*0-8050-1548-5*, Bks Young Read) H Holt & Co.

Caistor, Nicholas. Argentina. LC 91-7215. (Illus.). 96p. (gr. 6-11). 1991. PLB 22.80 (*0-8114-2443-X*) Raintree Steck-V.

Fox, Geoffrey. The Land & People of Argentina. LC 89-37811. (Illus.). 256p. (gr. 6 up). 1990. (Lipp Jr Bks); PLB 18.89 (*0-397-32381-6*, Lipp Jr Bks) HarpC Child Bks.

Gofen, Ethel C. Argentina. LC 90-23159. (Illus.). 128p. (gr. 5-9). 1991. PLB 21.95 (*1-85435-381-0*) Marshall Cavendish.

Hintz, Martin. Argentina. LC 85-2638. (Illus.). 127p. (gr. 4-6). 1985. PLB 20.55 (*0-516-02752-2*) Childrens.

Jacobsen, Karen. Argentina. LC 90-36526. (Illus.). 48p. (gr. k-4). 1990. PLB 12.85 (*0-516-01101-4*); pap. 4.95 (*0-516-41101-2*) Childrens.

Latin America, 6 vols. (Illus.). (gr. 5-9). 1991. Set. 131.70 (*1-85435-380-2*) Marshall Cavendish.

Lerner Publications, Department of Geography Staff, ed. Argentina in Pictures. (Illus.). 64p. (gr. 5 up). 1988. PLB 17.50 (*0-8225-1807-4*) Lerner Pubns.

Liebowitz, Sol. Argentina. (Illus.). 128p. (gr. 5 up). 1990. 14.95 (*0-7910-1106-2*) Chelsea Hse.

Morrison, Marion. Argentina. (Illus.). 48p. (gr. 4-8). 1989. lib. bdg. 14.95 (*0-382-09793-9*) Silver Burdett Pr.

Peterson, Marge & Peterson, Rob. Argentina: A Wild West Heritage. LC 89-11707. (Illus.). 128p. (gr. 5 up). 1990. text ed. 14.95 RSBE (*0-87518-413-8*, Dillon) Macmillan Child Grp.

ARGENTINE REPUBLIC–FICTION

Kalnay, Francis. Chucaro: Wild Pony of the Pampa. De Miskey, Julian, illus. 115p. 1993. pap. 6.95 (*0-8027-7387-7*) Walker & Co.

ARGUMENTATION

see Debates and Debating; Logic

ARISTOCRACY

see also Democracy

ARITHMETIC

Addition Wipe-off Book. 24p. (Orig.). (gr. 1 up). 1988. pap. 1.95 (*0-590-42012-7*) Scholastic Inc.

Allington, Richard L. Numbers. Garcia, Tom, illus. LC 79-19200. 32p. (gr. k-3). 1985. 9.95 (*0-8172-1278-7*); pap. 3.95 (*0-8114-8239-1*) Raintree Steck-V.

Anno, Mitsumasa. Anno's Magic Seed. LC 92-39309. 1994. write for info. (*0-399-22538-2*, Philomel Bks) Putnam Pub Group.

—Anno's Mysterious Multiplying Jar. Anno, Mitsumasa, illus. LC 82-22413. 48p. (gr. 3 up). 1983. 16.95 (*0-399-20951-4*, Philomel Bks) Putnam Pub Group.

Barner, Bob. Too Many Dinosaurs. LC 93-46523. (gr. 2 up). 1995. 6.95 (*0-553-37566-0*, Little Rooster) Bantam.

Bloom, Edgar B. It All Starts with Counting: A Short Guide to Old-Fashioned Arithmetic & Other Mathematical Concepts. Holliman, Mary C., ed. viii, 122p. (Orig.). (gr. 6-12). 1993. pap. 10.00 (*0-936015-26-8*) Pocahontas Pr.

Brazile, Lionel J., Jr. Arithmetic Summary Booklet. (Illus.). 16p. (Orig.). (gr. 1-9). 1990. pap. 12.95 (*0-9624016-0-9*) Scholar Pub Co.

Bucki, Lisa, et al. Mathemagic. (Illus., Orig.). 1992. pap. 19.95 (*0-672-30267-5*) Alpha Bks IN.

Burchard, Elizabeth. Arithmetic: In a Flash. 425p. (gr. 7-12). 1994. pap. 9.95 (*1-881374-16-5*) Flash Blasters.

Buschemeyer, Robin Q. Number Pal. Launching Pad Studios, Inc. Staff, illus. 40p. (Orig.). (ps-3). 1986. pap. 2.99 (*0-935609-02-4*) Eduplay.

Callaghan, Steven. Brainercise Mental Exercise Program: Arithmetic, Vol. 1, Bk. 8. large type ed. 25p. (gr. k up). 1991. comb binding 5.00 (*0-925395-23-4*) SGC Biomedical.

—Brainercise Mental Exercise Program: Arithmetic, Vol. 1, Bk. 7. large type ed. 25p. (gr. k up). 1991. comb binding 5.00 (*0-925395-22-6*) SGC Biomedical.

—Brainercise Mental Exercise Program: Arithmetic, Vol. 1, Bk. 9. large type ed. 25p. (gr. k up). 1991. comb binding 5.00 (*0-925395-29-3*) SGC Biomedical.

—Brainercise Mental Exercise Program: Arithmetic, Vol. 1, Bk. 10. large type ed. 25p. (gr. k up). 1991. comb binding 5.00 (*0-925395-30-7*) SGC Biomedical.

—Brainercise Mental Exercise Program: Arithmetic, Vol. 2, Bk. 1. large type ed. 25p. (gr. k up). 1991. comb binding 5.00 (*0-925395-27-7*) SGC Biomedical.

—Brainercise Mental Exercise Program: Arithmetic, Vol. 2, Bk. 3. large type ed. 25p. (gr. k up). 1991. comb binding 5.00 (*0-925395-32-3*) SGC Biomedical.

—Brainercise Mental Exercise Program: Arithmetic, Vol. 2, Bk. 2. large type ed. 25p. (gr. k up). 1991. comb binding 5.00 (*0-925395-31-5*) SGC Biomedical.

—Brainercise Mental Exercise Program: Arithmetic, Vol. 3, Bk. 1. large type ed. 25p. (gr. k up). 1991. comb binding 5.00 (*0-925395-28-5*) SGC Biomedical.

Daniel, Becky. Hooray for Addition Facts! (Illus.). 80p. (gr. 1-3). 1990. 9.95 (*0-86653-517-9*, GA1133) Good Apple.

—Hooray for Division Facts! (Illus.). 80p. (gr. 2-4). 1990. 9.95 (*0-86653-520-9*, GA1135) Good Apple.

—Hooray for Multiplication Facts! (Illus.). 80p. (gr. 2-4). 1990. 9.95 (*0-86653-519-5*, GA1136) Good Apple.

—Hooray for Subtraction Facts! (Illus.). 80p. (gr. 1-3). 1990. 9.95 (*0-86653-518-7*, GA1134) Good Apple.

Daniel, Becky & Daniel, Charlie. Arithmetrix. 64p. (gr. 5-8). 1980. 8.95 (*0-916456-75-7*, GA 188) Good Apple.

De Bie, Catherine F. Multiplication & Division Made Easy. Weigand, Betty, ed. (Illus.). 72p. (Orig.). 1990. pap. 10.95 (*0-9627585-0-7*) M & D Made Easy.

DeYoung, Lorie. Beginning Addition & Subtraction. Hoffman, Joan, ed. (Illus.). 32p. (gr. 2). 1993. wkbk. 1.99 (*0-938256-32-7*) Sch Zone Pub Co.

—Time, Money & Fractions. Hoffman, Joan, ed. (Illus.). 32p. (gr. 1-2). 1993. wkbk. 1.99 (*0-938256-44-0*) Sch Zone Pub Co.

Edens, Cooper. How Many Bears? LC 94-9371. (gr. k-3). 1994. 14.95 (*0-689-31923-1*, Atheneum) Macmillan Child Grp.

Evans, Karen. Beginning to Subtract. Nayer, Judith E., ed. McCarthy, Kathleen, illus. 32p. (gr. k-1). 1991. wkbk. 1.95 (*1-878624-56-3*) McClanahan Bk.

—Subtraction. Nayer, Judith E., ed. Kennedy, Anne & Wilson, Ann, illus. 32p. (gr. k-1). 1991. wkbk. 1.95 (*1-878624-58-X*) McClanahan Bk.

Faulkner, Keith. Simple Sums. (ps-3). 1994. 11.00 (*0-671-88555-3*, S&S BFYR) S&S Trade.

Fennell, Francis. Addition Skills. 80p. (Orig.). (ps-3). pap. 2.95 (*0-8431-2503-9*) Price Stern.

Gibson, Ray. Learning Games. (Illus.). 64p. (ps-1). 1993. pap. 8.95 (*0-7460-1296-9*, Usborne) EDC.

Giganti, Paul, Jr. Each Orange Had Eight Slices: Big Book Edition. Crews, Donald, illus. 32p. (ps up). 1994. pap. 18.95 (*0-688-13116-6*, Mulberry) Morrow.
Gregorich, Barbara. Addition & Subtraction: First Grade. Hoffman, Joan, ed. Koontz, Robin M., illus. 32p. (gr. 1). 1990. wkbk. 2.29 (*0-88743-182-8*) Sch Zone Pub Co.
—Addition & Subtraction: Second Grade. Hoffman, Joan, ed. Koontz, Robin M., illus. 32p. (gr. 2). 1990. wkbk. 2.29 (*0-88743-188-7*) Sch Zone Pub Co.
Gurau, Peter K. & Lieberthal, Edwin M. Fingermath. Gafney, Leo, ed. 192p. (gr. 3-8). 1980. text ed. 6.56 (*0-07-025223-8*) McGraw.
—Fingermath, Bk. 2. Gafney, Leo, ed. (Illus.). (gr. 2-6). 1980. text ed. 6.56 (*0-07-025222-X*) McGraw.
Harbin, Carey E. Fay, Jay & Adding Numbers. (Illus.). 29p. (Orig.). (ps-1). 1990. pap. text ed. 2.95 (*0-918995-04-3*) Voc-Offers.
Hewavisenti, Lakshmi. Measuring. LC 91-10767. (Illus.). 32p. (gr. k-4). 1991. PLB 11.90 (*0-531-17319-4*, Gloucester Pr) Watts.
Hilderbrand, Karen & Thompson, Kim. Addition. (Illus.). 48p. (gr. 3). 1991. wkbk. 6.99 (*0-9632249-2-1*) Twin Sisters.
—Division. (Illus.). 48p. (gr. 3). 1991. wkbk. 6.99 (*0-9632249-4-8*) Twin Sisters.
—Multiplication. (Illus.). 48p. (gr. 3). 1991. wkbk. 6.99 (*0-9632249-1-3*) Twin Sisters.
—Subtraction. (Illus.). 48p. (gr. 3). 1991. wkbk. 6.99 (*0-9632249-3-X*) Twin Sisters.

Hughes, Benjamin B. Multiplication Table by the "Method of Tricks" A Pictorially Rapid & Permanent Mastery. (Illus.). 24p. (gr. k up). 1994. pap. text ed. 10.00 (*1-885028-00-8*) Wings of Freedom.
Color. First copyrighted 1991. Powerful Conceptual Development. Hailed as the FASTEST METHOD EVER DEVISED...ANY child who can count forward to 30 & backward from 10 can, in only 4 flips of the page, excitedly & permanently master the Multiplication Table in only a couple of hours by this 1ST-TIME-EVER "revolutionary" ground-breaking strategy using cartoon picture mnemonics - a method first created by the author in 1990 for severe learning disabled children which has NEVER missed with ANY of the well over 1000 "academically challenged" children "emancipated" across 3 states. A 1991 Talk Show Sensation...Powerful enough for a National Award winning Elementary School Principal of the Year in Science to offer to promote the book nationally...Powerful enough for the largest school district in UTAH to not only offer to help publish the method but also fly the author down from ALASKA to showcase the method in classrooms for a solid 2-week period before a steady stream of key educators from throughout UTAH'S Salt Lake Valley...Powerful enough to induce others to subsequently try cartoon picture strategies of their own with perfectly predictable acclaim... Book follows author's EVERY CHILD A CHAMPION NATIONAL CAMPAIGN providing FREE inner-city "festival of success" clinics all across America. Teacher-Manuals, Posters, Flash-Cards, Games. Orders only: 1-800-MATH*JOY. Info: Brent Hughes, Times Table Tricks, Inc., P.O. Box 20355, Boulder, CO 80308-3355.
Publisher Provided Annotation.

Jenkins, Lee. Coin Stamp Mathematics. Merrick, Paul, illus. (Orig.). (gr. k-4). 1977. pap. 7.95 (*0-918932-05-X*) Activity Resources.
Jonson, Liz & Silliman, Emery. Beginning to Add. Nayer, Judith E., ed. Appleby, Ellen, illus. 32p. (gr. k-1). 1991. wkbk. 1.95 (*1-878624-55-5*) McClanahan Bk.
Larocque, Jean-Paul. Numbers Time. Larocque, Jean-Paul, illus. 17p. (gr. k-3). 1993. pap. 11.95 (*1-895583-62-4*) MAYA Pubs.
—What Is Two Plus Two. Larocque, Jean-Paul, illus. 12p. (gr. k-3). 1993. pap. 10.95 (*1-895583-63-2*) MAYA Pubs.
Lawrence, H. S. Addition & Subtraction: No Regrouping. Kifer, Kathy & Solar, Dahna, illus. (ENG & SPA.). 30p. (Orig.). (gr. 1-6). 1992. pap. 3.95 wkbk. (*0-931993-51-2*, GP-051) Garlic Pr OR.
—Addition: No Regrouping. Kifer, Kathy & Solar, Dahna, illus. (ENG & SPA.). 30p. (Orig.). (gr. 1-6). 1992. pap. 3.95 wkbk. (*0-931993-49-0*, GP-049) Garlic Pr OR.
—Multiplication: Factors 1-12. Kifer, Kathy & Solar, Dahna, illus. (ENG & SPA.). 30p. (Orig.). (gr. 3-6). 1992. pap. 3.95 wkbk. (*0-931993-52-0*, GP-052) Garlic Pr OR.
—Subtraction: No Regrouping. Kifer, Kathy & Solar, Dahna, illus. (ENG & SPA.). 30p. (Orig.). (gr. 1-6). 1992. pap. 3.95 wkbk. (*0-931993-50-4*, GP-050) Garlic Pr OR.
Laycock, Mary, et al. Skateboard Practice: Addition & Subtraction. new ed. Kyzer, Martha, illus. (gr. 1-2). 1978. pap. text ed. 7.95 (*0-918932-55-6*) Activity Resources.
Lieberman, Joe. Those Amazing Tables: Teaching Multiplication Through Patterns & Color Strips. (gr. 4-7). 1983. pap. 9.95 (*0-201-48019-0*) Addison-Wesley.
Lund, Charles. Tricks of the Trade with Cards. new ed. Laycock, Mary, ed. (gr. 2-9). 1978. pap. text ed. 7.95 (*0-918932-57-2*) Activity Resources.
Merriam, Eve. Twelve Ways to Get to Eleven. Karlin, Bernie, illus. LC 92-25810. 40p. (ps-1). 1993. pap. 14. 00 JRT (*0-671-75544-7*, S&S BFYR) S&S Trade.
Nodel, Maxine. Moral or Less: An Adventure in Addition & Subtraction. Nodel, Norman, illus. 32p. (ps-3). 1990. 8.95 (*0-922613-25-7*); pap. 6.95 wkbk. (*0-922613-26-5*); 4.95 (*0-922613-27-3*); cass. 9.00 (*0-922613-28-1*) Hachai Pubns.
Ockenga, Earl & Rucker, Walt. Subtracting from Eighteen or Less. Dawson, Dave, illus. 16p. (gr. 1). 1990. pap. text ed. 1.25 (*1-56281-135-5*, M135) Extra Eds.
—Subtracting from Ten or Less. Dawson, Dave, illus. 16p. (gr. 1). 1990. pap. text ed. 1.25 (*1-56281-110-X*, M110) Extra Eds.
—Sums Through Eighteen. Dawson, Dave, illus. 16p. (gr. 1). 1990. pap. text ed. 1.25 (*1-56281-130-4*, M130) Extra Eds.
—Sums Through Ten. Dawson, Dave, illus. 16p. (gr. 1). 1990. pap. text ed. 1.25 (*1-56281-105-3*, M105) Extra Eds.
—Telling Time. Dawson, Dave, illus. 16p. (gr. 1). 1990. pap. text ed. 1.25 (*1-56281-120-7*, M120) Extra Eds.
Parkis, Michael. Everything You Always Wanted to Know about Arithmetic. (gr. 4-8). 1987. 6.50 (*0-87879-804-8*, Ann Arbor Div) Acad Therapy.
Price, Gerry, illus. Fun Math Flip Book Series, 4 bks. (ps-3). 1994. No. 1: I Can Add! pap. 7.99 (*0-553-09564-1*); No. 2: I Can Subtract! pap. 7.99 (*0-553-09565-X*); No. 3: I Can Multiply! pap. 7.99 (*0-553-09566-8*); No. 4: I Can Divide! pap. 7.99 (*0-553-09567-6*) Bantam.
Rand, Ann & Rand, Paul. Little One. (Illus.). 32p. 1991. Repr. 16.95 (*0-8109-3558-9*) Abrams.
Rasmussen, Steven & Rasmussen, David. Key to Percents Series. Incl. Bk. 1: Percent Concepts. 45p. pap. text ed. 2.00 (*0-913684-57-0*); Bk. 2: Percents & Fractions. 45p. pap. text ed. 2.00 (*0-913684-58-9*); Bk. 3: Percents & Decimals. 45p. pap. text ed. 2.00 (*0-913684-59-7*); Answers & Notes (1-3), 38p. 2.30 (*0-913684-61-9*). (gr. 4-12). 1988. Key Curr Pr.
Rodriguez, David & Rodriguez, Judy. Times Tables the Fun Way Book for Kids: A Picture Method of Learning the Multiplication Facts. 2nd, rev. & enl. ed. Bagley, Val & Barwald, Diana, illus. LC 93-79769. 86p. (gr. 2-8). 1994. 19.95 (*1-883841-26-7*); student wkbk., 47p. 7.95 (*1-883841-27-5*); tchr's. manual, 136p. 24.95 (*1-883841-28-3*); flash cards 4.95 (*1-883841-29-1*) Key Pubs UT.
Salant, Michael A. Arithmetic Is Fun: The Arithmetic Example Handbook of Grade-School Math. LC 91-90203. (Illus.). 128p. (Orig.). (gr. 1-6). 1992. 16.95x (*0-9609288-5-5*); pap. 10.95xt glow in the dark spiral bdg. (*0-9609288-4-7*) M A Salant.
Schaffer, Frank, Publications Staff. Addition. (Illus.). 24p. (gr. 1-3). 1978. wkbk. 3.98 (*0-86734-007-X*, FS-3008) Schaffer Pubns.
Silliman, Emery & Jonson, Liz. Addition. Nayer, Judith E., ed. Mahan, Ben, illus. 32p. (gr. k-1). 1991. wkbk. 1.95 (*1-878624-57-1*) McClanahan Bk.
Smart, Margaret. Focus on Decimals, 2 vols. (Illus.). (gr. 7-9). 1977. Vol. 1. 7.50 (*0-918932-12-2*); Vol. 2. 7.50 (*0-918932-13-0*) Activity Resources.
Stuart, Marion W. Subtraction Wrap-ups: Individual Sets. (gr. 1-3). Date not set. text ed. write for info. learning aid (*0-943343-02-X*) Lrn Wrap-Ups.
The Subtraction Wipe-Off Book. 24p. (gr. 1 up). 1988. pap. 1.95 (*0-590-42042-9*) Scholastic Inc.
Thompson, Kim M. & Hilderbrand, Karen M. Addition. Kuzjak, Goran, illus. 24p. (gr. 1-4). 1993. wkbk. incl. audiocassette 9.98 (*1-882331-20-6*, TWIN 402) Twin Sisters.
—Division. Kuzjak, Goran, illus. 24p. (gr. 3-6). 1993. wkbk. incl. audiocassette 9.98 (*1-882331-22-2*, TWIN 404) Twin Sisters.
—A Little Rhythm, Rhyme & Read: Letters & Numbers. Kozjak, Goran, illus. 28p. (ps-1). 1993. Wkbk., incl. audio cass. 9.98 (*1-882331-15-X*) Twin Sisters.
—Multiplication. Kuzjak, Goran, illus. 24p. (gr. 2-6). 1993. wkbk. incl. audiocassette 9.98 (*1-882331-19-2*, TWIN 401) Twin Sisters.
—Rap with the Facts Twinset: Addition. Kuzjak, Goran, illus. 48p. (gr. 1-4). 1993. pap. 14.99 wkbk. incl. audiocassette & poster (*1-882331-04-4*, TWIN 300) Twin Sisters.
—Rap with the Facts Twinset: Division. Kuzjak, Goran, illus. 48p. 1993. pap. 14.99 wkbk. incl. audiocassette & poster (*1-882331-06-0*, TWIN 304) Twin Sisters.
—Rap with the Facts Twinset: Multiplication. Kuzjak, Goran, illus. 48p. (gr. 2-6). 1993. pap. 14.99 wkbk. incl. audiocassette & poster (*1-882331-03-6*, TWIN 301) Twin Sisters.
—Rap with the Facts Twinset: Subtraction. Kuzjak, Goran, illus. 48p. (gr. 1-4). 1993. pap. 14.99 wkbk. incl. audiocassette & poster (*1-882331-05-2*, TWIN 303) Twin Sisters.
—Subtraction. Kuzjak, Goran, illus. 24p. 1993. wkbk. incl. audiocassette 9.98 (*1-882331-21-4*, TWIN 403) Twin Sisters.
Time Life Inc. Editors. The Case of the Missing Zebra Stripes: Zoo Math. Crawford, Jean B., et al, eds. LC 92-16838. (Illus.). 64p. (gr. k-4). 1992. write for info. (*0-8094-9954-1*); lib. bdg. write for info. (*0-8094-9955-X*) Time-Life.
—How Do Octopi Eat Pizza Pie? Pizza Math. Crawford, Jean B., et al, eds. (Illus.). 64p. (gr. k-4). 1992. write for info. (*0-8094-9950-9*); lib. bdg. write for info. (*0-8094-9951-7*) Time-Life.
Tyler, J. & Bryant-Mole, K. Starting to Add. (Illus.). 24p. (ps up). 1989. pap. 3.50 (*0-7460-0455-9*, Usborne) EDC.
—Starting to Subtract. (Illus.). 24p. (ps up). 1989. pap. 3.50 (*0-7460-0456-7*, Usborne) EDC.
Weiss, Monica. Mmmm---Cookies! Simple Subtraction. Berlin, Rosemary, illus. LC 91-18648. 24p. (gr. k-2). 1992. PLB 10.59 (*0-8167-2486-5*); pap. text ed. 2.95 (*0-8167-2487-3*) Troll Assocs.
Wise, Beth A. My First Math Book. Morgado, Richard, illus. 32p. (ps). 1992. wkbk. 1.95 (*1-56293-172-5*) McClanahan Bk.

ARITHMETIC–STUDY AND TEACHING

see also Counting Books

Cron, Mary. Monster Math Workbook. Cherbak, Yvonne, illus. 48p. (Orig.). (gr. 1-3). 1993. pap. 2.95 (*1-56565-030-1*) Lowell Hse.
Gibson, Ray. Number Games. (Illus.). 32p. (ps-9). 1993. pap. 13.96 (*0-88110-651-8*, Usborne); pap. text ed. 5.95 (*0-7460-1294-2*, Usborne) EDC.
Musson, Gloria J. & Musson, Cyril D. RAPmetic, the Arithmetic Rap. Miller, Benjamin S., illus. 48p. (Orig.). (gr. 3 up). 1988. pap. text ed. 3.50 (*0-9619321-0-4*); cass. 6.50 (*0-9619321-1-2*) Sq One Pubns.
Rodriguez, David & Rodriguez, Judy. Times Tables the Fun Way: A Picture Method of Learning the Multiplication Facts. Bagley, Val & Barwald, Diana, illus. 86p. (gr. 2-8). 1992. 19.95 (*1-883841-25-9*) Key Pubs UT.

ARIZONA

Adventures in Arizona: An Illustrated History. Caillou, Aliza, ed. Carlson, Diane, illus. LC 91-65779. 48p. (Orig.). (gr. 4 up). 1991. pap. 6.95 (*0-9628329-3-6*) Thorne Enterprises.
Arizona Adventure: History for Boys & Girls. (gr. 4-9). 1972. text ed. 6.00 (*0-910152-00-4*) AZ Hist Foun.
Arizona Pathways: Study Guide. 32p. (Orig.). (gr. 6-8). 1990. wkbk. 9.95 (*0-911981-65-9*) Cloud Pub.
Arizona: Resource Library. (gr. 4-7). 20 bks. in carrying case 185.95 (*0-911981-66-7*) Cloud Pub.
Aylesworth, Thomas G. & Aylesworth, Virginia L. The West (Arizona, Nevada, Utah) (Illus.). 64p. (gr. 3 up). 1992. PLB 16.95 (*0-7910-1049-X*) Chelsea Hse.
Bly, Stephen A. Rivers in Arizona. 140p. (Orig.). (gr. 7-12). 1991. pap. 4.95 (*0-8474-6624-8*) Back to Bible.
Brew, Virginia & McCabe, Michael. Arizona: Studies. rev. ed. (Illus.). 160p. (gr. 4-6). 1994. text ed. 19.45 (*0-911981-58-6*) Cloud Pub.
Carole Marsh Arizona Books, 48 bks. 1994. lib. bdg. 1127.60 set (*0-7933-1276-0*); pap. 647.60 set (*0-7933-5126-X*) Gallopade Pub Group.
Cobb, Vicki. This Place Is Dry. Lavallee, Barbara, illus. (gr. 2-4). 1989. 12.95 (*0-8027-6854-7*); PLB 13.85 (*0-8027-6855-5*) Walker & Co.
Filbin, Dan. Arizona. (Illus.). 72p. (gr. 3-6). 1990. PLB 17.50 (*0-8225-2705-7*) Lerner Pubns.
Fradin, Dennis. Arizona: In Words & Pictures. LC 79-21480. (Illus.). 48p. (gr. 2-5). 1980. PLB 12.95 (*0-516-03903-2*); pap. 4.95 (*0-516-43903-0*) Childrens.
Fradin, Dennis B. Arizona - From Sea to Shining Sea. LC 93-12019. (Illus.). 64p. (gr. 3-5). 1993. PLB 16.45 (*0-516-03803-6*) Childrens.
Heinrichs, Ann. Arizona. LC 90-21118. (Illus.). 144p. (gr. 5-8). 1991. PLB 20.55 (*0-516-00449-2*) Childrens.
—Arizona. 200p. 1993. text ed. 15.40 (*1-56956-150-8*) W A T Braille.
McCabe, Michael. Arizona: Studies. (Illus.). 46p. (gr. 4-6). 1994. wkbk. 5.75 (*0-911981-59-4*) Cloud Pub.
—Arizona: Su Origen. (SPA., Illus.). (gr. 4-6). 1987. text ed. 16.45 (*0-911981-54-3*) Cloud Pub.
Marsh, Carole. Arizona: A(dama) to Z(oroaster) 1994. PLB 24.95 (*0-7933-7317-4*); pap. text ed. 14.95 (*0-7933-7316-6*); disk 29.95 (*0-7933-7318-2*) Gallopade Pub Group.

—Arizona & Other State Greats (Biographies) (Illus.). (gr. 3-12). 1994. PLB 24.95 (*1-55609-507-4*); pap. 14. 95 (*1-55609-506-6*); computer disk 29.95 (*0-7933-1373-2*) Gallopade Pub Group.

—Arizona Bandits, Bushwackers, Outlaws, Crooks, Devils, Ghosts, Desperadoes & Other Assorted & Sundry Characters! (Illus.). (gr. 3-12). 1994. PLB 24. 95 (*0-7933-0118-1*); pap. 14.95 (*0-7933-0117-3*); computer disk 29.95 (*0-7933-0119-X*) Gallopade Pub Group.

—Arizona Classic Christmas Trivia: Stories, Recipes, Activities, Legends, Lore & More! (Illus.). (gr. 3-12). 1994. PLB 24.95 (*0-7933-0121-1*); pap. 14.95 (*0-7933-0120-3*); computer disk 29.95 (*0-7933-0122-X*) Gallopade Pub Group.

—Arizona Coastales! (Illus.). (gr. 3-12). 1994. PLB 24.95 (*1-55609-503-1*); pap. 14.95 (*1-55609-502-3*); computer disk 29.95 (*0-7933-1369-4*) Gallopade Pub Group.

—Arizona Coastales! 1994. lib. bdg. 24.95 (*0-7933-7267-4*) Gallopade Pub Group.

—Arizona "Crinkum-Crankum" A Funny Word Book about Our State. (Illus.). 1994. lib. bdg. 24.95 (*0-7933-4816-1*); pap. 14.95 (*0-7933-4817-X*); disk 29. 95 (*0-7933-4818-8*) Gallopade Pub Group.

—Arizona Dingbats! Bk. 1: A Fun Book of Games, Stories, Activities & More about Our State That's All in Code! for You to Decipher. (Illus.). (gr. 3-12). 1994. PLB 24.95 (*0-7933-3779-8*); pap. 14.95 (*0-7933-3780-1*); computer disk 29.95 (*0-7933-3781-X*) Gallopade Pub Group.

—Arizona Festival Fun for Kids! (Illus.). (gr. 3-12). 1994. lib. bdg. 24.95 (*0-7933-3932-4*); pap. 14.95 (*0-7933-3933-2*); disk 29.95 (*0-7933-3934-0*) Gallopade Pub Group.

—The Arizona Hot Air Balloon Mystery. (Illus.). (gr. 2-9). 1994. 24.95 (*0-7933-2336-3*); pap. 14.95 (*0-7933-2337-1*); computer disk 29.95 (*0-7933-2338-X*) Gallopade Pub Group.

—Arizona Jeopardy! Answers & Questions about Our State! (Illus.). (gr. 3-12). 1994. PLB 24.95 (*0-7933-4085-3*); pap. 14.95 (*0-7933-4086-1*); computer disk 29.95 (*0-7933-4087-X*) Gallopade Pub Group.

—Arizona "Jography" A Fun Run Thru Our State! (Illus.). (gr. 3-12). 1994. PLB 24.95 (*1-55609-498-1*); pap. 14.95 (*1-55609-497-3*); computer disk 29.95 (*0-7933-1359-7*) Gallopade Pub Group.

—Arizona Kid's Cookbook: Recipes, How-to, History, Lore & More! (Illus.). (gr. 3-12). 1994. PLB 24.95 (*0-7933-0130-0*); pap. 14.95 (*0-7933-0129-7*); computer disk 29.95 (*0-7933-0131-9*) Gallopade Pub Group.

—The Arizona Mystery Van Takes Off! Book 1: Handicapped Arizona Kids Sneak Off on a Big Adventure. (Illus.). (gr. 3-12). 1994. 24.95 (*0-7933-4970-2*); pap. 14.95 (*0-7933-4971-0*); computer disk 29.95 (*0-7933-4972-9*) Gallopade Pub Group.

—Arizona Quiz Bowl Crash Course! (Illus.). (gr. 3-12). 1994. PLB 24.95 (*1-55609-505-8*); pap. 14.95 (*1-55609-504-X*); computer disk 29.95 (*0-7933-1368-6*) Gallopade Pub Group.

—Arizona Rollercoasters! (Illus.). (gr. 3-12). 1994. PLB 24.95 (*0-7933-5230-4*); pap. 14.95 (*0-7933-5231-2*); computer disk 29.95 (*0-7933-5232-0*) Gallopade Pub Group.

—Arizona School Trivia: An Amazing & Fascinating Look at Our State's Teachers, Schools & Students! (Illus.). (gr. 3-12). 1994. PLB 24.95 (*0-7933-0127-0*); pap. 14.95 (*0-7933-0126-2*); computer disk 29.95 (*0-685-45932-2*) Gallopade Pub Group.

—Arizona Silly Basketball Sportsmysteries, Vol. I. (Illus.). (gr. 3-12). 1994. PLB 24.95 (*0-7933-0124-6*); pap. 14. 95 (*0-7933-0123-8*); computer disk 29.95 (*0-7933-0125-4*) Gallopade Pub Group.

—Arizona Silly Basketball Sportsmysteries, Vol. II. (Illus.). (gr. 3-12). 1994. PLB 24.95 (*0-7933-1568-9*); pap. 14.95 (*0-7933-1569-7*); computer disk 29.95 (*0-7933-1570-0*) Gallopade Pub Group.

—Arizona Silly Football Sportsmysteries, Vol. I. (Illus.). (gr. 3-12). 1994. PLB 24.95 (*1-55609-501-5*); pap. 14. 95 (*1-55609-500-7*); computer disk 29.95 (*0-7933-1361-9*) Gallopade Pub Group.

—Arizona Silly Football Sportsmysteries, Vol. II. (Illus.). (gr. 3-12). 1994. PLB 24.95 (*0-7933-1362-7*); pap. 14. 95 (*0-7933-1363-5*); computer disk 29.95 (*0-7933-1364-3*) Gallopade Pub Group.

—Arizona Silly Trivia! (Illus.). (gr. 3-12). 1994. PLB 24. 95 (*1-55609-496-5*); pap. 14.95 (*1-55609-495-7*); computer disk 29.95 (*0-7933-1358-9*) Gallopade Pub Group.

—Arizona Timeline: A Chronology of Arizona History, Mystery, Trivia, Legend, Lore & More. (Illus.). (gr. 3-12). 1994. PLB 24.95 (*0-7933-5881-7*); pap. 14.95 (*0-7933-5882-5*); computer disk 29.95 (*0-7933-5883-3*) Gallopade Pub Group.

—Arizona's (Most Devastating!) Disasters & (Most Calamitous!) Catastrophies! (Illus.). (gr. 3-12). 1994. PLB 24.95 (*0-7933-0115-7*); pap. 14.95 (*0-7933-0114-9*); computer disk 29.95 (*0-7933-0116-5*) Gallopade Pub Group.

—Arizona's Unsolved Mysteries (& Their "Solutions") Includes Scientific Information & Other Activities for Students. (Illus.). (gr. 3-12). 1994. PLB 24.95 (*0-7933-5728-4*); pap. 14.95 (*0-7933-5729-2*); computer disk 29.95 (*0-7933-5730-6*) Gallopade Pub Group.

—Avast, Ye Slobs! Arizona Pirate Trivia. (Illus.). (gr. 3-12). 1994. PLB 24.95 (*0-7933-0136-X*); pap. 14.95 (*0-7933-0135-1*); computer disk 29.95 (*0-7933-0137-8*) Gallopade Pub Group.

—The Beast of the Arizona Bed & Breakfast. (Illus.). (gr. 3-12). 1994. PLB 24.95 (*0-7933-1365-1*); pap. 14.95 (*0-7933-1366-X*); computer disk 29.95 (*0-7933-1367-8*) Gallopade Pub Group.

—Bow Wow! Arizona Dogs in History, Mystery, Legend, Lore, Humor & More! (Illus.). (gr. 3-12). 1994. PLB 24.95 (*0-7933-3473-X*); pap. 14.95 (*0-7933-3474-8*); computer disk 29.95 (*0-7933-3475-6*) Gallopade Pub Group.

—Chill Out: Scary Arizona Tales Based on Frightening Arizona Truths. (Illus.). 1994. lib. bdg. 24.95 (*0-7933-4663-0*); pap. 14.95 (*0-7933-4664-9*); disk 29. 95 (*0-7933-4665-7*) Gallopade Pub Group.

—Christopher Columbus Comes to Arizona! Includes Reproducible Activities for Kids! (Illus.). (gr. 3-12). 1994. PLB 24.95 (*0-7933-3626-0*); pap. 14.95 (*0-7933-3627-9*); computer disk 29.95 (*0-7933-3628-7*) Gallopade Pub Group.

—The Hard-to-Believe-But-True! Book of Arizona History, Mystery, Trivia, Legend, Lore, Humor & More. (Illus.). (gr. 3-12). 1994. PLB 24.95 (*0-7933-0133-5*); pap. 14.95 (*0-7933-0132-7*); computer disk 29.95 (*0-7933-0134-3*) Gallopade Pub Group.

—If My Arizona Mama Ran the World! (Illus.). (gr. 3-12). 1994. PLB 24.95 (*0-7933-1370-8*); pap. 14.95 (*0-7933-1371-6*); computer disk 29.95 (*0-7933-1372-4*) Gallopade Pub Group.

—Jurassic Ark! Arizona Dinosaurs & Other Prehistoric Creatures. (gr. k-12). 1994. PLB 24.95 (*0-7933-7434-0*); pap. 14.95 (*0-7933-7435-9*); computer disk 29.95 (*0-7933-7436-7*) Gallopade Pub Group.

—Let's Quilt Arizona & Stuff It Topographically! (Illus.). (gr. 3-12). 1994. PLB 24.95 (*1-55609-499-X*); pap. 14. 95 (*1-55609-128-1*); computer disk 29.95 (*0-7933-1360-0*) Gallopade Pub Group.

—Let's Quilt Our Arizona County. 1994. lib. bdg. 24.95 (*0-7933-7119-8*); pap. text ed. 14.95 (*0-7933-7120-1*); disk 29.95 (*0-7933-7121-X*) Gallopade Pub Group.

—Let's Quilt Our Arizona Town. 1994. lib. bdg. 24.95 (*0-7933-6969-X*); pap. text ed. 14.95 (*0-7933-6970-3*); disk 29.95 (*0-7933-6971-1*) Gallopade Pub Group.

—Meow! Arizona Cats in History, Mystery, Legend, Lore, Humor & More! (Illus.). (gr. 3-12). 1994. PLB 24.95 (*0-7933-3320-2*); pap. 14.95 (*0-7933-3321-0*); computer disk 29.95 (*0-7933-3322-9*) Gallopade Pub Group.

—My First Book about Arizona. (gr. k-4). 1994. PLB 24. 95 (*0-7933-5575-3*); pap. 14.95 (*0-7933-5576-1*); computer disk 29.95 (*0-7933-5577-X*) Gallopade Pub Group.

—Uncle Rebus: Arizona Picture Stories for Computer Kids. (Illus.). (gr. k-3). 1994. PLB 24.95 (*0-7933-4510-3*); pap. 14.95 (*0-7933-4511-1*); disk 29. 95 (*0-7933-4512-X*) Gallopade Pub Group.

Salts, Roberta. Arizona Is for Kids. Fischer, Bruce, illus. 32p. (gr. 1-4). 1988. pap. 2.95 (*0-685-21928-3*) Double B Pubns.

Stacy, Darryl. Arizona: Gobierno y Ciudadania. (SPA., Illus.). 144p. (Orig.). (gr. 7-9). 1983. pap. text ed. 17. 95 (*0-911981-24-1*) Cloud Pub.

—Arizona: Government & Citizenship. rev. ed. (Illus.). 160p. (gr. 7-9). 1993. Repr. of 1990 ed. text ed. 18.45 (*0-911981-56-X*) Cloud Pub.

—Arizona: Government & Citizenship. rev. ed. (Illus.). 48p. (gr. 7-9). 1990. wkbk. 5.75 (*0-911981-57-8*) Cloud Pub.

Stacy, Darryl & McCabe, Michael. Arizona: Studies: Map Skills Program. (Illus.). 59p. (gr. 4-6). 1990. binder 45. 95 (*0-911981-53-5*) Cloud Pub.

Tegeler, Dorothy. Hello Arizona: The Arizona Activity Book. Hicks, Mark, illus. 32p. (Orig.). 1987. pap. 3.50 (*0-943169-07-0*) Fiesta Bks Inc.

Trimble, Marshall. Arizona: A Panoramic History of a Frontier State. LC 76-45265. 1977. pap. 14.95 (*0-385-12806-1*) Doubleday.

Turner Program Services, Inc. Staff & Clark, James I. Arizona. LC 85-9978. 48p. (gr. 3 up). 1985. PLB 19. 97 (*0-8174-4257-X*) Raintree Steck-V.

Wagoner, Jay J. Arizona! rev. ed. LC 79-15183. (Illus.). 270p. 1993. text ed. 19.95 (*0-87905-490-5*, Peregrine Smith) Gibbs Smith Pub.

Weaver, Dorothy H. Arizona A to Z. Wacker, Kay, illus. LC 93-38249. 32p. (Orig.). (gr. k up). 1994. pap. 6.95 (*0-87358-564-X*) Northland AZ.

ARIZONA–FICTION

Bock, Shelly V. Lonely Lyla. 1992. 7.95 (*0-533-09389-9*) Vantage.

Johnston, Annie F. The Little Colonel in Arizona. (gr. 5 up). 13.95 (*0-89201-033-9*) Zenger Pub.

Papagapitos, Karen. Jose's Basket. 1993. 6.95 (*0-9637328-1-1*) Kapa Hse Pr. JOSE'S BASKET is a touching portrayal of a family forced to be always on the move. Luis & Socorro Vasquez are migrant farm workers, who follow whatever crops need to be harvested. This continuous change of surrounding is very difficult on their four children. The parents try to make the transitions easier by anticipating all the new & exciting things that are sure to be waiting for them at the next stop. At one particular town, in Arizona, eight-year-old Jose (an excellent student & gifted writer) finds a school he never wants to leave. Of course, there does come a time when he must leave this new place & his wonderful teacher, Mrs. Ortega. By learning to piece together his adventures in every new place, much like his mother weaves reeds & grasses from the desert into her special basket (the grasses come from each place in which they pick crops), Jose is able to find the courage he needs to move on & stay in school. JOSE'S BASKET has been placed in the U.S. Department of Education's Library. Distributed by Baker & Taylor Books, 652 East Main St./P.O. Box 6920, Bridgewater, NJ 08807-0920.
Publisher Provided Annotation.

Smith, Kaitlin M. Arizona Is Hot. Smith, Kaitlin M., illus. 14p. (gr. k-3). 1992. pap. 10.95 (*1-895583-18-7*) MAYA Pubs.

ARKANSAS

Aylesworth, Thomas G. & Aylesworth, Virginia L. South Central (Louisiana, Arkansas, Missouri, Kansas, Oklahoma) (Illus.). 64p. (gr. 3 up). 1992. PLB 16.95 (*0-7910-1047-3*) Chelsea Hse.

Baker, T. Harri & Browning, Jane. An Arkansas History for Young People. (gr. 8). 1991. student wkbk. 28.00 (*1-55728-083-5*); write for info. tchr's. manual (*1-55728-201-3*) U of Ark Pr.

Carole Marsh Arkansas Books, 44 bks. 1994. lib. bdg. 1027.80 set (*0-7933-1277-9*); pap. 587.80 set (*0-7933-5128-6*) Gallopade Pub Group.

Cole, Alison. Renaissance. LC 93-21264. (Illus.). 64p. 1994. 16.95 (*1-56458-493-3*) Dorling Kindersley.

Di Piazza, Domenica. Arkansas. LC 93-33391. (Illus.). 72p. (gr. 3-6). 1994. PLB 17.50 (*0-8225-2742-1*) Lerner Pubns.

Fradin, Dennis. Arkansas: In Words & Pictures. Wahl, Richard, illus. LC 80-11995. 48p. (gr. 2-5). 1980. PLB 12.95 (*0-516-03904-0*) Childrens.

Fradin, Dennis B. Arkansas - From Sea to Shining Sea. LC 93-32677. (Illus.). 64p. (gr. 3-5). 1994. PLB 16.45 (*0-516-03804-4*) Childrens.

Heinrichs, Ann. Arkansas. LC 88-38529. (Illus.). 144p. (gr. 4 up). 1989. PLB 20.55 (*0-516-00450-6*) Childrens.

—Arkansas. 186p. 1993. text ed. 15.40 (*1-56956-155-9*) W A T Braille.

Marsh, Carole. Arkansas & Other State Greats (Biographies) (Illus.). (gr. 3-12). 1994. PLB 24.95 (*1-55609-494-9*); pap. 14.95 (*1-55609-493-0*); computer disk 29.95 (*0-7933-1389-9*) Gallopade Pub Group.

—Arkansas Bandits, Bushwackers, Outlaws, Crooks, Devils, Ghosts, Desperadoes & Other Assorted & Sundry Characters! (Illus.). (gr. 3-12). 1994. PLB 24. 95 (*0-7933-0142-4*); pap. 14.95 (*0-7933-0141-6*); computer disk 29.95 (*0-7933-0143-2*) Gallopade Pub Group.

—Arkansas Classic Christmas Trivia: Stories, Recipes, Activities, Legends, Lore & More! (Illus.). (gr. 3-12). 1994. PLB 24.95 (*0-7933-0145-9*); pap. 14.95 (*0-7933-0144-0*); computer disk 29.95 (*0-7933-0146-7*) Gallopade Pub Group.

—Arkansas Coastales! (Illus.). (gr. 3-12). 1994. PLB 24. 95 (*1-55609-490-6*); pap. 14.95 (*1-55609-489-2*); computer disk 29.95 (*0-7933-1385-6*) Gallopade Pub Group.

—Arkansas Coastales! 1994. lib. bdg. 24.95 (*0-7933-7268-2*) Gallopade Pub Group.

—Arkansas "Crinkum-Crankum" A Funny Word Book about Our State. (Illus.). 1994. lib. bdg. 24.95 (*0-7933-4819-6*); pap. 14.95 (*0-7933-4820-X*); disk 29. 95 (*0-7933-4821-8*) Gallopade Pub Group.

—Arkansas Dingbats! Bk. 1: A Fun Book of Games, Stories, Activities & More about Our State That's All in Code! for You to Decipher. (Illus.). (gr. 3-12). 1994. PLB 24.95 (*0-7933-3782-8*); pap. 14.95 (*0-7933-3783-6*); computer disk 29.95 (*0-7933-3784-4*) Gallopade Pub Group.

—Arkansas Festival for Kids! (Illus.). (gr. 3-12). 1994. lib. bdg. 24.95 (*0-7933-3935-9*); pap. 14.95 (*0-7933-3936-7*); disk 29.95 (*0-7933-3937-5*) Gallopade Pub Group.

—The Arkansas Hot Air Balloon Mystery. (Illus.). (gr. 2-9). 1994. 24.95 (*0-7933-2345-2*); pap. 14.95 (*0-7933-2346-0*); computer disk 29.95 (*0-7933-2347-9*) Gallopade Pub Group.

—Arkansas Jeopardy! Answers & Questions about Our State! (Illus.). (gr. 3-12). 1994. PLB 24.95 (*0-7933-4088-8*); pap. 14.95 (*0-7933-4089-6*); computer disk 29.95 (*0-7933-4090-X*) Gallopade Pub Group.

—Arkansas "Jography" A Fun Run Thru Our State! (Illus.). (gr. 3-12). 1994. PLB 24.95 (*1-55609-485-X*); pap. 14.95 (*1-55609-088-9*); computer disk 29.95 (*0-7933-1375-9*) Gallopade Pub Group.

—Arkansas Kid's Cookbook: Recipes, How-to, History, Lore & More! (Illus.). (gr. 3-12). 1994. PLB 24.95 (*0-7933-0154-8*); pap. 14.95 (*0-7933-0153-X*); computer disk 29.95 (*0-7933-0155-6*) Gallopade Pub Group.

—The Arkansas Mystery Van Takes Off! Book 1: Handicapped Arkansas Kids Sneak Off on a Big Adventure. (Illus.). (gr. 3-12). 1994. 24.95 (*0-7933-4973-7*); pap. 14.95 (*0-7933-4974-5*); computer disk 29.95 (*0-7933-4975-3*) Gallopade Pub Group.

—Arkansas Quiz Bowl Crash Course! (Illus.). (gr. 3-12). 1994. PLB 24.95 (*1-55609-492-2*); pap. 14.95 (*1-55609-491-4*); computer disk 29.95 (*0-7933-1384-8*) Gallopade Pub Group.

—Arkansas Rollercoasters! (Illus.). (gr. 3-12). 1994. PLB 24.95 (*0-7933-5233-9*); pap. 14.95 (*0-7933-5234-7*); computer disk 29.95 (*0-7933-5235-5*) Gallopade Pub Group.

—Arkansas School Trivia: An Amazing & Fascinating Look at Our State's Teachers, Schools & Students! (Illus.). (gr. 3-12). 1994. PLB 24.95 (*0-7933-0151-3*); pap. 14.95 (*0-7933-0150-5*); computer disk 29.95 (*0-7933-0152-1*) Gallopade Pub Group.

—Arkansas Silly Basketball Sportsmysteries, Vol. I. (Illus.). (gr. 3-12). 1994. PLB 24.95 (*0-7933-0149-1*); pap. 14.95 (*0-7933-0147-5*); computer disk 29.95 (*0-685-45933-0*) Gallopade Pub Group.

—Arkansas Silly Basketball Sportsmysteries, Vol. II. (Illus.). (gr. 3-12). 1994. PLB 24.95 (*0-7933-1571-9*); pap. 14.95 (*0-685-45934-9*); computer disk 29.95 (*0-7933-1573-5*) Gallopade Pub Group.

—Arkansas Silly Football Sportsmysteries, Vol. I. (Illus.). (gr. 3-12). 1994. PLB 24.95 (*1-55609-488-4*); pap. 14. 95 (*1-55609-487-6*); computer disk 29.95 (*0-7933-1377-5*) Gallopade Pub Group.

—Arkansas Silly Football Sportsmysteries, Vol. II. (Illus.). (gr. 3-12). 1994. PLB 24.95 (*0-7933-1378-3*); pap. 14. 95 (*0-7933-1379-1*); computer disk 29.95 (*0-7933-1380-5*) Gallopade Pub Group.

—Arkansas Silly Trivia! (Illus.). (gr. 3-12). 1994. PLB 24. 95 (*1-55609-484-1*); pap. 14.95 (*1-55609-083-8*); computer disk 29.95 (*0-7933-1374-0*) Gallopade Pub Group.

—Arkansas Timeline: A Chronology of Arkansas History, Mystery, Trivia, Legend, Lore & More. (Illus.). (gr. 3-12). 1994. PLB 24.95 (*0-7933-5884-1*); pap. 14.95 (*0-7933-5885-X*); computer disk 29.95 (*0-7933-5886-8*) Gallopade Pub Group.

—Arkansas's (Most Devastating!) Disasters & (Most Calamitous!) Catastrophies! (Illus.). (gr. 3-12). 1994. PLB 24.95 (*0-7933-0139-4*); pap. 14.95 (*0-7933-0138-6*); computer disk 29.95 (*0-7933-0140-8*) Gallopade Pub Group.

—Arkansas's Unsolved Mysteries (& Their "Solutions") Includes Scientific Information & Other Activities for Students. (Illus.). (gr. 3-12). 1994. PLB 24.95 (*0-7933-5731-4*); pap. 14.95 (*0-7933-5732-2*); computer disk 29.95 (*0-7933-5733-0*) Gallopade Pub Group.

—Avast, Ye Slobs! Arkansas Pirate Trivia. (Illus.). (gr. 3-12). 1994. PLB 24.95 (*0-7933-0160-2*); pap. 14.95 (*0-7933-0159-9*); computer disk 29.95 (*0-7933-0161-0*) Gallopade Pub Group.

—The Beast of the Arkansas Bed & Breakfast. (Illus.). (gr. 3-12). 1994. PLB 24.95 (*0-7933-1381-3*); pap. 14. 95 (*0-7933-1382-1*); computer disk 29.95 (*0-7933-1383-X*) Gallopade Pub Group.

—Bow Wow! Arkansas Dogs in History, Mystery, Legend, Lore, Humor & More! (Illus.). (gr. 3-12). 1994. PLB 24.95 (*0-7933-3476-4*); pap. 14.95 (*0-7933-3477-2*); computer disk 29.95 (*0-7933-3478-0*) Gallopade Pub Group.

—Chill Out: Scary Arkansas Tales Based on Frightening Arkansas Truths. (Illus.). 1994. lib. bdg. 24.95 (*0-7933-4666-5*); pap. 14.95 (*0-7933-4667-3*); disk 29. 95 (*0-7933-4668-1*) Gallopade Pub Group.

—Christopher Columbus Comes to Arkansas! Includes Reproducible Activities for Kids! (Illus.). (gr. 3-12). 1994. PLB 24.95 (*0-7933-3629-5*); pap. 14.95 (*0-7933-3630-9*); computer disk 29.95 (*0-7933-3631-7*) Gallopade Pub Group.

—The Hard-to-Believe-But-True! Book of Arkansas History, Mystery, Trivia, Legend, Lore, Humor & More. (Illus.). (gr. 3-12). 1994. PLB 24.95 (*0-7933-0157-2*); pap. 14.95 (*0-7933-0156-4*); computer disk 29.95 (*0-7933-0158-0*) Gallopade Pub Group.

—If My Arkansas Mama Ran the World! (Illus.). (gr. 3-12). 1994. PLB 24.95 (*0-7933-1386-4*); pap. 14.95 (*0-7933-1387-2*); computer disk 29.95 (*0-7933-1388-0*) Gallopade Pub Group.

—Jurassic Ark! Arkansas Dinosaurs & Other Prehistoric Creatures. (gr. k-12). 1994. PLB 24.95 (*0-7933-7437-5*); pap. 14.95 (*0-7933-7438-3*); computer disk 29.95 (*0-7933-7439-1*) Gallopade Pub Group.

—Let's Quilt Arkansas & Stuff It Topographically! (Illus.). (gr. 3-12). 1994. PLB 24.95 (*1-55609-486-8*); pap. 14.95 (*1-55609-078-1*); computer disk 29.95 (*0-7933-1376-7*) Gallopade Pub Group.

—Let's Quilt Our Arkansas County. 1994. lib. bdg. 24.95 (*0-7933-7122-8*); pap. text ed. 14.95 (*0-7933-7123-6*); disk 29.95 (*0-7933-7124-4*) Gallopade Pub Group.

—Let's Quilt Our Arkansas Town. 1994. lib. bdg. 24.95 (*0-7933-6972-X*); pap. text ed. 14.95 (*0-7933-6973-8*); disk 29.95 (*0-7933-6974-6*) Gallopade Pub Group.

—Meow! Arkansas Cats in History, Mystery, Legend, Lore, Humor & More! (Illus.). (gr. 3-12). 1994. PLB 24.95 (*0-7933-3323-7*); pap. 14.95 (*0-7933-3324-5*); computer disk 29.95 (*0-7933-3325-3*) Gallopade Pub Group.

—My First Book about Arkansas. (gr. k-4). 1994. PLB 24.95 (*0-7933-5578-8*); pap. 14.95 (*0-7933-5579-6*); computer disk 29.95 (*0-7933-5580-X*) Gallopade Pub Group.

—Uncle Rebus: Arkansas Picture Stories for Computer Kids. (Illus.). (gr. k-3). 1994. PLB 24.95 (*0-7933-4513-8*); pap. 14.95 (*0-7933-4514-6*); disk 29. 95 (*0-7933-4515-4*) Gallopade Pub Group.

Payne, Linda. Arkansas Historical Math Facts. LC 90-63448. 72p. (gr. 3-6). 1986. spiral bdg. 25.00 (*0-914546-84-8*) Rose Pub.

Thompson, Kathleen. Arkansas. LC 87-16372. 48p. (gr. 3 up). 1987. 19.97 (*0-8174-4494-7*) Raintree Steck-V.

Zodrow, Brenda. Arkansas Coloring Book. (Illus.). 54p. (gr. k-4). 1990. 4.50 (*1-55728-179-3*) U of Ark Pr.

ARKANSAS–FICTION

Crofford, Emily. A Matter of Pride. LaMarche, Jim, illus. LC 81-387. 48p. (gr. 2-6). 1991. Repr. of 1981 ed. PLB 17.50 (*0-87614-171-8*, AACR2) Carolrhoda Bks.

—A Place to Belong. LC 93-9289. 1993. 19.95 (*0-87614-808-9*) Carolrhoda Bks.

Harris, Kathleen M. The Wonderful Hay Tumble. Gackenbach, Dick, illus. LC 87-12305. 32p. (ps-2). 1988. 12.95 (*0-688-07151-1*); PLB 12.88 (*0-688-07152-X*, Morrow Jr Bks) Morrow Jr Bks.

Medearis, Mary. Big Doc's Girl. LC 84-45641. 142p. (gr. 7-12). 1985. pap. 7.95 (*0-87483-105-9*) August Hse.

Rhodes, Judy C. The Hunter's Heart. LC 92-47025. 192p. (gr. 5 up). 1993. SBE 14.95 (*0-02-773935-X*, Bradbury Pr) Macmillan Child Grp.

—The King Boy. LC 91-2159. 160p. (gr. 5-9). 1991. SBE 14.95 (*0-02-776115-0*, Bradbury Pr) Macmillan Child Grp.

ARMADILLOS

Lavies, Bianca. It's an Armadillo! LC 89-31821. (Illus.). 32p. (ps-2). 1989. 13.95 (*0-525-44523-4*, DCB) Dutton Child Bks.

Pembleton, Seliesa. The Armadillo. LC 91-43731. (Illus.). 60p. (gr. 4 up). 1992. text ed. 13.95 RSBE (*0-87518-507-X*, Dillon) Macmillan Child Grp.

Pugh, Ann, et al. Diggy Armadillo Goes to Fort Worth Stock Show & Rodeo, Bk. 2: Further Adventures: "Finding Rosita" Van Way Hampton, Cindy, illus. LC 93-73103. 54p. (gr. 3-6). 1993. staple bdg. 7.95 (*1-879465-02-7*) Diggy & Assocs.

Stuart, Dee. The Astonishing Armadillo. LC 92-25970. 1993. 19.95 (*0-87614-769-4*) Carolrhoda Bks.

—Astonishing Armadillo. (gr. 4-7). 1994. pap. 6.95 (*0-87614-630-2*) Carolrhoda Bks.

ARMAMENTS

see Disarmament

ARMED FORCES

see Soldiers

see names of countries and international organizations with the subdivision Armed Forces, e.g. U. S.–Armed Forces; etc.

ARMIES

see also Disarmament; Military Art and Science; Military Service, Compulsory; Soldiers; War;

also names of countries with the subhead Army (e.g. U. S. army; etc.); and headings beginning with the word Military

ARMORED CARS (TANKS)

see Tanks (Military Science)

ARMS, COATS OF

see Heraldry

ARMS AND ARMOR

see also Firearms; Ordnance

Armor. (Illus.). 64p. (gr. 3-9). 1990. PLB 16.95 (*1-85435-089-7*) Marshall Cavendish.

Byam, Michele. Arms & Armor. King, Dave, photos by. LC 87-26449. (Illus.). 64p. (gr. 5 up). 1988. 16.00 (*0-394-89622-X*); lib. bdg. 16.99 (*0-394-99622-4*) Knopf Bks Yng Read.

Gonen, Rivka. Charge! Weapons & Warfare in Ancient Times. LC 92-36772. 1993. lib. bdg. 22.95 (*0-8225-3201-8*, Runestone Pr) Lerner Pubns.

Gravett, Christopher. Arms & Armor. Hook, Richard, et al, illus. LC 94-7938. 32p. (gr. 4-6). 1994. PLB write for info. (*0-8114-6190-4*) Raintree Steck-V.

Harbor, B. Arms Trade. (Illus.). 48p. (gr. 5 up). 1988. PLB 18.60 (*0-86592-283-7*); 13.95 (*0-685-58315-5*) Rourke Corp.

Hofsinde, Robert. Indian Warriors & Their Weapons. Hofsinde, Robert, illus. LC 65-11041. (gr. 4-7). 1965. PLB 11.88 (*0-688-31613-1*) Morrow Jr Bks.

Yue, Charlotte & Yue, David. Armor. LC 93-50601. 1994. 14.95 (*0-395-68101-4*) HM.

ARMS CONTROL

see Disarmament

ARMSTRONG, DANIEL LOUIS, 1900-1971

Brown, Sandford. Louis Armstrong: Singing, Swinging Satchmo. LC 92-43192. (Illus.). 144p. (gr. 9-12). 1993. PLB 14.40 (*0-531-13028-2*) Watts.

—Louis Armstrong: Swinging, Singing Satchmo. (Illus.). (gr. 7-12). 1993. pap. 6.95 (*0-531-15680-X*) Watts.

Collier, James L. Louis Armstrong: An American Success Story. LC 84-42982. (Illus.). 176p. (gr. 5-9). 1985. SBE 14.95 (*0-02-722830-4*, Macmillan Child Bk) Macmillan Child Grp.

—Louis Armstrong: An American Success Story. LC 92-45767. (Illus.). 176p. (gr. 7 up). 1994. pap. 5.95 (*0-02-042555-4*, Aladdin) Macmillan Child Grp.

McKissack, Patricia & McKissack, Fredrick. Louis Armstrong: Jazz Musician. Ostendorf, Ned, illus. LC 91-12420. 32p. (gr. 1-4). 1991. lib. bdg. 12.95 (*0-89490-307-1*) Enslow Pubs.

Medearis, Angela S. Little Louis & the Jazz Band: The Story of Louis "Satchmo" Armstrong. Rich, Ann, illus. LC 93-23596. 1994. write for info. (*0-525-67424-1*, Lodestar Bks) Dutton Child Bks.

Woog, Adam. Louis Armstrong. LC 94-296. (gr. 5-8). 1995. 14.95 (*1-56006-059-X*) Lucent Bks.

ARMY

see Military Art and Science

ARMY LIFE

see Soldiers

ARMY SCHOOLS

see Military Education

ARMY VEHICLES

see Vehicles, Military

ARNOLD, BENEDICT, 1741-1801

Fritz, Jean. Traitor: The Case of Benedict Arnold. Andre, John, illus. (gr. 3-7). 1981. 15.95 (*0-399-20834-8*, Putnam) Putnam Pub Group.

—Traitor: The Case of Benedict Arnold. 192p. (gr. 5-9). 1989. pap. 4.99 (*0-14-032940-4*, Puffin) Puffin Bks.

Wade, Mary D. Benedict Arnold. LC 94-2574. 1994. write for info. (*0-531-20156-2*) Watts.

ARNOLD, BENEDICT, 1741-1801–FICTION

Rinaldi, Ann. Finishing Becca: A Story of Peggy Shippen & Benedict Arnold. (gr. 7 up). 1994. pap. 3.95 (*0-15-200879-9*); 10.95 (*0-15-200880-2*) HarBrace.

ART

see also Anatomy, Artistic; Animals in Art; Archeology; Architecture; Arts and Crafts; Blacks in Literature and Art; Christian Art and Symbolism; Collage; Collectors and Collecting; Drawing; Folk Art; Forgery of Works of Art; Gems; Graphic Arts; Illustration of Books; Painting; Photography, Artistic; Pictures; Portraits; Sculpture; Symbolism

Abell, ed. Make a Thousand Faces: Eye & Hand Coordination. (Illus.). 50p. (ps-k). 1993. 25.00 (*1-56611-062-9*); pap. 15.00 (*1-56611-063-7*) Jonas.

Allen, Dorothy S. Plaster & Bisque Art: Special Finishes. Cole, Tom, ed. LC 80-70317. (Illus.). 44p. (gr. 4 up). 1981. pap. 2.95 (*0-9605204-4-9*) Dots Pubns.

—Plaster & Bisque Art: The Soft Touch Technique. Cole, Tom, ed. LC 80-70317. (Illus.). 47p. (gr. 4 up). 1981. pap. 2.95 (*0-9605204-6-5*) Dots Pubns.

—Plaster & Bisque Art: With Transparent Watercolor. Cole, Tom, ed. LC 80-70317. (Illus.). 57p. (gr. 4 up). 1981. pap. 1.95 (*0-9605204-5-7*) Dots Pubns.

Allen, Dorothy S. & Cole, Tom. Plaster & Bisque Art: Mist, Museum Bronze, Pastel Chalk, Pearl & Suede Finishes. LC 80-70317. (Illus.). 52p. (gr. 4 up). 1981. pap. 2.95 (*0-9605204-3-0*) Dots Pubns.

Allison, Linda. Trash Artists Workshop. 96p. (gr. 3-6). 1994. 9.95 (*0-685-71611-2*, 750) W Gladden Found.

Angelou, Maya. My Painted House, My Friendly Chicken, & Me. Courtney-Clarke, Margaret, photos by. LC 93-45735. (Illus.). 48p. (ps-5). 1994. 16.00 (*0-517-59667-9*, Clarkson Potter) Crown Pub Group.

Armstrong, B. Build a Doodle, No. 1. 32p. (gr. k-4). 1985. 2.95 (*0-88160-124-1*, LW 133) Learning Wks.

—Build a Doodle, No. 2. 32p. (gr. k-4). 1985. 2.95 (*0-88160-125-X*, LW 134) Learning Wks.

Axelrod, Alan, commentary by. Songs of the Wild West. Fox, Dan, contrib. by. (Illus.). 128p. 1991. pap. 19.95 jacketed (*0-671-74775-4*, S&S BFYR) S&S Trade.

Aydelott, Jimmie. Art & Math Throughout the Year. (gr. 1-6). 1989. pap. 8.95 (*0-8224-0104-5*) Fearon Teach Aids.

Blansett, Mary L. & Schimminger, Lorraine. Put a Frog in Your Pocket. (Illus.). 112p. (gr. 3-6). 1985. guide 8.95 (*0-86530-085-2*, IP 85-2) Incentive Pubns.

Boy Scouts of America Staff. Cub Scout Academics: Art. (Illus.). 44p. 1991. pap. 1.35 (*0-8395-3031-5*, 33031) BSA.

Brackett, Karen. Beautiful Junk. 80p. 1994. 10.95 (*0-685-71610-4*, 751) W Gladden Found.

Brisson, Lynn. Three-D Art Projects That Teach. (Illus.). 80p. (gr. k-6). 1989. pap. text ed. 7.95 (*0-86530-084-4*, IP 166-1) Incentive Pubns.

Brooks, Rebecca. Inside Art: Culture History Expression, Bk. 1. Crawford, A. F., ed. (Illus.). 224p. (gr. 7). 1992. text ed. 44.40 (*0-87443-101-8*); tchr's. ed. 40.00 (*0-87443-103-4*) Benson.

Chacon, Rick. Big & Easy Art. Chacon, Rick, illus. 32p. (ps-1). 1986. wkbk. 5.95 (*1-55734-074-9*) Tchr Create Mat.

Chapman, Laura. Adventures in Art. (gr. 1-6). 1994. Bk. 1. text ed. 16.50 (*0-87192-251-7*); Bk. 2. text ed. 16.50 (*0-87192-252-5*); Bk. 3. text ed. 19.46 (*0-87192-253-3*); Bk. 1. tchr's. ed. 29.95 (*0-87192-257-6*); Bk. 2. tchr's. ed. 29.95 (*0-87192-258-4*); Bk. 3. tchr's. ed. 29.95 (*0-87192-259-2*) Davis Mass.

—Adventures in Art. (gr. 1-6). 1994. Bk. 4. text ed. 19.46 (*0-87192-254-1*); Bk. 5. text ed. 19.46 (*0-87192-255-X*); Bk. 6. text ed. 19.46 (*0-87192-256-8*); Bk. 4. tchr's. ed. 29.95 (*0-87192-260-6*); Bk. 5. tchr's. ed. 29.95 (*0-87192-261-4*); Bk. 6. tchr's. ed. 29.95 (*0-87192-262-2*) Davis Mass.

Cook, J. Understanding Modern Art. (Illus.). 64p. (gr. 5 up). 1992. PLB 13.96 (*0-88110-512-0*, Usborne); pap. 7.95 (*0-7460-0475-3*, Usborne) EDC.

Cracchiolo, Rachelle & Smith, Mary D. Quick Fun Art. (Illus.). 56p. (gr. k-3). 1977. wkbk. 5.95 (*1-55734-001-3*) Tchr Create Mat.

Cvach, Milos, text by. Robert Delaunay: The Eiffel Tower: An Art Play Book. Curtil, Sophie. (Illus.). 32p. (gr. 2 up). 1988. 17.95 (*0-8109-1141-8*) Abrams.

Daugherty, Franklin. Postmodern Times. LC 87-71793. 280p. 1988. 14.95 (*0-944284-00-0*) T C DeLeon.

Davidson, Rosemary. Take a Look: An Introduction to the Experience of Art. (Illus.). 128p. (gr. 4-7). 1994. 18.99 (*0-670-84478-0*) Viking Child Bks.

Evans, Joy. The Big Book of Art Centers. (Illus.). 64p. (gr. 1-4). 1992. pap. 11.95 incl. charts (*1-55799-221-5*, EMC307) Evan-Moor Corp.

—Creative Thinking Through Art, Vol. 1: Mixed Media. (Illus.). 64p. (gr. 2-5). 1993. pap. text ed. 11.95 (*1-55799-263-0*) Evan-Moor Corp.

Evans, Vicki. Be Like the Sun & Shine. (ENG, FRE & SPA., Illus.). 32p. (ps-5). 1993. pap. 9.00 (*0-9636367-0-7*) V Evans.

Find the Gifts. (gr. k-3). 1991. 5.98 (*0-8317-9729-0*) Smithmark.

Fleischman, Paul. Copier Creations: Using Copy Machines to Make Decals, Silhouettes, Flip Books, Films, & Much More! Cain, David, illus. LC 91-45413. 128p. (gr. 3 up). 1993. 14.00 (*0-06-021052-4*); PLB 13.89 (*0-06-021053-2*) HarpC Child Bks.

Florian, Douglas. A Painter. LC 92-29583. (Illus.). 32p. (ps up). 1993. 14.00 (*0-688-11872-0*); PLB 13.93 (*0-688-11873-9*) Greenwillow.

Foster, Tom. Color to Read, Vol. Aleph. LuBin, L., ed. Foster, Tom, illus. 72p. (ps-1). 1990. lib. bdg. write for info.; pap. write for info.; write for info. tchr's. ed. Lubin Pr.

Freeberg, Dolores. Graph Paper Art. Freeberg, Dolores, illus. 48p. (gr. 2-6). 1986. wkbk. 6.95 (*1-55734-052-8*) Tchr Create Mat.

Freeberg, Erling & Freeberg, Dolores. Challenging Graph Art. Freeberg, Erling & Freeberg, Dolores, illus. 48p. (gr. 2-6). 1987. wkbk. 6.95 (*1-55734-096-X*) Tchr Create Mat.

—Holiday Graph Art. Freeberg, Erling & Freeberg, Dolores, illus. 48p. (gr. 2-6). 1987. wkbk. 6.95 (*1-55734-093-5*) Tchr Create Mat.

—Patriotic Graph Art. Freeberg, Erling & Freeberg, Dolores, illus. 48p. (gr. 2-6). 1987. wkbk. 6.95 (*1-55734-094-3*) Tchr Create Mat.

—Simple Graph Art. Freeberg, Erling & Freeberg, Dolores, illus. 48p. (gr. k-1). 1987. wkbk. 6.95 (*1-55734-095-1*) Tchr Create Mat.

Frost, Joan. Art, Books & Children: Art Activities Based on Children's Literature. (Illus.). 88p. (gr. 1-6). 1984. spiral bdg. 13.95 (*0-938594-03-6*) Spec Lit Pr.

Gartenhaus, Alan. Start Exploring Masterpieces of American Art: A Fact-Filled Coloring Book. Driggs, Helen, illus. 128p. (Orig.). 1992. pap. 8.95 (*1-56138-083-0*) Running Pr.

Gogerty, Clare. Places in Art. Morris, Tony, illus. LC 94-8941. 1994. write for info. (*1-85435-767-0*) Marshall Cavendish.

Gregson, Bob. Take Part Art. (gr. 3-6). 1990. pap. 14.95 (*0-8224-6781-X*) Fearon Teach Aids.

Hodgson, Harriet. Artworks. Savage, Beth, illus. 64p. (gr. k-3). 1986. 6.95 (*0-912107-42-1*) Monday Morning Bks.

Hoeft, Pam. Holiday Art a la Carte. 112p. (gr. 4-8). 1982. 9.95 (*0-88160-049-0*, LW 235) Learning Wks.

Hoffman, Jennifer. Art Starts. Gregorich, Barbara, ed. (Illus.). 32p. (gr. 3 up). 1992. pap. 1.99 (*0-88743-261-1*, 02901) Sch Zone Pub Co.

—More Art Starts. Gregorich, Barbara, ed. (Illus.). 32p. (gr. 3 up). 1992. pap. 1.99 wkbk. (*0-88743-262-X*, 02902) Sch Zone Pub Co.

Hoobler, Dorothy. Images Across the Ages, 8 vols. 1994. Set. 127.68 (*0-8114-6384-2*) Raintree Steck-V.

Hunt, Lynn B. An Artist Game Bag. 2nd ed. Hunt, Lynn B., illus. 106p. (gr. 10 up). 1990. Repr. of 1936 ed. 39.95 (*0-381-20045-0*) Derrydale Pr.

Isaacson, Philip M. A Short Walk Around the Pyramids & Through the World of Art. LC 91-8854. (Illus.). 112p. (gr. 3-7). 1993. 20.00 (*0-679-81523-6*); PLB 20.99 (*0-679-91523-0*) Knopf Bks Yng Read.

Jones, Mary L. Woody Watches the Masters: Four Great Artists, Bk. 1. (Illus.). 36p. (gr. 3-7). 1985. 4.95 (*0-533-05814-7*) Vantage.

Junior Publishers of San Francisco Bay Area Book Council Staff, ed. Window to Our World: An International Collection of Kids' Art. Caduto, Michael J., intro. by. (Illus.). 82p. (Orig.). 1992. pap. 5.99 (*0-935701-03-6*) Foghorn Pr.

Keightley, Moy. Investigating Art: A Practical Guide for Young People. (Illus.). 160p. (gr. 7 up). 17.95x (*0-87196-973-4*) Facts on File.

Kirberger, R. M. Equine Art for Fun & Profit. 60p. 1991. wkbk. 19.95 (*1-880495-00-7*) Rhenaria.

Kontoyiannaki, Kosta & Smith, Kaitlin M. Art Ideas. Lewis, Glenn, intro. by. (Illus.). 55p. (gr. 1-12). 1991. pap. text ed. 15.95 (*0-9627882-4-4*) Bradley Mann.

Korea, Joan & Korea, Gene. Dog. Abell, ed. & illus. 50p. Date not set. 25.00 (*1-56611-048-3*); pap. 15.00 (*1-56611-049-1*) Jonas.

Kropa, Susie. Faces, Legs, & Belly Buttons. Kropa, Susie, illus. 80p. (ps). 1984. wkbk. 9.95 (*0-86653-239-0*, GA 564) Good Apple.

Laycock, Mary. Bucky for Beginners. Kyzer, Martha, illus. 64p. (Orig.). (gr. 4-12). 1984. pap. text ed. 7.95 (*0-918932-82-3*) Activity Resources.

McHugh, Christopher. Faces. LC 93-20400. (Illus.). 32p. (gr. 4-6). 1993. 14.95 (*1-56847-071-1*) Thomson Lrning.

—Food. LC 93-20399. (Illus.). 32p. (gr. 4-6). 1993. 14.95 (*1-56847-070-3*) Thomson Lrning.

—Water. LC 92-43266. (Illus.). 32p. (gr. 4-6). 1993. 14.95g (*1-56847-024-X*) Thomson Lrning.

Martin, Ana. Romanesque Art & Architecture. LC 93-3436. (Illus.). 36p. (gr. 3 up). 1993. PLB 14.95 (*0-516-08387-2*); pap. 6.95 (*0-516-48387-0*) Childrens.

Mayers, Florence C. A Russian ABC: Featuring Masterpieces from the Hermitage, St. Petersburg. (Illus.). 36p. 1992. 12.95 (*0-8109-1919-2*) Abrams.

Micklethwait, Lucy, selected by. A Child's Book of Art: Great Pictures, First Words. LC 93-54320. (Illus.). 64p. (gr. k up). 1993. 16.95 (*1-56458-203-5*) Dorling Kindersley.

Moon, Marjorie, ed. A Is for Art. (Illus., Orig.). (ps-2). 1988. pap. 10.95 (*0-317-91187-2*) M Moon.

My Journey Through Art: Create Your Own Masterpieces. 48p. (gr. 2 up). 1994. pap. 6.95 (*0-8120-1924-5*) Barron.

National Gallery of Art of London Staff. The ABCs of Art. (Illus.). 32p. 1994. 6.95 (*0-87663-631-8*) Universe.

National Gallery of Art Staff. The ABCs of Art: Wall Frieze. (ps-3). 1994. pap. 6.95 (*1-55550-912-6*) Universe.

Neal, Judith. Fun Projects for Kids: A Teacher's Guide to Classroom Art. Bellew, Mike, illus. LC 83-7657. 136p. (gr. k-6). 1983. PLB 15.95 (*0-516-00821-8*) Childrens.

Nelson, Andy. The Impressionists Coloring Book. Nelson, Andy, illus. 96p. (Orig.). (gr. 1-6). 1990. pap. 5.95 (*0-929636-06-6*) Culpepper Pr.

Nickerson, Betty, ed. All about Us - Nous Autres: Creative Writing & Painting by & for Young People. (ENG & FRE., Illus.). 36p. 1992. pap. 4.95 (*0-685-61052-7*) All About Us.

Nowlin, Susan & Sterling, Mary E. Think & Do Bulletin Boards. Wright, Terry, illus. 96p. (gr. k-4). 1988. wkbk. 10.95 (*1-55734-063-3*) Tchr Create Mat.

Peppin, Anthea. Nature in Art. LC 91-35014. (Illus.). 48p. (gr. 2-6). 1992. PLB 14.40 (*1-56294-173-9*); pap. 6.95 (*1-56294-817-2*) Millbrook Pr.

—Nature in Art. 1992. pap. 6.70 (*0-395-64555-7*) HM.

—People in Art. LC 91-34983. (Illus.). 48p. (gr. 2-6). 1992. PLB 14.40 (*1-56294-171-2*); pap. 6.95 (*1-56294-818-0*) Millbrook Pr.

—People in Art. (gr. 4-7). 1992. pap. 6.70 (*0-395-64556-5*) HM.

—Places in Art. LC 91-34978. (Illus.). 48p. (gr. 2-6). 1992. PLB 14.40 (*1-56294-172-0*); pap. 6.95 (*1-56294-819-9*) Millbrook Pr.

—Places in Art. (gr. 4-7). 1992. pap. 6.70 (*0-395-64557-3*) HM.

Pierce, Brenda H. Creative Art Picture Starters: General Subjects - Level II. Pierce, Brenda H., illus. 32p. (gr. 4-6). 1988. tchr's. ed. 3.95 (*0-922694-03-6*) Moons Creat Prods.

Richardson, Wendy & Richardson, Jack. Families: Through the Eyes of Artists. LC 90-34279. (Illus.). 48p. (gr. 4 up). 1991. PLB 15.40 (*0-516-09284-7*); pap. 7.95 (*0-516-49284-5*) Childrens.

Roehrig, Catherine. Fun with Hieroglyphs: From the Metropolitan Museum of Art. 1990. 19.95 (*0-670-83576-5*) Viking Child Bks.

Schnell, Louise. Seasonal Art. Evans, Carol, ed. Schnell, Louise, illus. 52p. (ps-3). 1988. wkbk. 5.95 (*0-915505-01-0*) Tchr Tested-Child.

Sefkow, Paula & Berger, Helen. All Children Create: Levels Four to Six, an Elementary Art Curriculum, Vol. II. Gutek, Rob, illus. LC 80-82018. 204p. (Orig.). (gr. 4-6). 1981. pap. 24.95x (*0-918452-25-2*) Learning Pubns.

Smith, Mary & Robison, Phyllis. Easy Art. Astrom, Lena, illus. 48p. (gr. k-3). 1982. wkbk. 5.95 (*1-55734-004-8*) Tchr Create Mat.

Spencer, Pat. Bulletin Boards Through the Year. Spencer, Pat, illus. 96p. (gr. k-4). 1988. wkbk. 10.95 (*1-55734-062-5*) Tchr Create Mat.

Spivak, Darlene E. Graph Art Puzzles. Wright, Theresa N., illus. 48p. (gr. 2-5). 1987. wkbk. 6.95 (*1-55734-068-4*) Tchr Create Mat.

Stern, Susan, created by. Keep on Looking. LC 92-52986. (Illus.). 64p. (Orig.). (gr. 2-6). 1992. pap. 9.95 (*1-56282-289-6*) Hyprn Child.

Striker, Susan. Build a Better Mousetrap. Striker, Susan, illus. 64p. (gr. 2 up). 1983. pap. 6.95 (*0-8050-2615-0*, Owl) H Holt & Co.

Sullivan, Charles, ed. Children of Promise: African-American Literature & Art for Young People. Campbell, Mary S., frwd. by. (Illus.). 128p. 1991. 24.95 (*0-8109-3170-2*) Abrams.

Sullivan, Dianna J. Big & Easy Art for Fall. Ecker, Beverly, illus. 48p. (ps-2). 1987. wkbk. 6.95 (*1-55734-082-X*) Tchr Create Mat.

—Big & Easy Art for Patriotic Holidays. Adkins, Lynda, illus. 48p. (ps-2). 1987. wkbk. 5.95 (*1-55734-085-4*) Tchr Create Mat.

—Big & Easy Art for Spring & Summer. Ecker, Beverly, illus. 64p. (ps-2). 1987. wkbk. 7.95 (*1-55734-084-6*) Tchr Create Mat.

—Big & Easy Art for Winter. Ecker, Beverly, illus. 48p. (ps-2). 1987. wkbk. 6.95 (*1-55734-083-8*) Tchr Create Mat.

—Big & Easy Community Helpers. Adkins, Lynda, illus. 48p. (ps-2). 1988. wkbk. 5.95 (*1-55734-106-0*) Tchr Create Mat.

—Holiday Art. Sullivan, Dianna J., illus. 48p. (gr. k-3). 1985. wkbk. 5.95 (*1-55734-007-2*) Tchr Create Mat.

—Milk Carton Art Projects. Adkins, Lynda, illus. 32p. (gr. 1-4). 1988. wkbk. 4.95 (*1-55734-099-4*) Tchr Create Mat.

Taylor, Anne. Math in Art. Taylor, Anne, illus. (Orig.). (gr. 1-9). 1974. pap. 7.95 (*0-918932-28-9*) Activity Resources.

Tekerian, Irisa & Watrous, Merrill. Art & Writing Throughout the Year. (gr. 1-6). 1988. pap. 15.95 (*0-8224-0499-0*) Fearon Teach Aids.

Terzian, Alexandra. The Kids' Multicultural Art Book: Art & Craft Experiences from Around the World. Trezzo-Braren Studio Staff, illus. 160p. (Orig.). (ps-6). 1993. pap. 12.95 (*0-913589-72-1*) Williamson Pub Co.

Triado, Juan-Ramon. The Key to Baroque Art. (Illus.). 80p. (gr. 8 up). 1990. PLB 21.50 (*0-8225-2056-7*) Lerner Pubns.

West-Naus, Roberta. Art Aardvark. (Illus.). 72p. (gr. 1-6). 1981. 7.95 (*0-88160-041-5*, LW 226) Learning Wks.

Wickham, Geoffrey. Rapid Perspective. (gr. 10 up). 9.95 (*0-85458-050-6*); pap. 7.95 (*0-85458-051-4*) Transatl Arts.

Williams, Helen. Stories in Art. LC 91-32185. (Illus.). 48p. (gr. 2-6). 1992. PLB 14.40 (*1-56294-174-7*); pap. 6.95 (*1-56294-820-2*) Millbrook Pr.

—Stories in Art. (gr. 4-7). 1992. pap. 6.70 (*0-395-64558-1*) HM.

Wolf, Gerald P. Child-Size Masterpieces - Transportation in America. (Orig.). (ps-6). 1992. pap. 12.95 (*0-939195-05-4*) Parent-Child Pr.

Woolf, Felicity. Picture This Century: An Introduction to Twentieth-Century Art. LC 92-9128. 1993. pap. 16.00 (*0-385-30852-3*) Doubleday.

Yenawine, Philip. Colors. (Illus.). (gr. 2-5). 1991. 14.95 (*0-385-30254-1*); PLB 14.99 (*0-385-30314-9*) Delacorte.

ART–ANALYSIS, INTERPRETATION, APPRECIATION

see Art–Study and Teaching

ART, ANCIENT

see also Art, Primitive

Prudhomme, Frances & Sternberg, Susan T. The Gift of the Greeks: Art & Civilization of Ancient Greece. 24p. (Orig.). (gr. 4-7). 1982. pap. 8.95 (*0-935213-04-X*) A M Huntington Art.

ART, APPLIED

see Art Industries and Trade

ART, CHRISTIAN

see Christian Art and Symbolism

ART, CLASSICAL

see Art, Greek

ART–CRITICISM

see Art Criticism

ART, DECORATIVE

Here are entered general works on the decoration and use of artistic objects. Works limited to the external ornamentation of objects are entered under Design, Decorative.

see also Decoration and Ornament; Enamel and Enameling; Furniture; Illustration of Books; Mosaics; Needlework; Pottery

Fabricant, Norman. Fun with Tattoo Art. (gr. 4-7). 1994. pap. 4.95 (*0-8167-3378-3*) Troll Assocs.

ART, ECCLESIASTICAL

see Christian Art and Symbolism

ART–EDUCATION

see Art–Study and Teaching

ART–FICTION

Agee, Jon. The Incredible Painting of Felix Clousseau. (Illus.). 32p. (ps up). 1988. 15.00 (*0-374-33633-4*) FS&G.

Blos, Sarah I. & Davis, Julie N. Katsu & the Kite. (Illus.). 14p. 1988. pap. 0.96 (*0-912303-43-3*) Michigan Mus.

Brooke, William J. A Brush with Magic. LC 92-41744. (Illus.). 160p. (gr. 3 up). 1993. 15.00 (*0-06-022973-X*); PLB 14.89 (*0-06-022974-8*) HarpC Child Bks.

Carrick, Donald. Morgan & the Artist. LC 84-14267. (Illus.). 32p. (ps-4). 1985. 14.45 (*0-89919-300-5*, Clarion Bks) HM.

Cohen, Miriam. No Good in Art. (gr. k-6). 1986. pap. 3.25 (*0-440-46389-0*, YB) Dell.

DePaola, Tomie. The Art Lesson. DePaola, Tomie, illus. 32p. (ps-3). 1994. pap. 5.95 (*0-399-22761-X*) Putnam Pub Group.

Drew, James. Rackstraw: The Magical Thoughts & Adventures of A Brilliant Young Art Mouse. George, Mary G., ed. Drew, James, illus. LC 93-71718. 168p. (gr. 2-9). 1994. 18.95 (*0-9625023-9-1*) Art Pr Intl.

Foster, Joanna. Cartons, Cans, & Orange Peels. (gr. 4-7). 1993. pap. 7.95 (*0-395-66504-3*, Clarion Bks) HM.

Guzzo, Sandra E. Miguel & the Santero. Sandoval, Richard C., illus. 32p. (Orig.). (gr. k-5). 1993. pap. text ed. 6.95 (*0-937206-30-X*) New Mexico Mag.

Hewitt, Sally. Busy Little Artist. 1990. 5.99 (*0-517-03604-5*) Random Hse Value.

Ingoglia, Gina. Art Class. LC 91-58786. (Illus.). 48p. (gr. k-3). 1992. 9.95 (*1-56282-047-8*); PLB 9.89 (*1-56282-227-6*) Disney Pr.

Koechlin, Lionel. Lulu & the Artist. (Illus.). 32p. (gr. k-2). 1991. 12.95 (*0-89565-741-4*) Childs World.
Leggat, Gillian. Artist & the Bully. (gr. 4-7). 1992. pap. 3.95 (*0-7910-2913-1*) Chelsea Hse.
Lehan, Daniel. This Is Not a Book about Dodos. Lehan, Daniel, illus. LC 91-794. 32p. (gr. k-3). 1992. 14.00 (*0-525-44878-0*, DCB) Dutton Child Bks.
—Wipe Your Feet! Lehan, Daniel, illus. LC 91-44145. 32p. (gr. k-3). 1993. 14.00 (*0-525-44992-2*, DCB) Dutton Child Bks.
Locker, Thomas. The Young Artist. (Illus.). 32p. (ps up). 1989. PLB 15.89 (*0-8037-0627-8*) Dial Bks Young.
McOmber, Rachel B., ed. McOmber Phonics Storybooks: String Art, Vol. 1. rev. ed. (Illus.). write for info. (*0-944991-96-3*) Swift Lrn Res.
—McOmber Phonics Storybooks: String Art, Vol. 2. rev. ed. (Illus.). write for info. (*0-944991-95-5*) Swift Lrn Res.
Mayhew, James. Katie's Picture Show. (ps-3). 1989. 14.95 (*0-553-05846-0*) Bantam.
Moon, Nicola. Lucy's Pictures. Ayliffe, Alex, illus. LC 94-11178. (gr. 7-9). Date not set. write for info. (*0-8037-1833-0*) Dial Bks Young.
Reed, Amy. Oliver's Art Adventure. 1993. 7.95 (*0-8062-4640-5*) Carlton.
Reese, Bob. Art. Reese, Bob, illus. LC 92-12187. 24p. (ps-2). 1992. PLB 9.75 (*0-516-05578-X*) Childrens.
Rylant, Cynthia. All I See. Catalanotto, Peter, illus. LC 88-42547. 32p. (gr. k-2). 1988. 15.95 (*0-531-05777-1*); PLB 15.99 (*0-531-08377-2*) Orchard Bks Watts.
Schick, Eleanor. Art Lessons. LC 86-243. (Illus.). 48p. (gr. k-3). 1987. 11.75 (*0-688-05120-0*); lib. bdg. 11.88 (*0-688-05121-9*) Greenwillow.
Sose, Bonnie. Little Artist: A Child's Art Book. 32p. (gr. 3 up). 11.00 (*0-685-65933-X*) Character Builders.

ART–FORGERIES
see Forgery of Works of Art

ART–GALLERIES AND MUSEUMS
Mayers, Florence C. ABC: the Alef-Bet Book: The Israel Museum, Jerusalem. LC 88-27501. (Illus.). 32p. (gr. k up). 1989. 12.95 (*0-8109-1885-4*) Abrams.

ART, GRAPHIC
see Graphic Arts

ART, GREEK
Prudhomme, Frances & Sternberg, Susan T. The Gift of the Greeks: Art & Civilization of Ancient Greece. 24p. (Orig.). (gr. 4-7). 1982. pap. 8.95 (*0-935213-04-X*) A M Huntington Art.

ART–HISTORY
Bracons, Jose. The Key to Gothic Art. (Illus.). 80p. (gr. 8 up). 1990. PLB 21.50 (*0-8225-2051-6*) Lerner Pubns.
Janson, H. W. & Janson, Anthony F. History of Art for Young People. 4th ed. (Illus.). 528p. 1992. 35.00 (*0-8109-3405-1*) Abrams.
McHugh, Christopher. People at Work. LC 93-20405. 32p. (gr. 4-6). 1993. 14.95 (*1-56847-111-4*) Thomson Lrning.
—Town & Country. LC 93-20401. (Illus.). 32p. (gr. 4-6). 1993. 14.95 (*1-56847-110-6*) Thomson Lrning.
Monteith, Jay. African Art: Activity Workbook. (Illus.). 24p. (Orig.). 1993. pap. text ed. 8.75 (*0-9627366-4-3*) Arts & Comns NY.
Paint & Painting. 48p. (gr. 3 up). 1994. 19.95 (*0-590-47636-X*) Scholastic Inc.
Raboff, Ernest. Diego Rodriquez de Silva y Velasquez. LC 87-17697. (Illus.). 32p. (gr. 1 up). 1988. pap. 7.95 (*0-06-446073-8*, Trophy) HarpC Child Bks.
—Henri Rousseau. LC 87-17700. (Illus.). 32p. (gr. 1 up). 1988. pap. 7.95 (*0-06-446069-X*, Trophy) HarpC Child Bks.
—Paul Gauguin. LC 87-17696. (Illus.). 32p. (gr. 1 up). 1988. pap. 5.95 (*0-06-446078-9*, Trophy) HarpC Child Bks.
—Paul Klee. LC 87-17699. (Illus.). 32p. (gr. 1 up). 1988. pap. 5.95 (*0-06-446065-7*, Trophy) HarpC Child Bks.

ART, INDIAN
see Indians of North America–Art

ART, PRIMITIVE
see also Cave Drawings; Folk Art; Indians of North America–Art;
also names of countries, cities, etc. with the subdivision Antiquities, e.g. U. S.–Antiquities; etc.
Terzi, Marinella. Prehistoric Rock Art. LC 92-7504. (Illus.). 36p. (gr. 3 up). 1992. PLB 14.95 (*0-516-08379-1*) Childrens.
—Prehistoric Rock Art. LC 92-7504. (Illus.). 36p. (gr. 3 up). 1993. pap. 6.95 (*0-516-48379-X*) Childrens.

ART–PSYCHOLOGY
Brommer, Gerald F. & Horn, George F. Art in Your World. 2nd ed. LC 84-73493. (Illus.). 256p. (gr. 7-8). 1985. text ed. 22.46 (*0-87192-168-5*, 168-5); tchr's. guide 10.95 (*0-685-01368-5*) Davis Mass.

ART, RENAISSANCE
Arenas, Jose F. The Key to Renaissance Art. (Illus.). 80p. (gr. 8 up). 1990. PLB 21.50 (*0-8225-2057-5*) Lerner Pubns.

ART–STUDY AND TEACHING
Atherton, Mary K., et al. Touch with Your Eyes! Frank, Phil, illus. 48p. (Orig.). (gr. k-8). 1982. pap. 4.50 (*0-9613069-0-4*) Orinda Art Coun.
Barry, Jan. Draw, Design & Paint. (Illus.). 144p. (gr. 2-6). 1990. 12.95 (*0-86653-536-5*, GA1142) Good Apple.
Bradley, Susannah. The Turbulent Triangle. Neary, Bryan, illus. 48p. (gr. 3-6). 1992. pap. 2.95 (*1-56680-001-3*) Mad Hatter Pub.
Cook, J. Understanding Modern Art. (Illus.). 64p. (gr. 5 up). 1992. PLB 13.96 (*0-88110-512-0*, Usborne); pap. 7.95 (*0-7460-0475-3*, Usborne) EDC.
FunFax Organizer. (Illus.). (gr. 3-6). 1992. 9.95 (*1-56680-000-5*) Mad Hatter Pub.
Greenberg, Jan & Jordan, Sandra. The Sculptor's Eye: Looking at Contemporary American Art. LC 92-16323. 1993. 19.95 (*0-385-30902-3*) Delacorte.
Heller, Ruth. Designs for Coloring Optical Art. (Illus.). 64p. 1992. pap. 3.95 (*0-448-03143-4*, G&D) Putnam Pub Group.
Hollingsworth, Patricia & Hollingsworth, Stephen F. Smart Art: Learning to Classify & Critique Art. (Illus.). 112p. (Orig.). (gr. 3-8). 1989. pap. text ed. 15. 95 (*0-913705-31-4*) Zephyr Pr AZ.
Maid, Amy. Mindscapes. LC 82-9904. 67p. (gr. 3-8). 1983. pap. 11.95x (*0-8290-1001-7*) Irvington.
Mayers, Florence C. A Russian ABC: Featuring Masterpieces from the Hermitage, St. Petersburg. (Illus.). 36p. 1992. 12.95 (*0-8109-1919-2*) Abrams.
Micklethwait, Lucy, selected by. & created by. I Spy Two Eyes: Numbers in Art. LC 92-35641. (Illus.). 48p. (ps up). 1993. 19.00 (*0-688-12640-5*); PLB 18.93 (*0-688-12642-1*) Greenwillow.
Molyneux, Lynn & Bucur, Mike. Your Own Thing: Individual Art Projects for Primary Grades. Bucur, Mike, illus. 160p. (gr. k-6). 1983. perfect bdg. 9.95 (*0-685-29140-5*) Trellis Bks Inc.
Savage, Stephen. Ancient Greek Monuments to Make: The Parthenon & the Theatre of Dionysos. Savage, Stephen, illus. Moon, Warren G., intro. by. (Illus.). 48p. (Orig.). (gr. 7 up). 1990. pap. 7.95 (*0-88045-096-7*) Stemmer Hse.
Time-Life Inc. Editors. Art & Music. Crawford, Jean, ed. (Illus.). 88p. (gr. k-3). 1994. write for info. (*0-8094-9474-4*); PLB write for info. (*0-8094-9475-2*) Time-Life.
Wygant, Foster. School Art in American Culture, 1820-1970. (Illus.). 240p. (Orig.). 1993. pap. 21.95 (*0-9610376-1-X*) Interwood Pr.
Yenawine, Philip. Lines. (Illus.). (gr. 2-5). 1991. 14.95 (*0-385-30253-3*); PLB 14.99 (*0-385-30313-0*) Delacorte.
—People. LC 92-11203. 1993. pap. 14.95 (*0-385-30901-5*) Dell.
—Places. LC 92-11202. 1993. 14.95 (*0-385-30900-7*) Dell.
—Shapes. (Illus.). (gr. 2-5). 1991. 14.95 (*0-385-30255-X*); PLB 14.99 (*0-385-30315-7*) Delacorte.
—Stories. (Illus.). (gr. 2-5). 1991. 14.95 (*0-385-30256-8*); PLB 14.99 (*0-385-30316-5*) Delacorte.

ART–VOCATIONAL GUIDANCE
Henderson, Kathy. Market Guide for Young Artists & Photographers. LC 90-39084. (Illus.). 176p. (Orig.). (gr. 3 up). 1990. pap. 12.95 (*1-55870-176-1*, 70068) Shoe Tree Pr.

ART ANATOMY
see Anatomy, Artistic

ART APPRECIATION
see Art–Study and Teaching; Art Criticism; Painting; Pictures

ART CRITICISM
Blanquet, Claire-Helene. Miro: Earth & Sky. LC 93-33680. 1994. write for info. (*0-7910-2813-5*) Chelsea Hse.
Blizzard, Gladys S. Come Look with Me: Animals in Art. LC 92-5357. 32p. (gr. 1-8). 1992. 13.95 (*1-56566-013-7*) Thomasson-Grant.
—Come Look with Me: Exploring Landscape Art with Children. LC 91-34320. (Illus.). 32p. (gr. 1-8). 1992. 13.95 (*0-934738-95-5*) Thomasson-Grant.
Gogerty, Clare. Stories in Art. Watkins, Lis, illus. LC 94-8957. 1994. write for info. (*1-85435-770-0*) Marshall Cavendish.
Hollingsworth, Patricia & Hollingsworth, Stephen F. Smart Art: Learning to Classify & Critique Art. (Illus.). 112p. (Orig.). (gr. 3-8). 1989. pap. text ed. 15. 95 (*0-913705-31-4*) Zephyr Pr AZ.
Judson, Bay, et al. Art Ventures: A Guide for Families to Ten Works of Art in the Carnegie Museum of Art. Koren, Edward, illus. LC 87-858. 24p. (Orig.). (gr. 4-6). 1987. pap. text ed. 5.95 (*0-88039-014-X*) Mus Art Carnegie.
Kennet, Frances. Looking at Painting. LC 89-7156. (Illus.). 48p. (gr. 4-8). 1990. 13.95 (*1-85435-102-8*) Marshall Cavendish.
Loumaye, Jacqueline. Chagall: My Town, Sad & Joyous. Goodman, John, tr. Boiry, Veronique, illus. LC 93-39109. 1994. write for info. (*0-7910-2807-0*) Chelsea Hse.
—Degas: The Painted Gesture. LC 93-33682. 1994. write for info. (*0-7910-2809-7*) Chelsea Hse.
Micklethwait, Lucy, selected by. I Spy a Lion: Animals in Art. LC 93-30017. 48p. 1994. 19.00 (*0-688-13230-8*); PLB 18.93 (*0-688-13231-6*) Greenwillow.
Richardson, Wendy & Richardson, Jack. Cities: Through the Eyes of Artists. LC 90-34277. 48p. (gr. 4 up). 1991. PLB 15.40 (*0-516-09282-0*); pap. 7.95 (*0-516-49282-9*) Childrens.
—Entertainers: Through the Eyes of Artists. LC 90-34278. 48p. (gr. 4 up). 1991. PLB 15.40 (*0-516-09283-9*); pap. 7.95 (*0-516-49283-7*) Childrens.
—Water: Through the Eyes of Artists. LC 90-34280. 48p. (gr. 4 up). 1991. PLB 15.40 (*0-516-09286-3*); pap. 7.95 (*0-516-49286-1*) Childrens.
Venezia, Mike. Jackson Pollock. Moss, Meg, contrib. by. LC 93-36699. (Illus.). 32p. (ps-4). 1994. PLB 12.85 (*0-516-02298-9*) Childrens.
—Michelangelo. Venezia, Mike, illus. LC 91-555. 32p. (ps-4). 1991. PLB 12.85 (*0-516-02293-8*); pap. 4.95 (*0-516-42293-6*) Childrens.
—Paul Klee. Venezia, Mike, illus. LC 91-12554. 32p. (gr. 4). 1991. PLB 12.85 (*0-516-02294-6*); pap. 4.95 (*0-516-42294-4*) Childrens.
Walker, Lou A. Roy Lichtenstein: The Artist at Work. Abramson, Michael, photos by. LC 93-2631. (Illus.). 48p. (gr. 3-7). 1994. 15.99 (*0-525-67435-7*, Lodestar Bks) Dutton Child Bks.

ART EDUCATION
see Art–Study and Teaching

ART FOGERIES
see Forgery of Works of Art

ART GALLERIES
see Art–Galleries and Museums

ART INDUSTRIES AND TRADE
see also Arts and Crafts; Folk Art
also special industries, trades, etc., e.g. Glass painting and staining; Leather Work
St. Tamara. Asian Crafts. St. Tamara, illus. LC 71-86983. (gr. 2-6). 1972. PLB 13.95 (*0-87460-148-7*) Lion Bks.

ART MUSEUMS
see Art–Galleries and Museums

ART OBJECTS
see also classes of art objects, e.g. Furniture; pottery; etc.

ART OBJECTS, FORGERY OF
see Forgery of Works of Art

ART SCHOOLS
see Art–Study and Teaching

ARTHUR, KING
see also Grail
Andronik, Catherine M. Quest for a King: Searching for the Real King Arthur. LC 88-7381. (Illus.). 160p. (gr. 5 up). 1989. SBE 13.95 (*0-689-31411-6*, Atheneum Child Bk) Macmillan Child Grp.
Brim, C. Arthur: Tales of the Young King. (Illus.). 32p. (gr. 2-6). 1989. 10.95 (*0-88625-236-9*) Durkin Hayes Pub.
Crawford, Tom. The Story of King Arthur. Green, John, illus. LC 94-3363. (gr. 4 up). 1994. pap. write for info. (*0-486-28347-X*) Dover.
Frost, Abigail. The Age of Chivalry. LC 89-17396. (Illus.). 48p. (gr. 4-8). 1990. PLB 13.95 (*1-85435-235-0*) Marshall Cavendish.
Green, Roger L. King Arthur & His Knights of the Round Table. (Orig.). (gr. 5-7). 1974. pap. 2.95 (*0-14-030073-2*) Viking Child Bks.
—King Arthur & His Knights of the Round Table. (gr. 5 up). 1990. pap. 3.99 (*0-14-035100-0*) Puffin Bks.
—King Arthur & His Knights of the Round Table. (gr. 5 up). 1993. 13.95 (*0-679-42311-7*, Everymans Lib Childs) Knopf.
Hastings, Selina. Sir Gawain & the Green Knight. Wijngaard, Juan, illus. LC 80-85379. 32p. (gr. 3-7). 1981. 16.00 (*0-688-00592-6*) Lothrop.
Hastings, Selina, retold by. Sir Gawain & the Loathly Lady. Wijngaard, Juan, illus. LC 85-63. 32p. (gr. k up). 1987. pap. 4.95 (*0-688-07046-9*, Mulberry) Morrow.
Heyer, Carol. Excalibur. Heyer, Carol, illus. LC 91-9100. 32p. (gr. k-4). 1991. 14.95 (*0-8249-8487-0*, Ideals Child) Hambleton-Hill.
Hodges, Margaret. The Kitchen Knight: A Tale of King Arthur. Hyman, Schart, illus. 1993. pap. 5.95 (*0-8234-1063-3*) Holiday.
Hodges, Margaret & Evernden, Margery. Of Swords & Sorcerers: The Adventures of King Arthur & His Knights. Frampton, David, illus. LC 91-40811. 112p. (gr. 5-7). 1993. SBE 14.95 (*0-684-19437-6*, Scribners Young Read) Macmillan Child Grp.
Howe, John, retold by. & illus. The Knight with the Lion: The Story of Yvain. LC 92-25940. 1995. 14.95 (*0-316-37583-7*) Little.
Lanier, Sidney. The Boy's King Arthur. Wyeth, N. C., illus. LC 73-13451. 336p. 1989. (Scribners Young Read); SBE 24.95 (*0-684-19111-3*, Scribner) Macmillan Child Grp.
Maccarone, Grace. The Sword in the Stone. (Illus.). 1992. pap. 2.95 (*0-590-45527-3*, 043, Cartwheel) Scholastic Inc.
Mallory, Thomas. King Arthur & His Knights of the Round Table. Lanier, Sidney & Pyle, Howard, eds. Florian, illus. 288p. (gr. 4-6). 1950. (G&D); 13.95 (*0-448-06016-7*, G&D) Putnam Pub Group.
Mockler, Anthony. King Arthur & His Knights. Harris, Nick, illus. 308p. 1987. jacketed 18.95 (*0-19-274531-X*) OUP.
Morpurgo, Michael. King Arthur. Foreman, Michael, illus. LC 93-33620. 1995. write for info. (*0-15-200080-1*) HarBrace.
O'Neill, Catherine. Let's Visit a Chocolate Factory. Parker, James W., illus. LC 87-3460. 32p. (gr. 2-4). 1988. PLB 10.79 (*0-8167-1161-5*); pap. text ed. 2.95 (*0-8167-1162-3*) Troll Assocs.
Perham, Molly, retold by. King Arthur & the Legends of Camelot. Heller, Julek, illus. 176p. (gr. 1 up). 1993. 22.00 (*0-670-84990-1*) Viking Child Bks.
Pyle, Howard. King Arthur. Hinkle, Don, ed. Tirtitilli, Jerry, illus. LC 87-15461. 48p. (gr. 3-6). 1988. PLB 12.89 (*0-8167-1213-1*); pap. 3.95 (*0-8167-1214-X*) Troll Assocs.
—King Arthur & the Magic Sword. LC 89-27793. 21p. (gr. 2-7). 1990. 13.95 (*0-8037-0824-6*) Dial Bks Young.
—Reader's Digest Best Loved Books for Young Readers: The Story of King Arthur & His Knights. Ogburn, Jackie, ed. Sweet, Darrell, illus. 208p. (gr. 4-12). 1989. 3.99 (*0-945260-31-8*) Choice Pub NY.

—The Story of King Arthur & His Knights. Pyle, Howard, illus. xviii, 313p. (gr. 7 up). pap. 6.95 (*0-486-21445-1*) Dover.
—The Story of Sir Lancelot & His Companions. (Illus.). 360p. (gr. 5 up). 1985. SBE 19.95 (*0-684-18313-7*, Scribners Young Read) Macmillan Child Grp.
—The Story of the Champions of the Round Table. Pyle, Howard, illus. xviii, 329p. (ps-4). 1968. pap. 7.95 (*0-486-21883-X*) Dover.
—The Story of the Champions of the Round Table. LC 84-13881. (Illus.). 348p. (gr. 7 up). 1984. RSBE 19.95 (*0-684-18171-1*, Scribners Young Read) Macmillan Child Grp.
—The Story of the Grail & the Passing of Arthur. Pyle, Howard, illus. LC 85-40302. 340p. (gr. 7 up). 1985. SBE 19.95 (*0-684-18483-4*, Scribners Young Read) Macmillan Child Grp.
—The Story of the Grail & the Passing of Arthur. unabr. ed. LC 92-29058. (Illus.). 272p. 1992. pap. text ed. 7.95 (*0-486-27361-X*) Dover.
Rojany, Lisa, adapted by. King Arthur's Camelot: A Pop-up Castle & Four Storybooks. Batki, Laszlo, illus. (ps up). 1993. Set, 12p. ea. 18.99 (*0-525-45026-2*, DCB) Dutton Child Bks.
Shannon, Mark. Gawain & the Green Knight. Shannon, David, illus. LC 93-13037. 32p. (ps-3). 1994. PLB 15.95 (*0-399-22446-7*, Putnam) Putnam Pub Group.
Storr, Catherine. The Sword in the Stone. Hunter, Susan, illus. LC 84-18293. 32p. (gr. 2-5). 1985. PLB 19.97 (*0-8172-2113-1*) Raintree Steck-V.
Talbott, Hudson. King Arthur: The Sword in the Stone. LC 90-28104. (Illus.). 56p. (gr. 5 up). 1991. 14.95 (*0-688-09403-1*); PLB 14.88 (*0-688-09404-X*) Morrow Jr Bks.
Tennyson, Alfred. Idylls of the King. (gr. 10 up). 1968. pap. 2.75 (*0-8049-0180-5*, CL-180) Airmont.
Twain, Mark. Connecticut Yankee in King Arthur's Court. LC 83-9162. (gr. 5 up). 1964. pap. 3.25 (*0-8049-0029-9*, CL-29) Airmont.
—A Connecticut Yankee in King Arthur's Court. new & abr. ed. Fago, John N., ed. Redondo, Francisco, illus. LC 83-9162. (gr. 4-12). 1977. pap. text ed. 2.95 (*0-88301-263-4*) Pendulum Pr.
—A Connecticut Yankee in King Arthur's Court. Hyman, Trina S., illus. LC 87-62879. 384p. (gr. 5 up). 1988. 19.95 (*0-688-06346-2*); signed ltd. ed. 100.00 (*0-688-08258-0*, Morrow Jr Bks) Morrow Jr Bks.
White, Terence H. The Sword in the Stone. Nolan, Dennis, illus. LC 92-24808. 256p. 1993. 18.95 (*0-399-22502-1*, Philomel Bks) Putnam Pub Group.
Winder, Blanche, ed. Stories of King Arthur. Gotlieb, Jules, illus. (gr. 4 up). 1968. pap. 1.95 (*0-8049-0167-8*, CL-167) Airmont.
Wray, Kit, as told by. & illus. King Arthur: A Hidden Picture Story. LC 91-76019. 32p. (ps-5). 1992. 7.95 (*1-56397-018-X*) Boyds Mills Pr.
Yolen, Jane, ed. Camelot. LC 92-39322. 1994. 21.95 (*0-399-22540-4*, Philomel Bks) Putnam Pub Group.

ARTHUR, KING–POETRY

Knowles, James, compiled by. King Arthur & His Knights. Rhead, Louis & Wheelwright, Rowland, illus. 416p. 1986. 12.99 (*0-517-61885-0*) Random Hse Value.
Riordan, James. Tales of King Arthur. Ambrus, Victor G., illus. LC 81-86152. 128p. (gr. 4-7). 1982. 14.95 (*1-56288-251-1*) Checkerboard.

ARTHURIAN ROMANCES

see Arthur, King

ARTIFICIAL INTELLIGENCE

Belgum, Erik. Artificial Intelligence: Opposing Viewpoints. LC 90-3519. (Illus.). 112p. (gr. 5-8). 1990. PLB 14.95 (*0-89908-085-5*) Greenhaven.

ARTIFICIAL SATELLITES

see also Space Vehicles

Baker, David. Earth Watch. (Illus.). 48p. (gr. 3-8). 1989. lib. bdg. 18.60 (*0-86592-372-8*); 13.95s.p. (*0-685-58641-3*) Rourke Corp.
Bendick, Jeanne. Artificial Satellites: Helpers in Space. (Illus.). 32p. (gr. k-2). 1991. PLB 12.90 (*1-56294-002-3*); pap. 4.95 (*1-878841-56-4*) Millbrook Pr.
Dudley, Mark. An Eye to the Sky. LC 91-33880. (Illus.). 48p. (gr. 5-6). 1992. text ed. 12.95 RSBE (*0-89686-691-2*, Crestwood Hse) Macmillan Child Grp.
Sabin, Francene. Rockets & Satellites. Maccabe, Richard, illus. LC 84-2738. 32p. (gr. 3-6). 1985. PLB 9.49 (*0-8167-0288-8*); pap. text ed. 2.95 (*0-8167-0289-6*) Troll Assocs.
Spizzirri Publishing Co. Staff. Satellites: An Educational Coloring Book. Spizzirri, Linda, ed. (Illus.). 32p. (gr. 1-8). 1986. pap. 1.75 (*0-86545-074-9*) Spizzirri.
Yost, Graham. Spies in the Sky. (Illus.). 144p. (gr. 8-12). 1989. lib. bdg. 16.95x (*0-8160-1942-8*) Facts on File.

ARTIFICIAL WEATHER CONTROL

see Weather Control

ARTILLERY

see also Ordnance

Nicholaus, J. Artillery. (Illus.). 48p. (gr. 3-8). 1989. lib. bdg. 18.60 (*0-86592-419-8*) Rourke Corp.

ARTISTIC ANATOMY

see Anatomy, Artistic

ARTISTIC PHOTOGRAPHY

see Photography, Artistic

ARTISTS

see also Architects; Art–Vocational Guidance; Black Artists; Painters; Sculptors; Women As Artists

Ball, Jacqueline A. & Conant, Catherine. Georgia O'Keeffe: Painter of the Desert. (Illus.). 64p. (gr. 3-7). PLB 14.95 (*1-56711-033-9*) Blackbirch.
Balsamo, Kathy. Exploring the Lives of Gifted People-The Arts. Johnson, Phyllis, illus. 80p. (gr. 4 up). 1987. pap. 8.95 (*0-86653-406-7*, GA1037) Good Apple.
Berman, Avis. James McNeill Whistler. LC 93-9453. 1993. 19.95 (*0-8109-3968-1*) Abrams.
Brommer, Gerald F. & Horn, George F. Art in Your World. 2nd ed. LC 84-73493. (Illus.). 256p. (gr. 7-8). 1985. text ed. 22.46 (*0-87192-168-5*, 168-5); tchr's. guide 10.95 (*0-685-01368-5*) Davis Mass.
Carle, Eric. The Art of Eric Carle. Carle, Eric, illus. LC 91-646. 124p. (gr. k up). 1993. pap. 29.95 (*0-88708-176-2*) Picture Bk Studio.
Collins, Pat L. I Am an Artist. Brickman, Robin, illus. LC 91-42071. 32p. (gr. k-3). 1992. 14.95 (*1-56294-702-8*); PLB 14.90 (*1-56294-082-1*) Millbrook Pr.
—I Am an Artist. (ps-3). 1994. pap. 7.95 (*1-56294-729-X*) Millbrook Pr.
Croll, Carolyn. The Man Who Painted Flowers. LC 93-42394. 1995. 14.95 (*0-399-22606-0*) Putnam Pub Group.
Cummings, Pat. Talking with Artists: Conversations with Victoria Chess, Pat Cummings, Leo & Diane Dillon, Richard Egielski, Lois Ehlert, Lisa Campbell Ernst, Tom Feelings, Steven Kellogg, Jerry Pinkney, Amy Schwartz, Lane Smith, Chris Van Allsburg, & David Wiesner. LC 91-9982. (Illus.). 96p. (gr. 4 up). 1992. SBE 18.95 (*0-02-724245-5*, Bradbury Pr) Macmillan Child Grp.
Cush, Cathie. Artists Who Created Great Works. (Illus.). 48p. (gr. 4-8). 1994. PLB write for info. (*0-8114-4933-5*) Raintree Steck-V.
Drucker, Malka. Frida Kahlo: Torment & Triumph in Her Life & Art. 1991. 16.50 (*0-553-07165-3*) Bantam.
Florian, Douglas. A Painter. LC 92-29583. (Illus.). 32p. (ps up). 1993. 14.00 (*0-688-11872-0*); PLB 13.93 (*0-688-11873-9*) Greenwillow.
Genius! The Artist & the Process, 6 bks. (Illus.). (gr. 7-9). 1990. 59.70 (*0-382-24030-8*); lib. bdg. 77.70 (*0-382-09902-8*) Silver Burdett Pr.
Glubok, Shirley. Painting. LC 93-8319. (Illus.). 256p. (gr. 4-6). 1994. SBE 24.95 (*0-684-19052-4*, Scribners Young Read) Macmillan Child Grp.
Gruen, John. Keith Haring. LC 93-46808. 1994. write for info. (*0-88682-664-0*) Creative Ed.
Hutchinson, Duane. Grotto Father: Artist-Priest of the West Bend Grotto. LC 89-39029. (Illus.). 64p. 1989. pap. 4.95 (*0-934988-20-X*) Foun Bks.
Hyman, Trina S. Self-Portrait: Trina Schart Hyman. Hyman, Trina S., illus. LC 80-26662. 32p. (gr. 4-7). 1989. PLB 15.89 (*0-06-022766-4*) HarpC Child Bks.
Kurtzman, Harvey. My Life As a Cartoonist. (Illus.). 1988. pap. 2.75 (*0-671-63453-4*, Minstrel Bks) PB.
Lipman, Jean & Aspinwall, Margaret. Alexander Calder & His Magical Mobiles. LC 81-1811. (Illus.). 96p. (ps up). 1981. 17.50 (*0-933920-17-2*) Hudson Hills.
Lyons, Mary E. Deep Blues: Bill Trayler, Self-Taught Artist. LC 93-23736. (gr. 3-6). 1994. 15.95 (*0-684-19458-9*, Scribner) Macmillan.
Meyer, Susan E. Edgar Degas. LC 94-8420. 1994. 19.95 (*0-8109-3220-2*) Abrams.
Moore, Reavis. Native Artists of Europe. (Illus.). 48p. (gr. 4-7). 1994. 14.95 (*1-56261-158-5*) John Muir.
Muller, Gerald. Gentle Giants. LC 87-24537. (Illus.). (gr. 6-9). 1988. pap. 7.95 (*0-8198-3045-3*) St Paul Bks.
Neimark, Anne E. Diego Rivera, Artist of the People. LC 91-25209. (Illus.). 128p. (gr. 3-7). 1992. 17.00 (*0-06-021783-9*); PLB 16.89 (*0-06-021784-7*) HarpC Child Bks.
Nickens, Bessie. Walking the Log: Memories of a Southern Childhood. LC 94-10803. (Illus.). 32p. (gr. 2 up). 1994. 14.95 (*0-8478-1794-6*) Rizzoli Intl.
Reef, Pat D. Dahlov Ipcar, Artist. (Illus.). 48p. (gr. 3-7). 1987. pap. 12.95 (*0-933858-20-5*) Kennebec River.
Richardson, Wendy & Richardson, Jack. Animals: Through the Eyes of Artists. LC 90-34276. (Illus.). 48p. (gr. 4 up). 1991. pap. 7.95 (*0-516-49281-0*) Childrens.
—Cities: Through the Eyes of Artists. LC 90-34277. 48p. (gr. 4 up). 1991. PLB 15.40 (*0-516-09282-0*); pap. 7.95 (*0-516-49282-9*) Childrens.
—Entertainers: Through the Eyes of Artists. LC 90-34278. 48p. (gr. 4 up). 1991. PLB 15.40 (*0-516-09283-9*); pap. 7.95 (*0-516-49283-7*) Childrens.
—The Natural World: Through the Eyes of Artists. LC 90-34281. (Illus.). 48p. (gr. 4 up). 1991. pap. 7.95 (*0-516-49285-3*) Childrens.
—Water: Through the Eyes of Artists. LC 90-34280. 48p. (gr. 4 up). 1991. PLB 15.40 (*0-516-09286-3*); pap. 7.95 (*0-516-49286-1*) Childrens.
Rowley, Patric. Artists: A Kansas Collection. Harper, Steve, photos by. (Illus.). 108p. (gr. 7-12). 1989. 34.95 (*0-9623079-0-4*) Artists Registry.
Ruth, Trevor & Ruth, Susan. Drawing My View. Ruth, Trevor & Ruth, Susan, illus. LC 93-11827. 1994. 4.95 (*0-383-03730-1*) SRA Schl Grp.
Sills, Leslie. Visions: Stories about Women Artists. Sills, Leslie & Levine, Abby, eds. LC 92-32909. (Illus.). 64p. (gr. 4 up). 1993. PLB 18.95 (*0-8075-8491-6*) A Whitman.
Tudor, Tasha. The Springs of Joy. Tudor, Tasha, illus. LC 79-66708. 64p. (ps up). 1988. SBE 12.95 (*0-02-689092-5*) Macmillan Child Grp.
Turner, Robyn M. Faith Ringgold. LC 92-42652. 32p. 1993. 15.95 (*0-316-85652-5*) Little.
—Georgia O'Keeffe. (ps-3). 1991. 15.95 (*0-316-85649-5*) Little.
Venezia, Mike. Botticelli. Venezia, Mike, illus. LC 90-21645. 32p. (ps-4). 1991. PLB 12.85 (*0-516-02291-1*); pap. 4.95 (*0-516-42291-X*) Childrens.
—Francisco Goya. Venezia, Mike, illus. LC 90-20887. 32p. (ps-4). 1991. PLB 12.85 (*0-516-02292-X*); pap. 4.95 (*0-516-42292-8*) Childrens.
—Georgia O'Keeffe. Venezia, Mike, illus. 32p. (ps-4). 1993. PLB 12.85 (*0-516-02297-0*); pap. 4.95 (*0-516-42297-9*) Childrens.
—Monet. Venezia, Mike, illus. LC 89-25452. 32p. (ps-4). 1990. PLB 12.85 (*0-516-02276-8*); pap. 4.95 (*0-516-42276-6*) Childrens.
—Van Gogh. Venezia, Mike, illus. LC 88-11842. 32p. (ps-4). 1988. PLB 12.85 (*0-516-02274-1*); pap. 4.95 (*0-516-42274-X*) Childrens.
Waldron, Ann. Claude Monet. (Illus.). 92p. 1991. 19.95 (*0-8109-3620-8*) Abrams.
Walker, Lou A. Roy Lichtenstein: The Artist at Work. Abramson, Michael, photos by. LC 93-2631. (Illus.). 48p. (gr. 3-7). 1994. 15.99 (*0-525-67435-7*, Lodestar Bks) Dutton Child Bks.

ARTISTS, AMERICAN

Abbott, Lawrence. I Stand in the Center of the Good: Interviews with Contemporary Native American Artists. LC 93-36892. (Illus.). 347p. 1994. text ed. 40.00 (*0-8032-1037-X*) U of Nebr Pr.
Berry, Michael. Georgia O'Keeffe. Horner, Matina, intro. by. (Illus.). 112p. (Orig.). (gr. 5 up). 1988. 17.95 (*1-55546-673-7*); pap. 9.95 (*0-7910-0420-1*) Chelsea Hse.
Bockris, Victor. Life & Death of Andy Warhol. (ps-3). 1990. pap. 14.95 (*0-553-34929-5*) Bantam.
Gherman, Beverly. Georgia O'Keeffe: The "Wideness & Wonder" of Her World. LC 93-21033. (Illus.). 144p. (gr. 7 up). 1994. pap. 5.95 (*0-02-040388-7*, Collier Young Ad) Macmillan Child Grp.
Laing, Martha. Grandma Moses: The Grand Old Lady of American Art. Rahmas, D. Steve, ed. LC 71-190231. 32p. (Orig.). (gr. 7-9). 1972. lib. bdg. 4.95 incl. catalog cards (*0-87157-513-2*) SamHar Pr.
Meryman, Richard. Andrew Wyeth. (Illus.). 92p. (gr. 7 up). 1991. 19.95 (*0-8109-3956-8*) Abrams.
Moore, Reavis. Native Artists of North America. Burton, LeVar, frwd. by. (Illus.). 48p. (gr. 4-7). 1993. 14.95 (*1-56261-105-4*) John Muir.
O'Neal, Zibby. Grandma Moses. 1987. pap. 4.99 (*0-14-032220-5*, Puffin) Puffin Bks.
—Grandma Moses: Painter of Rural America. Ruff, Donna, illus. (gr. 2-6). pap. 3.50 (*0-317-62289-7*, Puffin) Puffin Bks.
Peet, Bill. Bill Peet: An Autobiography. (gr. 4-7). 1994. pap. 9.95 (*0-395-68982-1*) HM.
Venezia, Mike. Jackson Pollock. Moss, Meg, contrib. by. LC 93-36699. (Illus.). 32p. (ps-4). 1994. PLB 12.85 (*0-516-02298-9*) Childrens.

ARTISTS, BLACK

see Black Artists

ARTISTS, BRITISH

Venezia, Mike. Edward Hopper. Venezia, Mike, illus. LC 90-2166. 32p. (ps-4). 1990. PLB 12.85 (*0-516-02277-6*); pap. 4.95 (*0-516-42277-4*) Childrens.

ARTISTS, DUTCH

Hughes, Andrew. Van Gogh. (Illus.). 32p. (gr. 5 up). 1994. 10.95 (*0-8120-6462-3*); pap. 5.95 (*0-8120-1999-7*) Barron.

ARTISTS–FICTION

Anholt, Laurence. Camille & the Sunflowers. (Illus.). 32p. (ps-2). 1994. 13.95 (*0-8120-6409-7*) Barron.
Auch, Mary J. Glass Slippers Give You Blisters. LC 88-45865. 176p. (gr. 3-7). 1989. 14.95 (*0-8234-0752-7*) Holiday.
Butenhoff, Lisa K. Nina's Magic. Thatch, Nancy R., ed. Butenhoff, Lisa K., illus. Melton, David, intro. by. LC 92-18293. (Illus.). 26p. (gr. 3-4). 1992. PLB 14.95 (*0-933849-40-0*) Landmark Edns.
Calders, Pere. Brush. Feitlowitz, Marguerite, tr. from SPA. Vendrell, Carme S., illus. 32p. (ps-3). 1988. pap. 6.95 (*0-916291-16-2*) Kane-Miller Bk.
Clarke, J. Riffraff. LC 92-9928. 96p. (gr. 9-12). 1992. 14.95 (*0-8050-1774-7*, Bks Young Read) H Holt & Co.
Cooney, Barbara. Hattie & the Wild Waves: A Story from Brooklyn. Cooney, Barbara, illus. LC 92-40723. 40p. 1993. pap. 4.99 (*0-14-054193-4*, Puffin) Puffin Bks.
Cormier, Robert. Tunes for Bears to Dance To. LC 92-2734. 112p. (gr. 5 up). 1992. 15.00 (*0-385-30818-3*) Delacorte.
Deeter, Catherine. Seymour Bleu: A Space Odyssey. LC 92-24525. (Illus.). 32p. (ps-3). Date not set. 15.00 (*0-06-021524-0*); PLB 14.89 (*0-06-021525-9*) HarpC Child Bks.
Dunrea, Olivier. The Painter Who Loved Chickens. LC 94-27562. 1995. 15.00 (*0-374-35729-3*) FS&G.
Edwards, Michelle. A Baker's Portrait. LC 90-41926. (Illus.). 32p. (gr. k up). 1991. 13.95 (*0-688-09712-X*); PLB 13.88 (*0-688-09713-8*) Lothrop.
—Eve & Smithy. LC 92-44166. (gr. 4 up). 1995. 15.00 (*0-688-11825-9*); lib. bdg. 14.93 (*0-688-11826-7*) Lothrop.
Harding, William H. Alvin's Famous No-Horse. Chesworth, Michael, illus. LC 92-13834. 64p. (gr. 2-4). 1992. alk. paper 14.95 (*0-8050-2227-9*, Redfeather BYR) H Holt & Co.
Johnson-Feelings, Dianne. The Painter Man. Granderson, Eddie, illus. LC 93-4063. 1993. write for info. (*0-89334-220-3*) Humanics Ltd.

Locker, Thomas. Miranda's Smile. LC 93-28050. (gr. 2 up). 1994. 15.99 (*0-8037-1688-5*); PLB 15.89 (*0-8037-1689-3*) Dial Bks Young.
—The Young Artist. (Illus.). 32p. 1993. pap. 4.99 (*0-14-054923-4*, Puff Pied Piper) Puffin Bks.
Nunes, Lygia B. My Friend the Painter. Pontiero, Giovanni, tr. from POR. 85p. (gr. 3-7). 1991. 13.95 (*0-15-256340-7*) HarBrace.
Porte, Barbara A. Chickens! Chickens! Henry, Greg, illus. LC 94-19552. 1995. write for info. (*0-531-06877-3*) Orchard Bks Watts.
Pullman, Philip. The Broken Bridge. LC 91-15893. 256p. (gr. 7 up). 1992. 15.00 (*0-679-81972-X*); PLB 15.99 (*0-679-91972-4*) Knopf Bks Yng Read.
Reeves, James. Mr. Horrox & the Gratch. Blake, Quentin, illus. LC 91-13326. 32p. (gr. 1-6). 1991. 13.95 (*0-922984-08-5*) Wellington IL.
Ross, Tom. Eggbert, the Slightly Cracked Egg. Barran, Rex, illus. 32p. (ps-3). 1994. 14.95 (*0-399-22416-5*) Putnam Pub Group.
Rylant, Cynthia. The Dreamer. Moser, Barry, illus. LC 93-19915. 32p. (ps-6). 1993. 14.95 (*0-590-47341-7*) Scholastic Inc.
Schreier, Joshua. Hank's Work. LC 92-15205. (ps-2). 1993. 13.50 (*0-525-44970-1*, DCB) Dutton Child Bks.
Shannon, Monica. Dobry. Katchamakoff, Atanas, illus. LC 92-31442. 176p. (gr. 5 up). 1993. pap. 4.99 (*0-14-036334-3*) Puffin Bks.
Stahl, Hilda. Hannah & the Daring Escape. LC 92-43994. 160p. (gr. 4-7). 1993. pap. 3.99 (*0-89107-714-6*) Crossway Bks.
Stewart, Celeste. Merry Berry. Weinberger, Jane & Black, Albert, eds. DeVito, Pamela, illus. LC 88-51280. 88p. (gr. 4-8). 1990. pap. 5.00 (*0-932433-53-7*) Windswept Hse.
Sugar & Garrison. Josiah True & the Art Maker. 1995. 14.00 (*0-671-88354-2*, S&S BFYR) S&S Trade.
Velthuijs, Max. Crocodile's Masterpiece. (Illus.). 32p. (ps-1). 1992. bds. 14.00 (*0-374-31658-9*) FS&G.
Wolkstein, Diane. Little Mouse's Painting. Begin, Maryjane, illus. LC 91-16017. 32p. (ps up). 1992. 15.00 (*0-688-07609-2*); PLB 14.93 (*0-688-07610-6*) Morrow Jr Bks.
Wooding, Sharon. The Painter's Cat. Wooding, Sharon, illus. 32p. (ps-3). 1994. 14.95 (*0-399-22414-9*) Putnam Pub Group.

ARTISTS, ITALIAN

Green, Jen. Michelangelo. (Illus.). 32p. (gr. 5 up). 1994. 10.95 (*0-8120-6461-5*); pap. 5.95 (*0-8120-1998-9*) Barron.
Mason, Antony. Leonardo Da Vinci. (Illus.). 32p. (gr. 5 up). 1994. 10.95 (*0-8120-6460-7*); pap. 5.95 (*0-8120-1997-0*) Barron.

ARTISTS, MEXICAN

Garza, Hedda. Frida Kahlo: Mexican Painter. (Illus.). (ps-3). 1994. PLB 18.95 (*0-7910-1698-6*, Am Art Analog); pap. 7.95 (*0-7910-1699-4*, Am Art Analog) Chelsea Hse.

ARTISTS, NEGRO

see Black Artists

ARTISTS, SPANISH

Blanquet, Claire-Helene. Miro: Earth & Sky. LC 93-33680. 1994. write for info. (*0-7910-2813-5*) Chelsea Hse.
Crisp, George. Salvador Dali: Spanish Painter. (Illus.). (ps-3). 1994. PLB 18.95 (*0-7910-1778-8*, Am Art Analog) Chelsea Hse.
Diego Rivera. (Illus.). 32p. (gr. 3-6). 1988. PLB 19.97 (*0-8172-2908-6*); pap. 4.95 (*0-8114-6764-3*) Raintree Steck-V.
Venezia, Mike. Salvador Dali. Venezia, Mike, illus. LC 92-35053. 32p. (ps-4). 1993. PLB 12.85 (*0-516-02296-2*); pap. 4.95 (*0-516-42296-0*) Childrens.

ARTISTS' MATERIALS

Sattler, Helen R. Recipes for Art & Craft Materials. rev. ed. Shohet, Marti, illus. LC 86-34271. 128p. (gr. 6 up). 1987. 14.00 (*0-688-07374-3*) Lothrop.
—Recipes for Art & Craft Materials. Shohet, Marti, illus. LC 93-26182. 144p. (gr. 5 up). 1994. pap. 4.95 (*0-688-13199-9*, Pub. by Beech Tree Bks) Morrow.

ARTS, GRAPHIC

see Graphic Arts

ARTS, USEFUL

see Technology

ARTS AND CRAFTS

see also Basket Making; Beadwork; Bookbinding; Decoration and Ornament; Enamel and Enameling; Folk Art; Glass Painting and Staining; Handicraft; Jewelry; Leather Work; Metalwork; Modeling; Mosaics; Needlework; Pottery; Stencil Work; Weaving; Wood Carving

Aulson, Pam. Crafty Ideas with Placemats. (Illus.). 24p. (gr. 6 up). 1979. pap. 3.00 (*0-9601896-3-7*) Patch As Patch.
Ball, W. W. Fun with String Figures. LC 76-173664. (Illus.). 89p. (gr. k-3). 1971. pap. 2.95 (*0-486-22809-6*) Dover.
Bonica, Diane. Writing & Art Go Hand in Hand. 80p. (gr. 2-6). 1988. pap. text ed. 7.95 (*0-86530-068-2*, IP 13-2) Incentive Pubns.
Brommer, Gerald F. Wire Sculpture & Other Three Dimensional Construction. LC 68-19999. (Illus.). 128p. (gr. 5-12). 1968. 15.95 (*0-87192-025-5*) Davis Mass.
Forte, Imogene. Arts & Crafts: From Things Around the House. LC 83-80961. (Illus.). 80p. (gr. k-6). 1983. pap. text ed. 3.95 (*0-86530-090-9*, IP909) Incentive Pubns.
—Nature Crafts. LC 84-62931. (Illus.). 80p. (gr. k-6). 1985. 3.95 (*0-86530-098-4*, IP 91-2) Incentive Pubns.
Gleason, Karan. Rainy Day Fun. Filkins, Vanessa, illus. 112p. (gr. k-4). 1987. pap. 10.95 (*0-86653-408-3*, GA1002) Good Apple.
Gregorich, Barbara. Chicken Scratch. Hoffman, Joan, ed. Alexander, Barbara, et al, illus. 32p. (Orig.). (ps-1). 1986. wkbk. 1.99 (*0-88743-127-5*) Sch Zone Pub Co.
Highlights Editors. Party Ideas with Crafts Kids Can Make. (Illus.). 48p. (Orig.). (gr. 1-6). 1981. pap. 2.95 (*0-87534-310-4*) Highlights.
Kerina, Jane. African Crafts. Feelings, Tom, illus. LC 69-18916. (gr. 2-6). 1970. PLB 13.95 (*0-87460-084-7*) Lion Bks.
MacKenzie, Joy. The Big Book of Bible Crafts & Projects. Flint, Russ, illus. 212p. (Orig.). (ps-4). 1981. pap. 15.99 (*0-310-70151-1*, 14019P) Zondervan.
Milord, Susan. Adventures in Art: Art & Crafts Experiences for 7- to 14-Year Olds. Williamson, Susan, ed. Milord, Susan, illus. LC 90-39031. 160p. (Orig.). (gr. 2-8). 1990. pap. 12.95 (*0-913589-54-3*) Williamson Pub Co.
More Super Search-a-Words. (gr. 2-5). 1987. pap. 1.79 (*0-671-64358-4*, Little Simon) S&S Trade.
Silbert, Linda P. & Silbert, Alvin J. Make My Own Book Kit Animals. (ps-2). 1984. wkbk. 4.98 (*0-89544-316-3*) Silbert Bress.
—Make My Own Book Kit Numbers. (ps-2). 1984. wkbk. 4.98 (*0-89544-318-X*) Silbert Bress.
—Make My Own Book Kit Shapes. (ps-2). 1984. wkbk. 4.98 (*0-89544-317-1*) Silbert Bress.
Simon, Seymour. The Paper Airplane Book. Byron, Barton, illus. (gr. 4-6). 1971. pap. 12.95 (*0-670-53797-7*) Viking Child Bks.
Zechlin, Katharina. Creative Enameling & Jewelry-Making. Kuttner, Paul, tr. LC 65-20877. (gr. 10 up). 1965. 6.95 (*0-8069-5062-5*); PLB 6.69 (*0-8069-5063-3*) Sterling.

ASHANTIS

McDermott, Gerald, retold by. & illus. Anansi the Spider: A Tale from the Ashanti. LC 76-150028. 48p. (ps-2). 1987. reinforced bdg. 15.95 (*0-8050-0310-X*, Bks Young Read); pap. 5.95 (*0-8050-0311-8*) H Holt & Co.

ASHE, ARTHUR, 1943-

Moutoussamy-Ashe, Jeanne. Daddy & Me. Moutoussamy-Ashe, Jeanne, photos by. LC 93-11513. (Illus.). 40p. (ps-3). 1993. 13.00 (*0-679-85096-1*); PLB 14.99 (*0-679-95096-6*) Knopf Bks Yng Read.
Quackenbush, Robert. Arthur Ashe & His Match with History. LC 93-14945. (gr. 5 up). 1994. pap. 14.00 (*0-671-86597-8*, S&S BFYR) S&S Trade.
—Arthur Ashe & His Match with History. (gr. 4-7). 1994. pap. 4.95 (*0-671-88182-5*, S&S BFYR) S&S Trade.
Weissberg, Ed. Arthur Ashe. King, Coretta Scott, intro. by. (Illus.). 112p. (gr. 5 up). 1991. lib. bdg. 17.95 (*0-7910-1115-1*) Chelsea Hse.

ASIA

see also Asia, Southeastern

Asia, 6 vols. (Illus.). (gr. 5-9). 1990. Set. 131.70 (*1-85435-293-8*) Marshall Cavendish.
Civilizations of Asia. (Illus.). 80p. (gr. 4 up). 1988. PLB 25.67 (*0-8172-3302-4*) Raintree Steck-V.
Coblence, Jean-Michel. Asian Civilizations. Lamb, Jane C., tr. from FRE. Ageorges, Veronique, illus. 77p. (gr. 7 up). 1988. 12.95 (*0-382-09483-2*) Silver Burdett Pr.
Corwin, Judith H. Asian Crafts. Rosoff, Iris, ed. LC 91-13500. (Illus.). 48p. (gr. 1-4). 1992. PLB 12.90 (*0-531-11013-3*) Watts.
Foster, Leila M. Bhutan. LC 88-37375. (Illus.). 128p. (gr. 5-9). 1989. PLB 20.55 (*0-516-02709-3*) Childrens.
Fyson, Nance L. People at Work in Sri Lanka. (gr. 6 up). 1988. 19.95 (*0-7134-5479-2*, Pub. by Batsford UK) Trafalgar.
Georges, D. V. Asia. LC 86-9631. (Illus.). 48p. (gr. k-4). 1986. PLB 12.85 (*0-516-01288-6*); pap. 4.95 (*0-516-41288-4*) Childrens.
Lerner Geography Department Staff, ed. Cyprus in Pictures. (Illus.). 64p. (gr. 5-12). 1992. PLB 17.50 (*0-8225-1910-0*) Lerner Pubns.
Major, John S. The Land & People of Mongolia. LC 89-37790. (Illus.). 224p. (gr. 6 up). 1990. (Lipp Jr Bks); (Lipp Jr Bks) HarpC Child Bks.
Marvis, Barbara J. Contemporary American Success Stories: Famous People of Asian Ancestry, Vol. I. LC 93-78991. 96p. (gr. 5-12). 1994. pap. 8.95 (*1-883845-06-8*) M Lane Pubs.
—Contemporary American Success Stories: Famous People of Asian Ancestry, Vol. II. LC 93-78991. 96p. (gr. 5-12). 1994. pap. text ed. 8.95 (*1-883845-07-6*) M Lane Pubs.
Sabin, Louis. Asia. Eitzen, Allan, illus. LC 84-10559. 32p. (gr. 3-6). 1985. PLB 9.49 (*0-8167-0274-8*); pap. text ed. 2.95 (*0-8167-0275-6*) Troll Assocs.
Schwartz, Linda. The Asian Question Collection. 120p. (gr. 4-8). 1994. 6.95 (*0-88160-215-9*, LW200) Learning Wks.

ASIA, CENTRAL

Thomas, Paul. The Central Asian States. Channon, John, contrib. by. LC 92-2239. (Illus.). 32p. (gr. 4-6). 1992. PLB 14.40 (*1-56294-307-3*) Millbrook Pr.

ASIA–DESCRIPTION AND TRAVEL

Levine, Bobbie & Lichter, Carolyn. A Child's Walk Through Asia. Wu, Marshall, illus. 25p. (gr. 2-6). 1984. spiral bdg. 1.50 (*0-912303-31-X*) Michigan Mus.

ASIA–HISTORY

Across Asia by Land. (Illus.). 128p. 1990. 17.95x (*0-8160-1874-X*) Facts on File.
Civilizations of the Middle East. (Illus.). 80p. (gr. 4 up). 1988. PLB 25.67 (*0-8172-3303-2*) Raintree Steck-V.
Diagram Visual Information Staff. Asian History on File. 288p. (gr. 5-10). 1994. 155.00x (*0-8160-2975-X*) Facts on File.
Frazee, Charles & Yopp, Hallie K. The Ancient World. Frazee, Kathleen & Lumba, Eric, illus. (gr. 6). 1990. text ed. 21.08 (*1-878473-51-4*); tchr's. ed. 27.08 (*1-878473-54-9*); wkbk. 3.00 (*1-878473-55-7*) Delos Pubns.
—Medieval & Early Modern Times. Frazee, Kathleen & Lumba, Eric, illus. (gr. 7). 1990. pap. text ed. 24.77 (*1-878473-56-5*); tchr's. ed. 30.77 (*1-878473-58-1*); wkbk. 3.00 (*0-685-58493-3*) Delos Pubns.

ASIA, SOUTHEASTERN

Bergquist, Laurence C. Destiny: A Southeast Asia Saga 1928-1953. (Illus.). 336p. 1994. 24.95 (*0-935553-06-1*, Dist. by Words To Go, Inc.) Pacifica Pr.
McGuire, William. Southeast Asians. LC 90-12996. (Illus.). (gr. 5-10). 1991. PLB 13.40 (*0-531-11108-3*) Watts.
Mason, Antony. Southeast Asia. (Illus.). 48p. (gr. 4-8). 1989. lib. bdg. 14.95 (*0-382-09796-3*) Silver Burdett Pr.
—Southeast Asia. LC 91-24807. (Illus.). 96p. (gr. 6-12). 1992. PLB 22.80 (*0-8114-2447-2*) Raintree Steck-V.
Rigg, Jonathan. Southeast Asia. LC 94-20444. 1995. write for info. (*0-8114-2788-9*) Raintree Steck-V.

ASIA, SOUTHEASTERN–FICTION

Ho, Minfong. The Clay Marble. 160p. (gr. 7 up). 1991. 14.95 (*0-374-31340-7*) FS&G.
Parenteau, John. Prisoner for Peace: Aung San Suu Kyi & Burma's Struggle for Democracy. LC 94-4100. (Illus.). 160p. (gr. 6 up). 1994. 18.95 (*1-883846-05-6*) M Reynolds.

ASIMOV, ISAAC, 1920-

Erlanger, Ellen. Isaac Asimov: Scientist & Storyteller. LC 86-10675. (Illus.). 56p. (gr. 4 up). 1986. PLB 13.50 (*0-8225-0482-0*) Lerner Pubns.

ASSASSINATION

see also names of persons and groups of persons with the subdivision Assassination, e.g. Presidents–U. S. –Assassination

ASSES AND MULES–FICTION

Amery, H. Hungry Donkey. (Illus.). 16p. (ps-3). 1992. pap. 3.95 (*0-7460-0586-5*) EDC.
Amstutz, Beverly. Benjamin & the Bible Donkeys. (Illus.). 36p. (gr. k-7). 1981. pap. 2.50x (*0-937836-03-6*) Precious Res.
Aspinall, Anthony. Misadventures of an Aging Mule. 400p. 1990. 34.95 (*0-233-98439-9*, Pub. by A Deutsch UK) Trafalgar.
Athey, Virginia. Zonkey, the Donkey. Rutherford, Donna, illus. 20p. (ps-2). 1993. pap. 6.50 saddle stitch (*0-922510-10-5*) Lucky Bks.
Baily, Jane B. Dottie, the Unfoolish Mule. Parker, Carolyn, illus. LC 90-93258. 32p. (Orig.). (gr. k-3). 1990. pap. 6.95 (*0-9626642-1-9*) J B Baily.
Brittain, Bill. Devil's Donkey. Glass, Andrew, illus. LC 80-7907. 128p. (gr. 3-7). 1982. pap. 3.95 (*0-06-440129-4*, Trophy) HarpC Child Bks.
Cheadle, J. A. A Donkey's Life: A Story for Children. Thomas, Toni, illus. LC 80-123421. iii, 88p. (Orig.). (gr. 2-6). 1979. pap. 3.50 (*0-9604244-0-7*) Heahstan Pr.
Jafa, Manorama. The Donkey on the Bridge. Bhusan, Rboti, illus. 24p. (Orig.). (gr. k-3). 1980. pap. 2.50 (*0-89744-209-1*, Pub. by Childrens Bk Trust IA) Auromere.
Lynch, Patricia. Turf Cutter's Donkey. 243p. (ps-8). 1988. pap. 6.95 (*1-85371-016-4*, Pub. by Poolbeg Press Ltd Eire) Dufour.
Milne, A. A. Eeyore Loses a Tail. Shepard, Ernest H., illus. 32p. 1993. incl. charm 13.99 (*0-525-45045-9*, DCB) Dutton Child Bks.
Piequet, Miriam. The Flying Mule Car. Anyone Can Read Staff, ed. Blanton, Betty, illus. 149p. (Orig.). (gr. 4-6). 1988. pap. 15.00 (*0-914275-11-9*) Anyone Can Read Bks.
Sehlin, Gunhild. Mary's Little Donkey: A Christmas Story for Young Children. Latham, Hugh & Mackan, Donald, trs. Verheijn, Jan, illus. (SWE.). 157p. (gr. 3-6). 1992. pap. 10.95 (*0-86315-064-0*, Pub. by Floris Bks UK) Gryphon Hse.
Weber, Kathryn. Molly Moonshine & Timothy. Downey, Jane, illus. 44p. (gr. 2-4). 1990. pap. 2.95 (*1-878438-01-8*) Ranch House Pr.

ASTROLOGY

see also Occult Sciences

Cowger, Barry D. Family Dynamics & Astrology. Green, Jeff, intro. by. (Illus.). 175p. (Orig.). (gr. 12). 1990. pap. 9.95 (*0-685-29119-7*) Envision Pub.
Dell, Pamela. Hotscopes: Aquarius 1994: Day-by-Day Horoscopes for Teens. 1993. pap. 3.95 (*0-307-22460-0*, Golden Pr) Western Pub.
—Hotscopes: Aries 1994: Day-by-Day Horoscopes for Teens. 1993. pap. 3.95 (*0-307-22450-3*, Golden Pr) Western Pub.
—Hotscopes: Cancer 1994: Day-by-Day Horoscopes for Teens. 1993. pap. 3.95 (*0-307-22453-8*, Golden Pr) Western Pub.
—Hotscopes: Capricorn 1994: Day-by-Day Horoscopes for Teens. 1993. pap. 3.95 (*0-307-22459-7*, Golden Pr) Western Pub.

—Hotscopes: Gemini 1994: Day-By-Day Horoscopes for Teens. 1993. pap. 3.95 (*0-307-22452-X*, Golden Pr) Western Pub.
—Hotscopes: Leo 1994: Day-by-Day Horoscopes for Teens. 1993. pap. 3.95 (*0-307-22454-6*, Golden Pr) Western Pub.
—Hotscopes: Libra 1994: Day-by-Day Horoscopes for Teens. 1993. pap. 3.95 (*0-307-22456-2*, Golden Pr) Western Pub.
—Hotscopes: Pisces 1994: Day-by-Day Horoscopes for Teens. 1993. pap. 3.95 (*0-307-22461-9*, Golden Pr) Western Pub.
—Hotscopes: Sagittarius 1994: Day-by-Day Horoscopes for Teens. 1993. pap. 3.95 (*0-307-22458-9*, Golden Pr) Western Pub.
—Hotscopes: Scorpio 1994: Day-by-Day Horoscopes for Teens. 1993. pap. 3.95 (*0-307-22457-0*, Golden Pr) Western Pub.
—Hotscopes: Taurus 1994: Day-by-Day Horoscopes for Teens. 1993. pap. 3.95 (*0-307-22451-1*, Golden Pr) Western Pub.
—Hotscopes: Virgo 1994: Day-by-Day Horoscopes for Teens. 1993. pap. 3.95 (*0-307-22455-4*, Golden Pr) Western Pub.
Gibson, Paul. How to Be Your Own Astrologer. (Illus.). 28p. (gr. 7 up). 1987. pap. text ed. 13.20 (*0-9619757-0-9*) R Osgood.
Harris, Paula. Pisces. 40p. (gr. 4). 1989. PLB 13.95 (*0-88682-254-8*) Creative Ed.
—Scorpio. 40p. (gr. 4). 1989. PLB 13.95 (*0-88682-260-2*) Creative Ed.
Lely, James A. Aquarius. 40p. (gr. 4). 1989. PLB 13.95 (*0-88682-258-0*) Creative Ed.
—Libra. 40p. (gr. 4). 1989. PLB 13.95 (*0-88682-262-9*) Creative Ed.
—Virgo. 40p. (gr. 4). 1989. PLB 13.95 (*0-88682-259-9*) Creative Ed.
Moore, Mary R. Zodiac: Exploring Human Qualities & Characteristics. rev. ed. LC 84-17977. (Illus.). 112p. (gr. 5 up). 1994. pap. 10.50 (*0-86647-080-8*) Pro Lingua.
Paul, Kathleen. Aries. 40p. (gr. 4). 1989. PLB 13.95 (*0-88682-255-6*) Creative Ed.
—Taurus. 40p. (gr. 4). 1989. PLB 13.95 (*0-88682-257-2*) Creative Ed.
Predicting: The Art of Astrology, Palmistry, Tarot & More. 256p. (Orig.). 1994. pap. text ed. 5.95 (*1-56138-465-8*) Running Pr.
Ross, Katharine. The Glow-in-the-Dark Zodiac Storybook. Marchesi, Stephen, illus. LC 92-61555. 24p. (gr. 3-7). 1993. 14.00 (*0-679-82470-7*) Random Bks Yng Read.
Royer, Mary P. Astrology: Opposing Viewpoints. LC 91-21657. (Illus.). 112p. (gr. 5-8). 1991. PLB 14.95 (*0-89908-090-1*) Greenhaven.
Schwartz, Alvin. Telling Fortunes: Love Magic, Dream Signs, & Other Ways to Learn the Future. Cameron, Tracey, illus. LC 85-45174. 128p. (gr. 4 up). 1987. 12.95 (*0-397-32132-5*, Lipp Jr Bks); PLB 12.89 (*0-397-32133-3*, Lipp Jr Bks) HarpC Child Bks.
Shaw, Dona. Astrology Carousel for Junior Astrologers. Shaw, Aaron, et al, illus. 101p. 1993. pap. text ed. 10.00x (*1-884776-02-7*) Lazuli Prods.
Swainson, Esme. Children: The Adventures of Rex & Zendah in the Zodiac. Rosicrucian Fellowship Staff, ed. (Illus.). 112p. (ps-8). 1981. pap. text ed. 4.95 (*0-911274-61-8*) Rosicrucian.
Taylor, Paula. Cancer. 40p. (gr. 4). 1989. PLB 13.95 (*0-88682-261-0*) Creative Ed.
—Capricorn. 40p. (gr. 4). 1989. PLB 13.95 (*0-88682-256-4*) Creative Ed.
—Gemini. 40p. (gr. 4). 1989. PLB 13.95 (*0-88682-252-1*) Creative Ed.
—Leo. 40p. (gr. 4). 1989. PLB 13.95 (*0-88682-253-X*) Creative Ed.
—Sagittarius. 40p. (gr. 4). 1989. PLB 13.95 (*0-88682-251-3*) Creative Ed.
Weber, Peter J. Zodiac Degrees. (Illus.). 128p. (Orig.). 1989. 14.95 (*0-940649-06-3*); pap. 9.95 (*0-940649-05-5*) Parnell Pub.

ASTRONAUTICS

see also Artificial Satellites; Interplanetary Voyages; Manned Space Flight; Outer Space; Rocketry; Space Flight; Space Flight to the Moon; Space Sciences; Space Vehicles

Alston, Edith. Let's Visit a Space Camp. Plunkett, Michael, illus. LC 89-34373. 32p. (gr. 2-4). 1990. lib. bdg. 10.79 (*0-8167-1743-5*); pap. text ed. 2.95 (*0-8167-1744-3*) Troll Assocs.
Baird, Anne. Space Camp: The Great Adventures for NASA Hopefuls. Koropp, Robert, photos by. Shepard, Alan B. & Buckbee, Edward O.frwd. by. LC 91-21587. (Illus.). 48p. (gr. 3 up). 1992. 14.00 (*0-688-10227-1*); PLB 13.93 (*0-688-10228-X*) Morrow Jr Bks.
Barrett, Norman S. The Picture World of Astronauts. LC 89-36497. (Illus.). 32p. (gr. k-4). 1990. PLB 12.40 (*0-531-14053-9*) Watts.
Cozic, Charles P., ed. Space Exploration: Opposing Viewpoints. LC 92-8149. (Illus.). 240p. (gr. 10 up). 1992. PLB 17.95 (*0-89908-197-5*); pap. text ed. 9.95 (*0-89908-172-X*) Greenhaven.
Dewaard, John. History of NASA: America's Voyage to the Stars. 1984. 12.98 (*0-671-06983-7*) S&S Trade.
Embury, Barbara & Crouch, Tom D. The Dream Is Alive: A Flight of Discovery Aboard the Space Shuttle. LC 90-55194. (Illus.). 64p. (gr. 3-7). 1991. 14.95 (*0-06-021813-4*) HarpC Child Bks.
Greene, Carol. Astronauts. LC 83-23142. (Illus.). 48p. (gr. k-4). 1984. PLB 12.85 (*0-516-01722-5*); pap. 4.95 (*0-516-41722-3*) Childrens.
Hawkes, Nigel. Into Space. LC 93-13468. (Illus.). 32p. (gr. 5-8). 1993. PLB 12.40 (*0-531-17416-6*, Gloucester Pr) Watts.
Hodges-Caballero, Jane. Air & Space Activities. rev. ed. LC 85-81658. 152p. (ps-3). 1993. pap. text ed. 17.95 (*0-685-65254-8*) Humanics Ltd.
Kent, Zachary. The Story of the Challenger Disaster. LC 86-6822. (Illus.). 32p. (gr. 3-6). 1986. PLB 12.30 (*0-516-04673-X*) Childrens.
Long, Kim. Astronaut Training Book for Kids. (Illus.). 160p. (gr. 5up). 1990. 15.95 (*0-525-67296-6*, Lodestar Bks) Dutton Child Bks.
McKay, David W. Space Science Projects for Young Scientists. 1989. pap. 6.95 (*0-531-15134-4*) Watts.
McPhee, Penelope & McPhee, Raymond. Your Future in Space: The U. S. Space Camp Training Program. Schulke, Flip & Schulke, Debra, photos by. McCandless, Bruce & Sullivan, Kathryn D.frwd. by. LC 86-9003. (Illus.). 128p. (gr. 7 up). 1986. pap. 14.95 (*0-517-56418-1*) Crown Bks Yng Read.
Mason, John. Spacecraft Technology. LC 89-17700. 1990. PLB 12.90 (*0-531-18328-9*, Pub. by Bookwright Pr) Watts.
Maynard, Christopher. Space. LC 92-32266. (Illus.). 32p. (gr. 1-4). 1993. 3.95 (*1-85697-897-4*, Kingfisher LKC) LKC.
Morris, Ting & Morris, Neil. Space. Levy, Ruth, illus. LC 93-24435. 32p. (gr. 2-4). 1994. PLB 12.90 (*0-531-14282-5*) Watts.
Rockwell, Anne & Brion, David. Space Vehicles. LC 93-43594. (Illus.). 24p. (ps-1). 1994. 13.99 (*0-525-45270-2*, DCB) Dutton Child Bks.
Shayler, David. Space. LC 94-7755. 1994. 16.00 (*0-679-84920-3*) Random.
Simon, Seymour. How to Be a Space Scientist in Your Own Home. Morrison, Bill, illus. LC 81-47759. (gr. 4-7). 1982. (Lipp Jr Bks); (Lipp Jr Bks) HarpC Child Bks.
Skurzynski, Gloria. Zero Gravity. LC 93-46735. (gr. 1-5). 1994. 14.95 (*0-02-782925-1*, Bradbury Pr) Macmillan Child Grp.
Stoff, Joshua. From Airship to Spaceship: Long Island Aviation & Spaceflight. LC 90-47647. (Illus.). 96p. (gr. 4-10). 1991. 15.00 (*1-55787-074-8*, NY71060, Empire State Bks); pap. 7.95 (*1-55787-075-6*, NY71059, Empire State Bks) Heart of the Lakes.
Wellington, Jerry. The Super Science Book of Space. Lloyd, Frances, illus. LC 93-24405. 32p. (gr. 4-8). 1993. 14.95 (*1-56847-129-7*) Thomson Lrning.
Williams, Brian. Pioneers of Flight. LC 90-9470. (Illus.). 48p. (gr. 4-8). 1990. PLB 11.95 (*0-8114-2755-2*) Raintree Steck-V.

ASTRONAUTICS–BIOGRAPHY

Behrens, June. Sally Ride, Astronaut: An American First. LC 83-23173. (Illus.). 32p. (gr. 2-5). 1984. PLB 11.80 (*0-516-03606-8*); pap. 3.95 (*0-516-43606-6*) Childrens.
Blacknall, Carolyn. Sally Ride: America's First Woman in Space. LC 84-12671. (Illus.). 80p. (gr. 3 up). 1985. text ed. 13.95 RSBE (*0-87518-260-7*, Dillon) Macmillan Child Grp.
Williams, Brian. Twenty Names in Space Exploration. LC 89-23901. (Illus.). 48p. (gr. 3-8). 1990. PLB 12.95 (*1-85435-256-3*) Marshall Cavendish.

ASTRONAUTICS–DICTIONARIES

Ressmeyer, Roger. Astronaut to Zodiac: A Young Stargazer's Alphabet. LC 92-9615. (Illus.). 32p. (gr. k-6). 1992. 15.00 (*0-517-58805-6*); PLB 15.99 (*0-517-58806-4*) Crown Bks Yng Read.
Simon, Seymour. Space Words: A Dictionary. Chewning, Randy, illus. LC 90-37402. 48p. (gr. 2-5). 1991. 15.00 (*0-06-022532-7*); PLB 14.89 (*0-06-022533-5*) HarpC Child Bks.

ASTRONAUTS

Barrett, Norman S. The Picture World of Astronauts. LC 89-36497. (Illus.). 32p. (gr. k-4). 1990. PLB 12.40 (*0-531-14053-9*) Watts.
Barton, Byron. I Want to Be an Astronaut. Barton, Byron, illus. LC 87-24311. 32p. (ps-1). 1988. 14.00 (*0-694-00261-5*, Crowell Jr Bks); PLB 13.89 (*0-690-04744-4*) HarpC Child Bks.
Behrens, June. I Can Be an Astronaut. LC 84-7601. (Illus.). 32p. (gr. k-3). 1984. PLB 11.80 (*0-516-01837-X*); pap. 3.95 (*0-516-41837-8*) Childrens.
—Puedo Ser un Astronauta (I Can Be an Astronaut) Kratky, Lada, tr. from ENG. LC 84-7601. (SPA., Illus.). 32p. (gr. k-3). 1984. PLB 11.80 (*0-516-31837-3*); pap. 3.95 (*0-516-51837-2*) Childrens.
Bernstein, Joanne E. & Blue, Rose. Judith Resnik: Challenger Astronaut. Gerber, Alan J., contrib. by. (Illus.). 144p. (gr. 5-9). 1990. 14.95 (*0-525-67305-9*, Lodestar Bks) Dutton Child Bks.
Billings, Charlene W. Christa McAuliffe: Pioneer Space Teacher. LC 86-13453. (Illus.). 64p. (gr. 6 up). 1986. lib. bdg. 15.95 (*0-89490-148-6*) Enslow Pubs.
Briggs, Carole S. Women in Space: Reaching the Last Frontier. (Illus.). 80p. (gr. 5 up). 1988. PLB 21.50 (*0-8225-1581-4*, First Ave Edns); pap. 5.95 (*0-8225-9547-8*, First Ave Edns) Lerner Pubns.
Burch, Jonathan. Astronauts. Stefoff, Rebecca, ed. LC 91-45925. (Illus.). 32p. (gr. 5-9). 1992. PLB 17.26 (*1-56074-041-8*) Garrett Ed Corp.
Burns, Khephra & Miles, William. Black Stars in Orbit: NASA's African-American Astronauts. LC 93-44624. (gr. 3 up). 1994. 18.95 (*0-15-200432-7*); pap. 8.95 (*0-15-200276-6*) HarBrace.
Ceasor, Ebraska D. Mae C. Jemison: First Black Female Astronaut. Durant, Charlotte & Pye, Ethel, eds. Johnson, Leonard J., illus. 40p. (Orig.). (ps-1). 1992. pap. 4.00 (*0-913678-22-8*) New Day Pr.
Charleston, Gordon. Armstrong Lands on the Moon. LC 93-32918. (Illus.). 32p. (gr. 4 up). 1994. text ed. 13.95 RSBE (*0-87518-530-4*, Dillon) Macmillan Child Grp.
Collins, Michael. Flying to the Moon: An Astronaut's Story. 2nd, rev. ed. LC 93-42001. 1994. pap. 4.50 (*0-374-42356-3*, Sunburst) FS&G.
Coords, Arthur E. The Space Apple Story: The Children's Tribute to the Seven Challenger Astronauts. (Illus.). 32p. (gr. 2-6). 1992. PLB 7.70 (*0-9631106-0-8*) A E Coords.
Fox, Mary V. Women Astronauts: Aboard the Space Shuttle. rev. ed. LC 87-10814. (Illus.). 144p. (gr. 7 up). 1987. lib. bdg. 13.98 (*0-671-64840-3*, J Messner); pap. 5.95 (*0-671-64841-1*) S&S Trade.
Gabriele. Astronauts & Spacecraft. 1985. pap. 1.95 (*0-911211-62-4*) Penny Lane Pubns.
Goodman, Mike. Astronauts. LC 89-31222. (Illus.). 48p. (gr. 5-6). 1989. RSBE 11.95 (*0-89686-430-8*, Crestwood Hse) Macmillan Child Grp.
Haskins, James & Benson, Kathleen. Space Challenger: The Story of Guion Bluford. LC 84-4251. (Illus.). 64p. (gr. 3-6). 1984. PLB 17.50 (*0-87614-259-5*) Carolrhoda Bks.
Haskins, Jim. Black Wings: The Story of African Americans in Aviation. LC 94-18623. Date not set. 13.95 (*0-590-45912-0*) Scholastic Inc.
I Can Be an Astronaut. 1992. 2.99 (*0-517-06742-0*) Random Hse Value.
Martin, Patricia S. Christine McAuliffe: Reach for the Stars. (Illus.). 24p. (gr. 1-4). 1987. PLB 14.60 (*0-86592-172-5*); Set. lib. bdg. 10.95s.p. (*0-685-67566-1*) Rourke Corp.
Moche, Dinah. The Astronauts. LC 78-54955. (Illus.). (ps-3). 1979. pap. 2.25 (*0-394-83901-3*) Random Bks Yng Read.
Naden, Corinne. Ronald McNair. King, Coretta Scott, intro. by. (Illus.). 112p. (gr. 5 up). 1991. lib. bdg. 17.95 (*0-7910-1133-X*) Chelsea Hse.
—Ronald McNair. (gr. 4-7). 1993. pap. 7.95 (*0-7910-1158-5*) Chelsea Hse.
Naden, Corinne J. & Blue, Rose. Christa McAuliffe: Teacher in Space. (Illus.). 48p. (gr. 2-4). 1991. PLB 12.90 (*1-56294-046-5*) Millbrook Pr.
Naden, Corrine J. Christa McAuliffe: A Teacher in Space. (gr. 4-7). 1992. pap. 4.95 (*1-878841-58-0*) Millbrook Pr.
Poskanzer, Susan C. What's It Like to Be an Astronaut. Eitzen, Allan, illus. LC 89-34393. 32p. (gr. k-3). 1990. PLB 10.89 (*0-8167-1793-1*); pap. text ed. 2.95 (*0-8167-1794-X*) Troll Assocs.
Schloss, Muriel. Mary Cleave, Astronaut. (gr. 5 up). 1990. 6.95 (*0-9621820-2-8*) Teachers Lab.
Shaw, Dena. Ronald McNair. LC 94-2759. 1994. pap. write for info. (*0-7910-2116-5*, Am Art Analog) Chelsea Hse.
Spangenburg, Ray & Moser, Diane. Space People from A to Z. 136p. 1990. 22.95x (*0-8160-1851-0*) Facts on File.
Stott, Carole. Into the Unknown. LC 88-25921. (Illus.). 48p. (gr. 5-7). 1989. PLB 12.90 (*0-531-19513-9*) Watts.
Westman, Paul. Neil Armstrong: Space Pioneer. LC 80-10832. (Illus.). 64p. (gr. 4 up). 1980. PLB 13.50 (*0-8225-0479-0*) Lerner Pubns.
Williams, Brian. Twenty Names in Space Exploration. LC 89-23901. (Illus.). 48p. (gr. 3-8). 1990. PLB 12.95 (*1-85435-256-3*) Marshall Cavendish.

ASTRONAUTS–FICTION

Barnes, Joyce A. The Baby Grand, the Moon in July, & Me. LC 93-17984. Date not set. write for info. (*0-8037-1586-2*); PLB write for info. (*0-8037-1600-1*) Dial Bks Young.
Eco, Umberto. The Three Astronauts. Carmi, Eugenio, illus. (gr. 1 up). 1989. 12.95 (*0-15-286383-4*, HB Juv Bks) HarBrace.
I Want to Be an Astronaut. (Illus.). (ps-k). 1991. write for info. (*0-307-12624-2*, Golden Pr) Western Pub.
Johnson, Larry D. & Mills, Jane L. Arnie the Astronaut. Hebert, Kim T., illus. LC 86-60353. 22p. (Orig.). (ps-1). 1986. pap. 4.50 (*0-938155-02-4*); pap. 12.00 set of 3 bks. (*0-685-13517-9*) Read A Bol.
Lovejoy, Pamela. If I Were An Astronaut. Lovejoy, Pamela, illus. 14p. (Orig.). (ps-2). 1994. pap. write for info. (*1-880038-18-8*) Learn-Abouts.
Moche, Dinah. If You Were an Astronaut. (Illus.). 24p. (ps-3). 1992. pap. write for info. (*0-307-11896-7*, 11896-02, Golden Pr) Western Pub.
Murphy, Elspeth C. Pug McConnell. LC 85-26922. 107p. (gr. 3-7). 1986. 4.99 (*0-89191-728-4*, Chariot Bks) Chariot Family.
North, Rick. Young Astronauts, No. 2. 1990. pap. 2.95 (*0-8217-3173-4*) Zebra.
—Young Astronauts No. 3. 1990. pap. 2.95 (*0-8217-3178-5*) Zebra.

ASTRONOMERS

Jackson, Garnet N. Benjamin Banneker, Scientist. Pate, Rodney, illus. LC 92-28799. 1992. write for info. (*0-8136-5228-6*); pap. write for info. (*0-8136-5701-6*) Modern Curr.

ASTRONOMICAL INSTRUMENTS

see also Telescope

ASTRONOMICAL PHYSICS

see Astrophysics

ASTRONOMICAL SPECTROSCOPY
see Astrophysics
ASTRONOMY
see also Almanacs; Astrology; Astrophysics; Life on Other Planets; Meteorites; Meteors; Moon; Outer Space; Planets; Seasons; Solar System; Space Sciences; Stars; Sun; Tides

Alley, David. Sky: All about Planets, Stars, Galaxies, Eclipses & More. Galiman, Ron, illus. 32p. 1993. pap. 5.95 (*1-895688-04-3*, Pub. by Greey dePencier CN) Firefly Bks Ltd.

Apfel, Necia H. Nebulae. LC 86-33765. (Illus.). 48p. (gr. 3-6). 1988. 17.00 (*0-688-07228-3*); PLB 16.93 (*0-688-07229-1*) Lothrop.

Asimov, Isaac. Ancient Astronomy. (gr. 4-7). 1991. pap. 4.95 (*0-440-40387-1*) Dell.

—Ask Isaac Asimov, 41 vols. (Illus.). 24p. (gr. 1-8). PLB 570.01 subscription set (*0-8368-0789-8*); PLB 14.60 ea., standing order (*0-8368-0788-X*) Gareth Stevens Inc.

—How Did We Find Out about Black Holes? Wool, David, illus. LC 73-4320. (gr. 5 up). 1978. PLB 12.85 reinforced (*0-8027-6337-5*) Walker & Co.

Asimov, Isaac, et al. Ancient Astronomy. rev. & updated ed. (Illus.). (gr. 3 up). 1995. PLB 17.27 (*0-8368-1191-7*) Gareth Stevens Inc.

Bendick, Jeanne. Artificial Satellites: Helpers in Space. (Illus.). 32p. (gr. k-2). 1991. PLB 12.90 (*1-56294-002-3*); pap. 4.95 (*1-878841-56-4*) Millbrook Pr.

—Comets & Meteors: Visitors from Space. (Illus.). 32p. (gr. k-2). 1991. PLB 12.90 (*1-56294-001-5*); pap. 4.95 (*1-878841-55-6*) Millbrook Pr.

Berger, Melvin & Berger, Gilda. Where Are the Stars During the Day? A Book about Stars. Sims, Blanche, illus. LC 92-18200. (gr. k-3). 1993. 12.00 (*0-8249-8644-X*, Ideals Child); pap. 4.50 (*0-8249-8607-5*) Hambleton-Hill.

Bloch, C. Planets: Outer Space Sticker Atlas. M. J. Studios Staff, illus. 32p. (gr. k-6). 1993. pap. 3.95 (*1-879424-13-4*) Nickel Pr.

Bonnet, Robert L. & Keen, G. Daniel. Space & Astronomy: Forty-Nine Science Fair Projects. 144p. 1991. 16.95 (*0-8306-3939-X*); pap. 9.95 (*0-8306-3938-1*) TAB Bks.

Boy Scouts of America. Astronomy. (Illus.). 80p. (gr. 6-12). 1983. pap. 1.85 (*0-8395-3303-9*, 33303) BSA.

Branley, Franklyn M. The Big Dipper. rev. ed. Coxe, Molly, illus. LC 90-31199. 32p. (ps-1). 1991. PLB 13.89 (*0-06-020512-1*) HarpC Child Bks.

—The Sky Is Full of Stars. Bond, Felicia, illus. LC 81-43037. 40p. (gr. k-3). 1983. pap. 4.95 (*0-06-445002-3*, Trophy) HarpC Child Bks.

—Star Guide. Eagle, Ellen, illus. LC 82-45928. 64p. (gr. 3-6). 1987. (Crowell Jr Bks); PLB 12.89 (*0-690-04351-1*, Crowell Jr Bks) HarpC Child Bks.

—Sun Dogs & Shooting Stars: A Skywatcher's Calendar. (Illus.). (gr. 5 up). 1980. 15.95 (*0-395-29520-3*) HM.

—Sun Dogs & Shooting Stars: A Skywatcher's Guide. 128p. 1993. pap. 3.50 (*0-380-71848-0*, Camelot) Avon.

—Superstar: The Supernova of Nineteen Eighty-Seven. Kelley, True, illus. LC 89-71164. 64p. (gr. 3-6). 1990. (Crowell Jr Bks); (Crowell Jr Bks) HarpC Child Bks.

Chandler, David. Exploring the Night Sky with Binoculars. Davis, Don, illus. 48p. (Orig.). 1983. pap. 4.95 (*0-9613207-0-2*) D Chandler.

Couper, H. & Henbest, Nigel. The Space Atlas: A Pictorial Guide to our Universe. 1992. 16.95 (*0-15-200598-6*, HB Juv Bks) HarBrace.

Definitely from out of Town. 48p. (gr. 4-5). 1991. PLB 11.95 (*1-56065-008-7*) Capstone Pr.

Dickinson, Terence. Exploring the Night Sky: The Equinox Astronomy Guide for Beginners. Bianchi, John, illus. 72p. (Orig.). (gr. 5 up). 1989. 17.95 (*0-920656-64-1*, Pub. by Camden Hse CN); pap. 9.95 (*0-920656-66-8*, Pub. by Camden Hse CN) Firefly Bks Ltd.

Discovery Atlas of Planets & Stars. LC 93-16805. 1993. write for info. (*0-528-83580-7*) Rand McNally.

Docekal, Eileen M. Sky Detective. (Illus.). 128p. (gr. 9-12). 1992. 14.95 (*0-8069-8404-X*) Sterling.

The Emperor of Time. 48p. (gr. 4-5). 1991. PLB 11.95 (*1-56065-013-3*) Capstone Pr.

Estalella, Robert. Our Satellite: The Moon. Ferron, Miquel, illus. LC 93-19897. (gr. 4-8). 1994. 12.95 (*0-8120-6369-4*); pap. 6.95 (*0-8120-1740-4*) Barron.

Exploring Space: From Ancient Legends to the Telescope to Modern Space Missions. LC 94-9646. (Illus.). 48p. (gr. 3 up). 1994. 19.95 (*0-590-47615-7*) Scholastic Inc.

Fowler, Allan. The Sun Is Always Shining Somewhere. (Illus.). 32p. (ps-2). 1991. PLB 10.75 (*0-516-04906-2*); pap. 3.95 (*0-516-44906-0*) Childrens.

Fradin, Dennis B. Astronomy. LC 82-19722. (Illus.). 48p. (gr. k-4). 1983. PLB 12.85 (*0-516-01673-3*); pap. 4.95 (*0-516-41673-1*) Childrens.

Gallant, Roy A. The Macmillan Book of Astronomy. Miller, Ron, et al, illus. LC 86-24158. 80p. (gr. 3-7). 1986. pap. 8.95 (*0-02-043230-5*, Aladdin) Macmillan Child Grp.

—Macmillan Book of Astronomy. LC 85-24158. (Illus.). 80p. (gr. 3-7). 1986. SBE 15.95 (*0-02-738040-8*, Macmillan Child Bk) Macmillan Child Grp.

Ganeri, Anita. Outdoor Science. LC 93-13125. (Illus.). 48p. (gr. 5 up). 1993. text ed. 13.95 RSBE (*0-87518-579-7*, Dillon) Macmillan Child Grp.

George, Michael. Galaxies. (gr. 5 up). 1993. PLB 18.95 (*0-88682-433-8*) Creative Ed.

—Stars. 1992. PLB 18.95 (*0-88682-400-1*) Creative Ed.

Graham, Ian. Astronomer. (Illus.). 32p. (gr. 5-8). 1991. PLB 12.40 (*0-531-17314-3*, Gloucester Pr) Watts.

—Astronomy. LC 94-13835. 1995. write for info. (*0-8114-3841-4*) Raintree Steck-V.

Gustafson, John R. Stars, Clusters, & Galaxies. LC 92-11228. (gr. 3-7). 1993. lib. bdg. 12.98 (*0-671-72536-X*, J Messner); pap. 6.95 (*0-671-72537-8*, J Messner) S&S Trade.

Harris, Richard. I Can Read About the Sun & Other Stars. Krasnoborski, William, illus. LC 76-54577. (gr. 2-4). 1977. pap. 2.50 (*0-89375-044-1*) Troll Assocs.

Heller, Robert, et al. Earth Science. 2nd ed. (Illus.). 1978. text ed. 32.24 (*0-07-028037-1*) McGraw.

Henbest, N. The Night Sky. (Illus.). 64p. (gr. 10 up). 1993. pap. 4.95 (*0-86020-284-4*) EDC.

Hirst, Robin & Hirst, Sally. My Place in Space. Harvey, Roland & Levine, Joe, illus. LC 89-37893. 40p. (ps-2). 1990. 13.95 (*0-531-05859-X*); PLB 13.99 (*0-531-08459-0*) Orchard Bks Watts.

How Do You Know That? 48p. (gr. 4-5). 1991. PLB 11.95 (*1-56065-014-1*) Capstone Pr.

Hubble, Edwin. Realm of the Nebulae. 1991. pap. 6.95 (*0-486-66762-6*) Dover.

Hunig, Klaus. Astro-Dome Book: 3-D Map of the Night Sky. Solensten, Lori, ed. Zerner, Amy & Drake, Charles, illus. Himelfarb, Donna, intro. by. 68p. (Orig.). (gr. 4 up). 1983. pap. 9.95 incl. Constellation Handbook (*0-913319-00-7*) Sunstone Pubns.

Jacobs, Francine. Cosmic Countdown: What Astronomers Have Learned about the Life of the Universe. Jastrow, Robert, frwd. by. LC 83-5535. (Illus.). 160p. (gr. 7 up). 1983. 9.95 (*0-87131-404-5*) M Evans.

Jobb, Jamie. The Night Sky Book. (gr. 5 up). 1977. pap. 9.95 (*0-316-46552-6*) Little.

Kelch, Joseph W. Small Worlds: Sixty Moons of Our Solar System. Steltenpohl, Jane, ed. (Illus.). 128p. (gr. 6-8). 1990. 13.95 (*0-671-70014-6*, J Messner); lib. bdg. 16.98 (*0-671-70013-8*) S&S Trade.

Kraus, John. Big Ear Two: Listening for Other-Worlds. (Illus.). 400p. (gr. 8 up). 1994. 24.95 (*1-882484-11-8*); pap. 14.95 (*1-882484-12-6*) CYGNUS-QUASAR Bks.

Lambert, David. Stars & Planets. Donohoe, Bill & Townsend, Tony, illus. LC 93-28282. 1994. PLB 19.97 (*0-8114-9246-X*) Raintree Steck-V.

Lancaster-Brown, Peter. Skywatch: Eyes-on Activities for Getting to Know the Stars, Planets & Galaxies. LC 92-40580. (Illus.). 128p. 1993. 14.95 (*0-8069-8627-1*) Sterling.

Lewellen, John. Moon, Sun & Stars. LC 81-7749. (Illus.). 48p. (gr. k-4). 1981. PLB 12.85 (*0-516-01637-7*); pap. 4.95 (*0-516-41637-5*) Childrens.

Lifestyles of the Big & Powerful. 48p. (gr. 4-5). 1991. PLB 11.95 (*1-56065-011-7*) Capstone Pr.

Liptak, Karen. Astronomy Basics. (Illus.). 48p. (gr. 3-7). 1986. 10.95 (*0-13-049966-8*) P-H.

Little People Big Book about Space. 64p. (ps-1). 1990. write for info. (*0-8094-7500-6*); lib. bdg. write for info. (*0-8094-7501-4*) Time-Life.

Looking for Little Green Men. 48p. (gr. 4-5). 1991. PLB 11.95 (*1-56065-009-5*) Capstone Pr.

Mackie, Dan. Space Tour. Hughes, Mark, illus. 32p. (gr. 5-9). 1985. pap. 5.95 (*0-88625-103-6*) Durkin Hayes Pub.

Magee, James E. Your Place in the Cosmos, Vol. I: A Layman's Book of Astronomy & the Mythology of the Eighty-Eight Celestial Constellations & Registry. Hevelius, Johannes, illus. 530p. 1985. text ed. 34.45 (*0-9614354-0-2*) Mosele & Assocs.

—Your Place in the Cosmos, Vol. II: A Layman's Book of Astronomy & the Mythology of the Eighty-Eight Celestial Constellations & Registry. Hevelius, Johannes, illus. 508p. 1988. text ed. 34.45 (*0-9614354-1-0*) Mosele & Assocs.

—Your Place in the Cosmos, Vol. III: A Layman's Book of Astronomy & the Mythology of the Eighty-Eight Celestial Constellations & Registry. Hevelius, Johannes, illus. 388p. 1992. text ed. 49.45 (*0-9614354-2-9*) Mosele & Assocs.

Marsh, Carole. Astronomy for Kids: Milky Way & Mars Bars. (Illus.). 1994. 24.95 (*0-7933-0012-6*); pap. 14.95 (*0-7933-0013-4*); computer disk 29.95 (*0-7933-0014-2*) Gallopade Pub Group.

Martin, Ernest L. The Star that Astonished the World. Griffith Observatory Sky & Telescope Staff, illus. 220p. (Orig.). (gr. 10). 1991. pap. 14.95x (*0-945657-88-9*) Acad Scriptural Knowledge.

Maurer, Richard. Junk in Space. (gr. 3 up). 1989. (S&S BFYR); pap. 5.95 (*0-671-67747-0*, S&S BFYR) S&S Trade.

Mayall, R. Newton, et al. Sky Observer's Guide. rev. ed. Polgreen, John, illus. (gr. 9 up). 1985. pap. write for info. (*0-307-24009-6*, Golden Pr) Western Pub.

Mayes, S. Why Is Night Dark? (Illus.). 24p. (gr. 1-4). 1990. lib. bdg. 11.96 (*0-88110-442-6*, Usborne); pap. 3.95 (*0-7460-0428-1*, Usborne) EDC.

Maynard, Christopher & Verdet, Jean-Pierre. The Universe. LC 94-9085. (Illus.). 128p. (gr. k-4). 1994. pap. 5.95 (*1-85697-527-4*, Kingfisher LKC) LKC.

Miotto, Enrico. The Universe: Origin & Evolution. LC 94-3839. 1994. write for info. (*0-8114-3334-X*) Raintree Steck-V.

Moche, Dinah. Astronomy Today: Planets, Stars, Space Exploration. McNaught, Harry, illus. LC 82-5211. 96p. (gr. 5 up). 1982. pap. 13.00 (*0-394-84423-8*) Random Bks Yng Read.

Moeschl, Richard. Exploring the Sky: Projects for Beginning Astronomers. rev. ed. LC 92-18863. (Illus.). 320p. (gr. 9-12). 1992. pap. 14.95 (*1-55652-160-X*) Chicago Review.

Muirden, James. About the Universe? LC 94-27356. (gr. 1-8). 1995. write for info. (*0-8114-3884-8*) Raintree Steck-V.

—Stars & Planets. LC 93-20104. (Illus.). 96p. (gr. 5 up). 1993. 15.95 (*1-85697-852-4*, Kingfisher LKC); pap. 9.95 (*1-85697-851-6*) LKC.

Myring, Lynn. Sun, Moon & Planets. (gr. 2-5). 1982. (Usborne-Hayes); pap. 3.95 (*0-86020-580-0*) EDC.

National Wildlife Federation Staff. Astronomy Adventures. (gr. k-8). 1991. pap. 7.95 (*0-945051-31-X*, 75022) Natl Wildlife.

Noffs, David & Noffs, Laurie. Harold Magazine, Bk. 5: Watching the Stars at Night. Noffs, Lauri A., illus. 24p. (Orig.). (gr. 5). 1987. wkbk. 2.50 (*0-929875-06-0*) Noffs Assocs.

Not Quite Planets. 48p. (gr. 4-5). 1991. PLB 11.95 (*1-56065-012-5*) Capstone Pr.

Ottewell, Guy. To Know the Stars. (Illus.). 41p. (gr. 3 up). 1983. pap. 7.00 (*0-934546-12-6*) Astron Wkshp.

Parker, Steve. Galileo & the Universe. Parker, Steve, illus. LC 91-28315. 32p. (gr. 3-7). 1992. 14.00 (*0-06-020735-3*) HarpC Child Bks.

Peacock, Graham & Ashton, Dennis. Astronomy. (Illus.). 32p. (gr. 2-4). 1994. 14.95 (*1-56847-191-2*) Thomson Lrning.

Raintree Publishers Staff. Astronomy. LC 87-28780. (Illus.). 64p. (Orig.). (gr. 5-9). 1988. PLB 11.95 (*0-8172-3080-7*) Raintree Steck-V.

Reigot, Betty P. A Book about Planets & Stars. (Illus.). 48p. (gr. 2-5). 1988. pap. 3.95 (*0-590-40593-4*) Scholastic Inc.

Rey, H. A. The Stars: A New Way to See Them. 3rd ed. (Illus.). (gr. 8 up). 1973. 16.45 (*0-395-08121-1*) HM.

Ridpath, Ian. Atlas of Stars & Planets. LC 92-32463. 80p. (gr. 5-10). 1993. 16.95 (*0-8160-2926-1*) Facts on File.

—Space. LC 91-7455. (Illus.). 48p. (gr. 5-8). 1991. PLB 13.90 (*0-531-19144-3*, Warwick) Watts.

Schatz, Dennis. Astronomy Activity Book. (gr. 4-7). 1991. pap. 6.95 (*0-671-70449-4*, Little Simon) S&S Trade.

Schultz, Charles., illus. Land & Space. LC 94-15492. (gr. 2 up). 1994. 9.99 (*0-517-11895-5*, Pub. by Derrydale Bks) Random Hse Value.

Schultz, Ron. Looking Inside Telescopes & the Night Sky. (Illus.). 48p. (Orig.). (gr. 3 up). Date not set. pap. 9.95 (*1-56261-072-4*) John Muir.

Scott, Carole. The Story of Astronomy. Forsey, Chris, illus. LC 91-36604. 32p. (gr. 1-4). 1993. PLB 11.89 (*0-8167-2703-1*); pap. text ed. 3.95 (*0-8167-2704-X*) Troll Assocs.

Simon, Seymour. Galaxies. LC 87-23967. (Illus.). 32p. (ps-3). 1988. 14.95 (*0-688-08002-2*); PLB 14.88 (*0-688-08004-9*, Morrow Jr Bks) Morrow Jr Bks.

—Galaxies. LC 87-23967. (Illus.). 32p. (gr. k up). 1991. pap. 5.95 (*0-688-10992-6*, Mulberry) Morrow.

—Look to the Night Sky: An Introduction to Star Watching. (Illus.). (gr. 5-12). 1979. pap. 6.99 (*0-14-049185-6*, Puffin) Puffin Bks.

Sims, Lesley. The Sun & Stars. LC 93-28280. 1994. PLB 18.99 (*0-8114-5505-X*) Raintree Steck-V.

Snowden, S. The Young Astronomer. (Illus.). 32p. (gr. 5-10). 1983. PLB 13.96 (*0-88110-028-5*); pap. 6.95 (*0-86020-651-3*) EDC.

Souza, Dorothy M. Northern Lights: Nature in Action Ser. LC 93-3027. 1993. 17.50 (*0-87614-799-6*) Carolrhoda Bks.

Space. (Illus.). 112p. (gr. 4-9). 1989. 18.95 (*1-85435-072-2*) Marshall Cavendish.

Speregen, Debra N. In the Sky Activity Book. (ps-3). 1994. pap. 1.95 (*0-590-47591-6*) Scholastic Inc.

Stacy, Tom. The Sun, Stars & Planets. Bull, Peter & Quigley, Sebastian, illus. 40p. (gr. 4-5). 1991. PLB 12.40 (*0-531-19107-9*, Warwick) Watts.

—Sun, Stars & Planets. Bull, Peter, illus. LC 90-42979. 40p. (Orig.). (gr. 2-5). 1991. pap. 4.99 (*0-679-80862-0*) Random Bks Yng Read.

Stephenson, Robert & Browne, Roger. Exploring Earth in Space. Hughes, Jenny, illus. LC 91-44198. 48p. (gr. 4-8). 1992. PLB 22.80 (*0-8114-2603-3*) Raintree Steck-V.

Stott, Carole. Night Sky. LC 93-644. (Illus.). 64p. (gr. 3-8). 1993. 9.95 (*1-56458-393-7*) Dorling Kindersley.

—Night Sky. (Illus.). (gr. 3-7). 1994. pap. 16.95 (*1-56458-685-5*) Dorling Kindersley.

Thompson, C. E. Glow-in-the-Dark Constellations: A Field Guide for Young Stargazers. Chewning, Randy, illus. 32p. (gr. 1-5). 1989. 11.95 (*0-448-09070-8*, G&D) Putnam Pub Group.

Time-Life Books Staff, ed. Space & Planets. 144p. 1991. write for info. (*0-8094-9650-X*); lib. bdg. write for info. (*0-8094-9651-8*) Time-Life.

Time Life Inc. Editors. The Search for the Mystery Planet: Space Math. Crawford, Jean B., ed. (Illus.). 64p. (gr. k-2). 1993. write for info. (*0-8094-9982-7*); lib. bdg. write for info. (*0-8094-9983-5*) Time-Life.

Unus, Iqbal J. Up in the Sky. (Illus.). 24p. (Orig.). (gr. 3-6). 1983. pap. 2.00 (*0-89259-054-8*) Am Trust Pubns.

Vancleave, Janice P. Janice Vancleave's Astronomy for Every Kid: 101 Easy Experiments That Really Work. 1991. text ed. 24.95 (*0-471-54285-7*); pap. text ed. 10.95 (*0-471-53573-7*) Wiley.

Weiss, Malcolm E. Sky Watchers of Ages Past. McFadden, Eliza, illus. (gr. 5-9). 1982. 14.45 (*0-395-29525-4*) HM.

Wilson, David A. Star Track. (Illus.). 152p. (Orig.). 1994. pap. 12.00 (*0-934852-38-3*) Lorien Hse.

Wilson, Lynn. What's Out There? A Book about Space. Billin-Frye, Paige, illus. LC 92-24469. 32p. (ps-3). 1993. lib. bdg. 7.99 (*0-448-40518-0*, G&D); pap. 2.25 (*0-448-40517-2*, G&D) Putnam Pub Group.

Wood, Robert W. Thirty-Nine Easy Astronomy Experiments. (Illus.). 160p. 1991. 16.95 (*0-8306-7597-3*, 3597); pap. 9.95 (*0-8306-3597-1*) TAB Bks.

Wroble, Lisa. Astronomy. Nolte, Larry, illus. 48p. (gr. 3-6). Date not set. PLB 12.95 (*1-56065-110-5*) Capstone Pr.

Wyler, Rose. The Starry Sky. Steltenpohl, Jane, ed. Petruccio, Steven, illus. 32p. (gr. k-2). 1989. PLB 11.98 (*0-671-66345-3*, J Messner); pap. 4.95 (*0-671-66349-6*) S&S Trade.

Zim, Herbert S. & Baker, Robert H. Stars. rev. ed. Irving, James G., illus. (gr. 6 up). 1985. pap. write for info. (*0-307-24493-8*, Golden Pr) Western Pub.

ASTRONOMY–DICTIONARIES

Ressmeyer, Roger. Astronaut to Zodiac: A Young Stargazer's Alphabet. LC 92-9615. (Illus.). 32p. (gr. k-6). 1992. 15.00 (*0-517-58805-6*); PLB 15.99 (*0-517-58806-4*) Crown Bks Yng Read.

Richardson, James. Science Dictionary of Space. Hunt, Joseph, illus. LC 91-16551. 48p. (gr. 3-7). 1992. lib. bdg. 11.59 (*0-8167-2524-1*); pap. 3.95 (*0-8167-2443-1*) Troll Assocs.

Simon, Seymour. Space Words: A Dictionary. Chewning, Randy, illus. LC 90-37402. 48p. (gr. 2-5). 1991. 15.00 (*0-06-022532-7*); PLB 14.89 (*0-06-022533-5*) HarpC Child Bks.

ASTROPHYSICS

Asimov, Isaac. Quasars, Pulsars & Black Holes. 1990. pap. 4.95 (*0-440-40353-7*) Dell.

Ehrlich, Robert. The Cosmological Milkshake: A Semi-Serious Look at the Size of Things. Ehrlich, Gary, illus. LC 93-28135. 1994. 24.00 (*0-8135-2045-2*) Rutgers U Pr.

ATHENS

Davis, William S. Day in Old Athens. LC 60-16707. (Illus.). (gr. 7 up). 1965. 20.00 (*0-8196-0111-X*) Biblo.

MacDonald, Fiona & Bergin, Mark. A Greek Temple. LC 92-10712. (Illus.). 48p. (gr. 5 up). 1992. 17.95 (*0-87226-361-4*) P Bedrick Bks.

ATHLETES

see also Black Athletes

Aaseng, Nathan. Athletes. LC 94-12469. 1995. write for info. (*0-8160-3019-7*) Facts on File.

—Carl Lewis: Legend Chaser. LC 84-23348. (Illus.). 56p. (gr. 4-9). 1985. PLB 13.50 (*0-8225-0496-0*) Lerner Pubns.

—Superstars Stopped Short. LC 81-12431. (Illus.). 80p. (gr. 4 up). 1982. PLB 11.95 (*0-8225-1326-9*) Lerner Pubns.

—True Champions: Great Athletes & Their Off-the-Field Heroics. LC 92-36942. (Illus.). 128p. (gr. 5 up). 1993. 14.95 (*0-8027-8246-9*); PLB 15.85 (*0-8027-8247-7*) Walker & Co.

Belfiglio, Val. Pride of the Southwest: Outstanding Athletes of the Southwest Conference. Carter, Bo, intro. by. (Illus.). 144p. (gr. 4-7). 1992. 14.95 (*0-89015-822-3*) Sunbelt Media.

Bernotas, Bob. Jim Thorpe. (Illus.). (gr. 5 up). 1993. PLB 17.95 (*0-7910-1722-2*) Chelsea Hse.

Boga, Steve. On Their Own: Adventure Athletes in Solo Sports, 3 bks. Kratoville, B. L., ed. (Illus.). (gr. 3-9). 1992. Set, 64p. ea. bk. pap. text ed. 11.00 (*0-87879-928-1*); wkbk. 12.50 (*0-87879-929-X*) High Noon Bks.

Breitenbucher, Cathy. Bonnie Blair: Speediest Skater. LC 94-5744. 1994. 17.50 (*0-8225-2883-5*); pap. 13.13 (*0-8225-9665-2*) Lerner Pubns.

Coffey, Wayne. Carl Lewis. (Illus.). 64p. (gr. 3-7). 1993. PLB 14.95 (*1-56711-006-1*) Blackbirch.

—Katarina Witt. (Illus.). 64p. (gr. 3-7). 1992. PLB 14.95 (*1-56711-001-0*) Blackbirch.

—Kip Keino. (Illus.). 64p. (gr. 3-7). 1992. PLB 14.95 (*1-56711-003-7*) Blackbirch.

Connolly, Pat. Coaching Evelyn: Fast, Faster, Fastest Woman in the World. LC 90-4835. (Illus.). 224p. (gr. 7 up). 1991. PLB 15.89 (*0-06-021283-7*) HarpC Child Bks.

Corrigan, Robert J. Tracking Heroes: Thirteen Track & Field Champions. LC 89-51039. 163p. (gr. 4-9). 1990. 8.95 (*1-55523-236-1*) Winston-Derek.

Fox, Fiona. How to Reach Your Favorite Star. LC 92-17291. (Illus.). 64p. (gr. 4-8). 1992. pap. 3.95 (*1-56288-330-5*) Checkerboard.

Frontier Press Company Staff. Lincoln Library of Sports Champions, 20 vols. 5th ed. LC 88-82571. (Illus.). 2560p. (gr. 4 up). 1989. Set. 439.00 (*0-912168-13-7*) Frontier Pr Co.

Great Athletes, 1992: Supplement, 3 vols. (gr. 6 up). 1994. Set. PLB 75.000 (*0-89356-819-8*) Salem Pr.

Harris, Jonathan. Drugged Athletes: The Crisis in American Sports. LC 86-29396. 204p. (gr. 5-9). 1987. SBE 14.95 (*0-02-742740-4*, Four Winds) Macmillan Child Grp.

Haskins, James. Sugar Ray Leonard. LC 82-15227. (Illus.). 160p. (gr. 4 up). 1982. 15.00 (*0-688-01436-4*) Lothrop.

Jennings, Jay. Moments of Courage. (Illus.). 64p. (gr. 5-7). 1991. PLB 10.95 (*0-382-24108-8*); pap. 5.95 (*0-382-24114-2*) Silver Burdett Pr.

Johnson, Rick L. Bo Jackson: Baseball-Football Superstar. LC 91-17910. (Illus.). 64p. (gr. 4-6). 1991. text ed. 13.95 RSBE (*0-87518-489-8*, Dillon) Macmillan Child Grp.

Knudson, R. R. Babe Didrikson: Athlete of the Century. Lewin, Ted, illus. 64p. (gr. 2-6). 1986. pap. 3.95 (*0-14-032095-4*, Puffin) Puffin Bks.

Lahey, David. Athletic Scholarships: Making Your Sports Pay. 200p. 1992. pap. 12.95 (*1-895629-06-3*, Pub. by Warwick Pub CN) Firefly Bks Ltd.

Littlefield, Bill. Champions: Their Glory & Beyond. Fuchs, Bernie, illus. Deford, Frank, frwd. by. LC 92-31390. 1993. 21.95 (*0-316-52805-6*) Little.

McMane, Fred & Wolf, Cathrine. The Worst Day I Ever Had. Hamann, Brad, illus. (gr. 3-7). 1991. pap. 8.95 (*0-316-55354-9*, Spts Illus Kids) Little.

Maitland, William J. Weight Training for Gifted Athletes. Mollen, Art, intro. by. LC 89-90833. (Illus.). 147p. (Orig.). (gr. 8 up). 1990. pap. 17.95 (*0-936759-01-1*) Maitland Enter.

Martin, Patricia S. Dale Murphy: Baseball's Gentle Giant. (Illus.). 24p. (gr. 1-4). 1987. PLB 14.60 (*0-86592-167-9*); 10.95 (*0-685-67567-X*) Rourke Corp.

Newman, Matthew. Mary Decker Slaney. LC 86-16525. (Illus.). 48p. (gr. 5-6). 1986. text ed. 11.95 RSBE (*0-89686-319-0*, Crestwood Hse) Macmillan Child Grp.

Nuwer, Hank. Sports Scandals. LC 93-26317. (Illus.). 196p. (gr. 9-12). 1994. PLB 13.90 (*0-531-11183-0*) Watts.

Oana, Katherine. The Sporting Way to Reading Comprehension. Cooper, William H., ed. Shuster, Dorarhye, illus. LC 84-51195. 68p. (Orig.). (gr. 3-8). 1984. 5.27 (*0-914127-17-9*) Univ Class.

O'Connor, Jim. Comeback! Four True Stories. Campbell, Jim, illus. LC 91-25028. 48p. (Orig.). (gr. 2-4). 1992. PLB 7,99 (*0-679-92666-6*); pap. 3.50 (*0-679-82666-1*) Random Bks Yng Read.

Oleksy, Walter. Sports Legends. (Illus.). 128p. (gr. 3-6). Date not set. 19.95 (*1-56065-121-0*) Capstone Pr.

Orr, Jack. Black Athlete: His Story in American History. Robinson, Jackie, intro. by. (gr. 6 up). 1969. PLB 14.95 (*0-87460-104-5*) Lion Bks.

Porter, A. P. Greg Lemond: Premier Cyclist. LC 89-13700. (gr. 4-7). 1991. pap. 4.95 (*0-8225-9584-2*) Lerner Pubns.

Rennert, Richard, ed. Book of Firsts: Sports Heroes. LC 93-18437. (Illus.). 1993. 13.95 (*0-7910-2055-X*, Am Art Analog); pap. 5.95 (*0-7910-2056-8*, Am Art Analog) Chelsea Hse.

Rogak, Lisa. Steroids: Dangerous Game. 64p. (gr. 5-10). 1992. PLB 15.95 (*0-8225-0048-5*) Lerner Pubns.

Salem Press Editors. The Twentieth Century: Great Athletes, 20 vols. (Illus.). 2924p. (gr. 6 up). 1992. lib. bdg. 400.00x (*0-89356-775-2*) Salem Pr.

Sanford, William R. & Green, Carl R. Babe Didrikson Zaharias. LC 91-44870. (Illus.). 48p. (gr. 5). 1993. text ed. 11.95 RSBE (*0-89686-736-6*, Crestwood Hse) Macmillan Child Grp.

Scott, Robert L. How to Market Your Student Athlete. (Illus.). 193p. (gr. 9 up). Date not set. wkbk. 19.95 (*0-9640318-0-9*) How Mrkt Stud Athlete.

Silverstein, Alvin, et al. Steroids: Big Muscles, Big Problems. LC 91-876. (Illus.). 112p. (gr. 6 up). 1992. lib. bdg. 17.95 (*0-89490-318-7*) Enslow Pubs.

Slater, Robert. The Jewish Child's Book of Sports Heroes. LC 92-40087. 1993. 14.95 (*0-8246-0360-5*) Jonathan David.

Solomon, Abbot N. Secrets of the Super Athletes: Tip for Fans & Players-Football. (Illus., Orig.). (gr. 7 up). 1982. pap. 1.95 (*0-440-97979-X*, LFL) Dell.

Sport Shots Boxed Set, No. 2: Contains Mini-Bios, 6 bks, Nos. 7-12. 1992. Set. 7.50 (*0-590-66108-6*) Scholastic Inc.

Strauss, Larry. How to Reach Your Favorite Sports Star. (gr. 4-7). 1993. pap. 2.95 (*0-307-22551-8*, Golden Pr) Western Pub.

Sullivan, George. Great Lives: Sports. LC 88-15673. (Illus.). 288p. (gr. 4-6). 1988. SBE 22.95 (*0-684-18510-5*, Scribners Young Read) Macmillan Child Grp.

Swanson, Gloria M. I've Got an Idea: The Story of Frederick McKinley Jones. (gr. 4-7). 1994. pap. 7.95 (*0-8225-9662-8*) Lerner Pubns.

White, Ellen E. Bo Jackson: Playing the Games. (Illus.). 96p. (Orig.). (gr. 3-7). 1990. pap. 2.95 (*0-590-44075-6*) Scholastic Inc.

ATHLETICS

see also Coaching (Athletics); Gymnastics; Olympic Games; Physical Education and Training; Sports; Track Athletics;

also names of specific athletic activities, e.g. Boxing; Rowing; etc.

Athletics. (Illus.). 22p. (gr. 6-12). 1964. pap. 1.85 (*0-8395-3324-1*, 33324) BSA.

Brunner, Rick, et al. Soviet Training & Recovery Methods: For Competitive Athletes. LC 90-62005. (Illus.). 200p. (Orig.). (gr. 10 up). 1990. pap. 18.95 (*0-9622039-2-0*) Sports Focus Pub.

Buchanan, David A. Greek Athletics. McLeish, Kenneth & McLeish, Valerie, eds. (Illus.). 48p. (gr. 7-12). 1976. pap. text ed. 9.00 (*0-582-20059-8*, 70659) Longman.

ATHLETICS–FICTION

Brown, F. K. Last Hurdle. Spier, Peter, illus. LC 87-29761. 202p. (gr. 3-9). 1988. Repr. of 1953 ed. 17.50 (*0-208-02212-0*, Linnet) Shoe String.

Bunting, Eve. Maggie the Freak. (Illus.). 64p. (gr. 3-8). 1992. 8.95 (*0-89565-775-9*) Childs World.

Cloverdale Press, Inc. Editors. Out of Bounds. 160p. (gr. 6 up). 1987. pap. 2.50 (*0-553-26338-2*, Starfire) Bantam.

Cloverdale Press, Inc. Editors, ed. Varsity Takedown Coach, No. 2. 128p. 1987. pap. 2.50 (*0-553-26209-2*) Bantam.

Crutcher, Chris. Athletic Shorts: Six Short Stories. 160p. (gr. 7 up). 1992. pap. 3.99 (*0-440-21390-8*, LFL) Dell.

Hallowell, Tommy. Varsity Coach. 128p. (Orig.). 1986. pap. 2.50 (*0-553-26033-2*, Starfire) Bantam.

Levy, Elizabeth. The Gymnasts' Gift. 112p. 1991. pap. 2.75 (*0-590-44693-2*) Scholastic Inc.

—The New Coach? 128p. (gr. 3-7). 1991. pap. 2.75 (*0-590-44695-9*) Scholastic Inc.

—Team Trouble. 128p. 1992. pap. 2.75 (*0-590-45252-5*) Scholastic Inc.

—The Winner. 128p. (gr. 3-6). 1989. pap. 2.50 (*0-590-41565-4*, Apple Paperbacks) Scholastic Inc.

Moloney, James. Dougy. 1993. pap. 10.95 (*0-7022-2499-5*, Pub. by Univ Queensland Pr AT) Intl Spec Bk.

Spinelli, Jerry. Maniac Magee. (gr. 4-7). 1990. 14.95 (*0-316-80722-2*, Joy St Bks) Little.

Teague, Sam. The King of Hearts' Heart. 192p. (gr. 3-7). 1987. 13.95 (*0-316-83427-0*) Little.

White, Terence. What Happened to Sherlock Holmes? as Set to Rest In... The Legend of Wilson-The Amazing Athlete. Blackburn, Francis, et al, eds. Meade, Javier & Jamieson, Lindsey, illus. Barton, Hill, intro. by. LC 83-51870. 102p. 1984. 9.95 (*0-9612698-0-4*) Seagull Pub Co.

ATLANTA BRAVES (BASEBALL TEAM)

Altanta Braves. (gr. 4-7). 1993. pap. 1.49 (*0-553-56428-5*) Bantam.

Goodman, Michael. Atlanta Braves. 48p. (gr. 4-10). 1992. PLB 14.95 (*0-88682-460-5*) Creative Ed.

ATLANTIC CABLE

see Cables, Submarine

ATLANTIC COAST

Hansen, Judith. Seashells in My Pocket: A Child's Nature Guide to Exploring the Atlantic Coast. 2nd ed. Sabaka, Donna, illus. LC 92-24397. 160p. (gr. 6 up). 1992. pap. 10.95 (*1-878239-15-5*) AMC Books.

ATLANTIC STATES

Aylesworth, Thomas G. & Aylesworth, Virginia L. Atlantic: Virginia, W. Virginia, District of Columbia. (Illus.). 64p. (gr. 3 up). 1991. lib. bdg. 16.95 (*0-7910-1041-4*) Chelsea Hse.

—Mid Atlantic: Pennsylvania - Delaware - Maryland. (Illus.). 64p. (gr. 3 up). 1991. lib. bdg. 16.95 (*0-7910-1040-6*) Chelsea Hse.

—The Mid-Atlantic (Pennsylvania, Delaware, Maryland) (Illus.). 67p. (Orig.). (gr. 3 up). 1988. 16.95 (*1-55546-554-4*); pap. 6.95 (*0-7910-0537-2*) Chelsea Hse.

Sagan, Miriam. The Middle Atlantic States. LC 93-49007. 1994. write for info. (*0-86625-508-7*) Rourke Pubns.

ATLANTIS

Abels, Harriette S. Lost City of Atlantis. LC 87-13440. (Illus.). 48p. (gr. 5-6). 1987. text ed. 12.95 RSBE (*0-89686-344-1*, Crestwood Hse) Macmillan Child Grp.

McMullen, David. Atlantis: The Missing Continent. LC 77-22138. (Illus.). 48p. (gr. 4 up). 1983. PLB 20.70 (*0-8172-1047-4*) Raintree Steck-V.

Stein, Wendy. Atlantis: Opposing Viewpoints. LC 88-24470. (Illus.). 112p. (gr. 5-8). 1989. PLB 14.95 (*0-89908-056-1*) Greenhaven.

ATLASES

see also Bible–Geography;

also names of countries, cities, etc. with the subdivision Maps, e.g. U. S.–Maps; etc.

American Map Corp. Staff. Scholastic World Atlas, No. 695520. (gr. 7-9). 1993. pap. 3.95 (*0-685-47443-7*) Am Map.

American Map Corp. Staff, ed. Atlas Mundial. (Illus.). (gr. 7-12). 1992. pap. 2.95 (*0-8416-9555-5*, 695555); Span. lang. ed. pap. write for info. Am Map.

Around the World: An Atlas of Maps & Pictures. LC 94-9997. 1994. 14.95 (*0-528-83691-9*) Rand McNally.

Atlas. (Illus.). 48p. (gr. k-3). 1994. write for info. (*1-56458-799-1*) Dorling Kindersley.

The Atlas of Ancient Worlds. LC 93-27041. 1994. 19.95 (*1-56458-471-2*) Dorling Kindersley.

Attmore, Stephen. Children's Atlas of the World. rev. ed. Fryer, George, illus. 32p. (gr. 1-3). 1994. pap. 5.95 (*0-8249-8662-8*, Ideals Child) Hambleton-Hill.

Bender, Lionel. Geography. LC 91-29406. (Illus.). 96p. (gr. 1-5). 1992. pap. 13.00 (*0-671-75996-5*, S&S BFYR); pap. 8.00 (*0-671-75997-3*, S&S BFYR) S&S Trade.

Children's Atlas of the United States. (gr. 5-9). 1989. 14.95 (*0-528-83362-6*); pap. write for info. (*0-528-83540-8*) Rand McNally.

Children's First Atlas. (Illus.). (gr. 2-6). 1985. 2.98 (*0-517-47997-4*) Random Hse Value.

Children's World Atlas. (Illus.). (gr. 5-9). 1991. 14.95 (*0-528-83455-X*) Rand McNally.

Delf, Brian, illus. Picture Atlas of the World. LC 92-37056. 1992. write for info. (*0-528-83564-5*) Rand McNally.

Discovery Atlas of Animals. LC 93-7252. 1993. write for info. (*0-528-83579-3*) Rand McNally.
Discovery Atlas of the United States. LC 93-18713. 1993. write for info. (*0-528-83578-5*) Rand McNally.
Discovery Atlas of the World. LC 93-12560. 1993. write for info. (*0-528-83577-7*) Rand McNally.
The Eyewitness Atlas of the World. LC 93-18572. 160p. (gr. k up). 1993. 24.95 (*1-56458-297-3*) Dorling Kindersley.
Fagan, Elizabeth G. Rand McNally Children's Atlas of World Wildlife. Wills, Jan, illus. LC 93-503. 1993. write for info. (*0-528-83581-5*) Rand McNally.
Family World Atlas. LC 93-48823. 1994. 9.95 (*0-528-83673-0*) Rand McNally.
Giant Children's Atlas of the World. 1993. pap. 27.95 (*0-528-83589-0*) Rand McNally.
Gorton, Julia. Student World Atlas. Price, Nicholas, illus. 48p. (gr. 3-6). 1994. 14.99 (*0-525-67491-8*, Lodestar Bks) Dutton Child Bks.
El Gran Atlas De los Chicos. (SPA.). 12p. 1992. pap. 203.76 incl. audio cass. & crayons (*1-56668-129-4*) Rincon Rodanthe.
Hammond. Discovering Maps: A Young Person's World Atlas. 1993. 11.95 (*0-8437-3414-0*) Hammond Inc.
Hammond Incorporated Staff. The World Atlas. LC 82-675036. (Illus.). 112p. (gr. 5 up). 1982. lib. bdg. 11.99 (*0-394-94663-4*); pap. 13.00 smyth-sewn (*0-394-84663-X*) Random Bks Yng Read.
It's a Big Big World. (gr. 1-6). 1992. English ed., incl. audio cass. & crayons. 16.98 (*2-89429-007-1*); Spanish ed., incl. audio cass. & crayons. 16.98 (*2-89429-009-8*) Rincon Rodanthe.
It's a Big, Big World Atlas. 12p. 1992. pap. 203.76 incl. audio cass. & crayons (*1-56668-140-5*) Rincon Rodanthe.
Lye, Keith. The Complete Atlas of the World. LC 94-19316. 1994. write for info. (*0-8114-5804-0*) Raintree Steck-V.
Mason, Antony. The Kingfisher First Picture Atlas. Woodcock, John & Fleury, Eugene, illus. LC 93-46855. 40p. (gr. 2-5). 1994. 12.95 (*1-85697-836-2*, Kingfisher LKC) LKC.
Middleton, Nick. Atlas of World Issues. (Illus.). 64p. (gr. 6 up). 1989. 16.95x (*0-8160-2022-1*) Facts on File.
Morris, Neil. The Golden Atlas for Children. Studio Illustratori Associati Boni Galante Staff, illus. 48p. (gr. 1-6). 1992. 8.95 (*0-307-17876-5*, 17876, Golden Pr) Western Pub.
—The Student's Activity Atlas. Walker, Roger, illus. 48p. (gr. 3 up). 1993. PLB 19.93 (*0-8368-1041-4*) Gareth Stevens Inc.
Morris, Scott, ed. Agriculture & Vegetation of the World. De Blij, Harm J., intro. by. LC 92-22290. (Illus.). 1993. 15.95 (*0-7910-1804-0*, Am Art Analog); pap. write for info. (*0-7910-1817-2*, Am Art Analog) Chelsea Hse.
—The Economy of the World. De Blij, Harm J., intro. by. LC 92-22291. (Illus.). 1993. 15.95 (*0-7910-1809-1*, Am Art Analog); pap. write for info. (*0-7910-1822-9*, Am Art Analog) Chelsea Hse.
—The Endangered World. De Blij, Harm J., intro. by. LC 92-22289. (Illus.). 1993. 15.95 (*0-7910-1806-7*, Am Art Analog); pap. write for info. (*0-7910-1819-9*, Am Art Analog) Chelsea Hse.
—Industry of the World. De Blij, Harm J., intro. by. LC 92-22288. (Illus.). 1993. 15.95 (*0-7910-1807-5*, Am Art Analog); pap. write for info. (*0-7910-1820-2*, Am Art Analog) Chelsea Hse.
—Languages of the World. De Blij, Harm J., intro. by. LC 92-22287. (Illus.). 1993. 15.95 (*0-7910-1811-3*, Am Art Analog); pap. write for info. (*0-7910-1824-5*, Am Art Analog) Chelsea Hse.
—The Military World. De Blij, Harm J., intro. by. LC 92-22286. (Illus.). 1993. 15.95 (*0-7910-1808-3*, Am Art Analog); pap. write for info. (*0-7910-1821-0*, Am Art Analog) Chelsea Hse.
—The Physical World. De Blij, Harm J., intro. by. LC 92-22285. (Illus.). 1993. 15.95 (*0-7910-1801-6*, Am Art Analog); pap. write for info. (*0-7910-1814-8*, Am Art Analog) Chelsea Hse.
—The Political World. De Blij, Harm J., intro. by. LC 92-22284. (Illus.). 1993. 15.95 (*0-7910-1802-4*, Am Art Analog); pap. write for info. (*0-7910-1815-6*, Am Art Analog) Chelsea Hse.
—Populations of the World. De Blij, Harm J., intro. by. LC 92-22283. (Illus.). 1993. 15.95 (*0-7910-1805-9*, Am Art Analog) Chelsea Hse.
—Religions of the World. De Blij, Harm J., intro. by. LC 92-22282. (Illus.). 1993. 15.95 (*0-7910-1810-5*, Am Art Analog); pap. write for info. (*0-7910-1823-7*, Am Art Analog) Chelsea Hse.
—Rocks & Minerals of the World. De Blij, Harm J., intro. by. LC 92-22910. (Illus.). 1993. 15.95 (*0-7910-1803-2*, Am Art Analog); pap. write for info. (*0-7910-1816-4*, Am Art Analog) Chelsea Hse.
Nichols, V. Notebook World Atlas. (Illus.). 16p. (gr. 5-12). 1993. pap. 1.95 (*1-879424-25-8*) Nickel Pr.
Olliver, Jane, ed. Doubleday Children's Atlas. LC 86-67523. (Illus.). 96p. (gr. k-6). 1987. pap. 14.00 (*0-385-23760-X*) Doubleday.
Perham, Molly & Steele, Philip. The Children's Illustrated World Atlas: A Young Person's Guide to the World. LC 93-70591. (Illus.). 56p. (gr. 1 up). 1993. 9.98 (*1-56138-331-7*) Courage Bks.
Petty, Kate. My First Atlas, Vol. 1. King, Colin, illus. (ps-8). 1991. 9.95 (*1-55782-361-8*, Pub. by Warner Juvenile Bks) Little.
Porter, Malcolm, contrib. by. The Dillon Press Children's Atlas. LC 93-15593. (Illus.). 96p. (gr. 5 up). 1993. text ed. 16.95 RSBE (*0-87518-606-8*, Dillon) Macmillan Child Grp.
Rand McNally & Company Staff. Rand McNally Children's Atlas of the World. rev. ed. LC 92-24028. (Illus.). (gr. 4-7). 1992. pap. 7.95 (*0-528-83541-6*) Rand McNally.
Rand McNally Staff. Children's Atlas of Earth Through Time. Fagan, Elizabeth, ed. (Illus.). 80p. 1990. 14.95 (*0-528-83415-0*) Rand McNally.
—Children's Atlas of the Universe. (Illus.). (gr. 3-7). 1990. 14.95 (*0-528-83408-8*) Rand McNally.
—Children's Atlas of World Wildlife. Fagan, Elizabeth, ed. Willis, Jan, illus. 96p. (gr. 3-7). 1990. 14.95 (*0-528-83409-6*) Rand McNally.
—First Atlas. Henley, Claire & Russell, Chris, illus. LC 93-37528. 1994. write for info. (*0-528-83679-X*) Rand McNally.
—Picture Atlas of the World. 1991. 19.95 (*0-528-83437-1*) Rand McNally.
—Rand McNally Animal Sticker Atlas. (Illus.). (ps-3). 1993. pap. 4.95 (*0-528-83586-6*) Rand McNally.
—Rand McNally Dinosaur Sticker Atlas. (Illus.). (ps-3). 1993. pap. 4.95 (*0-528-83585-8*) Rand McNally.
Reader's Digest Editors. Reader's Digest Children's World Atlas. rev. ed. LC 90-28667. (Illus.). 128p. (gr. 3-7). 1993. 20.00 (*0-89577-500-X*, Dist. by Random) RD Assn.
Rowland-Entwistle, Theodore. The Pop-up Atlas of the World. Jacobs, Philip & Peterkin, Mike, illus. 18p. (gr. 3 up). 1988. pap. 12.95 (*0-671-65898-0*, S&S BFYR) S&S Trade.
Snow, Alan. My First Atlas. 1992. 5.98 (*0-8317-0226-5*) Smithmark.
—My First Atlas. LC 91-24303. (Illus.). 32p. (gr. k-3). 1992. lib. bdg. 12.79 (*0-8167-2517-9*); pap. text ed. 4.95 (*0-8167-2518-7*) Troll Assocs.
Student's World Atlas. rev. ed. LC 93-41312. 1994. write for info. (*0-528-83699-4*) Rand McNally.
Tivers, Jacqueline & Day, Michael. The Viking Children's World Atlas: An Introductory Atlas for Young People. LC 83-675053. (Illus.). 48p. (gr. 4-6). 1983. pap. 9.95 (*0-670-21791-3*) Viking Child Bks.
—The Viking Children's World Atlas: An Introductory Atlas for Young People. rev. ed. LC 93-41434. (Illus.). 48p. (gr. k-5). 1994. 10.99 (*0-670-85481-6*) Viking Child Bks.
Tyler, Jenny. Children's Picture Atlas. (Illus.). 32p. (gr. 4-7). 1983. pap. 6.95 (*0-7460-1849-5*, Usborne) EDC.
Williams, Brian. The Kingfisher Reference Atlas: An A-Z Guide to Countries of the World. Porter, Malcolm, illus. LC 92-54829. 216p. 1993. 19.95 (*1-85697-838-9*, Kingfisher LKC) LKC.
Wood, Jenny & Munro, David. The Children's Atlas of People & Places. LC 92-28857. (Illus.). 96p. (gr. 2-6). 1993. PLB 18.90 (*1-56294-257-3*); pap. 10.95 (*1-56294-712-5*) Millbrook Pr.
World Atlas: A Resource for Students. (gr. 5-9). 1990. pap. 3.95 (*0-88463-480-9*) Nystrom.
World Book Editors, ed. The World Book Atlas. LC 93-60533. (Illus.). 432p. (gr. 7 up). 1993. PLB 89.00 (*0-7166-2696-9*) World Bk.
Wright, David & Wright, Jill. Facts on File Children's Atlas. updated ed. (Illus.). 96p. (gr. 6-10). 1991. 14.95 (*0-8160-2703-X*) Facts on File.
—The Facts on File Children's Atlas. LC 92-39432. 1993. write for info. (*0-8160-2925-3*) Facts on File.

ATLASES, HISTORICAL

Adams, Simon, et al. Illustrated Atlas of World History. LC 91-16652. (Illus.). 160p. (Orig.). (gr. 5 up). 1992. PLB 16.99 (*0-679-92465-5*); pap. 13.00 (*0-679-82465-0*) Random Bks Yng Read.
Children's Atlas of World History. (Illus.). (gr. 4-8). 1991. 14.95 (*0-528-83444-4*) Rand McNally.
Corbishley, Mike. Ancient Rome. (Illus.). 96p. 1989. 17.95 (*0-8160-1970-3*) Facts on File.
Powell, Anton. Ancient Greece. (Illus.). 96p. 1989. 17.95 (*0-8160-1972-X*) Facts on File.
Reader's Digest Editors. The Reader's Digest Children's Atlas of World History. LC 93-4320. (Illus.). (gr. 4-7). 1993. 20.00 (*0-89577-526-3*, Dist. by Random) RD Assn.

ATMOSPHERE

Here are entered works treating the body of air surrounding the earth as distinguished from the upper rarefied air. Works dealing with air as an element and of its chemical and physical properties are entered under Air.

see also Air; Meteorology

Amdur, Richard. The Fragile Earth. Train, Russell E., intro. by. LC 93-827. 1994. write for info. (*0-7910-1572-6*); pap. write for info. (*0-7910-1597-1*) Chelsea Hse.
Asimov, Isaac. How Did We Find Out about the Atmosphere? LC 84-27125. 64p. (gr. 5-9). 1985. 9.95 (*0-8027-6588-2*); PLB 12.85 (*0-8027-6580-7*) Walker & Co.
Behm, Barbara J., ed. Ask about the Earth & the Sky. (Illus.). 64p. (gr. 4-5). 1987. PLB 11.95 (*0-8172-2876-4*) Raintree Steck-V.
Bilger, Burkhard. Global Warming. (Illus.). 120p. (gr. 5 up). 1992. PLB 19.95 (*0-7910-1575-0*) Chelsea Hse.
Binato, Leonardo. What's Behind the Clouds? 12p. (ps-3). 1993. 4.95 (*1-56566-029-3*) Thomasson-Grant.
Branley, Franklyn M. Air Is All Around You. Keller, Holly, illus. LC 85-45405. 32p. (gr. k-3). 1987. incl. cassette 7.95 (*0-694-00202-X*, Trophy); pap. 4.50 (*0-06-445048-1*, Trophy) HarpC Child Bks.
Fisher, Marshall. The Ozone Layer. (Illus.). 111p. (gr. 5 up). 1992. lib. bdg. 19.95 (*0-7910-1576-9*) Chelsea Hse.
Fitzpatrick, Julie. In the Air. (Illus.). 30p. (gr. 3-5). 1991. 13.95 (*0-237-60207-5*, Pub. by Evans Bros Ltd) Trafalgar.
Gallant, Roy A. Rainbows, Mirages, & Sundogs. LC 86-23728. (Illus.). 112p. (gr. 3-7). 1987. SBE 14.95 (*0-02-737010-0*, Macmillan Child Bk) Macmillan Child Grp.
The Greenhouse Effect. (gr. 7-12). 1992. 24.95 (*0-7134-6500-X*, Pub. by Batsford UK) Trafalgar.
Hocking, Colin, et al. Global Warming & the Greenhouse Effect. Bergman, Lincoln & Fairwell, Kay, eds. Klofkorn, Lisa & Craig, Rose, illus. Hoyt, Richard, photos by. 168p. (gr. 7-10). 1990. pap. 15.00 (*0-912511-75-3*) Lawrence Science.
In the Air. 32p. (ps-3). 1994. 4.95 (*1-56458-732-0*) Dorling Kindersley.
Kallen, Stuart A. If the Sky Could Talk. LC 93-10177. 1993. 14.96 (*1-56239-185-2*) Abdo & Dghtrs.
Maury, Jean-Pierre. The Atmosphere. 80p. (gr. 8 up). 1989. pap. 4.95 (*0-8120-4213-1*) Barron.
Nardo, Don. Ozone. LC 91-6275. (Illus.). 112p. (gr. 5-8). 1991. PLB 14.95 (*1-56006-101-4*) Lucent Bks.
Neal, Philip. The Greenhouse Effect. (Illus.). 64p. (gr. 7-10). 1989. 19.95 (*0-85219-822-1*, Pub. by Batsford UK) Trafalgar.
Pearce, Q. L. Lightning & Other Wonders of the Sky. Steltenpohl, Jane, ed. Fraser, Mary A., illus. 64p. (gr. 4-6). 1989. PLB 12.98 (*0-671-68534-1*, J Messner); pap. 5.95 (*0-671-68648-8*) S&S Trade.
Sky & Earth. 88p. (ps-3). 1990. 15.93 (*0-8094-4837-8*); lib. bdg. 21.27 (*0-8094-4838-6*) Time-Life.
Stefoff, Rebecca. Extinction. (Illus.). 128p. (gr. 5 up). 1992. lib. bdg. 19.95 (*0-7910-1578-5*) Chelsea Hse.
Tivers, Jacqueline & Day, Michael. The Viking Children's World Atlas. LC 84-675391. (Illus.). (ps-7). 1985. pap. 5.99 (*0-14-031874-7*, Puffin) Puffin Bks.
Verdat, Jean-Pierre. The Sky: Stars & Night. Bogard, Vicki, tr. from FRE. Broutin, Christian, illus. LC 90-50776. 38p. (gr. k-5). 1991. 5.95 (*0-944589-32-4*, 324) Young Discovery Lib.
Verdet, Jean-Pierre. Livre du Ciel. (FRE.). 89p. (gr. 4-9). 1990. 13.95 (*2-07-039512-X*) Schoenhof.
Walker, Jane. The Ozone Hole. LC 92-37096. (gr. 4-7). 1993. 12.40 (*0-531-17405-0*, Gloucester Pr) Watts.
Ward, Alan. Sky & Weather. LC 92-369. 1993. 11.40 (*0-531-14176-4*) Watts.
West, David. Why Is the Sky Blue? And Answers to Questions You Always Wanted to Ask. (Illus.). 64p. 1992. 14.95 (*0-8120-6284-1*); pap. 8.95 (*0-8120-4884-9*) Barron.

ATMOSPHERE–POLLUTION

see Air–Pollution

ATMOSPHERE, UPPER

Duden, Jane. The Ozone Layer. LC 90-36297. (Illus.). 48p. (gr. 6). 1990. text ed. 12.95 RSBE (*0-89686-546-0*, Crestwood Hse) Macmillan Child Grp.
Hare, Tony. Ozone Layer. LC 89-81606. 1990. PLB 12.40 (*0-531-17218-X*, Gloucester Pr) Watts.
Neal, Philip. The Ozone Layer: Conservation 2000. (Illus.). 64p. (gr. 7-10). 1994. 24.95 (*0-7134-6713-4*, Pub. by Batsford UK) Trafalgar.
Petty, Kate. The Sky Above Us. (Illus.). 32p. (gr. 2-4). 1993. pap. 5.95 (*0-8120-1234-8*) Barron.

ATOLLS

see Coral Reefs and Islands

ATOMIC BOMB

Beyer, Don E. The Manhattan Project: America Makes the First Atomic Bomb. LC 90-13049. (Illus.). 128p. (gr. 7-12). 1991. PLB 13.90 (*0-531-11008-7*) Watts.
Farris, John. Hiroshima. McGovern, Brian, illus. LC 90-34064. 64p. (gr. 5-8). 1990. PLB 11.95 (*1-56006-015-8*) Lucent Bks.
Larsen, Rebecca. Oppenheimer & the Atomic Bomb. LC 88-16981. (Illus.). 192p. (gr. 6-12). 1988. PLB 14.40 (*0-531-10607-1*) Watts.
Morimoto, Junko. My Hiroshima. (Illus.). 32p. (ps-3). 1992. pap. 5.99 (*0-14-054524-7*, Puffin) Puffin Bks.
O'Neal, Michael. President Truman & the Atomic Bomb: Opposing Viewpoints. LC 90-35611. (Illus.). 112p. (gr. 5-8). 1990. PLB 14.95 (*0-89908-079-0*) Greenhaven.
Rummel, Jack. Robert Oppenheimer: Dark Prince. (Illus.). 144p. (gr. 7-12). 1992. lib. bdg. 16.95x (*0-8160-2598-3*) Facts on File.
Sherrow, Victoria. Hiroshima. LC 93-30428. 1994. text ed. 14.95 (*0-02-782467-5*, New Discovery Bks) Macmillan Child Grp.
Stein, Richard C. The Manhattan Project. LC 93-12686. (Illus.). 32p. (gr. 3-6). 1993. PLB 12.30 (*0-516-06670-6*); pap. 3.95 (*0-516-46670-4*) Childrens.

ATOMIC BOMB–FICTION

Miklowitz, Gloria D. After the Bomb. 156p. (gr. 7 up). 1987. pap. 2.95 (*0-590-43483-7*) Scholastic Inc.

ATOMIC BOMB–PHYSIOLOGICAL EFFECT

Coerr, Eleanor. Sadako. Young, Ed, illus. LC 92-41483. 48p. (gr. 1-4). 1993. TLB 16.95 (*0-399-21771-1*, Putnam) Putnam Pub Group.

ATOMIC NUCLEI

see Nuclear Physics

ATOMIC PILES

see Nuclear Reactors

ATOMIC POWER
see Nuclear Power
ATOMS
see also Nuclear Physics
Asimov, Isaac. How Did We Find Out about Atoms. LC 75-3910. 64p. (gr. 5-8). 1976. PLB 12.85 (*0-8027-6248-4*) Walker & Co.
Averous, Pierre. The Atom. (gr. 6 up). 1988. 4.95 (*0-8120-3837-1*) Barron.
Bains, Rae. Molecules & Atoms. Harriton, Chuck, illus. LC 84-2712. 32p. (gr. 3-6). 1985. PLB 9.49 (*0-8167-0284-5*); pap. text ed. 2.95 (*0-8167-0285-3*) Troll Assocs.
Mebane, Robert C. & Rybolt, Thomas R. Adventures with Atoms & Molecules, Bk. I: Chemistry Experiments for Young People. Perkins, Ronald I., intro. by. LC 85-10177. (Illus.). 82p. (gr. 4-9). 1985. lib. bdg. 16.95 (*0-89490-120-6*) Enslow Pubs.
—Adventures with Atoms & Molecules, Bk. II: Chemistry Experiments for Young People. Perkins, Ronald I., intro. by. LC 85-10177. (Illus.). 96p. (gr. 4-9). 1987. lib. bdg. 16.95 (*0-89490-164-8*) Enslow Pubs.
—Adventures with Atoms & Molecules, Bk. III: Chemistry Experiments for Young People. LC 85-10177. (Illus.). 96p. (gr. 4-9). 1991. lib. bdg. 16.95 (*0-89490-254-7*) Enslow Pubs.
—Adventures with Atoms & Molecules, Bk. IV: Chemistry Experiments for Young People. LC 85-10177. (Illus.). 96p. (gr. 4-9). 1992. lib. bdg. 16.95 (*0-89490-336-5*) Enslow Pubs.
Roxbee-Cox, P. Atoms & Molecules. (Illus.). 32p. (gr. 6-9). 1993. PLB 13.96 (*0-88110-589-9*); pap. 6.95 (*0-7460-0988-7*) EDC.
ATTENDANCE, SCHOOL
see School Attendance
ATTILA, 406?-453
Vardy, Steven B. Attila. (Illus.). 112p. (gr. 5 up). 1991. 17.95 (*1-55546-803-9*) Chelsea Hse.
ATTITUDE (PSYCHOLOGY)
see also Public Opinion
Shelton, Laura S. & Shapiro, Lawrence E. Take a Deep Breath: The Kids' Play-Away Stress Book. Beckett, Bob, illus. 100p. (Orig.). (gr. k-6). 1992. pap. 16.95 (*1-882732-02-2*) Ctr Applied Psy.
Simon, Norma. I Know What I Like. Leder, Dora, illus. LC 76-165822. (ps-2). 1971. PLB 11.95 (*0-8075-3507-9*) A Whitman.
ATTORNEYS
see Lawyers
AUCTIONS–FICTION
McCormick, Maxine. Pretty As You Please. LC 92-39310. 1994. 15.95 (*0-399-22536-6*, Philomel Bks) Putnam Pub Group.
AUDIO-VISUAL EDUCATION
Black, Kaye. Kidvid: Fun-Damentals of Video Instruction. Murray, Joe, illus. 96p. (Orig.). (gr. 4-8). 1989. pap. 15.95 (*0-913705-44-6*) Zephyr Pr AZ.
AUDUBON, JOHN JAMES, 1785-1851
Gleiter, Jan & Thompson, Kathleen. John J. Audubon. (Illus.). 32p. (gr. 2-5). 1987. PLB 19.97 (*0-8172-2675-3*) Raintree Steck-V.
Kastner, Joseph. John James Audubon. (Illus.). 92p. 1992. 19.95 (*0-8109-1918-4*) Abrams.
Kendall, Martha E. John James Audubon: Artist of the Wild. LC 92-11423. (Illus.). 48p. (gr. 2-4). 1993. PLB 12.90 (*1-56294-297-2*); pap. 5.95 (*1-56294-778-8*) Millbrook Pr.
Roop, Peter & Roop, Connie, eds. Capturing Nature: The Writings & Art of John James Audubon. Farley, Rick, illus. LC 92-15662. 48p. (gr. 5 up). 1993. 16.95 (*0-8027-8204-3*); PLB 17.85 (*0-8027-8205-1*) Walker & Co.
AUGUSTUS, EMPEROR OF ROME, 63 B.C.-14 A.D.
Poulton, Michael. Augustus & the Ancient Romans. Molan, Christine, illus. LC 92-5824. 63p. (gr. 6-7). 1992. PLB 24.26 (*0-8114-3350-1*) Raintree Steck-V.
AUSTIN, STEPHEN FULLER, 1793-1836
Wade, Mary D. Austin: The Son Becomes Father. Finney, Pat, illus. 64p. (gr. 3-5). 1993. 10.95 (*1-882539-08-7*); pap. 4.95 (*1-882539-09-5*); tchr's. guide 5.00 (*1-882539-10-9*) Colophon Hse.
AUSTRALIA
Arnold, Caroline. Australia Today. LC 87-10660. (Illus.). 96p. (gr. 4-9). 1987. PLB 10.90 (*0-531-10377-3*) Watts.
Australian External Territories. (Illus.). (gr. 5 up). 1989. 13.95 (*0-7910-0133-4*) Chelsea Hse.
Browne, Rollo. A Family in Australia. (Illus.). 32p. (gr. 2-5). 1987. PLB 13.50 (*0-8225-1671-3*) Lerner Pubns.
Cobb, Vicki. This Place Is Lonely: The Australian Outback. Lavallee, Barbara, illus. 32p. (Orig.). (gr. 2-5). 1994. 13.95 (*0-8027-6959-4*); lib. bdg. 14.85 (*0-8027-6960-8*); pap. 6.95 (*0-8027-7415-6*) Walker & Co.
Conforth, Kellie. A Picture Book of Australian Animals. Conforth, Kellie, illus. LC 91-18706. 24p. (gr. 1-4). 1992. PLB 9.59 (*0-8167-2470-9*); pap. 2.50 (*0-8167-2471-7*) Troll Assocs.
Cooper, Rod. Journey Through Australia. Camm, Martin, illus. LC 91-46173. 32p. (gr. 3-5). 1993. PLB 11.89 (*0-8167-2757-0*); pap. text ed. 3.95 (*0-8167-2758-9*) Troll Assocs.
Cranshaw, Peter. Australia. LC 88-18426. (Illus.). 48p. (gr. 4-8). 1988. PLB 14.95 (*0-382-09511-1*) Silver Burdett Pr.
Crump, Donald J., ed. Surprising Lands Down Under. (Illus.). 1989. 12.95 (*0-87044-714-9*); lib. bdg. 12.95 (*0-87044-719-X*) Natl Geog.
Dolce, Laura. Australia. (Illus.). 128p. (gr. 5 up). 1990. 14.95 (*0-7910-1105-4*) Chelsea Hse.
Georges, D. V. Australia. LC 86-9587. (Illus.). 48p. (gr. k-4). 1986. PLB 12.85 (*0-516-01290-8*); pap. 4.95 (*0-516-41290-6*) Childrens.
Gouck, Maura M. The Great Barrier Reef. LC 93-85. (SPA & ENG.). (gr. 2-6). 1993. 15.95 (*1-56766-008-8*) Childs World.
Kelly, Andrew. Australia. LC 90-38123. (Illus.). 32p. (gr. k-3). 1991. PLB 12.40 (*0-531-18381-5*, Pub. by Bookwright Pr) Watts.
Lepthien, Emilie U. Australia. LC 82-4541. (Illus.). (gr. 5-9). 1982. PLB 20.55 (*0-516-02751-4*) Childrens.
Mattern, Joanne. Australian Animals. LC 92-41033. (Illus.). 24p. (gr. k-2). 1993. 1.95 (*0-8167-3096-2*) Troll Assocs.
Morgan, Wendy. Ned Kelly Reconstructed. LC 93-48705. 1994. pap. write for info. (*0-521-43783-0*) Cambridge U Pr.
Nabhan, Martin. Australia. (Illus.). 64p. (gr. 7 up). 1990. lib. bdg. 17.27 (*0-86593-088-0*); PLB 12.95s.p. (*0-685-36362-7*) Rourke Corp.
Parker, Lewis K. Australia. LC 94-4249. 1994. write for info. (*1-55916-007-1*) Rourke Bk Co.
Powzyk, Joyce. Wallaby Creek. LC 84-29757. (Illus.). 32p. (gr. 1-4). 1985. PLB 12.88 (*0-688-05693-8*) Lothrop.
Rajendra, Vijeya. Australia. LC 91-15864. (Illus.). 128p. (gr. 5-9). 1991. PLB 21.95 (*1-85435-400-0*) Marshall Cavendish.
Santrey, Laurence. Australia. Eitzen, Allan, illus. LC 84-2636. 32p. (gr. 3-6). 1985. PLB 9.49 (*0-8167-0124-5*); pap. text ed. 2.95 (*0-8167-0125-3*) Troll Assocs.
Stanley-Baker, Penny. Australia: On the Other Side of the World. Valat, Pierre-Marie, illus. LC 87-34523. 38p. (gr. k-5). 1988. 5.95 (*0-944589-15-4*, 154) Young Discovery Lib.
Stark, Al. Australia: A Lucky Land. LC 87-13424. (Illus.). 152p. (gr. 5 up). 1988. text ed. 14.95 RSBE (*0-87518-365-4*, Dillon) Macmillan Child Grp.
Wilson, Barbara K. Acacia Terrace. 1990. 13.95 (*0-590-42885-3*) Scholastic Inc.
AUSTRALIA–FICTION
Adams, Jeanie. Going for Oysters. (ps-3). 1993. 14.95 (*0-8075-2978-8*) A Whitman.
Anderson, Honey & Reinholdt, Bill. Don't Cut down This Tree. Ruth, Trevor, illus. LC 92-21446. 1993. 3.75 (*0-383-03621-6*) SRA Schl Grp.
Baker, Jeannie. Window. LC 90-3922. (Illus.). 32p. (ps up). 1991. 14.00 (*0-688-08917-8*); PLB 13.93 (*0-688-08918-6*) Greenwillow.
Bound for Australia, No. 20. 144p. (Orig.). (gr. 7-12). 1987. pap. 2.50 (*0-553-26793-0*) Bantam.
Clarke, J. Al Capsella & the Watchdogs. LC 90-26090. 160p. (gr. 6 up). 1991. 14.95 (*0-8050-1598-1*, Bks Young Read) H Holt & Co.
—Al Capsella Takes a Vacation. 160p. (gr. 7 up). 1993. 14.95 (*0-8050-2685-1*, Bks Young Read) H Holt & Co.
—The Heroic Life of Al Capsella. LC 89-24629. 160p. (gr. 6 up). 1990. 14.95 (*0-8050-1310-5*, Bks Young Read) H Holt & Co.
Crew, Gary. No Such Country. LC 93-17619. 1994. pap. 15.00 (*0-671-79760-3*, S&S BFYR) S&S Trade.
—Strange Objects. LC 92-30519. 224p. (gr. 5-9). 1993. pap. 14.00 JR3 (*0-671-79759-X*, S&S BFYR) S&S Trade.
Culton, Wilma. Down at the Billabong. Crossett, Warren, illus. LC 92-31951. 1993. 3.75 (*0-383-03565-1*) SRA Schl Grp.
Disher, Garry. The Bamboo Flute. LC 92-39787. 96p. (gr. 3-6). 1993. 10.95 (*0-395-66595-7*) Ticknor & Flds Bks Yng Read.
Dumbleton, Mike. Dial-a-Croc. James, Ann, illus. LC 90-25385. 32p. (ps-2). 1991. 14.95 (*0-531-05945-6*); RLB 14.99 (*0-531-08545-7*) Orchard Bks Watts.
Gleitzman, Morris. Misery Guts. LC 92-22570. 1993. 12.95 (*0-15-254768-1*) HarBrace.
—Worry Warts. LC 92-22631. 1993. 12.95 (*0-15-299666-4*) HarBrace.
Kelleher, Victor. Del-Del. (gr. 7-10). 1992. 17.95 (*0-8027-8154-3*) Walker & Co.

Loder, Ann. The Wet Hat: And Other Stories from Beyond the Black Stump. Peters, Terry, illus. 102p. (Orig.). (gr. 4 up). 1993. pap. write for info. (*0-9636643-0-1*) A L Loder.
THE WET HAT, & OTHER STORIES FROM BEYOND THE BLACK STUMP is a collection of Australian short stories taken from the author's childhood & family album growing up on an Australian sheep ranch. The stories concern family pets; a gutsy pony, two heroic dogs; a kookaburra, (a native Australian bird), a chicken, & a tale about a tiny silkworm. There is a mystery story about a lost ring. Lastly, there is a humorous one. Each story is based on fact & is suitable for children from fourth to eighth grade, up. A dog is featured on the full color cover & there is a black & white illustration with each story. Order from: American Business Communications, 251 Michelle Ct., South San Francisco, CA 94080. FAX: (415) 952-3716 (att: Noel Loder). 415-952-8700.
Publisher Provided Annotation.

Marsden, John. Letters from the Inside. LC 93-41185. 1994. 13.95 (*0-395-68985-6*) HM.
Paterson, A. B. Man from Snowy River. (ps-3). 1992. pap. 7.95 (*0-207-15708-1*, Pub. by Angus & Robertson AT) HarpC.
Phipson, Joan. Hit & Run. 132p. (gr. 7 up). 1989. pap. 3.95 (*0-02-044665-9*, Collier Young Ad) Macmillan Child Grp.
Sheehan, Patty. Kylie's Concert. Maeno, Itoko, illus. 32p. 1993. 16.95 (*1-55942-046-4*, 7655); incl. video & tchr's. guide 79.95 (*1-55942-049-9*, 9374) Marshfilm.
Walker, Kate. Peter. LC 92-18948. 176p. (gr. 7 up). 1993. 13.95 (*0-395-64722-3*) HM.
Weir, Bob & Weir, Wendy. Baru Bay. LC 93-23325. (Illus.). 1995. incl. cassette 19.95 (*1-56282-622-0*); PLB 14.95 (*1-56282-623-9*) Hyprn Child.
Wrightson, Patricia. Balyet. LC 88-8298. 144p. (gr. 7 up). 1989. SBE 13.95 (*0-689-50468-3*, M K McElderry) Macmillan Child Grp.
AUSTRALIA–HISTORY
Wright, Judith. The Day the Mountain Played. Wright, Annette, illus. 1990. pap. 30.00x (*0-86439-080-7*, Pub. by Boolarong Pubns AT) St Mut.
AUSTRALIA–NATIVE RACES
Browne, Rollo. An Aboriginal Family. LC 84-19447. (Illus.). 32p. (gr. 2-5). 1985. PLB 13.50 (*0-8225-1655-1*) Lerner Pubns.
Nile, Richard. Australian Aborigines. LC 92-17044. (Illus.). 48p. (gr. 5-6). 1992. PLB 22.80 (*0-8114-2303-4*) Raintree Steck-V.
Rathe, Gustave. The Wreck of the Barque Stefano off the North West Cape of Australia in 1875. (Illus.). 160p. 1992. 17.00 (*0-374-38585-8*) FS&G.
Reynolds, J. Down under: Vanishing Cultures. 1992. 16.95 (*0-15-224182-5*, HB Juv Bks); pap. 8.95 (*0-15-224183-3*, HB Juv Bks) HarBrace.
Ward, Glenyse. Wandering Girl. LC 90-48825. 160p. (gr. 6 up). 1991. 14.95 (*0-8050-1634-1*, Bks Young Read) H Holt & Co.
AUSTRIA
Austria in Pictures. 64p. (gr. 5 up). 1991. PLB 17.50 (*0-8225-1888-0*) Lerner Pubns.
Boluch, Kathleen A. Julia's World, Pt. 1: Better Times. Christiansen, Lee & Selwyn, Paul, illus. 58p. 1990. 14.95 (*0-9626365-0-9*) Swarovski Amer Ltd.
Greene, Carol. Austria. LC 85-27994. (Illus.). 126p. (gr. 5-6). 1986. PLB 20.55 (*0-516-02756-5*) Childrens.
AUSTRIA–FICTION
The Sound of Music. 24p. (gr. 3 up). 1992. incl. cass., songbk., crayons 6.95, (*0-7935-1645-5*, 00850125) H Leonard.
The Sound of Music. 24p. (gr. 3 up). 1992. incl. songbk., recorder 9.95 (*0-7935-1422-3*, 00710355) H Leonard.
AUTHORS
see also Black Authors
also classes of writers (e.g. Novelists; Poets; etc.); and names of individual authors
Andronik, Catherine M. Kindred Spirit: A Biography of L. M. Montgomery, Creator of Anne of Green Gables. LC 92-25869. (Illus.). 176p. (gr. 5-9). 1993. SBE 15.00 (*0-689-31671-2*, Atheneum Child Bk) Macmillan Child Grp.
Berg, Julie. Maurice Sendak. LC 93-15738. 1993. 13.99 (*1-56239-225-5*) Abdo & Dghtrs.
Bruce, Harry. Maud: The Life of L. M. Montgomery. 1992. 17.00 (*0-553-08770-3*) Bantam.
Caisley, Raewyn. Raewyn's Got the Writing Bug Again. LC 93-24529. 1994. 4.25 (*0-383-03734-4*) SRA Schl Grp.
Campbell, Patricia J. Presenting Robert Cormier. 1990. pap. 4.95 (*0-440-20544-1*, LFL) Dell.
Collins, David R. To the Point: A Story about E. B. White. Johnson, Amy, illus. 56p. (gr. 3-6). 1989. 14.95 (*0-87614-345-1*); pap. 5.95 (*0-87614-508-X*) Carolrhoda Bks.

Commire, Anne, ed. Something about the Author: Facts & Pictures about Contemporary Authors & Illustrators of Books for Young People. Incl. Vol. 1. 1971. 85.00 (*0-8103-0050-8*); Vol. 2. 1972. 85.00 (*0-8103-0052-4*); Vol. 3. 1972. 85.00 (*0-8103-0054-0*); Vol. 4. 1973. 85.00 (*0-8103-0056-7*); Vol. 5. 1974. 85.00 (*0-8103-0058-3*); Vol. 6. 1974. 85.00 (*0-8103-0060-5*); Vol. 7. 1975. 85.00 (*0-8103-0062-1*); Vol. 8. 1976. 85.00 (*0-8103-0064-8*); Vol. 9. 1976. 85.00 (*0-8103-0066-4*); Vol. 10. 1976. 85.00 (*0-8103-0068-0*); Vol. 11. 1977. 85.00 (*0-8103-0070-2*); Vol. 12. 1977. 85.00 (*0-8103-0072-9*); Vol. 13. 1978. 85.00 (*0-8103-0094-X*); Vol. 14. 1978. 85.00 (*0-8103-0095-8*); Vol. 15. 1979. 85.00 (*0-8103-0096-6*); Vol. 16. 1979. 85.00 (*0-8103-0097-4*); Vol. 17. 1979. 85.00 (*0-8103-0098-2*); Vol. 18. 1980. 85.00 (*0-8103-0099-0*); Vol. 19. 1980. 85.00 (*0-8103-0051-6*); Vol. 20. 1980. 85.00 (*0-8103-0053-2*); Vol. 21. 1981. 85.00 (*0-8103-0093-1*); Vol. 22. 1981. 85.00 (*0-8103-0085-0*); Vol. 23. 1981. 85.00 (*0-8103-0086-9*); Vol. 24. 1981. 85.00 (*0-8103-0087-7*); Vol. 25. 1981. 85.00 (*0-8103-0084-2*); Vol. 26. 1982. 85.00 (*0-8103-0089-3*); Vol. 27. 1982. 85.00 (*0-8103-0083-4*); Vol. 28. 296p. 1982. 85.00 (*0-8103-0082-6*); Vol. 29. 328p. 1982. 85.00 (*0-8103-0081-8*). LC 72-27107. (gr. 7-12). Gale.

—Something about the Author: Facts & Pictures about Contemporary Authors & Illustrators of Books for Young People, Vol. 30. (Illus.). 304p. (gr. 9-12). 1983. 85.00 (*0-8103-0055-9*) Gale.

—Something about the Author: Facts & Pictures about Contemporary Authors & Illustrators of Books for Young People, Vol. 34. (Illus.). 224p. (gr. 9-12). 1984. 85.00 (*0-8103-0063-X*) Gale.

—Something about the Author: Facts & Pictures about Contemporary Authors & Illutrators of Books for Young People, Vol. 44. 300p. (gr. 9-12). 1986. 85.00 (*0-8103-2254-4*) Gale.

—Yesterday's Authors of Books for Children: Facts & Pictures about Authors & Illustrators of Books for Young People, 2 vols. (Illus.). (gr. 7-12). 1977. Vol. 1, 1977. 93.00 (*0-8103-0073-7*); Vol. 2, 1978. 93.00 (*0-8103-0090-7*) Gale.

Downing, Sybil & Barker, Jane. Crown of Life: The Story of Mary Roberts Rinehart. (Illus.). 192p. 1992. 19.50 (*1-879373-13-0*); pap. 9.95 (*1-879373-18-1*) R Rinehart.

Fleissner, Else M. Herman N. Hesse: Modern German Poet & Writer. Rahmas, D. Steve, ed. LC 70-190244. 32p. (Orig.). (gr. 7-12). 1972. lib. bdg. 4.95 incl. catalog cards (*0-87157-526-4*) SamHar Pr.

Gallo, Donald R., intro. by. Speaking for Ourselves, Too: More Autobiographical Sketches by Notable Authors of Books for Young Adults. 256p. (Orig.). (gr. 7-12). 1992. pap. 14.50 (*0-8141-4623-6*) NCTE.

Hurwitz, Johanna. Astrid Lindgren: Storyteller to the World. Dooling, Michael, illus. 64p. (gr. 2-6). 1989. pap. 10.95 (*0-670-82207-8*) Viking Child Bks.

Konigsburg, E. L., et al. In My Own Words Series, 4 vols. (Illus.). 512p. (gr. 5-7). 1990. s.p. 33.71 (*0-685-58837-8*, J Messner); (J Messner); (J Messner) S&S Trade.

Kresh, Paul. Isaac Bashevis Singer: The Story of a Storyteller. Scofield, Penrod, illus. LC 84-10271. 192p. (gr. 5 up). 1984. 13.95 (*0-525-67156-0*, Lodestar Bks) Dutton Child Bks.

Krull, Kathleen. Lives of the Writers: Comedies, Tragedies (& What the Neighbors Thought) Hewitt, Kathryn, illus. LC 93-32436. (gr. 3-7). 1994. 18.95 (*0-15-248009-9*, HB Juv Bks) HarBrace.

Lyon, Sue, ed. Great Writers of the English Language, 14 vols. LC 88-21077. (Illus.). 1450p. 1991. PLB 449.95 (*1-85435-000-5*) Marshall Cavendish.

Nunokawa, Jeff. Oscar Wilde. Duberman, Martin B., intro. by. LC 93-42397. 1994. write for info. (*0-7910-2311-7*) Chelsea Hse.

Otfinoski, Stephen. Nineteenth Century Writers. (Illus.). 128p. (gr. 7-12). 1991. 16.95x (*0-8160-2486-3*) Facts on File.

Peck, Richard. Anonymously Yours. 1991. 12.95 (*0-671-74162-4*, J Messner) S&S Trade.

Peet, Bill. Bill Peet: An Autobiography. Peet, Bill, illus. (gr. 3 up). 1989. 17.95 (*0-395-50932-7*) HM.

Perl, Lila. Isaac Bashevis Singer: The Life of a Storyteller. Ruff, Donna, illus. LC 93-45275. 1994. write for info. (*0-8276-0512-9*) JPS Phila.

Phillimore, J. Mansfield. (Illus.). 112p. (gr. 7 up). 1990. lib. bdg. 19.94 (*0-86593-020-1*); lib. bdg. 14.95s.p. (*0-685-46451-2*) Rourke Corp.

Quackenbush, Robert. Once upon a Time! A Story of the Brothers Grimm. LC 85-9410. (Illus.). 40p. (gr. 2-6). 1986. pap. 11.95 jacketed (*0-671-66296-1*, Little Simon) S&S Trade.

Rylant, Cynthia. Best Wishes. Ontal, Carlo, illus. 32p. (gr. 2-5). 1992. 12.95 (*1-878450-20-4*) R Owen Pubs.

Steinbauer, Janine. Katherine Mansfield. LC 93-10634. (gr. 6 up). 1994. 18.95 (*0-88682-623-3*) Creative Ed.

Yolen, Jane. A Letter from Phoenix Farm. Stemple, Jason, illus. 32p. (gr. 2-5). 1992. 12.95 (*1-878450-36-0*) R Owen Pubs.

AUTHORS, AMERICAN

Anderson, William. Laura Ingalls Wilder: A Biography. LC 91-33805. (Illus.). 240p. (gr. 3-7). 1992. 16.00 (*0-06-020113-4*); PLB 15.89 (*0-06-020114-2*) HarpC Child Bks.

Ashabranner, Brent. The Times of My Life: A Memoir. LC 90-40920. (gr. 4-7). 1990. 14.95 (*0-525-65047-4*, Cobblehill Bks) Dutton Child Bks.

Balee, Susan. Flannery O'Connor. LC 94-9377. 1994. write for info. (*0-7910-2418-0*); pap. write for info. (*0-7910-2419-9*) Chelsea Hse.

Becker, R. Margot. Ann M. Martin: The Story of the Author of the Baby-Sitters Club. (gr. 4-7). 1993. pap. 3.50 (*0-590-45877-9*) Scholastic Inc.

Berg, Julie. The Berenstains. LC 93-12959. 1993. 13.99 (*1-56239-224-7*) Abdo & Dghtrs.

—Beverly Cleary. Berg, Julie, illus. LC 93-12958. (gr. 6 up). 1993. 13.99 (*1-56239-222-0*) Abdo & Dghtrs.

—Tomie de Paola. Berg, Julie, illus. LC 93-12960. 1993. 13.95 (*1-56239-223-9*) Abdo & Dghtrs.

Brown, Margaret W. The Day Before Now. Blos, Joan W., ed. Allen, Thomas B., illus. LC 93-12814. (ps-2). 1994. pap. 15.00 (*0-671-79628-3*, S&S BFYR) S&S Trade.

Byars, Betsy C. The Moon & I. (Illus.). 112p. (gr. 7 up). 1992. 12.95 (*0-671-74166-7*, J Messner); lib. bdg. 14.98 (*0-671-74165-9*, J Messner) S&S Trade.

Carle, Eric. The Art of Eric Carle. Carle, Eric, illus. LC 91-646. 124p. (gr. k up). 1993. pap. 29.95 (*0-88708-176-2*) Picture Bk Studio.

Carpenter, Angelica S. L. Frank Baum: Royal Historian of Oz. (gr. 4-7). 1993. pap. 7.95 (*0-8225-9617-2*) Lerner Pubns.

Carpenter, Angelica S. & Shirley, Jean. L. Frank Baum: Royal Historian of Oz. (gr. 5 up). 1991. PLB 21.50 (*0-8225-4910-7*) Lerner Pubns.

Colwell, Lynn H. Erma Bombeck: Writer & Humorist. LC 91-40924. (Illus.). 112p. (gr. 6 up). 1992. lib. bdg. 17.95 (*0-89490-384-5*) Enslow Pubs.

Crews, Donald. Bigmama's. Crews, Donald, illus. LC 90-33142. 32p. (ps up). 1991. 15.00 (*0-688-09950-5*); PLB 14.93 (*0-688-09951-3*) Greenwillow.

Daly, John. Presenting S. E. Hinton. 1989. pap. 3.95 (*0-440-20482-8*, LFL) Dell.

Engel, Dean & Freedman, Florence B. Ezra Jack Keats: A Biography for Young Readers. (Illus.). 128p. (gr. 4-8). 1994. 14.95 (*1-881889-65-3*) Silver Moon.

Faber, Doris & Faber, Harold. Great Lives: American Literature. LC 94-10866. 1995. 22.95 (*0-684-19448-1*, Scribner) Macmillan.

Fox, Mary V. Bette Bao Lord: Novelist & Chinese Voice for Change. LC 92-36805. (Illus.). 152p. (gr. 4 up). 1993. PLB 14.40 (*0-516-03291-7*); pap. 5.95 (*0-516-43291-5*) Childrens.

Gallo, Donald R. Presenting Richard Peck. LC 89-32346. 176p. (gr. 8 up). 1989. text ed. 19.95x (*0-8057-8209-5*, Twayne) Macmillan.

Gentry, Tony. Alice Walker. King, Coretta Scott. (Illus.). 112p. (gr. 5 up). 1993. PLB 17.95 (*0-7910-1884-9*) Chelsea Hse.

Gherman, Beverly. E. B. White: Some Writer! LC 91-19012. (Illus.). 144p. (gr. 3-7). 1992. SBE 13.95 (*0-689-31672-0*, Atheneum Child Bk) Macmillan Child Grp.

Goble, Paul. Hau Kola - Hello Friend. Perrin, Gerry, photos by. LC 93-48167. (Illus.). 1994. 12.95 (*1-878450-44-1*) R Owen Pubs.

Gonzales, Doreen. Alex Haley: Author of "Roots" LC 93-44172. (Illus.). 128p. (gr. 6 up). 1994. lib. bdg. 17.95 (*0-89490-573-2*) Enslow Pubs.

—Madeleine L'Engle: Author of "A Wrinkle in Time" LC 91-3883. (Illus.). 112p. (gr. 4-6). 1991. text ed. 13.95 RSBE (*0-87518-485-5*, Dillon) Macmillan Child Grp.

Greene, Carol. Margaret Wise Brown: Author of Goodnight Moon. LC 92-34471. (Illus.). 48p. (gr. k-3). 1993. 12.85 (*0-516-04254-8*); pap. 4.95 (*0-516-44254-6*) Childrens.

Howe, James. Playing with Words. Craine, Michael, photos by. LC 93-48166. 1994. 12.95 (*1-878450-40-9*) R Owen Pubs.

Johnston, Norma. Louisa May: The World & Works of Louisa May Alcott. Cohn, Amy, ed. 256p. 1995. pap. 4.95 (*0-688-12696-0*, Beech Tree Bks) Morrow.

Kenan, Randall. James Baldwin. (Illus.). 1994. 19.95 (*0-7910-2301-X*, Am Art Analog) Chelsea Hse.

King, Sarah E. Maya Angelou: Greeting the Morning. (gr. 4-7). 1994. pap. 6.95 (*1-56294-725-7*) Millbrook Pr.

Knudson, R. R. The Wonderful Pen of May Swenson. LC 93-637. (Illus.). 112p. (gr. 3-7). 1993. SBE 13.95 (*0-02-750915-X*, Macmillan Child Bk) Macmillan Child Grp.

Lasky, Kathryn & Knight, Meribah. Searching for Laura Ingalls: A Reader's Journal. Knight, Christopher, illus. LC 92-26188. 48p. (gr. 2-6). 1993. RSBE 15.95 (*0-02-751666-0*, Macmillan Child Bk) Macmillan Child Grp.

Lewin, Ted. I Was a Teenage Professional Wrestler. Lewin, Ted, illus. LC 92-31523. 128p. (gr. 6-12). 1993. 16.95 (*0-531-05477-2*); RLB 16.99 (*0-531-08627-5*) Orchard Bks Watts.

—I Was a Teenage Professional Wrestler. (Illus.). 128p. (gr. 5-9). 1994. pap. 6.95 (*0-7868-1009-2*) Hyprn Ppbks.

Lyons, Mary. Keeping Secrets. 1995. write for info. (*0-8050-3065-4*) H Holt & Co.

Lyons, Mary E. Sorrow's Kitchen: The Life & Folklore of Zora Neale Hurston. LC 92-30600. (Illus.). 160p. (gr. 7 up). 1993. pap. 5.95 (*0-02-044445-1*, Collier Young Ad) Macmillan Child Grp.

McKissack, Patricia & McKissack, Fredrick. Lorraine Hansberry: Dramatist & Activist. Davis, Thulani, intro. by. LC 93-31086. 1994. 15.95 (*0-385-31164-8*) Delacorte.

Manfred, Frederick. Duke's Mixture. 260p. (gr. 8). 1994. pap. 15.95 (*0-931170-55-9*) Ctr Western Studies.

Mazer, Anne, intro. by. Going Where I'm Coming From: Personal Narrative of American Youth. (gr. 6 up). 1994. 15.95 (*0-89255-205-0*); pap. 6.95 (*0-89255-206-9*) Persea Bks.

Meigs, Cornelia. Invincible Louisa. LC 68-21174. (Illus.). (gr. 7 up). 1968. 17.95 (*0-316-56590-3*) Little.

Meltzer, Milton. Starting from Home: A Writer's Beginnings. (Illus.). 160p. (gr. 7 up). 1991. pap. 3.95 (*0-14-032299-X*, Puffin) Puffin Bks.

Mitchell, Mark. The Mustang Professor: The Story of J. Frank Dobie. Mitchell, Mark, illus. 96p. (gr. 4-7). 1993. 12.95 (*0-89015-823-1*) Sunbelt Media.

Nazel, Joseph. Langston Hughes. (Illus.). 192p. (Orig.). 1994. pap. 3.95 (*0-87067-591-5*, Melrose Sq) Holloway.

Otfinoski, Steven. Great Black Writers. LC 93-39871. (Illus.). 128p. (gr. 4-11). 1994. 16.95x (*0-8160-2906-7*) Facts on File.

Rylant, Cynthia. But I'll Be Back Again. LC 93-16188. (Illus.). 80p. (gr. 7 up). 1993. pap. 4.95 (*0-688-12653-7*, Pub. by Beech Tree Bks) Morrow.

Saidman, Anne. Stephen King: Master of Horror. (Illus.). 64p. (gr. 4-12). 1992. PLB 13.50 (*0-8225-0545-2*) Lerner Pubns.

Schoen, Celin V. Pearl Buck: Famed American Author of Oriental Stories. Rahmas, D. Steve, ed. LC 70-190247. 32p. (Orig.). (gr. 7-12). 1972. lib. bdg. 4.95 incl. catalog cards (*0-87157-530-2*) SamHar Pr.

Shirley, David. Alex Haley, Author. LC 93-16762. (Illus.). (gr. 5 up). 1994. PLB 18.95 (*0-7910-1979-9*, Am Art Analog); pap. write for info. (*0-7910-1980-2*, Am Art Analog) Chelsea Hse.

Sonder, Ben. The Tenement Writer: An Immigrant's Story. Rosner, Meryl, illus. LC 92-14400. 72p. (gr. 2-5). 1992. PLB 21.34 (*0-8114-7235-3*) Raintree Steck-V.

Spain, Valerie. Meet Maya Angelou. LC 94-1294. 96p. (Orig.). (gr. 2-6). 1995. pap. 3.50 (*0-679-86542-X*, Bullseye Bks) Random Bks Yng Read.

Stefoff, Rebecca. Herman Melville. LC 93-11751. 1994. PLB 15.00 (*0-671-86771-7*, J Messner); pap. write for info. (*0-671-86772-5*, J Messner) S&S Trade.

Stevens, Janet. Let's Make a Story: An Illustrator's Approach. LC 94-18976. Date not set. write for info. (*0-8234-1154-0*) Holiday.

Stevenson, James. Fun - No Fun. LC 93-18187. (Illus.). 32p. (gr. k up). 1994. 14.00 (*0-688-11673-6*); PLB 13.93 (*0-688-11674-4*) Greenwillow.

—July. Stevenson, James, illus. LC 88-37584. (gr. k up). 1990. 12.95 (*0-688-08822-8*); PLB 12.88 (*0-688-08823-6*) Greenwillow.

Stuart, Jesse. The Year of My Rebirth. 2nd ed. Gifford, James M. & Cunningham, Donald H., eds. Foster, Ruel E., intro. by. LC 90-62357. 392p. (gr. 7 up). 1991. 24.00 (*0-945084-17-X*) J Stuart Found.

Tomb, Eric. New England Authors. Conkle, Nancy, illus. 64p. (gr. 8). 1991. pap. text ed. 3.95 (*0-88388-149-7*) Bellerophon Bks.

Tomb, Eric & Knill, Henry. California Authors. Conkle, Nancy, illus. 68p. (gr. 1-9). pap. 3.95 (*0-88388-178-0*) Bellerophon Bks.

Tudor, Josh. Drawn from New England: A Portrait in Words & Pictures. LC 79-14230. (Illus.). 1979. 19.95 (*0-399-20835-6*, Philomel) Putnam Pub Group.

Uchida, Yoshiko. Invisible Thread. 1991. 12.95 (*0-671-74164-0*, J Messner) S&S Trade.

Verde, Thomas. Fiction Writers, 1900-1950. (Illus.). 128p. (gr. 7 up). 1993. PLB 16.95x (*0-8160-2573-8*) Facts on File.

Weidt, Maryann N. Oh, the Places He Went: A Story about Dr. Seuss - Theodore Seuss Geisel. Maguire, Kerry, illus. LC 93-41370. 1994. write for info. (*0-87614-823-2*); pap. write for info. (*0-87614-627-2*) Carolrhoda Bks.

Wheeler, Jill. Dr. Seuss. Wallner, Rosemary, ed. LC 92-16569. (gr. 4). 1992. PLB 13.99 (*1-56239-112-7*) Abdo & Dghtrs.

—Laura Ingalls Wilder. Wallner, Rosemary, ed. LC 92-16568. (gr. 4). 1992. PLB 13.99 (*1-56239-115-1*) Abdo & Dghtrs.

Yep, Laurence. Lost Garden. 1991. 12.95 (*0-671-74160-8*, J Messner); lib. bdg. 14.98 (*0-671-74159-4*) S&S Trade.

Zindel, Paul. The Pigman & Me. LC 91-35790. (Illus.). 178p. (gr. 7 up). 1992. 14.00 (*0-06-020857-0*); PLB 13.89 (*0-06-020858-9*) HarpC Child Bks.

AUTHORS, DANISH

Cote, Elizabeth. Hans Christian Andersen, Vida de Cuento de Hadas. Lazzarino, Luciano & Palacios, Argentina, illus. LC 92-9534. (SPA.). 1992. PLB 14.60 (*0-86593-186-0*); 10.95s.p. (*0-685-59299-5*) Rourke Corp.

AUTHORS, ENGLISH

Asbee, Sue. Woolf. (Illus.). 112p. (gr. 7 up). 1990. lib. bdg. 19.94 (*0-86593-019-8*); lib. bdg. 14.95s.p. (*0-685-46453-9*) Rourke Corp.

Brighton, Catherine. The Brontes: A Scene from the Childhood of Charlotte, Branwell, Emily, & Anne. LC 93-26097. 1994. 12.95 (*0-8118-0608-1*) Chronicle Bks.

Ferrell, Keith. George Orwell: The Political Pen. LC 84-25932. 192p. (gr. 7 up). 1984. 11.95 (*0-87131-444-4*) M Evans.

Greene, Carol. Rudyard Kipling: Author of the Jungle Books. LC 94-11940. (Illus.). 32p. (gr. 2-4). 1994. PLB 17.20 (*0-516-04266-1*); pap. 4.95 (*0-516-44266-X*) Childrens.

Guzzetti, Paula. A Family Called Bronte. LC 93-8101. (Illus.). 128p. (gr. 4 up). 1994. text ed. 13.95 RSBE (*0-87518-592-4*, Dillon) Macmillan Child Grp.

Wheeler, Jill. A. A. Milne: Creator of Winnie the Pooh. Wallner, Rosemary, ed. LC 92-16570. (gr. 4). 1992. PLB 13.99 (*1-56239-114-3*) Abdo & Dghtrs.

AUTHORS–FICTION

Christian, Mary B. Sebastian (Super Sleuth) & the Copycat Crime. McCue, Lisa, illus. LC 93-7038. 64p. (gr. 2-6). 1993. SBE 11.95 (*0-02-718211-8*, Macmillan Child Bk) Macmillan Child Grp.

Clarke, J. Riffraff. LC 92-9928. 96p. (gr. 9-12). 1992. 14.95 (*0-8050-1774-7*, Bks Young Read) H Holt & Co.

Kraus, Robert. The Adventures of Wise Old Owl. Kraus, Robert, illus. LC 92-20436. 32p. (ps-3). 1992. PLB 10.89 (*0-8167-2943-3*); pap. text ed. 2.95 (*0-8167-2944-1*) Troll Assocs.

Nixon, Joan L. If You Were a Writer. Degen, Bruce, illus. LC 88-402. 32p. (gr. k-3). 1988. RSBE 14.95 (*0-02-768210-2*, Four Winds) Macmillan Child Grp.

—The Name of the Game Was Murder. LC 92-8392. 1993. 15.00 (*0-385-30864-7*) Delacorte.

Pinkwater, Daniel. Author's Day. Pinkwater, Daniel, illus. LC 92-18154. 32p. (gr. k-3). 1993. RSBE 13.95 (*0-02-774642-9*, Macmillan Child Bk) Macmillan Child Grp.

Stafford, Jean. The Scarlet Letter. LC 92-44056. 1994. 13.95 (*0-88682-588-1*) Creative Ed.

Van Raven, Pieter. The Great Man's Secret. LC 88-29204. 176p. (gr. 7 up). 1989. SBE 13.95 (*0-684-19041-9*, Scribners Young Read) Macmillan Child Grp.

Williams, Barbara. Author & Squinty Gritt. LC 90-37021. 80p. (gr. 2-5). 1990. 12.95 (*0-525-44655-9*, DCB) Dutton Child Bks.

AUTHORS, FRENCH

Green, Julian. The War at Sixteen: Autobiography, Vol. 2. Cameron, Euan, tr. from FRE. LC 93-656. 224p. 1993. 24.95 (*0-7145-2969-9*) M Boyars Pubs.

Lazo, Caroline. Elie Wiesel. LC 93-44473. 1994. text ed. 13.95 (*0-87518-636-X*, Dillon) Macmillan Child Grp.

AUTHORS, LATIN AMERICAN

Dolan, Sean. Gabriel Garcia Marquez: Colombian Writer. LC 93-9478. (Illus.). 1994. 18.95 (*0-7910-1243-3*, Am Art Analog); pap. write for info. (*0-7910-1270-0*) Chelsea Hse.

Roman, Joseph. Pablo Neruda. (Illus.). (gr. 5 up). 1992. lib. bdg. 17.95 (*0-7910-1248-4*) Chelsea Hse.

Samuels, Steven. Jorge Luis Borges. (Illus.). (gr. 5 up). 1992. lib. bdg. 17.95 (*0-7910-1236-0*) Chelsea Hse.

AUTHORS, SCOTTISH

Greene, Carol. Robert Louis Stevenson: Author of A Child's Garden of Verses. (Illus.). 32p. (gr. 2-4). 1994. PLB 17.20 (*0-516-04265-3*); pap. 4.95 (*0-516-44265-1*) Childrens.

AUTHORSHIP

see also Drama–Technique; Fiction–Technique; Journalism

Bauer, Marion D. What's Your Story? A Young Person's Guide to Writing Fiction. 144p. (gr. 5 up). 1992. 13.45 (*0-395-57781-0*, Clarion Bks); pap. 6.70 (*0-395-57780-2*, Clarion Bks) HM.

Broekel, Ray. I Can Be an Author. LC 85-28050. (Illus.). 32p. (gr. k-3). 1986. PLB 11.80 (*0-516-01891-4*); pap. 3.95 (*0-516-41891-2*) Childrens.

Buhay, Debra. Black & White of Writing. 30p. (gr. 12). 1990. pap. 2.00 (*0-685-37411-4*) D Hockenberry.

Byars, Betsy C. The Moon & I. (Illus.). 112p. (gr. 7 up). 1992. 12.95 (*0-671-74166-7*, J Messner); lib. bdg. 14.98 (*0-671-74165-9*, J Messner) S&S Trade.

Caisley, Raewyn. Raewyn's Got the Writing Bug Again. LC 93-24529. 1994. 4.25 (*0-383-03734-4*) SRA Schl Grp.

Cameron, Eleanor. The Seed & the Vision: On the Writing & Appreciation of Children's Books. 400p. (gr. 10 up). 1993. 22.99 (*0-525-44949-3*, DCB) Dutton Child Bks.

Chimeric Inc. Staff. Illustory - Write & Illustrate Your Own Book! 12p. (gr. k-4). 19.95 (*0-9636796-0-0*) Chimeric.

Cook, Shirley & Carl, Kathy. Linking Literature & Writing. (Illus.). 240p. (gr. k-3). 1989. pap. text ed. 14.95 (*0-86530-064-X*, IP 166-5) Incentive Pubns.

Corbett, Paula. Fantasy Fling. 56p. (gr. 4-6). 1984. 7.95 (*0-88160-112-8*, LW 247) Learning Wks.

Cotter, Paulette & Johansen, Carol. Dream Scenes. 48p. (gr. 3-6). 1983. 5.95 (*0-88160-100-4*, LW 241) Learning Wks.

Daniel, Becky & Daniel, Charlie. Strain Your Brain. 48p. (gr. 4-6). 1980. 5.95 (*0-88160-032-6*, LW 217) Learning Wks.

Dickinson, Dof. Write from the Start. (Illus.). 136p. (Orig.). (gr. 3 up). 1988. pap. 20.00 (*0-333-47822-3*, Macmillan Ed UK) Players Pr.

Dresser, Norine. I Felt Like I Was from Another Planet: Writing from Personal Experience. (gr. 4-7). 1993. pap. 14.95 (*0-201-86058-9*) Addison-Wesley.

Ehrenhaft, George. The Writer's Survival Guide. 124p. (Orig.). (gr. 9-12). 1988. pap. text ed. 14.99, 8.99 per book for classroom sets (*0-87438-047-2*); tchr's. ed. 14.99 (*0-87438-048-0*) Media Basics.

Fearn, Leif. Developmental Writing & the Writing Kabyn. 70p. (gr. 2-9). 1981. 1.00 (*0-940444-07-0*) Kabyn.

Goble, Paul. Hau Kola - Hello Friend. Perrin, Gerry, photos by. LC 93-48167. (Illus.). 1994. 12.95 (*1-878450-44-1*) R Owen Pubs.

Goldman, Elizabeth & Farnan, Nancy J. Developing Writers in Grades 7-12. 294p. (gr. 7-12). 1985. 44.90 (*0-940444-23-2*) Kabyn.

Grant, Janet E. Young Person's Guide to Becoming a Writer. LC 91-19473. 152p. (Orig.). (gr. 6 up). 1993. pap. 8.95 (*1-55870-215-6*, 70125) Shoe Tree Pr.

Guiley, Rosemary E. Career Opportunities for Writers. rev. ed. 232p. (gr. 9-12). 1992. pap. 14.95 (*0-8160-2462-6*) Facts on File.

Guthrie, Donna. Young Author's Do-It-Yourself Book: How to Write, Illustrate, & Produce Your Own Book. (gr. 4-7). 1994. pap. 7.95 (*1-56294-723-0*) Millbrook Pr.

Guthrie, Donna, et al. The Young Author's Do-It-Yourself Book: How to Write, Illustrate, & Produce Your Own Book. Arnsteen, Katy K., illus. LC 93-9736. 64p. (gr. 2-4). 1994. PLB 15.40 (*1-56294-350-2*) Millbrook Pr.

Hamilton, Sally. Spin Your Wheels. 48p. (gr. 4-6). 1982. 5.95 (*0-88160-051-2*, LW 237) Learning Wks.

Hamley, Harold, ed. How to Write & Sell. 4th ed. 121p. (Orig.). (gr. 9-12). Repr. of 1989 ed. lib. bdg. 8.95 (*0-9621758-0-3*) Raconteurs.

Harner, David L. How to Publish a Tabloid Shopper. (Illus.). 248p. (Orig.). (gr. 12). 1989. pap. 22.95 (*0-685-26080-1*) Harner Pubns.

How to Write & Sell. 4th ed. 122p. (Orig.). (gr. 6-12). 1983. pap. 7.95 (*0-317-92526-1*) Raconteurs.

Howe, James. Playing with Words. Craine, Michael, photos by. LC 93-48166. 1994. 12.95 (*1-878450-40-9*) R Owen Pubs.

James, Elizabeth & Barkin, Carol. How to Write a Great School Report. Greenlaw, M. Jean, intro. by. LC 83-764. (Illus.). 167p. (gr. 3-5). 1983. PLB 11.93 (*0-688-02283-9*) Lothrop.

—How to Write a Great School Report. Greenlaw, M. Jean, intro. by. LC 83-764. (Illus.). 80p. (gr. 3 up). 1993. pap. 6.95 (*0-688-02278-2*, Pub. by Beech Tree Bks) Morrow.

—How to Write a Term Paper. Jacobs, Leland B., intro. by. LC 80-13734. 96p. (gr. 7 up). 1980. 11.88 (*0-688-00682-5*) Lothrop.

—How to Write Your Best Book Report. Doty, Roy, illus. LC 86-8597. 80p. (gr. 3-7). 1986. 14.93 (*0-688-05744-6*) Lothrop.

—How to Write Your Best Book Report. Doty, Roy, illus. LC 86-8597. 80p. (gr. 3 up). 1986. pap. 6.00 (*0-688-05743-8*, Pub. by Beech Tree Bks) Morrow.

Janeczko, Paul B., compiled by. Poetry from A to Z: A Guide for Young Writers. Bobak, Cathy, illus. LC 94-10528. (gr. 4-8). 1994. 15.95 (*0-02-747672-3*, Bradbury Pr) Macmillan Child Grp.

Joy, Flora. Shortcuts for Teaching Writing. 144p. (gr. 3-6). 1991. 12.95 (*0-86653-590-X*, GA1303) Good Apple.

Kaplan, Andrew. Careers for Wordsmiths. 1992. pap. 4.95 (*0-395-63563-2*) HM.

Lauritzen, Cyndi. Create & Write. 48p. (gr. 4-6). 1982. 5.95 (*0-88160-052-0*, LW 238) Learning Wks.

Lee, Betsy. Judy Blume's Story. LC 81-12494. (Illus.). 112p. (gr. 5 up). 1981. text ed. 11.95 RSBE (*0-87518-209-7*, Dillon) Macmillan Child Grp.

Livingston, Myra C. Poem-Making: Ways to Begin Writing Poetry. LC 90-5012. 176p. (gr. 4-8). 1991. 16.00 (*0-06-024019-9*); PLB 15.89 (*0-06-024020-2*) HarpC Child Bks.

McCabe, Robert E. & Goldman, Elizabeth. Getting Started in Developmental Writing. 100p. (gr. 2-9). 1982. 7.60 (*0-940444-17-8*) Kabyn.

Marsh, Carole. Write Your Own SportsMystery Kit. (Illus., Orig.). (gr. 3-12). 1994. pap. 24.00 (*0-935326-11-1*) Gallopade Pub Group.

Meltzer, Milton. Starting from Home: A Writer's Beginnings. (Illus.). 160p. (gr. 7 up). 1991. pap. 3.95 (*0-14-032299-X*, Puffin) Puffin Bks.

Moore, Jo E. Making Books with Beginning Writers. (Illus.). 48p. (gr. k-2). 1992. pap. 6.95 (*1-55799-225-8*, EMC262) Evan-Moor Corp.

—Shoe Box Centers Writing Activities: Shoe Box Centers. (Illus.). 64p. (gr. 1-3). 1992. pap. 7.95 (*1-55799-224-X*) Evan-Moor Corp.

Murtha, Philly. Writing: You Can Be an Author. Redpath, Ann, ed. 32p. (gr. 4 up). 1984. PLB 11.95 (*0-87191-998-2*) Creative Ed.

Naylor, Phyllis R. How I Came to Be a Writer. LC 86-32283. (Illus.). 144p. (gr. 4). 1987. pap. 4.95 (*0-689-71129-8*, Aladdin) Macmillan Child Grp.

O'Brien-Palmer, Michelle. Book-Write: A Creative Bookmaking Guide for Young Authors. Rubin, Shannon, illus. LC 91-68412. 128p. (gr. k-6). 1992. pap. 16.95 (*1-879235-01-3*) MicNik Pubns.

Ossorio, Joseph D., et al. Kid's Writing Society Membership Manual. (Illus.). 60p. (gr. 4-7). 1994. pap. 6.95 (*1-56721-071-6*) Twenty-Fifth Cent Pr.

—Under Twenty Writing Society Membership Manual. (Illus.). 72p. (gr. 8-12). 1994. pap. 8.95 (*1-56721-072-4*) Twenty-Fifth Cent Pr.

Peck, Richard. Write a Tale of Terror. (Illus.). 32p. (gr. 5-10). 1987. pap. 4.95 (*0-913839-60-4*) Bk Lures.

Polette, Nancy. The Best Ever Writing Models. (Illus.). 124p. (gr. 4-9). 1989. pap. 12.95 (*0-913839-78-7*) Bk Lures.

—The Research Project Book. 2nd ed. (Illus.). 128p. (gr. 4-9). 1992. pap. 12.95 (*1-879287-06-4*) Bk Lures.

—Write Your Own Fairy Tale. enl. ed. Dillon, Paul, illus. 48p. (Orig.). (gr. 3-7). 1993. pap. 5.95 (*1-879287-25-0*) Bk Lures.

Polon, Linda. Stir up a Story. 48p. (gr. 3-6). 1981. 5.95 (*0-88160-037-7*, LW 222) Learning Wks.

Preece, Alison & Cowden, Diane. Young Writers in the Making: Sharing the Process with Parents. LC 93-24636. 1993. pap. text ed. 15.00 (*0-435-08778-9*, 08778) Heinemann.

Rothstein, Evelyn, et al. Editing Writes, Blue Edition. Gompper, Gail, illus. (gr. 3-4). 1990. pap. 7.95 25 or more copies (*0-913935-46-8*) ERA-CCR.

—Editing Writes, Green Edition. Gompper, Gail, illus. (gr. 5-7). 1990. pap. 7.95 (*0-913935-47-6*) ERA-CCR.

—Editing Writes, Orange Edition. Gompper, Gail, illus. (gr. 2-8). 1990. pap. 7.95 25 or more copies (*0-913935-48-4*) ERA-CCR.

—Creative Writes, Bk. B. 34p. (gr. 5-12). 1984. pap. 14.95 (*0-913935-26-3*) ERA-CCR.

Schwartz, Linda. Creative Writing Rocket. 48p. (gr. 1-4). 1976. 5.95 (*0-88160-003-2*, LW 104) Learning Wks.

—The Creative Writing Roundup. 48p. (gr. 4-7). 1976. 5.95 (*0-88160-017-2*, LW 201) Learning Wks.

Sebranek, Patrick, et al. The Write Source: A Student Handbook. Krenzke, Chris, illus. 312p. (gr. 4-7). 1987. 8.95 (*0-939045-02-8*); text ed. 8.95 (*0-685-18820-5*); pap. text ed. 8.95 (*0-939045-03-6*) Write Source.

Shaw, Sally. Composition Capers. 48p. (gr. 4-6). 1982. 5.95 (*0-88160-044-X*, LW 229) Learning Wks.

Shubkagel, Judy F. Show Me How to Write an Experimental Science Fair Paper: A Fill-in-the-Blank Handbook. 44p. (gr. 4-8). 1993. wkbk. 9.95 (*1-883484-00-6*) Show Me How.
It is the "Writing of the Experimental Science Fair Paper that Drives Everybody Nuts!" This book was written by a science teacher to help 4th through 8th grade students, their parents & teachers know exactly what is expected on each page of the science fair paper. Included in this book is a complete science fair paper on a paper airplane project from the title page to the bibliography. Each section includes "a" & "b" pages. The "a" pages have three sections: the SAMPLE project, a REMINDER section, & an EXPLANATION of how to write each page. The REMINDER section includes helpful hints such as "You will need two copies of this page, one for the backboard & one for the notebook." The SAMPLE & EXPLANATION pages also emphasize & identify independent, dependent & constant variables. These variables are identified throughout the book with single, double, or dashed lines. Opposite the "a" pages are the "b" reproducible fill in the blank pages. Also included are sections on Variables, Selecting Topics, Using a Timeline, Backboard & Display & alternative charts & graphs. This book is very precise & complete... A MUST HAVE FOR FIRST TIME EXPERIMENTERS! Show Me How Publications. 15606 E. 44th St., Independence, MO 64055. Shubkagel (816) 373-7819.
Publisher Provided Annotation.

Spirack, Doris. Creative Writing Carousel. 48p. (gr. 4-6). 1982. 7.95 (*0-88160-086-5*, LW 239) Learning Wks.

Stevens, Carla. A Book of Your Own: Keeping a Diary or Journal. LC 92-33818. 1993. 14.95 (*0-89919-256-4*, Clarion Bks) HM.

Stevens, Janet. Let's Make a Story: An Illustrator's Approach. LC 94-18976. Date not set. write for info. (*0-8234-1154-0*) Holiday.

Story Time Stories That Rhyme Staff. Bean Sprouts - a How to Story Rhyme & Activity Workbook. Doyle, A., illus. 30p. (Orig.). (gr. 4-7). 1992. pap. text ed. 17.95 (*0-939476-82-7*, Pub. by Biblio Pr) Prosperity & Profits.

Tchudi, Susan & Tchudi, Stephen. The Young Writer's Handbook. LC 84-5312. 160p. (gr. 5 up). 1984. SBE 14.95 (0-684-18090-1, Scribners Young Read) Macmillan Child Grp.

AUTHORSHIP–FICTION

Giff, Patricia R. Write up a Storm. 1993. pap. 3.50 (0-440-40882-2) Dell.

Lee, Marie G. Saying Goodbye. LC 93-26092. 1994. write for info. (0-395-67066-7) HM.

Mooser, Stephen. The Things Upstairs. LC 93-50676. (Illus.). 144p. (gr. 3-6). 1994. pap. 2.95 (0-8167-3421-6) Troll Assocs.

Pinkwater, Daniel. Author's Day. Pinkwater, Daniel, illus. LC 92-18154. 32p. (gr. k-3). 1993. RSBE 13.95 (0-02-774642-9, Macmillan Child Bk) Macmillan Child Grp.

Suki: A Novel for Young People. 153p. (gr. 7-9). 6.50 (0-686-74923-5) ADL.

Who Wrote This Story? (Illus.). (ps-2). 1991. PLB 6.95 (0-8136-5163-8, TK3839); pap. 3.50 (0-8136-5663-X, TK3840) Modern Curr.

Williams, Barbara. Author & Squinty Gritt. LC 90-37021. 80p. (gr. 2-5). 1990. 12.95 (0-525-44655-9, DCB) Dutton Child Bks.

Wood, Marcia. Always, Julia. LC 91-40460. 128p. (gr. 5-9). 1993. SBE 13.95 (0-689-31728-X, Atheneum Child Bk) Macmillan Child Grp.

Zindel, Paul. David & Della. LC 93-12719. 176p. (gr. 7 up). 1993. 14.00 (0-06-023353-2); PLB 13.89 (0-06-023354-0) HarpC Child Bks.

AUTOBIOGRAPHIES

Borg, Mary. Writing Your Life: Autobiographical Writing Activities for Young People. Blackstone, Ann, illus. 46p. (gr. 5-12). 1989. pap. text ed. 14.95 (1-877673-09-9) Cottonwood Pr.

Bruzzone, Catherine & Morton, Lone. All about Me. Church, Caroline J., illus. 24p. (Orig.). (gr. k-3). 1993. pap. 3.95 (0-8249-8605-9, Ideals Child) Hambleton-Hill.

Euretig, Mary. I'm in the Spotlight! A Journal of Discovery for Young Writers. Bacchini, Lisa, illus. 160p. (Orig.). (gr. 1-5). 1993. pap. 11.95 (0-9628216-1-6) Dream Tree Pr.

Hanna, Ken. My Life & Times: For Whatever They're Worth. LC 88-51575. 128p. 1989. pap. 6.95 (1-55523-211-6) Winston-Derek.

Harris, Jennifer. What Was I Like? Childhood Memory Book Series, 6 bks, Set 1. Innes, George C., illus. (ps). 1992. Set. slipcased 49.95 (1-879956-12-8) Tintern Abbey.

—What Was I Like? Childhood Memory Book Series, 5 bks, Set 2. Innes, George C., illus. (gr. k-4). 1992. Set. slipcased 49.95 (1-879956-13-6) Tintern Abbey.

Hunter, Latoya. Diary of Latoya Hunter. LC 92-8384. 1992. 16.00 (0-517-58511-1, Crown) Crown Pub Group.

Konopka, Gisela. Courage & Love. (Orig.). (gr. 7 up). 1988. pap. 10.95 (0-9621328-0-2) G Konopka.

Little, Jean. Little by Little: A Writer's Education. (Illus.). 240p. (gr. 5-9). 1991. pap. 3.95 (0-14-032325-2, Puffin) Puffin Bks.

Oke, Janette. Spunky's Diary. 99p. (gr. 5-12). 1982. pap. 4.99 (0-934998-11-6) Bethel Pub.

Simpson, Anne. My Secret Diary. LC 92-20177. (Illus.). 64p. (gr. 4-6). 1992. pap. 2.95 (0-8167-2941-7) Troll Assocs.

Stevens, Carla. Book of Your Own: Keeping a Diary or Journal. (gr. 4-7). 1993. pap. 7.95 (0-395-67887-0, Clarion Bks) HM.

Woodward, Patricia. Journal Jumpstarts: Quick Topics & Tips for Journal Writing. rev. ed. 30p. (Orig.). (gr. 7-12). 1991. pap. text ed. 5.95 (1-877673-15-3) Cottonwood Pr.

AUTOGRAPHS

Owens, Tom. Collecting Sports Autographs: Fun & Profit from This Easy-to-Learn Hobby. 131p. (Orig.). (gr. 7 up). 1989. pap. 6.95 (0-933893-79-5) Bonus Books.

AUTOGRAPHS–COLLECTIONS

Frith, Michael. Autographs! I Collect Them! Frith, Michael, illus. LC 89-63064. 48p. (gr. 1-5). 1990. pap. 4.95 (0-679-80691-1) Random Bks Yng Read.

AUTOMATIC COMPUTERS

see Computers

AUTOMATIC CONTROL

see Automation

AUTOMATIC DATA PROCESSING

see Electronic Data Processing

AUTOMATIC INFORMATION RETRIEVAL

see Information Storage and Retrieval Systems

AUTOMATION

Asimov, Isaac. How Did We Find Out about Robots? Wool, David, illus. 64p. (gr. 4-7). 1984. PLB 10.85 (0-8027-6563-7) Walker & Co.

Paltrowitz, Donna & Paltrowitz, Stuart. Robotics. LC 83-13108. 64p. (gr. 7-11). 1983. (J Messner) S&S Trade.

AUTOMOBILE ACCIDENTS

see Traffic Accidents

AUTOMOBILE DRIVERS

American Automobile Association Staff. Sportsmanlike Driving. 9th ed. 352p. (gr. 9-12). 1987. text ed. 22.16 (0-07-001338-1); pap. text ed. 14.48 (0-07-001339-X); Student edition. write for info. (0-07-001361-6); Test booklet. write for info. (0-07-001363-2); Tchr's man. write for info. (0-07-001364-0) McGraw.

Grosshandler, Janet. Drugs & Driving. rev. ed. Rosen, Ruth, ed. (gr. 7-12). 1994. 14.95 (0-8239-2039-9) Rosen Group.

Knox, Jean M. Drinking, Driving & Drugs. (Illus.). 32p. (gr. 5 up). 1991. pap. 4.49 (1-55546-997-3) Chelsea Hse.

AUTOMOBILE DRIVERS–FICTION

Buller, Jon & Schade, Susan. Toad on the Road. Buller, Jon, illus. LC 91-4246. 32p. (Orig.). (ps-1). 1992. PLB 7.99 (0-679-92689-5); pap. 3.50 (0-679-82689-0) Random Bks Yng Read.

Cooney, Caroline B. Driver's Ed. LC 94-445. 1994. 15.95 (0-385-32087-6) Delacorte.

Coy, John. Night Driving. 1994. write for info. (0-8050-2931-1) H Holt & Co.

Holland, Alex N. Harvey Learns to Drive. Holland, Alex N., illus. 17p. (gr. k-3). 1992. pap. 10.95 (1-895583-52-7) MAYA Pubs.

Hyatt, Pat R. Coast to Coast with Alice. LC 94-25750. (gr. 1-8). 1995. write for info. (0-87614-789-9) Carolrhoda Bks.

Oxenbury, Helen. The Car Trip. Oxenbury, Helen, illus. 24p. (ps-1). 1994. pap. 3.99 (0-14-050377-3, Puff Pied Piper) Puffin Bks.

—The Important Visitor. Oxenbury, Helen, illus. 24p. (ps-1). 1994. pap. 3.99 (0-14-050379-X, Puff Pied Piper) Puffin Bks.

Smith, Matthew V. Jennie Learns to Drive. Smith, Matthew V., illus. 15p. (gr. k-3). 1992. pap. 12.95 (1-895583-30-6) MAYA Pubs.

Temple, Charles. Cadillac. Lockhart, Lynne, illus. LC 93-42387. 1995. write for info. (0-399-22654-0) Putnam Pub Group.

AUTOMOBILE DRIVING

see Automobile Drivers

AUTOMOBILE ENGINES

see Automobiles–Engines

AUTOMOBILE INDUSTRY AND TRADE–HISTORY

Wood, Tim. Racing Drivers. Stefoff, Rebecca, ed. LC 91-39098. (Illus.). 32p. (gr. 5-9). 1992. PLB 17.26 (1-56074-042-6) Garrett Ed Corp.

AUTOMOBILE RACING

see also Karts and Karting

Barrett, Norman S. Carros de Carrera. LC 90-70887. (SPA., Illus.). 32p. (gr. k-4). 1990. PLB 11.90 (0-531-07905-8) Watts.

Chirinian, Alain. Race Cars. (Illus.). 64p. (gr. 5-9). 1989. (J Messner); PLB 8.24s.p. (0-685-54167-3); pap. 3.71s.p. (0-685-47098-9) S&S Trade.

—Tough Wheels Series, 4 vols. (Illus.). 256p. (gr. 5-9). 1989. Set. PLB 43.92 (0-671-94096-1, J Messner); Set. PLB 32.94s.p. (0-685-54166-5); Set. pap. 14.85s.p. (0-685-47090-3) S&S Trade.

Connolly, Maureen. Dragsters. (Illus.). 48p. (gr. 3-6). 1992. PLB 12.95 (1-56065-074-5) Capstone Pr.

Denan, Jay. Burnout: Funny Car Races. LC 79-64700. (Illus.). 32p. (gr. 4-9). 1980. PLB 10.79 (0-89375-256-8); pap. 2.95 (0-89375-257-6) Troll Assocs.

—The Glory Ride, Road Racing. LC 79-52179. (Illus.). 32p. (gr. 4-9). 1980. PLB 10.79 (0-89375-254-1); pap. 2.95 (0-89375-255-X) Troll Assocs.

—Hot on Wheels: The Rally Scene. LC 79-64701. (Illus.). 32p. (gr. 4-9). 1980. PLB 10.79 (0-89375-258-4) Troll Assocs.

—Start Your Engines: Racing the Championship Trail. LC 79-64702. (Illus.). 32p. (gr. 4-9). 1980. PLB 10.79 (0-89375-260-6); pap. 2.95 (0-89375-261-4) Troll Assocs.

DiMino, Frank. Hot Rod Coloring Album. DiMino, Frank, illus. 32p. (Orig.). (gr. 1-6). 1993. pap. 4.50 (0-8431-3514-X, Troubador) Price Stern.

Dregni, Michael. Stock Car Racing. LC 93-44568. 1994. write for info. (1-56065-206-3) Capstone Pr.

Famous Sports Cars. (ps up). 1990. pap. 2.50 (0-89954-061-9) Antioch Pub Co.

Gifford, C. Racing Cars. (Illus.). 32p. (ps-3). 1994. PLB 13.96 (0-88110-701-8, Usborne); pap. 5.95 (0-7460-1654-9, Usborne) EDC.

—Racing Cars. (Illus.). 12p. (ps). 1994. bds. 4.50 (0-7460-1979-3, Usborne) EDC.

Graham, Ian. Racing Cars. LC 94-17294. 1995. write for info. (0-8120-6472-0) Barron.

Gregory, Stephen. Racing to Win: The Salt Flats. new ed. LC 75-21845. (Illus.). (gr. 5-10). 1976. PLB 10.79 (0-89375-010-7) Troll Assocs.

I Can Be a Race Car Driver. 1992. 2.99 (0-517-06741-2) Random Hse Value.

Jefferis, David & Lafferty, Peter. Checkered Flag! The History of the Racing Car. LC 90-32128. (Illus.). 32p. (gr. 5-8). 1991. PLB 12.40 (0-531-14122-5) Watts.

Naden, C. J. I Can Read About Racing Cars. LC 78-74658. (Illus.). (gr. 3-6). 1979. pap. 2.50 (0-89375-216-9) Troll Assocs.

Orr, Frank. Great Moments in Auto Racing. LC 73-18087. (Illus.). 160p. 1974. lib. bdg. 3.69 (0-394-92763-X) Random Bks Yng Read.

Robson, Denny A. Racing Cars. LC 92-9551. 1992. 11.90 (0-531-17380-1, Gloucester Pr) Watts.

Rubel, David. How to Drive an Indy Race Car. Keating, Edward, illus. 48p. (Orig.). (gr. 3 up). 1992. pap. 9.95 (1-56261-062-7) John Muir.

Schleifer, Jay. Bonneville! Quest for the Land Speed Record. LC 94-765. 1994. text ed. 14.95 (0-89686-817-6, Crestwood Hse) MacMillan Child Grp.

Sosa, Maria. Dragsters. LC 87-15568. (Illus.). 48p. (gr. 5-6). 1987. text ed. 11.95 RSBE (0-89686-350-6, Crestwood Hse) Macmillan Child Grp.

Stephenson, Sallie. Autocross Racing. LC 91-13635. (Illus.). 48p. (gr. 5). 1991. text ed. 12.95 RSBE (0-89686-692-0, Crestwood Hse) Macmillan Child Grp.

—Circle Track Racing. (Illus.). 48p. (gr. 5). 1991. text ed. 12.95 RSBE (0-89686-693-9, Crestwood Hse) Macmillan Child Grp.

—Rally Racing. LC 91-13641. (Illus.). 48p. (gr. 5). 1991. text ed. 12.95 RSBE (0-89686-694-7, Crestwood Hse) Macmillan Child Grp.

—Winston Cup Racing. (Illus.). 48p. (gr. 5). 1991. text ed. 12.95 RSBE (0-89686-695-5, Crestwood Hse) Macmillan Child Grp.

Sullivan, George. Racing Indy Cars. LC 91-19439. (Illus.). 64p. (gr. 4 up). 1992. 15.00 (0-525-65082-2, Cobblehill Bks) Dutton Child Bks.

AUTOMOBILE RACING–BIOGRAPHY

Garlits, Don & Yates, Brock. Big Daddy: The Autobiography of Don Garlits. 2nd, rev., enl. & updated ed. Smith, Donna G., ed. (Illus.). 354p. 1990. 50.00 (0-685-35751-1); pap. 9.95 (0-9626565-0-X) D Garlits.

AUTOMOBILE RACING–FICTION

Carlson, Nancy. Loudmouth George & the Big Race. LC 83-5191. (Illus.). 32p. (ps-3). 1983. PLB 13.50 (0-87614-215-3) Carolrhoda Bks.

Cowley, Joy. Screaming Mean Machine. (gr. 4-7). 1994. pap. 4.95 (0-590-48013-8) Scholastic Inc.

Felsen, Henry G. Crash Club. 208p. (gr. 9-12). 1990. pap. 25.00 slipcase, ltd. ed. (0-917473-06-X) G P Pub MI.

—Fever Heat. 224p. (gr. 9-12). 1990. pap. 25.00 slipcase, ltd. ed. (0-917473-09-4) G P Pub MI.

—Hot Rod. 160p. (gr. 9-12). 1990. pap. 25.00 slipcase, ltd. ed. (0-917473-11-6) G P Pub MI.

—Rag Top. 160p. (gr. 9-12). 1990. pap. 25.00 slipcase, ltd. ed. (0-917473-08-6) G P Pub MI.

—Road Rocket. 216p. (gr. 9-12). 1990. pap. 25.00 slipcase, ltd. ed. (0-917473-07-8) G P Pub MI.

—Street Rod. 160p. (gr. 9-12). 1990. pap. 25.00 slipcase, ltd. ed. (0-917473-10-8) G P Pub MI.

Jennings, Dana A. Me, Dad & No. 6. Sasaki, Goro, illus. LC 93-43640. 1995. write for info. (0-15-200085-2, Gulliver Bks) HarBrace.

Montgomery, Raymond A. Motocross Mania. (gr. 4-6). 1993. pap. 3.50 (0-553-56002-6) Bantam.

Seablom, Seth H. The Great Mukilteo to Friday Harbor Auto Race. Seablom, Seth H., illus. LC 75-38037. (gr. 1-3). 1976. pap. 2.00 (0-918800-00-5) Seablom.

Wahl, Jan. S.O.S. Bobomobile. 128p. 1995. pap. 3.99 (0-8125-2405-5) Tor Bks.

Wojciechowska, Maia. Dreams of the Indy Five Hundred. Karsky, A. K., illus. 52p. 1994. 14.50 (1-883740-11-8) Pebble Bch Pr Ltd.

AUTOMOBILE TOURING

see Automobiles–Touring

AUTOMOBILE TRUCKS

see Trucks

AUTOMOBILES

see also Buses; Trucks;

also names of automobiles, e.g. Ford Automobile

Andersen, T. J. Baja Cars. LC 87-29022. (Illus.). 48p. (gr. 5-6). 1988. text ed. 11.95 RSBE (0-89686-357-3, Crestwood Hse) Macmillan Child Grp.

Atkinson, Elizabeth. Monster Vehicles. 48p. (gr. 3-4). 1991. PLB 11.95 (1-56065-077-X) Capstone Pr.

Baxter, Leon. Famous Automobiles. 48p. (gr. 2-5). 1992. pap. 7.95 (0-8249-8559-1, Ideals Child) Hambleton-Hill.

Bendick, Jeanne. Eureka! It's an Automobile! Murdocca, Sal, illus. LC 91-34790. 48p. (gr. 2-6). 1992. PLB 15.40 (1-56294-057-0); pap. 5.95 (1-56294-700-1) Millbrook Pr.

Bouquet, Jeff S. Young Man's Guide to Autos: Basics, Operation, Safety & Maintenance. Kimmel, Nita, illus. 80p. 1991. 70.00x (1-56216-017-6); pap. 40.00x (1-56216-018-4) Systems Co.

Burt, Stephen. RVs & Vans. (Illus.). 48p. (gr. 3-6). 1992. PLB 12.95 (1-56065-071-0) Capstone Pr.

Butler, Daphne. First Look at Cars. LC 90-10265. (Illus.). 32p. (gr. 1-2). 1991. PLB 17.27 (0-8368-0503-8) Gareth Stevens Inc.

Car Classics Series, 6 bks. 1991. Set. 75.00s.p. (0-86593-141-0) Rourke Corp.

Cars. LC 91-58205. (Illus.). 64p. (gr. 6 up). 1992. 14.95 (1-56458-007-5); PLB 15.99 (1-56458-008-3) Dorling Kindersley.

Cars. LC 92-54272. (Illus.). 24p. (gr. k-3). 1993. 8.95 (1-56458-219-1) Dorling Kindersley.

Chirinian, Alain. Muscle Cars. Steltenpohl, Jane, ed. (Illus.). 64p. (gr. 5-9). 1989. (J Messner); PLB 8.24s.p. (0-685-47091-1); pap. 3.71s.p. (0-685-47092-X) S&S Trade.

—Weird Wheels. Steltenpohl, Jane, ed. (Illus.). 64p. (gr. 5-9). 1989. (J Messner); lib. bdg. 4.95 (0-671-68036-6); PLB 8.24s.p. (0-685-47095-4); pap. 3.71s.p. (0-685-47096-2) S&S Trade.

Chlad, Dorothy. When I Ride in a Car. LC 83-7382. (Illus.). 32p. (ps-2). 1983. pap. 3.95 (0-516-41987-0) Childrens.

Cole, Joanna. Cars & How They Go. Gibbons, Gail, illus. LC 82-45575. 32p. (gr. 2-6). 1983. (Crowell Jr Bks); PLB 13.89 (0-690-04262-0, Crowell Jr Bks) HarpC Child Bks.

—Cars & How They Go. Gibbons, Gail, illus. LC 82-45575. 32p. (gr. 2-6). 1986. pap. 4.95 (0-06-446052-5, Trophy) HarpC Child Bks.

Coleman, John. Your Book of Vintage Cars. Tucker, Harry, illus. (gr. 7 up). 1969. 7.95 (*0-571-08276-9*) Transatl Arts.

Cooper, J. Automobiles. 1991. 8.95s.p. (*0-86592-495-3*) Rourke Enter.

—Automoviles (Automobiles) 1991. 8.95s.p. (*0-86592-510-0*) Rourke Enter.

Coughlan, John. Experimental & Concept Cars. 48p. (gr. 3-10). 1994. PLB 17.27 (*1-56065-210-1*) Capstone Pr.

Craven. Jaguar: The King of Cats. 1991. 12.50s.p. (*0-86593-144-5*); PLB 16.67 (*0-685-59194-8*) Rourke Corp.

—Rolls-Royce: Leader in Luxury. 1991. 12.50s.p. (*0-86593-147-X*); lib. bdg. 16.67 (*0-685-59198-0*) Rourke Corp.

Craven, Linda & Craven, Jerry. Japanese Sports Cars. LC 93-14917. (Illus.). (gr. 5 up). 1993. write for info. (*0-86593-256-5*) Rourke Corp.

—Mustang: Ford's Wild Pony. LC 93-20243. (gr. 7-8). 1993. 17.26 (*0-86593-255-7*); 12.95s.p. (*0-685-66591-7*) Rourke Corp.

—Thunderbird: The High-Flying Ford. LC 93-219. 1993. write for info. (*0-86593-254-9*) Rourke Corp.

Creighton, Susan. Funny Cars. LC 87-29016. (Illus.). 48p. (gr. 5-6). 1988. text ed. 11.95 RSBE (*0-89686-362-X*, Crestwood Hse) Macmillan Child Grp.

Cruickshank, Gordon. Cars & How They Work. LC 92-7623. (Illus.). 64p. (gr. 3 up). 1992. 11.95 (*1-56458-142-X*) Dorling Kindersley.

Davies, Kay, et al. My Car. Pragoff, Fiona, photos by. (Illus.). 32p. (gr. 1 up). 1995. PLB 17.27 (*0-8368-1185-2*) Gareth Stevens Inc.

Dixon, Malcolm. Land Transportation. LC 90-22717. (Illus.). 48p. (gr. 5-8). 1991. 12.90 (*0-531-18412-9*, Pub. by Bookwright Pr) Watts.

Doerken, Nan. The First Family Car. 59p. (gr. 1-4). 1986. pap. 3.95 (*0-919797-53-9*) Kindred Pr.

Estrem, Paul. Rocket-Powered Cars. LC 87-22374. (Illus.). 48p. (gr. 5-6). 1987. text ed. 11.95 RSBE (*0-89686-352-2*, Crestwood Hse) Macmillan Child Grp.

Ford, Barbara. The Automobile: Inventions That Changed Our Lives. (gr. 3-7). 1987. 10.95 (*0-8027-6724-9*); PLB 11.85 (*0-8027-6725-7*) Walker & Co.

Graham, Ian. Cars. Gillah, Mick, illus. LC 93-19707. 32p. (gr. 4-6). 1993. PLB 19.97 (*0-8114-6162-9*) Raintree Steck-V.

Gunning, Thomas G. Dream Cars. LC 89-11738. (Illus.). 72p. (gr. 3 up). 1989. text ed. 14.95 RSBE (*0-87518-419-7*, Dillon) Macmillan Child Grp.

Haines. Ferrari: The Legend. 1991. 12.50s.p. (*0-86593-146-1*); lib. bdg. 16.67 (*0-685-66098-2*) Rourke Corp.

—Lamborghini: The Fastest. 1991. 12.50s.p. (*0-86593-145-3*); lib. bdg. 16.67 (*0-685-59195-6*) Rourke Corp.

—Mercedes: The First & the Best. 1991. 12.50s.p. (*0-86593-142-9*); lib. bdg. 16.67 (*0-685-59196-4*) Rourke Corp.

—Porsche: Fast & Beautiful. 1991. 12.50s.p. (*0-86593-143-7*); lib. bdg. 16.67 (*0-685-59197-2*) Rourke Corp.

Harris, Jack C. Dream Cars. LC 88-1827. (Illus.). 48p. (gr. 5-6). 1988. text ed. 11.95 RSBE (*0-89686-376-X*, Crestwood Hse) Macmillan Child Grp.

Immell, Myra H. Automobiles: Connecting People & Places. LC 93-4553. (gr. 5-8). 1994. 15.95 (*1-56006-226-6*) Lucent Bks.

Johnstone, Michael. Cars. Austin, illus. 32p. (gr. 1-4). 1994. 5.95 (*1-56458-681-2*) Dorling Kindersley.

Kanetzke, Howard W. The Story of Cars. rev. ed. LC 87-23231. (Illus.). 48p. (gr. 2-6). 1987. PLB 10.95 (*0-8172-3261-3*); pap. 4.49 (*0-8114-8217-0*) Raintree Steck-V.

Lanton, Sandy. Is That Our Car? Drum, Stacy, illus. 32p. (ps-2). Date not set. 11.95 (*1-56065-143-1*) Capstone Pr.

Leder, Jane M. Exotic Cars. LC 87-15572. (Illus.). 48p. (gr. 5-6). 1987. RSBE 11.95 (*0-89686-351-4*, Crestwood Hse) Macmillan Child Grp.

Lenski, Lois. Little Auto. Lenski, Lois, illus. LC 58-14239. (gr. k-3). 1980. 5.25 (*0-8098-1001-8*) McKay.

Lord, Trevor. Amazing Cars. King, Dave, photos by. LC 91-53138. (Illus.). 32p. (Orig.). (gr. 1-5). 1992. PLB 9.99 (*0-679-92766-2*); pap. 6.95 (*0-679-82766-8*) Knopf Bks Yng Read.

Machan, Wayne & Bruggen, Bill. The Corvair, 1960-1969. LC 89-63378. (Illus.). 128p. (Orig.). 1991. pap. 19.95 (*0-929758-07-2*) Beeman Jorgensen.

Marshall, Ray. The Car: Watch It Work by Operating the Moving Diagrams! Bradley, John F., ed. Marshall, Ray & Bradley, John F., illus. LC 83-40569. 10p. 1984. pap. 14.95 (*0-670-20371-8*) Viking Child Bks.

Martin, John. The World's Most Exotic Cars. 48p. (gr. 3-10). 1994. PLB 17.27 (*1-56065-209-8*) Capstone Pr.

The Motor Car. (ARA., Illus.). (gr. 5-12). 1980. 3.95x (*0-86685-209-3*) Intl Bk Ctr.

Nichols, V. Cars & Trucks Sticker Pad. M. J. Studios Staff, illus. 32p. (gr. k-6). 1993. pap. 2.95 (*1-879424-16-9*) Nickel Pr.

Olson, Norman. I Can Read About Trucks & Cars. LC 72-96957. (Illus.). (gr. 2-4). 1973. pap. 2.50 (*0-89375-055-7*) Troll Assocs.

Petty, Kate. New Car. Barber, Ed, photos by. (Illus.). 32p. (gr. 2 up). 1992. bds. 12.95 (*0-7136-3484-7*, Pub. by A&C Black UK) Talman.

Postcard Power! You Can Do Something for the Environment. (Illus.). 16p. (gr. 3-8). 1992. pap. 3.95 (*0-671-74476-3*, Little Simon) S&S Trade.

Putnam, Jeff. Hot Cars Poster Book. 32p. (gr. 3 up). 1992. pap. 3.99 (*0-87406-634-4*) Willowisp Pr.

Richardson, Joy. Cars. LC 93-42179. 1994. write for info. (*0-531-14325-2*) Watts.

Robertson, Sue & Punkus, Sue. Let's All Draw Cars, Trucks & Other Vehicles. (Illus.). 144p. (gr. 3-7). 1991. pap. 9.95 (*0-8230-2704-X*, Watson-Guptill Bks) Watson-Guptill.

Robinson, Scott. Indy Cars. LC 87-30509. (Illus.). 48p. (gr. 5-6). 1988. RSBE 11.95 (*0-89686-356-5*, Crestwood Hse) Macmillan Child Grp.

Rock, Maxine. The Automobile & The Environment. (Illus.). (gr. 5 up). 1992. lib. bdg. 19.95 (*0-7910-1592-0*) Chelsea Hse.

Rockwell, Anne. Cars. Rockwell, Anne, illus. LC 83-14080. 24p. (ps-1). 1984. 12.95 (*0-525-44079-8*, DCB) Dutton Child Bks.

—Cars. Rockwell, Anne, illus. LC 83-14080. 24p. (ps-1). 1986. pap. 3.95 (*0-525-44241-3*, DCB) Dutton Child Bks.

—Cars. 1994. pap. 4.50 (*0-14-054741-X*, Puff Unicorn) Puffin Bks.

Royston, Angela. Cars. LC 91-16122. (Illus.). 24p. (ps-k). 1991. pap. 6.95 POB (*0-689-71517-X*, Aladdin) Macmillan Child Grp.

Rutland, Jonathan. Amazing Fact Book of Cars. (Illus.). 32p. (gr. 4-8). 1987. PLB 14.95 (*0-87191-843-9*) Creative Ed.

Scarry, Richard. Richard Scarry's Cars. (Illus.). 24p. (ps-k). 1992. pap. write for info. (*0-307-11538-0*, 11538, Golden Pr) Western Pub.

—Richard Scarry's Cars & Trucks & Things That Go. (Illus.). (ps-2). 1974. write for info. (*0-307-15785-7*, Golden Bks) Western Pub.

Schleifer, Jay. Camaro. LC 92-3809. (Illus.). 48p. (gr. 5). 1993. text ed. 13.95 RSBE (*0-89686-696-3*, Crestwood Hse) Macmillan Child Grp.

—Corvette. LC 91-18096. (Illus.). 48p. (gr. 5). 1992. text ed. 13.95 RSBE (*0-89686-697-1*, Crestwood Hse) Macmillan Child Grp.

—Ferrari. LC 91-21374. (Illus.). 48p. (gr. 5). 1992. text ed. 13.95 RSBE (*0-89686-700-5*, Crestwood Hse) Macmillan Child Grp.

—Porsche. LC 91-31534. (Illus.). 48p. (gr. 5). 1992. text ed. 13.95 RSBE (*0-89686-703-X*, Crestwood Hse) Macmillan Child Grp.

Schultz, Charles, ed. Earth, Water, & Air. LC 94-15102. (Illus.). 1994. 9.99 (*0-517-11897-1*, Pub. by Derrydale Bks) Random Hse Value.

Sobol, Donald J. Encyclopedia Brown's Book of Wacky Cars. Enik, Ted, illus. LC 86-23556. 128p. (gr. 3-7). 1987. 11.95 (*0-688-06222-9*) Morrow Jr Bks.

Spizzirri Publishing Co. Staff. Automobiles: An Educational Coloring Book. Spizzirri, Linda, ed. Fuller, Glenn, et al, illus. 32p. (gr. 1-8). 1981. pap. 1.75 (*0-86545-032-3*) Spizzirri.

Steele, Philip. Cars & Trucks. LC 90-41180. (Illus.). 32p. (gr. 5-6). 1991. text ed. 3.95 RSBE (*0-89686-521-5*, Crestwood Hse) Macmillan Child Grp.

Tanta, S. What Makes a Car Go? (Illus.). 24p. (gr. k up). 1994. PLB 11.96 (*0-88110-704-2*, Usborne); pap. 3.95 (*0-7460-1650-6*, Usborne) EDC.

Things That Go. (Illus.). 16p. (ps-1). 1994. pap. 6.95 (*1-56458-523-9*) Dorling Kindersley.

Things That Go. (Illus.). 32p. (Orig.). (gr. 1-3). 1994. pap. 4.95 (*1-56458-549-2*) Dorling Kindersley.

Transformers GRT Car Rally. 1984. pap. 1.50 (*0-87135-015-7*) Marvel Entmnt.

Walker, Sloan & Vasey, Andrew. The Only Other Crazy Car Book. LC 83-6546. (Illus.). 48p. (gr. 4 up). 1984. 10.95 (*0-8027-6504-1*); PLB 11.85 (*0-8027-6517-3*) Walker & Co.

AUTOMOBILES–ACCIDENTS

see Traffic Accidents

AUTOMOBILES–DESIGN AND CONSTRUCTION

Parker, Steve. The Car. (Illus.). 32p. (gr. 5-8). 1993. PLB 12.40 (*0-531-17415-8*, Gloucester Pr) Watts.

Taylor, John. How Cars Are Made. LC 86-32878. (Illus.). 32p. (gr. 5-12). 1987. 12.95x (*0-8160-1689-5*) Facts on File.

AUTOMOBILES–DRIVING

see Automobile Drivers

AUTOMOBILES–ENGINES

Black, Wallace B. & Willis, Terri. Cars: An Environmental Challenge. LC 92-9797. (Illus.). 128p. (gr. 4-8). 1992. PLB 20.55 (*0-516-05504-6*) Childrens.

Carroll, Bill. Ford V8 Performance Guide. LC 76-16836. (Illus., Orig.). (gr. 7 up). 1972. 15.00 (*0-910390-17-7*) Auto Bk.

Coughlan, John. Eco Cars: Earth-Friendly Electric Cars. 48p. (gr. 3-10). 1994. PLB 17.27 (*1-56065-211-X*) Capstone Pr.

AUTOMOBILES–FICTION

Barracca, Debra & Barracca, Sal. A Taxi Dog Christmas. Ayers, Alan, illus. LC 91-44953. 40p. (ps-3). 1994. 14.99 (*0-8037-1360-6*); PLB 14.89 (*0-8037-1361-4*) Dial Bks Young.

Barry, Mark. Car Books & Puzzle. Barry, Mark, illus. (ps). 1993. Gift box set of 4 bks., 12p. ea. bds. 14.95 (*1-56828-039-4*) Red Jacket Pr.

Barry, Mark, illus. The City Car Book. 12p. (ps). 1992. 3.95 (*1-56828-004-1*) Red Jacket Pr.

—A Drive in the Country. 12p. (ps). 1992. 3.95 (*1-56828-006-8*) Red Jacket Pr.

—The Highway Car Book. 12p. (ps). 1992. 3.95 (*1-56828-005-X*) Red Jacket Pr.

Becker, Jim & Mayer, Andy. Where Does Little Car Go? 1992. 4.95 (*0-590-44911-7*, Cartwheel) Scholastic Inc.

Burningham, John. Mr. Gumpy's Motor Car. Burningham, John, illus. LC 75-4582. 48p. (ps-3). 1976. PLB 16.89 (*0-690-00799-X*, Crowell Jr Bks) HarpC Child Bks.

Cars & Trucks. (Illus.). 24p. (gr. k-2). 1988. 3.95 (*0-87449-501-6*) Modern Pub NYC.

Felsen, Henry G. Boy Gets Car. (Illus.). (gr. 7-11). 1968. lib. bdg. 5.39 (*0-394-90976-3*) Random Bks Yng Read.

Fisher, Barbara. Car Boy. Fisher, Barbara, illus. 29p. (Orig.). (gr. k-2). 1977. pap. 2.00 (*0-934830-02-9*) Ten Penny.

Flash the Ambulance. 1994. 3.99 (*0-517-10276-5*) Random Hse Value.

Fleming, Ian. Chitty-Chitty-Bang-Bang. Burningham, John, illus. LC 64-21282. 112p. (gr. 3-7). 1989. pap. 3.99 (*0-394-81948-9*) Knopf Bks Yng Read.

Garage Song. LC 91-393. 40p. 1991. pap. 13.95 jacketed (*0-671-73565-9*, Little Simon) S&S Trade.

Giffard, Hannah. Fast Car. Giffard, Hannah, illus. LC 92-62422. 12p. (ps). 1993. bds. 3.95 (*0-688-12444-5*, Tambourine Bks) Morrow.

Greenblat, Rodney A. Uncle Wizzmo's New Used Car. Greenblat, Rodney A., illus. LC 89-36577. 32p. (ps-3). 1990. 13.95 (*0-06-022097-X*); PLB 13.89 (*0-06-022098-8*) HarpC Child Bks.

—Uncle Wizzmo's New Used Car. LC 89-36577. (Illus.). 32p. (ps-3). 1992. pap. 4.95 (*0-06-443305-6*, Trophy) HarpC Child Bks.

Gregorich, Barbara. Beep, Beep. Hoffman, Joan, ed. Taber, Ed, illus. 16p. (Orig.). (gr. k-2). 1984. pap. 2.25 (*0-88743-007-4*, 06007) Sch Zone Pub Co.

—Beep, Beep. Hoffman, Joan, ed. (Illus.). 32p. (gr. k-2). 1992. pap. 3.95 (*0-88743-405-3*, 06057) Sch Zone Pub Co.

Hickle, Victoria. A Big Day for Brum. Mones, Isidre, illus. LC 92-45105. 32p. (ps-1). 1993. pap. 2.25 (*0-679-84494-5*) Random Bks Yng Read.

—Tire Trouble for Brum. Mones, Isidre, illus. 24p. (Orig.). (ps-k). 1993. pap. 1.50 (*0-679-84495-3*) Random Bks Yng Read.

Hillert, Margaret. The Birthday Car. (Illus.). (ps-k). 1966. PLB 6.95 (*0-8136-5031-3*, TK2278); pap. 3.50 (*0-8136-5531-5*, TK2279) Modern Curr.

Howland, Naomi. ABCDrive! A Car Trip Alphabet. LC 93-11530. (ps-1). 1994. 13.95 (*0-395-66414-4*, Clarion Bks) HM.

Jennings, Dana A. Me, Dad & No. 6. Sasaki, Goro, illus. LC 93-43640. 1995. write for info. (*0-15-200085-2*, Gulliver Bks) HarBrace.

Keefauver, John. The Three-Day Traffic Jam. LC 91-30583. 80p. (gr. 4-8). 1992. pap. 13.00 jacketed, 3-pc. bdg. (*0-671-75599-4*, S&S BFYR) S&S Trade.

Kowitt, Holly. The Fenderbenders Get Lost in America. 1991. pap. 2.95 (*0-590-44845-5*, Blue Ribbon Bks) Scholastic Inc.

Little Car. (ps-1). 2.49 (*0-517-48302-5*); pap. 2.49 (*0-517-46819-0*) Random Hse Value.

Maccarone, Grace. Cars! Cars! Cars! Carter, David A., illus. LC 94-18389. Date not set. 6.95 (*0-590-47572-X*) Scholastic Inc.

Mahy, Margaret. The Rattlebang Picnic. Kellogg, Steven, illus. LC 93-36294. (gr. 3 up). 1994. 14.99 (*0-8037-1318-5*); PLB 14.89 (*0-8037-1319-3*) Dial Bks Young.

Marshall, Val & Tester, Bronwyn. The Old Car. Axelsen, Stephen, illus. LC 92-27264. 1993. 3.75 (*0-383-03644-5*) SRA Schl Grp.

Montgomery, Raymond A. Behind the Wheel. 1992. pap. 3.25 (*0-553-29401-6*) Bantam.

Oxenbury, Helen. The Car Trip. Oxenbury, Helen, illus. 24p. (ps-1). 1983. 3.95 (*0-8037-0009-1*, 0383-120) Dial Bks Young.

Patrick, Denise L. The Car Washing Street. Ward, John, illus. LC 92-9229. 32p. (ps up). 1993. 14.00 (*0-688-11452-0*, Tambourine Bks); PLB 13.93 (*0-688-11453-9*, Tambourine Bks) Morrow.

Patron, Susan. Dark Cloud Strong Breeze. Catalanotto, Peter, illus. LC 93-4873. (gr. 5 up). 1994. write for info. (*0-531-06815-3*); PLB write for info. (*0-531-08665-8*) Orchard Bks Watts.

Paulsen, Gary. The Car. LC 93-41834. 1994. 13.95 (*0-15-292878-2*) HarBrace.

Peppe, Rodney. Huxley Pig's Model Car. (ps). 1991. pap. 8.95 (*0-385-30238-X*) Doubleday.

Ross, K. K. The Little Red Car. Alley, R. W., illus. LC 88-63930. 28p. (ps). 1990. 2.95 (*0-394-85376-8*) Random Bks Yng Read.

Rotunno, Rocco & Rotunno, Betsy. The Incredible Crash Dummies: The Dashboard Sandwich. (Illus.). 12p. (Orig.). (gr. 2-6). 1993. mixed media pkg. incl. stamp pad, stamps, box of 4 crayons 7.00 (*1-881980-06-5*) Noteworthy.

Santoro, Chris, illus. Lift the Hood, Find a Motor. LC 91-62581. 22p. (ps-k). 1993. 3.50 (*0-679-80903-1*) Random Bks Yng Read.

Smax, Willy. Benny the Breakdown Truck. Ludlow, Karen, illus. LC 93-50048. 64p. (gr. k-4). 1994. 16.00 (*0-517-59921-X*) Crown Bks Yng Read.

Spier, Peter. Tin Lizzie. Spier, Peter, illus. LC 74-1510. 48p. (gr. 3-5). 1990. 5.95 (*0-385-13342-1*); pap. 8.95 (*0-385-09470-1*) Doubleday.

Sutherland, Harry A. Dad's Car Wash. Chambliss, Maxie, illus. LC 93-28734. 32p. (ps-k). 1994. pap. 4.95 (*0-689-71807-1*, Aladdin) Macmillan Child Grp.

Tamboise, Pierre. A Trip by Torpedo. (Illus.). (gr. 3-8). 1992. PLB 8.95 (*0-89565-894-1*) Childs World.
Tucker, Sian. The Little Car. (Illus.). 10p. (ps-k). 1993. pap. 2.95 (*0-671-79737-9*, Little Simon) S&S Trade.
Wagner, Jenny. Motor Bill & the Lovely Caroline. Brooks, Ron, illus. LC 94-20241. Date not set. write for info. (*0-395-71547-4*) Ticknor & Flds Bks Yng Read.
Williams, Barbara. Author & Squinty Gritt. LC 90-37021. 80p. (gr. 2-5). 1990. 12.95 (*0-525-44655-9*, DCB) Dutton Child Bks.
Wilson, Nancy H. Helen & the Hudson Hornet. Young, Mary O., illus. LC 93-32321. 1995. 15.00 (*0-02-793076-9*, Maxwell Macmillan) Macmillan.
Wilson, Sarah. Garage Song. LC 91-393. (ps-3). 1994. pap. 4.95 (*0-671-88631-2*, Half Moon Bks) S&S Trade.

AUTOMOBILES–HISTORY

Coleman, John. Your Book of Veteran & Edwardian Cars. (gr. 7 up). 1972. 7.95 (*0-571-09375-2*) Transatl Arts.
Dale, Rodney. Early Cars. (Illus.). 64p. 1994. PLB 16.00 (*0-19-521002-6*) OUP.
Guttmacher, Peter. Jeep. LC 93-10476. (Illus.). 48p. (gr. 5-6). 1994. text ed. 13.95 RSBE (*0-89686-830-3*, Crestwood Hse) Macmillan Child Grp.
Haines, Shirley & Haines, Harry. BMW: Performance with Luxury. LC 92-43260. 1993. 17.26 (*0-86593-251-4*); 12.95s.p. (*0-685-66288-8*) Rourke Corp.
—Cadillac: Standard of the World. LC 92-42305. 1993. 17.26 (*0-86593-252-2*); 12.95s.p. (*0-685-66358-2*) Rourke Corp.
—Corvette: The American Sports Car. LC 93-18066. 1993. 17.26 (*0-86593-253-0*); 12.95s.p. (*0-685-66578-X*) Rourke Corp.
Parker, Steve. The Car. (Illus.). 32p. (gr. 5-8). 1993. PLB 12.40 (*0-531-17415-8*, Gloucester Pr) Watts.
Schleifer, Jay. Bugatti. LC 93-15491. (Illus.). 48p. (gr. 6 up). 1994. text ed. 13.95 RSBE (*0-89686-813-3*, Crestwood Hse) Macmillan Child Grp.
—Jaguar. LC 93-10529. (Illus.). 48p. (gr. 6 up). 1994. text ed. 13.95 RSBE (*0-89686-814-1*, Crestwood Hse) MacMillan Child Grp.
—Mercedes-Benz. LC 93-17505. (Illus.). 48p. (gr. 6 up). 1994. text ed. 13.95 RSBE (*0-89686-815-X*, Crestwood Hse) Macmillan Child Grp.
—Mustang. LC 91-27908. (Illus.). 48p. (gr. 5). 1992. text ed. 13.95 RSBE (*0-89686-699-8*, Crestwood Hse) Macmillan Child Grp.
—Thunderbird. LC 93-17241. (Illus.). 48p. (gr. 6 up). 1994. text ed. 13.95 RSBE (*0-89686-816-8*, Crestwood Hse) Macmillan Child Grp.
Simonds, Christopher. The Model T Ford. (Illus.). 64p. (gr. 5 up). 1991. PLB 12.95 (*0-382-24122-3*); pap. 7.95 (*0-382-24117-7*) Silver Burdett Pr.

AUTOMOBILES–LAWS AND REGULATIONS

see also Traffic Regulations

AUTOMOBILES–MODELS

Lutfy, Michael. Hot Wheels Race Team. (Illus.). 24p. (gr. 1 up). 1993. 7.95 (*0-8431-3472-0*, Troubador) Price Stern.
Sobol, Donald J. Encyclopedia Brown's Book of Wacky Cars. Enik, Ted, illus. 128p. (gr. 3-7). 1987. pap. 2.75 (*0-553-15512-1*, Skylark) Bantam.
Viemeister, Peter. Microcars. LC 82-90754. (Illus.). 136p. (Orig.). (gr. 5 up). 1982. pap. 10.95 (*0-9608598-0-2*) Hamiltons.
Young, Robert S. Miniature Vehicles. LC 92-33010. (Illus.). 72p. (gr. 5 up). 1993. text ed. 13.95 RSBE (*0-87518-518-5*, Dillon) Macmillan Child Grp.

AUTOMOBILES–MOTORS

see Automobiles–Engines

AUTOMOBILES–RACING

see Automobile Racing

AUTOMOBILES–REPAIRING

Florian, Douglas. An Auto Mechanic. LC 90-48809. (Illus.). 24p. (ps up). 1991. 13.95 (*0-688-10635-8*); PLB 13.88 (*0-688-10636-6*) Greenwillow.
—An Auto Mechanic. Florian, Douglas, illus. LC 93-28802. 24p. (ps up). 1994. pap. 4.95 (*0-688-13104-2*, Mulberry) Morrow.
Karwatka, Dennis, et al. Introductory Auto Mechanics. 608p. (gr. 9-12). 1986. text ed. 22.95 (*0-8219-0182-6*, 80452); wkbk. 6.95 (*0-8219-0183-4*, 80652); tchr's. guide 28.00 (*0-8219-0184-2*, 80902); transparency masters 89.00 (*0-8219-0489-2*, 80950) EMC.
Schaefer, Margaret A. Let's Build a Car. McRae, Patrick, illus. 32p. (gr. k-5). 1992. pap. 4.95 (*0-8249-8536-2*, Ideals Child) Hambleton-Hill.

AUTOMOBILES–REPAIRING–VOCATIONAL GUIDANCE

Broekel, Ray. I Can Be an Auto Mechanic. LC 85-11303. 32p. (gr. k-3). 1985. PLB 11.80 (*0-516-01885-X*); pap. 3.95 (*0-516-41885-8*) Childrens.

AUTOMOBILES–TOURING

Bingham, Mindy. Berta Benz & the Motorwagen. Maeno, Itoko, illus. 48p. (gr. 1-6). 1992. with dust jacket 14.95 (*0-911655-38-7*) Advocacy Pr.
Wood, Tim. Road Travel. LC 92-43978. (Illus.). 32p. (gr. 5-9). 1993. 14.95 (*1-56847-037-1*) Thomson Lrning.

AUTOSUGGESTION

see Hypnotism

AUTUMN

Allington, Richard L. & Krull, Kathleen. Autumn. Bond, Bruce, illus. LC 80-25190. 32p. (gr. k-3). 1985. pap. text ed. 3.95 (*0-8114-8242-1*) Raintree Steck-V.
Beach, Judy & Spencer, Kathleen. Minds-on Fun for Fall. (gr. k-4). 1991. pap. 9.95 (*0-86653-948-4*) Fearon Teach Aids.
Callinan, Karen. Autumn. Marden, Carol K., illus. 32p. (ps-2). Date not set. 11.95 (*1-56065-153-9*) Capstone Pr.
Chupick, Carol O. Celebrate Autumn. Grossman, Dan, illus. 144p. (gr. k-3). 1985. wkbk. 11.95 (*0-86653-264-1*, SS 838, Shining Star Pubns) Good Apple.
Fowler, Allan. Como Sabes Que Es Otono? How Do You Know It's Fall? LC 91-35060. (SPA., Illus.). 32p. (ps-2). 1992. PLB 10.75 (*0-516-34922-8*); pap. 3.95 (*0-516-54922-7*); big bk. 22.95 (*0-516-59623-3*) Childrens.
—How Do You Know It's Fall? LC 91-35060. (Illus.). 32p. (ps-2). 1992. PLB 10.75 (*0-516-04922-4*); PLB 22.95 big bk. (*0-516-49623-9*); pap. 3.95 (*0-516-44922-2*) Childrens.
Glover, Susanne & Grewe, Georgeann. A Splash of Fall. Grewe, Georgeann, illus. 128p. (gr. 2-5). 1987. pap. 11.95 (*0-86653-410-5*, GA1024) Good Apple.
Hirschi, Ron. Fall. Mangelsen, Thomas D., photos by. LC 90-19595. (Illus.). 32p. (ps-3). 1991. 14.00 (*0-525-65053-9*, Cobblehill Bks) Dutton Child Bks.
Maass, Robert. When Autumn Comes. Maass, Robert, photos by. LC 90-32069. (Illus.). 32p. (ps-2). 1990. 15. 95 (*0-8050-1259-1*, Owlet BYR) H Holt & Co.
Maestro, Betsy. Why Do Leaves Change Color? Krupinski, Loretta, illus. LC 93-9611. 32p. (gr. k-4). 1994. 15.00 (*0-06-022873-3*); PLB 14.89 (*0-06-022874-1*) HarpC Child Bks.
Markle, Sandra. Exploring Autumn. 160p. 1993. pap. 3.50 (*0-380-71910-X*, Camelot) Avon.
—Exploring Autumn: A Season of Science Activities, Puzzlers, & Games. Markle, Sandra, illus. LC 90-24209. 160p. (gr. 3-7). 1991. SBE 14.95 (*0-689-31620-8*, Atheneum Child Bk) Macmillan Child Grp.
Moncure, Jane B. Step into Fall: A New Season. Lexa-Senning, Susan, illus. LC 90-30637. 32p. (ps-2). 1990. PLB 19.95 (*0-89565-573-X*); PLB 13.95 (*0-685-56189-5*) Childs World.
Ottenheimer, Laurence. Livre de l'Automne. Galeron, Henri, illus. (FRE.). 90p. (gr. 4-9). 1983. 8.95 (*2-07-039506-5*) Schoenhof.
Pragoff, Fiona. Autumn. Pragoff, Fiona, illus. 20p. (ps). 1993. pap. 5.95 spiralbound (*0-689-71705-9*, Aladdin) Macmillan Child Grp.
Santrey, Louis. Autumn. Sabin, Francene, illus. LC 82-19396. 32p. (gr. 4-7). 1983. lib. bdg. 10.79 (*0-89375-905-8*); pap. text ed. 2.95 (*0-89375-906-6*) Troll Assocs.
Schweininger, Ann. Autumn Days. LC 93-16684. 32p. (ps-3). 1993. pap. 4.50 (*0-14-054055-5*, Puffin) Puffin Bks.
Simon, Seymour. Autumn Across America. Simon, Seymour, illus. LC 92-55043. 32p. (gr. 1-5). 1993. 14. 95 (*1-56282-467-8*); PLB 14.89 (*1-56282-468-6*) Hyprn Child.
Stone, Lynn M. Fall. LC 93-39057. 1994. write for info. (*1-55916-019-5*) Rourke Bk Co.
Thomson, Ruth. Autumn. LC 94-16940. (Illus.). 24p. (ps-3). 1994. PLB 14.40 (*0-516-07986-7*); pap. 4.95 (*0-516-47986-5*) Childrens.
Tresselt, Alvin R. Autumn Harvest. Duvoisin, Roger, illus. LC 51-8824. 32p. (gr. k-3). 1951. PLB 15.88 (*0-688-51155-4*) Lothrop.
Venino, Suzanne. What Happens in the Autumn? Crump, Donald J., ed. LC 82-47858. (ps-3). 1982. Set. 13.95 (*0-87044-452-2*); lib. bdg. 16.95 (*0-87044-465-4*) Natl Geog.
Webster, David. Fall. Steltenpohl, Jane, ed. Steadman, Barbara, illus. 48p. (gr. 2-4). 1989. (J Messner); pap. 5.95 (*0-671-65985-5*, J Messner) S&S Trade.
Zinkgraf, June & Bauman, Toni. Fall Fantasies. 240p. (gr. k-6). 1980. 15.95 (*0-916456-61-7*, GA 167) Good Apple.

AUTUMN–POETRY

Hull, Robert, ed. Poems for Autumn. LC 90-20590. (Illus.). 48p. (gr. 3-7). 1991. PLB 21.34 (*0-8114-7800-9*) Raintree Steck-V.

AVALANCHES

Facklam, Howard & Facklam, Margery. Avalanche! LC 90-45622. (Illus.). 48p. (gr. 5-6). 1991. text ed. 12.95 RSBE (*0-89686-598-3*, Crestwood Hse) Macmillan Child Grp.
Kramer, Stephen. Avalanche. Cone, Patrick, photos by. (Illus.). 48p. (gr. 1-4). 1991. PLB 17.50 (*0-87614-422-9*) Carolrhoda Bks.

AVIATION

see Aeronautics

AVIATORS

see Air Pilots

AZTECS

scc Indians of Mexico–Aztecs

B

BABIES

see Infants

BABOONS

Noble, Kate. Bubble Gum. Bass, Rachel, illus. 32p. (ps-3). 1992. 14.95 (*0-9631798-0-2*) Silver Seahorse.
Richmond, Gary. Barnaby Goes Wild, No. 7. (gr. 1-5). 1991. text ed. 6.99 (*0-8499-0914-7*) Word Inc.
Stone, Lynn. Baboons. (Illus.). 24p. (gr. k-5). 1990. lib. bdg. 11.94 (*0-86593-067-8*); lib. bdg. 8.95s.p. (*0-685-36315-5*) Rourke Corp.

BABY ANIMALS

see Animals–Infancy

BABY SITTERS

Anderson, Stephen E. Wee-Sitt Babysitting Guide. Trost, Ed, ed. Anderson, Stephen E., illus. (Orig.). (gr. 6-9). 1989. pap. 4.95 (*0-685-29145-6*) Chimurenga.
—Wee-Sitt Guide to Babysitting. Trost, Ed, ed. (Illus.). 21p. (Orig.). 1989. pap. text ed. 4.95 (*0-9624153-0-8*) Chimurenga.
Barkin, Carol & James, Elizabeth. The New Complete Babysitter's Handbook. Weston, Martha, illus. LC 93-39345. 1994. write for info. (*0-395-66557-4*, Clarion Bks); pap. write for info. (*0-395-66558-2*, Clarion Bks) HM.
Burgeson, Nancy. The Baby-Sitter's Guide. LC 91-14959. (Illus.). 32p. (gr. 5-9). 1991. pap. text ed. 1.95 (*0-8167-2467-9*) Troll Assocs.
Dayee, Frances S. Babysitting. LC 89-24773. (gr. 4-7). 1990. PLB 12.90 (*0-531-10908-9*) Watts.
Herzig, Alison C. & Mali, Jane L. Ten-Speed Babysitter. 144p. (gr. 2-9). 1988. pap. 2.95 (*0-8167-1368-5*) Troll Assocs.
Huff, Ocie B. The How-To's of Baby Sitting: A Baby Sitter's Handbook. 104p. (gr. 6-9). 1993. pap. 12.50 (*0-9633799-0-9*) Hlth Educ Srvs.

Hughey, Jodi. Basics to Baby-Sitting. Hughey, Jodi, illus. 30p. (Orig.). (gr. 5 up). 1994. pap. 5.95 (*1-885419-00-7*) Mtn-top Kip.
BASICS TO BABY-SITTING is designed as a how-to for those who love children & enjoy caring for them! The table of contents provides a look into BASICS TO BABY-SITTING & what it has to offer. INTRODUCTION briefly explains what is to be expected from BASICS TO BABY-SITTING. TWENTY-ONE HELPFUL HINTS is a list of ideas that can be done with the one(s) being watched. GETTING STARTED is a chapter on steps to be taken to start baby-sitting & who to baby-sit for. It is filled with thought-provoking ideas to help & be supportive. There are three short stories that follow: USING MY IMAGINATION, A WALKIN' EXPERIENCE & ONE CAT'S TALE. The stories are for entertaining & enjoyment. BASICS TO BABY-SITTING is written with enthusiasm. Each page is filled with support! How do you begin baby-sitting? Easy! With BASICS TO BABY-SITTING. For ordering, send check to: Mountain-top Kip Publications, P.O. Box 6, Dennison, OH 44621.
Publisher Provided Annotation.

Lansky, Vicki. Dear Babysitter Handbook. 60p. (gr. 7 up). 1990. pap. 3.95 (*0-916773-16-7*) Book Peddlers.
Loomis, Christine. My New Baby-Sitter. Ancona, George, photos by. LC 90-38527. (Illus.). 48p. (ps up). 1991. 13.95 (*0-688-09625-5*); PLB 13.88 (*0-688-09626-3*) Morrow Jr Bks.
Lowry, Lois. Taking Care of Terrific. LC 82-23331. 160p. (gr. 5 up). 1983. 14.95 (*0-395-34070-5*) HM.
Martin, Ann M. Baby-Sitters Club Guide to Baby-Sitting. (gr. 4-7). 1993. pap. 3.25 (*0-590-47686-6*) Scholastic Inc.
O'Keef, Richard D. How to Make More Money Babysitting: What Works, What Doesn't, & Why. LC 91-92960. (Illus.). 136p. (Orig.). (gr. 6-10). 1992. pap. 8.95 (*0-9630531-3-2*) Diamond Bks UT.
Salk, Lee & Litvin, Jay. How to Be a Super Sitter. 128p. (gr. 9 up). 1991. pap. 7.95 (*0-8442-8547-1*, VGM Career Bks) NTC Pub Grp.
Schneider, M. E. The Babysitter's Guide. (Orig.). (gr. 7-12). 1990. pap. 11.95 (*0-685-30792-1*) Marlin Pub.
Stuhring, Celeste. Kid Sitter Basics: A Handbook for Babysitters. (Illus.). 88p. 1994. pap. 11.00 (*0-933701-62-4*) Westport Pubs.

BABY SITTERS–FICTION

Alexander, Martha. Nobody Asked If I Wanted a Babysitter. (ps-3). 1993. pap. 3.99 (*0-14-054673-1*) Puffin Bks.
Benson, Rita. Looking after the Babysitter. Forss, Ian, illus. LC 93-26221. 1994. 4.25 (*0-383-03760-3*) SRA Schl Grp.
Black, Sonia & Brigandi, Pat. Baby-Sitters Club Notebook. (Illus.). (gr. 5 up). 1991. pap. 2.50 (*0-590-45074-3*) Scholastic Inc.

Blair, Cynthia. Warning: Baby-sitting May Be Hazardous to Your Health. 1993. pap. 3.99 (*0-449-70412-2*, Juniper) Fawcett.
Boyle, Kay. Winter Night. LC 92-44043. 1994. 13.95 (*0-88682-576-8*) Creative Ed.
Bradford, Jan. Caroline Zucker Meets Her Match. Ramsey, Marcy D., illus. LC 90-10813. 96p. (gr. 2-5). 1991. lib. bdg. 9.89 (*0-8167-2017-7*); pap. text ed. 2.95 (*0-8167-2018-5*) Troll Assocs.
Brandenberg, Franz. Leo & Emily & the Dragon. Aliki, illus. LC 83-14091. 56p. (gr. 1-3). 1984. 12.95 (*0-688-02531-5*); PLB 12.88 (*0-688-02532-3*) Greenwillow.
Brown Brothers & Sitter. 1985. incl. cass. 5.95 (*0-394-87662-8*) Random.
Brown, Fern G. Baby-Sitter on Horseback. (gr. 5 up). 1988. pap. 2.95 (*0-449-70283-9*, Juniper) Fawcett.
Brown, Marc T. Arthur Babysits. (Illus.). 32p. (ps-3). 1992. 14.95 (*0-316-11293-3*, Joy St Bks) Little.
Christelow, Eileen. Jerome the Babysitter. Christelow, Eileen, illus. LC 84-12738. 32p. (ps-3). 1987. pap. 4.95 (*0-89919-520-2*, Clarion Bks) HM.
Daniel, Kate. Babysitter's Nightmare. 1992. pap. 3.99 (*0-06-106773-3*, Harp PBks) HarpC.
Day, Alexandra. Good Dog Carl. LC 91-25274. (Illus.). 36p. (Orig.). (ps up). 1991. 11.95 (*0-671-75204-9*, Green Tiger) S&S Trade.
Endersby, Frank. The Baby Sitter. (gr. 4 up). 1981. 3.95 (*0-85953-271-2*) Childs Play.
Faucher, Elizabeth. Charles in Charge. 128p. (Orig.). (gr. 7 up). 1984. pap. 2.25 (*0-590-33550-2*, Point) Scholastic Inc.
Fletcher, Susan. Anti-Babysitter Plot. (gr. 4-7). 1994. pap. 2.95 (*0-590-46008-0*) Scholastic Inc.
Gorog, Judith. When Nobody's Home: Thirteen Tales for Tonight. LC 93-34595. 1994. 13.95 (*0-590-46862-6*) Scholastic Inc.
Green, Phyllis. Eating Ice Cream with a Werewolf. Stern, Patti, illus. LC 82-47727. 128p. (gr. 3-7). 1983. HarpC Child Bks.
Gregory, Valiska. Babysitting for Benjamin. Munsinger, Lynn, illus. LC 92-18373. 32p. (ps-3). 1993. 13.95 (*0-316-32785-9*) Little.
Grimes, N. Oh, Bother! Someone's Baby-Sitting! Disney's Winnie the Pooh Helping Hands Book. DiCiccio, Sue, illus. 24p. (ps-k). 1991. pap. write for info. (Golden Pr) Western Pub.
Hest, Amy. Nannies for Hire. Trivas, Irene, illus. LC 93-7040. 48p. (gr. 2 up). 1994. 15.00g (*0-688-12527-1*); PLB 14.93 (*0-688-12528-X*) Morrow Jr Bks.
Hodgeman, Ann. My Babysitter Has Fangs. Ashby, Ruth, ed. Pierard, John, illus. 128p. (Orig.). 1992. pap. 2.99 (*0-671-75868-3*, Minstrel Bks) PB.
Hodgman, Ann. My Babysitter Bites Again. Ashby, Ruth, ed. Pierard, John, illus. 144p. (Orig.). (gr. 3-6). 1993. pap. 2.99 (*0-671-79378-0*, Minstrel Bks) PB.
—My Babysitter Goes Bats. Ashby, Ruth, ed. 144p. (Orig.). 1994. pap. 3.50 (*0-671-88451-4*, Minstrel Bks) PB.
—My Babysitter Is a Vampire. Ashby, Ruth, ed. Pierard, John, illus. (Orig.). 1991. pap. 3.50 (*0-671-64751-2*, Minstrel Bks) PB.
Honeycutt, Natalie. Lydia Jane Bly & the Baby-Sitter Exchange. LC 92-46363. 128p. (gr. 2-6). 1993. SBE 13.95 (*0-02-744362-0*, Bradbury Pr) Macmillan Child Grp.
Hughes, Shirley. An Evening at Alfie's. Hughes, Shirley, illus. LC 84-11297. 32p. (ps-1). 1985. 14.95 (*0-688-04122-1*); PLB 14.88 (*0-688-04123-X*) Lothrop.
Jackson, Dave & Jackson, Neta. Secret Adventures Books, Episode 2: Snap. 100p. 1994. pap. 4.99 (*0-8054-4005-4*, 4240-05) Broadman.
Johnson, Angela. Shoes Like Miss Alice's. Page, Ken, illus. LC 93-4872. 1994. write for info. (*0-531-06814-5*); PLB write for info. (*0-531-08664-X*) Orchard Bks Watts.
Johnson, Dolores. What Kind of Baby-Sitter Is This? LC 90-42860. (Illus.). 32p. (gr. k-3). 1991. RSBE 13.95 (*0-02-747846-7*, Macmillan Child Bk) Macmillan Child Grp.
Johnson, Doug. Never Babysit the Hippopotamuses! Carter, Abby, illus. LC 93-18341. 32p. (ps-2). 1993. 14.95 (*0-8050-1873-5*, Bks Young Read) H Holt & Co.
Jukes, Mavis. Wild Iris Bloom. LC 90-24315. 192p. (gr. 5-9). 1992. 14.00 (*0-679-81891-X*) Knopf Bks Yng Read.
Keller, Beverly. Night the Baby-Sitter Didn't Come. (gr. 4-7). 1994. pap. 3.25 (*0-590-43726-7*) Scholastic Inc.
Kraus, Robert. Spider's Baby-Sitting Job. 1990. pap. 2.50 (*0-590-42445-9*) Scholastic Inc.
McAllister, Angela. The Babies of Cockle Bay. Jenkin-Pearce, Susie, illus. 32p. (ps-3). 1994. incl. dust jacket 13.95 (*0-8120-6424-0*); pap. 5.95 (*0-8120-1952-0*) Barron.
McKenna, Colleen O. The Brightest Light. 1992. 13.95 (*0-590-45347-5*, Scholastic Hardcover) Scholastic Inc.
Marshall, Val & Tester, Bronwyn. And Grandpa Sat on Friday. Spavern, Marilyn, illus. LC 92-34159. 1993. 4.25 (*0-383-03610-0*) SRA Schl Grp.
Martin, Ann M. Baby-Sitters at Shadow Lake Super Special. 1992. pap. 3.50 (*0-590-44962-1*) Scholastic Inc.
—Baby-Sitter's Club. (gr. 4 up). 1989. Set no. 5. pap. 11.00 (*0-590-63344-9*, SCHOLASTIC) Scholastic Inc.
—Baby-Sitters Club, Bks. 5-8. (gr. 4-7). 1990. pap. 13.00 boxed set (*0-590-63672-3*) Scholastic Inc.
—The Baby-Sitters Club, Bks. 9-12. (gr. 3-7). 1991. pap. 13.00 boxed set (*0-590-63701-0*) Scholastic Inc.
—The Baby-Sitters Club, Bks. 13-16. (gr. 3-7). 1991. pap. 13.00 boxed set (*0-590-63705-3*) Scholastic Inc.
—The Baby-Sitters Club, Bks. 17-20. (gr. 3-7). 1991. pap. 13.00 boxed set (*0-590-63704-5*) Scholastic Inc.
—The Baby-Sitters Club, Bks. 21-24. (gr. 3-7). 1991. pap. 13.00 boxed set (*0-590-63703-7*) Scholastic Inc.
—The Baby-Sitters Club, Bks. 25-28. (gr. 3-7). 1991. pap. 13.00 boxed set (*0-590-63702-9*) Scholastic Inc.
—Baby-Sitters Club, Bks. 29-32. (gr. 4-7). 1990. pap. 13.00 boxed set (*0-590-63583-2*) Scholastic Inc.
—Baby-Sitters Club, 4 vols, Bks. 33-36. (gr. 4-7). 1990. Boxed set. pap. 13.00 (*0-590-63669-3*) Scholastic Inc.
—Baby-Sitters Club, No. 45-48. (gr. 4-7). 1991. pap. 13.00 boxed set (*0-590-63963-3*) Scholastic Inc.
—The Baby-Sitters Little Sister, Bks. 9-12. (gr. 2-4). 1990. pap. 11.00 boxed set (*0-590-63668-5*) Scholastic Inc.
—Baby-Sitters on Board! (gr. 3-6). 1988. pap. 3.95 (*0-590-44240-6*) Scholastic Inc.
—The Baby-Sitters Remember. (gr. 4-7). 1994. pap. 3.95 (*0-590-47015-9*) Scholastic Inc.
—The BabySitters Club, 10 titles. large type ed. (gr. 4 up). 1993. Set. PLB 159.30 (*0-8368-1025-2*) Gareth Stevens Inc.
—Beware Dawn! 160p. 1991. pap. 3.25 (*0-590-44085-3*) Scholastic Inc.
—Claudia & Mean Janine. (gr. 4-7). 1987. pap. 3.50 (*0-590-43719-4*) Scholastic Inc.
—Claudia & Middle School. (gr. 4-7). 1991. pap. 3.25 (*0-590-44082-9*) Scholastic Inc.
—Claudia & the Bad Joke. 160p. (gr. 3-7). 1988. pap. 3.50 (*0-590-43510-8*) Scholastic Inc.
—Claudia & the Bad Joke. large type ed. 176p. (gr. 4 up). 1993. PLB 15.93 (*0-8368-1023-6*) Gareth Stevens Inc.
—Claudia & the Mystery at the Museum. 1993. pap. 3.50 (*0-590-47049-3*) Scholastic Inc.
—Claudia & the New Girl. large type ed. LC 93-15969. 176p. (gr. 4 up). 1993. PLB 15.93 (*0-8368-1016-3*) Gareth Stevens Inc.
—Claudia & the Phantom Phone Calls. 160p. (Orig.). (gr. 3-7). 1986. pap. 3.25 (*0-590-43513-2*) Scholastic Inc.
—Claudia: The Genius of Elm Street. 1991. pap. 3.25 (*0-590-44970-2*) Scholastic Inc.
—Claudia's Friend. (gr. 4-7). 1993. pap. 3.50 (*0-590-45665-2*) Scholastic Inc.
—Dawn & the Big Sleepover. (gr. 4-7). 1991. pap. 3.50 (*0-590-43573-6*) Scholastic Inc.
—Dawn & the Disappearing Dogs. (gr. 4-7). 1993. pap. 3.50 (*0-590-44960-5*) Scholastic Inc.
—Dawn & the We Kids Club. (gr. 4-7). 1994. pap. 3.50 (*0-590-47010-8*) Scholastic Inc.
—Dawn on the Coast. 1989. pap. 3.50 (*0-590-43900-6*) Scholastic Inc.
—Dawn Saves the Planet. 1992. 3.25 (*0-590-45658-X*, 052) Scholastic Inc.
—Dawn's Big Move. (gr. 4-7). 1993. pap. 3.50 (*0-590-47005-1*) Scholastic Inc.
—Dawn's Family Feud. (gr. 4-7). 1993. pap. 3.50 (*0-590-45666-0*) Scholastic Inc.
—Dawn's Wicked Stepsister. (gr. 4-7). 1990. pap. 3.25 (*0-590-42497-1*) Scholastic Inc.
—Get Well Soon, Mallory. (gr. 4-7). 1993. pap. 3.50 (*0-590-47007-8*) Scholastic Inc.
—Ghost at Dawn's House. 1993. pap. 3.50 (*0-590-43508-6*) Scholastic Inc.
—Good-Bye, Stacy, Good-Bye. large type ed. LC 93-4345. 176p. (gr. 4 up). 1993. PLB 15.93 (*0-8368-1017-1*) Gareth Stevens Inc.
—Goodbye Stacey, Goodbye. 1993. pap. 3.25 (*0-590-43386-5*) Scholastic Inc.
—Hello Mallory. 1993. pap. 3.25 (*0-590-43385-7*) Scholastic Inc.
—Hello, Mallory. large type ed. 176p. (gr. 4 up). 1993. PLB 15.93 (*0-8368-1018-X*) Gareth Stevens Inc.
—Jessi & the Awful Secret. (gr. 4-7). 1993. pap. 3.50 (*0-590-45663-6*) Scholastic Inc.
—Jessi & the Bad Baby-Sitter. 1993. pap. 3.50 (*0-590-47006-X*) Scholastic Inc.
—Jessi & the Dance School Phantom. 160p. (gr. 3-7). 1991. pap. 3.50 (*0-590-44083-7*, Apple Paperbacks) Scholastic Inc.
—Jessi and the Jewel Thieves: Baby-sitters Club Mystery Ser. (gr. 4-7). 1993. pap. 3.50 (*0-590-44959-1*) Scholastic Inc.
—Jessi's Baby Sitter. (gr. 4-7). 1990. pap. 3.50 (*0-590-43565-5*) Scholastic Inc.
—Jessi's Gold Medal. 1992. pap. 3.25 (*0-590-44964-8*, Apple Paperbacks) Scholastic Inc.
—Jessi's Horrible Prank. (gr. 4-7). 1994. pap. 3.50 (*0-590-47013-2*) Scholastic Inc.
—Jessi's Secret Language. 1993. pap. 3.50 (*0-590-44234-1*) Scholastic Inc.
—Jessi's Wish. (gr. 4 up). 1993. pap. 3.50 (*0-685-66003-6*) Scholastic Inc.
—Karen's Baby. (gr. 4-7). 1992. pap. 3.25 (*0-590-45649-0*) Scholastic Inc.
—Karen's Baby-Sitter. (gr. 4-7). 1994. pap. 2.95 (*0-590-47045-0*) Scholastic Inc.
—Karen's Big Top. (gr. 4-7). 1994. pap. 2.95 (*0-590-48229-7*) Scholastic Inc.
—Karen's Campout. (gr. 3-7). 1993. pap. 3.25 (*0-590-46911-8*) Scholastic Inc.
—Karen's Prize. 1990. pap. 2.95 (*0-590-43650-3*) Scholastic Inc.
—Karen's Snowy Day. (gr. 4-7). 1993. pap. 2.95 (*0-590-45650-4*) Scholastic Inc.
—Keep Out, Claudia! 160p. (gr. 3-7). 1992. pap. 3.50 (*0-590-45657-1*, Apple Paperbacks) Scholastic Inc.
—Kristy & the Baby Parade. 160p. (gr. 3-7). 1991. pap. 3.50 (*0-590-43574-4*) Scholastic Inc.
—Kristy & the Baby Parade. 154p. 1992. text ed. 12.32 (*1-56956-118-4*) W A T Braille.
—Kristy & the Copycat. (gr. 4-7). 1994. pap. 3.50 (*0-590-47012-4*) Scholastic Inc.
—Kristy and the Haunted Mansion. (gr. 4-7). 1993. pap. 3.50 (*0-590-44958-3*) Scholastic Inc.
—Kristy & the Missing Child: Baby-Sitters Club Mystery, No. 4. 160p. 1992. pap. 3.25 (*0-590-44800-5*) Scholastic Inc.
—Kristy & the Mother's Day Surprise. (gr. 4-7). 1989. pap. 3.50 (*0-590-43506-X*) Scholastic Inc.
—Kristy & the Snobs. 1993. pap. 3.50 (*0-590-43660-0*) Scholastic Inc.
—Kristy & the Snobs. large type ed. LC 93-15968. 176p. (gr. 4 up). 1993. PLB 15.93 (*0-8368-1015-5*) Gareth Stevens Inc.
—Kristy & the Vampires. (gr. 4-7). 1994. pap. 3.50 (*0-590-47053-1*) Scholastic Inc.
—Kristy & the Walking Disaster. 1993. pap. 3.50 (*0-590-43722-4*) Scholastic Inc.
—Kristy & the Walking Disaster. large type ed. 176p. (gr. 4 up). 1993. PLB 15.93 (*0-8368-1024-4*) Gareth Stevens Inc.
—Kristy and the Worst Kid Ever. (gr. 4-7). 1993. pap. 3.50 (*0-590-45664-4*) Scholastic Inc.
—Kristy for President. 160p. 1992. pap. 3.25 (*0-590-44967-2*) Scholastic Inc.
—Kristy's Great Idea. 1991. collector's ed. 9.95 (*0-590-44816-1*, Scholastic Hardcover) Scholastic Inc.
—Kristy's Great Idea. 1993. pap. 3.25 (*0-590-43388-1*) Scholastic Inc.
—Kristy's Mystery Admirer. (gr. 4-7). 1990. pap. 3.25 (*0-590-43567-1*) Scholastic Inc.
—Little Miss Stoneybrook & Dawn. 160p. (gr. 3-7). 1988. pap. 3.25 (*0-590-43717-8*) Scholastic Inc.
—Logan Bruno, Boy Baby-Sitter. (gr. 3-7). 1993. pap. 3.50 (*0-590-47118-X*) Scholastic Inc.
—Logan Likes Mary Anne! 1993. pap. 3.50 (*0-590-43387-3*) Scholastic Inc.
—Logan Likes Maryanne. 160p. (Orig.). (gr. 4-6). 1988. pap. 2.75 (*0-590-41124-1*, Apple Paperbacks) Scholastic Inc.
—Logan's Story (Special Edition Reader's Request) 1992. pap. 3.25 (*0-590-45575-3*, Apple Paperbacks) Scholastic Inc.
—Maid Mary Anne. (gr. 4-7). 1993. pap. 3.50 (*0-590-47004-3*) Scholastic Inc.
—Mallory & the Ghost Cat. 160p. 1992. pap. 3.25 (*0-590-44799-8*) Scholastic Inc.
—Mallory & the Secret Diary. (gr. 5 up). 1989. pap. 3.25 (*0-590-42500-5*, Apple Paperbacks) Scholastic Inc.
—Mallory & the Trouble with Twins. 1993. pap. 3.25 (*0-590-43507-8*) Scholastic Inc.
—Mallory Hates Boys (& Gym) 1992. 3.25 (*0-590-45660-1*) Scholastic Inc.
—Mallory on Strike. (gr. 4-7). 1991. pap. 3.50 (*0-590-44971-0*) Scholastic Inc.
—Mallory's Dream Horse. 160p. 1992. pap. 3.25 (*0-590-44965-6*) Scholastic Inc.
—Mary Anne & Miss Priss. (gr. 4-7). 1994. pap. 3.50 (*0-590-47011-6*) Scholastic Inc.
—Mary Anne & the Library Mystery. (gr. 4-7). 1994. pap. 3.50 (*0-590-47051-5*) Scholastic Inc.
—Mary Anne & the Search for Tigger. 1993. pap. 3.50 (*0-590-43347-4*) Scholastic Inc.
—Mary Anne & the Secret in the Attic. 160p. (gr. 3-7). 1992. pap. 3.25 (*0-590-44801-3*, Apple Paperbacks) Scholastic Inc.
—Mary Anne & Too Many Babies. 160p. 1992. pap. 3.25 (*0-590-44966-4*) Scholastic Inc.
—Mary Anne Saves the Day. 1993. pap. 3.50 (*0-590-43512-4*) Scholastic Inc.
—Mary Anne vs. Logan. (gr. 4-7). 1991. pap. 3.50 (*0-590-43570-1*) Scholastic Inc.
—Mary Anne's Bad Luck Mystery. 144p. (gr. 3-7). 1988. 3.50 (*0-590-43659-7*) Scholastic Inc.
—Mary Anne's Bad-Luck Mystery. large type ed. LC 93-4346. 176p. (gr. 4 up). 1993. PLB 15.93 (*0-8368-1021-X*) Gareth Stevens Inc.
—Mary Anne's Makeover. (gr. 4-7). 1993. pap. 3.50 (*0-590-45662-8*) Scholastic Inc.
—The Mystery at Claudia's House. 1992. 3.25 (*0-590-44961-3*) Scholastic Inc.
—New York, New York. (gr. 4-7). 1991. pap. 3.50 (*0-590-43576-0*) Scholastic Inc.
—Sea City, Here We Come! (gr. 3-7). 1993. pap. 3.95 (*0-590-45674-1*) Scholastic Inc.
—Secret Santa. LC 93-48981. 1994. 14.95 (*0-590-48295-5*) Scholastic Inc.
—Snowbound. 240p. 1991. pap. 3.95 (*0-590-44963-X*) Scholastic Inc.
—Stacey & the Cheerleaders. (gr. 4-7). 1993. pap. 3.50 (*0-590-47008-6*) Scholastic Inc.
—Stacey & the Mystery at the Mall. (gr. 4-7). 1994. pap. 3.50 (*0-590-47052-3*) Scholastic Inc.
—Stacey & the Mystery Money. (gr. 4-7). 1993. pap. 3.50 (*0-590-45696-2*) Scholastic Inc.
—Stacey's Big Crush. (gr. 4-7). 1993. pap. 3.50 (*0-590-45667-9*) Scholastic Inc.
—Stacey's Emergency. (gr. 4-7). 1991. pap. 3.50 (*0-590-43572-8*) Scholastic Inc.
—Stacey's Ex-Best Friend. 160p. 1992. pap. 3.25 (*0-590-44968-0*) Scholastic Inc.

—Stacey's Lie. (gr. 4-7). 1994. pap. 3.50 (*0-590-47014-0*) Scholastic Inc.
—Stacey's Mistake. 1993. pap. 3.50 (*0-590-43718-6*) Scholastic Inc.
—Stacey's Mistake. large type ed. LC 93-8086. 176p. (gr. 4 up). 1993. PLB 15.93 (*0-8368-1022-8*) Gareth Stevens Inc.
—Starring the Baby-Sitters Club. (gr. 4-7). 1992. pap. 3.95 (*0-590-45661-X*) Scholastic Inc.
—The Truth about Stacey. 1993. pap. 3.25 (*0-590-43511-6*) Scholastic Inc.
—Welcome Back, Stacey. (gr. 5 up). 1989. pap. 3.25 (*0-590-42501-3*, Apple Paperbacks) Scholastic Inc.
Miranda, Anne. Baby-Sit, Vol. 1. (ps). 1990. 9.95 (*0-316-57454-6*, Joy St Bks) Little.
Oh, Bother! Someone's Baby-Sitting! (Illus.). (ps-3). 1991. write for info. (*0-307-12634-X*, Golden Pr) Western Pub.
Pascal, Francine. Jessica the Babysitter. (gr. 4-7). 1991. pap. 2.99 (*0-553-15838-4*) Bantam.
Quackenbush, Robert. Henry Babysits. Quackenbush, Robert, illus. 48p. (ps-2). 1990. pap. 2.95 (*0-448-04338-6*, G&D) Putnam Pub Group.
—Henry Babysits. LC 93-15472. 1993. PLB 13.27 (*0-8368-0968-8*) Gareth Stevens Inc.
Roberts, Willo D. Baby-Sitting Is a Dangerous Job. LC 84-20445. 192p. (gr. 4-6). 1985. SBE 14.95 (*0-689-31100-1*, Atheneum Child Bk) Macmillan Child Grp.
—Baby-Sitting Is a Dangerous Job. 144p. 1987. pap. 3.99 (*0-449-70177-8*, Juniper) Fawcett.
Robertson, Keith. Henry Reed's Baby-Sitting Service. McCloskey, Robert, illus. (gr. 5-8). 1966. pap. 14.95 (*0-670-36825-3*) Viking Child Bks.
Ross, Anna. Say Bye-Bye. Gorbaty, Norman, illus. LC 90-52915. 24p. (ps). 1992. 3.95 (*0-394-85485-3*) Random Bks Yng Read.
Ross, Pat. M & M & the Bad News Babies. Hafner, Marylin, illus. 48p. (ps-3). 1985. pap. 3.95 (*0-14-031851-8*, Puffin) Puffin Bks.
Saunders, Susan. Patti's New Look. 80p. (Orig.). (gr. 4-6). 1988. pap. 2.50 (*0-590-40644-2*, Apple Paperbacks) Scholastic Inc.
Stahl, Hilda. Kathy's Baby-Sitting Hassle. 160p. (gr. 4-7). 1992. pap. 3.99 (*0-89107-659-X*) Crossway Bks.
Steel, Danielle. Max & the Baby-Sitter. Rogers, Jacqueline, illus. (ps-2). 1989. 8.95 (*0-385-29796-3*) Delacorte.
Stevens, Kathleen. The Beast & the Babysitter. Bowler, Ray, illus. LC 88-42917. 32p. (gr. 2-3). 1989. PLB 18.60 (*1-55532-929-2*) Gareth Stevens Inc.
Stine, R. L. The Baby-Sitter. 176p. (Orig.). (gr. 7 up). 1989. pap. 3.50 (*0-590-44236-8*, Point) Scholastic Inc.
Travers, Pamela L. Mary Poppins in Cherry Tree Lane. (gr. 3-7). 1992. 3.50 (*0-440-40637-4*, YB) Dell.
Tulloch, Richard. Being Bad for the Baby-Sitter. (gr. 4-7). 1994. pap. 2.95 (*0-590-46061-7*) Scholastic Inc.
Waggoner, Karen. Lemonade Babysitter. (ps-3). 1992. 14.95 (*0-316-91711-7*, Joy St Bks) Little.
Weyn, Suzanne. Baby-Sitter Go Home. 96p. 1992. pap. 2.75 (*0-590-43561-2*) Scholastic Inc.
—Checking In. LC 89-49703. 128p. (gr. 4-8). 1991. lib. bdg. 9.89 (*0-8167-2003-7*); pap. text ed. 2.95 (*0-8167-2004-5*) Troll Assocs.
—Liza's Lucky Break. LC 89-77117. 128p. (gr. 4-8). 1991. lib. bdg. 9.89 (*0-8167-2007-X*); pap. text ed. 2.95 (*0-8167-2008-8*) Troll Assocs.
—True Blue. LC 90-10830. 128p. (gr. 4-8). 1991. PLB 9.89 (*0-8167-2005-3*); pap. text ed. 2.95 (*0-8167-2006-1*) Troll Assocs.
White, Susan. Bad Baby-Sitter's Handbook. (gr. 4-7). 1992. pap. 2.99 (*0-440-40633-1*, YB) Dell.
Winthrop, Elizabeth. Bear's Christmas Surprise. Brewster, Patience, illus. LC 90-26414. 32p. (ps-3). 1991. reinforced 14.95 (*0-8234-0888-4*) Holiday.
Wolff, Virginia E. Make Lemonade. large type ed. LC 93-21003. (gr. 9-12). 1993. 15.95 (*0-7862-0056-1*) Thorndike Pr.
Wright, Susan K. Death by Babysitting. 168p. (Orig.). (gr. 4-8). 1994. pap. 5.95 (*0-8361-3694-2*) Herald Pr.

BACH, JOHANN SEBASTIAN, 1685-1750

Greene, Carol. Johann Sebastian Bach: Great Man of Music. Dobson, Steven, illus. LC 92-7373. 48p. (gr. k-3). 1992. PLB 12.85 (*0-516-04251-3*) Childrens.
—Johann Sebastian Bach: Great Man of Music. Dobson, Steven, illus. LC 92-7373. 48p. (gr. k-3). 1993. pap. 4.95 (*0-516-44251-1*) Childrens.
Patton, Barbara W. Introducing Johann Sebastian Bach. (Illus.). 48p. (Orig.). (gr. 3-9). 1992. pap. 6.95x (*1-878636-01-4*) Soundboard Bks.
Rachlin, Ann. Bach. Hellard, Susan, illus. LC 92-9520. 1992. 5.95 (*0-8120-4991-8*) Barron.

BACILLI

see Bacteriology

BACKPACKING

Boy Scouts of America Staff. Venture Backpacking. (Illus.). 82p. 1990. pap. 3.15 (*0-8395-3442-6*, 33442) BSA.
Holmes, Jimmy. Backpacking. (Illus.). 48p. (gr. 4-12). 1992. PLB 17.50 (*0-8225-2479-1*) Lerner Pubns.
Petersen, P. J. Nobody Else Can Walk It for You. LC 81-69669. 224p. (gr. 7 up). 1982. 12.95 (*0-385-28730-5*) Delacorte.
Tjepkema, Edith R. The Mountains of Paradise. 120p. (Orig.). (gr. 8-12). 1993. pap. 4.95 (*0-9620280-5-3*) Northland Pr.

BACTERIA

see Bacteriology

BACTERIOLOGY

see also Immunity; Microorganisms

Asimov, Isaac. How Did We Find Out about Germs. Wool, David, illus. LC 73-81402. 64p. (gr. 5-8). 1973. PLB 10.85 (*0-8027-6166-6*) Walker & Co.
Berger, Melvin. Germs Make Me Sick! Hafner, Marilyn, illus. LC 84-45334. 32p. (ps-3). 1985. (Crowell Jr Bks); PLB 14.89 (*0-690-04429-1*) HarpC Child Bks.
—Germs Make Me Sick! Hafner, Marylin, illus. LC 84-45334. 32p. (ps-3). 1987. (Trophy); pap. 4.95 (*0-06-445053-8*, Trophy) HarpC Child Bks.
—Germs Make Me Sick! Hafner, Marylin, illus. LC 93-27059. 1995. 15.00 (*0-06-024249-3*); PLB 14.89 (*0-06-024250-7*) HarpC Child Bks.
Facklam, Howard & Facklam, Margery. Bacteria. (Illus.). 64p. (gr. 5-8). 1994. bds. 15.95 (*0-8050-2857-9*) TFC Bks NY.
Friedman, Ellen. Bacteria. LC 94-3157. 40p. 1994. 18.95 (*0-88682-710-8*) Creative Ed.
LeMaster, Leslie J. Bacteria & Viruses. LC 84-27414. (Illus.). 48p. (gr. k-4). 1985. PLB 12.85 (*0-516-01937-6*) Childrens.
Rice, Judith A. Those Mean Nasty Dirty Downright Disgusting but...Invisible Germs. Merrill, Reed, illus. Gwaltney, Jack M., Jr. LC 89-34409. (Illus.). 32p. (Orig.). (ps-3). 1989. pap. 7.95 (*0-934140-46-4*) Redleaf Pr.
Sabin, Francene. Microbes & Bacteria. Acosta, Andres, illus. LC 84-2749. 32p. (gr. 3-6). 1985. PLB 9.49 (*0-8167-0232-2*); pap. text ed. 2.95 (*0-8167-0233-0*) Troll Assocs.

BACTERIOLOGY–HISTORY

Asimov, Isaac. How Did We Find Out about Germs. Wool, David, illus. LC 73-81402. 64p. (gr. 5-8). 1973. PLB 10.85 (*0-8027-6166-6*) Walker & Co.

BADEN-POWELL OF GILWELL, ROBERT STEPHENSON SMYTH BADEN-POWELL, 1ST BARON, 1857-1941

Brower, Pauline. Baden-Powell: Founder of the Boy Scouts. LC 89-33750. 32p. (gr. 2-4). 1989. PLB 11.80 (*0-516-04173-8*) Childrens.

BADGES OF HONOR

see Decorations of Honor

BADGERS–FICTION

Banks, Martin. Discovering Badgers. Caulkins, Janet, ed. (Illus.). 48p. (gr. 1-6). 1988. PLB 12.40 (*0-531-18225-8*, Pub. by Bookwright Pr) Watts.
Boyle, Doe & Thomas, Peter, eds. Earth Day Every Day: From an Original Article which Appeared in Ranger Rick Magazine, Copyright National Wildlife Federation. Beylon, Cathy, illus. LC 92-27292. 20p. (gr. k-3). 1993. 6.95 (*0-924483-82-2*); incl. audio tape 9.95 (*0-924483-85-7*); incl. audio tape & 13 inch plush toy 35.95 (*0-924483-86-5*); incl. 9 inch plush toy 21.95 (*0-924483-88-1*) Soundprints.
Brewster, Patience. Two Bushy Badgers. LC 92-40696. 1995. 14.95 (*0-316-10862-6*) Little.
Carlstrom, Nancy W. No Nap for Benjamin Badger. Nolan, Dennis, illus. LC 90-42564. 32p. (ps-1). 1991. RSBE 13.95 (*0-02-717285-6*, Macmillan Child Bk) Macmillan Child Grp.
Hoban, Russell. Baby Sister for Frances. Hoban, Lillian, illus. LC 92-32603. 32p. (ps-3). 1964. 15.00 (*0-06-022335-9*); PLB 14.89 (*0-06-022336-7*) HarpC Child Bks.
—A Bargain for Frances. Hoban, Lillian, illus. LC 91-12267. 64p. (gr. k-3). 1978. pap. 3.50 (*0-06-444001-X*, Trophy) HarpC Child Bks.
—Bedtime for Frances. Williams, Garth, illus. LC 60-8347. 32p. (gr. k-3). 1960. 14.00 (*0-06-022350-2*); PLB 13.89 (*0-06-022351-0*) HarpC Child Bks.
—Best Friends for Frances. Hoban, Lillian, illus. LC 92-38401. 32p. (ps-3). 1969. 15.00 (*0-06-022327-8*); PLB 14.89 (*0-06-022328-6*) HarpC Child Bks.
—Birthday for Frances. Hoban, Lillian, illus. LC 68-24321. 32p. (gr. k-3). 1968. 15.00 (*0-06-022338-3*); PLB 14.89 (*0-06-022339-1*) HarpC Child Bks.
—Bread & Jam for Frances. Hoban, Lillian, illus. LC 92-13622. 32p. (ps-3). 1965. 15.00 (*0-06-022359-6*); PLB 14.89 (*0-06-022360-X*) HarpC Child Bks.
—Bread & Jam for Frances. Hoban, Lillian, illus. LC 92-13622. 32p. (ps-3). 1986. pap. 4.95 (*0-06-443096-0*, Trophy) HarpC Child Bks.
Lewis, Naomi. Hare & Badger Go to Town. Ross, Tony, illus. 32p. (ps-1). 1987. 9.95 (*0-905478-94-0*, Pub. by Century UK) Trafalgar.
Maris, Ron. Hello, Baby Badger. (Illus.). 32p. (ps-1). Date not set. 16.95 (*1-85681-261-8*, Pub. by J MacRae UK) Trafalgar.
Sargent, Dave & Sargent, Pat. Buddy Badger. Sapaugh, Blaine, illus. 48p. (Orig.). (gr. k-8). 1993. text ed. 11.95 (*1-56763-036-7*); pap. text ed. 5.95 (*1-56763-037-5*) Ozark Pub.

BAHAISM

Baha'u'llah. Blessed Is the Spot. Stevenson, Anna, illus. LC 58-8815. (gr. k-2). 1958. 14.50 (*0-87743-014-4*, 352-040) Bahai.
Effendi, Shoghi. Your True Brother. Weinberg, Robert & Weinberg, Robertcompiled by. (Illus.). 24p. (Orig.). (gr. 8-10). 1991. pap. 7.50 (*0-85398-324-0*) G Ronald Pub.
Garst, Hitjo. From Mountain to Mountain: Stories about Baha'u'llah. McKinley, Olive, tr. from DUT. Parsons, Brian, illus. 138p. (gr. 3-4). 1988. 20.95 (*0-85398-265-1*) G Ronald Pub.
Heller, Wendy. My Name Is Nabil. (Illus.). 48p. (gr. 3-6). 1981. 11.95 (*0-933770-17-0*) Kalimat.
Lee, Anthony A. The Cornerstone: A Story About 'Abdu'l-Baha in America. Irvine, Rex J., illus. 24p. (Orig.). (gr. k-5). 1979. pap. 3.00 (*0-933770-01-4*) Kalimat.
—The Scottish Visitors: A Story about 'Abdu'l-Baha in Britain. Irving, Rex J., illus. 24p. (Orig.). (gr. k-5). 1981. pap. 3.00 (*0-933770-04-9*) Kalimat.
—The Unfriendly Governor. Irvine, Rex John, illus. 24p. (gr. k-5). 1980. pap. 3.00 (*0-933770-02-2*) Kalimat.

BAHAMAS

Greenfield, Eloise. Under the Sunday Tree. Ferguson, Amos, illus. LC 87-29373. 48p. (ps-1). 1988. PLB 14.89 (*0-06-022257-3*) HarpC Child Bks.
McCulla, Patricia E. Bahamas. (Illus.). 104p. (gr. 5 up). 1988. lib. bdg. 14.95 (*1-55546-191-3*) Chelsea Hse.

BAJA, CALIFORNIA–FICTION

Taylor, Theodore. Sweet Friday Island. LC 93-32435. (gr. 7 up). 1994. write for info. (*0-15-200009-7*); pap. write for info. (*0-15-200012-7*) HarBrace.

BAKERS AND BAKERIES

Curtis, Neil & Greenland, Peter. How Bread Is Made. (Illus.). 24p. (gr. 1-3). 1992. PLB 13.50 (*0-8225-2375-2*) Lerner Pubns.
Moncure, Jane B. What Was It Before It Was Bread? Hygaard, Elizabeth, illus. LC 85-11402. 32p. (ps-2). 1985. PLB 14.95 (*0-89565-323-0*) Childs World.
Whitmore, Arvella. Bread Winner. (gr. 4-7). 1990. 13.45 (*0-395-53705-3*) HM.
Ziegler, Sandra. A Visit to the Bakery. Pilot Productions Staff, photos by. LC 86-32647. (Illus.). 32p. (ps-3). 1987. PLB 11.45 (*0-516-01495-1*) Childrens.

BAKING

see also Bread; Cake

Anglund, Joan W. A Christmas Cookie Book. LC 77-78293. (Illus.). 1982. Repr. of 1977 ed. 3.95 (*0-915696-07-X*) Determined Prods.
Carlson, Anna L. & Wynne, Diana. My Brother & I Like Cookies. 2nd. ed. Wynne, Diana, illus. LC 80-81624. 96p. (Orig.). (gr. 1-7). 1983. pap. 4.95 (*0-939938-00-6*) Karwyn Ent.
Carlson, Faith. A Cookie Christmas. Carlson, Faith, illus. 28p. (Orig.). (ps-2). 1986. pap. 5.00 (*0-932591-05-1*) Baggeboda Pr.
Coyle, Rena. My First Baking Book. Arnold, Tedd, illus. LC 87-40646. 144p. (gr. 1-5). 1988. pap. 9.95 (*0-89480-579-7*, 1579) Workman Pub.
Drew, Helen. My First Baking Book. LC 91-10239. (Illus.). 48p. (gr. 2-6). 1991. 12.00 (*0-679-81545-7*); lib. bdg. 13.99 (*0-679-91545-1*) Knopf Bks Yng Read.
Oppenneer, Betsy. Betsy's Breads. rev. ed. (Illus.). 70p. (gr. 8 up). 1991. pap. 7.95 (*0-9627665-2-6*) Breadworks.
Rosin, Arielle. Eclairs & Brown Bears. Czap, Daniel, photos by. Collomb, Etienne. LC 93-24971. (Illus.). 60p. (gr. 3 up). 1994. 12.95 (*0-395-68380-7*) Ticknor & Flds Bks Yng Read.
Stephens, Fran. Baking Projects for Children. (Illus.). 128p. (ps-4). PLB 16.95 (*1-878363-62-X*) Forest Hse.
—Baking Projects for Children: Fun Foods to Make with Children from 4 to 10. Macdonald, Roland B. & Gray, Dan, illus. 128p. (gr. k-5). 1991. pap. 9.95 (*1-878767-10-0*) Murdoch Bks.

BAKING–FICTION

Addison-Wesley Staff. The Gingerbread Man Little Book. (Illus.). 16p. (gr. k-3). 1989. pap. text ed. 4.50 (*0-201-19054-0*) Addison-Wesley.
Allard, Harry. The Cactus Flower Bakery. Delaney, Ned, illus. LC 90-36565. 32p. (ps-3). 1993. pap. 4.95 (*0-06-443297-1*, Trophy) HarpC Child Bks.
Carle, Eric. Walter the Baker. LC 93-20124. (gr. 1-8). 1993. 15.95 (*0-88708-331-5*) Picture Bk Studio.
Chalmers, Mary. Take a Nap, Harry. Chalmers, Mary, illus. LC 89-77655. 32p. (ps-2). 1991. PLB 13.89 (*0-06-021244-6*) HarpC Child Bks.
Christelow, Eileen. Don't Wake up Mama! Another Five Little Monkeys Story. Christelow, Eileen, illus. 32p. (ps-3). 1992. 13.95 (*0-395-60176-2*, Clarion Bks) HM.
Cumpiano, Ina. Pan, Pan, Gran Pan (Small Book) Murdocca, Sal, illus. (SPA.). 16p. (Orig.). (gr. k-3). 1992. pap. text ed. 6.00 (*1-56334-085-2*) Hampton-Brown.
Elish, Dan. The Worldwide Dessert Contest. Gurney, John, illus. LC 87-24694. 208p. (gr. 4-6). 1988. 13.95 (*0-531-05752-6*); PLB 13.99 (*0-531-08352-7*) Orchard Bks Watts.
Gilson, Jamie. Can't Catch Me, I'm the Gingerbread Man. LC 80-39748. 192p. (gr. 5-9). 1981. 12.95 (*0-688-00435-0*); PLB 12.88 (*0-688-00436-9*) Lothrop.
Hayward, Linda. The Biggest Cookie in the World. Ewers, Joe, illus. LC 94-21151. 1995. write for info. (*0-679-87146-2*); PLB write for info. (*0-679-97146-7*) Random Bks Yng Read.
Hennessy, B. G. Jake Baked the Cake. Morgan, Mary, illus. 32p. (ps-3). 1992. pap. 3.99 (*0-14-050882-1*) Puffin Bks.
Lenihan, Edmund. Fionn MacCumhail & the Baking Hags. 128p. 1994. pap. 9.95 (*1-85635-071-1*, Pub. by Mercier Pr ER) Dufour.
McGuire, Leslie. Miss Mopp's Lucky Day. Silver, Jody, illus. LC 81-4879. 48p. (ps-3). 1982. 5.95 (*0-8193-1061-1*); PLB 5.95 (*0-8193-1062-X*) Parents.
McOmber, Rachel B., ed. McOmber Phonics Storybooks: The Cake. rev. ed. (Illus.). write for info. (*0-944991-44-0*) Swift Lrn Res.
Mayer, Marianna. Marcel the Pastry Chef. McDermott, Gerald, illus. 32p. (ps-3). 1991. 14.95 (*0-553-05192-X*) Bantam.

Morris, Ann. Bread, Bread, Bread: Big Book Edition. 32p. (gr. k up). 1993. pap. 18.95 (*0-688-12939-0*, Mulberry) Morrow.

Myers, Edward. Forri the Baker. Natchev, Alexi, photos by. LC 93-2468. 1994. write for info. (*0-8037-1396-7*, MR-291-AF); PLB write for info. (*0-8037-1397-5*) Dial Bks Young.

Nobisso, Josephine & Krajnc, Anton C. For the Sake of a Cake. LC 92-38391. (Illus.). 28p. 1993. 9.95 (*0-8478-1685-0*) Rizzoli Intl.
Here's a multi-species cautionary tale for people who know how to share the work - or those who SHOULD know! Written in droll verse & illustrated with subtle drawings of sophisticated wit & whimsical zaniness, FOR THE SAKE OF A CAKE tells the tale of a Koala & an Alligator, already in bed, who argue whose turn it is to get up to check the cake baking in the oven. No holds are barred & no punches pulled as each lays claim to having already done too much work. Who's right? As in life, the reader is never sure. But one thing is certain: unless they find a way to cooperate, they're putting their very lives in danger! Written by the author of GRANDPA LOVED, GRANDMA'S SCRAPBOOK, & SSH! THE WHALE IS SMILING, FOR THE SAKE OF A CAKE crosses over from the children's fiction section to adult gift books to food & specialty shops, setting a delicious example & offering a rare Viennese cake recipe at the end. Order from Rizzoli International, 300 Park Ave., New York, NY 10010-5399, 1-800-462-2357. *Publisher Provided Annotation.*

Rice, Eve. Benny Bakes a Cake. LC 80-17313. (Illus.). 32p. (gr. k-3). 1981. write for info. (*0-688-80312-1*); PLB write for info. (*0-688-84312-3*) Greenwillow.

—Benny Bakes a Cake. LC 80-17313. 32p. (ps-3). 1993. 14.00 (*0-688-11579-9*); PLB 13.93 (*0-688-11580-2*) Greenwillow.

Shafner, R. L. & Weisberg, Eric J. Mrs. Bretsky's Bakery. LC 92-44338. 1993. 13.50 (*0-8225-2102-4*) Lerner Pubns.

Speed, Toby. Hattie Baked a Wedding Cake. Hepworth, Cathy, illus. 32p. (ps-3). 1994. PLB 15.95 (*0-399-22342-8*) Putnam Pub Group.

Wolff, Ferida. Seven Loaves of Bread. Keller, Katie, illus. LC 92-34313. 32p. (ps up). 1993. 14.00 (*0-688-11101-7*, Tambourine Bks); PLB 13.93 (*0-688-11112-2*, Tambourine Bks) Morrow.

BALANCE OF NATURE

see Ecology

BALBOA, VASCO NUNEZ DE, 1475-1517

Ash, Maureen. Vasco Nunez de Balboa: Expedition to the Pacific Ocean. LC 90-2230. (Illus.). 128p. (gr. 3 up). 1990. PLB 20.55 (*0-516-03057-4*) Childrens.

BALL GAMES

see names of games, e.g. baseball; soccer

BALLADS

see also Folk Songs

Moser, Barry, retold by. & illus. Polly Vaughn: A Traditional British Ballad. 32p. (gr. 2 up). 1992. 15.95 (*0-316-58541-6*) Little.

Tate, Carole. Rhymes & Ballads of London. LC 72-90691. (Illus.). 32p. (gr. k-4). 1973. 6.95 (*0-87592-042-X*) Scroll Pr.

BALLET

see also Pantomimes

Ballenbera, Birdie. Looking at Ballet. LC 89-7176. (Illus.). 48p. (gr. 4-8). 1990. 13.95 (*1-85435-105-2*) Marshall Cavendish.

Craig, Janet. Ballet Dancer. Todd, Barbara, illus. LC 88-10043. 32p. (gr. k-3). 1989. PLB 10.89 (*0-8167-1434-7*); pap. text ed. 2.95 (*0-8167-1435-5*) Troll Assocs.

Dufort, Anthony. Ballet Steps. rev. & enlarged ed. LC 89-37078. (Illus.). 176p. (gr. 7 up). 1990. 18.00 (*0-517-57770-4*) Crown Bks Yng Read.

Edom, H. Starting Ballet. (Illus.). 32p. (gr. k-3). 1993. PLB 12.96 (*0-88110-634-8*); pap. 4.95 (*0-7460-0982-8*) EDC.

French, Vivian. One Ballerina Two. Ormerod, Jan, illus. LC 90-45969. 32p. (ps up). 1991. 13.95 (*0-688-10333-2*); PLB 13.88 (*0-688-10334-0*) Lothrop.

Frost, Erica. I Can Read about Ballet. LC 74-24927. (Illus.). (gr. 2-4). 1975. pap. 2.50 (*0-89375-063-8*) Troll Assocs.

Glassman, Bruce S. Mikhail Baryshnikov. (Illus.). 128p. (gr. 7-9). 1990. 9.95 (*0-382-24035-9*); PLB 12.95 (*0-382-09907-9*) Silver Burdett Pr.

Goodale, Katherine D. Pas de Trois, Fun with Ballet Words. Goodale, Kit, illus. Houlton, Loyce, intro. by. (Illus.). 25p. (Orig.). (gr. k-7). 1982. pap. 5.95 (*0-9609662-0-X*) Goodale Pub.

Gregory, Cynthia. Cynthia Gregory Dances Swan Lake. Swope, Martha, illus. 48p. (gr. 3-7). 1990. pap. 14.95 jacketed (*0-671-68786-7*, S&S BFYR) S&S Trade.

Jessel, Camilla. Life at the Royal Ballet School. Jessel, Camilla, illus. LC 79-12162. 143p. (gr. 4 up). 1979. 15.95 (*0-416-30191-6*, NO. 0137) Routledge Chapman & Hall.

Kanner, Catherine, illus. Fun with Ballet. 1992. incl. cass. 16.95 (*0-8362-4214-9*) Andrews & McMeel.

Kistler, Darci. Ballerina: My Story. Ashby, Ruth, ed. 128p. (Orig.). 1993. pap. 3.50 (*0-671-64437-8*, Minstrel Bks) PB.

Kuklin, Susan. Reaching for Dreams: A Ballet from Rehearsal to Opening Night. Kuklin, Susan, illus. LC 86-15356. (gr. 4-9). 1987. 12.95 (*0-688-06316-0*) Lothrop.

Maynard, Christopher. Ballet. LC 92-32055. 32p. (gr. 1-4). 1993. 3.95 (*1-85697-890-7*, Kingfisher LKC) LKC.

Menning, Viiu. Great Dancers. Conkle, Nancy & Neary, D., illus. (Orig.). (gr. 8). 1978. pap. 3.95 (*0-88388-065-2*) Bellerophon Bks.

Morris, Ann. Dancing to America. Kolnik, Paul, photos by. (Illus.). 40p. (gr. 2-7). 15.99 (*0-525-45128-5*) Dutton Child Bks.

—On Their Toes: A Russian Ballet School. Heyman, Ken, photos by. LC 91-11903. (Illus.). 48p. (gr. 3-7). 1991. SBE 14.95 (*0-689-31660-7*, Atheneum Child Bk) Macmillan Child Grp.

Riddell, Edwina. My First Ballet Class. LC 92-24450. (Illus.). 32p. (ps-2). 1993. 10.95 (*0-8120-6296-5*); pap. 5.95 (*0-8120-1674-2*) Barron.

Sanchez, Sharon S. About Ballet Performance. Bower, Adele, illus. 32p. (ps up). 1990. pap. 5.95 (*0-9626651-1-8*) Dance Data.

Sanchez, Sharon S., ed. About Ballet Class. Bower, Adele, illus. 32p. (Orig.). (ps up). 1990. pap. 5.95 (*0-9626651-0-X*) Dance Data.

Silver, Lynette. My Ballet Book. Smith, Kay, contrib. by. (Illus.). 64p. (gr. 5 up). 1993. pap. 6.95 (*1-875169-15-6*, Pub. by S Milner AT) Sterling.

Simon, Charnan. Evelyn Cisneros: Prima Ballerina. LC 90-40104. (Illus.). 32p. (gr. 2-4). 1990. PLB 11.80 (*0-516-04276-9*); pap. 3.95 (*0-516-44276-7*) Childrens.

Switzer, Ellen. The Nutcracker: A Story & A Ballet. Cara, Costas & Cara, Stephen, photos by. LC 85-7463. (Illus.). 112p. (gr. 4-6). 1985. SBE 16.95 (*0-689-31061-7*, Atheneum Child Bk) Macmillan Child Grp.

Tatchell, J. World of Ballet. (Illus.). 64p. (gr. 4 up). 1994. PLB 13.96 (*0-88110-707-7*, Usborne); pap. 8.95 (*0-685-72735-1*, Usborne) EDC.

Thomas, A. Ballet. (Illus.). 48p. (gr. 5 up). 1987. PLB 14. 96 (*0-88110-244-X*); pap. 7.95 (*0-7460-0085-5*) EDC.

Thomas, A., et al. Ballet & Dance. (Illus.). 96p. (gr. 5 up). 1987. pap. 12.95 (*0-7460-0201-7*) EDC.

Tichenor, Kay. Ballet. (Illus.). 32p. (Orig.). (gr. 1 up). 1976. pap. 4.50 (*0-8431-1718-4*, Troubador) Price Stern.

Verdy, Violette. Of Swans, Sugarplums & Satin Slippers. Brown, Marcia, illus. 80p. 1991. 15.95 (*0-590-43484-5*, Scholastic Hardcover) Scholastic Inc.

Winter, Ginny L. Ballet Book. Winter, Ginny L., illus. (gr. 1-5). 1962. 8.95 (*0-8392-3001-X*) Astor-Honor.

BALLET–FICTION

Alexander, Liza. I Want to Be a Ballet Dancer. (ps-3). 1993. pap. 2.25 (*0-307-13121-1*, Pub. by Golden Bks) Western Pub.

Andersen, Hans Christian. The Red Shoes. Iwasaki, Chihiro, illus. LC 82-61836. 36p. (gr. 3 up). 1991. pap. 15.95 (*0-907234-26-7*) Picture Bk Studio.

Asher, Sandy. Just Like Jenny. LC 82-70315. 160p. (gr. 5-9). 1986. pap. 2.50 (*0-440-94289-6*) Dell.

—Just Like Jenny. LC 82-70315. (gr. 4-6). 1982. pap. 12. 95 (*0-385-28496-9*) Delacorte.

Berenstain, Stan & Berenstain, Jan. The Berenstain Bears Gotta Dance. Berenstain, Stan & Berenstain, Jan, illus. LC 92-32565. 112p. (Orig.). (gr. 2-6). 1993. PLB 7.99 (*0-679-94032-4*); pap. 3.50 (*0-679-84032-X*) Random Bks Yng Read.

Betancourt, Jeanne. Kate's Turn. 192p. 1992. 13.95 (*0-590-43103-X*, Scholastic Hardcover) Scholastic Inc.

Bettina the Ballerina. 24p. (ps-3). 1991. write for info. (*0-307-14165-9*, 14165) Western Pub.

Brownrigg, Sheri. All Tutus Should Be Pink. Johnson, Meredith, illus. 32p. 1992. pap. 2.95 (*0-590-43904-9*, Cartwheel) Scholastic Inc.

—Best Friends Wear Pink Tutus. Johnson, Meredith, illus. LC 92-27569. 1993. write for info. (*0-590-46437-X*) Scholastic Inc.

Carlson, Nancy. Harriet's Recital. (Illus.). 32p. (ps-3). 1985. pap. 3.95 (*0-14-050464-8*, Puffin) Puffin Bks.

Charbonnet, Varela G. Ballet for Charlotte. 1994. 14.95 (*0-8050-3063-8*) H Holt & Co.

Chevance, Audrey. Tutu. Chevance, Audrey, illus. LC 91-3506. 32p. (ps-4). 1991. 13.95 (*0-525-44769-5*, DCB) Dutton Child Bks.

Cleary, Beverly. Ellen Tebbits. 160p. 1990. pap. 3.99 (*0-380-70913-9*, Camelot) Avon.

Cristaldi, Kathryn. Baseball Ballerina. Carter, Abby, illus. LC 90-20234. 48p. (Orig.). (gr. 1-3). 1992. PLB 7.99 (*0-679-91734-9*); pap. 3.50 (*0-679-81734-4*) Random Bks Yng Read.

Ettinger, Tom & Jaspersohn, William. My Ballet Book. (Illus.). 48p. (gr. 3-7). 1993. 10.95 (*0-694-00477-4*, Festival) HarpC Child Bks.

Eversole, Robyn H. The Magic House. Palagonia, Peter, illus. LC 91-17824. 32p. (ps-2). 1992. 13.95 (*0-531-05924-3*); lib. bdg. 13.99 (*0-531-08524-4*) Orchard Bks Watts.

Farrar, Susan C. Emily & Her Cavalier. Weinberger, Jane & Little, Carl, eds. LC 90-71373. (Illus.). 124p. 1991. 12.95g (*0-932433-76-6*); pap. 9.95 (*0-932433-77-4*) Windswept Hse.

—Samantha on Stage. Sanderson, Ruth, illus. 164p. (gr. 3 up). 1990. pap. 3.95 (*0-14-034328-8*, Puffin) Puffin Bks.

Gauch, Patricia L. Bravo, Tanya. Ichikawa, Satomi, illus. 40p. (ps-3). 1992. PLB 14.95 (*0-399-22145-X*, Philomel Bks) Putnam Pub Group.

—Tanya & Emily in a Dance for Two. Ichikawa, Satomi, illus. LC 93-5354. 40p. (ps-3). 1994. PLB 15.95 (*0-399-22688-5*, Philomel Bks) Putnam Pub Group.

Godden, Rumer. Listen to the Nightingale. 192p. (gr. 5 up). 1992. 15.00 (*0-670-84517-5*) Viking Child Bks.

Hall, Kirsten. Ballerina Girl. (Illus.). 28p. (ps-2). 1994. PLB 14.00 (*0-516-05363-9*); pap. text ed. 3.95 (*0-516-45363-7*) Childrens.

Heinzerling, Doris M. The Barefoot Ballerina. Nelson, Jane E., illus. 24p. (gr. k-1). 1993. write for info. (*1-879094-40-1*) Avonstoke Pr.

Hest, Amy. Maybe Next Year. LC 93-9627. (gr. 7 up). 1994. pap. 4.95 (*0-688-12491-7*, Pub. by Beech Tree Bks) Morrow.

Holabird, Katharine. Angelina Ballerina. Craig, Helen, illus. LC 83-8233. (ps-2). 1988. 15.00 (*0-517-55083-0*, Clarkson Potter) Crown Bks Yng Read.

Isadora, Rachel. My Ballet Class. LC 79-16297. (Illus.). 32p. (gr. k-3). 1980. 15.00 (*0-688-80253-2*) Greenwillow.

—Swan Lake. LC 88-29843. (Illus.). 32p. 1991. 14.95 (*0-399-21730-4*, Putnam) Putnam Pub Group.

Kirkland, Gelsey & Lawrence, Greg. Side Saddle Ballerina. Rogers, Jacqueline, illus. LC 93-20355. 1993. pap. 14.95 (*0-385-46978-0*) Doubleday.

Leggat, Bonnie-Alise. Punt, Pass & Point! Thatch, Nancy R., ed. Leggat, Bonnie-Alise, illus. Melton, David, intro. by. LC 92-17598. (Illus.). 26p. (gr. 3-5). 1992. PLB 14.95 (*0-933849-39-7*) Landmark Edns.

Lichtner, Schomer. Ballerina's Holiday. (Illus.). 76p. (Orig.). (gr. 5 up). 1979. pap. 4.95 (*0-941074-04-8*) Lichtner.

Little Ballerina. Date not set. pap. write for info. (*0-679-85904-7*) Random Bks Yng Read.

Malcolm, Jahnna N. Bad News Ballet, No. 7: The King & Us. 1990. pap. 2.75 (*0-590-43395-4*) Scholastic Inc.

Martin, Ann M. Jessi's Secret Language. large type ed. LC 93-15971. 176p. (gr. 4 up). 1993. PLB 15.93 (*0-8368-1020-1*) Gareth Stevens Inc.

O'Connor, Jane. Nina, Nina, Ballerina. DiSalvo-Ryan, DyAnne, illus. LC 92-24465. 32p. (ps-1). 1993. lib. bdg. 7.99 (*0-448-40512-1*, G&D); pap. 3.50 (*0-448-40511-3*, G&D) Putnam Pub Group.

Oxenbury, Helen. The Dancing Class. Oxenbury, Helen, illus. LC 82-19791. 24p. (ps-1). 1983. 5.95 (*0-8037-1651-6*, 0383-120) Dial Bks Young.

Richardson, Jean. Out of Step: The Twins Were So Alike. ..but So Different. Holmes, Dawn, illus. LC 92-39666. 28p. (ps-3). 1993. 12.95 (*0-8120-5790-2*); pap. 5.95 (*0-8120-1553-3*) Barron.

Ross, Katharine. The Little Ballerina. LC 92-42093. 1994. 2.50 (*0-679-84915-7*) Random Bks Yng Read.

San Souci, Robert D. The Firebird. LC 91-574. (Illus.). 32p. (ps-3). 1992. 14.00 (*0-8037-0799-1*); PLB 13.89 (*0-8037-0800-9*) Dial Bks Young.

Smath, Jerry. Up Goes Mr. Downs. LC 84-1199. (Illus.). 48p. (ps-3). 1985. 5.95 (*0-8193-1137-5*) Parents.

Streatfield, Noel. Ballet Shoes. Goode, Diane, illus. LC 89-24390. 288p. (gr. 4-9). 1991. gift ed. 15.00 (*0-679-80105-7*) Random Bks Yng Read.

Ure, Jean. What If They Saw Me Now? LC 83-14981. 160p. (gr. 7 up). 1984. 13.95 (*0-385-29317-8*) Delacorte.

Utz. A Delightful Day with Bella Ballet. LC 75-190267. (Illus.). 32p. (gr. 2-3). 1972. PLB 9.95 (*0-87783-056-8*); pap. 3.94 deluxe ed. (*0-87783-089-4*) Oddo.

Van Beek, Tom. Degas, the Ballet, & Me. Peters, Thea, illus. 48p. (gr. 2-7). 1993. 12.95 (*1-56288-424-7*) Checkerboard.

Weyn, Suzanne. Emma's Turn. Iskowitz, Joel, illus. LC 89-31348. 96p. (gr. 3-5). 1990. lib. bdg. 9.89 (*0-8167-1623-4*); pap. text ed. 2.95 (*0-8167-1624-2*) Troll Assocs.

—Stage Fright. Iskowitz, Joel, illus. LC 89-31349. 96p. (gr. 3-5). 1990. pap. text ed. 2.95 (*0-8167-1652-8*) Troll Assocs.

—Three for the Show. Iskowitz, Joel, illus. LC 89-34547. 96p. (gr. 3-5). 1990. pap. text ed. 2.95 (*0-8167-1656-0*) Troll Assocs.

BALLET–HISTORY

Garfunkel, Trudy. On Wings of Joy: The Story of Ballet from the 16th Century to Today. Villella, Edward, frwd. by. LC 93-41526. (Illus.). (gr. 7 up). 1994. 18.95 (*0-316-30412-3*) Little.

BALLETS–STORIES, PLOTS, ETC.
Hautzig, Deborah. The Story of the Nutcracker Ballet. Goode, Diane, illus. 32p. (ps-1). 1986. pap. 5.95 (*0-394-88296-2*) Random Bks Yng Read.
—The Story of the Nutcracker Ballet. Goode, Diane, illus. LC 85-30149. 32p. (ps-1). 1986. 2.25 (*0-394-88178-8*) Random Bks Yng Read.
Hodges, M. Constance. Alice in Danceland. Hodges, Del & Mavity, Dennis, photos by. Troxel, Rose, illus. (Orig.). (gr. 3-8). 1979. PLB 5.95 (*0-934856-00-1*) Delcon.
Horosko, Marian, retold by. Sleeping Beauty: The Ballet Story. Doney, Todd L., illus. LC 93-14399. 1994. 14.95 (*0-689-31885-5*, Atheneum) Macmillan.
Marcus, Leonard S. Petrouchka: A Ballet Cut-Out Book. Kendall, Jane F., illus. 16p. (gr. 3-6). 1983. pap. 12.95 cutout bk. (*0-87923-469-5*) Godine.
Meyerowitz, Joel. George Balanchine's the Nutcracker. (Illus.). 1993. 29.95 (*0-316-56921-6*) Little.
Riordan, James. Favorite Stories of the Ballet. Ambrus, Victor G., illus. Nureyev, Rudolf, frwd. by. LC 84-42778. (Illus.). 128p. (gr. 4 up). 14.95 (*1-56288-252-X*) Checkerboard.
Werner, Vivian, retold by. Petrouchka. Collier, John, illus. 32p. (gr. 5 up). 1992. 16.00 (*0-670-83607-9*) Viking Child Bks.
BALLOONS
see also Aeronautics
Adler, Irene. Ballooning: High & Wild. LC 75-23406. (Illus.). 32p. (gr. 5-10). 1976. PLB 10.79 (*0-89375-001-8*); pap. 2.95 (*0-89375-017-4*) Troll Assocs.
Bellville, Cheryl W. Flying in a Hot Air Balloon. LC 92-37390. 1993. 19.95 (*0-87614-750-3*) Carolrhoda Bks.
Carlisle, Madelyn. Let's Investigate Beautiful, Bouncy Balloons. (gr. 4-7). 1992. pap. 4.95 (*0-8120-4734-6*) Barron.
Cottrell, Leonard. Up in a Balloon. LC 69-17423. (Illus.). (gr. 8 up). 1970. 24.95 (*0-87599-142-4*) S G Phillips.
Fine, John C. Free Spirits in the Sky. LC 92-33443. (Illus.). 32p. (gr. 2-6). 1994. SBE 14.95 (*0-689-31705-0*, Atheneum Child Bk) Macmillan Child Grp.
Johnson, Neil. Fire & Silk: Flying in a Hot Air Balloon. (ps-3). 1991. 15.95 (*0-316-46959-9*) Little.
Kaner, Etta. Balloon Science. (gr. 4-7). 1990. pap. 9.57 (*0-201-52378-7*) Addison-Wesley.
—Balloon Science. (gr. 4-7). 1993. pap. 9.57 (*0-201-62640-3*) Addison-Wesley.
Lenssen, Ann. A Rainbow Balloon: A Book of Concepts. LC 91-31830. (Illus.). 32p. (ps-3). 1992. 13.50 (*0-525-65093-8*, Cobblehill Bks) Dutton Child Bks.
Marriott. Amazing Fact Book of Balloons. (Illus.). 32p. (gr. 4-8). 1987. PLB 14.95 (*0-87191-841-2*) Creative Ed.
Newman, Ed. Hot Air & Gas: The Basics of Balloons. Newman, Ed, illus. LC 92-70713. 52p. (Orig.). (gr. 4-12). 1992. pap. 6.95 (*0-9632038-0-0*) Greenway Pub.
Paulsen, Gary. Full of Hot Air: Launching, Floating High, & Landing. Heltshe, Mary A., photos by. LC 92-31327. (Illus.). 1993. 14.95 (*0-385-30887-6*) Delacorte.
Saunders, R. Balloon Voyager. (Illus.). 32p. (gr. 4 up). 1988. PLB 17.27 (*0-86592-870-3*); PLB 12.95s.p. (*0-685-58291-4*) Rourke Corp.
BALLOONS, DIRIGIBLE
see Airships
BALLOONS–FICTION
Adams, Adrienne. The Great Valentine's Day Balloon Race. 2nd ed. LC 93-46114. 1995. pap. 4.95 (*0-689-71847-0*, Aladdin) Macmillan Child Grp.
Bashful Bard. The Great Balloon Adventure. Bashful Bard, illus. LC 89-84961. 24p. (Orig.). (ps-1). 1989. pap. 3.99 (*1-877906-03-4*) Kenney Pubns.
Bonsall, Crosby N. Mine's the Best. Bonsall, Crosby, illus. LC 72-9863. 32p. (ps-2). 1973. PLB 13.89 (*0-06-020578-4*) HarpC Child Bks.
Coerr, Eleanor. The Big Balloon Race. Croll, Carolyn, illus. LC 91-13606. 64p. (gr. k-3). 1981. 13.00 (*0-06-021352-3*); PLB 12.89 (*0-06-021353-1*) HarpC Child Bks.
Darling, Benjamin. Robert & the Balloon Machine. Solliday, Tim, illus. 32p. 1991. 11.95 (*0-88138-120-9*, Green Tiger) S&S Trade.
Du Bois, William P. The Twenty-One Balloons. Du Bois, William P., illus. 184p. (gr. 5-9). 1986. pap. 3.99 (*0-14-032097-0*, Puffin) Puffin Bks.
Hayes, Sarah. The Grumpalump. Firth, Barbara, illus. 32p. (ps-2). 1991. 15.45 (*0-89919-871-6*, Clarion Bks) HM.
Lamorisse, Albert. Red Balloon. Lamorisse, Albert, photos by. LC 57-9229. (Illus.). 45p. (gr. 3-7). 1967. 13.95 (*0-685-01494-0*) Doubleday.
—The Red Balloon. LC 57-9229. (Illus.). 45p. (ps-3). 1978. (Zephyr-BFYR); pap. 7.95 (*0-385-14297-8*, Zephyr-BFYR) Doubleday.
Matthias, Catherine. Demasiados Globos (Too Many Balloons) Sharp, Gene, illus. LC 81-15520. (SPA.). 32p. (ps-2). 1990. pap. 2.95 (*0-516-53633-8*) Childrens.
—Too Many Balloons. Sharp, Gene, illus. LC 81-15520. 32p. (ps-2). 1982. PLB 10.25 (*0-516-03633-5*); pap. text ed. 2.95 (*0-516-43633-3*) Childrens.
May, Daryl & Bansemer, Roger. Rachael's Splendifilous Adventure. Little, Carl, ed. Bansemer, Roger, illus. LC 91-66032. 40p. (Orig.). (ps-4). 1992. PLB 10.95 (*0-932433-83-9*) Windswept Hse.
Mott, Evelyn C. Balloon Ride. Mott, Evelyn C., illus. 32p. (ps-1). 1991. 13.95 (*0-8027-8124-1*); PLB 14.85 (*0-8027-8126-8*) Walker & Co.
Myers, Bill. My Life As a Broken Bungee Cord. (gr. 4-7). 1993. pap. 4.99 (*0-8499-3404-4*) Word Inc.
Nolen, Jerdine. Harvey Potter's Balloon Farm. LC 91-38129. (ps-3). 1994. 15.00 (*0-688-07887-7*); 14.93 (*0-688-07888-5*) Lothrop.
O'Donnell, Elizabeth L. Are You Flying, Charlie Duncan? Milone, Karen, illus. LC 92-39876. 96p. (gr. 4 up). 1993. 14.00 (*0-688-09027-3*) Morrow Jr Bks.
Pene Du Bois, William. Twenty-One Balloons. Pene Du Bois, William, illus. 192p. (gr. 4-8). 1982. pap. 2.75 (*0-440-49183-5*, YB) Dell.
—The Twenty-One Balloons. Pene Du Bois, William, illus. (gr. 5-9). 1947. pap. 15.00 (*0-670-73441-1*) Viking Child Bks.
Roberts, Thom. Atlantic Free Balloon Race. (gr. 3-7). 1986. pap. 2.50 (*0-380-89868-3*, Camelot) Avon.
Scullard, Sue. The Great Round-the-World Balloon Race. Scullard, Sue, illus. LC 90-40590. 32p. (gr. 2-5). 1991. 12.95 (*0-525-44692-3*, DCB) Dutton Child Bks.
Shaffer, Dianna. The Man Who Loved Balloons. Shaffer, Dianna, illus. 32p. (ps-8). 1989. pap. text ed. 4.95 (*1-877995-02-9*) Koala Pub Co.
Smath, Jerry. Up Goes Mr. Downs. LC 93-13041. 1993. PLB 13.27 (*0-8368-0979-3*) Gareth Stevens Inc.
Vallet, Roxanne. The Balloon Book. Vallet, Roxanne, illus. 15p. (gr. 1-4). 1992. pap. 11.95 (*1-56606-008-7*) Bradley Mann.
Verne, Jules. Around the World in Eighty Days. 1990. pap. 3.25 (*0-590-43053-X*) Scholastic Inc.
Wade, Alan. I'm Flying! Mathers, Petra, illus. LC 88-31360. 40p. (gr. k-4). 1990. 13.95 (*0-394-84510-2*) Knopf Bks Yng Read.
Willard, Nancy. The Well-Mannered Balloon. D'Andrade, Diane, ed. Shekerjian, Hiag & Shekerjian, Regina, illus. 32p. (Orig.). (ps-3). 1991. pap. 3.95 (*0-15-294986-0*, HB Juv Bks) HarBrace.
Wilson, Sarah. Three in a Balloon. 1990. pap. 12.95 (*0-590-42631-1*) Scholastic Inc.
Wood, Audrey. Balloonia. Wood, Audrey, illus. LC 90-46602. 32p. (ps-2). 1981. 7.95 (*0-85953-122-8*, Pub. by Child's Play England); pap. 3.95 (*0-85953-320-4*, Pub. by Child's Play England) Childs Play.
BALLOT
see Elections
BALTIMORE–FICTION
Howard, Elizabeth F. Aunt Flossie's Hats (& Crab Cakes Later) Ransome, James E., illus. 32p. (ps-1). 1991. 14.95 (*0-395-54682-6*, Clarion Bks) HM.
—Chita's Christmas Tree. Cooper, Floyd, illus. LC 92-44482. 32p. (gr. k-2). 1993. pap. 4.95 (*0-689-71739-3*, Aladdin) Macmillan Child Grp.
—What's in Aunt Mary's Room? Lucas, Cedric, illus. LC 94-4985. Date not set. write for info. (*0-395-69845-6*, Clarion Bks) HM.
Lehne, Judith L. When the Ragman Sings. LC 93-20346. 128p. (gr. 3-7). 1993. 14.00 (*0-06-023316-8*); PLB 13.89 (*0-06-023317-6*) HarpC Child Bks.
BALTIMORE ORIOLES (BASEBALL TEAM)
Baltimore Orioles. (gr. 4-7). 1993. pap. 1.49 (*0-553-56407-2*) Bantam.
Rambeck, Richard. Baltimore Orioles. 48p. (gr. 4-10). 1992. PLB 14.95 (*0-88682-451-6*) Creative Ed.
BANANA
Western Promotional Books Staff. Bananas. (ps). 1994. 0.95 (*0-307-13461-X*) Western Pub.
BANDITS
see Robbers and Outlaws
BANDMASTERS
see Conductors (Music)
BANDS (MUSIC)
Kuribayashi, Pam. A Summer Madness. 79p. (Orig.). (gr. 10-12). 1988. pap. 5.95 (*0-685-22514-3*) Prairie Shark Pr.
Warner, Rachel. Our Steel Band. (Illus.). 25p. (gr. 2-4). 1991. 12.95 (*0-237-60143-5*, Pub. by Evans Bros Ltd) Trafalgar.
BANDS (MUSIC)–FICTION
Baer, Gene. Thump, Thump, Rat-a-Tat-Tat. Ehlert, Lois, illus. LC 88-28469. 32p. (ps-1). 1991. pap. 4.95 (*0-06-443265-3*, Trophy) HarpC Child Bks.
Birchman, David F. Brother Billy Bronto's Bygone Blues Band. O'Brien, John, illus. LC 90-2611. (ps-3). 1992. 14.00 (*0-688-10423-1*); PLB 13.93 (*0-688-10424-X*) Lothrop.
Block, Francesca L. Cherokee Bat & the Goat Guys. LC 91-30706. 112p. (gr. 7 up). 1992. 14.00 (*0-06-020269-6*); PLB 13.89 (*0-06-020270-X*) HarpC Child Bks.
Bowles, Brad. Grandma's Band. Chan, Anthony, illus. 48p. (gr. k-4). 1989. PLB 14.95 (*0-88045-112-2*) Stemmer Hse.
Brooks, Chelsea. A California Night's Dream. LC 94-17924. (gr. 5 up). 1994. pap. 2.95 (*0-02-041652-0*, Collier) Macmillan.
—Don't Forget to Write. LC 94-14181. (gr. 5 up). 1994. pap. 2.95 (*0-02-041651-2*) Macmillan Child Grp.
—Dreamers & Schemers. 1994. pap. 2.95 (*0-02-041653-9*, Aladdin) Macmillan Child Grp.
—Perfect Harmony. LC 93-12876. 160p. (Orig.). (gr. 5 up). 1993. pap. 2.95 (*0-02-041972-4*, Collier Young Ad) Macmillan Child Grp.
Finkelstein, Chaim. Cheery Bim Band 2: Let's Do It Again. LC 93-72269. 204p. (gr. 5-6). 1993. write for info. (*1-56062-209-1*) CIS Comm.
Giff, Patricia R. The Jingle Bells Jam. McCully, Emily A., illus. 80p. (Orig.). (gr. 1-4). 1992. pap. 3.25 (*0-440-40534-3*, YB) Dell.
—Meet the Lincoln Lions Band. McCully, Emily A., illus. 80p. (Orig.). (gr. 1-4). 1992. pap. 3.25 (*0-440-40516-5*, YB) Dell.
—Yankee Doodle Drumsticks. McCully, Emily A., illus. 80p. (Orig.). (gr. 1-4). 1992. pap. 3.25 (*0-440-40518-1*, YB) Dell.
Kidd, Ronald. Danny Dorfman's Dream Band, No. 3: The Case of the Missing Case. Jones, Bob, illus. LC 92-17208. 80p. (gr. 2-6). 1992. pap. 2.99 (*0-14-034988-X*) Puffin Bks.
—Danny Dorfman's Dream Band, No. 4: Rapunzel, Sort Of. Jones, Bob, illus. LC 92-16495. 80p. (gr. 2-6). 1992. pap. 3.50 (*0-14-034987-1*) Puffin Bks.
King, Virginia. The Band. Reynolds, Pat, illus. LC 92-21390. 1993. 2.50 (*0-383-03553-8*) SRA Schl Grp.
Kingsland, Robin. Bus Stop Bop. Ayliffe, Alex, illus. 32p. (ps-3). 1991. 14.95 (*0-670-83919-1*) Viking Child Bks.
Landis, James D. The Band Never Dances. LC 88-28401. 288p. (gr. 7 up). 1993. pap. 3.95 (*0-06-447075-X*, Trophy) HarpC Child Bks.
Mattox, Cheryl W. Let's Get the Rhythm of the Band. (ps-3). 1993. pap. 6.95 (*0-938971-97-2*) JTG Nashville.
Stortz, Diane. Alexander's Praise Time Band. Garris, Norma, illus. LC 92-32817. 28p. (ps-k). 1993. 4.99 (*0-7847-0036-2*, 24-03826) Standard Pub.
BANGLADESH
Bailey, Donna & Sproule, Anna. Bangladesh. LC 90-9652. (Illus.). 32p. (gr. 1-4). 1990. PLB 18.99 (*0-8114-2559-2*) Raintree Steck-V.
Laure, Jason. Bangladesh. LC 92-8891. (Illus.). 128p. (gr. 5-9). 1992. PLB 20.55 (*0-516-02609-7*) Childrens.
McClure, Vimala. Bangladesh: Rivers in a Crowded Land. LC 88-35911. (Illus.). 128p. (gr. 5 up). 1989. RSBE 14.95 (*0-87518-404-9*, Dillon) Macmillan Child Grp.
Nugent, Nicholas. Pakistan & Bangladesh. LC 92-10765. 96p. 1992. lib. bdg. 22.80 (*0-8114-2456-1*) Raintree Steck-V.
BANKING
see Banks and Banking
BANKS AND BANKING
see also Credit; Investments; Money
Dunnan, Nancy. Banking. Easton, Emily, ed. (Illus.). 128p. (gr. 12 up). 1990. lib. bdg. 9.95 (*0-382-09917-6*); pap. 5.95 (*0-382-24028-6*) Silver Burdett Pr.
BANKS AND BANKING–FICTION
Ille, Dorothy B. The Banker's Place. LC 92-63253. 82p. (gr. 6-11). 1993. 7.95 (*1-55523-591-3*) Winston-Derek.
BANKS AND BANKING–VOCATIONAL GUIDANCE
Haddock, Patricia. Careers in Banking & Finance. Rosen, Ruth, ed. (gr. 7-12). 1989. PLB 14.95 (*0-8239-0962-X*) Rosen Group.
BANNEKER, BENJAMIN, 1731-1806
Ferris, Jeri. What Are You Figuring Now? A Story about Benjamin Banneker. Johnson, Amy, illus. LC 88-7267. 56p. (gr. 3-6). 1988. PLB 14.95 (*0-87614-331-1*); pap. 4.95 (*0-685-19616-X*) Carolrhoda Bks.
—What Are You Figuring Now? A Story about Benjamin Banneker. Johnson, Amy, illus. 64p. (gr. 3-6). Repr. of 1988 ed. 4.95 (*0-87614-521-7*) Carolrhoda Bks.
Pinkney, Andrea D. Dear Benjamin Banneker. Pinkney, Brian, illus. LC 93-31162. (gr. 1-5). 1994. 14.95 (*0-15-200417-3*, Gulliver Bks) HarBrace.
BANNERS
see Flags
BANTING, SIR FREDERICK GRANT, 1891-1941
Pioneer. Frederick Banting. 1992. PLB 13.95 (*0-8050-2335-6*) H Holt & Co.
BAPTISM
Barnett, Robert J. Baptism: Who Needs It? 16p. (Orig.). (gr. 6 up). 1991. pap. text ed. 1.25 (*0-87227-171-4*) Reg Baptist.
Beutler, Cora. Baptism Journal, Boy. (Illus.). 28p. (Orig.). 1992. pap. 2.95 (*1-56684-005-8*, Sigma Pub) Pubs Wholesale.
Beutler, Cora R. Baptism Journal, Girl. (Illus.). 28p. (Orig.). 1992. pap. 2.95 (*1-56684-002-3*, Sigma Pub) Pubs Wholesale.
Clawson, Jan. Baptism: My Promise to Jesus. Fletcher, Amy, illus. 24p. (Orig.). (gr. 1-3). 1988. pap. 3.98 (*0-88290-298-9*) Horizon Utah.
England, Kathleen. Why We Are Baptized. LC 78-19180. (Illus.). 27p. (gr. 2-5). 1978. pap. 5.95 (*0-87747-893-7*) Deseret Bk.
Fogle, Jeanne S. Signs of God's Love: Baptism & Communion. Duckert, Mary J. & Lane, W. Ben, eds. Weidner, Bea, illus. 32p. (Orig.). (gr. 3-8). 1984. pap. 7.99 (*0-664-24636-2*, Geneva Pr) Westminster John Knox.
Halverson, Sandy. Preparing for Baptism. 48p. (gr. 1-3). 1983. pap. 5.98 (*0-88290-233-4*) Horizon Utah.
Todd, Richard E. Baptism. rev. ed. Miller, Alma E. & Kellner, Ron, illus. 26p. (gr. 2-6). 1993. wkbk. 2.45 (*0-9605324-1-2*) Crosswalk Res.
Todd, Richard E., ed. Baptism. Kellner, Ron, illus. 16p. (Orig.). (gr. 1-6). 1980. pap. 0.50 (*0-9605324-0-4*) Crosswalk Res.
Wittenback, Janet. God Makes Me His Child in Baptism. LC 85-7689. 24p. (gr. 2-5). 1985. pap. 2.99 (*0-570-04126-0*, 56-1537) Concordia.
BAPTISTS
see also Mennonites

for Children...& Their Parents! Mazellan, Ron, illus. LC 94-3054. (gr. k-7). 1994. 24.95 (*0-87227-180-3*) Reg Baptist.
"Who is God" "Why is night dark?" "How can I be perfect?" "What happens to people when they die?" If you've heard these questions, you know that answering them isn't always easy. I HAVE A QUESTION ABOUT GOD...: DOCTRINE FOR CHILDREN...& THEIR PARENTS! answers those questions & 53 more in a delightful format. Three children - 10-year-old Megan, 8-year-old Toph, & 4-year-old Bobbie - get into all kinds of situations & ask all kinds of questions. You'll start preschool with Bobbie, who can't wait to go to kindergarten & who never stops asking questions. You'll fly to Grandpa & Grandma's with Toph, who has never traveled by himself before. And you'll sympathize with Megan as she deals with a neighbor's injustice & with problems at school. As the kids discover the answers to their questions, usually with the help of their mom or dad, your kids will learn too. The questions fall into eight areas of Biblical teaching or doctrine: God, creation, the Bible, Jesus Christ, sin, salvation, church & the future. Each story includes a beautiful illustration by Ron Mazellan & a few questions to stimulate further thought & discussion. To order: 1-800-727-4440.
Publisher Provided Annotation.

Jackson, Mark. Ready Set Grow! A Faith & Practice Primer for Regular Baptists. LC 89-38819. (Illus.). 112p. (Orig.). 1989. pap. text ed. 4.95 (*0-87227-138-2*) Reg Baptist.
Johnson, Gordon G. Our Church: There's More to It Than You Think. Putman, Bob, adapted by. Ferris, Ron, illus. LC 83-82990. 72p. (gr. 5-6). 1993. wkbk. 5.99 (*0-935797-33-5*) Harvest IL.
The Shorter Catechism: A Baptist Version. 50p. (Orig.). (gr. 5 up). 1991. pap. 7.95 (*0-9622508-4-8*) Simpson NJ.

BAR
see Lawyers

BARBARY CORSAIRS
see Pirates

BARBARY STATES
see Africa, North

BARBECUE COOKING
see Outdoor Cookery

BARCELONA
Dunnan, Nancy. Barcelona. (Illus.). 64p. (gr. 3-7). PLB 14.95 (*1-56711-018-5*) Blackbirch.

BARNUM, PHINEAS TAYLOR, 1810-1891
Fleming, Alice. P. T. Barnum: The World's Greatest Showman. 128p. (gr. 4-7). 1993. 14.95 (*0-8027-8234-5*); PLB 15.85 (*0-8027-8235-3*) Walker & Co.
Price of Humbug: The Life of P. T. Barnum. LC 93-36724. (gr. 5-9). 1994. 15.95 (*0-689-31796-4*) Macmillan.
Tompert, Ann. P. T. Barnum: The Greatest Showman on Earth: A Biography of P. T. Barnum. LC 87-13600. (Illus.). 120p. (gr. 6 up). 1988. text ed. 13.95 RSBE (*0-87518-370-0*, Dillon) Macmillan Child Grp.

BARRIE, JAMES MATTHEW, BART., 1890-1937
Aller, Susan B. J. M. Barrie: The Magic Behind Peter Pan. LC 94-5452. (Illus.). 128p. (gr. 5 up). 1994. PLB 21.50 (*0-8225-4918-2*) Lerner Pubns.

BARRISTERS
see Lawyers

BARROWS
see also Mounds and Mound Builders

BARS AND RESTAURANTS
see Restaurants, Bars, etc.

BARTON, CLARA HARLOWE, 1821-1912
Bains, Rae. Clara Barton: Angel of the Battlefield. LC 81-23123. (Illus.). 48p. (gr. 4-6). 1982. PLB 10.79 (*0-89375-752-7*); pap. text ed. 3.50 (*0-89375-753-5*) Troll Assocs.
Boylston, Helen D. Clara Barton, Founder of American Red Cross. (Illus.). (gr. 4-6). 1963. lib. bdg. 11.99 (*0-394-90358-7*) Random Bks Yng Read.
Dubowski, Cathy E. Clara Barton: Healing the Wounds. (Illus.). 160p. (gr. 5 up). 1990. lib. bdg. 12.95 (*0-382-09940-0*); pap. 7.95 (*0-382-24049-9*) Silver Burdett Pr.
Klingel, Cynthia & Zadra, Dan. Clara Barton. (Illus.). 32p. 1987. PLB 14.95 (*0-88682-168-1*) Creative Ed.
Quackenbush, Robert. Clara Barton & Her Victory over Fear. LC 94-18168. 1995. 13.00 (*0-671-86598-6*, S&S BFYR) S&S Trade.
Rose, Mary C. Clara Barton: Soldier of Mercy. Johnson, E. Harper, illus. 80p. (gr. 2-6). 1991. Repr. of 1960 ed. lib. bdg. 12.95 (*0-7910-1403-7*) Chelsea Hse.
Sonneborn, Liz. Clara Barton. (Illus.). 72p. (gr. 3-5). 1991. lib. bdg. 12.95 (*0-7910-1565-3*) Chelsea Hse.
Stevenson, Augusta. Clara Barton: Founder of the American Red Cross. Giacoia, Frank, illus. LC 86-10750. 192p. (gr. 2-6). 1986. pap. 3.95 (*0-02-041820-5*, Aladdin) Macmillan Child Grp.

BARUCH, BERNARD MANNES, 1870-1965
Finke, Blythe F. Bernard M. Baruch: Speculator & Statesman. Rahmas, D. Steve, ed. LC 78-190249. 32p. (Orig.). (gr. 7-12). 1972. lib. bdg. 4.95 incl. catalog cards (*0-87157-532-9*) SamHar Pr.

BASEBALL
see also Little League Baseball; Softball
Aaseng, Nathan. You Are the Manager: Baseball. 112p. (gr. 5 up). 1984. pap. 1.95 (*0-440-99829-8*, LFL) Dell.
Almonte, Paul. Get Inside Baseball. LC 93-41625. (Illus.). 64p. (gr. 4-6). 1994. PLB 12.95 (*1-881889-55-6*) Silver Moon.
—Getting Inside Baseball. Salvini, Donna, illus. 64p. (gr. 4-6). 1994. pap. 6.95 (*1-881889-58-0*) Silver Moon.
Alvarez, Mark. The Official Baseball Hall of Fame Answer Book. (gr. 3 up). 1989. pap. 6.95 (*0-671-67377-7*, Little Simon) S&S Trade.
Arnow, Jan. Louisville Slugger: The Making of a Baseball Bat. Arnow, Jan, photos by. LC 84-7049. (Illus.). 48p. (gr. 3-7). 1984. 11.95 (*0-394-86297-X*, Pant Bks Young) Pantheon.
Aylesworth, Thomas G. The Kid's World Almanac of Baseball. Ripken, Cal, Jr., intro. by. LC 92-35867. 1993. pap. 7.95 (*0-88687-721-0*) Wrld Almnc.
Barden. Base Stealers. 1991. 12.50s.p. (*0-86593-126-7*) Rourke Corp.
Blackstone, Margaret. This Is Baseball. O'Brien, John, photos by. LC 92-22921. (Illus.). 32p. (ps-k). 1993. 14.95 (*0-8050-2390-9*, Bks Young Read) H Holt & Co.
Blumenthal, Howard J. You Can Do It! Careers in Baseball. LC 92-9542. 1993. 16.95 (*0-316-10095-1*) Little.
Broekel, Ray. Baseball. LC 81-38480. (Illus.). 48p. (gr. k-4). 1982. PLB 12.85 (*0-516-01616-4*); pap. 4.95 (*0-516-41616-2*) Childrens.
Carroll, Bob. The Major League Way to Play Baseball. (Illus.). 96p. (gr. 3 up). 1991. (S&S BFYR); pap. 5.95 (*0-671-70441-9*, S&S BFYR) S&S Trade.
—Official Baseball Hall of Fame Sticker Book of Records. 1990. pap. 7.95 (*0-671-69091-4*, Little Simon) S&S Trade.
Cawley, Sherry. Braves Fun Book I. 80p. (Orig.). 1986. pap. 3.95 (*0-937511-00-5*) Fun Bk Enter.
Cebulash, Mel. Baseball Players Do Amazing Things. (Illus.). (gr. 2-5). 1973. 8.95 (*0-394-82611-6*) Random Bks Yng Read.
Childress, Casey & McKenzie, Linda. A Beginner's Guide to Baseball Card Collecting: A Step-by-Step Guide for the Young Collector. LC 88-90757. (Illus.). 46p. (Orig.). (gr. 4-8). 1990. Repr. of 1988 ed. vinyl covers 7.95 (*0-9620167-0-5*) C Mack Pub.
Dagavarian, Debra A., ed. A Century of Children's Baseball Stories, No. 2. 200p. (Orig.). (gr. 5 up). 1993. 16.95 (*0-9625132-2-9*) Mecklermedia.
Darryl Strawberry Sports Shots. (ps-3). 1992. pap. 1.25 (*0-590-45843-4*) Scholastic Inc.
Downing, Joan. Baseball Is Our Game. LC 82-4418. (Illus.). (gr. k-3). 1982. pap. 3.95 (*0-516-43402-0*) Childrens.
Duden, Jane. Baseball. LC 91-7365. (Illus.). 48p. (gr. 5). 1991. text ed. 11.95 RSBE (*0-89686-625-4*, Crestwood Hse) Macmillan Child Grp.
Egan, Terry, et al. The Macmillan Book of Baseball Stories. LC 92-6447. (Illus.). 128p. (gr. 3 up). 1992. SBE 15.95 (*0-02-733280-2*, Macmillan Child Bk) Macmillan Child Grp.
Ettinger, Tom & Jaspersohn, William. My Baseball Book: A Write-in-Me Book for Young Players. (Illus.). 48p. (gr. 3-7). 1993. 10.95 (*0-694-00466-9*, Festival) HarpC Child Bks.
Feldman, Jay. Hitting. (Illus.). 96p. (gr. 5 up). 1991. (S&S BFYR); pap. 5.95 (*0-671-70442-7*, S&S BFYR) S&S Trade.

Ferroli, Stephen J. Disciple of a Master (How to Hit a Baseball to Your Potential) Dickenson, Ken, illus. Williams, Ted, frwd. by. (Illus.). 136p. (Orig.). (gr. 9-12). 1986. pap. 9.95 (*0-939905-00-0*) Line Drive.
Anyone attempting to learn one of the most difficult skills in sports - or charged with teaching it - will delight in DISCIPLE OF A MASTER, an A to Z guide that carefully outlines correct baseball batting technique in a lively & photo-filled text. By breaking the skill down into its component parts, author, hitter & expert teacher Steve Ferroli (Phys. Ed., Bridgewater State College, 1982) provides young athletes & coaches with precise instructions for building hitting ability, all the while creating an enthusiastic learning environment with every paragraph. "This book is remarkable & works on several levels." (Baseball Hobby News). His physical education & coaching background furnishing the biomechanical & kinesiological rationale, Ferroli covers the basics of stance, cocking action, stride, hip rotation & arm execution. This book teaches kids how to hit, leaving nothing uncovered, from bat selection to knowing what pitches deserve a batter's swing. Ferroli then packs this information into every page with insight, clarity & occasional humor. His strident belief is that batting potential is more a function of technique than raw talent, a belief for which he provides historical support, & one which opens up the enjoyment of the skill to a large segment of the student-athlete population. DISCIPLE OF A MASTER is endorsed & forwarded by Hall of Fame baseball player Ted Williams, who views it as an "extension & defense" of his own time-honored techniques. "Steve Ferroli teaches hitting exactly the way it should be taught." (Ted Williams). Lavishly illustrated & equally applicable to softball, it is full of drills practice suggestions designed to meet the needs of a wide variety of coaches, instructors & athletes, from physical education classes & intramurals to interscholastic competition. Send $9.95 to Line Drive Publishing, Box 2070, Hanover, MA 02339; 617-878-5035.
Publisher Provided Annotation.

Foley, Red. Red Foley's Best Baseball Book. (gr. 4-7). 1994. pap. 8.95 (*0-671-87577-9*, Little Simon) S&S Trade.
—Red Foley's Best Baseball Book Ever, 1993. (Illus.). 80p. (gr. 1 up). 1993. pap. 8.95 (*0-671-79732-8*, Little Simon) S&S Trade.
Ford, Jerry. The Grand Slam Collection: Have Fun Collecting Baseball Cards. (Illus.). 64p. (gr. 5-12). 1992. 15.95 (*0-8225-2350-7*); pap. 6.95 (*0-8225-9598-2*) Lerner Pubns.
Freeman, Mark. Squeeze Play. 144p. (gr. 7-9). 1989. pap. 3.99 (*0-345-35903-8*) Ballantine.
Greene, Carol. I Can Be a Baseball Player. LC 84-23222. (Illus.). 32p. (gr. k-3). 1985. PLB 11.80 (*0-516-01845-0*); pap. 3.95 (*0-516-41845-9*) Childrens.
—Puedo Ser Jugador de Beisbol (I Can Be a Baseball Player) Kratky, Lada, tr. LC 86-996. (SPA., Illus.). 32p. (gr. k-3). 1986. PLB 11.80 (*0-516-31845-4*); pap. 3.95 (*0-516-51845-3*) Childrens.
Gregory, Paul. Baseball & Softball. (Illus.). 80p. (gr. 10-12). 1992. pap. 6.95 (*0-7063-6667-0*, Pub. by Ward Lock UK) Sterling.
Gutelle, Andrew. All-Time Great World Series. Forbes, Bart, illus. LC 93-35668. 48p. (gr. 2-3). 1994. 7.99 (*0-448-40472-9*, G&D); pap. 3.50 (*0-448-40471-0*, G&D) Putnam Pub Group.
—Baseball's Best: Five True Stories. Spohn, Cliff, illus. LC 89-35413. 48p. (Orig.). (gr. 2-4). 1990. 3.50 (*0-394-80983-1*); lib. bdg. 7.99 (*0-394-90983-6*) Random Bks Yng Read.
Gutman, Bill. Baseball. LC 89-7377. (Illus.). 64p. (gr. 3-8). 1990. PLB 14.95 (*0-942545-84-2*) Marshall Cavendish.
—Sports Illustrated Strange & Amazing Baseball Stories. 128p. (gr. 5 up). 1990. pap. 2.99 (*0-671-70120-7*, Archway) PB.
Hall, Katy & Eisenberg, Lisa. Baseball Bloopers. Callen, Liz, illus. LC 89-62210. 96p. (Orig.). (gr. 2-6). 1991. pap. 2.95 (*0-679-80335-1*) Random Bks Yng Read.
Hollman, Fred. How to Profit from Baseball Card Collecting: A Basic Guide for the New Collector-Investor. Scherer, D. J., ed. 24p. (ps-12). 1991. 4.95 (*0-918734-36-3*) Reymont.
How to Play the All-Star Way, 6 vols. (gr. 4-7). 1994. Set. 89.64 (*0-8114-5782-6*) Raintree Steck-V.

Hurwitz, Johanna. Baseball Fever. Cruz, Ray, illus. LC 81-5633. 128p. (gr. 3 up). 1991. pap. 3.95 (*0-688-10495-9*, Pub. by Beech Tree Bks) Morrow.
Jacobs, William J. They Shaped the Game. LC 94-14007. (gr. 4-6). 1994. 15.95 (*0-684-19734-0*, Scribner) Macmillan.
Jarrett, William. Timetables of Sports History: Baseball. (Illus.). 96p. (gr. 6 up). 1989. 17.95 (*0-8160-1918-5*) Facts on File.
Kalb, Jonah. The Easy Baseball Book. Kossin, Sandy, illus. LC 75-44085. 64p. (gr. 2-5). 1976. 14.45 (*0-395-24385-8*) HM.
Kaplan, Jim. The Official Baseball Hall of Fame Book of Super Stars. (gr. 3 up). 1989. pap. 4.95 (*0-671-67379-3*, Little Simon) S&S Trade.
Kennedy, Trish & Schodorf, Timothy. Baseball Card Crazy. LC 92-14597. 80p. (gr. 4-6). 1993. SBE 11.95 (*0-684-19536-4*, Scribner Young Read) Macmillan Child Grp.
Koosman, Jerry. Jerry Koosman's Guide for Young Pitchers. Meyers, Susan, ed. Oster, Don, et al. (Illus., Orig.). (gr. 2-6). 1989. pap. 5.95 (*0-9618437-0-5*) Young Creations.
Macnow, Glen. Cal Ripken, Jr. Star Shortstop. LC 94-5544. (Illus.). 104p. (gr. 4-10). 1994. lib. bdg. 17.95 (*0-89490-485-X*) Enslow Pubs.
Maitland, William J. Young Ball Player's Guide to Safe Pitching: Ages Eight Thru Adult with Conditioning, Strengthening. (Illus.). 140p. (gr. 3 up). Date not set. pap. 14.95 (*0-936759-14-3*) Maitland Enter.
—Young Ballplayers Guide to Safe Pitching - Ages 8 through Adult. Barclay, John, ed. Molen, Art, intro. by. (Illus.). 150p. (gr. 4 up). 1991. pap. write for info. (*0-936759-02-X*) Maitland Enter.
Marx. Gold Gloves. 1991. 12.50s.p. (*0-86593-130-5*); PLB 16.67 (*0-685-59188-3*) Rourke Corp.
Mayers, Florence C. Baseball ABC. LC 94-1167. 1994. 12.95 (*0-8109-1938-9*) Abrams.
Nash, Bruce & Zullo, Allan. Baseball Hall of Shame Two: Young Fans' Edition. Clancy, Lisa, ed. 144p. (Orig.). 1991. pap. 2.99 (*0-671-73533-0*, Archway) PB.
Nolan Ryan Sports Shots. (ps-3). 1992. pap. 1.25 (*0-590-45844-2*) Scholastic Inc.
Norworth, Jack. Take Me Out to the Ballgame. LC 91-18555. (Illus.). 40p. (ps up). 1992. RSBE 14.95 (*0-02-735991-3*, Four Winds) Macmillan Child Grp.
Obojski, Robert. Baseball Bloopers & Diamond Oddities. LC 89-31270. (Illus.). 128p. 1991. pap. 4.95 (*0-8069-6981-4*) Sterling.
Plaut, David. Start Collecting Baseball Cards. LC 89-43016. (Illus.). 96p. (Orig.). (gr. 4 up). 1989. pap. 9.95 (*0-89471-762-6*) Running Pr.
Playbook! Baseball: You Are the Manager, You Call the Shots. (Illus.). (gr. 3-7). 1990. pap. 5.95 (*0-316-83624-9*, Spts Illus Kids) Little.
Rosenblum, Richard. Brooklyn Dodger Days. Rosenblum, Richard, illus. LC 90-36691. 32p. (gr. 1-5). 1991. SBE 13.95 (*0-689-31512-0*, Atheneum Child Bk) Macmillan Child Grp.
Schlossberg, Dan. Pitching. (Illus.). 96p. (gr. 5 up). 1991. pap. 12.95 (*0-671-73317-6*, S&S BFYR); pap. 5.95 (*0-671-70443-5*, S&S BFYR) S&S Trade.
The Secret of the Pros: How to Become a Baseball Card Dealer. 176p. (Orig.). (gr. 8 up). 1991. pap. 12.95 (*0-9631104-1-1*) M Cohen.
Shirts, Morris A. Warm up for Little League Baseball. rev. ed. MacDonald, Pat, ed. (Illus.). (gr. 3-6). 1990. pap. 2.99 (*0-671-70119-3*, Archway) PB.
Silvani, Harold. Baseball Card Grand Slam Curriculum Activities. Garcia, Joe, illus. 30p. (gr. 4-8). 1992. wkbk. 11.95 (*1-878669-52-4*) Crea Tea Assocs.
Sullivan, George. Baseball Kids. LC 89-29102. (Illus.). 64p. (gr. 5 up). 1990. 13.95 (*0-525-65023-7*, Cobblehill Bks) Dutton Child Bks.
Supraner, Robyn. I Can Read About Baseball. LC 74-24926. (Illus.). (gr. 2-4). 1975. pap. 2.50 (*0-89375-062-X*) Troll Assocs.
Teirstein, Mark A. Baseball. LC 93-23271. 1993. PLB 21.34 (*0-8114-5776-1*) Raintree Steck-V.
Turner, R. Dale. Baseball Yearbook. (Illus.). 35p. (gr. 2-12). 1991. spiral bdg. 9.95 (*0-9628939-0-0*) SeaWard Graph.
Walton, Rick. Off Base: Riddles about Baseball. (gr. 4-7). 1993. pap. 3.95 (*0-8225-9638-5*) Lerner Pubns.
Walton, Rick & Walton, Ann. Off Base: Riddles about Baseball. Burke, Susan S., illus. LC 92-19857. 1993. 11.95 (*0-8225-2338-8*) Lerner Pubns.
Weber, Bruce. Baseball Trivia and Fun Book. (gr. 4-7). 1993. pap. 2.50 (*0-590-47174-0*) Scholastic Inc.
—Bruce Weber's Inside Baseball 1992. (gr. 4-7). 1992. pap. 2.25 (*0-590-45627-X*, Apple Paperbacks) Scholastic Inc.
Weiner, Eric. The Kids Complete Baseball Catalogue. (Illus.). 256p. (gr. 5 up). 1990. (J Messner); pap. 12.95 (*0-671-70197-5*) S&S Trade.
Winfield, Dave. Ask Dave: Dave Winfield Answers Kids' Questions about Baseball & Life. LC 94-225. 1994. pap. 6.95 (*0-8362-8057-1*) Andrews & McMeel.

BASEBALL–BIOGRAPHY

Aaseng, Nathan. Baseball: It's Your Team. (gr. k-12). 1987. pap. 2.50 (*0-440-90507-9*, LFL) Dell.
—Dwight Gooden: Strikeout King. (Illus.). 56p. (gr. 4-9). 1988. PLB 13.50 (*0-8225-0478-2*, First Ave Edns); pap. 4.95 (*0-8225-9549-4*, First Ave Edns) Lerner Pubns.
—Jose Canseco: Baseball's Forty-Forty Man. (Illus.). 56p. (gr. 4-9). 1989. PLB 13.50 (*0-8225-0493-6*) Lerner Pubns.
—Jose Canseco: Baseball's Forty-Forty Man. 1991. pap. 4.95 (*0-8225-9586-9*) Lerner Pubns.
—Sports Great Kirby Puckett. LC 92-38433. (Illus.). 64p. (gr. 4-10). 1993. lib. bdg. 15.95 (*0-89490-392-6*) Enslow Pubs.
Aces of the Mound. (Illus.). 24p. (gr. 1 up). 1991. pap. 3.95 incl. stickers (*0-671-73635-3*, Little Simon) S&S Trade.
Aylesworth, Thomas G. Kids' World Almanac of Baseball. rev. ed. (gr. 4-7). 1993. 14.95 (*0-88687-722-9*) Wrld Almnc.
Balzar, Howard. Baseball Super Stars. Allison, B., intro. by. (Illus.). 23p. (Orig.). (gr. 1-8). 1990. pap. 2.50 (*0-943409-14-4*) Marketcom.
—Baseball Superstars. Allison, B., intro. by. 29p. (Orig.). 1991. pap. 4.95 (*0-943409-18-7*) Marketcom.
Barden. Base Stealers. 1991. 12.50s.p. (*0-86593-126-7*) Rourke Corp.
—MVPs. 1991. 16.67 (*0-86593-127-5*); 12.50s.p. (*0-685-66095-8*) Rourke Corp.
Baseball Heroes Series, 8 bks. 1991. Set. 100.00s.p. (*0-86593-125-9*) Rourke Corp.
Baseball Legends, 35 vols. (Illus.). (gr. 3 up). 1991. Set. PLB 493.35 (*0-7910-1163-1*, Am Art Analog) Chelsea Hse.
Bauleke, Ann. Kirby Puckett: Fan Favorite. LC 92-15271. 1993. 13.50 (*0-8225-0490-1*) Lerner Pubns.
—Kirby Puckett: Fan Favorite. (gr. 4-7). 1993. pap. 4.95 (*0-8225-9633-4*) Lerner Pubns.
—Rickey Henderson: Record Stealer. (Illus.). 48p. (gr. 4-9). 1991. PLB 13.50 (*0-8225-0541-X*) Lerner Pubns.
—Rickey Henderson: Record Stealer. (Illus.). 64p. (gr. 4-9). 1992. pap. 4.95 (*0-8225-9597-4*) Lerner Pubns.
Bjarkman, Peter. Warren Spahn. (Illus.). 1994. 14.95 (*0-7910-1191-7*, Am Art Analog) Chelsea Hse.
Bliss. Batting Champs. 1991. 12.50s.p. (*0-86593-129-1*) Rourke Corp.
—Home Run Leaders. 1991. 12.50s.p. (*0-86593-128-3*); PLB 16.67 (*0-685-66094-X*) Rourke Corp.
Bobby Bonilla. 1992. 1.25 (*0-590-46249-0*) Scholastic Inc.
Cox, Ted. Frank Thomas: The Big Hurt. LC 94-9914. (Illus.). 48p. (gr. 2-8). 1994. PLB 15.80 (*0-516-04386-2*); pap. 3.95 (*0-516-44386-0*) Childrens.
Curato, Guy, pseud. Batting One Thousand - Baseball's Leading Hitters: A Tribute to Lou Gehrig. LC 88-82916. 124p. (Orig.). (gr. 9). 1989. pap. write for info. (*0-9621591-0-7*) T Assicurato.
Devaney, John. Bo Jackson: A Star for All Seasons. 132p. 1992. 14.95 (*0-8027-8178-0*); PLB 15.85 (*0-8027-8179-9*) Walker & Co.
—Sports Great Roger Clemens. LC 89-7874. (Illus.). 64p. (gr. 4-10). 1990. lib. bdg. 15.95 (*0-89490-284-9*) Enslow Pubs.
Dickey, Glenn. Sports Great Kevin Mitchell. LC 92-24159. (Illus.). 64p. (gr. 4-10). 1993. lib. bdg. 15.95 (*0-89490-388-8*) Enslow Pubs.
Dunham, Montrew. Abner Doubleday, Young Baseball Pioneer. LC 93-45400. 1995. pap. 4.95 (*0-689-71788-1*, Aladdin) Macmillan Child Grp.
Gilbert, Thomas W. Roberto Clemente. (Illus.). 112p. (gr. 5 up). 1991. lib. bdg. 17.95 (*0-7910-1240-9*) Chelsea Hse.
Gire, Judy. A Boy & His Baseball: The Dave Dravecky Story. 32p. 1992. 14.99 (*0-310-58630-5*, Youth Bks) Zondervan.
Gowdey, David. Baseball Super Stars. Whitehead, Sam, illus. 64p. (gr. 7-12). 1994. pap. 8.95 (*0-448-40544-X*, G&D) Putnam Pub Group.
Green, Carl R. Orel Hershiser. LC 93-28044. (gr. 5 up). 1994. text ed. 13.95 (*0-89686-836-2*, Crestwood Hse) Macmillan.
Green, Carl R. & Ford, M. Roxanne. Deion Sanders. LC 93-951. (Illus.). 48p. (gr. 5-6). 1994. text ed. 13.95 RSBE (*0-89686-840-0*, Crestwood Hse) Macmillan Child Grp.
Greenberg, Keith. Nolan Ryan. LC 92-40311. 1993. 15.93 (*0-86592-002-8*); 11.95s.p. (*0-685-66273-X*) Rourke Enter.
Greene, Carol. Roy Campanella: Major-League Champion. LC 93-37878. (Illus.). 48p. (gr. k-3). 1994. PLB 12.85 (*0-516-04261-0*) Childrens.
Gutman, Bill. Jim Abbott: Star Pitcher. LC 92-7540. (Illus.). 48p. (gr. 3-6). 1992. PLB 13.40 (*1-56294-083-X*); pap. 4.95 (*1-56294-823-7*) Millbrook Pr.
—Jim Abbott: Star Pitcher. (gr. 4-7). 1992. pap. 4.95 (*0-395-64543-3*) HM.
Harvey, Miles. Barry Bonds: Baseball's Complete Player. LC 93-41053. (Illus.). 48p. (gr. 2-8). 1994. PLB 11.95 (*0-516-04381-1*) Childrens.
Hit Men. (Illus.). 24p. (gr. 1 up). 1991. pap. 3.95 incl. stickers (*0-671-73637-X*, Little Simon) S&S Trade.
Home Run Kings. (Illus.). 24p. (gr. 1 up). 1991. pap. 3.95 incl. stickers (*0-671-73636-1*, Little Simon) S&S Trade.
Italia, Bob. Baseball's Greatest Players. LC 93-13085. 1993. write for info. (*1-56239-241-7*) Abdo & Dghtrs.
Johnson, Rick L. Jim Abbott: Beating the Odds. (Illus.). 64p. (gr. 3 up). 1991. text ed. 13.95 RSBE (*0-87518-459-6*, Dillon) Macmillan Child Grp.
Kavanagh, Jack. Honus Wagner. (Illus.). 1994. 14.95 (*0-7910-1193-3*, Am Art Analog) Chelsea Hse.
—Rogers Hornsby. Murray, Jim, intro. by. (Illus.). 64p. (gr. 3 up). 1991. lib. bdg. 14.95 (*0-7910-1178-X*) Chelsea Hse.
—Shoeless Joe Jackson. LC 94-21264. 1995. write for info. (*0-7910-2170-X*) Chelsea Hse.
—Walter Johnson. (Illus.). 64p. (gr. 3 up). 1992. lib. bdg. 14.95 (*0-7910-1179-8*) Chelsea Hse.
Ken Griffey, Jr. 1992. 1.25 (*0-590-46112-5*) Scholastic Inc.
Klein, Dave. Stars of the Major Leagues. LC 73-18739. (Illus.). 160p. (gr. 7-12). 1974. lib. bdg. 3.69 (*0-394-92762-1*) Random Bks Yng Read.
Knapp, Ron. Sports Great Bobby Bonilla. LC 92-38431. (Illus.). 64p. (gr. 4-10). 1993. lib. bdg. 15.95 (*0-89490-417-5*) Enslow Pubs.
—Sports Great Orel Hershiser. LC 92-11329. (Illus.). 64p. (gr. 4-10). 1993. lib. bdg. 15.95 (*0-89490-389-6*) Enslow Pubs.
—Sports Great Will Clark. LC 92-521. (Illus.). 64p. (gr. 4-10). 1993. lib. bdg. 15.95 (*0-89490-390-X*) Enslow Pubs.
Kramer, S. A. Baseball's Greatest Pitchers. Campbell, Jim, illus. LC 91-27892. 48p. (Orig.). (gr. 2-4). 1992. PLB 7.99 (*0-679-92149-4*); pap. 3.50 (*0-679-82149-X*) Random Bks Yng Read.
Lace, William W. Sports Great Nolan Ryan. LC 92-41693. (Illus.). 64p. (gr. 4-10). 1993. lib. bdg. 15.95 (*0-89490-394-2*) Enslow Pubs.
Lee, Greg. Jim Abbott, Pitcher. LC 92-43251. 1993. 14.60 (*0-86593-258-1*); 10.95s.p. (*0-685-66274-8*) Rourke Corp.
Lonborg, Rosemary. The Quiet Hero - A Baseball Story. Houghton, Diane, illus. 32p. (gr. 2-6). 1993. perfect bound 7.95 (*0-8283-1958-8*) Branden Pub Co.
Lundgren, Hal. Ryne Sandberg: The Triple Threat. LC 85-29895. (Illus.). 48p. (gr. 2-8). 1986. pap. 3.95 (*0-516-44357-7*) Childrens.
Macht, Norm. Jimmie Foxx. Murray, Jim, intro. by. (Illus.). 64p. (gr. 3 up). 1991. PLB 14.95 (*0-7910-1175-5*) Chelsea Hse.
—Satchel Paige. Murray, Jim, intro. by. (Illus.). 64p. (gr. 3 up). 1991. lib. bdg. 14.95 (*0-7910-1185-2*) Chelsea Hse.
Macht, Norman L. Cy Young. (Illus.). 64p. (gr. 3 up). 1992. PLB 14.95 (*0-7910-1196-8*) Chelsea Hse.
—Reggie Jackson. Murray, Jim, intro. by. LC 94-228. (gr. 4 up). 1994. write for info. (*0-7910-2169-6*) Chelsea Hse.
Macnow, Glen. Sports Great Cal Ripken, Jr. LC 92-24158. (Illus.). 64p. (gr. 4-10). 1993. lib. bdg. 15.95 (*0-89490-387-X*) Enslow Pubs.
Martin, Patricia S. Dale Murphy: Baseball's Gentle Giant. (Illus.). 24p. (gr. 1-4). 1987. PLB 14.60 (*0-86592-167-9*); 10.95 (*0-685-67567-X*) Rourke Corp.
Marx. Gold Gloves. 1991. 12.50s.p. (*0-86593-130-5*); PLB 16.67 (*0-685-59188-3*) Rourke Corp.
—Relief Pitchers. 1991. 12.50s.p. (*0-86593-131-3*); lib. bdg. 16.67 (*0-685-66096-6*) Rourke Corp.
—Rookies. 1991. 12.50s.p. (*0-86593-132-1*); lib. bdg. 16.67 (*0-685-66097-4*) Rourke Corp.
Monroe, Judy. Dave Winfield. LC 87-30503. (Illus.). 48p. (gr. 5-6). 1988. RSBE 11.95 (*0-89686-370-0*, Crestwood Hse) Macmillan Child Grp.
Morgan, Bill. Sport Shots: Cal Ripken, Jr. (ps-3). 1994. pap. 1.25 (*0-590-48243-2*) Scholastic Inc.
Motomora, Mitchell. Specs: The True Story of Baseball Player George Toporcer. Barbaresi, Nina, illus. 24p. (ps-2). 1990. 17.10 (*0-8172-3585-X*); PLB 10.95 pkg. of 3 (*0-685-58557-3*) Raintree Steck-V.
Nabhan. Cy Young Winners. 1991. 12.50s.p. (*0-86593-133-X*) Rourke Corp.
Nash, Bruce & Zullo, Allan. More Little Big Leaguers: Amazing Boyhood Stories of Today's Baseball Stars. (Illus.). 96p. (gr. 1 up). 1991. pap. 7.95 incl. baseball cards (*0-671-73394-X*, Little Simon) S&S Trade.
Newman, Matthew. Dwight Gooden. LC 86-16527. (Illus.). 48p. (gr. 5-6). 1986. text ed. 11.95 RSBE (*0-89686-317-4*, Crestwood Hse) Macmillan Child Grp.
Nicholson, Lois. Cal Ripken, Jr. Quiet Hero. LC 93-22741. (Illus.). 112p. (gr. 4-8). 1993. bds. 12.95 (*0-87033-445-X*) Tidewater.
Puckett, Kirby. Be the Best You Can Be. Houle, Tim, illus. 40p. Date not set. 14.95 (*0-931674-20-4*) Waldman Hse Pr.
Rambeck, Richard. Jim Abbott. LC 92-43044. (SPA & ENG.). 32p. 1993. 14.95 (*1-56766-072-X*) Childs World.
Rappoport, Ken. Bobby Bonilla. LC 92-34583. (Illus.). 144p. (gr. 5 up). 1993. 14.95 (*0-8027-8255-8*); PLB 15.85 (*0-8027-8256-6*) Walker & Co.
—Nolan Ryan: The Ryan Express. LC 92-3244. (Illus.). 64p. (gr. 3 up). 1992. text ed. 13.95 RSBE (*0-87518-524-X*, Dillon) Macmillan Child Grp.
Record Breakers. (Illus.). 24p. (gr. 1 up). 1991. pap. 3.95 (*0-671-73634-5*, Little Simon) S&S Trade.
Reiser, Howard. Jim Abbott: All-American Pitcher. LC 93-7424. 48p. (gr. 2-8). 1993. PLB 11.95 (*0-516-04376-5*); pap. 3.95 (*0-516-44376-3*) Childrens.
—Ken Griffey, Jr. The Kid. LC 93-41054. (Illus.). 48p. (gr. 2-8). 1994. PLB 11.95 (*0-516-04384-6*) Childrens.
—Nolan Ryan: Strikeout King. LC 92-35741. (Illus.). 48p. (gr. 2-8). 1993. PLB 11.95 (*0-516-04365-X*); pap. 3.95 (*0-516-44365-8*) Childrens.
Roger Clemens. 1992. 1.25 (*0-590-46248-2*) Scholastic Inc.
Rolfe, John. Bo Jackson. (gr. 4-7). 1991. pap. 4.95 (*0-316-75457-9*, Spts Illus Kids) Little.
—Bo Jackson. (Illus.). 124p. (gr. 3-6). 1991. PLB 19.95 (*0-8225-3109-7*) Lerner Pubns.
—Jim Abbott. 144p. (gr. 3-6). 1991. PLB 19.95 (*0-8225-3108-9*) Lerner Pubns.

—Jim Abbott: Sports Illustrated Kids. (gr. 4-7). 1991. pap. 4.95 (0-316-75459-5, Spts Illus Kids) Little.
—Nolan Ryan. (Illus.). 144p. (gr. 3-7). 1992. pap. 4.95 (0-316-75462-5, Spts Illus Kids) Little.
Rosenthal, Bert. Dwight Gooden: King of the Ks. LC 85-11687. (Illus.). 48p. (gr. 2-8). 1985. pap. 3.95 (0-516-44348-8) Childrens.
Rothaus, James R. Bo Jackson. 32p. (gr. 2-6). 1991. 14.95 (0-89565-731-7) Childs World.
—Jose Canseco. 32p. 1991. 14.95 (0-89565-735-X) Childs World.
—Ken Griffey, Jr. 32p. 1991. 14.95 (0-89565-783-X) Childs World.
Rothaus, Jim. Cal Ripken. (ENG & SPA.). (gr. 2-6). 1992. PLB 14.95 (0-89565-867-4) Childs World.
—Kirby Puckett. (SPA & ENG.). (gr. 2-6). 1992. PLB 14.95 (0-89565-960-3) Childs World.
Savage, Jeff. Sports Great Jim Abbott. LC 92-522. (Illus.). 64p. (gr. 4-10). 1993. lib. bdg. 15.95 (0-89490-395-0) Enslow Pubs.
Scholz, Jackson. Fielder from Nowhere. 256p. (gr. 6 up). 1993. pap. 4.95 (0-688-12159-4, Pub. by Beech Tree Bks) Morrow.
Shannon, Mike. Willie Stargell. (Illus.). 64p. (gr. 3 up). 1992. lib. bdg. 14.95 (0-7910-1192-5) Chelsea Hse.
Stocker, Fern N. Billy Sunday: Baseball Preacher. (Orig.). (gr. 2-7). 1985. pap. text ed. 4.50 (0-8024-0442-1) Moody.
Sullivan, George. Pitchers: Twenty-Seven of Baseball's Greatest. LC 93-3007. (Illus.). 80p. (gr. 5 up). 1994. SBE 17.95 (0-689-31825-1, Atheneum Child Bk) Macmillan Child Grp.
—Sluggers! Twenty-Seven of Baseball's Greatest. LC 90-45817. (Illus.). 80p. (gr. 3 up). 1991. SBE 16.95 (0-689-31566-X, Atheneum Child Bk) Macmillan Child Grp.
Sullivan, Michael J. Top Ten Baseball Pitchers. LC 94-2157. (Illus.). 48p. (gr. 4-10). 1994. lib. bdg. 14.95 (0-89490-520-1) Enslow Pubs.
Thornley, Stew. Cal Ripken, Jr. Oriole Ironman. (gr. 4-7). 1992. 13.50 (0-8225-0547-9) Lerner Pubns.
—Deion Sanders: Prime Time Player. LC 92-45686. 1993. 13.50 (0-8225-0523-1) Lerner Pubns.
—Deion Sanders: Prime Time Player. (gr. 4-7). 1993. pap. 4.95 (0-8225-9648-2) Lerner Pubns.
Torres, John A. & Sullivan, Michael J. Sports Great Darryl Strawberry. LC 89-28918. (Illus.). 64p. (gr. 4-10). 1990. lib. bdg. 15.95 (0-89490-291-1) Enslow Pubs.
Tunis, John R. Highpockets. LC 75-175816. 192p. (gr. 5 up). 1990. pap. 4.95 (0-688-09288-8, Pub. by Beech Tree Bks) Morrow.
Weber, Bruce. Baseball Megastars, 1994. (gr. 4-7). 1994. pap. 3.95 (0-590-47448-0) Scholastic Inc.
—Sparky Anderson. LC 88-14985. (Illus.). 48p. (gr. 5-6). 1988. text ed. 11.95 RSBE (0-89686-379-4, Crestwood Hse) Macmillan Child Grp.
—Sport Shots: Barry Bonds. (ps-3). 1994. pap. 1.25 (0-590-48242-4) Scholastic Inc.
White, Sarah g. Like Father, Like Son: Baseball's Major League Families. (gr. 4-7). 1993. pap. 2.95 (0-590-46027-7) Scholastic Inc.
Woods, Bob. Sport Shots: John Olerud. (ps-3). 1994. pap. 1.25 (0-590-48240-8) Scholastic Inc.
Zennert, Richard. Hank Aaron. King, Coretta Scott, intro. by. (Illus.). 112p. (gr. 5 up). 1993. PLB 17.95 (0-7910-1859-8); pap. write for info. (0-7910-1888-1) Chelsea Hse.

BASEBALL–DICTIONARIES

Hollander, Zander, ed. The Baseball Book. rev. ed. LC 90-38060. (Illus.). 192p. (gr. 5 up). 1991. pap. 9.95 (0-679-81055-2) Random Bks Yng Read.

BASEBALL–FICTION

Aaseng, Nathan. Winning Season for the Braves. LC 82-72711. (gr. 3-7). 1988. pap. 4.99 (1-55513-950-7, Chariot Bks) Chariot Family.
Adler, David A. Cam Jansen & the Mystery of the Babe Ruth Baseball. Natti, Susanna, illus. (gr. 1-4). 1984. pap. 2.75 (0-440-41020-7, YB) Dell.
—Cam Jansen & the Mystery of the Babe Ruth Baseball. (gr. 4-7). 1991. pap. 3.99 (0-14-034895-6, Puffin) Puffin Bks.
Aiello. It's Your Turn at Bat. 1991. 0.85 (0-8050-2014-4) H Holt & Co.
Aiello, Barbara & Shulman, Jeffrey. It's Your Turn at Bat: Featuring Mark Riley. Barr, Loel, illus. 48p. (gr. 3-6). 1988. PLB 13.95 (0-8050-3070-0) TFC Bks NY.
Anderson, Peggy K. Safe at Home! LC 90-19133. 128p. (gr. 3-7). 1992. SBE 13.95 (0-689-31686-0, Atheneum Child Bk) Macmillan Child Grp.
Banks, Joann. Brandon's First Baseball Game. Robinson, Famous, illus. LC 90-63290. 37p. (Orig.). (ps-6). 1990. pap. text ed. 5.00 (0-9627951-0-0) JRBB Pubs.
Beatty, Patricia. Wait for Me, Watch for Me, Eula Bee. LC 78-12782. 224p. (gr. 5 up). 1990. Repr. of 1978 ed. 3.95 (0-688-10077-5, Pub. by Beech Tree Bks) Morrow.
Bee, Clair. Dugout Jinx. (Illus.). 208p. 1990. Repr. lib. bdg. 25.95x (0-89966-741-4) Buccaneer Bks.
Bonner. Two-Way Pitcher. (gr. 7 up). PLB 7.19 (0-8313-0008-6) Lantern.
Bowen, Robert S. Infield Flash. LC 69-14320. (gr. 7-12). 1969. PLB 11.93 (0-688-51007-8) Lothrop.
Buller, Jon & Schade, Susan. Twenty-Thousand Baseball Cards under the Sea. Buller, Jon, illus. LC 90-40704. 48p. (Orig.). (gr. 2-3). 1991. lib. bdg. 7.99 (0-679-91569-9); pap. 3.50 (0-679-81569-4) Random Bks Yng Read.
Carrier, Roch. El Jonron Mas Largo. Zeller, Beatriz, tr. Cohen, Sheldon, illus. LC 92-83961. (SPA.). 24p. (gr. 3 up). 1993. 14.95 (0-88776-304-9) Tundra Bks.
—The Longest Home Run. Fischman, Sheila, tr. from FRE. Cohen, Sheldon, illus. LC 92-62364. 24p. (gr. 3 up). 1993. 14.95 (0-88776-300-6) Tundra Bks.
—Le Plus Long Circuit (The Longest Home Run) Cohen, Sheldon, illus. LC 92-62362. (FRE.). 24p. (gr. 2 up). 1993. 14.95 (0-88776-301-4) Tundra Bks.
Cebulash, Mel. Batboy. Krych, Duane, illus. (gr. 3-8). 1992. PLB 8.95 (0-89565-882-8) Childs World.
Christopher, Matt. Baseball Pals. Henneberger, Robert, illus. (gr. 4-6). 1990. pap. 3.95 (0-316-14005-8) Little.
—Catcher with a Glass Arm. Caddell, Foster, illus. (gr. 4-6). 1985. pap. 3.95 (0-316-13985-8) Little.
—Centerfield Ballhawk. Beier, Ellen, illus. 64p. (gr. 2-4). 1992. 13.95 (0-316-14079-1) Little.
—Centerfield Ballhawk. (ps-3). 1994. 3.95 (0-316-14272-7) Little.
—Challenge at Second Base. Ramsey, Marcy, illus. 144p. (gr. 3-6). 1992. pap. 3.95 (0-316-14249-2) Little.
—Diamond Champs. (gr. 4-7). 1990. pap. 3.95 (0-316-14006-6) Little.
—The Dog That Pitched a No-Hitter. Vasconcellos, Daniel, illus. (gr. 1-3). 1988. 13.95 (0-316-14057-0) Little.
—Dog That Pitched a No-Hitter. (ps-3). 1993. pap. 3.95 (0-316-14103-8) Little.
—Hard Drive to Short. (gr. 4-7). 1991. pap. 3.95 (0-316-14071-6) Little.
—The Hit-Away Kid. (gr. 2-4). 1988. 12.95 (0-316-13995-5) Little.
—The Hit-Away Kid. (gr. 2-4). 1990. pap. 3.95 (0-316-14007-4) Little.
—The Kid Who Only Hit Homers. Kidder, Harvey, illus. (gr. 4-6). 1972. lib. bdg. 14.95 (0-316-13918-1) Little.
—The Kid Who Only Hit Homers. Kidder, Harvey, illus. 160p. (gr. 4 up). 1986. pap. 3.95 (0-316-13987-4) Little.
—Lefty's Lost Pitch. (Illus.). 13p. (gr. 3-6). 1991. incls. puzzle 12.95 (0-922242-18-6) Lombard Mktg.
—Long Stretch at First Base. (gr. 4-7). 1993. pap. 3.95 (0-316-14101-1) Little.
—Look Who's Playing First Base. Kidder, Harvey, illus. (gr. 4-6). 1987. pap. 3.95 (0-316-13989-0) Little.
—Lucky Baseball Bat. (ps-3). 1991. pap. 11.95 (0-316-14073-2) Little.
—Lucky Baseball Bat. (ps-3). 1993. pap. 3.95 (0-316-14260-3) Little.
—Man Out At First. LC 92-31130. 1993. 12.95 (0-316-14084-8) Little.
—Matt Christopher Baseball. (gr. 4-7). 1991. Boxed set 2. pap. 11.85 (0-316-14075-9) Little.
—Pressure Play. LC 92-37276. 1993. 15.95 (0-316-14098-8) Little.
—Return of the Home Run Kid. Casale, Paul, illus. 168p. (gr. 3-7). 1992. 14.95 (0-316-14080-5) Little.
—Return of the Home Run Kid. (gr. 4-7). 1994. 3.95 (0-316-14273-5) Little.
—The Spy on Third Base. Ulrich, George, illus. LC 88-8914. (gr. 2-4). 1988. 12.95 (0-316-13996-3) Little.
—Spy on Third Base, Vol. 1. (ps-3). 1990. pap. 3.95 (0-316-14008-2) Little.
—The Submarine Pitch. Ramsey, Marcy, illus. 144p. (gr. 3-6). 1992. pap. 3.95 (0-316-14250-6) Little.
—Supercharged Infield. (gr. 4-7). 1994. 3.95 (0-316-14277-8) Little.
—The Year Mom Won the Pennant. Caddell, Foster, illus. 160p. (gr. 4 up). 1986. pap. 3.95 (0-316-13988-2) Little.
—Zero's Slider. LC 93-21177. 1994. 13.95 (0-316-14270-0) Little.
Cohen, Barbara. Thank You, Jackie Robinson. Cuffari, Richard, illus. LC 87-29341. (gr. 3-6). 1988. PLB 15.00 (0-688-07909-1) Lothrop.
Cohen, Ron. My Dad's Baseball. LC 93-22938. (Illus.). 1994. 15.00 (0-688-12390-2); lib. bdg. 14.93 (0-688-12391-0) Lothrop.
Connell, David D. & Thurman, Jim. The Unnatural: A Mathnet Casebook. LC 93-18352. (gr. 4-7). 1993. text ed. write for info. (0-7167-6506-3, Sci Am Yng Rdrs) W H Freeman.
Cornwell, Anita. The Girls of Summer. Caines, Kelly, illus. LC 88-64051. 100p. (Orig.). (gr. 6 up). 1989. pap. 12.95 (0-938678-11-6) New Seed.
Cristaldi, Kathryn. Baseball Ballerina. Carter, Abby, illus. LC 90-20234. 48p. (Orig.). (gr. 1-3). 1992. PLB 7.99 (0-679-91734-9); pap. 3.50 (0-679-81734-4) Random Bks Yng Read.
Dagavarian, Debra. Century of Children's Baseball Stories. (gr. 4-7). 1990. pap. 7.95 (0-9625132-0-2) Stadium Bks.
Dagavarian, Debra A., ed. A Century of Children's Baseball Stories. 200p. 1992. lib. bdg. 16.95 (0-88736-832-8) Mecklermedia.
D'Andrea, Joseph C. If I Were a Baltimore Oriole. Wilson, Bill, illus. 24p. (Orig.). (ps-5). 1994. pap. 5.99 (1-878338-57-9) Picture Me Bks.
—If I Were a Boston Red Sox. Wilson, Bill, illus. 24p. (Orig.). (ps-5). 1994. pap. 5.99 (1-878338-58-7) Picture Me Bks.
—If I Were a Cleveland Indian. Wilson, Bill, illus. 24p. (Orig.). (ps-5). 1994. pap. 5.99 (1-878338-60-9) Picture Me Bks.
—If I Were a Houston Astro. Wilson, Bill, illus. 24p. (Orig.). (ps-5). 1994. pap. 5.99 (1-57151-202-0) Picture Me Bks.
—If I Were a Minnesota Twin. Wilson, Bill, illus. 24p. (Orig.). (ps-5). 1994. pap. 5.99 (1-878338-61-7) Picture Me Bks.
—If I Were a Philadelphia Phillie. Wilson, Bill, illus. 24p. (Orig.). (ps-5). 1994. pap. 5.99 (1-878338-62-5) Picture Me Bks.
—If I Were a Pittsburgh Pirate. Wilson, Bill, illus. 24p. (Orig.). (ps-5). 1994. pap. 5.99 (1-878338-63-3) Picture Me Bks.
—If I Were a Saint Louis Cardinal. Wilson, Bill, illus. 24p. (Orig.). (ps-5). 1994. pap. 5.99 (1-878338-65-X) Picture Me Bks.
Davis, Gibbs. Christy's Magic Glove. (ps-3). 1992. pap. 3.25 (0-553-15988-7) Bantam.
—Diamond Park Dinosaur. 1994. pap. 3.25 (0-553-48131-2, Skylark) Bantam.
—Lucky Socks. (gr. 4-7). 1991. pap. 2.99 (0-553-15865-1) Bantam.
—Major-League Melissa. (gr. 4-7). 1991. pap. 3.25 (0-553-15866-X) Bantam.
—Never Sink Nine, No. 5. 1992. pap. 3.25 (0-553-15996-8) Bantam.
—Pete the Magnificent. (ps-3). 1991. pap. 3.25 (0-553-15896-1) Bantam.
—Slugger Mike. (ps-3). 1991. pap. 3.25 (0-553-15883-X) Bantam.
Deuker, Carl. Heart of a Champion. LC 92-37231. 1993. 15.95 (0-316-18166-8, Joy St Bks) Little.
Dixon, Michael B., et al. Striking Out! (Orig.). (gr. k up). 1984. pap. 4.50 (0-87602-252-2) Anchorage.
Dolan, Ellen M. & Bolinske, Janet L., eds. Casey at the Bat. LC 87-61667. (Illus.). 32p. (Orig.). (gr. 1-3). 1987. text ed. 8.95 (0-88335-558-2); pap. text ed. 4.95 (0-88335-578-7) Milliken Pub Co.
Downing, Joan. El Beisbol Es Nuestro Juego (Baseball's Our Game) Kratky, Lada, tr. from ENG. Freeman, Tony, illus. LC 82-4418. (SPA.). 32p. (gr. k-3). 1984. pap. 3.95 (0-516-53402-5) Childrens.
Duffey, Betsy. Lucky in Left Field. LC 91-4579. (ps-3). 1992. pap. 13.00 (0-671-74687-1, S&S BFYR) S&S Trade.
Dygard, Thomas J. The Rookie Arrives. LC 87-26238. 208p. (gr. 7 up). 1988. 12.95 (0-688-07598-3) Morrow Jr Bks.
Economos, Chris. The New Kid. (Illus.). 32p. (gr. 1-4). 1989. PLB 18.99 (0-8172-3512-4); pap. 3.95 (0-8114-6715-5) Raintree Steck-V.
Ellis, Lucy. Pink Parrots, No. 3: Mixed Signals. (gr. 4-7). 1991. pap. 3.50 (0-316-18566-3, Spts Illus Kids) Little.
—Pink Parrots, No. 4: Fielder's Choice. (gr. 4-7). 1991. pap. 3.50 (0-316-12447-8, Spts Illus Kids) Little.

Ferguson, Marvin. Boys on the Gold Coast. 247p. (gr. 7-12). 1993. pap. 9.95 (1-882286-00-6) Parker Pub IL. Every chance they got, the boys (teenagers) played baseball on a corner lot with tattered balls & splintered bats. It was fun until Larry hit home runs that landed on the green canopies of the little shops across the street. After being kicked out of the neighborhood by the police, the boy's hopes & dreams were gone until "Pop," a retired janitor, showed them a real baseball park & helped them develop a team that eventually played the Chicago Cubs at Wrigley Field. VOYA (Voice of Youth Advocates-- New York), said in a recent review, "Overall a good book with a happy ending." This exciting story is intended for middle school (6th, 7th & 8th grades) boys & girls & fits nicely into whole language programs, teaching children that reading is fun, thus encouraging them to read more & learn valuable lessons. Also, many adults like to reminisce about the "Good Ole Days." Order from Baker & Taylor Books or from Parker Publishing, P.O. Box 386, Crystal Lake, IL 60039-0386.
Publisher Provided Annotation.

Franklin, Lance. Double Play. 144p. (gr. 6 up). 1987. pap. 2.50 (0-553-26526-1, Starfire) Bantam.
Freeman, Mark. Big League Break. 144p. (gr. 4 up). 1989. pap. 2.95 (0-345-35904-6) Ballantine.
—Play Ball. 144p. (gr. 4 up). 1989. pap. 2.95 (0-345-35902-X) Ballantine.
Gallina, Michael & Gallina, Jill. The Inside Pitch. (gr. k-6). 1989. 2.95 (0-931205-47-6); tchr's. ed. 14.95 (0-931205-46-8) Jenson Pubns.
Gault. The Home Run Kings. 1993. pap. 2.75 (0-590-45530-3) Scholastic Inc.

Giff, Patricia R. Left-Handed Shortstop. Morrill, Leslie, illus. 128p. (gr. k-6). 1989. pap. 3.50 (*0-440-44672-4*, YB) Dell.
—Left-Handed Shortstop. Morrill, Leslie, illus. (gr. 4-6). 1980. pap. 11.95 (*0-385-28533-7*); pap. 11.95 (*0-385-28534-5*) Delacorte.
—Ronald Morgan Goes to Bat. Natti, Susanna, illus. 32p. (gr. k-4). 1988. pap. 10.95 (*0-670-81457-1*) Viking Child Bks.
—Ronald Morgan Goes to Bat. Natti, Susanna, illus. 32p. (ps-3). 1990. pap. 3.99 (*0-14-050669-1*, Puffin) Puffin Bks.
Gordon, Sharon. Play Ball, Kate! Page, Don, illus. LC 81-4855. 32p. (gr. k-2). 1981. pap. text ed. 11.59 (*0-89375-525-7*); pap. 2.95 (*0-89375-526-5*) Troll Assocs.
Greenberg, Daniel A. The Great Baseball Card Hunt. Dodson, Bert, illus. Lewis, Glenn. (Illus.). 112p. (gr. 2-6). 1992. pap. 12.00 (*0-671-72927-6*, S&S BFYR); pap. 2.95 (*0-671-72931-4*, S&S BFYR) S&S Trade.
—The Missing Championship Ring. Dodson, Bert, illus. Lewis, Glenn. (Illus.). 112p. (gr. 2-6). 1992. (Little Simon); pap. 2.95 (*0-671-72933-0*, Little Simon) S&S Trade.
Grey, Zane. The Shortstop. Thorn, John, frwd. by. LC 91-24034. 240p. (gr. 7 up). 1992. Repr. of 1909 ed. 13.00 (*0-688-11088-6*) Morrow Jr Bks.
—The Young Pitcher. Thorn, John, frwd. by. LC 91-23670. 256p. (gr. 7 up). 1992. Repr. of 1911 ed. 13.00 (*0-688-11090-8*) Morrow Jr Bks.
Grubbs, Joan & Grubbs, Tori. PH - Little Leaguer: Little League Peewee Baseball. Abel, J., illus. 17p. (Orig.). (gr. 1-3). 1992. PLB 25.00 (*1-56611-549-3*); pap. 15.00 (*1-56611-009-2*) Jonas.
Halecroft, David. Wild Pitch. (Illus.). 128p. (gr. 3-7). 1991. pap. 2.95 (*0-14-034548-5*, Puffin) Puffin Bks.
Hallowell, Tommy. Duel on the Diamond. 128p. (gr. 3 up). 1990. pap. 3.50 (*0-14-032910-2*, Puffin) Puffin Bks.
—Duel on the Diamond. 1991. pap. 12.95 (*0-670-83729-6*) Viking Child Bks.
Hanft, Philip. Never Fear, Flip the Dip Is Here. Allen, Thomas B., illus. LC 90-3385. 32p. (ps-3). 1991. 12.95 (*0-8037-0897-1*); PLB 12.89 (*0-8037-0899-8*) Dial Bks Young.
Heller, Pete. Peppy Learns to Play Baseball. Kinsey, Thomas D., ed. Schaeffer, Bob, illus. 32p. (gr. k-5). pap. 3.95 (*0-932423-00-0*) Summa Bks.
Herman, Gail. Double-Header. Smath, Jerry, illus. LC 92-34175. 32p. (ps-1). 1993. PLB 7.99 (*0-448-40156-8*, G&D); pap. 3.50 (*0-448-40157-6*, G&D) Putnam Pub Group.
Herzig, Alison C. The Boonsville Bombers. Andreasen, Dan, illus. 96p. (gr. 3-7). 1993. pap. 3.99 (*0-14-034578-7*, Puffin) Puffin Bks.
Heymsfeld, Carla. Coaching Ms. Parker. O'Connor, Jane, illus. LC 91-28484. 96p. (gr. 3-5). 1992. SBE 12.95 (*0-02-743715-9*, Bradbury Pr) Macmillan Child Grp.
Hillert, Margaret. Play Ball. (Illus.). (ps-2). 1978. PLB 6.95 (*0-8136-5034-8*, TK2355); pap. 3.50 (*0-8136-5534-X*, TK2356) Modern Curr.
Hinds, Bill. Buzz Beamer's Out of This World Series. (Illus.). (gr. 3-7). 1991. pap. 3.95 (*0-316-36451-7*, Spts Illus Kids) Little.
Hiser, Constance. Dog on Third Base. Ewing, Carolyn, illus. LC 90-29062. 64p. (gr. 2-6). 1991. 13.95 (*0-8234-0898-1*) Holiday.
—Dog on Third Base. MacDonald, Pat, ed. Ewing, Carolyn S., illus. 80p. (gr. 2-4). 1993. pap. 2.99 (*0-671-78962-7*, Minstrel Bks) PB.
Hoff, Syd. The Littlest Leaguer. Hoff, Syd, illus. LC 75-25782. 48p. (gr. 2 up). 1979. (Little Simon) S&S Trade.
Hooks, William H. Mr. Baseball. (ps-3). 1991. 9.99 (*0-553-07315-X*); pap. 3.50 (*0-553-35303-9*) Bantam.
Hughes, Dean. Big Base Hit. Lyall, Dennis, illus. LC 89-37875. 96p. (Orig.). (gr. 2-6). 1990. PLB 9.99 (*0-679-90427-1*); pap. 2.95 (*0-679-80427-7*) Knopf Bks Yng Read.
—Play-Off, Bk. 13. Lyall, Dennis, illus. LC 90-49765. 112p. (Orig.). (gr. 2-6). 1991. pap. NLD (*0-679-81540-6*) Knopf Bks Yng Read.
—Stroke of Luck, Bk. 10. Lyall, Dennis, illus. LC 90-53313. 96p. (Orig.). (gr. 2-6). 1991. pap. 2.95 (*0-679-81537-6*) Knopf Bks Yng Read.
—Superstar Team, Bk. 9. Lyall, Dennis, illus. LC 90-53314. 96p. (Orig.). (gr. 2-6). 1991. pap. 2.95 (*0-679-81536-8*) Knopf Bks Yng Read.
—What a Catch! Lyall, Dennis, illus. LC 89-28876. 96p. (Orig.). (gr. 2-6). 1990. PLB 9.99 (*0-679-90429-8*); pap. 2.95 (*0-679-80429-3*) Knopf Bks Yng Read.
Hurwitz, Johanna. Baseball Fever. Cruz, Ray, illus. LC 81-5633. 128p. (gr. 4-6). 1981. 12.95 (*0-688-00710-4*); PLB 12.88 (*0-688-00711-2*, Morrow Jr Bks) Morrow Jr Bks.
—Baseball Fever. 128p. (gr. 4-7). 1983. pap. 2.95 (*0-440-40311-1*, YB) Dell.
Isadora, Rachel. Max. Isadora, Rachel, illus. LC 76-9088. 32p. (gr. k-3). 1976. RSBE 13.95 (*0-02-747450-X*, Macmillan Child Bk) Macmillan Child Grp.
Janney, Rebecca P. The Major League Mystery. LC 93-45633. 1994. 4.99 (*0-8499-3535-0*) Word Pub.
Jenkins, Jerry. The Secret Baseball Challenge. (Orig.). (gr. 7-12). 1986. pap. text ed. 4.99 (*0-8024-8232-5*) Moody.
Johnson, Neil. Batter Up. 1990. pap. 12.95 (*0-590-42729-6*) Scholastic Inc.
—Batter UP! 32p. 1992. pap. 3.95 (*0-590-42730-X*) Scholastic Inc.
Kelley, Shirley. The Rainy Day Blues. Herbst, Eric & Genee, Gloria, eds. Claridy, Jimmy, illus. King, B. B., intro. by. (Illus.). 32p. (ps-4). 1993. Incl. audio cass. 9.95 (*1-882436-01-6*) Better Pl Pub.
Kelly, Jeffrey A. The Basement Baseball Club. LC 86-27545. 160p. (gr. 3-5). 1987. 13.45 (*0-395-40774-5*) HM.
Kemp, Franklin. One Sane & the Crazy Nine. 1993. 10.95 (*0-8062-4770-3*) Carlton.
Kessler, Leonard. Here Comes the Strikeout. newly illus. ed. Kessler, Leonard, illus. LC 91-14717. 64p. (gr. k-3). 1965. 14.00 (*0-06-023155-6*); PLB 13.89 (*0-06-023156-4*) HarpC Child Bks.
—Here Comes the Strikeout. newly illus. ed. Kessler, Leonard, illus. LC 91-14720. 64p. (gr. k-3). 1978. pap. 3.50 (*0-06-444011-7*, Trophy) HarpC Child Bks.
—Old Turtle's Baseball Stories. Kessler, Leonard, illus. LC 81-6390. 56p. (gr. 1-3). 1982. 13.95 (*0-688-00723-6*); PLB 13.88 (*0-688-00724-4*) Greenwillow.
Kline, Suzy. Herbie Jones & the Monster Ball. Williams, Richard, illus. 112p. (gr. 2-6). 1988. 12.95 (*0-399-21569-7*, Putnam) Putnam Pub Group.
—Herbie Jones & the Monster Ball. Williams, Richard, illus. 128p. (gr. 3 up). 1990. pap. 3.99 (*0-14-034170-6*, Puffin) Puffin Bks.
Korman, Gordon. The Toilet Paper Tigers. LC 92-27277. 1993. 13.95 (*0-590-46230-X*) Scholastic Inc.
Kramer, S. A. At the Ball Game. La Padula, Thomas, illus. LC 93-31845. 32p. (Orig.). (ps-3). 1994. pap. 2.50 (*0-679-85291-3*) Random Bks Yng Read.
Kroll, Steven. Hit & Run Gang, No. 1: New Kid in Town. (ps-3). 1992. pap. 3.50 (*0-380-76407-5*, Camelot) Avon.
—Hit & Run Gang, No. 2: Playing Favorites. (gr. 4-7). 1992. pap. 3.50 (*0-380-76409-1*, Camelot) Avon.
—The Hit & Run Gang, No. 3: The Slump. 80p. (Orig.). (gr. 2). 1992. pap. 3.50 (*0-380-76408-3*, Camelot Young) Avon.
—The Hit & Run Gang, No. 5: Pitching Trouble. 96p. 1994. pap. 3.50 (*0-380-77366-X*, Camelot Young) Avon.
—The Hit & Run Gang, No. 6: You're Out! 96p. 1994. pap. 3.50 (*0-380-77367-8*, Camelot Young) Avon.
—The Hit & Run Gang: The Streak, No. 4. 80p. (Orig.). (gr. 2). 1992. pap. 3.50 (*0-380-76410-5*, Camelot Young) Avon.
Kusugak, Michael. Baseball Bats for Christmas. (JPN., Illus.). 24p. 1993. pap. 5.95 (*1-55037-314-5*, Pub. by Annick CN) Firefly Bks Ltd.
Latimer, Jim. Fox under First Base. McCue, Lisa, illus. LC 89-27576. 32p. (gr. k-2). 1991. SBE 13.95 (*0-684-19053-2*, Scribners Young Read) Macmillan Child Grp.
Lord, Betty B. In the Year of the Boar & Jackie Robinson. Simont, Marc, illus. LC 83-48440. 176p. (gr. 3-7). 1986. pap. 3.95 (*0-06-440175-8*, Trophy) HarpC Child Bks.
McConnachie, Brian. Elmer & the Chickens vs. the Big League. Stevenson, Harvey, illus. LC 91-2914. 32p. (ps-2). 1992. 14.00 (*0-517-57616-3*) Crown Bks Yng Read.
McCully, Emily A. Grandmas at Bat. McCully, Emily A., illus. LC 92-8318. 64p. (gr. k-3). 1993. 14.00 (*0-06-021031-1*); PLB 13.89 (*0-06-021032-X*) HarpC Child Bks.
McGee & Me! No. 8: Take Me Out of the Ball Game. 92p. pap. 3.99 (*0-8423-4113-7*) Tyndale.
McMullan, Kate. The Biggest Mouth in Baseball. DiVito, Anna, illus. LC 92-24467. 48p. (gr. 2-4). 1993. lib. bdg. 7.99 (*0-448-40516-4*, G&D); pap. 3.50 (*0-448-40515-6*, G&D) Putnam Pub Group.
McOmber, Rachel B., ed. McOmber Phonics Storybooks: Everyone Knows a Pitcher. rev. ed. (Illus.). write for info. (*0-944991-79-3*) Swift Lrn Res.
Manber, David. Zachary of the Wings. 88p. (gr. 9-12). 1993. PLB 10.95 (*1-879567-27-X*) Wonder Well.
Manes, Stephen. An Almost Perfect Game. LC 94-18192. 1995. 13.95 (*0-590-44432-8*) Scholastic Inc.
Marzollo, Jean. The Pizza Pie Slugger. Sims, Blanche, illus. LC 88-33379. 64p. (Orig.). (gr. 2-4). 1989. PLB 6.99 (*0-394-92881-4*); pap. 2.50 (*0-394-82881-X*) Random Bks Yng Read.
Michaels, Ski. The Baseball Bat. Guzzi, George, illus. LC 85-14065. 48p. (Orig.). (gr. 1-3). 1986. PLB 10.59 (*0-8167-0596-8*); pap. text ed. 3.50 (*0-8167-0597-6*) Troll Assocs.
Mochizuki, Ken. Baseball Saved Us. Lee, Dom, illus. LC 92-73215. 32p. (gr. k-8). 1993. 14.95 (*1-880000-01-6*) Lee & Low Bks.
Montgomery, Robert. Grand Slam. Reese, Ralph, illus. LC 89-5198. 176p. (gr. 5-8). 1991. PLB 9.89 (*0-8167-1988-8*); pap. text ed. 2.95 (*0-8167-1989-6*) Troll Assocs.
—Home Run! Reese, Ralph, illus. LC 89-5190. 176p. (gr. 5-8). 1991. PLB 9.89 (*0-8167-1986-1*); pap. text ed. 2.95 (*0-8167-1987-X*) Troll Assocs.
—The Show! Reese, Ralph, illus. LC 90-20586. 176p. (gr. 5-8). 1991. PLB 9.89 (*0-8167-1984-5*); pap. text ed. 2.95 (*0-8167-1985-3*) Troll Assocs.
Mooser, Stephen. Babe Ruth & the Home Run Derby. Ulrich, George, illus. 80p. (Orig.). (gr. 2-5). 1992. pap. 3.25 (*0-440-40486-X*, YB) Dell.
Morrison, Lillian. At the Crack of the Bat. LC 91-28946. (Illus.). 64p. (gr. 3-7). 1994. pap. 5.95 (*1-56282-670-0*) Hyprn Ppbks.
Myers, Walter D. Me, Mop, & the Moondance Kid. Pate, Rodney, illus. LC 88-6503. 128p. (gr. 3-7). 1988. 13.95 (*0-440-50065-6*) Delacorte.
—Mop, Moondance, & the Nagasaki Knights. LC 91-36824. 160p. (gr. 3-7). 1992. 14.00 (*0-385-30687-3*) Delacorte.
Nelson, Vaunda M. Mayfield Crossing. Jenkins, Leonard, illus. LC 92-10564. 96p. (gr. 3-7). 1993. 14.95 (*0-399-22331-2*, Putnam) Putnam Pub Group.
Nesbit, Jeffrey A. Absolutely Perfect Summer. 211p. (Orig.). (gr. 9-12). 1990. pap. 6.99 (*0-87788-005-0*) Shaw Pubs.
Otfinoski, Steven. The Stolen Signs. Dodson, Bert, illus. Lewis, Glenn. (Illus.). 112p. (gr. 2-6). 1992. (S&S BFYR); pap. 2.95 (*0-671-72930-6*, S&S BFYR) S&S Trade.
—Who Stole Home Plate? Dodson, Bert, illus. Lewis, Glenn. (Illus.). 112p. (gr. 2-6). 1992. (S&S BFYR); pap. 2.95 (*0-671-72932-2*, S&S BFYR) S&S Trade.
Parish, Peggy. Play Ball, Amelia Bedelia. Tripp, Wallace, illus. LC 71-85028. 64p. (gr. k-3). 1972. 14.00 (*0-06-024655-3*); PLB 13.89 (*0-06-024656-1*) HarpC Child Bks.

Peckinpah, Sandra L. Chester... the Imperfect All-Star. Moore, Trisha, illus. LC 92-74057. (gr. 1-5). 1993. PLB 15.95 (*0-9627806-1-8*); pap. text ed. 8.95 (*0-9627806-2-6*) Dasan Prodns. In classic fairy tale tradition, CHESTER...THE IMPERFECT ALL STAR tells the tale of a special angel in the Land Called Above whose passion is to play baseball with the angels' "Windrunner" team. Chester looks & feels different than the other angels because he has one leg shorter than the other. With the loving guidance of Coach Angel, he becomes the all star & is rewarded with his own unique place in the Land Called Below. A book for all the world's different & special children, for any child who has ever felt different, for their parents, siblings, & classmates. Addresses the problems such children experience, & foretells a happy ending. Fully illustrated in color, vocabulary included. To order call Cimino Publishing Group (516) 997-3721. *Publisher Provided Annotation.*

Pellowski, Michael J. Tour Troubles - Betty Cooper, Baseball Star. LC 91-58616. (Illus.). 256p. (Orig.). (gr. 4-8). 1992. pap. 3.99 (*1-56282-192-X*) Hyprn Child.
Petersen, P. J. Fireplug Is First Base. LC 89-25724. (Illus.). 64p. (gr. 2-5). 1990. 10.95 (*0-525-44587-0*, DCB) Dutton Child Bks.
—The Fireplug Is First Base. James, Betsy, illus. LC 92-18956. 64p. (gr. 2-5). 1992. pap. 3.99 (*0-14-036165-0*) Puffin Bks.
Plantos, T. Heather Hits Her First Home Run. (Illus.). 24p. (ps-8). 1989. pap. 4.95 (*0-88753-185-7*, Pub. by Black Moss Pr CN) Firefly Bks Ltd.
Prager, Annabelle. The Baseball Birthday Party. De Paola, Tomie, illus. LC 93-25258. 1995. write for info. (*0-679-84171-7*); PLB write for info. (*0-679-94171-1*) Random Bks Yng Read.
Real, Rory. A Baseball Dream. (Illus.). 32p. (ps-3). 1990. pap. 3.95 (*0-8120-4395-2*) Barron.
Sachs, Marilyn. Matt's Mitt & Fleet-Footed Florence. 80p. 1991. pap. 2.95 (*0-380-70963-5*, Camelot) Avon.
Scholz, Jackson. Batter Up. LC 92-32796. 256p. (gr. 5 up). 1993. 13.00 (*0-688-12485-2*) Morrow Jr Bks.
—Batter Up. LC 92-32796. 256p. (gr. 6 up). 1993. pap. 4.95 (*0-688-12158-6*, Pub. by Beech Tree Bks) Morrow.
Shannon, David A. How Georgie Radbourn Saved Baseball. LC 93-2475. (Illus.). 32p. 1994. 14.95 (*0-590-47410-3*, Blue Sky Press); pap. write for info. (*0-590-47411-1*, Blue Sky Press) Scholastic Inc.
Sharmat, Marjorie W. Nate the Great & the Stolen Base. (ps-3). 1994. pap. 3.50 (*0-440-40932-2*) Dell.
Sharp, Paul. Paul the Pitcher. LC 84-7011. (Illus.). 32p. (ps-2). 1984. PLB 10.25 (*0-516-02064-1*); pap. 2.95 (*0-516-42064-X*) Childrens.
—Ramon, el Lanzador (Paul the Pitcher) Sharp, Paul, illus. LC 84-7071. (SPA.). 32p. (ps-2). 1990. PLB 10.25 (*0-516-32064-5*); pap. 2.95 (*0-516-52064-4*) Childrens.
Slote, Alfred. Finding Buck McHenry. LC 90-39190. 256p. (gr. 3-7). 1991. 14.00 (*0-06-021652-2*); PLB 13.89 (*0-06-021653-0*) HarpC Child Bks.
—Finding Buck McHenry. LC 90-39190. 256p. (gr. 3-7). 1993. pap. 3.95 (*0-06-440469-2*, Trophy) HarpC Child Bks.
—Hang Tough, Paul Mather. LC 72-11531. 160p. (gr. 3-7). 1992. PLB 14.89 (*0-397-32509-6*, Lipp Jr Bks) HarpC Child Bks.

—Make-Believe Ball Player. Newsom, Tom, illus. LC 89-30598. 112p. (gr. 2-5). 1989. 13.00 (*0-397-32285-2*, Lipp Jr Bks); PLB 12.89 (*0-397-32286-0*, Lipp Jr Bks) HarpC Child Bks.
—Make-Believe Ball Player. LC 89-30598. 112p. (gr. 2-5). 1992. pap. 3.95 (*0-06-440425-0*, Trophy) HarpC Child Bks.
—Rabbit Ears. LC 81-47760. 128p. (gr. 4-7). 1983. pap. 3.95 (*0-06-440134-0*, Trophy) HarpC Child Bks.
Smith, Robert K. Bobby Baseball. Tiegreen, Alan, illus. (gr. 3-7). 1989. 13.95 (*0-385-29807-2*) Delacorte.
—Bobby Baseball. (gr. 4-7). 1991. pap. 3.50 (*0-440-40417-7*) Dell.
—Bobby Baseball. (gr. 4-7). 1991. pap. 3.25 (*0-440-80212-1*) Dell.
Spohn, David. Home Field. LC 92-5459. 1993. 10.00 (*0-688-11172-6*); lib. bdg. 9.93 (*0-688-11173-4*) Lothrop.
Springstubb, Tricia. With a Name Like Lulu, Who Needs More Trouble? Kastner, Jill, illus. (gr. 5-9). 1989. 14.95 (*0-385-29823-4*) Delacorte.
Stadler, John. Hooray for Snail! Stadler, John, illus. LC 83-46164. 32p. (ps-2). 1985. pap. 5.95 (*0-06-443075-8*, Trophy) HarpC Child Bks.
Stolz, Mary. Coco Grimes. LC 93-34153. 128p. (gr. 3-6). 1994. 14.00 (*0-06-024232-9*); PLB 13.89 (*0-06-024233-7*) HarpC Child Bks.
—Stealing Home. LC 92-5226. 160p. (gr. 3-6). 1992. 14.00 (*0-06-021154-7*); PLB 13.89 (*0-06-021157-1*) HarpC Child Bks.
Teague, Mark. The Field Beyond the Outfield. 32p. 1992. 14.95 (*0-590-45173-1*, Scholastic Hardcover) Scholastic Inc.
—Field Beyond the Outfield. (ps-3). 1994. pap. 4.95 (*0-590-45174-X*) Scholastic Inc.
Thayer, Ernest L. Casey at the Bat. Polacco, Patricia, illus. 32p. (ps-3). 1992. pap. 5.95 (*0-399-21884-X*, Sandcastle Bks) Putnam Pub Group.
Tunis, John R. Rookie of the Year. Brooks, Bruce & Bacom, Paulintro. by. 220p. (gr. 3-7). 1990. pap. 3.95 (*0-15-268880-3*, Odyssey) HarBrace.
—World Series. Bacon, Paul, illus. Brooks, Bruce, intro. by. (Illus.). 248p. (gr. 3-7). 1989. pap. 3.95 (*0-15-299646-X*, Odyssey) HarBrace.
Walker, Paul R. The Sluggers Club: A Sports Mystery. LC 92-28201. 1993. 13.95 (*0-15-276163-2*) HarBrace.
—Who Invented Baseball? LC 93-50898. (gr. 4 up). 1994. 10.99 (*0-679-84137-7*) Random Bks Yng Read.
Weaver. Farm Team. Date not set. 14.00 (*0-06-023588-8*); PLB 13.89 (*0-06-023589-6*) HarpC Child Bks.
Weaver, Will. Striking Out. LC 93-565. 288p. (gr. 5 up). 1993. 15.00 (*0-06-023346-X*); PLB 14.89 (*0-06-023347-8*) HarpC Child Bks.
Williams, Karen L. Baseball & Butterflies. 80p. 1990. 12.95 (*0-688-09489-9*) Lothrop.
Wojciechowska, Maia. Dreams of the World Series. Karsky, A. K., illus. 52p. 1994. 14.50 (*1-883740-09-6*) Pebble Bch Pr Ltd.
Zirpoli, Jane. Roots in the Outfield. LC 87-33900. (gr. 3-7). 1988. 13.45 (*0-395-45184-1*) HM.

BASEBALL–HISTORY

Brashler, William. The Story of Negro League Baseball. LC 93-36547. 144p. (gr. 3 up). 1994. 15.95 (*0-395-67169-8*); pap. 10.95 (*0-395-69721-2*) Ticknor & Flds Bks Yng Read.
Burleigh, Robert. Home Run. Wimmer, Mike, illus. LC 94-9975. 1995. 15.95 (*0-399-22814-4*, Philomel Bks) Putnam Pub Group.
Burns, Ken, et al. Twenty-Five Great Moments in Baseball. LC 94-1674. (Illus.). 64p. (gr. 3-7). 1994. 15.00 (*0-679-86751-1*); PLB 16.99 (*0-679-96751-6*) Knopf Bks Yng Read.
—Who Invented the Game? LC 94-9166. (Illus.). 64p. (gr. 3-7). 1994. 15.00 (*0-679-86750-3*); PLB 16.99 (*0-679-96750-8*) Knopf.
Cooper, Michael L. Playing America's Game: The Story of Negro League Baseball. (Illus.). 112p. (gr. 4-7). 1993. 15.99 (*0-525-67407-1*, Lodestar Bks) Dutton Child Bks.
Cornwell, Anita. The Girls of Summer. Caines, Kelly, illus. LC 88-64051. 100p. (Orig.). (gr. 6 up). 1989. pap. 12.95 (*0-938678-11-6*) New Seed.
Foley, Red. Red Foley's Cartoon History of Baseball. Whitehead, S. B., illus. 96p. (gr. 3 up). 1992. pap. 8.95 (*0-671-73627-2*, Little Simon) S&S Trade.
Frommer, Harvey. A Hundred & Fiftieth Anniversary Album of Baseball. LC 88-5740. (Illus.). 96p. (gr. 6-8). 1988. PLB 13.90 (*0-531-10588-1*) Watts.
Galt, Margot F. Up to the Plate: The All American Girls Professional Baseball League. LC 94-10636. 1994. 18.95 (*0-8225-3326-X*) Lerner Pubns.
Gardner, Robert & Shortelle, Dennis. The Forgotten Players: The Story of Black Baseball in America. LC 92-29618. 128p. (gr. 6 up). 1993. 12.95 (*0-8027-8248-5*); PLB 13.85 (*0-8027-8249-3*) Walker & Co.
Gutman, Bill. Great Moments in Baseball. Clancy, Lisa, ed. (Illus.). 128p. (gr. 5 up). 1989. pap. 2.99 (*0-671-67914-7*, Archway) PB.
Gutman, Dan. Baseball's Greatest Games. LC 93-31504. (Illus.). 160p. (gr. 4-7). 1994. 14.99 (*0-670-84604-X*) Viking Child Bks.
Hanmer, Trudy. The All-American Girls Professional Baseball League. LC 94-1233. 1994. text ed. 15.95 (*0-02-742595-9*, New Discovery Bks) Macmillan.
McKissack, Patricia C. & McKissack, Fredrick, Jr. Black Diamond: The Story of the Negro Baseball Leagues. LC 93-22691. (Illus.). 192p. (gr. 3-9). 1994. 13.95 (*0-590-45809-4*) Scholastic Inc.
Macy, Sue. A Whole New Ball Game: The Story of the All-American Girls Professional Baseball League. LC 92-31813. (Illus.). 144p. (gr. 7 up). 1993. 14.95 (*0-8050-1942-1*, Bks Young Read) H Holt & Co.
Nabhan. Cy Young Winners. 1991. 12.50s.p. (*0-86593-133-X*) Rourke Corp.
Nash, Bruce & Zullo, Allan. The Baseball Hall of Shame's Funtastic Trivia & Sticker Book. Maul, Bill, illus. 24p. (gr. 1 up). 1992. pap. 3.95 (*0-671-74439-9*, Little Simon) S&S Trade.
—The Sports Hall of Shame's Funtastic Trivia & Sticker Book. Maul, Bill, illus. 24p. (gr. 1 up). 1992. pap. 3.95 incl. 24 stickers (*0-671-74438-0*, Little Simon) S&S Trade.
Riley, James A., ed. Black Baseball Journal, Vol. 1, No. 1. (Illus.). 64p. (Orig.). 1990. pap. 6.95 (*0-9614023-5-0*) TK Pubs.
Rockwell, Bart. The World's Strangest Baseball Stories. LC 92-10120. (Illus.). 96p. (gr. 3-7). 1992. PLB 9.89 (*0-8167-2933-6*); pap. text ed. 2.95 (*0-8167-2850-X*) Troll Assocs.
Santos, Harry G. Town Team: The Folklore of Town Team Baseball. (Illus.). 120p. (Orig.). 1988. pap. 12.95 (*0-940151-09-X*) Statesman Exam.
Silverstein, Herma & Dunnahoo, Terry J. The Baseball Hall of Fame: The Halls of Fame. LC 93-6915. (Illus.). 48p. (gr. 5-6). 1994. text ed. 13.95 RSBE (*0-89686-849-4*, Crestwood Hse) Macmillan Child Grp.
Stotz, Carl E. A Promise Kept: The Story of the Founding of Little League Baseball. Loss, Kenneth D. & Zebrowski, Stephanie R., eds. (Illus.). 208p. (gr. 7-12). 1992. 16.95 (*1-880484-05-6*) Zebrowski Hist.

BASEBALL–POETRY

Morris, Willie. Prayer for the Opening of Little League Season. Moser, Barry, illus. LC 94-14471. 1994. write for info. (*0-15-200892-6*) HarBrace.
Sullivan, George. All about Baseball. (Illus.). 128p. (gr. 3 up). 1989. (Putnam); pap. 6.95 (*0-399-21734-7*, Putnam) Putnam Pub Group.
Thayer, Ernest L. Casey at the Bat. Hull, Jim, illus. Gardner, Martin, intro. by. (Illus.). 17.25 (*0-8446-5613-5*) Peter Smith.
—Casey at the Bat. LC 84-9891. (Illus.). (gr. 2-5). 1984. PLB 29.28 incl. cassette (*0-8172-2243-X*); PLB 19.97 (*0-8172-2121-2*) Raintree Steck-V.
—Casey at the Bat: A Ballad of the Republic, Sung in the Year 1888. Tripp, Wallace, illus. LC 77-21199. (gr. k-5). 1980. 14.95 (*0-399-21585-9*, Putnam); pap. 1.95 (*0-698-20486-7*, Putnam) Putnam Pub Group.
—Casey at the Bat: A Centennial Edition. Moser, Barry, illus. Hall, Donald, afterword by. LC 88-45285. (Illus.). 32p. (gr. 1 up). 1988. 14.95 (*0-87923-722-8*); pap. 9.95 (*0-87923-878-X*) Godine.

BASEBALL CLUBS

California Angels. (gr. 4-7). 1993. pap. 1.49 (*0-553-56414-5*) Bantam.
Colorado Rockies. (gr. 4-7). 1993. pap. 1.49 (*0-553-56430-7*) Bantam.
Florida Marlins. (gr. 4-7). 1993. pap. 1.49 (*0-553-56422-6*) Bantam.
Goodman, Michael. Houston Astros. (gr. 4-10). 1992. PLB 14.95 (*0-88682-459-1*) Creative Ed.
—Montreal Expos. 48p. (gr. 4-10). 1992. PLB 14.95 (*0-88682-457-5*) Creative Ed.
—Seattle Mariners. 48p. (gr. 4-10). 1992. PLB 14.95 (*0-88682-452-4*) Creative Ed.
Houston Astros. (gr. 4-7). 1993. pap. 1.49 (*0-553-56431-5*) Bantam.
Italia, Bob. The Toronto Blue Jays: World Champion of Baseball. LC 93-13084. 1993. 14.96 (*1-56239-239-5*) Abdo & Dghtrs.
Kansas City Royals. (gr. 4-7). 1993. pap. 1.49 (*0-553-56416-1*) Bantam.
Minnesota Twins. (gr. 4-7). 1993. pap. 1.49 (*0-553-56417-X*) Bantam.
Montreal Expos. (gr. 4-7). 1993. pap. 1.49 (*0-553-56423-4*) Bantam.
Rambeck, Richard. California Angels. 48p. (gr. 4-10). 1992. PLB 14.95 (*0-88682-449-4*) Creative Ed.
—Kansas City Royals. 48p. (gr. 4-10). 1992. PLB 14.95s.p. (*0-88682-440-0*) Creative Ed.
—Minnesota Twins. 48p. (gr. 4-10). 1992. PLB 14.95 (*0-88682-446-X*) Creative Ed.
—Toronto Blue Jays. 48p. (gr. 4-10). 1992. PLB 14.95 (*0-88682-442-7*) Creative Ed.
Seattle Mariners. (gr. 4-7). 1993. pap. 1.49 (*0-553-56419-6*) Bantam.
Texas Rangers. (gr. 4-7). 1993. pap. 1.49 (*0-553-56420-X*) Bantam.
Toronto Blue Jays. (gr. 4-7). 1993. pap. 1.49 (*0-553-56413-7*) Bantam.

BASIC (COMPUTER PROGRAM LANGUAGE)

Arthur, Gayle. Building with BASIC: A Programming Kit for Kids. (Illus., Orig.). (gr. k up). 1992. pap. 19.95 incl. disk (*0-672-30057-5*) Alpha Bks IN.
Ault, Rosalie S. BASIC Programming for Kids. LC 83-12773. (Illus.). 192p. (gr. 5 up). 1983. 10.95 (*0-685-06975-3*) HM.
Brenan, Kathleen M. & Mandell, Steven L. Introduction to Computers & Basic Programming. 2nd ed. 564p. (gr. 9-12). 1987. text ed. 32.75 (*0-314-32166-7*); Tchr's. manual. 15.95 (*0-314-43635-9*); wkbk. 9.50 (*0-314-36064-6*) West Pub.
Churchill, Eric R. BASIC Programming Flipper. 49p. (gr. 5 up). 1989. trade edition 5.95 (*1-878383-10-8*) C Lee Pubns.
Hurley, L. ZX-81 TS-1000: Programming for Young Programmers. (Illus.). 96p. (gr. 9up). 1983. pap. text ed. 9.95 (*0-07-031449-7*, BYTE Bks) McGraw.
Kallas, John L. BASIC. 252p. (Orig.). (gr. 8-12). 1985. pap. text ed. 14.99 (*0-89824-145-6*); 14.99 (*0-89824-167-7*) Trillium Pr.
Kemnitz, T. M. & Mass, Lynne. Kids Working with Computers: Acorn BASIC. (gr. 2-6). 1984. 4.99 (*0-89824-086-7*) Trillium Pr.
Kemnitz, Thomas M. & Mass, Lynne. Kids Working with Computers: The Apple BASIC Manual. Schlendorf, Lori, illus. 42p. (gr. 4-7). 1983. pap. 4.99 (*0-89824-092-1*) Trillium Pr.
—Kids Working with Computers: The Atari BASIC Manual. Schlendorf, Lori, illus. 48p. (gr. 4-7). 1983. pap. 4.99 (*0-89824-062-X*) Trillium Pr.
—Kids Working with Computers: The Texas Instruments BASIC Manual. Schlendorf, Lori, illus. 48p. (gr. 4-7). 1983. pap. 4.99 (*0-89824-059-X*) Trillium Pr.
—Kids Working with Computers: The Timex-Sinclair BASIC Manual. Schlendorf, Lori, illus. 48p. (gr. 4-7). 1983. pap. 4.99 (*0-89824-058-1*) Trillium Pr.
—Kids Working with Computers: TRS-80 BASIC Manual. Schlendorf, Lori, illus. 44p. (gr. 4-7). 1983. pap. 4.99 (*0-89824-055-7*) Trillium Pr.
Lipson, Shelley. It's BASIC: The ABC's of Computer Programming. Stapleton, Janice, illus. LC 81-20027. 48p. (gr. 4-6). 1982. 8.95 (*0-03-061592-5*, Bks Young Read); pap. 3.95 (*0-685-05626-0*) H Holt & Co.
Mackie, Dean & Mackie, David. BASIC. Migliore, Ron, illus. 48p. (gr. 1-5). 1985. pap. 3.95 (*0-88625-085-4*) Durkin Hayes Pub.
Simon, Seymour. The BASIC Book. Emberley, Barbara & Emberley, Ed E., illus. LC 85-42736. 32p. (gr. k-4). 1985. pap. 4.50 (*0-06-445015-5*, Trophy) HarpC Child Bks.
Spencer, Donald D. BASIC Programming. LC 82-17689. 224p. (gr. 8 up). 1983. 7.95 (*0-89218-062-5*, NO. 1133) Camelot Pub.
—Problem Solving with BASIC. LC 82-17875. 160p. (gr. 8 up). 1983. pap. 3.95x (*0-89218-075-7*, NO. 1135) Camelot Pub.

BASKET MAKING

Boy Scouts of America. Basketry. (Illus.). 32p. (gr. 6-12). 1986. pap. 1.85 (*0-8395-3313-6*, 33313) BSA.
Cary, Mara. Basic Baskets. LC 75-14222. 127p. 1975. HM.

BASKETBALL

Baize, Timothy. Broc: The Littlest Champion. LC 89-92510. (Illus.). 185p. (Orig.). (gr. 6-12). 1989. pap. 9.95 (*0-9625193-0-8*) T Baize.
Basketball Card Collecting Kit. 24p. 1992. pap. 4.95 incl. poster & basketball cards (*1-56156-162-2*) Kidsbks.
Basketball: Superstars & Superstats. 48p. (gr. 4-7). 1991. pap. 3.25 (*0-307-22362-0*) Western Pub.
Basketball You Call the Play. (gr. 4-7). 1991. pap. 3.25 (*0-307-22361-2*) Western Pub.
Bonvicini, Joan. Women's Basketball Drills: General Drills. (Orig.). (gr. 7 up). 1988. pap. 6.95 (*0-932741-59-2*) Championship Bks & Vid Prodns.
David Robinson Sports Shots. (ps-3). 1992. pap. 1.25 (*0-590-45840-X*) Scholastic Inc.
Frame, Laurence A. Sports Curriculum, Vol. 5: Basketmatics, with an Academic Emphasis upon Basketball. rev. ed. (Illus.). 100p. (gr. 4-8). 1993. pap. text ed. 30.00 (*1-884480-59-4*, TX-2-400-454); tchrs. ed. 2.00 (*0-685-70418-1*); wkbk. 28.00 (*0-685-70419-X*) Spts Curriculum.
Garrett, B. J. Who's on What? Basketball Trading Cards Reference Book, 1990-1991. Taylor, David S., illus. 100p. (Orig.). (gr. 3 up). 1993. pap. write for info. (*1-882816-00-5*) Eyes of August.
Grubbs, J. Angle Iron: The Junior High Team. Abell, J., ed. 50p. (gr. 6-8). 1988. PLB 25.00 (*1-56611-003-3*) Jonas.
Gutman, Bill. Basketball. LC 89-7606. (Illus.). 64p. (gr. 3-8). 1990. PLB 14.95 (*0-942545-92-3*) Marshall Cavendish.
Hanrahan, Brendan. NBA Dynamic Duos. (ps-3). 1993. pap. 2.25 (*0-307-12769-9*, Golden Pr) Western Pub.
Harris, Richard. I Can Read About Basketball. Milligan, John, illus. LC 76-54397. (gr. 2-5). 1977. pap. 2.50 (*0-89375-032-8*) Troll Assocs.
Henderson, Kathy. I Can Be a Basketball Player. LC 90-21648. 32p. (gr. k-3). 1991. PLB 11.80 (*0-516-01963-5*); pap. 3.95 (*0-516-41963-3*) Childrens.
Highlights for Children Staff. Basketball. Highlights for Children Staff, illus. 48p. (gr. 3-7). 1990. pap. 2.95 (*0-87534-353-8*) Highlights.
Inside Stuff: NBA Poster Book. (gr. 4-7). 1993. pap. 3.95 (*0-307-12416-9*, Golden Pr) Western Pub.
Italia, Bob. The Chicago Bulls: Basketball Champions. LC 93-35817. 1993. write for info. (*1-56239-237-9*) Abdo & Dghtrs.
Jarrett, William. TimeTables of Sports History: Basketball. (Illus.). 96p. 1990. 17.95x (*0-8160-1920-7*) Facts on File.
Larry Bird Sports Shots. (ps-3). 1992. pap. 1.25 (*0-590-45841-8*) Scholastic Inc.
Levin, Robert, ed. Y Basketball Dribblers Manual: For 5th-6th Grade Players. Barrett, Jerry, illus. 40p. (gr. 5-6). 1984. pap. text ed. 5.00 (*0-931250-84-6*, LYMC4666, Pub. by YMCA USA) Human Kinetics.

—Y Basketball Passers Manual: For 3rd-4th Grade Players. Barrett, Jery, illus. 36p. (gr. 3-4). 1984. pap. 5.00x (*0-931250-83-8*, LYMC4665, Pub. by YMCA USA) Human Kinetics.
Morris, Greggory. Basketball Basics. Engelland, Tim, illus. LC 75-34142. (gr. 2-6). 1979. 6.95 (*0-13-072256-1*, Pub. by Treehouse) P-H.
Nash, Bruce & Zullo, Allan. The Basketball Hall of Shame: Young Fans' Edition. Clancy, Lisa, ed. 160p. (Orig.). 1993. pap. 2.99 (*0-671-75356-8*, Archway) PB.
Rosenthal, Bert. Basketball. LC 82-19745. (Illus.). 48p. (gr. k-4). 1983. PLB 12.85 (*0-516-01674-1*); pap. 4.95 (*0-516-41674-X*) Childrens.
Ryan, Deborah. Women's Basketball Drills: Conditioning Drills. (Orig.). (gr. 7 up). 1988. pap. 6.95 (*0-932741-58-4*) Championship Bks & Vid Prodns.
Slam-Dunk Champions. (gr. 4-7). 1993. pap. 3.95 (*0-307-22364-7*, Golden Pr) Western Pub.
Slammin', Jammin', & Dunkin' (gr. 4-7). 1993. pap. 3.95 (*0-307-22365-5*, Golden Pr) Western Pub.
Smith, Alias & Pelkowski, Robert. Basketball: Rodney Rebound & Willie Dribble & DeeDee Dribble in The Runaway Basketball. 32p. (ps-3). 1989. pap. 3.95 (*0-8120-4241-7*) Barron.
Sullivan, George. All about Basketball. LC 91-10141. (Illus.). 1991. 13.99 (*0-399-61268-8*); pap. 7.95 (*0-399-21793-2*) Putnam Pub Group.
Summitt, Pat. Women's Basketball Drills: Offensive Drills. (Orig.). (gr. 7 up). 1988. pap. 6.95 (*0-932741-57-6*) Championship Bks & Vid Prodns.
Superstars & Super Stats. 48p. (gr. 3 up). 1992. pap. 3.95 incl. 6-pc. Skybox card (*0-307-22382-5*, 22382, Golden Pr) Western Pub.
Vancil, Mark. NBA Slam Dunk All-Stars. (ps-3). 1993. pap. 2.25 (*0-307-12768-0*, Golden Pr) Western Pub.
Walton, Rick & Walton, Ann. Hoop-La: Riddles about Basketball. Burke, Susan S., illus. LC 92-25771. 1993. 11.95 (*0-8225-2339-6*) Lerner Pubns.
Webb, Equilla A. An Amateur's Guide to Basketball Recruiting. 60p. (Orig.). (gr. 9-12). 1989. pap. text ed. 9.95 (*0-9624771-0-9*) Equilla Enterprises.
Withers, Tom. Basketball. LC 93-23275. 1993. PLB 21.34 (*0-8114-5779-6*) Raintree Steck-V.
Woodard, Lynette & Cook, Kevin. Shoot for the Stars Basketball Handbook, Vol. 1. Bunch, Lewis & Washington, Marian, eds. Hankins, Rod & Ray, Dan, illus. 60p. (gr. 9-12). 1989. text ed. write for info. Worldwide Sports.
YMCA of the U. S. A. Staff. Y Basketball Shooters Manual. Levin, Robert, ed. 44p. (gr. 7-9). 1985. pap. 5.00x (*0-931250-85-4*, LYMC4667, Pub. by YMCA USA) Human Kinetics.
You Call the Play. 48p. (gr. 3 up). 1992. pap. 3.95 incl. 6-pc. Skybox card (*0-307-22381-7*, 22381, Golden Pr) Western Pub.

BASKETBALL–BIOGRAPHY

Aaseng, Nathan. Sports Great David Robinson. LC 91-41532. (Illus.). 64p. (gr. 4-10). 1992. lib. bdg. 15.95 (*0-89490-373-X*) Enslow Pubs.
—Sports Great Michael Jordan. LC 92-11607. (Illus.). 64p. (gr. 4-10). 1992. lib. bdg. 15.95 (*0-89490-370-5*) Enslow Pubs.
Balzar, Howard. Basketball Super Stars. Allison, B., intro. by. (Illus.). 23p. (Orig.). (gr. 1-8). 1990. pap. 2.50 (*0-943409-15-2*) Marketcom.
Beahm, George. Michael Jordan: A Shooting Star. LC 93-46005. 1994. 14.95 (*0-8362-8048-2*) Andrews & McMeel.
Big Men: NBA Matchups. (gr. 4-7). 1993. pap. 2.95 (*0-307-20302-6*, Golden Pr) Western Pub.
Cohen, Neil. Shaquille O'Neal. McGarry, Steve, illus. (gr. 8 up). 1993. pap. 3.99 (*0-553-48158-4*) Bantam.
Cox, Ted. Shaquille O'Neal: Shaq Attack. LC 93-19781. (Illus.). 48p. (gr. 2-8). 1993. PLB 11.95 (*0-516-04379-X*); pap. 3.95 (*0-516-44379-8*) Childrens.
Dolan, Sean. Earvin "Magic" Johnson. King, Coretta Scott, intro. by. (Illus.). 112p. (gr. 5 up). 1993. PLB 17.95 (*0-7910-1774-5*) Chelsea Hse.
—Larry Bird. LC 94-5776. 1994. 14.95 (*0-7910-2427-X*) Chelsea Hse.
—Michael Jordan, Basketball Great. LC 93-16714. (Illus.). (gr. 5 up). 1994. PLB 18.95 (*0-7910-2150-5*, Am Art Analog); pap. write for info. (*0-7910-2151-3*, Am Art Analog) Chelsea Hse.
Frank, Steven. Magic Johnson. LC 94-5778. 1994. 14.95 (*0-7910-2430-X*) Chelsea Hse.
Goodman, Michael E. Magic Johnson. LC 88-20982. (Illus.). 48p. (gr. 5-6). 1988. text ed. 11.95 RSBE (*0-89686-382-4*, Crestwood Hse) Macmillan Child Grp.
Gowdey, David. Basketball Super Stars. Whitehead, Sam, illus. 64p. (gr. 1-4). 1994. pap. 8.95 (*0-448-40542-3*, G&D) Putnam Pub Group.
Green, Carl R. & Ford, M. Roxanne. David Robinson. LC 93-4976. (Illus.). 48p. (gr. 5-6). 1994. text ed. 13.95 RSBE (*0-89686-839-7*, Crestwood Hse) Macmillan Child Grp.
Greenberg, Keith E. Magic Johnson: Champion with a Cause. (Illus.). 64p. (gr. 4-9). 1992. PLB 13.50 (*0-8225-0546-0*) Lerner Pubns.
—Magic Johnson: Champion with a Cause. (gr. 4-7). 1992. pap. 4.95 (*0-8225-9612-1*) Lerner Pubns.
Gutman, Bill. Magic Johnson: Hero on & Off Court. LC 92-5002. (Illus.). 48p. (gr. 3-6). 1992. PLB 13.40 (*1-56294-287-5*); pap. 4.95 (*1-56294-825-3*) Millbrook Pr.
—Magic Johnson: Hero on & Off Court. (gr. 4-7). 1992. pap. 4.95 (*0-395-64546-8*) HM.
—Michael Jordan: Basketball Champ. LC 92-7541. (Illus.). 48p. (gr. 3-6). 1992. PLB 13.40 (*1-56294-085-6*); pap. 4.95 (*1-56294-827-X*) Millbrook Pr.
—Michael Jordan: Basketball Champ. (gr. 4-7). 1992. pap. 4.95 (*0-395-64545-X*) HM.
—Shaquille O'Neal: Basketball Sensation. LC 93-38971. (Illus.). 48p. (gr. 3-6). 1994. PLB 13.40 (*1-56294-460-6*) Millbrook Pr.
Harvey, Miles. Hakeem Olajuwon: The Dream. LC 94-14400. (Illus.). 48p. (gr. 2-8). 1994. PLB 15.80 (*0-516-04387-0*); pap. 3.95 (*0-516-44387-9*) Childrens.
Haskins, James. Sports Great Magic Johnson. rev. & expanded ed. LC 92-9188. (Illus.). 80p. (gr. 4-10). 1992. lib. bdg. 15.95 (*0-89490-348-9*) Enslow Pubs.
Herbert, Michael. Michael Jordan: The Bull's Air Power. rev. ed. LC 87-20868. 48p. (gr. 2 up). 1987. PLB 11.95 (*0-516-04362-5*); pap. 3.95 (*0-516-44362-3*) Childrens.
Jordan, Michael. Michael Jordan. (Illus.). (gr. 4-7). 1990. pap. 4.95 (*0-316-09229-0*, Spts Illus Kids) Little.
Kavanagh, Jack. Sports Great Larry Bird. LC 91-41525. (Illus.). 64p. (gr. 4-10). 1992. lib. bdg. 15.95 (*0-89490-368-3*) Enslow Pubs.
—Sports Great Patrick Ewing. LC 91-41531. (Illus.). 64p. (gr. 4-10). 1992. lib. bdg. 15.95 (*0-89490-369-1*) Enslow Pubs.
Knapp, Ron. Michael Jordan: Star Guard. LC 93-43744. (Illus.). 104p. (gr. 4-10). 1994. lib. bdg. 17.95 (*0-89490-482-5*) Enslow Pubs.
—Sports Great Hakeem Olajuwon. LC 91-41526. (Illus.). 64p. (gr. 4-10). 1992. lib. bdg. 15.95 (*0-89490-372-1*) Enslow Pubs.
—Sports Great Isiah Thomas. LC 91-41528. (Illus.). 64p. (gr. 4-10). 1992. lib. bdg. 15.95 (*0-89490-374-8*) Enslow Pubs.
—Top Ten Basketball Centers. (Illus.). 48p. (gr. 4-10). 1994. lib. bdg. 14.95 (*0-89490-515-5*) Enslow Pubs.
—Top Ten Basketball Scorers. (Illus.). 48p. (gr. 4-10). 1994. lib. bdg. 14.95 (*0-89490-516-3*) Enslow Pubs.
Lazenby, Roland. Georgetown, the Championships & Thompson. Blatty, William P., intro. by. (Illus.). 128p. (gr. 4-12). 1985. 19.95 (*0-913767-08-5*) Full Court VA.
Levin, Rich. Magic Johnson: Court Magician. rev. ed. LC 80-25814. (Illus.). 48p. (gr. 2-8). 1981. PLB 11.95 (*0-516-04313-7*); pap. 3.95 (*0-516-44313-5*) Childrens.
Lipsyte, Robert. Michael Jordan: A Life Above the Rim. Hite, John, illus. LC 93-50561. 96p. (gr. 5-9). 1994. 14.00 (*0-06-024234-5*); PLB 14.89 (*0-06-024235-3*) HarpC Child Bks.
—Michael Jordan: A Life above the Rim. Hite, John, illus. 96p. (gr. 5-9). 1994. pap. 3.95 (*0-06-446156-4*, Trophy) HarpC Child Bks.
Lovitt, Chip. Magic Johnson Sports Shots. 1991. pap. 1.25 (*0-590-47191-0*) Scholastic Inc.
—Michael Jordan. (gr. 4-7). 1993. pap. 3.25 (*0-590-46094-3*) Scholastic Inc.
—Sport Shots: Charles Barkley. (ps-3). 1994. pap. 1.25 (*0-590-48239-4*) Scholastic Inc.
—Sport Shots: Michael Jordan. (ps-3). 1994. pap. 1.25 (*0-590-48238-6*) Scholastic Inc.
McCune, Dan. Michael Jordan. LC 87-29021. (Illus.). 48p. (gr. 5-6). 1988. text ed. 11.95 RSBE (*0-89686-364-6*, Crestwood Hse) Macmillan Child Grp.
Macnow, Glen. David Robinson: Star Center. (Illus.). 104p. (gr. 4-10). 1994. lib. bdg. 17.95 (*0-89490-483-3*) Enslow Pubs.
—Sports Great Charles Barkley. LC 91-45827. (Illus.). 64p. (gr. 4-10). 1992. lib. bdg. 15.95 (*0-89490-386-1*) Enslow Pubs.
Make the Team: Basketball - A Slammin', Jammin' Guide to Super Hoops. (Illus.). (gr. 3-7). 1990. pap. 5.95 (*0-316-10749-2*) Little.
Michael Jordan. 1992. 1.25 (*0-590-46252-0*) Scholastic Inc.
Miller, Dawn. David Robinson: Backboard Admiral. (Illus.). 64p. (gr. 4-9). 1991. PLB 13.50 (*0-8225-0494-4*) Lerner Pubns.
—David Robinson: Backboard Admiral. 1992. pap. 4.95 (*0-8225-9600-8*) Lerner Pubns.
Morgan, Bill. The Magic: Earvin Johnson. 1992. 2.95 (*0-590-46050-1*, 063) Scholastic Inc.
Morgan, Terri & Thaler, Shuel. Chris Mullin: Sure Shot. LC 94-2704. (Illus.). 64p. (gr. 4-9). 1994. PLB 13.50 (*0-8225-2882-7*); pap. 4.95 (*0-8225-9664-4*) Lerner Pubns.
Nabhan, Marty. Fabulous Forwards. LC 92-9479. 1992. PLB 17.26 (*0-86593-161-5*); lib. bdg. 12.95s.p. (*0-685-59298-7*) Rourke Corp.
Nash, Bruce & Zullo, Allan. Little Basketball Big Leaguers: Amazing Boyhood Stories of Today's Basketball Stars. (Illus.). 96p. (gr. 1 up). 1991. pap. 7.95 (*0-671-73445-8*, Little Simon) S&S Trade.
Newberger, Joe & Hendricks, Elrod. The Ultimate Baseball Players Yearbook. Benscoter, Robert, illus. 96p. (gr. 3-9). 1991. wkbk. 12.95 (*0-9629307-0-9*) Batboy Pr.
Newman, Matthew. Larry Bird. LC 86-16524. (Illus.). 48p. (gr. 5-6). 1986. text ed. 11.95 RSBE (*0-89686-314-X*, Crestwood Hse) Macmillan Child Grp.
—Lynette Woodard. LC 86-19737. (Illus.). 48p. (gr. 5-6). 1986. text ed. 11.95 RSBE (*0-89686-316-6*, Crestwood Hse) Macmillan Child Grp.
—Patrick Ewing. LC 86-16522. (Illus.). 48p. (gr. 5-6). 1986. text ed. 11.95 RSBE (*0-89686-315-8*, Crestwood Hse) Macmillan Child Grp.
Olson, Eleanor. Wayne Estes: A Hero's Legacy. (Illus.). (gr. 7-12). 1991. pap. text ed. 6.00 (*0-9628317-0-0*) E Olson.
Paige, David. A Day in the Life of a School Basketball Coach. Smith, Bill, photos by. LC 80-54101. (Illus.). 32p. (gr. 4-8). 1981. PLB 11.79 (*0-89375-452-8*) Troll Assocs.
Patrick Ewing. 1992. 1.25 (*0-590-46247-4*) Scholastic Inc.
Petrucelli. Michael Jordan, Reading Level 2. (Illus.). 24p. (gr. 1-4). 1989. PLB 14.60 (*0-86592-428-7*); 10.95 (*0-685-58801-7*) Rourke Corp.
Playmakers: NBA Matchups. (gr. 4-7). 1993. pap. 2.95 (*0-307-20304-2*, Golden Pr) Western Pub.
Power Players: NBA Matchups. (gr. 4-7). 1993. pap. 2.95 (*0-307-20303-4*, Golden Pr) Western Pub.
Raber, Thomas R. Michael Jordan: Basketball Skywalker. LC 92-8277. 1992. 13.50 (*0-8225-0549-5*) Lerner Pubns.
Rappoport, Ken. Shaquille O'Neal. LC 93-38561. 128p. 1994. 15.95 (*0-8027-8294-9*); PLB 16.85 (*0-8027-8295-7*) Walker & Co.
Reiser, Howard. Patrick Ewing: Center of Attention. LC 94-14399. (Illus.). 48p. (gr. 2-8). 1994. PLB 15.80 (*0-516-04388-9*); pap. 3.95 (*0-516-44388-7*) Childrens.
—Scottie Pippen: Prince of the Court. LC 92-42023. (Illus.). 48p. (gr. 2-8). 1993. PLB 11.95 (*0-516-04366-8*); pap. 3.95 (*0-516-44366-6*) Childrens.
Rekela, George R. Hakeem Olajuwon: Tower of Power. LC 92-38905. 1993. lib. bdg. 13.50 (*0-8225-0518-5*); pap. 4.95 (*0-8225-9637-7*) Lerner Pubns.
Rolfe, John. David Robinson. (Illus.). (gr. 3-7). 1991. pap. 4.95 (*0-316-75461-7*, Spts Illus Kids) Little.
Rosenthal, Bert. Larry Bird: Cool Man on the Court. LC 80-27094. (Illus.). 48p. (gr. 2-8). 1981. pap. 3.95 (*0-516-44312-7*) Childrens.
Rothaus, James R. David Robinson. 32p. (gr. 2-6). 1991. 14.95 (*0-89565-784-8*) Childs World.
—Magic Johnson. (ENG & SPA.). 32p. (gr. 2-6). 1991. 14.95 (*0-89565-732-5*) Childs World.
—Michael Jordan. (SPA & ENG.). 32p. (gr. 2-6). 1991. 14.95 (*0-89565-733-3*) Childs World.
Rothaus, Jim. Karl Malone. (SPA & ENG.). (gr. 2-6). 1992. PLB 14.95 (*0-89565-961-1*) Childs World.
St. Pierre, Stephanie. Meet Shaquille O'Neal. Johnson, David, photos by. LC 93-1678. (Illus.). 112p. (gr. 3-5). 1993. pap. 3.50 (*0-679-85444-4*) Random Bks Yng Read.
Sanford, William R. & Green, Carl R. Kareem Abdul-Jabbar. LC 92-3592. (Illus.). 48p. (gr. 5). 1993. text ed. 11.95 RSBE (*0-89686-737-4*, Crestwood Hse) Macmillan Child Grp.
Schwabacher, Martin. Magic Johnson: Basketball Wizard. LC 93-16556. (Illus.). 1993. 13.95 (*0-7910-2037-1*, Am Art Analog); pap. write for info. (*0-7910-2038-X*, Am Art Analog) Chelsea Hse.
Scorers. (gr. 4-7). 1993. pap. 2.95 (*0-307-20301-8*, Golden Pr) Western Pub.
Sealy, Adrienne V. Little Tommy & the Basketball. Walker, Walt, illus. (gr. 2-6). 1980. 3.50x (*0-9602670-4-2*) Assn Family Living.
Sean, Dolan. Michael Jordan. LC 94-5779. 1994. 14.95 (*0-7910-2432-6*) Chelsea Hse.
Souders, Marilyn. Sport Shots: Shaquille O'Neal. (ps-3). 1994. pap. 1.25 (*0-590-48241-6*) Scholastic Inc.
Sullivan, Michael J. Chris Mullin: Star Forward. LC 93-32727. (Illus.). 104p. (gr. 4-10). 1994. lib. bdg. 17.95 (*0-89490-486-8*) Enslow Pubs.
Townsend, Brad. Shaquille O'Neal: Center of Attention. (gr. 4-7). 1994. pap. 4.95 (*0-8225-9655-5*) Lerner Pubns.
Vancil, Mark. NBA Slam Dunk All-Stars. (ps-3). 1993. pap. 2.25 (*0-307-12768-0*, Golden Pr) Western Pub.
White, Ellen E. Shaquille O'Neal. (gr. 8-12). 1994. pap. 2.95 (*0-590-47785-4*, Apple Paperbacks) Scholastic Inc.

BASKETBALL–FICTION

Burton, Elizabeth. Cinderfella & the Slam Dunk Contest. Offerdahl, Lynn, illus. 32p. (gr. 2-6). 1994. pap. 13.95 (*0-8283-1966-9*) Branden Pub Co.
Cebulash, Mel. Flippers Boy. Krych, Duane, illus. (gr. 3-8). 1992. PLB 8.95 (*0-89565-881-X*) Childs World.
Christopher, Matt. Johnny Long Legs. Kidder, Harvey, illus. 144p. (gr. 3-6). 1988. pap. 3.95 (*0-316-14065-1*) Little.
—No Arm in Left Field. Goto, Byron, illus. (gr. 4-6). 1987. lib. bdg. 15.95 (*0-316-13964-5*); pap. 3.95 (*0-316-13990-4*) Little.
Cooper, Ilene. Choosing Sides. (Illus.). 218p. (gr. 3-7). 1992. pap. 3.99 (*0-14-036097-2*, Puffin) Puffin Bks.
Cossi, Olga. The Magic Box. LC 89-8461. 192p. (gr. 12). 1990. 11.95 (*0-88289-748-9*) Pelican.
Dadey, Debbie & Jones, Marcia. Leprechauns Don't Play Basketball. 80p. 1992. pap. 2.75 (*0-590-44822-6*) Scholastic Inc.
D'Andrea, Joseph C. If I Were a Boston Celtic. Wilson, Bill, illus. 24p. (Orig.). (gr. k-5). Date not set. pap. 5.95 (*1-878338-45-5*) Picture Me Bks.
—If I Were a Charlotte Hornet. Wilson, Bill, illus. 24p. (Orig.). (ps-5). Date not set. pap. 5.95 (*1-878338-49-8*) Picture Me Bks.
—If I Were a Chicago Bull. Wilson, Bill, illus. 24p. (Orig.). (ps-5). Date not set. pap. 5.95 (*1-878338-42-0*) Picture Me Bks.

—If I Were a Cleveland Cavalier. Wilson, Bill, illus. 24p. (Orig.). (ps-5). Date not set. pap. 5.95 (*1-878338-50-1*) Picture Me Bks.
—If I Were a Denver Nugget. Wilson, Bill, illus. 24p. (Orig.). (gr. k-5). 1994. pap. 5.99 (*1-878338-66-8*) Picture Me Bks.
—If I Were a Detroit Piston. Wilson, Bill, illus. 24p. (Orig.). (gr. k-5). 1994. pap. 5.99 (*1-57151-102-4*) Picture Me Bks.
—If I Were a Los Angeles Clipper. Wilson, Bill, illus. 24p. (Orig.). (gr. k-5). 1994. pap. 5.99 (*1-57151-106-7*) Picture Me Bks.
—If I Were a Los Angeles Laker. Wilson, Bill, illus. 24p. (Orig.). (ps-5). Date not set. pap. 5.95 (*1-878338-44-7*) Picture Me Bks.
—If I Were a Miami Heat. Wilson, Bill, illus. 24p. (Orig.). (gr. k-5). 1994. pap. 5.99 (*1-57151-107-5*) Picture Me Bks.
—If I Were a New Jersey Net. Wilson, Bill, illus. 24p. (Orig.). (gr. k-5). 1994. pap. 5.99 (*1-57151-109-1*) Picture Me Bks.
—If I Were a New York Knick. Wilson, Bill, illus. 24p. (Orig.). (ps-5). Date not set. pap. 5.95 (*1-878338-43-9*) Picture Me Bks.
—If I Were a Philadelphia Seventy-Sixer. Wilson, Bill, illus. 24p. (Orig.). (gr. k-5). 1994. pap. 5.99 (*1-57151-110-5*) Picture Me Bks.
—If I Were a Phoenix Sun. Wilson, Bill, illus. 24p. (Orig.). (ps-5). Date not set. pap. 5.95 (*1-878338-46-3*) Picture Me Bks.
—If I Were a San Antonio Spur. Wilson, Bill, illus. 24p. (Orig.). (ps-5). Date not set. pap. 5.95 (*1-878338-48-X*) Picture Me Bks.
—If I Were an Atlanta Hawk. Wilson, Bill, illus. 24p. (Orig.). (gr. k-5). 1994. pap. 5.99 (*1-57151-100-8*) Picture Me Bks.
—If I Were an Orlando Magic. Wilson, Bill, illus. 24p. (Orig.). (ps-5). Date not set. pap. 5.95 (*1-878338-47-1*) Picture Me Bks.
Deuker, Carl. On the Devil's Court. 208p. (gr. 7 up). 1989. 15.95 (*0-316-18147-1*, Joy St Bks) Little.
Dygard, Thomas J. Outside Shooter. (Illus.). 192p. (gr. 5 up). 1991. pap. 3.99 (*0-14-034671-6*, Puffin) Puffin Bks.
—Rebound Caper. LC 82-18821. 176p. (gr. 7 up). 1983. 12.95 (*0-688-01707-X*) Morrow Jr Bks.
—Rebound Caper. 176p. (gr. 5 up). 1992. pap. 3.99 (*0-14-034913-8*) Puffin Bks.
—The Rebounder. LC 94-51257. 1994. write for info. (*0-688-12821-1*) Morrow Jr Bks.
—Tournament Upstart. LC 83-25039. 208p. (gr. 7 up). 1984. 9.50 (*0-688-02761-X*) Morrow Jr Bks.
Elish, Dan. Jason & the Baseball Bear. Stadler, John, illus. LC 89-23102. 160p. (gr. 3-5). 1990. 13.95 (*0-531-05868-9*); PLB 13.99 (*0-531-08468-X*) Orchard Bks Watts.
Freeman, Mark. Halfcourt Hero. 1989. 3.99 (*0-345-35911-9*) Ballantine.
Gorman, S. S. High-Fives: Slam Dunk. MacDonald, Patricia, ed. 128p. (Orig.). (gr. 3-6). 1990. pap. 2.99 (*0-671-70381-1*, Minstrel Bks) PB.
Grubbs, J. Angle Iron: Basketball. Abel, J., illus. 20p. (Orig.). 1992. pap. 15.00 (*1-56611-008-4*) Jonas.
Halecroft, David. Benched! 128p. (gr. 3-7). 1992. pap. 2.99 (*0-14-036038-7*) Puffin Bks.
Hallowell, Tommy. Jester in the Backcourt. 128p. (gr. 3 up). 1990. pap. 2.95 (*0-14-032911-0*, Puffin) Puffin Bks.
—Jester in the Backcourt. (gr. 4-7). 1991. 12.95 (*0-670-83732-6*) Viking Child Bks.
Hughes, Dean. On the Line. Lyall, Dennis, illus. LC 92-13788. 112p. (gr. 2-6). 1993. pap. 9.99 (*0-679-93490-1*); pap. NLD (*0-679-83490-7*) Knopf Bks Yng Read.
—One-Man Team. LC 93-44676. (Orig.). (gr. 4-9). 1994. PLB write for info. (*0-679-95441-4*, Bullseye Bks); pap. 3.99 (*0-679-85441-X*) Random Bks Yng Read.
—The Trophy. LC 93-42234. 128p. (gr. 3-7). 1994. 13.00 (*0-679-84368-X*); lib. bdg. cancelled (*0-679-94368-4*) Knopf Bks Yng Read.
Jackson, Alison. Blowing Bubbles with the Enemy. LC 93-2888. 120p. (gr. 3-7). 1993. 13.99 (*0-525-45056-4*, DCB) Dutton Child Bks.
—Crane's Rebound. Hearn, Diane D., illus. LC 90-20648. 128p. (gr. 3-7). 1991. 12.95 (*0-525-44722-9*, DCB) Dutton Child Bks.
—My Brother, the Star. LC 89-34480. 112p. (gr. 3-7). 1990. 12.95 (*0-525-44512-9*, DCB) Dutton Child Bks.
Jenkins, Jerry. The Scary Basketball Player. (Orig.). (gr. 7-12). 1986. pap. text ed. 4.99 (*0-8024-8233-3*) Moody.
Jones, Ron. B-Ball: The Team that Never Lost a Game. (gr. 5 up). 1990. 14.95 (*0-553-05867-3*) Bantam.
—B-Ball: The Team That Never Lost a Game. 1991. pap. 3.50 (*0-553-29404-0*) Bantam.
Kline, Suzy. Orp Goes to the Hoop. 96p. 1991. 13.95 (*0-399-21834-3*, Putnam) Putnam Pub Group.
—Orp Goes to the Hoop. 96p. (gr. 4). 1993. pap. 3.50 (*0-380-71829-4*, Camelot) Avon.
Lantz, Francess. Marissa's Dance. LC 93-43225. (Illus.). 128p. (gr. 3-7). 1994. pap. text ed. 2.95 (*0-8167-3475-5*) Troll Assocs.
Mallett, Jerry & Bartch, Marian. Clearly Old Ernie. 151p. (gr. 4-7). 1989. PLB 9.40 (*0-8000-3303-5*, 055786) Perma-Bound.
Marshall, Kirk. Fast Breaks. (gr. 4 up). 1989. pap. 3.99 (*0-345-35908-9*) Ballantine.
—Longshot Center. (gr. 4 up). 1989. pap. 3.95 (*0-345-35909-7*) Ballantine.
Marzollo, Jean. Slam Dunk Saturday. Sins, Blanche, illus. 64p. (Orig.). (gr. 2-4). 1994. PLB 7.99 (*0-679-92366-7*); pap. 2.99 (*0-679-82366-2*) Random Bks Yng Read.
Myers, Walter D. Hoops. LC 81-65497. 224p. (gr. 7 up). 1981. 13.95 (*0-385-28142-0*) Delacorte.
Provost, Gary. Good If It Goes. LC 89-18339. 160p. (gr. 4-7). 1990. pap. 3.95 (*0-689-71381-9*, Aladdin) Macmillan Child Grp.
Soto, Gary. Taking Sides. 138p. (gr. 3-7). 1991. 15.95 (*0-15-284076-1*, HB Juv Bks) HarBrace.
Stine, Megan & Stine, H. William. Long Shot, Bk. 10. LC 89-24355. 144p. (gr. 5 up). 1990. lib. bdg. 7.99 (*0-679-90526-X*) Random Bks Yng Read.
Tunis, John R. Yea! Wildcats. 319p. (gr. 3-7). 1989. pap. 3.95 (*0-15-299718-0*, Odyssey) HarBrace.
Wojciechowska, Maia. Dreams of the Hoop. Karsky, A. K., illus. 52p. 1994. 14.50 (*1-883740-10-X*) Pebble Bch Pr Ltd.

BASKETBALL–HISTORY

Duden, Jane & Osberg, Susan. Basketball. LC 90-28515. (Illus.). 48p. (gr. 5). 1991. text ed. 11.95 RSBE (*0-89686-627-0*, Crestwood Hse) Macmillan Child Grp.
The NBA Finals. 32p. (gr. 4). 1990. PLB 14.95 (*0-88682-314-5*) Creative Ed.
Rockwell, Bart. World's Strangest Basketball Stories. LC 92-25676. 1992. lib. bdg. 9.89 (*0-8167-2935-2*, Pub. by Watermill Pr); pap. 2.95 (*0-8167-2852-6*, Pub. by Watermill Pr) Troll Assocs.
Silverstein, Herma & Dunnahoo, Terry J. Basketball: The Halls of Fame. LC 93-448. (Illus.). 48p. (gr. 5-6). 1994. text ed. 13.95 RSBE (*0-89686-850-8*, Crestwood Hse) Macmillan Child Grp.

BASKETBALL CLUBS

Boyd, Brendan C., text by. Hoops: Behind the Scenes with the Boston Celtics. Horenstein, Henry, photos by. (Illus.). 128p. (gr. 3-7). 1989. (Spts Illus Kids); pap. 8.95 (*0-316-37309-5*) Little.
Goodman, Michael. Chicago Bulls. rev. ed. (Illus.). 32p. (gr. 5 up). 1993. PLB 14.95 (*0-88682-557-1*) Creative Ed.
—Dallas Mavericks. (Illus.). 32p. (gr. 4 up). 1993. PLB 14.95 (*0-88682-528-8*) Creative Ed.
Goodman, Michael E. Boston Celtics. rev. ed. (Illus.). 32p. (gr. 4 up). 1993. PLB 14.95 (*0-88682-530-X*) Creative Ed.
—Denver Nuggets. rev. ed. (Illus.). 32p. (gr. 4 up). 1993. PLB 14.95 (*0-88682-546-6*) Creative Ed.
—Houston Rockets. 32p. (gr. 4). 1993. PLB 14.95 (*0-88682-529-6*) Creative Ed.
—Los Angeles Lakers. rev. ed. (Illus.). 32p. (gr. 4 up). 1993. PLB 14.95 (*0-88682-542-3*) Creative Ed.
—New York Knicks. (Illus.). 32p. (gr. 4 up). 1993. PLB 14.95 (*0-88682-515-6*) Creative Ed.
—Philadelphia 76ers. rev. ed. (Illus.). 32p. (gr. 4 up). 1993. PLB 14.95 (*0-88682-544-X*) Creative Ed.
—Sacramento Kings. (Illus.). 32p. (gr. 4 up). 1993. PLB 14.95 (*0-88682-540-7*) Creative Ed.
—Seattle Supersonics. rev. ed. (Illus.). 32p. (gr. 4 up). 1993. PLB 14.95 (*0-88682-543-1*) Creative Ed.
Harris, Jack C. Milwaukee Bucks. (Illus.). 32p. (gr. 4 up). 1993. PLB 14.95 (*0-88682-541-5*) Creative Ed.
—New Jersey Nets. (gr. 5 up). 1993. PLB 14.95 (*0-88682-516-4*) Creative Ed.
McGuire, William. The Final Four (NCAA Basketball) 32p. (gr. 4). 1990. PLB 14.95 (*0-88682-310-2*) Creative Ed.
Rambeck, Richard. Atlanta Hawks. rev. ed. (Illus.). 32p. (gr. 4 up). 1993. PLB 14.95 (*0-88682-560-1*) Creative Ed.
—Cleveland Cavaliers. rev. ed. (Illus.). 32p. (gr. 4 up). 1993. PLB 14.95 (*0-88682-527-X*) Creative Ed.
—Detroit Pistons. rev. ed. (Illus.). 32p. (gr. 4 up). 1993. PLB 14.95 (*0-88682-521-0*) Creative Ed.
—Indiana Pacers. (Illus.). 32p. (gr. 4 up). 1993. PLB 14. 95 (*0-88682-522-9*) Creative Ed.
—Los Angeles Clippers. rev. ed. (Illus.). 32p. (gr. 4 up). 1993. PLB 14.95 (*0-88682-526-1*) Creative Ed.
—Phoenix Suns. rev. ed. (Illus.). 32p. (gr. 4 up). 1992. PLB 14.95 (*0-88682-520-2*) Creative Ed.
—Portland Trailblazers. (Illus.). 38p. (gr. 4 up). 1993. PLB 14.95 (*0-88682-518-0*) Creative Ed.
—San Antonio Spurs. (gr. 5 up). 1993. PLB 14.95 (*0-88682-519-9*) Creative Ed.
—Utah Jazz. 32p. (gr. 4). 1993. PLB 14.95 (*0-88682-525-3*) Creative Ed.
Zadra, Dan. Washington Bullets. 32p. (gr. 5 up). 1993. PLB 14.95 (*0-88682-523-7*) Creative Ed.

BAT

see Bats

BATES, KATHARINE LEE, 1859-1929

Glover, Janice. Katharine Lee Bates: Author of "America the Beautiful" Howard, Susie, illus. (Orig.). (gr. 3-6). 1993. pap. 7.95 (*1-883613-00-0*) Byte Size.
KATHARINE LEE BATES: AUTHOR OF "AMERICA THE BEAUTIFUL" is the true story of a small town girl who through her love of writing went on to pen the USA's favorite hymn. Miss Bates is a wonderful role model. "Janice Glover clearly weaves into her story incidents that inspired words of the popular song." "An encouragement to young writers." "Drawings offer detail & warmth." (Small Press). "Two thumbs up." (The Cape Codder). Glover, Janice. THOSE BILLINGTON BOYS: A PILGRIM STORY. Howard, Susie, illus. (gr. 3-6) PLC. 48 pg. 10.00 (1-883613-02-7) 1994. THOSE BILLINGTON BOYS: A PILGRIM STORY is the true account of two brother that were among the families that sailed on the Mayflower & settled Plimoth Plantation. Children will easily relate to the Billington brothers, age 7 & 9, who "continue to live in the pages of history for their adventures." (Author's Note). "A great improvement over the majority of books (on this subject)." (Plimoth Plantation). "Highly researched, well illustrated, fun account." (Fairfield Cnty, CT Educator). Also available from Byte Size Graphics Publishing: Carpenter, Karen & Howard, Susie. Illus. SOMETHING HAPPENED IN MY HOUSE: A JOURNEY OF CHILDREN'S GRIEF (With a Working Journal) PB. 32 pg. 9.95. (1-883613-01-9) 1993. For further information: Byte Size Graphics. 508-240-0795. FAX 508-240-7091. P.O. Box 826, No. Eastham, MA 02651.
Publisher Provided Annotation.

BATON TWIRLING

see Drum Majors

BATS

Arneson, D. J. Bats: A Nature-Fact Book. (Illus.). 32p. 1992. pap. 2.50 (*1-56156-147-9*) Kidsbks.
Bash, Barbara. Shadows of Night: The Hidden World of the Little Brown Bat. LC 92-22713. (Illus.). 32p. (gr. 1-5). 1993. 16.95 (*0-87156-562-5*) Sierra.
Bats. 1991. PLB 14.95 (*0-88682-337-4*) Creative Ed.
Cooper, Ann. Bats: Swift Shadows of the Twilight. Denver Museum of Art Staff, illus. 64p. (gr. 3-6). 1993. pap. text ed. 7.95x (*1-879373-52-1*) R Rinehart.
Earle, Ann. Bats: Let's Read & Find Out about Science Ser. Cole, Henry, illus. LC 93-11052. (gr. 4 up). Date not set. 15.00 (*0-06-023479-2*); PLB 14.89 (*0-06-023480-6*) HarpC Child Bks.
Fowler, Allan. Podria Ser un Mamifero - Libro Grande: (It Could Still Be a Mammal Big Book) LC 90-2161. (SPA., Illus.). 32p. (ps-2). 1993. 22.95 (*0-516-59463-X*) Childrens.
George, Michael. Bats. 32p. (gr. 2-6). 1991. 15.95 (*0-89565-712-0*) Childs World.
Gray, Susan H. Bats. LC 94-10468. (Illus.). 48p. (gr. k-4). 1994. PLB 17.20 (*0-516-01064-6*); pap. 4.95 (*0-516-41064-4*) Childrens.
Green, Carl R. & Sanford, William R. The Little Brown Bat. LC 85-22345. (Illus.). 48p. (gr. 5). 1986. text ed. 12.95 RSBE (*0-89686-267-4*, Crestwood Hse) Macmillan Child Grp.
Greenaway, Frank. Amazing Bats. Young, Jerry & Greenaway, Frank, photos by. LC 91-6517. (Illus.). 32p. (Orig.). (gr. 1-5). 1991. lib. bdg. 9.99 (*0-679-91518-4*); pap. 7.99 (*0-679-81518-X*) Knopf Bks Yng Read.
Halton, Cheryl M. Those Amazing Bats. LC 90-3959. (Illus.). 96p. (gr. 4 up). 1991. text ed. 13.95 RSBE (*0-87518-458-8*, Dillon) Macmillan Child Grp.
Harrison, Virginia & Riley, Helen. The World of Bats. LC 89-4471. (Illus.). 32p. (gr. 2-3). 1989. PLB 17.27 (*0-8368-0137-7*) Gareth Stevens Inc.
Johnson, Sylvia A. Bats. Masuda, Modoki, illus. LC 85-15999. 48p. (gr. 4 up). 1985. PLB 19.95 (*0-8225-1461-3*, First Ave Edns); pap. 5.95 (*0-8225-9500-1*, First Ave Edns) Lerner Pubns.
Julivert, Maria A. The Fascinating World of Bats. Studio, Marcel S., illus. 32p. (gr. 3-7). 1994. 11.95 (*0-8120-6429-1*); pap. 7.95 (*0-8120-1953-9*) Barron.
Kendall, Cindy. Bats. Bennish, Gracia, illus. Dudley, Dick, created by. LC 93-3114. (ps). 1994. 4.99 (*0-8037-1272-3*) Dial Bks Young.
Lovett, Sarah, text by. Extremely Weird Bats. (Illus.). 48p. (gr. 3 up). 1991. 9.95 (*1-56261-008-2*) John Muir.
Milton, Joyce. Bats & Other Creatures of the Night. Deal, Jim, illus. 32p. (Orig.). (ps-2). 1994. pap. 2.50 (*0-679-86213-7*) Random Bks Yng Read.

—Bats! Creatures of the Night. Moffatt, Judith, illus. LC 92-43198. 48p. (ps-1). 1993. 7.99g (*0-448-40194-0*, G&D); pap. 3.50 (*0-448-40193-2*, G&D) Putnam Pub Group.
Pringle, Laurence. Batman: Exploring the World of Bats. Tuttle, Merlin D., illus. LC 90-8679. 48p. (gr. 4-6). 1991. SBE 14.95 (*0-684-19232-2*, Scribners Young Read) Macmillan Child Grp.
Riley, Helen. The Bat in the Cave. Oxford Scientific Films Staff, photos by. LC 89-4469. (Illus.). 32p. (gr. 4-6). 1989. PLB 17.27 (*0-8368-0112-1*) Gareth Stevens Inc.
Selsam, Millicent E. & Hunt, Joyce. A First Look at Bats. 32p. (gr. 1-3). 1991. 11.95 (*0-8027-8135-7*); PLB 12.85 (*0-8027-8136-5*) Walker & Co.
Stone, Lynn M. Bats. LC 93-1535. 1993. write for info. (*0-86593-293-X*) Rourke Corp.
Stuart, Dee. Bats: Mysterious Flyers of the Night. (gr. 4-7). 1994. pap. 6.95 (*0-87614-631-0*) Carolrhoda Bks.
Tuttle, Merlin D. America's Neighborhood Bats: Understanding & Learning to Live in Harmony with Them. (Illus.). 104p. (gr. 10-12). 1988. 19.95 (*0-292-70403-8*); pap. 9.95 (*0-292-70406-2*) U of Tex Pr.
Warren, Elizabeth. I Can Read About Bats. LC 74-24928. (Illus.). (gr. 2-4). 1975. pap. 2.50 (*0-89375-064-6*) Troll Assocs.
Wexo, John B. Flyers. 24p. (gr. 3 up). 1991. PLB 14.95 (*0-88682-394-3*) Creative Ed.
Wilmot, Zoe. Bat. LC 93-77342. (ps). 1993. 3.99 (*0-89577-509-3*, Dist. by Random) RD Assn.

BATS–FICTION

Berg, Eric. Bernie's Safe Ideas. LC 93-8905. 1993. write for info. (*1-56071-324-0*) ETR Assocs.
—Five Special Senses. LC 93-8906. 1993. write for info. (*1-56071-328-3*) ETR Assocs.
—Try It, You'll Like It! LC 93-8907. 1993. write for info. (*1-56071-325-9*) ETR Assocs.
Block, Francesca L. Cherokee Bat & the Goat Guys. LC 91-20706. 128p. (gr. 7 up). 1993. pap. 3.95 (*0-06-447095-4*, Trophy) HarpC Child Bks.
Cannon, Janell. Stellaluna. LC 92-16439. 1993. 14.95 (*0-15-280217-7*) HarBrace.
Carlson, Natalie S. Spooky & the Wizard's Bats. Glass, Andrew, illus. LC 85-18020. 32p. (ps-1). 1986. 12.95 (*0-688-06280-6*); PLB 12.88 (*0-688-06281-4*) Lothrop.
Danziger, Paula. There's a Bat in Bunk Five. 160p. (gr. 5-9). 1988. pap. 3.99 (*0-440-40098-8*, LE) Dell.
Freeman, Don. Hattie the Backstage Bat. (Illus.). 32p. (Orig.). (ps-3). 1988. pap. 4.99 (*0-14-050893-7*, Puffin) Puffin Bks.
Freeman, Lydia & Freeman, Don. Pet of the Met. (Illus.). 64p. (Orig.). (ps-3). 1988. pap. 4.95 (*0-14-050892-9*, Puffin) Puffin Bks.
Gilson, Jamie. You Don't Know Beans about Bats. De Groat, Diane, illus. LC 93-559. 1994. write for info. (*0-395-67063-2*, Clarion Bks) HM.
Johnson, Norma T. Bats on the Bedstead. LC 86-27823. 128p. (gr. 3-7). 1987. 13.95 (*0-395-43022-4*) HM.
—Bats on the Bedstead. 128p. 1988. pap. 2.95 (*0-380-70540-0*, Camelot) Avon.
Lent, Blair. Bayberry Bluff. (ps-3). 1987. 13.45 (*0-395-35384-X*) HM.
Maestro, Betsy. Bats. Maestro, Giulio, illus. LC 93-26153. (gr. k-3). 1994. 14.95 (*0-590-46150-8*) Scholastic Inc.
Mollel, Tololwa M. A Promise to the Sun: A Story of Africa. Vidal, Beatriz, illus. 32p. (ps-3). 1992. 15.95 (*0-316-57813-4*, Joy St Bks) Little.
Searcy, Margaret Z. Tiny Bat & the Ball Game. Wise, Lu Celia, illus. LC 78-61367. (gr. 2-4). 1978. 7.50 (*0-916620-19-0*) Portals Pr.

BATTLE SHIPS

see Warships

BATTLES

Anderson, Dale. Battles That Changed the Modern World. Gerstle, Gary, contrib. by. LC 93-17028. (Illus.). 48p. (gr. 5-7). 1993. PLB 22.80 (*0-8114-4928-9*) Raintree Steck-V.

BATTLESHIPS

see Warships

BAY OF PIGS

see Cuba–History

BAZAARS

see Fairs

BEACHES

see Seashore

BEADWORK

Berry, Lori S. How to Bead Earrings: An Artistic Approach. Knight, Denise E., ed. LC 93-70575. (Illus.). 96p. (Orig.). 1993. perfect bdg. 10.95 (*0-943604-34-6*) Eagles View.

BEAGLE EXPEDITION, 1831-1836

Hyndley, Kate. The Voyage of the Beagle. Bull, Peter, illus. LC 88-28695. 32p. (gr. 5-9). 1989. PLB 11.90 (*0-531-18272-X*, Pub. by Bookwright Pr) Watts.

BEARS

Ahlstrom, Mark. The Polar Bear. LC 85-30900. (Illus.). 48p. (gr. 5). 1986. text ed. 12.95 RSBE (*0-89686-268-2*, Crestwood Hse) Macmillan Child Grp.
Ahlstrom, Mark E. The Black Bear. LC 85-22872. (Illus.). 48p. (gr. 5). 1985. text ed. 12.95 RSBE (*0-89686-276-3*, Crestwood Hse) Macmillan Child Grp.
Bailey, Jill. Polar Bear Rescue. Green, John, illus. LC 90-4490. 48p. (gr. 3-7). 1991. PLB 21.34 (*0-8114-2708-0*); pap. 4.95 (*0-8114-6556-X*) Raintree Steck-V.
Baker, Lucy. Polar Bears. (Illus.). 32p. (gr. 2-6). 1990. pap. 4.95 (*0-14-034435-7*, Puffin) Puffin Bks.
Banks, Martin. The Polar Bear on the Ice. Oxford Scientific Films Staff, photos by. LC 89-4472. (Illus.). 32p. (gr. 4-6). 1989. PLB 17.27 (*0-8368-0114-8*) Gareth Stevens Inc.
Berger, Melvin. The Big Bears. (Illus.). 16p. (ps-2). 1994. pap. text ed. 14.95 (*1-56784-015-9*) Newbridge Comms.
Betz, Dieter. The Bear Family. LC 91-42698. (Illus.). 60p. (gr. 2-6). 1992. 15.00 (*0-688-11647-7*, Tambourine Bks); PLB 14.93 (*0-688-11648-5*, Tambourine Bks) Morrow.
Bird, E. J. How Do Bears Sleep? Bird, E. J., illus. 32p. (ps-3). pap. 5.95 (*0-87614-522-5*) Carolrhoda Bks.
Bour, Laura. Bears. (Illus.). (ps). 1992. bds. 10.95 (*0-590-45270-3*, 038, Cartwheel) Scholastic Inc.
Brenner, Barbara & Garelick, May. Two Orphan Cubs. Kors, Erika, illus. (ps-1). 1989. 12.95 (*0-8027-6868-7*); PLB 13.85 (*0-8027-6869-5*) Walker & Co.
Bright, Michael. Polar Bear. LC 89-50446. (Illus.). 32p. (gr. 5-7). 1989. PLB 12.40 (*0-531-17180-9*, Gloucester Pr) Watts.
Brockman, Alfred. Bears. (ps-3). 1989. pap. 1.95 (*0-8167-1541-6*) Troll Assocs.
Calabro, Marian. Operation Grizzly Bear. Craighead, John, et al, illus. LC 88-37497. 112p. (gr. 5 up). 1989. SBE 13.95 (*0-02-716241-9*, Four Winds) Macmillan Child Grp.
Dodd, Lynley. Wake Up Bear. Dodd, Lynley, illus. LC 86-42798. 32p. (gr. 1-2). 1988. PLB 17.27 (*1-55532-124-0*) Gareth Stevens Inc.
Down, Mike. Bear. McAllister, David, illus. LC 91-44726. 32p. (gr. 4-6). 1993. text ed. 11.59 (*0-8167-2765-1*); tchr's. ed. 3.95 (*0-8167-2766-X*) Troll Assocs.
Fair, Jeff. Black Bear Magic for Kids. LC 91-50551. (Illus.). 48p. (gr. 3-4). 1992. PLB 18.60 (*0-8368-0760-X*) Gareth Stevens Inc.
Fowler, Allan. Please Don't Feed the Bears. LC 91-3130. 32p. (ps-2). 1991. PLB 10.75 (*0-516-04916-X*); PLB 22.95 big bk. (*0-516-49476-7*); pap. 3.95 (*0-516-44916-8*) Childrens.
Gabriele. Bears. 1985. pap. 1.95 (*0-911211-68-3*) Penny Lane Pubns.
Galdone, Paul, ed. & illus. The Three Bears. LC 78-158833. 32p. (ps-3). 1979. 14.45 (*0-395-28811-8*, Clarion Bks) HM.
George, Jean C. The Moon of the Bears. Parker, Ron, illus. LC 91-22557. 48p. (gr. 3-7). 1993. 15.00 (*0-06-022791-5*); PLB 14.89 (*0-06-022792-3*) HarpC Child Bks.
Gilks, Helen. Bears. Bale, Andrew, illus. LC 92-37693. 32p. (gr. 2-4). 1993. 15.95 (*0-395-66899-9*) Ticknor & Flds Bks Yng Read.
Graham, Ada & Graham, Frank. Bears in the Wild. Tyler, D. D., illus. LC 80-68732. 128p. (gr. 4-7). 1981. 8.95 (*0-440-00532-9*); PLB 8.44 (*0-440-00538-8*) Delacorte.
Greenaway, Theresa. Amazing Bears. King, Dave, photos by. LC 92-910. (Illus.). 32p. (Orig.). (gr. 1-5). 1992. PLB 9.99 (*0-679-92769-7*); pap. 7.99 (*0-679-82769-2*) Knopf Bks Yng Read.
Greene, Carol. Reading about the Grizzly Bear. LC 92-26803. (Illus.). 32p. (gr. k-3). 1993. lib. bdg. 13.95 (*0-89490-423-X*) Enslow Pubs.
Hall, Katy. Grizzly Riddles. LC 86-29275. 1989. 9.95 (*0-8037-0376-7*); PLB 9.89 (*0-8037-0377-5*) Dial Bks Young.
Harrison, Virginia & Banks, Martin. The World of Polar Bears. LC 89-4470. (Illus.). 32p. (gr. 2-3). 1989. PLB 17.27 (*0-8368-0139-3*) Gareth Stevens Inc.
Hart, Trish. There Are No Polar Bears down There. Hart, Trish, illus. LC 92-31949. 1993. 3.75 (*0-383-03597-X*) SRA Schl Grp.
Hoffman, Mary. Bear. LC 86-6775. (Illus.). 24p. (gr. k-5). 1986. PLB 9.95 (*0-8172-2396-7*); pap. 3.95 (*0-8114-6871-2*) Raintree Steck-V.
Hunt, Joni P. Bears. Leon, Vicki, ed. LC 93-9568. (Illus.). 48p. (Orig.). (gr. 5 up). 1993. pap. 9.95 perfect bdg. (*0-918303-31-1*) Blake Pub.
Johnston, Ginny & Cutchins, Judy. Andy Bear: A Polar Cub Grows Up at the Zoo. Noble, Constance, illus. LC 85-3095. 64p. (gr. 2-5). 1985. 13.00 (*0-688-05627-X*); lib. bdg. 12.88 (*0-688-05628-8*, Morrow Jr Bks) Morrow Jr Bks.
Kalas, Sybille. Polar Bear Family Book. (ps-3). 1991. pap. 15.95 (*0-88708-157-6*) Picture Bk Studio.
Kuchalla, Susan. Bears. Kelleher, Kathie, illus. LC 81-11368. 32p. (gr. k-2). 1982. PLB 11.59 (*0-89375-674-1*); pap. 2.95 (*0-89375-675-X*) Troll Assocs.
Lepthien, Emilie U. Polar Bears. LC 91-8892. 48p. (gr. k-4). 1991. PLB 12.85 (*0-516-01127-8*); pap. 4.95 (*0-516-41127-6*) Childrens.
McIntyre, Rick. Grizzly Cub: Five Years in the Life of a Bear. LC 90-35587. (Illus.). 104p. (Orig.). (gr. 4 up). 1990. pap. 14.95 (*0-88240-373-7*) Alaska Northwest.
Markert, Jenny. Polar Bears. 32p. (gr. 2-6). 1991. 15.95 (*0-89565-708-2*) Childs World.
Mattern, Joanne. Bears. Leeson, Tom & Leeson, Pat, illus. LC 92-20176. 24p. (gr. 4-7). 1992. (Pub. by Watermill Pr); pap. 1.95 (*0-8167-2952-2*, Pub. by Watermill Pr) Troll Assocs.
Moore, Jo E. & Tryon, Leslie. Bears Bears Bears. (Illus.). 48p. (gr. k-1). 1988. pap. 8.95 (*1-55799-130-8*) Evan-Moor Corp.
Namm, D. Little Bear. (Illus.). 28p. (ps-2). 1990. PLB 10.50 (*0-516-05356-6*); pap. 3.95 (*0-516-45356-4*) Childrens.
Nentl, Jerolyn. The Grizzly. LC 83-22354. (Illus.). 48p. (gr. 5). 1984. text ed. 12.95 RSBE (*0-89686-245-3*, Crestwood Hse) Macmillan Child Grp.
Ohanian, Susan. All about Bears. Ruth, Trevor, illus. LC 93-28988. 1994. 4.25 (*0-383-03735-2*) SRA Schl Grp.
Palmer, S. Osos Polares (Polar Bears) 1991. 8.95s.p. (*0-86592-673-5*) Rourke Enter.
—Polar Bears. (Illus.). 24p. (gr. k-5). 1989. lib. bdg. 11.94 (*0-86592-360-4*) Rourke Corp.
Patent, Dorothy H. Looking at Bears. Munoz, William, photos by. LC 94-1834. 40p. (gr. 1-3). 1994. 15.95 (*0-8234-1139-7*) Holiday.
Penny, Malcolm. Bears. LC 90-35063. (Illus.). 32p. (gr. 2-4). 1991. PLB 12.40 (*0-531-18368-8*, Pub. by Bookwright Pr) Watts.
—Let's Look At Bears. LC 89-7385. (ps-3). 1990. PLB 11.40 (*0-531-18321-1*, Pub. by Bookwright Pr) Watts.
Pettersson, Bertil. In the Bears' Forest. Murray, Steven T., tr. Fuller, Kathryn S., intro. by. (Illus.). 38p. 1991. bds. 11.95 (*91-29-59866-4*, Pub. by R & S Bks) FS&G.
Petty, Kate. Baby Animals: Bears. (Illus.). 24p. (ps-3). 1992. pap. 3.95 (*0-8120-4964-0*) Barron.
—Bears. LC 90-44447. (Illus.). 24p. (gr. k-3). 1991. PLB 10.90 (*0-531-17286-4*, Gloucester Pr) Watts.
Pfeffer, Pierre. Bears, Big & Little. Bogard, Vicki, tr. from FRE. Stephan, Franck, illus. LC 89-8883. 38p. (gr. k-5). 1989. 5.95 (*0-944589-23-5*, 023) Young Discovery Lib.
Polar Bears. 1991. PLB 14.95 (*0-88682-414-1*) Creative Ed.
Pringle, Laurence. Bearman: Exploring the World of Black Bears. Rogers, Lynn, illus. LC 89-5890. 48p. (gr. 5-7). 1989. 13.95 (*0-684-19094-X*, Scribners Young Read) Macmillan Child Grp.
—Bearman: Exploring the World of Black Bears. (Illus.). 49p. 1992. Braille. 3.92 (*1-56956-351-9*) W A T Braille.
Robinson, Fay. Real Bears & Alligators. Iosa, Ann W., illus. LC 92-10755. 32p. (ps-2). 1992. PLB 11.60 (*0-516-02374-8*) Childrens.
—Real Bears & Alligators. Iosa, Ann, illus. LC 92-10755. 32p. (ps-2). 1993. pap. 3.95 (*0-516-42374-6*) Childrens.
Robinson, Sandra C. The Everywhere Bear. (Illus.). 64p. (gr. 4-6). 1992. pap. 7.95 (*1-879373-07-6*) R Rinehart.
Rosenthal, Mark. Bears. LC 82-17910. (Illus.). 48p. (gr. k-4). 1983. PLB 12.85 (*0-516-01675-X*); pap. 4.95 (*0-516-41675-8*) Childrens.
Schmidt, Annemarie & Schmidt, Christian R. Bears & Their Forest Cousins. LC 91-9428. (Illus.). 32p. (gr. 4-6). 1991. PLB 18.60 (*0-8368-0684-0*) Gareth Stevens Inc.
Schneider, Jeff. My Friend the Polar Bear: An Ocean Magic Book. Spoon, Wilfred, illus. LC 90-61579. 12p. (ps). 1991. 4.95g (*1-877779-12-1*) Schneider Educational.
Stirling, Ian. Bears. Lang, Aubrey, photos by. (Illus.). 64p. (gr. 3-6). 1992. 14.95 (*0-87156-574-9*) Sierra.
Stone, L. Osos (Bears) 1991. 8.95s.p. (*0-86592-833-9*) Rourke Enter.
Stone, Lynn. Bears. (Illus.). 24p. (gr. k-5). 1990. lib. bdg. 11.94 (*0-86593-042-2*); lib. bdg. 8.95s.p. (*0-685-46449-0*) Rourke Corp.
Stone, Lynn M. Grizzlies. LC 93-22074. 1993. 19.95 (*0-87614-800-3*) Carolrhoda Bks.
Storms, John. Bonnie the Black Bear. Ooka, Dianne & Squellati, Liz, eds. Storms, Bob, illus. 24p. (Orig.). (gr. k-3). 1994. pap. 4.95 (*0-89346-794-4*) Heian Intl.
Tibbitts, Alison & Roocroft, Alan. Polar Bears. (Illus.). 24p. (ps-2). 1992. PLB 12.95 (*1-56065-104-0*) Capstone Pr.
Tracqui, Valerie. Polar Bear: Master of the Ice. (Illus.). 28p. (gr. 3-8). 1994. pap. 6.95 (*0-88106-432-7*) Charlesbridge Pub.
Wallace, Karen. Bears in the Forest. Frith, Barbara, illus. LC 93-39668. 32p. (ps up). 1994. 14.95 (*1-56402-336-2*) Candlewick Pr.
Whittaker, Bibby. Bears & Pandas. (Illus.). 32p. (gr. 4-6). 1991. 13.95 (*0-237-60171-0*, Pub. by Evans Bros Ltd) Trafalgar.
Wijngaard, Juan. Bear. Wijngaard, Juan, illus. LC 90-81897. 12p. (ps). 1991. bds. 3.95 (*0-517-58201-5*) Crown Bks Yng Read.
Wildlife Education, Ltd. Staff. Polar Bears. Espinoza, Rauol, et al, illus. 20p. (Orig.). (gr. k-12). 1985. pap. 2.75 (*0-937934-36-4*) Wildlife Educ.
—Polar Bears. Woods, Michael & Stuart, Walter, illus. 24p. 1992. 13.95 (*0-937934-85-2*) Wildlife Educ.
Yee, Patrick. Baby Bear. (Illus.). 12p. (ps). 1994. bds. 3.99 (*0-670-85288-0*) Viking Child Bks.

BEARS–FICTION

Ada, Alma F. Sale el Oso (Small Book) Myers, Amy, illus. (SPA.). 16p. (Orig.). (gr. k-3). 1992. pap. text ed. 6.00 (*1-56334-079-8*) Hampton-Brown.
Adair, Dick. The Story of Aloha Bear. Adair, Dick, illus. 24p. (ps-k). 1986. 7.95 (*0-89610-049-9*) Island Heritage.
Adinolfi, JoAnn. The Egyptian Polar Bear. Adinolfi, JoAnn, illus. 1994. 14.95 (*0-395-68074-3*) HM.
Ahlberg, Allan. The Bear Nobody Wanted. Ahlberg, Janet, illus. 144p. (gr. 3-7). 1993. 15.00 (*0-670-83982-5*) Viking Child Bks.

Alexander, Martha. And My Mean Old Mother Will Be Sorry, Blackboard Bear. Alexander, Martha, illus. LC 72-707. (gr. k-2). 1977. pap. 3.50 (*0-8037-0126-8*) Dial Bks Young.

—Blackboard Bear. Alexander, Martha, illus. (Orig.). (ps-2). 1988. pap. 3.50 (*0-8037-0629-4*) Dial Bks Young.

—Blackboard Bear. (ps-3). 1988. pap. 4.99 (*0-14-054609-X*) Dial Bks Young.

—Four Bears in a Box. (ps-3). 1992. 8.95 (*0-8037-1043-7*, Puff Pied Piper) Puffin Bks.

—I Sure Am Glad to See You, Blackboard Bear. LC 76-2280. (Illus.). (ps-3). 1976. Dial Bks Young.

—I Sure Am Glad to See You, Blackboard Bear. (Illus.). (ps-3). 1976. pap. 3.50 (*0-8037-4008-5*, Puff Pied Piper) Puffin Bks.

Allred, Gordon. Old Crackfoot. Brown, Margery, illus. (gr. 5 up). 1965. 8.95 (*0-8392-3051-6*) Astor-Honor.

Anholt, Catherine & Anholt, Laurence. Bear & Baby. Anholt, Laurence & Anholt, Catherine, illus. LC 92-54581. 24p. (ps). 1993. 5.95 (*1-56402-235-8*) Candlewick Pr.

Arnosky, Jim. Every Autumn Comes the Bear. Arnosky, Jim, illus. LC 92-30515. 32p. (ps-1). 1993. 14.95 (*0-399-22508-0*, Putnam) Putnam Pub Group.

Asch, Frank. Bear Shadow. Asch, Frank, illus. LC 82-18250. 32p. (ps-2). 1988. pap. 14.00 jacketed (*0-671-66279-1*, S&S BFYR); pap. 4.95 (*0-671-66866-8*, S&S BFYR) S&S Trade.

—Bear's Bargain. Asch, Frank, illus. LC 85-6355. (ps-2). 1989. pap. 12.95 jacketed (*0-671-66690-8*, S&S BFYR); pap. 4.95 (*0-671-67838-8*, S&S BFYR) S&S Trade.

—Bread & Honey. (Illus.). 48p. (ps-2). 1992. pap. 2.95 (*0-448-40319-6*, G&D) Putnam Pub Group.

—Milk & Cookies. LC 82-7962. (Illus.). 48p. (ps-3). 1982. 5.95 (*0-8193-1087-5*); PLB 5.95 (*0-8193-1088-3*) Parents.

—Moonbear. (gr. 4 up). 1993. 3.95 (*0-671-86743-1*, Little Simon) S&S Trade.

—Moonbear's Books. (gr. 3 up). 1993. 3.95 (*0-671-86744-X*, Little Simon) S&S Trade.

—Moonbear's Canoe. (ps-6). 1993. 3.95 (*0-671-86745-8*, Little Simon) S&S Trade.

—Moonbear's Friend. (ps-6). 1993. 3.95 (*0-671-86746-6*, Little Simon) S&S Trade.

—Mooncake. Asch, Frank, illus. 32p. 1986. pap. 4.95 (*0-671-66451-4*) S&S Trade.

—Popcorn. Asch, Frank, illus. LC 79-216. 48p. (ps-3). 1979. 5.95 (*0-8193-1001-8*); lib. bdg. 5.95 (*0-8193-1002-6*) Parents.

—Sand Cake. Asch, Frank, illus. LC 78-11183. 48p. (ps-3). 1979. 5.95 (*0-8193-0985-0*); lib. bdg. 5.95 (*0-8193-0986-9*) Parents.

—Sand Cake. LC 93-15452. 1993. PLB 13.27 (*0-8368-0973-4*) Gareth Stevens Inc.

Baker, Dianne. Ted Bear's Magic Swing. Krum, Ronda, illus. LC 91-65819. 32p. (gr. 1-3). 1992. 12.95 (*0-87159-162-6*) Unity Bks.

Ballenger, Sharon. Adventures of the Ballenger Bears. Colley, Molly, illus. 62p. (Orig.). (ps-6). 1992. Spiral bdg. pap. 11.95 (*1-880734-00-1*) SharLew Ent.

Ballet Bears Getting in Shape. (ps-3). 1987. pap. 2.50 (*0-89954-729-X*) Antioch Pub Co.

Bare Bear's New Clothes. 24p. (ps-1). 1986. 6.95 (*0-8431-1824-5*) Price Stern.

Barnes, Jill & Sueyoshi, Akiko. Great Day for Bears. Rubin, Caroline, ed. Japan Foreign Rights Centre Staff, tr. from JPN. Fujita, Miho, illus. LC 90-37753. 32p. (gr. k-3). 1990. PLB 14.60 (*0-944483-84-4*) Garrett Ed Corp.

Baron, Phil. The Do-Along Songbook. Forse, Ken, ed. High, David, et al, illus. 26p. (ps). 1986. 9.95 (*0-934323-34-8*); pre-programmed audio cass. tape incl. Alchemy Comms.

—The Mushroom Forest. Forsse, Ken & Becker, Mary, eds. Conley-Gorniak, Allyn & Armstrong, Julie A., illus. 26p. (ps). 1986. 9.95 (*0-934323-36-4*); pre-programmed audio cass. tape incl. Alchemy Comms.

Barr, Marilynn G. Bear Days. (Illus.). 48p. (ps-1). 1993. pap. 5.95 (*1-878279-55-6*) Monday Morning Bks.

Barton, Byron, retold by. & illus. The Three Bears. LC 90-43151. 32p. (ps-1). 1991. 15.00 (*0-06-020423-0*); PLB 14.89 (*0-06-020424-9*) HarpC Child Bks.

—Three Bears Big Book. LC 91-34151. 32p. (ps-1). 1994. pap. 19.95 (*0-06-443380-3*, Trophy) HarpC Child Bks.

Bazaldua, Barbara. Walt Disney's Winnie the Pooh & the Honey Pot Picnic. (ps-3). 1994. pap. 4.95 (*0-307-10365-X*, Golden Pr) Western Pub.

Beck, Martine. Wedding of Brown Bear & White Bear, Vol. 1. (ps-3). 1990. 12.95 (*0-316-08652-5*) Little.

Beck, Sara. Fanshen the Magic Bear. (Illus.). (gr. 1-5). 1973. 4.95 (*0-938678-01-9*) New Seed.

Bellows, Cathy. The Grizzly Sisters. LC 90-38787. (Illus.). 32p. (ps-3). 1991. RSBE 14.95 (*0-02-709032-9*, Macmillan Child Bk) Macmillan Child Grp.

Berenstain, Janice & Berenstain, Stan. The Berenstain Bears Get in a Fight. Berenstain, Janice & Berenstain, Stan, illus. LC 81-15866. 32p. (ps-1). 1982. pap. 2.25 (*0-394-85132-3*) Random Bks Yng Read.

—The Berenstain Bears Go to Camp. Berenstain, Janice & Berenstain, Stan, illus. LC 81-15864. 32p. (ps-1). 1982. pap. 2.50 (*0-394-85131-5*) Random Bks Yng Read.

Berenstain, Stan & Berenstain, Jan. The Berenstain Bears Accept No Substitutes. Berenstain, Stan & Berenstain, Jan, illus. 112p. (Orig.). (gr. 2-6). 1993. PLB 7.99 (*0-679-94035-9*); pap. 3.50 (*0-679-84035-4*) Random Bks Yng Read.

—The Berenstain Bears & the Bad Dream. (Illus.). 32p. (ps-1). 1992. incl. cassette 6.95 (*0-679-82761-7*) Random Bks Yng Read.

—The Berenstain Bears & the Drug Free Zone. Berenstain, Stan & Berenstain, Jan, illus. LC 92-31604. 112p. (Orig.). (gr. 2-6). 1993. PLB 7.99 (*0-679-93612-2*); pap. 3.50 (*0-679-83612-8*) Random Bks Yng Read.

—The Berenstain Bears & the Female Fullback. Berenstain, Stan & Berenstain, Jan, illus. 112p. (Orig.). (gr. 2-6). 1993. PLB 7.99 (*0-679-93611-4*); pap. 3.50 (*0-679-83611-X*) Random Bks Yng Read.

—The Berenstain Bears & the Galloping Ghost. Berenstain, Stan & Berenstain, Jan, illus. 112p. (Orig.). (gr. 2-6). 1994. 7.99 (*0-679-95815-0*); pap. 2.99 (*0-679-85815-6*) Random Bks Yng Read.

—The Berenstain Bears & The Green-Eyed Monster. LC 93-50109. (gr. 1 up). 1995. write for info. (*0-679-96434-7*) Random Bks Yng Read.

—The Berenstain Bears & the Nerdy Nephew. Berenstain, Stan & Berenstain, Jan, illus. LC 92-32564. 112p. (Orig.). (gr. 2-6). 1993. PLB 7.99 (*0-679-93610-6*); pap. 3.50 (*0-679-83610-1*) Random Bks Yng Read.

—The Berenstain Bears & the New Girl in Town. Berenstain, Jan & Berenstain, Stan, illus. LC 92-32570. 112p. (Orig.). (gr. 2-6). 1993. PLB 7.99 (*0-679-93613-0*); pap. 3.50 (*0-679-83613-6*) Random Bks Yng Read.

—The Berenstain Bears & the Red-Handed Thief. Berenstain, Stan & Berenstain, Jan, illus. 112p. (Orig.). (gr. 2-6). 1993. PLB 7.99 (*0-679-94033-2*); pap. 2.99 (*0-679-84033-8*) Random Bks Yng Read.

—The Berenstain Bears & the School Scandal Sheet. Berenstain, Stan & Berenstain, Jan, illus. 112p. (Orig.). (gr. 2-6). 1994. PLB 7.99 (*0-679-95812-6*); pap. 2.99 (*0-679-85812-1*) Random Bks Yng Read.

—The Berenstain Bears & the Trouble with Grownups. Berenstain, Stan & Berenstain, Jan, illus. LC 91-27430. 32p. (Orig.). (ps-1). 1992. PLB 5.99 (*0-679-93000-0*); pap. 2.25 (*0-679-83000-6*) Random Bks Yng Read.

—The Berenstain Bears & the Wheelchair Commando. Berenstain, Stan & Berenstain, Jan, illus. 112p. (Orig.). (gr. 2-6). 1993. PLB 7.99 (*0-679-94034-0*); pap. 3.50 (*0-679-84034-6*) Random Bks Yng Read.

—The Berenstain Bears & Too Much Pressure. Berenstain, Stan & Berenstain, Jan, illus. LC 92-6544. 32p. (Orig.). (ps-1). 1992. PLB 5.99 (*0-679-93671-8*); pap. 2.50 (*0-679-83671-3*) Random Bks Yng Read.

—The Berenstain Bears at Camp Crush. Berenstain, Stan & Berenstain, Jan, illus. 112p. (Orig.). (gr. 2-6). 1994. 7.99 (*0-679-96028-7*); pap. 2.99 (*0-679-86028-2*) Random Bks Yng Read.

—Berenstain Bears' Big Rummage Sale. 24p. (ps up). 1992. write for info. (*0-307-74020-X*, 64020) Western Pub.

—The Berenstain Bears Don't Pollute (Anymore) Berenstain, Stan & Berenstain, Jan, illus. 32p. (ps-1). 1993. incl. cass. 5.95 (*0-679-83889-9*) Random Bks Yng Read.

—The Berenstain Bears: Family Tree House. 2p. (ps-2). 1993. write for info. (*1-883366-06-2*) Yes Ent.

—The Berenstain Bears Gotta Dance. Berenstain, Stan & Berenstain, Jan, illus. LC 92-32565. 112p. (Orig.). (gr. 2-6). 1993. PLB 7.99 (*0-679-94032-4*); pap. 3.50 (*0-679-84032-X*) Random Bks Yng Read.

—The Berenstain Bears on Wheels. Berenstain, Stan & Berentstain, Jan, illus. 14p. (ps-k). 1992. bds. 3.99 (*0-679-83245-9*) Random Bks Yng Read.

—Eager Beavers: The Berenstain Bears. 16p. (ps-2). 1993. write for info. (*1-883366-02-X*) Yes Ent.

—Life with Pa Pa: The Berenstain Bears. 16p. (ps-2). 1993. write for info. (*1-883366-01-1*) Yes Ent.

—Mysterious Numbers: The Berenstain Bears. 16p. (ps-2). 1993. write for info. (*1-883366-00-3*) Yes Ent.

—Los Osos Berenstain dia de Mudanza. Guibert, Rita, tr. LC 93-37312. (SPA., Illus.). 32p. (ps-3). 1994. pap. 2.50 (*0-679-85430-4*) Random Bks Yng Read.

—Los Osos Berenstain en la Oscuridad. Guibert, Rita, tr. from ENG. Berenstain, Stan & Berenstain, Jan, illus. LC 91-51092. (SPA.). 32p. (ps-3). 1992. pap. 2.25 (*0-679-83471-0*) Random Bks Yng Read.

—Los Osos Berenstain, No Se Permiten Ninas. LC 93-29904. (SPA.). 32p. (ps-3). 1994. pap. 2.50 (*0-679-85431-2*) Random Bks Yng Read.

—Los Osos Berenstain y Demasiada Fiesta. Guibert, Rita, tr. Berenstain, Stan & Berenstain, Jan, illus. LC 92-45874. (SPA.). 32p. (ps-3). 1993. pap. 2.25 (*0-679-84745-6*) Random Bks Yng Read.

—Los Osos Berenstain y Demasiada Television. Guibert, Rita, tr. Berenstain, Stan & Berenstain, Jan, illus. LC 92-16251. (SPA.). 32p. (ps-3). 1993. pap. 2.25 (*0-679-84007-9*) Random Bks Yng Read.

—Los Osos Berenstain y el Cuarto Desordenado. Guibert, Rita, tr. from ENG. Berenstain, Stan & Berenstain, Jan, illus. LC 91-50191. (SPA.). 32p. (ps-3). 1992. pap. 2.25 (*0-679-83470-2*) Random Bks Yng Read.

—Los Osos Berenstain y la Ninera. Guibert, Rita, tr. Berenstain, Stan & Berenstain, Jan, illus. LC 92-46719. (SPA.). 32p. (ps-3). 1993. pap. 2.25 (*0-679-84746-4*) Random Bks Yng Read.

—Los Osos Berenstain y las Peleas Entre Amigos. Guibert, Rita, tr. Berenstain, Stan & Berenstain, Jan, illus. LC 92-14807. (SPA.). 32p. (ps-3). 1993. pap. 2.25 (*0-679-84006-0*) Random Bks Yng Read.

Berenstain, Stan & Berenstain, Janice. The Bear Detectives. Berenstain, Stan & Berenstain, Janice, illus. LC 75-1603. 48p. (gr. k-3). 1975. 6.95 (*0-394-83127-6*); lib. bdg. 7.99 (*0-394-93127-0*) Beginner.

—Bear Scouts. Berenstain, Stan & Berenstain, Janice, illus. LC 67-21919. 72p. (gr. k-3). 1967. 6.95 (*0-394-80046-X*) Beginner.

—Bears' Christmas. LC 79-117542. (Illus.). 72p. (gr. k-3). 1987. 6.95 (*0-394-80090-7*) Beginner.

—Bears in the Night. (Illus.). (ps-1). 1971. 6.95 (*0-394-82286-2*); lib. bdg. 7.99 (*0-394-92286-7*) Random Bks Yng Read.

—Bears on Wheels. LC 72-77840. (Illus.). (ps-1). 1969. 6.95 (*0-394-80967-X*); lib. bdg. 9.99 (*0-394-90967-4*) Random Bks Yng Read.

—Bears' Picnic. LC 66-10156. (Illus.). 72p. (gr. k-3). 1966. 6.95 (*0-394-80041-9*); lib. bdg. 7.99 (*0-394-90041-3*) Beginner.

—Bears' Vacation. Berenstain, Stan & Berenstain, Janice, illus. LC 68-28460. 72p. (gr. k-3). 1968. 6.95 (*0-394-80052-4*) Beginner.

—The Berenstain Bears & Mama's New Job. Berenstain, Stan & Berenstain, Jan, illus. LC 84-4787. 32p. (ps-1). 1984. lib. bdg. 5.99 (*0-394-96881-6*); pap. 2.25 (*0-394-86881-1*) Random Bks Yng Read.

—The Berenstain Bears & the Bad Dream. Berenstain, Stan & Berenstain, Janice, illus. LC 87-27295. 32p. (ps-1). 1988. lib. bdg. 5.99 (*0-394-97341-0*); pap. 2.25 (*0-394-87341-6*) Random Bks Yng Read.

—The Berenstain Bears & the Bad Habit. Berenstain, Stan & Berenstain, Janice, illus. LC 86-3205. 32p. (ps-1). 1987. lib. bdg. 5.99 (*0-394-97340-2*); pap. 2.25 (*0-394-87340-8*) Random Bks Yng Read.

—The Berenstain Bears & the Big Election. Berenstain, Stan & Berenstain, Janice, illus. LC 83-62399. 32p. (ps-3). 1984. pap. 1.50 (*0-394-86542-1*) Random Bks Yng Read.

—The Berenstain Bears & the Big Road Race. Berenstain, Stan & Berenstain, Janice, illus. LC 87-4581. 32p. (gr. k-3). 1987. lib. bdg. 5.99 (*0-394-99134-6*); pap. 2.25 (*0-394-89134-1*) Random Bks Yng Read.

—The Berenstain Bears & the Dinosaurs. Berenstain, Stan & Berenstain, Janice, illus. LC 84-60384. 32p. (ps-3). 1984. pap. 1.50 (*0-394-86883-8*) Random Bks Yng Read.

—The Berenstain Bears & the Double Dare. Berenstain, Stan & Berenstain, Janice, illus. LC 87-27296. 32p. (ps-1). 1988. lib. bdg. 5.99 (*0-394-99748-4*); pap. 2.25 (*0-394-89748-X*) Random Bks Yng Read.

—The Berenstain Bears & the Ghost of the Forest. Berenstain, Stan & Berenstain, Janice, illus. LC 88-42586. 32p. (Orig.). (gr. k-3). 1988. 2.50 (*0-394-80565-8*); lib. bdg. 5.99 (*0-394-90565-2*, Random Juv) Random Bks Yng Read.

—The Berenstain Bears & the Messy Room. Berenstain, Janice & Berenstain, Stan, illus. Lerner, Sharon, ed. 32p. (ps-2). 1983. lib. bdg. 5.99 (*0-394-95639-7*); pap. 2.50 (*0-394-85639-2*) Random Bks Yng Read.

—The Berenstain Bears & the Missing Dinosaur Bone. Berenstain, Stan & Berenstain, Janice, illus. LC 79-3458. 48p. (ps-3). 1980. 6.95 (*0-394-84447-5*); lib. bdg. 7.99 (*0-394-94447-X*) Beginner.

—The Berenstain Bears & the Missing Honey. Berenstain, Stan & Berenstain, Janice, illus. LC 87-4549. 32p. (ps-3). 1987. lib. bdg. 5.99 (*0-394-99133-8*); pap. 2.25 (*0-394-89133-3*) Random Bks Yng Read.

—The Berenstain Bears & the Prize Pumpkin. Berenstain, Stan & Berenstain, Janice, illus. LC 90-32865. 32p. (Orig.). (ps-1). 1990. lib. bdg. 5.99 (*0-679-90847-1*); pap. 2.25 (*0-679-80847-7*) Random Bks Yng Read.

—The Berenstain Bears & the Sitter. Berenstain, Stan & Berenstain, Janice, illus. LC 81-50046. 32p. (ps-1). 1981. lib. bdg. 5.99 (*0-394-94837-8*); pap. 2.25 (*0-394-84837-3*) Random Bks Yng Read.

—The Berenstain Bears & the Sitter. Berenstain, Stan & Berenstain, Janice, illus. 32p. (ps-1). 1987. 2.95 (*0-394-88890-1*) Random Bks Yng Read.

—The Berenstain Bears & the Slumber Party. Berenstain, Stan & Berenstain, Janice, illus. LC 89-35223. 32p. (Orig.). 1990. PLB 5.99 (*0-679-90419-0*); pap. 2.50 (*0-679-80419-6*) Random Bks Yng Read.

—The Berenstain Bears & the Spooky Old Tree. LC 77-93771. (Illus.). (ps-2). 1978. 6.95 (*0-394-83910-2*); lib. bdg. 7.99 (*0-394-93910-7*) Random Bks Yng Read.

—The Berenstain Bears & the Trouble with Friends. Berenstain, Stan & Berenstain, Janice, illus. LC 85-30165. 32p. (ps-1). 1987. lib. bdg. 5.99 (*0-394-97339-9*); pap. 2.50 (*0-394-87339-4*) Random Bks Yng Read.

—The Berenstain Bears & the Truth. LC 83-3304. (Illus.). 32p. (ps-k). 1983. lib. bdg. 5.99 (*0-394-95640-0*); pap. 2.25 (*0-394-85640-6*) Random Bks Yng Read.

—The Berenstain Bears & the Truth. Berenstain, Stan & Berenstain, Janice, illus. LC 83-3304. 32p. (ps-1). 1988. bk. & cassette pkg. 5.95 (*0-394-89771-4*) Random Bks Yng Read.

—The Berenstain Bears & the Week at Grandma's. Berenstain, Stan & Berenstain, Janice, illus. LC 85-25743. (ps-1). 1986. lib. bdg. 5.99 (*0-394-97335-6*); pap. 2.25 (*0-394-87335-1*) Random Bks Yng Read.

—The Berenstain Bears & the Wild, Wild Honey. LC 83-60057. (Illus.). 32p. (ps). 1983. pap. 1.50 (*0-394-85924-3*) Random Bks Yng Read.

—The Berenstain Bears & Too Much Birthday. Berenstain, Stan & Berenstain, Janice, illus. LC 85-14529. 32p. (ps-1). 1986. pap. 2.25 (*0-394-87332-7*) Random Bks Yng Read.

—The Berenstain Bears & Too Much Junk Food. Berenstain, Stan & Berenstain, Janice, illus. Lerner, Sharon, ed. LC 84-40393. 32p. (ps-2). 1985. lib. bdg. 5.99 (*0-394-97217-1*); pap. 2.25 (*0-394-87217-7*) Random Bks Yng Read.

—The Berenstain Bears & Too Much TV. Berenstain, Stan & Berenstain, Jan, illus. LC 83-22887. (gr. 3-6). 1984. lib. bdg. 5.99 (*0-394-96570-1*); pap. 2.25 (*0-394-86570-7*) Random Bks Yng Read.

—The Berenstain Bears & Too Much TV. Berenstain, Stan & Berenstain, Janice, illus. (ps-1). 1989. bk. & cassette 6.95 (*0-394-82894-1*) Random Bks Yng Read.

—The Berenstain Bears & Too Much Vacation. Berenstain, Stan & Berenstain, Janice, illus. LC 88-32094. 32p. (ps-1). 1990. Includes audio cassette. pap. 6.95 (*0-679-80311-4*) Random Bks Yng Read.

—The Berenstain Bears Are a Family. Berenstain, Stan & Berenstain, Janice, illus. LC 90-63082. 24p. (Orig.). (ps). 1991. 2.95 (*0-679-80746-2*) Random Bks Yng Read.

—The Berenstain Bears at the Super-Duper Market. Berenstain, Stan & Berenstain, Janice, illus. LC 90-63080. 24p. (Orig.). (ps). 1991. 2.95 (*0-679-80748-9*) Random Bks Yng Read.

—The Berenstain Bears' Bath Book. Berenstain, Stan & Berenstain, Janice, illus. 10p. (ps). 1985. vinyl 3.95 (*0-394-87116-2*) Random Bks Yng Read.

—The Berenstain Bears Blaze a Trail. Berenstain, Stan & Berenstain, Janice, illus. LC 87-4552. 32p. (ps-1). 1987. lib. bdg. 5.99 (*0-394-99132-X*); pap. 2.50 (*0-394-89132-5*) Random Bks Yng Read.

—The Berenstain Bears Don't Pollute (Anymore) Berenstain, Stan & Berenstain, Janice, illus. LC 91-9147. 32p. (Orig.). (ps-1). 1991. lib. bdg. 5.99 (*0-679-92351-9*); pap. 2.50 (*0-679-82351-4*) Random Bks Yng Read.

—Berenstain Bears Forget Their Manners. Berenstain, Stan & Berenstain, Janice, illus. LC 84-43156. 32p. (gr. k-3). 1985. lib. bdg. 5.99 (*0-394-97333-X*); pap. 2.50 (*0-394-87333-5*) Random Bks Yng Read.

—The Berenstain Bears Forget Their Manners. Berenstain, Stan & Berenstain, Janice, illus. 32p. (ps-1). 1986, pap. 6.95 with cassette (*0-394-88343-8*) Random Bks Yng Read.

—The Berenstain Bears' Four Seasons. Berenstain, Stan & Berenstain, Janice, illus. LC 90-63079. 24p. (Orig.). (ps). 1991. 2.95 (*0-679-80749-7*) Random Bks Yng Read.

—The Berenstain Bears Get in a Fight. Berenstain, Stan & Berenstain, Janice, illus. 32p. (ps-1). 1987. pap. 3.50 (*0-394-88893-6*) Random Bks Yng Read.

—The Berenstain Bears Get in a Fight. Berenstain, Stan & Berenstain, Janice, illus. 32p. (ps-1). 1988. pap. 5.95 bk. & cassette pkg. (*0-394-89778-1*) Random Bks Yng Read.

—The Berenstain Bears Get Stage Fright. Berenstain, Stan & Berenstain, Janice, illus. LC 85-25716. 32p. (gr. 3-6). 1986. lib. bdg. 5.99 (*0-394-97337-2*); pap. 2.25 (*0-394-87337-8*) Random Bks Yng Read.

—The Berenstain Bears Get the Gimmies. Berenstain, Stan & Berenstain, Janice, illus. LC 88-42587. 32p. (Orig.). (ps-1). 1988. lib. bdg. 5.99 (*0-394-90566-0*); pap. 2.25 (*0-394-80566-6*) Random Bks Yng Read.

—The Berenstain Bears Get the Gimmies. Berenstain, Stan & Berenstain, Janice, illus. LC 88-42587. 32p. (ps-1). 1990. Includes audio cassette. pap. 6.95 (*0-679-80313-0*); cass. incl. Random Bks Yng Read.

—The Berenstain Bears Go Fly a Kite. LC 83-60056. (Illus.). 32p. (ps-2). 1983. pap. 1.50 (*0-394-85921-9*) Random Bks Yng Read.

—The Berenstain Bears Go Out for the Team. Berenstain, Stan & Berenstain, Janice, illus. LC 85-30164. 32p. (ps-1). 1991. pap. 5.95 incls. cassette (*0-679-81495-7*) Random Bks Yng Read.

—The Berenstain Bears Go to Camp. Berenstain, Stan & Berenstain, Janice, illus. (ps-1). 1989. 5.95 (*0-394-82896-8*) Random Bks Yng Read.

—The Berenstain Bears Go to School. LC 77-79853. (Illus.). (ps-2). 1978. lib. bdg. 5.99 (*0-394-93736-8*); pap. 2.25 (*0-394-83736-3*) Random Bks Yng Read.

—The Berenstain Bears Go to the Doctor. Berenstain, Stan & Berenstain, Janice, illus. LC 81-50043. 32p. (ps-1). 1981. lib. bdg. 5.99 (*0-394-94835-1*); pap. 2.50 (*0-394-84835-7*) Random Bks Yng Read.

—The Berenstain Bears in the Dark. LC 82-5395. 32p. (ps-1). 1982. pap. 2.25 saddle-stitched (*0-394-85443-8*) Random Bks Yng Read.

—Berenstain Bears Learn about Strangers. Berenstain, Stan & Berenstain, Jan, illus. LC 84-43157. 32p. (ps-1). 1985. lib. bdg. 5.99 (*0-394-97334-8*); 2.25 (*0-394-87334-3*) Random Bks Yng Read.

—The Berenstain Bears Learn about Strangers. (Illus.). 32p. (ps-1). 1986. pap. 5.95 (*0-394-88346-2*) Random Bks Yng Read.

—The Berenstain Bears Meet Santa Bear. Berenstain, Stan & Berenstain, Janice, illus. LC 84-4829. 32p. (ps-1). 1989. pap. 5.95 incl. cassette (*0-394-85228-1*) Random Bks Yng Read.

—The Berenstain Bears' Moving Day. Berenstain, Stan & Berenstain, Janice, illus. LC 81-50044. 32p. (ps-1). 1981. lib. bdg. 5.99 (*0-394-94838-6*); pap. 2.50 (*0-394-84838-1*) Random Bks Yng Read.

—The Berenstain Bears' Nature Guide. Berenstain, Stan & Berenstain, Jan, illus. LC 75-8070. 72p. (ps-4). 1984. pap. 7.95 (*0-394-86602-9*) Random Bks Yng Read.

—The Berenstain Bears' New Baby. Berenstain, Stan & Berenstain, Janice, illus. 32p. (gr. 1-3). 1985. pap. 5.95 incl. cass. (*0-394-87661-X*) Random Bks Yng Read.

—The Berenstain Bears' Nursery Tales. (Illus.). (ps-1). 1973. pap. 2.25 (*0-394-82665-5*) Random Bks Yng Read.

—The Berenstain Bears on the Job. Berenstain, Stan & Berenstain, Janice, illus. LC 87-9739. 32p. (gr. k-3). 1987. lib. bdg. 5.99 (*0-394-99131-1*); pap. 2.50 (*0-394-89131-7*) Random Bks Yng Read.

—The Berenstain Bears on the Moon. Berenstain, Stan & Berenstain, Janice, illus. LC 84-20428. 48p. (ps-3). 1985. 6.95 (*0-394-87180-4*); lib. bdg. 7.99 (*0-394-97180-9*) Random Bks Yng Read.

—The Berenstain Bears Ready, Set, Go! Berenstain, Stan & Berenstain, Janice, illus. LC 88-42589. 32p. (Orig.). (gr. k-3). 1988. 2.25 (*0-394-80564-X*) Random Bks Yng Read.

—The Berenstain Bears Say Good Night. Berenstain, Stan & Berenstain, Janice, illus. LC 90-63081. 24p. (Orig.). (ps). 1991. 2.95 (*0-679-80747-0*) Random Bks Yng Read.

—The Berenstain Bears' Science Fair. Berenstain, Stan & Berenstain, Janice, illus. LC 76-8121. 72p. (ps-4). 1984. pap. 7.99 (*0-394-86603-7*) Random Bks Yng Read.

—The Berenstain Bears Shoot the Rapids. Berenstain, Stan & Berenstain, Janice, illus. LC 83-62400. 32p. (ps-3). 1984. pap. 1.50 (*0-394-86543-X*) Random Bks Yng Read.

—The Berenstain Bears' Take-Along Library. Berenstain, Stan & Berenstain, Janice, illus. Incl. The Berenstain Bears Visit the Dentist. 32p; The Berenstain Bears & Too Much TV. 32p; The Berenstain Bears & the Sitter. 32p; The Berenstain Bears in the Dark. 32p; The Berenstain Bears & the Messy Room. 32p. (Illus.). (ps-3). 1985. 11.50 (*0-394-87615-6*) Random Bks Yng Read.

—The Berenstain Bears to the Rescue. LC 83-60058. (Illus.). 32p. (ps-2). 1983. pap. 1.50 (*0-394-85923-5*) Random Bks Yng Read.

—The Berenstain Bears' Toy Time. (Illus.). 12p. (ps). 1985. 2.95 (*0-394-87449-8*) Random Bks Yng Read.

—The Berenstain Bears Trick or Treat. Berenstain, Stan & Berenstain, Janice, illus. LC 89-30884. 32p. (Orig.). (ps-1). 1989. PLB 5.99 (*0-679-90091-8*); pap. 2.50 (*0-679-80091-3*) Random Bks Yng Read.

—The Berenstain Bears Trick or Treat. Berenstain, Stan & Berenstain, Janice, illus. 32p. (ps-1). 1991. incl. 20-min. cassette 6.00 (*0-679-81497-3*) Random Bks Yng Read.

—The Berenstain Bears' Trouble at School. Berenstain, Stan & Berenstain, Janice, illus. LC 86-4999. 32p. (ps-1). 1987. pap. 2.50 (*0-394-87336-X*) Random Bks Yng Read.

—The Berenstain Bears' Trouble with Money. LC 83-3305. (Illus.). 32p. (ps-k). 1983. pap. 2.25 (*0-394-85917-0*) Random Bks Yng Read.

—The Berenstain Bears' Trouble with Pets. Berenstain, Stan & Berenstain, Janice, illus. LC 90-32956. 32p. (Orig.). (ps-1). 1990. lib. bdg. 5.99 (*0-679-90848-X*); pap. 2.50 (*0-679-80848-5*) Random Bks Yng Read.

—The Berenstain Bears Visit the Dentist. Berenstain, Stan & Berenstain, Janice, illus. LC 81-50045. 32p. (ps-1). 1981. lib. bdg. 5.99 (*0-394-94836-X*); pap. 2.50 (*0-394-84836-5*) Random Bks Yng Read.

—Big Honey Hunt. LC 62-15115. (Illus.). 64p. (gr. 1-2). 1962. 6.95 (*0-394-80028-1*) Beginner.

—He Bear, She Bear. Berenstain, Stan & Berenstain, Janice, illus. LC 74-5518. 48p. (ps-1). 1974. 6.95 (*0-394-82997-2*); lib. bdg. 7.99 (*0-394-92997-7*) Random Bks Yng Read.

—Inside, Outside, Upside Down. LC 68-28465. (Illus.). (ps-1). 1968. 6.95 (*0-394-81142-9*); lib. bdg. 7.99 (*0-394-91142-3*) Random Bks Yng Read.

Berg, Cami. Sky Bear. (Illus.). 40p. (ps up). 1994. 15.95 (*1-879244-87-X*) Windom Bks.

Bernier, Evariste. Baxter Bear & Moses Moose. Peterson, Dawn, illus. LC 90-61408. 48p. (gr. 1-4). 1990. 12.95 (*0-89272-287-8*) Down East.

Big Bear's Treasury, the Green Collection: A Family Treasury. LC 91-71859. (ps up). 1994. pap. 12.99 (*1-56402-363-X*) Candlewick Pr.

Big Bear's Treasury, Vol. 2: A Children's Anthology. LC 91-71859. 96p. (ps up). 1992. 19.95 (*1-56402-113-0*) Candlewick Pr.

Bill Martin Junior Library. 1993. PLB write for info. (*0-8050-3073-5*) H Holt & Co.

Bird, E. J. The Rainmakers. LC 92-29789. 1993. 19.95 (*0-87614-748-1*) Carolrhoda Bks.

Birney, Betty. Disney's Winnie the Pooh Helping Hands: Oh, Bother! Somebody's Grumpy! Baker, Darrell, illus. 24p. (ps-3). 1992. write for info. (*0-307-12667-6*, 12667) Western Pub.

—Oh, Brother! Someone's Jealous: Walt Disney's Winnie the Pooh Helping Hands. (ps-3). 1994. pap. 2.25 (*0-307-12820-2*, Golden Pr) Western Pub.

—Walt Disney's I Am Winnie the Pooh. (ps). 1994. 3.95 (*0-307-12456-8*, Golden Pr) Western Pub.

—Winnie the Pooh & the Missing Pots. Hicks, Russell, illus. 24p. (ps-2). 1992. write for info. (*0-307-12337-5*, 12337) Western Pub.

Bishop, Adela. The Christmas Polar Bear. Czapla, Carole, illus. 32p. (gr. k-3). 1991. 12.95 (*0-9625620-2-5*) DOT Garnet.
A selfish little bear living near the North Pole enlists the aid of the magic Rainbow Fish to ensure eternal summer - but with no winter, Santa's elves won't wake up to begin their Christmas toy-making. A change of heart, however, saves the season. The bear receives a magic coin from the fish that lets him turn snow bears into teddy bears - enough for every girl & boy on Santa's list - & then turns him into a polar bear, who can play all winter long. Lovingly illustrated, this is a Christmas story that can be read throughout the year.
Publisher Provided Annotation.

Bissett, Isabel. That's Dangerous. Tulloch, Coral, illus. LC 92-31947. 1993. 3.75 (*0-383-03596-1*) SRA Schl Grp.

Blocksma, Mary. The Best-Dressed Bear. Kalthoff, Sandra C., illus. LC 84-9565. 24p. (ps-2). 1984. pap. text ed. 3.95 (*0-516-41585-9*) Childrens.

—The Best Dressed Bear Big Book. (Illus.). 24p. (ps-2). 1989. PLB 22.95 (*0-516-49510-0*) Childrens.

Blueberry Bear. Kaler, Rebecca. 16p. (ps). 1993. 12.95 (*0-9634637-0-5*) Inquir Voices.

Boelts, Maribeth. Dry Days, Wet Nights. Parkinson, Kathy, illus. LC 93-28674. 1994. write for info. (*0-8075-1723-2*) A Whitman.

Bolliger, Max. Three Little Bears. Wilkon, Jozef, illus. (ps-3). 1987. 12.95 (*1-55774-006-2*) Modan-Adama Bks.

Bond, Michael. Bear Called Paddington. Fortnum, Peggy, illus. LC 60-9096. 128p. (gr. 3-7). 1968. pap. 3.50 (*0-440-40483-5*, YB) Dell.

—Bear Called Paddington. Fortnum, Peggy, illus. 128p. (gr. 1-5). 1960. 13.45 (*0-395-06636-0*) HM.

—The Hilarious Adventures of Paddington, 5 bks. Incl. A Bear Called Paddington; More about Paddington; Paddington at Large; Paddington at Work; Paddington Helps Out. (Illus.). 1986. Boxed set. pap. 14.75 (*0-440-43668-0*) Dell.

—More about Paddington. Fortnum, Peggy, illus. (gr. 4-6). 1962. 13.45 (*0-395-06640-9*) HM.

—Paddington Abroad. Fortnum, Peggy, illus. 128p. (gr. 2-6). 1992. pap. 3.25 (*0-440-47352-7*, YB) Dell.

—Paddington Abroad. Fortnum, Peggy, illus. LC 72-2753. 128p. (gr. 1-5). 1973. 14.45 (*0-395-14331-4*) HM.

—Paddington at the Circus. Lobban, John, illus. LC 91-44210. 32p. (ps-2). 1992. 8.95 (*0-694-00415-4*, Festival) HarpC Child Bks.

—Paddington at the Seashore. Lobban, John, illus. 28p. (ps). 1992. 2.95 (*0-694-00397-2*) HarpC Child Bks.

—Paddington at Work. Fortnum, Peggy, illus. LC 67-20372. (gr. 1-5). 1967. 13.95 (*0-395-06637-9*) HM.

—Paddington Bear. Lobban, John, illus. LC 91-29781. 32p. (ps-3). 1992. 8.95 (*0-694-00394-8*) HarpC Child Bks.

—Paddington Goes Shopping. Lobban, John, illus. 28p. (ps). 1992. 2.95 (*0-694-00395-6*) HarpC Child Bks.

—Paddington Goes to Town. 128p. (gr. 2-5). 1992. pap. 3.25 (*0-440-46793-4*, YB) Dell.

—Paddington Goes to Town. Fortnum, Peggy, illus. LC 68-28043. (gr. 1-5). 1977. 14.95 (*0-395-06635-2*) HM.

—Paddington Helps Out. Fortnum, Peggy, illus. 128p. (gr. 3-7). 1982. pap. 2.95 (*0-440-46802-7*, YB) Dell.

—Paddington Helps Out. Fortnum, Peggy, illus. (gr. 4-6). 1973. 13.45 (*0-395-06639-5*) HM.

—Paddington in the Kitchen. Lobban, John, illus. 28p. (ps). 1992. 2.95 (*0-694-00396-4*) HarpC Child Bks.

—Paddington Marches On. (Illus.). (gr. 4-6). 1965. 13.45 (*0-395-06642-5*) HM.

—Paddington Marches On. (gr. 4-7). 1991. pap. 3.25 (*0-440-46799-3*) Dell.

—Paddington Marches On. large type ed. Fortnum, Peggy, illus. 1993. 16.95 (*0-7451-1806-2*, Galaxy Child Lrg Print) Chivers N Amer.

—Paddington Meets the Queen. Lobban, John, illus. LC 92-24938. 32p. (ps-3). 1993. 3.95 (*0-694-00460-X*, Festival) HarpC Child Bks.

—Paddington on Stage. (gr. 4-7). 1992. pap. 3.25 (*0-440-46846-9*, YB) Dell.

—Paddington on Top. Fortnum, Peggy, illus. 128p. (gr. 1-5). 1975. 13.95 (*0-395-21897-7*) HM.

—Paddington on Top. 1991. pap. 3.25 (*0-440-46818-3*) Dell.

—Paddington Rides On! Lobban, John, illus. LC 92-24937. 32p. (ps-3). 1993. 3.95 (*0-694-00461-8*, Festival) HarpC Child Bks.

—Paddington Takes a Bath. Lobban, John, illus. 28p. (ps). 1992. 2.95 (*0-694-00398-0*) HarpC Child Bks.

—Paddington Takes the Test. 128p. (gr. k-6). 1982. pap. 1.95 (*0-440-47021-8*, YB) Dell.

—Paddington Takes to TV. (gr. 4-7). 1991. pap. 3.25 (*0-440-45930-3*) Dell.

—Paddington's Garden. Lobban, John, illus. LC 92-24527. 32p. (ps-3). 1993. 8.95 (*0-694-00462-6*, Festival) HarpC Child Bks.

Bonners, Susan. Panda. LC 78-50404. (Illus.). 32p. (ps-3). 1978. pap. 6.95 (*0-385-28772-0*); pap. 6.46 (*0-385-28775-5*) Delacorte.

Bornstein, Harry, et al. Don't Be a Grumpy Bear: A Coloring Book about Manners in Signed English. Miller, Ralph R., illus. 32p. (ps-2). 1986. pap. 3.95 (*0-930323-26-2*, Pub. by K Green Pubns) Gallaudet Univ Pr.

Bowden, Miriam. The Adventures of Paz in the Land of Numbers. Crum, Anna M., illus. LC 89-71741. 32p. (ps-3). 1992. 12.95 (*0-89334-150-9*, 150-9) Humanics Ltd.

Bracken, Carolyn, illus. Teddy Bear's Pockets. 8p. (ps). 1983. pap. 3.95 washable (*0-671-46448-5*, Little Simon) S&S Trade.

Bradman, Tony. A Bad Week for the Three Bears. Williams, Jenny, illus. LC 91-41871. 32p. (Orig.). (ps-1). 1993. pap. 2.25 (*0-679-83379-X*) Random Bks Yng Read.

Bray, Vivieene, illus. Little Bear's Bedtime. 10p. (ps-2). 1993. bds. 16.95 (*1-56293-317-5*) McClanahan Bk.

—Little Bear's Breakfast. 10p. (ps-2). 1993. bds. 16.95 (*1-56293-318-3*) McClanahan Bk.

Bread & Honey. (Illus.). 42p. (ps-3). 1992. PLB 13.26 (*0-8368-0880-0*); PLB 13.27 s.p. (*0-685-61512-X*) Gareth Stevens Inc.

Brett, Jan. Berlioz the Bear. LC 90-37634. (Illus.). 32p. 1991. 14.95 (*0-399-22248-0*, Putnam) Putnam Pub Group.

—Goldilocks & the Three Bears. (Illus.). 32p. (ps-3). 1990. pap. 6.95 (*0-399-22004-6*, Sandcastle Bks) Putnam Pub Group.

Briggs, Raymond. The Bear. LC 94-8734. (Illus.). 48p. (ps up). 1994. 20.00 (*0-679-86944-1*); PLB 20.99 (*0-679-96944-6*) Random Bks Yng Read.

Brimner, Larry D. Country Bear's Surprise. Councell, Ruth T., illus. LC 90-7717. 32p. (ps-2). 1991. PLB 12.99 (*0-531-08411-6*) Orchard Bks Watts.

Brown, Ruth. The Grizzly Revenge. Brown, Ruth, illus. 32p. (gr. 3-6). 1987. 15.95 (*0-86264-024-5*, Pub. by Anderson Pr UK) Trafalgar.

Bucknall, Caroline. One Bear All Alone. Bucknall, Caroline, illus. LC 85-6968. 32p. (ps-2). 1989. pap. 4.95 (*0-8037-0645-6*) Dial Bks Young.

—One Bear in the Hospital. Bucknall, Caroline, illus. LC 90-2994. 32p. (ps-2). 1991. 11.95 (*0-8037-0847-5*) Dial Bks Young.

—One Bear in the Picture. (Illus.). 32p. (ps-2). 1993. pap. 3.99 (*0-14-054591-3*) Puffin Bks.

Bunting, Eve. The Valentine Bears. Brett, Jan, illus. 32p. (gr. 3). 1985. 14.95 (*0-89919-138-X*, Clarion Bks); pap. 4.95 (*0-89919-313-7*, Clarion) HM.

Burgess, Thornton. The Adventures of Buster Bear. 1986. Repr. lib. bdg. 17.95 (*0-89966-525-X*) Buccaneer Bks.

—Buster Bear's Twins. 1992. Repr. lib. bdg. 17.95x (*0-89966-981-6*) Buccaneer Bks.

Burgess, Thornton W. The Adventures of Buster Bear. Kliros, Thea, adapted by. Cady, Harrison, illus. LC 92-36949. 96p. 1993. pap. 1.00 (*0-486-27564-7*) Dover.

—Adventures of Buster Bear. 19.95 (*0-8488-0354-X*) Amereon Ltd.

—Buster Bear's Twins. 19.95 (*0-8488-0396-5*) Amereon Ltd.

Burt, Denise. I'm Not a Bear. Ryan, Ron, photos by. (Illus.). 32p. (gr. k-5). 1987. pap. 5.95 (*0-944176-00-3*) Terra Nova.

Butler, Dorothy. My Brown Bear Barney. Fuller, Elizabeth, illus. LC 88-21199. 24p. (ps up). 1989. 14.00 (*0-688-08567-9*); PLB 13.93 (*0-688-08568-7*) Greenwillow.

Campbell, Janet, adapted by. Walt Disney's Winnie the Pooh & the Honey Tree. Kurtz, John, illus. LC 92-53442. 48p. (ps-4). 1993. 12.95 (*1-56282-379-5*) Disney Pr.

Candlewick Press Staff. Big Bear's Treasury, Vol. 3: A Children's Anthology. LC 91-71859. (Illus.). 96p. (ps up). 1994. 19.95 (*1-56402-309-5*) Candlewick Pr.

Caple, Kathy. Fox & Bear. Caple, Kathy, illus. 40p. (gr. k-3). 1992. 13.45 (*0-395-55634-1*) HM.

Carlson, Anna L. Homer Bear's Secret. 1st. ed. Wynne, Dianna, illus. 24p. (Orig.). (gr. k-4). 1983. pap. 1.95 (*0-939938-05-7*) Karwyn Ent.

Carlstrom, Nancy W. Better Not Get Wet, Jesse Bear. Degen, Bruce, illus. LC 87-10810. 32p. (ps-1). 1988. RSBE 13.95 (*0-02-717280-5*, Macmillan Child Bk) Macmillan Child Grp.

—Happy Birthday, Jesse Bear! Degen, Bruce, illus. LC 93-25180. (ps-1). 1994. 14.95 (*0-02-717277-5*, Macmillan Child Bk) Macmillan Child Grp.

—How Do You Say It Today, Jesse Bear? Degen, Bruce, illus. LC 91-21939. 32p. (ps-1). 1992. RSBE 13.95 (*0-02-717276-7*, Macmillan Child Bk) Macmillan Child Grp.

—It's About Time, Jesse Bear: And Other Rhymes. Degen, Bruce, illus. LC 88-8511. 32p. (ps-1). 1990. RSBE 13.95 (*0-02-717351-8*, Macmillan Child Bk) Macmillan Child Grp.

—Jesse Bear, What Will You Wear. Degen, Bruce, illus. LC 94-482. 1994. 19.95 (*0-689-71878-0*, Aladdin) Macmillan Child Grp.

Carson, Jo. The Great Shaking: An Account of the Earthquakes of 1811 & 1812. Parker, Robert A., illus. LC 93-4887. 1994. write for info. (*0-531-06809-9*); lib. bdg. write for info. (*0-531-08659-3*) Orchard Bks Watts.

Cartlidge, Michelle. Bear in the Forest. Cartlidge, Michelle, illus. 12p. (ps). 1991. bds. 3.50 (*0-525-44674-5*, DCB) Dutton Child Bks.

Casterline, Charlotte L. The Asthma Attack by Bo B. Bear. Brunza-Horn, Nanette, illus. (Orig.). (ps-6). 1988. pap. 5.95 (*0-9617218-2-0*) Info All Bk.

Christmas with the Santa Bears, A Christmas to Remember. (Illus.). 24p. 1987. (Honey Bear Bks); text ed. 3.95 (*0-87449-072-3*, Honey Bear Bks); text ed. 3.95 (*0-87449-112-6*, Honey Bear Bks) Modern Pub NYC.

Ciardi, John. Someone Could Win a Polar Bear. 64p. (ps-3). 1993. 13.95 (*1-56397-205-0*, Wordsong) Boyds Mills Pr.

Cooper, Helen. The Bear under the Stairs. Cooper, Helen, illus. LC 92-23840. (ps-2). 1993. 12.99 (*0-8037-1279-0*) Dial Bks Young.

Cormier, Robert. Tunes for Bears to Dance To. 1994. pap. 3.99 (*0-440-21903-5*) Dell.

Corral, Jeanie B. Scruffy 'n Me. 1994. 8.95 (*0-8062-4844-0*) Carlton.

Cosgrove, Stephen. Jingle Bear. James, Robin, illus. 32p. (Orig.). (gr. 1-4). 1985. pap. 2.95 (*0-8431-1440-1*) Price Stern.

Cosgrove, Stephen E. Fiddler. Edelson, Wendy, illus. 32p. (ps-3). 1990. PLB 14.95 (*0-89565-665-5*) Childs World.

Counhaye, Guy. The Chilly Bear. (Illus.). 32p. (gr. k-2). 1991. 12.95 (*0-89565-740-6*) Childs World.

Cowley, Stewart. Sleepy Bear. LC 93-77347. (Illus.). 22p. (ps). 1993. 6.99 (*0-89577-513-1*, Dist. by Random) RD Assn.

Curtiss, A. B. In the Company of Bears. Stone, Barbara, illus. 40p. (ps up). 1994. PLB 18.95 (*0-932529-72-0*) Oldcastle.
Available from the publisher, Tel. 619-489-0336, FAX: 619-747-1198, or from Baker & Taylor, Cogan Books, Pacific Pipeline, The Booksource, Quality Books, Koen. In a magical place which could be closer than you think, wise & wonderful polar bears have discovered the secret of time, "It is odd how a bear does nothing/Yet nothing is left undone." And the path to one's truth: "You need just your original face/ Without any pretending or fuss.../ When your're sad, you can sing your saddest songs/When you're mad you can beat the Chinese gongs." This is wonderful to read out loud! Bears know how to treat you special. They have time to chat, listen to your dreams & best of all they want you to "JUST BE YOURSELF." These venerable creatures understand that to reach any place of real importance, "You can't go by clock or by mile/You have to go by heart." This remarkable book spans all age levels. Simple but elegant poetic text & extravagant illustrations are showcased in this over-size, bear-wise treasure. As you turn the pages, an imposing bear silhouette moves ceremoniously along the rich pastel border. Library bound. Acid-free paper. Uncommonly splendid.
Publisher Provided Annotation.

Curwood, James O. Bear. Annaud, Jean-Jacques, intro. by. LC 89-13247. 208p. (gr. 3-11). 1992. 16.95 (*1-55704-054-0*); pap. 3.95 (*1-55704-131-8*) Newmarket.

Dabcovich, Lydia. Sleepy Bear. Dabcovich, Lydia, illus. 32p. (ps-2). 1982. 12.95 (*0-525-39465-6*, DCB) Dutton Child Bks.

—Sleepy Bear. Dabcovich, Lydia, illus. 32p. (ps-2). 1985. pap. 4.95 (*0-525-44196-4*, DCB) Dutton Child Bks.

—Sleepy Bear. (Illus.). 32p. (ps-1). 1993. pap. 17.99 (*0-14-054937-4*, Puff Unicorn) Puffin Bks.

Dalgliesh, Alice. The Bears on Hemlock Mountain. Sewell, Helen, illus. LC 89-27651. 64p. (gr. 1-4). 1990. Repr. of 1952 ed. RSBE 13.95 (*0-684-19169-5*, Scribners Young Read) Macmillan Child Grp.

—The Bears on Hemlock Mountain. 2nd ed. Sewell, Helen, illus. LC 91-40166. 64p. (gr. 1-3). 1992. pap. 3.95 (*0-689-71604-4*, Aladdin) Macmillan Child Grp.

Damon, Laura. Birthday Buddies. Aiello, Laurel, illus. LC 87-10866. 32p. (gr. k-2). 1988. PLB 11.59 (*0-8167-1091-0*); pap. text ed. 2.95 (*0-8167-1092-9*) Troll Assocs.

—Fun in the Snow. Paterson, Diane, illus. LC 87-10843. 32p. (gr. k-2). 1988. PLB 11.59 (*0-8167-1081-3*); pap. text ed. 2.95 (*0-8167-1082-1*) Troll Assocs.

Davies, Leah. Kelly Bear Beginnings, 5 bks. Hallett, Leah, illus. 176p. (ps-5). 1991. Set incl. Kelly Bear Feelings; Kelly Bear Behavior; Kelly Bear Health; Kelly Bear Activities; Kelly Bear Drug Awareness. pap. 29.95 (*0-9621054-7-3*) Kelly Bear Pr.

Davies, Leah G. Kelly Bear Behavior. Davies, Joy D., illus. LC 88-82603. 28p. (Orig.). (ps-3). 1988. pap. 4.50 (*0-9621054-1-4*) Kelly Bear Pr.

—Kelly Bear Feelings. rev. ed. Davies, Joy D., illus. LC 88-82577. 28p. (ps-3). 1988. pap. 4.50 (*0-9621054-0-6*) Kelly Bear Pr.

Day, Alexandra. Frank & Ernest on the Road. (Illus.). 48p. (ps-3). 1994. 14.95 (*0-590-45048-4*, Scholastic Hardcover) Scholastic Inc.

De Beer, Hans. Ahoy There, Little Polar Bear. De Beer, Hans, illus. LC 88-42533. 32p. (gr. k-3). 1988. 13.95 (*1-55858-028-X*) North-South Bks NYC.

—Ahoy There, Little Polar Bear. De Beer, Hans, illus. 32p. (gr. k-3). 1991. pap. 2.95 (*1-55858-109-X*) North-South Bks NYC.

—Kleiner Eisbar, Komm Bald Wieder! De Beer, Hans, illus. (GER.). 32p. (gr. k-3). 1992. 13.95 (*3-85825-316-2*) North-South Bks NYC.

—Kleiner Eisbar, Nimm Mich Mit! De Beer, Hans, illus. (GER.). 320p. (gr. k-3). 1992. 22.50 (*3-314-00344-7*, Bradford Bks) North-South Bks NYC.

—Little Polar Bear. De Beer, Hans, illus. LC 86-33208. 32p. (gr. k-3). 1989. 13.95 (*1-55858-024-7*); pap. 2.95 (*1-55858-030-1*) North-South Bks NYC.

—Little Polar Bear: A Pop-up Book. (Illus.). 32p. (gr. k-3). 1993. 15.95 (*1-55858-226-6*) North-South Bks NYC.

—Little Polar Bear Address Book. De Beer, Hans, illus. 128p. 1990. 7.95 (*1-55858-080-8*) North-South Bks NYC.

—Little Polar Bear & the Brave Little Hare. De Beer, Hans, illus. James, J. Alison, tr. from GER. LC 92-9803. (Illus.). 32p. (gr. k-3). 1992. 12.95 (*1-55858-179-0*); PLB 12.88 (*1-55858-180-4*) North-South Bks NYC.

—Little Polar Bear Finds a Friend. De Beer, Hans, illus. 32p. (gr. k-3). 1992. pap. 2.95 (*1-55858-144-8*) North-South Bks NYC.

De Brunhoff, Laurent. Babar Learns to Cook. De Brunhoff, Laurent, illus. LC 78-11769. (ps-3). 1979. 2.25 (*0-394-84108-5*) Random Bks Yng Read.

Deihl, Edna G. The Teddy Bear That Prowled at Night. Russell, Mary L., illus. 24p. (gr. k-3). 1991. pap. 7.95 (*0-88138-079-2*, Green Tiger) S&S Trade.

Dengler, Sandy. Smokey, a Simple Country Bear Who Made Good. Dengler, Sandy, illus. 31p. (gr. 3-5). 1987. pap. text ed. 3.00 (*0-914019-15-5*) NW Interpretive.

Dennie, Joseph C. & Weathers, Joseph. Smarty's New Friend. Bonnette, Charlotte A., ed. Williams, Vanessa R. & Washington, Mariama K., illus. LC 93-39652. 20p. (Orig.). (gr. 1-4). 1994. pap. 7.95 incl. cassette, Smarty's Drug Free Song (*1-877971-11-1*) Mid Atl Reg Pr.

Doerksen, Nan. Bears for Breakfast: The Thiessen Family Adventures. Penner, Kathy, illus. 34p. (ps-k). 1983. pap. 2.50 (*0-919797-07-5*) Kindred Pr.

Donnely, Marcus. Guffy the Bear. (Illus.). 32p. (ps). 1986. 4.50 (*0-938715-00-3*) Toy Works Pr.

Doray, Andrea. Boris Bear Remembers His Manners. Gress, Jonna C., ed. Claflin, Dale, illus. LC 91-78098. 18p. (Orig.). (gr. k-3). 1992. pap. 14.25 (*0-944943-06-3*, CODE 18437-5) Current Inc.

Douglass, Barbara. Good As New. Brewster, Patience, illus. LC 80-21406. 32p. (ps-1). 1982. 13.00 (*0-688-41983-6*); PLB 12.88 (*0-688-51983-0*) Lothrop.

Duchak, Kathleen D. The Three Bears. Lang, Anne D., illus. 28p. (ps). Date not set. 15.00 (*0-9640865-0-6*) Family Pubng.

Duffield, Francesca, illus. A Teddy Tale. LC 92-75612. 10p. (ps). 1993. 5.95 (*1-85697-918-0*, Kingfisher LKC) LKC.

Dyer, Jane, illus. Goldilocks & the Three Bears. 16p. (ps). 1984. 3.95 (*0-448-10213-7*, G&D) Putnam Pub Group.

Dyer, Ruth. Sam's Easy Reader Stories. LC 93-60261. (Illus.). 44p. (ps-3). 1994. pap. 4.95 (*1-55523-614-6*) Winston-Derek.

Eaton, Seymour. The Roosevelt Bears Go to Washington. Campbell, V. Floyd & Culver, R. K., illus. 192p. (gr. 6 up). 1981. pap. 4.50 (*0-486-24163-7*) Dover.

—The Roosevelt Bears: Their Travels & Adventures. Campbell, V. Floyd, illus. 192p. (gr. 1 up). 1979. pap. 5.95 (*0-486-23819-9*) Dover.

Edge, Nellie, adapted by. Osito, Osito. Zamora-Pearson, Marissa, tr. from ENG. Somerville, Sheila, illus. (SPA.). (ps-2). 1993. pap. text ed. 15.00 (*0-922053-26-X*) N Edge Res.

—Teddy Bear, Teddy Bear Big Book. Somerville, Sheila, illus. (ps-2). 1988. pap. text ed. 14.00 (*0-922053-04-9*) N Edge Res.

Elish, Dan. Jason & the Bear. 1992. pap. 3.50 (*0-553-15878-3*) Bantam.

Erickson, Gina C. & Foster, Kelli C. Bub & Chub. Gifford-Russell, Kerri, illus. 24p. (ps-2). 1992. pap. 3.50 (*0-8120-4859-8*) Barron.

Fair, Jeff. Bears for Kids. 48p. 1991. 14.95 (*1-55971-119-1*); pap. 6.95 (*1-55971-134-5*) NorthWord.

Falk, Barbara B. Grusha. Falk, Barbara B., illus. LC 92-14980. 32p. (ps-3). 1993. 15.00 (*0-06-021299-3*); PLB 14.89 (*0-06-021300-0*) HarpC Child Bks.

Farmer, Tony & Farmer, Lynne. How BIG Is an Elephant? LC 91-285. (gr. 3 up). 1991. 3.95 (*0-85953-516-9*) Childs Play.

—How HIGH Is the Moon? LC 91-19350. (gr. 4 up). 1991. 3.95 (*0-85953-517-7*) Childs Play.

Fast, Suellen M. Golden-Brown Baby Bear & the Three Sisters. Serman, Gina L., ed. 30p. (Orig.). (ps up). pap. 4.00 (*0-935281-11-8*) Daughter Cult.

Firmin, Peter. Boastful Mr. Bear. 1990. pap. 2.95 (*0-440-40371-5*, YB) Dell.

Flack, Marjorie. Ask Mr. Bear. Flack, Marjorie, illus. (ps-3). 1990. incl. cass. 19.95 (*0-87499-044-0*); pap. 12.95 incl. cass. (*0-87499-043-2*); Set; incl. 4 bks., cass., & guide. pap. 27.95 (*0-87499-045-9*) Live Oak Media.

Ford, Miela. Bear Play. LC 94-25739. (gr. 1-8). 1995. write for info. (*0-688-13832-2*); lib. bdg. write for info. (*0-688-13833-0*) Greenwillow.

Foreman, Donna. Story of the Christmas Bear. Blonski, Maribeth, illus. 40p. (gr. k-3). 1992. 7.95 (*1-880851-02-4*) Greene Bark Pr.

Freeman, Don. Beady Bear. (Illus.). (gr. 3-6). 1977. pap. 4.99 (*0-14-050197-5*, Puffin) Puffin Bks.

—Bearymore. (Illus.). (ps-3). 1979. pap. 3.95 (*0-14-050279-3*, Puffin) Puffin Bks.

—Bearymore. LC 76-94. (Illus.). 40p. (gr. k-3). 1976. 14.95 (*0-670-15174-2*) Viking Child Bks.

—Un Bosillo Para Corduroy: A Pocket for Corduroy. Freeman, Don, illus. (ENG & SPA.). 32p. (ps-3). 1992. RB 13.00 (*0-670-84483-7*) Viking Child Bks.

—Corduroy. (Illus.). (gr. k-1). 1993. pap. 3.99 (*0-14-050173-8*, Puffin); StoryTape 6.99 (*0-14-095114-8*, Puffin) Puffin Bks.

—A Pocket for Corduroy. (Illus.). (ps). 1993. pap. 3.99 (*0-14-050352-8*, Puffin); StoryTape 6.99 (*0-14-095124-5*) Puffin Bks.

Fuchs. Bear for All Seasons. 1993. 14.95 (*0-8050-2139-6*) H Holt & Co.

Gage, Wilson. Cully Cully & the Bear. LC 82-11715. (Illus.). (ps-3). 1983. PLB 14.93 (*0-688-01769-X*); pap. 3.95 (*0-688-07043-4*) Greenwillow.

Galdone, Paul. The Three Bears. Galdone, Paul, illus. LC 78-158833. 32p. (ps-3). 1985. pap. 5.95 (*0-89919-401-X*, Clarion Bks) HM.

Gallaz, Christophe. Threadbear. Vincent, Gabrielle, illus. 40p. (ps-3). 1993. 14.95 (*1-56846-085-6*) Creat Editions.

Gammell, Stephen. Wake up, Bear...It's Christmas! LC 81-5019. (Illus.). 32p. (ps up). 1990. pap. 4.95 (*0-688-09934-3*, Mulberry) Morrow.

Garcia-Bengochea, Debbie. Gumdrop the Christmas Bear. (Illus.). 34p. (Orig.). (ps-2). 1992. pap. 7.95 (*1-880525-00-3*) Masterson.

George, Jean C. The Grizzly Bear with the Golden Ears. Schoenherr, John, illus. LC 80-7908. 32p. (ps-3). 1982. PLB 13.89 (*0-06-021966-1*) HarpC Child Bks.

Gerrard, Anne. The Adventures of Christopher Bear & His Friends. (Illus.). 32p. (gr. 3). 1993. pap. 8.95 (*0-8059-3329-8*) Dorrance.

Gerstein, Mordicai. Anytime Mapleson & the Hungry Bears. Harris, Susan Y., illus. LC 89-34473. 32p. (ps-3). 1990. HarpC Child Bks.

Gikow, Louise. There's a Bear in the Woods. (ps-3). 1993. pap. 3.50 (*0-307-11568-2*, Golden Pr) Western Pub.

Gill, Shelly. Alaska's Three Bears. Cartwright, Shannon, illus. 32p. (ps-3). 1992. 13.95 (*0-934007-10-1*); pap. 7.95 (*0-934007-11-X*) Paws Four Pub.

Ginsburg, Mirra. Two Greedy Bears. LC 76-8819. (Illus.). 32p. (ps-3). 1990. pap. 3.95 (*0-689-71392-4*, Aladdin) Macmillan Child Grp.

—Two Greedy Bears: Adapted from a Hungarian Folktale. Aruego, Jose & Dewey, Ariane, illus. LC 76-8819. 32p. (ps-2). 1976. RSBE 13.95 (*0-02-736450-X*, Macmillan Child Bk) Macmillan Child Grp.

Gliori, Debi. Mr. Bear Babysits. (ps-3). 1994. 13.95 (*0-307-17506-5*, Artsts Writrs) Western Pub.

Goldilocks & the Three Bears. (Illus.). 64p. (ps-3). 1991. 11.95 (*0-916410-55-2*) A D Bragdon.

Goldilocks & the Three Bears. 32p. 1992. 4.95 (*0-8362-3025-6*) Andrews & McMeel.

Goldstein, Bobbye S. Bear in Mind: A Book of Bear Poems. DuBois, William P., illus. 32p. (ps-3). 1989. 12.95 (*0-670-81907-7*) Viking Child Bks.

Graham, Ada & Graham, Frank. Bears in the Wild. Tyler, D. D., illus. 176p. (gr. 4-8). 1983. pap. 2.25 (*0-440-40897-0*, YB) Dell.

Graham, Thomas. Mr. Bear's Boat. LC 87-24466. (Illus.). 32p. (ps-2). 1991. pap. 3.95 (*0-525-44739-3*, Puffin) Puffin Bks.

—Mr. Bear's Chair. Graham, Thomas, illus. LC 86-19920. 32p. (ps-2). 1990. 10.95 (*0-525-44300-2*, DCB); pap. 3.95 (*0-525-44651-6*, DCB) Dutton Child Bks.

Grandma Marian, pseud. Mrs. Pam Polar Bear. Sullo, Lorraine T., illus. 32p. (gr. k-2). 1989. 7.95 (*0-9614989-9-4*) Banmar Inc.

Green, Cecile. The Tale of Theodore Bear. Lysaker, Gene, illus. (gr. 1-2). 1978. pap. 1.25 (*0-89508-060-5*) Rainbow Bks.

Greenway, Jennifer, retold by. Goldilocks & the Three Bears. Miles, Elizabeth, illus. 1991. 6.95 (*0-8362-4900-3*) Andrews & McMeel.

Gretz, Susanna. Teddy Bears Cure a Cold. Sage, Alison, illus. LC 84-4015. 40p. (gr. k-3). 1985. RSBE 13.95 (*0-02-736960-9*, Four Winds) Macmillan Child Grp.

—Teddy Bears Cure a Cold. Sage, Alison, illus. 32p. (ps-2). 1986. pap. 3.95 (*0-590-43495-0*) Scholastic Inc.

—Teddy Bears' Moving Day. Gretz, Susanna, illus. LC 88-10365. 32p. (gr. k-3). 1988. pap. 3.95 (*0-689-71269-3*, Aladdin) Macmillan Child Grp.

—Teddy Bears Take the Train. Gretz, Susanna, illus. LC 87-8572. 32p. (gr. k-3). 1988. SBE 13.95 (*0-02-738170-6*, Four Winds) Macmillan Child Grp.

Greydanus, Rose. Bedtime Story. Cushman, Doug, illus. LC 86-30858. 32p. (gr. k-2). 1988. PLB 7.89 (*0-8167-0996-3*); pap. text ed. 1.95 (*0-8167-0997-1*) Troll Assocs.

Grimm, Jacob. King Grisly-Beard. (ps-3). 1987. pap. 2.95 (*0-374-44049-2*) FS&G.

Le Gros Ours Affame. (ps-3). pap. 5.95 (*0-85953-466-9*) Childs Play.

Gruber, Suzanne. Monster under My Bed. Britt, Stephanie, illus. LC 84-45687. 32p. (gr. k-2). 1985. PLB 10.89 (*0-8167-0456-2*); pap. text ed. 2.95 (*0-8167-0457-0*) Troll Assocs.

Hague, Kathleen. Alphabears: An ABC Book. Hague, Michael, illus. LC 83-26476. 32p. (ps-2). 1984. 12.95 (*0-8050-0841-1*, Bks Young Read) H Holt & Co.

—Alphabears: An ABC Book. Hague, Michael, illus. LC 83-26476. 32p. (ps-2). 1991. pap. 4.95 (*0-8050-1637-6*, Bks Young Read) H Holt & Co.

—Bear Hugs. Hague, Michael, illus. LC 88-28458. 64p. (ps-2). 1992. pap. 4.95 (*0-8050-2344-5*, Bks Young Read) H Holt & Co.

—Numbears: A Counting Book. Hague, Michael, illus. LC 85-27006. 32p. (ps-2). 1986. 12.95 (*0-8050-0309-6*, Bks Young Read) H Holt & Co.

—Numbears: Alphabears. Hague, Michael, illus. LC 85-27006. 32p. (ps-2). 1991. pap. 4.95 (*0-8050-1679-1*, Bks Young Read) H Holt & Co.

—Out of the Nursery, into the Night. Hague, Michael, illus. LC 86-14270. 32p. (ps-2). 1986. 13.95 (*0-8050-0088-7*, Bks Young Read) H Holt & Co.

Hanel, Wolfram. The Old Man & the Bear. Lanning, Rosemary, tr. Corderoc'h, Jean-Pierre, illus. LC 93-39757. 48p. (gr. 1-3). 1994. 12.95 (*1-55858-253-3*); PLB 12.88 (*1-55858-254-1*) North-South Bks NYC.

Harrison, Joanna. Dear Bear. LC 93-44730. 1994. 18.95 (*0-87614-839-9*) Carolrhoda Bks.

Harrison, Susan J. Christmas with the Bears. Harrison, Susan J., illus. 24p. (ps up). 1987. PLB 9.95 (*0-525-44329-0*, 0966-290, DCB) Dutton Child Bks.

Harte, Cheryl. Jingle Bear. Harte, Cheryl, illus. (ps). 1991. sponge-filled 5.95 (*0-679-80750-0*) Random Bks Yng Read.

Hasenau, F. A. Benjamin Visits the Jungle. LC 82-81827. (Illus.). (gr. k-2). 1982. 6.00 (*0-913042-14-5*) Holland Hse Pr.

Hayes, Sarah. This Is the Bear. Craig, Helen, illus. LC 92-53421. 32p. (ps). 1993. 12.95 (*1-56402-189-0*) Candlewick Pr.

—This Is the Bear. Craig, Helen, illus. LC 92-53421. 32p. (ps up). 1994. pap. 3.99 (*1-56402-270-6*) Candlewick Pr.

Hefter, Richard. Babysitter Bears. Hefter, Richard, illus. LC 83-8205. (gr. 3-6). 1983. 5.95 (*0-911787-08-9*) Optimum Res Inc.

—Bears Away from Home. Hefter, Richard, illus. LC 83-4149. (gr. 3-6). 1983. 5.95 (*0-911787-05-4*) Optimum Res Inc.

—Fast Food. Hefter, Richard, illus. LC 83-6734. (gr. 3-6). 1983. 5.95 (*0-911787-09-7*) Optimum Res Inc.

—Neat Feet. Hefter, Richard, illus. LC 83-8035. (gr. 3-6). 1983. 5.95 (*0-911787-07-0*) Optimum Res Inc.

—The Stickybear's Scary Night. (Illus.). 29p. (ps-1). 1984. 1.95 (*0-911787-41-0*) Optimum Res Inc.

—Where Is the Bear? Hefter, Richard, illus. LC 83-6296. 32p. (gr. 3-6). 1983. 5.95 (*0-911787-06-2*) Optimum Res Inc.

Heisch, Glan & Heisch, Elisabeth. The Cinnamon Bear: The Missing Star. Bishop, Kathryn, ed. Jackson, Jett & Arnoff, Julie, illus. Bishop, Kathryn, intro. by. 32p. 1992. PLB 13.95 (*1-880623-01-3*); pap. 8.95 (*1-880623-02-1*) Stiles-Bishop.

Heller, Nicholas. Mathilda the Dream Bear. LC 88-3830. (Illus.). 32p. (ps up). 1989. 12.95 (*0-688-08238-6*); PLB 12.88 (*0-688-08239-4*) Greenwillow.

Helmrath, M. O. & Bartlett, J. L. Bobby Bear & the Bees. LC 68-56806. (Illus.). 32p. (ps-1). 1968. PLB 12.35 prebound (*0-87783-003-7*); cassette 7.94x (*0-87783-177-7*) Oddo.

—Bobby Bear Finds Maple Sugar. LC 68-56805. (Illus.). 32p. (ps-1). 1968. PLB 12.35 prebound (*0-87783-005-3*) cassette 7.94x (*0-87783-178-5*) Oddo.

—Bobby Bear Goes Fishing. LC 68-56807. (Illus.). 32p. (ps-1). 1968. pap. 12.35 prebound (*0-87783-006-1*); cassette 7.94x (*0-87783-179-3*) Oddo.

—Bobby Bear in the Spring. LC 68-56810. (Illus.). 32p. (ps-1). 1968. PLB 12.35 prebound (*0-87783-007-X*); cassette 7.94x (*0-87783-180-7*) Oddo.

—Bobby Bear Series, 18 bks. (Illus.). (ps-1). Set. PLB 189.60 set (*0-87783-163-7*) 8 cassettes 63.52x (*0-87783-181-5*) Oddo.

—Bobby Bear's Halloween. LC 68-56808. (Illus.). 32p. (ps-1). 1968. PLB 9.95 (*0-87783-004-5*); cassette 7.94x (*0-87783-183-1*) Oddo.

—Bobby Bear's Rocket Ride. LC 68-56809. (Illus.). 32p. (ps-1). 1968. PLB 12.35 prebound (*0-87783-008-8*); cassette 7.94x (*0-87783-186-6*) Oddo.

Hill, Eric. Spot's Baby Sister: A Lift-the-Flap Book. Hill, Eric, illus. 22p. (ps-k). 1989. 11.95 (*0-399-21640-5*, Putnam) Putnam Pub Group.

Hissey, Jane. Jane Hissey Little Bear & Book Set. Hissey, Jane, illus. 12p. (ps). 1993. bds. 16.00 (*0-679-84762-6*) Random Bks Yng Read.

—Little Bear Lost. (Illus.). 32p. (ps-3). 1992. PLB 4.95 (*0-399-21760-6*, Philomel Bks) Putnam Pub Group.

—Little Bear's Day. Hissey, Jane, illus. LC 92-64017. 12p. (ps). 1993. bds. 3.99 (*0-679-84175-X*) Random Bks Yng Read.

—Little Bear's Trousers. (ps-2). 1987. 15.95 (*0-399-21493-3*, Philomel Bks) Putnam Pub Group.

—Little Bear's Trousers. (Illus.). 32p. (ps-3). 1992. PLB 5.95 (*0-399-21761-4*, Philomel Bks) Putnam Pub Group.

—Little Bear's Trousers: An Old Bear Story. (Illus.). 32p. (ps-3). 1990. pap. 5.95 (*0-399-22016-X*, Sandcastle Bks) Putnam Pub Group.

—Old Bear. Hissey, Jane, illus. 32p. (ps-3). 1989. pap. 5.95 (*0-399-22015-1*, Sandcastle Bks, Sandcastle Bks) Putnam Pub Group.

—Old Bear: Miniature Edition. (ps-3). 1992. 4.95 (*0-399-21764-9*, Philomel Bks) Putnam Pub Group.

—Old Bear Tales. Hissey, Jane, illus. LC 88-14155. 80p. 1988. 16.95 (*0-399-21642-1*, Philomel Bks) Putnam Pub Group.

Hobbs, Will. Beardance. LC 92-44874. 208p. (gr. 5-9). 1993. SBE 14.95 (*0-689-31867-7*, Atheneum Child Bk) Macmillan Child Grp.

Hoff, Syd. Bernard on His Own. Hoff, Syd, illus. LC 92-21770. 32p. (gr. k-3). 1993. 14.95 (*0-395-65226-X*, Clarion Bks) HM.

—Grizzwold. Hoff, Syd, illus. LC 64-14366. 64p. (gr. k-3). 1963. PLB 13.89 (*0-06-022481-9*) HarpC Child Bks.

Hofmann, Ginnie. One Teddy Bear Is Enough! Hofmann, Ginnie, illus. LC 88-18166. 32p. (Orig.). (ps-3). 1991. pap. 2.25 (*0-394-89582-7*) Random Bks Yng Read.

Hol, Coby. Tippy Bear & Little Sam. Hol, Coby, illus. LC 91-29672. 32p. (ps-k). 1992. 11.95 (*1-55858-138-3*); lib. bdg. 11.88 (*1-55858-149-9*) North-South Bks NYC.

—Tippy Bear Goes to a Party. Hol, Coby, illus. LC 91-8167. 32p. (ps-k). 1991. 11.95 (*1-55858-129-4*) North-South Bks NYC.

—Tippy Bear Hunts for Honey. Hol, Coby, illus. LC 91-10477. 32p. (ps-k). 1991. 11.95 (*1-55858-128-6*) North-South Bks NYC.

Houston, James R. Long Claws: An Arctic Adventure. (Illus.). 32p. (ps-3). 1992. pap. 4.99 (*0-14-054522-0*, Puffin) Puffin Bks.

Ingoglia, Gina. Three Bears. (ps-3). 1990. write for info. (*0-307-11594-1*) Western Pub.

Ingpen, Robert. The Age of Acorns. Ingpen, Robert, illus. LC 90-433. 28p. (gr. k-3). 1990. PLB 14.95 (*0-87226-436-X*, Bedrick Blackie) P Bedrick Bks.

—The Idle Bear. Ingpen, Robert, illus. LC 87-1187. 32p. (gr. k-3). 1987. PLB 12.95 (*0-87226-159-X*, Bedrick Blackie) P Bedrick Bks.

—The Miniature Idle Bear. LC 87-1187. (Illus.). 28p. (gr. k-3). 1989. 4.95 (*0-87226-418-1*, Bedrick Blackie) P Bedrick Bks.

Isenberg, Barbara & Wolf, Susan. The Adventures of Albert, the Running Bear. Gackenbach, Dick, illus. (gr. k-3). 1985. pap. 12.95 incl. cassette (*0-941078-88-4*); pap. 27.95 incl. cassette, 4 paperbacks guide (*0-941078-89-2*); PLB incl. cassette 19.95 (*0-941078-90-6*) Live Oak Media.

—The Adventures of Albert the Running Bear. Gachenbach, Dick, illus. LC 82-1311. 32p. (ps-3). 1982. (Clarion Bks); pap. 6.95 (*0-89919-125-8*, Clarion Bks) HM.

—Albert the Running Bear Gets the Jitters. De Groat, Diane, illus. 40p. (gr. k-4). 1987. 13.95 (*0-89919-517-2*, Clarion Bks); (Clarion Bks) HM.

Ivanovsky, Elisabeth. Little Treasury of Pierre Bear, 6 bks. 1992. Set. 5.99 (*0-517-08293-4*) Random Hse Value.

James, Thomas. Harry Helps Out. (Illus.). (gr. 1-2). 1972. pap. 1.95 (*0-89375-048-4*) Troll Assocs.

Janice. Little Bear Marches in the Saint Patrick's Day Parade. Mariana, illus. LC 67-15712. 40p. (gr. k-3). PLB 13.93 (*0-688-51075-2*) Lothrop.

—Little Bear's Christmas. Mariana, illus. LC 64-21191. (gr. k-3). 1964. PLB 13.93 (*0-688-51076-0*) Lothrop.

Jonas, Ann. Two Bear Cubs. Jonas, Ann, illus. LC 82-2860. 24p. (gr. k-3). 1982. PLB 14.88 (*0-688-01408-9*) Greenwillow.

Jones, Donna J. Barnabas Bear. Grove, Jason, illus. 32p. (gr. k-5). 1987. pap. 3.50 (*0-9617382-1-9*) Glacier Pub.

Joos, Louis, illus. Oregon's Journey. LC 93-11796. 40p. (gr. k-4). 1993. PLB 15.95 (*0-8167-3305-8*); pap. text ed. 3.95 (*0-8167-3306-6*) BrdgeWater.

Kahn, Peggy. The Care Bears' Book of ABC's. Bracken, Carolyn, illus. LC 82-18538. 40p. (ps-2). 1983. lib. bdg. 4.99 (*0-394-95808-X*) Random Bks Yng Read.

Kennedy, Jimmy. The Miniature Teddy Bear's Picnic. Theobalds, Prue, illus. LC 86-32111. 32p. (gr. k-3). 1989. 5.95 (*0-87226-417-3*, Bedrick Blackie) P Bedrick Bks.

—The Teddy Bears' Picnic. Day, Alexandra, illus. LC 91-24944. 40p. (ps-2). 1991. 13.00 (*0-671-75589-7*, Green Tiger); 19.95 (*0-671-74902-1*); incl. record 15.95 (*0-671-74903-X*) S&S Trade.

—The Teddy Bears' Picnic. Theobalds, Prue, illus. LC 86-32111. 32p. (ps-2). 1987. PLB 14.95 (*0-87226-153-0*, Bedrick Blackie); pap. 6.95 (*0-685-67547-5*) P Bedrick Bks.

—The Teddy Bears' Picnic. Theobalds, Prue, illus. LC 86-32111. 32p. 1990. pap. 6.95 (*0-87226-424-6*, Bedrick Blackie) P Bedrick Bks.

Kesey, Ken. Little Tricker the Squirrel Meets Big Double the Bear. Moser, Barry, illus. 1990. 14.95 (*0-670-81136-X*) Viking Child Bks.

Kidd, Ronald. Winnie the Pooh & Tigger Too! 24p. (ps up). 1992. write for info. (*0-307-14019-9*, 64019) Western Pub.

Kideckel, Marsha. The Too Big Bear. Macaulay, Kitty, illus. 24p. (Orig.). (ps-1). 1994. pap. 0.99 (*1-55037-347-1*, Pub. by Annick CN) Firefly Bks Ltd.

Kids Livin Life Staff. Homeless Hibernating Bear. (ps-3). 1993. pap. 7.95 (*1-882723-06-6*) Gold Leaf Pr.

Kletter, Lenore. Santabear's High Flying Adventure. (Illus.). 32p. (gr. 1-3). 1987. 12.99 (*0-9619204-0-8*) Santabear Bks.

Kolanovic, Dubravka. A Special Day. Thatch, Nancy R., ed. Kolanovic, Dubravka, illus. Melton, David, intro. by. LC 93-13419. (Illus.). 29p. (gr. k-2). 1993. PLB 14.95 (*0-933849-45-1*) Landmark Edns.

Kontoyiannaki, Kosta. Frankie Bear's Birthday Cake. Kontoyiannaki, Kosta, illus. 14p. (gr. 1-6). 1992. pap. 13.95 (*1-56606-004-4*) Bradley Mann.

Kotzwinkle, William. The Million Dollar Bear. Catrow, David, illus. LC 93-6262. 1995. write for info. (*0-679-85295-6*); PLB write for info. (*0-679-95295-0*) Knopf Bks Yng Read.

Kozikowski, Renate. Teddy Bears' Picnic. (Illus.). 32p. (ps-2). 1990. pap. 10.95 POB (*0-689-71362-2*, Aladdin) Macmillan Child Grp.

Kramer, Remi. How Lonestar Got His Name. rev. ed. Kramer, Remi, illus. 64p. (gr. 2-8). 1994. pap. 12.95 (*0-945887-08-6*); pap. 7.95 (*0-945887-12-4*) Northwind Pr. Winner: Top 100 Products of the Year, Best Illustration, Creativity Yearbook. "...a praiseworthy production from master storyteller Remi Kramer. His full-color illustrations are majestic statements of adventure & nature...very beautiful books that will thrill a youngster's eyes & heart." - The Book Reader. "...just the right touch of whimsy. His illustrations are rich & detailed." - The Statesman Review. "... non-stop adventures." - Award of Merit, Curriculum Product News. Universally praised as a book series that combines exceptional prose & unusually fine illustrations to tell the ongoing saga of a humble country bear who would rather be fishing but seems destined to become involved in thrilling, mystery-adventures filled with fun & excitement. Perhaps the Book Reader has said it best: "...it has to do with spaceships, mysterious caverns & finally coming home with a lump in your throat....will pull any child into the enchanted world of a bear, good heart & adventure." Available in hard & soft bindings. Hardbound editions: $12.95. Softbound editions: $7.95. Trade discount (3 cps. or more) 50%. To order, call 1-800-235-7756. *Publisher Provided Annotation.*

—The Legend of LoneStar Bear, Bk. One: How LoneStar Got His Name. Kramer, Remi, illus. 64p. 1988. PLB 12.95 (*0-945887-01-9*) Northwind Pr.

—The Legend of LoneStar Bear, Bk. Two: Soaring with Eagles. rev. ed. Kramer, Remi, illus. 72p. (gr. 2-8). 1994. 14.95 (*0-945887-02-7*); pap. 7.95 (*0-945887-14-0*) Northwind Pr.

Krueger, Ron, et al. Bearly There at All. French, Marty, illus. 26p. (ps up). 1988. incl. cassette 7.95 (*1-55578-912-9*) Worlds Wonder.

Kurland, Alexandra. Sara's Story: The Bear Nobody Wanted. (Illus.). 64p. (gr. k-4). 1988. 12.95 (*0-938209-34-5*) Bear Hollow Pr.

LaFleur, Tom & Brennan, Gale. Bingo the Bear. Kritchman-Knuteson, Joan, illus. 16p. (Orig.). (gr. k-6). 1981. pap. 1.25 (*0-685-02454-7*) Brennan Bks.

Lang, Aubrey. Rudy Visits the North. Hope, Muriel, illus. LC 91-75423. 40p. (ps-2). 1992. 14.95 (*1-56282-182-2*); PLB 14.89 (*1-56282-208-X*) Hyprn Child.

Lansky, Vicki. Koko Bear's Potty. 1986. pap. 3.99 (*0-553-34444-7*) Bantam.

—A New Baby at Koko Bear's House. reissued ed. Prince, Jane, illus. 32p. (Orig.). 1991. pap. 4.95 (*0-916773-22-1*) Book Peddlers.

Larson, Verna. Bearables of Bernie Bear. Pappas, Debra S., ed. Torres, Rene, illus. 30p. (Orig.). 1994. pap. 8.95 (*1-56550-022-9*) Vis Bks Intl.

Lasky, Kathryn. Cloud Eyes. Moser, Barry, illus. LC 93-37805. (gr. k-5). 1994. 14.95 (*0-15-219168-2*) HarBrace.

—Fourth of July Bear. Cogancherry, Helen, illus. LC 90-37422. 40p. (gr. k up). 1991. 13.95 (*0-688-08287-4*); PLB 13.88 (*0-688-08288-2*, Morrow Jr Bks) Morrow Jr Bks.

Latimer, Jim. James Bear & the Goose Gathering. Franco-Feeney, Betsy, illus. LC 92-26190. 32p. (gr. k-2). 1994. SBE 14.95 (*0-684-19526-7*, Scribners Young Read) Macmillan Child Grp.

—James Bear's Pie. Franco-Feeney, Betsy, illus. LC 90-36193. 32p. (ps-2). 1992. SBE 13.95 (*0-684-19226-8*, Scribners Young Read) Macmillan Child Grp.

Lebrun, Claude. Little Brown Bear Is Ill. Bour, Daniele, illus. 14p. (gr. k-3). 1982. 4.95 (*0-8120-5499-7*) Barron.

Lillie, Patricia. Floppy Teddy Bear. Baker, Karen L., illus. LC 93-26516. 32p. 1995. write for info. (*0-688-12570-0*); PLB write for info. (*0-688-12571-9*) Greenwillow.

Lind, Alan. Black Bear Cub. Lee, Katie, illus. Thomas, Peter, Jr., contrib. by. LC 93-31130. (Illus.). 32p. (gr. k-3). 1994. 11.95 (*1-56899-030-8*); incl. audiocassette 16.95 (*1-56899-050-2*); incl. audiocassette, 11" plush toy 39.95 (*1-56899-053-7*); incl. audiocassette, 6" plush toy 25.95 (*1-56899-052-9*); audiocassette avail. (*1-56899-051-0*) Soundprints.

Littleton, Mark. Escape of the Grizzly. LC 93-29408. 1994. pap. 3.99 (*1-56507-099-2*) Harvest Hse.

Lombardi, John R. Three Lost Bears. 1993. 7.95 (*0-533-10648-6*) Vantage.

L'Orso Affamato. (ps-3). 5.95 (*0-85953-554-1*) Childs Play.

Luttrell, Ida. The Bear Next Door. Stapler, Sarah, illus. LC 90-4153. 64p. (gr. k-3). 1991. PLB 11.89 (*0-06-024024-5*) HarpC Child Bks.

Lyon, David. The Crumbly Coast. LC 93-41083. 1995. write for info. (*0-385-32079-5*) Doubleday.

McClelland, Julia. This Baby. Brooks, Ron, illus. LC 92-43756. 1994. 13.95 (*0-395-66613-9*) HM.

McCloskey, Robert. Blueberries for Sal. McCloskey, Robert, illus. LC 48-4955. (ps-1). 1976. pap. 3.99 (*0-14-050169-X*, Puffin) Puffin Bks.

—Blueberries for Sal. McCloskey, Robert, illus. LC 48-4955. 56p. (ps-1). 1948. pap. 14.95 (*0-670-17591-9*) Viking Child Bks.

—Blueberries for Sal. (Illus.). 1993. pap. 6.99 incl. cassette (*0-14-095110-5*, Puffin) Puffin Bks.

McClung, Robert M. Major: The Story of a Black Bear. McClung, Robert M., illus. LC 87-26126. 64p. (gr. 9-12). 1988. Repr. of 1956 ed. lib. bdg. 15.00 (*0-208-02201-5*, Linnet) Shoe String.

—Samson: Last of the California Grizzlies. Hines, Bob, illus. LC 91-33350. 96p. (gr. 3-6). 1992. Repr. of 1973 ed. lib. bdg. 15.00 (*0-208-02327-5*, Pub. by Linnet) Shoe String.

McCue, Lisa, illus. Teddy Dresses. 1983. 2.95 (*0-671-45490-0*, Little Simon) S&S Trade.

McCully, Emily A. My Real Family. LC 92-46290. 1994. 13.95 (*0-15-277698-2*, Browndeer Pr) HarBrace.

—Speak up, Blanche! McCully, Emily A., illus. LC 90-36945. 32p. (gr. k-3). 1991. 15.00 (*0-06-024227-2*); PLB 14.89 (*0-06-024228-0*) HarpC Child Bks.

Mack, Stan. Ten Bears in My Bed: A Goodnight Countdown. Mack, Stan, illus. LC 74-151. 32p. (ps-1). 1974. lib. bdg. 11.99 (*0-394-92902-0*) Pantheon.

McKissack, Patricia & McKissack, Fredrick. The Three Bears. LC 85-12765. (Illus.). 32p. (ps-2). 1985. PLB 10.25 (*0-516-02364-0*); pap. 3.95 (*0-516-42364-9*) Childrens.

McKissack, Patricia C. & McKissack, Fredrick. Los Tres Osos: (The Three Bears) Bala, Virginia, illus. LC 85-12765. (SPA.). 32p. (ps-2). 1989. PLB 13.27 (*0-516-32364-4*); pap. 3.95 (*0-516-52364-3*) Childrens.

McPhail, David. The Bear's Toothache. (Illus.). 32p. (gr. k-3). 1972. lib. bdg. 14.95 (*0-316-56312-9*, Joy St Bks) Little.

—Henry Bear's Park. McPhail, David, illus. 48p. (gr. 1-3). 1976. lib. bdg. 14.95 (*0-316-56315-3*, Joy St Bks) Little.

—Lost, Vol. 1. (ps-3). 1990. 14.95 (*0-316-56329-3*, Joy St Bks) Little.

Magnus, Erica. My Secret Place. LC 93-8701. (Illus.). 1994. 14.00 (*0-688-11859-3*); PLB 13.93 (*0-688-11860-7*) Lothrop.

Mahan, Benton, illus. Goldilocks & the Three Bears. LC 80-27631. 32p. (gr. k-2). 1981. PLB 9.79 (*0-89375-470-6*); pap. text ed. 1.95 (*0-89375-471-4*) Troll Assocs.

Maison, Della. The Care Bears' Garden. Bracken, Carolyn, illus. LC 82-61566. 32p. (gr. 1-6). 1983. pap. 1.25 saddle-stitched (*0-394-85827-1*) Random Bks Yng Read.

Marilue. Bobby Bear & the Friendly Ghost. LC 85-61830. (Illus.). 32p. (ps-1). 1985. 6.95 (*0-87783-204-8*) Oddo.

—Bobby Bear at the Circus. Marilue, illus. LC 89-62708. 32p. (ps-2). 1990. PLB 12.95 (*0-87783-252-8*) Oddo.

—Bobby Bear Meets Cousin Boo. LC 80-82952. (Illus.). 32p. (ps-1). 1981. PLB 9.95 (*0-87783-155-6*) Oddo.

—Bobby Bear's Kite Contest. Marilue, illus. LC 87-62507. 32p. (ps-1). 1988. PLB 11.45 (*0-87783-219-6*) Oddo.

—Bobby Bear's Magic Show. Marilue, illus. LC 89-62707. 32p. (ps-2). 1990. PLB 12.95 (*0-87783-253-6*) Oddo.

—Bobby Bear's New Home. LC 78-190265. (Illus.). 32p. (ps-1). 1973. PLB 9.95 (*0-87783-054-1*); cassette 7.94x (*0-87783-184-X*) Oddo.

—Bobby Bear's Red Raft. LC 71-190266. (Illus.). 32p. (ps-1). 1973. PLB 9.95 (*0-87783-055-X*); cassette 7.94x (*0-87783-185-8*) Oddo.

Marks, Burton. Bear's Boat. (Illus.). 10p. (ps-3). 1993. 4.99 (*0-89577-516-6*, Dist. by Random) RD Assn.

Martin. Brown Bear Ltd. 1992. 100.00 (*0-8050-2308-9*) H Holt & Co.

Martin, Bill, Jr. Brown Bear, Brown Bear, What Do You See? Carle, Eric, illus. LC 83-12779. 24p. (ps-k). 1983. 14.95 (*0-8050-0201-4*, Bks Young Read) H Holt & Co.

—Polar Bear, Polar Bear, What Do You Hear? Carle, Eric, illus. 32p. (ps). 1991. 14.95 (*0-8050-1759-3*, Bks Young Read) H Holt & Co.

—Polar Bear, Polar Bear, What Do You Hear? Big Book. Carle, Eric, illus. LC 91-13322. 32p. (ps-2). 1992. pap. 18.95 (*0-8050-2346-1*, Bks Young Read) H Holt & Co.

Martin, Francesca, retold by. Honey Hunters. LC 91-58736. (Illus.). 32p. (ps up). 1994. pap. 5.99 (*1-56402-276-5*) Candlewick Pr.

Martin, Jeanne I. The Cinnamon Bear Who Wanted to Sing. Slater, Joann, illus. 24p. (Orig.). (gr. 1-5). 1986. saddle stitched 4.00 (*0-317-51971-9*) Satori Pr.

Matthews, Downs. Polar Bear Cubs. Guravich, Dan, photos by. LC 88-10284. (Illus.). 32p. (gr. 2-5). 1991. pap. 4.00 (*0-671-74493-3*, S&S BFYR) S&S Trade.

Mellen, Stephanie. A Bear in the Chair. Mellen, Stephanie, illus. LC 94-75065. 50p. (gr. k-2). 1994. pap. 6.95 (*0-9637414-1-1*) Meltec.

Meyer, Kathleen A. Bear, Your Manners Are Showing. Creative Studios 1, Inc. Staff, illus. 32p. (gr. k-2). 1987. 2.50 (*0-87403-271-7*, 3771) Standard Pub.

Michio Hoshino. The Grizzly Bear Family Book. Colligan-Taylor, Karen, tr. from JPN. (Illus.). 52p. (gr. 2 up). 1993. 15.95 (*0-88708-309-9*) Picture Bk Studio.

Milk & Cookies. (Illus.). 42p. (ps-3). 1992. PLB 13.27 (*0-8368-0878-9*) Gareth Stevens Inc.

Miller, Sherry. Lost in the Arctic with Pal Bear. Martinez, Jesse, illus. 32p. (Orig.). (gr. k-5). 1984. pap. 1.95 saddle-stitched (*0-913379-01-8*) Double M Pub.

Miller, Virginia. Eat Your Dinner! Miller, Virginia, illus. LC 91-58728. 32p. (ps up). 1992. 14.95 (*1-56402-121-1*) Candlewick Pr.

—On Your Potty! LC 90-49221. (Illus.). 32p. (ps up). 1991. 13.95 (*0-688-10617-X*); PLB 13.88 (*0-688-10618-8*) Greenwillow.

Milne, A. A. Christopher Robin Gives Pooh a Party. Shepard, Ernest H., illus. 32p. (ps up). 1992. incl. charm 13.95 (*0-525-44871-3*, DCB) Dutton Child Bks.

—The House at Pooh Corner. Shepard, Ernest H., illus. 192p. (ps up). 1988. 9.95 (*0-525-44444-0*, DCB) Dutton Child Bks.

—The House at Pooh Corner. Shepard, Ernest H., illus. LC 91-29462. 192p. (ps up). 1991. Full-color Gift Edition. 20.00 (*0-525-44774-1*, DCB) Dutton Child Bks.

—Pooh & Piglet Go Hunting. Shepard, Ernest H., illus. 32p. (ps up). 1992. incl. charm 13.95 (*0-525-44872-1*, DCB) Dutton Child Bks.

—Pooh & Some Bees. Cremins, Robert, illus. 10p. (ps up). 1987. 7.95 (*0-525-44339-8*, 0674-210, DCB) Dutton Child Bks.

—Pooh Goes Visiting. Cremins, Robert, illus. 10p. (ps up). 1987. 7.95 (*0-525-44337-1*, 0674-210, DCB) Dutton Child Bks.

—Pooh Goes Visiting. Shepard, Ernest H., illus. 32p. 1993. 4.99 (*0-525-45040-8*, DCB) Dutton Child Bks.

—Pooh Invents a New Game. Shepard, Ernest H., illus. 16p. (ps up). 1991. 7.95 (*0-525-44783-0*, DCB) Dutton Child Bks.

—Pooh's Library, 4 bks. Shepard, Ernest H., illus. (ps up). 1988. Set. 39.95 (*0-525-44451-3*, DCB) Dutton Child Bks.

—Pooh's Pot O'Honey, 4 vols. Shepard, Ernest H., illus. (ps up). 1985. Boxed Set. 10.95 (*0-525-37518-X*, DCB) Dutton Child Bks.

—A Treasury of Winnie-the-Pooh, 4 bks. Shepard, Ernest H., illus. Incl. Winnie-the-Pooh; The House at Pooh Corner; Now We Are Six; When We Were Very Young. (Illus.). 1987. Boxed set. pap. 13.00 (*0-440-49580-6*) Dell.

—Winnie-the-Pooh. (gr. k-6). 1988. pap. 5.95 (*0-440-40116-X*, Pub. by Yearling Classics) Dell.

—Winnie-the-Pooh. Shepard, Ernest H., illus. LC 91-26203. 176p. (ps up). 1991. Full-color Gift Edition. 20.00 (*0-525-44776-8*, DCB) Dutton Child Bks.

—Winnie-the-Pooh. Shepard, Ernest H., illus. 176p. 1992. pap. 3.99 (*0-14-036121-9*, Puffin) Puffin Bks.

—Winnie-the-Pooh: A Pop-Up Book. (Illus.). 12p. (ps up). 1984. 13.00 (*0-525-44119-0*, DCB) Dutton Child Bks.

—Winnie the Pooh & Some Bees. Shepard, Ernest H., illus. 32p. 1993. incl. charm 13.99 (*0-525-45044-0*, DCB) Dutton Child Bks.

—Winnie-the-Pooh's Little Book about Food. Shepard, Ernest H., illus. 10p. (ps up). 1992. 4.95 (*0-525-44875-6*, DCB) Dutton Child Bks.

—Winnie-the-Pooh's Little Book about Friends. Shepard, Ernest H., illus. 10p. (ps up). 1992. 4.95 (*0-525-44874-8*, DCB) Dutton Child Bks.

—Winnie-the-Pooh's Little Book about Parties. Shepard, Ernest H., illus. 10p. (ps up). 1992. 4.95 (*0-525-44876-4*, DCB) Dutton Child Bks.

—Winnie-the-Pooh's Little Book about Weather. Shepard, Ernest H., illus. 10p. (ps up). 1992. 4.95 (*0-525-44877-2*, DCB) Dutton Child Bks.
—Winnie the Pooh's Pop-up Theater Book. (Illus.). 12p. 1993. 15.95 (*0-525-44990-6*, DCB) Dutton Child Bks.
—Winnie-the-Pooh's Visitors Book. Shepard, Ernest H., illus. 128p. 1994. 13.99 (*0-525-45217-6*) Dutton Child Bks.
—Winny de Puh. (SPA.). 7.50 (*0-685-31015-9*) Santillana.
—Winny De Puh. (SPA., Illus.). 176p. (ps-3). 1992. 11.00 (*0-525-44986-8*, DCB) Dutton Child Bks.
—The World of Christopher Robin. Shepard, Ernest H., illus. 256p. (ps up). 1988. 17.50 (*0-525-44448-3*, DCB) Dutton Child Bks.
—The World of Pooh. Shepard, Ernest H., illus. 320p. (ps up). 1988. 17.50 (*0-525-44447-5*, DCB) Dutton Child Bks.
—The World of Pooh. (Illus.). (gr. 1-4). 1957. 13.95 (*0-525-43320-1*, 01258-370, Dutton); Incl. "World of Christopher" boxed 29.95 (*0-685-46952-2*, 01258-370) NAL-Dutton.
—The World of Winnie-the-Pooh, 2 bks. Shepard, Ernest H., illus. (ps up). 1988. Set. 33.95 (*0-525-44452-1*, DCB) Dutton Child Bks.
Minarik, Else. Father Bear Comes Home: (Papa Oso Vuele a Casa) (SPA.). 9.95 (*84-204-3048-X*) Santillana.
Minarik, Else H. Father Bear Comes Home. Sendak, Maurice, illus. LC 59-5794. 64p. (gr. k-3). 1959. 14.00 (*0-06-024230-2*); PLB 13.89 (*0-06-024231-0*) HarpC Child Bks.
—Father Bear Comes Home. Sendak, Maurice, illus. LC 59-5794. (ps-3). 1978. pap. 3.50 (*0-06-444014-1*, Trophy) HarpC Child Bks.
—A Kiss for Little Bear. Sendak, Maurice, illus. LC 68-16820. 32p. (ps-3). 1984. pap. 3.50 (*0-06-444050-8*, Trophy) HarpC Child Bks.
—A Kiss for Little Bear. unabr. ed. Sendak, Maurice, illus. (ps-3). 1991. pap. 6.95 incl. cassette (*1-55994-263-0*, Caedmon) HarperAudio.
—Kiss for Little Bear. 6p. 1992. Braille. 0.48 (*1-56956-271-7*) W A T Braille.
—Little Bear. Sendak, Maurice, illus. 64p. (gr. k-3). 1957. 14.00i (*0-06-024240-X*); PLB 13.89 (*0-06-024241-8*) HarpC Child Bks.
—Little Bear. unabr. ed. Sendak, Maurice, illus. (ps-3). 1990. pap. 6.95 incl. cassette (*1-55994-234-7*, Caedmon) HarperAudio.
—Little Bear, 3 bks. Sendak, Maurice, contrib. by. (Illus.). (gr. k-3). 1992. Boxed set. pap. 10.50 (*0-06-444197-0*, Trophy) HarpC Child Bks.
—Little Bear's Friend. Sendak, Maurice, illus. LC 60-6370. 64p. (gr. k-3). 1960. 14.00i (*0-06-024255-8*); PLB 13.89 (*0-06-024256-6*) HarpC Child Bks.
—Little Bear's Friend. Sendak, Maurice, illus. LC 60-6370. 64p. (ps-3). 1985. (Trophy); pap. 3.50 (*0-06-444051-6*, Trophy) HarpC Child Bks.
—Little Bear's Friend. unabr. ed. Sendak, Maurice, illus. (ps-3). 1990. pap. 6.95 incl. cassette (*1-55994-235-5*, Caedmon) HarperAudio.
—Little Bear's Visit. Sendak, Maurice, illus. LC 61-11451. 64p. (ps-3). 1961. 14.00 (*0-06-024265-5*); PLB 13.89 (*0-06-024266-3*) HarpC Child Bks.
—Little Bear's Visit. Sandal, Maurice, illus. LC 61-11451. 64p. (gr. k-3). 1979. pap. 3.50 (*0-06-444023-0*, Trophy) HarpC Child Bks.
—Little Bear's Visit. unabr. ed. Sendak, Maurice, illus. (ps-3). 1990. pap. 6.95 incl. cassette (*1-55994-236-3*, Caedmon) HarperAudio.
—Osito. LC 69-14452. (SPA., Illus.). 64p. (ps-3). 1969. PLB 10.89 (*0-06-024244-2*) HarpC Child Bks.
—Visita de Osito: (La Visita de Osito) Sendak, Maurice, illus. (SPA.). (gr. 1-6). pap. 9.50 (*84-204-3051-X*) Santillana.
Miyamoto, Tadao. Papa & Me. LC 94-1563. 1994. 18.95 (*0-87614-843-7*) Carolrhoda Bks.
Moncure, Jane B. Here We Go 'Round the Year. Hohag, Linda, illus. LC 87-13257. (SPA & ENG.). 32p. (ps-2). 1987. PLB 14.95 (*0-89565-402-4*) Childs World.
—Where Is Baby Bear? Friedman, Joy, illus. LC 87-12840. (SPA & ENG.). 32p. (ps-2). 1987. PLB 14.95 (*0-89565-405-9*) Childs World.
Mora, Emma. Gideon the Little Bear Cub. (Illus.). 30p. (ps-1). 1986. 3.95 (*0-8120-5728-7*) Barron.
Morey, Walt. Gentle Ben. 192p. (gr. 4 up). 1976. pap. 2.95 (*0-380-00743-6*, Camelot) Avon.
—Gentle Ben. Schoenherr, John, illus. LC 65-21290. 192p. (gr. 4 up). 1965. 12.95 (*0-525-30429-0*, DCB) Dutton Child Bks.
—Gentle Ben. Schoenherr, John, illus. 192p. (gr. 5 up). 1992. pap. 3.99 (*0-14-036035-2*, Puffin) Puffin Bks.
Moriwaki, Glenda. Love for Priscilla. Mendez, Gerardo, illus. 28p. (Orig.). (ps-3). 1991. pap. 4.95 (*0-9627956-7-4*) Meadora Pub.
Moss, Elaine. Polar. LC 89-2115. (Illus.). 32p. (ps up). 1990. 13.95 (*0-688-09176-8*); lib. bdg. 13.88 (*0-688-09177-6*) Greenwillow.
Mountain, Lee. Bobby Bear & Uncle Sam's Riddle. Marilue, illus. 32p. (ps-1). 1988. PLB 11.45 (*0-87783-221-8*) Oddo.
Mountain, Lee, et al. Goldilocks & the Three Bears. (Illus.). 16p. (gr. k-1). 1993. pap. 14.75 (*0-89061-739-2*) Jamestown Pubs.
Muntean, Michaela. Bicycle Bear. Cushman, Doug, illus. LC 83-3980. 48p. (ps-3). 1983. 5.95 (*0-8193-1103-0*); PLB 5.95 (*0-8193-1104-9*) Parents.
—Bicycle Bear. Cushman, Doug, illus. LC 93-15458. 1994. PLB 13.27 (*0-8368-0963-7*) Gareth Stevens Inc.
—Bicycle Bear Rides Again. Cushman, Doug, illus. LC 93-15470. 1995. 13.27 (*0-8368-0964-5*) Gareth Stevens Inc.
Murdocca, Sal. Christmas Bear. (gr. k-3). 1990. (Little Simon); pap. 3.95 (*0-671-70849-X*) S&S Trade.
Murphy, Jill. Peace at Last. Murphy, Jill, illus. LC 80-66743. 32p. (ps-2). 1980. 13.95 (*0-8037-6757-9*) Dial Bks Young.
—What Next, Baby Bear! Murphy, Jill, illus. LC 83-7316. 32p. (ps-2). 1984. 13.95 (*0-8037-0027-X*) Dial Bks Young.
—What Next, Baby Bear! Murphy, Jill, illus. LC 83-7316. 32p. (ps-2). 1986. pap. 3.95 (*0-685-37306-1*) Dial Bks Young.
—What Next, Baby Bear! LC 83-7316. (Illus.). 32p. (ps-3). 1992. pap. 17.99 giant size (*0-14-054539-5*, Puff Pied Piper) Puffin Bks.
Nesbit, Jeffrey A. The Legend of the Great Grizzly. LC 93-39765. 1994. pap. 4.99 (*0-8407-9254-9*) Nelson.
Newman, Nanette. There's a Bear in the Bath! Foreman, Michael, illus. LC 93-12877. 1994. 13.95 (*0-15-285512-2*) HarBrace.
Newton, Jill. Polar Scare. (Illus.). (ps-3). 1992. 15.00 (*0-688-11232-3*); PLB 14.93 (*0-685-75779-X*) Lothrop.
The Night Before Christmas, The Honey Bears' Christmas Surpris2. (Illus.). 24p. 1983. (Honey Bear Bks); text ed. 3.95 (*0-87449-028-6*, Honey Bear Bks); text ed. 3.95 (*0-87449-182-7*, Honey Bear Bks) Modern Pub NYC.
Nims, Bonnie L. Where Is the Bear at School? Tucker, Kathy, ed. Gill, Madelaine, illus. LC 89-37903. 24p. (ps-1). 1989. 11.95 (*0-8075-8935-7*) A Whitman.
—Where Is the Bear in the City? Mathews, Judith, ed. Gill, Madelaine, illus. LC 92-3390. 24p. (ps-1). 1992. 11.95g (*0-8075-8937-3*) A Whitman.
Oana, Katherine. Spacebear Lands on Earth. Baird, Tate, ed. Wallace, Dorathye, illus. LC 86-51210. 16p. (Orig.). (ps up). 1988. pap. 3.72 (*0-914127-26-8*) Univ Class.
Oetting, Rae. Bobby Bear's Birthday. Marilue, illus. LC 87-62508. 32p. (ps-1). 1988. PLB 11.45 (*0-87783-220-X*) Oddo.
Oppenheim, Joanne. Could It Be - Bank Street. (ps-3). 1990. PLB 9.99 (*0-553-05893-2*, Little Rooster); pap. 3.50 (*0-553-34924-4*) Bantam.
Osborne, Mary P., compiled by. Bears, Bears, Bears. Schmidt, Karen L., illus. 96p. (ps-2). 1990. pap. 14.95 (*0-671-69631-9*, S&S BYR) S&S Trade.
Owen, Annie. Goodnight Bear! Owen, Annie, illus. LC 93-79577. 14p. (ps). 1994. bds. 4.95 (*1-85697-945-8*, Kingfisher LKC) LKC.
Peabody, Paul. Blackberry Hollow. Peabody, Paul, illus. LC 92-8968. 160p. (gr. 3-7). 1993. 15.95 (*0-399-22500-5*, Philomel Bks) Putnam Pub Group.
Pene Du Bois, William. Bear Circus. (Illus.). (gr. k-2). 1987. pap. 3.95 (*0-14-050792-2*, Puffin) Puffin Bks.
—Gentleman Bear. LC 84-48320. (Illus.). 80p. (gr. k up). 1985. 14.95 (*0-374-32533-2*) FS&G.
—Gentleman Bear. (Illus.). 80p. (ps up). 1988. pap. 5.95 (*0-374-42536-1*) FS&G.
Pepin, Muriel. Little Bear's New Friend. Geneste, Marcelle, illus. LC 91-40652. 24p. (ps-3). 1992. 6.99 (*0-89577-417-8*, Dist. by Random) RD Assn.
Perron, Robert E. Bum & Carey Bear: A Christmas Tale. (Illus.). 48p. 1994. pap. 8.00 (*0-8059-3578-9*) Dorrance.
Piequet, Miriam. My Furry Bear. Anyone Can Read Staff, ed. Gregory, Miriam, illus. 43p. (Orig.). (gr. 3-5). 1985. 15.00 (*0-914275-02-X*) Anyone Can Read Bks.
Pirotta, Saviour. Chloe on the Jungle Gym. (ps-3). 1992. 13.95 (*0-8120-6269-8*); pap. 5.95 (*0-8120-4829-6*) Barron.
Pomerantz, Charlotte. Where's the Bear? Barton, Byron, illus. LC 83-1697. 32p. (ps-1). 1984. 15.00 (*0-688-01752-5*); PLB 14.93 (*0-688-01753-3*) Greenwillow.
Pooh's Big & Little Book. 14p. 1994. 8.98 (*1-57082-147-X*) Mouse Works.
Pooh's Treehouse. 1994. 15.98 (*1-57082-158-5*) Mouse Works.
Primavera, Elise. Ralph's Frozen Tale. LC 90-35521. 32p. 1991. 14.95 (*0-399-22252-9*, Putnam) Putnam Pub Group.
Propper. Bear, Reading Level 3-4. (Illus.). 28p. (gr. 2-5). 1983. PLB 16.67 (*0-86592-865-7*) Rourke Corp.
Pryor, Bonnie. Grandpa Bear's Christmas. Degen, Bruce, illus. LC 85-29707. 32p. (ps-1). 1986. 12.95 (*0-688-06063-3*); lib. bdg. 12.88 (*0-688-06064-1*) Morrow Jr Bks.
Reese, Bob. Bubba Bear. Reese, Bob, illus. (gr. k-6). 1986. 7.95 (*0-89868-173-1*); pap. 2.95 (*0-89868-174-X*) ARO Pub.
—Bubba Bear. Reese, Bob, illus. (gr. k-6). 1986. pap. 20.00 (*0-685-50871-4*) ARO Pub.
Reit, Seymour V. Rebus Bears-Bank Street. (ps-3). 1989. pap. 3.50 (*0-553-34689-X*) Bantam.
—The Rebus Bears: Level 1. Smith, Kenneth, illus. 1989. 9.99 (*0-553-05822-3*) Bantam.
Richardson, John. Bad Mood Bear. (ps). 1988. 6.95 (*0-8120-5871-2*) Barron.
Richardson, John & Richardson, John, illus. Ten Bears in a Bed. LC 91-26501. 22p. (ps-k). 1992. 13.95 (*1-56282-157-1*) Hyprn Child.
Rikys, Bodel. Red Bear. LC 91-9039. (Illus.). 32p. (ps). 1992. 11.00 (*0-8037-1048-8*) Dial Bks Young.
Roberts, Tom. Goldilocks. Kubinyi, Laszlo, illus. LC 93-6679. (ps-6). 1993. Incl. cassette. 9.95 (*0-88708-322-6*, Dist. by S&S Trade) Picture Bk Studio.
—Goldilocks & the Three Bears. Kubinyi, Laszlo, illus. 32p. (gr. k up). 1991. pap. 14.95 (*0-88708-146-0*, Rabbit Ears); pap. 19.95 incl. cass. (*0-88708-147-9*, Rabbit Ears) Picture Bk Studio.
Robinson, Fay. When Nicki Went Away. Iosa, Ann, illus. LC 92-13835. 32p. (ps-2). 1993. pap. 3.95 (*0-516-42376-2*) Childrens.
Rocklin, Joanne. Musical Chairs & Dancing Bears. De Matharel, Laure, illus. LC 92-41078. 32p. (ps-2). 1993. write for info. (*0-8050-2374-7*, Bks Young Read) H Holt & Co.
Rockwell, Anne. Come to Town. Rockwell, Anne, illus. LC 86-6217. 32p. (ps-1). 1987. (Crowell Jr Bks) HarpC Child Bks.
Root. Contrary Bear. Date not set. 15.00 (*0-06-025085-2*); PLB 14.89 (*0-06-025086-0*) HarpC Child Bks.
Root, Clive. Bamboo Bears. (Illus.). 112p. (Orig.). (gr. 8-12). 1990. pap. 17.95 (*0-920534-61-9*, Pub. by Hyperion Pr Ltd CN) Sterling.
Ross, Katharine. Fuzzy Teddy. McCue, Lisa, illus. LC 92-62263. 22p. (ps). 1993. 3.50 (*0-679-84643-3*) Random Bks Yng Read.
Rotunno, Rocco & Rotunno, Betsy. Little Bear's Best Birthday. Rotunno, Betsy, illus. 12p. (gr. 2-6). 1992. Mixed Media Pkg. incls. stamp pad, stamps & box of 4 crayons. 7.00 (*1-881980-00-6*) Noteworthy.
Rowinski, Kate. Ellie Bear & the Fly-Away Fly. Peterson, Dawn, illus. LC 93-25260. 32p. (gr. 1-4). 1993. 14.95 (*0-89272-335-1*) Down East.
—L. L. Bear's Island Adventure. Peterson, Dawn, illus. LC 92-71972. 32p. (ps-4). 1992. 14.95 (*0-89272-320-3*) Down East.
Russell, Georgina. Christmas Bear. Press, Jenny, illus. 28p. (ps-2). 1991. 8.95 (*0-7214-5331-7*, S808) Ladybird Bks.
Ryan, Will. Grundo Beach Party. Becker, Mary, ed. High, David, et al, illus. 26p. (ps). 1986. 9.95 (*0-934323-35-6*); pre-programmed audio cass. tape incl. Alchemy Comms.
—Lost in Boggley Woods. Becker, Mary, ed. High, David, et al, illus. 26p. (ps). 1986. 9.95 (*0-934323-38-0*); pre-programmed audio cass. tape incl. Alchemy Comms.
Ryder, Joanne. The Bear on the Moon. Lacey, Carol, illus. LC 89-13133. 32p. (gr. 1 up). 1991. 14.95 (*0-688-08109-6*); PLB 14.88 (*0-688-08110-X*) Morrow Jr Bks.
Sachs, Marilyn. The Bears' House. LC 86-29267. 80p. (gr. 4-7). 1987. 10.95 (*0-525-44286-3*, DCB) Dutton Child Bks.
—The Bears' House. 80p. (gr. 3-7). 1989. pap. 2.99 (*0-380-70582-6*, Camelot) Avon.
Sage, Kathleen A. Quakey Bear's Amazing Earthquake Adventure. 24p. (ps-3). 1992. pap. write for info. (*0-9630089-5-1*) Quakey Bear.
—Quakey Bear's Earthquake Lessons: A Gentle Earthquake Journey for Children. (ps-3). 1991. pap. write for info. (*0-9630089-0-0*) Quakey Bear.
Salzman, Yuri, illus. The Three Bears. 24p. (gr. 2-5). 1987. pap. write for info. (*0-307-10050-2*, Pub. by Golden Bks) Western Pub.
Sandin, Joan. Pioneer Bear: A Story That Really Happened. LC 93-48023. 1995. 3.50 (*0-679-86050-9*); PLB 7.99 (*0-679-96050-3*) Random.
Sargent, Dave & Sargent, Pat. Brutus the Bear. 64p. (gr. 2-6). 1992. pap. write for info. (*1-56763-006-5*) Ozark Pub.
Sargent, Pat. Barney the Bear Killer. Bowen, Jane, ed. Lenoir, Jane, illus. 120p. (Orig.). (gr. k-6). 1994. PLB 19.95 (*1-56763-054-5*); pap. 9.95 (*1-56763-055-3*) Ozark Pub.
Saul, Judy. Bobby Bear & the Band. LC 85-61831. (Illus.). 32p. (ps-1). 1985. 6.95 (*0-87783-203-X*) Oddo.
Saunders, Kathleen. The Manmade Bear. Woon, Kay, illus. 33p. (gr. 2-5). 1980. pap. 2.95 (*0-939666-11-1*) Yosemite Assn.
Scarry, Richard. Richard Scarry's The Three Bears. (Illus.). 28p. (ps). 1993. bds. 3.25 (*0-307-12524-6*, 12524, Golden Pr) Western Pub.
Scheffrin-Falk, Gladys. Another Celebrated Dancing Bear. Garrison, Barbara, illus. LC 89-13152. 32p. (gr. k-2). 1991. SBE 13.95 (*0-684-19164-4*, Scribners Young Read) Macmillan Child Grp.
Schindel, John. Who Are You? Watts, James, illus. LC 90-39850. 32p. (ps-3). 1991. SBE 13.95 (*0-689-50523-X*, M K McElderry) Macmillan Child Grp.
Schlachter, Rita. Bear Needs Help! LC 81-14052. (Illus.). 48p. (Orig.). (gr. 1-3). 1986. PLB 10.59 (*0-8167-0600-X*); pap. text ed. 3.50 (*0-8167-0601-8*) Troll Assocs.
Schoenherr, John. Bear. (Illus.). 32p. (ps-3). 1991. 14.95 (*0-399-22177-8*, Philomel Bks) Putnam Pub Group.
—Bear. Thomas, Peter, narrated by. Schoenherr, John, illus. 32p. (gr. k-3). 1991. incl. audiocassette tape & plush stuffed bear toy 44.95 (*0-924483-69-5*); incl. audiocassette tape 19.95 (*0-924483-34-2*) Soundprints.
Schroeder, Ruth E. The Honey Bee Bears in Bluer Than Blueberries. Dixon, David, illus. 22p. (gr. k-5). 1989. 8.95 (*0-685-26760-1*); PLB 8.95 (*0-685-26761-X*) R & D Bks.

Schumacher, Claire. A Big Chair for Little Bear. Schumacher, Claire, illus. LC 89-10968. 32p. (Orig.). (ps-1). 1990. pap. 2.25 (*0-679-80500-1*) Random Bks Yng Read.

Schwartz, Alvin. Fat Man in a Fur Coat: And Other Bear Stories. Christiana, David, illus. LC 84-4161. 167p. (gr. 3 up). 1984. 14.00 (*0-374-32291-0*) FS&G.

—Fat Man in a Fur Coat: And Other Bear Stories. Christiana, David, illus. (gr. 5 up). 1987. pap. 3.50 (*0-374-42273-7*) FS&G.

Sebastian, John. J.B.'s Harmonica. LC 91-35841. (ps-3). 1993. 13.95 (*0-15-240091-5*) HarBrace.

Shannon, George. Laughing All the Way. McLean, Meg, illus. LC 91-41135. 32p. (ps-3). 1992. 13.45 (*0-395-62473-8*) HM.

—Lizard's Song. Aruego, Jose & Dewey, Ariane, illus. LC 80-21432. 32p. (gr. k-3). 1981. 14.95 (*0-688-80310-5*); PLB 14.88 (*0-688-84310-7*) Greenwillow.

Sharmat, Marjorie W. One Terrific Thanksgiving. Obligado, Lilian, illus. LC 85-726. 32p. (ps-3). 1985. reinforced bdg. 14.95 (*0-8234-0569-9*) Holiday.

Shecter, Ben. When Will the Snow Trees Grow? Shecter, Ben, illus. LC 92-32557. 32p. (gr. k-3). 1993. 14.00 (*0-06-022897-0*); PLB 13.89 (*0-06-022898-9*) HarpC Child Bks.

Sheldon, Dyan. Love, Your Bear, Pete. Hurt-Newton, Tania, illus. LC 93-2883. (ps). 1994. 13.95 (*1-56402-332-X*) Candlewick Pr.

Shelton, Ingrid. Benji Bear's Adventure in the Thunderstorm. 31p. (ps-k). 1984. pap. 2.50 (*0-919797-09-1*) Kindred Pr.

—Benji Bear's Race. Block, Ruth W., illus. 35p. (Orig.). (ps-2). 1992. pap. 2.50 (*0-919797-74-1*) Kindred Pr.

—Benji Bear's Surprise Day. 30p. (ps-k). 1986. pap. 2.50 (*0-919797-54-7*) Kindred Pr.

Sibley, Brian, compiled by. The Pooh Book of Quotations. Shepard, Ernest H., illus. LC 91-2628. 128p. (ps up). 1991. 12.50 (*0-525-44824-1*, DCB) Dutton Child Bks.

Silsbe, Brenda. The Bears We Know. Ritchie, Scot, illus. 24p. (Orig.). (ps-2). 1989. pap. 0.99 (*1-55037-048-0*, Pub. by Annick CN) Firefly Bks Ltd.

Simon, Carly. Amy the Dancing Bear. Datz, Margot, illus. (ps-3). 1989. 15.00 (*0-385-26637-5*) Doubleday.

Slater, Teddy. Shopping with Samantha. Hearn, Diane D., illus. 24p. (ps-1). 1991. 4.95 (*0-671-72984-5*); PLB 6.95 (*0-671-72983-7*) Silver Pr.

Slater, Teddy, adapted by. Walt Disney's Winnie the Pooh & the Blustery Day. Langley, Bill & Wakeman, Diana, illus. LC 92-55130. 48p. (ps-k). 1993. 12.95 (*1-56282-488-0*) Disney Pr.

Smith, Wendy. Say Hello, Tilly. (ps-3). 1991. 13.95 (*0-553-07160-2*) Bantam.

Spanner, Helmut. Teddy Bear's Day. (Illus.). 12p. (ps-1). 1991. bds. 3.95 (*0-8431-0946-7*) Price Stern.

—What's Teddy Bear Doing? (Illus.). 12p. (ps-1). 1991. bds. 3.95 (*0-8431-0945-9*) Price Stern.

Stevenson, Jocelyn, compiled by. The Bear Brigade. (Illus.). 64p. (gr. 3-5). 1992. pap. 11.95 (*1-85158-400-5*, Pub. by Mnstream UK) Trafalgar.

Stickland, Henrietta. The Christmas Bear. Stickland, Paul, illus. LC 93-10157. 32p. (ps-3). 1993. 15.99 (*0-525-45062-9*, DCB) Dutton Child Bks.

Stickland, Paul. Bedtime Bear. (Illus.). 14p. (ps). 1994. 4.99 (*0-525-45146-3*) Dutton Child Bks.

—Birthday Bear. (Illus.). 14p. (ps). 1994. 4.99 (*0-525-45147-1*) Dutton Child Bks.

Stoddard, Sandol. Bedtime for Bear. Munsinger, Lynn, illus. LC 85-5259. 32p. (gr. k-3). 1985. pap. 4.80 (*0-395-47949-5*) HM.

Talkington, Bruce. Disney's Winnie the Pooh's Easter. Langley, Bill & Wakeman, Diana, illus. LC 92-53441. 32p. (ps-4). 1993. 10.95 (*1-56282-377-9*) Disney Pr.

—Disney's Winnie the Pooh's Halloween. Vaccaro Associates Staff, illus. LC 93-70934. 32p. (ps-4). 1993. 11.95 (*1-56282-540-2*) Disney Pr.

Tanner, Suzy-Jane. Bunnies & Bear Nature Box. (Illus.). 32p. (ps). 1992. 17.50 (*0-525-44924-8*, DCB) Dutton Child Bks.

Tashlin, Frank. Bear That Wasn't. (Illus.). v, 51p. (gr. 4 up). 1946. pap. 2.50 (*0-486-20939-3*) Dover.

Tate, Susan. Benny Bear Believes for A Healing. Henjum, Marian, illus. (Orig.). (gr. k-3). 1993. pap. 3.99 (*1-884395-00-7*) Clear Blue Sky.

Tejima, Keizaburo. The Bears' Autumn. Matsui, Susan, tr. from JPN. Tejima, Keizaburo, illus. LC 91-17118. 42p. (gr. 1-4). 1991. 12.95 (*0-671-74981-1*, Green Tiger) S&S Trade.

Theobalds, Prue. The Teddy Bears' Great Expedition. Theobalds, Prue, illus. LC 89-77039. 32p. (gr. k-3). 1990. PLB 12.95 (*0-87226-425-4*, Bedrick Blackie) P Bedrick Bks.

Three Bears. (FRE.). (gr. k-3). 4.25 (*0-685-28449-2*) Fr & Eur.

The Three Bears. 24p. (ps-3). 1988. 2.25 (*1-56288-150-7*) Checkerboard.

Tolhurst, Marilyn. Somebody & the Three Blairs. Abel, Simone, illus. LC 90-7747. 32p. (ps-1). 1991. 14.95 (*0-531-05878-6*); PLB 14.99 (*0-531-08478-7*) Orchard Bks Watts.

Tomkins, Jasper. Bear Sleep Soup. (ps-3). 1991. pap. 7.95 (*0-671-75278-2*, Green Tiger) S&S Trade.

—When a Bear Bakes a Cake. (ps-3). 1991. pap. 7.95 (*0-671-75277-4*, Green Tiger) S&S Trade.

Toussant, Eliza. Soddy Bear: The Persian Gulf War. Rasher, Steven, illus. 76p. (Orig.). (gr. 4 up). 1991. pap. 17.95 (*0-9630583-0-4*) E Toussant.

Trumble, Mike. Rupert & the Black Imp. (Illus.). 32p. (gr. k-3). 1992. (BBC-Parkwest); pap. 3.95 (*0-563-20741-8*, BBC-Parkwest) Parkwest Pubns.

—Rupert & the Dragon Sweets. (Illus.). 32p. (gr. k-3). 1992. (BBC-Parkwest); pap. 3.95 (*0-563-20745-0*, BBC-Parkwest) Parkwest Pubns.

—Rupert & the Hazlenut. (Illus.). 32p. (gr. k-3). 1992. (BBC-Parkwest); pap. 3.95 (*0-563-20743-4*, BBC-Parkwest) Parkwest Pubns.

—Rupert & the Secret Boat. (Illus.). 32p. (gr. k-3). 1992. (BBC-Parkwest); pap. 3.95 (*0-563-20736-1*, BBC-Parkwest) Parkwest Pubns.

Van Pallandt, Nicolas. The Butterfly Night of Old Brown Bear. (ps-3). 1992. bds. 15.00 jacketed (*0-374-31009-2*) FS&G.

Vincent, Gabrielle. Where Are You, Ernest & Celestine? Vincent, Gabrielle, illus. LC 85-17595. 28p. (gr. k-3). 1986. 11.75 (*0-688-06234-2*); PLB 14.93 (*0-688-06235-0*) Greenwillow.

Vyner, Sue. Arctic Spring. Vyner, Tim, illus. LC 92-32280. (ps-3). 1993. 13.99 (*0-670-84934-0*) Viking Child Bks.

Waddell, Martin. Can't You Sleep, Little Bear? Firth, Barbara, illus. LC 91-71858. 32p. (ps up). 1994. pap. 4.99 (*1-56402-262-5*) Candlewick Pr.

—Let's Go Home, Little Bear. Firth, Barbara, illus. LC 92-53003. 32p. (ps up). 1993. 14.95 (*1-56402-131-9*) Candlewick Pr.

—Little Mo. 1st U.S. ed. Barton, Jill, illus. LC 92-54410. 32p. (ps up). 1993. 14.95 (*1-56402-211-0*) Candlewick Pr.

Wahl, Jan. Humphrey's Bear. Joyce, William, illus. LC 85-5541. 32p. (ps-2). 1987. 15.95 (*0-8050-0332-0*, Bks Young Read) H Holt & Co.

—I Remember, Cried Grandma Pinky. Johnson, Arden, illus. LC 93-33806. 32p. (gr. k-2). 1994. PLB 14.95 (*0-8167-3456-9*); pap. text ed. 3.95 (*0-8167-3457-7*) BrdgeWater.

—Sylvester Bear Overslept. Lorenz, Lee, illus. LC 79-4095. 48p. (ps-3). 1979. 5.95 (*0-8193-1003-4*); PLB 5.95 (*0-8193-1004-2*) Parents.

Waldman, David K. How Teddy Bears Find Their Homes. Danner, Maggie, illus. LC 92-53786. 32p. (gr. k-2). 1994. casebound 12.95 (*0-945522-02-9*) Rebecca Hse.

Walt Disney Staff. Snuggle Up with Winnie the Pooh. (ps). 1993. 6.98 (*0-453-03104-8*) Mouse Works.

—Winnie the Pooh. 1992. 6.98 (*0-453-03014-9*) Mouse Works.

Ward, Lynd. Biggest Bear. (Illus.). 88p. (gr. k-3). 1952. 14.45 (*0-395-14806-5*) HM.

—The Biggest Bear. Ward, Lynd, illus. LC 52-8730. 80p. (gr. k-3). 1973. pap. 5.70 (*0-395-15024-8*, Sandpiper) HM.

Warren, Jean. The Bear & the Mountain: A Totline Teaching Tale. Shimono, Judy & Tourtillotte, Barbara, illus. LC 93-38781. 32p. (gr. 2-8). 1994. 12.95 (*0-911019-99-5*); pap. 5.95 (*0-911019-98-7*) Warren Pub Hse.

Waterston, Ellen. Barney's Joy. Pearce, Molly, illus. 32p. 1991. Repr. of 1990 ed. text ed. 14.95 (*0-9628129-2-7*) Sagebrush Bks.

Weber, Ane, et al. The Bear That Was Chicken. French, Marty, et al, illus. 26p. (ps up). 1986. Book & Cassette. 7.95 (*1-55578-101-2*) Worlds Wonder.

Weiss, Nicki. Where Does the Brown Bear Go? LC 87-36980. (Illus.). 24p. (ps up). 1989. 13.95 (*0-688-07862-1*); PLB 13.88 (*0-688-07863-X*) Greenwillow.

West, Cindy. Three Bears. (ps-3). 1993. pap. 1.50 (*0-307-11544-5*, Golden Pr) Western Pub.

Wickstrom, Thor. The Big Night Out. Wickstrom, Thor, illus. LC 91-46563. 32p. (ps-3). 1993. 13.99 (*0-8037-1170-0*); PLB 13.89 (*0-8037-1171-9*) Dial Bks Young.

Wildsmith, Brian. Bear's Adventure. Wildsmith, Brian, illus. LC 81-18814. 32p. (ps-2). 1982. 9.95 (*0-394-85295-8*) Pantheon.

—The Lazy Bear. (Illus.). 32p. (ps-1). 1987. pap. 7.50 (*0-19-272158-5*) OUP.

Willard, Nancy. Starlit Somersault Downhill. (ps-3). 1993. 15.95 (*0-316-94113-1*) Little.

Williams, Bill, illus. Winnie-the-Pooh All Year Long. 14p. (ps). 1981. write for info. (*0-307-12260-3*, Golden Bks) Western Pub.

Williams, Gloria L. Jelly for Alawishous. 1994. 7.95 (*0-533-10725-3*) Vantage.

Williams, Leslie. A Bear in the Air. Vendrell, Carme S., illus. LC 80-10290. 28p. (gr. k up). 1980. 7.95 (*0-916144-54-2*) Stemmer Hse.

Williams, Marcia. Joseph & His Magnificent Coat of Many Colors. LC 91-71843. (Illus.). 32p. (ps up). 1994. pap. 3.99 (*1-56402-265-X*) Candlewick Pr.

Wiltshire, Teri. The Tale of Gus the Grumbly Grizzly. Archer, Rebecca, illus. LC 92-46248. (ps). 1993. 8.95 (*1-85697-856-7*, Kingfisher LKC) LKC.

Winnie the Pooh. (Illus.). 48p. (ps-6). 1989. 5.99 (*0-517-67005-4*) Random Hse Value.

Winnie the Pooh. 96p. 1988. 6.98 (*1-57082-053-8*) Mouse Works.

Winter, Paula. The Bear & the Fly. Winter, Paula, illus. LC 76-2479. (ps-1). 1987. PLB 12.95 (*0-517-52605-0*) Crown Bks Yng Read.

Winthrop, Elizabeth. Bear & Mrs. Duck. Brewster, Patience, illus. LC 87-25129. 32p. (ps-3). 1988. reinforced bdg. 15.95 (*0-8234-0687-3*); pap. 5.95 (*0-8234-0843-4*) Holiday.

—Bear's Christmas Surprise. Brewster, Patience, illus. LC 90-26414. 32p. (ps-3). 1991. reinforced 14.95 (*0-8234-0888-4*) Holiday.

Wiseman, Bernard. Barber Bear. Wiseman, Bernard, illus. LC 86-27594. 48p. (gr. 1-3). 1987. pap. 11.95 (*0-316-94859-4*) Little.

Wolf, Jill. Edward the Easter Bear. (ps up). 1990. pap. 2.50 (*0-89954-140-2*) Antioch Pub Co.

Wolf, Jill & Moore, Clement C. Teddy Bears Night Before Christmas. Rudegeair, Jean, illus. 24p. (gr. 3-6). 1985. pap. 2.50 (*0-89954-330-8*) Antioch Pub Co.

Wolff, Ashley. Year of Beasts. LC 85-27419. (Illus.). 32p. (ps-1). 1989. pap. 3.95 (*0-525-44541-2*, DCB) Dutton Child Bks.

Wood, Audrey. Oh My Baby Bear! 32p. (ps-1). 1990. 12.95 (*0-15-257698-3*) HarBrace.

Wood, Bill. Marty the Marathon Bear. Kaluza, Mary K. & Carreiro, Bob, illus. Kauffman, Helen, photos by. 136p. (Orig.). (gr. 3-7). 1988. pap. text ed. 6.95 (*0-317-93376-0*) Rallysport Video Prodns.

Wood, Jakki. One Bear with Bees in His Hair. Wood, Jakki, illus. LC 90-43211. 32p. (ps-1). 1991. 13.95 (*0-525-44695-8*, DCB) Dutton Child Bks.

Woodman, Allen & Kirby, David. The Bear Who Came To Stay. Stevenson, Harvey, illus. LC 92-7799. 40p. (ps-3). 1994. RSBE 14.95 (*0-02-793397-0*, Bradbury Pr) Macmillan Child Grp.

Wouters, Anne. This Book Is for Us. Wouters, Anne, illus. LC 91-23742. 32p. (ps-1). 1992. 8.95 (*0-525-44882-9*, DCB) Dutton Child Bks.

Yee, Wong H. Big Black Bear. Yee, Wong H., illus. LC 92-40862. 1993. 14.95 (*0-395-66359-8*) HM.

Yektai, Niki. Hi Bears, Bye Bears. DeGroat, Diane, illus. LC 89-37554. 32p. (ps-1). 1990. 12.95 (*0-531-05858-1*); PLB 12.99 (*0-531-08458-2*) Orchard Bks Watts.

YES! Entertainment Corporation Staff, et al. Comes to Life Story Player & Berenstain Bears: Mysterious Numbers Book Set. 16p. (ps-2). 1993. write for info. (*1-883366-07-0*) YES Ent.

—Comes to Life Story Player (Phase I) & Berenstain Bears: Mysterious Numbers & Berenstain Bears Eager Beavers Books. 16p. (ps-2). 1993. write for info. (*1-883366-29-1*) YES Ent.

Young, Ruth. Golden Bear. Isadora, Rachel, illus. 32p. (ps-1). 1992. PLB 14.00 (*0-670-82577-8*) Viking Child Bks.

Zalben, Jane B. Happy Passover, Rosie. Zalben, Jane B., illus. LC 89-19979. 32p. (ps-2). 1990. 13.95 (*0-8050-1221-4*, Bks Young Read) H Holt & Co.

—Leo & Blossom's Sukkah. Zalben, Jane B., illus. LC 89-24596. 32p. (ps-2). 1990. 13.95 (*0-8050-1226-5*, Bks Young Read) H Holt & Co.

Ziefert, Harriet. Bear's Colors. Baum, Susan, illus. 12p. (ps). 1993. 4.50 (*0-694-00454-5*, Festival) HarpC Child Bks.

—Bear's Numbers. Baum, Susan, illus. 12p. (ps). 1993. 4.50 (*0-694-00455-3*, Festival) HarpC Child Bks.

—Bear's Shapes. Baum, Susan, illus. 12p. (ps). 1993. 4.50 (*0-694-00456-1*, Festival) HarpC Child Bks.

—Bear's Weather. Baum, Susan, illus. 12p. (ps). 1993. 4.50 (*0-694-00457-X*, Festival) HarpC Child Bks.

BEARS–PICTURES, ILLUSTRATIONS, ETC.

Barrett, Norman S. Osos. LC 90-71417. (SPA., Illus.). 32p. (gr. k-4). 1991. PLB 11.90 (*0-531-07917-1*) Watts.

Goldstein, Bobbye S. Bear in Mind: A Book of Bear Poems. DuBois, William P., illus. 32p. (ps-3). 1989. 12.95 (*0-670-81907-7*) Viking Child Bks.

Hefter, Richard. Bears at Work. Hefter, Richard, illus. LC 83-2192. 32p. (ps-1). 1983. 5.95 (*0-911787-00-3*) Optimum Res Inc.

—Jobs for Bears. Hefter, Richard, illus. LC 83-2197. 32p. (ps-1). 1983. 5.95 (*0-911787-02-X*) Optimum Res Inc.

—Lots of Little Bears. Hefter, Richard, illus. LC 83-2184. 32p. (ps-1). 1983. 5.95 (*0-911787-04-6*) Optimum Res Inc.

—The Stickybear Book of Weather. Hefter, Richard, illus. LC 83-2191. 32p. (ps-1). 1983. 5.95 (*0-911787-01-1*) Optimum Res Inc.

—Watch Out! Hefter, Richard, illus. LC 83-2190. 32p. (ps-1). 1983. 5.95 (*0-911787-03-8*) Optimum Res Inc.

Matthews, Downs. Polar Bear Cubs. (gr. 3). pap. 4.00 (*0-663-56236-8*) Silver Burdett Pr.

Menten, Ted, compiled by. The Teddy Bear Lover's Postcard Book. (Illus.). 64p. (Orig.). 1988. pap. 7.95 (*0-89471-646-8*) Running Pr.

Patent, Dorothy H. The Way of the Grizzly. Munoz, William, photos by. LC 86-17562. (Illus.). 64p. (gr. 4 up). 1987. 13.95 (*0-89919-383-8*, Clarion Bks); pap. 6.95 (*0-395-58112-5*, Clarion Bks) HM.

Ryder, Joanne. White Bear, Ice Bear. Rothman, Michael, illus. LC 87-36781. 32p. (gr. k-3). 1989. 13.95 (*0-688-07174-0*); PLB 13.88 (*0-688-07175-9*, Morrow Jr Bks) Morrow Jr Bks.

BEARS–POETRY

Hague, Kathleen. Bear Hugs. Hague, Michael, illus. LC 88-28458. 32p. (ps-2). 1989. 9.95 (*0-8050-0512-9*, Bks Young Read) H Holt & Co.

Marzollo, Jean. The Teddy Bear Book. Schweninger, Ann, illus. LC 87-24538. 32p. (ps-2). 1989. 11.95 (*0-8037-0524-7*); PLB 11.89 (*0-8037-0632-4*) Dial Bks Young.

BEASTS

see Animals

BEATLES, THE
Alico, Stella H. Elvis Presley - The Beatles. Cruz, E. R. & Guanlao, Ernie, illus. (gr. 4-12). 1979. pap. text ed. 2.95 (*0-88301-352-5*); wkbk 1.25 (*0-88301-376-2*) Pendulum Pr.
Hamilton, Sue. The Killing of a Rock Star: John Lennon. Hamilton, John, ed. LC 89-84907. (Illus.). 32p. (gr. 4). 1989. PLB 11.96 (*0-939179-59-8*) Abdo & Dghtrs.
Loewen, L. The Beatles. (Illus.). 112p. (gr. 5 up). 1989. lib. bdg. 18.60 (*0-86592-610-7*); lib. bdg. 13.95s.p. (*0-685-58616-2*) Rourke Corp.
Santrey, Laurence. John Lennon, Young Rock Star. Beier, Ellen, illus. LC 89-33938. 48p. (gr. 4-6). 1990. lib. bdg. 10.79 (*0-8167-1781-8*); pap. text ed. 3.50 (*0-8167-1782-6*) Troll Assocs.
BEAUTY, PERSONAL
see also Cosmetics; Costume; Hair
Hunt, Angela E. & Calenberg, Laura K. Beauty from the Inside Out: Becoming the Best You Can Be. Herron, Sandra & White, Kim, illus. LC 93-7132. 1993. pap. 12.99 (*0-8407-6789-7*) Nelson.
Johnson, Barbara L. Careers in Beauty Culture. Rosen, Ruth, ed. (gr. 7-12). 1989. PLB 14.95 (*0-8239-1002-4*) Rosen Group.
Jones, Barbara B. & Hawkes, Sharlene W. The Inside-Outside Beauty Book. LC 89-37561. (Illus.). 100p. (Orig.). (gr. 9 up). 1989. pap. 5.95 (*0-87579-271-5*) Deseret Bk.
Kyle, Jamie. Great Nails for Girls. (Illus.). 32p. (gr. 3 up). 1993. 17.95 (*1-56288-413-1*) Checkerboard.
McCombs, Barbara L. & Brannan, Linda. Good Grooming Habits. (Illus.). 32p. (Orig.). (gr. 7-12). 1990. Set. 10 wkbks. & tchr's. guide 44.95 (*1-56119-080-2*); tchr's. guide 1.95 (*1-56119-044-6*); software 39.95 (*1-56119-122-1*) Educ Pr MD.
McGlothin, Bruce. Great Grooming for Guys. Rosen, Ruth, ed. (gr. 7-12). 1993. 13.95 (*0-8239-1468-2*) Rosen Group.
Martin, Nancie S. Miss America: Through the Looking Glass. LC 85-13038. (Illus.). 128p. (gr. 5 up). 1985. (J Messner) S&S Trade.
Rourke, Arlene C. Los Manos y los Pies. LC 92-5661. (ENG & SPA.). 1992. 15.94 (*0-86625-290-8*); 11. 95s.p. (*0-685-59319-3*) Rourke Pubns.
Smith, Sandra L. Great Grooming for Girls. Rosen, Ruth, ed. (gr. 7-12). 1993. 13.95 (*0-8239-1469-0*) Rosen Group.
Vitkus, Jessica. Beauty & Fitness with "Saved by the Bell" LC 91-42583. (Illus.). 64p. (Orig.). (gr. 5 up). 1992. pap. 6.95 (*0-02-045425-2*, Collier Young Ad) Macmillan Child Grp.
Zeldis, Yona. Coping with Beauty, Fitness & Fashion. Rosen, Ruth, ed. Daven, Douglas, illus. LC 86-24850. 128p. (gr. 7 up). 1987. PLB 14.95 (*0-8239-0731-7*) Rosen Group.
BEAUTY CONTESTS–FICTION
Bradman, Tony. It Came from Outer Space. LC 91-17882. (Illus.). 32p. (ps-3). 1992. 12.00 (*0-8037-1098-4*) Dial Bks Young.
Cooney, Caroline B. Twenty Pageants Later. (gr. 4-7). 1993. pap. 3.99 (*0-553-29672-8*) Bantam.
Hiser, Constance. Sixth-Grade Star. LC 92-52856. 96p. (gr. 3-7). 1992. 13.95 (*0-8234-0967-8*) Holiday.
Janney, Rebecca P. Model Mystery. (gr. 4-7). 1993. pap. 4.99 (*0-8499-3835-X*) Word Inc.
Pascal, Francine. Miss Teen Sweet Valley. 1991. pap. 3.50 (*0-553-29060-6*) Bantam.
BEAVERS
Crump, Donald J., ed. Busy Beavers. (Illus.). (gr. k-4). 1988. Set. 13.95 (*0-87044-740-8*); Set. PLB 16.95 (*0-87044-745-9*) Natl Geog.
Dalmais. Beaver, Reading Level 3-4. (Illus.). 28p. (gr. 2-5). 1983. PLB 16.67 (*0-86592-859-2*) Rourke Corp.
George, William T. Beaver at Long Pond. George, Lindsay B., illus. Grammer, Red, contrib. by. (Illus.). 24p. (gr. k-3). 1989. incl. audiocassette tape & stuffed beaver toy 44.95 (*0-924483-70-9*); incl. audiocassette 19.95 (*0-924483-22-9*) Soundprints.
Hogan, Paula Z. The Beaver. Miyake, Yoshi, illus. LC 79-13305. 32p. (gr. 1-4). 1979. PLB 19.97 (*0-8172-1502-6*) Raintree Steck-V.
—The Beaver. LC 79-13305. (Illus.). 32p. (gr. 1-4). 1981. PLB 29.28 incl. cassette (*0-8172-1848-3*) Raintree Steck-V.
Lane, Margaret. The Beaver. Nockels, David, illus. LC 81-67074. 32p. (gr. k-4). 1993. 13.99 (*0-8037-0624-3*) Dial Bks Young.
—The Beaver. Nockels, David, illus. 32p. (gr. k-4). 1993. pap. 4.99 (*0-14-054925-0*, Puff Pied Piper) Puffin Bks.
Lepthien, Emilie U. Beavers. LC 92-14909. (Illus.). 48p. (gr. k-4). 1992. PLB 12.85 (*0-516-01131-6*) Childrens.
—Beavers. (Illus.). 48p. (gr. k-4). 1993. pap. 4.95 (*0-516-41131-4*) Childrens.
Murray, Peter. Beavers. (gr. 2-6). 1992. PLB 15.95 (*0-89565-844-5*) Childs World.
Nentl, Jerolyn. Beaver. LC 83-5323. (Illus.). 48p. (gr. 5). 1983. text ed. 12.95 RSBE (*0-89686-219-4*, Crestwood Hse) Macmillan Child Grp.
Ryden, Hope. The Beaver. (Illus.). 64p. 1992. pap. 9.95 (*1-55821-142-X*) Lyons & Burford.
Stone, L. Castores (Beavers) 1991. 8.95s.p. (*0-86592-832-0*) Rourke Enter.
Stone, Lynn. Beavers. (Illus.). 24p. (gr. k-5). 1990. lib. bdg. 11.94 (*0-86593-041-4*); lib. bdg. 8.95s.p. (*0-685-36338-4*) Rourke Corp.
Storms, John. Buddy the Beaver. Storms, Robert, illus. 24p. (Orig.). (gr. k-4). 1993. pap. 4.95 (*0-89346-529-1*) Heian Intl.
Wallace, Karen. Think of a Beaver. Manning, Mick, illus. LC 92-53132. 32p. (ps up). 1993. 14.95 (*1-56402-179-3*) Candlewick Pr.
BEAVERS–FICTION
Beavers Beware! 1992. pap. 9.99 (*0-553-07498-9*) Bantam.
Beavers Beware! 1992. pap. 3.99 (*0-553-35386-1*) Bantam.
Boyle, Doe & Thomas, Peter, eds. Operation Beaver: From an Original Article Which Appeared in Ranger Rick Magazine, Copyright National Wildlife Federation. Beylon, Cathy, illus. Luther, Sallie, contrib. by. LC 92-11869. (Illus.). 20p. (gr. k-3). 1992. 6.95 (*0-924483-57-1*); incl. audiocass. tape & 13" toy 35.95 (*0-924483-54-7*); incl. 9" toy 21.95 (*0-924483-55-5*); incl. audiocass. tape 9.95 (*0-924483-56-3*); write for info. audiocass. tape (*0-924483-81-4*) Soundprints.
Burgess, Thornton. Paddy the Beaver. 1986. Repr. lib. bdg. 17.95 (*0-89966-528-4*) Buccaneer Bks.
Burgess, Thornton W. Adventures of Paddy the Beaver. 18.95 (*0-8488-0379-5*) Amereon Ltd.
Carlson, Nancy. Take Time to Relax! LC 92-26584. 1993. pap. 4.99 (*0-14-054242-6*, Puffin) Puffin Bks.
—A Visit to Grandma's. LC 93-18607. (Illus.). 32p. (ps-3). 1993. pap. 4.99 (*0-14-054243-4*, Puffin) Puffin Bks.
Chottin, Ariane. Beaver Gets Lost. Geneste, Marcelle, illus. LC 91-40651. 24p. (ps-3). 1992. 6.99 (*0-89577-419-4*, Dist. by Random) RD Assn.
Coran, Pierre. The Lazy Beaver. (Illus.). 32p. (gr. k-2). 1991. 12.95 (*0-89565-743-0*) Childs World.
Dabcovich. Busy Beavers. 1993. pap. 28.67 (*0-590-72455-X*) Scholastic Inc.
Fisk, George W. Benny, the Lazy Beaver. Barker, Scott J., illus. LC 90-45200. 32p. 1991. 10.99 (*0-9620507-1-7*) Cosmic Concepts Pr.
George, William T. & George, Lindsay B. Beaver at Long Pond. LC 87-281. (Illus.). 24p. (ps-3). 1988. 14.00 (*0-688-07106-6*); lib. bdg. 13.88 (*0-688-07107-4*) Greenwillow.
Grandma Marian, pseud. Beni the Bashful Beaver. Kmiecik, Anne, illus. LC 87-71490. 32p. 1988. 6.95 (*0-9614989-1-9*) Banmar Inc.
Heine, Helme. The Pearl. Heine, Helme, illus. LC 88-3220. 32p. (gr. k-4). 1988. pap. 3.95 (*0-689-71262-6*, Aladdin) Macmillan Child Grp.
Kalas, Sybille & Kalas, Klaus. The Beaver Family Book. Crampton, Patricia, tr. LC 87-13914. (Illus.). (gr. k up). 1991. pap. 15.95 (*0-88708-050-2*) Picture Bk Studio.
MacDonald, Amy. Little Beaver & the Echo. Fox-Davies, Sarah, illus. 32p. 1990. 14.95 (*0-399-22203-0*, Putnam) Putnam Pub Group.
Michaels, Ski. Fun in the Sun. Paterson, Diane, illus. LC 85-14055. 48p. (Orig.). (gr. 1-3). 1986. PLB 10.59 (*0-8167-0568-2*); pap. text ed. 3.50 (*0-8167-0569-0*) Troll Assocs.
Minarik, Elsa H. Percy & the Five Houses. (ps-3). 1990. pap. 3.95 (*0-14-054209-4*, Puffin) Puffin Bks.
Minarik, Else H. Percy & the Five Houses. Stevenson, James, illus. LC 88-4804. 24p. (gr. k up). 1989. 11.95 (*0-688-08104-5*); PLB 11.88 (*0-688-08105-3*) Greenwillow.
Pryor, Bonnie. The Beaver Boys. Baker, Karen, illus. LC 90-38515. 40p. (ps up). 1992. 15.00 (*0-688-08702-7*); lib. bdg. 14.93 (*0-688-08703-5*) Morrow Jr Bks.
Sargent, Dave & Sargent, Pat. Billy Beaver. 64p. (gr. 2-6). 1992. pap. write for info. (*1-56763-004-9*) Ozark Pub.
Sharmat, Marjorie W. The Story of Bentley Beaver. Hoban, Lillian, illus. LC 82-47715. 64p. (gr. k-3). 1984. HarpC Child Bks.
Sign of the Beaver. 1984. pap. 2.75 (*0-440-77900-6*) Dell.
Speare, Elizabeth G. The Sign of the Beaver. 144p. (gr. 5 up). 1983. 13.45 (*0-395-33890-5*) HM.
—Sign of the Beaver. (gr. 4-7). 1993. pap. 1.99 (*0-440-21623-0*) Dell.
Stoller, Nettie. The Little Beaver Who Had No Tail. 1993. pap. 7.95 (*0-533-10516-1*) Vantage.
Thompson-Hoffman, Susan. Delver's Danger. Chapin, Tom, narrated by. Buzzanco, Eileen M., illus. LC 88-64152. 32p. (gr. 2-5). 1989. 11.95 (*0-924483-02-4*); incl. audiocassette 16.95 (*0-924483-05-9*); incl. audiocassette & toy combination 39.95 (*0-924483-08-3*); incl. audiocassette & small toy combination 25.95 (*0-924483-36-9*); write for info. audiocassette (*0-924483-11-3*) Soundprints.
Weiss, Clarence B. Grandpa Beaver: His Amazing Tales. Easson, Roger, ed. McKnight, Fred, illus. LC 87-20457. 98p. (Orig.). (gr. 5-12). 1987. pap. 6.95 (*0-942179-01-3*) Shelby Hse.
Wheeler, Bernelda. The Bannock. Bekkering, Herman, illus. LC 92-34255. 1993. 4.25 (*0-383-03617-8*) SRA Schl Grp.
BECKWOURTH, JAMES PIERSON, 1798-1867
Blassingame, Wyatt. Jim Beckwourth: Black Trapper & Indian Chief. (Illus.). 80p. (gr. 2-6). 1991. Repr. of 1973 ed. lib. bdg. 12.95 (*0-7910-1404-5*) Chelsea Hse.
Sabin, Louis. Jim Beckwourth: Adventures of a Mountain Man. Krupp, Marion, illus. LC 92-8717. 48p. (gr. 4-6). 1992. PLB 10.79 (*0-8167-2819-4*); pap. text ed. 3.50 (*0-8167-2820-8*) Troll Assocs.
BEDOUINS
King, John. Bedouin. LC 92-16506. (Illus.). 48p. (gr. 5-6). 1992. PLB 22.80 (*0-8114-2304-2*) Raintree Steck-V.
BEE
see Bees
BEES
see also Honey
Abels, Harriette S. Killer Bees. LC 87-14085. (Illus.). 48p. (gr. 5-6). 1987. text ed. 12.95 RSBE (*0-89686-342-5*, Crestwood Hse) Macmillan Child Grp.
Bailey, Jill. Life Cycle of a Bee. (ps-3). 1990. PLB 11.90 (*0-531-18316-5*, Pub. by Bookwright Pr) Watts.
Bennett, Geraldine M. Katrina Tells about Bee Stings. (Illus.). 34p. (Orig.). (gr. 2-8). Date not set. pap. 7.98 (*1-882786-16-5*) New Dawn NY.
Blau, Melinda E. Killer Bees. LC 77-10010. (Illus.). 48p. (gr. 4 up). 1983. PLB 20.70 (*0-8172-1055-5*) Raintree Steck-V.
Boy Scouts of America. Beekeeping. (Illus.). 56p. (gr. 6-12). 1983. pap. 1.85 (*0-8395-3362-4*, 33362) BSA.
Davis, Kathleen & Mayes, Dave. Killer Bees. LC 92-46894. (Illus.). 60p. (gr. 5 up). 1993. text ed. 13.95 RSBE (*0-87518-582-7*, Dillon) Macmillan Child Grp.
Eastman, David. I Can Read About Bees & Wasps. LC 78-73773. (Illus.). (gr. 2-5). 1979. pap. 2.50 (*0-89375-203-7*) Troll Assocs.
Fichter, George S. Bees, Wasps, & Ants. Kest, Kristin, illus. 36p. (gr. k-3). 1993. 4.95 (*0-307-11434-1*, 11434, Golden Pr) Western Pub.
Fischer-Nagel, Andreas & Fischer-Nagel, Heiderose. Life of the Honeybee. Fischer-Nagel, Andreas & Fischer-Nagel, Heiderose, illus. 48p. (gr. 2-5). 1986. pap. 6.95 (*0-87614-470-9*) Carolrhoda Bks.
Fischer-Nagel, Heiderose & Fischer-Nagel, Andreas. Life of the Honeybee. (Illus.). 48p. (gr. 2-5). 1987. pap. 6.95 (*0-685-18832-9*, First Ave Edns) Lerner Pubns.
Harrison, Virginia. The World of Honeybees. Oxford Scientific Films Staff, photos by. LC 89-33936. (Illus.). 32p. (gr. 2-3). 1989. PLB 17.27 (*0-8368-0142-3*) Gareth Stevens Inc.
Harwood, Lynne. Honeybees at Home. Harwood, Lynne, illus. LC 93-33552. 40p. (gr. 3-8). 1994. 16.95 (*0-88448-119-0*) Tilbury Hse.
Hawcock, David. Bee. Montgomery, Lee, illus. LC 93-85132. 12p. (ps-3). 1994. 5.99 (*0-679-85470-3*) Random Bks Yng Read.
Hogan, Paula Z. The Honeybee. Strigenz, Geri K., illus. LC 78-21165. 32p. (gr. 1-4). 1979. PLB 19.97 (*0-8172-1256-6*); pap. 4.95 (*0-8114-8179-4*); pap. 9.95 incl. cassette (*0-8114-8187-5*) Raintree Steck-V.
—The Honeybee. LC 78-21165. (Illus.). 32p. (gr. 1-4). 1984. PLB 29.28 incl. cassette (*0-8172-2229-4*) Raintree Steck-V.
Johnson, Sylvia A. A Beekeeper's Year. Von Ohlen, Nick, photos by. LC 93-10199. (Illus.). 1994. 14.95 (*0-316-46745-6*) Little.
Kahkonen, Sharon. Honey Bees. 32p. (gr. 1-4). 1989. PLB 18.99 (*0-8172-3508-6*); pap. 3.95 (*0-8114-6707-4*) Raintree Steck-V.
Lavies, Bianca. Killer Bees. (Illus.). 32p. (gr. 3-6). 1994. 16.99 (*0-525-45243-5*) Dutton Child Bks.
Lunn, Carolyn. A Buzz Is Part of a Bee. Dunnington, Tom, illus. LC 89-25434. 32p. (ps-2). 1990. PLB 10.25 (*0-516-02062-5*); pap. 2.95 (*0-516-42062-3*) Childrens.
Micucci, Charles, text by. & illus. Life & Times of the Honey Bee. LC 93-8135. 32p. (ps-3). 1995. 13.95g (*0-395-65968-X*) Ticknor & Flds Bks Yng Read.
Mitgutsch, Ali. From Blossom to Honey. Mitgutsch, Ali, illus. 24p. (ps-3). 1981. PLB 10.95 (*0-87614-146-7*) Carolrhoda Bks.
Oda, Hidetomo. Observing Bees & Wasps. Pohl, Kathy, ed. LC 85-28195. (Illus.). 32p. (gr. 3-7). 1986. PLB 10. 95 (*0-8172-2540-4*) Raintree Steck-V.
Otani, Takeshi. The Honeybee. Pohl, Kathy, ed. LC 85-28230. (Illus.). 32p. (gr. 3-7). 1986. text ed. 10.95 (*0-8172-2537-4*) Raintree Steck-V.
O'Toole, Christopher. The Honeybee in the Meadow. Oxford Scientific Films Staff, photos by. LC 89-33935. (Illus.). 32p. (gr. 4-6). 1989. PLB 17.27 (*0-8368-0117-2*) Gareth Stevens Inc.
Parramon, J. M. The Fascinating World of Bees. (Illus.). 48p. (gr. 3-7). 1991. pap. 6.95 (*0-8120-4720-6*) Barron.
Ross, Edward S. Yellowjackets. LC 92-42934. (gr. 2-6). 1993. 15.95 (*1-56766-017-7*) Childs World.
Scarffe, Bronwen. Busy Bees. Costeloe, Brenda, illus. LC 92-31958. 1993. 3.75 (*0-383-03558-9*) SRA Schl Grp.
Starosta, Paul. The Bee. (Illus.). 28p. (ps-4). 1993. pap. 6.95 (*0-88106-430-0*) Charlesbridge Pub.
Watts, Barrie. Honeybee. (Illus.). 25p. (gr. k-4). 1990. 5.95 (*0-382-24013-8*); PLB 7.95 (*0-382-24011-1*); 3.95 (*0-382-24343-9*) Silver Burdett Pr.
BEES–FICTION
Barbie the Bee. (Illus.). (ps-1). 2.98 (*0-517-46983-9*) Random Hse Value.
Bennett, Geraldine M. Katrina Tells about Bee Stings. (gr. k up). Date not set. pap. write for info. (*1-882786-07-6*) New Dawn NY.

it. The relationship of the bees to the Queen is discussed & the difference in her appearance. They also meet the drone in a funny episode that describes his appearance & his function in the hive. This is a very educational & amusing book about the bee & its activities inside & outside of the hive. How it gathers the pollen & the nectar & changes the nectar into honey. How & where it stores them both in the hive & how they make the comb that is used to store the honey, the pollen, & the brood. The author is a beekeeper of over 15 years & a former elementary teacher. Contact the Ashbrook Publishing, 10089 Bartholomew Rd., Chagrin Falls, Ohio 44022; 218-543-8369.
Publisher Provided Annotation.

Buzz the Bee Hunts for Flowers. LC 93-85490. 20p. (ps-1). 1994. 3.99 (*0-89577-570-0*) RD Assn.
Carratello, Patty. The Bee & the Seed. Spivak, Darlene, ed. Smythe, Linda, illus. 16p. (gr. k-2). 1987. wkbk. 1.95 (*1-55734-381-0*) Tchr Create Mat.
Cates, Joe W. Buzbee. Cates, Joe W., illus. 96p. (gr. 3-8). 1987. PLB write for info. (*0-942403-04-5*) J Barnaby Dist.
Cormier, Robert. The Bumblebee Flies Anyway. 256p. (gr. 5 up). 1991. pap. 3.99 (*0-440-90871-X*, LFL) Dell.
Fowler, Richard. Honeybee's Busy Day. LC 93-31152. 1994. 12.95 (*0-15-200055-0*, Gulliver Bks) HarBrace.
Frederick, Ruth. Where's Tommy? O'Connell, Ruth A., illus. 32p. (gr. 1-2). 1991. pap. 3.99 saddle stitch (*0-87403-806-5*, 24-03896) Standard Pub.
Haker, Loren F. The Li'l Rascals: Timmy & the Bees. (Illus.). 56p. (gr. 1-8). 1984. 7.95 (*0-9609964-0-0*); pap. 4.95 (*0-9609964-1-9*) Haker Books.
La Pierre, Keith C. The Wanna Beezzz. La Pierre, Keith C., illus. LC 93-78057. 34p. (ps-3). 1993. 8.95 (*0-9631513-1-2*); PLB write for info. (*0-9631513-2-0*) Lee Pub NY.
Lasky, Kathryn. Cloud Eyes. Moser, Barry, illus. LC 93-37805. (gr. k-5). 1994. 14.95 (*0-15-219168-2*) HarBrace.
Lobel, Arnold. The Rose in My Garden. Lobel, Anita, illus. LC 92-24588. 40p. (ps up). 1993. pap. 4.95 (*0-688-12265-5*, Mulberry) Morrow.
McOmber, Rachel B., ed. McOmber Phonics Storybooks: Me & the Bee. rev. ed. (Illus.). write for info. (*0-944991-46-7*) Swift Lrn Res.
Quinitchette, Lucille. Where Do Bumblebees Live? Shelley, Evelyn, illus. 13p. (Orig.). (gr. 4). 1994. pap. 5.95 (*0-9640122-1-9*) Pen & Pr Unltd.
Sand, George. The Mysterious Tale of Gentle Jack & Lord Bumblebee. Spirin, Gennady, illus. LC 87-30490. 80p. (ps up). 1988. Dial Bks Young.
Schwartz, Alvin. Busy Buzzing Bumblebees & Other Tongue Twisters. Meisel, Paul, illus. LC 91-4799. 64p. (gr. k-3). 1982. 14.00 (*0-06-025268-5*); PLB 13.89 (*0-06-025269-3*) HarpC Child Bks.
—Busy Buzzing Bumblebees & Other Tongue Twisters. Meisel, Paul, illus. LC 91-4800. 64p. (gr. k-3). 1982. pap. 3.50 (*0-06-444036-2*, Trophy) HarpC Child Bks.
Stockton, Frank R. The Bee-Man of Orn. Sendak, Maurice, illus. LC 85-45813. 48p. (ps up). 1987. Repr. of 1963 ed. 13.95 (*0-06-025818-7*); PLB 13.89 (*0-06-025819-5*) HarpC Child Bks.
—The Bee-Man of Orn. Sendak, Maurice, illus. LC 85-45813. 48p. (gr. 2 up). 1987. pap. 4.95 (*0-06-443125-8*, Trophy) HarpC Child Bks.
Williams, Effie M. A Hive of Busy Bees. (gr. 5 up). 1976. Repr. of 1939 ed. 3.40 (*0-686-15479-7*) Rod & Staff.

BEETHOVEN, LUDWIG VAN, 1770-1827

Greene, Carol. Ludwig Van Beethoven: Musical Pioneer. Dobson, Steven, illus. LC 89-15849. 48p. (gr. k-3). 1989. PLB 12.85 (*0-516-04208-4*); pap. 4.95 (*0-516-44208-2*) Childrens.
Loewen, L. Beethoven. (Illus.). 112p. (gr. 5 up). 1989. lib. bdg. 18.60 (*0-86592-609-3*); lib. bdg. 13.95s.p. (*0-685-58617-0*) Rourke Corp.
McHugh, Elisabet. Beethoven's Cat. (gr. k-6). 1991. pap. 3.50 (*0-440-40398-7*) Dell.
Sabin, Louis. Ludwig Van Beethoven: Young Composer. Beier, Ellen, illus. LC 91-18616. 48p. (gr. 4-6). 1992. PLB 10.79 (*0-8167-2511-X*); pap. text ed. 3.50 (*0-8167-2512-8*) Troll Assocs.
Sage, Alison. Play Beethoven. Gabby, Terry, illus. Bunting, Janet, contrib. by. (Illus.). 32p. (gr. 1-4). 1988. Incl. built-in 22-note electronic keyboard. 12.95 (*0-8120-5978-6*) Barron.
Tames, Richard. Ludwig Van Beethoven. LC 90-32377. (Illus.). 32p. 1991. PLB 12.40 (*0-531-14106-3*) Watts.
Thompson, Wendy. Ludwig Van Beethoven. (Illus.). 48p. (gr. 7up). 1991. 17.95 (*0-670-83678-8*) Viking Child Bks.

BEETLES

Beetles. (Illus.). 32p. (gr. 3-7). 1986. PLB 10.95 (*0-8172-2530-7*) Raintree Steck-V.
Heymann, Georgianne. Weevils. (Illus.). 32p. (gr. 3-7). 1986. PLB 10.95 (*0-8172-2713-X*) Raintree Steck-V.
Johnson, Sylvia A. Beetles. Kishida, Isao, illus. LC 82-7230. 48p. (gr. 4 up). 1982. lib. bdg. 19.95 (*0-8225-1476-1*) Lerner Pubns.
Murray, Peter. Beetles. LC 92-29742. (gr. 2-6). 1993. PLB 15.95 (*1-56766-000-2*) Childs World.
Oda, Hidetomo. The Diving Beetle. Pohl, Kathy, ed. LC 85-28300. (Illus.). 32p. (gr. 3-7). 1986. PLB 10.95 (*0-8172-2533-1*) Raintree Steck-V.
Ray, Stephen & Murdoch, Kathleen. Have You Ever Found a Beetle? Bruere, Julian, illus. LC 92-27265. 1993. 3.75 (*0-383-03627-5*) SRA Schl Grp.
Still, John. Amazing Beetles. Young, Jerry, illus. LC 91-6516. 32p. (Orig.). (gr. 1-5). 1991. lib. bdg. 9.99 (*0-679-91519-2*); pap. 6.95 (*0-679-81519-8*) Knopf Bks Yng Read.
Watts, Barrie. Beetles. 32p. (gr. k-4). 1991. pap. 4.95 (*0-531-15619-2*) Watts.

BEHAVIOR

see also Christian Life; Courage; Courtesy; Ethics; Etiquette; Friendship; Human Relations; Love; Patriotism; Self-Control; Self-Culture; Social Adjustment; Spiritual Life; Truthfulness and Falsehood

Adderholdt-Elliott, Miriam. Perfectionism: What's Bad about Being Too Good? Espeland, Pamela, ed. LC 86-81130. (Illus.). 136p. (gr. 7 up). 1987. pap. 8.95 (*0-915793-07-5*) Free Spirit Pub.
Albert, Burton, Jr. Mine, Yours, Ours. Axeman, Lois, illus. LC 77-9408. (ps-1). 1977. PLB 10.95 (*0-8075-5148-1*) A Whitman.
Alden, Laura. Houdini. Raskin, Betty, illus. LC 88-34126. 100p. (gr. 3-7). 1989. PLB 14.95 (*0-89565-456-3*) Childs World.
Anderson, David A. What You Can See, You Can Be! Jones, Don, illus. 48p. (Orig.). (gr. 3-8). 1988. 11.95 (*0-87516-603-2*) DeVorss.
Arnold, Tedd. Mother Goose's Words of Wit & Wisdom: A Book of Months. (Illus.). 64p. 1990. 14.95 (*0-8037-0825-4*); PLB 14.89 (*0-8037-0826-2*) Dial Bks Young.
Ayer, Eleanor. Determination. (gr. 7-12). 1991. PLB 14.95 (*0-8239-1226-4*) Rosen Group.
Banta, Robert. Grandpa Says: You Can Make It a Wonderful Life. LC 89-52115. 148p. (gr. 2-6). 1990. 7.95 (*1-55523-312-0*) Winston-Derek.
Barton, Charles D. Changes in Youth Morality: What Caused Them, No. 1. rev. ed. Barton, David, illus. 40p. 1988. pap. 3.00 (*0-317-93057-5*) Wallbuilders.
Bassett, Harmon. F. U. N.-D. A. T. E. S. with a Likeable You for Adolescents & Juveniles. rev. ed. LC 88-47848. 175p. (gr. 7-12). 1991. 19.50 (*1-55914-490-4*); pap. 14.50 (*1-55914-491-2*) ABBE Pubs Assn.
Beatty, Patricia. Behave Yourself, Bethany Brant. LC 86-12517. 160p. (gr. 5-9). 1986. 12.95 (*0-688-05923-6*) Morrow Jr Bks.

Beckett, Cheryl. Growing Up Inside Out. Barton, B. J., ed. Capalungo, Polly, illus. 167p. (Orig.). (gr. 11 up). 1994. pap. 10.95 (*0-9642255-0-6*) Higher States.
GROWING UP INSIDE OUT by Dr. Cheryl Thompson Beckett presents a powerful new approach to human development & consciousness. It sends a loud call to western developmental psychology to wake up & grow further. By presenting life as a multifaceted experience, it addresses how we grow & develop mentally, physically, emotionally & spiritually. The book shows the connection between consciousness & physiology while connecting modern western psychology & ancient, eastern Vedic psychology in order to outline life's adventure from conception to the highest consciousness. Dr. John Gray, (Men Are From Mars, Women Are From Venus) says, "This book sets the platform for working with relationships at their highest level." Freelance writer Susan Skog says, "I have read books on development & books on consciousness, but I have not found the two combined to give a vision for my children's growth & an inspiration for my own!" Dr. Beckett's intention is to expand & extend the continuum of development of western psychology. Her background as a mind/body health specialist includes M.S. in psychology, child development & consciousness & a Ph.D. in nutrition. She has over 20 years in working with children. She has taught in Spain, France, Switzerland & India. Order from: Baker & Taylor, & Big Horn Books (800-433-5995), East Mulberry, Ft. Collins, CO 80524 or from publisher directly: Higher States Publishing, 1917 Sheely Dr., Ft. Collins, CO 80526; 303-493-1495, 800-383-1616.
Publisher Provided Annotation.

Bennett, Geraldine M. Opening the Door to Your Inner Self: My Lessons. Bennett, Geraldine M., illus. LC 91-67122. 122p. (Orig.). (gr. 2 up). 1993. pap. 12.98 (*0-9630718-5-8*, 1-87122) New Dawn NY.
Berry, Joy. Every Kid's Guide to Good Manners. (Illus.). 48p. (gr. 3-7). 1987. 4.95 (*0-516-21420-9*) Childrens.
—Every Kid's Guide to Handling Disagreements. (Illus.). 48p. (gr. 3-7). 1987. 4.95 (*0-516-21421-7*) Childrens.
Berry, Ron, et al. Crassy the Crude Beastie: A Beastie Book about Manners. Bartholomew, illus. 48p. (ps-1). 1993. write for info. (*1-883761-03-4*) Fmly Life Prods.
—Fritter the Wasteful Beastie: A Beastie Book about Conserving Resources. Bartholomew, illus. 48p. (ps-1). 1993. write for info. (*1-883761-02-6*) Fmly Life Prods.
—Glumby the Grumbler: A Beastie Book about Being Grateful. Bartholomew, illus. 48p. (ps-1). 1993. write for info. (*1-883761-00-X*) Fmly Life Prods.
—Hogger the Hoarding Beastie: A Beastie Book about Sharing. Bartholomew, illus. 48p. (ps-1). 1993. write for info. (*1-883761-01-8*) Fmly Life Prods.
—Moogie the Messy Beastie: A Beastie Book about Being Neat. Bartholomew, illus. 48p. (ps-1). 1993. write for info. (*1-883761-05-0*) Fmly Life Prods.
—Scrappy the Squabbler: A Beastie Book about Getting along with Others. Bartholomew, illus. 48p. (ps-1). 1993. write for info. (*1-883761-04-2*) Fmly Life Prods.
Bertolini, Dewey. Secret Wounds & Silent Cries. rev. ed. LC 93-18867. 156p. 1993. pap. 7.99 (*1-56476-116-9*, Victor Books) SP Pubns.
—Sometimes I Really Hate You. 132p. 1991. pap. 4.99 (*0-89693-041-6*) SP Pubns.
Binford, Shari, et al, eds. Growing Up: New Challenges for a New Generation. 48p. 1991. pap. text ed. 11.95 (*1-878623-22-2*) Info Plus TX.
Bisignano, Judy. Relating. Tom, Darcy, illus. 64p. (gr. 3-8). 1985. wkbk. 8.95 (*0-86653-331-1*, GA 678) Good Apple.
Biskup, Michael D. & Cozic, Charles P., eds. Youth Violence. LC 92-23592. 200p. (gr. 10 up). 1992. PLB 16.95 (*1-56510-017-4*); pap. text ed. 9.95 (*1-56510-016-6*) Greenhaven.
Blackburn, Lynn B. I Know I Made It Happen: A Book about Children & Guilt. Johnson, Joy, ed. Borum, Shari, illus. 24p. (Orig.). (ps-6). 1990. pap. 3.50 (*1-56123-016-2*) Centering Corp.
Blair, L. E. Peer Pressure Girl Talk, No. 9. 1991. pap. 2.95 (*0-307-22009-5*) Western Pub.
Blake, James L. Common Sense in a Complex World: What Every Young Person Should Know. LC 88-72165. 192p. (Orig.). (gr. 8-11). 1989. pap. 8.95 (*0-9621230-0-5*) CSI Pub.
Bowman, John S. Sportmanship. (Illus.). 64p. (gr. 7-12,RL 4-6). 1990. PLB 14.95 (*0-8239-1110-1*) Rosen Group.
Boy Scouts of America Staff. Learning for Life: Fifth Grade. (Illus.). 168p. (gr. 5). 1991. pap. 5.00 (*0-8395-2130-8*, 32130) BSA.
—Learning for Life: First Grade. (Illus.). 139p. (gr. 1). 1991. pap. 5.00 (*0-8395-2126-X*, 32126) BSA.
—Learning for Life: Fourth Grade. (Illus.). 154p. (gr. 4). 1991. pap. 5.00 (*0-8395-2129-4*, 32129) BSA.
—Learning for Life: High School. (Illus.). 160p. (gr. 9-12). 1991. pap. 5.00 (*0-8395-2133-2*, 32133) BSA.
—Learning for Life: Junior High. (Illus.). 62p. (gr. 7-8). 1991. pap. 5.00 (*0-8395-2132-4*, 32132) BSA.
—Learning for Life: Kindergarten. (Illus.). 134p. (gr. k). 1991. pap. 5.00 (*0-8395-2125-1*, 32125) BSA.
—Learning for Life: Second Grade. (Illus.). 156p. (gr. 2). 1991. pap. 5.00 (*0-8395-2127-8*, 32127) BSA.
—Learning for Life: Sixth Grade. (Illus.). 162p. (gr. 6). 1991. pap. 5.00 (*0-8395-2131-6*, 32131) BSA.
—Learning for Life: Special Education. (Illus.). 130p. 1991. pap. 5.00 (*0-8395-2134-0*, 32134) BSA.
—Learning for Life: Third Grade. (Illus.). 136p. (gr. 3). 1991. pap. 5.00 (*0-8395-2128-6*, 32128) BSA.
Boyd, Selma & Boyd, Pauline. The How: Making the Best of a Mistake. Luks, Peggy, illus. LC 80-13513. 32p. (ps-3). 1981. 16.95 (*0-87705-176-3*) Human Sci Pr.
Boylan, Kristi M. Spenser's Important Work: Introducing Your Child To Day Care. Featherman, John, illus. 32p. (Orig.). 1993. pap. 7.99 (*1-883497-00-0*) Parent Track.
Bradley, R. C. Teaching for "Self-Directed" Living & Learning in Students - How to Help Students Get in Charge of Their Lives: "Self-Directed" Living & Learning. LC 90-85800. 224p. 1991. text ed. 19.95 (*0-9628624-0-1*) Bassi Bk.
Brady, Janeen. Show a Little Love. Grover, Nina, illus. 48p. (gr. k-6). 1981. songbk. 7.95 (*0-944803-26-1*); cassette 8.95 (*0-944803-28-8*) Brite Music.

—Standin' Tall Forgiveness. Wilson, Grant & Galloway, Neil, illus. 22p. (Orig.). (ps-6). 1981. pap. text ed. 1.50 activity bk. (*0-944803-39-3*); cassette & bk. 9.95 (*0-944803-40-7*) Brite Music.

—Standin' Tall Honesty. Wilson, Grant & Galloway, Neil, illus. 22p. (Orig.). (ps-6). 1981. pap. text ed. 1.50 activity bk. (*0-944803-37-7*); cassette & bk. 9.95 (*0-944803-38-5*) Brite Music.

—Standin' Tall Obedience. Wilson, Grant & Galloway, Neil, illus. 22p. (Orig.). (ps-6). 1981. pap. text ed. 1.50 activity bk. (*0-944803-35-0*); cassette & bk. 9.95 (*0-944803-36-9*) Brite Music.

Brady, Janeen & Woolley, Diane. Standin' Tall Dependability. Galloway, Neil, illus. 22p. (Orig.). (ps-6). 1984. pap. text ed. 1.50 activity bk. (*0-944803-59-8*); cassette & bk. 9.95 (*0-944803-60-1*) Brite Music.

—Standin' Tall Gratitude. Wilson, Grant, illus. 22p. (Orig.). (ps-6). 1982. pap. text ed. 1.50 activity bk. (*0-944803-48-2*); cassette & bk. 9.95 (*0-944803-49-0*) Brite Music.

—Standin' Tall Love. Wilson, Grant, illus. 22p. (Orig.). (ps-6). 1982. pap. text ed. 1.50 activity bk. (*0-944803-50-4*); cassette & bk. 9.95 (*0-944803-51-2*) Brite Music.

—Standin' Tall Self-Esteem. Wilson, Grant, illus. 22p. (Orig.). (ps-6). 1984. pap. text ed. 1.50 activity bk. (*0-944803-56-3*); cassette & bk. 9.95 (*0-944803-57-1*) Brite Music.

—Standin' Tall Service. Wilson, Grant, illus. 22p. (Orig.). (ps-6). 1984. pap. text ed. 1.50 activity bk. (*0-944803-52-0*); cassette & bk. 9.95 (*0-944803-53-9*) Brite Music.

Bright, Velma. What Would You Like to Be? Schultz, Patty, illus. 32p. (gr. 1). 1976. PLB 10.00 (*0-9605968-0-1*) Bright Bks.

Buerger, Jane. Obedience. rev. ed. Endres, Helen, illus. LC 80-39520. (SPA & ENG.). 32p. (ps-2). 1981. PLB 14.95 (*0-89565-206-4*) Childs World.

Burns, Marilyn. I Am Not a Short Adult: Getting Good at Being a Kid. (Illus.). (gr. 5 up). 1977. Little.

Caine, Geoffrey & Caiane, Renate N. Making Connections: Teaching & the Human Brain. 208p. (Orig.). (gr. 4-7). 1994. pap. 15.95 (*0-201-49088-9*) Addison-Wesley.

Cambridge, Barbara S. And This I Know: Affirmations for Children. rev. ed. Anderson, Lin, illus. 28p. 1987. pap. 6.95 (*0-317-91380-8*) CBridge Pubns.

Carlyle, Linda P. I Can Choose. 32p. 1992. pap. 5.95 (*0-8163-1082-3*) Pacific Pr Pub Assn.

Carswell, Evelyn & Bisignano, Judy. Living. Tom, Darcy, illus. 64p. (gr. 3-8). 1985. wkbk. 8.95 (*0-86653-332-X*, GA 679) Good Apple.

Cavanaugh, Joe & Dorn, Katie. Healing Hearts: A Young Person's Guide to Discovering the Goodness Within. Wright, Wendy, ed. (Illus.). 64p. (Orig.). (gr. 6 up). 1994. pap. text ed. 10.99 (*0-9640435-0-5*) Nantucket Pubng.

Joe Cavanaugh is a nationally recognized inspirational speaker specializing in youth issues. He was most recently featured on a PBS special, "Respectfully, Joe Cavanaugh," a program addressing self-esteem, values & goals of today's youth. HEALING HEARTS, his first book in a planned series, grew out of a need for young people to have a tool & ongoing journal to deal with these important issues. The testimonies of parents, teachers & students alike reiterate the power of his message. Tom E. McNellis, a parent, commented, "From a parent's perspective, Joe says so many things that we've wanted to say but are unable to say ourselves. He has a special talent & a very important message that should be heard by all." A junior high student's review says, "I learned a lot about my friends & about myself. I took away ideas & impressions that will last a lifetime." As Joe says on the first page of his book, "If I could sum up this book in a few words, it would be that its purpose is not to give you all the answers. Its purpose is to help you struggle through the questions. Questions about looking inside yourself & others & seeing the goodness more clearly." Call or write for information to order, Nantucket Publications, P.O. Box 1789, Minnetonka, MN 55345; 612-937-5492. This book is distributed by The Bookmen Inc. (800) 328-8411.
Publisher Provided Annotation.

Chaney, Casey. Ready, Willing & Terrified: A Coward's Guide to Risk-Taking. Moffett, Berdell & Rhiannon, Thea, eds. Craghead, Gary, illus. 144p. (Orig.). 1991. pap. 10.95 (*0-9626403-1-X*) Mocha Pub.

Chapian, Marie. Feeling Small... Walking Tall. 176p. (Orig.). (gr. 8 up). 1989. pap. 7.99 (*1-55661-029-7*) Bethany Hse.

Cohen, Susan & Cohen, Daniel. Teenage Competition: A Survival Guide. LC 86-24307. 156p. (gr. 7 up). 1986. 13.95 (*0-87131-487-8*) M Evans.

Cohn-Gilletly, Joanne. Ten Minutes with Me. 3rd ed. (Illus., Orig.). (gr. k-3). 1980. pap. 2.00 (*0-916634-05-1*) Double M Pr.

Coleman, William L. Entering the Teen Zone: Devotions to Guide You. LC 90-43092. 112p. (Orig.). (gr. 7-10). 1991. pap. 5.99 (*0-8066-2499-X*, 9-2499, Augsburg) Augsburg Fortress.

Community Intervention, Inc. Staff. Participant Guidebook: My Life... Right Now. (Illus.). 52p. (gr. 7-12). 1988. wkbk. 3.50 (*0-9613416-9-6*) Comm Intervention.

Cosby, Bill, et al. Changes: Becoming the Best You Can Be. rev. ed. Barr, Linda & Wojcicki, Marba, eds. Robison, Don, et al, illus. 196p. (gr. 6-8). 1988. pap. text ed. 6.85 (*0-933419-24-4*) Quest Intl.

Cosgrove, Stephen E. Ira Wordworthy. Edelson, Wendy, illus. 32p. (ps-3). 1990. PLB 14.95 (*0-89565-658-2*) Childs World.

—T. J. Flopp. Edelson, Wendy, illus. 32p. (ps-3). 1990. PLB 14.95 (*0-89565-660-4*) Childs World.

Cote. Curiosity, Reading Level 2. (Illus.). 32p. (gr. 1-4). 1989. PLB 15.94 (*0-86592-442-2*) Rourke Corp.

Crouthamel, Thomas G., Sr. It's OK. 2nd ed. Hasty, Patti, illus. LC 86-27694. 36p. (gr. 6 up). 1990. pap. 6.95 (*0-940701-18-9*) Keystone Pr.

Crowdy, Deborah. Pride. McCallum, Jodie, illus. LC 89-48107. (SPA & ENG.). 32p. (gr. k-3). 1990. PLB 14.95 (*0-89565-566-7*) Childs World.

Crum, Thomas F. Magic of Conflict Workshop for Young People. Heffernan, Cheryl, illus. (gr. 6-12). 1989. multi-media kit 49.95 (*1-877803-04-9*) AIKI Works.

Crutsinger, Carla. Teenage Connection: A Tool for Effective Teenage Communication. LC 87-73063. 225p. (gr. 7-12). 1987. pap. 13.95x (*0-944662-00-5*) Brainworks Inc.

Cummings, Rhoda & Fisher, Gary. The Survival Guide for Teenagers with LD: (Learning Differences) Espeland, Pamela, ed. LC 93-6798. (Illus.). 200p. (Orig.). (gr. 7 up). 1993. pap. 11.95 (*0-915793-51-2*); pap. 28.90 incl. audiocassettes (*0-915793-57-1*); audiocassettes 19.95 (*0-915793-56-3*) Free Spirit Pub.

Davenport, Terilyn A. Starting Out: Step-by-Step Guide for Teens Succeeding in the '90s. LC 93-87661. 320p. (Orig.). (gr. 11 up). 1994. 29.95 (*1-884573-09-6*); pap. 19.95 (*1-884573-10-X*) S-By-S Pubns.

Davis, Sandra P. That Special Touch. LC 89-92544. (Illus.). 140p. 1990. 39.95 (*0-9625232-0-8*) Special Touch.

Deaton, Wendy. My Own Thoughts on Stopping the Hurt. 32p. (gr. 2-6). 1993. wkbk. 5.95 (*0-89793-132-7*); write for info. practitioner packs (*0-89793-135-1*) Hunter Hse.

Delis-Abrams, Alexandra. ABC Feelings: A Coloring - Learning Book. rev. ed. Follendore, Joan, ed. Gurstein, Shari, illus. 64p. (gr. 3-8). 1991. pap. text ed. 7.95 (*1-879889-00-5*) Adage Pubns.

Dentemaro, Christine & Kranz, Rachel. Straight Talk about Student Life. LC 92-31488. 1993. write for info. (*0-8160-2735-8*) Facts on File.

Dolan, Edward F. Teenagers & Compulsive Gambling. LC 93-31956. (Illus.). 144p. (gr. 9-12). 1994. PLB 13.90 (*0-531-11100-8*) Watts.

Doud, Guy R. Stuff You Gotta Know: Straight Talk about Real-Life. LC 93-25113. (Illus.). 160p. (Orig.). (gr. 8-12). 1993. pap. 6.99 (*0-570-04622-X*) Concordia.

Eager, George B. Peer Pressure. Philbrook, Diana, illus. LC 93-80759. 144p. (gr. 6-12). 1994. 13.95 (*1-879224-17-8*); pap. 8.95 (*1-879224-13-5*) Mailbox.

Earle, Vana. Honesty. (Illus.). 64p. (gr. 7-12,RL 4-6). 1990. 14.95 (*0-8239-1109-8*) Rosen Group.

Educational Assessment Publishing Company Staff. Discover: Skills for Life, Level 8: Student Book. (Illus.). 240p. (gr. 8). 1991. text ed. 16.60 (*0-942277-32-5*) Am Guidance.

—Life Skills Handbook. (SPA., Illus.). 48p. (gr. 9-12). 1993. text ed. 6.00 wkbk. (*1-56269-090-6*); tchr's. manual, 72p. 9.00 (*1-56269-091-4*) Am Guidance.

—Parent - Child Learning Library: Honesty English Big Book. (Illus.). 32p. (gr. k-3). 1991. text ed. 16.95 (*0-942277-42-2*) Am Guidance.

—Parent - Child Learning Library: Honesty Spanish Big Book. (SPA., Illus.). 32p. (gr. k-3). 1991. text ed. 16.95 (*0-942277-41-4*) Am Guidance.

—Parent - Child Learning Library: Honesty Spanish Edition. (SPA., Illus.). 32p. (ps). 1991. text ed. 9.95 (*0-942277-87-2*) Am Guidance.

—Parent - Child Learning Library: Honesty. (Illus.). 32p. (ps-k). 1991. text ed. 9.95 (*0-942277-59-7*) Am Guidance.

—Parent - Child Learning Library: Responsibility English Big Book. (Illus.). 32p. 1991. text ed. 16.95 (*0-942277-44-9*) Am Guidance.

—Parent - Child Learning Library: Responsibility. (Illus.). 32p. (gr. k-3). 1991. text ed. 9.95 (*0-942277-58-9*) Am Guidance.

—Parent - Child Learning Library: Responsibility Spanish Big Book. (SPA., Illus.). 32p. (gr. k-3). 1991. text ed. 16.95 (*0-942277-45-7*) Am Guidance.

—Parent - Child Learning Library: Responsibility Spanish Edition. (SPA.). 32p. (ps). 1991. text ed. 9.95 (*0-942277-92-9*) Am Guidance.

—Skills for Life. (Illus.). (gr. 9-12). 1993. text ed. 18.50 (*1-56269-050-7*); tchr's. ed. 39.25 (*1-56269-051-5*); Total tchr. support system. 208.75 (*1-56269-052-3*) Am Guidance.

—Skills for Life. (Illus.). 48p. (gr. k). 1992. Spanish. text ed. 10.60 (*1-56269-000-0*); Spanish big bk., 64p. text ed. 76.95 (*1-56269-035-3*); Bilingual tchr's. ed., 80p. 31.21 (*1-56269-001-9*); Bilingual total tchr. support system, 168p. 92.35 (*1-56269-003-5*) Am Guidance.

—Skills for Life. (Illus.). 48p. (gr. 1). 1992. Spanish. text ed. 10.60 (*1-56269-005-1*); Spanish big bk., 64p. text ed. 76.95 (*1-56269-036-1*); Bilingual tchr's. ed., 96p. 31.21 (*1-56269-006-X*); Total tchr. support system, 168p. 92.35 (*1-56269-008-6*) Am Guidance.

—Skills for Life. (Illus.). 64p. (gr. 2). 1992. Spanish. text ed. 10.60 (*1-56269-010-8*); Bilingual tchr's. ed., 112p. 31.21 (*1-56269-011-6*); Bilingual total tchr. support system, 168p. 92.35 (*1-56269-013-2*) Am Guidance.

—Skills for Life. (Illus.). 80p. (gr. 3). 1992. Spanish. text ed. 11.45 (*1-56269-015-9*); Bilingual tchr's. ed., 112p. 34.18 (*1-56269-016-7*); 93.75 (*0-685-57572-1*) Bilingual total tchr. support system, 186p (*1-56269-018-3*) Am Guidance.

—Skills for Life. (Illus.). 116p. (gr. 4). 1992. Spanish. text ed. 11.45 (*1-56269-020-5*); Bilingual tchr's. ed., 116p. 34.18 (*1-56269-021-3*); Bilingual total tchr. support system, 216p. 93.75 (*0-685-57573-X*) Am Guidance.

—Skills for Life. (Illus.). 128p. (gr. 5). 1992. Spanish. text ed. 12.65 (*1-56269-025-6*); Bilingual tchr's. ed., 168p. 34.18 (*1-56269-026-4*); Bilingual total tchr. support system, 216p. 93.75 (*1-56269-028-0*) Am Guidance.

—Skills for Life. (Illus.). 144p. (gr. 6). 1992. Spanish. text ed. 13.65 (*1-56269-030-2*); Bilingual tchr's. ed., 168p. 34.18 (*1-56269-031-0*); Bilingual total tchr. support system, 224p. 93.75 (*1-56269-033-7*) Am Guidance.

Educational Assessment Publishing Co. Staff. Skills for Life. (Illus.). 240p. (gr. 7). 1992. Spanish. text ed. 16.60 (*1-56269-042-6*); Bilingual tchr's. ed., 256p. 39.25 (*1-56269-043-4*); Bilingual total tchr. support system, 396p. 208.15 (*1-56269-044-2*) Am Guidance.

Educational Assessment Publishing Company Staff. Skills for Life. (Illus.). 240p. (gr. 8). 1992. Spanish. text ed. 16.60 (*1-56269-045-0*); Bilingual tchr's. ed., 256p. 39.25 (*1-56269-046-9*); Bilingual total tchr. support system, 396p. 208.15 (*1-56269-047-7*) Am Guidance.

Elchoness, Monte. Why Do Kids Need Feelings? A Guide to Healthy Emotions. (Illus.). 96p. (Orig.). 1992. pap. 9.95 (*0-936781-07-6*) Monroe Pr.

Elliott, Paula. Every Day Can Feel Like Christmas: Color Your World with Love. Royall, Sandra, illus. 32p. (Orig.). 1991. pap. 4.95 (*1-879052-02-4*) Planetary Pubns.

Erickson, Mary. I Can Make God Glad! Reck, Sue, ed. Ebert, Len, illus. LC 93-33070. 32p. (ps-2). 1994. 9.99 (*0-7814-0102-X*, Chariot Bks) Chariot Family.

Erickson, P. C. Stand Tall. Pugh, Kayleen, illus. (Orig.). (gr. 4-8). 1978. pap. 2.95 (*0-89036-111-8*) Hawkes Pub Inc.

Evans, Pearl. Dancing with the Times: What's a Young Adult to Believe! Taylor, Richard, illus. 160p. (Orig.). (gr. 8 up). 1993. pap. 4.99 (*0-938453-05-X*) Small Helm Pr.

Everix, Nancy. More Windows to the World. Everix, Nancy, illus. 128p. (gr. 2-8). 1985. wkbk. 11.95 (*0-86653-316-8*, GA 640) Good Apple.

Father Flanagan's Boys' Home Staff. Basic Social Skills for Youth: A Handbook from Boys Town. Peter, Val J., intro. by. (Illus.). 38p. (Orig.). (gr. 6 up). 1992. pap. 3.95 (*0-685-68003-7*) Boys Town Pr.

Fiday, Beverly. Patience. Rigo, Christina L., illus. LC 86-12984. (SPA & ENG.). 32p. (ps-2). 1986. PLB 14.95 (*0-89565-358-3*) Childs World.

Fleming, Alice. What, Me Worry? How to Hang in When Your Problems Stress You Out. LC 91-31678. 96p. (gr. 7 up). 1992. SBE 13.95 (*0-684-19277-2*, Scribners Young Read) Macmillan Child Grp.

Frykman, John. The Hassle Handbook. rev. ed. LC 84-6851. (Illus.). 108p. 1988. 9.95 (*0-916147-02-9*) Regent Pr.

Gajewski, N. & Mayo, P. POW! Personal Power! (gr. 5-12). 1992. 39.00 (*0-930599-76-4*) Thinking Pubns.

Gajewski, Nancy & Mayo, Patty. SSS: Social Skill Strategies, Bk. A: A Curriculum for Adolescents. 336p. (gr. 5-12). 1989. pap. 33.00 (*0-930599-51-9*) Thinking Pubns.

Ganz, Yaffa. The Wonderful World We Live In. Ariel, Liat B., illus. 48p. (gr. k-6). 1989. 10.95 (*0-89906-964-9*); pap. 6.95 (*0-89906-965-7*) Mesorah Pubns.

Garnett, C. G. Great Adaptations in Life: Adapt to Life & Thrive: Children's Version, Vol. 1. (Illus., Orig.). (gr. k-6). 1993. pap. write for info. (*1-883709-21-0*) Gold Crest Pubns.

—Great Adaptations in Life: Adapt to Life & Thrive: Young Adult Version, Vol. 1. (Illus., Orig.). (gr. 7-12). 1993. pap. write for info. (*1-883709-11-3*) Gold Crest Pubns.

Gesme, Carole & Peterson, Larry. Help for Kids: Understanding Your Feelings about Moving. Schmoker, Lisa, ed. Lindstrom, Jack, illus. 56p. (gr. 1-12). 1992. spiral bound wkbk. 12.95 (*0-9633761-0-1*); spiral bound 8.95 (*0-9633761-1-X*) Pine Tr Pr MN.

Gibson, Christine R. & Hargrave, J. Michael. The Tator Tales: A Story & Activity Book on Handling Peer Pressure. Majewski, Chuck, illus. 51p. (gr. 3-5). 1988. pap. 6.95 (*0-9624285-0-7*) Tator Enterprises.

Girard, Linda W. Who Is a Stranger & What Should I Do? Levine, Abby, ed. Cogancherry, Helen, illus. LC 84-17313. 32p. (gr. 2-6). 1985. PLB 11.95 (*0-8075-9014-2*); pap. 4.95 (*0-8075-9016-9*) A Whitman.

Goffe, Toni. Bully for You. LC 91-9891. (gr. 4 up). 1991. 7.95 (*0-85953-365-4*); pap. 3.95 (*0-85953-355-7*) Childs Play.

Golant, Mitch & Crane, Bob. It's O. K. to Be Different. 128p. (gr. 1-5). 1988. pap. 4.95 (*0-8125-9462-2*) Tor Bks.

Goley. Cooperation, Reading Level 2. (Illus.). 32p. (gr. 1-4). 1989. PLB 15.94 (*0-86592-390-6*) Rourke Corp.

—Giving, Reading Level 2. (Illus.). 32p. (gr. 1-4). 1989. PLB 15.94 (*0-86592-392-2*); 11.95s.p. (*0-685-58782-7*) Rourke Corp.

—Joy, Reading Level 2. (Illus.). 32p. (gr. 1-4). 1989. PLB 15.74 (*0-86592-393-0*); 11.95s.p. (*0-685-58784-3*) Rourke Corp.

—Learning, Reading Level 2. (Illus.). 32p. (gr. 1-4). 1989. PLB 15.94 (*0-86592-396-5*); 11.95s.p. (*0-685-58785-1*) Rourke Corp.

—Responsibility, Reading Level 2. (Illus.). 32p. (gr. 1-4). 1989. PLB 14.60 (*0-86592-394-9*); 11.95s.p. (*0-685-58789-4*) Rourke Corp.

—Self Control, Reading Level 2. (Illus.). 32p. (gr. 1-4). 1989. PLB 15.94 (*0-86592-397-3*); 11.95s.p. (*0-685-58790-8*) Rourke Corp.

Goley, Elaine. Caring. (Illus.). 32p. (gr. 1-4). 1987. PLB 15.94 (*0-86592-381-7*); 11.95 (*0-685-67587-4*) Rourke Corp.

—Helping. (Illus.). 32p. (gr. 1-4). 1987. PLB 15.94 (*0-86592-384-1*); 11.95s.p. (*0-685-73889-2*) Rourke Corp.

—Honesty. (Illus.). 32p. (gr. 1-4). 1987. PLB 15.74 (*0-86523-857-X*); 11.95s.p. (*0-685-58144-6*) Rourke Corp.

—Kindness. (Illus.). 32p. (gr. 1-4). 1987. PLB 15.74 (*0-86592-383-3*); 11.95s.p. (*0-685-67579-3*) Rourke Corp.

—Learn the Value, 10 bks, Set I, Reading Level 2. (Illus.). 320p. (gr. 1-4). 1987. PLB 119.50s.p. (*0-685-58775-4*) Rourke Corp.

—Patience. (Illus.). 32p. (gr. 1-4). 1987. PLB 15.94 (*0-86592-379-5*); 11.95 (*0-685-67574-2*) Rourke Corp.

—Trust. (Illus.). 32p. (gr. 1-4). 1987. PLB 15.94 (*0-86592-378-7*); PLB 11.95s.p. (*0-685-67577-7*) Rourke Corp.

—Understanding Others. (Illus.). 32p. (gr. 1-4). 1987. PLB 15.94 (*0-86592-382-5*); PLB 11.95s.p. (*0-685-67588-2*) Rourke Corp.

Goley, Elaine, et al. Learn the Value, 18 bks, Set II, Reading Level 2. (Illus.). 576p. (gr. 1-4). 1989. Set. PLB 286.92 (*0-86592-391-4*); 215.10s.p. (*0-685-58776-2*) Rourke Corp.

Gordon, Michael. My Brother's a World-Class Pain: A Sibling's Guide to ADHD-Hyperactivity. Thomas, Sandra F., intro. by. Junco, Janet H., illus. 40p. (gr. 4 up). 1992. pap. 11.00 (*0-9627701-2-4*) GSI Pubns.

Gouge, Betty, et al. KidSkills Interpersonal Skill Series, Choices! Choices! Choices! Responsibility: Making & Living with Choices. Morse, J. Thomas, ed. Bleck, Linda & Bleck, Cathie, illus. LC 86-45001. 45p. (ps). 1986. PLB 8.95 (*0-934275-09-2*); bk. & cassette 11.95 (*0-934275-23-8*) Fam Skills.

—KidSkills Interpersonal Skill Series, My Feelings & Me: Feelings: Experiencing Feelings. Morse, J. Thomas, et al, eds. Bleck, Linda & Bleck, Cathie, illus. LC 85-81270. 44p. (ps). 1986. 8.95 (*0-934275-10-6*); bk. & cassette 11.95 (*0-934275-24-6*) Fam Skills.

—KidSkills Interpersonal Skill Series, The Rules at My House: Responsibility: Understanding & Accepting Limits. Morse, J. Thomas, et al, eds. Bleck, Linda & Bleck, Cathie, illus. 44p. (ps). 1986. PLB 8.95 (*0-934275-11-4*); bk. & cassette 11.95 (*0-934275-25-4*) Fam Skills.

—KidSkills Interpersonal Skill Series, Wonderful You: Self-Awareness: Accepting & Knowing Myself. Morse, J. Thomas, et al, eds. Bleck, Linda & Bleck, Cathie, illus. LC 85-81270. 42p. (ps). 1986. PLB 8.95 (*0-934275-12-2*); bk. & cassette 11.95 (*0-934275-26-2*) Fam Skills.

Grant, Robin R., Sr. RobinSays Try Womanhood Before Motherhood. 10p. 1992. pap. 2.25 (*0-9638384-0-7*, TX 3 303 786) RobinSays.

Greene, Leia A. The Bridge Between Two Worlds. Greene, Leia A., illus. 36p. (gr. k-12). 1992. pap. text ed. 4.95 (*1-880737-08-6*) Crystal Jrns.

—One Red Rose. Greene, Leia A., illus. (gr. k-12). 1992. pap. text ed. 4.95 (*1-880737-07-8*) Crystal Jrns.

Greenspan, Alice. Helping Is Fun. Hoha, Linda, illus. 32p. (gr. k-2). 1990. pasted 2.50 (*0-87403-027-7*, 24-03912) Standard Pub.

Grunsell, Angela. Bullying. LC 89-28332. (ps-3). 1990. PLB 11.40 (*0-531-17213-9*, Gloucester Pr) Watts.

Hafford, Jeanette N. Tiny's Self Help Books for Children. (Illus.). 18p. (Orig.). (gr. k-5). 1986. pap. 4.22 (*0-685-14506-9*) Tinys Self Help Bks.

Hall, Judy A. What Every Child Should Know & Do...for Surviving in the 90's: Big Book Version. Edwards, Juanita, ed. 24p. (gr. k-5). 1992. 18.95 (*0-9629597-3-1*) Personal Prods.

Harmon, Ed & Jarmin, Marge. Taking Charge of My Life: Choices, Changes & Me. Feign, Larry, illus. LC 88-988. 184p. (Orig.). (gr. 5-12). 1988. pap. 9.95 (*0-918588-10-3*) Barksdale Foun.

Harris, Gregg. The Twenty-One Rules of This House. rev. ed. 52p. 1993. pap. text ed. 11.00 (*0-923463-88-7*) Noble Pub Assocs.

Haubrich-Casperson, Jane & Van Nispen, Doug. Coping with Teen Gambling. LC 92-41549. 1993. 14.95 (*0-8239-1512-3*) Rosen Group.

Hazen, Barbara S. World, World, What Can I Do? LC 90-43764. 32p. (ps-3). 1991. 8.95 (*0-8192-1537-6*) Morehouse Pub.

Hochstatter, Daniel J., illus. Sammy's Excellent Real-Life Adventures. LC 92-40532. (gr. 5 up). 1993. 9.99 (*0-8407-9675-7*) Nelson.

Holland, Isabelle. Now Is Not Too Late. LC 79-22610. 160p. (gr. 4 up). 1991. pap. 3.95 (*0-688-10497-5*, Pub. by Beech Tree Bks) Morrow.

Hollis, Dave & Hollis, Dotty. Traditions of Honor. Woodburn, Mary S., ed. 297p. (Orig.). (gr. 8-12). 1994. pap. 12.95 (*0-9640894-1-6*) BPCOA. TRADITIONS OF HONOR is the first book to rewrite the "THREE R'S" of education to include RESPONSIBILITY, RESPECT & REPUTATION. It identifies, illustrates & examples the specific behaviors, beliefs & methods to easily instill & maintain the virtues of Honesty & Integrity, Self-discipline, Compassion, Life Long Learning, Friendship, Courage & Loyalty within our children. It deals directly with the realities of life & sets forth the rules of conduct to preserve our honor, dignity & fine reputation. It offers a soft but direct approach to resolving key issues & concerns between people, parents & peers. TRADITIONS OF HONOR sets forth the fundamental principles to building & maintaining a fine character in a highly changing & challenging world. A world that often places little or no value on the fine qualities of individuals. It helps our parents & children read through the many mixed messages of our world. TRADITIONS OF HONOR helps our children gain the kind of recognition & respect we all need & deserve for ourselves & our families. It is not a book of religious or political views & is strong in its convictions about basic rights & wrongs. It offers the fundamentals for responsible behavior.
Publisher Provided Annotation.

Holt, Janice M. Do I Like Myself? Coy, Venture, illus. LC 82-82332. 119p. (gr. 3-9). 1983. pap. 39.95 (*0-9608812-1-2*) Greenlf Pubns.

Hyde, Margaret O. Is This Kid "Crazy"? Understanding Unusual Behavior. LC 83-16916. 96p. (gr. 5-9). 1983. 12.00 (*0-664-32707-9*, Westminster) Westminster John Knox.

Hyde, Margaret O. & Forsyth, Elizabeth H. The Violent Mind. LC 91-18566. 144p. (gr. 9-12). 1991. PLB 14.40 (*0-531-11060-5*) Watts.

Institute for Women's Policy Research, The Young Women's Project Staff. The Young Women's Handbook: Beyond Surviving in the 90s. Moritz, Nadia, intro. by. 675p. (Orig.). (gr. 10 up). 1991. pap. 30.00 (*1-878428-05-5*) Inst Womens Policy Rsch.

Johnsen, Karen. The Trouble with Secrets. Forssell, Linda, illus. LC 85-51803. 32p. (Orig.). (ps-3). 1986. lib. bdg. 15.95 (*0-943990-23-8*); pap. 4.95 (*0-943990-22-X*) Parenting Pr.

Johnson, Daniel S. Creative Rebellion: Positive Options for Teens in the 90s. LC 91-61346. (Illus.). 160p. (gr. 6-12). 1991. pap. 11.95 (*0-922848-11-4*) Mystic Garden.

Johnson, Kendall. Turning Yourself Around: Self-Help Strategies for Troubled Teens. LC 92-4477. 224p. (gr. 7-12). 1992. 9.95 (*0-89793-092-4*) Hunter Hse.

Johnson, Linda C. Responsibility. (Illus.). 64p. (gr. 7-12, RL 4-6). 1990. PLB 14.95 (*0-8239-1107-1*) Rosen Group.

Johnson, Mary H. You Are Special: A Child's Guide for Successful Living. Bennefield, Robin M., ed. Carr, Walt, illus. 36p. (Orig.). (gr. 4-7). 1993. write for info. wkbk. (*0-911849-02-5*) Comptex Assocs Inc.

Jones, Bill. No Problem! 176p. 1992. pap. 4.99 (*0-89693-613-9*) SP Pubns.

Joyer, Mike & Roberts, Zack. One Hundred Excuses for Kids. Black, Cynthia, ed. Kerr, Kathleen, illus. 96p. (Orig.). 1990. pap. 4.95 (*0-941831-48-5*) Beyond Words Pub.

Kahaner, Ellen. Courage. (Illus.). 64p. (gr. 7-12,RL 4-6). 1990. PLB 14.95 (*0-8239-1112-8*) Rosen Group.

Kalb, Jonah & Viscott, David. What Every Kid Should Know. Kuchera, John & Margolis, Al, illus. 128p. (gr. 4-7). 1992. pap. 4.80 (*0-395-62983-7*, Sandpiper) HM.

Kalman, Bobbie. Come to My Place. (Illus.). 32p. (gr. k-2). 1985. 15.95 (*0-86505-062-7*); pap. 7.95 (*0-86505-086-4*) Crabtree Pub Co.

—Happy to Be Me. (Illus.). 32p. (gr. k-2). 1985. 15.95 (*0-86505-060-0*); pap. 7.95 (*0-86505-084-8*) Crabtree Pub Co.

Kaplan, Leslie S. Coping with Peer Pressure. rev. ed. 140p. 1993. lib. bdg. 14.95 (*0-8239-1650-2*) Rosen Group.

Keim, Will S. The Education of Character: Lesson for Beginners. Prosser, Donna, illus. Pittman, Bruce, intro. by. (Illus.). 96p. 1992. 14.95 (*0-9631834-0-0*) Viaticum Pr.

Kennemuth, Caroline. Kate Gleeson's What Shall I Do Today? (ps-3). 1993. pap. 1.95 (*0-307-10551-2*, Golden Pr) Western Pub.

—Kate Gleeson's Wonderful You. (ps-3). 1993. pap. 1.95 (*0-307-10550-4*, Golden Pr) Western Pub.

Kerr, M. E. Me Me Me Me Me: Not a Novel. LC 82-48521. 224p. (gr. 7 up). 1994. pap. 4.95 (*0-06-446163-7*, Trophy) HarpC Child Bks.

Kino Learning Center Staff & Sanders, Corinne. My Choices & Decisions. Mirocha, Kay, illus. 64p. (gr. 5-9). 1987. pap. 7.95 (*0-86653-421-0*, GA1031) Good Apple.

Kleckner. Humor, Reading Level 2. (Illus.). 32p. (gr. 1-4). 1989. PLB 15.74 (*0-86592-399-X*); lib. bdg. 11.95 (*0-685-58783-5*) Rourke Corp.

Lang, Denise V. But Everyone Else Looks So Sure of Themselves: A Guide to Surviving the Teen Years. LC 90-39087. (Illus.). 160p. (Orig.). (gr. 7 up). 1991. pap. 9.95 (*1-55870-177-X*, 70012) Shoe Tree Pr.

Lehrman, Fredric. Loving the Earth. (Illus.). 48p. (gr. 6-12). 1990. 14.95 (*0-89087-603-7*) Celestial Arts.

LeLoeuff, Jean. La Aventura de la Vida (The Adventure of Life) Puebla, Luis M., tr. Veronique, illus. (SPA.). 96p. (gr. 4 up). 1992. PLB 15.90 (*1-56294-177-1*) Millbrook Pr.

Lenett, Robin, et al. Sometimes It's O. K. to Tell Secrets! 128p. (Orig.). 1986. pap. 3.95 (*0-8125-9454-1*) Tor Bks.

Letch, Rachael. Special People. LC 90-48944. (gr. 4 up). 1990. 7.95 (*0-85953-360-3*); pap. 3.95 (*0-85953-350-6*) Childs Play.

Licata, Renora. Everything You Need to Know about Anger. rev. ed. (gr. 7-12). 1994. PLB 14.95 (*0-8239-2036-4*) Rosen Group.

Links, Marty & Knight, Marilyn. Yes I Can. (Illus.). 1990. 4.95 (*0-685-57229-3*); poster 4.95 (*0-685-57230-7*) Arts Pubns.

McAllister, Dawson. Please Don't Tell My Parents. 176p. 1992. pap. 8.99 (*0-8499-3311-0*) Word Inc.

McDonnell, Janet. Success. Hohag, Linda, illus. LC 88-4348. (SPA & ENG.). 32p. (ps-2). 1988. PLB 14.95 (*0-89565-376-1*) Childs World.

—Thankfulness. Hohag, Linda, illus. LC 88-2657. (SPA & ENG.). 32p. (ps-2). 1988. PLB 14.95 (*0-89565-375-3*) Childs World.

McElmurry, Mary A. Cooperating. Tom, Darcy, illus. 64p. (gr. 3-8). 1985. wkbk. 8.95 (*0-86653-334-6*, GA 680) Good Apple.

McGuire, J. Victor. No Negatives: A Positive Guide to Successful Leadership. Prado, Jan, ed. Giblin, Tom, pref. by. 130p. (Orig.). (gr. 9-12). 1989. pap. 7.95 wkbk. (*0-685-26846-2*) Spice Pr.

McMillan, Kate. Great Advice from Lila Fenwick. DeGroat, Diane, illus. LC 87-24513. 160p. (gr. 3-7). 1988. PLB 11.89 (*0-8037-0532-8*) Dial Bks Young.

Making Parents Proud. 48p. (gr. 6-8). 1990. pap. 8.99 (*1-55945-107-6*) Group Pub.

Mandino, Og. Og Mandino's Great Trilogy. 1993. 12.98 (*0-8119-0428-8*) Lifetime.

Manes, Stephen. Be a Perfect Person in Just Three Days. (ps-7). 1987. pap. 2.50 (*0-553-15367-6*) Bantam.

Margulies, Alice. Compassion. (Illus.). 64p. (gr. 7-12,RL 4-6). 1990. PLB 14.95 (*0-8239-1108-X*) Rosen Group.

Martin, Michael. The Good Behavior Book. Harris, Stephen & Brower, Nancy, eds. Shea, Mikki, illus. (Orig.). (ps up). 1988. pap. 10.95 (*0-9621191-7-2*) Behavior Products.

Maxfield, Michael & Maxfield, Myrica. The Sound of Success: Musical Motivation. 32p. 1992. 19.95 (*0-9634682-1-9*, 232822) Myrichael Way.

Mayo, Patty & Gajewski, Nancy. SSS: Social Skill Strategies, Book B: A Curriculum for Adolescents. Krause, Brad, illus. 350p. (Orig.). (gr. 5-12). 1989. pap. 33.00x (*0-930599-52-7*) Thinking Pubns.

Milios, Rita. Independent Living. Rosen, Ruth, ed. (gr. 7-12). 1992. 13.95 (*0-8239-1454-2*) Rosen Group.

Min, Kellet I. Modern Informative Nursery Rhymes: Values. Hansen, Heidi, illus. 32p. (Orig.). (ps-3). 1989. pap. 7.95 (*0-685-26431-9*) Rhyme & Reason.

Moncure, Jane B. Growing Strong Inside. Hohag, Linda, illus. LC 85-10341. 32p. (ps-2). 1985. PLB 14.95 (*0-89565-333-8*) Childs World.

—Happy Healthkins. Axeman, Lois, illus. LC 82-14794. (ps-2). 1982. PLB 13.95 (*0-89565-243-9*) Childs World.

—Honesty. rev. ed. Karch, Paul, illus. LC 80-39571. (ENG & SPA.). 32p. (ps-2). 1981. PLB 14.95 (*0-89565-203-X*) Childs World.

—Kindness. rev. ed. Hohag, Linda S., illus. LC 80-39535. (SPA & ENG.). 32p. (ps-2). 1981. PLB 14.95 (*0-89565-204-8*) Childs World.

Morse, J. Thomas, et al. KidSkills Interpersonal Skill Series, An Island Adventure: Self-Esteem: Being a Friend to Myself. Gouge, Betty, et al, eds. Bleck, Cathie, illus. LC 85-45429. 47p. (gr. 2-3). 1985. PLB 9.95 (*0-934275-01-7*); bk. & cassette 13.95 (*0-934275-14-9*) Fam Skills.

—KidSkills Interpersonal Skill Series, The Feeling Fun House: Feelings: Dealing with Feelings. Gouge, Betty, et al, eds. Bleck, Cathie, illus. LC 85-45423. 45p. (gr. 2-3). 1985. PLB 9.95 (*0-934275-03-3*); bk. & cassette 13.95 (*0-934275-17-3*) Fam Skills.

—KidSkills Interpersonal Skill Series, The Land of Listening: Listening: Getting & Giving Attention. Gouge, Betty, et al, eds. Bleck, Cathie, illus. LC 85-45429. 45p. (gr. 2-3). 1985. PLB 9.95 (*0-934275-00-9*); bk. & cassette 13.95 (*0-934275-15-7*) Fam Skills.

Murphy, Elspeth C. Sometimes I'm Good, Sometimes I'm Bad. Nelson, Jane, illus. 24p. (ps-2). 1981. pap. 3.99 (*0-89191-368-8*, 53686, Chariot Bks) Chariot Family.

Navarra, Tova. On My Own: Helping Kids Help Themselves. Kerr, Tom, illus. 128p. (gr. 2-8). 1993. pap. 6.95 (*0-8120-1563-0*) Barron.

—Playing It Smart: What to Do When You're on Your Own. Kerr, Tom, illus. 128p. (gr. 2-8). 1989. 12.95 (*0-8120-6131-4*) Barron.

Neilson, Stefan & Thoelke, Shay. Color Me Winning. (Illus.). 50p. (gr. 4-6). 1989. spiral bdg., adult wkbk. 20.00 (*1-880830-02-7*) Aeon-Hierophant.

Nelson, JoAnne. It's up to Me! Magnuson, Diana, illus. LC 93-9349. 1994. 5.95 (*0-935529-63-2*) Comprehen Health Educ.

Newbury, Kenneth. Life Skills Handbook. (Illus.). 48p. (gr. 9-12). 1993. text ed. 6.00 wkbk. (*1-56269-060-4*); tchr's. manual, 72p. 9.00 (*1-56269-061-2*) Am Guidance.

Nielsen, Shelly. Caring. Wallner, Rosemary, ed. LC 91-73044. 1992. 13.99 (*1-56239-064-3*) Abdo & Dghtrs.

—Manners. Wallner, Rosemary, ed. LC 91-73042. 1992. 13.99 (*1-56239-066-X*) Abdo & Dghtrs.

—Sharing. Wallner, Rosemary, ed. LC 91-73045. 1992. 13.99 (*1-56239-063-5*) Abdo & Dghtrs.

Noorlun, Lyle J. I Can-Can. 131p. (gr. 9 up). 1989. incl. cassette 16.95 (*1-877616-00-1*) Wholeness Intl.

O'Toole, Donna R. Growing Through Grief: A K-Twelve Curriculum to Help Young People Through All Kinds of Loss. rev. ed. McWhirter, Kore L., illus. 392p. (gr. k-12). 1989. pap. 59.95 3-ring bdr. (*1-878321-00-5*, Mntn Rainbow) Rainbow NC.

Oxenbury, Helen. Eating Out. (Illus.). 24p. (ps-1). 1994. pap. 3.99 (*0-14-054948-X*, Puff Pied Piper) Puffin Bks.

Packer, Alex J. Bringing up Parents: The Teenager's Handbook. Espeland, Pamela, ed. Pulver, Harry, Jr., illus. LC 92-36625. 272p. (gr. 7 up). 1993. pap. 12.95 (*0-915793-48-2*) Free Spirit Pub.

Palumbo, Thomas J. Thursday Think Time. Hyndman, Kathryn, illus. 64p. (gr. 3-8). 1985. wkbk. 8.95 (*0-86653-311-7*, GA 650) Good Apple.

Parsley, Bonnie M. The Choice Is Yours: A Teenager's Guide to Self-Discovery, Relationships, Values, & Spiritual Growth. 160p. (Orig.). 1992. pap. 9.00 (*0-671-75046-1*, Fireside) S&S Trade.

Pemberton, Nancy & Riehecky, Janet. Responsibility. Hohag, Linda, illus. LC 87-37557. (SPA & ENG.). 32p. (ps-2). 1988. PLB 14.95 (*0-89565-418-0*) Childs World.

Perez, Demetrio, Jr. Citizens Training Handbook-Manual de Formacion Ciudadana: Discipline-Moral-Covism-Urbanity. (SPA & ENG., Illus.). 315p. 1991. 25.00 (*0-9628780-0-6*) Ed Lncln-Mrt.

Peternel, Carolyn R. & Ahern, James. The I Like to Go to School Book. (Illus.). 36p. (Orig.). (gr. k-2). 1983. pap. 2.95 (*0-9612060-0-4*) Primary Progs.

Peterson, Lorraine. If the Devil Made You Do It, You Blew It. 192p. (Orig.). (gr. 8 up). 1989. pap. 7.99 (*1-55661-052-1*) Bethany Hse.

Petrucelli. Consideration, Reading Level 2. (Illus.). 32p. (gr. 1-4). 1989. PLB 15.94 (*0-86592-443-0*); lib. bdg. 11.95 (*0-685-58778-9*) Rourke Corp.

—Loyalty, Reading Level 2. (Illus.). 32p. (gr. 1-4). 1989. PLB 15.94 (*0-86592-441-4*); 11.95s.p. (*0-685-58786-X*) Rourke Corp.

Pincus, Debbie. Feeling Good about Yourself. (Illus.). 96p. (gr. 3-8). 1990. 10.95 (*0-86653-516-0*, GA 1139) Good Apple.

Plastow, John R. Football, Pizza & Success! 130p. (Orig.). (gr. 7-12). 1987. pap. 5.95 (*0-937382-03-5*) Rhinos Pr.

Plattner, Sandra S. Connecting with Myself. (ps-k). 1991. pap. 10.95 (*0-86653-986-7*) Fearon Teach Aids.

Powell, Richard. How to Deal with Parents. Snow, Alan, illus. LC 91-14997. 24p. (gr. k-3). 1992. lib. bdg. 9.59 (*0-8167-2418-0*); pap. text ed. 2.95 (*0-8167-2419-9*) Troll Assocs.

Prather, Hugh E., Jr. Circle of a Thought. 2nd, rev. ed. Helberg, Bob, ed. LC 87-73314. 80p. (gr. 9-12). 1987. pap. 7.95 (*0-944944-00-0*) Amethyst Aura.

Reef, Catherine. Think Positive: Cope with Stress. LC 93-3973. (gr. 4-7). 1993. 15.95 (*0-8050-2443-3*) TFC Bks NY.

Reihecky, Janet. Cooperation. Hutton, Kathryn, illus. LC 89-48284. (ENG & SPA.). 32p. (ps-2). 1990. PLB 14.95 (*0-89565-565-9*) Childs World.

Reilly, Jim, et al. Life & Works, 6 bks, Set II. (Illus.). 672p. (gr. 7 up). 1990. Set. PLB 119.64 (*0-86593-015-5*); Set. PLB 89.70s.p. (*0-685-36350-3*) Rourke Corp.

Riehecky, Janet. Good Sportsmanship. Rigo, Cristina, illus. LC 89-29663. (ENG & SPA.). 32p. (ps-2). 1990. PLB 14.95 (*0-89565-563-2*) Childs World.

—Sharing. Rigo, Christina, illus. LC 87-26811. (SPA & ENG.). 32p. (ps-2). 1988. PLB 14.95 (*0-89565-416-4*) Childs World.

Riley, Sue. Help! LC 77-16030. (Illus.). (ps-2). 1978. PLB 12.95 (*0-89565-012-6*) Childs World.

—Sharing. LC 77-16293. (Illus.). (ps-2). 1978. PLB 12.95 (*0-89565-015-0*) Childs World.

—Sorry. LC 77-16811. (Illus.). (ps-2). 1978. PLB 12.95 (*0-89565-013-4*) Childs World.

Ross, Sandra J. Visiting the Nicelies: A Lil'l Charmers Book. (Illus.). 60p. (Orig.). (gr. 3-7). 1991. pap. 5.95 (*1-881235-00-9*) Creat Opport.

Roth-Nelson, Stephanie. S. E. E. K. Self-Esteem Enhancement Kit. Zilis, Tom, illus. LC 93-29345. 176p. (Orig.). (gr. 6-12). 1993. pap. 14.95 (*0-942097-49-1*) BPPbks.

S.E.E.K. belongs in school & resource agency libraries. S.E.E.K. sparks discussion about emotions, helps teens practice self-respect & respect for others, deal with anger, examine their beliefs & values. Teens like its "short attention-span" concept, examples & illustrations. "With a refreshing & straightforward style, Roth-Nelson speaks to teens in a language they can understand. No issue is too sensitive or too weird: AIDS, sex, pregnancy, gangs, depression, school. This workbook will stimulate teens to look at themselves & their world in a new & empowering way. Educators, therapists & parents will also find much value here." (NAPRA). Middle, high school, health & special education teachers, counselors & dropout prevention & drug-free schools coordinators use S.E. E.K. U.S. & Canadian juvenile detention facilities & residential treatment centers use it, too. The 123-page Facilitator's Guide (ISBN 0-9642097-48-3, $29.95) makes S.E.E.K. perfect for groups. Session plans for each section offer 38 group activities using role playing, art, discussions, movies, field trips, planning, visualization activities & 42 reproducible masters for handouts. Guide & 10 non-consumable workbooks: $120. Training available, too. For information or to order, contact Roth-Nelson Consulting, Box 104, Louisville, CO 80027, 1-800-200-0367, or Bookpeople, Moving Books or DeVorss.

Publisher Provided Annotation.

Rubly-Burggraff, Roberta. Look Who's Drivin' the Bus. Robbins-Ptak, Elizabeth, illus. 150p. (Orig.). (gr. 9 up). 1993. pap. 29.95 (*0-937997-25-0*) Hi-Time Pub.

Samuelson, Rita. Sound Strategist. 86p. (gr. k-12). 1989. pap. 35.00 (*0-930599-50-0*) Thinking Pubns.

Sanders, Bill. Life, Sex & Everything in Between: Straight on Answers to the Questions That Trouble You Most. LC 90-49951. 160p. (Orig.). 1991. pap. 7.99 (*0-8007-5385-2*) Revell.

Sanders, Corinne. Choosing. Tom, Darcy, illus. 64p. (gr. 3-8). 1985. wkbk. 8.95 (*0-86653-333-8*, GA 677) Good Apple.

Schenkerman, Rona D. Growing up with Peer Pressure. 16p. (gr. 3-8). 1993. 1.95 (*1-56688-109-9*) Bur For At-Risk.

Schleifer, Jay. Citizenship. (Illus.). 64p. (gr. 7-12,RL 4-6). 1990. PLB 14.95 (*0-8239-1113-6*) Rosen Group.

Schliefer, Jay. The Work Ethic. (gr. 7-12). 1991. PLB 14.95 (*0-8239-1227-2*) Rosen Group.

Schmidt, Fran & Friedman, Alice. Creative Conflict Solving for Kids: Grades 3-4. 2nd ed. 90p. (gr. 3-4). 1993. Tchr's ed., incl. poster. 21.95 (*1-878227-17-3*); Wkbk. 11.95 (*0-685-64734-X*) Peace Educ.

—Peacemaking Skills for Little Kids. 2nd ed. (Illus.). 76p. (ps-2). 1993. Tchr's ed., incl. puppet, cass. & poster. 54.95 (*1-878227-16-5*); Wkbk. 11.95 (*1-878227-15-7*) Peace Educ.

Schwartz, Linda. What Would You Do? A Kid's Guide to Tricky & Sticky Situations. Armstrong, Beverly, illus. LC 90-63597. 184p. (gr. 3-7). 1991. pap. 9.95 (*0-88160-196-9*, LW294) Learning Wks.

Shank, Charles C. Wisdom Book for Children. 1993. pap. 7.95 (*0-8059-3356-5*) Dorrance.

Shapiro, Lawrence E. Jumpin' Jake Settles Down: A Workbook for Active Impulsive Kids. Shore, Hennie, ed. (Illus., Orig.). (gr. k-4). 1994. pap. 15.00 (*1-882732-11-1*) Ctr Applied Psy.

Sharma, Vijai P. Insane Jealousy: The Causes, Outcomes, & Solutions When Jealousy Gets Out of Hand: The Triangle of the Mind. Munro, Alistair, intro. by. 224p. (Orig.). (gr. 7-9). 1991. pap. text ed. 16.95 (*0-9628382-6-8*) Mind Pubns.

Shaw, Diana. Make the Most of a Good Thing: You! (gr. 5-9). 1986. (Joy St Bks) Little.

Siede, George & Preis, Donna, photos by. My Day: Active Minds. Schwager, Istar, contrib. by. (Illus.). 24p. (ps-3). 1992. PLB 9.95 (*1-56674-002-9*) Forest Hse.

Sims, Alicia M. Am I Still a Sister? 3th ed. Maus, Jim, illus. Sims, Darcie D., intro. by. LC 87-71613. (Illus.). 48p. (gr. k-9). 1993. pap. 5.00 (*0-9618995-0-6*) Big A NM.

Smith, Barry. A Child's Guide to Bad Behavior. Smith, Barry, illus. 32p. (ps). 1991. 9.70 (*0-395-57435-8*, Sandpiper) HM.

Smith, Wendell. The Roots of Character. (Illus.). 1987. tchr's. ed. 37.95 (*0-914936-90-5*); student wkbk., 176p. 11.95 (*0-914936-89-1*) Bible Temple.

Snider, Dee & Bashe, Philip. Dee Snider's Teenage Survival Guide. LC 86-32963. (gr. 6-12). 1987. (Dolp); pap. 8.95 (*0-385-23900-9*, Dolp) Doubleday.

Somers, Adele. Learn from Everyone! Practical Guidelines to Living. Somers, Stanley E., illus. 192p. (Orig.). (gr. 8 up). 1985. pap. 7.95 (*0-9615032-0-3*) World Relations Pr.

Squire-Buresh, Anne L. To Touch the Sky. LC 89-50050. 44p. (gr. k-3). 1989. 5.95 (*1-55523-224-8*) Winston-Derek.

Starbuck, Marnie. The Gladimals Practice Being Kind. (Illus.). 16p. 1990. 0.75 (*1-56456-209-3*, 479) W Gladden Found.

Students at Risk: Winning Colors Power Pack. (gr. 6-12). 1990. spiral bdg., tchr's. ed., 87p. 30.00 (*1-880830-10-8*); spiral bdg., wkbk., 56p. 20.00 (*1-880830-11-6*) Aeon-Hierophant.

Taylor-Gerdes, Elizabeth. Straight Up! A Teenager's Guide to Taking Charge of Your Life. Crouse, Jane, ed. Harris, Cortrell, illus. 110p. (gr. 7-12). 1994. pap. 9.95 (*1-885242-00-X*) Lindsey Pubng.

STRAIGHT UP! is a personal guide that provides teenagers the tools necessary to help them overcome the many barriers they face daily with courage & wisdom. Tools needed to help them expand their potential to be winners in life. Through timeless wisdom & practical tools, STRAIGHT UP! helps youths discover they have the personal power to take control of their lives in these forceful times. This book describes today's world with its great opportunities & pressure. It explains a teenager's role in this world. It also explains the important lessons that are passed on from their ancestors. STRAIGHT UP! discusses the 10 universal laws of mind & spirit that are operating in their lives at this very moment & at their command. It shows teens how to use these laws to enhance their lives regardless of race, gender, education or social status. STRAIGHT UP! is written by Dr. Elizabeth Taylor-Gerdes, a recognized leader in the fields of personal development, motivation & metaphysics. She

received her Master's Degree from the University of San Francisco & Doctorate from Union Institute in Cincinnati. She counsels & conducts workshops in self-esteem, personal management & professional development.
Publisher Provided Annotation.

Terkel, Susan N. Ethics. 144p. (gr. 5 up). 1992. 15.00 (*0-525-67371-7*, Lodestar Bks) Dutton Child Bks.
Thompson, Merita L. & Strange, Johanna. Discover: Skills for Life, Level K: Pupil Edition. (Illus.). 48p. (gr. k). 1991. text ed. 10.60 (*0-942277-00-7*) Am Guidance.
—Discover: Skills for Life, Level K: Spanish Home Worksheets. (SPA., Illus.). 7p. (gr. k). 1991. text ed. 7.55 (*0-942277-56-2*) Am Guidance.
—Discover: Skills for Life, Level K: Student Edition Big Book. (Illus.). 48p. (gr. k). 1991. text ed. 76.95 (*0-942277-88-0*) Am Guidance.
—Discover: Skills for Life, Level 1: Pupil Book. (Illus.). 48p. (gr. 1). 1991. text ed. 10.60 (*0-942277-04-X*) Am Guidance.
—Discover: Skills for Life, Level 1: Spanish Home Worksheets. (SPA., Illus.). 7p. (gr. 1). 1991. text ed. 7.55 (*0-942277-81-3*) Am Guidance.
—Discover: Skills for Life, Level 1: Student Edition Big Book. (Illus.). 64p. (gr. 1). 1991. text ed. 76.95 (*0-942277-43-0*) Am Guidance.
—Discover: Skills for Life, Level 2: Spanish Home Worksheet. (SPA., Illus.). 7p. (gr. 2). 1991. text ed. 7.55 (*0-942277-82-1*) Am Guidance.
—Discover: Skills for Life, Level 2: Student Book. (Illus.). 64p. (gr. 2). 1991. text ed. 10.60 (*0-942277-08-2*) Am Guidance.
—Discover: Skills for Life, Level 3: Spanish Home Worksheet. (SPA., Illus.). 7p. (gr. 3). 1991. text ed. 7.55 (*0-942277-83-X*) Am Guidance.
—Discover: Skills for Life, Level 3: Student Book. (Illus.). 80p. (gr. 3). 1991. text ed. 11.45 (*0-942277-12-0*) Am Guidance.
—Discover: Skills for Life, Level 4: Spanish Home Worksheets. (SPA., Illus.). 7p. (gr. 4). 1991. text ed. 7.55 (*0-942277-84-8*) Am Guidance.
—Discover: Skills for Life, Level 4: Student Book. (Illus.). 80p. (gr. 4). 1991. text ed. 11.45 (*0-942277-16-3*) Am Guidance.
—Discover: Skills for Life, Level 5: Spanish Home Worksheets. (SPA., Illus.). 7p. (gr. 5). 1991. text ed. 7.55 (*0-942277-85-6*) Am Guidance.
—Discover: Skills for Life, Level 5: Student Book. (Illus.). 128p. (gr. 5). 1991. text ed. 12.65 (*0-942277-20-1*) Am Guidance.
—Discover: Skills for Life, Level 6: Spanish Home Worksheets. (SPA., Illus.). 7p. (gr. 6). 1991. text ed. 7.55 (*0-942277-86-4*) Am Guidance.
—Discover: Skills for Life, Level 6: Student Book. (Illus.). 144p. (gr. 6). 1991. text ed. 13.65 (*0-942277-24-4*) Am Guidance.
—Skills for Life. (Illus.). 168p. (gr. 6). 1991. tchr's. ed. 34.18 (*0-942277-25-2*) Am Guidance.
Tindall, Judith & Salmon-White, Shirley. Peers Helping Peers Program for the Preadolescent: Student Workbook. LC 90-80478. x, 230p. (Orig.). (gr. 4-7). 1990. perforated 3-hole punched 15.95 (*1-55959-010-6*) Accel Devel.
Tindall, Judith A. Peer Power, Bk. 1: Strategies for the Professional Leader. 3rd ed. 200p. (Orig.). (gr. 7 up). 1994. pap. text ed. 16.95 (*1-55959-058-0*) Accel Devel.
—Peer Power, Bk. 1: Workbook. 3rd ed. 330p. (gr. 7 up). 1994. pap. 16.95 (*1-55959-057-2*) Accel Devel.
University of Mexico City Staff, tr. Mi Dia: Mentes Activas. Siede, George & Preis, Donna, photos by. Schwager, Istar, contrib. by. (SPA., Illus.). 24p. (ps-8). 1992. PLB 11.95 (*1-56674-038-X*) Forest Hse.
Vandenburg, Mary L. Coping with Being Shy. Rosen, Ruth, ed. (gr. 7-12). 1992. 14.95 (*0-8239-1425-9*) Rosen Group.
Van Kleef Douthit, Gretchen. Inside Out: My Book about Who I Am & How I Feel. 90p. 1991. perfect bdg. 8.00 (*0-89486-757-1*, T5151) Hazelden.
Venti, Pamela R. Why Should I? Asks Jeremy. Spiers, John, illus. 32p. (gr. 1-3). 1990. PLB 13.95 (*0-89565-700-7*) Childs World.
Walter, Nancy L. Inside of Me. Walter, Nancy L., photos by. (Illus.). 48p. (ps-3). 1993. pap. 19.95 (*0-9635127-9-X*) Naturally by Nan.
Wassermann, Selma & Wassermann, Jack. The Book of Deciding. Smith, Dennis, illus. LC 89-78073. (gr. k-3). 1990. lib. bdg. 12.85 (*0-8027-6952-7*); pap. 4.95 (*0-8027-9456-4*) Walker & Co.
—The Book of Judging. Smith, Dennis, illus. 32p. (gr. k-3). 1990. lib. bdg. 12.85 (*0-8027-6950-0*); pap. 4.95 (*0-8027-9455-6*) Walker & Co.
Wayman, Joe. Colors of My Rainbow. (Illus.). 36p. (gr. k-8). 1988. pap. 7.95 (*0-945799-03-9*) Audio cassette 9.95. Pieces of Lrning.
—I Like Me. (Illus.). 36p. (gr. k-8). 1988. pap. 7.95 (*0-945799-02-0*) Audio cassette 9.95. Pieces of Lrning.
Whitefeather, Willy. Willy Whitefeather's River Book for Kids. Whitefeather, Willy, illus. LC 93-38686. 128p. (Orig.). (gr. 1-8). 1994. pap. 11.95 (*0-943173-94-9*) Harbinger AZ.
Wirths, Claudine G. & Bowman-Kruhm, Mary. Where's My Other Sock? How to Get Organized & Drive Your Parents & Teachers Crazy. Coxe, Molly, illus. LC 88-39338. 128p. (gr. 5 up). 1989. (Crowell Jr Bks); PLB 13.89 (*0-690-04667-7*, Crowell Jr Bks) HarpC Child Bks.
Wise, C. Dexter, III. Be a Man: Reflections on the Meaning of Manhood in Our Day (An Outline) 30p. (Orig.). (gr. 6 up). 1988. pap. text ed. 5.00 (*0-685-22586-0*) Wise Works Inc.
—I Ain't Into That: (The Book) 48p. (Orig.). (gr. 6-12). 1987. pap. text ed. 5.00 (*0-685-22587-9*); 6.00 (*0-685-22588-7*) Wise Works Inc.
Young, Eleanor R. Basic Skills in Getting Around, No. 812542. (gr. 7-12). 1991. wkbk. 9.95 (*0-86703-192-1*) Opportunities Learn.
Young, Woody. Clockwise, Vol. One: Quotes on Life. White, Craig, illus. 50p. (Orig.). 1984. pap. text ed. 4.95 (*0-939513-01-3*) Joy Pub SJC.
—Smile Wise. White, Craig, illus. 48p. (Orig.). 1986. pap. text ed. 4.95 (*0-939513-21-8*) Joy Pub SJC.
Youngs, Bettie B. Problem Solving Skills for Children. 69p. (ps-4). 1989. 10.00 (*0-915190-93-1*, JP 9093-1) Jalmar Pr.

BEHAVIOR–FICTION

Aborn, Allyson. Everything I Do You Blame on Me: Why Should I? It's Not My Birthday! Shore, Hennie, ed. Goldman, Stu, illus. (Orig.). (gr. k-6). 1994. pap. 16.95 (*1-882732-10-3*) Ctr Applied Psy.
Ada, Alma F. The Gold Coin. Waldman, Neil, illus. LC 90-32806. 32p. (gr. k-3). 1991. SBE 14.95 (*0-689-31633-X*, Atheneum Child Bk) Macmillan Child Grp.
—The Gold Coin. Waldman, Neil, illus. Randall, Bernice, tr. from SPA. LC 93-14403. (Illus.). 32p. (gr. k-3). 1994. pap. 4.95 (*0-689-71793-8*, Aladdin) Macmillan Child Grp.
Adams, Pam, illus. If I Weren't Me. LC 90-46184. 24p. (ps-2). 1981. 9.95 (*0-85953-108-2*, Pub. by Child's Play England) Childs Play.
Adshead, Paul. Incredible Reversing Peppermints. (ps-3). 1993. 7.95 (*0-85953-514-2*) Childs Play.
Alexander, Martha. We Never Get to Do Anything. Alexander, Martha, illus. (ps-3). 1985. Dial Bks Young.
Alexander, Sue. Ellsworth & Millicent. Meier, David S., illus. LC 92-7705. 28p. (gr. k up). 1993. 14.95 (*0-88708-247-5*) Picture Bk Studio.
Allard, Harry. The Stupids Take Off. Marshall, James, illus. 32p. (gr. k-3). 1993. pap. 4.95 (*0-395-65743-1*) HM.
Anderson, Leone C. Surprise at Muddy Creek. Endres, Helen, illus. 32p. (gr. 1-3). 1990. PLB 13.95 (*0-89565-698-1*) Childs World.
Armstrong, Jennifer. Hugh Can Do. Root, Kimberly B., illus. LC 90-46275. 40p. (ps-4). 1992. 15.00 (*0-517-58218-X*); PLB 15.99 (*0-517-58219-8*) Crown Bks Yng Read.
—That Terrible Baby. Meddaugh, Susan, illus. LC 93-14727. 32p. 1994. 14.00 (*0-688-11832-1*, Tambourine Bks); PLB 13.93 (*0-688-11833-X*, Tambourine Bks) Morrow.
Arnold, Tedd. No Jumping on the Bed! Arnold, Tedd, illus. LC 86-13501. 32p. (ps-2). 1987. 14.00 (*0-8037-0038-5*); PLB 13.89 (*0-8037-0039-3*) Dial Bks Young.
Aruego, Jose & Dewey, Ariane. Rockabye Crocodile. LC 92-24587. 32p. (ps up). 1993. pap. 4.95 (*0-688-12333-3*, Mulberry) Morrow.
Ashforth, Camilla. Monkey Tricks. Ashforth, Camilla, illus. LC 92-53013. 32p. (ps up). 1993. 15.95 (*1-56402-170-X*) Candlewick Pr.
Aunt Zinnia & the Ogre. (Illus.). 32p. (gr. k-3). 1992. PLB 17.27 (*0-8368-0910-6*); PLB 17.27 s.p. (*0-685-61497-2*) Gareth Stevens Inc.
Awdry, W. A Cow on the Line & Other Thomas the Tank Engine Stories. Mitton, David & Permane, Terry, photos by. LC 91-21706. (Illus.). 32p. (Orig.). (ps-3). 1992. PLB 5.99 (*0-679-91977-5*); pap. 2.50 (*0-679-81977-0*) Random Bks Yng Read.
—Diesel's Devious Deed & Other Thomas the Tank Engine Stories. Mitton, David & Permane, Terry, photos by. LC 91-21133. (Illus.). 32p. (Orig.). (ps-3). 1992. PLB 5.99 (*0-679-91976-7*); pap. 2.50 (*0-679-81976-2*) Random Bks Yng Read.
—Duck Takes Charge. Mitton, David & Permane, Terry, photos by. LC 92-45564. (Illus.). 32p. (ps-2). 1993. 3.50 (*0-679-84763-4*) Random Bks Yng Read.
Baehr, Patricia. School Isn't Fair. Alley, R. W., illus. LC 91-38485. 32p. (ps-k). 1992. pap. 4.95 (*0-689-71544-7*, Aladdin) Macmillan Child Grp.
Baker, Carin G. Fight for Honor. 128p. (gr. 3-7). 1992. pap. 3.50 (*0-14-036024-7*) Puffin Bks.
Bancroft, Catherine & Gruenberg, Coale. That's Philomena. 1995. 15.00 (*0-02-708326-8*, Four Winds) Macmillan Child Grp.
Bartholomew. Jimmy & the White Lie. (Illus.). 32p. (gr. k-9). 1976. 4.99 (*0-570-03460-4*, 56-1341) Concordia.
Bauer, Marion D. On My Honor. LC 86-2679. 96p. (gr. 4-7). 1987. 12.95 (*0-89919-439-7*, Clarion Bks) HM.
Belloc, Hilaire. Matilda Who Told Lies. Kellogg, Steven, illus. LC 78-121812. 32p. (gr. k up). 1992. 13.00 (*0-8037-1101-8*) Dial Bks Young.
—Matilda Who Told Lies. Kellogg, Steven, illus. LC 78-121812. 32p. (ps up). 1992. pap. 3.99 (*0-14-054547-6*, Puff Pied Piper) Puffin Bks.
Berenstain, Stan & Berenstain, Jan. The Berenstain Bears & the Nerdy Nephew. Berenstain, Stan & Berenstain, Jan, illus. LC 92-32564. 112p. (Orig.). (gr. 2-6). 1993. PLB 7.99 (*0-679-93610-6*); pap. 3.50 (*0-679-83610-1*) Random Bks Yng Read.
—Los Osos Berenstain y Demasiada Fiesta. Guibert, Rita, tr. Berenstain, Stan & Berenstain, Jan, illus. LC 92-45874. (SPA.). 32p. (ps-3). 1993. pap. 2.25 (*0-679-84745-6*) Random Bks Yng Read.
—Los Osos Berenstain y Demasiada Television. Guibert, Rita, tr. Berenstain, Stan & Berenstain, Jan, illus. LC 92-16251. (SPA.). 32p. (ps-3). 1993. pap. 2.25 (*0-679-84007-9*) Random Bks Yng Read.
—Los Osos Berenstain y el Cuarto Desordenado. Guibert, Rita, tr. from ENG. Berenstain, Stan & Berenstain, Jan, illus. LC 91-50191. (SPA.). 32p. (ps-3). 1992. pap. 2.25 (*0-679-83470-2*) Random Bks Yng Read.
Best, Elizabeth. What Happened to Aunt Cordelia? Webb, Phillip, illus. LC 93-167. 1994. write for info. (*0-383-03725-5*) SRA Schl Grp.
Birney, Betty. Disney's Winnie the Pooh Helping Hands: Oh, Bother! Someone's Messy! Stevenson, Nancy, illus. 24p. (ps-3). 1992. pap. write for info. (*0-307-12690-0*, 12690, Golden Pr) Western Pub.
—Walt Disney's Winnie the Pooh Helping Hands: Oh, Bother! Someone Won't Share. Stevenson, Nancy, illus. 24p. (ps-3). 1993. pap. 1.95 (*0-307-12766-4*, 12766, Golden Pr) Western Pub.
Blau, Judith. Stop & Go Potty. Blau, Judith, illus. LC 92-61706. 6p. (ps). 1993. 6.99 (*0-679-84021-4*) Random Bks Yng Read.
Blume, Judy. It's Not the End of the World. (gr. k-6). 1986. pap. 3.25 (*0-440-44158-7*, YB) Dell.
—Then Again, Maybe I Won't. 164p. (gr. 5-8). 1986. pap. 3.99 (*0-440-48659-9*, YB) Dell.
Bobbi. T-Neck. 63p. 1992. pap. 5.95 (*0-9626608-4-1*) Magik NY.
Bornet, Vaughn D. It's a Dog's Life & I Like It! LC 91-78055. 40p. (gr. 3-8). 1991. pap. 8.95 (*0-9632366-0-1*) Bornet Bks.
Borovsky, Paul. Nico. Borovsky, Paul, illus. LC 92-13924. 32p. (ps-2). 1993. 14.00 (*0-517-58854-4*); PLB 14.99 (*0-517-58855-2*) Crown Bks Yng Read.
Boyd, Lizi. Half Wild & Half Child. (Illus.). 32p. (ps-3). 1991. pap. 3.95 (*0-14-050825-2*, Puffin) Puffin Bks.
Brenner, Barbara A. Group Soup. Munsinger, Lynn, illus. 32p. (ps-3). 1992. PLB 12.50 (*0-670-82867-X*) Viking Child Bks.
Broome, Errol. Tangles. James, Ann, illus. LC 93-30637. 112p. (gr. 3-7). 1994. 13.00 (*0-679-85713-3*) Knopf Bks Yng Read.
Brouwer, Sigmund. Race for the Part Street Treasure. 132p. 1991. pap. 4.99 (*0-89693-859-X*) SP Pubns.
Brown, Ruth. Copycat. LC 94-20451. (Illus.). 32p. (ps-1). 1994. 14.99 (*0-525-45326-1*, DCB) Dutton Child Bks.
Buchanan-Hedman, Pat. Patrick & Patty Go to Time Out. Koop, Christie, illus. 24p. (Orig.). (ps-5). 1991. 8.95 (*1-880121-50-6*) Three Cs Ent.
Buerger, Jane & Davis, Jenine. Helping. 32p. (ps-2). 1985. PLB 14.95 (*0-89565-302-8*) Childs World.
Byars, Betsy C. Bingo Brown & the Language of Love. (Illus.). 144p. (gr. 3-7). 1991. pap. 3.99 (*0-14-034141-2*, Puffin) Puffin Bks.
Calder, Lyn. Minnie 'n Me: The Perfect Bow. Shakespeare, Sue, illus. (ps-k). 1991. pap. write for info. (*0-307-10025-1*, Golden Pr) Western Pub.
Carl, Angela R. A Matter of Choice. Speirs, John, illus. 32p. (gr. 1-3). 1990. PLB 13.95 (*0-89565-699-X*) Childs World.
Carlson, Nancy. Life Is Fun! Carlson, Nancy, illus. 32p. (ps-3). 1993. reinforced bdg. 13.99 (*0-670-84206-0*) Viking Child Bks.
—Loudmouth George & the Sixth-Grade Bully. LC 83-7178. (Illus.). 32p. (ps-3). 1983. PLB 13.50 (*0-87614-217-X*) Carolrhoda Bks.
Carr, Jan. Dark Day, Light Night. Ransome, James, illus. LC 93-45932. 1995. write for info. (*0-7868-0018-6*); PLB write for info. (*0-7868-2014-4*) Hyprn Child.

Carroll, Louann. Journeys: The Adventures of Leaf. LC 92-13485. (Illus.). (gr. 1-8). 1992. pap. 9.95 (*1-880090-03-1*) Galde Pr. JOURNEYS is the simple yet profound tale of a distressed maple leaf whose tenuous hold on the tree is broken by the wind. Leaf's many adventures with Twig, Wind, Thornbush & Water teach her much about trust, choices, life, death, the wonder of friendship, & of living life bravely & to the fullest. When she falls from the tree, she believes her life is over, but when we read about a new bud on the same tree in the following springtime, we know that the spirit of the Leaf has been reborn in a new form. A story that children never grow tired of reading. Illustrated with black & white drawings by a 7th grade art class. Blank pages included for readers

to draw their own meaningful interpretations. JOURNEYS is a delightful story for young & old readers alike. "A morality tale for the '90s. JOURNEYS is filled with wisdom, love & humor. My children enjoyed it immensely."--Pat Miller, English Dept. Head, Fremont, CA. "JOURNEYS is an engaging story of one leaf's growth & education that symbolizes the greater dance of life we all share. The blank pages are wonderful places for children to share their own life's journey."--Kristine Grim, Educator, San Jose, CA. "A marvelous teaching tale that will tell children of the continuity of life while it entertains them with the journey of Leaf, a sympathetic, picturesque embodiment of Everyperson. Cast in a simple storyline that will reach the minds of the youngest of listeners & touch the hearts of the oldest of readers, JOURNEYS reminds us that there is no death, only a change of worlds."--Brad Steiger. Cassette tape available for listening to a dramatic reading of story. Available from Baker & Taylor or contact Galde Press, Inc., Publisher, P.O. Box 65611, St. Paul, MN 55165. Call 1-800-777-3454, FAX 612-891-6091.
Publisher Provided Annotation.

Cazet, Denys. Never Spit on Your Shoes. Cazet, Denys, illus. LC 89-35164. 32p. (ps-1). 1993. pap. 5.95 (*0-531-07039-5*) Orchard Bks Watts.

Civardi, Anne. Potty Time. Langley, Jonathan, illus. LC 87-21910. 24p. (ps). 1993. pap. 3.95 (*0-671-79618-6*, S&S BYR) S&S Trade.

Clark, Barbara R. Reflections. Davis, Ruby & Gerstung, Estella, eds. Clark, Carl R. & Williams, Cecil J. 72p. (Orig.). (gr. 4-12). 1982. pap. 4.95 (*0-686-37922-5*) Williams SC.

Cleary, Beverly. Ramona the Pest. 192p. (gr. 4-7). 1982. pap. 3.25 (*0-440-47209-1*, YB) Dell.

Clement, Claude. Be Careful, Little Antelope. Jensen, Patricia, adapted by. Pio, illus. LC 93-2950. 22p. (ps-3). 1993. 5.98 (*0-89577-504-2*, Readers Digest Kids) RD Assn.

Cohen, Miriam. So What? Hoban, Lillian, illus. LC 81-20101. 32p. (gr. k-3). 1982. PLB 15.93 (*0-688-01203-5*) Greenwillow.

Conford. Seven Days to a Brand New Life. 1993. pap. 2.95 (*0-685-66035-4*) Scholastic Inc.

Coplans, Peta. Dottie. Coplans, Peta, illus. LC 92-41955. 1994. write for info. (*0-395-66788-7*) HM.

Crary, Elizabeth. I'm Frustrated. LC 90-63870. (ps-3). 1992. PLB 16.95 (*0-943990-65-3*); pap. 5.95 (*0-943990-64-5*) Parenting Pr.

—I'm Mad. LC 90-63869. (ps-3). 1992. PLB 16.95 (*0-943990-63-7*); pap. 5.95 (*0-943990-62-9*) Parenting Pr.

—I'm Proud. LC 90-63871. (ps-3). 1992. PLB 16.95 (*0-943990-67-X*); pap. 5.95 (*0-943990-66-1*) Parenting Pr.

Crutcher, Chris. Staying Fat for Sarah Byrnes. large type ed. (gr. 9-12). 1993. 15.95 (*0-7862-0062-6*) Thorndike Pr.

Cummings, Carol. I'm Always in Trouble. Howatson, Melody, illus. 24p. (Orig.). (ps-3). 1991. pap. 3.99 (*0-9614574-5-7*) Teaching WA.

—Tattlin' Madeline. Howatson, Melody, illus. 24p. (Orig.). (ps-3). 1991. pap. 3.99 (*0-9614574-4-9*) Teaching WA.

—Win-Win Day. Howatson, Melody, illus. 24p. (Orig.). (ps-3). 1991. pap. 3.99 (*0-9614574-6-5*) Teaching WA.

—Won't You Ever Listen. Riddell, Russ, illus. 24p. (Orig.). (ps-3). 1992. pap. 5.99 (*0-9614574-7-3*) Teaching WA.

Cummings, Pat. Clean Your Room, Harvey Moon! Cummings, Pat, illus. LC 93-20571. 32p. (gr. k-2). 1994. pap. 4.95 (*0-689-71798-9*, Aladdin) Macmillan Child Grp.

Dahl, Roald. The Twits. Blake, Quentin, illus. 96p. (gr. 2-6). 1991. pap. 3.99 (*0-14-034640-6*, Puffin) Puffin Bks.

Dana, Katherine. Toodle D. Poodle. Shuster, Albert H., ed. LC 92-82386. (Illus.). 22p. (Orig.). 1992. pap. 5.52 (*0-914127-28-4*) Univ Class.

Daniells, Trenna. It's Okay to Be Different: Oliver's Adventures on Monkey Island. Braille International, Inc. Staff & Henry, James, illus. (Orig.). (gr. 2). 1992. pap. 10.95 (*1-56956-017-X*) W A T Braille.

Davies, Andrew. Conrad's War. 144p. (gr. 5 up). 1986. pap. 1.95 (*0-440-91452-3*, LFL) Dell.

Davies, Leah. Kelly Bear Beginnings, 5 bks. Hallett, Leah, illus. 176p. (ps-5). 1991. Set incl. Kelly Bear Feelings; Kelly Bear Behavior; Kelly Bear Health; Kelly Bear Activities; Kelly Bear Drug Awareness. pap. 29.95 (*0-9621054-7-3*) Kelly Bear Pr.

De Masco, Steve & Simmons, Alex. We Want to Win! Tiegreen, Alan, illus. LC 91-40935. 64p. (gr. 1-4). 1993. text ed. 9.59 (*0-8167-3100-4*); tchr's. ed. 2.50 (*0-8167-3101-2*) Troll Assocs.

Dobson, Danae. Forest Friends Learn to Be Kind. Morales, Cuitlahuac, illus. 32p. 1993. 7.99 (*0-8499-1016-1*) Word Inc.

—Forest Friends Learn to Share. Morales, Cuitlahuac, illus. 32p. (ps-k). 1993. 7.99 (*0-8499-0985-6*) Word Inc.

—Forest Friends Play Fair. Morales, Cuitlahuac, illus. 32p. (ps-k). 1993. 7.99 (*0-8499-0987-2*) Word Inc.

Doray, Andrea. Boris Bear Remembers His Manners. Gress, Jonna C., ed. Claflin, Dale, illus. LC 91-78098. 18p. (Orig.). (gr. k-3). 1992. pap. 14.25 (*0-944943-06-3*, CODE 18437-5) Current Inc.

Duffey, Betsy. Boy in the Doghouse. LC 90-47751. (Illus.). 96p. 1991. pap. 12.00 jacketed (*0-671-73618-3*, S&S BFYR) S&S Trade.

Eastman, Patricia. Sometimes Things Change. LC 83-10090. (Illus.). 32p. (ps-2). 1983. PLB 10.25 (*0-516-02044-7*); pap. 2.95 (*0-516-42044-5*) Childrens.

Egan, Tim. Chestnut Cove. LC 94-17367. (gr. 1-8). 1995. write for info. (*0-395-69823-5*) HM.

Eisberg, George L. & Ossorio, Nelson A. Why the One-Who-Is Has No Name. (Illus.). 60p. (gr. 4-6). 1994. pap. 6.95 (*1-56721-036-8*) Twnty-Fifth Cent Pr.

Eisberg, George L. & Rexford, Janis. Seven Elders. (Illus.). 48p. (gr. 3-6). 1994. pap. 6.95 (*1-56721-083-X*) Twnty-Fifth Cent Pr.

Eisberg, George L., et al. Mud Settling or Not to Do to Do. (Illus.). 48p. (gr. 3-5). 1994. pap. 6.95 (*1-56721-039-2*) Twnty-Fifth Cent Pr.

—To Get Full, Get Empty. (Illus.). 60p. (gr. 4-6). 1994. pap. 6.95 (*1-56721-042-2*) Twnty-Fifth Cent Pr.

—Flowers on the Road. (Illus.). 60p. (gr. 4-6). 1994. pap. 6.95 (*1-56721-029-5*) Twnty-Fifth Cent Pr.

Elias, Miriam L. Thanks to You! LC 94-44850. 1994. write for info. (*0-87306-663-4*); pap. write for info. (*0-87306-664-2*) Feldheim.

Fakih, Kimberly O. Grandpa Putter & Granny Hoe. Pearson, Tracy C., illus. 128p. (gr. 2-5). 1992. 13.00 (*0-374-32762-9*) FS&G.

Fassler, Joan. Don't Worry Dear. Kranz, Stewart, illus. LC 74-147124. 32p. (ps-3). 1971. 16.95 (*0-87705-055-4*) Human Sci Pr.

Frankel, Julie E. Oh No, Otis! Martin, Clovis, illus. LC 91-15328. 32p. (ps-2). 1991. PLB 10.25 (*0-516-02009-9*); pap. 2.95 (*0-516-42009-7*) Childrens.

Friedman, Arthur, illus. The Three Sillies. LC 80-27636. 32p. (gr. k-4). 1981. PLB 9.79 (*0-89375-486-2*); pap. text ed. 1.95 (*0-89375-487-0*) Troll Assocs.

Gaban, Jesus. Harry's Mealtime Mess. Colorado, Nani, illus. 16p. (ps-1). 1992. PLB 13.27 (*0-8368-0717-0*) Gareth Stevens Inc.

Gabhart, Ann. Bridge to Courage. 160p. (Orig.). (gr. 6). 1993. pap. 3.50 (*0-380-76051-7*, Flare) Avon.

Gantos, Jack. Not So Rotten Ralph. Rubel, Nicole, illus. LC 93-759. (gr. 4 up). 1994. 13.95 (*0-395-62302-2*) HM.

—Worse Than Rotten, Ralph. Rubel, Nicole, illus. (gr. k-3). 1982. 13.95 (*0-395-27106-1*); pap. 5.70 (*0-395-32919-1*) HM.

Gardner, Richard A. Dr. Gardner's Fables for Our Times. Myers, Robert, illus. LC 80-26098. 125p. (gr. k-6). 1981. 14.95 (*0-933812-06-X*) Creative Therapeutics.

—Dr. Gardner's Stories About the Real World, Vol. I. Lowenheim, Alfred, illus. LC 80-16542. 127p. (gr. k-6). 1980. Repr. of 1972 ed. PLB 14.95 (*0-933812-04-3*) Creative Therapeutics.

—Dr. Gardner's Stories About the Real World, Vol. II. Myers, Robert, illus. LC 80-16592. 95p. (gr. k-6). 1983. 14.95 (*0-933812-05-1*) Creative Therapeutics.

—Dr. Gardner's Stories about the Real World, Vol. I. LC 80-16542. (Illus.). 127p. (gr. k-6). 1980. pap. 4.99 (*0-933812-07-8*) Creative Therapeutics.

Gibala-Broxholm, Janice. Let Me Do It! Paterson, Diane, illus. LC 92-12856. 32p. (ps-k). 1994. RSBE 14.95 (*0-02-735827-5*, Bradbury Pr) Macmillan Child Grp.

Gifaldi, David. Gregory, Maw, & the Mean One. Glass, Andrew, illus. 144p. (gr. 7 up). 1992. 13.45 (*0-395-60821-X*, Clarion Bks) HM.

—Toby Scudder, Ultimate Warrior. LC 92-39532. 1993. 13.95 (*0-395-66400-4*, Clarion Bks) HM.

Gleitzman, Morris. Misery Guts. LC 92-22570. 1993. 12.95 (*0-15-254768-1*) HarBrace.

Godden, Rumer. Candy Floss. Hogrogian, Nonny, illus. 64p. (ps-3). 1991. 16.95 (*0-399-21807-6*, Philomel) Putnam Pub Group.

Gordon, Shirley. Me & the Bad Guys. Frascino, Edward, illus. 80p. (gr. 3-7). 1984. pap. 2.25 (*0-440-45520-0*, YB) Dell.

Goudge, Eileen. Too Much Too Soon. 160p. (gr. 7-12). 1984. pap. 2.25 (*0-440-98974-4*) Dell.

Grace, John. A Busy Day. Trotter, Stuart, illus. 28p. (ps-1). 1991. 3.95 (*0-7214-5333-3*, S914-2) Ladybird Bks.

—A Quiet Walk. Trotter, Stuart, illus. 28p. (ps-1). 1991. 3.95 (*0-7214-5332-5*, S914-1 SER.) Ladybird Bks.

Grady, Kitten S. Jiggsy's Necklace. Grady, Kitten S., illus. LC 87-62211. 40p. (gr. 1-6). 1987. 5.95 (*0-932433-34-0*) Windswept Hse.

Gravois, Jeanne M. Quickly, Quigley. Hill, Alison, illus. LC 93-1990. 32p. 1994. 14.00 (*0-688-13047-X*, Tambourine Bks); PLB 13.93 (*0-688-13048-8*, Tambourine Bks) Morrow.

Greaves, Margaret. Sarah's Lion. (ps-3). 1992. 13.95 (*0-8120-6279-5*) Barron.

Green, Kate. T-Bone's Tent. (Illus.). 32p. (gr. 1-4). 1992. 15.95 (*0-89565-782-1*) Childs World.

Greene, Carol. Wendy & the Whine. (Illus.). 32p. (gr. 1-4). 1987. pap. 4.99 (*0-570-04157-0*, 56-1615) Concordia.

Greene, Constance C. Double-Dare O'Toole. (gr. 4 up). 1990. pap. 3.95 (*0-14-034541-8*, Puffin) Puffin Bks.

—Isabelle Shows Her Stuff. 144p. (gr. 3-7). 1992. pap. 3.99 (*0-14-036029-8*) Puffin Bks.

Greenwald, Sheila. Give Us a Great Big Smile, Rosy Cole. Greenwald, Sheila, illus. 80p. (gr. 3 up). 1981. 14.95 (*0-316-32672-0*, Joy St Bks) Little.

—Rosy Cole: She Walks in Beauty. LC 93-40114. (gr. 5 up). 1994. 14.95 (*0-316-32743-3*) Little.

Grossman, Bill. The Guy Who Was Five Minutes Late. Glasser, Judy, illus. LC 89-36336. 32p. (ps-3). 1990. PLB 14.89 (*0-06-022269-7*) HarpC Child Bks.

Gunn, Robin J. Summer Promise. 171p. (Orig.). 1989. pap. 4.99 (*0-929608-13-5*) Focus Family.

Happiness Box. 1991. 8.95 (*1-56062-011-0*) CIS Comm.

Hargreaves, Roger. Mr. Bounce. 32p. (ps up). 1976. PLB 9.95 (*0-87191-814-5*) Creative Ed.

—Mr. Bump. 32p. (ps up). 1971. PLB 9.95 (*0-87191-815-3*) Creative Ed.

—Mr. Clumsy. 32p. (ps up). 1978. PLB 9.95 (*0-87191-817-X*) Creative Ed.

—Mr. Dizzy. 32p. (ps up). 1976. PLB 9.95 (*0-87191-906-0*) Creative Ed.

—Mr. Muddle. 32p. (ps up). 1976. PLB 9.95 (*0-87191-910-9*) Creative Ed.

—Mr. Strong. 32p. (ps up). 1976. PLB 9.95 (*0-87191-917-6*) Creative Ed.

—Mr. Tickle. 32p. (ps up). 1971. PLB 9.95 (*0-87191-759-9*) Creative Ed.

—Mr. Uppity. 32p. (ps up). 1972. PLB 9.95 (*0-87191-920-6*) Creative Ed.

Harper-Deiters, Cyndi. The Jonathan Michael Series. Ruggles, Robert & Ruggles, Grace, eds. Bowers, Helen M., illus. (Orig.). (gr. 2-5). 1993. pap. text ed. write for info. (*0-9632513-4-1*) Cntry Home.

Haseley, Dennis. Getting Him. LC 94-6421. (gr. 5 up). 1994. 16.00 (*0-374-32536-7*) FS&G.

Haugen, Tormod. Zeppelin. Diamond, Donna, illus. Jacobs, David R., tr. from NOR. LC 92-8319. (Illus.). 128p. (gr. 4-7). 1994. 15.00 (*0-06-020881-3*); PLB 14.89 (*0-06-020882-1*) HarpC Child Bks.

Hautzig, Esther. Riches. Diamond, Donna, illus. LC 89-26904. 32p. (gr. 3 up). 1992. PLB 13.89 (*0-06-022260-3*) HarpC Child Bks.

Heide, Florence P. Tales for the Perfect Child. Chess, Victoria, illus. 80p. (gr. 3-6). 1985. 15.00 (*0-688-03892-1*); PLB 14.93 (*0-688-03893-X*) Lothrop.

—Tales for the Perfect Child. (gr. 4-7). 1991. pap. 3.99 (*0-440-40463-0*) Dell.

Heitler, Susan M. David Decides about Thumbsucking: A Motivating Story for Children & an Informative Guide for Parents. Singer, Paula, illus. LC 85-61019. 52p. (ps-3). 1985. PLB 17.95 (*0-9614780-1-2*); pap. 9.95 (*0-9614780-0-4*) Reading Matters.

Hermes, Patricia. Nothing but Trouble, Trouble, Trouble. LC 93-13968. 160p. (gr. 3-7). 1994. 13.95 (*0-590-43499-3*) Scholastic Inc.

Himmelman, John. Wanted: Perfect Parents. LC 93-22201. (Illus.). 32p. (ps-3). 1993. PLB 13.95 (*0-8167-3028-8*); pap. write for info. (*0-8167-3029-6*) BrdgeWater.

Hird, Nancy E. Jessica Jacobs Did What? Stortz, Diane, ed. LC 94-2101. (Illus.). 48p. (Orig.). (ps-3). 1994. pap. 4.49 (*0-7847-0180-6*) Standard Pub.

Hoban, Russell. Jim Hedgehog's Supernatural Christmas. Lewin, Betsy, illus. 48p. (gr. 2-5). 1992. 12.70 (*0-395-56240-6*, Clarion Bks) HM.

Holland, Alex N. What It Means to Be a Bad Boy. Holland, Alex N., illus. 13p. (gr. k-3). 1992. pap. 4.95 (*1-895583-51-9*) MAYA Pubs.

Hollingsworth, Mary. Captain, the Countess & Cobbie the Swabby. LC 92-4714. (ps-3). 1992. pap. 8.99 (*0-7814-0967-5*, Chariot Bks) Chariot Family.

Honeycutt, Natalie. Juliet Fisher & the Foolproof Plan. LC 91-28119. 144p. (gr. 2-6). 1992. SBE 13.95 (*0-02-744845-2*, Bradbury Pr) Macmillan Child Grp.

Hooks, William H. Rough Tough Rowdy. Munsinger, Lynn, illus. 32p. (ps-3). 1992. PLB 12.50 (*0-670-82868-8*) Viking Child Bks.

Hopper, Nancy J. The Queen of Put-Down. LC 92-19559. 112p. (gr. 4-6). 1993. pap. 3.95 (*0-689-71670-2*, Aladdin) Macmillan Child Grp.

—The Seven & One-Half Sins of Stacey Kendall. (gr. 5-9). 1983. pap. 2.75 (*0-440-47736-0*, YB) Dell.

Horowitz, Jordan. Dennis the Menace. (ps-3). 1993. pap. 2.95 (*0-590-47399-9*) Scholastic Inc.

How to Keep a Secret. 1986. pap. 2.25 (*0-440-73483-5*) Dell.

Hughes, Dean. Find the Power! Lyall, Dennis, illus. LC 93-8037. 112p. (Orig.). (gr. 2-6). 1994. pap. 3.50 (*0-679-84359-0*) Random Bks Yng Read.

Hurwitz, Johanna. Class Clown. Hamanaka, Sheila, illus. LC 86-23624. 112p. (gr. 1-4). 1987. 12.95 (*0-688-06723-9*) Morrow Jr Bks.

Hutchins, Pat. Three-Star Billy. LC 93-26517. 32p. 1994. 15.00 (*0-688-13078-X*); lib. bdg. 14.93 (*0-688-13079-8*) Greenwillow.

Ikeda, Daisaku. The Princess & the Moon. McCaughrean, Geraldine, tr. from JPN. Wildsmith, Brian, illus. LC 92-148. 32p. (ps-3). 1992. 15.00 (*0-679-83620-9*); PLB 15.99 (*0-679-93620-3*) Knopf Bks Yng Read.

Ingle, Valorie L. The Power of Being Alone. (Illus.). (gr. k-4). 1994. write for info. (*1-883863-02-3*) Legend Prods.

—The Power of Forgiving. (Illus.). (gr. k-4). 1994. write for info. (*1-883863-04-X*) Legend Prods.

—The Power of Giving. (Illus.). (gr. k-4). 1993. PLB write for info. (*1-883863-01-5*) Legend Prods.

—The Power of Honesty. (Illus.). (gr. k-4). 1993. pap. write for info. (*1-883863-00-7*) Legend Prods.

—The Power of Hope. (Illus.). (gr. k-4). 1994. write for info. (*1-883863-05-8*) Legend Prods.

—The Power of Imagination. (Illus.). (gr. k-4). 1994. write for info. (*1-883863-09-0*) Legend Prods.

—The Power of Joy. (Illus.). (gr. k-4). 1994. write for info. (*1-883863-07-4*) Legend Prods.

—The Power of Love. (Illus.). (gr. k-4). 1994. write for info. (*1-883863-11-2*) Legend Prods.

—The Power of Patience & Understanding. (Illus.). (gr. k-4). 1994. write for info. (*1-883863-08-2*) Legend Prods.

—The Power of Sharing. (Illus.). (gr. k-4). 1994. write for info. (*1-883863-06-6*) Legend Prods.

—The Power of Sympathy. (Illus.). (gr. k-4). 1994. write for info. (*1-883863-03-1*) Legend Prods.

Jackson, Shirley. Charles. 1991. PLB 13.95s.p. (*0-88682-470-2*) Creative Ed.

Jensen, Patricia. A Funny Man. Becker, Wayne, illus. LC 92-36007. 1993. 3.95 (*0-590-46190-7*) Scholastic Inc.

Johnson, Scott. One of the Boys. LC 91-19262. 256p. (gr. 7 up). 1992. SBE 16.00 (*0-689-31520-1*, Atheneum Child Bk) Macmillan Child Grp.

—Overnight Sensation. LC 93-23084. 224p. (gr. 7 up). 1994. 16.95 (*0-689-31831-6*, Atheneum Child Bk) Macmillan Child Grp.

Keller, Holly. Geraldine's Blanket. Keller, Holly, illus. LC 83-14062. 32p. (ps-1). 1984. 13.95 (*0-688-02539-0*); PLB 13.88 (*0-688-02540-4*) Greenwillow.

—The New Boy. LC 90-41757. (Illus.). 24p. (ps up). 1991. 13.95 (*0-688-09827-4*); PLB 13.88 (*0-688-09828-2*) Greenwillow.

Keller, Wallace E. The Wrong Side of the Bed. (Illus.). 32p. (ps-1). 1993. 14.95 (*0-87663-799-3*) Universe.

Kelley, Shirley. The Good, the Bad & the Two Cookie Kid. Herbst, Eric & Genee, Gloria, eds. Claridy, Jimmy, illus. Cash, Johnny, intro. by. (Illus.). 32p. (ps-4). 1993. Incl. audio cass. 9.95 (*1-882436-02-4*) Better Pl Pub.

Klass, Sheila S. Kool Ada. (gr. 4-7). 1991. 13.95 (*0-590-43902-2*, Scholastic Hardcover) Scholastic Inc.

Kline, Suzy. Don't Touch! Tucker, Kathleen, ed. Leder, Dora, illus. LC 85-612. 32p. (ps-1). 1985. 13.95 (*0-8075-1707-0*) A Whitman.

Koller, Jackie F. Impy for Always. (ps-3). 1991. pap. 3.95 (*0-316-50149-2*) Little.

Konigsburg, E. L. Up from Jericho Tel. LC 85-20061. 192p. (gr. 5 up). 1986. SBE 15.95 (*0-689-31194-X*, Atheneum Child Bk) Macmillan Child Grp.

Kroll, Steven. Patrick's Tree House. Wilson, Roberta, illus. LC 93-4571. 64p. (gr. 2-5). 1994. RSBE 13.95 (*0-02-751005-0*, Macmillan Child Bk) Macmillan Child Grp.

Kubler, Annie. The Champion. LC 90-24246. (gr. 4 up). 1991. 3.95 (*0-85953-531-2*) Childs Play.

Lakin, Patricia. A Good Sport! Cushman, Doug, illus. LC 93-49845. 1994. write for info. (*0-8114-3870-8*) Raintree Steck-V.

Lasky, Kathryn. The Tantrum. McCarthy, Bobette, illus. LC 92-3701. 32p. (ps-1). 1993. RSBE 13.95 (*0-02-751661-X*, Macmillan Child Bk) Macmillan Child Grp.

Lester, Helen. Me First. Munsinger, Lynn, illus. LC 91-45808. 32p. (ps up). 1992. 13.45 (*0-395-58706-9*) HM.

Levene, Nancy S. Chocolate Chips & Trumpet Tricks. Reck, Sue, ed. LC 93-36195. 192p. (gr. 3-6). 1994. pap. 5.99 (*0-7814-0103-8*, Chariot Bks) Cook.

Leverich, Kathleen. Hilary & the Troublemakers. Lorraine, Walter, illus. LC 91-15234. 1992. 13.00 (*0-688-10857-1*) Greenwillow.

Levy, Elizabeth. Lizzie Lies a Lot. Wallner, John, illus. LC 75-32914. 80p. (gr. 4-6). 1976. 6.95 (*0-440-04919-9*); PLB 6.46 (*0-440-04920-2*) Delacorte.

—Lizzie Lies a Lot. 112p. (gr. 3-5). 1977. pap. 2.75 (*0-440-44714-3*, YB) Dell.

—Take Two, They're Small. (Orig.). (gr. k-6). 1986. pap. 2.95 (*0-440-48517-7*, YB) Dell.

Lewis, Beverley. The Six-Hour Mystery. Johnson, Meredith, illus. LC 93-35020. (gr. 4 up). 1993. 3.99 (*0-8066-2666-6*) Augsburg Fortress.

Lindgren, Barbro. Sam's Car. Eriksson, Eva, illus. LC 82-3437. 32p. (gr. k-3). 1982. 6.95 (*0-688-01263-9*) Morrow Jr Bks.

Lipniacka, Ewa. It's Mine! Bogdanowicz, Basia, illus. LC 92-33324. 1993. 6.95 (*1-56656-119-1*, Crocodile Bks) Interlink Pub.

Loves, June. I Know That. Smith, Craig, illus. LC 92-34262. 1993. 4.25 (*0-383-03633-X*) SRA Schl Grp.

Lowrey, Janette S. The Poky Little Puppy. Hansen, Rosanna, adapted by. Chandler, Jean, illus. 14p. (ps-k). 1992. bds. write for info. (*0-307-12333-2*, 12333, Golden Pr) Western Pub.

Lowry, Lois. Taking Care of Terrific. 176p. (gr. 4-7). 1984. pap. 3.99 (*0-440-48494-4*, YB) Dell.

Luttrell, Ida. Ottie Slockett. Fogelman, Phyllis J., ed. Krause, Ute, illus. LC 88-30884. 40p. (ps-3). 1990. 9.95 (*0-8037-0709-6*); PLB 9.89 (*0-8037-0711-8*) Dial Bks Young.

McCaughrean, Geraldine. A Pack of Lies. large type ed. 320p. (gr. 3 up). 1990. lib. bdg. 16.95x (*0-7451-1154-8*, Lythway Large Print) Hall.

McCrackin, Mark. A Winning Position. 96p. (gr. 7 up). 1982. pap. 1.50 (*0-440-99483-7*, LFL) Dell.

MacDonald, Betty. The Mrs. Piggle-Wiggle Treasury. Knight, Hilary, illus. LC 94-15040. 1994. 19.95 (*0-06-024812-2*); PLB 19.89 (*0-06-024813-0*) HarpC Child Bks.

Macdonald, Maryann. Rosie & the Poor Rabbits. Sweet, Melissa, illus. LC 92-42766. 32p. (ps-2). 1994. SBE 13.95 (*0-689-31832-4*, Atheneum Child Bk) Macmillan Child Grp.

McLean, Susan. Pennies for the Piper. 1993. pap. 4.50 (*0-374-45754-9*, Sunburst) FS&G.

Mahy, Margaret. The Horrendous Hullabaloo. MacCarthy, Patricia, illus. 28p. (ps-3). 1994. pap. 4.99 (*0-14-055322-3*) Puffin Bks.

Manes, Stephen. Be a Perfect Person. 1983. pap. 3.50 (*0-553-15580-6*) Bantam.

Maness, Malia. Curious Kimo. Hall, Pat, illus. LC 93-86143. 32p. (ps-3). 1993. 9.95 (*0-9633493-0-9*) Pacific Greetings.

Manley, Molly. Talkaty Talker. Marshall, Janet, illus. 24p. (ps-1). 1994. 9.95 (*1-56397-195-X*) Boyds Mills Pr.

Markoe, Merrill. Bad Dog, Bo! Markoe, Merrill, illus. LC 93-38684. 32p. (gr. k-3). 1994. PLB 13.95 (*0-8167-3462-3*); pap. text ed. 3.95 (*0-8167-3463-1*) BrdgeWater.

Martin, Jane R. & Marx, Patricia. Now Everybody Really Hates Me. Chast, Roz, illus. LC 92-13075. 32p. (ps-3). 1993. 14.00 (*0-06-021293-4*); PLB 13.89 (*0-06-021294-2*) HarpC Child Bks.

Martinez, Carol. Paco y Ana Aprenden Acerca de la Amabilidad. Stillman, Peter, illus. (SPA.). 32p. (Orig.). (gr. 2-4). 1988. pap. 1.50 (*0-311-38590-7*, Edit Mundo) Casa Bautista.

—Paco y Ana Aprenden Acerca de la Honradez. Stillman, Peter, illus. (SPA.). 32p. (Orig.). (gr. 2-4). 1988. pap. 1.50 (*0-311-38587-7*, Edit Mundo) Casa Bautista.

—Paco y Ana Aprenden Acerca de la Obediencia. Stillman, Peter, illus. (SPA.). 32p. (Orig.). (gr. 2-4). 1988. pap. 1.50 (*0-311-38588-5*, Edit Mundo) Casa Bautista.

Martini, Teri. Christmas for Andy. (gr. 3 up). 1991. pap. 3.95 (*0-8091-6603-8*) Paulist Pr.

Mason, Margo C. Ready, Alice? (ps-3). 1990. 9.99 (*0-553-05816-9*) Bantam.

Mather, Anne D. & Weldon, Louise B. The Cat at the Door: And Other Stories to Live By. Martin, Lyn, illus. 200p. (ps-4). 1991. pap. 12.00 perfect bdg. (*0-89486-758-X*, 5131A) Hazelden.

Matranga, Frances C. One Step at a Time. (Illus.). (gr. 4-7). 1987. pap. 3.99 (*0-570-03642-9*, 39-1126) Concordia.

Mawe, Sheelagh M. Dandelion: The Triumphant Life of a Misfit, a Story for All Ages. 165p. (Orig.). (gr. 4). 1994. pap. 6.95 (*0-9642168-0-9*) Totally Unique.
Dandelion is a lowly, mis-bred Irish farm horse. As is true of all creatures, she begins her life with a sense of her own worth. But little by little, the "circumstances" of her life erode that belief. Dandelion becomes dispirited & eventually gives up her dreams. Nevertheless, given a chance at freedom, she has wits enough to pursue it, only to find that "freedom" was not quite what she was looking for! Dandelion's subsequent journey leads her to her true destination. It leads her to herself. In this enchanting book, readers of all ages will find in Dandelion an inspirational symbol of all those who have overcome poverty, prejudice, background & self-doubt to make a resounding success of their lives. To order contact: TOTALLY UNIQUE THOUGHTS, A Division of TUT Enterprises, 1713 Acme St., Orlando, FL 32805-3603. 407-246-7040.
Publisher Provided Annotation.

Mayer, Mercer. All By Myself. Mayer & Mercer, illus. 24p. (ps-3). 1985. pap. write for info. (*0-307-11938-6*, Pub. by Golden Bks) Western Pub.

—Just Me & My Cousin. Mayer, Mercer, illus. 24p. (ps-3). 1992. pap. write for info. (*0-307-12688-9*, 12688, Golden Pr) Western Pub.

Miles, Betty. Just the Beginning. 148p. (gr. 3 up). 1978. pap. 2.50 (*0-380-01913-2*, Camelot) Avon.

Millman, Dan. Quest for the Crystal Castle. Bruce, T. Taylor, illus. LC 92-70302. 32p. (ps-5). 1992. 13.95 (*0-915811-41-3*) H J Kramer Inc.

Mills, Claudia. Dynamite Dinah. LC 91-20651. 128p. (gr. 3-7). 1992. pap. 3.95 (*0-689-71591-9*, Aladdin) Macmillan Child Grp.

Minarik, Else H. The Little Girl & the Dragon. Gourlault, Martine, illus. LC 90-38495. 24p. (ps up). 1991. 13.95 (*0-688-09913-0*); PLB 13.88 (*0-688-09914-9*) Greenwillow.

Mock, Dorothy K. The Big Secret: The Good News Kids Learn about Gentleness. Mitter, Kathy, illus. LC 93-6865. 32p. (Orig.). (ps-2). 1993. pap. 3.99 (*0-570-04744-7*) Concordia.

—God Is Everywhere: The Good News Kids Learn about Self-Control. Mitter, Kathy, illus. LC 93-22311. 32p. (Orig.). (ps-2). 1993. pap. 3.99 (*0-570-04745-5*) Concordia.

Moncure, Jane B. Caring for My Home. Connelly, Gwen, illus. 32p. (ps-2). 1990. PLB 12.95 (*0-89565-667-1*) Childs World.

—Caring for My Things. Collette, Rondi, illus. 32p. (ps-2). 1990. PLB 12.95 (*0-89565-670-1*) Childs World.

Morgan, Mary. Benjamin's Bugs. Morgan, Mary, illus. LC 93-22911. 44p. (ps-1). 1994. RSBE 12.95 (*0-02-767450-9*, Bradbury Pr) Macmillan Child Grp.

Moss, Thylias. I Want to Be. Pinkney, Jerry, illus. LC 92-28965. 32p. (ps-3). 1993. 14.99 (*0-8037-1286-3*); PLB 14.89 (*0-8037-1287-1*) Dial Bks Young.

Muntean, Michaela. We're Counting on You, Grover! Ewers, Joe, illus. (ps-k). 1991. write for info. (*0-307-12050-3*, Golden Pr) Western Pub.

Nagel, Karen B. The Three Young Maniacs & the Red Rubber Boots. Gullikson, Sandy, illus. LC 91-30842. 32p. (ps-3). 1993. 15.00 (*0-06-020777-9*); PLB 14.89 (*0-06-020778-7*) HarpC Child Bks.

Naylor, Phyllis R. All but Alice. LC 91-28722. 160p. (gr. 4-8). 1992. SBE 13.95 (*0-689-31773-5*, Atheneum Child Bk) Macmillan Child Grp.

—How Lazy Can You Get? (gr. 4-7). 1992. pap. 3.50 (*0-440-40608-0*) Dell.

Nobisso, Josephine & Krajnc, Anton C. For the Sake of a Cake. LC 92-38391. (Illus.). 28p. 1993. 9.95 (*0-8478-1685-0*) Rizzoli Intl.
Here's a multi-species cautionary tale for people who know how to share the work - or those who SHOULD know! Written in droll verse & illustrated with subtle drawings of sophisticated wit & whimsical zaniness, FOR THE SAKE OF A CAKE tells the tale of a Koala & an Alligator, already in bed, who argue whose turn it is to get up to check the cake baking in the oven. No holds are barred & no punches pulled as each lays claim to having already done too much work. Who's right? As in life, the reader is never sure. But one thing is certain: unless they find a way to cooperate, they're putting their very lives in danger! Written by the author of GRANDPA LOVED, GRANDMA'S SCRAPBOOK, & SSH! THE WHALE IS SMILING, FOR THE SAKE OF A CAKE crosses over from the children's fiction section to adult gift books to food & specialty shops, setting a delicious example & offering a rare Viennese cake recipe at the end. Order from Rizzoli International, 300 Park Ave., New York, NY 10010-5399, 1-800-462-2357.
Publisher Provided Annotation.

Norton, Ann. Brooke's Little Lies. 112p. (gr. 4-9). 1992. pap. 2.95 (*0-448-40491-5*, G&D) Putnam Pub Group.

O'Connell, June. Why Must I Choose? 143p. (gr. 5-8). 1992. pap. 2.75 (*0-87406-631-X*) Willowisp Pr.

O'Donnell, Elizabeth L. Are You Flying, Charlie Duncan? Milone, Karen, illus. LC 92-39876. 96p. (gr. 4 up). 1993. 14.00 (*0-688-09027-3*) Morrow Jr Bks.

—Patrick's Day. Rogers, Jacqueline, illus. LC 92-27421. 32p. (gr. k up). 1994. 15.00g (*0-688-07853-2*); PLB 14.93 (*0-688-07854-0*) Morrow Jr Bks.

Odor, Ruth S. Please. Indereiden, Nancy, illus. LC 79-25319. (ps-2). 1980. PLB 12.95 (*0-89565-115-7*) Childs World.

Oh, Bother! No One's Listening! (Illus.). (ps-3). 1991. write for info. (*0-307-12637-4*, Golden Pr) Western Pub.

Oh, Bother! Someone's Fibbing! (Illus.). (ps-3). 1991. write for info. (*0-307-12636-6*, Golden Pr) Western Pub.

Oh, Bother! Someone's Fighting! (Illus.). (ps-3). 1991. write for info. (*0-307-12635-8*, Golden Pr) Western Pub.

The Old Man & the Afternoon Cat. 42p. (ps-3). 1992. PLB 13.27 (*0-8368-0886-X*) Gareth Stevens Inc.

One Day Everything... (Illus.). (ps-2). 1991. pap. 3.50 (*0-8136-5962-0*, TK2353) Modern Curr.

Oppenheim, Joanne. One Gift Deserves Another. (Illus.). 32p. (ps-1). 1992. 13.00 (*0-525-44975-2*, DCB) Dutton Child Bks.

Oram, Hiawyn. Mine! Rees, Mary, illus. 16p. (ps-k). 1992. with dust jacket 12.95 (*0-8120-6303-1*); pap. 5.95 (*0-8120-4905-5*) Barron.

—Reckless Ruby. Ross, Tony, illus. LC 91-20124. 32p. (ps-2). 1992. 12.00 (*0-517-58744-0*) Crown Bks Yng Read.

Ossorio, Joseph D., et al. Poor, Rich & Happy. (Illus.). 60p. (gr. 4-6). 1994. pap. 6.95 (*1-56721-043-0*) Twnty-Fifth Cent Pr.

—Truth about the Chase. (Illus.). 60p. (gr. 4-6). 1994. pap. 6.95 (*1-56721-044-9*) Twnty-Fifth Cent Pr.

Ossorio, Nelson A. & Salvadeo, Michele B. Castles & Other Dreams. (Illus.). 60p. (gr. 4-6). 1994. pap. 6.95 (*1-56721-065-1*) Twnty-Fifth Cent Pr.

Parkison, Ralph F. Big Red & the Fence Post. Withrow, Marion O., ed. Bush, William, illus. 53p. (Orig.). (gr. 2-8). 1988. pap. write for info. Little Wood Bks.

—The Little Flea. Withrow, Marion O., ed. Bush, William, illus. 21p. (Orig.). (gr. 2-8). 1988. pap. write for info. Little Wood Bks.

Pavloff, George. The Man Who Was It. (Illus.). 72p. (gr. 1 up). 1990. 12.95 (*0-931474-39-6*) TBW Bks.

Pearson, Jack. Uncle Alphonso & the Frosty, Fibbing Dinosaurs. Julien, Terry, illus. LC 92-39373. 1993. pap. 4.49 (*0-7814-0100-3*, Chariot Bks) Chariot Family.

Petersen, P. J. I Hate Company. James, Betsy, illus. LC 94-2801. 48p. (gr. 2-4). 1994. 12.99 (*0-525-45329-6*, DCB) Dutton Child Bks.

Peterson, Lorraine. Falling Off Cloud Nine & Other High Places. Dugan, LeRoy, illus. LC 81-38465. 159p. (Orig.). (gr. 8-12). 1981. pap. 7.99 (*0-87123-167-0*) Bethany Hse.

—Radical Advice from the Ultimate Wiseguy. 192p. (Orig.). (gr. 8-12). 1990. pap. 7.99 (*1-55661-141-2*) Bethany Hse.

Pevsner, Stella. Cute Is a Four-Letter Word. 176p. (gr. 7 up). 1989. pap. 2.75 (*0-671-68845-6*, Archway) PB.

Pfeffer, Susan B. Just Between Us. 128p. (gr. k-6). 1981. pap. 2.25 (*0-440-44194-3*, YB) Dell.

Pienkowski, Jan. Small Talk. (Illus.). 10p. (ps up). 1983. 9.95 (*0-8431-0982-3*) Price Stern.

Plemons, Marti. Brooke & the Guilty Secret. (Illus.). 128p. (gr. 3-6). 1992. pap. 4.99 (*0-87403-938-X*, 24-03768) Standard Pub.

Pokeberry, P. J. The Secret of Hilhouse: An Adult Book for Teens. Mueller, Peggy, illus. Urie, Luanna, frwd. by. LC 93-60940. (Illus.). 96p. (Orig.). (gr. 4 up). 1993. pap. 8.95 (*0-943962-02-1*) Viewpoint Pr.

Potter, Beatrix. Peter Rabbit: Beatrix Potter Deluxe Pop Up. (Illus.). 1992. 4.99 (*0-517-07000-6*) Random Hse Value.

Potter, Katherine. Spike. LC 93-11476. 1994. 15.00 (*0-671-86733-4*, S&S BFYR) S&S Trade.

Pryor, Ainslie. The Baby Blue Cat Who Said No. (Illus.). 32p. (gr. 2-6). 1990. pap. 4.99 (*0-14-050768-X*, Puffin) Puffin Bks.

Quigley, Stacy. Do I Have To? Lexa, Susan, illus. Silverman, Manuel, intro. by. LC 85-24350. (Illus.). 32p. (gr. k-6). 1980. PLB 19.97 (*0-8172-1352-X*) Raintree Steck-V.

Radley, Gail. Special Strengths. Boddy, Joe, illus. 64p. (gr. 2-6). 1984. pap. 6.50 (*0-87743-702-5*, Pub. by Bellwood Pr) Bahai.

Rathman, Peggy. Ruby the Copycat. (ps-3). 1993. pap. 4.95 (*0-590-47423-5*) Scholastic Inc.

Rees, Claudia. The Bird with the Word Talks about Self-Control. Rees, Claudia, illus. (Orig.). (gr. 1-3). 1987. pap. 0.98 (*0-89274-451-0*) Harrison Hse.

Reinsma, Carol. The Shimmering Stone. Cori, Nathan, illus. 48p. (Orig.). (gr. k-3). 1994. pap. 3.99 (*0-7847-0007-9*, 24-03957) Standard Pub.

Roper, Gayle. The Puzzle of the Poison Pen. LC 94-6755. 1994. write for info. (*0-7814-1507-1*, Chariot Bks) Chariot Family.

Rylant, Cynthia. A Fine White Dust. LC 86-1003. 120p. (gr. 6-8). 1986. SBE 14.95 (*0-02-777240-3*, Bradbury Pr) Macmillan Child Grp.

Sarai. The Apple Tree That Would Not Let Go of Its Apples. Kozjak, Goran, illus. McNulty, Linda, intro. by. (Illus.). 28p. (Orig.). 1993. pap. 11.50 (*0-938837-13-3*) Behav Sci Ctr Pubs.

Sargent, Dave & Sargent, Pat. The Animal Pride Series. Sapaugh, Blaine, illus. (gr. 1-5). 1992. Set 1, 10 bks. PLB 107.55 (*1-56763-153-3*); Set 2, 10 bks. PLB 107.55 (*1-56763-155-X*); Sets 1 & 2. PLB 199.95 (*1-56763-157-6*); Set 1, 10 bks. pap. 53.55 (*1-56763-154-1*); Set 2, 10 bks. pap. 53.55 (*1-56763-156-8*); Sets 1 & 2. pap. 99.95 (*1-56763-158-4*) Ozark Pub.

Emerging from a small farm in the beautiful Ozark Mountains comes Farmer John's high/low series of twenty very mischievous animals, stories with connecting story lines, making up Dave & Pat Sargent's ANIMAL PRIDE SERIES. (Accelerated Reader) Creatively written using whole language, this series contains twenty short chapter books with large 18 point type, a moral that all ages can relate to, & an animal facts section at the end of each book. Written with encyclopedia-quality information on a 2.2-3.0 vocabulary level with the use of pen & ink illustrations to insure the popularity through the seventh grade, this series is often used with child development, school counseling, ESL, Chapter & special-education classrooms. Other popular titles for animal lovers include Pat Sargent's THE GRIZZLY (Booklist) from the Barney the Bear Killer Series (illustrated in color) & Dave Sargent's SPIKE THE BLACK WOLF (illustrated). Both written on a fourth grade vocabulary level with high interest levels, these very popular titles explore animal loyalty & are sure to capture the hearts of any age reader. THE GRIZZLY is the sequel to THE ANIMAL PRIDE SERIES (a must) & SPIKE THE BLACK WOLF has been nominated for various state awards. Ozark Publishing.
Publisher Provided Annotation.

Saroyan, William. The Parsley Garden. (gr. 4-12). 1989. 13.95 (*0-88682-355-2*, 97221-098) Creative Ed.

Scarffe, Bronwen. Alfred. Posey, Pam, illus. LC 92-21442. 1993. 3.75 (*0-383-03612-7*) SRA Schl Grp.

Scheidl, Gerda M. Loretta & the Little Fairy. Unzner-Fischer, Christa, illus. James, J. Alison, tr. from GER. LC 92-33832. (Illus.). 32p. (gr. 2-3). 1993. 13.95 (*1-55858-185-5*); PLB 13.88 (*1-55858-186-3*) North-South Bks NYC.

Schultz, Irene. The Woodland Gang & the Hidden Jewels. (Illus.). 128p. (gr. 3 up). 1984. pap. 4.95 (*0-685-25362-7*) Addison-Wesley.

Schwartz, Amy. Camper of the Week. LC 90-23033. (Illus.). 32p. (gr. k-2). 1991. 14.95 (*0-531-05942-1*); RLB 14.99 (*0-531-08542-2*) Orchard Bks Watts.

Scott, Elaine. Choices. Thompson, Ellen, illus. LC 88-34537. 192p. (gr. 7 up). 1989. 12.95 (*0-688-07230-5*) Morrow Jr Bks.

Sellers, Naomi. The Little Elephant Who Liked to Play. Mitsuhashi, Yoko, illus. LC 94-20299. 1994. write for info. (*0-382-24682-9*) Silver Burdett Pr.

Sendak, Maurice. Pierre: A Cautionary Tale. Sendak, Maurice, illus. LC 62-13315. 48p. (ps-3). 1991. pap. 3.95 (*0-06-443252-1*, Trophy) HarpC Child Bks.

Sharmat, Marjorie W. A Big Fat Enormous Lie. McPhail, David, illus. LC 77-15645. (ps-2). 1978. 13.00 (*0-525-26510-4*, DCB) Dutton Child Bks.

—Nate the Great & the Lost List. (Illus.). 48p. (gr. 1-4). 1976. 11.95 (*0-698-20646-0*, Coward) Putnam Pub Group.

Shigezawa, Ruth. Celeste: A Fable for All Ages. Altman, Robin W., illus. LC 93-72194. 28p. (gr. 2 up). 1993. 16.95 (*0-9637101-0-9*); pap. 7.95 (*0-9637101-1-7*) Cndlelght Pr.

Shles, Larry. The Adventure of the Squib Owl: Squib Ser. Shles, Larry, illus. 1988. pap. 7.95 (*0-915190-85-0*) Jalmar Pr.

Squib the Owl series, written & whimsically illustrated by Larry Shles, teaches self-esteem & personal & social responsibility as it entertains. The author uses the name Squib to personify the small vulnerable part of us all that struggles & at times feels helpless in an enormous world filled with emotions. This Series, five volumes, traces the adventures of this tiny owl as he struggles with his feelings searching at least for understanding. Each of the five titles explores a different vulnerability. MOTHS & MOTHERS, FEATHERS & FATHERS (explores feelings); HOOTS & TOOTS & HAIRY BRUTES (explores disabilities); ALIENS IN MY NEST (explores adolescent behavior); HUGS & SHRUGS (explores inner peace). The latest volume DO I HAVE TO GO TO SCHOOL TODAY? is great for the young reader who needs encouragement from teachers who accept him "just as he is". Brilliantly simple, yet realistically complex, Squib personifies each & every one of us. He is a reflection of what we are, & what we can become. Every reader who has struggled with life's limitations will recognize his own struggles & triumphs in the microcosm of Squib's forest world - in Squib we find a parable for all ages from 8-80.
Publisher Provided Annotation.

—Scooter's Tail of Terror: A Fable of Addiction & Hope. Ciconte, Marie, ed. (Illus.). 80p. (Orig.). (gr. 2 up). 1992. pap. 9.95 (*0-915190-89-3*, JP9089-3) Jalmar Pr.

Shufflebotham, Anne. Baby Bear Cub's Busy Day. LC 91-12965. (gr. 3 up). 1991. 5.99 (*0-85953-425-1*) Childs Play.

Slaughter, Hope. The Deeeeelicious Dragon. Heaney, Rhonda K., illus. LC 86-652. 32p. (ps-3). 1986. pap. 4.95 (*0-931093-05-8*) Red Hen Pr.

Slepian, Jan. Risk n' Roses. 176p. (gr. 6 up). 1990. 14.95 (*0-399-22219-7*, Philomel Bks) Putnam Pub Group.

Slightly Off-Center Writers Group, Ltd. Staff. Empty Bank & the Rich Shoemaker. (Illus.). 60p. (gr. 4-6). 1994. pap. 6.95 (*1-56721-024-4*) Twnty-Fifth Cent Pr.

—Getting What You Wish For. (Illus.). 60p. (gr. 4-6). 1994. pap. 6.95 (*1-56721-041-4*) Twnty-Fifth Cent Pr.

—Gift of Failure. (Illus.). 60p. (gr. 4-6). 1994. pap. 6.95 (*1-56721-034-1*) Twnty-Fifth Cent Pr.

—If You Have It, You Don't. (Illus.). 60p. (gr. 4-6). 1994. pap. 6.95 (*1-56721-037-6*) Twnty-Fifth Cent Pr.

—In All Directions. (Illus.). 48p. (gr. 3-5). 1994. pap. 6.95 (*1-56721-031-7*) Twnty-Fifth Cent Pr.

—The Last Drop into the Full Glass. (Illus.). 48p. (gr. 3-5). 1994. pap. 6.95 (*1-56721-038-4*) Twnty-Fifth Cent Pr.

—Look for the Spirit. (Illus.). 48p. (gr. 4-6). 1994. pap. 6.95 (*1-56721-086-4*) Twnty-Fifth Cent Pr.

—Master of Fear. (Illus.). 48p. (gr. 4-6). 1994. pap. 6.95 (*1-56721-032-5*) Twnty-Fifth Cent Pr.

—Proving It! (Illus.). 48p. (gr. 4-6). 1994. pap. 6.95 (*1-56721-035-X*) Twnty-Fifth Cent Pr.

—Reflections Make You Shine. (Illus.). 48p. (gr. 3-5). 1994. pap. 6.95 (*1-56721-045-7*) Twnty-Fifth Cent Pr.

—Show-Off. (Illus.). 48p. (gr. 3-5). 1994. pap. 6.95 (*1-56721-033-3*) Twnty-Fifth Cent Pr.

—Silent Speaker. (Illus.). 60p. (gr. 4-6). 1994. pap. 6.95 (*1-56721-028-7*) Twnty-Fifth Cent Pr.

—Thankless Gift. (Illus.). 60p. (gr. 3-5). 1994. pap. 6.95 (*1-56721-025-2*) Twnty-Fifth Cent Pr.

—Those Who Talk Big & Those Who Do Big. (Illus.). 60p. (gr. 4-6). 1994. pap. 6.95 (*1-56721-040-6*) Twnty-Fifth Cent Pr.

—When Is Enough Enough? (Illus.). 60p. (gr. 4-6). 1994. pap. 6.95 (*1-56721-030-9*) Twnty-Fifth Cent Pr.

—Wind's Lesson. (Illus.). 48p. (gr. 4-6). 1994. pap. 6.95 (*1-56721-087-2*) Twnty-Fifth Cent Pr.

Smith, Matthew V. When Not to Say Help. Smith, Matthew V., illus. 16p. (gr. k-3). 1992. pap. 11.95 (*1-895583-34-9*) MAYA Pubs.

—When to Say Help. Smith, Matthew V., illus. 18p. (gr. k-3). 1992. pap. 12.95 (*1-895583-33-0*) MAYA Pubs.

Snyder, Dianne. George & the Dragon Word. Lies, Brian, illus. 56p. (gr. 2-4). 1991. 13.45 (*0-395-55129-3*, Sandpiper) HM.

Some Things You Just Can't Do by Yourself. (Illus.). (ps-3). 1973. 4.95 (*0-938678-00-0*) New Seed.

Spinelli, Jerry. Fourth Grade Rats. (ps-3). 1991. 13.95 (*0-590-44243-0*, Scholastic Hardcover) Scholastic Inc.

Stahl, Hilda. Sendi Lee Mason & the Great Crusade. 128p. (gr. 2-5). 1991. pap. 4.99 (*0-89107-632-8*) Crossway Bks.

Starbuck, Marnie. The Gladimals Learn about Responsibility. 1991. pap. text ed. 0.75 (*1-56456-228-X*) W Gladden Found.

Steig, William. Abel's Island. Steig, William, illus. LC 75-35916. 128p. (gr. 1 up). 1976. 15.00 (*0-374-30010-0*) FS&G.

Stevenson, James. Worse Than the Worst. LC 93-239. (Illus.). 32p. (gr. k up). 1994. 14.00 (*0-688-12249-3*); PLB 13.93 (*0-688-12250-7*) Greenwillow.

Strasser, Todd. Wildlife. LC 86-19861. 224p. (gr. 7 up). 1987. pap. 14.95 (*0-385-29560-X*) Delacorte.

Streatfield, Noel. Dancing Shoes. 276p. (gr. 4-9). 1994. pap. 3.99 (*0-679-85428-2*) Random Bks Yng Read.

Stuart, Jesse. A Penny's Worth of Character. Miller, Jim W., et al, eds. Zornes, Rocky, illus. 62p. (gr. 3-6). 1988. 10.00 (*0-945084-03-X*) J Stuart Found.

Talbot, Marilyn. Shy Roland. (Illus.). 32p. (ps-k). 1994. 14.95 (*0-86264-405-4*, Pub. by Andersen Pr UK) Trafalgar.

Talley, Carol. Gumbo Goes Downtown. Maeno, Itoko, illus. LC 93-3551. 32p. (gr. 1-4). 1993. 16.95 (*1-55942-042-1*, 7654) Marshfilm.

Taylor, Livingston & Taylor, Maggie. Can I Be Good? Rand, Ted, illus. LC 92-23193. 1993. 14.95 (*0-15-200436-X*) HarBrace.

Tetz, Rosanne. Nina Can. 32p. 1993. pap. 5.95 (*0-8163-1111-0*) Pacific Pr Pub Assn.

Thaler, Mike. Upside down Day. 32p. (gr. k-3). 1986. pap. 2.95 (*0-380-89999-X*, Camelot) Avon.

Thomson, Pat. Best Pest. Firmin, Peter, illus. 32p. (ps-1). 1993. pap. 6.95 (*0-575-05156-6*, Pub. by Gollancz UK) Trafalgar.

Time Life Inc. Editors. Tales for a Stormy Day: A Book about Good Behavior. Kagan, Neil & Ward, Elizabeth, eds. (Illus.). (ps-2). 1992. write for info. (*0-8094-9307-1*); lib. bdg. write for info. (*0-8094-9308-X*) Time-Life.

Tolstoy, Leo. God Sees the Truth, but Waits. LC 85-29920. 32p. (gr. 4 up). 1986. PLB 13.95 (*0-88682-071-5*) Creative Ed.

Tytla, Milan. Come to Your Senses. McLeod, Chum, illus. 96p. 1993. pap. 9.95 (*1-55037-292-0*, Pub. by Annick CN) Firefly Bks Ltd.

Uchida, Yoshiko. The Best Bad Thing. 2nd ed. LC 83-2833. 128p. (gr. 4-7). 1993. pap. 4.95 (*0-689-71745-8*, Aladdin) Macmillan Child Grp.

Ulmer, Louise. The Man Who Learned to Give. (gr. k-2). 1977. pap. 1.99 (*0-570-06109-1*, 59-1227) Concordia.

Van der Beek, Deborah. Melinda & the Class Photograph. 28p. (gr. k-4). 1991. PLB 18.95 (*0-87614-694-9*) Carolrhoda Bks.

Van Laan, Nancy. A Mouse in My House. Priceman, Marjorie, illus. LC 89-15591. 32p. (ps-3). 1990. 9.95 (*0-679-80043-3*); PLB 10.99 (*0-679-90043-8*) Knopf Bks Yng Read.

Velde, Vande. Dragon's Bait. 1992. write for info. (*0-15-200726-1*, J Yolen Bks) HarBrace.

Waite, Michael P. Handy-Dandy Helpful Hal. LC 87-5275. (ps-2). 1987. text ed. 7.99 (*1-55513-221-9*, Chariot Bks) Chariot Family.

Walter, Lori J. The World According to Wally: It's All in How You See It. Kehl, Donald & Messoner, Dale, eds. Taylor, David S., illus. 30p. (Orig.). (gr. k-8). 1994. Incl. cass. pap. 13.95 (*0-9634833-2-3*) Rocking Bridge. Here's a heart-warming story that can be read & heard of how EVERYONE can change their lives by viewing life in a positive light. Wally's a cat who starts life by being deserted. His mother & 12 fellow kittens are sealed in a box & abandoned in a field in blistering heat. He's found by a pet shop owner, given to a mean man & angrily returned to the pet store. Wally's finally adopted by a nice couple. But there's a catch! The other cat in his new home hates him. But Wally risks his life to save this cat, thus turning him into a friend. Through his positive outlook, loving attitude & courage he makes friends & a new life for himself. It is a beautiful story of how he improves his life & the lives of everyone around him. WALLY's a quality children's book which features 30 full-color illustrations by award-winning artist David Scott Taylor. The digitally mastered cassette, produced by composer Donald James Kehl, features professional narration, six character voices, sound effects, two original orchestrated songs & full orchestral musical cues. To order: call 1-800-MY-WALLY (800-699-2559) or write WALLY, 2007 E. La Vieve, Tempe, AZ 85284.
Publisher Provided Annotation.

Walton, Rick. Will You Still Love Me? Teare, Brad, illus. LC 92-341. 32p. (ps). 1992. 11.95 (*0-87579-582-X*) Deseret Bk.

Wedell, Robert F. Rolf the Green Ghost. Warners, Sheila B., illus. 69p. (Orig.). (ps-8). 1988. pap. 4.95 (*0-685-30435-3*) Milrob Pr.

Weiss, Ellen. Oh Beans! Starring Jelly Bean. Hall, Susan, illus. LC 88-4904. 32p. (gr. k-3). 1989. PLB 8.79 (*0-8167-1404-5*); pap. text ed. 1.95 (*0-8167-1405-3*) Troll Assocs.

—Oh Beans! Starring Snap Bean. Hall, Susan, illus. LC 88-4900. 32p. (gr. k-3). 1989. PLB 8.79 (*0-8167-1410-X*) Troll Assocs.

—Oh Beans! Starring Vanilla Bean. Hall, Susan, illus. LC 88-4903. 32p. (gr. k-3). 1989. PLB 8.79 (*0-8167-1412-6*); pap. text ed. 1.95 (*0-8167-1413-4*) Troll Assocs.

Wells, Rosemary. Max & Ruby's First Greek Myth. Wells, Rosemary, illus. LC 92-30332. 32p. (ps-3). 1993. 11.99 (*0-8037-1524-2*); PLB 11.89 (*0-8037-1525-0*) Dial Bks Young.

What Have I Lost: Dial the Answer. 1992. pap. 3.99 (*0-517-06619-X*) Random Hse Value.

Wiggins, VeraLee. Shelby's Big Scare. LC 93-31363. 1994. 8.95 (*0-8163-1190-0*) Pacific Pr Pub Assn.

Wilhelm, Hans. Tyrone the Horrible. (ps). 1992. pap. 3.95 (*0-590-41472-0*) Scholastic Inc.

Williams, Sunnie. The Nomie Book: Growing up from Shy. Crisamore, Naomi, illus. 104p. (Orig.). (gr. 3-6). 1981. pap. 2.75 (*0-9605444-0-2*) Waking Light Pr.

Winner Takes All, No. 132. 192p. (Orig.). (gr. 7-12). 1987. pap. 2.50 (*0-553-26790-6*) Bantam.

Winterfeld, Henry. Trouble at Timpetill. Lattimore, Deborah N. & Hutchinson, William M., illus. 199p. (gr. 3-7). 1990. pap. 4.95 (*0-15-290786-6*, Odyssey) HarBrace.

Wolff, Virginia E. Make Lemonade. large type ed. LC 93-21003. (gr. 9-12). 1993. 15.95 (*0-7862-0056-1*) Thorndike Pr.

Wood, Audrey. Rude Giants. LC 91-13015. (Illus.). 32p. (ps-3). 1993. 13.95 (*0-15-269412-9*, HB Juv Bks) HarBrace.

—The Tickleoctopus. Wood, Don, illus. LC 93-26868. 1994. 14.95 (*0-15-287000-8*) HarBrace.

—Tugford Wanted to Be Bad. Wood, Don, illus. LC 83-318. 32p. (ps-3). 1983. pap. 4.95 (*0-15-291084-0*, Voyager Bks) HarBrace.

Woodard, Judy & Tucker, Martha. The Legend of the SunaKorn. LC 89-50138. 40p. 1989. 12.95 (*0-938021-41-9*) Turner Pub Ky.

Wright, Betty R. I Like Being Alone. Toht, Don, illus. Okun, Barbara F., intro. by. LC 80-25513. (Illus.). 32p. (gr. k-6). 1981. PLB 19.97 (*0-8172-1367-8*) Raintree Steck-V.

Wright, Kit. Tigerella. Bailey, Peter, illus. LC 93-34218. (ps-2). 1994. 14.95 (*0-590-48171-1*) Scholastic Inc.

Yee, Wong H. Big Black Bear. Yee, Wong H., illus. LC 92-40862. 1993. 14.95 (*0-395-66359-8*) HM.

Yolen, Jane. The Gift of Sarah Barker. 160p. (gr. 5 up). 1992. pap. 3.99 (*0-14-036027-1*) Puffin Bks.

BEHAVIOR–POETRY

Kennedy, X. J. Drat These Brats! Watts, James, illus. LC 92-33686. 48p. (gr. 3 up). 1993. SBE 12.95 (*0-689-50589-2*, M K McElderry) Macmillan Child Grp.

Min, Kellet I. Modern Informative Nursery Rhymes: Values, Book I. Hansen, Heidi, illus. LC 89-91719. 32p. (ps-3). 1989. pap. 7.95 (*0-9623411-3-4*) Rhyme & Reason.

Nielsen, Shelly. Playing Fair. Wallner, Rosemary, ed. LC 92-73043. 1992. 13.99 (*1-56239-065-1*) Abdo & Dghtrs.

Robson, Tom. Musical Wisdom: Songs & Drawings for the Child in Us All. James, Nancy V., illus. 88p. (Orig.). (gr. k-6). 1992. pap. 16.95 (*0-9633332-0-8*) Laughing Cat.

BEHAVIOR PROBLEMS (CHILDREN)

see Problem Children

BELGIUM

Belgium in Pictures. 64p. (gr. 5 up). 1991. PLB 17.50 (*0-8225-1889-9*) Lerner Pubns.

Goldstein, Frances. Children's Treasure Hunt Travel to Belgium & France. Goldstein, Frances, illus. LC 80-85012. 230p. (Orig.). (gr. k-12). 1981. pap. 6.95 (*0-933334-02-8*, Dist. by Hippocrene) Paper Tiger Pap.

Vandersteen, Willy. The Iron Flowerpotters. Lahey, Nicholas J., tr. from FLE. LC 76-49376. (Illus., Orig.). (gr. 3-8). 1977. pap. 2.50 (*0-915560-11-9*, 11) Hiddigeigei.

BELIEF AND DOUBT

Deverell, Catherine. Grandma Told Me So. (ps-k). 1988. 1.59 (*0-87403-386-1*, 2016) Standard Pub.

Teller, Hanoch. Courtrooms of the Mind: Stories & Advice on Judging Others Favorably. 2nd ed. 288p. (gr. 12). 1988. Repr. 11.95 (*0-9614772-4-5*) NYC Pub Co.

BELL, ALEXANDER GRAHAM, 1847-1922

Dunn, Andrew. Alexander Graham Bell. LC 90-2628. (Illus.). 48p. (gr. 5-7). 1991. PLB 12.40 (*0-531-18418-8*, Pub. by Bookwright Pr) Watts.

Farr, Naunerle C. Thomas Edison - Alexander Graham Bell. Taloac, Gerry & Trinidad, Angel, illus. (gr. 4-12). 1979. pap. text ed. 2.95 (*0-88301-357-6*); wkbk. 1.25 (*0-88301-381-9*) Pendulum Pr.

Lewis, Cynthia C. Hello, Alexander Graham Bell Speaking. (Illus.). 64p. (gr. 3 up). 1991. text ed. 13.95 RSBE (*0-87518-461-8*, Dillon) Macmillan Child Grp.

Pelta, Kathy. Alexander Graham Bell. (Illus.). 144p. (gr. 5-9). 1989. PLB 10.95 (*0-382-09529-4*) Silver Burdett Pr.

Rider Montgomery, Elizabeth. Alexander Graham Bell: Man of Sound. (Illus.). 80p. (gr. 2-6). 1993. Repr. of 1963 ed. lib. bdg. 12.95 (*0-7910-1423-1*) Chelsea Hse.

St. George, Judith. Dear Dr. Bell - Your Friend, Helen Keller. 172p. (gr. 5-9). 1992. 15.95 (*0-399-22337-1*, Putnam) Putnam Pub Group.

—Dear Dr. Bell...Your Friend, Helen Keller. LC 93-9304. 96p. (gr. 6 up). 1993. pap. text ed. 4.95 (*0-688-12814-9*, Pub. by Beech Tree Bks) Morrow.

Tames, Richard. Alexander Graham Bell. LC 89-29281. (Illus.). 32p. (gr. 5-8). 1990. PLB 12.40 (*0-531-14003-2*) Watts.

BELLS

Pienkowski, Jan. Door Bell. (Illus.). 10p. (ps up). 1992. incl. sound chip 13.95 (*0-8431-3452-6*) Price Stern.

BENCH, JOHNNY, 1947-

Shannon, Mike. Johnny Bench. (Illus.). 64p. (gr. 3 up). 1990. 14.95 (*0-7910-1168-2*) Chelsea Hse.

BERLIN, IRVING, 1888-

Streissguth, Tom. Say It with Music: A Story about Irving Berlin. Hagerman, Jennifer, illus. LC 93-4376. (gr. 4 up). 1993. 14.95 (*0-87614-810-0*) Carolrhoda Bks.

BERLIN

Ayer, Eleanor H. Berlin. LC 91-29721. (Illus.). 96p. (gr. 6 up). 1992. text ed. 14.95 RSBE (*0-02-707800-0*, New Discovery) Macmillan Child Grp.

Dudman, J. Division of Berlin. (Illus.). 80p. (gr. 7 up). 1988. PLB 18.60 (*0-86592-037-0*); 13.95s.p. (*0-685-58321-X*) Rourke Corp.

Steins, Richard. Berlin. (Illus.). 64p. (gr. 3-7). PLB 14.95 (*1-56711-019-3*) Blackbirch.

BERLIN–FICTION

Lutzeier, Elizabeth. The Wall. LC 92-52712. 160p. (gr. 5-9). 1992. 14.95 (*0-8234-0987-2*) Holiday.

BERLIN WALL (1961-)

Epler, Doris. The Berlin Wall: How It Rose & Why It Fell. LC 91-20610. (Illus.). 128p. (gr. 7 up). 1992. PLB 15.90 (*1-56294-114-3*); pap. 5.95 (*1-56294-835-0*) Millbrook Pr.

BERLIN WALL (1961-)–FICTION

Lutzeier, Elizabeth. The Wall. LC 92-52712. 160p. (gr. 5-9). 1992. 14.95 (*0-8234-0987-2*) Holiday.

BERMUDA TRIANGLE

Abels, Harriette S. Bermuda Triangle. LC 87-14029. (Illus.). 48p. (gr. 5-6). 1987. text ed. 12.95 RSBE (*0-89686-340-9*, Crestwood Hse) Macmillan Child Grp.

Collins, Jim. The Bermuda Triangle. LC 77-21808. (Illus.). 48p. (gr. 4 up). 1983. PLB 20.70 (*0-8172-1050-4*) Raintree Steck-V.

Gaffron, Norma. The Bermuda Triangle: Opposing Viewpoints. LC 94-555. (Illus.). 112p. (gr. 5-8). 1995. PLB 14.95 (*1-56510-217-7*) Greenhaven.

BERNADETTE SOUBIROUS, SAINT, 1844-1879

Urbide, Fernando & Engler, Dan. Bernadette: The Princess of Lourdes. CCC of America Staff, illus. 35p. (Orig.). (ps-6). 1990. incl. video 21.95 (*1-56814-004-5*); pap. text ed. 4.95 book (*0-685-62403-X*) CCC of America.

BERNARD DE CLAIRVAUX, SAINT, 1091-1153

Daughters of St. Paul. Bells of Conquest. LC 68-28105. (gr. 3-7). 1987. 3.00 (*0-8198-0228-X*); pap. 2.00 (*0-8198-1109-2*) St Paul Bks.

BERNSTEIN, LEONARD, 1918-

Deitch, Kenneth M. Leonard Bernstein: America's Maestro, With a Message from Issac Stern. Foley, Sheila, illus. Stern, Isaac, intro. by. LC 91-70821. (Illus.). 48p. (gr. 5-12). 1991. PLB 14.95 (*1-878668-03-X*); pap. 7.95 (*1-878668-07-2*) Disc Enter Ltd.

BERRA, LAWRENCE PETER, 1925-

Appel, Marty. Yogi Berra. (Illus.). 64p. (gr. 3 up). 1992. lib. bdg. 14.95 (*0-7910-1169-0*) Chelsea Hse.

BERRY, MARTHA MCCHESNEY, 1866-1942

Blackburn, Joyce. Martha Berry: A Woman of Courageous Spirit & Bold Dreams. 1992. pap. 8.95 (*1-56145-071-5*) Peachtree Pubs.

BEST BOOKS

see Books and Reading–Best Books

BETHUNE, MARY JANE (MCLEOD) 1875-1955

AESOP Enterprises, Inc. Staff & Crenshaw, Gwendolyn J. Mary McLeod Bethune: We've Come This Far by Faith. 14p. (gr. 3-12). 1991. pap. write for info. incl. cassette (*1-880771-08-X*) AESOP Enter.

Anderson, LaVere. Mary McLeod Bethune: Teacher with a Dream. (Illus.). 80p. (gr. 2-6). 1991. Repr. of 1976 ed. lib. bdg. 12.95 (*0-7910-1405-3*) Chelsea Hse.

Durant, Charlotte T. Miss Mary McLeod Bethune: The Life of a Beautiful African American Woman. Pye, Ethel, ed. Durant, Charlotte T., illus. 40p. (Orig.). (ps-1). 1992. pap. 4.00 (*0-913678-21-X*) New Day Pr.

Greene, Carol. Mary McLeod Bethune: Champion for Education. LC 92-37013. (Illus.). 48p. (gr. k-3). 1993. PLB 12.85 (*0-516-04255-6*); pap. 4.95 (*0-516-44255-4*) Childrens.

Greenfield, Eloise. Mary McLeod Bethune. Pinkney, Jerry, illus. LC 76-11522. 40p. (gr. 2-5). 1977. PLB 14.89 (*0-690-01129-6*, Crowell Jr Bks) HarpC Child Bks.

—Mary McLeod Bethune. Pinkney, Jerry, illus. LC 76-11522. 40p. (gr. 1-4). 1994. pap. 5.95 (*0-06-446168-8*, Trophy) HarpC Child Bks.

Halasa, Malu. Mary McLeod Bethune. King, Coretta Scott. (Illus.). 112p. (gr. 5 up). 1989. lib. bdg. 17.95x (*1-55546-574-9*) Chelsea Hse.

Kelso, Richard. Building a Dream: Mary Bethune's School. Heller, Debbe, illus. LC 92-18069. 46p. (gr. 2-5). 1992. PLB 19.97 (*0-8114-7217-5*) Raintree Steck-V.
McKissack, Patricia & McKissack, Fredrick. Mary McLeod Bethune. LC 92-12098. (Illus.). 32p. (gr. 3-6). 1992. PLB 12.30 (*0-516-06658-7*) Childrens.
—Mary McLeod Bethune. LC 92-12098. (Illus.). 32p. (gr. 3-6). 1993. pap. 3.95 (*0-516-46658-5*) Childrens.
—Mary McLeod Bethune: A Great Teacher. Ostendorf, Ned, illus. LC 91-8818. 32p. (gr. 1-4). 1991. lib. bdg. 12.95 (*0-89490-304-7*) Enslow Pubs.
McKissack, Patricia C. Mary McLeod Bethune: A Great American Educator. LC 85-12843. (Illus.). 111p. (gr. 4 up). 1985. PLB 14.40 (*0-516-03218-6*); pap. 5.95 (*0-516-43218-4*) Childrens.
Mary McLeod Bethune. (gr. 2-6). 1989. pap. 3.50 (*0-14-042219-6*, Puffin) Puffin Bks.
Meltzer, Milton. Mary McCleod Bethune. Marchesi, Stephen, illus. (gr. 2-6). 1988. pap. 3.50 (*0-317-69647-5*, Puffin) Puffin Bks.
Wolfe, Rinna E. Mary McLeod Bethune. Rich, Mary P., ed. LC 91-31660. (Illus.). 64p. (gr. 3-5). 1992. PLB 12. 90 (*0-531-20103-1*) Watts.

BEVERAGES

Charles, Oz. How Does Soda Get Into a Bottle? LC 87-11534. (Illus.). 32p. (gr. 1-5). 1988. pap. 9.95 (*0-671-63755-X*, S&S BFYR) S&S Trade.
Erlbach, Arlene. Soda Pop. LC 93-20106. 1993. 17.50 (*0-8225-2386-8*) Lerner Pubns.
Tchudi, Stephen. Soda Poppery: The History of Soft Drinks in America. LC 85-40289. 160p. (gr. 7 up). 1986. SBE 14.95 (*0-684-18488-5*, Scribners Young Read) Macmillan Child Grp.

BIBLE

Aprendamos de la Biblia: Learning about the Bible. (SPA.). 32p. 1987. pap. 1.50 (*0-311-26612-6*) Casa Bautista.
Backhouse, Robert. The Big Book of Bible Facts. LC 92-32366. 1993. 9.99 (*0-8407-7743-4*) Nelson.
Batchelor, Mary. Children's Bible in Three Hundred Sixty-Five Stories. Haysom, John, illus. 416p. (ps up). 1987. 15.95 (*0-7459-1333-4*) Lion USA.
Beall, Pamela C. & Nipp, Susan H. Wee Sing Bible Songs. Klein, Nancy, illus. 64p. (ps-2). 1986. pap. 2.95 (*0-8431-3806-8*); pap. 9.95 bk. & cass. (*0-8431-3795-9*) Price Stern.
Beck, Susan E. God Loves Me Bible. (ps). 1993. 7.99 (*0-310-91652-6*) Zondervan.
Beegle, Shirley. Bible Double Trouble Puzzles. Dilley, Romilda, illus. 64p. (gr. 5 up). 1992. wkbk. 6.99 (*0-87403-671-2*, 28-02791) Standard Pub.
The Beginning Reader's Bible. LC 93-42479. 1994. 6.99 (*0-8499-5086-4*) Word Pub.
The Bible for Beginning Readers. (Illus.). (gr. 3 up). 1991. text ed. 9.99 (*0-8499-0917-1*) Word Inc.
Biffi, Inos. The First Sacraments. Walsh, Kevin, tr. from ITA. Vignazia, Franco, illus. Martini, Carlo, intro. by. LC 88-80658. (Illus.). 94p. (gr. 4-9). 1989. 15.95 (*0-89870-206-2*) Ignatius Pr.
Blankenbaker, Frances. What the Bible Is All about for Young Explorers. LC 86-22488. (Illus.). 364p. (gr. 6-8). 1986. 12.99 (*0-8307-1179-1*, 5111647); pap. 8.99 (*0-8307-1162-7*, 5418877) Regal.
BMA Staff. The Bible ABCs: A Memory Book for Boys & Girls ages 3-5. Lautermilch, John, illus. 54p. (ps). 1980. pap. text ed. 4.95 (*0-89323-051-0*) Bible Memory.
Boldorini, Maria G., illus. My First Bible. 12p. (ps-1). 1994. 6.99 (*0-679-85621-8*) Random Bks Yng Read.
Chesto, Kathleen O. & Chesto, Elizabeth. Children's Scripture Puzzles: Reproducible Activities & Family Discussion for Sundays Through the Church Year (Cycle B) (Illus.). 116p. (Orig.). (gr. k-8). 1993. pap. 39.95 (*1-55612-619-0*) Sheed & Ward MO.
The Children's Bible. (Illus.). (gr. k-12). 1965. write for info. (*0-307-16520-5*, Golden Bks) Western Pub.
Coleman, William. Far Out Facts of the Bible. (gr. 3-7). 1989. pap. 3.69 (*1-55513-865-9*, Chariot Bks) Chariot Family.
Crain, Steve. Bible Fun Book, No. 8. 32p. (Orig.). (gr. k-4). 1981. pap. 1.19 oversized saddle stitched (*0-87123-772-5*) Bethany Hse.
Crisci, Elizabeth W. Five-Minute Bible Fun, Closing Activities. 96p. (ps-5). 1990. 10.95 (*0-86653-522-5*, SS1819, Shining Star Pubns) Good Apple.
Daniel, Sarah. Bible Rebus Quotes. 48p. (gr. 3 up). 1989. 7.95 (*0-86653-512-8*, SS890, Shining Star Pubns) Good Apple.
David C. Cook Publishing Staff. Awesome Real-Life Bible Devotions for Kids. LC 91-18215. (gr. 4-7). 1991. 9.99 (*1-55513-737-7*, Chariot Bks) Chariot Family.
—Just for Kids Bible: Selected Readings for Active Kids. LC 91-17565. (gr. 4-7). 1991. 13.99 (*1-55513-713-X*, Chariot Bks) Chariot Family.
—Lord Is My Shepherd: Bible Verses of Comfort & Encouragement for Children of All Ages. LC 91-17532. (ps-3). 1991. 8.99 (*1-55513-680-X*, Chariot Bks) Chariot Family.
De Fajardo, Vilma, ed. La Biblia Me Ensena. 96p. (ps). 1988. pap. 5.95 (*0-311-11454-7*) Casa Bautista.
God's Wonderful World: Activity Book. 24p. (gr. 3-7). 1991. pap. 2.29 (*1-55513-450-5*, 64501, Chariot Bks) Chariot Family.
The Good Word: New Century Version. 1128p. (gr. 7-12). 1991. pap. 14.99 (*0-8499-3267-X*) Word Inc.
Gregorowski, Christopher. Bible for Young People. (gr. 3 up). 1990. 6.98 (*1-55521-588-2*) Bk Sales Inc.
Herr, Amy, ed. Bible Nuture & Reader Series. rev. ed. (gr. 1-4). 1986. write for info. Rod & Staff.
International Children's Story Bible. (ps-3). 1993. 9.99 (*0-8499-1090-0*) Word Inc.
Jansen, Rick. Incredible NIV Bible Crosswords. 96p. 1992. pap. 3.99 (*0-310-60611-X*, Youth Bks) Zondervan.
Krein, Linda. Bible Crossword Fun. 48p. (gr. 3 up). 1990. 7.95 (*0-86653-547-0*, SS892, Shining Star Pubns) Good Apple.
—Bible Crosswords. Hyndman, Kathryn, illus. 48p. (gr. 3 up). 1986. wkbk. 7.95 (*0-86653-366-4*, SS 881, Shining Star Pubns) Good Apple.
Larsen, Sandy. Eye-Opening Bible Studies. 32p. (gr. 6-10). 1986. saddle-stitched 1.95 (*0-87788-247-9*) Shaw Pubs.
Latta, Richard. Bible Easter Puzzles. 48p. (gr. 3 up). 1988. 7.95 (*0-86653-427-X*, SS885, Shining Star Pubns) Good Apple.
Layton, Karen & Layton, Ron. Bible Word Fun. Hyndman, Kathryn, illus. 48p. (gr. 3 up). 1986. wkbk. 7.95 (*0-86653-367-2*, SS 882, Shining Star Pubns) Good Apple.
Ledyard, Gleason H., tr. Precious Moments Children's Bible: Easy-to-Read, New Life Version. Butcher, Samuel J., illus. LC 90-36671. 1424p. 1991. 24.99 (*0-8010-5664-0*); pap. 19.99 (*0-8010-5684-5*) Baker Bk.
Leone, Dee. Vacation Bible School Activities. 96p. (gr. 2-7). 1990. 10.95 (*0-86653-525-X*, SS1818, Shining Star Pubns) Good Apple.
—The World God Made. 48p. (ps-1). 1991. 7.95 (*0-86653-636-1*, SS1894, Shining Star Pubns) Good Apple.
Lindvall, Ella K. Bible Illustrated for Little Children. (Illus.). (ps-2). 1991. text ed. 9.99 (*0-8024-0569-X*) Moody.
Lovasik, Lawrence G. St. Joseph First Children's Bible. (ps-3). 1983. 4.95 (*0-89942-135-0*) Catholic Bk Pub.

Macias, Benjamin. One Hundred One Bible Riddles for All Ages. Macias, Daniel, illus. 112p. (Orig.). (gr. 1 up). 1993. pap. 7.95 (*0-9638277-1-5*) Fam of God.
This Bible riddle book is the most complete collection of fully illustrated Bible riddles for children, adolescents & adults. Each humorous Bible riddle has its own unique, creative & vivid illustration that perfectly describes the riddle. These Bible riddles have been shared with young & old & all agree that it is a treasure of wit & humor for ages to come. You will certainly find this Bible riddle book worthy of sharing with those who also have an appreciation for wholesome & clean riddles. In addition, this witty book can be used in children's activities & programs & young people can also incorporate it in their social activities. Parents can also share it as a gift to their children, knowing satisfactorily that the riddles are children oriented. This Bible riddle indeed is for all ages & ages to come. Family of God Publishing House, P.O. Box 758, Vista, CA 92083-0758. (619) 598-3629, FAX (619) 966-0312.
Publisher Provided Annotation.

MacKenthun, Carole & Dwyer, Paulinus. Faith. Filkins, Vanessa, illus. 48p. (gr. 2-7). 1986. wkbk. 7.95 (*0-86653-361-3*, SS 874, Shining Star Pubns) Good Apple.
—Goodness. Filkins, Vanessa, illus. 48p. (gr. 2-7). 1986. wkbk. 7.95 (*0-86653-363-X*, SS 875, Shining Star Pubns) Good Apple.
—Joy. Filkins, Vanessa, illus. 48p. (gr. 2-7). 1986. wkbk. 7.95 (*0-86653-360-5*, SS 873, Shining Star Pubns) Good Apple.
—Love. Filkins, Vanessa, illus. 48p. (gr. 2-7). 1986. wkbk. 7.95 (*0-86653-359-1*, SS 872, Shining Star Pubns) Good Apple.
—Patience. Filkins, Vanessa, illus. 48p. (gr. 2-7). 1986. wkbk. 7.95 (*0-86653-364-8*, SS 876, Shining Star Pubns) Good Apple.
—Peace. Filkins, Vanessa, illus. 48p. (gr. 2-7). 1986. wkbk. 7.95 (*0-86653-365-6*, SS 877, Shining Star Pubns) Good Apple.
McKenzie, Joy. Solving Bible Mysteries. 96p. 1994. pap. 9.99 (*0-310-59761-7*, Pub. by Youth Spec) Zondervan.
McKissack, Patricia & McKissack, Frederick. My Bible ABC Book. Merrill, Reed, illus. LC 87-70473. 32p. (Orig.). (ps-3). 1987. pap. 5.99 (*0-8066-2271-7*, 10-4588, Augsburg) Augsburg Fortress.
McMillan, Mary. Bible Story Bulletin Boards. 96p. (ps-3). 1988. 10.95 (*0-86653-430-X*, SS1828, Shining Star Pubns) Good Apple.
Malovitzki, Sinai. Parshas Lech. (YID., Illus.). 160p. 1987. tchr's. ed. 10.00 (*0-944704-03-4*) Sinai Heritage.
—Parshas Nitzuvim. (YID., Illus.). 150p. 1988. pap. 5.00 (*0-944704-61-1*) Sinai Heritage.
—Parshas Yisroy. (YID., Illus.). 400p. 1988. PLB 25.00 (*0-944704-19-0*) Sinai Heritage.
—Parshaw Va'Yeilech. (YID., Illus.). 95p. 1988. pap. 5.00 (*0-944704-62-X*) Sinai Heritage.
Meyer, David & Meyer, Alice. The Ten Commandments: An Illustrated Bible Passage for Young Children. Katsma, Candi, illus. LC 90-71557. 40p. (Orig.). (ps-4). 1991. pap. 11.95 incl. cassette (*1-879099-02-0*) Thy Word.
Meyer, David & Meyer, Alice, eds. First Corinthians Thirteen: An Illustrated Bible Chapter for Young Children. DeWind, June & Katsma, Candi, illus. LC 90-71555. 48p. (Orig.). (ps-4). 1990. pap. 12.95 incl. cassette (*1-879099-01-2*) Thy Word.
—Isaiah Fifty-Three: An Illustrated Bible Chapter for Young Children. Katsma, Candi, illus. LC 91-90827. 40p. (Orig.). (ps-4). 1992. pap. 11.95 incl. cassette (*1-879099-06-3*) Thy Word.
—Psalm One Hundred Thirty-Nine: An Illustrated Bible Chapter for Young Children. Crews, Terry, illus. LC 91-90825. 48p. (Orig.). (ps-4). 1991. pap. 12.95 incl. cassette (*1-879099-03-9*) Thy Word.
—Psalm Twenty-Three: An Illustrated Bible Chapter for Young Children. Katsma, Candi, illus. 32p. (Orig.). (ps-4). 1990. pap. 9.95 incl. cassette (*1-879099-00-4*) Thy Word.
Murdock, Michael D. The Teenager's One Minute Bible. Loy, Joy A., ed. 365p. (Orig.). 1991. pap. text ed. 5.95 (*1-56394-003-5*) Wisdom Intl.
My Very First Golden Bible. (ps-3). 1991. write for info. (*0-307-16557-4*, Golden Pr) Western Pub.
The New Adventure Bible: King James Version. 1600p. 1994. 19.99 (*0-310-93046-4*); indexed 25.99 (*0-310-93049-9*); pap. 15.99 (*0-310-93047-2*); pap. 21. 99 indexed (*0-310-93050-2*) Zondervan.
The New Adventure Bible: New International Version. 1600p. 1994. 19.99 (*0-310-91762-X*); indexed 25.99 (*0-310-91770-0*) Zondervan.
The New Adventure Bible: New International Version. 1600p. 1994. blue bonded leather 39.99 (*0-310-91767-0*); indexed, blue bonded leather 45.99 (*0-310-91775-1*) Zondervan.
The New Adventure Bible: New International Version. 1600p. 1994. burgundy bonded leather 39.99 (*0-310-91768-9*); indexed, burgundy bonded leather 45.99 (*0-310-91776-X*) Zondervan.
The New Adventure Bible: New Revised Standard Version. 1600p. 1994. 19.99 (*0-310-92395-6*); indexed 25.99 (*0-310-92397-2*); pap. 15.99 (*0-310-92396-4*); pap. 21.99 indexed (*0-310-92398-0*) Zondervan.
Persaud, Nancy. Bible Children Puzzles. 48p. (gr. 3 up). 1990. 7.95 (*0-86653-534-9*, SS891, Shining Star Pubns) Good Apple.
—Bible Number Puzzles. 48p. (gr. 3 up). 1989. 7.95 (*0-86653-491-1*, SS889, Shining Star Pubns) Good Apple.
Pliskin, Jacqueline J. The Bible Game & Workbook. 96p. 1990. pap. 5.95 (*0-944007-84-8*) Shapolsky Pubs.
Price, Cheryl. Bible Learning Centers. 96p. (gr. 2-6). 1989. 10.95 (*0-86653-498-9*, SS1817, Shining Star Pubns) Good Apple.
Que Linda es la Creacion: Beautiful Creation. (SPA & ENG.). 32p. 1987. pap. 1.50 (*0-311-26611-8*) Casa Bautista.
Rhoda, Michael D. Bible Favorites Activity Book. Gress, Jonna, ed. (Illus.). 6p. (ps-5). 1993. pap. 8.25 (*0-944943-41-1*, 22656-1) Current Inc.
Rogers, Barbara. God's Chosen King Activity Book. 88p. (Orig.). (ps-1). 1984. pap. 3.00 (*0-8361-3370-6*) Herald Pr.
Rossel, Seymour. Child's Bible: Lessons from the Writings & Prophets, Vol. 2. (gr. 3-5). 1989. pap. text ed. 8.50 (*0-318-42729-X*); tchr's. guide 14.95 (*0-87441-485-7*) Behrman.
Sanders, Nancy. Amazing Bible Puzzles: New Testament. (Illus.). 80p. (Orig.). (gr. 3-7). 1993. pap. 4.99 (*0-570-04749-8*) Concordia.
—Amazing Bible Puzzles: Old Testament. (Illus.). 80p. (Orig.). (gr. 3-7). 1993. pap. 4.99 (*0-570-04748-X*) Concordia.
Savary, Louis & Frankhausen, Edward. The Bible As Narrated by Jesus, the Storyteller. 1989. 9.95 (*0-88271-198-9*) Regina Pr.
Schlegl, William. Bible Trivia. Leedom, Valerie, illus. 48p. (gr. 3 up). 1986. wkbk. 7.95 (*0-86653-368-0*, SS 883, Shining Star Pubns) Good Apple.
Schwartaman, Sylvan D. & Spiro, Jack D. The Living Bible: A Topical Approach. (gr. 10-12). 5.00 (*0-8074-0097-1*, 161751) UAHC.
Shannon, Foster H. Green Leaf Bible Series, Year Five: The Growth of the Believing Community. 180p. (gr. 3 up). 1989. looseleaf 17.50 (*0-938462-09-1*) Green Leaf CA.
Snyder, Bernadette M. One Hundred Fifty Fun Facts Found in the Bible: For Kids of All Ages. Sharp, Chris, illus. LC 90-70802. 144p. (gr. 1-6). 1990. pap. 5.95 (*0-89243-330-2*) Liguori Pubns.

Soles, Henry, ed. Children of Color Holy Bible. Carter, Fred, et al, illus. 880p.

(gr. 2 up). 1993. write for info. (*0-9638127-0-X*) Child of Color. The new illustrated Holy Bible for Children of Color is designed for ALL of God's children of ALL ages. With its beautiful hardcover binding & authentically illustrated 4-color pictures, this Bible has appeal to a wide range of book lovers. Adults (men & women) ages 26-44 find this Bible their Bible of choice for themselves & their children ages 7-17. Churched & unchurched Bible buyers are regular respondents of a Children of Color Bible buyer survey. Responses usually come from the middle to upper income ranges & cross all denominational affiliations (Protestant & Catholic) & racial divides (African American, Hispanic, Caribbean). Over 1,000 pages of original King James version text serves as the foundation for over 40 illustrations of famous Bible stories. Also included are 13 traditional hymns & children's songs. This Bible also features 8 portraits of Blacks from the Bible & several lists, such as "Women of the Bible," "Children of the Bible," & "Miracles of the Bible," which make it easy to find favorite Bible passages. This Bible was featured on CNN recently & appears in the August edition of Essence magazine. To order contact: Children of Color Publishing, 345 Whitehall St. SW, Atlanta, GA 30303. (404) 215-9270, FAX (404) 215-9016 or (404) 215-9281.
Publisher Provided Annotation.

Steen, Shirley & Edwards, Anne. A Child's Bible: Old Testament & New Testament. (gr. 1-8). 1986. 11.95 (*0-8091-2867-5*) Paulist Pr.
Thomas, Mack. Bible Tells Me So: The Beginner's Guide to Loving & Understanding God's Word. (gr. k-5). 1992. 14.99 (*0-945564-20-1*, Gold & Honey) Questar Pubs.
—The First Step Bible. 448p. (ps). 1994. 14.99 (*0-88070-629-5*, Gold & Honey); cass. 7.99 (*0-88070-649-X*, Gold & Honey) Questar Pubs.
—My First Step Bible: Blue for Boys. 95p. (ps). 1992. 6.99 (*0-945564-48-1*, Gold & Honey) Questar Pubs.
—My First Step Bible: Pink for Girls. 95p. (ps). 1992. 6.99 (*0-945564-49-X*, Gold & Honey) Questar Pubs.
Thomas, Mack, ed. The Wonder Bible. 603p. (gr. 2-6). 1993. 16.99 (*0-945564-59-7*, Gold & Honey) Questar Pubs.
Vernon, Louise A. Bible Smuggler. LC 67-15994. (Illus.). 138p. (gr. 4-9). 1967. pap. 5.95 (*0-8361-1557-0*) Herald Pr.
Ward, Elaine M. Growing with the Bible. 64p. (Orig.). (gr. 1-6). 1986. pap. 7.95 (*0-940754-36-3*) Ed Ministries.
Wilson, Etta, ed. My Play a Tune Book: Twelve Favorite Bible Songs. Mahan, Benton, illus. 26p. (ps up). 1988. 12.95 (*0-687-27554-7*) JTG Nashville.
Woggon, Guillermo. Versiculos "Llave" Granberry, Nola, tr. (SPA., Illus.). 16p. (gr. 1-3). 1987. pap. 1.40 (*0-311-38565-6*) Casa Bautista.
Younger, Barbara & Flinn, Lisa. Making Scripture Stick. 108p. 1992. pap. 11.99 (*1-55945-093-2*) Group Pub.
The Youth Bible. 1991. duraflex bdg. 16.99 (*0-8499-3227-0*); 21.99 (*0-8499-0925-2*) Word Inc.

BIBLE–ANIMALS
see Bible–Natural History

BIBLE–ANTIQUITIES
Rogerson, John. The Bible. Evans, Gillian, ed. (Illus.). 96p. (gr. 6-9). 1993. 17.95 (*0-8160-2908-3*) Facts on File.
Thomas, Jerry D. Detective Zack & the Red Hat Mystery. LC 93-4322. 1993. 5.95 (*0-8163-1169-2*) Pacific Pr Pub Assn.
—Detective Zack & the Secrets in the Sand. LC 92-29931. 1993. 5.95 (*0-8163-1129-3*) Pacific Pr Pub Assn.

BIBLE–BIOGRAPHY
see also Apostles; Christian Biography; Prophets; Women in the Bible
Cassway, Esta. Prophets for Young People. LC 94-2498. 376p. 1994. 40.00 (*1-56821-148-1*) Aronson.
Colburn, Rhonda. The Story of Shadrach, Meshach & Abednego. Connelly, Gwen, illus. 24p. (ps-3). 1990. pap. 3.95 (*0-8249-8421-8*, Ideals Child) Hambleton-Hill.
Eisenberg, Ann. Bible Heroes I Can Be. Schanzer, Roz, illus. LC 89-48188. 24p. (ps). 1990. 12.95 (*0-929371-09-7*); pap. 4.95 (*0-929371-10-0*) Kar Ben.
Great Heroes of the Bible. (ps-3). 1992. pap. 4.99 (*0-529-07193-2*) World Bible.
Hershey, Katherine. Patriarchs. (Illus.). 51p. (gr. k-6). 1979. pap. text ed. 9.45 (*1-55976-005-2*) CEF Press.
Lingo, Susan L. & Downey, Melissa C. Abraham. Green, Roy, illus. 32p. (ps-7). 1992. wkbk. 3.99 (*0-87403-915-0*, 23-02525) Standard Pub.
—Daniel. Green, Roy, illus. 32p. (ps-7). 1992. wkbk. 3.99 (*0-87403-919-3*, 23-02529) Standard Pub.
—David. Green, Roy, illus. 32p. (ps-7). 1992. wkbk. 3.99 (*0-87403-918-5*, 23-02528) Standard Pub.
—Joshua. Green, Roy, illus. 32p. (ps-7). 1992. wkbk. 3.99 (*0-87403-917-7*, 23-02527) Standard Pub.
—Moses. Green, Roy, illus. 112p. (ps-7). 1992. wkbk. 3.99 (*0-87403-916-9*, 23-02526) Standard Pub.
Marquart, M. Jesus' Second Family. (gr. k-2). 1977. pap. 1.99 (*0-570-06111-3*, 59-1229) Concordia.
Rosenfeld, Dina. Kind Little Rivka. Lederer, Ilene W., illus. 32p. (ps-1). 1991. 8.95 (*0-922613-44-3*); pap. 6.95 (*0-922613-45-1*) Hachai Pubns.
Seger, Doris. Children of the Bible. Butcher, Sam & Geraldo, Esteban, illus. 64p. (gr. k-6). 1967. pap. text ed. 8.99 (*1-55976-028-1*) CEF Press.
Storr, Catherine. Abraham & Isaac. Rowe, Gavin, illus. LC 84-18076. 32p. (gr. k-4). 1985. 14.95 (*0-8172-1994-3*) Raintree Steck-V.
Wiersbe, Warren. Be Challenged! rev. ed. LC 82-12404. (gr. 7). 1982. pap. 4.50 (*0-8024-1080-4*) Moody.
Woods, Paul. Bible Heroes: Joseph, Esther, Mary & Peter. (Illus.). 48p. (gr. 6-8). 1992. pap. 8.99 (*1-55945-137-8*) Group Pub.
Yenne, Bill & Jacobs, Timothy, eds. The Story of Jonah. LC 93-24837. 1993. 6.99 (*0-8407-4915-5*); pap. 6.99 (*0-8407-4909-0*) Nelson.

BIBLE–BIRDS
see Bible–Natural History

BIBLE–BOTANY
see Bible–Natural History

BIBLE–COMMENTARIES
Adventures of the Kingdom Builders. LC 90-48194. (Illus.). 116p. 1990. pap. 2.99 (*0-8307-1464-2*, EL264) Regal.
Ashworth, L. E. Revelation: Signs of the Times. (Illus.). 240p. (Orig.). (gr. 10). 1990. pap. 5.95 (*0-9627415-0-7*) Advent Times.
Bilderback, Allen H. Revelation & Apocalyptic Symbols: Bible Stories of the Planets & Stars. Anderson, Cindy & Flippin, Terry, illus. 180p. (gr. 8 up). 1992. 24.95 (*0-9630710-1-7*); pap. 19.95 (*0-9630710-0-9*) ABCO Pub.
Blakeley, Given. What the Bible Says about the Kingdom of God. LC 88-71154. 466p. 1988. text ed. 13.95 (*0-89900-260-9*) College Pr Pub.
Chapman, Carl. Who Am I among So Many? An Autobiography Plus Special Articles: The Biggest Exception in the Bible, Paul's Thorn in the Flesh, & Not Discerning the Lord's Body. LC 88-92635. 132p. (Orig.). (gr. 9-12). 1989. pap. 4.99 (*0-9621529-0-0*) C Chapman.
Enriquez, Edmund C. The Golden Gospel: A Pictorial History of the Restoration. Enriquez, Edmund C., illus. 96p. (gr. 6-12). 1981. pap. 7.98 (*0-88290-198-2*) Horizon Utah.
Fields, Harvey J. A Torah Commentary for Our Times, Vol. 3: Numbers & Deuteronomy. Cormi, Giora, illus. LC 89-28478. (Orig.). (gr. 7-9). 1993. pap. text ed. 12.00x (*0-8074-0511-6*, 164020) UAHC.
Fischman, Joyce. Bible Work & Play, Vol. 1. rev. ed. Steinberger, Heidi, illus. 80p. (Orig.). (gr. 1-3). 1985. pap. text ed. 5.00 (*0-8074-0304-0*, 103620) UAHC.
Fox, F. Earle. Biblical Sexuality & the Battle for Science. LC 88-80409. 208p. (Orig.). (gr. 9-12). 1988. pap. 5.45 (*0-945778-00-7*) Emmaus Ministries.
George, Alan. My Wonderful Lord. Butcher, Sam & Hilterbrand, Greg, illus. 61p. (gr. k-6). 1987. pap. text ed. 8.99 (*1-55976-029-X*) CEF Press.
Luccarelli, Vincent, Jr. Job Revisited. LC 93-60359. 40p. (gr. 5 up). 1994. pap. 5.95 (*1-55523-616-2*) Winston-Derek.
MacKenthun, Carole. Biblical Bulletin Boards. Henson, Grace, illus. 48p. (gr. k-4). 1984. wkbk. 7.95 (*0-86653-197-1*, SS 814, Shining Star Pubns) Good Apple.
Miles, A. Marie. Bible: Chain of Truth. 168p. (gr. 5 up). pap. 2.00 (*0-686-29101-8*) Faith Pub Hse.
Nielson, John M. & Skillings, Otis. Bible Walk. 1980. 5.25 (*0-685-68193-9*, BCMB-492); cassette 10.98 (*0-685-68194-7*, BCTA-9016C); choral promo pack 6.00 (*0-685-68195-5*, BCL-9016C) Lillenas.
Nystrom, Carolyn. Holy Spirit in Me: Children's Bible Basics. (ps-3). 1993. 5.99 (*0-8024-7858-1*) Moody.
Potter, Jerold C. Books of the Bible. Bowen & Bowen Type Setters Staff, ed. 36p. 1988. pap. text ed. 1.50 (*0-925306-00-2*) WOFPPM.
Russell, Bob. Marriage by the Book: Biblical Models for Marriage Today. 112p. (Orig.). 1992. pap. 6.99 (*0-87403-906-1*, 29-03156) Standard Pub.
Schlegl, William. Bible Codes & Messages. (Illus.). 48p. (gr. 3 up). 1989. 7.95 (*0-86653-479-2*, SS887, Shining Star Pubns) Good Apple.
Sciacca, Fran & Sciacca, Jill. Good News in a Bad News World: Understanding the Gospel. 64p. 1992. pap. 3.99 saddle stitch bdg. (*0-310-48061-2*) Zondervan.
Shannon, Foster H. Green Leaf Bible Series Year Six: Songs & Promises. 184p. (gr. 3 up). 1992. thermobound 17.50 (*0-938462-10-5*) Green Leaf Ca.
Taggart, George. Bible Promises for Tiny Tots, III. Coffen, Richard W., ed. 32p. (Orig.). (ps). 1987. pap. 4.50 (*0-8280-0375-0*) Review & Herald.
Waller, Lynn. How Do We Know the Bible Is True? Reasons a Kid Can Believe It. 64p. (gr. 3-7). 1991. pap. 4.99 (*0-310-53821-1*, Youth Bks) Zondervan.
Weisheit, Eldon. The Gospel for Kids: Series C. (gr. 3-6). 1979. 7.99 (*0-570-03279-2*, 15-2723) Concordia.
Wilhelm, Hans. What Does God Do? 29p. 1987. write for info. (*0-8499-0712-8*) Word Inc.
Woods, Paul. Applying the Bible to Life. (Illus.). 48p. (gr. 6-8). 1991. pap. 8.99 (*1-55945-116-5*) Group Pub.

BIBLE–DICTIONARIES
Dictionary of the Bible. (gr. 2 up). 1994. pap. 5.95 (*0-685-74709-3*) Running Pr.
Layton, Karen & Layton, Ron. Bible Word Play. (Illus.). 48p. (gr. 3 up). 1989. 7.95 (*0-86653-472-5*, SS888, Shining Star Pubns) Good Apple.
McElrath, William N. Bible Dictionary for Young Readers. Fields, Don, illus. LC 65-15604. (gr. 4-6). 1965. 12.99 (*0-8054-4404-1*, 4244-04) Broadman.
—Mi Primer Diccionario Biblico. McElrath, Ruth G., tr. from ENG. Fields, Don, illus. (SPA.). 128p. (gr. 4-6). 1991. pap. 4.50 (*0-311-03656-2*) Casa Bautista.
Matthews, Velda & Beard, Ray. Basic Bible Dictionary. Korth, Bob, ed. Wahl, Dick, illus. 128p. (Orig.). (gr. 4-12). 1984. pap. 12.99 (*0-87239-720-3*, 2770) Standard Pub.
Wiersma, Debbie B. Precious Moments Children's Bible Dictionary. (Illus.). 160p. 1994. 14.99 (*0-8010-9736-3*) Baker Bk.
Wilson, Etta & Jones, Sally L. Bible Dictionary: A First Reference Book. Schindler, Stephen, illus. 24p. (gr. 3-5). 1993. text ed. 9.99 (*0-7847-0079-6*, 24-03619) Standard Pub.
Winder, Linda. My First Bible Dictionary: A Sticker-Fun Book. (Illus.). 48p. 1991. pap. 5.99 (*0-8010-9712-6*) Baker Bk.

BIBLE–DRAMA
see Mysteries and Miracle Plays

BIBLE–FESTIVALS
see Fasts and Feasts

BIBLE–FICTION
see Bible–History of Biblical Events–Fiction

BIBLE–FLOWERS
see Bible–Natural History

BIBLE–GARDENS
see Bible–Natural History

BIBLE–GEOGRAPHY
Hochstatter, Daniel J. Sammy's Fabulous Holy Land Travels: Sammy Visits the Land of the Bible. 1994. 9.99 (*0-7852-8281-5*) Nelson.
Hochstatter, Daniel J., illus. Sammy's Fabulous Holy Land Travels. LC 93-34525. 1994. 9.99 (*0-89528-281-X*) Nelson.
Rogerson, John. The Bible: Cultural Atlas for Young Children. LC 92-34670. 1993. write for info. (*0-8160-2923-7*) Facts on File.
Standard Bible Atlas. (Illus.). 32p. (Orig.). 1992. wkbk. 7.99 (*0-87403-840-5*, 14-03160) Standard Pub.
Stowell, Charlotte & Stowell, Gordon. Make a Bible Village. Stowell, Charlotte & Stowell, Gordon, illus. 28p. (gr. k-3). 1994. pap. 11.95 (*0-8192-1617-8*) Morehouse Pub.
Wilson, Etta & Jones, Sally L. Bible Atlas: A First Reference Book. Schindler, Stephen, illus. 24p. (gr. 3-5). 1993. text ed. 9.99 (*0-7847-0080-X*, 24-03620) Standard Pub.

BIBLE–HISTORY
Here are entered works on the origin, authorship and composition of the Bible as a book. Works dealing with historical events as described in the Bible are entered under Bible–History of Biblical Events.
Hoffman, Yair & Shamir, Ilana. The World of the Bible for Young Readers. (Illus.). 96p. (gr. 7 up). 1989. pap. 15.95 (*0-670-81739-2*) Viking Child Bks.
Hurlbut, Jesse L. Hurlbut's Story of the Bible. rev. ed. (Illus.). (gr. k-4). 1967. 29.99 (*0-310-26520-7*, 6524) Zondervan.
Teitelbaum, Eli. A Basic Guide to the Mishkan. rev. ed. Malowicky, Sinai, ed. & illus. 16p. (gr. 7-12). 1992. pap. text ed. write for info. (*1-878895-01-X*, A320) Torah Umesorah.
Thomas, Jerry D. Detective Zack & the Secret of Noah's Flood: Starburst. LC 92-5730. 128p. 1992. pap. 5.95 (*0-8163-1107-2*) Pacific Pr Pub Assn.
Todd, Richard E. Salvation. rev. ed. Miller, Alma E. & Kellner, Ron, illus. 26p. (gr. 2-6). 1993. wkbk. 2.45 (*0-9605324-6-3*) Crosswalk Res.
Unfred, David W. Dinosaurs & the Bible. LC 90-80887. (Illus.). 47p. (gr. 3-8). 1990. 12.99 (*0-910311-70-6*) Huntington Hse.

BIBLE–HISTORY OF BIBLICAL EVENTS
Adventures of the Early Church. (gr. 4-6). 1990. 1.55 (*0-89636-118-7*, JB 3C) Accent CO.
Cole, Babette & Van Der Meer, Ron. The Bible Beasties. (Illus.). 12p. 1993. 16.00 (*0-551-02595-6*, Pub. by HarperCollins UK) Harper SF.
Scepters, Swords, & Fire from Heaven. (gr. 4-6). 1990. 1.55 (*0-89636-113-6*, JB 2B) Accent CO.
Truit, Gloria A. Events of the Bible. (ps-3). 1992. pap. 1.89 (*0-570-06185-7*, 59-1312) Concordia.
Vincent, Mark. Untold Stories of Advent. LC 93-72479. 77p. (Orig.). 1993. pap. 10.95 (*0-87303-207-1*) Faith & Life.

Youngman, Bernard R. Patriarchs, Judges, & Kings. (gr. 8-12). 1984. pap. 9.95 (*0-7175-0414-X*) Dufour.

BIBLE–HISTORY OF BIBLICAL EVENTS–FICTION

Celestri, John. The Christian Crusader: The Quest Begins. 72p. (gr. 3-6). 1992. pap. 3.49 (*0-9634183-0-0*) CC Comics.

Children's Bible Stories to Read & Color: New Testament. (Illus.). 144p. 1991. pap. 2.49 (*0-517-68993-6*) Random Hse Value.

Frye, Chad. The Fun Bible Search Book...Find Rupert. Frye, Chad, illus. 32p. 1992. 12.95 (*1-55748-309-4*) Barbour & Co.

Grishaver, Joel L. Tanta Teva & the Magic Booth. Bleicher, David, illus. LC 93-13193. 1993. 11.95 (*1-881283-00-3*) Alef Design.

Head, Constance. The Man Who Carried the Cross for Jesus. (Illus.). (gr. k-4). 1979. 1.99 (*0-570-06124-5*, 59-1242) Concordia.

Jander, Martha. The Tower of Babel. Swisher, Elizabeth, illus. 24p. (Orig.). (gr. k-4). 1991. pap. 1.99 (*0-570-09026-1*) Concordia.

Lewis, Lee A. The Trouble with Dreams. LC 91-27503. 160p. (Orig.). (gr. 4-7). 1991. pap. 5.95 (*0-8361-3571-7*) Herald Pr.

Myers, Bill. The Tablet. Jorgenson, Andrea, illus. LC 92-34301. 160p. (Orig.). (gr. 3 up). 1992. pap. 5.99 (*1-55661-299-0*) Bethany Hse.

Rice, Tim & Webber, Andrew L. Joseph & the Amazing Technicolor Dreamcoat. Blake, Quentin, illus. 32p. (gr. k-3). 1993. pap. 11.95 (*1-85793-119-X*, Pub. by Pavilion UK) Trafalgar.

Ryan, John. Mabel & the Tower of Babel. Ryan, John, illus. 32p. (gr. 4-8). 1990. 9.99 (*0-7459-1742-9*) Lion USA.

Truitt, Gloria. Peter Set Free. Needham, James, illus. 24p. (gr. k-4). 1991. pap. 1.99 (*0-570-09027-X*) Concordia.

Van Horn, Brian & Van Horn, Chris. A Boy Full of Joy. Scott, Rita & Van Horn, Brian, illus. (ps-5). 1989. write for info. (*1-877765-01-5*) Lambgel Family.

—Lain Cain & Label Abel. Scott, Rita & Van Horn, Brian, illus. (gr. k-5). 1989. write for info. (*1-877765-02-3*) Lambgel Family.

—Leve Eve Believes Werpent the Serpent in the Garden of Eden. Scott, Rita & Van Horn, Brian, illus. (gr. k-5). 1989. write for info. (*1-877765-03-1*) Lambgel Family.

—Loah Noah & the Ark. Scott, Rita & Van Horn, Brian, illus. (gr. k-5). 1989. write for info. (*1-877765-04-X*) Lambgel Family.

BIBLE–INTERPRETATION

see Bible–Commentaries

BIBLE–INTRODUCTIONS

see Bible–Study

BIBLE–MAPS

see Bible–Geography

BIBLE–NATURAL HISTORY

Bible Discovery Collection: Animals. (Illus.). 64p. (gr. 4-6). 1992. 12.99 (*0-8423-1006-1*) Tyndale.

Bright & Beautiful. (Illus.). 8p. (ps). 1984. bds. 3.99 (*0-7459-1426-8*) Lion USA.

McKenzie, Marni S. Alphabet of Bible Creatures. Patterson, Karen T., illus. 56p. (ps-8). 1993. 14.95 (*1-882630-00-9*) Mercy Pr.

Paterson, John & Paterson, Katherine. Consider the Lilies: Flowers of the Bible. Dowden, Anne O., illus. LC 85-43603. 48p. (gr. 7 up). 1986. 14.00 (*0-690-04461-5*, Crowell Jr Bks) HarpC Child Bks.

Taylor, Paul S. The Great Dinosaur Mystery & the Bible. LC 89-81581. 63p. (gr. 4-8). 1990. 13.99 (*0-89636-264-7*, AC 215, Chariot Bks) Chariot Family.

Whitcomb, Norma A. Those Mysterious Dinosaurs: A Biblical Approach for Children, Their Parents & Their Teachers. 2nd ed. Job, Heather H., illus. Wyrtzen, Jack, frwd. by. (Illus.). 125p. (gr. 4 up). 1993. Spiral bdg. pap. 7.20x (*0-685-67781-8*); pap. text ed. 11.99 (*0-9635049-0-8*) Whitcomb Minist.

BIBLE–PARABLES

see Jesus Christ–Parables

BIBLE–PICTORIAL WORKS

Beers, V. Gilbert. My Picture Bible to See & to Share. 189p. (ps-4). 1982. text ed. 14.99 (*0-88207-818-6*, Sonflower Bks) SP Pubns.

—The Toddler's Bible. (ps). 1992. 14.99 (*0-89693-077-7*, Victor Books) SP Pubns.

Children's Illustrated Old Testament. (Illus.). (gr. 4-7). 1993. 14.95 (*0-15-238220-8*, HB Juv Bks) HarBrace.

Clark, Penny, illus. A Coloring Book of Bible Proverbs. 32p. (ps-5). 1988. 2.50 (*0-9618608-2-0*) Lynn's Bookshelf.

Decker, Barbara, ed. A Coloring Book of Bible Verses from the Epistles. Clark, Penny, illus. 32p. (ps-5). 1992. 2.50 (*0-9618608-9-8*) Lynn's Bookshelf.

Ellis, Joyce & Lynn, Claire. Bible Bees. Lautermilch, John, illus. 36p. (gr. k). 1981. 2.95 (*0-89323-049-9*) Bible Memory.

Farnsworth, Bill, illus. The Illustrated Children's Bible. LC 93-16222. (gr. 1-8). 1993. 19.95 (*0-15-232876-9*) HarBrace.

Gaines, M. C., ed. Picture Stories from the Bible: The Old Testament in Full-Color Comic-Strip Form. Cameron, Don, illus. LC 79-66064. 232p. (gr. 3-10). 1979. Repr. of 1943 ed. 12.95 (*0-934386-01-3*) Scarf Pr.

Hastings, Selina, retold by. The Children's Illustrated Bible. Thomas, Eric, illus. LC 93-30814. (gr. 3 up). 1994. 19.95 (*1-56458-472-0*) Dorling Kindersley.

Hook, Frances, illus. Frances Hook Picture Book. Hayes, Wanda. (Illus.). (gr. k-2). 1989. 10.99 (*0-87239-243-0*, 3548) Standard Pub.

Pittenger, Shari. Listen, Color & Learn: A Coloring Book for Family Devotions, Vol. I, Psalm 1-30. Pittenger, Shari, illus. Harris, Gregg, intro. by. 35p. (Orig.). (ps-6). 1989. pap. text ed. 4.95 (*0-923463-49-6*) Noble Pub Assocs.

Stoddard, Sandol. Doubleday Illustrated Children's Bible. Chen, Tony, illus. LC 82-45340. 384p. (gr. 4-6). 1983. pap. 25.00 (*0-385-18521-9*) Doubleday.

Stoner, Laura M. Acts - a Story Color Book. Huskey, Freeda, ed. Stoner, Laura M., illus. 80p. (Orig.). (gr. k-6). 1992. wkbk. 5.95 (*0-934426-46-5*) NAPSAC Reprods.

Taylor, Kenneth N. Bible in Pictures for Little Eyes. (Illus.). (ps-2). 1956. 14.99 (*0-8024-0595-9*) Moody.

Tudor, Tasha, illus. The Lord Is My Shepherd: The Twenty-Third Psalm. LC 79-27134. 32p. (gr. 2 up). 1989. 9.95 (*0-399-20756-2*, Philomel) Putnam Pub Group.

Turner, Teresa R. ABCs from the Book of Life. 32p. (gr. k-2). 1991. pap. 3.95 (*0-9633509-3-5*) T R Turner.

BIBLE–PLANTS

see Bible–Natural History

BIBLE–STUDY

Aderman, James. Is He the One? Fischer, William E., ed. Woodfin, James, illus. 64p. (gr. 9-12). 1985. pap. 3.95 leader's guide (*0-938272-21-7*); pap. 3.25 student's guide (*0-938272-20-9*) WELS Board.

The Adventure Bible. 1989. pap. 15.99 (*0-310-91919-3*) Zondervan.

Alex, Ben & Thomas, Mack. Beginners Bible Questions & Answer Book. (Illus.). 384p. (Orig.). (ps-5). 1992. 14.99 (*0-945564-21-X*, Gold & Honey) Questar Pubs.

Anglund, Joan W. God Is Love. (Illus.). (gr. 1 up). 5.95 (*0-317-13661-5*) Determined Prods.

Barkey, Tom. Forbid Not Prophecy. Mills, Dick, frwd. by. 125p. (Orig.). (gr. 8). 1991. pap. 5.95 (*0-9626910-1-1*) Power Comm Ch.

—God Is... My Strength. Mackall, Phyllis, ed. 86p. (Orig.). (gr. 8). 1990. pap. 6.95 (*0-9626910-0-3*) Power Comm Ch.

Beers, Gil & Hagler, Liz. The Early Reader's Bible. 527p. (ps-3). 1991. 15.99 (*0-945564-43-0*, Gold & Honey) Questar Pubs.

Beers, V. Gilbert. More Little Talks about God & You. LC 87-81042. 224p. (Orig.). (ps-3). 1987. pap. 9.99 (*0-89081-586-0*) Harvest Hse.

—My Picture Reading Bible to See & Share. (Illus.). 384p. 1994. 14.99 (*1-56476-297-1*, Victor Books) SP Pubns.

—Toddler's Bible Coloring Book - NT. (Illus.). 48p. (Orig.). 1994. pap. 1.99 (*1-56476-302-1*, Victor Books) SP Pubns.

—Toddler's Bible Coloring Book - OT. (Illus.). 48p. (Orig.). 1994. pap. 1.99 (*1-56476-301-3*, Victor Books) SP Pubns.

Bernstein, David. Parshas Beshalach. Shapiro, Sara, illus. (ENG & HEB.). 192p. (gr. 5-8). 1991. pap. text ed. 6.00 (*0-914131-96-6*, A148) Torah Umesorah.

Bible Guide: A Reader's Companion to the Bible. LC 93-85518. (Illus.). 320p. (Orig.). 1994. pap. 5.95 (*1-56138-379-1*) Running Pr.

Birky, Lela. Truth for Life Bible Studies. (gr. 7-9). 1965. pap. write for info. (*0-686-15481-9*) Rod & Staff.

Borchardt, Lois M. Learning about God's Love: Word-Picture Activities for Children in Grades 1 & 2. 48p. (gr. 1-2). 1986. pap. 2.99 (*0-570-04354-9*, 61-2017) Concordia.

Borenstein. Five-Minute Bible Games & Fun. (Illus.). 96p. (ps-3). 1992. 10.95 (*0-86653-698-1*, SS2828, Shining Star Pubns) Good Apple.

Britt, Stephanie M. My Little Memory Verses. (ps). 1994. 5.99 (*0-8499-1140-0*) Word Inc.

Brusselmans, Christiane, et al. Sunday: Book of Readings Adapted for Children, Year B. 176p. (ps-8). 1990. text ed. 49.95 (*0-929496-57-4*) Treehaus Comns.

—Sunday: Leaders Weekly Guidebook, Year B. 160p. (ps-8). 1990. text ed. 49.95 (*0-929496-58-2*) Treehaus Comns.

Burkhart, Joyce L. & Mercer, Deborah B. Scripture Concepts for Children Activity-Story Book: Building Godly Character, Vol. 2. Burkhart, Joyce L., illus. 43p. (ps-2). 1992. pap. 7.95 (*0-9633166-1-3*) Penta Ent.

—Scripture Concepts for Children Activity-Story Book, Vol. 1: Building Godly Self-Esteem. Burkhart, Joyce L., illus. 43p. (Orig.). (ps-2). 1991. pap. 7.95 (*0-9633166-0-5*) Penta Ent.

Burstein, Chaya M. The Mystery of the Coins. Burstein, Chaya M., illus. 160p. (Orig.). (gr. 4-6). 1988. pap. text ed. 9.95 (*0-8074-0350-4*, 123000); tchr's. guide 5.00 (*0-8074-0413-6*, 201442) UAHC.

Butcher, Sam. Bible Promises. (Illus.). 1992. 4.99 (*0-8407-4263-0*) Nelson.

—Itty Bitty Books: Precious Moments, 4 bks. (Illus.). 1992. Set. 19.99 (*0-8407-6882-6*) Nelson.

Cain, Clifford. Five-Minute Bible Object Lessons. (Illus.). 96p. (ps-5). 1992. 10.95 (*0-86653-694-9*, SS2824, Shining Star Pubns) Good Apple.

Campbell, Stan. The Saga Begins. 156p. (gr. 8 up). 1988. pap. 5.99 (*0-89693-656-2*, Victor Books) SP Pubns.

—That's the Way the Kingdom Crumbles. 144p. (gr. 8 up). 1988. pap. text ed. 5.99 (*0-89693-658-9*, Victor Books) SP Pubns.

—What's This World Coming To? 144p. (gr. 8 up). 1988. pap. text ed. 5.99 (*0-89693-865-4*, Victor Books) SP Pubns.

Carney, Mary L. Bible Knock-Knocks & Other Fun Stuff. LC 88-939. (ps-6). 1988. pap. 4.95 (*0-687-03180-X*) Abingdon.

Case, Riley B., et al. We Believe - Discovery. rev. ed. 64p. 1988. wkbk. 4.35 (*0-917851-26-9*) Bristol Hse.

Cavin, Diantha S. Scripture by Picture: Make Memorizing the Bible Fun & Easy. Cavin, Diantha S., illus. 78p. (Orig.). (ps-6). 1992. pap. 10.95 (*0-9628012-3-2*) Dexter KS.

Chick, Jack T. Rey de Reyes: La Biblia en Cuadros. (SPA., Illus.). 64p. (Orig.). 1989. pap. 2.25 (*0-937958-37-9*) Chick Pubns.

Chromey, Rick. Revelation. (Illus.). 48p. (gr. 9-12). 1992. pap. 8.99 (*1-55945-229-3*) Group Pub.

Clevenger, Ernest A., Jr. The Church. 104p. (gr. 3 up). 1990. pap. 4.75 (*0-88428-016-0*) Parchment Pr.

Complete Book of Bible Promises for Kids. 318p. (gr. 1-6). 1994. pap. 12.99 (*0-8423-0526-2*) Tyndale.

Complete Book of Bible Proverbs for Kids. 320p. (gr. 1-6). 1994. pap. 12.95 (*0-8423-0527-0*) Tyndale.

Corbin, Linda & Dys, Pat. Jesus Wins the Battle. (Illus., Orig.). (gr. 1-6). 1989. pap. 5.99 wkbk. (*0-87509-410-4*) Chr Pubns.

Costello, Gwen. A Bible Way of the Cross for Children. Curley, Ed, illus. 32p. (Orig.). (gr. 4-6). 1988. pap. 1.95 (*0-89622-353-1*) Twenty-Third.

Currier, Mary. Bible Memory Activity Book. (Illus.). 96p. (ps-4). 1993. pap. 7.99 (*0-8010-2578-8*) Baker Bk.

Daniel, Rebecca. Jesus: Birth to Ascension. (Illus.). 48p. (gr. k-6). 1992. 7.95 (*0-86653-695-7*, SS2825, Shining Star Pubns) Good Apple.

Daniel, Rebecca & Jones, Kathy. Night of Wonder Musical. (Illus.). 48p. (ps-7). 1992. incl. tape 16.95 (*0-685-50800-5*, SS2841, Shining Star Pubns); 7.95 (*0-86653-705-8*, SS2841, Shining Star Pubns); tape 10.95 (*0-685-50801-3*, SS2842, Shining Star Pubns) Good Apple.

—Noah & Company Musical. (Illus.). 48p. (ps-7). 1992. incl. tape 16.95 (*0-685-50798-X*, SS2839, Shining Star Pubns); 7.95 (*0-86653-704-X*, SS2839, Shining Star Pubns); tape 10.95 (*0-685-50799-8*, SS2840, Shining Star Pubns) Good Apple.

Daniel, Rebecca & Stegenga, Susan J. Christian Crafts from Cardboard Containers. (Illus.). 64p. (ps-5). 1992. 8.95 (*0-86653-703-1*, SS2833, Shining Star Pubns) Good Apple.

Darling, Kathy. Preschool Bible Crafts. (Illus.). 96p. (ps-1). 1992. 10.95 (*0-86653-699-X*, SS2829, Shining Star Pubns) Good Apple.

Daughters of St. Paul. The Bible for Young People. 142p. (gr. 4 up). 1988. pap. 5.00 (*0-8198-0212-3*) St Paul Bks.

DeGarmo, Eddie, et al. Go to the Top - Leave the Crowd Behind: 49 Readings Based on the Bible & DeGarmo & Key Lyrics. 88p. 1991. pap. 4.99 (*0-8307-1504-5*, S185202) Regal.

Dellinger, A. & Fletcher, S. Favorite Bible Verses. (ps-3). 1983. pap. 0.69 (*0-570-08310-9*, 56HH1442) Concordia.

Dockrey, Karen. I Thought You Were My Friend. 48p. (Orig.). 1994. pap. 2.99 (*1-56476-290-4*, Victor Books) SP Pubns.

—I Thought You Were My Friend: Leader's Guide. 96p. (Orig.). 1994. pap. 4.99 (*1-56476-281-5*, Victor Books) SP Pubns.

—What's a Kid Like Me Doing in a Family Like This? Leader's Book. 72p. (gr. 7-9). 1992. pap. 4.99 (*0-89693-113-7*) SP Pubns.

Ellis, Eric J. Bible Timeline Workbook: A Step-by-Step Learning Guide for Those Who Think that the Old Testament is Too Difficult to Piece Together. (Illus.). 240p. (gr. 7 up). 1994. pap. 10.00 transparencies (*1-886001-01-4*); sprial bdg. 12.00 (*1-886001-02-2*) Crnstone Pr.

The Explorer's Study Bible. (Illus.). (gr. 3-6). 1991. 19.99 (*0-8407-1598-6*); pap. 15.99 (*0-8407-1597-8*) Nelson.

Fields, Harvey J., ed. A Torah Commentary for Our Times: Genesis, Vol. I. Carmi, Giora, illus. LC 89-28478. (gr. 7 up). 1990. pap. text ed. 12.00 (*0-8074-0308-3*, 164000) UAHC.

Fochman, Joyce. Bible Work & Play, Vol. 3. rev. ed. Lemelman, Martin, illus. 80p. 1986. pap. 5.00 wkbk. (*0-8074-0305-9*, 103640) UAHC.

Fogle, Jeanne S. Teaching the Bible with Puppets. LC 89-50563. (Illus.). 1989. tchr's. ed. 9.95 (*0-89622-405-8*) Twenty-Third.

Following God's Trailblazers: Kings & Prophets 14 Lessons, Vol. 4. (gr. 3-9). 1958. pap. text ed. 4.25 (*0-86508-033-X*); figures/text 14.45 (*0-86508-034-8*) BCM Pubn.

Forbes, Milton L. Out of the Mists of Time: Who Wrote the Bible & Why. LC 91-91561. 125p. 1992. pap. 4.95 (*0-9623700-2-9*) Mtntop Bks.

Freehof, Lillian S. Bible Legends: An Introduction to Midrash, Vol. 2: Exodus. Schwartz, Howard, ed. Tarlow, Phyllis, illus. 160p. (gr. 4-6). 1988. pap. text ed. 6.95 (*0-8074-0412-8*, 123060) UAHC.

Freeman, W. B. Nelson's Super Book of Bible Activities for Kids, Bk. 5. (ps-3). 1994. pap. 8.99 (*0-8407-9194-1*) Nelson.

Fromer, Margaret & Nystrom, Carolyn. Acts 13-28: Missions Accomplished. DeVelasco, Joe, illus. 93p. (gr. 7-12). 1979. saddle-stitched tchr's. ed. 4.99 (*0-87788-011-5*); saddle- stitched student ed. 3.99 (*0-87788-010-7*) Shaw Pubs.

Gaines, M. C., ed. Picture Stories from the Bible: The Old Testament in Full-Color Comic-Strip Form. Cameron, Don, illus. LC 79-66064. 222p. (gr. 3-10). 1979. Repr. of 1943 ed. 12.95 (*0-934386-01-3*) Scarf Pr.

Giampa, Linda. New Testament Activity Book. Giampa, Linda, illus. 32p. (Orig.). (gr. k-3). 1992. pap. 2.99 (*0-570-04725-0*) Concordia.

Goldman, Russ. Learning the Bible Through Puzzles. 38p. 1992. pap. write for info. (*1-882185-00-5*) Crnrstone Pub.

Great Devotional Classics, 29 bklts. 1160p. 1975. Set. pap. 14.95 (*0-8358-0332-5*) Upper Room.

Group Publishing, Inc. Editors. Angels, Demons, Miracles & Prayer. (Illus.). 48p. (gr. 9-12). 1993. pap. 8.99 (*1-55945-235-8*) Group Pub.

—Dealing with Life's Pressures. (Illus.). 48p. (gr. 9-12). 1993. pap. 8.99 (*1-55945-232-3*) Group Pub.

—Doing Your Best. (Illus.). 48p. (gr. 6-8). 1993. pap. 8.99 (*1-55945-142-4*) Group Pub.

—Psalms. (Illus.). 48p. (gr. 9-12). 1993. pap. 8.99 (*1-55945-234-X*) Group Pub.

—The Thirteen Most Important Bible Lessons for Teenagers. LC 93-13436. 100p. 1993. pap. 12.99 (*1-55945-261-7*) Group Pub.

Grunze, Richard. Searching in God's Word-New Testament. Most, Richard, illus. 142p. (gr. 5-6). 1986. 4.95 (*0-938272-41-1*) WELS Board.

—Searching in God's Word-Old Testament. Most, Richard, illus. 140p. (gr. 5-6). 1986. 4.95 (*0-938272-40-3*) WELS Board.

Haas, Lois J. Tiny Steps of Faith Series. 1985. pap. text ed. 3.50 (*0-86508-010-0*) BCM Pubn.

Haidle, David & Haidle, Helen. He Is My Shepherd: The Twenty-Third Psalm for Children. Davis, Deena, ed. Haidle, David & Haidle, Helen, illus. LC 89-31428. 27p. (ps-3). 1989. 8.99 (*0-88070-278-8*, Gold & Honey) Questar Pubs.

Heath, Lou & Taylor, Beth. Reading My Bible in Fall. LC 85-30947. (Orig.). (gr. 1-6). 1986. pap. 4.99 (*0-8054-4322-3*) Broadman.

—Reading My Bible in Spring. (Orig.). (gr. 3-6). 1987. pap. 4.99 (*0-8054-4320-7*) Broadman.

—Reading My Bible in Summer. (Orig.). (gr. 3-6). 1987. pap. 4.99 (*0-8054-4321-5*) Broadman.

—Reading My Bible in Winter. LC 85-30940. (Orig.). (gr. 1-6). 1986. pap. 4.99 (*0-8054-4323-1*) Broadman.

Hillam, Corbin. Bible Story Clip & Copy Patterns. (Illus.). 96p. (ps-3). 1992. 10.95 (*0-86653-693-0*, SS2823, Shining Star Pubns) Good Apple.

—The Big Bible Story Coloring Book. (Illus.). 240p. (ps-3). 1992. 8.95 (*0-86653-700-7*, SS2830, Shining Star Pubns) Good Apple.

Horn, Geoffrey & Cavanaugh, Arthur. Bible Stories for Children. Stewart, Arvis, illus. LC 79-27811. 336p. (gr. 1-5). 1980. SBE 14.95 (*0-02-554060-2*, Macmillan Child Bk) Macmillan Child Grp.

Hornock, Marcia. Preschool ABC Bible Heroes. (Illus.). 96p. (ps-1). 1992. 10.95 (*0-86653-697-3*, SS2827, Shining Star Pubns) Good Apple.

Horton, Stanley M. What the Bible Says about the Holy Spirit. Zimmerman, Thomas F., frwd. by. LC 75-43154. 316p. (gr. 12). 1976. pap. 8.95 (*0-88243-647-3*, 02-0647) Gospel Pub.

Jordan, Bernice C. Acts: 14 Lessons, Vol. 1. (gr. 3-9). 1954. pap. text ed. 4.25 (*0-86508-039-9*); figure text 11.50 (*0-86508-040-2*) BCM Pubn.

—Acts: 15 Lessons, Vol. 2. (gr. 3-9). 1954. pap. text ed. 4.25 (*0-86508-041-0*); figure text 11.50 (*0-86508-042-9*) BCM Pubn.

—Fighting Giants: Joshua-Solomon 14 Lessons, Vol. 3. (gr. 3-9). 1957. pap. text ed. 4.25 (*0-86508-031-3*); figures/text 14.45 (*0-86508-032-1*) BCM Pubn.

—Footsteps to God: Six Basic Bible Truth Lessons. (Illus.). (gr. 3-9). 1970. pap. text ed. 8.50 (*0-86508-025-9*) BCM Pubn.

—Genesis: Fifteen Lessons, Vol. 1. (gr. 3-9). 1960. pap. text ed. 4.25 (*0-86508-027-5*); figures/text 14.45 (*0-86508-028-3*) BCM Pubn.

—God's Storehouse: Exodus 16 Lessons, Vol. 2. (Illus.). (gr. 3-9). 1961. pap. text ed. 4.25 (*0-86508-029-1*); text/figures 14.45 (*0-86508-030-5*) BCM Pubn.

—Gospels: Fourteen Lessons, Vol. 1. (gr. 3-9). 1955. pap. text ed. 4.25 (*0-86508-035-6*); figures/text 14.45 (*0-86508-036-4*) BCM Pubn.

—Gospels: Fourteen Lessons, Vol. 2. (gr. 3-9). 1956. pap. text ed. 4.25 (*0-86508-037-2*); figures/text 14.45 (*0-86508-038-0*) BCM Pubn.

The King & the Beast: Contemporary English Version. 1991. 15.99 (*0-8407-2028-9*); pap. 10.99 (*0-8407-2027-0*) Nelson.

Kizer, Kathryn. God Made... Sealy, Kathy, illus. (Orig.). (ps). 1988. pap. 3.50 (*0-936625-43-0*, New Hope AL) Womans Mission Union.

Kroecker, Beth. Bible ABC: Primer Pages. 30p. (gr. 1-6). 1987. lib. bdg. 39.95 (*0-88946-040-X*) E Mellen.

Lang, Stephen J. The Illustrated Book of Bible Trivia. (Illus.). 1991. PLB 12.99 (*0-8423-1613-2*) Tyndale.

Larsen, Dale & Larsen, Sandy. It's Up to Me: Choosing God's Way. (Illus.). 32p. (gr. 4-6). 1989. saddle-stitched camper ed. 1.50 (*0-87788-404-8*); saddle-stitched counselor ed. 3.50 (*0-87788-405-6*) Shaw Pubs.

—Joseph: From Pit to Pyramid. (Illus.). 32p. (gr. 4-6). 1989. saddle-stitched camper ed. 1.50 (*0-87788-435-8*); saddle-stitched counselor ed. 3.50 (*0-87788-436-6*) Shaw Pubs.

Larsen, Sandy. Choosing: Which Way Do I Go? (Illus.). 32p. (gr. 7-10). 1985. saddle-stitched camper ed. 1.50 (*0-87788-115-4*); saddle-stitched counselor ed. 3.50 (*0-87788-116-2*) Shaw Pubs.

—Forgiving: Lightening Your Load. (Illus.). 32p. (gr. 6-8). 1985. saddle-stitched campers ed. 1.50 (*0-87788-279-7*); saddle-stitched counselor ed. 3.50 (*0-87788-280-0*) Shaw Pubs.

Larsen, Sandy & Larsen, Dale. Celebrating Creation: Exploring God's World. 32p. (gr. 7-10). 1988. Camper. saddle-stitched 1.50 (*0-87788-109-X*); Counselor. saddle-stitched 3.50 (*0-87788-110-3*) Shaw Pubs.

Lashbrook, Marilyn. It's Not My Fault: Man's Big Mistake. Sharp, Chris, illus. LC 90-60459. 32p. (gr. k-3). 1990. 5.95 (*0-86606-439-7*, 870) Roper Pr.

—Too Bad, Ahab! Naboth's Vineyard. Sharp, Chris, illus. LC 90-60457. 32p. (gr. k-3). 1990. 5.95 (*0-86606-441-9*, 872) Roper Pr.

Lebovics, Adel. What Will the World Be Like? Nodoz, Norman, illus. 32p. (ps-1). 1993. 8.95 (*0-922613-56-7*); Russian translation. 8.95 (*0-922613-58-3*); Italian translation. 8.95 (*0-922613-59-1*); pap. 6.95 (*0-922613-57-5*) Hachai Pubns.

LeFever, Marlene. Survival Kit for Growing Christians. 32p. (gr. 4-6). 1988. saddle-stitched camper 1.50 (*0-87788-796-9*); saddle-stitched counselor 3.50 (*0-87788-797-7*) Shaw Pubs.

Link, Mark. Path Through Scripture. (Illus.). 288p. (gr. 9-12). 1987. pap. 13.50 (*0-89505-402-7*, 21095) Tabor Pub.

—Path Through Scripture: Teacher's Resource Manual. 328p. (gr. 9-12). 1987. 26.20 (*0-89505-403-5*, 253X1) Tabor Pub.

—The Seventh Trumpet: Teacher's Manual. 207p. (gr. 9-12). 1978. 20.95 (*0-89505-030-7*, 21005) Tabor Pub.

Lockman, Vic. Reading & Understanding the Bible. Lockman, Vic, illus. 56p. (gr. 6). 1992. stapled 5.95 (*0-936175-18-4*) V Lockman.

Loehrlein, Myrna & Nylin, Dawn. Preschool Bible Lessons. 96p. (ps-1). 1990. 10.95 (*0-86653-541-1*, SS1875, Shining Star Pubns) Good Apple.

Lost & Found. (Illus.). 60p. (gr. k-6). 1971. pap. text ed. 8.99 (*1-55976-025-7*) CEF Press.

Lynn, Claire. B-I-B-L-E That's the Book for Me! Lautermilch, John, illus. 18p. (Orig.). (ps-1). 1981. pap. 1.00 (*0-89323-013-8*) Bible Memory.

MacKenzie, Joy. The Big Book of Bible Crafts & Projects. Flint, Russ, illus. 212p. (Orig.). (ps-4). 1981. pap. 15.99 (*0-310-70151-1*, 14019P) Zondervan.

Manley, Deborah. Bible Times. 48p. 1990. 4.99 (*0-517-69616-9*) Random Hse Value.

Martin, Ernest L. The Original Bible Restored. 2nd ed. (Illus.). 336p. (gr. 10). 1991. pap. text ed. 14.95 (*0-945657-89-7*) Acad Scriptural Knowledge.

Matheny, James F. & Matheny, Marjorie B. Is There a Russian Connection? An Exposition of Ezekiel 37 & 39. 76p. (Orig.). 1987. pap. 3.95 (*0-939422-01-8*) Jay & Assocs.

Maves, Paul & Maves, Carolyn. Finding Your Way Through the Bible: Revised NRSV Edition. 176p. (Orig.). (gr. 2-5). 1992. pap. 4.95 (*0-687-13046-8*) Abingdon.

Miller, Calvin. Apples, Snakes & Bellyaches. (gr. 4-7). 1993. pap. 10.99 (*0-8499-3526-1*) Word Inc.

Miller, Linda F. An Introduction to the Literature & Personalities of the Bible. 89p. (gr. 7-12). 1985. curriculum guide 14.00 (*1-881678-10-5*) CRIS.

Morris, C. Spencer & Beers, V. Gilbert. Beginners ABC Bible Memory Book. 287p. (Orig.). (ps-3). 12.99 (*0-945564-41-4*, Gold & Honey) Questar Pubs.

Mufassir, Sulayman. Biblical Studies from a Muslim Perspective. Obaba, Al I., ed. 49p. (Orig.). 1991. pap. text ed. 2.00 (*0-916157-61-X*) African Islam Miss Pubns.

My Bible Study Notebook. 1992. 5.95 (*1-55748-280-2*) Barbour & Co.

My First Bible Fun Book. (Illus.). 1992. 6.95 (*1-55748-265-9*) Barbour & Co.

Nelson, P. C. Bible Doctrines. Zimmerman, Thomas F., intro. by. LC 81-82738. 128p. (gr. 9-12). 1981. pap. 2.95 (*0-88243-479-9*, 02-0479) Gospel Pub.

Newman, Shirley. Introduction to Kings, Later Prophets & Writings, Vol. 3. Rossel, Seymour, ed. Hoban, Brom, illus. 160p. (Orig.). (gr. 4-5). 1981. pap. text ed. 6.95x (*0-87441-336-2*); wkbk. by Morris Sugarman 3.95 (*0-685-00733-2*); tchr's ed. 14.95x (*0-685-41994-0*) Behrman.

Nystrom, Carolyn. Angels & Me. (Illus.). (ps-2). 1984. pap. 4.99 (*0-8024-6150-6*) Moody.

—Jesus Is No Secret: Children's Bible Basics. (Illus.). (gr. 3-7). 1994. 5.99 (*0-8024-7865-4*) Moody.

—Mark: God on the Move. 96p. (gr. 7-12). 1978. saddle-stitched tchr's. ed. 4.99 (*0-87788-312-2*); student ed. 3.99 (*0-87788-311-4*) Shaw Pubs.

—What Is the Bible? 32p. (ps-2). 1994. 5.99 (*0-8024-7864-6*) Moody.

O'Connor, Francine M. Wait & Wonder. (Illus.). 16p. (gr. 1-3). 1991. pap. 1.95 (*0-89243-419-8*); incl. tchr's. packet 9.95 (*0-89243-418-X*) Liguori Pubns.

Orange, Tom. Scripture Bulletin Boards. 96p. (gr. 2-7). 1987. 10.95 (*0-86653-397-4*, SS1826, Shining Star Pubns) Good Apple.

Overholtzer, Ruth. Wordless Book Visualized. (Illus.). 54p. (gr. k-6). 1979. pap. text ed. 8.99 (*1-55976-027-3*) CEF Press.

Pearson, Mary Rose. Bible Object Lessons. (gr. 1-6). 1991. packet 4.95 (*0-89636-303-1*) Accent CO.

Pennock, Michael F. Discovering the Promise of the Old Testament. LC 91-76778. (Illus.). 224p. (Orig.). (gr. 9-12). 1992. pap. text ed. 8.95 student text (*0-87793-472-X*); tchr's. manual 12.95 (*0-87793-473-8*) Ave Maria.

—Living the Message of the New Testament. LC 91-77474. (Illus.). 216p. (Orig.). (gr. 9-12). 1992. pap. text ed. 8.95 student text (*0-87793-469-X*); tchr's. manual 12.95 (*0-87793-468-1*) Ave Maria.

Pingry, Patricia. The Story of Samson & His Great Strength. Sheets, Leslie, illus. 24p. (Orig.). (ps-1). 1994. pap. 3.95 (*0-8249-8655-5*, Ideals Child) Hambleton-Hill.

—The Story of the Garden of Eden. Ragland, Teresa, illus. 24p. (Orig.). (ps-1). 1994. pap. 3.95 (*0-8249-8654-7*, Ideals Child) Hambleton-Hill.

Piper, John. What's the Difference? Manhood & Womanhood According to the Bible. Elliot, Elisabeth, frwd. by. 64p. (Orig.). 1990. pap. 3.50 (*0-89107-562-3*) Crossway Bks.

Plueddemann, Jim. Keeping Cool in a Crazy World. (Illus.). 32p. (gr. 4-6). 1988. saddle-stitched camper 1.50 (*0-87788-454-4*); saddle-stitched counselor 3.50 (*0-87788-455-2*) Shaw Pubs.

Raney, Nancy. The Big Bible Broadcast. (Illus.). 144p. (gr. 1-6). 1989. 24.95 (*1-55513-870-5*, 68700) Cook.

Respess, Kathryn. The Children of Israel: A Workbook Introduction to Ancient Israel. 124p. (gr. 9-12). 1984. student wkbk. 22.00 (*1-881678-08-3*) CRIS.

Rinehart, Paula. Never Too Small for God. 56p. (gr. 2-6). 1989. pap. 5.00 (*0-89109-270-6*) NavPress.

—One of a Kind. 64p. (gr. 2-6). 1989. pap. 5.00 (*0-89109-269-2*) NavPress.

—Stuck Like Glue. 48p. (gr. 2-6). 1988. pap. 5.00 (*0-89109-268-4*) NavPress.

Roper, Harlin J. In the Beginning God: Genesis - Exodus 18. 64p. 1989. Repr. wkbk. 4.50 (*0-86606-350-1*, 1) Roper Pr.

Rowland, Beth, ed. Lively Bible Lessons for Kindergarten. LC 92-16301. 1992. 11.99 (*1-55945-097-5*) Group Pub.

Rutan, Debbie. Big Promises for Little People. 30p. 1991. pap. 3.95 (*0-685-39073-X*) Green & White Pub.

Scheets, Thomas M. The Bible Says: A Look at Opposing Claims. LC 88-62605. 64p. (Orig.). 1989. pap. 4.95 (*1-55612-239-X*) Sheed & Ward MO.

Schramm, Mary. A Look at God's Book. (Illus.). 42p. (gr. k-6). 1973. pap. text ed. 14.99 (*1-55976-148-2*) CEF Press.

Segal, Lore. The Book of Adam to Moses. Baskin, Leonard, illus. LC 87-2581. 144p. (gr. k up). 1987. lib. bdg. 14.99 (*0-394-96757-7*) Knopf Bks Yng Read.

Shannon, Foster H. Green Leaf Bible Series, Year Four. 180p. (gr. 3 up). 1988. looseleaf 17.50 (*0-938462-08-3*) Green Leaf CA.

—The Green Leaf Bible Series: Heroes of the Bible, Year One. 174p. (gr. 3 up). 1982. pap. 15.00 (*0-938462-06-7*) Green Leaf CA.

Shearer, Jody M. Challenging Racism: Fast Lane Bible Studies. Hall, Eddy, ed. Friesen, Jim, illus. 42p. (Orig.). (gr. 7-9). 1993. pap. 9.95 saddle stitch (*0-87303-210-1*) Faith & Life.

Sikora, Pat. Small Group Bible Studies: How to Lead Them. 224p. (Orig.). 1991. pap. 9.99 (*0-87403-858-8*, 18-03218) Standard Pub.

Simpson, Dale. A Study in Wisdom. Majewski, Joy, illus. 22p. (gr. k-5). 1993. pap. 4.00 (*1-880892-48-0*) Fam Lrng Ctr.

Simpson, Susie M. Understanding the Bible According to Granny: Themes from Genesis. Majewski, Joy, illus. 133p. (gr. 1 up). 1992. pap. 10.00 (*1-880892-46-4*) Fam Lrng Ctr.

Smith, Anne. Thank You, God. 24p. (Orig.). (ps). 1988. pap. text ed. 1.75 (*0-936625-44-9*) Womans Mission Union.

Smith, Josie, tr. from ENG. El Joven y las Misiones - Missions Bible Study for Youth. (SPA., Illus.). 62p. (Orig.). (gr. 10 up). 1991. pap. 3.10 (*0-311-11068-1*) Casa Bautista.

Stadler, Richard H. Living As a Winner. Fischer, William E., ed. Woodfin, James, illus. 64p. (gr. 9-12). 1985. pap. 2.95 leaders guide (*0-938272-23-3*); pap. 2.95 students guide (*0-938272-22-5*) WELS Board.

Stohl, Anita. Christian Crafts Yarn Art. (Illus.). 64p. (ps-5). 1992. 8.95 (*0-86653-701-5*, SS2831, Shining Star Pubns) Good Apple.

Stolpe, Norman. Coming Attractions. (Illus.). 116p. (Orig.). (gr. 9-12). 1991. pap. text ed. 8.35 (*0-930265-94-7*); tchr's. ed. 10.45 (*0-930265-95-5*) CRC Pubns.

The Student Bible. (gr. 10 up). 1992. 26.99 (*0-310-90916-3*) Zondervan.

Taylor, Kent. Bible in Pictures for Little Eyes. (gr. 2 up). Date not set. 18.99 (*0-8024-0685-8*) Moody.

The Teen Study Bible. (gr. 7-11). 1993. 22.99 (*0-310-91672-0*); 16.99 (*0-310-91673-9*) Zondervan.

Tiner, John H. Find-the-Word Puzzles: Wisdom & Praise. Rector, Andy, ed. 48p. (Orig.). (gr. 5 up). 1993. pap. 3.99 (*0-7847-0061-3*, 28-02797) Standard Pub.

Tirabassi, Becky. Quietimes Student Prayer: Notebook. 264p. (gr. 10 up). 1991. pap. 7.99 filler (*0-8407-9122-4*) Nelson.

Tudor, Tasha, illus. And It Was So: Words from the Scripture. 2nd, rev. ed. LC 87-16130. 48p. (ps up). 1988. 12.00 (*0-664-32724-9*, Westminster) Westminster John Knox.

Vander Vennen, Mark. Take Six: Behind the Scenes with the Parables. 64p. (Orig.). (gr. 9-12). 1992. pap. text ed. 3.25 (*0-685-60748-8*, 1210-3051); leader's guide 7.25 (*1-56212-011-5*, 1210-3054) CRC Pubns.

Vos Wezeman, Phyllis & Wiessner, Colleen A. Mary's Memories. 38p. (Orig.). (gr. 1-6). 1989. pap. 5.95 (*0-940754-72-X*) Ed Ministries.

Webb, Joan C. Devotions for Little Boys & Girls: Old Testament. McCallum, Joanne V., illus. 112p. (Orig.). (ps-k). 1992. pap. 5.99 (*0-87403-681-X*, 12-02821) Standard Pub.

Weinberg, Shnayer. Targilon for Haschalas Chumash: A Chumash Workbook for Beginners. (Illus.). 130p. (Orig.). pap. text ed. 5.50 (*1-878895-00-1*, A135) Torah Umesorah.

Weisheit, Eldon. The Gospel for Little Kids. 1980. pap. 5.99 (*0-570-03811-1*, 12-2920) Concordia.

Wendland, Ernst H. God's Mission in the New Testament. Fischer, William E., ed. 40p. (Orig.). 1986. pap. 2.50 (*0-938272-55-1*) WELS Board.

Westberg, Barbara. Rhymes, Riddles & Reasons, Vol. 2: Exodus Through Judges. Agnew, Tim, illus. LC 90-38218. 224p. (Orig.). (gr. 3-7). 1992. pap. 7.99 (*0-932581-76-5*) Word Aflame.

Willingham, David. One Large Order of Faith to Go. Stoub, Paul, illus. Smit, Harvey A., intro. by. (Illus.). 99p. (Orig.). (gr. 6-8). 1991. pap. text ed. 6.25 (*1-56212-012-3*, 1701-0480) CRC Pubns.

Woychuk, N. A. I Am: Memory Book for Pre-Schoolers. Jones, Mary E., illus. 33p. (Orig.). (ps). 1988. pap. 7.95 (*1-880960-10-9*) Script Memory Fl.

Younger, Barbara & Flinn, Lisa. Making Scripture Stick. 108p. 1992. pap. 11.99 (*1-55945-093-2*) Group Pub.

Youngman, Bernard R. Spreading the Gospel. (gr. 8-12). 1979. pap. 9.95 (*0-7175-0420-4*) Dufour.

BIBLE–THEOLOGY

see Theology

BIBLE–USE

McElrath, William N. Bible Guidebook. LC 72-79174. 144p. (gr. 3-6). 1972. 12.99 (*0-8054-4410-6*) Broadman.

BIBLE–ZOOLOGY

see Bible–Natural History

BIBLE. NEW TESTAMENT

Anderson, Julian G. The New Testament in Everyday American English. rev. ed. RKB Studios Staff, illus. x, 886p. (gr. 10 up). 1989. pap. 4.95 (*0-685-27817-4*) Anderson Bks.

Berry, Michael & Berry, Nora. Seek & Ye Shall Find New Testament. (ps-3). 1992. 12.99 (*0-929216-74-1*) HSH Edu Media Co.

Booth, Julianne. Books of the New Testament. (gr. k-4). 1981. pap. 1.89 (*0-570-06150-4*, 59-1305) Concordia.

Bundschuh, Rick. The Church. LC 88-9692. (Illus.). 154p. (Orig.). (gr. 9-12). 1988. pap. 5.99 (*0-8307-1182-1*, S184102) Regal.

Campbell, Stan. Growing Pains: The Church Hits the Road. 144p. (gr. 9-12). 1989. pap. 5.99 (*0-89693-384-9*, Victor Books) SP Pubns.

Dastrup, Linda. I Am a Child of God: My Gospel Principles Book. 14p. (gr. 1-7). 1985. wkbk. 3.95 (*0-9621898-2-0*) Creative Changes.

George, Alan. First Christians. Butcher, Sam, illus. 56p. (gr. k-6). 1991. pap. text ed. 9.45 (*1-55976-023-0*) CEF Press.

The Gospel of John: Jesus' Teachings. 48p. (gr. 9-12). 1990. pap. 8.99 (*1-55945-208-0*) Group Pub.

Hillmann, W. Children's Bible. 95p. (ps-8). 1959. pap. 4.95 (*0-8146-0120-0*) Liturgical Pr.

Jones, Eugene P. Which Was, Which Is, Which Is to Come. (Illus.). 105p. (Orig.). 1989. pap. 24.95 (*0-925039-00-4*) River-Light Pub.

Kelly, Paul. First & Second Corinthians: Christian Discipleship. (Illus.). 48p. (gr. 9-12). 1992. pap. 8.99 (*1-55945-230-7*) Group Pub.

Larsen, Rayola C. Alphabet Talk: Gospel Rhymes for Each Letter of the Alphabet. Perry, Lucille R., illus. LC 89-83429. 32p. (Orig.). (gr. k-3). 1989. pap. 4.98 (*0-88290-147-8*) Horizon Utah.

Lysne, Mary. New Testament Match Up. Lysne, Mary E., illus. 32p. 1991. pap. 1.99 saddle stitch (*0-87403-876-6*, 25-02506) Standard Pub.

Mehew, Randall & Mehew, Karen. Gospel Basic Busy Book, Vol. I. Christopherson, Jerry, illus. 100p. 1989. pap. text ed. 6.95 (*0-910613-13-3*) Millenial Pr.

New Testament: Activity Book. 24p. (gr. 3-7). 1991. pap. 2.29 (*1-55513-452-1*, 64527, Chariot Bks) Chariot Family.

New Testament Psalms Proverbs. 1968. pap. 4.50 (*0-8361-1279-2*) Herald Pr.

Segraves, Daniel. Hair Length in the Bible: A Study of First Corinthians 11: 2-16. LC 89-37912. 80p. (Orig.). 1989. pap. 5.99 (*0-932581-57-9*) Word Aflame.

Simon, Mary M. Thank you, Jesus: Luke 17: 11-19; Jesus Heals Ten Men with Leprosy. Jones, Dennis, illus. LC 93-36192. 32p. (gr. 1-3). 1994. pap. 3.99 (*0-570-04762-5*) Concordia.

Smith, Joyce M. Demons, Doubters & Dead Men. 64p. (Orig.). (gr. 4-7). 1986. 2.95 (*0-8423-0542-4*) Tyndale.

Stoner, Laura M. Acts - a Story Color Book. Huskey, Freeda, ed. Stoner, Laura M., illus. 80p. (Orig.). (gr. k-6). 1992. wkbk. 5.95 (*0-934426-46-5*) NAPSAC Reprods.

Taylor, Kenneth N. El Nuevo Testamento en Cuadros Para Ninos. (SPA.). 72p. 1991. 7.99 (*0-8254-1708-2*) Kregel.

Truitt, Gloria A. People of the New Testament: Arch Book Supplement. LC 59-1311. 1983. pap. 1.99 (*0-570-06173-3*) Concordia.

Vos Wezeman, Phyllis & Wiessner, Colleen A. The Mosaic of Mary & Martha. 29p. (Orig.). (gr. 1-6). 1989. pap. 5.95 (*0-940754-73-8*) Ed Ministries.

Wilson, Terry C. The Same: II Timothy 2: 2. 250p. (Orig.). (gr. 12). 1989. pap. 30.00 (*0-685-28038-1*) T C Wilson.

BIBLE. OLD TESTAMENT

Bachrach, Kalman. Olami Sefer Rishon, Bk. 1. rev. ed. Krukman, Tsvi, illus. (HEB.). 59p. (gr. 2). 1943. pap. text ed. 2.00x (*1-878530-14-3*) K Bachrach Co.

—Olami Sefer Sheini, Bk. 2. rev. ed. Krukman, Tsvi, illus. (HEB.). 71p. (gr. 3-4). 1950. pap. text ed. 2.00x (*1-878530-15-1*) K Bachrach Co.

—Olami Sefer Shlishi, Bk. 3. Gutman, Nachum, illus. (HEB.). 92p. (gr. 4-6). 1936. pap. text ed. 2.00x (*1-878530-16-X*) K Bachrach Co.

Berry, Michael & Berry, Nora. Seek & Ye Shall Find Old Testament. (ps-3). 1992. 12.99 (*0-929216-78-4*) HSH Edu Media Co.

Booth, Julianne. Books of the Old Testament. (ps-3). 1988. pap. 1.89 (*0-570-06151-2*) Concordia.

Daniel, Rebecca. Famous Old Testament Heroes. 48p. (ps-6). 1990. 7.95 (*0-86653-528-4*, SS858, Shining Star Pubns) Good Apple.

Davis, Susan. When God Lived in a Tent. (Illus.). (ps-1). 1978. 1.95 (*0-8127-0181-X*) Review & Herald.

Eisenberg, Ann. Bible Heroes I Can Be. Schanzer, Roz, illus. LC 89-48188. 24p. (ps). 1990. 12.95 (*0-929371-09-7*); pap. 4.95 (*0-929371-10-0*) Kar Ben.

Falk, Aaron. The Torah for Children. Nodel, Norman, illus. LC 92-28623. 32p. (gr. k-4). 1993. 12.95 (*1-880582-06-6*); pap. 9.95 (*1-880582-07-4*) Judaica Pr.

Genesis - God's Beginnings. (ps-3). 1992. pap. 4.99 (*0-529-07192-4*) World Bible.

Giampa, Linda. Old Testament Activity Book. Giampa, Linda, illus. 32p. (gr. k-3). 1992. pap. 2.99 (*0-570-04724-2*) Concordia.

Haan, Sheri D. The First Woman: Bible Stories in Rhythm & Rhyme. Hochstatter, Dan, illus. 80p. (ps-3). 1992. 6.99 (*0-8010-4368-9*) Baker Bk.

Hillmann, W. Children's Bible. 95p. (ps-8). 1959. pap. 4.95 (*0-8146-0120-0*) Liturgical Pr.

Lysne, Mary. Old Testament Match Up. Lysne, Mary E., illus. 32p. 1991. pap. 1.99 saddle stitch (*0-87403-875-8*, 25-02505) Standard Pub.

Nappa, Amy. Exodus: Following God. (Illus.). 48p. (gr. 9-12). 1992. pap. 8.99 (*1-55945-226-9*) Group Pub.

Newland, Mary R. The Hebrew Scriptures: The Biblical Story of God's Promise to Israel & Us. Nagel, Stephan, ed. Abrahamson, Evie, illus. 261p. (Orig.). (gr. 10-11). 1990. pap. text ed. 12.00 (*0-88489-231-X*); tchr's. ed. 18.95 (*0-88489-232-8*) St Marys.

Orthner, Donald P. Wellsprings of Life: Understanding Proverbs. Thompson, Del, illus. Minnick, Mark, pref. by. (Illus.). xii, 228p. (Orig.). (gr. 9 up). 1989. pap. 7.95 (*0-317-93833-9*) Adon Bks.

Osborne, Richard, compiled by. Proverbs for Kids from the Book. VanRoon, Terry & Kielesinski, Chris, illus. 320p. (gr. k). 1987. 12.99 (*0-8423-4975-8*) Tyndale.

Roper, Harlin J. In the Beginning God: Genesis - Exodus 18. 64p. (gr. 7-12). 1988. Repr. wkbk. 4.50 (*0-86606-362-5*, 1Y) Roper Pr.

—In the Beginning God: Genesis - Exodus 18. (Illus.). 64p. (gr. 4-6). 1989. Repr. of 1956 ed. wkbk. 4.50 (*0-86606-374-9*, 1J) Roper Pr.

Smith, Cindy. Amazing Stories from Genesis. 96p. 1992. pap. 13.99 (*1-55945-094-0*) Group Pub.

Smith, Kathy B. Old Testament Sticker Book. M. J. Studios Staff, illus. 32p. (Orig.). (gr. k-6). 1993. pap. 3.95 (*1-879424-63-0*) Nickel Pr.

Stolpe, Norman D. Genesis: The Beginnings. (Illus.). 48p. (gr. 6-8). 1991. pap. 8.99 (*1-55945-111-4*) Group Pub.

Truitt, Gloria A. People of the Old Testament. LC 59-1310. (gr. k-4). 1983. pap. 1.99 (*0-570-06172-5*) Concordia.

BIBLE. OLD TESTAMENT–BIOGRAPHY

Joshua at Jericho. 1989. text ed. 3.95 cased (*0-7214-5263-9*) Ladybird Bks.

Kolbrek, Loyal. The Day God Made It Rain. (gr. k-2). 1977. pap. 1.99 (*0-570-06108-3*, 59-1226) Concordia.

Lashbrook, Marilyn. The Weak Strongman: Samson. Sharp, Chris, illus. LC 90-60456. 32p. (gr. k-3). 1990. 5.95 (*0-86606-442-7*, 873) Roper Pr.

Neff, Lavonne. God's Gift Baby. (gr. k-4). 1977. pap. 1.89 (*0-570-06113-X*, 59-1230) Concordia.

Parry, Linda & Parry, Alan. Jacob & Esau. Parry, Linda & Parry, Alan, illus. LC 90-80555. 24p. (Orig.). (ps-2). 1990. pap. 1.99 (*0-8066-2490-6*, 9-2490, Augsburg) Augsburg Fortress.

—Miriam & Moses. Parry, Linda & Parry, Alan, illus. LC 90-80556. 24p. (Orig.). (ps-2). 1990. pap. 1.95 (*0-8066-2489-2*, 9-2489, Augsburg) Augsburg Fortress.

Rosenfeld, Dina. Kind Little Rivka. Englin, A., tr. from ENG. Winn-Lederer, Ilene, illus. (RUS.). 32p. (ps-1). 1993. 8.95 (*0-922613-29-X*) Hachai Pubns.

Simon, Mary M. The Hide-&-Seek Prince: Second Kings 11-12: 16: Joash. Jones, Dennis, illus. LC 93-35606. 32p. (Orig.). (gr. 1-3). 1994. pap. 3.99 (*0-570-04740-4*) Concordia.

—Hurray for the Lord's Army! Judges 6: 11 - 7: 22 (Gideon) Jones, Dennis, illus. LC 93-35604. 32p. (Orig.). (gr. 1-3). 1994. pap. 3.99 (*0-570-04739-0*) Concordia.

Vos Wezeman, Phyllis & Wiessner, Colleen A. A Day with David. 30p. (Orig.). (gr. 1-6). 1988. pap. 5.95 (*0-940754-57-6*) Ed Ministries.

—Gleanings from Ruth. 25p. (Orig.). (gr. 1-6). 1988. pap. 5.95 (*0-940754-61-4*) Ed Ministries.

—Joseph's Jigsaw. 50p. (Orig.). (gr. 1-6). 1988. pap. 5.95 (*0-940754-59-2*) Ed Ministries.

BIBLE. O. T. PSALMS

Clayton, C. Sing a Song of Gladness. (Illus.). 32p. (gr. k-4). 1974. pap. 1.99 (*0-570-06087-7*, 59-1302) Concordia.

Keller, W. Phillip. A Child's Look at the Twenty-Third Psalm. Jarrett, Lauren, illus. LC 84-13718. 96p. (gr. 3 up). 1985. pap. 7.95 (*0-385-15457-7*, Galilee) Doubleday.

Pittenger, Shari. Listen, Color & Learn: A Coloring Book for Family Devotions, Vol. I, Psalm 1-30. Pittenger, Shari, illus. Harris, Gregg, intro. by. 35p. (Orig.). (ps-6). 1989. pap. text ed. 4.95 (*0-923463-49-6*) Noble Pub Assocs.

BIBLE AS LITERATURE

see also Religious Literature

BIBLE CLASSES

see Bible–Study

BIBLE PLAYS

see Mysteries and Miracle Plays

BIBLE STORIES

Abraham, Angela & Abraham, Ken. The Hosanna Bible. Anderson, Terry, et al, illus. LC 93-593. 448p. (ps-3). 1993. 15.99 (*0-8499-1036-6*) Word Inc.

Abram Talked with God. 24p. (gr. 2-5). 1985. 5.95 (*0-570-08950-6*, 56-1541) Concordia.

Adams, Georgie. The Bible Storybook. Utton, Peter, photos by. LC 93-40682. 1994. write for info. (*0-8037-1760-1*) Dial Bks Young.

Adventures with Judah Lion & Lucy Lamb. (Orig.). 1991. pap. 3.95 (*0-570-05100-2*, 31-4804) Concordia.

Amstutz, Beverly. Benjamin & the Bible Donkeys. (Illus.). 36p. (gr. k-7). 1981. pap. 2.50x (*0-937836-03-6*) Precious Res.

Antioch. Away in the Manger. (ps-3). 1991. pap. 2.50 (*0-89954-153-4*) Antioch Pub Co.

Bach, Alice. Miriam's Well. 1991. 16.00 (*0-385-30435-8*) Delacorte.

Bach, Alice & Exum, J. Cheryl. Moses' Ark: Stories from the Bible. Dillon, Leo D. & Dillon, Diane, illus. (gr. 4-8). 1989. 14.95 (*0-685-30899-5*) Delacorte.

Baden, Robert. Adam & His Family. (Illus.). 24p. (gr. k-4). 1986. pap. 1.99 (*0-570-06198-9*, 59-1421) Concordia.

Baehr, Kingsley M. Hope in a Scarlet Rope. LC 94-9000. 1994. 6.99 (*0-8423-1345-1*) Tyndale.

Batchelor, Mary. The Children's Bible in Three Hundred Sixty-Five Stories: Red Gift Edition. (Illus.). 416p. (gr. k up). 1988. 26.95 (*0-7459-1019-X*) Lion USA.

—Children's Bible in Three Hundred Sixty-Five Stories: White Gift Edition. (Illus.). 416p. (gr. k up). 1988. 26. 95 (*0-7459-1375-X*) Lion USA.

—The Lion Book of Bible Stories & Prayers. (Illus.). 96p. (gr. 1-5). 1989. 11.95 (*0-85648-239-0*) Lion USA.

Baumann, Kurt, retold by. The Story of Jonah. Reed, Allison, illus. LC 86-62522. 32p. (gr. k-3). 1987. 13.95 (*1-55858-050-6*) North-South Bks NYC.

Baw, Cindy & Brownlow, Paul C. Children of the Bible: Exciting Stories about Children in the Bible. (Illus.). (ps-3). 1984. 8.99 (*0-915720-19-1*) Brownlow Pub Co.

Beers, Gil & Hagler, Liz. The Early Reader's Bible. 527p. (ps-3). 1991. 15.99 (*0-945564-43-0*, Gold & Honey) Questar Pubs.

Beers, V. Gilbert. Growing up with God's Friends. Endres, Helen, illus. LC 87-81046. 94p. (Orig.). (ps-7). 1987. 12.99 (*0-89081-528-3*) Harvest Hse.

—Growing up with Jesus. Endres, Helen, illus. LC 87-81043. 94p. (Orig.). (ps-7). 1987. 12.99 (*0-89081-525-9*) Harvest Hse.

Beers, V. Gilbert & Beers, Ronald A. The Big Book of All-Time Favorite Bible Stories. Hochstatter, Daniel J., illus. LC 92-8306. 1992. 12.99 (*0-8407-9165-8*) Nelson.

—Little People in Tough Spots: Bible Answers for Young Children. (Illus.). 144p. 1992. 7.99 (*0-8407-9157-7*) Nelson.

Berg, Jean H., retold by. The Story of Peter. Palm, Felix, illus. 40p. (Orig.). (gr. k-3). 1990. pap. 9.95 incl. audiocassette (*0-87510-216-6*) Christian Sci.

Bergey, Alyce. David & Jonathan. (Illus.). 24p. (gr. k-4). 1987. pap. 1.89 (*0-570-09006-7*, 59-1434) Concordia.

—Young Jesus in the Temple. (Illus.). 24p. (gr. k-4). 1986. pap. 1.99 saddlestitched (*0-570-06203-9*, 59-1426) Concordia.

Bibee, John. The Journey of Wishes. Turnbaugh, Paul, illus. LC 93-8173. 187p. (Orig.). (gr. 4-8). 1993. pap. 6.99 (*0-8308-1207-5*, 1207) InterVarsity.

The Bible: God's Wonderful Book. 10p. (gr. 1-8). 1968. pap. text ed. 4.50 (*0-86508-150-6*) BCM Pubn.

Bible Stories & Activities for Children. 1991. pap. 5.95 (*0-687-03183-4*) Abingdon.

Bible Stories: Four of the Greatest Tales Ever Told. LC 93-85528. (Illus.). 128p. 1994. 4.95 (*1-56138-376-7*) Running Pr.

Bible Stories to Read & Color. (Illus.). 388p. (ps-4). pap. 9.95 (*1-55748-069-9*) Barbour & Co.

Biffi, Inos. The Story of the Eucharist. Drury, John, tr. from ITA. Vignazia, Franco, illus. LC 85-82173. 125p. (gr. 5 up). 1986. 17.95 (*0-89870-089-2*) Ignatius Pr.

Billy Goat Escapes. 1991. 0.79 (*0-8307-1058-2*, 5608605) Regal.

Blanchette, Rick. Where Do You Park an Ark? LC 94-9714. 1994. write for info. (*0-8423-1346-X*) Tyndale.
Bourgeois, Jean-Francois. Los Ninos de la Biblia. Maecha, Alberto, ed. Landgraff, Michael, illus. (SPA.). 40p. (gr. 3-5). 1984. pap. write for info. (*0-942504-11-9*) Overcomer Pr.
Brown, Christopher, as told by. Favorite Bible Stories, Vol. 3. 1989. pap. 2.50 (*0-89954-597-1*) Antioch Pub Co.
Brunson, Dorothy. Easy-to-Teach Bible Picture Lessons: All about Jesus. Brewer, Karen, ed. Bolton, Barbara, contrib. by. 40p. (Orig.). (ps). 1994. pap. 9.99 (*0-7847-0244-6*, 13-42044) Standard Pub.
Bull, Norman. Church of Jesus Grows. (gr. 2-7). 1979. 10.95 (*0-7175-0454-9*) Dufour.
—Prophets of the Jews. (gr. 2-7). 1984. pap. 10.95 (*0-7175-0979-6*) Dufour.
Burstein, Chaya. Benjy's Bible Trails. LC 90-25421. (Illus.). 32p. (gr. 1-5). 1992. pap. 3.95 (*0-929371-27-5*) Kar Ben.
The Camel's Journey. 1991. 0.79 (*0-8307-1057-4*, 5608602) Regal.
Caswell, Helen. Parable of the Bridesmaids. Caswell, Helen, illus. 24p. (ps-3). 1992. 11.95 (*0-687-30022-3*) Abingdon.
—Parable of the Good Samaritan. Caswell, Helen, illus. 24p. (ps-3). 1992. 11.95 (*0-687-30023-1*) Abingdon.
Chapman, Geoffrey. Book of Gospels. (Illus.). 672p. 1985. 95.00 (*0-225-66351-1*) Harper SF.
Chariot Family Staff. Noah's Ark. Tallarico, Tony, illus. 1987. plastic 6.47 (*1-55513-653-2*, 56531, Chariot Bks) Chariot Family.
Ching Yee, Janice. God's Busiest Angels. (Illus.). (gr. k-6). 1975. pap. 3.00 (*0-931420-09-1*) Pi Pr.
—God's Naughtiest Angels. (Illus.). (gr. k-6). 1974. pap. 3.00 (*0-931420-08-3*) Pi Pr.
The Christmas Donkey. 1991. 0.79 (*0-8307-1061-2*, 5608614) Regal.
Coe, Joyce. Jesus Rides into Jerusalem. (Illus.). 24p. (gr. k-4). 1987. pap. 1.99 (*0-570-09007-5*, 59-1435) Concordia.
Coleman, Sheila S. The Best Story about Jesus. Ham, John, illus. 32p. (gr. k-2). 1989. pasted 2.50 (*0-87403-602-X*, 3862) Standard Pub.
Coleman, William. Brave & Bashful. LC 88-37131. (gr. 3-7). 1989. pap. 3.69 (*0-89191-988-0*, Chariot Bks) Chariot Family.
—Kings & Critters. LC 88-36957. (gr. 3-7). 1989. pap. 3.69 (*0-89191-989-9*, Chariot Bks) Chariot Family.
Cook, Erwin W. A Boy of Nazareth. 1994. pap. 4.95 (*0-533-10728-8*) Vantage.
Couch, Frank. Children's Bible in Story. Codd, Michael, illus. 320p. 1989. 12.95 (*0-8249-8355-6*, Ideals Child) Hambleton-Hill.
Crain, Steve. Bible Fun Book, No. 7. 32p. (Orig.). (gr. k-4). 1981. oversized saddle stitched 1.19 (*0-87123-766-0*) Bethany Hse.
Crompton, T., illus. The Good Samaritan: Retold by Catherine Storr. 32p. (gr. k-4). 1984. 14.65 (*0-8172-1988-9*, Raintree Childrens Books Belitha Press Ltd. - London) Raintree Steck-V.
Crowder, Susan. The Great Flood. Crowder, Susan, illus. 28p. (Orig.). 1988. pap. 2.50 (*0-912927-27-5*, X027) St John Kronstadt.
—The Three Children in the Furnace. Crowder, Susan, illus. 37p. (Orig.). 1984. pap. 2.50 (*0-912927-11-9*, X011) St John Kronstadt.
Dampier, Joseph H. Workbook on Christian Doctrine. 64p. (Orig.). (gr. 6 up). 1943. pap. 3.99 (*0-87239-072-1*, 3343) Standard Pub.
David C. Cook Publishing Staff. My Own Little Bible: Storybook. (ps-3). 1991. 6.99 (*1-55513-682-6*, Chariot Bks) Chariot Family.
—My Own Little Bible: Storybook. (ps-3). 1991. simulated leather, gift boxed 12.99 (*1-55513-753-9*, Chariot Bks) Chariot Family.
Davidson, Alice J. Alice in Bibleland Storybooks: Prayers & Graces. Marshall, Victoria, illus. 32p. (gr. 3 up). 1986. 5.50 (*0-8378-5078-9*) Gibson.
—Alice in Bibleland Storybooks: Story of David & Goliath. Marshall, Victoria, illus. 32p. (gr. 3 up). 1985. 5.50 (*0-8378-5070-3*) Gibson.
—Alice in Bibleland Storybooks: Story of Daniel & the Lions. Marshall, Victoria, illus. 32p. (gr. 3 up). 1986. 5.50 (*0-8378-5079-7*) Gibson.
—Alice in Bibleland Storybooks: Story of Baby Jesus. Marshall, Victoria, illus. 32p. (gr. 3 up). 1985. 5.50 (*0-8378-5072-X*) Gibson.
—Alice in Bibleland Storybooks: Story of Baby Moses. Marshall, Victoria, illus. 32p. (gr. 3 up). 1985. 5.50 (*0-8378-5071-1*) Gibson.
—Alice in Bibleland Storybooks: Story of Jonah. Marshall, Victoria, illus. 32p. (gr. 3 up). 1984. 5.50 (*0-8378-5068-1*) Gibson.
—Alice in Bibleland Storybooks: Story of Noah. Marshall, Victoria, illus. 32p. (gr. 3 up). 1984. 5.50 (*0-8378-5067-3*) Gibson.
—Alice in Bibleland Storybooks: Story of the Loaves & Fishes. Marshall, Victoria, illus. 32p. (ps-3). 1985. 5.50 (*0-8378-5073-8*) Gibson.
—Alice in Bibleland Storybooks: The Lord's Prayer. (Illus.). (gr. 3 up). 1989. 5.50 (*0-8378-1868-0*) Gibson.
—Alice in Bibleland Storybooks: The Story of Isaac & Rebeckah. (Illus.). (gr. 3 up). 1989. 5.50 (*0-8378-1852-4*) Gibson.
—Alice in Bibleland Storybooks: The Story of Jesus & His Disciples. (Illus.). (gr. 3 up). 1989. 5.50 (*0-8378-1860-5*) Gibson.
—Alice in Bibleland Storybooks: The Story of Ruth & Naomi. (Illus.). (gr. 3 up). 1989. 5.50 (*0-8378-1855-9*) Gibson.
—Alice in Bibleland Storybooks: The Story of Exodus. (Illus.). (gr. 3 up). 1989. 5.50 (*0-8378-1849-4*) Gibson.
—Alice in Bibleland Storybooks: The Story of Joshua. (Illus.). (gr. 3 up). 1989. 5.50 (*0-8378-1850-8*) Gibson.
—Alice in Bibleland Storybooks: The Story of Esther. (Illus.). (gr. 3 up). 1989. 5.50 (*0-8378-1851-6*) Gibson.
—Alice in Bibleland Storybooks: The Story of Paul. (Illus.). (gr. 3 up). 1989. 5.50 (*0-8378-1853-2*) Gibson.
—Alice in Bibleland Storybooks: The Story of the Good Samaritan. (Illus.). (gr. 3 up). 1989. 5.50 (*0-8378-1854-0*) Gibson.
—Alice in Bibleland Storybooks: The Story of the Lost Sheep. (Illus.). (gr. 3 up). 1989. 5.50 (*0-8378-1865-6*) Gibson.
—Alice in Bibleland Storybooks: The Story of the Prodigal Son. (Illus.). (gr. 3 up). 1989. 5.50 (*0-8378-1848-6*) Gibson.
—Alice in Bibleland Storybooks: The Story of the Tower of Babel. (Illus.). (gr. 3 up). 1989. 5.50 (*0-8378-1866-4*) Gibson.
Davoll, Barbara. The Potluck Supper. Hockerman, Dennis, illus. 1988. 4.95 (*0-685-22774-X*); book & cassette 7.95 (*0-685-22775-8*) Zondervan.
—The Shiny Red Sled. Hockerman, Dennis, illus. 24p. 1989. text ed. 6.99 (*0-89693-498-5*, Victor Books); cassette 9.99 (*0-89693-031-9*) SP Pubns.
The Deadly Pretender. (Illus.). (gr. 2-5). 1992. pap. 4.99 (*0-87509-506-2*) Chr Pubns.
Dean, Bessie. Paul's Letters of Love. (Illus.). 72p. (Orig.). (gr. k-5). 1981. pap. 5.98 (*0-88290-170-2*) Horizon Utah.
De Brincat, Matthew. Salt & Light. 56p. (gr. 6up). 1983. pap. 3.00 (*0-911423-00-1*) Bible-Speak.
Decker, Marjorie A. Rock-a-Bye Stories of Jesus (Christian Mother Goose) (ps-3). 1993. 7.99 (*0-529-10003-7*) World Bible.
Dede, Vivian H. Elizabeth's Christmas Story. LC 59-1430. (Illus.). 24p. (gr. k-4). 1987. pap. 1.99 (*0-570-09002-4*, 59-1430) Concordia.
De Graaf, Anne. Believing the Truth. (Illus.). 32p. 1989. 4.95 (*0-310-52770-8*) Zondervan.
—Following the Messiah. (Illus.). 32p. 1989. 4.95 (*0-310-52740-6*) Zondervan.
De La Mare, Walter. Stories from the Bible: From the Garden of Eden to the Promised Land. Ardizzone, Edward, illus. 418p. (gr. 3 up). 1985. pap. 8.95 (*0-571-11086-X*) Faber & Faber.
Dellinger, A. & Fletcher, S. N. T. Stories. (ps-3). 1983. pap. 0.69 (*0-570-08312-5*, 56HH1444) Concordia.
—O. T. Heroes. (ps-3). 1983. pap. 0.69 (*0-570-08311-7*, 56HH1443) Concordia.
De Paola, Tomie. Noah & the Ark. De Paola, Tomie, illus. 40p. (Orig.). (ps-4). 1985. pap. 5.95 (*0-685-07222-3*) Harper SF.
—Tomie De Paola's Book of Bible Stories. 128p. 1990. 19.95 (*0-399-21690-1*, Putnam) Putnam Pub Group.
DeVries, Betty. One Hundred One Bible Activity Sheets. 144p. (ps up). 1983. pap. 8.99 (*0-8010-2931-7*) Baker Bk.
Doney, Meryl. How the Bible Came to Us. (Illus.). 48p. (gr. 8 up). 1985. 13.95 (*0-85648-574-8*) Lion USA.
Draper, Edythe. Wonder. 448p. (gr. 1-4). 1984. 8.99 (*0-8423-8385-9*) Tyndale.
Duckworth, Liz. God's Great Creation. (Illus.). 6p. 1994. pop-up bk. 3.99 (*1-56476-169-X*, Victor Books) SP Pubns.
Dyck, Peter J. Storytime Jamboree. Neidigh, Sherry, illus. 176p. (Orig.). (gr. 1 up). 1994. pap. 6.95 (*0-8361-3667-5*) Herald Pr.
Egermeier, Elsie E. Egermeier's Bible Story Book. 5th ed. Uptton, Clive, illus. LC 68-23397. (gr. k-6). 1969. 14.95 (*0-87162-006-5*, D2005); deluxe ed. 15.95 (*0-87162-007-3*, D2006); pap. 8.95 (*0-87162-229-7*, D2008) Warner Pr.
—Egermeier's Favorite Bible Stories. (gr. k-1). 1965. 9.95 (*0-87162-014-6*, D3695) Warner Pr.
Enns, Peter. Stories to Remember: David, God's Champion. Ligon, Terry, illus. 32p. (ps-5). 1987. pap. 2.98 (*0-943593-04-2*); cassette 5.98 (*0-943593-06-9*); coloring bk. 0.98 (*0-943593-05-0*) Kids Intl Inc.
—Stories to Remember: Here Comes Jesus. Ligon, Terry, illus. 32p. (ps-5). 1987. pap. 2.98 (*0-943593-12-3*); coloring bk. 0.98 (*0-943593-13-1*); cassette 5.98 (*0-943593-14-X*) Kids Intl Inc.
Enns, Peter & Forsberg, Glen. Daniel & the Lions & Five Other Stories. Friesen, John H., illus. 24p. (ps-5). 1985. book & cassette 4.95 (*0-936215-04-6*) STL Intl.
—Jesus Is Alive! & Five Other Stories. Friesen, John H., illus. 24p. (ps-5). 1985. book & cassette 4.95 (*0-936215-06-2*) STL Intl.
—Six Stories of Jesus. Friesen, John H., illus. 24p. (ps-5). 1985. 4.95 (*0-936215-05-4*); cassette incl. STL Intl.
Enns, Peter & Ligon, Terry. Stories to Remember: Look What God Made. (Illus.). 32p. (ps-5). 1987. pap. 2.98 (*0-943593-00-X*); coloring bk. 0.98 (*0-943593-01-8*); cassette 5.98 (*0-943593-02-6*) Kids Intl Inc.
Erickson, Mary. God Can Do Anything. LC 92-33128. 1993. 9.99 (*0-7814-0001-5*, Chariot Bks) Chariot Family.
Evans, Shirlee. Tree Tall to the Rescue. Ponter, James, illus. LC 87-8615. 144p. (Orig.). (gr. 4-9). 1987. pap. 4.50 (*0-8361-3444-3*) Herald Pr.
Falk, Cathy A. Easy-to-Teach Bible Picture Lessons: Look What God Made. Brewer, Karen, ed. Bolton, Barbara, contrib. by. (Illus.). 40p. (Orig.). (ps). 1994. pap. 9.99 (*0-7847-0241-1*, 13-42041) Standard Pub.
Farnsworth, Bill, illus. The Illustrated Children's Bible. LC 93-16222. (gr. 1-8). 1993. 19.95 (*0-15-232876-9*) HarBrace.
Fed by Ravens. 1991. 0.79 (*0-8307-1059-0*, 5608608) Regal.
The First Christmas. LC 93-24835. 1993. 6.99 (*0-8407-4916-3*); pap. 6.99 (*0-8407-4912-0*) Nelson.
Fletcher, Sarah. My Bible Story Book. LC 73-91810. (Illus.). 72p. (ps-3). 1974. 9.99 (*0-570-03423-X*, 56-1171) Concordia.
—My Stories about Jesus. Kueker, Don, illus. 32p. (ps-3). 1974. pap. 2.89 (*0-570-03427-2*, 56-1182) Concordia.
Frank, Penny. Daniel in the Lion's Den. (Illus.). 24p. (gr. 1 up). 1987. 3.99 (*0-85648-752-X*) Lion USA.
—David & Goliath. (Illus.). 24p. (gr. 1 up). 1986. 3.99 (*0-85648-743-0*) Lion USA.
—Elijah & the Prophets of Baal. (Illus.). 24p. (gr. 1-4). 1987. 3.99 (*0-85648-747-3*) Lion USA.
—Gideon Fights for God. (Illus.). 24p. (gr. 1-4). 1987. 3.99 (*0-85648-738-4*) Lion USA.
—Jeremiah & the Great Disaster. (Illus.). 24p. (gr. 1-4). 1987. 3.99 (*0-85648-750-3*) Lion USA.
—Jesus on Trial. (Illus.). 24p. (gr. 1 up). 1987. 3.99 (*0-85648-772-4*) Lion USA.
—Jesus the Teacher. (Illus.). 24p. (gr. 1 up). 1987. 3.99 (*0-85648-760-0*) Lion USA.
—Jonah Runs Away. (Illus.). 24p. (gr. 1-4). 1987. 3.99 (*0-85648-755-4*) Lion USA.
—King David. (Illus.). 24p. (gr. 1 up). 1987. 3.99 (*0-85648-744-9*) Lion USA.
—Mary, Martha & Lazarus. (Illus.). 24p. (gr. 1-4). 1987. 3.99 (*0-85648-769-4*) Lion USA.
—Naaman's Dreadful Secret. (Illus.). 24p. (gr. 1 up). 1987. 3.99 (*0-85648-748-1*) Lion USA.
—Nehemiah's Greatest Day. (Illus.). (gr. 1 up). 1987. pap. 3.99 (*0-85648-754-6*) Lion USA.
—Paul & Friends. (Illus.). 24p. (gr. 1 up). 1987. 3.99 (*0-85648-776-7*) Lion USA.
—Paul the Prisoner. (Illus.). 24p. (gr. 1-4). 1987. 3.99 (*0-85648-777-5*) Lion USA.
—The Story of the Two Brothers. (Illus.). 24p. (gr. 4 up). 1987. 3.99 (*0-85648-765-1*) Lion USA.
Fryechad. My Bible White. (ps). 1993. 4.97 (*1-55748-395-7*) Barbour & Co.
Fuchshuber, Annegert, illus. Augsburg Story Bible. LC 92-2527. 272p. (gr. 3-7). 1992. lib. bdg. 19.99 (*0-8066-2607-0*, 9-2607, Augsburg) Augsburg Fortress.
Gahr, Anna F. Short Stories of God's Blessings. 36p. (gr. 2-8). 1992. pap. text ed. 12.00 (*1-883702-08-9*) Aiello Grp.
Gambill, Henrietta, ed. All Creatures Great & Small: Bible Pop-Up. (Illus.). 10p. (ps). 1994. 3.99 (*0-7847-0205-5*, 24-03145) Standard Pub.
—I Can Draw Bible Stories. (Illus.). 32p. 1994. pap. 4.99 (*0-7847-0220-9*, 24-03250) Standard Pub.
—Now the Day Is Over: Bible Pop-Up. (Illus.). 10p. (ps). 1994. 3.99 (*0-7847-0206-3*, 24-03146) Standard Pub.
—Through the Bible in a Year Puzzles for Grade Schoolers. (Illus.). 192p. (gr. 4-6). 1994. pap. 7.99 (*0-7847-0239-X*, 28-02783) Standard Pub.
Garrison, Eileen & Albanese, Gayle. Eucharistic Manual for Children. Dickinson, Charles, illus. LC 84-60217. 28p. (gr. 1-8). 1984. pap. 4.75 (*0-8192-1343-8*) Morehouse Pub.
Geller, Norman. The First Seven Days. (Illus.). 32p. (gr. 1-4). 1983. pap. 6.95 (*0-915753-00-6*) N Geller Pub.
Gellman, Marc. Does God Have a Big Toe? Stories about Stories in the Bible. De Mejo, Oscar, illus. LC 89-1893. 96p. (gr. 4 up). 1989. 16.00 (*0-06-022432-0*); PLB 15.89 (*0-06-022433-9*) HarpC Child Bks.
Gibson, Katherine. The Tall Book of Bible Stories. reissued ed. Chaiko, Ted, illus. LC 57-10952. 128p. (ps-3). 1957. 9.95 (*0-06-021935-1*) HarpC Child Bks.
Gill, Anne. Tiny Bible Tales, 4 bks. McDougall, Kathleen, illus. (ps-2). 1994. Set. 19.95 (*0-8167-3317-1*) BrdgeWater.
God Leads His People. 96p. (gr. 4-6). 1991. 1.70 (*0-89636-304-X*, JB3A) Accent CO.
God's Chosen People. 96p. (gr. 4-6). 1990. 1.55 (*0-89636-272-8*, JB2A) Accent CO.
Graham, Bill. God's Promise. Wyrick, Monica, illus. 18p. (ps). 1991. 10.95 (*1-879680-11-4*) About You.
Grant, Amy. Heart to Heart. 96p. 1989. 10.99 (*0-8499-0710-1*) Word Inc.
Grant, Myrna. Ivan & the American Journey. LC 88-71170. (gr. 3-7). 1988. 4.99 (*0-88419-221-0*, Creation Hse) Strang Comms Co.
—Ivan & the Hidden Bible. LC 88-71169. (gr. 3-7). 1988. 4.99 (*0-88419-222-9*, Creation Hse) Strang Comms Co.
—Ivan & the Secret in the Suitcase. LC 88-71168. (gr. 3-7). 1988. 4.99 (*0-88419-223-7*, Creation Hse) Strang Comms Co.
Greene, Carol. The Easter Women. (Illus.). 24p. (gr. k-4). 1987. pap. 1.99 (*0-570-09003-2*, 59-1431) Concordia.
—My Bible Stories: The Hop-Aboard Handbook & Sing-along Cassette. (Illus.). 64p. (Orig.). (ps). 1993. pap. 13.99 (*0-570-04752-8*) Concordia.
Grimes, Rich. Satchel Stories: Ammon's Courage. Hiller, Annie, ed. Grimes, Rich, illus. 4p. (ps). 1992. text ed. 8.95 (*0-9623915-0-6*) Jackson Pub.
—Satchel Stories: David & Goliath. Hiller, Annie, ed. Grimes, Rich, illus. 4p. (ps). 1992. text ed. 8.95 (*1-56713-002-X*) Jackson Pub.

—Satchel Stories: Dinosaurs. Hiller, Annie, ed. Grimes, Rich, illus. 4p. (ps). 1992. text ed. 8.95 (1-56713-003-8) Jackson Pub.

—Satchel Stories: Jesus Blessing the Children. Hiller, Annie, ed. Grimes, Rich, illus. 4p. (ps). 1992. text ed. 8.95 (1-56713-001-1) Jackson Pub.

—Satchel Stories: Laban's Sword. Hiller, Annie, ed. Grimes, Rich, illus. 4p. (ps). 1992. text ed. 8.95 (0-9623915-8-1) Jackson Pub.

—Satchel Stories: Nephi's Broken Bow. Hiller, Annie, ed. Grimes, Rich, illus. 4p. (ps). 1992. text ed. 8.95 (1-56713-000-3) Jackson Pub.

—Satchel Stories: The Brother of Jared. Hiller, Annie, ed. Grimes, Rich, illus. 4p. (ps). 1992. text ed. 8.95 (0-9623915-9-X) Jackson Pub.

—Satchel Stories: Whales. Hiller, Annie, ed. Grimes, Rich, illus. 4p. (ps). 1992. text ed. 8.95 (1-56713-004-6) Jackson Pub.

Groth, Lynn. With You, Dear Child, in Mind. 16p. (Orig.). (ps). 1985. pap. 1.25 (0-938272-77-2) Wels Board.

Haan, Sheri D. Precious Moments Stories from the Bible. Butcher, Samuel, illus. LC 78-97507. 288p. (gr. 1-6). 1987. 14.99 (0-8010-4311-5) Baker Bk.

Hall, Sarabel. Hannah Hummingbird. Lobley, Robert E., illus. LC 88-30357. 16p. (Orig.). (gr. 1-3). 1989. pap. 6.95 (0-86534-131-1) Sunstone Pr.

Harmon, ed. Prayertime Bible Stories. LC 91-35647. 1992. 7.99 (0-7814-0045-7, Chariot Bks) Chariot Family.

Hartman, Bob. Angels, Angels All Around. Rayevsky, Robert, illus. 96p. (gr. 1-5). 1993. 15.95 (0-7459-2623-1) Lion USA.

Head, Constance. Jeremiah & the Fall of Jerusalem. (Illus.). 24p. (gr. k-4). 1986. pap. 1.99 saddlestitched (0-570-06201-2, 59-1424) Concordia.

Henley, Karyn. The Beginner's Bible: Timeless Children's Stories. Davis, Dennas, illus. 528p. (ps-3). 1989. 16.99 (0-945564-31-7, Gold & Honey) Questar Pubs.

Hochstatter, Daniel J., illus. Sammy's Tree-Mendous Christmas Adventure. LC 93-22314. 1993. 9.99 (0-8407-9234-4) Nelson.

Hollenbeck, Beatrice. God's Word & Me, Vol. 1. (Illus.). 82p. (gr. k-6). 1971. pap. text ed. 12.99 (1-55976-018-4) CEF Press.

—God's Word & Me, Vol. 2. (Illus.). 70p. (gr. k-6). 1971. pap. text ed. 12.99 (1-55976-019-2) CEF Press.

Hollingsworth, Mary. Kids Life Bible Storybook. 1994. 15.99 (0-7814-0126-7, Bible Discovery) Chariot Family.

—My Very First Book of Bible Heroes. Incrocci, Rick, illus. LC 93-7292. 1993. 4.99 (0-8407-9230-1) Nelson.

Hollingsworth, T. R. Ezra of Galilee. 80p. (Orig.). (gr. 3-6). 1987. pap. text ed. 6.95 (0-9617668-0-8) Hollybridge Pubns.

Horton, Edna C. & Hadley, Roberta. El Cuidado de Dios. Villasenor, Emma Z., tr. (Illus.). (gr. 1-3). 1989. pap. 1.40 (0-311-38555-9) Casa Bautista.

Hunt, P. Bible Stories from the Old Testament. (Illus.). (gr. k-5). 4.98 (0-517-43909-3) Random Hse Value.

Hunter, Emily. The Bible-Time Nursery Rhyme Book. 96p. 1988. 12.99 (0-89081-404-X) Harvest Hse.

Hurlbut, Jesse L. The Bedtime Bible Story Book. Sortor, Toni, ed. Arbuckle, Kathy, illus. 1989. text ed. 17.95 (1-55748-096-6); pap. text ed. 9.95 (1-55748-095-8); leather bdg. 24.95 (1-55748-113-X) Barbour & Co.

—The Bedtime Bible Story Book. Sortor, Toni, ed. (Illus.). (gr. k up). 1993. pap. 8.95 (1-55748-264-0) Barbour & Co.

Hutson, Joan. Hail Mary. Huston, Joan, illus. 28p. (ps). 1987. 3.95 (0-8198-3324-X) St Paul Bks.

—It's Important. Hutson, Joan, illus. 48p. (ps). 1987. 3.95 (0-8198-3615-X) St Paul Bks.

—My Happy Ones. Hutson, Joan, illus. 32p. (ps). 1987. 3.95 (0-8198-4723-2) St Paul Bks.

Hutton, Warwick. Adam & Eve: The Bible Story. Hutton, Warwick, illus. LC 86-27690. 32p. 1987. SBE 14.95 (0-689-50433-0, M K McElderry) Macmillan Child Grp.

Iguchi, Bunshu. The Tiny Sheep. Iguchi, Bunshu, illus. 24p. (ps up). 1986. 10.00 (0-8170-1108-0) Judson.

Illustrated Bible Stories for Children. 1987. 4.98 (0-671-07535-7, BOOKTHRIFT) S&S Trade.

In His Steps. (gr. 3 up). pap. 2.50 perfect bdg. (1-55748-137-7) Barbour & Co.

International Children's Story Bible. (Illus.). 240p. 1990. 9.99 (0-8499-0784-5) Word Inc.

Kaiser, Judith B. Quick-Line Stories for Young Children. 1975. spiral bdg. 3.95 (0-916406-12-1) Accent CO.

Kauffman, Suzanne. God Comforts His People: Activity Book. Converse, James, illus. 84p. (Orig.). (gr. k-6). 1986. pap. 3.00 (0-8361-3411-7) Herald Pr.

Kendall, Joan. The Story of Samuel. (gr. k-4). 1984. 1.59 (0-87162-271-8, D8500) Warner Pr.

Kennedy, Pamela. Now I'm One. Reck, Sue, ed. Gale, Bill, illus. LC 93-79573. 10p. (ps). Date not set. 3.99 (0-7814-0151-8, Chariot Bks) Chariot Family.

—Now I'm Three. Reck, Sue, ed. Gale, Bill, illus. LC 93-79575. 10p. (ps). Date not set. 3.99 (0-7814-0153-4, Chariot Bks) Chariot Family.

—Now I'm Two. Reck, Sue, ed. Gale, Bill, illus. LC 93-79574. 10p. (ps). Date not set. 3.99 (0-7814-0152-6, Chariot Bks) Chariot Family.

Kingsley, Stuart. My Name Is Jesus. (Illus.). 44p. (gr. 3 up). 1988. 6.95 (1-55523-127-6) Winston-Derek.

Klein, Lee. Are There Stripes in Heaven. 32p. 1994. pap. 4.95t (0-8091-6618-6) Paulist Pr.

Knecht, F. J. Child's Bible History. Schumacher, Philip, tr. (Illus.). (gr. 5). 1973. pap. 4.00 (0-89555-005-9) TAN Bks Pubs.

Knoles, Deborah. Easy-to-Teach Bible Picture Lessons: Kids Like Me. Brewer, Karen, ed. Bolton, Barbara, contrib. by. (Illus.). 40p. (Orig.). (ps). 1994. pap. 9.99 (0-7847-0242-X, 13-4242) Standard Pub.

Kolbrek, Loyal. The Day God Made It Rain. (gr. k-2). 1977. pap. 1.99 (0-570-06108-3, 59-1226) Concordia.

—Paul Believes in Jesus. (Illus.). 24p. (gr. k-4). 1987. pap. 1.99 (0-570-09008-3, 59-1436) Concordia.

Kostich, Beverly E. Stepping into the Bible. LC 87-34169. (ps-6). 1988. pap. 2.95 (0-687-40060-0) Abingdon.

Larcombe, Jennifer R. Through-the-Bible Storybook. 1992. 19.99 (0-310-56380-1, Youth Bks) Zondervan.

Larsen, Dan. Jesus. (gr. 3 up). 1992. 9.95 (1-55748-274-8) Barbour & Co.

Lashbrook, Marilyn. God, Please Send Fire: Elijah & the Prophets of Baal. Sharp, Chris, illus. LC 90-60458. 32p. (gr. k-3). 1990. 5.95 (0-86606-440-0, 871) Roper Pr.

Leale, Judy. Three-Minute Bible Stories. Beckett, Sheilah, illus. 32p. 1992. 9.95 (1-56156-152-5) Kidsbks.

Lehman, Elsie E. God Sends His Son Activity Book. 80p. (Orig.). (gr. 3-9). 1987. pap. 3.00 (0-8361-3429-X) Herald Pr.

—God's Wisdom & Power Activity Book. 80p. (ps-1). 1985. pap. 3.00 (0-8361-3391-9) Herald Pr.

Lehn, Cornelia. God Keeps His Promise: A Bible Story Book for Young Children. Darwin, Beatrice, illus. LC 76-90377. (gr. k-4). 1970. 12.95 (0-87303-291-8) Faith & Life.

Lepon, Shoshana. The Ten Tests of Abraham. Forst, Siegmund, illus. 32p. (Orig.). (gr. k-4). 1986. pap. 5.95 (0-910818-67-3) Judaica Pr.

Linde, Lavaun & Quishenberry, Mary. Daniel & the Big Cats: Level One. Maniscalco, Joe, illus. 32p. (gr. 1). 1986. pap. text ed. 4.99 (0-945107-04-8) Bradshaw Pubs.

—God Adds Oil: Level Two. Maniscalco, Joe, illus. 32p. (Orig.). (gr. 1). 1988. pap. text ed. 4.99 (0-945107-05-6) Bradshaw Pubs.

—I Will Help: Level One. Maniscalco, Joe, illus. 32p. (Orig.). (gr. 1). 1986. pap. text ed. 4.99 (0-945107-01-3) Bradshaw Pubs.

—Jonah's Ride: Level Two. Maniscalco, Joe, illus. 32p. (Orig.). (gr. 1). 1988. pap. text ed. 4.99 (0-945107-09-9) Bradshaw Pubs.

—The Lad's Bag: Level One. Maniscalco, Joe, illus. 32p. (gr. 1). 1986. pap. text ed. 4.99 (0-945107-03-X) Bradshaw Pubs.

—Mom & the Lad: Level One. Maniscalco, Joe, illus. 32p. (gr. 1). 1986. pap. text ed. 4.99 (0-945107-02-1) Bradshaw Pubs.

—Not a Bed: Level One. Maniscalco, Joe, illus. 32p. (Orig.). (gr. 1). 1986. pap. text ed. 4.99 (0-945107-00-5) Bradshaw Pubs.

—Seven Dips: Level Two. Maniscalco, Joe, illus. 32p. (Orig.). (gr. 1). 1988. pap. text ed. 4.99 (0-945107-08-0) Bradshaw Pubs.

—Three Brave Men: Level Two. Maniscalco, Joe, illus. 32p. (Orig.). (gr. 1). 1988. pap. text ed. 4.99 (0-945107-07-2) Bradshaw Pubs.

—Zacchaeus' Cash Bag: Level Two. Maniscalco, Joe, illus. 32p. (Orig.). (gr. 1). 1988. pap. text ed. 4.99 (0-945107-06-4) Bradshaw Pubs.

Lindvall, Ella K. Read-Aloud Bible Stories, Vol. 1. LC 82-2114. 160p. (ps-2). 1982. 17.99 (0-8024-7163-3) Moody.

—Read Aloud Bible Stories, Vol. 3. (ps-2). 1990. 17.99 (0-8024-7165-X) Moody.

Linville, Barbara. Christy's Pouting Again. McCallum, Joanne, created by. & illus. 32p. (gr. k-2). 1989. 2.99 (0-87403-627-5, 3891) Standard Pub.

—Joey's Too Much TV. McCallum, Joanne, created by. & illus. 32p. (gr. k-2). 1989. 2.99 (0-87403-628-3, 3892) Standard Pub.

—Tommy's Afraid to Try. McCallum, Joanne, created by. & illus. 32p. (gr. k-2). 1989. 2.99 (0-87403-630-5) Standard Pub.

Little Donkey's Big Day. 1991. 0.79 (0-8307-1062-0, 5608617) Regal.

Little, Emily. David & the Giant. Wilhelm, Hans, illus. LC 86-22079. 48p. (ps-1). 1987. lib. bdg. 7.99 (0-394-98867-1); pap. 3.50 (0-394-88867-7) Random Bks Yng Read.

Lockwood, Barbara & McAuley, Marilyn. Bible Surprises. LC 87-71384. (ps). 1992. bds. 4.99 (1-55513-120-4, Chariot Bks) Chariot Family.

The Lost Sheep Is Found. 1991. 0.79 (0-8307-1064-7, 5608629) Regal.

Lovik, Craig J. The Exodus. (Illus.). 24p. (gr. k-4). 1987. pap. 1.99 (0-570-09001-6, 59-1429) Concordia.

Lucas, Daryl. Children. Durham, Robert C., illus. 18p. (gr. 2). 1992. 7.99 (0-8423-1013-4) Tyndale.

—Heroes. Durham, Robert C., illus. 18p. (gr. 2). 1992. 8.99 (0-8423-1009-6) Tyndale.

—Heroines. Durham, Robert C., illus. 18p. (gr. 2). 1992. 8.99 (0-8423-1012-6) Tyndale.

—Prophets. Durham, Robert C., illus. (gr. 2). 1992. 8.99 (0-8423-1011-8) Tyndale.

McCall, Yvonne H. The Story of Jacob, Rachel & Leah. (Illus.). 24p. (gr. k-4). 1986. pap. 1.99 saddlestitched (0-570-06205-5, 59-1428) Concordia.

McElroy. Jesus Forgives Peter. 24p. (Orig.). (gr. k-4). 1985. pap. 1.99 (0-570-06192-X, 59-1293) Concordia.

MacHaster, Eve B. God Comforts His People. Converse, James, illus. LC 95-835. 176p. (Orig.). (gr. 3 up). 1985. pap. 5.95 (0-8361-3393-5) Herald Pr.

Mackall, Dandi D. Jesus Loves Me. (ps-3). 1994. pap. 4.99 (0-8066-2695-X, Augsburg) Augsburg Fortress.

Macmaster, Eve. God Gives the Land. Converse, James, photos by. LC 83-182. (Illus.). 168p. (Orig.). (ps-1). 1983. pap. 5.95 (0-8361-3332-3) Herald Pr.

—God Rescues His People: Stories of God & His People: Exodus, Leviticus, Numbers & Deuteronomy. Converse, James, illus. LC 82-2849. 176p. (Orig.). (ps-1). 1982. pap. 5.95 (0-8361-1994-0) Herald Pr.

—God's Chosen King. Converse, James, illus. LC 83-12736. 190p. (Orig.). (gr. 5-6). 1983. pap. 5.95 (0-8361-3344-7) Herald Pr.

—God's Justice. Converse, James, illus. LC 84-20514. 168p. (Orig.). (ps-1). 1984. pap. 5.95 (0-8361-3381-1) Herald Pr.

—God's Wisdom & Power. Converse, James, illus. LC 84-8974. 168p. (Orig.). (gr. 3-8). 1984. pap. 5.95 (0-8361-3362-5) Herald Pr.

MacMaster, Eve B. God Builds His Church. Converse, James, illus. LC 87-2875. 184p. (Orig.). (gr. 3 up). 1987. pap. 5.95 (0-8361-3446-X) Herald Pr.

—God Sends His Son. Converse, James, illus. LC 86-18342. 160p. (Orig.). (gr. 3-9). 1986. pap. 5.95 (0-8361-3420-6) Herald Pr.

—God's Suffering Servant. Converse, James, illus. LC 86-19526. 120p. (Orig.). (gr. 3-9). 1987. pap. 5.95 (0-8361-3422-2) Herald Pr.

Mains, Karen B. & Mains, David. Tales of the Kingdom. Stockman, Jack, illus. 112p. (gr. 1 up). 1983. 16.99 (0-89191-560-5) Cook.

Mann, Victor. He Remembered to Say "Thank You" (Illus.). 32p. (ps-4). 1976. pap. 1.99 (0-570-06103-2, 59-1221) Concordia.

Marquardt, Mervin A. The Temptation of Jesus. (Illus.). 24p. (gr. k-4). 1986. pap. 1.99 saddlestitched (0-570-06204-7, 59-1427) Concordia.

Marquart, M. Jesus' Second Family. (gr. k-2). 1977. pap. 1.99 (0-570-06111-3, 59-1229) Concordia.

Marshall, Catherine. Catherine Marshall's Story Bible. 200p. (ps-5). 1985. pap. 10.95 (0-380-69961-3) Avon.

Martin, Bill. Fit for the King. Haynes, Glenda, ed. Sweeney, Hazel, illus. 384p. (Orig.). (gr. 7 up). 1985. pap. 11.50 (0-89114-154-5) Baptist Pub Hse.

Martin, Mildred A. Storytime with the Millers. Baker, Anthony, illus. 96p. (Orig.). (ps-3). 1992. pap. 4.50 (0-9627643-1-0) Green Psturs Pr.

—Wisdom & the Millers: Proverbs for Children. 2nd ed. Burkholder, Edith, illus. 159p. (gr. 2-8). 1993. 9.50 (0-685-68129-7); pap. 6.00 (0-9627643-5-3) Green Psturs Pr.

Marxhausen, Evelyn. Simeon & the Baby Jesus. (Illus.). 24p. (gr. k-4). 1986. pap. 1.99 saddlestitched (0-570-06202-0, 59-1425) Concordia.

Maschke, Ruby A. Bible Puzzles for Children. 64p. (gr. 4-6). 1986. pap. 8.00 (0-8170-1095-5) Judson.

Matthews, Graham P., Jr. Children's Bible Stories with Questions. LeDee, Kim, illus. LC 93-19623. (gr. 3 up). 1993. write for info. (0-910683-18-2) Townsnd-Pr.

Miller, Sarah W. Bible Dramas for Older Boys & Girls. LC 75-95409. (gr. 3-6). 1970. pap. 4.99 (0-8054-7506-0) Broadman.

Mitchell, Robert E. Jesus the Good Shepherd. (Illus.). 24p. (ps-2). 1989. pap. 1.99 (0-570-09018-0, 59-1441) Concordia.

Moeri, Louise. Save Queen of Sheba. 112p. 1990. pap. 3.50 (0-380-71154-0, Camelot) Avon.

Molan, Chris, illus. Joseph the Dream Teller: Retold by Catererine Storr. 32p. (gr. k-4). 1984. 14.65 (0-8172-1989-7, Raintree Children's Books Belitha Press Ltd. - London) Raintree Steck-V.

Mueller, A. C. My Good Shepherd Bible Story Book. LC 70-89876. (gr. 3-5). 1969. bds. 15.99 (0-570-03400-0, 56-1126) Concordia.

Mueller, Virginia. Jacob's Ladder. LC 59-1444. (Illus.). 24p. (ps-4). 1990. pap. 1.99 (0-570-09021-0) Concordia.

Muir, Virginia J. The One Year Bible Story Book. Hook, Richard & Hook, Frances, illus. 384p. (gr. 5 up). 1988. 12.99 (0-8423-2631-6) Tyndale.

My Very Own Bible. 1991. 5.99 (0-89081-918-1) Harvest Hse.

Neff, Lavonne. God's Gift Baby. (gr. k-4). 1977. pap. 1.89 (0-570-06113-X, 59-1230) Concordia.

New International Version of Bible Staff. The Lost Boy. (Illus., Orig.). 1986. pap. 4.95 (0-918789-07-9) FreeMan Prods.

—The Stowaway. (Illus., Orig.). 1986. pap. 4.95 (0-918789-09-5) FreeMan Prods.

Noah & the Flood. 1992. pap. 9.99 (0-553-08133-0) Bantam.

Nystrom, Carolyn. Angels & Me: Children's Bible Basics. (ps-3). 1994. 5.99 (0-8024-7863-8) Moody.

—Children's Bible Basics Ser, 11 bks. Hanna, Wayne, illus. (ps-2). Set. pap. 54.89 (0-8024-5988-9) Moody.

O'Neal, Debbie T. My Read-&-Do Bible Storybook. Ebert, Len, illus. LC 89-15184. 128p. (Orig.). (gr. 3-8). 1989. pap. 14.99 kivar (0-8066-2431-0, 9-2431) Augsburg Fortress.

Oppenheim, Shulamith L. Iblis: An Islamic Tale. Young, Ed, illus. LC 92-15060. 1994. 15.95 (0-15-238016-7) HarBrace.

Ottow, Harriett. Ruth's Adventures in Israel. LC 87-51493. 44p. (gr. k-2). 1988. 5.95 (1-55523-133-0) Winston-Derek.

Overholtzer, Ruth. Joshua. Butcher, Sam & Anderasen, Norma, illus. 62p. (gr. k-6). 1987. pap. text ed. 9.45 (*1-55976-012-5*) CEF Press.

Owen, Barbara. God Hears Me. (ps-3). 1994. pap. 4.99 (*0-8066-2696-8*, Augsburg) Augsburg Fortress.

Parker, Gary. Life Before Birth. (Orig.). (gr. 1-8). 1987. 10.95 (*0-89051-117-9*) Master Bks.

Parry, Alan & Parry, Linda. The Beginning. (Illus.). 24p. (ps). 1990. pap. 0.99 (*0-8066-2473-6*, 9-2473) Augsburg Fortress.

—Caleb & Katie's Big Book of Bible Adventures. (Illus.). 64p. (gr. k-5). 1993. 12.99 (*0-8499-0982-1*) Word Inc.

—The Farmer & the Seed. Parry, Alan, illus. 24p. (ps). 1990. pap. 0.99 (*0-8066-2474-4*, 9-2474) Augsburg Fortress.

—Joseph & His Coat. Parry, Alan, illus. 24p. (ps). 1990. pap. 0.99 (*0-8066-2476-0*, 9-2476) Augsburg Fortress.

Pavlat, Leo. Bible Stories: From the Old & New Testament. (gr. 1 up). 1994. 12.98 (*0-7858-0013-1*) Bk Sales Inc.

Petach, Heidi. Jonah: The Inside Story. Petach, Heidi, illus. 32p. (gr. k-2). 1989. 2.50 (*0-87403-594-5*, 3854) Standard Pub.

Pfrimmer, Mildred. Books to Learn & Live by, 5 bks. Incl. Bk. The ABC's of Creation.; Bk. 2. The ABC's of the Flood.; Bk. 3. The Aardvark in the Art.; Bk. 4. Elephant in Eden.; Bk. 5. The Tale of the Whale.. (gr. 3-9). 1977. Set. 17.50 (*0-685-80546-8*) Triumph Pub.

Phillips, Cheryl & Harvey, Bonnie C., eds. My Jesus Pocketbook of God's Fruit. Fulton, Ginger A., illus. LC 83-50194. 32p. (ps-3). 1983. pap. 0.69 (*0-937420-08-5*) Stirrup Assoc.

Phillips, Cheryl M. & Harvey, Bonnie C., eds. My Jesus Pocketbook of the Lord's Prayer. Fulton, Ginger A., illus. LC 83-50193. 32p. (ps-3). 1983. pap. 0.69 (*0-937420-07-7*) Stirrup Assoc.

Pilling, Ann. Before I Go to Sleep: A Collection of Bible Stories, Poems & Prayers for Children. Denton, Kady M., illus. LC 89-7816. 96p. 1990. PLB 15.99 (*0-517-58019-5*) Crown Bks Yng Read.

Pilling, Ann, retold by. The Kingfisher Children's Bible. Denton, Kady M., illus. LC 92-42679. 1993. 18.95 (*1-85697-840-0*, Kingfisher LKC) LKC.

Pingry, Patricia. Story of Daniel & the Lions. Britt, Stephanie, illus. 24p. (Orig.). (ps-3). 1988. pap. 3.95 (*0-8249-8179-0*, Ideals Child) Hambleton-Hill.

—Story of Johan & the Big Fish. Venturi-Pickett, Stacy, illus. 24p. (Orig.). (ps-3). 1988. pap. 3.95 (*0-8249-8181-2*, Ideals Child) Hambleton-Hill.

Pliskin, Jacqueline J. The Bible Story Activity Book. Pliskin, Jacqueline J., illus. 96p. (gr. 1-4). 1990. pap. 5.95 (*0-944007-67-8*) Shapolsky Pubs.

Polyzoides, G. Stories from the Old Testament. (GRE., Illus.). 71p. (gr. 5 up). 4.00 (*0-686-80434-1*) Divry.

Promises for Kids from the Book. 320p. (gr. 1 up). 1988. 12.99 (*0-8423-5053-5*) Tyndale.

Randall, Louise A. Bible Heroes: Stories for Children Ages One to Six. Pardew, Louise, illus. LC 87-82112. 56p. (ps). 1988. pap. 4.98 (*0-88290-316-0*) Horizon Utah.

—Scripture Stories for Tiny Tots: Read-Aloud Stories from the Bible for Children 1 to 6. LC 83-83429. 38p. (Orig.). (gr. k-3). 1983. pap. 4.98 (*0-88290-209-1*) Horizon Utah.

Rathert, Donna R. Job. (Illus.). 24p. (ps-2). 1989. pap. 1.99 (*0-570-09017-2*, 59-1440) Concordia.

Raub, Joyce. Cain & Abel. (Illus.). 24p. (gr. k-4). 1986. pap. 1.99 saddlestitched (*0-570-06199-7*, 59-1422) Concordia.

Ray, Jane, illus. The Story of Christmas: Words from the Gospels of Matthew & Luke. LC 91-11357. 32p. (ps up). 1991. 15.95 (*0-525-44768-7*, DCB) Dutton Child Bks.

Read with Me Bible: An NIV Story Bible for Children. (ps-3). 1993. 16.99 (*0-310-91662-3*) Zondervan.

Rector, Andy. Five Minutes 'til Bedtime: Twelve Quick-' As-a-Wink Bible Stories. Patterson, Kathleen, illus. 32p. (Orig.). 1993. pap. 5.99 (*0-87401-110-8*, 24-03670) Standard Pub.

Regehr, Lydia. Bible Riddles of Birds & Beasts & Creeping Things. (Illus.). 36p. (Orig.). (gr. 7-12). 1982. pap. 1.25 (*0-89323-030-8*) Bible Memory.

Reid, John C. Parables from Nature: Earthly Stories with Heavenly Meanings. 2nd ed. Foley, Timothy, illus. 96p. (gr. k-4). 1991. pap. 7.99 (*0-8028-4052-3*) Eerdmans.

Reinsma, Carol & Bruno, Bonnie. The Young Reader's Bible. Stortz, Diane, ed. (Illus.). 448p. (ps-3). 1994. 17.99 (*0-7847-0161-X*) Standard Pub.

Richards, Larry. Talkable Bible Stories: Helping Your Kids Apply God's Word to Their Lives. (Illus.). 256p. (ps-3). 1994. pap. 9.99 (*0-8007-5505-7*) Revell.

Roberts, Jim & Scheck, Joann. Bible Pop-O-Rama Books, 2 vols. Incl. The Brightest Star. 5.99 (*0-8066-1601-6*, 10-0915). (Illus.). 12p. (gr. 3 up). 1978. (Augsburg) Augsburg Fortress.

Robertson, Jenny. Enciclopedia de Historias Biblicas. LaValle, Maria T., tr. King, Gordon, illus. (SPA.). 272p. (gr. 3-5). 1984. 17.00 (*0-311-03671-6*) Casa Bautista.

Rogers, Barbara. God Rescues His People Activity Book. 72p. (Orig.). (ps-1). 1983. pap. 3.00 (*0-8361-3338-2*) Herald Pr.

Sattgast, L. J. Good Morning, Jesus, Good Night, Jesus. Reck, Sue, ed. (Illus.). 48p. (ps-2). Date not set. 7.99 (*0-7814-0194-1*, Chariot Bks) Chariot Family.

Schoolland, Marian M. Marian's Big Book of Bible Stories. (gr. k-4). 1947. 19.99 (*0-8028-5003-0*) Eerdmans.

Silverthorne, Sandy. All-Time Awesome Bible Search. Silverthorne, Sandy, illus. 32p. (Orig.). (ps up). 1991. 11.99 (*0-89081-920-3*) Harvest Hse.

—The Great Bible Adventure. Silverthorne, Sandy, illus. LC 90-36385. 32p. (Orig.). (ps-8). 1990. 11.99 (*0-89081-842-8*) Harvest Hse.

Simcox, Helen E. For All the World. (ps-3). 1994. 14.99 (*0-8066-2712-3*, Fortress Pr) Augsburg Fortress.

Simon, Mary M. God's Children Pray. 1989. 5.99 (*0-570-04173-2*, 56-1633) Concordia.

Simonelic, Ken. Effy & the Little Glass Soldier. LC 91-16066. (Orig.). (gr. 5-9). 1991. pap. 3.00 (*0-915541-83-1*) Star Bks Inc.

Spier, Peter. Noah's Ark. Spier, Peter, illus. LC 76-43630. 44p. (gr. k-3). 1977. PLB 15.95 (*0-385-09473-6*) Doubleday.

Standard Publishing Staff. Favorite Bible Stories Chalkboard Book. (ps-3). 1991. 9.99 (*0-87403-723-9*) Standard Pub.

Steiner, Rudolf. And It Came to Pass: An Old Testament, Reader for Children. 1973. lib. bdg. 79.95 (*0-87968-556-5*) Krishna Pr.

Stirrup Associates, Inc. Staff. My Jesus Pocketbook of Li'l Critters. Phillips, Cheryl M., ed. Sherman, Erin, illus. LC 82-63139. 32p. (Orig.). (ps-3). 1983. pap. text ed. 17.50 spiral bdg. (*0-937420-05-0*) Stirrup Assoc.

—My Jesus Pocketbook of Manners. Phillips, Cheryl M., ed. Sherman, Erin, illus. LC 82-63141. 32p. (ps-3). 1983. pap. 0.69 (*0-937420-06-9*) Stirrup Assoc.

—My Jesus Pocketbook of the 23rd Psalm. Phillips, Cheryl M., ed. LC 82-63140. (Illus.). 32p. (Orig.). (ps-3). 1983. pap. text ed. 0.69 (*0-937420-04-2*) Stirrup Assoc.

Stoddard, Sandol. A Child's First Bible. Chen, Tony, illus. 96p. (ps-3). 1991. 15.99 (*0-8037-0941-2*) Dial Bks Young.

Stohs, Anita R. Children of the Bible Activity Book. (Illus.). 32p. (Orig.). 1993. pap. 3.49 (*0-570-04750-1*) Concordia.

—Everyday Fun with Jesus Activity Book. (Illus.). 48p. (Orig.). 1994. pap. 4.99 (*0-570-04751-X*) Concordia.

The Storks & the King. 1991. 0.79 (*0-8307-1060-4*, 5608612) Regal.

Storr, Catherine, retold by. Miracles by the Sea. Molan, Christine, illus. LC 82-23022. 32p. (gr. k-4). 1983. 14.65 (*0-8172-1983-8*) Raintree Steck-V.

—The Prodigal Son. Rowe, Gavin, illus. LC 82-23011. 32p. (gr. k-4). 1983. 14.65 (*0-8172-1982-X*) Raintree Steck-V.

Stowell, Gordon. Jesus Alimenta. Stowell, Gordon, illus. De Martinez, Violeta S., tr. from SPA. (Illus.). 24p. (ps). 1988. pap. 0.75 (*0-311-38614-8*) Casa Bautista.

—Jesus Ama. Stowell, Gordon, illus. De Martinez, Violeta S., tr. from SPA. (Illus.). 24p. (ps). 1984. pap. 0.75 (*0-311-38611-3*) Casa Bautista.

—Jesus & the Fisherman. (Illus.). 14p. (gr. 1-5). 1982. pap. 0.79 (*0-8307-0831-6*, 5608150) Regal.

—Jesus Cuenta. Stowell, Gordon, illus. De Martinez, Violeta S., tr. from SPA. (Illus.). 24p. (ps). 1984. pap. 0.75 (*0-311-38613-X*) Casa Bautista.

—Jesus Ensena. Stowell, Gordon, illus. De Martinez, Violeta S., tr. from SPA. (Illus.). 24p. (ps). 1984. pap. 0.75 (*0-311-38609-1*) Casa Bautista.

—Jesus Feeds the People. (Illus.). 14p. (gr. 1-5). 1982. pap. 0.79 (*0-8307-0832-4*, 5608167) Regal.

—Jesus Heals. (Illus.). 14p. (gr. 1-5). 1982. pap. 0.79 (*0-8307-0828-6*, 5608122) Regal.

—Jesus Llama. Stowell, Gordon, illus. De Martinez, Violeta S., tr. from SPA. (Illus.). 24p. (ps). 1984. pap. 0.75 (*0-311-38612-1*) Casa Bautista.

—Jesus Loves. 14p. (gr. 1-5). 1982. pap. 0.79 (*0-8307-0830-8*, 5608145) Regal.

—Jesus Nace. De Martinez, Violeta S., tr. from SPA. (Illus.). 24p. (ps). 1984. pap. 0.75 (*0-311-38608-3*) Casa Bautista.

—Jesus Sana. Stowell, Gordon, illus. De Martinez, Violeta S., tr. from ENG. (Illus.). 24p. (ps-1). 1984. pap. 0.75 (*0-311-38610-5*) Casa Bautista.

—Jesus Teaches. (Illus.). 14p. 1982. pap. 0.79 (*0-8307-0829-4*, 5608138) Regal.

—Jesus Tells Some Stories. (Illus.). 14p. (gr. 1-5). 1982. pap. 0.79 (*0-8307-0833-2*, 5608176) Regal.

—Jesus Vive. Stowell, Gordon, illus. De Martinez, Violeta S., tr. from SPA. (Illus.). 24p. (ps-1). 1984. pap. 0.75 (*0-311-38615-6*) Casa Bautista.

Swartz, Susan S. All God's Creatures. (ps-3). 1994. pap. 4.99 (*0-8066-2687-9*) Augsburg Fortress.

Tangvald, Christine H. Yea, Hooray! The Son Came Home Today, & Other Bible Stories about Wisdom. Sasaki, Ellen J., illus. LC 93-9244. 1993. 7.99 (*0-7814-0927-6*, Chariot Bks) Chariot Family.

Tate, Susan. Petal Pals Children's Stories, 4 bks. (gr. k-3). 1993. pap. 15.96 (*1-884395-07-4*) Clear Blue Sky.

Taylor, Kenneth. The Book for Children. 640p. 1985. 12. 99 (*0-8423-2145-4*) Tyndale.

Taylor, Kenneth N. Boy Helps Jesus. (ps-3). 1994. 3.99 (*0-8423-1292-7*) Tyndale.

—Catholic Family-Time Bible Stories in Pictures. (Illus.). 307p. (gr. 3-6). 1993. 14.95 (*0-87973-882-0*, 882) Our Sunday Visitor.

—Good Neighbor. (ps-3). 1994. 3.99 (*0-8423-5947-8*) Tyndale.

—Very Special Baby. (ps-3). 1994. 3.99 (*0-8423-1301-X*) Tyndale.

Taylor, Kenneth N., ed. My First Bible Stories in Pictures. Hook, Robert & Hook, Frances, illus. Lockwood, Robert P., intro. by. 272p. (gr. 1-3). 1990. 14.95 (*0-87973-245-8*, 245); 10.95 (*0-87973-246-6*, 246) Our Sunday Visitor.

Thomas, Nelson. Children of God: Read along Story Book in Contemporary English Version. (ps-3). 1993. 9.99 (*0-8407-8479-1*) Nelson.

Thomas Nelson Publishers Staff. Bible Stories, Bk. 3. (gr. 2 up). 1993. 6.99 (*0-8407-4911-2*) Nelson.

Turner, Philip. The Bible Story. Wildsmith, Brian, illus. 142p. 1987. 19.95 (*0-19-273104-1*) OUP.

Two by Two. 1991. 0.79 (*0-8307-1063-9*, 5608622) Regal.

Ulmer, Louise. Samuel, the Judge. (Illus.). 24p. (gr. k-4). 1986. pap. 1.99 saddlestitched (*0-570-06200-4*, 59-1423) Concordia.

Vos, Catherine F. The Child's Story Bible. (Illus.). 432p. (gr. 3 up). 1983. Repr. of 1934 ed. PLB 19.99 (*0-8028-5011-1*) Eerdmans.

Waddy, Lawrence. First Bible Stories. Mitchell, Mark, illus. LC 93-34710. 80p. (Orig.). (ps-3). 1994. pap. 7.95 (*0-8091-6613-5*) Paulist Pr.

Wallace, Lew. Ben Hur. Larson, Dan, ed. Bohl, Al, illus. 224p. (Orig.). (gr. 6 up). 1990. pap. text ed. 2.50 (*1-55748-114-8*) Barbour & Co.

Walton, John & Walton, Kim. Daniel & the Lions. LC 86-72322. (Illus.). (ps). 1987. pap. 3.49 (*1-55513-045-3*, Chariot Bks) Chariot Family.

—God & the World He Made. LC 86-70677. (Illus.). (ps). 1986. pap. 3.49 (*1-55513-030-5*, Chariot Bks) Chariot Family.

—Tiny Tots Bible Story Book. Craig, Alice, illus. (ps). 1993. 14.99 (*0-7814-0834-2*, Chariot Bks) Chariot Family.

Waybill, Marjorie. God's Justice: Activity Book. 88p. (Orig.). (ps-1). 1985. pap. 3.00 (*0-8361-3397-8*) Herald Pr.

White, J. Edson. Best Stories from the Best Book: And Thou Shalt Teach Them Diligently Unto Thy Children. (Illus.). 160p. (gr. 5 up). 1990. pap. 8.95 (*0-945460-06-6*) Upward Way.

Willis, Doris. Tell Me a Bible Story. LC 90-22423. 1991. pap. 3.95 (*0-687-03126-5*) Abingdon.

Wilson, Etta. Daniel & the Lions. (Illus.). 1992. bds. 3.49 (*0-8007-7123-0*) Revell.

—Jesus & the Donkey. (Illus.). 1992. bds. 3.49 (*0-8007-7125-7*) Revell.

Winthrop, Elizabeth, adapted by. He Is Risen: The Easter Story. Mikolaycak, Charles, illus. LC 84-15869. 32p. (gr. 4-6). 1985. reinforced bdg. 15.95 (*0-8234-0547-8*) Holiday.

Wolf, Bob. Uncle Bob's Bible Stories. Lautermilch, John, illus. 108p. (Orig.). (gr. 4-8). 1982. pap. 1.50 (*0-89323-028-6*) Bible Memory.

Woods, Paul. Miracles! (Illus.). 48p. (gr. 6-8). 1991. pap. 8.99 (*1-55945-117-3*) Group Pub.

Woody, Marilyn J. A Child's Book of Angels: Stories from the Bible about God's Special Messengers. LC 92-12862. 1992. 10.99 (*1-55513-756-3*, Chariot Bks) Chariot Family.

Wunnenberg, Helen. Three Questions. (Illus.). 12p. (gr. k-6). 1983. visualized song 3.99 (*3-90117-027-8*) CEF Press.

Ziefert, Harriet. Animals of the Bible. Galli, Letizia, illus. LC 93-38568. 1995. write for info. (*0-385-32084-1*) Doubleday.

BIBLE STORIES–N.T.

Alexander, Pat. My Own Book of Bible Stories. (Illus.). 128p. 1983. 9.99 (*0-85648-541-1*) Lion USA.

Alexander, Pat, as told by. My Own Book of Bible Stories. 2nd ed. Cox, Carolyn, illus. LC 92-36252. 128p. (gr. k-3). 1993. text ed. 14.95 (*0-7459-2635-5*) Lion USA.

Anastasio, Dina. Joy to the World! Paterson, Bettina, illus. 32p. (ps-3). 1992. (G&D); pap. 2.25 (*0-448-40479-6*, G&D) Putnam Pub Group.

Backhouse, Halcyon. The Incredible Journey. LC 92-33820. (Illus.). 1993. 9.99 (*0-8407-9403-7*) Nelson.

Berg, Jean H. The Story of Jesus. Krush, Beth & Krush, Joe, illus. 40p. (Orig.). (gr. k-3). 1977. pap. 9.95 incl. audiocassette (*0-87510-185-2*) Christian Sci.

Burgess, Beverly C. Seedtime Stories: Bedtime Stories with Poems & Devotionals. Mckee, Vici, illus. (Orig.). (gr. 2-6). 1991. pap. 4.95 (*1-879470-01-2*) Burgess Pub.

Caswell, Helen. Loaves & Fishes. LC 93-25308. 24p. 1993. 11.95 (*0-687-22526-4*) Abingdon.

—Parable of the Sower. LC 90-23200. (ps-3). 1991. 11.95 (*0-687-30020-7*) Abingdon.

Concordia Staff. Boy Who Gave His Lunch Away: John 6: 1-15. 1993. pap. 1.99 (*0-570-06027-3*) Concordia.

—Night the Angels Sang: Luke 2: 8-20. (ps-3). 1993. pap. 1.99 (*0-570-06095-8*) Concordia.

Daniel, Rebecca. Book I-His Birth. McClure, Nancee, illus. 32p. (gr. 2-7). 1984. wkbk. 6.95 (*0-86653-213-7*, SS 824, Shining Star Pubns) Good Apple.

—Book IV-the Teacher. McClure, Nancee, illus. 32p. (gr. 2-7). 1984. wkbk. 7.95 (*0-86653-225-0*, SS 827, Shining Star Pubns) Good Apple.

—Book VI-His Miracles. McClure, Nancee, illus. 32p. (gr. 2-7). 1984. wkbk. 7.95 (*0-86653-227-7*, SS 829, Shining Star Pubns) Good Apple.

—Book VII-His Parables. McClure, Nancee, illus. 32p. (gr. 2-7). 1984. wkbk. 7.95 (*0-86653-228-5*, SS 830, Shining Star Pubns) Good Apple.

—Book XI-His Last Hours. McClure, Nancee, illus. 32p. (gr. 2-7). 1984. wkbk. 7.95 (*0-86653-232-3*, SS 834, Shining Star Pubns) Good Apple.
—Book XII-His Resurrection. McClure, Nancee, illus. 32p. (gr. 2-7). 1984. wkbk. 7.95 (*0-86653-233-1*, SS 835, Shining Star Pubns) Good Apple.
Dean, Bessie. Stories Jesus Told. 72p. 1979. pap. 5.98 (*0-88290-132-X*) Horizon Utah.
Decker, Barbara, ed. A Coloring Book of Bible Verses from the Epistles. Clark, Penny, illus. 32p. (Orig.). 1989. coloring bk 2.50 (*0-9618608-4-7*) Lynn's Bookshelf.
Dudley-Smith, Timothy. The Lion Book of Stories of Jesus. (Illus.). 96p. (gr. 1-5). 1989. 11.95 (*0-85648-906-9*) Lion USA.
Erickson, Mary E. Miracle in the Morning: The Wonderful Story of Easter. LC 92-20260. 1993. 10.99 (*0-7814-0779-6*, Chariot Bks) Chariot Family.
Frank, Penny. A Baby Called John. Morris, Tony, et al, illus. 24p. (ps-3). 3.99 (*0-85648-756-2*) Lion USA.
—Come Down, Zacchaeus! Morris, Tony, et al, illus. 24p. (ps-3). 3.99 (*0-85648-768-6*) Lion USA.
—The First Easter. (ps-3). 1987. 3.99 (*0-85648-773-2*) Lion USA.
—The First Easter. Haysom, John & Morris, Tony, illus. Burow, Daniel, contrib. by. LC 92-31640. 1992. 6.95 (*0-7459-2607-X*) Lion USA.
—Good News for Everyone. Morris, Tony, et al, illus. 24p. (ps-3). 3.99 (*0-85648-774-0*) Lion USA.
—Jesus Gives the People Food. (ps-3). 1988. 3.99 (*0-85648-761-9*) Lion USA.
—Jesus' Special Friends. Morris, Tony, et al, illus. 24p. (ps-3). 3.99 (*0-85648-759-7*) Lion USA.
—People Jesus Met. Morris, Tony, et al, illus. 24p. (ps-3). 3.99 (*0-85648-770-8*) Lion USA.
—Story of the Good Samaritan. (ps-3). 1985. 3.99 (*0-85648-763-5*) Lion USA.
—The Story of the Great Feast. Morris, Tony, et al, illus. 24p. (ps-3). 3.99 (*0-85648-766-X*) Lion USA.
—The Story of the Lost Sheep. Morris, Tony, et al, illus. 24p. (ps-3). 3.99 (*0-85648-767-8*) Lion USA.
—The Story of the Sower. Morris, Tony, et al, illus. 24p. (ps-3). 3.99 (*0-85648-764-3*) Lion USA.
Fryar, Jane. The Easter Day Surprise. (Illus.). 24p. (Orig.). (ps-4). 1993. pap. 1.99 (*0-570-09033-4*) Concordia.
—Jesus Enters Jerusalem. (Illus.). 24p. (Orig.). (ps-4). 1993. pap. 1.99 (*0-570-09032-6*) Concordia.
Gangwer, Rosalie M. Jesus Calms the Storm: Matthew 8, 23-27 & Mark 4, 35-41 for the Beginning Reader. Mitter, Kathryn, illus. LC 93-17472. 32p. (ps-3). 1993. 6.50 (*0-8198-3955-8*) St Paul Bks.
Glavich, Mary K. A Child's Book of Miracles. LC 94-2378. (gr. 3 up). 1994. 2.50 (*0-8294-0802-9*) Loyola.
—A Child's Book of Parables. LC 94-2383. 1994. 2.50 (*0-8294-0801-0*) Loyola.
Hegg, Tom. The Mark of the Maker. Hanson, Warren, illus. 46p. (gr. 4 up). 1991. 10.95 (*0-931674-18-2*) Waldman Hse Pr.
Jackson, Dave & Jackson, Neta, eds. Best Loved Bible Stories. 1993. pap. 9.99 (*0-7814-0136-4*, Bible Discovery) Chariot Family.
Jesus Loves Us. (Illus.). 32p. (Orig.). 1993. pap. 1.99 (*0-570-04757-9*) Concordia.
Keffer, Louis. Interactive Bible Stories for Children: New Testament. LC 93-41547. (gr. 2 up). 1994. 12.99 (*1-55945-291-9*) Group Pub.
Knecker, Don, illus. The First Christmas According to Luke. 32p. (ps-4). 1993. incl. dust jacket 15.99 (*0-570-04753-6*) Concordia.
Kondeatis, Christos. Scenes from the Life of Jesus Christ: A Three-Dimensional Bible Storybook. LC 94-1732. (gr. 1 up). 1994. 19.95 (*0-8037-1786-5*) Dial Bks Young.
Lashbrook, Marilyn. Don't Rock the Boat: The Story of the Miraculous Catch. Britt, Stephanie M., illus. LC 88-63779. 32p. (ps). 1989. 5.95 (*0-86606-435-4*, 867) Roper Pr.
—Nothing to Fear: Jesus Walks on Water. Sharp, Chris, illus. LC 90-61060. 32p. (gr. k-3). 1991. 5.95 (*0-86606-443-5*, 874) Roper Pr.
—Now I See: The Story of the Man Born Blind. Britt, Stephanie M., illus. LC 88-62520. 32p. (ps). 1989. 5.95 (*0-86606-437-0*, 869) Roper Pr.
Lattimore, Deborah N. The Sailor Who Captured the Sea: A Story of the Book of Kells. Lattimore, Deborah N., illus. LC 89-26937. 40p. (gr. 2-5). 1991. PLB 15.89 (*0-06-023711-2*) HarpC Child Bks.
Lewis, Shari. One-Minute Bible Stories: New Testament. (ps). 1991. pap. 4.99 (*0-440-40628-5*, YB) Dell.
Lysne, Mary. Read the Pictures: Fun from the New Testament, Bk. 1. Lysne, Mary E., illus. 32p. (gr. k-3). 1991. pap. 1.99 saddle stitch (*0-87403-879-0*, 23-02509) Standard Pub.
—Read the Pictures: More Fun from the New Testament, Bk. 2. Lysne, Mary E., illus. 32p. (gr. k-3). 1991. pap. 1.99 saddle stitch (*0-87403-880-4*, 23-02510) Standard Pub.
Moxley, Sheila, illus. The Christmas Story: A Lift-the-Flap Advent Calendar. LC 92-29520. 24p. 1993. 15.99 (*0-8037-1351-7*) Dial Bks Young.
Odor, Ruth S. The Very Special Visitors. Clarke, Karen, illus. 28p. (ps). 1992. 2.50 (*0-87403-955-X*, 24-03595) Standard Pub.
O'Neal, Debbie T. & Rosato, Amelia. The Lost Coin. Rosato, Amelia, illus. LC 92-46610. 14p. 1993. 7.00 (*0-8170-1194-3*) Judson.
—The Lost Sheep. Rosato, Amelia, illus. LC 92-46612. 14p. 1993. 7.00 (*0-8170-1193-5*) Judson.
Parry, Alan. The Lost Coin. (Illus.). 24p. (ps-k). 1994. 3.99 (*0-8499-1088-9*) Word Inc.
—The Lost Pearl. (Illus.). 24p. (ps-k). 1994. 3.99 (*0-8499-1087-0*) Word Inc.
—The Lost Son. (Illus.). 24p. (ps-k). 1994. 3.99 (*0-8499-1086-2*) Word Inc.
Pipe, Rhona. The Easter Story. Spencely, Annabel, illus. LC 92-13325. 1993. 7.99 (*0-8407-3420-4*) Nelson.
Quaglini, Juliana. The Night of the Shepherds: A Christmas Experience. Flanagan, Anne J., tr. from ITA. De Vico, Elvira, illus. LC 93-25027. 32p. (Orig.). (gr. 4 up). 1993. pap. 3.95 (*0-8198-5128-0*) St Paul Bks.
Rector, Andy. Quick-As-a-Wink New Testament Bedtime Stories. Patterson, Kathleen, illus. 12p. (ps). 1993. bds. 4.99 (*0-7847-0112-1*, 24-03102) Standard Pub.
Sattgast, L. J. My Very First Bible - New Testament. Flint, Russ, illus. (Orig.). (ps-3). 1989. 16.99 (*0-89081-756-1*) Harvest Hse.
Sheldon, Charles. In His Steps. Larsen, Dan, adapted by. (gr. 3 up). 1992. 9.95 (*1-55748-275-6*) Barbour & Co.
Simon, Mary M. Come to Jesus: Jesus Blesses the Children. Jones, Dennis, illus. 24p. (Orig.). (ps-1). 1992. pap. 2.49 (*0-570-04707-2*) Concordia.
—The First Christmas: Luke 2: 1-20: The Birth of Jesus. Jones, Dennis, illus. LC 92-21372. 32p. (Orig.). (gr. 1-3). 1993. pap. 3.99 (*0-570-04741-2*) Concordia.
—Follow That Star. Jones, Dennis, illus. 24p. (ps-1). 1990. pap. 2.49 (*0-570-04177-5*) Concordia.
—Row the Boat. Jones, Dennis, illus. 24p. (ps-1). 1990. pap. 2.49 (*0-570-04186-4*, 56-1645) Concordia.
—Send a Baby: Birth of John the Baptist. Jones, Dennis, illus. 24p. (Orig.). (ps-1). 1992. pap. 2.49 (*0-570-04706-4*) Concordia.
—Through the Roof. Jones, Dennis, illus. LC 93-36193. 32p. (Orig.). (gr. 1-3). 1994. pap. 3.99 (*0-570-04734-X*) Concordia.
—Too Tall, Too Small. Jones, Dennis, illus. 24p. (ps-1). 1990. pap. 2.49 (*0-570-04185-6*) Concordia.
—A Walk on the Waves: Matthew 14: 13-32: Jesus Walks on the Water. Jones, Dennis, illus. LC 92-21374. 32p. (Orig.). (gr. 1-3). 1993. pap. 3.99 (*0-570-04735-8*) Concordia.
—Where Is Jesus? Easter. Jones, Dennis, illus. 24p. (Orig.). (ps-1). 1991. pap. 2.49 (*0-570-04703-X*) Concordia.
Standard Publishing Staff. First Christmas: A Picture Window Book. (ps). 1992. 6.99 (*0-87403-883-9*, 24-03793) Standard Pub.
Stortz, Diane. Five Small Loaves & Two Small Fish. Stites, Joe, illus. 28p. (ps). 1992. 2.50 (*0-87403-953-3*, 24-03593) Standard Pub.
—No Problem! Stuart, Don, illus. 28p. (ps) 1992. 2.50 (*0-87403-954-1*, 24-03594) Standard Pub.
—Zaccheus Meets Jesus. Fagan, Todd, illus. 28p. (ps). 1992. 2.50 (*0-87403-958-4*, 24-03598) Standard Pub.
Stowell, Gordon. Dorcas. Lerin, S. D. de, tr. from ENG. (Illus.). 24p. (gr. 1). 1978. pap. 0.75 (*0-311-38517-6*, Edit Mundo) Casa Bautista.
—Juan el Bautista. Lerin, S. D., tr. from ENG. (Illus.). 24p. (gr. 1). 1981. pap. 0.75 (*0-311-38515-X*, Edit Mundo) Casa Bautista.
—Pablo. Lerin, S. D., tr. from ENG. (Illus.). 24p. (gr. 1). 1981. pap. 0.75 (*0-311-38518-4*, Edit Mundo) Casa Bautista.
—Pedro. Lerin, S. D., tr. from ENG. (Illus.). 24p. (gr. 1). 1981. pap. 0.75 (*0-311-38516-8*, Edit Mundo) Casa Bautista.
Stump, Gladys S. Paul. (Illus.). (gr. 1). 1978. pap. 1.95 (*0-8127-0165-8*) Review & Herald.
Taylor, Kenneth N. Stories about Jesus. Munger, Nancy, illus. LC 94-4083. 112p. 1994. 7.99 (*0-8423-6093-X*) Tyndale.
Taylor, Mark A. Breakfast with Jesus. Stiles, Andy, illus. 28p. (ps). 1993. PLB 4.99 (*0-7847-0037-0*, 24-03827) Standard Pub.
Tester, Sylvia. Jesus & the Children. Pistone, Nancy, illus. 12p. (ps). 1992. deluxe ed. 4.99 (*0-87403-993-2*, 24-03113) Standard Pub.
Truitt, Gloria. The Raising of Jairus' Daughter. (Illus.). 24p. (gr. k-4). 1990. pap. 1.99 (*0-570-09023-7*, 59-1446) Concordia.
Wangerin, Walter, Jr. A Penny Is Everything. (Illus.). 32p. (gr. 1-4). 1974. pap. 1.99 (*0-570-06084-2*, 59-1204) Concordia.
Welcome Jesus. (Illus.). 32p. (Orig.). 1993. pap. 1.99 (*0-570-04754-4*) Concordia.
Whalin, Terry. Never Too Busy. Faltico, Mary L., illus. 28p. (ps-k). 1993. 4.99 (*0-7847-0038-9*, 24-03828) Standard Pub.
—A Strange Place to Sing. LC 94-7171. (gr. 4 up). 1994. write for info. (*0-7847-0273-X*) Standard Pub.
Whipple, Janis M., ed. Jesus for Little Ones: Illustrated Bible Stories for Children. Caswell, Helen, illus. LC 94-8886. 160p. (ps-3). 1994. 12.99 (*0-8054-4011-9*, 4240-11) Broadman.
Wildsmith, Brian. An Easter Story. Wildsmith, Brian, illus. LC 93-25097. 40p. (ps-3). 1994. 15.00 (*0-679-84727-8*) Knopf Bks Yng Read.
Winstone, Harold. Gospel for Young Christians. Lescanff, Jacques, illus. 192p. (gr. 3-6). 1985. 3.95 (*0-225-27392-6*) Harper SF.
Yenne, Bill, retold by. The Story of Easter. LC 93-37475. (Illus.). 1994. write for info. (*0-7852-8332-3*); pap. write for info. (*0-7852-8328-5*) Nelson.

BIBLE STORIES–O.T.

Abraham. 1991. 0.79 (*0-8307-1416-2*, 5608900) Regal.
Alexander, Matilda. Judges. (Illus.). 57p. (gr. k-6). 1981. pap. text ed. 9.45 (*1-55976-016-8*) CEF Press.
Alexander, Pat, as told by. My Own Book of Bible Stories. 2nd ed. Cox, Carolyn, illus. LC 92-36252. 128p. (gr. k-3). 1993. text ed. 14.95 (*0-7459-2635-5*) Lion USA.
All the Animals. (ps-1). 1990. bds. 6.99 (*0-7459-1838-7*) Lion USA.
Amoss, Berthe. David & Goliath. (Illus.). 10p. (ps-7). 1989. pap. 2.95 (*0-922589-12-7*) More Than Card.
—Jonah. (Illus.). 10p. (ps-7). 1989. pap. 2.95 (*0-922589-09-7*) More Than Card.
—Noah. (Illus.). 10p. (ps-7). 1989. pap. 2.95 (*0-922589-10-0*) More Than Card.
Animals Two by Two. (ps-1). 1990. bds. 6.99 (*0-7459-1839-5*) Lion USA.
Araten, Harry. Two by Two: Favorite Bible Stories. Araten, Harry, illus. LC 90-46841. 32p. (gr. k-3). 1991. pap. 7.95 (*0-929371-54-2*) Kar Ben.
Arch Books Staff. Abraham, Sarah, & the Promised Son: Genesis 17, 18: 1-15, 21: 1-7. 1993. pap. 1.99 (*0-570-06183-0*) Concordia.
—Garden & a Promise: Genesis 1-3. (ps-3). 1992. pap. 1.99 (*0-570-06072-9*) Concordia.
—Story of Noah's Ark: Genesis 6: 5-9: 17. (ps-3). 1993. pap. 1.99 (*0-570-06009-5*) Concordia.
Aronoff, Daisy P. ABC Bible & Holiday Stories. Danciger, Leila N., illus. 58p. (ps-7). 1992. pap. 15.95 (*1-878612-28-X*) Sunflower Co.
Bach, Alice & Exum, J. Cheryl. Moses & Noah's Ark: Stories from the Bible. Dillon, Leo D. & Dillon, Diane, illus. LC 89-1069. 181p. 1989. 14.95 (*0-385-29778-5*) Delacorte.
Baden, Robert. Caleb, God's Special Spy. (Illus.). 24p. (Orig.). (ps-4). 1993. pap. 1.99 (*0-570-09031-8*) Concordia.
Barrett, John, et al. Stories of God's Love: Creation, Noah's Ark, Christmas, Joshua & the Wall of Jericho. Haines, Bill, illus. (ps-2). 1990. 9.99 (*1-55513-399-1*, 63990, Chariot Bks) Chariot Family.
—Stories of People Who Loved God: Jonah, Daniel, David, Esther. Haines, Bill, illus. (ps-2). 1991. 9.99 (*1-55513-539-0*, 65391, Chariot Bks) Chariot Family.
Because God Said So. (gr. 4-6). 1990. 1.55 (*0-89636-114-4*, JB 3B) Accent CO.
Beers, V. Gilbert & Beers, Ronald A. Bible Stories to Live by, Old Testament. De Jonge, Reint, illus. 96p. (gr. k-3). 1991. 12.99 (*0-8407-3506-5*) Nelson.
Berg, Jean H. Daniel in the Lions' Den. Darwin, Beatrice, illus. Jareaux, Robin, contrib. by. (Illus.). 32p. (Orig.). (gr. k-3). 1973. pap. 9.95 incl. audiocassette (*0-87510-178-X*) Christian Sci.
—Joseph & His Brothers. Krush, Beth & Krush, Joe, illus. 32p. (Orig.). (gr. k-3). 1976. pap. 9.95 incl. audiocassette (*0-87510-104-6*) Christian Sci.
—Nehemiah Builds the Wall. Madden, Don, illus. 32p. (Orig.). (gr. k-3). 1978. pap. 9.95 incl. audiocassette (*0-87510-114-3*) Christian Sci.
—Noah & the Ark. Madden, Don, illus. 32p. (Orig.). (gr. k-3). 1974. pap. 9.95 incl. audiocassette (*0-87510-180-1*) Christian Sci.
Bergey, Alyce. World God Made: Genesis 1-2. (ps-3). 1965. pap. 1.99 (*0-570-06011-7*) Concordia.
Blair, Grandpa. The Gospel Rag: Adam & Eve Straight Up. 2nd ed. 16p. (gr. 11 up). 1992. 5.95 (*0-930366-71-9*) Northcountry Pub.
Brent, Isabelle. Noah's Ark. 1992. 12.95 (*0-316-10837-5*) Little.
Brown, Rodney. Noah's Great Adventure. (Illus.). 20p. 1993. 15.95 (*1-883909-00-7*) Wisdom Tree.
Cassway, Esta. Five Books of Moses for Young People. LC 92-8013. 248p. 1992. 40.00 (*0-87668-451-7*) Aronson.
Caswell, Helen. Daniel & His Friends. LC 93-25305. 24p. 1993. 11.95 (*0-687-10085-2*) Abingdon.
Chaikin, Miriam. Exodus. Mikolaycak, Charles, illus. LC 85-27361. 32p. (gr. 1-4). 1987. reinforced bdg. 15.95 (*0-8234-0607-5*) Holiday.
—Joshua in the Promised Land. Frampton, David, illus. (gr. 3-6). 1990. pap. 6.70 (*0-395-54797-0*, Clarion Bks) HM.
Chaikin, Miriam, retold by. Children's Bible Stories: From Genesis to Daniel. Gilbert, Yvonne, illus. LC 90-42588. 96p. (gr. 1-5). 1993. 17.99 (*0-8037-0956-0*); PLB 17.89 (*0-8037-0990-0*) Dial Bks Young.
Child's Bible: Old Testament: Rewritten for Children by Anne Edwards. LC 78-51444. 384p. (gr. 1-8). 1978. pap. 4.95 (*0-8091-2117-4*) Paulist Pr.
Citrin, Paul J. Joseph's Wardrobe. (Illus.). (gr. 4-6). 1987. pap. 6.95 (*0-8074-0319-9*, 123924) UAHC.
The Creation. (ps-2). 1976. incl. tape 5.99 (*0-89191-804-3*, 98046, Chariot Bks) Chariot Family.
Daniel. (ps-2). 1976. incl. tape 5.99 (*0-89191-800-0*, 98004, Chariot Bks) Chariot Family.
Daniel, Rebecca. Moses & the Ten Commandments. (Illus.). 16p. (ps-3). 1992. 16.95 (*0-86653-644-2*, SS2810, Shining Star Pubns) Good Apple.
David. (ps-2). 1979. incl. tape 5.99 (*0-89191-803-5*, 98038, Chariot Bks) Chariot Family.
Enns, Peter & Forsberg, Glen. Adam & Eve & Five Other Stories. Friesen, John H., illus. 24p. (ps-5). 1985. book & Cassette 4.95 (*0-936215-01-1*) STL Intl.
—David & Goliath & Five Other Stories. Friesen, John H., illus. 24p. (ps-5). 1985. book & Cassette 4.95 (*0-936215-03-8*) STL Intl.

—Joseph the Dreamer & Five Other Stories. Friesen, John H., illus. 24p. (ps-5). 1985. book & cassette 4.95 (*0-936215-02-X*) STL Intl.

Fisher, Leonard E., adapted by. & illus. David & Goliath. LC 92-24063. 32p. (ps-3). 1993. reinforced bdg. 15.95 (*0-8234-0997-X*) Holiday.

Fisher, Leonard E., illus. & adapted by. The Seven Days of Creation. LC 81-2952. 32p. (ps-3). 1981. reinforced bdg. 14.95 (*0-8234-0398-X*) Holiday.

Fletcher, Sarah. My Stories about God's People. Kueker, Don, illus. 32p. (ps-3). 1974. pap. 2.89 (*0-570-03426-4*, 56-1181) Concordia.

Frank, Penny. Abraham, Friend of God. (ps-3). 1984. 3.99 (*0-85648-729-5*) Lion USA.

—Adam & Eve. (ps-3). 1988. 3.99 (*0-85648-727-9*) Lion USA.

—Adam & Eve. Haysom, John & Morris, Tony, illus. Burow, Daniel, contrib. by. LC 92-29470. 1992. 6.95 (*0-7459-2609-6*) Lion USA.

—God Speaks to Samuel. Morris, Tony, et al, illus. 24p. (ps-3). 3.99 (*0-85648-741-4*) Lion USA.

—In the Beginning. (ps-3). 1988. 3.99 (*0-85648-726-0*) Lion USA.

—In the Beginning. Haysom, John, illus. LC 92-31617. 1992. 6.95 (*0-7459-2608-8*) Lion USA.

—Isaac Finds a Wife. Morris, Tony, et al, illus. 24p. (ps-3). 3.99 (*0-85648-730-9*) Lion USA.

—Jacob & Esau. (ps-3). 1988. 3.99 (*0-85648-731-7*) Lion USA.

—Joseph & the King of Egypt. Morris, Tony, et al, illus. 24p. (ps-3). 3.99 (*0-85648-733-3*) Lion USA.

—Joseph the Dreamer. Morris, Tony, et al, illus. 24p. (ps-3). 3.99 (*0-85648-732-5*) Lion USA.

—A King for Israel. Morris, Tony, et al, illus. 24p. (ps-3). 3.99 (*0-85648-742-2*) Lion USA.

—King Nebuchadnezzar's Golden Statue. Morris, Tony, et al, illus. 24p. (ps-3). 3.99 (*0-85648-751-1*) Lion USA.

—Let My People Go! Morris, Tony, et al, illus. 24p. (ps-3). 3.99 (*0-85648-735-X*) Lion USA.

—Noah & the Great Flood. (ps-3). 1988. 3.99 (*0-85648-728-7*) Lion USA.

—The Princess & the Baby. (ps-3). 1988. 3.99 (*0-85648-734-1*) Lion USA.

—Queen Esther Saves Her People. Morris, Tony, et al, illus. 24p. (ps-3). 3.99 (*0-85648-753-8*) Lion USA.

—Ruth's New Family. Morris, Tony, et al, illus. 24p. (ps-3). 3.99 (*0-85648-740-6*) Lion USA.

—Samson the Strong Man. (ps-3). 1985. 3.99 (*0-85648-739-2*) Lion USA.

Freehof, Lillian S. Bible Legends: An Introduction to Midrash, Vol. 1: Genesis. Schwartz, Howard, ed. (gr. 4-6). 1987. pap. text ed. 6.95 (*0-8074-0357-1*, 123050) UAHC.

Gaines, M. C., ed. Picture Stories from the Bible: The Old Testament in Full-Color Comic-Strip Form. Cameron, Don, illus. LC 79-66064. 222p. (gr. 3-10). 1979. Repr. of 1943 ed. 12.95 (*0-934386-01-3*) Scarf Pr.

Geisert, Arthur. After the Flood. LC 93-758. 1994. 16.95 (*0-395-66611-2*) HM.

George, Alan. Paul, God's Servant. (Illus.). 88p. (gr. k-6). 1992. pap. text ed. write for info. (*1-55976-036-2*) CEF Press.

Guernsey, Paul. Noah & the Ark. Lohstoeter, Lori, illus. 40p. (gr. k up). 1993. incl. cass. 19.95 (*0-88708-293-9*, Rabbit Ears); 14.95 (*0-88708-292-0*, Rabbit Ears) Picture Bk Studio.

Head, Constance. The Story of Deborah. (Illus.). (gr. k-3). 1978. 1.99 (*0-570-06116-4*, 59-1234) Concordia.

Henderson, Felicity. My Little Box of Bible Friends. (ps-1). 1991. 10.95 (*0-7459-2012-8*) Lion USA.

Hershey, Katherine. Daniel, Strong in the Lord. (Illus.). (gr. k-6). 1992. pap. text ed. 9.45 (*1-55976-035-4*) CEF Press.

Hickman, Martha W. And God Created Squash: How the World Began. Levine, Abby, ed. Ferri, Giuliano, illus. LC 92-22654. 32p. (ps-3). 1993. PLB 14.95 (*0-8075-0340-1*) A Whitman.

Hollenbeck, Beatrice. Esther. (Illus.). 53p. (gr. k-6). 1964. pap. text ed. 9.45 (*1-55976-014-1*) CEF Press.

Hollender, Betty R. Bible Stories for Little Children, Bk. 1. rev. ed. Bearson, Lee, illus. 80p. (Orig.). (gr. 1-3). 1985. pap. text ed. 6.00 (*0-8074-0309-1*, 103100) UAHC.

—Bible Stories for Little Children, Vol. 2. rev. ed. (Illus.). 80p. (gr. 1-3). 1987. pap. text ed. 6.00 (*0-8074-0324-5*, 103101) UAHC.

—Bible Stories for Little Children, Vol. 3. rev. ed. (Illus.). 80p. (gr. 1-3). 1988. pap. text ed. 6.00 (*0-8074-0416-0*, 103102) UAHC.

—Bible Stories for Little Children, Vol. 4. rev. ed. (Illus.). 80p. (gr. 1-3). 1989. pap. text ed. 6.00 (*0-8074-0418-7*, 103103) UAHC.

Jenkins, Lee. Daniel: A Melodrama. Jenkins, Todd, illus. Greeno, Ron, frwd. by. (Illus.). 32p. (Orig.). (ps-3). 1993. pap. 6.95 (*1-883952-02-6*) Hse of Steno.

Jonah. (ps-2). 1976. incl. tape 5.99 (*0-89191-799-3*, 97998, Chariot Bks) Chariot Family.

Jonas, Ann. Aardvarks, Disembark! (Illus.). 40p. (ps-3). 1994. pap. 4.99 (*0-14-055309-6*) Puffin Bks.

Joshua. (ps-2). 1979. incl. tape 5.99 (*0-89191-610-5*, 26104, Chariot Bks) Chariot Family.

Keffer, Louis. Interactive Bible Stories for Children: Old Testament. LC 93-41548. (gr. 2 up). 1994. 12.99 (*1-55945-190-4*) Group Pub.

Kolatch, Alfred J. Classic Bible Stories for Jewish Children. Araten, Harry, illus. LC 93-10165. 72p. (gr. 3 up). 1994. 14.95 (*0-8246-0362-1*) Jonathan David.

Kondeatis, Christos. Bible Stories of the Old Testament. (ps-6). 1993. pap. 18.00 (*0-671-87573-6*, S&S BFYR) S&S Trade.

Lashbrook, Marilyn. I Don't Want to: The Story of Jonah. Britt, Stephanie M., illus. LC 87-60264. 32p. (ps). 1987. 5.95 (*0-86606-428-1*, 844) Roper Pr.

—The Wall That Did Not Fall: The Story of Rahab's Faith. Britt, Stephanie M., illus. LC 87-63420. 32p. (ps). 1988. 5.95 (*0-86606-433-8*, 864) Roper Pr.

Lenski, Lois. Mr. & Mrs. Noah. LC 48-5989. (Illus.). 48p. (ps-1). 1962. PLB 12.89 (*0-690-54562-2*, Crowell Jr Bks) HarpC Child Bks.

Leone, Dee. The Stories of Noah & Joseph. (Illus.). 48p. (ps-1). 1992. 7.95 (*0-86653-645-0*, SS2811, Shining Star Pubns) Good Apple.

Lepon, Shoshana. Noah & the Rainbow. Friedman, Aaron, illus. LC 92-26431. (gr. k-4). 1993. 11.95 (*1-880582-04-X*); pap. 8.95 (*1-880582-05-8*) Judaica Pr.

Levinger, Elma E. Beautiful Garden & Other Bible Tales. Robinson, Jessie B., illus. (gr. 3-5). 6.95 (*0-8197-0253-6*) Bloch.

Lewis, Shari. One-Minute Bible Stories: Old Testament. Ewing, Carolyn S., illus. LC 86-2011. 48p. (ps-3). 1986. PLB 10.00 (*0-385-19565-6*); pap. 7.99 (*0-385-19566-4*) Doubleday.

—One-Minute Bible Stories: Old Testament. (ps). 1991. pap. 4.99 (*0-440-40627-7*, YB) Dell.

Lysne, Mary. Read the Pictures: Fun from the Old Testament, Bk. 1. Lysne, Mary E., illus. 32p. (gr. k-3). 1991. pap. 1.99 saddle stitch (*0-87403-877-4*, 23-02507) Standard Pub.

—Read the Pictures: More Fun from the Old Testament, Bk. 2. Lysne, Mary E., illus. 32p. (gr. k-3). 1991. pap. 1.99 saddle stitch (*0-87403-878-2*, 23-02508) Standard Pub.

McDonough, Yona Z. Eve & Her Sisters: Women of the Old Testament. Zeldis, Malcah, illus. LC 93-9378. 32p. (gr. k up). 1994. 15.00 (*0-688-12512-3*); PLB 14.93 (*0-688-12513-1*) Greenwillow.

Madgwick, Wendy. Behold! Spot-the-Difference Bible Stories. Alles, Hemesh, illus. LC 93-5506. 48p. (gr. k-3). 1994. 12.00 (*0-679-85333-2*) Random Bks Yng Read.

Metaxas, Eric. David & Goliath. Fraser, Douglas, illus. 40p. (gr. k up). 1993. incl. cass. 19.95 (*0-88708-295-5*, Rabbit Ears); 14.95 (*0-88708-294-7*, Rabbit Ears) Picture Bk Studio.

Miller, Susan M. Esther. (gr. 3 up). 1992. pap. 2.50 perfect bdg. (*1-55748-260-8*) Barbour & Co.

Mills, Peter. Daniel's Adventure with the Lions. 24p. 1994. 7.95 (*0-687-10084-4*) Abingdon.

Neusner, Jacob. Meet Our Sages. Hellmuth, Jim, illus. LC 80-12771. 128p. (gr. 5-8). 1980. pap. text ed. 5.95x (*0-87441-327-3*) Behrman.

Noah. (ps-2). 1976. incl. tape 6.99 (*0-89191-801-9*, 98012, Chariot Bks) Chariot Family.

Noah & the Ark. LC 93-14131. 1993. TR. 6.99 (*0-8407-4914-7*); MM. 6.99 (*0-8407-4910-4*) Nelson.

Noah's Ark & Other Old Testament Stories. (ps-2). 1989. 9.99 (*1-55513-812-8*, Chariot Bks) Chariot Family.

Nofziger, Harold H., illus. And It Was Good. 36p. (ps up). 1993. 12.95 (*0-8361-3634-9*) Herald Pr.

O'Connor, Francine M. ABCs of the Old Testament...for Children. Boswell, Kathryn, illus. 32p. (gr. 1-5). 1989. pap. 3.95 (*0-89243-310-8*) Liguori Pubns.

Olive, Teresa. Joseph & His Brothers. (Illus.). 24p. (Orig.). (ps-4). 1993. pap. 1.99 (*0-570-09030-X*) Concordia.

Paamoni, Zev. Aaron, the High Priest. (Illus.). (gr. 5-10). 1970. 3.00 (*0-914080-27-X*) Shulsinger Sales.

—Benjamin, the Littlest Brother. (Illus.). (gr. 5-10). 1970. 3.00 (*0-914080-28-8*) Shulsinger Sales.

—Yitzchak, Son of Abraham. (Illus.). (gr. 5-10). 1970. 4.00 (*0-914080-25-3*) Shulsinger Sales.

Patterson, Geoffrey. Jonah & the Whale. (Illus.). (ps-3). 1992. 14.00 (*0-688-11238-2*); PLB 13.93 (*0-688-11239-0*) Lothrop.

Paxton, Lenore & Siadi, Phillip. His Name Was David, Around the World: The Story of David & Goliath. Snavely, Linda W., illus. 32p. (ps-4). Date not set. pap. 7.95 coloring bk.-cassette pkg. (*1-880449-07-2*) Wrldkids Pr.

—Noah & the Ark: Around the World. (Illus.). 24p. (ps-4). 1993. pap. 7.95 coloring bk.-cassette pkg. (*1-880449-06-4*) Wrldkids Pr.

Pipe, Rhona. Daniel & the Lions' Den. Spencely, Annabel, illus. LC 92-12073. 1993. 7.99 (*0-8407-3422-0*) Nelson.

—Samson the Strong Man. Press, Jenny, illus. LC 92-13326. (gr. 1 up). 1993. 7.99 (*0-8407-3421-2*) Nelson.

—When Time Began. Press, Jenny, illus. LC 92-13321. 1993. 7.99 (*0-8407-3419-0*) Nelson.

Pipe, Rhona & Hunt. Where's Noah? An Interactive Bible Storybook. (ps-3). 1993. 7.99 (*1-56507-144-1*) Harvest Hse.

Rector, Andy. Quick-As-a-Wink Old Testament Bedtime Bible Stories. Patterson, Kathleen, illus. 12p. (ps). 1993. bds. 4.99 (*0-7847-0111-3*, 24-03101) Standard Pub.

Reid, Barbara. Two by Two. LC 92-9013. (Illus.). 32p. (gr. k-3). 1993. 14.95 (*0-590-45869-8*) Scholastic Inc.

Rosenfeld, Dina. David the Little Shepherd. Lederer, Ilene W., illus. 32p. (ps-1). 1995. 8.95 (*0-922613-67-2*) Hachai Pubns.

Ruth. (gr. 3 up). pap. 2.50 perfect bdg. (*1-55748-173-3*) Barbour & Co.

Ryan, John. Jonah, a Whale of a Tale. Ryan, John, illus. 32p. (gr. 1-7). 1992. 11.95 (*0-7459-2150-7*) Lion USA.

Sand, Dee. The Amazing Floating Zoo, Bk. 2. LC 93-70743. (Illus.). 60p. (Orig.). (gr. 2-5). 1993. pap. 4.99 (*0-87509-530-5*) Chr Pubns.

Schorsch, Laurence, retold by. David & Goliath. Schories, Pat, illus. 24p. (ps-3). 1992. 4.95 (*1-56288-221-X*) Checkerboard.

—Noah's Ark. Schories, Pat, illus. 24p. (ps-3). 1992. 4.95 (*1-56288-223-6*) Checkerboard.

—The Story of Jonah. Hu, Ying-Hwa, illus. 24p. (ps-3). 1992. 4.95 (*1-56288-222-8*) Checkerboard.

—The Story of Joseph. Sperling, Tom, illus. 24p. (ps-3). 1992. 4.95 (*1-56288-224-4*) Checkerboard.

Simon, Mary M. Daniel & the Tattletales: Daniel 6: Daniel in the Lions' Den. Jones, Dennis, illus. LC 92-31887. 32p. (Orig.). (gr. 1-3). 1993. pap. 3.99 (*0-570-04733-1*) Concordia.

—The Hide-&-Seek Prince: Second Kings 11-12: 16: Joash. Jones, Dennis, illus. LC 93-35606. 32p. (Orig.). (gr. 1-3). 1994. pap. 3.99 (*0-570-04740-4*) Concordia.

—Hide the Baby: The Birth of Moses. Jones, Dennis, illus. 24p. (Orig.). (ps-1). 1991. pap. 2.49 (*0-570-04702-1*) Concordia.

—Hurray for the Lord's Army! Judges 6: 11 - 7: 22 (Gideon) Jones, Dennis, illus. LC 93-35604. 32p. (Orig.). (gr. 1-3). 1994. pap. 3.99 (*0-570-04739-0*) Concordia.

—Jibber-Jabber: The Tower of Babel. Jones, Dennis, illus. 24p. (Orig.). (ps-1). 1992. pap. 2.49 (*0-570-04705-6*) Concordia.

—The No-Go King: Exodus 5-15: The Exodus. Jones, Dennis, illus. LC 92-31888. 32p. (Orig.). (gr. 1-3). 1993. pap. 3.99 (*0-570-04732-3*) Concordia.

—Toot! Toot! Jones, Dennis, illus. 24p. (ps-1). 1990. pap. 2.49 (*0-570-04184-8*) Concordia.

—Whoops! Jonah. Jones, Dennis, illus. 24p. (Orig.). (ps-1). 1992. pap. 2.49 (*0-570-04704-8*) Concordia.

Standard Publishing Staff. Jonah & the Big Fish: A Picture Window Book. (ps). 1992. 6.99 (*0-87403-882-0*) Standard Pub.

—Noah's Ark Picture Window Book. (ps). 1992. 6.99 (*0-87403-884-7*, 24-03794) Standard Pub.

—Story of Creation: A Picture Window Book. (ps). 1992. 6.99 (*0-87403-881-2*, 24-03791) Standard Pub.

Stewart, Dana. The Happy Times Players Present - The Story of Creation. McCallum, Jodie, illus. 12p. (ps). 1993. 4.99 (*0-7847-0127-X*, 23-02219) Standard Pub.

—The Happy Times Players Present - The Story of Noah's Ark. McCallum, Jodie, illus. 12p. (ps). 1993. 4.99 (*0-7847-0128-8*, 23-02220) Standard Pub.

Stowell, Gordon. Abraham. Lerin, S. D., tr. from ENG. (Illus.). 24p. (gr. 1). 1981. pap. 0.75 (*0-311-38511-7*, Edit Mundo) Casa Bautista.

—Jonas. Lerin, S. D., tr. from ENG. (Illus.). 24p. (gr. 1). 1978. pap. 0.75 (*0-311-38514-1*, Edit Mundo) Casa Bautista.

—Rut. Lerin, S. D., tr. from ENG. (Illus.). 24p. (gr. 1). 1981. pap. 0.75 (*0-311-38513-3*, Edit Mundo) Casa Bautista.

Stump, Gladys S. Elisha's Room. (Illus.). (gr. 1). 1978. pap. 1.95 (*0-8127-0162-3*) Review & Herald.

Tangvald, Christine H. Too Little - Too Big, & Other Bible Stories about Faith. Girouard, Patrick, illus. LC 93-42082. (gr. 2 up). 1994. write for info. (*0-7814-0928-4*, Chariot Bks) Chariot Family.

Tanvald, Christine H. The Big Big Big Boat, & Other Bible Stories about Obedience. Girouard, Patrick, illus. LC 93-9234. 1993. 7.99 (*0-7814-0926-8*, Chariot Bks) Chariot Family.

Taylor, Kenneth N. My First Bible for Tots: Creation. (Illus.). 12p. (ps). 1992. bds. 3.99 (*0-8423-1696-5*) Tyndale.

—My First Bible for Tots: David & Goliath. (Illus.). 12p. (ps). 1992. bds. 3.99 (*0-8423-1697-3*) Tyndale.

—The Old Testament in Pictures for Little Eyes. 240p. 1993. pap. 7.99 (*0-8024-0683-1*) Moody.

Theobalds, Prue. Noah & the Animals. Theobalds, Prue, illus. LC 92-45630. 34p. (gr. 4 up). 1993. 12.95 (*0-87226-507-2*, Bedrick Blackie) P Bedrick Bks.

Thomas Nelson Publishers Staff. David & Goliath. LC 93-24836. (gr. 2 up). 1993. 6.99 (*0-8407-4913-9*) Nelson.

Thomsen, Paul. The Mystery of the Ark. (Illus.). 80p. (Orig.). (gr. 4 up). 1991. pap. 4.95 (*1-56121-029-3*) Wolgemuth & Hyatt.

The Times of Joshua & the Judges. (gr. 4-6). 1990. 1.55 (*0-89636-112-8*, JB 1B) Accent CO.

Waldman, Sarah. Light: The First Seven Days. LC 92-8767. (ps-3). 1993. 14.95 (*0-15-220870-4*) HarBrace.

Wengrov, Charles. Tales of the Prophet Samuel. (Illus.). (gr. 5-10). 1969. 4.00 (*0-914080-22-9*) Shulsinger Sales.

Wilkon, Piotr. Noah's Ark. Wilkon, Jozef, illus. LC 92-2687. 32p. (gr. k-3). 1992. 14.95 (*1-55858-158-8*); PLB 14.88 (*1-55858-159-6*) North-South Bks NYC.

Winder, Linda. Noah. 1993. 5.99 (*0-7814-0122-4*, Chariot Bks) Chariot Family.

Wolkstein, Diane. Esther's Story. Wijngaard, Juan, illus. LC 94-15473. 1995. write for info. (*0-688-12127-6*) Morrow Jr Bks.

Yenne, Bill, retold by. Joseph & the Coat of Many Colors. LC 93-37474. (Illus.). 1994. write for info. (*0-7852-8330-7*); pap. write for info. (*0-7852-8326-9*) Nelson.

—Joshua & the Battle of Jericho. LC 93-35873. (gr. 3 up). 1994. write for info. (*0-7852-8331-5*); pap. write for info. (*0-7852-8327-7*) Nelson.

—The Story of Moses. LC 93-37476. 1994. write for info. (*0-7852-8329-3*); pap. write for info. (*0-7852-8325-0*) Nelson.

Yenne, Bill & Jacobs, Timothy, eds. The Story of Jonah. LC 93-24837. 1993. 6.99 (*0-8407-4915-5*); pap. 6.99 (*0-8407-4909-0*) Nelson.

BIBLE STUDY

see Bible–Study

BIBLICAL ARCHEOLOGY

see Bible–Antiquities

BIBLICAL CHARACTERS

see Bible–Biography

BIBLIOGRAPHY–BEST BOOKS

see Books and Reading–Best Books

BIBLIOGRAPHY–REFERENCE BOOKS

see Reference Books

BICYCLE RACING–FICTION

Christopher, Matt. Dirt Bike Runaway. Stewart, Edgar, illus. LC 83-13538. 160p. (gr. 4-6). 1989. 14.95 (*0-316-13956-4*); pap. 3.95 (*0-316-14002-3*) Little.

Crews, Donald. Bicycle Race. LC 84-27912. (Illus.). 24p. (ps-1). 1985. 16.00 (*0-688-05171-5*); lib. bdg. 15.93 (*0-688-05172-3*) Greenwillow.

Crowley, Michael. Shack & Back. (ps-3). 1993. 14.95 (*0-316-16231-0*) Little.

Schwartz, David. Supergrandpa. (Illus.). (ps-3). 1991. 13.95 (*0-688-09898-3*); 13.88 (*0-688-09899-1*) Lothrop.

BICYCLES AND BICYCLING

see also Motorcycles

Abramowski, Dwain. Mountain Bikes. LC 90-31879. (Illus.). 64p. (gr. 5-8). 1990. PLB 12.90 (*0-531-10871-6*) Watts.

Allen, Bob. Mountain Biking. (Illus.). 48p. (gr. 4-12). 1992. PLB 17.50 (*0-8225-2476-7*) Lerner Pubns.

Barnes, F. A. & Kuehne, Tom. Canyon Country: Mountain Biking. LC 87-73014. (Illus.). 144p. (Orig.). (gr. 7 up). 1988. pap. 8.00 (*0-9614586-5-8*) Canyon Country Pubns.

Boy Scouts of America. Cycling. (Illus.). 40p. (gr. 6-12). 1984. pap. 1.85 (*0-8395-3277-6*, 33277) BSA.

Boy Scouts of America Staff. Venture Freestyle Biking. (Illus.). 52p. 1990. pap. 3.15 (*0-8395-3447-7*, 3447) BSA.

Chlad, Dorothy. Bicycles Are Fun to Ride. Halverson, Lydia, illus. LC 83-23234. 32p. (ps-2). 1984. pap. 3.95 (*0-516-41975-7*) Childrens.

—Es Divertido Andar en Bicicleta (Bicycles Are Fun to Ride) Kratky, Lada, tr. Halverson, Lydia, illus. LC 85-23263. (SPA.). 32p. (ps-2). 1986. pap. 3.95 (*0-516-51975-1*) Childrens.

Cook, J. Mountain Bikes. (Illus.). 48p. (gr. 6-10). 1990. lib. bdg. 12.96 (*0-88110-426-4*, Usborne); pap. 5.95 (*0-7460-0520-2*, Usborne) EDC.

Dolan, Edward F., Jr. Bicycle Touring & Camping. American, Youth Hostels, intro. by. LC 81-21962. 192p. (gr. 7 up). 1982. (J Messner); pap. 5.75 (*0-685-05841-7*) S&S Trade.

Erlbach, Arlene. Bicycles. LC 93-34457. (Illus.). 48p. (gr. 2-5). 1994. 18.95 (*0-8225-2388-4*) Lerner Pubns.

Evans, Jeremy. Off-Road Biking. LC 91-13629. (Illus.). 48p. (gr. 5-6). 1992. text ed. 13.95 RSBE (*0-89686-687-4*, Crestwood Hse) Macmillan Child Grp.

Italia, Robert. Mountain Biking. Wallner, Rosemary, ed. LC 91-73023. 32p. 1991. PLB 9.95 (*1-56239-074-0*) Abdo & Dghtrs.

Jennings, Gordon. Minibikes! Coker, Paul, Jr., illus. (gr. 5 up). 1979. P-H.

Kent, J. Racing Bikes. (Illus.). 48p. (gr. 6-10). 1990. (Usborne); pap. 5.95 (*0-7460-0518-0*) EDC.

Klingel, Cynthia. Bicycle Safety. (Illus.). 32p. (ps-3). 1986. PLB 12.95 (*0-88682-085-5*) Creative Ed.

Lafferty, Peter & Jefferis, David. Pedal Power: The History of Bicycles. LC 89-29307. (Illus.). 32p. (gr. 5-8). 1990. PLB 12.40 (*0-531-14084-9*) Watts.

Langley, James. The New Bike Book: How to Get the Most Out of Your New Bicycle. LC 89-81204. (Illus.). 128p. (Orig.). 1990. pap. 4.95 (*0-933201-28-1*) Bicycle Books.

Lord, Trevor. Amazing Bikes. Downs, Peter, photos by. LC 92-911. (Illus.). 32p. (Orig.). (gr. 1-5). 1992. PLB 9.99 (*0-679-92772-7*); pap. 7.99 (*0-679-82772-2*) Knopf Bks Yng Read.

Maestro, Betsy. Bike Trip. Maestro, Giulio, illus. LC 90-35935. 32p. (gr. k-4). 1992. 16.00 (*0-06-022731-1*); PLB 15.89 (*0-06-022732-X*) HarpC Child Bks.

Motorcycles: Superfacts. 1992. 4.99 (*0-517-07323-4*) Random Hse Value.

Nielsen, Nancy J. Bicycle Racing. LC 87-30489. (Illus.). 48p. (gr. 5-6). 1988. text ed. 11.95 RSBE (*0-89686-361-1*, Crestwood Hse) Macmillan Child Grp.

Petty, Kate. New Bike. Barber, Ed, photos by. (Illus.). 32p. (gr. 2 up). 1992. bds. 12.95 (*0-7136-3482-0*, Pub. by A&C Black UK) Talman.

Porter, A. P. Greg LeMond: Premier Cyclist. (Illus.). 56p. (gr. 4-9). 1990. PLB 13.50 (*0-8225-0476-6*) Lerner Pubns.

—Greg Lemond: Premier Cyclist. LC 89-13700. (gr. 4-7). 1991. pap. 4.95 (*0-8225-9584-2*) Lerner Pubns.

Scioscia, Mary. Bicycle Rider. Young, Ed, illus. LC 82-47702. 48p. (gr. 2-6). 1983. PLB 14.89 (*0-06-025223-5*) HarpC Child Bks.

Seidl, Herman. Mountain Bikes: Maintaining, Repairing & Upgrading. LC 92-18773. (Illus.). 128p. (gr. 4 up). 1992. 16.95 (*0-8069-8764-2*) Sterling.

—Mountain Bikes: Maintaining, Repairing & Upgrading. (Illus.). 128p. (gr. 10-12). 1993. pap. 10.95 (*0-8069-8765-0*) Sterling.

Thomson, H. E. The Tour of the Forest Bike Race: A Guide to Bicycle Racing & the Tour de France. LC 90-80062. (Illus.). 64p. (Orig.). (gr. 5 up). 1990. 9.95 (*0-933201-35-4*) Bicycle Books.

Todd, Armor. The Marin Mountain Bike Guide. 2nd ed. Todd, Linda, illus. 80p. (gr. 9-12). 1989. pap. 8.95t (*0-9623537-0-1*) A Todd.

Van der Plas, Rob. Roadside Bicycle Repairs: The Simple Guide to Fixing Your Bike. 2nd ed. Van der Plas, Rob, illus. LC 89-81203. 128p. 1990. pap. 4.95 (*0-933201-27-3*) Bicycle Books.

Van Der Plas, Robert. Mountain Bike Handbook. LC 91-13643. (Illus.). 128p. (gr. 10-12). 1992. pap. 10.95 (*0-8069-8425-2*) Sterling.

Wheels! The Kids' Bike Book. (Illus.). (gr. 3-7). 1990. (Spts Illus Kids); pap. 9.95 (*0-316-81624-8*) Little.

Wiley, Jack. Unicycles & Artistic Bicycles Illustrated. LC 86-61015. (Illus.). 168p. (gr. 7 up). 1986. pap. 26.95 (*0-913999-15-6*) Solipaz Pub Co.

BICYCLES AND BICYCLING–FICTION

Barbot, Daniel. A Bicycle for Rosaura. Fuenmayor, Morella, illus. 24p. (ps-3). 1991. 9.95 (*0-916291-34-0*) Kane-Miller Bk.

Berenstain, Stan & Berenstain, Janice. Bike Lesson. LC 64-11460. (Illus.). 64p. (ps-1). 1964. 6.95 (*0-394-80036-2*); lib. bdg. 7.99 (*0-394-90036-7*) Random Bks Yng Read.

Bibee, John. The Magic Bicycle. LC 83-240. (Illus.). 215p. (Orig.). (gr. 4-9). 1983. pap. 6.99 (*0-87784-348-1*, 348) InterVarsity.

Brown, Marc T. D. W. Rides Again! LC 93-7192. 1993. 12.95 (*0-316-11356-5*) Little.

Christopher, Matt. Tight End. (gr. 4-6). 1986. write for info.; pap. 3.95 (*0-316-14054-6*) Little.

Crawford, Ron. Bike. LC 92-42986. 1993. 12.00 (*0-671-87002-5*, Green Tiger); pap. 3.95 (*0-671-87003-3*, Green Tiger) S&S Trade.

Fraser, Sheila. I Can Ride a Bike. Kopper, Lisa, illus. 24p. (ps-3). 1991. 5.95 (*0-8120-6227-2*) Barron.

Gillespie, Bonita. Peggy's Problem. Cover, Marilyn, illus. 35p. (gr. 3-8). 1987. 6.95 (*1-55523-058-X*) Winston-Derek.

Glass, Andrew. Charles T. McBiddle. LC 91-29026. (ps-3). 1993. 15.00 (*0-385-30554-0*) Doubleday.

Holabird, Katharine. Angelina's Birthday Surprise. Craig, Helen, illus. LC 89-3513. 32p. (ps-2). 1989. 15.00 (*0-517-57325-3*, Clarkson Potter) Crown Bks Yng Read.

Jakob, Donna. My Bike. (Illus.). 32p. (ps-2). 1994. 13.95 (*1-56282-454-6*); PLB 13.89 (*1-56282-455-4*) Hyprn Child.

Johnston, Tony & Karas, G. Brian. Three Little Bikers. LC 93-39249. (Illus.). 40p. (ps-2). 1994. 8.99 (*0-679-84701-4*); 9.99 (*0-679-94701-9*) Knopf.

Krulik, Nancy E. Ralph Troll's New Bicycle. (Illus.). 1992. 2.50 (*0-590-45924-4*, 047) Scholastic Inc.

Leeuwenburg, Charles. Captain Boz & the Rusty Bicycle. 1994. 7.95 (*0-533-10818-7*) Vantage.

Lewis, Rob. The White Bicycle. LC 88-45092. (Illus.). 32p. (ps up). 1988. 12.00 (*0-374-38384-7*) FS&G.

Liebler, John. Frog Counts to Ten. LC 93-40116. (Illus.). 32p. (gr. k-3). 1994. 13.90 (*1-56294-436-3*) Millbrook Pr.

Lloyd, Errol. Sasha & the Bicycle Thieves. (Illus.). 42p. (gr. 2-4). 1989. 3.95 (*0-8120-6141-1*) Barron.

McLeod, Emilie W. The Bear's Bicycle. McPhail, David, illus. 32p. (gr. k-3). 1986. lib. bdg. 14.95 (*0-316-56203-3*, Joy St Bks); pap. 5.95 (*0-316-56206-8*, Joy St Bks) Little.

McMillan, Bruce. The Remarkable Riderless Runaway Tricycle. rev. ed. (Illus.). 48p. (gr. k-4). 1985. pap. 10.00 (*0-934313-00-8*) Apple Isl Bks.

McOmber, Rachel B., ed. McOmber Phonics Storybooks: Pete's Bike Ride. rev. ed. (Illus.). write for info. (*0-944991-40-8*) Swift Lrn Res.

Miles, Betty. I Would If I Could. 120p. (gr. 3-6). 1983. pap. 2.95 (*0-380-63438-4*, Camelot) Avon.

Moore, Peggy S. The Case of the Missing Bike & Other Things. 2nd, rev. ed. Adome, Afua, illus. 40p. (Orig.). (gr. 4-6). 1992. pap. 5.95 (*0-9613078-1-1*) Detroit Black.

Muntean, Michaela. Bicycle Bear Rides Again. Cushman, Doug, illus. LC 93-15470. 1995. 13.27 (*0-8368-0964-5*) Gareth Stevens Inc.

Packard, Edward. Superbike. (gr. 4-7). 1992. pap. 3.25 (*0-553-29294-3*) Bantam.

Petrie, Catherine. Hot Rod Harry. Sharp, Paul, illus. LC 81-15549. 32p. (ps-2). 1982. PLB 10.25 (*0-516-03493-6*); pap. text ed. 2.95 (*0-516-43493-4*) Childrens.

Robinet, Harriette G. Ride the Red Cycle. (Illus.). (gr. 1-5). 1980. 13.45 (*0-395-29183-6*) HM.

Rogers, Mary. The Twins' First Bike. 34p. (gr. 1). 1992. pap. text ed. 23.00 big bk. (*1-56843-019-1*); pap. text ed. 4.50 (*1-56843-069-8*) BGR Pub.

Russell, David A. Superbike. 180p. (gr. 4-7). 1993. 3.95 (*1-883174-00-7*) High Octane.

Sachs, Betsy. Mountain Bike Madness. Dann, Penny, illus. LC 93-29929. (gr. 2-4). 1994. PLB 7.99 (*0-679-93395-6*); pap. 2.99 (*0-679-83395-1*) Random Bks Yng Read.

Say, Allen. The Bicycle Man. Say, Allen, illus. 48p. (gr. k-3). 1982. 14.45 (*0-395-32254-5*); 11.95 (*0-685-05704-6*) HM.

Scioscia, Mary. Bicycle Rider. Young, Ed, illus. LC 82-47702. 48p. (gr. 2-6). 1993. pap. 3.95 (*0-06-443295-5*, Trophy) HarpC Child Bks.

Smith, Matthew V. Harold Gets a New Bike. Smith, Matthew V., illus. 12p. (gr. k-3). 1993. pap. 11.95 (*1-56606-014-1*) Bradley Mann.

Stott, Dorothy. Little Duck's Bicycle Ride. Stott, Dorothy, illus. LC 90-19425. 32p. (ps-k). 1991. 10.95 (*0-525-44728-8*, DCB) Dutton Child Bks.

Thomas, Jane R. Wheels. LC 85-18404. (ps-3). 1986. 12.95 (*0-317-39001-5*, Clarion Bks) HM.

—Wheels. McCully, Emily A., illus. LC 85-13291. 32p. (ps-3). 1986. 14.95 (*0-89919-410-9*, Clarion Bks) HM.

Tuffy's Bike Race. (Illus.). 40p. (gr. k-5). 1994. pap. 4.95 (*0-685-71588-4*, 524) W Gladden Found.

Vinje, Marie. The New Bike. Hoffman, Joan, ed. (Illus.). 32p. (gr. k-2). 1992. pap. 3.95 (*0-88743-426-6*, 06078) Sch Zone Pub Co.

—The New Bike. Hoffman, Joan, ed. (Illus.). 16p. (gr. k-2). 1992. pap. 2.25 (*0-88743-265-4*, 06032) Sch Zone Pub Co.

Wahl, Jan. The Furious Flycycle. 96p. 1994. pap. 3.95 (*0-8125-2404-7*) Tor Bks.

Warner, Gertrude C. Bicycle Mystery. Cunningham, David, illus. LC 79-126428. 128p. (gr. 2-7). 1971. PLB 10.95 (*0-8075-0708-3*); pap. 3.50 (*0-8075-0709-1*) A Whitman.

Wojciechowska, Maia. Dreams of Cycling. Karsky, A. K., illus. 52p. 1994. 14.50 (*1-883740-13-4*) Pebble Bch Pr Ltd.

Wolff, Ashley. Stella & Roy. Wolff, Ashley, illus. LC 92-27005. 32p. (ps-k). 1993. 12.99 (*0-525-45081-5*, DCB) Dutton Child Bks.

Woodruff, Elvira. Disappearing Bike Shop. (gr. 4-7). 1994. pap. 3.50 (*0-440-40938-1*) Dell.

Zach, Cheryl. Benny & the Crazy Contest. LC 90-43903. (Illus.). 80p. (gr. 2-6). 1991. SBE 12.95 (*0-02-793705-4*, Bradbury Pr) Macmillan Child Grp.

BIGOTRY

see Toleration

BILINGUAL BOOKS–FRENCH-ENGLISH

Annable, Toni & Kaspar, Maria H. The Four Seasons. Viola, Amy, tr. Lumetta, Lawrence, illus. 80p. (Orig.). (gr. 5 up). 1992. Set. pap. text ed. 8.95 (*1-882828-09-7*) Vol. 1: English-Spanish, Las Cuatro Estaciones. Vol. 2: English-French, Les Quatre Saisons. Kasan Imprints.

—The Runaway Match, 2 vols. Viola, Amy, tr. 48p. (Orig.). (gr. 2 up). 1992. pap. 8.95 Set (*1-882828-10-0*) Vol. 1: English-Spanish, La Cerrilla Fugitiva. Vol. 2: English-Spanish, L'Allumette Fugutive. Kasan Imprints.

—Sherm the Worm. Viola, Amy, tr. (Illus.). 96p. (Orig.). (gr. k up). 1992. Set. pap. 8.95 (*1-882828-08-9*) Vol. 1 English-Spanish, Lozano el Gusano. Vol. 2 English-French, Valere le Ver. Kasan Imprints.

—The Silver Tree. Viola, Amy, tr. (Illus.). 80p. (Orig.). (gr. 6 up). 1992. Set. pap. 8.95 (*1-882828-11-9*) Vol. 1 English-Spanish, El Arbol de Plata. Vol. 2 English-French, L'Arbre Argente. Kasan Imprints.

De Brunhoff, Laurent. Babar's French Lessons. (Illus.). (ps). 1963. 11.00 (*0-394-80587-9*); lib. bdg. 5.99 (*0-394-90587-3*) Random Bks Yng Read.

Morton, Lone. Goodnight Everyone (Bonne Nuit a Tous) Wood, Jakki, illus. Bougard, Marie-Therese, tr. from FRE. LC 94-2434. (ENG & FRE., Illus.). 28p. (ps up). 1994. 6.95 (*0-8120-6453-4*) Barron.

—I'm Too Big (Je Suis Trop Gros) Weatherill, Steve, illus. Helie, Ide M., tr. from FRE. McCourt, Ella, concept by. LC 94-561. (ENG & FRE., Illus.). 28p. (ps up). 1994. 6.95 (*0-8120-6454-2*) Barron.

Renyi Bilingual Picture Dictionary. (FRE & ENG.). 192p. (ps-12). 19.95 (*1-878363-42-5*) Forest Hse.

Root, Betty. Three Hundred First Words - Premiers Mots. Dann, Geoff, photos by. (ENG & FRE.). 156p. (ps). 1993. 9.95 (*0-8120-6357-0*) Barron.

Strub, Susanne. My Dog, My Sister, & I (Mon Chien, Ma Soeur, et Moi) Strub, Susanne, illus. LC 92-22063. (ENG & FRE.). 32p. (ps up). 1993. 14.00 (*0-688-12010-5*, Tambourine Bks); PLB 13.93 (*0-688-12011-3*, Tambourine Bks) Morrow.

BILINGUAL BOOKS–GERMAN-ENGLISH

Renyi Bilingual Picture Dictionary. (GER & ENG.). 192p. (ps-12). 19.95 (*1-878363-43-3*) Forest Hse.

BILINGUAL BOOKS–ITALIAN-ENGLISH

Renyi Bilingual Picture Dictionary. (ITA & ENG.). 192p. (ps-12). 18.95 (*1-878363-46-8*) Forest Hse.

BILINGUAL BOOKS–PORTUGUESE-ENGLISH

Renyi Bilingual Picture Dictionary. (POR & ENG.). 192p. (ps-12). 19.95 (*1-878363-52-2*) Forest Hse.

BILINGUAL BOOKS–RUSSIAN-ENGLISH

Renyi Bilingual Picture Dictionary. (RUS & ENG.). 192p. (ps-12). 19.95 (*1-878363-53-0*) Forest Hse.

BILINGUAL BOOKS–SPANISH-ENGLISH

Ada, Alma F. Mediopollito: Half-Chicken: A New Version of a Traditional Story. Zubizarreta, Rosalma, tr. Howard, Kim, illus. LC 93-41088. (ENG & SPA.). 1995. write for info. (*0-385-32044-2*) Doubleday.

Ancona, George. The Pinatamaker: El Pinatero. LC 93-2389. (gr. 5 up). 1994. 16.95 (*0-15-261875-9*) HarBrace.

Annable, Toni & Kaspar, Maria H. The Four Seasons. Viola, Amy, tr. Lumetta, Lawrence, illus. 80p. (Orig.). (gr. 5 up). 1992. Set. pap. text ed. 8.95 (*1-882828-09-7*) Vol. 1: English-Spanish, Las Cuatro Estaciones. Vol. 2: English-French, Les Quatre Saisons. Kasan Imprints.

—The Runaway Match, 2 vols. Viola, Amy, tr. 48p. (Orig.). (gr. 2 up). 1992. pap. 8.95 Set (*1-882828-10-0*) Vol. 1: English-Spanish, La Cerrilla Fugitiva. Vol. 2: English-Spanish, L'Allumette Fugutive. Kasan Imprints.

—Sherm the Worm. Viola, Amy, tr. (Illus.). 96p. (Orig.). (gr. k up). 1992. Set. pap. 8.95 (*1-882828-08-9*) Vol. 1 English-Spanish, Lozano el Gusano. Vol. 2 English-French, Valere le Ver. Kasan Imprints.

—The Silver Tree. Viola, Amy, tr. (Illus.). 80p. (Orig.). (gr. 6 up). 1992. Set. pap. 8.95 (*1-882828-11-9*) Vol. 1 English-Spanish, El Arbol de Plata. Vol. 2 English-French, L'Arbre Argente. Kasan Imprints.

Barchas, Sarah. Pinata! Bilingual Songs for Children. 24p. (gr. k-6). 1991. Incl. audio cass. pap. 12.95 (*0-9632621-0-6*) High Haven Mus.
Hispanic culture & language are celebrated in 17 original songs in this 40 minute cassette with illustrated lyrics book. The songs evoke pride in traditions, holidays & contributions of Hispanic culture & people; explore basic concepts & joy in reading; share delight & value in knowing two languages & paving the way for three. These bilingual songs have Spanish & English interwoven, or in alternating verses, or in separate language versions making them accessible to speakers of either or both languages. Young people can lean on the language they know best & stretch to the language they seek to acquire. PINATA! can be used for any context inviting second language acquisition (ESL, SSL, bilingual) & any context inviting multicultural awareness & valuing of Hispanic culture. It can be used to integrate with the curriculum in social studies, language arts & music, including history & biography. It can enhance acceptance & understanding of self & others. "Fun for sing-alongs in schools with Spanish-speaking students, where Spanish is taught, or as an enrichment for multicultural studies." (ESLC, Brodart, 1994). Ordering information: High Haven Music, P.O. Box 246, Sonoita, AZ 85637-0246.
Publisher Provided Annotation.

Benjamin, Alan. Let's Eat: Vamos a Comer. (SPA & ENG.). (ps). 1992. pap. 2.95 (*0-671-76927-8*, Little Simon) S&S Trade.

—Let's Play: Vamos a Jugar. (ENG & SPA.). (ps). 1992. pap. 2.95 (*0-671-76928-6*, Little Simon) S&S Trade.

—Let's Take a Walk: Vamos a Caminar. (ENG & SPA.). (ps). 1992. pap. 2.95 (*0-671-76929-4*, Little Simon) S&S Trade.

—What Color? Que Color? (ENG & SPA.). (ps). 1992. pap. 2.95 (*0-671-76930-8*, Little Simon) S&S Trade.

Blanco, Alberto. Angel's Kite. Morales, Rodolfo, illus. Bellm, Dan, tr. from SPA. LC 93-42285. (ENG & SPA., Illus.). 1994. 13.95 (*0-89239-121-9*) Childrens Book Pr.

Chang, Monica. The Mouse Bride: La Novia Raton. Zeller, Beatriz, tr. from CHI. Liu, Lesley, illus. (SPA & ENG.). 32p. (gr. 2-4). 1994. 16.95 (*957-32-2150-0*) Pan Asian Pubns.
After a village cat terrorizes the tiny mice's community, the mouse leader searches for a mighty husband that will protect his daughter. Although he first seeks the Sun, the Cloud, the Wind, & the Wall to wed his mouse daughter, the husband that eventually wins her hand is a touching choice that provides the perfect ending to this ancient Taiwanese folktale. This charming story is accompanied by detailed, award-winning illustrations that show the life, traditions & costumes of rural Taiwan. This book is a guaranteed classic. Also available in English/ Chinese, Vietnamese, Korean, Thai, Tagalog, Khmer, Lao & Hmong. For grades 2-4. Please specify the language when ordering. Available exclusively from: Pan Asian Publications (USA) Inc., 29564 Union City Blvd., Union City, CA 94587. Order toll free: 1-800-853-ASIA, FAX: (510) 475-1489.
Publisher Provided Annotation.

—Story of the Chinese Zodiac: El Zodiaco Chino. Zeller, Beatriz, tr. from CHI. Lee, Arthur, illus. (ENG & SPA.). 32p. (gr. 2-4). 1994. 16.95 (*957-32-2143-8*) Pan Asian Pubns.
How were the twelve animals chosen for the Chinese Zodiac? And why is the rat the first one on the list? These questions, & others, are answered in this hilarious version of the ancient Chinese Zodiac legend. The breathtaking, colorful, "paper cut-out" illustrations that accompany this story will enrapture the young readers as the rollicking story will appear to leap out before their very eyes! STORY OF THE CHINESE ZODIAC is guaranteed to be a popular choice. Also available in English/Chinese, Vietnamese, Korean, Thai, Tagalog, Khmer, Lao & Hmong. For grades 2-4. Please specify the languages when ordering. Available exclusively from: Pan Asian Publications (USA) Inc., 29564 Union City Blvd., Union City, CA 94587. Order toll free: 1-800-853-ASIA, FAX: (510) 475-1489.
Publisher Provided Annotation.

Cisneros, Sandra. Hairs: Pelitos. Ybanez, Terry, illus. LC 93-32775. (ps-3). 1994. 15.00 (*0-679-86171-8*, Apple Soup Bks); PLB 15.99 (*0-679-96171-2*, Apple Soup Bks) Knopf Bks Yng Read.

Deru, Myriam & Alen, Paule. The Birthday Surprise. (SPA & ENG., Illus.). 32p. (ps-1). 1991. 5.99 (*0-517-65556-X*) Random Hse Value.

—My First Day at School. (SPA & ENG., Illus.). 32p. (ps-1). 1991. 5.99 (*0-517-65557-8*) Random Hse Value.

Dr. Seuss. The Cat in the Hat - el Gato Ensombrerado. Dr. Seuss, illus. (ENG & SPA.). 72p. (ps-3). 1993. incl. cass. 6.95 (*0-679-84329-9*) Random Bks Yng Read.

Emberley, Rebecca. Let's Go: A Book in Two Languages - Vamos: un Libro en Dos Lenguas. LC 92-37278. (ENG & SPA.). 1993. 15.95 (*0-316-23450-8*) Little.

—My Day: A Book in Two Languages - Mi Dia: un Libro en Dos Lenguas. LC 92-37277. (ENG & SPA.). 1993. 15.95 (*0-316-23454-0*) Little.

—My House Mi Casa. (ps-3). 1993. pap. 5.95 (*0-316-23448-6*) Little.

Fry, Ed. Paseo en Barco de Vela - Sailboat Ride. (ENG & SPA., Illus.). 24p. (gr. k-1). 1992. pap. 23.75 (*0-89061-721-X*) Jamestown Pubs.

—El Viento Fuerte - the Big Wind. (ENG & SPA., Illus.). 24p. (gr. k-1). 1992. pap. 23.75 (*0-89061-722-8*) Jamestown Pubs.

Gonzaleź, Lucia M., retold by. The Bossy Gallito: A Traditional Cuban Folk Tale. Delacre, Lulu, illus. LC 93-15541. 32p. (ps-2). 1994. 14.95 (*0-590-46843-X*) Scholastic Inc.

Griego, Margo C., et al. Tortillitas Para Mama: And Other Nursery Rhymes, Spanish & English. LC 81-4823. (Illus.). 32p. (ps-2). 1988. pap. 5.95 (*0-8050-0317-7*, Owlet BYR) H Holt & Co.

Hammond, Anna & Matunis, Joe. This Home We Have Made: Esta Casa Que Memos Hecho. Mendell, Olga K., tr. LC 92-28954. (ENG & SPA.). 24p. (ps-3). 1993. 14.00 (*0-517-59339-4*, Crown) Crown Bks Yng Read.

Hao, Kuang-ts'ai. Dance, Mice, Dance! Bailen, Ratones, Bailen! Zeller, Beatriz, tr. from CHI. Tartarotti, Stefano, illus. (ENG & SPA.). 32p. (gr. 2-4). 1994. 16.95 (*1-57227-001-2*) Pan Asian Pubns.
DANCE, MICE, DANCE! is an entertaining story about a magical flute player who becomes proud & lazy after being highly praised by the townspeople. Although the town folk soon desert him because of his bad ways, the town mice befriend him & teach him the value of his talent & the importance of friendship. Readers will also enjoy the whimsical illustrations that accompany this worthwhile story. Based on THE PIED PIPER OF HAMELIN. Also available in English/ Chinese, Vietnamese, Korean, Thai, Tagalog, Khmer, Lao & Hmong. For grades 2-4. Please specify language when ordering. Available exclusively from: Pan Asian Publications (USA) Inc., 29564 Union City Blvd., Union City, CA 94587. Order toll free: 1-800-853-ASIA, FAX: (510) 475-1489.
Publisher Provided Annotation.

—The Emperor & the Nightingale: El Emperador y el Ruisenor. Zeller, Beatriz, tr. from CHI. Chang, Shih-ming, illus. (ENG & SPA.). 32p. (gr. 2-4). 1994. 16.95 (*1-57227-019-5*) Pan Asian Pubns.
What price will an emperor, who wants to live forever, pay for immortality? Will he give up his favorite horse? His kingdom, perhaps? The answers to these questions are poignantly shown through this haunting & inspiring story about an emperor who ultimately decides to forsake immortality for the love of something greater than himself. This story is illustrated in dreamy details that enhance the story's lyrical power. Readers of all ages will be touched by the messages of love & life offered in THE EMPEROR & THE NIGHTINGALE. Based on Andersen's THE EMPEROR & THE NIGHTINGALE. Also available in English/Chinese, Vietnamese, Korean, Thai, Tagalog, Khmer, Lao & Hmong. For grades 2-4. Please specify the languages when ordering. Available exclusively from: Pan Asian Publications (USA) Inc., 29564 Union City Blvd., Union City, CA 94587. Order toll free: 1-800-853-ASIA, FAX: (510) 475-1489.
Publisher Provided Annotation.

—The Giant & the Spring: El Gigante y el Nino Primavera. Zeller, Beatriz, tr. from CHI. Wang, Eva, illus. (ENG & SPA.). 32p. (gr. 2-4). 1994. 16.95 (*1-57227-010-1*) Pan Asian Pubns.
What happens when a lonely Giant captures Spring & won't let it go? In this tale, the themes of selfishness & sharing are explored & the Giant's eventual realization of his error, coupled with his freeing of Spring, touchingly illustrate the value of making the right choice. The delicate illustrations in this book portray the gentle, although misguided nature of the Giant & the resilence of little Spring. Young readers will delight in the Giant's journey from greediness to generosity. Based on THE SELFISH GIANT by Oscar Wilde. Also available in English/Chinese, Vietnamese, Korean, Thai, Tagalog, Khmer, Lao &

Hmong. For grades 2-4. Please specify language when ordering. Available exclusively from: Pan Asian Publications (USA) Inc., 29564 Union City Blvd., Union City, CA 94587. Order toll free: 1-800-853-ASIA, FAX: (510) 475-1489.
Publisher Provided Annotation.

—Seven Magic Brothers: Siete Hermanos Magicos. Zeller, Beatriz, tr. from CHI. Wang, Eva, illus. (ENG & SPA.). 32p. (gr. 2-4). 1994. 16.95 (*957-32-2165-9*) Pan Asian Pubns.
SEVEN MAGIC BROTHERS is a tale about the adventures of seven superpowered brothers who triumph through their cooperation. This tale illustrates the strength of brotherhood & loyalty. Young readers are guaranteed to be inspired by the message of unity & delighted by the brothers' exciting adventures. Young readers are sure to be delighted by the rich & detailed illustrations that accompany this exciting tale. Also available in English/Chinese, Vietnamese, Korean, Thai, Tagalog, Khmer, Lao & Hmong. For grades 2-4. Please specify the language when ordering. Available exclusively from: Pan Asian Publications (USA) Inc., 29564 Union City Blvd., Union City, CA 94587. Order toll free 1-800-853-ASIA, FAX: (510) 475-1489.
Publisher Provided Annotation.

Hofer, Grace & Day, Rachel. Oyen Ninos, Listen Children. Day, Rachel, tr. Moncus, Stephen, illus. 96p. (gr. 4-7). 1993. 12.95 (*0-89015-865-7*) Sunbelt Media.

Koplow, Lesley. Tanya & the Tobo Man: A Story for Children Entering Therapy. LC 91-85. (SPA & ENG., Illus.). 32p. (ps-4). 1991. 16.95 (*0-945354-34-7*); pap. 6.95 (*0-945354-33-9*) Magination Pr.

Lomas Garza, Carmen. Family Pictures: Cuadros de familia. (SPA & ENG., Illus.). 32p. (gr. 1-7). 1993. pap. 5.95 (*0-89239-108-1*) Childrens Book Pr.

MacArthur, Barbara. Canten Navidad. Jensen, Robert, illus. (ENG & SPA.). 15p. (Orig.). (ps-12). 1993. pap. 12.95 incl. cass. (*1-881120-09-0*) Frog Pr WI.

Mora, Pat. Listen to the Desert - Que Dice el Desierto? Mora, Francisco X., illus. LC 93-31463. (ENG & SPA.). (ps-2). 1994. 14.95 (*0-395-67292-9*, Clarion Bks) HM.

Morton, Lone. Goodnight Everyone (Buenos Noches a Todos) Wood, Jakki, photos by. LC 94-2433. (ENG & SPA., Illus.). 28p. (ps up). 1994. 6.95 (*0-8120-6452-6*) Barron.

—I'm Too Big (Soy Demasiado Grande) Weatherill, Steve, illus. McCourt, Ella, concept by. LC 94-563. (ENG & SPA., Illus.). 28p. (ps up). 1994. 6.95 (*0-8120-6451-8*) Barron.

Mountain, Lee. El Fuego del Dragon - Dragon Fire. (ENG & SPA., Illus.). 23p. (gr. k-1). 1992. pap. 23.75 (*0-89061-720-1*) Jamestown Pubs.

—Pelea con Dragon - Dragon Fight. (ENG & SPA., Illus.). 24p. (gr. k-1). 1992. pap. 23.75 (*0-89061-719-8*) Jamestown Pubs.

Paulsen, Gary. Sisters Hermanas. 1993. 10.95 (*0-15-275323-0*, HB Juv Bks); pap. 3.95 (*0-15-275324-9*) HarBrace.

Read & Color Book Series. (Illus.). Date not set. pap. write for info. (*0-86545-223-7*) Spizzirri.
This series of educational read & color books features realistic illustrations & text. Over 100 titles cover interesting topics about everything from Dinosaurs, Indians & Space to many species of animals. ($1.95 pap.). 48 titles from the series are available on cassette with music & sound effects added. ($5.95). These museum curator approved books are a "must have" for anyone with children or grandchildren & an eye for superior quality at a reasonable price. For the younger child: an entire line of activity & workbooks that help make it fun to learn the ABCs, counting, & reading words. ($2.95 pap.). Many titles are available bilingually in English & Spanish. ($2.95 pap.). All titles 32 p. (Preschool to 5th gr.). For your store call our wholesale division toll free at 1-800-325-9819. Schools & libraries call toll free at 1-800-322-9819.
Publisher Provided Annotation.

Reid, Elizabeth. Bilingual ABC: Spanish & English. (SPA & ENG., Illus.). 64p. (gr. k-3). 1995. pap. text ed. 2.50 (*0-9627080-6-2*) In One EAR.

—Moms & Dads - Mamis y Papis: Bilingual Coloring Book. (SPA & ENG., Illus.). 64p. (gr. 1-4). 1992. pap. 1.95 (*0-9627080-5-4*) In One EAR.

Renyi Bilingual Picture Dictionary. (SPA & ENG.). 192p. (ps-12). 19.95 (*1-878363-54-9*) Forest Hse.

Rey, H. A. Jorge el Curioso. (SPA., Illus.). (gr. k-3). 1961. 13.95 (*0-395-17075-3*) HM.

Ricklen, Neil, illus. My Family: Mi Familia. LC 93-30661. (ENG & SPA.). 14p. (ps-k). 1994. pap. 3.95 (*0-689-71771-7*, Aladdin) Macmillan Child Grp.

Rodriguez, Gina M. Green Corn Tamales - Tamales de Elote. (SPA & ENG., Illus.). 40p. 1994. 14.95 (*0-938243-00-4*) Hispanic Bk Dist.

Root, Betty. Three Hundred First Words - Palabras Primeras. Dann, Geoff, photos by. (ENG & SPA.). 156p. (ps). 9.95 (*0-8120-6358-9*) Barron.

Simon, Norma. What Do I Do: English - Spanish Edition. Lasker, Joe, illus. LC 74-79544. 40p. (ps-2). 1969. PLB 13.95 (*0-8075-8823-7*) A Whitman.

—What Do I Say. Lasker, Joe, illus. LC 67-17420. (ENG & SPA.). (ps-2). 1967. 13.95 (*0-8075-8828-8*); PLB 13. 95 (*0-8075-8826-1*) A Whitman.

Tallon, Robert, illus. ABCDEFGHIJKLMNOPQRSTUVWXYZ. LC 76-86987. (ENG & SPA.). 64p. (gr. k-2). 1969. PLB 15. 95 (*0-87460-131-2*) Lion Bks.

Volkmer, Jane A. Song of Chirimia - La Musica de la Chirimia: A Guatemalan Folktale - Folklore Guatemalteco. Volkmer, Jame A., illus. (SPA & ENG.). 40p. (ps-4). 1990. PLB 18.95 (*0-87614-423-7*) Carolrhoda Bks.

Wei Jiang & Cheng An Jiang. La Heroina Hua Mulan--The Legend of Mu Lan: Una Leyenda De la Antigua China--A Heroine of Ancient China. (SPA & ENG., Illus.). 32p. (gr. 1 up). 1992. pap. 6.95 (*1-878217-15-1*) Victory Press.

Williams, Letty. Little Red Hen: La Pequena Gallina Roja. Williams, Herb, illus. LC 78-75684. (ENG & SPA.). (ps-3). 1972. (Pub. by Treehouse) P-H.

BILL OF RIGHTS
see U. S. Constitution–Amendments

BILLBOARDS
see Signs and Signboards

BILLIARDS

Denn, Jon. Rack 'em Daddy! By the Pied Piper of Pool. Denn, et al, illus. LC 92-73955. 128p. (Orig.). (gr. 3). 1992. pap. 13.95 (*0-9634187-5-0*) Colburn Pr.

Lawson, James R., ed. The Pool Player's National Pocket Billiards Directory. 1991. pap. 19.95 (*0-945071-50-7*) Lawco.

BILLS OF CREDIT
see Credit; Paper Money

BILLY THE KID

Green, Carl R. & Sanford, William R. Billy the Kid. LC 91-18124. (Illus.). 48p. (gr. 4-10). 1992. lib. bdg. 14.95 (*0-89490-364-0*) Enslow Pubs.

BIMETALLISM
see Gold; Silver

BINDING OF BOOKS
see Bookbinding

BINGHAM, HIRAM, 1875-1956

Steele, Philip. The Incas & Machu Picchu. LC 92-42283. (Illus.). 32p. (gr. 6-8). 1993. text ed. 13.95 RSBE (*0-87518-536-3*, Dillon) Macmillan Child Grp.

BIOBIBLIOGRAPHY
see Authors

BIOCHEMISTRY
see also Molecular Biology

Aronson, Billy. They Came from DNA: Mysteries of Science. (gr. 4-7). 1993. text ed. 17.95 (*0-7167-9006-8*) W H Freeman.

BIOGEOGRAPHY
see Anthropogeography; Geographical Distribution of Animals and Plants

BIOGRAPHY
see also Autobiographies; Christian Biography; Heraldry; Portraits
also names of classes of persons (e.g. Artists; Authors; Musicians; etc.); names of countries, cities, etc. and special subjects with the subdivision Biography (e.g. U. S. –Biography; Blacks–Biography; Religions–Biography; Woman–Biography; etc.) and names of persons for biographies of individuals

Alighieri, Dante & Sean. Echoes of Wolves. 30p. 1992. pap. write for info. (*0-9634867-3-X*) Peyto Pub.

Berenstain, Michael. Who Am I? A First Book of Famous People. Berenstain, Michael, illus. 40p. (gr. 2-4). 1992. write for info. (*0-307-11551-8*, 11551, Golden Pr) Western Pub.

Bliven, Bruce, Jr. American Revolution. (Illus.). (gr. 4-6). 1963. lib. bdg. 9.99 (*0-394-90383-8*) Random Bks Yng Read.

Clarke, Brenda. Caring for Others. LC 89-26296. (Illus.). 48p. (gr. 4-8). 1990. PLB 11.95 (*0-8114-2751-X*) Raintree Steck-V.

Cruise, Beth & Schleifer, Jay. Dustin Diamond: Teen Star. (Illus.). 96p. (Orig.). (gr. 5 up). 1993. pap. 3.50 (*0-02-044975-5*, Collier Young Ad) Macmillan Child Grp.

Delisle, Jim. Kidstories: Biographies of Twenty Young People You'd Like to Know. Espeland, Pamela, ed. LC 91-18363. (Illus.). 176p. (Orig.). (gr. 3 up). 1991. pap. 9.95 (*0-915793-34-2*) Free Spirit Pub.

Drimmer, Fredrick. Born Different: Amazing Stories of Very Special People. 1991. pap. 3.50 (*0-553-15897-X*) Bantam.

Goodwin, Bob & Hayes, Dympna. Famous Lives. Kelly, Teri, ed. (Illus.). 48p. (gr. 4). 1987. PLB 14.65 (*0-88625-171-0*); pap. 5.95 (*0-88625-150-8*) Durkin Hayes Pub.

Gudeman, Janice. Creative Encounters with Creative People. Beebe, Mark & Filkins, Vanessa, illus. 144p. (gr. 4 up). 1984. wkbk. 12.95 (*0-86653-258-7*, GA 623) Good Apple.

—Learning from the Lives of Amazing People. 144p. (gr. 4 up). 1988. wkbk. 12.95 (*0-86653-446-6*, GA1055) Good Apple.

Harris, Laurie L., ed. Biography Today: Profiles of People of Interest to Young Readers, 1992. 498p. 1993. PLB 46.00 annual cumulation (*1-55888-139-5*) Omnigraphics Inc.

Hawthorne, Nathaniel. True Stories from History & Biography. Charvat, William, et al, eds. LC 73-150220. 380p. (gr. 5 up). 1972. 49.50 (*0-8142-0157-1*) Ohio St U Pr.

Hokett, Norene. Main Street Was Two Blocks Long. LC 93-29407. 192p. (gr. 9 up). 1993. 16.95 (*1-55853-263-3*) Rutledge Hill Pr.

Hurwitz, Johanna. Astrid Lindgren. Dooling, Michael, illus. 64p. (gr. 2-6). 1991. 3.95 (*0-14-032692-8*) Puffin Bks.

Lee, Betsy. Judy Blume's Story. LC 81-12494. (Illus.). 112p. (gr. 5 up). 1981. text ed. 11.95 RSBE (*0-87518-209-7*, Dillon) Macmillan Child Grp.

Lewis, Barbara A. Kids with Courage: True Stories about Young People Making a Difference. Espeland, Pamela, ed. LC 91-46726. 184p. (gr. 5-12). 1992. pap. 10.95 (*0-915793-39-3*); write for info. tchr's. guide (*0-915793-40-7*) Free Spirit Pub.

Lyons, Mary E. Master of Mahogany: The Story of Tom Day, Free Black Cabinetmaker. Bridges, Jim, photos by. LC 93-37900. (gr. 3-6). 1994. 15.95 (*0-684-19675-1*, Scribner) Macmillan.

McLeish, Kenneth & McLeish, Valerie. Famous People. LC 90-37910. (Illus.). 96p. (gr. 3-6). 1991. PLB 14.89 (*0-8167-2238-2*); pap. text ed. 6.95 (*0-8167-2239-0*) Troll Assocs.

Marzollo, Jean. My First Book of Biographies. Trivas, Irene, illus. LC 92-27623. (gr. k-4). 1994. 14.95 (*0-590-45014-X*) Scholastic Inc.

Mayberry, Jodine. Leaders Who Changed the Twentieth Century. LC 93-19032. (Illus.). 48p. (gr. 5-7). 1993. PLB 22.80 (*0-8114-4926-2*) Raintree Steck-V.

Morgan, et al. What Made Them Great Series, 8 bks. (Illus.). 832p. (gr. 5-8). 1990. Set. PLB 79.60 (*0-382-09983-4*); Set. pap. 47.60 (*0-382-09984-2*) Silver Burdett Pr.

Older, Jules. Ben & Jerry...The Real Scoop! Severance, Lyn, illus. LC 92-39649. 80p. (Orig.). (gr. 3-8). 1993. pap. 6.95 (*1-881527-04-2*) Chapters Pub.

Pelton, Jeanette. Folks I Wish I'd Known. Pelton, Dan, ed. Pelton, Fawn, illus. 75p. (gr. 5-8). 1993. pap. 4.00 (*1-879564-05-X*) Long Acre Pub.

People Who Have Helped the World, 32 bks. (Illus.). (gr. 5-8). Complete set. PLB 637.86 (*1-55532-837-7*) Gareth Stevens Inc.

People Who Made a Difference, 18 bks. (Illus.). (gr. 3-8). Complete set. PLB 358.80 (*0-8368-0914-9*) Gareth Stevens Inc.

Pollard, Michael. People Who Care. Stefoff, Rebecca, ed. LC 91-36502. (Illus.). 48p. (gr. 5-8). 1992. PLB 19.93 (*1-56074-035-3*) Garrett Ed Corp.

—Thinkers. Stefoff, Rebecca, ed. LC 91-33296. (Illus.). 48p. (gr. 5-8). 1992. PLB 19.93 (*1-56074-036-1*) Garrett Ed Corp.

Reef, Catherine. Black Fighting Men: A Proud History. (Illus.). 80p. (gr. 4-7). 1994. bds. 14.95 (*0-8050-3106-5*) TFC Bks NY.

Sargent, Dave. Callie. 160p. 1992. pap. write for info. (*1-56763-002-2*) Ozark Pub.

—An Uphill Climb. 344p. 1992. PLB write for info. (*1-56763-000-6*); pap. write for info. (*1-56763-001-4*) Ozark Pub.

Silvani, Harold. Famous People - Men. 30p. (gr. 4-8). 1975. wkbk. 6.95 (*1-878669-24-9*, 4005) Crea Tea Assocs.

Sinnott, Susan. Extraordinary Asian-Pacific Americans. LC 93-12678. (Illus.). 260p. (gr. 4 up). 1993. PLB 24. 65 (*0-516-03152-X*) Childrens.

Start, Debra. A Shining Star. 24p. (gr. 1-4). 1994. PLB 6.95 (*1-881907-11-2*) Two Bytes Pub.

Tallarico, Tony. I Didn't Know That about Famous People & Places. (Illus.). 32p. 1992. 9.95 (*1-56156-114-2*) Kidsbks.

Vasquez, Ely P., et al. The Story of Ana: La Historia de Ana. Guzman, Elia, illus. (SPA & ENG., Illus.). 28p. (Orig.). (gr. 3-6). 1985. PLB 8.95 (*0-932727-15-8*); pap. 3.95 (*0-932727-01-8*) Hope Pub Hse.

Wilkinson, Philip & Dineen, Jacqueline. People Who Changed the World. Ingpen, Robert, illus. LC 93-31357. 1994. write for info. (*0-7910-2764-3*); pap. write for info. (*0-7910-2789-9*) Chelsea Hse.

BIOLOGICAL CHEMISTRY

see Biochemistry

BIOLOGY

see also Adaptation (Biology); Anatomy; Cells; Color of Animals; Embryology; Evolution; Fresh-Water Biology; Genetics; Life (Biology); Marine Biology; Microbiology; Natural History; Physiology; Reproduction; Sex; Zoology

Bailey, Jill & Seddon, Tony. Mimicry & Camouflage. 64p. (gr. 5 up). 1988. 15.95x (*0-8160-1657-7*) Facts on File.

Becker, Maurice. Biology Flipper. (Illus.). 49p. (gr. 5 up). 1988. Repr. of 1977 ed. 15.95 (*1-878383-05-1*) C Lee Pubns.

Berman, William. How to Dissect. 4th ed. LC 83-27510. (Illus.). 224p. (Orig.). (gr. 8 up). 1985. P-H.

Burchard, Elizabeth. Biology: In a Flash. 480p. (gr. 7-12). 1994. pap. 9.95 (*1-881374-00-9*) Flash Blasters.

Burnie, David. Dictionary of Nature. LC 93-30696. (gr. 3 up). 1994. 19.95 (*1-56458-473-9*) Dorling Kindersley.

—Life. LC 93-33101. (gr. 3 up). 1994. 15.95 (*1-56458-477-1*) Dorling Kindersley.

Chisholm, J. Biology. Beeson, D., illus. 48p. (gr. 3-6). 1984. pap. 6.95 (*0-86020-707-2*) EDC.

Cleeve, Roger. The Living World. Steltenpohl, Jane, ed. (Illus.). 32p. (gr. 3-5). 1990. lib. bdg. 10.98 (*0-671-68627-5*, J Messner); pap. 4.95 (*0-671-68630-5*) S&S Trade.

Day, M. H. Fossil History of Man. 3rd ed. Head, J. J., ed. LC 84-70785. (Illus.). 16p. (gr. 10 up). 1984. pap. 2.75 (*0-89278-432-6*, 45-9632) Carolina Biological.

Edwards, Gabrielle I. & Cimmino, Marion. Laboratory Techniques for High Schools: A Work-Text of Biomedical Methods. 3rd ed. 246p. (gr. 10-12). 1994. pap. text ed. 11.95 (*0-8120-1978-4*) Barron.

Hanauer, Ethel. Biology Experiments for Children. LC 68-9305. (Illus.). 96p. (gr. 5 up). 1969. pap. 2.95 (*0-486-22032-X*) Dover.

Jepson, Maud. Illustrated Biology, 2 pts. (Illus.). (gr. 8-12). Animals, Pt. 2. 6.95x (*0-7195-0734-0*) Transatl Arts.

Koenig, Herbert G., et al. Life Science: A Concise Competency Review. rev. ed. Gamsey, Wayne, ed. Fairbanks, Eugene B., illus. 96p. (gr. 7-12). 1991. pap. text ed. 4.11 (*0-935487-42-5*) N & N Pub Co.

Lanham, Url N. Origins of Modern Biology. LC 68-24478. 273p. (gr. 11-12). 1971. text ed. 46.50x (*0-231-02872-5*); pap. text ed. 18.00x (*0-231-08660-1*) Col U Pr.

LeMaster, Leslie J. Cells & Tissues. LC 85-6695. (Illus.). 45p. (gr. k-3). 1985. PLB 12.85 (*0-516-01266-5*) Childrens.

Martin, Linda. Watch Them Grow. LC 93-25426. (Illus.). 48p. (ps-1). 1994. 14.95 (*1-56458-458-5*) Dorling Kindersley.

Morgan, Nina. The Human Cycle. LC 93-5265. (Illus.). 32p. (gr. 2-5). 1993. 12.95 (*1-56847-094-0*) Thomson Lrning.

Myers, Jack. How Do We Dream? And Other Questions about Your Body. (Illus.). 64p. (gr. 1-7). 1994. 7.95 (*1-56397-400-2*) Boyds Mills Pr.

Palmer, J. D. Biological Rhythms & Living Clocks. 2nd ed. Head, J. J., ed. LC 84-70786. (Illus.). 16p. (gr. 10 up). 1984. pap. 2.75 (*0-89278-192-0*, 45-9692) Carolina Biological.

—Human Biological Rhythms. Head, J. J., ed. Khoury, Diana, illus. LC 81-67983. 16p. (gr. 10 up). 1983. pap. 2.75 (*0-89278-304-4*, 45-9704) Carolina Biological.

Parker, Steve. The Living World. Hull, Richard, illus. 48p. (gr. 3-6). 1992. pap. 2.95 (*1-56680-011-0*) Mad Hatter Pub.

Ricciuti, Edward. The Our Living World Resource Guide & Reference. (Illus.). 64p. (gr. 4-8). 1994. PLB 16.95 (*1-56711-057-6*) Blackbirch.

Ricciuti, Edward R. Microorganisms: The Unseen World. Gonzalez, Pedro J., illus. Behler, John, intro. by. LC 93-44544. (Illus.). 64p. (gr. 4-8). 1994. PLB 16.95 (*1-56711-040-1*) Blackbirch.

St. Pierre, Rita B. Biology Dictionary. 2nd ed. LC 92-35770. 1992. write for info. (*0-89420-291-X*) Natl Book.

Seddon, Tony & Bailey, Jill. Living World. LC 86-16800. (Illus.). 160p. (gr. 3 up). 1987. pap. 12.95 (*0-385-23754-5*) Doubleday.

Simon, Norma. Why Am I Different? (ps-3). 1993. pap. 4.95 (*0-8075-9076-2*) A Whitman.

Spear. Life Science: All Creatures Great & Small. (gr. 7-9). 1991. text ed. 10.00 (*0-89824-534-6*); manual 5.00 (*0-89824-535-4*) Trillium Pr.

Stephenson, Robert & Browne, Roger. Exploring Variety of Life. Clay, Marilyn, illus. LC 92-34357. 48p. (gr. 4-8). 1992. PLB 22.80 (*0-8114-2606-8*) Raintree Steck-V.

Stockley, C. Dictionary of Biology. (Illus.). 128p. (gr. 6 up). 1987. PLB 15.96 (*0-88110-229-6*); pap. 9.95 (*0-86020-819-2*) EDC.

Taylor, Barbara. Meadow. Taylor, Kim & Burton, Jane, photos by. LC 92-52821. (Illus.). 32p. (gr. 2-5). 1992. 9.95 (*1-56458-129-2*) Dorling Kindersley.

Taylor, Kim. Too Clever to See. (gr. 2-5). 1991. 9.95 (*0-385-30216-9*) Delacorte.

Tesar, Jenny. Humans. (Illus.). 64p. (gr. 4-8). 1994. PLB 16.95 (*1-56711-048-7*) Blackbirch.

Treays, R. Essential Biology. (Illus.). 64p. 1992. PLB 12.96 (*0-88110-585-6*); pap. 5.95 (*0-7460-0743-4*) EDC.

Wilbur, Richard. Opposites. D'Andrade, Diane, ed. (Illus.). 39p. (ps up). 1991. 11.95 (*0-15-258720-9*) HarBrace.

Zoehfeld. What's Alive. 1995. 15.00 (*0-06-023443-1*); PLB 14.89 (*0-06-023444-X*) HarpC Child Bks.

BIOLOGY–ECOLOGY

see Ecology

BIOLOGY–EXPERIMENTS

Harlow, Rosie & Morgan, Gareth. Energy & Growth. Kuo Kang Chen & Fitzsimmons, Cecilia, illus. 40p. (gr. 5-8). 1991. PLB 12.90 (*0-531-19124-9*, Warwick) Watts.

Tant, Carl. Science Fair Spelled W-I-N. Crask, Tammy & Setzer, Debra, illus. 112p. (Orig.). (gr. 7-12). 1992. pap. 14.95 (*1-880319-02-0*) Biotech.

Tocci, Salvatore. Biology Projects for Young Scientists. 1989. pap. 6.95 (*0-531-15127-1*) Watts.

—Biology Projects for Young Scientists. LC 87-10432. (Illus.). 128p. (gr. 7-12). 1987. PLB 13.90 (*0-531-10429-X*) Watts.

VanCleave, Janice. A-Plus Projects in Biology: Winning Science Fair Ideas. 240p. 1993. text ed. 22.95 (*0-471-58629-3*); pap. text ed. 12.95 (*0-471-58628-5*) Wiley.

Vancleave, Janice P. Biology for Every Kid: One Hundred & One Easy Experiments That Really Work. 1990. pap. text ed. 10.95 (*0-471-50381-9*) Wiley.

Ward, Alan. Experimenting with Science about Yourself. Flax, Zena, illus. 48p. (gr. 2-7). 1991. lib. bdg. 12.95 (*0-7910-1512-2*) Chelsea Hse.

Wood, Robert W. Thirty-Nine Easy Animal Biology Experiments. (Illus.). 160p. (gr. 3-8). 1991. 9.70 (*0-8306-6594-3*, 3594); pap. 9.95 (*0-8306-3594-7*) TAB Bks.

BIOLOGY, MARINE

see Marine Biology

BIOLOGY, MOLECULAR

see Molecular Biology

BIOLOGY–STUDY AND TEACHING

Davis, Mary P. Action Biology - Advanced Placement. (Illus.). 540p. (gr. 11-12). 1988. pap. text ed. 21.33 (*0-931054-18-4*) Clark Pub.

—Action Biology - for the First Year. (Illus.). 494p. (gr. 10). 1988. pap. text ed. 21.33 (*0-931054-19-2*) Clark Pub.

Reep, Marianna L. & Plass, Richard M. New York State Regents Biology Laboratory Manual. (Illus.). 138p. (gr. 8-11). 1989. 5.95 (*0-685-29317-3*) Amer Scholastic.

BIOLOGY–VOCATIONAL GUIDANCE

Czerneda, Julie. Great Careers for People Interested in Living Things, 6 vols. LC 93-78080. (Illus.). 48p. (gr. 6-9). 1993. 16.95 (*0-8103-9387-5*, 102105, UXL) Gale.

Sipiera, Paul P. I Can Be a Biologist. LC 91-39243. (Illus.). 32p. (gr. k-3). 1992. PLB 11.80 (*0-516-01966-X*); pap. 3.95 (*0-516-41966-8*) Childrens.

BIOLUMINESCENCE

Barkan, Joanne. Creatures That Glow. (gr. 9-12). 1991. PLB 13.99 (*0-385-41979-1*) Doubleday.

Presnall, Judith J. Animals That Glow. LC 92-25529. 1993. PLB 12.90 (*0-531-20071-X*) Watts.

BIONICS

Gross, Cynthia S. The New Biotechnology: Putting Microbes to Work. LC 88-18823. (Illus.). 96p. (gr. 5 up). 1988. PLB 21.50 (*0-8225-1583-0*) Lerner Pubns.

Morris, Beryl. Biotechnology. LC 93-41597. 1992. pap. write for info. (*0-521-43785-7*) Cambridge U Pr.

BIOTECHNOLOGY

see Bionics

BIPLANES

see Airplanes

BIRD HOUSES

Naether, Carl & Vriends, Matthew M. Building an Aviary. (Illus.). 160p. (gr. 8 up). 1989. PLB 12.95 (*0-685-28494-8*, PS-763) TFH Pubns.

Robin Bird House. 1993. 9.95 (*1-56828-049-1*) Red Jacket Pr.

Wren Bird House. 1993. 9.95 (*1-56828-050-5*) Red Jacket Pr.

BIRD WATCHING

see Birds

BIRDS

see also Birds of Prey; Water Birds

Ames, Felicia. The Bird You Care For. 1970. pap. 1.75 (*0-451-07527-7*, E7527, Sig) NAL-Dutton.

Animals, Birds & Fish. (Illus.). (ps-5). 3.50 (*0-7214-8003-9*); Ser. S50. wkbk. B 1.95 (*0-317-04633-0*) Ladybird Bks.

Armstrong, B. Birds. 32p. (gr. 1-6). 1988. 3.95 (*0-88160-161-6*, LW 266) Learning Wks.

Arnold, Caroline. Flamingo. Hewett, Richard, photos by. LC 90-19186. (Illus.). 48p. (gr. 2 up). 1991. 13.95 (*0-688-09411-2*); PLB 13.88 (*0-688-09412-0*) Morrow Jr Bks.

Arnosky, Jim. Crinkleroot's Guide to Knowing the Birds. Arnosky, Jim, illus. LC 91-38234. 32p. (gr. k-5). 1992. RSBE 14.95 (*0-02-705857-3*, Bradbury Pr) Macmillan Child Grp.

—Crinkleroot's 25 Birds Every Child Should Know. Arnosky, Jim, illus. LC 92-36059. 32p. (gr. k-3). 1993. RSBE 12.95 (*0-02-705859-X*, Bradbury Pr) Macmillan Child Grp.

Austin, Oliver L., Jr. Families of Birds. Rev. ed. Singer, Arthur, illus. (gr. 9 up). 1985. pap. write for info. (*0-307-13669-8*); pap. write for info. (*0-307-24015-0*, Golden Pr) Western Pub.

Bailey, Jill & Seddon, Tony. Birds of Prey. (Illus.). 64p. (gr. 5 up). 1988. 15.95x (*0-8160-1655-0*) Facts On File.

Baines, Chris. The Nest. Ives, Penny, illus. LC 89-77653. 24p. (ps-3). 1990. 7.95 (*0-940793-55-5*, Crocodile Bks) Interlink Pub.

Bare, Colleen S. Who Comes to the Water Hole? Bare, Colleen S., photos by. LC 91-7915. (Illus.). 32p. (ps-3). 1991. 13.95 (*0-525-65073-3*, Cobblehill Bks) Dutton Child Bks.

Barrett, Norman S. Flightless Birds. LC 90-42382. (Illus.). 32p. (gr. k-4). 1991. PLB 11.90 (*0-531-14112-8*) Watts.

Bash, Barbara. Urban Roosts: Where Birds Nest in the City. Bash, Barbara, illus. (gr. 1-5). 1990. 15.95 (*0-316-08306-2*) Little.

Baskin-Salzberg, Anita & Salzberg, Allen. Flightless Birds. LC 93-9553. (Illus.). 64p. (gr. 4-6). 1993. PLB 12.90 (*0-531-20117-1*) Watts.

Bender, Lionel. Birds & Mammals. Khan, Aziz, illus. LC 87-82896. 40p. (gr. 6-8). 1988. PLB 12.40 (*0-531-17091-8*, Gloucester Pr) Watts.

Birds. 32p. (Orig.). (ps-1). 1984. pap. 1.25 (*0-8431-1516-5*) Price Stern.

Birds Activity Book. (Illus.). (ps-6). pap. 2.95 (*0-565-01030-1*, Pub. by Natural Hist Mus) Parkwest Pubns.

Birds & How They Live. LC 91-58204. (Illus.). 64p. (gr. 3 up). 1992. 11.95 (*1-879431-97-1*); PLB 12.99 (*1-879431-98-X*) Dorling Kindersley.

Birds of Arizona. (Illus.). 32p. (gr. 3 up). 1994. pap. 1.00 (*0-935810-13-7*) Primer Pubs.

Birds of North America. (Illus.). 64p. (gr. 7 up). 1992. pap. 4.95 (*0-7460-1145-8*, Usborne) EDC.

Bizette, Genevieve, illus. Nell's Aviary. (ps). 1993. Gift box set of 4 bks., 12p. ea. incl 4 hanging birds. bds. 14.95 (*1-56828-038-6*) Red Jacket Pr.

Boice, Tara. If You Find a Baby Bird: How to Protect & Care for Wild Baby Birds. 36p. (gr. 4-9). 1992. pap. 7.95 (*0-9631916-0-8*) Seawind Pub.

Bonsignori, Martina. Baby Birds. Torriani, Graziella, illus. 18p. (ps-k). 1992. bds. 3.95 (*1-56397-153-4*) Boyds Mills Pr.

Boy Scouts of America. Bird Study. (Illus.). 64p. (gr. 6-12). 1984. pap. 1.85 (*0-8395-3282-2*, 33282) BSA.

Bremmer. How Birds Live. (gr. 4-6). 1981. (Usborne-Hayes); PLB 13.96 (*0-88110-082-X*); pap. 6.95 (*0-86020-157-0*) EDC.

Brown, Mary B. Wings along the Waterway. LC 91-18559. (Illus.). 80p. (gr. 3-6). 1992. 17.95 (*0-531-05981-2*); lib. bdg. 17.99 (*0-531-08581-3*) Orchard Bks Watts.

Burgess, Thornton W. Burgess Bird Book for Children. 24.95 (*0-8488-0404-X*) Amereon Ltd.

Burnie, David. Bird. Chadwick, Peter, photos by. LC 87-26441. (Illus.). 64p. (gr. 5 up). 1988. 16.00 (*0-394-89619-X*); lib. bdg. 16.99 (*0-394-99619-4*) Knopf Bks Yng Read.

Burton, Maurice. Birds. (Illus.). 64p. (gr. 4-7). 1985. 15.95x (*0-8160-1063-3*) Facts on File.

Butterfield, Moira. Bird. Johnson, Paul, illus. 24p. (ps-1). 1992. pap. 3.95 (*0-671-75892-6*, Little Simon) S&S Trade.

Caitlin, Stephen. Amazing World of Birds. Snyder, Joel, illus. LC 89-4968. 32p. (gr. 2-4). 1990. PLB 11.59 (*0-8167-1747-8*); pap. text ed. 2.95 (*0-8167-1748-6*) Troll Assocs.

Casey, Denise. Big Birds. Gilmore, Jackie, photos by. LC 92-17275. (Illus.). 48p. (gr. 1-5). 1993. 14.99 (*0-525-65121-7*, Cobblehill Bks) Dutton Child Bks.

Cherayeff, Catherine & Richardson, Nan. Feathery Facts. Cherayeff, Catherine, concept by. LC 94-2479. 1995. 10.95 (*0-15-200110-7*) HarBrace.

Ching, Patrick & Ching, Patrick. Beautiful Birds of Hawaii Coloring Book. (Illus.). 32p. (ps-2). 1992. pap. 3.95 (*1-880188-43-0*) Bess Pr.

Cole, Joanna. A Bird's Body. Wexler, Jerome, illus. LC 82-6446. 48p. (gr. k-3). 1982. 12.95 (*0-688-01470-4*); lib. bdg. 12.88 (*0-688-01471-2*, Morrow Jr Bks) Morrow Jr Bks.

Compass Productions Staff. Baffling Bird Behavior. Mirocha, Paul, illus. 10p. (gr. k-4). 1992. 5.95 (*0-694-00410-3*, Festival) HarpC Child Bks.

Cox & Cork. Birds. (gr. 2-5). 1980. (Usborne-Hayes); PLB 11.96 (*0-88110-072-2*); pap. 3.95 (*0-86020-475-8*) EDC.

Culver, Todd A. Discover Birds. (Illus.). 48p. (gr. 3-6). 1992. PLB 14.95 (*1-878363-66-2*, HTS Bks) Forest Hse.

Doris, Ellen. Ornithology. Rubenstein, Len, photos by. LC 93-61888. (Illus.). 63p. 1994. 15.95 (*0-500-19008-9*) Thames Hudson.

Forsyth, Adrian & Aziz, Laurel. Exploring the World of Birds: An Equinox Guide to Avian Life. (Illus.). 72p. (gr. 4 up). 1990. 15.95 (*0-920656-98-6*, Pub. by Camden Hse CN); pap. 9.95 (*0-920656-94-3*, Pub. by Annick CN) Firefly Bks Ltd.

Fowler, Allan. It Could Still Be a Bird. LC 90-2206. (Illus.). 32p. (ps-2). 1990. PLB 10.75 (*0-516-04901-1*); pap. 22.95 big bk. (*0-516-49461-9*); pap. 3.95 (*0-516-44901-X*) Childrens.

—Podria Ser un Pajaro: It Could Still Be a Bird. LC 90-2206. (SPA.). 32p. (ps-2). 1991. PLB 10.75 (*0-516-34901-5*); pap. 3.95 (*0-516-54901-4*) Childrens.

Friskey, Margaret. Birds We Know. LC 81-7745. (Illus.). 48p. (gr. k-4). 1981. PLB 12.85 (*0-516-01609-1*); pap. 4.95 (*0-516-41609-X*) Childrens.
Ganeri, A. Bird Facts. (Illus.). 48p. (gr. 3-7). 1991. lib. bdg. 12.96 (*0-88110-530-9*, Usborne); pap. 5.95 (*0-7460-0619-5*, Usborne) EDC.
Ganeri, Anita. Birds. Kline, Marjory, ed. (Illus.). 32p. (gr. 5-8). 1993. PLB 12.40 (*0-531-17362-3*, Gloucester Pr) Watts.
—Jungle Birds. Lings, Steve & Weston, Steve, illus. LC 93-19869. 32p. (gr. 4-6). 1993. PLB 19.97 (*0-8114-6160-2*) Raintree Steck-V.
George, Michael. Birds. 32p. (gr. 2-6). 1991. 15.95 (*0-89565-702-3*) Childs World.
Greenberg, Russell. El Sur de Mexico: Cruce de Caminos para las Pajaros Migratorios: Southern Mexico: Crossroads for Migratory Birds. Zickefoose, Julie, et al, illus. (ENG & SPA.). 32p. 1990. pap. 3.00 (*1-881230-01-5*) Smiths Migratory.
Greenberg, Russell & Lumpkin, Susan. Birds over Troubled Forests. Zickefooser, Julie, illus. 32p. (Orig.). 1991. pap. 5.00 (*1-881230-00-7*) Smiths Migratory.
Haley, Neale. Birds for Pets & Pleasure. Carroll, Pamela, illus. LC 80-68740. 224p. (gr. 7 up). 1981. PLB 8.95 (*0-385-28053-X*); pap. 4.95 (*0-440-00475-6*) Delacorte.
Hall, George. Hot Wings of the World. (Illus.). 24p. (Orig.). 1990. pap. 2.50 (*0-942025-86-5*) Kidsbks.
Harner, David L. Attracting & Feeding Wild Birds in the Prescott Area. (Illus.). 96p. (Orig.). (gr. 12). 1989. pap. 3.95 (*0-685-26081-X*) Harner Pubns.
Harris, Alan, ed. Birds. LC 92-54484. 1993. write for info. (*1-56458-216-7*) Dorling Kindersley.
Hiller, Ilo. Introducing Birds to Young Naturalists: From Texas Parks & Wildlife Magazine. LC 89-4398. (Illus.). (gr. 6). 1989. 9.00 (*0-89096-412-2*); pap. 4.50 (*0-89096-410-6*) Tex A&M Univ Pr.
Hirschi, Ron. What Is a Bird? Walker, Galen B., photos by. (Illus.). (ps-4). 1987. 10.95 (*0-8027-6720-6*); PLB 11.85 (*0-8027-6721-4*) Walker & Co.
—Where Do Birds Live? Walker, Galen B., photos by. (Illus.). (ps-4). 1987. 10.95 (*0-8027-6722-2*); PLB 11.85 (*0-8027-6723-0*) Walker & Co.
Hornblow, Leonora & Hornblow, Arthur. Birds Do the Strangest Things. Singer, Alan D., illus. LC 90-8583. 64p. (gr. 2-4). 1991. pap. 3.95 (*0-679-81159-1*) Random Bks Yng Read.
Hoyt, George & Hoyt, Doris. A Bird's-Eye View of California. Atkinson, Mary, illus. 48p. (Orig.). (gr. k-4). 1989. pap. 4.95 (*0-9622364-4-6*) Adona Pub.
Illustrated Encyclopedia of Wildlife, Vol. 6: The Birds, Pt. I. 208p. (gr. 7 up). 1990. lib. bdg. write for info. (*1-55905-042-X*) Grey Castle.
Illustrated Encyclopedia of Wildlife, Vol. 7: The Birds, Pt. II. 208p. (gr. 7 up). 1990. lib. bdg. write for info. (*1-55905-043-8*) Grey Castle.
Illustrated Encyclopedia of Wildlife, Vol. 8: The Birds, Pt. III. 208p. (gr. 7 up). 1990. lib. bdg. write for info. (*1-55905-044-6*) Grey Castle.
Jennings, Terry. Birds. LC 89-455. (Illus.). 32p. (gr. 3-6). 1989. pap. 4.95 (*0-516-48436-2*) Childrens.
Jones, Teri C. Birds. (Illus.). 64p. (gr. k-4). 1992. PLB 13.75 (*1-878363-81-6*, HTS Bks) Forest Hse.
Julivert, Maria A. Fascinating World of Birds. Arrendondo, Francisco, illus. LC 92-5684. (gr. 4-7). 1992. pap. 7.95 (*0-8120-1378-6*) Barron.
Kelly, Michael. Your First Lovebird. (Illus.). 34p. (Orig.). 1991. pap. 1.95 (*0-86622-069-0*, YF-112) TFH Pubns.
Kuchalla, Susan. Birds. Britt, Gary, illus. LC 81-11412. 32p. (gr. k-2). 1982. lib. bdg. 11.59 (*0-89375-656-3*); pap. 2.95 (*0-89375-657-1*) Troll Assocs.
Lantier-Sampon, Patricia. Birds. LC 91-50345. (Illus.). 24p. (ps-2). 1991. PLB 15.93 (*0-8368-0541-0*) Gareth Stevens Inc.
Legg, Gerald. Amazing Tropical Birds. Young, Jerry, photos by. LC 91-6515. (Illus.). 32p. (Orig.). (gr. 1-5). 1991. lib. bdg. 9.99 (*0-679-91520-6*); pap. 6.95 (*0-679-81520-1*) Knopf Bks Yng Read.
Lerner, Carol. Backyard Birds of Winter. LC 94-3036. 1994. write for info. (*0-688-12819-X*); PLB write for info. (*0-688-12820-3*) Morrow Jr Bks.
Lohr, J. E. Your First Cockatiel. (Illus.). 36p. (Orig.). 1991. pap. 1.95 (*0-86622-060-7*, YF-104) TFH Pubns.
Lovett, Sarah. Extremely Weird Birds. (gr. 3 up). 1992. pap. 9.95 (*1-56261-040-6*) John Muir.
Mabie, Grace. A Picture Book of Water Birds. Pistolesi, Roseanna, illus. LC 91-34129. 24p. (gr. 1-4). 1992. PLB 9.59 (*0-8167-2436-9*); pap. text ed. 2.50 (*0-8167-2437-7*) Troll Assocs.
McKean, Barb. Birds. Migliore, Ron, illus. 32p. (gr. 3-7). 1985. pap. 3.50 (*0-88625-116-8*) Durkin Hayes Pub.
MacPherson, Mary. Birdwatch: A Young Person's Introduction to Birding. Douglas, Virginia, illus. 144p. (Orig.). (gr. 6 up). 1989. pap. 9.95 (*0-920197-57-4*, Pub. by Summerhill CN) Sterling.
Markle, Sandra. Outside & Inside Birds. LC 93-38910. (ps-3). 1994. 15.95 (*0-02-762312-2*, Bradbury Pr) Macmillan Child Grp.

Mason, B. J., Jr. Elliott B. in Birds of a Feather. Moore, Kevin R., illus. Dibler-Mason, Betty J., intro. by. (Illus.). 66p. (Orig.). (gr. 2-4). 1993. Incl. audio cass. pap. 14.95 (*0-9640707-0-7*) Color-Me Storybks. Most of us are aware that the general makeup of the domestic cat is to watch & chase birds. But did you ever hear of a cat that actually takes care of them? Color-Me Storybooks introduces its first in a series of characters that aid in accelerating learning & reinforcing family values - initially, through a friendly cat named Elliott B. that teaches children about wild birds. In fact, he even owns his own wild bird store! Elliott B. dedicates his life to educating school children & the community about the habits & habitats of wild birds through an exchange of dialogue about our feathery friends. "It cleverly combines visual, auditory & tactile learning," states Professional Educator & President of King Tree Book Company, Deer Park, Washington, Craig Palmer. "...good visual stimulation...bold print," adds Special Education Professor, Denton, Texas, Dr. Claude Cheek. Librarian Marsha Barker, Happy Hill Farm Academy, Granbury, Texas, found her students to be "fascinated & drawn to Elliott B...materials are wonderful... excellent for use in teaching across the curriculum...recommend to any early elementary educator." Sixty-six pages of educational fun that includes coloring, a glossary & sheet music. Schedule storytime & character appearance. Call 214-495-8225. *Publisher Provided Annotation.*

Mayes, S. How Does a Bird Fly? (Illus.). 24p. (gr. 1 up). 1991. PLB 11.96 (*0-88110-546-5*, Usborne); pap. 3.95 (*0-7460-0694-2*, Usborne) EDC.
Mitchell, Victor. Birds. Mitchell, Victor, illus. 16p. (gr. k up). 1988. pap. 1.99 (*0-7459-1467-5*) Lion USA.
National Wildlife Federation Staff. Birds, Birds, Birds. (gr. k-8). 1991. pap. 7.95 (*0-945051-32-8*, 75004) Natl Wildlife.
Noreen, George W. Your First Finch. (Illus.). 36p. (Orig.). 1991. pap. 1.95 (*0-86622-062-3*, YF-106) TFH Pubns.
North American Birdlife. (Illus.). 32p. (Orig.). (gr. 1-6). 1972. pap. 4.50 (*0-8431-1730-3*) Price Stern.
O'Connor, Karen. The Feather Book. LC 90-2959. (Illus.). 60p. (gr. 4 up). 1991. text ed. 14.95 RSBE (*0-87518-445-6*, Dillon) Macmillan Child Grp.
Orr, Richard. The Bird Atlas. Orr, Richarad, illus. LC 93-18225. 64p. (gr. 4 up). 1993. 19.95 (*1-56458-327-9*) Dorling Kindersley.
Ostriches. 1991. PLB 14.95s.p. (*0-88682-338-2*) Creative Ed.
Owen, Oliver S. From Egg to Robin. LC 94-7793. 1994. write for info. (*1-56239-293-X*) Abdo & Dghtrs.
Owens, Mary B. Counting Cranes. (ps-3). 1993. 14.95 (*0-316-67719-1*) Little.
Parramon, J. M. My First Visit to the Aviary. Sales, G., illus. 32p. (ps). 1990. pap. 4.95 (*0-8120-4303-0*) Barron.
Pasca, Sue-Rhee. Your First Canary. (Illus.). 36p. (Orig.). 1991. pap. 1.95 (*0-86622-059-3*, YF-103) TFH Pubns.
Patent, Dorothy H. Feathers. Munoz, William, photos by. (Illus.). 64p. (gr. 5 up). 1992. 15.00 (*0-525-65081-4*, Cobblehill Bks) Dutton Child Bks.
Perry, Philip & Weiss, Ellen. Facts America: Birds. LC 92-9403. (Illus.). 64p. (gr. 2-6). 1993. 7.98 (*0-8317-2315-7*) Smithmark.
Petersen, Candyce A. Eggbert the Robin. Stoffregen, Jill A., illus. LC 92-12894. 24p. (ps-3). Date not set. 11.95 (*1-56065-099-0*) Capstone Pr.
Pine, Jonathan. Backyard Birds. Zickefoose, Julie, illus. LC 91-45184. 48p. (gr. 2-5). 1993. 12.00 (*0-06-021039-7*); PLB 11.89 (*0-06-021040-0*) HarpC Child Bks.
—Backyard Birds. Zickefoose, Julie, illus. LC 91-45184. 48p. (gr. 2-5). 1993. pap. 7.95 (*0-06-446150-5*, Trophy) HarpC Child Bks.
Polette, Nancy. Birds in Literature. (Illus.). 48p. (gr. k-3). 1990. pap. 5.95 (*0-913839-86-8*) Bk Lures.
Reid, Struan. Bird World. (Illus.). 64p. (gr. 4-6). 1991. PLB 15.40 (*1-56294-009-0*) Millbrook Pr.
Ricciuti, Edward. Birds. (Illus.). 64p. (gr. 4-8). 1993. PLB 16.95 (*1-56711-038-X*) Blackbirch.
—Birds. Simpson, Bill, illus. 64p. (gr. 4-8). 1993. jacketed 14.95 (*1-56711-053-3*) Blackbirch.
Richardson, Joy. Birds. LC 93-18558. (Illus.). 32p. (gr. 2-4). 1993. PLB 11.40 (*0-531-14262-0*) Watts.
Rockwell, Anne. Our Yard Is Full of Birds. Rockwell, Lizzy, illus. LC 90-30436. 32p. (ps-2). 1992. RSBE 13.95 (*0-02-777273-X*, Macmillan Child Bk) Macmillan Child Grp.
Roop, Peter & Roop, Connie, eds. Capturing Nature: The Writings & Art of John James Audubon. Farley, Rick, illus. LC 92-15662. 48p. (gr. 5 up). 1993. 16.95 (*0-8027-8204-3*); PLB 17.85 (*0-8027-8205-1*) Walker & Co.
Rupp, Rebecca. Everything You Never Learned about Birds. Domm, Jeffrey C., illus. LC 94-21014. 1995. pap. 14.95 (*0-88266-345-3*) Storey Comm Inc.
Sanford, Bill & Green, Carl. The Dodo. LC 89-7867. (Illus.). 48p. (gr. 5-6). 1989. text ed. 12.95 RSBE (*0-89686-455-3*, Crestwood Hse) Macmillan Child Grp.
Santrey, Laurence. Birds. Johnson, Pamela, illus. LC 84-2731. 32p. (gr. 3-6). 1985. PLB 9.49 (*0-8167-0192-X*); pap. text ed. 2.95 (*0-8167-0193-8*) Troll Assocs.
Schafer, Susaan. The Turkey Vulture. LC 93-44534. 1994. text ed. 13.95 (*0-87518-604-1*, Dillon) Macmillan Child Grp.
Schultz, Ellen. I Can Read About Birds. LC 78-73775. (Illus.). (gr. 2-4). 1979. pap. 2.50 (*0-89375-204-5*) Troll Assocs.
Sea Birds. 1991. PLB 14.95 (*0-88682-416-8*) Creative Ed.
Selsam, Millicent E. & Hunt, Joyce. A First Look at Birds. Springer, Harriet, illus. LC 73-81404. 32p. (gr. 2-4). 1973. PLB 12.85 (*0-8027-6164-X*) Walker & Co.
Sill, Cathryn. About Birds: A Guide for Children. Sill, John, illus. 40p. (ps-3). 1991. 14.95 (*1-56145-028-6*) Peachtree Pubs.
Singer, Arthur & Singer, Alan, illus. State Birds. Buckley, Virginia, text by. LC 86-2209. 64p. (gr. 4 up). 1986. 16.95 (*0-525-67177-3*, Lodestar Bks); pap. 5.95 (*0-525-67314-8*, Lodestar Bks) Dutton Child Bks.
Smith, William J. Birds & Beasts. Hnizdovsky, Jacques, illus. (gr. k up). 1990. 18.95 (*0-87923-865-8*) Godine.
Snedden, Robert. What Is a Bird? Oxford Scientific Films, photos by. (Illus.). 32p. (gr. 2-5). 1993. 13.95 (*0-87156-539-0*) Sierra.
Spizzirri Publishing Co. Staff. Birds: Educational Coloring Book. Spizzirri, Linda, ed. Goodman, Marlene, et al, illus. 32p. (gr. 1-8). 1981. pap. 1.75 (*0-86545-026-9*) Spizzirri.
—Prehistoric Birds: An Educational Coloring Book. Spizzirri, Linda, ed. Spizzirri, Peter M., illus. 32p. (gr. 1-8). 1981. pap. 1.75 (*0-86545-023-4*) Spizzirri.
Spizzirri Publishing, Inc. Staff. Endangered Birds: An Educational Coloring Book. Spizzirri, Linda, ed. (Illus.). 32p. (gr. k-5). 1992. pap. 1.75 (*0-86545-171-0*) Spizzirri.
Steele, Philip. Birds. LC 90-42015. (Illus.). 32p. (gr. 5-6). 1991. text ed. 3.95 RSBE (*0-89686-583-5*, Crestwood Hse) Macmillan Child Grp.
—Birds. (gr. 4-7). 1991. lib. bdg. 4.95 (*0-671-72244-1*, J Messner) S&S Trade.
Sterry, Paul. Seabirds. Lings, Steve, illus. 1994. PLB 19.97 (*0-8114-6188-2*) Raintree Steck-V.
Stockley, C., et al. Ornithology. (Illus.). 48p. (gr. 4-12). 1993. PLB 13.96 (*0-88110-514-7*, Usborne); pap. 7.95 (*0-7460-0685-3*, Usborne) EDC.
Stone, Lynn. Bird Discovery Library, 6 bks, Reading Level 2. (Illus.). 144p. (gr. k-5). 1989. Set. PLB 71.64 (*0-86592-320-5*) Rourke Corp.
Stone, Lynn M. Vultures. LC 88-30196. (Illus.). 24p. (gr. 2-4). 1989. PLB 11.94 (*0-86592-324-8*); PLB 8.95s.p. (*0-685-58506-9*) Rourke Corp.
—Vultures. LC 92-26721. 1993. 19.95 (*0-87614-768-6*) Carolrhoda Bks.
Tinbergen, Niko. Kleew. (Illus.). 48p. (gr. 4 up). 1991. 10.95 (*1-55821-122-5*) Lyons & Burford.
Wallace, Ian, et al. Bird Life. Quinn, David, et al, illus. 32p. (gr. 4-7). 1985. lib. bdg. 13.96 (*0-88110-172-9*); pap. 5.95 (*0-86020-841-9*) EDC.
Watts, Barrie. Birds' Nest. (Illus.). 25p. (gr. k-4). 1991. 5.95 (*0-382-09443-3*); PLB 7.95 (*0-382-09439-5*); pap. 3.95 (*0-382-24015-4*) Silver Burdett Pr.
Weidensaul, Scott. Descubre Aves. University of Mexico City Staff, tr. from SPA. O'Neill, Pablo M. & Robare, Lorie, illus. 48p. (gr. 3-8). 1993. PLB 16.95 (*1-56674-047-9*, HTS Bks) Forest Hse.
—A Kid's First Book of Birdwatching. (Illus.). 64p. (ps up). 1990. incl. cassette 18.95 (*0-89471-826-6*) Running Pr.
Weston, A. A Step-by-Step Book about Lovebirds. (Illus.). 64p. (gr. 9-12). 1988. pap. 3.95 (*0-86622-456-4*, SK-016) TFH Pubns.
Wexo, John B. Flyers. 24p. (gr. 3 up). 1991. PLB 14.95 (*0-88682-394-3*) Creative Ed.
Wildsmith, Brian. Birds by Brian Wildsmith. (Illus.). (gr. k-4). 1967. pap. 7.50 (*0-19-272117-8*) OUP.
Wood, A. J. Beautiful Birds. Ward, Helen, illus. LC 90-85907. 24p. (ps-1). 1991. 8.95 (*1-878093-47-9*) Boyds Mills Pr.
Wright, Lynn F. The Prison Bird. Donaho, K. Blythe, illus. LC 91-75180. 24p. (gr. 1-4). 1991. 12.95 (*1-881519-01-5*) WorryWart.
Zim, Herbert S. & Gabrielson, Ira N. Birds. Irving, James G., illus. 160p. (gr. 7 up). 1987. PLB 4.95 (*0-307-24053-3*); pap. write for info. (Golden Pr) Western Pub.

BIRDS, AQUATIC

see Water Birds

BIRDS–EGGS AND NESTS

Babson, Jane F. The Nest on the Porch. Babson, Jane F., illus. LC 88-51084. 32p. (Orig.). (ps up). 1989. pap. 4.95 (*0-940787-01-6*) Winstead Pr.
Bennett, Paul. Making a Nest. LC 93-49800. (Illus.). 32p. 1994. 14.95 (*1-56847-204-8*) Thomson Lrning.

Curran, Eileen. Birds Nests. Johnson, Pamela, illus. LC 84-8658. 32p. (gr. k-2). 1985. PLB 11.59 (*0-8167-0341-8*); pap. text ed. 2.95 (*0-8167-0342-6*) Troll Assocs.

Czajkowski, Alexandre M. Birds & Their Nests. (ps-3). 1994. 5.95 (*0-944589-49-9*) Young Discovery Lib.

Demuth, Patricia B. Cradles in the Trees: The Story of Bird Nests. LC 93-9114. (Illus.). 32p. (ps-3). 1994. RSBE 14.95 (*0-02-728466-2*) Macmillan Child Grp.

Reidel, Marlene. From Egg to Bird. Reidel, Marlene, illus. 24p. (ps-3). 1981. PLB 10.95 (*0-87614-159-9*) Carolrhoda Bks.

Selsam, Millicent E., et al. A First Look at Birds' Nest. Springer, Harriett, illus. LC 84-15238. 32p. (gr. 1-4). 1984. lib. bdg. 9.85 (*0-8027-6565-3*) Walker & Co.

BIRDS–FICTION

Ada, Alma F. El Panuelo de Seda. (SPA., Illus.). 24p. 1993. 16.95x (*1-56492-105-0*) Laredo.

Aiken, Joan. Nightbirds on Nantucket. 243p. (gr. k-6). 1981. pap. 1.75 (*0-440-96370-2*, YB) Dell.

Alden, Laura. Nightingale's Adventure in Alphabet Town. McCallum, Jodie, illus. LC 92-1069. 32p. (ps-2). 1992. PLB 11.80 (*0-516-05414-7*) Childrens.

Allen, Constance. My Name Is Big Bird. Swanson, Maggie, illus. 24p. (ps-k). 1992. pap. write for info. (*0-307-11533-X*, 11533, Golden Pr) Western Pub.

Andersen, Hans Christian. The Nightingale. Zwerger, Lisbeth, illus. LC 84-9492. (gr. 1 up). 1991. pap. 14.95 (*0-907234-57-7*) Picture Bk Studio.

—The Nightingale. Bell, Anthea, tr. from DAN. Zwerger, Lisbeth, illus. LC 92-6632. 28p. (gr. 4 up). 1993. Repr. Mini-bk. 4.95 (*0-88708-269-6*) Picture Bk Studio.

Aroner, Miriam & Haas, Shelly O. The Kingdom of Singing Birds. LC 92-39382. 1993. 13.95 (*0-929371-43-7*); pap. 5.95 (*0-929371-44-5*) Kar Ben.

Avi. Blue Heron. LC 91-4308. 192p. (gr. 5-9). 1992. SBE 14.95 (*0-02-707751-9*, Bradbury Pr) Macmillan Child Grp.

Baker, Jeannie. Home in the Sky. Baker, Jeannie, illus. 32p. (ps-3). 1993. pap. 4.95 (*0-590-44704-1*) Scholastic Inc.

Baker, Keith. The Dove's Letter. Baker, Keith, illus. LC 87-8530. 32p. (ps-3). 1988. 14.95 (*0-15-224133-7*, HB Juv Bks) HarBrace.

Bang, Molly. The Paper Crane. Bang, Molly, illus. LC 84-13546. 32p. (gr. k-3). 1985. 15.00 (*0-688-04108-6*); lib. bdg. 14.93 (*0-688-04109-4*) Greenwillow.

Barber, Noel. Buzzard Is My Best Friend. 1981. 12.95 (*0-02-507260-9*) Macmillan.

Barquist, Larry E. The Little Bird That Couldn't Fly. 1993. 7.95 (*0-533-10456-4*) Vantage.

Bedard, Michael. The Nightingale. Ricci, Regolo, illus. (gr. k-4). 1992. 14.95 (*0-395-60735-3*, Clarion Bks) HM.

Berenstain, Stan & Berenstain, Janice. After the Dinosaurs. Berenstain, Stan & Berenstain, Janice, illus. LC 88-42588. 32p. (Orig.). (gr. k-3). 1988. lib. bdg. 5.99 (*0-394-90518-0*); (Random Juv) Random Bks Yng Read.

Berliner, Franz. Miserable Marabou. Hedlund, Irene, illus. LC 89-30852. 23p. (gr. k-3). 1989. PLB 18.60 (*0-8368-0094-X*) Gareth Stevens Inc.

Bizette, Genevieve. The Cardinal. Bizette, Genevieve, illus. 12p. (ps). 1992. 3.95 (*1-56828-011-4*) Red Jacket Pr.

—The Dove. Bizette, Genevieve, illus. 12p. (ps). 1992. 3.95 (*1-56828-009-2*) Red Jacket Pr.

—Nell's Aviary. (ps). 1992. 11.95 (*1-56828-013-0*) Red Jacket Pr.

—The Seagull. Bizette, Genevieve, illus. 12p. (ps). 1992. 3.95 (*1-56828-010-6*) Red Jacket Pr.

Bowman, Margret & Millhouse, Nicholas. Blue-Footed Booby: Bird of the Galapagos. Bowman, Margret, illus. LC 85-27617. 32p. (gr. 1-7). 1986. 11.95 (*0-8027-6628-5*); lib. bdg. 11.85 (*0-8027-6629-3*) Walker & Co.

Braff Brodzinsky, Anne. The Mulberry Bird: Story of an Adoption. LC 86-2460. (Illus.). 48p. (gr. k-5). 1986. 10.95 (*0-9609504-5-1*) Perspect Indiana.

Bragg, Ruth. Mrs. Muggle's Sparkle. Bragg, Ruth, illus. LC 89-31371. 28p. (ps up). 1991. pap. 15.95 (*0-88708-106-1*) Picture Bk Studio.

Breneman, Steven B. Fly Away Home. LC 84-6252. 74p. (Orig.). (gr. 2-6). 1984. pap. 8.50 (*0-87743-183-3*, Pub. by Bellwood Pr) Bahai.

Briggs, Jean P. Birds Have a Barbecue. 1994. 7.95 (*0-8062-4847-5*) Carlton.

Bulla, Clyde R. White Bird. Cook, Donald, illus. LC 89-70231. 64p. (Orig.). (gr. 2-4). 1990. lib. bdg. 6.99 (*0-679-90662-2*); pap. 2.50 (*0-679-80662-8*) Random Bks Yng Read.

Bunting, Eve. Fly Away Home. Giblin, James C., ed. Himler, Ronald, illus. 32p. (ps-2). 1991. 13.95 (*0-395-55962-6*, Clarion Bks) HM.

—Fly Away Home. Himler, Ronald, illus. 32p. (gr. k-3). 1993. pap. 5.70 (*0-395-66415-2*, Clarion Bks) HM.

—The Followers. (Illus.). 64p. (gr. 3-8). 1992. 8.95 (*0-89565-764-3*) Childs World.

Burgess, Thornton. The Adventures of Ol'Mistah Buzzard. 1992. Repr. lib. bdg. 17.95x (*0-89966-995-6*) Buccaneer Bks.

Burgess, Thornton W. Adventures of Sammy Jay. 15.95 (*0-8488-0381-7*) Amereon Ltd.

Burnett, Frances H. The Troubles of Queen Silver-Bell: As Told by Queen Crosspatch. Cady, Harrison, illus. 56p. (gr. 3-6). 1992. 4.99 (*0-517-07247-5*, Pub. by Derrydale Bks) Random Hse Value.

Calvert, Patricia. The Snowbird. 192p. (gr. 7 up). 1982. pap. 1.95 (*0-451-13353-6*, AE1354, Sig Vista) NAL-Dutton.

Campbell, Louise A. & Bowers, Grace A. Muffin, The Maine Puffin. Mason, MacAdam L., illus. 40p. (Orig.). (gr. k-3). 1988. pap. 9.95 (*0-9621949-0-5*) Muffin Enter.

Cannon, Janell. Stellaluna. LC 92-16439. 1993. 14.95 (*0-15-280217-7*) HarBrace.

Cavanaugh, Kate. Pete Goes to Grand Island. Kiner, K. C., illus. 24p. 1992. pap. 5.95 (*0-9622353-3-4*) KAC.

Charles, Veronika M. The Crane Girl. LC 92-50843. (Illus.). 32p. (ps-1). 1993. 14.95 (*0-531-05485-3*) Orchard Bks Watts.

Chipangu, Florita. Bird Meets Fish. Donovan, Bob, illus. 36p. 1993. pap. 2.50 (*1-878181-07-6*) Discovery Comics.

Clair, Bevan. Run Roadrunner. LC 80-82912. (ps-6). 1980. pap. 1.50 (*0-686-30719-4*) B A Scott.

Climo, Shirley. King of the Birds. Heller, Ruth, illus. LC 87-47693. 32p. (gr. k-3). 1988. (Crowell Jr Bks); PLB 14.89 (*0-690-04623-5*) HarpC Child Bks.

—King of the Birds. Heller, Ruth, illus. LC 87-47693. 32p. (gr. k-3). 1991. pap. 4.95 (*0-06-443273-4*, Trophy) HarpC Child Bks.

Cole, Brock. The Winter Wren. LC 84-1583. (Illus.). 32p. (gr. 2 up). 1984. 15.00 (*0-374-38454-1*, Sunburst) FS&G.

—The Winter Wren. LC 84-1583. (Illus.). 32p. (gr. 2 up). 1988. pap. 4.95 (*0-374-48408-2*) FS&G.

Cooke, Tom, illus. Hide-&-Seek with Big Bird: A Sesame Street Book. LC 89-64284. 14p. (ps). 1991. bds. 3.99 (*0-679-80785-3*) Random Bks Yng Read.

Cosgrove, Stephen. The Nosey Birds. Steelhammer, Ilona, illus. 24p. (gr. k-2). 1990. PLB 11.95 (*1-878363-22-0*) Forest Hse.

Czernecki, Stefan & Rhodes, Timothy. The Hummingbirds' Gift. LC 93-19369. (Illus.). 32p. (gr. k-4). 1994. 14.95 (*1-56282-604-2*); PLB 14.89 (*1-56282-605-0*) Hyprn Child.

Damjan, Mischa. The False Flamingoes. Steadman, Ralph, illus. LC 70-105399. 32p. (ps-3). 7.95 (*0-87592-016-0*) Scroll Pr.

Day, David. Aska's Birds. 1992. pap. 15.00 (*0-385-25388-5*) Doubleday.

DeCremer, Shirley. Freddie the Frog. Overton, Amy, illus. LC 92-33094. 16p. Date not set. 14.95 (*0-935343-03-2*) Peartree.

De Paola, Tomie. Bill & Pete. De Paola, Tomie, illus. LC 78-5330. (gr. k-2). 1978. 14.95 (*0-399-20646-9*, Putnam); (Putnam) Putnam Pub Group.

Dodd, Lynley. Slinky Malinki, Open the Door. LC 93-21180. 1994. 17.27 (*0-8368-1074-0*) Gareth Stevens Inc.

Eastman, Philip D. Are You My Mother? LC 60-13495. (Illus.). 64p. (gr. 1-2). 1966. 6.95 (*0-394-80018-4*); lib. bdg. 7.99 (*0-394-90018-9*) Beginner.

—Best Nest. Eastman, Philip D., illus. LC 68-28459. 72p. (gr. k-3). 1968. 6.95 (*0-394-80051-6*); lib. bdg. 7.99 (*0-394-90051-0*) Beginner.

Ehlert, Lois. Feathers for Lunch. 33p. (ps-3). 1990. 13.95 (*0-15-230550-5*) HarBrace.

Elish, Dan. The Great Squirrel Uprising. Cazet, Denys, illus. LC 91-27145. 128p. (gr. 4 up). 1992. 14.95 (*0-531-05995-2*); lib. bdg. 14.99 (*0-531-08595-3*) Orchard Bks Watts.

Erickson, Gina C. & Foster, Kelli C. Sometimes I Wish. Russell, Kerri G., illus. 24p. (ps-2). 1991. pap. 3.50 (*0-8120-4681-1*) Barron.

Estrada, Zilia C. If I Were a Bird. Estrada, Zilia C., illus. (Orig.). (gr. 1 up). 1988. pap. write for info. Blue Flame Pr.

Farmer, Penelope. The Summer Birds. large type ed. 176p. (gr. 3 up). 1990. lib. bdg. 14.95x (*0-7451-1066-5*, Lythway Large Print) Hall.

Fender, Kay. Odette: A Springtime in Paris. Dumas, Philippe, illus. 32p. (ps-3). 1991. 10.95 (*0-916291-33-2*) Kane-Miller Bk.

Fox, Mem. Wilfrid Gordon McDonald Partridge. Vivas, Julie, illus. 32p. (gr. k-4). 1989. pap. 7.95 (*0-916291-26-X*) Kane-Miller Bk.

Gahr, Anna F. Ballet of Birds. 16p. (gr. k-6). 1994. pap. text ed. 12.00 (*1-883702-07-0*) Aiello Grp.

Garland, Sarah. Polly's Puffin. LC 88-24348. (Illus.). 24p. (ps up). 1989. 11.95 (*0-688-08748-5*); PLB 13.88 (*0-688-08749-3*) Greenwillow.

Gaw, Robyn. Chick-in-a-Box. Cooper-Brown, Jean, illus. LC 93-11735. 1994. 4.25 (*0-383-03799-9*) SRA Schl Grp.

Ginsburg, Mirra, adapted by. The Old Man & His Birds. Ruff, Donna, illus. LC 93-26705. 24p. 1994. 15.00 (*0-688-04603-7*); PLB 14.93 (*0-688-04604-5*) Greenwillow.

Gunn, Robin J. Mrs. Rosey Posey & the Empty Nest. LC 92-12955. (gr. k-3). 1993. pap. 4.99 (*0-7814-0329-4*, Chariot Bks) Chariot Family.

Hague, Kathleen. The Legend of the Veery Bird. Hague, Michael, illus. LC 84-19732. 32p. (ps up). 1985. 13.95 (*0-15-243824-6*, HB Juv Bks) HarBrace.

Hanen, Joyce. Yellow Bird & Me. LC 85-484. 128p. (gr. 3-7). 1991. pap. 5.95 (*0-395-55388-1*, Clarion Bks) HM.

Hao, Kuang-ts'ai. The Emperor & the Nightingale. Chang, Shih-ming, illus. (ENG & CHI.). 32p. (gr. 2-4). 1994. 14.95 (*1-57227-018-7*) Pan Asian Pubns.

—The Emperor & the Nightingale. Chang, Shih-ming, illus. (ENG & VIE.). 32p. (gr. 2-4). 1994. 16.95 (*1-57227-020-9*) Pan Asian Pubns.

—The Emperor & the Nightingale. Chang, Shih-ming, illus. (ENG & KOR.). 32p. (gr. 2-4). 1994. 16.95 (*1-57227-021-7*) Pan Asian Pubns.

—The Emperor & the Nightingale. Chang, Shih-ming, illus. (ENG & THA.). 32p. (gr. 2-4). 1994. 16.95 (*1-57227-022-5*) Pan Asian Pubns.

—The Emperor & the Nightingale. Chang, Shih-ming, illus. (ENG & TAG.). 32p. (gr. 2-4). 1994. 16.95 (*1-57227-023-3*) Pan Asian Pubns.

—The Emperor & the Nightingale. Chang, Shih-ming, illus. (ENG & CAM.). 32p. (gr. 2-4). 1994. 16.95 (*1-57227-024-1*) Pan Asian Pubns.

—The Emperor & the Nightingale. Chang, Shih-ming, illus. (ENG & LAO.). 32p. (gr. 2-4). 1994. 16.95 (*1-57227-025-X*) Pan Asian Pubns.

—The Emperor & the Nightingale. Chang, Shih-ming, illus. (ENG & KOR.). 32p. (gr. 2-4). 1994. 16.95 (*1-57227-026-8*) Pan Asian Pubns.

—The Emperor & the Nightingale: El Emperador y el Ruisenor. Zeller, Beatriz, tr. from CHI. Chang, Shih-ming, illus. (ENG & SPA.). 32p. (gr. 2-4). 1994. 16.95 (*1-57227-019-5*) Pan Asian Pubns.

What price will an emperor, who wants to live forever, pay for immortality? Will he give up his favorite horse? His kingdom, perhaps? The answers to these questions are poignantly shown through this haunting & inspiring story about an emperor who ultimately decides to forsake immortality for the love of something greater than himself. This story is illustrated in dreamy details that enhance the story's lyrical power. Readers of all ages will be touched by the messages of love & life offered in THE EMPEROR & THE NIGHTINGALE. Based on Andersen's THE EMPEROR & THE NIGHTINGALE. Also available in English/Chinese, Vietnamese, Korean, Thai, Tagalog, Khmer, Lao & Hmong. For grades 2-4. Please specify the languages when ordering. Available exclusively from: Pan Asian Publications (USA) Inc., 29564 Union City Blvd., Union City, CA 94587. Order toll free: 1-800-853-ASIA, FAX: (510) 475-1489.

Publisher Provided Annotation.

Hautzig, Deborah, adapted by. Big Bird Visits the Dodos. Mathieu, Joe, illus. LC 84-43051. 32p. (ps-3). 1985. lib. bdg. 5.99 (*0-394-97373-9*) Random Bks Yng Read.

—Follow That Bird. LC 84-43052. (Illus.). 48p. (gr. 1-4). 1985. lib. bdg. 7.99 (*0-394-97225-2*) Random Bks Yng Read.

Herman, Gail. Big Bird Visits Granny Bird. Nicklaus, Carol, illus. LC 90-60822. 32p. (Orig.). (ps-3). 1991. pap. 1.50 (*0-679-81050-1*) Random Bks Yng Read.

Hoffman, Beverly. Skipper & Jade: A Love Story. LC 90-71859. 44p. 1991. pap. 6.95 (*1-55523-411-9*) Winston-Derek.

Hoffman, Beverly & Fiorilla, Sal J. A Flower for Iggey. Hoffman, Beverly & Robinson, Michael D., illus. LC 92-85530. 150p. (Orig.). (gr. 3-6). 1993. 12.95 (*0-9634122-1-3*); cass. musical tape avail. Feather Fables.

Holling, Holling C. Seabird. Holling, Holling C., illus. (gr. 4-6). 1978. pap. 7.70 (*0-395-26681-5*) HM.

The Ice Bird. 32p. (gr. 1 up). 1981. pap. 4.50 (*0-941402-01-0*) Devon Pub.

In Songbird Jungle. (ps-k). 1993. 3.99 (*0-89577-480-1*, Dist. by Random) RD Assn.

Ingoglia, Gina. Sylvester & Tweety: What a Mess. (ps-3). 1990. write for info. (*0-307-11595-X*) Western Pub.

Ishii, Momoko. Tongue-Cut Sparrow. Paterson, Katherine, tr. Akaba, Suekichi, illus. LC 86-29314. 40p. (ps-3). 1987. 13.95 (*0-525-67199-4*, Lodestar Bks) Dutton Child Bks.

Ivy, Richard. The Whooptie Whooptie Whatie Whatiee Bird. 28p. (ps-6). 1993. pap. 8.50 (*1-884095-00-3*) Ivy Hill Pubs.

Jeffers, Susan. Wild Robin. Jeffers, Susan, illus. LC 76-21343. 40p. (ps-3). 1986. pap. 4.95 (*0-525-44244-8*, DCB) Dutton Child Bks.

Johnson, Angela. Mama Bird, Baby Birds. Mitchell, Rhonda, illus. LC 93-46415. 12p. (ps). 1994. 4.95 (*0-531-06848-X*) Orchard Bks Watts.

Johnston, Tony. Old Lady & the Birds. LC 91-45124. (ps-3). 1994. 14.95 (*0-15-257769-6*, HB Juv Bks) HarBrace.

Kasza, Keiko. A Mother for Choco. Kasza, Keiko, illus. 32p. (ps-1). 1992. PLB 14.95 (*0-399-21841-6*, Putnam) Putnam Pub Group.

Keller, Holly. Island Baby. LC 91-32491. (Illus.). 32p. (ps-8). 1992. 14.00 (*0-688-10579-3*); PLB 13.93 (*0-688-10580-7*) Greenwillow.

Kittredge, Sonya. Chickadee Rescue. Weinberger, Jane, ed. Kittredge, Sonya, photos by. (Illus.). 32p. (Orig.). (ps-3). 1993. pap. 7.95 (*0-932433-78-2*) Windswept Hse.

Klein, Gerda W. Peregrinations: Adventures with the Green Parrot. Chabela, Elizabeth H., illus. LC 86-80966. 48p. (gr. 3-4). 1986. 12.95 (*0-9616699-0-X*); pap. 5.95 (*0-9616699-1-8*) CHB Goodyear Comm.

Kleven, Elisa. The Lion & the Little Red Bird. LC 91-36691. (Illus.). 32p. (ps-2). 1992. 13.50 (*0-525-44898-5*, DCB) Dutton Child Bks.

Knutson, Barbara. How the Guinea Fowl Got Her Spots. (ps-3). 1991. pap. 6.95 (*0-87614-537-3*) Carolrhoda Bks.

Kveton, Steven. The Legend of Fredbird. Koehler, Ed, illus. 16p. (Orig.). (ps up). 1986. pap. text ed. 2.95 (*0-9616799-0-5*) Water St Missouri.

Langton, Jane. Fledgling. LC 79-2008. 192p. (gr. 3-7). 1980. PLB 13.89 (*0-06-023679-5*) HarpC Child Bks.

Lasky, Kathryn. She's Wearing a Dead Bird on Her Head. Catrow, David, illus. LC 94-18204. Date not set. write for info. (*0-7868-0065-8*); pap. write for info. (*0-7868-2052-7*) Hyprn Child.

Laurin, Anne. Perfect Crane. Mikolaycak, Charles, illus. LC 80-7912. 32p. (gr. 1-4). 1981. PLB 13.89 (*0-06-023744-9*) HarpC Child Bks.

Lawson, Amy. The Talking Bird & the Story Pouch. Brown, Craig M., illus. LC 86-45493. 96p. (gr. 5up). 1987. HarpC Child Bks.

Leeper, Fran. Journey of the Sparrows. (gr. 4-7). 1993. pap. 3.50 (*0-440-40785-0*) Dell.

Lerner, Sharon. Big Bird's Copycat Day: A Step 1 Book. Jacquet, Jean-Pierre & Mathieu, Joe, illus. LC 84-6869. 32p. (ps-2). 1984. lib. bdg. 7.99 (*0-394-96912-X*); pap. 3.50 (*0-394-86912-5*) Random Bks Yng Read.

Lewis, Jean. Sweet Dreams, Tweety. (ps-3). 1993. pap. 1.95 (*0-307-10552-0*, Golden Pr) Western Pub.

Linn, James R. The Little Green Hummingbird. Huston, Dwayne L., ed. Benedict, Jennifer S., illus. LC 92-75969. 44p. (gr. 3). 1993. pap. 7.98 (*1-882798-01-5*) Erth & Sky Pub.

Lionni, Leo. Inch by Inch. (Illus.). (gr. k-1). 1962. 10.95 (*0-8392-3010-9*) Astor-Honor.

—Inch by Inch. Cohn, Amy, ed. LC 94-6483. (Illus.). 32p. (ps up). 1994. pap. 4.95 (*0-688-13283-9*, Mulberry) Morrow.

—Pulgada a Pulgada. (SPA., Illus.). (gr. k-1). 1961. 10.95 (*0-8392-3030-3*) Astor-Honor.

Livingston, P. Gullible the Seagull. (Illus., Orig.). (gr. k-6). 1992. pap. 9.95 (*0-9629860-2-X*) Sound Pub WA.

London, Jonathan. Condor's Egg. Chaffee, James, illus. Mesta, Robert, afterword by. LC 93-31001. (Illus.). 32p. 1994. 13.95 (*0-8118-0260-4*) Chronicle Bks.

The Lunettes. rev. ed. 50p. 1992. PLB 25.00 (*1-56611-005-X*); pap. 15.00 (*1-56611-849-2*) Jonas.

McConnachie, Brian. Elmer & Chickens vs. Big Bird. 1993. pap. 3.99 (*0-517-11135-7*) Random Hse Value.

Maddern, Eric. Rainbow Bird. (gr. 4-8). 1993. 14.95 (*0-316-54314-4*) Little.

Manzano, Roy R. Pelly's Exciting Adventures. (Illus.). 1993. 9.95 (*0-533-10526-9*) Vantage.

Martchenko, Michael. Bird Feeder Banquet. Martchenko, Michael, illus. 24p. (Orig.). (gr. k-3). 1990. 14.95 (*1-55037-147-9*, Pub. by Annick CN); pap. 4.95 (*1-55037-146-0*, Pub. by Annick CN) Firefly Bks Ltd.

Marzilli, Vincent, II. Return of the Nighthawks. Marzilli, Roanne O., illus. 56p. (Orig.). (gr. k-6). 1987. pap. 7.95 (*0-9617809-1-6*) Vincent Marzilli.

Meddaugh, Susan. Tree of Birds. Meddaugh, Susan, illus. 32p. (gr. k-3). 1990. 13.45 (*0-395-53147-0*) HM.

—Tree of Birds. (ps-3). 1994. pap. 4.95 (*0-395-68978-3*) HM.

Meeker, Clare H. The Tale of Two Rice Birds. Lamb, Christine, illus. 32p. (ps up). 1994. 14.95 (*1-57061-008-8*) Sasquatch Bks.

Meeks, Arone R. Enora & the Black Crane. LC 92-32123. 1993. 14.95 (*0-590-46375-6*) Scholastic Inc.

Mister Tom. Fuzzy Buzzard. Bretlinger, Ted, illus. 32p. (gr. 2-4). 1978. write for info. Oddo.

Moncure, Jane B. Happy Birthday, Word Bird. Hohag, Linda, illus. LC 83-15256. 32p. (ps-2). 1983. PLB 14.95 (*0-89565-256-0*) Childs World.

—Hi, Word Bird. Hohag, Linda S., illus. LC 80-15919. 32p. (ps-2). 1981. PLB 14.95 (*0-89565-159-9*) Childs World.

—Word Bird Asks: What? What? What? Gohman, Vera, illus. LC 83-15258. 32p. (gr. k-2). 1983. PLB 14.95 (*0-89565-258-7*) Childs World.

—Word Bird Builds a City. Gohman, Vera, illus. LC 83-15275. 32p. (ps-2). 1983. PLB 14.95 (*0-89565-257-9*) Childs World.

—Word Bird's Circus Surprise. Hohag, Linda, illus. LC 80-29528. 32p. (gr. k-2). 1981. PLB 14.95 (*0-89565-162-9*) Childs World.

—Word Bird's Shapes. Hohag, Linda, illus. LC 83-15255. 32p. (gr. k-2). 1983. PLB 14.95 (*0-89565-255-2*) Childs World.

Mondo. Morning of the Bright Bird. Akinlana, Marcus, illus. 48p. 1993. pap. 8.95 (*0-88378-136-0*) Third World.

Moore, Beverly. Echo's Song. Moore, Beverly, illus. 40p. (gr. k-3). 1993. PLB 13.95g (*0-9637288-7-3*) River Walker Bks.

El Nuevo Nido de Big Bird. (SPA.). (ps-3). 1993. pap. 4.95 (*0-307-52060-9*, Golden Pr) Western Pub.

Nystrom, Carolyn. The Lark Who Had No Song. McElrath-Eslick, Lori, illus. 32p. (ps-6). 1991. 11.95 (*0-7459-1879-4*) Lion USA.

Oana, Katherine. Lori Lamb. Baird, Tate, ed. Burtick, Lyn M., illus. 16p. (Orig.). (ps-k). 1989. pap. 4.52 (*0-914127-09-8*) Univ Class.

O'Huigin, Sean. King of the Birds. Dixon, Tom, illus. 36p. (ps-5). 1992. pap. 4.95 (*0-88753-168-7*, Pub. by Black Moss Pr CN) Firefly Bks Ltd.

Oriev, Uri. Island on Bird Street. (gr. 4-7). 1992. pap. 4.95 (*0-395-61623-9*) HM.

Ostheeren, Ingrid. Jonathan Mouse & the Baby Bird. Mathieu, Agnes, illus. Lanning, Rosemary, tr. from GER. LC 91-6614. (Illus.). 32p. (gr. k-3). 1991. 14.95 (*1-55858-108-1*) North-South Bks NYC.

Parkison, Ralph F. The Little Girl, the Lillipop, & the Green Bird, Bk. 1. Withrow, Marion O., ed. Bush, William, illus. 31p. (Orig.). (gr. 2-6). 1988. pap. 4.25 (*0-929949-00-5*) Little Wood Bks.

Patent, Dorothy H. Whooping Crane. (gr. 4-7). 1993. pap. 6.95 (*0-395-66505-1*, Clarion Bks) HM.

Pearson, Susan. Lenore's Big Break. Carlson, Nancy, illus. 32p. (gr. k up). 1992. PLB 14.00 (*0-670-83474-2*) Viking Child Bks.

Peet, Bill. Fly Homer Fly. Peet, Bill, illus. (gr. k-3). 1976. 14.95 (*0-395-24536-2*); pap. 4.80 (*0-395-28005-2*) HM.

Pellowski, Michael J. Maxwell Finds a Friend. Kennedy, Anne, illus. LC 85-14085. 48p. (Orig.). (gr. 1-3). 1986. PLB 10.59 (*0-8167-0586-0*); pap. text ed. 3.50 (*0-8167-0587-9*) Troll Assocs.

Percy, Graham. Max & the Very Rare Bird. (Illus.). 32p. 1991. 15.95 (*0-89565-786-4*) Childs World.

Plum, K. D. Fly Away Home. Dugan, Karen, illus. 26p. (ps). 1994. 10.95 (*0-8431-3687-1*) Price Stern.

Pochocki, Ethel. The Gypsies' Tale. Kelly, Laura, illus. LC 93-3320. (gr. 4 up). 1994. pap. 15.00 (*0-671-79934-7*, S&S BFYR) S&S Trade.

Potter, Beatrix. Madame Trotte-Menu. (FRE., Illus.). 58p. 1990. 9.95 (*0-7859-3634-3*, 2070561054) Fr & Eur.

—Panache Petitgris. (FRE.). 59p. 1990. 10.95 (*2-07-056102-X*) Schoenhof.

Rees, Claudia. The Bird with the Word Talks about Self-Control. Rees, Claudia, illus. (Orig.). (gr. 1-3). 1987. pap. 0.98 (*0-89274-451-0*) Harrison Hse.

Richmond, Gary. The Early Bird. 32p. 1992. 7.99 (*0-8499-0924-4*) Word Inc.

Roberts, Sarah. Don't Cry, Big Bird. Leigh, Tom, illus. LC 81-4075. 40p. (gr. k-2). 1981. 4.95 (*0-394-84868-3*) Random Bks Yng Read.

—Don't Cry, Big Bird. Leigh, Tom, illus. LC 81-4075. 40p. (ps-3). 1993. pap. 2.99 (*0-679-83950-X*) Random Bks Yng Read.

Rockwell, Norman. Willie Was Different. Rockwell, Norman, illus. LC 94-8785. 1994. write for info. (*0-936399-61-9*) Berkshire Hse.

Rogers, Mary. Baby Birds. 33p. (ps-k). 1992. pap. text ed. 23.00 big bk. (*1-56843-003-5*); pap. text ed. 4.50 (*1-56843-053-1*) BGR Pub.

Rohmann, Eric. Time Flies. LC 93-28200. (Illus.). 32p. (ps-4). 1994. 15.00 (*0-517-59598-2*); lib. bdg. 15.99 (*0-517-59599-0*) Crown Bks Yng Read.

Ross, Anna. Big Bird's Big Bike. Cooke, Tom, illus. LC 92-60305. 22p. (ps). 1993. 3.25 (*0-679-83271-8*) Random Bks Yng Read.

Rossetti, Christina. Fly Away, Fly Away over the Sea. Watts, Bernadette, illus. LC 90-42738. 32p. (ps-k). 1991. 14.95 (*1-55858-101-4*) North-South Bks NYC.

Rotton, Wendy & Salvadeo, Michele B. The Ill-Tempered Crane. (Illus.). 48p. (gr. 3-5). 1994. pap. 6.95 (*1-56721-060-0*) Twnty-Fifth Cent Pr.

Santos, Elsie S. The Master of Song. Santos, Duarte S., illus. 44p. (Orig.). (ps-1). 1984. pap. 4.95 (*0-914151-02-9*) E S Santos.

Santos, Nina D. Strangers on the Mountain. 128p. 1991. pap. 22.00x (*0-85088-665-1*, Pub. by Gomer Pr UK) St Mut.

Scholes, Katherine. The Landing: A Night of Birds. Wong, David, illus. 72p. (gr. 4 up). 1989. 12.95 (*0-385-26191-8*, Zephyr-BFYR) Doubleday.

—The Landing: A Night of Birds. Wong, David, illus. 71p. (gr. 4-7). 1994. 14.95 (*0-85572-165-0*, Pub. by Hill Content Pubng AT) Seven Hills Bk Dists.

Schutzer, Dena. Polka & Dot. Schutzer, Dena, illus. LC 93-29935. 1994. 14.00 (*0-679-84192-X*); PLB 14.99 (*0-679-94192-4*) Knopf Bks Yng Read.

Searcy, Margaret Z. Race of Flitty Hummingbird & Flappy Crane. (Illus.). (gr. 2-4). 1980. 7.50 (*0-916620-21-2*) Portals Pr.

Sesame Street: A Bird's Best Friend. 24p. (ps-3). 1991. write for info. (*0-307-14155-1*, 14155) Western Pub.

Sesame Street: Big Bird's Adventure. 24p. (ps-3). 1991. write for info. (*0-307-14170-5*, 14170) Western Pub.

Sesame Street: Early Bird on Sesame Street. 24p. (ps-3). 1991. write for info. (*0-307-14169-1*, 14169) Western Pub.

Sherwood, Jonathan & Farrington, Liz. Red Poppies for a Little Bird. McGovern, Brian, illus. 40p. (gr. k-4). 1993. 14.95 (*1-56844-005-7*) Enchante Pub.

Silver, Jody. Rupert, Polly & Daisy. Silver, Jody, illus. LC 83-24979. 48p. (ps-3). 1984. 5.95 (*0-8193-1124-3*) Parents.

Smith, Duane. Heritage Revealed Series for Younger Readers, 3 Bks. 1994. Set. pap. 13.95 (*1-886218-00-5*); The Legend of the Golden Hawk. pap. 4.95 (*0-9632074-1-5*); Journey to Clay Mountain. pap. 4.95 (*0-9632074-2-3*); Lost on Victoria Lake. pap. 4.95 (*0-9632074-3-1*) Azimuth Ga. Introducing THE HERITAGE REVEALED SERIES FOR YOUNGER READERS! These three stories of cultural understanding & identity from the author of the critically acclaimed novel, THE NUBIAN, are designed for children ages 7 through 14. THE LEGEND OF THE GOLDEN HAWK: A wild hawk becomes trapped in a game preserve. During his capture he loses his memory, & struggles with the despair of his captivity until he is miraculously rescued by the faithfulness of his brother. JOURNEY TO CLAY MOUNTAIN: A small village at the base of a mountain range is dominated by the shadows from the largest of these, the Clay Mountain. The villagers toil in frustration until a young boy discovers the wonderful secret of the Clay Mountain, a secret which has been hidden for centuries. LOST...ON VICTORIA LAKE: Two children are cast adrift in their father's fishing boat during a storm. They are rescued by the guidance & provision of their royal ancestors, who appear to the children in a series of magnificent visions. For order information, call 1-800-373-5000 or write to the Azimuth Press, 3002 Dayna Dr, College Park, GA 30349. *Publisher Provided Annotation.*

Smucker, Anna E. Outside the Window. Schuett, Stacey, illus. LC 92-33452. 1994. 15.00 (*0-679-84023-0*); PLB 15.99 (*0-679-94023-5*) Knopf Bks Yng Read.

Snell, Gordon. Cruncher Sparrow's Flying School. O'Cleary, Michael, illus. 76p. (Orig.). (gr. 2-6). 1991. pap. 6.95 (*1-85371-163-2*, Pub. by Poolbeg Pr ER) Dufour.

Snyder, Zilpha K. And Condors Danced. LC 87-5364. 216p. (gr. 4-6). 1987. 14.95 (*0-385-29575-8*) Delacorte.

—And Condors Danced. 224p. (gr. k-6). 1989. pap. 3.50 (*0-440-40153-4*, YB) Dell.

Sobel, Barbara. The Little Bird. Neulinger, Karen, illus. LC 86-81462. 32p. (gr. k-2). 1986. PLB 7.59 (*0-87386-018-7*); pap. 1.95 (*0-87386-014-4*) Jan Prods.

Sommers, Tish. A Bird's Best Friend. Swanson, Maggie, illus. 32p. (ps-k). 1986. write for info. (*0-307-12018-X*, Pub. by Golden Bks) Western Pub.

Stobbs, William. Who Killed Cock Robin? (Illus.). 28p. (ps up). 1990. bds. 12.95 (*0-19-279862-6*) OUP.

Stolp, Hans. Golden Bird. (gr. 4-7). 1992. pap. 3.50 (*0-440-40611-0*) Dell.

Talbert, Marc. Dead Birds Singing. (gr. 7 up). 1988. pap. 2.95 (*0-440-20036-9*, LFL) Dell.

Tate, Suzanne. Salty Seagull: A Tale of an Old Salt. Melvin, James, illus. LC 92-60375. 28p. (Orig.). (gr. k-3). 1992. pap. 3.95 (*1-878405-06-3*) Nags Head Art.

Thackray, Patricia. Fanny McFancy: A Passion for Fashion. Forrest, Sandra, illus. LC 91-16447. 40p. 1991. 12.95 (*0-671-74980-3*, Green Tiger) S&S Trade.

Thomas, Carol. When the Nightingale Sings. Lilly, Charles, illus. LC 92-6045. 160p. (gr. 7 up). 1994. pap. 3.95 (*0-06-440524-9*, Trophy) HarpC Child Bks.

Tibo, Gilles. Simon et la Petite Plume Cassee. LC 94-60138. (FRE., Illus.). 24p. (gr. k-4). 1994. 10.95 (*0-88776-341-3*) Tundra Bks.

—Simon Finds a Feather. LC 94-60134. (Illus.). 24p. (gr. k-4). 1994. 10.95 (*0-88776-340-5*) Tundra Bks.

Tilly, Jim. Puffin: A Journey Home. Sagan, Alexander, illus. 32p. 1993. 14.95 (*0-9635083-3-4*) Misty Mtn.

Tolan, Stephanie. A Time to Fly Free. LC 90-31676. 176p. (gr. 3-7). 1990. pap. 3.95 (*0-689-71420-3*, Aladdin) Macmillan Child Grp.

Tolstoy, Leo. Varya & Her Greenfinch. Klein, Erika, illus. (ps-2). 1988. 7.95 (*0-86315-043-8*, 20238) Gryphon Hse.

Torres, Leyla. Gorrion Del Metro: Subway Sparrow. (ps-3). 1993. pap. 15.00 (*0-374-32756-4*) FS&G.

—Subway Sparrow. LC 92-55104. (ENG, SPA & POL.). 1993. 15.00 (*0-374-37285-3*) FS&G.

Tusa, Tricia. Maebelle's Suitcase. Tusa, Tricia, illus. LC 86-12434. 32p. (gr. k-3). 1987. SBE 13.95 (*0-02-789250-6*, Macmillan Child Bk) Macmillan Child Grp.

Van den Berg, Marinus. The Three Birds: A Story for Children about the Loss of a Loved One. LC 93-38734. (Illus.). 24p. (ps-3). 1994. pap. 8.95 (*0-945354-59-2*) Magination Pr.

—The Three Birds: A Story for Children about the Loss of a Loved One. Ireland, Sandra, illus. LC 93-38211. 32p. (ps up). 1994. PLB 17.27 (*0-8368-1072-4*) Gareth Stevens Inc.

Vesey, Amanda. Duncan & the Bird. LC 92-37335. 1993. 18.95 (*0-87614-785-6*) Carolrhoda Bks.

Weinberger, Jane. Cory the Cormorant. LC 91-68128. (Illus.). 40p. (ps-4). 1992. pap. 9.95 (*0-932433-92-8*) Windswept Hse.

—Stormy. Kardas, Alek, illus. LC 85-62021. 54p. (gr. 1-6). 1985. 5.95 (*0-932433-13-8*) Windswept Hse.

Wender, Leon. Little Brown Roadrunner: Who Did It Herself. O'Connor, Claiborne, illus. LC 92-72166. 24p. (Orig.). (gr. 1-3). 1992. pap. text ed. 4.00 (*0-938513-14-1*) Amador Pubs.

West, Colin. Go Tell It to the Toucan. West, Colin, illus. (ps-3). 1990. PLB 8.95 (*0-553-05889-4*, Little Rooster) Bantam.

Wetterer, Margaret K. The Boy Who Knew the Language of the Birds. Wright, Beth, illus. 48p. (gr. k-4). 1991. PLB 17.50 (*0-87614-652-3*) Carolrhoda Bks.

Wetzel, Rick & Swanson, Maggie. Un Cuento Para la Hora De Dormir De Big Bird. Guibert, Rita, tr. from ENG. Wetzel, Rick & Swanson, Maggie, illus. LC 92-3815. (SPA.). 32p. (ps-3). 1992. pap. 2.25 (*0-679-83500-8*) Random Bks Yng Read.

Whittemore, E. M. Delia, the Bluebird of Mulberry Bend. 1980. pap. 2.99 (*0-88019-017-5*) Schmul Pub Co.

Widman, Christine. The Hummingbird Garden. Ransome, James, illus. LC 91-27338. 32p. (gr. k-3). 1993. RSBE 14.95 (*0-02-792761-X*, Macmillan Child Bk) Macmillan Child Grp.

Wiggin, Kate D. The Birds' Christmas Carol. (Orig.). (gr. k-6). 1988. pap. 3.50 (*0-440-40121-6*, Pub. by Yearling Classics) Dell.

Wildsmith, Brian. The Apple Bird. (Illus.). 16p. 1987. pap. 2.95 (*0-19-272136-4*) OUP.

Williams, Julie S. And the Birds Appeared. Burningham, Robin Y., illus. 32p. (ps-3). 1988. 8.95 (*0-8248-1194-1*, Kolowalu Bk) UH Pr.

Wren. 1923. pap. 1.75 (*0-440-79704-7*) Dell.

Ziefert, Harriet. Finding Robin Redbreast. 1988. pap. 4.95 (*0-14-050839-2*, Puffin) Puffin Bks.

BIRDS–FLIGHT

see Flight

BIRDS–HABITS AND BEHAVIOR

Arnold, Caroline. Ostriches & Other Flightless Birds. Hewett, Richard R., illus. 48p. (gr. 2-5). 1990. PLB 19.95 (*0-87614-377-X*) Carolrhoda Bks.

Cousteau Society Staff. Albatross. LC 92-34179. (Illus.). (ps-1). 1993. pap. 3.95 POB (*0-671-86565-X*, Little Simon) S&S Trade.

Hoffman, Mary. Bird of Prey. LC 86-17832. (Illus.). 24p. (gr. k-5). 1987. PLB 9.95 (*0-8172-2701-6*); pap. 3.95 (*0-8114-6872-0*) Raintree Steck-V.

Horton, et al. Amazing Fact Book of Birds. (Illus.). 32p. 1987. PLB 14.95 (*0-87191-842-0*) Creative Ed.

Johnson, Sylvia A. Albatrosses of Midway Island. Lanting, Frans, illus. 48p. (gr. 2-5). 1990. PLB 19.95 (*0-87614-391-5*) Carolrhoda Bks.

Kalman, Bobbie. Birds at My Feeder. (Illus.). 56p. (gr. 3-4). 1987. 15.95 (*0-86505-167-4*); pap. 7.95 (*0-86505-187-9*) Crabtree Pub Co.

Losito, Linda, et al. Birds: Aerial Hunters. (Illus.). 96p. 1989. 17.95x (*0-8160-1963-0*) Facts on File.

—Birds: The Plant- & Seed-Eaters. (Illus.). 96p. 1989. 17.95x (*0-8160-1964-9*) Facts on File.

MacDonald, Sandra. Birds at the Sanctuary. 8p. (gr. k-2). 1993. pap. write for info. (*1-882563-03-4*) Lamont Bks.

Moncure, Jane B. Life Cycles: The Singing Mailbox. Lexa-Senning, Susan, illus. LC 89-24000. 32p. (ps-2). 1990. PLB 14.95 (*0-89565-552-7*) Childs World.

Morris, Dean. Birds. rev. ed. LC 87-16672. (Illus.). 48p. (gr. 2-6). 1987. PLB 10.95 (*0-8172-3203-6*) Raintree Steck-V.

Raintree Publishers Staff. Birds. LC 87-28786. (Illus.). 64p. (Orig.). (gr. 5-9). 1988. PLB 11.95 (*0-8172-3084-X*) Raintree Steck-V.

BIRDS–MIGRATION

Gans, Roma. Bird Migration. Date not set. 13.95 (*0-06-020224-6*, HarpT); PLB 13.89 (*0-06-020225-4*, HarpT) HarpC.

Grubbs, J., ed. Where Do the Birds Go When It Storms. Abell, J. & Abell, J., illus. (gr. 1-3). 1992. lib. bdg. 25.00 (*1-56611-012-2*); pap. 15.00 (*0-685-66201-2*) Jonas.

Oram, Liz & Baker, R. Robin. Bird Migration. LC 91-12120. (Illus.). 48p. (gr. 4-8). 1992. PLB 22.80 (*0-8114-2925-3*) Raintree Steck-V.

Peters, L. This Way Home. (gr. 4 up). 1994. 14.95 (*0-8050-1368-7*) H Holt & Co.

BIRDS–PICTURES, ILLUSTRATIONS, ETC.

Gise, Joanne. A Picture Book of Birds. Pistolesi, Roseanna, illus. LC 89-37328. 24p. (gr. 1-4). 1990. lib. bdg. 9.59 (*0-8167-1898-9*); pap. text ed. 2.50 (*0-8167-1899-7*) Troll Assocs.

Kindersley, Dorling. Birds. Kindersley, Dorling, illus. LC 92-8601. 24p. (ps-k). 1992. pap. 7.95 POB (*0-689-71644-3*, Aladdin) Macmillan Child Grp.

Reilly, Pauline. Echidna. Rolland, Will, illus. 32p. (Orig.). 1993. pap. 6.95 (*0-86417-285-0*, Pub. by Kangaroo Pr AT) Seven Hills Bk Dists.

—Galah. Rolland, Will, illus. 32p. (Orig.). 1993. pap. 6.95 (*0-86417-346-6*, Pub. by Kangaroo Pr AT) Seven Hills Bk Dists.

—Kiwi. Rolland, Will, illus. 32p. (Orig.). 1993. pap. 6.95 (*0-86417-488-8*, Pub. by Kangaroo Pr AT) Seven Hills Bk Dists.

—Kookabura That Helps at the Nest. Rolland, Will, illus. 32p. (Orig.). 1993. pap. 6.95 (*0-86417-119-6*, Pub. by Kangaroo Pr AT) Seven Hills Bk Dists.

—Lyrebird That Is Too Busy to Dance. Rolland, Will, illus. 32p. (Orig.). 1993. pap. 6.95 (*0-86417-086-6*, Pub. by Kangaroo Pr AT) Seven Hills Bk Dists.

—Mallefowl: The Incubator Bird. Rolland, Will, illus. 32p. (Orig.). 1993. pap. 6.95 (*0-86417-317-2*, Pub. by Kangaroo Pr AT) Seven Hills Bk Dists.

BIRDS–POETRY

Carter, Ann, compiled by. Birds, Beasts, & Fishes: A Selection of Animal Poems. Cartwright, Reg, illus. Carter, Ann, intros. by. LC 90-21493. (Illus.). 64p. (ps up). 1991. SBE 16.95 (*0-02-717776-9*, Macmillan Child Bk) Macmillan Child Grp.

O'Malley, Kevin. Who Killed Cock Robin? LC 92-40340. (Illus.). (gr. k-3). 1993. 15.00 (*0-688-12430-5*); PLB 14.93 (*0-688-12431-3*) Lothrop.

Smith, John F. The Song of the Whango-Whee. Colon, Odette E., illus. Hannaford, Joey, contrib. by. (Illus.). 24p. (ps-5). 1993. 14.95 (*1-884375-00-6*) Chinky-Po Tree.

BIRDS–PROTECTION

Heilman, Joan R. Bluebird Rescue: A Harrowsmith Country Life Nature Guide. rev. ed. LC 91-40618. (Illus.). 48p. (gr. 10 up). 1992. lib. bdg. 16.95 (*0-944475-27-2*); pap. 6.95 (*0-944475-24-8*) Camden Hse Pub.

Maynard, Thane. Saving Endangered Birds: Ensuring a Future in the Wild. (Illus.). 56p. (gr. 5-7). 1993. 15.95 (*0-531-15260-X*); PLB 15.90 (*0-531-11094-X*) Watts.

BIRDS' EGGS

see Birds–Eggs and Nests

BIRDS' NESTS

see Birds–Eggs and Nests

BIRDS OF PREY

see also names of birds of prey, e.g. Eagles, etc.

Barrett, Norman S. Birds of Prey. LC 90-46306. (Illus.). 32p. (gr. k-4). 1991. PLB 11.90 (*0-531-14151-9*) Watts.

Birds of Prey. 1991. PLB 14.95 (*0-88682-332-3*) Creative Ed.

Gray, Ian. Birds of Prey. LC 90-33768. (Illus.). 32p. (gr. 2-4). 1991. PLB 12.40 (*0-531-18367-X*, Pub. by Bookwright Pr) Watts.

Hoffman, Mary. Bird of Prey. LC 86-17832. (Illus.). 24p. (gr. k-5). 1987. PLB 9.95 (*0-8172-2701-6*); pap. 3.95 (*0-8114-6872-0*) Raintree Steck-V.

Parry-Jones, Jemima. Amazing Birds of Prey. Dunning, Mike, photos by. LC 92-909. (Illus.). 32p. (Orig.). (gr. 1-5). 1992. PLB 9.99 (*0-679-92771-9*); pap. 7.99 (*0-679-82771-4*) Knopf Bks Yng Read.

Selsam, Millicent E. & Hunt, Joyce. A First Look at Owls, Eagles, & Other Hunters of the Sky. Springer, Harriet, illus. 32p. (gr. 6-9). 1986. 10.95 (*0-8027-6625-0*); PLB 10.85 (*0-8027-6642-0*) Walker & Co.

Stone, Lynn. Birds. LC 92-34485. 1993. 12.67 (*0-86625-440-4*); 9.50s.p. (*0-685-66270-5*) Rourke Pubns.

Stone, Lynn M. Birds of Prey. LC 82-17909. (Illus.). 48p. (gr. k-4). 1983. PLB 12.85 (*0-516-01676-8*); pap. 4.95 (*0-516-41676-6*) Childrens.

Wildlife Education, Ltd. Staff. Birds of Prey. Goldman, Kenneth, et al, illus. 20p. (Orig.). (gr. 5 up). 1980. pap. 2.75 (*0-937934-01-1*) Wildlife Educ.

BIRMINGHAM, ALABAMA

White, Marjorie L. Downtown Discovery Tour. rev. ed. (Illus.). 44p. (Orig.). (gr. 3-9). 1984. pap. 5.00 (*0-317-42237-5*) Birmingham Hist Soc.

White, Marjorie L. & Shannon, Katherine. Five Points Heritage Hike Guide. (Illus.). 32p. (Orig.). (gr. 3-9). 1983. pap. 2.00 (*0-685-11943-2*) Birmingham Hist Soc.

BIRTH

see Childbirth

BIRTH CONTROL

Benson, Michael. Coping with Birth Control. rev. ed. Benson, Roger, ed. (gr. 4-7). 1992. PLB 14.95 (*0-8239-1489-5*) Rosen Group.

Emmens, Carol A. The Abortion Controversy. 128p. 1987. lib. bdg. 5.95 (*0-671-64209-X*, J Messner); lib. bdg. 12.98 (*0-671-62284-6*) S&S Trade.

Terkel, Susan N. Abortion: Facing the Issues. Rosoff, Iris, ed. LC 88-14288. (Illus.). 160p. (gr. 7 up). 1988. PLB 13.40 (*0-531-10565-2*) Watts.

Watson, Jane W. World in Danger - Too Many People! (Illus.). 80p. (Orig.). (gr. 4-6). 1994. pap. 8.95 (*1-56474-099-4*) Fithian Pr.

Whitelaw, Nancy. Margaret Sanger: Every Child a Wanted Child. LC 93-13635. (Illus.). 160p. (gr. 4 up). 1994. text ed. 13.95 RSBE (*0-87518-581-9*, Dillon) Macmillan Child Grp.

BIRTHDAYS

De Beer, Hans. Little Polar Bear Birthday Book. De Beer, Hans, illus. 120p. 1990. 7.95 (*1-55858-081-6*) North-South Bks NYC.

Fass, Bernie & Caggiano, Rosemary. Happy Birthday Party Time. 48p. (gr. k-6). 1976. pap. 14.95 (*0-86704-002-5*) Clarus Music.

Gibbons, Gail. Happy Birthday! LC 86-297. (Illus.). 32p. (ps-3). 1986. reinforced bdg. 15.95 (*0-8234-0614-8*) Holiday.

Green, Laurel & Beck, Trudy. My Birthday Memories. Nebeker, Kinde, illus. (ps-12). 1985. 5.00 (*0-9613079-1-9*) Greenbeck.

Haywood, Carolyn. Happy Birthday from Carolyn Haywood. (gr. 2-4). 1987. pap. 2.95 (*0-8167-1040-6*) Troll Assocs.

Jenny, Gerri. Birthday Parties for Children: Activities, Games, Cakes & Fun for Children from 4-10. Macdonald, Roland B. & Gray, Dan, illus. 128p. (gr. k-5). 1991. pap. 9.95 (*1-878767-15-1*) Murdoch Bks.

Moncure, Jane B. Our Birthday Book. Endres, Helen, illus. LC 86-30976. 32p. (ps-3). 1987. PLB 13.95 (*0-89565-349-4*) Childs World.

Montgomery, Lucy M. Anne of Green Gables Birthday Book. Mills, Lauren, illus. 1990. 8.95 (*0-7704-2362-0*) Bantam.

Motomora, Mitchell. Happy Birthday! (Illus.). 32p. (gr. 1-4). 1989. PLB 18.99 (*0-8172-3510-8*); pap. 3.95 (*0-8114-6706-6*) Raintree Steck-V.

Murphy, Elspeth C. It's My Birthday, God: Psalm 90. Nelson, Jane, illus. (ps-2). 1983. misc. format 3.99 (*0-89191-580-X*, Chariot Bks) Chariot Family.

Neilson, Gena, illus. It's Your Birthday. (ps-1). 1986. spiral bdg. 9.95 (*0-937763-03-9*) Lauri Inc.

Paxton, Lenore & Siadi, Phillip. Happy B-I-R-T-H-DAY: A Sing, Color, 'n Say Fun Book-Tape Package. Lindsay, Warren & Huntoon, Cathy, illus. 32p. (ps-3). 1992. pap. 6.95 incl. tape (*1-880449-02-1*) Wrldkids Pr.

Perl, Lila. Candles, Cakes, & Donkey Tails: Birthday Symbols & Celebrations. De Larrea, Victoria, illus. LC 84-5803. 80p. (gr. 3-6). 1984. (Clarion Bks) HM.

Smith, Dian G. Happy Birthday to Me! A Four-Year Record Book for Birthday Boys & Girls. Franc-Nohain, Marie M., illus. 48p. (gr. 2-5). 1989. 9.95 (*0-684-19046-X*, Scribners Young Read) Macmillan Child Grp.

Vowles, Andrew & Illingworth, Lynn. My Birthday Book. Williams, Harland, illus. 32p. (gr. 1-5). 1985. pap. 2.95 (*0-88625-061-7*) Durkin Hayes Pub.

Ziefert, Harriet. What's a Birthday? Schumacher, Claire, illus. 16p. (ps-k). 1993. 5.95 (*0-694-00380-8*, Festival) HarpC Child Bks.

BIRTHDAYS–FICTION

Ada, Alma F. Serafina's Birthday. Bates, Louise, illus. LC 91-15389. 32p. (ps-2). 1992. SBE 13.95 (*0-689-31516-3*, Atheneum Child Bk) Macmillan Child Grp.

Allen, Helen S. A Birthday Letter to Lynn: Mandy Learns to Make a Cake. 16p. (ps). 1992. pap. text ed. 5.00 (*1-881907-04-X*) Two Bytes Pub.

Anderson, Honey & Reinholtd, Bill. Getting the Mail. Fleming, Leanne, illus. LC 92-34338. 1993. 3.75 (*0-383-03624-0*) SRA Schl Grp.

Anholt, Laurence & Anholt, Catherine. Can You Guess? A Lift-the-Flap Birthday Party Book. 16p. (ps-1). 1993. pap. 4.99 (*0-14-054951-X*, Puffin) Puffin Bks.

Argent, Kerry. Happy Birthday, Wombat! A Lift-the-Flap Book. (ps). 1991. 11.95 (*0-316-05097-0*, Joy St Bks) Little.

Awdry, W. Happy Birthday, Thomas! A Step 1 Book - Preschool-Gr 1. Bell, Owain, illus. LC 89-49649. 32p. (Orig.). (ps-1). 1990. lib. bdg. 7.99 (*0-679-90809-9*); pap. 3.50 (*0-679-80809-4*) Random Bks Yng Read.

Bailey, Bobbi M. Emma's Happy Birthday Piano. DeFazio, Deborah, illus. 36p. (gr. k-4). 1991. pap. 7.95 (*0-9625005-1-8*) Wee Pr.

Barker, Marjorie. Magical Hands. Yoshi, illus. LC 89-31373. 32p. (ps up). 1991. pap. 14.95 (*0-88708-103-7*) Picture Bk Studio.

Barklem, Jill. The Brambley Hedge Birthday Book. Barklem, Jill, illus. 128p. (gr. k up). 1994. 12.95 (*0-399-22669-9*, Philomel) Putnam Pub Group.

Barnett, Ada, et al. Eddycat Attends Sunshine's Birthday Party. Hoffmann, Mark, illus. LC 92-56881. 1993. PLB 17.27 (*0-8368-0943-2*) Gareth Stevens Inc.

Barrett, Judi. Benjamin's 365 Birthdays. 2nd ed. Barrett, Ron, illus. LC 92-2497. 40p. (ps-1). 1992. pap. 4.95 (*0-689-71635-4*, Aladdin) Macmillan Child Grp.

are excellent." - E. Paul Torrance, Georgia Studies of Creative Behavior. "Pixel encourages the child to enjoy childhood. The imaginary world of children is recreated in this ageless story." (Educat Curriculum Product Review) To order: Pixel Products & Pub., RD #2, Box C110, Lock Haven, PA 17745. Trade discounts. Libraries/ schools/bookstores 40%. Distributors 50%. $1.75 P&H. Add $.50 for each additional book.
Publisher Provided Annotation.

Bender, Robert. The Preposterous Rhinoceros, or, Alvin's Beastly Birthday. LC 93-14200. 1994. 14.95 (*0-8050-2806-4*) H Holt & Co.

Berenstain, Stan & Berenstain, Jan. The Berenstain Bears & The Green-Eyed Monster. LC 93-50109. (gr. 1 up). 1995. write for info. (*0-679-96434-7*) Random Bks Yng Read.

Berenstain, Stan & Berenstain, Janice. The Berenstain Bears & Too Much Birthday. Berenstain, Stan & Berenstain, Janice, illus. LC 85-14529. 32p. (ps-1). 1986. pap. 2.25 (*0-394-87332-7*) Random Bks Yng Read.

Blocksma, Mary. Grandma Dragon's Birthday. Kalthoff, Sandra C., illus. LC 82-19851. 24p. (ps-2). 1983. pap. 3.95 (*0-516-41582-4*) Childrens.

The Bonnie Little Birthday Book. (ps-3). 6.95 (*0-87741-005-4*) Makepeace Colony.

Bradford, Clare. Birthday Wishes. Rees, Genevieve, illus. LC 93-20804. 1994. 4.25 (*0-383-03737-9*) SRA Schl Grp.

Brown, Marc T. Arthur's Birthday. (ps-3). 1991. pap. 4.95 (*0-316-11074-4*) Little.

Bunting, Eve. Flower Garden. Hewitt, Kathryn, illus. LC 92-25766. 1994. 13.95 (*0-15-228776-0*) HarBrace.

Cameron, Ann. Julian, Dream Doctor. Strugnell, Ann, illus. LC 89-37562. 64p. (Orig.). (gr. 2-4). 1993. PLB 7.99 (*0-679-90524-3*); pap. 2.99 (*0-679-80524-9*) Random Bks Yng Read.

—Julian, Dream Doctor. 46p. 1992. text ed. 3.68 (*1-56956-116-8*) W A T Braille.

Carlstrom, Nancy W. Happy Birthday, Jesse Bear! Degen, Bruce, illus. LC 93-25180. (ps-1). 1994. 14.95 (*0-02-717277-5*, Macmillan Child Bk) Macmillan Child Grp.

Carrick, Carol. Paul's Christmas Birthday. Carrick, Donald, illus. LC 77-28408. 32p. (gr. k-3). 1978. PLB 13.88 (*0-688-84159-7*) Greenwillow.

Cartlidge, Michelle. Mouse Birthday. Cartlidge, Michelle, illus. 24p. (ps). 1994. 4.99 (*0-525-45237-0*) Dutton Child Bks.

Caseley, Judith. Three Happy Birthdays. LC 88-18788. (Illus.). 32p. (ps up). 1989. 12.95 (*0-688-08179-7*); PLB 12.88 (*0-688-08180-0*) Greenwillow.

—Three Happy Birthdays. LC 92-24583. 40p. (gr. 1 up). 1993. pap. 4.95 (*0-688-11699-X*, Mulberry) Morrow.

Cazet, Denys. A Fish in His Pocket. LC 87-5462. (Illus.). 32p. (ps-2). 1991. pap. 4.95 (*0-531-07021-2*) Orchard Bks Watts.

Charlip, Remy & Miller, Mary B. Handtalk Birthday: A Number & Story Book in Sign Language. Ancona, George, illus. LC 86-22755. 48p. (ps up). 1987. SBE 15.95 (*0-02-718080-8*, Four Winds) Macmillan Child Grp.

Christelow, Eileen. Don't Wake up Mama! Another Five Little Monkeys Story. Christelow, Eileen, illus. 32p. (ps-3). 1992. 13.95 (*0-395-60176-2*, Clarion Bks) HM.

Clarke, Gus. How Many Days to My Birthday? LC 91-53022. (Illus.). 32p. (ps up). 1992. 14.00 (*0-688-11236-6*); PLB 13.93 (*0-688-11237-4*) Lothrop.

Cohen, Barbara. Make a Wish, Molly. Jones, Jan N., illus. LC 93-17901. 1994. 14.95 (*0-385-31079-X*) Delacorte.

Cummings, Pat. Carousel. Cummings, Pat, illus. LC 93-8708. 32p. (ps-3). 1994. RSBE 14.95 (*0-02-725512-3*, Bradbury Pr) Macmillan Child Grp.

Davidson, Nicole. Surprise Party. 192p. (Orig.). (gr. 5). 1993. pap. 3.50 (*0-380-76996-4*, Flare) Avon.

De Brunhoff, Laurent. Babar's Birthday Surprise. LC 74-123071. (Illus.). 36p. (ps-2). 1970. Repr. of 1970 ed. 12.00 (*0-394-80591-7*) Random Bks Yng Read.

Delton, Judy. Birthday Bike for Brimhall. (ps-3). 1991. pap. 2.99 (*0-440-40461-4*) Dell.

—Birthday Bike for Brimhall. LC 83-21025. (Illus.). 56p. (gr. k-4). 1985. 14.95 (*0-87614-256-0*) Carolrhoda Bks.

Devlin, Wende & Devlin, Harry. Cranberry Birthday. Devlin, Wende & Devlin, Harry, illus. LC 88-294. 40p. (gr. k-3). 1988. RSBE 13.95 (*0-02-729210-X*, Four Winds) Macmillan Child Grp.

—Cranberry Birthday. Devlin, Harry, illus. LC 92-23541. 40p. (ps-3). 1993. pap. 4.95 (*0-689-71697-4*, Aladdin) Macmillan Child Grp.

Dhanjal, Beryl. Sarah's Birthday Surprise. (Illus.). 25p. (gr. 2-4). 1991. 15.95 (*0-237-60158-3*, Pub. by Evans Bros Ltd) Trafalgar.

Dicks, Terrance. Goliath's Birthday. Littlewood, Valerie, illus. 52p. (gr. 2-5). 1992. pap. 3.50 (*0-8120-4821-0*) Barron.

Disney, Walt, Productions Staff. The Mickey Mouse Birthday Book. LC 78-55911. (Illus.). (ps-3). 1978. 3.95 (*0-394-83963-3*); lib. bdg. 4.99 (*0-394-93963-8*) Random Bks Yng Read.

Dorflinger, Carolyn. Tomorrow Is Mom's Birthday. Trapani, Iza, illus. LC 93-19607. 32p. (ps-3). 1994. reinforced smythe sewn 14.95 (*1-879085-84-4*) Whsprng Coyote Pr.

Drew, David. When I Turned Six. Gouldthorpe, Peter, illus. LC 93-26929. 1994. 4.25 (*0-383-03784-0*) SRA Schl Grp.

Dr. Seuss. Happy Birthday to You. Dr. Seuss, illus. (gr. 1-5). 1959. 14.00 (*0-394-80076-1*); PLB 13.99 (*0-394-90076-6*) Random Bks Yng Read.

Duncan, Lois. Birthday Moon. (ps-3). 1991. pap. 3.95 (*0-14-050876-7*, Puffin) Puffin Bks.

Eisenberg, Lisa. Happy Birthday, Lexie. 144p. (gr. 3-7). 1991. 12.95 (*0-670-83553-6*) Viking Child Bks.

—Happy Birthday, Lexie. 144p. (gr. 3-7). 1993. pap. 3.99 (*0-14-034568-X*) Puffin Bks.

ETR Associates Staff. Ellie's Birthday. Paley, Nina, illus. LC 92-8358. 1992. write for info. (*1-56071-106-X*) ETR Assocs.

Ferguson, Virginia & Durkin, Peter. Waiting. Fleming, Leanne, illus. LC 92-34336. 1993. 3.75 (*0-383-03663-1*) SRA Schl Grp.

Fitzgerald, John & Fitzgerald, Lyn. Barnaby's Birthday. Posey, Pam, illus. LC 92-34275. 1993. 14.00 (*0-383-03618-6*) SRA Schl Grp.

Fitzhugh, Louise. I Am Four. Bonners, Susan, illus. LC 82-70309. 48p. (ps-k). 1982. pap. 8.95 (*0-385-28444-6*); pap. 8.89 (*0-385-28445-4*) Delacorte.

—I Am Three. Natti, Susanna, illus. LC 81-15218. 48p. (ps). 1982. 8.95 (*0-440-04035-3*); PLB 8.89 (*0-440-04039-6*) Delacorte.

Flack, Marjorie. Ask Mr. Bear. Flack, Marjorie, illus. LC 58-8370. 32p. (ps-1). 1971. pap. 4.95 (*0-02-043090-6*, Aladdin) Macmillan Child Grp.

Fleetwood, Jennie. Happy Birthday: Nine Birthday Stories. Willow, illus. 96p. (gr. 2-4). 1993. 16.95 (*0-460-88050-0*, Pub. by J M Dent & Sons) Trafalgar.

Fleischman, Paul. The Birthday Tree. Sewall, Marcia, illus. LC 78-22155. 32p. (gr. k-3). 1991. pap. 4.50 (*0-06-443246-7*, Trophy) HarpC Child Bks.

Frankel, Julie E. Oh No, Otis! Martin, Clovis, illus. LC 91-15328. 32p. (ps-2). 1991. PLB 10.25 (*0-516-02009-9*); pap. 2.95 (*0-516-42009-7*) Childrens.

Freeman, Chester D. & McGuire, John E. Runaway Bear. Kuper, Rachel, illus. LC 93-16893. 32p. (gr. k-3). 1993. 14.95 (*0-88289-956-2*); ltd. boxed signed ed. 29. 95 (*1-56554-016-6*) Pelican.

Gardner, Sally. The Little Nut Tree. Gardner, Sally, illus. LC 93-26714. 32p. 1994. 14.00 (*0-688-13297-9*, Tambourine Bks) Morrow.

Gay, Marie-Louise. Willy Nilly. Levine, Abby, ed. Gay, Marie-Louise, illus. LC 90-12376. 32p. (gr. 1-3). 1990. 13.95 (*0-8075-9119-X*) A Whitman.

Giff, Patricia R. Happy Birthday, Ronald Morgan! Natti, Susanna, illus. 32p. (Orig.). (ps-3). 1988. pap. 4.99 (*0-14-050668-3*, Puffin) Puffin Bks.

Girard, Linda. You Were Born on Your Very First Birthday. Tucker, Kathy, ed. LC 82-13700. (Illus.). 32p. (ps-3). 1983. PLB 13.95 (*0-8075-9455-5*); pap. 5.95 (*0-8075-9456-3*) A Whitman.

Glyman, Caroline A. The Birthday Present. Biser, Dee, illus. LC 92-23390. 32p. (gr. k-3). 1992. PLB 12.95 (*1-878363-79-4*) Forest Hse.

Goble, Paul, retold by. & illus. Iktomi & the Boulder: A Plains Indian Story. LC 87-35789. 32p. (ps-2). 1991. pap. 4.95 (*0-531-07023-9*) Orchard Bks Watts.

Goennel, Heidi. It's My Birthday. Goennel, Heidi, illus. LC 91-30231. 32p. (ps-1). 1992. 14.00 (*0-688-11421-0*, Tambourine Bks); PLB 13.93 (*0-688-11422-9*, Tambourine Bks) Morrow.

Gordon, Sharon. Surprise Party. Hall, Susan, illus. LC 81-4869. 32p. (gr. k-2). 1981. PLB 11.59 (*0-89375-521-4*); pap. 2.95 (*0-89375-522-2*) Troll Assocs.

Gracia, Debbie. My Birthday on Christmas Day. Aragon, Hilda, illus. 30p. (Orig.). (ps-7). 1980. pap. 3.75 (*0-915347-05-9*) Pueblo Acoma Pr.

Gregory, Valiska. Happy Burpday, Maggie McDougal! Porter, Pat, illus. 64p. (gr. 2-4). 1992. 11.95 (*0-316-32777-8*) Little.

Griffey, Harriet. Birthday Time: Toddler's World. King, Colin, illus. 28p. (ps-1). 1992. 3.50 (*0-7214-1479-6*, 928-2) Ladybird Bks.

Hallinan, P. K. Today Is Your Birthday! (Illus.). 24p. (Orig.). (ps-3). 1991. pap. 4.95 perfect bdg. (*0-8249-8493-5*, Ideals Child) Hambleton-Hill.

Happy, Elizabeth. Bailey's Birthday. Chase, Andra, illus. LC 93-32519. 32p. (gr. 1-4). 1994. 16.95 (*1-55942-059-6*, 7658); video, tchr's. guide & storybook 79.95 (*1-55942-062-6*, 9377) Marshfilm.

Harrison, Troon. The Long Weekend. Foreman, Michael, illus. LC 93-307. (gr. k). 1994. 14.95 (*0-15-248842-1*) HarBrace.

Hautzig, Deborah. Grover's Bad Dream. Mathieu, Joe, illus. LC 90-32085. 40p. (ps-3). 1990. 4.95 (*0-679-80898-1*); lib. bdg. 6.99 o.s.i (*0-679-90898-6*) Random Bks Yng Read.

—Happy Birthday Little Witch. Brown, Marc, illus. 1985. pap. 3.50 (*0-394-87365-3*) Random Bks Yng Read.

Heide, Florence P. Treehorn's Wish. Gorey, Edward, illus. LC 83-6240. 64p. (gr. 3-6). 1984. reinforced bdg 8.95 (*0-8234-0493-5*) Holiday.

Hill, Eric. Spot's Birthday Party. (Illus.). (ps-k). 1982. 11. 95 (*0-399-20903-4*, Putnam) Putnam Pub Group.

Hillert, Margaret. The Birthday Car. (Illus.). (ps-k). 1966. PLB 6.95 (*0-8136-5031-3*, TK2278); pap. 3.50 (*0-8136-5531-5*, TK2279) Modern Curr.

Hissey, Jane. Ruff. LC 93-48613. (Illus.). 32p. (ps-3). 1994. 16.00 (*0-679-86042-8*) Random Bks Yng Read.

Hoban, Russell. A Birthday for Frances. Hoban, Lillian, illus. LC 68-24321. (ps-2). 1976. pap. 5.95 (*0-06-443007-3*, Trophy) HarpC Child Bks.

Holabird, Katharine. Angelina's Birthday Surprise. Craig, Helen, illus. LC 89-3513. 32p. (ps-2). 1989. 15.00 (*0-517-57325-3*, Clarkson Potter) Crown Bks Yng Read.

Horowitz, Lynn R. Lulu Turns Four. Urbahn, Clara, illus. 32p. (ps-k). 1993. 13.95 (*0-9625620-5-X*) DOT Garnet. A little chimp named Lulu is about to celebrate her fourth birthday, & like every small person in the process of getting bigger, she wonders if she'll master the challenges: standing by herself all the time; going to the doctor without feeling afraid; sharing happily with her little sister; eating bugs & green leaves like the grownups. Release from her fears comes in the form of a birthday present from her mother, a helpless kitten who needs Lulu to help her grow up, in this charming book about the responsibilities--& the pleasures--of birthdays. LYNN HOROWITZ, a Yale graduate with a Masters in education, is the author of two previous books for young readers, THE GOOD BAD WOLF & MANOS A LA OBRA. She lives in Berkeley, California. CLARA URBAHN, an artist & illustrator of children's books, lives in Nantucket, Massachusetts. To order: DOT*GARNET, 2225 Eighth Avenue, Oakland, CA 94606. (510) 834-6063, FAX 834-7516.
Publisher Provided Annotation.

Howe, James. Creepy-Crawly Birthday. Morrill, Leslie, illus. LC 90-35370. 48p. (gr. k up). 1991. 13.95 (*0-688-09687-5*); PLB 13.88 (*0-688-09688-3*) Morrow Jr Bks.

—Creepy-Crawly Birthday. 48p. 1992. pap. 5.99 (*0-380-75984-5*, Camelot) Avon.

Hurd, Thacher. Little Mouse's Birthday Cake. Hurd, Thacher, illus. LC 91-11919. 32p. (ps-1). 1994. pap. 3.95 (*0-06-443353-6*, Trophy) HarpC Child Bks.

Hutchins, Pat. Happy Birthday, Sam. LC 78-1295. (Illus.). 32p. (gr. k-3). 1978. PLB 13.88 (*0-688-84160-0*) Greenwillow.

—Happy Birthday, Sam. LC 78-1295. (Illus.). 32p. (ps up). 1991. pap. 3.95 (*0-688-10482-7*, Mulberry) Morrow.

—Happy Birthday, Sam Peter. LC 84-18058. (Illus.). 32p. (ps-1). 1985. pap. 3.50 (*0-14-050339-0*, Puffin) Puffin Bks.

Inkpen, Mick. Kipper's Birthday. LC 92-28202. 1993. PLB write for info. (*0-15-200503-X*) HarBrace.

Ireland, Shep. Wesley & Wendell: Happy Birthday. Ireland, Shep, illus. 40p. (gr. 1). 1991. lib. bdg. 4.75 (*0-8378-0333-0*) Gibson.

Jonas, Ann. The Thirteenth Clue. LC 91-34586. (Illus.). 32p. (ps-6). 1992. 14.00 (*0-688-09742-1*); PLB 13.93 (*0-688-09743-X*) Greenwillow.

Keats, Ezra J. Letter to Amy. Keats, Ezra J., illus. LC 68-24329. (gr. k-3). 1968. 15.00 (*0-06-023108-4*); PLB 14.89 (*0-06-023109-2*) HarpC Child Bks.

Kendall, Martha E. Pinata Party. (Illus.). 24p. (gr. k-3). 1993. pap. 2.50 (*0-87406-654-9*) Willowisp Pr.

Ketteman, Helen. Not Yet, Yvette. Mathews, Judith, ed. Trivas, Irene, illus. LC 91-19608. 24p. (ps-2). 1992. PLB 11.95 (*0-8075-5771-4*) A Whitman.

Kline, Suzy. Herbie Jones & the Birthday Showdown. 96p. (gr. 2-6). 1993. 14.95 (*0-399-22600-1*, Putnam) Putnam Pub Group.

Komaiko, Leah. Broadway Banjo Bill. LC 91-29382. (ps-3). 1993. 15.00 (*0-385-30524-9*) Doubleday.

Krauss, Ruth. Birthday Party. Sendak, Maurice, illus. (gr. k-3). 1978. PLB 11.89 (*0-06-023330-3*) HarpC Child Bks.

Lacoe, Addie. Just Not the Same. Estrada, Pau, illus. LC 91-44041. 32p. (ps-3). 1992. 14.45 (*0-395-59347-6*) HM.

Levy, Elizabeth. Something Queer at the Birthday Party. Gerstein, Mordicai, illus. 48p. (gr. 1-4). 1992. pap. 2.99 (*0-440-40687-0*, YB) Dell.

Little, Jean. One to Grow On. (gr. 4-7). 1991. pap. 3.95 (*0-14-034667-8*, Puffin) Puffin Bks.

Lorian, Nicole. A Birthday Present for Mama: A Step Two Book. Miller, J. P., illus. LC 83-26849. (ps-2). 1984. pap. 3.50 (*0-394-86755-6*) Random Bks Yng Read.

Lowry, Lois. Attaboy, Sam! De Groat, Diane, illus. 128p. (gr. 2-6). 1992. 13.45 (*0-395-61588-7*) HM.

McGovern, Ann. Happy Silly Birthday to Me. Dreamer, Sue, illus. 32p. (gr. k-3). 1994. pap. 2.50 (*0-590-46365-9*, Cartwheel Bks) Scholastic Inc.

Mackall, Dandi D. Kay's Birthday Surprise. Mathers, Dawn, illus. LC 89-82554. 32p. (ps-2). 1990. pap. 5.99 (*0-8066-2467-1*, 9-2467) Augsburg Fortress.

Madenski, Melissa. In My Mother's Garden. Speidel, Sandra, illus. LC 93-40112. 1995. 15.95 (*0-316-54326-8*) Little.

Magorian, James. Griddlemort Loses His Birthday. LC 88-71604. (Illus.). 32p. (gr. 1-4). 1988. pap. 3.00 (*0-930674-29-4*) Black Oak.

Mahy, Margaret. The Birthday Burglar & a Very Wicked Headmistress. Chamberlain, Margaret, illus. LC 92-46599. 144p. (gr. 5 up). 1993. pap. 4.95 (*0-688-12470-4*, Pub. by Beech Tree Bks) Morrow.

Mariana. Miss Flora McFlimsey's Birthday. rev. ed. Mariana, illus. LC 86-15269. 40p. (ps-2). 1987. 11.95 (*0-688-04537-5*) Lothrop.

Mealy, Virginia T. Happy Birthday Author. (Illus.). 128p. (gr. k-4). 1986. pap. 12.95 (*0-913839-50-7*) Bk Lures.

Mickey's Birthday Surprise. (Illus.). 24p. (ps-2). 1991. write for info. (*0-307-74003-X*, Golden Pr) Western Pub.

Moncure, Jane B. What's So Special about Today? It's My Birthday. Williams, Jenny, illus. LC 87-21907. 32p. (ps-2). 1987. PLB 14.95 (*0-89565-414-8*) Childs World.

Mora, Pat. A Birthday Basket for Tia. Lang, Cecily, illus. LC 91-15753. 32p. (ps-1). 1992. RSBE 13.95 (*0-02-767400-2*, Macmillan Child Bk) Macmillan Child Grp.

—A Birthday Basket for Tia. Lang, Cecily, illus. (gr. k-4). 1993. 13.95 (*0-685-64816-8*); audio cass. 11.00 (*1-882869-78-8*) Read Advent.

—Pablo's Tree. Mora, Francisco X., illus. LC 92-27145. 32p. (ps-1). 1994. RSBE 14.95 (*0-02-767401-0*, Macmillan Child Bk) Macmillan Child Grp.

—Uno, Dos, Tres: One, Two, Three. Lavallee, Barbara, illus. LC 94-15337. (ps-3). Date not set. write for info. (*0-395-67294-5*, Clarion Bks) HM.

Morgan, Michaela. Dinostory. Kelley, True, illus. LC 90-44935. 32p. (ps-4). 1991. 13.95 (*0-525-44726-1*, DCB) Dutton Child Bks.

Munsch, Robert. El Cumpleanos de Mariela: Moira's Birthday. Martchenko, Michael, illus. (SPA.). 32p. (ps-1). 1992. pap. 5.95 (*1-55037-269-6*, Pub. by Annick CN) Firefly Bks Ltd.

—Moira's Birthday. Martchenko, Michael, illus. 32p. (gr. k-3). 1987. 12.95 (*0-920303-85-4*, Pub. by Annick CN); pap. 4.95 (*0-920303-83-8*, Pub. by Annick CN) Firefly Bks Ltd.

—Moira's Birthday. (CHI., Illus.). 32p. 1993. pap. 5.95 (*1-55037-301-3*, Pub. by Annick CN) Firefly Bks Ltd.

Myers, Laurie. Garage Sale Fever. Howell, Kathleen C., illus. LC 92-40342. 80p. (gr. 2-5). 1993. 13.00 (*0-06-022905-5*); PLB 12.89 (*0-06-022908-X*) HarpC.

Nightingale, Sandy. I'm a Little Monster. Nightingale, Sandy, illus. LC 94-18345. 1995. write for info. (*0-15-200309-6*) HarBrace.

Noble, Trinka H. Jimmy's Boa & the Big Splash Birthday Bash. Kellog, Steven, illus. LC 88-10933. 32p. (ps-3). 1989. 13.95 (*0-8037-0539-5*); PLB 13.89 (*0-8037-0540-9*) Dial Bks Young.

—Jimmy's Boa & the Big Splash Birthday Bash. Kellogg, Steven, illus. 32p. (ps-3). 1993. pap. 4.99 (*0-14-054921-8*, Puff Pied Piper) Puffin Bks.

O'Keefe, Susan H. A Bug from Aunt Tillie. LC 91-3094. 32p. (Orig.). 1991. pap. 3.95 (*0-8091-6602-X*) Paulist Pr.

Osband, Gillian. Boysie's First Birthday. Allen, Jonathan, illus. 32p. (gr. k-2). 1990. PLB 14.95 (*0-87614-404-0*) Carolrhoda Bks.

Ostrovsky, Alexsandr. Birthday (Den Rosdenia) Ostrovsky, Alexsandr, illus. (RUS.). 16p. (Orig.). 1982. pap. 14.95 (*0-934393-17-6*) Rector Pr.

Oxenbury, Helen. The Birthday Party. (Illus.). 24p. (ps-1). 1993. pap. 3.99 (*0-14-054947-1*, Puff Pied Piper) Puffin Bks.

—It's My Birthday. LC 93-39667. (Illus.). 24p. (ps up). 1994. 9.95 (*1-56402-412-1*) Candlewick Pr.

Ozman. Jennifer's Birthday Present. LC 73-87798. (Illus.). 32p. (gr. k-3). 1974. PLB 9.95 (*0-87783-125-4*); pap. 3.94 deluxe ed. (*0-87783-126-2*) Oddo.

Pearson, Susan. Happy Birthday Grampie. Dillon, Leo D., ed. Dillon, Diane, illus. LC 86-31105. 32p. (ps-3). 1987. PLB 10.89 (*0-8037-3458-1*) Dial Bks Young.

Peck, Robert N. Little Soup's Birthday. (ps-3). 1991. pap. 2.99 (*0-440-40551-3*, YB) Dell.

Percy, Graham. Meg & Her Circus Tricks. (Illus.). 32p. 1991. 15.95 (*0-89565-785-6*) Childs World.

Peters, Sharon. Feliz Cumpleanos. Harvey, Paul, illus. (SPA.). 32p. (gr. k-2). 1981. PLB 7.89 (*0-89375-553-2*); pap. 1.95 (*0-685-04948-5*) Troll Assocs.

Pfeffer, Susan B. Twin Surprises. Carter, Abby, illus. 64p. (gr. 2-4). 1991. 13.95 (*0-8050-1850-6*, Redfeather BYR) H Holt & Co.

Pittman, Helena C. A Dinosaur for Gerald. Pittman, Helena C., illus. 32p. (gr. k-3). 1990. PLB 18.95 (*0-87614-431-8*) Carolrhoda Bks.

Polacco, Patricia. Some Birthday! LC 90-10381. (Illus.). 40p. (ps-2). 1991. pap. 14.95 jacketed, 3-pc. bdg. (*0-671-72750-8*, S&S BFYR) S&S Trade.

—Some Birthday. (ps-6). 1993. pap. 5.95 (*0-671-87170-6*, S&S BFYR) S&S Trade.

Pomerantz, Charlotte. The Half-Birthday Party. DeSalvo-Ryan, DyAnne, illus. LC 84-4963. 48p. (gr. 1-4). 1984. 13.95 (*0-89919-273-4*, Clarion Bks) HM.

Porte, Barbara A. Harry's Birthday. Abolafia, Yossi, illus. LC 93-18189. 48p. (gr. k up). 1994. 14.00 (*0-688-12142-X*); PLB 13.93 (*0-688-12143-8*) Greenwillow.

Prager, Annabelle. The Surprise Party. De Paola, Tomie, illus. LC 87-20649. 48p. (Orig.). (gr. 1-3). 1988. 3.50 (*0-394-89596-7*); PLB 7.99 (*0-394-99596-1*) Random Bks Yng Read.

Pryor, Bonnie. Birthday Blizzard. Delaney, Molly, illus. LC 92-1713. 32p. (gr. k up). 1993. 15.00 (*0-688-09423-6*); PLB 14.93 (*0-688-09424-4*) Morrow Jr Bks.

Quackenbush, Robert. Henry's Important Date. LC 93-7772. 1993. PLB 13.27 (*0-8368-0969-6*) Gareth Stevens Inc.

Regan, Dian C. The Class with the Summer Birthdays. Guevara, Susan, illus. LC 90-19670. 80p. (gr. 2-4). 1992. pap. 4.95 (*0-8050-2327-5*, Redfeather BYR) H Holt & Co.

Ricklen, Neil, photos by. Baby's Birthday. (Illus.). 24p. (ps). 1991. pap. 4.95 casebound, padded cover (*0-671-73880-1*, Little Simon) S&S Trade.

Roberts, Bethany. The Two O'Clock Secret. Grant, Christy, ed. Kramer, Robin, illus. LC 92-6405. 32p. (ps-2). 1993. 13.95g (*0-8075-8159-3*) A Whitman.

Robins, Dorothy. Katie's Birthday Wish. LC 88-81467. (Illus.). 32p. (Orig.). (ps-2). 1988. pap. 8.95 (*0-937124-18-4*) Kimbo Educ.

Rotunno, Rocco & Rotunno, Betsy. Little Bear's Best Birthday. Rotunno, Betsy, illus. 12p. (gr. 2-6). 1992. Mixed Media Pkg. incls. stamp pad, stamps & box of 4 crayons. 7.00 (*1-881980-00-6*) Noteworthy.

Russo, Marisabina. Only Six More Days. (Illus.). 32p. (ps-3). 1992. pap. 3.99 (*0-14-054473-9*) Puffin Bks.

Rylant, Cynthia. Birthday Presents. Stevenson, Sucie, illus. LC 87-5485. 32p. (ps-1). 1987. 13.95 (*0-531-05705-4*); PLB 13.99 (*0-531-08305-5*) Orchard Bks Watts.

—Birthday Presents. LC 87-5485. (Illus.). 32p. (ps-1). 1991. pap. 4.95 (*0-531-07026-3*) Orchard Bks Watts.

—Henry & Mudge & the Best Day Ever. Stevenson, Sucie, illus. LC 93-35939. 1995. 14.00 (*0-02-778012-0*, Bradbury Pr) Macmillan Child Grp.

Sabin, Louis. Birthday Surprise. Magine, John, illus. LC 81-2632. 32p. (gr. k-2). 1981. PLB 11.59 (*0-89375-527-3*); pap. text ed. 2.95 (*0-89375-528-1*) Troll Assocs.

Samuels, Barbara. Happy Birthday, Dolores. LC 88-15469. (Illus.). 32p. (ps-1). 1989. 13.95 (*0-531-05791-7*); PLB 13.99 (*0-531-08391-8*) Orchard Bks Watts.

Sawicki, Norma J. Something for Mom. Weston, Martha, illus. LC 86-34421. 32p. (ps-1). 1987. PLB 12.93 (*0-688-05590-7*) Lothrop.

Schulte, Elaine L. Twelve Candles Club. (gr. 4-7). 1994. pap. 4.99 (*0-685-74698-4*) Bethany Hse.

Scovel, Karen & Hunter, Ted. Joe's Earthday Birthday. Whitney, Jean, illus. 32p. (Orig.). (gr. 2-4). 1992. PLB 16.95 (*0-943990-85-8*); pap. 5.95 (*0-943990-84-X*) Parenting Pr.

Seymour, Peter. The Happy Birthday Book: A Party-Time Book with Lights & Music. Ewing, Carolyn, illus. 12p. (ps-1). 1992. pap. 10.95 POB (*0-689-71585-4*, Aladdin) Macmillan Child Grp.

Shafner, R. L. & Weisberg, Eric J. Mrs. Bretsky's Bakery. LC 92-44338. 1993. 13.50 (*0-8225-2102-4*) Lerner Pubns.

Shaw, Janet. Happy Birthday Kirsten! A Springtime Story. Thieme, Jeanne, ed. Graef, Renne, illus. 72p. (gr. 2-5). 1987. PLB 12.95 (*0-937295-88-4*); pap. 5.95 (*0-937295-33-7*) Pleasant Co.

Simon, Carly. The Nightime Chauffeur. Datz, Margot, illus. LC 92-44934. 1993. pap. 16.00 (*0-385-47009-6*) Doubleday.

Spurr, Elizabeth. The Biggest Birthday Cake in the World. Grove, Karen, ed. Litzinger, Rosanne, illus. LC 89-19901. 32p. (ps-3). 1991. 14.95 (*0-15-207150-4*) HarBrace.

Steptoe, John. Birthday. Steptoe, John, illus. LC 72-182782. 32p. (ps-2). 1991. 14.95 (*0-8050-1849-2*, Bks Young Read) H Holt & Co.

Stine, R. L. The Surprise Party. (Orig.). (gr. 6-9). 1990. pap. 3.99 (*0-671-73561-6*, Archway) PB.

Tafuri, Nancy. The Barn Party. LC 94-25356. 1995. write for info. (*0-688-04616-9*); write for info. (*0-688-04617-7*) Greenwillow.

Taylor, Linda L. The Lettuce Leaf Birthday Letter. Durrell, Julie, illus. LC 93-16906. 1994. 13.99 (*0-8037-1454-8*); PLB 13.89 (*0-8037-1455-6*) Dial Bks Young.

Thaler, Mike. Never Mail an Elephant. Smath, Jerry, illus. LC 93-14395. 32p. (ps-3). 1993. PLB 9.89 (*0-8167-3018-0*); pap. text ed. 2.50 (*0-8167-3019-9*) Troll Assocs.

Theriot, David. Leola et la pirogue. Easterling, Mae L., illus. (FRE.). 39p. (gr. 3). 1979. pap. text ed. 1.25 (*0-911409-03-3*) Natl Mat Dev.

Toretta-Fuentes, June. Maria's Secret. Machlin, Mikki, illus. LC 92-9866. 32p. 1992. pap. 3.95 (*0-8091-6606-2*) Paulist Pr.

Tripp, Valerie. Happy Birthday Molly! A Springtime Story. Thieme, Jeanne, ed. Gaadt, David, illus. 72p. (gr. 2-5). 1987. PLB 12.95 (*0-937295-90-6*); pap. 5.95 (*0-937295-37-X*) Pleasant Co.

—Happy Birthday Samantha! A Springtime Story. Thieme, Jeanne, ed. Grace, Robert & Niles, Nancy, illus. 72p. (gr. 2-5). 1987. PLB 12.95 (*0-937295-89-2*); pap. 5.95 (*0-937295-35-3*) Pleasant Co.

Tyler, Linda W. The Sick-in-Bed Birthday. Davis, Susan, illus. 32p. (ps-3). 1990. pap. 3.95 (*0-14-050783-3*, Puffin) Puffin Bks.

Van der Meer, Ron. The Birthday Cake: A Lift-the-Flap Pop-up Book. Van der Meer, Ron, illus. LC 91-62464. 14p. (ps-1). 1993. 8.99 (*0-679-82849-4*) Random Bks Yng Read.

Waite, Michael. Gilly Greenweed's Gift for Granny. LC 91-37443. (ps-3). 1992. pap. 7.99 (*0-7814-0035-X*, Chariot Bks) Chariot Family.

Weber, Jil. A Happy Birthday Surprise! 1992. pap. 2.50 (*1-878689-12-6*) Frajil Farms.

Weiss, Monica. Birthday Cake Candles, Counting. Berlin, Rosemary, illus. LC 91-16033. 24p. (gr. k-2). 1992. PLB 10.59 (*0-8167-2496-2*); pap. text ed. 2.95 (*0-8167-2497-0*) Troll Assocs.

Whittington, Mary K. The Patchwork Lady. Yolen, Jane, ed. Dyer, Jane, illus. 32p. (ps-3). 1991. 13.95 (*0-15-259580-5*) HarBrace.

Wild, Margaret. The Slumber Party. Cox, David, illus. LC 92-39783. 32p. (ps-2). 1993. PLB 13.95 (*0-395-66598-1*) Ticknor & Flds Bks Yng Read.

Willard, Nancy. High Rise Glorious Skittle Skat Roarious Sky Pie Angel Food Cake. Watson, Richard J., illus. 54p. (gr. 3 up). 1990. 15.95 (*0-15-234332-6*) HarBrace.

Wilson, Sarah. Uncle Albert's Flying Birthday. LC 90-36158. (Illus.). 40p. (ps-3). 1993. pap. 7.95 (*0-671-79847-2*, S&S BYR) S&S Trade.

Wormell, Mary. Hilda Hen's Happy Birthday. LC 94-21020. 1995. write for info. (*0-15-200299-5*) HarBrace.

Ziefert, Harriet. The Small Potatoes & the Birthday Party. 64p. (gr. k-6). 1985. pap. 7.95 (*0-440-48035-3*, YB) Dell.

—Where's My Easter Egg? Brown, Richard, illus. LC 84-62004. (gr. 2-6). 1985. pap. 5.99 (*0-14-050537-7*, Puffin) Puffin Bks.

Zion, Gene. No Roses for Harry! Graham, Margaret B., illus. LC 58-7752. 32p. (ps-3). 1976. pap. 4.95 (*0-06-443011-1*, Trophy) HarpC Child Bks.

BIRTHDAYS–POETRY

Damon, Laura. Birthday Buddies. Aiello, Laurel, illus. LC 87-10866. 32p. (gr. k-2). 1988. PLB 11.59 (*0-8167-1091-0*); pap. text ed. 2.95 (*0-8167-1092-9*) Troll Assocs.

Goldstein, Bobbye S. Birthday Rhymes, Special Times. (ps-3). 1993. 15.00 (*0-385-30419-6*) Doubleday.

Hopkins, Lee B., selected by. Happy Birthday. Knight, Hilary, illus. 40p. (ps-2). 1991. pap. 11.95 jacketed (*0-671-70973-9*, S&S BFYR) S&S Trade.

Metaxes, Eric. The Birthday ABC. Raglin, Tim, illus. LC 93-46896. 1995. 14.00 (*0-671-88306-2*, S&S BFYR) S&S Trade.

Shearer, Marilyn J. Annie's Birthday Party: Learning Colors & Shapes. Truax, Nancy, illus. 16p. (Orig.). (ps-6). 1989. 19.95 (*0-685-30095-1*); pap. 10.95 (*0-685-30096-X*) L Ashley & Joshua.

BISMARCK (BATTLESHIP)

Ballard, Robert D. Exploring the Bismarck: The Real-Life Quest to Find Hitler's Greatest Battleship. (gr. 4-7). 1993. pap. 6.95 (*0-590-44269-4*) Scholastic Inc.

Exploring the Bismarck. 64p. 1991. 15.95 (*0-590-44268-6*, Scholastic Hardcover) Scholastic Inc.

BISON

Green, Carl R. & Sanford, William R. The Bison. LC 85-6624. (Illus.). 48p. (gr. 5). 1985. text ed. 12.95 RSBE (*0-89686-275-5*, Crestwood Hse) Macmillan Child Grp.

Lepthien, Emilie U. Buffalo. LC 89-457. (Illus.). 48p. (gr. k-4). 1989. PLB 12.85 (*0-516-01161-8*); pap. 4.95 (*0-516-41161-6*) Childrens.

Sanford, William R. & Green, Carl R. The Cape Buffalo. LC 86-32859. (Illus.). 48p. (gr. 5). 1987. text ed. 12.95 RSBE (*0-89686-321-2*, Crestwood Hse) Macmillan Child Grp.

Stone, Lynn. African Buffalo. (Illus.). 24p. (gr. k-5). 1990. lib. bdg. 11.94 (*0-86593-052-X*); lib. bdg. 8.95s.p. (*0-685-36344-9*) Rourke Corp.

Stone, Lynn M. Back from the Edge: The American Bison. LC 90-38385. (Illus.). 48p. (gr. 4-6). 1991. PLB 16.67 (*0-86593-101-1*); PLB 12.50s.p. (*0-685-59353-3*) Rourke Corp.

Taylor, Dave. The Bison & the Great Plains. (Illus.). 32p. (gr. 3-4). 1990. PLB 15.95 (*0-86505-366-9*); pap. 7.95 (*0-86505-396-0*) Crabtree Pub Co.

BISON–FICTION

Kershen, L. Michael. Why Buffalo Roam. Hansen, Monica, illus. Kershen, Drew L., intro. by. (Illus.). 32p. (gr. k-4). 1992. PLB 15.00 (*0-88045-043-6*) Stemmer Hse.

McClung, Robert M. Shag: Last of the Plains Buffalo. Darling, Louis, illus. LC 91-7508. 96p. (gr. 3-7). 1991. Repr. of 1960 ed. PLB 15.00 (*0-208-02313-5*, Linnet) Shoe String.

Pinkwater, Jill. Buffalo Brenda. LC 91-14806. 208p. (gr. 3-7). 1992. pap. 3.95 (*0-689-71586-2*, Aladdin) Macmillan Child Grp.

Schnell, Robert W. Bonko. Wilkon, Jozef, illus. LC 77-99446. 28p. (ps-3). 8.95 (*0-87592-008-X*) Scroll Pr.

Slote, Alfred. Finding Buck McHenry. LC 90-39190. 256p. (gr. 3-7). 1991. 14.00 (*0-06-021652-2*); PLB 13.89 (*0-06-021653-0*) HarpC Child Bks.

Wallace, Bill. Buffalo Gal. LC 91-28243. 192p. (gr. 5 up). 1992. 14.95 (*0-8234-0943-0*) Holiday.

BLACK ACTORS

Bergman, Carol. Sidney Poitier. King, Coretta Scott, intro. by. (Illus.). 112p. (Orig.). (gr. 5 up). 1988. 17.95 (*1-55546-605-2*); pap. 9.95 (*0-7910-0209-8*) Chelsea Hse.

Haskins, James S. Black Theater in America. LC 81-43874. (Illus.). 160p. (gr. 7 up). 1991. PLB 14.89 (*0-690-04129-2*, Crowell Jr Bks) HarpC Child Bks.

BLACK AMERICANS

see Blacks

BLACK ARTISTS

Everett, Gwen & National Museum of American Art Staff. Li'l Sis & Uncle Willie: A Story Based on the Life & Paintings of William H. Johnson. Johnson, William H., illus. LC 91-14800. 32p. (ps-3). 1992. Repr. of 1991 ed. 13.95 (*0-8478-1462-9*) Rizzoli Intl.

Moore, Reavis. Native Artists of Africa. 48p. (gr. 4-7). 1994. 14.95 (*1-56261-147-X*) John Muir.

Parks, James D. Robert S. Duncanson: Nineteenth Century Black Romantic Painter. 1990. 12.95 (*0-87498-011-9*) Assoc Pubs DC.

Sose, Bonnie. Little Artist. (ps-3). 1993. Afro American Version. 11.00 (*0-9615279-1-9*); White Version. 11.00 (*0-9615279-2-7*) Character Builders.

BLACK ATHLETES

Aaseng, Nathan. Florence Griffith Joyner: Dazzling Olympian. (Illus.). 56p. (gr. 4-9). 1989. PLB 13.50 (*0-8225-0495-2*) Lerner Pubns.

Biracree, Tom. Wilma Rudolph. Horner, Matina, intro. by. (Illus.). 112p. (Orig.). (gr. 5 up). 1988. 17.95 (*1-55546-675-3*); pap. 9.95 (*0-7910-0217-9*) Chelsea Hse.

Fremon, David. The Negro Baseball Leagues. LC 94-2389. (gr. 5 up). 1994. text ed. 15.95 (*0-02-735695-7*, New Discovery Bks) MacMillan Child Grp.

Haskins. The Negro Leagues. 1993. 16.95 (*0-8050-2207-4*) H Holt & Co.

Knapp, Ron. Sports Great Bo Jackson. LC 89-29059. (Illus.). 64p. (gr. 4-10). 1990. lib. bdg. 15.95 (*0-89490-281-4*) Enslow Pubs.

Macht, Norm. Satchel Paige. Murray, Jim, intro. by. (Illus.). 64p. (gr. 3 up). 1991. lib. bdg. 14.95 (*0-7910-1185-2*) Chelsea Hse.

Margolies, Jacob. The Negro Leagues: The Story of Black Baseball. (Illus.). 144p. (gr. 7-12). 1993. pap. 19.86 (*0-531-11130-X*) Watts.

—The Negro Leagues: The Story of Black Baseball. (Illus.). (gr. 7-12). 1994. pap. 6.95 (*0-531-15694-X*) Watts.

Press, David P. A Multicultural Portrait of Professional Sports. LC 93-10316. 1993. 18.95 (*1-85435-661-5*) Marshall Cavendish.

Rothaus, James R. Barry Sanders. 32p. (gr. 2-6). 1991. 14.95 (*0-89565-737-6*) Childs World.

—Bo Jackson. 32p. (gr. 2-6). 1991. 14.95 (*0-89565-731-7*) Childs World.

—David Robinson. 32p. (gr. 2-6). 1991. 14.95 (*0-89565-784-8*) Childs World.

—Ken Griffey, Jr. 32p. 1991. 14.95 (*0-89565-783-X*) Childs World.

—Magic Johnson. (ENG & SPA.). 32p. (gr. 2-6). 1991. 14.95 (*0-89565-732-5*) Childs World.

—Michael Jordan. (SPA & ENG.). 32p. (gr. 2-6). 1991. 14.95 (*0-89565-733-3*) Childs World.

BLACK AUTHORS

Bishop, Jack. Ralph Ellison. King, Coretta Scott, intro. by. (Illus.). 112p. (Orig.). (gr. 5 up). 1988. 17.95 (*1-55546-585-4*); pap. 9.95 (*0-7910-0202-0*) Chelsea Hse.

Colbert, Roz. Zora Neale Hurston. (Illus.). 80p. (gr. 3-5). 1993. PLB 12.95 (*0-7910-1766-4*) Chelsea Hse.

Dolan, Sean. Chiang Kai-Shek. Schlesinger, Arthur M., Jr., intro. by. (Illus.). 112p. (gr. 5 up). 1989. lib. bdg. 17.95 (*0-87754-517-0*) Chelsea Hse.

Lyons, Mary E. Sorrow's Kitchen: The Life & Folklore of Zora Neale Hurston. LC 90-8058. (Illus.). 160p. (gr. 7 up). 1990. SBE 14.95 (*0-684-19198-9*, Scribners Young Read) Macmillan Child Grp.

Shuker, Nancy. Maya Angelou. Easton, Emily, ed. (Illus.). 128p. (gr. 7-9). 1990. 12.95 (*0-382-09908-7*); 9.95 (*0-382-24036-7*); PLB 17.98s.p. (*0-685-74290-3*) Silver Burdett Pr.

Walker, Alice. Langston Hughes, American Poet. rev. ed. Deeter, Catherine, illus. LC 92-28540. 48p. (gr. 3-6). Date not set. 15.00 (*0-06-021518-6*); PLB 14.89 (*0-06-021519-4*) HarpC Child Bks.

Wilson, M. L. Chester Himes. King, Coretta Scott, intro. by. LC 87-30961. (Illus.). 112p. (Orig.). (gr. 5 up). 1988. 17.95 (*1-55546-591-9*); pap. 9.95 (*0-7910-0212-8*) Chelsea Hse.

Yates, Janelle. Zora Neale Hurston: A Storyteller's Life. Adams, David, illus. 104p. (gr. 4 up). 1991. pap. 9.95 (*0-9623380-7-9*) Ward Hill Pr.

BLACK DEATH

see Plague

BLACK FOLKLORE

Bang, Molly. Wiley & the Hairy Man: Adapted from an American Folk Tale. Bang, Molly G., illus. LC 75-38581. 64p. (gr. 1-4). 1976. RSBE 11.95 (*0-02-708370-5*, Macmillan Child Bk) Macmillan Child Grp.

Hamilton, Virginia. The People Could Fly: American Black Folktales. Dillon, Leo & Dillon, Diane, illus. LC 85-25020. 192p. 1993. pap. 10.00 (*0-679-84336-1*) Knopf Bks Yng Read.

—The People Could Fly: American Black Folktales. Dillon, Leo & Dillon, Diane, illus. Jones, James E., contrib. by. 192p. 1994. pap. 15.00 incl. cass. (*0-679-85465-7*) Knopf Bks Yng Read.

Harris, Joel C. Complete Tales of Uncle Remus. Chase, Richard, ed. (Illus.). 832p. (gr. 7 up). 1955. 35.00 (*0-395-06799-5*) HM.

—Favorite Uncle Remus. Van Santvoord, George & Coolidge, Archibald C., eds. Van Santvoord, George & Coolidge, Archibald C., illus. 320p. (gr. 4-8). 1973. 17.45 (*0-395-06800-2*) HM.

Jensen, Patricia A. John Henry & His Mighty Hammer. Litzinger, Roseanne, illus. LC 93-4810. 32p. (gr. k-2). 1993. PLB 11.59 (*0-8167-3156-X*); pap. text ed. 2.95 (*0-8167-3157-8*) Troll Assocs.

Kessler, Brad. Brer Rabbit & Boss Lion. Mayer, Bill, illus. 40p. (gr. k up). 1993. incl. cass. 19.95 (*0-88708-274-2*, Rabbit Ears); 14.95 (*0-88708-273-4*, Rabbit Ears) Picture Bk Studio.

Lester, Julius, as told by. The Last Tales of Uncle Remus. Pinkney, Jerry, illus. LC 93-7531. (ps-4). 1994. 16.99 (*0-8037-1303-7*); PLB 16.89 (*0-8037-1304-5*) Dial Bks Young.

Norman, Floyd E. Afro-Classic Folk Tales, Bk. 1: A Rattlesnake Tale. Stewart, Lyn, ed. Norman, Floyd, illus. Sullivan, Leo, intro. by. (Illus.). 28p. (Orig.). (gr. 4-7). 1992. pap. 9.95 (*1-881368-00-9*) Vignette.

San Souci, Robert D., retold by. Two White Pebbles. LC 93-43952. 1995. write for info. (*0-8037-1640-0*); PLB write for info. (*0-8037-1641-9*) Dial Bks Young.

Young, Richard & Young, Judy D. African-American Folktales. 176p. 1993. 18.95 (*0-87483-308-6*); pap. 9.95 (*0-87483-309-4*) August Hse.

BLACK HAWK, SAUK CHIEF, 1767-1838

Oppenheim, Joanne. Black Hawk, Frontier Warrior. new ed. LC 78-18049. (Illus.). 48p. (gr. 4-6). 1979. PLB 10.59 (*0-89375-157-X*); pap. 3.50 (*0-89375-147-2*) Troll Assocs.

BLACK LITERATURE–COLLECTIONS

Strickland, Dorothy S., ed. Listen Children, an Anthology of Black Literature. 1992. 16.75 (*0-8446-6582-7*) Peter Smith.

BLACK MAGIC

see Witchcraft

BLACK MUSICIANS

De Veaux, Alexis. Don't Explain: A Song of Billie Holiday. 151p. (gr. 9 up). 1988. pap. 7.95 (*0-86316-132-4*) Writers & Readers.

Frankl, Ron. Charlie Parker. King, Coretta Scott, intro. by. (Illus.). 112p. (gr. 5 up). 1992. lib. bdg. 17.95 (*0-7910-1134-8*); pap. write for info. (*0-7910-1159-3*) Chelsea Hse.

Gentry, Tony. Dizzy Gillespie: Musician. King, Coretta Scott, intro. by. (Illus.). 112p. (gr. 5 up). 1994. PLB 18.95 (*0-7910-1127-5*, Am Art Analog); pap. write for info. (*0-7910-1152-6*, Am Art Analog) Chelsea Hse.

Greenberg, Keith E. Whitney Houston. (Illus.). 32p. (gr. 4-9). 1988. lib. bdg. 13.50 (*0-8225-1619-5*) Lerner Pubns.

Haskins, James S. Black Music in America: A History Through Its People. LC 85-47885. (Illus.). 224p. (gr. 7 up). 1987. (Crowell Jr Bks); PLB 15.89 (*0-690-04462-3*, Crowell Jr Bks) HarpC Child Bks.

Jerome, Leah. Tevin Campbell. (Illus.). 48p. 1992. 1.49 (*0-440-21431-9*) Dell.

Kliment, Bud. Count Basie. King, Coretta Scott, intro. by. (Illus.). 112p. (gr. 5 up). 1992. lib. bdg. 17.95 (*0-7910-1118-6*) Chelsea Hse.

—Ella Fitzgerald. King, Coretta Scott, intro. by. (Illus.). 112p. (Orig.). (gr. 5 up). 1989. 17.95 (*1-55546-586-2*); pap. 9.95 (*0-7910-0220-9*) Chelsea Hse.

Kriss Kross. (gr. 4-7). 1992. pap. 1.49 (*0-440-21525-0*) Dell.

Mabery, D. L. Janet Jackson. (Illus.). 48p. (gr. 4-9). 1988. pap. 13.50 (*0-8225-1618-7*) Lerner Pubns.

—This Is Michael Jackson. LC 84-10043. (Illus.). 48p. (gr. 4-9). 1984. PLB 13.50 (*0-8225-1600-4*) Lerner Pubns.

Mitchell, Barbara. Raggin' A Story about Scott Joplin. Mitchell, Hetty, illus. 64p. (gr. 3-6). 1987. PLB 14.95 (*0-87614-310-9*) Carolrhoda Bks.

Palmer, Leslie. Lena Horne. King, Coretta Scott. (Illus.). 112p. (gr. 5 up). 1989. lib. bdg. 17.95x (*1-55546-594-3*) Chelsea Hse.

Patterson, Charles. Marian Anderson. LC 88-10695. (Illus.). 160p. (gr. 7 up). 1988. PLB 14.40 (*0-531-10568-7*) Watts.

Preston, Kitty. Scott Joplin. King, Coretta Scott, intro. by. (Illus.). 112p. (Orig.). (gr. 5 up). 1988. 17.95 (*1-55546-598-6*); pap. 9.95 (*0-7910-0205-5*) Chelsea Hse.

Raso, Anne M. Kris Kross Krazy. (gr. 4-7). 1992. pap. 3.50 (*0-553-56179-0*) Bantam.

Shay, Regan. Boyz II Men. (gr. 4-7). 1992. pap. 1.49 (*0-440-21475-0*) Dell.

Still, Judith A. Little David Had No Fear. Phillips, Ted, Jr., illus. (Orig.). (gr. 6-8). 1990. write for info. (*1-877873-03-9*); pap. write for info. Master-Player Lib.

Tanenhaus, Sam. Louis Armstrong. King, Coretta Scott, intro. by. (Illus.). 112p. (gr. 5 up). 1989. text ed. 17.95 (*1-55546-571-4*); pap. 9.95 (*0-7910-0221-7*) Chelsea Hse.

Wallner, Rosemary. M. C. Hammer. LC 91-73039. 202p. 1991. 12.94 (*1-56239-054-6*) Abdo & Dghtrs.

—Michael Jackson. LC 91-73036. 202p. 1991. 12.94 (*1-56239-057-0*) Abdo & Dghtrs.

BLACK MUSLIMS

Halasa, Malu. Elijah Muhammad. King, Coretta Scott, intro. by. (Illus.). (gr. 5 up). 1990. 17.95 (*1-55546-602-8*) Chelsea Hse.

BLACK POETRY

Adoff, Arnold, ed. My Black Me: A Beginning Book of Black Poetry. LC 73-16445. 96p. (gr. 3 up). 1974. 12.95 (*0-525-35460-3*, DCB) Dutton Child Bks.

—My Black Me: A Beginning Book of Black Poetry. (Illus.). 96p. (gr. 4-7). 1994. 14.99 (*0-525-45216-8*, DCB) Dutton Child Bks.

—The Poetry of Black America: Anthology of the Twentieth Century. Brooks, Gwendolyn, intro. by. LC 72-76518. 576p. (gr. 7 up). 1973. 25.00 (*0-06-020089-8*); PLB 24.89 (*0-06-020090-1*) HarpC Child Bks.

Green, Barbara-Marie, et al. More Poetic Thoughts: By Love Pain Hope Poet, Barbara-Marie Green & Others. 70p. (Orig.). 1993. pap. 5.50 (*1-883414-01-6*) Bar JaMae.

Hudson, Wade, compiled by. Pass It On: African-American Poetry for Children. Cooper, Floyd, illus. LC 92-16034. 32p. (gr. k-4). 1993. 14.95 (*0-590-45770-5*) Scholastic Inc.

Miller, May. Dust of Uncertain Journey. LC 75-40977. 67p. (gr. 9-12). 1975. pap. 5.00 (*0-916418-05-7*) Lotus.

Nelson, Johnnierence. Positive Passage: Everyday Kwanzaa Poems. (Illus.). 48p. (Orig.). (gr. 1 up). 1991. pap. 6.00 (*0-9623205-1-X*) House Nia.

Oliver, Elizabeth M. Black Mother Goose Book. 2nd ed. Stockett, Thomas A., illus. LC 81-83427. 48p. (gr. k-3). Repr. of 1981 ed. 12.95 (*0-912444-35-5*) DARE Bks.

Saccone, Vivian R. ABCs of What Is Black. Saccone, Vivian R., illus. LC 92-84105. 44p. (ps-3). 1994. pap. 5.95 (*1-55523-583-2*) Winston-Derek.

White, Paulette C. Love Poem to a Black Junkie. 37p. (gr. 7-12). 1975. pap. 4.00x (*0-916418-04-9*) Lotus.

BLACKBOARD DRAWING

see Crayon Drawing

BLACKS

African-American Almanac, 3 vols. 576p. (gr. 6-9). 1994. Set. 84.00 (*0-8103-9239-9*, 021503, UXL); Vol. 1. write for info. (*0-8103-9240-2*, UXL); Vol. 2. write for info. (*0-8103-9241-0*, UXL); Vol. 3. write for info. (*0-8103-9242-9*, UXL) Gale.

African-American Reference Library, 10 vols. (gr. 6-9). 1993. Set & free index. 195.00 (*0-8103-9230-5*, 021500, UXL) Gale.

Banks, Valerie J. Kwanzaa: An African Celebration. (Illus.). 16p. 1991. pap. 3.00 (*0-685-59710-5*) Sala Enterp.

—Kwanzaa Coloring Book. 6th ed. (ENG & SWA., Illus.). 46p. (gr. k-8). 1992. pap. 5.95 (*0-9622340-6-0*) Sala Enterp.

Barrett, Anna P. Juneteenth. rev. ed. Goodman, Frances B., ed. Costner, Howard, illus. 64p. (gr. k-8). 1993. pap. 9.95 (*0-89896-111-4*) Larksdale.

Bellegarde. Black Heroes & Heroines, Bk 5: Benjamin Banneker's Great Achievements. 64p. (gr. 5 up). 1985. 8.95 (*0-918340-14-4*) Bell Ent.

Bibliotheca Press Staff. Black English, Chocolate Slang: or English Too??? 15p. (gr. 9-12). 1989. pap. text ed. 4.00 (*0-318-42724-9*, Pub. by Biblio Pr Ga) Prosperity & Profits.

Chandler, Ann. Black Women: A Salute to Black Inventors. rev. ed. Ivery, Evelyn L., ed. Chandler, Alton, et al, illus. Chandler, Alton, intro. by. 24p. (gr. 3-7). 1992. pap. text ed. 1.50 (*1-877804-06-1*) Chandler White.

Cwiklik, Robert. Stokely Carmichael & Black Power. LC 92-11560. (Illus.). 32p. (gr. 2-4). 1993. PLB 12.90 (*1-56294-276-X*); pap. 4.95 (*1-56294-839-3*) Millbrook Pr.

Daniel, Becky. Portraits in Black. (Illus.). 96p. (gr. 4-7). 1990. 10.95 (*0-86653-531-4*, GA1147) Good Apple.

Farrand, Vernell C. & Farrand, Brent. Afro-Bets Activity & Enrichment Guide: Book of Black Heroes from A to Z. 1989. pap. 7.95 (*0-940975-05-X*) Just Us Bks.

Haber, Louis. Black Pioneers of Science & Invention. (gr. 5 up). 1992. pap. 5.95 (*0-15-208566-1*, HB Juv Bks) HarBrace.

Hancock, Sibyl. Famous Firsts of Black Americans. Haynes, Jerry, illus. LC 82-612. 128p. (gr. 3-9). 1983. 11.95 (*0-88289-240-1*) Pelican.

Haskins, James S. Black Dance in America: A History Through Its People. LC 89-35529. (Illus.). 240p. (gr. 7 up). 1990. 15.00 (*0-690-04657-X*, Crowell Jr Bks); (Crowell Jr Bks) HarpC Child Bks.

—Black Theater in America. LC 81-43874. (Illus.). 160p. (gr. 7 up). 1991. PLB 14.89 (*0-690-04129-2*, Crowell Jr Bks) HarpC Child Bks.

Haskins, Jim. Outward Dreams: Black Inventors & Their Inventions. (gr. 7 up). 1992. pap. 3.50 (*0-553-29480-6*, Starfire) Bantam.

Howell, Ann C. Communication: A Salute to Black Inventors. rev. ed. Ivery, Evelyn L., ed. Chandler, Alton, et al, illus. Chandler, Alton, intro. by. 24p. (gr. 3-7). 1992. pap. text ed. 1.50 (*1-877804-05-3*) Chandler White.

—Food: A Salute to Black Inventors. rev. ed. Ivery, Evelyn L., ed. Venable, James, et al, illus. Chndler, Alton, intro. by. 24p. (gr. 3-7). 1992. pap. text ed. 1.50 (*1-877804-01-0*) Chandler White.

—Old West: A Salute to Black Inventors. rev. ed. Ivery, Evelyn L., ed. Chandler, Alton, et al, illus. Chandler, Alton, pref. by. 24p. (gr. 3-7). 1992. pap. text ed. 1.50 (*1-877804-03-7*) Chandler White.
—Safety: A Salute to Black Inventors. rev. ed. Ivery, Evelyn L., ed. Chandler, Alton, et al, illus. Chandler, Alton H., intro. by. 24p. (gr. 3-7). 1992. pap. text ed. 1.50 (*1-877804-02-9*) Chandler White.
—Transportation - Food - Safety - Old West - Working Easier - Communication - Black Women: A Salute to Black Inventors. rev. ed. Ivery, Evelyn L., ed. Chandler, Alton, et al, illus. 24p. (gr. 3-7). 1992. pap. text ed. 10.50 (*1-877804-10-X*) Chandler White.
—Transportation: A Salute to Black Inventors. rev. ed. Ivery, Evelyn L., ed. Venable, James, et al, illus. Chandler, Alton, intro. by. 24p. (gr. 3-7). 1992. pap. text ed. 1.50 (*1-877804-00-2*) Chandler White.
—Working Easier: A Salute to Black Inventors. rev. ed. Ivery, Evelyn L., ed. Chandler, Alton, et al, illus. Chandler, Alton, intro. by. 24p. (gr. 3-7). 1992. pap. text ed. 1.50 (*1-877804-04-5*) Chandler White.
Johnson, Cathleen. People You Should Know: Famous Black Americans. 86p. (gr. 4). 1991. write for info. wkbk. (*0-9631180-0-5*) Perspect NC.
Johnson, James Weldon. Lift Every Voice & Sing. Catlett, Elizabeth, illus. 36p. 1993. 14.95 (*0-8027-8250-7*); PLB 15.85 (*0-8027-8251-5*) Walker & Co.
—Lift Ev'ry Voice & Sing. Gilchrist, Jan S., illus. LC 92-32283. (ps up). 1995. 14.95 (*0-590-46982-7*) Scholastic Inc.
Johnson, Zenobia M. Afro-American Copy Color Fun. (Illus.). 32p. (Orig.). (ps-1). 1979. wkbk. 3.00 (*0-9617411-2-0*) Z M Johnson.
—Black Footprints. (Illus.). 32p. (Orig.). (gr. 4-7). 1979. wkbk. 3.50 (*0-9617411-1-2*) Z M Johnson.
Kunjufu, Jawanza. Lessons from History: A Celebration in Blackness. 108p. (gr. 1-5). 1987. 12.95 (*0-913543-05-5*); pap. 6.95 (*0-913543-04-7*) African Am Imag.
—Lessons from History: A Celebration in Blackness. 116p. (gr. 6-12). 1987. 13.95 (*0-913543-07-1*); pap. 7.95 (*0-913543-06-3*) African Am Imag.
Meissel, Chris. Young Children Rap to Learn about Famous African-Americans. Keeling, Jan, ed. Eaddy, Susan, illus. 80p. (Orig.). 1993. pap. text ed. 8.95 (*0-86530-265-0*) Incentive Pubns.
Miller, Robert. Cowboys. Leonard, Richard, illus. 104p. (gr. 4-7). 1992. PLB 8.95 (*0-382-24079-0*); pap. 4.95 (*0-382-24084-7*) Silver Burdett Pr.
Myers, Walter D. Now Is Your Time! The African-American Struggle for Freedom. 391p. 1993. text ed. 31.28 (*1-56956-381-0*) W A T Braille.
Papi, Liza. Carnavalia! African-Brazilian Folklore & Crafts. LC 93-38451. (Illus.). 48p. 1994. 16.95 (*0-8478-1779-2*) Rizzoli Intl.
Perry, Rufus L. The Cushite: Or the Children of Ham (the Negro Race) Obaba, Al I., ed. 49p. (Orig.). 1991. pap. text ed. 4.00 (*0-916157-32-6*) African Islam Miss Pubns.
Roberts, Paulette & Whaley, Jeanette. Seeds for Progress. LC 89-52122. (Illus.). 140p. 1990. pap. 12.95 (*1-55523-309-0*) Winston-Derek.
Robinson, Dorothy. The Legend of Africania. Temple, Herbert, illus. LC 74-4781. 32p. (gr. k-5). 1974. 10.95 (*0-87485-037-1*) Johnson Chi.
Shakelford, Jane D. My Happy Days. (Illus.). 1990. 7.95 (*0-87498-004-6*) Assoc Pubs DC.
Smead, Howard. The Afro-Americans. Moynihan, Daniel P., intro. by. (Illus.). 120p. (gr. 5 up). 1989. lib. bdg. 17.95 (*0-87754-854-4*); pap. 9.95 (*0-7910-0256-X*) Chelsea Hse.
Sullivan, Charles, ed. Children of Promise: African-American Literature & Art for Young People. Campbell, Mary S., frwd. by. (Illus.). 128p. 1991. 24.95 (*0-8109-3170-2*) Abrams.
Sutton, Charyn, ed. Grio "The Praise Singer" The 1987 Chronicle of Afro-American Heritage, Vol. III. Massey, Cal, et al, illus. 80p. (Orig.). (gr. k-12). 1988. pap. text ed. 9.95 (*0-936509-00-7*); 183.25 (*0-936509-01-5*) Enteracom Inc.
Westridge Young Writers Workshop Staff. Kids Explore America's African-American Heritage. (Illus.). 112p. (Orig.). (gr. 3 up). Date not set. pap. 8.95 (*1-56261-090-2*) John Muir.
Whiting, Helen A. Negro Art, Music, & Rhyme. Jones, Lois M., illus. (gr. 2). 1990. 4.25 (*0-87498-005-4*) Assoc Pubs DC.

BLACKS–BIOGRAPHY

Adler, David A. A Picture Book of Harriet Tubman. Byrd, Samuel, illus. LC 91-19628. 32p. (ps-3). 1992. reinforced bdg. 15.95 (*0-8234-0926-0*) Holiday.
Adoff, Arnold. Malcolm X. Wilson, John, illus. LC 70-94787. 48p. (gr. 2-5). 1970. PLB 14.89 (*0-690-51414-X*, Crowell Jr Bks) HarpC Child Bks.
African America: Heralding a Heritage. 9.95 (*0-932991-05-X*) Place In the Woods.
African-American Biography, 4 vols. 832p. (gr. 6-9). 1993. Set. 112.00 (*0-8103-9234-8*, 021502, UXL) Gale.
Akinsheye, Dexter. African American Inventor Math Pack Workbook. Akinsheye, Dayo, ed. Akinsheye, Addae, illus. 20p. (Orig.). (gr. 2-5). 1992. pap. text ed. 2.50 (*1-877835-53-6*) TD Pub.
—Discovering American History. Akinsheye, Dayo, ed. Griffin, Charles, illus. 20p. (Orig.). (gr. 2-3). 1992. pap. 4.99 (*1-877835-70-6*) TD Pub.
Altman, Susan. Extraordinary Black Americans from Colonial to Contemporary Times. LC 88-11977. (Illus.). 240p. (gr. 4 up). 1989. PLB 24.65 (*0-516-00581-2*) Childrens.
Banta, Melissa. Colin Powell. LC 94-8349. 1994. write for info. (*0-7910-1770-2*); pap. write for info. (*0-7910-2142-4*) Chelsea Hse.
Bauleke, Ann. Rickey Henderson: Record Stealer. (Illus.). 48p. (gr. 4-9). 1991. PLB 13.50 (*0-8225-0541-X*) Lerner Pubns.
Beaton, Margaret. Oprah Winfrey: TV Talk Show Host. LC 90-2150. (Illus.). (gr. 4 up). 1990. PLB 14.40 (*0-516-03270-4*) Childrens.
Bellegarde, Ida R. Black Heroes & Heroines, Bk. 4. LC 79-51798. 64p. (gr. 5 up). 1984. 8.95 (*0-918340-13-6*) Bell Ent.
Bernotas, Bob. Amiri Baraka (Le Roi Jones) King, Coretta Scott, intro. by. (Illus.). 112p. (gr. 5 up). 1991. lib. bdg. 17.95 (*0-7910-1117-8*) Chelsea Hse.
Brown, Eric. Different Shades of Courage: A Coloring & Activities Book of African American Achievement, Vol. 1. Sheen, Jen, ed. (Illus.). 53p. (Orig.). (gr. 4 up). 1993. pap. 9.95 (*0-9636468-0-X*) Little Tike.
Brown, Kevin. Romare Bearden. King, Coretta Scott, intro. by. (Illus.). 112p. (gr. 5 up). 1993. PLB 17.95 (*0-7910-1119-4*) Chelsea Hse.
Burchard, Peter. Charlotte Forten: A Black Teacher in the Civil War. LC 94-18305. (Illus.). 96p. (gr. 4-7). 1995. 16.00 (*0-517-59242-8*); PLB write for info. (*0-517-59243-6*) Crown Bks Yng Read.
Carwell, Hattie. Blacks in Science: Astrophysicist to Zoologist. Earls, Julian, intro. by. (Illus.). 96p. (gr. 8 up). 1988. pap. 7.00 (*0-682-48911-5*); 10.00 (*0-685-22950-5*) H Carwell.
Ceasor, Ebraska, et al. Blacks in Ohio: Seven Portraits. McCluskey, John, ed. (Orig.). (gr. 7-12). 1976. pap. 5.00 (*0-913678-13-9*) New Day Pr.
Ceasor, Ebraska D. Mae C. Jemison: First Black Female Astronaut. Durant, Charlotte & Pye, Ethel, eds. Johnson, Leonard J., illus. 40p. (Orig.). (ps-1). 1992. pap. 4.00 (*0-913678-22-8*) New Day Pr.
Colbert, Roz. Zora Neale Hurston. (Illus.). 80p. (gr. 3-5). 1993. PLB 12.95 (*0-7910-1766-4*) Chelsea Hse.
Daniel, Sadie L. Women Builders. rev. & enl. ed. Perry, Thelma D., contrib. by. 1990. 12.95 (*0-87498-084-4*); pap. 10.95 (*0-87498-085-2*) Assoc Pubs DC.
Davis, Russell H. Black Americans in Cleveland. (Illus.). 1990. pap. 10.00 (*0-87498-075-5*) Assoc Pubs DC.
Dominy, Jeannine. Katherine Dunham. (Illus.). 112p. (gr. 5 up). 1992. lib. bdg. 17.95 (*0-7910-1123-2*) Chelsea Hse.
Donovan, Richard X. Black Scientists of America. Sorrels, Judith, illus. 134p. (gr. 6 up). 1990. pap. 10.95 (*0-89420-265-0*, 297000) Natl Book.
Dunham, Montrew. Langston Hughes: Young Poet. LC 93-21128. 1995. pap. 4.95 (*0-689-71787-3*, Aladdin) Macmillan Child Grp.
—Mahalia Jackson: Young Gospel Singer. LC 93-34072. 1995. pap. 4.95 (*0-689-71786-5*, Aladdin) Macmillan Child Grp.
Equiano, Olaudah. The Kidnapped Prince: The Life of Olaudah Equiano. Cameron, Ann, adapted by. Gates, Henry L., Jr., intro. by. LC 93-29914. (Illus.). 144p. (gr. 4-9). 1995. 16.00 (*0-679-85619-6*); pap. write for info. (*0-679-95619-0*) Knopf Bks Yng Read.
Everett, Gwen & National Museum of American Art Staff. Li'l Sis & Uncle Willie: A Story Based on the Life & Paintings of William H. Johnson. Johnson, William H., illus. LC 91-14800. 32p. (ps-3). 1992. Repr. of 1991 ed. 13.95 (*0-8478-1462-9*) Rizzoli Intl.
Ferris, Jeri. Walking the Road to Freedom: A Story about Sojourner Truth. Hanson, Peter E., illus. 64p. (gr. 3-6). 1989. pap. 5.95 (*0-87614-505-5*, First Ave Edns) Lerner Pubns.
Finke, Blythe F. Angela Davis: Traitor or Martyr of the Freedom of Expression? Rahmas, D. Steve, ed. LC 77-190246. 32p. (Orig.). (gr. 7-12). 1972. lib. bdg. 4.95 incl. catalog cards (*0-87157-528-0*) SamHar Pr.
Fleming, Beatrice J. & Pryde, Marion J. Distinguished Negroes Abroad. rev. ed. (Illus.). (gr. 1-6). 1990. 21.95 (*0-87498-002-X*) Assoc Pubs DC.
Fogelson, Genia. Harry Belafonte. rev. ed. (ps up). 1991. pap. 3.95 (*0-87067-571-0*, BH571) Holloway.
Folsom, Franklin. Black Cowboy: The Life & Legend of George McJunkin. 3rd ed. (Illus.). 162p. 1992. pap. 7.95 (*1-879373-14-9*) R Rinehart.
Fraser, Alison. Walter White. King, Coretta Scott, intro. by. (Illus.). 112p. (gr. 5 up). 1991. 17.95 (*1-55546-617-6*); pap. 9.95 (*0-7910-0253-5*) Chelsea Hse.
Freedman, Florence B. Two Tickets to Freedom: The True Story of Ellen & William Craft, Fugitive Slaves. Keats, Ezra J., illus. 96p. (gr. 4 up). 1989. 12.95 (*0-87226-330-4*); pap. 5.95 (*0-87226-221-9*) P Bedrick Bks.
Fullen, M. K. Pathblazers: Eight People Who Made a Difference. Waldman, Selma, illus. 64p. (Orig.). (gr. 3-10). 1992. 12.95 (*0-940880-35-0*); pap. 6.95 (*0-940880-36-9*) Open Hand.
Gaines, Edith M., et al. Black Image Makers. Adrine-Robinson, Kenyette, ed. Belanger, Ray, et al, illus. Gregory, Dick, frwd. by. (Orig.). (gr. 5-9). 1988. pap. 5.00 (*0-913678-17-1*) New Day Pr.
Goldman, Martin S. Nat Turner: And the Southampton Revolt of 1831. LC 91-36618. (Illus.). 160p. (gr. 9-12). 1992. PLB 14.40 (*0-531-13011-8*) Watts.
Gonzales, Doreen. Alex Haley: Author of "Roots" LC 93-44172. (Illus.). 128p. (gr. 6 up). 1994. lib. bdg. 17.95 (*0-89490-573-2*) Enslow Pubs.
Greene, Carol. Thurgood Marshall: First Black Supreme Court Justice. LC 91-4798. (Illus.). 48p. (gr. k-3). 1991. PLB 12.85 (*0-516-04225-4*); pap. 4.95 (*0-516-44225-2*) Childrens.
Greenfield, Eloise. Childtimes: A Three-Generation Memoir. Little, Lessie J., illus. LC 77-26581. 192p. (gr. 4-6). 1993. pap. 5.95 (*0-06-446134-3*, Trophy) HarpC Child Bks.
Guy, Rosa. Edith Jackson. (gr. 7 up). 1992. pap. 3.50 (*0-440-21137-9*) Dell.
Haber, Louis. Black Pioneers of Science & Invention. LC 77-109090. (Illus.). 181p. (gr. 5 up). 1970. 17.95 (*0-15-208565-3*, HB Juv Bks) HarBrace.
Hart, Philip S. Flying Free: America's First Black Aviators. Lindbergh, Reeve, frwd. by. (Illus.). 72p. (gr. 5 up). 1992. 19.95 (*0-8225-1598-9*) Lerner Pubns.
Harvey, Miles. Hakeem Olajuwon: The Dream. LC 94-14400. (Illus.). 48p. (gr. 2-8). 1994. PLB 15.80 (*0-516-04387-0*); pap. 3.95 (*0-516-44387-9*) Childrens.
Haskins, James & Benson, Kathleen. Space Challenger: The Story of Guion Bluford. LC 84-4251. (Illus.). 64p. (gr. 3-6). 1984. PLB 17.50 (*0-87614-259-5*) Carolrhoda Bks.
Haskins, Jim. One More River to Cross: The Story of Twelve Black Americans. (gr. 8-12). 1994. pap. 3.50 (*0-590-42897-7*) Scholastic Inc.
—One More River to Cross: Twelve Black Americans. 160p. 1992. 13.95 (*0-590-42896-9*, Scholastic Hardcover) Scholastic Inc.
—Outward Dreams: Black Inventors & Their Inventions. 128p. (gr. 7). 1991. 13.95 (*0-8027-6993-4*); PLB 14.85 (*0-8027-6994-2*) Walker & Co.
Hayden, Robert. Nine African-American Inventors. rev. ed. (Illus.). 171p. (gr. 5-8). 1992. Repr. of 1972 ed. PLB 14.95 (*0-8050-2133-7*) TFC Bks NY.
—Seven African-American Scientists. rev. ed. (Illus.). 173p. (gr. 5-8). 1992. Repr. of 1970 ed. PLB 14.95 (*0-8050-2134-5*) TFC Bks NY.
Hayden, Robert C. Eleven African-American Doctors. rev. ed. (Illus.). 208p. (gr. 5-8). 1992. Repr. of 1976 ed. PLB 14.95 (*0-8050-2135-3*) TFC Bks NY.
Haynes, Richard M. Ida B. Wells. LC 92-22192. (Illus.). 128p. (gr. 7-10). 1992. PLB 22.80 (*0-8114-2325-5*) Raintree Steck-V.
Herzel, Catherine B. She Made Many Rich: Sister Emma Francis of the Virgin Islands. Youngblood, Paul, illus. (Illus.). 24p. (gr. 6 up). 1990. pap. 4.50 (*0-935357-06-8*) CRIC Prod.
Hudson, Wade & Wesley, Valerie W. Afro-Bets Book of Black Heroes from A to Z: An Introduction to Important Black Achievers. LC 87-82951. (Illus.). 64p. (gr. 3-6). 1988. pap. 7.95 (*0-940975-02-5*) Just Us Bks.
Igus, Toyomi, et al. Book of Black Heroes, Vol. 2: Great Women in the Struggle. LC 91-90098. 112p. (gr. 4-8). 1991. lib. bdg. 17.95 (*0-940975-27-0*); pap. 10.95 (*0-940975-26-2*) Just Us Bks.
Italia, Bob. Anita Hill. LC 93-4615. 40p. 1993. 12.94 (*1-56239-259-X*) Abdo & Dghtrs.
—Clara Hale: Mother to Those Who Needed One. Wallner, Rosie, ed. LC 93-15261. 1993. 12.94 (*1-56239-235-2*) Abdo & Dghtrs.
Jackson, Garnet N. Elijah McCoy, Inventor. Thomas, Gary, illus. LC 92-28797. 1992. 56.50 (*0-8136-5230-8*); pap. 28.50 (*0-8136-5703-2*) Modern Curr.
—Garrett Morgan, Inventor. Hudson, Thomas, illus. LC 92-28801. 1992. write for info. (*0-8136-5231-6*); pap. write for info. (*0-8136-5704-0*) Modern Curr.
Jakoubek, Robert. Adam Clayton Powell, Jr. King, Coretta Scott, intro. by. (Illus.). 112p. 1988. lib. bdg. 17.95x (*1-55546-606-0*); pap. 9.95 (*0-7910-0213-6*) Chelsea Hse.
James Rapier: Mini Play. (gr. 5 up). 1977. 6.50 (*0-89550-360-3*) Stevens & Shea.
Johnson, Jacqueline. Stokely Carmichael: The Story of Black Power. Gallin, Richard, ed. Young, Andrew, intro. by. (Illus.). 128p. (gr. 5 up). 1990. lib. bdg. 12.95 (*0-382-09920-6*); pap. 7.95 (*0-382-24056-1*) Silver Burdett Pr.
Johnson, LaVerne C. Bessie Coleman: Writer. Perry, Craig R., illus. LC 92-35255. 1992. 3.95 (*0-922162-95-6*) Empak Pub.
—Heritage Kids Volume Set: George Washington Carver: Bessie Coleman: Harriet Tubman: Jean Baptiste DuSable. Perry, Craig P., illus. LC 92-35256. 1992. 3.95 (*0-922162-90-5*); Set. write for info. (*0-922162-99-9*) Empak Pub.
Jones, Margaret. Martin Luther King, Jr. Scott, R., illus. LC 68-9483. 36p. (gr. 2-4). 1968. PLB 11.80 (*0-516-03524-X*); pap. 3.95 (*0-516-43524-8*) Childrens.
King, Coretta Scott, intro. by. Black Americans of Achievement Series, 25 vols, No. 2. (Illus.). 1991. Set. lib. bdg. 448.75 (*0-7910-1112-7*) Chelsea Hse.
Klots, Steve. Ida Wells-Barnett, Civil Rights Leader. LC 93-14250. (gr. 5 up). 1994. write for info. (*0-7910-1885-7*); pap. write for info. (*0-7910-1914-4*) Chelsea Hse.
—Richard Allen. KIng, Coretta Scott, intro. by. (Illus.). 112p. (gr. 5 up). 1991. lib. bdg. 17.95 (*1-55546-570-6*) Chelsea Hse.
Koral, April. Florence Griffith Joyner: Track & Field Star. LC 91-32827. (Illus.). 64p. (gr. 3-6). 1992. PLB 12.90 (*0-531-20061-2*) Watts.

Lawler, Mary. Marcus Garvey. King, Coretta Scott, intro. by. (Illus.). 112p. (Orig.). (gr. 5 up). 1988. 17.95 (*1-55546-587-0*); pap. 9.95 (*0-7910-0203-9*) Chelsea Hse.

Lee, George L. Worldwide Interesting People: One Hundred Sixty-Two History Makers of African Descent. LC 91-50939. (Illus.). 144p. 1992. lib. bdg. 19.95 (*0-89950-670-4*) McFarland & Co.

Liss, Howard. Great Black Americans in Science. (Illus.). 160p. (gr. 3-9). 1990. lib. bdg. 14.95 (*0-87460-392-7*) Lion Bks.

McBrier, Vivian F. R. Nathaniel Dett: His Life & Works (1882-1943) 1990. 15.95 (*0-87498-092-5*) Assoc Pubs DC.

McCafferty, Jim. Holt & the Cowboys. Davis, Florence S., illus. LC 93-16618. 40p. (gr. 4-8). 1993. 12.95 (*0-88289-985-6*) Pelican.

Machamer, Gene. The Illustrated Black American Profiles. Sager, Linda C., ed. LC 90-82937. (Illus.). 192p. (Orig.). 1991. pap. 9.95 (*0-9627369-0-2*) Carlisle Pr.

McKissack, Patricia & McKissack, Fredrick. African-American Inventors. LC 93-42625. (Illus.). 96p. (gr. 4-6). 1994. PLB 17.90 (*1-56294-468-1*) Millbrook Pr.

—Carter G. Woodson: The Father of Black History. Ostendorf, Ned, illus. LC 91-8813. 32p. (gr. 1-4). 1991. lib. bdg. 12.95 (*0-89490-309-8*) Enslow Pubs.

—Great African Americans Series, 18 bks. (Illus.). (gr. 1-4). Set. lib. bdg. 233.10 (*0-89490-376-4*) Enslow Pubs.

—Ida B. Wells-Barnett: A Voice Against Violence. Ostendorf, Ned, illus. LC 90-49848. 32p. (gr. 1-4). 1991. lib. bdg. 12.95 (*0-89490-301-2*) Enslow Pubs.

—Madam C. J. Walker: Self-Made Millionaire. LC 92-6189. (Illus.). 32p. (gr. 1-4). 1992. lib. bdg. 12.95 (*0-89490-311-X*) Enslow Pubs.

—Mary Church Terrell: Leader for Equality. Ostendorf, Ned, illus. LC 91-3083. 32p. (gr. 1-4). 1991. lib. bdg. 12.95 (*0-89490-305-5*) Enslow Pubs.

Marzollo, Jean. Happy Birthday, Martin Luther King. Pinkney, J. Brian, illus. LC 91-42137. 32p. (ps-3). 1993. 14.95 (*0-590-44065-9*) Scholastic Inc.

May, Chris. Bob Marley. (Illus.). 64p. (gr. 5-9). 1991. 11.95 (*0-317-04244-0*, Pub. by Evans Bros Ltd) Trafalgar.

Medearis, Angela S. Come This Far to Freedom: A History of African Americans. Shaffer, Terea D., illus. LC 92-31251. 144p. (gr. 3-7). 1993. SBE 14.95 (*0-689-31522-8*, Atheneum Child Bk) Macmillan Child Grp.

Millender, Dharathula H. Crispus Attucks: Black Leader of Colonial Patriots. Morrow, Gray, illus. LC 86-10779. 192p. (gr. 2-6). 1986. pap. 3.95 (*0-02-041810-8*, Aladdin) Macmillan Child Grp.

Miller, Robert H. The Story of "Stagecoach" Mary Fields. Hanna, Cheryl, illus. LC 93-46286. 1994. write for info. (*0-382-24394-3*) Silver.

Miller, Vousette T. Color Me Beautiful Color Me Black. (Illus.). 32p. (ps-6). 1988. wkbk. 4.00 (*0-9619641-0-3*) Vous Etes Tres Belle.

Mills, Earl. Dorothy Dandridge. rev. ed. 1991. pap. 3.95 (*0-87067-580-X*) Holloway.

Mumford, Donald & Mumford, Esther. From Africa to the Arctic: Five Explorers. Lee, Nancy, illus. 48p. (gr. 1-3). 1992. 9.95 (*0-9605670-6-2*) Ananse Pr.

Mumford, Esther H. The Man Who Founded a Town. Kim, Jody, illus. 32p. (Orig.). (gr. 2-5). 1990. 8.95 (*0-9605670-2-X*); pap. 4.95 (*0-9605670-3-8*) Ananse Pr.

Naden, Corinne. Ronald McNair. King, Coretta Scott, intro. by. (Illus.). 112p. (gr. 5 up). 1991. lib. bdg. 17.95 (*0-7910-1133-X*) Chelsea Hse.

Northup, Solomon. Twelve Years a Slave: Excerpts from the Narrative of Solomon Northup. abr. ed. Lucas, Alice, ed. (Illus.). 48p. (Orig.). (gr. 5-12). Date not set. pap. text ed. 25.00 incl. 3 audio tapes (*0-936434-39-2*, Pub. by Zellerbach Fam Fund); pap. text ed. 5.00 tchr's. guide (*0-936434-59-7*) SF Study Ctr.

Excerpts in print & on audiotape from the true story of Solomon Northup, a free African American from New York who was kidnapped & sold into slavery in Louisiana. He lived as a slave for 12 years before regaining his freedom in 1853. Northup told of his harrowing experiences in a full-length book which Frederick Douglass called truth that is "stranger than fiction." African American actor/singer Wendell Brooks dramatically retells this moving story, enhancing the text by singing work songs & spirituals from the period. Actor Ossie Davis calls it "a powerful work. I recommend it without reservation." Reviewed in SLJ, 5/93, p. 71. BOOKLIST, 5/15/93, p. 1716, calls this 48-page illustrated excerpt: "excellent primary source material for the study of slavery in the United States." Also recorded on three 30-minute audiocassettes, TWELVE YEARS A SLAVE is excellent for schools, fifth grade through junior college. Also for church groups, other adult settings. Make checks payable to Many Cultures Publishing, P.O. Box 425646, San Francisco, CA 94142-5646. Toll Free 1-800-484-4173, ext. 1073, FAX 415-626-7276. California purchasers add sales tax.

Publisher Provided Annotation.

Obaba, Al-Imam. Adam Clayton Powell, Jr. (Illus.). 43p. (Orig.). 1989. pap. 3.95 (*0-916157-06-7*) African Islam Miss Pubns.

—Marcus Mosiah Garvey, Jr. Great Nubian Quiz. (Illus.). 43p. (Orig.). 1989. pap. 3.95 (*0-916157-15-6*) African Islam Miss Pubns.

Orr, Jack. Black Athlete: His Story in American History. Robinson, Jackie, intro. by. (gr. 6 up). 1969. PLB 14.95 (*0-87460-104-5*) Lion Bks.

Peters, Margaret W. The Ebony Book of Black Achievement. rev. ed. Ferguson, Cecil L., illus. LC 79-128544. 128p. (gr. 4-8). 1974. Repr. 10.95 (*0-87485-040-1*) Johnson Chi.

Picott, J. Rupert, ed. Walter Washington. 1990. 5.95 (*0-87498-094-1*) Assoc Pubs DC.

Pogrund, Benjamin. Nelson Mandela. LC 91-50541. (Illus.). 68p. (gr. 3-4). 1992. PLB 19.93 (*0-8368-0621-2*) Gareth Stevens Inc.

Pollack, Jill S. Shirley Chisholm. LC 93-31175. (Illus.). 64p. (gr. 5-8). 1994. PLB 12.90 (*0-531-20168-6*) Watts.

Porter, A. P. Jump at de Sun: The Story of Zora Neale Hurston. (gr. 4-7). 1992. pap. 6.95 (*0-87614-546-2*) Carolrhoda Bks.

Potter, Joan & Claytor, Constance. African-American Firsts: Famous, Little-Known, & Unsung Triumphs of Blacks in America. Munoz, Alison, illus. LC 93-84716. 352p. (Orig.). (gr. 7 up). 1994. pap. 14.95 (*0-9632476-1-1*) Pinto Pr.

Press, Skip. Natalie & Nat King Cole. LC 94-22429. 1995. text ed. 13.95 (*0-89686-879-6*, Crestwood Hse) Macmillan Child Grp.

Reef, Catherine. Benjamin Davis, Jr. (Illus.). 80p. (gr. 4-7). 1992. PLB 14.95 (*0-8050-2137-X*) TFC Bks NY.

Reiser, Howard. Patrick Ewing: Center of Attention. LC 94-14399. (Illus.). 48p. (gr. 2-8). 1994. PLB 15.80 (*0-516-04388-9*); pap. 3.95 (*0-516-44388-7*) Childrens.

Rennert, Richard, ed. Shapers of America. LC 92-39962. 1993. 13.95 (*0-7910-2053-3*, Am Art Analog); pap. 5.95 (*0-7910-2054-1*, Am Art Analog) Chelsea Hse.

Richardson, Ben & Foley, William A. Great Black Americans. LC 75-12841. (Illus.). 352p. (gr. 7 up). 1990. PLB 17.89 (*0-690-04791-6*, Crowell Jr Bks) HarpC Child Bks.

Ross, H. K. Black American Women, No. 3. (Illus.). 160p. (gr. 6-12). 1990. PLB 14.95 (*0-87460-365-X*) Lion Bks.

Rothaus, Jim. Karl Malone. (SPA & ENG.). (gr. 2-6). 1992. PLB 14.95 (*0-89565-961-1*) Childs World.

—Kirby Puckett. (SPA & ENG.). (gr. 2-6). 1992. PLB 14.95 (*0-89565-960-3*) Childs World.

Santrey, Laurence. Young Frederick Douglass: Fight for Freedom. Dodson, Bert, illus. LC 82-15993. 48p. (gr. 4-6). 1983. PLB 10.79 (*0-89375-857-4*); pap. text ed. 3.50 (*0-89375-858-2*) Troll Assocs.

Scally, M. A. Walking Proud. 1990. 12.95 (*0-87498-100-X*) Assoc Pubs DC.

Schroeder, Alan. Josephine Baker. King, Coretta Scott, intro. by. (Illus.). 128p. (gr. 5 up). 1991. lib. bdg. 17.95 (*0-7910-1116-X*) Chelsea Hse.

Scott, Victoria & Jones, Ernest. Sylvia Stark: A Pioneer. Lewis, Karen, illus. 64p. (Orig.). (gr. 4-12). 1992. PLB 12.95 (*0-940880-37-7*); pap. 6.95 (*0-940880-38-5*) Open Hand.

Shapiro, Miles. Maya Angelou, Author. King, Coretta Scott, intro. by. (Illus.). 112p. (gr. 5 up). 1994. PLB 18.95 (*0-7910-1862-8*, Am Art Analog); pap. write for info. (*0-7910-1891-1*, Am Art Analog) Chelsea Hse.

Shirley, David. Satchel Paige. King, Coretta Scott, intro. by. (Illus.). 112p. (gr. 5 up). 1993. PLB 17.95 (*0-7910-1880-6*); pap. write for info. (*0-7910-1983-7*) Chelsea Hse.

Siegel, Beatrice. The Year They Walked: Rosa Parks & the Montgomery Bus Boycott. LC 91-14078. (Illus.). 128p. (gr. 4-7). 1992. SBE 13.95 (*0-02-782631-7*, Four Winds) Macmillan Child Grp.

Simmons-Henry, Linda, et al. The Heritage of Blacks in North Carolina. (gr. 6-12). 1990. 60.00 (*0-912081-12-0*) Delmar Co.

Sklansky, Jeff. James Farmer. (Illus.). 112p. (gr. 5 up). 1992. lib. bdg. 17.95 (*0-7910-1126-7*) Chelsea Hse.

Stwertka, Eve. Duke Ellington: A Life of Music. LC 93-21267. (Illus.). (gr. 9-12). 1994. PLB 14.40 (*0-531-13035-5*) Watts.

Super, Neil. Daniel "Chappie" James. (Illus.). 80p. (gr. 4-7). 1992. PLB 14.95 (*0-8050-2138-8*) TFC Bks NY.

Sweet, Dovie D. Red Light, Green Light: The Life of Garrett Morgan & His Invention of the Stop Light. 4th ed. (Orig.). (gr. 1-6). 1988. pap. 5.00 (*0-682-49088-1*) Kitwardo Pubs.

Tames, Richard. Nelson Mandela. LC 90-43956. (Illus.). 32p. 1991. PLB 12.40 (*0-531-14124-1*) Watts.

Thomas. Alex Haley Boyhood Years. Date not set. 15.00 (*0-06-023417-2*); PLB 14.89 (*0-06-023418-0*) HarpC Child Bks.

Thomas, Anika D. Life in the Ghetto. Thatch, Nancy R., ed. Thomas, Anika D., illus. Melton, David, intro. by. LC 91-13944. (Illus.). 26p. (gr. 5 up). 1991. PLB 14.95 (*0-933849-34-6*) Landmark Edns.

Thompson, Cliff. Charles Chesnutt. King, Coretta Scott, intro. by. (Illus.). 112p. (gr. 5 up). 1993. PLB 17.95 (*1-55546-578-1*) Chelsea Hse.

Thompson-Peters, Flossie E. Dynamic Black Americans. Green, Kenneth L., illus. 32p. (gr. 1-8). 1988. pap. 4.70 (*1-880784-07-6*) Atlas Pr.

DYNAMIC BLACK AMERICANS, a biographical series, is written by Flossie E. Thompson-Peters in lilting, rhythmic verse. Young readers find these books exciting as well as informative. Ideal as core literature, choral reading, dramatizations & read-aloud books. JAN, THE SHOEMAN, Jan Matzeliger (inventor); BENJAMIN BANNEKER, 3rd ed. (1994) (pioneer urban planner); JEAN BAPTISTE DuSABLE (founder of Chicago), New Spanish edition available 2/94; MALCOLM X; HARRIET TUBMAN (freedom fighter & Civil War heroine); & DANIEL HALE WILLIAMS (first successful open heart surgeon). Ages 7-14, Appropriate for elementary grades & selected secondary & ESL students. DYNAMIC BLACK AMERICAN SERIES. ISBN 1-880784-07-6. $4.70 per copy. $23.50 for series (6 books). Paperback. THE SHEPHERD, A BIOGRAPHY of Dr. Arthur A. Peters, by Flossie Thompson-Peters, is about a community activist, civil rights leader & Los Angeles minister who started a church in 1943 & became a great influence in the civic, spiritual & political life of the African-American community of Los Angeles. "The book is of historical significance & is of more than local interest." - L.A. Times Book Review. Photographs. General interest. Hardcover, 251 pages. $10.00. ISBN 1-880784-00-9. MARTIN LUTHER KING, JR. is a biography by Flossie Thompson-Peters in poetic, rhythmic style. The life of Dr. King is chronicled from childhood, through trials & triumphs, to his tragic end, with emphasis upon his lasting influence. Ages 8 to adult. 94 pages. $7.50 ISBN 1-880784-06-8. Jesse J. Peters, President. Atlas Press, P.O. Box 56282, Los Angeles, CA 90008. (213) 295-3036.

Publisher Provided Annotation.

—La Historia De Jean Baptiste DuSable: El Padre De Chicago. Nolasco-Carrandi, Guadalupe, tr. from ENG. Clo, Kathy, illus. (SPA.). 32p. (gr. 3-8). 1994. pap. 4.70 (*1-880784-09-2*) Atlas Pr.

Thornley, Stew. Deion Sanders: Prime Time Player. (gr. 4-7). 1993. pap. 4.95 (*0-8225-9648-2*) Lerner Pubns.

Towle, Wendy. The Real McCoy: The Life of an African-American Inventor. Clay, Wil, illus. LC 91-38895. 32p. (gr. k-4). 1993. 14.95 (*0-590-43596-5*) Scholastic Inc.

Travis, Dempsey J. I Refuse to Learn to Fail. (Illus.). 75p. (gr. 3-6). 1991. 15.00 (*0-941484-12-2*) Urban Res Pr.

Turner, Glennette T. Take a Walk in Their Shoes: Biographies of Fourteen Outstanding African Americans - with Skits about Each to Act Out. Fax, Elton C., illus. LC 92-19524. 176p. (gr. 3-7). 1992. pap. 5.99 (*0-14-036250-9*) Puffin Bks.

Turner, Robyn M. Faith Ringgold. LC 92-42652. 32p. 1993. 15.95 (*0-316-85652-5*) Little.

Van Steenwyk, Elizabeth. Ida B. Wells-Barnett: Woman of Courage. LC 88-31376. (Illus.). 112p. (gr. 7-12). 1992. PLB 14.40 (*0-531-13014-2*) Watts.

Washington, Booker T. Up from Slavery. Andrews, C. A., intro. by. (gr. 5 up). 1967. pap. 2.50 (*0-8049-0157-0*, CL-157) Airmont.

Weisbrot, Robert. Father Divine. (Illus.). 120p. (gr. 5 up). 1992. lib. bdg. 17.95 (*0-7910-1122-4*) Chelsea Hse.

Wesley, Charles H. Richard Allen: An Apostle of Freedom. 1990. 12.95 (*0-87498-078-X*); pap. 9.95 (*0-87498-079-8*) Assoc Pubs DC.

Williams, Jean. Matthew Henson: Polar Adventurer. LC 93-6101. (Illus.). 64p. (gr. 5-8). 1994. PLB 12.90 (*0-531-20006-X*) Watts.

Wisniewski, David. Sundiata: Lion King of Mali. Wisniewski, David, illus. 32p. (gr. k-4). 1992. 15.95 (*0-395-61302-7*, Clarion Bks) HM.

Witcover, Paul. Zora Neale Hurston. King, Coretta Scott, intro. by. (Illus.). 112p. (gr. 5 up). 1991. PLB 17.95 (*0-7910-1129-1*) Chelsea Hse.

Woods, Geraldine. Oprah Winfrey. LC 91-7818. (Illus.). 80p. (gr. 3 up). 1991. text ed. 13.95 RSBE (*0-87518-463-4*, Dillon) Macmillan Child Grp.

Woodson, Carter G. African Heroes & Heroines. (Illus.). 1990. 12.95 (*0-87498-077-1*); pap. 9.95 (*0-87498-076-3*) Assoc Pubs DC.

Yates, Janelle. Zora Neale Hurston: A Storyteller's Life. enl. ed. Adams, David, illus. 98p. (gr. 4 up). 1993. PLB 14.95 (*0-9623380-3-6*); pap. 9.95 (*0-9623380-1-X*) Ward Hill Pr.

Yount, Lisa. Black Scientists. (Illus.). (gr. 5-12). 1991. lib. bdg. 16.95x (*0-8160-2549-5*) Facts on File.

BLACKS–CIVIL RIGHTS

Bullard, Sara. Free At Last: A History of the Civil Rights Movement & Those Who Died in the Struggle. Bond, Julian, intro. by. LC 92-38174. (Illus.). 112p. 1993. PLB 20.00 (*0-19-508381-4*) OUP.

Cwiklik, Robert. Stokely Carmichael & Black Power. LC 92-11560. (Illus.). 32p. (gr. 2-4). 1993. PLB 12.90 (*1-56294-276-X*); pap. 4.95 (*1-56294-839-3*) Millbrook Pr.

Douglass, Frederick. Why Is the Negro Lynched. Obaba, Al I., ed. 49p. (Orig.). 1991. pap. text ed. 7.95 (*0-916157-78-4*) African Islam Miss Pubns.

Ella Baker. (Illus.). 128p. (gr. 5-8). 1990. lib. bdg. 12.95 (*0-382-09931-1*); pap. 7.95 (*0-382-24066-9*) Silver Burdett Pr.

Fireside, Harvey & Fuller, Sarah B. Brown vs. Board of Education: Equal Schooling for All. LC 93-5897. (Illus.). 104p. (gr. 6 up). 1994. lib. bdg. 17.95 (*0-89490-469-8*) Enslow Pubs.

Haskins, James S. The March on Washington. LC 92-13626. (Illus.). 128p. (gr. 5 up). 1993. 15.00 (*0-06-021289-6*); PLB 14.89 (*0-06-021290-X*) HarpC Child Bks.

The History of the Civil Rights Movement, 9 bks. (Illus.). (gr. 5-8). 1990. Set, 128p. ea. lib. bdg. 116.55 (*0-382-09919-2*); pap. 71.55 (*0-382-24055-3*) Silver Burdett Pr.

Jones, Margaret. Martin Luther King, Jr. Scott, R., illus. LC 68-9483. 36p. (gr. 2-4). 1968. PLB 11.80 (*0-516-03524-X*); pap. 3.95 (*0-516-43524-8*) Childrens.

Kelso, Richard. Walking for Freedom: The Montgomery Bus Boycott. Newton, Michael, illus. LC 92-18080. 52p. (gr. 2-5). 1992. PLB 19.97 (*0-8114-7218-3*) Raintree Steck-V.

Kosof, Anna. The Civil Rights Movement & Its Legacy. LC 89-9166. (Illus.). 112p. (gr. 7-12). 1989. PLB 13.40 (*0-531-10791-4*) Watts.

Levine, Ellen. Freedom's Children: Young Civil Rights Activists Tell Their Own Stories. 224p. 1993. 16.95 (*0-399-21893-9*) Putnam Pub Group.

McKissack, Patricia & McKissack, Fredrick. The Civil Rights Movement in America from 1865 to the Present. 2nd ed. LC 86-9636. (Illus.). 352p. (gr. 4 up). 1991. 30.85 (*0-516-00579-0*) Childrens.

Millender, Dharathula H. Martin Luther King, Jr. Young Man with a Dream. Fiorentino, Al, illus. LC 86-10739. 192p. (gr. 2-6). 1986. pap. 3.95 (*0-02-042010-2*, Aladdin) Macmillan Child Grp.

Myers, Walter D. Now Is Your Time! The African-American Struggle for Freedom. LC 91-314. (Illus.). 320p. (gr. 6 up). 1992. pap. 10.95 (*0-06-446120-3*, Trophy) HarpC Child Bks.

Powledge, Fred. We Shall Overcome: Heroes of the Civil Rights Movement. LC 92-25184. (Illus.). 224p. (gr. 7 up). 1993. SBE 16.95 (*0-684-19362-0*, Scribners Young Read) Macmillan Child Grp.

Senna, Carl. The Black Press & the Struggle for Civil Rights. (Illus.). 176p. (gr. 7-12). 1993. PLB 13.90 (*0-531-11036-2*) Watts.

—The Black Press & the Struggle for Civil Rights. (Illus.). (gr. 7-12). 1994. pap. 6.95 (*0-531-15693-1*) Watts.

Walter, Mildred P. Mississippi Challenge. LC 92-6718. (Illus.). 224p. (gr. 6 up). 1992. SBE 18.95 (*0-02-792301-0*, Bradbury Pr) Macmillan Child Grp.

BLACKS–CIVIL RIGHTS–FICTION

Moore, Yvette. Freedom Songs. LC 92-20289. 176p. (gr. 7 up). 1992. pap. 3.99 (*0-14-036017-4*) Puffin Bks.

BLACKS–DRAMA

Turner, Glennette T. Take a Walk in Their Shoes: Biographies of Fourteen Outstanding African Americans - with Skits about Each to Act Out. Fax, Elton C., illus. LC 92-19524. 176p. (gr. 3-7). 1992. pap. 5.99 (*0-14-036250-9*) Puffin Bks.

BLACKS–EDUCATION

see also Segregation in Education

Carroll, Joan. The Black College Career Guide. 140p. (gr. 9-12). 1992. pap. 6.95 (*1-881223-00-0*) Zulema Ent.

Cherry, Charles W., II. Excellence Without Excuse: The Black Student's Guide to Academic Excellence. LC 91-35248. (gr. 7 up). 1993. 24.95 (*1-56385-497-X*); pap. 13.95 (*1-56385-498-8*) Intl Schol Pr.

Hodge-Wright, Toni, et al, eds. The Handbook of Historically Black Colleges & Universities, Premier Edition 1992-94: Comprehensive Profiles & Photos of Black Colleges & Universities. Evans, Christine, et al, illus. LC 92-71364. 248p. (gr. 10 up). 1992. 19.95 (*0-9632669-0-X*) Jireh & Assocs.

Jackson, Garnet N. Frederick Douglass, Freedom Fighter. Holliday, Keaf, illus. LC 92-28777. 1992. 56.40 (*0-8136-5229-4*); pap. 28.50 (*0-8136-5702-4*) Modern Curr.

Lusane, Clarence. The Struggle for Equal Education. (Illus.). 160p. (gr. 7-12). 1992. PLB 13.90 (*0-531-11121-0*) Watts.

Picott, J. Rupert. A Quarter Century of the Black Experience in Elementary & Secondary Education, 1950-1975. 1990. 9.95 (*0-87498-087-9*) Assoc Pubs DC.

Woodson, Carter G. Mis-Education of the Negro. 1990. pap. 12.95 (*0-87498-001-1*) Assoc Pubs DC.

BLACKS–EDUCATION–FICTION

Bauldock, Gerald. Reaching for the Moon. LC 88-92848. 303p. (Orig.). (gr. 7-12). 1989. pap. text ed. 14.95 (*0-9621728-0-4*) B-Dock Pr.

Clifton, Fred. Darl. (Illus.). 104p. (gr. 2-6). 1973. 12.00 (*0-89388-098-1*) Okpaku Communications.

De Gree, Melvin. Brickhouse Dreams: Young Benjamin E. Mays. Davis, Beverly, illus. 140p. (Orig.). (gr. 3-10). 1992. pap. 11.95 (*0-9632895-0-0*) Trail of Success.

Hudson, Cheryl W. & Ford, Bernette G. Bright Eyes, Brown Skin. Ford, George, illus. LC 90-81648. 24p. (ps-2). 1990. 12.95 (*0-940975-10-6*); pap. 6.95 (*0-940975-23-8*) Just Us Bks.

BLACKS–EMPLOYMENT

Marsh, Carole. The Best Book of Black Biographies. (gr. 3-12). 1994. PLB 24.95 (*1-55609-330-6*); pap. 14.95 (*1-55609-329-2*); computer disk 29.95 (*1-55609-331-4*) Gallopade Pub Group.

—Black Business. (gr. 4-12). 1994. PLB 24.95 (*1-55609-327-6*); pap. 14.95 (*1-55609-326-8*); computer disk 29.95 (*1-55609-328-4*) Gallopade Pub Group.

BLACKS–FICTION

Armstrong, Jennifer. Steal Away. LC 91-18504. 224p. (gr. 6 up). 1992. 15.95 (*0-531-05983-9*); lib. bdg. 15.99 (*0-531-08583-X*) Orchard Bks Watts.

Armstrong, William H. Sounder. LC 70-85030. (Illus.). 128p. (gr. 6 up). 1969. 14.00 (*0-06-020143-6*); PLB 13.89 (*0-06-020144-4*) HarpC Child Bks.

—Sounder. Barkley, James, illus. LC 70-85030. 128p. (gr. 6 up). 1972. pap. 3.95 (*0-06-440020-4*, Trophy) HarpC Child Bks.

Banks, Jacqueline T. New One. (gr. 4-7). 1994. 13.95 (*0-395-66610-4*) HM.

Barber, Barbara E. Saturday at The New You. Rich, Anna, illus. LC 93-5165. 1994. 14.95 (*1-880000-06-7*) Lee & Low Bks.

Barrett, Anna P. The Middlebatchers: Throw a Party for the Marriage of Hetty Wish & Lester Leg, Vol. 1. Darst, Shelia S., ed. Russell, Dave, illus. 118p. (Orig.). (gr. 3-7). 1984. pap. 7.95 (*0-89896-105-X*) Larksdale.

Barrett, William E. Lilies of the Field. Silverman, Burt, illus. LC 62-8085. (gr. 7 up). 1967. 3.95 (*0-685-01491-6*, Im); pap. 3.95 (*0-385-07246-5*, Im) Doubleday.

Belton, Sandra. From Miss Ida's Porch. Cooper, Floyd, illus. LC 92-31239. 40p. (gr. 2-5). 1993. RSBE 14.95 (*0-02-708915-0*, Four Winds) Macmillan Child Grp.

Binch, Caroline. Gregory Cool. LC 93-11845. (gr. 3 up). 1994. 14.99 (*0-8037-1577-3*) Dial Bks Young.

Bolden, Tonya, ed. Rites of Passage: Stories about Growing up by Black Writers from Around the World. Johnson, Charles, frwd. by. LC 93-31304. 240p. (gr. 5 up). 1993. 16.95 (*1-56282-688-3*) Hyprn Child.

Bonham, Frank. Mystery of the Fat Cat. Smith, Alvin, illus. 160p. (gr. 5-9). 1971. pap. 1.25 (*0-440-46226-6*, YB) Dell.

Bontemps, Arna W. & Hughes, Langston. Popo & Fifina. Campbell, E. Simms, illus. Rampersad, Arnold & Rampersad, Arnoldintro. by. (Illus.). 120p. 1993. jacketed 14.95 (*0-19-508765-8*) OUP.

Boyd, Candy D. Forever Friends. 192p. (gr. 5-9). 1986. pap. 4.99 (*0-14-032077-6*, Puffin) Puffin Bks.

Braby, Marie. The Longest Wait. Ward, John, illus. LC 94-24875. 1995. write for info. (*0-531-06871-4*); PLB write for info. (*0-531-08721-2*) Orchard Bks Watts.

Brady, Jennifer. Jambi & the Lions. Thatch, Nancy R., ed. Brady, Jennifer, illus. Melton, David, intro. by. LC 92-17593. (Illus.). 26p. (gr. 3-5). 1992. PLB 14.95 (*0-933849-41-9*) Landmark Edns.

Burgess, Barbara H. Oren Bell. 1991. 15.00 (*0-385-30325-4*) Delacorte.

Byars, Betsy C. The Burning Questions of Bingo Brown. LC 87-21022. 160p. (gr. 3-7). 1988. pap. 14.00 (*0-670-81932-8*) Viking Child Bks.

Campbell, Tammie L. Honey Brown in Search of Her Identity, Vol. 1. Jammer, Cornelius C., Jr., illus. Moon, Felicia, intro. by. (Illus.). 24p. (Orig.). (gr. k-5). 1990. pap. 4.95 (*0-9623947-0-X*) T L Campbell.

Carter, Donna R. Music in the Family. Harris, Cortrell J., illus. 32p. (gr. k-3). 1994. pap. write for info. (*1-885242-01-8*) Lindsey Pubng. Growing up with music Oliver had one wish--to play in his family's band. He strives to become a good musician but discovers it will take much more than talent. This story helps us learn about different instruments & musical styles like gospel, blues, jazz & reggae. This is a story about perseverance & one boy's triumph to make his dream come true.
Publisher Provided Annotation.

Ceasor, Frank, Sr. & Gaines, Edith. Can You Count?; Carpetbaggers in Action; Mr. Impossible. 2nd ed. McCluskey, John A., ed. Pryor, Ernest, et al, illus. (gr. 4-7). 1993. pap. 3.00 (*0-913678-27-9*) New Day Pr.

Chapman, Cheryl. Snow on Snow on Snow. St. James, Synthia, illus. 1994. write for info. (*0-8037-1456-4*); PLB write for info. (*0-8037-1457-2*) Dial Bks Young.

Chapman, Christina. Treasure in the Attic. Hoggan, Pat, illus. LC 92-35814. 32p. (gr. 4-6). 1992. PLB 19.97 (*0-8114-3582-2*) Raintree Steck-V.

Chocolate, Debbi & Hudson, Wade. NEATE: To the Rescue. LC 92-72004. 112p. (Orig.). (gr. 5 up). 1992. pap. 3.95 (*0-940975-42-4*) Just Us Bks.

Clifton, Lucille. Everett Anderson's Christmas Coming. Gilchrist, Jan S., illus. LC 91-2041. 32p. (ps-4). 1991. 14.95 (*0-8050-1549-3*, Bks Young Read) H Holt & Co.

—Everett Anderson's Year. rev. ed. Grifalconi, Ann, illus. LC 92-4683. 32p. (ps-2). 1992. 14.95 (*0-8050-2247-3*, Bks Young Read) H Holt & Co.

Connelly, Bernardine. Follow the Drinking Gourd. Buchanan, Yvonne, illus. LC 93-19247. 1993. 14.95 (*0-88708-336-6*, Rabbit Ears); incl. cass. 19.95 (*0-88708-335-8*, Rabbit Ears) Picture Bk Studio.

Cousins, Linda. Huggy Bean: A Desert Adventure. (Illus.). 28p. 1992. pap. 5.95 (*0-936073-12-8*) Gumbs & Thomas.

—Huggy Bean & the Origin of the Magic Kente Cloth. (Illus.). 28p. 1991. pap. 5.95 (*0-936073-11-X*) Gumbs & Thomas.

—Huggy Bean: We Happened upon a Beautiful Place. (Illus.). 28p. 1992. pap. 5.95 (*0-936073-13-6*) Gumbs & Thomas.

Crews, Donald. Shortcut. LC 91-36312. (Illus.). 32p. (ps-6). 1992. 14.00 (*0-688-06436-1*); PLB 13.93 (*0-688-06437-X*) Greenwillow.

Davis, Ossie. Just Like Martin. LC 91-4672. 1992. pap. 14.00 (*0-671-73202-1*, S&S BFYR) S&S Trade.

Dean, Jeffrey J. & Dean, Debra A. The Amazing Adventures of Abiola. Ferguson, Dwayne J., illus. LC 93-30332. 32p. (gr. 6-9). 1994. 12.95 (*0-86543-409-3*); pap. 5.95 (*0-86543-410-7*) Africa World.

Dhondy, Farrukh. Black Swan. LC 92-30425. 208p. (gr. 6 up). 1993. 14.95 (*0-395-66076-9*) HM.

Dotson, Williette D. Visions: The Story of a Black Girl Determined to Make It Despite the Odds. 190p. (gr. 9 up). 1993. text ed. 18.95 (*0-9635032-0-0*) SAC Pr.

Draper, Sharon. Tears of a Tiger. LC 94-10278. (gr. 7 up). 1994. 14.95 (*0-689-31878-2*, Atheneum) Macmillan.

Duncan, Alice F. Willie Jerome. LC 94-10444. 1995. 15. 00 (*0-02-733208-X*) Macmillan Child Grp.

Echewa, T. O. How Tables Came to Umu Madu. LC 88-83368. (Illus.). 90p. (gr. 5 up). 19.95 (*0-86543-127-2*); pap. 7.95 (*0-86543-128-0*) Africa World.

Falwell, Cathryn. Feast for Ten. Falwell, Cathryn, illus. LC 92-35512. 32p. (ps-3). 1993. 14.95 (*0-395-62037-6*, Clarion Bks) HM.

Farmer, Nancy. Do You Know Me. Jackson, Shelley, illus. 112p. (gr. 3-7). 1994. pap. 3.99 (*0-14-036946-5*) Puffin Bks.

—The Ear, the Eye & the Arm. LC 93-11814. 320p. (gr. 7 up). 1994. 16.95 (*0-531-06829-3*); lib. bdg. 16.99 RLB (*0-531-08679-8*) Orchard Bks Watts.

Faux, Ruth. Golden Dawn. Turechek, Lou, illus. LC 93-61636. 192p. (Orig.). (gr. 7 up). 1994. pap. 6.95 (*1-878893-43-2*) Telcraft Bks.

Feelings, Tom. Tommy Traveller in the World of Black History. (gr. 4-7). 1993. pap. 6.95 (*0-86316-211-8*) Writers & Readers.

Felder, Pamela T. I'm Black & I'm Beautiful. Slade, John, ed. Rice, Kendrick, illus. 14p. (Orig.). 1993. pap. 3.50 (*0-9638310-0-3*) Pams Unique.

Gray, Nigel. I'll Take You to Mrs. Cole! Foreman, Michael, illus. 32p. (ps-3). 1992. 12.95 (*0-916291-39-1*) Kane-Miller Bk.

Greenfield, Eloise. Daydreamers. Feelings, Tom, illus. (gr. k up). 1981. 13.95 (*0-8037-2137-4*) Dial Bks Young.

—Koya Delaney & the Good Girl Blues. 176p. 1992. 13. 95 (*0-590-43300-8*, Scholastic Hardcover) Scholastic Inc.

Grifalconi, Ann. Electric Yancy. LC 94-14596. 1995. write for info. (*0-688-13187-5*); PLB write for info. (*0-688-13188-3*) Lothrop.

Guy, Rosa. Billy the Great. Binch, Caroline, illus. LC 92-34704. 32p. (gr. k-3). 1992. 15.00 (*0-385-30666-0*) Delacorte.

—The Music of Summer. (gr. 7 up). 1991. 14.00 (*0-685-52466-3*) Delacorte.
—The Music of Summer. 1992. pap. 15.00 (*0-385-30599-0*) Doubleday.
Haarhoff, Dorian. Desert December. Vermeulen, Leon, illus. 32p. (ps-3). 1992. 13.95 (*0-395-61300-0*, Clarion Bks) HM.
Hamilton, V. Drylongso. Pinkney, J., illus. 1992. write for info. (*0-15-224241-4*, HB Juv Bks) HarBrace.
Hamilton, Virginia. Bells of Christmas. 59p. (ps up). 1989. 17.95 (*0-15-206450-8*) HarBrace.
—M. C. Higgins, the Great. LC 72-92439. 288p. (gr. 7 up). 1974. SBE 15.95 (*0-02-742480-4*, Macmillan Child Bk) Macmillan Child Grp.
—White Romance. 233p. (gr. 7 up). 1989. pap. 3.95 (*0-15-295888-6*, Odyssey) HarBrace.
—Zeely. Shimin, Symeon, illus. LC 67-10266. 128p. (gr. 5-7). 1968. SBE 13.95 (*0-02-742470-7*, Macmillan Child Bk) Macmillan Child Grp.
—Zeely. 2nd ed. LC 92-28769. (Illus.). 128p. (gr. 3-7). 1993. pap. 3.95 (*0-689-71695-8*, Aladdin) Macmillan Child Grp.
Havill, Juanita. Jamaica & Brianna. O'Brien, Anne S., illus. LC 92-36508. 1993. 13.95 (*0-395-64489-5*) HM.
Hayes, Sarah. Happy Christmas, Gemma. Ormerod, Jan, illus. LC 85-23674. 32p. (ps-1). 1986. 13.95 (*0-688-06508-2*) Lothrop.
Heo, Yumi. Father's Rubber Shoes. LC 94-21961. (gr. 1-8). 1995. write for info. (*0-531-06873-0*); PLB write for info. (*0-531-08723-9*) Orchard Bks Watts.
Higginsen, Vy & Bolden, Tonya. Mama, I Want to Sing. 1992. 13.95 (*0-590-44201-5*, Scholastic Hardcover) Scholastic Inc.
Hill, Elizabeth S. Evan's Corner. (ps-3). 1991. 13.00 (*0-670-82830-0*) Viking Child Bks.
Hoffman, Mary. Amazing Grace. (ps-3). 1991. 14.00 (*0-8037-1040-2*) Dial Bks Young.
Hoobler, Dorothy & Hoobler, Thomas. Next Stop, Freedom: The Story of a Slave Girl. Hanna, Cheryl, illus. 64p. (gr. 4-6). 1991. 5.95 (*0-382-24152-5*); PLB 7.95 (*0-382-24145-2*); pap. 3.95 (*0-382-24347-1*) Silver Burdett Pr.
Hooks, William H. The Ballad of Belle Dorcas. Pinkney, Brian, illus. LC 89-2715. 48p. (gr. 2-7). 1990. 13.95 (*0-394-84645-1*); lib. bdg. 14.99 (*0-394-94645-6*) Knopf Bks Yng Read.
Howard, Ellen. When Daylight Comes. LC 85-7963. 192p. (gr. 5-9). 1985. SBE 14.95 (*0-689-31133-8*, Atheneum Child Bk) Macmillan Child Grp.
Howe, Quincy. Streetsmart. LC 93-1397. 112p. (gr. 6-12). 1993. pap. 6.95 (*0-932765-42-4*, 1325-93); tchr's. guide 5.95 (*0-685-70875-6*, 1326-93) Close Up.
Hru, Dakari. Joshua's Masai Mask. Rich, Anna, illus. LC 92-73219. 32p. (gr. k-4). 1993. 14.95 (*1-880000-02-4*) Lee & Low Bks.
Hudson, Cheryl W. & Ford, Bernette G. Bright Eyes, Brown Skin. Ford, George, illus. LC 90-81648. 24p. (ps-2). 1990. 12.95 (*0-940975-10-6*); pap. 6.95 (*0-940975-23-8*) Just Us Bks.
Hudson, Wade. Afro-Bets Kids: I'm Gonna Be! Blair, Culverson, illus. LC 92-72000. 32p. (Orig.). (ps up). 1992. pap. 6.95 (*0-940975-40-8*) Just Us Bks.
Hudson, Wade, et al. Jamal's Busy Day. LC 90-81646. (Illus.). 24p. (gr. 1-3). 1991. lib. bdg. 12.95 (*0-940975-21-1*); pap. 6.95 (*0-940975-24-6*) Just Us Bks.
Hughes, Langston. Thank You M'am. 1991. PLB 13.95 (*0-88682-478-8*) Creative Ed.
Hulbert, Jay & Kantor, Sid. Armando Asked "Why?" Hoggan, Pat, illus. 24p. (ps-2). 1990. PLB 17.10 (*0-8172-3576-0*); pap. 4.95 (*0-8114-6739-2*) Raintree Steck-V.
Humphrey, Margo. The River That Gave Gifts. LC 78-61980. (Illus.). (gr. 2-9). 1987. 13.95 (*0-89239-027-1*) Childrens Book Pr.
Igus, Toyomi. When I Was Little. Bond, Higgins, illus. LC 92-72006. 32p. (Orig.). (gr. 1 up). 1992. 14.95 (*0-940975-32-7*); pap. 6.95 (*0-940975-33-5*) Just Us Bks.
Isadora, Rachel. At the Crossroads. Isadora, Rachel, illus. 32p. (ps up). 1994. pap. 4.95 (*0-688-13103-4*, Mulberry) Morrow.
—Over the Green Hills. LC 91-12761. 32p. (ps up). 1992. 14.00 (*0-688-10509-2*); PLB 13.93 (*0-688-10510-6*) Greenwillow.
Johnson, Dolores. Now Let Me Fly: The Story of a Slave Family. Johnson, Dolores, illus. LC 92-33683. 32p. (gr. k-5). 1993. RSBE 14.95 (*0-02-747699-5*, Macmillan Child Bk) Macmillan Child Grp.
—What Kind of Baby-Sitter Is This? LC 90-42860. (Illus.). 32p. (gr. k-3). 1991. RSBE 13.95 (*0-02-747846-7*, Macmillan Child Bk) Macmillan Child Grp.
Johnson-Feelings, Dianne. The Painter Man. Granderson, Eddie, illus. LC 93-4063. 1993. write for info. (*0-89334-220-3*) Humanics Ltd.
Johnston, Brenda A., et al. Stories from Black History Series II, 3 bks. 2nd ed. McCluskey, John A., ed. (Illus.). (gr. 4-7). 1993. Set. pap. 8.00 (*0-913678-24-4*) New Day Pr.
Jones, Jay S. Rosalia, Be Proud. Jones, MariaElena G., illus. 41p. (gr. k-6). 1992. 14.95 (*0-9632040-0-9*); PLB 14.95 (*0-9632040-1-7*) Integrity Inst.
Keats, Ezra J. Silba por Willie: (Whistle for Willie) (SPA., Illus.). 40p. (ps-1). 1992. 14.00 (*0-670-84395-4*) Viking Child Bks.
Knight, Ginny. Jessie Helps a Wish. Knight, Ginny, illus. 1991. 3.00 (*0-940248-82-4*) Guild Pr.
Kroll, Virginia. Africa Brothers & Sisters. French, Vanessa & French, Vanessa, illus. LC 91-20346. 32p. (ps-2). 1993. RSBE 14.95 (*0-02-751166-9*, Four Winds) Macmillan Child Grp.
—Masai & I. Carpenter, Nancy, illus. LC 91-24561. 32p. (gr. k-2). 1992. RSBE 14.95 (*0-02-751165-0*, Four Winds) Macmillan Child Grp.
Lewin, Hugh. Jafta: The Homecoming. Kopper, Lisa, illus. LC 93-12945. 32p. (ps-2). 1994. 8.99 (*0-679-84722-7*); PLB 9.99 (*0-679-94722-1*) Knopf Bks Yng Read.
Lipsyte, Robert. The Brave. LC 90-25396. 208p. (gr. 7 up). 1991. 15.00 (*0-06-023915-8*); PLB 14.89 (*0-06-023916-6*) HarpC Child Bks.
Maartens, Maretha. Paper Bird: A Novel of South Africa. 144p. (gr. 4-9). 1991. 13.45 (*0-395-56490-5*, Clarion Bks) HM.
McDaniels, William. Abdul & the Designer Tennis Shoes. 1990. pap. 6.95 (*0-913543-15-2*) African Am Imag.
McKissack, Patricia. The Dark-Thirty: Southern Tales of the Supernatural. Pinkney, Brian, illus. LC 92-3021. 128p. (gr. 3-7). 1992. 15.00 (*0-679-81863-4*); PLB 15. 99 (*0-679-91863-9*) Knopf Bks Yng Read.
Martin, Ann M. Jessi's Secret Language. large type ed. LC 93-15971. 176p. (gr. 4 up). 1993. PLB 15.93 (*0-8368-1020-1*) Gareth Stevens Inc.
Mathis, Sharon B. Listen for the Fig Tree. 176p. (gr. 7 up). 1990. pap. 4.99 (*0-14-034364-4*, Puffin) Puffin Bks.
Medearis, Angela S. Annie's Gifts. Richa, Anna, illus. LC 92-71998. 32p. (gr. 1-4). 1993. 14.95 (*0-940975-30-0*); pap. 6.95 (*0-940975-31-9*) Just Us Bks.
—Dancing with the Indians. Byrd, Samuel, illus. LC 90-28666. 32p. (ps-3). 1991. reinforced 14.95 (*0-8234-0893-0*) Holiday.
Mennen, Ingrid. One Round Moon & a Star for Me. Daly, Niki, illus. LC 93-9628. 32p. (ps-2). 1994. 14.95 (*0-531-06804-8*); PLB 14.99 (*0-531-08654-2*) Orchard Bks Watts.
Meyer, Carolyn. White Lilacs. LC 92-30503. 1993. write for info. (*0-15-200641-9*) HarBrace.
—White Lilacs. (gr. 4-7). 1993. pap. 3.95 (*0-15-295876-2*, HB Juv Bks) HarBrace.
Morninghouse, Sundaira. Habari Gani? What's the News? Kim, Jody, illus. 32p. (gr. k-4). 1992. 14.95 (*0-940880-39-3*) Open Hand.
Myers, Walter D. Mop, Moondance, & the Nagasaki Knights. LC 91-36824. 160p. (gr. 3-7). 1992. 14.00 (*0-385-30687-3*) Delacorte.
—The Mouse Rap. LC 89-36419. 192p. (gr. 5-9). 1990. 14.00 (*0-06-024343-0*); PLB 13.89 (*0-06-024344-9*) HarpC Child Bks.
—The Righteous Revenge of Artemis Bonner. LC 91-42401. 144p. (gr. 5-9). 1992. 14.00 (*0-06-020844-9*); PLB 13.89 (*0-06-020846-5*) HarpC Child Bks.
Naidoo, Beverley. Journey to Jo'burg: A South African Story. reissued ed. Velasquez, Eric, illus. LC 85-45508. 96p. (gr. 4-7). 1986. 14.00 (*0-397-32168-6*, Lipp Jr Bks); PLB 13.89 (*0-397-32169-4*) HarpC Child Bks.
Patrick, Denise L. Red Dancing Shoes. Ransome, James E., illus. LC 91-32666. 32p. (ps up). 1993. 14.00 (*0-688-10392-8*, Tambourine Bks); PLB 13.93 (*0-688-10393-6*, Tambourine Bks) Morrow.
Pepper Bird Staff. Copasetic: Adventures of Bojangles Robinson. Rose, Ann C., illus. 48p. (Orig.). (gr. 4-7). 1993. pap. 3.95 (*1-56817-000-9*) Pepper Bird.
Perales, Andre P. Fanfou dans les Bayous: The Adventures of a Bilingual Elephant in Louisiana. Jarlov, Christian, illus. LC 82-15148. 40p. (gr. 1-7). 1982. pap. 5.95 (*0-88289-378-5*); cassette 11.95 (*0-88289-410-2*) Pelican.
Perkins, Charles D. Swinging on a Rainbow. Hamilton, Charles, illus. LC 91-78393. 32p. (gr. 1-4). 1992. 14.95 (*0-86543-286-4*); pap. 6.95 (*0-86543-287-2*) Africa World.
Petry, Ann. Tituba of Salem Village. LC 64-20691. 272p. (gr. 5 up). 1991. pap. 3.95 (*0-06-440403-X*, Trophy) HarpC Child Bks.
Pickney, Gloria J. The Sunday Outing. Pickney, Jerry, illus. LC 93-25383. (gr. k-4). 1994. 14.99 (*0-8037-1198-0*); PLB 14.89 (*0-8037-1199-9*) Dial Bks Young.
Piercy, Patricia A. The Great Encounter: A Special Meeting Before Columbus. Wilkerson, Napoleon, illus. 47p. (gr. 1-7). 1991. pap. 5.95 (*0-913543-26-8*) African Am Imag.
Pirotta, Saviour. Follow That Cat! Melnyczuk, Peter, illus. LC 92-38287. 32p. (gr. k-3). 1993. 13.99 (*0-525-45125-0*, DCB) Dutton Child Bks.
Polacco, Patricia. Mrs. Katz & Tush. 1992. 15.00 (*0-553-08122-5*, Little Rooster) Bantam.
Prather, Ray. Fish & Bones. LC 91-44227. 272p. (gr. 5-9). 1992. 14.00 (*0-06-025121-2*); PLB 14.89 (*0-06-025122-0*) HarpC Child Bks.
Pruitt, Pamela, et al. Henry Box Brown; Struggle for Freedom; Wildfire. 2nd ed. McCluskey, John A., ed. Howard, Cecelia, et al, illus. (Orig.). (gr. 4-7). 1993. pap. 3.00 (*0-913678-25-2*) New Day Pr.
Pullman, Philip. The Broken Bridge. LC 91-15893. 256p. (gr. 7 up). 1992. 15.00 (*0-679-81972-X*); PLB 15.99 (*0-679-91972-4*) Knopf Bks Yng Read.
Raschka, Chris. Yo! Yes? LC 92-25644. (Illus.). 32p. (ps-1). 1993. 14.95 (*0-531-05469-1*); PLB 14.99 (*0-531-08619-4*) Orchard Bks Watts.
Richemont, Enid. The Magic Skateboard. Ormerod, Jan, illus. LC 92-53010. 80p. (gr. 3-6). 1993. 13.95 (*1-56402-132-7*) Candlewick Pr.
Ringgold, Faith. Aunt Harriet's Underground in the Sky. Ringgold, Faith, illus. LC 92-20072. 32p. (ps-4). 1993. 16.00 (*0-517-58767-X*); lib. bdg. 17.99 (*0-517-58768-8*) Crown Bks Yng Read.
—Tar Beach. Ringgold, Faith, illus. LC 90-40410. 32p. (ps-3). 1991. 16.00 (*0-517-58030-6*); lib. bdg. 16.99 (*0-517-58031-4*) Crown Bks Yng Read.
Rochman, Hazel, ed. Somehow Tenderness Survives: Stories of Southern Africa. LC 88-916. 208p. (gr. 7 up). 1990. pap. 3.95 (*0-06-447063-6*, Trophy) HarpC Child Bks.
Rodriguez, Anita. Aunt Martha & the Golden Coin. Rodrigues, Anita, illus. LC 92-7316. 32p. (ps-2). 1993. 14.00 (*0-517-59337-8*, Clarkson Potter); PLB 14.99 (*0-517-59338-6*, Clarkson Potter) Crown Bks Yng Read.
Rosales, Melodye. Double Dutch & the Voodoo Shoes: An Urban Folktale. Rosales, Melodye, illus. LC 91-13153. 32p. (ps-3). 1991. PLB 13.85 (*0-516-05133-4*); pap. 5.95 (*0-516-45133-2*) Childrens.
Rosen, Michael J. Elijah's Angel. Robinson, A., illus. 1992. 13.95 (*0-15-225394-7*, HB Juv Bks) HarBrace.
—A School for Pompey Walker. Robinson, Aminah B., illus. LC 94-6240. 1995. write for info. (*0-15-200114-X*, HB Juv Bks) Harbrace.
Roy, J. Soul Daddy. 1992. 16.95 (*0-15-277193-X*, HB Juv Bks) HarBrace.
Sacks, Margaret. Themba. Clay, Wil, illus. LC 92-9754. 48p. (gr. 2-5). 1992. 12.00 (*0-525-67414-4*, Lodestar Bks) Dutton Child Bks.
Samton, Sheila. Amazing Aunt Agatha. Bandk, Yvette, illus. 24p. (ps-2). 1990. PLB 17.10 (*0-8172-3575-2*); pap. 4.95 (*0-8114-6737-6*) Raintree Steck-V.
Schorsh, Laurence. Grandma's Visit. Pollard, Nan, illus. 32p. (ps-3). 1990. 4.95 (*1-56288-049-7*) Checkerboard.
Schroeder, Alan. Carolina Shout! Fuchs, Bernie, illus. LC 94-17125. (gr. 1-8). 1995. PLB write for info. (*0-8037-1678-8*); write for info. (*0-8037-1676-1*) Dial Bks Young.
Shepard, Mary L. & Gaines, Edith. Forty Acres; Little Jess & the Circus; Jubilee Day. 2nd ed. McCluskey, John A., ed. Smith, Ron & Murchison, Leon, illus. (gr. 4-7). 1993. pap. 3.00 (*0-913678-26-0*) New Day Pr.
Sloan, Phyllis J. Postcard from Heaven. Knight, Ginny, illus. 1990. 3.00 (*0-940248-81-6*) Guild Pr.
Smalls-Hector, Irene. Dawn & the Round-to-It. Geter, Tyrone, illus. LC 93-19731. 1994. pap. 15.00 (*0-671-87166-8*, S&S BFYR) S&S Trade.
—Irene & the Big, Fine Nickel, Vol. 1. (ps-3). 1991. 15. 95 (*0-316-79871-1*) Little.
—Irene Jennie & the Christmas Masquerade: The Johnkankus. Goodnight, Paul, illus. LC 93-7037. 1994. 15.95 (*0-316-79878-9*) Little.
Smothers, Ethel F. Down in the Piney Woods. LC 91-328. 144p. (gr. 5-9). 1992. 14.00 (*0-679-80360-2*); PLB 14.99 (*0-679-90360-7*) Knopf Bks Yng Read.
Steptoe, John. Baby Says. ALC Staff, ed. LC 92-11524. (Illus.). 28p. (ps up). 1992. pap. 3.95 (*0-688-11855-0*, Mulberry) Morrow.
Stolz, Mary. Go Fish. Cummings, Pat, illus. LC 90-4860. 80p. (gr. 2-6). 1991. 13.00 (*0-06-025820-9*); PLB 12. 89 (*0-06-025822-5*) HarpC Child Bks.
—Stealing Home. LC 92-5226. 160p. (gr. 3-6). 1992. 14. 00 (*0-06-021154-7*); PLB 13.89 (*0-06-021157-1*) HarpC Child Bks.
Taylor, Mildred D. Let the Circle Be Unbroken. LC 81-65854. 432p. (gr. 7 up). 1981. 15.95 (*0-8037-4748-9*) Dial Bks Young.
—Mississippi Bridge. LC 89-27898. (Illus.). 64p. 1990. 14.00 (*0-8037-0426-7*); PLB 13.89 (*0-8037-0427-5*) Dial Bks Young.
—The Road to Memphis. 304p. (gr. 5-9). 1992. pap. 3.99 (*0-14-036077-8*, Puffin) Puffin Bks.
—Roll of Thunder, Hear My Cry. Pinkney, Jerry, illus. LC 76-2287. (gr. 6 up). 1976. 15.00 (*0-8037-7473-7*) Dial Bks Young.
—Roll of Thunder, Hear My Cry. large type ed. 304p. 1989. Repr. of 1976 ed. lib. bdg. 15.95 (*1-55736-140-1*, Crnrstn Bks) BDD LT Grp.
Temple, Frances. Taste of Salt: A Story of Modern Haiti. LC 92-6716. 192p. (gr. 7-12). 1992. 14.95 (*0-531-05459-4*); PLB 14.99 (*0-531-08609-7*) Orchard Bks Watts.
Thomas, Joyce C. Marked by Fire. 160p. (gr. 7 up). 1982. pap. 3.99 (*0-380-79327-X*, Flare) Avon.
Thurman, Wallace. Blacker the Berry. Larson, Charles R., ed. O'Daniel, Thurman B., illus. (gr. 11 up). 1970. pap. 7.00 (*0-02-054750-1*, Collier Young Ad) Macmillan Child Grp.
Turner, Glennette T. Running for Our Lives. Byrd, Samuel, illus. LC 93-28430. 208p. (gr. 3-7). 1994. 15. 95 (*0-8234-1121-4*) Holiday.
Vigna, Judith. Black Like Kyra, White Like Me. Tucker, Kathleen, ed. Vigna, Judith, illus. LC 92-1203. 32p. (gr. 2-6). 1992. 13.95g (*0-8075-0778-4*) A Whitman.
Voigt, Cynthia. Come a Stranger. 240p. (gr. 6 up). 1991. pap. 3.95 (*0-449-70246-4*, Juniper) Fawcett.
Wagner, Jane. J. T. Parks, Gordon, photos by. (Illus.). 128p. (gr. 3-8). 1972. pap. 3.99 (*0-440-44275-3*, YB) Dell.
Walker, A. & Deeter, Catherine. Finding the Green Stone. 32p. (ps up). 1991. 16.95 (*0-15-227538-X*, HB Juv Bks) HarBrace.
Walter, Mildred P. Mariah Keeps Cool. LC 89-23981. 144p. (gr. 3-7). 1990. SBE 13.95 (*0-02-792295-2*, Bradbury Pr) Macmillan Child Grp.

Wampamba, Mazzi. The Kingdom of the South: The Long Journey. Nobles, Henry, Jr., illus. (gr. 1-4). 1992. pap. 3.95 (*1-56411-045-1*) Untd Brothers.

Washington, Vivian E. I Am Somebody, I Am Me: A Black Child's Credo. Stockett, Thomas & Washington, Luther, illus. 35p. (Orig.). (gr. 2-6). 1986. pap. 8.50 (*0-935132-07-4*) C H Fairfax.

Waters, Linda F. Slices of Chocolate Lives. 176p. (Orig.). 1993. pap. 4.95 (*0-9630887-0-X*) Ethnic Bks.

Welty, Eudora. A Worn Path. 1991. PLB 13.95 (*0-88682-471-0*) Creative Ed.

Whitley, Shirley H. Sometimes Life Ain't Sweet: Stories of Rural Black Youth. 72p. (Orig.). (gr. 4-9). 1993. pap. 7.95 (*0-9637271-0-9*) I B Bold Pubns.

Wilkinson, Brenda. Ludell. LC 75-9390. 176p. (gr. 7 up). 1975. PLB 14.89 (*0-06-026492-6*) HarpC Child Bks.

—Ludell. LC 75-9390. 176p. (gr. 5 up). 1992. pap. 3.95 (*0-06-440419-6*, Trophy) HarpC Child Bks.

—Ludell & Willie. LC 76-18402. (gr. 7 up). 1977. PLB 13.89 (*0-06-026488-8*) HarpC Child Bks.

Williams, Michael. Crocodile Burning. 192p. (gr. 7 up). 1992. 15.00 (*0-525-67401-2*, Lodestar Bks) Dutton Child Bks.

Williams, S. Working Cotton. Byard, C., ed. 1992. 14.95 (*0-15-299624-9*, HB Juv Bks) HarBrace.

Williamson, Mel & Ford, George. Walk on. (Illus.). 32p. (gr. 3 up). 1972. 11.95 (*0-89388-042-6*) Okpaku Communications.

Wilson, Beth P. Jenny. Johnson, Delores, illus. LC 89-8135. 32p. (gr. k-3). 1990. RSBE 13.95 (*0-02-793120-X*, Macmillan Child Bk) Macmillan Child Grp.

Worth, Bonnie. The Lean, Green Urkel Machine. (gr. 4-7). 1992. pap. 3.25 (*0-440-40739-7*, YB) Dell.

Yarbrough, Camille. Cornrows. Byard, Carole, illus. (gr. 2-6). 1992. pap. 6.95 (*0-698-20709-2*, Sandcastle Bks) Putnam Pub Group.

—Tamika & the Wisdom Rings. Rich, Anna, illus. LC 93-39477. 112p. (Orig.). (gr. 1-4). 1994. PLB 9.99 (*0-679-92749-2*); pap. 2.99 (*0-679-82749-8*) Random Bks Yng Read.

BLACKS–HISTORY

Ben-Jochannan, Yosef. Black Man of the Nile & His Family. LC 89-61274. 381p. 1990. pap. 24.95 (*0-933121-26-1*) Black Classic.

Chronology of African-American History, 2 vols. LC 93-38944. 320p. (gr. 6-9). 1993. Set 55.00 (*0-8103-9231-3*, 021501, UXL) Gale.

Davis, Julia A. African-American History for Young Readers. 2nd ed. (Illus.). 336p. (gr. 5-9). 1992. 30.00 (*0-9631110-5-1*) Epps-Alford.

—The Children's Picture Book of African American History. (Illus.). 150p. (ps-5). 1992. 20.00 (*0-9631110-3-5*) Epps-Alford.

Diuguid, Norah M., et al. The History of the Helping Hand Club. 1990. 8.95 (*0-87498-010-0*) Assoc Pubs DC.

Douglass, Frederick. Why Is the Negro Lynched. Obaba, Al I., ed. 49p. (Orig.). 1991. pap. text ed. 7.95 (*0-916157-78-4*) African Islam Miss Pubns.

Dunnigan, Alice A. The Fascinating Story of Black Kentuckians: Their Heritage & Tradition. 1990. 29.45 (*0-87498-088-7*); index 8.00 (*0-87498-089-5*) Assoc Pubs DC.

Garrett, Beatrice. A Bite of Black History: A Collective of Narrative & Short Poems of Afro-American History for Juveniles & Young Adults. LC 91-74117. 72p. (gr. 6 up). 1991. 14.95 (*0-9629887-1-5*); pap. 9.95 (*0-9629887-0-7*) Bosck Pub Hse.

Garrett, Romeo B. The Presidents & the Negro. 1990. 24. 45 (*0-87498-013-5*) Assoc Pubs DC.

Giles, Lucille. Color Me Brown. rev. ed. Holmes, Louis F., illus. 47p. (gr. k-6). 1974. pap. 5.00 (*0-87485-017-7*) Johnson Chi.

Halliburton, Warren J. Historic Speeches of African Americans. LC 92-39318. (Illus.). 192p. (gr. 9-12). 1993. PLB 13.90 (*0-531-11034-6*) Watts.

—Historic Speeches of African Americans. (Illus.). (gr. 7-12). 1993. pap. 6.95 (*0-531-15677-X*) Watts.

Hansen, Joyce. Between Two Fires: Black Soldiers in the Civil War. (Illus.). (gr. 7-12). 1993. pap. 6.95 (*0-531-15676-1*) Watts.

Harriso, Alferdteen. A History of the Most Worshipful Stringer Grand Lodge. 1990. 15.95 (*0-87498-090-9*) Assoc Pubs DC.

Haskins, James S. Black Dance in America: A History Through Its People. LC 89-35529. (Illus.). 240p. (gr. 7 up). 1992. pap. 6.95 (*0-06-446121-1*, Trophy) HarpC Child Bks.

Haskins, Jim. Against All Opposition: Black Explorers in America. 128p. 1992. 13.95 (*0-8027-8137-3*); PLB 14. 85 (*0-8027-8138-1*) Walker & Co.

Hine, Darlene C. From the Scottsboro Case to the Breaking of Baseball's Color Barrier, 1931-1947. LC 93-16016. (Illus.). (gr. 7 up). 1994. 18.95 (*0-7910-2251-X*, Am Art Analog); pap. 7.95 (*0-7910-2677-9*, Am Art Analog) Chelsea Hse.

Hornsby, Alton, Jr. & Straub, Deborah G. African American Chronology, Vol. 1: 1492-1972. LC 93-38944. 1993. write for info. (*0-8103-9232-1*, UXL) Gale.

—African American Chronology, Vol. 2: 1973-1993. LC 93-38944. 1993. write for info. (*0-8103-9233-X*, UXL) Gale.

Howell, Ann C. Conscious Choices of African-Americans During the American Revolution. Ivery, Evelyn L., ed. Still, Wayne A. & Chandler, Alton, illus. Barboza, Maurice A., intro. by. 32p. (Orig.). (gr. 3-7). 1991. pap. text ed. 2.50 (*1-877804-09-6*) Chandler White.

Johnston, Brenda A., et al. Stories from Black History Series II, 3 bks. 2nd ed. McCluskey, John A., ed. (Illus.). (gr. 4-7). 1993. Set. pap. 8.00 (*0-913678-24-4*) New Day Pr.

Just Us Books Editors. Black History Month Activity & Enrichment Handbook. LC 90-60068. 24p. (gr. 3-12). 1990. 8.95 (*0-940975-25-4*); pap. 6.50 (*0-940975-14-9*) Just Us Bks.

Keyla Activity Book: Bessie Coleman. 24p. (gr. 4-6). 1993. pap. text ed. 4.95 (*1-882962-09-5*) Keyla.

Keyla Activity Book: Garrett Morgan. 24p. (gr. 4-6). 1992. pap. text ed. 4.95 (*1-882962-04-4*) Keyla.

Keyla Activity Book: Kwanzaa. 24p. (gr. 4-6). 1992. pap. text ed. 4.95 (*1-882962-00-1*) Keyla.

Keyla Activity Book: Lewis H. Latimer. 24p. (gr. 4-6). 1993. pap. text ed. 4.95 (*1-882962-08-7*) Keyla.

Keyla Activity Book: Madame C.J. Walker. 24p. (gr. 4-6). 1992. pap. text ed. 4.95 (*1-882962-02-8*) Keyla.

Keyla Activity Book: Mansa Musa. 32p. (ps). 1993. pap. text ed. 6.99 (*1-882962-06-0*) Keyla.

Keyla Activity Book: Sunni Ali Ber. 24p. (gr. 4-6). 1993. pap. text ed. 4.95 (*1-882962-07-9*) Keyla.

Lester, Julius. Long Journey Home: Stories from Black History. LC 75-181791. 160p. (gr. 6 up). 1993. 13.99 (*0-8037-4953-8*) Dial Bks Young.

—To Be a Slave. Feelings, Tom, illus. LC 68-28738. (gr. 7-12). 1968. 14.95 (*0-8037-8955-6*) Dial Bks Young.

McKenzie, Edna C. Freedom in the Midst of a Slave Society. 1990. 12.50 (*0-87498-003-8*) Assoc Pubs DC.

McPherson, James M. Marching Toward Freedom: Blacks in the Civil War, 1861-1865. (Illus.). 128p. (gr. 7-12). 1990. 16.95x (*0-8160-2337-9*) Facts on File.

Marsh, Carole. Black "Jography" The Paths of Our Black Pioneers. (gr. 3-12). 1994. PLB 24.95 (*1-55609-321-7*); pap. 14.95 (*1-55609-320-9*); computer disk 29.95 (*1-55609-322-5*) Gallopade Pub Group.

—Black Trivia, A-Z. (gr. 3-12). 1994. PLB 24.95 (*1-55609-318-7*); pap. 14.95 (*1-55609-317-9*); computer disk 29.95 (*1-55609-319-5*) Gallopade Pub Group.

—The Color Purple & All That Jazz. (gr. 3-12). 1994. PLB 24.95 (*1-55609-315-2*); pap. 14.95 (*1-55609-314-4*); computer disk 29.95 (*1-55609-316-0*) Gallopade Pub Group.

Martinello, Marian L. & Sance, Melvin M. A Personal History: The Afro-American Texans. (Illus.). 104p. (gr. 5-8). 8.95 (*0-86701-005-3*) U of Tex Inst Tex Culture.

Medearis, Angela S. Come This Far to Freedom: A History of African Americans. Shaffer, Terea D., illus. LC 92-31251. 144p. (gr. 3-7). 1993. SBE 14.95 (*0-689-31522-8*, Atheneum Child Bk) Macmillan Child Grp.

—Our People. Bryant, Micheal, illus. LC 92-44499. 32p. (gr. k-3). 1994. SBE 14.95 (*0-689-31826-X*, Atheneum Child Bk) Macmillan Child Grp.

Meltzer, Milton. The Black Americans: A History in Their Own Words. rev. ed. LC 83-46160. (Illus.). 320p. (gr. 7 up). 1984. (Crowell Jr Bks); PLB 15.89 (*0-690-04418-6*, Crowell Jr Bks) HarpC Child Bks.

—The Black Americans: A History in Their Own Words, 1619-1983. rev. ed. LC 83-46160. (Illus.). 320p. (gr. 7 up). 1987. pap. 9.95 (*0-06-446055-X*, Trophy) HarpC Child Bks.

Metcalf, Doris. African Americans: Their Impact on U. S. History. (Illus.). 240p. (gr. 5-9). 1992. 16.95 (*0-86653-670-1*, GA1345) Good Apple.

Miller, Robert. Buffalo Soldiers. Leonard, Richard, illus. 104p. (gr. 4-7). 1992. PLB 8.95 (*0-382-24080-4*); pap. 4.95 (*0-382-24085-5*) (*0-685-47034-2*) Silver Burdett Pr.

—Mountain Men. Leonard, Richard, illus. 104p. (gr. 4-7). 1991. PLB 8.95 (*0-382-24082-0*); pap. 4.95 (*0-382-24087-1*) Silver Burdett Pr.

—Pioneers. Leonard, Richard, illus. 104p. (gr. 4-7). 1991. PLB 8.95 (*0-382-24081-2*); pap. 4.95 (*0-382-24086-3*) Silver Burdett Pr.

—Reflections of a Black Cowboy Series, 4 vols. Leonard, Richard, illus. 416p. (gr. 4-7). 1991. Set. PLB 35.80 (*0-382-24078-2*); Set. pap. 19.80 (*0-382-24083-9*) Silver Burdett Pr.

Myers, Walter D. Now Is Your Time! The African-American Struggle for Freedom. LC 91-314. (Illus.). 304p. (gr. 6 up). 1992. 18.00 (*0-06-024370-8*); PLB 17.89 (*0-06-024371-6*) HarpC Child Bks.

Nardo, Don. Braving the New World, 1619-1784: From the Arrival of the Enslaved Africans to the End of the American Revolution. LC 94-2963. (gr. 7 up). 1994. write for info. (*0-7910-2259-5*); pap. write for info. (*0-7910-2685-X*) Chelsea Hse.

Our Black Heritage, 8 vols. (gr. 4-12). 1994. PLB 24.95 (*0-7933-6793-X*); pap. 14.95 (*0-7933-6794-8*); disk 29. 95 (*0-7933-6795-6*) Gallopade Pub Group.

Picott, R. & Ridley, W. N. History of the Restitution Fund Commission of the Episcopal Diocese of Pennsylvania, a Challenge. 1990. 15.95 (*0-87498-091-7*) Assoc Pubs DC.

Piggins, Carol A. A Multicultural Portrait of the Civil War. LC 93-10319. 1993. 18.95 (*1-85435-660-7*, Pub. by M Cavendish Bks UK) Marshall Cavendish.

Read & Color Black History. (Illus.). 1992. 2.25 (*0-9634154-0-9*) R & C Black Hist.

Riley, James A., ed. Black Baseball Journal, Vol. 1, No. 1. (Illus.). 64p. (Orig.). 1990. pap. 6.95 (*0-9614023-5-0*) TK Pubs.

Roy, Jessie H. & Turner, Geneva C. Pioneers of Long Ago. Jones, Lois M., illus. 1990. 12.95 (*0-87498-008-9*) Assoc Pubs DC.

Sealy, Adrienne V. The Color Your Way into Black History Book. Abantu Industries, illus. 78p. (gr. 2-5). 1980. wkbk. 4.00 (*0-9602670-6-9*) Assn Family Living.

Stevenson, Lisbeth G. African-American History: Heroes in Hardship. (Illus.). 352p. (Orig.). (gr. 8-9). 1991. pap. text ed. 12.50 (*0-944348-01-7*) Cambdgport Pr.

Turner, Morrie. All God's Chillun Got Soul. 64p. (gr. 6). 1980. pap. 7.00 (*0-8170-0892-6*) Judson.

Wesley, Charles H. Neglected History. 1990. 5.95 (*0-87498-012-7*) Assoc Pubs DC.

Woodson, Carter G. The History of the Negro Church. (Illus.). 1990. 17.95 (*0-87498-000-3*) Assoc Pubs DC.

—The Negro in Our History. rev. ed. Wesley, Charles H., contrib. by. 1990. 19.95 (*0-87498-080-1*); pap. 15.95 (*0-87498-081-X*) Assoc Pubs DC.

Wright, Courtni C. Wagon Train: A Black Family's Westward Journey in 1865. Griffith, Gershom, illus. LC 94-18975. Date not set. write for info. (*0-8234-1152-4*) Holiday.

BLACKS–MONTGOMERY, ALABAMA

Stein, R. Conrad. The Story of the Montgomery Bus Boycott. Greene, Nathan, illus. LC 85-31349. 32p. (gr. 3-6). 1986. pap. 3.95 (*0-516-44697-5*) Childrens.

BLACKS–MORAL AND SOCIAL CONDITIONS

Hough, Judith. Mary Mack - A Paper Doll Circa 1895: Color Decorate Authentic Fashions & Ethnic Costumes. Hough, Judith, illus. 26p. (gr. 2-6). 1992. pap. 7.95 (*0-9633769-1-8*) Touch The Sky.

BLACKS–POLITICS AND SUFFRAGE

Brimmer, Andrew F. Economic Development: International & African Perspectives. 1990. 15.95 (*0-87498-093-3*) Assoc Pubs DC.

Cwiklik, Robert. Stokely Carmichael & Black Power. LC 92-11560. (Illus.). 32p. (gr. 2-4). 1993. PLB 12.90 (*1-56294-276-X*); pap. 4.95 (*1-56294-839-3*) Millbrook Pr.

Jakoubek, Robert. Adam Clayton Powell, Jr. King, Coretta Scott, intro. by. (Illus.). 112p. 1988. lib. bdg. 17.95x (*1-55546-606-0*); pap. 9.95 (*0-7910-0213-6*) Chelsea Hse.

BLACKS–SEGREGATION

see also Segregation in Education

BLACKS–SEGREGATION–FICTION

Blume, Judy. Iggie's House. LC 70-104340. 128p. (gr. 4-6). 1982. SBE 13.95 (*0-02-711040-0*, Bradbury Pr) Macmillan Child Grp.

BLACKS–SOUTHERN STATES

Jones, Maxine D. & McCarthy, Kevin. African-Americans in Florida: An Illustrated History. LC 93-27737. (Illus.). (gr. 4-8). 1993. PLB 24.95 (*1-56164-030-1*); pap. 17.95 (*1-56164-031-X*) Pineapple Pr.

BLACKS–THE WEST

Brenner, Barbara A. Wagon Wheels. newly illus. ed. Bolognese, Don, illus. LC 92-18780. 64p. (gr. k-3). 1978. 14.00 (*0-06-020668-3*); PLB 13.89 (*0-06-020669-1*) HarpC Child Bks.

Katz, William L. The Black West. rev. ed. LC 87-28067. (Illus.). 352p. (gr. 8-12). 1987. 29.95 (*0-940880-17-2*); pap. 15.95 (*0-940880-18-0*) Open Hand.

BLACKS–WESTERN STATES

Hamilton, Sue L. Los Angeles Riots. Hamilton, John, ed. LC 92-28400. 1992. 11.96 (*1-56239-149-6*) Abdo & Dghtrs.

BLACKS AS SOLDIERS

Browne Pfeifer, Kathryn. Henry O. Flipper. (Illus.). 80p. (gr. 4-7). 1993. PLB 14.95 (*0-8050-2351-8*) TFC Bks NY.

Cox, Clinton. The Forgotten Heroes: The Story of the Buffalo Soldiers. LC 92-36622. 176p. 1993. 14.95 (*0-590-45121-9*) Scholastic Inc.

Mettger, Zak. Till Victory Is Won: Black Soldiers in the Civil War. (Illus.). 96p. (gr. 5-9). 1994. 16.99 (*0-525-67412-8*, Lodestar Bks) Dutton Child Bks.

Reef, Catherine. The Buffalo Soldiers. (Illus.). 80p. (gr. 4-7). 1993. PLB 14.95 (*0-8050-2372-0*) TFC Bks NY.

—Civil War Soldiers. (Illus.). 80p. (gr. 4-7). 1993. PLB 14.95 (*0-8050-2371-2*) TFC Bks NY.

Super, Neil. Vietnam War Soldiers. (Illus.). 80p. (gr. 4-7). 1993. PLB 14.95 (*0-8050-2307-0*) TFC Bks NY.

BLACKS IN LITERATURE AND ART

Moll, Patricia B. Children & Books I: African American Storybooks & Activities for all Children. 218p. (ps-3). 1991. pap. 14.95 (*0-9616511-2-1*); spiral bdg. 14.95 (*0-9616511-3-X*) Hampton Mae.

Strickland, Michael & Strickland, Dorothy. Families: Poems Celebrating the African American Experience. Ward, John, illus. LC 93-61162. 32p. (ps-3). 1994. 14. 95 (*1-56397-288-3*) Boyds Mills Pr.

Walter, Mildred P. Trouble's Child. LC 84-16387. 128p. (gr. 4 up). 1985. 11.95 (*0-688-04214-7*) Lothrop.

BLACKWELL, ELIZABETH, 1821-1910

Baker, Rachel. The First Woman Doctor. Copelman, Evelyn, illus. 192p. (gr. 4-6). 1987. pap. 2.95 (*0-590-44767-X*) Scholastic Inc.

Brown, Jordan. Elizabeth Blackwell. Horner, Matina S., intro. by. (Illus.). 112p. (gr. 5 up). 1989. 17.95 (*1-55546-642-7*) Chelsea Hse.

Greene, Carol. Elizabeth Blackwell: First Woman Doctor. Dobson, Steven, illus. LC 90-20001. 48p. (gr. k-3). 1991. PLB 12.85 (*0-516-04217-3*); pap. 4.95 (*0-516-44217-1*) Childrens.
Klingel, Cindy. Women of America: Elizabeth Blackwell. rev. ed. (gr. 2-4). 1987. PLB 14.95 (*0-88682-169-X*) Creative Ed.
Latham, Jean L. Elizabeth Blackwell: Pioneer Woman Doctor. Gold, Ethel, illus. 80p. (gr. 2-6). 1991. Repr. of 1975 ed. lib. bdg. 12.95 (*0-7910-1406-1*) Chelsea Hse.
Sabin, Francene. Elizabeth Blackwell: The First Woman Doctor. LC 81-23140. (Illus.). 48p. (gr. 4-6). 1982. PLB 10.79 (*0-89375-756-X*); pap. text ed. 3.50 (*0-89375-757-8*) Troll Assocs.
Schleichert. Elizabeth Blackwell. 1991. 14.95 (*0-8050-2064-0*) H Holt & Co.
Schleichert, Elizabeth. The Life of Elizabeth Blackwell. Castro, Antonio, illus. 80p. (gr. 4-7). 1991. PLB 13.95 (*0-941477-66-5*) TFC Bks NY.

BLAKE, WILLIAM, 1757-1827

Willard, Nancy. A Visit to William Blake's Inn. Provensen, Nancy & Provensen, Martin, illus. LC 80-27403. 44p. (ps-3). 1982. pap. 5.95 (*0-15-293823-0*, Voyager Bks) HarBrace.

BLIND

Adler, David A. A Picture Book of Helen Keller. Wallner, John & Wallner, Alexandra, illus. LC 89-77510. 32p. (ps-3). 1990. reinforced bdg. 15.95 (*0-8234-0818-3*) Holiday.
Alexander, Sally. Mom Can't See Me. Ancona, George, illus. LC 89-13241. 48p. (gr. 1-5). 1990. RSBE 14.95 (*0-02-700401-5*, Macmillan Child Bk) Macmillan Child Grp.
Alexander, Sally H. Taking Hold: My Journey into Blindness. LC 94-12302. (gr. 5 up). 1994. 13.95 (*0-02-700402-3*) Macmillan Child Grp.
Bergman, Thomas. Seeing in Special Ways: Children Living with Blindness. LC 88-42970. (Illus.). 56p. (gr. 4-5). 1989. PLB 18.60 (*1-55532-915-2*) Gareth Stevens Inc.
Birch, Beverley. Louis Braille: Bringer of Hope to the Blind. Lantier, Patricia, adapted by. LC 90-9969. (Illus.). 64p. (gr. 3-4). 1991. PLB 19.93 (*0-8368-0454-6*) Gareth Stevens Inc.
Hunter, Edith F. Child of the Silent Night. Holmes, Bea, illus. LC 94-26217. 1995. pap. write for info. (*0-688-13794-6*) Morrow.
Keller, Helen A. Story of My Life. LC 54-11951. (Illus.). (gr. 7 up). 1954. 15.95 (*0-385-04453-4*) Doubleday.
Landau, Elaine. Blindness. (Illus.). 64p. (gr. 5-8). 1994. bds. 15.95 (*0-8050-2992-3*) TFC Bks NY.
Parkinson, Robert W. Growing up on Purpose. 73p. 1989. Braille. Braille ed. 5.84 (*1-56956-248-2*) W A T Braille.
St. George, Judith. Dear Dr. Bell - Your Friend, Helen Keller. 172p. (gr. 5-9). 1992. 15.95 (*0-399-22337-1*, Putnam) Putnam Pub Group.
—Dear Dr. Bell...Your Friend, Helen Keller. LC 93-9304. 96p. (gr. 6 up). 1993. pap. text ed. 4.95 (*0-688-12814-9*, Pub. by Beech Tree Bks) Morrow.

BLIND–BIOGRAPHY

Gibson, William. The Miracle Worker. (gr. 6-9). 1984. pap. 4.50 (*0-553-24778-6*) Bantam.
Hall, Candace C. Shelley's Day: The Day of a Legally Blind Child. Hall, Candace C., illus. 24p. (Orig.). (gr. k-6). 1980. pap. 2.95 (*0-9603840-0-6*) Andrew Mtn Pr.
Keller, Helen. Story of My Life. Barnett, M. R., intro. by. (gr. 8 up). 1965. pap. 2.95 (*0-8049-0070-1*, CL-70) Airmont.

BLIND, DOGS FOR THE

see Guide Dogs

BLIND–EDUCATION

Daniells, Trenna. One to Grow On! Series. James, Henry, tr. (Illus., Orig.). (gr. 1-2). 1992. Per vol., incl. audio cass. pap. 10.95 (*1-56956-000-5*) W A T Braille.
Offered on audio-cassettes for several years, this popular children's series is now available in a format ideal for blind children who are developing their braille reading skills. Each of the 16 titles is produced in grade 1 & grade 2 braille plus print, so reading can be shared by blind & sighted children, parents & educators. The 30-minute audio-cassette, with music & sound effects, is included, allowing children to practice reading skills independently. The ONE TO GROW ON! series promotes self-responsibility & encourages high self-esteem. Children relate to & identify with the characters, which helps develop the determination & courage to approach life with a positive & successful attitude. Each adventure is filled with fun-loving characters, depicted in braille graphics to stimulate the imagination. Available in grade 1 & grade 2 braille. I Don't Want to Be a Lion Anymore!: Be True to Yourself. Gr. 1 ISBN 1-56956-001-3, Gr. 2 ISBN 1-56956-026-9; The Keeper of Dreams: No More Nightmares. Gr. 1, ISBN 1-56956-002-1, Gr. 2 ISBN 1-56956-027-7; When Jokes Aren't Fun: The Hyena Who Teased Too Much. Gr. 1 ISBN 1-56956-003-X, Gr. 2 ISBN 1-56956-028-5; Maylene the Mermaid: All Things Change. Gr. 1 ISBN 1-56956-004-8, Gr. 2 ISBN 1-56956-029-3; Travis & the Dragon: Accepting Others As They Are. Gr. 1 ISBN 1-56956-005-6, Gr. 2 ISBN 1-56956-030-7; Cody Caterpillar Turns Over a New Leaf: Taking the Problem Out of Bedtime. Gr. 1 ISBN 1-56956-006-4, Gr. 2 ISBN 1-56956-031-5; Timothy Chicken Learns to Lead: Don't Blame Others. Gr. 1 ISBN 1-56956-007-2, Gr. 2 ISBN 1-56956-016-1; Oliver's Adventures on Monkey Island: It's Okay to Be Different. Gr. 1 ISBN 1-56956-008-0, Gr. 2 ISBN 1-56956-017-X. To Order, contact Jeri Brubaker, Braille International, Inc., 3290 S.E. Slater St., Stuart, FL 34997; 1-800-336-3142.
Publisher Provided Annotation.

Hunter, Edith F. Child of the Silent Night: The Story of Laura Bridgman. Holmes, Bea, illus. 128p. (gr. 2-5). 1963. 14.45 (*0-395-06835-5*) HM.

BLIND–FICTION

Barrett, Mary B. Sing to the Stars. Speidel, Sandra, illus. LC 92-41773. 1994. 15.95 (*0-316-08224-4*) Little.
Condra, Estelle. See the Ocean. Crockett-Blassingame, Linda, illus. LC 94-4234. 1994. reinforced bdg. 14.95 (*1-57102-005-5*, Ideas Child) Hambleton-Hill.
Garfield, James B. Follow My Leader. Greiner, Robert, illus. LC 57-1611. 192p. (gr. 4-6). 1957. pap. 13.95 (*0-670-32332-2*) Viking Child Bks.
Goldin, Barbara D. Cakes & Miracles: A Purim Tale. Weihs, Erika, illus. LC 92-25848. 1993. pap. 4.99 (*0-14-054871-8*) Puffin Bks.
Karim, Roberta. Mandy Sue Day. Ritz, Karen, illus. LC 93-34671. 1994. 14.95 (*0-395-66155-2*, Clarion Bks) HM.
Kipling, Rudyard. Light That Failed. (gr. 8 up). 1969. pap. 1.50 (*0-8049-0199-6*, CL-199) Airmont.
Little, Jean. From Anna. Sandin, Joan, illus. LC 72-76505. 208p. (gr. 4-6). 1973. pap. 3.95 (*0-06-440044-1*, Trophy) HarpC Child Bks.
MacLachlan, Patricia. Through Grandpa's Eyes. Ray, Deborah K., illus. LC 79-2019. 48p. (gr. 2-4). 1971. PLB 13.89 (*0-06-022560-2*) HarpC Child Bks.
Moon, Nicola. Lucy's Pictures. Ayliffe, Alex, illus. LC 94-11178. (gr. 7-9). Date not set. write for info. (*0-8037-1833-0*) Dial Bks Young.
Napoli, Donna J. Shark Shock. LC 93-43975. (Illus.). 192p. (gr. 3-7). 1994. 13.99 (*0-525-45267-2*, DCB) Dutton Child Bks.
Pascal, Francine. Jessica's Blind. 1994. pap. 3.50 (*0-553-48108-8*) Bantam.
Peck, Richard. Through a Brief Darkness. 144p. (gr. 7 up). 1989. pap. 3.25 (*0-440-98809-8*, LFL) Dell.
Slightly Off-Center Writers Group, Ltd. Staff. Blind Man's Dog. (Illus.). 60p. (gr. 3-6). 1994. pap. 6.95 (*1-56721-048-1*) Twnty-Fifth Cent Pr.
Taylor, Theodore. Cay. LC 69-15161. 160p. (gr. 6-9). 1987. pap. 15.95 (*0-385-07906-0*) Doubleday.
Whelan, Gloria. Hannah. Bowman, Leslie, illus. LC 92-24243. 64p. (gr. 2-4). 1993. RLB 11.99 (*0-679-91397-1*); pap. 2.99 (*0-679-82698-X*) Random Bks Yng Read.
Yolen, Jane. The Seeing Stick. Charlip, Remy & Maraslis, Demetra, illus. LC 75-6946. 32p. (gr. k up). 1975. PLB 14.89 (*0-690-00596-2*, Crowell Jr Bks) HarpC Child Bks.

BLIND–REHABILITATION

see Blind–Education

BLOCK PRINTING

see Wood Engraving

BLOOD

LeMaster, Leslie J. Your Heart & Blood. LC 84-7604. (Illus.). 48p. (gr. k-4). 1984. PLB 12.85 (*0-516-01933-3*); pap. 4.95 (*0-516-41933-1*) Childrens.
Parker, Steve. The Heart & Blood. rev. ed. (Illus.). 48p. (gr. 5 up). 1991. pap. 6.95 (*0-531-24604-3*) Watts.
Ross, Dennis W. Blood. LC 87-70225. (Illus.). 16p. (Orig.). (gr. 10 up). 1988. pap. text ed. 2.75 (*0-89278-184-X*, 45-9784) Carolina Biological.
Showers, Paul. Drop of Blood. Madden, Don, illus. LC 67-23672. (gr. k-3). 1967. PLB 12.89 (*0-690-24526-2*, Crowell Jr Bks) HarpC Child Bks.
—A Drop of Blood. rev. ed. Madden, Don, illus. LC 88-3623. 32p. (gr. k-4). 1989. (Crowell Jr Bks); PLB 13.89 (*0-690-04717-7*, Crowell Jr Bks) HarpC Child Bks.
Wolfe, Rinna E. Charles Richard Drew, M. D. (Illus.). 64p. (gr. 3-6). 1991. PLB 12.90 (*0-531-20021-3*) Watts.

BLOOD–CIRCULATION

Avraham, Regina. The Circulatory System. Koop, C. Everett, intro. by. (Illus.). 112p. (gr. 6-12). 1989. 18.95 (*0-7910-0013-3*) Chelsea Hse.
Bailey, Donna. All about the Heart & Blood. LC 90-10052. (Illus.). 48p. (gr. 2-6). 1990. PLB 20.70 (*0-8114-2779-X*) Raintree Steck-V.
Bryan, Jenny. The Pulse of Life: The Circulatory System. LC 92-36410. (Illus.). 48p. (gr. 5 up). 1993. text ed. 13.95 RSBE (*0-87518-566-5*, Dillon) Macmillan Child Grp.
Heart & Blood. 48p. (gr. 5-8). 1988. PLB 10.95 (*0-382-09700-9*) (*0-685-24608-6*) Silver Burdett Pr.
Parramon, Merce. How Our Blood Circulates. (Illus.). 1994. 13.95 (*0-7910-2127-0*, Am Art Analog) Chelsea Hse.
Silverstein, Alvin & Silverstein, Virginia. Circulatory System. (Illus.). 96p. (gr. 5-8). 1994. bds. 16.95 (*0-8050-2833-1*) TFC Bks NY.

BLOOD–DISEASES

Payne, Mary. Up & down the Blood Sugar Trail. Berry, Cathy, illus. Smith, Lendon H., intro. by. (Illus., Orig.). (gr. k-4). 1987. pap. 1.98 (*0-9619326-0-0*) MstrWorks Pub.

BLUE JAYS–FICTION

Hurwitz, Johanna. Yellow Blue Jay. Carrick, Donald, illus. LC 85-25868. 128p. (gr. 2-5). 1986. 11.95 (*0-688-06078-1*) Morrow Jr Bks.

BLY, NELLIE

see Cochrane, Elizabeth, 1867-1922

BOAT RACING

Jackson, Al & Tardy, Gene. Drag Boat Racing: The National Championships. (Illus.). 48p. (gr. 3-7). 1973. PLB 6.89x (*0-914844-05-9*); pap. 3.95 (*0-914844-06-7*) J Alden.

BOATBUILDING

London, Johnathan. Old Salt, Young Salt. LC 94-14593. 1995. write for info. (*0-688-12975-7*); PLB write for info. (*0-688-12976-5*) Lothrop.
Williams, John. Simple Science Projects with Water. LC 91-50549. (Illus.). 32p. (gr. 2-4). 1992. PLB 17.27 (*0-8368-0771-5*) Gareth Stevens Inc.

BOATING

see Boats and Boating

BOATS AND BOATING

see also Boatbuilding; Canoes and Canoeing; Houseboats; Motorboats; Rowing; Sailing; Ships; Steamboats; Submarines

Barton, Byron. Boats. Barton, Byron, illus. LC 85-47900. 32p. (ps-k). 1986. 4.95 (*0-694-00059-0*, Crowell Jr Bks); PLB 13.89 (*0-690-04536-0*) HarpC Child Bks.
Boating with Cap'n Bob & Matey: An Encyclopedia for Kids of All Ages. LC 88-62045. (Illus.). 32p. (gr. 1-9). 1989. casebound 12.95 (*0-931595-03-7*, Dist. by The Talman Co) Seascape Enters.
Boats. LC 91-58216. (Illus.). 24p. (ps-3). 1992. 8.95 (*1-56458-006-7*) Dorling Kindersley.
Butler, Daphne. First Look at Boats. LC 90-10256. (Illus.). 32p. (gr. 1-2). 1991. PLB 17.27 (*0-8368-0502-X*) Gareth Stevens Inc.
Cooper, J. Boats & Ships. 1991. 8.95s.p. (*0-86592-492-9*) Rourke Enter.
—Botes y Barcos (Boats & Ships) 1991. 8.95s.p. (*0-86592-474-0*) Rourke Enter.
Gibbons, Gail. Boat Book. Gibbons, Gail, illus. LC 82-15851. 32p. (ps-3). 1983. reinforced bdg. 15.95 (*0-8234-0478-1*); pap. 5.95 (*0-8234-0709-8*) Holiday.
Hamilton-MacLaren, Alistair. Water Transportation. LC 91-16195. (Illus.). 48p. (gr. 4-8). 1992. PLB 12.90 (*0-531-18414-5*, Pub. by Bookwright Pr) Watts.
Hutchinson, Gillian. The Story of Boats. James, John, illus. LC 91-39010. 32p. (gr. 1-4). 1993. PLB 11.89 (*0-8167-2705-8*); pap. text ed. 3.95 (*0-8167-2706-6*) Troll Assocs.
Jeunesse, Gallimard, created by. Boats. Broutin, Christian, illus. LC 92-41414. 1993. 11.95 (*0-590-47131-7*) Scholastic Inc.
Kindersley, Dorling. Ships & Boats. LC 91-25687. (Illus.). 24p. (ps-k). 1992. pap. 7.95 POB (*0-689-71566-8*, Aladdin) Macmillan Child Grp.
Let's Discover Ships & Boats. LC 80-22959. (Illus.). 80p. (gr. k-6). 1983. per set 199.00 (*0-8172-1774-6*); 14.95 ea. Raintree Steck-V.
Matthews, Rupert. Let's Look At Ships & Boats. LC 89-9710. (ps-3). 1990. PLB 11.40 (*0-531-18322-X*, Pub. by Bookwright Pr) Watts.
Mollica, Anthony & Northup, Bill. Those Wonderful Chriscraft Speedboats. (Illus.). 28p. 1992. wkbk. 3.95 (*1-883029-02-3*) CHP NY.
Mollica, Tony & Northup, Bill. Those Wonderful Garwood Speedboats. (Illus.). 28p. 1992. wkbk. 3.95 (*1-883029-01-5*) CHP NY.
—Those Wonderful Old Racing Boats. (Illus.). 28p. 1992. wkbk. 3.95 (*1-883029-00-7*) CHP NY.
—Touring the One Thousand Islands. (Illus.). 28p. 1993. wkbk. 3.95 (*1-883029-03-1*) CHP NY.

Mosenthal, Basil. Young Sailor: An Introduction to Sailing & the Sea. (Illus.). 48p. (gr. 8 up). 1993. 13.95 (*0-924486-61-9*) Sheridan.

Motorboating. (Illus.). 64p. (gr. 6-12). 1962. pap. 1.85 (*0-8395-3294-6*, 33294) BSA.

Oppenheim, Joanne. Row, Row, Row Your Boat. O'Malley, Kevin, illus. LC 92-29015. 1993. 9.99 (*0-553-09498-X*) Bantam.

Robbins, Ken. Boats. 1989. pap. 12.95 (*0-590-41157-8*) Scholastic Inc.

Rockwell, Anne. Boats. Rockwell, Anne, illus. LC 82-2420. 24p. (ps). 1985. 12.95 (*0-525-44004-6*, DCB); (DCB) Dutton Child Bks.

—Boats. (Illus.). 24p. 1994. pap. 4.99 (*0-14-054988-9*, Puff Unicorn) Puffin Bks.

Rowing. (Illus.). 48p. (gr. 6-12). 1981. pap. 1.85 (*0-8395-3392-6*, 33290) BSA.

Ruane, J. Boats, Boats, Boats. (Illus.). 28p. (ps-2). 1990. 10.50 (*0-516-05351-5*); pap. 3.95 (*0-516-45351-3*) Childrens.

Sargent, Ruth. The Nautical Alphabet. Carlson, Kathleen, illus. 32p. (ps-1). 1984. saddle-stitched 3.95 (*0-89272-190-1*) Down East.

Scarry, Richard. Richard Scarry's Boats. (Illus.). 24p. (ps-k). 1992. pap. write for info. (*0-307-11537-2*, 11537, Golden Pr) Western Pub.

Schultz, Charles, ed. Earth, Water, & Air. LC 94-15102. (Illus.). 1994. 9.99 (*0-517-11897-1*, Pub. by Derrydale Bks) Random Hse Value.

Ships & Boats. (Illus.). 80p. (gr. k-6). 1986. pap. 23.32 (*0-8172-2593-5*) Raintree Steck-V.

Small-Boat Sailing. (Illus.). 80p. (gr. 6-12). 1989. pap. 1.85 (*0-8395-3319-5*, 33319) BSA.

Steele, Philip. Boats. LC 90-41177. (Illus.). 32p. (gr. 5-6). 1991. text ed. 11.95 RSBE (*0-89686-522-3*, Crestwood Hse) Macmillan Child Grp.

Thomas, A. Things That Float. (Illus.). 24p. (gr. 2-4). 1987. pap. 3.95 (*0-7460-0102-9*) EDC.

BOATS AND BOATING–FICTION

Carratello, Patty. My Old Gold Boat. Spivak, Darlene, ed. Smythe, Linda, illus. 16p. (gr. k-2). 1988. wkbk. 1.95 (*1-55734-383-7*) Tchr Create Mat.

Conrad, Pam. Taking the Ferry Home. LC 87-45856. 224p. (gr. 7 up). 1988. PLB 11.89 (*0-06-021318-3*) HarpC Child Bks.

Cooper, Marva. Livingston's Vision. (Illus.). (gr. 1-7). 3.95 (*1-882185-08-0*) Crnrstone Pub.

Crane, Stephen. The Open Boat. Johnson, V. C., illus. 64p. (gr. 6 up). 1982. PLB 13.95s.p. (*0-87191-826-9*) Creative Ed.

Day, Alexandra. River Parade. (Illus.). 32p. (gr. 3-7). 1992. pap. 3.99 (*0-14-054158-6*, Puffin) Puffin Bks.

DeCremer, Shirley. Freddie the Frog. Overton, Amy, illus. LC 92-33094. 16p. Date not set. 14.95 (*0-935343-03-2*) Peartree.

Doherty, Berlie. Snowy. Bowen, Keith, illus. LC 91-47519. 32p. (ps-3). 1993. 14.00 (*0-8037-1343-6*) Dial Bks Young.

Drew, David. Two More. Jacobs, Elizabeth, illus. LC 92-31957. 1993. 3.75 (*0-383-03600-3*) SRA Schl Grp.

Fisher, Barbara. Harmony Hurricane Muldoon. Fisher, Barbara, illus. 22p. (Orig.). (gr. 3-5). 1979. pap. 2.00 (*0-934830-09-6*) Ten Penny.

Fisher, Leonard E. Sailboat Lost. Fisher, Leonard E., illus. LC 90-21504. 32p. (ps up). 1991. 15.95 (*0-02-735351-6*, Macmillan Child Bk) Macmillan Child Grp.

Hager, Betty. Marcie & the Shrimp Boat Adventure. LC 93-44488. 112p. (gr. 3-7). 1994. pap. 4.99 (*0-310-38421-4*) Zondervan.

Haskell, Bess C. The Hunky Dory. Poole, Ann, illus. 41p. (Orig.). (gr. 4 up). 1991. pap. 10.95 (*0-9626857-2-0*) Coastwise Pr.

—The Raft. Fetz, Ingrid, illus. (gr. 5 up). 1988. write for info. (*0-933858-26-4*) Kennebec River.

Helldorfer, Mary C. Sailing to the Sea. Krupinski, Loretta, illus. 32p. (ps-3). 1991. 13.95 (*0-670-83520-X*) Viking Child Bks.

—Sailing to the Sea. Krupinski, Loretta, illus. 32p. (ps-3). 1993. pap. 4.99 (*0-14-054317-1*, Puffin) Puffin Bks.

Hest, Amy. A Sort-of Sailor. Rockwell, Lizzie, illus. LC 89-38252. 32p. (gr. k-3). 1990. RSBE 13.95 (*0-02-743641-1*, Four Winds) Macmillan Child Grp.

Hillert, Margaret. Away Go the Boats. (Illus.). (ps-k). 1981. PLB 6.95 (*0-8136-5073-9*, TK2270); pap. 3.50 (*0-8136-5573-0*, TK2271) Modern Curr.

—Yellow Boat. (Illus.). (ps-k). 1966. PLB 6.95 (*0-8136-5033-X*, TK2388); pap. 3.50 (*0-8136-5533-1*, TK2389) Modern Curr.

Hobbs, Will. Downriver. LC 90-1044. 208p. (gr. 7 up). 1991. SBE 14.95 (*0-689-31690-9*, Atheneum Child Bk) Macmillan Child Grp.

Johnson, Pamela. A Mouse's Tale. D'Andrade, Diane, ed. (Illus.). 32p. (ps-3). 1991. 11.95 (*0-15-256032-7*) HarBrace.

Kingman, Lee. The Luck of the Miss L. LC 92-24600. 160p. (gr. 5 up). 1993. pap. 4.95 (*0-688-11779-1*, Pub. by Beech Tree Bks) Morrow.

Marshall, James. Speedboat. (ps-3). 1994. pap. 4.95 (*0-395-68977-5*) HM.

Mazel, Charles. Heave Ho: My Little Green Book of Seasickness. 1992. pap. 7.95 (*0-07-041165-4*) McGraw.

Moncure, Jane B. Nanny Goat's Boat. Friedman, Joy, illus. LC 87-12839. (SPA & ENG.). 32p. (ps-2). 1987. PLB 14.95 (*0-89565-404-0*) Childs World.

Monfried, Lucia. The Daddie's Boat. LC 89-25689. (Illus.). 32p. (ps-3). 1990. 12.95 (*0-525-44584-6*, DCB) Dutton Child Bks.

Morgan, A. Nicole's Boat. (Illus.). 24p. (ps-8). 1986. 12.95 (*0-920303-60-9*, Pub. by Annick CN); pap. 4.95 (*0-920303-61-7*, Pub. by Annick CN) Firefly Bks Ltd.

Mowat, Farley. The Boat That Wouldn't Float. 1984. pap. 3.99 (*0-553-27788-X*) Bantam.

Murez, Diane. A Day on the Boat with Captain Betty. Murez, Steve, illus. LC 92-11428. 32p. (gr. 2 up). 1993. RSBE 14.95 (*0-02-767430-4*, Macmillan Child Bk) Macmillan Child Grp.

Nakawatari, Harutaka. The Sea & I. (Illus.). 32p. (ps-3). 1992. 15.00 (*0-374-36428-1*) FS&G.

O'Hearn, Michael. Hercules the Harbor Tug. (Illus.). 32p. (ps-4). 1994. 15.95 (*0-88106-889-6*); PLB 16.00 (*0-88106-890-X*); pap. 7.95 (*0-88106-888-8*) Charlesbridge Pub.

Peck, Robert N. Soup Ahoy. Robinson, Charles, illus. LC 93-14097. 144p. (gr. 2-6). 1994. 15.00 (*0-679-84978-5*); PLB 15.99 (*0-679-94978-X*) Knopf Bks Yng Read.

Rosenbaum, Eliza. Friends Afloat. Pidgeon, Jean, illus. LC 92-39029. 24p. (gr. 2-3). 1992. PLB 19.97 (*0-8114-3584-9*) Raintree Steck-V.

Samton, Sheila W. Jenny's Journey. (Illus.). 32p. (ps-3). 1991. 13.95 (*0-670-83490-4*) Viking Child Bks.

—Jenny's Journey. LC 92-40724. (Illus.). 32p. (ps-3). 1993. pap. 4.99 (*0-14-054308-2*, Puffin) Puffin Bks.

Stevenson, James. Watching the Boat Come In. 1995. write for info. RTE (*0-688-13745-8*) Greenwillow.

Swolgaard, Carole. Sailboat Coloring Guide: A Great Five Star Super Deluxe Coloring Book. Seablom, Victoria, ed. Seablom, Seth H., illus. 32p. (Orig.). (gr. 1-6). 1979. pap. 2.50 saddle stitched (*0-918800-07-2*) Seablom.

Temple, Charles. Shanty Boat. Hall, Melanie, illus. LC 92-46025. 1994. 14.95 (*0-395-66163-3*) HM.

Tubby, I. M., pseud. I'm a Little Tugboat. (Illus.). 10p. (ps up). 1982. pap. 3.95 vinyl (*0-671-44434-4*, Little Simon) S&S Trade.

Tucker, Sian. The Little Boat. (Illus.). 10p. (ps-k). 1993. pap. 2.95 (*0-671-79736-0*, Little Simon) S&S Trade.

Vigor, John. Danger, Dolphins, & Ginger Beer. LC 92-26182. (Illus.). 192p. (gr. 3-7). 1993. SBE 14.95 (*0-689-31817-0*, Atheneum Child Bk) Macmillan Child Grp.

Wise, Francis H. & Wise, Joyce M. Red Sail. (Illus.). (ps-1). 1978. pap. 1.50 (*0-915766-40-X*) Wise Pub.

Young, Ruth. Daisy's Taxi. Sewall, Marcia, illus. LC 90-7735. 32p. (ps-1). 1991. 13.95 (*0-531-05921-9*); PLB 13.99 (*0-531-08521-X*) Orchard Bks Watts.

BOATS AND BOATING–HISTORY

Kentley, Eric. Boat. Stevenson, Jim, photos by. LC 91-53136. (Illus.). 64p. (gr. 5 up). 1992. 16.00 (*0-679-81678-X*); PLB 16.99 (*0-679-91678-4*) Knopf Bks Yng Read.

Lincoln, Margaret. Amazing Boats. Dunning, Mike & Moller, Ray, photos by. LC 92-3045. (Illus.). 32p. (Orig.). (gr. 1-5). 1992. PLB 9.99 (*0-679-92770-0*); pap. 7.99 (*0-679-82770-6*) Knopf Bks Yng Read.

BODY, HUMAN

see Anatomy; Physiology

BODY AND MIND

see Mind and Body

BODY WEIGHT CONTROL

see Weight Control

BOGS

see Marshes

BOLIVAR, SIMON, 1783-1830

Adler, David A. A Picture Book of Simon Bolivar. Casilla, Robert, illus. LC 91-19419. 32p. (ps-3). 1992. reinforced bdg. 14.95 (*0-8234-0927-9*) Holiday.

De Varona, Frank. Simon Bolivar: Latin American Liberator. LC 92-19459. (Illus.). 32p. (gr. 2-4). 1993. PLB 12.90 (*1-56294-278-6*); pap. 4.95 (*1-56294-812-1*) Millbrook Pr.

BOLIVIA

Blair, David N. The Land & People of Bolivia. LC 89-39721. (Illus.). 224p. (gr. 6 up). 1990. (Lipp Jr Bks); PLB 15.89 (*0-397-32383-2*, Lipp Jr Bks) HarpC Child Bks.

Ikuhara, Yoshiyuki. Children of the World: Bolivia. LC 87-42616. (Illus.). (gr. 5-6). 1988. PLB 21.26 (*1-55532-321-9*) Gareth Stevens Inc.

Jacobsen, Karen. Bolivia. LC 91-8889. 48p. (gr. k-4). 1991. PLB 12.85 (*0-516-01122-7*); pap. 4.95 (*0-516-41122-5*) Childrens.

Lerner Publications, Department of Geography Staff, ed. Bolivia in Pictures. (Illus.). 64p. (gr. 5 up). 1987. PLB 17.50 (*0-8225-1808-2*) Lerner Pubns.

Morrison, Marion. Bolivia. LC 88-10877. (Illus.). 128p. (gr. 5-9). 1988. PLB 20.55 (*0-516-02705-0*) Childrens.

St. John, Jetty. A Family in Bolivia. LC 86-21034. (Illus.). 32p. (gr. 2-5). 1986. PLB 13.50 (*0-8225-1670-5*) Lerner Pubns.

Schimmel, Karen. Bolivia. (Illus.). 112p. (gr. 5 up). 1991. 14.95 (*0-7910-1109-7*) Chelsea Hse.

BOLSHEVISM

see Communism

BOMBS, FLYING

see Guided Missiles

BONDS

see also Investments; Stocks

BONES

Bones & Skeletons. 8.95 (*1-56458-041-5*) Dorling Kindersley.

Gross, Ruth B. A Book about Your Skeleton. Bjorkman, Steve, illus. LC 93-49824. (ps-4). 1994. 2.95 (*0-590-48312-9*, Cartwheel) Scholastic Inc.

How Many Bones Do I Have? 1991. 3.99 (*0-517-05891-X*) Random Hse Value.

Johnson, Jinny. Skeletons: An Inside Look at Animals. Gray, Elizabeth, illus. LC 94-62. (gr. 3 up). 1994. 16.95 (*0-89577-604-9*) RD Assn.

Murray, Peter. Your Bones: An Inside Look at Skeletons. LC 92-7460. (Illus.). (gr. 1-8). 1992. PLB 14.95 (*0-89565-968-9*) Childs World.

Saunderson, Jane. Muscles & Bones. Farmer, Andrew & Green, Robina, illus. LC 90-42882. 32p. (gr. 4-6). 1992. lib. bdg. 11.89 (*0-8167-2088-6*); pap. text ed. 3.95 (*0-8167-2089-4*) Troll Assocs.

Ward, Brian. Bones & Joints: And Their Care. LC 90-46111. (Illus.). 32p. (gr. 5-8). 1991. PLB 12.40 (*0-531-14175-6*) Watts.

BONHEUR, ROSA, 1822-1889

Turner, Robyn M. Rosa Bonheur. (ps-3). 1991. 15.95 (*0-316-85648-7*) Little.

—Rosa Bonheur: Portraits of Women Artists for Children. (gr. 4-7). 1993. pap. 6.95 (*0-316-85653-3*) Little.

BOOK ILLUSTRATION

see Illustration of Books

BOOK INDUSTRIES AND TRADE

see also Bookbinding; Paper Making and Trade; Printing; Publishers and Publishing

Evans, Joy & Moore, Jo E. How to Make Books with Children, Vol. II. (Illus.). 96p. (gr. 1-6). 1991. pap. 9.95 (*1-55799-212-6*) Evan-Moor Corp.

Evans, Joy, et al. Making Big Books with Children. (Illus.). 64p. (gr. k-2). 1989. pap. 11.95 (*1-55799-165-0*) Evan-Moor Corp.

Moore, Jo E., et al. Making Seasonal Big Books with Children. (Illus.). 64p. (gr. k-3). 1990. pap. 11.95 (*1-55799-194-4*, EMC304) Evan-Moor Corp.

BOOK TRADE

see Book Industries and Trade; Publishers and Publishing

BOOKBINDING

Aliki. How a Book Is Made. Aliki, illus. LC 85-48156. 32p. (gr. k-4). 1988. pap. 5.95 (*0-06-446085-1*, Trophy) HarpC Child Bks.

BOOKS

see also Authors; Illustration of Books; Libraries; Printing; Publishers and Publishing;

also headings beginning with the word Book

Aliki. How a Book Is Made. Aliki, illus. LC 85-48156. 32p. (gr. 2 up). 1986. 14.00 (*0-690-04496-8*, Crowell Jr Bks); PLB 13.89 (*0-690-04498-4*, Crowell Jr Bks) HarpC Child Bks.

Carroll, Jeri & Dunlavy, Kathy. My Very First Books to Make & Read. 144p. (ps-2). 1990. 11.95 (*0-86653-557-8*, GA1163) Good Apple.

Greene, Carol. How a Book Is Made. (gr. 5-9). 1988. PLB 12.85 (*0-516-01216-9*) Childrens.

McClymont, Diane. Books. Young, Richard, ed. LC 91-20532. (Illus.). 32p. (gr. 3-5). 1991. PLB 15.93 (*1-56074-010-8*) Garrett Ed Corp.

Merrison, Tim. Books. Stefoff, Rebecca, ed. LC 90-13868. (Illus.). 32p. (gr. 4-8). 1991. PLB 17.26 (*0-944483-96-8*) Garrett Ed Corp.

Robins, Deri & Stowell, Charlotte. Making Books. Robins, Jim, illus. LC 93-48560. 1994. PLB 10.95 (*1-85697-517-7*, Kingfisher LKC); pap. 5.95 (*1-85697-518-5*) LKC.

Sterling, Mary E. Making Big & Little Books. Apodaca, Blanca & Vasconcelles, Keith, illus. 80p. (Orig.). (gr. k-3). 1991. wkbk. 8.95 (*1-55734-133-8*) Tchr Create Mat.

BOOKS–FICTION

Brillhart, Julie. Story Hour - Starring Megan! Levine, Abby, ed. Brillhart, Julie, illus. LC 91-19523. 32p. (ps-2). 1992. PLB 13.95 (*0-8075-7628-X*) A Whitman.

Diaz, Jorge. The Rebellious Alphabet. Jorfald, Ivind S., illus. Fox, Geoffrey, tr. LC 93-12697. (Illus.). 32p. (gr. 7 up). 1993. 14.95 (*0-8050-2765-3*, Bks Young Read) H Holt & Co.

Facklam, Margery. The Trouble with Mothers. 144p. (gr. 5). 1991. pap. 2.95 (*0-380-71139-7*, Camelot) Avon.

Furtado, Jo. Sorry, Miss Folio! Joos, Frederic, illus. 32p. (ps-3). 1988. 10.95 (*0-916291-18-9*) Kane-Miller Bk.

Green, Kate. Little Bookmobile. 1986. pap. 7.95 (*0-385-23633-6*) Doubleday.

Hentoff, Nat. The Day They Came to Arrest the Book. 160p. (gr. 7 up). 1983. pap. 3.99 (*0-440-91814-6*, LFL) Dell.

Lakin, Patricia. Get Ready to Read! Cushman, Doug, illus. LC 93-49842. 1994. write for info. (*0-8114-3866-X*) Raintree Steck-V.

Lasky, Kathryn. Memoirs of a Book Bat. (gr. 4 up). 1994. 10.95 (*0-15-215727-1*) HarBrace.

Levinson, Nancy S. Clara & the Bookwagon. Croll, Carolyn, illus. LC 86-45773. 64p. (gr. k-3). 1991. pap. 3.50 (*0-06-444134-2*, Trophy) HarpC Child Bks.

Lindbergh, Anne M. Travel Far, Pay No Fare. LC 91-35886. 192p. (gr. 5-8). 1992. 14.00 (*0-06-021775-8*); PLB 13.89 (*0-06-021776-6*) HarpC Child Bks.

McPhail, David. Fix-It. McPhail, David, illus. LC 83-16459. 24p. (ps-k). 1984. 11.00 (*0-525-44093-3*, DCB) Dutton Child Bks.

Minsberg, David. The Bookmonster. Matheis, Shelley, illus. 32p. (ps-k). 1981. 7.50 (*0-940674-00-9*); incl. bookmonster doll 27.95 (*0-685-03087-3*) Littlebee.

Polette, Nancy. Bartering with Books. (Illus.). 48p. (gr. 4-7). 1992. pap. 5.95 (*1-879287-16-1*) Bk Lures.

Tilton, Martha. I Am a Library Book. Shuster, Albert, ed. (Illus.). 14p. (Orig.). (ps). 1993. pap. 0.89 (*0-914127-22-5*) Univ Class.

BOOKS–HISTORY

Brookfield, Karen. Book. Fordes, Laurence, illus. 64p. (gr. 5 up). 1993. 15.00 (*0-679-84012-5*); PLB 15.99 (*0-679-94012-X*) Knopf Bks Yng Read.

Knowlton, Jack. Books & Libraries. Barton, Harriett, illus. LC 89-70804. 48p. (gr. 2-5). 1991. PLB 14.89 (*0-06-021610-7*) HarpC Child Bks.

BOOKS AND READING

see also Children's Literature; Libraries; Reference Books

Berksen, Barbara. Island of the Blue Dolphins: A Study Guide. (gr. 4-7). 1984. tchr's. ed. & wkbk. 14.95 (*0-88122-088-4*) LRN Links.

Brophy, Susan. The Fighting Ground: A Study Guide. (gr. 4-7). 1988. tchr's. ed. & wkbk. 14.95 (*0-88122-082-5*) LRN Links.

Carruth, Gordon, ed. The Young Reader's Companion. LC 93-6662. (Illus.). 610p. (gr. 4 up). 1993. 39.95 (*0-8352-2765-0*) Bowker.
"...a great reference book...an entertaining reading experience on its own...teachers & parents (will) find this a valuable addition to their reference shelves." - RUSS WALSH, READING SPECIALIST & NEWSLETTER EDITOR, PARENTAL INVOLVEMENT (S.I.G.) INT'L READING ASSOCIATION. "...a wonderful book. I cannot imagine any school librarian, or indeed any person charged with finding good things for young people to read, who would not insist on owning a copy." - CHARLES VAN DORAN, AUTHOR, THE HISTORY OF KNOWLEDGE. This authoritative single-volume encyclopedia helps young readers understand the characters, plots, & allusions in the books they read. Whether used as a reference book or simply for leisurely browsing, THE YOUNG READER'S COMPANION helps expand their reading skills, & can also be used by librarians, parents, & teachers to help select appropriate material for kids. The book contains over 2,000 entries, arranged alphabetically for easy access. Entries are approximately 200 words long, & designate the appropriate reading level - either "Middle Reader" or "Young Adult." A variety of topics are covered, including; * literary characters (Homer Price, Adam Dalgleish) * mythological & legendary figures (Hercules, Davy Crockett, Babe Ruth) * famous authors (Thomas Hardy, Alex Haley, A.A. Milne, John Updike) * classic titles (DEATH OF A SALESMAN, the ILIAD, GULLIVER'S TRAVELS) * frequently used words, phrases, symbols, & concepts (mad as a hatter, abracadabra, raven, Eden, the cross, butterfingers, irony). Author entries include dates of birth & death, major works, aspects of the author's life reflected in his or her boos, & short excerpts of their writings. Entries for works of fiction include publication date & a synopsis of the plot. Fictional characters are described in detail; the works in which they appear are listed as well. Entries are extensively cross-referenced, suggestions for further reading are provided, & numerous illustrations are interspersed throughout.
Publisher Provided Annotation.

Collaci, Dorothy. The Contender: A Study Guide. 1989. tchr's. ed. & wkbk. 14.95 (*0-88122-059-0*) LRN Links.

Davis, Bea. Cam Jansen & the Mystery of the Dinosaur Bones: A Study Guide. (gr. 1-3). 1986. tchr's. ed. & wkbk. 14.95 (*0-88122-068-X*) LRN Links.

Davis, Beatrice G. All of a Kind Family: A Study Guide. (gr. 3-6). 1984. tchr's. ed. & wkbk. 14.95 (*0-88122-072-8*) LRN Links.

Davis, Beatrice G., et al. Black Boy: A Study Guide. (gr. 9-12). 1984. tchr's. ed. & wkbk. 14.95 (*0-88122-105-8*) LRN Links.

De Saint Mars, Dominique. Max Doesn't Like to Read. LC 92-17998. (gr. 2-4). 1992. PLB 8.95 (*0-89565-979-4*) Childs World.

Direct, R. F. Reading Books for Pay. rev. ed. 192p. (gr. 12). 1989. pap. text ed. 45.00 (*0-945661-09-6*) PASE Pubns.

Feldman, Enid. Freaky Friday: A Study Guide. (gr. 4-7). 1988. tchr's. ed. & wkbk. 14.95 (*0-88122-083-3*) LRN Links.

Foltzer, Monica. A Sound Track to Reading. 3rd ed. 52p. (gr. 3 up). 1985. pap. text ed. 3.80 (*0-9607918-4-1*, 764921) St Ursula.

Fradken, Ada. The Enormous Egg: A Study Guide. (gr. 4-6). 1986. tchr's. ed. & wkbk. 14.95 (*0-685-31133-3*) LRN Links.

Friedland, Joyce & Kessler, Rikki. The Big Wave: A Study Guide. (gr. 4-6). 1982. tchr's. ed. & wkbk. 14.95 (*0-88122-000-0*) LRN Links.

—Bless the Beasts & the Children: A Study Guide. 1983. tchr's. ed. & wkbk. 14.95 (*0-88122-023-X*) LRN Links.

—Bridge to Teribithia: A Study Guide. (gr. 4-6). 1982. tchr's. ed. & wkbk. 14.95 (*0-88122-001-9*) LRN Links.

—Busybody Nora: A Study Guide. (gr. 2-4). 1982. tchr's. ed. & wkbk. 14.95 (*0-88122-002-7*) LRN Links.

—Girl Who Owned a City: A Study Guide. (gr. 4-6). 1982. tchr's. ed. & wkbk. 14.95 (*0-88122-003-5*) LRN Links.

Fuhler, Carol. Caddie Woodlawn: A Study Guide. (gr. 4-7). 1988. tchr's. ed. & wkbk. 14.95 (*0-88122-079-5*) Lrn Links.

Grifalconi, Ann. Electric Yancy. LC 94-14596. 1995. write for info. (*0-688-13187-5*); PLB write for info. (*0-688-13188-3*) Lothrop.

Gross, Edward, ed. Above & Below: A Guide to Beauty & the Beast. (Illus.). 112p. (Orig.). (gr. 9-12). 1990. pap. 12.95 (*0-9627508-0-8*) Image NY.

James, Elizabeth & Barkin, Carol. How to Write Your Best Book Report. Doty, Roy, illus. LC 86-8597. 80p. (gr. 3-7). 1986. 14.93 (*0-688-05744-6*) Lothrop.

—How to Write Your Best Book Report. Doty, Roy, illus. LC 86-8597. 80p. (gr. 3 up). 1986. pap. 6.00 (*0-688-05743-8*, Pub. by Beech Tree Bks) Morrow.

Knowlton, Jack. Books & Libraries. Barton, Harriett, illus. LC 89-70804. 48p. (gr. 2-5). 1993. pap. 5.95 (*0-06-446153-X*, Trophy) HarpC Child Bks.

Kroll, Carol. The Hobbit: A Study Guide. 1983. tchr's. ed. & wkbk. 14.95 (*0-88122-036-1*) LRN Links.

Leavitt, Joy. Adventures of Huckleberry Finn: A Study Guide. (gr. 10-12). 1983. tchr's. ed. & wkbk. 14.95 (*0-88122-020-5*) LRN Links.

—Adventures of Tom Sawyer: A Study Guide. (gr. 7-12). 1984. tchr's. ed. & wkbk. 14.95 (*0-88122-103-1*) LRN Links.

—All Quiet on the Western Front: A Study Guide. 1983. tchr's. ed. & wkbk. 14.95 (*0-88122-035-3*) LRN Links.

—Death of a Salesman: A Study Guide. (gr. 10-12). 1984. tchr's. ed. & wkbk. 14.95 (*0-88122-113-9*) LRN Links.

Levine, Gloria. Anne of Green Gables: A Study Guide. (gr. 6-8). 1989. tchr's. ed. & wkbk. 14.95 (*0-88122-056-6*) LRN Links.

—Fantastic Mr. Fox: A Study Guide. (gr. 3-5). 1985. tchr's. ed. & wkbk. 14.95 (*0-88122-076-0*) LRN Links.

Marsh, Norma. The Chocolate Touch: A Study Guide. (gr. 2-4). 1989. tchr's. ed. & wkbk. 14.95 (*0-88122-043-4*) Lrn Links.

—A Gift for Mama: A Study Guide. (gr. 2-4). 1989. tchr's. ed. & wkbk. 14.95 (*0-88122-045-0*) LRN Links.

Meyer, Mary. Fahrenheit 451: A Study Guide. 1984. tchr's. ed. & wkbk. 14.95 (*0-88122-114-7*) LRN Links.

Nebraska Library Commission Staff. Our Books, Our Wings: Books that Nebraskans Read & Treasure. 300p. (Orig.). (gr. 7). 1989. pap. 8.95 (*0-685-29054-9*) NE Library Commission.

Norris, Crystal. Flowers for Algernon: A Study Guide. (gr. 9-11). 1985. tchr's. ed. & wkbk. 14.95 (*0-88122-115-5*) LRN Links.

—Great Expectations: A Study Guide. (gr. 9-12). 1987. tchr's. ed. & wkbk. 14.95 (*0-88122-116-3*) LRN Links.

Polette, Nancy. Books to Begin On. (Illus.). 48p. (ps-1). 1994. pap. 5.95 (*1-879287-28-5*) Bk Lures.

—Multi-Cultural Literature: Books & Activities. Dillon, Paul, illus. 48p. (Orig.). (gr. 3-6). 1993. pap. 5.95 (*1-879287-22-6*) Bk Lures.

—Novel Booktalks. 144p. (Orig.). (gr. 4-8). 1992. pap. 9.95 (*1-879287-18-8*) Bk Lures.

—Picture Booktalks. 144p. (gr. 1-3). 1992. pap. 9.95 (*1-879287-17-X*) Bk Lures.

The Private & Personal Reading Journal. 16p. (gr. 3-7). 1989. pap. 3.50 (*0-8352-2842-8*) Bowker.

Robertson, Debbie. Blast off with Book Reports. Barry, Pat, illus. 64p. (gr. 3-8). 1985. wkbk. 7.95 (*0-86653-327-3*, GA 682) Good Apple.

Sheff, Alice. Be a Perfect Person in Just Three Days: A Study Guide. (gr. 1-3). 1989. tchr's. ed. & wkbk. 14.95 (*0-88122-044-2*) LRN Links.

—Freckle Juice: A Study Guide. (gr. 1-4). 1988. tchr's. ed. & wkbk. 14.95 (*0-88122-066-3*) LRN Links.

Thorne, Randy. Quick & Short Book Reports. Sussman, Ellen, intro. by. (Illus.). 56p. (gr. 3-5). 1990. pap. 6.95 (*0-933606-86-9*, MS-690) E Sussman Educ.

Tretler, Marcia. Alan & Naomi: A Study Guide. (gr. 4-6). 1989. tchr's. ed. & wkbk. 14.95 (*0-88122-055-8*) LRN Links.

—Anne Frank: The Diary of a Young Girl: A Study Guide. (gr. 6-10). 1987. tchr's. ed. & wkbk. 14.95 (*0-88122-104-X*) LRN Links.

—Call It Courage: A Study Guide. (gr. 4-7). 1987. tchr's ed. & wkbk. 14.95 (*0-88122-080-9*) Lrn Links.

—The Cay: A Study Guide. (gr. 4-7). 1986. tchr's. ed. & wkbk. 14.95 (*0-88122-081-7*) LRN Links.

—From the Mixed-up Files of Mrs. Basil E. Frankweiler: A Study Guide. (gr. 4-7). 1987. tchr's. ed. & wkbk. 14. 95 (*0-88122-084-1*) LRN Links.

Tuchman, Anita. The Black Pearl: A Study Guide. (gr. 7-12). 1984. tchr's. ed. & wkbk. 14.95 (*0-88122-106-6*) LRN Links.

Villanella, Rosemary. Charlie & the Chocolate Factory: A Study Guide. (gr. 4-6). 1989. tchr's. ed. & wkbk. 14.95 (*0-88122-047-7*) LRN Links.

BOOKS AND READING FOR CHILDREN

see Children–Books and Reading

BOOKS AND READING–BEST BOOKS

Anderson, Vicki. Fiction Index for Readers Ten to Sixteen: Subject Access to Over 8200 Books (1960-1990) LC 91-50954. 488p. (gr. 7-12). 1992. PLB 35. 00x (*0-89950-703-4*) McFarland & Co.

Bodart, Joni R. One Hundred World Class Thin Books: or What to Read When Your Book Report Is Due Tomorrow. 300p. (gr. 7-12). 1993. PLB 27.50 (*0-87287-986-0*) Libs Unl.

Dibner, Ellen J. & Gustafson, Ronald. Book Finders for Kids: The "Easy to Use" Subject Guide to Finding Non-fiction Books in a Library. Dibner, Ellen J. & Gustafson, Ronald, illus. LC 88-61646. 16p. (Orig.). (gr. 2-8). 1988. pap. 2.95 (*0-9620888-0-3*) Point Publications.

Moll, Patricia B. Children & Books I: African American Storybooks & Activities for all Children. 218p. (ps-3). 1991. pap. 14.95 (*0-9616511-2-1*); spiral bdg. 14.95 (*0-9616511-3-X*) Hampton Mae.

Webb, C. Anne, et al, eds. Your Reading: A Booklist for Junior High & Middle School Students. 9th ed. LC 93-8652. 225p. (Orig.). (gr. 6-9). 1993. pap. 16.95 (*0-8141-5942-7*) NCTE.

Wurth, Shirley, ed. Books for You: A Booklist for Senior High Students. 11th ed. 257p. (Orig.). (gr. 9-12). 1992. pap. 16.95 (*0-8141-0365-0*) NCTE.

BOOKS FOR CHILDREN

see Children's Literature

BOONE, DANIEL, 1734-1820

Brandt, Keith. Daniel Boone: Frontier Adventures. Lawn, John, illus. LC 82-15915. 48p. (gr. 4-6). 1983. PLB 10. 79 (*0-89375-843-4*); pap. text ed. 3.50 (*0-89375-844-2*) Troll Assocs.

Cavan, Seamus. Daniel Boone & the Opening of the Ohio Country. Goetzmann, William H., ed. Collins, Michael, intro. by. (Illus.). 112p. (gr. 5 up). 1991. lib. bdg. 18.95 (*0-7910-1309-X*) Chelsea Hse.

Farr, Naunerle C. Davy Crockett-Daniel Boone. Carrillo, Fred & Redondo, Nestor, illus. (gr. 4-12). 1979. pap. text ed. 2.95 (*0-88301-351-7*); wkbk. 1.25 (*0-88301-375-4*) Pendulum Pr.

Greene, Carol. Daniel Boone: Man of the Forests. Dobson, Steven, illus. LC 89-25346. 48p. (gr. k-3). 1990. PLB 12.85 (*0-516-04210-6*); pap. 4.95 (*0-516-44210-4*) Childrens.

Hargrove, Jim. Daniel Boone: Pioneer Trailblazer. LC 85-13309. (Illus.). 124p. (gr. 5-7). 1985. PLB 14.40 (*0-516-03215-1*) Childrens.

Lawlor, Laurie. Daniel Boone. Tucker, Kathleen, ed. LC 87-27373. (Illus.). 160p. (gr. 4-8). 1989. PLB 12.95 (*0-8075-1462-4*) A Whitman.

Retan, Walter. The Story of Daniel Boone. DeJohn, Marie, illus. 112p. (Orig.). (gr. 2-5). 1992. pap. 3.25 (*0-440-40711-7*, YB) Dell.

Stevenson, Augusta. Daniel Boone: Young Hunter & Tracker. Doremus, Robert, illus. LC 86-10795. 192p. (gr. 2-6). 1986. pap. 3.95 (*0-02-041830-2*, Aladdin) Macmillan Child Grp.

Wilkie, Katharine E. Daniel Boone: Taming the Wilds. Johnson, E. Harper, illus. 72p. (gr. 2-6). 1991. Repr. of 1960 ed. PLB 12.95 (*0-7910-1407-X*) Chelsea Hse.

Zadra, Dan. Frontiersmen in America: Daniel Boone. rev. ed. (gr. 2-4). 1988. 14.95 (*0-88682-191-6*) Creative Ed.

BOONE, DANIEL, 1734-1820–FICTION

Gleiter, Jan & Thompson, Kathleen. Daniel Boone. LC 84-9816. (Illus.). (gr. 2-5). 1984. PLB 19.97 (*0-8172-2120-4*); PLB 29.28 incl. cassette (*0-8172-2242-1*); pap. 23.95 incl. cassette (*0-8172-2273-1*) Raintree Steck-V.

BOOTS

see Shoes and Shoe Industry

BORDER LIFE

see Frontier and Pioneer Life

BORNEO–FICTION

Myers, Christopher A. & Myers, Lynne B. Forest of the Clouded Leopard. LC 93-350. (gr. 4 up). 1994. write for info. (*0-395-67408-5*) HM.

BOSTON

Byers, Helen. Kidding Around Boston: A Young Person's Guide. 2nd ed. Blakemore, Sally, illus. 64p. (gr. 3 up). 1993. pap. 9.95 (*1-56261-092-9*) John Muir.

Hughes, Richard. Bound for Boston. Wheeler, Jill, ed. Lowery, Carol, illus. LC 88-71730. 48p. (gr. 4). 1989. lib. bdg. 10.95 (*0-939179-44-X*) Abdo & Dghtrs.
Moffat, Susan D. Kids Explore Boston: The Very Best Kids' Activities Within an Easy Drive of Boston. (gr. 4 up). 1994. pap. 10.95 (*1-55850-392-7*) Adams Inc MA.
Monke, Ingrid. Boston. LC 88-20202. (Illus.). 60p. (gr. 3 up). 1988. text ed. 13.95 RSBE (*0-87518-382-4*, Dillon) Macmillan Child Grp.

BOSTON–FICTION

Farber, Norma. As I Was Crossing Boston Common. Lobel, Arnold, illus. LC 75-6520. 32p. (ps-2). 1991. pap. 3.95 (*0-525-44781-4*, Puffin) Puffin Bks.
Forbes, Esther. Johnny Tremain. Ward, Lynd, illus. (gr. 7-9). 1943. 13.45 (*0-395-06766-9*) HM.
Howells, William Dean. Rise of Silas Lapham. Hillerich, R. L., intro. by. (gr. 11 up). 1968. pap. 2.95 (*0-8049-0165-1*, CL-165) Airmont.
Hughes, Dean. Lucky Fights Back. LC 91-31416. 150p. (Orig.). (gr. 3-6). 1991. pap. text ed. 4.95 (*0-87579-559-5*) Deseret Bk.
Lasky, Kathryn. I Have an Aunt on Marlborough Street. Guevara, Susan, illus. LC 91-279. 32p. (gr. k-3). 1992. RSBE 13.95 (*0-02-751701-2*, Macmillan Child Bk) Macmillan Child Grp.
—Prank. (gr. 6 up). 1986. pap. 2.75 (*0-440-97144-6*, LFL) Dell.
Lent, Blair. Molasses Flood. Lent, Blair, illus. LC 92-1125. 32p. (ps-3). 1992. 14.45 (*0-395-45314-3*) HM.
Lowry, Lois. Taking Care of Terrific. LC 82-23331. 160p. (gr. 5 up). 1983. 14.95 (*0-395-34070-5*) HM.
Marquand, John P. The Late George Apley: A Novel in the Form of a Memoir. (gr. 7 up). 1937. 18.95 (*0-685-03075-X*) Little.
Rinaldi, Ann. The Fifth of March. 1993. pap. 3.95 (*0-15-227517-7*, HB Juv Bks) HarBrace.
—Fifth of March: A Story of the Boston Massacre. 1993. 10.95 (*0-15-200343-6*) HarBrace.

BOSTON–HISTORY

Dunnahoo, Terry. Boston's Freedom Trail. LC 94-470. 1994. text ed. 14.95 (*0-87518-623-8*, Dillon) Macmillan Child Grp.
O'Connor, Thomas H. Bibles, Brahmins, & Bosses: A Short History of Boston. 3rd, rev. ed. (Illus.). 271p. (Orig.). 1991. 12.00 (*0-89073-082-2*) Boston Public Lib.
Stein, R. Conrad. The Story of the Boston Tea Party. LC 83-27319. (Illus.). (gr. 3-6). 1984. PLB 12.30 (*0-516-04666-7*); pap. 3.95 (*0-516-44666-5*) Childrens.

BOSTON RED SOX (BASEBALL TEAM)

Boston Red Socks. (gr. 4-7). 1993. pap. 1.49 (*0-553-56408-0*) Bantam.
Lally, Dick. Boston Red Sox. 1991. pap. 2.99 (*0-517-05790-5*) Random Hse Value.
Rambeck, Richard. Boston Red Sox. 48p. (gr. 4-10). 1992. PLB 14.95s.p. (*0-88682-450-8*) Creative Ed.

BOSTON TEA PARTY, 1773–FICTION

Knight, James E. Boston Tea Party, Rebellion in the Colonies. Wenzel, David, illus. LC 81-23077. 32p. (gr. 5-9). 1982. PLB 11.59 (*0-89375-734-9*); pap. text ed. 2.95 (*0-89375-735-7*) Troll Assocs.
Seabrooke, Brenda. The Chester Town Tea Party. Smith, Nancy, illus. 30p. (gr. k-5). 1991. 8.95 (*0-87033-422-0*) Tidewater.

BOTANY

see also Flowers; Fruit; Leaves; Plant Physiology; Plants; Plants, Fossil; Seeds; Shrubs; Trees; Vegetables

Back, Christine. Bean & Plant. LC 86-9634. (Illus.). 25p. (gr. 2-5). 1986. PLB 7.95 (*0-382-09286-4*); pap. 3.95 (*0-382-24014-6*) Silver Burdett Pr.
Baker, Wendy & Haslam, Andrew. Plants: A Creative Hands-on Approach to Science. LC 92-24559. (Illus.). 48p. (gr. 2-5). 1993. pap. 12.95 POB (*0-689-71664-8*, Aladdin) Macmillan Child Grp.
Be a Plant Detective. 40p. (gr. 2 up). 1989. 3.99 (*0-517-68912-X*) Random Hse Value.
Bonnet, Robert L. & Keen, G. Daniel. Botany: Forty-Nine More Science Fair Projects. (Illus.). 170p. (gr. 4-7). 1990. 16.95 (*0-8306-7416-0*, 3416); pap. 9.95 (*0-8306-3416-9*) TAB Bks.
Boy Scouts of America. Botany. (Illus.). 64p. (gr. 6-12). 1983. pap. 1.85 (*0-8395-3379-9*, 33379) BSA.
The Carnival. (Illus.). (ps-5). 3.50 (*0-7214-0634-3*) Ladybird Bks.
Catherall, Ed. Exploring Plants. LC 91-40544. (Illus.). 48p. (gr. 4-8). 1992. PLB 22.80 (*0-8114-2601-7*) Raintree Steck-V.
Cooper, J. The Earth's Garden Series, 6 bks. 1991. Set. 53.70s.p. (*0-86592-619-0*) Rourke Enter.
—Spanish Language Books, Set 3: Los Jardines de la Tierra (The Earth's Garden, 6 bks. 1991. 53.70s.p. (*0-86592-496-1*) Rourke Enter.
Damon, Laura. Wonders of Plants & Flowers. Miyaki, Yoshi, illus. LC 89-5003. 32p. (gr. 2-4). 1990. PLB 11.59 (*0-8167-1761-3*); pap. text ed. 2.95 (*0-8167-1762-1*) Troll Assocs.
Dietl, Ulla. The Plant-&-Grow Project Book. LC 93-24788. (Illus.). 48p. (gr. 2-10). 1993. 12.95 (*0-8069-0456-9*) Sterling.
Forsthoefel, John & Ransick, Gary. Discovering Botany. Sellers, Marci, illus. 84p. (gr. 3-6). 1982. 9.95 (*0-88047-005-4*, 8206) DOK Pubs.
Fustec, Fabienne. Plants. (Illus.). 128p. (ps-3). 1993. 7.00 (*0-679-84161-X*); PLB 11.99 (*0-679-94161-4*) Random Bks Yng Read.
Ganeri, Anita. Plant Science. LC 92-36738. (Illus.). 48p. (gr. 5 up). 1993. text ed. 13.95 RSBE (*0-87518-580-0*, Dillon) Macmillan Child Grp.
Garassino, Alessandro. Plants: Origin & Evolution. LC 94-3838. 1994. write for info. (*0-8114-3332-3*) Raintree Steck-V.
Hershey, David R. Plant Biology Science Projects. LC 94-12934. 1995. write for info. (*0-471-04983-2*) Wiley.
Hoover, Evalyn, et al. The Budding Botanist: Investigations with Plants. Winkleman, Gretchen & Hillen, Judith, eds. Mercier, Sheryl, illus. 109p. (Orig.). (gr. 3-6). 1993. pap. text ed. 14.95 (*1-881431-40-1*, 1213) AIMS Educ Fnd.
Kerrod, Robin. Plant Life. Evans, Ted, illus. LC 93-50186. (gr. 2 up). 1994. 16.95 (*1-85435-627-5*) Marshall Cavendish.
Peissel, Michel & Allen, Missy. Dangerous Flora. (Illus.). 112p. (gr. 5 up). 1993. PLB 19.95 (*0-7910-1786-9*, Am Art Analog) Chelsea Hse.
Plant Life. LC 92-34975. 1993. write for info. (*0-8094-9712-3*); PLB write for info. (*0-8094-9713-1*) Time-Life.
Pope, Joyce. Plants & Flowers. Pantry, Stuart, illus. LC 91-45378. 32p. (gr. 3-6). 1993. PLB 11.59 (*0-8167-2779-1*); pap. text ed. 3.95 (*0-8167-2780-5*) Troll Assocs.
—Practical Plants. 64p. 1990. 15.95x (*0-8160-2424-3*) Facts on File.
Stidworthy, John. Plants & Seeds. LC 89-26047. 1990. PLB 12.40 (*0-531-17220-1*, Gloucester Pr) Watts.
Wood, Robert W. Thirty-Nine Easy Plant Biology Experiments. 160p. 1991. 16.95 (*0-8306-1941-0*, 5003); pap. 9.95 (*0-8306-1935-6*) TAB Bks.

BOTANY–ANATOMY

Wexler, Jerome. Wonderful Pussy Willows. Wexler, Jerome, photos by. LC 91-32262. (Illus.). 32p. (ps-3). 1992. 14.50 (*0-525-44867-5*, DCB) Dutton Child Bks.

BOTANY–ECOLOGY

see also Desert Plants

Pope, Joyce. Plant Partnerships. LC 90-32395. (Illus.). 62p. (gr. 6 up). 1991. PLB 15.95 (*0-8160-2422-7*) Facts on File.
Sussman, Susan & James, Robert. Big Friend, Little Friend: A Book about Symbiosis. (Illus.). 32p. (gr. 2-5). 1989. 13.95 (*0-395-49701-9*) HM.

BOTANY, ECONOMIC

see also Cotton; Grasses; Plants, Edible; Weeds

BOTANY, FOSSIL

see Plants, Fossil

BOTANY–GEOGRAPHICAL DISTRIBUTION

see Geographical Distribution of Animals and Plants

BOTANY, MEDICAL

Dowden, Anne O. Poisons in Our Path: Plants That Harm & Heal. Dowden, Anne O., illus. LC 92-9518. 64p. 1994. 17.00 (*0-06-020861-9*); PLB 16.89 (*0-06-020862-7*) HarpC Child Bks.

BOTANY–PHYSIOLOGY

see Plant Physiology

BOTANY–STRUCTURE

see Botany–Anatomy

BOTANY–VOCATIONAL GUIDANCE

Higginson, Mel. Scientists Who Study Plants. LC 94-6998. 1994. write for info. (*0-86593-373-1*) Rourke Corp.

BOTANY OF THE BIBLE

see Bible–Natural History

BOTTICELLI, SANDRO, 1447?-1510

Venezia, Mike. Botticelli. Venezia, Mike, illus. LC 90-21645. 32p. (ps-4). 1991. PLB 12.85 (*0-516-02291-1*); pap. 4.95 (*0-516-42291-X*) Childrens.

BOUNTY (SHIP)–FICTION

Bligh, William. Mutiny on Board HMS Bounty. Teitel, N. R., intro. by. (gr. 8 up). 1965. pap. 1.95 (*0-8049-0088-4*, CL-88) Airmont.

BOURKE-WHITE, MARGARET, 1906-1971

Ayer, Eleanor H. Margaret Bourke-White: Photographing the World. LC 91-39800. (Illus.). 112p. (gr. 5 up). 1992. text ed. 13.95 RSBE (*0-87518-513-4*, Dillon) Macmillan Child Grp.
Daffron, Carolyn. Margaret Bourke-White. Horner, Matina, intro. by. (Illus.). 112p. (Orig.). (gr. 5 up). 1988. 17.95 (*1-55546-644-3*); pap. 9.95 (*0-7910-0411-2*) Chelsea Hse.
Dunham, Montrew. Margaret Bourke-White, Young Photographer. LC 93-46159. 1995. pap. 4.95 (*0-689-71785-7*, Aladdin) Macmillan Child Grp.
Keller, Emily. Margaret Bourke-White: A Photographer's Life. LC 92-44382. (gr. 4-9). 1993. 21.50 (*0-8225-4916-6*) Lerner Pubns.

BOW AND ARROW

see also Archery

BOWDITCH, NATHANIEL, 1773-1838

Latham, Jean L. Carry on, Mr. Bowditch. Cosgrove, John O., illus. LC 55-5219. 256p. (gr. 6 up). 1973. pap. 5.70 (*0-395-13713-6*, Sandpiper) HM.
—Carry on, Mr. Bowditch. Cosgrove, John O., illus. (gr. 6 up). 1955. 14.95 (*0-395-06881-9*) HM.

BOWED INSTRUMENTS

see Stringed Instruments

BOXERS

Dolan, Terrance. Julio Cesar Chavez. LC 93-43867. (gr. 4-7). 1993. write for info. (*0-7910-2021-5*) Chelsea Hse.
Famous Fighters-Coloring Book. 1985. pap. 3.95 (*0-88388-064-4*) Bellerophon Bks.
Green, Carl R. Oscar de la Hoya. LC 93-33583. 1994. text ed. 13.95 (*0-89686-835-4*, Crestwood Hse) Macmillan Child Grp.
Lipsyte, Robert. Free to Be Muhammad Ali. LC 77-25640. (gr. 5 up). 1978. PLB 14.89 (*0-06-023902-6*) HarpC Child Bks.
—Joe Louis: A Champ for all America. Hite, John, illus. LC 93-48767. 96p. (gr. 5-9). 1994. PLB 14.89 (*0-06-023410-5*) HarpC Child Bks.
—Joe Louis: A Champ for All America. LC 93-48767. (Illus.). 96p. (gr. 5-9). 1994. pap. 3.95 (*0-06-446155-6*, Trophy) HarpC Child Bks.
Sanford, William R. & Green, Carl R. Muhammad Ali. LC 91-42181. (Illus.). 48p. (gr. 5). 1993. text ed. 11.95 RSBE (*0-89686-739-0*, Crestwood Hse) Macmillan Child Grp.
Taylor, Bob. Oscar de la Hoya. LC 93-7813. 1993. write for info. (*0-86592-175-X*) Rourke Enter.

BOXING

Conklin, Thomas. Muhammad Ali: The Fight for Respect. 1992. pap. 5.95 (*0-395-63556-X*) HM.
Jakoubek, Robert. Jack Johnson. King, Coretta Scott, intro. by. (Illus.). 112p. (gr. 5 up). 1990. PLB 17.95 (*0-7910-1113-5*) Chelsea Hse.
Rosenthal, Bert. Sugar Ray Leonard: The Baby-faced Boxer. LC 82-4472. (Illus.). 48p. (gr. 2-8). 1982. pap. 3.95 (*0-516-44326-7*) Childrens.
Sender. Requiem por un Campesino. (gr. 7-12). 1972. pap. 6.95 (*0-88436-055-5*, 70273) EMC.
Sipe, Daniel. Kickboxing. 48p. (gr. 3-10). 1994. PLB 17.27 (*1-56065-203-9*) Capstone Pr.

BOXING–FICTION

Carrier, Roch. The Boxing Champion. Cohen, Sheldon, illus. LC 90-70133. 24p. (gr. 3 up). 1991. 14.95 (*0-88776-249-2*) Tundra Bks.
—The Boxing Champion. Cohen, Sheldon, illus. 24p. (gr. 3 up). 1993. pap. 6.95 (*0-88776-308-1*) Tundra Bks.
Cebulash, Mel. Muscle-Bound. Krych, Duane, illus. (gr. 3-8). 1992. PLB 8.95 (*0-89565-883-6*) Childs World.
Gifford, Griselda. The Story of Ranald. 104p. (gr. 5-8). 1990. pap. 6.95 (*0-86241-094-0*, Pub. by Cnngt Pub Ltd) Trafalgar.
Lipsyte, Robert. The Brave. LC 90-25396. 208p. (gr. 7 up). 1991. 15.00 (*0-06-023915-8*); PLB 14.89 (*0-06-023916-6*) HarpC Child Bks.
—The Chief. LC 92-54502. 240p. (gr. 7 up). 1993. 15.00 (*0-06-021064-8*); PLB 14.89 (*0-06-021068-0*) HarpC Child Bks.
Lynch, Chris. Shadow Boxer. LC 92-47490. 224p. (gr. 5 up). 1993. 14.00 (*0-06-023027-4*); PLB 13.89 (*0-06-023028-2*) HarpC Child Bks.
Peck, Robert N. Dukes. LC 84-4272. 128p. (gr. 5-9). 1984. 9.95 (*0-910923-06-X*) Pineapple Pr.

BOXING–HISTORY

Blady, Ken. The Jewish Boxers' Hall of Fame. LC 88-29367. (Illus.). (gr. 7 up). 1989. 14.95 (*0-933503-87-3*) Shapolsky Pubs.

BOY SCOUTS

Baden-Powell, Robert. My Adventures As a Spy. Baden-Powell, Robert, illus. 132p. (Orig.). 1993. pap. 16.95 (*0-9632054-8-X*) Stevens Pub.
—Scouting for Boys: A Handbook for Instruction in Good Citizenship. Baden-Powell, Robert, illus. 273p. (Orig.). 1992. pap. 17.95 (*0-9632054-1-2*) Stevens Pub.
Birkby, Robert C. Boy Scout Handbook. 10th ed. (Illus.). 672p. (gr. 6-12). 1992. 5.00 (*0-685-48068-2*, 33229) BSA.
Boy Scouts of America. Cub Scout Songbook. (Illus.). 80p. (gr. 3-5). 1969. pap. 2.40x (*0-8395-3222-9*, 33222) BSA.
Boy Scouts of America Staff. Explorer Leader Handbook. (Illus.). 186p. (gr. 4-9). 1991. pap. 8.25 (*0-8395-4637-8*, 34637) BSA.
—Scoutmaster Handbook. (Illus.). 272p. 1992. pap. 6.50 (*0-8395-3002-1*, 33002) BSA.
Cave, Edward. The Boy Scout's Hike Book. 243p. (gr. 10). 1992. pap. 12.95 (*0-9632054-0-4*) Stevens Pub.
Fish & Wildlife Management. 40p. (Orig.). (gr. 6-12). 1990. pap. 1.85 (*0-8395-3307-1*, 33307) BSA.
Lord Baden-Powell. Rovering to Success: A Guide for Young Manhood. Lord Baden-Powell, illus. 247p. (Orig.). 1992. pap. 16.95 (*0-9632054-3-9*) Stevens Pub.
Murphy, Claire R. Friendship Across Arctic Waters: Alaskan Cub Scouts Visit Their Soviet Neighbors. Mason, Charles, photos by. (Illus.). 48p. (gr. 3-8). 1991. 15.95 (*0-525-67348-2*, Lodestar Bks) Dutton Child Bks.
Orienteering. (Illus.). 32p. (gr. 6-12). 1992. pap. 1.85 (*0-8395-3385-3*, 33385) BSA.
Sheldon, Bill, compiled by. & frwd. by. The Boy Scout Collector's Bibliography. 254p. (Orig.). (gr. 6-12). 1987. pap. 13.50 for info. (*0-9616668-0-3*) B Sheldon.

BOY SCOUTS–FICTION

Delton, Judy. Pee Wee Scout Backpack, 6 vols. (gr. 4-7). 1990. pap. 15.00 (*0-440-36014-5*) Dell.
—Pee Wees on Parade. Tiegreen, Alan, illus. 80p. (ps-3). 1992. pap. 3.25 (*0-440-40700-1*, YB) Dell.

BOY SCOUTS–HANDBOOKS, MANUALS, ETC.

Boy Scouts of America. Sea Exploring Manual. 272p. (gr. 6-12). 1987. pap. 12.85 (*0-8395-3229-6*, 33239) BSA.
Boy Scouts of America Staff. Cub Scout Sports: Fishing. 40p. (Orig.). (gr. 2-5). 1988. pap. 1.35 (*0-8395-4086-8*, 34086) BSA.
—Junior Leader Handbook. (Illus.). 168p. 1990. pap. 2.25 (*0-8395-3500-7*, 33500) BSA.
—My Scout Advancement Trail. (Illus.). 16p. (Orig.). (gr. 5). 1990. pap. 0.95 (*0-8395-3424-8*, 33424) BSA.
—Order of the Arrow Handbook. rev. ed. (Illus.). 96p. (gr. 6 up). 1990. pap. 1.85 (*0-8395-4996-2*, 34996) BSA.

Den Chief Handbook. (Illus.). 128p. (gr. 6-12). 1980. pap. 3.20x (*0-8395-3211-3*, 33211) BSA.
Wolf Cub Scout Book. rev. ed. (Illus.). 224p. (gr. 2). 1986. pap. 3.50 (*0-8395-3234-2*, 33234) BSA.

BOYLE, ROBERT, 1627-1691

Tiner, John H. Robert Boyle: Trailblazer of Science. (Illus.). (gr. 3-6). 1989. pap. 6.95 (*0-88062-155-9*) Mott Media.

BOYS

see also Boy Scouts; Newsboys; Youth

Brooks, Bruce. Boys Will Be. 128p. (gr. 6 up). 1993. 14.95 (*0-8050-2420-4*, Bks Young Read) H Holt & Co.
—Boys Will Be. LC 94-3599. 1995. pap. write for info. (*0-7868-1026-2*) Hyprn Ppbks.
Buck, Pearl S. The Big Wave. LC 85-45402. (Illus.). 80p. (gr. 3-6). 1986. pap. 3.95 (*0-06-440171-5*, Trophy) HarpC Child Bks.
Cleary, Beverly. Otis Spofford. 192p. 1990. pap. 3.99 (*0-380-70919-8*, Camelot) Avon.
Deaton, Wendy. My Own Thoughts: A Growth & Recovery Workbook for Young Boys. 32p. (gr. 2-6). 1993. wkbk. 5.95 (*0-89793-131-9*); practitioner packs 15.95 (*0-89793-134-3*) Hunter Hse.
Stanley, George E. Hershell Cobwell & the Miraculous Tattoo. 128p. 1991. pap. 2.95 (*0-380-75897-0*, Camelot) Avon.

BOYS–EMPLOYMENT

see Child Labor

BOYS–FICTION

Abbott, Jennie. The Boy Who Remembered Everything. Badenhop, Mary, illus. LC 87-14986. 96p. (gr. 5-8). 1988. PLB 9.89 (*0-8167-1183-6*); pap. text ed. 2.95 (*0-8167-1184-4*) Troll Assocs.
Abell, J. Drink Water People, Hard to Fake. (Illus.). 50p. (Orig.). (gr. 5 up). 1993. 25.00 (*1-56611-081-5*); pap. 15.00 (*1-56611-082-3*) Jonas.
Acker, Toni. Tobey: A Tale of Transition. Verrier, Claude, illus. 40p. (gr. 7-12). 1987. pap. 5.95 (*0-942953-00-2*) Wonder Works Studio.
Adamek, Maurine R. I'll Do Better Tomorrow, I Promise. Schubert, Annalee, illus. LC 92-11169. 32p. 1992. pap. 6.99 (*0-9628579-3-9*) Vision WY.
Adventures of Tom Sawyer. 1993. pap. text ed. 6.50 (*0-582-09677-4*, 79814) Longman.
Ahlberg, Allan. Woof! Wegner, Fritz, illus. LC 86-40009. 155p. (gr. 3-7). 1986. pap. 11.95 (*0-670-80832-6*) Viking Child Bks.
Aiello, Barbara & Shulman, Jeffrey. Hometown Hero: Featuring Scott Whittaker. Barr, Loel, illus. 48p. (gr. 3-6). 1989. PLB 13.95 (*0-941477-04-5*) TFC Bks NY.
Albert, Burton. Where Does the Trail Lead? Pinkney, Brian, illus. LC 90-21450. 40p. (ps-3). 1993. pap. 5.95 (*0-671-79617-8*, S&S BFYR) S&S Trade.
Alcott, Louisa May. Jo's Boys. 352p. (gr. 4-6). 1984. pap. 2.25 (*0-14-035015-2*, Puffin) Puffin Bks.
—Jo's Boys. Stern, Madelain, afterword by. 304p. (gr. 7-12). 1987. pap. 2.25 (*0-451-52089-0*, Sig Classics) NAL-Dutton.
—Jo's Boys. 344p. 1992. pap. 3.25 (*0-590-45178-2*, Apple Classics) Scholastic Inc.
—Little Men. (Illus.). 384p. (gr. 4 up). 1982. pap. 6.95 (*0-448-11018-0*, G&D) Putnam Pub Group.
—Little Men. 384p. (Orig.). (gr. 4-6). 1987. pap. 3.25 (*0-590-41279-5*, Apple Paperbacks) Scholastic Inc.
Alexander, Lloyd. Marvelous Misadventures of Sebastian. (gr. 4-7). 1991. pap. 3.50 (*0-440-40549-1*, YB) Dell.
Allen, Sandra & Dlugokinski, Eric. Ben's Secret. 28p. (gr. k-6). 1992. pap. 9.95 (*1-882801-00-8*) Feelings Factory.
Amis, Kingsley. We Are All Guilty. 96p. (gr. 7 up). 1992. 14.00 (*0-670-84268-0*) Viking Child Bks.
Amouse, Phil A. A Jonah Day. (Illus.). 32p. (gr. 4-7). 1992. pap. 5.99 (*1-56121-071-4*) Wolgemuth & Hyatt.
Appleton, Victor. Fire Biker. Greenberg, Anne, ed. 160p. 1992. pap. 2.99 (*0-671-75652-4*, Archway) PB.
—The Microbots. Greenberg, Anne, ed. 160p. (Orig.). 1992. pap. 2.99 (*0-671-75651-6*) PB.
Apps, Roy. The Secret Summer of Daniel Lyons. large type ed. (gr. 1-8). 1994. sewn 16.95 (*0-7451-2088-1*, Galaxy Child Lrg Print) Chivers N Amer.
Armstrong, Nancy M. Navajo Long Walk. Livers-Lambert, Paulette, illus. 100p. (gr. 4-8). 1994. pap. 7.95 (*1-879373-56-4*) R Rinehart.
Arrick, Fran. Where'd You Get the Gun, Billy? 1992. pap. 3.50 (*0-553-28935-7*) Bantam.
Asimov, Isaac & Sturgeon, Theodore. The Ugly Little Boy & The Widget, the Wadget, & Boff. 1989. 3.50 (*0-8125-5966-5*) Tor Bks.
Assaf, Yael. Pete & the Vegetable Soup. Kriss, David, tr. from HEB. Elchanan, illus. 24p. (Orig.). (ps). 1992. pap. text ed. 3.00x (*1-56134-160-6*) Dushkin Pub.
—Pete y la Sopa de Verduras. Writer, C. C. & Nielsen, Lisa C., trs. Elchanan, illus. (SPA.). 24p. (Orig.). (ps). 1992. pap. text ed. 3.00x (*1-56134-170-3*) Dushkin Pub.
Auch, Mary J. Mom Is Dating Weird Wayne. LC 88-45275. 160p. (gr. 4-7). 1988. 14.95 (*0-8234-0720-9*) Holiday.
Avi. The Fighting Ground. Thompson, Ellen, illus. LC 82-47719. 160p. (gr. 5 up). 1984. (Lipp Jr Bks); PLB 13.89 (*0-397-32074-4*, Lipp Jr Bks) HarpC Child Bks.
—The Fighting Ground. LC 82-47719. 160p. (gr. 4 up). 1987. pap. 3.95 (*0-06-440185-5*, Trophy) HarpC Child Bks.
—Sometimes I Think I Hear My Name. Adams, Jeanette, illus. LC 81-38421. 160p. (gr. 7 up). 1982. Pantheon.
Ayme, Marcel. Paon. Sabatier, C. & Sabatier, R., illus. (FRE.). 1985. pap. 8.95 (*2-07-031087-6*) Schoenhof.
Babbitt, Natalie. Herbert Rowbarge. LC 82-18274. 216p. (gr. 9 up). 1982. 15.00 (*0-374-32959-1*); pap. 3.95, 1984 (*0-374-51852-1*, Sunburst) FS&G.
Bach, Alice. The Bully of Library Place. (Orig.). 1988. pap. 2.95 (*0-440-40030-9*, YB) Dell.
Baer, Judy. Journey to Nowhere. LC 88-63462. 144p. (Orig.). (gr. 6 up). 1989. pap. 3.99 (*1-55661-067-X*) Bethany Hse.
Bagdon, Paul. Scrapper John: Showdown at Burnt Rock. 128p. (Orig.). (gr. 6). 1992. pap. 3.50 (*0-380-76417-2*, Camelot) Avon.
Baillie, Allan. Bad Boys. (gr. 4-7). 1994. pap. 2.95 (*0-590-48258-0*) Scholastic Inc.
Baker, Carin G. Girl Trouble. 144p. (gr. 3-7). 1992. pap. 3.50 (*0-14-036074-3*, Puffin) Puffin Bks.
—Road Warriors. 144p. (gr. 3-7). 1992. pap. 3.50 (*0-14-036076-X*, Puffin) Puffin Bks.
Baker, Jeannie. Window. (Illus.). 32p. (ps-3). 1993. pap. 4.99 (*0-14-054830-0*) Puffin Bks.
Balis, Andrea & Reiser, Robert. P. J. (gr. k-6). 1987. pap. 2.95 (*0-440-46880-9*, YB) Dell.
Balloon Magic. (Illus.). (ps-2). 1991. PLB 6.95 (*0-8136-5194-8*, TK7259); pap. 3.50 (*0-8136-5694-X*, TK7260) Modern Curr.
Bang, Molly G. Wiley & the Hairy Man: Adapted from an American Folk Tale. Bang, Molly G., illus. LC 87-2540. 64p. (gr. 1-4). 1987. pap. 3.95 (*0-689-71162-X*, Aladdin) Macmillan Child Grp.
Bar, Amos. Gary el Jardinero. Writer, C. C. & Nielsen, Lisa C., trs. Elchanan, illus. (SPA.). 24p. (Orig.). (ps). 1992. pap. text ed. 3.00x (*1-56134-172-X*) Dushkin Pub.
Baram, Bella. La Gata Que Buscaba un Hogar. Writer, C. C. & Nielsen, Lisa C., trs. Elchanan, illus. (SPA.). 24p. (Orig.). (ps). 1992. pap. text ed. 3.00x (*1-56134-150-9*) Dushkin Pub.
Barrie, J. M. Peter Pan. Shebar, Susan, ed. Lewis, T., illus. LC 87-15480. 48p. (gr. 2-6). 1988. PLB 12.89 (*0-8167-1199-2*); pap. text ed. 3.95 (*0-8167-1200-X*) Troll Assocs.
Bates, Betty. Tough Beans. Morrill, Leslie, illus. 96p. (gr. 3-7). 1992. pap. 3.50 (*0-440-40689-7*, YB) Dell.
Batmanglij, M. & Batmanglij, N. The Wonderful Story of Zaal. Franta, illus. LC 86-12665. 48p. (gr. 4 up). 1986. 18.50 (*0-934211-01-9*) Mage Pubs Inc.
Battanyi-Petose, Laura. Downtown Boy. 1993. pap. 3.50 (*0-06-106154-9*, Harp PBks) HarpC.
Bautista, Bezalie P. The Boy Who Looked Different. Saprid, Pearle R., illus. 24p. (Orig.). (gr. k-2). 1990. pap. 3.50x (*971-10-0406-2*, Pub. by New Day Pub PI) Cellar.
Bawden, Nina. The Finding. LC 84-25069. 160p. (gr. 3 up). 1985. 13.95 (*0-688-04979-6*) Lothrop.
Baylor, Byrd. Amigo. Williams, Garth, illus. 48p. (gr. 1-3). 1989. pap. 4.95 (*0-689-71299-5*, Aladdin) Macmillan Child Grp.
Beatty, Patricia. Charley Skedaddle. 192p. 1988. pap. 2.95 (*0-8167-1317-0*) Troll Assocs.
Becker, Shirley. Buddy's Shadow. Fargo, Todd, illus. 32p. (ps-2). 1992. Repr. of 1991 ed. 13.95 (*0-944727-19-0*) Jason & Nordic Pubs.
Bellerophon Books Staff. Billy Yank. (gr. 4-7). 1992. pap. 3.95 (*0-88388-155-1*) Bellerophon Bks.
Benchley, Nathaniel. George the Drummer Boy. Bolognese, Don, illus. LC 76-18398. 64p. (gr. k-3). 1987. pap. 3.50 (*0-06-444106-7*, Trophy) HarpC Child Bks.
Bennett, Cherie. Sunset Sensation. 224p. (Orig.). 1994. pap. 3.99 (*0-425-14253-1*) Berkley Pub.
—Too Many Boys, No. 1. 128p. (Orig.). 1994. pap. 3.50 (*0-425-14252-3*) Berkley Pub.
Bennett, Geraldine M. Conrad's Dilemma. (gr. 5 up). Date not set. pap. write for info. (*1-882786-06-8*) New Dawn NY.
—Conrad's Dilemma: A Helpful Dream. (Illus.). 34p. (Orig.). (gr. 2-8). Date not set. pap. 7.98 (*1-882786-15-7*) New Dawn NY.
Bergman, Tamar. The Boy from over There. Halkin, Hillel, tr. from HEB. LC 87-36634. 192p. (gr. 3-7). 1988. 13.45 (*0-395-43077-1*) HM.
—Boy from over There. (gr. 4-7). 1992. pap. 3.95 (*0-395-64370-8*) HM.
Berry, Steve. The Boy Who Wouldn't Speak. Betteridge, Deirdre, illus. 32p. 1992. PLB 14.95 (*1-55037-231-9*, Pub. by Annick CN); pap. 4.95 (*1-55037-230-0*, Pub. by Annick CN) Firefly Bks Ltd.
Bite, Jon. His Bark Is Worse Than His Bite. Abell, ed. & illus. 50p. (Orig.). (gr. 3-7). 1993. PLB 25.00 (*1-56611-075-0*); pap. 15.00 (*1-56611-076-9*) Jonas.
Blatchford, Claire. Una Sorpresa para Reggie. Writer, C. C. & Nielsen, Lisa C., trs. Eagle, Mike, illus. (SPA.). 24p. (Orig.). (ps). 1992. pap. text ed. 3.00x (*1-56134-151-7*) Dushkin Pub.
Blegvad, Lenore. Anna Banana & Me. Blegvad, Erik, illus. LC 86-22220. 32p. (ps-3). 1987. pap. 3.95 (*0-689-71114-X*, Aladdin) Macmillan Child Grp.
Blos, Joan. Brothers of the Heart. LC 87-1089. 176p. (gr. 7 up). 1987. pap. 3.95 (*0-689-71166-2*, Aladdin) Macmillan Child Grp.
—Brothers of the Heart: A Story of the Northwest, 1837-1838. LC 85-40293. 176p. (gr. 5 up). 1985. SBE 14.95 (*0-684-18452-4*, Scribners Young Read) Macmillan Child Grp.
Blos, Joan W. Old Henry. Gammell, Stephen, illus. LC 86-21745. 32p. (ps-4). 1987. lib. bdg. 13.95 (*0-688-06399-3*); 13.88 (*0-688-06400-0*) Morrow Jr Bks.
Bobbi. Matthew's Dream. Simbrom, Janine C., illus. 51p. 1993. pap. 5.95 (*0-9626608-6-8*) Magik NY.
Bonsall, Crosby N. And I Mean It, Stanley. LC 73-14324. (Illus.). 32p. (ps-1). 1984. pap. 3.50 (*0-06-444046-X*, Trophy) HarpC Child Bks.
—Who's a Pest? Bonsall, Crosby N., illus. LC 62-13310. 64p. (gr. k-3). 1986. pap. 3.50 (*0-06-444099-0*, Trophy) HarpC Child Bks.
Bosch, Carl. Bully on the Bus. Strecker, Rebekah, illus. LC 88-42650. 64p. (Orig.). (gr. 2-5). 1988. PLB 16.95 (*0-943990-43-2*); pap. 5.95 (*0-943990-42-4*) Parenting Pr.
Boulden, Jim. Glad to Be Me. Fountain, Phil, illus. 32p. (Orig.). (gr. 1-6). 1993. pap. 4.95 (*1-878076-26-4*) Boulden Pub.
Bourgeois, Paulette. Franklin Fibs. (Illus.). 1992. pap. 3.95 (*0-590-44647-9*) Scholastic Inc.
—Franklin Is Bossy. (ps-3). 1994. pap. 3.95 (*0-590-47757-9*) Scholastic Inc.
The Boy Not Say Name. (Illus.). (ps-2). 1991. PLB 6.95 (*0-8136-5041-0*, TK2280); pap. 3.50 (*0-8136-5541-2*, TK2281) Modern Curr.
Bradbury, Ray. Dandelion Wine. (gr. 6 up). 1985. pap. 5.50 (*0-553-27753-7*) Bantam.
Breslin, Theresa. Simon's Challenge. 112p. (gr. 3-5). 1994. pap. 6.95 (*0-86241-270-6*, Pub. by Cnngt UK) Trafalgar.
Bridgers, Sue E. Notes for Another Life. LC 81-1673. 256p. (gr 7 up). 1981. Repr. of 1981 ed. lib. bdg. 13.99 (*0-394-94889-0*) Knopf Bks Yng Read.
Bridwell, Norman. Clifford's Good Deeds. 1991. pap. 5.95 incl. cassette (*0-590-63824-6*) Scholastic Inc.
Briggs, Raymond. Jim & the Beanstalk. Briggs, Raymond, illus. 40p. (ps-2). 1989. pap. 5.95 (*0-698-20641-X*, Sandcastle Bks) Putnam Pub Group.
Brimner, Larry D. Elliot Fry's Goodbye. Fernandes, Eugenie, illus. 32p. (ps-3). 1994. 14.95 (*1-56397-113-5*) Boyds Mills Pr.
Brittain, Bill. The Fantastic Freshman. LC 87-35051. 160p. (gr. 5-9). 1988. PLB 12.89 (*0-06-020719-1*) HarpC Child Bks.
Brown, Jeff. Clement Aplati. Ross, Tony, illus. (FRE.). 79p. 1989. pap. 10.95 (*2-07-031196-1*) Schoenhof.
Brown, Margaret W. David's Little Indian. Charlip, Remy, illus. 48p. (gr. 2-5). 1989. Repr. of 1954 ed. 10.95 (*0-929077-02-4*, Hopscotch Bks); PLB 10.95 (*0-317-92547-4*, Hopscotch Bks) Watermark Inc.
Brown, Tricia. Hello, Amigos! Ortiz, Fran, photos by. LC 86-9882. (Illus.). 48p. (ps-2). 1992. 15.95 (*0-8050-0090-9*, Owlet BYR); pap. 5.95 (*0-8050-1891-3*) H Holt & Co.
Browne, Anthony. Willy the Wimp. Browne, Anthony, illus. LC 84-14320. 32p. (ps-2). 1989. Repr. of 1985 ed. 5.99 (*0-394-82610-8*) Knopf Bks Yng Read.
Brumpton, Karen B. Freeman Earns a Bike. Feldman, Roper, illus. LC 84-60947. 32p. (ps-4). 1984. 10.95 (*0-917487-00-1*) McVie Pub.
Buchan, Stuart. Guys Like Us. (gr. k-12). 1989. pap. 2.95 (*0-440-20244-2*, LFL) Dell.
Bulla, Clyde R. The Cardboard Crown. Chessare, Michele, illus. LC 83-45049. 96p. (gr. 2-5). 1984. (Crowell Jr Bks); (Crowell Jr Bks) HarpC Child Bks.
—The Chalk Box Kid. Allen, Thomas B., illus. LC 87-4683. 64p. (gr. 2-4). 1987. PLB 6.99 (*0-394-99102-8*); pap. 2.99 (*0-394-89102-3*) Random Bks Yng Read.
Bulla, Dale. The Magic Box. Arkenberg, Rebecca N., illus. 24p. (gr. 2-6). 1993. 12.95 (*1-884197-00-0*) N Horizon Educ.
Burgess, Barbara H. Oren Bell. (ps-3). 1993. pap. 3.50 (*0-440-40747-8*) Dell.
Burnett, Frances H. Little Lord Fauntleroy. (Illus.). 252p. 1981. Repr. PLB 21.95x (*0-89966-288-9*) Buccaneer Bks.
—Little Lord Fauntleroy. (gr. k-6). 1986. pap. 4.95 (*0-440-44764-X*, Pub. by Yearling Classics) Dell.
Burningham, John. John Patrick Norman McHennessey: The Boy Who Was Always Late. (Illus.). 32p. (ps-3). 1987. 14.95 (*0-517-56805-5*) Crown Bks Yng Read.
Burton, Virginia L. Mike Mulligan & His Steam Shovel. (gr. 3 up). 1993. pap. 7.95 incl. cass. (*0-395-45738-6*) HM.
Buscaglia, Leo F. A Memory for Tino. Newsom, Carol, illus. 50p. (ps up). 1988. 12.95 (*1-55642-020-X*) SLACK Inc.
Busters Big Chase. 1990. 5.98 (*1-55521-690-0*) Bk Sales Inc.
Butterworth, W. E. Leroy & the Old Man. 168p. (gr. 7 up). 1989. pap. 3.25 (*0-590-42711-3*) Scholastic Inc.
Byars, Betsy C. The Burning Questions of Bingo Brown. 176p. (gr. 3 up). 1990. pap. 3.99 (*0-14-032479-8*, Puffin) Puffin Bks.
—Cracker Jackson. 160p. (gr. 5-9). 1986. pap. 3.95 (*0-14-031881-X*, Puffin) Puffin Bks.
—The Eighteenth Emergency. Grossman, Robert, illus. LC 72-91399. 128p. (gr. 4-6). 1973. pap. 12.95 (*0-670-29055-6*) Viking Child Bks.
—The T. V. Kid. large type ed. 312p. (gr. 4-7). 1990. 15.95 (*0-7451-1179-3*) G K Hall.
Caines, Jeannette. I Need a Lunch Box. Cummings, Pat, illus. LC 85-45829. 32p. (ps-1). 1993. 15.00i (*0-06-020984-4*); PLB 14.89 (*0-06-020985-2*) HarpC Child Bks.
Calhoun, Mary. Jack & the Whoopee Wind. Gackenbach, Dick, illus. LC 86-1630. 32p. (ps-3). 1987. 13.95 (*0-688-06137-0*); lib. bdg. 13.88 (*0-688-06138-9*, Morrow Jr Bks) Morrow Jr Bks.

Calif, Ruth. The Over-the-Hill Ghost. Holub, Joan, illus. LC 87-30523. 160p. (gr. 3-8). 1988. 10.95 (*0-88289-667-9*) Pelican.

Cameron, Ann. Julian, Secret Agent. Allison, Diane W., illus. LC 88-4428. 64p. (Orig.). (gr. 2-4). 1988. lib. bdg. 6.99 (*0-394-91949-1*); pap. 2.50 (*0-394-81949-7*) Random Bks Yng Read.

—Julian's Glorious Summer. Leder, Dora, illus. LC 86-33828. 64p. (gr. 2-4). 1987. 2.99 (*0-394-89117-1*); lib. bdg. 6.99 (*0-394-99117-6*) Random Bks Yng Read.

Cannon, A. E. Will the Real Cal Cameron Please Stand Up? (gr. 7 up). 1988. write for info. Delacorte.

Cardinal, Catherine S. Charlotte Pug: (The Walnut War) (Illus.). (gr. k-5). 1994. pap. 3.40 (*0-9630655-2-1*) Garden Gate.
Introducing CHARLOTTE PUG (The Walnut War) written by Catherine S. Cardinal who has brought to you MUD GRAPE PIE & THE BUTTON BOX. CHARLOTTE PUG deals with an age old conflict between the boys & the girls. This serious & sometimes comical situation has a positive conclusion & leaves the reader with a thought provoking lesson. The author's first collection, MUD GRAPE PIE, is a compilation of tales which deal with a fanciful herb garden & its fairy-like caretaker, Princess Jill. The Princess & her friends have many adventures, each one imparting a lesson about the herbs & imposing a moral applicable to life. THE BUTTON BOX (a gathering place for all sorts of odds & ends) holds a collection of stories. Liza, Mary, Gladys, Sampson, Katie, & Grandpa Arthur are characters that are kept in this volume as is the assortment of buttons in the button box. Order from: Garden Gate Publishing, 1655 Washington Ave., Vincennes, IN 47591. Tel. 812-882-2626.
Publisher Provided Annotation.

Carlson, Nancy. Arnie & the Stolen Markers. (Illus.). 32p. (ps-3). 1989. pap. 3.95 (*0-14-050707-8*, Puffin) Puffin Bks.

—Loudmouth George & The New Neighbors. Carlson, Nancy, illus. (gr. k-3). 1987. incl. cassette 19.95 (*0-87499-034-3*); pap. 12.95 incl. cassette (*0-87499-032-7*); 4 paperbacks, cassette & guide 27.95 (*0-87499-033-5*) Live Oak Media.

Carlson, Rick. Danny Buys a Blobit Value: Truthfulness. 32p. 1992. pap. 1.95 saddle stitched (*0-310-58142-7*, Youth Bks) Zondervan.

Carratello, Patty. This Is Fred. Spivak, Darlene, ed. Brostrom, Eileen, illus. 16p. (gr. k-2). 1988. wkbk. 1.95 (*1-55734-391-8*) Tchr Create Mat.

—Will Bill? Spivak, Darlene, ed. Olsen, Shirley, illus. 16p. (gr. k-2). 1988. wkbk. 1.95 (*1-55734-388-8*) Tchr Create Mat.

Carrick, Carol. Stay Away from Simon. Carrick, Donald, illus. LC 84-14289. 64p. (gr. 2-5). 1985. 12.95 (*0-89919-343-9*, Clarion Bks) HM.

—Stay Away from Simon! Carrick, Donald, illus. (gr. 3-6). 1989. pap. 5.70 (*0-89919-849-X*, Clarion Bks) HM.

—What a Wimp! Carrick, Donald, illus. LC 82-9597. (gr. 3-6). 1988. pap. 3.95 (*0-89919-703-5*, Clarion Bks) HM.

Cartwright, Hal V. Granny Boy & the Puny Warbler. Matheson, Hedda, illus. LC 92-71096. 48p. (Orig.). (gr. 4). 1992. pap. 8.50 (*0-923687-16-5*) Celo Valley Bks.

Caruso, Joseph G. Adam's Diary. (Illus.). 26p. (Orig.). (gr. k up). 1989. pap. 4.00 (*0-88680-313-6*); Piano-Vocal Score 15.00 (*0-88680-314-4*); royalty on application 60.00 (*0-685-58566-2*) I E Clark.

Cateland, Grace. Joey Forever. 1993. pap. 3.99 (*0-553-56611-3*) Bantam.

Cathcart, Pamela B. History Hunt at Cold Harbor. Andrus, Michael J., frwd. by. (Illus.). 95p. (Orig.). 1994. 19.95 (*0-931563-15-1*); pap. 6.95 (*0-931563-14-3*) Wishing Rm.

Caudill, Rebecca. Did You Carry the Flag Today, Charley? Grossman, Nancy, illus. LC 66-11422. 96p. (gr. 2-4). 1971. reinforced bdg. 15.95 (*0-8050-1201-X*, Bks Young Read); 3.95 (*0-03-086620-0*) H Holt & Co.

Cavanaugh, Kate. Pete & His Elves Series. Kiner, K. C., illus. 28p. 1992. Set. pap. write for info. (*0-9622353-4-2*) KAC.

Cavanna, Betty. Boy Next Door. (gr. 4-7). 1992. pap. 2.50 (*0-8167-1270-0*) Troll Assocs.

Chambers, Barry. Willy the Hit Man. 94p. (gr. 4-8). 1992. pap. 6.25 (*1-880384-01-9*) Coldwater Pr.

Chapman, Carol. The Tale of Meshka the Kvetch. Lobel, Arnold, illus. LC 80-11225. 32p. (gr. k-3). 1989. pap. 3.95 (*0-525-44494-7*, DCB) Dutton Child Bks.

Chapouton, Anne-Marie. Billy the Brave. Bell, Anthea, tr. from FRE. Claverie, Jean, illus. LC 85-63307. 32p. (gr. k-2). 1986. 8.95 (*1-55858-070-0*) North-South Bks NYC.

Chappell, James A. Little Johnny Raindrop. Shaw, Charles, illus. LC 88-2173. 32p. (ps-3). 1988. 12.95 (*0-938349-28-7*) State House Pr.

Chardiet, Bernice & Maccarone, Grace. Martin & the Teacher's Pet. Karas, Brian, illus. 48p. 1992. pap. 2.50 (*0-590-44931-1*) Scholastic Inc.

Chetwin, Grace. Gom on Windy Mountain. LC 85-18166. (Illus.). 224p. (gr. 6 up). 1986. 12.95 (*0-688-05767-5*) Lothrop.

Chief Little Summer & Warm Night Rain. The Misfit. 300p. (gr. 8-12). 1991. 10.95 (*1-880440-03-2*) Piqua Pr.

—Reflections on a Rainy April Day. 23p. (gr. 1-5). 1991. 7.95 (*1-880440-02-4*) Piqua Pr.

Christian, Mary B. Sebastian & the Bone to Pick Mystery. 64p. 1986. pap. 2.25 (*0-553-15385-4*, Skylark) Bantam.

—Singin' Somebody Else's Song. LC 88-12000. 192p. (gr. 7 up). 1988. SBE 14.95 (*0-02-718500-1*, Macmillan Child Bk) Macmillan Child Grp.

Christopher, Matt. Johnny Long Legs. Kidder, Harvey, illus. 144p. (gr. 3-6). 1988. pap. 3.95 (*0-316-14065-1*) Little.

—Long Shot For Paul. (gr. 3-7). 1990. pap. 3.95 (*0-316-14244-1*) Little.

Clark, Eleanor B. Kitty's Cousins. 1993. 7.95 (*0-533-10569-2*) Vantage.

Clarke, Norman. Patrick in Person. Julian-Otte, Vanessa, illus. 130p. (gr. 3 up). 1992. bds. 16.95 laminated (*0-571-16225-8*) Faber & Faber.

Cleary, Beverly. Henry & Beezus. 1923. pap. 1.75 (*0-440-73295-6*) Dell.

—Henry & Ribsy. 1923. pap. 1.75 (*0-440-73296-4*) Dell.

—Henry & the Paper Route. Darling, Louis, illus. LC 57-8562. (gr. 3-7). 1957. 15.95 (*0-688-21380-4*); PLB 15.80 (*0-688-31380-9*) Morrow Jr Bks.

—Henry & the Paper Route. 192p. 1990. pap. 3.99 (*0-380-70921-X*, Camelot) Avon.

—Henry & the Paper Route. 1923. pap. 1.75 (*0-440-73298-0*) Dell.

—Henry Huggins, 4 vols. (gr. 4-7). 1990. Boxed set. pap. 14.00 (*0-380-71206-7*, Camelot) Avon.

—Henry Huggins. 1923. pap. 1.75 (*0-440-73551-3*) Dell.

—Henry Huggins Clubhouse, 6 vols. (gr. 4-7). 1990. pap. 19.50 boxed set (*0-440-36015-3*) Dell.

—Runaway Ralph. LC 77-95786. (Illus.). (gr. 3-7). 1970. 14.95 (*0-688-21701-X*); PLB 14.88 (*0-688-31701-4*, Morrow Jr Bks) Morrow Jr Bks.

Clendenin, Mary J. Gonzalo, Coronado's Shepherd Boy. Roberts, Melissa, ed. (Illus.). 128p. (gr. 4-7). 1990. 10.95 (*0-89015-700-6*, Pub. by Panda Bks) Sunbelt Media.

Clifford, Eth. I Hate Your Guts, Ben Brooster. 144p. 1990. pap. 2.75 (*0-590-43534-5*) Scholastic Inc.

—The Man Who Sang in the Dark. Owen, Mary B., illus. 96p. (gr. 2-5). 1987. 13.95 (*0-395-43664-8*) HM.

Clifton. Everett Anderson's Nine Month Long. LC 78-2402. (ps-2). 1988. pap. 4.95 (*0-8050-0295-2*, Bks Young Read) H Holt & Co.

Clifton, Lucille. The Boy Who Didn't Believe in Spring. Turkle, Brinton, illus. LC 87-27145. 32p. (ps-3). 1988. pap. 4.95 (*0-525-44365-7*, 0383-120, DCB) Dutton Child Bks.

—Everett Anderson's Nine Month Long. Grifalconi, Ann, illus. LC 78-2402. 32p. (ps-2). 1978. 13.95 (*0-8050-0287-1*, Bks Young Read) H Holt & Co.

—Some of the Days of Everett Anderson. Ness, Evaline, illus. LC 78-98922. 32p. (ps-2). 1988. 13.95 (*0-8050-0290-1*, Bks Young Read) H Holt & Co.

—Some of the Days of Everett Anderson. 32p. (ps-2). 1987. pap. 5.95 (*0-8050-0289-8*, Bks. Young Read) H Holt & Co.

Cohen, Miriam. Starring First Grade. Hoban, Lillian, illus. LC 84-5929. 32p. (gr. k-3). 1985. PLB 15.93 (*0-688-04030-6*) Greenwillow.

Comstock, Esther J. Vallejo & the Four Flags. Comstock, Floyd B., illus. LC 79-21636. xvi, 142p. (gr. 4). 1988. 12.50 (*0-933994-01-X*); pap. 8.75 (*0-933994-07-9*) Comstock Bon.

Conlin, Susan & Friedman, Susan L. Nathan's Day. Smith, M. Kathryn, illus. LC 90-62679. 32p. (Orig.). (ps-k). 1991. lib. bdg. 16.95 (*0-943990-61-0*); pap. 5.95 (*0-943990-60-2*) Parenting Pr.

Conrad, Pam. Pedro's Journal. 1992. pap. 2.95 (*0-590-46206-7*, 058, Apple Paperbacks) Scholastic Inc.

Conversions. (gr. 3-7). 1992. pap. 3.99 (*0-553-48032-4*) Bantam.

Cook, Olive R. Trails to Poosey. Sammel, Chelsea, illus. Cook, George R., intro. by. LC 86-8602. (Illus.). 200p. (Orig.). (gr. 3-6). 1986. pap. 5.95 (*0-930079-01-9*) Misty Hill Pr.

Cooney, Barbara. Island Boy. LC 88-175. (ps-3). 1988. pap. 15.00 (*0-670-81749-X*) Viking Child Bks.

Cooper, Susan. The Dark Is Rising. LC 86-3647. 256p. (gr. 7 up). 1986. pap. 3.95 (*0-689-71087-9*, Aladdin) Macmillan Child Grp.

—Greenwitch. LC 86-3324. 148p. (gr. 4-7). 1986. pap. 3.95 (*0-689-71088-7*, Collier Young Ad) Macmillan Child Grp.

—The Grey King. LC 86-3613. 176p. (gr. 6 up). 1986. pap. 3.95 (*0-689-71089-5*, Collier Young Ad) Macmillan Child Grp.

—Silver on the Tree. LC 86-3341. 288p. (gr. 6 up). 1987. pap. 3.95 (*0-689-71152-2*, Collier Young Ad) Macmillan Child Grp.

Corbin, William. Me & the End of the World. LC 90-2355. 256p. (gr. 5-9). 1991. pap. 15.00 jacketed, 3-pc. bdg. (*0-671-74223-X*, S&S BFYR) S&S Trade.

Corral, Jeanie B. Scruffy 'n Me. 1994. 8.95 (*0-8062-4844-0*) Carlton.

Cretan, Gladys. Joey's Head. Sims, Blanche, illus. LC 90-41592. 48p. (gr. 2-4). 1993. pap. 3.95 (*0-671-86699-0*, Half Moon Bks) S&S Trade.

Cross, Gillian. Roscoe's Leap. LC 87-45328. 160p. (gr. 7 up). 1987. 14.95 (*0-8234-0669-5*) Holiday.

Crump, Fred, Jr. Pedro's Patio: El Patio de Pedro. Johns, Leticia G., tr. from ENG & SPA. Crump, Fred, Jr., illus. LC 94-76371. 41p. (ps-5). 1994. pap. 6.95 (*1-55523-700-2*) Winston-Derek.

Crutcher, Chris. The Crazy Horse Electric Game. LC 86-14592. 160p. (gr. 7 up). 1987. 10.25 (*0-688-06683-6*) Greenwillow.

Cummings, Pat. Clean Your Room, Harvey Moon! Cummings, Pat, illus. LC 89-23863. 32p. (ps-2). 1991. RSBE 14.95 (*0-02-725511-5*, Bradbury Pr) Macmillan Child Grp.

Curry, Jane L. Me, Myself & I. LC 87-2681. 160p. (gr. 7 up). 1987. SBE 14.95 (*0-689-50429-2*, M K McElderry) Macmillan Child Grp.

Dahl, Roald. Boy: Tales of Childhood. LC 85-117335. (Illus.). 176p. (gr. 3 up). 1984. 16.00 (*0-374-37374-4*) FS&G.

—Boy: Tales of Childhood. (gr. 4-6). 1986. pap. 4.99 (*0-14-031890-9*, Puffin) Puffin Bks.

—Charlie & Chocolate Factory, Vol. 1. (gr. 4-7). 1977. pap. 2.75 (*0-553-15248-3*) Bantam.

—Charlie & the Chocolate Factory. 176p. (ps up). 1988. pap. 4.50 (*0-14-032869-6*, Puffin) Puffin Bks.

—Charlie & the Chocolate Factory. large type ed. 174p. 1989. Repr. of 1964 ed. lib. bdg. 13.95 (*1-55736-154-1*, Crnrstn Bks) BDD LT Grp.

—Charlie & the Chocolate Factory: A Play. George, Richard R., adapted by. 320p. (gr. 3-7). 1983. pap. 3.50 (*0-14-031125-4*, Puffin) Puffin Bks.

—Charlie & the Chocolate Factory: (Charlie y la Fabrica de Chocolate) (SPA.). 8.95 (*968-6026-71-1*) Santillana.

—Charlie & the Great Glass Elevator. 176p. 1988. pap. 4.50 (*0-14-032870-X*, Puffin) Puffin Bks.

—Charlie & the Great Glass Elevator: The Further Adventures of Charlie Bucket & Willie Wonka, the Chocolate-Maker Extraordinaire. Schindelman, Joseph, illus. (gr. k-7). 1972. 15.00 (*0-394-82472-5*); lib. bdg. 15.99 (*0-394-92472-X*) Knopf Bks Yng Read.

—Danny, Champion of the World. (gr. 3 up). 1984. pap. 2.75 (*0-553-15505-9*) Bantam.

—Danny, the Champion of the World. 208p. (gr. 3 up). 1988. pap. 4.50 (*0-14-032873-4*, Puffin) Puffin Bks.

—James & the Giant Peach. 112p. 1988. pap. 4.50 (*0-14-032871-8*, Puffin) Puffin Bks.

—James & the Giant Peach. large type ed. (gr. 4-7). 1989. lib. bdg. 14.95 (*1-55736-155-X*, Crnrstn Bks) BDD LT Grp.

—James & the Giant Peach. 128p. 1990. Repr. lib. bdg. 19.95x (*0-89966-702-3*) Buccaneer Bks.

—James & the Giant Peach. 1984. pap. 2.95 (*0-553-15317-X*) Bantam.

—James & the Giant Peach: A Play. 128p. (gr. 3-7). 1983. pap. 3.50 (*0-14-031464-4*, Puffin) Puffin Bks.

—The Wonderful Story of Henry Sugar & Six More. large type, rev. ed. 280p. 1989. lib. bdg. 14.95 (*1-85089-984-3*, Crnrstn Bks) BDD LT Grp.

Dana, Barbara. Necessary Parties. LC 85-45267. 352p. (gr. 7 up). 1986. PLB 14.89 (*0-06-021409-0*) HarpC Child Bks.

—Zucchini. Christelow, Eileen, illus. LC 80-8448. 128p. (gr. 3-6). 1982. PLB 13.89 (*0-06-021395-7*) HarpC Child Bks.

Davis, Gibbs. Pete the Magnificent. (ps-3). 1991. pap. 3.25 (*0-553-15896-1*) Bantam.

—Slugger Mike. (ps-3). 1991. pap. 3.25 (*0-553-15883-X*) Bantam.

Davoll, Barbara. A Pack of Lies. Hockerman, Dennis, illus. 24p. 1989. pap. 6.99 (*0-89693-497-7*, Victor Books); cassette 9.99 (*0-89693-030-0*) SP Pubns.

De Brissac, Elvire. Grabuge et l'Indomptable Amelie. Lapointe, Claude, illus. (FRE.). 144p. (gr. 3-7). 1990. pap. 11.95 (*2-07-031212-7*) Schoenhof.

Deich, Joy. J. P.'s Pumpkin Patch: Too Many Pumpkins. 32p. (gr. k-4). 1993. pap. 2.95 (*0-9629698-5-0*) Aaron Lake Pub.

Delton, Judy. I Never Win! Gilchrist, Cathy, illus. LC 80-27618. 32p. (gr. k-4). 1981. PLB 14.95 (*0-87614-139-4*) Carolrhoda Bks.

—Lucky Dog Days. 80p. (gr. k-3). 1988. pap. 3.25 (*0-440-40063-5*, YB) Dell.

—That Mushy Stuff. (Orig.). (gr. k-6). 1989. pap. 3.25 (*0-440-40176-3*, YB) Dell.

Demarest, Chris L. My Little Red Car. Demarest, Chris L., illus. 32p. (ps-1). 1992. PLB 14.95 (*1-878093-86-X*) Boyds Mills Pr.

Demas-Bliss, C. Matthew's Meadow. Lewin, T., illus. 1992. 14.95 (*0-15-200759-8*, HB Juv Bks) HarBrace.

Demi. Watch Harry Grow! Demi, illus. LC 84-60109. 26p. (ps-1). 1984. bds. 3.50 (*0-394-86857-9*) Random Bks Yng Read.

Dennis, John J. The Boy Who Could Not Fly. 64p. (gr. 4-8). pap. 7.95 (*0-9629036-0-4*) Grow Up Hlthy.

Dennis the Menace. (ps-3). 1993. pap. 2.95 (*0-8167-3147-0*) Troll Assocs.

Denzel, Justin. Boy of the Painted Cave. 160p. (gr. 3-7). 1988. 14.95 (*0-399-21559-X*, Philomel Bks) Putnam Pub Group.

De Paola, Tomie. Michael Bird Boy. LC 74-23563. (Illus.). 32p. (gr. k-4). 1998. pap. 12.95 jacketed (*0-671-66468-9*, S&S BFYR); pap. 5.95 (*0-671-66469-7*, S&S BFYR) S&S Trade.

Depaola, Tomie. Tom. (Illus.). 32p. (ps-3). 1993. PLB 14.95 (*0-399-22417-3*, Putnam) Putnam Pub Group.

Derwent, Lavinia. The Boy from Sula. 158p. (gr. 5-7). 1989. pap. 6.95 (*0-86241-111-4*, Pub. by Cnngt Pub Ltd) Trafalgar.

De Segur. Francois le Bossu. Bayard, Emile, illus. (FRE.). 250p. (gr. 5-10). 1981. pap. 9.95 (*2-07-033196-2*) Schoenhof.

Detemple, DeeDee. Cresnowatsofitz. LC 94-60118. (Illus.). 44p. (gr. k-3). 1994. pap. 6.95 (*1-55523-685-5*) Winston-Derek.

Deuker, Carl. On the Devil's Court. 256p. 1991. pap. 3.50 (*0-380-70879-5*, Flare) Avon.

Dickens, Charles. David Copperfield. (Illus.). 32p. (gr. 6 up). 1994. 9.95 (*0-9638463-1-0*, Crtoon Mdia); pap. 3.99 (*0-9638463-0-2*) Cethial Commns.

—Great Expectations. 464p. (gr. 5 up). 1992. pap. 3.50 (*0-14-035130-2*, Puffin) Puffin Bks.

—Great Expectations. LC 92-50184. 536p. 1992. 5.98 (*1-56138-170-5*) Courage Bks.

—Oliver Twist. abr. ed. 137p. 1962. pap. text ed. 5.95 (*0-582-53014-8*) Longman.

—Oliver Twist. Nyborg, Randy, illus. 373p. 1992. Repr. PLB 29.95 (*1-87776-769-7*) Regal Pubns.

Dickens, Frank. Albert Herbert Hawkins: The Naughtiest Boy in the World. Dickens, Frank, illus. LC 72-149044. 32p. (ps-3). 7.95 (*0-87592-000-4*) Scroll Pr.

Diggle, Giles. Roosters. 192p. (gr. 7 up). 1992. 18.95 (*0-571-16512-5*) Faber & Faber.

Diggs, Lucy. Everyday Friends. (gr. 5 up). 1987. pap. 2.95 (*0-8167-1047-3*) Troll Assocs.

Dinardo, Jeffrey. Timothy & the Night Noises. LC 86-9383. 1998. pap. 11.95 (*0-671-66807-2*, Little Simon); pap. 2.25 (*0-671-70298-X*, Little Simon) S&S Trade.

Dixon, Franklin W. Case of the Counterfeit Criminals. Winkler, Ellen, ed. 160p. (Orig.). 1992. pap. 3.99 (*0-671-73061-4*, Minstrel Bks) PB.

—Sabotage at Sports City. Winkler, Ellen, ed. 160p. (Orig.). 1992. pap. 3.99 (*0-671-73062-2*, Minstrel Bks) PB.

—Time Bomb. Greenberg, Anne, ed. 224p. (Orig.). 1992. pap. 3.75 (*0-671-75661-3*, Archway) PB.

Dodson, Lamar. Be My Daddy. 1992. 12.95 (*0-533-10200-6*) Vantage.

Doyle, Brian. Easy Avenue. 122p. (gr. 4-7). 1991. pap. 4.95 (*0-88899-124-X*, Pub. by Groundwood-Douglas & McIntyre CN) Firefly Bks Ltd.

Drescher, Joan. Max & Rufus. Drescher, Joan, illus. (gr. k-3). 1982. HM.

Driscoll, Jack. Skylight. LC 91-10593. 192p. (gr. 7 up). 1991. 14.95 (*0-531-05961-8*); RLB 14.99 (*0-531-08561-9*) Orchard Bks Watts.

Dubelaar, Thea. Looking for Vincent. Bruijn, Ruud, illus. 56p. (gr. 2-8). 1992. 9.95 (*1-56288-300-3*) Checkerboard.

Dubowski, Cathy E. Cave Boy. Dubowski, Mark, illus. LC 87-23427. 32p. (ps-1). 1988. lib. bdg. 7.99 (*0-394-99571-6*); pap. 3.50 (*0-394-89571-1*) Random Bks Yng Read.

Duckett, Gary. The Return of Talatu'u. LC 86-40285. 150p. (gr. 4-6). 1987. 7.95 (*1-55523-022-9*) Winston-Derek.

Duckworth, Marion. BJ Bernard Grows up. Chase, Andra, illus. 28p. (ps-k). 1993. 4.99 (*0-7847-0065-6*, 24-03845) Standard Pub.

Duder, Tessa. In Lane Three, Alex Archer. 1991. pap. 3.99 (*0-553-29020-7*) Bantam.

Duffey, Betsy. A Boy in the Doghouse. Morrill, Leslie, illus. LC 90-47751. 96p. (gr. 2-6). 1993. pap. 2.95 (*0-671-86698-2*, Half Moon Bks) S&S Trade.

—The Math Wiz. Wilson, Janet, illus. (gr. 4-7). 1990. 12.00 (*0-670-83422-X*) Viking Child Bks.

—The Math Wiz. Wilson, Janet, illus. 80p. (gr. 2-5). 1993. pap. 3.99 (*0-14-034477-2*) Puffin Bks.

Eastman, P. D. Corre, Perro, Corre! Mlawer, Teresa, tr. (Illus.). 64p. (gr. 1-2). 1992. 8.95 (*1-880507-02-1*) Lectorum Pubns.

Edens, Cooper. The Story Cloud. Grant, Kenneth L., illus. LC 91-13315. 48p. (ps-1). 1991. jacketed, reinforced bdg. 16.00 (*0-671-74823-8*, Green Tiger) S&S Trade.

Egielski. Buz. Date not set. 15.00 (*0-06-023566-7*); PLB 14.89 (*0-06-023567-5*) HarpC Child Bks.

Erb, Hazel R. Ole Bill. 1994. 7.95 (*0-8062-4934-X*) Carlton.

Erickson, Gina & Foster, Kelli C. Matthew's Brew. Gifford, Kerri, illus. 24p. (gr. k-3). 1994. pap. 3.50 (*0-8120-1922-9*) Barron.

Erickson, Gina C. & Foster, Kelli C. Dwight & the Trilobite. Gifford, Kerri, illus. 24p. (ps-3). 1994. pap. 3.50 (*0-8120-1839-7*) Barron.

Ernst, Lisa C. Sam Johnson & the Blue Ribbon Quilt. LC 82-9980. (Illus.). 32p. (gr. k up). 1992. pap. 3.95 (*0-688-11505-5*, Mulberry) Morrow.

Ethridge, Kenneth. Toothpick. 128p. (gr. 7 up). 1988. pap. 2.50 (*0-8167-1316-2*) Troll Assocs.

Ets, Marie H. In the Forest. (Illus.). (ps-2). 1976. pap. 3.95 (*0-14-050180-0*, Puffin) Puffin Bks.

—Just Me. (Illus.). (gr. k-2). 1978. pap. 4.99 (*0-14-050325-0*, Puffin) Puffin Bks.

Fabian, Stella. Is Your Heart Happy? Is Your Body Strong? (Orig.). (gr. 6). 1992. pap. 3.75 (*0-685-52888-X*) Brighton & Lloyd.

Fassler, Joan. The Man of the House. Landa, Peter, illus. LC 73-80122. 32p. (ps-3). 1975. 16.95 (*0-87705-010-4*) Human Sci Pr.

Fenner, Carol. Randall's Wall. LC 90-46490. 96p. (gr. 4-7). 1991. SBE 13.95 (*0-689-50518-3*, M K McElderry) Macmillan Child Grp.

Fenton, Edward. Duffy's Rocks. (gr. k-12). 1989. pap. 3.25 (*0-440-20242-6*, LFL) Dell.

Ferguson, Alane. Cricket & the Crackerbox Kid. 192p. (gr. 5). 1992. pap. 3.50 (*0-380-71341-1*, Camelot) Avon.

Fern, Eugene. Pepito's Story. LC 90-23639. (ps-3). 1993. pap. 4.99 (*0-553-37163-0*) Bantam.

Feuer, Elizabeth. One Friend to Another. LC 87-45363. 192p. (gr. 6 up). 1987. 15.00 (*0-374-35642-4*) FS&G.

Fitzgerald, John D. The Great Brain Does It Again. Mayer, Mercer, illus. LC 74-18600. (gr. 4-7). 1975. PLB 11.89 (*0-8037-5066-8*) Dial Bks Young.

—The Great Brain Reforms. 176p. (gr. k-6). 1975. pap. 3.50 (*0-440-44841-7*, YB) Dell.

—The Great Brain Reforms. LC 72-7601. (Illus.). 176p. (gr. 4-7). 1973. PLB 11.89 (*0-8037-3068-3*) Dial Bks Young.

—Me & My Little Brain. Mayer, Mercer, illus. LC 71-153732. (gr. 4-7). 1985. PLB 11.89 (*0-8037-5532-5*) Dial Bks Young.

—The Return of the Great Brain. 180p. (gr. 3-5). 1975. pap. 3.99 (*0-440-45941-9*, YB) Dell.

Fleischman, Paul. Saturnalia. LC 89-36380. 128p. (gr. 7 up). 1992. pap. 3.95 (*0-06-447089-X*, Trophy) HarpC Child Bks.

Fleischman, Sid. The Whipping Boy. Sis, Peter, illus. (gr. 2-5). 1987. pap. 2.95 (*0-8167-1038-4*) Troll Assocs.

—The Whipping Boy. large type ed. (Illus.). 104p. 1989. lib. bdg. 15.95 (*1-55736-115-0*, Crnrstn Bks) BDD LT Grp.

—The Whipping Boy. 95p. 1992. text ed. 7.60 (*1-56956-123-0*) W A T Braille.

Fleisher, Gila M. Dan Goes to First Grade. Kriss, David, tr. from HEB. Eagle, Mike, illus. 24p. (Orig.). (ps). 1992. pap. text ed. 3.00x (*1-56134-166-5*) Dushkin Pub.

—Daniel Entra Al Primer Grado. Writer, C. C. & Nielsen, Lisa C., trs. Eagle, Mike, illus. (SPA.). 24p. (Orig.). (ps). 1992. pap. text ed. 3.00x (*1-56134-176-2*) Dushkin Pub.

Fleming, Virginia. Be Good to Eddie Lee. Cooper, Floyd, illus. 32p. (ps-3). 1993. PLB 14.95 (*0-399-21993-5*, Philomel Bks) Putnam Pub Group.

Foley, Brian J. The Adventures of Mustard. 1993. 7.95 (*0-533-10662-1*) Vantage.

Foreman, Michael. War Boy: A Country Childhood. Foreman, Michael, illus. 96p. (gr. 3 up). 1990. 16.95 (*1-55970-049-1*) Arcade Pub Inc.

Fosburgh, Liza. Mrs. Abercorn & the Bunce Boys. 128p. (gr. k-6). 1989. pap. 2.75 (*0-440-40154-2*, YB) Dell.

Fox, Paula. A Likely Place. Ardizzone, Edward, illus. LC 87-5542. 64p. (gr. 2-6). 1987. Repr. SBE 13.95 (*0-02-735761-9*, Macmillan Child Bk) Macmillan Child Grp.

—Maurice's Room. Fetz, Ingrid, illus. LC 87-19504. 64p. (gr. 2-6). 1988. pap. 3.95 (*0-689-71216-2*, Aladdin) Macmillan Child Grp.

—Portrait of Ivan. Lambert, Saul, illus. LC 87-1109. 144p. (gr. 6-8). 1987. pap. 3.95 (*0-689-71167-0*, Aladdin) Macmillan Child Grp.

—The Stone-Faced Boy. LC 86-22204. 112p. (gr. 4-6). 1987. pap. 3.95 (*0-689-71127-1*, Aladdin) Macmillan Child Grp.

Frame, Laurence A. The New Window, la Ventana Nueva, Vol. 1. Frame, Laurence A., illus. (ENG & SPA.). 30p. (gr. 2-8). 1994. pap. 12.00 (*1-884480-54-3*) Spts Curriculum.

French, Michael. Soldier Boy. (gr. 7 up). 1990. pap. 2.95 (*0-553-28609-9*, Starfire) Bantam.

Frost, Dorothy R. Dad! Why'd You Leave Me? (Illus.). 96p. (Orig.). (gr. 3-6). 1992. pap. 4.95 (*0-8361-3592-X*) Herald Pr.

Gabhart, Ann. Bridge to Courage. 160p. (Orig.). (gr. 6). 1993. pap. 3.50 (*0-380-76051-7*, Flare) Avon.

Gackenbach, Dick. Harry & the Terrible Whatzit. Gackenbach, Dick, illus. LC 76-40205. 32p. (ps-3). 1984. pap. 4.95 (*0-89919-223-8*, Clarion Bks) HM.

Gaither, Alfred L. Wilbert's First Day. Black, Gerald, illus. 24p. (Orig.). Date not set. pap. write for info. (*0-9626882-0-7*) Alegator Bks.

Gallo, Donald R. Presenting Richard. 1993. pap. 4.99 (*0-440-21888-8*) Dell.

Garcia Sanchez, J. L. El Nino Gigante (The Giant Child) Sole, Carme, illus. (SPA.). 32p. (gr. k-2). 1988. 9.95 (*84-372-1346-0*) Santillana.

Garden, Nancy. Mystery of the Secret Marks. 192p. (gr. 3 up). 1989. 15.00 (*0-374-35021-3*) FS&G.

Garner, Alan. Elidor. (gr. 4-7). 1993. pap. 3.99 (*0-440-40763-X*) Dell.

Geller, Beverly. The Upsherin: Ephraim's First Haircut. 44p. Date not set. 8.95 (*0-935063-70-6*) CIS Comm.

George, Jean C. Water Sky. George, Jean C., illus. LC 86-45496. 224p. (gr. 6 up). 1987. 13.00 (*0-06-022198-4*); PLB 12.89 (*0-06-022199-2*) HarpC Child Bks.

Gerber, Merrill J. Handsome As Anything. 176p. 1992. pap. 2.95 (*0-590-43020-3*, Point) Scholastic Inc.

Gerrard, Roy. Mik's Mammoth. (Illus.). 32p. (gr. k-3). 1990. 15.00 (*0-374-31891-3*) FS&G.

Giblin, James C. Chimney Sweeps. Tomes, Margot, illus. LC 81-43878. 64p. (gr. 4-8). 1982. (Crowell Jr Bks); (Crowell Jr Bks) HarpC Child Bks.

Giff, Patricia R. Matthew Jackson Meets the Wall. (gr. 4-7). 1991. pap. 3.50 (*0-440-40547-5*, YB) Dell.

—The Rootin' Tootin' Bugle Boy. (ps-3). 1993. pap. 3.25 (*0-440-40757-5*) Dell.

—Watch Out, Ronald Morgan. Natti, Susanna, illus. 32p. (gr. k-4). 1986. pap. 4.99 (*0-14-050638-1*, Puffin) Puffin Bks.

Gilliland, Hap. Flint's Rock. Livers-Lambert, Pauline, illus. LC 94-65093. 144p. (Orig.). (gr. 4 up). 1994. pap. 8.95 (*1-879373-82-3*) R Rinehart.

Gilson, Jamie. Harvey, the Beer Can King. (Illus.). (gr. 4-6). 1988. pap. 2.50 (*0-671-67423-4*, Minstrel Bks) PB.

—Hello, My Name Is Scrambled Eggs. Wallner, John, illus. (gr. 3-6). 1991. pap. 3.99 (*0-671-74104-7*, Minstrel Bks) PB.

—Hobie Hanson, Greatest Hero of the Mall. Riggio, Anita, illus. LC 89-2343. 160p. (gr. 3-6). 1989. 12.95 (*0-688-08968-2*) Lothrop.

—Hobie Hanson, You're Weird. LC 86-15241. 170p. (gr. 4-7). 1987. 12.95 (*0-688-06700-X*) Lothrop.

—Hobie Hanson, You're Weird. MacDonald, Pat, ed. Primavera, Elise, illus. 176p. (gr. 3-6). 1990. pap. 3.50 (*0-671-73752-X*, Minstrel Bks) PB.

Giorda. William the Last. (Illus.). (gr. 3-8). 1992. PLB 8.95 (*0-89565-884-4*) Childs World.

Glazier, Lyle. Summer for Joey. LC 86-63092. 256p. 1987. pap. 9.95 (*0-912395-08-7*) Millers River Pub Co.

Gleason, Richard. Sprout. LC 86-51074. (Illus.). 84p. (gr. 3-8). 1987. 7.95 (*1-55523-052-0*) Winston-Derek.

Goedecke, Christopher J. The Wind Warrior: The Training of a Karate Champion. Hausherr, Rosmarie, illus. LC 91-6405. 64p. (gr. 3-9). 1992. RSBE 15.95 (*0-02-736262-0*, Four Winds) Macmillan Child Grp.

Goode, Diane. I Hear a Noise. Goode, Diane, illus. LC 87-3060. 32p. (ps-1). 1992. pap. 3.99 (*0-525-44884-5*, Puffin Bks) Puffin Bks.

Grabarits, Anne C. Kathy Needs Comfort & Timmy's New Outlook. (Illus.). 30p. 1993. saddlestitched 4.95 (*0-8059-3424-3*) Dorrance.

Graeber, Charlotte T. Fudge. Harness, Cheryl, illus. LC 86-7353. 128p. (gr. 1-4). 1987. 12.95 (*0-688-06735-2*) Lothrop.

—Fudge. 1989. pap. 2.99 (*0-671-70288-2*, Minstrel Bks) PB.

Graham, Amanda. Educating Arthur. Gynell, Donna, illus. LC 87-42756. 32p. (gr. 2-3). 1988. PLB 18.60 (*1-55532-411-8*) Gareth Stevens Inc.

Gray Boy Renegade Dog on Loose. 96p. (gr. 4-7). 1990. pap. 2.95 (*0-8167-1820-2*) Troll Assocs.

Greene, Bette. Get on out of Here, Philip Hall. 144p. (gr. 4-7). 1984. pap. 2.75 (*0-440-43038-0*, YB) Dell.

Greene, Constance C. Just Plain Al. (gr. k-6). 1988. pap. 2.95 (*0-440-40073-2*, YB) Dell.

Greenfield, Eloise. Daydreamers. Feelings, Tom, illus. LC 80-27262. (gr. k up). 1985. pap. 4.95 (*0-8037-0167-5*) Dial Bks Young.

—Nathaniel Talking. (gr. 4-7). 1993. pap. 6.95 (*0-86316-201-0*) Writers & Readers.

Gretz, Susanna. Roger Loses His Marbles. Gretz, Susanna, illus. LC 88-3753. 32p. (ps-2). 1988. 11.95 (*0-8037-0565-4*) Dial Bks Young.

—Roger Takes Charge! LC 86-24061. (Illus.). 32p. (ps-2). 1987. 12.95 (*0-8037-0121-7*) Dial Bks Young.

—Roger Takes Charge. 1990. pap. 3.95 (*0-8037-0742-8*, Puff Pied Piper) Puffin Bks.

Grey, Zane. The Shortstop. LC 91-24034. 240p. (gr. 6 up). 1992. pap. 4.95 (*0-688-11261-7*, Pub. by Beech Tree Bks) Morrow.

—The Young Pitcher. LC 91-23670. 256p. (gr. 6 up). 1992. pap. 4.95 (*0-688-11262-5*, Pub. by Beech Tree Bks) Morrow.

Gripe, Maria. Elvis & His Secret. Gripe, Harald, illus. 208p. (gr. 3-7). 1979. pap. 1.50 (*0-440-42434-8*, YB) Dell.

Grubbs, Joan J., et al. Books for Young Gentlemen. rev. ed. Grubbs, Joan, illus. 50p. (gr. 6-8). 1993. 22.00 (*1-56611-024-6*); PLB 25.00 (*1-56611-071-8*); pap. 15.00 (*0-685-65770-1*) Jonas.

Gutman, Bill. Smitty. (gr. 7-12). 1988. PLB 2.95 (*0-89872-301-9*) Turman Pub.

Guy, Lucien. Scatterbrain Sam. (Illus.). 32p. (gr. 3-5). 1991. 12.95 (*0-89565-754-6*) Childs World.

Guy, Rosa. Billy the Great. (ps-3). 1994. pap. 4.99 (*0-440-40920-9*) Dell.

—New Guys Around the Block. (gr. 7 up). 1992. 3.50 (*0-685-57133-5*, LFL) Dell.

—The Ups & Downs of Carl Davis III. (gr. 5 up). 1989. 13.95 (*0-385-29724-6*) Delacorte.

—Ups & Downs of Carl Davis the Third. (gr. 4-7). 1993. pap. 3.50 (*0-440-40744-3*) Dell.

Haas, Dorothy. Burton & the Giggle Machine. Bobak, Cathy, illus. LC 91-25411. 160p. (gr. 5-8). 1992. SBE 13.95 (*0-02-738203-6*, Bradbury Pr) Macmillan Child Grp.

Haggerty, Mary E. Una Grieta en la Pared. Gonzalez, Tomas, tr. De Anda, Ruben, illus. LC 93-38626. (SPA.). 32p. (gr. k-3). 1994. 14.95 (*1-88000-009-1*); pap. 5.95 (*1-88000-012-1*) Lee & Low Bks.

Hagstrom, Amy. Strong & Free. Hagstrom, Amy, illus. LC 87-3942. 24p. (gr. 1 up). 1987. PLB 14.95 (*0-933849-15-X*) Landmark Edns.

Hal Finds a Home. (Illus.). (ps-2). 1991. PLB 6.95 (*0-685-50734-3*, TK38812); pap. 3.50 (*0-8136-5676-1*, TK38822) Modern Curr.
Hale, Irina. Boxman. Hale, Irina, illus. 32p. (ps-1). 1992. 12.00 (*0-670-84287-7*) Viking Child Bks.
Hall, Lynn. Danger Dog. LC 86-13914. 112p. (gr. 4-7). 1986. SBE 13.95 (*0-684-18680-2*, Scribners Young Read) Macmillan Child Grp.
—Danza! LC 88-8047. 192p. (gr. 5-7). 1989. pap. 3.95 (*0-689-71289-8*, Aladdin) Macmillan Child Grp.
Hamilton, Dorothy. Busboys at Big Bend. Ponter, James, illus. LC 74-8689. 112p. (gr. 8-12). 1974. o. p. 4.95 (*0-8361-1744-1*); pap. 3.95 (*0-8361-1745-X*) Herald Pr.
Hamilton, Virginia. Junius over Far. LC 84-48344. 288p. (gr. 7 up). 1985. PLB 14.89 (*0-06-022195-X*) HarpC Child Bks.
—M. C. Higgins, the Great. LC 87-6330. 288p. (gr. 7 up). 1987. pap. 3.95 (*0-02-043490-1*, Collier Young Ad) Macmillan Child Grp.
Hamsa, Bobbie. Fast Draw Freddie (Rookie Readers) LC 83-23931. (Illus.). 32p. (ps-2). 1984. lib. bdg. 10.25 (*0-516-02046-3*); pap. 2.95 (*0-516-42046-1*) Childrens.
Handler, Kalindi. The Boy Behind the Counter. 160p. (Orig.). (gr. 7 up). 1989. pap. 2.50 (*0-380-75646-3*, Flare) Avon.
Hannam, Charles. A Boy in Your Situation. 216p. (gr. 7-9). 1989. pap. 9.95 (*0-233-98279-5*, Pub. by A Deutsch England) Trafalgar.
Hansen, Joyce. Home Boy. 1994. pap. 4.95 (*0-395-69625-9*, Clarion Bks) HM.
Harbo, Gary. Bad Bart's Revenge: Advanced Reader. Harbo, Gary & Wallace, Shawn, illus. 35p. (gr. 1-4). 1991. text ed. 8.95 (*1-884149-03-0*) Kutie Kari Bks.
Harrell, John. Here Comes Maurice: A Musical for One Puppet. (Illus.). 15p. (gr. 6 up). 1987. Incls. cassette. pap. 10.95 (*0-9615389-6-1*) York Hse.
Harris, Mark J. Solay. LC 92-33012. 160p. (gr. 4-7). 1993. SBE 13.95 (*0-02-742655-6*, Bradbury Pr) Macmillan Child Grp.
Harrison, David. The Boy Who Counted Stars. Lewin, Betsy, illus. LC 92-61632. 32p. (gr. 1-5). 1994. 14.95 (*1-56397-125-9*) Boyds Mills Pr.
Hartman, Bob. Johnny Thumbs. Kolding, Max, illus. 48p. (Orig.). (gr. 1-3). 1993. pap. 3.99 (*0-7847-0093-1*, 24-03943) Standard Pub.
Hartman, Dale S. Jarad's Special Visitor. Whitaker, Kate, ed. DeVito, Pam, illus. LC 93-61631. 40p. (Orig.). (ps-2). 1994. pap. 5.95 (*1-883650-12-7*) Windswept Hse.
Hastings. Rufus & Christopher Series, 3 vols. (Illus.). (gr. 2-4). Set. PLB 29.95 (*0-87783-168-8*); Set. pap. 11.82 deluxe edition (*0-87783-169-6*); cassettes 23.82x (*0-87783-234-X*) Oddo.
Haugaard, Erik. The Death of Mr. Angel. 167p. (gr. 9-12). 1992. 13.95 (*1-879373-26-2*) R Rinehart.
Haugaard, Erik C. A Boy's Will. (gr. 4-7). 1990. pap. 5.95 (*0-395-54962-0*) HM.
—Cromwell's Boy. (gr. 4-7). 1990. pap. 5.95 (*0-395-54975-2*) HM.
Hautzig, Deborah. Grover's Lucky Jacket. Chartier, Normand, illus. LC 89-30102. 40p. (ps-3). 1989. PLB 6.99 (*0-679-90077-2*); pap. 4.95 (*0-679-80077-8*) Random Bks Yng Read.
Hawes, Louise. Nelson Malone Meets the Man from Mush-Nut. (gr. 3-7). 1988. pap. 2.50 (*0-380-70508-7*, Camelot) Avon.
Hawkins, Tommy. The Voice Underneath the Pillow. LC 91-41233. (Illus.). 80p. (ps-3). 1992. 12.00g (*1-880691-17-5*) Blackbird MI.
Hawks, Robert. The Richest Kid in the World. 144p. (Orig.). 1992. pap. 2.99 (*0-380-76241-2*, Camelot) Avon.
—The Richest Kid in the World: The Sixty Billion Dollar Fugitive. 160p. (Orig.). (gr. 5). 1992. pap. 3.50 (*0-380-76242-0*, Camelot) Avon.
Hayes, D. W. Shorty Gordy. LC 91-65922. (Illus.). (gr. k-3). 1992. 7.95 (*1-55523-449-6*) Winston-Derek.
Haynes, Betsy. Against Sinclair. 1984. pap. 2.75 (*0-553-15712-4*) Bantam.
Haywood, Carolyn. Eddie's Menagerie. 192p. (gr. 2-4). 1987. pap. 2.95 (*0-8167-1042-2*) Troll Assocs.
Heide, Florence P. The Problem with Pulcifer. Glasser, Judy, illus. LC 81-48606. 64p. (gr. 2 up). 1992. pap. 3.95 (*0-688-11570-5*, Mulberry) Morrow.
Herlihy, Dirlie. Ludie's Song. LC 87-30305. 224p. (gr. 5 up). 1988. 14.95 (*0-8037-0533-6*) Dial Bks Young.
Hermes, Patricia. Kevin Corbett Eats Flies. Newsom, Carol, illus. LC 85-27086. 160p. (gr. 3-7). 1986. 13.95 (*0-15-242290-0*, HB Juv Bks) HarBrace.
Hernandez, Betsy, et al. The Boy Who Wanted the Moon. Hilliard, Cindy & French, Marty, illus. 26p. (ps up). 1986. Book & Cassette. 7.95 (*1-55578-100-4*); cass. incl. Worlds Wonder.
Herold, Ann B. The Hard Life of Seymour E. Newton. 96p. (Orig.). (gr. 2-5). 1990. pap. 5.95 (*0-8361-3532-6*) Herald Pr.
Hickey, Tony. Joe in the Middle. 205p. 1988. pap. 5.95 (*1-85371-021-0*, Pub. by Poolbeg Press Ltd Eire) Dufour.
—Spike & the Professor. Ballagh, Robert, illus. LC 89-51005. 160p. (Orig.). (gr. 4-7). 1989. pap. 5.95 (*1-85371-039-3*, Pub. by Poolbeg Press Ltd Eire) Dufour.
Highwater, Jamake. Eyes of Darkness. LC 82-187. 192p. (gr. 6 up). 1985. 13.00 (*0-688-41993-3*) Lothrop.
Hill, Fred D. Christopher & Cumulus Cloud. Young, Elaine & Hill, Charlotte, eds. Rhiney, Sharon, illus. LC 90-80285. 28p. (Orig.). (gr. k-4). 1990. pap. 5.95 (*0-9620182-1-X*) Charill Pubs.
Hilts, Len. Timmy O-Dowd & the Big Ditch: A Story of the Glory Days on the Old Erie Canal. 91p. (gr. 3-7). 1988. 13.95 (*0-15-200606-0*, Gulliver Bks) HarBrace.
Hoban, Gordon. Handy Andrews: A Novel. LC 91-90475. 176p. (Orig.). 1991. pap. 14.95 (*0-944204-11-2*) Omniun.
Hoban, Lillian. Arthur's Funny Money. Hoban, Lillian, illus. LC 80-7903. 64p. (gr. k-3). 1987. incl. cassette 5.98 (*0-694-00173-2*, Trophy); pap. 3.50 (*0-06-444048-6*, Trophy) HarpC Child Bks.
—Arthur's Halloween Costume. LC 83-49465. (Illus.). 64p. (gr. k-3). 1986. pap. 3.50 (*0-06-444101-6*, Trophy) HarpC Child Bks.
—Arthur's Loose Tooth. Hoban, Lillian, illus. LC 85-42611. 64p. (ps-3). 1985. PLB 13.89 (*0-06-022354-5*) HarpC Child Bks.
Hochman, Doris Z. Kid Koala's Fun Book. Hochman, Doris Z., illus. 44p. (gr. 2-5). 1991. wkbk. 6.95 (*1-878070-00-2*) Three Elves Pr.
Hodges, Candri. When I Grow Up. Yoder, Dot, illus. 32p. (gr. k-4). Date not set. PLB 13.95 (*0-944727-27-1*); pap. 6.95 (*0-944727-26-3*) Jason & Nordic Pubs.
Hodgman, Ann. Stinky Stanley. MacDonald, Pat, ed. Cymerman, John E., illus. 128p. (Orig.). (gr. 3-6). 1993. pap. 2.99 (*0-671-78548-6*, Minstrel Bks) PB.
—Stinky Stanley Stinks Again. MacDonald, Pat, ed. Cymerman, John E., illus. 128p. (Orig.). 1993. pap. 2.99 (*0-671-78560-5*, Minstrel Bks) PB.
Hoffmann, Henry. Slovenly Peter: or Cheerful Stories & Funny Pictures for Good Little Folks. (Illus.). 88p. 1991. Repr. PLB 25.95x (*0-89966-765-1*) Buccaneer Bks.
Hofmann, Ginnie. Who Wants an Old Teddy Bear? Hofmann, Ginnie, illus. LC 80-10445. 32p. (ps-3). 1980. lib. bdg. 5.99 (*0-394-93925-5*); pap. 2.25 (*0-394-83925-0*) Random Bks Yng Read.
Holabird, Katharine. Alexander & the Dragon. Craig, Helen, illus. 24p. (ps-2). 1988. 14.00 (*0-517-56996-5*, Clarkson Potter) Crown Bks Yng Read.
Holcomb, Nan. Andy Finds a Turtle. Yoder, Dot, illus. 32p. (ps-2). 1992. Repr. of 1988 ed. 13.95 (*0-944727-13-1*) Jason & Nordic Pubs.
—Andy Opens Wide. Yoder, Dot, illus. 32p. (ps-2). 1992. Repr. of 1990 ed. 13.95 (*0-944727-17-4*) Jason & Nordic Pubs.
—Danny & the Merry-Go-Round. Lucia, Virginia, illus. 32p. (ps-2). 1992. Repr. of 1988 ed. 13.95 (*0-944727-11-5*) Jason & Nordic Pubs.
—Patrick & Emma Lou. Yoder, Dot, illus. 32p. (ps-3). 1992. Repr. of 1989 ed. 13.95 (*0-944727-14-X*) Jason & Nordic Pubs.
—A Smile from Andy. Yoder, Dot, illus. 32p. (ps-3). 1992. Repr. of 1989 ed. 13.95 (*0-944727-15-8*) Jason & Nordic Pubs.
Holland, Isabelle. The Man Without a Face. LC 71-37736. 144p. (gr. 7 up). 1987. pap. 3.95 (*0-06-447028-8*, Trophy) HarpC Child Bks.
Holt, S. Marie. Mike Goes to the North Pole. Holt, Shirley, illus. 28p. (gr. k-5). 1993. 21.95x (*0-9613476-6-X*) Shirlee.
Honeycutt, Natalie. The Best-Laid Plans of Jonah Twist. LC 88-7288. 128p. (gr. 3-5). 1988. SBE 13.95 (*0-02-744850-9*, Bradbury Pr) Macmillan Child Grp.
—The Best-Laid Plans of Jonah Twist. 128p. (gr. 2). 1990. pap. 2.95 (*0-380-70762-4*, Camelot) Avon.
Hooks, William H. Mr. Bubble Gum: Level 3. Meisel, Paul, illus. 1989. 9.99 (*0-553-05834-7*) Bantam.
—Mr. Bubblegum-Bank Street. (ps-3). 1989. pap. 3.50 (*0-553-34694-6*) Bantam.
Horenstein, Henry. Sam Goes Trucking. Horenstein, Henry, illus. (ps-3). 1989. 14.45 (*0-395-44313-X*) HM.
Horenstein, Henry, photos by. Mike Goes Trucking. 1988. write for info. HM.
Horowitz, Jordan. Dennis the Menace. (ps-3). 1993. pap. 2.95 (*0-590-47399-9*) Scholastic Inc.
—Dennis the Menace. (gr. 4-7). 1993. pap. 2.95 (*0-590-48219-X*) Scholastic Inc.
—Home Alone Two: Lost in New York Picture Book Adaptation. (Illus.). 1992. 2.95 (*0-590-45719-5*) Scholastic Inc.
Hort, Lenny. The Boy Who Held Back the Sea. Locker, Thomas, illus. LC 86-32893. 1987. 15.00 (*0-8037-0406-2*); PLB 14.89 (*0-8037-0407-0*) Dial Bks Young.
Horton, Randy. Fraud, Fame, Alien Life Forms. Parker, Liz, ed. Taylor, Marjorie, illus. 45p. (Orig.). (gr. 6-12). 1992. pap. text ed. 2.95 (*1-56254-053-X*) Saddleback Pubns.
Howe, E. W. The Moonlight Boy. 1988. Repr. of 1886 ed. lib. bdg. 59.00x (*0-7812-1288-X*) Rprt Serv.
Hudson, Wade, et al. Jamal's Busy Day. LC 90-81646. (Illus.). 24p. (gr. 1-3). 1991. lib. bdg. 12.95 (*0-940975-21-1*); pap. 6.95 (*0-940975-24-6*) Just Us Bks.
Hughes, Dean. Family Pose. LC 88-28501. 192p. (gr. 3-7). 1989. SBE 14.95 (*0-689-31396-9*, Atheneum Child Bk) Macmillan Child Grp.
—Nutty Knows All. LC 88-886. 160p. (gr. 3-7). 1988. SBE 13.95 (*0-689-31410-8*, Atheneum Child Bk) Macmillan Child Grp.
Hughes, Shirley. Alfie Gets in First. LC 81-8427. (Illus.). 32p. (ps up). 1987. pap. 4.95 (*0-688-07036-1*, Mulberry) Morrow.
—An Evening at Alfie's. LC 84-11297. (Illus.). 32p. (ps up). 1992. pap. 3.95 (*0-688-11520-9*, Mulberry) Morrow.
Hughes, Thomas. Tom Brown's School Days. Andrew, C., intro. by. (gr. 7 up). 1968. pap. 1.95 (*0-8049-0174-0*, CL-174) Airmont.
—Tom Brown's Schooldays. 288p. (gr. 4-6). 1984. pap. 3.50 (*0-14-035022-5*, Puffin) Puffin Bks.
Hunt, Angela E. Howie Hugemouth. Newton-King, Laurie, illus. 28p. (ps-k). 1993. 4.99 (*0-7847-0066-4*, 24-03846) Standard Pub.
Hurd, Edith T. Johnny Lion's Book. Hurd, Clement, illus. LC 65-14490. 64p. (gr. k-3). 1985. pap. 3.50 (*0-06-444074-5*, Trophy) HarpC Child Bks.
Hurwitz, Johanna. Aldo Applesauce. Wallner, John, illus. 128p. (gr. 3-5). 1989. pap. 3.99 (*0-14-034083-1*, Puffin) Puffin Bks.
—Aldo Ice Cream. Wallner, John, illus. 128p. (gr. 3-7). 1989. pap. 3.99 (*0-14-034084-X*, Puffin) Puffin Bks.
—Much Ado about Aldo. Wallner, John, illus. 96p. (gr. 3-7). 1989. pap. 3.99 (*0-14-034082-3*, Puffin) Puffin Bks.
—Rip-Roaring Russell. Hoban, Lillian, illus. LC 83-1019. 96p. (ps-1). 1983. 12.95 (*0-688-02347-9*); lib. bdg. 12.88 (*0-688-02348-7*, Morrow Jr Bks) Morrow Jr Bks.
—Rip-Roarring Russell. Hoban, Lillian, illus. 96p. (gr. 2-5). 1989. pap. 3.99 (*0-14-032939-0*, Puffin) Puffin Bks.
—Russell Rides Again. Hoban, Lillian, illus. 96p. (gr. 2-5). 1989. pap. 3.99 (*0-14-032941-2*, Puffin) Puffin Bks.
—Russell Sprouts. Hoban, Lillian, illus. LC 87-5494. 80p. (ps-2). 1987. 12.95 (*0-688-07165-1*); lib. bdg. 12.88 (*0-688-07166-X*, Morrow Jr Bks) Morrow Jr Bks.
—Russell Sprouts. Hoban, Lillian, illus. 80p. (gr. 2-5). 1989. pap. 3.99 (*0-14-032942-0*, Puffin) Puffin Bks.
Hutchins, Pat. You'll Soon Grow into Them, Titch. Hutchins, Pat, illus. LC 82-11755. 32p. (gr. k-3). 1983. 16.00 (*0-688-01770-3*); PLB 15.93 (*0-688-01771-1*) Greenwillow.
Ibbitson, John. The Wimp. 96p. 1986. pap. text ed. 4.50 (*0-8219-0237-7*, 35358); wkbk. 1.20 (*0-8219-0238-5*, 35721) EMC.
Ingle, Valorie L. The Power of Helping. (Illus.). (gr. k-4). 1994. write for info. (*1-883863-10-4*) Legend Prods.
Isadora, Rachel. Newsboy. (Illus.). 24p. 1995. write for info. (*0-688-11389-3*); PLB write for info. (*0-688-11390-7*) Greenwillow.
Jackson, Alison. My Brother, the Star. LC 89-34480. 112p. (gr. 3-7). 1990. 12.95 (*0-525-44512-9*, DCB) Dutton Child Bks.
Jackson, Dave & Jackson, Neta. The Bandit of Ashley Downs. 128p. (Orig.). 1993. pap. 4.99 (*1-55661-270-2*) Bethany Hse.
—The Hidden Jewel. 128p. (Orig.). (gr. 3-7). 1992. pap. 4.99 (*1-55661-245-1*) Bethany Hse.
James, Sara. Bootsflat: Boots & the Spooky House. (Illus.). 24p. (ps). 1993. 3.98 (*0-8317-0605-8*) Smithmark.
—Bootsflat: Boots Goes to School. (Illus.). 24p. (ps). 1993. 3.98 (*0-8317-0606-6*) Smithmark.
Jander, Martha. Philip & the Ethiopian. (Illus.). 24p. (gr. k-4). 1990. pap. 1.99 (*0-570-09024-5*, 59-1447) Concordia.
Jefferies, Richard. Bevis. 384p. (gr. 4-6). 1984. pap. 2.25 (*0-14-035026-8*, Puffin) Puffin Bks.
Jeram, Anita. Bill's Belly Button. (ps-3). 1991. 14.95 (*0-316-46114-8*) Little.
—It Was Jake. (ps-3). 1991. 14.95 (*0-316-46120-2*) Little.
Johnson, Crockett. Harold's Fairy Tale. reissue ed. Johnson, Crockett, illus. LC 56-8147. 64p. (ps-1). 1986. PLB 12.89 (*0-06-022976-4*) HarpC Child Bks.
—A Picture for Harold's Room. Johnson, Crockett, illus. LC 60-6372. 64p. (ps-3). 1985. pap. 3.50 (*0-06-444085-0*, Trophy) HarpC Child Bks.
Johnson, Donald E. Jamie: A Novel. (Illus.). 104p. (Orig.). (gr. 6-8). 1993. pap. 8.95 (*1-56474-052-8*) Fithian Pr.
Johnson, Phyllis. The Boy Toy. Shiffman, Lena, illus. 32p. (gr. k-3). 1988. pap. 5.95 (*0-914996-26-6*) Lollipop Power.
Johnston, Annie F. Joel: A Boy of Galilee. Coven, Peggy, illus. Slater, Rosalie J., intro. by. LC 92-75820. (Illus.). 254p. (gr. 4-8). 1992. pap. 12.00 (*0-912498-11-0*) F A C E.
Jones, Diana W. Eight Days of Luke. LC 88-220. 160p. (gr. 7 up). 1988. Repr. of 1975 ed. 11.95 (*0-688-08006-5*) Greenwillow.
—The Lives of Christopher Chant. LC 87-24540. (gr. 7 up). 1988. 11.95 (*0-688-07806-0*) Greenwillow.
—The Lives of Christopher Chant. LC 87-24540. 240p. (gr. 4-7). 1990. pap. 3.50 (*0-394-82205-6*) Random Bks Yng Read.
Jones, Rebecca. Germy Blew It. 112p. (gr. 2-9). 1988. pap. 2.95 (*0-8167-1314-6*) Troll Assocs.
Jones, Rebecca C. Germy Blew It Again. LC 88-22696. 124p. (gr. 2-4). 1988. 13.95 (*0-8050-0905-1*, Bks Young Read) H Holt & Co.
Joyce, William. George Shrinks. Joyce, William, illus. LC 83-47697. 32p. (ps-2). 1987. pap. 4.95 (*0-06-443129-0*, Trophy) HarpC Child Bks.
K, King. Rainbow Chase. 1992. 10.95 (*0-533-10031-3*) Vantage.
Kaaki, Lisa. The Awakening. Zhou, Hoda D., illus. 30p. (Orig.). (gr. 1-4). 1991. pap. 3.50 (*0-89259-118-8*) Am Trust Pubns.
Kaplan, Lee. Four Eyes. LC 90-71708. 44p. (gr. 1-3). 1991. 5.95 (*1-55523-402-X*) Winston-Derek.

Kaplan, Marjorie. Henry & the Boy Who Thought Numbers Were Fleas. Chang, Heidi, illus. LC 90-43852. 80p. (gr. 2-4). 1991. SBE 12.95 (*0-02-749351-2*, Four Winds) Macmillan Child Grp.

Kassel, April. Slow Joe. Block, Lori, illus. Sargent, Dave, intro. by. (Illus.). 36p. (Orig.). (gr. k-8). 1993. text ed. 12.95 (*1-56763-067-7*); pap. text ed. 5.95 (*1-56763-068-5*) Ozark Pub.

Kassirer, Sue. The Gingerbread Boy. Williams, Jennie, illus. 24p. (Orig.). (ps-k). 1993. pap. 1.50 (*0-679-84795-2*) Random Bks Yng Read.

Katz, Illana & Ritvo, Edward. Joey & Sam: Autism. (ps-3). 1993. pap. 9.95 (*1-882388-06-2*) Real Life Strybks.

Keats, Ezra J. Goggles! Keats, Ezra J., illus. LC 86-28718. 40p. (gr. k-3). 1987. pap. 4.95 (*0-689-71157-3*, Aladdin) Macmillan Child Grp.

—Pet Show! Keats, Ezra J., illus. LC 86-17225. 40p. (gr. k-3). 1987. pap. 4.95 (*0-689-71159-X*, Aladdin) Macmillan Child Grp.

—Peter's Chair. LC 67-4816. (Illus.). 32p. (ps-3). 1983. pap. 4.95 (*0-06-443040-5*, Trophy) HarpC Child Bks.

—Peter's Chair Big Book. Keats, Ezra J., illus. LC 67-4816. 32p. (ps-3). 1993. pap. 19.95 (*0-06-443325-0*, Trophy) HarpC Child Bks.

—The Snowy Day. (Illus.). (ps-k). 1976. pap. 4.99 (*0-14-050182-7*, Puffin) Puffin Bks.

Kennedy, William P. Charlie Malarkey & the Belly Button Machine. (ps-3). 1990. pap. 4.95 (*0-14-054239-6*, Puffin) Puffin Bks.

Kent, Jack. Joey Runs Away. LC 85-3673. (Illus.). 32p. (gr. k-4). 1989. (S&S BFYR); pap. 5.95 (*0-671-67936-8*, S&S BFYR) S&S Trade.

Kerr, M. E. Dinky Hocker Shoots Smack. LC 72-80366. 208p. (gr. 7 up). 1989. pap. 2.95 (*0-06-447006-7*, Trophy) HarpC Child Bks.

—Fell. LC 86-45776. 160p. (gr. 7 up). 1987. PLB 14.89 (*0-06-023268-4*) HarpC Child Bks.

Kezzeiz, Ediba. When I Grow up. Shishani, Ami, illus. 17p. (Orig.). (ps-1). 1991. pap. 3.50 ea. (*0-89259-116-1*) Am Trust Pubns.

Kharms, Daniil. The Story of a Boy Named Will, Who Went Sledding Down the Hill. Radunsky, Vladimir, illus. Gambrell, Jamey, tr. from RUS. LC 93-16612. (Illus.). 32p. (gr. k-3). 1993. 14.95 (*1-55858-214-2*); lib. bdg. 14.88 (*1-55858-215-0*) North-South Bks NYC.

Killien, Christi. Artie's Brief: The Whole Truth & Nothing But. 112p. 1990. pap. 2.95 (*0-380-71108-7*, Camelot) Avon.

—Rusty Fertlanger, Lady's Man. LC 87-31001. 144p. (gr. 5-9). 1988. 13.95 (*0-395-46762-4*) HM.

King, Larry L. Because of Lozo Brown. Schwartz, Amy, illus. LC 88-3952. (ps-3). 1988. 11.95 (*0-670-81031-2*) Viking Child Bks.

Kline, Suzy. Herbie Jones. Williams, Richard, illus. LC 84-24915. 96p. (gr. 2-6). 1985. 13.95 (*0-399-21183-7*, Putnam) Putnam Pub Group.

—Herbie Jones & the Dark Attic. Williams, Richard, illus. 112p. (gr. 2-6). 1992. 14.95 (*0-399-21838-6*, Putnam) Putnam Pub Group.

—Horrible Harry & the Ant Invasion. Remkiewicz, Frank, illus. 64p. (gr. 2-5). 1989. pap. 11.00 (*0-670-82469-0*) Viking Child Bks.

—Horrible Harry & the Green Slime. Remkiewicz, Frank, illus. 64p. (gr. 2-5). 1989. pap. 10.95 (*0-670-82468-2*) Viking Child Bks.

—Orp & the Chop Suey Burgers. 96p. (gr. 4). 1992. pap. 3.50 (*0-380-71359-4*, Camelot) Avon.

—What's the Matter with Herbie Jones? Williams, Richard, illus. (gr. 3-7). pap. 3.95 (*0-317-62246-3*, Puffin) Puffin Bks.

Klingsheim, Arild. Julius. (gr. 4-7). 1991. pap. 4.95 (*0-440-40431-2*) Dell.

Koff, Richard M. Christopher. 160p. 1985. pap. text ed. 2.25 (*0-553-15363-3*) Bantam.

Korman, Gordon. I Want to Go Home! 192p. (Orig.). (gr. 3-7). 1991. pap. 3.25 (*0-590-44210-4*) Scholastic Inc.

Kraus, Joanna H. Tall Boy's Journey. (gr. 4-7). 1993. pap. 5.95 (*0-87614-616-7*) Carolrhoda Bks.

Kraus, Robert. Herman the Helper. Aruego, Jose & Dewey, Ariane, illus. LC 73-9319. (ps). 1987. pap. 12.95 jacketed (*0-671-66887-0*, S&S BFYR); pap. 5.95 (*0-671-66270-8*, S&S BFYR) S&S Trade.

—Leo the Late Bloomer. Reissue. ed. Aruego, Jose, illus. LC 70-159154. 32p. (gr. k-3). 1971. 16.00 (*0-87807-042-7*, Crowell Jr Bks); PLB 15.89 (*0-87807-043-5*) HarpC Child Bks.

Krensky, Stephen. Lionel at Large. Natti, Susanna, illus. (gr. 1-4). 1993. pap. 3.25 (*0-14-036542-7*, Puffin) Puffin Bks.

—Lionel in the Fall. Natti, Susanna, illus. LC 86-32876. 48p. (ps-3). 1987. 9.95 (*0-8037-0384-8*); PLB 9.89 (*0-8037-0385-6*) Dial Bks Young.

—Lionel in the Fall. Natti, Susanna, illus. (gr. 1-4). 1993. pap. 3.25 (*0-14-036545-1*, Puffin) Puffin Bks.

—Lionel in the Spring. Natti, Susanna, illus. LC 88-30885. 48p. (ps-3). 1992. pap. 3.99 (*0-14-036117-0*, Dial Easy to Read) Puffin Bks.

Kroll, Steven. Andrew Wants a Dog. Delany, Molly, illus. LC 91-25637. 64p. (gr. 2-4). 1993. pap. 2.95 (*1-56282-521-6*) Hyprn Ppbks.

—One Tough Turkey. Wallner, John, illus. LC 82-2925. 32p. (ps-3). 1982. reinforced bdg. 14.95 (*0-8234-0457-9*) Holiday.

Krulik, Nancy E. Home Alone Two: Lost in New York, Kevin's Christmas Vacation Scrapbook. 1992. 2.95 (*0-590-46187-7*) Scholastic Inc.

Krumgold, Joseph. And Now Miguel. Charlot, Jean, illus. LC 53-8415. 245p. (gr. 5 up). 1984. pap. 3.95 (*0-06-440143-X*, Trophy) HarpC Child Bks.

—Onion John. Shimin, Symeon, illus. LC 59-11395. 248p. (gr. 5 up). 1984. pap. 3.95 (*0-06-440144-8*, Trophy) HarpC Child Bks.

Kunhardt, Edith. Where's Peter? LC 86-27061. (Illus.). 24p. (ps-3). 1988. 11.95 (*0-688-07204-6*); lib. bdg. 11.88 (*0-688-07205-4*) Greenwillow.

Kurelek, William. A Prairie Boy's Summer. Kurelek, William, illus. 48p. (gr. 5 up). 1975. 14.95 (*0-88776-058-9*); pap. 6.95 (*0-88776-116-X*) Tundra Bks.

—A Prairie Boy's Winter. Kurelek, William, illus. LC 73-8913. 48p. (gr. k-3). 1984. 14.45 (*0-395-17708-1*); pap. 6.70 (*0-395-36609-7*) HM.

Kurtz, Shirley. The Boy & the Quilt. Benner, Cheryl A., illus. LC 91-74050. 32p. (ps-5). 1991. pap. 6.95 (*1-56148-009-6*) Good Bks PA.

Kuskin, Karla. Paul. Avery, Milton, illus. LC 93-29424. 48p. (gr. 1 up). 1994. 16.95 (*0-06-023568-3*); PLB 16.89 (*0-06-023573-X*) HarpC Child Bks.

LaFarge, Oliver. Laughing Boy. 245p. 1981. Repr. PLB 24.95 (*0-89966-367-2*) Buccaneer Bks.

La Farge, Oliver. Laughing Boy. 259p. 1981. Repr. PLB 21.95 (*0-89967-041-5*) Harmony Raine.

Landstrom, Olof & Landstrom, Lena. Will Gets a Haircut. LC 93-660. (Illus.). 1993. Repr. 13.00 (*91-29-62075-9*, Pub. by R & S Bks) FS&G.

Lane, Daniel. Billy's Choice. 1993. 7.95 (*0-8062-4620-0*) Carlton.

Langerman, Jean. No Carrots for Harry! Remkiewicz, Frank, illus. LC 89-3373. (ps-3). 1989. 5.95 (*0-8193-1190-1*) Parents.

Lappin, Peter. Dominic Savio: Teenage Saint. 2nd ed. LC 54-11044. 155p. (gr. 5-10). 1989. 1.95 (*0-685-30656-9*); pap. write for info. Don Bosco Multimedia.

Lattimore, Deborah N. The Flame of Peace: A Tale of the Aztecs. Lattimore, Deborah N., illus. LC 86-26934. 48p. (gr. k-3). 1987. PLB 12.89 (*0-06-023709-0*) HarpC Child Bks.

Lattimore, Eleanor F. Little Pear. (Illus.). 1992. Repr. PLB 14.95x (*0-89966-917-4*) Buccaneer Bks.

—Little Pear. (gr. 1-4). 1992. 17.25 (*0-8446-6576-2*) Peter Smith.

Lawhead, Steve. Howard Had a Hot Air Ballon. Lawhead, Steve, illus. 32p. (gr. k-3). 1988. 7.99 (*0-7459-1268-0*) Lion USA.

Leaf, Munro. Robert Francis Weatherbee. LC 87-26046. (Illus.). 75p. (ps-3). 1988. Repr. of 1935 ed. PLB 14.50 (*0-208-02211-2*, Linnet) Shoe String.

Lear, Edward. How Pleasant to Know Mr. Lear! LC 82-80822. (Illus.). 136p. (gr. 4-6). 1982. 14.95 (*0-8234-0462-5*) Holiday.

Leech, Bryan J. John Jeremy Colton. LC 93-2472. (Illus.). 32p. (ps-3). 1994. 14.95 (*1-56282-650-6*); PLB 14.89 (*1-56282-651-4*) Hyprn Child.

Lelchuk, Alan. On Home Ground. Nacht, Merle, illus. LC 87-8496. 72p. (gr. 5 up). 1987. 9.95 (*0-15-200560-9*, Gulliver Bks) HarBrace.

Lester, Alison. Clive Eats Alligators. (ps). 1991. pap. 4.80 (*0-395-58408-6*) HM.

Lewis, Linda. Is There Life after Boys? 165p. (gr. 5-7). 1990. pap. 2.95 (*0-671-69559-2*, Archway) PB.

—Pre-Teen Means Inbetween. MacDonald, Pat, ed. 160p. (Orig.). (gr. 3-6). 1993. pap. 2.99 (*0-671-74535-2*, Minstrel Bks) PB.

Lim, Sing. West Coast Chinese Boy. LC 79-67110. (Illus.). 64p. (gr. 5 up). 1991. pap. 7.95 (*0-88776-270-0*) Tundra Bks.

Lindgren, Barbro. Sam's Potty. Eriksson, Eva, illus. LC 86-864. 32p. (ps-k). 1986. 6.95 (*0-688-06603-8*) Morrow Jr Bks.

—Sam's Wagon. Eriksson, Eva, illus. LC 86-865. 32p. (ps-k). 1986. 6.95 (*0-688-05802-7*) Morrow Jr Bks.

Lindquist, Susan H. Walking the Rim. LC 91-76966. 144p. (gr. 7 up). 1992. 14.95 (*1-56397-098-8*) Boyds Mills Pr.

Lipsyte, Robert. The Chemo Kid. LC 91-55500. 176p. (gr. 7 up). 1993. pap. 3.95 (*0-06-447101-2*, Trophy) HarpC Child Bks.

—One Fat Summer. LC 76-49746. (gr. 7 up). 1977. PLB 14.89 (*0-06-023896-8*) HarpC Child Bks.

—The Summerboy. 160p. 1984. pap. 2.25 (*0-553-24130-3*) Bantam.

Little, Jean. Different Dragons. (gr. 3-6). 1987. pap. 14.95 (*0-670-80836-9*) Viking Child Bks.

—Different Dragons. Fernandez, Laura, illus. 144p. (gr. 3-7). 1989. pap. 3.95 (*0-14-031998-0*, Puffin) Puffin Bks.

Livingston, Myra C. A Circle of Seasons. Fisher, Leonard E., illus. LC 81-20305. 32p. (ps-3). 1982. reinforced bdg. 15.95 (*0-8234-0452-8*); pap. 5.95 (*0-8234-0656-3*) Holiday.

Locker, Thomas. Boy Who Held Back the Sea. (ps-3). 1991. pap. 4.95 (*0-8037-1049-6*, Puff Pied Piper) Puffin Bks.

Lonergan, Carroll V. Brave Boys of Old Fort Ticonderoga. LC 87-22144. (gr. 6 up). 1987. write for info., 192 p. (*0-932334-57-1*, Empire State Bks); pap. 7.95, 144 p. (*1-55787-018-7*, NY16028, Empire State Bks) Heart of the Lakes.

Lowry, Lois. Rabble Starkey. (gr. k-6). 1988. pap. 3.50 (*0-440-40056-2*, YB) Dell.

—Your Move, J. P. (gr. 4-7). 1991. 3.50 (*0-685-50680-0*, Pub. by Yearling Classics) Dell.

Lubcker, Donna H. Sameer's Journey. Parado, Arturo H., illus. 40p. (Orig.). (gr. 3-5). 1992. pap. 10.00 (*0-9633803-3-8*) Jasmine Studios.

Lyons, Pam. A Boy Called Simon. (Orig.). (gr. k-12). 1987. pap. 2.50 (*0-440-91094-3*, LFL) Dell.

McArthur, Nancy. The Plant That Ate Dirty Socks. 128p. (Orig.). 1988. pap. 3.50 (*0-380-75493-2*, Camelot) Avon.

Macaulay, Craig. Dix Hommes et une Echelle. (ps-3). 1993. pap. 5.95 (*1-55037-342-0*, Pub. by Annick CN) Firefly Bks Ltd.

McBrier, Michael. Getting Oliver's Goat. Sims, Blanche, illus. LC 87-13870. 96p. (gr. 3-6). 1988. PLB 9.89 (*0-8167-1145-3*); pap. text ed. 2.95 (*0-8167-1146-1*) Troll Assocs.

—Oliver & the Amazing Spy. Sims, Blanche, illus. LC 87-13793. 96p. (gr. 3-6). 1988. PLB 9.89 (*0-8167-1143-7*); pap. text ed. 2.95 (*0-8167-1144-5*) Troll Assocs.

—Oliver Smells Trouble. Sims, Blanche, illus. LC 87-13954. 96p. (gr. 3-6). 1988. PLB 9.89 (*0-8167-1149-6*); pap. text ed. 2.95 (*0-8167-1150-X*) Troll Assocs.

—Oliver's Barnyard Blues. Sims, Blanche, illus. LC 87-13864. 96p. (gr. 3-6). 1988. PLB 9.89 (*0-8167-1147-X*); pap. text ed. 2.95 (*0-8167-1148-8*) Troll Assocs.

McCann, Helen. What Do We Do Now, George? Eagle, Ellen, illus. LC 91-2329. 160p. (gr. 4-7). 1993. pap. 2.95 (*0-671-86691-5*, Half Moon Bks) S&S Trade.

McCay, Winsor. The Complete Little Nemo in Slumberland, Vols. I-IV: 1905-1911. Marschall, Richard, intro. by. (Illus.). 96p. (gr. 6 up). 1991. 139.80 (*0-924359-00-5*) Remco Wrldserv Bks.

McClain, Margaret S. Bellboy: A Muletrain Journey. Stuart, Sara B., illus. LC 89-61681. 154p. (gr. 5 up). 1990. 14.95 (*0-9622468-1-6*) NM Pub Co.

McCloskey, Robert. Homer Price. McCloskey, Robert, illus. (gr. 4-6). 1943. pap. 14.00 (*0-670-37729-5*) Viking Child Bks.

McCrum, Robert. The World Is a Banana. large type ed. 171p. 1992. 16.95 (*0-7451-1611-6*, Galaxy Child Lrg Print) Chivers N Amer.

MacDonald, Elizabeth. John's Picture. (ps-3). 1991. 13.95 (*0-670-83579-X*) Viking Child Bks.

MacDonald, George. At the Back of the North Wind. Mills, Lauren, illus. LC 87-45455. 320p. 1988. 18.95 (*0-87923-703-1*) Godine.

Macdonald, Maryann. Sam's Worries. Riches, Judith, illus. LC 91-71379. 32p. (ps-2). 1994. pap. 4.95 (*1-56282-522-4*) Hyprn Ppbks.

McEvoy, Seth & Wartik, Nancy. Albert's Riddle. (Illus.). 224p. (gr. 6-8). 1989. 9.95 (*0-318-37482-X*) Kipling Pr.

McGovern, Ann. Nicholas Bentley Stoningpot III. reissue ed. De Paola, Tomie, illus. 32p. (ps-3). 1992. PLB 14.95 (*1-56397-104-6*) Boyds Mills Pr.

McKenzie, Ellen K. A Bowl of Mischief. LC 92-24246. 240p. (gr. 4-7). 1992. 14.95 (*0-8050-2090-X*, Bks Young Read) H Holt & Co.

—Stargone John. Low, William, illus. LC 90-34119. 64p. (gr. 2-4). 1992. pap. 4.95 (*0-8050-2069-1*, Redfeather BYR) H Holt & Co.

McKinney, Cecilia B. Clif's Special Day. 1994. 7.95 (*0-8062-4867-X*) Carlton.

McKissack, Patricia C. Mirandy & Brother Wind. Pinkney, Jerry, illus. LC 87-349. 32p. (ps-3). 1988. 15.00 (*0-394-88765-4*); lib. bdg. 15.99 (*0-394-98765-9*) Knopf Bks Yng Read.

MacLachlan, Patricia. Arthur, for the Very First Time. Bloom, Lloyd, illus. LC 79-2007. 128p. (gr. 3-6). 1989. pap. 3.95 (*0-06-440288-6*, Trophy) HarpC Child Bks.

—Arthur for the Very First Time. large type ed. 160p. 1990. Repr. lib. bdg. 15.95 (*1-55736-169-X*, Crnrstn Bks) BDD LT Grp.

McMillan, Bruce. Eating Fractions. 1993. pap. 19.95 (*0-590-72732-X*) Scholastic Inc.

McOmber, Rachel B., ed. McOmber Phonics Storybooks: Ben in Bed. rev. ed. (Illus.). write for info. (*0-944991-29-7*) Swift Lrn Res.

—McOmber Phonics Storybooks: Ben Will Get Well. rev. ed. (Illus.). write for info. (*0-944991-30-0*) Swift Lrn Res.

—McOmber Phonics Storybooks: Max. rev. ed. (Illus.). write for info. (*0-944991-01-7*) Swift Lrn Res.

—McOmber Phonics Storybooks: Max is Six. rev. ed. (Illus.). write for info. (*0-944991-43-2*) Swift Lrn Res.

—McOmber Phonics Storybooks: Max Ran. rev. ed. (Illus.). write for info. (*0-944991-02-5*) Swift Lrn Res.

—McOmber Phonics Storybooks: Max the Grand. rev. ed. (Illus.). write for info. (*0-944991-57-2*) Swift Lrn Res.

Mac's Choice Workbook. (gr. 1-7). 1994. 5.50 (*0-685-71620-1*, 716W) W Gladden Found.

Mahy, Margaret. The Boy Who Was Followed Home. Kellogg, Steven, illus. 32p. (ps-3). 1983. pap. 4.95 (*0-8037-0903-X*) Dial Bks Young.

—Boy Who Was Followed Home. (ps-3). 1983. pap. 4.95 (*0-14-054614-6*) Dial Bks Young.

Mallett, Jerry & Bartch, Marian. Good Old Ernie. 127p. (gr. 4-7). 1978. PLB 7.50 (*0-8479-1992-7*, 120716) Perma-Bound.

—Poor Old Ernie. 96p. (gr. 4-7). 1988. Repr. of 1983 ed. PLB 8.40 (*0-8479-9036-2*, 239600) Perma-Bound.

Mandrell, Louise. Eddie Finds a Hero: A Story about the Meaning of Memorial Day. (ps-3). 1993. 12.95 (*1-56530-037-8*) Summit TX.

Mandrell, Louise & Collins, Ace. Jonathan's Gift. 32p. 1992. 12.95 (*1-56530-012-2*) Summit TX.
Manes, Stephen. Be a Perfect Person in Just Three Days! Huffman, Tom, illus. 64p. (gr. 3-6). 1982. 14.95 (*0-89919-064-2*, Clarion Bks) HM.
Mannino, Marc P. & Mannino, Angelica L. La Cola Magica de Marjorie. Norman-Grumbley, Patricia, tr. from ENG. Mannino, Angelica L., illus. LC 93-86116. (SPA.). 32p. (Orig.). (gr. k-3). 1993. pap. 7.95 (*0-9638340-1-0*) Sugar Sand.
Marchant, Brian & Marchant, Heather. A Boy Named Chong. 40p. (gr. k-9). 1993. pap. 11.95 (*1-885298-00-5*); video 14.95 (*1-885298-01-3*) Project Chong.
Marsh, Carole. Columbia Lastname: The Schwarzchild Radius, Bk. 1. (Orig.). (gr. 4 up). 1994. PLB 24.95 (*1-55609-284-9*); pap. text ed. 14.95 (*0-935326-62-6*) Gallopade Pub Group.
Marshall, James. The Cut-Ups. Marshall, James, illus. 32p. (ps-3). 1986. pap. 3.95 (*0-14-050637-3*, Puffin) Puffin Bks.
Marshall, Janet P. Ohmygosh My Pocket. Marshall, Janet P., illus. 24p. (ps-k). 1992. bds. 7.95 (*1-56397-044-9*) Boyds Mills Pr.
Martin, Charles E. Sams Saves the Day. Martin, Charles E., illus. LC 86-19594. 32p. (gr. k-3). 1987. 11.75 (*0-688-06814-6*); lib. bdg. 11.88 (*0-688-06815-4*) Greenwillow.
Martin, George. Wild Oakie. LC 92-85412. 76p. (gr. 2-6). 1993. 6.95 (*1-55523-552-2*) Winston-Derek.
Martin, Rafe. Will's Mammoth. Grammell, Stephen, illus. 32p. (ps-3). 1989. 15.95 (*0-399-21627-8*, Putnam) Putnam Pub Group.
Marzollo, Jean. Cannonball Chris. Sims, Blanche, illus. LC 86-31512. 48p. (gr. 2-3). 1987. pap. 3.50 (*0-394-88512-0*, Random Juv) Random Bks Yng Read.
Masland, Skip. William Willya & the Washing Machine. Sheppard, Scott O., illus. 40p. (gr. k-5). 1993. 15.95 (*1-883016-01-0*) Moonglow Pubns.
Matas, Carol. Daniel's Story. 144p. (gr. 4-7). 1993. pap. 3.95 (*0-590-46588-0*) Scholastic Inc.
Matthews, Judith & Robinson, Fay. Nathaniel Willy, Scared Silly. Natchev, Alexi, illus. LC 92-4052. 32p. (ps-3). 1994. RSBE 15.00 (*0-02-765285-8*, Bradbury Pr) Macmillan Child Grp.
Matthews, Phoebe. The Boy on the Cover. (gr. 7 up). 1988. pap. 2.75 (*0-380-75407-X*, Flare) Avon.
Matthias, Catherine. Out the Door. Neill, Eileen M., illus. LC 81-17060. 32p. (ps-2). 1982. PLB 10.25 (*0-516-03560-6*); pap. 2.95 (*0-516-43560-4*) Childrens.
Mauser, Pat R. A Bundle of Sticks. Owens, Gail, illus. LC 87-1074. 176p. (gr. 3-6). 1987. pap. 3.95 (*0-689-71169-7*, Aladdin) Macmillan Child Grp.
Mayer, Mercer. A Boy, a Dog & a Frog. Mayer, Mercer, illus. LC 67-22254. 32p. (ps-2). 1985. pap. 3.50 (*0-8037-0769-X*) Dial Bks Young.
—Boy, a Dog, & a Frog. (ps-3). 1992. pap. 3.50 (*0-14-054611-1*) Viking Child Bks.
—Bubble Bubble. rev. ed. Mayer, Mercer, illus. 48p. 1992. pap. 5.95 (*1-879920-03-4*) Rain Bird Prods.
Mayne, William. Gideon Ahoy! (gr. 5-9). 1989. pap. 13.95 (*0-440-50126-1*) Delacorte.
Mazer, Norma F. C My Name Is Cal. 144p. 1990. 13.95 (*0-590-41833-5*, Point); pap. 2.95 (*0-685-49598-1*, Point) Scholastic Inc.
Mazer, Norma F. & Mazer, Harry. The Solid Gold Kid. (gr. 7 up). 1989. pap. 3.50 (*0-553-27851-7*, Starfire) Bantam.
Merriam, Eve. Fighting Words. Small, David, illus. 32p. (gr. k up). 1992. 15.00 (*0-688-09676-X*); PLB 14.93 (*0-688-09677-8*) Morrow Jr Bks.
Meyer, Carolyn. The Problem with Sidney. (gr. 7 up). 1990. pap. 2.95 (*0-553-28803-2*, Starfire) Bantam.
—The Two Faces of Adam. 1991. pap. 2.99 (*0-553-28859-8*) Bantam.
Milligan, Bryce. With the Wind, Kevin Dolan. LC 86-70018. (Illus.). 194p. (gr. 7 up). 1992. pap. 7.95 (*0-931722-45-4*) Corona Pub.
Milne, A. A. World of Christopher Robin. (gr. 1-4). 1958. Boxed with "World of Pooh" 29.95 (*0-525-43348-1*, Dutton) NAL-Dutton.
Milne, Teddy. Anthony. LC 86-62446. 197p. (Orig.). (gr. 5 up). 1986. pap. 5.00 (*0-938875-01-9*) Pittenbruach Pr.
Molver, Eileen. Lindiwi Finds a Way. (gr. 4-7). 1992. pap. 4.95 (*0-7910-2915-8*) Chelsea Hse.
Moncure, Jane B. John's Choice. Halverson, Lydia, illus. LC 82-19897. 32p. (gr. 1-3). 1982. 13.95 (*0-89565-252-8*) Childs World.
—Terry's Turn-Around. Endres, Helen, illus. LC 82-19898. 32p. (gr. 3-4). 1982. write for info. (*0-89565-250-1*); PLB 13.95 (*0-685-57929-8*) Childs World.
Moody, Ralph. Man of the Family. 1976. 24.95 (*0-8488-1436-3*) Amereon Ltd.
Moore, Elaine. Who Let Girls in the Boys' Locker Room? LC 94-820. (Illus.). 144p. (gr. 3-6). 1994. pap. text ed. 2.95 (*0-8167-3439-9*) Troll Assocs.
Moore, Inga. Oh, Little Jack. Moore, Inga, illus. LC 91-71827. 32p. (ps-3). 1994. pap. 4.99 (*1-56402-273-0*) Candlewick Pr.
Moore, Ruth N. Where the Eagles Fly. 104p. (Orig.). (gr. 4-7). 1994. pap. 5.95 (*0-8361-3664-0*) Herald Pr.
Morgan, A. Matthew & the Midnight Money Van. (Illus.). 24p. (ps-8). 1987. PLB 14.95 (*0-920303-75-7*, Pub. by Annick CN); pap. 4.95 (*0-920303-72-2*, Pub. by Annick CN) Firefly Bks Ltd.
—Matthew & the Midnight Tow Truck. (Illus.). 24p. (ps-8). 1984. 12.95 (*0-920303-00-5*, Pub. by Annick CN); pap. 4.95 (*0-920303-01-3*, Pub. by Annick CN) Firefly Bks Ltd.
—Matthew & the Midnight Turkeys. (Illus.). 24p. (ps-8). 1985. PLB 14.95 (*0-920303-36-6*, Pub. by Annick CN); pap. 4.95 (*0-920303-37-4*, Pub. by Annick CN) Firefly Bks Ltd.
Morgan, Allen. Andrew & the Wild Bikes. Beinicke, Steve, illus. 32p. (ps-2). 1990. 12.95 (*1-55037-083-9*, Pub. by Annick CN); pap. 4.95 (*1-55037-082-0*, Pub. by Annick CN) Firefly Bks Ltd.
Morgan, Lenore. Peter's Pockets. LC 65-27622. (Illus.). 32p. (gr. k-2). 1968. PLB 9.95 (*0-87783-029-0*) Oddo.
Morton, Jane. No Place for Cal. 112p. (Orig.). 1989. pap. 2.75 (*0-380-75548-3*, Camelot) Avon.
Munsch, Robert. Boy in the Drawer. Martchenko, Michael, illus. 32p. (gr. k-3). 1982. 12.95 (*0-920236-34-0*, Pub. by Annick CN); pap. 4.95 (*0-920236-36-7*, Pub. by Annick CN) Firefly Bks Ltd.
—The Boy in the Drawer. Martchenko, Michael, illus. 24p. (ps-1). 1987. pap. 0.99 (*0-920303-50-1*, Pub. by Annick CN) Firefly Bks Ltd.
—The Boy in the Drawer. (CHI., Illus.). 32p. 1993. pap. 5.95 (*1-55037-296-3*, Pub. by Annick CN) Firefly Bks Ltd.
—Jonathan Cleaned Up. Martchenko, Michael, illus. 24p. (ps-1). 1986. pap. 0.99 (*0-920236-21-9*, Pub. by Annick CN) Firefly Bks Ltd.
—Jonathan Cleaned up - Then He Heard a Sound. (CHI., Illus.). 32p. 1993. pap. 5.95 (*1-55037-300-5*, Pub. by Annick CN) Firefly Bks Ltd.
—Mateo y la Grua de Medianoche: (Matthew & the Midnight Tow Truck) Langer, Shirley, tr. Martchenko, Michael, illus. (SPA.). 32p. 1991. pap. 5.95 (*1-55037-190-8*, Pub. by Annick CN) Firefly Bks Ltd.
—Mortimer. Martchenko, Michael, illus. 24p. (ps-1). 1986. pap. 0.99 (*0-920236-68-5*, Pub. by Annick CN) Firefly Bks Ltd.
—Mortimer. (CHI., Illus.). 32p. 1993. pap. 5.95 (*1-55037-302-1*, Pub. by Annick CN) Firefly Bks Ltd.
—El Muchacho en la Gaveta: The Boy in the Drawer. Martchenko, Michael, illus. (SPA.). 32p. (ps-2). 1989. pap. 5.95 (*1-55037-097-9*, Pub. by Annick CN) Firefly Bks Ltd.
Murphy, Jill. Jeffrey Strangeways. Murphy, Jill, illus. LC 91-71844. 144p. (gr. 3-6). 1994. pap. 4.50 (*1-56402-283-8*) Candlewick Pr.
Myers, Tim. Let's Call Him Lau-Wiliwili-Humuhumu-Nukunuku-Nukunuku-Apua'a-'oi'oi. (ps-3). 1993. pap. 5.95 (*1-880188-66-X*) Bess Pr.
Myers, Walter D. The Outside Shot. (gr. k-12). 1987. pap. 3.99 (*0-440-96784-8*, LFL) Dell.
Namioka, Lensey. Yang the Youngest & His Terrible Ear. (gr. 4-7). 1994. pap. 3.50 (*0-440-40917-9*) Dell.
Narahashi, Keiko. I Have a Friend. Narahashi, Keiko, illus. LC 86-27628. 32p. (ps-3). 1987. SBE 13.95 (*0-689-50432-2*, M K McElderry) Macmillan Child Grp.
Nash, Margaret & Brodley, Sue. Josh's Expedition. (Illus.). 32p. (ps-1). 1993. 17.95 (*0-370-31572-3*, Pub. by Bodley Head UK) Trafalgar.
Nasta, Cynthia V. Peter & His Pick-up Truck: An Arizona Children's Tale. Zilka, Pat, illus. LC 89-80352. 24p. (ps-8). 1989. PLB 6.95 (*0-9622064-1-5*); pap. 6.95 (*0-9622064-2-3*) Little Buckaroo.
Naylor, Phyllis R. Beetles, Lightly Toasted. LC 87-911. 144p. (gr. 3-7). 1987. SBE 13.95 (*0-689-31355-1*, Atheneum Child Bk) Macmillan Child Grp.
—The Boy with the Helium Head. Choroa, Kay, illus. (ps-3). 1992. 3.50 (*0-440-40644-7*, YB) Dell.
—The Year of the Gopher. LC 86-17317. 224p. (gr. 7 up). 1987. SBE 14.95 (*0-689-31333-0*, Atheneum Child Bk) Macmillan Child Grp.
Nelson, Ray, Jr. & Kelly, Doug. The Seven Seas of Billy's Bathtub. (Illus.). 48p. (gr. 1-5). 1993. 12.95 (*1-883772-00-1*) Flying Rhino.
Neugeboren, Jay. Poli - a Mexican Boy in Early Texas. Leamon, Tom, illus. LC 88-64094. 120p. (gr. 7 up). 1992. pap. 7.95 (*0-931722-74-8*) Corona Pub.
Ngumy, James. Boy Who Rode a Lion. (ps-3). 1992. pap. 2.95 (*0-7910-2907-7*) Chelsea Hse.
Nixon, Joan L. The Gift. Glass, Andrew, illus. LC 87-22764. 96p. (gr. 3-7). 1988. pap. 3.95 (*0-689-71217-0*, Aladdin) Macmillan Child Grp.
—Specter. 1993. pap. 3.99 (*0-440-97740-1*) Dell.
Nobens, C. A. Montgomery's Time Zone. Nobens, C. A., illus. 32p. (ps-4). 1990. PLB 18.95 (*0-87614-398-2*) Carolrhoda Bks.
Nolan, Dennis. Wolf Child. Nolan, Dennis, illus. LC 88-35955. 40p. (gr. 1-5). 1989. RSBE 14.95 (*0-02-768141-6*, Macmillan Child Bk) Macmillan Child Grp.
O'Callaghan, Myrnie. A Boy Called Mish Mash. LC 91-92177. 100p. (Orig.). (gr. 5-8). 1991. pap. 9.95 (*0-9630075-0-5*) Creole Connect.
O'Callaghan, Patricia. Andrew: A fable of Flight. LC 94-60117. (Illus.). 44p. (gr. k-3). 1994. 6.95 (*1-55523-686-3*) Winston-Derek.
Oden, Fay. Calvin & His Video Camera. 1993. 7.95 (*0-8062-4565-4*) Carlton.
Odom, Melissa W. No Regard Beauregard & the Golden Rule. Rice, James, illus. LC 87-36118. 132p. (gr. k-6). 1988. 12.95 (*0-88289-686-5*) Pelican.
O'Donnell, Elizabeth L. Maggie Doesn't Want to Move. Schwartz, Amy, illus. LC 86-23684. 32p. (gr. k-3). 1987. RSBE 13.95 (*0-02-768830-5*, Pub. by Four Winds Pr) Macmillan Child Grp.
Ofek, Uriel. Cuidado! Patos Cruzando. Writer, C. C. & Nielsen, Lisa C., trs. Elchanan, illus. (SPA.). 24p. (Orig.). (ps). 1992. pap. text ed. 3.00x (*1-56134-155-X*) Dushkin Pub.
Oke, Janette. Maury Had a Little Lamb. Mann, Brenda, illus. 137p. (Orig.). (gr. 3 up). 1989. pap. 4.99 (*0-934998-34-5*) Bethel Pub.
—Spring's Gentle Promise. LC 89-22. 224p. (Orig.). (gr. 4 up). 1989. pap. 6.99 (*1-55661-059-9*) Bethany Hse.
Oliver, Clarence. 1992. pap. 3.50 (*0-553-15993-3*) Bantam.
Oliver, Diana. Sam the Spy. LC 93-85236. 132p. (Orig.). (gr. 3-7). 1994. pap. 3.50 (*0-679-85698-6*) Random Bks Yng Read.
Oliver Twist. (SPA.). 1990. casebound 3.50 (*0-7214-1398-6*) Ladybird Bks.

Olsen, Carol. Left-Over Louie. 2nd ed. (Illus.). 168p. (Orig.). 1993. 29.95 (*1-883078-75-X*); pap. 11.95 (*1-883078-76-8*) Gig Harbor Pr. Louie Twitwhistle of Surly Lagoon stars in this delightful book for all ages. Students in the Pacific Northwest entered their classmate Louie in a National Contest, proposing him as a new character for a children's series. They won first place, making LEFT-OVER LOUIE a legend in his own time. His clothes are out of style & his pant legs drag the floor. He wears a battle helmet to school & keeps a magpie for a pet. His idea of a hot lunch is a powdered doughnut & coffee. He does General MacArthur imitations at recess & dreams of being an Antarctic explorer. He recycles, digs up artifacts in his backyard, & dabbles in politics. Louie visits a nursing home where he meets a special veteran. Touched by his loneliness & fear around him, he pledges, "I shall return!" He rallies some classmates to build bridges of friendship. A very true & very funny "main course" in how to sensitize children & adults to the needs of others. Also available in the Left-over Louie series - SLIME: SLUGS HAVE FEELINGS TOO. Teachers! Librarians! Parents! Don't be left out! Order today! Gig Harbor Press, Box 2059, Gig Harbor, WA 98335, 206-858-8819.
Publisher Provided Annotation.

Oram, Hiawyn. Angry Arthur. Kitamura, Satoshi, illus. LC 88-31695. 32p. (ps-1). 1989. (DCB); pap. 3.95 (*0-525-44472-6*) Dutton Child Bks.
—Boy Wants a Dinosaur. (ps-3). 1993. pap. 4.95 (*0-374-40889-0*) FS&G.
—Ned & the Joybaloo. Kitamura, Satoshi, illus. 28p. (ps up). 1989. 11.95 (*0-374-35501-0*) FS&G.
Orczy, Emmuska. Beau Brocade. 275p. (gr. 4 up). 1980. Repr. of 1905 ed. lib. bdg. 13.95x (*0-89968-194-8*) Lightyear.
Ormondroyd, Edward. Theodore. Larrecq, John M., illus. LC 66-10352. 40p. (ps-3). 1984. pap. 5.95 (*0-395-36610-0*) HM.
Ossorio, Nelson A. & Salvadeo, Michele B. Boy of la Mancha. (Illus.). 60p. (gr. 4-6). 1994. pap. 6.95 (*1-56721-068-6*) Twnty-Fifth Cent Pr.
Otis, Sharon & Walker, Lois. Jeffrey's Laugh. Hawk, Lee, illus. Goldman, Howard, intro. by. (Illus., Orig.). (ps-6). 1987. wkbk. 6.50 (*0-9617737-2-3*) Total Lrn.
Palmer, Bernard. Danny Orlis, No. 3: The Race Against Time. 128p. 1989. pap. 4.99 (*0-8423-0560-2*) Tyndale.
—Danny Orlis, No. 4: The Showdown. 128p. 1989. pap. 4.99 (*0-8423-0557-2*) Tyndale.
—Danny Orlis, No. 6: The Sacred Ruins. 128p. 1989. pap. 4.99 (*0-8423-0561-0*) Tyndale.
Parish, Peggy. Good Hunting, Blue Sky. Watts, James, illus. LC 84-43143. 64p. (gr. k-3). 1988. PLB 14.89 (*0-06-024662-6*) HarpC Child Bks.
Park, Barbara. Dear God, Help! Love, Earl. LC 92-20909. 108p. (gr. 3-7). 1994. pap. 3.99 (*0-679-85395-2*) Random Bks Yng Read.
Parkinson, Curtis. Tom Foolery. Bobak, Cathy, illus. LC 92-7852. 32p. (ps-2). 1993. RSBE 13.95 (*0-02-770025-9*, Bradbury Pr) Macmillan Child Grp.
Pascal, Francine. Bossy Steven. (ps-3). 1991. pap. 2.99 (*0-553-15881-3*) Bantam.
—The Hand-Me-Down Kid. 176p. (gr. 3-7). 1990. pap. 2.75 (*0-590-43391-1*) Scholastic Inc.
—Starring Winston. (gr. 4-7). 1990. pap. 2.99 (*0-553-15836-8*) Bantam.

—Steven's in Love. 1992. pap. 3.25 (*0-553-15943-7*) Bantam.
—Sweet Valley Kids, No. 29: Andy & the Alien. (ps-3). 1992. pap. 2.99 (*0-553-15925-9*) Bantam.
Paterson, Katherine. Jacob Have I Loved. (gr. 7 up). 1981. pap. 2.95 (*0-380-56499-8*, Flare) Avon.
Paton Walsh, Jill. Gaffer Samson's Luck. Cole, Brock, illus. 128p. (gr. 3-7). 1990. pap. 3.50 (*0-374-42513-2*, Sunburst) FS&G.
Patterson, Nancy R. The Shiniest Rock of All. Jerome, Karen A., illus. 80p. (gr. 3 up). 1991. 13.00 (*0-374-36805-8*) FS&G.
Paulsen, Brendan P. The Luck of the Irish. Connelly, Gwen, illus. (gr. 2-4). 1988. 19.97 (*0-8172-2752-0*) Raintree Steck-V.
Paulsen, Gary. Boy Who Owned the School. (gr. 4-7). 1991. pap. 3.50 (*0-440-40524-6*, YB) Dell.
—Popcorn Days & Buttermilk Nights. 112p. (gr. 5-9). 1989. pap. 3.99 (*0-14-034204-4*, Puffin) Puffin Bks.
Pearson, Kit. The Lights Go on Again. 202p. (gr. 5-9). 1994. 13.99 (*0-670-84919-7*) Viking Child Bks.
Peck, Richard. Something for Joey. 1983. pap. 3.99 (*0-553-27199-7*) Bantam.
Peet, Bill. Huge Harold. Peet, Bill, illus. (gr. k-3). 1982. pap. 4.80 (*0-395-32923-X*) HM.
Pef. Ivre de Francais. (FRE.). 48p. (gr. 1-5). 1986. pap. 7.95 (*2-07-031246-1*) Schoenhof.
Pelham, David. Sam's Surprise. (Illus.). 22p. (ps-4). 1992. 9.95 (*0-525-44947-7*, DCB) Dutton Child Bks.
Persall, Holli C. The Magic Corn. Haley, Laura M., illus. 24p. (gr. k-4). 1990. 10.95 (*0-9628486-0-3*) Rhyme Time.
Pete, Jacelen D. Just Another Busy Day. (Illus.). 32p. 1989. 8.95 (*0-934601-93-3*) Peachtree Pubs.
Petersen, P. J. Good-Bye to Good Ol' Charlie. LC 86-2016. 168p. (gr. 7 up). 1987. pap. 14.95 (*0-385-29483-2*) Delacorte.
Petrie, Catherine. Hot Rod Harry Big Book. (Illus.). 32p. (ps-2). 1991. PLB 22.95 (*0-516-49516-X*) Childrens.
Pfeffer, Susan B. The Year without Michael. 176p. (gr. 7-12). 1987. 16.00 (*0-553-05430-9*, Starfire) Bantam.
—The Year without Michael. (gr. 7-12). 1988. pap. 3.99 (*0-553-27373-6*, Starfire) Bantam.
Pike, Christopher. Christopher Pike, 4 vols. 1990. pap. 11.80 boxed (*0-671-96377-5*) S&S Trade.
Pingry, Patricia. Story of Joseph & a Dream Come True. Spence, James, illus. 24p. (Orig.). (ps-3). 1988. pap. 3.95 (*0-8249-8182-0*, Ideals Child) Hambleton-Hill.
Pinkwater, Daniel M. The Snarkout Boys & the Baconburg Horror. 1985. pap. 2.50 (*0-451-13581-4*, Sig Vista) NAL-Dutton.
Pitts, Paul. The Shadowman's Way. 128p. (Orig.). (gr. 5). 1992. pap. 3.50 (*0-380-76210-2*, Camelot) Avon.
Plum, Carol T. Peter Can't Wait. Most, Andee, illus. 32p. (gr. k-3). 1991. 9.95 (*0-87973-006-4*, 6); pap. 5.95 (*0-87973-007-2*, 7) Our Sunday Visitor.
Polikoff, Barbara G. Life's a Funny Proposition, Horatio. 112p. (gr. 3-7). 1994. pap. 3.99 (*0-14-036644-X*) Puffin Bks.
Polisar, Barry L. The Trouble with Ben. Clark, David, illus. 32p. (gr. k-4). 1992. 14.95 (*0-938663-13-5*) Rainbow Morn.
Porte, Barbara A. Harry's Mom. 1990. pap. 2.95 (*0-440-40362-6*, YB) Dell.
—Harry's Visit. (Orig.). (gr. k-6). 1990. pap. 2.95 (*0-440-40331-6*, YB) Dell.
Porter, Bruce. Bill & the Burning Bush. Porter, Bruce, illus. 40p. (Orig.). (gr. 1 up). 1987. pap. 3.95 (*0-939925-12-5*) R C Law & Co.
—Butch & the Bad Baloney. Porter, Bruce, illus. 40p. (Orig.). (gr. 1 up). 1987. pap. 3.95 (*0-939925-15-X*) R C Law & Co.
—Jonah Gets the Jitters. Porter, Bruce, illus. 40p. (Orig.). (gr. 3 up). 1987. pap. 3.95 (*0-939925-14-1*) R C Law & Co.
—Samuel & the Strange Sound. Porter, Bruce, illus. 40p. (Orig.). (gr. 3 up). 1987. pap. 3.95 (*0-939925-13-3*) R C Law & Co.
—Squirt & the Super Soldier. Porter, Bruce, illus. 40p. (Orig.). (gr. 3 up). 1987. pap. 3.95 (*0-939925-16-8*) R C Law & Co.
Porter, Stratton. Freckless. (Orig.). 1988. pap. 4.95 (*0-440-40050-3*, Pub by Yearning Classics) Dell.
Potash, Dorothy. El Cuento de Ned y Su Nariz. Sperling, Thomas, illus. (SPA.). 24p. (ps-4). 1993. PLB 13.95 (*1-879567-24-5*, Valeria Bks) Wonder Well.
Potter, Beatrx. Petit-Jean des Villes. (FRE., Illus.). 58p. 1990. 9.95 (*0-7859-3632-7*, 2070560953) Fr & Eur.
Poulin, Stephane. Benjamin & the Pillow Saga. Poulin, Stephane, illus. 1990. 14.95 (*1-550370-69-3*, Pub. by Annick CN); pap. 5.95 (*1-550370-68-5*, Pub. by Annick CN) Firefly Bks Ltd.
Poynor, Alice. East to the Shifting Sands. 190p. (Orig.). (gr. 6-9). 1992. pap. 4.95 (*981-3009-05-5*) OMF Bks.
Press, Skip. Cliffhanger. Parker, Liz, ed. Taylor, Marjorie, illus. 45p. (Orig.). (gr. 6-12). 1992. pap. text ed. 2.95 (*1-56254-055-6*) Saddleback Pubns.
Priestley, Dinah. Hector the Bully. Smith, Wendy, illus. 24p. (ps-3). 1989. PLB 17.50 (*0-87614-356-7*) Carolrhoda Bks.
Prokofiev, Sergei. Peter & the Wolf. Carlson, Maria, tr. Mikolaycak, Charles, illus. (gr. 2-5). 1987. incl. cassette 19.95 (*0-87499-074-2*); pap. 12.95 incl. cassette (*0-87499-073-4*); 4 paperbacks, cassette & guide 27.95 (*0-87499-075-0*) Live Oak Media.
Puig, Evelyn. Chico the Street Boy. Johnson, W. Cameron, illus. 85p. (gr. 4-8). 1991. 3.95 (*0-901269-79-4*) Grosvenor USA.
Quarantine at Alexander Abraham's. (gr. 3-7). 1992. pap. 3.99 (*0-553-48031-6*) Bantam.
Quin-Harken, Janet. Billy & Ben: The Terrible Two. Newsom, Carol, illus. 1992. pap. 3.50 (*0-553-48022-7*) Bantam.
Quintilone, Paul M. Brian Has a Winning Day. (gr. 3-5). 1988. pap. write for info. (*0-9616980-2-0*) Quintilone Ent.
Rabe, Tish. My Name Is Ernie. Swanson, Maggie, illus. (ps-k). 1991. pap. write for info. (*0-307-11513-5*, Golden Pr) Western Pub.
Rapp, Adam. Missing the Piano. 160p. (gr. 7 up). 1994. 14.99 (*0-670-95340-7*) Viking Child Bks.
Rawlings, Marjorie K. The Yearling. 2nd ed. Shenton, Edward, illus. LC 86-20743. 448p. (gr. 5 up). 1988. pap. 5.95 (*0-02-044931-3*, Collier Young Ad) Macmillan Child Grp.
Rayner, Mary. Oh, Paul! Rayner, Mary, illus. 42p. (gr. 2-4). 1989. 3.95 (*0-8120-6145-4*) Barron.
Reader, Dennis. I Want One! (ps-3). 1992. pap. 4.95 (*0-8249-8581-8*, Ideals Child) Hambleton-Hill.
Reece, Colleen L. Escape from Fear. Wheeler, Penny E., ed. 96p. (Orig.). (gr. 6-9). 1988. pap. 4.95 (*0-8280-0441-2*) Review & Herald.
Reece, June E. Jimmy & the Sun Drop. Reece, June E., intro. by. Richardson, Nichole, illus. 24p. (Orig.). (ps-3). 1992. pap. 3.50 (*0-9631934-0-6*) Sun Drop.
Reeder, Carolyn. Moonshiner's Son. LC 92-39570. 208p. (gr. 3-7). 1993. SBE 14.95 (*0-02-775805-2*, Macmillan Child Bk) Macmillan Child Grp.
Reichley, David. Jasper & Sam. Reichley, David, illus. (gr. 4-6). 1992. 14.95 (*1-879260-04-2*) Evanston Pub.
Renauld, Christiane. A Pal for Martin. (Illus.). 32p. (gr. 3-5). 1991. 12.95 (*0-89565-756-2*) Childs World.
Reuter, Bjarne. Buster's World. LC 89-11919. 160p. (gr. 4 up). 1989. 12.95 (*0-525-44475-0*, DCB) Dutton Child Bks.
Rey, H. A. Curious George Gets a Medal. Rey, H. A., illus. LC 57-7206. 48p. (gr. k-3). 1974. pap. 4.80 (*0-395-18559-9*, Sandpiper) HM.
El Rey Leon. (SPA.). 96p. 1994. 6.98 (*0-685-72087-X*) Mouse Works.
Richter, Hans P. Friedrich. (gr. 6 up). 1992. 17.25 (*0-8446-6573-8*) Peter Smith.
Riecken, Nancy. Andrew's Own Place. Aubrey, Meg K., illus. LC 92-22953. 1993. 14.95 (*0-395-64723-1*) HM.
Riley, Janeway. Us...& Our Good Stuff. (Illus.). 176p. 1993. 19.95 (*0-9637378-1-3*) Janeway Riley.
Roberts, Willo D. What Are We Going to Do about David? LC 92-4726. 176p. (gr. 3-7). 1993. SBE 14.95 (*0-689-31793-X*, Atheneum Child Bk) Macmillan Child Grp.
Robertson, Keith. Henry Reed, Inc. McCloskey, Robert, illus. 240p. (gr. 4-6). 1989. pap. 4.99 (*0-14-034144-7*, Puffin) Puffin Bks.
—Henry Reed's Baby-Sitting Service. 206p. (gr. 2-5). 1974. pap. 3.25 (*0-440-43565-X*, YB) Dell.
—Henry Reed's Baby-Sitting Service. McCloskey, Robert, illus. 208p. (gr. 4-6). 1989. pap. 3.99 (*0-14-034146-3*, Puffin) Puffin Bks.
—Henry Reed's Big Show. McCloskey, Robert, illus. (gr. 4-6). 1970. pap. 14.95 (*0-670-36839-3*) Viking Child Bks.
—Henry Reed's Big Show. McCloskey, Robert, illus. 208p. (gr. 4-7). 1978. pap. 2.50 (*0-440-43570-6*, YB) Dell.
—Henry Reed's Journey. LC 63-8522. 224p. (gr. 2-5). 1974. pap. 3.25 (*0-440-43555-2*, YB) Dell.
—Henry Reed's Journey. McCloskey, Robert, illus. 224p. (gr. 4-6). 1989. pap. 4.99 (*0-14-034145-5*, Puffin) Puffin Bks.
Robinson, Nancy K. Just Plain Cat. LC 82-18258. 128p. (gr. 3-6). 1984. SBE 13.95 (*0-02-777350-7*, Four Winds) Macmillan Child Grp.
Robson, Jenny. Winner's Magic. (ps-3). 1992. pap. 2.95 (*0-7910-2906-9*) Chelsea Hse.
Rochman, Hazel, ed. Somehow Tenderness Survives: Stories of Southern Africa. LC 88-916. 208p. (gr. 7 up). 1990. pap. 3.95 (*0-06-447063-6*, Trophy) HarpC Child Bks.
Rodgers, A. Mary. A Billion for Boris. LC 74-3586. 192p. (gr. 5 up). 1974. PLB 13.89 (*0-06-025054-2*) HarpC Child Bks.
Rodgers, Elizabeth. Ollie Goes to School. (Illus.). 32p. (ps-2). 1992. pap. 2.50 (*0-590-44785-8*, Cartwheel) Scholastic Inc.
Rodowsky, Colby. H, My Name Is Henley. LC 82-12164. 184p. (gr. 5 up). 1982. 14.00 (*0-374-32831-5*) FS&G.
Roe, Cheryl A. Tym, the Turtle Boy. Hilliard, Peg, illus. 52p. (Orig.). (ps-3). 1989. pap. write for info. (*0-9624183-0-7*) Timeless Sales.
Rogers, Jean. Dinosaurs Are 568. Hafner, Marylin, illus. LC 88-5501. 96p. (gr. 3 up). 1988. 10.95 (*0-688-07931-8*) Greenwillow.
Rollini, Art. When Will Summer Come? Balla, Laszlo, illus. LC 90-70904. 21p. (ps-6). 1991. pap. 5.95 (*1-55523-354-6*) Winston-Derek.
Romain, Trevor. The Boy Who Swallowed a Rainbow. Romain, Trevor, illus. 32p. (ps-5). 1993. 13.95 (*1-880092-05-0*, Dist. by Publishers Distribution Service) Bright Bks TX.
Roney, Lonzell. A Whale of a Tale. 1994. 7.95 (*0-8062-4807-6*) Carlton.
Ross, Andrea. Seymour. LC 81-71758. 24p. (gr. 2-3). 1992. pap. 3.50x (*0-943864-64-X*) Davenport.
Rosy. Basil. (ps-3). 1993. 13.95 (*0-307-17502-2*, Artsts Writrs) Western Pub.
Rudner, Barry. The Littlest Tall Fellow. Carraro, J. M., ed. Fahsbender, Thomas, illus. 28p. (gr. k-6). 1989. pap. 5.95 (*0-925928-00-3*) Tiny Thought.
Russell, Barbara T. Last Left Standing. 1995. 13.95g (*0-395-71037-5*) Ticknor & Flds Bks Yng Read.
Ryan, Mary C. Frankie's Run. (gr. 3-7). 1987. 12.95 (*0-316-76370-5*) Little.
—Me Two. 192p. 1993. pap. 3.50 (*0-380-71826-X*, Camelot) Avon.
Ryland, Cynthia. Soda Jerk. Calatanotto, Peter, illus. 64p. (gr. 7 up). 1993. pap. 3.95 (*0-688-12654-5*, Pub. by Beech Tree Bks) Morrow.
Rylant, Cynthia. Henry & Mudge & the Careful Cousin: The Thirteenth Book of Their Adventures. Stevenson, Sucie, illus. LC 92-12851. 48p. (gr. 1-3). 1994. RSBE 13.95 (*0-02-778021-X*, Bradbury Pr) Macmillan Child Grp.
—Henry & Mudge & the Long Weekend. Stevenson, Sucie, illus. LC 90-26799. 40p. (gr. 1-3). 1992. RSBE 12.95 (*0-02-778013-9*, Bradbury Pr) Macmillan Child Grp.
—Henry & Mudge & the Wild Wind. Stevenson, Sucie, illus. LC 91-12644. 40p. (gr. 1-3). 1993. RSBE 12.95 (*0-02-778014-7*, Bradbury Pr) Macmillan Child Grp.
—Henry & Mudge: Book & Toy. (Illus.). 48p. (ps-3). 1992. pap. 19.95 (*0-689-71648-6*, Aladdin) Macmillan Child Grp.
Sachar, Louis. Johnny's in the Basement. 128p. (Orig.). (gr. 4-7). 1983. pap. 3.99 (*0-380-83451-0*, Camelot) Avon.
—Johnny's in the Basement. 128p. (gr. 2-6). 1990. Repr. of 1981 ed. PLB 12.99 (*0-679-90411-5*) Random Bks Yng Read.
—Marvin Redpost: Why Pick on Me? Hughes, Neal, illus. LC 92-12858. 80p. (Orig.). (gr. 1-4). 1993. PLB 9.99 (*0-679-91947-3*); pap. 2.99 (*0-679-81947-9*) Random Bks Yng Read.
—There's a Boy in the Girl's Bathroom. Greenstein, Mina, designed by. LC 86-20100. 224p. (gr. 5 up). 1987. lib. bdg. 13.99 (*0-394-98570-2*) Knopf Bks Yng Read.
—There's a Boy in the Girls' Bathroom. LC 86-20100. 208p. (gr. 3-7). 1988. Repr. of 1987 ed. 3.50 (*0-394-80572-0*) Knopf Bks Yng Read.
Sachs, Betsy. The Boy Who Ate Dog Biscuits. Apple, Margot, illus. LC 89-3905. 64p. (gr. 2-4). 1989. pap. 2.99 (*0-394-84778-4*) Random Bks Yng Read.
Sadako & the Paper. 1986. pap. 2.25 (*0-440-77465-9*) Dell.
Sadler, Marilyn. Alistair Underwater. 1990. pap. 13.95 jacketed (*0-671-69406-5*, S&S BFYR) S&S Trade.
Salem, Lynn & Stewart, Josie. Martian Goo. Tiefenthal, Colleen, illus. 8p. (gr. 1). 1993. pap. 3.50 (*1-880612-13-5*) Seedling Pubns.
—Now He Knows. Poirier, Kathleen, illus. 12p. (gr. 1). 1993. pap. 3.50 (*1-880612-06-2*) Seedling Pubns.
Sampson, Emma S. Billy & the Major. 300p. 1992. Repr. lib. bdg. 21.95x (*0-89966-921-2*) Buccaneer Bks.
San Souci, Robert D. The Boy & the Ghost. Pinkney, J. Brian, illus. (ps-3). 1989. pap. 13.95 jacketed (*0-671-67176-6*, S&S BFYR) S&S Trade.
Sant, Thomas. The Amazing Adventures of Albert & His Flying Machine. De Rosa, Dee, illus. 160p. (gr. 4-7). 1990. 13.95 (*0-525-67302-4*, Lodestar Bks) Dutton Child Bks.
Sargent, Dave. Spike. 199p. 1992. write for info. Ozark Pub.
Sargent, Sara. Weird Henry Berg. 1986. pap. 2.50 (*0-440-79346-7*) Dell.
Saul, Carol P. Peter's Song. De Groat, Diane, illus. LC 91-24674. 40p. (ps-1). 1992. pap. 14.00 jacketed (*0-671-73812-7*, S&S BFYR) S&S Trade.
Scarboro, Elizabeth. The Secret Language of the SB. 128p. (gr. 3-7). 1992. pap. 3.99 (*0-14-034310-5*, Puffin) Puffin Bks.
Scheidl, Gerda M. Four Candles for Simon. Pfister, Marcus, illus. LC 86-33199. 32p. (gr. k-3). 1987. 13.95 (*1-55858-065-4*) North-South Bks NYC.
Schertle, Alice. In My Treehouse. Dunham, Meredith, illus. LC 82-10016. 32p. (gr. k-3). 1983. 11.95 (*0-688-01638-3*) Lothrop.
—William & Grandpa. Stevenson, D., ed. Dabcovich, Lydia, illus. LC 88-666. 32p. (gr. k-3). 1988. 12.95 (*0-688-07580-0*); PLB 12.88 (*0-688-07581-9*) Lothrop.
Schrag, J. O. Nicholas. Ediger, Kristin, illus. 35p. (Orig.). (gr. k-3). 1991. pap. 7.95 (*0-945530-05-6*) Wordsworth KS.
Schwartz, Frederick J. The Adventures of Rondy. Olson, Wayne, ed. Kuehn, Christopher, illus. 148p. (gr. k-7). 1985. 7.95 (*0-9616638-0-4*) Rondy Pubns.
Scott, Ann H. Sam. Shimin, Symeon, illus. 40p. (ps-8). 1992. PLB 14.95 (*0-399-22104-2*, Philomel Bks) Putnam Pub Group.
Scovel, Karen & Hunter, Ted. Joe's Earthday Birthday. Whitney, Jean, illus. 32p. (Orig.). (gr. 2-4). 1992. PLB 16.95 (*0-943990-85-8*); pap. 5.95 (*0-943990-84-X*) Parenting Pr.
Seals, Angela D. D.U.D.LEY. 1992. 7.95 (*0-533-09734-7*) Vantage.
Seldon, George. The Cricket in Times Square. large type ed. 192p. 1990. Repr. PLB 15.95 (*1-55736-170-3*, Crnrstn Bks) BDD LT Grp.
Sempe, Jean-Jacques. Marcellin Caillou. (FRE.). 162p. (gr. 5-10). 1990. pap. 8.95 (*2-07-033561-5*) Schoenhof.
Sempe, Jean-Jacques & Goscinny, R. Recres du Petit Nicolas. (FRE.). 181p. (gr. 5-10). 1987. pap. 9.95 (*2-07-033468-6*) Schoenhof.

Sendak, Maurice. Kenny's Window. Sendak, Maurice, illus. LC 56-5148. 64p. (ps up). 1989. pap. 4.95 (*0-06-443209-2*, Trophy) HarpC Child Bks.
—The Night Kitchen: (La Cocina de Noche) Sendak, Maurice, illus. (SPA.). (gr. 1-6). 14.95 (*84-204-4570-3*) Santillana.
—Where the Wild Things Are: (Donde Viven los Monstruos) Sendak, Maurice, illus. (SPA.). (gr. 1-6). 22.95 (*84-204-3022-6*) Santillana.
Sewall, Marcia. People of the Breaking Day. Sewall, Marcia A., illus. LC 89-18194. 48p. (gr. 1 up). 1990. SBE 15.95 (*0-689-31407-8*, Atheneum Child Bk) Macmillan Child Grp.
Sharmat, Marjorie W. Nate the Great. Simont, Marc, illus. 48p. (gr. 1-4). 1986. 12.95 (*0-698-20627-4*, Coward) Putnam Pub Group.
—Nate the Great Goes Down. (ps-3). 1991. pap. 3.50 (*0-440-40438-X*) Dell.
Sharmat, Mitchell. Gregory, the Terrible Eater. Aruego, Jose & Dewey, Ariane, illus. 32p. (gr. k-3). 1984. pap. 3.95 (*0-590-43350-4*) Scholastic Inc.
Sharp, Paul. Paul the Pitcher Big Book. (Illus.). 32p. (ps-2). 1991. PLB 22.95 (*0-516-49518-6*) Childrens.
Sheldon, Dyan & De Lyman, Alicia G. Jack & Alice. (Illus.). 32p. (gr. k-2). 1992. 15.95 (*0-09-173638-2*, Pub. by Hutchinson UK) Trafalgar.
Shepard, Eva & Lehman, Celia. Nzuzi & the Spell. Hofstetter, Virginia, illus. LC 92-60935. 160p. (gr. 2-8). 1992. pap. 6.95 (*1-878893-22-X*) Telcraft Bks.
Shepard, Steven. Fogbound. Thatch, Nancy R., ed. Shepard, Steven, illus. Melton, David, intro. by. LC 93-13422. (Illus.). 29p. (gr. 5-8). 1993. PLB 14.95 (*0-933849-43-5*) Landmark Edns.
Shirley, Joseph. The Very Special Place. Mosteller, Rosella, illus. 32p. (Orig.). (gr. k-4). 1992. pap. 10.95 incl. cass. (*0-9632816-0-7*) NISIS.
Shusterman, Neal. What Daddy Did. 240p. (gr. 7 up). 1993. pap. 3.95 (*0-06-447094-6*, Trophy) HarpC Child Bks.
Shute, Linda. Momotaro the Peach Boy. LC 85-9997. (Illus.). 32p. (ps-3). 1986. 14.95 (*0-688-05863-9*) Lothrop.
Shyer, Marlene F. Welcome Home, Jellybean. LC 87-19483. 160p. (gr. 3-7). 1988. pap. 3.95 (*0-689-71213-8*, Aladdin) Macmillan Child Grp.
Sidney, Margaret. Ben Pepper. 1992. Repr. PLB 25.95x (*0-89966-969-7*) Buccaneer Bks.
Sierra, Patricia. A Boy I Never Knew. 128p. (gr. 7 up). 1988. pap. 2.50 (*0-380-75208-5*, Flare) Avon.
Simon, Seymour. Einstein Anderson Lights up the Sky. Winkowski, Fred, illus. (gr. 3-7). pap. 3.95 (*0-317-62300-1*, Puffin) Puffin Bks.
—Einstein Anderson, Science Sleuth. Winkowski, Fred, illus. 80p. (gr. 3-7). 1986. pap. 3.99 (*0-14-032098-9*, Puffin) Puffin Bks.
—Einstein Anderson Shocks His Friends. Winkowski, Fred, illus. 80p. (gr. 3-7). 1986. pap. 3.95 (*0-14-032099-7*, Puffin) Puffin Bks.
Singer, A. L. Home Alone Two: Lost in New York Mass Market Novelization. 1992. 3.25 (*0-590-45718-7*) Scholastic Inc.
Sinykin, Sheri C. The Shorty Society. 144p. (gr. 5 up). 1994. 14.99 (*0-670-85248-1*) Viking Child Bks.
Slightly Off-Center Writers Group, Ltd. Staff. Young Christopher. (Illus.). 72p. (gr. 4-6). 1994. pap. 6.95 (*1-56721-082-1*) Twnty-Fifth Cent Pr.
Slote, Alfred. Hang Tough, Paul Mather. reissue ed. LC 72-11531. 160p. (gr. 3-7). 1985. pap. 3.95 (*0-06-440153-7*, Trophy) HarpC Child Bks.
—Matt Gargan's Boy. LC 74-26669. 160p. (gr. 3-7). 1985. pap. 3.95 (*0-06-440154-5*, Trophy) HarpC Child Bks.
—My Robot Buddy. LC 85-45393. (Illus.). 96p. (gr. 2-5). 1986. pap. 3.95 (*0-06-440165-0*, Trophy) HarpC Child Bks.
—Omega Station. Kramer, Anthony, illus. LC 85-45395. 160p. (gr. 2-5). 1986. pap. 3.95 (*0-06-440167-7*, Trophy) HarpC Child Bks.
—The Trading Game. LC 89-12851. 208p. (gr. 3-7). 1992. pap. 3.95 (*0-06-440438-2*, Trophy) HarpC Child Bks.
Smath, Jerry. Leon's Prize. LC 87-25800. (Illus.). 40p. (ps-3). 1987. 5.95 (*0-8193-1169-3*) Parents.
Smith, Derek. Hard Cash. 184p. (gr. 5 up). 1992. 15.95 (*0-571-16174-X*) Faber & Faber.
Smith, Duncan. Fred & the Rocket. (Illus.). 32p. 1993. 10.95 (*0-237-51145-2*, Pub. by Evans Bros Ltd) Trafalgar.
—Fred the Ted. (Illus.). 25p. (gr. k-2). 1991. 11.95 (*0-237-51101-0*, Pub. by Evans Bros Ltd) Trafalgar.
—Fred under the Bed. (Illus.). 25p. (gr. k-2). 1991. 11.95 (*0-237-51112-6*, Pub. by Evans Bros Ltd) Trafalgar.
Smith, Janice L. It's Not Easy Being George: Stories about Adam Joshua (& His Dog) Gackenbach, Dick, illus. LC 88-33075. 128p. (gr. 1-4). 1991. pap. 3.50 (*0-06-440338-6*, Trophy) HarpC Child Bks.
—The Kid Next Door & Other Headaches: Stories about Adam Joshua. Gackenbach, Dick, illus. LC 83-47689. 160p. (gr. 1-4). 1984. PLB 12.89 (*0-06-025793-8*) HarpC Child Bks.
Smith, K. Skeeter. (gr. 6 up). 1989. 14.95 (*0-395-49603-9*) HM.
Smith, Matthew V. Harvey Takes a Ride to the Park. Smith, Matthew V., illus. 15p. (gr. k-3). 1992. pap. 10.95 (*1-895583-05-5*) MAYA Pubs.
—Jimmy's Day Off. Smith, Matthew V., illus. 16p. (gr. k-3). 1994. pap. 12.95 (*1-895583-64-0*) MAYA Pubs.
—Ralph's Funtime. Smith, Matthew V., illus. 17p. (gr. k-3). 1992. pap. 19.95 (*1-895583-08-X*) MAYA Pubs.
Smith, Mildred S. Where Is Jeffrey's Yo-Yo? (Illus.). 56p. (ps-12). 1988. 8.50 (*0-9612296-5-9*) Williams SC.
Smith, Robert D. Tommy's Father. 32p. (gr. 2). 1991. pap. 8.95 (*1-880404-03-6*) Bkwrights.
Smith, Robert K. Mostly Michael. Coville, Katherine, illus. LC 86-19618. 192p. (gr. 4-6). 1987. pap. 13.95 (*0-385-29545-6*) Delacorte.
—Mostly Michael. 192p. (gr. k-6). 1988. pap. 3.99 (*0-440-40097-X*, YB) Dell.
Smitt, Elizabeth. Lucca & Chester's Big Fight. (Illus.). 32p. (ps-2). 1995. 14.95 (*0-395-70930-X*) Ticknor & Flds Bks Yng Read.
Smurthwaite, Donald. The Search for Wallace Whipple. LC 93-46245. (gr. 8-12). 1994. pap. 6.95 (*0-87579-830-6*) Deseret Bk.
Snyder, Dianne. Boy of the Three-Year Nap. (ps-3). 1993. pap. 4.95 (*0-395-66957-X*) HM.
Snyder, Dianne, retold by. The Boy of the Three-Year Nap. Say, Allen, illus. LC 87-30674. 32p. (ps-3). 1988. 16.95 (*0-395-44090-4*) HM.
Sobel, Barbara. Jake Finds a Penny. Ziffer, Louise, illus. LC 86-81370. 32p. (gr. k-2). 1986. PLB 7.59 (*0-87386-019-5*); pap. 1.95 (*0-87386-015-2*) Jan Prods.
Sonnenschein, Harriet. Harold's Runaway Nose. 40p. (ps). 1991. pap. 2.25 (*0-671-74075-X*, S&S BFYR) S&S Trade.
Speare, Jean. A Candle for Christmas. Blades, Ann, illus. LC 86-61560. 32p. (gr. k-4). 1987. SBE 13.95 (*0-689-50417-9*, M K McElderry) Macmillan Child Grp.
Spinelli, Jerry. Maniac Magee. LC 89-27144. 192p. (gr. 3-7). 1992. pap. 3.95 (*0-06-440424-2*, Trophy) HarpC Child Bks.
Standish, Burt L. Frank Merriwell Down South. Rudman, Jack, ed. (gr. 9 up). Date not set. 9.95 (*0-8373-9305-1*); pap. 3.95 (*0-8373-9005-2*) F Merriwell.
—Frank Merriwell in Europe. Rudman, Jack, ed. (gr. 9 up). Date not set. 9.95 (*0-8373-9308-6*); pap. 3.95 (*0-8373-9008-7*) F Merriwell.
—Frank Merriwell's Bravery. Rudman, Jack, ed. (gr. 9 up). Date not set. 9.95 (*0-8373-9306-X*); pap. 3.95 (*0-8373-9006-0*) F Merriwell.
—Frank Merriwell's Hunting Tour. Rudman, Jack, ed. (gr. 9 up). Date not set. 9.95 (*0-8373-9307-8*); pap. 3.95 (*0-8373-9007-9*) F Merriwell.
—Frank Merriwell's Schooldays. Rudman, Jack, ed. (gr. 9 up). 1970. 9.95 (*0-8373-9309-4*); pap. 3.95 (*0-8373-9009-5*) F Merriwell.
—Frank Merriwell's Sports Afield. Rudman, Jack, ed. (gr. 9 up). Date not set. 9.95 (*0-8373-9310-8*); pap. 3.95 (*0-8373-9010-9*) F Merriwell.
—Frank Merriwell's Trip West. Rudman, Jack, ed. (gr. 9 up). Date not set. 9.95 (*0-8373-9304-3*); pap. 3.95 (*0-8373-9004-4*) F Merriwell.
Stanley, Monty M. They Call Me a Delinquent. 91p. (Orig.). (gr. 5-12). 1989. 8.95 (*0-9622667-1-X*) Illini Pubns.
Stan-Padilla, Viento. Dream Feather. Stan-Padilla, Viento, illus. LC 87-17823. 60p. (Orig.). (gr. 2 up). 1987. pap. 11.95 (*0-913990-57-4*) Book Pub Co.
Steel, Danielle. Freddie's First Night Away. (ps-3). 1992. pap. 2.99 (*0-440-40574-2*) Dell.
—Freddie's Trip. (ps-3). 1992. pap. 2.99 (*0-440-40573-4*) Dell.
Steig, William. Dominico. (gr. 4-7). 1994. 15.00 (*0-374-31823-9*, Mirasol); pap. 4.95 (*0-374-41927-2*, Mirasol) FS&G.
—Sylvester & the Magic Pebble. (Illus.). 32p. (ps-3). 1988. (Little Simon); (S&S BFYR) S&S Trade.
—Sylvester & the Magic Pebble. Steig, William, illus. 32p. (ps-1). 1988. Bk. & cassette. pap. 8.95 (*0-671-67144-8*, S&S BFYR) S&S Trade.
Stein, Aidel. Do Not Disturb. 154p. (Orig.). (gr. 6-8). 1994. pap. 7.95 (*1-56871-037-2*) Targum Pr.
Stephens, Michael. Eddy the Great. (gr. 4-7). 1994. pap. 5.95 (*1-86373-392-2*, Pub. by Allen & Unwin Aust Pty AT) IPG Chicago.
Stevens, Jan R. Carlos & the Squash Plant: Carlos y la Planta Calabaza. Arnold, Jeanne, illus. LC 92-82137. (SPA & ENG.). 32p. (gr. k). 1993. 14.95 (*0-87358-559-3*) Northland AZ.
Stevenson, James. Monty. Stevenson, James, illus. LC 78-11409. 32p. (ps up). 1992. pap. 4.95 (*0-688-11288-9*, Mulberry) Morrow.
—The Supreme Souvenir Factory. LC 87-33390. (Illus.). 56p. (gr. 1-4). 1988. 13.95 (*0-688-07782-X*) Greenwillow.
Stiles, Martha B. James the Vinepuller. (ps-3). 1992. 14.95 (*0-87614-047-9*) Carolrhoda Bks.
Stolz, Mary. The Bully of Barkham Street. Shortall, Leonard, illus. LC 68-2661. 224p. (gr. 3-7). 1985. pap. 3.95 (*0-06-440159-6*, Trophy) HarpC Child Bks.
—The Explorer of Barkham Street. McCully, Emily A., illus. LC 84-48339. 192p. (gr. 4-6). 1985. 15.00 (*0-06-025976-0*) HarpC Child Bks.
—The Explorer of Barkham Street. McCully, Emily A., illus. LC 84-48339. 192p. (gr. 3-7). 1987. pap. 3.95 (*0-06-440210-X*, Trophy) HarpC Child Bks.
Strasser, Todd. Home Alone Movie Tie-In. 1991. pap. 2.95 (*0-590-44668-1*) Scholastic Inc.
—Home Alone Two: Lost in New York Digest Novelization. 1992. 3.25 (*0-590-45717-9*) Scholastic Inc.
Taber, Anthony. The Boy Who Stopped Time. Taber, Anthony, illus. LC 92-398. 32p. (ps-3). 1993. SBE 13.95 (*0-689-50460-8*, M K McElderry) Macmillan Child Grp.
Talbot, John. Hasn't He Grown! (Illus.). 32p. (ps-2). 1989. 13.95 (*0-86264-232-9*, Pub. by Anderson Pr UK) Trafalgar.
Tamar, Erika. It Happened at Cecilia's. LC 88-28502. 144p. (gr. 6-9). 1989. SBE 13.95 (*0-689-31478-7*, Atheneum Child Bk) Macmillan Child Grp.
Taylor, Theodore. The Cay. 144p. (gr. 6). 1977. pap. 3.99 (*0-380-00142-X*, Camelot) Avon.
Tetz, Resanne. Andrew Can. 32p. 1992. pap. 5.95 (*0-8163-1063-7*) Pacific Pr Pub Assn.
Thaler, Mike. How Far Will a Rubber Band Stretch. 1990. pap. 13.95 (*0-671-69361-1*, S&S BFYR) S&S Trade.
Thayer, Jane. The Puppy Who Wanted a Boy. McCue, Lisa, illus. LC 85-15465. 48p. (ps up). 1988. pap. 4.95 (*0-688-08293-9*, Mulberry) Morrow.
Thompson, Julian F. Herb Seasoning. 1990. pap. 12.95 (*0-590-43023-8*) Scholastic Inc.
Tibo, Gilles. Simon & the Wind. Tibo, Gilles, illus. LC 89-50777. 24p. (gr. k-4). 1989. 10.95 (*0-88776-234-4*) Tundra Bks.
—Simon et le Vent d'Automne. Tibo, Gilles, illus. LC 89-50776. (FRE.). 24p. (gr. k-4). 1989. 10.95 (*0-88776-235-2*) Tundra Bks.
Titherington, Jeanne. A Place for Ben. Titherington, Jeanne, illus. LC 86-7656. 24p. (ps-3). 1987. 11.95 (*0-688-06493-0*); PLB 11.88 (*0-688-06494-9*) Greenwillow.
Tolstoy, Leo. Shoemaker Martin. Watts, Bernadette, illus. Hanhart, Brigitte, adapted by. LC 86-60489. (Illus.). 32p. (gr. k-3). 1986. 14.95 (*1-55858-044-1*) North-South Bks NYC.
Tomlinson, Theresa. Riding the Waves. LC 92-3942. (Illus.). 144p. (gr. 4-8). 1993. SBE 13.95 (*0-02-789207-7*, Macmillan Child Bk) Macmillan Child Grp.
Townsend, Tom. Trader Wooly & the Secret of the Lost Nazi Treasure. Roberts, Melissa, ed. (Illus.). 120p. (gr. 4-7). 1987. 10.95 (*0-89015-602-6*, Pub. by Panda Bks); pap. 5.95 (*0-89015-634-4*) Sunbelt Media.
Troll Press Staff. Home Alone Two: Lost in New York. (gr. 4-7). 1992. pap. 2.50 (*0-8167-2847-X*) Troll Assocs.
Tunis, John R. The Kid from Tomkinsville. Bacon, Paul, illus. Brooks, Bruce, intro. by. (Illus.). 278p. (gr. 3-7). 1989. pap. 3.95 (*0-15-242567-5*, Odyssey) HarBrace.
Twain, Mark. Adventures of Huckleberry Finn. facsimile ed. (Illus.). 366p. 1990. Repr. of 1885 ed. miniature 60.00 (*1-878582-01-1*) Childs Min Bk Co.
—Adventures of Huckleberry Finn. (Illus.). (gr. 4-7). 1991. pap. 6.50 (*0-582-03585-6*) Longman.
—The Adventures of Tom Sawyer. facsimile ed. (Illus.). 267p. 1990. Repr. of 1876 ed. miniature 60.00 (*1-878582-00-3*) Childs Min Bk Co.
—Adventures of Tom Sawyer. 1991. pap. text ed. 6.50 (*0-582-03588-0*) Longman.
—Adventures of Tom Sawyer. 320p. 1992. 9.49 (*0-8167-2546-2*); pap. 2.95 (*0-8167-2547-0*) Troll Assocs.
—Adventures of Tom Sawyer. 1993. pap. 2.95 (*0-590-43352-0*) Scholastic Inc.
Twain, Mark, pseud. Aventures de Tom Sawyer. Lapointe, Claude, illus. (FRE.). 296p. (gr. 5-10). 1987. pap. 9.95 (*2-07-033449-X*) Schoenhof.
—Huckleberry Finn. Vogel, Nathaele, illus. (FRE.). 380p. (gr. 5-10). 1990. pap. 10.95 (*2-07-033230-6*) Schoenhof.
—Huckleberry Finn. (gr. 4-7). 1993. pap. 4.95 (*0-8114-6826-7*) Raintree Steck-V.
—Tom Sawyer. (gr. 4-7). 1993. pap. 4.95 (*0-8114-6843-7*) Raintree Steck-V.
Twain, Mark. Tom Sawyer. 1994. 4.98 (*0-8317-1646-0*) Smithmark.
Twain, Mark & Ploog, Michael. Tom Sawyer. (Illus.). 52p. Date not set. pap. 4.95 (*1-57209-007-3*) Classics Int Ent.
Ulmer, Louise. The Son Who Said He Wouldn't. (gr. k-4). 1981. pap. 1.99 (*0-570-06145-8*, 59-1262) Concordia.
Umansky, Kaye & Chamberlain, Margaret. Pass the Jam, Jim! (Illus.). 32p. (ps-1). 1993. 17.95 (*0-370-31662-2*, Pub. by Bodley Head UK) Trafalgar.
Ungerer, Tomi. Orlando. (ps-3). 1993. pap. 3.99 (*0-440-40594-7*) Dell.
Uri, Galila B. The Milah Chair. 250p. (gr. 7). 1992. write for info. (*1-56062-143-5*); pap. write for info. (*1-56062-144-3*) CIS Comm.
Vallet, Roxanne. Ralph Gets a Prize. Vallet, Roxanne, illus. 12p. (gr. k-3). 1993. pap. text ed. 12.95 (*1-56606-017-6*) Bradley Mann.
Van Antwerp, T. Cooper. Hereafter Rising. Graves, Helen, ed. LC 88-50121. 190p. (gr. 3-10). 1988. 8.95 (*1-55523-139-X*) Winston-Derek.
Van Denend, G. Mark in the Closet. Vreeman, J., ed. (Illus.). 16p. (Orig.). 1985. pap. 3.95 (*0-918789-01-X*) FreeMan Prods.
Van De Wetering, Janwillem. Hugh Pine. (Illus.). 96p. (gr. 3 up). 1980. 14.45 (*0-395-29459-2*) HM.
—Hugh Pine. ALC Staff, ed. Munsinger, Lynn, illus. LC 80-13652. 88p. (gr. 2 up). 1992. pap. 3.95 (*0-688-11799-6*, Pub. by Beech Tree Bks) Morrow.
—Hugh Pine & Something Else. ALC Staff, ed. Munsinger, Lynn, illus. LC 88-35801. 80p. (gr. 2 up). 1992. pap. 3.95 (*0-688-11800-3*, Pub. by Beech Tree Bks) Morrow.

—Hugh Pine & the Good Place. ALC Staff, ed. Munsinger, Lynn, illus. LC 86-3108. 72p. 1992. pap. 3.95 (*0-688-11801-1*, Pub. by Beech Tree Bks) Morrow.

Vann, Donna R. Roberto & the Fountain of Lights. (Illus.). 32p. (gr. 4 up). 1988. 8.99 (*0-7459-1277-X*) Lion USA.

Vincent, Gabrielle. Feel Better, Ernest! LC 87-21074. (Illus.). 32p. (ps-3). 1988. Repr. of 1988 ed. 11.95 (*0-688-07725-0*); lib. bdg. 13.88 (*0-688-07726-9*) Greenwillow.

Viorst, Judith. Alexander & the Terrible, Horrible, No Good, Very Bad Day. Cruz, Ray, illus. LC 72-75289. 32p. (gr. k-4). 1972. RSBE 13.95 (*0-689-30072-7*, Atheneum Child Bk) Macmillan Child Grp.

—Alexander & the Terrible, Horrible, No Good, Very Bad Day. Cruz, Ray, illus. LC 87-1087. 32p. (gr. k-4). 1987. pap. 3.95 (*0-689-71173-5*, Aladdin) Macmillan Child Grp.

—Alexander Who Used to Be Rich Last Sunday. LC 77-1579. (Illus.). 32p. (ps-4). 1987. pap. 3.95 (*0-689-71199-9*, Aladdin) Macmillan Child Grp.

—The Good-Bye Book. Chorao, Kay, illus. LC 91-19916. 32p. (ps-1). 1992. pap. 4.95 (*0-689-71581-1*, Aladdin) Macmillan Child Grp.

Vivelo, Jackie. Reading to Matthew. Saflund, Birgitta, illus. LC 93-84912. 40p. (gr. 3-8). 1993. 15.95 (*1-879373-60-2*) R Rinehart.

Voight, Cynthia. David & Jonathan. 1994. pap. 3.95 (*0-590-45166-9*) Scholastic Inc.

Voigt, Cynthia. Dicey's Song. large type ed. 334p. 1990. Repr. lib. bdg. 15.95 (*1-55736-166-5*, Crnrstn Bks) BDD LT Grp.

Waber, Bernard. Bernard. Waber, Bernard, illus. 48p. (gr. k-3). 1986. 13.45 (*0-395-31865-3*); pap. 5.70 (*0-395-42648-0*) HM.

—Ira Sleeps Over. (gr. 3 up). 1993. pap. 7.95 incl. cass. (*0-395-45949-4*) HM.

—Lyle Finds His Mother. LC 74-5336. (Illus.). 48p. (gr. k-3). 1974. 14.95 (*0-395-19489-X*) HM.

Wahl, Jan. How the Children Stopped the Wars. O'Keefe, Maureen, illus. LC 93-2479. 96p. 1993. Repr. of 1969 ed. 15.95 (*1-883672-00-7*) Tricycle Pr.

Wallace, Bill. Beauty. LC 88-6422. 192p. (gr. 3-7). 1988. 14.95 (*0-8234-0715-2*) Holiday.

—Snot Stew. McCue, Lisa, illus. 96p. 1990. pap. 3.50 (*0-671-69335-2*, Minstrel Bks) PB.

Walter, Mildred P. Justin & the Best Biscuits in the World. Stock, Catherine, illus. LC 86-7148. 128p. (gr. 3-7). 1986. 14.00 (*0-688-06645-3*) Lothrop.

—My Mama Needs Me. Cummings, Pat, illus. LC 82-12654. 32p. (ps-1). 1983. 15.00 (*0-688-01670-7*); PLB 14.93 (*0-688-01671-5*) Lothrop.

Washington, Anthony. Young Run Away. Adoma, Afua, illus. (Orig.). (gr. 3-6). 1984. pap. 2.98 (*0-9613078-2-X*) Detroit Black.

Watkins, Tracy D. Patrick the Pelaganty. Herbrechtsmeier, Keith, ed. Jones, Jerry D., illus. LC 93-83730. 40p. (ps-3). 1993. 8.99 (*1-883261-00-7*) Pelaganty.

Weaks, Charles. Leon's Big Day. rev. ed. 1993. 6.95 (*0-8062-4747-9*) Carlton.

Weber, Bernard. Ira Says Goodbye. (ps-3). 1991. pap. 5.95 (*0-395-58413-2*) HM.

Weil, Jennifer C. & Farrington, Liz. William's Gift. Hui-Han Liu, illus. 40p. (gr. k-4). 1994. 14.95 (*1-56844-007-3*) Enchante Pub.

Weinberger, Jane. That's What Counts. Margit Studio, illus. LC 87-50549. 40p. (gr. k-4). 1988. pap. 5.95 (*0-932433-33-2*) Windswept Hse.

Wells, Rosemary. Don't Spill It Again, James. LC 77-71513. (Illus.). 48p. (ps-3). 1990. 8.95 (*0-8037-2118-8*); pap. 3.95 (*0-8037-0831-9*) Dial Bks Young.

—Shy Charles. Wells, Rosemary, illus. LC 87-27247. 32p. (ps-3). 1988. 11.95 (*0-8037-0563-8*); PLB 11.89 (*0-8037-0564-6*) Dial Bks Young.

Westmoreland, Ronald P. The Wild Horses of Hidden Valley. Roberts, Melissa, ed. (Illus.). 96p. (gr. 4-7). 1990. 8.95 (*0-89015-717-0*) Sunbelt Media.

Wetterer, Margaret K. The Boy Who Knew the Language of the Birds. Wright, Beth, illus. 48p. (gr. k-4). 1991. PLB 17.50 (*0-87614-652-3*) Carolrhoda Bks.

When the Boys Ran Home. 1983. pap. 2.50 (*0-440-79450-1*) Dell.

When the Boys Ran the House. Newsom, Carol, illus. 160p. (gr. 3-7). 1983. pap. 3.25 (*0-440-49450-8*, YB) Dell.

Wilhelm, Hans. Tyrone the Double Dirty Rotten Cheater. (Illus.). 1992. pap. 3.95 (*0-590-44080-2*) Scholastic Inc.

Willey, Margaret. Saving Lenny. (gr. 7 up). 1990. 13.95 (*0-553-05850-9*, Starfire) Bantam.

Williams, Barbara. Albert's Toothache. Chorao, Kay, illus. LC 74-4040. 32p. (ps-1). 1988. pap. 3.95 (*0-525-44363-0*, 0383-120, DCB) Dutton Child Bks.

Wilson, Johnniece M. Robin on His Own. 160p. 1992. pap. 2.95 (*0-590-41809-2*, Apple Paperbacks) Scholastic Inc.

Wilson, Sarah. The Day That Henry Cleaned His Room. (ps-3). 1990. pap. 13.95 (*0-671-69202-X*, S&S BFYR) S&S Trade.

Winfield, Arthur. Rover Boys at College. 191p. 1981. Repr. PLB 12.95x (*0-89966-330-3*) Buccaneer Bks.

Winthrop, Elizabeth. Luke's Bully. Porter, Pat G., illus. 64p. (gr. 2-5). 1992. pap. 3.99 (*0-14-034329-6*, Puffin) Puffin Bks.

—Tough Eddie. Hoban, Lillian, illus. LC 84-13664. 32p. (ps-2). 1989. pap. 3.95 (*0-525-44496-3*, DCB) Dutton Child Bks.

Wiseman, David. Jeremy Visick. (gr. 5 up). 1981. 13.95 (*0-395-30449-0*) HM.

—Jeremy Visick. (gr. 4-7). 1990. pap. 5.95 (*0-395-56153-1*) HM.

Wolff, Virginia E. Probably Still Nick Swansen. 144p. (gr. 6 up). 1988. 13.95 (*0-8050-0701-6*, Bks Young Read) H Holt & Co.

Wood, Audrey. Elbert's Bad Word. Wood, Audrey & Wood, Don, illus. LC 86-7557. 32p. (ps-3). 1988. 13. 95 (*0-15-225320-3*, HB Juv Bks) HarBrace.

Wood, John. Charlie & the Stinking Ragbags. (Illus., Orig.). (gr. 4-6). 1991. pap. 8.95 (*0-86327-298-3*, Pub. by Wolfhound Pr EIRE) Dufour.

Woodson, Frank. Mean Waters. Parker, Liz, ed. Taylor, Marjorie, illus. 45p. (Orig.). (gr. 6-12). 1992. pap. text ed. 2.95 (*1-56254-059-9*) Saddleback Pubns.

Wyeth, Sharon D. Boys Wanted. (gr. k-6). 1989. pap. 2.95 (*0-440-40224-7*, YB) Dell.

Yep, Laurence. Butterfly Boy. (ps-3). 1993. 16.00 (*0-374-31003-3*) FS&G.

Yorinks, Arthur. Hey, Al. Egielski, Richard, illus. LC 86-80955. 32p. (gr. k up). 1986. 15.00 (*0-374-33060-3*) FS&G.

—It Happened in Pinsk. Egielski, Richard, illus. LC 83-1727. 32p. (ps up). 1983. 14.00 (*0-374-33651-2*) FS&G.

Zalben, Jane B. Earth to Andrew O. Blechman. Zalben, Jane B., illus. (gr. 3-7). 1989. 14.00 (*0-374-31916-2*) FS&G.

Zaldivar, Raquel P. Roberto Goes Fishing - Roberto Va de Pesca. Bubiera, Sandra S., illus. 32p. (gr. 1-3). 1992. 12.95 (*1-880507-00-5*) Lectorum Pubns.

Ziefert, Harriet. Good Luck, Bad Luck. James, Lillie, illus. 32p. (ps-3). 1992. 8.95 (*0-670-84275-3*) Viking Child Bks.

—Harry Goes to Fun Land. LC 88-82400. (Illus.). 32p. (ps-3). 1989. pap. 8.95 (*0-670-82664-2*) Viking Child Bks.

—Harry Goes to Fun Land. Smith, Mavis, illus. LC 88-62146. 32p. (ps-3). 1989. pap. 3.50 (*0-14-050980-1*, Puffin) Puffin Bks.

—Harry's Bath. 1990. 9.95 (*0-553-05863-0*, Little Rooster) Bantam.

—Stitches. Aitken, Amy, illus. LC 93-6553. (ps-2). 1993. pap. 3.25 (*0-14-036553-2*, Puffin) Puffin Bks.

—Three Wishes. Jacobson, David, illus. 32p. (ps-3). 1993. pap. 3.50 (*0-14-054556-5*) Puffin Bks.

—Tim & Jim Take Off. Mandel, Suzy, illus. 32p. (ps-3). 1990. pap. 3.50 (*0-14-054222-1*, Puffin) Puffin Bks.

Zindel, Paul. The Amazing & Death-Defying Diary of Eugene Dingman. LC 82-47712. 224p. (gr. 7 up). 1987. 14.00 (*0-06-026862-X*); PLB 13.89 (*0-06-026863-8*) HarpC Child Bks.

Zolotow, Charlotte. But Not Billy. Chorao, Kay, illus. LC 82-47703. 32p. (ps-k). 1983. 12.95 (*0-06-026963-4*) HarpC Child Bks.

—My Grandson Lew. Pene Du Bois, William, illus. LC 73-1433. 32p. (ps-3). 1985. pap. 3.95 (*0-06-443066-9*, Trophy) HarpC Child Bks.

—Over & Over. Reissue. ed. Williams, Garth, illus. LC 56-8149. 32p. (ps-3). 1987. PLB 15.89 (*0-06-026956-1*) HarpC Child Bks.

—Someone New. Blegvad, Erik, illus. LC 77-11838. (ps-3). 1978. PLB 14.89 (*0-06-027018-7*) HarpC Child Bks.

—Timothy Too! (ps-3). 1986. 13.45 (*0-395-39378-7*) HM.

BOYS–POETRY

Derwent, Lavinia. Sula. 160p. (gr. 5-7). 1989. pap. 6.95 (*0-86241-068-1*, Pub. by Cnngt Pub Ltd) Trafalgar.

BRADY, MATHEW B., 1823?-1896

Sullivan, George. Mathew Brady: His Life & Photographs. LC 93-28354. (Illus.). 1994. write for info. (*0-525-65186-1*, Cobblehill Bks) Dutton Child Bks.

BRAHMS, JOHANNES, 1833-1897

Rachlin, Ann. Brahms. Hellard, Susan, illus. 24p. (gr. k-3). 1993. pap. 5.95 (*0-8120-1542-8*) Barron.

BRAILLE, LOUIS, 1809-1852

Davidson, Margaret. Louis Braille, l'Enfant de la Nuit. Dahar, Andre, illus. (FRE.). 103p. (gr. 3-7). 1990. pap. 10.95 (*2-07-031225-9*) Schoenhof.

—Louis Braille: The Boy Who Invented Books for the Blind. Compere, Janet, illus. 80p. 1991. pap. 2.75 (*0-590-44350-X*) Scholastic Inc.

BRAIN

see also Dreams; Mind and Body; Nervous System; Psychology; Sleep

Asimov, Isaac. How Did We Find Out about the Brain. (gr. 5 up). 1987. 10.95 (*0-8027-6736-2*); PLB 11.85 (*0-8027-6737-0*) Walker & Co.

August, Paul. Brain Function. Mendelson, Jack H. & Mello, Nancyintro. by. (Illus.). 128p. (gr. 5 up). 1988. lib. bdg. 19.95x (*1-55546-204-9*) Chelsea Hse.

Bailey, Donna. All about Your Brain. LC 90-41008. (Illus.). 48p. (gr. 2-6). 1990. PLB 20.70 (*0-8114-2778-1*) Raintree Steck-V.

Barrett, Susan L. It's All in Your Head: A Guide to Understanding Your Brain & Boosting Your Brain Power. rev. ed. Espeland, Pamela, ed. Urbanovic, Jackie, illus. LC 92-18090. 160p. (gr. 3-7). 1992. pap. 9.95 (*0-915793-45-8*) Free Spirit Pub.

Bruun, Ruth D. & Bruun, Bertel. Brain: What It Is, What It Does. Brunn, Peter, illus. LC 88-21182. 64p. 1989. 12.95 (*0-688-08453-2*); PLB 12.88 (*0-688-08454-0*) Greenwillow.

Bryan, Jenny. Mind & Matter. LC 93-71714. (Illus.). 48p. (gr. 5 up). 1993. text ed. 13.95 RSBE (*0-87518-588-6*, Dillon) Macmillan Child Grp.

Kennedy, Philip R. Get a Move on, Neuron! Kennedy, Philip R., illus. LC 92-97171. 42p. (Orig.). (gr. 5-8). 1992. pap. text ed. 10.00 (*0-9635701-0-2*); Tchr's. ed. 12.00 (*0-9635701-1-0*) Your Chlds Neuro.

LeMaster, Leslie J. Your Brain & Nervous System. LC 84-7635. (Illus.). 48p. (gr. k-4). 1984. PLB 12.85 (*0-516-01931-7*); pap. 4.95 (*0-516-41931-5*) Childrens.

Mathers, Douglas. Brain. Farmer, Andrew & Green, Robina, illus. LC 90-42883. 32p. (gr. 4-6). 1992. PLB 11.89 (*0-8167-2090-8*); pap. 3.95 (*0-8167-2091-6*) Troll Assocs.

Metos, Thomas H. The Human Mind: How We Think & Learn. (Illus.). 128p. (gr. 9-12). 1990. PLB 13.40 (*0-531-10885-6*) Watts.

Moore, Adam. Broken Arrow Boy. Thatch, Nancy R., ed. Melton, David, intro. by. LC 90-5933. (Illus.). 26p. (gr. 3-8). 1990. PLB 14.95 (*0-933849-24-9*) Landmark Edns.

Parker, Steve. The Brain & Nervous System. rev. ed. (Illus.). 48p. (gr. 5-8). 1991. pap. 6.95 (*0-531-24600-0*) Watts.

—Learning a Lesson: How You See, Think & Remember. LC 89-77860. (Illus.). 32p. (gr. k-4). 1991. PLB 11.40 (*0-531-14087-3*) Watts.

Powledge, Tabitha M. Your Brain: How You Got It & How It Works. LC 94-14273. (gr. 6-8). 1994. 14.95 (*0-684-19659-X*, Scribner) Macmillan.

Schultz, Ron. Looking Inside the Brain. (Illus.). 48p. (Orig.). (gr. 3 up). 1992. pap. 9.95 (*1-56261-064-3*) John Muir.

Silverstein, Alvin & Silverstein, Virginia B. The World of the Brain. LC 86-31007. (Illus.). 192p. (gr. 7up). 1986. 12.95 (*0-688-05777-2*) Morrow Jr Bks.

Simon, Seymour. Professor I. Q. Explores the Brain. (Illus.). 48p. (gr. 4-7). 1993. 13.95 (*1-878093-27-4*) Boyds Mills Pr.

Smith, Kathie B. & Crenson, Victoria. Thinking. Storms, Robert S., illus. LC 87-5886. 24p. (gr. k-3). 1988. PLB 10.59 (*0-8167-1016-3*); pap. text ed. 2.50 (*0-8167-1017-1*) Troll Assocs.

Stafford, Patricia. Your Two Brains. Tunney, Linda, illus. LC 85-28575. 96p. (gr. 3-7). 1986. SBE 13.95 (*0-689-31142-7*, Atheneum Child Bk) Macmillan Child Grp.

Tyler. Brain Puzzles. (gr. 2-5). 1980. (Usborne-Hayes); PLB 12.96 (*0-88110-051-X*); pap. 4.50 (*0-86020-437-5*) EDC.

BRASS INSTRUMENTS

see Wind Instruments

BRAVERY

see Courage

BRAZIL

Ashford, Moyra. Brazil. LC 90-19250. (Illus.). 96p. (gr. 6-12). 1991. PLB 22.80 (*0-8114-2436-7*) Raintree Steck-V.

Bailey, Donna & Sproule, Anna. Brazil. LC 90-30534. (Illus.). 32p. (gr. 1-4). 1990. PLB 18.99 (*0-8114-2560-6*) Raintree Steck-V.

Bender, Evelyn. Brazil. (Illus.). 112p. (gr. 5 up). 1990. 14. 95 (*0-7910-1108-9*) Chelsea Hse.

Carpenter, Mark. Brazil: An Awakening Giant. LC 87-13417. (Illus.). 128p. (gr. 5 up). 1988. text ed. 14.95 RSBE (*0-87518-366-2*, Dillon) Macmillan Child Grp.

Cobb, Vicki. This Place Is Wet. Lavallee, Barbara, illus. 32p. (gr. 2-4). 1989. 12.95 (*0-8027-6880-6*); PLB 13. 85 (*0-8027-6881-4*) Walker & Co.

Cross, Wilbur. Brazil. LC 84-7602. (Illus.). 128p. (gr. 5-9). 1984. PLB 20.55 (*0-516-02753-0*) Childrens.

Haverstock, Nathan A. Brazil in Pictures. rev. ed. (Illus.). 64p. (gr. 5 up). 1987. PLB 17.50 (*0-8225-1802-3*) Lerner Pubns.

Jacobsen, Karen. Brazil. LC 89-10042. 48p. (gr. k-4). 1989. PLB 12.85 (*0-516-01171-5*); pap. 4.95 (*0-516-41171-3*) Childrens.

Lewington, Anna. Antonio's Rain Forest. Parker, Edward, photos by. (Illus.). 48p. (gr. 2-5). 1993. 21.50 (*0-87614-749-X*) Carolrhoda Bks.

Morrison, Marion. Brazil. LC 93-26100. 1993. PLB 22.80 (*0-8114-1842-1*) Raintree Steck-V.

Papi, Liza. Carnavalia! African-Brazilian Folklore & Crafts. LC 93-38451. (Illus.). 48p. 1994. 16.95 (*0-8478-1779-2*) Rizzoli Intl.

Richard, Christopher. Brazil. LC 90-22471. (Illus.). 128p. (gr. 5-9). 1991. PLB 21.95 (*1-85435-382-9*) Marshall Cavendish.

Waterlow, Julia. Brazil. LC 91-48018. (Illus.). 48p. (gr. 5-8). 1992. PLB 13.90 (*0-531-18439-0*, Pub. by Bookwright Pr) Watts.

BRAZIL–FICTION

Gerson, Mary-Joan, retold by. How Night Came from the Sea: A Story from Brazil. Golembe, Carla, illus. LC 93-20054. (ps-3). 1994. 15.95 (*0-316-30855-2*, Joy St Bks) Little.

Lewin, Ted. Amazon Boy. Lewin, Ted, illus. LC 92-15798. 32p. (gr. k-3). 1993. RSBE 14.95 (*0-02-757383-4*, Macmillan Child Bk) Macmillan Child Grp.

Nunes, Lygia B. My Friend the Painter. Pontiero, Giovanni, tr. from POR. 85p. (gr. 3-7). 1991. 13.95 (*0-15-256340-7*) HarBrace.

BREAD

see also Baking

Baskerville, Judith. Bread. Stefoff, Rebecca, ed. Barber, Ed, photos by. LC 91-18189. (Illus.). 32p. (gr. 3-5). 1991. PLB 15.93 (*1-56074-001-9*) Garrett Ed Corp.

Curtis, Neil & Greenland, Peter. How Bread Is Made. (Illus.). 24p. (gr. 1-3). 1992. PLB 13.50 (*0-8225-2375-2*) Lerner Pubns.

Devlin, Wende & Devlin, Harry. Cranberry Thanksgiving. Devlin, Harry, illus. LC 80-17070. 48p. (ps-3). 1984. Repr. of 1971 ed. RSBE 13.95 (*0-02-729930-9*, Four Winds) Macmillan Child Grp.

Garrett, Norman A. Great Bread Machine Recipes. LC 92-16781. 128p. (gr. 10-12). 1992. pap. 6.95 (*0-8069-8724-3*) Sterling.

—Quick & Delicious Bread Machine Recipes. LC 91-37674. 128p. (gr. 10-12). 1993. pap. 6.95 (*0-8069-8812-6*) Sterling.

Gershator, David. Bread Is for Eating. 1995. write for info. (*0-8050-3173-1*) H Holt & Co.

Mitgutsch, Ali. From Grain to Bread. Mitgutsch, Ali, illus. LC 80-28592. 24p. (ps-3). 1981. PLB 10.95 (*0-87614-155-6*) Carolrhoda Bks.

Moncure, Jane B. What Was It Before It Was Bread? Hygaard, Elizabeth, illus. LC 85-11402. 32p. (ps-2). 1985. PLB 14.95 (*0-89565-323-0*) Childs World.

Morris, Ann. Bread, Bread, Bread. Heyman, Ken, photos by. LC 82-26677. (Illus.). 32p. (ps-2). 1989. 14.95 (*0-688-06334-9*); PLB 14.88 (*0-688-06335-7*) Lothrop.

—Bread, Bread, Bread. Heyman, Ken, photos by. LC 92-25547. (Illus.). 32p. (gr. k up). 1993. pap. 4.95 (*0-688-12275-2*, Mulberry) Morrow.

Oppenneer, Betsy. Betsy's Breads. rev. ed. (Illus.). 70p. (gr. 8 up). 1991. pap. 7.95 (*0-9627665-2-6*) Breadworks.

Robbins, Ken. Make Me a Peanut Butter Sandwich & a Glass of Milk. (Illus.). (ps up). 1992. 14.95 (*0-590-43550-7*, 023, Scholastic Hardcover) Scholastic Inc.

Story of Bread. (ARA., Illus.). (gr. 3-5). 1987. 3.95x (*0-86685-226-3*) Intl Bk Ctr.

Turner, Dorothy. Bread. Yates, John, illus. 32p. (gr. 1-4). 1989. PLB 14.95 (*0-87614-359-1*) Carolrhoda Bks.

BREATHING

see Respiration

BRIDAL CUSTOMS

see Marriage Customs and Rites

BRIDGE (GAME)

Goodwin, Jude & Ellison, Don. Teach Me to Play: A First Book of Bridge. (gr. 3-9). 1988. PLB 10.95 (*0-944705-03-0*); pap. 10.95 (*0-944705-01-4*) Pando Pubns.

Marsh, Carole. Six Puppy Feet: Bridge for Kids. (Illus.). (gr. k-12). 1994. 24.95 (*1-55609-157-5*); pap. 14.95 (*0-935326-13-8*) Gallopade Pub Group.

BRIDGER, JAMES, 1804-1881

Luce, Willard & Luce, Celia. Jim Bridger: Man of the Mountains. Parrish, George I., Jr., illus. 80p. (gr. 2-6). 1991. Repr. of 1966 ed. lib. bdg. 12.95 (*0-7910-1454-1*) Chelsea Hse.

BRIDGES

see also names of cities with the subdivision Bridges (e.g. New York City–Bridges) also names of bridges, e.g. Brooklyn Bridge

Ardley, Neil. Bridges. Stefoff, Rebecca, ed. LC 90-40247. (Illus.). 48p. (gr. 4-7). 1990. PLB 17.26 (*0-944483-74-7*) Garrett Ed Corp.

Carlisle, Norman & Carlisle, Madelyn. Bridges. LC 82-17874. (Illus.). 48p. (gr. k-4). 1983. PLB 12.85 (*0-516-01677-6*) Childrens.

Chambers. Tollbridge. 1995. 15.00 (*0-06-023598-5*); PLB 14.89 (*0-06-023599-3*) HarpC Child Bks.

Cooper, J. Bridges. 1991. 8.95s.p. (*0-86592-628-X*) Rourke Enter.

—Puentes (Bridges) (SPA.). 1991. 8.95s.p. (*0-86592-934-3*) Rourke Enter.

Dunn, Andrew. Bridges. LC 93-6832. 32p. (gr. 5-8). 1993. 13.95 (*1-56847-028-2*) Thomson Lrning.

Fitzpatrick, Julie. Towers & Bridges. (Illus.). 30p. (gr. 3-5). 1991. 13.95 (*0-237-60213-X*, Pub. by Evans Bros Ltd) Trafalgar.

Gaff, Jackie. Buildings, Bridges & Tunnels. Fisher, Michael, et al, illus. LC 91-212. 40p. (Orig.). (gr. 2-5). 1991. pap. 3.99 (*0-679-80865-5*) Random Bks Yng Read.

Kent, Zachary. The Story of the Brooklyn Bridge. LC 88-16220. (Illus.). 32p. (gr. 3-6). 1988. pap. 3.95 (*0-516-44739-4*) Childrens.

Mitgutsch, Ali. From Cement to Bridge. Mitgutsch, Ali, illus. LC 81-334. 24p. (ps-3). 1981. PLB 10.95 (*0-87614-148-3*) Carolrhoda Bks.

Pelta, Kathy. Bridging the Golden Gate. (Illus.). 96p. (gr. 4-8). 1987. PLB 15.95 (*0-8225-1707-8*); pap. 5.95 (*0-8225-9521-4*) Lerner Pubns.

Richardson, Joy. Bridges. LC 93-30058. (Illus.). 32p. (gr. 2-4). 1994. PLB 11.40 (*0-531-14289-2*) Watts.

Robbins, Ken. Bridges. (Illus.). 1991. 13.95 (*0-8037-0929-3*); PLB 13.89 (*0-8037-0930-7*) Dial Bks Young.

Sheppard, Jeff. I Know a Bridge. Sorensen, Henri, illus. LC 93-2656. 32p. (ps-k). 1993. RSBE 14.95 (*0-02-782457-8*, Macmillan Child Bk) Macmillan Child Grp.

Spangenburg, Ray & Moser, Diane. The Story of America's Bridges. (Illus.). 96p. (gr. 6-9). 1991. lib. bdg. 18.95x (*0-8160-2259-3*) Facts on File.

Wilson, Forrest. Bridges Go from Here to There. (Illus.). 80p. 1993. 14.95 (*0-89133-206-5*) Preservation Pr.

BRIDGES–FICTION

Lobel, Anita. Sven's Bridge. LC 91-29544. (Illus.). 32p. (ps-4). 1992. 14.00 (*0-688-11251-X*); PLB 13.93 (*0-688-11252-8*) Greenwillow.

McCully, Emily A. Crossing the New Bridge. McCully, Emily A., illus. LC 93-16047. 32p. (ps-3). 1994. PLB 15.95 (*0-399-22618-4*, Putnam) Putnam Pub Group.

Massi, Jeri. The Bridge. (Illus.). 122p. (Orig.). (gr. 2-4). 1986. pap. 4.95 (*0-89084-348-1*) Bob Jones Univ Pr.

Mead, Alice. Crossing the Starlight Bridge. 128p. (gr. 3-6). 1994. SBE 14.95 (*0-02-765950-X*, Bradbury Pr) Macmillan Child Grp.

Taylor, Mildred D. Mississippi Bridge. 53p. 1992. Braille. 4.24 (*1-56956-373-X*) W A T Braille.

BRIDGMAN, LAURA DEWEY, 1829-1889

Hunter, Edith F. Child of the Silent Night: The Story of Laura Bridgman. Holmes, Bea, illus. 128p. (gr. 2-5). 1963. 14.45 (*0-395-06835-5*) HM.

BRIGANDS

see Robbers and Outlaws

BRITAIN, BATTLE OF, 1940

Black, Wallace B. & Blashfield, Jean F. Battle of Britain. LC 90-46579. (Illus.). 48p. (gr. 5-6). 1991. text ed. 4.95 RSBE (*0-89686-553-3*, Crestwood Hse) Macmillan Child Grp.

BRITISH COLUMBIA

Bowers, Vivien. British Columbia. LC 94-25539. 1995. write for info. (*0-8225-2755-3*) Lerner Pubns.

LeVert, Suzanne. British Columbia. (Illus.). 64p. (gr. 3 up). 1991. lib. bdg. 16.95 (*0-7910-1033-3*) Chelsea Hse.

Nanton, Isabel. British Columbia. (Illus.). 144p. (gr. 4 up). 1993. PLB 20.55 (*0-516-06619-6*) Childrens.

BRITISH IN THE U. S.

Cornelius, James. The English Americans. (Illus.). 112p. (gr. 5 up). 1991. 17.95 (*0-87754-874-9*) Chelsea Hse.

BRITISH IN THE U. S.–FICTION

Weisberg, Valerie H. Three Jolly Stories Include: Three Jollys, Jollys Visit L. A., Jolly Gets Mugged: An ESL Adult-Child Reader. Kolino, Olga, illus. 76p. (Orig.). (gr. 4 up). 1985. pap. text ed. 6.95x (*0-9610912-4-X*) V H Pub.

BROADCASTING

see Radio Broadcasting; Television Broadcasting

BROCK, SIR ISAAC, 1769-1812

Berton, Pierre. The Death of Isaac Brock. (Illus.). 84p. (gr. 5 up). 1992. pap. 5.95 (*0-7710-1426-0*, Pub. by McClelland & Stewart CN) Firefly Bks Ltd.

BRONTE, CHARLOTTE, 1816-1855

Martin, C. Brontes. (Illus.). 112p. (gr. 7 up). 1989. lib. bdg. 19.94 (*0-86592-299-3*); 14.95s.p. (*0-685-58635-9*) Rourke Corp.

BRONTE, EMILY JANE, 1818-1848

Martin, C. Brontes. (Illus.). 112p. (gr. 7 up). 1989. lib. bdg. 19.94 (*0-86592-299-3*); 14.95s.p. (*0-685-58635-9*) Rourke Corp.

BROOKLYN

Greenberg, Keith E. Out of the Gang. (Illus.). 40p. (gr. 4-8). 1992. PLB 17.50 (*0-8225-2553-4*) Lerner Pubns.

BROOKLYN–FICTION

Blos, Joan W. Brooklyn Doesn't Rhyme. Birling, Paul, illus. LC 93-31589. 96p. (gr. 3-6). 1994. SBE 12.95 (*0-684-19694-8*, Scribners Young Read) Macmillan Child Grp.

Brown, Kay. Willy's Summer Dream. 132p. (gr. 7 up). 1989. 13.95 (*0-15-200645-1*, Gulliver Bks) HarBrace.

Gottlieb, Dale. My Stories by Hildy Calpurnia Rose. Gottlieb, Dale, illus. LC 90-46096. 40p. (ps-4). 1991. 14.00 (*0-679-81150-8*) Knopf Bks Yng Read.

Hest, Amy. How to Get Famous in Brooklyn. Sawaya, Linda D., illus. LC 93-35920. 1995. 14.00 (*0-02-743655-1*, Four Winds) Macmillan Child Grp.

McCloskey, Kevin. Mrs. Fitz's Flamingos. LC 90-2278. (Illus.). (ps-3). 1992. 14.00 (*0-688-10474-6*); PLB 13.93 (*0-688-10475-4*) Lothrop.

Orden, J. Hannah. In Real Life. LC 92-31359. 192p. (gr. 7 up). 1993. pap. 3.99 (*0-14-034039-4*) Puffin Bks.

Rush, Ken. The Seltzer Man. Rush, Ken, illus. LC 91-40905. 32p. (ps-3). 1993. RSBE 14.95 (*0-02-777917-3*, Macmillan Child Bk) Macmillan Child Grp.

Woodson, Jacqueline. Between Madison & Palmetto. LC 92-38783. (gr. 1-6). 1993. 13.95 (*0-385-30906-6*) Delacorte.

BROOKLYN BRIDGE–FICTION

Simpson, Louise M. The Quinns. LC 92-62014. 80p. Date not set. pap. 5.00 (*1-56002-230-2*, Univ Edtns) Aegina Pr.

BROOKLYN DODGERS (BASEBALL TEAM)

Cohen, Barbara. Thank You, Jackie Robinson. Cuffari, Richard, illus. LC 87-29341. (gr. 3-6). 1988. PLB 15.00 (*0-688-07909-1*) Lothrop.

Green, Carl R. & Sanford, William R. Jackie Robinson. LC 91-23921. (Illus.). 48p. (gr. 5). 1992. text ed. 11.95 RSBE (*0-89686-743-9*, Crestwood Hse) Macmillan Child Grp.

BROTHERS AND SISTERS

Bailey, Debbie. Brothers. Huszar, Susan, photos by. (Illus.). 14p. 1993. text ed. 4.95 (*1-55037-274-2*, Pub. by Annick CN) Firefly Bks Ltd.

—Hermanas - Sisters. Huszar, Susan, illus. (SPA.). 14p. 1993. 4.95 (*1-55037-307-2*, Pub. by Annick CN) Firefly Bks Ltd.

—Hermanos - Brothers. Huszar, Susan, illus. (SPA.). 14p. 1993. 4.95 (*1-55037-308-0*, Pub. by Annick CN) Firefly Bks Ltd.

—Sisters. Huszar, Susan, illus. 14p. 1993. text ed. 4.95 (*1-55037-275-0*, Pub. by Annick CN) Firefly Bks Ltd.

Bode, Janet. Truce: Ending the Sibling War. 144p. (gr. 8-12). 1991. PLB 13.90 (*0-531-10996-8*) Watts.

Cavanaugh, Kate. Pete's Lost. Kiner, K. C., illus. 24p. (Orig.). 1991. pap. 4.95 (*0-9622353-2-6*) KAC.

Coleman, William L. Getting Along with Brothers & Sisters. 1994. 5.99 (*0-8066-2669-0*) Augsburg Fortress.

Collman, Barbera J. Kid's Book to Welcome a New Baby: A Fun Activity Book of Things to Do & to Learn for a "Big Brother" or "Big Sister" (Illus.). 96p. (Orig.). 1992. pap. 8.95 (*0-943400-65-1*) Marlor Pr.

Crouthamel, Thomas G., Sr. It's OK. 2nd ed. Hasty, Patti, illus. LC 86-27694. 36p. (gr. 6 up). 1990. pap. 6.95 (*0-940701-18-9*) Keystone Pr.

Gordon, Michael. My Brother's a World-Class Pain: A Sibling's Guide to ADHD-Hyperactivity. Thomas, Sandra F., intro. by. Junco, Janet H., illus. 40p. (gr. 4 up). 1992. pap. 11.00 (*0-9627701-2-4*) GSI Pubns.

Hawkins-Walsh, Elizabeth. Katie's Premature Brother. Johnson, Joy, ed. Borum, Shari, illus. 24p. (Orig.). (ps). 1990. pap. 2.85 (*1-56123-005-7*) Centering Corp.

Landau, Elaine. Sibling Rivalry: Brothers & Sisters at Odds. (Illus.). 64p. (gr. 4-6). 1994. 13.90 (*1-56294-328-6*) Millbrook Pr.

Marshak, Samuel. The Month Brothers: A Slavic Tale. Whitney, Thomas P., tr. from RUS. Stanley, Diane, illus. LC 82-7927. 32p. (gr. k up). 1983. PLB 12.88 (*0-688-01510-7*) Morrow Jr Bks.

Monroe, Betsy. Sibling Scrapbook: An Activity Book for the New Big Brother & Big Sister. Monroe, Betsy, illus. 24p. (Orig.). (gr. k-4). 1989. pap. write for info. (*1-878083-00-7*) Color Me Well.

Nilsson, Lennart & Swanberg, Lena K. How Was I Born? James, Clare, tr. LC 94-11908. (Illus.). 1994. 18.95 (*0-385-31357-8*) Delacorte.

Peterson, Jeanne W. I Have a Sister, My Sister Is Deaf. Ray, Deborah K., illus. LC 76-24306. (gr. k-3). 1977. PLB 13.89 (*0-06-024702-9*) HarpC Child Bks.

Powell, Richard. How to Deal with Babies. Snow, Alan, illus. LC 91-3461. 24p. (gr. k-3). 1992. lib. bdg. 9.59 (*0-8167-2420-2*); pap. text ed. 2.95 (*0-8167-2421-0*) Troll Assocs.

Roos, Stephen. My Horrible Secret. Newsom, Carol, illus. 128p. (Orig.). (gr. 4-7). 1991. pap. 3.25 (*0-440-43956-6*, YB) Dell.

Rosenberg, Maxine B. Brothers & Sisters. Ancona, George, photos by. (Illus.). 32p. (gr. k-3). 1991. 14.45 (*0-395-51121-6*, Clarion Bks) HM.

Schlitt, RaRa S. Robert Nathaniel's Tree. Armstrong, Camilla B., illus. 36p. (gr. k up). 1993. 14.95 (*0-9630017-3-6*) Light-Bearer.

Senisi, Ellen. Brothers & Sisters. LC 92-42912. 1993. 12.95 (*0-590-46419-1*) Scholastic Inc.

Stein, Sara B. That New Baby. LC 73-15271. (Illus.). 48p. (gr. 1 up). 1974. 12.95 (*0-8027-6175-5*) Walker & Co.

Super, Gretchen. Sisters & Brothers. De Kiefte, Kees, illus. 48p. (gr. k-3). 1992. PLB 15.95 (*0-8050-2219-8*) TFC Bks NY.

BROTHERS AND SISTERS–FICTION

Adams, Edward B., ed. Two Brothers & Their Magic Gourds. Dong-Ho, Choi, illus. 32p. (gr. 3). 1981. 8.95 (*0-8048-1474-0*, Pub. by Seoul Intl Tourist SK) C E Tuttle.

Adler, C. S. Tuna Fish Thanksgiving. 160p. (gr. 5-9). 1992. 13.45 (*0-395-58829-4*, Clarion Bks) HM.

Adler, Katie & McBride, Rachael. For Sale: One Sister--Cheap! Venezia, Mike, illus. LC 86-11723. 32p. (ps-3). 1986. pap. 3.95 (*0-516-43476-4*) Childrens.

Alcott, Louisa May. Jack & Jill. (Illus.). 352p. (gr. 5 up). 1991. pap. 2.95 (*0-14-035128-0*, Puffin) Puffin Bks.

—Quatre Filles du Docteur March. Rozier, J. & Gaudriault, M., illus. (FRE.). (gr. 5-10). 1900. 10.95 (*2-07-033413-9*) Schoenhof.

Alexander, Martha. Good Night, Lily. Alexander, Martha, illus. LC 92-53005. 14p. (ps). 1993. 4.95 (*1-56402-164-5*) Candlewick Pr.

—Lily & Willy. Alexander, Martha, illus. LC 92-53004. 14p. (ps). 1993. 4.95 (*1-56402-163-7*) Candlewick Pr.

—Nobody Asked Me If I Wanted a Baby Sister. Alexander, Martha, illus. LC 78-153731. (ps-2). 1971. 10.95 (*0-8037-6401-4*); PLB 10.89 (*0-8037-6402-2*) Dial Bks Young.

—Where's Willy? Alexander, Martha, illus. LC 92-53006. 14p. (ps). 1993. 4.95 (*1-56402-161-0*) Candlewick Pr.

—Willy's Boot. Alexander, Martha, illus. LC 92-53007. 14p. (ps). 1993. 4.95 (*1-56402-162-9*) Candlewick Pr.

Aliki. Jack & Jake. Aliki, illus. LC 85-9911. 32p. (ps-1). 1986. 11.75 (*0-688-06099-4*); PLB 11.88 (*0-688-06100-1*) Greenwillow.

Allen, Pamela. I Wish I Had a Pirate Suit. LC 92-12295. (gr. 4 up). 1993. 3.99 (*0-14-050988-7*) Puffin Bks.

Alpert, Lou. Max & the Great Blueness. Alpert, Lou, illus. LC 92-23313. 32p. (ps-3). 1993. smythe sewn reinforced 13.95 (*1-879085-38-0*) Whsprng Coyote Pr.

Ames, Mildred. The Dancing Madness: A Novel. LC 80-65831. 144p. (gr. 7 up). 1980. 8.95 (*0-385-28113-7*) Delacorte.

story provides an opportunity for both adults & children to share their thoughts & feelings about being different or being treated unfairly, fighting, & then making up. The story has a delightful style that both children & adults will enjoy.
Publisher Provided Annotation.

Andres, Katherine. Humphrey & Ralph. Day, Brant, illus. LC 93-11478. (ps-1). 1994. 14.00 (*0-671-88129-9*, S&S BFYR) S&S Trade.
Applegate, Katherine. My Sister's Boyfriend. 1992. pap. 3.50 (*0-06-106717-2*, Harp PBks) HarpC.
Armstrong, Jennifer. That Terrible Baby. Meddaugh, Susan, illus. LC 93-14727. 32p. 1994. 14.00 (*0-688-11832-1*, Tambourine Bks); PLB 13.93 (*0-688-11833-X*, Tambourine Bks) Morrow.
Asch, Frank & Vagin, Vladimir. Dear Brother. 32p. 1992. 13.95 (*0-590-43107-2*, Scholastic Hardcover) Scholastic Inc.
Auch, Mary J. Monster Brother. LC 93-41746. (Illus.). 32p. (ps-3). 1994. reinforced bdg. 15.95 (*0-8234-1095-1*) Holiday.
—Pick of the Litter. LC 87-25205. 160p. (gr. 3-7). 1988. 14.95 (*0-8234-0692-X*) Holiday.
Aver, Kate. Joey's Way. Himler, Ronald, illus. LC 92-7830. 48p. (gr. 1-4). 1992. SBE 13.95 (*0-689-50552-3*, M K McElderry) Macmillan Child Grp.
Avery, Gillian. Maria Escapes. Snow, Scott, illus. LC 91-36730. 272p. (gr. 4-8). 1992. pap. 15.00 jacketed, 3-pc. bdg. (*0-671-77074-8*, S&S BFYR) S&S Trade.
Axelsen, Stephen & Axelsen, Jenny. Little Sisters. Axelsen, Stephen & Axelsen, Jenny, illus. LC 92-34261. 1993. 4.25 (*0-383-03637-2*) SRA Schl Grp.
Ayres, Becky H. Per & the Dala Horse. Gilbert, Yvonne, illus. LC 93-38596. 1995. write for info. (*0-385-32075-2*) Doubleday.
Baczewski, Paul C. Just for Kicks. LC 90-30528. 192p. (gr. 6 up). 1990. 13.95 (*0-397-32465-0*, Lipp Jr Bks); PLB 13.89 (*0-397-32466-9*, Lipp Jr Bks) HarpC Child Bks.
Baer, Judy. Never Too Late. 144p. (Orig.). 1993. pap. 3.99 (*1-55661-329-6*) Bethany Hse.
Baillie, Allan. Adrift. 128p. (gr. 3-7). 1992. 14.00 (*0-670-84474-8*) Viking Child Bks.
—Little Brother. 144p. (gr. 5 up). 1994. pap. 3.99 (*0-14-036862-0*) Puffin Bks.
Balderose, Nancy W. Once upon a Pony: A Mountain Christmas. LC 92-13814. 32p. 1992. 12.95 (*0-8192-7000-8*); pap. write for info. (*0-8192-7001-6*) Morehouse Pub.
Bambara, Toni C. Raymond's Run. (gr. 4-9). 1989. 13.95 (*0-88682-351-X*, 97222-098) Creative Ed.
Bancroft, Catherine & Gruenberg, Coale. That's Philomena. 1995. 15.00 (*0-02-708326-8*, Four Winds) Macmillan Child Grp.
Barrie, Barbara. Adam Zigzag. LC 93-8735. 1994. 14.95 (*0-385-31172-9*) Delacorte.
Bartone, Elisa. Peppe the Lamplighter. LC 92-1397. (Illus.). (ps-3). 1993. 14.00 (*0-688-10268-9*); PLB 13.93 (*0-688-10269-7*) Lothrop.
Bassett, Lisa. Koala Christmas. Bassett, Jeni, illus. LC 90-47628. 32p. (ps-2). 1991. 12.95 (*0-525-65065-2*, Cobblehill Bks) Dutton Child Bks.
Bechard, Margaret. My Sister, My Science Report. 96p. (gr. 3-7). 1990. pap. 11.95 (*0-670-83290-1*) Viking Child Bks.
—My Sister, My Science Report. 96p. (gr. 3-7). 1992. pap. 4.99 (*0-14-034408-X*, Puffin) Puffin Bks.
Benson, Rita. What Angela Needs. McClelland, Linda, illus. LC 92-34266. 1993. 14.00 (*0-383-03666-6*) SRA Schl Grp.
Berenstain, Stan & Berenstain, Jan. The Berenstain Bears Gotta Dance. Berenstain, Stan & Berenstain, Jan, illus. LC 92-32565. 112p. (Orig.). (gr. 2-6). 1993. PLB 7.99 (*0-679-94032-4*); pap. 3.50 (*0-679-84032-X*) Random Bks Yng Read.
—Los Osos Berenstain, No Se Permiten Ninas. LC 93-29904. (SPA.). 32p. (ps-3). 1994. pap. 2.50 (*0-679-85431-2*) Random Bks Yng Read.
Berenstain, Stan & Berenstain, Janice. The Berenstain Bears: No Girls Allowed. Berenstain, Stan & Berenstain, Janice, illus. LC 85-18246. 32p. (ps-1). 1986. pap. 2.50 (*0-394-87331-9*) Random Bks Yng Read.
Berg, Eric. Baby Makes Four. LC 93-8909. 1993. write for info. (*1-56071-327-5*) ETR Assocs.
Birdseye, Tom. Tucker. LC 89-46243. 120p. (gr. 3-7). 1990. 13.95 (*0-8234-0813-2*) Holiday.
—Waiting for Baby. Leedy, Loreen, illus. LC 90-29076. 32p. (ps-3). 1991. reinforced 14.95 (*0-8234-0892-2*) Holiday.
Blackman, Malorie. Girl Wonder & the Terrific Twins. Toft, Lis, illus. LC 92-27667. (gr. 2-5). 1993. 12.99 (*0-525-45065-3*, DCB) Dutton Child Bks.
Blume, Judy. Here's to You, Rachel Robinson. LC 93-9631. 208p. (gr. 5 up). 1993. 14.95 (*0-531-06801-3*); PLB 14.99 (*0-531-08651-8*) Orchard Bks Watts.
—Pain & the Great One. (ps-3). 1985. pap. 4.99 (*0-440-40967-5*) Dell.
—Superfudge. 176p. (gr. 2-6). 1981. pap. 3.99 (*0-440-48433-2*, YB) Dell.
—Superfudge. LC 80-10439. 176p. (gr. 3-6). 1980. 13.00 (*0-525-40522-4*, DCB) Dutton Child Bks.
—Superfudge. large type ed. 239p. (gr. 2-6). 1987. Repr. of 1980 ed. lib. bdg. 14.95 (*1-55736-014-6*, Crnrstn Bks) BDD LT Grp.
—Tales of a Fourth Grade Nothing. Doty, Roy, illus. LC 70-179050. 128p. (gr. 2-5). 1972. 11.95 (*0-525-40720-0*, DCB) Dutton Child Bks.
Bonsall, Crosby N. The Day I Had to Play with My Sister. Bonsall, Crosby N., illus. LC 72-76507. 32p. (ps-2). 1972. PLB 13.89 (*0-06-020576-8*) HarpC Child Bks.
Bosse, Malcolm. The Examination. LC 94-50955. (gr. 7 up). 1994. 17.00 (*0-374-32234-1*) FS&G.
Boyd, Lizi. Sam Is My Half Brother. (Illus.). 32p. (ps-2). 1990. pap. 11.95 (*0-670-83046-1*) Viking Child Bks.
—Sam Is My Half Brother. (Illus.). 32p. (ps-3). 1992. pap. 3.99 (*0-14-054190-X*, Puffin) Puffin Bks.
Bradman, Tony. Billy & the Baby. (ps-3). 1992. 11.95 (*0-8120-6328-7*); pap. 5.95 (*0-8120-1387-5*) Barron.
—The Bluebeards: Peril at the Pirate School. Murphy, Rowan B., illus. 64p. (gr. 2-5). 1990. pap. 2.95 (*0-8120-4502-5*) Barron.
Brandenberg, Franz. I Wish I Was Sick, Too! Aliki, illus. LC 75-46610. 32p. (gr. k-3). 1976. PLB 15.88 (*0-688-84047-7*) Greenwillow.
Brenner, Barbara. Rosa & Marco & the Three Wishes. Halsey, Megan, illus. LC 90-26855. 32p. (gr. 1-3). 1992. RSBE 12.95 (*0-02-712315-4*, Bradbury Pr) Macmillan Child Grp.
Brink, Carol R. Magical Melons. Davis, Marguerite, illus. LC 90-144. 208p. (gr. 3-7). 1990. pap. 3.95 (*0-689-71416-5*, Aladdin) Macmillan Child Grp.
Brisson, Pat. Your Best Friend, Kate. Brown, Rick, illus. LC 91-15245. 40p. (gr. 1-7). 1992. pap. 4.50 (*0-689-71545-5*, Aladdin) Macmillan Child Grp.
Brown, Laurene K. Rex & Lilly Family Time. Brown, Marc T., illus. LC 93-24162. 1995. lib. bdg. 12.95 (*0-316-11385-9*) Little.
Brown, Marc T. D. W. Just Big Enough. LC 92-19947. 1993. 11.95 (*0-316-11305-0*, Joy St Bks) Little.
—D. W. Rides Again! LC 93-7192. 1993. 12.95 (*0-316-11356-5*) Little.
Browne, Anthony. The Tunnel. Browne, Anthony, illus. (gr. 4-8). 1990. 14.00 (*0-394-84582-X*); lib. bdg. 12.99 (*0-394-94582-4*) Random Bks Yng Read.
Buckley, Helen. Take Care of Things, Edward Said. Coville, Katherine, illus. LC 88-1578. 32p. (ps up). 1991. 13.95 (*0-688-07731-5*); PLB 13.88 (*0-688-07732-3*) Lothrop.
Bulla, Clyde R. Keep Running, Allen! Ichikawa, Satomi, illus. LC 77-23311. (gr. k-2). 1978. PLB 14.89 (*0-690-01375-2*, Crowell Jr Bks) HarpC Child Bks.
Burgess, Barbara H. Oren Bell. 1991. 15.00 (*0-385-30325-4*) Delacorte.
Byars, Betsy C. Bingo Brown, Gypsy Lover. 160p. (gr. 3 up). 1990. 12.95 (*0-670-83322-3*) Viking Child Bks.
—Bingo Brown, Gypsy Lover. 128p. (gr. 3-7). 1992. pap. 3.99 (*0-14-034518-3*) Puffin Bks.
Callen, Larry. Contrary Imaginations. LC 90-33181. (Illus.). 128p. (gr. 6 up). 1991. 12.95 (*0-688-09961-0*) Greenwillow.
Calvert, Patricia. Writing to Richie. LC 94-14458. (gr. 4-6). 1994. 14.95 (*0-684-19764-2*, Scribner) Macmillan.
Cameron, Ann. The Stories Huey Tells. LC 94-6221. (gr. 2 up). 1995. write for info. (*0-679-86732-5*); PLB write for info. (*0-679-96732-X*) Knopf Bks Yng Read.
Cannon, A. E. Shadow Brothers. 1992. pap. 3.50 (*0-440-21167-0*) Dell.
Caple, Kathy. The Coolest Place in Town. Caple, Kathy, illus. 32p. (gr. k-3). 1990. 13.45 (*0-395-51523-8*) HM.
—The Wimp. LC 94-7121. 1994. 14.95 (*0-395-63115-7*) HM.
Caraher, Kim. There's a Bat on the Balcony. Sofilas, Mark, illus. LC 92-34260. 1993. 4.25 (*0-383-03660-7*) SRA Schl Grp.
Carlson, Natalie S. A Brother for the Orphelines. (gr. k-6). 1969. pap. 2.75 (*0-440-40827-X*, YB) Dell.
Carlstrom, Nancy W. Wishing at Dawn in Summer. Allison, Diane W., illus. (ps-2). 1993. 14.95 (*0-316-12854-6*) Little.
Caseley, Judith. Harry & Arney. LC 93-20787. 1994. write for info. (*0-688-12140-3*) Greenwillow.
Chall, Marsha W. Mattie. LC 91-3042. (ps-3). 1992. 11.00 (*0-688-09730-8*) Lothrop.
Chase, Alyssa. Jomo & Mata. Chase, Andra, illus. LC 93-25206. 32p. (gr. 1-4). 1993. 16.95 (*1-55942-051-0*, 7656); video, tchr's. guide & storybook 79.95 (*1-55942-054-5*, 9375) Marshfilm.
Church, Kristine. My Brother John. Niland, Kilmeny, illus. LC 90-25868. 32p. (ps-3). 1991. 12.95 (*0-688-10800-8*, Tambourine Bks); PLB 12.88 (*0-688-10801-6*, Tambourine Bks) Morrow.
Clark, Sue A. The Rainbow Tree. Clark, Gary B., ed. (Illus.). 18p. (gr. 4-7). 1990. write for info. Point View Pr.
Clifford, Eth. Will Somebody Please Marry My Sister? (gr. 4-7). 1993. pap. 2.95 (*0-590-46624-0*) Scholastic Inc.
Collins, Pat L. Don't Tease the Guppies. Hafner, Marylin, illus. LC 92-25336. 32p. (ps-1). 1994. 14.95 (*0-399-22530-7*) Putnam Pub Group.
Collis, Annabel. You Can't Catch Me! LC 92-54486. 1993. 13.95 (*0-316-15237-4*) Little.
Conford, Ellen. Royal Pain. (gr. 4-7). 1990. pap. 2.95 (*0-590-43821-2*) Scholastic Inc.
Conlon-McKenna, Marita. Under the Hawthorn Tree: Children of the Famine. LC 92-18955. 160p. (gr. 5 up). 1992. pap. 3.99 (*0-14-036031-X*) Puffin Bks.
Cook, Jean T. Hugs for Our New Baby. (Illus.). (ps-2). 1987. 5.99 (*0-570-04165-1*, 56-1622) Concordia.
Cooney, Caroline B. Whatever Happened to Janie? LC 92-32334. 208p. 1993. 15.95 (*0-385-31035-8*) Delacorte.
Cooper, Susan. Danny & the Kings. Smith, Joseph A., illus. LC 92-22744. 32p. (ps-3). 1993. SBE 14.95 (*0-689-50577-9*, M K McElderry) Macmillan Child Grp.
Corcoran, Barbara. The Hideaway. LC 86-28849. 128p. (gr. 5-9). 1987. SBE 13.95 (*0-689-31353-5*, Atheneum Child Bk) Macmillan Child Grp.
Coxe, Molly. Whose Footprints? Coxe, Molly, illus. LC 89-70850. 40p. (ps-1). 1990. (Crowell Jr Bks); (Crowell Jr Bks) HarpC Child Bks.
Craig, Helen. Susie & Alfred in a Busy Day in Town. Craig, Helen, illus. LC 93-21181. 32p. (Orig.). 1994. pap. 4.99 (*1-56402-380-X*) Candlewick Pr.
Cretan, Gladys. Joey's Head. Sims, Blanche, illus. LC 90-41592. 48p. (gr. 2-4). 1991. pap. 13.95 jacketed (*0-671-73201-3*, S&S BFYR) S&S Trade.
Cuckoo Sister. 1986. 14.95 (*0-440-50231-4*) Dell.
Cupo, Hortense. No Way Out but Through. LC 93-29519. Date not set. 4.95 (*0-8198-5130-2*) St Paul Bks.
Cutler, Jane. No Dogs Allowed. (gr. 4-7). 1992. 14.00 (*0-374-35526-6*) FS&G.
Dahl, Tessa. The Same but Different. Robins, Arthur, illus. 32p. (ps-3). 1993. pap. 3.99 (*0-14-054823-8*) Puffin Bks.
Davis, Deborah. My Brother Has AIDS. (gr. 4-8). 1994. 14.95 (*0-689-31922-3*, Atheneum) Macmillan.
Davis, Jenny. Anchovy Breath to Zoo Food: One Hundred Seventy-Five Names I Call My Brother When I'm Mad. Taylor, B. K., illus. 80p. (Orig.). 1994. pap. 3.50 (*0-380-77135-7*, Camelot) Avon.
Day, Lara. My Brother & I. 15p. (ps-k). 1992. pap. text ed. 23.00 big bk. (*1-56843-004-3*); pap. text ed. 4.50 (*1-56843-054-X*) BGR Pub.
Deaver, Julie R. First Wedding, Once Removed. LC 90-4184. 224p. (gr. 5-9). 1990. PLB 13.89 (*0-06-021427-9*) HarpC Child Bks.
Degen, Bruce. Teddy Bear Towers. Degen, Bruce, illus. LC 90-31937. 32p. (ps-1). 1991. HarpC Child Bks.
Delton, Judy. Angel in Charge. Morrill, Leslie, illus. LC 84-27862. 152p. (gr. 2-5). 1985. 13.45 (*0-395-37488-X*) HM.
—Angel's Mother's Baby. (gr. 4-7). 1992. pap. 3.25 (*0-440-40586-6*) Dell.
De Saint Mars, Dominique. Lily Fights with Max. LC 92-18000. (gr. 2-4). 1992. PLB 8.95 (*0-89565-980-8*) Childs World.
—Max Doesn't Like to Read. LC 92-17998. (gr. 2-4). 1992. PLB 8.95 (*0-89565-979-4*) Childs World.
—Max Is Shy. LC 92-17996. (gr. 2-4). 1992. 8.95 (*0-685-60114-5*) Childs World.
Desaix, Deborah D. In the Back Seat. (ps-3). 1993. 14.00 (*0-374-33639-3*) FS&G.
Devlin, Wende & Devlin, Harry. A New Baby in Cranberryport. LC 93-45819. (ps-1). 1994. pap. 2.95 (*0-689-71780-6*, Aladdin) Macmillan Child Grp.
Dodds, Bill. My Sister Annie. 96p. (gr. 4-7). 1993. 14.95 (*1-56397-114-3*) Boyds Mills Pr.
Dorris, Michael. Morning Girl. LC 92-52989. 80p. (gr. 3 up). 1994. 3.50 (*1-56282-661-1*) Hyprn Ppbks.
Drescher, Joan. The Birth-Order Blues. Drescher, Joan, illus. 32p. (ps-3). 1993. RB 13.99 (*0-670-83621-4*) Viking Child Bks.
Drew, David. Something Silver, Something Blue. Roennfeldt, Robert, illus. LC 92-34256. 1993. 4.25 (*0-383-03654-2*) SRA Schl Grp.
Dunbar, Fiona. My Secret Brother. (Illus.). 32p. (ps-1). 1994. 17.95 (*0-09-176402-5*, Pub. by Hutchinson UK) Trafalgar.
Duncan, Alice F. Willie Jerome. LC 94-10444. 1995. 15.00 (*0-02-733208-X*) Macmillan Child Grp.
Edelman, Elaine. I Love My Baby Sister: Most of the Time. Watson, Wendy, illus. LC 85-574. 24p. (ps-3). 1985. pap. 3.95 (*0-14-050547-4*, Puffin) Puffin Bks.
Elwood, Roger. The Frankenstein Project. (gr. 3-7). 1991. pap. 4.99 (*0-8499-3303-X*) Word Inc.
Ephron, Delia. The Girl Who Changed the World. LC 92-42444. 160p. (gr. 3-6). 1993. 13.95 (*0-395-66139-0*) Ticknor & Flds Bks Yng Read.
Erickson, Gina K. Bat's Surprise. (ps-3). 1993. pap. 3.95 (*0-8120-1735-8*) Barron.
Evans, David. The Famous Hooper Brothers. Labby, Sherman, illus. 101p. (Orig.). 1988. pap. 15.95 (*0-929422-00-7*) Jonah Pr.
Falwell, Cathryn. Nicky & Alex. Falwell, Cathryn, illus. 32p. (ps). 1992. 5.95 (*0-395-56915-X*, Clarion Bks) HM.
Feldman, Eve B. That Cat! Ransome, James E., illus. LC 94-280. 1994. write for info. (*0-688-13310-X*, Tambourine Bks) Morrow.
Ferguson, Alane. The Practical Joke War. LC 90-45578. 144p. (gr. 3-7). 1991. SBE 13.95 (*0-02-734526-2*, Bradbury Pr) Macmillan Child Grp.
Fine, Anne. The Book of the Banshee. LC 91-23715. (gr. 7 up). 1992. 13.95 (*0-316-28315-0*) Little.
Fitzgerald, John. The Baby Brother. Power, Margaret, illus. LC 93-2803. 1994. write for info. (*0-383-03677-1*) SRA Schl Grp.
Fleming, Leanne, illus. The Quiet World. LC 93-111. 1994. write for info. (*0-383-03671-2*) SRA Schl Grp.
Flieger, Pat. The Fog's Net. Gamper, Ruth, illus. LC 93-31512. 1994. 14.95 (*0-395-68194-4*) HM.

Flynn, Mary J. If a Seahorse Wore a Saddle. Flynn, Mary J., illus. 48p. (Orig.). (ps-1). 1991. pap. 10.95 (*0-9623072-3-8*) S Ink WA.

Fox, Paula. Lily & the Lost Boy. LC 87-5778. 160p. (gr. 6-8). 1987. 12.95 (*0-531-05720-8*); PLB 12.99 (*0-531-08320-9*) Orchard Bks Watts.

—Lily & the Lost Boys. large type, unabr. ed. 230p. (gr. 5-7). 1989. lib. bdg. 13.95x (*0-8161-4725-6*) G K Hall.

—Western Wind. LC 93-9629. 208p. (gr. 5 up). 1993. 14.95 (*0-531-06802-1*); PLB 14.99 (*0-531-08652-6*) Orchard Bks Watts.

Fran, Renee & Freshman, Floris, illus. What Happened to Mommy? 32p. (Orig.). (ps-6). 1994. pap. 5.95 (*0-9640250-0-0*) Eastman NY.

Franklin, Jonathan. Don't Wake the Baby. (Illus.). 32p. (ps-1). 1991. bds. 13.95 jacketed (*0-374-31826-3*) FS&G.

Friend, Catherine. Sawfin Stickleback. (Illus.). 32p. (ps-3). 1994. 13.95 (*1-56282-473-2*); PLB 13.89 (*1-56282-474-0*) Hyprn Child.

Fromm, Pete. Monkey Tag. LC 93-34593. (gr. 4-7). 1994. 14.95 (*0-590-46525-2*) Scholastic Inc.

Galbraith, Kathryn O. Roommates & Rachel. Graham, Mark, illus. LC 90-34768. 48p. (gr. 1-4). 1991. SBE 12.95 (*0-689-50520-5*, M K McElderry) Macmillan Child Grp.

Garland, Sarah. Billy & Belle. Garland, Sarah, illus. 32p. (ps-3). 1992. 13.00 (*0-670-84396-2*) Viking Child Bks.

Gehret, Jeanne. I'm Somebody Too. 159p. (gr. 4-7). 1992. text ed. 16.00 (*0-9625136-7-9*); pap. 12.00 (*0-9625136-6-0*) Verbal Images Pr. "This juvenile fiction...held my interest throughout. It is the story of sibling rivalry exacerbated by the younger sib Ben's condition known as attention deficit disorder or ADD. His older sister Emily represses her own needs & resentments as a people-pleaser & tries to keep conflict to a minimum...This is a fictionalized account of their struggles as a family, the growing crisis & the final resolution as the family seeks treatment...The therapy sessions are very well done by someone who knows what therapy is all about... engaging fiction...invaluable to the general public...a valuable addition to bibliotherapy programs involving professionals in schools & public libraries. Many parents as well as children will benefit from reading the book."--Small Press. "In addition to a good story, Gehret offers a few pages on how siblings can deal with frustration."--School Library Journal. A companion to Jeanne Gehret's bestselling picture book EAGLE EYES: A CHILD'S GUIDE TO PAYING ATTENTION (1991), which introduced the same family through the tale of scatterbrained Ben. I'M SOMEBODY TOO. 159 pages. Ages 9 to 12. Paperback $12.00 (ISBN 0-9625136-6-0); Hardcover $16.00 (ISBN 0-9625136-7-9). Verbal Images Press, 19 Fox Hill Dr., Fairport, NY 14450. *Publisher Provided Annotation.*

Geller, Mark. Who's on First? LC 91-46184. 64p. (gr. 6 up). 1992. 14.00 (*0-06-021084-2*); PLB 13.89 (*0-06-021085-0*) HarpC Child Bks.

George, Jean C. On the Far Side of the Mountain. LC 89-25988. 176p. (gr. 3-7). 1990. 15.00 (*0-525-44563-3*, DCB) Dutton Child Bks.

Gerstein, Mordicai. The Gigantic Baby. Levin, Arnie, illus. LC 90-35537. 32p. (gr. k-3). 1991. PLB 14.89 (*0-06-022106-2*) HarpC Child Bks.

Getz, David. Thin Air. LC 90-34137. 128p. (gr. 6 up). 1990. 14.95 (*0-8050-1379-2*, Bks Young Read) H Holt & Co.

Gillespie, Bonita. Peggy's Problem. Cover, Marilyn, illus. 35p. (gr. 3-8). 1987. 6.95 (*1-55523-058-X*) Winston-Derek.

Gilson, Jamie. You Cheat! Chambliss, Maxie, illus. LC 91-13886. 64p. (gr. 1-4). 1992. SBE 13.95 (*0-02-735993-X*, Bradbury Pr) Macmillan Child Grp.

Givens, Terryl. Dragon Scales & Willow Leaves. Portwood, Andrew, illus. LC 93-665. Date not set. write for info. (*0-399-22619-2*, Putnam) Putnam Pub Group.

Glaser, Linda. Keep Your Socks on, Albert! Ward, Sally G., illus. LC 91-19387. 48p. (ps-2). 1992. 11.00 (*0-525-44838-1*, DCB) Dutton Child Bks.

Gliori, Debi. My Little Brother. Gliori, Debi, illus. LC 91-58748. 32p. (ps up). 1992. 13.95 (*1-56402-079-7*) Candlewick Pr.

Gorman, Carol. Brian's Footsteps. Koehler, Ed, illus. LC 93-38322. 96p. (Orig.). (gr. 4-7). 1994. pap. 3.99 (*0-570-04629-7*) Concordia.

Grahame, Kenneth. Dream Days. Parrish, Maxfield, illus. LC 92-44589. 1993. 18.95 (*0-89815-546-0*) Ten Speed Pr.

—The Golden Age. Parrish, Maxfield, illus. LC 92-44992. 1993. 18.95 (*0-89815-545-2*) Ten Speed Pr.

Grant, Eva. Will I Ever Be Older? Lexa, Susan, illus. Hollingsworth, Charles E., intro. by. LC 80-24782. (Illus.). (gr. k-6). 1981. PLB 19.97 (*0-8172-1363-5*) Raintree Steck-V.

Greenfield, Eloise. She Come Bringing Me That Little Baby Girl. Steptoe, John L., illus. LC 74-8104. 32p. (ps-3). 1993. pap. 5.95 (*0-06-443296-3*, Trophy) HarpC Child Bks.

—Sister. Barnett, Moneta, illus. LC 73-22182. 96p. (gr. 5-8). 1987. pap. 3.95 (*0-06-440199-5*, Trophy) HarpC Child Bks.

Grifalconi, Ann. Not Home: Somehow, Somewhere, There Must Be Love: A Novel. LC 94-16708. 1995. 14.95 (*0-316-32905-3*) Little.

Grimm, Jacob & Grimm, Wilhelm K. Hansel & Gretel. Jeffers, Susan, illus. LC 80-15079. 32p. (gr. k up). 1986. pap. 4.95 (*0-8037-0318-X*) Dial Bks Young.

Haarhoff, Dorian. Desert December. Vermeulen, Leon, illus. 32p. (ps-3). 1992. 13.95 (*0-395-61300-0*, Clarion Bks) HM.

Hager, Betty. Marcie & the Shrimp Boat Adventure. LC 93-44488. 112p. (gr. 3-7). 1994. pap. 4.99 (*0-310-38421-4*) Zondervan.

Hallinan, P. K. We're Very Good Friends, My Brother & I. Hallinan, P. K., illus. 24p. (ps-2). 1990. 4.95 (*0-8249-8469-2*, Ideals Child) Hambleton-Hill.

Hamilton, Gail. Family Rivalry. (gr. 4-6). 1993. pap. 3.99 (*0-553-48042-1*) Bantam.

Hamilton, Virginia. Justice & Her Brothers. (gr. 4-7). 1992. 17.25 (*0-8446-6577-0*) Peter Smith.

Hanrahan, Brendan. My Sisters Love My Clothes. (Illus.). 32p. (gr. 1-4). 1992. 12.95 (*0-9630181-0-8*) Perry Heights.

Harvey, Jayne. Great-Uncle Dracula & the Dirty Rat. Carter, Abby, illus. LC 92-39018. 64p. (gr. 2-4). 1993. PLB 6.99 (*0-679-93457-X*); pap. 2.50 (*0-679-83457-5*) Random Bks Yng Read.

Hassett, John & Hassett, Ann. We Got My Brother at the Zoo. LC 92-1681. 1993. 14.95 (*0-395-62429-0*) HM.

Havill, Juanita. Jennifer, Too. LC 93-6319. (Illus.). 56p. (gr. 2-5). 1994. 11.95 (*1-56282-618-2*); PLB 11.89 (*1-56282-619-0*) Hyprn Child.

Herrick, Amy. Kimbo's Marble. Gazsi, Edward S., illus. LC 91-18988. 48p. (gr. 1-5). 1993. 16.00 (*0-06-020373-0*); PLB 15.89 (*0-06-020374-9*) HarpC Child Bks.

Hersom, Kathleen. The Half Child. LC 90-24079. 176p. (gr. 5-9). 1991. pap. 13.95 jacketed, 3-pc. bdg. (*0-671-74225-6*, S&S BFYR) S&S Trade.

Heymans, Annemie & Heymans, Margriet. The Princess in the Kitchen Garden. (Illus.). 48p. (ps-3). 1993. bds. 16.00 (*0-374-36122-3*) FS&G.

Hill, Kirkpatrick. Toughboy & Sister. LC 90-31297. 128p. (gr. 3-7). 1990. SBE 13.95 (*0-689-50506-X*, M K McElderry) Macmillan Child Grp.

—Toughboy & Sister. 128p. (gr. 3-7). 1992. pap. 3.99 (*0-14-034866-2*) Puffin Bks.

Hill, Sue K. Night Travelers. Lopez, Angelo, illus. LC 93-93872. 64p. (gr. 4 up). 1994. pap. 9.00 (*1-56002-335-X*, Univ Edtns) Aegina Pr.

Hines, Anna G. They Really Like Me! LC 87-24211. (Illus.). 24p. (ps up). 1989. 11.95 (*0-688-07733-1*); PLB 11.88 (*0-688-07734-X*) Greenwillow.

Hinton, Susie E. Tex. 192p. (gr. k up). 1989. pap. 3.99 (*0-440-97850-5*, LFL) Dell.

Hoban, Lillian. Arthur's Prize Reader. Hoban, Lillian, illus. LC 77-25637. 64p. (ps-3). 1978. PLB 13.89 (*0-06-022380-4*) HarpC Child Bks.

Holabird, Katharine. Angelina's Baby Sister. (ps-2). 1991. 14.00 (*0-517-58600-2*, Clarkson Potter) Crown Bks Yng Read.

Hooks, William H. Mr. Baseball. (ps-3). 1991. 9.99 (*0-553-07315-X*); pap. 3.50 (*0-553-35303-9*) Bantam.

—Mr. Dinosaur. Meisel, Paul, illus. LC 92-33476. 1994. (Little Rooster); pap. 3.99 (*0-553-37234-3*, Little Rooster) Bantam.

Hopkins, Lee B. Mama & Her Boys. Marchesi, Stephen, illus. LC 91-23399. 176p. (gr. 5 up). 1993. pap. 13.00 JRT (*0-671-74986-2*, S&S BFYR) S&S Trade.

Horowitz, Ruth. Mommy's Lap. LC 90-32626. (ps-3). 1993. 13.00 (*0-688-07235-6*); PLB 12.93 (*0-688-07236-4*) Lothrop.

Howard, Elizabeth F. Mac & Marie & the Train Toss Surprise. Carter, Gail G., illus. LC 92-17918. 32p. (ps-2). 1993. RSBE 14.95 (*0-02-744640-9*, Four Winds) Macmillan Child Grp.

Howard, Ellen. The Cellar. Mulvihill, Patricia, illus. LC 90-23190. 64p. (gr. 2-4). 1992. SBE 12.95 (*0-689-31724-7*, Atheneum Child Bk) Macmillan Child Grp.

Howard, Megan. My Sister Stole My Boyfriend. LC 93-85683. 144p. (Orig.). (gr. 3-9). 1994. pap. 3.99 (*0-679-85703-6*) Random Bks Yng Read.

Howe, James. Pinky & Rex Get Married. Sweet, Melissa, illus. LC 89-406. 48p. (gr. k-3). 1990. SBE 11.95 (*0-685-58512-3*, Atheneum Child Bk); 12.95 (*0-689-31453-1*, Atheneum Childrens Bks) Macmillan Child Grp.

—There's a Dragon in My Sleeping Bag. Rose, David S., illus. LC 93-26572. 1994. 14.95 (*0-689-31873-1*, Atheneum Child Bk) Macmillan Child Grp.

Hughes, Shirley. The Big Alfie & Annie Rose Storybook. Hughes, S., illus. LC 88-11149. 64p. (ps-1). 1989. 15.00 (*0-688-07672-6*); PLB 14.88 (*0-688-07673-4*) Lothrop.

Hurwitz, Johanna. Aldo Ice Cream. Wallner, John, illus. LC 80-24371. 128p. (gr. 4-6). 1981. 13.95 (*0-688-00375-3*); PLB 13.88 (*0-688-00374-5*, Morrow Jr Bks) Morrow Jr Bks.

—New Neighbors for Nora. reissued ed. Hoban, Lillian, illus. LC 90-47882. 80p. (ps). 1991. Repr. of 1979 ed. 12.95 (*0-688-09947-5*); PLB 12.88 (*0-688-09948-3*, Morrow Jr Bks) Morrow Jr Bks.

—Nora & Mrs. Mind-Your-Own Business. reissued ed. Hoban, Lillian, illus. LC 90-47997. 80p. (ps up). 1991. Repr. of 1977 ed. 12.95 (*0-688-09945-9*); PLB 12.88 (*0-688-09946-7*, Morrow Jr Bks) Morrow Jr Bks.

—Russell & Elisa. Hoban, Lillian, illus. LC 88-37578. 96p. (gr. k up). 1989. 11.95 (*0-688-08792-2*); lib. bdg. 11.88 (*0-688-08793-0*, Morrow Jr Bks) Morrow Jr Bks.

—Russell & Elisa. (gr. 4 up). 1990. pap. 3.99 (*0-14-034406-3*, Puffin) Puffin Bks.

—School's Out. Hamanaka, Sheila, illus. LC 90-13446. 128p. (gr. 2 up). 1991. 12.95 (*0-688-09938-6*) Morrow Jr Bks.

—Superduper Teddy. Hoban, Lillian, illus. 80p. (gr. 2-5). 1991. pap. 3.95 (*0-14-034593-0*, Puffin) Puffin Bks.

Hutchins, Hazel. Katie's Babbling Brother. Ohi, Ruth, illus. 24p. (gr. k-3). 1991. PLB 14.95 (*1-55037-153-3*, Pub. by Annick CN); pap. 4.95 (*1-55037-156-8*, Pub. by Annick CN) Firefly Bks Ltd.

Hutchins, Pat. Silly Billy! LC 91-32561. (Illus.). 32p. (ps-6). 1992. 14.00 (*0-688-10817-2*); PLB 13.93 (*0-688-10818-0*) Greenwillow.

—Tidy Titch. LC 90-38483. (Illus.). 32p. (ps up). 1991. 15.00 (*0-688-09963-7*); PLB 14.93 (*0-688-09964-5*) Greenwillow.

—Titch. Hutchins, Pat, illus. LC 92-1642. 40p. (ps-1). 1993. pap. 4.95 (*0-689-71688-5*, Aladdin) Macmillan Child Grp.

Inkiow, Dimiter. Me & Clara & Casimir the Cat. Reiner, Walter & Reiner, Traudl, illus. LC 78-31316. (gr. 1-4). 1979. 2.95 (*0-394-84124-7*) Pantheon.

Ireland, Shep. Wesley & Wendell: At Home. Ireland, Shep, illus. 40p. (gr. 1). 1991. lib. bdg. 4.75 (*0-8378-0330-6*) Gibson.

—Wesley & Wendell: Happy Birthday. Ireland, Shep, illus. 40p. (gr. 1). 1991. lib. bdg. 4.75 (*0-8378-0333-0*) Gibson.

—Wesley & Wendell: In the Garden. Ireland, Shep, illus. 40p. (gr. 1). 1991. lib. bdg. 4.75 (*0-8378-0331-4*) Gibson.

—Wesley & Wendell: Vacation. Ireland, Shep, illus. 40p. (gr. 1). 1991. lib. bdg. 4.75 (*0-8378-0332-2*) Gibson.

Jewell, Nancy. Two Silly Trolls. Thiesing, Lisa, illus. LC 90-4387. 64p. (gr. k-3). 1992. 14.00 (*0-06-022829-6*); PLB 13.89 (*0-06-022830-X*) HarpC Child Bks.

Johnson, Angela. Do Like Kyla. Ransome, James E., illus. LC 89-16229. 32p. (ps-2). 1990. 14.95 (*0-531-05852-2*); PLB 14.99 (*0-531-08452-3*) Orchard Bks Watts.

—One of Three. Soman, David, illus. LC 90-29316. 32p. (ps-1). 1991. 14.95 (*0-531-05955-3*); RLB 14.99 (*0-531-08555-4*) Orchard Bks Watts.

Johnson, Terry C. Slither McCreep & His Brother, Joe. Chess, Victoria, illus. 1992. 13.95 (*0-15-276100-4*, HB Juv Bks) HarBrace.

Johnston, Julie. Hero of Lesser Causes. LC 92-37268. 1993. 15.95 (*0-316-46988-2*, Joy St Bks) Little.

—Hero of Lesser Causes. 192p. (gr. 5 up). 1994. pap. 3.99 (*0-14-036998-8*) Puffin Bks.

Just Me & My Little Brother. (Illus.). (ps-3). 1991. write for info. (*0-307-12628-5*, Golden Pr) Western Pub.

Kalman, Maira. Hey Willy, See the Pyramids. (ps-3). 1990. pap. 4.95 (*0-14-050840-6*, Puffin) Puffin Bks.

Katz, Illana & Ritvo, Edward. Joey & Sam: A Heartwarming Storybook about Autism, a Family, & a Brother's Love. Borowitz, Franz, illus. LC 92-38812. 40p. (gr. k-6). 1993. smythe sewn 16.95 (*1-882388-00-3*) Real Life Strybks.

Keats, Ezra J. Peter's Chair Big Book. Keats, Ezra J., illus. LC 67-4816. 32p. (ps-3). 1993. pap. 19.95 (*0-06-443325-0*, Trophy) HarpC Child Bks.

Kehret, Peg. Danger at the Fair. LC 94-16873. 1995. write for info. (*0-525-65182-9*, Cobblehill Bks) Dutton Child Bks.

Kelleher, Victor. Del-Del. (gr. 7-10). 1992. 17.95 (*0-8027-8154-3*) Walker & Co.

Keller, Holly. Geraldine's Baby Brother. LC 93-34491. (ps up). 1994. 15.00 (*0-688-12005-9*); PLB 14.93 (*0-688-12006-7*) Greenwillow.

—What Alvin Wanted. LC 88-34917. (Illus.). 32p. (ps up). 1990. 12.95 (*0-688-08933-X*); lib. bdg. 12.88 (*0-688-08934-8*) Greenwillow.

Kellogg, Steven. Much Bigger Than Martin. Kellogg, Steven, illus. LC 75-2799. 32p. (ps-3). 1976. 12.95 (*0-8037-5809-X*); PLB 11.89 (*0-8037-5810-3*) Dial Bks Young.

Kerr, M. E. Linger. LC 92-30988. 224p. (gr. 7 up). 1993. 15.00 (*0-06-022879-2*); PLB 14.89 (*0-06-022882-2*) HarpC Child Bks.
—Night Kites. LC 85-45386. 192p. (gr. 7 up). 1986. PLB 14.89 (*0-06-023254-4*) HarpC Child Bks.
Komaiko, Leah. Where Can Daniel Be? Cazet, Denys, illus. LC 93-49393. 32p. (ps-1). 1994. 15.95 (*0-531-06850-1*); PLB 15.99 (*0-531-08700-X*) Orchard Bks Watts.
Konigsburg, E. L. From the Mixed-Up Files of Mrs. Basil E. Frankweiler. LC 86-25903. (Illus.). 176p. (gr. 4-7). 1987. pap. 3.95 (*0-689-71181-6*, Aladdin) Macmillan Child Grp.
Kordon, Klaus. Brothers Like Friends. Crawford, Elizabeth D., tr. from GER. 192p. (gr. 5 up). 1992. 14.95 (*0-399-22137-9*, Philomel Bks) Putnam Pub Group.
Kramer, S. A. At the Ball Game. La Padula, Thomas, illus. LC 93-31845. 32p. (Orig.). (ps-3). 1994. pap. 2.50 (*0-679-85291-3*) Random Bks Yng Read.
Krasilovsky, Phyllis. The Very Little Boy. (Illus.). (ps). 1992. pap. 4.95 (*0-590-44762-9*, 030, Cartwheel) Scholastic Inc.
—The Very Little Girl. (Illus.). (ps). 1992. pap. 4.95 (*0-590-44761-0*, 029, Cartwheel) Scholastic Inc.
Kroll, Steven. The Squirrels' Thanksgiving. Bassett, Jeni, illus. LC 89-77513. 32p. (ps-3). 1991. reinforced 14.95 (*0-8234-0823-X*) Holiday.
Kroll, Virginia L. Helen the Fish. Mathews, Judith, ed. Weidner, Teri, illus. LC 91-17230. 32p. (gr. k-3). 1992. PLB 13.95 (*0-8075-3194-4*) A Whitman.
Kubler, Annie. When I Grow Up. LC 91-27125. 1992. 5.95 (*0-85953-505-3*) Childs Play.
Landis, James D. The Sisters Impossible. 160p. 1981. pap. 2.50 (*0-553-26013-8*) Bantam.
Lasky, Kathryn. Prank. (gr. 6 up). 1986. pap. 2.75 (*0-440-97144-6*, LFL) Dell.
—Voice in the Wind: A Starbuck Family Adventure. (gr. 4-7). 1993. 16.95 (*0-15-294102-9*, HB Juv Bks); pap. 6.95 (*0-15-294103-7*) HarBrace.
Lawrence, James. Binky Brothers, Detectives. Kessler, Leonard, illus. LC 68-10374. (gr. k-3). 1978. pap. 3.50 (*0-06-444003-6*, Trophy) HarpC Child Bks.
Lawson, A. Star Baby. Apple, Margot, illus. 1992. 15.95 (*0-15-200905-1*, HB Juv Bks) HarBrace.
Le Guin, Ursula K. A Ride on the Red Mare's Back. Downing, Julie, illus. LC 91-21677. 48p. (gr. 1-4). 1992. 15.95 (*0-531-05991-X*); PLB 15.99 (*0-531-08591-0*) Orchard Bks Watts.
Leroe, Ellen. Leap Frog Friday. DeRosa, Dee, illus. LC 92-8284. 48p. (gr. 2-5). 1992. 12.00 (*0-525-67370-9*, Lodestar Bks) Dutton Child Bks.
Levine, Abby. Ollie Knows Everything. Munsinger, Lynn, illus. LC 93-29600. 1994. write for info. (*0-8075-6020-0*) A Whitman.
Levine, Arthur A. All the Lights in the Night. Ransome, James, illus. LC 90-47496. 32p. (ps-3). 1991. 14.95 (*0-688-10107-0*, Tambourine Bks); PLB 14.88 (*0-688-10108-9*, Tambourine Bks) Morrow.
Levinson, Riki. Me Baby! Hafner, Marylin, illus. LC 90-40372. 32p. (ps-1). 1991. 13.95 (*0-525-44693-1*, DCB) Dutton Child Bks.
Levy, Elizabeth. School Spirit Sabotage: A Brian & Pea Brain Mystery. Ulrich, George, illus. LC 93-23029. 96p. 1994. 14.00 (*0-06-023407-5*); PLB 13.89 (*0-06-023408-3*) HarpC Child Bks.
Lewis, Kim. The Last Train. LC 93-32370. (Illus.). 32p. (ps up). 1994. 14.95 (*1-56402-343-5*) Candlewick Pr.
Lindgren, Astrid. The Children on Troublemaker Street. Wikland, Ilon, illus. LC 91-15647. 112p. (gr. 1-4). 1991. pap. 3.50 (*0-689-71515-3*, Aladdin) Macmillan Child Grp.
Lindman, Maj. Snipp, Snapp, Snurr & the Big Farm. (Illus.). 32p. 1993. Repr. lib. bdg. 14.95x (*1-56849-004-6*) Buccaneer Bks.
—Snipp, Snapp, Snurr & the Big Surprise. (Illus.). 32p. 1993. Repr. lib. bdg. 14.95x (*1-56849-003-8*) Buccaneer Bks.
—Snipp, Snapp, Snurr & the Buttered Bread. (Illus.). 32p. 1993. Repr. lib. bdg. 14.95x (*1-56849-002-X*) Buccaneer Bks.
—Snipp, Snapp, Snurr & the Gingerbread. (Illus.). 30p. 1991. pap. 10.95x (*0-89966-829-1*) Buccaneer Bks.
—Snipp, Snapp, Snurr & the Magic Horse. (Illus.). 32p. 1993. Repr. lib. bdg. 14.95x (*1-56849-001-1*) Buccaneer Bks.
—Snipp, Snapp, Snurr & the Red Shoes. (Illus.). 32p. 1993. Repr. lib. bdg. 14.95x (*1-56849-000-3*) Buccaneer Bks.
—Snipp, Snapp, Snurr & the Reindeer. (Illus.). 32p. 1993. Repr. lib. bdg. 14.95x (*1-56849-005-4*) Buccaneer Bks.
—Snipp, Snapp, Snurr & the Seven Dogs. (Illus.). 32p. 1993. Repr. lib. bdg. 14.95x (*1-56849-007-0*) Buccaneer Bks.
—Snipp, Snapp, Snurr & the Yellow Sled. (Illus.). 30p. 1991. pap. 10.95x (*0-89966-828-3*) Buccaneer Bks.
—Snipp, Snapp, Snurr Learn to Swim. (Illus.). 32p. 1993. Repr. lib. bdg. 14.95x (*1-56849-006-2*) Buccaneer Bks.
Lipniacka, Ewa. Asleep at Last. Bogdanowicz, Basia, illus. LC 92-33326. 1993. 6.95 (*1-56656-118-3*, Crocodile Bks) Interlink Pub.
—It's Mine! Bogdanowicz, Basia, illus. LC 92-33324. 1993. 6.95 (*1-56656-119-1*, Crocodile Bks) Interlink Pub.
Little, Jean. Listen for the Singing. LC 90-40250. 272p. (gr. 4-7). 1991. pap. 3.95 (*0-06-440394-7*, Trophy) HarpC Child Bks.
—Listen for the Singing. LC 90-40019. 272p. (gr. 4-7). 1991. PLB 14.89 (*0-06-023910-7*) HarpC Child Bks.
Lowry, Lois. The One Hundredth Thing about Caroline. 160p. (gr. k-6). 1985. pap. 3.50 (*0-440-46625-3*, YB) Dell.
Lynch, Chris. Gypsy Davey. 160p. (gr. 7 up). 1994. 14.00 (*0-06-023586-1*); PLB 13.89 (*0-06-023587-X*) HarpC Child Bks.
—Shadow Boxer. LC 92-47490. 224p. (gr. 5 up). 1993. 14.00 (*0-06-023027-4*); PLB 13.89 (*0-06-023028-2*) HarpC Child Bks.
McAllister, Angela. The Snow Angel. Fletcher, Claire, illus. LC 92-44155. 1993. 14.00 (*0-688-04569-3*) Lothrop.
McCully, Emily A. I & Sproggy. (gr. 4 up). 1990. pap. 3.95 (*0-14-034542-6*, Puffin) Puffin Bks.
McDaniel, Becky B. Katie Couldn't. Axeman, Lois, illus. LC 85-11666. 30p. (gr. 1-2). 1985. PLB 10.25 (*0-516-02069-2*); pap. 2.95 (*0-516-42069-0*) Childrens.
—Katie Did It. LC 83-7260. (Illus.). 32p. (ps-2). 1983. PLB 10.25 (*0-516-02043-9*); pap. 2.95 (*0-516-42043-7*) Childrens.
Macdonald, Maryann. No Room for Francie. Christelow, Eileen, illus. LC 94-8596. 1995. write for info. (*0-7868-0032-1*); lib. bdg. write for info. (*0-7868-2027-6*) Hyprn Child.
McDonald, Megan. The Great Pumpkin Switch. Lewin, Ted, illus. LC 91-39660. 32p. (ps-2). 1992. 14.95 (*0-531-05450-0*); PLB 14.99 (*0-531-08600-3*) Orchard Bks Watts.
McGuigan, Mary A. Cloud Dancer. LC 93-5562. 128p. (gr. 6-8). 1994. SBE 14.95 (*0-684-19632-8*, Scribners Young Read) Macmillan Child Grp.
McIntire, Jamie. Santa's Christmas Surprise. Henry, Steve, illus. LC 93-24843. (gr. k-3). 1993. pap. text ed. 2.95 (*0-8167-3257-4*) Troll Assocs.
McKay, Hilary. The Exiles. McKeating, Eileen, illus. LC 91-38220. 208p. (gr. 4-7). 1992. SBE 14.95 (*0-689-50555-8*, M K McElderry) Macmillan Child Grp.
Macken, Walter. Flight of the Doves. LC 91-3922. 1992. pap. 14.00 (*0-671-73801-1*, S&S BFYR) S&S Trade.
Mcphail, David. Sisters. 32p. (ps-3). 1990. pap. 3.95 (*0-15-275320-6*, Voyager Bks) HarBrace.
Mahy, Margaret. Seven Chinese Brothers. Tseng, Jean & Mou-sien Tseng, illus. (ps-3). 1990. pap. 13.95 (*0-590-42055-0*) Scholastic Inc.
—Seven Chinese Brothers. 1992. pap. 3.95 (*0-590-42057-7*) Scholastic Inc.
—Tangled Fortunes. Young, Marian, illus. LC 93-32202. 1994. 14.95 (*0-385-32066-3*) Delacorte.
Manes, Stephen. An Almost Perfect Game. LC 94-18192. 1995. 13.95 (*0-590-44432-8*) Scholastic Inc.
—Chocolate-Covered Ants. 1990. 13.95 (*0-590-40960-3*) Scholastic Inc.
Marcus, Irene W. & Marcus, Paul. Scary Night Visitors: A Story for Children with Bedtime Fears. Jeschke, Susan, illus. LC 90-41919. 32p. (ps-2). 1990. 16.95 (*0-945354-26-6*); pap. 6.95 (*0-945354-25-8*) Magination Pr.
—Scary Night Visitors: A Story for Children with Bedtime Fears. Jeschke, Susan, illus. LC 92-56874. 1993. PLB 17.27 (*0-8368-0935-1*) Gareth Stevens Inc.
Margolis, Richard J. Secrets of a Small Brother. Carrick, Donald, illus. LC 84-3478. 40p. (gr. 1-4). 1984. RSBE 12.95 (*0-02-762280-0*, Macmillan Child Bk) Macmillan Child Grp.
Marshall, James. The Cut-ups. (Illus.). 32p. (gr. 3-8). 1984. pap. 14.00 (*0-670-25195-X*) Viking Child Bks.
Martin, Ann M. Inside Out. LC 83-18631. 160p. (gr. 4-9). 1984. 13.95 (*0-8234-0512-5*) Holiday.
—Karen's Brothers. (gr. 4-7). 1991. pap. 2.75 (*0-590-43643-0*) Scholastic Inc.
Mason, Margo C. Are We There Yet? (ps-3). 1990. 9.99 (*0-553-05870-3*) Bantam.
—Are We There Yet? (ps-3). 1990. pap. 3.50 (*0-553-34886-8*) Bantam.
Matarasso, Janet. Angela's New Sister. Chamberlain, Margaret, illus. 24p. 1988. 11.95 (*0-521-35640-7*) Cambridge U Pr.
May, Kara. Big Brave Brother Ben. LC 91-530234. (Illus.). (ps-3). 1992. 14.00 (*0-688-11235-8*); PLB 13.93 (*0-688-11234-X*) Lothrop.
Mayhew, James. Dare You! LC 92-18862. 1993. 13.45 (*0-395-65013-5*, Clarion Bks) HM.
Mazer, Norma F. D, My Name Is Danita. (gr. 7 up). 1991. 13.95 (*0-590-43655-4*) Scholastic Inc.
—Three Sisters. (gr. 7 up). 1991. pap. 2.95 (*0-590-43817-4*, Point) Scholastic Inc.
Metzger, Lois. Barry's Sister. LC 91-23738. 240p. (gr. 5 up). 1992. SBE 15.95 (*0-689-31521-X*, Atheneum Child Bk) Macmillan Child Grp.
—Barry's Sister. LC 93-7760. 240p. (gr. 5 up). 1993. pap. 4.50 (*0-14-036484-6*, Puffin) Puffin Bks.
Miklowitz, Gloria D. The Love Bombers. LC 80-65836. 160p. (gr. 7 up). 1980. pap. 8.95 (*0-385-28545-0*) Delacorte.
Mills, Claudia. Boardwalk with Hotel. 144p. (gr. 7-12). 1986. pap. 2.50 (*0-553-15397-8*, Skylark) Bantam.
—A Visit to Amy-Claire. Hamanaka, Sheila, illus. LC 91-280. 32p. (gr. k-3). 1992. RSBE 14.95 (*0-02-766991-2*, Macmillan Child Bk) Macmillan Child Grp.
Milton, John. Comus. Hyman, Trina S., illus. Hodges, Margaret, adapted by. LC 94-13618. (Illus.). (gr. 1-8). 1995. write for info. (*0-8234-1146-X*) Holiday.
Mischief on Daisy Hill. (Illus.). 32p. (ps-3). Date not set. 12.95 (*0-915696-15-0*) Determined Prods.
Moers, Hermann. Hugo's Baby Brother. Wilkon, Jozef, illus. Lanning, Rosemary, tr. from GER. LC 91-7775. (Illus.). 32p. (gr. k-3). 1992. 14.95 (*1-55858-137-5*); lib. bdg. 14.88 (*1-55858-146-4*) North-South Bks NYC.
Mohr, Carole. Freud & Freud, Inc. (gr. 4-7). 1991. pap. 2.75 (*0-553-15915-1*) Bantam.

Moll, Linda J. A Poison Tree: A Children's Fairy Tale. Moll, Linda J., illus. 40p. (gr. 1 up). 1994. PLB 12.95 (*0-9641641-1-6*) Punking Pr.
A POISON TREE is a children's fairy tale set in Ireland's countryside. Ian McGonagle feels rage for his wee brother, Malachy, after discovering his younger sibling ruined his birthday surprise. Ian vows revenge & calls on the evil fairies for help. Indeed, the evil fairies come with a black seed from which a poison tree will grow. But what happens next is not what Ian expected. Find out how sibling anger turns into forgiveness & how brotherly love prevails in this enchanting Irish fairy tale. A POISON TREE is a charming story for any child learning the sometimes difficult skill of getting along with others. Parents, caregivers, & teachers will find A POISON TREE a valuable social tool in the family, neighborhood or classroom. Children love the comical antics of the fairies & sit in anticipation of A POISON TREE's climactic ending. Teachers will find A POISON TREE a wonderful source for introducing literary devices & techniques to young scholars. A POISON TREE is rich in simile, metaphor, alliteration, rhyming verse,...Illustrations include quaint silhouettes & the text which is scripted in modified 4th-century celtic lettering. A Celtic knotwork border frames the page & completes the beauty of the book. To order A POISON TREE, contact Christopher Moll, P.O. Box 25, Williamson, NY 14589; 315-589-5119.
Publisher Provided Annotation.

Moncure, Jane B. Caring for My Baby Sister. Martin, Clovis, illus. 32p. (ps-2). 1990. PLB 12.95 (*0-89565-669-8*) Childs World.
—My Baby Brother Needs a Friend. Hook, Frances, illus. LC 78-21935. (ps-3). 1979. PLB 14.95 (*0-89565-019-3*) Childs World.
—What's So Special about Lauren? She's My Baby Sister. Williams, Jenny, illus. LC 87-21927. 32p. (ps-2). 1987. PLB 14.95 (*0-89565-413-X*) Childs World.
Moore, Robin. The Bread Sister of Sinking Creek. LC 89-36400. 160p. (gr. 4-7). 1992. pap. 3.95 (*0-06-440357-2*, Trophy) HarpC Child Bks.
Morpurgo, Michael. Twist of Gold. LC 92-25928. 246p. (gr. 5-9). 1993. 14.99 (*0-670-84851-4*) Viking Child Bks.
Mulford, Philippa G. The World Is My Eggshell. LC 85-16198. (gr. 7 up). 1986. pap. 14.95 (*0-385-29432-8*) Delacorte.
Murdocca, Sal. Baby Wants the Moon. LC 94-14517. 1994. write for info. (*0-688-13664-8*); PLB write for info. (*0-688-13665-6*) Lothrop.
Murphy, Catherine F. Songs in the Silence. LC 93-26947. 192p. (gr. 3-7). 1994. SBE 14.95 (*0-02-767730-3*, Macmillan Child Bk) Macmillan Child Grp.
Myers, Anna. Rosie's Tiger. LC 94-50814. 1994. write for info. (*0-8027-8305-8*) Walker & Co.
Myers, Edward. Climb or Die. LC 93-44861. 192p. (gr. 5-9). 1994. 14.95 (*0-7868-0026-7*); PLB 14.89 (*0-7868-2021-7*) Hyprn Child.
Myers, Walter D. Darnell Rock Reporting. LC 94-8666. 1994. 14.95 (*0-385-32096-5*) Delacorte.
Napoli, Donna J. Shark Shock. LC 93-43975. (Illus.). 192p. (gr. 3-7). 1994. 13.99 (*0-525-45267-2*, DCB) Dutton Child Bks.
Naylor, Phyllis R. Boys Against Girls. LC 93-37683. (Illus.). 1994. 14.95 (*0-385-32081-7*) Delacorte.
—Boys Start the War. LC 92-249. (gr. 4-7). 1993. 14.95 (*0-385-30814-0*) Doubleday.
—The Fear Place. LC 93-38891. (gr. 3-7). 1994. 14.95 (*0-689-31866-9*, Atheneum Child Bk) Macmillan Child Grp.

—The Girls Got Even. LC 92-43047. 1993. 13.95 (*0-385-31029-3*) Delacorte.

Nesbit, Edith. The Railway Children. 1993. 12.95 (*0-679-42534-9*, Everymans Lib) Knopf.

—Railway Children. (gr. 4 up). 1993. pap. 3.25 (*0-553-21415-2*, Bantam Classics) Bantam.

Nesbit, Jeffrey A. The Puzzled Prodigy. (Orig.). (gr. 3-6). 1992. pap. 4.99 (*0-89693-075-0*, Victor Books) SP Pubns.

—Struggle with Silence. 129p. 1991. pap. 4.99 (*0-89693-132-3*) SP Pubns.

Newman, Nanette. Sharing. 1990. 13.95 (*0-385-41104-9*) Doubleday.

Nixon, Joan L. When I am Eight. Gackenbach, Dick, photos by. LC 93-20023. (gr. 1-3). 1994. 13.99 (*0-8037-1499-8*) Dial Bks Young.

—When I Am Eight. LC 93-20023. (ps-3). 1994. 13.89 (*0-8037-1500-5*) Dial Bks Young.

O'Connor, Karen. The Green Team: The Adventures of Mitch & Molly. Chapin, Patrick O., illus. LC 92-24643. 80p. (Orig.). (gr. 1-4). 1993. pap. 4.99 (*0-570-04726-9*) Concordia.

—The Water Detectives: The Adventures of Mitch & Molly. Chapin, Patrick O., illus. LC 92-24649. 80p. (Orig.). (gr. 1-4). 1993. pap. 4.99 (*0-570-04727-7*) Concordia.

O'Donnell, Elizabeth L. Maggie Doesn't Want to Move. LC 89-18207. (Illus.). 32p. (gr. k-3). 1990. pap. 3.95 (*0-689-71375-4*, Aladdin) Macmillan Child Grp.

Oppel, Kenneth. Dead Water Zone. LC 92-37282. 1993. 14.95 (*0-316-65102-8*, Joy St Bks) Little.

Oppenheim, Joanne. Left & Right. Litzinger, Rosanne, illus. LC 87-22939. 153p. (ps-3). 1989. 13.95 (*0-15-200505-6*, Gulliver Bks) HarBrace.

—One Gift Deserves Another. (Illus.). 32p. (ps-1). 1992. 13.00 (*0-525-44975-2*, DCB) Dutton Child Bks.

Paris, Nancy M. My Brother Is Different. (Illus.). (gr. 1-4). 1992. 6.95 (*1-55523-512-3*) Winston-Derek.

Parish, Peggy. Willy Is My Brother. 1989. pap. 12.95 (*0-440-50221-7*) Dell.

Park, Barbara. Junie B. Jones & a Little Monkey Business. Brunkus, Denise, illus. LC 92-56706. 80p. (Orig.). (gr. 1-4). 1993. PLB 9.99 (*0-679-93886-9*); pap. 2.99 (*0-679-83886-4*) Random Bks Yng Read.

—Operation: Dump the Chump. Sauber, Rob, illus. LC 81-8147. 128p. (gr. 3-6). 1982. lib. bdg. 10.99 (*0-394-95179-4*) Knopf Bks Yng Read.

—Operation: Dump the Chump. 112p. (gr. 3-7). 1983. pap. 2.75 (*0-380-63974-2*, Camelot) Avon.

Pascal, Francine. The Hand-Me-Down Kid. LC 79-5462. (gr. 5-9). 1980. pap. 12.95 (*0-670-35969-6*) Viking Child Bks.

—The Long, Lost Brother. 1991. pap. 3.25 (*0-553-29214-5*) Bantam.

Paterson, Katherine. Flip-Flop Girl. 128p. (gr. 3-7). 1994. 13.99 (*0-525-67480-2*, Lodestar Bks) Dutton Child Bks.

Pearson, Susan. Monnie Hates Lydia. Paterson, Diane, illus. LC 75-9198. 32p. (ps-3). 1985. Dial Bks Young.

Percy, Graham. Meg & the Great Race. Percy, Graham, illus. LC 92-44851. (ps-3). 1993. 15.95 (*1-56766-077-0*) Childs World.

Petersen, P. J. The Amazing Magic Show. Williams-Andriani, Renee, illus. LC 93-34861. (gr. 2-5). 1994. 14.00 (*0-671-86581-1*, S&S BFYR) S&S Trade.

—Corky & the Brothers Cool. LC 84-15579. 192p. (gr. 7 up). 1985. 14.95 (*0-318-18244-0*) Delacorte.

—I Want Answers & a Parachute. DiVito, Anna, illus. LC 92-38262. (gr. 6 up). 1993. pap. 13.00 (*0-671-86577-3*, S&S BFYR) S&S Trade.

Pevsner, Stella. And You Give Me a Pain, Elaine. LC 78-5857. 192p. (gr. 6 up). 1979. 13.45 (*0-395-28877-0*, Clarion Bks) HM.

—I'm Emma, I'm a Quint. LC 92-36952. 1993. 13.95 (*0-395-64166-7*, Clarion Bks) HM.

Pfeffer, Susan B. Family of Strangers. 1992. 16.00 (*0-553-08364-3*) Bantam.

—The Riddle Streak. Chesworth, Michael, illus. 64p. (gr. 2-4). 1993. 14.95 (*0-8050-2147-7*, Bks Young Read) H Holt & Co.

—Sybil at Sixteen. (gr. 7 up). 1989. 13.95 (*0-553-05842-8*) Bantam.

Pickett, Anola. Old Enough for Magic. Delaney, Ned, illus. LC 88-30320. 64p. (gr. k-3). 1989. PLB 13.89 (*0-06-024732-0*) HarpC Child Bks.

—Old Enough for Magic. Delaney, Ned, illus. LC 88-30320. 64p. (gr. k-3). 1993. pap. 3.50 (*0-06-444161-X*, Trophy) HarpC Child Bks.

Prenzlau, Sheryl. Changing Places. (Illus.). 112p. (gr. 3-5). 1994. pap. 6.95 (*1-56871-044-5*) Targum Pr.

Pryor, Bonnie. Jumping Jenny. Riggio, Anita, illus. 192p. (gr. 2 up). 1992. 14.00 (*0-688-09684-0*) Morrow Jr Bks.

Pyrnelle, Louise-Clarke. Diddie, Dumps & Tot. (Illus.). 117p. (gr. 4-8). 1963. 14.95 (*0-911116-17-6*) Pelican.

Rabin, Staton. Casey over There. Shed, Greg, illus. LC 92-30322. 1994. 14.95 (*0-15-253186-6*) HarBrace.

Reiss, Kathryn. The Glass House People. 1992. 16.95 (*0-15-231040-1*, HB Juv Bks) HarBrace.

Remkiewicz, Frank. GreedyAnna. LC 91-149230. (ps-3). 1992. pap. 14.00 (*0-688-10294-8*); PLB 13.93 (*0-688-10295-6*) Lothrop.

Ringgold, Faith. Aunt Harriet's Underground in the Sky. Ringgold, Faith, illus. LC 92-20072. 32p. (ps-4). 1993. 16.00 (*0-517-58767-X*); lib. bdg. 17.99 (*0-517-58768-8*) Crown Bks Yng Read.

Rispin, Karen. Ambush at Amboseli. LC 93-37801. 1994. 4.99 (*0-8423-1295-1*) Tyndale.

Roberts, Willo D. To Grandmother's House We Go. LC 89-34972. 192p. (gr. 3-7). 1990. SBE 14.95 (*0-689-31594-5*, Atheneum Child Bk) Macmillan Child Grp.

Roche, P. K. Webster & Arnold Go Camping. (Illus.). 32p. (ps-3). 1991. pap. 3.95 (*0-14-050806-6*, Puffin) Puffin Bks.

Rodda, Emily. The Timekeeper. Young, Noela, illus. LC 92-31512. 160p. (gr. 5 up). 1993. 14.00 (*0-688-12448-8*) Greenwillow.

Roe, Eileen. Con Mi Hermano with My Brother. Casilla, Robert, illus. LC 90-33983. 32p. (ps-3). 1991. RSBE 14.00 (*0-02-777373-6*, Bradbury Pr) Macmillan Child Grp.

Rogers, Mary. Big Brother. 19p. (gr. k). 1992. pap. text ed. 23.00 big bk. (*1-56843-010-8*); pap. text ed. 4.50 (*1-56843-060-4*) BGR Pub.

Roos, Stephen. My Horrible Secret. Newsom, Carol, illus. LC 82-14954. 128p. (gr. 4-6). 1983. pap. 10.95 (*0-385-29246-5*) Delacorte.

Root, Phyllis. Moon Tiger. Young, Ed, illus. LC 85-7572. 32p. (ps-2). 1985. 14.95 (*0-8050-0896-9*, Bks Young Read) H Holt & Co.

Ross, Christine. Lily & the Present. Ross, Christine, illus. LC 91-41134. 28p. (ps-3). 1992. 13.95 (*0-395-61127-X*) HM.

Roy, J. Soul Daddy. 1992. 16.95 (*0-15-277193-X*, HB Juv Bks) HarBrace.

Russo, Marisabina. I Don't Want to Go Back to School. LC 93-5479. 32p. 1994. 15.00 (*0-688-04601-0*); PLB 14.93 (*0-688-04602-9*) Greenwillow.

—Only Six More Days. (Illus.). 32p. (ps-3). 1992. pap. 3.99 (*0-14-054473-9*) Puffin Bks.

Ryan, Mary E. Me, My Sister, & I. LC 92-368. 1992. pap. 15.00 (*0-671-73851-8*, S&S BFYR) S&S Trade.

—My Sister Is Driving Me Crazy. LC 90-41263. 224p. (gr. 5-9). 1991. pap. 15.00 jacketed, 3-pc. bdg. (*0-671-73203-X*, S&S BFYR) S&S Trade.

—My Sister Is Driving Me Crazy. LC 90-41263. 224p. (gr. 5-9). 1993. pap. 3.95 (*0-671-86694-X*, Half Moon Bks) S&S Trade.

Sachs, Marilyn. What My Sister Remembered. LC 91-32263. 120p. (gr. 5-9). 1992. 15.00 (*0-525-44953-1*, DCB) Dutton Child Bks.

Samuels, Barbara. Faye & Dolores. Samuels, Barbara, illus. LC 87-1419. 40p. (ps-3). 1987. pap. 4.95 (*0-689-71154-9*, Aladdin) Macmillan Child Grp.

Sandoval, Dolores. Be Patient, Abdul. Sandoval, Dolores, illus. LC 93-34224. 1995. 14.95 (*0-689-50607-4*, M K McElderry) Macmillan Child Grp.

Sanschagrin, Joceline. Lollypop's Baby Sister. (Illus.). 16p. (ps). 1993. bds. 5.95 (*2-921198-45-2*, Pub. by Les Edits Herit CN) Adams Inc MA.

Savage, Cindy. My Sister, the Pig, & Me. (Illus.). 142p. (gr. 3-5). 1992. pap. 2.50 (*0-87406-638-7*) Willowisp Pr.

Schnitter, Jane. William Is My Brother. LC 90-21364. (Illus.). 32p. (ps-3). 1991. 10.95 (*0-944934-03-X*) Perspect Indiana.

Scott, Michael. Gemini Game. LC 93-39972. 160p. 1994. 14.95 (*0-8234-1092-7*) Holiday.

Service, Pamela F. Stinker from Space. (gr. 6 up). 1989. pap. 3.99 (*0-449-70330-4*, Juniper) Fawcett.

—Stinker from Space. 105p. 1992. text ed. 8.40 (*1-56956-122-2*) W A T Braille.

Sheldon, Dyan. My Brother Is a Visitor from Another Planet. Brazell, Derek, illus. LC 92-53420. 96p. (gr. 3-6). 1993. 13.95 (*1-56402-141-6*) Candlewick Pr.

Shelton, Rick. Hoggle's Christmas. Gates, Donald, illus. LC 92-37861. 80p. (gr. 2-6). 1993. 12.99 (*0-525-65129-2*, Cobblehill Bks) Dutton Child Bks.

Shreve, Susan. Wait for Me. De Groat, Diane, illus. LC 91-30233. 112p. (gr. 3 up). 1992. 13.00 (*0-688-11120-3*, Tambourine Bks) Morrow.

Shulman, Dee. Dora's New Brother. (Illus.). 32p. (ps-1). 1994. 19.95 (*0-370-31814-5*, Pub. by Bodley Head UK) Trafalgar.

Sidney, Margaret. Five Little Peppers & Their Friends. 1992. Repr. PLB 25.95x (*0-89966-970-0*) Buccaneer Bks.

—Five Little Peppers in the Little Brown House. 1992. Repr. PLB 25.95x (*0-89966-968-9*) Buccaneer Bks.

Simon, Shirley. Benny's Baby Brother. Gregorich, Barbara, ed. (Illus.). 16p. (Orig.). (gr. k-2). 1985. pap. 2.25 (*0-88743-016-3*, 06016) Sch Zone Pub Co.

Siracusa, Catherine. Bingo, the Best Dog in the World. Levitt, Sidney, illus. LC 90-4400. 64p. (gr. k-3). 1991. 11.95 (*0-06-025812-8*); PLB 11.89 (*0-06-025813-6*) HarpC Child Bks.

Skifton, Chrys. God's Country Kids: The Adventure Begins. White, James W., ed. Barber, Jeannie, illus. LC 94-71146. 57p. (gr. k-6). 1994. 22.00 (*0-9640794-7-X*) Celebration Pr.
"This book is a breath of fresh air. We share the innocence of children as they show us the world about them through their eyes in a time travel adventure. It is a subtle testament to the way the world should be family oriented, moral, ethical. Give yourself a treat & step out of the adult world into that of the child. This children's book is for all ages." - James Wm. White, Director of the LaCrosse Public Library & The Winding Rivers Library System. This is the first book of a beautifully illustrated series. It introduces two brothers & their sister. This is a fantasy adventure. Each chapter has a different adventure that is educational as well as magical. To order contact: Celebration Press, P.O. Box 693, Onalaska, WI 54650 or call 608-783-3561 or (800) HY-CHRYS. Also available from Baker & Taylor & The Bookmen.
Publisher Provided Annotation.

Skurzynski, Gloria. Caught in the Moving Mountains. (Illus.). 144p. (gr. 7 up). 1994. pap. 4.95 (*0-688-12945-5*, Pub. by Beech Tree Bks) Morrow.

Sleator, William. Fingers. 208p. (Orig.). (gr. 7). 1990. pap. 3.50 (*0-553-25004-3*, Starfire) Bantam.

Slier, Debby. Brothers & Sisters. 12p. (ps). 1989. 2.95 (*1-56288-146-9*) Checkerboard.

Slote, Elizabeth. Ana & Bold Berto. LC 93-37534. 1995. write for info. (*0-688-12980-3*, Tambourine Bks); PLB write for info. (*0-688-12981-1*, Tambourine Bks) Morrow.

Smothers, Ethel F. Down in the Piney Woods. LC 91-328. 144p. (gr. 5-9). 1992. 14.00 (*0-679-80360-2*); PLB 14.99 (*0-679-90360-7*) Knopf Bks Yng Read.

Snyder, Carol. One Up, One Down. Chambliss, Maxie, illus. LC 93-36282. 1995. 16.00 (*0-689-31828-6*, Atheneum) Macmillan.

Springer, Nancy. Toughing It. LC 93-42231. (gr. 7 up). 1994. 10.95 (*0-15-200008-9*); pap. 4.95 (*0-15-200011-9*) Harbrace.

Stahl, Hilda. Kathy's New Brother. LC 92-9135. 160p. (gr. 4-7). 1992. pap. 3.99 (*0-89107-682-4*) Crossway Bks.

—Roxie's Mall Madness. LC 93-22575. 160p. (Orig.). (gr. 6-9). 1993. pap. 3.99 (*0-89107-753-7*) Crossway Bks.

Steptoe, John. Baby Says. ALC Staff, ed. LC 92-11524. (Illus.). 28p. (ps up). 1992. pap. 3.95 (*0-688-11855-0*, Mulberry) Morrow.

Stevenson, James. Worse Than Willy! Stevenson, James, illus. LC 83-14201. 32p. (gr. k-3). 1984. 10.25 (*0-688-02596-X*); PLB 10.88 (*0-688-02597-8*) Greenwillow.

Stevenson, Sucie. Do I Have to Take Violet? Stevenson, Sucie, illus. 32p. (ps-3). 1992. pap. 3.99 (*0-440-40682-X*, YB) Dell.

Stimson, Joan. Big Panda, Little Panda. Rutherford, Meg, illus. LC 93-36235. 32p. (ps-2). 1994. 12.95 (*0-8120-6404-6*); pap. 4.95 (*0-8120-1691-2*) Barron.

Stine, R. L. The Stepsister. large type ed. (gr. 6 up). Date not set. PLB 14.60 (*0-8368-1162-3*) Gareth Stevens Inc.

Streatfeild, Noel. Gemma & Sisters. (Orig.). (gr. k-6). 1987. pap. 3.25 (*0-440-42862-9*, YB) Dell.

Stren, P. For Sale: One Brother. Stren, P., illus. LC 91-73821. 32p. (gr. 1-4). 1993. 13.95 (*1-56282-126-1*); PLB 13.89 (*1-56282-127-X*) Hyprn Child.

Strub, Susanne. My Dog, My Sister, & I (Mon Chien, Ma Soeur, et Moi) Strub, Susanne, illus. LC 92-22063. (ENG & FRE.). 32p. (ps up). 1993. 14.00 (*0-688-12010-5*, Tambourine Bks); PLB 13.93 (*0-688-12011-3*, Tambourine Bks) Morrow.

Sutton, Esther. Kid Sisters Super Special, No. 7: Growing Up. 136p. (Orig.). (gr. 3-5). 1993. pap. 7.95 (*1-56871-035-6*) Targum Pr.

Sweeney, Joyce. Shadow: A Novel. LC 93-32215. 1994. 15.95 (*0-385-32051-5*) Delacorte.

Swindells, Robert. Fallout. ALC Staff, ed. LC 84-22362. 160p. (gr. 7 up). 1992. pap. 3.95 (*0-688-11778-3*, Pub. by Beech Tree Bks) Morrow.

Testa, Maria. Thumbs Up, Rico! Paterson, Diane, illus. 1994. write for info. (*0-8075-7906-8*) A Whitman.

Tolan, Stephanie S. Who's There? LC 94-15384. 1994. write for info. (*0-688-04611-8*) Morrow Jr Bks.

Tomioka, Chiyoko. Rise & Shine, Mariko-Chan! Tsuchida, Yoshiharu, illus. 32p. (ps-1). 1992. pap. 3.95 (*0-590-45507-9*) Scholastic Inc.

Tsutsui, Yoriko. Anna in Charge. Hayashi, Akiko, illus. 32p. (ps-1). 1989. pap. 11.95 (*0-670-81672-8*) Viking Child Bks.

—Anna's Special Present. Hayashi, Akiko, illus. 32p. (ps-3). 1990. pap. 3.95 (*0-14-054219-1*, Puffin) Puffin Bks.

Van Leeuwen, Jean. Oliver & Amanda & the Big Snow. Schweninger, Ann, illus. LC 93-48598. 1995. write for info. (*0-8037-1762-8*); lib. bdg. write for info. (*0-8037-1763-6*) Dial Bks Young.

—Oliver & Amanda's Halloween. Schweninger, Ann, illus. LC 91-30941. 48p. (ps-3). 1992. 11.00 (*0-8037-1237-5*); PLB 10.89 (*0-8037-1238-3*) Dial Bks Young.

Venezia, Mike. How to Be an Older Brother or Sister. Venezia, Mike, illus. LC 85-27977. 32p. (ps-3). 1986. PLB 11.30 (*0-516-03494-4*); pap. 3.95 (*0-516-43494-2*) Childrens.

Vigor, John. Danger, Dolphins, & Ginger Beer. LC 92-26182. (Illus.). 192p. (gr. 3-7). 1993. SBE 14.95 (*0-689-31817-0*, Atheneum Child Bk) Macmillan Child Grp.
Violette's Daring Adventure. (Illus.). 32p. (gr. k-3). 1992. PLB 17.27 (*0-8368-0912-2*) Gareth Stevens Inc.
Viorst, Judith. I'll Fix Anthony. Lobel, Arnold, illus. LC 78-77942. (ps-3). 1969. 14.00i (*0-06-026306-7*); PLB 13.89 (*0-06-026307-5*) HarpC Child Bks.
—Sunday Morning. 2nd ed. Knight, Hilary, illus. LC 92-16928. 40p. (ps-3). 1992. RSBE 13.95 (*0-689-31794-8*, Atheneum Child Bk) Macmillan Child Grp.
—Sunday Morning. 2nd ed. Knight, Hilary, illus. LC 92-29561. 32p. (gr. k-3). 1993. pap. 3.95 (*0-689-71702-4*, Aladdin) Macmillan Child Grp.
Voigt, Cynthia. The Vandemark Mummy. LC 91-7311. 244p. (gr. 5-9). 1991. SBE 15.95 (*0-689-31476-0*, Atheneum Child Bk) Macmillan Child Grp.
Wallace, Bill. Snot Stew. McCue, Lisa, illus. LC 88-31976. 96p. (gr. 3-7). 1989. 13.95 (*0-8234-0745-4*) Holiday.
Walter, Mildred P. Two & Too Much. LC 88-14888. (Illus.). 32p. (ps-2). 1990. RSBE 13.95 (*0-02-792290-1*, Bradbury Pr) Macmillan Child Grp.
Walters-Lucy, Jean. Look Ma, I'm Flying. Tabesh, Delight, ed. & illus. LC 92-13953. 48p. (Orig.). (ps-5). 1992. pap. 6.95 perfect bdg. (*0-941992-28-4*) Los Arboles Pub.
Walton, Sherry. Books Are for Eating. LC 89-11749. (Illus.). 24p. (ps-1). 1990. 11.95 (*0-525-44554-4*, DCB) Dutton Child Bks.
Warner, Gertrude C. The Castle Mystery. (gr. 4-7). 1993. 10.95 (*0-8075-1078-5*); pap. 3.50 (*0-8075-1079-3*) A Whitman.
—The Mystery in Washington, D.C. (gr. 4-7). 1994. 10.95 (*0-8075-5409-X*); pap. 3.75 (*0-8075-5410-3*) A Whitman.
—The Mystery on the Ice. (gr. 4-7). 1993. 10.95 (*0-8075-5414-6*); pap. 3.50 (*0-8075-5413-8*) A Whitman.
Wartski, Maureen C. My Brother Is Special. 144p. (gr. 7 up). 1981. pap. 3.50 (*0-451-15856-3*, Sig) NAL-Dutton.
Watkins, Yoko K. My Brother, My Sister, & I. LC 93-23535. 224p. (gr. 6 up). 1994. SBE 16.95 (*0-02-792526-9*, Bradbury Pr) Macmillan Child Grp.
Watson, Harvey. Bob War & Poke. 144p. (gr. 5-9). 1991. 13.45 (*0-395-57038-7*, Sandpiper) HM.
Weiss, Monica. Birthday Cake Candles, Counting. Berlin, Rosemary, illus. LC 91-16033. 24p. (gr. k-2). 1992. PLB 10.59 (*0-8167-2496-2*); pap. text ed. 2.95 (*0-8167-2497-0*) Troll Assocs.
—How Many? How Much? Measuring. Berlin, Rosemary, illus. LC 91-3992. 24p. (gr. k-2). 1992. PLB 10.59 (*0-8167-2500-4*); pap. text ed. 2.95 (*0-8167-2501-2*) Troll Assocs.
—Pop! ABC Letter & Sounds: Learning the Alphabet. Berlin, Rosemary, illus. LC 91-18704. 24p. (gr. k-2). 1992. PLB 10.59 (*0-8167-2492-X*); pap. text ed. 2.95 (*0-8167-2493-8*) Troll Assocs.
Weiss, Nicki. A Family Story. Weiss, Nicki, illus. LC 85-27231. 24p. (ps-3). 1987. 11.75 (*0-688-06504-X*); PLB 11.88 (*0-688-06505-8*) Greenwillow.
—Princess Pearl. Weiss, Nicki, illus. LC 85-17699. 24p. (gr. k-3). 1986. 11.75 (*0-688-05894-9*); PLB 11.88 (*0-688-05895-7*) Greenwillow.
Welcher, Rosalind. My Brother Says There's a Monster Living in Our Toilet. Welcher, Rosalind, illus. 96p. (Orig.). 1987. pap. 6.95 (*0-939775-01-8*) West Hill Pr.
Wells, Rosemary. Max & Ruby's First Greek Myth. Wells, Rosemary, illus. LC 92-30332. 32p. (ps-3). 1993. 11.99 (*0-8037-1524-2*); PLB 11.89 (*0-8037-1525-0*) Dial Bks Young.
—Max & Ruby's Midas: Another Greek Myth. LC 94-11181. Date not set. write for info. (*0-8037-1782-2*); PLB write for info. (*0-8037-1783-0*) Dial Bks Young.
—Max's Dragon Shirt. Wells, Rosemary, illus. LC 90-43755. 32p. (ps-2). 1991. 12.00 (*0-8037-0944-7*); lib. bdg. 10.89 (*0-8037-0945-5*) Dial Bks Young.
—Waiting for the Evening Star. Jeffers, Susan, illus. LC 92-30492. 40p. (gr. k-3). 1993. 15.00 (*0-8037-1398-3*); PLB 14.89 (*0-8037-1399-1*) Dial Bks Young.
Wersba, Barbara. You'll Never Guess the End. LC 91-24771. 144p. (gr. 7 up). 1992. 14.00 (*0-06-020448-6*); PLB 13.89 (*0-06-020449-4*) HarpC Child Bks.
Westwood, Chris. Brother of Mine. LC 92-32020. (gr. 5 up). 1993. write for info. (*0-395-66137-4*, Clarion Bks) HM.
Whitaker, Alexander. Dream Sister. 160p. (gr. k-6). 1989. pap. 2.95 (*0-440-40156-9*, YB) Dell.
Wiesner, David. Hurricane. Wiesner, David, illus. (gr. k-3). 1990. 14.95 (*0-395-54382-7*, Clarion Bks) HM.
Williams, Barbara. Mitzi & the Terrible Tyrannosaurus Rex. McCully, Emily A., illus. 112p. (gr. 3-7). 1983. pap. 1.95 (*0-440-45673-8*, YB) Dell.
Wilson, Jodi L. When I Grow Up. Anderson, Kari A., illus. 32p. (Orig.). (gr. 1-3). Date not set. pap. 4.95x (*0-9628335-0-9*) Wilander Pub.
Wilson, Johnniece M. Oh, Brother. 128p. (gr. 3-7). 1989. pap. 2.95 (*0-590-41001-6*, Apple Paperbacks) Scholastic Inc.
Wilson, Nancy H. Bringing Nettie Back. 144p. 1994. pap. 3.50 (*0-380-72256-9*, Camelot) Avon.
Winter, Susan. I Can. Winter, Susan, illus. LC 92-54384. 24p. (ps-1). 1993. 9.95 (*1-56458-197-7*) Dorling Kindersley.
—Me Too. Winter, Susan, illus. LC 92-54383. 24p. (ps-1). 1993. 9.95 (*1-56458-198-5*) Dorling Kindersley.
Wisler, G. Clifton. Jericho's Journey. LC 92-36701. 144p. (gr. 5-9). 1993. 13.99 (*0-525-67428-4*, Lodestar Bks) Dutton Child Bks.
Wittman, Sally. Stepbrother Sabotage. McCully, Emily A., illus. LC 89-26804. 80p. (gr. 2-5). 1991. pap. 3.95 (*0-06-440408-0*, Trophy) HarpC Child Bks.
Wood, June R. A Share of Freedom. LC 94-6578. 256p. 1994. 15.95 (*0-399-22767-9*, Putnam) Putnam Pub Group.
Woodruff, Elvira. The Magnificent Mummy Maker. LC 93-7870. 160p. (gr. 4-7). 1994. 13.95 (*0-590-45742-X*) Scholastic Inc.
—Tubtime. Stevenson, Sucie, illus. LC 89-36609. 32p. (ps-3). 1990. reinforced bdg. 14.95 (*0-8234-0777-2*) Holiday.
Wright, Betty R. The Ghost of Popcorn Hill. Ritz, Karen, illus. LC 92-16391. 96p. (gr. 3-7). 1993. 14.95 (*0-8234-1009-9*) Holiday.
—The Scariest Night. LC 91-55030. 166p. (gr. 3-7). 1991. 14.95 (*0-8234-0904-X*) Holiday.
Wyeth, Sharon D. Lisa, We Miss You. 1990. pap. 2.95 (*0-440-40393-6*) Dell.
Yaccarino, Dan. Big Brother Mike. Yaccarino, Dan, illus. LC 92-72017. 32p. (ps-2). 1993. 13.95 (*1-56282-329-9*); PLB 13.89 (*1-56282-330-2*) Hyprn Child.
Yorinks, Arthur. Oh, Brother. Egielski, Richard, illus. 40p. (ps up). 1991. pap. 5.95 (*0-374-45598-8*, Sunburst) FS&G.
Young, Alida E. Is My Sister Dying? 144p. (Orig.). (gr. 5-8). 1991. pap. 2.99 (*0-87406-541-0*) Willowisp Pr.
Zalben, Jane B. Buster Gets Braces. Zalben, Jane B., illus. LC 91-13967. 32p. (ps-2). 1992. 15.95 (*0-8050-1682-1*, Bks Young Read) H Holt & Co.
Zolotow, Charlotte. Big Sister & Little Sister. Alexander, Martha, illus. LC 66-8268. 32p. (gr. k-3). 1990. pap. 4.95 (*0-06-443217-3*, Trophy) HarpC Child Bks.

BROWN, JAMES NATHANIEL, 1936-

Loewen, L. James Brown. (Illus.). 112p. (gr. 5 up). 1989. lib. bdg. 18.60 (*0-86592-607-7*); 13.95 (*0-685-58615-4*) Rourke Corp.

BROWN, JOHN, 1800-1859

Barrett, Tracy. Harper's Ferry: The Story of John Brown's Raid. LC 92-39810. (Illus.). 64p. (gr. 4-6). 1993. PLB 15.40 (*1-56294-380-4*); pap. 5.95 (*1-56294-745-1*) Millbrook Pr.
Collins, James L. John Brown & the Fight Against Slavery. (Illus.). 32p. (gr. 2-4). 1991. PLB 12.90 (*1-56294-043-0*); pap. 4.95 (*1-878841-72-6*) Millbrook Pr.
Everett, Gwen. John Brown: One Man Against Slavery. Lawrence, Jacob, illus. LC 92-41973. 32p. (gr. 5 up). 1993. 15.95 (*0-8478-1702-4*) Rizzoli Intl.
Potter, Robert R. John Brown: Militant Abolitionist. Shenton, James P., illus. LC 94-17020. 1994. write for info. (*0-8114-2378-6*) Raintree Steck-V.
Scott, John A. & Scott, Robert A. John Brown of Harper's Ferry. (Illus.). 192p. (gr. 5 up). 1988. 16.95x (*0-8160-1347-0*) Facts on File.

BRUEGEL, PIETER, THE ELDER, 1525?-1569

Muhlberger, Richard, text by. What Makes a Bruegel a Bruegel? (Illus.). 48p. (gr. 5 up). 1993. 9.95 (*0-670-85203-1*) Viking Child Bks.
Venezia, Mike. Pieter Bruegel. Venezia, Mike, illus. LC 92-4810. 32p. (ps-4). 1992. PLB 12.85 (*0-516-02279-2*) Childrens.
—Pieter Bruegel. Venezia, Mike, illus. LC 92-4810. 32p. (ps-4). 1993. pap. 4.95 (*0-516-42279-0*) Childrens.

BRYAN, WILLIAM JENNINGS, 1860-1925

Allen, Robert. William Jennings Bryan. (gr. 3-6). 1992. pap. 6.95 (*0-88062-160-5*) Mott Media.

BUCCANEERS

see also Pirates

BUCCANEERS–FICTION

Pyle, Howard. Tales of Pirates & Buccaneers. Pyle, Howard, illus. LC 93-44689. 1994. write for info. (*0-517-10162-9*) Random Hse Value.

BUCHANAN, JAMES, PRESIDENT U. S. 1791-1868

Brill, Marlene T. James Buchanan. LC 88-10884. (Illus.). 100p. (gr. 3 up). 1988. PLB 14.40 (*0-516-01358-0*) Childrens.
Collins, David R. James Buchanan: Fifteenth President of the United States. Young, Richard G., ed. LC 89-39948. (Illus.). 128p. (gr. 5-9). 1990. PLB 17.26 (*0-944483-62-3*) Garrett Ed Corp.

BUCK, PEARL (SYDENSTRICKER), 1892-1973

LaFarge, Ann. Pearl Buck. Horner, Matina, intro. by. (Illus.). 112p. (gr. 5 up). 1988. lib. bdg. 17.95 (*1-55546-645-1*) Chelsea Hse.
Mitchell, Barbara. Between Two Worlds: A Story about Pearl Buck. Ritz, Karen, illus. 56p. (gr. 3-6). 1988. PLB 14.95 (*0-87614-332-X*) Carolrhoda Bks.
Schoen, Celin V. Pearl Buck: Famed American Author of Oriental Stories. Rahmas, D. Steve, ed. LC 70-190247. 32p. (Orig.). (gr. 7-12). 1972. lib. bdg. 4.95 incl. catalog cards (*0-87157-530-2*) SamHar Pr.

BUDDHA AND BUDDHISM

Burland, Cottie A. Way of the Buddha. (gr. 3-7). 1988. pap. 10.95 (*0-7175-0590-1*) Dufour.
Connolly, Holly & Connolly, Peter. Buddhism. Cole, W. Owen, ed. (Illus.). 140p. (Orig.). (gr. 9 up). 1992. pap. 14.95x (*1-871402-07-7*, Pub. by S Thornes UK) Dufour.
Gibb, Christopher. The Dalai Lama: The Leader of the Exiled People of Tibet & Tireless Worker for World Peace. LC 89-43119. (Illus.). 68p. (gr. 5-6). 1990. PLB 19.93 (*0-8368-0224-1*) Gareth Stevens Inc.
Landaw, Jonathan. The Story of Buddha. Basu, R. K., illus. (gr. 3-10). 1979. 7.95 (*0-89744-140-0*) Auromere.
Landaw, Jonathan & Brooke, Janet. Prince Siddhartha. rev. ed. (Illus.). 144p. (gr. 1-8). 1993. 15.95 (*0-86171-016-9*) Wisdom MA.
Morgan, Peggy. Being a Buddhist. (Illus.). 72p. (gr. 7-10). 1989. 19.95 (*0-7134-6015-6*, Pub. by Batsford UK) Trafalgar.
Raimondo, Lois. The Little Lama of Tibet. LC 93-13627. (Illus.). 40p. (ps-4). 1994. 14.95 (*0-590-46167-2*) Scholastic Inc.
Roth, Susan L. Buddha. LC 93-8240. 1994. 15.95 (*0-385-31072-2*) Doubleday.
Rowe, W. W. The Buddha's Question. LC 93-13993. 1994. 9.95 (*1-55939-020-4*) Snow Lion.
Snelling, John. Buddhist Festivals. (Illus.). 48p. (gr. 3-8). 1987. PLB 15.94 (*0-86592-980-7*); 11.95s.p. (*0-685-67596-3*) Rourke Corp.
Stewart, Whitney. To the Lion Throne. (Illus.). 60p. (Orig.). (gr. 3 up). 1990. PLB 8.95 (*0-937938-75-0*) Snow Lion.
Swann, Jivan. Tantra: A Handbook for Spiritual Lovers. Westley, Christine, ed. (Illus.). 32p. 1989. pap. 6.00 (*0-9622052-1-4*) Turtle Prints.
Wangu, Madhu B. Buddhism. (Illus.). 128p. (gr. 7-12). 1992. bds. 17.95x (*0-8160-2442-1*) Facts on File.
Zerner, Amy, illus. Zen ABC. LC 92-22940. 1993. 14.95 (*0-8048-1806-1*) C E Tuttle.

BUDDHA AND BUDDHISM–FICTION

Dharma Realm Buddhist University Faculty. Human Roots: Buddhist Stories for Young Readers, Vol. 2. (Illus.). 140p. (Orig.). (gr. 3 up). 1984. pap. 5.00 (*0-88139-017-8*) Buddhist Text.
Hesse, Hermann. Siddhartha. (gr. 10-12). 1982. pap. 3.99 (*0-553-20884-5*) Bantam.
Pharma Realm Buddhist University Faculty Staff, compiled by. Human Roots: Buddhist Stories for Young Readers, Vol. 1. (Illus.). 95p. (Orig.). (gr. 3 up). 1982. pap. 5.00 (*0-88139-500-5*) Buddhist Text.

BUDGERIGARS

Hearne, T. Parakeets. (Illus.). 32p. (gr. 2-5). 1989. lib. bdg. 15.94 (*0-86625-182-0*); 11.95 (*0-685-58611-1*) Rourke Corp.
Lohr, J. E. Your First Budgerigar. (Illus.). 36p. (Orig.). 1991. pap. 1.95 (*0-86622-058-5*, YF-102) TFH Pubns.
Vrbova, Zuza. Budgerigars. McAulay, Robert, illus. 48p. (gr. 2 up). 1990. PLB 9.95 (*0-86622-556-0*, J-006) TFH Pubns.

BUDGERIGARS–FICTION

Burch, Robert. Traveling Bird. (gr. 1-4). 1959. 9.95 (*0-8392-3038-9*) Astor-Honor.

BUDGETS, HOUSEHOLD

see also Finance, Personal

BUDGETS, PERSONAL

see Finance, Personal

BUFFALO, AMERICAN

see Bison

BUFFALOES–FICTION

Bouton, Bud. B Is for Buffalo. (Illus.). 64p. (gr. 1 up). 1994. 15.95 (*1-879244-03-9*) Windom Bks.
Goble, Paul. Buffalo Woman. LC 83-15704. (Illus.). 32p. (gr. k up). 1984. RSBE 14.95 (*0-02-737720-2*, Bradbury Pr) Macmillan Child Grp.
Grimsdell, Jeremy. Kalinzu. LC 92-45573. (Illus.). 32p. (ps-3). 1993. 14.95 (*1-85697-886-9*, Kingfisher LKC) LKC.
Reese, Bob. Buffa Buffalo. Reese, Bob, illus. (gr. k-6). 1986. 7.95 (*0-89868-175-8*); pap. 2.95 (*0-89868-176-6*) ARO Pub.

BUGLE–FICTION

Baker, Olaf. Where the Buffaloes Begin. Gammell, Stephen, illus. LC 85-5682. 48p. (ps-4). 1989. 14.95 (*0-670-82760-6*); pap. 5.99 (*0-14-050560-1*) Viking Child Bks.

BUGS

see Insects

BUILDING

see also Architecture; Carpentry; Engineering; Masonry

Allen, Judy. What Is a Wall, After All? Baron, Alan, illus. LC 92-54623. 32p. (ps up). 1993. PLB 14.95 (*1-56402-218-8*) Candlewick Pr.
Balterman, Lee. Girders & Cranes: A Skyscraper Is Built. Levine, Abby, ed. Balterman, Lee, illus. LC 90-37028. 32p. (gr. k-4). 1991. PLB 14.95 (*0-8075-2923-0*) A Whitman.
Barber, Nicola. Building for Tomorrow. LC 92-24925. (Illus.). 48p. (gr. 5). 1992. PLB 22.80 (*0-8114-2805-2*) Raintree Steck-V.
Barbey, Dorine. Giant Works: Underground, over Water, in the Air. Favreau, Luc, illus. 40p. (gr. k-5). 1993. PLB 9.95 (*1-56674-059-2*, HTS Bks) Forest Hse.
Bare, Colleen S. This Is a House. Bare, Colleen S., photos by. (Illus.). 32p. (gr. 1-5). 1992. 14.00 (*0-525-65090-3*, Cobblehill Bks) Dutton Child Bks.
Barton, Byron. Building a House. LC 80-22674. (Illus.). (ps up). 1990. pap. 4.95 (*0-688-09356-6*, Mulberry) Morrow.
Cash, Terry. Bricks. Stefoff, Rebecca, ed. Barber, Ed, photos by. LC 90-40249. (Illus.). 32p. (gr. 3-5). 1990. PLB 15.93 (*0-944483-68-2*) Garrett Ed Corp.
Daniel, Kira. Home Builder. Smolinski, Dick, illus. LC 88-10354. 32p. (gr. k-3). 1989. PLB 10.89 (*0-8167-1420-7*); pap. text ed. 2.95 (*0-8167-1421-5*) Troll Assocs.
Darling, David. Spiderwebs to Skyscrapers: The Science of Structure. LC 91-4001. (Illus.). 60p. (gr. 4-6). 1991. text ed. 13.95 RSBE (*0-87518-478-2*, Dillon) Macmillan Child Grp.

Evans, David & Williams, Claudette. Building Things. LC 93-7066. (Illus.). 32p. (gr. k-4). 1993. 9.95 (*1-56458-344-9*) Dorling Kindersley.
Gaff, Jackie. Buildings, Bridges & Tunnels. Fisher, Michael, et al, illus. LC 91-212. 40p. (Orig.). (gr. 2-5). 1991. pap. 3.99 (*0-679-80865-5*) Random Bks Yng Read.
Hawkes, Nigel. Structures & Buildings. (Illus.). 32p. (gr. 5-8). 1994. bds. 13.95 (*0-8050-3418-8*) TFC Bks NY.
Isaacson, Phillip M. Round Buildings, Square Buildings & Buildings That Wiggle Like a Fish. Isaacson, Phillip M., illus. LC 87-16967. 128p. (gr. 5 up). 1994. 14.95 (*0-394-89382-4*); pap. 13.00 (*0-679-80649-0*) Knopf Bks Yng Read.
Lambert, Mark. Building Technology. LC 90-25054. (Illus.). 48p. (gr. 5-8). 1991. 12.90 (*0-531-18399-8*, Pub. by Bookwright Pr) Watts.
Macaulay, David. Unbuilding. (gr. k-3). 1987. pap. 7.70 (*0-395-45425-5*) HM.
Mills, Jane L. & Johnson, Larry D. Build Like Me. Hebert, Kim T., illus. LC 86-60362. 13p. (Orig.). (ps). 1986. pap. 4.00 (*0-938155-01-6*); pap. 12.00 set of 3 bks. (*0-685-13524-1*) Read A Bol.
Mitgutsch, Ali. From Clay to Bricks. Mitgutsch, Ali, illus. LC 80-29567. 24p. (ps-3). 1981. PLB 10.95 (*0-87614-149-1*) Carolrhoda Bks.
Nash, Paul. Super Structures. Harris, Peter, ed. LC 89-12009. (Illus.). 32p. (gr. 2-4). 1989. PLB 13.26 (*0-944483-37-2*) Garrett Ed Corp.
Rickard, Graham. Building Homes. (Illus.). 32p. (gr. 2-5). 1989. 13.50 (*0-8225-2129-6*) Lerner Pubns.
Rowe, Julian & Perham, Molly. Build It Strong! LC 94-16941. (Illus.). 32p. (gr. 1-4). 1994. PLB 18.60 (*0-516-08138-1*); pap. 4.95 (*0-516-48138-X*) Childrens.
Royston, Angela. Buildings, Bridges & Tunnels. Shone, Rob, illus. LC 90-13023. 40p. (gr. 4-5). 1991. PLB 12. 40 (*0-531-19108-7*, Warwick) Watts.
Royston, Angela & Thompson, Graham. Monster Building Machines. 24p. (ps-2). 1990. 9.95 (*0-8120-6174-8*) Barron.
Wood, Richard. The Builder Through History. Smith, Tony, illus. LC 93-24398. 48p. (gr. 5-8). 1994. 15.95 (*1-56847-102-5*) Thomson Lrning.
Zubrowski, Bernie. Structures. 64p. (gr. 5-8). 1993. pap. text ed. 9.95 (*0-938587-35-8*) Cuisenaire.

BUILDING–FICTION

Avi. The Barn. LC 94-6920. 112p. (gr. 4-6). 1994. 13.95 (*0-531-06861-7*); PLB 13.99 (*0-531-08711-5*) Orchard Bks Watts.
Grossman, Bill. The Banging Book. Zimmerman, Robert, illus. LC 94-18689. 1995. 15.00 (*0-06-024497-6*, Festival); write for info. HarpC Child Bks.
Hughes, Shirley. The Big Concrete Lorry: A Tale of Trotter Street. Hughes, Shirley, illus. LC 89-8051. 32p. (ps-1). 1990. 13.95 (*0-688-08534-2*) Lothrop.
Hurle, Garry. The Most Important Building in Town. Moir, Mali, illus. 54p. (gr. 1-6). 1994. 11.95 (*0-85572-210-X*, Pub. by Hill Content Pubng AT) Seven Hills Bk Dists.
Krasilovsky, Phyllis. The Man Who Was Too Lazy to Fix Things. Cymerman, John E., illus. LC 91-435. 32p. (ps-3). 1992. 15.00 (*0-688-10394-4*, Tambourine Bks); PLB 14.93 (*0-688-10395-2*, Tambourine Bks) Morrow.
Macaulay, David. Unbuilding. (Illus.). (gr. 3 up). 1980. 15.45 (*0-395-29457-6*) HM.
Martin, Juliet. A Puzzle. Kelly, Geoff, illus. LC 93-18051. 1994. write for info. (*0-383-03710-7*) SRA Schl Grp.
Reasoner, Chuck. The Big Busy Building. Lassen, Cary P., illus. 10p. (ps up). 1994. bds. 12.95 (*0-8431-3659-6*) Price Stern.
Steinbaum, Michael & Warmbold, Jean. The Tumble-Down Tower. Balkovek, James, illus. (ps-4). 1993. pap. 9.95 (*0-8449-4254-5*); FRE Translation Tool, "Trans-it" 4.95 (*0-8449-4297-9*); CHI Translation Tool, "Trans-it" 4.95 (*0-8449-4299-5*); GER Translation Tool, "Trans-it" 4.95 (*0-8449-4298-7*); SPA Translation Tool, "Trans-it" 4.95 (*0-8449-4296-0*) Good Morn Tchr.
Tryon, Leslie. Albert's Alphabet. Tryon, Leslie, illus. LC 90-38883. 40p. (ps-1). 1991. SBE 14.95 (*0-689-31642-9*, Atheneum Child Bk) Macmillan Child Grp.
—Albert's Alphabet. 1st ed. LC 93-48408. (ps-2). 1994. pap. 4.95 (*0-689-71799-7*, Aladdin) Macmillan Child Grp.
Wood, Leslie. My House. (Illus.). 16p. (ps up). 1988. pap. 2.95 (*0-19-272186-0*) OUP.

BUILDING–REPAIR AND RECONSTRUCTION

Jackson, Thomas C. Hammers, Nails, Planks & Paint. Chewning, Randy, illus. 32p. (ps-3). 1994. pap. 2.50 (*0-590-44642-8*, Cartwheel) Scholastic Inc.

BUILDING–VOCATIONAL GUIDANCE

Lytle, Elizabeth S. Exploring Careers in the Construction Industry. Rosen, Ruth, ed. (gr. 7-12). 1992. PLB 14.95 (*0-8239-1405-4*) Rosen Group.

BUILDING REPAIR

see Building–Repair and Reconstruction

BUILDINGS–MAINTENANCE AND REPAIR

see Building–Repair and Reconstruction

BUILDINGS–REMODELING

see Building–Repair and Reconstruction

BULGARIA

Bulgaria. (Illus.). (gr. 7-12). 12.95 (*0-685-21877-5*, 047939) Know Unltd.
Bulgaria in Pictures. LC 93-23080. 64p. (gr. 5 up). 1994. PLB 18.95 (*0-8225-1890-2*) Lerner Pubns.
Popescu, Julian. Bulgaria. (Illus.). 96p. (gr. 5 up). 1988. 14.95 (*1-55546-177-8*) Chelsea Hse.

BULGARIA–FICTION

Shannon, Monica. Dobry. Katchamakoff, Atanas, illus. LC 92-31442. 176p. (gr. 5 up). 1993. pap. 4.99 (*0-14-036334-3*) Puffin Bks.

BULLFIGHTS

Say, Allen. El Chino. Say, Allen, illus. 32p. (gr. 2-8). 1990. 14.45 (*0-395-52023-1*) HM.

BULLFIGHTS–FICTION

Leaf, Munro. El Cuento de Ferdinando: The Story of Ferdinand. Lawson, Robert, illus. Belpre, Pura, tr. (SPA., Illus.). 72p. (ps-3). 1990. pap. 4.50 (*0-14-054253-1*, Puffin) Puffin Bks.
—El Cuento de Ferdinando: (The Story of Ferdinand) Belpre, Pura, tr. Lawson, Robert, illus. (SPA.). (gr. k-3). 1990. Set; incl. 4 bks., guide, & cass. incl. cass. 19.95 (*0-87499-189-7*); pap. 12.95 incl. cass. (*0-87499-188-9*); pap. 27.95 (*0-87499-191-9*) Live Oak Media.
—The Story of Ferdinand. Lawson, Robert, illus. LC 36-19452. (gr. k-3). 1936. pap. 13.00 (*0-670-67424-9*) Viking Child Bks.
—The Story of Ferdinand. Lawson, Robert, illus. 1993. pap. 6.99 incl. cassette (*0-14-095115-6*, Puffin) Puffin Bks.
The Story of Ferdinand. (ps-3). 1988. pap. 6.95 (*0-14-095071-0*, Puffin) Puffin Bks.
Vandersteen, Willy. The Tender-Hearted Matador: Duck, Lambik, or Your Goose Is Cooked! Lahey, Nicholas J., tr. LC 75-8494. (Illus.). 56p. (Orig.). (gr. 3 up). 1976. pap. 2.50 (*0-915560-10-0*, 10) Hiddigeigei.
Wojciechowska, Maia. Shadow of a Bull. LC 91-27716. 160p. (gr. 3-7). 1992. pap. 3.95 (*0-689-71567-6*, Aladdin) Macmillan Child Grp.

BULLION

see Gold; Money; Silver

BUNCHE, RALPH JOHNSON, 1904-1971

McKissack, Patricia & McKissack, Fredrick. Ralph J. Bunche: Peacemaker. Ostendorf, Ned, illus. LC 90-49849. 32p. (gr. 1-4). 1991. lib. bdg. 12.95 (*0-89490-300-4*) Enslow Pubs.

BUNYAN, JOHN, 1628-1688

Dengler, Sandy. John Bunyan: Writer of Pilgrim's Progress. (Orig.). (gr. 2-7). 1986. pap. text ed. 4.50 (*0-8024-4352-4*) Moody.

BUNYAN, PAUL

Anderson, J. I. I Can Read About Paul Bunyan. Snyder, Joel, illus. LC 76-54494. (gr. 2-5). 1977. pap. 2.50 (*0-89375-041-7*) Troll Assocs.
Emberley, Barbara. The Story of Paul Bunyan. Emberley, Ed E., illus. LC 93-11791. 1994. pap. 14.00 (*0-671-88557-X*, S&S BFYR) S&S Trade.
—The Story of Paul Bunyan. Emberley, Ed, illus. LC 93-11791. 1994. pap. 5.95 (*0-671-88647-9*, Half Moon Bks) S&S Trade.
Gleeson, Brian. Paul Bunyan. Meyerowitz, Rick, illus. LC 90-8558. 32p. (gr. k up). 1991. pap. 14.95 (*0-88708-142-8*, Rabbit Ears); pap. 19.95 incl. cass. (*0-88708-143-6*, Rabbit Ears) Picture Bk Studio.
—Paul Bunyan. Meyerowitz, Rick, illus. 64p. 1993. Repr. of 1990 ed. incl. cass. 9.95 (*0-88708-303-X*, Rabbit Ears); 5.95 (*0-88708-302-1*, Rabbit Ears) Picture Bk Studio.
Gleiter, Jan & Thompson, Kathleen. Paul Bunyan & Babe the Blue Ox. LC 84-9786. (Illus.). 32p. (gr. k-5). 1984. PLB 19.97 (*0-8172-2119-0*); PLB 29.28 incl. cassette (*0-8172-2241-3*); pap. 23.95 incl. cassette (*0-8172-2272-3*) Raintree Steck-V.
Helldorfer, M. C. Moon Trouble. Hunt, Jonathan, illus. LC 92-22233. 32p. (gr. k-5). 1994. RSBE 15.95 (*0-02-743517-2*, Bradbury Pr) Macmillan Child Grp.
Jensen, Patricia A. Paul Bunyan & His Blue Ox. Pidgeon, Jean L., illus. LC 93-24802. 32p. (gr. k-2). 1993. PLB 11.59 (*0-8167-3162-4*); pap. text ed. 2.95 (*0-8167-3163-2*) Troll Assocs.
Kellogg, Steven. Paul Bunyan: Big Book Edition. Kellogg, Steven, illus. 32p. (ps up). 1993. pap. 18.95 (*0-688-12610-3*, Mulberry) Morrow.
McCormick, Dell J. Paul Bunyan Swings His Axe. McCormick, Dell J., illus. LC 36-33409. (gr. 4-6). 1936. 11.95 (*0-87004-093-6*) Caxton.
—Tall Timber Tales: More Paul Bunyan Stories. Livesley, Lorna, illus. LC 39-20778. (gr. 4-6). 1939. 11.95 (*0-87004-094-4*) Caxton.
Paul Bunyan. (Illus.). 20p. (ps up). 1992. write for info. incl. long-life batteries (*0-307-74712-3*, 64712, Golden Pr) Western Pub.
Rounds, Glen. Ol' Paul, The Mighty Logger. LC 75-22163. (Illus.). 96p. (gr. 4-6). 1976. 15.95 (*0-8234-0269-X*); pap. 5.95 (*0-8234-0713-6*) Holiday.
Sabin, Louis. Paul Bunyan. Smolinski, Dick, illus. LC 84-2747. 32p. (gr. 3-6). 1985. PLB 9.49 (*0-8167-0254-3*); pap. text ed. 2.95 (*0-8167-0255-1*) Troll Assocs.
Shephard, Esther. Paul Bunyan. Kent, Rockwell, illus. LC 85-5448. 233p. (gr. 7 up). 1985. 12.95 (*0-15-259749-2*, HB Juv Bks) HarBrace.
Turney, Ida V. Paul Bunyan, the Work Giant. (Illus.). (gr. 3 up). 1969. 7.95 (*0-8323-0163-9*) Binford Mort.

BURBANK, LUTHER, 1849-1926

Luther Burbank: Mini-Play. (gr. 5 up). 1978. 6.50 (*0-89550-330-1*) Stevens & Shea.

BURGLARS

see Robbers and Outlaws

BURIAL

see Cemeteries; Funeral Rites and Ceremonies; Mounds and Mound Builders

BURIED CITIES

see Cities and Towns, Ruined, Extinct, etc.

BURIED TREASURE

Alwin-Hill, Raymond. Treasure Island. LC 91-52607. (Orig.). 1991. pap. 6.00 (*0-88734-412-7*) Players Pr.
Colby, C. B. World's Best Lost Treasure Stories. LC 91-14377. (Illus.). 96p. (gr. 3-10). 1992. pap. 3.95 (*0-8069-8421-X*) Sterling.
Deem, James M. How to Hunt Buried Treasure. Kelley, True, illus. LC 91-21749. 192p. (gr. 3-7). 1992. 15.45 (*0-395-58799-9*) HM.
Donnelly, Judy. True-Life Treasure Hunts. La Padula, Thomas, illus. 48p. (Orig.). (gr. 2-4). 1993. PLB 7.99 (*0-679-93980-6*); pap. 3.50 (*0-679-83980-1*) Random Bks Yng Read.
Gennings, S. Atocha Treasure. (Illus.). 32p. (gr. 4 up). 1988. PLB 17.27 (*0-86592-874-6*); PLB 12.95s.p. (*0-685-58293-0*) Rourke Corp.
Gibbons, Gail. Sunken Treasure. Gibbons, Gail, illus. LC 87-30114. 32p. (gr. 1-5). 1988. 14.00 (*0-690-04734-7*, Crowell Jr Bks); PLB 14.89 (*0-690-04736-3*) HarpC Child Bks.
—Sunken Treasure. Gibbons, Gail, illus. LC 87-30114. 32p. (gr. 1-5). 1990. pap. 4.95 (*0-06-446097-5*, Trophy) HarpC Child Bks.
Green, Harriet H. & Martin, Sue G. Treasure Hunts. 144p. (gr. 4-7). 1983. wkbk. 12.95 (*0-86653-115-7*, GA 469) Good Apple.
Incredible Buried Treasure. 32p. (ps-k). 1994. 4.95 (*1-56458-728-2*) Dorling Kindersley.
Kane, Penny. A Hidden Treasure. LC 89-50049. 87p. (gr. 8-11). 1989. pap. 5.95 (*1-55523-226-4*) Winston-Derek.
Lazo, Caroline E. Missing Treasure. (Illus.). 48p. (gr. 5-6). 1990. text ed. 11.95 RSBE (*0-89686-510-X*, Crestwood Hse) Macmillan Child Grp.
Nesbit, Edith. Story of the Treasure Seekers. (gr. 4-6). 1987. pap. 2.25 (*0-685-03990-0*, Puffin) Puffin Bks.
Schultz, Ron. Looking Inside Sunken Treasure. (Illus.). 48p. (gr. 3 up). Date not set. pap. 9.95 (*1-56261-074-0*) John Muir.
Tykr, J. Treasure Trails. (ps-3). 1993. pap. 4.95 (*0-7460-1321-3*, Usborne) EDC.

BURIED TREASURE–FICTION

Adimora-Ezeigbo, Akachi. Buried Treasure. (ps-3). 1992. pap. 2.95 (*0-7910-2908-5*) Chelsea Hse.
Bailey, Harold P. The Quadruple of the Merry Folbolly: or The Golden Adventure. 1993. 11.95 (*0-533-10590-0*) Vantage.
Barron, T. A. The Merlin Effect. LC 93-36234. 280p. (gr. 5-9). 1994. 16.95 (*0-399-22689-3*, Philomel Bks) Putnam Pub Group.
Bellairs, John. The Treasure of Alpheus Winterborn. 192p. (gr. 3-8). 1985. pap. 2.75 (*0-553-15527-X*, Skylark) Bantam.
Biggar, Joan R. Treasure at Morning Gulch. (Illus.). 152p. (Orig.). (gr. 5-8). 1991. pap. 3.99 (*0-570-04193-7*) Concordia.
Brouwer, Sigmund. Race for the Part Street Treasure. 132p. 1991. pap. 4.99 (*0-89693-859-X*) SP Pubns.
Bulla, Clyde R. Ghost Town Treasure. Freeman, Don, illus. 96p. (gr. 2-5). 1994. pap. 3.99 (*0-14-036732-2*) Puffin Bks.
Buller, Jon & Schade, Susan. Twenty-Thousand Baseball Cards under the Sea. Buller, Jon, illus. LC 90-40704. 48p. (Orig.). (gr. 2-3). 1991. lib. bdg. 7.99 (*0-679-91569-9*); pap. 3.50 (*0-679-81569-4*) Random Bks Yng Read.
Byars, Betsy C. Seven Treasure Hunts. Barrett, Jennifer, illus. LC 90-32043. 80p. (gr. 2-6). 1991. 14.00 (*0-06-020885-6*); PLB 13.89 (*0-06-020886-4*) HarpC Child Bks.
—The Seven Treasure Hunts. Barrett, Jennifer, illus. LC 90-32043. 80p. (gr. 2-6). 1992. pap. 3.95 (*0-06-440435-8*, Trophy) HarpC Child Bks.
Carris, Joan D. A Ghost of a Chance. Henry, Paul, illus. 160p. (gr. 3-7). 1992. 14.95 (*0-316-13016-8*) Little.
Clements, Bruce. The Treasure of Plunderell Manor. 192p. (gr. 7 up). 1991. pap. 3.95 (*0-374-47962-3*) FS&G.
Coleman, William. Chesapeake Charlie & Blackbeard's Treasure. LC 80-70573. 128p. (Orig.). (gr. 5-9). 1981. pap. 3.99 (*0-87123-116-6*) Bethany Hse.
Connell, David D. & Thurman, Jim. The Map With a Gap. LC 93-37779. 1994. text ed. write for info. (*0-7167-6527-6*); pap. text ed. write for info. (*0-7167-6523-3*) W H Freeman.
Cox, Leona D. Secret of the Two Bar Four Ranch. Giles, David N., illus. LC 93-81079. 160p. (gr. 6-12). 1994. pap. 11.95 (*0-9627680-6-5*) Inkwell CA.
Deem, Jmes M. How to Hunt Buried Treasure. 192p. 1994. pap. 3.99 (*0-380-72176-7*, Camelot) Avon.
Drew, David. Ah, Treasure! Tulloch, Coral, illus. LC 92-21455. 1993. 3.75 (*0-383-03611-9*) SRA Schl Grp.
Flood, E. L. Secret in the Moonlight: Welcome Inn. LC 93-50936. (Illus.). 144p. (gr. 3-6). 1994. pap. 2.95 (*0-8167-3427-5*) Troll Assocs.
Fox, J. N. Young Indiana Jones & the Pirates' Loot. LC 93-46831. 132p. (Orig.). (gr. 3-7). 1994. pap. 3.99 (*0-679-86433-4*, Bullseye Bks) Random Bks Yng Read.
Garrett, Sandra G. & Williams, Philip C. The Pirate's Treasure. LC 93-33877. 1994. write for info. (*0-86625-506-0*) Rourke Pubns.
Gaskin, Carol. Secret of the Royal Treasure. 144p. (Orig.). 1986. pap. 2.50 (*0-553-25729-3*) Bantam.
Gave, Marc. Disney's Goof Troop: Max's Treasure Hunt. (Illus.). 24p. (ps-3). 1992. pap. write for info. (*0-307-12762-1*, 12762, Golden Pr) Western Pub.

Goodman, Julius. Treasure Diver. 128p. (gr. 5-9). 1984. pap. 2.25 (*0-553-25764-1*) Bantam.
Griffin, Peni R. The Treasure Bird. Gowing, Toby, illus. LC 91-42773. 144p. (gr. 4-7). 1992. SBE 13.95 (*0-689-50554-X*, M K McElderry) Macmillan Child Grp.
—The Treasure Bird. 144p. (gr. 3-7). 1994. pap. 3.99 (*0-14-036653-9*) Puffin Bks.
Hager, Betty. Old Jake & the Pirate's Treasure. Dawkins, Ron, illus. LC 93-44489. 112p. (gr. 3-7). 1994. pap. 4.99 (*0-310-38401-X*) Zondervan.
Hope, Laura L. Bobbsey Twins' Big Adventure at Home. 120p. (gr. 1-4). 1990. 4.50 (*0-448-09134-8*, G&D) Putnam Pub Group.
Karr, Kathleen. Gideon & the Mummy Professor. 1993. 16.00 (*0-374-32563-4*) FS&G.
Katz, Welwyn W. Whalesinger. LC 90-34091. 212p. (gr. 7 up). 1991. SBE 14.95 (*0-689-50511-6*, M K McElderry) Macmillan Child Grp.
Kennedy, Richard. Amy's Eyes. Egielski, Richard, illus. LC 82-48841. 448p. (ps up). 1985. 15.00 (*0-06-023219-6*) HarpC Child Bks.
Kroll, Steven. Second Chance. 80p. (Orig.). 1994. pap. 3.50 (*0-380-77368-6*, Camelot Young) Avon.
Leslie-Spinks, Tim. Treasures of Trinkamalee. (gr. 4-7). 1993. 15.95 (*1-55037-320-X*, Pub. by Annick CN) Firefly Bks Ltd.
Macken, Walter. Island of the Great Yellow Ox. LC 90-22515. 192p. (gr. 5-9). 1991. pap. 14.00 jacketed, 3-pc. bdg. (*0-671-73800-3*, S&S BFYR) S&S Trade.
MacLachlan, Patricia. Unclaimed Treasures. LC 83-47714. 128p. (gr. 5-7). 1987. pap. 3.95 (*0-06-440189-8*, Trophy) HarpC Child Bks.
McOmber, Rachel B., ed. McOmber Phonics Storybooks: The Confection Connection. rev. ed. (Illus.). write for info. (*0-944991-73-4*) Swift Lrn Res.
Masterman-Smith, Virginia. The Treasure Trap. Litzinger, Roseanne, illus. LC 91-45217. 208p. (gr. 3-7). 1992. pap. 3.95 (*0-689-71578-1*, Aladdin) Macmillan Child Grp.
Micocci, Harriet. Captain Orkle's Treasure. Dora, illus. (gr. 3-7). 1961. 10.95 (*0-8392-3003-6*) Astor-Honor.
Morris, Dave. Buried Treasure. (gr. 4 up). 1990. pap. 2.95 (*0-440-40391-X*) Dell.
Myers, Walter D. The Righteous Revenge of Artemis Bonner. LC 91-42401. 144p. (gr. 5-9). 1992. 14.00 (*0-06-020844-9*); PLB 13.89 (*0-06-020846-5*) HarpC Child Bks.
Nesbit, Edith. Story of the Treasure Seekers. (gr. 4-6). 1987. pap. 2.25 (*0-685-03990-0*, Puffin) Puffin Bks.
Orton, Helen F. The Treasure in the Little Trunk. Ball, Robert, illus. 208p. (gr. 4). 1989. pap. text ed. 5.95 (*0-685-29125-1*) Niagara Cnty Hist Soc.
Packard, Edward. Sunken Treasure. 1982. 6.95 (*0-553-05018-4*) Bantam.
Parish, Peggy. Key to the Treasure. 160p. (gr. k-6). 1980. pap. 3.50 (*0-440-44438-1*, YB) Dell.
—Pirate Island Adventure. 176p. (gr. k-6). 1981. pap. 3.50 (*0-440-47394-2*, YB) Dell.
Pascal, Francine. The Case of the Hidden Treasure. (gr. 1-3). 1993. pap. 3.25 (*0-553-48064-2*) Bantam.
Richards, Dorothy F. Marty Finds a Treasure. Karch, Paul, illus. LC 82-19906. 32p. (gr. 1-3). 1983. lib. bdg. 13.95 (*0-89565-251-X*) Childs World.
Ryan, John. Pugwash & the Buried Treasure. (Illus.). 32p. (gr. k-2). 1994. 19.95 (*0-370-30338-5*, Pub. by Bodley Head UK) Trafalgar.
Saunders, Susan. Lauren's Treasure. 96p. (gr. 3-7). 1988. pap. 2.50 (*0-590-41695-2*) Scholastic Inc.
Schubert, Ingrid & Schubert, Dieter. Wild Will. LC 93-2484. 1993. 17.50 (*0-87614-816-X*) Carolrhoda Bks.
Schwartz, Alvin. Gold & Silver, Silver & Gold: Tales of Hidden Treasure. 1993. pap. 8.95 (*0-374-42583-3*, Sunburst) FS&G.
Shulevitz, Uri. The Treasure. (Illus.). 32p. (gr. k-3). 1986. pap. 5.95 (*0-374-47955-0*, Sunburst) FS&G.
Sobol, Donald J. Encyclopedia Brown & the Case of the Treasure Hunt. Owens, Gail, illus. LC 87-22048. 96p. (gr. 3-7). 1988. 12.95 (*0-688-06955-X*) Morrow Jr Bks.
Sohl, Marcia & Dackerman, Gerald. Treasure Island. 16p. (gr. 4-10). 1976. pap. 2.95 (*0-88301-106-9*); pap. 1.25 student activity bk. (*0-88301-185-9*) Pendulum Pr.
Stevenson, Robert Louis. Treasure Island. (gr. 7 up). 1962. pap. 2.95 (*0-8049-0002-7*, CL-2) Airmont.
—Treasure Island. (Illus.). (gr. 1-9). 1947. deluxe ed. 13.95 (*0-448-06025-6*, G&D) Putnam Pub Group.
—Treasure Island. 224p. (gr. 2-5). 1984. pap. 2.95 (*0-14-035016-0*, Puffin) Puffin Bks.
—Treasure Island. Craft, Kinuko Y., illus. Edwards, Jane, adapted by. LC 79-24100. (Illus.). (gr. 4-12). 1983. PLB 20.70 (*0-8172-1655-3*) Raintree Steck-V.
—Treasure Island. Wyeth, N. C., illus. LC 81-8788. 273p. (gr. 3 up). 1981. SBE 24.95 (*0-684-17160-0*, Scribners Young Read) Macmillan Child Grp.
—Treasure Island. write for info. S&S Trade.
—Treasure Island. Letley, Emma, ed. (gr. 7-12). 1985. pap. 3.95 (*0-19-281681-0*) OUP.
—Treasure Island. (gr. 7 up). 1965. pap. 1.75 (*0-451-51917-5*, Sig Classics) NAL-Dutton.
—Treasure Island. (gr. k-6). 1986. 7.98 (*0-685-16845-X*, 618168) Random Hse Value.
—Treasure Island. reissued ed. Norby, Lisa, adapted by. Fernandez, Fernando, illus. LC 89-70039. 96p. (Orig.). (gr. 2-6). 1990. PLB 5.99 (*0-679-90402-6*, Bullseye Bks); pap. 2.99 (*0-679-80402-1*, Bullseye Bks) Random Bks Yng Read.
—Treasure Island. 272p. 1990. pap. 2.50 (*0-8125-0508-5*) Tor Bks.
—Treasure Island. Peake, Mervyn, illus. LC 92-53174. 240p. 1992. 12.95 (*0-679-41800-8*, Evrymans Lib Childs Class) Knopf.
—Treasure Island. McNaughton, Colin, illus. LC 93-18941. 272p. (gr. 4-8). 1993. 15.95 (*0-8050-2773-4*, Bks Young Read) H Holt & Co.
—Treasure Island. Price, Norman, illus. LC 93-50905. 1994. write for info. (*0-448-40562-8*, G&D) Putnam Pub Group.
Stover, Marjorie. Midnight in the Dollhouse. Levine, Abby, ed. Loccisano, Karen, illus. LC 89-37904. 160p. (gr. 3-6). 1990. 11.95 (*0-8075-5124-4*) A Whitman.
Treasure Island. (Illus.). 352p. (gr. 3-9). 1981. pap. 7.95 (*0-448-11025-3*, G&D) Putnam Pub Group.
Treasure Island. (Illus.). 24p. (Orig.). (gr. k up). 1993. pap. 2.50 (*1-56144-103-1*, Honey Bear Bks) Modern Pub NYC.
Warner, Gertrude C., created by. The Haunted Cabin Mystery. (Illus.). (gr. 2-7). 1991. 10.95g (*0-8075-3179-0*); pap. 3.50g (*0-8075-3178-2*) A Whitman.
Werenko, Lisa V. It Zwibble & the Hunt for the Rain Forest Treasure. 1992. pap. 2.50 (*0-590-44841-2*) Scholastic Inc.
Wood, A. J. The Treasure Hunt. Downer, Maggie, illus. LC 92-5515. 32p. (ps-4). 1992. 13.95 (*1-56566-018-8*) Thomasson-Grant.

BURMA

San Suu Kyi Sung. Burma. (Illus.). 96p. (gr. 5 up). 1988. 14.95 (*0-222-00979-9*) Chelsea Hse.
Saw Myat Yin. Burma. LC 89-25463. (Illus.). 128p. (gr. 5-9). 1991. PLB 21.95 (*1-85435-299-7*) Marshall Cavendish.
Wright, David K. Burma. LC 90-21265. (Illus.). 128p. (gr. 5-9). 1991. PLB 20.55 (*0-516-02725-5*) Childrens.

BURNETT, FRANCES HODGSON, 1849-1924

Carpenter, Angelica S. Frances Hodgson Burnett: Beyond the Secret Garden. (gr. 4-7). 1992. pap. 6.95 (*0-8225-9610-5*) Lerner Pubns.
Carpenter, Angelica S. & Shirley, Jean. Frances Hodgson Burnett: Beyond the Secret Garden. (Illus.). 128p. (gr. 5 up). 1990. PLB 21.50 (*0-8225-4905-0*) Lerner Pubns.

BURTON, SIR RICHARD FRANCIS, 1821-1890

Simon, Charnan. Richard Burton: Explorer of Arabia & Africa. LC 90-20814. (Illus.). 128p. (gr. 3 up). 1991. PLB 20.55 (*0-516-03062-0*) Childrens.

BURYING GROUNDS

see Cemeteries

BUS DRIVERS

Stamper, Judith. What's It Like to Be a Bus Driver. Garcia, T. R., illus. LC 89-34388. 32p. (gr. k-3). 1990. lib. bdg. 10.89 (*0-8167-1795-8*); pap. text ed. 2.95 (*0-8167-1796-6*) Troll Assocs.

BUS DRIVERS–FICTION

Lakin, Patricia. Up a Tree. Cushman, Doug, illus. LC 93-49847. 1994. write for info. (*0-8114-3868-6*) Raintree Steck-V.

BUSES

Chlad, Dorothy. Riding on a Bus. LC 85-12750. (Illus.). 32p. (ps-2). 1985. pap. 3.95 (*0-516-41979-X*) Childrens.

BUSES–FICTION

Anderson, Rachel. The Bus People. LC 92-1506. 96p. (gr. 5 up). 1992. 13.95 (*0-8050-2297-X*, Bks Young Read) H Holt & Co.
Appleby, Ellen. Wheels on the Bus. (Illus.). 24p. (ps-k). 1993. 9.00 (*0-307-74815-4*, 64815, Golden Pr) Western Pub.
Awdry, W. Thomas the Tank Engine & the Great Race. Bell, Owain, illus. 7p. (ps-k). 1989. bds. 7.00 with plastic wheels (*0-679-80000-X*) Random Bks Yng Read.
Beveridge, Barbara. Over the Marble Mountain. Mancini, Rob, illus. LC 92-27097. (gr. 4 up). 1993. 2.50 (*0-383-03589-9*) SRA Schl Grp.
Bowes, Clare. The Hippo Bus. Bowes, Clare, illus. LC 92-34264. 1993. 14.00 (*0-383-03629-1*) SRA Schl Grp.
Champlin, Dale, illus. The Wheels on the Bus Big Book. (ps-2). 1988. pap. text ed. 14.00 (*0-922053-15-4*) N Edge Res.
Cole, Joanna. The Magic School Bus at the Waterworks. (gr. 1-4). 1986. 13.95 (*0-590-43739-9*, Scholastic Hardcover) Scholastic Inc.
—The Magic School Bus Inside the Earth. Degen, Bruce, illus. 1989. pap. 3.95 (*0-590-40760-0*, Scholastic Hardcover) Scholastic Inc.
—The Magic School Bus Inside the Human Body. Deger, Bruce, illus. (ps-3). 1990. pap. 3.95 (*0-590-41427-5*, Scholastic Hardcover) Scholastic Inc.
Crews, Donald. School Bus. Crews, Donald, illus. LC 83-18681. 32p. (gr. k-3). 1984. 15.00 (*0-688-02807-1*); PLB 14.93 (*0-688-02808-X*) Greenwillow.
—School Bus. LC 92-43766. (Illus.). 32p. (ps up). 1993. pap. text ed. 3.95 (*0-688-12267-1*, Mulberry) Morrow.
Eldrid, Brenda M. The Little School Bus That Talked. Beckes, Shirley, illus. 24p. (ps-2). 1992. pap. 0.99 (*1-56293-113-X*) McClanahan Bk.
Fuller, Ted. Barney the Bus. Weinberger, Jane, ed. DeVito, Pamela, illus. LC 88-51276. 48p. (ps-4). 1989. pap. 7.95 (*0-932433-49-9*) Windswept Hse.
Giffard, Hannah. Red Bus. Giffard, Hannah, illus. LC 92-62424. 12p. (ps). 1993. bds. 3.95 (*0-688-12443-7*, Tambourine Bks) Morrow.
Gomi, Taro. Bus Stops. Gomi, Taro, illus. LC 88-10193. 32p. (ps-1). 1988. 10.95 (*0-87701-551-1*) Chronicle Bks.
Grosset & Dunlap Staff. Wheels on the Bus. Smath, Jerry, illus. 18p. (ps). 1991. bds. 2.95 (*0-448-40124-X*, G&D) Putnam Pub Group.
Hutchins, Pat. Follow That Bus! Hutchins, Laurence, illus. LC 76-21822. 112p. (gr. 3-7). 1988. pap. 2.95 (*0-394-80792-8*) Knopf Bks Yng Read.
Johnson, John E., illus. Here Comes the Bus. 14p. (gr. 2-5). 1985. 4.99 (*0-394-87544-3*) Random Bks Yng Read.
Kingsland, Robin. Bus Stop Bop. Ayliffe, Alex, illus. 32p. (ps-3). 1991. 14.95 (*0-670-83919-1*) Viking Child Bks.
Kovalski, Maryann. Wheels on the Bus. Kovalski, Maryann, illus. (ps-4). 1990. pap. 4.95 (*0-316-50259-6*, Joy St Bks) Little.
Lakin, Patricia. Up a Tree. Cushman, Doug, illus. LC 93-49847. 1994. write for info. (*0-8114-3868-6*) Raintree Steck-V.
Muntean, Michaela. The Very Bumpy Bus Ride. Wiseman, Bernard, illus. LC 81-16905. 48p. (ps-3). 1982. 5.95 (*0-8193-1079-4*); 5.95 (*0-8193-1080-8*) Parents.
—The Very Bumpy Bus Ride. Wiseman, Bernard, illus. LC 93-13042. 1993. PLB 13.27 (*0-8368-0980-7*) Gareth Stevens Inc.
Neville, Kathleen. Yellowbuddy: The Runaway School Bus. (gr. 4-7). 1993. pap. 8.95 (*0-933905-22-X*) Claycomb Pr.
Rogers, Mary. Daniel's First Bus Ride. 30p. (gr. k). 1992. pap. text ed. 23.00 big bk. (*1-56843-008-6*); pap. text ed. 4.50 (*1-56843-058-2*) BGR Pub.
Stevens, Florence & Lamont-Clarke, Ginette. Et Si L'Autobus Nous Oublie? Ouellet, Odile, illus. LC 90-70136. 24p. (ps-2). 1990. 12.95 (*0-88776-252-2*); pap. 6.95 (*0-88776-260-3*) Tundra Bks.
—What If the Bus Doesn't Come? Ouellet, Odile, illus. LC 90-70135. 24p. (ps-2). 1990. 12.95 (*0-88776-251-4*); pap. 6.95 (*0-88776-259-X*) Tundra Bks.
Wiseman, Bernard. The Big Yellow School Bus. LC 91-58787. (Illus.). 48p. (gr. k-3). 1992. 9.95 (*1-56282-048-6*); PLB 9.89 (*1-56282-226-8*) Disney Pr.
Zelinsky, Paul O. The Wheels on the Bus: With Pictures that Move. 16p. (ps). 1990. 14.95 (*0-525-44644-3*, DCB) Dutton Child Bks.
Ziefert, Harriet. Jason's Bus Ride. Taback, Simms, illus. (ps-2). 1993. pap. 3.25 (*0-14-036536-2*, Puffin) Puffin Bks.

BUSH, GEORGE, 1924-

Deegan, Paul J. George Bush. Wallner, Rosemary, ed. LC 91-73077. (gr. 4 up). 1991. 13.99 (*1-56239-024-4*) Abdo & Dghtrs.
Pemberton, William E. George Bush. LC 92-46768. 1993. 19.93 (*0-86625-478-1*); 14.95s.p. (*0-685-66539-9*) Rourke Pubns.
Sandak, Cass R. The Bushes. LC 91-11153. (Illus.). 48p. (gr. 5). 1991. text ed. 4.95 RSBE (*0-89686-632-7*, Crestwood Hse) Macmillan Child Grp.
Stefoff, Rebecca. George H. W. Bush: Forty-First President of the United States. Iraq War. Young, Richard G., ed. LC 91-30666. (Illus.). 140p. (gr. 5-9). 1992. PLB 17.26 (*1-56074-033-7*) Garrett Ed Corp.

BUSINESS

see also Advertising; Banks and Banking; Credit; Economic Conditions; Manufactures; Merchants; Occupations; Salesmen and Salesmanship; Small Business

Aaseng, Nathan. Close Calls: From the Brink of Ruin to Business Success. (Illus.). 80p. (gr. 5 up). 1990. PLB 18.95 (*0-8225-0682-3*) Lerner Pubns.
American Business. (Illus.). 48p. (gr. 6-12). 1975. pap. 1.85 (*0-8395-3325-X*, 33325) BSA.
Business Kids Staff. The Business Kit. Ashemimry, Nasir M., intro. by. (Illus.). 129p. (gr. 8-12). 1989. tchr's. ed. 14.95 (*0-9625075-1-2*); kit of 5 booklets 49.95 (*0-9625075-0-4*) Lemonade Kids.
Carroll, Jeri & Wells, Candace. Founders. Foster, Tom, illus. 64p. (ps-3). 1986. wkbk. 7.95 (*0-86653-345-1*, GA 695) Good Apple.
Cook, J. Business. 48p. (gr. 6 up). 1987. pap. 6.95 (*0-86020-934-2*) EDC.
Greenberg, Keith E. Ben & Jerry: Ice Cream for Everyone! (Illus.). 48p. (gr. 2-5). 1994. PLB 12.95 (*1-56711-064-9*) Blackbirch.
Lamancusa, Joe. Kid Cash: Creative Money-Making Ideas. (gr. 4-7). 1993. pap. 9.95 (*0-8306-4265-X*) TAB Bks.
Menzies, Linda. Teen's Guide to Business: The Secret to a Successful Enterprise. 1992. pap. 7.95 (*0-942361-50-4*) MasterMedia Ltd.
Sheffer, Susannah, ed. Earning Our Own Money: Homeschoolers 13 & under Describe How They Have Earned Money. Linn, Emily, tr. (Illus.). 28p. (Orig.). (gr. 1 up). 1991. pap. text ed. 3.95 (*0-913677-09-4*) Holt Assocs.
Shniderman, Jeffrey & Hurwitz, Sue. Applications: A Guide to Filling Out All Kinds of Forms. LC 93-7911. 1993. 13.95 (*0-8239-1609-X*) Rosen Group.
Winitz, Harris. Business, Bk. 2. Baker, Syd, illus. 50p. (Orig.). (gr. 7 up). 1986. pap. text ed. 22.00 incl. cass. (*0-939990-46-6*) Intl Linguistics.
Wood, Heather. One Hundred One Marvelous Money-Making Ideas for Kids. 128p. (Orig.). 1995. pap. 3.99 (*0-8125-2060-2*) Tor Bks.

BUSINESS–BIOGRAPHY

Aaseng, Nathan. The Unsung Heroes: Unheralded People Who Invented Famous Products. (Illus.). 80p. (gr. 5 up). 1989. 18.95 (*0-8225-0676-9*) Lerner Pubns.

Burford, Betty. Chocolate by Hershey: A Story about Milton S. Hershey. Chantland, Loren, illus. LC 93-43638. 1994. 14.95 (*0-87614-830-5*) Carolrhoda Bks.

Canadeo, Anne. Ralph Lauren: Master of Fashion. Young, Richard G., ed. LC 91-32777. (Illus.). 64p. (gr. 4-8). 1992. PLB 17.26 (*1-56074-021-3*) Garrett Ed Corp.

—Sam Walton: The Giant of Wal-Mart. Young, Richard G., ed. LC 91-32776. (Illus.). 64p. (gr. 4-8). 1992. PLB 17.26 (*1-56074-025-6*) Garrett Ed Corp.

Collins, David R. Lee Iacocca: Chrysler's Good Fortune. Young, Richard G., ed. LC 91-31989. (Illus.). 64p. (gr. 4-8). 1992. PLB 17.26 (*1-56074-017-5*) Garrett Ed Corp.

—Phillip H. Knight: Running with Nike. Young, Richard G., ed. LC 91-32316. (Illus.). 64p. (gr. 4-8). 1992. PLB 17.26 (*1-56074-020-5*) Garrett Ed Corp.

Falkof, Lucille. John H. Johnson: The Man from Ebony. Young, Richard G., ed. LC 91-32775. (Illus.). 64p. (gr. 4-8). 1992. PLB 17.26 (*1-56074-018-3*) Garrett Ed Corp.

Goldish, Meish. Levi Strauss. LC 93-11997. (gr. 1-8). 1993. 15.93 (*0-86592-070-2*); 11.95s.p. (*0-685-66542-9*) Rourke Enter.

Greenberg, Keith. Sam Walton. LC 92-45123. 1993. 15.93 (*0-86592-047-8*); 11.95s.p. (*0-685-66419-8*) Rourke Enter.

Haddock, Patricia. Lee Iacocca: Standing up for America: A Biography of Lee Iacocca. LC 86-32965. (Illus.). 128p. (gr. 6 up). 1987. text ed. 13.95 RSBE (*0-87518-362-X*, Dillon) Macmillan Child Grp.

Italia, Bob. H. Ross Perot: The Man Who Woke up America. LC 93-3682. 1993. 12.94 (*1-56239-236-0*) Abdo & Dghtrs.

Koopman, Anne. Charles P. Lazarus: The Titan of Toys R Us. Young, Richard G., ed. LC 91-32054. (Illus.). 64p. (gr. 4-8). 1992. PLB 17.26 (*1-56074-022-1*) Garrett Ed Corp.

Mascola. Ray Kroc, Reading Level 2. (Illus.). 24p. (gr. 1-4). 1989. PLB 14.60 (*0-86592-433-3*); 10.95s.p. (*0-685-58802-5*) Rourke Corp.

Mayberry, Jodine. Business Leaders Who Built Financial Empires. (Illus.). 48p. (gr. 4-8). 1994. PLB write for info. (*0-8114-4934-3*) Raintree Steck-V.

Rozakis, Laurie. Mary Kay. LC 92-45124. 1993. 15.93 (*0-86592-040-0*); 11.95s.p. (*0-685-66418-X*) Rourke Enter.

Spiesman, Harriet. John Scully: Building the Apple Dream. Young, Richard G., ed. LC 91-28542. (Illus.). 64p. (gr. 4-8). 1992. PLB 17.26 (*1-56074-023-X*) Garrett Ed Corp.

Stefoff, Rebecca. Ted Turner: Television's Triumphant Tiger. Young, Richard G., ed. LC 91-32774. (Illus.). 64p. (gr. 4-8). 1992. PLB 17.26 (*1-56074-024-8*) Garrett Ed Corp.

Tippins, Sherill. Donna Karan: Designing an American Dream. Young, Richard G., ed. LC 91-32784. (Illus.). 64p. (gr. 4-8). 1992. PLB 17.26 (*1-56074-019-1*) Garrett Ed Corp.

—Michael Eisner: Fun for Everyone. Young, Richard G., ed. LC 91-28544. (Illus.). 64p. (gr. 4-8). 1992. PLB 17.26 (*1-56074-014-0*) Garrett Ed Corp.

Zickgraf, Ralph. William H. Gates: From Whiz Kid to Software King. Young, Richard G., ed. LC 91-32056. (Illus.). 64p. (gr. 4-8). 1992. PLB 17.26 (*1-56074-016-7*) Garrett Ed Corp.

BUSINESS, CHOICE OF

see Vocational Guidance

BUSINESS–FICTION

Aiello, Barbara & Shulman, Jeffrey. Business Is Looking Up: Featuring Renaldo Rodriguez. Barr, Loel, illus. 48p. (gr. 3-6). 1988. PLB 13.95 (*0-8050-3136-7*) TFC Bks NY.

Barbour, Karen. Little Nino's Pizzeria. 32p. (ps-3). 1990. pap. 4.95 (*0-15-246321-6*, Voyager Bks) HarBrace.

Ginny, Susan. Uncle Lester's Lemonade Lure. Ginny, Susan, illus. 15p. (Orig.). (gr. 2-3). 1988. pap. 4.95 (*0-9621556-0-8*) SYF Enter.
Fictional story of a small town store owner whose business spirit enables him to survive advanced competition in his local hardware store.
Publisher Provided Annotation.

Herman, Charlotte. Max Malone Makes a Million. Smith, Cat B., illus. LC 90-46373. 64p. (gr. 2-4). 1992. pap. 4.95 (*0-8050-2328-3*, Redfeather BYR) H Holt & Co.

Klevin, Jill R. The Turtle Street Trading Co. Edwards, Linda S., illus. LC 82-70312. 144p. (gr. 4-6). 1982. 11.95 (*0-385-29043-8*); PLB 11.95 (*0-685-05625-2*) Delacorte.

—Turtles Together Forever! Edwards, Linda S., illus. LC 82-70313. 160p. (gr. 4-6). 1982. pap. 9.95 (*0-385-29045-4*); pap. 9.89 (*0-385-29046-2*) Delacorte.

Merrill, Jean. The Toothpaste Millionaire. Palmer, Jan, illus. LC 73-22055. 96p. (gr. 2-5). 1974. 13.95 (*0-395-18511-4*) HM.

Naylor, Phyllis R. Eddie, Incorporated. Sims, Blanche, illus. LC 79-22589. (gr. 4-6). 1980. SBE 13.95 (*0-689-30754-3*, Atheneum Child Bk) Macmillan Child Grp.

Pearson, Tracey C. Storekeeper. (ps-3). 1991. pap. 3.95 (*0-8037-1052-6*, Puff Pied Piper) Puffin Bks.

Robertson, Keith. Henry Reed, Inc. McCloskey, Robert, illus. (gr. 4-6). 1958. pap. 14.95 (*0-670-36796-6*) Viking Child Bks.

Shefelman, Janice. A Peddler's Dream. Shefelman, Tom, illus. LC 91-35285. 32p. (gr. 2-5). 1992. 14.45 (*0-395-60904-6*) HM.

Spinelli, Jerry. Bathwater Gang Gets down to Business. (ps-3). 1992. 12.95 (*0-316-80808-3*) Little.

Van Leeuwen, Jean. Benjy in Business. Apple, Margot, illus. LC 82-22158. 112p. (gr. 2-6). 1983. Dial Bks Young.

BUSINESS–HISTORY

Aaseng, Nathan. The Rejects: People & Products That Outsmarted the Experts. (Illus.). 80p. (gr. 5 up). 1989. 18.95 (*0-8225-0677-7*) Lerner Pubns.

BUSINESS, SMALL

see Small Business

BUSINESS–VOCATIONAL GUIDANCE

Menzies, Linda, et al. A Teen's Guide to Business: The Secrets to a Successful Enterprise. large type ed. LC 93-30254. (gr. 9-12). 1993. 15.95 (*0-7862-0061-8*) Thorndike Pr.

BUSINESS COLLEGES

see Business Education

BUSINESS DEPRESSIONS

see Depressions; Economic Conditions

BUSINESS EDUCATION

Gilabert, Frank. Business Career Planning Series, 5 bks. (Orig.). (gr. 12). Date not set. Set. pap. 55.00 (*1-884194-05-2*); The Biz Careers Finance Guide: How to Improve Your Business Knowledge about Finance, 100p. pap. 14.95 (*1-884194-02-8*); The Biz Careers Accounting Guide: How to Improve Your Business Knowledge about Accounting, 100p. pap. 14.95 (*1-884194-01-X*); The Biz Careers Planning Guide: How to Prepare for Your Business Career, 70p. pap. 9.95 (*1-884194-00-1*); The Business Careers Information Systems Guide: How to Improve Your Business Knowledge about Information Systems, 100p. pap. 14.95 (*1-884194-03-6*); The Biz Careers Marketing Guide: How to Improve Your Business Knowledge about Marketing, 100p. pap. 14.95 (*1-884194-04-4*) Biz Careers.

Spencer, Jean. Exploring Careers in the Electronic Office. rev. ed. Rosen, Ruth, ed. (gr. 7-12). 1989. PLB 14.95 (*0-8239-1009-1*) Rosen Group.

BUSINESS ENGLISH

see English Language–Business English

BUSINESS ETHICS

see also Success

BUSINESS LETTERS

see also English Language–Business English

BUSINESS SCHOOLS

see Business Education

BUTTERFLIES

see also Caterpillars; Moths

Beaty, Dave. Moths & Butterflies. LC 92-29741. (Illus.). (gr. 2-6). 1993. 15.95 (*1-56766-001-0*) Childs World.

Berenstain, Michael. Michael Berenstain's Butterfly Book. Berenstain, Michael, illus. 24p. (ps-k). 1992. pap. write for info. laminated covers (*0-307-10023-5*, 10023, Golden Pr) Western Pub.

Berger, Melvin. A Butterfly Is Born. (Illus.). 16p. (ps-2). 1993. pap. text ed. 14.95 (*1-56784-012-4*) Newbridge Comms.

Butterfield, Moira. Butterfly. Johnson, Paul, illus. 24p. (ps-1). 1992. pap. 3.95 (*0-671-75894-2*, Little Simon) S&S Trade.

Butterflies. (Illus.). 32p. (ps-1). 1986. pap. 1.25 (*0-8431-1523-8*) Price Stern.

Butterflies. 1991. PLB 14.95s.p. (*0-88682-421-4*) Creative Ed.

Butterflies & Moths. 8.95 (*1-56458-038-5*) Dorling Kindersley.

Cox & Cork. Butterflies & Moths. (gr. 2-5). 1980. PLB 11.96 (*0-88110-073-0*); pap. 3.95 (*0-86020-477-4*) EDC.

Cutts, David. Look - a Butterfly. Conner, Eulala, illus. LC 81-11369. 32p. (gr. k-2). 1982. PLB 11.59 (*0-89375-662-8*); pap. text ed. 2.95 (*0-89375-663-6*) Troll Assocs.

Dunn, Gary. Descubre Mariposas. University of Mexico City Staff, tr. from SPA. O'Neill, Pablo M. & Robare, Lorie, illus. 48p. (gr. 3-8). 1993. PLB 16.95 (*1-56674-048-7*, HTS Bks) Forest Hse.

Dunn, Opal. Butterfly Match & Patch Book. (ps). 1992. 4.99 (*0-440-40613-7*, YB) Dell.

Echols, Jean C. Hide a Butterfly. Bergman, Lincoln & Fairwell, Kay, eds. Baker, Lisa H. & Klofkorn, Lisa, illus. Callaway, Jane, et al, photos by. 28p. (Orig.). (gr. 1-3). 1986. pap. 8.50 (*0-912511-23-0*) Lawrence Science.

Faber, Betty L. Discover Butterflies. (Illus.). 48p. (gr. 3-6). 1992. PLB 14.95 (*1-878363-67-0*, HTS Bks) Forest Hse.

Feltwell, John. Butterflies & Moths. LC 92-54313. (Illus.). 64p. (gr. 3 up). 1993. 9.95 (*1-56458-227-2*) Dorling Kindersley.

Fichter, George S. Butterflies & Moths. Kest, Kristin, illus. 36p. (gr. k-3). 1993. 4.95 (*0-307-11435-X*, 11435, Golden Pr) Western Pub.

Fischer-Nagel, Heiderose & Fischer-Nagel, Andreas. Life of the Butterfly. Simon, Noel, tr. from GER. Fischer-Nagel, Heiderose & Fischer-Nagel, Andreas, photos by. (Illus.). 48p. (gr. 2-5). 1987. lib. bdg. 19.95 (*0-87614-244-7*); pap. 6.95 (*0-87614-484-9*) Carolrhoda Bks.

Florian, Douglas. Discovering Butterflies. LC 89-37816. 32p. (ps-2). 1990. pap. 3.95 (*0-689-71376-2*, Aladdin) Macmillan Child Grp.

Fowler, Allan. It Could Still Be a Butterfly. LC 94-10470. (Illus.). 32p. (ps-2). 1994. PLB 14.40 (*0-516-06028-7*); pap. 3.95 (*0-516-46028-5*) Childrens.

Gattis, L. S., III. Butterflies & Moths for Pathfinders: A Basic Youth Enrichment Skill Honor Packet. (Illus.). 20p. (Orig.). (gr. 5 up). 1987. pap. 5.00 tchr's. ed. (*0-936241-31-4*) Cheetah Pub.

George, Jean C. The Moon of the Monarch Butterflies. Mak, Kam, illus. LC 91-33152. 48p. (gr. 3-7). 1993. 15.00 (*0-06-020816-3*); PLB 14.89 (*0-06-020817-1*) HarpC Child Bks.

Gibbons, Gail. Monarch Butterfly. Gibbons, Gail, illus. LC 89-1880. 32p. (ps-3). 1989. reinforced bdg. 15.95 (*0-8234-0773-X*) Holiday.

—Monarch Butterfly. Gibbons, Gail, illus. LC 89-1880. 32p. (ps-3). 1991. pap. 5.95 (*0-8234-0909-0*) Holiday.

Hariton, Anca. Butterfly Story. Hariton, Anca, illus. LC 94-19377. (ps-k). 1995. write for info (*0-525-45212-5*) Dutton Child Bks.

Heiligman. From Caterpillar to Butterfly. 1995. 14.00 (*0-06-024264-7*); PLB 13.89 (*0-06-024268-X*) HarpC Child Bks.

Hogan, Paula Z. The Butterfly. LC 78-26827. (Illus.). 32p. (gr. 1-4). 1979. PLB 19.97 (*0-8172-1252-3*); pap. 4.95 (*0-8114-8176-X*); pap. 9.95 incl. cassette (*0-8114-8184-0*) Raintree Steck-V.

—The Butterfly. LC 78-26827. (Illus.). 32p. (gr. k-3). 1984. PLB 29.28 incl. cassette (*0-8172-2226-X*) Raintree Steck-V.

Howe, James. I Wish I Were a Butterfly. LC 86-33635. (gr. k up). 1994. pap. 5.95 (*0-15-238013-2*) HarBrace.

Josephson, Judith P. The Monarch Butterfly. LC 88-10871. (Illus.). 48p. (gr. 5). 1988. text ed. 12.95 RSBE (*0-89686-389-1*, Crestwood Hse) Macmillan Child Grp.

Julivert, Maria A. The Fascinating World of Butterflies & Moths. Marcel Socias Studio Staff & Arridondo, F., illus. 32p. (gr. 3-7). 11.95 (*0-8120-6282-5*) Barron.

Kendall, Cindy. Butterflies. Bennish, Gracia, illus. Dudley, Dick. LC 93-3117. (ps). 1994. pap. 3.95 (*0-8037-1275-8*) Dial Bks Young.

Knight, Christopher, photos by. Monarchs. Lasky, Kathryn, text by. LC 92-33972. (Illus.). 1993. 16.95 (*0-15-255296-0*); pap. 8.95 (*0-15-255297-9*) HarBrace.

Lavies, Bianca. Monarch Butterflies, Mysterious Travelers. (Illus.). 32p. (gr. 3-6). 1993. 14.99 (*0-525-44905-1*, DCB) Dutton Child Bks.

Lepthien, Emilie U. Monarch Butterflies. LC 89-456. (Illus.). 48p. (gr. k-4). 1989. PLB 12.85 (*0-516-01165-0*); pap. 4.95 (*0-516-41165-9*) Childrens.

Lhommedieu, Arthur J. Metamorphoses: Butterfly. (ps-3). 1993. 5.95 (*0-85953-170-8*) Childs Play.

Ling, Mary. Butterfly. LC 92-52808. (Illus.). 24p. (ps-1). 1992. 7.95 (*1-56458-112-8*) Dorling Kindersley.

Mattern, Joanne. A Picture Book of Butterflies & Moths. Pistolesi, Roseanna, illus. LC 92-5225. 24p. (gr. 1-4). 1992. PLB 9.59 (*0-8167-2796-1*); pap. 2.50 (*0-8167-2797-X*) Troll Assocs.

Mitchell, Robert & Zim, Herbert S. Butterflies & Moths. Durenceau, Andre, illus. (gr. 5 up). 1964. PLB write for info. (*0-307-24052-5*); pap. write for info. (Golden Pr) Western Pub.

Mitchell, Victor. Butterflies. (Illus.). 16p. (gr. k up). 1988. pap. 1.99 (*0-7459-1466-7*) Lion USA.

Morris, Dean. Butterflies & Moths. rev. ed. LC 87-16666. (Illus.). 48p. (gr. 2-6). 1987. PLB 10.95 (*0-8172-3204-4*) Raintree Steck-V.

Oda, Hidetomo. Butterflies. Pohl, Kathy, ed. LC 85-28196. (Illus.). 32p. (gr. 3-7). 1986. text ed. 10.95 (*0-8172-2531-5*) Raintree Steck-V.

—The Swallowtail Butterfly. Pohl, Kathy, ed. LC 85-28229. (Illus.). 32p. (gr. 3-7). 1986. PLB 10.95 (*0-8172-2542-0*) Raintree Steck-V.

Opler, Paul. Butterflies East & West: A Book to Color. Strawn, Susan, illus. 96p. (Orig.). (gr. 1-6). 1993. pap. 8.95 (*1-879373-45-9*) R Rinehart.

Opler, Paul & Strawn, Susan. Butterflies of Eastern North America: A Coloring Album & Activity Book. Strawn, Susan, illus. (gr. 1-6). 1989. pap. 4.95 (*0-911797-53-X*) R Rinehart.

Ossorio, Nelson A. & Salvadeo, Michele B. To Be Beautiful: or The Story of the Butterfly. (Illus.). 48p. (gr. 3-5). 1994. pap. 6.95 (*1-56721-046-5*) Twnty-Fifth Cent Pr.

Parramon, J. M. The Fascinating World of Butterflies. (Illus.). 48p. (gr. 3-7). 1991. pap. 7.95 (*0-8120-4722-2*) Barron.

Petersen, Candyce A. Beauty the Butterfly. Stoffregen, Jill A., illus. 24p. (ps-3). Date not set. 11.95 (*1-56065-097-4*) Capstone Pr.

Porter, Keith. Discovering Butterflies & Moths. (Illus.). 48p. (gr. 2 up). 1990. pap. 4.95 (*0-531-18364-5*, Pub. by Bookwright Pr) Watts.

Reidel, Marlene. From Egg to Butterfly. Reidel, Marlene, illus. LC 81-204. 24p. (ps-3). 1981. PLB 10.95 (*0-87614-153-X*) Carolrhoda Bks.

Robson, Denny. Butterflies & Moths. (Illus.). 32p. (gr. 4-6). 1991. 13.95 (*0-237-60170-2*, Pub. by Evans Bros Ltd) Trafalgar.

Rotter, Charles. Monarchs. (gr. 2-6). 1992. PLB 15.95 (*0-89565-840-2*) Childs World.
Rowan, James P. Butterflies & Moths. LC 83-7216. (Illus.). 48p. (gr. k-4). 1983. PLB 12.85 (*0-516-01692-X*); pap. 4.95 (*0-516-41692-8*) Childrens.
Sabin, Louis. Amazing World of Butterflies & Moths. Helmer, Jean C., illus. LC 81-7504. 32p. (gr. 2-4). 1982. PLB 11.59 (*0-89375-560-5*); pap. text ed. 2.95 (*0-89375-561-3*); cassette 9.95 (*0-685-04943-4*) Troll Assocs.
Saintsing, David. The World of Butterflies. LC 86-5706. (Illus.). 32p. (gr. 2-3). 1986. 17.27 (*1-55532-072-4*) Gareth Stevens Inc.
Still, John. Amazing Butterflies & Moths. Young, Jerry, photos by. LC 90-19234. (Illus.). 32p. (Orig.). (gr. 1-5). 1991. PLB 9.99 (*0-679-91515-X*); pap. 7.99 (*0-679-81515-5*) Knopf Bks Yng Read.
Watts, Barrie. Butterflies & Moths. LC 90-46301. (Illus.). 32p. (gr. k-4). 1991. PLB 11.40 (*0-531-14160-8*); pap. 4.95 (*0-531-15617-6*) Watts.
—Butterfly & Caterpillar. LC 86-10050. (Illus.). 25p. (gr. k-4). 1991. 5.95 (*0-382-09291-0*); 3.95 (*0-382-09958-3*); PLB 9.98 (*0-382-09282-1*) Silver Burdett Pr.
Whalley, Mary & Whalley, Paul. Butterfly in the Garden. LC 86-5705. (Illus.). 32p. (gr. 4-6). 1986. PLB 15.93 (*1-55532-068-6*) Gareth Stevens Inc.
Whalley, Paul. Butterfly & Moth. Keates, Colin, et al, photos by. LC 88-1574. (Illus.). 64p. (gr. 5 up). 1988. 16.00 (*0-394-89618-1*); lib. bdg. 16.99 (*0-394-99618-6*) Knopf Bks Yng Read.
Whyte, Malcolm. Butterflies. (Illus.). 32p. (Orig.). (gr. 1-4). 1989. pap. 2.95 (*0-8431-1962-4*, Troubador) Price Stern.
Zappler, Liz. A Day in the Life of the Monarch Butterfly. Eakin, Ed, ed. Morris, Aaron, illus. 48p. (gr. 2-6). 1989. 8.85 (*0-89015-616-6*) Sunbelt Media.

BUTTERFLIES–FICTION

Andersdatter, Karla M. Follow the Blue Butterfly. Koff, Deborah, illus. (gr. 4-8). 1980. 6.00 (*0-935430-00-8*) In Between.
Carle, Eric & Carle, Eric. The Very Hungry Caterpillar Board Book. (Illus.). 26p. (ps). 1994. bds. 7.95 (*0-399-22690-7*, Philomel) Putnam Pub Group.
Dickson, Sandy L. The Story of Smartworms: The Journey Begins. Barrow, Madeline H., ed. Dixon, David, illus. 34p. (gr. k-5). 1989. write for info.; PLB write for info.; pap. write for info. Smartworm Corp.
Fisher, Lucretia. The Butterfly & the Stone. Jardine, Thomas, illus. LC 80-29260. 48p. (Orig.). (ps up). 1981. pap. 3.95 (*0-916144-69-0*) Stemmer Hse.
Fontenot, Mary A. Clovis Crawfish & Petit Papillon. Graves, Keith, illus. LC 83-27325. 32p. (ps-3). 1985. Repr. 12.95 (*0-88289-448-X*) Pelican.
Hartmann, Lorice. Who Will Fly with Butterfly? (Illus.). 48p. (gr. k-3). 1977. pap. 8.95 (*0-912760-51-6*) Valkyrie Pub Hse.
Holland, Alex N. Alice's Amazing Butterfly. Holland, Alex N., illus. 15p. (gr. 1-3). 1992. pap. 11.95 (*1-56606-001-X*) Bradley Mann.
Hunt, Joni P. A Shimmer of Butterflies. Leon, Vicki, ed. (Illus.). 40p. (Orig.). (gr. 5 up). 1992. pap. 7.95 (*0-918303-30-3*) Blake Pub.
Klass, David. California Blue. LC 93-13705. 224p. (gr. 7 up). 1994. 13.95 (*0-590-46688-7*) Scholastic Inc.
Lawrence, Louise. Calling B for Butterfly. LC 81-48648. 224p. (gr. 7 up). 1988. pap. 3.95 (*0-06-447036-9*, Trophy) HarpC Child Bks.
Oana. Timmy Tiger & the Butterfly Net. LC 80-82954. (Illus.). 32p. (ps-4). 1981. PLB 9.95 (*0-87783-160-2*) Oddo.
On Butterfly Farm. LC 92-62556. 20p. (ps-k). 1993. 3.99 (*0-89577-478-X*, Dist. by Random) RD Assn.
Osborne, Mary P. Spider Kane & the Mystery under the May-Apple. Chess, Victoria, illus. LC 90-33524. 128p. (gr. 1-7). 1992. 13.00 (*0-679-80855-8*); PLB 13.99 (*0-679-90855-2*) Knopf Bks Yng Read.
Pellowski, Michael J. Professor Possum's Great Adventure. Durrell, Julie, illus. LC 88-1281. 48p. (Orig.). (gr. 1-4). 1988. PLB 10.59 (*0-8167-1341-3*); pap. text ed. 3.50 (*0-8167-1342-1*) Troll Assocs.
Prior, R. W. The Great Monarch Butterfly Chase. Glick, Beth, illus. LC 92-7423. 32p. (ps-3). 1993. RSBE 14.95 (*0-02-775145-7*, Bradbury Pr) Macmillan Child Grp.
Sundgaard, Arnold. The Lamb & the Butterfly. Carle, Eric, illus. LC 88-60092. 32p. (ps-2). 1988. 14.95 (*0-531-05779-8*); PLB 14.99 (*0-531-08379-9*) Orchard Bks Watts.
Trella, Phyllis. Butterflies Have Grandparents, Too. Trella, Phyllis, illus. LC 82-73691. 48p. (gr. 2-6). write for info. (*0-914201-02-6*) Cheeruppet.
Trott, Betty. Breathe on Me Butterflies. McGrew, Michelle, illus. LC 93-60232. 44p. (gr. k-3). 1994. pap. 8.95 (*1-55523-603-0*) Winston-Derek.
Van Pallandt, Nicolas. The Butterfly Night of Old Brown Bear. (ps-3). 1992. bds. 15.00 jacketed (*0-374-31009-2*) FS&G.
Vinje, Marie. Hanna's Butterfly. Hoffman, Joan, ed. (Illus.). 32p. (gr. k-2). 1992. pap. 3.95 (*0-88743-428-2*, 06080) Sch Zone Pub Co.
—Hanna's Butterfly. Hoffman, Joan, ed. (Illus.). 16p. (gr. k-2). 1992. pap. 2.25 (*0-88743-267-0*, 06034) Sch Zone Pub Co.
West, Tracy. The Butterflies of Freedom. (gr. 6 up). 1988. pap. 2.25 (*0-317-69512-6*) S&S Trade.
Yoshi. The Butterfly Hunt. Yoshi, illus. LC 90-7361. 32p. (gr. k up). 1991. pap. 14.95 (*0-88708-137-1*) Picture Bk Studio.
—The Butterfly Hunt. Yoshi, illus. LC 92-6631. 28p. (gr. k). 1993. Repr. Mini-bk. 4.95 (*0-88708-270-X*) Picture Bk Studio.

BUTTONS

Wayne-Von Konigslow, Andrea & Granfield, Linda. The Make-Your-Own Button Book. LC 93-15230. (Illus.). 40p. (gr. k-5). 1994. pap. 12.95 (*1-56282-486-4*) Hyprn Child.

BUYERS GUIDES

see Consumer Education; Shopping

BY-PRODUCTS

see Waste Products

BYZANTINE EMPIRE

Major, John S. The Silk Route. Fieser, Stephen, illus. LC 92-38169. 1994. 15.00 (*0-06-022924-1*); PLB 14.89 (*0-06-022926-8*) HarpC.
Polyzoides, G. History of Byzantine & Modern Greece. (GRE., Illus.). (gr. 4-6). 4.00 (*0-686-79635-7*) Divry.

C

CABEZA DE VACA, ALVAR NUNEZ, 1490?-1557–FICTION

Baker, Betty. Walk the World's Rim. LC 65-11458. 192p. (gr. 5 up). 1965. PLB 14.89 (*0-06-020381-1*) HarpC Child Bks.

CABINET OFFICERS–U. S.

Mulford, Carolyn. Elizabeth Dole: Public Servant. LC 91-25395. (Illus.). 144p. (gr. 6 up). 1992. lib. bdg. 18.95 (*0-89490-331-4*) Enslow Pubs.
Patrick, Diane. The Executive Branch. LC 94-963. 1994. write for info. (*0-531-20179-1*) Watts.

CABINET WORK

see also Woodwork

CABINS

see Log Cabins

CABLES, SUBMARINE

Nathan, Adele G. First Transatlantic Cable. (Illus.). (gr. 5-9). 1963. lib. bdg. 8.99 (*0-394-90388-9*) Random Bks Yng Read.

CABOT, JOHN, 1461-1498

Goodnough, David. John Cabot & Son. LC 78-18054. (Illus.). 48p. (gr. 4-7). 1979. PLB 10.59 (*0-89375-172-3*); pap. 3.50 (*0-89375-164-2*) Troll Assocs.

CABRINI, FRANCES XAVIER, SAINT, 1850-1917

Windeatt, Mary F. St. Frances Cabrini. Harmon, Gedge, illus. 32p. (gr. 1-5). 1989. Repr. of 1954 ed. wkbk. 3.00 (*0-89555-375-9*) TAN Bks Pubs.

CACTUS

Bash, Barbara. Desert Giant: The World of the Saguaro Cactus. Bash, Barbara, illus. 32p. (gr. 1-5). 1989. 15.95 (*0-316-08301-1*) Little.
Cactus of Arizona. (Illus.). 32p. (gr. 3 up). 1994. pap. 1.00 (*0-935810-15-3*) Primer Pubs.
Cooper, J. Cactos (Cactus) 1991. 8.95s.p. (*0-86592-546-1*) Rourke Enter.
—Cactus. 1991. 8.95s.p. (*0-86592-622-0*) Rourke Enter.
Guiberson, Brenda Z. Cactus Hotel. Lloyd, Megan, illus. LC 90-41748. 32p. (ps-2). 1991. 15.95 (*0-8050-1333-4*, Bks Young Read) H Holt & Co.
Haselton, Scott E. Cactus & Succulents & How to Grow Them. (gr. 6-12). 1983. 1.25 (*0-9605656-1-2*) Desert Botanical.
Lerner, Carol. Cactus. Lerner, Carol, illus. LC 91-35678. 32p. 1992. 15.00 (*0-688-09636-0*); PLB 14.93 (*0-688-09637-9*) Morrow Jr Bks.
Madgwick, Wendy. Cacti & Other Succulents. LC 91-14934. (Illus.). 48p. (gr. 5-9). 1992. PLB 21.34 (*0-8114-2737-4*) Raintree Steck-V.
Milios, Rita. A Desert Cactus Comes to Life. Stoffregen, Jill A., illus. LC 92-12895. 24p. (ps-3). Date not set. 11.95 (*1-56065-168-7*) Capstone Pr.
Overbeck, Cynthia. Cactus. Hani, Shabo, illus. LC 82-211. 48p. (gr. 4 up). 1982. lib. bdg. 19.95 (*0-8225-1469-9*, First Ave Edns); pap. 5.95 (*0-8225-9556-7*, First Ave Edns) Lerner Pubns.
Storad, Conrad J. Saguaro Cactus. Jansen, Paula, photos by. LC 93-38913. 48p. (gr. 2-3). 1994. PLB 18.95 (*0-8225-3002-3*) Lerner Pubns.

CAESAR, CAIUS JULIUS, 100-44 B.C.

Wells, Reuben F. With Caesar's Legions. LC 60-16709. (Illus.). (gr. 7-11). 1951. 18.00 (*0-8196-0110-1*) Biblo.
Whitehead, Albert C. The Standard Bearer: A Story of Army Life in the Time of Caesar. (Illus.). (gr. 7-11). 1943. 20.00 (*0-8196-0116-0*) Biblo.

CAESAR, CAIUS JULIUS, 100-44 B.C.–DRAMA

Shakespeare, William. Julius Caesar. Rudzik, O. H., intro. by. (Illus.). (gr. 9 up). 1965. pap. 1.95 (*0-8049-1004-9*, S4) Airmont.
—Julius Caesar. Shaw, Charlie, illus. Stewart, Diana, adapted by. LC 80-16406. (Illus.). 48p. (gr. 4 up). 1983. PLB 20.70 (*0-8172-1664-2*) Raintree Steck-V.

CAFETERIAS

see Restaurants, Bars, etc.

CAKE

Drew, Helen. My First Baking Book. LC 91-10239. (Illus.). 48p. (gr. 2-6). 1991. 12.00 (*0-679-81545-7*); lib. bdg. 13.99 (*0-679-91545-1*) Knopf Bks Yng Read.
Meijer, Marie, created by. The Bake-a-Cake Book: Beat the Batter, Measure the Flour, Bake a Cake with the Cakebakers. Ramel, Charlotte, illus. LC 93-40877. (ps-3). 1994. 16.95 (*0-8118-0693-6*) Chronicle Bks.
Mrs. Beeton's Complete Book of Cakes & Biscuits. (Illus.). 336p. (gr. 10-12). 1992. 27.95 (*0-7063-6806-1*, Pub. by Ward Lock UK) Sterling.

CALCULATING MACHINES

see also Computers

Bloom, Marjorie W. & Galton, Grace C. Estimate! Calculate! Evaluate! Calculator Activities for the Middle Grades. (gr. 4-7). 1990. pap. 9.50 (*0-201-48032-8*) Addison-Wesley.
Jacobs, Russell F. Problem Solving with the Calculator. 3rd ed. (Illus.). 168p. (gr. 6-12). 1990. pap. text ed. 8.95 (*0-918272-18-1*); tchr's. guide-answer key 2.50 (*0-918272-19-X*) Jacobs.
Michunas, Lynn. Kalculator Kids. 64p. (gr. 3-7). 1982. 8.95 (*0-86653-076-2*, GA 410) Good Apple.
Wyler, Rose & Elting, Mary. Math Fun: With Pocket Calculator. LC 91-16265. (Illus.). 64p. (gr. 4-7). 1992. PLB 10.98 (*0-671-74308-2*, J Messner); pap. 5.95 (*0-671-74309-0*, J Messner) S&S Trade.

CALCULUS

Cohen, Donald. Calculus by & for Young People: (Ages 7, Yes 7 & Up) Cohen, Donald, illus. 177p. (Orig.). (gr. 2 up). 1988. pap. 12.00 spiral bdg. (*0-9621674-0-1*) D Cohen Mathman.
—Calculus by & for Young People: (Ages 7, Yes 7 & Up) rev. ed. Honda, Noriko, tr. (Illus.). 177p. (gr. 1 up). 1989. English ed. spiral bdg. 13.95 (*0-9621674-1-X*); Japanese ed. pap. write for info. (*0-9621674-7-9*); package, incl. bk., worksheets, & 2 videotapes 110.00 (*0-9621674-9-5*) Worksheets (*0-9621674-5-2*) Videotape 1: Infinite Series by & for 6 Year Olds & Up (*0-9621674-2-8*) Videotape 2: Iteration with 6 to 11 Year Olds (*0-9621674-4-4*) D Cohen Mathman.
Reichman, Barry. The Pre-Calculus & Calculus Workbook & Videotape. 100p. (gr. 6-12). 1990. 225.00 (*0-685-38398-9*) Video Tutorial Serv.
Research & Education Association Staff. High School Pre-Calculus Tutor. (gr. 9-12). 1994. 12.95 (*0-87891-910-4*) Res & Educ.

CALENDARS

see also Almanacs

Advent Calendar. 1993. 9.95 (*1-56828-048-3*) Red Jacket Pr.
Ball, Sara. The Teddy Bear Book of Days. (Illus.). (gr. 4-12). 1992. 15.00 (*1-56021-185-7*) W J Fantasy.
Branley, Franklyn M. Keeping Time. Van Rynbach, Iris, illus. LC 92-6783. 1993. 13.95 (*0-395-47777-8*) HM.
Bushwick, Nathan. Understanding the Jewish Calendar. 114p. (gr. 9-12). 1989. 9.95 (*0-940118-17-3*) Moznaim.
Busy Week. (ps). 1990. text ed. 3.95 cased (*0-7214-5271-X*) Ladybird Bks.
De Beer, Hans. Little Polar Bear Birthday Book. De Beer, Hans, illus. 120p. 1990. 7.95 (*1-55858-081-6*) North-South Bks NYC.
Fisher, Leonard E. Calendar Art: Thirteen Days, Weeks, Months, Years from Around the World. Fisher, Leonard E., illus. LC 86-25835. 64p. (ps up). 1987. SBE 15.95 (*0-02-735350-8*, Four Winds) Macmillan Child Grp.
Grewe, Georgeann & Glover, Susanne. Calendar Companions for Fall. Grewe, Georgeann, illus. 128p. (gr. 1-6). 1984. wkbk. 11.95 (*0-317-43005-X*, GA 534) Good Apple.
—Calendar Companions for Spring. Grewe, Georgeann, illus. 128p. (gr. 1-6). 1984. wkbk. 11.95 (*0-86653-171-8*, GA 536) Good Apple.
—Calendar Companions for Winter. Grewe, Georgeann, illus. 128p. (gr. 1-6). 1984. wkbk. 11.95 (*0-86653-168-8*, GA 535) Good Apple.
Hughes, Paul. The Days of the Week. Harris, Peter, ed. Burn, Jeffery, illus. LC 89-11758. 62p. (gr. 4-7). 1989. PLB 17.26 (*0-944483-32-1*) Garrett Ed Corp.
Lipkind, William. Days to Remember. Snyder, Jerome, illus. (gr. 3 up). 1961. 10.95 (*0-8392-3006-0*) Astor-Honor.
Martinet, Jeanne. The Year You Were Born, 1983. Lanfredi, Judy, illus. LC 91-31605. 56p. 1992. PLB 13.93 (*0-688-11078-9*, Tambourine Bks); pap. 7.95 (*0-688-11077-0*, Tambourine Bks) Morrow.
Milne, A. A. Winnie-the-Pooh's Calendar Book 1988. Shepard, Ernest H., illus. (ps up). 1987. spiral bd. 4.95 (*0-525-44311-8*, Dutton) NAL-Dutton.
Packard, Mary, retold by. The Nutcracker Story Book Set & Advent Calendar, 24 bks. Brooks, Nan, illus. 96p. 1993. miniature ed. 16.95 (*1-56305-503-1*, 3503) Workman Pub.
Rockwell, Anne. Bear Child's Book of Special Days. LC 89-1633. (Illus.). 32p. (ps-1). 1989. 12.95 (*0-525-44508-0*, DCB) Dutton Child Bks.
Rosenberg, Amye. My Calendar. 66p. (gr. 1-2). 1984. pap. text ed. 4.25 (*0-87441-385-0*) Behrman.
Spizman, Robyn. Bulletin Boards: Ideas for Holidays & Special Days. Pesiri, Evelyn, illus. 64p. (gr. k-6). 1984. wkbk. 7.95 (*0-86653-211-0*, GA 567) Good Apple.
—Bulletin Boards: Seasonal Ideas & Activities. Pesiri, Evelyn, illus. 64p. (gr. k-6). 1984. wkbk. 7.95 (*0-86653-218-8*, GA 568) Good Apple.

CALHOUN, JOHN CALDWELL, 1782-1850

Brown, Warren. John C. Calhoun. (Illus.). 112p. (gr. 5 up). 1993. 18.95 (*0-7910-1727-3*, Am Art Analog); pap. write for info. (*0-7910-1728-1*, Am Art Analog) Chelsea Hse.

Durwood, Thomas A. John C. Calhoun & the Roots of War. (Illus.). 160p. (gr. 5 up). 1990. lib. bdg. 12.95 (*0-382-09936-2*); pap. 7.95 (*0-382-24045-6*) Silver Burdett Pr.

CALIFORNIA

Aylesworth, Thomas G. & Aylesworth, Virginia L. Pacific: California, Hawaii. (gr. 3 up). 1992. lib. bdg. 16.95 (*0-7910-1050-3*) Chelsea Hse.

Bellerophon Books Staff. Story of California: 1849 to Present, Vol. 2. (gr. 4-7). 1992. pap. 3.95 (*0-88388-171-3*) Bellerophon Bks.

Brown, Richard, illus. Gulliver's Travels: A Kid's Guide to Southern California. 135p. (gr. 1 up). 1988. 6.95 (*0-318-33430-5*, Gulliver Bks) HarBrace.

—A Kid's Guide to Southern California. 135p. (gr. 1 up). 1988. pap. 6.95 (*0-15-200457-2*, Gulliver Bks) HarBrace.

Brown, Vinson & Livezey, Robert. The Sierra Nevadan Wildlife Region. 3rd, rev. ed. (Illus.). 192p. (gr. 4 up). 1962. pap. 8.95 (*0-911010-02-5*) Naturegraph.

California: Raices Nativas. (SPA., Illus.). 64p. (gr. 4-6). 1990. pap. text ed. 12.45 (*0-911981-09-8*) Cloud Pub.

Carole Marsh California Books, 46 bks. 1994. lib. bdg. 1077.70 set (*0-7933-1278-7*); pap. 617.70 set (*0-7933-5130-8*) Gallopade Pub Group.

Carpenter, Allan. California. LC 77-21101. (Illus.). 96p. (gr. 4 up). 1978. PLB 16.95 (*0-516-04105-3*) Childrens.

Endo, Terry, ed. Children's Yellow Pages: Orange County, 1986-87 Edition. Goldstein, Howard, illus. 200p. (Orig.). (gr. k up). 1986. pap. 6.95 (*0-938789-00-7*) Teruko Inc.

Fradin, Dennis. California en Palabras y Fotos: California: In Words & Pictures. LC 86-21526. (Illus.). 48p. (gr. 2-6). 1986. pap. 4.95 (*0-516-53905-1*) Childrens.

—California: In Words & Pictures. Ulm, Robert, illus. LC 76-50600. 48p. (gr. 2-5). 1977. PLB 12.95 (*0-516-03905-9*) Childrens.

Fradin, Dennis B. California - De Mar a Mar: (California - From Sea to Shining Sea) LC 92-12944. (SPA., Illus.). 64p. (gr. 3-5). 1993. PLB 16.45 (*0-516-33805-6*); pap. 5.95 (*0-516-53805-5*) Childrens.

—California - from Sea to Shining Sea. LC 92-12944. (Illus.). 64p. (gr. 3-5). 1992. PLB 16.45 (*0-516-03805-2*); pap. 5.95 (*0-516-43805-0*) Childrens.

Gales, Donald M. Handbook of Wildflowers, Weeds, Wildlife & Weather of the South Bay & Palos Verdes (California) 3rd, rev. ed. 240p. (gr. 8 up). 1988. pap. 12.00 (*0-317-89904-X*) D M Gales.

Gray, Anne. The Wonderful World of San Diego. 2nd ed. LC 74-76733. (Illus.). (gr. 4 up). 1975. pap. 3.95 (*0-88289-081-6*) Pelican.

Greenberg, Janet. California. LC 94-1038. 1994. write for info. (*0-86625-511-7*) Rourke Pubns.

Head, W. S. The California Chaparral: An Elfin Forest. LC 75-24239. 96p. (gr. 4 up). 1972. 15.95 (*0-87961-003-4*); pap. 7.95 (*0-87961-002-6*) Naturegraph.

Hedgpeth, Joel. Common Seashore Life of Southern California. Hinton, Sam, illus. 64p. (gr. 4 up). 1961. 14.95 (*0-911010-63-7*); pap. 6.95 (*0-911010-62-9*) Naturegraph.

Herda, D. J. Historical America: The Southwestern States. LC 92-28206. (Illus.). 64p. (gr. 5-8). 1993. PLB 15.40 (*1-56294-123-2*) Millbrook Pr.

Houston, Juanita. Our Golden California - Student Workbook. (Illus.). (gr. 4-6). 1991. pap. 14.95 student wkbk. (*0-88280-097-3*); tchr's. guide 19.95 (*0-88280-098-1*) ETC Pubns.

Hoyt, George & Hoyt, Doris. A Bird's-Eye View of California. Atkinson, Mary, illus. 48p. (Orig.). (gr. k-4). 1989. pap. 4.95 (*0-9622364-4-6*) Adona Pub.

Lavaroni, Charles. California: Roots. 144p. (gr. 4-6). 1984. pap. text ed. 11.45 (*0-911981-04-7*) Cloud Pub.

Lewis, Judy & Yarbrough, Jane. California People & Places. (Illus.). 32p. (gr. 4). 1991. study prints 260.00 (*1-879748-01-0*) Calif Perf Prods.

McCabe, Michael & Brew, Virginia. California: Roots. 28p. (gr. 4-6). 1991. Repr. of 1983 ed. tchr's. ed. 7.95 (*0-911981-07-1*) Cloud Pub.

—California: Roots. (Illus.). 59p. (gr. 4-6). 1983. wkbk. 5.25 (*0-911981-05-5*) Cloud Pub.

Marsh, Carole. Avast, Ye Slobs! California Pirate Trivia. (Illus.). (gr. 3-12). 1994. PLB 24.95 (*0-7933-0184-X*); pap. 14.95 (*0-7933-0183-1*); computer disk 29.95 (*0-7933-0185-8*) Gallopade Pub Group.

—The Best of the California Bed & Breakfast. (Illus.). (gr. 3-12). 1994. PLB 24.95 (*0-7933-1397-X*); pap. 14.95 (*0-7933-1398-8*); computer disk 29.95 (*0-7933-1399-6*) Gallopade Pub Group.

—Bow Wow! California Dogs in History, Mystery, Legend, Lore, Humor & More! (Illus.). (gr. 3-12). 1994. PLB 24.95 (*0-7933-3479-9*); pap. 14.95 (*0-7933-3480-2*); computer disk 29.95 (*0-7933-3481-0*) Gallopade Pub Group.

—California & Other State Greats (Biographies) (Illus.). (gr. 3-12). 1994. PLB 24.95 (*1-55609-521-X*); pap. 14.95 (*1-55609-520-1*); computer disk 29.95 (*0-7933-1405-4*) Gallopade Pub Group.

—California Bandits, Bushwackers, Outlaws, Crooks, Devils, Ghosts, Desperadoes & Other Assorted & Sundry Characters! (Illus.). (gr. 3-12). 1994. PLB 24.95 (*0-7933-0166-1*); pap. 14.95 (*0-7933-0165-3*); computer disk 29.95 (*0-7933-0167-X*) Gallopade Pub Group.

—California Classic Christmas Trivia: Stories, Recipes, Activities, Legends, Lore & More! (Illus.). (gr. 3-12). 1994. PLB 24.95 (*0-7933-0169-6*); pap. 14.95 (*0-7933-0168-8*); computer disk 29.95 (*0-7933-0170-X*) Gallopade Pub Group.

—California Coastales! (Illus.). (gr. 3-12). 1994. PLB 24.95 (*1-55609-517-1*); pap. 14.95 (*1-55609-516-3*); computer disk 29.95 (*0-7933-1401-1*) Gallopade Pub Group.

—California Coastales! 1994. lib. bdg. 24.95 (*0-7933-7269-0*) Gallopade Pub Group.

—California "Crinkum-Crankum" A Funny Word Book about Our State. (Illus.). 1994. lib. bdg. 24.95 (*0-7933-4822-6*); pap. 14.95 (*0-7933-4823-4*); disk 29.95 (*0-7933-4824-2*) Gallopade Pub Group.

—California Dingbats! Bk. 1: A Fun Book of Games, Stories, Activities & More about Our State That's All in Code! for You to Decipher. (Illus.). (gr. 3-12). 1994. PLB 24.95 (*0-7933-3785-2*); pap. 14.95 (*0-7933-3786-0*); computer disk 29.95 (*0-7933-3787-9*) Gallopade Pub Group.

—California Festival Fun for Kids! (Illus.). (gr. 3-12). 1994. lib. bdg. 24.95 (*0-7933-3938-3*); pap. 14.95 (*0-7933-3939-1*); disk 29.95 (*0-7933-3940-5*) Gallopade Pub Group.

—The California Hot Air Balloon Mystery. (Illus.). (gr. 2-9). 1994. 24.95 (*0-7933-2354-1*); pap. 14.95 (*0-7933-2355-X*); computer disk 29.95 (*0-7933-2356-8*) Gallopade Pub Group.

—California Jeopardy! Answers & Questions about Our State! (Illus.). (gr. 3-12). 1994. PLB 24.95 (*0-7933-4091-8*); pap. 14.95 (*0-7933-4092-6*); computer disk 29.95 (*0-7933-4093-4*) Gallopade Pub Group.

—California "Jography" A Fun Run Thru Our State! (Illus.). (gr. 3-12). 1994. PLB 24.95 (*1-55609-511-2*); pap. 14.95 (*1-55609-510-4*); computer disk 29.95 (*0-685-45935-7*) Gallopade Pub Group.

—California Kid's Cookbook: Recipes, How-to, History, Lore & More! (Illus.). (gr. 3-12). 1994. PLB 24.95 (*0-7933-0178-5*); pap. 14.95 (*0-7933-0177-7*); computer disk 29.95 (*0-7933-0179-3*) Gallopade Pub Group.

—The California Mystery Van Takes Off! Book 1: Handicapped California Kids Sneak Off on a Big Adventure. (Illus.). (gr. 3-12). 1994. 24.95 (*0-7933-4976-1*); pap. 14.95 (*0-7933-4977-X*); computer disk 29.95 (*0-7933-4978-8*) Gallopade Pub Group.

—California Quiz Bowl Crash Course! (Illus.). (gr. 3-12). 1994. PLB 24.95 (*1-55609-519-8*); pap. 14.95 (*1-55609-518-X*); computer disk 29.95 (*0-7933-1400-3*) Gallopade Pub Group.

—California Rollercoasters! (Illus.). (gr. 3-12). 1994. PLB 24.95 (*0-7933-5236-3*); pap. 14.95 (*0-7933-5237-1*); computer disk 29.95 (*0-7933-5238-X*) Gallopade Pub Group.

—California School Trivia: An Amazing & Fascinating Look at Our State's Teachers, Schools & Students! (Illus.). (gr. 3-12). 1994. PLB 24.95 (*0-7933-0175-0*); pap. 14.95 (*0-7933-0174-2*); computer disk 29.95 (*0-7933-0176-9*) Gallopade Pub Group.

—California Silly Basketball Sportsmysteries, Vol. I. (Illus.). (gr. 3-12). 1994. PLB 24.95 (*0-7933-0172-6*); pap. 14.95 (*0-7933-0171-8*); computer disk 29.95 (*0-7933-0173-4*) Gallopade Pub Group.

—California Silly Basketball Sportsmysteries, Vol. II. (Illus.). (gr. 3-12). 1994. PLB 24.95 (*0-7933-1574-3*); pap. 14.95 (*0-7933-1575-1*); computer disk 29.95 (*0-7933-1576-X*) Gallopade Pub Group.

—California Silly Football Sportsmysteries, Vol. I. (Illus.). (gr. 3-12). 1994. PLB 24.95 (*1-55609-515-5*); pap. 14.95 (*1-55609-514-7*); computer disk 29.95 (*0-7933-1396-1*) Gallopade Pub Group.

—California Silly Football Sportsmysteries, Vol. II. (Illus.). (gr. 3-12). 1994. PLB 24.95 (*0-7933-1394-5*); pap. 14.95 (*0-7933-1395-3*); computer disk 29.95 (*0-685-74235-0*) Gallopade Pub Group.

—California Silly Trivia! (Illus.). (gr. 3-12). 1994. PLB 24.95 (*1-55609-509-0*); pap. 14.95 (*1-55609-508-2*); computer disk 29.95 (*0-7933-1390-2*) Gallopade Pub Group.

—California's (Most Devastating!) Disasters & (Most Calamitous!) Catastrophies! (Illus.). (gr. 3-12). 1994. PLB 24.95 (*0-7933-0163-7*); pap. 14.95 (*0-7933-0162-9*); computer disk 29.95 (*0-7933-0164-5*) Gallopade Pub Group.

—Chill Out: Scary California Tales Based on Frightening California Truths. (Illus.). 1994. lib. bdg. 24.95 (*0-7933-4669-X*); pap. 14.95 (*0-7933-4670-3*); disk 29.95 (*0-7933-4671-1*) Gallopade Pub Group.

—Christopher Columbus Comes to California! Includes Reproducible Activities for Kids! (Illus.). (gr. 3-12). 1994. PLB 24.95 (*0-7933-3632-5*); pap. 14.95 (*0-7933-3633-3*); computer disk 29.95 (*0-7933-3634-1*) Gallopade Pub Group.

—The Hard-to-Believe-But-True! Book of California History, Mystery, Trivia, Legend, Lore, Humor & More. (Illus.). (gr. 3-12). 1994. PLB 24.95 (*0-7933-0181-5*); pap. 14.95 (*0-7933-0180-7*); computer disk 29.95 (*0-7933-0182-3*) Gallopade Pub Group.

—If My California Mama Ran the World! (Illus.). (gr. 3-12). 1994. PLB 24.95 (*0-7933-1402-X*); pap. 14.95 (*0-7933-1403-8*); computer disk 29.95 (*0-7933-1404-6*) Gallopade Pub Group.

—Jurassic Ark! California Dinosaurs & Other Prehistoric Creatures. (gr. k-12). 1994. PLB 24.95 (*0-7933-7440-5*); pap. 14.95 (*0-7933-7441-3*); computer disk 29.95 (*0-7933-7442-1*) Gallopade Pub Group.

—Let's Quilt California & Stuff It Topographically! (Illus.). (gr. 3-12). 1994. PLB 24.95 (*1-55609-513-9*); pap. 14.95 (*1-55609-512-0*); computer disk 29.95 (*0-7933-1392-9*) Gallopade Pub Group.

—Let's Quilt Our California County. 1994. lib. bdg. 24.95 (*0-7933-7125-2*); pap. text ed. 14.95 (*0-7933-7126-0*); disk 29.95 (*0-7933-7127-9*) Gallopade Pub Group.

—Let's Quilt Our California Town. 1994. lib. bdg. 24.95 (*0-7933-6975-4*); pap. text ed. 14.95 (*0-7933-6976-2*); disk 29.95 (*0-7933-6977-0*) Gallopade Pub Group.

—Meow! California Cats in History, Mystery, Legend, Lore, Humor & More! (Illus.). (gr. 3-12). 1994. PLB 24.95 (*0-7933-3326-1*); pap. 14.95 (*0-7933-3327-X*); computer disk 29.95 (*0-7933-3328-8*) Gallopade Pub Group.

—Uncle Rebus: California Picture Stories for Computer Kids. (Illus.). (gr. k-3). 1994. PLB 24.95 (*0-7933-4516-2*); pap. 14.95 (*0-7933-4517-0*); disk 29.95 (*0-7933-4518-9*) Gallopade Pub Group.

O'Connor, Karen. San Diego. (Illus.). 60p. (gr. 3 up). 1990. text ed. 13.95 RSBE (*0-87518-439-1*, Dillon) Macmillan Child Grp.

Ogintz, Eileen. Sunny Southern California: Everything That's Fun to Do & See for Kids - & Parents Too! (Illus.). 96p. (Orig.). 1994. pap. 9.95 (*0-06-258542-8*) HarpC West.

Oliver, Dana M. California Game Book. Oliver, Rice D., ed. (Illus.). 32p. (gr. 4-12). 1993. pap. 7.00 (*0-936778-69-5*) Calif Weekly.

Oliver, Rice D. California Student Resource File. (Illus.). 158p. (gr. 4). 1993. 25.00 (*0-936778-66-0*) Calif Weekly.

—Student Atlas of California. 3rd ed. (Illus.). 72p. (gr. 4 up). 1988. 7.95 (*0-936778-98-9*); tchr's ed. 8.95 (*0-936778-99-7*) Calif Weekly.

—Student Atlas of California. 4th, rev. ed. (Illus.). 66p. (gr. 4-8). 1993. pap. text ed. 11.00 (*0-936778-63-6*); tchr's. ed. 13.00 (*0-936778-64-4*) Calif Weekly.

Pelta, Kathy. California. LC 93-1497. (Illus.). 72p. (gr. 3-6). 1993. lib. bdg. 17.50 (*0-8225-2738-3*) Lerner Pubns.

Riegel, Martin P. Ghost Ports of the Pacific, Vol. I: California. LC 89-90772. (Illus.). 52p. (Orig.). 1989. 11.00 (*0-944871-18-6*); pap. 4.95 (*0-944871-19-4*) Riegel Pub.

Salts, Bobbi, ed. California Is for Kids! An Activity Book. Parker, Steve, illus. 32p. (gr. 1-6). 1990. pap. 2.95 (*0-929526-04-X*) Double B Pubns.

Seablom, Seth H. The California Coloring Guide. (Illus.). 32p. (gr. 1-6). 1979. pap. 2.50 (*0-918800-05-6*) Seablom.

Stack, Mary E. San Diego, California: The Travel Guide for Kids. Koch, Richard L., illus. 32p. (gr. k-4). 1991. pap. 4.95 (*0-945600-06-2*) Colormore Inc.

Stein, R. Conrad. California. 209p. 1993. text ed. 15.40 (*1-56956-174-5*) W A T Braille.

Thompson, Kathleen. California. LC 87-16395. 48p. 1987. 19.97 (*0-8174-4621-4*) cancelled 3/4" video (*0-86514-237-8*) Raintree Steck-V.

Todd, Armor. The Marin Mountain Bike Guide. 2nd ed. Todd, Linda, illus. 80p. (gr. 9-12). 1989. pap. 8.95t (*0-9623537-0-1*) A Todd.

White, Don. Poop Decks & Periwinkles: Emily & Jason Explore San Diego. LC 91-66464. 112p. (gr. 3-6). 1991. pap. 12.95 (*0-942259-06-8*) Westerfield Enter.

Wills, Charles A. A Historical Album of California. LC 93-35015. (Illus.). 64p. (gr. 4-8). 1994. PLB 15.90 (*1-56294-479-7*); pap. 6.95 (*1-56294-759-1*) Millbrook Pr.

CALIFORNIA–BIOGRAPHY

Mirko, Vincent W. Grandpa Says. 300p. (Orig.). (gr. 10). 1989. pap. 25.00 (*0-9623257-0-8*) Millsmont Pub.

Yep, Laurence. The Lost Garden. (Illus.). 128p. (gr. 5-7). 1991. 14.98 (*0-685-58838-6*, J Messner); 9.71s.p. (*0-685-47021-0*, J Messner); pap. 12.95 (*0-685-58839-4*, J Messner); pap. 11.24s.p. (*0-685-47022-9*, J Messner) S&S Trade.

—Lost Garden. 1991. 12.95 (*0-671-74160-8*, J Messner); lib. bdg. 14.98 (*0-671-74159-4*) S&S Trade.

CALIFORNIA–FICTION

Bader, Bonnie. Golden Quest. LC 93-16461. 64p. (Orig.). (gr. 3-5). 1993. PLB 12.95 (*1-881889-30-0*) Silver Moon.

Beatty, Patricia. The Nickel Plated Beauty. LC 92-27683. 272p. (gr. 5 up). 1993. pap. 4.95 (*0-688-12279-5*, Pub. by Beech Tree Bks) Morrow.

Brooks, Chelsea. Dreamers & Schemers. 1994. pap. 2.95 (*0-02-041653-9*, Aladdin) Macmillan Child Grp.

Chambers, Vickie. In the Silence of the Hills. Taylor, LaVonne, ed. (Illus.). (gr. 9-12). 1994. write for info. (*0-9627735-1-4*) Excllnc Entrps.

Chase, Alyssa. Tessa on Her Own. Maeno, Itoko, illus. 32p. (gr. 1-4). 1994. 16.95 (*1-55942-064-2*, 7656) Marshfilm.

Cleary, Beverly. The Luckiest Girl. LC 58-6667. 228p. (gr. 7 up). 1958. PLB 12.88 (*0-688-31741-3*) Morrow Jr Bks.

Fleischman, Sid. By the Great Horn Spoon. Von Schmidt, Eric, illus. (gr. 4-6). 1988. 16.95 (*0-316-28577-3*, Joy St Bks); pap. 5.95 (*0-316-28612-5*, Joy St Bks) Little.

Gates, Doris. Blue Willow. Lantz, Paul, illus. LC 40-32435. 176p. (gr. 4-7). 1940. pap. 14.00 (*0-670-17557-9*) Viking Child Bks.

Gray, Genevieve. How Far, Felipe? Grifalconi, Ann, illus. LC 77-11846. 64p. (gr. k-3). 1978. PLB 11.89 (*0-06-022108-9*) HarpC Child Bks.
Gunn, Robin J. Summer Promise. 171p. (Orig.). 1989. pap. 4.99 (*0-929608-13-5*) Focus Family.
Harte, Bret. Outcasts of Poker Flat & Other Stories. (gr. 8 up). 1964. pap. 1.95 (*0-8049-0051-5*, CL51) Airmont.
Hoobler, Dorothy & Hoobler, Thomas. Treasure in the Stream: The Story of a Gold Rush Girl. Carpenter, Nancy, illus. 64p. (gr. 4-6). 1991. 5.95 (*0-382-24151-7*); PLB 7.95 (*0-382-24144-4*); pap. 3.95 (*0-382-24346-3*) Silver Burdett Pr.
Katz, Welwyn W. Whalesinger. LC 90-34091. 212p. (gr. 7 up). 1991. SBE 14.95 (*0-689-50511-6*, M K McElderry) Macmillan Child Grp.
Kelso, Mary J. Goodbye, Bodie. Kelso, Mary J., illus. 120p. (Orig.). (gr. 6 up). 1989. pap. 6.95 (*0-9621406-1-9*) MarKel Pr.
Krensky, Stephen. The Iron Dragon Never Sleeps. Fulweiler, Frank, illus. LC 93-31167. 1994. 13.95 (*0-385-31171-0*) Delacorte.
Lowell, Susan. I Am Lavina Cumming. Mirocha, Paul, illus. LC 93-24155. 200p. (gr. 2-6). 1993. 14.95 (*0-915943-39-5*); pap. 6.95 (*0-915943-77-8*) Milkweed Ed.
Norris, Frank. Octopus. (gr. 11 up). 1968. pap. 1.95 (*0-8049-0179-1*, CL-179) Airmont.
O'Dell, Scott. Island of the Blue Dolphins. (gr. 7 up). 1960. 14.95 (*0-395-06962-9*) HM.
Petersen, P. J. Liars. LC 91-28490. 176p. (gr. 5-9). 1992. pap. 15.00 jacketed, 3-pc. bdg. (*0-671-75035-6*, S&S BFYR) S&S Trade.
Politi, Leo. Song of the Swallows. reissue ed. LC 49-8215. (Illus.). 32p. (gr. 1-4). 1987. SBE 14.95 (*0-684-18831-7*, Scribners Young Read) Macmillan Child Grp.
Schulte, Elaine L. Melanie & the Modeling Mess. LC 93-45377. 1994. 4.99 (*1-55661-254-0*) Bethany Hse.
Singer, Marilyn. California Demon. LC 92-52981. 160p. (gr. 5-9). 1992. 14.95 (*1-56282-298-5*); PLB 14.89 (*1-56282-299-3*) Hyprn Child.
Singleton, Linda J. Spring Break. LC 94-4570. (gr. 7 up). 1994. 3.95 (*1-56565-144-8*) Lowell Hse Juvenile.
Snyder, Zilpha K. Cat Running. LC 94-447. 1994. 14.95 (*0-385-31056-0*) Delacorte.
—The Egypt Game. Raible, Alton, illus. LC 67-10467. 224p. (gr. 4-6). 1972. SBE 16.00 (*0-689-30006-9*, Atheneum Child Bk) Macmillan Child Grp.
—Velvet Room. Raible, Alton, illus. LC 65-10474. 224p. (gr. 3-7). 1972. (Atheneum Childrens Bk); pap. 1.95 (*0-685-00576-3*) Macmillan Child Grp.
Soto, Gary. Baseball in April & Other Stories. 137p. (gr. 3-7). 1991. pap. 4.95 (*0-15-205721-8*, Odyssey) HarBrace.
—Crazy Weekend. LC 93-13967. 144p. (gr. 3-7). 1994. 13.95 (*0-590-47814-1*) Scholastic Inc.
—The Pool Party. Casilla, Robert, illus. LC 92-34407. 1993. 13.95 (*0-385-30890-6*) Delacorte.
Staples, Donna. Arena Beach. LC 92-36302. 1993. 14.95 (*0-395-65366-5*) HM.
Steinbeck, John. Of Mice & Men. (gr. 9-12). 1970. pap. 2.75 (*0-553-26675-6*) Bantam.
Taylor, T. Maria: A Christmas Story. 1992. 13.95 (*0-15-217763-9*, HB Juv Bks) HarBrace.
Thoene, Brock & Thoene, Bodie. Cannons of the Comstock. 224p. 1992. pap. 7.99 (*1-55661-166-8*) Bethany Hse.

CALIFORNIA–GOLD DISCOVERIES

Blake, Arthur & Dailey, Pamela. The Gold Rush of 1849: Staking a Claim in California. LC 94-25773. 1995. write for info. (*1-562-94483-5*) Millbrook Pr.
Blumberg, Rhoda. The Great American Gold Rush. LC 89-736. (Illus.). 144p. (gr. 5 up). 1989. SBE 17.95 (*0-02-711681-6*, Bradbury Pr) Macmillan Child Grp.
Coerr, Eleanor. Chang's Paper Pony. Croll, Carolyn & Ray, Deborah K., illus. LC 87-45679. 64p. (gr. k-3). 1993. pap. 3.50 (*0-06-444163-6*, Trophy) HarpC Child Bks.
Gold Rush Stories: Mini-Play. (gr. 5 up). 1978. 6.50 (*0-89550-331-X*) Stevens & Shea.
Lake, A. L. Gold Fever. (Illus.). 32p. (gr. 3-8). 1990. PLB 18.00 (*0-86625-374-2*); PLB 13.50s.p. (*0-685-34710-9*) Rourke Corp.
Lyngheim, Linda. Gold Rush Adventure. Garber, Phyllis, illus. LC 87-82679. 96p. (gr. 3-6). 1988. 12.95 (*0-915369-03-6*); pap. 9.95 (*0-915369-02-8*) Langtry Pubns.
McNeer, May. The California Gold Rush. LC 87-4685. 160p. (gr. 5-9). 1987. pap. 4.99 (*0-394-89177-5*) Random Bks Yng Read.
Rawls, Jim. Dame Shirley & the Gold Rush. Holder, John, illus. LC 92-18083. (gr. 2-5). 1992. PLB 19.97 (*0-8114-7222-1*) Raintree Steck-V.
Van Steenwyk, Elizabeth. The California Gold Rush: West with the Forty-Niners. (Illus.). 64p. (gr. 5-8). 1991. PLB 12.90 (*0-531-20032-9*) Watts.
Wade, L. California: The Rush for Gold. 1991. 11.95s.p. (*0-86592-467-8*) Rourke Enter.

CALIFORNIA–HISTORY

Blake, Arthur & Dailey, Pamela. The Gold Rush of 1849: Staking a Claim in California. LC 94-25773. 1995. write for info. (*1-562-94483-5*) Millbrook Pr.
Boule, Mary N. The Missions: California's Heritage, No. 1: Mission San Diego de Alcala. Grim, Ellen & De Batuc, Alfredo, illus. 24p. (Orig.). (gr. 4-6). 1988. pap. 3.50 (*1-877599-00-X*) Merryant Pubs.
—The Missions: California's Heritage, No. 10: Mission Santa Barbara. Grim, Ellen & De Batuc, Alfredo, illus. 24p. (Orig.). (gr. 4-6). 1988. pap. 3.50 (*1-877599-09-3*) Merryant Pubs.
—The Missions: California's Heritage, No. 11: Mission la Purisima Concepcion. Grim, Ellen & De Batuc, Alfredo, illus. 24p. (Orig.). (gr. 4-6). 1988. pap. 3.50 (*1-877599-10-7*) Merryant Pubs.
—The Missions: California's Heritage, No. 12: Mission Santa Cruz. Grim, Ellen & De Batuc, Alfredo, illus. 24p. (Orig.). (gr. 4-6). 1988. pap. 3.50 (*1-877599-11-5*) Merryant Pubs.
—The Missions: California's Heritage, No. 13: Mission Nuestra Senora de la Soledad. Grim, Ellen & De Batuc, Alfredo, illus. 20p. (Orig.). (gr. 4-6). 1988. pap. 3.50 (*1-877599-12-3*) Merryant Pubs.
—The Missions: California's Heritage, No. 14: Mission San Jose. Grim, Ellen & De Batuc, Alfredo, illus. 28p. (Orig.). (gr. 4-6). 1988. pap. 3.50 (*1-877599-13-1*) Merryant Pubs.
—The Missions: California's Heritage, No. 15: Mission San Juan Bautista. Grim, Ellen & De Batuc, Alfredo, illus. 24p. (Orig.). (gr. 4-6). 1988. pap. 3.50 (*1-877599-14-X*) Merryant Pubs.
—The Missions: California's Heritage, No. 16: Mission San Miguel Arcangel. Grim, Ellen & De Batuc, Alfredo, illus. 24p. (Orig.). (gr. 4-6). 1988. pap. 3.50 (*1-877599-15-8*) Merryant Pubs.
—The Missions: California's Heritage, No. 17: Mission San Fernando Rey de Espana. Grim, Ellen & De Batuc, Alfredo, illus. 24p. (Orig.). (gr. 4-6). 1988. pap. 3.50 (*1-877599-16-6*) Merryant Pubs.
—The Missions: California's Heritage, No. 18: Mission San Luis Rey de Francia, 21 Bks. De Batuc, Alfredo & Grim, Ellen, illus. 24p. (Orig.). (gr. 4). 1988. pap. 3.50 (*1-877599-17-4*) Merryant Pubs.
—The Missions: California's Heritage, No. 19: Mission Santa Ines. Grim, Ellen & De Batuc, Alfredo, illus. 24p. (Orig.). (gr. 4-6). 1988. pap. 3.50 (*1-877599-18-2*) Merryant Pubs.
—The Missions: California's Heritage, No. 2: Mission San Carlos Borromeo de Carmelo. Grim, Ellen & De Batuc, Alfredo, illus. 24p. (Orig.). (gr. 4-6). 1988. pap. 3.50 (*1-877599-01-8*) Merryant Pubs.
—The Missions: California's Heritage, No. 20: Mission San Rafael Arcangel. Grim, Ellen & De Batuc, Alfredo, illus. 24p. (Orig.). (gr. 4-6). 1988. pap. 3.50 (*1-877599-19-0*) Merryant Pubs.
—The Missions: California's Heritage, No. 21: Mission San Francisco Solano. Grim, Ellen & De Batuc, Alfredo, illus. 24p. (Orig.). (gr. 4-6). 1988. pap. 3.50 (*1-877599-20-4*) Merryant Pubs.
—The Missions: California's Heritage, No. 3: Mission San Antonio de Padua. Grim, Ellen & De Batuc, Alfredo, illus. 24p. (Orig.). (gr. 4-6). 1988. pap. 3.50 (*1-877599-02-6*) Merryant Pubs.
—The Missions: California's Heritage, No. 4: Mission San Gabriel Arcangel. Grim, Ellen & De Batuc, Alfredo, illus. 24p. (Orig.). (gr. 4-6). 1988. pap. 3.50 (*1-877599-03-4*) Merryant Pubs.
—The Missions: California's Heritage, No. 5: Mission San Luis Obispo de Tolosa. Grim, Ellen & De Batuc, Alfredo, illus. 24p. (Orig.). (gr. 4-6). 1988. pap. 3.50 (*1-877599-04-2*) Merryant Pubs.
—The Missions: California's Heritage, No. 6: Mission San Francisco de Asis. Grim, Ellen & De Batuc, Alfredo, illus. 24p. (Orig.). (gr. 4-6). 1988. pap. 3.50 (*1-877599-05-0*) Merryant Pubs.
—The Missions: California's Heritage, No. 7: Mission San Juan Capistrano. Grim, Ellen & De Batuc, Alfredo, illus. 24p. (Orig.). (gr. 4-6). 1988. pap. 3.50 (*1-877599-06-9*) Merryant Pubs.
—The Missions: California's Heritage, No. 8: Mission Santa Clara de Asis. Grim, Ellen & De Batuc, Alfredo, illus. 24p. (Orig.). (gr. 4-6). 1988. pap. 3.50 (*1-877599-07-7*) Merryant Pubs.
—The Missions: California's Heritage, No. 9: Mission San Buenaventura. Grim, Ellen & De Batuc, Alfredo, illus. 24p. (Orig.). (gr. 4-6). 1988. pap. 3.50 (*1-877599-08-5*) Merryant Pubs.
Brewton, Barney. California Studies. (gr. 4). 1987. text incl. activity program 229.00 (*0-318-41079-6*) Southwinds Pr.
Brock, John M. An Illustrated History of Kern County. Ambriz, Don & Reed, Libby, illus. 83p. (gr. 3-8). 1976. pap. 5.00 (*0-943500-05-2*) Kern Historical.
California Missions Fact Cards. (Illus.). 24p. (gr. 3-6). 1992. looseleaf binder 22.00 (*0-9634017-3-4*); card set 18.00 (*0-9634017-7-7*) Toucan Valley.
Coerr, Eleanor. Chang's Paper Pony. Croll, Carolyn & Ray, Deborah K., illus. LC 87-45679. 64p. (gr. k-3). 1993. pap. 3.50 (*0-06-444163-6*, Trophy) HarpC Child Bks.
De Ruiz, Dana C. To Fly with the Swallows: A Story of Old California. Heller, Debbe, illus. LC 92-14416. 53p. (gr. 2-5). 1992. PLB 21.34 (*0-8114-7234-5*) Raintree Steck-V.
Knill, Harry. The Story of Early California to 1849, Vol. 1. Archambault, Alan, illus. 48p. (Orig.). (gr. 4 up). 1988. pap. 3.95 (*0-88388-129-2*) Bellerophon Bks.
Lyngheim, Linda. Gold Rush Adventure. Garber, Phyllis, illus. LC 87-82679. 96p. (gr. 3-6). 1988. 12.95 (*0-915369-03-6*); pap. 9.95 (*0-915369-02-8*) Langtry Pubns.
—The Indians & the California Missions. rev. ed. Garber, Phyllis, illus. LC 84-80543. 160p. (gr. 4-6). 1990. 14.95 (*0-915369-04-4*); pap. 10.95 (*0-915369-00-1*) Langtry Pubns.
McNeer, May. The California Gold Rush. LC 87-4685. 160p. (gr. 5-9). 1987. pap. 4.99 (*0-394-89177-5*) Random Bks Yng Read.
Margolin, Malcolm, ed. Native Ways: California Indian Stories & Memories. (Illus.). 128p. (gr. 4-6). 1994. pap. 7.95 (*0-930588-73-8*) Heyday Bks.
Marsh, Carole. California Timeline: A Chronology of California History, Mystery, Trivia, Legend, Lore & More. (Illus.). (gr. 3-12). 1994. PLB 24.95 (*0-7933-5887-6*); pap. 14.95 (*0-7933-5888-4*); computer disk 29.95 (*0-7933-5889-2*) Gallopade Pub Group.
—California's Unsolved Mysteries (& Their "Solutions") Includes Scientific Information & Other Activities for Students. (Illus.). (gr. 3-12). 1994. PLB 24.95 (*0-7933-5734-9*); pap. 14.95 (*0-7933-5735-7*); computer disk 29.95 (*0-7933-5736-5*) Gallopade Pub Group.
—My First Book about California. (gr. k-4). 1994. PLB 24.95 (*0-7933-5581-8*); pap. 14.95 (*0-7933-5582-6*); computer disk 29.95 (*0-7933-5583-4*) Gallopade Pub Group.
Myrick, David F. Montecito & Santa Barbara, Vol. 2. LC 87-30188. (Illus.). 320p. (gr. 11). 1991. 54.95 (*0-87046-100-1*, Pub. by Trans-Anglo) Interurban.
Nicholson, Loren. Old Picture Postcards: A Historic Journey along California's Central Coast. (Illus.). 144p. (Orig.). (gr. 9-12). 1989. pap. 12.95 (*0-9623233-1-4*) CA HPA.
Oliver, Rice D. Lone Woman of Ghalas-Hat: The True Story of the Island of the Blue Dolphins. (Illus.). 48p. (gr. 4-8). 1986. PLB 9.95x (*0-936778-96-2*); pap. 3.95x (*0-936778-95-4*) Calif Weekly.
O'Rourke, Everett V. The Highest School in California: A Story of Bodie, California. O'Rourke, Michael E., photos by. (Illus.). 32p. (Orig.). (gr. 1-4). 1978. 4.00 (*0-685-22567-4*) E ORourke.

Osterman, Joe. The Old El Toro Reader: A Guide to the Past. Walker, Doris & Osterman, Tim, eds. Schepp, Warren & Dodton, Deborah, illus. LC 92-96902. 112p. (Orig.). (gr. 3-4). 1992. pap. 9.95 (*1-881129-02-0*) Old El Toro Pr.
As "easy-read" history of a section of Orange County in southern California, THE READER is a combination children's history, an illustrated history, & a preservationist document. Although its focus is on a specific local area, it presents a "microcosm" of lifestyles that have been present in the ever-increasing move toward urbanization. THE CALIFORNIANS MAGAZINE based an article on the changes & impact of various cultures, Native Americans through Anglo, on this work. Simple one-page chapters & 140 pictures plus captions, along with maps & charts, combine to present a basic picture for children & adults alike. "It is absolutely great! It communicates to kids, to teachers, everyone." - Ellen Lee, author. Available from publisher. Write to "Old" El Toro Press, 10950 S. Valley View Ave., Whittier, CA 90604.
Publisher Provided Annotation.

Rawls, James J. Never Turn Back: Father Serra's Mission. Guzzi, George, illus. LC 92-12814. 52p. (gr. 2-5). 1992. PLB 19.97 (*0-8114-7221-3*) Raintree Steck-V.
Reinstedt, Randall A. One-Eyed Charley: The California Whip. Bergez, John, ed. LC 90-81382. (Illus.). 84p. (gr. 3-6). 1990. casebound 12.95 (*0-933818-23-8*); pap. 8.95 (*0-933818-77-7*) Ghost Town.
—Tales & Treasures of California's Missions. Bergez, John, ed. LC 92-73253. (Illus.). 120p. (gr. 3-6). 1992. casebound 13.95 (*0-933818-24-6*); pap. 10.95 (*0-933818-79-3*) Ghost Town.
Serpico, Phil. Santa Fe Route to the Pacific. Serpico, Phil, illus. LC 87-46360. 150p. (gr. 6 up). 1988. 25.00 (*0-88418-000-X*) Omni Hawthorne.
Stienecker, David. A Mission Padre. LC 94-743. (gr. 4 up). 1994. write for info. (*1-55916-040-3*) Rourke Bk Co.
Van Steenwyk, Elizabeth. The California Gold Rush: West with the Forty-Niners. (Illus.). 64p. (gr. 5-8). 1991. PLB 12.90 (*0-531-20032-9*) Watts.
Wade, L. California: The Rush for Gold. 1991. 11.95s.p. (*0-86592-467-8*) Rourke Enter.

CALISTHENICS
see Gymnastics; Physical Education and Training

CALLIGRAPHY
see Writing

CAMBISTRY
see Weights and Measures

CAMBODIA

Baillie, Allan. Little Brother. 144p. (gr. 3-7). 1992. 14.00 (*0-670-84381-4*) Viking Child Bks.

Canesso, Claudia. Cambodia. (Illus.). 96p. (gr. 6 up). 1989. lib. bdg. 14.95 (*1-55546-798-9*) Chelsea Hse.

Chandler, David P. The Land & People of Cambodia. LC 90-5907. (Illus.). 224p. (gr. 6 up). 1991. 19.00 (*0-06-021129-6*); PLB 18.89 (*0-06-021130-X*) HarpC Child Bks.

Diep, Bridgette. Trip Through Cambodia. Vaing, Jocelang, illus. LC 73-159478. 32p. (ps-3). 8.95 (*0-87592-054-3*) Scroll Pr.

Graff, Nancy P. Where the River Runs: A Portrait of a Refugee Family. Howard, Richard, photos by. LC 92-24184. (Illus.). 80p. 1993. 16.95 (*0-316-32287-3*) Little.

Roland, Donna. Grandfather's Stories from Cambodia. (gr. k-3). 1984. pap. 4.95x (*0-941996-05-0*); tchr's ed. 5.50 (*0-685-55724-3*) Open My World.

—More of Grandfather's Stories from Cambodia. (gr. 1-3). 1984. pap. 4.95x (*0-941996-06-9*); tchr's. ed. 5.50 (*0-941996-14-X*) Open My World.

CAMELS

Arnold, Caroline. Camel. Hewett, Richard, illus. LC 91-26805. 48p. (gr. 2 up). 1992. 15.00 (*0-688-09498-8*); PLB 14.93 (*0-688-09499-6*) Morrow Jr Bks.

Bailey, Donna. Camels. LC 90-22109. (Illus.). 32p. (gr. 1-4). 1992. PLB 18.99 (*0-8114-2644-0*) Raintree Steck-V.

Green, Carl R. & Sanford, William R. The Camel. LC 88-5957. (Illus.). 48p. (gr. 5-6). 1988. RSBE 12.95 (*0-89686-385-9*, Crestwood Hse) Macmillan Child Grp.

Markert, Jenny. Camels. 32p. (gr. 2-6). 1991. 15.95 (*0-89565-719-8*) Childs World.

Nexo, John B. Camels. 24p. (gr. 3). 1989. PLB 14.95 (*0-88682-222-X*) Creative Ed.

Wildlife Education, Ltd. Staff. Camels. Orr, Richard, illus. 20p. (gr. 5 up). 1984. pap. 2.75 (*0-937934-24-0*) Wildlife Educ.

CAMELS–FICTION

Hendry, Diana. Camel Called April. (ps-3). 1991. 10.95 (*0-688-10193-3*) Lothrop.

Holt-Fortin, Cher. The Ayyam-i Ha Camel. Irvine, Rex J., illus. 48p. (Orig.). (gr. 2-6). 1989. 9.95 (*0-933770-73-1*) Kalimat.

Peet, Bill. Pamela Camel. (Illus.). (gr. 4-8). 1986. pap. 5.95 (*0-395-41670-1*, Sandpiper) HM.

Perinchief, Robert. Hamel the Camel: A Different Mammal. Nordensten, Ellen H., illus. 21p. (ps-5). 1993. 12.95 (*1-882809-00-9*) Perry Pubns.

Ramakrishnan, Prema. King Kamel. Joshi, Jagdish, illus. 24p. (Orig.). (gr. k-3). 1980. pap. 2.50 (*0-89744-210-5*, Pub. by Childrens Bk Trust IA) Auromere.

Tworkov, Jack. The Camel Who Took a Walk. (Illus.). 32p. (gr. k-3). 1974. 13.95 (*0-525-27393-X*, DCB); (DCB) Dutton Child Bks.

—The Camel Who Took a Walk. Duvoisin, Roger, illus. 32p. (ps-3). 1989. pap. 3.95 (*0-525-44476-9*, DCB) Dutton Child Bks.

CAMERAS

Hewett, Joan. Camera. (gr. 4-7). 1990. pap. 6.95 (*0-395-54788-1*, Clarion Bks) HM.

Jervis, Alastair. Camera Technology. LC 90-44515. (Illus.). 48p. (gr. 5-8). 1991. PLB 12.90 (*0-531-18385-8*, Pub. by Bookwright Pr) Watts.

Jeunesse, Gallimard, et al, eds. The Camera: Snapshots, Movies, Videos, & Cartoons. Valat, Pierre-Marie, illus. LC 92-41412. 1993. 11.95 (*0-590-47129-5*) Scholastic Inc.

McPartland, Scott. Edwin Land. LC 93-22077. (gr. 7-8). 1993. 15.93 (*0-86592-150-4*); 11.95s.p. (*0-685-66592-5*) Rourke Enter.

Roberts. Fun with Sun Prints & Box Cameras. 1981. 8.95 (*0-679-20629-9*) McKay.

CAMP COOKING

see Outdoor Cookery

CAMPAIGNS, POLITICAL

see Politics, Practical

CAMPAIGNS, PRESIDENTIAL

see Presidents–U. S.–Election

CAMPANELLA, ROY, 1921-

Greene, Carol. Roy Campanella: Major-League Champion. LC 93-37878. (Illus.). 48p. (gr. k-3). 1994. PLB 12.85 (*0-516-04261-0*) Childrens.

Tackach, James. Roy Campanella. Murray, Jim, intro. by. (Illus.). 64p. (gr. 3 up). 1991. lib. bdg. 14.95 (*0-7910-1170-4*) Chelsea Hse.

CAMPING

see also Backpacking; Outdoor Cookery; Outdoor Life; Wilderness Survival

Boy Scouts of America. Camping. (Illus.). 96p. (gr. 6-12). 1984. pap. 1.85 (*0-8395-3256-3*, 33256) BSA.

Camping & Walking. (Illus.). 128p. (gr. 3 up). 1987. PLB 15.96 (*0-88110-287-3*); pap. 9.95 (*0-7460-0129-0*) EDC.

Cooke, Tom, illus. Hide & Seek Camping Trip: A Sesame Street Book. LC 89-61021. 14p. (ps). 1990. bds. 3.99 (*0-679-80138-3*) Random Bks Yng Read.

Evans, Jeremy. Camping & Survival. LC 91-39143. (Illus.). 48p. (gr. 5-6). 1992. text ed. 13.95 RSBE (*0-89686-686-6*, Crestwood Hse) Macmillan Child Grp.

Felt, Freddi. My Going to Camp Book. Fredman, Foan, illus. 40p. (gr. 1-6). 1988. 5.95 (*0-9616875-2-5*) F & F Pub.

Fraser, Judith & Herman, Jon. Careful Campers Coloring Book: A Children's Guide to Caring for Nature's Wonders. (Illus.). 32p. (Orig.). (gr. 1-3). 1990. pap. text ed. 2.00 (*0-914019-26-0*) NW Interpretive.

Griffin, Steven A. & Griffin, Elizabeth M. Camping for Kids. LC 93-47641. (Illus.). 96p. (gr. k-8). 1994. pap. 7.95 (*1-55971-228-7*) NorthWord.

McManus, Patrick F. Kid Camping from Aaaaiii! to Zip. Doty, Roy, illus. LC 79-13152. (gr. 3-8). 1979. 12.95 (*0-688-41910-0*) Lothrop.

Pioneering. (Illus.). 48p. (gr. 6-12). 1974. pap. 1.85 (*0-8395-3382-9*, 33377) BSA.

Queen, Margaret M. So You're off to Summer Camp: A Trunk Load of Tips for a Fun-Filled Camp Adventure. Matens, Margaret H., illus. LC 93-77129. 136p. (gr. 2-12). 1993. 14.95 (*1-882959-55-8*); perfect bdg. 6.95 (*1-882959-50-7*) Foxglove TN.

CAMPING–FICTION

Allen, Julia. My First Camping Trip. Reese, Bob, illus. (gr. k-3). 1987. 7.95 (*0-89868-181-2*); pap. 2.95 (*0-685-50867-6*) ARO Pub.

—My First Camping Trip. Reese, Bob, illus. (gr. k-3). 1987. pap. 20.00 (*0-89868-182-0*) ARO Pub.

Aunt Eeebs. The Happy Campers. Aunt Eeebs, illus. 24p. (Orig.). (ps-2). 1991. pap. write for info. (*1-878908-02-2*) Rivercrest Indus.

Bauer, Marion D. A Taste of Smoke. LC 92-32585. (gr. 5 up). 1993. 13.95 (*0-395-64341-4*, Clarion Bks) HM.

—When I Go Camping with Grandma. Garns, Allen, illus. LC 93-33809. 32p. (gr. k-3). 1995. PLB 14.95 (*0-8167-3448-8*); pap. text ed. 4.95 (*0-8167-3449-6*) BrdgeWater.

Brown, Mary K. Let's Go Camping with Mr. Sillypants. LC 94-15991. 1995. write for info. (*0-517-59773-X*); PLB write for info. (*0-517-59774-8*) Crown Pub Group.

Carrick, Carol. Sleep Out. Carrick, Donald, illus. LC 72-88539. 32p. (gr. 1-3). 1979. (Clarion Bks); pap. 4.95 (*0-89919-083-9*, Clarion) HM.

Cartwright, Pauline. Home. Tulloch, Coral, illus. LC 93-20062. 1994. write for info. (*0-383-03695-X*) SRA Schl Grp.

Dadey, Debbie & Jones, Marcia. Werewolves Don't Go to Summer Camp. 128p. (gr. 2-5). 1991. pap. 2.50 (*0-590-44061-6*) Scholastic Inc.

Davoll, Barbara. The Camping Caper. Hockerman, Dennis, illus. 24p. 1993. 6.99 (*1-56476-162-2*, Victor Books) SP Pubns.

Gauthier, Bertrand. Zachary in Camping Out. Sylvestre, Daniel, illus. LC 93-15457. 1993. 15.93 (*0-8368-1012-0*) Gareth Stevens Inc.

Gondosch, Linda. Camp Kickapoo. Lincoln, Patricia H., illus. LC 92-28060. 128p. (gr. 4-6). 1993. 13.99 (*0-525-67373-3*, Lodestar Bks) Dutton Child Bks.

Gould, Deborah. Camping in the Temple of the Sun. Paterson, Diane, illus. LC 91-16358. 32p. (gr. k-5). 1992. RSBE 13.95 (*0-02-736355-4*, Bradbury Pr) Macmillan Child Grp.

Greer, Gary & Ruddick, Robert. This Island Isn't Big Enough for the Four of Us! LC 86-47750. 160p. (gr. 3-7). 1989. pap. 3.95 (*0-06-440203-7*, Trophy) HarpC Child Bks.

Greer, Gery & Ruddick, Robert. This Island Isn't Big Enough for the Four of Us. LC 86-47750. 160p. (gr. 3-7). 1987. 14.00 (*0-690-04612-X*, Crowell Jr Bks); PLB 13.89 (*0-690-04614-6*, Crowell Jr Bks) HarpC Child Bks.

Guild, Anne V. Mickey Mouse in Let's Go...on a Camping Caper. Scholefield, Ron, et al, illus. 26p. (ps up). 1987. pap. 14.95 (*1-55578-803-3*) Worlds Wonder.

Henkes, Kevin. Bailey Goes Camping. Henkes, Kevin, illus. LC 84-29027. 24p. (ps-1). 1985. 14.00 (*0-688-05701-2*); lib. bdg. 13.93 (*0-688-05702-0*) Greenwillow.

Hill, Kirkpatrick. Winter Camp. LC 92-41200. (Illus.). 192p. (gr. 3-7). 1993. SBE 14.95 (*0-689-50588-4*, M K McElderry) Macmillan Child Grp.

Hoban, Lillian. Arthur's Camp-Out. Hoban, Lillian, illus. LC 91-27528. 64p. (gr. k-3). 1993. 14.00 (*0-06-020525-3*); PLB 13.89 (*0-06-020526-1*) HarpC Child Bks.

Howe, James. Pinky & Rex & the Double-Dad Weekend. Sweet, Melissa, illus. LC 94-9384. 1995. 14.00 (*0-689-31871-5*, Atheneum) Macmillan.

Kahrimanis, Leola. Blue Hills Robbery. Roberts, M., ed. (Illus.). 128p. (gr. 6-8). 1991. 10.95 (*0-89015-753-7*) Sunbelt Media.

Kaye, Marilyn. Color War! 128p. (Orig.). (gr. 3 up). 1989. pap. 3.50 (*0-380-75702-8*, Camelot) Avon.

—Too Many Counselors. 128p. 1990. pap. 2.95 (*0-380-75913-6*, Camelot) Avon.

Kleitsch, Christel & Kelley, True. It Happened at Pickle Lake. (Illus.). 64p. (gr. 2-5). 1993. 11.99 (*0-525-45058-0*, DCB) Dutton Child Bks.

Koontz, Robin M. Chicago & the Cat: The Camping Trip. Koontz, Robin M., illus. LC 92-46685. 32p. (gr. k-3). 1994. 12.99 (*0-525-65137-3*, Cobblehill Bks) Dutton Child Bks.

L'Engle, Madeleine. The Moon by Night. LC 63-9072. 224p. (gr. 7 up). 1963. 16.00 (*0-374-35049-3*) FS&G.

Levy, Elizabeth. Dracula Is a Pain in the Neck. Gerstein, Mordicai, illus. LC 82-47707. 80p. (gr. 2-6). 1983. PLB 12.89 (*0-06-023823-2*) HarpC Child Bks.

Locker, Thomas. Where the River Begins. LC 84-1709. (Illus.). 32p. (gr. k-3). 1984. 16.95 (*0-8037-0089-X*); PLB 14.89 (*0-8037-0090-3*) Dial Bks Young.

McArthur, Nancy. The Adventure of the Backyard Sleepout. 80p. 1992. pap. 2.75 (*0-590-45033-6*) Scholastic Inc.

McKenna, Colleen O. Camp Murphy. (gr. 4-7). 1994. pap. 3.25 (*0-590-45808-6*) Scholastic Inc.

Martin, Ann M. Bummer Summer. LC 82-48755. 160p. (gr. 5-9). 1983. 14.95 (*0-8234-0483-8*) Holiday.

Muntean, Michaela. Baby Fozzie Goes Camping. Wilson, Ann, illus. 26p. (ps up). 1987. 12.95 (*1-55578-604-9*) Worlds Wonder.

Nagel, Karen B. Norfin Trolls Campout Adventure. (ps-3). 1993. pap. 2.50 (*0-590-46630-5*) Scholastic Inc.

Naylor, Phyllis R. The Fear Place. LC 93-38891. (gr. 3-7). 1994. 14.95 (*0-689-31866-9*, Atheneum Child Bk) Macmillan Child Grp.

Nesbit, Jeffrey A. The Lost Canoe. 130p. 1991. pap. 4.99 (*0-89693-130-7*) SP Pubns.

O'Connor, Jane. Amy's (Not So) Great Camp-Out. Long, Laurie S., illus. LC 92-45881. 64p. (gr. 1-4). 1993. 7.99 (*0-448-40167-3*, G&D); pap. 3.95 (*0-448-40166-5*, G&D) Putnam Pub Group.

Parish, Peggy. Amelia Bedelia Goes Camping. LC 84-7979. (Illus.). 56p. (gr. 1-3). 1985. 12.95 (*0-688-04058-6*); PLB 12.88 (*0-688-04057-8*) Greenwillow.

Paulsen, Gary. Dunc & Amos & the Red Tatoos, No. 12. (gr. 4-7). 1993. pap. 3.50 (*0-440-40790-7*) Dell.

Petersen, P. J. I Hate Camping. Remkiewicz, Frank, illus. LC 90-39650. 80p. (gr. 4-7). 1991. 13.00 (*0-525-44673-7*, DCB) Dutton Child Bks.

—I Hate Camping. Remkiewicz, Frank, illus. 96p. (gr. 2-5). 1993. pap. 3.99 (*0-14-036446-3*, Puffin) Puffin Bks.

Roche, P. K. Webster & Arnold Go Camping. (Illus.). 32p. (ps-3). 1991. pap. 3.95 (*0-14-050806-6*, Puffin) Puffin Bks.

Sadler, Marilyn. P. J. Funnybunny Camps Out: A Step One Book. Bollen, Roger, illus. LC 92-6156. 32p. (Orig.). (ps-3). 1994. PLB 7.99 (*0-679-93269-0*); pap. 3.50 (*0-679-83269-6*) Random Bks Yng Read.

Schneider, Howie. Amos Camps Out: A Couch Adventure in the Woods. (ps-3). 1992. 14.95 (*0-316-77402-2*, Joy St Bks) Little.

Schwartz, Joel L. Upchuck Summer. Degen, Bruce, illus. 144p. (gr. 3-7). 1983. pap. 3.50 (*0-440-49264-5*, YB) Dell.

Schwartz, Linda. Camp Mail from Me. 32p. (gr. 3-6). 1994. 4.95 (*0-88160-225-6*, LW320) Learning Wks.

—My Camp Memories. LC 93-86210. 32p. (gr. 3-6). 1994. 4.95 (*0-88160-226-4*, LW321) Learning Wks.

Seton, Ernest T. Two Little Savages. (Illus.). 286p. (gr. 4-8). 1903. pap. 6.95 (*0-486-20985-7*) Dover.

Sheldon, Dyan. Harry on Vacation. Heap, Sue, illus. LC 92-52999. 144p. (gr. 3-6). 1993. 13.95 (*1-56402-127-0*) Candlewick Pr.

Singer, Marilyn. In My Tent. McCully, Emily A., illus. LC 91-16115. 32p. (gr. k-3). 1992. RSBE 14.95 (*0-02-782701-1*, Macmillan Child Bk) Macmillan Child Grp.

Spindle's Picnic. 1989. 2.99 (*0-517-69123-X*) Random Hse Value.

Sumiko. My Summer Vacation. Sumiko, illus. LC 89-43164. 32p. (Orig.). (ps-1). 1993. pap. 2.25 (*0-679-80525-7*) Random Bks Yng Read.

Tafuri, Nancy. Do Not Disturb. LC 86-357. (Illus.). 24p. (ps-3). 1987. 11.75 (*0-688-06541-4*); PLB 11.88 (*0-688-06542-2*) Greenwillow.

Taylor, Theodore. Sweet Friday Island. LC 93-32435. (gr. 7 up). 1994. write for info. (*0-15-200009-7*); pap. write for info. (*0-15-200012-7*) HarBrace.

Tyrone Goes Camping. (Illus.). 40p. (gr. k-5). 1994. pap. 4.95 (*0-685-71585-X*, 521) W Gladden Found.

Vallet, Muriel. Camping Is Exciting. Vallet, Muriel, illus. 19p. (gr. k-3). 1992. pap. 13.95 (*1-895583-48-9*) MAYA Pubs.

—Dad, Can We Go Camping Tonight? Vallet, Muriel, illus. 16p. (gr. 1-6). 1992. pap. 13.95 (*1-56606-003-6*) Bradley Mann.

Weinberg, Shifra. Regards from Camp 2: Deepwater Dilemma. LC 93-72270. (gr. 5-8). 1993. write for info. (*1-56062-200-8*) CIS Comm.

Weiss, Ellen. Oh Beans! Starring Half-Baked Bean. Hall, Susan, illus. LC 88-4901. 32p. (gr. k-3). 1989. PLB 8.79 (*0-8167-1402-9*); pap. text ed. 1.95 (*0-8167-1403-7*) Troll Assocs.

Westcott, A. & Symons, C. Whispering River. LC 78-108727. (Illus.). 48p. (gr. 3-5). 1970. PLB 10.95 (*0-87783-049-5*); pap. 3.94 deluxe ed (*0-87783-116-5*) Oddo.

White, Stephen. Barney & Baby Bop: A Tent Too Full. Dowdy, Linda, ed. McKee, Darren & Alger, Bill, illus. LC 93-77870. 24p. (ps-1). 1993. pap. 2.25 (*1-57064-009-2*) Barney Pub.

Williams, Vera B. Three Days on a River in a Red Canoe. LC 80-23893. (Illus.). 32p. (gr. k-3). 1981. 14.95 (*0-688-80307-5*); PLB 14.88 (*0-688-84307-7*) Greenwillow.

Wittmann, Patricia. Scrabble Creek. Poydar, Nancy, illus. LC 92-10810. 32p. (gr. k-3). 1993. RSBE 14.95 (*0-02-793225-7*, Macmillan Child Bk) Macmillan Child Grp.

Ziefert, Harriet. Harry Goes to Day Camp. Smith, Mavis, illus. (ps-2). 1994. pap. 3.25 (*0-14-037000-5*) Puffin Bks.

CAMPS–FICTION

Ames, Diane. The Buddy System. 1992. pap. 3.50 (*0-06-106075-5*, Harp PBks) HarpC.

—Campfire Secrets. 1992. pap. 3.50 (*0-06-106076-3*, Harp PBks) HarpC.
—Summer Fling. 1992. pap. 3.50 (*0-06-106074-7*, Harp PBks) HarpC.
Angell, Judie. In Summertime, It's Tuffy. 192p. (gr. 5 up). 1979. pap. 2.25 (*0-440-94051-6*, LFL) Dell.
Brown, Marc T. Arthur Goes to Camp. Brown, Marc T., illus. LC 81-15588. 32p. (ps-3). 1984. 14.95 (*0-316-11218-6*, Joy St Bks); pap. 4.95 (*0-316-11058-2*, Joy St Bks) Little.
Carlson, Nancy. Arnie Goes to Camp. 1988. pap. 11.95 (*0-670-81549-7*) Viking Child Bks.
Chesworth, Michael. Archibald Frisby. 1994. 15.00 (*0-374-30392-4*) FS&G.
Cocca-Leffler, Maryann. What a Pest! Cocca-Leffler, Maryann, illus. 32p. (ps-1). 1994. 7.99 (*0-448-40399-4*, G&D); pap. 3.50 (*0-448-40393-5*, G&D) Putnam Pub Group.
Conford, Ellen. Hail, Hail Camp Timberwood. Owens, Gail, illus. LC 78-18715. (gr. 3-7). 1978. 14.95 (*0-316-15291-9*) Little.
Cummings, Pat. Petey Moroni's Camp Runamok Diary. Cummings, Pat, illus. LC 91-45774. 32p. (gr. k-5). 1992. SBE 14.95 (*0-02-725513-1*, Bradbury Pr) Macmillan Child Grp.
Cushman, Doug. Camp Big Paw. Cushman, Doug, illus. LC 89-26867. 64p. (gr. k-3). 1990. PLB 13.89 (*0-06-021368-X*) HarpC Child Bks.
—Camp Big Paw. LC 89-26867. (Illus.). 64p. (gr. k-3). 1993. pap. 3.50 (*0-06-444166-0*, Trophy) HarpC Child Bks.
Danziger, Paula. There's a Bat in Bunk Five. LC 80-64833. 160p. (gr. 7 up). 1980. pap. 10.95 (*0-385-29013-6*) Delacorte.
Delton, Judy. My Mom Made Me Go to Camp. (gr. 1-3). 1993. pap. 2.99 (*0-553-37251-3*) Bantam.
—My Mom Made Me Go to Camp. 1993. pap. 2.99 (*0-440-40838-5*) Dell.
Duffey, Betsy. Lucky on the Loose. Morrill, Leslie, illus. LC 92-21421. 1993. pap. 13.00 (*0-671-86424-6*, S&S BFYR) S&S Trade.
Fearnehough, Mary E. Camp Adventure. LC 92-59948. 108p. (gr. 4-8). 1993. pap. 5.95 (*1-55523-576-X*) Winston-Derek.
Feuer, Elizabeth. Camp Bugaboo. LC 93-34212. 1994. 15.00 (*0-374-31020-3*) FS&G.
Fort, Donny. Church Camp. 144p. 1992. pap. 6.99 (*0-310-54861-6*, Pub. by Zondervan Bks) Zondervan.
Galbraith, Kathryn O. Roommates Again. Graham, Mark, illus. LC 93-8709. 48p. (ps-2). 1994. SBE 14.95 (*0-689-50592-2*, M K McElderry) Macmillan Child Grp.
—Roommates Again. Graham, Mark, illus. LC 93-8709. 48p. (gr. 1-4). 1994. SBE 12.95 (*0-689-50597-3*, M K McElderry) Macmillan Child Grp.
Gitenstein, Judy. Summer Camp. 64p. (Orig.). (gr. 2-4). 1984. pap. 2.75 (*0-553-15562-8*, Skylark) Bantam.
Hallowell, Tommy. Shot from Midfield. 112p. (gr. 3 up). 1990. pap. 3.50 (*0-14-032912-9*, Puffin) Puffin Bks.
Himmelman, John. Lights Out! LC 93-33811. (Illus.). 32p. (gr. k-3). 1995. PLB 14.95 (*0-8167-3450-X*); pap. text ed. 4.95 (*0-8167-3451-8*) BrdgeWater.
Howe, James. Pinky & Rex Go to Camp. Sweet, Melissa, illus. LC 91-16123. 48p. (ps-3). 1992. SBE 12.95 (*0-689-31718-2*, Atheneum Child Bk) Macmillan Child Grp.
—Pinky & Rex Go to Camp. 48p. (gr. 2-8). 1993. pap. 3.99 (*0-380-72082-5*, Camelot Young) Avon.
Jones Gunn, Robin. Seventeen Wishes. LC 93-11278. 1993. write for info. (*1-56179-169-5*) Focus Family.
Kaye, Marilyn. Camp Sunnyside Friends, No. 13: Big Sister Blues. 128p. (Orig.). 1991. pap. 2.95 (*0-380-76551-9*, Camelot) Avon.
—Camp Sunnyside Friends, No. 17: Camp Spaghetti. 128p. (Orig.). (gr. 4). 1992. pap. 3.50 (*0-380-76556-X*, Camelot) Avon.
—Looking for Trouble. 128p. (gr. 4). 1990. pap. 2.95 (*0-380-75909-8*, Camelot) Avon.
—The New & Improved Sarah. 144p. (Orig.). 1990. pap. 2.95 (*0-380-76180-7*, Camelot) Avon.
—A Witch in Cabin Six. 128p. (gr. 3-4). 1990. pap. 2.95 (*0-380-75912-8*, Camelot) Avon.
Keller, Beverly. Camp Trouble. (gr. 4-7). 1993. pap. 2.95 (*0-590-43728-3*) Scholastic Inc.
Levinson, Nancy S. Your Friend Natalie Popper. 112p. (gr. 5-9). 1991. 13.95 (*0-525-67307-5*, Lodestar Bks) Dutton Child Bks.
Littke, Lael. There's a Snake at Girls' Camp. LC 94-751. (Orig.). (gr. 3-7). 1994. pap. 4.95 (*0-87579-845-4*) Deseret Bk.
Logue, Mary. The Missing Statue of Minnehaha. (gr. 3-8). 1992. PLB 8.95 (*0-89565-902-6*) Childs World.
McPhail, David. Pig Pig Goes to Camp. (ps-3). 1987. pap. 4.99 (*0-14-054778-9*) Dutton Child Bks.
Mallett, Jerry & Bartch, Marian. Goodbye to Camp Crumb. Smith, Mark D., illus. 59p. (gr. 2-5). 1986. PLB 7.50 (*0-8479-9929-7*, 120950) Perma-Bound.
Marcey, Sally. Choice Adventures, No. 11: The Silverlake Stranger. LC 92-36889. 1993. 4.99 (*0-8423-5048-9*) Tyndale.
Marshall, James. The Cut-ups at Camp Custer. (Illus.). 32p. (ps-3). 1989. pap. 12.95 (*0-670-82051-2*) Viking Child Bks.
Massey Weddle, Linda. T. J. & the Big Trout River Vandals. LC 91-14678. 94p. (Orig.). (gr. 4-7). 1991. pap. 3.95 (*0-87227-148-X*, RBP5180) Reg Baptist.
—T. J. & the Somebody Club. LC 92-5342. 108p. 1992. 3.95 (*0-87227-176-5*, RBP5210) Reg Baptist.
Myers, Bill. My Life As a Smashed Burrito with Extra Hot Sauce. 1993. pap. 4.99 (*0-8499-3402-8*) Word Inc.
Park, Barbara. Buddies. (gr. 7 up). 1986. pap. 2.95 (*0-380-69992-3*, Flare) Avon.

Schwartz, Amy. Camper of the Week. LC 90-23033. (Illus.). 32p. (gr. k-2). 1991. 14.95 (*0-531-05942-1*); RLB 14.99 (*0-531-08542-2*) Orchard Bks Watts.
Schwartz, Joel L. Upchuck Summer's Revenge. 1990. 13.95 (*0-385-29978-8*) Doubleday.
Smith, Jane D. Mary by Myself. LC 93-47457. 128p. (gr. 3 up). 1994. 14.00 (*0-06-024517-4*); PLB 13.89 (*0-06-024518-2*) HarpC Child Bks.
Spinelli, Jerry. Who Ran My Underwear up the Flagpole? 1992. 2.95 (*0-590-46278-4*, Apple Paperbacks) Scholastic Inc.
Stine, Megan & Stine, H. William. Camp Zombie. LC 93-33748. 1994. write for info. (Bullseye Bks) Random Bks Yng Read.
—Camp Zombie. 108p. (Orig.). (gr. 2-6). 1994. pap. 2.99 (*0-679-85640-4*) Random Bks Yng Read.
Stoltz, Donald R. Bunk One. Costa, Gwen, ed. LC 90-22976. 100p. (Orig.). 1991. pap. 13.95 (*0-87949-346-1*) Ashley Bks.
Thaler, Mike. Camp Rotten Time. Lee, Jared, illus. LC 93-3231. 32p. (ps-3). 1993. PLB 9.79 (*0-8167-3024-5*); pap. 2.95 (*0-8167-3025-3*) Troll Assocs.
Thomas, Jerry D. Detective Zack & the Mystery at Thunder Mountain. LC 93-41480. (gr. 4 up). 1994. 5.95 (*0-8163-1212-5*) Pacific Pr Pub Assn.
Thompson, Jonathon J., Jr. Away at Camp. 20p. (gr. 1-6). 1992. 3.00 (*0-933479-11-5*) Thompson.
Van Leeuwen, Jean. The Great Summer Camp Catastrophe. DeGroat, Diane, illus. LC 91-18487. 192p. (gr. 2-6). 1992. 13.00 (*0-8037-1106-9*); PLB 12.89 (*0-8037-1107-7*) Dial Bks Young.
Weinberg, Shifra. Regards from Camp, No. 3. LC 93-72599. 110p. (gr. 6). 1993. 11.95 (*1-56062-232-6*) CIS Comm.
Ziefert, Harriet. Harry Goes to Day Camp. (Illus.). 32p. (ps-2). 1990. pap. 8.95 (*0-670-83201-4*) Viking Child Bks.
—Harry Goes to Day Camp. Smith, Mavis, illus. 32p. (ps-3). 1990. pap. 3.50 (*0-14-054223-X*, Puffin) Puffin Bks.

CANADA

Ayer, Elizabeth. Canada. (Illus.). 64p. (gr. 7 up). 1990. lib. bdg. 17.27 (*0-86593-091-0*); lib. bdg. 12.95s.p. (*0-685-36363-5*) Rourke Corp.
Aziz, Laurel & Edwards, Frank B. Ottawa: A Kid's Eye View. Kraulis, J. A., illus. 72p. 1993. text ed. 19.95 (*0-921285-27-2*, Pub. by Bungalo Bks CN); pap. 9.95 (*0-921285-26-4*, Pub. by Bungalo Bks CN) Firefly Bks Ltd.
Bailey, Donna. Canada. LC 91-21292. (Illus.). 32p. (gr. 1-4). 1992. PLB 18.99 (*0-8114-2568-1*); pap. 3.95 (*0-8114-7181-0*) Raintree Steck-V.
Bakken, Edna. Alberta. LC 91-951144. (Illus.). 144p. (gr. 5-8). 1992. PLB 20.55 (*0-516-06611-0*) Childrens.
Barnes, Michael. Ontario. LC 94-20253. Date not set. PLB write for info. (*0-8225-2754-5*) Lerner Pubns.
Bender, Lionel. Canada. (Illus.). 48p. (gr. 4-8). 1987. PLB 14.95 (*0-382-09508-1*) Silver Burdett Pr.
Canada. 2nd ed. (gr. 6 up). 1993. pap. write for info. (*1-878867-30-X*, Compass Amrcn) Fodors Travel.
Emmond, Ken. Manitoba. LC 91-951136. (Illus.). 144p. (gr. 4 up). 1992. PLB 20.55 (*0-516-06612-9*) Childrens.
Flint, David. Canada. LC 92-43923. (Illus.). 32p. (gr. 3-4). 1993. PLB 19.24 (*0-8114-2939-3*) Raintree Steck-V.
Haaland, Lynn. Acadia Seacoast: A Guidebook for Appreciation. Mills, Louise & Johnson, Mercy, eds. Swensson, Dale I. & Welles, T., illus. 32p. (Orig.). (gr. k up). 1984. pap. 3.00 (*0-915189-01-1*) Oceanus.
Hancock, Lyn. Northwest Territories. (Illus.). 144p. (gr. 4 up). 1992. PLB 20.55 (*0-516-06615-3*) Childrens.
Harrison, Ted. O Canada. LC 92-39800. 32p. (gr. k-2). 1993. PLB 14.95 (*0-395-66075-0*) Ticknor & Flds Bks Yng Read.
Haskins, Jim. Count Your Way Through Canada. Michaels, Steve, illus. 24p. (gr. 1-4). 1989. 17.50 (*0-87614-350-8*); pap. 5.95 (*0-87614-515-2*) Carolrhoda Bks.
Kalman, Bobbie. Canada Celebrates Multiculturalism. LC 93-34136. (Illus.). 32p. (Orig.). (gr. 3-6). 1993. PLB 15.95 (*0-86505-220-4*); pap. 7.95 (*0-86505-300-6*) Crabtree Pub Co.
Kessler, Deirdre. Prince Edward Island. (Illus.). 144p. (gr. 4 up). 1992. PLB 20.55 (*0-516-06616-1*) Childrens.
Law, Kevin J. Canada. (Illus.). (gr. 5 up). 1988. 14.95 (*0-222-00912-8*) Chelsea Hse.
—Canada. (Illus.). 128p. (gr. 5 up). 1990. lib. bdg. 14.95 (*0-7910-1101-1*) Chelsea Hse.
Lerner Publications, Department of Geography Staff. Canada in Pictures. (Illus.). 64p. (gr. 5 up). 1989. PLB 17.50 (*0-8225-1870-8*) Lerner Pubns.
LeVert, Suzanne. Alberta. (Illus.). 64p. (gr. 3 up). 1991. lib. bdg. 16.95 (*0-7910-1026-0*) Chelsea Hse.
—Canada: Facts & Figures. (Illus.). (gr. 3 up). 1992. PLB 16.95 (*0-7910-1035-X*) Chelsea Hse.
—Dominion of Canada. (Illus.). (gr. 3 up). 1992. lib. bdg. 16.95 (*0-7910-1034-1*) Chelsea Hse.
—Let's Discover Canada, 14 bks. (Illus.). (gr. 3 up). 1991. PLB 237.30 (*0-7910-1021-X*) Chelsea Hse.
—Manitoba. (Illus.). 64p. (gr. 3 up). 1991. lib. bdg. 16.95 (*0-7910-1025-2*) Chelsea Hse.
—New Brunswick. (Illus.). (gr. 3 up). 1992. lib. bdg. 16.95 (*0-7910-1029-5*) Chelsea Hse.
—Newfoundland. (Illus.). (gr. 3 up). 1992. lib. bdg. 16.95 (*0-7910-1027-9*) Chelsea Hse.
—Nova Scotia. (Illus.). (gr. 3 up). 1992. lib. bdg. 16.95 (*0-7910-1028-7*) Chelsea Hse.
—Ontario. Berton, Pierre, intro. by. (Illus.). 64p. (gr. 3 up). 1991. lib. bdg. 16.95 (*0-7910-1022-8*) Chelsea Hse.
—Prince Edward Island. (Illus.). 69p. (gr. 3 up). 1991. lib. bdg. 16.95 (*0-7910-1023-6*) Chelsea Hse.
—Saskatchewan. (Illus.). 64p. (gr. 3 up). 1991. lib. bdg. 17.95 (*0-7910-1024-4*) Chelsea Hse.
—Yukon. (Illus.). (gr. 3 up). 1992. lib. bdg. 16.95 (*0-7910-1032-5*) Chelsea Hse.
Lotz, Jim. Nova Scotia. LC 91-951128. (Illus.). 144p. (gr. 4 up). 1992. PLB 20.55 (*0-516-06613-7*) Childrens.
MacKay, Kathryn. Ontario. (Illus.). 144p. (gr. 5-8). 1992. PLB 20.55 (*0-516-06614-5*) Childrens.
Malcolm, Andrew H. The Land & People of Canada. LC 90-47560. (Illus.). 240p. (gr. 6 up). 1991. 17.95 (*0-06-022494-0*); PLB 17.89 (*0-06-022495-9*) HarpC Child Bks.
Manson, Ainslie. A Dog Came, Too: A True Story. Blades, Ann, illus. LC 91-44891. 32p. (gr. 1-5). 1993. SBE 13.95 (*0-689-50567-1*, M K McElderry) Macmillan Child Grp.
Margoshes, David. Saskatchewan. (Illus.). 144p. (gr. 4 up). 1992. PLB 20.55 (*0-516-06618-8*) Childrens.
Paltrowitz, Stuart & Paltrowitz, Donna. Content Area Reading Skills-Competency Canada: Main Idea. (Illus.). (gr. 4). 1987. pap. text ed. 3.25 (*0-89525-853-6*) Ed Activities.
Pang Guek Cheng. Canada. LC 93-11018. (gr. 5 up). 1993. 21.95 (*1-85435-579-1*) Marshall Cavendish.
Parker, Lewis K. Canada. LC 93-42778. 1994. write for info. (*1-55916-002-0*) Rourke Bk Co.
Sabin, Louis. Canada. Eitzen, Allan, illus. LC 84-40437. 32p. (gr. 3-6). 1985. PLB 9.49 (*0-8167-0302-7*); pap. text ed. 2.95 (*0-8167-0303-5*) Troll Assocs.
Schemenauer, Elma. Canada. LC 94-11943. (Illus.). 48p. (gr. k-4). 1994. PLB 17.20 (*0-516-01065-4*); pap. 4.95 (*0-516-41065-2*) Childrens.
Shepherd, J. Canada. LC 87-14626. (Illus.). 128p. (gr. 5-9). 1987. PLB 20.55 (*0-516-02757-3*) Childrens.
Sunday, Jane. Canada. LC 92-10767. 96p. 1992. lib. bdg. 22.80 (*0-8114-2455-3*) Raintree Steck-V.
Wright, David K. Canada. Wright, David K., photos by. LC 89-43197. (Illus.). 64p. (gr. 5-6). 1991. PLB 21.26 (*0-8368-0256-X*) Gareth Stevens Inc.
Wright, Sarah B. Islands of the Northeastern United States & Eastern Canada. (Illus.). 224p. (Orig.). 1990. pap. text ed. 9.95 (*0-934601-99-2*) Peachtree Pubs.

CANADA–BIOGRAPHY

Canadian Childhoods: A Tundra Anthology. LC 88-50262. (Illus.). (gr. 4-8). 1989. 24.95 (*0-88776-208-5*) Tundra Bks.
Kalman, Bobbie. Canada - the Land. LC 93-23516. (Illus.). 32p. (Orig.). (gr. 3-6). 1993. PLB 15.95 (*0-86505-217-4*); pap. 7.95 (*0-86505-297-2*) Crabtree Pub Co.
—Canada - the People. LC 93-34328. (Illus.). 32p. (Orig.). (gr. 3-6). 1993. PLB 15.95 (*0-86505-218-2*); pap. 7.95 (*0-86505-298-0*) Crabtree Pub Co.
MacKinnon, Christy. Silent Observer. (Illus.). 48p. 1993. 15.95 (*1-56368-022-X*, Pub. by K Green Pubns) Gallaudet Univ Pr.
Paulita, Mary. Half-Pint on Guadalcanal: A Saga of Heroism, Commitment & Love. Gehring, Frederick P., frwd. by. (Illus.). 144p. (Orig.). (gr. 8). 1993. pap. 10.00 (*0-9631198-1-8*) Marist Miss Sis.
Tykal, Jack B. Etienne Provost: Man of the Mountains. Smith, Monte, ed. Smith, Ralph L., illus. Gowans, Fred, intro. by. LC 89-80549. (Illus.). 256p. (gr. 9 up). 1989. 15.95 (*0-943604-24-9*); pap. 9.95 perfect bdg. (*0-943604-23-0*) Eagles View.

Williams, A. Susan. Canada. LC 91-9534. (Illus.). 32p. (gr. k-4). 1991. 12.40 (*0-531-18390-4*, Pub. by Bookwright Pr) Watts.

CANADA–DISCOVERY AND EXPLORATION
see America–Discovery and Exploration

CANADA–FICTION

Blades, Ann. Mary of Mile 18. LC 74-179430. (Illus.). (gr. 1-4). 1971. pap. 6.95 (*0-88776-059-7*) Tundra Bks.

Buchanan, Dawna L. The Falcon's Wing. LC 91-22545. 144p. (gr. 5 up). 1992. 13.95 (*0-531-05986-3*); lib. bdg. 13.99 (*0-531-08586-4*) Orchard Bks Watts.

Ferris, Sean. Children of the Great Muskeg. (Illus.). 84p. (gr. 3-5). 1991. pap. 12.95 (*0-88753-128-8*, Pub. by Black Moss Pr CN) Firefly Bks Ltd.

Freedman, Benedict & Freedman, Nancy. Mrs. Mike. (gr. 7 up). 1984. pap. 3.95 (*0-425-10328-5*) Berkley Pub.

Garrigue, Sheila. The Eternal Spring of Mr. Ito. LC 93-30356. 176p. (gr. 3-7). 1994. pap. 3.95 (*0-689-71809-8*, Aladdin) Macmillan Child Grp.

Halvorson, Marilyn. Hold on, Geronimo. LC 87-25656. 240p. (gr. 7 up). 1988. pap. 14.95 (*0-385-29665-7*) Delacorte.

Hemon, Louis. Maria Chapdelaine. Brown, Alan, tr. from FRE. Tibo, Gilles, illus. Carrier, Roch, intro. by. LC 89-50775. (Illus.). 96p. (gr. 6 up). 1989. Repr. of 1914 ed. 29.95 (*0-88776-236-0*) Tundra Bks.

Heneghan, James. Torn Away. (Illus.). 192p. (gr. 7 up). 1994. 14.99 (*0-670-85180-9*) Viking Child Bks.

Houston, James R. River Runners: A Tale of Hardship & Bravery. 160p. (gr. 5 up). 1992. pap. 4.50 (*0-14-036093-X*, Puffin) Puffin Bks.

Hughes, Monica. The Crystal Drop. LC 92-27706. (gr. 5-9). 1993. pap. 14.00 JR3 (*0-671-79195-8*, S&S BFYR) S&S Trade.

Jam, Teddy. The Year of Fire. Wallace, Ian, illus. LC 92-2882. 48p. (gr. 1-5). 1993. SBE 14.95 (*0-689-50566-3*, M K McElderry) Macmillan Child Grp.

Kinsey-Warnock, Natalie. Wilderness Cat. Graham, Mark, illus. LC 90-24250. 32p. (ps-3). 1992. 14.00 (*0-525-65068-7*, Cobblehill Bks) Dutton Child Bks.

Lingard, Joan. Between Two Worlds. 192p. (gr. 7 up). 1991. 14.95 (*0-525-67360-1*, Lodestar Bks) Dutton Child Bks.

London, Jonathan. The Sugaring-off Party. Pelletier, Gilles, illus. LC 93-21911. 1994. write for info. (*0-525-45187-0*, DCB) Dutton Child Bks.

Lunn, Janet. The Root Cellar. 230p. (gr. 7 up). 1985. pap. 3.99 (*0-14-031835-6*, Puffin) Puffin Bks.

Montgomery, Lucy M. Anne of Green Gables, 3 vols. (gr. 7-12). 1987. Boxed Set. pap. 8.85 (*0-553-33307-0*); pap. 8.85 (*0-553-30838-6*) Bantam.

Mowat, Farley. Lost in the Barrens. (Illus.). (gr. 7 up). 1956. 15.95 (*0-316-58638-2*, Joy St Bks) Little.

Oke, Janette. When Breaks the Dawn. large type ed. 219p. (gr. 4 up). 1986. pap. 8.99 (*0-87123-895-0*) Bethany Hse.

—When Comes the Spring. LC 85-11261. 224p. (Orig.). (gr. 6). 1985. pap. 6.99 (*0-87123-795-4*) Bethany Hse.

—When Hope Springs New. large type ed. 216p. (gr. 4 up). 1986. pap. 8.99 (*0-87123-675-3*) Bethany Hse.

CANADA–HISTORY

Berton, Pierre. Canada under Siege. (Illus.). 88p. (gr. 5-8). 1992. pap. 5.99 (*0-7710-1431-7*, Pub. by McClelland & Stewart CN) Firefly Bks Ltd.

Thompson, Roy J. C. Wings of the Canadian Armed Forces 1913-1992. rev. ed. Thompson, Roy J. C., ed. Braham, Bob, intro. by. (Illus.). 200p. 1992. pap. text ed. 17.95 (*1-878973-04-5*) Hse History.

CANADA–HISTORY–TO 1763 (NEW FRANCE)

Coulter, Tony. Jacques Cartier, Samuel de Champlain, & the Explorers of Canada. Goetzmann, William H., ed. Collins, Michael, intro. by. (Illus.). 112p. (gr. 6-12). 1993. PLB 18.95 (*0-7910-1298-0*, Am Art Analog); pap. write for info. (*0-7910-1521-1*, Am Art Analog) Chelsea Hse.

Jacobs, William J. La Salle: A Life of Boundless Adventure. LC 93-29699. (Illus.). 64p. (gr. 5-8). 1994. PLB 12.90 (*0-531-20141-4*) Watts.

CANADA–SOCIAL LIFE AND CUSTOMS

Hausherr, Rosmarie. The City Girl Who Went to Sea. Hausherr, Rosmarie, illus. LC 89-27236. 80p. (gr. 3-6). 1990. SBE 14.95 (*0-02-743421-4*, Four Winds) Macmillan Child Grp.

Kalman, Bobbie. Canada - the Culture. LC 93-34384. (Illus.). 32p. (Orig.). (gr. 3-6). 1993. PLB 15.95 (*0-86505-219-0*); pap. 7.95 (*0-86505-299-9*) Crabtree Pub Co.

Stone, Lynn. Villages. LC 93-16152. 1993. write for info. (*0-86625-448-X*) Rourke Pubns.

CANADA. ROYAL CANADIAN MOUNTED POLICE–FICTION

Freedman, Benedict & Freedman, Nancy. Mrs. Mike. (gr. 7 up). 1984. pap. 3.95 (*0-425-10328-5*) Berkley Pub.

CANADIAN INDIANS
see Indians of North America–Canada

CANADIAN POETRY–COLLECTIONS

Booth, David, selected by. Doctor Knickerbocker & Other Rhymes. Kovalski, Maryann, illus. LC 92-46266. 80p. (gr. 3 up). 1993. 16.95 (*0-395-67168-X*) Ticknor & Flds Bks Yng Read.

Lauture, Denize. Father & Son. Green, Jonathan, illus. 32p. (ps-3). 1993. 14.95 (*0-399-21867-X*, Philomel Bks) Putnam Pub Group.

Lee, Dennis. The Ice Cream Store. (Illus.). (ps). 1992. 14.95 (*0-590-45861-2*, 002, Scholastic Hardcover) Scholastic Inc.

Little, Jean. Hey, World, Here I Am! Truesdell, Sue, illus. LC 88-10987. 96p. (gr. 3-7). 1989. PLB 12.89 (*0-06-024006-7*) HarpC Child Bks.

CANALS

Cooper, J. Canales (Canals) (SPA.). 1991. 8.95s.p. (*0-86592-923-8*) Rourke Enter.

—Canals. 1991. 8.95s.p. (*0-86592-638-7*) Rourke Enter.

McNeese, Tim. America's Early Canals. LC 91-41353. (Illus.). 48p. (gr. 5). 1993. text ed. 11.95 RSBE (*0-89686-730-7*, Crestwood Hse) Macmillan Child Grp.

Oxlade, Chris. Canals & Waterways. Pyke, Jeremy, illus. Chillmaid, Marty, photos by. LC 93-49749. (Illus.). 1994. write for info. (*0-531-14331-7*) Watts.

Spangenburg, Ray & Moser, Diane. The Story of America's Canals. (Illus.). 96p. (gr. 6-12). 1992. bds. 18.95x (*0-8160-2256-9*) Facts on File.

CANALS–FICTION

Curry, Jane L. What the Dickens! 160p. (gr. 5 up). 1993. pap. 3.99 (*0-14-036284-3*, Puffin) Puffin Bks.

Selberg, Ingrid. Our Changing World: A Moving Parts Book. Miller, Andrew, illus. 12p. (ps-8). 1992. 12.95 (*0-399-20869-0*, Philomel Bks) Putnam Pub Group.

CANARIES–FICTION

Carly, Robin. Scary Canary, No. 1. 1994. pap. 2.99 (*0-553-37328-5*, Little Rooster) Bantam.

—Scary Canary, No. 2. 1994. pap. 2.99 (*0-553-37329-3*, Little Rooster) Bantam.

Frost, Erica. The Story of Matt & Mary. Schumacher, Claire, illus. LC 85-14011. 48p. (Orig.). (gr. 1-3). 1986. PLB 10.59 (*0-8167-0602-6*); pap. text ed. 3.50 (*0-8167-0603-4*) Troll Assocs.

Lofting, Hugh. Doctor Dolittle & the Green Canary. Lofting, Hugh, illus. (gr. 4 up). 1989. 14.95 (*0-318-41607-7*) Delacorte.

—Dr. Dolittle's Canary. 1989. pap. 14.95 (*0-440-50141-5*) Dell.

Redhead, Janet S. Something Special for Miss Margery. Forss, Ian, illus. LC 93-6632. 1994. write for info (*0-383-03673-9*) SRA Schl Grp.

CANCER

Bergman, Thomas. One Day at a Time: Children Living with Leukemia. LC 88-42972. (Illus.). 48p. (gr. 4-5). 1989. PLB 18.60 (*1-55532-913-6*) Gareth Stevens Inc.

Chamberlain, Shannin. My ABC Book of Cancer. (Illus.). 40p. (Orig.). (ps-8). 1991. pap. 6.95 (*0-912184-07-8*) Synergistic Pr.

Coughlan & Carnegie. Pride of the River: The Forceful Story. Doonican, Val, illus. 1990. pap. 30.00x (*0-86439-046-7*, Pub. by Boolarong Pubns AT) St Mut.

Fingert, Howard J. Cancer Therapy. Head, J. J., ed. Steffen, Ann T., illus. LC 86-72194. 16p. (Orig.). (gr. 10 up). 1987. pap. text ed. 2.75 (*0-89278-370-2*, 45-9770) Carolina Biological.

Fradin, Dennis. Cancer. (gr. 5-9). 1988. 12.85 (*0-516-01210-X*); pap. 4.95 (*0-516-41210-8*) Childrens.

Gaes, Jason. My Book for Kids with Cansur: A Child's Autobiography of Hope. LC 87-60794. (Illus.). 32p. (gr. 1-7). 1987. 12.95 (*0-937603-04-X*) Melius Pub.

Gire, Judy. A Boy & His Baseball: The Dave Dravecky Story. 32p. 1992. 14.99 (*0-310-58630-5*, Youth Bks) Zondervan.

Gravelle, Karen & Bertram, John. Teenagers Face-to-Face with Cancer. LC 86-8608. 96p. (gr. 7 up). 1986. lib. bdg. 12.98 (*0-671-54549-3*, J Messner) S&S Trade.

Greenberg, Jan. No Dragons to Slay. LC 83-17200. 152p. (gr. 7 up). 1983. 14.00 (*0-374-35528-2*) FS&G.

Hyde, Margaret O. & Hyde, Lawrence E. Cancer in the Young: A Sense of Hope. LC 84-27126. 96p. (gr. 9 up). 1985. 10.00 (*0-664-32722-2*, Westminster) Westminster John Knox.

Landau, Elaine. Cancer. (Illus.). 64p. (gr. 5-8). 1994. bds. 15.95 (*0-8050-2990-7*) TFC Bks NY.

Little, Jean. Mama's Going to Buy You a Mockingbird. LC 84-20877. 208p. (gr. 4-6). 1985. pap. 13.95 (*0-670-80346-4*) Viking Child Bks.

Monroe, Judy. Leukemia. LC 90-33663. (Illus.). 48p. (gr. 5-6). 1990. text ed. 12.95 RSBE (*0-89686-532-0*, Crestwood Hse) Macmillan Child Grp.

Parkinson, Carolyn S. My Mommy Has Cancer. Verstraete, Elaine, illus. 20p. (Orig.). (ps-4). 1992. pap. 8.95 (*0-9630287-0-7*) Solace Pub.
MY MOMMY HAS CANCER is a caring, informative & beautifully written book by Carolyn Stearns Parkinson to help young children understand what cancer is. The exceptional, warm, four-color illustrations by Elaine Verstraete are original water paintings of REAL people. The combination of the story & the illustrations help adults & children talk about this difficult subject & what their unique needs & concerns are. This book meets a crucial need for young children & their families, as one parent said, "It helped us to say the words we could not find to say." The book is being used in hospitals, schools, libraries & homes. "Carolyn Stearns Parkinson's book MY MOMMY HAS CANCER provides an excellent & necessary addition to the children's literature explaining illness. The beauty & sensitivity of both Carolyn Parkinson's words & Elaine Verstraete's color illustrations create a gentle ambiance in which children, from their own perspective, can learn about cancer, its emotional impact & its treatment. This is a superb book for parents to read with their children," by Michael H. Henrichs, Ph.D., Founder & Director of Kids Adjusting Through Support, Inc., Clinical, Child & School Psychologist, Cl. Assoc. Professor of Psychiatry & Oncology. To order, contact: Solace Publishing Inc., P.O. Box 567, Folsom, CA 95763-0567; 916-984-9015.
Publisher Provided Annotation.

Robins, Perry. Play It Safe in the Sun. Podwal, Michael, illus. 40p. 1994. pap. 9.95 (*0-9627688-1-2*) Skin Cancer Fndtn.
PLAY IT SAFE IN THE SUN is the first book on sun safety written especially for children. This practical guide tells children everything they need to know about year-round sun protection & early detection of skin cancer. With 40 pages of reading fun, 18 clever full-color illustrations & entertaining puzzles, the book has an interactive learning format that challenges children & stimulates group participation. Reproduction masters are included for a "sunword" puzzle, a sun-sense test & a coloring page. With warmth & humor, Dr. Robins discusses skin cancer, ozone depletion, the danger of tanning machines, use of sunscreens, as well as a range of other objects related to sun protection & skin health. Written by the president & founder of the Foundation & illustrated by 10-year-old artist Michael Podwal, this book is ideal for reading at home with the entire family & for use in classrooms, camps & clubs, doctor's offices & child care facilities. To order, send $9.95 plus $2.50, shipping & handling, (check, money order, MasterCard or VISA). Special discount: 25 copies/$174.
Publisher Provided Annotation.

Rodgers, Joann. Cancer. (Illus.). 112p. (gr. 6 up). 1990. 18.95 (*0-7910-0059-1*) Chelsea Hse.

Silverstein, Alvin & Silverstein, Virginia B. Cancer: Can It Be Stopped? new, rev. ed. LC 86-45500. (Illus.). 128p. (gr. 7 up). 1987. 12.95 (*0-397-32202-X*, Lipp Jr Bks); (Lipp Jr Bks) HarpC Child Bks.

Strauss, Linda. Coping When a Parent Has Cancer. Rosen, Ruth, ed. LC 88-18539. (gr. 7 up). 1988. PLB 14.95 (*0-8239-0785-6*) Rosen Group.

Terkel, Susan N. & Brazz, Marlene L. Understanding Cancer. Shaw, Annette, illus. LC 92-38715. 64p. (gr. k-4). 1993. PLB 12.40 (*0-531-11085-0*) Watts.

Yount, Lisa. Cancer. LC 91-23547. (Illus.). 112p. (gr. 5-8). 1991. PLB 14.95 (*1-56006-125-1*) Lucent Bks.

CANDLEMAS

Johnson, Crockett. Will Spring Be Early or Will Spring Be Late? Johnson, Crockett, illus. LC 59-9424. 48p. (gr. k-3). 1961. PLB 13.89 (*0-690-89423-6*, Crowell Jr Bks) HarpC Child Bks.

CANDLES

Constable, David. Candlemaking. (Illus.). 80p. (Orig.). 1993. pap. 16.95 (*0-85532-683-2*, Pub. by Search Pr UK) A Schwartz & Co.

Faraday, Michael. Faraday's Chemical History of a Candle. (Illus.). (gr. 7-11). 1988. pap. 9.95 (*1-55652-035-2*) Chicago Review.

CANDY
see Confectionery
CANNED GOODS
see Canning and Preserving
CANNING AND PRESERVING
Mitgutsch, Ali. From Fruit to Jam. Mitgutsch, Ali, illus. LC 81-58. 24p. (ps-3). 1981. PLB 10.95 (*0-87614-154-8*) Carolrhoda Bks.
CANNON
see Ordnance
CANOES AND CANOEING
Bailey, Donna. Canoeing. LC 90-23055. (Illus.). 32p. (gr. 1-4). 1991. PLB 18.99 (*0-8114-2903-2*); pap. 3.95 (*0-8114-4706-5*) Raintree Steck-V.
Barrett, Norman S. Canoeing. Franklin Watts Ltd., ed. LC 86-51222. (Illus.). 32p. (ps-3). 1988. PLB 11.90 (*0-531-10349-8*) Watts.
Boy Scouts of America Staff. Canoeing. (Illus.). 88p. (gr. 6-12). 1989. pap. 1.85 (*0-8395-3308-X*, 33308) BSA.
—Venture Whitewater. (Illus.). 70p. 1990. pap. 3.15 (*0-8395-3465-5*, 33465) BSA.
Evans, Jeremy. Whitewater Kayaking. LC 91-39142. (Illus.). 48p. (gr. 5-6). 1992. text ed. 13.95 RSBE (*0-89686-685-8*, Crestwood Hse) Macmillan Child Grp.
Fox, Alan. Kayaking. LC 92-5548. 1993. 17.50 (*0-8225-2482-1*) Lerner Pubns.
Penzler, Otto. Danger! White Water. LC 75-21844. (Illus.). 32p. (gr. 5-10). 1976. PLB 10.79 (*0-89375-004-2*) Troll Assocs.
Speltz, Bob. A Real Runabouts Review of Canoes. 72p. (Orig.). 1991. pap. 12.95 (*0-932299-08-3*) R G Speltz.
CANOES AND CANOEING–FICTION
Delval, Marie-Helene. The Apple-Tree Canoe. (Illus.). 48p. (gr. 3-8). 1990. 8.95 (*0-89565-805-4*) Childs World.
Kraus, Robert, ed. & illus. Wise Old Owl's Canoe Trip Adventure. LC 91-39014. 32p. (ps-3). 1993. text ed. 10.89 (*0-8167-2947-6*); 2.95 (*0-8167-2948-4*) Troll Assocs.
Mason, Jane. River Day. Sorensen, Henri, illus. LC 93-26573. 32p. (gr. k-3). 1994. RSBE 14.95 (*0-02-762869-8*, Macmillan Child Bk) Macmillan Child Grp.
Roddy, Lee. The Dangerous Canoe Race. (Orig.). (gr. 3-6). 1990. pap. 4.99 (*0-929608-62-3*) Focus Family.
Williams, Vera B. Three Days on a River in a Red Canoe. LC 80-23893. (Illus.). 32p. (gr. k-3). 1981. 14.95 (*0-688-80307-5*); PLB 14.88 (*0-688-84307-7*) Greenwillow.
CAPE COD
Dalton, J. W. The Life Savers of Cape Cod. Ackerman, Frank, intro. by. (Illus.). 176p. 1991. pap. 8.95 (*0-940160-49-8*) Parnassus Imprints.

Shortsleeve, Kevin. The Story of Cape Cod. Shortsleeve, Brian F., ed. Iwanowski, Elka, illus. 64p. (Orig.). (gr. k-3). 1993. pap. 9.75 (*0-9622782-1-1*) Cape Cod Life Mag. THE STORY OF CAPE COD by Kevin Shortsleeve & Illustrated by Elka Iwanowski. Children's book in rhyming verse of the history of Cape Cod. 64 pages, paperbound. (Gr. k-3) 1993, $9.75 (0-9622782-1-1). Call or write for information. To order: Cape Cod Life, Inc., 1370 Rt. 28-A, P.O. Box 767, Cataumet, MA 02534. 508-564-4466.
Publisher Provided Annotation.

CAPE COD–FICTION
Adkins, Jan. A Storm Without Rain. LC 92-24601. 192p. (gr. 7 up). 1993. pap. 3.95 (*0-688-11852-6*, Pub. by Beech Tree Bks) Morrow.
Adler, C. S. The Lump in the Middle. 160p. 1991. pap. 3.50 (*0-380-71176-1*, Camelot) Avon.
—Mismatched Summer. 144p. 1991. 14.95 (*0-399-21776-2*, Putnam) Putnam Pub Group.
Chenoweth, Russ. Shadow Walkers. LC 92-18798. 176p. (gr. 5 up). 1993. SBE 13.95 (*0-684-19447-3*, Scribner Young Read) Macmillan Child Grp.
CAPITAL PUNISHMENT
Flanders, Stephen A. Capital Punishment. 240p. (gr. 9-12). 1991. 22.95x (*0-8160-1912-6*) Facts on File.
Hays, Scott. Capital Punishment. (Illus.). 64p. (gr. 7 up). 1990. lib. bdg. 17.27 (*0-86593-074-0*); lib. bdg. 12.95s.p. (*0-685-36322-8*) Rourke Corp.
Herda, D. J. Furman vs. Georgia: The Death Penalty Case. LC 93-37512. (Illus.). 104p. (gr. 6 up). 1994. lib. bdg. 17.95 (*0-89490-489-2*) Enslow Pubs.
Landau, Elaine. Teens & the Death Penalty. LC 91-23351. 112p. (gr. 6 up). 1992. lib. bdg. 17.95 (*0-89490-297-0*) Enslow Pubs.
Nardo, Don. Death Penalty. LC 92-20366. (Illus.). 112p. (gr. 5-8). 1992. PLB 14.95 (*1-56006-132-4*) Lucent Bks.
O'Sullivan, Carol. Death Penalty: Identifying Propaganda Techniques. LC 89-11033. (Illus.). 32p. (gr. 3-6). 1990. PLB 10.95 (*0-89908-636-5*) Greenhaven.
Siegel, Mark, et al, eds. Capital Punishment: An Effective Punishment? 56p. 1991. pap. text ed. 11.95 (*1-878623-18-4*) Info Plus TX.
Steins, Richard. The Death Penalty: Is It Justice? (Illus.). 64p. (gr. 5-8). 1993. PLB 14.95 (*0-8050-2571-5*) TFC Bks NY.
CAPITALISTS AND FINANCIERS
Marsh, Carole. The Big Rio of Ross Perot! 1994. lib. bdg. 24.95 (*0-7933-6942-8*); pap. text ed. 14.95 (*0-7933-6943-6*); disk 29.95 (*0-7933-6941-X*) Gallopade Pub Group.
Mayberry, Jodine. Business Leaders Who Built Financial Empires. (Illus.). 48p. (gr. 4-8). 1994. PLB write for info. (*0-8114-4934-3*) Raintree Steck-V.
CAR WHEELS
see Wheels
CARBON 14 DATING
see Radiocarbon Dating
CARCINOMA
see Cancer
CARD GAMES
see Cards
CARD TRICKS
see also Fortune Telling
Bailey, Vanessa. Card Tricks: Games & Projects for Children. LC 90-32666. (Illus.). 32p. (gr. k-4). 1990. PLB 11.90 (*0-531-17255-4*, Gloucester Pr) Watts.
Charles, Kirk. Amazing Card Tricks. LC 92-5482. (Illus.). (gr. 2-6). 1992. PLB 14.95 (*0-89565-965-4*) Childs World.
Croxton, William L. Amazing Card Tricks Made Easy to Do. rev. ed. (Illus.). 64p. (gr. 4 up). 1990. pap. 4.95 (*0-9623230-0-4*) WLC Enterprises.
Gravatt, Glenn. Fifty Modern Card Tricks You Can Do! 50p. (Orig.). (gr. 7 up). 1977. pap. 3.00 (*0-915926-07-5*) Magic Ltd.
—Fifty More Modern Card Tricks. Walker, Barbara, ed. 60p. (gr. 7 up). 1979. 4.00 (*0-915926-33-4*) Magic Ltd.
Johnson, Stephanie. Hoppin' Magic: My First Card & Coin Magic Tricks. Manwaring, Kerry, illus. 32p. 1993. pap. 5.95 (*1-56565-089-1*) Lowell Hse.
Longe, Bob. World's Best Card Tricks. LC 90-46641. (Illus.). 128p. 1992. pap. 4.95 (*0-8069-8233-0*) Sterling.
CARDIAC DISEASES
see Heart–Diseases
CARDINALS
Roseman, Kenneth. The Cardinal's Snuffbox. Negron, Bill, illus. 128p. (gr. 4-6). 1982. pap. text ed. 7.95 (*0-8074-0059-9*, 140060) UAHC.
CARDS
see also Card Tricks; Fortune Telling
Cole, Joanna & Calmenson, Stephanie. Crazy Eights: And Other Card Games. Tiegreen, Alan, illus. LC 93-5427. 80p. (gr. 2 up). 1994. 15.00 (*0-688-12199-3*); PLB 14.93 (*0-688-12200-0*); pap. 6.95 (*0-688-12201-9*, Pub. by Beech Tree Bks) Morrow Jr Bks.
Collis, Len. Card Games for Children. Carter, Terry & George, Bob, illus. 96p. (ps up). 1989. pap. 5.95 (*0-8120-4290-5*) Barron.
Golick, Margaret. Deal Me In: Children's Card Games. rev. ed. 190p. 1988. 8.95 (*0-88432-253-X*, B53739) Audio-Forum.
Grube, Karl W. Cribbage d'Etroit. Grube, Karl W., illus. 129p. (gr. 3 up). Date not set. 29.95 (*0-685-63059-5*); tchr's. ed. 49.95 (*0-685-63060-9*) Intl Gamester.
—Cribbage in Schools Program. Grube, Karl W., illus. 29p. (gr. 3 up). Date not set. pap. text ed. 10.00 tchr's. guide (*0-685-63061-7*) Intl Gamester.
—Lake Huron Poker. Grube, Karl W., illus. 124p. (gr. 3 up). Date not set. pap. text ed. 29.95 (*0-685-63062-5*); tchr's. ed. 49.95 (*0-685-63063-3*) Intl Gamester.
—Lake Michigan Poker. Grube, Karl W., illus. 132p. (gr. 3 up). Date not set. pap. text ed. 29.95 (*0-685-63064-1*); tchr's. ed. 49.95 (*0-685-63065-X*) Intl Gamester.
Grube, Karl W. & Grube, Kathryn. Lake Superior Cribbage. Grube, Kathryn, illus. 112p. (gr. 3 up). Date not set. pap. text ed. 29.95 (*0-685-63057-9*); tchr's. ed. 49.95 (*0-685-63058-7*) Intl Gamester.
MacColl, Gail. The Book of Cards for Kids. LC 91-50962. (ps-3). 1992. pap. 10.95 (*1-56305-240-7*) Workman Pub.
McCoy, Elin. Cards for Kids: Games, Tricks & Amazing Facts. Huffman, Tom, illus. LC 91-11373. 160p. (gr. 1-7). 1991. SBE 13.95 (*0-02-765461-3*, Macmillan Child Bk) Macmillan Child Grp.
Old Karankawa Indian Card Game. (gr. 1 up). 1984. 5.95 (*0-937460-53-2*) Hendrick-Long.
Schreiner, Nikki B., et al. The Whole World Kit: American Dream Activity Cards. Weathers, Susan, et al, illus. 60p. (gr. 4-8). 1990. pap. text ed. 215.00 (*1-879218-29-1*) Touch & See Educ.
Wergin, Joseph P. & Smith, Beatrice S. Poker for Kids. Grube, Karl W., intro. by. 1993. pap. 12.50 (*0-685-63089-7*); tchr's. ed. 20.00 (*0-685-63090-0*) Intl Gamester.
—Poker for Kids & Everyone Else. Grube, Karl W., intro. by. 124p. 1992. pap. 10.00 (*0-685-60627-9*); tchr's. ed. 20.00 (*0-685-60628-7*) Intl Gamester.
CARDS, GREETING
see Greeting Cards
CAREER STORIES
see Vocational Stories
CAREERS
see Occupations; Professions; Vocational Guidance; see subject headings with the subdivision Vocational Guidance
CARIBBEAN AREA
Anduze, A. L. Caribbean Crosswords. LC 93-70926. (Illus.). 64p. (gr. 5-12). Date not set. pap. 8.95 (*0-932831-10-9*) Eastern Caribbean Inst.
Antigua & Barbuda. (Illus.). (gr. 5 up). 1988. 14.95 (*0-7910-0151-2*) Chelsea Hse.
Broberg, Merle. Barbados. (Illus.). 96p. (gr. 5 up). 1989. lib. bdg. 14.95 (*1-55546-792-X*) Chelsea Hse.
Dominica. (Illus.). (gr. 5 up). 1988. 13.95 (*0-7910-0152-0*) Chelsea Hse.
Eisenberg, Joyce. Grenada. (Illus.). 88p. (gr. 5 up). 1988. lib. bdg. 14.95 (*1-55546-777-6*) Chelsea Hse.
Haverstock, Nathan A. The Dominican Republic in Pictures. (Illus.). 64p. (gr. 5 up). 1988. PLB 17.50 (*0-8225-1812-0*) Lerner Pubns.
Lessac, Frane. Caribbean Alphabet. Lessac, Frane, illus. LC 93-15833. 32p. 1994. 15.00 (*0-688-12952-8*, Tambourine Bks); PLB 14.93 (*0-688-12953-6*, Tambourine Bks) Morrow.
Mason, Antony. The Caribbean. (Illus.). 48p. (gr. 4-8). 1989. PLB 14.95 (*0-382-09823-4*) Silver Burdett Pr.
Presilla, Maricel. Feliz Nochebuena Feliz Navidad: Christmas Feasts of the Hispanic Caribbean. (gr. 2-6). 1994. 15.95 (*0-8050-2512-X*) H Holt & Co.
Springer, Eintou P. The Caribbean. rev ed. (Illus.). 48p. (gr. 5 up). 1987. PLB 12.95 (*0-382-09469-7*) Silver Burdett Pr.
Sunshine, Catherine H. & Menkart, Deborah, eds. Caribbean Connections: Overview of Regional History. (Illus., Orig.). (gr. 7-12). 1991. pap. text ed. 16.00 (*1-878554-06-9*) Netwrk of Educ.
Walker, Cas. The Caribbean. (Illus.). 32p. (gr. 4-6). 1991. 17.95 (*0-237-60189-3*, Pub. by Evans Bros Ltd) Trafalgar.
CARIBBEAN AREA–FICTION
Ada, Alma F., et al. Choices & Other Stories from the Caribbean. LC 92-43134. 1993. pap. 6.95 (*0-377-00257-7*) Friendship Pr.
Buffett, Jimmy. Jolly Man. LC 87-8573. (gr. 4 up). 1993. pap. 4.95 (*0-15-240538-0*, HB Juv Bks) HarBrace.
Carlstrom, Nancy W. Baby-O. Stevenson, Sucie, illus. 32p. (ps-3). 1992. 14.95 (*0-316-12851-1*) Little.
Cooper, Marva. Livingston's Vision. (Illus.). (gr. 1-7). 3.95 (*1-882185-08-0*) Crnrstone Pub.
Gershator, Phyllis. Rata-Pata-Scata-Fata: A Caribbean Story. Meade, Holly, illus. LC 92-40695. 1994. 14.95 (*0-316-30470-0*, Joy St Bks) Little.
Hodge, Merle. For the Life of Laetitia. 1993. 15.00 (*0-374-32447-6*) FS&G.
Hulser, Andrea. Henry in the Caribbean. Hulser, Andrea, illus. 40p. 1993. pap. 14.95 (*0-89825-007-2*) Pub Resces PR.
Linden, Ann M. One Smiling Grandma: A Caribbean Counting Book. Russell, Lynne, illus. LC 91-30826. 32p. (ps-3). 1992. 15.00 (*0-8037-1132-8*) Dial Bks Young.
Powell, Pamela. The Turtle Watchers. LC 92-5822. 160p. (gr. 3-7). 1992. 13.00 (*0-670-84294-X*) Viking Child Bks.
Taylor, Theodore. Timothy of the Cay: A Prequel-Sequel. 192p. (gr. 4-7). 1993. 13.95 (*0-15-288358-4*, HB Juv Bks) HarBrace.
CARIBOU
Harris, Lorle K. The Caribou. LC 88-18953. (Illus.). 60p. (gr. 3 up). 1989. text ed. 13.95 RSBE (*0-87518-391-3*, Dillon) Macmillan Child Grp.
Lepthien, Emilie U. Reindeer. LC 93-33513. (Illus.). 48p. (gr. k-4). 1994. PLB 12.85 (*0-516-01059-X*) Childrens.
Miller, Debbie S. A Caribou Journey. Van Zyle, Jon, illus. LC 93-9777. (gr. 2-5). 1994. 15.95 (*0-316-57380-9*) Little.
Nentl, Jerolyn. The Caribou. LC 83-26254. (Illus.). 48p. (gr. 5). 1984. text ed. 12.95 RSBE (*0-89686-244-5*, Crestwood Hse) Macmillan Child Grp.
Owens, Mary B. A Caribou Alphabet. McCollough, Mark, contrib. by. (Illus.). 40p. (gr. k-6). 1988. 16.95 (*0-937966-25-8*) Tilbury Hse.
CARICATURES
see Cartoons and Caricatures
CARILLONS
see Bells
CARLSBAD CAVERNS
Petersen, David. Carlsbad Caverns National Park. LC 93-36997. (Illus.). 48p. (gr. k-4). 1994. PLB 12.85 (*0-516-01051-4*) Childrens.
CARNEGIE, ANDREW, 1835-1919
Bowman, John. Andrew Carnegie. Furstinger, Nancy, ed. (Illus.). 128p. (gr. 7-10). 1989. PLB 7.95 (*0-382-09582-0*) Silver Burdett Pr.
CARNIVALS
see Festivals
CAROLS
Absolon, Mary. A Song at Christmas. Morris, Tony, illus. 64p. (gr. 3-8). 1991. 9.99 (*0-7459-1951-0*) Lion USA.
Amery, H., compiled by. Christmas Carols. (Illus.). 64p. (ps up). 1990. (Usborne); pap. 7.95 (*0-7460-0432-X*, Usborne) EDC.
Bishop, Roma, illus. Christmas Songs & Prayers for Children. 32p. (ps). 1993. 3.98 (*0-8317-5168-1*) Smithmark.
Cancion De Navidad. (SPA.). 1990. casebound 3.50 (*0-7214-1397-8*) Ladybird Bks.
Chamberlain, Sarah, illus. Friendly Beasts: A Traditional Christmas Carol. LC 91-2115. 24p. (ps-2). 1991. 13.95 (*0-525-44773-3*, DCB) Dutton Child Bks.
Christmas Sing-Along. (Illus.). 5p. (gr. k-3). 1991. 9.95 (*0-8167-2454-7*) Troll Assocs.

Christmas Songs. 32p. (gr. 3 up). 1992. Incl. cass., songbk., crayons. 6.95 (*0-7935-1083-X*, 00850117) H Leonard.
Cooper, Don. Merry Christmas Songs & Games. Fritz, Ronald, illus. 32p. (ps-3). 1989. pap. 5.95 incl. cassette (*0-394-82230-7*) Random Bks Yng Read.
Davie, Helen, illus. Sing with Me Christmas Carols. 24p. (ps up). 1987. pap. 5.95 incl. cassette (*0-394-89060-4*) Random Bks Yng Read.
De Brebeuf, Jean. Huron Carol. Tyrrell, Frances, illus. LC 91-35965. 32p. (ps-6). 1992. 15.00 (*0-525-44909-4*, DCB) Dutton Child Bks.
De Paola, Tomie. Tomie DePaola's Book of Christmas Carols. DePaola, Tomie, illus. LC 86-755157. 82p. (gr. 1 up). 1987. 19.95 (*0-399-21432-1*, Putnam) Putnam Pub Group.
Disney's Christmas Favorites. 16p. 1992. Incl. xylotone. 14.95 (*0-7935-1392-8*, 00824003) H Leonard.
Forrester, Maureen, selected by. Joy to the World! Tyrrell, Frances, illus. Heller, Charles, contrib. by. (Illus.). 32p. 1993. reinforced bdg. 14.99 (*0-525-45169-2*, DCB) Dutton Child Bks.
Gick, Georg J. & Swinger, Marlys. Shepherd's Pipe Songs from the Holy Night: A Christmas Cantata for Children's Voices or Youth Choir. Choral ed. Maendel, Maria A. & Maendel, Maria M., illus. Clement, J. T., intro. by. LC 71-85805. 64p. (gr. k up). 1969. pap. 3.50 (*0-87486-011-3*); cassette 7.00 (*0-87486-049-0*) Plough.
Goode, Diane, illus. Christmas Carols. LC 82-62169. 32p. (ps up). 1988. pap. 1.50 (*0-394-81940-3*) Random Bks Yng Read.
—Diane Goode's Christmas Magic: Poems & Carols. LC 92-6366. 32p. (Orig.). (ps-3). 1992. PLB 5.99 (*0-679-92427-2*); pap. 2.25 (*0-679-82427-8*) Random Bks Yng Read.
Hague, Michael. Jingle Bells. Hague, Michael, illus. LC 90-32066. 32p. (ps up). 1990. 4.95 (*0-8050-1413-6*, Bks Young Read) H Holt & Co.
Hague, Michael, illus. Deck the Halls. LC 90-25628. 32p. (ps up). 1991. 4.95 (*0-8050-1007-6*, Bks Young Read) H Holt & Co.
—O Christmas Tree. LC 90-25527. 32p. (ps up). 1991. 4.95 (*0-8050-1538-8*, Bks Young Read) H Holt & Co.
—We Wish You a Merry Christmas. LC 90-32067. 32p. (gr. k up). 1990. 4.95 (*0-8050-1006-8*, Bks Young Read) H Holt & Co.
Harrison, Susan, illus. My First Book of Christmas Carols. 24p. 1992. pap. 3.95 (*0-8249-8568-0*, Ideals Child) Hambleton-Hill.
Jennings, Linda. My Christmas Book of Stories & Carols. 1991. 5.99 (*0-517-05189-3*) Random Hse Value.
Kimura, Hideo M. Sing, Pick & Strum Nineteen Christmas Carols with Your Ukulele. (Illus.). 74p. (Orig.). 1992. pap. 12.95 (*0-917822-27-7*) Heedays.
Langstaff, John & Langstaff, Nancy. The Christmas Revels Songbook. (Illus.). 160p. 1985. pap. 14.95 (*0-87923-927-1*) Godine.
MacArthur, Barbara. Chantez Noel. Jensen, Robert, illus. (ENG & FRE.). 14p. (ps-12). 1993. pap. 12.95 incl. cass. (*1-881120-10-4*) Frog Pr WI.
—Singen Weihnachten. Jensen, Robert, illus. (GER.). 14p. (Orig.). (ps-12). 1993. pap. 12.95 (*1-881120-12-0*) Frog Pr WI.
Mayr-Pletschen, Heide, illus. A Christmas Carol Book. (gr. 3 up). 2.75 (*0-685-24603-5*) Merry Thoughts.
Morehead, Ruth J., illus. Christmas Is Coming with Ruth J. Morehead's Holly Babes: A Book of Poems & Songs. LC 89-3717. 32p. (Orig.). (ps-1). 1990. pap. 2.25 (*0-679-80075-1*) Random Bks Yng Read.
Nayer, Judy, ed. My First Book of Christmas Carols. Severn, Jeff, illus. 24p. (ps-2). 1991. pap. 0.99 (*1-56293-117-2*) McClanahan Bk.
Race, Donna. Jolly Old St. Nicholas: A Holiday Book with Lights & Music. LC 91-43087. (Illus.). 12p. (ps-1). 1992. pap. 11.95 POB (*0-689-71622-2*, Aladdin) Macmillan Child Grp.
Raffi. Raffi's Christmas Treasury: 14 Illustrated Songs & Musical Arrangements. Westcott, Nadine B., illus. (ps up). 1988. PLB 17.95 (*0-517-56806-3*) Crown Bks Yng Read.
Retan, Walter, compiled by. I Love Christmas: A Wonderful Collection of Christmas Stories, Poems, Carols, & More. Ewing, Carolyn, illus. 96p. (gr. k up). 1992. write for info. (*0-307-15875-6*, 15875, Golden Pr) Western Pub.
Rey, H. A. We Three Kings & Other Carols. Rey, H. A., illus. 22p. (ps). 1994. Repr. of 1944 ed. spiral 9.95 (*0-694-00661-0*, Festival) HarpC Child Bks.
Richardson, Jean. Stephen's Feast. Englander, Alice, illus. (ps-3). 1991. 15.95 (*0-316-74435-2*) Little.
Roth, Kevin. Songs for a Merry Christmas. Bollinger, Kristine, illus. 24p. (Orig.). (ps-1). 1992. pap. 9.95 incl. cass. (*0-679-83253-X*) Random Bks Yng Read.
Running Press Staff, ed. KIDZ Merry Christmas Car Songbook & Audiocassette. (Illus.). 80p. (gr. 1 up). 1991. incl. audiocassette 9.95 (*1-56138-051-2*) Running Pr.
Scarry, Richard. Richard Scarry's Favorite Christmas Carols. 1991. 22.25 (*1-55987-050-8*) J B Comns.
Schindler, Stephen D., illus. The Twelve Days of Christmas. LC 90-22389. 24p. (ps up). 1991. 2.95 (*0-694-00363-8*) HarpC Child Bks.
Schorsch, Lawrence, compiled by. The Real Mother Goose Book of Christmas Carols. 1993. 9.95 (*1-56288-405-0*) Checkerboard.
Schulte, Karl, compiled by. Christmas Carols. Dolce, J. Ellen, illus. 1990. pap. write for info. (*0-307-02979-4*, Golden Pr) Western Pub.
Schwartz, Carol. First Noel (Pop Up) 1991. 3.95 (*0-8037-1015-1*) Dial Bks Young.
—Friendly Beasts (Pop Up) 1991. 3.95 (*0-8037-1018-6*) Dial Bks Young.
—Twelve Days of Christmas (Pop Ups) 1991. 3.95 (*0-8037-1017-8*) Dial Bks Young.
Tennyson, Noel, illus. Christmas Carols: A Treasury of Holiday Favorites with Words & Pictures. LC 83-60412. 24p. (gr. 1-5). 1983. 2.95 (*0-394-86125-6*) Random Bks Yng Read.
Wax, Wendy, compiled by. A Treasury of Christmas Poems, Carols, & Games to Share. Spier, John, illus. (ps-1). 1992. 10.00 (*0-440-40731-1*) Dell.
Wilburn, Kathy, illus. My Favorite Christmas Carols. LC 90-22390. 24p. (ps up). 1991. 2.95 (*0-694-00366-2*) HarpC Child Bks.
Wilson, Etta, ed. My Play a Tune Book: Christmas Songs. Harrison, Susan, illus. 26p. (gr. k up). 1987. 15.95 (*0-938971-05-0*) JTG Nashville.
Zharkova, Olga, illus. We Three Kings. LC 92-38571. 1993. 14.95 (*0-590-46433-7*) Scholastic Inc.

CARPENTRY

Here are entered works dealing with the construction of a wooden building or the wooden portion of any building. Works that treat the making and finishing of fine woodwork, such as furniture or interior details, are entered under Cabinet Work.
see also Building; Woodwork
Chadwick, Charley G., et al. Wall Framing. Harrington, Lois G., ed. Smith, George W., Jr. & Edwards, Jason, illus. 72p. (Orig.). (gr. 10-12). 1989. pap. text ed. 8.00 (*0-89606-266-X*, 701); tchr's. key 3.00 (*0-685-27030-0*, 701TK) Am Assn Voc Materials.
Florian, Douglas. A Carpenter. LC 90-30752. (Illus.). 24p. (ps up). 1991. 13.95 (*0-688-09760-X*); PLB 13.88 (*0-688-09761-8*) Greenwillow.
Leavitt, Jerome E. Easy Carpentry Projects for Children. 96p. (gr. 2 up). 1986. pap. 3.95 (*0-486-25057-1*) Dover.
Lillegard, Dee. I Can Be a Carpenter. LC 86-9676. (Illus.). 32p. (gr. k-3). 1986. PLB 11.80 (*0-516-01884-1*); pap. 3.95 (*0-516-41884-X*) Childrens.
Martin, John H. A Day in the Life of a Carpenter. Wells, Sarah, illus. LC 84-2420. 32p. (gr. 4-8). 1985. PLB 11.79 (*0-8167-0093-1*); pap. text ed. 2.95 (*0-8167-0094-X*) Troll Assocs.

CARPENTRY–FICTION

Hesse, Karen. Sable. 1994. 14.95 (*0-8050-2416-6*) H Holt & Co.
Kinens, Janis J. The Old Woodcutter. Kinens, Janis J., illus. LC 88-81904. 32p. (gr. k-12). 1988. PLB 12.95 (*0-9620999-0-2*); 12.95 (*0-9620999-1-0*) Guzzy Pr.

CARPETS

see also Weaving

CARRIERS, AIRCRAFT

see Aircraft Carriers

CARS (AUTOMOBILES)

see Automobiles

CARS, ARMORED (TANKS)

see Tanks (Military Science)

CARSON, CHRISTOPHER, 1809-1868

Gleiter, Jan & Thompson, Kathleen. Kit Carson. Whipple, Rick, illus. 32p. (gr. 2-5). 1987. PLB 19.97 (*0-8172-2650-8*) Raintree Steck-V.
Zadra, Dan. Frontiersmen in America: Kit Carson. rev. ed. (gr. 2-4). 1988. 14.95 (*0-88682-189-4*) Creative Ed.

CARSON, RACHEL, 1907-1964

Accorsi, William. Rachel Carson. LC 92-43760. (Illus.). 32p. (ps-3). 1993. reinforced bdg. 15.95 (*0-8234-0994-5*) Holiday.
Foster, Leila M. The Story of Rachel Carson & the Environmental Movement. LC 90-2208. (Illus.). 32p. (gr. 3-6). 1990. pap. 3.95 (*0-516-44753-X*) Childrens.
Goldberg, Jake. Rachel Carson. (Illus.). 72p. (gr. 3-5). 1991. lib. bdg. 12.95 (*0-7910-1566-1*) Chelsea Hse.
Greene, Carol. Rachel Carson: Friend of Nature. Dobson, Steven, illus. LC 91-39446. 48p. (gr. k-3). 1992. PLB 12.85 (*0-516-04229-7*) Childrens.
—Rachel Carson: Friend of Nature. Dobson, Steven, illus. LC 91-39446. 48p. (gr. k-3). 1993. pap. 4.95 (*0-516-44229-5*) Childrens.
Harlan, Judith. Rachel Carson: Sounding the Alarm: A Biography of Rachel Carson. LC 88-35909. (Illus.). 128p. (gr. 5 up). 1989. text ed. 13.95 RSBE (*0-87518-407-3*, Dillon) Macmillan Child Grp.
Henricksson, John. Rachel Carson: The Environmental Movement. (Illus.). 96p. (gr. 7 up). 1991. PLB 15.40 (*1-878841-16-5*); pap. 5.95 (*1-56294-833-4*) Millbrook Pr.
Jezer, Marty. Rachel Carson. Horner, Matina, intro. by. (Illus.). 112p. (gr. 5 up). 1988. lib. bdg. 17.95 (*1-55546-646-X*) Chelsea Hse.
Kudlinski, Kathleen V. Rachel Carson: Pioneer of Ecology. Lewin, Ted, illus. 64p. (gr. 2-7). 1988. pap. 10.95 (*0-670-81488-1*) Viking Child Bks.
—Rachel Carson: Pioneer of Ecology. Lewin, Ted, illus. 64p. (gr. 2-6). 1989. pap. 3.99 (*0-14-032242-6*, Puffin) Puffin Bks.
Latham, Jean L. Rachel Carson: Who Loved the Sea. (Illus.). 80p. (gr. 2-6). 1991. Repr. of 1973 ed. PLB 12.95 (*0-7910-1408-8*) Chelsea Hse.
Luthor. Rachel Carson. Date not set. PLB write for info. (*0-8050-2291-0*) H Holt & Co.
Presnall, Judith J. Rachel Carson. LC 93-49487. (Illus.). 112p. (gr. 5-8). 1994. 14.95 (*1-56006-052-2*) Lucent Bks.
Ransom, Candice F. Listening to Crickets: A Story about Rachel Carson. Haas, Shelly O., illus. (gr. 3-6). 1993. 14.95 (*0-87614-727-9*) Carolrhoda Bks.
—Listening to Crickets: A Story about Rachel Carson. (gr. 4-7). 1993. pap. 5.95 (*0-87614-615-9*) Carolrhoda Bks.
Reef, Catherine. Rachel Carson: The Wonder of Nature. Raymond, Larry, illus. 68p. (gr. 4-7). 1992. PLB 14.95 (*0-941477-38-X*) TFC Bks NY.
Ring, Elizabeth. Rachel Carson: Caring for the Earth. LC 91-37644. (Illus.). 48p. (gr. 2-4). 1992. PLB 12.90 (*1-56294-056-2*); pap. 4.95 (*1-56294-798-2*) Millbrook Pr.
—Rachel Carson: Caring for the Earth. (gr. 4-7). 1992. pap. 4.95 (*0-395-64730-4*) HM.
Sabin, Francene. Rachel Carson: Friend of the Earth. Miyake, Yoshi, illus. LC 92-5825. 48p. (gr. 4-6). 1992. PLB 10.79 (*0-8167-2821-6*); pap. text ed. 3.50 (*0-8167-2822-4*) Troll Assocs.
Wadsworth, Ginger. Rachel Carson: Voice for the Earth. (Illus.). 128p. (gr. 5 up). 1991. PLB 21.50 (*0-8225-4907-7*) Lerner Pubns.

CARTER, JIMMY, PRESIDENT U. S. 1924-

Richman, Daniel A. James E. Carter: Thirty-Ninth President of the United States. Young, Richard G., ed. LC 88-24562. (Illus.). (gr. 5-9). 1989. PLB 17.26 (*0-944483-24-0*) Garrett Ed Corp.
Smith, Betsy C. Jimmy Carter, President. LC 86-5589. (Illus.). 128p. (gr. 10 up). 1986. 12.95 (*0-8027-6650-1*); PLB 13.85 (*0-8027-6652-8*) Walker & Co.
Wade, Linda R. James Carter. LC 89-33754. 100p. (gr. 3 up). 1989. PLB 14.40 (*0-516-01372-6*) Childrens.

CARTIER, JACQUES, 1491-1557

Coulter, Tony. Jacques Cartier, Samuel de Champlain, & the Explorers of Canada. Goetzmann, William H., ed. Collins, Michael, intro. by. (Illus.). 112p. (gr. 6-12). 1993. PLB 18.95 (*0-7910-1298-0*, Am Art Analog); pap. write for info. (*0-7910-1521-1*, Am Art Analog) Chelsea Hse.
Humble, Richard. The Voyages of Jacques Cartier. LC 92-6266. 1993. 12.40 (*0-531-14216-7*) Watts.

CARTOGRAPHY

see Map Drawing; Maps

CARTOONS AND CARICATURES

see also Comic Books, Strips, etc.
Benjamin, Carol L. Cartooning for Kids. Benjamin, Carol L., illus. LC 81-43876. 80p. (gr. 3-7). 1982. PLB 13.89 (*0-690-04208-6*, Crowell Jr Bks) HarpC Child Bks.
Benson, Rita. Looking after the Babysitter. Forss, Ian, illus. LC 93-26221. 1994. 4.25 (*0-383-03760-3*) SRA Schl Grp.
Brown, Charlene & Davis, Carolyn. Comic Strip Fun. (Illus.). 64p. (Orig.). (gr. k up). 1989. pap. 3.95 (*0-929261-29-1*, BA04) W Foster Pub.
Browne, Dik. Hi & Lois: Dawg Day Afternoon. 128p. 1986. pap. 1.95 (*0-8125-6908-3*) Tor Bks.
Burness, Tad. Joshua. Burness, Tad, illus. 90p. (Orig.). (gr. 3 up). 1987. pap. 4.95 (*1-55523-082-2*) Winston-Derek.
Byars, Betsy C. The Cartoonist. 128p. (gr. k-6). 1981. pap. 1.95 (*0-440-41046-0*, YB) Dell.
David, Mark. Cartooning for Kids: A Step-by-Step Guide to Creating Your Own Cartoons. (gr. 4-7). 1993. pap. 3.95 (*0-207-17144-0*, Pub. by Angus & Robertson AT) HarpC.
De Goscinny, Rene. Asterix & Caesar's Gift. 1977. pap. 9.95x (*0-317-00093-4*) Intl Lang.
—Asterix & Cleopatra. Uderzo, illus. 1976. pap. 9.95x (*0-340-17220-7*) Intl Lang.
—Asterix & the Big Fight. Uderzo, illus. 1976. pap. 9.95x (*0-340-19167-8*) Intl Lang.
—Asterix & the Cauldron. Uderzo, illus. 1976. pap. 9.95x (*0-340-22711-7*) Intl Lang.
—Asterix & the Chieftain's Shield. (Illus.). 1977. pap. 9.95x (*0-340-22710-9*) Intl Lang.
—Asterix & the Golden Sickle. Uderzo, illus. 1976. pap. 9.95 (*0-340-21209-8*) Intl Lang.
—Asterix & the Goths. Uderzo, illus. 1976. pap. 9.95x (*0-917201-54-X*) Intl Lang.
—Asterix & the Great Crossing. Uderzo, illus. 1976. pap. 9.95x (*0-340-21589-5*) Intl Lang.
—Asterix & the Laurel Wreath. Uderzo, illus. 1976. pap. 9.95x (*0-340-20699-3*) Intl Lang.
—Asterix & the Roman Agent. Uderzo, illus. 1976. pap. 9.95x (*0-340-19168-6*) Intl Lang.
—Asterix & the Soothsayer. Uderzo, illus. 1976. pap. 9.95 (*0-340-20697-7*) Intl Lang.
—Asterix at the Olympic Games. Uderzo, illus. 1976. pap. 9.95x (*0-340-19169-4*) Intl Lang.
—Asterix aux Jeux Olympiques. (FRE.). (gr. 7-9). 1990. 19.95 (*0-8288-5109-3*, FC884) Fr & Eur.
—Asterix Chez les Bretons. (FRE.). (gr. 7-9). 1990. 19.95 (*0-8288-5108-5*, FC880) Fr & Eur.
—Asterix Chez les Helvetes. (FRE., Illus.). (gr. 7-9). 1990. 19.95 (*0-8288-5110-7*, FC889) Fr & Eur.
—Asterix en Hispanie. (FRE., Illus.). (gr. 7-9). 1990. 19.95 (*0-8288-5111-5*, FC887) Fr & Eur.
—Asterix et Cleopatre. (FRE.). (gr. 7-9). 1990. 19.95 (*0-8288-5112-3*, FC878) Fr & Eur.
—Asterix et la Serpe d'or. (FRE., Illus.). (gr. 3-8). 1990. 19.95 (*0-8288-4939-0*) Fr & Eur.
—Asterix et le Chaudron. (FRE., Illus.). (gr. 7-9). 1990. 19.95 (*0-8288-5113-1*, FC885) Fr & Eur.

—Asterix et les Goths. (FRE.). (gr. 7-9). 1990. 19.95 (*0-8288-5114-X*, FC875) Fr & Eur.
—Asterix et les Normands. (FRE.). (gr. 7-9). 1990. 19.95 (*0-8288-5115-8*, FC881) Fr & Eur.
—Asterix Gladiateur. (FRE.). (gr. 7-9). 1990. 19.95 (*0-8288-5116-6*, FC876) Fr & Eur.
—Asterix in Britain. Uderzo, illus. 1976. pap. 9.95x (*0-340-17221-5*) Intl Lang.
—Asterix in Spain. Uderzo, illus. 1976. pap. 9.95x (*0-340-18326-8*) Intl Lang.
—Asterix in Switzerland. Uderzo, illus. 1976. pap. 9.95x (*0-340-19270-4*) Intl Lang.
—Asterix la Zizanie. (FRE., Illus.). (gr. 7-9). 1990. 19.95 (*0-8288-5117-4*, FC888) Fr & Eur.
—Asterix le Gaulois. (FRE.). (gr. 7-9). 1990. 19.95 (*0-8288-5118-2*, FC873) Fr & Eur.
—Asterix Legionnaire. (FRE.). (gr. 7-9). 1990. 19.95 (*0-8288-5119-0*, FC882) Fr & Eur.
—Asterix the Gladiator. Uderzo, illus. 1976. pap. 9.95x (*0-340-18320-9*) Intl Lang.
—Asterix the Legionary. Uderzo, illus. 1976. pap. 9.95x (*0-340-18321-7*) Intl Lang.
—The Mansion of the Gods. Uderzo, illus. 1976. pap. 9.95 (*0-340-19269-0*) Intl Lang.
De Goscinny, Rene & Uderzo, M. El Adivino. (SPA., Illus.). 19.95 (*0-8288-6082-3*, S26630) Fr & Eur.
—Der Arvernerschild. (GER., Illus.). 19.95 (*0-8288-4914-5*) Fr & Eur.
—Asterix als Gladiator. (GER., Illus.). (gr. 7-10). 1992. 19.95 (*0-8288-4923-4*) Fr & Eur.
—Asterix als Legionar. (GER., Illus.). (gr. 7-10). 1992. 19.95 (*0-8288-4924-2*) Fr & Eur.
—Asterix & Caesar's Gift. (Illus.). (gr. 7-10). 1990. 19.95 (*0-8288-4915-3*) Fr & Eur.
—Asterix & Cleopatra. (Illus.). (gr. 7-10). 1990. 19.95 (*0-8288-4916-1*) Fr & Eur.
—Asterix & the Big Fight. (Illus.). (gr. 7-10). 1990. 19.95 (*0-8288-4917-X*) Fr & Eur.
—Asterix & the Chieftain's Shield. (Illus.). (gr. 7-10). 1990. 19.95 (*0-8288-4918-8*) Fr & Eur.
—Asterix & the Laurel Wreath. (Illus.). (gr. 7-10). 1990. 19.95 (*0-8288-4920-X*) Fr & Eur.
—Asterix & the Normans. (Illus.). (gr. 7-10). 1990. 19.95 (*0-8288-4921-8*) Fr & Eur.
—Asterix & the Roman Agent. (Illus.). (gr. 7-10). 1990. 19.95 (*0-8288-4922-6*) Fr & Eur.
—Asterix apud Gothos. (LAT., Illus.). (gr. 7-10). 1990. PLB 19.95 (*0-8288-4925-0*) Fr & Eur.
—Asterix at the Olympic Games. (Illus.). (gr. 7-10). 1990. 19.95 (*0-8288-4926-9*) Fr & Eur.
—Asterix auf Korsika. (GER., Illus.). (gr. 7-10). 1990. PLB 19.95 (*0-8288-4927-7*) Fr & Eur.
—Asterix bei den Briten. (GER., Illus.). (gr. 7-10). 1990. PLB 19.95 (*0-8288-4928-5*) Fr & Eur.
—Asterix bei den Olympischen Spielen. (GER., Illus.). (gr. 7-10). 1990. PLB 19.95 (*0-8288-4929-3*) Fr & Eur.
—Asterix bei den Schweizern. (GER., Illus.). (gr. 7-10). 1990. PLB 19.95 (*0-8288-4930-7*) Fr & Eur.
—Asterix chez les Belges. (FRE., Illus.). (gr. 7-10). 1990. 19.95 (*0-8288-4931-5*) Fr & Eur.
—Asterix der Gallier. (GER., Illus.). (gr. 7-10). 1990. PLB 19.95 (*0-8288-4932-3*) Fr & Eur.
—Asterix el Galo. (SPA., Illus.). (gr. 7-10). 19.95 (*0-8288-4933-1*) Fr & Eur.
—Asterix en Bretana. (SPA., Illus.). (gr. 7-10). 1990. PLB 19.95 (*0-8288-4934-X*) Fr & Eur.
—Asterix en Corcega. (SPA., Illus.). (gr. 7-10). 1990. PLB 19.95 (*0-8288-4935-8*) Fr & Eur.
—Asterix en Corse. (FRE., Illus.). (gr. 7-10). 1990. 19.95 (*0-8288-4936-6*) Fr & Eur.
—Asterix en Helvecia. (SPA., Illus.). (gr. 7-10). 1990. PLB 19.95 (*0-8288-4937-4*) Fr & Eur.
—Asterix en los Juegos Olimpicos. (SPA., Illus.). (gr. 7-10). 1990. PLB 19.95 (*0-8288-4938-2*) Fr & Eur.
—Asterix Gallus. (LAT., Illus.). (gr. 7-10). 1990. lib. bdg. 19.95 (*0-8288-4941-2*) Fr & Eur.
—Asterix Gladiador. (SPA., Illus.). (gr. 7-10). 1990. PLB 19.95 (*0-8288-4942-0*) Fr & Eur.
—Asterix in Spain. (Illus.). 1990. 19.95 (*0-8288-4945-5*) Fr & Eur.
—Asterix in Spanien. (GER., Illus.). 1990. PLB 19.95 (*0-8288-4946-3*) Fr & Eur.
—Asterix in Switzerland. (Illus.). 1990. PLB 19.95 (*0-8288-4947-1*) Fr & Eur.
—Asterix iter Gallicum. (LAT., Illus.). 1990. PLB 19.95 (*0-8288-4948-X*) Fr & Eur.
—Asterix Legionario. (SPA., Illus.). 1990. PLB 19.95 (*0-8288-4949-8*) Fr & Eur.
—Asterix the Gaul. (Illus.). 1990. 19.95 (*0-8288-4950-1*) Fr & Eur.
—Asterix the Gladiator. (Illus.). 1990. 19.95 (*0-8288-4951-X*) Fr & Eur.
—Asterix the Legionary. (Illus.). 1990. 19.95 (*0-8288-4952-8*) Fr & Eur.
—Asterix und die Goten. (GER., Illus.). 1990. PLB 19.95 (*0-8288-4953-6*) Fr & Eur.
—Asterix und Kleopatra. (GER., Illus.). 1990. PLB 19.95 (*0-8288-4954-4*) Fr & Eur.
—Asterix y Cleopatra. (SPA., Illus.). 1990. PLB 19.95 (*0-8288-4955-2*) Fr & Eur.
—Asterix y el Caldero. (SPA., Illus.). 1990. PLB 19.95 (*0-8288-4956-0*) Fr & Eur.
—Asterix y los Godos. (SPA., Illus.). 1990. PLB 19.95 (*0-8288-4957-9*) Fr & Eur.
—Asterix y los Normandos. (SPA., Illus.). 1990. PLB 19.95 (*0-8288-4958-7*) Fr & Eur.
—Le Cadeau de Cesar. (FRE., Illus.). 1990. 19.95 (*0-8288-4959-5*) Fr & Eur.
—The Caldron. (Illus.). 1990. 19.95 (*0-8288-4960-9*) Fr & Eur.
—La Cizana. (SPA., Illus.). 19.95 (*0-8288-4961-7*) Fr & Eur.
—El Combate de los Jefes. (SPA., Illus.). 19.95 (*0-8288-4962-5*) Fr & Eur.
—Les Douze Travaux d'Asterix. (FRE., Illus.). 1990. 19.95 (*0-8288-4964-1*) Fr & Eur.
—El Escudo Arverno. (SPA., Illus.). 19.95 (*0-8288-4965-X*) Fr & Eur.
—Falx Aurea. (LAT., Illus.). 19.95 (*0-8288-4966-8*) Fr & Eur.
—Das Geschenk Casars. (GER., Illus.). 19.95 (*0-8288-4967-6*) Fr & Eur.
—The Golden Sickle. (Illus.). 1990. 19.95 (*0-8288-4968-4*) Fr & Eur.
—Die Goldene Sichel. (GER., Illus.). 19.95 (*0-8288-4969-2*) Fr & Eur.
—La Gran Travesia. (SPA., Illus.). 19.95 (*0-8288-5124-7*) Fr & Eur.
—La Grande Traversee. (FRE., Illus.). 1990. 19.95 (*0-8288-4970-6*) Fr & Eur.
—Die Grosse Uberfahrt. (GER., Illus.). 19.95 (*0-8288-4972-2*) Fr & Eur.
—La Hoz de Oro. (SPA., Illus.). 19.95 (*0-8288-4973-0*) Fr & Eur.
—Der Kampf der Hauptlinge. (GER., Illus.). 19.95 (*0-8288-4974-9*) Fr & Eur.
—Der Kupferkessel. (GER., Illus.). 19.95 (*0-8288-4975-7*) Fr & Eur.
—Los Laureles del Cesar. (SPA., Illus.). 19.95 (*0-8288-4976-5*) Fr & Eur.
—Les Lauriers de Cesar. (FRE., Illus.). 1990. 19.95 (*0-8288-4977-3*) Fr & Eur.
—Die Lorbeeren des Casar. (GER., Illus.). 19.95 (*0-8288-4978-1*) Fr & Eur.
—The Mansions of the Gods. (Illus.). 1990. 19.95 (*0-8288-4979-X*) Fr & Eur.
—Die Normannen. (GER., Illus.). 19.95 (*0-8288-4980-3*) Fr & Eur.
—El Regalo del Cesar. (SPA., Illus.). 19.95 (*0-8288-4900-5*) Fr & Eur.
—La Residencia de los Dioses. (SPA., Illus.). 19.95 (*0-8288-4901-3*) Fr & Eur.
—Der Seher. (GER., Illus.). 19.95 (*0-8288-5125-5*) Fr & Eur.
—La Serpe d'Or. (FRE., Illus.). 1990. 19.95 (*0-8288-4904-8*) Fr & Eur.
—The Soothsayer. (Illus.). 1990. 19.95 (*0-8288-4905-6*) Fr & Eur.
—Streit Um Asterix. (GER., Illus.). 19.95 (*0-8288-4906-4*) Fr & Eur.
—Tour de France. (GER., Illus.). 1990. 19.95 (*0-8288-4907-2*) Fr & Eur.
—Le Tour de Gaulle. (FRE., Illus.). 19.95 (*0-8288-4908-0*) Fr & Eur.
—Die Trabantenstadt. (GER., Illus.). 19.95 (*0-8288-4910-2*) Fr & Eur.
—La Vuelta a la Galia. (SPA., Illus.). 19.95 (*0-8288-4911-0*) Fr & Eur.
—La Zizanie. (FRE., Illus.). 1990. 19.95 (*0-8288-4912-9*) Fr & Eur.
De Kay, James T. Left-Handed Kids. LC 89-36893. (Illus.). 96p. 1989. pap. 5.95 (*0-87131-591-2*) M Evans.
Edens, Cooper. With Secret Friends. LC 91-23642. (Illus.). 48p. (gr. 7-12). 1992. signed & numbered 20.00 (*0-671-75593-5*, Green Tiger); pap. 8.00 (*0-671-74970-6*, Green Tiger) S&S Trade.
Edwards, Don. Cartooning. Stieglitz, Cliff, ed. Edwards, Don, illus. 64p. (Orig.). (gr. 7 up). 1993. pap. 12.95 (*0-9637336-0-5*) Airbrush Act.
Gautier, Dick. The Career Cartoonist: A Step-by-Step Guide to Presenting & Selling Your Artwork. 128p. (Orig.). 1992. pap. 10.95 (*0-399-51732-4*, Perigee Bks) Berkley Pub.
Herge. The Castafiore Emerald. (gr. k up). 1975. pap. 7.95 (*0-316-35842-8*, Joy St Bks) Little.
Hinds, Bill. Buzz Beamer's Radical Olympics. Hinds, Bill, illus. 32p. (gr. 3-7). 1992. pap. 4.95 (*0-316-36452-5*, Spts Illus Kids) Little.
Hodge, Anthony. Cartooning. Hodge, Anthony, illus. LC 91-34409. 32p. (gr. 5-9). 1992. PLB 12.40 (*0-531-17322-4*, Gloucester Pr) Watts.
Hoff, Syd. How to Draw Cartoons. (Illus.). 32p. (Orig.). (gr. k-3). 1991. pap. 1.95 (*0-590-40689-2*) Scholastic Inc.
Italia, Robert. The Simpsons. Wallner, Rosemary, ed. LC 91-73050. 1991. 13.95 (*1-56239-051-1*) Abdo & Dghtrs.
—Teenage Mutant Ninja Turtles. Wallner, Rosemary, ed. LC 91-73051. 1991. 13.95 (*1-56239-050-3*) Abdo & Dghtrs.
Johnston, Lynn. Is This "One of Those Days," Daddy? Johnston, Lynn, illus. LC 82-72417. 128p. (gr. 5 up). 1982. pap. 8.95 (*0-8362-1197-9*) Andrews & McMeel.
Keane, Bill. Look Who's Here. 1987. pap. 3.99 (*0-449-13276-5*, GM) Fawcett.
Ketcham, Hank. Dennis the Menace: Everybody's Little Helper. (Illus.). 128p. 1984. pap. 1.95 (*0-449-12732-X*, GM) Fawcett.
—Dennis the Menace: Little Man in a Big Hurry. (Illus.). 128p. 1984. pap. 1.95 (*0-449-12778-8*, Gm) Fawcett.
—Dennis the Menace: Make-Believe Angel. (Illus.). 1981. pap. 1.95 (*0-449-13902-6*, GM) Fawcett.
—Dennis the Menace: Teacher's Threat. (Illus.). 1981. pap. 1.50 (*0-449-13643-4*, GM) Fawcett.
—Dennis the Menace: Voted Most Likely. (Illus.). (gr. 7 up). 1982. pap. 1.75 (*0-449-13747-3*, GM) Fawcett.
—Dennis the Menace: Where the Action Is. (Illus.). 128p. 1981. pap. 1.50 (*0-449-13669-8*, GM) Fawcett.
—Dennis the Menace: Your Friendly Neighborhood Kid. (Illus.). 1979. pap. 1.25 (*0-449-13778-3*, GM) Fawcett.
Lightfoot, Marge. Cartooning for Kids. Lightfoot, Marge, illus. 64p. 1993. 16.95 (*1-895688-03-5*, Pub. by Greey dePencier CN); pap. 8.95 (*0-920775-84-5*, Pub. by Greey dePencier CN) Firefly Bks Ltd.
Lockman, Vic. Machines. Lockman, Vic, illus. 48p. (Orig.). (gr. 8 up). 1992. pap. 5.95 stapled (*0-936175-20-6*) V Lockman.
—Miracle Art: Trick Cartoons. Lockman, Vic, illus. 48p. (Orig.). (gr. 8 up). 1992. pap. 5.95 stapled (*0-936175-19-2*) V Lockman.
Mascola. Charles Schulz, Reading Level 2. (Illus.). 24p. (gr. 1-4). 1989. PLB 14.60 (*0-86592-429-5*) Rourke Corp.
Mercadoocasio, Gwen. How to Draw Comics. LC 94-1837. 1994. 5.95 (*0-681-00424-X*) Longmeadow Pr.
Mickey Mouse et Monte Cristo. (FRE.). (gr. 3-8). 6.25 (*0-685-28446-8*) Fr & Eur.
Newell, Peter S. Topsys & Turvys. (Illus.). 76p. (gr. 3-7). pap. 3.50 (*0-486-21231-9*) Dover.
Parker, Steve. Draw Partner: How to Draw Wild West Cartoons for Kids. Parker, Steve, illus. 32p. (gr. 1-6). 1990. pap. 2.95 (*0-929526-08-2*) Double B Pubns.
Ryan, Tom K. Let'er Rip Tumbleweeds. (Illus.). 128p. 1981. pap. 1.50 (*0-449-13894-1*, GM) Fawcett.
Schultz, Ron. Looking Inside Cartoon Animation. (Illus.). 48p. (Orig.). (gr. 3 up). 1992. pap. 9.95 (*1-56261-066-X*) John Muir.
Schulz, Charles M. Apuros Escolares. (SPA., Illus.). (gr. 3-8). 1.50 (*0-685-28419-0*) Fr & Eur.
—Summers Fly, Winters Walk. (Illus.). 128p. 1991. pap. 5.95 (*0-8050-1692-9*, Owl Bks) H Holt & Co.
—There's No One Like You, Snoopy: Selected Cartoons from "You're You, Charlie Brown, Vol. I. (Illus.). (gr. 1-5). 1985. pap. 2.95 (*0-449-20776-5*, Crest) Fawcett.
—Your Choice, Snoopy. 1987. pap. 2.95 (*0-449-21327-7*, Crest) Fawcett.
Sesame Street Staff. Sesame Street Storybook. (Illus.). (ps-4). 1971. 5.95 (*0-394-82332-X*); lib. bdg. 5.99 (*0-394-92332-4*) Random Bks Yng Read.
Smythe, Reginald. Watch Your Step, Andy Capp. (Illus.). (gr. 4 up). 1979. pap. 1.25 (*0-449-13562-4*, P3562, GM) Fawcett.
Tatchell, J. & Evans, C. Young Cartoonist. 72p. (gr. 5 up). 1987. pap. 8.95 (*0-7460-0083-9*) EDC.
Thurber, James. Many Moons. Slobodkin, Louis, illus. LC 43-51250. 46p. (gr. 3-7). 1973. pap. 5.95 (*0-15-656980-9*, Voyager Bks) HarBrace.
Tollison, Hal. Cartoon Fun. (Illus.). 64p. (Orig.). (gr. k up). 1989. pap. 3.95 (*1-56010-033-8*, BA07) W Foster Pub.
Viska, Peter. Animation Book. (gr. 4-7). 1994. pap. 5.95 (*0-590-47573-8*) Scholastic Inc.
Walt Disney Staff. Alice in Wonderland. 1988. 6.98 (*0-8317-0287-7*) Viking Child Bks.
Walt Disney's Silly Symphonies. (Illus.). 128p. 1992. 5.95 (*1-56138-156-X*) Running Pr.

CARVER, GEORGE WASHINGTON, 1864?-1943

Adair, Gene. George Washington Carver. King, Coretta Scott, intro. by. (Illus.). 112p. (Orig.). (gr. 5 up). 1989. 17.95 (*1-55546-577-3*); pap. 9.95 (*0-7910-0234-9*) Chelsea Hse.
AESOP Enterprises, Inc. Staff & Crenshaw, Gwendolyn J. George Washington Carver: A Scientist Glorifying the Glories of Nature. 16p. (gr. 3-12). 1991. pap. write for info. incl. cassette (*1-880771-04-7*) AESOP Enter.
Aliki. A Weed Is a Flower: The Life of George Washington Carver. Aliki, illus. 32p. (ps-3). 1988. pap. 14.00 (*0-671-66118-3*, S&S BFYR); pap. 5.95 (*0-671-66490-5*, S&S BFYR) S&S Trade.
Benitez, Mirna. George Washington Carver, Plant Doctor. 32p. 1989. PLB 18.99 (*0-8172-3522-1*); pap. 3.95 (*0-8114-6719-8*) Raintree Steck-V.
Coil, Suzanne M. George Washington Carver. (Illus.). 64p. (gr. 5-8). 1990. PLB 12.90 (*0-531-10864-3*) Watts.
Collins, David. George Washington Carver. Van Seversen, Joe, illus. 131p. (gr. 3-6). 1981. pap. 6.95 (*0-915134-90-X*) Mott Media.
Gray, James M. George Washington Carver. Gallin, Richard, ed. (Illus.). 144p. (gr. 5-9). 1990. PLB 10.95 (*0-382-09964-8*); pap. 6.95 (*0-382-09969-9*) Silver Burdett Pr.
Greene, Carol. George Washington Carver: Scientist & Teacher. Dobson, Steven, illus. LC 92-7374. 48p. (gr. k-3). 1992. PLB 12.85 (*0-516-04250-5*) Childrens.
—George Washington Carver: Scientist & Teacher. Dobson, Steven, illus. LC 92-7374. 48p. (gr. k-3). 1993. pap. 4.95 (*0-516-44250-3*) Childrens.
Johnson, LaVerne C. George Washington Carver: Writer. Perry, Craig R., illus. LC 92-35254. (gr. 6-9). 1992. pap. 3.95 (*0-922162-91-3*) Empak Pub.
Luthor. George W. Carver. Date not set. PLB write for info. (*0-8050-2271-6*) H Holt & Co.
McKissack, Patricia & McKissack, Fredrick. George Washington Carver: The Peanut Scientist. Ostendorf, Ned, illus. LC 91-8814. 32p. (gr. 1-4). 1991. lib. bdg. 12.95 (*0-89490-308-X*) Enslow Pubs.
Means, Florence. Carvers' George. LC 90-59179. (Illus.). 160p. (gr. 6-10). 1991. PLB 13.95 (*1-55905-075-6*) Marshall Cavendish.

Mitchell, Barbara. A Pocketful of Goobers: A Story about George Washington Carver. Hanson, Peter, illus. 64p. (gr. 3-6). 1986. PLB 14.95 (*0-87614-292-7*) Carolrhoda Bks.

Moore, Eva. Story of George Washington Carver. 1990. pap. 2.95 (*0-590-42660-5*) Scholastic Inc.

Nicholson, Lois. George Washington Carver: Scientist. (Illus.). 80p. 1993. 13.95 (*0-7910-1763-X*, Am Art Analog) Chelsea Hse.

Nicholson, Louis P. George Washington Carver. LC 93-38515. 1994. write for info. (*0-7910-2108-4*); pap. write for info. (*0-7910-2114-9*) Chelsea Hse.

Rogers, Teresa. George Washington Carver: Nature's Trailblazer. Raymond, Larry, illus. 72p. (gr. 4-7). 1992. PLB 14.95 (*0-8050-2115-9*) TFC Bks NY.

CARVING, WOOD

see Wood Carving

CASALS, PABLO, 1876-1973

Garza, Hedda. Pablo Casals. (gr. 4-7). 1992. pap. 7.95 (*0-7910-1261-1*) Chelsea Hse.

Hargrove, Jim. Pablo Casals: Cellist of Conscience. LC 90-21047. (Illus.). 152p. (gr. 4 up). 1991. PLB 14.40 (*0-516-03272-0*); pap. 5.95 (*0-516-43272-9*) Childrens.

CASH, JOHNNY

Loewen, L. Johnny Cash. (Illus.). 112p. (gr. 5 up). 1989. lib. bdg. 18.60 (*0-86592-608-5*); 13.95s.p. (*0-685-58613-8*) Rourke Corp.

CASSATT, MARY, 1845-1926

Cain, Michael. Mary Cassatt. Horner, Matina, intro. by. (Illus.). 112p. (gr. 5 up). 1989. lib. bdg. 17.95 (*1-55546-647-8*) Chelsea Hse.

Meyer, Susan E. Mary Cassatt. (Illus.). 80p. (gr. 7 up). 1990. 19.95 (*0-8109-3154-0*) Abrams.

Plain, Nancy. Mary Cassatt, the Life of an Artist. LC 93-46578. 1994. text ed. 13.95 (*0-87518-597-5*, Dillon) Macmillan Child Grp.

Turner, Robyn M. Mary Cassatt: Portraits of Women Artists for Children. (gr. 4-7). 1992. 16.95 (*0-316-85650-9*) Little.

Venezia, Mike. Mary Cassatt. Venezia, Mike, illus. LC 90-2165. 32p. (ps-4). 1990. PLB 12.85 (*0-516-02278-4*); pap. 4.95 (*0-516-42278-2*) Childrens.

CASTLES

Campbell, Elizabeth. Castle Hopping in the U. K. with Elizabeth. (Illus.). 60p. (Orig.). (gr. 9-12). 1988. pap. 12.95 (*0-9618324-0-1*) EFC Pub.

Castle. LC 93-30158. 32p. 1994. 16.95 (*1-56458-467-4*) Dorling Kindersley.

Clements, Gillian. The Truth about Castles. Clements, Gillian, illus. 40p. (gr. 2-6). 1990. PLB 18.95 (*0-87614-401-6*) Carolrhoda Bks.

—Truth about Castles. (gr. 4-7). 1991. pap. 6.95 (*0-87614-552-7*) Carolrhoda Bks.

Cooper, J. Castillos (Castles) (SPA.). 1991. 8.95s.p. (*0-86592-937-8*) Rourke Enter.

—Castles. 1991. 8.95s.p. (*0-86592-629-8*) Rourke Enter.

Evangelista, Gloria. Castle. Wenzel, David, illus. LC 93-87111. 24p. (Orig.). (ps up). 1995. pap. 7.99 (*0-679-86195-5*) Random Bks Yng Read.

Gee, Robyn, ed. Castle Times. McCaig, Rob & Ashman, Iain, illus. 24p. (gr. 3-6). 1982. pap. 4.50 (*0-86020-621-1*) EDC.

Graham, Rickard. Norman Castles. LC 89-34447. 1990. PLB 10.90 (*0-531-18323-8*, Pub. by Bookwright Pr) Watts.

Gravett, Christopher. Castle. LC 93-32594. (Illus.). 1994. 16.00 (*0-679-86000-2*); PLB 16.99 (*0-679-96000-7*) Knopf Bks Yng Read.

Incredible Knights & Castles. 32p. (ps-k). 1994. 4.95 (*1-56458-730-4*) Dorling Kindersley.

James, Alan. Castles & Mansions. (Illus.). 32p. (gr. 2-5). 1989. 13.50 (*0-8225-2128-8*) Lerner Pubns.

Macaulay, David. Castle. Macaulay, David, illus. LC 77-7159. 80p. (gr. 1 up). 1977. 16.95 (*0-395-25784-0*); pap. 7.70 (*0-395-32920-5*) HM.

MacDonald, Fiona. A Medieval Castle: Inside Story. Bergin, Mark, illus. 48p. (gr. 5 up). 1990. 17.95 (*0-87226-340-1*) P Bedrick Bks.

Maynard, Christopher. Castles. LC 92-32844. 32p. (gr. 1-4). 1993. 3.95 (*1-85697-891-5*, Kingfisher LKC) LKC.

Moss, Miriam. Forts & Castles. Forsey, Chris, illus. LC 93-11167. 32p. (gr. 4-6). 1993. PLB 19.97 (*0-8114-6157-2*) Raintree Steck-V.

O'Dell, Scott. The Castle in the Sea. 192p. (gr. 7up). 1983. 13.95 (*0-395-34831-5*) HM.

Osband, Gillian. Castles. Andrew, Robert, illus. LC 91-60082. 16p. 1991. 15.95 (*0-531-05949-9*) Orchard Bks Watts.

Penner, Lucille R. Knights & Castles. Bell, Owain, illus. LC 93-45710. (gr. 4 up). 1994. PLB 2.50 (*0-679-85095-3*) Random.

Rom, Christine S. Creepy Castles. LC 89-28986. (Illus.). 48p. (gr. 5-6). 1990. text ed. 11.95 RSBE (*0-89686-505-3*, Crestwood Hse) Macmillan Child Grp.

Sea Castles, Unit 9. (gr. 3). 1991. 7.45 (*0-88106-770-9*) Charlesbridge Pub.

Spellman, Linda. Castles, Codes, Calligraphy. 112p. (gr. 4-6). 1984. 9.95 (*0-88160-103-9*, LW 904) Learning Wks.

Thibault, Dominique. Long Ago in a Castle. Farre, Marie, illus. 40p. (gr. k-5). 1993. PLB 9.95 (*1-56674-071-1*, HTS Bks) Forest Hse.

CASTLES–FICTION

Allen, Laura J. Rollo & Tweedy & the Ghost at Dougal Castle. LC 89-26921. (Illus.). 64p. (gr. k-3). 1992. 13.00 (*0-06-020106-1*); PLB 13.89 (*0-06-020107-X*) HarpC Child Bks.

Carlson, Natalie S. The Orphelines in the Enchanted Castle. (gr. k-6). 1988. pap. 2.75 (*0-440-40015-5*, YB) Dell.

Cook, Lyn. The Secret of Willow Castle. Goodwin, Judith, illus. 236p. (Orig.). (gr. 3-10). 1984. pap. 7.95 (*0-920656-30-7*, Pub. by Camden Hse CN) Firefly Bks Ltd.

Graves, Robert. An Ancient Castle. Graves, Elizabeth, illus. Thomas, William D., afterword by. LC 81-17204. (Illus.). 72p. (gr. 7 up). 1981. 13.95 (*0-935576-06-1*); pap. 8.95 (*0-935576-33-9*) Kesend Pub Ltd.

Hayes, Sarah. Crumbling Castle. LC 91-58723. 80p. (gr. 3-6). 1994. pap. 3.99 (*1-56402-274-9*) Candlewick Pr.

Kaufman, Gershen. Journey to a Magic Castle. Jeffery, Megan E., illus. LC 91-78278. 30p. (gr. 5-8). 1993. pap. write for info. incl. worksheets (*0-916634-14-0*) Double M Pr.

Lawson, Julie. Kate's Castle. (ps-3). 1994. pap. 6.95 (*0-19-541001-7*) OUP.

Light, John. Snap Happy. LC 91-36610. (gr. 4 up). 1991. 3.95 (*0-85953-504-5*) Childs Play.

McGuire, Leslie. Eureeka's Castle: Magellan Saves the Day. Brannon, Tom, illus. (ps-k). 1991. pap. 1.25 (*0-307-11512-7*, Golden Pr) Western Pub.

Marsh, Carole. Castle Hayne. (Illus.). 60p. (gr. 4-12). 1994. PLB 19.95 (*1-55609-159-1*); pap. 14.95 (*1-55609-241-5*) Gallopade Pub Group.

Montgomery, Lucy M. The Blue Castle. (gr. 7 up). 1989. pap. 3.50 (*0-553-28051-1*, Starfire) Bantam.

Muchnik, Michoel. The Cuckoo Clock Castle of Shir. LC 79-55560. (Illus.). (ps-3). 1980. 8.95 (*0-8197-0476-8*) Bloch.

Nesbit, Edith. Enchanted Castle. 179p. 1981. Repr. PLB 16.95x (*0-89967-035-0*) Harmony Raine.

Nolan, Dennis. The Castle Builder. Nolan, Dennis, illus. LC 86-23784. 32p. (gr. k-3). 1987. RSBE 13.95 (*0-02-768240-4*, Macmillan Child Bk) Macmillan Child Grp.

O'Dell, Scott. The Castle in the Sea. 160p. (gr. 7 up). 1984. pap. 3.50 (*0-449-70123-9*, Juniper) Fawcett.

Osborne, Mary P. The Knight at Dawn. Murdocca, Sal, illus. LC 92-13075. 80p. (Orig.). (gr. 1-4). 1993. PLB 9.99 (*0-679-92412-4*); pap. 2.99 (*0-679-82412-X*) Random Bks Yng Read.

Skwarek, Skip. In the Deep Dark Dungeon. Compass Productions Staff, illus. LC 91-45515. 10p. (gr. k-4). 1992. 4.95 (*0-8037-1187-5*) Dial Bks Young.

Warner, Gertrude C. The Castle Mystery. (gr. 4-7). 1993. 10.95 (*0-8075-1078-5*); pap. 3.50 (*0-8075-1079-3*) A Whitman.

Weissman, Anne. The Castle of Chuchurumbel: El Castillo de Churchurumbel. Bailyn, Susan, illus. (ENG & SPA.). 19p. (gr. k-2). 1987. 8.95 (*968-6217-00-2*) Hispanic Bk Dist.

Winthrop, Elizabeth. The Battle for the Castle. LC 92-54490. 160p. (gr. 3-7). 1993. 14.95 (*0-8234-1010-2*) Holiday.

—The Castle in the Attic. Hyman, Trina S., illus. LC 85-5607. 192p. (gr. 4-7). 1985. 14.95 (*0-8234-0579-6*) Holiday.

—The Castle in the Attic. 192p. 1986. pap. 2.95 (*0-553-15433-8*) Bantam.

Zimmerman, Marjorie. The Mystery of the Old Castle. LC 88-6936. (gr. 3-7). 1988. pap. 4.99 (*1-55513-584-6*, Chariot Bks) Chariot Family.

CASTRO, FIDEL, 1927-

Bentley, Judith. Fidel Castro. 128p. (gr. 4-7). 1991. lib. bdg. 13.98 (*0-671-70198-3*, J Messner); pap. 7.95 (*0-671-70199-1*) S&S Trade.

Beyer, Don E. Castro! LC 92-34534. (Illus.). 176p. (gr. 7-12). 1993. PLB 14.40 (*0-531-13027-4*) Watts.

Brown, Warren. Fidel Castro: Cuban Revolutionary. LC 93-25211. (Illus.). 128p. (gr. 7 up). 1994. 15.90 (*1-56294-385-5*) Millbrook Pr.

Kurland, Gerald. Fidel Castro: Communist Dictator of Cuba. Rahmas, D. Steve, ed. 32p. (Orig.). (gr. 7-12). 1972. lib. bdg. 4.95 incl. catalog cards (*0-87157-536-1*) SamHar Pr.

Madden, Paul. Fidel Castro. LC 92-46482. 1993. 19.93 (*0-86625-479-X*); 14.95s.p. (*0-685-67776-1*) Rourke Pubns.

CAT

see Cats

CATASTROPHES

see Disasters

CATERPILLARS

see also Butterflies; Moths

Aunt Peggy. Caterpillar. Beeching, Mark, illus. 24p. 1992. pap. 6.95 (*0-9636185-0-4*); Coloring bk. 2.95 (*0-9636185-3-9*) Aunt Peggys Pub.

—Caterpillar. 2nd ed. Beeching, Mark, illus. 24p. (ps-k). 1994. 13.95 (*0-9636185-2-0*) Aunt Peggys Pub. A beautifully illustrated, twenty-four page picture book for children ages 2 to 6 yrs. In this book there are three words that explain the working of nature--COCOON--HIBERNATE--& METAMORPHOSIS. Available in: HARDCOVER (0-9636185-0-4, $6.95), PAPERBACK (0-9636185-2-0, $13.95), COLORING BOOK (0-9636185-3-9, $2.95), or "FUN PACK"--PAPERBACK/COLOR BOOK (0-9636185-4-7, $8.95). Order from: Aunt Peggy's Publishing, P.O. Box 395, Lowell, IN 46356. 219-696-8707. *Publisher Provided Annotation.*

—Caterpillar: Fun Pack. Beeching, Mark, illus. 24p. (ps-k). 1994. Set, Story bk. & color bk. 8.95 (*0-9636185-4-7*) Aunt Peggys Pub.

Facklam, Margery. Creepy, Crawly Caterpillars. Facklim, Paul, illus. LC 93-41443. 1995. 14.95 (*0-316-27391-0*) Little.

French, Vivian. Caterpillar, Caterpillar. Voake, Charlotte, illus. LC 92-544006. 32p. (ps up). 1993. 14.95 (*1-56402-206-4*) Candlewick Pr.

Hariton, Anca. Butterfly Story. Hariton, Anca, illus. LC 94-19377. (ps-k). 1995. write for info (*0-525-45212-5*) Dutton Child Bks.

Watts, Barrie. Caterpillars. 32p. (gr. k-4). 1991. pap. 4.95 (*0-531-15620-6*) Watts.

CATERPILLARS–FICTION

Bartlett, Jaye. Caterpillar Had a Dream: A Poetic Story about Dreams Coming True. (Illus.). 1991. 8.95 (*1-878064-02-9*) TLC Bks.

—Caterpillar Had a Dream: A Story about Dreams Coming True. Dubina, Alan, illus. 38p. (Orig.). (ps up). 1990. PLB 11.95 incl. cassette (*1-878064-00-2*) New Age CT.

Brown, Bernice. The Magic Caterpillar. Eberspacher, Jeff, ed. Brown, Bernice, illus. 48p. (gr. k-3). 1992. PLB 9.95 casebound (*1-877740-19-5*); pap. 5.50 (*1-877740-20-9*) Nel-Mar Pub.

Brown, Ruth. If at First You Do Not See. Brown, Ruth, illus. LC 82-15527. 48p. (ps-2). 1983. 14.95 (*0-8050-1053-X*, Bks Young Read) H Holt & Co.

Carle, Eric. La Chenille Affamee. (FRE., Illus.). 32p. (ps up). 1992. PLB 16.95 (*0-399-21870-X*, Philomel Bks) Putnam Pub Group.

—The Very Hungry Caterpillar. Carle, Eric, illus. LC 70-82764. (ps-2). 1981. 15.95 (*0-399-20853-4*, Philomel) Putnam Pub Group.

—The Very Hungry Caterpillar. Carle, Eric, illus. 32p. (ps up). 1986. miniature ed. 4.95 (*0-399-21301-5*, Putnam) Putnam Pub Group.

—The Very Hungry Caterpillar: Mini & Plush Package. Carle, Eric, illus. 32p. (ps-3). 1991. 13.95 (*0-399-22049-6*, Philomel) Putnam Pub Group.

Cosgrove, Stephen. The Dream Tree. James, Robin, illus. 32p. (Orig.). (gr. 1-4). 1974. pap. 2.95 (*0-8431-0553-4*) Price Stern.

Daniells, Trenna. Taking the Problems Out of Bedtime. Braille International, Inc. Staff & Henry, James, illus. (Orig.). (gr. 2). 1992. pap. 10.95 (*1-56956-031-5*) W A T Braille.

DeLuise, Dom. Charlie the Caterpillar. Santoro, Christopher, illus. LC 90-31557. 40p. (ps-1). 1990. pap. 13.95 jacketed (*0-671-69358-1*, S&S BFYR) S&S Trade.

—Charlie the Caterpillar. Santoro, Christopher, illus. LC 90-31557. 40p. (ps-1). 1993. pap. 4.95 (*0-671-79607-0*, S&S BFYR) S&S Trade.

Denslow, Sharon P. Woollybear Good-Bye. Cote, Nancy, illus. LC 94-10188. (ps-3). 1994. 14.95 (*0-02-728687-8*, Four Winds) Macmillan Child Grp.

Dickson, Sandy L. The Story of Smartworms: The Journey Begins. Barrow, Madeline H., ed. Dixon, David, illus. 34p. (gr. k-5). 1989. write for info.; PLB write for info.; pap. write for info. Smartworm Corp.

Haas, James. Charles Caterpillar. Kendzia, Mary C., ed. Uzanus, Phil, illus. 32p. (Orig.). 1992. pap. 4.95 (*0-89622-530-5*) Twenty-Third.

Perugini, Donna. The Flight of Orville Wright Caterpillar. (Illus.). 32p. (Orig.). (gr. k-6). 1983. pap. 3.98 (*0-89274-297-6*) Harrison Hse.

CATHEDRALS

Ancona, George. Stone Cutters, Carvers & the Cathedral. LC 94-10549. 1995. write for info. (*0-688-12056-3*); lib. bdg. write for info. (*0-688-12057-1*) Lothrop.

Gandiol-Coppin, Brigitte. Cathedrals: Stone upon Stone. Bogard, Vicki, tr. from FRE. Thibault, Dominique, illus. LC 89-5361. 38p. (gr. k-5). 1989. 5.95 (*0-944589-24-3*, 024) Young Discovery Lib.

Macaulay, David. Cathedral. (Illus.). (gr. k up). 1981. pap. 7.70 (*0-395-31668-5*) HM.

—Cathedral: The Story of Its Construction. LC 73-6634. (Illus.). 80p. (gr. 1-5). 1973. 15.45 (*0-395-17513-5*) HM.

Macdonald, Fiona. A Medieval Cathedral. James, John, illus. 48p. (gr. 5 up). 1994. 17.95 (*0-87226-350-9*); pap. 8.95 (*0-87226-266-9*) P Bedrick Bks.

Perdrizet, Marie-Pierre. The Cathedral Builders. Raycraft, Mary B., tr. from FRE. Krahenbuhl, Eddy, illus. LC 91-24233. 64p. (gr. 4-6). 1992. PLB 15.40 (*1-56294-162-3*) Millbrook Pr.

CATHER, WILLA SILBERT, 1873-1947

Keene, Ann T. Willa Cather. LC 93-45743. 1994. write for info. (*0-671-86760-1*, J Messner); pap. write for info. (*0-671-86761-X*, J Messner) S&S Trade.

CATHOLIC CHURCH

Bishops' Committee for Pastoral Research Staff & National Conference of Catholic Bishops Staff. The Sexual Challenge: Growing up Christian. 16p. (Orig.). (gr. 9-12). 1990. pap. 0.95 (*1-555-86364-7*) US Catholic.

Cronin, Gaynell B. & Bellina, Joan. Together at Mass. Murtagh, Betty, illus. LC 87-70417. 32p. (Orig.). (ps-2). 1987. pap. 2.95 (*0-87793-357-X*) Ave Maria.

Cura, M. J., et al. A Path Through Advent for Children 1993. (Illus.). 48p. 1993. pap. 1.00 (*0-915531-05-4*) OR Catholic.

—A Path Through Lent for Children 1994. (Illus.). 48p. (gr. 3-7). 1994. pap. 1.00 (*0-915531-08-9*) OR Catholic.

Donze, Mary T. I Can Pray the Mass. (SPA & ENG., Illus.). 48p. (gr. 2-4). 1993. pap. text ed. 2.95 (*0-89243-513-5*) Liguori Pubns.

Koch, Carl. The Catholic Church: Journey, Wisdom, & Mission. rev. ed. Allaire, Barbara & Wilt, Michael, eds. (Illus.). 336p. (gr. 11-12). 1994. pap. text ed. 13.50 (*0-88489-298-0*); tchr's. ed. 24.95 (*0-88489-299-9*) St Marys.

Kwatera, Michael. The Ministry of Servers. Stuckenschneider, Placid, illus. 48p. (Orig.). (gr. 6-8). 1982. pap. 1.95 (*0-8146-1300-4*) Liturgical Pr.

Leichner, Jeannine T. Joy Joy, the Mass: Our Family Celebration. (Illus.). (gr. k-3). 1978. pap. 2.95 (*0-87973-350-0*); Spanish Edition. 2.95 (*0-87973-348-9*, 348) Our Sunday Visitor.

McPhee, John, ed. Tu Fe. Diaz, Olimpia, tr. (SPA.). (gr. 9-12). 1979. pap. 3.95 (*0-89243-124-5*, 48290) Liguori Pubns.

Mazar, Peter, ed. Take-Me-Home: Notes on the Church Year for Children. (Illus.). 128p. (Orig.). (gr. 1-8). 1991. pap. 15.00 (*0-929650-52-2*) Liturgy Tr Pubns.

Nelson, Yvette. Celebrating the Eucharist. Proof Positive-Farrowlyne Associates, Inc. Staff, illus. 73p. (Orig.). (gr. 7-8). 1992. pap. text ed. 2.80 (*0-88489-269-7*); tchr's. ed. 6.00 (*0-88489-270-0*) St Marys.

O'Connor, Francine. You & God: Friends Forever - A Faith Book for Catholic Children. (Illus.). 64p. (gr. 1-4). 1993. pap. text ed. 2.95 (*0-89243-515-1*) Liguori Pubns.

O'Connor, Francine M. ABCs of the Mass...for Children. Boswell, Kathryn, illus. 32p. (Orig.). (ps-4). 1988. pap. 3.95 (*0-89243-291-8*) Liguori Pubns.

O'Connor, Francine M. & Boswell, Kathryn. The ABCs of the Rosary. (Illus.). 32p. (gr. 1-4). 1984. pap. 3.95 (*0-89243-221-7*) Liguori Pubns.

Paltro, Piera. I Believe: The Profession of Faith or Creed. Daughters of St. Paul Staff, tr. from ITA. Curti, Anna M., illus. 29p. (Orig.). (gr. k-3). 1992. pap. 2.50 (*0-8198-3664-8*) St Paul Bks.

—My Mass. Daughters of St. Paul Staff, tr. from ITA. Curti, Anna M., illus. 31p. (Orig.). (gr. k-3). 1992. pap. 2.50 (*0-8198-4765-8*) St Paul Bks.

Pennock, Michael. Forming a Catholic Conscience. LC 90-84839. (Illus.). 208p. (Orig.). (gr. 9-12). 1991. pap. text ed. 8.95 (*0-87793-444-4*); tchr's. ed., 168 pgs. 11.95 (*0-87793-445-2*) Ave Maria.

—The Sacraments: Celebrating the Signs of God's Love. LC 92-75347. (Illus.). 240p. (Orig.). (gr. 9-12). 1993. pap. 9.95 (*0-87793-503-3*); 13.95 (*0-87793-504-1*) Ave Maria.

Senger, Mary C. Let's Learn about the Church & Celebrate Its Message. (Illus.). 64p. (gr. 4-6). 1990. pap. 4.95 (*0-8146-1888-X*) Liturgical Pr.

Stadler, Bernice & Reese, Nancy. Celebrations of the Word for Children: Cycle C. LC 88-90102. 104p. (Orig.). (gr. 3-8). 1988. pap. text ed. 9.95 (*0-89622-362-0*) Twenty-Third.

Talbert. Stations of the Cross. Date not set. 15.00 (*0-06-023383-4*); PLB 14.89 (*0-06-023384-2*) HarpC Child Bks.

Windeatt, Mary F. Catholic Story Coloring Books. Harmon, Gedge, illus. 32p. (gr. 1-5). 1989. Repr. of 1954 ed. Set of 24. 48.00 (*0-89555-381-3*) TAN Bks Pubs.

—Pauline Jaricot: Foundress of the Living Rosary & the Society for the Propagation of the Faith. Grout, Paul A., illus. LC 93-60214. 244p. 1993. pap. 10.00 (*0-89555-425-9*) TAN Bks Pubs.

—St. Dominic Savio. Harmon, Gedge, illus. 32p. (gr. 1-5). 1989. Repr. of 1954 ed. wkbk. 3.00 (*0-89555-370-8*) TAN Bks Pubs.

Winkler, Jude. Mass for Children. (ps-3). 14.95 (*0-89942-215-2*) Catholic Bk Pub.

Zilonka, Paul. God's Living Word. 1990. pap. 4.50 (*0-89942-146-6*) Catholic Bk Pub.

CATHOLIC CHURCH–DICTIONARIES

O'Connor, Francine M. ABCs of the Sacraments...for Children. Nolte, Larry, illus. 32p. (gr. k-3). 1989. pap. 3.95 (*0-89243-298-5*) Liguori Pubns.

CATHOLIC CHURCH–DOCTRINAL AND CONTROVERSIAL WORKS

Biffi, Inos. The Apostles' Creed. Vignazia, Franco, illus. LC 93-39151. 48p. 1994. pap. 9.99 (*0-8028-3756-5*) Eerdmans.

—Prayer. Vignazia, Franco, illus. LC 93-41090. 48p. (Orig.). 1994. pap. 9.99 (*0-8028-3759-X*) Eerdmans.

—The Sacraments. Vignazia, Franco, illus. LC 93-39150. 32p. 1994. pap. 9.99 (*0-8028-3757-3*) Eerdmans.

—The Ten Commandments. Vignazia, Franco, illus. LC 93-39147. 32p. 1994. pap. 9.99 (*0-8028-3758-1*) Eerdmans.

Canon & Howe, G. E. Stories from The Catechist: Nine Hundred Seven Traditional Catholic Stories Illustrating the Truths of the Catholic Catechism. LC 82-50589. 387p. 1989. pap. 15.00 (*0-89555-184-5*) Tan Bks Pubs.

Center for Learning Network. Fundamentalism: A Catholic Response. 98p. (gr. 9-12). 1992. pap. text ed. 12.95 (*1-56077-062-7*) Ctr Learning.

Credo: A Catholic Catechism. 296p. (gr. 7-12). 1984. pap. 8.95 (*0-225-66343-0*) Harper SF.

Pennock, Michael. Being Catholic: Believing, Living, Praying. LC 93-73883. (Illus.). 288p. (Orig.). (gr. 10-12). 1994. pap. text ed. 11.95 (*0-87793-527-0*); tchr's. ed., 232p. 15.95 (*0-87793-528-9*) Ave Maria.

Redemptorist Pastoral Publication Staff. How You Live with Jesus: Catechism for Today's Young Catholic. LC 81-80097. 96p. (gr. 4-6). 1981. pap. 4.95 (*0-89243-137-7*) Liguori Pubns.

—Jesus Loves You: A Catholic Catechism for the Primary Grades. LC 82-8000658. 96p. (gr. 1-3). 1982. pap. 5.95 (*0-89243-157-1*) Liguori Pubns.

CATHOLIC CHURCH–FICTION

Benard, Robert. A Catholic Education. (gr. k-12). 1987. pap. 3.50 (*0-440-91124-9*, LFL) Dell.

Cormier, Robert. Other Bells for Us to Ring. Ray, Deborah K., illus. 144p. (gr. 4-7). 1992. pap. 3.99 (*0-440-40717-6*, YB) Dell.

Hooker, Irene H. & Brindle, Susan A. The Caterpillar That Came to Church - la Oruga Que Fue a Misa: A Story of the Eucharist - Un Cuento de la Eucaristia. Lademan, Miriam A., ed. Houtman, Jane F. & De Martinez, Luz M., trs. Hooker, Irene H. & Brindle, Susan A., illus. LC 92-63219. (ENG & SPA.). 64p. (Orig.). 1993. 9.95 (*0-87973-874-X*, 874); pap. 7.95 (*0-87973-875-8*, 875) Our Sunday Visitor.

Mandrell, Louise. End of the Rainbow: A Story about the Meaning of St. Patrick's Day. (gr. 4-7). 1993. 12.95 (*1-56530-047-5*) Summit TX.

CATHOLIC CHURCH–HISTORY

Gardiner, Harold C. Edmund Campion: Hero of God's Underground. Goudket, Rose, illus. LC 91-76073. 180p. 1992. pap. 9.95 (*0-89870-387-5*) Ignatius Pr.

Hanley, Boniface. With Minds of Their Own: Eight Women Who Made a Difference. LC 91-72117. (Illus.). 232p. (Orig.). (gr. 7-12). 1991. pap. 9.95 (*0-87793-454-1*) Ave Maria.

Pennock, Michael. The Catholic Church Story. LC 90-64153. (Illus.). 224p. (Orig.). (gr. 9-12). 1991. pap. text ed. 8.95 (*0-87793-447-9*); tchr's. ed. 12.95 (*0-87793-448-7*) Ave Maria.

CATHOLIC CHURCH–MISSIONS

Gray, Charlotte. Mother Teresa. LC 88-2226. (Illus.). 68p. (gr. 5-6). 1990. pap. 7.95 (*0-8192-1523-6*) Morehouse Pub.

—Mother Teresa: Servant to the World's Suffering People. Ullstein, Susan, adapted by. LC 89-49750. (Illus.). 64p. (gr. 3-4). 1990. PLB 19.93 (*0-8368-0393-0*) Gareth Stevens Inc.

Holland, Margaret. Mother Teresa. (Illus.). 48p. (gr. 3-5). 1992. pap. 2.99 (*0-87406-585-2*) Willowisp Pr.

Pond, Mildred M. Mother Teresa. (Illus.). 80p. (gr. 3-5). 1992. lib. bdg. 12.95 (*0-7910-1755-9*) Chelsea Hse.

Tames, Richard. Mother Teresa. (Illus.). 32p. (gr. 5 up). 1991. pap. 5.95 (*0-531-24613-2*) Watts.

CATHOLIC LITERATURE

Bitney, James & Nelson, Yvette. Welcome to the Way, Jr. High Student Edition. (Illus.). 80p. (Orig.). (gr. 6-8). 1989. pap. text ed. 7.88 (*0-89505-585-6*, T2512) Tabor Pub.

—Welcome to the Way, Sr. High Student Edition. (Illus.). 80p. (gr. 9-12). 1989. pap. text ed. 7.88 (*0-89505-580-5*, T2513) Tabor Pub.

Catechist Guide. (gr. 7). 1993. 15.95 (*0-7829-0340-1*, 88175) Tabor Pub.

Catechist Guide. (gr. 7). 1993. 15.95 (*0-7829-0341-X*, 88176) Tabor Pub.

Catechist Guide. (gr. 8). 1993. 15.95 (*0-7829-0345-2*, 88185) Tabor Pub.

Catechist Guide. (gr. 8). 1993. 15.95 (*0-7829-0346-0*, 88186) Tabor Pub.

Catechist Guide. (gr. 1). 1992. 15.95 (*0-7829-0012-7*, 88012) Tabor Pub.

Catechist Guide. (gr. 1). 1992. 15.95 (*0-7829-0013-5*, 88013) Tabor Pub.

Catechist Guide. (gr. 2). 1992. 15.95 (*0-7829-0017-8*, 88022) Tabor Pub.

Catechist Guide. (gr. 2). 1992. 15.95 (*0-7829-0018-6*, 88023) Tabor Pub.

Catechist Guide. (gr. 3). 1992. 15.95 (*0-7829-0022-4*, 88032) Tabor Pub.

Catechist Guide. (gr. 3). 1992. 15.95 (*0-7829-0023-2*, 88033) Tabor Pub.

Catechist Guide. (gr. 4). 1992. 15.95 (*0-7829-0027-5*, 88042) Tabor Pub.

Catechist Guide. (gr. 4). 1992. 15.95 (*0-7829-0028-3*, 88043) Tabor Pub.

Catechist Guide. (gr. 5). 1992. 15.95 (*0-7829-0032-1*, 88052) Tabor Pub.

Catechist Guide. (gr. 5). 1992. 15.95 (*0-7829-0033-X*, 88053) Tabor Pub.

Catechist Guide. (gr. 6). 1992. 15.95 (*0-7829-0037-2*, 88062) Tabor Pub.

Catechist Guide. (gr. 6). 1992. 15.95 (*0-7829-0038-0*, 88063) Tabor Pub.

Children's Book. annotated ed. (gr. 1). 1992. 11.95 (*0-7829-0011-9*, 88011) Tabor Pub.

Children's Book. annotated ed. (gr. 2). 1992. 11.95 (*0-7829-0016-X*, 88021) Tabor Pub.

Children's Book. annotated ed. (gr. 3). 1992. 11.95 (*0-7829-0021-6*, 88031) Tabor Pub.

Children's Book. annotated ed. (gr. 4). 1992. 11.95 (*0-7829-0026-7*, 88041) Tabor Pub.

Children's Book. annotated ed. (gr. 5). 1992. 11.95 (*0-7829-0031-3*, 88051) Tabor Pub.

Children's Book. annotated ed. (gr. 6). 1992. 11.95 (*0-7829-0036-4*, 88061) Tabor Pub.

Living Waters Five Child's Book. (gr. 5). 1992. 7.95 (*0-7829-0030-5*, 88050) Tabor Pub.

Living Waters Four Child's Book. (gr. 4). 1992. 7.95 (*0-7829-0025-9*, 88040) Tabor Pub.

Living Waters One Child's Book. (gr. 1). 1992. 7.95 (*0-7829-0010-0*, 88010) Tabor Pub.

Living Waters Six Child's Book. (gr. 6). 1992. 7.95 (*0-7829-0035-6*, 88060) Tabor Pub.

Living Waters Three Child's Book. (gr. 3). 1992. 7.95 (*0-7829-0020-8*, 88030) Tabor Pub.

Living Waters Two Child's Book. (gr. 2). 1992. 7.95 (*0-7829-0015-1*, 88020) Tabor Pub.

Mangieri, Rose M. My Companion to Know, Love, & Serve. LC 73-158919. (Illus.). 85p. (Orig.). (ps-1). 1977. pap. 5.50 (*0-913382-45-0*, 103-7) Prow Bks-Franciscan.

Snyder, Bernadette M. Three Hundred Sixty-Five Fun Facts for Catholic Kids. LC 89-84983. 144p. (Orig.). (gr. 4-12). 1989. pap. 5.95 (*0-89243-309-4*) Liguori Pubns.

CATLIN, GEORGE, 1796-1872

Sufrin, Mark. George Catlin: Painter of the Indian West. Catlin, George, illus. LC 90-19813. 160p. (gr. 5-9). 1991. SBE 14.95 (*0-689-31608-9*, Atheneum Child Bk) Macmillan Child Grp.

CATS

Abell-Grubbs, J. Socks Changes His Mind: (The White House Cat, Bk. II. Abell, ed. & illus. (gr. 1 up). 1993. PLB 25.00 (*1-56611-043-2*); pap. 15.00 (*1-56611-044-0*) Jonas.

Ames, Felicia. The Cat You Care For. 1968. pap. 3.50 (*0-451-13041-3*, Sig) NAL-Dutton.

Aymar, Brant, ed. The Personality of the Cat. (Illus.). 352p. 1989. 8.99 (*0-517-00016-4*) Random Hse Value.

Bantam Staff. Kitten: Baby Animal. (ps). 1994. 4.99 (*0-553-09550-1*) Bantam.

Barrett, Norman S. Cats. LC 89-29347. (Illus.). 32p. (gr. k-4). 1990. PLB 11.90 (*0-531-14041-5*) Watts.

Brenner, Barbara & Chardiet, Bernice. Where's That Cat. Schwartz, Carol, illus. LC 93-40722. 1994. write for info. (*0-590-45216-9*) Scholastic Inc.

Bryant, Donna. My Cat Buster. Wood, Jakki, illus. 20p. (ps-3). 1991. 8.95 (*0-8120-6211-6*) Barron.

Burdett, Alice. Nature's Savage Cats. LC 92-33536. 1993. 14.99 (*0-8037-1608-7*) Dial Bks Young.

Burton, Jane. Ginger the Kitten. LC 89-11417. (Illus.). 32p. (gr. 2-3). 1989. PLB 17.27 (*0-8368-0213-6*) Gareth Stevens Inc.

Burton, Jane, photos by. See How They Grow: Kitten. (Illus.). 24p. (gr. k-3). 1991. 6.95 (*0-525-67343-1*, Lodestar Bks) Dutton Child Bks.

Clutton-Brock, Juliet. Cat. King, Dave, photos by. LC 91-9399. (Illus.). 64p. (gr. 5 up). 1991. 16.00 (*0-679-81458-2*); lib. bdg. 16.99 (*0-679-91458-7*) Knopf Bks Yng Read.

Cole, Joanna. My New Kitten. Miller, Margaret, photos by. LC 94-20295. (Illus.). Date not set. write for info. (*0-688-12901-3*); PLB write for info. (*0-688-12902-1*) Morrow Jr Bks.

Cowley, Stewart. Five Little Kittens: A Magic Window Book. Davies, Kate, illus. LC 92-60794. 22p. (ps). 1992. 6.99 (*0-89577-454-2*, Dist. by Random) RD Assn.

Curtis, Alice P. Every Cat Should Have a Home. (Illus.). 60p. (Orig.). 1992. pap. write for info. (*0-9612126-0-8*) A P Walmsley.

De Bourgoing, Pascale. Cats. (Illus.). 1992. bds. 10.95 (*0-590-45269-X*, 039, Cartwheel) Scholastic Inc.

De Paola, Tomie. The Kids' Cat Book. LC 79-2090. (Illus.). 32p. (ps-3). 1979. reinforced bdg. 15.95 (*0-8234-0365-3*); pap. 5.95 (*0-8234-0534-6*) Holiday.

Dupont, Marie. Your First Kitten. (Illus.). 36p. (Orig.). 1991. pap. 1.95 (*0-86622-061-5*, YF-118) TFH Pubns.

Edney, Andrew. ASPCA Complete Cat Care Manual. LC 92-52783. (Illus.). 192p. 1992. 24.95 (*1-56458-064-4*) Dorling Kindersley.

Eisler, Colin. Cats Know Best. Ivory, Leslie A., illus. LC 87-15653. 32p. (ps up). 1988. 13.95 (*0-8037-0503-4*); PLB 13.89 (*0-8037-0560-3*) Dial Bks Young.

Evans, Mark. Kitten. LC 92-52827. (Illus.). 48p. (gr. 2 up). 1992. 9.95 (*1-56458-126-8*) Dorling Kindersley.

Fontanel, Beatrice. Cats, Big & Little. Bogard, Vicki, tr. from FRE. Logvinoff, Anne, illus. LC 90-50772. 38p. (gr. k-5). 1991. 5.95 (*0-944589-27-8*, 278) Young Discovery Lib.

Fowler, Allan. It Could Still Be a Cat. (Illus.). 32p. (ps-2). 1993. PLB 10.75 (*0-516-06015-5*); pap. 3.95 (*0-516-46015-3*) Childrens.

Galeron, Henri, illus. Chat. (FRE.). (ps-1). 1989. 13.95 (*2-07-035703-1*) Schoenhof.

Garrick, Elizabeth. Camelot World: The Mysterious Cat. 128p. (Orig.). 1990. pap. 2.95 (*0-380-76038-X*, Camelot) Avon.

Hains, Harriet. Our New Kitten. LC 92-52813. (Illus.). 24p. (ps-1). 1993. 9.95 (*1-56458-117-9*) Dorling Kindersley.

photos by. (Illus.). 300p. (gr. 6 up). 1992. pap. 14.95 (*0-9631549-0-7*) Tiger Isld Pr.
Here is the riveting, lavishly illustrated saga of how actress Tippi Hedren, in the process of making a feature film as a plea to save wildlife, came to share her home & hearth with its "stars" - some hundred lions, tigers, leopards, cheetahs, & cougars - on a 180 acre preserve in California. Over a hundred photos bring the big cats, & the humans who worked, lived, raised them from cubs & sometimes slept with them, vividly to life. "An exciting read.. ."--Library Journal. "An intriguing tale of obsession..."--Kirkus Review. "This is a rare & captivating book... fascinating, unusual & engrossing"--John Barkham Reviews. "Animal lovers will have difficulty putting Hedren's book down..."--Charleston Evening Post. To order: Tiger Island Press, 6867 Soledad Cyn Rd., Acton, CA 93510.
Publisher Provided Annotation.

Herriot, James. The Christmas Day Kitten. (Illus.). 32p. (gr. 3 up). 1993. pap. 6.95 (*0-312-09767-0*) St Martin.
—Oscar, Cat-about-Town. Brown, Ruth, illus. 32p. (gr. 1-3). 1993. pap. 6.95 (*0-312-09130-3*) St Martin.
Hirschi, Ron. What Is a Cat? Younker, Linda Q., illus. 32p. (gr. 1-3). 1991. 13.95 (*0-8027-8122-5*); PLB 14.85 (*0-8027-8123-3*) Walker & Co.
—Where Do Cats Live? Younker, Linda Q., illus. 32p. (gr. 1-3). 1991. 13.95 (*0-8027-8109-8*); PLB 14.85 (*0-8027-8110-1*) Walker & Co.
Houk, Randy. Jasmine. Houk, Randy, illus. 32p. (gr. k-3). 1993. 14.95 (*1-882728-01-7*); read-along cass. 7.95 (*1-882728-04-1*) Benefactory.
Howard, Tom. The Love of Cats. (Illus.). 96p. 1992. Repr. 12.98 (*0-8317-1203-1*) Smithmark.
James, Betsy. He Wakes Me. David, Helen K., illus. LC 90-28920. 32p. (ps-1). 1991. RLB 14.99 (*0-531-08554-6*) Orchard Bks Watts.
Jameson, P. Cats. (Illus.). 32p. (gr. 2-5). 1989. lib. bdg. 15.94 (*0-86625-183-9*) Rourke Corp.
Johnson, Esther G. Cats in My Life from Granny to Ginger. Johnson, Dagny, illus. 103p. (gr. 9-12). 1990. pap. 7.95 (*0-9629143-0-4*) Skyehill Pubns.
Kappeler, Markus. Big Cats. (Illus.). 32p. (gr. 4-6). 1991. PLB 18.60 (*0-8368-0685-9*) Gareth Stevens Inc.
Kotes, F. F. A Kitty to Love: A Child's Guide to Cat Care. 40p. (Orig.). (gr. 3-8). 1993. pap. 9.95 (*1-878500-02-3*, Valley Hse Bk) Martin Mgmt.
Lawrence, Elizabeth H. Miss Muffin. 1993. 7.95 (*0-8062-4616-2*) Carlton.
Levchuk, Helen. The Dingles. Bianchi, John, illus. 24p. (ps-2). 1991. pap. 4.95 (*0-88899-044-8*, Pub. by Groundwood-Douglas & McIntyre CN) Firefly Bks Ltd.
Levine, Arthur A. The Boy Who Drew Cats: A Japanese Folktale. LC 91-46232. (ps-3). 1994. 16.00 (*0-8037-1172-7*); 15.89 (*0-8037-1173-5*) Dial Bks Young.
Levine, Caroline. Riddles to Tell Your Cat. Grant, Christy, ed. Seltzer, Meyer, illus. 32p. (gr. 1-4). 1992. PLB 8.95 (*0-8075-7006-0*) A Whitman.
Little Cats. 1991. PLB 14.95 (*0-88682-413-3*) Creative Ed.
Lumpkin, Susan. Big Cats. LC 92-26838. (Illus.). 72p. (gr. 6-9). 1993. 17.95 (*0-8160-2847-8*) Facts on File.
—Small Cats. LC 92-26837. (Illus.). 72p. (gr. 6-9). 1993. 17.95 (*0-8160-2848-6*) Facts on File.
McHattie, Grace. Going Live! Cat Book. (Illus.). 94p. 1992. pap. 3.95 (*0-563-20880-5*, BBC-Parkwest) Parkwest Pubns.
McPherson, Mark. Caring for Your Cat. Bernstein, Marianne, illus. LC 84-223. 48p. (gr. 3-7). 1985. PLB 9.89 (*0-8167-0115-6*); pap. text ed. 2.95 (*0-8167-0116-4*) Troll Assocs.
Markert, Jenny. Wildcats. 32p. (gr. 2-6). 1991. 15.95 (*0-89565-704-X*) Childs World.
Marsh, Carole. Meow! Alabama Cats in History, Mystery, Legend, Lore, Humor & More! (Illus.). (gr. 3-12). 1994. PLB 24.95 (*0-7933-3314-8*); pap. 14.95 (*0-7933-3315-6*); computer disk 29.95 (*0-7933-3316-4*) Gallopade Pub Group.
—Meow! Alaska Cats in History, Mystery, Legend, Lore, Humor & More! (Illus.). (gr. 3-12). 1994. PLB 24.95 (*0-7933-3317-2*); pap. 14.95 (*0-7933-3318-0*); computer disk 29.95 (*0-7933-3319-9*) Gallopade Pub Group.
—Meow! Arizona Cats in History, Mystery, Legend, Lore, Humor & More! (Illus.). (gr. 3-12). 1994. PLB 24.95 (*0-7933-3320-2*); pap. 14.95 (*0-7933-3321-0*); computer disk 29.95 (*0-7933-3322-9*) Gallopade Pub Group.
—Meow! Arkansas Cats in History, Mystery, Legend, Lore, Humor & More! (Illus.). (gr. 3-12). 1994. PLB 24.95 (*0-7933-3323-7*); pap. 14.95 (*0-7933-3324-5*); computer disk 29.95 (*0-7933-3325-3*) Gallopade Pub Group.
—Meow! California Cats in History, Mystery, Legend, Lore, Humor & More! (Illus.). (gr. 3-12). 1994. PLB 24.95 (*0-7933-3326-1*); pap. 14.95 (*0-7933-3327-X*); computer disk 29.95 (*0-7933-3328-8*) Gallopade Pub Group.
—Meow! Colorado Cats in History, Mystery, Legend, Lore, Humor & More! (Illus.). (gr. 3-12). 1994. PLB 24.95 (*0-7933-3329-6*); pap. 14.95 (*0-7933-3330-X*); computer disk 29.95 (*0-7933-3331-8*) Gallopade Pub Group.
—Meow! Connecticut Cats in History, Mystery, Legend, Lore, Humor & More! (Illus.). (gr. 3-12). 1994. PLB 24.95 (*0-7933-3332-6*); pap. 14.95 (*0-7933-3333-4*); computer disk 29.95 (*0-7933-3334-2*) Gallopade Pub Group.
—Meow! Delaware Cats in History, Mystery, Legend, Lore, Humor & More! (Illus.). (gr. 3-12). 1994. PLB 24.95 (*0-7933-3335-0*); pap. 14.95 (*0-7933-3336-9*); computer disk 29.95 (*0-7933-3337-7*) Gallopade Pub Group.
—Meow! Florida Cats in History, Mystery, Legend, Lore, Humor & More! (Illus.). (gr. 3-12). 1994. PLB 24.95 (*0-7933-3341-5*); pap. 14.95 (*0-7933-3342-3*); computer disk 29.95 (*0-7933-3343-1*) Gallopade Pub Group.
—Meow! Georgia Cats in History, Mystery, Legend, Lore, Humor & More! (Illus.). (gr. 3-12). 1994. PLB 24.95 (*0-7933-3344-X*); pap. 14.95 (*0-7933-3345-8*); computer disk 29.95 (*0-7933-3346-6*) Gallopade Pub Group.
—Meow! Hawaii Cats in History, Mystery, Legend, Lore, Humor & More! (Illus.). (gr. 3-12). 1994. PLB 24.95 (*0-7933-3347-4*); pap. 14.95 (*0-7933-3348-2*); computer disk 29.95 (*0-7933-3349-0*) Gallopade Pub Group.
—Meow! Idaho Cats in History, Mystery, Legend, Lore, Humor & More! (Illus.). (gr. 3-12). 1994. PLB 24.95 (*0-7933-3350-4*); pap. 14.95 (*0-7933-3351-2*); computer disk 29.95 (*0-7933-3352-0*) Gallopade Pub Group.
—Meow! Illinois Cats in History, Mystery, Legend, Lore, Humor & More! (Illus.). (gr. 3-12). 1994. PLB 24.95 (*0-7933-3353-9*); pap. 14.95 (*0-7933-3354-7*); computer disk 29.95 (*0-7933-3355-5*) Gallopade Pub Group.
—Meow! Indiana Cats in History, Mystery, Legend, Lore, Humor & More! (Illus.). (gr. 3-12). 1994. PLB 24.95 (*0-7933-3356-3*); pap. 14.95 (*0-7933-3357-1*); computer disk 29.95 (*0-7933-3358-X*) Gallopade Pub Group.
—Meow! Iowa Cats in History, Mystery, Legend, Lore, Humor & More! (Illus.). (gr. 3-12). 1994. PLB 24.95 (*0-7933-3359-8*); pap. 14.95 (*0-7933-3360-1*); computer disk 29.95 (*0-7933-3361-X*) Gallopade Pub Group.
—Meow! Kansas Cats in History, Mystery, Legend, Lore, Humor & More! (Illus.). (gr. 3-12). 1994. PLB 24.95 (*0-7933-3362-8*); pap. 14.95 (*0-7933-3363-6*); computer disk 29.95 (*0-7933-3364-4*) Gallopade Pub Group.
—Meow! Kentucky Cats in History, Mystery, Legend, Lore, Humor & More! (Illus.). (gr. 3-12). 1994. PLB 24.95 (*0-7933-3365-2*); pap. 14.95 (*0-7933-3366-0*); computer disk 29.95 (*0-7933-3367-9*) Gallopade Pub Group.
—Meow! Louisiana Cats in History, Mystery, Legend, Lore, Humor & More! (Illus.). (gr. 3-12). 1994. PLB 24.95 (*0-7933-3368-7*); pap. 14.95 (*0-7933-3369-5*); computer disk 29.95 (*0-7933-3370-9*) Gallopade Pub Group.
—Meow! Maine Cats in History, Mystery, Legend, Lore, Humor & More! (Illus.). (gr. 3-12). 1994. PLB 24.95 (*0-7933-3371-7*); pap. 14.95 (*0-7933-3372-5*); computer disk 29.95 (*0-7933-3373-3*) Gallopade Pub Group.
—Meow! Maryland Cats in History, Mystery, Legend, Lore, Humor & More! (Illus.). (gr. 3-12). 1994. PLB 24.95 (*0-7933-3374-1*); pap. 14.95 (*0-7933-3375-X*); computer disk 29.95 (*0-7933-3376-8*) Gallopade Pub Group.
—Meow! Massachusetts Cats in History, Mystery, Legend, Lore, Humor & More! (Illus.). (gr. 3-12). 1994. PLB 24.95 (*0-7933-3377-6*); pap. 14.95 (*0-7933-3378-4*); computer disk 29.95 (*0-7933-3379-2*) Gallopade Pub Group.
—Meow! Michigan Cats in History, Mystery, Legend, Lore, Humor & More! (Illus.). (gr. 3-12). 1994. PLB 24.95 (*0-7933-3380-6*); pap. 14.95 (*0-7933-3381-4*); computer disk 29.95 (*0-7933-3382-2*) Gallopade Pub Group.
—Meow! Minnesota Cats in History, Mystery, Legend, Lore, Humor & More! (Illus.). (gr. 3-12). 1994. PLB 24.95 (*0-7933-3383-0*); pap. 14.95 (*0-7933-3384-9*); computer disk 29.95 (*0-7933-3385-7*) Gallopade Pub Group.
—Meow! Mississippi Cats in History, Mystery, Legend, Lore, Humor & More! (Illus.). (gr. 3-12). 1994. PLB 24.95 (*0-7933-3386-5*); pap. 14.95 (*0-7933-3387-3*); computer disk 29.95 (*0-7933-3388-1*) Gallopade Pub Group.
—Meow! Missouri Cats in History, Mystery, Legend, Lore, Humor & More! (Illus.). (gr. 3-12). 1994. PLB 24.95 (*0-7933-3389-X*); pap. 14.95 (*0-7933-3390-3*); computer disk 29.95 (*0-7933-3391-1*) Gallopade Pub Group.
—Meow! Montana Cats in History, Mystery, Legend, Lore, Humor & More! (Illus.). (gr. 3-12). 1994. PLB 24.95 (*0-7933-3392-X*); pap. 14.95 (*0-7933-3393-8*); computer disk 29.95 (*0-7933-3394-6*) Gallopade Pub Group.
—Meow! Nebraska Cats in History, Mystery, Legend, Lore, Humor & More! (Illus.). (gr. 3-12). 1994. PLB 24.95 (*0-7933-3395-4*); pap. 14.95 (*0-7933-3396-2*); computer disk 29.95 (*0-7933-3397-0*) Gallopade Pub Group.
—Meow! Nevada Cats in History, Mystery, Legend, Lore, Humor & More! (Illus.). (gr. 3-12). 1994. PLB 24.95 (*0-7933-3398-9*); pap. 14.95 (*0-7933-3399-7*); computer disk 29.95 (*0-685-41935-5*) Gallopade Pub Group.
—Meow! New Hampshire Cats in History, Mystery, Legend, Lore, Humor & More! (Illus.). (gr. 3-12). 1994. PLB 24.95 (*0-7933-3400-4*); pap. 14.95 (*0-7933-3401-2*); computer disk 29.95 (*0-7933-3402-0*) Gallopade Pub Group.
—Meow! New Jersey Cats in History, Mystery, Legend, Lore, Humor & More! (Illus.). (gr. 3-12). 1994. PLB 24.95 (*0-7933-3404-7*); pap. 14.95 (*0-685-48034-8*); computer disk 29.95 (*0-7933-3406-3*) Gallopade Pub Group.
—Meow! New Mexico Cats in History, Mystery, Legend, Lore, Humor & More! (Illus.). (gr. 3-12). 1994. PLB 24.95 (*0-7933-3407-1*); pap. 14.95 (*0-7933-3408-X*); computer disk 29.95 (*0-7933-3409-8*) Gallopade Pub Group.
—Meow! New York Cats in History, Mystery, Legend, Lore, Humor & More! (Illus.). (gr. 3-12). 1994. PLB 24.95 (*0-7933-3410-1*); pap. 14.95 (*0-7933-3411-X*); computer disk 29.95 (*0-7933-3412-8*) Gallopade Pub Group.
—Meow! North Carolina Cats in History, Mystery, Legend, Lore, Humor & More! (Illus.). (gr. 3-12). 1994. PLB 24.95 (*0-7933-3413-6*); pap. 14.95 (*0-7933-3414-4*); computer disk 29.95 (*0-7933-3415-2*) Gallopade Pub Group.
—Meow! North Dakota Cats in History, Mystery, Legend, Lore, Humor & More! (Illus.). (gr. 3-12). 1994. PLB 24.95 (*0-7933-3416-0*); pap. 14.95 (*0-7933-3417-9*); computer disk 29.95 (*0-7933-3418-7*) Gallopade Pub Group.
—Meow! Ohio Cats in History, Mystery, Legend, Lore, Humor & More! (Illus.). (gr. 3-12). 1994. PLB 24.95 (*0-7933-3419-5*); pap. 14.95 (*0-7933-3420-9*); computer disk 29.95 (*0-7933-3421-7*) Gallopade Pub Group.
—Meow! Oklahoma Cats in History, Mystery, Legend, Lore, Humor & More! (Illus.). (gr. 3-12). 1994. PLB 24.95 (*0-7933-3422-5*); pap. 14.95 (*0-7933-3423-3*); computer disk 29.95 (*0-7933-3424-1*) Gallopade Pub Group.
—Meow! Oregon Cats in History, Mystery, Legend, Lore, Humor & More! (Illus.). (gr. 3-12). 1994. PLB 24.95 (*0-7933-3425-X*); pap. 14.95 (*0-7933-3426-8*); computer disk 29.95 (*0-7933-3427-6*) Gallopade Pub Group.
—Meow! Pennsylvania Cats in History, Mystery, Legend, Lore, Humor & More! (Illus.). (gr. 3-12). 1994. PLB 24.95 (*0-7933-3428-4*); pap. 14.95 (*0-7933-3429-2*); computer disk 29.95 (*0-7933-3430-6*) Gallopade Pub Group.
—Meow! Rhode Island Cats in History, Mystery, Legend, Lore, Humor & More! (Illus.). (gr. 3-12). 1994. PLB 24.95 (*0-7933-3431-4*); pap. 14.95 (*0-7933-3432-2*); computer disk 29.95 (*0-7933-3433-0*) Gallopade Pub Group.
—Meow! South Carolina Cats in History, Mystery, Legend, Lore, Humor & More! (Illus.). (gr. 3-12). 1994. PLB 24.95 (*0-7933-3434-9*); pap. 14.95 (*0-7933-3435-7*); computer disk 29.95 (*0-7933-3436-5*) Gallopade Pub Group.
—Meow! South Dakota Cats in History, Mystery, Legend, Lore, Humor & More! (Illus.). (gr. 3-12). 1994. PLB 24.95 (*0-7933-3437-3*); pap. 14.95 (*0-7933-3438-1*); computer disk 29.95 (*0-7933-3439-X*) Gallopade Pub Group.
—Meow! Tennessee Cats in History, Mystery, Legend, Lore, Humor & More! (Illus.). (gr. 3-12). 1994. PLB 24.95 (*0-7933-3440-3*); pap. 14.95 (*0-7933-3441-1*); computer disk 29.95 (*0-7933-3442-X*) Gallopade Pub Group.
—Meow! Texas Cats in History, Mystery, Legend, Lore, Humor & More! (Illus.). (gr. 3-12). 1994. PLB 24.95 (*0-7933-3443-8*); pap. 14.95 (*0-7933-3444-6*); computer disk 29.95 (*0-7933-3445-4*) Gallopade Pub Group.
—Meow! Utah Cats in History, Mystery, Legend, Lore, Humor & More! (Illus.). (gr. 3-12). 1994. PLB 24.95 (*0-7933-3446-2*); pap. 14.95 (*0-7933-3447-0*); computer disk 29.95 (*0-7933-3448-9*) Gallopade Pub Group.
—Meow! Vermont Cats in History, Mystery, Legend, Lore, Humor & More! (Illus.). (gr. 3-12). 1994. PLB 24.95 (*0-7933-3449-7*); pap. 14.95 (*0-7933-3450-0*); computer disk 29.95 (*0-7933-3451-9*) Gallopade Pub Group.

—Meow! Virginia Cats in History, Mystery, Legend, Lore, Humor & More! (Illus.). (gr. 3-12). 1994. PLB 24.95 (*0-7933-3452-7*); pap. 14.95 (*0-7933-3453-5*); computer disk 29.95 (*0-7933-3454-3*) Gallopade Pub Group.
—Meow! Washington Cats in History, Mystery, Legend, Lore, Humor & More! (Illus.). (gr. 3-12). 1994. PLB 24.95 (*0-7933-3455-1*); pap. 14.95 (*0-7933-3456-X*); computer disk 29.95 (*0-7933-3457-8*) Gallopade Pub Group.
—Meow! Washington DC Cats in History, Mystery, Legend, Lore, Humor & More! (Illus.). (gr. 3-12). 1994. PLB 24.95 (*0-7933-3338-5*); pap. 14.95 (*0-7933-3339-3*); computer disk 29.95 (*0-7933-3340-7*) Gallopade Pub Group.
—Meow! West Virginia Cats in History, Mystery, Legend, Lore, Humor & More! (Illus.). (gr. 3-12). 1994. PLB 24.95 (*0-7933-3458-6*); pap. 14.95 (*0-7933-3459-4*); computer disk 29.95 (*0-7933-3460-8*) Gallopade Pub Group.
—Meow! Wisconsin Cats in History, Mystery, Legend, Lore, Humor & More! (Illus.). (gr. 3-12). 1994. PLB 24.95 (*0-7933-3461-6*); pap. 14.95 (*0-7933-3462-4*); computer disk 29.95 (*0-7933-3463-2*) Gallopade Pub Group.
—Meow! Wyoming Cats in History, Mystery, Legend, Lore, Humor & More! (Illus.). (gr. 3-12). 1994. PLB 24.95 (*0-7933-3464-0*); pap. 14.95 (*0-7933-3465-9*); computer disk 29.95 (*0-7933-3466-7*) Gallopade Pub Group.
Mattern, Joanne. Picture Book of Cats. Pistolesi, Roseanna, illus. LC 90-42548. 24p. (gr. 1-4). 1991. PLB 9.59 (*0-8167-2146-7*); pap. 2.50 (*0-8167-2147-5*) Troll Assocs.
Milton, Joyce. Big Cats. Duran, Silvia, illus. LC 94-7361. 1994. write for info. (*0-448-40565-2*, G&D); pap. write for info. (*0-448-40564-4*, G&D) Putnam Pub Group.
Morris, Dean. Cats. rev. ed. LC 87-16699. (Illus.). 48p. (gr. 2-6). 1987. PLB 10.95 (*0-8172-3205-2*) Raintree Steck-V.
Naples, Marge. A Step-by-Step Book about Siamese Cats. (Illus.). 64p. (gr. 9-12). 1988. pap. 3.95 (*0-86622-473-4*, SK-021) TFH Pubns.
Nottridge, Rhoda. Let's Look At Big Cats. (ps-3). 1990. PLB 11.40 (*0-531-18285-1*, Pub. by Bookwright Pr) Watts.
Overbeck, Cynthia. Cats. Yoshino, Shin, illus. LC 83-17530. 48p. (gr. 4 up). 1983. PLB 19.95 (*0-8225-1480-X*) Lerner Pubns.
Owl Magazine Editors, ed. The Kids' Cat Book. (Illus.). 96p. (gr. 3 up). 1992. pap. 9.95 (*0-920775-51-9*, Pub. by Greey de Pencier CN) Firefly Bks Ltd.
Parsons, Alexandra. Amazing Cats. Young, Jerry, photos by. LC 90-31885. (Illus.). 32p. (Orig.). (gr. 1-5). 1990. lib. bdg. 9.99 (*0-679-90690-8*); pap. 7.99 (*0-679-80690-3*) Knopf Bks Yng Read.
Petersen-Fleming, Judy & Fleming, Bill. Puppy Care & Critters, Too! Ringold-Reiss, Debra, photos by. LC 93-23129. (Illus.). 40p. 1993. 15.00 (*0-688-12565-4*, Tambourine Bks); PLB 14.93 (*0-688-12566-2*, Tambourine Bks) Morrow.
Petty, Kate. Baby Animals: Kittens. (Illus.). 24p. (ps-3). 1992. pap. 3.95 (*0-8120-4967-5*) Barron.
—Cats. (Illus.). 24p. (ps-3). 1993. pap. 3.95 (*0-8120-1485-5*) Barron.
—Gatos. Thompson, George, illus. LC 90-71414. (SPA.). 24p. (gr. k-4). 1991. PLB 10.90 (*0-531-07916-3*) Watts.
Pfloog, Jan. Asi Son los Gatitos! (Kittens are Like That) Pfloog, Jan, illus. Saunders, Paola B., tr. LC 93-19920. (Illus.). 32p. (ps-3). 1993. pap. 2.25 (*0-679-84719-7*) Random Bks Yng Read.
—Kittens Are Like That. Pfloog, Jan, illus. LC 75-36469. 32p. (ps-1). 1976. 2.25 (*0-394-83243-4*) Random Bks Yng Read.
Piers, Helen. Taking Care of Your Cat. (Illus.). 32p. 1992. pap. 4.95 (*0-8120-4873-3*) Barron.
Posell, Elsa. Cats. LC 82-23484. (Illus.). 48p. (gr. k-4). 1983. PLB 12.85 (*0-516-01671-7*) Childrens.
Rees, Yvonne. Cats. (Illus.). 64p. 1991. 4.99 (*0-517-05153-2*) Random Hse Value.
Richards, Dorothy S. The World of Cats. (Illus.). 64p. 1989. 7.99 (*0-517-69085-3*) Random Hse Value.
Roach, Margaret J. I Love You, Charles Henry: Cats & Dogs in My Life. Moore, Susan & Craft, Page, eds. Moore, Susan J., illus. (gr. 1-6). 1994. pap. 13.50 (*1-882666-02-X*) M Roach & Assocs.
Ryden, Hope, photos by & text by. Your Cat's Wild Cousins. (Illus.). 48p. (gr. 2-5). 1992. 16.00 (*0-525-67354-7*, Lodestar Bks) Dutton Child Bks.
Schwartz, Alvin. Stories to Tell a Cat. Huerta, Catherine, illus. LC 91-37257. 80p. (gr. 4 up). 1992. 15.00 (*0-06-020850-3*); PLB 14.89 (*0-06-020851-1*) HarpC Child Bks.
Scott, Mary. A Picture Book of Wild Cats. Pistolesi, Roseanna, illus. LC 91-16500. 24p. (gr. 1-4). 1992. PLB 9.59 (*0-8167-2430-X*); pap. 2.50 (*0-8167-2431-8*) Troll Assocs.
Selsam, Millicent E. How Kittens Grow. 1992. pap. 2.50 (*0-590-44784-X*) Scholastic Inc.
Selsam, Millicent E. & Hunt, Joyce. First Look at Cats. Springer, Harriett, illus. LC 80-7673. 32p. (gr. 1-4). 1981. 7.95 (*0-8027-6398-7*); PLB 9.85 (*0-8027-6399-5*) Walker & Co.
Simon, Seymour. Big Cats. Simon, Seymour, illus. LC 90-36374. 40p. (gr. k-3). 1991. 17.00 (*0-06-021646-8*); PLB 16.89 (*0-06-021647-6*) HarpC Child Bks.
—Big Cats. LC 90-36374. (Illus.). 40p. (gr. k-3). 1994. pap. 5.95 (*0-06-446119-X*, Trophy) HarpC Child Bks.
Spinelli, Eileen. Cats. (Illus.). 64p. (gr. k-4). 1992. PLB 12.95 (*1-878363-82-4*, HTS Bks) Forest Hse.
—Kittens. (Illus.). 64p. (gr. k-4). 1992. PLB 13.75 (*1-878363-86-7*, HTS Bks) Forest Hse.
Stolz, Mary. Cat Walk. Blegvad, Erik, illus. LC 82-47576. 128p. (gr. 3-7). 1983. HarpC Child Bks.
Stone, Lynn. Big Cat Discover Library, 6 bks, Reading Level 2. (Illus.). (gr. k-5). 1989. Set. PLB 71.64 (*0-86592-500-3*) Rourke Corp.
—Wild Cats. LC 92-34499. 1993. 12.67 (*0-86625-441-2*); 9.50s.p. (*0-685-66272-1*) Rourke Pubns.
Stroble, Bill. Frisky Kitties: My Book of What God Made. (ps). 1989. bds. 6.99 (*1-55513-732-6*, Chariot Bks) Chariot Family.
Tanaka, Shelley. The Cat Lover's Diary. Fanelli, Jenny, ed. Baron, Elaine, photos by. Reynolds, Nancy L. & Macpherson, Elaine, illus. 176p. (gr. 5 up). 1984. pap. 8.95 (*0-394-86613-4*) Random Bks Yng Read.
Vrbova, Zuza. Kittens. McAulay, Robert, illus. 48p. (gr. 2 up). 1990. PLB 9.95 (*0-86622-553-6*, J-003) TFH Pubns.
Waverly, Barney. How Big? How Fast? How Hungry? A Book about Cats. Henry, Steve, illus. 24p. (ps-2). 1990. PLB 17.10 (*0-8172-3582-5*); PLB 10.95 pkg. of 3 (*0-685-58552-2*) Raintree Steck-V.
Wildlife Education, Ltd. Staff. Big Cats. Meltzer, Dave, et al, illus. 20p. (Orig.). (gr. 5 up). 1981. pap. 2.75 (*0-937934-04-6*) Wildlife Educ.
—Little Cats. Orr, Richard & Stuart, Walter, illus. 200p. (gr. 5 up). 1983. pap. 2.75 (*0-937934-16-X*) Wildlife Educ.
—Little Cats. Orr, Richard & Stuart, Walter, illus. 24p. 1992. 13.95 (*0-937934-82-8*) Wildlife Educ.
Wilkinson, Sally. Cats Are People Too: By PattySue, Herself. 47p. (Orig.). (gr. 5 up). 1989. pap. 6.95 (*0-9623354-5-2*) OP Inc.
Winston, Peggy D. Wild Cats. Crump, Donald J., ed. LC 81-47742. 32p. (ps-3). 1981. lib. bdg. 16.95 (*0-87044-401-8*) Natl Geog.
Wolff, George. I Can Read About Cats & Kittens. LC 72-96959. (Illus.). (gr. 2-4). 1973. pap. 2.50 (*0-89375-056-5*) Troll Assocs.

CATS–FICTION

Abercrombie, Barbara. Charlie Anderson. Graham, Mark, illus. LC 89-2449. 32p. (ps-4). 1990. SBE 13.95 (*0-689-50486-1*, M K McElderry) Macmillan Child Grp.
—Michael & the Cats. Graham, Mark, illus. LC 92-23950. 32p. (ps-2). 1993. SBE 13.95 (*0-689-50543-4*, M K McElderry) Macmillan Child Grp.
Ahlberg, Allan. The Black Cat. Amstutz, Andre, illus. LC 92-45621. 32p. (gr. k up). 1993. pap. text ed. 4.95 (*0-688-12679-0*, Mulberry) Morrow.
Albee, Jo. The Lost Kitten. Goldberg, Grace, illus. 24p. (ps-2). 1992. pap. 0.99 (*1-56293-111-3*) McClanahan Bk.
Alden, L. Cat's Adventure in Alphabet Town. McCallum, J., illus. LC 91-3605. 32p. (ps-2). 1992. PLB 11.80 (*0-516-05403-1*) Childrens.
Alexander, Lloyd. The Cat Who Wished to Be a Man. 120p. (gr. 4-7). 1977. (DCB); (DCB) Dutton Child Bks.
—Cat Who Wished to Be a Man. (gr. 4-7). 1992. pap. 3.50 (*0-440-40580-7*) Dell.
Aliki. Tabby: A Story in Pictures. Aliki, illus. LC 94-18523. 1995. 14.00 (*0-06-024915-3*); PLB 13.89 (*0-06-024916-1*) HarpC.
Allen, Jonathan. Purple Sock, Pink Sock. Allen, Jonathan, illus. LC 91-43379. 12p. (ps). 1992. 3.95 (*0-688-11782-1*, Tambourine Bks) Morrow.
Allen, Pamela. My Cat Maisie. (Illus.). 32p. (ps-3). 1991. 12.95 (*0-670-83251-0*) Viking Child Bks.
—My Cat Maisie. (Illus.). 32p. (ps-3). 1993. pap. 4.99 (*0-14-054237-X*, Puffin) Puffin Bks.
Amery, H. Kitten's Day Out. (Illus.). 16p. (ps-3). 1992. pap. 3.95 (*0-7460-1415-5*) EDC.
Andrews & McMeel Inc. Staff. Tom & Jerry Friends to the End. (ps-3). 1993. 14.95 (*1-878685-26-0*) Turner Pub GA.
Anello, Christine. Farmyard Cat. (ps-3). 1990. pap. 3.95 (*0-86896-392-5*, Pub. by Ashton Scholastic AT) Heinemann.
Antle, Nancy. The Good Bad Cat. Gregorich, Barbara, ed. (Illus.). 16p. (Orig.). (gr. k-2). 1985. pap. 2.25 (*0-88743-012-0*, 06012) Sch Zone Pub Co.
—The Good Bad Cat. Gregorich, Barbara, ed. (Illus.). 32p. (gr. k-2). 1992. pap. 3.95 (*0-88743-410-X*, 06062) Sch Zone Pub Co.
Apablasa, Bill. Rhymin' Simon & the Mystery of the Fat Cat. Thiesing, Lisa, illus. LC 90-21054. 64p. (gr. 2-5). 1991. 10.95 (*0-525-44702-4*, DCB) Dutton Child Bks.
Archambault, John & Martin, Bill, Jr. A Beautiful Feast for a Big King Cat. Degen, Bruce, illus. LC 92-32331. 32p. (ps-3). 1994. 13.00 (*0-06-022903-9*); PLB 12.89 (*0-06-022904-7*) HarpC Child Bks.
Arnold, Marsha D. Heart of a Tiger. Henterly, Jamichael, illus. LC 94-17126. (gr. 1-8). 1995. write for info. (*0-8037-1695-8*); PLB write for info. (*0-8037-1696-6*) Dial Bks Young.
Asare, Meshack. Cat in Search of a Friend. LC 86-10583. (Illus.). 32p. (ps-5). 1986. 10.95 (*0-916291-07-3*, Cranky Nell Bk) Kane-Miller Bk.
Asch, Frank & Vagin, Vladimir. Here Comes the Cat! Asch, Frank & Vladimir, Vagin, illus. 1991. pap. 3.95 (*0-590-41854-8*) Scholastic Inc.
Averill, Esther. Fire Cat. Averill, Esther, illus. LC 60-10234. 64p. (gr. k-3). 1960. PLB 13.89 (*0-06-020196-7*) HarpC Child Bks.
—The Fire Cat. LC 60-10234. (Illus.). 64p. (gr. k-3). 1983. pap. 3.50 (*0-06-444038-9*, Trophy) HarpC Child Bks.
—Jenny's Birthday Book. Averill, Esther, illus. LC 54-6589. 32p. (gr. k-3). 1954. PLB 14.89 (*0-06-020251-3*) HarpC Child Bks.
—The School for Cats & Jenny's Moonlight Adventure. Averill, Esther, illus. (gr. k-3). 1990. pap. 2.95 (*0-553-15362-5*) Bantam.
Axworthy, Anni. Along Came Toto. Axworthy, Anni, illus. LC 92-52992. 32p. (ps-3). 1993. 12.95 (*1-56402-172-6*) Candlewick Pr.
Ayme, Marcel. Patte du Chat. Sabatier, Roland, illus. (FRE.). 72p. (gr. 1-5). 1990. pap. 9.95 (*2-07-031200-3*) Schoenhof.
Babbitt, Natalie. Nellie: A Cat on Her Own. Babbitt, Natalie, illus. (ps up). 1989. 14.00 (*0-374-35506-1*) FS&G.
—Nellie: A Cat on Her Own. (Illus.). (ps-3). 1992. pap. 4.95 (*0-374-45496-5*, Sunburst) FS&G.
Bahous, Sally. Sitti & the Cats. LC 98-80262. 24p. (gr. 3-6). 1993. 13.95x (*1-879373-61-0*) R Rinehart.
Baillie, Marilyn. My Cat. (ps-3). 1994. pap. 6.95 (*0-316-07688-0*) Little.
Baker, Barbara & Winborn, Martha. Digby & Kate Again. (Illus.). (gr. k-3). 1994. pap. 3.25 (*0-14-036665-2*) Puffin Bks.
Baker, Leslie. The Antique Store Cat. Baker, Leslie, illus. 32p. (ps-3). 1992. 14.95 (*0-316-07837-9*) Little.
—Third Story Cat. (ps-3). 1990. pap. 4.95 (*0-316-07836-0*) Little.
Balian, Lorna. Amelia's Nine Lives. Balian, Lorna, illus. 32p. (ps-3). 1987. Repr. of 1986 ed. 7.50 (*0-687-37096-5*) Humbug Bks.
—Amelia's Nine Lives. Balian, Lorna, illus. 32p. (ps-3). 1986. PLB 13.95 (*0-687-01250-3*) Humbug Bks.
Ball, Jacqueline A. A Kitten Named Cuddles. (gr. 4-7). 1991. pap. 2.95 (*0-06-106038-0*, PL) HarpC.
A Balloon for Katie Kitten. 28p. (ps-2). 1992. 3.95 (*0-7214-5308-2*, S915-1) Ladybird Bks.
Baram, Bella. The Cat Who Looked for a House. Kriss, David, tr. from HEB. Elchanan, illus. 24p. (Orig.). (ps). 1992. pap. text ed. 3.00x (*1-56134-140-1*) Dushkin Pub.
Barber, Antonia. The Mousehole Cat. Bayley, Nicola, illus. LC 90-31533. 40p. (gr. k-3). 1990. SBE 14.95 (*0-02-708331-4*, Macmillan Child Bk) Macmillan Child Grp.
Bare, Colleen S. Critter: The Class Cat. (Illus.). 32p. (ps-2). 1993. pap. 3.99 (*0-14-055266-9*, Puff Unicorn) Puffin Bks.
Barkan, Joanne. That Fat Hat. Swanson, Maggie, illus. LC 92-7414. 1992. 2.95 (*0-590-45643-1*) Scholastic Inc.
Barnes, Peter W. Nat, Nat, the Nantucket Cat. Arciero, Susan, illus. 30p. 1993. 15.95 (*0-9637688-0-8*) Vacation Spot.
Bauer, Marion D. Ghost Eye. 1992. 12.95 (*0-590-45298-3*, Scholastic Hardcover) Scholastic Inc.
Bayley, Nicola. Copycats. Bailey, Nicole, illus. LC 91-58722. 96p. (ps up). 1992. 14.95 (*1-56402-114-9*) Candlewick Pr.
Bell, Clare. Ratha & Thistle-Chaser. LC 89-36807. 240p. (gr. 7 up). 1990. SBE 14.95 (*0-689-50462-4*, M K McElderry) Macmillan Child Grp.
Bennett, Geraldine M. Katrina Tells of Healing a Kitten. (gr. k up). Date not set. pap. write for info. New Dawn NY.
Bennett, Marian. God Made Kittens. (Illus.). 24p. (ps). 1980. 2.50 (*0-87239-404-2*, 3636) Standard Pub.
Berenzy, A. Puss in Boots. 1994. 14.95 (*0-8050-1284-2*) H Holt & Co.
Bingham, Mindy. Minou. Maeno, Itoko, illus. LC 86-26539. 64p. (gr. k-6). 1987. 14.95 (*0-911655-36-0*) Advocacy Pr.
The Birthday Party Prize. 28p. (ps-2). 1992. 3.95 (*0-7214-5310-4*, S915-3 SER.) Ladybird Bks.
Bissell, LeClair & Watherwax, Richard. The Cat Who Drank Too Much. (ENG & SPA., Illus.). 48p. (gr. 4 up). 1982. pap. 5.00 (*0-911153-00-4*) Spanish ed., 03/1984 (*0-911153-01-2*) Bibulophile Pr.
Blacker, Terence. You're Under Arrest, Ms. Wiz. Goffe, Toni, illus. 64p. (gr. 2-5). 1990. pap. 2.95 (*0-8120-4499-1*) Barron.
Blau, Judith. Kitten Mitten's Stocking. Blau, Judith, illus. 7p. (ps). 1992. incl. puppet 5.99 (*0-679-83046-4*) Random Bks Yng Read.
Blume, Judy. The Pain & the Great One. Trivas, Irene, illus. LC 84-11009. 32p. (gr. k-3). 1984. RSBE 14.95 (*0-02-711100-8*, Bradbury Pr) Macmillan Child Grp.
Boivin, Kelly. Where Is Mittens? Martin, Clovis, illus. LC 90-2220. 32p. (ps-2). 1990. PLB 10.25 (*0-516-02060-9*); pap. 2.95 (*0-516-42060-7*) Childrens.
Borton, Lady. Fat Chance! Ray, Deborah K., illus. 32p. (ps-3). 1993. 14.95 (*0-399-21963-3*, Philomel) Putnam Pub Group.
Bradbury, Thomas E. Scraggly's New Home. Goyette, Ron & Funk, Nancy C., trs. (Illus.). 32p. (Orig.). (gr. k-5). 1987. pap. text ed. write for info. (*0-9618945-0-4*) Tern Pubns.
Braun, Lilian J. The Cat Who Sniffed Glue. 1989. pap. 4.99 (*0-515-09954-6*) Jove Pubns.
Broome, Errol. Tangles. James, Ann, illus. LC 93-30637. 112p. (gr. 3-7). 1994. 13.00 (*0-679-85713-3*) Knopf Bks Yng Read.

Brouillard, Anne. Three Cats. LC 91-34180. (Illus.). 32p. 1992. 6.98 (0-934738-97-1) Thomasson-Grant.

Brown, Margaret W. A Pussycat's Christmas. new ed. Mortimer, Anne, illus. LC 93-4424. 32p. (gr. k-4). 1994. 14.00 (0-06-023532-2); PLB 13.89 (0-06-023533-0) HarpC Child Bks.

—Sneakers: Seven Stories About a Cat. Charlot, Jean, illus. (ps-3). 1985. PLB 14.89 (0-06-020767-1) HarpC Child Bks.

Brown, Ruth. Copycat. LC 94-20451. (Illus.). 32p. (ps-1). 1994. 14.99 (0-525-45326-1, DCB) Dutton Child Bks.

—Our Cat Flossie. Brown, Ruth, illus. LC 86-19895. 32p. (ps-1). 1990. pap. 3.95 (0-525-44608-7, DCB) Dutton Child Bks.

Bryan, Ashley. The Cat's Purr. LC 84-21534. (Illus.). 48p. (ps-3). 1985. SBE 12.95 (0-689-31086-2, Atheneum Child Bk) Macmillan Child Grp.

Brychta, Alex. The Arrow. (ps-k). 1987. 2.95 (0-19-272166-6) OUP.

Buchanan, Doris A. Mr. Grumpuss. 1991. 7.95 (0-533-09546-8) Vantage.

Buckman, Mary. Magical Muriel. LC 90-60453. (Illus., Orig.). (gr. k-2). 1991. pap. text ed. 12.95 (1-879414-07-4) Mary Bee Creat.

Bulla, Clyde R. The Valentine Cat. Weisgard, Leonard, illus. LC 94-18353. 64p. (gr. k-3). 1995. pap. text ed. 2.25 (0-8167-3599-9) Troll Assocs.

Burke, Roma N. Whiskers, a Kitten's Story. LC 87-62417. 120p. (gr. 3-8). 1988. pap. 8.95 (0-88100-058-2) Natl Writ Pr.

Burnford, Sheila. The Incredible Journey. 1985. pap. 3.99 (0-553-15616-0) Bantam.

—The Incredible Journey. 1984. pap. 3.99 (0-553-27442-2) Bantam.

Burns, Theresa. You're Not My Cat. Burns, Theresa, illus. LC 88-8388. 32p. (ps-3). 1989. (Lipp Jr Bks) HarpC Child Bks.

Butler, Beverly. Ghost Cat. 1988. pap. 2.75 (0-590-43443-8, Scholastic) Scholastic Inc.

Calhoun, Mary. Henry the Sailor Cat. Ingraham, Erick, illus. LC 92-29794. 40p. (gr. k up). 1994. 15.00g (0-688-10840-7); PLB 14.93 (0-688-10841-5) Morrow Jr Bks.

—High-Wire Henry. Ingraham, Erick, illus. LC 89-35642. 40p. (gr. k up). 1991. 13.95 (0-688-08983-6); PLB 13.88 (0-688-08984-4, Morrow Jr Bks) Morrow Jr Bks.

—The Witch of Hissing Hill. McCaffery, Janet, illus. LC 64-15475. (gr. k-3). 1964. PLB 13.88 (0-688-31762-6) Morrow Jr Bks.

—Wobble the Witch Cat. Duvoisin, Roger, illus. LC 58-5018. 32p. (gr. k-3). 1958. PLB 13.88 (0-688-31621-2) Morrow Jr Bks.

Calmenson, Stephanie. Tom & Jerry: The Movie--Digest Novelization. (gr. 4-7). 1993. pap. 3.25 (0-590-47115-5) Scholastic Inc.

Carle, Eric. Have You Seen My Cat? LC 87-15262. (Illus.). (ps up). 1991. pap. 14.95 (0-88708-054-5) Picture Bk Studio.

—Have You Seen My Cat? Carle, Eric, illus. 1991. pap. 3.95 (0-590-44461-1, Blue Ribbon Bks) Scholastic Inc.

Carlson, Natalie S. Spooky & the Bad Luck Raven. Glass, Andrew, illus. LC 87-15471. (ps-1). 1988. 12.95 (0-688-07650-5); lib. bdg. 12.88 (0-688-07651-3) Lothrop.

—Spooky & the Witch's Goat. Glass, Andrew, illus. LC 88-21628. 32p. (gr. k-4). 1989. 12.95 (0-688-08540-7); PLB 12.88 (0-688-08541-5) Lothrop.

Carris, Joan D. Witch Cat. (gr. 5 up). 1986. pap. 2.95 (0-440-49477-X, YB) Dell.

Casey, P. My Cat Jack. LC 93-39669. 32p. (ps up). 1994. 14.95 (1-56402-410-5) Candlewick Pr.

Cassedy, Sylvia. Best Cat Suit of All. LC 87-24659. (ps-3). 1991. 10.95 (0-8037-0516-6); PLB 10.89 (0-8037-0517-4) Dial Bks Young.

The Cat & the Rat EV, Unit 6. (gr. 2). 1991. 5-pack 21.25 (0-88106-750-4) Charlesbridge Pub.

Cat, Christopher & Cullen, Countee. My Lives & How I Lost Them. Owens, Nubia, illus. Strickland, Dorothy, frwd. by. LC 92-46738. (Illus.). 174p. (gr. 3-5). 1993. 7.95 (0-8136-7209-0) Silver Burdett Pr.

The Cat in the Hat. Date not set. write for info. (0-679-86348-6) Random Bks Yng Read.

The Cat Who Learned to Sail. LC 89-64308. (Illus.). 32p. (gr. 4-8). 1991. 13.95 (0-931595-07-X); pap. 7.95 (0-931595-04-5) Seascape Enters.

Cauley, Lorinda B. Puss in Boots. LC 86-7629. (Illus.). 32p. (ps-3). 1988. 13.95 (0-15-264227-7, HB Juv Bks); pap. 3.95 (0-15-264228-5) HarBrace.

Cebulash, Mel. Catnapper. (gr. 3-8). 1992. PLB 8.95 (0-89565-878-X) Childs World.

Cech, John. The Southernmost Cat. Osborn, Kathy, illus. LC 93-40671. 1995. 14.00 (0-02-717885-4) Macmillan Child Grp.

Chalmers, Mary. Merry Christmas, Harry. new ed. LC 90-27516. (Illus.). 32p. (ps-2). 1992. 13.00 (0-06-022739-7) HarpC Child Bks.

Charles, Donald. El Ano de Gato Galano (Calico Cat's Year) Kratky, Lada, tr. from GER. Charles, Donald, illus. (SPA.). 32p. (ps-3). 1984. PLB 11.80 (0-516-33461-1); pap. 3.95 (0-516-53461-0) Childrens.

—Calico Cat at School. LC 81-6096. (Illus.). 32p. (ps-3). 1981. pap. 3.95 (0-516-43445-4) Childrens.

—Cuenta con Gato Galano (Count on Calico Cat) Kratky, Lada, tr. from ENG. Charles, Donald, illus. LC 74-8007. (SPA.). 32p. (ps-3). 1984. pap. 3.95 (0-516-53479-3) Childrens.

—Gata Galano Observa los Colores: Calico Cat Looks at Colors. LC 75-12948. (SPA., Illus.). 32p. (ps-3). 1992. PLB 11.80 (0-516-33437-9); pap. 3.95 (0-516-53437-8) Childrens.

—El Libro de Ejercicios de Gato Galano (Calico Cat's Exercise Book) Kratky, Lada, tr. from ENG. Charles, Doanld, illus. LC 82-9640. (SPA.). 32p. (ps-3). 1984. pap. 3.95 (0-516-53457-2) Childrens.

—Mira las Formas con Gato Galano (Calico Cat Looks at Shapes) LC 75-12947. (SPA., Illus.). 32p. (ps-3). 1987. PLB 11.80 (0-516-33436-0); pap. 3.95 (0-516-53436-X) Childrens.

Chenoweth, Margaret. Scaredy Cat Finds a Home. (ps-3). 1991. pap. 2.50 (0-89954-515-7) Antioch Pub Co.

Cherry, Lynne. Archie, Follow Me. LC 89-77160. (Illus.). 32p. (ps-1). 1990. 12.95 (0-525-44647-8, DCB) Dutton Child Bks.

The Christmas Kitten: Timeless Tales. 1992. 4.99 (0-517-06968-7) Random Hse Value.

Cleary, Beverly. Socks. Darwin, Beatrice, illus. LC 72-10298. 160p. (gr. 3-7). 1973. 11.95 (0-688-20067-2); PLB 11.88 (0-688-30067-7, Morrow Jr Bks) Morrow Jr Bks.

Clement, Claude. Kitty's Special Job. Raquois, Olivier, illus. LC 91-46233. 22p. (ps-3). 1992. 6.99 (0-89577-427-5, Readers Digest Kids) RD Assn.

Cline, Paul. Grummit's Day. 1991. 12.95 (0-9625261-3-4) Medlicott Pr.

—My Mother's Hands. 1991. pap. 5.95 (0-9625261-2-6) Medlicott Pr.

Clymer, Susan. Nine Lives of Adventure-Cat. (gr. 4-7). 1994. pap. 2.75 (0-590-47149-X) Scholastic Inc.

Coatsworth, Elizabeth. The Cat Who Went to Heaven. Ward, Lynd, illus. LC 58-10917. 72p. (gr. 4-6). 1967. RSBE 15.00 (0-02-719710-7, Macmillan Child Bk) Macmillan Child Grp.

—The Cat Who Went to Heaven. rev. ed. Ward, Lynd & Jael, illus. LC 90-175. 80p. (gr. 3-7). 1990. pap. 3.95 (0-689-71433-5, Aladdin) Macmillan Child Grp.

Coffelt, N. Good Night, Sigmund! 1992. 13.95 (0-15-200464-5, HB Juv Bks) HarBrace.

Coffelt, Nancy. The Dog Who Cried Woof. LC 94-5653. 1994. write for info. (0-15-200201-4, Gulliver Bks) HarBrace.

Coil, Suzanne M. Mabel. Mayfield, Shannon, illus. Gilbert, Peaches, created by. LC 94-9791. (Illus.). 32p. (gr. 4-7). 1994. 15.95 (0-87905-602-9) Gibbs Smith Pub.

Cook, Veronica L. Mike the Copycat: Adventures & Stories of Cat Tails. Cook, Veronica L., illus. 50p. (Orig.). (ps up). 1989. pap. text ed. write for info. Ronnie Two Pub.

Coon, Alma S. Amy, Ben, & Catalpa the Cat: A Fanciful Story of This & That. Owens, Gail, illus. 40p. (ps-2). 1990. 8.95 (0-87935-079-2) Williamsburg.

Cooper, Helen. The House Cat. LC 93-34217. (ps-2). 1994. 15.95 (0-590-48172-X) Scholastic Inc.

Coran, Pierre. The Crying Cat. (Illus.). 32p. (gr. k-2). 1991. 18.50 (0-89565-745-7); 12.95s.p. (0-685-55072-9) Childs World.

Corlett, William. The Gondolier's Cat. Turska, Krystyna, illus. 32p. (ps-1). 1994. 19.95 (0-340-54165-2, Pub. by Hodder & Stoughton UK) Trafalgar.

Corrin, Ruth. Mr. Cat. Hurford, John, illus. LC 91-20236. 32p. (ps-3). 1991. 13.95 (0-940793-89-X, Crocodile Bks) Interlink Pub.

Cosgrove, Stephen. Fanny. James, Robin, illus. 32p. (Orig.). (gr. 1-4). 1986. pap. 2.95 (0-8431-1460-6) Price Stern.

Coxon, Michele. The Cat Who Lost His Purr. Coxon, Michele, illus. 32p. (gr. k-3). 1991. 12.95 (0-87226-453-X, Bedrick Blackie) P Bedrick Bks.

Coxon, Michelle. Who Will Play with Me? Coxon, Michelle, illus. LC 91-40498. 32p. (gr. k-3). 1992. PLB 12.95 (0-87226-469-6, Bedrick Blackie) P Bedrick Bks.

Craig, Janet. Muffy & Fluffy: The Kittens Who Didn't Agree. Hall, Susan, illus. LC 87-16227. 32p. (gr. k-2). 1988. PLB 7.89 (0-8167-1227-1); pap. text ed. 1.95 (0-8167-1228-X) Troll Assocs.

Crozat, Francois. I Am a Little Cat. (Illus.). 28p. (ps-k). 1992. 8.95 (0-8120-6277-9); miniature version o.p. 2.95 (0-8120-6287-6) Barron.

Cutler, Ebbitt. If I Were a Cat I Would Sit in a Tree. Arnold, Rist, illus. 28p. (gr. k-4). 1985. text ed. 7.95 (0-88776-177-1, Dist. by U of Toronto Pr) Tundra Bks.

Danner, Thomas. Lazy Cat. Crozat, Francois, illus. 28p. (ps-3). 1994. 12.95 (1-56397-353-7) Boyds Mills Pr.

Danziger, Paula. The Cat Ate My Gymsuit. 160p. (gr. 5 up). 1980. pap. 3.99 (0-440-41612-4, YB) Dell.

—The Cat Ate My Gymsuit. 145p. 1992. Braille. 11.60 (1-56956-336-5) W A T Braille.

Dass, Baba H. Cat & Sparrow. Rich, Andrea, illus. LC 81-51915. 32p. (gr. k-3). 1982. 6.95 (0-918100-06-2) Sri Rama.

Davis. Silk Ball. Date not set. 15.00 (0-06-024279-5); PLB 14.89 (0-06-024288-4) HarpC Child Bks.

Davis, Jim. Garfield's Furry Tales. (ps-3). 1994. pap. 6.95 (0-8167-3432-1) Troll Assocs.

—Garfield's Tales of Mystery. (ps-3). 1994. pap. 6.95 (0-8167-3436-4) Troll Assocs.

Davis, Marion M. Sam Predicts a Storm. Johnson, Anne, illus. 35p. (Orig.). 1991. pap. 6.95 (0-9622221-1-9) Starboard Cove.

—Sam the Royal Cat, No. 1. Starboard Cove Publishing Staff, ed. Johnston, Anne, illus. 35p. (Orig.). 1989. pap. 5.95x (0-9622221-0-0) Starboard Cove.

Dean, Robyn. A Black Cat Named Smokey: On Vacation. Dean, Robyn, illus. LC 92-93502. 64p. (Orig.). (gr. k-3). 1992. pap. 7.95 (0-9633466-0-1) Zyxalon Pr.

Deeter, Catherine. Seymour Bleu: A Space Odyssey. LC 92-24525. (Illus.). 32p. (ps-3). Date not set. 15.00 (0-06-021524-0); PLB 14.89 (0-06-021525-9) HarpC Child Bks.

DeJong, Meindert. The Easter Cat. Hoban, Lillian, illus. LC 90-24407. 128p. (gr. 3-7). 1991. pap. 3.95 (0-689-71468-8, Aladdin) Macmillan Child Grp.

Delton, Judy. Kitty from the Start. LC 86-21481. (gr. 3-5). 1987. 13.95 (0-395-42847-5) HM.

Derby, Sally. Jacob & the Stranger. Gore, Leonid, illus. LC 93-11022. 32p. (ps-3). 1994. 11.95 (0-395-66897-2) Ticknor & Flds Bks Yng Read.

De Regniers, Beatrice S. So Many Cats. Weiss, Ellen, illus. LC 85-3739. 32p. (ps-3). 1985. (Clarion Bks); pap. 4.95 (0-89919-700-0, Clarion Bks) HM.

De Vinck, Christopher. Augusta & Trab. LC 93-7897. 144p. (gr. 3-7). 1993. SBE 13.95 (0-02-729945-7, Four Winds) Macmillan Child Grp.

Dicks, Terrance. A Cat Called Max: Magnificent Max. Goffe, Toni, illus. 64p. (gr. 3-6). 1990. pap. 2.95 (0-8120-4427-4) Barron.

—A Cat Called Max: Max & the Quiz Kids. Goffe, Toni, illus. 64p. (gr. 2-5). 1990. pap. 2.95 (0-8120-4501-7) Barron.

—A Cat Called Max: Max's Amazing Summer. Goffe, Toni, illus. 52p. (gr. 3-6). 1992. pap. 3.50 (0-8120-4819-9) Barron.

Disney, Walt. Aristocats. 1988. 5.99 (0-517-66195-0) Random Hse Value.

—Oliver & Company. (ps-3). 1990. 6.98 (0-453-03009-2) Viking Child Bks.

Dodd, Lynley. Hairy Maclary's Show Business. LC 91-50554. (Illus.). 32p. (gr. 1-2). 1992. PLB 17.27 (0-8368-0763-4) Gareth Stevens Inc.

—The Minister's Cat, ABC. LC 93-36139. 1994. 17.27 (0-8368-1073-2) Gareth Stevens Inc.

—Slinky Malinki, Open the Door. LC 93-21180. 1994. 17.27 (0-8368-1074-0) Gareth Stevens Inc.

Drake, John. The Beginning of the River: Herman's Quest. Kortekaas, Kelly, illus. 48p. (gr. k-5). 1992. 16.95 (0-9633574-0-9) Little Turtle.

Dr. Seuss. The Cat in the Hat. Dr. Seuss, illus. 64p. (ps-1). 1987. book & cassette 7.95 (0-394-89218-6) Random Bks Yng Read.

—The Cat in the Hat - el Gato Ensombrerado. Dr. Seuss, illus. (ENG & SPA.). 72p. (ps-3). 1993. incl. cass. 6.95 (0-679-84329-9) Random Bks Yng Read.

—Cat in the Hat Comes Back. Dr. Seuss, illus. LC 58-9017. 72p. (gr. k-3). 1958. 6.95 (0-394-80002-8); lib. bdg. 7.99 (0-394-90002-2) Random Bks Yng Read.

—The Cat in the Hat Comes Back. (ps-1). 1986. pap. 6.95 incl. cassette (0-394-88327-6) Random Bks Yng Read.

Dubanevich, Arlene. Tom's Tail. (ps-3). 1990. 13.95 (0-670-83021-6) Viking Child Bks.

—Tom's Tail. LC 92-8615. (gr. 4 up). 1992. 4.50 (0-14-054177-2) Puffin Bks.

Duel, Debra. William's Story. Ryan, Donna, illus. 72p. (Orig.). (gr. k-8). 1992. pap. 9.95 (1-880812-02-9) S Ink WA.

Dueland, Joy. Barn Kitten, House Kitten. (Illus.). (gr. 2-8). 1978. pap. 3.50 (0-931942-00-4) Phunn Pubs.

—Dear Tabby. (Illus.). (gr. 4-8). 1978. pap. 2.50 (0-931942-02-0) Phunn Pubs.

—Kitten in the Manger. (Illus.). 32p. (gr. 2-8). 1981. pap. 6.95 (0-685-08286-5) Phunn Pubs.

Dunn, Judy. The Little Kitten. Dunn, Phoebe, photos by. LC 82-16711. (Illus.). 32p. (ps-4). 1983. 2.25 (0-394-85818-2) Random Bks Yng Read.

Edge, Nellie, adapted by. I've Got a Cat Big Book. Saylor, Melissa, illus. (ps-2). 1988. pap. text ed. 14.00 (0-922053-13-8) N Edge Res.

—Yo Tengo un Gato. Zamora-Pearson, Marissa, tr. from ENG. Saylor, Melissa, illus. (SPA.). (ps-2). 1993. pap. text ed. 15.00 (0-922053-29-4) N Edge Res.

Edmiston, Jim. Mizzy & the Tigers. (ps-3). 1992. pap. 5.95 (0-8120-4828-8) Barron.

Ehlert, Lois. Feathers for Lunch. 33p. (ps-3). 1990. 13.95 (0-15-230550-5) HarBrace.

Eisler, Colin. Cats Know Best. LC 87-15653. (Illus.). 32p. 1992. pap. 4.99 (0-8037-1139-5, Puff Pied Piper) Puffin Bks.

Elliott, Lisa E. Old Friends & New Friends, Old Kitties & New Kitties. Caroland, Mary, ed. LC 90-71002. 44p. (gr. k-3). 1991. 5.95 (1-55523-364-3) Winston-Derek.

Ellison, Jean F. Justine...It's Time. Collier, Bobbie, contrib. by. LC 93-83722. (Illus.). 24p. (Orig.). (gr. 2-8). 1993. 12.95 (0-9637825-1-7); pap. 4.95 (0-9637825-0-9) Spotlght News.

Erickson, John. The Case of the Missing Cat: Discover the Land of Enchantment. (Illus.). 144p. 1990. 11.95 (0-87719-186-7); pap. 6.95 (0-87719-185-9); 2 cass. 15.95 (0-87719-187-5) Gulf Pub.

Estes, Eleanor. Pinky Pye. Ardizzone, Edward, illus. LC 75-31581. 192p. (gr. 3-7). 1976. pap. 4.95 (0-15-671840-5, Voyager Bks) HarBrace.

Everitt, Betsy. Frida the Wondercat. 32p. (ps-3). 1990. 13.95 (0-15-229540-2) HarBrace.

—Fride the Wondercat. (ps-3). pap. 4.95 (0-15-229541-0, HB Juv Bks) HarBrace.

Feldman, Eve B. That Cat! Ransome, James E., illus. LC 94-280. 1994. write for info. (0-688-13310-X, Tambourine Bks) Morrow.

Flack, Marjorie. Angus & the Cat. 40p. (ps-k). 1989. PLB 13.99 (*0-685-01488-6*); pap. 12.95 (*0-685-01489-4*) Doubleday.
—Angus & the Cat. 1989. (Zephyr-BFYR) Doubleday.
Foley, Louise M. Poison! Said the Cat, No. 3. 192p. 1992. pap. 3.50 (*0-425-12898-9*) Berkley Pub.
Foreman, Mark. Sid the Kitten. (Illus.). 32p. (ps-2). 1989. 13.95 (*0-86264-218-3*, Pub. by Anderson Pr UK) Trafalgar.
Foreman, Michael. Cat & Canary. LC 84-9568. (Illus.). 32p. (ps-3). 1987. pap. 5.99 (*0-8037-0133-0*) Dial Bks Young.
Foster, Lucile. Lucy the Cat. 1993. 7.95 (*0-8062-4774-6*) Carlton.
Four Fierce Kittens. 1992. 13.95 (*0-590-45535-4*, Scholastic Hardcover) Scholastic Inc.
Fox, Frances M. The Little Cat That Could Not Sleep. Hughes, Shirley, illus. LC 72-89335. 32p. (gr. k-4). 1973. 7.95 (*0-87592-030-6*) Scroll Pr.
Fox, Paula. One-Eyed Cat. Trivas, Irene, illus. LC 84-10964. 192p. (gr. 6-8). 1984. SBE 14.95 (*0-02-735540-3*, Bradbury Pr) Macmillan Child Grp.
—One-Eyed Cat. (gr. k-6). 1985. pap. 3.99 (*0-440-46641-5*, YB) Dell.
—One Eyed Cat. (gr. 4-7). 1993. pap. 1.99 (*0-440-21625-7*) Dell.
Fremantle, Anne. Island of Cats. Sapieha, Christine, illus. (gr. 1-4). 1964. 12.95 (*0-8392-3011-7*) Astor-Honor.
Freschet, Bernice. Furlie Cat. Lewin, Betsy, illus. LC 85-11656. 32p. (ps-3). 1986. 12.95 (*0-688-05917-1*) Lothrop.
Frost, Erica. A Kitten for Rosie. Fiammenghi, Gioia, illus. LC 85-14126. 48p. (Orig.). (gr. 1-3). 1986. PLB 10.59 (*0-8167-0650-6*); pap. text ed. 3.50 (*0-8167-0651-4*) Troll Assocs.
—The Story of Matt & Mary. Schumacher, Claire, illus. LC 85-14011. 48p. (Orig.). (gr. 1-3). 1986. PLB 10.59 (*0-8167-0602-6*); pap. text ed. 3.50 (*0-8167-0603-4*) Troll Assocs.
Gag, Wanda & Gag, Wanda. Millions of Cats. (Illus.). 112p. (gr. k-3). 1977. 9.95 (*0-698-20091-8*, Sandcastle); pap. 4.95 (*0-698-20637-1*, Sandcastle Bks) Putnam Pub Group.
Galdone, Paul. King of the Cats: A Ghost Story. Galdone, Paul, illus. LC 79-16659. (gr. k-3). 1985. pap. 4.95 (*0-89919-400-1*, Clarion Bks) HM.
—Puss in Boots. Galdone, Paul, illus. LC 75-25505. 32p. (ps-4). 1979. 13.45 (*0-395-28808-8*, Clarion Bks) HM.
—Puss in Boots. LC 75-25505. 32p. (gr. k-3). 1983. pap. 4.95 (*0-89919-192-4*, Clarion Bks) HM.
—Puss 'N Boots. (ps-3). 1987. incl. cass. 6.95 (*0-317-64571-4*, Clarion Bks) HM.
Gallagher, Jennifer A. The Fine Red Cat. (Illus.). 32p. (gr. 3-5). 1993. 14.95 (*1-880851-10-5*) Greene Bark Pr.
Gantos, Jack. Happy Birthday, Rotten Ralph. Rubel, Nicole, illus. 32p. (ps-3). 1990. 13.45 (*0-395-53766-5*) HM.
—Not So Rotten Ralph. Rubel, Nicole, illus. LC 93-759. (gr. 4 up). 1994. 13.95 (*0-395-62302-2*) HM.
—Rotten Ralph. Rubel, Nicole, illus. LC 75-34101. 48p. (gr. k-3). 1976. 13.95 (*0-395-24276-2*); pap. 4.50 (*0-685-02307-9*) HM.
—Rotten Ralph. Rubel, Nicole, illus. (gr. k-3). 1980. pap. 4.80 (*0-395-29202-6*, Sandpiper) HM.
—Rotten Ralph's Rotten Christmas. Rubel, Nicole, illus. LC 84-664. 32p. (ps-3). 1984. 13.95 (*0-395-35380-7*); pap. 17.95 incl. doll (*0-395-45346-1*); pap. 4.80 (*0-395-45685-1*) HM.
—Rotten Ralph's Trick or Treat. Rubel, Nicole, illus. LC 86-7276. 32p. (gr. k-3). 1986. 13.45 (*0-395-38943-7*) HM.
—Worse Than Rotten, Ralph. Rubel, Nicole, illus. (gr. k-3). 1982. 13.95 (*0-395-27106-1*); pap. 5.70 (*0-395-32919-1*) HM.
Garber, Barbara J. Me & Daffodil. Garber, Barbara J., illus. LC 92-61375. 66p. 1993. pap. 8.00 (*1-56002-212-4*, Univ Edtns) Aegina Pr.
Garfield: Food for Thought. (Illus.). 1987. pap. 2.95 (*0-440-82192-4*) Dell.
La Gata a la Que le Gustaba el Rojo. (Illus.). 8p. (gr. 1). 1993. pap. 3.50 (*1-880612-26-7*) Seedling Pubns.
Los Gatitos. (SPA.). (ps-3). 1993. pap. 2.25 (*0-307-70079-8*, Golden Pr) Western Pub.
El Gato Con Botas. (SPA.). (ps-3). 1993. pap. 4.95 (*0-307-72197-3*, Golden Pr) Western Pub.
Gee, R. & Borton, P. Cat & Mouse in Space. (Illus.). 24p. (ps up). 1994. PLB 11.95 (*0-88110-708-5*, Usborne); pap. 3.95 (*0-7460-1417-1*, Usborne) EDC.
Gelman, Rita G. Hello Cat You Need a Hat. 1993. pap. 28.67 (*0-590-71915-7*) Scholastic Inc.
Gerstein, Mordicai. The New Creatures. LC 90-4128. (Illus.). 32p. (ps-3). 1991. PLB 14.89 (*0-06-022167-4*) HarpC Child Bks.
Ghigna, Charles. Good Cats, Bad Cats. Catrow, David, illus. LC 92-52984. 40p. 1992. 7.95 (*1-56282-292-6*); PLB 10.89 (*1-56282-293-4*) Hyprn Child.
Gibson, R. Cat & Mouse Get a Pet. (Illus.). 24p. (ps up). 1994. PLB 11.96 (*0-88110-697-6*, Usborne); pap. 3.95 (*0-7460-1419-8*, Usborne) EDC.
Gilchrest, Guy. My Mom's Okay. Gilchrest, Guy, illus. LC 91-10722. 24p. (ps-3). 1991. 5.95 (*1-56288-088-8*) Checkerboard.
Gillis, Everett A. Goldie. Gillis, Paul, illus. 64p. (Orig.). (gr. 3-7). 1982. pap. 8.00 (*0-938328-02-6*) Pisces Pr TX.
Gleeson, Kate. Kate Gleeson's Three Little Kittens. (ps). 1993. bds. 2.25 (*0-307-06122-1*, Pub. by Golden Bks) Western Pub.
Golden, Nora. Comical Celtic Cat. (gr. 1 up). 1984. 13.95 (*0-85105-901-5*, Pub. by Colin Smythe Ltd Britain) Dufour.
Goldsboro, Bobby. Bobby Goldsboro's A Cat Named Bob. 16p. (ps-2). 1993. write for info. (*1-883366-33-X*) YES Ent.
Goldsmith, Melissa. In a Cat State of Mind. Goldsmith, Melissa, illus. LC 90-403394. 120p. (Orig.). (gr. 2-11). 1990. 17.95 (*0-938921-06-1*); pap. text ed. 6.95 (*0-938921-07-X*) Tigertail Ent.
Gordon, Gaelyn. Duckat. (ps). 1992. 13.95 (*0-590-45455-2*, Scholastic Hardcover) Scholastic Inc.
Gormley, Beatrice. Sky Guys to White Cat. McCully, Emily A., illus. LC 91-364. 144p. (gr. 3-6). 1991. 12. 95 (*0-525-44743-1*, DCB) Dutton Child Bks.
Graboff, Abner. In a Cat's Eye. (Illus.). (gr. 7 up). 1976. pap. 5.00 (*0-912846-25-9*) Bookstore Pr.
Greaves, Margaret. Henry's Wild Morning. O'Brien, Teresa, illus. LC 90-3554. 40p. (ps-3). 1991. 13.95 (*0-8037-0907-2*) Dial Bks Young.
Green, Krister. Lisi & the Kittens. Coughlin, Ramona, tr. from SWE. Martin, Lisi, illus. 28p. (gr. 3-5). 1990. 12. 95g (*0-940607-07-7*) Pictura NJ.
Greene, Carol. The Old Ladies Who Liked Cats. Krupinski, Loretta, illus. LC 90-4443. 32p. (gr. k-3). 1991. 15.00 (*0-06-022104-6*); PLB 14.89 (*0-06-022105-4*) HarpC Child Bks.
—The Old Ladies Who Liked Cats. Krupinski, Loretta, illus. LC 90-4443. 32p. (gr. k-3). 1994. pap. 4.95 (*0-06-443354-4*, Trophy) HarpC Child Bks.
Greenwood, Pamela D. I Found Mouse. Plecas, Jennifer, illus. LC 93-46427. (ps). 1994. 14.95 (*0-395-65478-5*, Clarion Bks) HM.
Grubbs, J. Socks, the Cat Who Moved to Washington. Abell, J., ed. Grubbs, J., illus. 50p. (gr. 1-4). 1993. PLB 25.00 (*1-56611-022-X*); pap. 15.00 (*1-56611-047-5*) Jonas.
Grubbs, Joan P. The Cat Who Returned Nine Times. Abell, ed. & illus. 50p. (Orig.). (gr. 1-4). 1993. 25.00 (*1-56611-060-2*); pap. 15.00 (*0-685-68773-2*) Jonas.
Haas, Jessie. Chipmunk! Smith, Joseph A., illus. LC 92-30080. 24p. (ps up). 1993. 14.00 (*0-688-11874-7*); PLB 13.93 (*0-688-11875-5*) Greenwillow.
Hale, Kathleen. Orlando's Evening Out. Hale, Kathleen, illus. 32p. (ps-3). 1992. 15.95 (*0-7232-3652-6*) Warne.
—Orlando's Home Life. (Illus.). 32p. (ps-3). 1992. 16.00 (*0-7232-3653-4*) Warne.
Hall, Donald. I Am the Dog, I Am the Cat. Moser, Barry, illus. LC 93-28060. (gr. 1 up). 1994. 15.99 (*0-8037-1504-8*); PLB 15.89 (*0-8037-1505-6*) Dial Bks Young.
Hall, M. The Naughty Kitten. 1994. 11.95 (*1-881116-57-3*) ICAN Pr.
Hamer, Sylvia. C. B. & the Pink Pointe Shoes. Hamer, Sylvia, illus. LC 87-70557. 32p. (Orig.). (gr. 3-4). 1987. pap. 9.95 (*0-942479-00-9*) Anderson Pr.
Hanus, Karen. One-Eyed Cat: A Study Guide. Friedland, Joyce & Kessler, Rikki, eds. (gr. 5-8). 1991. pap. text ed. 14.95 (*0-88122-580-0*) LRN Links.
Hathorn, Libby. Looking for Felix. Culio, Ned, illus. LC 92-34259. 1993. 4.25 (*0-383-03638-0*) SRA Schl Grp.
—Way Home. Rogers, Gregory, illus. LC 93-48030. 32p. (gr. 1-5). 1994. 15.00 (*0-517-59909-0*) Crown Bks Yng Read.
Hausherr, Rosmarie. My First Kitten. Hausherr, Rosmarie, illus. LC 85-42804. 48p. (gr. 1-4). 1985. RSBE 13.95 (*0-02-743420-6*, Four Winds) Macmillan Child Grp.
Hautzig, Deborah. Ernie & Bert's New Kitten. Mathieu, Joe, illus. LC 89-10583. 40p. (ps-3). 1990. 4.95 (*0-679-80420-X*) Random Bks Yng Read.
—Ernie & Bert's New Kitten. Mathieu, Joe, illus. LC 89-10583. 40p. (ps-3). 1993. pap. 2.99 (*0-679-83954-2*) Random Bks Yng Read.
Hawkins, Colin & Hawkins, Jacqui. Pat the Cat. LC 82-18104. (Illus.). (ps-1). 1986. 9.95 (*0-399-20957-3*, Putnam) Putnam Pub Group.
Hawkins, Laura. The Cat That Could Spell Mississippi. LC 92-8025. 160p. (gr. 3-5). 1992. 13.95 (*0-395-61627-1*) HM.
Hayes, Sarah. The Cats of Tiffany Street. Hayes, Sarah, illus. LC 91-58720. 32p. (ps up). 1992. 13.95 (*1-56402-094-0*) Candlewick Pr.
Hayward, Stan. The Shutterbug. Godfrey, Bob, illus. (ps-5). 1987. pap. 2.25 (*0-671-63776-2*) S&S Trade.
Heathcliff Pigs Out. (Illus.). 1985. pap. 0.95 (*0-440-82008-1*) Dell.
Heathcliff: Wanted. (Illus.). 1987. pap. 0.95 (*0-440-82119-3*) Dell.
Heathcliff's Vacation. (Illus.). 1986. pap. 1.25 (*0-440-82041-3*) Dell.
Heckert, Connie. Dribbles. Sayles, Elizabeth, illus. LC 92-24846. 1993. 14.45 (*0-395-62336-7*, Clarion Bks) HM.
Heilbroner, Joan. Tom the TV Cat: A Step Two Book. Murdocca, Sal, illus. LC 83-24600. 48p. (ps-2). 1984. lib. bdg. 7.99 (*0-394-96708-9*); pap. 3.50 (*0-394-86708-4*) Random Bks Yng Read.
Heinz, Brian J. Alley Cat. (gr. 4 up). 1993. 14.95 (*0-385-31042-0*) Doubleday.
Hendry, Diana, ed. Back Soon. Thompson, Carol, illus. LC 93-45590. 32p. (gr. k-3). 1994. PLB 13.95 (*0-8167-3487-9*); pap. text ed. 3.95 (*0-8167-3488-7*) BrdgeWater.
Here, Kitty, Kitty! 14p. (ps). 1993. bds. 2.99 (*0-679-84908-4*) Random Bks Yng Read.
Herriot, James. Moses the Kitten. Barrett, Peter, illus. LC 84-50930. 32p. (ps up). 1984. 13.00 (*0-312-54905-9*) St Martin.
—Moses the Kitten. Barrett, Peter, illus. 1991. pap. 6.95 (*0-312-06419-5*) St Martin.
Heupel, DuWayne. Kitten in the Country. Craig, Michael, illus. 32p. (gr. 1-2). 1993. text ed. 10.95 (*1-882841-05-0*) Educare CO.
Hoban, Julia. Buzby. Himmelman, John, illus. LC 89-29408. 64p. (gr. k-3). 1990. PLB 11.89 (*0-06-022398-7*) HarpC Child Bks.
—Buzby. Himmelman, John, illus. LC 89-29408. 64p. (gr. k-3). 1992. pap. 3.50 (*0-06-444152-0*, Trophy) HarpC Child Bks.
—Buzby to the Rescue. Himmelman, John, illus. LC 91-46085. 64p. (gr. k-3). 1993. 14.00 (*0-06-021025-7*); PLB 13.89 (*0-06-021024-9*) HarpC Child Bks.
Hoban, Tana. One Little Kitten. LC 78-31862. (Illus.). 24p. (gr. k-3). 1979. 16.00 (*0-688-80222-2*); PLB 15. 93 (*0-688-84222-4*) Greenwillow.
—One Little Kitten. LC 78-31862. (Illus.). 24p. (ps up). 1992. pap. 3.95 (*0-688-11506-3*, Mulberry) Morrow.
Hoff, Syd. Captain Cat. Hoff, Syd, illus. LC 91-27518. 48p. (ps-2). 1993. 14.00 (*0-06-020527-X*); PLB 13.89 (*0-06-020528-8*) HarpC Child Bks.
Hogrogian, Nonny. The Cat Who Loved to Sing. LC 86-27358. (Illus.). 40p. (ps-2). 1988. lib. bdg. 13.99 (*0-394-99004-8*) Knopf Bks Yng Read.
Hollingsworth, Mary. Charlie & the Shabby Tabby. (Illus.). (ps-3). 1989. 5.99 (*0-915720-26-4*) Brownlow Pub Co.
Holt, S. Marie. Mike Moves to the City. Holt, Shirley, illus. 28p. (gr. k-5). 1992. 21.95x (*0-9613476-5-1*) Shirlee.
Horowitz, Jordan. Tom & Jerry: The Movie. (ps-3). 1993. pap. 2.95 (*0-590-47116-3*) Scholastic Inc.

Horowitz, Lynn R. Lulu Turns Four. Urbahn, Clara, illus. 32p. (ps-k). 1993. 13.95 (*0-9625620-5-X*) DOT Garnet. A little chimp named Lulu is about to celebrate her fourth birthday, & like every small person in the process of getting bigger, she wonders if she'll master the challenges: standing by herself all the time; going to the doctor without feeling afraid; sharing happily with her little sister; eating bugs & green leaves like the grownups. Release from her fears comes in the form of a birthday present from her mother, a helpless kitten who needs Lulu to help her grow up, in this charming book about the responsibilities--& the pleasures--of birthdays. LYNN HOROWITZ, a Yale graduate with a Masters in education, is the author of two previous books for young readers, THE GOOD BAD WOLF & MANOS A LA OBRA. She lives in Berkeley, California. CLARA URBAHN, an artist & illustrator of children's books, lives in Nantucket, Massachusetts. To order: DOT*GARNET, 2225 Eighth Avenue, Oakland, CA 94606. (510) 834-6063, FAX 834-7516. *Publisher Provided Annotation.*

Howe, James. The Celery Stalks at Midnight. Morrill, Leslie H., illus. 128p. (gr. 3-7). 1984. pap. 3.99 (*0-380-69054-3*, Camelot) Avon.
—Creepy-Crawly Birthday. Morrill, Leslie, illus. LC 90-35370. 48p. (gr. k up). 1991. 13.95 (*0-688-09687-5*); PLB 13.88 (*0-688-09688-3*) Morrow Jr Bks.
—Hot Fudge. Morrill, Leslie, illus. LC 89-13468. 48p. (gr. k up). 1990. 13.95 (*0-688-08237-8*); PLB 13.88 (*0-688-09701-4*, Morrow Jr Bks) Morrow Jr Bks.
—Nighty-Nightmare. Morrill, Leslie, illus. LC 86-22334. 128p. (gr. 3-7). 1987. SBE 13.95 (*0-689-31207-5*, Atheneum Child Bk) Macmillan Child Grp.
—Rabbit Cadabra! Daniel, Alan, illus. LC 91-34656. 48p. (gr. k up). 1993. 15.00 (*0-688-10402-9*); PLB 14.93 (*0-688-10403-7*) Morrow Jr Bks.
—Return to Howliday Inn. Daniels, Alan, illus. LC 91-29505. 176p. (gr. 3-7). 1992. SBE 13.95 (*0-689-31661-5*, Atheneum Child Bk) Macmillan Child Grp.
Hubbell, Andra. Supercat. Dally, Tim, illus. LC 88-63735. 16p. (ps-3). 1989. PLB 16.95 (*0-9621759-1-9*); PLB 11.95 (*0-317-93727-8*) Rochester Pub Lib Dist.
Huck, Charlotte. Princess Furball. Lobel, Anita, illus. LC 88-18780. 40p. (ps up). 1989. 14.00 (*0-688-07837-0*); PLB 13.93 (*0-688-07838-9*) Greenwillow.
Hutchins, Hazel. And You Can Be the Cat. Ohi, Ruth, illus. 24p. (ps-3). 1992. PLB 14.95 (*1-55037-219-X*, Pub. by Annick CN); pap. 4.95 (*1-55037-216-5*, Pub. by Annick CN) Firefly Bks Ltd.

Incredible Journey. 1985. pap. 1.50 (*0-440-82001-4*) Dell.
Ingoglia, Gina. Sylvester & Tweety: What a Mess. (ps-3). 1990. write for info. (*0-307-11595-X*) Western Pub.
Irland, Nancy B. Very Strange Story of Blaze the Cat. (gr. 4-7). 1991. pap. 2.99 (*0-8163-1046-7*) Pacific Pr Pub Assn.
Ivory, Lesley A. Meet My Cats. (Illus.). 32p. 1994. pap. 5.99 (*0-14-054920-X*, Puff Pied Piper) Puffin Bks.
Ivory, Leslie A. The Birthday Cat. Ivory, Leslie A., illus. LC 93-129. 32p. (ps-3). 1993. 15.00 (*0-8037-1622-2*) Dial Bks Young.
—Cats in the Sun. LC 90-43068. (Illus.). 32p. 1992. miniature ed. 5.95 (*0-8037-1242-1*) Dial Bks Young.
—Meet My Cats. (gr. 2 up). 1989. 13.95 (*0-8037-0602-2*) Dial Bks Young.
—Meet My Cats. LC 89-1526. (Illus.). 32p. 1992. miniature ed. 5.95 (*0-8037-1241-3*) Dial Bks Young.
Jacobs, Joseph. King of the Cats. Galdone, Paul, illus. LC 79-16659. 32p. (ps-3). 1980. 14.45 (*0-395-29030-9*, Clarion Bks) HM.
Jessel, Camilla. Kitten Book. LC 91-71841. (Illus.). 32p. (ps up). 1994. pap. 4.99 (*1-56402-278-1*) Candlewick Pr.
Johansen, Hanna. A Tomcat's Tale. LC 90-39067. (Illus.). 144p. (gr. 5 up). 1991. 13.95 (*0-525-44583-8*, DCB) Dutton Child Bks.
Johnson, Audean, illus. Soft as a Kitten. 14p. (ps). 1982. bds. 8.00 (*0-394-85517-5*) Random Bks Yng Read.
Johnson, Debra A. I Dreamed I Was--a Kitten. LC 94-5655. (gr. k up). 1994. write for info. (*1-56239-302-2*) Abdo & Dghtrs.
Johnson, Eleanor. Pirate, the Lighthouse Cat. (gr. 2-5). 1986. pap. 6.95 (*0-930096-77-0*) G Gannett.
Johnston, Johanna & Johnston, Abigail. Great Gravity the Cat. rev. ed. Mathis, Melissa B., illus. LC 88-13351. 64p. (gr. 3-7). 1989. lib. bdg. 15.00 (*0-208-02223-6*, Linnet) Shoe String.
Johnston, Norma. Whisper of the Cat. 192p. (Orig.). 1988. pap. 2.95 (*0-553-26947-X*, Starfire) Bantam.
Johnston, Tony. Old Lady & the Birds. LC 91-45124. (ps-3). 1994. 14.95 (*0-15-257769-6*, HB Juv Bks) HarBrace.
Jones, Cordelia. Cat Called Camouflage. LC 79-166339. (Illus.). (gr. 7 up). 1971. 21.95 (*0-87599-189-0*) S G Phillips.
Joos, Frederic & Joos, Francoise. Puss in Palace. (Illus.). 32p. (gr. k-2). 1990. 13.95 (*0-86264-235-3*, Pub. by Anderson Pr UK) Trafalgar.
Joosse, Barbara M. Anna & the Cat Lady. Mayo, Gretchen W., illus. LC 91-12510. 176p. (gr. 3-7). 1992. 14.00 (*0-06-020242-4*) HarpC Child Bks.
—Nobody's Cat. Sewall, Marcia, illus. LC 91-37619. 32p. (gr. k-3). 1992. 15.00 (*0-06-020834-1*); PLB 14.89 (*0-06-020835-X*) HarpC Child Bks.
Jung, Minna. William's Ninth Life. Rosenberry, Vera, illus. LC 92-44520. 32p. (ps-2). 1993. 14.95 (*0-531-05492-6*); PLB 14.99 (*0-531-08642-9*) Orchard Bks Watts.
Jungman, Ann. When the People Are Away. Birch, Linda, illus. 32p. (ps-3). 1993. 12.95 (*1-56397-202-6*) Boyds Mills Pr.
Kamen, Gloria. Second-Hand Cat. Kamen, Gloria, illus. LC 91-250. 32p. (gr. k-3). 1992. SBE 13.95 (*0-689-31631-3*, Atheneum Child Bk) Macmillan Child Grp.
Kantenwein, Louise. Boss Cat. 1993. 7.95 (*0-533-10628-1*) Vantage.
Karen & the Little Lost Kitten. (Illus.). 24p. (ps-2). 1982. 5.95 (*0-8431-0641-7*) Price Stern.
Karlin, Bernie. Meow! (Illus.). 32p. (ps-3). 1993. pap. 2.50 (*0-671-79603-8*, Little Simon) S&S Trade.
Keats, Ezra J. Hi, Cat! 2nd ed. Keats, Ezra J., illus. LC 87-37433. 40p. (gr. k-4). 1988. pap. 4.95 (*0-689-71258-8*, Aladdin) Macmillan Child Grp.
—Hi, Cat! (gr. k-3). 1990. incl. cass. 19.95 (*0-87499-180-3*); pap. 12.95 incl. cass. (*0-87499-179-X*); Set; incl. 4 bks., cass., & guide. pap. 27.95 (*0-685-38540-X*) Live Oak Media.
—Kitten for a Day. Keats, Ezra J., illus. LC 92-40563. 32p. (ps-1). 1993. pap. 4.95 (*0-689-71737-7*, Aladdin) Macmillan Child Grp.
Kellogg, Steven. A Rose for Pinkerton. Kellogg, Steven, illus. LC 81-65848. 32p. (ps-3). 1981. 14.00 (*0-8037-7502-4*); PLB 12.89 (*0-8037-7503-2*) Dial Bks Young.
Kern, Phyllis F. Bumble Cat: How She Came to Be. Kern, Phyllis F., illus. 32p. (gr. k-3). 1985. HM.
Kerr. The Alamo Cat. (Illus.). 64p. (gr. 4-6). 1988. 10.95 (*0-89015-639-5*, Pub. by Panda Bks) Sunbelt Media.
Kersell, Jim. The Little Kitten's Very Scary Day. (Illus.). 24p. (gr. k-3). 1992. pap. 1.99 (*0-87406-641-7*) Willowisp Pr.
Kettner, Christine. An Ordinary Cat. Kettner, Christine, illus. LC 90-19441. 32p. (ps-3). 1991. HarpC Child Bks.
Khalsa, Dayal K. The Snow Cat. Khalsa, Dayal K., illus. LC 92-8988. 32p. (ps-2). 1992. 14.00 (*0-517-59183-9*, Clarkson Potter) Crown Bks Yng Read.
Kingett, Robert P. P. W. Liveaboard Cat. (Illus.). 48p. (Orig.). 1988. pap. write for info. Catalina Creations.
Kinsey-Warnock, Natalie. Wilderness Cat. Graham, Mark, illus. LC 90-24250. 32p. (ps-3). 1992. 14.00 (*0-525-65068-7*, Cobblehill Bks) Dutton Child Bks.
Kipling, Rudyard. Cat That Walked by Himself. LC 90-34357. 1989. 11.95 (*0-85953-276-3*) Childs Play.
—The Cat Who Walked by Himself. LC 90-34357. 1990. pap. 5.95 (*0-85953-309-3*) Childs Play.
Koci, Marta. Katie's Kitten. LC 82-60893. (Illus.). 28p. (ps-2). 1991. pap. 14.95 (*0-907234-21-6*) Picture Bk Studio.
—Katie's Kitten. (Illus.). 28p. (gr. k up). 1991. pap. 4.95 (*0-88708-181-9*) Picture Bk Studio.
Koda-Callan, Elizabeth. The Cat Next Door. (Illus.). 40p. (ps-3). 1993. 12.95 (*1-56305-502-3*, 3502) Workman Pub.
Koontz, Robin M. Chicago & the Cat. Koontz, Robin M., illus. LC 91-34863. 32p. (gr. k-3). 1993. 12.00 (*0-525-65097-0*, Cobblehill Bks) Dutton Child Bks.
—Chicago & the Cat: The Camping Trip. Koontz, Robin M., illus. LC 92-46685. 32p. (gr. k-3). 1994. 12.99 (*0-525-65137-3*, Cobblehill Bks) Dutton Child Bks.
—Chicago & the Cat: The Halloween Party. Koontz, Robin M., illus. LC 93-27043. 32p. (gr. k-3). 1994. 12. 99 (*0-525-65138-1*, Cobblehill Bks) Dutton Child Bks.
Kreloff, Elliot, illus. My Big Kitten Book. (ps-k). 1993. Set, lg. bk. 12p., small bk. 6p. bds. 4.95 (*1-56293-360-4*) McClanahan Bk.
Krensky, Stephen. Fraidy Cats. Lewin, Betsy, illus. LC 92-35360. (gr. 3 up). 1993. 2.95 (*0-590-46438-8*) Scholastic Inc.
Kroll, Steven. Branigan's Cat & the Halloween Ghost. Ewing, Carolyn, illus. LC 89-77509. 32p. (ps-3). 1990. reinforced 14.95 (*0-8234-0822-1*) Holiday.
Kyte, Dennis. Mattie - Cataragus. 1988. pap. 13.95 (*0-385-24403-7*) Doubleday.
Latimer, Heather. Curse of the Painted Cats: A Romantic Suspense Novel. 250p. 1989. 18.95 (*0-943698-03-0*); pap. 4.95 (*0-943698-04-9*); talking bk. with 2 audio cassettes, 3 hrs. 15.95 (*0-943698-06-5*) Papyrus Pubs.
Lattimore, Deborah N. The Winged Cat: A Tale of Ancient Egypt. Lattimore, Deborah N., illus. LC 90-38441. 40p. (gr. 2-5). 1992. 15.00 (*0-06-023635-3*); PLB 14.89 (*0-06-023636-1*) HarpC Child Bks.
Lawton, Helen. Moggy the Mouser. McAllan, Marina, illus. LC 93-6571. 1994. write for info. (*0-383-03702-6*) SRA Schl Grp.
Lear, Edward. The Owl & the Pussycat. (ps-1). 1989. 13. 95 (*0-89919-505-9*, Clarion Bks); pap. 4.95 (*0-89919-854-6*, Clarion Bks) HM.
Le Guin, Ursula K. Catwings. Schindler, Stephen D., illus. LC 87-33104. 48p. (gr. 2-5). 1988. 11.95 (*0-531-05759-3*); PLB 11.99 (*0-531-08359-4*) Orchard Bks Watts.
LeGuin, Ursula K. Catwings. Schindler, Stephen D., illus. 64p. (gr. 2-5). 1992. pap. 2.95 (*0-590-46072-2*) Scholastic Inc.
Le Guin, Ursula K. Catwings Return. Schindler, Stephen D., illus. LC 88-17902. 56p. (gr. 2-5). 1989. 11.95 (*0-531-05803-4*); PLB 11.99 (*0-531-08403-5*) Orchard Bks Watts.
LeGuin, Ursula K. Catwings Return. Schindler, Stephen D., illus. 64p. (gr. 2-5). 1992. pap. 2.95 (*0-590-46074-9*) Scholastic Inc.
Le Guin, Ursula K. Wonderful Alexander & the Catwings. Schindler, S. D., illus. LC 93-49397. 48p. (gr. k-3). 1994. 12.95 (*0-531-06851-X*); PLB 12.99 (*0-531-08701-8*) Orchard Bks Watts.
Leman, Jill. Sleepy Kittens. Leman, Martin, illus. LC 93-24232. 32p. 1994. 14.00 (*0-688-13288-X*, Tambourine Bks); PLB 13.93 (*0-688-13289-8*, Tambourine Bks) Morrow.
Leman, Martin. The Little Cats ABC Book. LC 93-26272. 1994. 13.00 (*0-671-88612-6*) S&S Trade.
Lemans, Martin. Curiouser & Curiouser Cats. (Illus.). 32p. (ps-2). 1993. 16.95 (*0-575-04707-0*, Pub. by Gollancz UK) Trafalgar.
Leonard, Marcia. Midnight Cat. 1989. bds. 2.95 (*0-8167-1887-3*) Troll Assocs.
Leonard, Marcia, adapted by. Your First Adventure: Little Kitten Sleeps Over, No. 9. adpt. ed. Schmidt, Karen L., illus. 32p. 1987. pap. 2.50 (*0-553-15472-9*) Bantam.
LeRoy, Gen. Taxi Cat & Huey. Ritz, Karen, illus. LC 90-27383. 144p. (gr. 3-7). 1992. 14.00 (*0-06-021768-5*); PLB 13.89 (*0-06-021769-3*) HarpC Child Bks.
Leverich, Kathleen. Brigid, Bewitched. Andreasen, Dan, illus. LC 93-43221. 80p. (Orig.). (gr. 1-4). 1994. PLB 9.99 (*0-679-95433-3*); pap. 2.99 (*0-679-85433-9*) Random Bks Yng Read.
Lewis, J. Patrick. The Fat-Cats at Sea. Chess, Victoria, illus. 40p. (ps-3). 1994. 15.00 (*0-679-82639-4*, Apple Soup Bks); PLB 15.99 (*0-679-92639-9*, Apple Soup Bks) Knopf Bks Yng Read.
Lindgren, Barbro. Sam's Ball. LC 83-722. (Illus.). 32p. (ps-k). 1983. 6.95 (*0-688-02359-2*) Morrow Jr Bks.
Lindstrom, Eva. The Cat Hat. Croall, Stephen, tr. from SWE. (Illus.). 40p. (gr. 1-4). 1989. 12.95 (*0-916291-23-5*); pap. 6.95 (*0-916291-24-3*) Kane-Miller Bk.
Lisle, Janet T. The Dancing Cats of Applesap. Shefts, Joelle, illus. 1985. pap. 2.50 (*0-553-15348-X*, Skylark) Bantam.
—Looking for Juliette. LC 94-6922. 128p. (gr. 3-5). 1994. 14.95 (*0-531-06870-6*); PLB 14.99 (*0-531-08720-4*) Orchard Bks Watts.
The Little Cat & the Greedy Old Woman: Story & Pictures. LC 94-16526. 1995. 14.95 (*0-689-50611-2*) Macmillan Child Grp.
Little Kittens Dress-up. 28p. (ps-2). 1992. 3.95 (*0-7214-5312-0*, S915-5) Ladybird Bks.
Little, Mary E. Old Cat & the Kitten. LC 93-30376. 128p. (gr. 3-7). 1994. pap. 3.95 (*0-689-71800-4*, Aladdin) Macmillan Child Grp.
Livingston, Myra C., ed. Dog Poems. Morrill, Leslie, illus. LC 89-2061. 32p. (ps-3). 1990. reinforced 12.95 (*0-8234-0776-4*) Holiday.
London, Jonathan. Hip Cat. Hubbard, Woodleigh, illus. LC 93-1179. 1993. 13.95 (*0-8118-0315-5*) Chronicle Bks.
Loveland, Nicole. Boogins Gets a Basket. (Illus.). 32p. (ps-2). 1984. PLB 4.95 (*0-917107-00-4*) Cat-Tales Pr.
McClintock, Barbara. The Heartaches of a French Cat. LC 88-45289. (Illus.). 48p. 1989. 14.95 (*0-87923-757-0*) Godine.
McCue, Lisa, illus. Kitty's Colors. (ps-2). 1983. pap. 2.95 (*0-671-45489-7*, Little Simon) S&S Trade.
McHugh, Elisabet. Beethoven's Cat. (gr. k-6). 1991. pap. 3.50 (*0-440-40398-7*) Dell.
McLerran, Alice. I Want to Go Home. Kastner, Jill, illus. LC 91-9599. 32p. (ps-3). 1992. 15.00 (*0-688-10144-5*, Tambourine Bks); PLB 14.93 (*0-688-10145-3*, Tambourine Bks) Morrow.
Magellan, Mauro. Max, the Apartment Cat. Magellan, Mauro, illus. LC 88-32067. 32p. 1989. 12.95 (*0-89334-117-7*) Humanics Ltd.
Mahy, Margaret. The Three-Legged Cat. Allen, Jonathan, illus. 32p. (ps-3). 1993. 13.99 (*0-670-85015-2*) Viking Child Bks.
Makris, Kathryn. The Five Cat Club. 176p. (Orig.). (gr. 5 up). 1994. pap. 3.50 (*0-380-77049-0*, Camelot Young) Avon.
Mandel, Peter. Red Cat, White Cat. (ps-2). 1994. 14.95 (*0-8050-2929-X*) H Holt & Co.
Mannin, Ethel. The Saga of Sammy-Cat. Kesteven, Peter, illus. (gr. 1-3). 1969. Repr. of 1969 ed. 2.59 (*0-08-013397-5*, Pergamon Pr) Elsevier.
Maril, Nadja. Me, Molly Midnight, the Artist's Cat. Maril, Herman, illus. LC 77-22708. 40p. (gr. k up). 1977. 9.95 (*0-916144-15-1*); pap. 3.95 (*0-916144-16-X*) Stemmer Hse.
—Runaway Molly Midnight, the Artist's Cat. Maril, Herman, illus. LC 80-17097. 40p. (gr. k up). 1980. 9.95 (*0-916144-62-3*) Stemmer Hse.
Marshall, Val & Tester, Bronwyn. The Cat's Whiskers. Knuckey, Cam, illus. LC 93-11737. 1994. 4.25 (*0-685-69328-7*) SRA Schl Grp.
Martin, Ann M. Karen's Kittens. 1992. pap. 2.75 (*0-590-45645-8*) Scholastic Inc.
Martin, Bengt. Olaf the Ship's Cat. Friberger, Anna, illus. 32p. (ps-3). 1992. 7.95 (*1-56288-266-X*) Checkerboard.
Martin, David. Lizzie & Her Kitty. Gliori, Debi, illus. LC 92-54405. 24p. (ps). 1993. 5.95 (*1-56402-058-4*) Candlewick Pr.
Marzollo, Jean. Halloween Cats. (ps-3). 1992. pap. 2.50 (*0-590-46026-9*) Scholastic Inc.
—Three Little Kittens. Thornton, Shelley, illus. 32p. (Orig.). (ps-k). 1986. pap. 2.50 (*0-590-43713-5*) Scholastic Inc.
Matthews, Morgan. Fish for Supper. Miller, Susan, illus. LC 85-14056. 48p. (Orig.). (gr. 1-3). 1986. PLB 10.59 (*0-8167-0588-7*); pap. text ed. 3.50 (*0-8167-0589-5*) Troll Assocs.
Matthias, Catherine. I Love Cats. LC 83-7215. (Illus.). 32p. (ps-2). 1983. PLB 10.25 (*0-516-02041-2*); pap. 2.95 (*0-516-42041-0*) Childrens.
Mayer, Mercer. Great Cat Chase. (ps-3). 1994. pap. 5.95 (*1-879920-07-7*) Rain Bird Prods.
Mayerson, Evelyn W. The Cat Who Escaped from Steerage. LC 90-32890. 80p. (gr. 4-6). 1990. SBE 13. 95 (*0-684-19209-8*, Scribners Young Read) Macmillan Child Grp.
Micucci, Charles. A Little Night Music. Micucci, Charles, illus. LC 88-505. 32p. (ps-3). 1989. 10.95 (*0-688-07900-8*); PLB 10.88 (*0-688-07901-6*, Morrow Jr Bks) Morrow Jr Bks.
Miller, Edna. Patches Finds a New Home. Miller, Edna, illus. (ps-4). 1989. pap. 12.95 jacketed (*0-671-66266-X*, S&S BFYR) S&S Trade.
—Patches Finds a New Home. LC 87-32355. (Illus.). 40p. (gr. k-4). 1993. pap. 5.95 (*0-671-79677-1*, S&S BFYR) S&S Trade.
Miller, Minnie T. Grandma's Tiny Kitty. 130p. (gr. k-3). 1975. 5.95 (*0-87881-014-5*) Mojave Bks.
Minarik, Else H. What If? LC 86-7649. (Illus.). 24p. (ps-2). 1987. 11.75 (*0-688-06473-6*); PLB 11.88 (*0-688-06474-4*) Greenwillow.
Mishica, Clare. Fraidy Cat Finds a Friend. Stortz, Diane, ed. (Illus.). 28p. (ps-k). 1994. 5.49 (*0-7847-0202-0*) Standard Pub.
Moncure, Jane B. Caring for My Kitty. Rigo, Christina, illus. 32p. (ps-2). 1990. PLB 12.95 (*0-89565-666-3*) Childs World.
Moore, Inga. Six-Dinner Sid. LC 90-42749. (Illus.). 32p. (ps-3). 1993. pap. 4.95 (*0-671-79613-5*, S&S BFYR) S&S Trade.
Mora, Pat. A Birthday Basket for Tia. Lang, Cecily, illus. LC 91-15753. 32p. (ps-1). 1992. RSBE 13.95 (*0-02-767400-2*, Macmillan Child Bk) Macmillan Child Grp.
Moss, Helen. Silky, the Woods Cat. Arkinstall, Eva, illus. 80p. (gr. 2-4). 1993. 10.95 (*0-89015-867-3*) Sunbelt Media.
Muntean, Michaela. The Old Man & the Afternoon Cat. Weissman, Bari, illus. LC 81-11047. 48p. (ps-3). 1982. 5.95 (*0-8193-1071-9*); PLB 5.95 (*0-8193-1072-7*) Parents.
Nannini, Roger, illus. Josephine's Toy Shop: A Look-&-Play Book with a Special Fold-Out Toy Shop. (ps-2). 1991. 15.95 (*0-8037-1004-6*) Dial Bks Young.

Nethery, Mary. Hannah & Jack. Morgan, Mary, illus. LC 93-4651. 1995. 15.95 (*0-02-768125-4*, Bradbury Pr) Macmillan Child Grp.

Neville, Emily C. It's Like This, Cat. Weiss, Emil, illus. LC 62-21292. 192p. (gr. 5-9). 1964. 15.00 (*0-06-024390-2*); PLB 14.89 (*0-06-024391-0*) HarpC Child Bks.

Newberry, Clare T. April's Kittens. Newberry, Clare T., illus. LC 40-32442. 32p. (gr. k-3). 1940. 17.00 (*0-06-024400-3*); PLB 16.89 (*0-06-024401-1*) HarpC Child Bks.

—Kittens ABC. reissue ed. Date not set. 14.95 (*0-06-024450-X*); PLB 14.89 (*0-06-024451-8*) HarpC Child Bks.

Newman, Al. Fraid E. Cat. Doody, Jim, illus. LC 93-77687. 32p. (ps-3). 1993. 13.95 (*0-89334-215-7*); pap. 4.95 (*0-89334-219-X*) Humanics Ltd.

Newman, Nanette. Spider the Horrible Cat. Foreman, Michael, illus. LC 92-17242. 1993. write for info. (*0-15-277972-8*) HarBrace.

Newton, Jill. Cat-Fish. LC 91-42858. (Illus.). 32p. (ps up). 1992. 14.00 (*0-688-11423-7*); PLB 13.93 (*0-688-11424-5*) Lothrop.

Nicklaus, Carol. Come Dance with Me. Nicklaus, Carol, illus. 32p. (ps-1). 1991. PLB 5.95 (*0-671-73503-9*); pap. 2.95 (*0-671-73507-1*) Silver Pr.

Nightingale, Sandy. Cat's Knees & Bee's Whiskers. Nightingale, Sandy, illus. LC 92-39811. 1993. 14.95 (*0-15-215364-0*) HarBrace.

Nizer, Louis. Catspaw. (gr. 4 up). Date not set. pap. 4.99 (*0-517-11076-8*) Random Hse Value.

Nodset, Joan L. Come Here, Cat. Kellog, Steven, illus. LC 92-39005. (ps-3). 1973. 10.00 (*0-06-024557-3*); PLB 9.89 (*0-06-024558-1*) HarpC Child Bks.

Noonan, Diana. Fat Cat Tompkin. Smith, Craig, illus. LC 92-34273. 1993. 3.75 (*0-383-03623-2*) SRA Schl Grp.

Nordqvist, Sven. Festus & Mercury Go Camping. LC 92-43181. 1993. 18.95 (*0-87614-802-X*) Carolrhoda Bks.

Norman, Philip R. Dancing Dogs. LC 93-2533. 1995. 14.95 (*0-316-61208-1*) Little.

Norton, Miriam. Kitten Who Thought He Was a Mouse. (ps-3). 1993. 11.95 (*0-307-17553-7*, Artsts Writrs) Western Pub.

Oana, Katy D. Shasta & the Shebang Machine. Stephens, Jacquelyn S., illus. LC 77-18350. (gr. k-2). 1978. PLB 5.95 (*0-89508-066-4*) Rainbow Bks.

Oke, Janette. The Prodigal Cat. 160p. (Orig.). (gr. 3). 1984. pap. 4.99 (*0-934998-19-1*) Bethel Pub.

Okimoto, Jean D. Blumpoe Grumpoe Meets Arnold C, Vol. 1. (ps-3). 1990. 13.95 (*0-316-63811-0*, Joy St Bks) Little.

The Old Man & the Afternoon Cat. 42p. (ps-3). 1992. PLB 13.27 (*0-8368-0886-X*) Gareth Stevens Inc.

Oldfield, Margaret J. Fat Cat & Ebenezer Geezer: The Teeny Tiny Mouse. 2nd ed. Oldfield, Margaret J., illus. (gr. k-2). 1980. pap. 3.00 (*0-934876-13-4*) Creative Storytime.

One Eyed Cat. 1986. pap. 3.25 (*0-440-76641-9*) Dell.

Oppenheim, Joanne. Do You Like Cats? Newsom, Carol, illus. LC 92-14113. 1993. 9.99 (*0-553-09116-6*, Little Rooster); pap. 3.99 (*0-553-37107-X*, Little Rooster) Bantam.

Ormerod, Jan. Come Back, Kittens: A Hide & Seek Book with See-Through Pages. Ormerod, Jan, illus. LC 91-30426. 32p. (ps up). 1992. 13.00 (*0-688-09134-2*) Lothrop.

Osband, Gillian. Boysie's Kitten. Allen, Jonathan, illus. 32p. (ps-2). 1990. PLB 14.95 (*0-87614-403-2*) Carolrhoda Bks.

Ossorio, Joseph D. & Salvadeo, Michele B. How Did Cats Get Their Tails. (Illus.). 48p. (gr. 2-4). 1994. pap. 6.95 (*1-56721-055-4*) Twnty-Fifth Cent Pr.

Outlet Staff. Tabby Cat Wants That. 1991. 3.99 (*0-517-05682-8*) Random Hse Value.

Packard, Mary. Christmas Kitten. (Illus.). 28p. (ps-2). 1994. PLB 14.00 (*0-516-05364-7*) Childrens.

Palazzo-Craig, Janet. Case of the Missing Cat. Shire, Ellen, illus. LC 77-7635. 48p. (gr. 2-4). 1982. PLB 10.89 (*0-89375-594-X*); pap. text ed. 3.50 (*0-89375-595-8*) Troll Assocs.

Pank, Rachel. Sonia & Barnie & the Noise in the Night. 1991. pap. 13.95 (*0-590-44657-6*) Scholastic Inc.

—Under the Blackberries. 1992. 13.95 (*0-590-45481-1*, Scholastic Hardcover) Scholastic Inc.

Parker, A. E. The Case of the Invisible Cat. (gr. 4-7). 1992. pap. 2.95 (*0-590-45632-6*) Scholastic Inc.

Parnall, Peter. Marsh Cat. Parnall, Peter, illus. LC 90-25733. 128p. (gr. 3 up). 1991. SBE 13.95 (*0-02-770120-4*, Macmillan Child Bk) Macmillan Child Grp.

Patterson, Francine. Koko's Kitten. Cohn, Ronald H., photos by. 50p. (gr. k up). 1985. pap. 13.95 (*0-590-40952-2*) Scholastic Inc.

El Perro y el Gato (Dog & Cat) (SPA., Illus.). 28p. (ps-2). 1991. PLB 11.55 (*0-516-35353-5*); pap. 3.95 (*0-516-55353-4*) Childrens.

Peters, Sharon. Five Little Kittens. Rosenberg, Amye, illus. LC 81-2317. 32p. (gr. k-2). 1981. PLB 11.59 (*0-89375-503-6*); pap. 2.95 (*0-89375-504-4*) Troll Assocs.

Peterson, Cliff & Peterson, Anne. The Adventures of Sir Wellington Boots. 1993. 7.95 (*0-533-10328-2*) Vantage.

Pilkey, Dav. Dragon's Fat Cat. LC 91-16369. (Illus.). 48p. (gr. 1-3). 1992. 12.95 (*0-531-05982-0*); lib. bdg. 12.99 (*0-531-08582-1*) Orchard Bks Watts.

—Kat Kong. LC 92-14483. (ps-3). 1993. 10.95 (*0-15-242036-3*); pap. 5.95 (*0-15-242037-1*) HarBrace.

—When Cats Dream. LC 91-31355. (Illus.). 32p. (ps-2). 1992. 14.95 (*0-531-05997-9*); PLB 14.99 (*0-531-08597-X*) Orchard Bks Watts.

Pinkwater, Daniel. The Wuggie Norple Story. De Paola, Tomie, illus. LC 88-878. 40p. (gr. k-4). 1988. pap. 4.50 (*0-689-71257-X*, Aladdin) Macmillan Child Grp.

Pirotta, Saviour. Follow That Cat! Melnyczuk, Peter, illus. LC 92-38287. 32p. (gr. k-3). 1993. 13.99 (*0-525-45125-0*, DCB) Dutton Child Bks.

Pittman, Helena C. Miss Hindy's Cats: Picture Book. (ps-3). 1991. pap. 6.95 (*0-87614-538-1*) Carolrhoda Bks.

Poe, Edgar Allan. The Black Cat. Redpath, Ann, ed. Delessert, Etienne, illus. 32p. (gr. 9 up). 1985. PLB 13.95s.p. (*0-88682-001-4*) Creative Ed.

—The Black Cat. rev. ed. (gr. 9-12). 1989. Repr. of 1902 ed. multi-media kit 35.00 (*0-685-31130-9*) Balance Pub.

Polacco, Patricia. Mrs. Katz & Tush. 1992. 15.00 (*0-553-08122-5*, Little Rooster) Bantam.

—Tikvah Means Hope. (ps-3). 1994. 15.95 (*0-385-32059-0*) Doubleday.

Polette, Nancy. Little Old Woman & the Hungry Cat. LC 88-18788. (Illus.). 24p. (ps up). 1989. 12.95 (*0-688-08314-5*); PLB 12.88 (*0-688-08315-3*) Greenwillow.

Polushkin, Maria. Kitten in Trouble. Levin, Betsy, illus. LC 85-5753. 32p. (ps-k). 1988. RSBE 13.95 (*0-02-774740-9*, Bradbury Pr) Macmillan Child Grp.

Potter, Beatrix. The Complete Adventures of Tom Kitten. (ps-3). 1987. pap. 5.95 (*0-14-050503-2*, Puffin) Puffin Bks.

—El Cuento del Gato Tomas. (SPA., Illus.). 64p. 1988. 4.95 (*0-7232-3565-1*) Warne.

—The Roly-Poly Pudding. 80p. (gr. 1 up). 1986. pap. 2.75 (*0-486-25099-7*) Dover.

—The Roly-Poly Pudding. LC 93-34679. (Illus.). 1994. 6.95 (*0-681-45606-X*) Longmeadow Pr.

—The Tale of Tom Kitten. (Illus.). 58p. (gr. k up). 1983. pap. 1.75 (*0-486-24502-0*) Dover.

—The Tale of Tom Kitten. Atkinson, Allen, illus. 1983. pap. 2.25 (*0-553-15224-6*) Bantam.

—The Tale of Tom Kitten. Frenck, Hal, illus. LC 87-40285. 24p. (ps up). 1990. incl. audio cassettes 6.95 (*1-55782-018-X*, Pub. by Warner Juvenile Bks) Little.

—The Tale of Tom Kitten. (Illus.). (ps-3). 1987. 5.95 (*0-7232-3467-1*); pap. 2.25 (*0-7232-3492-2*) Warne.

—The Tale of Tom Kitten. Routledge, Patricia, read by. (ps-3). 1992. pap. 6.95 bk. & tape (*0-7232-3670-4*) Warne.

—Tale of Tom Kitten. 1988. bds. 2.99 (*0-517-65278-1*) Random Hse Value.

—The Tale of Tom Kitten. (Illus.). 32p. (ps-3). 1994. pap. 3.99 (*0-14-054296-5*) Puffin Bks.

—Tom Chaton. (FRE.). 58p. 1980. 10.95 (*2-07-056071-6*) Schoenhof.

—Tom Chaton. (FRE., Illus.). 58p. 1980. 9.95 (*0-7859-3626-2*, 2070560715) Fr & Eur.

—Tom Kitten: Beatrix Potter Deluxe Pop Up. (Illus.). 1992. 4.99 (*0-517-06998-9*) Random Hse Value.

—Tom Kitten's Playtime. (Illus.). 24p. (ps). 1994. bds. 2.99 (*0-7232-4092-2*) Warne.

Potter, Beatrix, created by. Tom Kitten. Marsh, T. F., et al, illus. 24p. (gr. 2-4). 1992. PLB 10.95 (*1-56674-010-X*, HTS Bks) Forest Hse.

Potter, Maureen. Theatre Cat. 64p. 1986. 11.95 (*0-86278-085-3*, Pub. by O'Brien Press Ltd Eire) Dufour.

Poulin, Stephane. Can You Catch Josephine? Poulin, Stephane, illus. LC 87-50374. 24p. (gr. k-4). 1988. 12.95 (*0-88776-198-4*); pap. 6.95 (*0-88776-214-X*) Tundra Bks.

—Peux-tu Attraper Josephine? LC 87-50375. (FRE., Illus.). 24p. (Orig.). (gr. k-4). 1988. 12.95 (*0-88776-199-2*); pap. 6.95 (*0-88776-225-5*) Tundra Bks.

Price, Susan. The Ghost Drum: A Cat's Tale. LC 86-46032. 176p. (gr. 5 up). 1987. 15.00 (*0-374-32538-3*) FS&G.

Provensen, Alice & Provensen, Martin. An Owl & Three Pussycats. LC 93-44747. (gr. k-3). 1994. 16.95 (*0-15-200183-2*, Browndeer Pr) HarBrace.

Pryor, Ainslie. The Baby Blue Cat & the Dirty Dog Brothers. (Illus.). (ps-3). 1987. 11.95 (*0-670-81781-3*) Viking Child Bks.

—Baby Blue Cat & the Smiley Worm Doll. (ps). 1990. 11.95 (*0-670-83531-5*) Viking Child Bks.

—The Baby Blue Cat & the Whole Batch of Cookies. (Illus.). 32p. (ps-1). 1989. 11.95 (*0-670-81782-1*) Viking Child Bks.

—The Baby Blue Cat & the Whole Batch of Cookies. (Illus.). 32p. (ps-1). 1991. pap. 3.95 (*0-14-050770-1*, Puffin) Puffin Bks.

—The Baby Blue Cat Who Said No. (Illus.). 32p. (gr. 2-6). 1990. pap. 4.99 (*0-14-050768-X*, Puffin) Puffin Bks.

Purdy, Carol. Mrs. Merriwether's Musical Cat. Mathers, Petra, illus. LC 92-43934. 32p. (ps-3). 1994. PLB 15.95 (*0-399-22543-9*, Putnam) Putnam Pub Group.

Puss in Boots. (Illus.). 24p. (Orig.). (gr. k-3). 1993. pap. 2.50 (*1-56144-297-6*, Honey Bear Bks) Modern Pub NYC.

Puss 'n Boots. (FRE.). (gr. k-3). 9.95 (*0-685-28440-9*) Fr & Eur.

Radke, Martha E. The Cat Who Conducted with His Tail. Tootill, Ginger, illus. LC 81-90803. 28p. (Orig.). (ps-3). 1982. pap. 1.95 (*0-9607994-0-0*) G E Radke.

Radzinski, Kandy, illus. The Twelve Cats of Christmas. 32p. 1992. 9.95 (*0-8118-0102-0*) Chronicle Bks.

Rayburn, Cherie. Where's Kitty? Luedecke, Beverly, illus. 12p. (ps-5). 1994. pap. 8.25 (*0-944943-45-4*, 23304-5) Current Inc.

Reiser, Lynn. Bedtime Cat. LC 90-30751. (Illus.). 24p. (ps up). 1991. 13.95 (*0-688-10025-2*); PLB 13.88 (*0-688-10026-0*) Greenwillow.

—Dog & Cat. LC 90-3553. (Illus.). 24p. (ps up). 1991. 13.95 (*0-688-09892-4*); PLB 13.88 (*0-688-09893-2*) Greenwillow.

Richardson, Jean. Dino, the Ding Bat Cat. Peterson, Nancy G., illus. LC 92-17736. 48p. (gr. 1-3). 1992. 12.95 (*0-89015-869-X*) Sunbelt Media.

Risom, Ole. I Am a Kitten. Szekeres, Cyndy, illus. 26p. (ps). 1993. bds. 3.95 (*0-307-12169-0*, 12169, Golden Pr) Western Pub.

Roberts, Bethany. Cat Parade! Greenseid, Diane, illus. LC 93-26726. 1995. write for info. (*0-395-67893-5*, Clarion Bks) HM.

—Halloween Mice! Cushman, Doug, illus. LC 93-17192. 1994. write for info. (*0-395-67064-0*, Clarion Bks) HM.

Robertus, Polly. The Dog Who Had Kittens. Stevens, Janet, illus. LC 90-39174. 32p. (ps-3). 1991. reinforced bdg. 14.95 (*0-8234-0860-4*); pap. 5.95 (*0-8234-0974-0*) Holiday.

Robinson, Nancy K. Just Plain Cat. LC 82-18258. 128p. (gr. 3-6). 1984. SBE 13.95 (*0-02-777350-7*, Four Winds) Macmillan Child Grp.

—Just Plain Cat. reissue ed. 1992. pap. 2.95 (*0-590-45850-7*, Apple Paperbacks) Scholastic Inc.

Rockwell, Anne, as told by. & illus. Puss in Boots & Other Stories. LC 87-14976. 96p. (gr. k-4). 1988. SBE 16.95 (*0-02-777781-2*, Macmillan Child Bk) Macmillan Child Grp.

Rodriguez, Agatha A. Catability. Medina, Mary L., illus. 20p. (Orig.). 1990. pap. text ed. 7.95g (*0-933196-04-0*) Bilingue Pubns.

Roe, JoAnn. Marco the Manx Series, 3 bks. Runestrand, Meredith & Mayo, Steve, illus. (gr. k-5). Set. write for info. (*0-931551-06-4*); Fisherman Cat, 1988. PLB 10.95 (*0-931551-02-1*); Alaska Cat. PLB 10.95 (*0-931551-05-6*); Castaway Cat. pap. 5.95 (*0-931551-03-X*); Fisherman Cat, 1988. pap. 6.95 (*0-931551-01-3*); Alaska Cat. pap. 6.95 (*0-931551-04-8*) Montevista Pr.

—Samurai Cat: Marco the Manx Ser. (Illus.). 64p. (gr. k-5). 1993. PLB 11.95 (*0-931551-08-0*); pap. 6.95 (*0-931551-07-2*) Montevista Pr.

Roennfeldt, Mary. What's That Noise? Roennfeldt, Robert, illus. LC 91-16215. 32p. (ps-1). 1992. 13.95 (*0-531-05972-3*); lib. bdg. 13.99 (*0-531-08572-4*) Orchard Bks Watts.

Roos, Kelley & Roos, Stephen. The Incredible Cat Caper. (gr. 3-6). 1986. pap. 2.75 (*0-440-44084-X*, YB) Dell.

Rose, Agatha. Hide-&-Seek in the Yellow House. Spohn, Kate, illus. 32p. (ps-1). 1992. PLB 14.00 (*0-670-84383-0*) Viking Child Bks.

Rose, David S. Maynard's Dreams. Rose, David S., illus. LC 92-43146. 32p. (ps-3). 1993. SBE 14.95 (*0-689-31847-2*, Atheneum Child Bk) Macmillan Child Grp.

Rosenbluth, Rosalyn. Scaredy-Cat Kitten. Borgo, Deborah, illus. 24p. (ps-2). 1993. pap. text ed. 0.99 (*1-56293-352-3*) McClanahan Bk.

Ross, Katharine. Fuzzy Kitten. McCue, Lisa, illus. LC 92-62262. 22p. (ps-3). 1993. 3.50 (*0-679-84644-1*) Random Bks Yng Read.

Ross, Tony. I Want a Cat. (Illus.). 26p. (ps up). 1989. 13.00 (*0-374-33621-0*) FS&G.

—I Want a Cat. (Illus.). 26p. (ps up). 1991. pap. 4.95 (*0-374-43544-8*) FS&G.

Roy, Claude. Chat Qui Parlait Malgre Lui. Glaseur, Willi, illus. (FRE.). 87p. (gr. 5-10). 1982. pap. 8.95 (*2-07-033615-8*) Schoenhof.

Rubinstein, Gillian. Dog in, Cat Out. James, Ann, illus. LC 92-39785. 32p. (ps-k). 1993. PLB 13.95 (*0-395-66596-5*) Ticknor & Flds Bks Yng Read.

Rushton, Willie. Every Cat in the Book. (Illus.). 64p. (gr. 3-5). 1994. 19.95 (*1-85793-199-8*, Pub. by Pavilion UK) Trafalgar.

Rylant, Cynthia. Henry & Mudge & the Happy Cat. Stevenson, Sucie, illus. LC 88-18855. 48p. (gr. 1-3). 1990. RSBE 13.95 (*0-02-778008-2*, Bradbury Pr) Macmillan Child Grp.

—Henry & Mudge & the Happy Cat: The Eighth Book of Their Adventures. Stevenson, Sucie, illus. LC 93-10797. 48p. (gr. 1-3). 1994. pap. 3.95 (*0-689-71791-1*, Aladdin) Macmillan Child Grp.

—Mr. Putter & Tabby Pick the Pears. Howard, Arthur, illus. LC 94-11259. 1995. write for info. (*0-15-200245-6*) HarBrace.

—Mr. Putter & Tabby Pour the Tea. Howard, Arthur, illus. LC 93-21470. (ps-6). 1994. 10.95 (*0-15-256255-9*) HarBrace.

—Mr. Putter & Tabby Pour the Tea. (ps-3). 1994. pap. 4.95 (*0-15-200901-9*, HB Juv Bks) HarBrace.

—Mr. Putter & Tabby Walk the Dog. Howard, Arthur, illus. LC 93-21467. (ps-6). 1994. 10.95 (*0-15-256259-1*) HarBrace.

St. Pierre, Stephanie. The Three Little Kittens. Regan, Dana, illus. 12p. (ps). 1994. bds. 4.95 (*0-448-40459-1*, G&D) Putnam Pub Group.

—Valentine Kittens. 1990. pap. 3.95 (*0-590-63481-X*) Scholastic Inc.

Saki. Tobermory. 32p. (gr. 6). 1990. PLB 13.95 (*0-88682-305-6*) Creative Ed.

Salem, Lynn & Stewart, Josie. The Cat Who Loved Red. (Illus.). 8p. (gr. 1). 1992. pap. 3.50 (1-880612-03-8) Seedling Pubns.

Sampson, Fay. Pangur Ban. (Illus.). 128p. (Orig.). (gr. 4-8). 1989. pap. 4.99 (0-85648-580-2) Lion USA.

—Serpent of Senargad. (Illus.). 128p. (gr. 4-8). 1989. pap. 4.99 (0-7459-1520-5) Lion USA.

—Shape-Shifter. (Illus.). 128p. (gr. 4-8). 1989. pap. 4.99 (0-7459-1347-4) Lion USA.

San Souci, Robert D. The White Cat. Spirin, Gennady, illus. LC 88-19698. 32p. (ps-3). 1990. 15.95 (0-531-05809-3); PLB 15.99 (0-531-08409-4) Orchard Bks Watts.

Sara. Across Town. LC 90-7982. (Illus.). 32p. (ps-2). 1991. 13.95 (0-531-05932-4); PLB 13.99 (0-531-08532-5) Orchard Bks Watts.

Sargent, Dave & Sargent, Pat. Bobby Bobcat. 64p. (gr. 2-6). 1992. pap. write for info. (1-56763-012-X) Ozark Pub.

Sathre, Vivian. Mouse Chase. Schumaker, Ward, illus. LC 94-17010. Date not set. write for info. (0-15-200105-0) HarBrace.

Saunders, Susan. Mystery Cat, Bk. 1. (Orig.). (ps-3). 1986. pap. 2.25 (0-553-15377-3, Skylark) Bantam.

—Mystery Cat & the Chocolate Trap. 96p. (Orig.). 1986. pap. 2.25 (0-553-15415-X, Skylark) Bantam.

Scamell, Ragnhild. Solo Plus One. Martland, Elizabeth, illus. 32p. (ps-3). 1992. 13.95 (0-316-77242-9) Little.

Scaredy Kitten. 28p. (ps-2). 1992. 3.95 (0-7214-5309-0, S915-2) Ladybird Bks.

Scarry, Richard. Richard Scarry's the Cat Family Takes a Trip. (Illus.). 24p. (ps-3). 1992. write for info. (0-307-12760-5, 12760) Western Pub.

—Richard Scarry's the Cat Family's Busy Day. (Illus.). 24p. (ps-3). 1992. write for info. (0-307-12761-3, 12761) Western Pub.

Schertle, Alice. That Olive! Wheeler, Cindy, illus. LC 84-10025. 32p. (ps-1). 1986. PLB 11.88 (0-688-04091-8) Lothrop.

Schlein, Miriam. The Way Mothers Are: Thirtieth Anniversary Edition. rev. ed. Tucker, Kathy, ed. Lasker, Joe, illus. LC 92-21516. 32p. (ps-k). 1993. PLB 13.95 (0-8075-8691-9) A Whitman.

Schmidt, Annie M. Minnie. Salway, Lance, tr. from DUT. LC 93-35924. 1994. pap. 6.95 (0-915943-95-6) Milkweed Ed.

Schoch, Tim. Cat Attack. (gr. 3-7). 1988. pap. 2.75 (0-380-75520-3, Camelot) Avon.

Schreiber-Wicke, Edith. Cats' Carnival. Laimgruber, Monika, illus. LC 85-45964. 24p. 1986. 13.95 (0-87923-627-2) Godine.

Schurr, Cathleen. The Shy Little Kitten. reissued ed. Tenggren, Gustaf, illus. 24p. (ps-k). 1992. write for info. (0-307-00145-8, 312-10, Golden Pr) Western Pub.

Segal, Lore. The Story of Mrs. Lovewright & Purrless Her Cat. reissued ed. Zelinsky, Paul, illus. LC 84-25011. 40p. (ps up). 1993. 14.00 (0-394-86817-X) Knopf Bks Yng Read.

Seidler, Ann & Slepian, Jan. The Cat Who Wore a Pot on Her Head. Martin, Richard E., illus. 32p. (gr. k-3). 1987. pap. 3.95 (0-590-43708-9) Scholastic Inc.

Selden, George. Harry Kitten & Tucker Mouse. Williams, Garth, illus. LC 83-16530. 64p. (gr. 2-5). 1986. 14.00 (0-374-32860-9) FS&G.

—Harry Kitten & Tucker Mouse. (gr. k-6). 1989. pap. 3.50 (0-440-40124-0, YB) Dell.

Sesame Street Staff. Grover's New Kitten. Barrett, John E., photos by. LC 81-50538. (Illus.). 14p. (ps). 1981. bds. 3.95 (0-394-84872-1) Random Bks Yng Read.

Sharmat, Marjorie W. School Bus Cat. (gr. 4-7). 1990. pap. 2.99 (0-06-106024-0, PL) HarpC.

Sheldon, Dyan. Harry on Vacation. Heap, Sue, illus. LC 92-52999. 144p. (gr. 3-6). 1993. 13.95 (1-56402-127-0) Candlewick Pr.

Silverman, Erica. Mrs. Peachtree & the Eighth Avenue Cat. Beier, Ellen, illus. LC 92-16973. 32p. (ps-3). 1994. RSBE 15.00 (0-02-782684-8, Macmillan Child Bk) Macmillan Child Grp.

Simon, Norma. The Baby House. Samuels, Barbara, illus. LC 94-6637. 1995. 14.00 (0-671-87044-0, S&S BFYR) S&S Trade.

—Oh, That Cat! Leder, Dora, illus. LC 85-15546. 32p. (ps-4). 1986. 11.95 (0-8075-5919-9) A Whitman.

Slater, Helen. Fuzzy Friends: Cuddle the Kitten. (Illus.). 10p. 1993. 3.95 (0-681-41812-5) Longmeadow Pr.

Slavin, Bill & Tucker, Kathleen, eds. The Cat Came Back. Slavin, Bill, illus. 32p. (gr. 1-6). 1992. 13.95g (0-8075-1097-1) A Whitman.

Slepian, Jan. The Broccoli Tapes. (gr. 3-7). 1989. 14.95 (0-399-21712-6, Philomel Bks) Putnam Pub Group.

—Broccoli Tapes. 225p. 1992. text ed. 18.00 (1-56956-201-6) W A T Braille.

The Smart Little Cat. (Illus.). (ps-2). 1991. PLB 6.95 (0-8136-5172-7, TK3879); pap. 3.50 (0-8136-5672-9, TK3880) Modern Curr.

Smith. Help! There's a Cat Washing Here. (ps-7). 1987. pap. 2.50 (0-553-15374-9, Skylark) Bantam.

Smith, Glenna C. The Little Mouse Was a Grouch. Jordan, Alton, ed. (Illus.). (gr. k-3). 1981. (Read Res); pap. text ed. 20.00 (0-89868-106-5) ARO Pub.

Smith, Linda J. Cat's Wedding. LC 89-7422. (Illus.). 32p. (gr. k-2). 1989. 12.95 (0-8249-8402-1, Ideals Child) Hambleton-Hill.

—Three Little Kittens. Smith, Linda J., illus. LC 90-5102. 32p. (ps-3). 1991. 13.95 (0-8249-8490-0, Ideals Child) Hambleton-Hill.

Smith, Matthew V. Flip the Cat. Smith, Matthew V., illus. 10p. (gr. k-3). 1993. pap. 10.95 (1-56606-013-3) Bradley Mann.

Sneed, Brad. Lucky Russell. (Illus.). 32p. (ps-3). 1992. 14.95 (0-399-22329-0, Putnam) Putnam Pub Group.

Snyder, Phillip C. Pa Pong: A Siamese Kitty. Mohrman, Janet S., illus. 28p. (ps-1). 1981. pap. text ed. 3.95 (0-940560-03-8) Custom Hse.

Sommers, Maxine S. Texas Cool Cat Coloring Book. Bircham, Don, illus. 10p. (Orig.). (gr. k-1). 1991. pap. 1.95 size: 8 1/2" x 11" (0-943991-20-X) Pound Sterling Pub.

Sorenson, Jody. The Secret Letters of Mama Cat. LC 87-25333. 122p. (gr. 5-8). 1988. 12.95 (0-8027-6779-6); PLB 13.85 (0-8027-6791-5) Walker & Co.

Soto, Gary. Chato's Kitchen. Guevara, Susan, illus. LC 93-43503. 1995. write for info. (0-399-22658-3, Putnam) Putnam Pub Group.

Spier, Peter. Peter Spier's Little Cats. LC 82-45494. (Illus.). 14p. (ps-1). 1984. 2.50 (0-385-18197-3) Doubleday.

Spirn, Michele. The Cat Who Couldn't Meow. (ps-1). 1988. 8.49 (0-87386-054-3); incl. cassette 16.99 (0-685-25195-0); pap. 1.95 (0-87386-050-0); pap. 9.95 incl. cassette (0-685-25196-9) Jan Prods.

Spohn, Kate. Clementine's Winter Wardrobe. LC 89-42531. (Illus.). 32p. (ps-1). 1989. 13.95 (0-531-05841-7); PLB 13.99 (0-531-08441-8) Orchard Bks Watts.

Stahl, Hilda. Sendi Lee Mason & the Stray Striped Cat. LC 90-80621. 128p. (Orig.). (gr. 2-5). 1990. pap. 4.95 (0-89107-580-1) Crossway Bks.

Stanley, Diane. Siegfried. (ps-3). 1991. 15.00 (0-553-07022-3) Bantam.

Steadman, Ralph. No Room to Swing a Cat. (Illus.). 32p. (gr. k-2). 1990. 15.95 (0-86264-241-8, Pub. by Anderson Pr UK) Trafalgar.

Steenstra, Virginia G. Best Cat. 1993. 7.95 (0-8062-4608-1) Carlton.

Steiber, Ellen. Fangs of Evil. LC 93-44043. 108p. (Orig.). (gr. 2-6). 1994. pap. 2.99 (0-679-85466-5, Bullseye Bks) Random Bks Yng Read.

Stevens, Janet. How the Manx Cat Lost Its Tail. (ps-8). 1992. pap. 4.95 (0-15-236766-7) HarBrace.

Stevenson, James. Will You Please Feed Our Cat? Stevenson, James, illus. LC 86-11927. 32p. (gr. k-3). 1987. 11.75 (0-688-06847-2); lib. bdg. 11.88 (0-688-06848-0) Greenwillow.

Stewart, Linda. Sam the Cat Detective. (gr. 4-7). 1993. pap. 2.95 (0-590-46145-1) Scholastic Inc.

Stolz, Mary. CatWalk. Blegvad, Erik, illus. LC 82-47576. 128p. (gr. 3-7). 1985. pap. 3.95 (0-06-440155-3, Trophy) HarpC Child Bks.

—The Weeds & the Weather. Watson, N. Cameron, illus. LC 93-240. 40p. (gr. k up). 1994. 14.00 (0-688-12289-2); PLB 13.93 (0-688-12290-6) Greenwillow.

Storr, Catherine, as told by. Dick Whittington. LC 85-16904. (Illus.). 32p. (gr. 2-5). 1985. PLB 19.97 (0-8172-2507-2) Raintree Steck-V.

Stott, Dorothy. Kitty & Me. (gr. 4 up). 1993. 9.99 (0-525-45075-0, DCB) Dutton Child Bks.

Strub, Susanne. My Cat & I. Strub, Susanne, illus. LC 92-21839. 32p. (ps up). 1993. 14.00 (0-688-12008-3, Tambourine Bks); PLB 13.93 (0-688-12009-1, Tambourine Bks) Morrow.

Stufgis, Matthew. Tosca's Surprise. Mortimer, Anne, illus. 32p. (ps-3). 1994. pap. 4.50 (0-14-055270-7, Puff Pied Piper) Puffin Bks.

Sturgis, Matthew. Tosca's Christmas. Mortimer, Anne, illus. 32p. (ps-3). 1992. pap. 3.99 (0-14-054840-8, Puff Pied Piper) Puffin Bks.

—Tosca's Surprise. Mortimer, Anne, illus. LC 90-38731. 32p. (ps-3). 1991. 11.95 (0-8037-0946-3) Dial Bks Young.

Su, Lucy. Jinzi & Minzi Are Friends. Su, Lucy, illus. LC 91-58738. 24p. (ps up). 1992. 5.95 (1-56402-051-7) Candlewick Pr.

—Jinzi & Minzi at the Playground. Su, Lucy, illus. LC 91-58740. 24p. (ps up). 1992. 5.95 (1-56402-052-5) Candlewick Pr.

Supraner, Robyn. The Cat Who Wanted to Fly. Goodman, Joan E., illus. LC 85-14119. 48p. (Orig.). (gr. 1-3). 1986. PLB 10.59 (0-8167-0612-3); pap. text ed. 3.50 (0-8167-0613-1) Troll Assocs.

—Kitty: A Cat's Diary. Paterson, Diane, illus. LC 85-14023. 48p. (Orig.). (gr. 1-3). 1986. PLB 10.59 (0-8167-0574-7); pap. text ed. 3.50 (0-8167-0575-5) Troll Assocs.

Sweeney, Joyce. Shadow: A Novel. LC 93-32215. 1994. 15.95 (0-385-32051-5) Delacorte.

Tamar, Erika. It Happened at Cecilia's. LC 91-8171. 144p. (gr. 7 up). 1991. pap. 3.95 (0-02-045395-7, Collier Young Ad) Macmillan Child Grp.

Tan, Amy. The Chinese Siamese Cat. Schields, Gretchen, illus. LC 93-24008. (gr. k-3). 1994. 16.95 (0-02-788835-5, Macmillan Child Bk) Macmillan Child Grp.

Taylor, Mildred D. The Gold Cadillac. Hays, Michael, illus. LC 86-11526. 48p. (gr. 2-6). 1987. 12.95 (0-8037-0342-2); PLB 12.89 (0-8037-0343-0) Dial Bks Young.

Taylor, Theodore. Sniper. LC 89-7415. 227p. (gr. 7 up). 1989. 15.95 (0-15-276420-8) HarBrace.

Teague, Mark. The Trouble with the Johnsons. (Illus.). (gr. k-3). 1989. pap. 12.95 (0-590-42394-0) Scholastic Inc.

Thaler, Mike. Catzilla. (gr. 4-7). 1991. pap. 2.95 (0-671-73297-8) S&S Trade.

—My Cat Is Going to the Dogs. Lee, Jared, illus. LC 93-18596. 32p. (ps-3). 1993. PLB 9.79 (0-8167-3022-9); pap. 2.95 (0-8167-3023-7) Troll Assocs.

Thompson, Emily. Imagine: A Million Kittens for Elmo. (ps-3). 1993. pap. 2.25 (0-307-13122-X, Golden Pr) Western Pub.

—Rosita's Calico Cat. Brannon, Tom, illus. 24p. (ps-3). 1994. pap. 2.25 (0-307-13127-0, Pub. by Golden Bks) Western Pub.

Three Little Kittens. (Illus.). (ps-1). 1985. 2.99 (0-517-47898-6) Random Hse Value.

Titus, Eve. The Kitten Who Couldn't Purr. Fechner, Amrei, illus. LC 90-13418. 32p. (ps up). 1991. Repr. 12.95 (0-688-09363-9); PLB 12.88 (0-688-09364-7, Morrow Jr Bks) Morrow Jr Bks.

Tom Kitten. (Illus.). (ps-2). 1.95 (0-7214-5219-1) Ladybird Bks.

Turkle, Brinton. Do Not Open. Turkle, Brinton, illus. LC 80-10289. 32p. (ps-2). 1981. pap. 13.95 (0-525-28785-X, 01258-370, DCB) Dutton Child Bks.

Turnbull, Ann. Queen Cat. (gr. 4-7). 1992. pap. 2.99 (0-440-40511-4, YB) Dell.

Underhill, Liz. Miss McTaffety's Cats. (Illus.). 32p. (ps-1). 1994. 19.95 (0-224-03040-X, Pub. by Jonathan Cape UK) Trafalgar.

Uspenski, Eduard. Uncle Fedya, His Dog, & His Cat. Shpitalnik, Vladimir, illus. Heim, Michael, tr. from RUS. LC 92-44491. (Illus.). 144p. (gr. 1-5). 1993. 14.00 (0-679-82064-7) Knopf Bks Yng Read.

Vagin, Vladimir & Asch, Frank. Here Comes the Cat! Vagin, Vladimir & Asch, Frank, illus. LC 88-3083. (gr. k-3). 1989. pap. 11.95 (0-590-41859-9) Scholastic Inc.

Viorst, Judith. The Tenth Good Thing about Barney. Blegvad, Eric, illus. LC 71-154764. 32p. (gr. k-4). 1971. SBE 13.95 (0-689-20688-7, Atheneum Child Bk) Macmillan Child Grp.

Wahl, Jan. Dracula's Cat. LC 77-27051. (Illus.). (ps-3). 1981. 6.95 (0-685-03842-4); pap. 2.50 (0-685-03843-2) P-H.

—Dracula's Cat & Frankenstein's Dog. Chorao, Kay, illus. (ps-2). 1990. pap. 13.95 (0-671-70820-1) S&S Trade.

—My Cat Ginger. Naava, illus. LC 91-31883. 32p. (ps-2). 1992. 14.00 (0-688-10722-2, Tambourine Bks); PLB 13.93 (0-688-10723-0, Tambourine Bks) Morrow.

—Tim Kitten & the Red Cupboard. 1990. pap. 2.25 (0-671-70296-3, S&S BFYR) S&S Trade.

Wallace, Bill. Snot Stew. McCue, Lisa, illus. LC 88-31976. 96p. (gr. 3-7). 1989. 13.95 (0-8234-0745-4) Holiday.

Walsh, Abigail M. Momma Cat. Dowling, Marilyn, illus. LC 90-823. 112p. (gr. 2 up). 1990. 6.95 (0-934745-16-1) Acadia Pub Co.

Walsh, Jill P. Pepi & the Secret Names. French, Fiona, illus. LC 93-48620. 1994. 15.00 (0-688-13428-9) Lothrop.

Walter, Lori J. The World According to Wally: It's All in How You See It. Kehl, Donald & Messoner, Dale, eds. Taylor, David S., illus. 30p. (Orig.). (gr. k-8). 1994. Incl. cass. pap. 13.95 (0-9634833-2-3) Rocking Bridge. Here's a heart-warming story that can be read & heard of how EVERYONE can change their lives by viewing life in a positive light. Wally's a cat who starts life by being deserted. His mother & 12 fellow kittens are sealed in a box & abandoned in a field in blistering heat. He's found by a pet shop owner, given to a mean man & angrily returned to the pet store. Wally's finally adopted by a nice couple. But there's a catch! The other cat in his new home hates him. But Wally risks his life to save this cat, thus turning him into a friend. Through his positive outlook, loving attitude & courage he makes friends & a new life for himself. It is a beautiful story of how he improves his life & the lives of everyone around him. WALLY's a quality children's book which features 30 full-color illustrations by award-winning artist David Scott Taylor. The digitally mastered cassette, produced by composer Donald James Kehl, features professional narration, six character voices, sound effects, two original orchestrated songs & full orchestral musical cues. To order: call 1-800-MY-WALLY (800-699-2559) or write WALLY, 2007 E. La Vieve,

Tempe, AZ 85284.
Publisher Provided Annotation.

Walters, Catherine. Max & Minnie. Walters, Catherine, illus. 32p. 1994. 12.95 (*0-87226-377-0*) P Bedrick Bks.
Wardlaw, Lee. The Tales of Grandpa Cat. LC 92-39797. 32p. (gr. 2 up). 1994. 14.99 (*0-8037-1511-0*); PLB 14. 89 (*0-8037-1512-9*) Dial Bks Young.
Wareing, Eleanor J. The Cat Who Was Named Twice. Lynn, Susan K., illus. 141p. (Orig.). (gr. 3-6). 1990. pap. 6.95 (*0-9629175-0-8*) E J Wareing.
Weinberger, Jane. Fanny & Sarah. 2nd ed. MacDonald, Karen, illus. LC 84-51987. 40p. (gr. k-4). 1986. pap. 3.95 (*0-932433-02-2*) Windswept Hse.
—Tabitha Jones. 2nd ed. Jones, Renata S., illus. 40p. (Orig.). (ps-4). 1985. pap. 3.95 (*0-932433-07-3*) Windswept Hse.
Weininger, Rachel. Nightshade. Sawyer, Barbara, illus. LC 88-63135. 64p. (Orig.). (gr. 4-6). 1989. pap. 5.95 (*0-931093-11-2*) Red Hen Pr.
Weiss, Ellen & Friedman, Mel. The Curse of the Calico Cat. Zimmer, Dirk, illus. LC 93-42552. 64p. (Orig.). (gr. 2-4). 1994. PLB 7.99 (*0-679-95405-8*); pap. 2.99 (*0-679-85405-3*) Random Bks Yng Read.
Westall, Robert. Blitzcat. (gr. 7 up). 1989. pap. 12.95 (*0-590-42770-9*) Scholastic Inc.
—Blitzcat. 240p. (gr. 7 up). 1990. pap. 3.25 (*0-590-42771-7*) Scholastic Inc.
—The Witness. Williams, Sophy, illus. 32p. 1994. 14.99 (*0-525-45331-8*) Dutton Child Bks.
—Yaxley's Cat. 208p. 1992. 13.95 (*0-590-45175-8*, Scholastic Hardcover) Scholastic Inc.
What Does Kitty See? 20p. (ps). 1993. 4.99 (*0-89577-486-0*, Dist. by Random) RD Assn.
Whatling, R. C. The Cat Story. 16p. (gr. 7-10). 1986. 35. 00x (*0-7223-2012-4*, Pub. by A H Stockwell England) St Mut.
Wheeler, Cindy. Bookstore Cat. LC 89-42635. 1994. 3.50 (*0-394-84109-3*); PLB 7.99 (*0-394-94109-8*) Random.
Wild, Margaret. The Very Best of Friends. Vivas, Julie, illus. 30p. (ps-3). 1990. 13.95 (*0-15-200625-7*, Gulliver Bks) HarBrace.
Wildsmith, Brian. Giddy Up. 16p. (ps-k). 1987. pap. 2.95 (*0-19-272183-6*) OUP.
—If I Were You. 16p. (ps-k). 1987. pap. 2.95 (*0-19-272182-8*) OUP.
Wilkon, Piotr. The Brave Little Kittens. Wilkon, Jozef, illus. Graves, Helen, tr. from GER. LC 90-44095. (Illus.). 32p. (ps-k). 1991. 14.95 (*1-55858-103-0*) North-South Bks NYC.
Williams, S. P. Ginger Goes on a Diet. Garafano, Marie, illus. LC 92-28950. 1993. 13.95 (*0-395-66077-7*) HM.
Willis, Jeanne. Earth Tigerlets, As Explained by Professor Xargle. Ross, Tony, illus. LC 90-19346. 32p. (ps-2). 1991. 13.95 (*0-525-44732-6*, DCB) Dutton Child Bks.
Wilson, A. N. Tabitha. Fox-Davies, Sarah, illus. LC 88-19820. 48p. (gr. 3 up). 1989. 14.95 (*0-531-05813-1*); PLB 14.99 (*0-531-08413-2*) Orchard Bks Watts.
Wilson, Yvonne M. Kitten Without A Name. (Illus.). 23p. (gr. 1-2). 1982. pap. 1.00 (*0-686-97302-X*) Bible Memory.
Wiseman, Bernard. Cats! Cats! Cats! Wiseman, Bernard, illus. LC 83-27288. 48p. (ps-3). 1984. 5.95 (*0-8193-1127-8*) Parents.
—Cats! Cats! Cats! LC 93-15455. (Illus.). 1993. PLB 13. 27 (*0-8368-0965-3*) Gareth Stevens Inc.
Witches Four. 42p. (ps-3). 1993. PLB 13.27 (*0-8368-0893-2*) Gareth Stevens Inc.
Wolff, Ashley. Only the Cat Saw. (gr. k-3). 1985. 13.95 (*0-399-21698-7*, Putnam) Putnam Pub Group.
Wood, Leslie. Sam's Big Day. 16p. (ps-k). 1987. 2.95 (*0-19-272165-8*) OUP.
Wooding, Sharon. The Painter's Cat. Wooding, Sharon, illus. 32p. (ps-3). 1994. 14.95 (*0-399-22414-9*) Putnam Pub Group.
Worland, Denyse. Playtime. Kelly, Geoff, illus. LC 92-31077. 1993. 4.25 (*0-383-03590-2*) SRA Schl Grp.
Wright, Betty R. The Cat Next Door. Owens, Gail, illus. LC 90-29080. 32p. (ps-3). 1991. reinforced 14.95 (*0-8234-0896-5*) Holiday.
Wynne-Jones, Tim. Zoom at Sea. Beddows, Eric, illus. LC 92-14738. 32p. (ps-2). 1993. 15.00 (*0-06-021448-1*); PLB 14.89 (*0-06-021449-X*) HarpC Child Bks.
—Zoom Away. Beddows, Eric, illus. LC 92-41171. 32p. (ps-2). 1993. 15.00 (*0-06-022962-4*); PLB 14.89 (*0-06-022963-2*) HarpC.
—Zoom Upstream. Beddows, Eric, illus. LC 93-22162. 32p. (ps-2). 1994. 15.00 (*0-06-022977-2*, HarpT); PLB 14.89 (*0-06-022978-0*, HarpT) HarpC.
Young, Ed. Up a Tree: A Wordless Picture Book. Young, Ed, illus. LC 82-47733. 32p. (ps-3). 1983. PLB 14.89 (*0-06-026814-X*) HarpC Child Bks.
Zapata, Crystal. Cat That Barked. rev. ed. LC 88-36660. (gr. 2-6). 1989. 4.00 (*0-915541-71-8*) Star Bks Inc.
Ziefert, Harriet. Cat Games. Schumacher, Claire, illus. LC 87-25805. 32p. (Orig.). (ps-3). 1988. pap. 3.50 (*0-14-050809-0*, Puffin) Puffin Bks.
—Dr. Cat. Mandel, Suzy, illus. LC 88-62152. 32p. (ps-3). 1989. pap. 3.50 (*0-14-050985-2*, Puffin) Puffin Bks.
Zistel, Era. A Cat Called Christopher. (Illus.). 88p. (Orig.). (gr. 4 up). 1991. pap. 9.95 (*0-9617426-7-4*) J N Townsend.
—Wintertime Cat. rev. ed. Zistel, Era, illus. 64p. 1988. pap. 5.95 (*0-9617426-4-X*) J N Townsend.

CATS–PICTURES, ILLUSTRATIONS, ETC.
Christensen, N. Good Night, Little Kitten. (Illus.). 28p. (ps-2). 1990. 10.50 (*0-516-05354-X*); pap. 3.95 (*0-516-45354-8*) Childrens.
Cole, Joanna. A Cat's Body. Wexler, Jerome, illus. LC 81-22386. 48p. (gr. k-3). 1982. lib. bdg. 12.88 (*0-688-01054-7*, Morrow Jr Bks) Morrow Jr Bks.
Gorey, Edward, illus. Category. LC 86-10938. (ps up). 1986. Repr. 8.95 (*0-685-13444-X*) Modan-Adama Bks.
How to Draw Cats. (Illus.). 32p. 1992. PLB 12.96 (*0-88110-580-5*); pap. 4.95 (*0-7460-0996-8*) EDC.
Isaak, Betty. Classifying Cat. Armstrong, Bev, illus. 24p. (ps). 1982. wkbk. 2.95 (*0-88160-087-3*, LW 123) Learning Wks.
Spizzirri Publishing Co. Staff & Spizzirri, Linda. Cats: An Educational Coloring Book. (Illus.). 32p. (gr. k-5). 1985. pap. 1.75 (*0-86545-069-2*) Spizzirri.

CATS–POETRY
Beisner, Monika. Catch That Cat! A Picture Book of Rhymes & Puzzles. (Illus.). 32p. 1990. 15.00 (*0-374-31226-5*) FS&G.
Eliot, T. S. Mr. Mistoffelees with Mungojerrie & Rumpelteazer. Howton, Louise, ed. Le Cain, Errol, illus. 32p. (ps up). 1991. 13.95 (*0-15-256230-3*) HarBrace.
Farjeon, Eleanor. Cats Sleep Anywhere. Jenkins, Mary P., illus. LC 89-77611. 32p. (ps-1). 1990. (Lipp Jr Bks); (Lipp Jr Bks) HarpC Child Bks.
Field, Eugene. The Gingham Dog & the Calico Cat. Street, Janet, illus. 32p. (ps up). 1993. pap. 5.95 (*0-399-22517-X*, Philomel Bks) Putnam Pub Group.
Wheeler, Benson. I, Becky Barrymore. Barrymore, Lionel, illus. (gr. 3 up). 8.95 (*0-8315-0036-0*) Speller.
Wilson, Jean A. Caz & His Cat: Now We Like the Night. Wilson, Richard C., illus. 32p. 1994. 14.95 (*1-884739-00-8*) Wahr.
Yolen, Jane. Raining Cats & Dogs. LC 91-24295. (ps-3). 1993. 14.95 (*0-15-265488-7*, HB Juv Bks) HarBrace.

CATS–TRAINING
Tilden, Ruth. Cat Tricks: Pop-up Kittycats. (ps-3). 1994. pap. 7.95 (*0-671-88305-4*, Little Simon) S&S Trade.

CATTLE
see also Cows; Dairying; Livestock; Veterinary Medicine
Chorlian, Ruth W. Long Trail of the Texas Longhorns. 80p. (gr. 4-7). 1986. 9.95 (*0-89015-540-2*, Pub. by Panda Bks) Sunbelt Media.

CATTLE–FICTION
McKelvey, David. Maverick the Lucky Longhorn. McKelvey, David, illus. 32p. (gr. k-3). 1986. lib. bdg. 10.95 (*0-931722-48-9*); pap. 3.95 (*0-931722-47-0*) Corona Pub.
Scott, Ann H. A Brand is Forever. Himler, Ronald, illus. 48p. (gr. k-3). 1993. 12.95 (*0-395-60118-5*, Clarion Bks) HM.

CAVE DRAWINGS
Terzi, Marinella. Prehistoric Rock Art. LC 92-7504. (Illus.). 36p. (gr. 3 up). 1992. PLB 14.95 (*0-516-08379-1*) Childrens.
—Prehistoric Rock Art. LC 92-7504. (Illus.). 36p. (gr. 3 up). 1993. pap. 6.95 (*0-516-48379-X*) Childrens.

CAVE DWELLERS
Gunzi, Christiane. Cave Life. Greenaway, Frank, photos by. LC 92-53490. (Illus.). 32p. (gr. 2-5). 1993. 9.95 (*1-56458-212-4*) Dorling Kindersley.

CAVE DWELLERS–FICTION
Brennan, J. H. Shiva Accused: An Adventure of the Ice Age. LC 90-25888. 288p. (gr. 5 up). 1991. 16.95 (*0-06-020741-8*) HarpC Child Bks.
Little Treasury of the Flintstones, 6 vols. 1989. Boxed set. 5.99 (*0-517-65855-0*, Chatham River Pr) Random Hse Value.

CAVELL, EDITH LOUISA, 1865-1915
Richardson, Nigel. Edith Cavell. (Illus.). 64p. (gr. 5-9). 1991. 11.95 (*0-237-60020-X*, Pub. by Evans Bros Ltd) Trafalgar.

CAVES
Bendick, Jeanne. Caves. 1995. write for info. (*0-8050-2764-5*) H Holt & Co.
Brandt, Keith. Caves. Schneider, Rex, illus. LC 84-2573. 32p. (gr. 3-6). 1985. PLB 9.49 (*0-8167-0142-3*); pap. text ed. 2.95 (*0-8167-0143-1*) Troll Assocs.
Gans, Roma. Caves. Maestro, Giulio, illus. LC 76-4881. 40p. (gr. k-3). 1962. PLB 14.89 (*0-690-01070-2*, Crowell Jr Bks) HarpC Child Bks.
Gibbons, Gail. Caves & Caverns. LC 92-760. (gr. 4-7). 1993. 14.95 (*0-15-226820-0*, HB Juv Bks) HarBrace.
Greenberg, Judith E. & Carey, Helen H. Caves. Miyake, Yoshi, illus. 32p. (gr. 2-4). 1990. PLB 10.95 (*0-8172-3750-X*) Raintree Steck-V.
Kerbo, Ronal C. Caves. LC 81-4514. (Illus.). 48p. (gr. 3 up). 1981. pap. 4.95 (*0-516-47638-6*) Childrens.
Kramer, Stephen. Caves. Day, Kenrick L., photos by. LC 93-42136. 1994. 17.50 (*0-87614-447-4*) Carolrhoda Bks.
McFall, Christie. America Underground. LC 91-8951. (Illus.). 80p. (gr. 5 up). 1992. 14.00 (*0-525-65079-2*, Cobblehill Bks) Dutton Child Bks.
Morris, Deborah. Trapped In A Cave! A True Story. LC 92-40731. 1993. 7.99 (*0-8054-4003-8*) Broadman.
Naden, C. J. I Can Read About Caves. new ed. LC 78-66271. (Illus.). (gr. 2-5). 1979. pap. 2.50 (*0-89375-205-3*) Troll Assocs.
Rigby, Susan. Caves. Burns, Robert, illus. LC 91-45082. 32p. (gr. 4-6). 1993. PLB 11.59 (*0-8167-2749-X*); pap. text ed. 3.95 (*0-8167-2750-3*) Troll Assocs.
Schultz, Ron. Looking Inside Caves & Caverns. Gadbois, Nick & Aschwanden, Peter, illus. (gr. 4-7). 1993. pap. 9.95 (*1-56261-126-7*) John Muir.
Silver, Donald M. One Small Square: Cave. LC 93-36570. (Illus.). 1993. text ed. write for info. (*0-7167-6514-4*) W H Freeman.
Wood, Jenny. Caves: An Underground Wonderland. LC 90-55463. (Illus.). 32p. (gr. 3-4). 1991. PLB 17.27 (*0-8368-0469-4*) Gareth Stevens Inc.

CAVES–FICTION
Henken, Heidi. Cobb's Cave. Kratoville, Betty L., ed. (Illus.). 64p. (gr. 3-9). 1989. PLB 4.95 (*0-87879-655-X*) High Noon Bks.
McCusker, Paul. The Secret Cave of Robinwood. (gr. 4-7). 1991. pap. 4.99 (*1-56179-102-4*) Focus Family.
Misla, Victor M. The Treasure of Camuy's Cave. Misla, Victor M., illus. 30p. (Orig.). (gr. 6-7). 1987. pap. 5.00 (*0-9626870-1-4*) NW Monarch Pr.
Petersen, P. J. How Can You Hijack a Cave? (gr. k up). 1990. pap. 3.25 (*0-440-20583-2*, LFL) Dell.
Steiner, Barbara. Ghost Cave. 135p. (gr. 3-7). 1990. 13.95 (*0-15-230752-4*) HarBrace.
Zuniega, Thelma M. The Haunted Cave. (Illus.). (ps-3). 1972. 3.00 (*0-686-09535-9*, Pub. by New Day Pub PI) Cellar.

CELLS
see also D N A; Embryology
Balkwill, Fran. Cell Wars. (gr. 4-7). 1994. pap. 8.95 (*0-87614-637-X*) Carolrhoda Bks.
—Cells Are Us. Rolph, Mic, illus. 32p. (gr. 3-6). 1993. 17.50 (*0-87614-762-7*) Carolrhoda Bks.
—Cells Are Us. (gr. 4-7). 1994. pap. 8.95 (*0-87614-636-1*) Carolrhoda Bks.
Bender, Lionel. Atoms & Cells. LC 89-26066. (ps-3). 1990. PLB 12.40 (*0-531-17219-8*, Gloucester Pr) Watts.
George, Michael. Cells. (gr. 4-7). 1993. 15.95 (*1-56846-057-0*) Creat Editions.
LeMaster, Leslie J. Cells & Tissues. LC 85-6695. (Illus.). 45p. (gr. k-3). 1985. PLB 12.85 (*0-516-01266-5*) Childrens.
Miller, Kenneth. Energy & Life. Head, J. J., ed. Steffen, Ann T., illus. LC 86-72192. 16p. (Orig.). (gr. 10 up). 1988. pap. text ed. 2.75 (*0-89278-168-8*, 45-9768) Carolina Biological.
Moner, John G. The Animal Cell. Head, J. J., ed. Steffen, Ann T., illus. LC 83-70597. 32p. (gr. 10 up). 1987. pap. text ed. 3.00 (*0-89278-347-8*, 45-9747) Carolina Biological.
Young, John K. Cells: Amazing Forms & Functions. LC 90-34262. (Illus.). 128p. (gr. 9-12). 1990. PLB 13.40 (*0-531-10880-5*) Watts.

CELLS, ELECTRIC
see Electric Batteries

CELTS
Briais, Bernard. Celts. LC 91-15842. (Illus.). 48p. (gr. 4-8). 1991. PLB 13.95 (*1-85435-266-0*) Marshall Cavendish.
Corbishley, Mike. The Celts. (Illus.). (gr. 2-6). pap. 3.95 (*0-7141-1387-5*, Pub. by Brit Mus UK) Parkwest Pubns.
—The Celts Activity Book. (Illus.). 16p. 1994. pap. 5.95 (*0-500-27763-X*) Thames Hudson.

CEMETERIES
Reef, Catherine. Arlington National Cemetery. LC 91-17183. (Illus.). 72p. (gr. 4-6). 1991. text ed. 14.95 RSBE (*0-87518-471-5*, Dillon) Macmillan Child Grp.

CEMETERIES–FICTION
Rodowsky, Colby. The Gathering Room. LC 81-5360. 186p. (gr. 5 up). 1981. 14.00 (*0-374-32520-0*) FS&G.

CENTRAL AFRICA
see Africa, Central

CENTRAL AMERICA
Brandt, Keith. Mexico & Central America. Eitzen, Allan, illus. LC 84-2668. 32p. (gr. 3-6). 1985. PLB 9.49 (*0-8167-0264-0*); pap. text ed. 2.95 (*0-8167-0265-9*) Troll Assocs.
Griffiths, J. Crisis in Central America. (Illus.). 80p. (gr. 7 up). 1988. PLB 18.60 (*0-86592-034-6*) Rourke Corp.
Hernandez, Xavier. San Rafael: A Central American City Through the Ages. Ballonga, Jordi & Escofet, Josep, illus. LC 91-39906. 64p. (gr. 4-7). 1992. 17.45 (*0-395-60645-4*) HM.
Morrison, Marion. Central America. (Illus.). 48p. (gr. 4-8). 1989. lib. bdg. 14.95 (*0-382-09824-2*) Silver Burdett Pr.
—Central America. LC 92-14537. 96p. 1992. lib. bdg. 22. 80 (*0-8114-2458-8*) Raintree Steck-V.
Schrock, Sadie. Belize-Land by the Carib Sea. (gr. 3). 1991. 2.95 (*0-87813-539-1*) Christian Light.
—Nature Study of Belize. (gr. 3). 1991. pap. 2.95 (*0-87813-538-3*) Christian Light.
Siy, Alexandra. The Eeyou: People of Eastern James Bay. LC 92-34887. (Illus.). 80p. (gr. 5 up). 1993. text ed. 14.95 RSBE (*0-87518-549-5*, Dillon) Macmillan Child Grp.
Wekesser, Carol, et al, eds. Central America: Opposing Viewpoints. LC 90-13922. (Illus.). 240p. (gr. 10 up). 1990. PLB 17.95 (*0-89908-484-2*); pap. text ed. 9.95 (*0-89908-459-1*) Greenhaven.

CENTRAL STATES
see Middle West

CEREBRAL PALSY
Aaseng, Nathan. Cerebral Palsy. (Illus.). 112p. (gr. 9-12). 1991. PLB 13.40 (*0-531-12529-7*) Watts.
Bergman, Thomas. Going Places: Children Living with Cerebral Palsy. Bergman, Thomas, illus. LC 90-48266. 48p. (gr. 4-5). 1991. PLB 18.60 (*0-8368-0199-7*) Gareth Stevens Inc.

Gould, Marilyn. Golden Daffodils. LC 84-40758. 172p. (gr. 4 up). 1991. PLB 12.95 (*0-9632305-3-0*); pap. 6.95 (*0-9632305-1-4*) Allied Crafts.

CEREMONIES

see Etiquette; Manners and Customs; Rites and Ceremonies

CERTAINTY

see Belief and Doubt; Probabilities

CERVANTES SAAVEDRA, MIGUEL DE, 1547-1616

Miguel de Cervantes. (Illus.). 112p. (gr. 6-12). 1993. PLB 17.95 (*0-7910-1238-7*); pap. write for info. (*0-7910-1265-4*) Chelsea Hse.

Milton, Joyce. Don Quixote (Miguel de Cervantes) (gr. 9-12). 1985. pap. 2.50 (*0-8120-3512-7*) Barron.

CEYLON

Lerner Publications, Department of Geography Staff, ed. Sri Lanka in Pictures. (Illus.). 64p. (gr. 5 up). 1988. 17.50 (*0-8225-1853-8*) Lerner Pubns.

CEYLON–FICTION

Williams, Harry. Twins of Ceylon. Paton, Jane, illus. LC 65-12044. (gr. 6-9). 1965. 12.95 (*0-8023-1108-3*) Dufour.

CEZANNE, PAUL, 1839-1906

Mason, Antony. Cezanne. (Illus.). 32p. (gr. 5 up). 1994. 10.95 (*0-8120-6459-3*); pap. 5.95 (*0-8120-1293-3*) Barron.

CHAGALL, MARC, 1899-

Bober, Natalie S. Marc Chagall: Painter of Dreams. Rosenberry, Vera, illus. LC 91-25463. 124p. (gr. 4-8). 1991. 14.95 (*0-8276-0379-7*) JPS Phila.

Greenfeld, Howard. Marc Chagall. (Illus.). 80p. (gr. 7 up). 1990. 19.95 (*0-8109-3152-4*) Abrams.

Loumaye, Jacqueline. Chagall: My Town, Sad & Joyous. Goodman, John, tr. Boiry, Veronique, illus. LC 93-39109. 1994. write for info. (*0-7910-2807-0*) Chelsea Hse.

CHAIRS

Giblin, James C. Be Seated: A Book About Chairs. LC 92-25073. (Illus.). 136p. (gr. 3-7). 1993. 15.00 (*0-06-021537-2*); PLB 14.89 (*0-06-021538-0*) HarpC Child Bks.

CHAIRS–FICTION

Gauthier, Leanne, et al. Joey's Chair. 36p. (gr. k-2). Date not set. 14.95 (*0-9640296-0-X*) Downunder Design.

Smith, Maggie. My Grandma's Chair. LC 90-2278. (ps-3). 1992. 14.00 (*0-688-10663-3*); PLB 13.93 (*0-688-10664-1*) Lothrop.

Williams, Vera B. A Chair for My Mother. Williams, Vera B., illus. LC 81-7010. 32p. (gr. k-3). 1982. 15.00 (*0-688-00914-X*); PLB 14.93 (*0-688-00915-8*) Greenwillow.

CHAKA, ZULU CHIEF, 1787?-1828

Stanley, Diane & Vennema, Peter. Shaka: King of the Zulus. Stanley, Diane, illus. LC 93-11730. 40p. (gr. k up). 1994. pap. 4.95 (*0-688-13114-X*, Mulberry) Morrow.

CHAMBERLAIN, WILTON NORMAN, 1936-

Frankl, Ron. Wilt Chamberlain. LC 94-5775. 1994. 14.95 (*0-7910-2428-8*) Chelsea Hse.

CHAMELEONS

Martin, James. Chameleons: Dragons in the Trees. Wolfe, Art, photos by. LC 91-8736. (Illus.). 36p. (gr. 1-5). 1991. 13.00 (*0-517-58388-7*); lib. bdg. 13.99 (*0-517-58389-5*) Crown Bks Yng Read.

Murray, Peter. Chameleons. LC 92-41543. (gr. 2-6). 1993. 15.95 (*1-56766-016-9*) Childs World.

Schnieper, Claudia. Chameleons. Meier, Max, photos by. (Illus.). 48p. (gr. 2-5). 1989. 19.95 (*0-87614-341-9*); pap. 6.95 (*0-87614-520-9*) Carolrhoda Bks.

Walton, Marilyn J. Chameleon's Rainbow. Salzman, Yuri, illus. LC 84-17760. 32p. (gr. 3-6). 1985. PLB 14.65 (*0-940742-45-4*); incl cassette 27.99 (*0-8172-2285-5*) Raintree Steck-V.

CHAMPLAIN, SAMUEL DE, 1567-1635

Coulter, Tony. Jacques Cartier, Samuel de Champlain, & the Explorers of Canada. Goetzmann, William H., ed. Collins, Michael, intro. by. (Illus.). 112p. (gr. 6-12). 1993. PLB 18.95 (*0-7910-1298-0*, Am Art Analog); pap. write for info. (*0-7910-1521-1*, Am Art Analog) Chelsea Hse.

Jacobs, William J. Champlain: A Life of Courage. LC 93-31176. (Illus.). 64p. (gr. 5-8). 1994. PLB 12.90 (*0-531-20112-0*) Watts.

Zadra, Dan. Explorers of America: Champlain. rev. ed. (gr. 2-4). 1988. PLB 14.95 (*0-88682-181-9*) Creative Ed.

CHANCELLORSVILLE, BATTLE OF, 1863

Kent, Zachary. The Battle of Chancellorsville. LC 94-9486. (Illus.). 1994. PLB 16.40 (*0-516-06679-X*); pap. 3.95 (*0-516-46679-8*) Childrens.

CHANGE, SOCIAL

see Social Change

CHAPLIN, CHARLES SPENCER, 1889-

Brown, Pam. Charlie Chaplin: Comic Genius Who Brought Laughter & Hope to Millions. LC 88-27568. (Illus.). 64p. (gr. 5-6). 1991. PLB 19.93 (*1-55532-838-5*) Gareth Stevens Inc.

CHAPMAN, JOHN, 1774-1845

Greene, Carol. John Chapman: The Man Who Was Johnny Appleseed. LC 91-12649. (Illus.). 48p. (gr. k-3). 1991. PLB 12.85 (*0-516-04223-8*); pap. 4.95 (*0-516-44223-6*) Childrens.

Le Sueur, Meridel. Little Brother of the Wilderness: The Story of Johnny Appleseed. LC 87-80574. (Illus.). 68p. (gr. 5 up). 1987. Repr. of 1947 ed. 9.95 (*0-930100-21-2*) Holy Cow.

Sabin, Louis. Johnny Appleseed. Smolinski, Dick, illus. LC 84-2732. 32p. (gr. 3-6). 1985. PLB 9.49 (*0-8167-0220-9*); pap. text ed. 2.95 (*0-8167-0221-7*) Troll Assocs.

CHAPMAN, JOHN, 1774-1845–FICTION

Glass, Andrew. Folks Call Me Appleseed John. LC 93-41046. 1995. write for info. (*0-385-32045-0*) Doubleday.

Hunt, Irene. Trail of Apple Blossoms. Partridge, Sherri, illus. LC 92-46739. 64p. (gr. 4-6). 1993. PLB 12.95 (*0-382-24359-5*); 10.95 (*0-382-24368-4*) Silver Burdett Pr.

Ingoglia, Gina. Johnny Appleseed & the Planting of the West. LC 92-52978. (Illus.). 80p. (gr. 1-4). 1992. PLB 12.89 (*1-56282-259-4*); pap. 3.50 (*1-56282-258-6*) Disney Pr.

Moore, Eva. Johnny Appleseed. (Orig.). (gr. 2-3). pap. 2.50 (*0-590-40297-8*) Scholastic Inc.

CHAPMAN, JOHN JAY, 1862-1933

Aliki. La Historia de Johnny Appleseed. Mlawer, Teresa, tr. (Illus.). 32p. (gr. k-2). 1992. 9.95 (*0-9625162-6-0*) Lectorum Pubns.

CHARACTER EDUCATION

American Institute for Character Education Staff. Character Education Curriculum: The Happy Life Series plus Living with Me & Others Including Our Rights & Responsibilities, Levels A-F. (Illus.). (gr. 1-7). 1984. Set. 820.00 (*0-685-09646-7*) Level A, 124p. tchr's. ed. 95.00 (*0-913413-01-1*); Level B, 127p. tchr's ed. 95.00 (*0-913413-02-X*); Level C, 148p. tchr's. ed. 95.00 (*0-913413-03-8*); Level D, 152p. tchr's ed. 95.00 (*0-913413-04-6*); Level E, 160p. tchr's ed. 95.00 (*0-913413-05-4*); Level F, 6th gr. tchr's ed. 95.00 (*0-685-09647-5*); Level G, Middle School#Level K, Kindergarten with film strips. 125. 00 (*0-685-09648-3*) Char Ed Inst.

Aronoff, Daisy P. ABC Bible & Holiday Stories. Danciger, Leila N., illus. 58p. (ps-7). 1992. pap. 15.95 (*1-878612-28-X*) Sunflower Co.

Kylie's Song. (gr. 1-4). 1989. incl. activity guide & video 79.95 (*0-925159-87-5*, 9351) Marshfilm.

Mendoza, George. Hunter I Might Have Been. (Illus.). (gr. 3-5). 1968. 10.95 (*0-8392-3064-8*) Astor-Honor.

Mitchell, Joyce S. Free to Choose: Decision Making for Young Men. LC 76-5589. (gr. 7 up). 1976. 8.95 (*0-440-02723-3*) Delacorte.

Plum, Joan. I Am Special Fun Book. 32p. (Orig.). (ps-2). 1989. pap. 2.95 (*0-87973-055-2*, 55) Our Sunday Visitor.

Ross, Sandra J. Visiting the Nicelies: A Lil'l Charmers Book. (Illus.). 60p. (Orig.). (gr. 3-7). 1991. pap. 5.95 (*1-881235-00-9*) Creat Opport.

Rudner, Barry. The Handstand. Fahsbender, Thomas, illus. 32p. 1991. pap. 5.95 (*0-925928-05-4*) Tiny Thought.

—Will I Still Have to Make My Bed In The Morning? (Illus.). 32p. 1991. pap. 5.95 (*0-925928-10-0*) Tiny Thought.

Schmidt, Fran & Friedman, Alice. Come in Spaceship Earth. Heyne, Chris, illus. 61p. (Orig.). (gr. 4-9). 1990. Incl. poster. pap. text ed. 21.95 (*1-878227-06-8*) Peace Educ.

—Creative Conflict Solving for Kids: Grades 5-9. 2nd., rev. ed. Cranford, Kay K., et al, illus. 80p. (gr. 4-9). 1985. Incl. poster. pap. text ed. 21.95 (*1-878227-00-9*) Peace Educ.

—Creative Conflict Solving for Kids: Grades 3-4. 90p. (Orig.). (gr. 3-4). 1991. Incl. poster. 21.95 (*1-878227-10-6*); Set of 5, 24p. 11.95 (*1-878227-11-4*) Peace Educ.

—Fighting Fair: Dr. Martin Luther King Jr. for Kids. rev. ed. Heyne, Chris, illus. (gr. 4-9). 1990. Set. pap. text ed. 74.95 69 p., incl. poster, video (*1-878227-02-5*); tchr's. ed., incl. poster 19.95 (*1-878227-07-6*); Set of 5. wkbk., 48p. 11.95 (*1-878227-08-4*) Peace Educ.

—Peacemaking Skills for Little Kids. Le Shane, Phyllis, contrib. by. (Illus.). 76p. (Orig.). (gr. k-2). 1988. pap. text ed. 54.95 incl. poster, puppet, cassette (*1-878227-03-3*) Peace Educ.

Schmidt, Fran, et al. Mediation for Kids. 2nd ed. (Illus.). 68p. (gr. 4-12). 1992. Incl. poster. 21.95 (*1-878227-13-0*); Set of 5, 28p. 11.95 (*1-878227-14-9*) Peace Educ.

Teller, Hanoch. Above the Bottom Line: Stories & Advice on Integrity. 416p. (gr. 8 up). 1988. write for info. (*0-9614772-5-3*) NYC Pub Co.

CHARACTER EDUCATION–FICTION

Bobo, Carmen P. Sarah's Growing-up Summer. LC 88-62111. 52p. 1989. 6.95 (*1-55523-187-X*) Winston-Derek.

Cosgrove, Stephen. The Grumpling. (Illus.). 32p. (Orig.). (gr. 1-4). 1989. pap. 3.95 (*0-8431-2739-2*) Price Stern.

—Poppyseed. (Illus.). 32p. (Orig.). (gr. 1-4). 1989. pap. 2.95 (*0-8431-2738-4*) Price Stern.

—Tickle's Tail. (Illus.). 32p. (Orig.). (gr. 1-4). 1989. pap. 2.95 (*0-8431-2736-8*) Price Stern.

Dyson, Kymberli M. Clyde, the Cloud Who Always Cried. (Illus.). 28p. (Orig.). (gr. k-4). 1994. Saddle-stitched. 5.00 (*1-885282-00-1*) This Little. CLYDE, THE CLOUD WHO ALWAYS CRIED is this little light's first tale in a 14-book series for children. Written in verse, each "fable" introduces one of God's creations who must learn to overcome a negative characteristic, i.e. TERENCE THE TATTLING TREE, WENDY THE WHINING TREE, SEYMOUR THE SELFISH SEA, et al. Each story is charmingly illustrated with characters who are easily identifiable by children & adults alike. CLYDE develops low self-esteem from his jealousy towards SUSANNA THE SUN. Through a series of events which affect the world around him, God helps CLYDE realize his individuality & unique purpose in life. As with each book in this series, the priority of God in each character's lesson is illustrated in a non-judgmental, nondogmatic fashion. Volume discounts are available from the publisher. Also available is a T-shirt delightfully displaying all the characters from THIS LITTLE LIGHT series. (One size fits all children & one size fits all adults). To order contact: this little light publishing, P.O. Box 70481, Pasadena, CA 91117, (818) 791-1484 or (800) 814-4774.

Publisher Provided Annotation.

Hegg, Tom. The Mark of the Maker. Hanson, Warren, illus. 46p. (gr. 4 up). 1991. 10.95 (*0-931674-18-2*) Waldman Hse Pr.

Knudson, R. R. You Are the Rain. LC 73-15397. 160p. (gr. 7 up). 1974. pap. 5.95 (*0-440-08759-7*) Delacorte.

Parkison, Ralph F. The Little Girl & the Inchworm. Withrow, Marion O., ed. Bush, William, illus. 75p. (Orig.). (gr. 2-8). 1988. pap. write for info. Little Wood Bks.

—Santa's Wheat Kernels. Withrow, Marion O., ed. Bush, William, illus. 60p. (Orig.). (gr. 2-8). 1988. pap. write for info. Little Wood Bks.

Rudner, Barry. Nonsense. Fahsbender, Thomas, illus. (gr. k-6). 1991. 5.95 (*0-925928-04-6*) Tiny Thought.

Rummel, Mary. God's Love for Happiness: A Return to Family Values. Dirks, Nathan & Brandt, Bill, illus. LC 92-91032. 64p. (Orig.). (gr. k up). 1992. pap. 9.95 (*0-9635091-0-1*) Olive Brnch.

CHARACTERS AND CHARACTERISTICS IN LITERATURE

see also Blacks in Literature and Art; Children in Literature and Art

Ada, Alma F. Dear Peter Rabbit: Querido Pedrin. Zubizarreta, Rosa, tr. Tryon, Leslie, illus. LC 93-8459. 40p. (ps-3). 1994. English ed. SBE 14.95 (*0-689-31850-2*, Atheneum Child Bk); Spanish ed. SBE 14.95 (*0-689-31915-0*, Atheneum Child Bk) Macmillan Child Grp.

CHARLEMAGNE, 742-814

Frost, Abigail. The Age of Chivalry. LC 89-17396. (Illus.). 48p. (gr. 4-8). 1990. PLB 13.95 (*1-85435-235-0*) Marshall Cavendish.

CHARLEMAGNE, 742-814–FICTION

Westwood, Jennifer. Stories of Charlemagne. LC 74-12435. (gr. 6 up). 1976. 21.95 (*0-87599-213-7*) S G Phillips.

CHARLESTON, SOUTH CAROLINA–FICTION

Smith, Bruce. The Silver Locket: A Charleston Christmas Storybook. Smith, Bruce, illus. LC 94-78135. 110p. (Orig.). (ps up). 1994. pap. 11.95 (*0-9642620-0-2*) Marsh Wind Pr. Children's tales of the joy of the Christmas season set against a backdrop of America's most charming city. Share the wonder of a small boy who greets one of Claus' reindeer beneath the foggy, moss-shrouded oaks of Charleston's historic Battery; Meet Butter the golden retriever, who nurses an injured teal back to health in the marshes along the Ashley River; Ride cobbled streets with Magnolia, the carriage horse who refuses to pull without a carriage filled with children; Discover the magic of The Silver Locket, in which two young girls share a wondrous Charleston snowfall & learn the true meaning of the season.

CHARMS–POETRY

Roy, Cal. What Every Young Wizard Should Know. Roy, Cal, illus. (gr. 2 up). 1963. 8.95 (*0-8392-3043-5*) Astor-Honor.

CHARTOGRAPHY

see Map Drawing; Maps

CHASE, THE

see Hunting

CHATEAUX

see Castles

CHAUCER, GEOFFREY, 1340?-1400

Oetting. The Chieftain of Chaucer. LC 73-87806. (Illus.). 32p. (gr. 2-5). 1974. PLB 9.95 (*0-87783-137-8*); pap. 3.94 deluxe ed. (*0-87783-138-6*) Oddo.

CHAVEZ, CESAR ESTRADA

Cesar Chavez: Mini Play. (gr. 5 up). 1978. 5.00 (*0-89550-305-0*) Stevens & Shea.

Conord, Bruce W. Cesar Chavez: Union Leader. (Illus.). 80p. (gr. 3-5). 1993. 13.95 (*0-7910-1757-5*, Am Art Analog); pap. 4.95 (*0-7910-1999-3*, Am Art Analog) Chelsea Hse.

De Ruiz, Dana C. & Larios, Richard. La Causa: The Migrant Farmworkers' Story. Gutierrez, Rudy, illus. LC 92-12806. 92p. (gr. 2-5). 1992. PLB 21.34 (*0-8114-7231-0*) Raintree Steck-V.

Franchere, Ruth. Cesar Chavez. Thollander, Earl, illus. LC 85-42999. 48p. (gr. 2-5). 1986. pap. 4.95 (*0-06-446023-1*, Trophy) HarpC Child Bks.

—Cesar Chavez. LC 78-101927. (Illus.). 40p. (gr. 2-5). 1970. PLB 14.89 (*0-690-18384-4*, Crowell Jr Bks) HarpC Child Bks.

Holmes, Burnham. Cesar Chavez. LC 92-18225. (Illus.). 128p. (gr. 7-10). 1992. PLB 22.80 (*0-8114-2326-3*) Raintree Steck-V.

Roberts, Naurice. Cesar Chavez & La Causa. LC 85-27980. (Illus.). 32p. (gr. 2-4). 1986. PLB 11.80 (*0-516-03484-7*); pap. 3.95 (*0-516-43484-5*) Childrens.

—Cesar Chavez y la Causa. 32p. (gr. 2-5). 1986. pap. 3.95 (*0-516-53484-X*) Childrens.

CHECKERS

Pike, Robert W. Winning Checkers for Kids of All Ages. Nelson, Scott, illus. 64p. (Orig.). (gr. 3-8). 1993. pap. 9.95 (*0-9635300-0-3*) C&M Pub MA.

CHEERS AND CHEERLEADING

Cooney, Caroline B. Cheerleader. 1991. pap. 3.25 (*0-590-44316-X*, Point) Scholastic Inc.

Egbert, Barbara. Cheerleading & Songleading. LC 80-52322. (Illus.). 128p. (gr. 9 up). 1980. pap. 9.95 (*0-8069-8950-5*) Sterling.

Haller, Lynda. Cheerleader U. S. A. - Tryouts to Triumph. 68p. (gr. 1-12). 1989. pap. 10.00 spiral bdg. (*0-317-93086-9*) Cheertime USA.

—More Cheers & Chants. rev. ed. Whitman, Rick, photos by. (Illus.). 39p. (Orig.). (gr. 3-12). 1988. pap. text ed. 8.00 (*0-685-22930-0*); cassette 6.00 (*0-9614174-5-5*) Cheertime USA.

Phillips, Betty L. Go! Fight! Win! The NCA Guide for Cheerleaders. Herkimer, Lawrence R., illus. Shepherd, Francis, photos by. LC 79-53607. (Illus.). 160p. (gr. 7 up). 1981. PLB 11.80 (*0-440-02957-0*); pap. 9.95 (*0-385-29336-4*) Delacorte.

CHEETAHS

Arnold, Caroline. Cheetah. Hewett, Richard, photos by. LC 88-39940. (Illus.). 48p. (gr. 2 up). 1989. 12.95 (*0-688-08143-6*); PLB 12.88 (*0-688-08144-4*) Morrow Jr Bks.

—Cheetah. ALC Staff, ed. LC 88-39940. (Illus.). 48p. (gr. 3 up). 1992. pap. 5.95 (*0-688-11696-5*, Mulberry) Morrow.

Cheetahs. 1991. PLB 14.95s.p. (*0-88682-417-6*) Creative Ed.

Dupont, Philippe & Tracqui, Valerie. The Cheetah: Animal Close-Ups. (Illus.). 28p. (ps-3). 1992. pap. 6.95 (*0-88106-425-4*) Charlesbridge Pub.

Georgeanne, Irvine. Wild & Wonderful Big Cats at the San Diego Zoo. LC 93-47529. (gr. 3 up). 1995. 16.00 (*0-671-87191-9*, S&S BFYR) S&S Trade.

Kappeler, Markus. Big Cats. (Illus.). 32p. (gr. 4-6). 1991. PLB 18.60 (*0-8368-0685-9*) Gareth Stevens Inc.

Markert, Jenny. Cheetahs. 32p. (gr. 2-6). 1991. 15.95 (*0-89565-716-3*) Childs World.

Ossorio, Nelson A., et al. To Run Like the Wind: or The Wisdom of the Cheetah. (Illus.). 48p. (gr. 4-6). 1994. pap. 6.95 (*1-56721-047-3*) Twnty-Fifth Cent Pr.

Stone, L. Cheetahs. (Illus.). 24p. (gr. k-5). 1989. lib. bdg. 11.94 (*0-86592-503-8*) Rourke Corp.

Zingg, Eduard. Trumpa, the Cheetah. Italia, Bob, ed. LC 93-10263. (gr. 4 up). 1993. 14.96 (*1-56239-214-X*) Abdo & Dghtrs.

CHEMICAL ELEMENTS

Newton, David E. Chemical Elements. LC 93-30044. (Illus.). 128p. (gr. 9-12). 1994. PLB 13.40 (*0-531-12501-7*) Watts.

Parramon Editorial Team Staff. Los Elementos. (Illus.). 96p. (ps-1). 1994. 16.95 (*0-8120-6441-0*) Barron.

CHEMICAL ENGINEERING

see also Metallurgy

CHEMICAL INDUSTRIES

Here are entered works about industries based mainly on chemical processes. Works on the manufacture of chemicals as such are entered under Chemicals.

see also names of industries, e.g. Paper Making and Trade; etc.

CHEMICALS

Jennings, Terry. Everyday Chemicals. LC 88-22888. (Illus.). 32p. (gr. 3-6). 1989. pap. 4.95 (*0-516-48401-X*) Childrens.

Landau, Elaine. Chemical & Biological Warfare. 128p. (gr. 5-9). 1991. 14.95 (*0-525-67364-4*, Lodestar Bks) Dutton Child Bks.

CHEMISTRY

see also Biochemistry; Color; Explosives; Fire; Pharmacy; Poisons

also headings beginning with the word Chemical

Asimov, Isaac. Ask Isaac Asimov, 41 vols. (Illus.). 24p. (gr. 1-8). PLB 570.01 subscription set (*0-8368-0789-8*); PLB 14.60 ea., standing order (*0-8368-0788-X*) Gareth Stevens Inc.

Barber, Jacqueline. Chemical Reactions. Bergman, Lincoln & Fairwell, Kay, eds. Baker, Lisa H. & Craig, Rose, illus. Barber, Jacqueline, et al, photos by. 24p. (Orig.). (gr. 7-10). 1986. pap. 8.50 (*0-912511-13-3*) Lawrence Science.

—Crime Lab Chemistry. rev. ed. Bergman, Lincoln & Fairwell, Kay, eds. (Illus.). 10p. (gr. 4-8). 1989. pap. 8.50 (*0-912511-16-8*) Lawrence Science.

Bronstein, Leona B. & McGrain, Eleanore. Chemistry Flipper. 49p. (gr. 7 up). 1989. Repr. of 1978 ed. trade edition 5.95 (*1-878383-06-X*) C Lee Pubns.

Burchard, Elizabeth. Chemistry: In a Flash. 464p. (gr. 7-12). 1994. pap. 9.95 (*1-881374-01-7*) Flash Blasters.

Challand, Helen J. Experiments with Chemistry. LC 88-11862. (Illus.). 48p. (gr. k-4). 1988. PLB 12.85 (*0-516-01151-0*) Childrens.

Chemistry. (Illus.). 48p. (gr. 6-12). 1973. pap. 1.85 (*0-8395-3367-5*, 33367) BSA.

Chishom, J. & Lynnington, M. Chemistry. Ashman, Iain, illus. 48p. (gr. 6 up). 1983. PLB 13.96 (*0-86020-710-2*); pap. 6.95 (*0-86020-709-9*) EDC.

Cobb, Vicki. Chemically Active! Experiments You Can Do at Home. Cobb, Theo, illus. LC 83-49490. 160p. (gr. 5-8). 1985. (Lipp Jr Bks); PLB 14.89 (*0-397-32080-9*, Lipp Jr Bks) HarpC Child Bks.

Conway, Lorraine. Chemistry Concepts. Akins, Linda, illus. 64p. (gr. 5 up). 1983. wkbk. 7.95 (*0-86653-100-9*, GA 460) Good Apple.

Cunningham, A. Essential Chemistry. (Illus.). 64p. 1992. lib. bdg. 12.96 (*0-88110-508-2*, Usborne); pap. 5.95 (*0-7460-0727-2*) EDC.

Evans, David & Williams, Claudette. Make It Change. LC 92-52815. (Illus.). 32p. (gr. k-3). 1992. 9.95 (*1-56458-119-5*) Dorling Kindersley.

Hoyt, Marie A. Workbook Game Sheets for Kitchen Chemistry & Front Porch Physics. Green, Victor D. & Loor, Robin, illus. 44p. (Orig.). (gr. 3-8). 1983. pap. text ed. 4.00 (*0-914911-02-3*) Educ Serv Pr.

Kranepool, Harry A. New Investigations in Modern Chemistry. Plass, Richard M., ed. (Illus.). 1989. lab manual & wkbk., 270p. 9.95 (*0-685-29318-1*) Lab manual, 116p. 5.95 (*0-685-74152-4*); Lab reports, 154p. 5.95 (*0-685-74153-2*) Amer Scholastic.

Licata, David P. Advanced Placement Chemistry Student Handbook. (gr. 10-12). 1993. pap. text ed. 12.95 (*0-9636095-0-5*) Licatas Edutype.

Newmark, Ann. Chemistry. LC 92-54480. (Illus.). 64p. (gr. 7 up). 1993. 15.95 (*1-56458-231-0*) Dorling Kindersley.

Rapp, George, Jr. & Erickson, Laura L. Earth's Chemical Clues: The Story of Geochemistry. LC 89-7914. (Illus.). 64p. (gr. 6 up). 1990. lib. bdg. 15.95 (*0-89490-153-2*) Enslow Pubs.

Russo, Tom. Microchemistry: For High School Chemistry. rev. ed. Stone, Harry, ed. (Illus.). 90p. (gr. 9-12). 1990. lab manual 15.80 (*1-877960-05-5*, 4-400) Kemtec Educ.

Time Life Books Staff. Structure of Matter. 1992. 18.95 (*0-8094-9662-3*) Time-Life.

Wertheim, J. & Oxlade, C. Dictionary of Chemistry. (Illus.). 128p. (gr. 6 up). 1987. PLB 15.96 (*0-88110-230-X*); pap. 9.95 (*0-86020-821-4*) EDC.

Zubrowski, Bernie. Inks, Food Colors, & Papers. Vantage Art Staff, illus. 80p. (gr. 5-8). 1993. pap. text ed. 10.95 (*0-685-68097-5*) Cuisenaire.

CHEMISTRY, BIOLOGICAL

see Biochemistry

CHEMISTRY–EXPERIMENTS

Challand, Helen J. Activities in the Physical Sciences. LC 83-26224. (Illus.). 96p. (gr. 5 up). 1984. PLB 13.95 (*0-516-00504-9*) Childrens.

Cobb, Vicki. Chemically Active: Experiments You Can Do at Home. Cobb, Theo, illus. LC 83-49490. 160p. (gr. 6-8). 1990. pap. 4.95 (*0-06-446101-7*, Trophy) HarpC Child Bks.

Gardner, Robert. Famous Experiments You Can Do. LC 90-34043. (Illus.). 144p. (gr. 9-12). 1990. PLB 13.90 (*0-531-10883-X*) Watts.

—Kitchen Chemistry: Science Experiments to Do at Home. Steltenpohl, Jane, ed. (Illus.). 136p. (gr. 4-8). 1989. lib. bdg. 13.98 (*0-671-67776-4*, J Messner); lib. bdg. 5.95 (*0-671-67576-1*); PLB 8.99s.p. (*0-685-47082-2*); pap. 3.71s.p. (*0-685-47083-0*) S&S Trade.

—Science Projects about Chemistry. LC 94-959. (Illus.). 128p. (gr. 6 up). 1994. lib. bdg. 17.95 (*0-89490-531-7*) Enslow Pubs.

Hoyt, Marie A. Kitchen Chemistry & Front Porch Physics. Finkler, C. Etana, illus. 60p. (Orig.). (gr. 3-8). 1983. pap. 5.00 (*0-914911-00-7*) Educ Serv Pr.

Johnson, May. Chemistry Experiments. King, Colin, illus. 64p. (gr. 3-6). 1983. lib. bdg. 11.96 (*0-88110-161-3*); pap. 4.95 (*0-86020-527-4*) EDC.

Kramer, Alan. How to Make a Chemical Volcano. LC 89-8994. 1989. 12.95 (*0-531-15120-4*); PLB 12.90 (*0-531-10771-X*) Watts.

Lyon, Sue & Lyon, Sue, eds. Science in Action: Fun with Chemistry. rev. ed. Berman, Paul, created by. LC 92-36324. (gr. 4-9). 1993. write for info. (*0-86307-340-9*) Marshall Cavendish.

Mebane, Robert C. & Rybolt, Thomas R. Adventures with Atoms & Molecules, Bk. I: Chemistry Experiments for Young People. Perkins, Ronald I., intro. by. LC 85-10177. (Illus.). 82p. (gr. 4-9). 1985. lib. bdg. 16.95 (*0-89490-120-6*) Enslow Pubs.

—Adventures with Atoms & Molecules, Bk. II: Chemistry Experiments for Young People. Perkins, Ronald I., intro. by. LC 85-10177. (Illus.). 96p. (gr. 4-9). 1987. lib. bdg. 16.95 (*0-89490-164-8*) Enslow Pubs.

—Adventures with Atoms & Molecules, Bk. III: Chemistry Experiments for Young People. LC 85-10177. (Illus.). 96p. (gr. 4-9). 1991. lib. bdg. 16.95 (*0-89490-254-7*) Enslow Pubs.

—Adventures with Atoms & Molecules, Bk. IV: Chemistry Experiments for Young People. LC 85-10177. (Illus.). 96p. (gr. 4-9). 1992. lib. bdg. 16.95 (*0-89490-336-5*) Enslow Pubs.

Mullin, Virginia L. Chemistry Experiments for Children. Case, Bernard, illus. LC 68-9306. (gr. 3-10). 1968. pap. 3.50 (*0-486-22031-1*) Dover.

Newton, David E. Consumer Chemistry Projects for Young Scientists. LC 90-48499. (Illus.). 128p. (gr. 9-12). 1991. PLB 13.90 (*0-531-11011-7*) Watts.

Science in Action: The Marshall Cavendish Guide to Projects & Experiments, 6 vols. LC 87-36819. 288p. (gr. 4-9). 1989. Set. 89.95 (*0-86307-020-5*) Marshall Cavendish.

VanCleave, Janice. A-Plus Projects in Chemistry: Winning Science Fair Ideas. 240p. (gr. 7 up). 1993. text ed. 22.95 (*0-471-58631-5*); pap. text ed. 12.95 (*0-471-58630-7*) Wiley.

Wood, Robert W. Thirty-Nine Easy Chemistry Experiments. (Illus.). 160p. 1991. 16.95 (*0-8306-7596-5*, 3596); pap. 9.95 (*0-8306-3596-3*) TAB Bks.

Wyler, Rose. Science Fun with a Homemade Chemistry Set. Stewart, Pat, illus. LC 86-21868. 48p. (gr. 2-4). 1987. lib. bdg. 11.38 (*0-671-55575-8*, J Messner); lib. bdg. 4.95 (*0-671-55570-7*); PLB 8.54s.p. (*0-685-47072-5*); pap. 3.71s.p. (*0-685-47073-3*) S&S Trade.

CHEMISTRY, INORGANIC

see also Metals

CHEMISTRY, MEDICAL AND PHARMACEUTICAL

see also Drugs; Pharmacy; Poisons

CHEMISTRY, ORGANIC–SYNTHESIS

see also Plastics; Polymers and Polymerization

CHEMISTRY, PHYSICAL AND THEORETICAL

see also Atoms; Crystallography; Molecules; Nuclear Physics; Polymers and Polymerization; Thermodynamics

CHEMISTRY, TECHNICAL

see also Canning and Preserving; Chemicals; Waste Products

also names of specific industries and products, e.g. Clay Industries

CHEMISTRY–VOCATIONAL GUIDANCE

Sipiera, Paul. I Can Be a Chemist. LC 92-5807. (Illus.). 32p. (gr. k-3). 1992. PLB 11.80 (*0-516-01965-1*) Childrens.

—I Can Be a Chemist. LC 92-5807. (Illus.). 32p. (gr. k-3). 1993. pap. 3.95 (*0-516-41965-X*) Childrens.

Woodburn, John H. Chemistry. (Illus.). 160p. (gr. 6 up). 1987. 13.95 (*0-8442-6137-8*, VGM Career Bks); pap. 10.95 (*0-8442-6138-6*, VGM Career Bks) NTC Pub Grp.

CHEMISTS

see also Chemistry–Vocational Guidance

Newton, David E. Linus Pauling: Scientist & Advocate. LC 93-31719. (Illus.). 128p. 1994. 16.95x (*0-8160-2959-8*) Facts on File.

Parker, Steve. Marie Curie & Radium. LC 92-3616. (Illus.). 32p. (gr. 3-7). 1992. 14.00 (*0-06-020847-3*); PLB 13.89 (*0-06-021472-4*) HarpC Child Bks.

—Marie Curie & Radium. Parker, Steve, illus. LC 92-3616. 32p. (gr. 3-7). 1992. pap. 5.95 (*0-06-446143-2*, Trophy) HarpC Child Bks.

St. Pierre, Stephanie. Gertrude Elion. LC 93-22315. (gr. 7-8). 1993. 15.93 (*0-86592-130-X*); 11.95s.p. (*0-685-66593-3*) Rourke Enter.

CHESS

Bain, John A. Chess Tactics for Students. Mitchell, Robert P., ed. (Illus.). 228p. (Orig.). (gr. 2-12). 1994. pap. 14.95 (*0-9639614-0-3*); tchr's. ed. 14.95 (*0-9639614-1-1*) Lrning Plus.

Caldwell, S. Playing Chess. (Illus.). 64p. (gr. 5 up). 1987. PLB 12.96 (*0-88110-288-1*); pap. 6.95 (*0-7460-0135-5*) EDC.

Carroll, David. Make Your Own Chess Set. Carroll, David, photos by. (Illus.). (gr. 5 up). 1978. (Pub. by Treehouse) P-H.

James, Richard. Move One! A Chess Course for Beginners. (Illus.). 144p. (Orig.). (gr. 1-4). 1991. pap. 13.95 (*0-571-14063-7*) Faber & Faber.

Keene, Raymond. The Simon & Schuster Pocket Book of Chess. LC 88-30555. (gr. 4 up). 1989. (S&S BFYR); pap. 7.95 (*0-671-67924-4*, S&S BFYR) S&S Trade.

Lombardy, William & Marshall, Bette. Chess for Children Step by Step: A New, Easy Way to Learn the Game. (Illus.). 1977. 18.95i (*0-316-53091-3*); pap. 18.95i (*0-316-53090-5*) Little.

Marsh, Carole. Go Queen Go! Chess for Kids. (Illus.). 48p. (gr. k-12). 1994. 24.95 (*1-55609-160-5*); pap. 14. 95 (*0-935326-14-6*) Gallopade Pub Group.

Norwood, D. Chess Puzzles. (Illus.). 64p. (gr. 5 up). 1992. PLB 12.96 (*0-88110-464-7*); pap. text ed. 6.95 (*0-7460-0950-X*) EDC.

Watts, L. & Varley, C. Advanced Chess. (Illus.). 32p. (gr. 5 up). 1991. lib. bdg. 12.96 (*0-88110-503-1*, Usborne); pap. 6.95 (*0-7460-0617-9*, Usborne) EDC.

—Better Chess. (Illus.). 64p. (gr. 5 up). 1993. pap. 9.95 (*0-7460-1437-6*) EDC.

CHESS–FICTION

Baggiani, J. M. & Tewell, V. M. The Chess Set & Other Stories. Birt, Jane L., illus. 21p. (gr. 2-3). 1966. pap. 3.50 (*0-934329-07-9*) Baggiani-Tewell.

Bochak, John. The Gamemaster. Bochak, Grayce, photos by. LC 94-14182. 1995. 14.00 (*0-02-710961-5*, Four Winds) Macmillan Child Grp.

Kontoyiannaki, Elizabeth. Dad, Play Chess with Me. Kontoyiannaki, Elizabeth, illus. 13p. (gr. k-3). 1993. pap. 12.95 (*1-56606-015-X*) Bradley Mann.

Robinson, Nancy K. Countess Veronica. 176p. (gr. 3-7). 1994. 13.95 (*0-590-44485-9*, Scholastic Hardcover) Scholastic Inc.

Sutcliff, Rosemary. Chess-Dream in a Garden. Thompson, Ralph, illus. LC 92-54595. 48p. (ps up). 1993. 16.95 (*1-56402-192-0*) Candlewick Pr.

CHIANG, KAI-SHEK, 1896-

Daley, William. The Chinese Americans. Moynihan, Daniel P., intro. by. (Illus.). 112p. (gr. 5 up). 1988. lib. bdg. 17.95 (*0-87754-867-6*) Chelsea Hse.

CHICAGO

Aylesworth, Thomas & Aylesworth, Virginia. Chicago. (Illus.). 64p. (gr. 3-7). PLB 14.95 (*1-56711-020-7*) Blackbirch.

Davis, James E. & Hawke, Sharryl D. Chicago. (Illus.). 64p. (gr. 4-9). 1990. PLB 11.95 (*0-8172-3025-4*) Raintree Steck-V.

Davis, Lauren. Kidding Around Chicago: A Young Person's Guide. 2nd ed. Blakemore, Sally, illus. 64p. (gr. 3 up). 1993. pap. 9.95 (*1-56261-094-5*) John Muir.

Gary Grimm & Associates Staff. Chicago for Kids: Of All Ages. rev. ed. Filkins, Vanessa, illus. 32p. (gr. k-8). Repr. of 1985 ed. wkbk. 4.00 (*1-56490-001-0*) G Grimm Assocs.

—Let's Color Chicago. Filkins, Vanessa, illus. 40p. (Orig.). (ps-6). 1993. wkbk. 4.00 (*1-56490-000-2*) G Grimm Assocs.

Kurland, Gerald. Richard Daley: The Strong Willed Mayor of Chicago. Rahmas, D. Steve, ed. LC 70-190236. 32p. (Orig.). (gr. 7-12). lib. bdg. 4.95 incl. catalog cards (*0-87157-518-3*) SamHar Pr.

Pfeiffer, Christine. Chicago. LC 88-20199. (Illus.). 60p. (gr. 3 up). 1988. text ed. 13.95 RSBE (*0-87518-385-9*, Dillon) Macmillan Child Grp.

Stewart, G. Chicago. (Illus.). 48p. (gr. 5 up). 1989. lib. bdg. 15.94 (*0-86592-538-0*); lib. bdg. 11.95s.p. (*0-685-58587-5*) Rourke Corp.

Thomson, Ruth. Chicago. LC 94-12308. (gr. 1 up). 1994. write for info. (*0-516-07996-4*) Childrens.

CHICAGO–FICTION

Cuneo, Mary L. Anne Is Elegant. LC 92-42417. 176p. (gr. 4 up). 1993. 15.00 (*0-06-022992-6*); PLB 14.89 (*0-06-022993-4*) HarpC Child Bks.

Deaver, Julie R. You Bet Your Life. LC 92-28211. 224p. (gr. 7 up). 1993. 15.00 (*0-06-021516-X*); PLB 14.89 (*0-06-021517-8*) HarpC Child Bks.

Herman, Charlotte. Summer on Thirteenth Street. LC 91-21156. 188p. (gr. 3-7). 1991. 13.95 (*0-525-44642-7*, DCB) Dutton Child Bks.

Monsell, Mary E. A Fish Named Yum: Mr. Spin, Vol. IV. Christelow, Eileen, illus. LC 93-25731. 64p. (gr. 1-4). 1994. SBE 13.95 (*0-689-31882-0*, Atheneum Child Bk) Macmillan Child Grp.

—The Spy Who Came North from the Pole: Mr. Pin, Vol. III. Christelow, Eileen, illus. LC 92-24646. 64p. (gr. 1-4). 1993. SBE 12.95 (*0-689-31754-9*, Atheneum Child Bk) Macmillan Child Grp.

Nixon, Joan L. Land of Promise. LC 92-28591. (gr. 4-7). 1993. 16.00 (*0-553-08111-X*) Bantam.

Sinclair, Upton. The Jungle. (gr. 11 up). 1965. pap. 2.95 (*0-8049-0086-8*, CL-86) Airmont.

Summer of Dreams: The Story of a World's Fair Girl. 64p. (gr. 4-6). 1993. incl. jacket 5.95 (*0-382-24335-8*); lib. bdg. 7.95 (*0-382-24332-3*); pap. 3.95 (*0-382-24354-4*) Silver Burdett Pr.

CHICAGO–HISTORY

Johnson, LaVerne C. Jean Baptiste DuSable: Writer. Perry, Craig R., illus. LC 92-35252. 1992. 3.95 (*0-922162-93-X*) Empak Pub.

Murphy, Jim. The Great Fire. LC 94-9963. 1995. 15.95 (*0-590-47267-4*) Scholastic Inc.

Roberts, Naurice. Harold Washington: Mayor with a Vision. LC 87-7247. (Illus.). 32p. (gr. 2-4). 1988. PLB 11.80 (*0-516-03657-2*); pap. 3.95 (*0-516-43657-0*) Childrens.

Simon, Charnan. The Story of the Haymarket Riot. LC 88-22803. (Illus.). 32p. (gr. 3-6). 1988. pap. 3.95 (*0-516-44740-8*) Childrens.

Stein, R. Conrad. The Story of the Chicago Fire. Wahl, Richard, illus. LC 81-15543. 32p. (gr. 3-6). 1982. pap. 3.95 (*0-516-44633-9*) Childrens.

Thompson-Peters, Flossie E. The Story of Jean Baptiste DuSable: Father of Chicago. Clo, Kathy, illus. 32p. (Orig.). (gr. 3-9). 1986. pap. text ed. 4.70 (*1-880784-03-3*) Atlas Pr.

Warburton, Lois. The Chicago Fire. LC 89-33554. (Illus.). 64p. (gr. 5-8). 1989. PLB 11.95 (*1-56006-002-6*) Lucent Bks.

CHICAGO CUBS (BASEBALL TEAM)

Chicago Cubs. (gr. 4-7). 1993. pap. 1.49 (*0-553-56421-8*) Bantam.

Goodman, Michael. Chicago Cubs. 48p. (gr. 4-10). 1992. PLB 14.95 (*0-88682-464-8*) Creative Ed.

Lally, Dick. The Chicago Cubs. 1991. pap. 2.99 (*0-517-05791-3*) Random Hse Value.

CHICAGO WHITE SOX (BASEBALL TEAM)

Chicago White Sox. (gr. 4-7). 1993. pap. 1.49 (*0-553-56415-3*) Bantam.

Kavanagh, Jack. Shoeless Joe Jackson. LC 94-21264. 1995. write for info. (*0-7910-2170-X*) Chelsea Hse.

Rambeck, Richard. Chicago White Sox. 48p. (gr. 4-10). 1992. PLB 14.95 (*0-88682-448-6*) Creative Ed.

CHICHESTER, FRANCIS CHARLES, 1901-

Galdone, Paul. Little Red Hen. (ps-3). 1987. incl. cass. 6.95 (*0-317-64569-2*, Clarion Bks) HM.

CHICKENS–FICTION

Addison-Wesley Staff. La Gallinita Roja Big Book. (SPA., Illus.). 16p. (gr. k-3). 1989. pap. text ed. 31.75 (*0-201-19936-X*) Addison-Wesley.

—La Gallinita Roja, Spanish Little Book. (SPA., Illus.). 16p. (gr. k-3). 1989. pap. text ed. 4.50 (*0-201-19708-1*) Addison-Wesley.

—The Little Red Hen Little Book. (Illus.). 16p. (gr. k-3). 1989. pap. 4.50 (*0-201-19364-7*) Addison-Wesley.

Adshead, Paul. The Chicken That Could Swim. LC 90-34358. (ps-3). 1990. 11.95 (*0-85953-294-1*); pap. 5.95 (*0-85953-346-8*) Childs Play.

Alonso, Fernando. Little Red Hen - La Gallina Paulina. Gimeno, J. M., illus. (SPA & ENG.). 26p. (gr. k-2). 1989. Spanish ed. 5.25 (*0-88272-467-3*); English ed. 5.25 (*0-88272-468-1*) Santillana.

Auch, Mary J. The Easter Egg Farm. Auch, Mary J., illus. LC 91-15681. 32p. (ps-3). 1992. reinforced bdg. 15.95 (*0-8234-0917-1*) Holiday.

Barber, Antonia. Gemma & the Baby Chick. Littlewood, Karin, illus. 32p. (ps-3). 1993. 14.95 (*0-590-45479-X*) Scholastic Inc.

Bassett, Jeni, photos by & text by. The Chicks' Trick. LC 93-18471. 1994. write for info. (*0-525-65152-7*, Cobblehill Bks) Dutton Child Bks.

Bond, Felicia. The Chicks' Christmas. LC 82-45918. (Illus.). 32p. (ps-3). 1988. (Crowell Jr Bks); PLB 11.89 (*0-690-04333-3*) HarpC Child Bks.

Bourgeois, Paulette. Too Many Chickens! (ps-3). 1991. 12.95 (*0-316-10358-6*) Little.

Boutiaul, Claudine. The Hen with the Wooden Leg. (Illus.). 32p. (gr. 3-5). 1991. 12.95 (*0-89565-751-1*) Childs World.

Bray, Marian. World's Biggest Chicken. LC 92-7556. 1992. pap. 4.99 (*1-55513-929-9*) Cook.

Brown, Margaret W. Little Chicken. Weisgard, Leonard, illus. LC 43-16942. 32p. (ps-3). 1943. 13.00 (*0-06-020739-6*); PLB 12.89 (*0-06-020740-X*) HarpC Child Bks.

Burgess, Beverly C. Chicken Little. (Orig.). (gr. 1-3). 1987. 3.98 (*0-89274-414-6*) Harrison Hse.

Byars, Betsy C. Good-Bye, Chicken Little. LC 78-19829. 112p. (gr. 5 up). 1990. pap. 3.95 (*0-06-440291-6*, Trophy) HarpC Child Bks.

Casey, Patricia. Cluck, Cluck. LC 87-30435. (Illus.). 32p. (ps-1). 1988. 12.95 (*0-688-07767-6*) Lothrop.

Castoldi, Maggiorina. Chirpy the Chick. 30p. (ps-1). 1987. 3.95 (*0-8120-5819-4*) Barron.

Chicken Licken. (ARA.). (gr. 2-4). 1987. 3.95x (*0-86685-299-9*); incl. cassette 12.00x (*0-685-02568-3*) Intl Bk Ctr.

Clement, Claude. Be Patient, Little Chick. Jensen, Patricia, adapted by. Erost, illus. LC 93-2951. 22p. (ps-3). 1993. 5.98 (*0-89577-503-4*, Readers Digest Kids) RD Assn.

—The Hungry Duckling. Geneste, Marcelle, illus. LC 91-40648. 24p. (ps-3). 1992. 6.99 (*0-89577-418-6*, Dist. by Random) RD Assn.

Coerr, Eleanor. The Josefina Story Quilt. Degen, Bruce, illus. LC 85-45260. 64p. (gr. k-3). 1986. 14.00 (*0-06-021348-5*); PLB 13.89 (*0-06-021349-3*) HarpC Child Bks.

Cole, Joanna. A Chick Hatches. LC 76-29017. (Illus.). 48p. (gr. k-3). 1976. PLB 13.88 (*0-688-32087-2*) Morrow Jr Bks.

Coltman, Paul. Tinker Jim. (ps-3). 1992. 15.00 (*0-374-37611-5*) FS&G.

Cutler, Ivor. Doris. Munoz, Claudio, illus. LC 92-5923. 32p. (gr. k-3). 1992. PLB 14.00 (*0-688-11939-5*, Tambourine Bks) Morrow.

Czernecki, Stefan & Rhodes, Timothy. Nina's Treasures. LC 90-36592. (Illus.). 56p. (gr. 1-6). 1990. pap. 14.95 (*0-920534-65-1*) Sterling.

Dabcovich, Lydia. Mrs. Huggins & Her Hen Hannah. Dabcovich, Lydia, illus. LC 85-4406. 24p. (ps-2). 1988. 12.95 (*0-525-44203-0*, DCB); pap. 3.95 (*0-525-44368-1*, DCB) Dutton Child Bks.

Daniells, Trenna. Don't Blame Others: Timothy Chicken Learns to Lead. Braille International, Inc. Staff & Henry, James, illus. (Orig.). (gr. 1). 1992. pap. 10.95 (*1-56956-007-2*) W A T Braille.

D'Aulaire, Ingri. Don't Count Your Chicks. (ps-3). 1993. pap. 4.99 (*0-440-40771-0*) Dell.

Delaney, Ned. Cosmic Chickens. Delaney, Ned, illus. LC 86-19398. 48p. (ps-3). 1988. HarpC Child Bks.

Dunrea, Olivier. The Broody Hen. LC 91-29377. (Illus.). 32p. (ps-3). 1992. 15.00 (*0-385-30597-4*) Doubleday.

—The Painter Who Loved Chickens. LC 94-4243. 1995. 14.95 (*0-02-733209-8*) Macmillan.

—The Painter Who Loved Chickens. LC 94-27562. 1995. 15.00 (*0-374-35729-3*) FS&G.

Edwards, Michelle. Chicken Man. (Illus.). (gr. k-3). 1991. 13.95 (*0-688-09708-1*); PLB 13.88 (*0-688-09709-X*) Lothrop.

—Chicken Man. Edwards, Michelle, illus. LC 93-11728. 32p. (ps up). 1994. pap. 4.95 (*0-688-13106-9*, Mulberry) Morrow.

Ehrlich, Amy. Buck-Buck the Chicken. Alley, R. W., illus. LC 86-31639. 48p. (gr. 1-3). 1987. pap. 3.50 (*0-394-88804-9*) Random Bks Yng Read.

Ernst, Lisa C. Zinnia & Dot. (Illus.). 32p. (ps-3). 1992. 14.00 (*0-670-83091-7*) Viking Child Bks.

Fine, Anne. The True Story of Harrowing Farm. Fisher, Cynthia, illus. LC 92-33935. 1993. 12.95 (*0-316-28316-9*, Joy St Bks) Little.

Fox, Mem. Hattie & the Fox. Mullins, Patricia, illus. LC 91-41727. 32p. (ps-2). 1992. pap. 4.95 (*0-689-71611-7*, Aladdin) Macmillan Child Grp.

Giffard, Hannah. Hens Say Cluck. Giffard, Hannah, illus. LC 92-62425. 12p. (ps). 1993. bds. 3.95 (*0-688-12442-9*, Tambourine Bks) Morrow.

Gilman, Phoebe. Little Blue Hen. 1993. pap. 28.67 (*0-590-73273-0*) Scholastic Inc.

Ginsburg, Mirra. The Chick & the Duckling. Suteyev, V., tr. from RUS. Aruego, Jose & Dewey, Ariane, illus. LC 74-18873. 32p. (ps-1). 1972. RSBE 14.95 (*0-02-735940-9*, Macmillan Child Bk) Macmillan Child Grp.

—Good Morning, Chick. Barton, Byron, illus. LC 80-11352. 32p. (ps). 1980. 14.00 (*0-688-80284-2*); PLB 13.93 (*0-688-84284-4*) Greenwillow.

—Good Morning, Chick. Barton, Byron, illus. 32p. (ps up). 1993. Repr. text ed. 4.95 (*0-688-12666-9*, Tupelo Bks) Morrow.

Gregorich, Barbara. Nine Men Chase a Hen. Hoffman, Joan, ed. (Illus.). 32p. (gr. k-2). 1992. pap. 3.95 (*0-88743-407-X*, 06059) Sch Zone Pub Co.

Hall, Nancy A. Los Pollitos Dicen the Baby Chicks Sing: Traditional Games, Nursery Rhymes, & Songs From. (ps-3). 1994. 15.95 (*0-316-34010-3*) Little.

Hare, Eric B. Pip Pip the Naughty Chicken. 31p. 1989. pap. 6.95 incl. cassette (*0-8163-0806-3*) Pacific Pr Pub Assn.

Hens. 1989. 3.50 (*0-685-49867-0*) Blue Q.

Hoban, Julia. Quick Chick. Hoban, Lillian, illus. LC 88-30894. 32p. (ps-2). 1989. 9.95 (*0-525-44490-4*, DCB) Dutton Child Bks.

El Hombiccito Galleta. (SPA.). (ps-3). 1993. pap. 5.95 (*0-307-91592-1*, Golden Pr) Western Pub.

Hutchins, Pat. Rosie's Walk. Hutchins, Pat, illus. LC 87-17550. 32p. (ps-k). 1971. pap. 4.95 (*0-02-043750-1*, Aladdin) Macmillan Child Grp.

Jensen, Patricia. Be Patient, Little Chick. (ps-3). 1994. 6.99 (*0-89577-580-8*, Readers Digest Kids) RD Assn.

Jeschke, Susan. Sidney. LC 74-13188. (Illus.). (ps-3). 1979. reinforced bdg. o.p. 4.95 (*0-03-013536-2*, Bks Young Read); pap. 2.95 (*0-03-048966-0*) H Holt & Co.

Kellog, Steven. Chicken Little. LC 84-25519. (Illus.). (gr. 1 up). 1987. pap. 4.95 (*0-688-07045-0*, Mulberry) Morrow.

King-Smith, Dick. Pretty Polly. Peck, Marshall, illus. LC 91-42449. 128p. (gr. 2-7). 1992. o.s.i 14.00 (*0-517-58606-1*); PLB 14.99 (*0-517-58607-X*) Crown Bks Yng Read.

Kiser, SuAnn. Hazel Saves the Day. Day, Betsy, illus. LC 92-34782. 1994. write for info. (*0-8037-1488-2*); PLB write for info. (*0-8037-1489-0*) Dial Bks Young.

Kneen, Maggie, illus. The Great Egg Hunt. LC 93-27272. 1993. 13.95 (*0-8118-0552-2*) Chronicle Bks.

Kratky, Lada J. La Gallinita, el Gallo y el Frijol. Yerkes, Lane, illus. (SPA.). 24p. (Orig.). (gr. k-3). 1992. pap. text ed. 6.00 small bk. (*1-56334-081-X*) Hampton-Brown.

Kurtz, Shirley. Birthday Chickens. (gr. 4-7). 1994. pap. 6.95 (*1-56148-110-6*) Good Bks PA.

Kwitz, Mary D. Little Chick's Friend Duckling. Degen, Bruce, illus. LC 90-5027. 32p. (ps-2). 1992. 13.00 (*0-06-023638-8*); PLB 13.89 (*0-06-023639-6*) HarpC Child Bks.

Landa, Norbert. Rabbit & Chicken Play Hide & Seek. Turk, Hanne, illus. LC 90-33484. (ps). 1992. bds. 4.95 (*0-688-09970-X*, Tambourine Bks) Morrow.

—Rabbit & Chicken Play with Colors. Turk, Hanne, illus. LC 90-33485. (ps). 1992. bds. 4.95 (*0-688-09969-6*, Tambourine Bks) Morrow.
Lane, Megan H. Something to Crow About. (ps-2). 1990. 10.95 (*0-8037-0697-9*); PLB 10.89 (*0-8037-0698-7*) Dial Bks Young.
Lewis, Sherry L. My Trip to the Big Chicken. LC 93-80806. 32p. 1993. pap. write for info. (*0-9639319-0-3*) K S Jewels.
Little Chick's Easter Treasure. (Illus.). (ps-3). 1991. pap. 4.95 (*0-88101-113-4*) Unicorn Pub.
The Little Red Hen. (ARA., Illus.). (gr. 1-3). 1987. Set. incl. cass. 14.95x (*0-685-02575-6*) Intl Bk Ctr.
The Little Red Hen. (Illus.). (ps-k). 1991. PLB 6.95 (*0-8136-5045-3*, TK2332); pap. 3.50 (*0-8136-5545-5*, TK2333) Modern Curr.
Macaulay, David. Why the Chicken Crossed the Road. (Illus.). 32p. (gr. 4-6). 1987. 13.45 (*0-395-44241-9*, Clarion Bks) HM.
—Why the Chicken Crossed the Road. 1991. pap. 4.80 (*0-395-58411-6*) HM.
McConnachie, Brian. Elmer & the Chickens vs. the Big League. Stevenson, Harvey, illus. LC 91-2914. 32p. (ps-2). 1992. 14.00 (*0-517-57616-3*) Crown Bks Yng Read.
McKelvey, David. Bobby the Mostly Silky. LC 83-73327. (Illus.). 32p. (gr. 1-3). 1984. lib. bdg. 10.95 (*0-931722-28-4*); pap. 3.95 (*0-931722-27-6*) Corona Pub.
McKissack, Patricia & McKissack, Fredrick. La Gallinita Roja: The Little Red Hen. LC 86-20801. (Illus.). 32p. (ps-2). 1986. PLB 10.25 (*0-516-32363-6*); pap. 4.95 (*0-516-52363-5*) Childrens.
—The Little Red Hen. Hockerman, Dennis, illus. LC 85-12760. (ps-2). 1985. PLB 10.25 (*0-516-02363-2*); pap. 3.95 (*0-516-42363-0*) Childrens.
McOmber, Rachel B., ed. McOmber Phonics Storybooks: A Red Hen. rev. ed. (Illus.). write for info. (*0-944991-25-4*) Swift Lrn Res.
—McOmber Phonics Storybooks: Hen Pox. rev. ed. (Illus.). write for info. (*0-944991-28-9*) Swift Lrn Res.
Mathers, Petra. Maria Theresa. Mathers, Petra, illus. LC 84-48346. 32p. (ps-3). 1985. PLB 13.89 (*0-06-024112-8*) HarpC Child Bks.
Min, Laura. Mrs. Sato's Hens. 8p. (ps-k). 1994. text ed. 3.95 (*0-673-36193-4*) GdYrBks.
Mountain, Lee, et al. The Little Red Hen. (Illus.). 12p. (gr. k-1). 1991. pap. 18.75 (*0-89061-941-7*) Jamestown Pubs.
O'Connor, Jane & O'Connor, Robert. Super Cluck. Lloyd, Megan, illus. LC 90-32832. 64p. (ps-3). 1991. 11.95 (*0-06-024594-8*); PLB 13.89 (*0-06-024595-6*) HarpC Child Bks.
—Super Cluck. Lloyd, Megan, illus. LC 90-32832. 64p. (gr. k-3). 1993. pap. 3.50 (*0-06-444162-8*, Trophy) HarpC Child Bks.
Pearson, Kit. The Sky Is Falling. 256p. (gr. 3-7). 1990. pap. 15.00 (*0-670-82849-1*) Viking Child Bks.
Pinkwater, Daniel M. Hoboken Chicken Emergency. LC 76-41910. (Illus.). 94p. (gr. k-3). 1990. pap. 12.95 jacketed (*0-671-73980-8*, S&S BFYR); pap. 4.95 (*0-671-66447-6*, S&S BFYR) S&S Trade.
Pomerantz, Charlotte. Here Comes Henny. Parker, Nancy W., illus. LC 93-5480. 24p. 1994. 14.00 (*0-688-12355-4*); PLB 13.93 (*0-688-12356-2*) Greenwillow.
Porte, Barbara A. Chickens! Chickens! Henry, Greg, illus. LC 94-19552. 1995. write for info. (*0-531-06877-3*) Orchard Bks Watts.
Quackenbush, Robert. Sherlock Chick & the Peekaboo Mystery. Quackenbush, Robert, illus. LC 87-3591. 48p. (ps-3). 1987. 5.95 (*0-8193-1149-9*) Parents.
Rausiri, Supa. The Beautiful Chick. Rodriguez, Gloria F., ed. Chang, Phillip, illus. Pinta, Thanom, tr. (Illus.). (gr. k-2). 1979. pap. 3.00x (*0-686-26620-X*, Pub. by New Day Pub PI) Cellar.
Reiser, Lynn. The Surprise Family. LC 93-16249. (Illus.). 32p. (ps up). 1994. 14.00 (*0-688-11671-X*); PLB 13.93 (*0-688-11672-8*) Greenwillow.
Roddie, Shen. Chicken Pox. Cony, Frances, illus. LC 92-53851. 1993. 14.95 (*0-316-75347-5*, Joy St Bks) Little.
Rutman, Shereen. My Wet Hen. Mahan, Ben, illus. 16p. (ps). 1993. wkbk. 2.25 (*1-56293-324-8*) McClanahan Bk.
Scarry, Richard. Richard Scarry's The Little Red Hen. (Illus.). 28p. (ps). 1993. bds. 3.25 (*0-307-12523-8*, 12523, Golden Pr) Western Pub.
Schmidt, Karen L., illus. Chicken Little. 18p. (ps). 1986. 3.95 (*0-448-10223-4*, G&D) Putnam Pub Group.
—The Little Red Hen. 16p. (ps). 1984. 3.95 (*0-448-10218-8*, G&D) Putnam Pub Group.
Sharpe, Susan. Chicken Bucks. LC 92-5049. 144p. (gr. 5-8). 1992. SBE 13.95 (*0-02-782353-9*, Bradbury Pr) Macmillan Child Grp.
Sheldon, Dyan. Harry & Chicken. Heap, Sue, illus. LC 91-71851. 80p. (gr. 3-6). 1994. pap. 3.99 (*1-56402-275-7*) Candlewick Pr.
Sherlock Chick & the Giant Egg Mystery. (Illus.). 42p. (ps-3). 1993. PLB 13.27 (*0-8368-0897-5*) Gareth Stevens Inc.
Sherlock Chick's First Case. 42p. (ps-3). 1993. PLB 13.27 (*0-8368-0892-4*) Gareth Stevens Inc.
Smee, Nicola. Three Little Chicks. (Illus.). 10p. (ps). 1994. bds. 6.95 (*0-590-48079-0*, Cartwheel) Scholastic Inc.
Stoeke, Janet M. A Hat for Minerva Louise. LC 94-2139. (Illus.). 24p. (ps-1). 1994. 12.99 (*0-525-45328-8*) Dutton Child Bks.
—Minerva Louise. LC 87-24458. (Illus.). 24p. (ps-1). 1992. pap. 3.99 (*0-14-054544-1*, Puff Unicorn) Puffin Bks.
Swan, Walter. Brenda the Cow & the Little White Hen. Swan, Deloris, ed. Asch, Connie, illus. 16p. (Orig.). (gr. 2-3). 1989. pap. 1.50 (*0-927176-02-5*) Swan Enterp.
Sweet, Melissa, illus. Little Chick. 24p. (ps). 1994. bds. 2.95 (*0-448-40555-5*, G&D) Putnam Pub Group.
Tripp, Valerie. Sillyhen's Big Surprise. Martin, Sandra K., illus. LC 89-35758. 24p. (ps-2). 1989. pap. 3.95 (*0-516-41522-0*) Childrens.
—La Sorpresa de Gallinita (Sillyhen's Big Surprise) Martin, Sandra K., illus. LC 89-35758. (SPA.). 24p. (ps-2). 1990. pap. 3.95 (*0-516-51522-5*) Childrens.
Wallace, Karen. My Hen is Dancing. Jeram, Anita, illus. LC 93-930. 32p. (ps up). 1994. 14.95 (*1-56402-303-6*) Candlewick Pr.
Wells, Rosemary. Max's Chocolate Chicken. Wells, Rosemary, illus. LC 88-14954. 32p. (ps-2). 1989. 9.95 (*0-8037-0585-9*); PLB 9.89 (*0-8037-0586-7*) Dial Bks Young.
Williams, Garth. Chicken Book. (ps). 1992. pap. 3.99 (*0-440-40600-5*) Dell.
Wormell, Christopher. A Number of Animals. (Illus.). 32p. (ps-12). 1993. 19.95 (*1-56846-083-X*) Creat Editions.
Wormell, Mary. Hilda Hen's Happy Birthday. LC 94-21020. 1995. write for info. (*0-15-200299-5*) HarBrace.
—Hilda Hen's Search. (ps-1). 1994. 13.95 (*0-15-200069-0*) HarBrace.
Zemach, Margot. The Little Red Hen: An Old Story. Zemach, Margot, illus. LC 83-14159. 32p. (ps-3). 1983. 14.00 (*0-374-34621-6*) FS&G.
—Little Red Hen: An Old Story. (ps-3). 1993. pap. 4.95 (*0-374-44511-7*, Sunburst) FS&G.
Zimmerman. Pollita Chiquita. (SPA.). 1993. pap. 28.67 (*0-590-73225-0*) Scholastic Inc.
Zimmerman, H. Werner. Henny Penny. 1989. pap. 9.95 (*0-590-42390-8*) Scholastic Inc.

CHIEF JUSTICES
see Judges

CHILD ABUSE
see also Child Molesting

Alexander, Debra W. All My Feelings. 23p. (gr. k-5). 1992. 3.95 (*1-56688-055-6*) Bur For At-Risk.
—Don't Go. 16p. (gr. k-5). 1992. 3.95 (*1-56688-057-2*) Bur For At-Risk.
—I Can't Remember. 16p. (gr. k-5). 1992. 3.95 (*1-56688-059-9*) Bur For At-Risk.
—It Happened to Me. 24p. (gr. k-5). 1992. 3.95 (*1-56688-058-0*) Bur For At-Risk.
—Something Bad Happened. 16p. (gr. k-5). 1992. 3.95 (*1-56688-056-4*) Bur For At-Risk.
—The World I See. 24p. (gr. k-5). 1992. 3.95 (*1-56688-054-8*) Bur For At-Risk.
Anderson, Deborah & Finne, Martha. Liza's Story: Neglect & the Police. Swofford, Jeanette, illus. LC 85-25379. 48p. (gr. 1-4). 1986. text ed. 11.95 RSBE (*0-87518-323-9*, Dillon) Macmillan Child Grp.
Bass, Ellen. I Like You to Make Jokes with Me, But I Don't Want You to Touch Me. 2nd ed. Lemieux, Margo, illus. Salgado, Maria A., tr. (ENG & SPA., Illus.). 28p. 1993. pap. 6.95 (*0-914996-27-4*) Lollipop Power.
Bliss, Jonathan. Child Abuse. (Illus.). 64p. (gr. 7 up). 1990. lib. bdg. 17.27 (*0-86593-081-3*); lib. bdg. 12.95s.p. (*0-685-46438-5*) Rourke Corp.
Check, William A. Child Abuse. (Illus.). 104p. (gr. 6-12). 1990. lib. bdg. 18.95 (*0-7910-0043-5*); pap. 9.95 (*0-7910-0509-7*) Chelsea Hse.
Coalition for Child Advocacy Staff. Touching. Bergsma, Jody, illus. 32p. (Orig.). (ps). 1985. pap. 5.95 (*0-934671-00-1*) Whatcom Cty Opp.
Cooney, Judith. Coping with Sexual Abuse. rev. ed. Rosen, R., ed. 118p. (gr. 7-12). 1991. PLB 14.95 (*0-8239-1336-8*); leader's guide 5.95 (*0-8239-0846-1*) Rosen Group.
Daisy: A Book about Child Abuse. (ps-3). 1991. pap. 4.95 (*0-87614-543-8*) Carolrhoda Bks.
DeKoster, Katie & Swisher, Karin L., eds. Child Abuse: Opposing Viewpoints. LC 93-9240. 1994. lib. bdg. 17.95 (*1-56510-056-5*); pap. 9.95 (*1-56510-055-7*) Greenhaven.
Delaney, Richard J. & McNerney, Terry. The Long Journey Home. McNerney, Terry, illus. 44p. (Orig.). (gr. 1-8). 1994. pap. text ed. 7.95 (*0-9629849-2-2*) R J Delaney.
Elias, Susan C. Strong & Safe: A Children's Guide to Self Protection. Wise, Caroline, illus. 60p. (Orig.). (gr. 1-3). 1989. pap. 8.95 (*0-317-93904-1*) Womansource.
Engelmann, Jeanne. Wonder What I Feel Today? A Coloring Book about Feelings. Barton, Patrice, illus. 16p. (gr. k-5). 1991. pap. 1.50 (*0-89486-744-X*, 5177B) Hazelden.
Gil, Eliana M. I Told My Secret: A Book for Kids Who Were Abused. Haskell, Sally, illus. 16p. (Orig.). (gr. 3 up). 1986. pap. 2.00 (*0-9613205-1-6*) Launch Pr.
Grimm, Carol & Montgomery, Becky. T Is for Touching. (gr. k up). 1985. manual & 3-filmstrip series o.p. 79.00 (*0-317-40553-5*); manual & videotape one half inch 79.95 (*0-914633-09-0*); manual & videotape three quarter inch o.p. 95.00 (*0-914633-08-2*); write for info. manual (*0-914633-05-8*) Rape Abuse Crisis.
Gross, Cheryl & Werz, Ed. The Sock Club: Real & Fake. 16p. (gr. k-4). 1992. 0.95 (*1-56688-049-1*) Bur For At-Risk.
—The Sock Club: What Could Happen. 16p. (gr. k-4). 1992. 0.95 (*1-56688-051-3*) Bur For At-Risk.
Harvey & Watson-Russell. So, You Have to Go to Court! A Child's Guide to Testifying As a Witness in Child Abuse Cases. 3rd ed. 48p. 1991. pap. 10.00 (*0-409-90611-5*) Butterworth Legal Pubs.
Hyde, Margaret O. Know about Abuse. 93p. 1992. 13.95 (*0-8027-8176-4*); PLB 14.85 (*0-8027-8177-2*) Walker & Co.
Ito, Tom. Child Abuse. (Illus.). (gr. 5-8). 1994. 14.95 (*1-56006-115-4*) Lucent Bks.
Jessie. Please Tell! A Child's Story About Sexual Abuse. Jessie, illus. 32p. (ps-7). 1991. pap. 8.00 (*0-89486-776-8*, 5169A) Hazelden.
Krause, Elaine. For Pete's Sake, Tell! Sullivan, Linda, illus. 54p. (Orig.). (gr. k-3). 1983. pap. text ed. 3.95 (*0-930359-02-X*) Krause Hse.
—Speak up, Say No! 3rd ed. Sullivan, Linda, illus. 40p. (ps-3). 1989. pap. text ed. 3.95 (*0-930359-01-1*) Krause Hse.
Landau, Elaine. Child Abuse: An American Epidemic. rev. ed. 128p. (gr. 7 up). 1990. lib. bdg. 12.98 (*0-671-68874-X*, J Messner); lib. bdg. 5.95 (*0-671-68875-8*) S&S Trade.

Lehman, Yvette K. Know & Tell: A Workbook for Parents & Children on How to Prevent Child Abuse. 2nd ed. (ENG, SPA, CHI.). 46p. (ps-4). 1993. Wkbk. 9.00 (*0-9638555-0-6*) Y K Lehman.
KNOW & TELL is a workbook for parents & young children on the prevention of child abuse. Parents & children learn the necessary skills to help children remain safe at home & away. This book has been widely acclaimed by specialists in the field of Prevention & Education... "The method used is guiding parents in making their own safety rules then teaching the rules in a participatory fashion. The information is solid, age approprate & applicable to all families...Parents & staff highly recommend." - Dr. Barbara Scales, Educator, Administrate, Child Study Center, U. Cal. Berkeley. "This is clearly one of the best children's books on the subject. I though the language was appropriate, the concepts simple yet important & the tone very positive & friendly. Dr. Eliana Gil, Training & Consulting Services, Rockland, MD. "...a useful building block for child's safety...Child predators often go for the path of least resistance - a child who has not been trained about personal parameters. KNOW & TELL gives a structure by which parents can help their children build these parameters in a thought-provoking way." - Denise Etchart Cooper, Ex. Dir., Kevin Collins Foundation for Missing Children, San Francisco.
Publisher Provided Annotation.

—Know & Tell: A Workbook for Parents & Children on How to Prevent Child Abuse. 2nd ed. Naeb, Yuli, tr. from CHI. Colloms, Alisa, illus. 46p. (ps-4). 1993. 9.00 (*0-9638555-2-2*) Y K Lehman.
—Saber y Decir: El Manual Para Padres e Hijos Sobre Como Prevenir el Abuso a los Ninos. 2nd ed. Chavez, Vivian & Costas, Gloria, trs. from ENG. Colloms, Alisa, illus. 46p. (ps-4). 1993. wkbk. 9.00 (*0-9638555-1-4*) Y K Lehman.
Morgan, Marcia K. My Feelings. 2nd ed. Hilty, Christi S., illus. (ps-5). 1984. pap. text ed. 3.95 (*0-930413-00-8*, TX-1-361-947) Equal Just Con.
Mufson, Susan. Straight Talk about Child Abuse. 1993. pap. 3.99 (*0-440-21349-5*) Dell.
Mufson, Susan & Kranz, Rachel. Straight Talk about Child Abuse. 128p. 1991. 16.95x (*0-8160-2376-X*) Facts on File.
Nasta, Phyllis. Aaron Goes to the Shelter: A Story & Workbook Guide about Abuse, Placement & Protective Services. Williams, Mary L., illus. 37p. (Orig.). (gr. k-6). 1992. pap. text ed. 5.95 (*1-880702-01-0*) Whole Child.
Rape & Abuse Crisis Center Staff. Red Flag Green Flag People. Freed, Kecia S., illus. 28p. (gr. k up). 1985. pap. 4.00 wkbk. (*0-914633-10-4*) Rape Abuse Crisis.

Stark, Evan. Everything You Need to Know about Sexual Abuse. rev. ed. (Illus.). 64p. (gr. 7-12). 1993. 14.95 (*0-8239-1611-1*) Rosen Group.

Stewart, Gail. Child Abuse. LC 89-1386. (Illus.). 48p. (gr. 5-6). 1989. text ed. 12.95 RSBE (*0-89686-442-1*, Crestwood Hse) Macmillan Child Grp.

Tipp, Stacey. Child Abuse: Detecting Bias. LC 91-22101. (Illus.). 32p. (gr. 4-7). 1991. PLB 10.95 (*0-89908-611-X*) Greenhaven.

Wakcher, Bridget. Child Abuse: Is It Happening to You? Show, Michael, illus. 32p. (Orig.). (gr. 1 up). 1984. pap. 3.50 (*0-930363-00-0*) Teknek.

Ward, Fred & Ward, Betty. About Sexual Abuse: A Program for Teens & Young Adults. Olszewski, Lema J. & Wolff, Kathy, eds. 85p. (Orig.). (gr. 9 up). 1990. pap. text ed. 9.95 (*1-55896-175-5*) Unitarian Univ.

White, Laurie A. & Spencer, Steven L. Take Care with Yourself: A Young Person's Guide to Understanding, Preventing & Healing from the Hurts of Child Abuse. Cohen, Alice E., illus. 36p. (Orig.). (gr. k-7). 1983. English edition. pap. 5.95 (*0-9612024-0-8*); pap. Spanish edition avail. White & Spencer.

CHILD ABUSE–FICTION

Amstutz, Beverly. Touch Me Not! (Illus.). 20p. (ps-7). 1983. pap. 2.50x (*0-937836-09-5*) Precious Res.

Boulden, Jim & Boulden, Joan. Secrets That Hurt. Winter, Peter, illus. 32p. (Orig.). (gr. 1-6). 1993. pap. 4.95 (*1-878076-28-0*) Boulden Pub.

—Tough Times. Fountain, Phil, illus. 32p. (Orig.). (gr. 1-6). 1993. pap. 4.95 (*1-878076-29-9*) Boulden Pub.

Kent, Lisa. Hilde Knows: Someone Cries for the Children. Machlin, Mikki, illus. 48p. (Orig.). (gr. 1-7). 1994. pap. 6.95 (*1-880396-38-6*, JP9638-6) Jalmar Pr. Hilde, a wire-haired dachshund, is kidnapped from her happy home & held for ransom by a cruel man & his wife. In their home, Hilde sees how treacherous humans can be to their own child, Marybelle. Hilde becomes the little girl's only friend & confidant. When they are rescued, Marybelle finds love & happiness in a new home & Hilde is reunited with her family. This story, told by Hilde, helps children look at a scary subject, child abuse, from a safe distance & viewpoint: through the eyes of a dog. This removes the onus of self-identification, allowing easy transference by the young reader or audience. HILDE KNOWS reinforces the safety rules we try to teach our children in a unique way & helps children heal & find safety. It clearly demonstrates the dangers of succumbing to temptation, taking bad advice from a friend, & accepting gifts from a stranger. The book includes pages written by Dr. Stanley D. Machlin, a psychiatrist, outlining how caring adults can use the book with a child. Unshaded drawings invite children to color & draw - an important tool in therapeutic settings. Both problem & solution are presented in this meaningful little book. *Publisher Provided Annotation.*

Ross, Ramon R. Harper & Moon. LC 92-17216. (Illus.). 192p. (gr. 4 up). 1993. SBE 14.95 (*0-689-31803-0*, Atheneum Child Bk) Macmillan Child Grp.

Shreve, Susan. Lucy Forever & Miss Rosetree, Shrinks. LC 86-29513. 128p. (gr. 3-7). 1988. pap. 2.95 (*0-394-80570-4*) Knopf Bks Yng Read.

Springer, Nancy. The Boy on a Black Horse. LC 92-27158. 176p. (gr. 5-9). 1994. SBE 14.95 (*0-689-31840-5*, Atheneum Child Bk) Macmillan Child Grp.

Stahl, Hilda. Chelsea's Special Touch. LC 92-37203. 160p. (gr. 4-7). 1993. 3.99 (*0-89107-712-X*) Crossway Bks.

Winston-Hiller, Randy. Some Secrets Are For Sharing. Cleaveland, C. A. & McCreary, Jane, illus. 33p. (Orig.). (gr. 4 up). 1986. pap. 5.95 (*0-910223-08-4*) MAC Pub.

CHILD AND PARENT

see Parent and Child

CHILD AUTHORS

Here are entered works on children as authors and works written by children.

Allen County Police Officers Assn., compiled by. Kids Talk to Kids. 75p. (gr. 6-12). 1990. pap. write for info. (*0-9614659-6-4*) Cuchullain Pubns.

CHILD ARTISTS

Here are entered works on children as artists and on works of art by children.

Small, Carol B. Art Concepts for Children. Small, Carol B., illus. LC 89-14917. 112p. (Orig.). (gr. 6 up). 1989. pap. 8.95 (*0-938267-04-3*) Bold Prodns.

CHILD BIRTH

see Childbirth

CHILD DEVELOPMENT

see Child Study; Children–Growth

CHILD LABOR

see also Newsboys

Coil, Suzanne M. Struggle for Child Labor Laws. (Illus.). 64p. (gr. 5-8). 1995. bds. 15.95 (*0-8050-2986-9*) TFC Bks NY.

Freedman, Russell. Kids at Work: Lewis Hine & the Crusade Against Child Labor. Hine, Lewis, photos by. LC 93-5989. (Illus.). 1994. 16.95 (*0-395-58703-4*, Clarion Bks) HM.

Meltzer, Milton. Cheap Raw Material: How Our Youngest Workers Are Exploited & Abused. LC 93-31478. (Illus.). 192p. (gr. 7 up). 1994. 14.99 (*0-670-83128-X*) Viking Child Bks.

CHILD MOLESTING

Bean, Barbara & Bennett, Shari. The Me Nobody Knows: A Guide for Teen Survivors. LC 93-12624. 200p. 1993. pap. 9.95 (*0-02-902015-8*) Free Pr.

Benedict, Helen. Safe, Strong & Streetwise: The Teenager's Guide to Preventing Sexual Assault. (Illus.). 192p. (gr. 7 up). 1987. pap. 6.95 (*0-87113-100-5*) Little.

Cooney, Judith. Coping with Sexual Abuse. rev. ed. Rosen, R., ed. 118p. (gr. 7-12). 1991. PLB 14.95 (*0-8239-1336-8*); leader's guide 5.95 (*0-8239-0846-1*) Rosen Group.

Deaton, Wendy & Johnson, Kendall. No More Hurt. 32p. (gr. 4-6). 1991. wkbk. 5.95 (*0-89793-083-5*); practitioner packs 15.95 (*0-89793-085-1*) Hunter Hse.

Girard, Linda W. My Body Is Private. Tucker, Kathleen, ed. LC 84-17220. (Illus.). 32p. (ps-3). 1984. PLB 11.95 (*0-8075-5320-4*); pap. 4.95 (*0-8075-5319-0*) A Whitman.

Hodgson, Harriet. Power Plays: How Teens Can Pull the Plug on Sexual Harassment. 140p. 1993. pap. 8.95 (*0-925190-67-5*) Deaconess Pr.

Hyde, Margaret O. Sexual Abuse: Let's Talk about It. rev. & enl. ed. Forsyth, Elizabeth H., intro. by. LC 87-133328. 112p. (gr. 5 up). 1987. 10.00 (*0-664-32725-7*) Westminster John Knox.

Jessie. Por Favor, Di! Un Cuento Para Ninos Sobre el Abuso Sexual. Jessie, illus. 32p. (ps-7). 1993. pap. 8.00 (*0-89486-943-4*, 1474A) Hazelden.

Larson, Priscilla. Stranger Danger. 1991. 2.99 (*0-8423-6599-0*) Tyndale.

McCoy, Sandy. Something Happened to Me: Helping a Child to Become a Sexual Abuse Survivor. 18p. (ps-2). 1993. 4.95 (*1-882811-01-1*) Skyline Pubns.

Meyer, Linda D. Safety Zone: A Book Teaching Children Abduction Prevention Skills. Megale, Marina & Walsh, John. (Illus.). 32p. (Orig.). (gr. k-6). 1984. PLB 9.00 (*0-9603516-8-X*) Franklin Pr WA.

Porett, Jane. When I Was Little Like You. Lipczenko, Susan D., illus. LC 93-13974. 1993. 12.95 (*0-87868-530-8*) Child Welfare.

Reid, Kathryn G. & Fortune, Marie M. Preventing Child Sexual Abuse: A Curriculum for Children Ages 9-12. LC 89-33084. (Illus.). 96p. (Orig.). 1989. pap. 9.95 (*0-8298-0810-8*) Pilgrim OH.

Russell, Pamela & Stone, Beth. Do You Have a Secret? How to Get Help for Scary Secrets. McKee, Mary, illus. LC 85-27986. 36p. (Orig.). (ps-2). 1986. pap. 6.95 (*0-89638-098-X*) Hazelden.

Sanford, Doris. Something Must Be Wrong with Me. Evans, Graci, illus. 28p. (ps-6). 1993. 7.99 (*0-88070-469-1*, Gold & Honey) Questar Pubs.

Satullo, Jane, et al. It Happens to Boys Too... Bookless, Nan, illus. 35p. (ps-6). pap. 8.95 (*0-9618618-0-0*) RCC-Berkshires Pr.

Sweet, Phyllis. Something Happened to Me. Lindquist, Barbara, illus. LC 81-83422. (gr. 2-5). 1985. pap. 4.95 (*0-941300-00-5*) Mother Courage.

Terkel, Susan N. & Rench, Janice E. Feeling Safe, Feeling Strong: How to Avoid Sexual Abuse & What to Do If It Happens to You. LC 84-9664. (Illus.). 72p. (gr. 4-8). 1984. PLB 15.95 (*0-8225-0021-3*) Lerner Pubns.

Ward, Fred & Ward, Betty. About Sexual Abuse: A Program for Teens & Young Adults. Olszewski, Lema J. & Wolff, Kathy, eds. 85p. (Orig.). (gr. 9 up). 1990. pap. text ed. 9.95 (*1-55896-175-5*) Unitarian Univ.

CHILD MOLESTING–FICTION

Asher, Sandy. Things Are Seldom What They Seem. LC 82-72819. 144p. (gr. 7up). 1983. pap. 11.95 (*0-385-29250-3*) Delacorte.

Caines, Jeannette. Chilly Stomach. Cummings, Pat, illus. LC 85-45250. 32p. (ps-2). 1986. HarpC Child Bks.

Cole, Barbara S. Don't Tell a Soul. Rosen, R., ed. 175p. (gr. 7-12). 1987. PLB 12.95 (*0-8239-0701-5*) Rosen Group.

Grant, Cynthia D. Uncle Vampire. LC 92-44455. 160p. (gr. 8 up). 1993. SBE 13.95 (*0-689-31852-9*, Atheneum Child Bk) Macmillan Child Grp.

Howard, Ellen. Gilly's Secret. LC 92-44896. 128p. (gr. 3-7). 1993. pap. 3.95 (*0-689-71746-6*, Aladdin) Macmillan Child Grp.

Jukes, Mavis. Wild Iris Bloom. LC 90-24315. 192p. (gr. 5-9). 1992. 14.00 (*0-679-81891-X*) Knopf Bks Yng Read.

Katz, Illana. Sarah: Sexual Abuse. (ps-3). 1994. PLB 16.95 (*1-882388-07-0*); pap. 9.95 (*1-882388-08-9*) Real Life Strybks.

Kelley, Barbara. Harpo's Horrible Secret. Block, Lori, illus. Sargent, Dave, intro. by. (Illus.). 120p. (Orig.). (gr. k-8). 1993. text ed. 16.95 (*1-56763-058-8*); pap. text ed. 8.95 (*1-56763-059-6*) Ozark Pub.

Koenig, Andrea. Thumbelina: The Journal of a Young Girl. Chodos-Irvine, Margaret, illus. LC 93-30652. 320p. (gr. 7 up). Date not set. 15.00 (*0-06-023338-9*); PLB 14.89 (*0-06-023339-7*) HarpC Child Bks.

Lowery, Linda. Laurie Tells. Karpinski, John E., illus. LC 93-9786. (gr. 4 up). 1994. 18.95 (*0-87614-790-2*) Carolrhoda Bks.

MacLean, John. Mac. 192p. (gr. 7 up). 1987. 13.45 (*0-395-43080-1*) HM.

Nathanson, Laura. The Trouble with Wednesdays. 176p. (gr. 7-12). 1987. pap. 2.95 (*0-553-26337-4*, Starfire) Bantam.

Nelson, Theresa. The Beggars' Ride. LC 90-52515. 256p. (gr. 6-12). 1992. 15.95 (*0-531-05896-4*); PLB 15.99 (*0-531-08496-5*) Orchard Bks Watts.

Page, Carole G. Hallie's Secret. 144p. 1987. pap. text ed. 4.99 (*0-8024-3476-2*) Moody.

Polese, Carolyn. Promise Not to Tell. Barrett, Jennifer, illus. LC 84-19767. 66p. (gr. 3 up). 1985. 16.95 (*0-89885-239-0*) Human Sci Pr.

—Promise Not to Tell. Barrett, Jennifer, illus. LC 92-24599. 64p. (gr. 4 up). 1993. pap. 3.95 (*0-688-12026-1*, Pub. by Beech Tree Bks) Morrow.

Sanford, Doris. I Can't Talk about It: A Child's Book about Sexual Abuse. Evans, Graci, illus. LC 86-831. 24p. (gr. k-6). 1986. 7.99 (*0-88070-149-8*, Gold & Honey) Questar Pubs.

Voigt, Cynthia. If She Hollers. LC 93-43519. (gr. 7 up). 1994. 14.95 (*0-590-46714-X*) Scholastic Inc.

Wachter, Oralee. No More Secrets for Me. Aaron, Jane, illus. (gr. 1-4). 1984. pap. 6.95 (*0-316-91491-6*) Little.

Woodson, Jacqueline. I Hadn't Meant to Tell You This. LC 93-8733. 1994. 14.95 (*0-385-32031-0*) Delacorte.

CHILD PSYCHOLOGY

see Child Study

CHILD STUDY

Here are entered works on the psychology, personality, habits, mental development, etc., of the child.

see also Adolescence; Kindergarten; Parent and Child; Play; Problem Children

Anglund, Joan W. Childhood Is a Time of Innocence: Twentieth Anniversary Edition. LC 65-20974. (Illus.). 32p. (gr. k up). 1984. Repr. of 1964 ed. 6.95 (*0-15-216952-0*, HB Juv Bks) HarBrace.

Berry, Joy. About Change & Moving. Bartholomew, illus. 48p. (gr. 3 up). 1990. PLB 12.30 (*0-516-02951-7*) Childrens.

—About Dependence & Separation. (Illus.). 48p. (gr. 3 up). 1990. 12.30 (*0-516-02957-6*); pap. 4.95 (*0-516-42957-4*) Childrens.

—About Handling Traumatic Experiences. (Illus.). 48p. (gr. 3 up). 1990. 12.30 (*0-516-02958-4*); pap. 4.95 (*0-516-42958-2*) Childrens.

Bibeau, Simone. Developing the Early Learner: Level 1. rev. ed. Kruck, Gerry, illus. 64p. (ps-2). 1983. pap. text ed. 4.95 (*0-940406-01-2*) Perception Pubns.

—Developing the Early Learner: Level 2. rev. ed. Kruck, Gerry, illus. 64p. (ps-2). 1983. pap. text ed. 4.95 (*0-940406-02-0*) Perception Pubns.

—Developing the Early Learner: Level 3. rev. ed. Kruck, Gerry, illus. 64p. (ps-2). 1983. pap. text ed. 4.95 (*0-940406-03-9*) Perception Pubns.

—IQ Booster Kit: Developing the Early Learner Levels 1-4. Kruck, Gerry, illus. 256p. (ps-2). 1983. pap. text ed. 85.00 (bks. & cassettes) (*0-940406-05-5*) Perception Pubns.

Brown, Sam E. Gentle Rain & Loving Sun: Activities for Developing a Healthy Self-Concept in Young Children. LC 91-72221. xii, 380p. (Orig.). 1992. pap. text ed. 29.95 (*1-55959-031-9*) Accel Devel.

Coleman, William L. Today I Feel Shy. LC 83-9216. 128p. (Orig.). (gr. 3-4). 1983. pap. 6.99 (*0-87123-588-9*) Bethany Hse.

Fleming, Alice. What to Say When You Don't Know What to Say. LC 82-5782. 128p. (gr. 7 up). 1982. SBE 13.95 (*0-684-17626-2*, Scribners Young Read) Macmillan Child Grp.

Hendryx, Brian, illus. One Hundred One Wacky Facts about Kids. 96p. 1992. pap. 1.95 (*0-590-44890-0*) Scholastic Inc.

Kaufman, Gershen & Raphael, Lev. Stick up for Yourself! Every Kid's Guide to Personal Power & Positive Self-Esteem. LC 89-28642. (Illus.). 96p. (gr. 2-7). 1990. pap. 8.95 (*0-915793-17-2*) Free Spirit Pub.

Kehoe, Patricia. Something Happened & I'm Scared to Tell: A Book for Young Children Victims of Abuse. Deach, Carol, illus. LC 86-62032. 32p. (Orig.). (ps-1). 1987. PLB 15.95 (*0-943990-29-7*); pap. 4.95 (*0-943990-28-9*) Parenting Pr.

Lane, Kristi. Feelings Are Real: Intermediate Workbook. vii, 48p. (gr. 4-6). 1991. 6.95 (*1-55959-016-5*) Accel Devel.

—Feelings Are Real: Primary Workbook. viii, 40p. (gr. 2-3). 1991. 6.95 (*1-55959-015-7*) Accel Devel.

Little People Big Book About Ourselves. 64p. (ps-1). 1989. write for info. (*0-8094-7458-1*); PLB write for info. (*0-8094-7459-X*) Time-Life.

McCoy, Diana L. The Secret: A Child's Story of Sex Abuse, Ages 7-10. Brown, Wynne, illus. Sgroi, Suzanne, intro. by. 32p. (Orig.). (gr. 2-5). 1986. pap. text ed. 6.00 (*0-9619250-1-9*) Magic Lantrn.

Quinn, Patricia O. & Stern, Judith M. The "Putting on the Brakes" Activity Book for Young People with ADHD. Russell, Neil, illus. 88p. (gr. 3-8). 1993. pap. 14.95 (*0-945354-57-6*) Magination Pr.
—Putting on the Brakes: Young People's Guide to Understanding Attention Deficit Hyperactivity Disorder (ADHD) LC 91-20390. (gr. 4-7). 1991. pap. 8.95 (*0-945354-32-0*) Magination Pr.
Sanchez, Gail J. & Gerbino, Mary. Overeating: Let's Talk about It. Raap, Cynthia, illus. LC 85-25388. 120p. (gr. 4 up). 1987. RSBE 9.95 (*0-87518-371-9*, Dillon) Macmillan Child Grp.
Sealy, Adrienne V. No Hill Is Too High. Holder, Stanley, illus. (gr. 2-5). 1978. PLB 4.95 (*0-9602670-0-X*) Assn Family Living.
Simon, Norma. I Am Not a Crybaby. Cogancherry, Helen, illus. 32p. (ps-3). 1991. pap. 3.95 (*0-14-054216-7*, Puffin) Puffin Bks.
Wittels, Harriet & Greisman, Joan. Things I Hate! LC 73-11053. (Illus.). 32p. (ps-3). 1973. 16.95 (*0-87705-096-1*) Human Sci Pr.

CHILD WELFARE

Here are entered works on the aid, support, and protection of children, by the state or by private welfare organizations.
see also Child Labor; Children–Care and Hygiene; Children–Hospitals; Juvenile Delinquency; Playgrounds

Amstutz, Beverly. Sharing Is Fun. Amstutz, Beverly, illus. 24p. (gr. k-7). 1979. pap. 2.50x (*0-937836-00-1*) Precious Res.
Berry, Joy. Every Kid's Guide to Laws That Relate to Kids in the Community. (Illus.). 48p. (gr. 3-7). 1987. 5.95 (*0-516-21423-3*) Childrens.
—Every Kid's Guide to the Juvenile Justice System. (Illus.). 48p. (gr. 3-7). 1987. 5.95 (*0-516-21422-5*) Childrens.
Fierstein, Jeff. Kid Contracts. 32p. (gr. 4-8). 1982. 6.95 (*0-86653-091-6*, GA 442) Good Apple.
Fundamental of Child Care Study Aid. 1974. pap. 2.50 (*0-87738-047-3*) Youth Ed.
Gay, Kathlyn. Day Care: Looking for Answers. LC 91-18141. (Illus.). 128p. (gr. 6 up). 1992. lib. bdg. 17.95 (*0-89490-324-1*) Enslow Pubs.
Hallinan, P. K. I Know There's a Power. Hallinan, P. K., illus. 28p. 1991. pap. 5.00 (*0-89486-780-6*, 5441B) Hazelden.
O'Connor, Karen. Homeless Children. LC 89-37553. (Illus.). 96p. (gr. 5-8). 1989. PLB 14.95 (*1-56006-109-X*) Lucent Bks.
Rape & Abuse Crisis Center Staff. Annie. rev. ed. Freed, Kecia S., illus. 21p. (ps up). 1985. pap. text ed. 2.50 (*0-914633-03-1*) Rape Abuse Crisis.
Sanford, Doris. Lisa's Parents Fight. Davis, Deena, ed. Evans, Graci, illus. LC 89-31409. 28p. (gr. k-4). 1989. 6.99 (*0-88070-301-6*, Gold & Honey) Questar Pubs.

CHILD WELFARE–FICTION

Sanford, Doris. Don't Make Me Go Back, Mommy. Evans, Graci, illus. (gr. k-6). 1990. 7.99 (*0-88070-367-9*, Gold & Honey) Questar Pubs.
Stanek, Muriel. Don't Hurt Me, Mama. Fay, Ann, ed. LC 83-16771. (Illus.). 32p. (gr. 1-3). 1983. PLB 11.95 (*0-8075-1689-9*) A Whitman.

CHILDBIRTH

see also Pregnancy

Allinson, Elaine S. Daniel's Question: A Cesarean Birth Story. DeBiase, Judith, illus. 13p. (ps-5). 1981. staple bdg. 2.95 (*0-9606960-0-8*) Willow Tree NY.
Bently, Judith. Brides, Midwives, & Widows. (Illus.). 96p. (gr. 5-8). 1995. bds. 16.95 (*0-8050-2994-X*) TFC Bks NY.
Birth & Growth. 48p. (gr. 5-8). 1988. PLB 10.95 (*0-382-09708-4*) Silver Burdett Pr.
Brooks, Robert. So That's How I Was Born. Perl, Susan, illus. LC 81-20859. 48p. (ps-2). 1993. pap. 4.95 (*0-671-78344-0*, S&S BYR) S&S Trade.
Brown, Fern G. Teen Guide to Childbirth. (Illus.). 64p. (gr. 7 up). 1990. pap. 4.95 (*0-531-15208-1*) Watts.
Cole, Joanna. How You Were Born. LC 83-17314. (ps up). 1984. pap. 4.95 (*0-688-05801-9*, Mulberry) Morrow.
—How You Were Born. rev. ed. Miller, Margaret, photos by. LC 92-23970. (Illus.). 48p. (ps up). 1994. pap. 4.95 (*0-688-12061-X*, Mulberry) Morrow.
—How You Were Born: Illustrated with Photographs. rev. ed. Miller, Margaret, photos by. LC 92-23970. (Illus.). 48p. (ps up). 1993. 15.00 (*0-688-12059-8*); PLB 14.93 (*0-688-12060-1*) Morrow Jr Bks.
Frasier, Debra. On the Day You Were Born. Johnston, Allyn, ed. Frasier, Debra, illus. 32p. (ps up). 1991. 13. 95 (*0-15-257995-8*) HarBrace.
Ganeri, Anita. Birth & Growth. (Illus.). 32p. (gr. 2-4). 1994. PLB 18.99 (*0-8114-5519-X*) Raintree Steck-V.
Gee, R. Babies. 48p. (gr. 5-10). 1986. PLB 13.96 (*0-88110-336-5*); pap. 6.95 (*0-86020-839-7*) EDC.
Kipfer, Barbara A. One Thousand Four-Hundred Things for Kids to Be Happy About. (ps-3). 1994. pap. 8.95 (*1-56305-238-5*) Workman Pub.
Malecki, Maryann. Mom & Dad & I Are Having a Baby! Malecki, Maryann, illus. LC 82-81707. 70p. (Orig.). (ps-3). 1982. pap. 6.95 (*0-937604-03-8*) Pennypress.
Nilsson, Lennart & Swanberg, Lena K. How Was I Born? James, Clare, tr. LC 94-11908. (Illus.). 1994. 18.95 (*0-385-31357-8*) Delacorte.
Prot, Viviane A. The Story of Birth. Bogard, Vicki, tr. from FRE. Gaudriault, Rozier, illus. LC 90-50777. 38p. (gr. k-5). 1991. 5.95 (*0-944589-34-0*, 340) Young Discovery Lib.
Rushton, Lucy. Birth Customs. LC 92-42174. (Illus.). 32p. (gr. 4-8). 1993. 13.95 (*1-56847-030-4*) Thomson Lrning.
Schoen, Mark. Bellybuttons Are Navels. (Illus.). 40p. (ps-k). 1990. 12.95 (*0-8290-2409-3*) Irvington.

CHILDREN–ADOPTION

see Adoption

CHILDREN–BOOKS AND READING

Here are entered works on the reading interests of children, or lists of books read by or recommended for children. Collections of works published for children are entered under Children's Literature.

Bernhardt, Edythe. ABCs of Thinking with Caldecott Books. Polette, Nancy. (Illus.). 124p. (gr. 1-4). 1988. pap. 12.95 (*0-913839-70-1*) Bk Lures.
Cleary, Florence D. Discovering Books & Libraries: A Handbook for Students in the Middle & Upper Grades. 2nd ed. LC 76-55368. 196p. (gr. 7-12). 1977. pap. 10.00 (*0-8242-0594-4*) Wilson.
Cole, Joanna. Hungry, Hungry Sharks: A Step Two Book. Wynne, Patricia, illus. LC 85-2218. 48p. (gr. 1-3). 1986. lib. bdg. 7.99 (*0-394-97471-9*); pap. 3.50 (*0-394-87471-4*) Random Bks Yng Read.
Dickson, Sue. Off We Go. rev. ed. Portadino, Norma, illus. 112p. (gr. k-3). 1985. pap. 4.97 (*1-55574-001-4*, WB-130) CBN Publishing.
—Raceway. rev. ed. Portadino, Norma, illus. 96p. (gr. k-3). 1984. pap. 4.97 (*1-55574-002-2*, WB-140) CBN Publishing.

Gillespie, John T. & Lembo, Diana L. Introducing Books: A Guide for the Middle Grades. LC 74-94512. 318p. 1970. 29.95 (*0-8352-0215-1*) Bowker.

Global Beat. 34p. 1992. pap. 5.00 (*0-87104-715-2*, Branch Libraries) NY Pub Lib.
Hawthorne, Terri B. & Brown, Diane B. GAIA Celebration for Children: A Workshop & Activities Book. Brown, Diane B., illus. 32p. 1990. pap. 5.99 (*0-929404-02-5*) Tara Educ Servs.
I Am Big Book. (Illus.). 32p. (ps-3). 1990. pap. 22.95 (*0-516-49454-6*) Childrens.
Kowalczyk, Carolyn. Purple Is Part of the Rainbow. Sharp, Gene, illus. LC 85-11693. 32p. (ps-2). 1985. PLB 10.25 (*0-516-02068-4*); pap. 2.95 (*0-516-42068-2*) Childrens.
Lowry, Lois. Anastasia Has the Answers. (gr. 5 up). 1986. 14.95 (*0-395-41795-3*) HM.
Miles, Miska. Annie & the Old One. Parnall, Peter, illus. (gr. 1-3). 1985. pap. 7.95 (*0-316-57120-2*) Little.
Polette, Nancy. The ABCs of Books & Thinking Skills. (Illus.). 144p. (gr. 1-8). 1987. pap. 14.95 (*0-913839-61-2*) Bk Lures.
—The Book Bag. (Illus.). 64p. 1986. pap. 7.95 (*0-913839-46-9*) Bk Lures.
—Novel Thinking. (Illus.). 128p. (gr. 6-12). 1987. pap. 12.95 (*0-913839-47-7*) Bk Lures.
—Reader's Almanac. (Illus.). 148p. (gr. 4-8). 1985. pap. 14.95 (*0-913839-44-2*) Bk Lures.
Polette, Nancy & O'Neal, Kathleen. The Crosby Bonsall Thinking Book. (Illus.). 32p. 1987. pap. 4.95 (*0-913839-65-5*) Bk Lures.
Polette, Nancy & Polette, Keith. Readers Theatre. (Illus.). 48p. (gr. 4-8). 1986. pap. 5.95 (*0-913839-56-6*) Bk Lures.
Rape & Abuse Crisis Center Staff. Annie. rev. ed. Freed, Kecia S., illus. 21p. (ps up). 1985. pap. text ed. 2.50 (*0-914633-03-1*) Rape Abuse Crisis.
Ringstad, M. Adventures on Library Shelves. Pearson, C., illus. LC 68-16398. 48p. (gr. 2 up). 1967. PLB 12.35 prebound (*0-87783-001-0*) Oddo.
Shelton, Helen, ed. Bibliography of Books for Children, 1988-89. LC 89-345. 112p. (ps-6). 1989. 15.00 (*0-87173-118-5*) ACEI.
Sutherland, Zena, ed. The Best in Children's Books: The University of Chicago Guide to Children's Literature, 1973-1978. LC 79-24331. (gr. 12 up). 1980. lib. bdg. 25.00x (*0-226-78059-7*) U Ch Pr.
White, Valerie. Choosing Your Children's Books: Beginning Readers 5 to 8 Years Old. White, Trevor, illus. 32p. (Orig.). (gr. k-3). 1993. pap. 4.95 (*1-882726-00-6*) Bayley & Musgrave.

Zuckert, Ellen R., ed. The KIDSTUFF Survey: Parents Rate Toys, Books, Videotapes, Music & Software for Kids under Six. 2nd, rev. ed. Rosenblatt, Barbara G., illus. 240p. (ps-1). 1993. pap. 9.95 (*0-9634785-1-6*) Cove Pt Pr.
The revised edition of The KIDSTUFF Survey is the only comprehensive guide to toys, books, videotapes, music & software for kids under six based on the views of parents nationwide. It is a unique resource; unlike other product guides, the ratings in The KIDSTUFF Survey are drawn exclusively on parents' & kids' experience with more than 1000 items over the course of months & years. There are concise product descriptions, parents' comments' & price information included to help parents & grandparents choose the best items for kids in the market today. The KIDSTUFF Survey also features the "A Lists" of the best products in each category by age group. In addition, the book contains information on more than 50 mail-order catalogues, toll-free telephone numbers of all major toy manufacturers & extensive indexes to help people choose the products they want. The KIDSTUFF Survey, featured in newspaper articles & radio talk shows around the country, is an indispensable guide that brings together the views of parents on toys, books, videotapes, music & software for kids under six.
Publisher Provided Annotation.

CHILDREN–CARE AND HYGIENE

Here are entered general works on the physical care of children. Works limited to their physical care in school are entered under School Hygiene.

see also Baby Sitters; Children–Diseases; Children–Hospitals; Health Education; Nurses and Nursing

Carroll, Teresa P. Mommy Breastfeeds Our Baby. Gray, Linda, illus. (Orig.). (ps). 1990. pap. 4.95 (*0-9626614-0-6*) NuBaby AL.

Glaser, Nily. Be Street Smart - Be Safe: Raising Safety Minded Children. Kids Against Crime Organization Staff, et al, illus. LC 93-80451. 96p. (Orig.). (gr. k-6). 1994. pap. 9.95 (*0-9632663-2-2*) Gan Pub.
THE MOST COMPREHENSIVE & ENJOYABLE GUIDE TO ONE OF TODAY'S MOST CONCERNING ISSUES: CHILD SAFETY!--WRITTEN BY A VETERAN EDUCATOR. Using rhyme & delightful illustrations, Careful Lee the hound teaches children grades K-6 to: *Differentiate between safe & unsafe situations, without making them fearful *Say an unequivocal NO! when faced by a potentially dangerous situation *Refuse to cooperate with those trying to tempt them. *Distance themselves from unsafe places & people *Use common sense & trust their intuition. "...(This) work is truly important in the fight against crime."--Office of Pete Wilson, Governor of California. "This safety book is long over due!...It is very comprehensive, well thought-out, creative & POSITIVE...It provides a sound foundation that is a must for every home that has children."--Susan Rifkin, School Principal. "This book must be in the hands of every parent & child...A great help in teaching children to minimize potential danger... Important Work!"--Huguette Salti, M.D., Pediatrician. "...a great tool... offers a delightful way to teach children, parents & teachers how to be safety smart...I highly recommend this book to every child, parent & teacher." --Police Sgt. Walter Snyder. May be ordered from publisher 909-381-8844, or Baker & Taylor.
Publisher Provided Annotation.

Hafford, Jeannette N. Help Mates for Your Playmates. (Illus.). 18p. (ps-7). 1986. pap. 4.22 (*0-9616549-1-0*) Tinys Self Help Bks.

Lindsay, Jeanne W. Teens Parenting - Your Baby's First Year: A How-to-Parent Book Especially for Teenage Parents. rev. ed. LC 91-21513. (Illus.). 192p. (gr. 6 up). 1991. text ed. 15.95 (*0-930934-53-9*); pap. text ed. 9.95 (*0-930934-52-0*) wkbk. 2.50 (*0-930934-64-4*) Morning Glory.

Lindsay, Jeanne W. & McCullough, Sally. Teens Parenting - Discipline from Birth to Three: How to Prevent & Deal with Discipline Problems with Babies & Toddlers. LC 91-3711. (Illus.). 192p. (Orig.). (gr. 6 up). 1991. text ed. 15.95 (*0-930934-55-5*); pap. text ed. 9.95 (*0-930934-54-7*); wkbk. 2.50 (*0-930934-66-0*) Morning Glory.

Long, Lynette. On My Own: The Kids' Self Care Book. Hall, Joann, illus. LC 84-463. 160p. (Orig.). (gr. 1-7). 1984. pap. 7.95 (*0-87491-735-2*) Acropolis.

Noble, Elizabeth & Sorger, Leo. The Joy of Being a Boy. 115p. 1994. pap. 4.95 (*0-9641183-0-0*) New Life Images. The first book to reassure the young boy & his family that for his penis to remain intact as nature intended is the BEST way. Circumcision is the only surgical procedure where the decision to operate is made solely by parents who know little about the structure & function of the penis & foreskin. In simple words & photographs, THE JOY OF BEING A BOY explains these facts. It is an essential reading for: families with young boys, doctor's offices, libraries, day care centers & schools. This book will educate those who blindly follow tradition or believe in such medical fallacies that surgery is necessary for cleanliness & disease prevention. Even physicians often do not know that the foreskin should be left alone until it naturally retracts in childhood. The United States is the only country that circumcises most male infants for non-ritualistic reasons. According to the Universal Declaration of Human Rights & the United Nations Convention on the Rights of the Child "no-one shall be subjected to torture or to cruel, inhuman or degrading treatment or punishment." As well as psychological harm, for the adult male an average of twelve square inches of erogenous tissue is lost by this medically-unnecessary genital mutilation.
Publisher Provided Annotation.

CHILDREN–CHARITIES, PROTECTION, ETC.
see Child Welfare
CHILDREN, DELINQUENT
see Juvenile Delinquency
CHILDREN–DISCIPLINE
see Children–Management
CHILDREN–DISEASES
see also Children–Hospitals;
also names of diseases e.g. Diptheria; etc.

Boston, Linda M. Huff & Puff & Me. 2nd ed. 1988. 15.00 (*0-941549-09-7*) Creative Hlth.

Buckel, Marian C. & Buckel, Tiffany. Mom, I Have a Staring Problem: A True Story of Petit Mal Seizures & the Hidden Problem It Can Cause: Learning Disability. LC 92-90113. (Illus.). 1992. pap. 3.95 saddle stitch (*0-317-04291-2*) M C Buckel.

Hathaway, Joe & Hathaway, Nancy. How John Was Unique. 12p. (Orig.). (gr. k-3). 1984. pap. text ed. 3.95 (*0-918335-01-9*) Natl Marfan Foun.

Houlton, Betsy. Tad & Me: How I Found Out about Fetal Alcohol Syndrome. Hanson, Eric, illus. 24p. (gr. 6-12). 1991. pap. 1.75 (*0-89486-739-3*, 5513B) Hazelden.

Landau, Elaine. Dyslexia. (Illus.). 64p. (gr. 5-8). 1991. PLB 12.90 (*0-531-20030-2*) Watts.

Moe, Barbara. Coping with Eating Disorders. (gr. 7-12). 1991. PLB 14.95 (*0-8239-1343-0*) Rosen Group.

Nourse, Alan E. Lumps, Bumps, & Rashes: A Look at Kids' Diseases. rev. ed. LC 90-32785. (Illus.). 64p. (gr. 5-8). 1990. PLB 12.90 (*0-531-10865-1*) Watts.

Ogden, John A. The Medibears Guide to the Doctor's Exam: For Children & Parents. Ogden, Ethel F., illus. (gr. k-5). 1991. 10.95 (*0-8130-1082-9*) U Press Fla.

Ostrow, William & Ostrow, Vivian. All about Asthma. Levine, Abby, ed. Sims, Blanche, illus. LC 89-5254. 32p. (gr. 2-6). 1989. PLB 11.95 (*0-8075-0276-6*); pap. 4.95 (*0-8075-0275-8*) A Whitman.

Tartakoff, Katy. My Stupid Illness. Shields, Laurie, illus. 54p. Repr. of 1991 ed. wkbk. 14.95 (*0-9629365-4-5*) Childrens Lgcy.

CHILDREN–DISEASES–FICTION

Aiello, Barbara & Shulman, Jeffrey. A Portrait of Me: Featuring Christine Kontos. (Illus.). 48p. (gr. 3-6). 1989. PLB 13.95 (*0-941477-05-3*) TFC Bks NY.

Arnothy. I Am Fifteen: And I Don't Want to Die. 1993. pap. 2.95 (*0-590-44630-4*) Scholastic Inc.

Bess, Clayton. The Mayday Rampage. DiCicco, Dan, illus. LC 92-74268. 208p. (gr. 9-12). 1993. 14.95 (*1-882405-00-5*); pap. 7.95 (*1-882405-01-3*); 3 audiocassettes, incl. AIDS curriculum unit w/ tchr's. guide 21.95 (*1-882405-02-1*) Lookout Pr.

Blume, Judy. Deenie. 144p. (gr. 7 up). 1991. pap. 3.99 (*0-440-93259-9*, LFL) Dell.

Charlip, Remy & Supree, Burton. Mother Mother I Feel Sick Send for the Doctor Quick Quick Quick. (Illus.). 1993. pap. 14.95x (*1-56849-172-7*) Buccaneer Bks.

Cherry, Lynne. Who's Sick Today? (Illus.). 24p. (ps-1). 1993. pap. 3.99 (*0-14-054839-4*) Puffin Bks.

Gehret, Jeanne. I'm Somebody Too. 159p. (gr. 4-7). 1992. text ed. 16.00 (*0-9625136-7-9*); pap. 12.00 (*0-9625136-6-0*) Verbal Images Pr. "This juvenile fiction...held my interest throughout. It is the story of sibling rivalry exacerbated by the younger sib Ben's condition known as attention deficit disorder or ADD. His older sister Emily represses her own needs & resentments as a people-pleaser & tries to keep conflict to a minimum...This is a fictionalized account of their struggles as a family, the growing crisis & the final resolution as the family seeks treatment...The therapy sessions are very well done by someone who knows what therapy is all about... engaging fiction...invaluable to the general public...a valuable addition to bibliotherapy programs involving professionals in schools & public libraries. Many parents as well as children will benefit from reading the book."--Small Press. "In addition to a good story, Gehret offers a few pages on how siblings can deal with frustration."--School Library Journal. A companion to Jeanne Gehret's bestselling picture book EAGLE EYES: A CHILD'S GUIDE TO PAYING ATTENTION (1991), which introduced the same family through the tale of scatterbrained Ben. I'M SOMEBODY TOO. 159 pages. Ages 9 to 12. Paperback $12.00 (ISBN 0-9625136-6-0); Hardcover $16.00 (ISBN 0-9625136-7-9). Verbal Images Press, 19 Fox Hill Dr., Fairport, NY 14450.
Publisher Provided Annotation.

Getz, David. Thin Air. LC 90-34137. 128p. (gr. 3-7). 1992. pap. 3.95 (*0-06-440422-6*, Trophy) HarpC Child Bks.

Girard, Linda W. Alex, the Kid with AIDS. Levine, Abby, ed. Sims, Blanche, illus. LC 89-77592. 32p. (gr. 2-5). 1991. PLB 13.95 (*0-8075-0245-6*); pap. 5.95 (*0-8075-0247-2*) A Whitman.

Haines, Rashelle. Jimmy's Last Wish: A Story about Forever. Alvarado, Carol, illus. 32p. 1992. 22.95 (*0-944963-23-4*); PLB 20.95 (*0-944963-32-3*); audio tape 9.95 (*0-944963-20-X*) Glastonbury Pr.

Jones, Shelley D. When Laughing Isn't Funny. (Illus.). 1990. 6.95 (*0-533-08541-1*) Vantage.

Kelley, True. I've Got Chicken Pox. Kelley, True, illus. LC 93-11685. 1994. write for info. (*0-525-45185-4*) Dutton Child Bks.

Laird, Elizabeth. Loving Ben. (gr. 5 up). 1989. 14.95 (*0-385-29810-2*) Delacorte.

London, Jonathan. The Lion Who Had Asthma. Levine, Abby, ed. Westcott, Nadine B., illus. LC 91-16553. 32p. (ps-1). 1992. PLB 13.95 (*0-8075-4559-7*) A Whitman.

McAllister, Angela. The Ice Palace. Barrett, Angela, illus. LC 93-45255. 1994. 15.95 (*0-399-22784-9*, Putnam) Putnam Pub Group.

MacLachlan, Patricia. The Sick Day. Du Bois, William P., illus. LC 78-11686. (gr. k-3). 1979. 6.95 (*0-394-83876-9*) Pantheon.

Orr, Wendy. Aa-Choo! Ohi, Ruth, illus. 32p. (ps-3). 1992. PLB 14.95 (*1-55037-209-2*, Pub. by Annick CN); pap. 4.95 (*1-55037-208-4*, Pub. by Annick CN) Firefly Bks Ltd.

Osofsky, Audrey. My Buddy. Rand, Ted, illus. LC 92-3028. 32p. (gr. k-3). 1992. 14.95 (*0-8050-1747-X*, Bks Young Read) H Holt & Co.

Roberts, Willo D. Sugar Isn't Everything: A Support Book, in Fiction Form, for the Young Diabetic. LC 86-17275. 208p. (gr. 4 up). 1987. SBE 14.95 (*0-689-31316-0*, Atheneum Child Bk) Macmillan Child Grp.

—Sugar Isn't Everything: A Support Book, in Fiction Form, for the Young Diabetic. LC 88-3358. 192p. (gr. 3-7). 1988. pap. 3.95 (*0-689-71225-1*, Aladdin) Macmillan Child Grp.

Roddie, Shen. Chicken Pox. Cony, Frances, illus. LC 92-53851. 1993. 14.95 (*0-316-75347-5*, Joy St Bks) Little.

Sinykin, Sheri C. Apart at the Seams. 120p. (gr. 6-12). 1991. pap. 3.95 perfect bdg. (*0-89486-733-4*, 5138A) Hazelden.

Starkman, Neal. Z's Gift. Ellen, G. & Sasaki, Joy, illus. LC 88-71483. 52p. (Orig.). (gr. 4-6). 1988. pap. 7.00 (*0-935529-08-X*) Comprehen Health Educ.

Ziefert, Harriet. So Sick. Nicklaus, Carol, illus. LC 85-1957. 32p. (ps-1). 1985. pap. 3.50 (*0-394-87580-X*) Random Bks Yng Read.

CHILDREN–EDUCATION
see Education, Elementary
CHILDREN, EMOTIONALLY DISTURBED
see Problem Children
CHILDREN–EMPLOYMENT
see Child Labor
CHILDREN–FICTION

Acierno, Maria. Children of Flight Pedro Pan. 80p. (gr. 4-6). 1994. PLB 12.95 (*1-881889-52-1*) Silver Moon.

Allen, Julia. My First Job. Reese, Bob, illus. (gr. k-3). 1987. 7.95 (*0-89868-184-7*); pap. 2.95 (*0-89868-183-9*) ARO Pub.

—My First Phone Call. Reese, Bob, illus. (gr. k-3). 1987. 7.95 (*0-89868-189-8*); pap. 2.95 (*0-89868-190-1*) ARO Pub.

—Thirty Word My First Series, 6 bks. Reese, Bob, illus. (gr. k-3). 1987. Set. 47.70 (*0-89868-237-1*); Set. pap. 29.50 (*0-89868-236-3*) ARO Pub.

Anglund, Joan W. A Child's Year. (Illus.). 24p. (ps-k). 1992. write for info. (*0-307-00141-5*, 312-06, Golden Pr) Western Pub.

Anholt, Catherine & Anholt, Laurence. All about You. (Illus.). 32p. (ps). 1992. 14.00 (*0-670-84488-8*) Viking Child Bks.

—Bear & Baby. Anholt, Laurence & Anholt, Catherine, illus. LC 92-54581. 24p. (ps). 1993. 5.95 (*1-56402-235-8*) Candlewick Pr.

—Kids. Anholt, Catherine & Anholt, Laurence, illus. LC 91-58739. 32p. (ps up). 1992. 13.95 (*1-56402-097-5*) Candlewick Pr.

—Kids. LC 91-58739. (Illus.). 32p. (ps up). 1994. pap. 4.99 (*1-56402-269-2*) Candlewick Pr.

—Toddlers. Anholt, Catherine & Anholt, Laurence, illus. LC 92-54588. 24p. (ps). 1993. 5.95 (*1-56402-242-0*) Candlewick Pr.

Babbitt, Lucy C. Children of the Maker. LC 88-45482. 208p. (gr. 6 up). 1988. 15.00 (*0-374-31245-1*) FS&G.

Bannerman, Helen. The Story of Little Black Quasha. (Illus.). 56p. (ps-4). 1990. Repr. of 1908 ed. 10.95 (*0-9616844-3-7*) Greenhouse Pub.

—The Story of Little Black Quibba. (Illus.). 68p. (ps-4). 1990. Repr. of 1902 ed. 10.95 (*0-9616844-4-5*) Greenhouse Pub.

Barrett, John M. No Time for Me: Learning to Live with Busy Parents. Servello, Joe, illus. LC 78-21257. 32p. (ps-3). 1985. 16.95 (*0-87705-385-5*) Human Sci Pr.

Barrett, Judi. Cloudy with a Chance of Meatballs. Barrett, Ron, illus. (gr. 2-5). 1985. pap. 12.95 incl. cassette (*0-941078-91-4*); PLB incl. cassette 19.95 (*0-941078-93-0*); incl. cassette, 4 paperbacks guide 27.95 (*0-941078-92-2*) Live Oak Media.

Beatty, Patricia. Lupita Manana. LC 81-505. (gr. 7-9). 1981. PLB 12.93 (*0-688-00359-1*) Morrow Jr Bks.

Bennett, Cherie. Sunset Scandal. 224p. (Orig.). (gr. 4-7). 1992. pap. 3.99 (*0-425-13385-0*) Berkley Pub.

—Sunset Whispers. 224p. (Orig.). 1992. pap. 3.99 (*0-425-13386-9*) Berkley Pub.

Bernard, Patricia. Kangaroo Kids. 1992. pap. 3.50 (*0-553-15959-3*) Bantam.

Birenbaum, Barbara. The Hidden Shadow. Birenbaum, Barbara, illus. LC 86-12187. 54p. (gr. 1-4). 1986. 10.95 (*0-935343-42-3*); pap. 5.95 (*0-935343-43-1*) Peartree.

Bonsall, Crosby N. The Case of the Scaredy Cats. LC 75-159039. (Illus.). 64p. (ps-3). 1984. pap. 3.50 (*0-06-444047-8*, Trophy) HarpC Child Bks.

Bornstein, Ruth L. The Seedling Child. LC 86-19581. (Illus.). 28p. (ps-2). 1987. 12.95 (*0-15-272459-1*) HarBrace.

Bowen, Richard. The First Helping. Bowen, Richard, illus. (gr. k-6). 1993. pap. 9.95 (*1-56883-009-2*) Colonial Pr AL.

Brancato, Robin F. Come Alive at 505. LC 79-19144. 224p. (gr. 7 up). 1980. 8.95 (*0-394-84294-4*); lib. bdg. 8.99 (*0-394-94294-9*) Knopf Bks Yng Read.

Brinckloe, Julie. Fireflies. LC 85-26767. (Illus.). 32p. (gr. k-2). 1986. pap. 3.95 (*0-689-71055-0*, Aladdin) Macmillan Child Grp.

Burgess, Thornton W. Mother West Wind's Children. Cady, Harrison, illus. 156p. (ps-3). 1985. pap. 8.95 (*0-316-11657-2*) Little.

Busch, Wilhelm. Max & Moritz. Klein, H. Arthur, ed. 216p. (Orig., Bilingual Eng & Ger). (gr. 3-6). 1962. pap. 4.95 (*0-486-20181-3*) Dover.
Carlson, Nancy. Loudmouth George & the Cornet. Carlson, Nancy, illus. (gr. k-3). 1986. pap. 12.95 incl. cassette (*0-87499-011-4*); PLB incl. cassette 19.95 (*0-87499-013-0*); incl. cassette 4 paperbacks guide 27.95 (*0-87499-012-2*) Live Oak Media.
—Loudmouth George & the Sixth Grade Bully. LC 84-18120. (Illus.). 32p. (ps-3). 1985. pap. 3.95 (*0-14-050510-5*, Puffin) Puffin Bks.
Caseley, Judith. Ada Potato. LC 87-19738. (Illus.). 24p. (ps up). 1989. 11.95 (*0-688-07742-0*); PLB 11.88 (*0-688-07743-9*) Greenwillow.
Clapp, Patricia C. Witches' Children. (gr. 5-9). 1987. pap. 4.99 (*0-14-032407-0*, Puffin) Puffin Bks.
Cleary, Beverly. Henry & Beezus. Darling, Louis, illus. LC 52-5930. 192p. (gr. 3-7). 1952. 13.95 (*0-688-21383-9*); PLB 13.88 (*0-688-31383-3*, Morrow Jr Bks) Morrow Jr Bks.
—Jean & Johnny. 224p. (gr. 6-9). 1981. pap. 2.95 (*0-440-94358-2*, LE) Dell.
—Ramona Quimby, Age Eight. Tiegreen, Alan, illus. LC 80-28425. 192p. (gr. 4-6). 1981. 13.95 (*0-688-00477-6*); PLB 13.88 (*0-688-00478-4*) Morrow Jr Bks.
Conrad, Pam. Staying Nine. LC 87-45862. (Illus.). 80p. (gr. 2-5). 1990. pap. 3.95 (*0-06-440377-7*, Trophy) HarpC Child Bks.
Cooper, Susan. The Dark Is Rising Sequence Box, 5 bks. (gr. 7 up). 1993. Boxed set. pap. 19.75 (*0-02-042565-1*, Aladdin) Macmillan Child Grp.
—Seaward. LC 86-23234. 180p. (gr. 5 up). 1987. pap. 3.95 (*0-02-042190-7*, Collier Young Ad) Macmillan Child Grp.
Corbett, Scott. The Lemonade Trick. Galdone, Paul, illus. 96p. (gr. 4-6). 1988. pap. 2.95 (*0-590-32197-8*, Apple Paperbacks) Scholastic Inc.
Cosgrove, Stephen. Feather Fin. James, Robin, illus. LC 84-15057. 32p. (Orig.). (gr. 1-4). 1983. pap. 2.95 (*0-8431-0593-3*) Price Stern.
Crew, Linda. Children of the River. (gr. 7 up). 1991. pap. 3.99 (*0-440-21022-4*, LFL) Dell.
DeClements, Barthe. No Place for Me. (gr. 5-9). 1987. pap. 12.95 (*0-670-81908-5*) Viking Child Bks.
Delton, Alan T., illus. Huckleberry Hash. 1990. pap. 2.95 (*0-440-40325-1*, YB) Dell.
Delton, Judy. Angel's Mother's Baby. Apple, Margot, illus. 144p. (gr. 2-5). 1989. 13.45 (*0-395-50926-2*) HM.
—Merry Merry Huckleberry. Tiegreen, Alan, illus. (Orig.). 1990. pap. 2.95 (*0-440-40365-0*, Pub. by Yearling Classics) Dell.
Drescher, Joan. I'm in Charge. Drescher, Joan, illus. (gr. 1-3). 1981. 9.95 (*0-316-19330-5*, Pub. by Atlantic Pr) Little.
Duncan, Lois. Wonder Kid Meets the Evil Lunch Snatcher. (gr. 2-4). 1990. pap. 2.95 (*0-316-19561-8*) Little.
Dunrea, Olivier. Ravena. (ps-3). 1992. 3.99 (*0-440-40645-5*, YB) Dell.
Ellis, Terry. The Legend of Willow Wood Springs. LC 85-63828. (Illus.). 180p. (Orig.). (gr. 4 up). 1989. pap. 4.75 (*0-915677-30-X*) Roundtable Pub.
Engh, M. J. House in the Snow. 144p. 1990. pap. 2.75 (*0-590-42658-3*) Scholastic Inc.
Enns, Peter & Forsberg, Glen. Stories That Live, 6 vols. Friesen, John H., illus. 144p. (ps-5). 1985. books & cassettes 29.70 (*0-936215-00-3*) STL Intl.
Ferguson, Alane. The Practical Joke War. 96p. (gr. 4-8). 1993. pap. 3.50 (*0-380-71721-2*, Camelot) Avon.
Ferris, Jean. Looking for Home. 176p. (gr. 8 up). 1989. 15.00 (*0-374-34649-6*) FS&G.
Field, Rachel. Prayer for a Child. Jones, Elizabeth O., illus. LC 84-70991. 32p. (ps-k). 1984. pap. 3.95 (*0-02-043070-1*, Aladdin) Macmillan Child Grp.
Finley, Martha. Elsie's Children. 243p. 1981. Repr. PLB 25.95x (*0-89966-336-2*) Buccaneer Bks.
Fishman, Richard A. The Sandlot Summit. Sutter, Richard, illus. LC 85-63032. 197p. (Orig.). (gr. 4-9). 1985. pap. 3.95 (*0-9615884-0-3*) Sunlakes Pub.
Flowers, Sandra H. Leslie: Maybe I'll Be. Allred, David & Leonard, Camille, eds. Maudsley, Kenith, illus. 24p. (Orig.). (gr. 1-4). Date not set. pap. 1.00 (*0-9630029-4-5*) Community Comm.
Freedman, Russell. Children of the Wild West. LC 83-5133. (Illus.). 128p. (gr. 3-6). 1983. 15.95 (*0-89919-143-6*, Clarion Bks) HM.
Garcia Sanchez, J. L. El Nino Gigante (The Giant Child) Sole, Carme, illus. (SPA.). 32p. (gr. k-2). 1988. 9.95 (*84-372-1346-0*) Santillana.
Giff, Patricia R. Spectacular Stone Soup. 80p. (Orig.). (gr. k-6). 1989. pap. 3.50 (*0-440-40134-8*, YB) Dell.
—Today Was a Terrible Day. Natti, Susanna, illus. 1980. 11.95 (*0-670-71830-0*) Viking Child Bks.
Gipson, Fred. Savage Sam. (gr. 1-5). 1976. pap. 6.00 (*0-06-080377-0*, P377, PL) HarpC.
Girzone, Joseph F. Joshua & the Children, 2 Vols. 1991. pap. 17.95 (*0-02-019891-4*, Collier Young Rd) Macmillan Child Grp.
Goble, Paul. The Lost Children: The Boys Who Were Neglected. Goble, Paul, illus. LC 91-44283. 40p. (ps-12). 1993. SBE 14.95 (*0-02-736555-7*, Bradbury Pr) Macmillan Child Grp.
Gorman, Carol. Chelsey & the Green-Haired Kid. (gr. 5 up). 1987. 13.45 (*0-395-41854-2*) HM.
Grant, Eva. Will I Ever Be Older? (ps-3). 1993. pap. 3.95 (*0-8114-5206-9*) Raintree Steck-V.
Grosset & Dunlap Staff. I'm So Big! (Illus.). 18p. (ps). 1991. bds. 2.95 (*0-448-40122-3*, G&D) Putnam Pub Group.
Harte, Kathleen M. There's Lots That I Can Do. Harte, Kathleen M., illus. LC 92-43904. 32p. (ps-k). 1993. pap. 2.25 (*0-679-84798-7*) Random Bks Yng Read.
Hastings. Rufus & Christopher & the Box of Laughter. LC 77-190270. (Illus.). 32p. (gr. 2-4). 1972. PLB 9.95 (*0-87783-060-6*); pap. 3.94 deluxe ed. (*0-87783-106-8*); cassette 7.94x (*0-87783-196-3*) Oddo.
Heron, Jean O. Voyage d'Alice ou Comment Sont Nes les Droits de l'Enfant. Dumas, Philippe, illus. (FRE.). 151p. (gr. 3-7). 1990. pap. 11.95 (*2-07-031245-3*) Schoenhof.
Higgins, Betty. Witch Watch. Sun Star Publications Staff, ed. Yazzie, Johnson, illus. August, Clara & Schatt, Paulintro. by. (Illus.). 24p. (Orig.). (gr. 3-8). 1986. pap. 2.95 (*0-937787-05-1*) Sun Star Pubns.
Hutchins, Pat. You'll Soon Grow into Them, Titch. Hutchins, Pat, illus. LC 82-11755. 32p. (ps up). 1992. pap. 4.95 (*0-688-11507-1*, Mulberry) Morrow.
Jarrow, Gail. The Two-ton Secret. 144p. (gr. 5). 1989. pap. 2.95 (*0-380-75904-7*, Camelot) Avon.
Johnson, Sue. At Grandma's House: Story Book for Young Children in Sign Language. Herigstad, Joni, illus. 28p. 1985. pap. 4.50 (*0-916708-14-4*) Modern Signs.
Kamins, Tamar. The B. Y. Times Kid Sisters: The "I-Can't-Cope-Club, No. 1. 1992. pap. 5.95 (*0-944070-84-1*) Targum Pr.
—The B. Y. Times Kid Sisters: The Treehouse Kids, No. 2. 1992. pap. 5.95 (*0-944070-92-2*) Targum Pr.
Kaye, Marilyn. Looking for Trouble. 128p. (gr. 4). 1990. pap. 2.95 (*0-380-75909-8*, Camelot) Avon.
Keats, Ezra J. Apartment Three. LC 85-26791. (Illus.). 32p. (gr. 1-5). 1986. pap. 3.95 (*0-689-71059-3*, Aladdin) Macmillan Child Grp.
Kerr, M. E. The Son of Someone Famous. LC 73-14338. 240p. (gr. 7 up). 1991. pap. 3.95 (*0-06-447069-5*, Trophy) HarpC Child Bks.
Kimmelman, Leslie. Frannie's Fruits. Mathers, Petra, illus. LC 88-17637. 32p. (ps-3). 1989. PLB 14.89 (*0-06-023164-5*) HarpC Child Bks.
King-Smith, Dick. The Cuckoo Child. Bowman, Leslie, illus. LC 92-72029. 128p. (gr. 3-6). 1993. 13.95 (*1-56282-350-7*); PLB 13.89 (*1-56282-351-5*) Hyprn Child.
Kitzinger, Sheila. Being Born. Nilsson, Lennart, illus. (ps-1). 1992. pap. 11.95 (*0-399-22225-1*, Putnam) Putnam Pub Group.
Klein, Leah. The B. Y. Times: Here We Go Again, No. 9. 1992. pap. 7.95 (*0-944070-90-6*) Targum Pr.
—The B. Y. Times: Summer Daze, No. 8. pap. 7.95 (*0-944070-83-3*) Targum Pr.
—The B. Y. Times: The New Kids, No. 10. 1992. pap. 7.95 (*0-944070-91-4*) Targum Pr.
Klevin, Jill R. Turtles Together Forever! Edwards, Linda S., illus. LC 82-70313. 160p. (gr. 4-6). 1982. pap. 9.95 (*0-385-29045-4*); pap. 9.89 (*0-385-29046-2*) Delacorte.
Knox, Jeri A. Introducing Nikki & Kiana. LC 93-77322. 82p. (Orig.). (gr. 6-10). 1993. pap. text ed. 7.00 (*1-880679-03-5*) Mtn MD.
Konigsburg, E. L. Journey to an 800 Number. LC 81-10829. 144p. (gr. 5-9). 1982. SBE 13.95 (*0-689-30901-5*, Atheneum Child Bk) Macmillan Child Grp.
Krensky, Stephen. Los Hios de la Tierra y el Cielo: Children of the Earth & Sky. (ps-3). 1993. pap. 4.95 (*0-590-46861-8*) Scholastic Inc.
Landsman, Sandra G. I'm Special: An Experiential Workbook for the Child in Us All. Landman, Rodney G., illus. (gr. k up). 1986. pap. 6.95 (*0-935571-02-7*) Treehouse.
Lasky, Kathryn. A Baby for Max. Knight, Christopher G., illus. LC 86-22131. 48p. (ps-2). 1987. pap. 4.95 (*0-689-71118-2*, Aladdin) Macmillan Child Grp.
Lazewnik, Libby. Baker's Dozen: The Inside Story, No. 5. 1992. ppt. 7.95 (*0-944070-93-0*) Targum Pr.
Levene, Nancy. Peanut Butter & Jelly Secrets. LC 87-5247. (gr. 3-6). 1987. pap. 4.99 (*1-55513-303-7*, Chariot Bks) Chariot Family.
—Salty Scarecrow Solution. LC 89-31274. (gr. 3-6). 1989. pap. 4.99 (*1-55513-523-4*, Chariot Bks) Chariot Family.
—Shoelaces & Brussel Sprouts. LC 87-5267. (gr. 3-6). 1987. pap. 4.99 (*1-55513-301-0*, Chariot Bks) Chariot Family.
—T-Bone Trouble. LC 90-32906. (gr. 3-6). 1990. pap. 4.99 (*1-55513-765-2*, Chariot Bks) Chariot Family.
Lewis, Luevester. Jackie. Jolly, Cheryl, illus. (gr. k-5). 1970. pap. 1.00 (*0-685-42384-0*) Third World.
Lindgren, Astrid. The Children of Noisy Village. (gr. 3-7). 1988. pap. 3.95 (*0-14-032609-X*, Puffin) Puffin Bks.
—Mischievous Meg. Bothmer, Gerry, tr. Domanska, Janina, illus. LC 85-575. (ps-k). 1985. pap. 4.99 (*0-14-031954-9*, Puffin) Puffin Bks.
Lovejoy, Pamela. Rainbow Children. Lovejoy, Pamela, illus. 7p. (Orig.). 1994. pap. text ed. write for info. (*1-880038-19-6*) Learn-Abouts.
Low, Joseph. Mice Twice. LC 85-26768. (Illus.). 32p. (ps-3). 1986. pap. 4.95 (*0-689-71060-7*, Aladdin) Macmillan Child Grp.
Lowry, Lois. Rabble Starkey. (gr. 5 up). 1987. 13.95 (*0-395-43607-9*) HM.
McBrier, Page. Spaghetti Breath. 128p. (gr. 4). 1989. pap. 2.50 (*0-380-75782-6*, Camelot) Avon.
—Under Twelve Not Allowed. 128p. (gr. 4). 1989. pap. 2.50 (*0-380-75780-X*, Camelot) Avon.
McCloskey, Robert. Centerburg Tales. (Illus.). (gr. 1-3). 1977. pap. 4.99 (*0-14-031072-X*, Puffin) Puffin Bks.
McDowell, Mildred. The Little People. Whitaker, Arleen, illus. Harman, Sandra L., intro. by. LC 72-133255. (Illus.). 44p. (gr. 1-2). 1971. 2.50 (*0-87884-002-8*) Unicorn Ent.
McPhail, David. The Dream Child. McPhail, David, illus. LC 84-18755. 32p. (ps-3). 1988. pap. 4.95 (*0-525-44366-5*, 0383-120, DCB) Dutton Child Bks.
McRae, Patrick, illus. Here Comes Peter Cottontail. 24p. (Orig.). (ps-3). 1986. pap. 3.95 (*0-8249-8106-5*, Ideals Child) Hambleton-Hill.
Magnus, Erica. Around Me. Pearson, Susan, ed. Magnus, Erica, illus. LC 90-26459. 32p. (ps-3). 1992. 13.00 (*0-688-09756-1*); PLB 12.93 (*0-688-09753-7*) Lothrop.
Marshall, James. George & Martha. Marshall, James, illus. LC 74-184250. 48p. (gr. k-3). 1972. 14.95 (*0-395-16619-5*) HM.
Matthews, Morgan. Silly Sidney. Kolding, Richard M., illus. LC 85-14063. 48p. (Orig.). (gr. 1-3). 1986. PLB 10.59 (*0-8167-0610-7*); pap. text ed. 3.50 (*0-8167-0611-5*) Troll Assocs.
—Which Way, Hugo? Miller, Susan, illus. LC 85-14132. 48p. (Orig.). (gr. 1-3). 1986. PLB 10.59 (*0-8167-0648-4*); pap. text ed. 3.50 (*0-8167-0649-2*) Troll Assocs.
Mayer, Gina. Just Me in the Tub. (ps-3). 1994. pap. 2.25 (*0-307-12816-4*, Golden Pr) Western Pub.
Miles, Betty. The Real Me. LC 74-160. 144p. (gr. 3 up). 1974. lib. bdg. 9.99 (*0-394-92838-5*) Knopf Bks Yng Read.
—The Trouble with Thirteen. LC 78-31678. 112p. (gr. 3-7). 1989. pap. 2.95 (*0-394-82043-6*) Knopf Bks Yng Read.
Moncure, Jane B. Now I Am Five! Endres, Helen, illus. LC 83-25264. 32p. (ps-2). 1984. pap. 3.95 (*0-516-41879-3*) Childrens.
—Now I Am Four! Hutton, Kathryn, illus. LC 83-25270. 32p. (ps-2). 1984. pap. 3.95 (*0-516-41878-5*) Childrens.
—Now I Am Three! Hohag, Linda, illus. LC 83-20892. 32p. (ps). 1984. pap. 3.95 (*0-516-41877-7*) Childrens.
—Now I Am Two! Hutton, Kathryn, illus. LC 83-20891. 32p. (ps). 1984. pap. 3.95 (*0-516-41876-9*) Childrens.
Montgomery. Railway Children. 1994. 14.95 (*0-8050-3129-4*) H Holt & Co.
Moody, Ralph. Little Britches. 1976. 24.95 (*0-8488-1105-4*) Amereon Ltd.
Morgenstern, Susie. Oukele la Tele. Pef, illus. (FRE.). 54p. (gr. 1-5). 1991. pap. 9.95 (*2-07-031190-2*) Schoenhof.
Mulford, Philippa G. Everything I Hoped For. 192p. (Orig.). (gr. 8-12). 1990. pap. 2.95 (*0-380-76074-6*, Flare) Avon.
Murphy, Jill. Peace at Last. Murphy, Jill, illus. LC 80-66743. 32p. (ps-2). 1982. pap. 3.95 (*0-8037-6964-4*) Dial Bks Young.
Naylor, Phyllis R. Boys Start the War - The Girls Get Even. (gr. 4-7). 1994. pap. 4.99 (*0-440-40971-3*) Dell.
Nelson, Theresa. Devil Storm. LC 87-5493. 224p. (gr. 5-7). 1987. 12.95 (*0-531-05711-9*); PLB 12.99 (*0-531-08311-X*) Orchard Bks Watts.
Nesbit, Edith. Five Children & It. 182p. 1981. Repr. PLB 21.95 (*0-89967-036-9*) Harmony Raine.
—The Railway Children. (gr. 5-8). 1988. 16.00 (*0-8446-6345-X*) Peter Smith.
Newbery Library Award Staff. The Newbery Library Award. Incl. The Twenty-One Balloons. Pene Du Bois, William; The Witch of Blackbird Pond. Speare, Elizabeth; Johnny Tremain. Forbes, Esther; Island of the Blue Dolphins. O'Dell, Scott. (gr. 5 up). 1983. pap. 12.30 boxed set (*0-440-46256-8*) Dell.
Nobleman, Louis R. Second-Hand Dreams. Nobleman, Louis R., illus. (gr. k-6). 1993. pap. 9.95 (*1-56883-010-6*) Colonial Pr AL.
O'Brien, Richard. Evil. (Orig.). (gr. 7 up). 1989. pap. 3.50 (*0-440-20226-4*) Dell.
O'Brien, Robert C. Mrs. Frisby & the Rats of NIMH. 248p. (gr. 3-7). 1986. pap. 3.95 (*0-689-71068-2*, Aladdin) Macmillan Child Grp.
Pascal, Francine. Surprise! Surprise! (ps-3). 1989. pap. 2.99 (*0-553-15758-2*, Skylark) Bantam.
—Sweet Valley. 1992. pap. 3.25 (*0-553-15945-3*) Bantam.
—Sweet Valley Clean-Up. 1992. pap. 2.99 (*0-553-15923-2*) Bantam.
—Sweet Valley Kids. 1992. pap. 2.75 (*0-685-52277-6*) Bantam.
—Sweet Valley Kids. 1992. pap. 2.75 (*0-685-52278-4*) Bantam.
—Sweet Valley Twins. 1992. pap. 3.25 (*0-553-15953-4*) Bantam.
Paton Walsh, Jill. A Chance Child. (Illus.). 192p. (gr. 5 up). 1991. pap. 3.95 (*0-374-41174-3*, Sunburst) FS&G.
Peet, Bill. Jennifer & Josephine. Peet, Bill, illus. (gr. k-3). 1980. 14.95 (*0-395-18225-5*); pap. 5.95 (*0-395-29608-0*) HM.
Pef. Livre de Nattes. (FRE.). 78p. (gr. 1-5). 1990. pap. 7.95 (*2-07-031240-2*) Schoenhof.
Perkins, Al. Tubby & the Lantern. LC 70-158390. (Illus.). (gr. k-2). 1971. lib. bdg. 4.99 (*0-394-92297-2*) Beginner.
Pfeffer. Kid Power Strikes Back. 1993. pap. 2.75 (*0-590-44427-1*) Scholastic Inc.
Prevert, Jacques. Contes pour Enfants pas Sages. Henriquez, Elsa, illus. (FRE.). 88p. (gr. 1-5). 1990. pap. 12.95 (*2-07-031181-3*) Schoenhof.

Quackenbush, Robert. Henry's Important Date. Quackenbush, Robert, illus. LC 81-5026. 48p. (ps-3). 1982. 5.95 (*0-8193-1067-0*); PLB 5.95 (*0-8193-1068-9*) Parents.

Ray, Satyajit. Phatik Chand. Ray, Lila, tr. from BEN. 108p. (gr. 6-8). 1984. pap. 8.00 (*0-86578-230-X*) Ind-US Inc.

Reepen, Ronald. Lefty Meets Hefty. Reepen, Ronald, illus. 40p. (gr. 2-7). 1987. 6.95 (*0-930905-02-4*) Platypus Bks.

Reid, Mary. How Have I Grown? Speirs, John, illus. LC 93-44811. 1993. write for info. standard (*0-590-49757-X*); write for info. big bk. (*0-590-72911-X*) Scholastic Inc.

Rey, H. A. Anybody at Home? (Illus.). 24p. (gr. k-3). 1942. pap. 2.10 (*0-395-07045-7*, Sandpiper) HM.

Roberts, Willo D. Don't Hurt Laurie! Sanderson, Ruth, illus. LC 76-46569. 176p. (gr. 4-6). 1977. SBE 14.95 (*0-689-30571-0*, Atheneum Child Bk) Macmillan Child Grp.

Rodgers, Mary. Freaky Friday. LC 74-183158. 156p. (gr. 5-8). 1972. 14.00 (*0-06-025048-8*); PLB 13.89 (*0-06-025049-6*) HarpC Child Bks.

Roos, Stephen. The Terrible Truth: Secrets of a Sixth-Grader. Newsom, Carol, illus. LC 83-5253. 128p. (gr. 4-6). 1983. 12.95 (*0-385-29306-2*) Delacorte.

Rosenberg, Maxine B. Making a New Home in America. Ancona, George, illus. LC 85-11642. 48p. (gr. 1-4). 1986. 13.95 (*0-688-05824-8*); PLB 13.88 (*0-688-05825-6*) Lothrop.

Rosholt, Malcolm & Rosholt, Margaret. The Child of Two Mothers. Larson, Lynn, illus. LC 83-63177. 108p. (gr. 4 up). 1983. PLB 9.95x (*0-910417-03-2*) Rosholt Hse.

Ross, Tony. I'm Coming to Get You! LC 84-5831. (Illus.). 32p. (ps-2). 1987. pap. 4.95 (*0-8037-0434-8*) Dial Bks Young.

Roy, Claude. Enfantasques. (FRE.). (gr. 5-10). 1979. pap. 6.95 (*2-07-033087-7*) Schoenhof.

Rylant, Cynthia. Children of Christmas: Stories for the Season. Schindler, Stephen D., illus. LC 87-1690. 48p. (gr. 3 up). 1987. 13.95 (*0-531-05706-2*); PLB 13.99 (*0-531-08306-3*) Orchard Bks Watts.

Sanchez, J. L. & Pacheco, M. A. La Nina Invisible (The Invisible Girl) Wensell, Uliises, illus. (SPA.). 42p. (gr. k-2). 1988. write for info. (*84-372-1829-2*) Santillana.

Sargent, Sarah. Weird Henry Berg. 160p. (gr. 5 up). 1981. pap. 2.25 (*0-440-49346-3*, YB) Dell.

Schulz, Charles M. Apuros Escolares. (SPA., Illus.). (gr. 3-8). 1.50 (*0-685-28419-0*) Fr & Eur.

Schwartz, Amy. Bea & Mr. Jones. Schwartz, Amy, illus. 30p. (ps-3). 1983. pap. 3.95 (*0-14-050439-7*, Puffin) Puffin Bks.

Schwartz, Linda. My Book about Me. LC 93-86207. 32p. (gr. 1-6). 1994. 4.95 (*0-88160-235-3*, LW330) Learning Wks.

Sealey, Patricia. Nothing Ever Happens Here. (ps-3). 1992. pap. 3.95 (*0-7910-2903-4*) Chelsea Hse.

Seymour, Peter. You Can Be Anything. (Illus.). 24p. (ps-2). 1986. 5.95 (*0-8431-1462-2*) Price Stern.

Sharmat, Marjorie W. A Big Fat Enormous Lie. McPhail, David, illus. LC 77-15645. 32p. (ps-2). 1986. pap. 3.99 (*0-525-44242-1*, DCB) Dutton Child Bks.

Shyer, Marlene F. Here I Am, an Only Child. Carrick, Donald, illus. LC 87-1112. 32p. (ps-3). 1987. pap. 3.95 (*0-689-71156-5*, Aladdin) Macmillan Child Grp.

Sidney, Margaret. Five Little Peppers & How They Grew. LC 89-62372. 288p. (gr. 4 up). 1990. pap. 2.95 (*0-14-035127-2*, Puffin) Puffin Bks.

Soto, Gary. Small Faces. (gr. 4-7). 1993. 3.50 (*0-440-21553-6*) Dell.

Stanley, Diane. The Good-Luck Pencil. Degen, Bruce, illus. LC 85-13122. 32p. (gr. k-2). 1986. RSBE 13.95 (*0-02-786800-1*, Four Winds) Macmillan Child Grp.

Stein, Aidel. Baker's Dozen: Stars in Their Eyes, No. 4. 1992. pap. 7.95 (*0-944070-85-X*) Targum Pr.

Streatfeild, Noel. Thursday's Child. (Orig.). (gr. 5 up). 1986. pap. 3.50 (*0-440-48687-4*, YB) Dell.

Supraner, Robyn. Amazing Mark. Levy, Pam, illus. LC 85-14070. 48p. (Orig.). (gr. 1-3). 1986. PLB 10.59 (*0-8167-0644-1*); pap. text ed. 3.50 (*0-8167-0645-X*) Troll Assocs.

—No Room for a Sneeze! Trivas, Irene, illus. LC 85-14164. 48p. (Orig.). (gr. 1-3). 1986. PLB 10.59 (*0-8167-0656-5*); pap. text ed. 3.50 (*0-8167-0657-3*) Troll Assocs.

Tafuri, Nancy. The Ball Bounced. LC 87-37582. (Illus.). 24p. (ps up). 1989. 11.95 (*0-688-07871-0*) Greenwillow.

Thomasson, Merry F. I Can Help. (ps). 1992. 9.95 (*0-9615407-7-X*) Merrybooks VA.

Thompson, Julian F. Simon Pure. 336p. (gr. 10-12). 1987. pap. 12.95x (*0-590-40507-1*, Scholastic Hardcover) Scholastic Inc.

Tournier, Michel. Barbedor. Lemoine, Georges, illus. (FRE.). 48p. (gr. 3-7). 1990. pap. 8.95 (*2-07-031172-4*) Schoenhof.

Utz. The Simple Pink Bubble That Ended the Trouble with Jonathan Hubble. LC 78-190273. (Illus.). 32p. (gr. 2-3). 1972. PLB 9.95 (*0-87783-062-2*); pap. 3.94 deluxe ed. (*0-87783-108-4*) Oddo.

Vail. A Kid's Best Friend. 1993. pap. 2.95 (*0-590-42787-3*) Scholastic Inc.

Vallet, Roxanne. Children Can Be Scarry. Vallet, Roxanne, illus. 14p. (gr. k-3). 1993. pap. 12.95 (*1-56606-018-4*) Bradley Mann.

Van der Meer, Ron & Van der Meer, Atie. Jumping Children. (gr. 4 up). 1989. 4.95 (*0-85953-262-3*) Childs Play.

Vaughan, Marcia K. Wombat Stew. Lofts, Pamela, illus. LC 85-63492. 32p. (ps-3). 1985. 8.95 (*0-382-09211-2*); 4.95s.p. (*0-382-24356-0*) Silver Burdett Pr.

Von Olfers, Sibylle. The Story of the Root Children. Von Olfers, Sibylle, illus. (GER.). 32p. (ps-3). 1992. Repr. of 1906 ed. 12.95 (*0-86315-106-X*, Pub. by Floris Bks UK) Gryphon Hse.

Von Rosenberg, Marjorie. Max & Martha: Children from Germany in the Texas Hill Country. (Illus.). 48p. (gr. 4-7). 1986. 8.95 (*0-89015-539-9*, Pub. by Panda Bks) Sunbelt Media.

Waber, Bernard. Ira Sleeps Over. Waber, Bernard, illus. LC 72-75605. 48p. (gr. k-3). 1973. 13.45 (*0-395-13893-0*) HM.

—You're a Little Kid with a Big Heart. (Illus.). (gr. k-3). 1980. 14.95 (*0-395-29163-1*) HM.

Walker, Mort & Browne, Dik. Hi & Lois: Trixie a la Mode. 128p. 1986. pap. 1.95 (*0-8125-6904-0*) Tor Bks.

Walsh, Jill P. A Chance Child. 144p. (gr. 7 up). 1980. pap. 1.95 (*0-380-48561-3*, 48561-3, Flare) Avon.

Ward, Ken. Twelve Kids One Cow: Ken Ward's World. Ward, Ken, illus. 36p. 1989. pap. 4.95 (*1-55037-076-6*, Pub. by Annick CN) Firefly Bks Ltd.

Weiss, Ann E. Good Neighbors? (gr. 5-8). 1985. 12.95 (*0-317-38803-7*) HM.

White, Ellen E. White House Autumn. (Orig.). (gr. 7 up). 1985. pap. 2.95 (*0-380-89780-6*, Flare) Avon.

Will & Nicolas. Finders Keepers. Mordvinoff, Nicolas, illus. LC 51-12326. 32p. (gr. k-4). 1989. pap. 3.95 (*0-15-630950-5*, Voyager Bks) HarBrace.

Williams, Barbara. The Crazy Gang Next Door. LC 90-1350. 160p. (gr. 3-7). 1992. pap. 3.95 (*0-06-440391-2*, Trophy) HarpC Child Bks.

Yep, Laurence. The Serpent's Children. LC 82-48855. 288p. (gr. 7 up). 1984. PLB 13.89 (*0-06-026812-3*) HarpC Child Bks.

Yolen, Jane. Children of the Wolf. 144p. (gr. 7 up). 1993. pap. 3.99 (*0-14-036477-3*, Puffin) Puffin Bks.

Yourcenar, Marguerite. Comment Wang-Fo Fut Sauve. Lemoine, Georges, illus. (FRE.). 48p. (gr. 3-7). 1990. pap. 7.95 (*2-07-031178-3*) Schoenhof.

CHILDREN–GROWTH

Ames, Evelyn E. & Trucano, Lucille. Becoming Male & Female. LC 88-63796. (Illus.). 116p. (gr. 9-12). 1988. pap. text ed. 12.00 (*0-935529-05-5*) Comprehen Health Educ.

Harris, Robbie & Levy, Elizabeth. Before You Were Three: How You Began to Walk, Talk, Explore & Have Feelings. Gordillo, Henry E., photos by. LC 76-5587. 160p. (gr. 1 up). 1981. pap. 7.95 (*0-440-00471-3*) Delacorte.

Kino Learning Center Staff, et al. My Changing Body. Mirocha, Kay, illus. 64p. (gr. 5-9). 1987. pap. 7.95 (*0-86653-420-2*, GA1030) Good Apple.

—My Journal of Personal Growth. Mirocha, Kay, illus. 64p. (gr. 5-9). 1987. pap. 7.95 (*0-86653-418-0*, GA 1028) Good Apple.

Kirk, Pat & Brown, Alice. Bear Buddies: A Child Learns to Make Friends. (Illus.). (ps-2). 1986. 4.99 (*0-915720-55-8*) Brownlow Pub Co.

—Bear Up: A Child Learns to Handle Ups & Downs. (Illus.). (ps-2). 1986. 4.99 (*0-915720-51-5*) Brownlow Pub Co.

—Bearing Burdens: A Child Learns to Help. (Illus.). (ps-2). 1986. 4.99 (*0-915720-54-X*) Brownlow Pub Co.

—Love Bears All Things: A Child Learns to Love. (Illus.). (ps-2). 1986. 4.99 (*0-915720-50-7*) Brownlow Pub Co.

Knoepfel, Marilyn & Farber, Betty. Look, I'm Growing Up. Hutton, Kathryn, illus. 32p. (gr. k-2). 1991. pasted 2.50 (*0-87403-819-7*, 24-03919) Standard Pub.

Moyer, Inez. Responding to Infants. LC 83-71345. 200p. (Orig.). (ps). 1983. pap. 18.95 (*0-513-01769-0*) Denison.

Ortiz, Simon. The Importance of Childhood. Gracia, Fred D., illus. 16p. (Orig.). (ps-7). 1982. pap. 3.75 (*0-915347-01-6*) Pueblo Acoma Pr.

Phifer, Kate G. Tall & Small: A Book about Height. Kendrick, Dennis, illus. LC 86-32401. 96p. (gr. 5 up). 1987. 11.95 (*0-8027-6684-6*); PLB 12.85 (*0-8027-6685-4*) Walker & Co.

Sealy, Adrienne V. Mama, Watch Out - I'm Growing Up. (Illus.). (gr. 2-5). 1978. PLB 4.95x (*0-9602670-1-8*) Assn Family Living.

Thiry, Joan. Discovering the Whole You. Sititra, illus. 64p. (Orig.). (gr. 5-6). 1991. pap. text ed. 6.00 (*0-935046-05-4*); tchr's. edition 14.00 (*0-935046-06-2*) Chateau Thierry.

Tucker, Nicholas. Childhood. LC 90-21867. (Illus.). 64p. (gr. 5-9). 1991. PLB 11.95 (*0-8114-7804-1*) Raintree Steck-V.

Wingfield, Jack & Wingfield, Angela. Growing up Now. (Illus.). 48p. (gr. 4-8). 1992. 14.95 (*0-7459-1537-X*) Lion USA.

Yemm, Marta. Years to Grow. LC 81-68369. (Illus.). 600p. (Orig.). (ps-k). 1981. pap. 31.95 (*0-513-01724-0*) Denison.

CHILDREN–HEALTH

see Children–Care and Hygiene

CHILDREN–HOSPITALS

see also Child Welfare; Children–Diseases

Alsop, Peter, et al. In the Hospital. 64p. (Orig.). (gr. k-6). 1989. pap. 12.98g (*1-877942-00-6*, MS503) Moose Schl Records.

Going to the Hospital. (Illus.). 32p. (ps). 1990. 2.99 (*0-517-69197-3*) Random Hse Value.

Krall, Charlotte B. & Jim, Judith M. Fat Dog's First Visit: A Child's View of the Hospital. Hull, Nancy, ed. & illus. LC 87-2745. 28p. (Orig.). (ps-3). 1987. pap. text ed. 4.00 (*0-939838-23-0*) Pritchett & Hull.

Livingston, Carole & Ciliotta, Claire. Why Am I Going to the Hospital? Walter, Paul, illus. (gr. 1 up). 1981. 12. 00 (*0-8184-0316-0*) Carol Pub Group.

Rosenstock, Judith D. & Rosenstock, Harvey A. Your Hospital Stay...It'll Be Okay. Sorg, James M., illus. 36p. (Orig.). (gr. 1-5). 1988. pap. 4.95 (*0-9622172-0-4*) D Miller Fndtn.

CHILDREN–MANAGEMENT

Here are entered books on child training and discipline. These books may include psychological matter such as is entered under Child Study, but their content and purpose are more practical. Books on management of children in school are entered under School Discipline.

see also Baby Sitters; Character Education; Problem Children

Allison, Alida. The Toddler's Potty Book. (Illus.). 32p. (Orig.). (ps). 1985. pap. 3.95 (*0-8431-0673-5*) Price Stern.

Leonard, Marcia. Getting Dressed. 1988. pap. 3.95 (*0-553-05467-8*) Bantam.

Mohr-Stephens, Judy. Please Understand Us! Is the World As I See It?; My Little World Book; Open Minded Kids!; Fence Me In...with Understanding, 33 vols. Riegert, Evelyn, ed. Bruce, Michael, illus. 500p. (gr. k-8). 1990. Set. 139.95 (*0-935323-00-7*) Barrington Hse.

Monroe, Judy. Latchkey Children. LC 89-1383. (Illus.). 48p. (gr. 5-6). 1989. text ed. 12.95 RSBE (*0-89686-438-3*, Crestwood Hse) Macmillan Child Grp.

Rogers, Fred. Going to the Potty. Judkis, Jim, illus. 32p. (ps-2). 1986. (Putnam); pap. 5.95 (*0-399-21297-3*, Putnam) Putnam Pub Group.

Siegel, Felicia S. Let's Stop Fighting...Let's Start Playing. 42p. (gr. 2-8). 1988. comb. bdg. 4.95 (*0-9631627-0-5*) Social Skills.

Smith, Michael W. & Ridenour, Fritz. Old Enough to Know. 111p. 1989. 6.99 (*0-8499-3162-2*) Word Inc.

Spizman, Robyn F. Lollipop Grapes & Clothespin Critters: Quick, On-the-Spot Remedies for Restless of Children 2-10. LC 84-24548. 160p. (ps-5). 1985. pap. 8.61 (*0-201-06497-9*) Addison-Wesley.

Take a Bath. 1988. pap. 3.95 (*0-553-05464-3*) Bantam.

CHILDREN–MANAGEMENT–FICTION

Gregory, Kim. Close at Hand. Marks, Theresa, illus. LC 91-93065. 36p. (Orig.). (ps-3). 1992. pap. text ed. 10. 98 incl. wristband with interchangeable snap-on theme lids (*0-9630898-0-3*) K T Kids.

Lampert, Emily. A Little Touch of Monster. Kroupa, Melanie, illus. LC 85-26847. 32p. (ps-3). 1986. lib. bdg. 12.95 (*0-316-51287-7*, 512877, Joy St Bks) Little.

Soderstrom, Mary. Maybe Tomorrow I'll Have a Good Time. Wein, Charlotte E., illus. LC 80-25357. 32p. (ps-3). 1981. 16.95 (*0-89885-012-6*) Human Sci Pr.

CHILDREN–PICTURES, ILLUSTRATIONS, ETC.

Ricklen, Neil, photos by. Baby Inside. (Illus.). 24p. (ps). 1991. pap. 4.95 casebound, padded cover (*0-671-73878-X*, Little Simon) S&S Trade.

Trezise, Percy. Children of the Great Lake. (ps-3). 1993. 10.00 (*0-207-17677-9*, Pub. by Angus & Robertson AT) HarpC.

The United Nations Celebrates Children: A Postcard Book. 36p. (Orig.). 1993. pap. 7.95 (*1-881889-43-2*) Silver Moon.

CHILDREN–PSYCHOLOGY

see Child Study

CHILDREN–RELIGIOUS LIFE

Abdu'l-Baha. Tablet of the Heart: God & Me. Fisher, Betty J. & Lundberg, Leslie, eds. Ostovar, Terry, illus. Oldziey, Pepper P., contrib. by. (Illus.). (ps-2). 1987. PLB 15.95 (*0-87743-207-4*) Bahai.

Aisenberg, Gino & Montes, Elizabeth. Bursting with Joy - Una Celebracion! (Illus., Orig.). (gr. 1-8). 1992. tchr's. ed. 15.95 (*1-55944-025-2*) Franciscan Comns.

Anderson, Debby. Jesus Loves the Little Children. LC 92-74367. (ps). 1993. deluxe ed. 4.99 (*0-7814-0687-0*, Chariot Bks) Chariot Family.

Angers, JoAnn M. My Beginning Mass Book. Read, Maryann, illus. 48p. (Orig.). (gr. 1-4). 1978. pap. 1.95 (*0-89622-082-6*) Twenty-Third.

Bitney, James. First Communion: A Parish Celebration Family Book. 48p. 1993. pap. text ed. 6.30 (*1-55944-038-4*) Franciscan Comns.

Blackwell, Muriel F. How Do I Become a Christian? LC 89-34347. (gr. 4-6). 1991. 7.99 (*0-8054-4341-X*) Broadman.

Brandt, Catharine. We Light the Candles: Devotions Related to Family Use of the Advent Wreath. 40p. pap. 4.99 (*0-8066-1544-3*, 10-15443, Augsburg) Augsburg Fortress.

Burgess, Beverly Capps. How Can I Please You God? McKee, Vicki, illus. 29p. (Orig.). 1989. pap. text ed. 4.00 (*0-9618975-1-1*) Annette Capps.

Canfield, Anita. The Young Woman & Her Self-Esteem. 93p. (gr. 7-12). 1990. pap. 4.95 (*0-87579-365-7*) Deseret Bk.

Cantoni, Louise B. Leaving Matters to God. Gomez-Milan, Francis, illus. LC 92-9984. 164p. (gr. 3-8). 1984. 3.00 (*0-8198-4424-1*) St Paul Bks.

Carlyle, Linda P. God & Joseph & Me. 25p. 1992. 6.95 (*0-8163-1092-0*) Pacific Pr Pub Assn.

—Grandma Stepped on Fred. 25p. 1992. 6.95 (*0-8163-1094-7*) Pacific Pr Pub Assn.
—Max Moves In. 26p. 1992. 6.95 (*0-8163-1095-5*) Pacific Pr Pub Assn.
—Rescued from the River. 25p. 1992. 6.95 (*0-8163-1093-9*) Pacific Pr Pub Assn.
Caswell, Helen. God Makes Us Different. LC 87-33466. (ps-3). 1988. pap. 5.95 (*0-687-15336-0*) Abingdon.
Center for Learning Network. Connections: A Summer Bible Program for Children. 78p. (gr. k-3). 1990. pap. text ed. 12.95 (*1-56077-053-8*) Ctr Learning.
Chamberlain, Eugene. Carol Beth Learns about Following Jesus. LC 89-38428. (gr. 1-3). 1991. 6.99 (*0-8054-4340-1*) Broadman.
Chariot Books Staff. Please. (ps). 1993. 3.29 (*0-7814-0107-0*, Chariot Bks) Chariot Family.
—Sorry. (ps). 1993. 3.29 (*0-7814-0105-4*, Chariot Bks) Chariot Family.
—Thank You. (ps). 1993. 3.29 (*0-7814-0106-2*, Chariot Bks) Chariot Family.
Coleman, William. Animals That Show & Tell. LC 85-15122. 144p. (gr. 2-7). 1985. pap. 6.99 (*0-87123-807-1*) Bethany Hse.
—Before You Tuck Me In. LC 85-26703. 128p. (Orig.). (ps-k). 1986. pap. 6.99 (*0-87123-830-6*) Bethany Hse.
—The Warm Hug Book. LC 85-6175. 128p. (Orig.). (ps). 1985. pap. 6.99 (*0-87123-794-6*) Bethany Hse.
Colton, Ann R. Precepts for the Young. 66p. (gr. 1-8). 1959. pap. 2.50 (*0-917187-15-6*) A R Colton Fnd.
Cooper, Charlotte. Fifty Object Stories for Children. (ps-4). 1988. pap. 5.99 (*0-8010-2523-0*) Baker Bk.
Corbin, Linda & Dys, Pat. Jesus Teaches Me. Fieser, Stephen, illus. 35p. (gr. 1-6). 1987. wkbk. 5.99 (*0-87509-389-2*) Chr Pubns.
Daughters of St. Paul. Gamble for God. Mayer, Maxine, illus. LC 83-10087. 132p. (gr. 3-8). 1984. 3.00 (*0-8198-3033-X*) St Paul Bks.
Davis, Cos H., Jr. I'm Big Enough. LC 89-24027. (ps-3). 1991. 6.99 (*0-8054-4342-8*) Broadman.
Dean, Bessie. God Hears My Prayers. (Illus.). 24p. (ps-3). 1993. pap. 3.98 (*0-88290-110-9*) Horizon Utah.
—I'm Happy When I'm Good. (Illus.). 24p. (ps-3). 1979. pap. 3.98 (*0-88290-109-5*) Horizon Utah.
De Graaf, Anne. Healing Minds & Bodies. (Illus.). 32p. 1989. 4.95 (*0-310-52730-9*) Zondervan.
—Jesus Touches People. (Illus.). 32p. 1989. 4.95 (*0-310-52750-3*) Zondervan.
Dellinger, A. & Fletcher, S. Proverbs. 16p. (ps-3). 1983. pap. 0.69 (*0-570-08309-5*, 56HH1441) Concordia.
—Table Prayers. (ps-3). 1983. pap. 0.69 (*0-570-08316-8*, 56HH1448) Concordia.
Dellinger, Annetta. Ann Elizabeth Signs With Love. (ps-2). 1991. 8.99 (*0-570-04192-9*, 56-1651) Concordia.
Dellinger, Annetta E. Adopted & Loved Forever. (Illus.). (ps-2). 1987. 5.99 (*0-570-04167-8*, 56-1624) Concordia.
Doerken, Nan. The First Family Car. 59p. (gr. 1-4). 1986. pap. 3.95 (*0-919797-53-9*) Kindred Pr.
Dvir, Azriel & Mashat, Mazal. My Little Siddur. 68p. 8.95 (*0-915361-87-6*) Modan-Adama Bks.
Dyson, Clegg & Dyson, Betty. Follow Me. 44p. (Orig.). (gr. 3-7). Date not set. pap. 4.99 (*1-884553-15-X*) Discipleshp.
Edward, S. S. Miracle of the Shoebox Baby. 64p. (gr. 5-12). 1993. pap. 8.95 (*1-883500-23-0*) RAMSI Bks.
Erickson, Mary. I Can Make God Glad! Reck, Sue, ed. Ebert, Len, illus. LC 93-33070. 32p. (ps-2). 1994. 9.99 (*0-7814-0102-X*, Chariot Bks) Chariot Family.
Fittro, Pat, ed. Adventures with God: A Year of Devotional Activities for Kids, 2 bks. (Illus.). (gr. 8 up). 1993. Bk. 1, 88p. pap. 5.99 (*0-7847-0083-4*, 12-02823) Bk. 2, 88p. pap. 5.99 (*0-7847-0084-2*, 12-02829) Standard Pub.
Flanagan, Anne J. Children's Way of the Cross. Smolinski, Dick, illus. 39p. (Orig.). (gr. 2-6). 1992. pap. 1.50 (*0-8198-6954-6*) St Paul Bks.
Fogle, Jeanne S. Seasons of God's Love: The Church Year. Duckert, Mary J. & Lane, Ben, eds. Widener, Bea, illus. LC 88-6414. 32p. 1988. pap. 7.99 (*0-664-25032-7*, Geneva Pr) Westminster John Knox.
Foreman, Rosmarie. God Created. 32p. 1986. pap. text ed. 1.25 (*1-882449-12-6*) Messenger Pub.
Gambill, Henrietta. Are You Listening? Axeman, Lois, illus. LC 85-10349. 32p. (gr. k-2). 1985. PLB 14.95 (*0-89565-332-X*) Childs World.
Gesch, Roy C. Confirmed in Christ. (gr. 7 up). 1983. pap. 2.99 (*0-570-03911-8*, 12-2852) Concordia.
Gibson, Eva. Listening to My Heart. 160p. (Orig.). 1990. special spiral bdg. 10.99 (*1-55661-132-3*) Bethany Hse.
God Made Only One Me. (ps-4). 1987. Set. 10.95 (*0-570-04155-4*, 56-1608); pap. 5.99 (*0-570-04148-1*) Concordia.
Hageman, Marybeth. Thank You, God, for Me. (Illus.). (ps). 1987. pap. 2.50 (*0-570-09114-4*, 56-1589) Concordia.
Hall, Susan T. Perfect Pals God Made for Me. (Illus.). (ps). 1989. 7.49 (*1-55513-933-7*, Chariot Bks) Chariot Family.
Halverson, Delia T. Oak Street Chonicles & the Good News: Everyday Life & Christian Faith. Dotts, M. Franklin, ed. (Illus., Orig.). 1989. pap. 4.95 tchr's. ed., 48p. (*0-687-75340-6*); student ed., 40p. 3.75 (*0-687-75339-2*) Abingdon.
Hansel, Tim. Real Heroes Eat Hamburgers. Harmon, Jeannie & Davis, Cathy, eds. LC 89-9952. 64p. (gr. 3-7). 1989. pap. 4.99 (*1-55513-334-7*, Chariot Bks) Chariot Family.
—Real Heroes Wear Jeans. Harmon, Jeannie & Davis, Cathy, eds. LC 89-9953. 64p. (gr. 3-7). 1989. pap. 4.99 (*1-55513-333-9*, Chariot Bks) Chariot Family.
Heide, F. God & Me. (Illus.). 32p. (ps). 1987. pap. 3.99 (*0-570-07792-3*, 56-1316) Concordia.
Hibschman, Barbara. A Heart for Imbabura. (Illus.). 30p. (gr. 5 up). 1992. pap. 3.99 (*0-87509-487-2*) Chr Pubns.
Houk, Margaret. That Very Special Person - Me. 136p. (Orig.). 1990. pap. 6.95 (*0-8361-3514-8*) Herald Pr.
Iakovina, Theodore. A Special Gift to God. Buchmiller, Therese, illus. 38p. (gr. k-4). 1986. PLB write for info. Amnos Pubns.
Jackson, Carol. Jesus & Me. Plunkett, Mark W., ed. Steele, Martha, illus. 320p. (gr. 1-2). 1993. pap. 24.99 (*0-87403-850-2*, 13-42031) Standard Pub.
Jackson, James W. A Steward-ship Adventure: Christianomics for Kids. (Illus.). 24p. (Orig.). (gr. 3-6). 1988. wkbk. 2.95 (*1-55513-840-3*, 68403) Cook.
Jones, Rebecca C. I Am Not Afraid. (Illus.). (ps). 1987. pap. 2.50 (*0-570-09113-6*, 56-1588) Concordia.
Jones, Sally L. Friends of God. Pistone, Nancy, illus. 10p. (ps-3). 1993. text ed. 10.99 (*0-7847-0047-8*, 24-03657) Standard Pub.
—In the Beginning. Pistone, Nancy, illus. 10p. (ps-3). 1993. text ed. 10.99 (*0-7847-0046-X*, 24-03656) Standard Pub.
Josef, Marion. We Thank God. Mayfield, Ana M., illus. 28p. (Orig.). (gr. k-4). 1993. pap. 0.95 (*0-8198-8267-4*) St Paul Bks.
Kraft, Victoreen. Are You Afraid. Chappell, David & Bates, Steve, illus. 20p. (gr. k-6). 1983. pap. text ed. 4.25 (*1-55976-139-3*) CEF Press.
Lecciones y Actividades Misioneras para Ninos de 3 y 4 anos, No. 1. (SPA.). 96p. (ps). 1988. pap. 3.50 (*0-311-12039-3*) Casa Bautista.
Lecciones y Actividades Misioneras para Ninos de 5 a 6 Anos, No. 2. (SPA.). 96p. (gr. k-1). 1987. pap. text ed. 3.50 (*0-311-12033-4*) Casa Bautista.
Lecciones y Actividades Misioneras para Ninos de 7 a 8 Anos, No. 2. (SPA.). 96p. (gr. 2-3). 1987. pap. 3.50 (*0-311-12034-2*) Casa Bautista.
McKissack, Patricia & McKissack, Fredrick. God Made Something Wonderful. Ching, illus. LC 89-84938. 32p. (Orig.). (gr. 3-5). 1989. pap. 5.99 (*0-8066-2434-5*, 9-2434) Augsburg Fortress.
McMillan, Mary. Christian Parties for Spring & Summer. (Illus.). 96p. (ps-3). 1989. 10.95 (*0-86653-473-3*, SS1814, Shining Star Pubns) Good Apple.
Mapstone, Edna. Footsteps of Faith. Means, Gary & Cook, Beth A., illus. 32p. (Orig.). (gr. 1-5). 1993. wkbk. 3.99 (*0-87509-528-3*) Chr Pubns.
Marxhausen, J. If I Should Die-If I Should Live. (Illus.). 48p. (ps). 1987. pap. 4.99 (*0-570-07793-1*, 56HH1317) Concordia.
Meyzlisch, Saul, ed. A Child's Passover Haggadah. (Illus.). 76p. (gr. 1-6). 1987. 9.95 (*0-915361-70-1*) Modan-Adama Bks.
Mignolli, Marisa. Hosanna to You, Jesus! A Palm Sunday Experience. Benigni, M. Luisa, illus. 32p. (Orig.). (ps-3). 1993. pap. 3.95 (*0-8198-3368-1*) St Paul Bks.
Mishica, Clare. Billions of Bugs. Loman, Roberta K., illus. 28p. (ps). 1993. 4.99 (*0-7847-0039-7*, 24-03829) Standard Pub.
Murphy, Elspeth C. Do You See Me God? Duca, Bill, illus. LC 88-27445. 32p. (ps). 1989. text ed. 9.99 (*1-55513-457-2*, Chariot Bks) Chariot Family.
—God You Fill Us up with Joy. LC 86-4140. (Illus.). (ps-2). 1987. pap. 3.99 (*1-55513-037-2*, Chariot Bks) Cook.
Niquette, Alan & Niquette, Beth. Building Your Christian Defense System. (Orig.). (gr. 9-12). 1988. pap. text ed. 6.99 (*1-55661-015-7*); tchr's. guide 7.99 (*1-55661-016-5*) Bethany Hse.
Owens, Carolyn. Color Me...Cuddly! McLaughlin, Dorthy, illus. 32p. (ps-4). 1982. pap. 1.19 (*0-87123-695-8*) Bethany Hse.
Peterson, Lorraine. Dying of Embarassment & Living to Tell about It. LC 87-35334. 224p. (Orig.). (gr. 9-12). 1988. pap. 7.99 (*0-87123-967-1*) Bethany Hse.
Plantinga, Cornelius, Jr. A Sure Thing. LC 86-8280. (Illus.). 300p. (gr. 8-10). 1986. text ed. 14.95 (*0-930265-27-0*); tchr's. manual 11.95 (*0-930265-28-9*) CRC Pubns.
Programas y Actividades para Muchachos y Jovencitos, No. 4. (SPA.). 96p. (gr. 4-10). 1987. pap. text ed. 3.50 (*0-311-12036-9*) Casa Bautista.
Programas y Actividades para Ninas y Jovencitas, No. 4. 96p. (gr. 4-10). 1987. pap. text ed. 3.50 (*0-311-12035-0*) Casa Bautista.
Raburn, Terry. Starting Blocks: Running the Race A-G Style. LC 88-80813. 128p. (Orig.). (gr. 7 up). 1988. pap. 2.95 (*0-88243-860-3*, 02-0860); tchr's. guide 4.50 (*0-88243-200-1*, 32-0200) Gospel Pub.
Richardson, Arleta. Sixteen & Away from Home. LC 85-438. (gr. 3-7). 1985. pap. 3.99 (*0-89191-933-3*, 59337, Chariot Bks) Chariot Family.
Robinson, J. H. & Robinson, R. D. Involving Children in One Hundred Four Sunday School Openings. 72p. 1983. pap. 5.99 (*0-570-03912-6*, 12HH2851) Concordia.
Rossel, Seymour. A Child's Bible: The Torah & Its Lessons. (gr. 1 up). 1988. text & activity bk., 160pps. 8.50 (*0-87441-466-0*); tchr's guide, 96pps. 14.95 (*0-87441-467-9*) Behrman.
Russell, Bob. When Life's a Zoo: God Still Loves You. Underwood, Jonathan, ed. 160p. (Orig.). 1993. pap. 5.99 (*0-7847-0078-8*, 11-39958) Standard Pub.
Sanford, Doris. Help! Fire! Escaping with My Life. Evans, Graci & Evans, Gracie, illus. 32p. 1992. 9.99 (*0-88070-520-5*, Gold & Honey) Questar Pubs.
—My Friend, the Enemy: Surviving a Prison Camp. Evans, Graci, illus. 32p. 1992. 9.99 (*0-88070-518-3*, Gold & Honey) Questar Pubs.
—No Longer Afraid: Living with Cancer. Evans, Graci, illus. 1992. 9.99 (*0-88070-519-1*, Gold & Honey) Questar Pubs.
—Yes, I Can: Challenging Cerebral Palsy. Heaney, Liz, ed. Evans, Gracie, illus. 32p. 1992. 9.99 (*0-88070-510-8*, Gold & Honey) Questar Pubs.
Schrader, D. Take My Hands. (gr. k-8). 1981. 5.99 (*0-570-04035-3*, 61HH1019) Concordia.
Schreivogel, Paul A. More Prayers for Small Children: About Big & Little Things. Goldsborough, June, illus. LC 88-83018. 32p. (Orig.). (gr. 1 up). 1988. pap. 5.99 (*0-8066-2381-0*, 10-4547, Augsburg) Augsburg Fortress.
Sheehan, Pauline. God Hugs? Sheehan, Pauline, illus. 20p. (Orig.). 1986. pap. 3.95 (*0-9617018-0-3*) Sheehan Indus.
Simpson, Winifred R. I Can Help Mommy. (Illus.). (ps). 1987. pap. 2.50 (*0-570-09112-8*, 56-1587) Concordia.
Stafford, Tim. Do You Sometimes Feel Like a Nobody? 144p. 1991. pap. 7.99 (*0-310-71131-2*, Campus Life) Zondervan.
Swanson, Steve, et al. Faith Prints: Youth Devotions for Every Day of the Year. LC 85-13466. 224p. (Orig.). (gr. 8 up). 1985. pap. 7.99 (*0-8066-2178-8*, 10-2189, Augsburg) Augsburg Fortress.
Swartzentruber. God Made Me in a Good Way. 1976. 2.50 (*0-686-18183-2*) Rod & Staff.
—We Should Be Thankful. 1976. 2.50 (*0-686-18188-3*) Rod & Staff.
Truitt, Gloria A. People of the Bible & Their Prayers. (Illus.). 24p. (ps-4). 1987. pap. 1.99 (*0-570-09005-9*, 59-1433) Concordia.
Ureta, Floreal & Malve, Eduardo. Vive Lo Que Crees! - Live What You Believe! (SPA.). 96p. 1990. pap. 3.50 (*0-311-12349-X*) Casa Bautista.
VanderZee, Leonard. Can I Call after Midnight. 76p. (Orig.). (gr. 10-12). 1989. pap. text ed. 17.95 leader's guide (*0-930265-70-X*) CRC Pubns.
Van Seters, Virginia A. Twenty-Six Object Talks for Children's Worship. Briggs, Richard, illus. 48p. 1988. pap. 3.99 (*0-87403-497-3*, 2877) Standard Pub.
Wade, Evelyn A. God Is Here, I'm Not Afraid. Rogers, Kathy, illus. LC 88-83019. 32p. (Orig.). 1988. pap. 5.99 (*0-8066-2382-9*, 10-2646, Augsburg) Augsburg Fortress.
Walking with God: Daily Bread. (gr. k-4). 1972. pap. text ed. 6.99 (*1-55976-300-0*) CEF Press.
Weber, Rhiannon. Signposts from Proverbs: An Introduction to Proverbs. Evans, Lawrence L., illus. 128p. (Orig.). 1988. spiral bdg. 9.95 (*0-85151-517-7*) Banner of Truth.

CHILDREN–TRAINING
see Children–Management

CHILDREN, BOOKS AND READING FOR
see Children–Books and Reading

CHILDREN IN AFRICA

Children of the World: Nigeria. LC 89-43199. (Illus.). 64p. (gr. 5-6). 1989. PLB 21.26 (*0-8368-0258-6*) Gareth Stevens Inc.
Drum & Spear Collective Staff. Children of Africa: A Coloring Book. Drum & Spear Collective Staff, illus. LC 92-63013. 24p. (ps-3). 1993. pap. 5.95 (*0-88378-076-3*) Third World.
Feelings, Muriel. Moja Means One: A Swahili Counting Book. Feelings, Tom, illus. LC 76-134856. (ps-3). 1987. 13.95 (*0-8037-5776-X*); PLB 13.89 (*0-8037-5777-8*) Dial Bks Young.
Pelnar, Tom & Weber, Valerie, eds. Tanzania. Nakamura, Haruko, photos by. LC 88-42890. (Illus.). 64p. (gr. 5-6). 1989. PLB 21.26 (*1-55532-210-7*) Gareth Stevens Inc.
Rogers, Barbara R. Zambia. Rogers, Stillman, photos by. LC 89-43178. (Illus.). 64p. (gr. 5-6). 1991. PLB 21.26 (*0-8368-0257-8*) Gareth Stevens Inc.
Weber, Valerie & Rateliff, John D., eds. Egypt. Komatsu, Yoshio, photos by. LC 87-42579. (Illus.). 64p. (gr. 5-6). 1991. PLB 21.26 (*1-55532-209-3*) Gareth Stevens Inc.

CHILDREN IN AFRICA–FICTION

Black History Series 1, 6 bks. Incl. Vol. 1. George Abraham Jefferson Thinks about Freedom. Smith, Martha. 15p. (gr. 2-3) (*0-913678-01-5*); Vol. 2. Terrible Tuesday. Gaines, Edith. 13p. (gr. 2-3) (*0-913678-02-3*); Vol. 3. Free; The Contraption; The First Freedom Ride. Gaines, Edith & Smith, Martha. 40p. (gr. 3-4) (*0-913678-03-1*); Vol. 4. I Cannot Be a Traitor; the Cannon That Talked Back. Johnston, Brenda & Woodrich, Mary. 31p. (gr. 4-5) (*0-913678-04-X*); Vol. 5. Adventures of Olaudah, the African Boy; Move Feet Move. Hartman, Suzanne & Shepard, Mary. 35p. (gr. 5-6) (*0-913678-05-8*); Vol. 6. The Disguise. Shepard, Mary. 15p. (gr. 5-6) (*0-913678-06-6*). (Illus.). (gr. 2-6). 1988. Set. pap. 8.00x (*0-913678-00-7*) New Day Pr.

CHILDREN IN ART
see Children in Literature and Art

CHILDREN IN ASIA

Coerr, Eleanor B. Sadako & the Thousand Paper Cranes. Himler, Ronald, illus. LC 76-9872. (gr. 3-5). 1977. 14.95 (*0-399-20520-9*, Putnam) Putnam Pub Group.

Harkonen, Reijo. The Children of China. Pitkanen, Matti A., illus. 40p. (gr. 3-6). 1990. PLB 19.95 (*0-87614-394-X*) Carolrhoda Bks.
—The Children of Nepal. Pitkanen, Matti A., illus. 48p. (gr. 3-6). 1990. PLB 19.95 (*0-87614-395-8*) Carolrhoda Bks.
Kamatsu, Yoshio. Children of the World: Bhutan. LC 88-21051. (Illus.). 64p. (gr. 5-6). 1988. PLB 21.26 (*1-55532-867-9*) Gareth Stevens Inc.
Kubota, Makota. Children of the World: South Korea. LC 86-42804. (Illus.). 64p. (gr. 5-6). 1987. PLB 21.26 (*1-55532-168-2*) Gareth Stevens Inc.
Miyazima, Yasuhiko. Children of the World: China. LC 87-42576. (Illus.). 64p. (gr. 5-6). 1988. PLB 21.26 (*1-55532-207-7*) Gareth Stevens Inc.
Morieda, Takashi. Children of the World: Burma. LC 86-42799. (Illus.). 64p. (gr. 5-6). 1987. PLB 21.26 (*1-55532-159-3*) Gareth Stevens Inc.
Nurland, Patricia. Vietnam. Vu Viet Dung, photos by. LC 89-43178. (Illus.). 64p. (gr. 5-6). 1991. PLB 21.26 (*0-8368-0230-6*) Gareth Stevens Inc.
Oshihara, Yuzuro. Children of the World: Malaysia. LC 86-42802. (Illus.). 64p. (gr. 5-6). 1987. PLB 21.26 (*1-55532-160-7*) Gareth Stevens Inc.
Ryuichi, Hirokawa. Children of the World: Jordan. LC 87-42618. (Illus.). 64p. (gr. 5-6). 1987. PLB 21.26 (*1-55532-224-7*) Gareth Stevens Inc.
Sumio, Uchiyama. Children of the World: India. LC 87-42577. (Illus.). 64p. (gr. 5-6). 1988. PLB 21.26 (*1-55532-208-5*) Gareth Stevens Inc.
Watanabe, Hitomi. Children of the World: Nepal. LC 86-42806. (Illus.). 64p. (gr. 5-6). 1987. PLB 21.26 (*1-55532-166-6*) Gareth Stevens Inc.

CHILDREN IN ASIA–FICTION

McCunn, Ruthanne L. Pie-Biter. Tang, You-Shah, illus. (CHI & ENG.). 32p. (gr. k up). 1983. English ed. 11. 95 (*0-932538-09-6*); Chinese ed. 11.95 (*0-932538-10-X*) Design Ent SF.

CHILDREN IN AUSTRALIA

Children of the World: Australia. LC 87-42617. (Illus.). 64p. (gr. 5-6). 1987. PLB 21.26 (*1-55532-222-0*) Gareth Stevens Inc.

CHILDREN IN CANADA

Harvey & Watson-Russell. So, You Have to Go to Court! A Child's Guide to Testifying As a Witness in Child Abuse Cases. 3rd ed. 48p. 1991. pap. 10.00 (*0-409-90611-5*) Butterworth Legal Pubs.
Tanobe, Miyuki. Quebec, I Love You: Je t'Aime. Tanobe, Miyuki, illus. 48p. (gr. 5 up). 1971. pap. 6.95 (*0-88776-156-9*) Tundra Bks.
Watson-Russell & Harvey. So, You've Been Busted! A Guide to Court Procedures for Adolescents Charged under the Young Offenders Act. 48p. 1989. pap. 10.00 (*0-409-80985-3*) Butterworth Legal Pubs.
Wright, David K. Canada. Wright, David K., photos by. LC 89-43197. (Illus.). 64p. (gr. 5-6). 1991. PLB 21.26 (*0-8368-0256-X*) Gareth Stevens Inc.

CHILDREN IN CHINA–FICTION

Lewis, Elizabeth F. Young Fu of the Upper Yangtze. new ed. Young, Ed, illus. LC 72-91654. 268p. (gr. 4-6). 1973. 18.95 (*0-8050-0549-8*, Bks Young Read) H Holt & Co.

CHILDREN IN EUROPE

Bjener, Tamiko. Children of the World: Finland. LC 87-42580. (Illus.). 64p. (gr. 5-6). 1987. PLB 21.26 (*1-55532-218-2*) Gareth Stevens Inc.
—Children of the World: Sweden. LC 86-42803. (Illus.). 64p. (gr. 5-6). 1987. PLB 21.26 (*1-55532-164-X*) Gareth Stevens Inc.
Children of the World: Yugoslavia. LC 88-21053. (Illus.). 64p. (gr. 5-6). 1988. PLB 21.26 (*1-55532-219-0*) Gareth Stevens Inc.
Drighi, Laura. Children of the World: Italy. LC 87-42640. (Illus.). 64p. (gr. 5-6). 1988. PLB 21.26 (*1-55532-404-5*) Gareth Stevens Inc.
Holland, Gini. Poland. LC 89-43181. (Illus.). 64p. (gr. 5-6). 1992. PLB 21.26 (*0-8368-0233-0*) Gareth Stevens Inc.
Nebor, Leos. Children of the World: Czechoslovakia. LC 87-42638. (Illus.). 64p. (gr. 5-6). 1988. PLB 21.26 (*1-55532-216-6*) Gareth Stevens Inc.
Taylor-Boyd, Susan & Brown, Julie, eds. U. S. S. R. Miyajina, Yasuhiko, photos by. LC 88-42891. (Illus.). 64p. (gr. 5-6). 1989. PLB 21.26 (*1-55532-215-8*) Gareth Stevens Inc.
Tolan, Sally & Sherwood, Rhoda I., eds. France. Pierre, Philippe, photos by. LC 88-42889. (Illus.). 64p. (gr. 5-6). 1990. PLB 21.26 (*1-55532-212-3*) Gareth Stevens Inc.
Yakoyama, Masami. Children of the World: Spain. LC 86-42808. (Illus.). 64p. (gr. 5-6). 1987. PLB 21.26 (*1-55532-163-1*) Gareth Stevens Inc.

CHILDREN IN FOREIGN COUNTRIES

Ackley, Meredith & Weber, Valerie, eds. Children of the World: Japan. LC 89-11493. (Illus.). 64p. (gr. 5-6). 1989. PLB 21.26 (*0-8368-0121-0*) Gareth Stevens Inc.
Adelman, Deborah. The Children of Perestroika Come of Age: Young People of Moscow Talk about Life in the New Russia. LC 90-25104. 200p. 1994. text ed. 30.00 (*1-56324-286-9*); pap. 16.95 (*1-56324-287-7*) M E Sharpe.
Children of the World, 30 vols, Set I. 1920p. (gr. 5-6). 1986. Set. PLB 638.00 (*1-55532-923-3*) Gareth Stevens Inc.
My Home Country, 12 bks. (gr. 2-8). 1992. Complete set. PLB 223.20 s.p. (*0-8368-0845-2*) Gareth Stevens Inc.
O'Brien, John & Taylor-Boyd, Susan, eds. Children of the World: England. Kato, Setsvo, photos by. LC 89-4462. (Illus.). 64p. (gr. 5-6). 1989. PLB 21.26 (*1-55532-211-5*) Gareth Stevens Inc.
Tozuks, Takako. Children of the World: Turkey. Reitci, Rita & Sherwood, Rhoda I., eds. Tozuka, Takako, photos by. LC 88-32745. (Illus.). 64p. (gr. 5-6). 1989. PLB 21.26 (*1-55532-851-2*) Gareth Stevens Inc.

CHILDREN IN ISLANDS OF THE PACIFIC

Bjener, Tamiko. Children of the World: Philippines. LC 86-42805. (Illus.). 64p. (gr. 5-6). 1987. PLB 21.26 (*1-55532-167-4*) Gareth Stevens Inc.
Tozuka, Takako. Children of the World: Indonesia. LC 86-42807. (Illus.). 64p. (gr. 5-6). 1987. PLB 21.26 (*1-55532-165-8*) Gareth Stevens Inc.
Yanagi, Akinobu. Children of the World: New Zealand. LC 86-42801. (Illus.). 64p. (gr. 5-6). 1987. PLB 21.26 (*1-55532-162-3*) Gareth Stevens Inc.

CHILDREN IN ISLANDS OF THE PACIFIC–FICTION

Oetting. Keiki of the Islands. LC 71-108728. (Illus.). 96p. (gr. 3 up). 1970. PLB 10.95 (*0-87783-018-5*); pap. 3.94 deluxe ed. (*0-87783-096-7*) Oddo.
Olsen, E. A. Killer in the Trap. Le Blanc, L., illus. LC 68-16399. 48p. (gr. 3 up). 1970. PLB 10.95 (*0-87783-019-3*); pap. 3.94 deluxe ed. (*0-87783-097-5*); cassette 10.60x (*0-87783-190-4*) Oddo.
Poploff, Michelle. Busy O'Brien & the Great Bubblegum Blowout. MacDonald, Pat, ed. Carter, Abby, illus. 96p. 1992. pap. 2.99 (*0-671-74082-2*, Minstrel Bks) PB.
Wallace, Bill. Totally Disgusting. MacDonald, Pat, ed. 128p. 1992. pap. 2.99 (*0-671-75416-5*, Minstrel Bks) PB.

CHILDREN IN LITERATURE AND ART

Bjork, Christina. The Other Alice: The Story of Alice Liddell & Alice in Wonderland. Eriksson, Inga-Karin, illus. Sandlin, Joan, tr. from SWE. LC 93-662. (Illus.). 1993. 18.00 (*91-29-62242-5*, Pub. by R & S Bks) FS&G.

CHILDREN IN NORTH AMERICA

Ikuhara, Yoshiyuki. Children of the World: Mexico. LC 86-42800. (Illus.). 64p. (gr. 5-6). 1987. PLB 21.26 (*1-55532-161-5*) Gareth Stevens Inc.

CHILDREN IN SOUTH AMERICA

Ikuhara, Yoshiyuki. Children of the World: Brazil. LC 87-42579. (Illus.). 64p. (gr. 5-6). 1987. PLB 21.26 (*1-55532-221-2*) Gareth Stevens Inc.

CHILDREN IN THE U. S.

Children of the World, 30 vols, Set I. 1920p. (gr. 5-6). 1986. Set. PLB 638.00 (*1-55532-923-3*) Gareth Stevens Inc.
Etkin, Linda & Willoughby, Bebe, eds. America's Children: Stories, Poems, & Real-Life Adventures of Children Through Our Nation's History. (Illus.). 96p. (gr. 2-7). 1992. write for info. (*0-307-15876-4*, 15876, Golden Pr) Western Pub.
Kronenwetter, Michael. Under Eighteen: Knowing Your Rights. LC 93-6605. (Illus.). 112p. (gr. 6 up). 1993. lib. bdg. 17.95 (*0-89490-434-5*) Enslow Pubs.

CHILDREN IN THE U. S.–FICTION

Oke, Janette. New Kid in Town. Mann, Brenda, illus. 125p. (Orig.). (gr. 3 up). 1983. pap. 4.99 (*0-934998-16-7*) Bethel Pub.
Williams, Cecil & Mirikitani, Janice, eds. I Have Something to Say about This Big Trouble: Children of the Tenderloin Speak Out. (Illus.). 128p. (Orig.). (gr. 3-7). 1989. pap. 9.95 (*0-9622574-1-9*) Glide Word.

CHILDREN'S BOOKS

see Children's Literature

CHILDREN'S DISEASES

see Children–Diseases

CHILDREN'S HOSPITALS

see Children–Hospitals

CHILDREN'S LIBRARIES

see Libraries, Children's

CHILDREN'S LITERATURE

Here are entered collections of works of a cross-genre nature, e.g., Poetry and Prose. Works on the reading interests of children, and or lists of books read by or recommended for children are entered under Children–Books and Reading.

see also Children–Books and Reading; Fairy Tales; Libraries, Children'S; Picture Books; Plays; Poetry; Stories

Barkan, Joanne, et al. The Muppet Babies in Let's Imagine....A Trip to the Stars. Chauhan, Man har, illus. 26p. (ps up). 1987. pap. 14.95 (*1-55578-806-8*) Worlds Wonder.
—The Muppet Babies in Let's Imagine...The Missing Toy's Adventure. Wilson, Ann, illus. 26p. (ps up). 1987. pap. 14.95 (*1-55578-805-X*) Worlds Wonder.
—The Muppet Babies in Let's Imagine...What Happened in the Nursery. Venning, Sue, illus. (ps up). 1987. pap. 14.95 (*1-55578-808-4*) Worlds Wonder.
Barken, Joanne, et al. The Muppet Babies in Let's Imagine...Music Everywhere. Brannon, Tom, illus. 26p. (ps up). 1987. pap. 14.95 (*1-55578-807-6*) Worlds Wonder.
Beginners Bookshelf, 8 vols. (ps-3). 79.95 (*0-685-09844-3*) Ency Brit Inc.
Berger, Larry B. & Lithwick, Dahlia, eds. I Will Sing Life: Voices from the Hole in the Wall Gang Camp. Benson, Robert, photos by. Newman, Paul, intro. by. (Illus.). 288p. 1992. 22.95 (*0-316-09273-8*) Little.
Bolinske, Janet L., ed. Big Bug Big Book Package, 6 bks. (Illus.). (gr. k-1). 1987. Set of 6 bks., 24 pgs. ea. bk. spiral bdg. 80.00 (*0-88335-760-7*) Milliken Pub Co.
—Children's Classics Big Book Package, 6 bks. (Illus.). (gr. 1-3). 1987. Set of 6 bks., 32 pgs. ea. bk. spiral bdg. 80.00 (*0-88335-540-X*) Milliken Pub Co.
—Children's Classics Hardcover Package, 18 bks. (Illus., Orig.). (gr. 1-3). 1987. Set, 32p. ea. 145.00 (*0-88335-550-7*) Milliken Pub Co.
—Children's Classics Softcover Package, 18 bks. (Illus., Orig.). (gr. 1-3). 1987. Set, 32p. ea. pap. 80.00 (*0-88335-570-1*) Milliken Pub Co.
Brown, J. Aaron, ed. The Rock-a-Bye Collection, Vols. 1 & 2. rev. ed. Vienneau, Jim, illus. 14p. (ps). 1990. Vol. 1. 12.95 (*0-927945-03-7*) Vol. 2 (*0-927945-04-5*) Someday Baby.
Cohn, Amy, selected by. From Sea to Shining Sea. Bang, Molly, et al, illus. LC 92-30598. 416p. 1993. 29.95 (*0-590-42868-3*) Scholastic Inc.
Cole, Joanna & Calmenson, Stephanie. The Laugh Book. Hafner, Marilyn, illus. LC 85-13113. 320p. (gr. 2-6). 1986. 17.00 (*0-385-18559-6*) Doubleday.
Coleman, Michael. The Much Better Story Book: Stories, Poems & Illustrations from Children & Bestselling Authors & Artists. (Illus.). 192p. (gr. 3-5). 1994. pap. 7.95 (*0-09-911531-X*, Pub. by Hutchinson UK) Trafalgar.
Frost, Joan. Art, Books & Children: Art Activities Based on Children's Literature. (Illus.). 88p. (gr. 1-6). 1984. spiral bdg. 13.95 (*0-938594-03-6*) Spec Lit Pr.
Graf, Virginia, ed. The Friendship Tree & Other Stories for Children by Children. Yourell, Pamela, illus. (Orig.). (gr. 3-8). Date not set. pap. 9.50 (*1-882788-03-6*) VanGar Pubs.
Guess What I'm Thinking Of. 32p. (gr. 2-6). 1994. 4.95 (*0-685-71577-9*, 513) W Gladden Found.
Hammer, Roger A. My Own Book! Reading Is Fundamental (RIF) 20th Anniversary. Schlosser, Cy, illus. LC 86-30410. 128p. (gr. 3-12). 1987. pap. 14.95 (*0-932991-50-5*) Place in the Woods.
Harvey, Gail. Read to Me, Grandma. 1993. pap. 8.99 (*0-517-09348-0*) Random Hse Value.
—Read to Me, Grandpa. 1993. pap. 8.99 (*0-517-09349-9*) Random Hse Value.
Henderson, Kathy, selected by. The Bedtime Book. Ives, Penny, illus. LC 92-9413. (ps-3). 1992. 14.95 (*0-8120-6295-7*) Barron.
Janger, Kathie, ed. Rainbow Collection, 1990-91: Stories & Poetry by Young People. Sarecky, Melody, illus. DeVito, Danny, intro. by. (Illus.). 160p. (Orig.). (gr. 1-8). 1991. pap. 6.00 (*0-929889-07-X*) Young Writers Contest Found.
Kidd, Ron. The Nutcracker. Reinert, Rick, illus. 48p. (gr. k-6). 1985. 6.95 (*0-8249-8095-6*, Ideals Child) Hambleton-Hill.
Landau, Elaine. On the Streets: The Lives of Adolescent Prostitutes. LC 86-21825. 112p. (gr. 9 up). 1987. lib. bdg. 12.98 (*0-671-62135-1*, J Messner) S&S Trade.
Lewis, Shari & O'Kun, Lan. One-Minute Bedtime Stories. Cumings, Art, illus. LC 79-8024. 48p. (ps-3). 1982. pap. 10.00 (*0-385-15292-2*) Doubleday.
Magill, Frank N., ed. Masterplots II: American Fiction Supplement, 2 vols. (gr. 9-12). 1994. Set. PLB 185.00 (*0-89356-719-1*) Salem Pr.
Mahy, Margaret. Bubble Trouble: And Other Poems & Stories. Mahy, Margaret, illus. LC 92-3540. 80p. (gr. 3-7). 1992. SBE 13.95 (*0-689-50557-4*, M K McElderry) Macmillan Child Grp.
My Own Book of Special Things. 32p. (ps-4). 1994. 4.95 (*0-685-71920-0*, 511) W Gladden Found.
My Own Book of Wishes. 32p. (ps-4). 1994. 4.95 (*0-685-71919-7*, 510) W Gladden Found.
Newbery Medal Collection, 5 vols, No. 3. (gr. 4 up). 1988. Boxed. pap. 16.25 (*0-440-36003-X*) Dell.
Pena, Sylvia C., ed. Kikiriki: Stories & Poems in English & Spanish for Children. 2nd ed. LC 81-68072. (ENG & SPA., Illus.). 116p. (Orig.). (gr. k-6). 1989. pap. 8.50 (*0-685-34571-8*) Arte Publico.
Perez, N. A. One Special Year. LC 84-25258. 200p. (gr. 6-9). 1985. 13.95 (*0-395-36693-3*) HM.
Rudin, Ellen, ed. Young Authors of America, Vol. 1. (Illus.). 102p. (gr. 5-8). 1988. pap. 0.60 (*0-440-84003-1*) Dell.
Russell, William F., selected by. Classics to Read Aloud to Your Children. LC 84-7033. 320p. (ps-5). 1984. 20. 00 (*0-517-55404-6*, Crown) Crown Pub Group.
Schoch, Tim. Summer Camp Creeps. 160p. (Orig.). (gr. 3-7). 1987. pap. 2.95 (*0-380-75343-X*, Camelot) Avon.
Shoemaker, Mrs. J. W., compiled by. Young Folks Recitations: Designed for Young People of Fourteen Years; Containing Selections in Prose & Poetry; Together with Some Short Dialogues & Tableaux. LC 73-2839. (gr. 8-10). 1973. Repr. of 1884 ed. 14.00 (*0-8369-6413-6*) Ayer.
Stanek, Lou W. Thinking Like a Writer. 128p. (Orig.). (gr. 4 up). 1994. PLB 9.99 (*0-679-96217-4*); pap. 5.99 (*0-679-86217-X*) Random Bks Yng Read.
Story Time Staff. Home Schooling with Educational Story Rhymes. Story Time Staff, illus. 50p. (gr. 6-9). 1993. binder 21.95 (*1-56820-108-7*) Story Time.
—Rhyme Theatre - Story Rhyme Plays & Skits. 60p. 1994. binder 19.95 (*1-56820-117-6*) Story Time.
Stroyer, Paul. Treasure Chest of Tales. (Illus.). (gr. 3 up). 1959. 12.95 (*0-8392-3039-7*) Astor-Honor.
Taylor, Kenneth. Stories for the Children's Hour. 2nd ed. (gr. 1-8). 1987. pap. 7.99 (*0-8024-2227-6*) Moody.

Treasury of Disney Little Golden Books. (ps-2). 1972. write for info. (*0-307-17865-X*, Golden Bks) Western Pub.

Trelease, Jim, ed. Hey! Listen to This: Stories to Read-Aloud. 240p. (Orig.). (gr. k-4). 1992. 22.00 (*0-670-83691-5*, Viking); pap. 11.00 (*0-14-014653-9*) Viking Child Bks.

Veitch, Carol J. & Crawford, Jane. More Literature Puzzles for Elementary & Middle Schools. Mannerberg, Patricia A., illus. LC 86-7161. xiii, 90p. (gr. 1-7). 1986. pap. text ed. 15.50 (*0-87287-518-0*) Libs Unl.

Weber, Chris, ed. Treasures, No. 2: Stories & Art by Students in Oregon. Kimmel, Eric, intro. by. 256p. (Orig.). (gr. k-12). 1988. pap. 11.95 (*0-9616058-1-2*) OR Students Writing.

Witter, Evelyn, et al. More Stories Worth Reading. Penovich, Geraldine & Penovich, Beatrice A., eds. (Illus.). 1989. write for info. Printemps Bks.

Zorn, Steven, as told by. Mostly Ghostly: Eight Spooky Tales to Chill Your Bones. Brodley, John, illus. LC 91-71087. 56p. (gr. 2 up). 1991. 9.98 (*1-56138-033-4*) Courage Bks.

CHILDREN'S LITERATURE–BIBLIOGRAPHY

Editorial America, S. A. Staff. Los Cuentos Infantiles Mas Famosos Del Mundo. Del Real, Maria E., ed. (SPA., Illus.). 464p. (Orig.). (ps-8). 1990. pap. write for info. (*0-944499-93-7*) Editorial Amer.

Lynn, Ruth N., ed. Fantasy Literature for Children & Young Adults: An Annotated Bibliography. 4th, rev. & updated ed. (gr. 3 up). 1994. 50.00 (*0-8352-3456-8*) Bowker.

Miller, Heather S. Children & Gardens: An Annotated Bibliography of Children's Garden Books, 1829-1988. Miasek, Meryl A., ed. 60p. (Orig.). pap. write for info. (*0-9621791-1-6*) CBHL Inc.

Scarry, Richard. Richard Scarry's Storybook Dictionary. LC 99-901821. (Illus.). (gr. k-2). 1966. write for info. (*0-307-15548-X*, Golden Bks) Western Pub.

Shelton, Helen, ed. Bibliography of Books for Children, 1988-89. LC 89-345. 112p. (ps-6). 1989. 15.00 (*0-87173-118-5*) ACEI.

White, Valerie. Choosing Your Children's Books: Beginning Readers 5 to 8 Years Old. White, Trevor, illus. 32p. (Orig.). (gr. k-3). 1993. pap. 4.95 (*1-882726-00-6*) Bayley & Musgrave.

CHILDREN'S LITERATURE–HISTORY AND CRITICSIM

Gross, Edward, ed. Above & Below: A Guide to Beauty & the Beast. (Illus.). 112p. (Orig.). (gr. 9-12). 1990. pap. 12.95 (*0-9627508-0-8*) Image NY.

Hadlow, Ruth, et al. Children's Books Too Good to Miss. 8th ed. (gr. 1-6). 1992. write for info. (*0-9616276-0-3*) Lucas Comns.

CHILDREN'S READING

see Children's Literature; Reading

CHILE

Dwyer, Chris. Chile. (Illus.). 128p. (gr. 5 up). 1990. 14.95 (*0-7910-1102-X*) Chelsea Hse.

Galvin, Irene F. Chile: Land of Poets & Patriots. LC 89-28747. (Illus.). 128p. (gr. 5 up). 1990. text ed. 14.95 RSBE (*0-87518-421-9*, Dillon) Macmillan Child Grp.

Hintz, Martin. Chile. LC 84-23104. (Illus.). 128p. (gr. 5-9). 1985. PLB 20.55 (*0-516-02755-7*) Childrens.

Jacobsen, Karen. Chile. LC 90-20818. (Illus.). 48p. (gr. k-4). 1991. PLB 12.85 (*0-516-01111-1*); pap. 4.95 (*0-516-41111-X*) Childrens.

Lerner Publications, Department of Geography Staff, ed. Chile in Pictures. (Illus.). 64p. (gr. 5 up). 1988. PLB 17.50 (*0-8225-1809-0*) Lerner Pubns.

Mihalik, Paul A. Patagonia Profile. (Illus.). 93p. (Orig.). (gr. 7-12). 1985. pap. text ed. 9.95 (*0-9615916-0-9*) Padre Pio Pubs.

Winter, Jane K. Chile. LC 90-22472. (Illus.). 128p. (gr. 5-9). 1991. PLB 21.95 (*1-85435-383-7*) Marshall Cavendish.

CHIMES

see Bells

CHIMPANZEES

Birnbaum, Bette. Jane Goodall & the Wild Chimpanzees. (Illus.). 32p. (gr. 1-4). 1989. PLB 18.99 (*0-8172-3509-4*); pap. 3.95 (*0-8114-6709-0*) Raintree Steck-V.

Butterworth, Christine & Bailey, Donna. Chimpanzees. LC 90-9928. (Illus.). 32p. (gr. 1-4). 1990. PLB 18.99 (*0-8114-2642-4*); pap. 3.95 (*0-8114-4615-8*) Raintree Steck-V.

Chimpanzees. 1991. PLB 14.95 (*0-88682-340-4*) Creative Ed.

DaVolls, Linda. Tano & Binti: Two Chimpanzees Return to the Wild. DaVolls, Andy, illus. LC 93-25403. (gr. k-3). 1994. 14.95 (*0-395-68701-2*, Clarion Bks) HM.

Fromer, Julie. Jane Goodall: Living with the Chimps. Castro, Antonio, illus. 72p. (gr. 4-7). 1992. PLB 14.95 (*0-8050-2116-7*) TFC Bks NY.

Fuchs, Carol. Jane Goodall: The Chimpanzee's Friend. LC 93-6506. 1993. 14.60 (*0-86593-262-X*); 10.95s.p. (*0-685-66546-1*) Rourke Corp.

Goodall, Jane. The Chimpanzee Family Book. Neugebauer, Michael, illus. LC 88-33359. 72p. (ps up). 1991. pap. 17.95 (*0-88708-090-1*) Picture Bk Studio.

—My Life with Chimpanzees. (Illus.). 128p. (gr. 4-6). 1988. pap. 3.50 (*0-671-66095-0*, Minstrel Bks) PB.

Luthor. Jane Goodall. Date not set. PLB write for info. (*0-8050-2272-4*) H Holt & Co.

McCormick, Maxine. Chimpanzee. LC 89-28272. (Illus.). 48p. (gr. 5). 1990. text ed. 12.95 (*0-89686-514-2*, Crestwood Hse) Macmillan Child Grp.

Petty, Kate. Baby Animals: Chimpanzees. (Illus.). 24p. (ps-3). 1992. pap. 3.95 (*0-8120-4965-9*) Barron.

—Chimpanzees. (gr. 4-7). 1990. PLB 10.90 (*0-531-17193-0*, Gloucester Pr) Watts.

Stone, Lynn. Chimpanzees. (Illus.). 24p. (gr. k-5). 1990. lib. bdg. 11.94 (*0-86593-064-3*); lib. bdg. 8.95s.p. (*0-685-36316-3*) Rourke Corp.

CHIMPANZEES–FICTION

Armstrong, Jennifer. That Champion Chimp. (gr. 4-7). 1990. pap. 2.75 (*0-553-15828-7*) Bantam.

Blaustein, Muriel. Jim Chimp's Story. LC 91-18001. (Illus.). 40p. (ps-2). 1992. pap. 14.00 jacketed (*0-671-74779-7*, S&S BFYR) S&S Trade.

Browne, Anthony. Willy & Hugh. Browne, Anthony, illus. LC 90-4938. 32p. (ps-3). 1991. 13.00 (*0-679-81446-9*); lib. bdg. 13.99 (*0-679-91446-3*) Knopf Bks Yng Read.

Hoban, Lillian. Arthur's Camp-Out. Hoban, Lillian, illus. LC 91-27528. 64p. (gr. k-3). 1993. 14.00 (*0-06-020525-3*); PLB 13.89 (*0-06-020526-1*) HarpC Child Bks.

—Arthur's Christmas Cookies. unabr. ed. (Illus.). (ps-3). 1990. pap. 6.95 incl. cassette (*1-55994-217-7*, Caedmon) HarperAudio.

—Arthur's Funny Money. unabr. ed. (Illus.). (ps-3). 1990. pap. 6.95 incl. cassette (*1-55994-218-5*, Caedmon) HarperAudio.

—Arthur's Honey Bear. unabr. ed. (Illus.). (ps-3). 1990. pap. 6.95 incl. cassette (*1-55994-219-3*, Caedmon) HarperAudio.

—Arthur's Loose Tooth. Hoban, Lillian, illus. LC 85-42611. 64p. (gr. k-3). 1987. pap. 3.50 (*0-06-444093-1*, Trophy) HarpC Child Bks.

—Arthur's Pen Pal. unabr. ed. (Illus.). (ps-3). 1990. pap. 6.95 incl. cassette (*1-55994-238-X*, Caedmon) HarperAudio.

—Arthur's Prize Reader. unabr. ed. (Illus.). (ps-3). 1990. pap. 6.95 incl. cassette (*1-55994-220-7*, Caedmon) HarperAudio.

Rabe, Berniece. Where's Chimpy? Tucker, Kathleen, ed. Schmidt, Diane, photos by. LC 87-37259. (Illus.). 32p. (ps-2). 1988. PLB 13.95 (*0-8075-8928-4*); pap. 5.95 (*0-8075-8927-6*) A Whitman.

CHINA

Bliss, Jonathan. China. (Illus.). 64p. (gr. 7 up). 1990. lib. bdg. 17.27 (*0-86593-090-2*); lib. bdg. 12.95s.p. (*0-685-36364-3*) Rourke Corp.

Brill, Marlene T. Mongolia. LC 91-34172. 128p. (gr. 5-9). 1992. PLB 20.55 (*0-516-02605-4*) Childrens.

Busuttil, Joelle. Behind the Wall of China. Bogard, Vicki, tr. from FRE. Quentin, Laurence, illus. LC 92-969. (gr. k-5). 1992. 5.95 (*0-944589-42-1*) Young Discovery Lib.

Charley, Catherine. China. LC 94-15613. 1995. write for info. (*0-8114-2789-7*) Raintree Steck-V.

China (People's Republic of) (Illus.). 128p. (gr. 5 up). 1991. 14.95 (*0-7910-1368-5*) Chelsea Hse.

China: Teacher's Guide. (gr. 4-7). 1991. 18.00 (*0-8172-3479-9*) Raintree Steck-V.

Conklin, Paul, et al, photos by. Land of Yesterday, Land of Tomorrow: Discovering Chinese Central Asia. Ashabranner, Brent, text by. (Illus.). 96p. (gr. 5 up). 1992. 16.00 (*0-525-65086-5*, Cobblehill Bks) Dutton Child Bks.

De Bruycker, Daniel & Dauber, Maximilien. China. Walker, Maureen, tr. from FRE. (Illus.). 76p. (gr. 5 up). 1994. 13.95 (*0-8120-6426-7*); pap. 7.95 (*0-8120-1865-6*) Barron.

Dudley, William & Swisher, Karin, eds. China. LC 88-24296. (Illus.). 250p. (gr. 10 up). 1988. lib. bdg. 17.95 (*0-89908-439-7*); pap. text ed. 9.95 (*0-89908-414-1*) Greenhaven.

Ferroa, Peggy. China. LC 91-15865. (Illus.). 128p. (gr. 5-9). 1991. PLB 21.95 (*1-85435-399-3*) Marshall Cavendish.

Fisher, Leonard E. The Great Wall of China. Fisher, Leonard E., illus. LC 85-15324. 32p. (gr. 1-5). 1986. RSBE 15.95 (*0-02-735220-X*, Macmillan Child Bk) Macmillan Child Grp.

Flint, David. China. LC 93-15794. (Illus.). 32p. (gr. 3-4). 1993. PLB 19.24 (*0-8114-3421-4*) Raintree Steck-V.

Fyson, Nance L. & Greenhill, Richard. A Family in China. LC 84-19426. (Illus.). 32p. (gr. 2-5). 1985. PLB 13.50 (*0-8225-1653-5*) Lerner Pubns.

Haskins, Jim. Count Your Way Through China. (Illus.). 24p. (gr. 1-4). 1987. lib. bdg. 17.50 (*0-87614-302-8*) Carolrhoda Bks.

Johnson, Neil. Step into China. Johnson, Neil, illus. LC 87-20266. 32p. (gr. 3-6). 1988. lib. bdg. 9.98 (*0-671-64338-X*, J Messner); pap. 5.95 (*0-671-65852-2*) S&S Trade.

Kalman, Bobbie. China - the Culture. (Illus.). 32p. (gr. 4-5). 1989. PLB 15.95 (*0-86505-209-3*); pap. 7.95 (*0-86505-289-1*) Crabtree Pub Co.

—China - The Land. (Illus.). 32p. (gr. 4-5). 1989. PLB 15.95 (*0-86505-207-7*); pap. 7.95 (*0-86505-287-5*) Crabtree Pub Co.

—China - The People. (Illus.). 32p. (gr. 4-5). 1989. PLB 15.95 (*0-86505-208-5*); pap. 7.95 (*0-86505-288-3*) Crabtree Pub Co.

Keeler, Stephen. Passport to China. LC 93-38982. 1994. write for info. (*0-531-14320-1*) Watts.

Lazo, Caroline. The Terra Cotta Army of Emperor Qin. LC 92-26189. (Illus.). 80p. (gr. 6 up). 1993. text ed. 14.95 RSBE (*0-02-754631-4*, New Discovery) Macmillan Child Grp.

Lerner Publications, Department of Geography Staff, ed. China in Pictures. (Illus.). 64p. (gr. 5 up). 1989. 17.50 (*0-8225-1859-7*) Lerner Pubns.

Martell, Mary H. The Ancient Chinese. LC 92-9052. (Illus.). 64p. (gr. 6 up). 1993. text ed. 14.95 RSBE (*0-02-730653-4*, New Discovery) Macmillan Child Grp.

Merton, D. & Yun-Kan, Shio. China: The Land & Its People. rev. ed. LC 85-72107. (Illus.). 48p. (gr. 5 up). 1991. PLB 12.95 (*0-382-24242-4*) Silver Burdett Pr.

Odijk, Pamela. The Chinese. (Illus.). 48p. (gr. 5-8). 1991. PLB 12.95 (*0-382-09894-3*) Silver Burdett Pr.

Sabin, Louis. Ancient China. Frenck, Hal, illus. LC 84-2729. 32p. (gr. 3-6). 1985. PLB 9.49 (*0-8167-0316-7*); pap. text ed. 2.95 (*0-8167-0317-5*) Troll Assocs.

Seablom, Seth H. China Coloring Guide. (Illus.). 32p. (gr. 1-6). 1979. pap. 2.50 (*0-918800-06-4*) Seablom.

Stewart, Gail B. China. LC 90-35497. (Illus.). 48p. (gr. 6-7). 1990. text ed. 12.95 RSBE (*0-89686-538-X*, Crestwood Hse) Macmillan Child Grp.

Tan, Jennifer. Food in China. LC 88-31644. (Illus.). 32p. (gr. 3-6). 1989. lib. bdg. 15.94 (*0-86625-338-6*); 11.95s.p. (*0-685-58502-6*) Rourke Corp.

Terzi, Marinella. The Chinese Empire. LC 92-7509. (Illus.). 36p. (gr. 3 up). 1992. PLB 14.95 (*0-516-08377-5*) Childrens.

Tolhurst, Marilyn. China. (Illus.). 48p. (gr. 4-8). 1987. PLB 14.95 (*0-382-09510-3*) Silver Burdett Pr.

Tsow, Ming. Chinese Spring Festival. (Illus.). 25p. (gr. 2-4). 1991. 12.95 (*0-237-60137-0*, Pub. by Evans Bros Ltd) Trafalgar.

—A Day with Ling. (Illus.). 25p. (gr. 2-4). 1991. 12.95 (*0-237-60117-6*, Pub. by Evans Bros Ltd) Trafalgar.

Twist, Clint. Marco Polo: Overland to Medieval China. LC 93-30744. 1994. PLB 22.80 (*0-8114-7251-5*) Raintree Steck-V.

Waterlow, Julia. China. LC 90-25276. (Illus.). 32p. (gr. k-4). 1991. 12.40 (*0-531-18393-9*, Pub. by Bookwright Pr) Watts.

—China. LC 93-20428. (Illus.). 32p. (gr. 5-8). 1994. PLB 12.40 (*0-531-14271-X*) Watts.

Yu, Ling. A Family in Taiwan. (Illus.). 32p. (gr. 2-5). 1990. PLB 13.50 (*0-8225-1685-3*) Lerner Pubns.

Zurlo, Tony. China: The Dragon Awakes. LC 94-8015. 1994. text ed. 14.95 (*0-87518-596-7*, Dillon Pr) Macmillan Child Grp.

CHINA–BIOGRAPHY

Foster, Leila M. Nien Cheng: Courage in China. LC 92-9333. (Illus.). 152p. (gr. 4 up). 1992. PLB 14.40 (*0-516-03279-8*); pap. 5.95 (*0-516-43279-6*) Childrens.

Hoobler, Dorothy & Hoobler, Thomas. Chinese Portraits. Bruck, Victoria, illus. LC 92-13617. 96p. (gr. 7-8). 1992. PLB 22.80 (*0-8114-6375-3*) Raintree Steck-V.

—Zhou Enlai. Schlesinger, Arthur M., Jr., intro. by. (Illus.). 112p. (gr. 5 up). 1986. 17.95 (*0-87754-516-2*) Chelsea Hse.

Hope, Irene. Ai-Chan's Secret. 1989. pap. 2.95 (*9971-972-85-9*) OMF Bks.

Kurland, Gerald. Mao Tse-Tung: Founder of Communist China. Rahmas, D. Steve, ed. LC 75-190232. 32p. (Orig.). (gr. 7-12). 1972. lib. bdg. 4.95 incl. catalog cards (*0-87157-514-0*) SamHar Pr.

Song Nan Zhang. A Little Tiger in the Chinese Night. Song Nan Zhang, illus. LC 93-60336. 48p. (gr. 6-9). 1993. 19.95 (*0-88776-320-0*) Tundra Bks.

Steele, Philip. China. LC 93-25237. (Illus.). 32p. (gr. 4 up). 1994. text ed. 13.95 RSBE (*0-89686-771-4*, Crestwood Hse) Macmillan Child Grp.

CHINA–FICTION

Adams, Fern. China's Daughter. 134p. (Orig.). (gr. 7-12). 1991. pap. 4.95 (*0-8474-6623-X*) Back to Bible.

Bosse, Malcolm. The Examination. LC 94-50955. (gr. 7 up). 1994. 17.00 (*0-374-32234-1*) FS&G.

Brooke, William J. A Brush with Magic. LC 92-41744. (Illus.). 160p. (gr. 3 up). 1993. 15.00 (*0-06-022973-X*); PLB 14.89 (*0-06-022974-8*) HarpC Child Bks.

Carle, Eric. The Secret Birthday Message: Miniature Edition. Carle, Eric, illus. LC 91-8306. 26p. (ps-3). 1991. 4.95 (*0-06-020102-9*) HarpC Child Bks.

Chang, Margaret & Chang, Raymond. In the Eye of War. LC 89-38027. 208p. (gr. 4-7). 1990. SBE 14.95 (*0-689-50503-5*, M K McElderry) Macmillan Child Grp.

Clyde, Ahmad. Cheng Ho's Voyage. Durkee, Noura, illus. LC 81-66951. 32p. (Orig.). (gr. 3-7). 1981. pap. 2.00 (*0-89259-021-1*) Am Trust Pubns.

Cooley, Regina F. The Magic Christmas Pony. Hansen, Han H., illus. LC 91-76342. 36p. (gr. 1-5). 1991. 19.95 (*1-880450-04-6*) Capstone Pub.

DeJong, Meindert. House of Sixty Fathers. Sendak, Maurice, illus. LC 56-8148. 192p. (gr. 5-8). 1956. PLB 14.89 (*0-06-021481-3*) HarpC Child Bks.

Demi. The Artist & the Architect. Demi, illus. LC 90-40936. 32p. (ps-2). 1991. 15.95 (*0-8050-1580-9*, Bks Young Read) H Holt & Co.

Fabian, Erika. Adventures in Splendid China. (Illus.). 64p. (gr. 4 up). 1994. 16. 95 (*0-9638417-0-X*) Eriako Assocs. ADVENTURES IN SPLENDID CHINA: Five children, Billy, an African-American; Pablo, a Mexican-American; Amy & Kirk, two Caucasians; & Ying, a girl from Hong Kong, join the legendary Monkey King on a magical journey in China. Through the people they meet, they learn about Chinese beliefs, customs, & art such as why brides wear red, why the horse-head violin is played in Mongolia, & why tigers are friends of the Yi people. This is an entertaining as well as educational book to be enjoyed by anyone curious about China. Charming, full-color illustrations combined with photography make each page a visual surprise. Ages 9 & up. 64 p. hardback. January 1994. $16.95. ISBN 0-9638417-0-X. COSTUMES OF SPLENDID CHINA: A paper doll book that features full-color regional costumes from China. Five American children of various ethnic backgrounds & the Monkey King of China, each has three pre-cut outfits. Included is a booklet describing each costume & some customs from each region, which the children can collate & keep, plus a full-color map of China that highlights these locations. Ages 6 & up. 24 p. March 1994 $6.95. ISBN 0-9638417-1-8. Orders for both books may be placed by contacting: The Book People, (800) 999-4650 or The Distributors, (800) 955-7032, or China Books Phone (415) 282-2994. FAX (415) 282-0094. *Publisher Provided Annotation.*

Flack, Marjorie. Story about Ping. Wiese, Kurt, illus. LC 33-29356. (ps-2). 1933. pap. 14.00 (*0-670-67223-8*) Viking Child Bks.

Flack, Marjorie & Wiese, Kurt. The Story about Ping. (Illus.). 1993. pap. 6.99 incl. cassette (*0-14-095117-2*, Puffin) Puffin Bks.

Fritz, Jean. China Homecoming. Fritz, Michael, photos by. LC 84-24775. (Illus.). 144p. (gr. 5 up). 1985. 15.95 (*0-399-21182-9*, Putnam) Putnam Pub Group.

Frost, Lesley. Digging Down to China. Hudnut, R., illus. 64p. (gr. 1-4). 1968. 9.95 (*0-8159-5306-2*) Devin.

Guo, Tony & Cheung, Euphine. Er-Lang & the Suns: A Tale from China. Edwards, Karl, illus. 24p. (Orig.). (gr. k-4). 1994. big bk. 21.95 (*1-879531-11-9*); PLB 9.95 (*1-879531-42-9*); pap. 4.95 (*1-879531-21-6*) Mondo Pubng.

Handforth, Thomas. Mei Li. Handforth, Thomas, illus. 48p. (gr. k-3). 1955. PLB 14.95 (*0-385-07401-8*) Doubleday.

Hillman, E. Min-Yo & the Moon Dragon. Wallner, J., illus. 1992. 14.95 (*0-15-254230-2*, HB Juv Bks) HarBrace.

Hwa-I Publishing Co., Staff. Chinese Children's Stories, Vol. 10: The Money Tree, The Coxcomb. Ching, Emily, et al, eds. Wonder Kids Publications Staff, tr. from CHI. Hwa-I Publishing Co., Staff, illus. LC 90-60792. 28p. (gr. 3-6). 1991. Repr. of 1988 ed. 7.95x (*1-56162-010-6*) Wonder Kids.

—Chinese Children's Stories, Vol. 100: From Rice into Flowers, The Shy Rainbow. Ching, Emily, et al, eds. Wonder Kids Publications Staff, tr. from CHI. Hwa-I Publishing Co., Staff, illus. LC 90-60811. 28p. (gr. 3-6). 1991. Repr. of 1988 ed. 7.95x (*1-56162-100-5*) Wonder Kids.

—Chinese Children's Stories, Vol. 12: The Snail & the Ox, Sparrows Can't Walk. Ching, Emily, et al, eds. Wonder Kids Publications Staff, tr. from CHI. Hwa-I Publishing Co., Staff, illus. LC 90-60793. 28p. (gr. 3-6). 1991. Repr. of 1988 ed. 7.95x (*1-56162-012-2*) Wonder Kids.

—Chinese Children's Stories, Vol. 13: Rooster Summons the Sun, The White-Haired Bird. Ching, Emily, et al, eds. Wonder Kids Publications Staff, tr. from CHI. Hwa-I Publishing Co., Staff, illus. LC 90-60793. 28p. (gr. 3-6). 1991. Repr. of 1988 ed. 7.95x (*1-56162-013-0*) Wonder Kids.

—Chinese Children's Stories, Vol. 14: Weasel Steals the Chickens, Why is the Crow Black? Ching, Emily, et al, eds. Wonder Kids Publications Staff, tr. from CHI. Hwa-I Publishing Co., Staff, illus. LC 90-60793. 28p. (gr. 3-6). 1991. Repr. of 1988 ed. 7.95x (*1-56162-014-9*) Wonder Kids.

—Chinese Children's Stories, Vol. 15: Jiggle in the Wind, The Bat Can't See the Sun. Ching, Emily, et al, eds. Wonder Kids Publications Staff, tr. from CHI. Hwa-I Publishing Co., Staff, illus. LC 90-60793. 28p. (gr. 3-6). 1991. Repr. of 1988 ed. 7.95x (*1-56162-015-7*) Wonder Kids.

—Chinese Children's Stories, Vol. 17: The Monkey & the Fire, Lazy Wife & the Bread Ring. Ching, Emily, et al, eds. Wonder Kids Publications Staff, tr. from CHI. Hwa-I Publishing Co., Staff, illus. LC 90-60794. 28p. (gr. 3-6). 1991. Repr. of 1988 ed. 7.95x (*1-56162-017-3*) Wonder Kids.

—Chinese Children's Stories, Vol. 18: The Little Bamboo Pole, The Wise Old Man. Ching, Emily, et al, eds. Wonder Kids Publications Staff, tr. from CHI. Hwa-I Publishing Co., Staff, illus. LC 90-60794. 28p. (gr. 3-6). 1991. Repr. of 1988 ed. 7.95x (*1-56162-018-1*) Wonder Kids.

—Chinese Children's Stories, Vol. 19: Crow Moves Away, Baby Lion & Baby Rhino. Ching, Emily, et al, eds. Wonder Kids Publications Staff, tr. from CHI. Hwa-I Publishing Co., Staff, illus. LC 90-60794. 28p. (gr. 3-6). 1991. Repr. of 1988 ed. 7.95x (*1-56162-019-X*) Wonder Kids.

—Chinese Children's Stories, Vol. 20: Ah-Liu Picks Corn, Cuckoo's Winter. Ching, Emily, et al, eds. Wonder Kids Publications Staff, tr. from CHI. Hwa-I Publishing Co., Staff, illus. LC 90-60794. 28p. (gr. 3-6). 1991. Repr. of 1988 ed. 7.95x (*1-56162-020-3*) Wonder Kids.

—Chinese Children's Stories, Vol. 22: The Steal a Bell, The Dropout. Ching, Emily, et al, eds. Wonder Kids Publications Staff, tr. from CHI. Hwa-I Publishing Co., Staff, illus. LC 90-60796. 28p. (gr. 3-6). 1991. Repr. of 1988 ed. 7.95x (*1-56162-022-X*) Wonder Kids.

—Chinese Children's Stories, Vol. 23: Dummy Afa, The Fox in a Tiger's Suit. Ching, Emily, et al, eds. Wonder Kids Publications Staff, tr. from CHI. Hwa-I Publishing Co., Staff, illus. LC 90-60796. 28p. (gr. 3-6). 1991. Repr. of 1988 ed. 7.95x (*1-56162-023-8*) Wonder Kids.

—Chinese Children's Stories, Vol. 24: Running Fifty vs. One-Hundred Strides, Atu Yanks the Rice Seedlings. Ching, Emily, et al, eds. Wonder Kids Publications Staff, tr. from CHI. Hwa-I Publishing Co., Staff, illus. LC 90-60796. 28p. (gr. 3-6). 1991. Repr. of 1988 ed. 7.95x (*1-56162-024-6*) Wonder Kids.

—Chinese Children's Stories, Vol. 25: The Blindmen & the Elephant, Little Frog in the Well. Ching, Emily, et al, eds. Wonder Kids Publications Staff, tr. from CHI. Hwa-I Publishing Co., Staff, illus. LC 90-60796. 28p. (gr. 3-6). 1991. Repr. of 1988 ed. 7.95x (*1-56162-025-4*) Wonder Kids.

—Chinese Children's Stories, Vol. 26: Celebrating New York, Miss Yuan-Tsau. Ching, Emily, et al, eds. Wonder Kids Publications Staff, tr. from CHI. (Illus.). 28p. (gr. 3-6). 1991. Repr. of 1988 ed. 7.95 (*1-56162-026-2*) Wonder Kids.

—Chinese Children's Stories, Vol. 27: Sky-Mending Festival, Decorative Paper for Graves. Ching, Emily, et al, eds. Wonder Kids Publications Staff, tr. from CHI. Hwa-I Publishing Co., Staff, illus. LC 90-60797. 28p. (gr. 3-6). 1991. Repr. of 1988 ed. 7.95x (*1-56162-027-0*) Wonder Kids.

—Chinese Children's Stories, Vol. 28: Mih-Ro River, The Herder & the Seamstress. Ching, Emily, et al, eds. Wonder Kids Publications Staff, tr. from CHI. Hwa-I Publishing Co., Staff, illus. LC 90-60797. 28p. (gr. 3-6). 1991. Repr. of 1988 ed. 7.95x (*1-56162-028-9*) Wonder Kids.

—Chinese Children's Stories, Vol. 29: Moon Cake, Fei's Adventure. Ching, Emily, et al, eds. Wonder Kids Publications Staff, tr. from CHI. Hwa-I Publishing Co., Staff, illus. LC 90-60797. 28p. (gr. 3-6). 1991. Repr. of 1988 ed. 7.95x (*1-56162-029-7*) Wonder Kids.

—Chinese Children's Stories, Vol. 30: La-Ba Porridge, The Stove God. Ching, Emily, et al, eds. Wonder Kids Publications Staff, tr. from CHI. Hwa-I Publishing Co., Staff, illus. LC 90-60797. 28p. (gr. 3-6). 1991. Repr. of 1988 ed. 7.95x (*1-56162-030-0*) Wonder Kids.

—Chinese Children's Stories, Vol. 32: Dumplings, Ham. Ching, Emily, et al, eds. Wonder Kids Publications Staff, tr. from CHI. Hwa-I Publishing Co., Staff, illus. LC 90-60798. 28p. (gr. 3-6). 1991. Repr. of 1988 ed. 7.95x (*1-56162-032-7*) Wonder Kids.

—Chinese Children's Stories, Vol. 33: Noodles over the Bridge, Steamed Bread. Ching, Emily, et al, eds. Wonder Kids Publications Staff, tr. from CHI. Hwa-I Publishing Co., Staff, illus. LC 90-60798. 28p. (gr. 3-6). 1991. Repr. of 1988 ed. 7.95x (*1-56162-033-5*) Wonder Kids.

—Chinese Children's Stories, Vol. 34: The Stuffed Steamed Bao, Miss Freckle's Tofu. Ching, Emily, et al, eds. Wonder Kids Publications Staff, tr. from CHI. Hwa-I Publishing Co., Staff, illus. LC 90-60798. 28p. (gr. 3-6). 1991. Repr. of 1988 ed. 7.95x (*1-56162-034-3*) Wonder Kids.

—Chinese Children's Stories, Vol. 35: Monks' Beef Stew, Yue's Tofu Store. Ching, Emily, et al, eds. Wonder Kids Publications Staff, tr. from CHI. Hwa-I Publishing Co., Staff, illus. LC 90-60798. 28p. (gr. 3-6). 1991. Repr. of 1988 ed. 7.95x (*1-56162-035-1*) Wonder Kids.

—Chinese Children's Stories, Vol. 37: Confucius' Bookkeeping, The Scissors Shop. Ching, Emily, et al, eds. Wonder Kids Publications Staff, tr. from CHI. Hwa-I Publishing Co., Staff, illus. LC 90-60799. 28p. (gr. 3-6). 1991. Repr. of 1988 ed. 7.95x (*1-56162-037-8*) Wonder Kids.

—Chinese Children's Stories, Vol. 38: The Peace Drum, Comb. Ching, Emily, et al, eds. Wonder Kids Publications Staff, tr. from CHI. Hwa-I Publishing Co., Staff, illus. LC 90-60799. 28p. (gr. 3-6). 1991. Repr. of 1988 ed. 7.95x (*1-56162-038-6*) Wonder Kids.

—Chinese Children's Stories, Vol. 39: Brush Pen, Duan's Ink-Slab. Ching, Emily, et al, eds. Wonder Kids Publications Staff, tr. from CHI. Hwa-I Publishing Co., Staff, illus. LC 90-6079. 28p. (gr. 3-6). 1991. Repr. of 1988 ed. 7.95x (*1-56162-039-4*) Wonder Kids.

—Chinese Children's Stories, Vol. 40: The Ink-Stick, Shiuan Paper. Ching, Emily, et al, eds. Wonder Kids Publications Staff, tr. from CHI. Hwa-I Publishing Co., Staff, illus. LC 90-60799. 28p. (gr. 3-6). 1991. Repr. of 1988 ed. 7.95x (*1-56162-040-8*) Wonder Kids.

—Chinese Children's Stories, Vol. 42: Tiger Seeks a Master, Why Are Cats Afraid of Dogs? Ching, Emily, et al, eds. Wonder Kids Publications Staff, tr. from CHI. Hwa-I Publishing Co., Staff, illus. LC 90-60800. 28p. (gr. 3-6). 1991. Repr. of 1988 ed. 7.95x (*1-56162-042-4*) Wonder Kids.

—Chinese Children's Stories, Vol. 43: The Bunny's Tail, Fox, Monkey, Rabbit & Horse. Ching, Emily, et al, eds. Wonder Kids Publications Staff, tr. from CHI. Hwa-I Publishing Co., Staff, illus. LC 90-60800. 28p. (gr. 3-6). 1991. Repr. of 1988 ed. 7.95x (*1-56162-043-2*) Wonder Kids.

—Chinese Children's Stories, Vol. 44: Snake's Lost Drum, Ox & Buffalo Change Clothes. Ching, Emily, et al, eds. Wonder Kids Publications Staff, tr. from CHI. Hwa-I Publishing Co., Staff, illus. LC 90-60800. 28p. (gr. 3-6). 1991. Repr. of 1988 ed. 7.95x (*1-56162-044-0*) Wonder Kids.

—Chinese Children's Stories, Vol. 45: The Goat & the Camel, The Wolf & the Pig. Ching, Emily, et al, eds. Wonder Kids Publications Staff, tr. from CHI. Hwa-I Publishing Co., Staff, illus. LC 90-60800. 28p. (gr. 3-6). 1991. Repr. of 1988 ed. 7.95x (*1-56162-045-9*) Wonder Kids.

—Chinese Children's Stories, Vol. 47: The Crane-Riding Immortal, Lyu Dungbin & Guanyin. Ching, Emily, et al, eds. Wonder Kids Publications Staff, tr. from CHI. Hwa-I Publishing Co., Staff, illus. LC 90-60801. 28p. (gr. 3-6). 1991. Repr. of 1988 ed. 7.95x (*1-56162-047-5*) Wonder Kids.

—Chinese Children's Stories, Vol. 48: Sir Thunder & Lady Lightning, The Door Guards. Ching, Emily, et al, eds. Wonder Kids Publications Staff, tr. from CHI. Hwa-I Publishing Co., Staff, illus. LC 90-60801. 28p. (gr. 3-6). 1991. Repr. of 1988 ed. 7.95x (*1-56162-048-3*) Wonder Kids.

—Chinese Children's Stories, Vol. 49: The Slippery Nose Deity, Under the Moonlight. Ching, Emily, et al, eds. Wonder Kids Publications Staff, tr. from CHI. Hwa-I Publishing Co., Staff, illus. LC 90-60801. 28p. (gr. 3-6). 1991. Repr. of 1988 ed. 7.95x (*1-56162-049-1*) Wonder Kids.

—Chinese Children's Stories, Vol. 50: Zung Kuei & the Little Ghost, Earth God & Earth Goddess. Ching, Emily, et al, eds. Wonder Kids Publications Staff, tr. from CHI. Hwa-I Publishing Co., Staff, illus. LC 90-60801. 28p. (gr. 3-6). 1991. Repr. of 1988 ed. 7.95x (*1-56162-050-5*) Wonder Kids.

—Chinese Children's Stories, Vol. 52: Joining the Army, Beating up the Tiger. Ching, Emily, et al, eds. Wonder Kids Publications Staff, tr. from CHI. Hwa-I Publishing Co., Staff, illus. LC 90-60802. 28p. (gr. 3-6). 1991. Repr. of 1988 ed. 7.95x (*1-56162-052-1*) Wonder Kids.

—Chinese Children's Stories, Vol. 53: Meeting an Angel, The Child in the Deer Skin. Ching, Emily, et al, eds. Wonder Kids Publications Staff, tr. from CHI. Hwa-I Publishing Co., Staff, illus. LC 90-60802. 28p. (gr. 3-6). 1991. Repr. of 1988 ed. 7.95x (*1-56162-053-X*) Wonder Kids.

—Chinese Children's Stories, Vol. 54: The Story of Shun, Village of Filial Piety. Ching, Emily, et al, eds. Wonder Kids Publications Staff, tr. from CHI. Hwa-I Publishing Co., Staff, illus. LC 90-60802. 28p. (gr. 3-6). 1991. Repr. of 1988 ed. 7.95x (*1-56162-054-8*) Wonder Kids.

—Chinese Children's Stories, Vol. 55: Two Baskets of Mulberries, Trun's Little Daughter. Ching, Emily, et al, eds. Wonder Kids Publications Staff, tr. from CHI. Hwa-I Publishing Co., Staff, illus. LC 90-60802. 28p. (gr. 3-6). 1991. Repr. of 1988 ed. 7.95x (*1-56162-055-6*) Wonder Kids.

—Chinese Children's Stories, Vol. 57: The Little-Boy God, A Rooster's Egg. Ching, Emily, et al, eds. Wonder Kids Publications Staff, tr. from CHI. Hwa-I Publishing Co., Staff, illus. LC 90-60803. 28p. (gr. 3-6). 1991. Repr. of 1988 ed. 7.95x (*1-56162-057-2*) Wonder Kids.

—Chinese Children's Stories, Vol. 58: Three Princes & the Firewood, Wang's Memory. Ching, Emily, et al, eds. Wonder Kids Publications Staff, tr. from CHI. Hwa-I Publishing Co., Staff, illus. LC 90-60803. 28p. (gr. 3-6). 1991. Repr. of 1988 ed. 7.95x (*1-56162-058-0*) Wonder Kids.

—Chinese Children's Stories, Vol. 59: A Tankful of Water, The Little Hero. Ching, Emily, et al, eds. Wonder Kids Publications Staff, tr. from CHI. Hwa-I Publishing Co., Staff, illus. LC 90-60803. 28p. (gr. 3-6). 1991. Repr. of 1988 ed. 7.95x (*1-56162-059-9*) Wonder Kids.

—Chinese Children's Stories, Vol. 60: Weighing an Elephant, The Distant Homeland. Ching, Emily, et al, eds. Wonder Kids Publications Staff, tr. from CHI. Hwa-I Publishing Co., Staff, illus. LC 90-60803. 28p. (gr. 3-6). 1991. Repr. of 1988 ed. 7.95x (*1-56162-060-2*) Wonder Kids.

—Chinese Children's Stories, Vol. 62: To Catch the Suns, Two Quarrelsome Brothers. Ching, Emily, et al, eds. Wonder Kids Publications Staff, tr. from CHI. Hwa-I Publishing Co., Staff, illus. LC 90-60804. 28p. (gr. 3-6). 1991. Repr. of 1988 ed. 7.95x (*1-56162-062-9*) Wonder Kids.

—Chinese Children's Stories, Vol. 63: To Speak or Not, The Dark Village. Ching, Emily, et al, eds. Wonder Kids Publications Staff, tr. from CHI. Hwa-I Publishing Co., Staff, illus. LC 90-60804. 28p. (gr. 3-6). 1991. Repr. of 1988 ed. 7.95x (*1-56162-063-7*) Wonder Kids.

—Chinese Children's Stories, Vol. 64: Why Is the Sky So High?, Turning into Stone. Ching, Emily, et al, eds. Wonder Kids Publications Staff, tr. from CHI. Hwa-I Publishing Co., Staff, illus. LC 90-60804. 28p. (gr. 3-6). 1991. Repr. of 1988 ed. 7.95x (*1-56162-064-5*) Wonder Kids.

—Chinese Children's Stories, Vol. 65: Lugging Mountains, What's a Life Span? Ching, Emily, et al, eds. Wonder Kids Publications Staff, tr. from CHI. Hwa-I Publishing Co., Staff, illus. LC 90-60804. 28p. (gr. 3-6). 1991. Repr. of 1988 ed. 7.95x (*1-56162-065-3*) Wonder Kids.

—Chinese Children's Stories, Vol. 67: The After-Meal Bell, Passing the Three Gorges. Ching, Emily, et al, eds. Wonder Kids Publications Staff, tr. from CHI. Hwa-I Publishing Co., Staff, illus. LC 90-60805. 28p. (gr. 3-6). 1991. Repr. of 1988 ed. 7.95x (*1-56162-067-X*) Wonder Kids.

—Chinese Children's Stories, Vol. 68: The Donkey-Riding Poet, The Backyard Song. Ching, Emily, et al, eds. Wonder Kids Publications Staff, tr. from CHI. Hwa-I Publishing Co., Staff, illus. LC 90-60805. 28p. (gr. 3-6). 1991. Repr. of 1988 ed. 7.95x (*1-56162-068-8*) Wonder Kids.

—Chinese Children's Stories, Vol. 69: The Young Family, Tsuei's Beautiful Bride. Ching, Emily, et al, eds. Wonder Kids Publications Staff, tr. from CHI. Hwa-I Publishing Co., Staff, illus. LC 90-60805. 28p. (gr. 3-6). 1991. Repr. of 1988 ed. 7.95x (*1-56162-069-6*) Wonder Kids.

—Chinese Children's Stories, Vol. 7: Dragon Eye & Cassia Circle, The Conceited Barber. Ching, Emily, et al, eds. Wonder Kids Publications Staff, tr. from CHI. Hwa-I Publishing Co., Staff, illus. LC 90-60792. 28p. (gr. 3-6). 1991. Repr. of 1988 ed. 7.95x (*1-56162-007-6*) Wonder Kids.

—Chinese Children's Stories, Vol. 70: Ji's Jokes, The Scrooge. Ching, Emily, et al, eds. Wonder Kids Publications Staff, tr. from CHI. Hwa-I Publishing Co., Staff, illus. LC 90-60805. 28p. (gr. 3-6). 1991. Repr. of 1988 ed. 7.95x (*1-56162-070-X*) Wonder Kids.

—Chinese Children's Stories, Vol. 72: The Lotus Child, The Ghost in the Basin. Ching, Emily, et al, eds. Wonder Kids Publications Staff, tr. from CHI. Hwa-I Publishing Co., Staff, illus. LC 90-60806. 28p. (gr. 3-6). 1991. Repr. of 1988 ed. 7.95x (*1-56162-072-6*) Wonder Kids.

—Chinese Children's Stories, Vol. 73: Walking through Walls, Who Is the Real Lord Ji? Ching, Emily, et al, eds. Wonder Kids Publications Staff, tr. from CHI. Hwa-I Publishing Co., Staff, illus. LC 90-60806. 28p. (gr. 3-6). 1991. Repr. of 1988 ed. 7.95x (*1-56162-073-4*) Wonder Kids.

—Chinese Children's Stories, Vol. 74: Chaos in the Heavenly Palace, Eating the Ginseng Fruit. Ching, Emily, et al, eds. Wonder Kids Publications Staff, tr. from CHI. Hwa-I Publishing Co., Staff, illus. LC 90-60806. 28p. (gr. 3-6). 1991. Repr. of 1988 ed. 7.95x (*1-56162-074-2*) Wonder Kids.

—Chinese Children's Stories, Vol. 75: Tang's Strange Journey, Dwarfs & Giants. Ching, Emily, et al, eds. Wonder Kids Publications Staff, tr. from CHI. Hwa-I Publishing Co., Staff, illus. LC 90-60806. 28p. (gr. 3-6). 1991. Repr. of 1988 ed. 7.95x (*1-56162-075-0*) Wonder Kids.

—Chinese Children's Stories, Vol. 77: Sir Guan's Big Red Face, Turning Cranes into Words. Ching, Emily, et al, eds. Wonder Kids Publications Staff, tr. from CHI. Hwa-I Publishing Co., Staff, illus. LC 90-60807. 28p. (gr. 3-6). 1991. Repr. of 1988 ed. 7.95x (*1-56162-077-7*) Wonder Kids.

—Chinese Children's Stories, Vol. 78: Tang Buohu's Drawings, The General & the Water Tank. Ching, Emily, et al, eds. Wonder Kids Publications Staff, tr. from CHI. Hwa-I Publishing Co., Staff, illus. LC 90-60807. 28p. (gr. 3-6). 1991. Repr. of 1988 ed. 7.95x (*1-56162-078-5*) Wonder Kids.

—Chinese Children's Stories, Vol. 79: Black-Faced Sir Bao, Doctor Hwa-Tuo. Ching, Emily, et al, eds. Wonder Kids Publications Staff, tr. from CHI. Hwa-I Publishing Co., Staff, illus. LC 90-60807. 28p. (gr. 3-6). 1991. Repr. of 1988 ed. 7.95x (*1-56162-079-3*) Wonder Kids.

—Chinese Children's Stories, Vol. 8: The Millets Won't Go Home, The Immortal Palm. Ching, Emily, et al, eds. Wonder Kids Publications Staff, tr. from CHI. Hwa-I Publishing Co., Staff, illus. LC 90-60792. 28p. (gr. 3-6). 1991. Repr. of 1988 ed. 7.95x (*1-56162-008-4*) Wonder Kids.

—Chinese Children's Stories, Vol. 80: The Dwarf Minister, The Fabulous Chimera's Gift. Ching, Emily, et al, eds. Wonder Kids Publications Staff, tr. from CHI. Hwa-I Publishing Co., Staff, illus. LC 90-60807. 28p. (gr. 3-6). 1991. Repr. of 1988 ed. 7.95x (*1-56162-080-7*) Wonder Kids.

—Chinese Children's Stories, Vol. 82: The Fish Minister, The Hidden Sword. Ching, Emily, et al, eds. Wonder Kids Publications Staff, tr. from CHI. Hwa-I Publishing Co., Staff, illus. LC 90-60808. 28p. (gr. 3-6). 1991. Repr. of 1988 ed. 7.95x (*1-56162-082-3*) Wonder Kids.

—Chinese Children's Stories, Vol. 83: The Revenge of Chao's Orphan, Tien's Wonderful Strategies. Ching, Emily, et al, eds. Wonder Kids Publications Staff, tr. from CHI. Hwa-I Publishing Co., Staff, illus. LC 90-60808. 28p. (gr. 3-6). 1991. Repr. of 1988 ed. 7.95x (*1-56162-083-1*) Wonder Kids.

—Chinese Children's Stories, Vol. 84: Who Is the Real Liu Bong?, Kong Borrows the East Wind. Ching, Emily, et al, eds. Wonder Kids Publications Staff, tr. from CHI. Hwa-I Publishing Co., Staff, illus. LC 90-60808. 28p. (gr. 3-6). 1991. Repr. of 1988 ed. 7.95x (*1-56162-084-X*) Wonder Kids.

—Chinese Children's Stories, Vol. 85: The Battle of the Fei River, The Princess' Engagement. Ching, Emily, et al, eds. Wonder Kids Publications Staff, tr. from CHI. Hwa-I Publishing Co., Staff, illus. LC 90-60808. 28p. (gr. 3-6). 1991. Repr. of 1988 ed. 7.95x (*1-56162-085-8*) Wonder Kids.

—Chinese Children's Stories, Vol. 86: From Crows into Bricks, Two Treasured Swords. Ching, Emily, et al, eds. Wonder Kids Publications Staff, tr. from CHI. (Illus.). 28p. (gr. 3-6). 1991. Repr. of 1988 ed. 7.95 (*1-56162-086-6*) Wonder Kids.

—Chinese Children's Stories, Vol. 87: Fan Bridge & Escape Alley, The Stream of Flowers. Ching, Emily, et al, eds. Wonder Kids Publications Staff, tr. from CHI. Hwa-I Publishing Co., Staff, illus. LC 90-60809. 28p. (gr. 3-6). 1991. Repr. of 1988 ed. 7.95x (*1-56162-087-4*) Wonder Kids.

—Chinese Children's Stories, Vol. 88: Five Stone Goats, Six-Foot Street. Ching, Emily, et al, eds. Wonder Kids Publications Staff, tr. from CHI. Hwa-I Publishing Co., Staff, illus. LC 90-60809. 28p. (gr. 3-6). 1991. Repr. of 1988 ed. 7.95x (*1-56162-088-2*) Wonder Kids.

—Chinese Children's Stories, Vol. 89: Peach Blossom Cave, Mt. Lee. Ching, Emily, et al, eds. Wonder Kids Publications Staff, tr. from CHI. Hwa-I Publishing Co., Staff, illus. LC 90-60809. 28p. (gr. 3-6). 1991. Repr. of 1988 ed. 7.95x (*1-56162-089-0*) Wonder Kids.

—Chinese Children's Stories, Vol. 9: The Story of Rice, The Cows & the Trumpet. Ching, Emily, et al, eds. Wonder Kids Publications Staff, tr. from CHI. Hwa-I Publishing Co., Staff, illus. LC 90-60792. 28p. (gr. 3-6). 1991. Repr. of 1988 ed. 7.95x (*1-56162-009-2*) Wonder Kids.

—Chinese Children's Stories, Vol. 90: The Dragon Who Puts out Fires, The Golden Hairpin Well. Ching, Emily, et al, eds. Wonder Kids Publications Staff, tr. from CHI. Hwa-I Publishing Co., Staff, illus. LC 90-60809. 28p. (gr. 3-6). 1991. Repr. of 1988 ed. 7.95x (*1-56162-090-4*) Wonder Kids.

—Chinese Children's Stories, Vol. 92: White-Rice Magic Cave, Sun-Moon Lake. Ching, Emily, et al, eds. Wonder Kids Publications Staff, tr. from CHI. Hwa-I Publishing Co., Staff, illus. LC 90-60810. 28p. (gr. 3-6). 1991. Repr. of 1988 ed. 7.95x (*1-56162-092-0*) Wonder Kids.

—Chinese Children's Stories, Vol. 93: Mt. Anvil & the Sword Well, Two Waters. Ching, Emily, et al, eds. Wonder Kids Publications Staff, tr. from CHI. Hwa-I Publishing Co., Staff, illus. LC 90-60810. 28p. (gr. 3-6). 1991. Repr. of 1988 ed. 7.95x (*1-56162-093-9*) Wonder Kids.

—Chinese Children's Stories, Vol. 94: Muddy Water Stream, Sister Lakes & Brother Trees. Ching, Emily, et al, eds. Wonder Kids Publications Staff, tr. from CHI. Hwa-I Publishing Co., Staff, illus. LC 90-60810. 28p. (gr. 3-6). 1991. Repr. of 1988 ed. 7.95x (*1-56162-094-7*) Wonder Kids.

—Chinese Children's Stories, Vol. 95: Half-Shield Mountain, The Adopted Daughter Lake. Ching, Emily, et al, eds. Wonder Kids Publications Staff, tr. from CHI. Hwa-I Publishing Co., Staff, illus. LC 90-60810. 28p. (gr. 3-6). 1991. Repr. of 1988 ed. 7.95x (*1-56162-095-5*) Wonder Kids.

—Chinese Children's Stories, Vol. 97: Tiger Aunty, Ah-Long & Ah-Hwa. Ching, Emily, et al, eds. Wonder Kids Publications Staff, tr. from CHI. Hwa-I Publishing Co., Staff, illus. LC 90-60811. 28p. (gr. 3-6). 1991. Repr. of 1988 ed. 7.95x (*1-56162-097-1*) Wonder Kids.

—Chinese Children's Stories, Vol. 98: Ai-Yu Jello, Granny & the Fox. Ching, Emily, et al, eds. Wonder Kids Publications Staff, tr. from CHI. Hwa-I Publishing Co., Staff, illus. LC 90-60811. 28p. (gr. 3-6). 1991. Repr. of 1988 ed. 7.95x (*1-56162-098-X*) Wonder Kids.

—Chinese Children's Stories, Vol. 99: The Underground People, Half-Street Lai. Ching, Emily, et al, eds. Wonder Kids Publications Staff, tr. from CHI. Hwa-I Publishing Co., Staff, illus. LC 90-60811. 28p. (gr. 3-6). 1991. Repr. of 1988 ed. 7.95x (*1-56162-099-8*) Wonder Kids.

Jackson, Dave. Shanghaied to China. (gr. 4-7). 1993. pap. 4.99 (*1-55661-271-0*) Bethany Hse.

Jaynes, Ruth. Yo-Ho & Kim. 58p. (gr. 1-6). 1965. 2.50 (*0-89986-386-8*) Oriental Bk Store.

—Yo-Ho & Kim at Sea. 58p. (gr. 1-6). 1965. 2.50 (*0-89986-387-6*) Oriental Bk Store.

Kendall, Carol. Sweet & Sour: Tales from China. (gr. 4-7). 1990. pap. 5.70 (*0-395-54798-9*, Clarion Bks) HM.

Lattimore, Deborah N. The Dragon's Robe. Lattimore, Deborah N., illus. LC 89-34512. 32p. (gr. 1-5). 1990. 15.00 (*0-06-023719-8*); PLB 14.89 (*0-06-023723-6*) HarpC Child Bks.

Lattimore, Eleanor F. Little Pear. Lattimore, Eleanor F., illus. LC 31-22069. (gr. 2-5). 1968. pap. 3.95 (*0-15-652799-5*, Voyager Bks) HarBrace.

—Little Pear. D'Andrade, Diane, ed. (Illus.). 106p. (Orig.). (gr. 2-5). 1991. pap. 4.95 (*0-15-246685-1*, HB Juv Bks) HarBrace.

—Little Pear & His Friends. (Illus.). 129p. (Orig.). (gr. 2-5). 1991. pap. 4.95 (*0-15-246863-3*, HB Juv Bks) HarBrace.

Lawson, Julie. The Dragon's Pearl. Morin, Paul, illus. 32p. (gr. k-3). 1993. 15.45 (*0-395-63623-X*, Clarion Bks) HM.

Lewis, Elizabeth F. Young Fu of the Upper Yangtze. (gr. k-6). 1990. pap. 3.99 (*0-440-49043-X*, YB) Dell.

Lim, Genny. Wings for Lai Ho. Lew, Gordon, tr. Ja, Andrea, illus. 48p. (Orig.). (gr. 5-8). 1982. pap. 5.95 (*0-934788-01-4*) E-W Pub Co.

Lobel, Arnold. Ming Lo Moves the Mountain. (ps-3). 1986. pap. 3.95 (*0-590-42902-7*) Scholastic Inc.

—Ming Lo Moves the Mountain. LC 92-47364. (Illus.). 32p. (ps up). 1993. pap. text ed. 4.95 (*0-688-10995-0*, Mulberry) Morrow.

—Ming Lo Moves the Mountain. Lobel, Arnold, illus. (gr. k-4). 1993. 14.95 (*0-685-64815-X*); audio cass. 11.00 (*1-882869-76-1*) Read Advent.

McCay, William. Young Indiana Jones & the Face of the Dragon. 132p. (gr. 3-7). 1994. pap. 3.50 (*0-679-85092-9*) Random Bks Yng Read.

Mahy, Margaret. Seven Chinese Brothers. Tseng, Jean & Mou-sien Tseng, illus. (ps-3). 1990. pap. 13.95 (*0-590-42055-0*) Scholastic Inc.

Neville, Emily C. The China Year. LC 90-39899. 256p. (gr. 5-9). 1991. PLB 15.89 (*0-06-024384-8*) HarpC Child Bks.

Paterson, Katherine. Rebels of the Heavenly Kingdom. LC 83-1529. 224p. (gr. 12 up). 1983. 11.95 (*0-525-66911-6*, Lodestar Bks) Dutton Child Bks.

Pittman, Helena C. A Grain of Rice. LC 84-4670. (Illus.). (gr. k-4). 1986. lib. bdg. 12.95 (*0-8038-9289-6*) Hastings.

Pyne, K. D. All the Way to China. Whitten, Jessie, illus. 16p. (ps). 1993. saddle-stitch 4.95 (*1-882185-06-4*) Crnrstone Pub.

Scott, Mavis. Little Ho & the Golden Kites. Reynolds, Pat, illus. 32p. (Orig.). (gr. k-2). 1993. pap. 6.95 (*0-04-442242-3*, Pub. by Allen & Unwin Aust Pty AT) IPG Chicago.

Singer, Marilyn. The Painted Fan. Ma, Wenhai, illus. LC 92-29796. 40p. 1994. 15.00g (*0-688-11742-2*); lib. bdg. 14.93 (*0-688-11743-0*) Morrow Jr Bks.

Tan, Amy. The Chinese Siamese Cat. Schields, Gretchen, illus. LC 93-24008. (gr. k-3). 1994. 16.95 (*0-02-788835-5*, Macmillan Child Bk) Macmillan Child Grp.

—The Moon Lady. Schields, Gretchen, illus. LC 91-22321. 32p. (gr. 1 up). 1992. RSBE 16.95 (*0-02-788830-4*, Macmillan Child Bk) Macmillan Child Grp.

Tseng, Grace. The Brocade. Tseng, Jean & Tseng, Mou-sien, illus. LC 94-9757. 1994. write for info. (*0-688-12515-8*); lib. bdg. write for info. (*0-688-12516-6*) Lothrop.

Va, Leong. A Letter to the King. Anderson, James, tr. from CHI. Va, Leong, illus. LC 91-9469. 32p. (gr. k-3). 1991. 14.95 (*0-06-020079-0*); PLB 14.89 (*0-06-020070-7*) HarpC Child Bks.

Vander Els, Betty. Leaving Point. LC 87-23710. 176p. (gr. 7-12). 1987. 15.00 (*0-374-34376-4*) FS&G.

Vollbracht, James. The Way of the Circle. Foleen, Chris, illus. LC 92-45871. 48p. (gr. 4-8). 1993. pap. 6.95 (*0-915166-76-3*) Impact Pubs Cal.

Wolff, Ferida. The Emperor's Garden. Osborn, Kathy, illus. LC 93-14751. 1994. 15.00 (*0-688-11651-5*, Tambourine Bks); PLB 14.93 (*0-688-11652-3*) Morrow.

Wolkstein, Diane. White Wave: A Chinese Tale. Young, Ed, illus. LC 78-4781. (gr. 2 up). 1979. (Crowell Jr Bks) HarpC Child Bks.

Wonder Kids Publications Group Staff (USA) & Hwa-I Publishing Co., Staff. Animal Tales: Chinese Children's Stories, Vols. 11-15. Ching, Emily, et al, eds. Wonder Kids Publication Staff, tr. from CHI. Hwa-I Publishing Co., Staff, illus. LC 90-60793. 28p. (gr. 3-6). 1991. Repr. of 1988 ed. Five vol. set, 28p. ea. bk. 39.75 (*0-685-58702-9*) Wonder Kids.

—Chinese Sites: Chinese Children's Stories, Vols. 86-90. Ching, Emily, et al, eds. Wonder Kids Publications Staff, tr. from CHI. Hwa-I Publishing Co., Staff, illus. LC 90-60809. (gr. 3-6). 1991. Repr. of 1988 ed. Five vol. set, 28p. ea. bk. 39.75 (*0-685-58717-7*) Wonder Kids.

—Festivals: Chinese Children's Stories, Vols. 26-30. Ching, Emily, et al, eds. Wonder Kids Publications Staff, tr. from CHI. Hwa-I Publishing Co., Staff, illus. LC 90-60797. (gr. 3-6). 1991. Repr. of 1988 ed. Five vol. set, 28p. ea. bk. 39.75 (*0-685-58705-3*) Wonder Kids.

—Filial Piety: Chinese Children's Stories, Vols. 51-55. Ching, Emily, et al, eds. Wonder Kids Publications Staff, tr. from CHI. Hwa-I Publishing Co., Staff, illus. LC 90-60802. (gr. 3-6). 1991. Repr. of 1988 ed. Five vol. set, 28p. ea. bk. 39.75 (*0-685-58710-X*) Wonder Kids.

—Folklore: Chinese Children's Stories, Vols. 1-5. Ching, Emily, et al, eds. Wonder Kids Publications Staff, tr. from CHI. Hwa-I Publishing Co., Staff, illus. LC 90-60791. 28p. (gr. 3-6). 1991. Repr. of 1988 ed. Five vol. set, 28p. ea. bk. 39.75 (*0-685-58701-0*); Set (100 vols.) 795.00 (*1-56162-120-X*) Wonder Kids.

—Heroes: Chinese Children's Stories, Vols. 76-80. Ching, Emily, et al, eds. Wonder Kids Publications Staff, tr. from CHI. Hwa-I Publishing Co., Staff, illus. LC 90-60807. (gr. 3-6). 1991. Repr. of 1988 ed. Five vol. set, 28p. ea. bk. 39.75 (*0-685-58715-0*) Wonder Kids.

—Historical Accounts: Chinese Children's Stories, Vols. 81-85. Ching, Emily, et al, eds. Wonder Kids Publications Staff, tr. from CHI. Hwa-I Publishing Co., Staff, illus. LC 90-60808. (gr. 3-6). 1991. Repr. of 1988 ed. Five vol. set, 28p. ea. bk. 39.75 (*0-685-58716-9*) Wonder Kids.

—Idioms: Chinese Children's Stories, Vols. 21-25. Ching, Emily, et al, eds. Wonder Kids Publications Staff, tr. from CHI. Hwa-I Publishing Co., Staff, illus. LC 90-60796. (gr. 3-6). 1991. Repr. of 1988 ed. Five vol. set, 28p. ea. bk. 39.75 (*0-685-58704-5*) Wonder Kids.

—Literature: Chinese Children's Stories, Vols. 66-70. Ching, Emily, et al, eds. Wonder Kids Publications Staff, tr. from CHI. Hwa-I Publishing Co., Staff, illus. LC 90-60805. (gr. 3-6). 1991. Repr. of 1988 ed. Five vol. set, 28p. ea. bk. 39.75 (*0-685-58713-4*) Wonder Kids.

—Popular Narratives: Chinese Children's Stories, Vols. 71-75. Ching, Emily, et al, eds. Wonder Kids Publications Staff, tr. from CHI. Hwa-I Publishing Co., Staff, illus. LC 90-60806. (gr. 3-6). 1991. Repr. of 1988 ed. Five vol. set, 28p. ea. bk. 39.75 (*0-685-58714-2*) Wonder Kids.

—Taiwanese Sites: Chinese Children's Stories, Vols. 91-95. Ching, Emily, et al, eds. Wonder Kids Publications Staff, tr. from CHI. Hwa-I Publishing Co., Staff, illus. LC 90-60810. (gr. 3-6). 1991. Repr. of 1988 ed. Five vol. set, 28p. ea. bk. 39.75 (*0-685-58718-5*) Wonder Kids.

—Twelve Beasts & the Years: Chinese Children's Stories, Vols. 41-45. Ching, Emily, et al, eds. Wonder Kids Publications Staff, tr. from CHI. Hwa-I Publishing Co., Staff, illus. LC 90-60800. (gr. 3-6). 1991. Repr. of 1988 ed. Five vol. set, 28p. ea. bk. 39.75 (*0-685-58708-8*) Wonder Kids.

—Wonder Kids: Chinese Children's Stories, Vols. 56-60. Ching, Emily, et al, eds. Wonder Kids Publications Staff, tr. from CHI. Hwa-I Publishing Co., Staff, illus. LC 90-60803. (gr. 3-6). 1991. Repr. of 1988 ed. Five vol. set, 28p. ea. bk. 39.75 (*0-685-58711-8*) Wonder Kids.

Yep, Laurence. The Junior Thunder Lord. Van Nutt, Robert, illus. LC 93-33805. 32p. (gr. k-3). 1994. PLB 15.95 (*0-8167-3454-2*); pap. text ed. 4.95 (*0-8167-3455-0*) BrdgeWater.

CHINA–FOREIGN RELATIONS

Lawson, Don. The Eagle & the Dragon: The History of U.S.-China Relations. LC 85-47531. (Illus.). 192p. (gr. 7 up). 1985. (Crowell Jr Bks); (Crowell Jr Bks) HarpC Child Bks.

CHINA–HISTORY

Burland, Cottie A. Ancient China. Puulton, Yvonne, illus. (gr. 4-8). 1974. Repr. of 1960 ed. 10.95 (*0-7175-0018-7*) Dufour.

Carter, Alden R. China Past - China Future. LC 93-13537. 1994. 13.90 (*0-531-11161-X*) Watts.

Cotterell, Arthur. Ancient China. Brightling, Geoff & Hills, Alan, photos by. (Illus.). 64p. (gr. 5 up). 1994. PLB 17.99 (*0-679-96167-4*); 16.00 (*0-679-86167-X*) Knopf Bks Yng Read.

Foster, Leila M. Nien Cheng: Courage in China. LC 92-9333. (Illus.). 152p. (gr. 4 up). 1992. PLB 14.40 (*0-516-03279-8*); pap. 5.95 (*0-516-43279-6*) Childrens.

Goff, Denise. Early China. (Illus.). 32p. (gr. 4-6). 1991. 13.95 (*0-237-60169-9*, Pub. by Evans Bros Ltd) Trafalgar.

Hwa-I Publishing Co., Staff. Chinese Children's Stories, Vol. 81: The Emperor vs. the Rebel, The Queen & the Fire. Ching, Emily, et al, eds. Wonder Kids Publications Staff, tr. from CHI. (Illus.). 28p. (gr. 3-6). 1991. Repr. of 1988 ed. 7.95 (*1-56162-081-5*) Wonder Kids.

McLean, Virginia O. Chasing the Moon to China. Cheairs, Nancy & Robinson, Susan, illus. Mitler, Ellen, et al, photos by. LC 87-60411. 40p. (gr. k-6). 1987. PLB 15.95 incl. record (*0-9606046-1-8*) Redbird.

McLenighan, Valjean. China: A History to Nineteen Forty-Nine. LC 83-14260. (Illus.). 128p. (gr. 5-9). 1983. PLB 20.55 (*0-516-02754-9*) Childrens.

Major, John S. The Silk Route. Fieser, Stephen, illus. LC 92-38169. 1994. 15.00 (*0-06-022924-1*); PLB 14.89 (*0-06-022926-8*) HarpC.

Marrin, Albert. Mao Tse-Tung & His China. LC 93-3799. 288p. (gr. 7 up). 1993. pap. 5.99 (*0-14-036478-1*, Puffin) Puffin Bks.

Nicholson, Robert & Watts, Claire. La Antigua China: Hechos, Historias, Actividades. Araluce, Jose R., tr. (SPA., Illus.). 32p. (gr. 6-10). 1993. 14.95x (*1-56492-093-3*) Laredo.

Pischel, Enrica C. China from the 7th to 19th Century. Berselli, Remo & Bacchin, Giorgio, illus. LC 93-40124. 1994. PLB 25.67 (*0-8114-3329-3*) Raintree Steck-V.

Ross, Frank, Jr. Oracles Bones, Stars & the Wheelbarrows: Ancient Chinese Science & Technology. 1990. pap. 4.80 (*0-395-54967-1*) HM.

Teague, Ken. Growing up in Ancient China. Hook, Richard, illus. LC 91-14879. 32p. (gr. 3-5). 1993. PLB 11.89 (*0-8167-2715-5*); pap. text ed. 3.95 (*0-8167-2716-3*) Troll Assocs.

Terzi, Marinella. The Chinese Empire. LC 92-7509. 36p. (gr. 3 up). 1993. pap. 6.95 (*0-516-48377-3*) Childrens.

Waterlow, Julia. The Ancient Chinese. LC 93-42771. (Illus.). 32p. (gr. 4-6). 1994. 14.95 (*1-56847-169-6*) Thomson Lrning.

CHINA (PEOPLE'S REPUBLIC OF CHINA)

Abell. Drawing an Interest on the Bank on China. (Illus.). 50p. (Orig.). (gr. 5 up). 1993. PLB 25.00 (*1-56611-083-1*); pap. 15.00 (*1-56611-085-8*) Jonas.

Busuttil, Joelle. Behind the Wall of China. Quentin, Laurence, illus. 40p. (gr. k-5). 1993. PLB 9.95 (*1-56674-057-6*, HTS Bks) Forest Hse.

Jacobsen, Karen. China. LC 90-2200. (Illus.). 48p. (gr. k-4). 1990. PLB 12.85 (*0-516-01102-2*); pap. 4.95 (*0-516-41102-0*) Childrens.

Major, John S. The Land & People of China. LC 88-23427. (Illus.). 288p. (gr. 6 up). 1989. (Lipp Jr Bks); PLB 18.89 (*0-397-32337-9*, Lipp Jr Bks) HarpC Child Bks.

Thomas, Graham. Timeline: People's Republic of China. (Illus.). 72p. (gr. 7 up). 1990. 19.95 (*0-85219-791-8*, Pub. by Batsford UK) Trafalgar.

CHINA (PEOPLE'S REPUBLIC OF CHINA) –FICTION

McLenighan, Valjean. People's Republic of China. LC 84-7025. (Illus.). 128p. (gr. 5-9). 1984. PLB 20.55 (*0-516-02781-6*) Childrens.

CHINA (PEOPLE'S REPUBLIC OF CHINA) –HISTORY

Finney, Susan & Kindle, Patricia. China: Then & Now. 64p. (gr. 4-8). 1988. wkbk. 8.95 (*0-86653-458-X*, GA1062) Good Apple.

Ross, Stewart. China since Nineteen Forty-Five. LC 87-3500. (Illus.). 64p. (gr. 7-12). 1989. PLB 13.40 (*0-531-18220-7*, Pub. by Bookwright Pr) Watts.

CHINA (PEOPLE'S REPUBLIC OF CHINA) –SOCIAL LIFE AND CUSTOMS

Li Shufen, ed. Legends of Ten Chinese Traditional Festivals. Zhan, Tong, illus. 54p. (gr. 1-3). 1992. pap. 8.95 (*0-8351-2560-2*) China Bks.

McLean, Virginia O. Chasing the Moon to China. Cheairs, Nancy & Robinson, Susan, illus. Mitler, Ellen, et al, photos by. LC 87-60411. 40p. (gr. k-6). 1987. PLB 15.95 incl. record (*0-9606046-1-8*) Redbird.

Rau, Margaret. Young Women in China. LC 88-31045. (Illus.). 160p. (gr. 6 up). 1989. lib. bdg. 18.95 (*0-89490-170-2*) Enslow Pubs.

Sing, Rachel. Chinese New Year's Dragon. (ps-3). 1994. pap. 4.95 (*0-671-88602-9*, Half Moon Bks) S&S Trade.

Stepanchuk, Carol. Red Eggs & Dragon Boats: Celebrating Chinese Festivals. LC 93-85733. 48p. (gr. 3-8). 1993. 16.95 (*1-881896-08-0*) Pacific View Pr.

CHINA (PORCELAIN)

see Porcelain

CHINAWARE

see Porcelain

CULTURAL CHANGE

see Social Change

CHINESE IN SAN FRANCISCO–FICTION

Yep, Laurence. Child of the Owl. LC 76-24314. 224p. (gr. 7 up). 1977. PLB 12.89 (*0-06-026743-7*) HarpC Child Bks.

—Dragonwings. LC 74-2625. 256p. (gr. 7 up). 1975. PLB 14.89 (*0-06-026738-0*) HarpC Child Bks.

—Dragonwings. large type ed. 282p. 1990. Repr. of 1975 ed. lib. bdg. 15.95 (*1-55736-168-1*, Crnrstn Bks) BDD LT Grp.

CHINESE IN THE U. S.

Bandon, Alexandra. Chinese Americans. LC 93-32711. (Illus.). 112p. (gr. 6 up). 1994. text ed. 14.95 RSBE (*0-02-768149-1*, New Discovery Bks) Macmillan Child Grp.

Brownstone, David M. The Chinese-American Heritage. (Illus.). 144p. 1988. 16.95x (*0-8160-1627-5*) Facts on File.

Chin, Steven A. Dragon Parade: A Chinese New Year Story. Tseng, Mou-Sien, illus. LC 92-18079. 32p. (gr. 2-5). 1992. PLB 18.51 (*0-8114-7215-9*) Raintree Steck-V.

Daley, William. Chinese Americans. (gr. 4-7). 1993. pap. 8.95 (*0-7910-0260-8*) Chelsea Hse.

Dell, Pamela. I. M. Pei, Designer of Dreams. LC 92-36903. (Illus.). 32p. (gr. 2-4). 1993. PLB 11.80 (*0-516-04186-X*); pap. 3.95 (*0-516-44186-8*) Childrens.

Fox, Mary V. Bette Bao Lord: Novelist & Chinese Voice for Change. LC 92-36805. (Illus.). 152p. (gr. 4 up). 1993. PLB 14.40 (*0-516-03291-7*); pap. 5.95 (*0-516-43291-5*) Childrens.

Hamilton, Leni. Clara Barton. Horner, Matina, intro. by. (Illus.). 112p. (gr. 5 up). 1988. lib. bdg. 17.95 (*1-55546-641-9*) Chelsea Hse.

Hargrove, Jim. Dr. An Wang: Computer Pioneer. LC 92-35061. (Illus.). 152p. (gr. 4 up). 1993. PLB 14.40 (*0-516-03290-9*); pap. 5.95 (*0-516-43290-7*) Childrens.

Hoobler, Dorothy & Hoobler, Thomas. The Chinese American Family Album. Lord, Betty B., intro. by. (Illus.). 128p. 1994. 19.95 (*0-19-509123-X*); lib. bdg. 22.95 (*0-19-508130-7*) OUP.

Krull, Kathleen. City Within a City: How Kids Live in New York's Chinatown. Hautzig, David, photos by. LC 93-15846. 1994. write for info. (*0-525-67437-3*, Lodestar Bks) Dutton Child Bks.

Lee, Kathleen. American Origins: Tracing Our Chinese Roots. LC 93-35616. (Illus.). 48p. (gr. 4-7). 1994. 12.95 (*1-56261-159-3*) John Muir.

McCunn, Ruthanne L. An Illustrated History of the Chinese in America. LC 79-50114. (Illus.). 136p. (gr. 5 up). 1979. pap. 7.95 (*0-932538-02-9*) Design Ent SF.

MacMillan, Dianne M. Chinese New Year. LC 93-46183. (Illus.). 48p. (gr. 1-4). 1994. lib. bdg. 14.95 (*0-89490-500-7*) Enslow Pubs.

Martinello, Marian & Field, William T., Jr. Who Are the Chinese Texans? Ricks, Thorn, illus. 84p. (Orig.). (gr. 5-8). 8.95 (*0-933164-36-X*); pap. 5.95 (*0-933164-46-7*) U of Tex Inst Tex Culture.

Mayberry, Jodine. Chinese. Daniels, Roger, contrib. by. LC 90-17223. (Illus.). 64p. (gr. 5-8). 1990. PLB 13.40 (*0-531-10977-1*) Watts.

Ng, Franklin. Chinese Amerian Struggle for Equality. LC 92-7472. 1992. 22.60 (*0-86593-181-X*); lib. bdg. 16.95s.p. (*0-685-59290-1*) Rourke Corp.

Sinnott, Susan. Chinese Railroad Workers. LC 94-50. 1994. write for info. (*0-531-20169-4*) Watts.

Wilson. Chinese Americans. 1991. 13.95s.p. (*0-86593-135-6*) Rourke Corp.

Wu, Dana Y. & Tung, Jeffrey D. The Chinese-American Experience. LC 92-15649. (Illus.). 64p. (gr. 4-6). 1993. PLB 15.40 (*1-56294-271-9*) Millbrook Pr.

Yep, Laurence. The Lost Garden. (Illus.). 128p. (gr. 5-7). 1991. 14.98 (*0-685-58838-6*, J Messner); 9.71s.p. (*0-685-47021-0*, J Messner); pap. 12.95 (*0-685-58839-4*, J Messner); pap. 11.24s.p. (*0-685-47022-9*, J Messner) S&S Trade.

—Lost Garden. 1991. 12.95 (*0-671-74160-8*, J Messner); lib. bdg. 14.98 (*0-671-74159-4*) S&S Trade.

CHINESE IN THE U. S.–FICTION

Brown, Tricia. Chinese New Year. Ortiz, Fran, photos by. LC 87-8532. (Illus.). 48p. (ps-2). 1987. 14.95 (*0-8050-0497-1*, Bks Young Read) H Holt & Co.

Chan, Jennifer L. One Small Girl. Lee, Wendy K., illus. LC 92-35423. 32p. (gr. k-2). 1993. 12.95 (*1-879965-05-4*) Polychrome Pub.

Goldin, Barbara D. Red Means Good Fortune: A Story of San Francisco's Chinatown. Ma, Wenhai, illus. 64p. (gr. 2-6). 1994. PLB 12.99 (*0-670-85352-6*) Viking Child Bks.

Joe, Jeanne. Ying-Ying: Pieces of a Childhood. Caigoy, Faustino, illus. 112p. (Orig.). (gr. 4 up). 1982. pap. 4.95 (*0-934788-02-2*) E-W Pub Co.

Krensky, Stephen. The Iron Dragon Never Sleeps. Fulweiler, Frank, illus. LC 93-31167. 1994. 13.95 (*0-385-31171-0*) Delacorte.

Levitin, Sonia. The Golem & the Dragon Girl. LC 92-27665. 176p. (gr. 3-7). 1993. 14.99 (*0-8037-1280-4*); PLB 14.89 (*0-8037-1281-2*) Dial Bks Young.

Namioka, Lensey. April & the Dragon Lady. LC 93-27958. 1994. write for info. (*0-15-276644-8*, Browndeer Pr) HarBrace.
—Yang the Youngest & His Terrible Ear. De Kiefte, Kees, illus. 112p. (gr. 3-7). 1992. 15.95 (*0-316-59701-5*, Joy St Bks) Little.
Nunes, Susan M. The Last Dragon. Soentpiet, Chris K., illus. LC 93-30631. 1996. write for info. (*0-395-67020-9*, Clarion Bks) HM.
Porte, Barbara A. Leave That Cricket Be, Alan Lee. Ruff, Donna, illus. LC 92-29401. 32p. (ps up). 1993. 14.00 (*0-688-11793-7*); PLB 13.93 (*0-688-11794-5*) Greenwillow.
Tedrow, T. L. Land of Promise. LC 92-28222. 1992. 4.99 (*0-8407-7735-3*) Nelson.
Waters, Kate. Lion Dancer: Ernie Wan's Chinese New Year. (ps-3). 1991. pap. 3.95 (*0-590-43047-5*) Scholastic Inc.
Weyn, Suzanne. Chloe Mania! LC 93-42853. (Illus.). 128p. (gr. 4-8). 1994. PLB 9.89 (*0-8167-3233-7*); pap. text ed. 2.95 (*0-8167-3234-5*) Troll Assocs.
Yamate, Sandra S. Char Siu Bao Boy. (Illus.). 32p. (gr. k-4). 1991. 12.95 (*1-879965-00-3*) Polychrome Pub.
Yee, Paul. Roses Sing on New Snow: A Delicious Tale. Chan, Harvey, illus. LC 91-755. 32p. (ps-3). 1992. RSBE 13.95 (*0-02-793622-8*, Macmillan Child Bk) Macmillan Child Grp.
—Tales from Gold Mountain: Stories of the Chinese in the New World. Ng, Simon, illus. LC 89-12643. 64p. (ps up). 1990. RSBE 15.95 (*0-02-793621-X*, Macmillan Child Bk) Macmillan Child Grp.
Yep, Laurence. Child of the Owl. LC 76-24314. 224p. (gr. 7 up). 1990. pap. 3.95 (*0-06-440336-X*, Trophy) HarpC Child Bks.
—Dragon's Gate. LC 92-43649. 288p. (gr. 7 up). 1993. 15.00 (*0-06-022971-3*); PLB 14.89 (*0-06-022972-1*) HarpC Child Bks.
—The Star Fisher. 160p. (gr. 5 up). 1992. pap. 3.99 (*0-14-036003-4*, Puffin) Puffin Bks.

CHINESE LANGUAGE

Chang, Florence C. China Is Farther Than the Sun? A Beginning Chinese-English Reader. LC 80-68256. (Illus.). 51p. (gr. 3-4). 1980. pap. 5.50x incl. wkbk. (*0-936620-00-5*) Ginkgo Hut.
—Maomao & Mimi. Chang, Tao-Yuan, illus. LC 81-80784. 80p. (Orig.). (gr. 5-6). 1981. pap. 4.15x incl. exercises (*0-936620-05-6*) Ginkgo Hut.
—Puppy's Tail. Chang, Tao-Yuan, illus. LC 81-82176. 72p. (Orig.). (gr. 1-2). 1981. pap. 4.15x incl. exercises (*0-936620-06-4*) Ginkgo Hut.
—With Sound & Color: An Intermediate Chinese-English Reader. Chai, Florence, illus. LC 80-68257. 71p. (Orig.). (gr. 7-9). 1980. pap. 6.00x (wkbk. incl.) (*0-936620-01-3*) Ginkgo Hut.
Goldstein, Peggy. Long Is a Dragon: Chinese Writing for Children. LC 90-81148. (Illus.). 32p. (gr. 3-8). 1991. PLB 15.95 (*1-881896-01-3*) Pacific View Pr.
Lee, Huy-Voun. At the Beach. LC 93-25462. (Illus.). 1994. 14.95 (*0-8050-2768-8*) H Holt & Co.
Murray, D. M. & Wong, T. W. Noodle Words: An Introduction to Chinese & Japanese Characters. LC 79-147179. (Illus.). (gr. 9 up). 1971. pap. 6.95 (*0-8048-0948-8*) C E Tuttle.
Sheheen, Dennis, illus. A Child's Picture English-Chinese Dictionary. (gr. k-6). 1987. Repr. 9.95 (*1-55774-001-1*) Modan-Adama Bks.

CHINESE LITERATURE–COLLECTIONS

Ramos, Lindsey. Four Chinese Children's Stories. Troupe, Connie, illus. 1991. 14.95 (*0-9628563-0-4*) Lttle Peop Pr.

CHIPMUNKS–FICTION

Berenstain, Michael. Peat Moss & Ivy's Backyard Adventure. Berenstain, Michael, illus. LC 85-43097. 32p. (ps-3). 1986. pap. 1.95 (*0-394-87604-0*) Random Bks Yng Read.
Gruber, Suzanne. Chatty Chipmunk's Nutty Day. Cushman, Doug, illus. LC 84-8665. 32p. (gr. k-2). 1985. PLB 11.59 (*0-8167-0360-4*); pap. text ed. 2.95 (*0-8167-0440-6*) Troll Assocs.
Haas, Jessie. Chipmunk! Smith, Joseph A., illus. LC 92-30080. 24p. (ps up). 1993. 14.00 (*0-688-11874-7*); PLB 13.93 (*0-688-11875-5*) Greenwillow.
Oana, Katherine. Chirpy Chipmunk. Baird, Tate, ed. Butrick, Lyn M., illus. LC 88-51854. 16p. (Orig.). (ps). 1989. pap. 4.52 (*0-914127-08-X*) Univ Class.
Ryder, Joanne. Chipmunk Song. Cherry, Lynne, illus. LC 86-19786. 32p. (ps-3). 1987. 13.95 (*0-525-67191-9*, Lodestar Bks); pap. 4.95 (*0-525-67312-1*, Lodestar Bks) Dutton Child Bks.
Sherrow, Victoria. Chipmunk at Hollow Tree Lane. Davis, Allen, illus. Komisar, Alexi, contrib. by. LC 93-27267. (Illus.). 32p. (ps-2). 1994. 14.95 (*1-56899-028-6*); incl. audiocassette 19.95 (*1-56899-043-X*); incl. 9" plush toy 29.95 (*1-56899-042-1*); mini-sized bk. 4.50 (*1-56899-029-4*); mini-sized bk., incl. 6" plush toy 12.95 (*1-56899-044-8*); audiocassette avail. (*1-56899-041-3*) Soundprints.
Teitelbaum, Michael. Alvin & the Chipmunks: Alvin's Daydreams. YES! Entertainment Corporation Staff, ed. 16p. (ps-2). 1993. write for info. (*1-883366-18-6*) YES Ent.

CHISHOLM, SHIRLEY

Hicks, Nancy. The Honorable Shirley Chisholm: Congresswoman from Brooklyn. (gr. 7 up). PLB 12.95 (*0-87460-259-9*) Lion Bks.
Pollack, Jill S. Shirley Chisholm. LC 93-31175. (Illus.). 64p. (gr. 5-8). 1994. PLB 12.90 (*0-531-20168-6*) Watts.

CHIVALRY

see also Arthur, King; Civilization, Medieval; Crusades; Feudalism; Heraldry; Knights and Knighthood

Bulfinch, Thomas. Age of Chivalry. (gr. 8 up). 1965. pap. 1.95 (*0-8049-0061-2*, CL-61) Airmont.
The End of Chivalry. 64p. (gr. 4-8). 1990. 14.95 (*0-86307-996-2*) Marshall Cavendish.
Westwood, Jennifer. Stories of Charlemagne. LC 74-12435. (gr. 6 up). 1976. 21.95 (*0-87599-213-7*) S G Phillips.

CHIVALRY–FICTION

De Cervantes Saavedra, Miguel. Don Quixote. (gr. 11 up). 1967. pap. 2.75 (*0-8049-0153-8*, CL-153) Airmont.
Green, Roger L. King Arthur & His Knights of the Round Table. (Orig.). (gr. 5-7). 1974. pap. 2.95 (*0-14-030073-2*) Viking Child Bks.
Lewis, Naomi, tr. Proud Knight, Fair Lady: The Twelve Lais of Marie de France. Barrett, Angela, illus. 128p. (gr. 5 up). 1989. pap. 19.95 (*0-670-82656-1*) Viking Child Bks.
Pyle, Howard. Men of Iron. Bennet, C. L., intro. by. (Illus.). (gr. 6 up). 1965. pap. 3.50 (*0-8049-0093-0*, CL-93) Airmont.

CHOCOLATE

Alessandrini, Jean. Mystery & Chocolate. (Illus.). (gr. 3-8). 1992. PLB 8.95 (*0-89565-898-4*) Childs World.
Blair, Cynthia. Chocolate Is My Middle Name. (gr. 7 up). 1992. pap. 3.99 (*0-449-70400-9*, Juniper) Fawcett.
Burford, Betty. Chocolate by Hershey: A Story about Milton S. Hershey. Chantland, Loren, illus. LC 93-43638. 1994. 14.95 (*0-87614-830-5*) Carolrhoda Bks.
Busenberg, Bonnie. Vanilla, Chocolate, & Strawberry: The Story of Your Favorite Flavors. LC 93-15101. 1993. 23.95 (*0-8225-1573-3*) Lerner Pubns.
Catling, Patrick S. The Chocolate Touch. Apple, Margot, illus. LC 78-31100. 96p. (gr. 4-6). 1979. Repr. of 1952 ed. PLB 11.88 (*0-688-32187-9*) Morrow Jr Bks.
Dahl, Roald. Charlie & the Chocolate Factory. large type ed. 174p. 1989. Repr. of 1964 ed. lib. bdg. 13.95 (*1-55736-154-1*, Crnrstn Bks) BDD LT Grp.
Dineen, Jacqueline. Chocolate. (Illus.). 32p. (gr. 1-4). 1991. PLB 14.95 (*0-87614-657-4*) Carolrhoda Bks.
Mitgutsch, Ali. From Cacao Bean to Chocolate: Translation of Vom Kakao Zur Schokolade. Mitgutsch, Ali, illus. LC 80-29588. 24p. (ps-3). 1981. PLB 10.95 (*0-87614-147-5*) Carolrhoda Bks.
Pinder, Polly. Polly Pinder's Chocolate Cookbook. Pinder, Polly, illus. Search Studios Staff, photos by. (Illus.). 144p. (gr. 7 up). 1988. 24.95 (*0-85532-603-4*, Pub. by Search Pr UK) A Schwartz & Co.

CHOICE OF BOOKS

see Books and Reading; Books and Reading–Best Books

CHOICE OF PROFESSION

see Vocational Guidance

CHOPIN, FREDERIC FRANCOIS, 1810-1849

Patton, Barbara. Introducing Frederic Chopin. (Illus., Orig.). (gr. 3-9). 1990. pap. 6.95x (*1-878636-00-6*) Soundboard Bks.
Rachlin, Ann. Chopin. Hellard, Susan, illus. 24p. (gr. k-3). 1993. pap. 5.95 (*0-8120-1543-6*) Barron.
Tames, Richard. Frederic Chopin. LC 90-38304. 1991. 12.40 (*0-531-14179-9*) Watts.

CHOREOGRAPHY

see Ballet; Dancing

CHRIST

see Jesus Christ

CHRISTENING

see Baptism

CHRISTIAN ART AND SYMBOLISM

see also Bible–Pictorial Works; Cathedrals; Jesus Christ–Art

Beard, Frank. Bible Symbols of the Bible in Pictures. 1985. pap. 7.99 (*0-88019-170-8*) Schmul Pub Co.
Currier, Mary. Christian Crafts from Paper Plates. 64p. (ps-5). 1989. 8.95 (*0-86653-494-6*, SS1880, Shining Star Pubns) Good Apple.
Hillam, Corbin. Christian Clip & Copy Time-Savers. 96p. (ps up). 1990. 10.95 (*0-86653-553-5*, SS1822, Shining Star Pubns) Good Apple.
Jones, Lois S. Crucifixion & Resurrection. Jones, Preston, ed. (gr. 10-12). 1994. pap. 5.00 (*1-882238-04-4*); Incl. video cass. 59.95 (*1-882238-03-6*) Swan-Jones Prod.
Schneck, Susan. Christian Clip & Copy Art. 96p. (ps-8). 1989. 10.95 (*0-86653-503-9*, SS1816, Shining Star Pubns) Good Apple.
Stegenga, Susan J. Christian Crafts - Paper Bag Puppets. 64p. (ps-5). 1990. 8.95 (*0-86653-552-7*, SS1881, Shining Star Pubns) Good Apple.

CHRISTIAN BIOGRAPHY

see also Apostles; Cardinals; Clergy; Missionaries; Pilgrim Fathers; Popes; Saints

Aaseng, Nathan. Billy Graham. 112p. (gr. 3-7). 1993. 4.99 (*0-310-39841-X*, Pub. by Youth Spec) Zondervan.
African Triumph. LC 67-29693. (gr. 3-7). 1978. 3.00 (*0-8198-0225-5*); pap. 2.00 (*0-8198-0226-3*) St Paul Bks.
Benton, John. Kari. 192p. (gr. 7-12). 1984. pap. 3.50 (*0-8007-8491-X*) J Benton Bks.
Bonniwell, William R. The Life of Blessed Margaret of Castello. LC 83-70524. 113p. (gr. 8). 1983. pap. 6.00 (*0-89555-213-2*) TAN Bks Pubs.
Carson, Ben. Ben Carson. Murphy, Cecil & Asseng, Nathancontrib. by. 112p. (gr. 3-9). 1992. pap. 4.99 (*0-310-58641-0*, Pub. by Youth Spec) Zondervan.
Daughters of St. Paul. God's Secret Agent. LC 67-24026. (gr. 4-9). 1967. 3.00 (*0-8198-0236-0*); pap. 2.00 (*0-8198-3036-4*) St Paul Bks.
Dawson, Canon. Heroines of Missionary Adventures, Vols. 1-2. 1979. Vol. 1. pap. 4.99 (*0-88019-039-6*) Vol. 2. pap. 4.99 (*0-88019-040-X*) Schmul Pub Co.
Dravecky, Dave & Stafford, Tim. Dave Dravecky. 112p. (gr. 3-9). 1993. pap. 4.99 (*0-310-58651-8*, Youth Bks) Zondervan.
Evens, Lori H. Movin' Mountains. 176p. (Orig.). 1991. pap. 7.95 (*0-929292-21-9*) Hannibal Bks.
Flores, Kathy. Beauty for Ashes. Cox, Gail, ed. Gobble, Janice, illus. Malvido, Lalo, photos by. 37p. (Orig.). 1990. pap. 3.98 (*0-9626862-0-4*) K Flores Min.
Hanley, Boniface. With Minds of Their Own: Eight Women Who Made a Difference. LC 91-72117. (Illus.). 232p. (Orig.). (gr. 7-12). 1991. pap. 9.95 (*0-87793-454-1*) Ave Maria.
Heroes of the Cross, All for Jesus, Vol. 8. pap. 4.99 (*0-88019-162-7*) Schmul Pub Co.
Higgins, Bill. God's Faithful Goose: John Hus. (gr. 3-6). 1994. pap. 8.95 (*1-883405-02-5*) Grey Pilgrim.
Hockett, Betty M. Mud on Their Wheels: The Life-Story of Vern & Lois Ellis. Loewen, Janelle, illus. LC 88-81703. 80p. (Orig.). (gr. 3-6). 1988. pap. 3.50 (*0-943701-14-7*) George Fox Pr.
Hostetler, Paul. A Wing & a Prayer. Pierce, Glen, ed. Phipps, Weston & Deyhle, Karen, illus. LC 92-75502. 159p. (Orig.). 1993. pap. 7.95 (*0-916035-58-1*) Evangel Indiana.
Lappin, Peter. The Falcon & the Dove: The Story of Laura Vicuna. (Illus.). 180p. (gr. 9-12). 1985. pap. 4.95 (*0-89944-067-3*) Don Bosco Multimedia.
—General Mickey. 167p. (Orig.). (gr. 5-10). 1977. pap. 2.95 (*0-89944-029-0*) Don Bosco Multimedia.
McFarlan, Donald. White Queen: Mary Slessor. 1982. pap. 3.95 (*0-87508-632-2*) Chr Lit.
Mohan, Claire J. A Red Rose for Frania: A Story of the Young Life of Francis Siedliska. Thomer, Susannah, illus. (gr. 4-7). 1989. PLB 5.95 (*0-9621500-8-8*) Young Sparrow Pr.
Morris, Deborah. Real Kids, Real Adventures. LC 94-11741. 112p. (gr. 3-10). 1994. 5.99 (*0-8054-4051-8*, 4240-51) Broadman.
O'Grady, Jim. Dorothy Day: With Love for the Poor. (Illus.). 128p. (gr. 4 up). 1993. pap. 10.95 (*0-9623380-6-0*) Ward Hill Pr.
Payne, Mary A. Russell's Journal: Trust. (Illus.). 48p. (gr. k-4). 1993. 7.95 (*0-8059-3334-4*) Dorrance.
Richardson, Arleta. A Heart for God in India. Payne, Peggy & Yoder, Tamra, eds. Ortega, Jennifer, illus. 52p. (Orig.). (gr. 4-6). 1989. pap. 4.00 (*0-89367-144-4*) Light & Life.
Root, Loretta P. Outflowing Love: Auntie-Bai, Effie Southworth's Life. Benson, Mary C., ed. Benson, John, illus. 124p. (Orig.). 1989. pap. 5.95 (*0-89367-142-8*) Light & Life.
Roth, David & Maifair, Linda L. Colin Powell. 112p. (gr. 3-7). 1993. 4.99 (*0-310-39851-7*, Pub. by Youth Spec) Zondervan.
Scott. Slave Ship Captain: John Newton. 1989. pap. 3.95 (*0-87508-623-3*) Chr Lit.
Smith, Melanie. Master-Minded: Ten Stories of Contemporary Servants. Nelson, Becky, ed. 91p. (Orig.). (gr. 7-12). 1992. pap. text ed. 4.95 (*1-56309-046-5*, New Hope) Womans Mission Union.

Frederic Handel, Mahalia Jackson, Stonewall Jackson, Johannes Kepler, Francis Scott Key, Jason Lee, Robert E. Lee, Abraham Lincoln, Samuel F. B. Morse, Isaac Newton, Florence Nightingale, Louis Pasteur, Samuel Francis Smith, Billy Sunday, Teresa of Calcutta, George Washington, Daniel Webster, Susanna Wesley, Wright Brothers. For more information on ordering the SOWERS SERIES or other fine Mott Media products call or write: MOTT MEDIA, 1000 E. HURON, MILFORD, MI 48381. (810) 685-8773.
Publisher Provided Annotation.

Stocker, Fern N., et al. Preteen Biography Series, 6 bks. (gr. 2-7). Set. pap. 27.00 (*0-8024-6668-0*) Moody.

Swift, Catherine. Eric Liddell. 176p. (gr. 8 up). 1990. 4.99 (*1-55661-150-1*) Bethany Hse.

Tada, Joni E. Joni's Story. Musser, Joe & Maifair, Linda L.contrib. by. 112p. (gr. 3-9). 1992. pap. 4.99 (*0-310-58661-5*, Pub. by Youth Spec) Zondervan.

Tallach, John. They Shall Be Mine. 128p. (gr. 9-12). 1981. pap. 7.95 (*0-85151-320-4*) Banner of Truth.

Tozer, A. W. Let My People Go: The Life of Robert A. Jaffray. rev. ed. LC 90-80076. 128p. 1990. pap. 7.99 (*0-87509-427-9*) Chr Pubns.

White, Kathleen. Jim Elliott. 128p. (gr. 8 up). 1990. Repr. 4.99 (*1-55661-125-0*) Bethany Hse.

Williamson, Denise. River of Danger: A Story of Samuel Kirkland. 112p. (gr. 4-7). 1990. pap. 6.95 (*1-56121-027-7*) Wolgemuth & Hyatt.

Wilson Story, Bettie. Gospel Trailblazer: The Exciting Story of Francis Asbury. 128p. (gr. 4-6). 1984. pap. 3.95 (*0-687-15652-1*) Abingdon.

Windeatt, Mary F. Blessed Kateri Tekakwitha. Harmon, Gedge, illus. 32p. (gr. 1-5). 1989. Repr. of 1954 ed. wkbk. 3.00 (*0-89555-378-3*) TAN Bks Pubs.

CHRISTIAN DOCTRINE

see Theology

CHRISTIAN EDUCATION

see Religious Education

CHRISTIAN ETHICS

Biffi, Inos. The Ten Commandments. Vignazia, Franco, illus. LC 93-39147. 32p. 1994. pap. 9.99 (*0-8028-3758-1*) Eerdmans.

Butterworth, Nick & Inkpen, Mick, illus. Who Made Me? Doney, Malcolm, text by. LC 92-20748. 1992. write for info. (*0-551-01476-8*) Zondervan.

Carr, Dan. Cheating. (Illus.). (gr. k-4). 1984. pap. 0.99 (*0-570-08725-2*, 56-1469) Concordia.

—Hurting Others. (Illus.). (gr. k-4). 1984. pap. 0.99 (*0-570-08727-9*, 56-1471) Concordia.

—Lying. (Illus.). (gr. k-4). 1984. pap. 0.99 (*0-570-08732-5*, 56-1476) Concordia.

—My Bad Temper. (Illus.). (gr. 1-3). 1984. pap. 0.99 (*0-570-08730-9*, 56-1474) Concordia.

—Paying Attention. (Illus.). (gr. k-4). 1984. pap. 0.99 (*0-570-08729-5*, 56-1473) Concordia.

—Sharing. (Illus.). (gr. k-4). 1984. pap. 0.99 (*0-570-08728-7*, 56-1472) Concordia.

—Stealing. (Illus.). (gr. k-4). 1984. pap. 0.99 (*0-570-08731-7*, 56-1475) Concordia.

—Vandalism. (Illus.). (gr. k-4). 1984. pap. 0.99 (*0-570-08726-0*, 56-1470) Concordia.

Chappell, Stephen. Dragons & Demons, Angels & Eagles: Morality Tales for Teens. LC 89-63202. 128p. (Orig.). 1990. pap. 6.95 (*0-89243-314-0*) Liguori Pubns.

Christenson, Larry. The Wonderful Way That Babies Are Made. LC 82-12813. 48p. (Orig.). (ps up). 1982. 11.99 (*0-87123-627-3*) Bethany Hse.

Roeda, Jack. Decisions. 2nd ed. Stoub, Paul, illus. Smith, Harvey A., intro. by. (Illus.). 80p. (gr. 9-12). 1992. pap. text ed. 6.50 (*0-930265-96-3*, 1240-4920); tchr's. manual 8.50 (*1-56212-000-X*, 1240-4940); session guides 4.95 (*0-685-60757-7*, 1240-4910) CRC Pubns.

Sciacca, Fran & Sciacca, Jill. What Really Matters? Setting Priorities. 64p. 1992. pap. 3.99 saddle stitch bdg. (*0-310-48091-4*) Zondervan.

Tighe, Mike. I Was Afraid I'd Lose My Soul to a Chocolate Malt... And Other Stories of Everyday Spirituality. LC 89-63837. (Illus.). 96p. (Orig.). 1990. pap. 2.95 (*0-89243-316-7*) Liguori Pubns.

Weakland, Rembert G. Letters to Teens: Hopeful Words from an Archbishop. 48p. (Orig.). (gr. 8-12). 1988. pap. 1.75 (*0-89243-290-X*) Liguori Pubns.

Yorgason, Blaine & Yorgason, Brenton. The Problem with Immorality. 43p. 1990. pap. text ed. 3.50 (*0-929985-15-X*) Jackman Pubng.

Young, Douglas. A Primer of Christianity & Ethics. Hunting, Constance, ed. 200p. (Orig.). (gr. 9-12). 1985. pap. 12.95 (*0-913006-34-3*) Puckerbrush.

CHRISTIAN LIFE

see also Children–Religious Life; Christian Ethics; Faith; Love; Prayer; Religious Education; Spiritual Life

Aaseng, Nathan. I'm Learning, Lord, but I Still Need Help: Story Devotions for Boys. LC 81-65652. 112p. (Orig.). (gr. 3-7). 1981. pap. 5.99 (*0-8066-1888-4*, 10-3202, Augsburg) Augsburg Fortress.

—I'm Searching, Lord, but I Need Your Light. LC 82-72644. 112p. (gr. 3-6). 1983. pap. 5.99 (*0-8066-1950-3*, 10-3203, Augsburg) Augsburg Fortress.

—Which Way Are You Leading Me, Lord? Bible Devotions for Boys. LC 84-21562. 112p. (Orig.). (gr. 3-7). 1984. pap. 5.99 (*0-8066-2113-3*, 10-7099, Augsburg) Augsburg Fortress.

Adams, David. Life after High School. (Illus.). 48p. (gr. 9-12). 1991. pap. 8.99 (*1-55945-220-X*) Group Pub.

—Movies, Music, TV & Me. (Illus.). 48p. (gr. 9-12). 1991. pap. 8.99 (*1-55945-213-7*) Group Pub.

—Today's Lessons from Yesterday's Prophets. (Illus.). 48p. (gr. 9-12). 1992. pap. 8.99 (*1-55945-227-7*) Group Pub.

Adams, Nate. Energizers. 192p. 1993. pap. 8.99 (*0-310-37371-9*, Pub. by Youth Spec) Zondervan.

Armed & Dangerous: Answers for Teens from the Bible! pap. 7.95 (*1-55748-242-X*) Barbour & Co.

Barrett, Joanne, et al. Zeroes into Heroes. (gr. 3-6). 1990. 5.25 (*0-685-68191-2*, BCMB-628); cassette 10.98 (*0-685-68192-0*, BCTA-9130C) Lillenas.

Bartel, Marvin. My Own Picture Book about Getting Older. Bartel, Marvin, illus. LC 89-80248. 43p. (ps-7). 1989. wkbk. 4.95 (*0-87303-135-0*) Faith & Life.

Bartz, Paul A. Letting God Create Your Day, Vol. 1, No. 1: Scripts from the International Broadcast Creation Moments. 84p. (Orig.). 1989. pap. write for info. Colorsong Prodns.

Beckman, Beverly. Senses in God's World. 24p. (ps). 1986. 6.99 (*0-570-04150-3*, 56-1604) Concordia.

Beckmann, Beverly. Emotions in God's World. 24p. (ps-1). 1986. 6.99 (*0-570-04149-X*, 56-1610) Concordia.

—Seasons in God's World. Bowser, Carolyn E., illus. 24p. (gr. 2-5). 1985. 6.99 (*0-570-04127-9*, 56-1538) Concordia.

Beers, V. Gilbert. Friends Are Helpers. Eubank, Mary G., illus. 12p. (ps-2). 1991. bds. 3.99 (*0-8010-0997-9*) Baker Bk.

—Friends Give Good Gifts. Eubank, Mary G., illus. 12p. (ps-2). 1991. bds. 3.99 (*0-8010-0998-7*) Baker Bk.

—Friends Play Together. Eubank, Mary G., illus. 12p. (ps-2). 1991. bds. 3.99 (*0-8010-0999-5*) Baker Bk.

—Friends Share. Eubank, Mary G., illus. 12p. (ps-2). 1991. bds. 3.99 (*0-8010-0996-0*) Baker Bk.

—Precious Moments Through-the-Day Stories. Butcher, Samuel J., illus. LC 90-1265. 256p. 1991. 14.99 (*0-8010-0992-8*) Baker Bk.

Beers, V. Gilbert & Beers, Ronald A. Growing God's Way to See & Share. 192p. (gr. 7 up). 1987. pap. 14. 99 (*0-89693-801-8*, Victor Books) SP Pubns.

—Little People in Tough Spots: Bible Answers for Young Children. (Illus.). 144p. 1992. 7.99 (*0-8407-9157-7*) Nelson.

Bennett, Marian. God Made Puppies. Beegle, Shirley, ed. Arthur, Lorraine, illus. 24p. (ps-3). 1994. pap. 1.89 (*0-7847-0256-X*) Standard Pub.

Bentley, Victor. Possessing Truth in Balance & Anatomy of a Backslider. LC 89-8945. 128p. (Orig.). 1989. pap. 5.99 (*0-932581-48-X*) Word Aflame.

Benton, John. Sheila. 192p. (gr. 7-12). 1982. pap. 3.50 (*0-8007-8419-7*) J Benton Bks.

Bernstein, Bob. Thinking Numbers. 96p. (gr. 2-7). 1989. 10.95 (*0-86653-506-3*, GA1094) Good Apple.

Berry, John R. Good Words for New Christians. (Orig.). (gr. 6-12). 1987. pap. 2.95 (*0-9616900-0-3*) J R Berry.

Berry, Roger L. Into All the World. (gr. 4). 1991. 17.50 (*0-87813-925-7*) Christian Light.

Bertolini, Dewey. Secret Wounds & Silent Cries. rev. ed. LC 93-18867. 156p. 1993. pap. 7.99 (*1-56476-116-9*, Victor Books) SP Pubns.

—Sometimes I Really Hate You. 132p. 1991. pap. 4.99 (*0-89693-041-6*) SP Pubns.

Bibee, John. The Only Game in Town. Turnbaugh, Paul, illus. LC 88-9369. 209p. (ps-6). 1988. pap. 6.99 (*0-8308-1202-4*, 1202) InterVarsity.

Bible, Ken, compiled by. A Pocketful of Praise. (gr. 3-7). 1987. songbk. 3.75 (*0-685-68220-X*, BCMB-574); double-length cassette, split-channel 12.98 (*0-685-68221-8*, BCTA-9085C) Lillenas.

—Primary Praise. 1990. songbk. 6.50 (*0-685-68214-5*, BCMB-620); double-length split-channel cassette 12. 98 (*0-685-68215-3*, BCTA-9122C) Lillenas.

Bishops' Committee for Pastoral Research Staff & National Conference of Catholic Bishops Staff. The Sexual Challenge: Growing up Christian. 16p. (Orig.). (gr. 9-12). 1990. pap. 0.95 (*1-555-86364-7*) US Catholic.

Bitney, James & Nelson, Yvette. Welcome to the Family. 112p. (gr. 4-6). 1988. student ed. 8.95 (*0-89505-658-5*, T18X1) Tabor Pub.

Bonnici, Roberta L. I'm Scared to Witness! Clore, Chuck, illus. 48p. (Orig.). (gr. 9-12). 1979. pap. 1.50 (*0-88243-931-6*, 02-0931); leader's guide 3.95 (*0-88243-330-X*, 02-0330) Gospel Pub.

—Your Right to Be Different. Clore, Chuck, illus. 48p. (gr. 9-12). 1982. pap. 1.50 (*0-88243-842-5*, 02-0842); leader's guide 3.95 (*0-88243-333-4*, 02-0333) Gospel Pub.

Boone, Debby & Ferrer, Gabriel. Tomorrow Is a Brand New Day. (Illus.). 32p. (Orig.). (ps-3). 1989. 11.99 (*0-89081-770-7*) Harvest Hse.

Booth, Patsy R. If I Could Talk to God, I'd Say: Directed Discovery Journal. 102p. (gr. 4 up). 1994. 10.95 (*1-884393-24-1*) Cedar Tree.

Borchers, Deena. Changing the World. (Illus.). 48p. (gr. 9-12). 1993. pap. 8.99 (*1-55945-236-6*) Group Pub.

Boyce, Kim & Abraham, Ken. In Focus: Devotions to Help You Make Sense Out of a Senseless World. LC 92-31299. (Illus.). 1993. pap. 7.99 (*0-7814-0814-8*, Chariot Bks) Chariot Family.

—In Process: Devotions to Help You Develop Your Faith. Reck, Sue, ed. LC 93-32713. 160p. (gr. 7-12). 1994. pap. 7.99 (*0-7814-0822-9*, Chariot Bks) Cook.

Britton, Colleen. Celebrate Communion. 79p. (gr. 1-6). 1984. pap. 9.95 (*0-940754-26-6*) Ed Ministries.

Brown, Kevin & Mitsch, Ray. The Quest. LC 92-26406. 1993. 9.99 (*0-8407-4560-5*) Nelson.

Browning, James. Read the Label Carefully: Separating New Age & Christianity. Nelson, Becky, ed. 22p. (Orig.). (gr. 7-12). 1992. pap. text ed. 1.95 (*1-56309-062-7*, Wrld Changers Res) Womans Mission Union.

Buchanan, Jami L. Letters to My Little Sisters. LC 84-27612. (Orig.). (gr. 7-8). 1985. pap. 5.99 (*0-8307-0999-1*, S185100) Regal.

Cachiaras, Dot. Sharing Makes Me Happy. Beegle, Shirley, ed. Arthur, Lorraine, illus. 24p. (ps-3). 1994. pap. 1.89 (*0-7847-0264-0*) Standard Pub.

Cake, J. C. Good Knight Stories. Stickler, Ruth, ed. 190p. (gr. 1 up). 1967. pap. 5.95 (*0-932785-49-2*) Philos Pub.

Campbell, Stan. Higher Love. 96p. 1991. pap. 2.99 student bk. (*0-89693-790-9*) SP Pubns.

Cantwell, Lee G. Cross Currents. LC 93-12389. x, 244p. (Orig.). (gr. 8-12). 1993. pap. 9.95 (*0-87579-672-9*) Deseret Bk.

Carney, Mary L. There's an Angel in My Locker. 112p. (Orig.). (gr. 7-9). 1986. pap. 6.99 (*0-310-28471-6*, 11341P, Pub. by Youth Spec.) Zondervan.

Ceckowski, Karen. The Joy of Serving. (Illus.). 48p. (gr. 9-12). 1991. pap. 8.99 (*1-55945-210-2*) Group Pub.

Center for Learning Network. My Journey, My Prayer. 96p. (gr. 9-12). 1991. pap. text ed. 5.95 (*1-56077-128-3*) Ctr Learning.

Chamberlain, Martha E. Surviving Junior High. LC 88-2937. 296p. (Orig.). (gr. 7-9). 1988. pap. 9.95 (*0-8361-3462-1*) Herald Pr.

Chapian, Marie. The Secret Place of Strength. 208p. (Orig.). 1991. 10.99 (*1-55661-219-2*) Bethany Hse.

Chappell, David, illus. Five Things God Cannot Do. 16p. (gr. k-6). 1989. pap. text ed. 4.25 (*1-55976-129-6*) CEF Press.

Cherry, Leon P. First Call. 48p. 1992. pap. 2.95 (*1-882185-02-1*) Crnrstone Pub.

Chesney, Sandy. The Zapped Tadpole & More. 93p. (gr. 4 up). 1991. pap. 4.99 (*0-8163-1029-7*) Pacific Pr Pub Assn.

Children's Day & Rally Day Program Builder, No. 5. 2p. (gr. k-6). 1965. 4.25 (*0-685-68750-3*, BCMP-105) Lillenas.

Chromey, Rick. Christians in a Non-Christian World. (Illus.). 48p. (gr. 9-12). 1992. pap. 8.99 (*1-55945-224-2*) Group Pub.

—Turning Depression Upside Down. (Illus.). 48p. (gr. 9-12). 1992. pap. 8.99 (*1-55945-135-1*) Group Pub.

Clapp, Steve & Berman, Julie S. Repairing Christian Lifestyles. 2nd, rev. ed. (Illus.). 80p. (gr. 6-12). 1992. wkbk. 24.95 (*0-87178-737-7*) Brethren.

Clemmer Steiner, Susan. God Has No Favorites. Shelley, Maynard, ed. LC 89-84827. 97p. (Orig.). (gr. 8-12). 1989. pap. 4.95 (*0-87303-134-2*) Faith & Life.

Coleman. Straight Answers for Kids. LC 91-41504. (gr. 4-8). 1992. pap. 9.99 (*1-55513-336-3*, Chariot Bks) Chariot Family.

Coleman, Willaim L. What You Should Know about Accepting People Who Aren't Like You. 1994. 5.99 (*0-8066-2637-2*, Augsburg) Augsburg Fortress.

Coleman, William. Earning Your Wings. LC 84-6299. 140p. (gr. 7 up). 1984. pap. 6.99 (*0-87123-311-8*) Bethany Hse.

—Getting Ready for Our New Baby. LC 84-432. 112p. (ps-2). 1984. pap. 6.99 (*0-87123-295-2*) Bethany Hse.

Coleman, William L. Cupid is Stupid! How to Fall in Love Without Falling on Your Face. LC 91-21852. 164p. (Orig.). (gr. 9 up). 1991. pap. 7.99 (*0-8308-1335-7*, 1335) InterVarsity.

—Entering the Teen Zone: Devotions to Guide You. LC 90-43092. 112p. (Orig.). (gr. 7-10). 1991. pap. 5.99 (*0-8066-2499-X*, 9-2499, Augsburg) Augsburg Fortress.

—Getting Along with Brothers & Sisters. 1994. 5.99 (*0-8066-2669-0*) Augsburg Fortress.

Connolly, Francis X. St. Philip of the Joyous Heart. Rethi, Lili, illus. LC 92-74761. 189p. (gr. 5-8). 1993. pap. 9.95 (*0-89870-431-6*) Ignatius Pr.

Corbin, Linda & Dys, Pat. Jesus Is God's Son. (Orig.). (gr. 1-6). 1988. pap. 4.99 (*0-87509-404-X*) Chr Pubns.

Cordova, Laura. God Made Me Special. 64p. (ps-3). 1989. 8.95 (*0-86653-496-2*, SS1857, Shining Star Pubns) Good Apple.

Crabtree, Jack. Play It Safe. 210p. (Orig.). 1993. pap. 8.99 (*1-56476-110-X*, Victor Books) SP Pubns.

Crary, Elizabeth. Mommy Don't Go. Megale, Marina, illus. LC 85-63759. 32p. (Orig.). (ps-2). 1986. lib. bdg. 15.95 (*0-943990-27-0*); pap. 4.95 (*0-943990-26-2*) Parenting Pr.

Cronin, Gaynell B. The Forgiveness of the Lord. LC 93-72557. (Illus.). 64p. (Orig.). (gr. 2-3). 1993. pap. 4.50 (*0-87793-516-5*); director's manual, 40p. 4.50 (*0-87793-518-1*); family bk., 60 p. 3.50 (*0-87793-515-7*) Ave Maria.

—The Table of the Lord. LC 86-70131. (Illus., Orig.). (gr. 1-3). 1986. Child's Bk, 104 pgs. pap. text ed. 4.50 (*0-87793-299-9*); Director's Manual, 168 pgs. spiral 9.75 (*0-87793-325-1*); Family Bk., 96p. 3.50 (*0-87793-326-X*) Ave Maria.

Crook, Carol. Enter-Praise-Worship. (Illus.). 9p. (Orig.). (gr. 7 up). 1988. pap. 0.75x (*0-939399-03-2*) Bks of Truth.

—Thoughts Turn to Actions. 7p. (Orig.). (gr. 5 up). 1989. pap. 0.75x (*0-939399-10-5*) Bks of Truth.

Cummings, Margaret A. Touched by AIDS. Butler, Cathy, ed. 22p. (Orig.). (gr. 7-12). 1992. pap. text ed. 1.95 (*1-56309-024-4*, Wrld Changers Res) Womans Mission Union.

Cutts, Grace. Let My People Go. 29p. (ps-2). 1991. 3.99 (*0-87509-450-3*) Chr Pubns.

—On Call. 30p. (ps-2). 1991. 3.99 (*0-87509-452-X*) Chr Pubns.

Cutts, Gracie. Weak Thing in Moni Land. 29p. (ps-2). 1991. 3.99 (*0-87509-451-1*) Chr Pubns.

Daniel, Rebecca. Count God's Blessings. 48p. (ps-1). 1991. 9.95 (*0-86653-626-4*, SS1889, Shining Star Pubns) Good Apple.

—God's Colorful World. 48p. (ps-1). 1991. 9.95 (*0-86653-630-2*, SS1888, Shining Star Pubns) Good Apple.

Darling, Kathy. Preschool Christian Value Lessons. 96p. (ps-1). 1991. 10.95 (*0-86653-627-2*, SS1891, Shining Star Pubns) Good Apple.

Davidson, Robert G. God Doesn't Make Junk. (gr. 9-12). 1990. 8.00 (*0-940754-93-2*, 8242) Ed Ministries.

—Youth Programming Workbook. 40p. (Orig.). 1989. pap. 8.50 (*0-940754-67-3*) Ed Ministries.

Davis, Ken. How to Live with Your Parents Without Losing Your Mind. (gr. 7 up). 1988. pap. 7.99 (*0-310-32331-2*, 11791P, Pub. by Youth Spec) Zondervan.

—Jumper Fables. 1994. pap. 8.99 (*0-310-40011-2*) Zondervan.

DeGrote-Sorensen, Barbara. Everybody Needs a Friend: A Young Christian Book for Girls. LC 86-32152. 112p. (Orig.). (gr. 3-7). 1987. pap. 5.99 (*0-8066-2247-4*, 10-2120, Augsburg) Augsburg Fortress.

De Jonge, Joanne. Trash Can Review. Foley, Timothy, illus. 64p. (Orig.). 1992. pap. 7.99 (*0-8028-5071-5*) Eerdmans.

De La Cruz Aymes, Maria, et al. Growing with God's Forgiveness & I Celebrate Reconcilation. 72p. (gr. 1-3). 1985. pap. text ed. 6.39 (*0-8215-2371-6*); tchr's. ed. 9.00 (*0-8215-2373-2*); parent pack (10 booklets) 18.66 (*0-8215-2375-9*) Sadlier.

—Growing with the Bread of Life & My Mass Book. 72p. (gr. 1-3). 1985. pap. text ed. 6.39 (*0-8215-2370-8*); tchr's. ed. 9.00 (*0-8215-2372-4*); parent pack (10 booklets) 18.66 (*0-8215-2374-0*) Sadlier.

Dickson, Charles. Beating the Chemical Cop-Out. Nelson, Becky, ed. 22p. (Orig.). (gr. 7-12). 1992. pap. text ed. 1.95 (*1-56309-036-8*, Wrld Changers Res) Womans Mission Union.

—Please Help Me Hold On. Nelson, Becky, ed. 22p. (Orig.). (gr. 7-12). 1992. pap. text ed. 1.95 (*1-56309-037-6*, Wrld Changers Res) Womans Mission Union.

Dobson, James. Preparing for Adolescence. rev. ed. Mills, Kathi, ed. LC 89-30455. 175p. 1989. pap. 7.99 (*0-8307-1258-5*, 5419314); 4.99 (*0-8307-1384-0*, 5018928) Regal.

Dockrey, Karen. It's Not Fair! Through Grief to Healing. Nelson, Becky, ed. 22p. (Orig.). (gr. 7-12). 1992. pap. text ed. 1.95 (*1-56309-035-X*, Wrld Changers Res) Womans Mission Union.

Doney, Meryl. Discovering Out of Doors. (Illus.). 28p. (ps-3). 1979. pap. 2.99 (*0-85648-175-0*) Lion USA.

Donze, Mary T. I Can Pray the Rosary! Donze, Mary T., illus. 48p. (Orig.). (gr. 2-4). 1991. pap. 2.95 (*0-89243-335-3*) Liguori Pubns.

Doolittle, Robert. Searching Young Hearts: Adolescent Sexuality & Spirituality. Stamschror, Robert, ed. (Illus.). 72p. (gr. 7-12). 1993. stitched 8.95 (*0-88489-292-1*) St Marys.

Doud, Guy. God Loves Me - So What! 192p. (Orig.). 1992. pap. 6.99 (*0-570-04572-X*) Concordia.

Doud, Guy R. Stuff You Gotta Know: Straight Talk about Real-Life. LC 93-25113. (Illus.). 160p. (Orig.). (gr. 8-12). 1993. pap. 6.99 (*0-570-04622-X*) Concordia.

Doward, Jan S. Finding the Right Path. 96p. (gr. 5 up). 1990. pap. 6.95 (*0-8163-0938-8*) Pacific Pr Pub Assn.

Duplex, Mary. Trouble with a Capital T. 96p. 1992. pap. 7.95 (*0-8163-1057-2*) Pacific Pr Pub Assn.

Duplex, Mary H., et al. Quiet Times with Jesus. LC 92-20278. (ps). 1992. pap. 9.95 (*0-8280-0678-4*) Review & Herald.

Eager, George B. Love, Dating & Marriage. Wetmore, Gordon, et al, illus. LC 86-90552. 136p. (Orig.). (gr. 6-12). 1987. pap. 6.95 (*0-9603752-5-2*) Mailbox.

Eberle, Sarah. What Is Love? Beegle, Shirley, ed. Speer, Tammie L., illus. 24p. (ps-3). 1994. pap. 1.89 (*0-7847-0266-7*) Standard Pub.

Eder, Enelle G. & Pulham, Grace. Growing in God's Garden - the Greatest Show on Earth: Four Theme-Related Programs to Use with Children, 2 vols. in 1. LC 88-83338. (Illus.). 112p. (gr. 3-6). 1989. tchr's. ed. 9.50 (*0-88243-555-8*, 02-0555) Gospel Pub.

Ege, Christine. Words for the World: Including God's Word for the World. Herbert, Janet, illus. LC 91-90681. 136p. (gr. k-8). 1992. text ed. 35.00 incl. 1 8-cass. tape album (*1-884161-01-4*) Comprehen Lang.

Erickson, Mary. I Can Make God Glad! Reck, Sue, ed. Ebert, Len, illus. LC 93-33070. 32p. (ps-2). 1994. 9.99 (*0-7814-0102-X*, Chariot Bks) Chariot Family.

Eubank, Mary G. & Hollingsworth, Mary. King's Workers. 1990. write for info. (*0-8499-0827-2*) Word Inc.

Evenhouse, Bill. Reasons One, Sects & Cults with Non-Christian Roots. rev. ed. 120p. 1991. 5.75 (*0-930265-97-1*); tchr's. manual, 60p. 5.75 (*1-56212-007-7*) CRC Pubns.

Everett, Betty S. I Want to Be Like You, Lord: Bible Devotion for Girls. LC 84-21563. 112p. (Orig.). (gr. 7-10). 1984. pap. 5.99 (*0-8066-2112-5*, 10-3196, Augsburg) Augsburg Fortress.

—Who Am I, Lord? LC 82-72645. 112p. (Orig.). (gr. 3-6). 1983. pap. 5.99 (*0-8066-1951-1*, 10-7072, Augsburg) Augsburg Fortress.

Fajardo, David, compiled by. Pero...Debo Dejarlo Todo? But...Should I Give up Everything? (SPA.). 64p. (Orig.). (gr. 11 up). 1990. pap. text ed. 2.50 (*0-311-12340-6*) Casa Bautista.

Faulkner, Linda M. The Young Christian's Puzzle Book: For Becoming a Grown-up Christian. (Illus.). 40p. (gr. 5-7). 1992. pap. 3.50 (*0-88243-828-X*, 02-0828) Gospel Pub.

Fawcett, Cheryl & Newman, Robert C. I Have a Question about God... Doctrine for Children...& Their Parents! Mazellan, Ron, illus. LC 94-3054. (gr. k-7). 1994. 24.95 (*0-87227-180-3*) Reg Baptist.
"Who is God" "Why is night dark?" "How can I be perfect?" "What happens to people when they die?" If you've heard these questions, you know that answering them isn't always easy. I HAVE A QUESTION ABOUT GOD...: DOCTRINE FOR CHILDREN...& THEIR PARENTS! answers those questions & 53 more in a delightful format. Three children - 10-year-old Megan, 8-year-old Toph, & 4-year-old Bobbie - get into all kinds of situations & ask all kinds of questions. You'll start preschool with Bobbie, who can't wait to go to kindergarten & who never stops asking questions. You'll fly to Grandpa & Grandma's with Toph, who has never traveled by himself before. And you'll sympathize with Megan as she deals with a neighbor's injustice & with problems at school. As the kids discover the answers to their questions, usually with the help of their mom or dad, your kids will learn too. The questions fall into eight areas of Biblical teaching or doctrine: God, creation, the Bible, Jesus Christ, sin, salvation, church & the future. Each story includes a beautiful illustration by Ron Mazellan & a few questions to stimulate further thought & discussion. To order: 1-800-727-4440.
Publisher Provided Annotation.

Fenske, S. H. My Life in Christ: A Momento of My Confirmation. LC 76-5729. (gr. 8 up). 1976. pap. 2.95 (*0-8100-0056-3*, 16N0514) Northwest Pub.

Fettke, Tom & Rebuck, Linda. Miracle after Miracle. 1982. 5.25 (*0-685-68201-3*, BCMB-505); cassette 10.98 (*0-685-68202-1*, BCTA-9032C) Lillenas.

Fields, Doug. If Life Is a Piece of Cake, Why Am I Still Hungry? (Orig.). (gr. 7 up). 1989. pap. 5.99 (*0-89081-718-9*) Harvest Hse.

Finding the Light in Deep Water & Dark Times: Especially for Youth. 1992. pap. 6.95 (*0-88494-839-0*) Bookcraft Inc.

Fischer, John. True Believers Don't Ask Why. 192p. (Orig.). (gr. 11-12). 1989. 12.99 (*1-55661-055-6*) Bethany Hse.

Fitzgerald, Annie. Dear God, Bless Our Food. LC 84-71372. 16p. (Orig.). (ps-4). 1984. pap. 1.99 (*0-8066-2108-7*, 10-1859, Augsburg) Augsburg Fortress.

—Dear God, Good Morning. LC 84-71377. 16p. (Orig.). (ps-4). 1984. pap. 1.99 (*0-8066-2104-4*, 10-1860, Augsburg) Augsburg Fortress.

—Dear God, Good Night. LC 84-71374. 16p. (ps-4). 1984. pap. 1.99 (*0-8066-2105-2*, 10-1861, Augsburg) Augsburg Fortress.

—Dear God, I Just Love Birthdays. LC 84-71371. 16p. (Orig.). (ps-4). 1984. pap. 1.99 (*0-8066-2107-9*, 10-1862, Augsburg) Augsburg Fortress.

—Dear God, Thanks for Friends. LC 84-71873. 16p. (Orig.). (ps-4). 1984. pap. 1.99 (*0-8066-2109-5*, 10-1863, Augsburg) Augsburg Fortress.

—Dear God, Thanks for Making Me Me. LC 83-71368. 16p. (Orig.). (ps-4). 1984. pap. 1.99 (*0-8066-2106-0*, 10-1864, Augsburg) Augsburg Fortress.

Flanagan, John. Kids 'n Values: A Handbook for Helping Kids Discover Christian Values. LC 91-62268. (Illus.). 144p. (gr. 2-7). 1992. pap. text ed. 11.95 (*0-89243-411-2*) Liguori Pubns.

Flex Sessions: Family, Sharing the Faith & Moral Choices. 144p. (gr. 9-12). 1993. pap. 12.99 (*1-56476-140-1*, Victor Books) SP Pubns.

Flex Sessions: Service, Stewardship & Stress. 144p. (gr. 9-12). 1993. pap. 12.99 (*1-56476-139-8*, Victor Books) SP Pubns.

Foss, Allen J. Living in God's Grace: Apostles' Creed - Sacraments. Rinden, David, ed. 266p. (gr. 6-8). 1989. pap. 5.95 (*0-943167-06-X*) Faith & Fellowship Pr.

—Walking in God's Truth: Ten Commandments-Lord's Prayer. rev. ed. Rinden, David, intro. by. Heiman, Lori, illus. 276p. (gr. 6-8). 1989. pap. text ed. 5.95 (*0-943167-04-3*) Faith & Fellowship Pr.

Frades, Ernesto. The Happy Valley of the Elves: A Terry Turtle Adventure. Frades, Ernesto, illus. 48p. (Orig.). (gr. k-3). 1990. pap. write for info. (*0-9624929-1-4*) Little Great Whale.

Frank, Penny. Enemies All Around. (Illus.). 24p. (gr. 1 up). 1986. 3.99 (*0-85648-749-X*) Lion USA.

Franks, Tom. Born to Raze Hell. 112p. (Orig.). 1989. pap. 5.95 (*1-877717-00-2*) Mercedes Ministries.

Freeman, Hobart E. Biblical Thinking & Confession: The Key to Victorious Living 365 Days a Year. (Orig.). 1990. pap. write for info (*1-878725-36-X*) Faith Min & Pubns.

Fretz, Clarence Y. You & Your Bible-You & Your Life. (gr. 8). 1968. pap. 4.10x (*0-87813-902-8*); tchr's. guide 16.00x (*0-87813-903-6*) Christian Light.

Friedrich, Elizabeth. The Story of God's Love. 144p. (gr. 6-9). 1985. 9.99 (*0-570-04122-8*, 56-1533) Concordia.

Gage, Rodney. Let's Talk about AIDS & Sex. LC 92-30853. 1992. 5.99 (*0-8054-6073-X*) Broadman.

Gambill, Henrietta, ed. God's Love... Acetate Window Book, No. 2. (Illus.). 16p. 1994. 6.99 (*0-7847-0152-0*, 24-03702) Standard Pub.

—Little Lost Lamb. (Illus.). 18p. 1994. 7.99 (*0-7847-0234-9*, 24-03120) Standard Pub.

—Little Panda. (Illus.). 18p. 1994. 7.99 (*0-7847-0233-0*, 24-03119) Standard Pub.

—Little Puppy. (Illus.). 18p. 1994. 7.99 (*0-7847-0236-5*, 24-03126) Standard Pub.

—The Lord Is My Shepherd: Little Moving Picture Book. (Illus.). 10p. (ps). 1994. 3.99 (*0-7847-0207-1*, 24-03147) Standard Pub.

—My Family: Acetate Window Book, No. 1. (Illus.). 16p. 1994. 6.99 (*0-7847-0151-2*, 24-03701) Standard Pub.

—Who Made Frogs? (Illus.). 18p. 1994. 7.99 (*0-7847-0235-7*, 24-03125) Standard Pub.

Gambill, Henrietta D. Dinosaurs in God's World Long Ago. Beegle, Shirley, ed. Boddy, Joe, illus. 24p. (ps-3). 1994. pap. 1.89 (*0-7847-0253-5*) Standard Pub.

Gillespie, Mike. Caring for God's Creation. (Illus.). 48p. (gr. 6-8). 1991. pap. 8.99 (*1-55945-121-1*) Group Pub.

—Feelings: Frazzled, Frenzied & Frantic. Clark, Brian, ed. Day, Bruce, illus. 96p. (gr. 4 up). 1994. pap. 12.99 (*0-87403-766-2*) Standard Pub.

—Making Good Decisions. (Illus.). 48p. (gr. 9-12). 1991. pap. 8.99 (*1-55945-209-9*) Group Pub.

Gilmore, Charles F. Handbook for Living: The Christian Life. rev. & enl. ed. (Illus.). 94p. 1993. pap. 4.95 (*0-9627630-4-7*) Light & Living.

Gilroy, Mark. Christlike Leadership. (Illus.). 48p. (gr. 9-12). 1993. pap. 8.99 (*1-55945-231-5*) Group Pub.

—Exploring Ethical Issues. (Illus.). 48p. (gr. 9-12). 1992. pap. 8.99 (*1-55945-225-0*) Group Pub.

Gire, Judy. A Boy & His Baseball: The Dave Dravecky Story. 32p. 1992. 14.99 (*0-310-58630-5*, Youth Bks) Zondervan.

God Guides Us. (Illus.). (gr. 4). 1992. pap. text ed. 6.20 (*0-8294-0672-7*); tchr's. ed. 17.95 (*0-8294-0674-3*) Loyola.

God Is Good. LC 73-5752. (Illus.). 138p. (gr. 1). 1992. pap. text ed. 5.60 (*0-8294-0657-3*); tchr's. ed. 17.95 (*0-8294-0659-X*) Loyola.

God Is Near. LC 92-72746. 32p. 1992. pap. 4.99 (*0-8066-2634-8*, 9-2634) Augsburg Fortress.

God Made Me. LC 92-72745. 32p. 1992. 4.99 (*0-8066-2633-X*, 9-2633) Augsburg Fortress.

Godwin, Jeff. What's Wrong with Christian Rock? LC 90-85347. (Illus.). (gr. 7-12). 1990. pap. 8.95 (*0-937958-36-0*) Chick Pubns.

Going, Nancy. Materialism. (Illus.). 48p. (gr. 6-8). 1992. pap. 8.99 (*1-55945-130-0*) Group Pub.

Gorman, Cinda. Growing up Christian in a Sexy World. 50p. (Orig.). (gr. 5-6). 1989. pap. 8.50 (*0-940754-78-9*) Ed Ministries.

Grimley, Mildred H. Mattie Loves All. Wine, Jeanine M., illus. 22p. (gr. 1-5). 1985. 5.95 (*0-87178-552-8*) Brethren.

Gundersen, Ben. Memory Verse Bulletin Boards. 96p. (ps-7). 1988. 10.95 (*0-86653-426-1*, SS1827, Shining Star Pubns) Good Apple.

Hageman, Marybeth. I Want to Be Like Jesus. LC 89-80615. 32p. (Orig.). 1989. pap. 5.99 (*0-8066-2419-1*, 9-2419) Augsburg Fortress.

Hamilton, Dorothy. The Castle. Graber, Esther R., illus. LC 75-15599. 112p. (gr. 4-8). 1975. pap. 3.95 (*0-8361-1776-X*) Herald Pr.

Haney, Joy. Behold the Nazarite Woman. Agnew, Tim, illus. LC 90-30639. 96p. (Orig.). 1990. pap. 5.99 (*0-932581-63-3*) Word Aflame.

—May I Wash Your Feet. Agnew, Tim, illus. LC 91-21855. 100p. (Orig.). 1991. pap. 5.99 (*0-932581-87-0*) Word Aflame.

Hansel, Tim. Through the Wilderness of Loneliness. LC 91-6290. 128p. 1991. 12.99 (*1-55513-290-1*, 62901, Life Journey) Chariot Family.

Harding, Susan. Tell Me about God: Simple Studies in the Doctrine of God for Children. (Illus.). 64p. (ps-4). 1985. pap. 7.95 (*0-85151-510-X*) Banner of Truth.

Harner, Ruth. Send Someone to Tell Me. Smith, Dale, illus. 16p. (gr. k-6). 1988. pap. text ed. 4.25 (*1-55976-135-0*) CEF Press.

Hartman, Bob. Who Brought the Bread? Stortz, Diane, ed. (Illus.). 32p. (gr. 1-3). 1994. 12.99 (*0-7847-0188-1*) Standard Pub.

—Who Wrecked the Roof? Stortz, Diane, ed. (Illus.). 32p. (gr. 1-8). 1994. 12.99 (*0-7847-0189-X*) Standard Pub.

Haskin, Dorothy. The One Who Was Different. Butcher, Sam, illus. 16p. (gr. k-6). 1983. pap. text ed. 4.25 (*1-55976-130-X*) CEF Press.

Have You Got a Minute, GOD? Prayers by Teens. (Illus.). 30p. (Orig.). (gr. 7-12). 1990. pap. 2.00 (*0-937997-15-3*) Hi-Time Pub.

Hayhurst, L. W. The Christian Boy, 4 vols. 1964. Vol. 1. pap. 2.50 (*0-685-74299-7*, CB100); Vol. 2. pap. 2.50 (*0-685-74300-4*, CB200); Vol. 3. pap. 2.50 (*0-685-74301-2*, CB300); Vol. 4. pap. 2.50 (*0-685-74302-0*, CB400) Quality Pubns.

Hayhurst, Mamie W. The Christian Girl, 4 vols. 1964. Vol. 1. pap. 2.50 (*0-685-74303-9*, CG100); Vol. 2. pap. 2.50 (*0-685-74304-7*, CG200); Vol. 3. pap. 2.50 (*0-685-75590-8*, CG300); Vol. 4. pap. 2.50 (*0-685-74306-3*, CG400) Quality Pubns.

Heerey, Frances C. First Holy Communion. 1988. pap. 3.95 (*0-88271-057-5*) Regina Pr.

Hernandez, Frank & Hernandez, Betsy. Hide em in Your Heart: Activity Book. Dugan, Terry & Slonim, David, illus. 40p. (Orig.). (ps-6). 1991. pap. 7.95 (*0-917143-06-X*) Sparrow TN.

Hershey, Katerine. The Message of a Star. Bates, Stephen & Williamson, Kevin, illus. 9p. (gr. k-6). 1982. pap. 4.25 (*1-55976-133-4*) CEF Press.

Hershey, Katherine. The Christian Soldier. Biel, Bill, et al, illus. 10p. (gr. k-6). 1981. pap. text ed. 4.25 (*1-55976-138-5*) CEF Press.

—A Shepherd for You. (Illus.). 22p. (gr. k-6). 1988. pap. text ed. 4.25 (*1-55976-149-0*) CEF Press.

Higgins, John. Meet God! A Young Christian's Handbook for Knowing God. LC 88-80294. (Illus.). 128p. (gr. 4-6). 1988. 6.50 (*0-88243-488-8*, 02-0488) Gospel Pub.

Hillis, Don W. Stories of Love that Lasts. 80p. (gr. 9-12). 1980. pap. 1.00 (*0-89323-015-4*) Bible Memory.

Hogan, Jan. Gladdys Makes Peace. Wine, Jeanine M., illus. 22p. (gr. 1-5). 1985. 9.95 (*0-87178-313-4*) Brethren.

Hollingsworth, Mary. My Very First Book of Bible Lessons. LC 93-9641. 1993. pap. 4.99 (*0-8407-9227-1*) Nelson.

—My Very First Book of Bible Words. LC 93-21843. 1993. 4.99 (*0-8407-9226-3*) Nelson.

Horie, Michiaki & Horie, Hildegard. Steps to Inner Freedom. Huff, Dawn, tr. from GER. Paff, Mike, illus. 120p. (Orig.). (gr. 7 up). 1987. pap. 5.95 (*0-939925-06-0*) R C Law & Co.

Horlacher, Bill & Horlacher, Kathy. I'm Glad I'm Your Grandma. Beegle, Shirley, ed. Hutton, Kathryn, illus. 24p. (ps-3). 1994. pap. 1.89 (*0-7847-0260-8*) Standard Pub.

How the Dyaks Learned to Give. 20p. (gr. k-6). 1986. pap. text ed. 4.25 (*1-55976-140-7*) CEF Press.

Howard, Barbara. Journey of Joy. 157p. (gr. 5 up). 1990. pap. text ed. 11.00 (*0-8309-0562-6*) Herald Hse.

Huddleston, Steve. What Is God's Purpose for Me? (Illus.). 48p. (gr. 6-8). 1992. pap. 8.99 (*1-55945-132-7*) Group Pub.

Hunt, Angela E. Pulling Yourself Together When Your Parents Are Pulling Apart. LC 94-11147. (gr. 3 up). 1995. write for info. (*0-8423-5104-3*) Tyndale.

Hutchcraft, Doug & Hutchcraft, Ronald P. Letters from the College Front: Guys' Edition. (Illus.). 80p. (gr. 9-12). 1993. 8.99 (*0-8010-4379-4*) Baker Bk.

Hutson, Joan. I'm Glad I Am: Christian Affirmations for Children. Hutson, Joan, illus. LC 92-10627. 48p. (Orig.). (gr. 1-4). 1992. pap. 3.95 (*0-8198-3623-0*) St Paul Bks.

Image, Vols. I, II & III. (gr. 7). 1993. 8.50 (*0-7829-0347-9*, 88070) Tabor Pub.

Image. annotated ed. (gr. 7). 1993. 11.95 (*0-7829-0349-5*, 88170) Tabor Pub.

Incredible Meetings for Kids Grades 4-6. 128p. (gr. 4-6). 1991. pap. 12.99 (*0-89693-927-8*) SP Pubns.

Jackson, Neta. Loving One Another. Gavitt, Anne, illus. 192p. (ps-2). 1993. 10.99 (*0-945564-66-X*, Gold & Honey) Questar Pubs.

Jafolla, Mary-Alice. The Simple Truth. LC 81-69084. 109p. 1993. pap. 9.95 (*0-87159-199-5*) Unity Bks.

Javernick, Ellen. Celebrate the Christian Family. Mohler, Sarah, illus. 144p. (gr. k-6). 1987. pap. 11.95 (*0-86653-391-5*, SS 844, Shining Star Pubns) Good Apple.

Jay, Ruth J. Learning from God's Animals. Ratzlaff, Lynette, illus. 36p. (Orig.). (ps-k). 1981. pap. 2.99 (*0-934998-04-3*) Bethel Pub.

—Learning from God's Birds. Ratzlaff, Lynette, illus. 34p. (Orig.). (ps-k). 1981. pap. 2.99 (*0-934998-05-1*) Bethel Pub.

Johanning, Jolynn. God Made All of Me: Activities for Young Children. (Illus.). 120p. 1992. pap. text ed. 11.95 (*0-89390-210-1*) Resource Pubns.

Johnson, Betty. Gifts & Rewards. Butcher, Sam, illus. 13p. (gr. k-6). 1981. pap. text ed. 4.25 (*1-55976-137-7*) CEF Press.

—Teach Me Now, Vol. I. (Illus.). 80p. (ps). 1981. pap. text ed. 24.99 kit (*1-55976-108-3*) CEF Press.

—Teach Me Now, Vol. II. (Illus.). 90p. (ps). 1982. pap. text ed. 24.99 kit (*1-55976-109-1*) CEF Press.

—Teach Me Now, Vol. III. (Illus.). 80p. (ps). 1983. pap. text ed. 24.99 kit (*1-55976-110-5*) CEF Press.

—Teach Me Now, Vol. IV. (Illus.). 87p. (ps). 1984. pap. text ed. 24.99 kit (*1-55976-111-3*) CEF Press.

Johnson, Greg & Shellenberger, Susie. Keeping Your Cool While Sharing Your Faith. LC 93-7532. (Illus.). 1993. 7.99 (*0-8423-7036-6*) Tyndale.

Johnson, Kevin. Can I Be a Christian Without Being Weird? LC 92-15804. 1992. pap. 6.99 (*1-55661-281-8*) Bethany Hse.

Johnson, Lois W. You're My Best Friend, Lord. LC 76-3866. 112p. (Orig.). (gr. 4-7). 1976. pap. 5.99 (*0-8066-1541-9*, 10-7490, Augsburg) Augsburg Fortress.

Johnstone, Jill. You Can Change the World. 128p. (gr. 3-7). 1993. Printed caseside. pap. 14.99 (*0-310-40041-4*, Pub. by Youth Spec) Zondervan.

Jones, Bill. No Problem! 176p. 1992. pap. 4.99 (*0-89693-613-9*) SP Pubns.

Jones, Chris. What Do I Do Now Lord? LC 76-3860. 112p. (Orig.). (gr. 4-7). 1976. pap. 5.99 (*0-8066-1539-7*, 10-7044, Augsburg) Augsburg Fortress.

Jones, Rebecca C. I Am Not Afraid. (Illus.). (ps). 1987. pap. 2.50 (*0-570-09113-6*, 56-1588) Concordia.

Joy, Flora. Creative Writing Booklets. 64p. (gr. k-6). 1985. 7.95 (*0-86653-274-9*, GA626) Good Apple.

—Creative Writing Booklets, No. 2. 64p. (gr. k-6). 1985. 7.95 (*0-86653-284-6*, GA629) Good Apple.

Kauffman, Suzanne. God's Suffering Servant Activity Book. 64p. 1988. pap. 3.00 (*0-8361-3450-8*) Herald Pr.

Kelemen, Julie. Advent Is for Children. 64p. (Orig.). (gr. 3 up). 1988. pap. 2.95 (*0-89243-292-6*) Liguori Pubns.

Kelley, Gail & Hershberger, Carol. Come Mime with Me: A Guide to Preparing Scriptural Dramas for Children. LC 86-62621. (Illus.). 104p. (gr. 1 up). 1987. 10.95 (*0-89390-089-3*) Resource Pubns.

Kelly, Paul. Forgiveness. (Illus.). 48p. (gr. 9-12). 1992. pap. 8.99 (*1-55945-223-4*) Group Pub.

Kemper, Kristen. Co-Workers in Creation: First Steps in Ecology. 68p. (Orig.). (gr. 1-6). 1991. pap. 9.95 (*1-877871-19-2*) Ed Ministries.

Kesler, Jay & Stafford, Tim. Making Life Make Sense: Answers to Hard Questions about God & You. 176p. 1991. pap. 7.99 (*0-310-71191-6*, Campus Life) Zondervan.

Kesler, Jay L. Challenges for the College Bound: Advice & Encouragement from a College President. LC 93-36779. 160p. (gr. 12). 1994. 8.99 (*0-8010-5262-9*) Baker Bk.

Kile, Joan. God's Mustard Seed, Vol. 1. Ragland, Teresa, illus. 32p. (ps-5). 1993. PLB 15.00 (*0-9636314-0-3*) Musty the Mustard.

Klaus, Sandra. Life Is Valuable. Hilterbrand, Greg, illus. (gr. k-6). 1987. pap. 4.25 (*1-55976-152-0*) CEF Press.

—Pythons & Book Reports. Bates, Steve, illus. 51p. (gr. k-6). 1987. pap. text ed. 6.99 (*1-55976-178-4*) CEF Press.

Klein, Patricia, ed. Growing up Born Again. LC 87-26393. (Illus.). 160p. (gr. 10 up). 1987. pap. 7.99 (*0-8007-5259-7*) Revell.

Knauer, Daryl. The Boy Who Couldn't. Stortz, Diane, ed. (Illus.). 28p. (ps-k). 1994. 5.49 (*0-7847-0199-7*) Standard Pub.

Laemmlen, Ann & Owen, Jackie. The Articles of Faith Learning Book. 171p. (gr. 3-6). 1990. pap. 7.95 wkbk. (*0-87579-400-9*) Deseret Bk.

Landis, Mary M. Health for the Glory of God. (gr. 4-5). 1976. write for info. (*0-686-15484-3*); tchr's. ed. avail. (*0-686-15485-1*) Rod & Staff.

Larsen, Dale & Larsen, Sandy. Discovering Myself: Who Am I Anyway? (Illus.). 32p. (Orig.). (gr. 7-10). 1987. Camper Ed. saddle-stitched 1.50 (*0-87788-178-2*); Counselor Ed. saddle-stitched 3.50 (*0-87788-179-0*) Shaw Pubs.

—Got a License, but Where Do I Go? Devotions for Teens on the Move. LC 87-36576. 112p. (Orig.). (gr. 8-12). 1988. pap. 5.99 (*0-87788-295-9*) Shaw Pubs.

Lashbrook, Marilyn. Digging for Buried Treasure. Bates, Steve, illus. 12p. (gr. k-6). 1984. pap. text ed. 4.25 (*1-55976-141-5*) CEF Press.

—God Speaks to Me. Bates, Stephen, illus. 52p. (gr. k-6). 1985. pap. text ed. 8.99 (*1-55976-030-3*) CEF Press.

Lawson, Michael & Skipp, David. Sexo y Mas: Guia Para la Juventud. (SPA., Illus.). 110p. (Orig.). (gr. 10-12). 1988. pap. 2.95 (*0-945792-02-6*) Editorial Unilit.

LeFever, Marlene. God's Special Creation--Me! (Illus.). 48p. (Orig.). (gr. 4-6). 1987. Camper Ed. pap. 1.50 (*0-87788-313-0*); Counselor Ed. pap. 3.50 (*0-87788-314-9*) Shaw Pubs.

Lehman, Paula D. Journey with Justice. Hull, Eddy & Shelly, Maynard, eds. Dirks, Ray, illus. LC 90-81509. 100p. (Orig.). 1990. pap. 7.95 (*0-87303-139-3*) Faith & Life.

Leichner, Jeannine T. Called to His Supper. (Illus.). 64p. (Orig.). (gr. 1-3). 1990. pap. 3.95 (*0-87973-138-9*, 138) Our Sunday Visitor.

LeJeune, Shonda. God Is. LeJeune, Shonda, illus. 32p. (Orig.). (gr. 3-8). 1993. pap. 8.95 (*0-87516-659-8*) DeVorss.

Let the Lord Have His Way. (Illus.). (gr. k-6). 1973. visualized song 3.50 (*3-90117-013-8*) CEF Press.

Libby, Larry. Someday Heaven. 48p. 13.99 (*0-945564-77-5*, Gold & Honey) Questar Pubs.

—Somewhere Angels. 48p. (gr. k-5). 1994. 13.99 (*0-88070-651-1*, Gold & Honey) Questar Pubs.

Linam, Gail. God's Fall Gifts. Hester, Ron, illus. (ps). 1992. pap. 3.95 (*0-8054-4159-X*, 4241-59) Broadman.

Link, Mark. Challenge. 160p. (gr. 9-12). 1987. 6.95 (*0-89505-654-2*, 22014) Tabor Pub.

Linn, Joseph. Can You Imagine? 1983. songbk. 5.95 (*0-685-68206-4*, BCMB-519); coloring bk. 0.75 (*0-685-68207-2*, BCMU-728); cassette 12.98 (*0-685-68208-0*, BCTA-9045C) Lillenas.

Lipson, Greta & Greenberg, Bernice. Extra! Extra! Read All about It! 160p. (gr. 4-8). 1981. 12.95 (*0-86653-006-1*, GA234) Good Apple.

Littleton, Mark. Fillin' Up. Evans, Graci, illus. 168p. 1992. 8.99 (*0-945564-72-4*, Gold & Honey) Questar Pubs.

—Tunin' Up: Daily Jammin' for Tight Relationships. Heaney, Liz, ed. 208p. 1992. pap. 8.99 (*0-88070-454-3*, Gold & Honey) Questar Pubs.

Living for God: Daily Bread. (Illus.). (gr. k-4). 1977. pap. 6.99 (*1-55976-325-6*) CEF Press.

Livingston, J. B. If I Were a Teenager: Pupil Book, 4 vols. 1966. pap. 2.50 (*0-685-74307-1*) Quality Pubns.

Loman, Roberta K., illus. All about Hands. 28p. (ps). 1992. 2.50 (*0-87403-951-7*, 24-03591) Standard Pub.

The Lord Is My Shepherd. (Illus.). (gr. k-6). 1963. visualized song 4.99 (*3-90117-004-9*) CEF Press.

Lost & Found Kit. (gr. k-6). 1978. 19.99 (*1-55976-105-9*) CEF Press.

Loth, Paul. The Bible Tells Me So. LC 93-18723. 1993. 7.99 (*0-8407-9232-8*) Nelson.

Loth, Paul J. First Steps. LC 92-11389. 1992. 7.99 (*0-8407-9167-4*) Nelson.

Loveland Comm. Staff. Discover Animals. 1992. 4.49 (*1-55513-910-8*, Chariot Bks) Chariot Family.

—Discover Colors. 1992. 4.49 (*1-55513-916-7*, Chariot Bks) Chariot Family.

—Discover Families. 1992. 4.49 (*1-55513-911-6*, Chariot Bks) Chariot Family.

—Discover Sizes & Shapes. 1992. 4.49 (*1-55513-909-4*, Chariot Bks) Chariot Family.

Lowry, James W. In the Whale's Belly & Other Martyr Stories. (Illus.). (gr. 7 up). 1981. pap. 4.70 (*0-87813-513-8*) Christian Light.

Lynn, Claire, compiled by. Build on the Rock. Lautermilch, John & Fearber, Sharon, illus. 52p. (Orig.). (ps-7). 1979. pap. 1.25 (*0-89323-000-6*, 707) Bible Memory.

Lynn, Daryl, et al. Evident Progress. 60p. (Orig.). 1991. pap. 2.25 (*0-89323-046-4*) Bible Memory.

Lynn, David. More High School Talksheets: Fifty All-New Creative Discussions for High School Youth Groups. 112p. 1992. pap. 9.99 (*0-310-57491-9*, Pub. by Youth Spec) Zondervan.

—More Junior High Talksheets: Fifty All-New Creative Discussions for Junior High Youth Groups. 112p. 1992. pap. 9.99 (*0-310-57481-1*, Pub. by Youth Spec) Zondervan.

—More Zingers. 1990. pap. 8.99 (*0-310-52521-7*) Zondervan.

Lynn, David & Lynn, Kathy. More Zingers for First to Third Graders. 64p. (gr. 1-3). 1993. Saddle stitch. pap. 7.99 (*0-310-37231-3*, Pub. by Youth Spec) Zondervan.

—Zingers for First to Third Graders: 12 Real-Life Character Builders. 64p. (gr. 1-3). 1993. Saddle stitch. pap. 7.99 (*0-310-37221-6*, Pub. by Youth Spec) Zondervan.

McAllister, Dawson. Discussion Manual for Student Relationships, Vol. 2. Lamb, Jim, illus. (gr. 5-12). 1976. pap. 8.75 (*0-923417-07-9*) Shepherd Minst.

—Discussion Manual for Student Relationships, Vol. 3. Lamb, Jim, illus. (gr. 5-12). 1978. pap. 8.75 (*0-923417-08-7*) Shepherd Minst.

—How to Know If You're Really in Love. LC 93-40906. 1994. 8.99 (*0-8499-3312-9*) Word Pub.

—Please Don't Tell My Parents. 176p. 1992. pap. 8.99 (*0-8499-3311-0*) Word Inc.

—Student Relationships, Vol. 1. (gr. 5-12). 1981. pap. 6.95 tchr's. guide (*0-923417-18-4*) Shepherd Minst.

McAllister, Dawson & Kimmel, Tim. Student Relationships, Vol. 2. (gr. 5-12). 1981. pap. 6.95 tchr's. guide (*0-923417-04-4*) Shepherd Minst.

MacAllister, Dawson & Kimmel, Tim. Student Relationships, Vol. 3. (gr. 5-12). 1981. pap. 6.95 tchr's. guide (*0-923417-19-2*) Shepherd Minst.

McAllister, Dawson & Miller, John. Discussion Manual for Student Discipleship, Vol. 2. Lamb, Jim, illus. (gr. 5-12). 1978. pap. 8.50 (*0-923417-16-8*) Shepherd Minst.

McAllister, Dawson & Sharp, Floyd. Handbook for Financial Faithfulness. (Illus.). (gr. 5-12). 1974. pap. 6.95 (*0-923417-17-6*) Shepherd Minst.

McAllister, Dawson & Webster, Dan. Discussion Manual for Student Discipleship, Vol. 1. Lamb, Jim, illus. (gr. 5-12). 1975. pap. 8.50 (*0-923417-15-X*) Shepherd Minst.

—Discussion Manual for Student Relationships, Vol. 1. Lamb, Jim, illus. (gr. 5-12). 1975. pap. 8.75 (*0-923417-06-0*) Shepherd Minst.

McAuley. God Hears Everything. LC 91-72357. 1992. 4.99 (*1-55513-715-6*, Chariot Bks) Chariot Family.

—God Made Fireflies. LC 91-72356. 1992. 4.99 (*1-55513-716-4*, Chariot Bks) Chariot Family.

McCullough, Steven. Becoming Responsible. (Illus.). 48p. (gr. 6-8). 1991. pap. 8.99 (*1-55945-109-2*) Group Pub.

Machado, Antonio A., et al. Our Lady at Fatima: Prophecies of Tragedy or Hope for America & the World? LC 85-70673. (Illus.). 128p. (Orig.). (gr. 8). 1986. pap. 7.95 (*1-877-90510-0*) Am Soc Defense TFP.

McIntosh, Scott. How to Be an Angel: The Book the Devil Did Not Want Published. (Illus.). 80p. (Orig.). 1993. pap. 9.95 (*0-9632879-1-5*) McIntosh Pubns.

McKissack, Patricia A. Lights Out, Christopher. Bartholomew, illus. LC 84-71375. 32p. (Orig.). (ps-1). 1984. pap. 5.99 (*0-8066-2110-9*, 10-3870, Augsburg) Augsburg Fortress.

McKissack, Patricia C. It's the Truth, Christopher. Bartholomew, illus. LC 84-71376. 32p. (Orig.). (ps-1). 1984. pap. 5.99 (*0-8066-2111-7*, 10-3457, Augsburg) Augsburg Fortress.

McMillan, Mary. Christian Celebrations for Autumn & Winter. 96p. (gr. 2-7). 1990. 10.95 (*0-86653-546-2*, SS1821, Shining Star Pubns) Good Apple.

Maddox, Linda G. Step Toward Freedom. LC 88-8154. (Orig.). (gr. 12). 1991. 7.99 (*0-8054-5070-X*) Broadman.

Mahany, Patricia S. Hurry up, Noah. Beegle, Shirley, ed. Pollard, Nan, illus. 24p. (ps-3). 1994. pap. 1.89 (*0-7847-0257-8*) Standard Pub.

Marshall, Peter, et al. The Light & the Glory for Children. LC 92-11727. (Illus.). 160p. (Orig.). (gr. 4-7). 1992. pap. 9.99 (*0-8007-5448-4*) Revell.

Martin, John D. Living Together on God's Earth. (gr. 3). 1974. 15.00x (*0-87813-915-X*); tchr's. guide 19.65x (*0-87813-910-9*) Christian Light.

Matranga, Frances C. I'm Glad I'm Me! Beegle, Shirley, ed. McCallum, Joanne, illus. 24p. (ps-3). 1994. pap. 1.89 (*0-7847-0259-4*) Standard Pub.

—The Perfect Friend. 80p. (Orig.). (gr. 5-7). 1985. pap. 3.99 (*0-570-04112-0*, 56-1523) Concordia.

Mattozzi, Patti. Little Lessons for Little Learners: Heaven. (gr. 3 up). 1991. 4.50 (*0-8378-1986-5*) Gibson.

Maxwell, Arthur S. & Holloway, Cheryl W. Uncle Arthur's Storytime. Mull, Christy, et al, illus. 128p. 1989. 29.90 (*1-877773-03-4*) Family Media.

—Uncle Arthur's Storytime, Vol. 1. Tank, Darrel, et al, illus. 128p. 1989. PLB 29.90 (*1-877773-01-8*) Family Media.

—Uncle Arthur's Storytime, Vol. 2. Mull, Christ, et al, illus. 128p. 1989. PLB 29.90 (*1-877773-02-6*) Family Media.

Maxwell, Cassandre. Bright Star, Bright Star, What Do You See? Maxwell, Cassandre, illus. LC 89-82551. 32p. (ps-k). 1990. pap. 5.99 (*0-8066-2462-0*, 9-2462) Augsburg Fortress.

Mazak, Lisa. One, Two, Three, Jesus Loves Me. (Illus.). (gr. k-6). 1982. illustrated song 3.99 (*3-90117-018-9*) CEF Press.

Mehew, Randall & Mehew, Karen. Gospel Basic Busy Book, Vol. II. Bales, Marcia, illus. 100p. 1990. pap. text ed. 6.95 (*0-910613-08-7*) Millenial Pr.

Middleton, Barth & Middleton, Sally. Living God's Way. Bates, Steve, illus. 64p. (gr. k-6). 1985. pap. text ed. 11.99 (*1-55976-031-1*) CEF Press.

—Loving God's Way. Bates, Stephen, illus. 55p. (gr. k-6). 1988. pap. text ed. 7.50 (*1-55976-033-8*) CEF Press.

Miller, R. Edward. The Flaming Flame. 95p. (Orig.). (gr. 12). 1973. pap. 2.50 (*0-945818-03-3*) Peniel Pubns.

—I Looked & I Saw Mysteries. Schisler, Jack, intro. by. 106p. (gr. 12). 1988. pap. 3.50 (*0-945818-01-7*) Peniel Pubns.

—I Looked & I Saw the Lord. Schisler, Jack, intro. by. 95p. (Orig.). (gr. 12). 1988. pap. 3.50 (*0-945818-00-9*) Peniel Pubns.

—I Looked & I Saw Visions of God. 147p. (Orig.). (gr. 12). 1974. pap. 3.50 (*0-945818-06-8*) Peniel Pubns.

—I Looked & Saw the Heavens Opened... 96p. (Orig.). (gr. 12). 1972. pap. 3.50 (*0-945818-05-X*) Peniel Pubns.

—The Prince & the Three Beggars. 33p. (Orig.). (gr. 12). 1975. pap. 2.00 (*0-945818-04-1*) Peniel Pubns.

—Secrets of the Kingdom. 180p. (Orig.). (gr. 10). 1989. pap. 5.25 (*0-945818-08-4*) Peniel Pubns.

—Thy God Reigneth. Frodsham, Stanley, intro. by. 58p. (gr. 12). 1964. pap. 2.50 (*0-945818-02-5*) Peniel Pubns.

—Victory in Adversity. 168p. (Orig.). (gr. 10). 1988. pap. 4.95 (*0-945818-07-6*) Peniel Pubns.

Mills, Charles. My Talents for Jesus; When I Grow Up. LC 92-26393. 1993. 8.95 (*0-8163-1115-3*) Pacific Pr Pub Assn.

Moore, Joseph. Learning to Serve - Serving to Learn: A Christian Service Program for Students. LC 94-70327. 112p. (Orig.). (gr. 9-12). 1993. pap. text ed. 3.95 (*0-87793-526-2*); tchr's. ed., 128p. 10.95 (*0-87793-531-9*) Ave Maria.

Morgan, Les. Pulling Weeds. Hartley, Fred, frwd. by. LC 88-93031. 124p. (Orig.). (gr. 9-12). 1989. pap. 5.99 (*0-87509-414-7*) Chr Pubns.

Morris-McKinsey, Jill, ed. Religiously Speaking: Plays & Poems for Children's Church. 48p. (Orig.). 1992. pap. 7.98 (*1-877588-03-2*) Creatively Yours.

Morrow, Roger & Glenn, Monica. Let's Talk. 160p. (Orig.). (gr. 7-12). 1991. pap. 4.95 (*0-8474-6625-6*) Back to Bible.

Mueller, Charles S. & Bardill, Donald R. Thank God, I'm a Teenager. rev. ed. LC 88-6215. (Illus.). 144p. (gr. 7-12). 1988. pap. 8.99 (*0-8066-2351-9*, 10-6242, Augsburg) Augsburg Fortress.

Mueller, Virginia. What Is Faith? Beegle, Shirley, ed. Hutton, Kathryn, illus. 24p. (ps-3). 1994. pap. 1.89 (*0-7847-0265-9*) Standard Pub.

Murdock, Michael D. The God-Book. Loy, Joy A., ed. 250p. (Orig.). 1991. pap. text ed. 4.95 (*1-56394-004-3*) Wisdom Intl.

Myers, Bill. More Hot Topics. 144p. 1989. pap. 5.99 (*0-89693-670-8*) SP Pubns.

Nally, Susan & Lee, Liz. How to Feel Most Excellent! About Who You Are (& Really Enjoy It) LC 93-48685. (gr. 6 up). 1994. 7.99 (*0-8054-4008-9*) Broadman.

Napa, Amy. Dealing with Disappointment. (Illus.). 48p. (gr. 6-8). 1992. pap. 8.99 (*1-55945-139-4*) Group Pub.

Nappa, Mike. Accepting Other: Beyond Barriers & Stereotypes. (Illus.). 48p. (gr. 6-8). 1992. pap. 8.99 (*1-55945-126-2*) Group Pub.

—Reaching Out to a Hurting World. (Illus.). 48p. (gr. 6-8). 1992. pap. 8.99 (*1-55945-140-8*) Group Pub.

Norman, Louise. God's Power Versus Satan's Power: Christian Life Lessons. Snader, Barbara, illus. 64p. (Orig.). (gr. 1-8). 1985. pap. text ed. 12.50 (*0-86508-062-3*) BCM Pubn.

Nye, Julie. Every Perfect Gift. Vogt, Carla, ed. Weikel, Cheryl, illus. 201p. (Orig.). (gr. 9 up). 1990. pap. 4.95 (*0-89084-499-2*) Bob Jones Univ Pr.

Nystrom, Carolyn & Floding, Matthew. Relationships: Face to Face. (Illus.). 64p. (Orig.). (gr. 7 up). 1986. saddle-stitched student ed. 3.99 (*0-87788-722-5*); saddle-stitched tchr's. ed. 4.99 (*0-87788-723-3*) Shaw Pubs.

O'Connell, Frances H. Giving & Growing: A Student's Guide for Service Projects. Stamschror, Robert P., ed. Mediawerks Staff, illus. 79p. (Orig.). (gr. 7-12). 1990. text ed. 3.50 stitched (*0-88489-224-7*); tchr's. ed. 3.95 (*0-88489-225-5*) St Marys.

Odor, Harold & Odor, Ruth. Becoming a Christian. Greene, Tom, illus. 16p. (gr. 3-7). 1985. 0.99 (*0-87239-901-X*, 3301) Standard Pub.

Odor, Ruth S. A Child's Book of Manners. Beegle, Shirley, ed. McCallum, Joanne, illus. 24p. (ps-3). 1994. pap. 1.89 (*0-7847-0252-7*) Standard Pub.

Oke, Janette. Love Comes Softly, 4 bks, Vols. 1-4. 1993. Set. 27.99 (*1-55661-777-1*) Bethany Hse.

—Love Comes Softly, 4 bks, Vols. 5-8. 1993. Set. 27.99 (*1-55661-778-X*) Bethany Hse.

—Love's Unending Legacy. large type ed. LC 84-18412. 224p. (gr. 4 up). 1985. pap. 8.99 (*0-87123-855-1*) Bethany Hse.

—Winter Is Not Forever. large type ed. LC 88-2882. 224p. (gr. 4 up). 1988. 6.99 (*1-55661-002-5*); pap. 8.99 (*1-55661-008-4*) Bethany Hse.

The One Year Book of Devotions for Kids. LC 93-15786. 1993. pap. 10.99 (*0-8423-5088-8*) Tyndale.

O'Neal, Esther. Knowing Christ. (Illus.). 64p. (gr. k-6). 1962. pap. text ed. 8.99 (*1-55976-026-5*) CEF Press.

Orange, Tom & McClure, Nancee. Bulletin Boards That Bless. 48p. (gr. 4-8). 1984. wkbk. 7.95 (*0-86653-201-3*, SS 821, Shining Star Pubns) Good Apple.

Our Fathers World. (gr. 2). 1982. 4.60 (*0-686-37694-3*) Rod & Staff.

Overholtzer, Ruth P. Life of Peter. Beerhorst, Adrian, illus. 21p. (gr. k-6). 1964. pap. text ed. 9.45 (*1-55976-013-3*) CEF Press.

Page, Carole G. Neeley Never Said Good-By. (Orig.). (gr. 7 up). 1984. pap. 4.99 (*0-8024-8454-9*) Moody.

Palmer, Glenda. Blue Galoshes in Spring: God's Wonderful World of Seasons. LC 92-34716. (Illus.). 1993. pap. 4.99 (*0-7814-0710-9*, Chariot Bks) Chariot Family.

—P Is for Pink Polliwogs: God's Wonderful World of Letters. LC 92-34715. (Illus.). 1993. pap. 4.99 (*0-7814-0708-7*, Chariot Bks) Chariot Family.

—Two Enormous Elephants: God's Wonderful World of Numbers. LC 92-34714. (Illus.). 1993. pap. 4.99 (*0-7814-0709-5*, Chariot Bks) Chariot Family.

Parry, Cindy. Activities That Build Young Women, Vol. 2. 48p. 1993. pap. 6.98 (*0-88290-457-4*) Horizon Utah.

Pearson, Mary R. All about God. LC 93-7692. 1993. 8.99 (*0-8423-1215-3*) Tyndale.

Pennock, Michael. Being Catholic: Believing, Living, Praying. LC 93-73883. (Illus.). 288p. (Orig.). (gr. 10-12). 1994. pap. text ed. 11.95 (*0-87793-527-0*); tchr's. ed., 232p. 15.95 (*0-87793-528-9*) Ave Maria.

—The Sacraments: Celebrating the Signs of God's Love. LC 92-75347. (Illus.). 240p. (Orig.). (gr. 9-12). 1993. pap. 9.95 (*0-87793-503-3*); 13.95 (*0-87793-504-1*) Ave Maria.

Perry, Cindy. Activities That Build Young Women, Vol. 1. 48p. 1993. pap. 6.98 (*0-88290-456-6*) Horizon Utah.

Peterson, Lorraine. Anybody Can Be Cool, but Awesome Takes Practice. LC 88-19454. (Illus.). 192p. (Orig.). (gr. 9-12). 1988. pap. 7.99 (*1-55661-040-8*) Bethany Hse.

Pick a Pack of Praise. (gr. 3-6). 1988. songbk. 6.50 (*0-685-68211-0*, BCMB-594); singers ed. 2.95 (*0-685-68212-9*, BCMB-594A); double-length split-channel cassette 12.98 (*0-685-68213-7*, BCTA-9100C) Lillenas.

Pinkston, William S., Jr. With Wings As Eagles. (Illus.). 127p. (gr. 2). 1983. pap. 6.94 (*0-89084-231-0*) Bob Jones Univ Pr.

Plueddemann, Jim. Ready! Get Set! Grow! (Illus.). 48p. 1987. Camper Ed. saddle-stitched 1.50 (*0-87788-715-2*); Counselor Ed. saddle-stitched 3.50 (*0-87788-716-0*) Shaw Pubs.

Potter, Velma M. God Flies Benny's Flag. Russell, Jervis F., ed. (Illus.). 235p. (gr. 4 up). 1989. pap. 12.95 (*0-939116-20-0*) Frontier OR.

Preschool Praise. 1988. wire-ring bdg. 6.50 (*0-8341-9083-4*, BCMB-586); split-channel cassette, double-length 12.98 (*0-685-68210-2*, BCTA-9096C) Lillenas.

Price, Brena. Giving, Christian Stewardship: Teaching Bks. Ressler, William, illus. 14p. (gr. 1-8). 1971. pap. text ed. 4.50 (*0-86508-154-9*) BCM Pubn.

Price, Cheryl. Memory Verse Motivators. 96p. (ps-5). 1990. 10.95 (*0-86653-550-0*, SS1823, Shining Star Pubns) Good Apple.

Price, Nelson L. Only the Beginning. LC 79-55662. (gr. 10 up). 1980. 7.99 (*0-8054-5331-8*, 4253-31) Broadman.

Pride, Mary. Baby Doe. (Illus.). 48p. 1990. 8.95 (*0-943497-94-9*) Wolgemuth & Hyatt.

Pudaite, Rochunga. Horizons Never End. Lombard, Lynette, illus. 20p. (gr. k-6). 1988. pap. text ed. 4.25 (*1-55976-144-X*) CEF Press.

Quest, Vols. I, II & III. (gr. 8). 1993. 8.50 (*0-7829-0348-7*, 88080) Tabor Pub.

Quest. annotated ed. (gr. 8). 1993. 11.95 (*0-7829-0353-3*, 88180) Tabor Pub.

Quigley, Betty. Our Master's Prayers: A Brief Story of Jesus' Life Based on His Prayers. Thurman, Nadine, pref. by. (Illus.). 160p. 1991. 12.50 (*0-9626735-1-X*); pap. 7.50 (*0-9626735-3-6*) Rabeth Pub Co.

Rebuck, Linda & Fettke, Tom. Gettin' Ready for the Miracle. 1985. 4.95 (*0-685-71358-X*, BCMC-57); cassette 10.98 (*0-685-71359-8*, BCTA-9071C) Lillenas.

—To Tell the Truth. 1985. 5.25 (*0-685-68203-X*, BCMB-546); cassette 10.98 (*0-685-68204-8*, BCTA-9065C) Lillenas.

Rector, Andy. The Secret Room. Stortz, Diane, ed. (Illus.). 48p. (Orig.). (ps-3). 1994. pap. 4.49 (*0-7847-0179-2*) Standard Pub.

Reid, Mary C. Come to the Mountain With Me. LC 92-73011. 32p. 1992. pap. 4.99 (*0-8066-2631-3*, 9-2631) Augsburg Fortress.

Repp, Gloria. His Best for God. (Illus.). 24p. (gr. k-6). 1989. pap. text ed. 4.25 (*1-55976-150-4*) CEF Press.

Richmond, Gary. Barnaby Goes Wild, No. 7. (gr. 1-5). 1991. text ed. 6.99 (*0-8499-0914-7*) Word Inc.

—Henry & the Great Flood. 32p. 1990. write for info. (*0-8499-0745-4*) Word Inc.

—Zookeeper Looks at Monkeys. 1991. pap. 3.99 (*0-8499-0861-2*) Word Inc.

—Zookeeper Looks at Mother & Baby Animals. 1991. pap. 3.99 (*0-8499-0863-9*) Word Inc.

Ridenour, Fritz. How to Be a Christian Without Being Religious. 166p. 1991. 5.99 (*0-8307-1026-4*, S182104); leader's guide 14.99 (*0-8307-1511-8*, SH215) Regal.

Robbins, Duffy. It's How You Play the Game. 132p. 1991. pap. 4.99 (*0-89693-856-5*) SP Pubns.

Roberts, Donald. Grace: God's Special Gift. (gr. 1-4). 1982. pap. 3.99 (*0-570-04060-4*, 56-1363) Concordia.

Roeda, Jack. Decisions. 2nd ed. Stoub, Paul, illus. Smith, Harvey A., intro. by. (Illus.). 80p. (gr. 9-12). 1992. pap. text ed. 6.50 (*0-930265-96-3*, 1240-4920); tchr's. manual 8.50 (*1-56212-000-X*, 1240-4940); session guides 4.95 (*0-685-60757-7*, 1240-4910) CRC Pubns.

Rogers, Ethel T. Thanks, God! 1985. 7.95 (*0-685-68222-6*, BCMB-551) Lillenas.

Runk, Wesley T. Standing Up for Jesus. (gr. k-4). 1985. 4.50 (*0-89536-725-4*, 5809) CSS OH.

S-A-L-V-A-T-I-O-N. (gr. k-6). 1971. illustrated song 2.99 (*3-90117-012-X*) CEF Press.

St. Clair, Barry & Jones, Bill. Love: Making It Last. 140p. (Orig.). 1993. pap. 5.99 (*1-56476-188-6*, Victor Books) SP Pubns.

St. Clair, Barry & Naylor, Keith. Taking Your Campus for Christ. 112p. (Orig.). 1993. pap. 4.99 (*1-56476-201-7*, Victor Books) SP Pubns.

Salladay, Susan. I Want a Puppy! (Illus.). 48p. (gr. 1-3). 1992. pap. 2.99 (*0-8423-1645-0*) Tyndale.

Salvation, Learning about God's Plan. 19p. (Orig.). (gr. 1-8). 1974. pap. text ed. 4.50 (*0-86508-151-4*) BCM Pubn.

Sanders, Bill. Hot & Cool: A Daily Calendar. (Illus.). 380p. (Orig.). (gr. 9-12). 1993. spiral bdg. 9.99 (*0-8007-7211-3*) Revell.

—Life, Sex & Everything in Between: Straight on Answers to the Questions That Trouble You Most. LC 90-49951. 160p. (Orig.). 1991. pap. 7.99 (*0-8007-5385-2*) Revell.

—Stand Tall: Learning to Really Love Yourself. LC 92-13985. 160p. (Orig.). 1992. pap. 7.99 (*0-8007-5452-2*) Revell.

—Stand Up: Making Peer Pressure Work for You. LC 93-18504. 200p. (Orig.). 1993. pap. 7.99 (0-8007-5458-1) Revell.

Sanford, Doris. For Your Own Good. Evans, Graci, illus. 24p. (gr. k-6). 1993. 7.99 (0-88070-604-X, Gold & Honey) Questar Pubs.

—It Won't Last Forever. Evans, Graci, illus. 28p. (gr. k-6). 1993. 7.99 (0-88070-605-8, Gold & Honey) Questar Pubs.

Sapp, Kathy. I Am a Part of Something Big. (Illus.). 306p. (Orig.). (gr. 4-6). 1989. pap. text ed. 3.50 (0-936625-66-X, New Hope AL) Womans Mission Union.

Sattgast. God Made Me Most Wonderfully. LC 91-7288. 1992. 7.99 (1-55513-556-0, Chariot Bks) Chariot Family.

Sattgast, L. J. Look What God Made! Smith, Julie, ed. McDonnell, Janet, illus. LC 94-9201. 32p. (ps-2). Date not set. 5.99 (0-7814-0184-4, Chariot Bks) Chariot Family.

Sattgast, Linda. When Stars Come Out. 120p. (ps-k). 1994. 9.99 (0-88070-641-4, Gold & Honey) Questar Pubs.

Sayler, Mary H. First Days in High School: Devotions to Cheer You On. 208p. 1994. 8.99 (0-8054-5372-5, 4253-72) Broadman.

Schmidt, J. David. More Graffiti: Devotions for Guys. LC 83-24523. (Illus.). 128p. (Orig.). (gr. 7-12). 1984. pap. 7.99 (0-8007-5142-6) Revell.

Schmidt, John. You & God Together...Friends Forever. 36p. (ps-2). 1994. PLB 6.95 (1-881907-12-0) Two Bytes Pub.

Schulte, Elaine. Twelve Candles, 4 vols, Vols. 1-4. 1993. Set. 19.99 (1-55661-781-X) Bethany Hse.

Sciacca, Fran & Sciacca, Jill. Are Families Forever? Understanding Your Family. 64p. 1992. pap. 3.99 saddle stitch bdg. (0-310-48071-X) Zondervan.

—Burgers, Fries, & a Friend to Go: Making Friends. 64p. 1992. pap. 3.99 saddle stitch bdg. (0-310-48041-8) Zondervan.

—Cliques & Clones. (gr. 7 up). 1987. pap. 3.95 (0-89066-100-6) World Wide Pubs.

—Cliques & Clones: Facing Peer Pressure. 64p. 1992. pap. 3.99 saddle stitch bdg. (0-310-48031-0) Zondervan.

—Does Anyone Else Feel This Way? Conquering Loneliness & Depression. 64p. 1992. pap. 3.99 saddle stitch bdg. (0-310-48021-3) Zondervan.

—Does God Live Here Anymore? 1988. pap. 3.95 (0-89066-113-8) World Wide Pubs.

—Good News for a Bad News World. 1989. pap. 3.95 (0-685-25653-7) World Wide Pubs.

—Good News in a Bad News World: Understanding the Gospel. 64p. 1992. pap. 3.99 saddle stitch bdg. (0-310-48061-2) Zondervan.

—Is This the Real Thing? What Love Is & Isn't. 64p. 1992. pap. 3.99 saddle stitch bdg. (0-310-48081-7) Zondervan.

—Learning to Hope in a Wish-Filled World. 1988. pap. 3.95 (0-89066-111-1) World Wide Pubs.

—So What's Wrong with a Big Nose? 1988. pap. 3.95 (0-89066-112-X) World Wide Pubs.

—So What's Wrong with a Big Nose? Building Self-Esteem. 64p. 1992. pap. 3.99 saddle stitch bdg. (0-310-48051-5) Zondervan.

—Some Assembly Required. 1989. pap. 3.95 (0-685-25748-7) World Wide Pubs.

—Some Things Are Never Discounted. 1988. pap. 3.95 (0-89066-114-6) World Wide Pubs.

Searle-Barnes, Bonita. Air. (Illus.). 32p. (gr. k-3). 1993. 6.99 (0-7459-2694-0) Lion USA.

—Light. (Illus.). 32p. (gr. k-3). 1993. 6.99 (0-7459-2695-9) Lion USA.

—Sound. (Illus.). 32p. (gr. k-3). 1993. 6.99 (0-7459-2692-4) Lion USA.

—Water. (Illus.). 32p. (gr. k-3). 1993. 6.99 (0-7459-2693-2) Lion USA.

—The Wonder of God's World: Air. Smithson, Colin, illus. LC 92-44575. 1993. 6.99 (0-7459-2021-7) Lion USA.

—The Wonder of God's World: Light. Smithson, Colin, illus. LC 92-44275. 1993. 6.99 (0-7459-2022-5) Lion USA.

—The Wonder of God's World: Water. Smithson, Colin, illus. LC 92-44274. 1993. 6.99 (0-7459-2024-1) Lion USA.

Serratt, Mary L. Light Journey: Adventures in Personal Witnessing. Nelson, Becky, ed. 32p. (gr. 7-12). 1993. pap. text ed. 4.95 (1-56309-063-5) Womans Mission Union.

Shackelford, Robert D. Benefits of Righteousness. 73p. (Orig.). (gr. 9-12). 1988. pap. 3.95 (0-9618308-2-4) R Shackelford.

Sharing the Light in the Wilderness: Favorite Talks from Especially for Youth. LC 93-2985. x, 193p. (Orig.). (gr. 8-12). 1993. pap. 5.95 (0-87579-717-2) Deseret Bk.

Shaw, Rick. Competition. (Illus.). 48p. (gr. 6-8). 1992. pap. 8.99 (1-55945-133-5) Group Pub.

Shellenberger, Susie. Straight Ahead: Twenty-Eight Devotionals for Teen Disciples. 32p. 1987. pap. 1.95 (0-8341-1199-3) Beacon Hill.

Shepherd, Linda E. Kara's Quest. LC 93-26476. Date not set. 7.99 (0-8407-9680-3) Nelson.

—Ryan's Trials. LC 93-25995. (gr. 9-12). Date not set. pap. 7.99 (0-8407-9681-1) Nelson.

Sheppard, Sandy. Avaricious Ardvarks & Other Alphabet Tongue Twisters. Stortz, Diane, ed. (Illus.). 28p. (ps-k). 1994. 5.49 (0-7847-0200-4) Standard Pub.

Simon, Mary M. My First Diary. Dorenkamp, Michelle, illus. 80p. (Orig.). (gr. 2-5). 1992. pap. 4.99 (0-570-04721-8) Concordia.

Simpson, Winifred R. I Can Help Mommy. (Illus.). (ps). 1987. pap. 2.50 (0-570-09112-8, 56-1587) Concordia.

Six Wonderful Things. 14p. (gr. k-6). 1976. pap. text ed. 4.25 (1-55976-126-1) CEF Press.

Smart, Janette & Camsey, Terry. Get on Board, Children. Skillings, Otis, contrib. by. 1976. 5.25 (0-8341-9133-4, BCMB-410); song charts 29.95 (0-685-68199-8, BCMU-710); cassette 10.98 (0-685-68200-5, BCTA-7137C) Lillenas.

Smith, Jane D. The Tabernacle. Butcher, Sam, illus. 38p. (gr. k-6). 1972. pap. text ed. 9.45 (1-55976-022-2) CEF Press.

Smith, Julie, ed. Sleepytime, Anytime with God. LC 94-4610. (Illus.). 384p. (ps-2). Date not set. 15.99 (0-7814-0174-7, Chariot Bks) Chariot Family.

Smith, Michael W. & Ridenour, Fritz. Old Enough to Know. large type ed. 111p. (gr. 7 up). 1989. pap. 12.99 (0-8499-3163-0) Word Inc.

So What's a Christian Anyway? 31p. 1989. pap. 1.99 (0-8307-1397-2, EL235) Regal.

Soaries, Buster. My Family Is Driving Me Crazy. 132p. 1991. pap. 4.99 (0-89693-939-1) SP Pubns.

Sorensen, David A. The Friendship Olympics: A Young Christian Book for Boys. LC 86-32259. 112p. (gr. 3-7). 1987. pap. 5.99 (0-8066-2248-2, 10-2430, Augsburg) Augsburg Fortress.

—Me, Myself, & God. LC 89-49096. 112p. (Orig.). (gr. 3-7). 1990. pap. 5.99 (0-8066-2442-6, 9-2442) Augsburg Fortress.

Sose, Bonnie. Designed by God So I Must Be Special. Sose, Bonnie, illus. 24p. (ps-2). 1991. 10.95 (0-9615279-6-X); Afro-American version available. 10.95 (0-9615279-4-3) Character Builders.

Speck, Greg. Living for Jesus When the Party's Over. 1991. pap. 7.99 (0-8024-4791-0) Moody.

Sprague, Gary. My Parents Got a Divorce. LC 91-43023. 1992. pap. 7.99 (0-7814-0486-X, Chariot Bks) Chariot Family.

Stafford, Tim. Love, Sex & the Whole Person: Everything You Want to Know. 280p. 1991. pap. 9.99 (0-310-71181-9, Campus Life) Zondervan.

Stagg, Mildred A. & Lamb, Cecile. Song of the Seed. Faltico, Mary L., illus. 28p. (ps). 1992. 2.50 (0-87403-956-8, 24-03596) Standard Pub.

Stanphill, Ira F. Happiness Is the Lord. (Illus.). (gr. k-6). 1987. visualized song 5.99 (3-90117-011-1) CEF Press.

Stenbock, Evelyn, compiled by. Children's Day Program Builder, No. 6. 32p. 1970. 4.25 (0-685-68749-X, BCMP-106) Lillenas.

—Children's Day Program Builder, No. 7. 32p. 1974. 4.25 (0-685-68748-1, BCMP-107) Lillenas.

—Children's Day Program Builder, No. 8. 32p. 1977. 4.25 (0-685-68747-3, BCMP-108) Lillenas.

—Children's Day Program Builder, No. 9. 32p. 1979. 4.25 (0-685-68746-5, BCMP-109) Lillenas.

Stenbock, Evelyn, ed. Twenty for Teens. 1980. 4.25 (0-8341-9090-7, BCMP-611) Lillenas.

Stephens, Andrea. Stressed-Out but Hangin' Tough. LC 89-10676. 160p. (Orig.). (gr. 8-12). 1989. pap. 7.99 (0-8007-5326-7) Revell.

Stephens, Andrea & Stephens, Bill. Prime Time: Devotions for Girls. LC 90-22459. (Orig.). 1992. pap. 7.99 (0-8007-5390-9) Revell.

—Prime Time: Devotions for Guys. LC 91-6638. (Orig.). 1992. pap. 7.99 (0-8007-5391-7) Revell.

—Ready for Prime Time: Devotions for Girls. LC 92-31717. 176p. (Orig.). 1993. pap. 7.99 (0-8007-5459-X) Revell.

—Ready for Prime Time: Devotions for Guys. LC 92-31721. 176p. (Orig.). 1993. pap. 7.99 (0-8007-5460-3) Revell.

Stevens, Margaret M. Stepping Stones for Boys & Girls. Stevens, David S., illus. (gr. 5 up). 1977. pap. 4.50 (0-87516-248-7) DeVorss.

Stewart, Kristine K. God Made Me Special. Beegle, Shirley, ed. Arthur, Lorraine, illus. 24p. (ps-3). 1994. pap. 1.89 (0-7847-0255-1) Standard Pub.

Stirrup Associates, Inc. Staff. Beautiful Attitudes Matthew 5: 3-12. Phillips, Cheryl M. & Harvey, Bonnie C., eds. Fulton, Ginger A., illus. LC 84-50914. 32p. (ps). 1984. pap. 1.49 (0-937420-17-4) Stirrup Assoc.

Stortz, Diane, ed. Good-Morning Babies. Garris, Norma, illus. 12p. (ps). 1994. bds. 5.99 (0-7847-0156-3, 24-03106) Standard Pub.

—Good-Night Babies. Garris, Norma, illus. 12p. (ps). 1994. bds. 5.99 (0-7847-0155-5, 24-03105) Standard Pub.

—Playtime Babies. Garris, Norma, illus. 12p. (ps). 1994. bds. 5.99 (0-7847-0157-1, 24-03107) Standard Pub.

Stuchbury, Dianne. Listen! Stuchbury, Dianne, illus. 24p. (ps-1). 1991. 4.99 (0-7459-2001-2) Lion USA.

—Look! Stuchbury, Dianne, illus. 24p. (ps-1). 1991. 4.99 (0-7459-2000-4) Lion USA.

—Taste & Smell! Stuchbury, Dianne, illus. 24p. (ps-1). 1991. 4.99 (0-7459-2003-9) Lion USA.

—Touch! Stuchbury, Dianne, illus. 24p. (ps-1). 1991. 4.99 (0-7459-2002-0) Lion USA.

Super Meetings for Kids Grades 4-6. 128p. (gr. 4-6). 1991. pap. 12.99 (0-89693-926-X) SP Pubns.

Swanson, Steve. Is There Life after High School? Making Decisions about Your Future. LC 90-15499. 112p. (Orig.). (gr. 9 up). 1991. pap. 5.99 (0-8066-2500-7, 9-2500, Augsburg) Augsburg Fortress.

Tate, Mimi. The Belly Button Brigade. 1974. pap. 2.15 (0-685-47446-1, BBB01) Quality Pubns.

Taylor, Laurie. How Could This Happen? Dealing with Crisis Pregnancy. Nelson, Becky, ed. 20p. (Orig.). (gr. 7-12). 1992. pap. text ed. 1.95 (1-56309-034-1, Wrld Changers Res) Womans Mission Union.

Ten Best Object Lessons. (Illus.). 5p. (gr. k-6). 1956. pap. text ed. 1.25 (1-55976-146-6) CEF Press.

Terrific Meetings for Kids Grades 4-6. 128p. (gr. 4-6). 1991. pap. 12.99 (0-89693-930-8) SP Pubns.

Theresa of Avila. Majestic Is Your Name. rev. ed. Hazard, David, ed. 144p. 1993. pap. 6.99 (1-55661-336-9) Bethany Hse.

Thoene, Bodie. Zion Covenant, 3 bks, Bks. 1-3. 1993. Set. 32.99 (1-55661-779-8) Bethany Hse.

—Zion Covenant, 3 bks, Bks. 4-6. 1993. Set. 33.99 (1-55661-780-1) Bethany Hse.

Thomas, Mack. Let's Make Jesus Happy. 256p. (ps-2). 1993. 12.99 (0-945564-76-7, Gold & Honey) Questar Pubs.

—What Would Jesus Do? Mortenson, Denis, illus. 253p. (ps-2). 1991. 12.99 (0-945564-05-8, Gold & Honey) Questar Pubs.

Thomas, Mack, adapted by. A Tale of Two Princes - Eckart Zur Nieden. 32p. (ps-2). 12.99 (0-88070-598-1, Gold & Honey) Questar Pubs.

Through the Roof! (gr. 2-5). 1991. promo pk. shrinkwrapped, incl. leader's ed., singer's ed. & listening tape 19.95 (0-687-41915-8); singer's ed., 16p. 2.25 (0-687-41914-X); spiral bdg. leader's ed., 64p. 10.95 (0-687-41911-5); listening tape 9.95 (0-687-41912-3); instrumental accompanist tape 29.95 (0-687-41913-1) Abingdon.

Timmer, John. Once upon a Time: Story Sermons for Children. 144p. 1992. pap. 8.99 (0-310-58621-6, Pub. by Minister Res Lib) Zondervan.

Todd, Richard E. Church. Miller, Alma E. & Kellner, Ron, illus. 26p. (gr. 2-6). 1993. wkbk. 2.45 (0-9605324-4-7) Crosswalk Res.

—Communion. rev. ed. Miller, Alma E. & Kellner, Ron, illus. 26p. (gr. 2-6). 1993. wkbk. 2.45 (0-9605324-3-9) Crosswalk Res.

Tracy, Wesley D. What's a Nice God Like You Doing in a Place Like This? 120p. 1990. pap. 5.95 (0-8341-1371-6) Beacon Hill.

Trahey, Jerome. Building Self-Esteem: A Workbook for Teens. Guelzow, Diane, illus. 176p. (Orig.). (gr. 7-12). 1992. pap. 16.95 (0-89390-231-4) Resource Pubns.

Trueblood, Becki. Best for Me. 1991. pap. 4.99 (0-8163-1050-5) Pacific Pr Pub Assn.

Tyndale Staff. One Year Book of Devotions for Kids. (gr. 4-7). 1993. pap. 10.99 (0-8423-5087-X) Tyndale.

Vivir la Misa. (SPA.). (gr. 6). 1986. pap. text ed. 2.75 (0-8198-8007-8) St Paul Bks.

Vivo en El Espiritu. (ENG & SPA.). (gr. 5). 1985. pap. text ed. 2.75 (0-8198-8006-X) St Paul Bks.

Vos Wezeman, Phyllis & Fournier, Jude D. Counting the Days: Twenty-Five Ways. 51p. (Orig.). 1989. pap. 9.95 (0-940754-77-0) Ed Ministries.

Vos Wezeman, Phyllis & Wiessner, Colleen A. Fabric of Faith. Chase, Judith, illus. 47p. (Orig.). (gr. 4-8). 1990. pap. 7.50 (1-877871-04-4) Ed Ministries.

Wallace, Jeffery S. Discovering the Four Seasons. Bittner, Bob, ed. LC 92-43796. (Illus.). 128p. (gr. 3-6). 1993. pap. 7.99 (0-7459-2617-7) Lion USA.

Wallis, Reginald. The New Venture. (gr. 3-7). 1935. pap. 0.85 (0-87213-914-X) Loizeaux.

Wamberg, Steve & Wamberg, Annie. Building Better Friendships. (Illus.). 48p. (gr. 6-8). 1992. pap. 8.99 (1-55945-138-6) Group Pub.

—Can Christians Have Fun? (Illus.). 48p. (gr. 6-8). 1992. pap. 8.99 (1-55945-134-3) Group Pub.

Ward, Elaine M. Being with God: Advent Devotions. Lenzen, Diane, illus. 32p. (Orig.). (gr. 1-6). 1988. pap. 4.50 (0-940754-66-5) Ed Ministries.

—Gifts of the Spirit. 59p. (Orig.). (gr. 9-12). 1988. pap. 9.95 (0-940754-64-9) Ed Ministries.

—In the Summertime: What's There to Do? 1990. pap. 5.95 (0-940754-98-3) Ed Ministries.

—Movers of Mountains. 88p. (Orig.). (gr. 7-12). 1984. pap. 12.95 (0-940754-24-X, 8196) Ed Ministries.

Warfield, B. B. Faith & Life. 458p. (gr. 7 up). 1991. 23.95 (0-85151-585-1) Banner of Truth.

Warren, Mary P. Lord, I'm Back Again: Story Devotions for Girls. LC 81-65651. 112p. (Orig.). 1981. pap. 5.99 (0-8066-1887-6, 10-4098, Augsburg) Augsburg Fortress.

Watson, Elaine. Busy Feet. Loman, Roberta K., illus. 28p. (ps). 1992. 2.50 (0-87403-952-5, 24-03592) Standard Pub.

Waybill, Marjorie. God's Family Activity Book. 64p. (Orig.). (ps-1). 1983. pap. 3.00 (0-8361-3336-6) Herald Pr.

Weinandy, Tom. What Must I Do? 32p. (Orig.). (gr. 8 up). 1988. pap. text ed. 9.95 10-pk. (0-932085-07-5) Word Among Us.

Weisheit, E. Sixty-One Worship Talks for Children. rev. ed. LC 68-20728. (gr. 3-6). 1975. pap. 7.99 (0-570-03714-X, 12-2616) Concordia.

We're in This Together, Lord. LC 92-30987. 112p. (gr. 3-7). 1992. pap. 5.99 (0-8066-2649-6, 9-2649) Augsburg Fortress.

Whitmer, Lisa H. & Hutchcraft, Ronald P. Letters from the College Front: Girls' Edition. 96p. (gr. 9-12). 1993. 8.99 (*0-8010-9722-3*) Baker Bk.

Wiersbe, Warren. Be Challenged! rev. ed. LC 82-12404. (gr. 7). 1982. pap. 4.50 (*0-8024-1080-4*) Moody.

Wiessner, Colleen A. & Vos Wezeman, Phyllis. Flavors of Faith. 70p. (gr. 1-6). 1991. pap. 7.50 (*1-877871-27-3*, 5873) Ed Ministries.

Wiggin, Eric & Wiggin, Kate D. Rebecca of Sunnybrook Farm: The Child. Boddy, Joe, illus. 224p. 1990. pap. 9.95 (*0-943497-95-7*) Wolgemuth & Hyatt.

Wilde, Gary. Handling Conflict. (Illus.). 48p. (gr. 6-8). 1991. pap. 8.99 (*1-55945-125-4*) Group Pub.

Wiley, Chris. The Little Commission Handbook. 27p. 1991. pap. 1.95 (*0-8341-1421-6*) Beacon Hill.

Wilhelm, Carolyn. Early Childhood Bulletin Boards. 96p. (ps-1). 1987. 10.95 (*0-86653-393-1*, SS1825, Shining Star Pubns) Good Apple.

Willey, Henry N., Jr. I'm Not Too Little. (Illus.). 8p. (gr. k-6). 1984. visualized song 3.50 (*3-90117-028-6*) CEF Press.

Williams, Bradley B. Out of the Miry Clay. (Orig.). 1989. pap. 5.95 (*0-9620486-0-7*) B B Williams.

Williamson, Kevin, illus. Heaven How to Get There. 6p. (gr. k-6). 1964. pap. text ed. 2.65 (*1-55976-125-3*) CEF Press.

Winder, Linda. My First Question & Answer Book: A Sticker-Fun Book. (Illus.). 48p. 1991. pap. 5.99 (*0-8010-9713-4*) Baker Bk.

Wirths, Claudine G. & Bowman-Kruhm, Mary. How to Get up When Schoolwork Gets You Down. LC 93-3050. 1993. pap. 5.99 (*0-7814-0118-6*, Chariot Bks) Chariot Family.

Witnessing, Telling Others about Jesus. 15p. (gr. 1-8). 1972. pap. text ed. 4.50 (*0-86508-155-7*) BCM Pubn.

Wood, Randy. God, I Need to Talk! Nelson, Becky, ed. 26p. (gr. 7-12). 1993. pap. text ed. 4.95 (*1-56309-066-X*) Womans Mission Union.

Woods, Paul. Miracles! (Illus.). 48p. (gr. 6-8). 1991. pap. 8.99 (*1-55945-117-3*) Group Pub.

Worrall, Joyce. God Is So Great. Nielsen, Deborah B., illus. 19p. (gr. k-6). 1985. pap. text ed. 4.25 (*1-55976-132-6*) CEF Press.

Younger, Carol. Overcoming Insecurities. (Illus.). 48p. (gr. 9-12). 1991. pap. 8.99 (*1-55945-221-8*) Group Pub.

Yount, Christine. Responding to Injustice. (Illus.). 48p. (gr. 9-12). 1991. pap. 8.99 (*1-55945-214-5*) Group Pub.

Your Hand in Mine. 1988. 7.95 (*0-89954-778-8*) Antioch Pub Co.

The Youth Bible. 1991. duraflex bdg. 16.99 (*0-8499-3227-0*); 21.99 (*0-8499-0925-2*) Word Inc.

CHRISTIAN LIFE–FICTION

Ackerman, Karen. Walking with Clara Belle. Mason, Debbie, illus. 40p. (gr. k-3). Date not set. 9.95 (*0-8198-8243-7*) St Paul Bks.
Ages 5-8. How old is "old?" Children are brought to a special appreciation of the elderly through this charming treatment of friendship. The child who goes "walking with Clara Belle" can develop positive attitudes towards aging - & loving relationships with the aged. "This charming experience of a little girl with her elderly next-door neighbor can be an eye-opener in helping children to develop positive attitudes toward aging. The story encourages love & deep regard for the aged in a world that seems to do its best to downplay the goodness of getting old. This book can help parents & teachers explore attitudes toward aging & the aged with children in kindergarten through third grade. The illustrations lend themselves to questions." - Ruth Charlesworth, THE VERMONT CATHOLIC TRIBUNE. To order, please call (800) 876-4463.
Publisher Provided Annotation.

Ada, Alma F., et al. Choices & Other Stories from the Caribbean. LC 92-43134. 1993. pap. 6.95 (*0-377-00257-7*) Friendship Pr.

Andrews, Dorothy W. God's World & Johnny. (gr. 5 up). 1983. pap. 4.45 (*0-318-01335-5*) Rod & Staff.

At the Back of the North Wind. (Illus.). (gr. 3 up). pap. 2.50 perfect bdg. (*1-55748-188-1*) Barbour & Co.

Bacher, June M. Love Follows the Heart. (Orig.). (gr. 9-12). 1990. pap. 3.99 (*1-56507-248-0*) Harvest Hse.

Baer, Judy. Cedar River Daydreams, Bks. 1-5. (Orig.). 1991. Giftset. 19.99 (*1-55661-763-1*) Bethany Hse.

—Cedar River Daydreams, Bks. 6-10. (Orig.). 1991. Giftset. 19.99 (*1-55661-764-X*) Bethany Hse.

—Dear Judy, What's It Like at Your House? 160p. (Orig.). (gr. 7-10). 1992. pap. 7.99 (*1-55661-291-5*) Bethany Hse.

—Lonely Girl. 144p. (Orig.). (gr. 7-10). 1992. pap. 3.99 (*1-55661-280-X*) Bethany Hse.

—More Than Friends. 144p. (gr. 7-10). 1992. pap. 3.99 (*1-55661-298-2*) Bethany Hse.

—No Turning Back. 144p. (Orig.). 1991. 3.99 (*1-55661-216-8*) Bethany Hse.

—Second Chance. 144p. (Orig.). (gr. 7-10). 1991. 3.99 (*1-55661-217-6*) Bethany Hse.

—Something Old, Something New. 144p. (Orig.). (gr. 7-9). 1991. pap. 3.99 (*1-55661-183-8*) Bethany Hse.

—Special Kind of Love. 1993. pap. 3.99 (*1-55661-367-9*) Bethany Hse.

Bagley, Pat. If You Were a Boy in the Time of the Nephites. Bagley, Pat, illus. 48p. (gr. 3-6). 1989. pap. 4.95 (*0-87579-250-2*) Deseret Bk.

—If You Were a Girl in the Time of the Nephites. Bagley, Pat, illus. 48p. (gr. 3-6). 1989. pap. 4.95 (*0-87579-249-9*) Deseret Bk.

Baldry, Cherith. Rite of Brotherhood. Reck, Sue, ed. 160p. (gr. 8-12). Date not set. pap. 4.99 (*0-7814-0094-5*, Chariot Bks) Chariot Family.

Ball, Karen. Choice Adventures: Hazardous Homestead. 160p. (gr. 4-8). 1992. pap. text ed. 4.99 (*0-8423-5032-2*) Tyndale.

—The Overnight Ordeal. LC 93-40182. 1994. 4.99 (*0-8423-5134-5*) Tyndale.

Barger, Eric. From Rock to Rock. LC 87-70776. (Illus.). 190p. 1990. pap. 8.99 (*0-910311-61-7*) Huntington Hse.

Bauman, Elizabeth H. Coals of Fire. LC 53-12197. (Illus.). (gr. 5-9). 1954. 4.95 (*0-8361-1957-6*) Herald Pr.

Bedley, Janet. Promises Broken, Promises Kept. LC 91-6306. 224p. 1991. pap. 6.99 (*1-55513-609-5*, 36095, Life Journey) Chariot Family.

Beers, V. Gilbert. Precious Moments Read-Aloud Stories, Bk. 1. Wiersma, Debbie B., ed. Butcher, Samuel J., tr. (Illus.). 256p. (gr. 4 up). 1991. 11.99 (*0-8010-1015-2*) Baker Bk.

Bell, Christina. The Boy with a Toucan in His Heart. 160p. 1990. 39.00x (*0-85439-397-8*, Pub. by St Paul Pubns UK) St Mut.

Biggar, Joan R. Shipwreck on the Lights. 160p. (Orig.). (gr. 5-8). 1992. pap. 3.99 (*0-570-04710-2*) Concordia.

Blanchette, Rick. Choice Adventure: Class Project Showdown. LC 92-30501. 1993. 4.99 (*0-8423-5047-0*) Tyndale.

Blount, Lucy D. The Story of Lucy What's-Her-Name! And Your Name Too! Long, Woodie, illus. 48p. 1992. Spiral bdg. pap. 12.00 (*0-9630017-2-8*) Light-Bearer.

Bly, Stephen. Coyote True. LC 92-8224. 128p. 1992. pap. 4.99 (*0-89107-680-8*) Crossway Bks.

—You Can Always Trust a Spotted Horse. LC 92-46667. 128p. (Orig.). (gr. 4-7). 1993. pap. 4.99 (*0-89107-716-2*) Crossway Bks.

Bohl, Al. Zaanan: The Ransom of Renaissance. (Illus.). 224p. (gr. 9-12). 1990. pap. text ed. 2.50 (*1-55748-136-9*) Barbour & Co.

Bolton, Martha. On the Loose...the Cafeteria Lady. pap. 6.99 (*1-56179-280-2*) Focus Family.

—What's Growing under Your Bed? 1986. 8.50 (*0-685-68720-1*, BCMP-634) Lillenas.

Briscoe, Jill. Harrow Sparrow. Cummings, Ann L., illus. 143p. (gr. 6). 1989. pap. write for info. Jilcoe.

Briscoe, Stuart & Briscoe, Jill. How Much Does God Know? Marinin, Sally, illus. 12p. 1993. pap. 2.99 (*0-8010-1040-3*) Baker Bk.

—Is God Ever Naughty? Marinin, Sally, illus. 12p. 1993. pap. 2.99 (*0-8010-1041-1*) Baker Bk.

—Where Is God? Marinin, Sally, illus. 12p. 1993. pap. 2.99 (*0-8010-1038-1*) Baker Bk.

Brouwer, Sigmund. Barbarians from the Isle. 132p. (gr. 5-8). 1992. pap. 4.99 (*0-89693-116-1*) SP Pubns.

—The Downtown Desperadoes. 132p. 1991. pap. 4.99 (*0-89693-860-3*) SP Pubns.

—Race for the Part Street Treasure. 132p. 1991. pap. 4.99 (*0-89693-859-X*) SP Pubns.

—Wings of an Angel. 132p. (gr. 5-8). 1992. pap. 4.99 (*0-89693-115-3*) SP Pubns.

Bunyan, John. The Pilgrim's Progress. Larsen, Dan, ed. Bohl, Al, illus. 224p. (gr. 4-8). 1989. pap. text ed. 2.50 (*1-55748-099-0*) Barbour & Co.

—The Pilgrim's Progress. Larsen, Dan, adapted by. (gr. 3 up). 1992. 9.95 (*1-55748-276-4*) Barbour & Co.

Burgess, Beverly C. God Is Never to Busy to Listen. Linder, Elizabeth, illus. (Orig.). (gr. 1-3). 1987. pap. 1.98 (*0-89274-457-X*) Harrison Hse.

Carney, Mary L. Angel in My Backpack. 128p. (gr. 7-9). 1987. pap. 6.99 (*0-310-28501-1*, 11342P, Pub. by Youth Spec.) Zondervan.

Carraway, Mary. Jill. LC 85-71473. 144p. (Orig.). (gr. 6-9). 1985. pap. 3.99 (*0-87123-847-0*) Bethany Hse.

—Wendy. LC 87-72793. 160p. (Orig.). (gr. 9-12). 1988. pap. 3.99 (*0-87123-942-6*) Bethany Hse.

Children Around the World: Activity Book. 24p. (gr. 3-7). 1991. pap. 2.29 (*1-55513-451-3*, 64519, Chariot Bks) Chariot Family.

Chisholm, Gloria. Jocelyn. LC 87-72794. 176p. (Orig.). (gr. 9-12). 1988. pap. 3.99 (*0-87123-846-2*) Bethany Hse.

Christian, Mary B. But Everybody Does It: Peer Pressure. Brubaker, Lee W., illus. LC 85-17112. 72p. (Orig.). (gr. 4-7). 1986. pap. 3.99 (*0-570-03636-4*, 39-1098) Concordia.

Clarkson, Margaret. Susie's Babies: A Clear & Simple Explanation of the Everyday Miracle of Birth. 72p. 1992. pap. 7.99 (*0-8028-4053-1*) Eerdmans.

Clement, Jane T. The Sparrow. 4th ed. Hutterian Brethren Staff, ed. Mow, Kathy, illus. Moody, Ruby, intro. by. LC 68-21133. (Illus.). 212p. (gr. 4 up). 1992. pap. 10.00 (*0-87486-009-1*) Plough.

Coman, Carolyn. Tell Me Everything. 1993. 15.00 (*0-374-37390-6*) FS&G.

Conley, Lucy A. Tattletale Sparkie. (gr. 3 up). 1983. 7.70 (*0-318-01337-1*) Rod & Staff.

Cook, Jean T. Hugs for Our New Baby. (Illus.). (ps-2). 1987. 5.99 (*0-570-04165-1*, 56-1622) Concordia.

Courtney, Jane. Where Have All the Colours Gone? Lathwell, Alan, illus. 1990. 29.00x (*0-85439-407-9*, Pub. by St Paul Pubns UK) St Mut.

Craig, Lynn. New Friends in New Places. LC 94-1929. 1994. pap. 4.99 (*0-8407-9239-5*) Nelson.

—Summer of Choices. LC 94-4504. 1994. pap. 4.99 (*0-8407-9241-7*) Nelson.

Davoll, Barbara. Hare-Brained Habit. (gr. 4-7). 1993. pap. 6.99 (*0-8024-2705-7*) Moody.

—A Sticky Mystery. Hockerman, Dennis, illus. 24p. 1989. 6.99 (*0-89693-485-3*); cassette 9.99 (*0-89693-033-5*) SP Pubns.

—Upstairs Connection. (gr. 4-7). 1993. pap. 6.99 (*0-8024-2704-9*) Moody.

Davoll, Barbara & Hockerman, Dennis. A Short Tail. 24p. 1989. 6.99 (*0-89693-499-3*); cassette 9.99 (*0-89693-032-7*) SP Pubns.

Decker, Marjorie. Christian Mother Goose Humpty Dumpty. (ps). 1989. 3.99 (*0-529-06683-1*) World Bible.

—Christian Mother Goose Little Bo Peep. (ps). 1989. 3.99 (*0-529-06687-4*) World Bible.

—Christian Mother Goose Little Miss Muffet. (ps). 1989. 3.99 (*0-529-06686-6*) World Bible.

—Christian Mother Goose: Little Tommy Tucker. (ps). 1989. 3.99 (*0-529-06685-8*) World Bible.

—Christian Mother Goose Piano Book. (gr. k-4). 1989. 8.99 (*0-529-06692-0*) World Bible.

—Christian Mother Goose Pop-Up Bedtime Rhymes. (ps). 1989. 6.99 (*0-529-06688-2*) World Bible.

—Christian Mother Goose Pop-Up Favorite Rhymes. (ps). 1989. 6.99 (*0-529-06691-2*) World Bible.

—Christian Mother Goose Pop-Up Happy Rhymes. (ps). 1989. 6.99 (*0-529-06690-4*) World Bible.

DeGrote, Barbara. Take the Pizza & Run: And Other Stories for Children about Stewardship. Martens, Ray, illus. 32p. 1992. pap. 5.99 (*0-8066-2599-6*, 10-25996) Augsburg Fortress.

De Grote-Sorensen, Barbara. Who's That in My Mirror? LC 89-49097. 112p. (Orig.). (gr. 3-7). 1990. pap. 5.99 (*0-8066-2441-8*, 9-2441) Augsburg Fortress.

Dellinger, Annetta. The Jesus Tree. Morris, Susan S., illus. 32p. (ps-2). 1991. 7.99 (*0-570-04191-0*) Concordia.

Demsky, Andrew. Five Hundred Degrees in the Shade: Every Teen Feels the Heat. LC 93-15564. 1993. 8.95 (*0-8163-1162-5*) Pacific Pr Pub Assn.

Dick, Lois Hoadley. False Coin, True Coin. LC 92-39280. 1993. write for info. (*0-89084-664-2*) Bob Jones Univ Pr.

Dobson, Danae. Woof & the Big Fire. 32p. 1990. write for info. (*0-8499-8362-2*) Word Inc.

—Woof, the Seeing-Eye Dog. 32p. 1990. write for info. (*0-8499-8363-0*) Word Inc.

Doleski, Teddi. The Hurt. (Illus.). 32p. (gr. 2-5). 1983. pap. 3.95 (*0-8091-6551-1*) Paulist Pr.

Doney, Meryl. The Very Worried Sparrow. Geldart, William, illus. 32p. (ps-6). 1991. 11.95 (*0-7459-1919-7*) Lion USA.

Dostoyevsky, Fyodor. The Heavenly Christmas Tree. (gr. 5 up). 1992. PLB 13.95 (*0-88682-492-3*) Creative Ed.

Duplex, Mary H. Mystery at Maple Street Park. LC 93-28466. 1994. 7.95 (*0-8163-1187-0*) Pacific Pr Pub Assn.

Dyck, Peter J. Shalom at Last. Neidigh, Sherry, illus. 128p. (Orig.). 1992. pap. 5.95 (*0-8361-3615-2*) Herald Pr.

Dyson, Kymberli M. Clyde, the Cloud Who Always Cried. (Illus.). 28p. (Orig.). (gr. k-4). 1994. Saddle-stitched. 5.00 (*1-885282-00-1*) This Little. CLYDE, THE CLOUD WHO ALWAYS CRIED is this little light's first tale in a 14-book series for children. Written in verse, each "fable" introduces one of God's creations who must learn to overcome a negative characteristic, i.e. TERENCE THE TATTLING TREE, WENDY THE WHINING TREE, SEYMOUR THE SELFISH SEA, et al. Each story is charmingly illustrated with characters who are easily identifiable by children & adults alike. CLYDE develops low self-esteem from his jealousy towards SUSANNA THE SUN. Through a series of events which affect the world

around him, God helps CLYDE realize his individuality & unique purpose in life. As with each book in this series, the priority of God in each character's lesson is illustrated in a non-judgmental, nondogmatic fashion. Volume discounts are available from the publisher. Also available is a T-shirt delightfully displaying all the characters from THIS LITTLE LIGHT series. (One size fits all children & one size fits all adults). To order contact: this little light publishing, P.O. Box 70481, Pasadena, CA 91117, (818) 791-1484 or (800) 814-4774.
Publisher Provided Annotation.

Eavey, Louise. A Child's Shining Pathway. Murphy, Emmy L., illus. (ps-1). 1976. pap. 1.95 (*0-915374-08-0*, 08-0) Rapids Christian.
Enns, Peter. God Is Good. Ligon, Terry, illus. 24p. (ps-5). 1985. 4.95 (*0-936215-21-6*); cassette incl. STL Intl.
—Jesus Loves Me. Ligon, Terry, illus. 24p. (ps-5). 1985. 4.95 (*0-936215-23-2*); cassette incl. STL Intl.
—Special Friends. Ligon, Terry, illus. 24p. (ps-5). 4.95 (*0-936215-22-4*); cassette incl. STL Intl.
Enscoe, Lawrence G. & Enscoe, Andrea J., eds. You Can Get There from Here. 1990. 9.95 (*0-685-68697-3*, BCMP-655) Lillenas.
Eubank, Mary G. & Hollingsworth, Mary. King's Alphabet. (ps-3). 1990. write for info. (*0-8499-0713-6*) Word Inc.
—King's Manners. (ps-3). 1990. write for info. (*0-8499-0826-4*) Word Inc.
Finlay, Alice S. A Gift from the Sea for Laura Lee. 48p. (gr. k-2). 1993. pap. 3.99 (*0-310-59871-0*, Pub. by Youth Spec) Zondervan.
—Laura Lee & the Little Pine Tree. 48p. (gr. k-2). 1993. pap. 3.99 (*0-310-59861-3*, Pub. by Youth Spec) Zondervan.
—Laura Lee & the Monster Sea. 48p. (gr. k-2). 1993. pap. 3.99 (*0-310-59841-9*, Pub. by Youth Spec) Zondervan.
Fischer, John. Saint Ben. 288p. (Orig.). 1993. pap. 8.99 (*1-55661-259-1*) Bethany Hse.
Forever Friends. LC 91-12471. 144p. 1991. pap. 4.99 (*0-8066-2535-X*, 9-2535) Augsburg Fortress.
Fort, Donny. Church Camp. 144p. 1992. pap. 6.99 (*0-310-54861-6*, Pub. by Zondervan Bks) Zondervan.
Fraser. Mystery at Deepwood Bay. LC 91-30621. 1992. pap. 4.99 (*1-55513-717-2*, Chariot Bks) Chariot Family.
Fraser, W. Courage on Mirror Mountain. LC 89-31978. 128p. (gr. 3-7). 1989. pap. 4.99 (*1-55513-039-9*, Chariot Bks) Chariot Family.
—Mystery on Mirror Mountain. LC 89-9757. 112p. (gr. 3-7). 1989. pap. 4.99 (*1-55513-588-9*, Chariot Bks) Chariot Family.
Fraser, Wynnette. Invasion on Mirror Mountain. Reck, Sue, ed. LC 93-32678. 128p. (gr. 4-6). 1994. pap. 4.99 (*0-7814-0104-6*, Chariot Bks) Cook.
Frost, Marie. Hattie's Adventures. 1994. pap. 4.99 (*1-56179-261-6*) Focus Family.
—Hattie's Faraway Family. 1994. pap. 4.99 (*1-56179-215-2*) Focus Family.
—Hattie's Holiday Fun. 1994. pap. 4.99 (*1-56179-216-0*) Focus Family.
—Meet Hattie. 1994. pap. 4.99 (*1-56179-214-4*) Focus Family.
Frost, Marie & Hanson, Bonnie C. Hattie's Cry for Help. (Illus.). 1992. pap. 5.99 (*1-56121-104-4*) Wolgemuth & Hyatt.
Fryar, Jane. The Locked-In Friend. Wilson, Deborah, illus. 32p. (ps-2). 1991. 7.99 (*0-570-04195-3*) Concordia.
Fuentes, Vilma M. Pearl Makers: Six Stories about Children in the Philippines. (Illus., Orig.). (gr. 1-6). 1989. 4.95 (*0-377-00191-0*) Friendship Pr.
Gilbert, Lela. The Journey with the Golden Book. (Illus.). 1992. pap. 6.99 (*1-56121-070-6*) Wolgemuth & Hyatt.
Gillett. The Great Reptile Race. 1992. pap. 4.99 (*1-55513-538-2*, Chariot Bks) Chariot Family.
Good, Bertha. Carlos of North Road Camp: And Other Stories & Poems. 2nd ed. 167p. (gr. 2-4). 1993. pap. 5.50 (*0-9627643-6-1*) Green Psturs Pr.
Good Little Books for Good Little Children Staff. God Made Me. 12p. (ps). 1986. 3.25 (*0-8378-5207-2*) Gibson.
—The Little Lost Lamb. 12p. (ps). 1986. 3.25 (*0-8378-5206-4*) Gibson.
Gorman, Carol. Biggest Bully in Brookdale. (Illus.). 80p. (gr. 2-4). 1992. pap. 3.99 (*0-570-04713-7*) Concordia.
—Brian's Footsteps. Koehler, Ed, illus. LC 93-38322. 96p. (Orig.). (gr. 4-7). 1994. pap. 3.99 (*0-570-04629-7*) Concordia.
—The Great Director. Nappi, Rudi, illus. LC 93-20228. 60p. (Orig.). (gr. 2-4). 1993. pap. 3.99 (*0-570-04746-3*) Concordia.
—It's Not Fair. (Illus.). 80p. (Orig.). (gr. 2-4). 1992. pap. 3.99 (*0-570-04714-5*) Concordia.
—Million Dollar Winner. Koehler, Ed, illus. LC 93-36935. 96p. (Orig.). (gr. 4-7). 1994. pap. 3.99 (*0-570-04630-0*) Concordia.
—Nobody's Friend. Nappi, Rudy, illus. LC 92-24936. 60p. (Orig.). (gr. 1-4). 1993. pap. 3.99 (*0-570-04729-3*) Concordia.
—The Richest Kid in the World. Nappi, Rudy, illus. LC 92-24935. 60p. (Orig.). (gr. 1-4). 1993. pap. 3.99 (*0-570-04728-5*) Concordia.
—Skin Deep. Nappi, Rudy, illus. LC 93-20230. 60p. (gr. 2-4). 1993. pap. 3.99 (*0-570-04747-1*) Concordia.
—The Taming of Roberta Parsley. Koehler, Ed, illus. LC 93-38312. 96p. (Orig.). (gr. 4-7). 1994. pap. 3.99 (*0-570-04628-9*) Concordia.
Greegor, Katherine. Trouble - of the Northwest Territory. Cummins, Lisa, illus. LC 92-61031. 100p. (Orig.). (gr. 3-8). 1992. pap. 5.95 (*0-9633091-7-X*) Promise Land Pubs.
Griffith, Connie. Mysterious Rescuer. LC 93-8421. 128p. (Orig.). 1994. pap. 4.99 (*0-8010-3865-0*) Baker Bk.
—Secret Behind Locked Doors. LC 93-8420. 128p. (gr. 5-8). 1994. pap. 5.99 (*0-8010-3864-2*) Baker Bk.
—The Shocking Discovery. 128p. (gr. 6-8). 1994. pap. 5.99 (*0-8010-3866-9*) Baker Bk.
Groomer, Vera. Dibe Yahzi. (ps). 1980. pap. 1.95 (*0-8127-0260-3*) Review & Herald.
Guenther, Gloria. Gift of Love. 174p. (gr. 3-6). 1989. pap. 3.95 (*0-919797-58-X*) Kindred Pr.
Gunn, Robin J. Mrs. Rosey-Posey & the Chocolate Cherry Treat. Duca, Bill, illus. LC 89-25417. 32p. (ps-2). 1991. pap. 4.99 (*1-55513-370-3*, 33704, Chariot Bks) Chariot Family.
—Mrs. Rosey Posey & the Empty Nest. LC 92-12955. (gr. k-3). 1993. pap. 4.99 (*0-7814-0329-4*, Chariot Bks) Chariot Family.
—Mrs. Rosey-Posey & the Treasure Hunt. Duca, Bill, illus. LC 89-25244. 32p. (ps-2). 1991. pap. 4.99 (*1-55513-372-X*, 33720, Chariot Bks) Chariot Family.
—Sweet Dreams. LC 94-6239. 1994. write for info. (*1-56179-255-1*) Focus Family.
Haffey, Richard. H. R. Cornelius Learns about Love: A Commandments Book for Children. (Illus.). 20p. (Orig.). (gr. 2-5). 1985. pap. 2.95 (*0-89622-235-7*) Twenty-Third.
Hamilton, Kersten. Natalie Jean & Tag-along Tessa. 1991. 2.99 (*0-8423-4621-X*) Tyndale.
—Natalie Jean & the Flying Machine. 1991. 2.99 (*0-8423-4620-1*) Tyndale.
—Natalie Jean & the Haints' Parade. 1991. 2.99 (*0-8423-4622-8*) Tyndale.
—Natalie Jean Goes Hog Wild. 1991. 2.99 (*0-8423-4623-6*) Tyndale.
Hartman, Bob. The One & Only Delgado Cheese: A Tale of Talent, Fame, & Friendship. Nelson, Donna K., illus. LC 92-29059. 40p. (gr. k-3). 1993. 13.95 (*0-7459-2405-0*) Lion USA.
Harwell, Ivy E. The Servant. Ellison, Chris, illus. 180p. (Orig.). (gr. 12 up). 1994. pap. 8.99 (*1-882671-09-0*) Wrds of Life.
Helldorfer, Mary C. Clap Clap! Speidel, Sandra, illus. 32p. (ps-2). 1993. reinforced bdg. 13.99 (*0-670-85155-8*) Viking Child Bks.
Hendrickson, Julie. Carefree Play, Summer Day. Burris, Priscilla, illus. LC 93-35480. 1994. 4.99 (*0-7852-8216-5*) Nelson.
Henry, Kim. Two Prayers for Patches. Stortz, Diane, ed. LC 94-1122. (Illus.). 28p. (ps-k). 1994. 5.49 (*0-7847-0201-2*) Standard Pub.
Henry, Marie. Hannah Whitall Smith. (Orig.). 1993. pap. 8.99 (*1-55661-316-4*) Bethany Hse.
Hess, Donna. In Search of Honor. 153p. (Orig.). (gr. 9 up). 1991. pap. 4.95 (*0-89084-595-6*) Bob Jones Univ Pr.
Hoehne, Marcia. A Place of My Own. LC 92-44336. 128p. (Orig.). (gr. 4-7). 1993. pap. 4.99 (*0-89107-718-9*) Crossway Bks.
Hoff, B. J. Song of the Silent Harp. 400p. (Orig.). (gr. 9-12). 1991. 9.99 (*1-55661-110-2*) Bethany Hse.
Hollingsworth, Mary. Parrots, Pirates & Walking the Plank. LC 92-8089. (ps-3). 1992. pap. 8.99 (*0-7814-0668-4*, Chariot Bks) Chariot Family.
Hostetler, Marian. We Knew Paul. 128p. (Orig.). (gr. 4-8). 1992. pap. 4.95 (*0-8361-3589-X*) Herald Pr.
Hughes, Ann K. Mary, Martha, Lottie & You. Gross, Karen, ed. 32p. (Orig.). (gr. 1-6). 1992. pap. text ed. 3.95 (*1-56309-045-7*) Womans Mission Union.
Hughes, Robert D. Gabriel's Trumpet. (Orig.). Date not set. pap. 6.99 (*0-8054-6059-4*) Broadman.
Hunt, Angela E. Cassie Perkins: A Dream to Cherish. 176p. (gr. 4-8). 1992. pap. 4.99 (*0-8423-1064-9*) Tyndale.
—The Chance of a Lifetime. LC 92-20635. 1993. pap. 4.99 (*0-8423-1118-1*) Tyndale.
Hutchens, Paul. Sugar Creek Gang Series, 36 bks. (gr. 2-7). Set. pap. 142.65 (*0-8024-4836-4*) Moody.
Hutson, Joan. Legend of the Nine Talents. Hutson, Joan, illus. LC 92-26957. 1992. 4.95 (*0-8198-4468-3*) St Paul Bks.
Irland, Nancy B. Very Strange Story of Blaze the Cat. (gr. 4-7). 1991. pap. 2.99 (*0-8163-1046-7*) Pacific Pr Pub Assn.
Jackson, Dave & Jackson, Neta. The Chimney Sweep's Ransom. 128p. (Orig.). 1992. pap. 4.99 (*1-55661-268-0*) Bethany Hse.
—Escape from the Slave Traders. LC 92-11170. 128p. (Orig.). (gr. 3-7). 1992. pap. 4.99 (*1-55661-263-X*) Bethany Hse.
—Kidnapped by River Rats. Jackson, Julian, illus. 144p. (Orig.). (gr. 3-7). 1991. pap. 4.99 (*1-55661-220-6*) Bethany Hse.
—The Queen's Smuggler. Jackson, Julian, illus. 144p. (Orig.). (gr. 3-7). 1991. pap. 4.99 (*1-55661-221-4*) Bethany Hse.
—Secret Adventures Books, Episode 2: Snap. 100p. 1994. pap. 4.99 (*0-8054-4005-4*, 4240-05) Broadman.
Jenkins, Jerry B. Dallas O'Neil & the Baker Street Sports Club Series, 8 bks. (gr. 2-7). Set. pap. 39.92 (*0-8024-2164-4*) Moody.
—Dallas O'Neil Mysteries Ser, 8 bks. (gr. 2-7). Set. pap. 39.92 (*0-8024-8389-5*) Moody.
Jenks, Graham. Every Mom Is Special. Burris, Priscilla, illus. 1994. 4.99 (*0-7852-8215-7*) Nelson.
Johnson, Gwen L. Matthew's Journey into the Deep. (Illus.). 144p. (gr. 3-9). 1993. pap. 6.99 (*0-9639527-0-6*) Triton Enter.
Johnson, Lois W. Grandpa's Stolen Treasure. LC 92-30093. 144p. (Orig.). (gr. 3-8). 1992. pap. 5.99 (*1-55661-239-7*) Bethany Hse.
—Mysterious Hideaway: Adventures of the Northwoods. (gr. 4-7). 1992. pap. 5.99 (*1-55661-238-9*) Bethany Hse.
—Trouble at Wild River. 144p. (Orig.). (gr. 3-8). 1991. pap. 5.99 (*1-55661-144-7*) Bethany Hse.
—Vanishing Footprints. 144p. (Orig.). (ps-8). 1991. pap. 5.99 (*1-55661-103-X*) Bethany Hse.
Jones Gunn, Robin. Seventeen Wishes. LC 93-11278. 1993. write for info. (*1-56179-169-5*) Focus Family.
—Yours Forever. 160p. (Orig.). (gr. 7-11). 1990. pap. 4.99 (*0-929608-90-9*) Focus Family.
Jordan, James L. Ricky's Last Chance. 104p. (gr. 4-6). 1991. pap. 3.95 (*0-9630534-0-X*) Living Water.
Jorgensen, Dan. Kelli's Choice. LC 90-2693. 144p. (gr. 7 up). 1991. pap. 4.99 (*1-55513-773-3*, 37739, Chariot Bks) Chariot Family.
Jost, Esther. Tyinya Farzhi. 30p. (gr. 1-4). 1990. pap. 4.50 (*0-921788-07-X*) Kindred Pr.
Kaetler, Sarah. More Stories from Grandpa's Rocking Chair. Kaetler, Sarah, illus. 73p. (gr. 3-6). 1991. pap. 4.95 (*0-919797-75-X*) Kindred Pr.
Keefer, Mikal. I Like Sunday School! Stites, Joe, illus. 28p. (ps-k). 1993. 4.99 (*0-7847-0040-0*, 24-03830) Standard Pub.
Keller, Kent. The Mayan Mystery. LC 93-48838. (Illus.). 1994. 4.99 (*0-8423-5132-9*) Tyndale.
Kent, Renee. Kelli's Discovery. (Illus.). 64p. (Orig.). (gr. 4-6). 1989. pap. text ed. 3.50 (*0-936625-71-6*, New Hope AL) Womans Mission Union.
—Yes, You Can, Kelli! McClain, Cindy, ed. 109p. (Orig.). (gr. 1-6). 1991. pap. text ed. 3.50 (*1-56309-012-0*, New Hope AL) Womans Mission Union.
Kerr, M. E. What I Really Think of You. LC 81-47735. 224p. (gr. 7 up). 1991. pap. 3.50 (*0-06-447062-8*, Trophy) HarpC Child Bks.
Kiemel Anderson, Ann. God's Little Dreamer. Lane, Sandy, illus. LC 90-33475. 32p. (ps-8). 1990. 10.99 (*0-89081-785-5*) Harvest Hse.
Klassen, Julie. The Adventures of Heart Longing. LC 86-82881. 128p. (gr. 1-6). 1987. pap. 2.95 (*0-88243-557-4*, 02-0557) Gospel Pub.
Klaus, Sandra. Chris Finds the Answer. Bates, Stephen, illus. 20p. (gr. k-6). 1988. pap. text ed. 4.25 (*1-55976-127-X*) CEF Press.
Klusmeyer, Joann. What about Me? (Illus.). (gr. 4-7). 1987. 3.99 (*0-570-03641-0*, 39-1125) Concordia.
Koenig, Norma E. The Runaway Heart. (Orig.). (gr. 4-6). 1981. pap. 4.95 (*0-377-00112-0*) Friendship Pr.
Landis, Mary. Anthony Gets Ready for Church. 1990. pap. 2.15 (*0-317-02906-1*) Rod & Staff.
Lansing, Karen E. Time to Be a Friend. LC 92-13010. 96p. (gr. 4-8). 1993. pap. 4.95 (*0-8361-3614-4*) Herald Pr.
Lapka, Fay S. The Sea, the Song & the Trumpetfish. 160p. (Orig.). (gr. 7-12). 1991. pap. 6.99 (*0-87788-754-3*) Shaw Pubs.
Larsen, Dan. David Livingstone. (gr. 3 up). 1992. pap. 2.50 perfect bdg. (*1-55748-259-4*) Barbour & Co.
Laurie, Lucy. A Day in the Country. 1990. 29.00x (*0-85439-374-9*, Pub. by St Paul Pubns UK) St Mut.
Lehn, Cornelia. I Heard Good News Today. Schlegel, Ralph A., illus. Oyer, Lora S., intro. by. LC 83-80401. (Illus.). 148p. (gr. 1-6). 1983. 12.95 (*0-87303-073-7*) Faith & Life.
Leppard, Lois G. Mandie & the Fiery Rescue. 160p. (Orig.). (gr. 3-7). 1993. pap. 3.99 (*1-55661-289-3*) Bethany Hse.
—Mandie & the Jumping Juniper. 160p. (Orig.). (gr. 3-7). 1991. 3.99 (*1-55661-200-1*) Bethany Hse.
—Mandie & the Medicine Man, Bk. 6. LC 85-73426. 150p. (Orig.). (gr. 4-8). 1986. pap. 3.99 (*0-87123-891-8*) Bethany Hse.
—Mandie & the Mysterious Bells, Bk. 10. LC 87-72792. 160p. (Orig.). (gr. 4-8). 1988. pap. 3.99 (*1-55661-000-9*) Bethany Hse.
—Mandie & the Mysterious Fisherman. (gr. 4-7). 1992. pap. 3.99 (*1-55661-235-4*) Bethany Hse.
—Mandie & the Singing Chalet. 160p. (Orig.). (ps-8). 1991. pap. 3.99 (*1-55661-198-6*) Bethany Hse.
—Mandie & the Windmill's Message. 160p. (Orig.). (gr. 3-7). 1992. pap. 3.99 (*1-55661-288-5*) Bethany Hse.
Levene. The Fastest Car in the County. LC 91-33539. (gr. 3-6). 1992. pap. 4.99 (*1-55513-395-9*, Chariot Bks) Chariot Family.
—The Pet That Never Was. LC 91-33518. 1992. pap. 4.99 (*1-55513-394-0*, Chariot Bks) Chariot Family.

Levene, Nancy S. Chocolate Chips & Trumpet Tricks. Reck, Sue, ed. LC 93-36195. 192p. (gr. 3-6). 1994. pap. 5.99 (*0-7814-0103-8*, Chariot Bks) Cook.
—Crocodile Meatloaf. LC 92-32615. (ps-6). 1993. pap. 4.99 (*0-7814-0000-7*, Chariot Bks) Chariot Family.
—Hero for a Season. Reck, Sue, ed. LC 93-21126. 96p. (gr. 3-6). 1994. pap. 4.99 (*0-7814-0702-8*, Chariot Bks) Cook.
—Master of Disaster. LC 94-17356. Date not set. write for info. (*0-7814-0089-9*, Chariot Bks) Chariot Family.
Lewis, Beverly. California Christmas. 160p. (gr. 6-9). 1994. pap. 4.99 (*0-310-43321-5*) Zondervan.
—Holly's First Love. LC 92-47055. 1993. pap. 2.99 (*0-310-38051-0*) Zondervan.
—Secret Summer Heart. 160p. (gr. 6-9). 1993. pap. 4.99 (*0-310-38061-8*, Pub. by Youth Spec) Zondervan.
Lewis, C. S. Screwtape Letters the Christian Classic Series. (gr. 4-7). 1993. pap. 9.99 (*0-8407-6261-5*) Nelson.
Littleton, Mark. Secrets of Moonlight Mountain. 1993. pap. 3.99 (*1-56507-960-4*) Harvest Hse.
—Tree Fort Wars. LC 92-44181. (gr. 4 up). 1993. pap. 5.99 (*1-555-13764-4*, Chariot Bks) Chariot Family.
—Winter Thunder. LC 92-5433. 1993. pap. 3.99 (*1-56507-008-9*) Harvest Hse.
Lloyd, Jeremy. Woodland Gospels: According to Captain Beaky & His Band. Percy, Graham, illus. LC 83-20790. 63p. (gr. k up). 1984. pap. 4.95 (*0-571-14285-0*) Faber & Faber.
London, Carolyn. Stolen Ice Cream Bar. Nielson, Deborah, illus. 12p. (gr. k-6). 1981. pap. text ed. 4.25 (*1-55976-151-2*) CEF Press.
Long, Kathy. Hallelujah the Clown: A Story of Blessing & Discovery. Boddy, Joe, illus. LC 92-70384. 32p. (ps-k). 1992. pap. 4.99 (*0-8066-2560-0*, 9-2560, Augsburg) Augsburg Fortress.
Lord, Wendy. Gorilla on the Midway. LC 93-1051. 1994. pap. 4.99 (*0-7814-0892-X*, Chariot Bks) Chariot Family.
—Pickle Stew. LC 93-19018. 1994. pap. 4.49 (*0-7814-0886-5*, Chariot Bks) Chariot Family.
Luttrell, Wanda. Home on Stoney Creek. LC 93-47084. (gr. 4 up). 1994. write for info. (*0-7814-0901-2*) Chariot Family.
—Stranger in Williamsburg. LC 94-20574. 1995. write for info. (*0-7814-0902-0*, Chariot Bks) Chariot Family.
McCullough, Mary F. The City: Sights, Sounds, & Smells. McClain, Cindy, ed. (Illus.). 32p. (Orig.). (ps). 1991. pap. text ed. 3.95 (*0-936625-96-1*, New Hope AL) Womans Mission Union.
McCusker, Paul. Behind the Locked Door. (gr. 3-7). 1993. pap. 4.99 (*1-56179-133-4*) Focus Family.
—Lights Out at Camp What-a-Nut. 150p. (gr. 3-7). 1993. pap. 4.99 (*1-56179-134-2*) Focus Family.
MacDonald, George. The Adventures of Ranald Bannerman. rev. ed. Phillips, Michael, ed. 192p. (gr. 3 up). 1991. 10.99 (*1-55661-223-0*) Bethany Hse.
—At the Back of the North Wind. rev. ed. Phillips, Michael, ed. 176p. (ps-2). 1991. 10.99 (*1-55661-196-X*) Bethany Hse.
—The Lost Princess: A Double Story. Sadler, Glenn E., ed. Oberdieck, Bernhard, illus. 144p. 1992. text ed. 21.99 (*0-8028-5070-7*) Eerdmans.
McDowell, John & Hostetler, Bob. The Love Killer. LC 93-25122. (gr. 6 up). 1993. 8.99 (*0-8499-3509-1*) Word Pub.
McDowell, Josh. Under Siege. 192p. 1992. pap. 8.99 (*0-8499-3363-3*) Word Inc.
McEwan, Elaine K. Murphy's Mansion. Norton, LoraBeth, ed. 96p. (gr. 3-6). Date not set. pap. 4.99 (*0-7814-0160-7*, Chariot Bks) Chariot Family.
—Operation Garbage: A Josh McIntire Book. LC 92-43761. 1993. pap. 4.99 (*0-7814-0121-6*, Chariot Bks) Chariot Family.
—Underground Hero. LC 92-27104. (gr. 3-6). 1993. pap. 4.99 (*0-7814-0113-5*, Chariot Bks) Chariot Family.
McFarlan, Donald. Wizard of the Great Lakes. (gr. 5-9). 1979. pap. 3.95 (*0-87508-631-4*) Chr Lit.
McKissack, Patricia. Give It with Love, Christopher: Christopher Learns about Gifts & Giving. Batholomew, illus. LC 87-73524. 32p. (ps-3). 1988. pap. 5.99 (*0-8066-2354-3*, 10-2554, Augsburg) Augsburg Fortress.
—Speak Up, Christopher: Christopher Learns the Difference Between Right & Wrong. Bartholomew, illus. LC 87-73523. 32p. (ps-6). 1988. pap. 5.99 (*0-8066-2355-1*, 10-5966, Augsburg) Augsburg Fortress.
Marcey, Sally. Choice Adventures, No. 11: The Silverlake Stranger. LC 92-36889. 1993. 4.99 (*0-8423-5048-9*) Tyndale.
Marshall, Donald R. The Enchantress of Crumbledown. LC 90-81830. 229p. (gr. 3-6). 1990. 9.95 (*0-87579-352-5*) Deseret Bk.
Martin, Mildred A. Missionary Stories & the Millers. Burkholder, Edith, illus. 208p. (gr. 3 up). 1993. pap. 6.00 (*0-9627643-4-5*) Green Psturs Pr.
—Prudence & the Millers. 190p. (Orig.). (gr. 3-8). 1993. 9.50 (*0-9627643-9-6*); pap. 6.00 (*0-9627643-8-8*) Green Psturs Pr.
Massey Weddle, Linda. T. J. & the Big Trout River Vandals. LC 91-14678. 94p. (Orig.). (gr. 4-7). 1991. pap. 3.95 (*0-87227-148-X*, RBP5180) Reg Baptist.
—T. J. & the Nobody House. LC 90-8702. 95p. (Orig.). (gr. 3-7). 1990. pap. text ed. 3.95 (*0-87227-145-5*, RBP5174) Reg Baptist.
—T. J. & the Somebody Club. LC 92-5342. 108p. 1992. 3.95 (*0-87227-176-5*, RBP5210) Reg Baptist.
Matranga, Frances C. One Step at a Time. (Illus.). (gr. 4-7). 1987. pap. 3.99 (*0-570-03642-9*, 39-1126) Concordia.
Mattozzi, Patti. Little Lessons for Little Learners: Angels. 32p. (gr. 2 up). 1989. pap. 4.50 (*0-8378-1843-5*) Gibson.
—Little Lessons for Little Learners: Prayer. 32p. (gr. 1 up). 1989. 4.50 (*0-8378-1844-3*) Gibson.
May, D. J. Mr. Marble's Moose. LC 93-1494. 1993. 9.99 (*0-8499-1068-4*) Word Pub.
Meyer, Kathleen A. Bear, Your Manners Are Showing. Beegle, Shirley, ed. Boerke, Carole, illus. 24p. (ps-3). 1994. pap. 1.89 (*0-7847-0251-9*) Standard Pub.
Miller, Marianne M. Too Busy: A Days of the Week Story. Wray, Rhonda, ed. Miller, Marianne M., illus. LC 93-11657. 36p. (Orig.). (gr. k-3). 1993. pap. 9.95 (*0-916260-96-8*, B114) Meriwether Pub.
Minar, Barbra. Lamper's Meadow. 160p. (gr. 4-7). 1992. pap. 6.99 (*0-89107-663-8*) Crossway Bks.
The Misadventures of Curtis Greene. 96p. (gr. 4-6). 1991. 1.70 (*0-89636-275-2*, JB4A) Accent CO.
Mishica, Clare. Charlie the Champ. (Illus.). 48p. (gr. k-3). 1994. pap. 3.99 (*0-7847-0138-5*, 24-03958) Standard Pub.
—The Penquin's Big Win. (Illus.). 48p. (Orig.). (gr. k-3). 1994. pap. 3.99 (*0-7847-0139-3*, 24-03959) Standard Pub.
Mock, Dorothy. Aqua Kid Saves the Day: The Good News Kids Learn about Peace. (Illus.). 32p. (Orig.). (ps-2). 1992. pap. 3.99 (*0-570-04718-8*) Concordia.
—Fire Truck Friends: The Good News Kids Learn about Joy. (Illus.). 32p. (Orig.). (ps-2). 1992. pap. 3.99 (*0-570-04717-X*) Concordia.
—One Big Family: The Good News Kids Learn about Kindness. Mitter, Kathy, illus. LC 92-27012. 32p. (Orig.). (ps-2). 1993. pap. 3.99 (*0-570-04737-4*) Concordia.
—Springtime Special: The Good News Kids Learn about Patience. Mitter, Kathy, illus. LC 92-27010. 32p. (Orig.). (ps-2). 1993. pap. 5.99 (*0-570-04736-6*) Concordia.
—The Trouble with Trevor: The Good News Kids Learn about Goodness. Mitter, Kathy, illus. LC 92-27013. 32p. (Orig.). (ps-2). 1993. pap. 3.99 (*0-570-04738-2*) Concordia.
—Worms for Winston: The Good News Kids Learn about Love. (Illus.). 32p. (Orig.). (ps-2). 1992. pap. 5.99 (*0-570-04716-1*) Concordia.
Mock, Dorothy K. The Big Secret: The Good News Kids Learn about Gentleness. Mitter, Kathy, illus. LC 93-6865. 32p. (Orig.). (ps-2). 1993. pap. 3.99 (*0-570-04744-7*) Concordia.
—God Is Everywhere: The Good News Kids Learn about Self-Control. Mitter, Kathy, illus. LC 93-22311. 32p. (Orig.). (ps-2). 1993. pap. 3.99 (*0-570-04745-5*) Concordia.
—The Thanksgiving Parade: The Good News Kids Learn about Faithfulness. Mitter, Kathy, illus. LC 93-2988. 32p. (Orig.). (ps-2). 1993. pap. 3.99 (*0-570-04743-9*) Concordia.
Modica, Terry A. The Dark Secret of the Ouija. Bohl, Al, illus. 224p. (gr. 9-12). 1990. pap. text ed. 2.50 (*1-55748-138-5*) Barbour & Co.
Morgan, Trudy. Where's Alex Best? LC 93-35925. 1994. write for info. (*0-8280-0736-5*) Review & Herald.
Morpugo, Michael. The War of Jenkins' Ear. LC 94-7602. 1995. 15.95 (*0-399-22735-0*, Philomel Bks) Putnam Pub Group.
Morris, Gilbert. The Dixie Widow. 302p. (Orig.). (gr. 9-12). 1991. text ed. 8.99 (*1-55661-115-3*) Bethany Hse.
—The Rustlers of Panther Gap. LC 94-7128. (gr. 3-7). 1994. pap. 4.99 (*0-8423-4393-8*) Tyndale.
Mueller, Charles. Almost Adult: Devotions for 9-12 Year Olds. LC 92-27014. 160p. (Orig.). (gr. 4-7). 1993. pap. 6.99 (*0-570-04598-3*) Concordia.
Murphy, Elspeth C. Julie Chang. LC 85-27989. 107p. (gr. 3-7). 1986. 4.99 (*0-89191-720-9*, 57208, Chariot Bks) Chariot Family.
—The Mystery of the Clumsy Juggler. LC 89-39821. 48p. (gr. 2-4). 1991. pap. 3.99 (*1-55513-897-7*, 38976, Chariot Bks) Chariot Family.
—The Mystery of the Hidden Egg. LC 89-29863. 48p. (gr. 2-4). 1991. pap. 3.99 (*1-55513-915-9*, 39156, Chariot Bks) Chariot Family.
—Pug McConnell. LC 85-26922. 107p. (gr. 3-7). 1986. 4.99 (*0-89191-728-4*, Chariot Bks) Chariot Family.
Myers, Bill. The Experiment. Jorgenson, Andrea, illus. 160p. (Orig.). (gr. 3 up). 1991. pap. 5.99 (*1-55661-214-1*) Bethany Hse.
—My Life As a Broken Bungee Cord. (gr. 4-7). 1993. pap. 4.99 (*0-8499-3404-4*) Word Inc.
—My Life As a Smashed Burrito with Extra Hot Sauce. 1993. pap. 4.99 (*0-8499-3402-8*) Word Inc.
—My Life As a Tornado Test Target. (gr. 4-7). 1994. pap. 4.99 (*0-8499-3538-5*) Word Inc.
—My Life As Alien Monster Bait. (gr. 3-7). 1993. pap. 4.99 (*0-8499-3403-6*) Word Inc.
—My Life As Crocodile Junk Food. (gr. 3-7). 1993. pap. 4.99 (*0-8499-3405-2*) Word Inc.
—My Life As Dinosaur Dental Floss. (gr. 4-7). 1994. pap. 4.99 (*0-8499-3537-7*) Word Inc.
—The Portal. Jorgenson, Andrea, illus. 160p. (Orig.). (gr. 3 up). 1991. pap. 5.99 (*1-55661-163-3*) Bethany Hse.
Myers, Bill & West, Robert. The Blunder Years. LC 93-964. (Illus.). 1993. 3.99 (*0-8423-4117-X*) Tyndale.
Myers, Bill & West, Robert E. Beauty in the Least. LC 93-14026. 1993. 3.99 (*0-8423-4124-2*) Tyndale.
Neeves, D'Reen, illus. God Cares for Me. 12p. (ps-2). 1991. bds. 6.99 (*0-7459-2059-4*) Lion USA.
Nehemias, Paulette. A Tree in Sprocket's Pocket: Stories about God's Green Earth. Harris, Jim, illus. LC 92-26033. 128p. (Orig.). (gr. 3-5). 1993. pap. 4.99 (*0-570-04730-7*) Concordia.
—Wiggler's Worms: Stories about God's Green Earth. Harris, Jim, illus. LC 92-28486. 128p. (Orig.). (gr. 3-5). 1993. pap. 4.99 (*0-570-04731-5*) Concordia.
Nesbit, Jeff. Cougar Chase. LC 93-40145. 1994. pap. 4.99 (*0-8407-9255-7*) Nelson.
—Mountaintop Rescue. LC 93-49796. (gr. 4 up). 1994. pap. 4.99 (*0-8407-9257-3*) Nelson.
—Setting the Trap. LC 93-41025. 1994. pap. 4.99 (*0-8407-9256-5*) Nelson.
Nesbit, Jeffrey A. Crosscourt Winner. 132p. 1991. pap. 4.99 (*0-89693-129-3*) SP Pubns.
—The Legend of the Great Grizzly. LC 93-39765. 1994. pap. 4.99 (*0-8407-9254-9*) Nelson.
—The Lost Canoe. 130p. 1991. pap. 4.99 (*0-89693-130-7*) SP Pubns.
—The Reluctant Runaway. 120p. 1991. pap. 4.99 (*0-89693-131-5*) SP Pubns.
—Struggle with Silence. 129p. 1991. pap. 4.99 (*0-89693-132-3*) SP Pubns.
—A War of Words. LC 92-27663. (Illus.). 1992. pap. 4.99 (*0-89693-076-9*, Victor Books) SP Pubns.
Newton, Lucilda A. Big Peanuts in Trouble. (ps-3). 1976. pap. 2.50 (*0-915374-18-8*, 18-8) Rapids Christian.
Noonan, Janet & Calvert, Jacquelyn. Berries for the Queen. LC 92-32336. (ps-2). 1994. 8.99 (*0-7814-0903-9*, Chariot Bks) Chariot Family.
—A Crown for Sir Conrad. LC 92-32337. 1994. 8.99 (*0-7814-0317-0*, Chariot Bks) Chariot Family.
O'Connor, Karen. The Green Team: The Adventures of Mitch & Molly. Chapin, Patrick O., illus. LC 92-24643. 80p. (Orig.). (gr. 1-4). 1993. pap. 4.99 (*0-570-04726-9*) Concordia.
Oestreicher, James. Choice Adventures: Monumental Discovery. 160p. 1992. pap. 4.99 (*0-8423-5030-6*) Tyndale.
Oke, Janette. Julia's Last Hope. large type ed. 224p. (Orig.). (gr. 8 up). 1990. pap. 9.99 (*1-55661-157-9*) Bethany Hse.
—When Breaks the Dawn. LC 86-3405. 250p. (Orig.). (gr. 4 up). 1986. pap. 6.99 (*0-87123-882-9*) Bethany Hse.
—A Woman Named Damaris. large type ed. 224p. (Orig.). (gr. 9 up). 1991. pap. 9.99 (*1-55661-226-5*) Bethany Hse.
O'Leary, Daniel J. & Dalton, Kathleen. Where Is God? Sabatte, Frank, illus. (gr. 4 up). 1991. pap. 2.95 (*0-8091-6598-8*) Paulist Pr.
Oliver, Barbara. Mission Stories for Young Children. 48p. (Orig.). (gr. 1-3). 1990. pap. 2.95 (*0-936625-93-7*, New Hope AL) Womans Mission Union.
Otto, Carolyn. First Church. 1994. write for info. (*0-8050-2554-5*) H Holt & Co.
Page, Carole G. Bouquet of Good-Byes. 1992. pap. 4.99 (*0-8024-8180-9*) Moody.
—Change of Plans. 1992. pap. 4.99 (*0-8024-8179-5*) Moody.
—Heather's Choice. LC 82-3417. 128p. (gr. 7 up). 1982. pap. 4.99 (*0-8024-8453-0*) Moody.
—Taste of Fame. (gr. 2-6). 1992. pap. 4.99 (*0-8024-8178-7*) Moody.
Pearson. Uncle Alphonso & the Greedy Green Dinosuar. LC 90-20340. 1992. pap. 4.99 (*1-55513-424-6*, Chariot Bks) Chariot Family.
—Uncle Alphonso & the Puffy Proud Dinosaur. LC 90-32442. 1992. pap. 4.99 (*1-55513-562-5*, Chariot Bks) Chariot Family.
Pearson, Jack. Uncle Alphonso & the Frosty, Fibbing Dinosaurs. Julien, Terry, illus. LC 92-39373. 1993. pap. 4.49 (*0-7814-0100-3*, Chariot Bks) Chariot Family.
Pearson, Mary Rose. Three Cheers for Big Ears. Park, Julie, illus. 48p. (gr. 2). 1992. pap. 2.99 (*0-8423-1043-6*) Tyndale.
Petersen, Ken. Choice Adventures: Quarterback Sneak. 160p. (gr. 4-8). 1992. pap. 4.99 (*0-8423-5029-2*) Tyndale.
Petersen, Randy. The Appalachian Ambush. LC 93-40183. 1994. 4.99 (*0-8423-5133-7*) Tyndale.
Peterson, Lorraine. If You Really Trust Me, Why Can't I Stay Out Longer? 224p. (Orig.). 1991. pap. 7.99 (*1-55661-212-5*) Bethany Hse.
Phillips, Michael & Pella, Judith. Treasure of Stonewycke. LC 88-7531. 352p. (Orig.). (gr. 11 up). 1988. pap. 8.99 (*0-87123-902-7*) Bethany Hse.
Plemons, Marti. Georgie & the New Kid. (Illus.). 128p. (gr. 3-6). 1992. pap. 4.99 (*0-87403-687-9*, 24-03727) Standard Pub.
—Josh & the Guinea Pig. (Illus.). 128p. (gr. 3-6). 1992. pap. 4.99 (*0-87403-686-0*, 24-03726) Standard Pub.
—Megan & the Owl Tree. (Illus.). 128p. (gr. 3-6). 1992. pap. 4.99 (*0-87403-685-2*, 24-03725) Standard Pub.
—Scott & the Ogre. (Illus.). 128p. (gr. 3-6). 1992. pap. 4.99 (*0-87403-688-7*, 24-03728) Standard Pub.
Porter, Barbara J. Grandpa & Me & the Wishing Star. Marsh, Dilleen, illus. LC 90-81831. 32p. (ps). 1990. 10.95 (*0-87579-269-3*) Deseret Bk.
Proctor, R. P. Motor Bike Mayhem. LC 93-38898. 1994. 4.99 (*0-8423-5131-0*) Tyndale.

Rebuck, Linda, et al, eds. Twinkle & the All-Star Angel Band. 1992. singer's activity bk. 3.95 (*0-685-68510-1*, BCMC-78); director ed. bk. 9.95 (*0-685-68511-X*, BCMC-78A); cassette 10.98 (*0-685-68512-8*, BCTA-9142C) Lillenas.

Reid, Mary C. Come to the Island With Me. LC 92-73012. 32p. 1992. pap. 4.99 (*0-8066-2632-1*, 9-2632) Augsburg Fortress.

Reinsma, Carol. The Picnic Caper. Cori, Nathan, illus. LC 93-29567. 48p. (Orig.). (gr. k-3). 1994. pap. 3.99 (*0-7847-0006-0*, 24-03956) Standard Pub.

—A Place in the Palace. Cori, Nathan, illus. 48p. (Orig.). (gr. 1-3). 1993. pap. 3.99 (*0-7847-0095-8*, 24-03945) Standard Pub.

—The Secret of the Ring in the Offering. Schneider, Jennifer, illus. 48p. (Orig.). (gr. 1-3). 1993. pap. 3.99 (*0-7847-0094-X*, 24-03944) Standard Pub.

—The Shimmering Stone. Cori, Nathan, illus. 48p. (Orig.). (gr. k-3). 1994. pap. 3.99 (*0-7847-0007-9*, 24-03957) Standard Pub.

Repp, Gloria. A Question of Yams: A Missionary Story Based on True Events. Daniels, Karen, ed. Bruckner, Roger, illus. 67p. (Orig.). (gr. 2-4). 1992. pap. 4.95 (*0-89084-614-6*) Bob Jones Univ Pr.

Richardson, Arleta. The Grandma's Attic Storybook. LC 92-33823. 1993. pap. 9.99 (*0-7814-0070-8*, Chariot Bks) Chariot Family.

—Looking for Home. LC 92-46259. 1993. pap. 4.99 (*0-7814-0921-7*, Chariot Bks) Chariot Family.

—Stories from the Growing Years. LC 90-20123. (gr. 3-7). 1991. pap. 3.99 (*1-55513-819-5*, 38190, Chariot Bks) Chariot Family.

—Whistle-Stop West. LC 92-46260. 1993. pap. 4.99 (*0-7814-0922-5*, Chariot Bks) Chariot Family.

Richmond, Gary. Backyard Safari. (ps-3). 1990. write for info. (*0-8499-0741-1*) Word Inc.

—The Forgotten Friend. (gr. 1-5). 1991. text ed. 6.99 (*0-8499-0913-9*) Word Inc.

—Miss Otter Goes to the Movies. 1990. 6.99 (*0-8499-0743-8*) Word Inc.

—Prodigal Wolf. 1990. 6.99 (*0-8499-0746-2*) Word Inc.

—A Scary Night at the Zoo. 1990. write for info. (*0-8499-0742-X*) Word Inc.

Rispin, Karen. Ambush at Amboseli. LC 93-37801. 1994. 4.99 (*0-8423-1295-1*) Tyndale.

—Anika's Mountain. LC 93-31345. (Illus.). 1994. pap. 4.99 (*0-8423-1219-6*) Tyndale.

—Sabrina the Schemer. LC 93-39634. 1994. 4.99 (*0-8423-1296-X*) Tyndale.

Robbins, Duffy. Have I Got News for You! 112p. 1993. pap. 6.99 (*0-310-37461-8*, Pub. by Youth Spec) Zondervan.

Roddy, Lee. High Country Ambush. 176p. (Orig.). (gr. 3-8). 1992. pap. 5.99 (*1-55661-287-7*) Bethany Hse.

—Mystery of the Phantom Gold. 176p. (Orig.). (gr. 3-8). 1991. pap. 5.99 (*1-55661-210-9*) Bethany Hse.

—Night of the Vanishing Lights. 1994. pap. 4.99 (*1-56179-256-X*) Focus Family.

—Terror in the Sky. 176p. (Orig.). (ps-8). 1991. pap. 5.99 (*1-55661-096-3*) Bethany Hse.

Roland, Timothy. Detective Dan & the Flying Frog Mystery. 48p. (gr. 2-5). 1993. pap. 3.99 (*0-310-38121-5*, Pub. by Youth Spec) Zondervan.

—Detective Dan & the Gooey Gumdrop Mystery. 48p. (gr. 2-5). 1993. pap. 3.99 (*0-310-38111-8*, Pub. by Youth Spec) Zondervan.

—Detective Dan & the Missing Marble Mystery. 2nd, abr., & rev. ed. 48p. (gr. 2-5). 1993. pap. 3.99 (*0-310-38091-X*, Pub. by Youth Spec) Zondervan.

—Detective Dan & the Puzzling Pizza Mystery. 48p. (gr. 2-5). 1993. pap. 3.99 (*0-310-38101-0*, Pub. by Youth Spec) Zondervan.

Roper, Gayle. The Puzzle of the Poison Pen. LC 94-6755. 1994. write for info. (*0-7814-1507-1*, Chariot Bks) Chariot Family.

—A Race to the Finish. LC 90-21160. 128p. (gr. 3-7). 1991. pap. 4.99 (*1-55513-816-0*, 38166, Chariot Bks) Chariot Family.

Rue, Nancy. Home by Another Way. (gr. 9-12). 1991. pap. 8.95 (*0-89107-633-6*) Crossway Bks.

St. John, Maddie, et al. A Story from Widg. St. John, Maddie, illus. LC 90-71987. 64p. (Orig.). (gr. k-3). 1992. pap. 6.00 (*1-56002-047-4*) Aegina Pr.

St. John, Patricia. Patricia St. John Books, 10 bks. (gr. 2-7). Set. 46.96 (*0-8024-0726-9*) Moody.

—The Secret at Pheasant Cottage. LC 78-24384. (gr. 6-8). 1979. pap. 4.50 (*0-8024-7683-X*) Moody.

—Secret of the Fourth Candle. LC 81-22400. 128p. 1981. pap. 4.50 (*0-8024-7681-3*) Moody.

—Where the River Begins. LC 80-12304. 128p. (Orig.). (gr. 5-8). pap. 4.50 (*0-8024-8124-8*) Moody.

Sarlas-Fontana, Jane. Spero Learns of Palm Sunday & Jesus' Love. 28p. (ps-4). 1993. pap. 5.95 (*0-9638336-0-X*) Spero & Me.

Schulte, Elaine. Eternal Passage. 1989. pap. 7.99 (*1-55513-988-4*, 39883, Life Journey) Chariot Family.

—Golden Dreams. 1989. pap. 7.99 (*1-55513-987-6*, 39875, Life Journey) Chariot Family.

—Off to a New Start. LC 88-35035. (gr. 3-7). 1989. pap. 4.99 (*1-55513-771-7*, Chariot Bks) Chariot Family.

—With Wings As Eagles. LC 90-6305. 1990. pap. 7.99 (*1-55513-989-2*, 39891, Life Journey) Chariot Family.

Schulte, Elaine L. A Colton Cousins Adventure: Susannah Strikes Gold. 144p. 1992. pap. 5.99 (*0-310-54611-7*, Youth Bks) Zondervan.

—Daniel Colton Kidnapped: Daniel Strikes a Bad Bargain - Now He Must Outsmart His Captors. (Illus.). 144p. (gr. 3-7). 1993. pap. 5.99 (*0-310-57261-4*, Pub. by Youth Spec) Zondervan.

—Melanie & the Modeling Mess. LC 93-45377. 1994. 4.99 (*1-55661-254-0*) Bethany Hse.

Seebo, Donna D. God's Kiss: Mrs. Seebo's Fables. 32p. 1993. incl. cassette 19.95 (*1-883164-01-X*) Cassette (*1-883164-02-8*) Delphi Intl.

Seek, Vesta. Danger for Old Ruff. Wilson, Deborah G., illus. LC 89-25240. 32p. (ps-2). 1991. pap. 4.99 (*1-55513-360-6*, 33605, Chariot Bks) Chariot Family.

—Old Ruff & the Mother Bird. Wilson, Deborah G., illus. LC 89-25264. 32p. (ps-2). 1991. pap. 4.99 (*1-55513-361-4*, 33613, Chariot Bks) Chariot Family.

Sensenig, Janet. Daryl Borrows a Brother. 166p. 1989. 6.70 (*0-317-02911-8*) Rod & Staff.

Shaffer, Betty. Lisa. LC 82-72149. 141p. (Orig.). (gr. 8-12). 1982. pap. 3.99 (*0-87123-316-9*) Bethany Hse.

Sharp, Christopher. Bad Mouth Christopher. (gr. 1-4). 1980. pap. 4.99 (*0-570-03482-5*, 56-1703) Concordia.

Simpson, Winifred R. Hello, World, You're Mine? (Illus.). (gr. 4-7). 1987. pap. 3.99 (*0-570-03643-7*, 39-1127) Concordia.

Skoglund, Elizabeth. Harold's Dog Horace Is Scared of the Dark. Bjorkman, Dale, illus. 48p. (gr. 2). 1992. pap. 2.99 (*0-8423-1047-9*) Tyndale.

Skold, Betty W. Lord, I Have a Question: Story Devotions for Girls. LC 79-50079. 112p. (gr. 3-6). 1979. pap. 5.99 (*0-8066-1718-7*, 10-4096, Augsburg) Augsburg Fortress.

Slattery, Kathryn. Grandma, I'll Miss You: A Child's Story about Death & New Life. LC 92-18984. 1993. 14.99 (*0-7814-0937-3*, Chariot Bks) Chariot Family.

Smee, Doug. Acting Up! 1990. 8.50 (*0-8341-9076-1*, BCMP-661) Lillenas.

Smith, David B. Bucky Gets Busted. LC 93-37921. 1993. write for info. (*0-8280-0807-8*) Review & Herald.

—Watching the War. LC 93-48994. 1994. write for info. (*0-8280-0790-X*) Review & Herald.

Smith, Marjorie. I Like My Teacher: You Know Why? Gross, Karen, ed. 24p. (Orig.). (ps). 1992. pap. text ed. 3.95 (*1-56309-055-4*, New Hope) Womans Mission Union.

Snelling, Lauraine. Call for Courage. LC 92-16240. 160p. (Orig.). (gr. 7-10). 1992. pap. 5.99 (*1-55661-260-5*) Bethany Hse.

—Eagles' Wings. 160p. (Orig.). (gr. 7-10). 1991. pap. 5.99 (*1-55661-203-6*) Bethany Hse.

—Go for the Glory. 160p. (Orig.). (gr. 7-10). 1991. pap. 5.99 (*1-55661-218-4*) Bethany Hse.

—The Race. 176p. (Orig.). (gr. 7-9). 1991. pap. 5.99 (*1-55661-161-7*) Bethany Hse.

Snider, Catherine. Mommy Loves Jesus. Arnsteen, Katy K., illus. LC 93-13354. 24p. (Orig.). (ps-6). 1993. pap. 3.95 (*0-8198-4731-3*) St Paul Bks.

Sollitt, Kenneth. Our Changing Lives. 182p. 1986. pap. 6.95 (*0-940652-04-8*) Sunrise Bks.

Sometimes It's Hard to Be Friends. LC 87-38204. 24p. (ps-1). 1988. pap. 4.99 (*1-55513-892-6*, Chariot Bks) Chariot Family.

Sorenson, Stephen. Growing up Is an Adventure, Lord. LC 92-27056. 112p. (gr. 3-7). 1992. pap. 5.99 (*0-8066-2647-X*, 9-2647) Augsburg Fortress.

—Growing up Isn't Easy, Lord: Story Devotions for Boys. LC 79-50080. 112p. (gr. 3-6). 1979. pap. 5.99 (*0-8066-1713-6*, 10-2904, Augsburg) Augsburg Fortress.

Souter, John. Choice Adventures: Abandoned Gold Mine. 160p. (gr. 4-8). 1992. pap. 4.99 (*0-8423-5031-4*) Tyndale.

Spears-Stewart, Reta. Toby's Big Truck Adventure. LC 92-35750. 1993. 7.95 (*0-8163-1141-2*) Pacific Pr Pub Assn.

Stafford, Tim. John Porter in Big Trouble. (Illus.). 32p. (gr. 2-8). 1990. 11.95 (*0-7459-1807-7*) Lion USA.

Stahl, Hilda. Big Trouble for Roxie. 160p. (gr. 4-7). 1992. pap. 3.99 (*0-89107-658-1*) Crossway Bks.

—Chelsea & the Outrageous Phone Bill. 160p. (gr. 4-7). 1992. pap. 3.99 (*0-89107-657-3*) Crossway Bks.

—Chelsea's Special Touch. LC 92-37203. 160p. (gr. 4-7). 1993. 3.99 (*0-89107-712-X*) Crossway Bks.

—Daisy Punkin: Meet Daisy Punkin. 128p. (gr. 2-5). 1991. pap. 4.99 (*0-89107-617-4*) Crossway Bks.

—Elizabeth Gail & the Mystery of the Hidden Key, No. 20. (gr. 4-7). 1992. pap. 4.99 (*0-8423-0816-4*) Tyndale.

—Elizabeth Gail & the Secret of the Gold Charm, No. 21. (gr. 4-7). 1992. pap. 4.99 (*0-8423-0817-2*) Tyndale.

—Hannah & the Daring Escape. LC 92-43994. 160p. (gr. 4-7). 1993. pap. 3.99 (*0-89107-714-6*) Crossway Bks.

—Hannah & the Snowy Hideaway. LC 93-8295. 160p. (Orig.). (gr. 6-9). 1993. pap. 3.99 (*0-89107-748-0*) Crossway Bks.

—Kayla O'Brian & the Runaway Orphans. 128p. (gr. 4-7). 1991. pap. 4.95 (*0-89107-631-X*) Crossway Bks.

—Mystery at Bellwood Estate. LC 92-41738. 160p. (gr. 4-7). 1993. pap. 3.99 (*0-89107-713-8*) Crossway Bks.

—Roxie's Mall Madness. LC 93-22575. 160p. (Orig.). (gr. 6-9). 1993. pap. 3.99 (*0-89107-753-7*) Crossway Bks.

—Sadie Rose & the Champion Sharpshooter. 128p. (gr. 4-7). 1991. pap. 4.99 (*0-89107-630-1*) Crossway Bks.

—Sadie Rose & the Mad Fortune Hunters. LC 90-80619. 128p. (Orig.). (gr. 4-7). 1990. pap. 4.99 (*0-89107-578-X*) Crossway Bks.

—Sadie Rose & the Mysterious Stranger. 128p. (Orig.). (gr. 6-9). 1993. pap. 4.99 (*0-89107-747-2*) Crossway Bks.

—Sendi Lee Mason & the Great Crusade. 128p. (gr. 2-5). 1991. pap. 4.99 (*0-89107-632-8*) Crossway Bks.

—Tough Choices for Roxie. LC 92-37055. 160p. (gr. 4 up). 1993. pap. 3.99 (*0-89107-711-1*) Crossway Bks.

Starry Night. LC 93-15030. write for info. (*1-56179-163-6*) Focus Family.

Stephenson, Jean. Dogwood Stew & Catnip Tea. LC 92-40804. 160p. (Orig.). (gr. 4-7). 1993. pap. 4.99 (*0-89107-717-0*) Crossway Bks.

Stickland, Henrietta. The Christmas Bear. Stickland, Paul, illus. LC 93-10157. 32p. (ps-3). 1993. 15.99 (*0-525-45062-9*, DCB) Dutton Child Bks.

Stiles, Louise. Little Tree. Torvik, Brian, illus. 32p. (gr. 3 up). 1987. pap. 5.95 (*0-88144-051-5*) Christian Pub.

Stone, Maggie R. The Portrait, Bk. I. Schatz, Bud, intro. by. 161p. (Orig.). (gr. 5-12). 1990. pap. 5.95 (*0-685-38818-2*) M R Stone Minst.

Stortz, Diane. Alexander's Praise Time Band. Garris, Norma, illus. LC 92-32817. 28p. (ps-k). 1993. 4.99 (*0-7847-0036-2*, 24-03826) Standard Pub.

—Barnaby Mouse, Detective, & the Mystery of the Big Book. Girouard, Patrick, illus. LC 93-14425. 28p. (ps). 1994. 4.99 (*0-7847-0004-4*, 24-03870) Standard Pub.

Stover, Jo A. They Didn't Use Their Heads. Stover, Jo A., illus. 45p. (ps). 1990. pap. 4.95 (*0-89084-546-8*) Bob Jones Univ Pr.

Stowell, Gordon. God Knows. 14p. (gr. 1-5). 1984. mini-bk. 0.79 (*0-8307-0959-2*, 5608425) Regal.

—Help Me. 14p. (gr. 1-5). 1984. mini-bk. 0.79 (*0-8307-0961-4*, 5608444) Regal.

—I Like. 14p. (ps-2). 1984. mini-bk. 0.79 (*0-8307-0962-2*, 5608579) Regal.

—I'm Sorry. 14p. (gr. 1-5). 1984. mini-bk. 0.79 (*0-8307-0957-6*, 5608400) Regal.

—It's Fun. (gr. 1-5). 1984. mini-bk. 0.79 (*0-8307-0956-8*, 5608392) Regal.

—Please God. 14p. (gr. 1-5). 1984. mini-bk. 0.79 (*0-8307-0954-1*, 5608381) Regal.

—Thank You God. 14p. (gr. 1-7). 1984. mini-bk. 0.79 (*0-8307-0960-6*, 5608436) Regal.

Strawn, Kathy. Help! They Don't Read Yet. Gross, Karen, ed. 32p. (Orig.). (ps). 1992. pap. text ed. 3.95 (*1-56309-056-2*) Womans Mission Union.

Tada, Joni E. Darcy. LC 87-35712. (gr. 3-7). 1988. pap. 4.99 (*1-55513-809-8*, Chariot Bks) Chariot Family.

Tada, Joni E. & Jensen, Steve. Darcy & the Meanest Teacher in the World. LC 92-33075. (gr. 3-7). 1993. pap. 4.99 (*0-7814-0885-7*, Chariot Bks) Chariot Family.

—Darcy's Dog Dilemma. Norton, LoraBeth, ed. LC 93-36330. 128p. (gr. 4-8). 1994. pap. 4.99 (*0-7814-0167-4*, Chariot Bks) Cook.

Tangvald, Christine. Guess What? We're Moving. LC 87-34107. 24p. (ps-2). 1988. 7.99 (*1-55513-481-5*, Chariot Bks) Chariot Family.

—Someone I Love Died. LC 87-31474. 24p. (ps-2). 1988. 7.99 (*1-55513-490-4*, Chariot Bks) Chariot Family.

—We Have a New Baby. LC 87-35457. 24p. (ps-2). 1988. 7.99 (*1-55513-503-X*, Chariot Bks) Chariot Family.

Tate, Susan. Petal Pals Children's Stories, 4 bks. (gr. k-3). 1993. pap. 15.96 (*1-884395-07-4*) Clear Blue Sky.

Taylor, Maureen. Without Warning. LC 91-12470. 144p. 1991. pap. 4.99 (*0-8066-2538-4*, 9-2538) Augsburg Fortress.

Tetz, Rosanne. Nina Can. 32p. 1993. pap. 5.95 (*0-8163-1111-0*) Pacific Pr Pub Assn.

Thoene, Brock & Thoene, Bodie. Gold Rush Prodigal. 224p. (Orig.). (gr. 9-12). 1991. pap. 7.99 (*1-55661-162-5*) Bethany Hse.

—Shooting Star. LC 93-16175. 224p. (Orig.). 1993. pap. 7.99 (*1-55661-320-2*) Bethany Hse.

Thomas, Jerry D. Detective Zack & the Mystery at Thunder Mountain. LC 93-41480. (gr. 4 up). 1994. 5.95 (*0-8163-1212-5*) Pacific Pr Pub Assn.

Thomson, Andy. Renegade in the Hills. Moore, Rebecca, ed. True, Stephanie, illus. 135p. (Orig.). (gr. 5-8). 1989. pap. 4.95 (*0-89084-494-1*) Bob Jones Univ Pr.

Trent, John, et al. The Treasure Tree. 128p. (gr. k-3). 1992. 14.99 (*0-8499-0936-8*) Word Inc.

Trout. Joshua Mouse Lends a Hand. 1992. 6.99 (*0-7814-0010-4*, Chariot Bks) Chariot Family.

—Sheldon Squirrel Learns to Share. 1992. 6.99 (*0-7814-0011-2*, Chariot Bks) Chariot Family.

Uhing, M. James. Windows of a Heart. Lauer, Alphonse, ed. Reyes, Augustine, illus. 72p. 1993. pap. 5.00 (*1-56788-013-4*, 20-002) BMH Pubns.

Unruh, Sophia. Lenka of Emma Creek. Shelly, Maynard, ed. Unruh, Arch, illus. LC 89-81282. 32p. (Orig.). (ps-7). 1989. pap. 9.95 (*0-87303-136-9*) Faith & Life.

Van Horn, Brian & Van Horn, Chris. No Time in a Jam. Scott, Rita & Van Horn, Brian, illus. (gr. 2-8). 1989. write for info. (*1-877765-05-8*) Lambgel Family.

Vann, Donna R. Stefan's Secret Fear. Haysom, John, illus. 32p. (gr. 4-8). 1990. 11.95 (*0-7459-1307-5*) Lion USA.

Voelker, Joyce. Dear Terry. (Illus.). 97p. (Orig.). (gr. 3-6). 1990. pap. 4.95 (*0-89084-526-3*) Bob Jones Univ Pr.

Waite, Michael P. Miggy & Tiggy. LC 87-5251. 32p. (ps-2). 1987. 8.99 (*1-55513-220-0*, Chariot Bks) Chariot Family.

—Suzy Swoof. LC 87-5269. (ps-2). 1987. 7.99 (*1-55513-219-7*, Chariot Bks) Chariot Family.

Wald, Ann. Choice Adventure: Counterfeit Collection. LC 92-36279. 1993. 4.99 (*0-8423-5049-7*) Tyndale.

Watkins, Dawn. Zoli's Legacy, Pt. 1: Inheritance. (Illus.). 190p. (Orig.). (gr. 7-12). 1991. pap. 4.95 (*0-89084-596-4*) Bob Jones Univ Pr.

—Zoli's Legacy, Pt. 2: Bequest. 142p. (Orig.). (gr. 7-12). 1991. pap. 4.95 (*0-89084-597-2*) Bob Jones Univ Pr.
Watkins, Dawn L. Pulling Together. Cooper, Carolyn, ed. Pflug, Kathy, illus. 135p. (Orig.). (gr. 2-4). 1992. pap. 4.95 (*0-89084-609-X*) Bob Jones Univ Pr.
Watson, Wayne. Watercolour Ponies. (gr. 4 up). 1992. 12.99 (*0-8499-0976-7*) Word Inc.
Weaver, Anna. Eyes for Benny. (gr. 6 up). 1984. 7.45 (*0-318-01331-2*) Rod & Staff.
Webster-Seek, Vesta. Old Ruff & Life on the Farm. LC 92-12956. (gr. k-3). 1993. pap. 4.99 (*0-7814-0966-7*, Chariot Bks) Chariot Family.
Weyland, Jack. Jack Weyland. 672p. (gr. 9-12). 1992. Boxed set incls. Stephanie, Sara, Whenever I Hear Your Name, Sam, & Charly. pap. 16.00 (*0-87579-596-X*) Deseret Bk.
—Sam. LC 81-682. 168p. (gr. 9-12). 1992. pap. 4.95 (*0-87579-122-0*) Deseret Bk.
—Sara, Whenever I Hear Your Name. LC 86-29071. 168p. (gr. 9-12). 1992. pap. 4.95 (*0-87579-621-4*) Deseret Bk.
—Stephanie. LC 88-17541. 224p. (gr. 9-12). 1992. pap. 4.95 one of boxed set (*0-87579-622-2*) Deseret Bk.
What on Earth Are You Doing for Heaven's Sake? 1990. 5.95 (*0-8378-2061-8*) Gibson.
Wiggin, Kate D. Mother Carey's Chickens. Coven, Peggy, illus. Adams, Carole G., intro. by. Stephens, Alice B., illus. 368p. (gr. 4-8). 1991. pap. 14.00 (*0-912498-10-2*) F A C E.
Wiggins, VeraLee. Julius, the Perfectly Pesky Pet Parrot. LC 93-14254. 1994. 7.95 (*0-8163-1173-0*) Pacific Pr Pub Assn.
—Shelby's Best Friend. LC 93-27279. 1994. 8.95 (*0-8163-1189-7*) Pacific Pr Pub Assn.
—Shelby's Big Prayer. LC 93-11939. 1994. 8.95 (*0-8163-1188-9*) Pacific Pr Pub Assn.
—Shelby's Big Scare. LC 93-31363. 1994. 8.95 (*0-8163-1190-0*) Pacific Pr Pub Assn.
Wilhelm, Hans. Waldo, Tell Me about Christ. Wilhelm, Hans, illus. 40p. (gr. 3 up). 1988. 4.95 (*0-8378-1812-5*) Gibson.
—Waldo, Tell Me about God. Wilhelm, Hans, illus. 40p. (gr. 3 up). 1988. 4.95 (*0-8378-1809-5*) Gibson.
—Waldo, Tell Me about Guardian Angels. Wilhelm, Hans, illus. 40p. (gr. 3 up). 1988. 4.95 (*0-8378-1811-7*) Gibson.
—Waldo, Tell Me about Me. Wilhelm, Hans, illus. 40p. (gr. 3 up). 1988. 4.95 (*0-8378-1810-9*) Gibson.
Williams, Ginny. Second Chances. (gr. 5-9). Date not set. pap. 10.99 (*1-56507-184-0*) Harvest Hse.
Williams, Karen S. Best Friends Are for Keeps. LC 92-10988. 1992. write for info. (*0-8280-0660-1*) Review & Herald.
Williamson, Denise. The King's Reward: A Story of Vincent DePaul. 130p. (gr. 5 up). 1991. pap. 5.95 (*1-56121-059-5*) Wolgemuth & Hyatt.
Wilson, Neil S. Choice Adventures, No. 9: The Tall Ship Shakedown. LC 92-30500. 1993. 4.99 (*0-8423-5046-2*) Tyndale.
Woodson, Meg. Turn It into Glory. Holmes, Marjorie, intro. by. 224p. (gr. 9 up). 1991. 13.99 (*1-55661-178-1*) Bethany Hse.
Wright, Christine. My Sister Katie: How She Sees God's World. Hull, Biz, illus. LC 90-81702. 32p. 1990. text ed. 7.99 (*0-8066-2497-3*, 9-2497) Augsburg Fortress.
Wright, Dan. Way Cool Comic, No. 1, Pt. 1. 27p. 1993. 1.95 (*0-685-70279-0*) Bristol Hse.
—Way Cool Comic, No. 1, Pt. 2. 27p. 1993. 1.95 (*0-917851-64-1*) Bristol Hse.
Yates, Elizabeth. Journeyman. rev. ed. (Illus.). 161p. (gr. 9 up). 1990. pap. 4.95 (*0-89084-535-2*) Bob Jones Univ Pr.
Young, Philip G. The World That Was. Brumagin, Wayne, ed. Campbell, Susan, illus. 121p. (Orig.). (gr. 4 up). 1993. pap. 8.95 (*1-880451-03-4*) Rainbows End.
Zaanan: Conflict on Cada Maylon. (gr. 3 up). pap. 2.50 perfect bdg. (*1-55748-190-3*) Barbour & Co.

CHRISTIAN SCIENCE

Beringer, Joan E. God's Gifts. Leder, Dora, illus. LC 81-82908. 32p. (gr. k-3). 1984. 8.95 (*0-87510-160-7*) Christian Sci.
Dueland, Joy. Filled up Full. (Illus.). 30p. (Orig.). (gr. k-3). 1974. pap. 4.95 (*0-87510-100-3*) Christian Sci.
—My Best Friend. (Illus.). 27p. (Orig.). (gr. k-3). 1972. pap. 4.95 (*0-87510-081-3*) Christian Sci.

CHRISTIAN SYMBOLISM

see Christian Art and Symbolism

CHRISTIAN UNITY

Rosen, Ruth, ed. Jesus for Jews. Owens, Nate, illus. LC 87-20343. 336p. (Orig.). (gr. 12). 1987. 13.95 (*0-9616148-3-8*); pap. 7.95 (*0-9616148-4-6*); pap. 4.95 mass market (*0-9616148-2-X*) Purple Pomegranate.

CHRISTIANITY

see also Church; God; Jesus Christ; Missions; Protestantism; Reformation; Theology;
also names of Christian churches and sects (e.g. Catholic church; Huguenots; etc.) and headings beginning with the words Christian and Church

Bertolini, Dewey. Sometimes I Really Hate You. 132p. 1991. pap. 4.99 (*0-89693-041-6*) SP Pubns.
Brown, Alan & Perkins, Judy. Christianity. (Illus.). 68p. (gr. 7-9). 1989. 19.95 (*0-7134-5319-2*, Pub. by Batsford UK) Trafalgar.
Darmani, Lawrence. African Youth Speak. (Illus.). 32p. (Orig.). (gr. 9-12). 1994. pap. 4.95 (*0-377-00271-2*) Friendship Pr.
Josef, Marion. God Loves Us. Mayfield, Ana M., illus. 32p. (Orig.). (ps-1). 1993. pap. 3.95 (*0-8198-3037-2*) St Paul Bks.
Landis, Mary. God's Wonderful Trees. 1990. pap. 2.15 (*0-317-02907-X*) Rod & Staff.
—God's Wonderful Water. 1990. pap. 2.15 (*0-317-02908-8*) Rod & Staff.
—My Thank You Book. 1990. pap. 2.15 (*0-317-02909-6*) Rod & Staff.
Lynch, Patricia A. Christianity. (Illus.). 128p. (gr. 7-12). 1991. 17.95x (*0-8160-2441-3*) Facts on File.
Michka, Nikolas & Michka, Vera. Azbuka. (RUS., Illus.). 70p. 1994. write for info. (*1-885024-00-2*) Slavic Christian.
Nystrom, Carolyn. What Is a Christian? Children's Bible Basics. (ps). 1992. 5.99 (*0-8024-7854-9*) Moody.
Orr, Leonard D. Physical Immortality. (gr. 7 up). 1988. pap. 10.00 (*0-945793-01-4*) Inspir Univ.
Orr, Lernard D. Breath Awareness: Breath Awareness for Public Schools, Medical Profession. (gr. 7 up). 1988. pap. 10.00 (*0-945793-02-2*) Inspir Univ.
Paterson, Katherine. Who Am I? Milanowski, Stephanie, illus. 96p. (Orig.). 1992. pap. 8.99 (*0-8028-5072-3*) Eerdmans.
Play! Think! Grow! Two Hundred Thirty-Four Activities for Christian Growth. 264p. (Orig.). (ps-1). 1992. pap. 19.95 (*0-687-13498-6*) Abingdon.
Sciacca, Fran & Sciacca, Jill. No Pain, No Gain. 1989. pap. 3.95 (*0-685-25654-5*) World Wide Pubs.
—Warning: This Christian Is Highly Explosive! 1989. pap. 3.95 (*0-685-25655-3*) World Wide Pubs.
Walters, David. Being a Christian. Odell, Dave, illus. 40p. (Orig.). (gr. 2-10). Date not set. write for info. wkbk. (*0-9629559-2-2*) Good News Min.
Watkins, Morris. Global Christianity. 64p. (Orig.). (gr. 7 up). 1987. pap. 6.95 (*0-939925-08-7*) R C Law & Co.
Windeatt, Mary F. The Brown Scapular. Harmon, Gedge, illus. 32p. (gr. 1-5). 1989. Repr. of 1954 ed. wkbk. 3.00 (*0-89555-380-5*) TAN Bks Pubs.
—The Rosary. Harmon, Gedge, illus. 32p. (gr. 1-5). 1989. Repr. of 1954 ed. wkbk. 3.00 (*0-89555-379-1*) TAN Bks Pubs.

CHRISTIANITY–HISTORY

see Church History

CHRISTIANITY AND SCIENCE

see Religion and Science

CHRISTMAS

see also Christmas–Fiction; Christmas Entertainments; Christmas Plays; Christmas Poetry; Jesus Christ–Nativity; Santa Claus

ABC Christmas Book. (Illus.). 20p. (ps-5). 1986. pap. 4.00 (*0-914510-16-9*) Evergreen.
Actividades Navidenas: Christmas Activities. 32p. 1987. pap. 1.50 (*0-311-26613-4*) Casa Bautista.
Anderson, Joan. Christmas on the Prairie. Ancona, George, illus. LC 85-4095. 48p. (gr. 2-6). 1985. 14.95 (*0-89919-307-2*, Clarion Bks) HM.
Angel, Marie. Woodland Christmas. 1991. 12.95 (*0-8037-1088-7*) Dial Bks Young.
Anglund, Joan W. A Christmas Cookie Book. LC 77-78293. (Illus.). 1982. Repr. of 1977 ed. 3.95 (*0-915696-07-X*) Determined Prods.
—Christmas Is a Time of Giving. Anglund, Joan W., illus. LC 61-10106. 28p. (ps up). 1961. 9.95 (*0-15-217863-5*, HB Juv Bks) HarBrace.
—Christmas Is Love. (Illus.). 32p. (ps up). 1988. 7.95 (*0-15-200425-4*, Gulliver Bks) HarBrace.
Applegate, Katherine. Disney's Christmas with All the Trimmings: Original Stories & Crafts from Mickey Mouse & Friends. Wilson, Phil, illus. 64p. (ps-3). 1994. 12.95 (*0-7868-3003-4*) Disney Pr.
Barth, Edna. Holly, Reindeer, & Colored Lights: The Story of the Christmas Symbols. Arndt, Ursula, illus. LC 71-157731. 96p. (gr. 3-6). 1981. pap. 5.95 (*0-89919-037-5*, Clarion Bks) HM.
Batchelor, Mary. Lion Christmas Book. (Illus.). 96p. (Orig.). 1988. pap. 7.99 (*0-7459-1511-6*) Lion USA.
Beaton, Jane, et al. Family Celebrations: Advent & Christmas. 64p. 1984. pap. 2.95 (*0-8146-1389-6*) Liturgical Pr.
Benjamin, Alan. Christmas Wishes. 16p. 1989. pap. 3.95 (*0-671-68268-7*, Little Simon) S&S Trade.
Bohatta, Ida. The Little Advent Book. (Illus.). (ps-3). 1992. 4.00 (*1-56021-139-3*) W J Fantasy.
The Book of Christmas. 144p. (gr. 7 up). 1986. 19.93 (*0-8094-5261-8*); lib. bdg. 25.93 (*0-8094-5262-6*) Time-Life.
Bradbury, Lynne. The First Christmas: Bible Stories. Williams, Jenny, illus. 28p. (ps-2). 1989. 3.95 (*0-7214-5197-7*, S846-1 SER.) Ladybird Bks.
Branley, Franklyn M. The Christmas Sky. rev. ed. Fieser, Stephen, illus. LC 89-71210. 48p. (gr. 3-7). 1990. 14.95 (*0-690-04770-3*, Crowell Jr Bks); PLB 14.89 (*0-690-04772-X*, Crowell Jr Bks) HarpC Child Bks.
Brent, Isabelle. The Christmas Story. (Illus.). 1989. 13.95 (*0-8037-0730-4*) Dial Bks Young.
Bridwell, Norman. The Witch's Christmas. Bridwell, Norman, illus. 32p. (gr. k-3). 1986. pap. 1.95 (*0-590-40434-2*) Scholastic Inc.
Brokaw, Meredith & Gilbar, Annie. The Penny Whistle Christmas Party Book: Including Hanukkah, New Year's, & Twelfth Night Family Parties. Weber, Jill, illus. 128p. (Orig.). 1991. (Fireside); pap. 12.00 (*0-671-73794-5*, Fireside) S&S Trade.
Brown, Ann. Handmade Christmas Gifts That Are Actually Usable. Small, Carol B., illus. LC 87-31993. 75p. (Orig.). (gr. k-6). 1987. pap. 6.95 (*0-938267-03-5*) Bold Prodns.
Capote, Truman. A Christmas Memory. Peck, Beth, illus. LC 88-36452. 48p. (gr. 2 up). 1989. 17.00 (*0-679-80040-9*) Knopf Bks Yng Read.
Carlson. A Christmas Lullaby. 24p. (gr. k-4). 1985. pap. 1.99 (*0-570-06195-4*, 59-1296) Concordia.
Carol Time. (ps). 1977. 2.95 (*0-86112-234-8*, Pub. by Brimax Bks) Borden.
Carvin, Ruth. Color It Christmas: With Three Christmas Posters. Carvin, Ruth, illus. 8p. (gr. 3 up). 1987. write for info. Carvin Pub.
Cassat, Julie. What I Like Best about Christmas. Rigo, Christina, illus. 14p. (gr. 4-7). 1989. pap. text ed. 5.95 (*0-927106-02-7*) Prod Concept.
Chamberlain, Margaret, illus. The Little Christmas Fold-Out Book. 28p. (ps-4). 1991. accordian bk. 4.99 (*0-7459-2121-3*) Lion USA.
Chariot Staff. Christmas Pop-up Counting Book. (ps). 1993. 9.99 (*0-7814-0127-5*, Chariot Bks) Chariot Family.
—My Jesus Pocketbook Christmas Is Coming. LC 93-71225. (ps-3). 1993. pap. 0.69 (*0-7814-0143-7*, Chariot Bks) Chariot Family.
Cherkerzian, Diane. Christmas Fun: Holiday Crafts & Treats. Eitzen, Allen, illus. LC 92-75840. 32p. (ps-5). 1994. 4.95 (*1-56397-277-8*); prepack 14.95 (*1-56397-278-6*) Boyds Mills Pr.
The Children's Christmas Woodbook. (ps). 1986. bds. 9.95 (*0-8120-5753-8*) Barron.
A Child's Christmas. (Illus.). 32p. 1989. pap. text ed. 10.95 (*0-929648-62-5*) Galison.
Chorao, Kay, compiled by. & illus. Baby's Christmas Treasury. LC 90-45872. 48p. (ps). 1991. 10.00 (*0-679-80198-7*); lib. bdg. 10.99 (*0-679-90198-1*) Random Bks Yng Read.
Christmas Creche Pop-up Book. (Illus.). (ps-3). 1992. 15.00 (*1-56021-159-8*) W J Fantasy.
Christmas Is Coming. (ps-k). 1990. bds. 3.95 (*0-7214-9133-2*) Ladybird Bks.
Christmas: One Hundred Seasonal Favorites. 248p. (gr. 4-12). 1985. 17.95 (*0-88188-158-9*, 00361399) H Leonard.
The Christmas Robin. 1989. 3.95 (*0-7214-5255-8*) Ladybird Bks.
Church, Francis P. Yes, Virginia, There Is a Santa Claus. Allison, Christine, intro. by. LC 92-12268. 1992. 10.00 (*0-385-30854-X*) Delacorte.
Cocca-Leffler, Maryann. Count the Days Till Christmas. Cocca-Leffler, Maryann, illus. LC 92-82915. 16p. (ps-3). 1993. pap. 3.95 (*0-590-46929-0*, Cartwheel) Scholastic Inc.
Cooney. Christmas. Date not set. 15.00 (*0-06-023433-4*); PLB 14.89 (*0-06-023434-2*) HarpC Child Bks.
Corwin, Judith H. Christmas Around the World. LC 93-6567. (gr. 3 up). 1995. lib. bdg. 13.00 (*0-671-87239-7*, J Messner); lib. bdg. 6.95 (*0-671-87240-0*) S&S Trade.
—Christmas Fun. Corwin, Judith H., illus. 64p. (gr. 3 up). 1982. lib. bdg. 10.98 (*0-671-45944-9*, J Messner); lib. bdg. 5.95 (*0-671-49583-6*); PLB 7.71s.p. (*0-685-47052-0*); pap. 4.46s.p. (*0-685-47053-9*) S&S Trade.
Daniel, Becky. Christmas Story (Book & Frieze) 16p. (ps-3). 1990. incl. tchr's. guide 16.95 (*0-86653-555-1*, SS1876, Shining Star Pubns) Good Apple.
Daniel, Frank, illus. Christmas. 20p. (ps). 1993. pap. 3.95 (*0-689-71734-2*, Aladdin) Macmillan Child Grp.
Davidson, Amanda. Teddy's Christmas Cut-Out. 16p. (gr. 4-7). 1990. pap. 2.50 (*0-8167-2197-1*) Troll Assocs.
De Reina, Casiodoro & De Valera, Cipriano, eds. La Natividad. rev. ed. Vivas, Julie, illus. LC 93-46976. (SPA.). 1994. 4.95 (*0-15-200184-0*) HarBrace.
Doll, F., et al. Preparing Young Children for Christmas 1993. (Illus.). 48p. 1993. pap. 1.00 (*0-915531-06-2*) OR Catholic.
Domanska, Janina, illus. The First Noel. LC 85-27084. 24p. (ps up). 1986. 11.75 (*0-688-04324-0*); PLB 11.88 (*0-688-04325-9*) Greenwillow.
Doray, Andrea. What Do We Want for Christmas? A Giving & Sharing Book. Gress, Jonna, ed. Farley, Becky, illus. LC 93-73679. 16p. (ps-1). 1994. pap. 7.20 (*0-944943-40-3*, 23302-7) Current Inc.
Duden, Jane. Christmas. LC 89-28520. (Illus.). 48p. (gr. 5-6). 1990. text ed. 12.95 RSBE (*0-89686-497-9*, Crestwood Hse) Macmillan Child Grp.
Englehart, Steve. Christmas Countdown: A Story a Day for 25 Days for Everyone Who Just Can't Wait 'til Christmas. Waldman, Bryna, illus. 64p. (Orig.). 1993. pap. 5.99 (*0-380-76842-9*, Camelot) Avon.
Erickson, Mary E. Christmas Star Sight & Sound. (ps-3). 1992. 12.99 (*0-87403-990-8*, 24-03690) Standard Pub.
Ewing, Carolyn, illus. Jingle Bells: A Holiday Book with Lights & Music. 10p. (ps-1). 1990. pap. 10.95 (*0-689-71431-9*, Aladdin) Macmillan Child Grp.
Faggella, Kathy. My Christmas: A Photolog Book. 48p. (ps-3). 1993. 9.95 (*1-55670-330-9*) Stewart Tabori & Chang.
Ferguson, Dwayne. Afro-Bets Kids Christmas Fun: An Activity & Coloring Book. Ferguson, Dwayne, illus. LC 92-72003. 48p. (gr. k-3). 1992. pap. 2.95 (*0-940975-41-6*) Just Us Bks.
Ferris, Lynn B., illus. A Classic Treasury of Christmas. LC 91-19276. 48p. 1991. 13.95 (*0-8249-8524-9*, Ideals Child); incl. cassette 17.95 (*0-8249-7453-0*) Hambleton-Hill.
The First Christmas. (ps). 1983. 2.95 (*0-86112-198-8*, Pub. by Brimax Bks) Borden.
The First Christmas. 1991. 4.99 (*0-517-06128-7*) Random Hse Value.

The First Christmas. LC 93-24835. 1993. 6.99 (*0-8407-4916-3*); pap. 6.99 (*0-8407-4912-0*) Nelson.
First Christmas (Christmas Mini-Carousels in Three Dimensional Format) 1992. carousel pop-up 4.95 (*0-8431-3437-2*) Price Stern.
Fittro, Pat, ed. Christmas Programs for Children. 48p. (ps up). 1994. pap. 3.50 (*0-7847-0216-0*, 21-08609) Standard Pub.
—Standard Christmas Program Book: Includes Thanksgiving Material. 48p. (Orig.). 1994. pap. 3.50 (*0-7847-0215-2*, 21-08655) Standard Pub.
Five Christmas Programs for Children. 1976. 4.25 (*0-685-68611-6*, BCMC-32) Lillenas.
Fogartie, Arthur F. The Sixteenth Manger. 64p. 1987. pap. 7.00 (*0-8170-1119-6*) Judson.
Fradin, Dennis B. Christmas. LC 89-25634. (Illus.). 48p. (gr. 1-4). 1990. lib. bdg. 14.95 (*0-89490-258-X*) Enslow Pubs.
Gabriele. Christmas Arts & Crafts. 1985. pap. 1.95 (*0-911211-76-4*) Penny Lane Pubns.
—Christmas Traditions. 1985. pap. 1.95 (*0-911211-78-0*) Penny Lane Pubns.
—The Night Before Christmas. 1985. pap. 1.95 (*0-911211-77-2*) Penny Lane Pubns.
Gertz, Susan E. Hanukkah & Christmas at My House. Gertz, Susan E., illus. LC 91-73702. 32p. (ps-6). 1992. pap. 6.95 (*0-9630934-0-1*) Willow & Laurel.
Gibbons, Gail. Christmas Time. LC 82-1038. (Illus.). 32p. (ps-3). 1982. reinforced bdg. 15.95 (*0-8234-0453-6*); pap. 5.95 (*0-8234-0575-3*) Holiday.
—Christmas Time. Gibbons, Gail, illus. (gr. k-3). 1985. PLB incl. cassette 19.95 (*0-941078-84-1*); pap. 12.95 incl. Cassette (*0-941078-82-5*); PLB 27.95 incl. cassette, 4 paperbacks, guide (*0-317-40160-2*) Live Oak Media.
Giblin, James C. The Truth about Santa Claus. LC 85-47541. (Illus.). 96p. (gr. 3-7). 1985. (Crowell Jr Bks); PLB 15.89 (*0-690-04484-4*, Crowell Jr Bks) HarpC Child Bks.
Gibson, K. & Gee, R. Christmas. (Illus.). 32p. (ps-3). 1992. pap. 5.95 (*0-7460-1030-3*) EDC.
Gibson, Roxie C. Hey, God! What Is Christmas. Gibson, James, illus. LC 82-60192. 64p. (gr. 3-5). 1982. 4.95 (*0-938232-09-6*, 32752) Winston-Derek.
Goffin, Josse, text by. & illus. The Christmas Story. LC 94-4134. 12p. (ps). 1994. 8.95 (*0-395-70929-6*) Ticknor & Flds Bks Yng Read.
Goode, Diane. Diane Goode's American Christmas. Goode, Diane, illus. LC 89-25605. 80p. (ps up). 1990. 14.95 (*0-525-44620-6*, DCB) Dutton Child Bks.
Goode, Diane, illus. Diane Goode's Little Library of Christmas Classics. 32p. (gr. 1 up). 1983. boxed set 7.95 (*0-394-85229-X*) Random Bks Yng Read.
Graham-Barber, Lynda. Ho! Ho! Ho! The Complete Book of Christmas Words. Lewin, Betsy, illus. LC 92-6715. 128p. (gr. 4-7). 1993. SBE 14.95 (*0-02-736933-1*, Bradbury Pr) Macmillan Child Grp.
Gray, Carole, illus. Christmas Nativity Diorama. (ps-1). 1992. pap. 9.95 case, shrinkwrapped (*0-671-78513-3*, S&S BFYR) S&S Trade.
Greene, Carol. Waiting for Christmas: Stories & Activities for Advent. Swisher, Elizabeth, illus. LC 87-70474. 32p. (Orig.). (ps-5). 1987. pap. 5.99 (*0-8066-2264-4*, 10-6915, Augsburg) Augsburg Fortress.
Hallinan, P. K. Today Is Christmas. Hallinan, P. K., illus. 24p. (ps-3). 1993. PLB 11.45 (*1-878363-93-X*) Forest Hse.
Hansen, Lee. My Christmas Counting Book. (ps-3). 1993. pap. 4.95 (*0-307-10361-7*, Golden Pr) Western Pub.
Harrison, Susan. AlphaZoo Christmas. Harrison, Susan, illus. LC 93-20351. 40p. (ps-2). 1993. 13.95 (*0-8249-8623-7*, Ideals Child); PLB 14.00 (*0-8249-8632-6*) Hambleton-Hill.
—Twelve Days of Christmas. Harrison, Susan, illus. 24p. (ps-3). 1989. pap. 2.95 (*0-8249-8391-2*, Ideals Child) Hambleton-Hill.
Hawthorne, Terri B. & Brown, Diane B. Winter Solstice Celebrations Through the Ages: A Coloring Book for All Ages. Brown, Diane B., illus. 32p. 1990. pap. 5.99 (*0-929404-01-7*) Tara Educ Servs.
Haywood, Carolyn. Merry Christmas from Eddie. (gr. 2-4). 1987. pap. 2.95 (*0-8167-1041-4*) Troll Assocs.
Herman, Emmi S. Christmas KidDoodles, Bk. 1. Sims, Deborah, illus. 64p. (Orig.). (ps-2). 1991. pap. 0.99 activity pad (*1-56293-153-9*) McClanahan Bk.
—KidDoodles, Bk. 1. Boyd, Patti, illus. 64p. (ps-2). 1991. pap. 0.99 activity pad (*1-878624-50-4*) McClanahan Bk.
Herriot, James. The Christmas Day Kitten. (Illus.). 32p. (gr. 3 up). 1993. pap. 6.95 (*0-312-09767-0*) St Martin.
Hershey, Katherine. A Very Special Day. Seals, Thelma, et al, illus. 21p. (gr. k-6). 1980. 4.25 (*1-55976-131-8*) CEF Press.
Hierstein-Morris, Jill. Christmas: Facts & Fun. Hierstein-Morris, Jill, illus. 72p. (Orig.). (gr. 1 up). 1990. pap. 9.95 (*1-877588-02-4*) Creatively Yours.
Hinke, George, illus. Christmas Memories: A Family Album of Christmas Celebrations. 48p. 1993. 17.95 (*0-8249-8567-2*, Ideals Child) Hambleton-Hill.
Houts, Amy. An A-B-C Christmas. Munger, Nancy, illus. 28p. (ps-k). 1993. 4.99 (*0-7847-0063-X*, 24-03843) Standard Pub.
Johnson, Florence. Santa's ABC. (ps-3). 1993. pap. 4.95 (*0-307-10360-9*, Golden Pr) Western Pub.
Johnson, Paul, illus. Christmas Prayers. 16p. (ps). 1993. bds. 2.98 (*0-8317-4277-1*) Smithmark.
Jones, Kathy. Celebrate Christmas. Filkins, Vanessa, illus. 144p. (gr. k-6). 1985. wkbk. 11.95 (*0-86653-279-X*, SS 840, Shining Star Pubns) Good Apple.
Kalman, Bobbie. Early Christmas. (Illus.). 64p. (gr. 4-5). 1981. 15.95 (*0-86505-001-5*); pap. 7.95 (*0-86505-003-1*) Crabtree Pub Co.
—We Celebrate Christmas. (Illus.). 56p. (gr. 3-4). 1985. 15.95 (*0-86505-040-6*); pap. 7.95 (*0-86505-050-3*) Crabtree Pub Co.
Kelley, Emily. Christmas around the World. Kiedrowski, Priscilla, illus. 48p. (gr. k-4). 1986. lib. bdg. 14.95 (*0-87614-249-8*) Carolrhoda Bks.
—Christmas Around the World. Kiedrowski, Priscilla, illus. 48p. (ps-4). 1986. pap. 5.95 (*0-87614-453-9*, First Ave Edns) Lerner Pubns.
Kennedy, Pamela. Prayers at Christmastime. Britt, Stephanie M., illus. 24p. (ps-k). 1990. 3.95 (*0-8249-8480-3*, Ideals Child) Hambleton-Hill.
Kinin, Claudia. My Christmas Book of Numbers. (ps-3). 1993. 6.95 (*0-307-13721-X*, Golden Pr) Western Pub.
Klug, Ron & Klug, Lyn, eds. The Christian Family Christmas Book. LC 87-1391. (Illus.). 128p. (ps-7). 1987. text ed. 14.99 (*0-8066-2270-9*, 10-1113, Augsburg) Augsburg Fortress.
Knecker, Don, illus. The First Christmas According to Luke. 32p. (ps-4). 1993. incl. dust jacket 15.99 (*0-570-04753-6*) Concordia.
Kunin, Claudia. My Christmas Alphabet. (ps-3). 1993. 6.95 (*0-307-13720-1*, Golden Pr) Western Pub.
Kurelek, William. A Northern Nativity. Kurelek, William, illus. (gr. 4 up). 1976. 14.95 (*0-88776-099-6*); pap. 7.95 (*0-685-04960-4*) Tundra Bks.
Langstaff, John. What a Morning! The Christmas Story in Black Spirituals. Bryan, Ashley, illus. LC 87-750130. 32p. 1987. SBE 14.95 (*0-689-50422-5*, M K McElderry) Macmillan Child Grp.
Lankford, Mary D. Christmas Around the World. Dugan, Karen, illus. LC 93-38566. 1994. write for info. (*0-688-12166-7*); PLB write for info. (*0-688-12167-5*) Morrow Jr Bks.
Lanza, Barbara. First Christmas Pop-up Book. (ps-3). 1993. 6.95 (*0-307-12464-9*, Golden Pr) Western Pub.
LaPlaca, Annette. How Long 'til Christmas? The Kid's Book of Holiday Fun. Bryer, Debbie, illus. 48p. (Orig.). (gr. 3-6). 1993. pap. 4.99 saddle-stitch (*0-87788-369-6*) Shaw Pubs.
Leet, Frank R. When Santa Was Late. Winfrey, Buford A., illus. 24p. (ps-4). 1990. 3.95 (*0-8249-8483-8*, Ideals Child) Hambleton-Hill.
Leone, Dee. Christmas A-Z. 96p. (gr. 2-7). 1989. 10.95 (*0-86653-499-7*, SS1892, Shining Star Pubns) Good Apple.
Low, Alice, compiled by. The Family Read-Aloud Christmas Treasury. Brown, Marc T., illus. (ps up). 1989. 17.95 (*0-316-53371-8*, Joy St Bks) Little.
Ludlow, Angela. The Fun at Christmas Book. (Illus.). 32p. (gr. 4-8). 1991. pap. 5.99 (*0-7459-1877-8*) Lion USA.
McCreary, Jane. Story of Christmas: A Trim a Tree Story Six Wonderful Ornaments Tell the Christmas Story. (ps-3). 1992. 10.99 (*0-87403-866-9*, 24-03556) Standard Pub.
Mackall, Dandi D. Christmas Gifts That Didn't Need Wrapping. Mathers, Dawn, illus. LC 89-82553. 32p. (ps-2). 1990. pap. 5.99 (*0-8066-2466-3*, 9-2466) Augsburg Fortress.
McKissack, Patricia & McKissack, Frederick. The Children's ABC Christmas. Rogers, Kathy, illus. LC 87-73525. 32p. (ps-6). 1988. pap. 5.99 (*0-8066-2356-X*, 10-1046, Augsburg) Augsburg Fortress.
McKissack, Patricia & McKissack, Fredrick. From Heaven Above: The Story of Christmas Proclaimed by the Angels. Knutson, Barbara, illus. LC 92-70385. 32p. (ps-2). 1992. pap. 4.99 (*0-8066-2609-7*, 9-2609, Augsburg) Augsburg Fortress.
McKissack, Patricia C. & McKissack, Frederick. Christmas in the Big House, Christmas in the Quarters. Thompson, John, illus. LC 92-33831. (gr. 3-8). 1994. 15.95 (*0-590-43027-0*) Scholastic Inc.
Marsh, Carole. Minnesota Classic Christmas Trivia: Stories, Recipes, Activities, Legends, Lore & More! (Illus.). (gr. 3 up). 1994. PLB 24.95 (*0-7933-0626-4*); pap. 14.95 (*0-7933-0625-6*); computer disk 29.95 (*0-7933-0627-2*) Gallopade Pub Group.
Marzollo, Jean & Wick, Walter. I Spy Christmas. 1992. bds. 12.95 (*0-590-45846-9*, Cartwheel) Scholastic Inc.
May, Darcy. Twelve Days of Christmas. 12p. 1993. 9.95 (*1-55670-336-8*) Stewart Tabori & Chang.
Moncure, Jane B. Our Christmas Book. rev. ed. Stasiak, Krystyna & Connelly, Gwen, illus. LC 85-29132. 32p. (ps-3). 1986. PLB 13.95 (*0-89565-341-9*) Childs World.
Moore, Clement. Night Before Christmas Pop-Ups. 1991. 4.99 (*0-517-06127-9*) Random Hse Value.
Moore, Clement C. The Night Before Christmas. Holt, Shirley, illus. 28p. 16.95 (*0-9613476-2-7*) Shirlee.
—The Night Before Christmas. LC 89-42998. (Illus.). 80p. 1989. 4.95 (*0-89471-754-5*) Running Pr.
Munro, Roxie. Christmastime in New York City. (Illus.). 32p. (ps-3). 1994. pap. 5.99 (*0-14-050462-1*) Puffin Bks.
My Big Christmas Book. 1988. 5.98 (*0-671-07565-9*) S&S Trade.
My Christmas Activity Book. 1990. 3.99 (*0-517-03709-2*) Random Hse Value.
My Christmas Present. (ps-k). 1990. bds. 3.95 (*0-7214-9128-6*) Ladybird Bks.
My First Christmas Book. (ps-k). 1990. bds. 3.95 (*0-7214-9093-X*) Ladybird Bks.
National Gallery of Art Staff. A Renaissance Christmas. (Illus.). 64p. 1991. 19.95 (*0-8212-1875-1*) Bulfinch Pr.
Nielsen, Shelly. Christmas. Wallner, Rosemary, ed. LC 91-73034. 1992. 13.99 (*1-56239-067-8*) Abdo & Dghtrs.
Nora, Clarke. The Christmas Collection. Rouwntree, Julia, et al, illus. 24p. (ps up). 1992. 9.95 (*1-85697-833-8*, Kingfisher LKC) LKC.
Ogilvy, Carol & Tinkham, Trudy. Classy Christmas Concerts. Renard, Jan, illus. 112p. (gr. k-7). 1986. wkbk. 10.95 (*0-86653-349-4*, GA 795) Good Apple.
O'Leary, Sean C. Christmas Wonder: From Ireland - For Children: Craftwork, Lore, Poems, Songs & Stories. LC 89-50972. (Illus.). 98p. (Orig.). 1989. pap. 12.95 (*0-86278-177-9*, Pub. by O'Brien Press Ltd Eire) Dufour.
Osborn, Susan T. & Tangvald, Christine H. Children Around the World Celebrate Christmas! McCallum, Jodie, illus. LC 93-6683. (gr. 4 up). 1993. 10.99 (*0-87403-799-9*, 24-03664) Standard Pub.
Parks, Joe E. Christmas Around the World. 1981. 4.95 (*0-685-68526-8*, BCMC-45); cassette 10.98 (*0-685-68527-6*, BCTA-9034C) Lillenas.
Patterson, Don. A Child's Trip to Christmas in Santa Fe: A Photographic Documentary. LC 91-62868. (Illus.). 120p. (gr. k-3). 1991. 29.95 (*0-9629093-2-7*) MyndSeye.
Paxton, Lenore & Siadi, Phillip. Christmas Time of Year: A Sing, Color, 'n Say Fun Book-Tape Package. Lindsay, Warren & Huntoon, Cathy, illus. 32p. (ps-3). 1992. pap. 6.95 (*1-880449-04-8*) Wrldkids Pr.
Peraza, Michael, illus. Disney's the Little Mermaid: An Under the Sea Christmas: A Holiday Songbook. LC 93-70939. 48p. 1993. 9.95 (*1-56282-504-6*) Disney Pr.
Pistolesi, Roseanna. Let's Celebrate Christmas: A Book of Drawing Fun. Pistolesi, Roseanna, illus. LC 87-61376. 32p. (gr. 2-6). 1988. PLB 10.65 (*0-8167-1133-X*); pap. text ed. 1.95 (*0-8167-1134-8*) Troll Assocs.
Pomaska, Anna. The Little Christmas Activity Book. (ps up). 1988. pap. 1.00 (*0-486-25679-0*) Dover.
Presilla, Maricel. Feliz Nochebuena Feliz Navidad: Christmas Feasts of the Hispanic Caribbean. (gr. 2-6). 1994. 15.95 (*0-8050-2512-X*) H Holt & Co.
Quaglini, Juliana. The Night of the Shepherds: A Christmas Experience. Flanagan, Anne J., tr. from ITA. De Vico, Elvira, illus. LC 93-25027. 32p. (Orig.). (gr. 4 up). 1993. pap. 3.95 (*0-8198-5128-0*) St Paul Bks.
Ray, Jane, illus. La Historia de Navidad. LC 91-578. (SPA.). 32p. (ps up). 1991. 16.00 (*0-525-44830-6*, DCB) Dutton Child Bks.
Rhoda, Michael D. A Christmas Surprise! Gress, Jonna, ed. 10p. (ps-1). 1994. write for info. (*0-944943-43-8*, CODE 23303-6) Current Inc.
Robbins, Ruth. Baboushka & the Three Kings. Sidjakov, Nicholas, illus. LC 60-15036. (ps up). 1960. 13.45 (*0-395-27673-X*, Pub. by Parnassus) HM.
Rollins, Charlemae, ed. Christmas Gif' An Anthology of Christmas Poems, Songs, & Stories, Written by & about Black People. Bryan, Ashley, illus. Baker, Augusta, intro. by. LC 92-18976. (Illus.). 128p. 1993. PLB 14.43 (*0-688-11668-X*) Morrow Jr Bks.
Sadie Fields Productions Staff. Christmas Long Ago. (Illus.). 14p. 1992. 15.95 (*0-399-21839-4*, Putnam) Putnam Pub Group.
Santa Is Coming. (ps). 1983. 2.95 (*0-86112-229-1*, Pub. by Brimax Bks) Borden.
Santa's Christmas Activity Book. 1992. 3.99 (*0-517-07695-0*) Random Hse Value.
Scarry, Patricia M. Sweet Smell of Christmas. Miller, J. P., illus. 32p. (ps-2). 1970. write for info. (*0-307-13527-6*, Golden Bks) Western Pub.
Shapes of Christmas. (gr. k-2). 1991. pap. 3.95 (*0-8167-2188-2*) Troll Assocs.
Silverman, Jerry. Christmas Songs. (Illus.). 64p. (gr. 5 up). 1992. PLB 15.95 (*0-7910-1832-6*, Am Art Analog); pap. 7.95 (*0-7910-1848-2*, Am Art Analog) Chelsea Hse.
Simon, Mary M. A Silent Night: Hear Me Read Bible Stories Ser. (Illus.). 24p. (ps-1). 1991. pap. 2.49 (*0-570-04700-5*, 56-1659) Concordia.
Smith, Elva S., compiled by. Christmas in Legend & Story: A Book for Boys & Girls Illustrated from Famous Paintings. Hazeltine, Alice I., compiled by. LC 72-39390. (gr. 7 up). Repr. of 1915 ed. 18.00 (*0-8369-6353-9*) Ayer.
Stamper, Judith. Christmas Holiday Grab Bag. Regan, Dana, illus. LC 92-13226. 48p. (gr. 2-5). 1992. PLB 11.89 (*0-8167-2908-5*); pap. text ed. 3.95 (*0-8167-2909-3*) Troll Assocs.
Starlight Christmas Package. 1990. pap. 2.75 (*0-553-61163-1*) Bantam.
Story of Christmas for Children. LC 89-11048. (Illus.). (ps-3). 1989. 2.95 (*0-8249-8254-1*, Ideals Child) Hambleton-Hill.
Sullivan, Dianna. Christmas Activities from Around the World. Walhood, Darlene, illus. 48p. (gr. 1-4). 1985. wkbk. 6.95 (*1-55734-008-0*) Tchr Create Mat.
Trent, Robbie. The First Christmas. rev. ed. Simont, Marc, illus. LC 89-29729. 32p. (ps-2). 1990. pap. 3.50 (*0-06-443249-1*, Trophy) HarpC Child Bks.
—First Christmas Board Book. Simont, Marc, illus. LC 89-29729. 26p. (ps). 1992. 4.95 (*0-694-00423-5*, Festival) HarpC Child Bks.
Troll Staff. Christmas Around the World. 12p. (ps-3). 1991. pap. 2.95 (*0-8167-2189-0*) Troll Assocs.

Tuchman, Gail. Christmas KidDoodles, Bk. 3. Nethery, Susan, illus. 64p. (Orig.). (ps-2). 1991. pap. 0.99 activity pad (*1-56293-155-5*) McClanahan Bk.
Tudor, Tasha. Take Joy: The Tasha Tudor Christmas Book. Tudor, Tasha, illus. LC 66-10645. (gr. k up). 1980. 18.95 (*0-399-20766-X*, Philomel) Putnam Pub Group.
Vesey, Susan & Doney, Meryl. The Christmas Activity Book (Mini) (Illus.). 48p. (gr. 1-6). 1990. pap. 0.99 (*0-7459-1507-8*) Lion USA.
Vittitow, Mary L. & Liu, Sarah. Fun Things for Kids at Christmastime. Vittitow, Mary L., illus. 64p. (gr. 1-4). 1991. pap. 7.99 wkbk. (*0-87403-843-X*, 28-03063) Standard Pub.
Wamberg, Steve & Wamberg, Annie. Christmas: A Fresh Look. (Illus.). 48p. (gr. 6-8). 1991. pap. 8.99 (*1-55945-124-6*) Group Pub.
Watson, Carol. My Little Christmas Box, 4 bks. (Illus.). 32p. (ps-3). 1990. Set. casebound 10.95 (*0-7459-1837-9*) Lion USA.
Welcome Jesus. (Illus.). 32p. (Orig.). 1993. pap. 1.99 (*0-570-04754-4*) Concordia.
Wever, Hinke B. Little Lights in the Darkness: Stories & Activities for Advent & Christmas. Vilain, Frederic, tr. from GER. Muller, Anna-Hermine, illus. LC 90-42800. 99p. (Orig.). 1990. pap. 9.95 (*0-8198-4444-6*) St Paul Bks.
Wilkes, Angela. My First Christmas Activity Book. LC 94-638. (Illus.). 48p. 1994. 12.95 (*1-56458-674-X*) Dorling Kindersley.
Willis, Ted. A Problem for Mother Christmas. Bennett, Jill, illus. 160p. (gr. 3-5). 1991. 17.95 (*0-575-03884-5*, Pub. by Gollancz England) Trafalgar.
Wise, Beth A. Christmas KidDoodles, Bk. 2. Hoffman, Judy, illus. 64p. (Orig.). (ps-2). 1991. pap. 0.99 activity pad (*1-56293-154-7*) McClanahan Bk.
—Christmas KidDoodles, Bk. 4. Boyd, Patti, illus. 64p. (Orig.). (ps-2). 1991. pap. 0.99 activity pad (*1-56293-156-3*) McClanahan Bk.
—KidDoodles, Bk. 4. Nethery, Susan, illus. 64p. (Orig.). (ps-2). 1991. pap. 0.99 activity pad (*1-878624-53-9*) McClanahan Bk.
Wolf, Tony. The First Christmas Book. (ps-2). 1992. 20.00 (*1-56021-198-9*) W J Fantasy.
Woody, Marilyn. First Christmas High Chair Devotions. LC 92-75291. (ps). 1993. pap. 6.99 (*0-7814-0064-3*, Chariot Bks) Chariot Family.
World Book Editors, ed. Christmas in Germany. LC 93-60510. (Illus.). 80p. (gr. 5 up). 1993. PLB write for info. (*0-7166-0893-6*) World Bk.
World Book Staff, ed. Christmas in Russia. LC 92-64394. (Illus.). 80p. (gr. 6 up). 1992. write for info. (*0-7166-0892-8*) World Bk.
—Christmas in the Holy Land. LC 87-50393. (Illus.). 80p. (gr. 6 up). 1992. write for info. (*0-7166-2009-X*) World Bk.

CHRISTMAS–DRAMA
see Christmas Plays

CHRISTMAS–FICTION

Adams, Adrienne. The Christmas Party. Adams, Adrienne, illus. LC 78-16230. 32p. (ps-3). 1978. SBE 13.95 (*0-684-15930-9*, Scribners Young Read) Macmillan Child Grp.
—The Christmas Party. 2nd ed. Adams, Adrienne, illus. LC 91-42159. 32p. (ps-3). 1992. pap. 3.95 (*0-689-71630-3*, Aladdin) Macmillan Child Grp.
Ahlberg, Janet & Ahlberg, Allan. Jolly Christmas Postman. (Illus.). 1991. 17.95 (*0-316-02033-8*) Little.
Aiken, Lewis R. Haunting Christmas Tales. 1993. pap. 2.95 (*0-590-46025-0*) Scholastic Inc.
Alexander, Andrea. Why Do Mice Celebrate Christmas? And Other Fun Questions of the Season. Alexander, Andrea, illus. 64p. (Orig.). (ps-5). 1991. pap. 13.95 (*0-9628006-0-0*) Zenon Pub.
Alexander, Liza. Imagine: Big Bird Meets Santa Claus. (ps-3). 1993. pap. 2.25 (*0-307-13119-X*, Golden Pr) Western Pub.
Aliki. Christmas Tree Memories. Aliki, illus. LC 90-45575. 32p. (ps-3). 1991. 15.00 (*0-06-020007-3*); PLB 14.89 (*0-06-020008-1*) HarpC Child Bks.
—Christmas Tree Memories. Aliki, illus. LC 90-45575. 32p. (gr. k-3). 1994. pap. 5.95 (*0-06-443369-2*, Trophy) HarpC Child Bks.
Allen, Dennis & Allen, Nan. Rip Van Christmas. 1991. 4.95 (*0-685-68513-6*, BCMC-74); cassette 10.98 (*0-685-68514-4*, BCTA-9134C) Lillenas.
Allen, Nan & Allen, Dennis. Case of the Missing Christmas. 1988. 4.95 (*0-685-68521-7*, BCMC-65); cassette 10.98 (*0-685-68522-5*, BCTA-9095C) Lillenas.
Aloia, Gregory F. The Legend of the Golden Straw: A Christmas Story. (ps-4). 1989. 14.95 (*0-8294-0631-X*) Loyola.
Ames, Mildred. Grandpa Jake & the Grand Christmas. LC 90-8527. 112p. (gr. 5-7). 1990. SBE 13.95 (*0-684-19241-1*, Scribners Young Read) Macmillan Child Grp.
Amstutz, Beverly. Too Big for the Bag. (Illus.). (gr. k-7). 1981. pap. 2.50x (*0-937836-05-2*) Precious Res.
Anderson, Debbie S. Daniel & the Sand Angel: A Florida Christmas Story. Broderick, Michael, illus. 32p. (Orig.). (ps-4). 1988. pap. 9.95 (*0-936417-11-0*) Axelrod Pub.
Anglund, Joan W. Christmas Candy Book. (Illus.). 1983. 5.95 (*0-915696-63-0*) Determined Prods.
Aoki, Hisako. Santa's Favorite Story. 2nd ed. Gantschev, Ivan, illus. LC 82-60895. 28p. (gr. k up). 1991. pap. 4.95 (*0-88708-153-3*) Picture Bk Studio.
Aoki, Hisako & Gantschev, Ivan. Santa's Favorite Story. LC 82-60895. (Illus.). 28p. (ps up). 1991. pap. 14.95 (*0-907234-16-X*) Picture Bk Studio.
Appleby, Ellen. In the Gingerbread House. (Illus.). 5p. 1993. bds. 3.98 (*0-8317-9654-5*) Smithmark.
Arico, Diane, ed. A Season of Joy: Favorite Stories & Poems for Christmas. San Souci, Daniel, illus. LC 86-29059. 64p. (gr. k-3). 1987. Doubleday.
Armstrong, Beverly. Christmas Capers. (Illus.). 24p. (gr. 2-6). 1987. 4.95 (*0-88160-151-9*, LW264) Learning Wks.
Askinosie, Barbra. A Star for Christmas. (Illus.). 26p. (ps-1). 1988. pap. 2.95 incl. sticker pgs. (*0-671-66870-6*, Little Simon) S&S Trade.
Atwell, David L. Sleeping Moon. Atwell, Debby, illus. LC 94-270. 1994. 14.95 (*0-395-68677-6*) HM.
Awiakta, Marilou. Rising Fawn & the Fire Mystery. Bringle, Beverly, illus. Easson, Roger R., ed. LC 83-13824. (Illus.). 48p. (Orig.). (gr. 5 up). 1984. pap. 11.95 (*0-918518-29-6*) Iris Pr.
Bailey, Bobbi M. The Christmas Tree That Cried. (Illus.). 36p. (gr. k-6). 1982. 11.95 (*0-9625005-0-X*) Wee Pr.
Baird, Anne. The Christmas Lamb. Baird, Anne, illus. LC 88-5137. 32p. (ps-2). 1989. 12.95 (*0-688-07774-9*); (Morrow Jr Bks) Morrow Jr Bks.
Balch, Glenn. Christmas Horse. Crowell, Pers, illus. Woodward, Tim, intro. by. (Illus.). 1990. pap. 9.95 (*0-931659-10-8*) Limberlost Pr.
Balderose, Nancy W. Once upon a Pony: A Mountain Christmas. LC 92-13814. 32p. 1992. 12.95 (*0-8192-7000-8*); pap. write for info. (*0-8192-7001-6*) Morehouse Pub.
Barracca, Debra & Barracca, Sal. A Taxi Dog Christmas. Ayers, Alan, illus. LC 91-44953. 40p. (ps-3). 1994. 14.99 (*0-8037-1360-6*); PLB 14.89 (*0-8037-1361-4*) Dial Bks Young.
Barry, Robert. Mr. Willowby's Christmas Tree. (Illus.). 32p. 1992. Repr. PLB 16.95x (*0-89966-935-2*) Buccaneer Bks.
—Mr. Willowby's Christmas Tree. Barry, Robert, illus. 32p. (ps-2). 1992. pap. 4.99 (*0-440-40726-5*, YB) Dell.
Bassett, Lisa. Koala Christmas. Bassett, Jeni, illus. LC 90-47628. 32p. (ps-2). 1991. 12.95 (*0-525-65065-2*, Cobblehill Bks) Dutton Child Bks.
Baum, L. Frank. The Life & Adventures of Santa Claus. (gr. 2-6). 1985. 4.98 (*0-517-42062-7*) Random Hse Value.
—The Life & Adventures of Santa Claus. Apple, Max, afterword by. 160p. 1994. pap. 2.95 (*0-451-52064-5*, Sig Classics) NAL-Dutton.
—The Life & Adventures of Santa Claus. (Illus.). 1993. Repr. PLB 18.95x (*1-56849-175-1*) Buccaneer Bks.
Beachy, J. Wayne. The Extraordinary Ordinary Christmas Matoaca, 1870. Hawkins, Beverly, illus. 20p. (Orig.). (gr. 5). 1984. pap. 2.50 (*0-9608084-2-6*) B Hawkins Studio.
Bemelmans, Ludwig. Madeline's Christmas. LC 85-40092. (Illus.). 32p. (ps-3). 1985. pap. 14.00 (*0-670-80666-8*) Viking Child Bks.
—Madeline's Christmas. (ps-3). 1988. pap. 4.50 (*0-14-050666-7*, Puffin) Puffin Bks.
—Madeline's Christmas. (Illus.). (ps-3). 1993. pap. 6.99 incl. cassette (*0-14-095108-3*, Puffin) Puffin Bks.
Bernardini, Robert. Southern Love for Christmas. Rice, James, illus. 32p. (gr. k-3). 1993. 14.95 (*0-88289-974-0*) Pelican.
—A Southern Time Christmas. Rice, James, illus. LC 91-12467. 32p. 1991. 14.95 (*0-88289-828-0*) Pelican.
The Best Christmas Stories Ever. 1992. 2.95 (*0-590-45168-5*, Apple Classics) Scholastic Inc.
Bibee, John. The Last Christmas. LC 90-4870. (Illus.). 204p. (Orig.). (gr. 3-8). 1990. pap. 6.99 (*0-8308-1204-0*, 1204) InterVarsity.
Billingsley, Veteria & Billingsley, Derrell. The First Christmas Gift. 1977. 4.25 (*0-685-68603-5*, BCMC-33) Lillenas.
Birenbaum, Barbara. The Lighthouse Christmas. Birenbaum, Barbara & Sapp, Patt, illus. LC 90-7284. 48p. (Orig.). (gr. k-5). 1991. 10.95 (*0-935343-26-1*); pap. 5.95 (*0-935343-25-3*) Peartree.

Bishop, Adela. The Christmas Polar Bear. Czapla, Carole, illus. 32p. (gr. k-3). 1991. 12.95 (*0-9625620-2-5*) DOT Garnet.
A selfish little bear living near the North Pole enlists the aid of the magic Rainbow Fish to ensure eternal summer - but with no winter, Santa's elves won't wake up to begin their Christmas toy-making. A change of heart, however, saves the season. The bear receives a magic coin from the fish that lets him turn snow bears into teddy bears - enough for every girl & boy on Santa's list - & then turns him into a polar bear, who can play all winter long. Lovingly illustrated, this is a Christmas story that can be read throughout the year.
Publisher Provided Annotation.

Bivens, Christopher, illus. The Perfect Tree & Favorite Christmas Carols. Ingram, John W., ed. Bivins, Christopher, illus. LC 90-34514. 48p. (ps-2). 1990. 4.95 (*0-88101-104-5*) Unicorn Pub.
Bivens, Tom. The Perfect Tree. Bivens, Chris, illus. 48p. (ps-2). 1991. 6.95 (*0-88101-179-7*) Unicorn Pub.
Black, Auguste R. The Year That Santa Goofed & Other Short Stories. Sherentz, Michael & Horton, Terri, illus. 22p. (Orig.). (gr. 1-5). 1990. pap. 2.95 (*0-9628010-2-X*) A R Black.
Blacke, Terry L. & Rider, Debra. Pabulum Pig: The Yule Swine. Blacke, Terry L., illus. LC 91-68193. 41p. (gr. 4). 1992. pap. 7.98 (*0-9630718-2-3*) New Dawn NY.
Boddy, Joe, illus. A Christmas Carol. 48p. (ps-2). 1992. 5.95 (*0-88101-263-7*) Unicorn Pub.
—Countdown to Christmas. 48p. (ps). 1992. 6.95 (*0-88101-230-0*) Unicorn Pub.
Bokich, Obren. Christmas Card for Mr. McFizz. (Illus.). 40p. (gr. k-6). 1991. 11.95 (*0-88138-097-0*, Green Tiger) S&S Trade.
Bolte, Carl E., Jr. Elvin: The Little Black Elf. Turner, Vernon K., ed. LC 87-28960. 150p. (Orig.). 1988. pap. 8.95 (*0-89865-554-4*) Donning Co.
Borden, Louise. Just in Time for Christmas. Lewin, Ted, illus. LC 93-40082. (ps-3). 1994. 14.95 (*0-590-45355-6*) Scholastic Inc.
Bosca, Francesca. Caspar & the Star. Ferri, Giuliano, illus. 40p. (gr. 1-8). 1991. 12.95 (*0-7459-2120-5*) Lion USA.
Bowen, Sally. Down by the Christmas Stream. Wasmer, Kristina, illus. 38p. 1992. pap. 10.95 (*0-9633546-0-4*, Dist. by BookWorld Services, Inc.) Bowen & Assocs.
Braced, Knyla. The Christmas Long Stocking. Abell, ed. & illus. 50p. (Orig.). (gr. 1-6). 1993. PLB 25.00 (*1-56611-078-5*); pap. 15.00 (*1-56611-077-7*) Jonas.
Bracken, Carolyn, illus. Santa's Pockets. (ps). 1983. pap. 3.95 (*0-671-47660-2*, Little Simon) S&S Trade.
Breathed, Berkeley. A Wish for Wings That Work: An Opus Christmas Story. Breathed, Berkeley, illus. 32p. 1991. 14.95 (*0-316-10758-1*) Little.
Bredin, Henrietta. Christmas Eve. LC 92-1235. 1992. 5.95 (*0-85953-145-7*) Childs Play.
Brett, Jan. Christmas Trolls. Brett, Jan, illus. LC 93-10106. 32p. (ps-3). 1993. PLB 15.95 (*0-399-22507-2*, Putnam) Putnam Pub Group.
—Twelve Days of Christmas. (Illus.). 32p. 1990. 14.95 (*0-399-22037-2*, Putnam) Putnam Pub Group.
—The Wild Christmas Reindeer. Brett, Jan, illus. 32p. (ps-3). 1990. 14.95 (*0-399-22192-1*, Putnam) Putnam Pub Group.
Briggs, Raymond. Father Christmas Goes on Holiday. LC 77-1980. (Illus.). 32p. (gr. k-3). 1977. pap. 3.95 (*0-14-050187-8*, Puffin) Puffin Bks.
Broger, Achim, retold by. The Santa Clauses. Krause, Ute, illus. LC 86-2147. 28p. (ps-3). 1986. 11.95 (*0-8037-0266-3*) Dial Bks Young.
—The Santa Clauses. Krause, Ute, illus. LC 86-2147. 28p. (ps-3). 1988. pap. 3.95 (*0-8037-0557-3*) Dial Bks Young.
Brooke, Roger. Santa's Christmas Journey. LC 84-9796. (Illus.). 32p. (gr. k-5). 1984. PLB 19.97 (*0-8172-2116-6*); PLB 29.28 incl. cassette (*0-8172-2244-8*) Raintree Steck-V.
—Santa's Christmas Journey. (ps-3). 1993. pap. 4.95 (*0-8114-8356-8*) Raintree Steck-V.
Brown. On Christmas Eve. 1995. 15.00 (*0-06-023648-5*); PLB 14.89 (*0-06-023649-3*) HarpC Child Bks.
Brown, Marc T. Arthur's Christmas. Brown, Marc T., illus. LC 84-4373. (ps-3). 1985. 14.95 (*0-316-11180-5*, Joy St Bks); pap. 4.95 (*0-316-10993-2*) Little.
Brown, Margaret W. Christmas in the Barn. Cooney, Barbara, illus. LC 52-7858. 32p. (gr. k-3). 1961. PLB 13.89 (*0-690-19272-X*, Crowell Jr Bks) HarpC Child Bks.
—A Pussycat's Christmas. new ed. Mortimer, Anne, illus. LC 93-4424. 32p. (gr. k-4). 1994. 14.00 (*0-06-023532-2*); PLB 13.89 (*0-06-023533-0*) HarpC Child Bks.
Bruni, Mary A. Rosita's Christmas Wish. Ricks, Thom, illus. LC 85-52040. 48p. (gr. k-8). 1985. 13.95 (*0-935857-00-1*); ltd. ed. 125.00 (*0-935857-03-6*); write for info. (*0-935857-09-5*); pap. write for info. (*0-935857-01-X*); pap. write for info. (*0-935857-10-9*) Texart.
Bruni, Mary-Ann S. El Sueno de Rosita. De Castro, Rogelio, tr. from ENG. Ricks, Thom, illus. (SPA.). 48p. (gr. k-8). 1987. 13.95 (*0-935857-02-8*); pap. write for info. (*0-935857-04-4*) (*0-935857-11-7*) (*0-935857-12-5*) Texart.
Bryant, Bonnie. Starlight Christmas. (gr. 4-7). 1990. pap. 3.50 (*0-553-15832-5*) Bantam.
Burch, Robert. Christmas with Ida Early. LC 83-5792. 144p. (gr. 3-7). 1983. pap. 12.95 (*0-670-22131-7*) Viking Child Bks.
—Christmas with Ida Early. LC 85-5680. 158p. (gr. 3-7). 1985. pap. 4.99 (*0-14-031971-9*, Puffin) Puffin Bks.
—Renfroe's Christmas: A Novel by Robert Burch. Negri, Rocco, illus. LC 92-44773. 56p. (gr. 4-6). 1993. Repr. of 1971 ed. 14.95 (*0-8203-1553-2*) U of Ga Pr.
Bures, Ruth A. Here Comes Christmas. 40p. (gr. k-8). 1982. pap. 14.95 (*0-86704-008-4*) Clarus Music.
Burningham, John. Harvey Slumfenberger's Christmas Present. Burningham, John, illus. LC 92-54957. 32p. (ps up). 1993. 16.95 (*1-56402-246-3*) Candlewick Pr.
Burton, Tim. The Nightmare Before Christmas. Burton, Tim, illus. LC 92-54867. 40p. 1993. 15.95 (*1-56282-411-2*); PLB cancelled (*1-56282-412-0*) Hyprn Child.

Buscaglia, Leo F. Seven Stories of Christmas Love. Newsom, Tom, illus. 110p. 1987. 12.95 (1-55642-019-6) SLACK Inc.

Butcher, Samuel. Precious Moments Christmas Story. (ps-3). 1991. 7.25 (0-307-15506-4) Western Pub.

Butterworth, Nick. Nativity Play. (ps-3). 1991. pap. 3.99 (0-440-40541-6, YB) Dell.

Campbell, Louisa. Gargoyles' Christmas. Taylor, Bridget S., illus. LC 94-4035. 32p. (gr. k-2). 1994. 15.95 (0-87905-587-1) Gibbs Smith Pub.

Capek, Jindra. A Child Is Born. Capek, Jindra, illus. (gr. 5 up). 1987. 12.95 (1-55774-007-0) Modan-Adama Bks.

Capocy, Edward J. The Magic of Christmas. rev. ed. Capocy, Edward J., illus. 48p. 1991. 14.00 (1-880210-00-2); PLB 18.00 (1-880210-01-0); pap. 4.50 (1-880210-02-9); coloring bk. 2.29 (1-880210-03-7) Am Classic Ent.

Capote, Truman. A Christmas Memory. Delessert, Etienne, illus. 40p. (gr. 4 up). 1984. PLB 13.95 (0-87191-956-7) Creative Ed.

Carey, Karla. Julie & Jackie at Christmas-Time: The Narration & Music Book. Nolan, Dennis, illus. 69p. 1990. pap. 18.95 complete pkg. (0-685-35761-9); pap. 9.95 (1-55768-201-1); cassette 9.95 (0-685-35762-7) LC Pub.

Carlson, Anna L. The Mouse Family's Christmas. 1st. ed. (Illus.). 24p. (Orig.). (gr. k-4). 1983. pap. 1.95 (0-939938-04-9) Karwyn Ent.

Carlsruh, Dan K. The Cannibals of Sunset Drive. LC 92-40568. 144p. (gr. 3-7). 1993. SBE 13.95 (0-02-717110-8, Macmillan Child Bk) Macmillan Child Grp.

Carrier, Lark. A Christmas Promise. LC 86-12356. (Illus.). 36p. (ps up). 1991. pap. 15.95 (0-88708-032-4) Picture Bk Studio.

Carty, Margaret F. Christmas in Vermont: Three Stories. Langley, Marilynn, illus. LC 83-62750. 48p. (Orig.). (gr. 5 up). 1983. pap. 2.95 (0-933050-21-6) New Eng Pr VT.

Catalanotto, Peter. Christmas Always. LC 90-28712. (Illus.). 32p. (ps-1). 1991. 14.95 (0-531-05946-4); RLB 14.99 (0-531-08546-5) Orchard Bks Watts.

Caudill, Rebecca. A Certain Small Shepherd. Pene Du Bois, William, illus. LC 65-17604. 48p. (gr. 2-4). 1971. reinforced bdg. 14.95 (0-8050-1323-7, Bks Young Read) H Holt & Co.

Cavendish, Maxwell P. The True Story of Christmas. LeBaudour, RoseMarie, illus. 56p. (Orig.). (gr. 4 up). 1991. pap. 15.00 (0-9628016-2-3) Gentian Servs.

Cazet, Denys. Christmas Moon. Cazet, Denys, illus. LC 84-10969. 32p. (ps-2). 1984. RSBE 13.95 (0-02-717810-2, Bradbury Pr) Macmillan Child Grp.

Chalmers, Mary. A Christmas Story. Chalmers, Mary, illus. LC 56-8143. 24p. (ps-1). 1962. Repr. of 1956 ed. PLB 12.89 (0-06-021191-1) HarpC Child Bks.

—Merry Christmas, Harry. new ed. LC 90-27516. (Illus.). 32p. (ps-2). 1992. 13.00 (0-06-022739-7) HarpC Child Bks.

Charman, Andrew. Lonely Christmas Tree. (ps-3). 1992. pap. 5.95 (0-671-78452-8, Little Simon) S&S Trade.

Chartier, Normand, illus. Jingle Bells. 1986. pap. 2.25 (0-671-63022-9, Little Simon) S&S Trade.

Chisholm, Sarah. My Christmas Angel. (ps). 1993. pap. 5.99 (0-8066-2601-1) Augsburg Fortress.

Chmielarz, Sharon. Down at Angel's. Kastner, Jill, illus. LC 93-11020. 32p. (ps-2). 1994. 14.95g (0-395-65993-0) Ticknor & Flds Bks Yng Read.

Christmas at the Zoo Pop Up. 10p. (ps-3). 1990. 3.95 (0-8167-2185-8) Troll Assocs.

A Christmas Carol. (Illus.). 24p. (gr. k-2). 1991. 3.95 (1-56144-071-X, Honey Bear Bks) Modern Pub NYC.

A Christmas Carol. 24p. (gr. k-3). 1992. pap. 2.50 (1-56144-161-9, Honey Bear Bks) Modern Pub NYC.

Christmas Pop-up Set: The First Christmas Tree, Silent Night, The Shepherd's Christmas, Santa's Toy Shop, 4 bks. 1993. Boxed set. 14.95 (0-307-16300-8, Artsts Writrs) Western Pub.

A Christmas Story. LC 78-66026. (gr. 4 up). 1978. 4.95 (0-934038-00-7) Perish Pr.

Christmas with the Santa Bears, A Christmas to Remember. (Illus.). 24p. 1987. (Honey Bear Bks); text ed. 3.95 (0-87449-072-3, Honey Bear Bks); text ed. 3.95 (0-87449-112-6, Honey Bear Bks) Modern Pub NYC.

Chubby Chums Christmas Tree: Christmas Wishes; Wheels That Work; A Little Book of Colors, 3 bks. 12p. (ps). 1992. Boxed Set. pap. 7.95 incl. Christmas ornament (0-671-79043-9, Little Simon) S&S Trade.

Chubby Chums Snowman: Jingle Bells; Opposites; Things I Like to Eat, 3 bks. 12p. (ps). 1992. Boxed Set. pap. 7.95 incl. Christmas ornament (0-671-79042-0, Little Simon) S&S Trade.

Ciaravino, John. A Christmas Dream. LC 88-51890. (Illus.). 44p. (gr. k-3). 1989. 5.95 (1-55523-215-9) Winston-Derek.

Civardi, Annie. The Secrets of Santa. Scruton, Clive, illus. LC 91-130. 32p. (ps-1). 1991. pap. 13.95 jacketed (0-671-74270-1, S&S BFYR) S&S Trade.

Clemons, Jack. Gruesome John Frederick: A Tale of Christmas. Hamel, Tom, illus. LC 87-71713. 73p. (Orig.). (gr. 4-5). 1988. pap. 6.00 (0-916383-30-X) Aegina Pr.

Clifton, Lucille. Everett Anderson's Christmas Coming. Gilchrist, Jan S., illus. LC 91-2041. 32p. (ps-4). 1991. 14.95 (0-8050-1549-3, Bks Young Read) H Holt & Co.

Climo, Shirley. Cobweb Christmas. Lasker, Joe, illus. LC 81-43879. 32p. (ps-3). 1982. (Crowell Jr Bks); PLB 14.89 (0-690-04216-7) HarpC Child Bks.

Codor, Dick & Teitelbaum, Michael. Follow that Sleigh: The Reindeer Who Saved Christmas. Oren, Rony, contrib. by. (Illus.). (gr. k-5). 1990. 9.95 (0-944007-51-1) Shapolsky Pubs.

Cohen, Barbara. The Christmas Revolution. De Groat, Diane, illus. LC 86-21340. 96p. (gr. 3-6). 1987. 12.95 (0-688-06806-5) Lothrop.

—Christmas Revolution. 1993. pap. 3.50 (0-440-40871-7) Dell.

Collington, Peter. On Christmas Eve. Collington, Peter, illus. LC 90-4202. 32p. 1990. 14.95 (0-679-80830-2) Knopf Bks Yng Read.

Coltharp, Barbara. Colonel Neverfail's Christmas. Sandifer, Shannon & Woolfolk, Doug, eds. Turner, James, illus. (Orig.). (gr. 1-3). 1981. 7.95 (0-86518-019-9) Moran Pub Corp.

Compton, Kenn. Happy Christmas to All! Compton, Kenn, illus. LC 90-29078. 32p. (ps-3). 1991. reinforced 14.95 (0-8234-0890-6) Holiday.

Compton, Patricia A. Terrible Eek. (ps-6). 1993. pap. 5.95 (0-671-87169-2, S&S BFYR) S&S Trade.

Connolly, Brian A. Bradley's Christmas Adventure. Diamanti, Gina, illus. 38p. (Orig.). (gr. 1-6). 1989. pap. 7.95 (0-9624282-0-5) Steele Hollow.

Cooley, Regina F. The Magic Christmas Pony. Hansen, Han H., illus. LC 91-76342. 36p. (gr. 1-5). 1991. 19.95 (1-880450-04-6) Capstone Pub.

Cooper, Susan. Danny & the Kings. Smith, Joseph A., illus. LC 92-22744. 32p. (ps-3). 1993. SBE 14.95 (0-689-50577-9, M K McElderry) Macmillan Child Grp.

—The Dark Is Rising. Cober, Alan, illus. LC 72-85916. 232p. (gr. 5 up). 1973. SBE 15.95 (0-689-30317-3, M K McElderry) Macmillan Child Grp.

Cork, Sarah G. The Bottlestopper's Christmas Tree Farm. (Illus.). 50p. (gr. k-3). 1991. pap. 4.95 (0-943487-35-8) Sevgo Pr.

Corrin, Sara & Corrin, Stephen, eds. The Faber Book of Christmas Stories. Bennet, Jill, illus. LC 84-13552. 150p. (gr. 3-7). 1984. pap. 9.95 (0-571-13348-7) Faber & Faber.

Corrin, Sarah & Corrin, Stephen, eds. Round the Christmas Tree. (gr. 3-7). pap. 3.95 (0-317-62263-3, Puffin) Puffin Bks.

Cosgrove, Stephen. Button Breaker. (ps-3). 1992. pap. 3.95 (0-307-13450-4) Western Pub.

—Prancer. Heyer, Carol, illus. LC 89-83843. 32p. (gr. k-7). 1990. 14.95 (1-55868-019-5); pap. 5.95 (1-55868-020-9); pap. 12.95 incl. audio (1-55868-041-1) Gr Arts Ctr Pub.

Cothen, Joe. Come to Bethlehem: The Christmas Story. Seago, Robert, illus. LC 75-25503. 64p. (gr. 4 up). 1975. 8.95 (0-88289-098-0) Pelican.

Crabtree, Cathy L. & Fowler, Joanne. Poor Me & the Magic of Christmas. rev. ed. Sanor, Peggy, illus. LC 89-84463. 20p. (gr. 2-3). 1989. pap. text ed. 5.95 (0-9622719-0-X) Lavender Pr.

Craig, Janet. Little Christmas Star. Miller, Susan, illus. LC 87-10936. 32p. (gr. k-2). 1988. PLB 11.59 (0-8167-1097-X); pap. text ed. 2.95 (0-8167-1098-8) Troll Assocs.

Craig, Janet A. A Letter to Santa. Rader, Laura, illus. LC 93-2214. 32p. (gr. k-2). 1993. PLB 11.59 (0-8167-3252-3); pap. text ed. 2.95 (0-8167-3253-1) Troll Assocs.

Crawford, Ron. Bike. LC 92-42986. 1993. 12.00 (0-671-87002-5, Green Tiger); pap. 3.95 (0-671-87003-3, Green Tiger) S&S Trade.

Crespi, Francesca, illus. Santa Claus Is Coming! 8p. (ps-2). 1987. pap. 3.95 (0-8050-0472-6, Bks Young Read) H Holt & Co.

—Silent Night. 8p. (ps-2). 1987. pap. 3.95 (0-8050-0471-8, Bks Young Read) H Holt & Co.

Crew, Linda. Nekomah Creek Christmas. Robinson, Charles, illus. LC 94-478. 1994. 14.95 (0-385-32047-7) Delacorte.

Cruise, Beth. Mistletoe Magic. 1994. pap. 3.95 (0-02-042794-8, Aladdin) Macmillan Child Grp.

Crump, Patricia. Jesus' Stocking. Thomas, Ira, illus. 1990. 2.95 (0-8091-6591-0) Paulist Pr.

Cruz, Manuel & Cruz, Ruth. A Chicano Christmas Story. Cruz, Manuel, illus. LC 80-69444. (SPA.). 48p. (Orig.). (ps-5). 1981. pap. text ed. 3.95 (0-86624-000-4, RM7) Bilingual Ed Serv.

Curry, Jane L. The Christmas Knight. DiSalvo-Ryan, DyAnne, illus. LC 92-2277. 32p. (gr. k-4). 1993. SBE 14.95 (0-689-50572-8, M K McElderry) Macmillan Child Grp.

Curtin, Michael. The League Against Christmas. 256p. 1990. 21.95 (0-233-98382-1, Pub. by A Deutsch England) Trafalgar.

Cushman. Aunt Eater's Mystery Xmas. 1995. 14.00 (0-06-023579-9); PLB 13.89 (0-06-023580-2) HarpC Child Bks.

—Mouse & Mole & the Christmas Walk. 1994. text ed. write for info. (0-7167-6560-8) W H Freeman.

Cutting, Michael. The Little Crooked Christmas Tree. Broda, Ron, illus. 24p. 1991. 13.95 (0-590-45204-5, Scholastic Hardcover) Scholastic Inc.

Cuyler, Margery. The Christmas Snowman. Westerman, Johanna, illus. 32p. (ps-3). 1992. 14.95 (1-55970-066-1) Arcade Pub Inc.

Czernecki, Stefan & Rhodes, Timothy. Pancho's Pinata. Czernecki, Stefan, illus. LC 92-7325. 40p. (gr. k-4). 1992. 14.95 (1-56282-277-2); PLB 14.89 (1-56282-278-0) Hyprn Child.

Daniel, Mark, compiled by. Child's Christmas Treasury. LC 87-36527. (Illus.). 112p. (ps up). 1988. 15.95 (0-8037-0484-4) Dial Bks Young.

Davidson, Amanda. Teddy's Countdown to Christmas. 16p. (gr. 4-7). 1990. pap. 2.50 (0-8167-2198-X) Troll Assocs.

Davies, Valentine. Miracle on Thirty-Fourth Street. De Paola, Tomie, illus. (gr. k up). 1984. 16.95 (0-15-254526-3, HB Juv Bks) HarBrace.

Day, Alexandra. Carl's Christmas. Day, Alexandra, illus. 32p. 1990. bds. 12.95 (0-374-31114-5) FS&G.

De Angeli, Marguerite. The Lion in the Box. De Angeli, Marguerite, illus. 80p. (gr. 2-5). 1992. pap. 3.50 (0-440-40740-0, YB) Dell.

Dear Santa. (Illus.). 5p. (gr. k-3). 1991. 9.95 (0-8167-2455-5) Troll Assocs.

De Brunhoff, Jean. Babar & Father Christmas. De Brunhoff, Jean, illus. 40p. (gr. k-3). 1987. 16.95 (0-394-89265-8) Random Bks Yng Read.

—Babar & Father Christmas. De Brunhoff, Jean, illus. LC 90-61863. 48p. 1991. 4.95 (0-679-81483-3) Random Bks Yng Read.

Dedieu, Thierry. The Little Christmas Soldier. Dedieu, Thierry, illus. LC 92-40172. 32p. (ps-2). 1993. 15.95 (0-8050-2612-6, Bks Young Read) H Holt & Co.

Deedy, Carmen A. Treeman. Ponte, Douglas J., illus. LC 93-1667. 1993. 16.95 (1-56145-077-4) Peachtree Pubs.

Delamare, David. The Christmas Secret. LC 91-12779. (Illus.). 40p. (ps-2). 1991. jacketed, reinforced bdg. 15.00 (0-671-74822-X, Green Tiger) S&S Trade.

Delamare, David, illus. Nutcracker. 48p. (gr. 1-5). 1992. 12.95 (0-88101-235-1) Unicorn Pub.

—Nutcracker. 48p. (ps-3). 1992. 4.95 (0-88101-244-0) Unicorn Pub.

Dellinger, Annetta. The Jesus Tree. Morris, Susan S., illus. 32p. (ps-2). 1991. 7.99 (0-570-04191-0) Concordia.

Delton, Judy. No Time for Christmas. Mitchell, Anastasia, illus. 48p. (gr. k-4). 1988. PLB 14.95 (0-87614-327-3) Carolrhoda Bks.

—A Pee Wee Christmas. 80p. (Orig.). (gr. k-6). 1988. pap. 3.25 (0-440-40067-8, YB) Dell.

—The Perfect Christmas Gift. McCue, Lisa, illus. LC 91-6549. 32p. (gr. k-3). 1992. RSBE 13.95 (0-02-728471-9, Macmillan Child Bk) Macmillan Child Grp.

Demi. Demi's Dozen X-Mas. 1994. pap. write for info. (0-8050-3245-2) H Holt & Co.

Dennis, Martin C. Will Arnold See Christmas? 1993. 7.95 (0-533-10404-1) Vantage.

Denton, Kady M. Christmas Boot. (ps). 1990. 12.95 (0-316-18091-2) Little.

De Paola, Tomie. An Early American Christmas. De Paola, Tomie, illus. LC 86-3102. 32p. (ps-3). 1987. reinforced bdg. 15.95 (0-8234-0617-2); pap. 5.95 (0-8234-0979-1) Holiday.

—The First Christmas. (Illus.). 6p. (ps-1). 1984. 16.95 (0-399-21070-9, Putnam) Putnam Pub Group.

—Jingle the Christmas Clown. (Illus.). 40p. (ps-3). 1992. 15.95 (0-399-22338-X, Putnam) Putnam Pub Group.

—Merry Christmas, Strega Nona. De Paola, Tomie, illus. LC 86-4639. 32p. (ps-3). 1986. 14.95 (0-15-253183-1, HB Juv Bks) HarBrace.

Devlin, Wende & Devlin, Harry. Cranberry Christmas. Devlin, Harry, illus. LC 80-16971. 40p. (ps-3). 1984. Repr. of 1976 ed. RSBE 13.95 (0-02-729900-7, Four Winds) Macmillan Child Grp.

—Cranberry Christmas. Devlin, Wende & Devlin, Harry, illus. LC 91-1988. 40p. (gr. k-3). 1991. pap. 3.95 (0-689-71510-2, Aladdin) Macmillan Child Grp.

Dewoody, Darrel W. & Dewoody, Betty N. C. T. the Living Christmas Tree. Plunkett, Kathleen, illus. (gr. k-6). 1989. write for info. Old Amer Pr.

Dickens, Charles. Charles Dickens' A Christmas Carol. Richardson, I. M., ed. Kendall, Jane F., illus. LC 87-11270. 32p. (gr. 2-6). 1988. PLB 9.79 (0-8167-1053-8); pap. text ed. 1.95 (0-8167-1054-6) Troll Assocs.

—Christmas Books. Glancy, Ruth, intro. by. 520p. 1989. pap. 7.95 (0-19-281790-6) OUP.

—Christmas Carol. LC 85-15815. (gr. 7 up). 1963. pap. 2.25 (0-8049-0026-4, CL-26) Airmont.

—A Christmas Carol. LC 85-15815. 191p. 1981. Repr. PLB 15.95x (0-89966-344-3) Buccaneer Bks.

—A Christmas Carol. LC 85-15815. 150p. 1980. Repr. PLB 15.95 (0-89967-017-2) Harmony Raine.

—A Christmas Carol. Imsand, Marcel, illus. LC 85-15815. 78p. (gr. 4 up). 1984. PLB 13.95s.p. (0-87191-955-9) Creative Ed.

—A Christmas Carol. Kennedy, Pam, ed. Flint, Russ, illus. 32p. (gr. k-6). 1985. pap. 2.95 (0-8249-8099-9, Ideals Child) Hambleton-Hill.

—A Christmas Carol. Zwerger, Lisbeth, illus. LC 88-15161. 60p. (gr. 5 up). 1991. pap. 19.95 (0-88708-069-3) Picture Bk Studio.

—A Christmas Carol. Innocenti, Roberto, illus. LC 90-1335. 152p. 1990. 30.00 (1-55670-161-6) Stewart Tabori & Chang.

—A Christmas Carol. Rice, James, illus. & retold by. 48p. 14.95 (0-88289-812-4) Pelican.

—A Christmas Carol. 128p. (gr. 4-7). 1987. pap. 2.75 (0-590-43527-2) Scholastic Inc.

—Christmas Carol. Sturrock, Walt, illus. 1990. 11.95 (0-88101-108-8) Unicorn Pub.

—A Christmas Carol. 1990. pap. 2.50 (*0-8125-0434-8*) Tor Bks.

—A Christmas Carol. Boddy, Joe, illus. LC 91-9054. 48p. (ps-2). 1991. Animal version. 6.95 (*0-88101-160-6*) Unicorn Pub.

—Christmas Carol. 1992. pap. 10.70 (*0-395-60726-4*) HM.

—A Christmas Carol. Innocenti, Roberto, illus. 152p. (gr. 1-12). 1990. lib. bdg. 25.00 RLB smythe-sewn (*0-88682-327-7*, 97200-098) Creative Ed.

—Christmas Carol: Xmas Treasury Pop-Ups. 1993. pap. 4.99 (*0-517-08787-1*) Random Hse Value.

Dickens, Charles & Staton, Joe. A Christmas Carol. (Illus.). 52p. Date not set. pap. 4.95 (*1-57209-016-2*) Classics Int Ent.

Dicks, Terrance. Goliath's Christmas. Littlewood, Valerie, illus. 64p. (gr. 2-4). 1987. PLB 7.95 (*0-8120-5843-7*); pap. 2.95 (*0-8120-3878-9*) Barron.

Dinardo, Jeffrey. Henry's Christmas, No. 4. 1993. pap. 3.25 (*0-440-40873-3*) Dell.

Donnelly, Liza. Dinosaurs' Christmas. 32p. 1991. 12.95 (*0-590-44797-1*, Scholastic Hardcover) Scholastic Inc.

Dostoyevsky, Fyodor. The Heavenly Christmas Tree. (gr. 5 up). 1992. PLB 13.95 (*0-88682-492-3*) Creative Ed.

Dreamer, Sue. A Teddy Bear Christmas. Dreamer, Sue, illus. 10p. (ps-1). 1992. bds. 7.95 (*1-56397-121-6*) Boyds Mills Pr.

Dr. Seuss. How the Grinch Stole Christmas. Dr. Seuss, illus. (gr. k-3). 1957. 11.00 (*0-394-80079-6*); PLB 11. 99 (*0-394-90079-0*) Random Bks Yng Read.

Dubowski, Cathy E. Scrooge: Adapted from Charles Dickens' "A Christmas Carol" Dubowski, Mark, illus. LC 94-661. 48p. (gr. 1-3). 1994. PLB 7.99 (*0-448-40222-X*, G&D); pap. 3.50 (*0-448-40221-1*, G&D) Putnam Pub Group.

Duffey, Betsy. Lucky Christmas. Morrill, Leslie, illus. LC 93-41092. (gr. 2-5). 1994. pap. 13.00 (*0-671-86425-4*, S&S BFYR) S&S Trade.

Duntze, Dorothee. The Twelve Days of Christmas. Duntze, Dorothee, illus. LC 91-32359. 32p. (gr. k-3). 1992. 14.95 (*1-55858-151-0*); PLB 14.88 (*1-55858-152-9*) North-South Bks NYC.

Duvoisin, Roger. Petunia's Christmas. Duvoisin, Roger, illus. (gr. k-3). 1963. lib. bdg. 12.99 (*0-394-90868-6*) Knopf Bks Yng Read.

Edens, Cooper. Santa Cows. Lane, Daniel, illus. LC 91-57. 40p. (gr. 2 up). 1991. jacketed, reinforced bdg. 14. 00 (*0-671-74863-7*, Green Tiger) S&S Trade.

Edler, Timothy J. Crawfish-Man's Night Befo' Christmas. (Illus.). 40p. (gr. k-8). 1984. pap. 10.00 (*0-931108-12-8*) Little Cajun Bks.

—Santa's Cajun Christmas Adventure. (Illus.). 48p. (gr. k-8). 1981. pap. 6.00 (*0-931108-07-1*) Little Cajun Bks.

Eisen, Armand. A Visit to Christmasland: A Storybook with a Real Charm Bracelet. Lisi, Victoria, illus. 32p. 1993. incl. bracelet 12.95 (*0-8362-4506-7*) Andrews & McMeel.

Eisen, Armand, ed. The Classic Christmas Treasury for Children. LC 89-43004. (Illus.). 56p. (gr. 3 up). 1990. 9.98 (*0-89471-769-3*) Courage Bks.

Eisenberg, Lisa. Lexie on Her Own. 128p. (gr. 3-7). 1992. 13.00 (*0-670-84489-6*) Viking Child Bks.

Emerson, Zack. Tis the Season. 256p. 1991. pap. 2.95 (*0-590-44593-6*) Scholastic Inc.

Enright, Elizabeth. A Christmas Tree for Lydia. Zimdars, Berta, illus. 32p. (gr. 4 up). 1986. PLB 13.95 (*0-88682-063-4*) Creative Ed.

Ets, Marie H. & Labastida, Aurora. Nine Days to Christmas. Ets, Marie H., illus. (ps-2). 1959. pap. 13. 95 (*0-670-51350-4*) Viking Child Bks.

Eure, Wesley. Red Wings of Christmas. Paolillo, Ronald G., illus. LC 92-5457. 160p. (gr. 3-7). 1992. 19.95 (*0-88289-902-3*); audiocassette 14.95 (*0-88289-998-8*) Pelican.

Ewing, Juliana H. Old Father Christmas: Based on a Story by Juliana Horatia Ewing. Doherty, Berlie, retold by. Meloni, Maria T., illus. LC 92-43820. 42p. (ps-3). 1993. 12.95 (*0-8120-6354-6*) Barron.

Fass, Bernie & Wolfson, Mack. Christmas on Main Street. 48p. (gr. 3-12). 1986. pap. 16.95 (*0-86704-036-X*); student bk. 2.95 (*0-86704-037-8*) Clarus Music.

Fearrington, Ann. Christmas Night Lights. LC 94-25768. 1995. 13.95 (*0-395-71036-7*) Ticknor & Fields.

Ferris, Lynn B., illus. A Classic Treasury of Christmas. LC 91-19276. 48p. 1991. 13.95 (*0-8249-8524-9*, Ideals Child); incl. cassette 17.95 (*0-8249-7453-0*) Hambleton-Hill.

Find Frosty as He Sings Christmas Carols. 1991. 7.98 (*1-56173-162-5*) Pubns Intl Ltd.

Find Santa Claus as He Brings Christmas Joy. 1991. 7.98 (*1-56173-161-7*) Pubns Intl Ltd.

Find the Gifts on the Twelve Days of Christmas. 1991. 7.98 (*1-56173-164-1*) Pubns Intl Ltd.

Find the Nutcracker in His Christmas Ballet. 1991. 7.98 (*1-56173-163-3*) Pubns Intl Ltd.

Fisher, Barbara. Philpin's Tree. (Illus.). 12p. (Orig.). (gr. 1-3). 1977. pap. 2.00 (*0-934830-00-2*) Ten Penny.

Fisher, Maxine P. The Country Mouse & the City Mouse: "Christmas Is Where the Heart Is" Smath, Jerry, illus. LC 93-26488. 48p. (ps-2). 1994. 13.00 (*0-679-84684-0*) Random Bks Yng Read.

Fisher, Nell. A Handbell for Hans. 1990. 2.95 (*0-8378-1885-0*) Gibson.

Fisher, Sally. The Christmas Journey. Sardo, Douglas, illus. 40p. (ps-7). 1993. 19.99 (*0-670-85039-X*) Viking Child Bks.

Fix, Philippe. A Village Christmas. 1991. 8.95 (*0-525-44748-2*) Dutton Child Bks.

Flucke, Paul. The Secret of the Gifts. Yoe, Craig, illus. LC 92-5679. 32p. 1992. 11.99 (*0-8308-1841-3*, 1841) InterVarsity.

Folmer, A. P. Barnabys First Christmas. 1989. pap. 5.95 (*0-590-42892-6*) Scholastic Inc.

Foreman, Donna. Story of the Christmas Bear. Blonski, Maribeth, illus. 40p. (gr. k-3). 1992. 7.95 (*1-880851-02-4*) Greene Bark Pr.

Fox, Naomi. A Christmas Carol. Fox, Neal, illus. 24p. (ps-2). 1993. pap. 9.95 (*1-882179-06-4*) Confetti Ent.

—A Difficult Kind of Christmas. Fox, Neal, illus. 24p. (ps-2). 1993. pap. text ed. 9.95 (*1-882179-04-8*) Confetti Ent.

French, Vivian, abridged by. Charles Dicken's "A Christmas Carol" Benson, Patrick, illus. LC 93-54577. 48p. (ps up). 1993. 15.95 (*1-56402-204-8*) Candlewick Pr.

Fun with Rudolph. 1993. 5.99 (*0-307-16351-2*, Artsts Writrs) Western Pub.

Funakoshi, Canna. One Christmas. Izawa, Yohji, illus. LC 90-7445. 40p. (gr. k up). 1991. pap. 12.95 (*0-88708-140-1*) Picture Bk Studio.

Gambill, Henrietta D. Little Christmas Animals. LC 94-10000. 1994. 1.89 (*0-7847-0274-8*) Standard Pub.

Gammell, Stephen. Wake up, Bear...It's Christmas! Gammell, Stephen, illus. LC 81-5019. 32p. (ps-3). 1981. PLB 14.93 (*0-688-00693-0*) Lothrop.

—Wake up, Bear...It's Christmas! LC 81-5019. (Illus.). 32p. (ps up). 1990. pap. 4.95 (*0-688-09934-3*, Mulberry) Morrow.

Gantschev, Ivan. The Christmas Teddy Bear. Clements, Andrew, adapted by. LC 93-20121. (gr. 4 up). 1993. write for info. (*0-88708-333-1*) Picture Bk Studio.

—The Christmas Teddy Bear. Gantschev, Ivan, illus. Clements, Andrew, adapted by. LC 94-10270. (Illus.). (gr. k-3). 1994. 14.95 (*1-55858-349-1*); PLB 14.88 (*1-55858-348-3*) North-South Bks NYC.

Gantz, David. The Biggest Christmas Tree. 32p. 1991. pap. 2.50 (*0-590-44026-8*) Scholastic Inc.

Garcia-Bengochea, Debbie. Gumdrop the Christmas Bear. (Illus.). 34p. (Orig.). (ps-2). 1992. pap. 7.95 (*1-880525-00-3*) Masterson.

Gardam, Catharine. The Animals' Christmas. Rowe, Gavin, illus. LC 90-5538. 32p. (gr. k-4). 1990. SBE 13. 95 (*0-689-50502-7*, M K McElderry) Macmillan Child Grp.

Gauthier, Bertrand. Zachary in the Wawabongbong. Sylvestre, Daniel, illus. LC 93-15456. 1993. 15.93 (*0-8368-1011-2*) Gareth Stevens Inc.

Gebhardt, Catherine. A Perfect Christmas for Kate Leary. LC 90-70222. 44p. (gr. k-3). 1990. pap. 5.95 (*1-55523-331-7*) Winston-Derek.

George, William T. Christmas at Long Pond. George, Lindsay B., illus. LC 91-31475. 32p. (ps-8). 1992. 14. 00 (*0-688-09214-4*); PLB 13.93 (*0-688-09215-2*) Greenwillow.

Gibbons, Gail. Christmas on an Island. LC 93-50111. (gr. 3 up). 1994. write for info. (*0-688-09678-6*); PLB write for info. (*0-688-09679-4*) Morrow Jr Bks.

Giff, Patricia R. The Jingle Bells Jam. McCully, Emily A., illus. 80p. (Orig.). (gr. 1-4). 1992. pap. 3.25 (*0-440-40534-3*, YB) Dell.

Gikow, Louise. Baby Kermit's Christmas. (ps-3). 1993. 5.95 (*0-307-13722-8*, Golden Pr) Western Pub.

—Muppet Christmas Carol. (ps-3). 1993. pap. 2.25 (*0-307-12795-8*, Golden Pr) Western Pub.

Gili, Phillida. The Nutcracker: A Pop-Up Book. LC 91-77288. (Illus.). 12p. (ps up). 1992. 15.95 (*0-694-00414-6*, Festival) HarpC Child Bks.

Gimbel, Cheryl & Maners, Wendelin. Why Does Santa Celebrate Christmas? Lovelady, J., ed. (Illus.). 36p. (gr. k up). 1990. 12.95 (*0-915190-67-2*, JP9067-2) Jalmar Pr.

Godden, Rumer. The Story of Holly & Ivy. Cooney, Barbara, illus. LC 84-25799. 32p. (ps-5). 1985. pap. 15.00 (*0-670-80622-6*) Viking Child Bks.

Goldsmith, Howard. The Christmas Star. Appleget, Byron, illus. 48p. (ps-5). 1994. write for info. saddlestitch (*0-9642651-8-4*); PLB write for info. (*0-9642651-1-7*); text ed. write for info. (*0-9642651-2-5*); pap. 6.95 (*0-9642651-3-3*); pap. text ed. write for info. (*0-9642651-4-1*); tchr's. ed. avail. (*0-9642651-5-X*); wkbk. avail. (*0-9642651-6-8*); lab manual avail. (*0-9642651-7-6*) Reading Video. Sad & lonely that no one answered its signal, TWINKLE, THE CHRISTMAS STAR decides to take a trip in the sky to try & find a friend. Exciting & unexpected adventures await him in the vast sky. The adventures of TWINKLE make a heartwarming story with endearing pictures that most certainly will capture the hearts of young readers. Howard Goldsmith was an Arthur Rackham Predoctoral Fellow at the University of Michigan, where he received a M.A. He is the author of about forty-five juvenile books for all ages. In addition, his stories have appeared in Disney Adventures, Scholastic, Child Life, Highlights for Children, Weekly Reader, Ideals, & others. To order contact "The" Reading Video, Inc., P.O. Box 42761, Indianapolis, IN 46241. Retail Price $6.95.
Publisher Provided Annotation.

Gordon, Shirley. Crystal's Christmas Carol. Frascino, Edward, illus. LC 87-33487. 40p. (gr. k-3). 1989. HarpC Child Bks.

Goudge, Eileen. Hawaiian Christmas. (gr. 6 up). 1986. pap. 2.95 (*0-440-93649-7*, LFL) Dell.

Grambling, Lois G. Elephant & Mouse Get Ready for Christmas. Maze, Deborah, illus. 32p. 1990. with dust jacket 12.95 (*0-8120-6185-3*) Barron.

Graves, Carolyn. Skip-a-Star: The Legend of the Christmas Snow. 2nd ed. (Illus.). 32p. (gr. 2-4). 1993. Set, audio cass. & bk. 9.95 (*1-882716-03-5*); Bk. pap. text ed. 4.95 (*1-882716-05-1*); write for info. audio cassette (*1-882716-04-3*) PAVE.

Green, Michelle Y. Willie Pearl Series. 1992. write for info. (*0-9627697-6-2*) W Ruth Co.

Greenberg, Kenneth R. The Adventures of Tusky & His Friends: A Christmas Mystery. Pearson, Allison K., illus. 63p. (gr. k-3). 1991. PLB 14.95 (*1-879100-01-0*) Tusky Enterprises.

Greenberg, Martin. Newbery Christmas. (gr. 4-7). 1991. 16.95 (*0-385-30485-4*) Delacorte.

Greenburg, Dan. Young Santa. Miller, Warren, illus. LC 93-7482. 80p. 1993. pap. 4.99 (*0-14-034773-9*, Puffin) Puffin Bks.

Greene, George W. Christmas Books & Ornaments. Hatter, Laurie, illus. (ps). 1993. Gift box set of 4 bks., 12p. ea. bds. 14.95 (*1-56828-041-6*) Red Jacket Pr.

—Hamlet Trims His Tree. Hatter, Laurie, illus. 12p. (ps). 1993. 4.95 (*1-56828-023-8*) Red Jacket Pr.

—Margaret's Christmas Stocking. Hatter, Laurie, illus. 12p. (ps). 1993. 4.95 (*1-56828-022-X*) Red Jacket Pr.

Grubbs, Joan. A Sweet Potato: A Christmas Story. Abell, J., ed. (Orig.). (gr. 2-5). 1993. PLB 25.00 (*1-56611-021-1*); pap. 15.00 (*1-56611-040-8*) Jonas.

Guback, Georgia. The Carolers. LC 90-41756. (Illus.). 32p. 1992. 14.00 (*0-688-09772-3*); PLB 13.93 (*0-688-09773-1*) Greenwillow.

Haarhoff, Dorian. Desert December. Vermeulen, Leon, illus. 32p. (ps-3). 1992. 13.95 (*0-395-61300-0*, Clarion Bks) HM.

Hall, Donald. Lucy's Cristmas. McMurdy, Michael, illus. LC 92-46292. (gr. k-3). 1994. 14.95 (*0-15-276870-X*, Browndeer Pr) HarBrace.

Hall, Lynn. Here Comes Zelda Claus: And Other Holiday Disasters. 149p. (gr. 3-7). 1989. 13.95 (*0-15-233790-3*) HarBrace.

Hall, Tom T. Christmas & the Old House. Seeley, Laura L., illus. 48p. 1989. incl. audio 21.00 (*0-934601-91-7*) Peachtree Pubs.

Hamilton, Dorothy. Christmas for Holly. Graber, Esther R., illus. LC 72-141831. 112p. (gr. 4-9). 1971. pap. 3.95 (*0-8361-1658-5*) Herald Pr.

Hamilton, Mary M. Christmas Magic: A Modern Christmas Fable. Miles, Leona & Kelly, Robert T., eds. Babcock, Patricia, illus. 208p. 1989. lib. bdg. 15. 95 (*0-317-93677-8*) Havet Pr.

Hamilton, Virginia. Bells of Christmas. 59p. (ps up). 1989. 17.95 (*0-15-206450-8*) HarBrace.

Happy House Staff. Hurry up, Santa. 1992. 0.60 (*0-394-82496-2*) Random.

Harder, Geraldine & Harder, Milton. Christmas Goose. Shelly, Maynard, ed. Dyck, Lavonne, illus. LC 90-84535. 80p. (Orig.). (gr. k-6). 1990. pap. 5.95 (*0-87303-146-6*) Faith & Life.

Harris, Christine. Oliver All Alone. Walters, Catherine, illus. LC 94-20453. 36p. (ps-2). 1994. 12.99 (*0-525-45340-7*, DCB) Dutton Child Bks.

Harris, Leon. Night Before Christmas - in Texas, That Is. Wohlberg, Meg, illus. (gr. k-7). 1977. Repr. of 1952 ed. 9.95 (*0-88289-175-8*) Pelican.

Harvey, Brett. My Prairie Christmas. Ray, Deborah K., illus. LC 90-55104. 32p. (ps-3). 1990. reinforced 14.95 (*0-8234-0827-2*) Holiday.

—My Prairie Christmas. Ray, Deborah K., illus. 1993. pap. 5.95 (*0-8234-1064-1*) Holiday.

Haskett, William P. Grandpa Haskett Presents: Original New Christmas Stories for the Young & Young-at-Heart. Haskett, M. R., ed. Haskett, Merelaine, illus. Haskett, M. R., intro. by. (Illus.). 20p. (Orig.). (ps-2). 1982. pap. 3.00g (*0-9609724-0-4*) Haskett Spec.

Hautzig, Deborah, ed. The Christmas Story: Based on the Gospels According to St. Matthew & St. Luke. Beckett, Sheilah, illus. LC 83-60411. 24p. (ps-2). 1983. 3.99 (*0-394-86124-8*) Random Bks Yng Read.

Hawthorne, Grace & Mayfield, Larry. Christmas Fever. 1981. 4.95 (*0-685-68515-2*, BCMC-42); cassette 10.98 (*0-685-68516-0*, BCTA-9022C) Lillenas.

Hayes, Joe. The Wise Little Burro. Jelinek, Lucy, illus. 48p. (Orig.). (gr. k-6). 1991. pap. 5.95 (*0-939729-20-2*) Trails West Pub.

Hayes, Sarah. Happy Christmas, Gemma. Ormerod, Jan, illus. LC 85-23674. 32p. (ps-1). 1986. 13.95 (*0-688-06508-2*) Lothrop.

—Happy Christmas, Gemma. ALC Staff, ed. Ormerod, Jan, illus. LC 85-23674. 32p. (ps up). 1992. pap. 4.95 (*0-688-11702-3*, Mulberry) Morrow.

Haywood, Carolyn. Merry Christmas from Betsy. (gr. k-6). 1989. pap. 3.25 (*0-440-40187-9*, YB) Dell.

—Merry Christmas from Eddie. Durrell, Julie, illus. LC 86-2466. 112p. (gr. 1-4). 1986. 12.95 (*0-688-05828-0*) Morrow Jr Bks.

Hazen, Barbara S. Rudolph the Red-Nosed Reindeer. Scarry, Richard, illus. 24p. (ps-1). 1985. Repr. of 1958 ed. write for info. (*0-307-10203-3*, Pub. by Golden Bks) Western Pub.

Heath, Amy. Sofie's Role. Hamanaka, Sheila, illus. LC 91-33488. 40p. (gr. k-2). 1992. RSBE 14.95 (*0-02-743505-9*, Four Winds) Macmillan Child Grp.

Hegg, Tom. A Cup of Christmas Tea. Hanson, Warren, illus. 46p. 1982. 10.95 (*0-931674-08-5*) Waldman Hse Pr.

Hendry, Diana. Why Father Christmas Was Late for Hartlepool. Heap, Sue, illus. 32p. (gr. k-2). 1994. 16. 95 (*1-85681-108-5*, Pub. by J MacRae UK) Trafalgar.

Henley, Claire, illus. The Baby in the Manger. 10p. (ps-1). 1992. bds. 6.99 (*0-7459-2181-7*) Lion USA.

Herriot, James. Christmas Day Kitten. Brown, Ruth, illus. LC 86-13890. (ps up). 1986. 12.95 (*0-312-13407-X*) St Martin.

Highlights for Children Editors. Tis the Season: Holiday Stories from Highlights. (Illus.). 96p. (Orig.). (gr. 2-5). 1993. pap. 2.95 (*1-56397-279-4*) Boyds Mills Pr.

Hildebrandt, Greg. A Christmas Treasury. (Illus.). 72p. 1984. 11.95 (*0-88101-107-X*) Unicorn Pub.

Hildebrandt, Greg & Hildebrandt, Greg, illus. Twas the Night Before Christmas: And Other Holiday Favorites. LC 90-10976. 48p. (gr. k-2). 1990. 4.95 (*0-88101-103-7*) Unicorn Pub.

Hill, Eric. Spot's First Christmas: Mini Edition. (Illus.). 22p. (ps). 1992. 4.95 (*0-399-22410-6*, Putnam) Putnam Pub Group.

Hill, Susan. Glass Angels. Littlewood, Valerie & Littlewood, Valerie, illus. LC 91-58731. 96p. (gr. 3-6). 1992. 16.95 (*1-56402-111-4*) Candlewick Pr.

—King of Kings. Lawrence, John, illus. LC 92-54624. 32p. (ps up). 1993. 14.95 (*1-56402-210-2*) Candlewick Pr.

Hisako Aoki. Santa's Favorite Story. Gantschev, Ivan, illus. 24p. 1991. pap. 4.95 (*0-590-44454-9*, Blue Ribbon Bks) Scholastic Inc.

Hoban, Lillian. Arthur's Christmas Cookies. unabr. ed. (Illus.). (ps-3). 1990. pap. 6.95 incl. cassette (*1-55994-217-7*, Caedmon) HarperAudio.

Hoban, Russell. Emmet Otter's Jug Band Christmas. (Illus.). 42p. 1992. Repr. PLB 11.95x (*0-89966-951-4*) Buccaneer Bks.

Hoffman, E. T. The Nutcracker. Angus, Fay, adapted by. Welply, Michael, illus. (gr. 2 up). 1989. pap. 18.00 casebound, pop-up (*0-671-68617-8*, Little Simon) S&S Trade.

—The Nutcracker: Xmas Treasury Pop-Up. 1993. pap. 4.99 (*0-517-08788-X*) Random Hse Value.

Hoffman, Robert B., Jr. Christmas Trees. Birdsall, Josh, illus. 62p. (Orig.). (gr. 3 up). 1991. pap. 9.95 (*0-9633156-0-9*) R B Hoffman.

Hol, Coby. Tippy Bear's Christmas. LC 91-45679. (Illus.). 32p. (ps-k). 1992. 11.95 (*1-55858-156-1*); PLB 11.88 (*1-55858-157-X*) North-South Bks NYC.

Holabird, Katharine. Angelina's Christmas. Craig, Helen, illus. LC 85-12389. 32p. (gr. 1 up). 1986. 15.00 (*0-517-55823-8*, Clarkson Potter) Crown Bks Yng Read.

—Christmas with Angelina. Craig, Helen, illus. LC 92-80523. 6p. (ps-k). 1992. bds. 5.99 (*0-679-83485-0*) Random Bks Yng Read.

Hollands, Judith. An Elf for Christmas. MacDonald, Patricia, ed. De Rosa, Dee, illus. 80p. (Orig.). (gr. 2-5). 1990. pap. 2.99 (*0-671-70170-3*, Minstrel Bks) PB.

Hollingsworth, Mary. Christmas in Happy Forest. (Illus.). (ps-2). 1990. 6.99 (*1-877719-05-6*) Brownlow Pub Co.

Hooks, William H. The Mighty Santa Fe. Thomas, Angela T., illus. LC 92-17026. 32p. (gr. k-3). 1993. RSBE 14.95 (*0-02-744432-5*, Macmillan Child Bk) Macmillan Child Grp.

Hooper, Maureen. The Christmas Drum. Paterson, Diane, illus. LC 93-73308. 32p. (ps-3). 1994. 14.95 (*1-56397-105-4*) Boyds Mills Pr.

Hornidge, Marilis. Christmas Tales. Weinberger, Jane, ed. DeVito, Pamela, illus. LC 88-51378. 72p. (gr. 1-6). 1988. pap. 7.95 (*0-932433-50-2*) Windswept Hse.

Houston, Gloria. Littlejim's Gift: An Appalachian Christmas Story. Allen, Thomas B., illus. LC 93-41736. 32p. (gr. 1-5). 1994. PLB 15.95 (*0-399-22696-6*, Philomel Bks) Putnam Pub Group.

Houston, Gloria M. The Year of the Perfect Christmas Tree: An Appalachian Story. Cooney, Barbara, illus. LC 87-245515. 32p. (ps-3). 1988. 14.95 (*0-8037-0299-X*); PLB 14.89 (*0-8037-0300-7*) Dial Bks Young.

Hover, M. Here Comes Santa Claus. Santoro, Christopher, illus. 14p. (ps). 1982. write for info. (*0-307-12267-0*, Golden Bks.) Western Pub.

Howard, Elizabeth F. Chita's Christmas Tree. Cooper, Floyd, illus. LC 92-44482. 32p. (gr. k-2). 1993. pap. 4.95 (*0-689-71739-3*, Aladdin) Macmillan Child Grp.

Howe, James. The Fright Before Christmas. Morrill, Leslie, illus. LC 87-26280. 48p. (gr. k-3). 1988. 13.95 (*0-688-07664-5*); PLB 13.88 (*0-688-07665-3*, Morrow Jr Bks) Morrow Jr Bks.

—The Fright Before Christmas. Morrill, Leslie H., illus. 48p. 1989. pap. 5.95 (*0-380-70445-5*, Camelot) Avon.

Huang, Benrei, illus. Pop-up Merry Christmas. 14p. (ps-1). 1992. 3.95 (*0-448-40253-X*, G&D) Putnam Pub Group.

—Pop-up Santa's Workshop. 14p. (ps-1). 1992. 3.95 (*0-448-40252-1*, G&D) Putnam Pub Group.

Hudson, Mary C. Christmas Birds. (Illus.). 12p. (gr. k-5). 1992. pap. 5.95 (*0-685-70143-3*) M C Hudson.

—Povorina. (Illus.). 16p. (gr. k-5). 1989. pap. 5.95 (*0-9627745-0-2*) M C Hudson.

Hughes, Dean. Lucky's Mud Festival. LC 91-34494. 141p. (Orig.). (gr. 3-6). 1991. pap. text ed. 4.95 (*0-87579-566-8*) Deseret Bk.

Humphrey, L. Spencer. The Nutcracker. 32p. 1994. pap. 2.95 (*0-8125-2322-9*) Tor Bks.

Hyman, Trina S. How Six Found Christmas. Hyman, Trina S., illus. LC 91-70462. 32p. (ps-3). 1991. reinforced bdg. 13.95 (*0-8234-0914-7*) Holiday.

Ideals Staff. Jolly Old Santa Claus. Hinke, George, illus. 24p. (gr. k-3). 1985. pap. 2.95 (*0-89542-448-7*, Ideals Child) Hambleton-Hill.

Impey, Rose. Letter to Santa Claus. (ps-3). 1991. pap. 3.99 (*0-440-40544-0*, YB) Dell.

Ingle, Annie. The Smallest Elf. Smath, Jerry, illus. LC 90-30388. 32p. (Orig.). (ps-1). 1990. pap. 2.25 (*0-679-80846-9*) Random Bks Yng Read.

Ireland, Shep. Merry Christmas. Ireland, Shep, illus. 1992. 4.75 (*0-8378-3799-5*) Gibson.

Ives, Penny. Mrs. Santa Claus. 1993. pap. 3.99 (*0-440-40877-6*) Dell.

Jane, Pamela. Noelle of the Nutcracker. Brett, Jan, illus. 64p. (gr. 2-5). 1986. 13.95 (*0-395-39969-6*) HM.

Janice. Little Bear's Christmas. Mariana, illus. LC 64-21191. (gr. k-3). 1964. PLB 13.93 (*0-688-51076-0*) Lothrop.

Jeffers, Susan. Silent Night. (Illus.). 1992. pap. 4.99 (*0-525-44431-9*, DCB) Dutton Child Bks.

Jeffs, Stephanie. The Little Christmas Tree. Barker, Chris, illus. 16p. (ps-8). 1991. 12.95 (*0-7459-2118-3*) Lion USA.

Jennings, Linda. My Christmas Book of Stories & Carols. 1991. 5.99 (*0-517-05189-3*) Random Hse Value.

Jewell, Nancy. Christmas Lullaby. Vitale, Stefano, illus. LC 93-38786. 1994. 14.95 (*0-395-66586-8*, Clarion Bks) HM.

Joey's Special Christmas Gift. (Illus.). 26p. (ps-1). 1988. pap. 2.95 incl. sticker pgs. (*0-671-66869-2*) S&S Trade.

Johnson, Allen, Jr. The Christmas Tree Express. Keetle, Lisbeth, illus. (gr. 4-8). Date not set. 12.95 (*1-878561-21-9*) Seacoast AL.

Johnson, Eileen B. Gregory Matoose: The Christmas Wish. 16p. (gr. k-6). 1991. text ed. 9.95 (*1-881617-00-9*) Teapot Tales.

Johnson, Russell. Trouble at Christmas. Watts, Bernadette, illus. LC 90-28988. 32p. (gr. k-3). 1991. 14.95 (*1-55858-116-2*) North-South Bks NYC.

Johnston, Annie F. The Little Colonel's Christmas Vacation. (gr. 5 up). 13.95 (*0-89201-035-5*) Zenger Pub.

Jones, Jo. Amanda's Tree. Kuse, James A., ed. (gr. 3-6). 1979. pap. 2.95 (*0-89542-514-9*) Jo-Jo Pubns.

—Amanda's Tree. Vansant, Jo, illus. (gr. 3-6). 1977. pap. 3.50 (*0-9602266-0-5*) Jo-Jo Pubns.

Joseph, Daniel M. All Dressed Up & Nowhere to Go. (ps-3). 1993. 14.95 (*0-395-60196-7*) HM.

Joseph, Lynn. An Island Christmas. Stock, Catherine, illus. 32p. (ps-3). 1992. 14.45 (*0-395-58761-1*, Clarion Bks) HM.

Joyce, William. Santa Calls. Joyce, William, illus. LC 92-52691. 40p. (ps up). 1993. 18.00 (*0-06-021133-4*); PLB 17.89 (*0-06-021134-2*); ltd. ed. 125.00 (*0-06-023355-9*) HarpC Child Bks.

Jurie, Jeri. Bizzy Bubbles: Santa's Littlest Elf. Fahs, Anita, illus. LC 77-82535. (gr. k-6). 1977. 10.95x (*0-686-01311-5*); pap. 6.95x (*0-686-01312-3*) Al Fresco.

Kahn, Peggy. Christmastime at Santa's Workshop. Paris, Pat, illus. 14p. (ps-3). 1992. 7.99 (*0-679-82451-0*) Random Bks Yng Read.

Kaye, Marilyn. Camp Sunnyside Friends Christmas Special: The Spirit of Sunnyside. 128p. (Orig.). 1992. pap. 3.50 (*0-380-76921-2*, Camelot) Avon.

Keller, Holly. A Bear for Christmas. Keller, Holly, illus. LC 85-12645. 32p. (ps-3). 1986. 11.75 (*0-688-05988-0*); PLB 11.88 (*0-688-05989-9*) Greenwillow.

Kellogg, Steven. The Christmas Witch. Kellogg, Steven, illus. LC 91-32688. 40p. (gr. k-3). 1992. 15.00 (*0-8037-1268-5*); PLB 14.89 (*0-8037-1269-3*) Dial Bks Young.

Kessler, Leonard. That's Not Santa! LC 93-39653. (ps-4). 1994. 2.95 (*0-590-48140-1*) Scholastic Inc.

Kimball, Richard S. A Christmas Wrinkle. LC 88-16310. (Illus.). 48p. (Orig.). (gr. 3 up). 1988. pap. 4.95 (*0-944443-01-X*) Green Timber.

A different holiday story...for ages eight to adult. Yes, there is a Santa Claus. He lives in each of us who will give him room. That's the message in this Christmas coming-of-age story. Dan, aged 10, is troubled during the holiday season by the contrast between Christmas glitter & the human suffering he discovers not just from the news but in his own backyard, visited daily by a bag lady searching the family garbage cans. Prospects for a pleasant Christmas become dimmer still when Dan's younger sister begins to doubt the magic of Santa Claus. In the cold & dark of earliest Christmas morning, Dan turns from worry to action, rekindles the warmth of Christmas, & sees its meaning by new light. Charcoal drawings throughout the text add warmth & depth of feeling to the story. Full color cover. Paperback, $4.95. Call or write for information to order, Green Timber Publications, P.O. Box 3884, Portland, ME 04104. 207-797-4180.
Publisher Provided Annotation.

Kinard, Lee. Harriet Tubman's Famous Christmas Eve Raid. LC 93-60260. (Illus.). 44p. (gr. k-3). 1993. 10.95 (*1-55523-612-X*) Winston-Derek.

Kingman, Lee. The Best Christmas. Cooney, Barbara, illus. (gr. 2-5). 1984. 16.50 (*0-8446-6160-0*) Peter Smith.

—The Best Christmas. Cooney, Barbara, illus. LC 92-21152. 96p. (gr. 5 up). 1993. pap. 4.95 (*0-688-11838-0*, Pub. by Beech Tree Bks) Morrow.

Kismaric, Carole, adapted by. A Gift from Saint Nicholas. Mikolaycak, Charles, illus. LC 87-8797. 32p. (ps-3). 1988. reinforced bdg. 15.95 (*0-8234-0674-1*) Holiday.

Kline, Suzy. Horrible Harry & the Christmas Surprise. Remkiewicz, Frank, illus. LC 93-15137. 64p. (gr. 2-5). 1993. pap. 2.99 (*0-14-034452-7*, Puffin) Puffin Bks.

Knapp, Toni, ed. The Gossamer Tree: A Christmas Fable. Brown, Craig M., illus. LC 88-90759. 32p. (Orig.). (gr. 2 up). 1988. 14.95 (*1-882092-00-7*); pap. 8.95 (*1-882092-02-3*) Travis Ilse.

Kneen. Twelve Days of Christmas: A Revolving Picture Book. (Illus.). 12p. (ps-6). 1992. 13.95 (*0-525-44654-0*, DCB) Dutton Child Bks.

Kneen, Maggie. Who's Getting Ready for Christmas? Kneen, Maggie, illus. LC 93-11061. (gr. 4-7). 1993. 13.95 (*0-8118-0470-4*) Chronicle Bks.

Knight, Hilary. Christmas Nutshell Library, 4 bks. Knight, Hilary, illus. Incl. Angels & Berries & Candy Canes; Christmas Stocking Story (*0-06-023205-6*); Firefly in a Fir Tree (*0-06-023190-4*); The Night Before Christmas. LC 63-18904. (Illus.). (gr. 1 up). 1963. Set. 11.00 (*0-06-023165-3*) HarpC Child Bks.

Krahn, Fernando. How Santa Had a Long & Difficult Journey Delivering His Presents. (gr. k-6). 1988. pap. 3.95 (*0-440-40118-6*, YB) Dell.

Kraus, Robert. Daddy Long Ears Christmas Surprise. 1989. 4.95 (*0-671-68150-8*, Little Simon) S&S Trade.

—Wise Old Owl's Christmas Adventure. LC 93-25544. (Illus.). 32p. (ps-3). 1993. PLB 10.89 (*0-8167-2945-X*); pap. text ed. 2.95 (*0-8167-2946-8*) Troll Assocs.

Krementz, Jill. A Very Young Circus Flyer. (gr. k-6). 1987. pap. 6.95 (*0-440-49216-5*, YB) Dell.

Kreysa, Francis J. The Year Christmas Almost Stopped. 1st. ed. Woodard, Chris, illus. 106p. (gr. 4-7). 1982. pap. 3.00 (*0-9611398-0-3*) Kreysa.

Kroeber, Theodora. Green Christmas. Larrecq, John M., illus. LC 67-26304. (gr. k-2). 1967. 6.95 (*0-87466-047-5*, Pub. by Parnassus) HM.

Kunhardt, Edith. Danny's Christmas Star. LC 88-18785. (Illus.). 24p. (ps up). 1989. 12.95 (*0-688-07905-9*); PLB 12.88 (*0-688-07906-7*) Greenwillow.

Kusugak, Michael A. Baseball Bats for Christmas. Krykorka, Vladyana, illus. 24p. (gr. k-3). 1990. 15.95 (*1-55037-145-2*, Pub. by Annick CN); pap. 5.95 (*1-55037-144-4*, Pub. by Annick CN) Firefly Bks Ltd.

Lagerlof, Selma. The Legend of the Christmas Rose. Mikolaycak, Charles, illus. Greene, Ellin, retold by. LC 89-77511. (Illus.). 32p. (ps up). 1990. reinforced 15.95 (*0-8234-0821-3*) Holiday.

Lambert, Jonathan. Twelve Days of Christmas. (ps-3). 1992. pap. 12.00 (*0-671-78396-3*, S&S BFYR) S&S Trade.

Lapka, Fay S. The Sea, the Song & the Trumpetfish. 160p. (Orig.). (gr. 7-12). 1991. pap. 6.99 (*0-87788-754-3*) Shaw Pubs.

La Rochelle, David. A Christmas Guest. Skoro, Martin, illus. 32p. (ps-3). 1988. PLB 18.95 (*0-87614-325-7*); pap. 5.95 (*0-87614-506-3*) Carolrhoda Bks.

Latino, Frank. The Legend of Holly Boy: The Holly Boy. Hood, Jack, illus. 38p. (Orig.). (gr. 9-12). 1994. 15.95 (*0-9640474-0-3*); pap. 7.95 (*0-9640474-1-1*) F Latino Pub Co.

Leeuwen, Jean Van. The Great Christmas Kidnapping Caper. (gr. 3-7). 1976. pap. 2.50 (*0-440-43220-0*, YB) Dell.

Leighton, Maxinne R. An Ellis Island Christmas. Nolan, Dennis, illus. 32p. (gr. 1-4). 1992. 15.00 (*0-670-83182-4*) Viking Child Bks.

Lemoine, Charles A. Santa Clawfish. Lemoine, Charles A., illus. 32p. (Orig.). 1986. pap. 3.20 (*0-941327-00-0*) Charles A Lemoine.

Lemoine, Georges, illus. The Christmas Story According to St. Luke. 32p. 1978. PLB 13.95 (*0-87191-957-5*) Creative Ed.

L'Engle, Madeleine. The Twenty-Four Days Before Christmas. (gr. k-6). 1987. pap. 3.50 (*0-440-40105-4*, YB) Dell.

Leppard, Lois G. Mandie & the Holiday Surprise, Bk. 11. LC 88-71502. 160p. (gr. 3-6). 1988. pap. 3.99 (*1-55661-036-X*) Bethany Hse.

Lewis, Beverly. California Christmas. 160p. (gr. 6-9). 1994. pap. 4.99 (*0-310-43321-5*) Zondervan.

Lewis, J. Patrick. The Christmas of the Reddle Moon. Kelley, Gary, illus. LC 93-28049. (gr. 3 up). 1994. 15. 99 (*0-8037-1566-8*); PLB 15.89 (*0-8037-1567-6*) Dial Bks Young.

Lewis, Shari. One Minute Christmas. 1993. pap. 4.99 (*0-440-40856-3*) Dell.

—One Minute Christmas Stories. Palmer, Jan, illus. Matthews, Gerry, contrib. by. LC 86-29146. (Illus.). 48p. (gr. k-3). 1987. pap. 7.95 (*0-385-23424-4*) Doubleday.

Lewison, Wendy. Christmas Cookies. Morgan, Mary, illus. 24p. (ps). 1993. bds. 2.95 (*0-448-40554-7*, G&D) Putnam Pub Group.

Lindgren, Astrid. Christmas in Noisy Village. LC 64-21473. 32p. (ps-3). 1981. pap. 3.99 (*0-14-050344-7*, Puffin) Puffin Bks.

—Lotta's Christmas Surprise. Wikland, Ilon, illus. 32p. (ps-3). 1990. 13.95 (*91-29-59782-X*, Pub. by R & S Bks) FS&G.

Lisi, Victoria, illus. March of the Wooden Soldiers. 48p. (ps-2). 1992. 5.95 (*0-88101-261-0*) Unicorn Pub.

Little Brown Staff. George Balanchine's the Nutcracker, Vol. 1: A Keepsake Edition. (gr. 4-7). 1993. 8.95 (*0-316-23154-1*) Little.

Lockhart, Barbara. Christmas Tall Books, 3 bks. Lockhart, Lynne, illus. 36p. (ps). 1993. Set, incl. snowman. bds. 14.95 (*1-56828-044-0*) Red Jacket Pr.

—The Christmas Tree. Lockhart, Lynne, illus. 12p. (ps). 1993. 4.95 (*1-56828-025-4*) Red Jacket Pr.

Long, Ron E. & Barrett, Joanne. Hark, the Herald Angel. Fettke, Tom, contrib. by. 1983. 4.95 (*0-685-68531-4*, BCMC-48); cassette 10.98 (*0-685-68532-2*, BCTA-9039C) Lillenas.

Lunn, Janet. One Hundred Shining Candles. Grater, Lindsay, illus. LC 90-8892. 32p. (gr. 2-4). 1991. SBE 13.95 (*0-684-19280-2*, Scribners Young Read) Macmillan Child Grp.

Luton, Mildred. Christmas Time in the Mountains. Peattie, Gary, illus. 44p. (Orig.). (gr. 1-6). 1981. pap. 5.00 (*0-87516-434-X*) DeVorss.

Lyman, et al. Pee Wee Saves Christmas. Curtis, Peggy H., illus. 80p. 1983. 14.95 (*0-317-03904-0*) Imagination Dust.

McAllister, Mimi. Christmas at Gump's. McAllister, Mimi & Becker, Richard, illus. LC 90-60435. 48p. 1990. 16.95 (*0-9624887-4-7*) C Salway Pr.

McClure, Gillian. Christmas Donkey: A New Version of the Nativity Story. (ps-3). 1993. 15.00 (*0-374-31261-3*) FS&G.

McCue, Lisa, illus. Corduroy's Christmas. Freeman, Don & Hennessy, B. G.concept by. (Illus.). 16p. (ps-1). 1992. 10.95 (*0-670-84477-2*) Viking Child Bks.

McCully, Emily A. The Christmas Gift. LC 87-45758. (Illus.). 32p. (ps-1). 1992. pap. 3.95 (*0-06-443307-2*, Trophy) HarpC Child Bks.

MacDonald, George. The Christmas Stories of George MacDonald. LC 81-68187. (gr. 3-7). 1981. 12.99 (*0-89191-491-9*, 54916, Chariot Bks) Chariot Family.

McIntire, Jamie. Santa's Christmas Surprise. Henry, Steve, illus. LC 93-24843. (gr. k-3). 1993. pap. text ed. 2.95 (*0-8167-3257-4*) Troll Assocs.

McKenna, Colleen O. Merry Christmas Miss McConnell. (ps-3). 1990. 12.95 (*0-590-43554-X*, Scholastic Hardcover) Scholastic Inc.

—Merry Christmas, Miss McConnell. 160p. 1991. pap. 2.95 (*0-590-43555-8*, Apple Paperbacks) Scholastic Inc.

McMullan, Kate. Nutcracker Noel. McMullan, Jim, illus. LC 93-77115. 32p. (ps up). 1993. 15.00 (*0-06-205039-7*); PLB 14.89 (*0-06-205040-0*) HarpC Child Bks.

McPhail, David. Santa's Book of Names. LC 92-37279. 1993. 14.95 (*0-316-56335-8*, Joy St Bks) Little.

McQuilkin, Frank. Forgottenville: The Town That Arrested Santa Claus. Doros Animations, Inc., illus. 48p. (gr. k-7). 1982. 11.95 (*0-941316-00-9*) TSM Books.

Maggio, Rosalie. The Music Box Christmas. LC 90-38529. 128p. (gr. 5 up). 1990. 12.95g (*0-688-08851-1*) Morrow Jr Bks.

Manushkin, Fran. The Perfect Christmas Picture. Weinhaus, Karen A., illus. LC 79-2678. 64p. (ps-3). 1987. pap. 3.50 (*0-06-444112-1*, Trophy) HarpC Child Bks.

Marie, Nancy. Country Christmas. Ryan, Delores, illus. 36p. (gr. k-5). 1979. 5.95 (*0-941595-00-5*) Heldreth Pub.

Marilue. Bobby Bear's Christmas. LC 77-83628. (Illus.). 32p. (ps-1). 1978. PLB 9.95 (*0-87783-142-4*); cassette o.p. 7.94x (*0-87783-182-3*) Oddo.

Markham, Marion M. The Christmas Present Mystery. McCully, Emily A., illus. 64p. 1990. pap. 2.95 (*0-380-70966-X*, Camelot) Avon.

Marsh, Carole. The Fortune Cookie Christmas. (Illus., Orig.). (gr. 3 up). 1994. 24.95 (*1-55609-285-7*); pap. 14.95 (*0-935326-53-7*) Gallopade Pub Group.

Marshall, D. J. A Little Duck's Christmas Wish. 1992. 6.95 (*0-533-08777-5*) Vantage.

Marshall, James. Merry Christmas Space Case. 1989. pap. 4.95 (*0-8037-0653-7*, Dial) Doubleday.

Martin, Ann M. Secret Santa. LC 93-48981. 1994. 14.95 (*0-590-48295-5*) Scholastic Inc.

Martini, Teri. Christmas for Andy. (gr. 3 up). 1991. pap. 3.95 (*0-8091-6603-8*) Paulist Pr.

—Feliz Navidad, Pablo. McNichols, William H., illus. (gr. 4 up). 1990. 2.95 (*0-8091-6597-X*) Paulist Pr.

Masek, Linda E. Mag-ni-fi-cat & the Christmas Tree Mystery. 1992. 10.95 (*0-533-10173-5*) Vantage.

Mathias, Beverley. A Treasury of Christmas Stories. Aldous, Kate, illus. LC 93-50708. 160p. (ps-3). 1994. write for info. (*1-85697-985-7*, Kingfisher LKC) LKC.

May, Robert. Rudolph the Red Nosed Reindeer. LC 91-156221. (ps-3). 1990. 9.95 (*1-55709-139-0*) Applewood.

May, Robert L. Rudolph's Second Christmas. Emberley, Michael, illus. LC 92-18416. (ps-3). 1992. 9.95 (*1-55709-192-7*) Applewood.

Mayer, Mercer. Merry Christmas Mom & Dad. Mayer, Mercer, illus. 24p. (ps-3). 1982. pap. write for info. (*0-307-11886-X*, Golden Bks.) Western Pub.

Mayo, Virginia. Dont' Forget Me Santa Claus. (ps). 1993. 12.95 (*0-8120-6391-0*) Barron.

Menotti, Gian-Carlo. Amahl & the Night Visitors. Lemieux, Michele, illus. LC 84-27196. 64p. (ps up). 1986. 15.00 (*0-688-05426-9*); lib. bdg. 14.88 (*0-688-05427-7*, Morrow Jr Bks) Morrow Jr Bks.

Merriam, Eve. The Christmas Box. Small, David, illus. LC 85-5666. 32p. (ps-3). 1985. 12.95 (*0-688-05255-X*); lib. bdg. 12.88 (*0-688-05256-8*, Morrow Jr Bks) Morrow Jr Bks.

Merry Xmas Library. 1991. pap. 11.25 (*0-679-81418-3*) Random Bks Yng Read.

Mickey's Christmas Party. 10p. 1994. 6.98 (*1-57082-157-7*) Mouse Works.

Miles, Calvin. Calvin's Christmas Wish. Johnson, Dolores, illus. 32p. (ps-3). 1993. 13.99 (*0-670-84295-8*) Viking Child Bks.

Miller, Lynne, ed. Ten Tales of Christmas. 112p. (gr. 4-6). 1988. pap. 2.50 (*0-590-41447-X*) Scholastic Inc.

Miller, Paul M. Christmas Comes to Lone Star Gulch. Linn, Joseph, contrib. by. 1989. 4.95 (*0-8341-9157-1*, BCMC-67); song charts 29.95 (*0-685-68524-1*, BCMC-67C); cassette 10.98 (*0-685-68525-X*, BCTA-9106C) Lillenas.

Mills, Reita. Santa's Ups & Downs. 1992. 6.95 (*0-533-10307-X*) Vantage.

Moerbeek, Kees. Night Before Christmas. 12p. (ps up). 1992. 9.95 (*0-8431-3445-3*) Price Stern.

Moeri, Louise. Star Mother's Youngest Child. Hyman, Trina S., illus. 48p. (ps-2). 1980. 14.45 (*0-395-21406-8*, Sandpiper); pap. 5.95 (*0-395-29929-2*) HM.

Montgomery, Raymond A. & Gillig. Home in Time for Christmas. 1987. pap. 2.99 (*0-553-15709-4*) Bantam.

Moore, Clement C. The Night Before Christmas. Hague, Michael, illus. LC 80-84842. 12p. (gr. k up). 1981. 12. 95 (*0-8050-0900-0*, Bks Young Read) H Holt & Co.

—The Night Before Christmas. Lobel, Anita, illus. LC 84-4342. 32p. (ps-5). 1984. 12.00 (*0-394-86863-3*); lib. bdg. 12.99 (*0-394-96863-8*) Knopf Bks Yng Read.

—The Night Before Christmas. De Paola, Tomie, illus. (gr. k-3). 1984. incl. cassette 19.95 (*0-317-07112-2*); pap. 12.95 incl. cassette (*0-941078-37-X*); incl. 4 bks., cassette, & guide 27.95 (*0-685-08869-3*) Live Oak Media.

—The Night Before Christmas. Tien, illus. 32p. (ps-1). 1986. pap. 5.95 (*0-671-62209-9*, Little Simon) S&S Trade.

—The Night Before Christmas: Or: Account of a Visit from St. Nicholas. Bevis, Phillip & Irwin, Colin, eds. Henley, Clark, illus. 22p. 1984. 150.00 (*0-923980-03-2*) Arundel Pr.

—Two Little Christmas Classics. Goode, Diane, illus. 32p. (ps up). 1989. pap. 4.95 incl. cassette (*0-394-84629-X*) Random Bks Yng Read.

Moore, J. Thomas. Night after Christmas. (gr. k up). 1990. pap. 5.95 (*0-925928-07-0*) Tiny Thought.

Moore, John T., et al. Christmas Classics for Children. (ps-k). 1981. 14.99 (*0-570-04058-2*, 56-1351) Concordia.

Moore, Ruth N. The Christmas Surprise. Eitzen, Allen, illus. 160p. (Orig.). (gr. 4-8). 1989. pap. 5.95 (*0-8361-3499-0*) Herald Pr.

Mora, Francisco X. La Gran Fiesta. Mora, Francisco X., illus. LC 92-44365. 32p. (ps-k). 1993. PLB 15.00 (*0-917846-19-2*, 95518) Highsmith Pr.

Morehead, Ruth J. The Christmas Story with Holly Babes. Morehead, Ruth J., illus. LC 85-32305. 32p. (ps-1). 1987. 2.25 (*0-394-88051-X*); cassette pkg. 5.95 (*0-394-89058-2*) Random Bks Yng Read.

Morehead, Ruth J., illus. A Christmas Countdown with Ruth J. Morehead's Holly Babes. LC 90-61905. 22p. (ps). 1991. bds. 2.95 (*0-679-81417-5*) Random Bks Yng Read.

Morris, Dixie G. Who is Santa? Medrano, JoAnn, illus. Robinson, Deborah L., intro. by. (Illus.). 25p. (Orig.). (ps-3). 1988. spiral bdg. 7.50 (*0-929946-04-9*) L P T C.

Narney, Dean. The Christmas Tree That Ate My Mother. 1992. 2.95 (*0-590-44881-1*, Apple Paperbacks) Scholastic Inc.

Naylor, Phyllis R. Keeping a Christmas Secret. Shiffman, Lena, illus. LC 93-12248. 32p. (gr. k-2). 1993. pap. 4.95 (*0-689-71760-1*, Aladdin) Macmillan Child Grp.

—Old Sadie & the Christmas Bear. LC 84-2995. (Illus.). 32p. (ps-2). 1984. RSBE 13.95 (*0-689-31052-8*, Atheneum Child Bk) Macmillan Child Grp.

Nelson-Erichsen, Jean. Copito: The Christmas Chihuahua. Atcheson, Marguerite, illus. Davenport, May, intro. by. LC 82-72080. (Illus.). 80p. (gr. k-5). 1982. pap. 3.50x (*0-943864-07-0*) Davenport.

Nerlove, Miriam. Christmas. Tucker, Kathy, ed. Nerlove, Miriam, illus. LC 89-70737. 24p. (ps-1). 1990. 11.95 (*0-8075-1148-X*) A Whitman.

—Christmas: An Albert Whitman Prairie Book. (ps-3). 1993. pap. 4.95 (*0-8075-1147-1*) A Whitman.

Nielsen-McLellan, Karen L. Ginger Bear's Christmas Cookie Mystery. Nielsen-McLellan, Karen L., illus. 32p. (ps-1). 1992. 12.95 (*0-9634851-0-5*) Scand Descent.

A Christmas mystery! Elves, cookies & Santa Claus's baker all rushing to make ginger bear cookies for the holiday stockings of all the "good" boys & girls of the world. A hard covered children's book with full-color illustrations & jacket. The highly animated story revolves around a bear named Ginger Bear who does all the baking for Santa Claus at the North Pole. During the holiday season, the orders for the "special" ginger bear cookies out number Ginger Bear's capabilities to produce the cookies. A sequence of mysterious events are set in motion by two elves, Dunlap & Otis. All is resolved by a trio of cookies who come to life & bake enough cookies to fill all the stockings on Santa's list. To enhance & delight, edible ginger bear cookies are available as well as a 16" plush bear dressed like Ginger Bear. Order through: Scandinavian Descent, Inc., 5917 Camelback Ct., Indianapolis, IN 46250. (317) 576-9900.
Publisher Provided Annotation.

The Night Before Christmas. (Illus.). 24p. (gr. k-2). 1991. 3.95 (*1-56144-070-1*, Honey Bear Bks) Modern Pub NYC.

The Night Before Christmas, The Honey Bears' Christmas Surpris2. (Illus.). 24p. 1983. (Honey Bear Bks); text ed. 3.95 (*0-87449-028-6*, Honey Bear Bks); text ed. 3.95 (*0-87449-182-7*, Honey Bear Bks) Modern Pub NYC.

Night Santa Got Stuck. 13p. (gr. k-3). 1991. pap. 2.95 (*0-8167-2193-9*) Troll Assocs.

Nixon, Joan L. The Christmas Eve Mystery. Fay, Ann, ed. Cummins, Jim, illus. LC 81-345. 32p. (gr. 1-3). 1981. PLB 8.95 (*0-8075-1150-1*) A Whitman.

—That's the Spirit, Claude. Pearson, Tracey C., illus. 32p. (ps-3). 1992. 13.00 (*0-670-83434-3*) Viking Child Bks.

Njoku, Scholastica I. The Miracle of a Christmas Doll. McKay, Suzanne, illus. 29p. (gr. k up). 1986. perfect bdg. 5.95x (*0-9617833-0-3*) S I NJOKU.

Noble, Trinka H. Apple Tree Christmas. Noble, Trinka H., illus. LC 84-1901. 32p. (ps-2). 1988. 13.50 (*0-8037-0102-0*); PLB 12.89 (*0-8037-0103-9*) Dial Bks Young.

Nordqvist, Sven. Merry Christmas, Festus & Mercury. (Illus.). 24p. (ps-3). 1989. PLB 18.95 (*0-87614-383-4*) Carolrhoda Bks.

—Tomten's Christmas Porridge. Haug, Arden, tr. from SWE. Nordquist, Sven, illus. 28p. (gr. 1-6). 1991. 14. 95 (*0-9615394-2-9*) Skandisk.

Novak, Matt. The Last Christmas Present. Novak, Matt, illus. LC 92-44513. 32p. (ps-1). 1993. 14.95 (*0-531-05495-0*); PLB 14.99 (*0-531-08645-3*) Orchard Bks Watts.

The Nutcracker. 24p. (gr. k-3). 1992. pap. 2.50 (*1-56144-162-7*, Honey Bear Bks) Modern Pub NYC.

The Nutcracker, The Twelve Days of Christmas, A Christmas for Santa, The Christmas Kitten. (Illus.). 24p. (gr. 1 up). 1988. text ed. 4.95 (*0-87449-504-0*, Honey Bear Bks); text ed. 4.95 (*0-87449-505-9*, Honey Bear Bks); text ed. 4.95 (*0-87449-506-7*, Honey Bear Bks); text ed. 4.95 (*0-87449-507-5*, Honey Bear Bks) Modern Pub NYC.

Oakley, Graham. Church Mice at Christmas. Oakley, Graham, illus. LC 80-14518. 40p. (gr. k-3). 1980. SBE 13.95 (*0-689-30797-7*, Atheneum Child Bk) Macmillan Child Grp.

O'Donnell, William F. Mother Santa Clauss Stories. 1976. 16.95 (*0-8488-1116-X*) Amereon Ltd.

O. Henry. The Gift of the Magi. King, Kevin, illus. 32p. (gr. 5 up). 1988. pap. 12.95 (*0-671-64706-7*, Little Simon) S&S Trade.

—The Gift of the Magi. Sauber, Robert, illus. LC 91-7313. 48p. (gr. 1-6). 1991. 9.95 (*0-88101-116-9*) Unicorn Pub.

—The Gift of the Magi. Zwerger, Lisbeth, illus. LC 92-6632. 28p. 1992. pap. 5.95 (*0-88708-276-9*) Picture Bk Studio.

—The Gift of the Magi: A Special Christmas Edition. rev. ed. Marshall, Rita, illus. 32p. (gr. 4 up). 1984. PLB 13.95 (*0-87191-954-0*) Creative Ed.

O'Keefe, Susan H. A Season for Giving. Keating, Pamela T., illus. 1990. 2.95 (*0-8091-6592-9*) Paulist Pr.

Old-Fashioned Christmas (Christmas Mini-Carousel in Three Dimensional Format) 1992. 4.95 (*0-8431-3438-0*) Price Stern.

Olson, Arielle N. Hurry Home, Grandma! Dabcovich, Lydia, illus. LC 84-1529. 32p. (ps-1). 1984. 9.95 (*0-525-44113-1*, DCB) Dutton Child Bks.

Oppenheimer, Evelyn. Tilli Comes to Texas. Haverfield, Mary, illus. LC 86-3089. 40p. (gr. k-3). 1986. PLB 9.95 (*0-937460-21-4*) Hendrick-Long.

Ottum, Bob & Wood, JoAnne. Santa's Beard Is Soft & Warm. Ruth, Rod, illus. (ps). 1974. write for info. (*0-307-12148-8*, Golden Bks) Western Pub.

Packard, Mary. Christmas Kitten. (Illus.). 28p. (ps-2). 1994. PLB 14.00 (*0-516-05364-7*) Childrens.

Palacios, Argentina. Christmas for Chabelita. Lohstoeter, Lori, illus. LC 94-9833. 32p. (gr. k-3). 1994. PLB 14.95 (*0-8167-3545-X*); pap. text ed. 3.95 (*0-8167-3541-7*) BrdgeWater.

Palangi, Paula. Last Straw. LC 91-44346. (ps-3). 1992. pap. 9.99 (*0-7814-0562-9*, Chariot Bks) Chariot Family.

Palumbo, Nancy. Penelope P'Nutt & the Spirit of Christmas: Penelope P'Nutt et L'Ambiance De Noel. Weaver, Judith, illus. 16p. (gr. k-6). 1989. wkbk. 5.95 (*0-927024-03-9*) Crayons Pubns.

—Penelope P'Nutt & the Spirit of Christmas: Penelope P'Nutt y el Espiritu de la Navidad. Weaver, Judith, illus. 16p. (gr. k-6). 1989. wkbk. 5.95 (*0-927024-02-0*) Crayons Pubns.

Paris, Pat. On Christmas Day. (Illus.). 10p. (ps). 1991. pap. 4.95 casebound (*0-671-74173-X*, Little Simon) S&S Trade.

Parish, Peggy. Merry Christmas, Amelia Bedelia. Sweat, Lynn, illus. LC 85-24919. 64p. (gr. 1-4). 1986. 13.00 (*0-688-06101-X*); PLB 12.93 (*0-688-06102-8*) Greenwillow.

Parker, Ann N. A Christmas Trilogy. Vickery, Diane, illus. (gr. k-4). 1988. pap. 3.95 (*0-943487-14-5*) Sevgo Pr.

Pascal, Francine. The Case of the Christmas Thief. (ps-3). 1992. pap. 3.25 (*0-553-48063-4*) Bantam.

—Christmas Ghost. (gr. 7-12). 1990. pap. write for info. Bantam.

—A Christmas Without Elizabeth. (gr. 4-7). 1993. pap. 3.99 (*0-553-15947-X*) Bantam.

—The Magic Christmas. (gr. 4-7). 1992. pap. 3.99 (*0-553-48051-0*) Bantam.

Paterson, Bettina, illus. Merry ABC. 24p. (ps). 1993. bds. 2.95 (*0-448-40553-9*, G&D) Putnam Pub Group.

Paterson, Cynthia & Paterson, Brian. The Foxwood Surprise. (Illus.). 32p. (ps-3). 1988. 6.95 (*0-8120-5986-7*) Barron.

Paterson, Katherine. Angels & Other Strangers: Family Christmas Stories. LC 79-63797. 128p. (gr. 1 up). 1979. 14.00 (*0-690-03992-1*, Crowell Jr Bks) HarpC Child Bks.

—Angels & Other Strangers: Family Christmas Stories. LC 79-63797. (gr. 7 up). 1988. pap. 3.95 (*0-06-440283-5*, Trophy) HarpC Child Bks.

—Angels & Other Strangers: Family Christmas Stories. LC 79-63797. 128p. (gr. 7 up). 1991. PLB 13.89 (*0-690-04911-0*, Crowell Jr Bks) HarpC Child Bks.

Patterson, Nancy R. The Christmas Cup. Bowman, Leslie W., illus. LC 88-29112. 80p. (gr. 3-5). 1989. 13.95 (*0-531-05821-2*); PLB 13.99 (*0-531-08421-3*) Orchard Bks Watts.

—The Christmas Cup. 80p. 1991. pap. 2.95 (*0-590-43870-0*, Apple Paperbacks) Scholastic Inc.

Patti, Joyce. The First Christmas. (Illus.). 18p. (ps up). 1990. 13.95 (*0-525-44606-0*, DCB) Dutton Child Bks.

Paulsen, Gary. A Christmas Sonata. Bowman, Leslie W., illus. LC 90-46891. 80p. (gr. 3-7). 1992. 14.95 (*0-385-30441-2*) Delacorte.

Pearson, Susan. The Day Porkchop Climbed the Christmas Tree. Brown, Richard, illus. (ps up). 1998. pap. 9.95 (*0-671-66370-4*, S&S BFYR); (S&S BFYR) S&S Trade.

—Karin's Christmas Walk. Noble, Trinka H., illus. LC 80-11739. 32p. (ps-3). 1980. Dial Bks Young.

—Karin's Christmas Walk. Noble, Trinka H., illus. LC 80-11739. 32p. (ps-3). 1983. pap. 4.95 (*0-8037-0020-2*) Dial Bks Young.

Pearson, Tracey C., illus. We Wish You a Merry Christmas. LC 82-22224. 32p. (ps up). 1983. 8.95 (*0-8037-9368-5*); pap. 3.95 (*0-8037-0310-4*) Dial Bks Young.

Peet, Bill. Countdown to Christmas. Peet, Bill, illus. LC 72-78394. 48p. (gr. k-8). 1972. (Golden Gate); PLB 15.93 (*0-516-08716-9*) Childrens.

Pepper, Dennis, ed. An Oxford Book of Christmas Stories. Brown, Judy, illus. 224p. (gr. 3 up). 1988. pap. 10.95 1988 (*0-19-278124-3*) OUP.

Perron, Robert E. Bum & Carey Bear: A Christmas Tale. (Illus.). 48p. 1994. pap. 8.00 (*0-8059-3578-9*) Dorrance.

Peterkin, Julia. A Plantation Christmas. Hendrickson, David, illus. LC 72-4563. (gr. 7 up). Repr. of 1934 ed. 10.50 (*0-8369-9119-2*) Ayer.

Peters, Lauren. Problems at the North Pole. Thatch, Nancy R., ed. Melton, David, intro. by. LC 90-5929. (Illus.). 26p. (ps-2). 1990. PLB 14.95 (*0-933849-25-7*) Landmark Edns.

Peters, Sharon. The Tiny Christmas Elf. Durrell, Julie, illus. LC 86-30849. 32p. (gr. k-2). 1988. PLB 7.89 (*0-8167-0988-2*); pap. text ed. 1.95 (*0-8167-0989-0*) Troll Assocs.

Peterson, Carolyn S. & Fenton, Ann D. Christmas Story Programs. Sterchele, Christina L., illus. (ps-6). 1981. 10.00 (*0-913545-01-5*) Moonlight FL.

Pfister, Marcus. The Christmas Star. Pfister, Marcus, illus. James, J. Alison, tr. from GER. LC 93-15143. (Illus.). 32p. (gr. k-3). 1993. 16.95 (*1-55858-203-7*); lib. bdg. 16.88 (*1-55858-204-5*) North-South Bks NYC.

Pickthall, Marjorie. The Worker in Sandalwood: A Christmas Eve Miracle. Tyrrell, Frances, illus. LC 94-548. 32p. (gr. k-4). 1994. 14.99 (*0-525-45332-6*) Dutton Child Bks.

Pierce, Catherine D. Christmas Thief. Gallagher, Jane, illus. (Orig.). (ps-k). 1988. pap. text ed. 4.50 (*0-9621397-0-X*) C D Pierce.

Pilkey, Dav. Dragon's Merry Christmas. LC 91-1996. (Illus.). 48p. (gr. 1-3). 1991. 12.95 (*0-531-05957-X*); RLB 12.99 (*0-531-08557-0*) Orchard Bks Watts.

Pilkington, Brian. Grandpa Claus. Pilkington, Brian, illus. 28p. (ps-3). 1990. PLB 19.95 (*0-87614-436-9*) Carolrhoda Bks.

Pipe, Rhona. One Christmas Night. Smith, Julie, ed. Downer, Maggie, illus. 24p. (ps-3). Date not set. green cover 4.99 (*0-7814-1511-X*, Chariot Bks); red cover 4.99 (*0-7814-1510-1*, Chariot Bks) Chariot Family.

Pippen, Christie. A Very Scraggly Christmas Tree. Beckes, Shirley V., illus. (gr. 2-4). 1988. 19.97 (*0-8172-2754-7*) Raintree Steck-V.

Pippen, Christine. Very Scraggly Christmas Tree. (ps-3). 1993. pap. 4.95 (*0-8114-5214-X*) Raintree Steck-V.

Plume, Ilse. The Christmas Witch. Plume, Ilse, illus. LC 91-71380. 32p. (gr. k-3). 1993. pap. 4.95 (*1-56282-524-0*) Hyprn Ppbks.

Pochocki, Ethel F. The Fox Who Found Christmas. Bell, Thomas P., illus. LC 90-82095. 56p. (Orig.). 1990. pap. 5.95 (*0-87793-431-2*) Ave Maria.

Porter, Connie. Addy's Surprise: A Christmas Story. Rosales, Melodye, illus. Graef, Renee, contrib. by. LC 93-5162. (Illus.). 1993. 12.95 (*1-56247-080-9*); pap. 5.95 (*1-56247-079-5*) Pleasant Co.

Porter-Chase, Mary. The Return of Sinta Claus: A Family Winter Solstice Tale. Walsh, Lloyd, illus. (Orig.). (gr. 3-12). 1991. pap. 6.00 (*0-9630798-0-8*) Samary Pr.

Portlock, Rob. My Dad Ran over a Frog. Portlock, Rob, illus. LC 92-11584. 32p. (Orig.). (ps-1). 1992. pap. 4.99 (*0-8308-1901-0*, 1901) InterVarsity.

Potter, Beatrix. Peter Rabbit's Christmas Book. (ps-3). 1990. pap. 5.95 (*0-7232-3778-6*) Warne.

—The Tailor of Gloucester. (Illus.). 60p. 1993. deluxe ed. 16.00 (*0-7232-4094-9*) Warne.

—Tailor of Gloucester. (Illus.). 36p. (ps-3). 1993. 4.99 (*0-7232-4137-6*) Warne.

—The Tailor or Gloucester Christmas Activity Book. (Illus.). 36p. (ps-3). 1993. 4.99 (*0-7232-4136-8*) Warne.

Prelutsky, Jack. It's Christmas. Hafner, Marylin, illus. 48p. (Orig.). (gr. k-3). 1986. 2.75 (*0-590-44048-9*); incl. cassette 5.95 (*0-590-63171-3*) Scholastic Inc.

Price, Moe. Reindeer Christmas. (ps-3). 1993. 15.95 (*0-15-266199-9*, HB Juv Bks) HarBrace.

Pryor, Bonnie. Merry Christmas, Amanda & April. De Groat, Diane, illus. LC 89-39723. 32p. (ps up). 1990. 13.95 (*0-688-07544-4*); PLB 13.88 (*0-688-07545-2*, Morrow Jr Bks) Morrow Jr Bks.

Quattrocki, Carolyn. Frosty's Snowy Day. Spellman, Susan & Graves, Linda, illus. 24p. (ps-4). 1992. PLB 10.95 (*1-56674-022-3*) Forest Hse.

—The Little Drummer Boy. Spellman, Susan & Graves, Linda, illus. 24p. (ps-4). 1992. PLB 10.95 (*1-56674-023-1*) Forest Hse.

—The Nutcracker. Spellman, Susan & Graves, Linda, illus. 24p. (ps-4). 1992. PLB 10.95 (*1-56674-024-X*) Forest Hse.

—Rudolph's Adventure. Spellman, Susan & Graves, Linda, illus. 24p. (ps-4). 1992. PLB 10.95 (*1-56674-025-8*) Forest Hse.

—Santa Claus Is Coming to Town. Spellman, Susan & Graves, Linda, illus. 24p. (ps-4). 1992. PLB 10.95 (*1-56674-026-6*) Forest Hse.

Quindlen, Anna. The Tree That Came to Stay. Carpenter, Nancy, illus. LC 91-31957. 32p. (ps-4). 1992. 14.00 (*0-517-58145-0*) Crown Bks Yng Read.

Rabe, Berniece. The First Christmas Candy Cane: A Legend. LC 94-6197. 1994. write for info. (*0-681-00441-X*) Longmeadow Pr.

Radzinski, Kandy. The Twelve Cats of Christmas. 32p. 1992. 9.95 (*0-8118-0102-0*) Chronicle Bks.

Ragland, Teresa B., illus. Cooking in the Kitchen with Santa. 32p. (ps up). 1992. PLB 11.95 (*1-56674-028-2*) Forest Hse.

Ramsey, Leola M. Beth, the Little Bethlehem Star: The Christmas Story. 23p. 1991. 3.50 (*0-9629541-0-1*) LMR Prodns.

—Chris: The Naughty Christmas Tree. 26p. 1992. 3.50 (*0-9629541-1-X*) LMR Prodns.

Ransom, Candice F. One Christmas Dawn. Fiore, Peter, illus. LC 93-39751. 32p. (gr. k-3). 1995. PLB 14.95 (*0-8167-3384-8*); pap. text ed. 4.95 (*0-8167-3385-6*) BrdgeWater.

Rappaport, Doreen. Mrs. Santa's Christmas Present. LC 88-81465. (Illus.). 32p. (Orig.). (ps-2). 1988. pap. 8.95 (*0-937124-19-2*) Kimbo Educ.

Razzi, Jim, adapted by. Disney's Mickey's Christmas Carol. LC 91-58970. (Illus.). 1992. 12.95 (*1-56282-238-1*); PLB 12.89 (*1-56282-236-5*) Disney Pr.

—Disney's Mickey's Christmas Carol. LC 92-58971. (Illus.). 1992. pap. 3.50 (*1-56282-239-X*) Disney Pr.

Rebuck, Linda, et al. Not a Creature Was Stirring. (gr. 2 up). 1990. 4.95 (*0-685-68517-9*, BCMC-72); cassette 10.98 (*0-685-68518-7*, BCTA-9119C) Lillenas.

Reiser, Lynn. Christmas Counting. LC 91-32501. (Illus.). 32p. (ps-4). 1992. 14.00 (*0-688-10676-5*); PLB 13.93 (*0-688-10677-3*) Greenwillow.

Rice, Helen S. The Story of the Christmas Guest. (Illus.). 34p. 1991. pap. 9.95x (*0-89966-842-9*) Buccaneer Bks.

Rice, James. Cajun Night Before Christmas Coloring Book. 32p. (gr. k-4). 1976. pap. 2.75 (*0-88289-138-3*) Pelican.

Richardson, I. M. Story of the Christmas Rose. De Kiefte, Kees, illus. LC 87-13817. 32p. (gr. k-4). 1988. PLB 9.79 (*0-8167-1069-4*); pap. text ed. 1.95 (*0-8167-1070-8*) Troll Assocs.

Ricklen, Neil, photos by. Baby's Christmas. (Illus.). 24p. (ps). 1991. pap. 4.95 casebound, padded cover (*0-671-73881-X*, Little Simon) S&S Trade.

Rigg, Lucy. Baby's Christmas. 1990. 2.95 (*0-8378-1883-4*) Gibson.

—Little Christmas Treasure Books: Christmas Joys. (Illus.). (gr. 2 up). 1989. 2.95 (*0-8378-1870-2*) Gibson.

Riggio, Anita. A Moon in My Teacup. Riggio, Anita, illus. 32p. (ps-3). 1993. PLB 14.95 smythe sewn (*1-56397-008-2*) Boyds Mills Pr.

Roberts, Bethany. Waiting-for-Christmas Stories. Stapler, Sarah, illus. LC 93-11480. 1994. 13.95 (*0-395-67324-0*) HM.

Robinson, Ann. Cappy Claus. Hall, Constance, illus. 16p. (ps-6). 1992. pap. 4.95 (*0-9633373-0-0*) Chameleon FL.

Robinson, Barbara. The Best Christmas Pageant Ever. Brown, Judith G., illus. LC 72-76501. 96p. (gr. 3 up). 1972. 14.00 (*0-06-025043-7*); PLB 13.89 (*0-06-025044-5*) HarpC Child Bks.

—The Best Christmas Pageant Ever. Brown, Judith G., illus. LC 72-76501. 96p. (gr. 3 up). 1988. pap. 31.60 (*0-06-440278-9*, Trophy); pap. 3.95 (*0-685-44099-0*) HarpC Child Bks.

Rock, Gail. The House Without a Christmas Tree. Gehm, Charles, illus. LC 74-162. 96p. (gr. 2 up). 1974. lib. bdg. 9.99 (*0-394-92833-4*) Knopf Bks Yng Read.

—The House Without a Christmas Tree. (gr. 4-6). 1985. pap. 2.95 (*0-440-43394-0*, YB) Dell.

Rockwell, Norman, illus. Home for Christmas: An Advent Book. 1993. 13.99 (*0-525-44894-2*, DCB) Dutton Child Bks.

Rogers, Jacqueline. The Christmas Pageant. (Illus.). 32p. (ps-3). 1992. pap. 5.95 (*0-448-40256-4*, G&D) Putnam Pub Group.

Rogers, Jean. King Island Christmas. Munoz, Rie, illus. LC 84-25865. 32p. (gr. k-3). 1985. 13.00 (*0-688-04236-8*); lib. bdg. 12.93 (*0-688-04237-6*) Greenwillow.

Roos, Rogers. Crocodile Christmas. 1993. pap. 3.50 (*0-440-40872-5*) Dell.

Roos, Stephen. Crocodile Christmas: The Pet Lovers Club. Rogers, Jacqueline, illus. LC 91-47079. 128p. (gr. 3-6). 1992. 14.00 (*0-385-30681-4*) Delacorte.

Rosen, Michael J. Elijah's Angel. Robinson, A., illus. 1992. 13.95 (*0-15-225394-7*, HB Juv Bks) HarBrace.

Ross, Bill, illus. Silly Christmas Scenes. (ps-3). 1991. pap. 3.50 (*0-8249-8523-0*, Ideals Child) Hambleton-Hill.

Ross, Pat. M & M & the Santa Secrets. (Illus.). 1987. pap. 3.99 (*0-14-032222-1*, Puffin) Puffin Bks.

Roth, Susan L. Another Christmas. Roth, Susan L., illus. LC 91-33148. 32p. (gr. k). 1992. 15.00 (*0-688-09942-4*); PLB 14.93 (*0-688-09943-2*) Morrow Jr Bks.

Rotunno, Rocco & Rotunno, Betsy. How Snowshoe Saves Christmas. (Illus.). 12p. (Orig.). (gr. 2-6). 1993. mixed media pkg. incl. stamp pad, stamps, box of 4 crayons 7.00 (*1-881980-05-7*) Noteworthy.

—The Story of Christmas Tree Lane. (Illus.). 12p. (Orig.). (gr. 2-6). 1993. mixed media pkg. incl. stamp pad, stamps, box of 4 crayons 7.00 (*1-881980-04-9*) Noteworthy.

Russell, Georgina. Christmas Bear. Press, Jenny, illus. 28p. (ps-2). 1991. 8.95 (*0-7214-5331-7*, S808) Ladybird Bks.

Ryder, Joanne. First Grade Elves. Lewin, Betsy, illus. LC 93-25543. 32p. (ps-2). 1993. PLB 9.79 (*0-8167-3010-5*); pap. text ed. 2.95 (*0-8167-3011-3*) Troll Assocs.

Rylant, Cynthia. Children of Christmas: Stories for the Season. Schindler, Stephen D., illus. LC 87-1690. 48p. (gr. 3 up). 1993. pap. 5.95 (*0-531-07042-5*) Orchard Bks Watts.

—Mr. Putter & Tabby Bake the Cake. Howard, Arthur, illus. LC 94-9557. (gr. 1-5). 1994. 10.95 (*0-15-200205-7*); pap. 4.95 (*0-15-200214-6*) HarBrace.

Sabin, Fran & Sabin, Lou. The Great Santa Claus Mystery. Trivas, Irene, illus. LC 81-7530. 48p. (gr. 2-4). 1982. PLB 10.89 (*0-89375-602-4*); pap. text ed. 3.50 (*0-89375-603-2*) Troll Assocs.

Sadie Fields Productions Staff. On Christmas Eve. Ives, Penny, illus. 14p. 1992. 16.95 (*0-399-22148-4*, Putnam) Putnam Pub Group.

San Souci, Robert D. Christmas Ark. (gr. 4-7). 1991. 16.00 (*0-385-24836-9*) Doubleday.

Santa's New Sleigh. 10p. (gr. k-2). 1991. pap. 3.95 (*0-8167-2187-4*) Troll Assocs.

Santa's Take-along Library, 5 bks. (ps-3). 1992. Boxed set incls. The Christmas Story, Christmas Is Coming, The Smallest Elf, The Story of the Nutcracker Ballet, & The Night Before Christmas, 32p. ea. pap. 11.50 (*0-679-83864-3*) Random Bks Yng Read.

Santa's Workshop (Christmas Mini-Carousel in Three Dimensional Format) 1992. pop-up 4.95 (*0-8431-3439-9*) Price Stern.

Santoro, Christopher, illus. Rudolph the Red-Nosed Reindeer. LC 86-62550. 14p. (ps-1). 1987. 5.95 (*0-394-88923-1*) Random Bks Yng Read.

Sarlas-Fontana, Jane. The Adventures of Spero the Orthodox Church Mouse: The Nativity of Our Lord Christ's Birth. Simic, Tim, illus. 20p. (ps-4). 1992. pap. 6.95 (*0-937032-91-3*) Light&Life Pub Co MN.

Say, Allen. Tree of Cranes. Say, Allen, illus. 32p. (gr. k-3). 1991. 16.45 (*0-395-52024-X*, Sandpiper) HM.

Scholey, Arthur. Dickens Christmas Carol Show. 1979. 5.00 (*0-87602-119-4*) Anchorage.

Schotter, Roni. Efan the Great. Pate, Rodney, illus. LC 84-25070. 32p. (gr. 2-5). 1986. 12.95 (*0-688-04986-9*); PLB 12.88 (*0-688-04987-7*) Lothrop.

Schulz, Charles M. Snoopy & the Twelve Days of Christmas. (gr. 1 up). 9.95 (*0-317-13662-3*) Determined Prods.

Schur, Maxine R. Samantha's Surprise: A Christmas Story. Thieme, Jeanne, ed. Niles, Nancy & Lusk, Nancy N, illus. 72p. (gr. 2-5). 1986. PLB 12.95 (*0-937295-86-8*); pap. 5.95 (*0-937295-22-1*) Pleasant Co.

Schwartz, Carol. Little Juggler (Pop-Up) 1991. 3.95 (*0-8037-1020-8*) Dial Bks Young.

—Visit from Saint Nicholas (Pop Up) 1991. 3.95 (*0-8037-1019-4*) Dial Bks Young.

Scott, Beverly A. Santa's New Suit Funbook. (ps-6). 1973. pap. 3.00 (*0-686-11715-8*) B A Scott.

Scott, Bob. The Ugly Christmas Tree. MacDonald, Hugh, illus. LC 92-93614. 24p. (Orig.). (gr. 3-8). 1993. 7.95 (*0-9621201-1-1*); pap. 4.95 (*0-9621201-2-X*) B Scott Bks.

Sehlin, Gunhild. Mary's Little Donkey: A Christmas Story for Young Children. Latham, Hugh & Mackan, Donald, trs. Verheijn, Jan, illus. (SWE.). 157p. (gr. 3-6). 1992. pap. 10.95 (*0-86315-064-0*, Pub. by Floris Bks UK) Gryphon Hse.

Sharmat, Marjorie W. I'm Santa Claus & I'm Famous. Hafner, Marylin, illus. LC 90-55106. 32p. (ps-4). 1990. reinforced 14.95 (*0-8234-0826-4*) Holiday.

Sharp, Evelyn. Child's Christmas. 1991. 12.99 (*0-517-03369-0*) Random Hse Value.

Sharp, Mary. Bobbi Saves Christmas! Skar, Cynthia S., illus. 28p. (Orig.). (gr. 1-4). 1981. pap. 1.89 (*0-9603200-1-6*) Bobbi Ent.

Shaver, Beth. Little Friggles...the Search for Christmas. 21p. 1992. Personalized. text ed. 12.95 (*1-883842-03-4*); text ed. 7.95 (*1-883842-02-6*) Kids at Heart.

Shaw, Janet. Kirsten's Surprise: A Christmas Story. Thieme, Jeanne, ed. Graef, Renee, illus. 72p. (gr. 2-5). 1986. PLB 12.95 (*0-937295-85-X*); pap. 5.95 (*0-937295-19-1*) Pleasant Co.

Sheehan, Chris. Christmas Magic. LC 94-75616. (Illus.). 5p. (ps up). 1994. 16.95 (*1-85697-528-2*, Kingfisher LKC) LKC.

Sheppard, Dorothy M. & Sheppard, Jack G. Jo Jo the Elf Meets Santa's Enemy. Roxbury, David, et al, illus. 65p. (gr. 1-6). Date not set. PLB 12.95 (*0-9634300-1-7*); pap. 7.95 (*0-9634300-0-9*) D & J Arts Pubs. JO JO THE ELF MEETS SANTA'S ENEMY, a children's fantasy, opens a new frontier for Santa & a loveable elf named Jo Jo. Jo Jo is a woods elf from the Black Forest of Germany who sails with Santa on Christmas Eve to protect him from an evil wizard named Natanzo. Natanzo is determined to steal Santa's bag, which has special magical powers that any wizard would crave to possess. Jo Jo battles giant birds, monsters, dragons, & Natanzo, Master of Evil in order to save Santa's bag, so toys can be delivered to all the children of the world. It's an adventure from start to finish, as Jo Jo fights to defeat evil. He not only wins his battles, but is guaranteed to win the hearts of all ages & emerge to become a new Christmas hero for all time. This exciting book, with 27 beautiful full-color illustrations, will encourage children to read. How to order info: Baker & Taylor Books.
Publisher Provided Annotation.

Shpakow, Tanya. On the Way to Christmas. Shpakow, Tanya, illus. LC 90-5373. 40p. (ps-2). 1991. 15.00 (*0-679-81796-4*); lib. bdg. 15.99 (*0-679-91796-9*) Knopf Bks Yng Read.

Shura. Winter Dreams, Christmas Love. 1993. pap. 3.50 (*0-685-66037-0*) Scholastic Inc.

Siegenthaler, Kathrin. Santa Claus & the Woodcutter. Pfister, Marcus, illus. Crawford, Elizabeth, tr. LC 87-32203. (Illus.). 32p. (gr. k-3). 1988. 13.95 (*1-55858-027-1*) North-South Bks NYC.

Sight & Sound Staff. Santa's Narrow Escape Christmas Sound Story. (ps). 1991. 30.50 (*0-88704-205-8*) Sight & Sound.

Simon, Carly. Boy of the Bells. Datz, Margot, illus. 1990. 14.95 (*0-385-41587-7*); PLB 15.99 (*0-385-41736-5*) Doubleday.

Skocz, Anita J. Crystal Star Angel. Christy, Cynthia, illus. 48p. 1994. pap. 5.95t (*0-8091-6617-8*) Paulist Pr.

Slate, Joseph. How Little Porcupine Played Christmas. Bond, Felicia, illus. LC 81-43884. 32p. (ps-3). 1982. (Crowell Jr Bks) HarpC Child Bks.

—Who Is Coming to Our House? Wolff, Ashley, illus. LC 87-7319. 32p. (ps-1). 1988. PLB 14.95 (*0-399-21537-9*, Putnam) Putnam Pub Group.

Smalls-Hector, Irene. Irene Jennie & the Christmas Masquerade: The Johnkankus. Goodnight, Paul, illus. LC 93-7037. 1994. 15.95 (*0-316-79878-9*) Little.

Smith, Bruce. The Silver Locket: A Charleston Christmas Storybook. Smith, Bruce, illus. LC 94-78135. 110p. (Orig.). (ps up). 1994. pap. 11.95 (*0-9642620-0-2*) Marsh Wind Pr. Children's tales of the joy of the Christmas season set against a backdrop of America's most charming city. Share the wonder of a small boy who greets one of Claus' reindeer beneath the foggy, moss-shrouded oaks of Charleston's historic Battery; Meet Butter the golden retriever, who nurses an injured teal back to health in the marshes along the Ashley River; Ride cobbled streets with Magnolia, the carriage horse who refuses to pull without a carriage filled with children; Discover the magic of The Silver Locket, in which two young girls share a wondrous Charleston snowfall & learn the true meaning of the season. Ten stories by award-winning journalist, poet, & writer Bruce Smith - the Charleston correspondent for the Associated Press whose stories about Charleston & the South Carolina coast have been published throughout the South, across the nation & around the world. 110 page, perfect bound trade paperback. Illustrated with black & white renderings of Charleston scenes. Cover illuminated in silver, red & black. $11.95 retail. To order: Marsh Wind Press, Box 1596, Mount Pleasant, SC 29465. 803-884-5957.
Publisher Provided Annotation.

Smith, George S. The Christmas Eve Cattle Drive. Bacon, Eliza, illus. 32p. (gr. 1-4). 1991. pap. 3.95 (*0-89015-820-7*) Sunbelt Media.

Smith, Janice L. There's a Ghost in the Coatroom: Adam Joshua's Christmas. Gackenbach, Dick, illus. LC 90-23068. 96p. (gr. 1-4). 1991. 12.95 (*0-06-022863-6*); PLB 12.89 (*0-06-022864-4*) HarpC Child Bks.

Smithson, T. K. How Reindeer Fly. LC 93-85737. 24p. (ps-3). 1993. pap. 8.50 (*1-884291-00-7*) Stardust NC.

Snowman's Christmas Surprise. 12p. (ps). 1991. pap. 2.95 (*0-8167-2190-4*) Troll Assocs.

Society of Brothers Staff, ed. Behold That Star: A Christmas Anthology: A Collection of Fifteen Christmas Stories. 3rd ed. Maendel, Maria A., illus. LC 67-25968. 368p. (gr. 4 up). 1966. 17.00 (*0-87486-003-2*) Plough.

Solotareff, Gregoire. Noel's Christmas Secret. 1989. 13.95 (*0-374-35544-4*) FS&G.

Soto, Gary. Too Many Tamales. Martinez, Ed, illus. 32p. (ps-3). 1993. 14.95 (*0-399-22146-8*, Putnam) Putnam Pub Group.

Speare, Jean. A Candle for Christmas. Blades, Ann, illus. LC 86-61560. 32p. (gr. k-4). 1987. SBE 13.95 (*0-689-50417-9*, M K McElderry) Macmillan Child Grp.

Speirs, John, illus. The Twelve Days of Christmas. 24p. (Orig.). (ps-3). 1992. pap. 4.99 (*0-679-82730-7*) Random Bks Yng Read.

Spier, Peter. Peter Spier's Christmas! Spier, Peter, illus. LC 80-2875. 40p. (ps up). 1983. PLB 13.95 (*0-385-13184-4*); pap. 14.95 (*0-385-13183-6*) Doubleday.

—Peter Spier's Christmas! Spier, Peter, illus. 48p. (ps-5). 1992. 4.99 (*0-440-40730-3*, YB) Dell.

Spohn, Kate. Christmas at Anna's. Spohn, Kate, illus. 32p. (ps-3). 1993. 13.99 (*0-670-84895-6*) Viking Child Bks.

Squeaky Sneaker Books Staff. Mystery of the Crazy Christmas Angel. (ps-3). 1993. pap. 3.95 (*1-56233-177-9*, Squeaky Sneaker) Star Song TN.

Stack, Richard L. The Doggonest Christmas. Stack, Charles W., illus. 48p. (gr. k-6). 1989. 16.95 (*0-9605400-6-7*) Four Seas Bk. In THE DOGGONEST CHRISTMAS, Josh is only a mutt, but he dreams of being something better. He lives with Miss Elly, a kind lady who believes in dreams & helps him seek his fortune. The little dog triumphs over pessimism, both for himself & his doubting friends. This endearing story is a classic & is enjoyed by all ages. In the sequel, DOGGONEST VACATION (0-9628262-0-0), Josh travels to Maryland, where he meets Trevor, a Chesapeake Bay Retriever who doesn't want to be a hunting dog. Josh teaches his new friend to believe in himself & to trust others. In DOGGONEST PUPPY LOVE (0-9628262-1-9), Josh falls in love with Millie, the first dog. He & Miss Elly travel to Washington, D.C., where Josh & Millie have an exciting adventure. The story proves the power of faith. Josh, Mr. Stack's real life friend, has followed these titles with his autobiography, JOSH, THE STORY OF THE WONDER DOG (0-9628262-5-1). This is the true story of how Josh wandered into the author's life & changed the course of history. For information about school visits, or to order, call Windmill Press at 1-800-932-6112.
Publisher Provided Annotation.

Sterchele, Christina L., illus. Twelve Days of Christmas. (ps-6). 1981. 3.50 (*0-913545-07-4*) Moonlight FL.

Stevenson, James. The Night after Christmas. LC 81-1022. (Illus.). 32p. (gr. k-3). 1981. 15.00 (*0-688-00547-0*); PLB 14.93 (*0-688-00548-9*) Greenwillow.

—The Oldest Elf. LC 94-25355. 1995. write for info. (*0-688-13755-5*); write for info. (*0-688-13756-3*) Greenwillow.

—The Worst Person's Christmas. LC 90-39716. (Illus.). 32p. (ps up). 1991. 14.00 (*0-688-10210-7*); PLB 13.88 (*0-688-10211-5*) Greenwillow.

Stevenson, Sucie. Christmas Eve. Stevenson, Sucie, illus. 32p. (ps-2). 1992. pap. 4.99 (*0-440-40729-X*, YB) Dell.

Stock, Catherine. Christmas Time. Stock, Catherine, illus. LC 89-71249. 32p. (ps-1). 1990. SBE 11.95 (*0-02-788403-1*, Bradbury Pr) Macmillan Child Grp.

—Christmas Time. Stock, Catherine, illus. LC 92-42225. 32p. (ps-1). 1993. pap. 3.95 (*0-689-71725-3*, Aladdin) Macmillan Child Grp.

Stone, Jon & Bailey, Joe. Christmas Eve on Sesame Street. Mathieu, Joe, illus. LC 81-50247. 64p. (ps-2). 1981. 7.95 (*0-394-84733-4*); (Random Juv) Random Bks Yng Read.

Stortz, Diane. A One-Two-Three Christmas. Munger, Nancy, illus. 28p. (ps-k). 1993. 4.99 (*0-7847-0064-8*, 24-03844) Standard Pub.

Story of Christmas. (ps-2). 1978. incl. tape 6.99 (*0-89191-602-4*, 26021, Chariot Bks) Chariot Family.

Story Time Stories That Rhyme Staff. Christmas Stories That Rhyme. Story Time Stories That Rhyme Staff, illus. 39p. (gr. 4-7). 1992. binder 19.95 (*1-56820-015-3*) Story Time.

Stout, Robert T. The Noorps Are Coming. Stout, Robert T., illus. 32p. (ps-6). 1982. pap. 3.95 (*0-911049-05-3*) Yuletide Intl.

Sturgis, Matthew. Tosca's Christmas. Mortimer, Anne, illus. 1989. 11.95 (*0-8037-0722-3*) Dial Bks Young.

—Tosca's Christmas. Mortimer, Anne, illus. 32p. (ps-3). 1992. pap. 3.99 (*0-14-054840-8*, Puff Pied Piper) Puffin Bks.

Summers, Jack L. The Christmas People. LC 88-51480. 180p. 1988. 7.95 (*1-55523-208-6*) Winston-Derek.

Tanner, Suzy-Jane. Twelve Days of Christmas. Tanner, Suzy-Jane, illus. 31p. (ps). 1993. Repr. 4.95 (*1-882607-11-2*) Merrybooks VA.

Taylor, T. Maria: A Christmas Story. 1992. 13.95 (*0-15-217763-9*, HB Juv Bks) HarBrace.

Tazewell. Littlest Angel. new ed. 32p. 1991. 15.95 (*0-516-09218-9*) Childrens.

Tazewell, Charles. The Littlest Angel. 32p. (gr. k-4). 1985. pap. 6.95 (*0-89542-923-3*, Ideals Child) Hambleton-Hill.

—The Littlest Angel. Micich, Paul, illus. LC 91-2442. 32p. (gr. k-4). 1991. 14.95 (*0-8249-8516-8*, Ideals Child) Hambleton-Hill.

Teddy Bear's Christmas. (gr. k-2). 1991. pap. 2.95 (*0-8167-2191-2*) Troll Assocs.

Tews, Susan. Gingerbread Doll. 32p. (ps-3). 1993. 14.95 (*0-395-56438-7*, Clarion Bks) HM.

Thacker, Nola. Till's Christmas. 144p. 1991. 13.95 (*0-590-43542-6*, Scholastic Hardcover) Scholastic Inc.

—Till's Christmas. 1992. 2.95 (*0-590-43543-4*, Apple Paperbacks) Scholastic Inc.

Tharlet, Eve. Christmas Won't Wait. Clements, Andrew, tr. from FRE. (Illus.). (gr. k up). 1991. pap. 14.95 (*0-88708-151-7*) Picture Bk Studio.

Thomas, Dylan. A Child's Christmas in Wales. Hyman, Trina S., illus. LC 85-766. 48p. (gr. 4-6). 1985. reinforced bdg. 14.95 (*0-8234-0565-6*) Holiday.

—A Conversation about Christmas. 1991. PLB 13.95 (*0-88682-468-0*) Creative Ed.

Thomas, Joan G. The Christmas Angel. Thomas, Joan G., illus. 20p. (gr. 1-5). 1988. pap. 3.95 (*0-8192-1429-9*) Morehouse Pub.

Thompson, R. W., Jr. The Christmas Eve Tradition. Keitz, Roderick K., illus. 16p. (ps-3). 1993. PLB 8.95 (*0-9636442-1-1*) N Pole Chron.

Thomson, Clarence. The Little Pine Tree's Christmas Dream. Laughlin, Denise D., illus. LC 93-5301. 32p. (Orig.). (gr. 1-6). 1993. pap. 4.95 (*0-8091-6614-3*) Paulist Pr.

Tift, Tom. Santa & the Captain: A Mystic Christmas Tale. Clover, Barbara, illus. LC 89-81337. 24p. (Orig.). (gr. 2-4). 1989. pap. 6.95 (*0-9624607-0-2*) Hickory Ridge Pr.

Tolstoy, Leo. Papa Panov's Special Day. 2nd ed. Molder, Mig, retold by. Morris, Tony, illus. 32p. 1988. 11.95 (*0-7459-1358-X*) Lion USA.

Tompert, Ann. A Carol for Christmas. Kelly, Laura, illus. LC 94-9039. (gr. k-3). 1994. 14.95 (*0-02-789402-9*) Macmillan.

—The Silver Whistle. Peck, Beth, illus. LC 88-1446. 32p. (gr. k-3). 1988. RSBE 14.95 (*0-02-789160-7*, Macmillan Child Bk) Macmillan Child Grp.

Tornqvist, Rita. The Christmas Carp. Kilburn, Greta, tr. Tornqvist, Marit, illus. 32p. (gr. k-3). 1990. 13.95 (*91-29-59784-6*, Pub. by R & S Bks) FS&G.

Tripp, Valerie. Molly's Surprise: A Christmas Story. Thieme, Jeanne, ed. Payne, C. F., illus. 72p. (gr. 2-5). 1986. PLB 12.95 (*0-937295-87-6*); pap. 5.95 (*0-937295-25-6*) Pleasant Co.

Trivas, Irene. Emma's Christmas: An Old Song Re-sung & Pictured. LC 88-1640. (Illus.). 32p. (ps-2). 1988. 14.95 (*0-531-05780-1*); PLB 14.99 (*0-531-08380-2*) Orchard Bks Watts.

—Emma's Christmas: An Old Song Re-sung & Pictured. LC 88-1640. (Illus.). 32p. (ps-2). 1992. pap. 5.95 (*0-531-07022-0*) Orchard Bks Watts.

Troll Staff. Christmas Countdown. 10p. (ps). 1991. pap. 3.95 (*0-8167-2183-1*) Troll Assocs.

Trosclair. A Cajun Night Before Christmas. Jacobs, Howard, ed. Rice, James, illus. LC 74-151725. 48p. (gr. 6-12). 1973. 12.95 (*0-88289-002-6*) Pelican.

Tudor, Tasha. Becky's Christmas. Tudor, Tasha, illus. LC 91-61679. 46p. (gr. 3 up). with autograph 25.00 (*0-9621753-5-8*) Jenny Wren Pr.

—Dolls' Christmas. Tudor, Tasha, illus. LC 59-12744. (gr. k-3). 1979. 6.95 (*0-8098-1026-3*); pap. 4.95 (*0-8098-2912-6*) McKay.

Turner, Barbie C. Hark the Herald Angels Sing. (ps-6). 1993. pap. 17.00 (*0-671-87146-3*, S&S BFYR) S&S Trade.

Turner, Thomas N. Hillbilly Night Afore Christmas. Rice, James, illus. LC 83-4120. 32p. (gr. 1-6). 1983. 12.95 (*0-88289-367-X*) Pelican.

The Twelve Days of Christmas. (Illus.). 24p. (gr. k-3). 1992. pap. 2.50 (*1-56144-164-3*, Honey Bear Bks) Modern Pub NYC.

Two-Minute Christmas Stories. (Illus.). 36p. (ps-1). 1989. write for info. (*0-307-12188-7*, Pub. by Golden Bks) Western Pub.

Tyler, Linda W. After Christmas Tree. (ps-3). 1990. 12.95 (*0-670-83045-3*) Viking Child Bks.

—The After-Christmas Tree. Davis, Susan, illus. LC 92-8616. (gr. 4 up). 1992. 3.99 (*0-14-054191-8*) Puffin Bks.

Ungerer, Tomi. Christmas Eve at the Mellops. Ungerer, Tomi, illus. 32p. (gr. k-3). 1992. pap. 3.99 (*0-440-40728-1*, YB) Dell.

Upton, Richard & Fair, Sharon. The Search for the Smell of Christmas. Buerkle, Bonnie K., illus. 32p. 1992. 14.95x (*0-9633348-0-8*) Aromatique.

Uttley, Alison. Stories for Christmas. Lines, Kathleen, ed. Rowes, Gavin, illus. 128p. (gr. 3-7). 1991. pap. 4.95 (*0-571-16321-1*) Faber & Faber.

Van Allsburg, Chris. Polar Express. Van Allsburg, Chris, illus. LC 85-10907. 32p. (gr. 2 up). 1985. 17.45 (*0-395-38949-6*) HM.

Van DeWeyer, Robert & Spenceley, Annabel. The Shepherd's Son. LC 92-40284. 24p. (gr. k-3). 1993. 10.00 (*0-8170-1188-9*) Judson.

Van Dyke, Henry. The Other Wise Man. Kennedy, Pamela, adapted by. Barrett, Robert, illus. 32p. (ps-3). 1992. pap. 4.95 (*0-8249-8564-8*, Ideals Child) Hambleton-Hill.

Van Leeuwen, Jean. The Great Christmas Kidnapping Caper. Kellogg, Steven, illus. LC 75-9201. 144p. (gr. 2-6). 1975. 12.95 (*0-685-01454-1*) Dial Bks Young.

—The Great Christmas Kidnapping Caper. Kellogg, Steven, illus. 172p. (gr. 3 up). 1990. pap. 3.99 (*0-14-034287-7*, Puffin) Puffin Bks.

—Oliver & Amanda's Christmas. Schweninger, Ann, illus. 9.95 (*0-685-29542-7*) Dial Bks Young.

—Oliver & Amanda's Christmas. 1989. 9.95 (*0-8037-0636-7*); PLB 9.89 (*0-8037-0647-2*) Dial Bks Young.

—Oliver & Amanda's Christmas. Schweninger, Ann, illus. 56p. (ps-3). 1992. pap. 3.99 (*0-14-054566-2*, Dial Easy to Read) Puffin Bks.

VanRynbach, Iris. Cecily's Christmas. LC 87-34083. (Illus.). 32p. (ps-1). 1988. 11.95 (*0-688-07832-X*); lib. bdg. 11.88 (*0-688-07833-8*) Greenwillow.

Vernon, Judy L. All Ears: A Christmas Story. 25p. (Orig.). (gr. 2-8). 1989. pap. 4.95 (*0-9617776-4-8*) J Vernon.

Verschuren, Ineke, compiled by. The Christmas Story Book. 430p. (gr. 4-8). Repr. of 1986 ed. 29.50 (*0-86315-077-2*, Pub. by Floris Bks UK) Gryphon Hse.

Vincent, Gabrielle. Merry Christmas, Ernest & Celestine. Vincent, Gabrielle, illus. LC 83-14155. 32p. (gr. k-3). 1984. PLB 11.88 (*0-688-02605-2*); 12.00 (*0-688-02606-0*) Greenwillow.

Vreeman, J. We Wish You a Merry Christmas. (Illus.). 16p. (Orig.). 1985. pap. 3.95 (*0-918789-02-8*) FreeMan Prods.

Waddell, Martin. Daisy's Christmas. 1993. pap. 3.99 (*0-440-40876-8*) Dell.

Wahl, Jan. Emily Rosebush's Snowflake: A Christmas Story. Wahl, Jan, illus. LC 94-22713. 32p. (gr. k-3). 1995. pap. 2.25 (*0-8167-3573-5*, Whistlestop) Troll Assocs.

Wainwright, Richard M. Poofin: The Cloud That Cried on Christmas. Crompton, Jack, illus. 40p. 1989. Repr. 13.00g (*0-9619566-1-5*) Family Life.

Waldman, Bryna, illus. The First Christmas. 48p. 1992. 9.95 (*0-88101-229-7*) Unicorn Pub.

—The First Christmas. 48p. 1992. 12.95 (*0-88101-239-4*) Unicorn Pub.

Waldrop, Ruth. Santa Grows up in Mother Goose Land. Hendrix, Hurston H., illus. 34p. (ps-3). 1986. pap. 4.95 (*0-9616894-0-4*); cassette incl. RuSk Inc.

Wallace, Bill. The Christmas Spurs. LC 90-55111. 128p. (gr. 3-7). 1990. 14.95 (*0-8234-0831-0*) Holiday.

—The Christmas Spurs. MacDonald, Patricia, ed. De Rosa, Dee, illus. 128p. (gr. 3-7). 1991. pap. 3.50 (*0-671-74505-0*, Minstrel Bks) PB.

Walt Disney Company Staff. Disney's Christmas Stories. (Illus.). (ps-1). 1989. Contains "Donald Duck's Christmas Tree," "Santa's Toy Shop," & "Mickey's Christmas Carol" write for info. (*0-307-15750-4*, Golden Pr) Western Pub.

—Reindeer Round-Up: A Merry Christmas at the North Pole. Walt Disney Company Staff, illus. 26p. (ps up). 1988. 19.95 (*1-55578-313-9*) Worlds Wonder.

Walter, Mildred P. Have a Happy... Byard, Carole, illus. LC 88-8962. 144p. (gr. 3-6). 1989. 10.95 (*0-688-06923-1*) Lothrop.

Warren, Jean. Huff & Puff's Foggy Christmas: A Totline Teaching Tale. Cubley, Kathleen, ed. Piper, Molly & Ekberg, Jean, illus. LC 93-38780. 32p. (Orig.). (ps-2). 1994. 12.95 (*0-911019-97-9*); pap. text ed. 5.95 (*0-911019-96-0*) Warren Pub Hse.

Waterston, Ellen. Barney's Joy. Pearce, Molly, illus. 32p. 1991. Repr. of 1990 ed. text ed. 14.95 (*0-9628129-2-7*) Sagebrush Bks.

Watson, Clyde. How Brown Mouse Kept Christmas. Watson, Wendy, illus. LC 80-18532. 32p. (ps-3). 1980. 10.00 (*0-374-33494-3*) FS&G.

Wedell, Robert F. Rolf & the Rainbow Christmas. M. J. Art Concepts Staff, illus. LC 89-91971. 133p. (Orig.). 1989. pap. 5.00 (*0-9625221-1-2*) Milrob Pr.

Wells, Joel. The Manger Mouse. Anderson, Annette B., illus. (gr. k-5). 1990. 15.95 (*0-88347-255-4*) Thomas More.

Wells, Rosemary. Max's Christmas. Wells, Rosemary, illus. LC 85-27547. 32p. (ps-2). 1986. 9.95 (*0-8037-0289-2*); PLB 9.89 (*0-8037-0290-6*) Dial Bks Young.

Wells, Ruth & Van Dyke, Henry, eds. The Other Wise Man. Moser, Barry, illus. LC 93-16259. (ps-8). 1993. 16.95 (*0-88708-329-3*) Picture Bk Studio.

Welser, Matthew W. God Promised Us a Savior. (Illus.). 24p. (ps-4). 1989. pap. 1.99 (*0-570-09019-9*, 59-1442) Concordia.

West, Irene C. Most Loved Christmas Stories. 96p. (gr. k-10). 1992. pap. 7.95 (*0-9632452-7-9*) Design Pub UT.

Westall, Robert. Christmas Spirit: Two Stories. Lawrence, John, illus. LC 94-9847. (gr. 3 up). 1994. 14.00 (*0-374-31260-5*) FS&G.

Wiggin, Kate D. The Birds' Christmas Carol. (Illus.). (gr. 4-6). 14.95 (*0-395-07205-0*) HM.

—The Birds' Christmas Carol. (Illus.). 69p. 1990. Repr. of 1886 ed. 15.95 (*0-9616844-6-1*) Greenhouse Pub.

Wilder, Laura Ingalls. A Little House Christmas: Holiday Stories from the Little House Books. Williams, Garth, illus. LC 93-24537. 96p. (gr. 3-7). 1994. 18.95 (*0-06-024269-8*); PLB 18.89 (*0-06-024270-1*) HarpC Child Bks.

Wilder, Laura Ingalls, adapted by. Christmas in the Big Woods. Graef, Renee, illus. LC 94-14478. 1995. 12.00 (*0-06-024752-5*, HarpT); PLB 11.89 (*0-06-024753-3*) HarpC Child Bks.

Wildsmith, Brian. A Christmas Story. Wildsmith, Brian, illus. LC 89-7959. 32p. (ps-3). 1989. 15.95 (*0-679-80074-3*) Knopf Bks Yng Read.

—A Christmas Story. Wildsmith, Brian, illus. LC 89-7959. (ps-3). 1993. 6.99 (*0-679-84726-X*) Knopf Bks Yng Read.

Wilhelm, Hans. Schnitzel's First Christmas. (Illus.). 1989. pap. 13.95 jacketed (*0-671-67977-5*, S&S BFYR) S&S Trade.

—Schnitzel's First Christmas. LC 89-5858. (Illus.). 40p. (ps-1). 1991. pap. 5.00 (*0-671-74494-1*, S&S BFYR) S&S Trade.

—Waldo, Tell Me about Christmas. (Illus.). 40p. (gr. 3 up). 1989. 4.95 (*0-8378-1846-X*) Gibson.

Wilkins, Joyce R. & Hawkins, Edeltraud. The Animal Market. LC 93-25202. 1993. 8.95 (*1-880373-06-8*) Pictorial Herit.

Windsor, Patricia. The Christmas Killer. 192p. 1991. 13.95 (*0-590-43311-3*, Scholastic Hardcover) Scholastic Inc.

—The Christmas Killer. 1992. pap. 3.25 (*0-590-43310-5*) Scholastic Inc.

—Very Weird & Moogly Christmas. (gr. 4-7). 1991. pap. 3.25 (*0-440-40528-9*, YB) Dell.

Winter, Alice S. Christmas Memories. 1994. 7.95 (*0-533-10785-7*) Vantage.

Winter, Jeanette. The Christmas Tree Ship. LC 93-36341. (Illus.). 32p. (ps up). 1994. PLB 14.95 (*0-399-22693-1*, Philomel Bks) Putnam Pub Group.

Winthrop, Elizabeth. Bear's Christmas Surprise. Brewster, Patience, illus. LC 90-26414. 32p. (ps-3). 1991. reinforced 14.95 (*0-8234-0888-4*) Holiday.

—A Child Is Born: The Christmas Story. Mikolaycak, Charles, photos by. LC 82-11728. (Illus.). 32p. (ps-3). 1983. reinforced bdg. 15.95 (*0-8234-0472-2*) Holiday.

Wolf, Jill & Moore, Clement C. Teddy Bears Night Before Christmas. Rudegeair, Jean, illus. 24p. (gr. 3-6). 1985. pap. 2.50 (*0-89954-330-8*) Antioch Pub Co.

Wolff, Ashley. Year of Beasts. LC 85-27419. (Illus.). 32p. (ps-1). 1989. pap. 3.95 (*0-525-44541-2*, DCB) Dutton Child Bks.

World's Best Christmas Stories. LC 93-27249. (Illus.). 80p. (gr. 4-6). 1993. pap. 1.95 (*0-8167-3142-X*, Pub. by Watermill Pr) Troll Assocs.

Worley, Daryl. Billy & the Christmas Present. Daab, John, illus. 32p. (gr. 2-4). 1989. 9.95 (*0-924067-01-2*) Tyke Corp.

Worth, Valerie. At Christmastime. Frasconi, Antonio, illus. LC 92-52693. 32p. (gr. k up). 1992. 15.00 (*0-06-205019-2*); PLB 14.89 (*0-06-205020-6*) HarpC Child Bks.

Yeomans, Thomas. For Every Child a Star: A Christmas Story. De Paola, Tomie, illus. LC 84-499. 32p. (ps-3). 1986. reinforced bdg. 14.95 (*0-8234-0526-5*) Holiday.

Yolen, Jane, ed. Hark! A Christmas Sampler. De Paola, Tomie, illus. LC 90-42865. 128p. 1991. 19.95 (*0-399-21853-X*, Putnam) Putnam Pub Group.

Yorinks, Arthur. Christmas in July. Egielski, Richard, illus. LC 91-55244. 32p. (ps-3). 1991. 14.95 (*0-06-020256-4*); PLB 14.89 (*0-06-020257-2*) HarpC Child Bks.

Young, William E. Ringle & Dingle: Santa's Christmas Elves. Hillenbach, Patricia, illus. 32p. (Orig.). 1991. pap. 5.95 (*0-9628122-1-8*) Pautuxet Pubns.

Zeplin, Zeno. Great Texas Christmas Legends. 2nd ed. Jones, Judy, illus. 156p. (gr. 4 up). 1987. 15.95 (*0-9615760-2-2*); pap. 7.95 (*0-9615760-3-0*) Nel-Mar Pub.

Ziefert, Harriet. Nicky's Christmas Surprise. Brown, Richard, illus. LC 85-5681. 20p. (ps). 1985. pap. 5.99 (*0-14-050555-5*, Puffin) Puffin Bks.

—Scooter's Christmas. Brown, Richard, illus. 16p. (ps-k). 1993. 10.95 (*0-694-00484-7*, Festival) HarpC Child Bks.

Zolotow, Charlotte. The Beautiful Christmas Tree. Robbins, Ruth, illus. 32p. (gr. k-3). 1983. 13.95 (*0-395-27676-4*); pap. 4.95 (*0-395-34925-7*) HM.

CHRISTMAS–POETRY
see Christmas Poetry
CHRISTMAS CARDS
see Greeting Cards
CHRISTMAS CAROLS
see Carols
CHRISTMAS COOKERY

Corwin, Judith H. Christmas Around the World. LC 93-6567. (gr. 3 up). 1995. lib. bdg. 13.00 (*0-671-87239-7*, J Messner); lib. bdg. 6.95 (*0-671-87240-0*) S&S Trade.
—Christmas Crafts. LC 93-6366. (Illus.). (gr. k-4). Date not set. PLB write for info. (*0-531-11149-0*) Watts.
Presilla, Maricel. Feliz Nochebuena Feliz Navidad: Christmas Feasts of the Hispanic Caribbean. (gr. 2-6). 1994. 15.95 (*0-8050-2512-X*) H Holt & Co.

CHRISTMAS DECORATIONS

Barth, Edna. Holly, Reindeer, & Colored Lights: The Story of the Christmas Symbols. Arndt, Ursula, illus. LC 71-157731. 96p. (gr. 3-6). 1979. 15.45 (*0-395-28842-8*, Calrion Bks) HM.
Berger, Thomas. The Christmas Craft Book. Lawson, Polly, tr. (Illus.). 86p. 1990. pap. 12.95 (*0-86315-110-8*, Pub. by Floris Bks UK) Gryphon Hse.
Christmas Decorations: Make & Color Your Own. (ps-3). 1989. pap. 1.95 (*0-89375-645-8*) Troll Assocs.
Corwin, Judith H. Christmas Around the World. LC 93-6567. (gr. 3 up). 1995. lib. bdg. 13.00 (*0-671-87239-7*, J Messner); lib. bdg. 6.95 (*0-671-87240-0*) S&S Trade.
—Christmas Crafts. LC 93-6366. (Illus.). (gr. k-4). Date not set. PLB write for info. (*0-531-11149-0*) Watts.
Crespi, Francesca. Christmas Decorations. 16p. 1992. pap. 7.95 (*0-8249-8529-X*, Ideals Child) Hambleton-Hill.
Crowther, Robert. Punchout Christmas Decorations. 1989. pap. 5.95 (*0-671-68400-0*) S&S Trade.
Cusick, Dawn. Fabric Lovers' Christmas Scrapcrafts. LC 93-10659. (Illus.). 128p. (gr. 10-12). 1993. 24.95 (*0-8069-0437-2*, Pub. by Lark Bks) Sterling.
Delamare, David, illus. Twelve Days of Christmas. 48p. 1992. 12.95 (*0-88101-238-6*) Unicorn Pub.
De Paola, Tomie. The Family Christmas Tree Book. LC 80-12081. (Illus.). 32p. (ps-3). 1980. reinforced bdg. 15.95 (*0-8234-0416-1*); pap. 5.95 (*0-8234-0535-4*) Holiday.
Fowler, Virginia. Christmas Crafts & Customs Around the World. Fowler, Virginia, illus. LC 84-9770. 180p. (gr. 5 up). 1988. (S&S BFYR); (S&S BFYR) S&S Trade.
Green, Jen. Making Masks & Crazy Faces. LC 92-9813. 1992. 12.40 (*0-531-17365-8*, Gloucester Pr) Watts.
Greene, George W. Christmas Books & Ornaments. Hatter, Laurie, illus. (ps). 1993. Gift box set of 4 bks., 12p. ea. bds. 14.95 (*1-56828-041-6*) Red Jacket Pr.
Henderson, Kathy. Christmas Trees. LC 89-859. (Illus.). 48p. (gr. k-4). 1989. PLB 12.85 (*0-516-01162-6*); pap. 4.95 (*0-516-41162-4*) Childrens.
Kingshead Corporation Staff. Cut, Color & Create: Make Your Own: Christmas Garland. Kingshead Corporation Staff, illus. 24p. (ps-2). 1987. pap. 2.97 (*1-55941-020-5*) Kingshead Corp.
—Cut, Color & Create: Make Your Own: Christmas Ornaments. Kingshead Corporation Staff, illus. 24p. (gr. 2 up). 1987. pap. 2.97 (*1-55941-018-3*) Kingshead Corp.
—Cut, Color & Create: Make Your Own: Christmas Snowflakes. Kingshead Corporation Staff, illus. 24p. (gr. 3 up). 1987. pap. 2.97 (*1-55941-019-1*) Kingshead Corp.
—Cut, Color & Create: Make Your Own: Easy Christmas Ornaments. Kingshead Corporation Staff, illus. 24p. (ps-2). 1987. pap. 2.97 (*1-55941-016-7*) Kingshead Corp.
—Cut, Color & Create: Make Your Own: Farm. Kingshead Corporation Staff, illus. 24p. (ps-4). 1987. pap. 2.97 (*1-55941-007-8*) Kingshead Corp.
—Cut, Color & Create: Make Your Own: Masks. Kingshead Corporation Staff, illus. 24p. (ps-4). 1988. pap. 2.97 (*0-685-22520-8*) Kingshead Corp.
—Cut, Color & Create: Make Your Own: Number People. Kingshead Corporation Staff, illus. 24p. (ps-3). 1987. pap. 2.97 (*1-55941-004-3*) Kingshead Corp.
—Cut, Color & Create: Make Your Own: Number Blocks. Kingshead Corporation Staff, illus. 24p. (ps-3). 1987. pap. 2.97 (*1-55941-006-X*) Kingshead Corp.
LaRose-Weaver, Diane & Cusick, Dawn. Fireside Christmas: Celebrate the Holidays with More Than 120 Festive Projects to Make. LC 92-37316. (Illus.). 160p. (gr. 8 up). 1992. 26.95 (*0-8069-8378-7*, Pub. by Lark Bks) Sterling.
Malone, Maggie. Christmas Scrapcrafts. (Illus.). 136p. (gr. 5-10). 1992. pap. 12.95 (*0-8069-6805-2*) Sterling.
Munro, Roxie. Christmastime in New York City. (Illus.). 32p. (ps-3). 1994. pap. 5.99 (*0-14-050462-1*) Puffin Bks.
Murray, Anna. My Christmas Craft Book. 1993. 9.99 (*0-307-16750-X*) Western Pub.
National Gallery, London. Christmas Decorations. (Illus.). (gr. 8 up). 1993. pap. 12.95 (*0-316-59890-9*) Little.
Robins, Deri & Buchanan, George. Santa's Sackful of Best Christmas Ideas. LC 92-41103. 32p. (gr. 2-6). 1993. pap. 5.95 (*1-85697-919-9*, Kingfisher LKC) LKC.
Robson, Denny A. Christmas: Activities & Projects. LC 92-3214. 1992. 11.90 (*0-531-17333-X*, Gloucester Pr) Watts.
Supraner, Robyn. Merry Christmas: Things to Make & Do. Barto, Renzo, illus. LC 80-23884. 48p. (gr. 1-5). 1981. PLB 11.89 (*0-89375-422-6*); pap. 3.50 (*0-89375-423-4*) Troll Assocs.
Taylor, Carol. Christmas Naturals: Ornaments, Wreaths & Decorations. LC 91-17552. (Illus.). 128p. (gr. 8 up). 1992. pap. 14.95 (*0-8069-8361-2*) Sterling.
Walton, Sally & Walton, Stewart. Christmas Stencils. (Illus.). (gr. 1 up). 1993. pap. 6.95 (*0-688-12942-0*, Tupelo Bks) Morrow.
Wegrzecki, Lester L. Christmas Decoration: Eggshell-Wydmuszki. Chrypinski, Anna, intro. by. (Illus., Orig.). (gr. 4 up). 1987. pap. write for info. (*0-9620774-0-2*) L L Wegrzecki.

CHRISTMAS ENTERTAINMENTS
see also Christmas Plays

Bishop, Roma, illus. Christmas Songs & Prayers for Children. 32p. (ps). 1993. 3.98 (*0-8317-5168-1*) Smithmark.
Chancellor, Betty. A Child's Christmas Cookbook. Obering, Kay & Nast, Thomas, illus. 40p. (Orig.). (gr. 1-8). 1969. pap. 4.00 (*0-914510-00-2*) Evergreen.
Christmas Delights. 12p. (gr. 1-6). 1971. pap. 3.25 (*0-914510-02-9*) Evergreen.
Elish, Dan. My Christmas Stocking: Stories, Songs, Poems, Recipes, Crafts & Fun for Kids. Bernardin, James, illus. Palubniak, Nancy, photos by. (Illus.). 80p. (ps-3). 1993. 9.98 (*0-8317-5173-8*) Smithmark.
Folmer, A. P. Fabulous Christmas Fun Book. (gr. 4-7). 1993. pap. 3.95 (*0-590-46476-0*) Scholastic Inc.
Hill, G. L. The Best Birthday: A Christmas Entertainment for Children. (gr. 5-6). 13.95 (*0-89190-404-2*, Pub. by Am Repr) Amereon Ltd.
Menotti, Gian-Carlo. Amahl & the Night Visitors. Lemieux, Michele, illus. LC 84-27196. 64p. (ps up). 1986. 15.00 (*0-688-05426-9*); lib. bdg. 14.88 (*0-688-05427-7*, Morrow Jr Bks) Morrow Jr Bks.
The New Christmas Fun Book. (Illus.). 32p. (gr. 1-7). 1992. pap. 5.99 (*0-7459-2247-3*) Lion USA.
Schlegl, William. Bible Christmas Puzzles. Van Kanegan, Jeff, illus. 48p. (gr. 3 up). 1987. pap. 7.95 (*0-86653-409-1*, SS 884, Shining Star Pubns) Good Apple.
Thomas, Dylan. A Child's Christmas in Wales. Ardizzone, Edward, illus. LC 80-66216. 48p. 1980. 14. 95 (*0-87923-339-7*); pap. 9.95 (*0-87923-529-2*) Godine.
Wax, Wendy, compiled by. A Treasury of Christmas Poems, Carols, & Games to Share. Spier, John, illus. (ps-1). 1992. 10.00 (*0-440-40731-1*) Dell.
Webster, George P. & Nast, Thomas. Santa Claus & His Works. (Illus.). 12p. (gr. 1-8). 1972. pap. 3.25 (*0-914510-03-7*) Evergreen.
York, Carol B. Christmas Dolls. (gr. 4-7). 1993. pap. 2.75 (*0-590-42435-1*) Scholastic Inc.
Zwebner, Janet. The Follow That Sleigh Christmas Activity Book. 48p. (gr. 1-5). 1990. wkbk. 5.95 (*0-944007-62-7*) Shapolsky Pubs.

CHRISTMAS PLAYS

Dramas Navidenos para Ninos. 32p. (Orig.). (gr. 3-6). 1991. pap. 1.75 (*0-311-08226-2*) Casa Bautista.
Groff, Phylis. The Christmas Nightingale. 1935. 4.50 (*0-87602-115-1*) Anchorage.
Jordan, Myra J. & Grant, Roy E. Santa's Problem. (Illus.). 30p. (Orig.). (ps-1). 1980. pap. 5.00 (*0-914562-08-8*) Merriam-Eddy.
Kamerman, Sylvia E., ed. The Big Book of Christmas Plays. LC 88-15691. (gr. 4-12). 1988. 18.95 (*0-8238-0288-4*) Plays.
—Christmas Play Favorites for Young People. (Orig.). (gr. 4-12). 1982. pap. 12.00 (*0-8238-0257-4*) Plays.
King, Martha B. A Christmas Carol. 1941. 4.50 (*0-87602-114-3*) Anchorage.
McCaslin, Nellie. A Miracle in the Christmas City. LC 93-2602. 16p. 1993. pap. 5.00 play script (*0-88734-437-2*) Players Pr.
Menotti, Gian-Carlo. Amahl & the Night Visitors. Lemieux, Michele, illus. LC 84-27196. 64p. (ps up). 1986. 15.00 (*0-688-05426-9*); lib. bdg. 14.88 (*0-688-05427-7*, Morrow Jr Bks) Morrow Jr Bks.
Pickett, Margaret E. What's Keeping You, Santa? A Christmas Musical Program Package. Brown, Blanche M., illus. 74p. (gr. k-12). 1983. Incl Production Guide with choir arranged songs, cass of songs, thirty slides from bk. 49.95 (*0-913939-01-3*) TP Assocs.
Snyder, J. L. What Christmas Means to Me. Powell, Terry, illus. 43p. (gr. 8-12). 1989. pap. text ed. 2.50 (*0-87227-134-X*) Reg Baptist.
Weedn, Flavia & Weedn, Lisa. Flavia & the Christmas Legacy. (Illus.). 52p. 1990. 16.00 (*0-929632-11-7*) Applause Inc.

CHRISTMAS POETRY
see also Carols

Arico, Diane, ed. A Season of Joy: Favorite Stories & Poems for Christmas. San Souci, Daniel, illus. LC 86-29059. 64p. (gr. k-3). 1987. Doubleday.
Artell, Mike, illus. Twas the Night Before Christmas. LC 93-37281. (ps-1). 1994. pap. 10.95 (*0-689-71801-2*, Aladdin) Macmillan Child Grp.
Ashley, Jill. Riddles about Christmas. Brook, Bonnie, ed. Gray, Rob, illus. 32p. (ps-3). 1990. 4.95 (*0-671-70554-7*); PLB 6.95 (*0-671-70552-0*); 2.50 (*0-382-24383-8*) Silver Pr.
Brannon, Tom, illus. Jim Henson's Muppet Babies' Christmas Book. 48p. (ps-2). 1992. 6.95 (*0-307-15955-8*, 15955, Golden Pr) Western Pub.
Brett, Jan. The Twelve Days of Christmas. (Illus.). 32p. 1990. 14.95 (*0-399-22197-2*, Putnam) Putnam Pub Group.
Cancion De Navidad. (SPA.). 1990. casebound 3.50 (*0-7214-1397-8*) Ladybird Bks.
Cloonan, Paula, illus. The Twelve Days of Christmas. 24p. (gr. k-3). 1990. PLB 14.95 (*0-87226-438-6*, Bedrick Blackie) P Bedrick Bks.
Counihan, Claire. Twelve Days of Christmas. 1989. pap. 2.50 (*0-590-42918-3*) Scholastic Inc.
Delamare, David, illus. Twelve Days of Christmas. 48p. 1992. 5.95 (*0-88101-264-5*) Unicorn Pub.
—Twelve Days of Christmas (Fairy Tale Classic) 48p. 1992. 9.95 (*0-88101-228-9*) Unicorn Pub.
Duncan, Beverly K. Christmas in the Stable. (Illus.). 32p. (ps up). 1990. 14.95 (*0-15-217758-2*) HarBrace.
Goode, Diane, illus. Diane Goode's Christmas Magic: Poems & Carols. LC 92-6366. 32p. (Orig.). (ps-3). 1992. PLB 5.99 (*0-679-92427-2*); pap. 2.25 (*0-679-82427-8*) Random Bks Yng Read.
Harrison, Michael & Stuart-Clark, Christopher, eds. The Oxford Book of Christmas Poems. (Illus.). 160p. (gr. 3 up). 1988. 18.00 (*0-19-276051-3*); pap. 10.95 (*0-19-276080-7*) OUP.
Hildebrandt, Greg, illus. Twas the Night Before Christmas: Includes Christmas Carols & The Nativity. 48p. 1985. 6.95 (*0-88101-181-9*) Unicorn Pub.
Jerris, Tony. The Littlest Spruce. Weinberger, Tanya, illus. 20p. (Orig.). (ps up). 1991. pap. 9.95 (*0-9630107-1-9*) Little Spruce.
Kearney, Jill. A Fishmas Carol. LC 94-6198. 1994. write for info. (*0-681-00582-3*) Longmeadow Pr.
Kennedy, X. J. The Beasts of Bethlehem. McCurdy, Michael, illus. LC 91-38417. 48p. (gr. 1 up). 1992. SBE 13.95 (*0-689-50561-2*, M K McElderry) Macmillan Child Grp.
Livingston, Myra C. Poems of Christmas. LC 80-13627. 132p. (gr. 5 up). 1980. SBE 14.95 (*0-689-50180-3*, M K McElderry) Macmillan Child Grp.
Livingston, Myra C., selected by. Christmas Poems. Hyman, Trina S., illus. LC 83-18559. 32p. (ps-3). 1984. reinforced bdg. 14.95 (*0-8234-0508-7*) Holiday.
Marshall, James. The Night Before Christmas. (Illus.). 1992. 4.95 (*0-590-45977-5*, Blue Ribbon Bks) Scholastic Inc.
Mitchell, Julie, compiled by. A Christmas Garland. Orr, Kathy, illus. 40p. 1991. lib. bdg. 8.95 (*0-8378-2069-3*) Gibson.
Moore, Clement C. Disney Babies the Night Before Christmas. LC 91-58969. (Illus.). 1992. incls. 6 ornaments 11.95 (*1-56282-244-6*) Disney Pr.
—The Grandma Moses Night before Christmas. 2nd ed. Moses, Grandma, illus. LC 90-24145. 32p. 1991. 15. 00 (*0-679-81526-0*); lib. bdg. 15.99 (*0-679-91526-5*) Random Bks Yng Read.
—The Night Before Christmas. Trimby, Elisa, illus. LC 77-71994. (gr. 1 up). 1977. pap. 5.95 (*0-385-13615-3*) Doubleday.
—The Night Before Christmas. (Illus.). 16p. (gr. 1-8). 1970. pap. 4.00 (*0-914510-01-0*) Evergreen.
—The Night Before Christmas. De Paola, Tomie, illus. LC 80-11758. 32p. (ps up). 1980. reinforced bdg. 15. 95 (*0-8234-0414-5*); pap. 6.95 (*0-8234-0417-X*) Holiday.
—The Night Before Christmas. Gorsline, Douglas, illus. 32p. (ps-1). 1985. incl. cassette 5.95 (*0-394-87658-X*) Random Bks Yng Read.
—The Night Before Christmas. LC 87-15343. (Illus.). 48p. (gr. k-3). 1988. PLB 12.89 (*0-8167-1209-3*); pap. text ed. 3.95 (*0-8167-1210-7*) Troll Assocs.
—The Night Before Christmas. Goode, Diane, illus. LC 82-62171. 32p. 1988. pap. 1.50 (*0-394-81938-1*) Random Bks Yng Read.
—The Night Before Christmas. Foreman, Michael, illus. LC 88-50097. (ps up). 1988. pap. 11.95 (*0-670-82388-0*) Viking Child Bks.
—The Night Before Christmas. Amoss, Berthe, illus. 10p. (ps-7). 1989. pap. 3.95 (*0-922589-06-2*) More Than Card.
—The Night Before Christmas. LC 89-42998. (Illus.). 80p. 1989. 4.95 (*0-89471-754-5*) Running Pr.
—The Night Before Christmas. Harness, Cheryl, illus. LC 88-35019. 40p. (ps-8). 1990. 6.99 (*0-394-82698-1*) Random Bks Yng Read.
—The Night Before Christmas. Clonan, Paula, illus. LC 89-6560. 28p. (gr. k-3). 1990. PLB 12.95 (*0-87226-416-5*, Bedrick Blackie) P Bedrick Bks.
—The Night Before Christmas. Rice, James, illus. LC 89-34789. 32p. 1990. 14.95 (*0-88289-755-1*) Pelican.
—The Night Before Christmas. Tudor, Tasha, illus. LC 75-8858. 64p. (ps-1). 1990. SBE 12.95 (*0-02-767643-9*, Macmillan Child Bk) Macmillan Child Grp.
—Night Before Christmas. 1989. pap. 2.25 (*0-671-68408-6*, Little Simon) S&S Trade.
—The Night Before Christmas. Watson, Wendy, illus. 32p. (ps-1). 1990. 13.95 (*0-395-53624-3*, Clarion Bks) HM.
—The Night Before Christmas. Marshall, James, illus. 32p. (ps-3). 1989. pap. 5.95 incl. cass. (*0-590-63489-5*); pap. 2.50 (*0-590-42758-X*) Scholastic Inc.
—The Night Before Christmas. Regan, Dana, illus. LC 90-22388. 24p. (ps up). 1991. 2.95 (*0-694-00365-4*) HarpC Child Bks.
—Night Before Christmas. (Illus.). 24p. (ps-2). 1985. 2.95 (*0-89542-498-3*, Ideals Child) Hambleton-Hill.

—The Night Before Christmas. Ferris, Lynn B., illus. 24p. 1991. 6.95 (*0-8362-4917-8*) Andrews & McMeel.
—The Night Before Christmas. Marshall, James, illus. 32p. 1991. 13.95 (*0-590-45075-1*, Scholastic Hardcover) Scholastic Inc.
—The Night Before Christmas. Patti, Joyce, illus. LC 92-9084. 12p. 1992. 9.95 (*1-55670-274-4*) Stewart Tabori & Chang.
—Night Before Christmas. (ps). 1992. 4.50 (*0-553-37118-5*) Bantam.
—The Night Before Christmas. Hirashima, Jean, illus. LC 92-27138. 32p. (ps-3). 1993. pap. 2.25 (*0-448-40482-6*, G&D) Putnam Pub Group.
—Night Before Christmas. (ps-3). 1986. 4.95 (*0-307-13750-3*) Western Pub.
—The Night Before Christmas. (ps-3). 1993. pap. 5.95 (*0-395-66508-6*, Clarion Bks) HM.
—The Night Before Christmas: A Pop-Up Book. Harris, Denise & Cote, Nancy, illus. Costello, Linda, designed by. (ps-1). 1993. 9.95 (*1-56397-003-1*) Boyds Mills Pr.
—The Night Before Christmas Board Book. Regan, Dana, illus. LC 91-46766. 26p. (ps). 1992. 4.95 (*0-694-00424-3*) HarpC Child Bks.
—Night Before Christmas Coloring Book. 1986. pap. 2.95 (*0-671-62959-X*, Little Simon) S&S Trade.
—Twas the Night Before Christmas. (Illus.). 24p. (gr. k-3). 1992. pap. 2.50 (*1-56144-163-5*, Honey Bear Bks) Modern Pub NYC.
—Twas the Night Before Christmas. 1992. pap. 3.95 (*0-395-64374-0*) HM.
—Twas the Night Before Christmas. Downing, Julie, illus. LC 93-40243. (ps up). 1994. 14.95 (*0-02-767646-3*, Bradbury Pr) Macmillan Child Grp.
—Twas the Night Before Christmas: A Visit from St. Nicholas. Smith, Jessie W., illus. (ps-2). 1912. 14.95 (*0-395-06952-1*) HM.
—A Visit from St. Nicholas. Hader, Berta & Hader, Elmer, illus. LC 93-33703. (gr. 2 up). 1994. pap. write for info. (*0-486-27978-2*) Dover.
Nedobeck, Don, illus. Nedobecks Twelve Days of Christmas. (gr. 1-8). 1988. Repr. lib. bdg. 9.95 (*0-944314-02-3*) New Wrinkle.
The Night Before Christmas. 1984. pap. 3.95 (*0-671-50952-7*, Little Simon) S&S Trade.
The Night Before Christmas. 1989. 3.95 (*0-7214-5205-1*) Ladybird Bks.
Niland, Kilmeny. A Bellbird in a Flame Tree: The Twelve Days of Christmas. LC 90-25869. 32p. (ps-3). 1991. 12.95 (*0-688-10797-4*, Tambourine Bks); PLB 12.88 (*0-688-10798-2*) Morrow.
Nister, Ernest. Ernest Nister's Book of Christmas. Intervisual Staff, illus. 12p. 1991. 12.95 (*0-399-21799-1*, Philomel) Putnam Pub Group.
O'Brien, John. The Twelve Days of Christmas. (Illus.). 32p. 1993. 14.95 (*1-56397-142-9*) Boyds Mills Pr.
Paraskevas, Betty. A Very Kroll Christmas. Paraskevas, Michael, illus. LC 93-41624. (ps up). 1994. 14.95 (*0-15-292883-9*) HarBrace.
Prelutsky, Jack. It's Christmas. Hafner, Marilyn, illus. LC 81-1100. 48p. (gr. 1-3). 1981. 15.00 (*0-688-00439-3*); PLB 14.93 (*0-688-00440-7*) Greenwillow.
Quattrocki, Carolyn. Twas the Night Before Christmas. Spellman, Susan & Graves, Linda, illus. 24p. (ps-4). 1992. PLB 10.95 (*1-56674-027-4*) Forest Hse.
Retan, Walter, compiled by. I Love Christmas: A Wonderful Collection of Christmas Stories, Poems, Carols, & More. Ewing, Carolyn, illus. 96p. (gr. k up). 1992. write for info. (*0-307-15875-6*, 15875, Golden Pr) Western Pub.
Rice, James. La Nochebuena South of the Border. Smith, Ana, tr. Rice, James, illus. LC 93-13002. (ENG & SPA.). 32p. (gr. k-3). 1993. 14.95 (*0-88289-966-X*) Pelican.
Stewart, Pat. Away in a Manger. (Illus.). 32p. (gr. 3 up). 1989. 6.95 (*0-02-689338-X*) Checkerboard.
Taylor, Jane. Twinkle, Twinkle, Little Star. 1992. 10.95 (*0-590-45566-4*, Cartwheel) Scholastic Inc.
Teasdale, Sara. Christmas Carol. Gottlieb, Dale, illus. 32p. (ps-2). 1993. 14.95 (*0-8050-2695-9*, Bks Young Read) H Holt & Co.
Teichman, Mary, illus. Merry Christmas: A Victorian Verse. LC 92-29870. 32p. (ps up). 1993. 10.00 (*0-06-022889-X*); PLB 9.89 (*0-06-022892-X*) HarpC Child Bks.
Trosclair. Cajun Night Before Christmas: Full-Color Edition. Jacobs, Howard, ed. Rice, James, illus. LC 92-8375. 48p. (gr. k-3). 1992. 14.95 (*0-88289-940-6*); boxed ed. 25.00 (*0-88289-947-3*); audio 9.95 (*0-88289-914-7*) Pelican.
Turner, Ann. The Christmas House. Calder, Nancy E., illus. LC 93-12740. 32p. (gr. k-3). 1994. 15.00 (*0-06-023429-6*); PLB 14.89 (*0-06-023432-6*) HarpC Child Bks.
Wax, Wendy, compiled by. A Treasury of Christmas Poems, Carols, & Games to Share. Spier, John, illus. (ps-1). 1992. 10.00 (*0-440-40731-1*) Dell.
Wilner, Isabel. B Is for Bethlehem: A Christmas Alphabet. Kleven, Elisa, illus. LC 89-49481. 32p. (ps up). 1990. 13.95 (*0-525-44622-2*, DCB) Dutton Child Bks.
Zabar, Abbie. A Perfectly Irregular Christmas Tree. Zabar, Abbie, illus. 40p. 1991. 14.00 (*0-517-58608-8*, C Potter Bks) Crown Pub Group.

CHRISTOLOGY
see Jesus Christ

CHRONOLOGY
see Calendars; Time

CHRONOLOGY, HISTORICAL
Alvarez Del Real, Maria E., ed. Fechas Que Han Hecho Historia. (SPA., Illus.). 320p. (Orig.). 1988. pap. 5.00x (*0-944499-41-4*) Editorial Amer.
Martinet, Jeanne. The Year You Were Born, 1983. Lanfredi, Judy, illus. LC 91-31605. 56p. 1992. PLB 13.93 (*0-688-11078-9*, Tambourine Bks); pap. 7.95 (*0-688-11077-0*, Tambourine Bks) Morrow.

CHURCH
see also Christian Unity; Christianity
Borchers, Deena. What is the Church? (Illus.). 48p. (gr. 9-12). 1992. pap. 8.99 (*1-55945-222-6*) Group Pub.
Caswell, Helen. My Big Family at Church. LC 88-30630. 1989. pap. 5.95 (*0-687-27533-4*) Abingdon.
Cooper, Harold. Believing Truth about the Church. (Illus.). 80p. (gr. 8-9). 1975. pap. 3.50 (*0-89114-070-0*); P. 64. tchr's. ed. 1.50 (*0-89114-071-9*) Baptist Pub Hse.
Huyser-Honig, Joan & Huyser-Honig, Steve. The Church Serves. 86p. (Orig.). (gr. 7-8). 1987. pap. text ed. 7.25 (*0-930265-38-6*); tchr's. ed. 8.95 (*0-930265-39-4*) CRC Pubns.
Lenters, William R. The Church Cares. 77p. (Orig.). (gr. 7-8). 1987. pap. text ed. 7.25 (*0-930265-32-7*); tchr's. ed 8.95 (*0-930265-33-5*) CRC Pubns.
Martens, Sheri. Adam & Andrea Learn & Grow: Understanding Church Words from a Kid's Viewpoint. Penner, Kathy, illus. 80p. (ps-5). 1989. pap. 7.95 (*0-919797-81-4*) Kindred Pr.
O'Keefe, Susan H. Who Will Miss Me If I Don't Go to Church? Keating, Pam, illus. LC 92-28347. 32p. 1993. pap. 3.95 (*0-8091-6608-9*) Paulist Pr.
Richards, H. J. The Mass for Children. 28p. (Orig.). 1991. pap. 2.95 (*0-8146-2038-8*) Liturgical Pr.
Robertson, Everett, ed. Puppet Scripts for Use at Church, No. 2. LC 78-72843. (gr. k up). 1980. 7.99 (*0-8054-7519-2*) Broadman.
Waybill, Marjorie. God Builds His Church: Activity Book. Converse, James, illus. 72p. (Orig.). (gr. 4-5). 1988. pap. 3.00 (*0-8361-3457-5*) Herald Pr.
Willis, Doris. I Like to Come to My Church. (ps). 1990. 3.95 (*0-687-03122-2*) Abingdon.

CHURCH AND STATE
see also Religious Liberty
Barton, Charles D. The Myth of Separation. 296p. (Orig.). (gr. 7 up). 1989. pap. 7.95 (*0-925279-04-8*) Wallbuilders.
Gay, Kathlyn. Church & State: Government & Religion in the United States. LC 91-34753. (Illus.). 128p. (gr. 7 up). 1992. PLB 15.90 (*1-56294-063-5*) Millbrook Pr.
Sherrow, Victoria. Separation of Church & State. LC 91-39770. (Illus.). 144p. (gr. 7-12). 1992. PLB 13.90 (*0-531-13000-2*) Watts.
Weiss, Ann E. God & Government: The Separation of Church & State. 160p. (gr. 5-9). 1982. 9.95 (*0-395-32085-2*) HM.
—God & Government: The Separation of Church & State. 1990. pap. 4.80 (*0-395-54977-9*) HM.

CHURCH ARCHITECTURE
see also Cathedrals; Churches

CHURCH BELLS
see Bells

CHURCH BIOGRAPHY
see Christian Biography

CHURCH DENOMINATIONS
see Sects

CHURCH FESTIVALS
see Fasts and Feasts

CHURCH HISTORY
see also Church and State; Jews; Missions; Popes; Protestantism; Reformation; Sects
also names of countries, states, etc. with the subdivision Church History (e.g. U. S.–Church History; etc.)
Griswold, Millie H. Promises to Keep: Simplified Edition. 24p. 1985. write for info. wkbk. (*1-881909-14-X*) Advent Christ Gen Conf.
Halverson, Sandy. Church History Activity Book: Creative Scripture Learning Experiences about the Restoration for Children 4-12. 36p. (Orig.). (gr. 3-6). 1983. pap. 5.98 (*0-88290-213-X*) Horizon Utah.
Huston, David A. The Light of the Pentecost: A Unique Historical Account of the New Testament Church. Penton, Ben, illus. (gr. 7 up). 1989. pap. 5.95 (*0-932345-03-4*) Antioch Publishes.
Johnson, George, et al. The Story of the Church. LC 80-51329. 521p. (gr. 9). 1980. pap. 16.50 (*0-89555-156-X*) Tan Bks Pubs.
Rondthaler, Katharine B. Tell Me a Story. Holder, Elizabeth j., illus. 64p. (ps-5). pap. 4.00 (*1-878422-06-5*) Moravian Ch in Amer.
Sidwell, Mark, ed. Faith of Our Fathers: Scenes from Church History. 216p. (Orig.). (gr. 9 up). 1989. pap. 6.95 (*0-89084-492-5*) Bob Jones Univ Pr.
Traketellas, Demetrios. Growing in the Knowledge of Christ. 18p. (gr. 12). 1987. pap. 1.25 (*0-917651-43-X*) Holy Cross Orthodox.
Wenger, Rachelle & Wenger, Renee. Word of God, Priceless Treasure. Wenger, Ray M., ed. Wenger, Rachelle & Wenger, Renee, illus. 64p. (Orig.). (gr. 3-6). 1993. pap. 5.99 (*0-9634616-1-3*) Plumb Line Pr.

CHURCH HISTORY–FICTION
Lecomte, Eva. Paula, the Waldensian. Strong, W. M., tr. (gr. 3-7). 1942. pap. 5.99 (*0-87213-511-X*) Loizeaux.

CHURCH HISTORY–REFORMATION
see Reformation

CHURCH MUSIC
see also Carols; Hymns
Advance Cal-Tech Inc. Let's Praise & Play: Children's Christian Mini-Piano Book. Kung, Edward, ed. Mc Kig, Susan, illus. Childe, Laura, intro. by. (Illus.). 36p. (ps-6). text ed. write for info. (*0-943759-00-5*) Advance Cal Tech.
Benoit, David & Graff, Charles G. Theft by Deception. (Illus.). 12p. (Orig.). (gr. 7 up). 1987. pap. text ed. 1.50 (*0-923105-08-5*) Glory Ministries.
Bible, Ken, compiled by. Sing a Song of Scripture. (gr. 3-7). 1986. 6.50 (*0-8341-9050-8*, BCMB-558); Vols. 1 & 2. double-cassette pack 19.98 (*0-685-68217-X*, BCTA-9075B); Vol. 1. cassette 12.98 (*0-685-68218-8*, BCTA-9074C); Vol. 2. cassette 12.98 (*0-685-68219-6*, BCTA-9075C) Lillenas.
Howard, Julie. Walk on the Water. 24p. (Orig.). 1990. pap. 5.95 (*0-8146-2011-6*) Liturgical Pr.
Lenski, Lois. Sing for Peace. 16p. (ps-2). 1985. pap. 1.50 (*0-8361-3396-X*) Herald Pr.
Nicol, Mary M. & Roth, Pamela K., eds. Ready, Set... Sing! (Songs for Sunday & Everyday) 96p. (Orig.). 1989. pap. 9.00 (*0-8170-1155-2*) Judson.
Ogilvy, Carol & Tinkham, Trudy. Primary Christmas Concerts. 112p. (gr. k-3). 1989. 10.95 (*0-86653-485-7*, GA1091) Good Apple.
Salvation Song Index. 6p. (gr. k-6). 1957. pap. 0.50 (*1-55976-204-7*) CEF Press.
Sing! (gr. 4-6). 1980. 6.50 (*0-8341-9002-8*, BCMB-484); Vol. 1. double-length cassette 12.98 (*0-685-68229-3*, BCTA-9028C); Vol. 2. double-length cassette 12.98 (*0-685-68230-7*, BCTA-9029C) Lillenas.
Songbook for Living Waters, Vol. I. 1993. 24.95 (*0-7829-0384-3*, 88090) Tabor Pub.
Songbook for Living Waters, Vol. II. 1993. 24.95 (*0-7829-0385-1*, 88091) Tabor Pub.
Songs of God & Me. 1980. 5.75 (*0-8341-9099-0*, BCMB-483); Vol. 1. double-length cassette 12.98 (*0-685-68226-9*, BCTA-9026C); Vol. 2. double-length cassette 12.98 (*0-685-68227-7*, BCTA-9027C) Lillenas.
Songs to Grow On. 1980. 6.50 (*0-685-68223-4*, BCMB-482); double-length cassette 12.98 (*0-685-68224-2*, BCTA-9025C) Lillenas.
Weishei, Eldon. Psalms for Teens. 128p. (Orig.). 1993. pap. 6.99 (*0-570-04599-1*) Concordia.

CHURCH OF CHRIST OF LATTER DAY SAINTS
see Mormons and Mormonism

CHURCH OF CHRIST, SCIENTIST
see Christian Science

CHURCH UNITY
see Christian Unity

CHURCHES
Here are entered general descriptive and historical works on churches which cannot be entered under Church Architecture. Works relating to the churches of a city are entered under the name of the city with the subdivision Churches.
see also Cathedrals
Stainer, Tom & Sutton, Harry. Cathedrals. McEwan, Joseph, illus. 32p. (gr. 4-6). 1992. pap. 4.95 (*0-563-34161-0*, BBC-Parkwest) Parkwest Pubns.

CHURCHES–FICTION
Barrett, William E. Lilies of the Field. Silverman, Burt, illus. LC 62-8085. (gr. 7 up). 1967. 3.95 (*0-685-01491-6*, Im); pap. 3.95 (*0-385-07246-5*, Im) Doubleday.
Cole, Robin H. Pablo & the Miracle of Saint Anton. Cole, Robin H., illus. LC 89-37973. 48p. 1990. pap. 3.95 (*0-8091-6590-2*) Paulist Pr.
Murphy, Elspeth C. Mary Jo Bennett. LC 85-17059. 107p. (Orig.). (gr. 3-7). 1985. pap. 4.99 (*0-89191-711-X*, 57117, Chariot Bks) Chariot Family.
Stoddard, Sandol. God's Little House. 32p. 1984. pap. 1.95 (*0-8091-6553-8*) Paulist Pr.
Tester, Sylvia. Where Are We Going Today? Chase, Andra, illus. 12p. (ps). 1992. deluxe ed. 4.99 (*0-87403-996-7*, 24-03116) Standard Pub.
Wilson, Neil. Choice Adventures, No. 1: The Mysterious Old Church. (gr. 4-7). 1991. pap. 4.99 (*0-8423-5025-X*) Tyndale.

CHURCHILL, SIR WINSTON LEONARD SPENCER, 1874-1965
Driemen, J. E. Winston Churchill: An Unbreakable Spirit. LC 89-26029. (Illus.). 128p. (gr. 5 up). 1990. text ed. 13.95 RSBE (*0-87518-434-0*, Dillon) Macmillan Child Grp.
Italia, Bob. Winston Churchill. Walner, Rosemary, ed. LC 90-82615. (Illus.). 32p. (gr. 4). 1990. PLB 11.96 (*0-939179-78-4*) Abdo & Dghtrs.
Williams, Brian. Winston Churchill. (Illus.). 32p. (gr. 3-8). 1988. PLB 10.95 (*0-86307-925-3*) Marshall Cavendish.

CHURCHYARDS
see Cemeteries

CID CAMPEADOR
Koslow, Philip. El Cid: Spanish Military Leader. LC 92-33377. (Illus.). 1993. PLB 18.95 (*0-7910-1239-5*, Am Art Analog); pap. write for info. (*0-7910-1266-2*, Am Art Analog) Chelsea Hse.
McCaughrean, Geraldine. El Cid. Ambrus, Victor G., illus. 128p. (gr. 5 up). 1989. 19.95 (*0-19-276077-7*) OUP.

CINCINNATI REDS (BASEBALL TEAM)
Cincinnati Reds. (gr. 4-7). 1993. pap. 1.49 (*0-553-56429-3*) Bantam.
Goodman, Michael. Cincinnati Reds. 48p. (gr. 4-10). 1992. Net. PLB 14.95s.p. (*0-88682-462-1*) Creative Ed.

CINEMATOGRAPHY, TRICK

Rimner, I. Movies - FX. (Illus.). 48p. (gr. 3-8). 1989. PLB 18.60 (*0-86592-453-8*); 13.95 (*0-685-58294-9*) Rourke Corp.

CIPHERS

see also Cryptography; Writing

Albert, Burton, Jr. Code Busters! Levine, Abby, ed. Warshaw, Jerry, illus. LC 84-2935. 32p. (gr. 3-6). 1985. 11.95 (*0-8075-1235-4*) A Whitman.

Ashton, Christina. Codes & Ciphers: Hundreds of Unusual & Secret Ways to Send Messages. (Illus.). 112p. (Orig.). (gr. 7 up). 1993. pap. 7.95 (*1-55870-292-X*, 70204) Betterway Bks.

Garden, Nancy. The Kid's Code & Cipher Book. Gomez, Victoria, illus. LC 80-10434. 176p. (gr. 5 up). 1981. 10.95 (*0-03-053856-4*, Bks Young Read); 4.95 (*0-03-059267-4*) H Holt & Co.

—The Kid's Code & Cipher Book. LC 91-30453. (Illus.). 163p. (gr. 6-12). 1991. Repr. of 1981 ed. PLB 17.50 (*0-208-02341-0*, Linnet) Shoe String.

Mango, Karin N. Codes, Ciphers & Other Secrets. LC 88-5638. (Illus.). 96p. (gr. 4-6). 1988. PLB 10.90 (*0-531-10575-X*) Watts.

Nelson, Nigel. Codes. De Saulles, Tony, illus. LC 93-40962. 32p. (gr. k-2). 1994. 12.95 (*1-56847-157-2*) Thomson Lrning.

Spellman, L. Codes. 40p. (gr. 4-8). 1992. 6.95 (*0-88160-253-1*, LW1402) Learning Wks.

Wrixon, Fred B. Codes & Ciphers: An A to Z of Covert Communication, from the Clay Tablet to the Microdot. (Illus.). 288p. 1992. pap. 18.00 (*0-13-277047-4*) P-H Gen Ref & Trav.

CIPHERS–FICTION

Bonsall, Crosby N. The Case of the Double Cross. LC 80-7768. (Illus.). 64p. (gr. k-3). 1980. PLB 13.89 (*0-06-020603-9*) HarpC Child Bks.

Janeczko, Paul B. Loads of Codes & Secret Ciphers. LC 84-5791. (Illus.). 144p. (gr. 5-9). 1984. SBE 13.95 (*0-02-747810-6*, Macmillan Child Bk) Macmillan Child Grp.

CIRCULATION OF THE BLOOD

see Blood–Circulation

CIRCUMNAVIGATION

see Voyages around the World

CIRCUS

see also Animals–Training

Caggiano, Rosemary & Martinez, Larry. The Circus. 48p. (gr. k-6). 1978. pap. 14.95 (*0-86704-000-9*) Clarus Music.

Chwast, Seymour. The Twelve Circus Rings. LC 92-13576. 1993. write for info. (*0-15-200627-3*) HarBrace.

Cushman, Kathleen. Circus Dreams: The Making of a Circus Artist. (gr. 4-7). 1990. 15.95 (*0-316-16561-1*, Joy St Bks) Little.

Doty, Roy. Wonderful Circus Parade. (ps). 1991. pap. 4.95 (*0-671-72842-3*, Little Simon) S&S Trade.

Harmer, Mabel. Circus. LC 81-7709. (Illus.). 48p. (gr. k-4). 1981. PLB 12.85 (*0-516-01610-5*) Childrens.

Hoban, Tana. Round & Round & Round. Hoban, Tana, illus. LC 82-11984. 32p. (gr. k-3). 1983. 14.95 (*0-688-01813-0*); PLB 14.88 (*0-688-01814-9*) Greenwillow.

Johnson, John E., illus. Here Comes the Circus. 14p. (gr. 2-5). 1985. 4.99 (*0-394-87543-5*) Random Bks Yng Read.

Johnson, Neil. Big-Top Circus. LC 93-40274. 1995. write for info. (*0-8037-1602-8*); PLB write for info. (*0-8037-1603-6*) Dial Bks Young.

Laslo, Cynthia. The Rosen Photo Guide to a Career in the Circus. (Illus.). (gr. 7-12). 1988. lib. bdg. 12.95 (*0-8239-0819-4*) Rosen Group.

Magic of the Circus. (ps-1). pap. 2.49 (*0-517-48305-X*) Random Hse Value.

Patterson, Jose. A Circus Child. (Illus.). 25p. (gr. 2-4). 1991. 12.95 (*0-237-60132-X*, Pub. by Evans Bros Ltd) Trafalgar.

Price of Humbug: The Life of P. T. Barnum. LC 93-36724. (gr. 5-9). 1994. 15.95 (*0-689-31796-4*) Macmillan.

Schmidt, Diane. I Am a Jesse White Tumbler. Tucker, Kathy, ed. Schmidt, Diane, photos by. LC 89-16590. (Illus.). 40p. (gr. 2-8). 1990. 13.95 (*0-8075-3444-7*) A Whitman.

CIRCUS–FICTION

Adler, David A. Cam Jansen & the Mystery of the Circus Clown. Natti, Susanna, illus. LC 82-50363. 64p. (gr. 2-4). 1983. pap. 10.95 (*0-670-20036-0*) Viking Child Bks.

Barkan, Joanne. Animal Car. Ong, Christina, illus. 12p. (ps). 1993. pap. 3.50 (*0-689-71676-1*, Aladdin) Macmillan Child Grp.

—Circus Locomotive. Ong, Christina, illus. 12p. (ps). 1993. pap. 3.50 (*0-689-71674-5*, Aladdin) Macmillan Child Grp.

—Clown Caboose. Ong, Christina, illus. 12p. (ps). 1993. pap. 3.50 (*0-689-71675-3*, Aladdin) Macmillan Child Grp.

—Performers' Car. Ong, Christina, illus. 12p. (ps). 1993. pap. 3.50 (*0-689-71673-7*, Aladdin) Macmillan Child Grp.

Bell, Clarisa. El Circo. Sanchez, Jose R., illus. (SPA.). 24p. (Orig.). (gr. 2-6). 1992. PLB 9.95x (*1-56492-078-X*) Laredo.

Bond, Michael. Paddington at the Circus. Lobban, John, illus. LC 91-44210. 32p. (ps-2). 1992. 8.95 (*0-694-00415-4*, Festival) HarpC Child Bks.

Bonfills, Bolette. Peter Joins the Circus. Mogensen, Jan, illus. 24p. (ps-2). 1994. 9.95 (*1-56656-154-X*, Crocodile Bks) Interlink Pub.

Brown, Marc. Arthur's Chicken Pox. LC 93-22996. 1994. 15.95 (*0-316-11384-0*) Little.

Burningham, John. Cannonball Simp. Burningham, John, illus. LC 93-32369. 32p. (ps up). 1994. 15.95 (*1-56402-338-9*) Candlewick Pr.

Bushnell, Jack. Circus of the Wolves. Parker, Robert A., illus. LC 93-8092. 1994. 15.00 (*0-688-12554-9*); lib. bdg. 14.93 (*0-688-12555-7*) Lothrop.

Carey, Karla. Julie & Jackie at the Circus: The Narration & Music Book. Nolan, Dennis, illus. 57p. 1990. pap. 18.95 complete pkg. (*0-685-35759-7*); pap. 9.95 (*1-55768-202-X*); cassette 9.95 (*0-685-35760-0*) LC Pub.

Chatterton, Martin. Silly Circus! Chatterton, Martin, illus. 32p. (ps up). 1994. pap. 2.99 (*1-56402-405-9*) Candlewick Pr.

Christian, Mary B. Sebastian, Super-Sleuth, & the Flying Elephant. McCue, Lisa, illus. LC 94-14434. (gr. 2-6). 1994. 11.95 (*0-02-718252-5*) Macmillan.

Claesson, Stig. Sophie the Circus Princess. Henstra, Friso, illus. Stevens, Susanna, tr. from SWE. LC 93-16780. (Illus.). 1995. 14.00 (*0-671-87008-4*, Green Tiger) S&S Trade.

Cole, Ronald P. Sawdust "Fair Dinkum" LC 92-91125. 88p. 1993. pap. 8.00 (*1-56002-256-6*, Univ Edtns) Aegina Pr.

Cox, Julia. The Adventures of Boo, Vol. 2: Circus. Ortland, Stephen, illus. 32p. 1992. write for info. (*0-9627586-2-0*) Mango Entrps.

Daniel, Jennifer. Animal Shapes. Stinga, Frank, illus. 12p. (ps). Date not set. 2.95 (*1-56828-059-9*) Red Jacket Pr.

—Big Clown, Small Clown. Stinga, Frank, illus. 12p. (ps). Date not set. 2.95 (*1-56828-061-0*) Red Jacket Pr.

—The Circus Train Gift Pack. Stinga, Frank, illus. 48p. (ps). Date not set. Set. bds. 9.95 4 bks. (*1-56828-063-7*) Red Jacket Pr.

—The Colorful Locomotive. Stinga, Frank, illus. 12p. (ps). Date not set. 2.95 (*1-56828-062-9*) Red Jacket Pr.

—Side Show One, Two, Three. Stinga, Frank, illus. 12p. (ps). Date not set. 2.95 (*1-56828-060-2*) Red Jacket Pr.

De Bello, Rosario. Gina's Saturday Adventure. De Bello, Rosario, illus. LC 93-5845. 32p. (ps-3). 1994. pap. 4.95 (*0-8091-6612-7*) Paulist Pr.

De Paola, Tomie. Jingle the Christmas Clown. (Illus.). 40p. (ps-3). 1992. 15.95 (*0-399-22338-X*, Putnam) Putnam Pub Group.

Dr. Seuss. If I Ran the Circus. Dr. Seuss, illus. (gr. k-3). 1956. 14.00 (*0-394-80080-X*); lib. bdg. 10.99 (*0-394-90080-4*) Random Bks Yng Read.

Dumbo's Circus. 1985. 4.95 (*0-553-05403-1*) Bantam.

Ehlert, Lois. Circus. Ehlert, Lois, illus. LC 91-12067. 40p. (ps-1). 1992. 15.00 (*0-06-020252-1*); PLB 14.89 (*0-06-020253-X*) HarpC Child Bks.

Ehrlich, Amy. Lucy's Winter Tale. Howell, Troy, illus. LC 88-25740. 32p. (gr. k). 1992. 14.00 (*0-8037-0659-6*); PLB 13.89 (*0-8037-0661-8*) Dial Bks Young.

Eldadah, Basil. The Greatest Act. 84p. 1989. pap. 5.95 (*0-915957-05-1*) Amana Corp.

Ernst, Lisa C. Ginger Jumps. Ernst, Lisa C., illus. LC 89-38706. 32p. (ps-2). 1990. RSBE 14.95 (*0-02-733565-8*, Bradbury Pr) Macmillan Child Grp.

Falk, Barbara B. Grusha. Falk, Barbara B., illus. LC 92-14980. 32p. (ps-3). 1993. 15.00 (*0-06-021299-3*); PLB 14.89 (*0-06-021300-0*) HarpC Child Bks.

Freeman, Don. Bearymore. (Illus.). (ps-3). 1979. pap. 3.95 (*0-14-050279-3*, Puffin) Puffin Bks.

—Bearymore. LC 76-94. (Illus.). 40p. (gr. k-3). 1976. 14.95 (*0-670-15174-2*) Viking Child Bks.

Garland, Michael. Circus Girl. Garland, Michael, illus. LC 92-22270. 32p. (ps-3). 1993. 14.99 (*0-525-45069-6*, DCB) Dutton Child Bks.

Goennel, Heidi. The Circus. LC 91-448. (Illus.). 32p. (ps-3). 1992. 15.00 (*0-688-10883-0*, Tambourine Bks); PLB 14.93 (*0-688-10884-9*, Tambourine Bks) Morrow.

Haywood, Carolyn. Eddie's Friend Boodles. Stock, Catherine, illus. LC 91-3212. (gr. 1 up). 1991. 12.95 (*0-688-09028-1*) Morrow Jr Bks.

Hillert, Margaret. Circus Fun. (Illus.). (ps-k). 1969. PLB 6.95 (*0-8136-5011-9*, TK2284); pap. 3.50 (*0-8136-5511-0*, TK2285) Modern Curr.

Hol, Coby. Bela, Etoile du Cirque. Hol, Coby, illus. (FRE.). 32p. (gr. k-3). 1992. 14.95 (*3-314-20724-7*) North-South Bks NYC.

—Bela Wird Zirkuspony. Hol, Coby, illus. (GER.). 32p. (gr. k-3). 1992. 14.95 (*3-314-00533-4*) North-South Bks NYC.

Hughes, Francine, adapted by. The Wildest Show on Earth. (Illus.). (ps-3). 1993. pap. 2.50 (*0-448-40447-8*, G&D); pap. 5.95 incl. cass. tape (*0-448-40449-4*, G&D) Putnam Pub Group.

Johnson, Crockett. Harold's Circus. LC 59-5318. (ps-3). 1959. PLB 11.89 (*0-06-022966-7*) HarpC Child Bks.

Joos, Louis, illus. Oregon's Journey. LC 93-11796. 40p. (gr. k-4). 1993. PLB 15.95 (*0-8167-3305-8*); pap. text ed. 3.95 (*0-8167-3306-6*) BrdgeWater.

Kaghan, Joan. The Billy Goat Show. 32p. 1993. 14.00 (*0-374-30711-3*) FS&G.

Kalman, Maira. Roarr! Calder's Circus. (ps-3). 1993. pap. 16.95 (*0-385-30916-3*) Doubleday.

Littleton, Mark. Escape of the Grizzly. LC 93-29408. 1994. pap. 3.99 (*1-56507-099-2*) Harvest Hse.

Lustig, Loretta, illus. The Pop-Up Book of the Circus. LC 78-68789. (ps-3). 1979. 8.99 (*0-394-84134-4*) Random Bks Yng Read.

McCully, Emily A. Mirette on the Highwire. (Illus.). 32p. (ps-3). 1992. 14.95 (*0-399-22130-1*, Putnam) Putnam Pub Group.

Marilue. Bobby Bear at the Circus. Marilue, illus. LC 89-62708. 32p. (ps-2). 1990. PLB 12.95 (*0-87783-252-8*) Oddo.

Miranda, Anne. The Elephant at the Waldorf. Vanderbeek, Don, illus. LC 93-33804. 32p. (gr. k-3). 1995. PLB 14.95 (*0-8167-3452-6*); pap. text ed. 3.95 (*0-8167-3453-4*) BrdgeWater.

Moncure, Jane B. Word Bird's Circus Surprise. Hohag, Linda, illus. LC 80-29528. 32p. (gr. k-2). 1981. PLB 14.95 (*0-89565-162-9*) Childs World.

Montenegro, Laura. Sweet Tooth. LC 93-49643. 1994. write for info. (*0-395-68078-6*) HM.

Norman, Jane & Beazley, Frank. Tick-i-ty Ted Joins the Circus. 24p. (ps-3). 1993. pap. write for info. (*1-883585-01-5*) Pixanne Ent.

Otis, James. Toby Tyler. 152p. 1981. Repr. PLB 21.95x (*0-89966-363-X*) Buccaneer Bks.

—Toby Tyler. 188p. 1981. Repr. PLB 19.95 (*0-89967-037-7*) Harmony Raine.

—Toby Tyler, or, Ten Weeks with a Circus. (gr. 4 up). 1990. pap. 3.50 (*0-440-40358-8*) Dell.

Packard, Edward. The Circus. 64p. 1983. pap. 2.25 (*0-553-15426-5*) Bantam.

Pare, R. Circus Days. (Illus.). 24p. (ps-8). 1988. PLB 14.95 (*1-55037-021-9*, Pub. by Annick CN); pap. 4.95 (*1-55037-020-0*, Pub. by Annick CN) Firefly Bks Ltd.

Paulsen, Gary. Dunc & Amos Hit the Big Top. (gr. 4-7). 1993. pap. 3.25 (*0-440-40756-7*) Dell.

Peet, Bill. Ella. (Illus.). 48p. (gr. k-3). 1964. 13.45 (*0-395-17577-1*) HM.

Pellowski, Michael. Clara Joins the Circus. Kelley, True, illus. LC 80-25602. 48p. (ps-3). 1981. 5.95 (*0-8193-1057-3*); PLB 5.95 (*0-8193-1058-1*) Parents.

Peppe, Rodney. Thumbprint Circus. Peppe, Rodney, illus. 32p. (ps-1). 1992. pap. 3.99 (*0-440-40692-7*, YB) Dell.

Percy, Graham. Meg & Her Circus Tricks. (Illus.). 32p. 1991. 15.95 (*0-89565-785-6*) Childs World.

Pittau, Francisco. Tightrope Walker. LC 92-54429. (ps-3). 1993. 13.00 (*0-688-12379-1*) Lothrop.

Piumini, Roberto. The Saint & the Circus. Holmes, Olivia, tr. from ITA. Root, Barrett V., illus. LC 90-23481. 32p. (ps-3). 1991. 14.95 (*0-688-10377-4*, Tambourine Bks); PLB 14.88 (*0-688-10378-2*, Tambourine Bks) Morrow.

Rey, H. A. See the Circus. (Illus.). (gr. k-3). 1956. pap. 2.10 (*0-395-07068-6*, Sandpiper) HM.

Saroyan, William. The Circus. Zimdars, Berta, illus. 32p. (gr. 4 up). 1986. PLB 13.95 (*0-88682-066-9*) Creative Ed.

Smucker, Barbara. Incredible Jumbo. 1991. 12.95 (*0-670-82970-6*) Viking Child Bks.

Spier, Peter. Peter Spier's Circus! Spier, Peter, illus. LC 90-23282. 48p. (ps-3). 1992. pap. 16.00 (*0-385-41969-4*) Doubleday.

Stern, Peter. Whompers & Whammies: The Great Circus War. LC 91-26083. (ps-3). 1994. 14.00 (*0-688-10775-3*); 13.93 (*0-688-10776-1*) Lothrop.

Vandersteen, Willy. The Circus Baron. Lahey, Nicholas J., tr. from FLE. LC 75-8497. (Illus.). 56p. (Orig.). (gr. 3 up). 1976. pap. 2.50 (*0-915560-21-6*, 21) Hiddigeigei.

Vincent, Gabrielle. Ernest & Celestine at the Circus. LC 88-23220. (Illus.). 32p. (ps up). 1989. 11.95 (*0-688-08684-5*); PLB 11.88 (*0-688-08685-3*) Greenwillow.

Weil, Lisl. Let's Go to the Circus. Weil, Lisl, illus. LC 87-25201. 32p. (ps-3). 1988. reinforced bdg. 13.95 (*0-8234-0693-8*) Holiday.

Wersba, Barbara. Let Me Fall Before I Fly. Hoys, James, illus. LC 86-2686. 48p. (gr. 6 up). 1986. PLB 13.95 (*0-88682-057-X*) Creative Ed.

Winn, Chris. Archie's Acrobats. (Illus.). 32p. (gr. k-3). 1990. pap. 6.95 (*0-575-04481-0*, Pub. by Gollancz England) Trafalgar.

Wiseman, Bernard. Morris & Boris at the Circus. Wiseman, Bernard, illus. LC 87-45682. 64p. (gr. k-3). 1988. 14.00 (*0-06-026477-2*); PLB 13.89 (*0-06-026478-0*) HarpC Child Bks.

—Morris & Boris at the Circus. Wiseman, Bernard, illus. LC 87-45682. 64p. (gr. k-3). 1990. pap. 3.50 (*0-06-444143-1*, Trophy) HarpC Child Bks.

Wolff, Mia. Catcher. LC 93-33802. (ps-2). 1994. 15.00 (*0-374-31227-3*) FS&G.

CIRCUS–HISTORY

Duncan, Lois. The Circus Comes Home. Steinmetz, Joseph J., photos by. LC 92-7481. (Illus.). 1993. 16.95 (*0-385-30689-X*) Doubleday.

CIRCUS–PICTURES, ILLUSTRATIONS, ETC.

Circus. (gr. 2 up). 1991. pap. 1.47 (*1-56297-092-5*, GS-32) Lee Pubns KY.

Count Ten Circus Friends. (Illus.). 6p. (gr. k-2). 1988. bds. 6.95 (*0-87449-455-9*) Modern Pub NYC.

Machotka, Hana. Magic Ring: A Year With The Big Apple Circus. Machotka, Hana, illus. Binder, Paul, intro. by. LC 87-28230. (Illus.). 80p. (gr. 3 up). 1988. 13.95 (*0-688-07449-9*); pap. 8.95 (*0-688-08222-X*) Morrow Jr Bks.

CITIES AND TOWNS

Here are entered works on cities and towns. For works on large cities and their surrounding areas use Metropolitan Areas. General works on the government of cities are entered under Municipal Government. General works on local government other than that of cities are entered under Local Government.

Barr, Roger. Cities. (Illus.). (gr. 5-8). 1994. 14.95 (*1-56006-158-8*) Lucent Bks.

Baylor, Byrd. The Best Town in the World. Himler, Ronald, illus. LC 83-9033. 32p. (gr. 1-3). 1983. SBE 14.95 (*0-684-18035-9*, Scribners Young Read) Macmillan Child Grp.

Brown, Craig. City Sounds. LC 90-25632. (Illus.). 24p. (ps-4). 1992. 14.00 (*0-688-10028-7*); PLB 13.93 (*0-688-10029-5*) Greenwillow.

Cities. 44p. (gr. k-5). 1988. pap. 2.95 (*0-8431-2248-X*) Price Stern.

Costa-Pace, Rosa. The City. LC 93-17918. (Illus.). 1994. 13.95 (*0-7910-2101-7*, Am Art Analog) Chelsea Hse.

Cozic, Charles P., ed. America's Cities: Opposing Viewpoints. LC 92-40708. (Illus.). 264p. (gr. 10 up). 1993. PLB 17.95 (*0-89908-195-9*); pap. text ed. 9.95 (*0-89908-170-3*) Greenhaven.

Doney, Meryl. Discovering the City. (Illus.). 32p. (gr. k-2). pap. 2.99 (*0-85648-259-5*) Lion USA.

Geography Department. Street Smart! Cities in Ancient Times. LC 94-632. (gr. 5 up). 1994. write for info. (*0-8225-3208-5*, Runestone Pr) Lerner Pubns.

Hernandez, Xavier. San Rafael: A Central American City Through the Ages. Ballonga, Jordi & Escofet, Josep, illus. LC 91-39906. 64p. (gr. 4-7). 1992. 17.45 (*0-395-60645-4*) HM.

Kalman, Bobbie. I Live in a City. (Illus.). 32p. (gr. 2-3). 1986. 15.95 (*0-86505-070-8*); pap. 7.95 (*0-86505-092-9*) Crabtree Pub Co.

Lenski, Lois. Sing a Song of People. Laroche, Giles, photos by. (ps-3). 1987. pap. 15.95 (*0-316-52074-8*) Little.

Little People Big Book about Where We Live. 64p. (ps-1). 1990. write for info. (*0-8094-7483-2*); PLB write for info. (*0-8094-7484-0*) Time-Life.

Macaulay, David. Underground. Macaulay, David, illus. (gr. 1 up). 1976. 16.95 (*0-395-24739-X*); pap. 8.70 (*0-395-34065-9*) HM.

McSharry, Patra & Rosen, Roger, eds. Urbanities: Visions of the Metropolis. (gr. 7-12). 1993. 16.95 (*0-8239-1387-2*); pap. 8.95 (*0-8239-1388-0*) Rosen Group.

Maestro, Betsy. Delivery Van: Words for Town & Country. Maestro, Giulio, illus. 32p. (ps-2). 1990. 14.95 (*0-395-51119-4*, Clarion Bks) HM.

—Taxi: A Book of City Words. Maestro, Giulio, illus. LC 88-22867. (ps-2). 1989. 13.95 (*0-89919-528-8*, Clarion Bks) HM.

—Taxi: A Book of City Words. Maestro, Giulio, illus. LC 88-22867. (ps-3). 1990. pap. 5.70 (*0-395-54811-X*, Clarion Bks) HM.

Maestro, Betsy & DelVecchio, Ellen. Big City Port. Maestro, Giulio, illus. LC 85-4339. 32p. (gr. k-3). 1984. RSBE 14.95 (*0-02-762110-3*, Four Winds) Macmillan Child Grp.

Malfatti, Patrizia, tr. Look Around the City. Montanari, Donata, illus. 16p. (ps-3). 1993. bds. 11.95 (*0-448-40187-8*, G&D) Putnam Pub Group.

Mazer, Norma F. Downtown. LC 84-91105. 192p. (gr. 7 up). 1984. 11.95 (*0-688-03859-X*) Morrow Jr Bks.

More about Carpinteria As It Was, Vol 2. LC 79-83931. (gr. 11 up). 1982. 9.95 (*0-9608826-1-8*) Papillon Pr.

O'Connor, Karen & Crowdy, Deborah. Let's Take a Walk in the City. Axeman, Lois, illus. LC 86-20746. 32p. (ps-2). 1986. PLB 14.95 (*0-89565-355-9*) Childs World.

Provensen, Alice & Provensen, Martin. Town & Country. LC 93-44749. (gr. k-3). 1994. 16.95 (*0-15-200182-4*, Browndeer Pr) HarBrace.

Reynolds, Tony. Cities in Crisis. (Illus.). 48p. (gr. 5 up). 1990. lib. bdg. 18.60 (*0-86592-118-0*); lib. bdg. 13.95s.p. (*0-685-36376-7*) Rourke Corp.

Ross, Katharine. The Little City Book. Miller, Edward, illus. LC 93-84942. 28p. (ps). 1994. 3.25 (*0-679-85290-5*) Random Bks Yng Read.

Sanchez, Isidro & Peris, Carme. City Sports. 32p. (ps-1). 1992. pap. 5.95 (*0-8120-4866-0*) Barron.

Steele, Philip. City Through the Ages. Lapper, Ivan, et al, illus. LC 91-37350. 32p. (gr. 3-6). 1993. PLB 11.89 (*0-8167-2727-9*); pap. text ed. 3.95 (*0-8167-2728-7*) Troll Assocs.

This Is How We Live in the Town. (ps-k). 1992. 8.00 (*1-56021-095-8*) W J Fantasy.

Wright, David K. A Multicultural Portrait of Life in the Cities. LC 93-10318. 1993. 18.95 (*1-85435-659-3*) Marshall Cavendish.

Yepsen, Roger. City Trains: Moving Through America's Cities by Rail. Yepsen, Roger, illus. LC 92-2395. 96p. (gr. 3-7). 1993. SBE 14.95 (*0-02-793675-9*, Macmillan Child Bk) Macmillan Child Grp.

CITIES AND TOWNS–FICTION

Asch, Frank & Vagin, Vladimir. Dear Brother. 32p. 1992. 13.95 (*0-590-43107-2*, Scholastic Hardcover) Scholastic Inc.

Bat-Ami, Miriam. When the Frost Is Gone. Ramsey, Marcy D., illus. LC 92-26181. 80p. (gr. 5 up). 1994. SBE 13.95 (*0-02-708497-3*, Macmillan Child Bk) Macmillan Child Grp.

Bell, William. Forbidden City. (gr. 7 up). 1990. 14.95 (*0-553-07131-9*, Starfire); pap. 3.99 (*0-553-28864-4*, Starfire) Bantam.

Berends, Polly B. The Case of the Elevator Duck. Allison, Diane, illus. LC 88-23971. 64p. (gr. 2-4). 1989. PLB 7.99 (*0-394-92646-3*); pap. 2.50 (*0-394-82646-9*) Random Bks Yng Read.

Bertrand, Lynne. Who Sleeps in the City? Jaekel, Susan, illus. 24p. (ps). 1994. 9.95 (*1-881527-48-4*) Chapters Pub.

Best, Cari. Taxi! Taxi! Gottlieb, Dale, illus. LC 92-32249. 1994. 14.95 (*0-316-09259-2*) Little.

Blegvad, Lenore. Once upon a Time & Grandma. Blegvad, Lenore, illus. LC 92-7407. 32p. (ps-3). 1993. SBE 14.95 (*0-689-50548-5*, M K McElderry) Macmillan Child Grp.

Buehner, Caralyn & Buehner, Mark. The Escape of Marvin the Ape. LC 91-10795. (Illus.). 32p. (ps-3). 1992. 14.00 (*0-8037-1123-9*); PLB 13.89 (*0-8037-1124-7*) Dial Bks Young.

Burstein, Fred. The Dancer. Auclair, Joan, illus. LC 91-41429. 40p. (ps-3). 1993. RSBE 14.95 (*0-02-715625-7*, Bradbury Pr) Macmillan Child Grp.

Cartwright, Pauline. Home. Tulloch, Coral, illus. LC 93-20062. 1994. write for info. (*0-383-03695-X*) SRA Schl Grp.

Casey, Barbara W. Leilani Zan. LC 90-71707. 113p. (gr. 9-12). 1992. 7.95 (*1-55523-405-4*) Winston-Derek.

Christopher, John. The City of Gold & Lead. LC 67-21245. 224p. (gr. 5-9). 1970. SBE 14.95 (*0-02-718380-7*, Macmillan Child Bk) Macmillan Child Grp.

The Citiscapes Series. Date not set. Big Bks. pap. 23.00 (*1-56843-024-8*); Little Bks. 4.50 (*0-685-62346-7*) BGR Pub.

Colman, Hila. Nobody Told Me What I Need to Know. LC 84-8673. 176p. (gr. 7 up). 1984. 11.95 (*0-688-03869-7*) Morrow Jr Bks.

Craft, Ruth. The Day of the Rainbow. Daly, Niki, illus. 32p. (ps-3). 1991. pap. 4.95 (*0-14-050935-6*, Puffin) Puffin Bks.

Craig, Helen. Susie & Alfred in a Busy Day in Town. Craig, Helen, illus. LC 93-21181. 32p. (Orig.). 1994. pap. 4.99 (*1-56402-380-X*) Candlewick Pr.

Cunningham, Linda. The Copper Angel of Piper's Mill & How She Saved Her Town. Goldberg, Grace, illus. 4p. (gr. 3-5). 1989. 12.95 (*0-89272-274-6*) Down East.

DiSalvo-Ryan, DyAnne. City Green. LC 93-27117. 1994. write for info. (*0-688-12786-X*); PLB write for info. (*0-688-12787-8*) Morrow Jr Bks.

Eskridge, Ann E. The Sanctuary. 144p. 1994. 13.99 (*0-525-65168-3*, Cobblehill Bks) Dutton Child Bks.

Fields, Julia. The Green Lion of Zion Street. Pinkney, Jerry, illus. LC 92-24571. 32p. (gr. k-3). 1993. pap. 4.95 (*0-689-71693-1*, Aladdin) Macmillan Child Grp.

Finsand, Mary J. The Town That Moved. 1991. pap. 2.99 (*0-440-40489-4*) Dell.

Florian, Douglas. City Street. Florian, Douglas, illus. LC 89-28694. 32p. (ps up). 1990. 14.00 (*0-688-09543-7*); PLB 13.93 (*0-688-09544-5*) Greenwillow.

Fox, Paula. Maurice's Room. reissued ed. Fetz, Ingrid, illus. LC 85-7200. 64p. (gr. 2-6). 1985. SBE 13.95 (*0-02-735490-3*, Macmillan Child Bk) Macmillan Child Grp.

—The Village by the Sea. (gr. k-6). 1990. pap. 3.99 (*0-440-40299-9*, Pub. by Yearling Classics) Dell.

Giff, Patricia R. Shark in School. LC 93-39016. (gr. 1 up). 1994. 14.95 (*0-385-32029-9*) Delacorte.

Ginny, Susan. Uncle Lester's Lemonade Lure. Ginny, Susan, illus. 15p. (Orig.). (gr. 2-3). 1988. pap. 4.95 (*0-9621556-0-8*) SYF Enter.
Fictional story of a small town store owner whose business spirit enables him to survive advanced competition in his local hardware store.
Publisher Provided Annotation.

Goldberg, Whoopi. Alice. Rocco, John, illus. LC 92-15935. 48p. 1992. 15.00 (*0-553-08990-0*) Bantam.

Gould, Marilyn. Graffiti Wipeout. LC 91-90783. 112p. (gr. 5 up). 1992. pap. 6.95 (*0-9632305-0-6*) Allied Crafts.

Griffin, Peni R. The Brick House Burglars. LC 93-22914. 144p. (gr. 4-7). 1994. SBE 14.95 (*0-689-50579-5*, M K McElderry) Macmillan Child Grp.

Henwood, Simon. The Hidden Jungle. (Illus.). 32p. (ps-3). 1992. 15.00 (*0-374-33070-0*) FS&G.

Hest, Amy. Ruby's Storm. Cote, Nancy, illus. LC 92-31242. 32p. (ps-2). 1994. RSBE 14.95 (*0-02-743160-6*, Four Winds) Macmillan Child Grp.

Hillert, Margaret. City Fun. (Illus.). (ps-k). 1981. PLB 6.95 (*0-8136-5071-2*, TK2286); pap. 3.50 (*0-8136-5571-4*, TK2287) Modern Curr.

Holman, Felice. Secret City, U. S. A. LC 89-39841. 208p. (gr. 5-9). 1990. SBE 14.95 (*0-684-19168-7*, Scribners Young Read) Macmillan Child Grp.

Holt, S. Marie. Mike Moves to the City. Holt, Shirley, illus. 28p. (gr. k-5). 1992. 21.95x (*0-9613476-5-1*) Shirlee.

Hopkins, Lee B. Mama. Marchesi, Stephen, illus. LC 91-24712. 112p. (gr. 2-8). 1992. pap. 13.00 jacketed, 3-pc. bdg. (*0-671-74985-4*, S&S BFYR) S&S Trade.

—Mama & Her Boys. Marchesi, Stephen, illus. LC 91-23399. 176p. (gr. 5 up). 1993. pap. 13.00 JRT (*0-671-74986-2*, S&S BFYR) S&S Trade.

Hurwitz, Johanna. Hurray for Ali Baba Bernstein. Owens, Gail, illus. LC 88-19107. 112p. (gr. 3-7). 1989. 11.95 (*0-688-08241-6*); PLB 11.88 (*0-688-08242-4*, Morrow Jr Bks) Morrow Jr Bks.

—Nora & Mrs. Mind-Your-Own-Business. Jeschke, Susan, illus. LC 76-54283. 64p. (gr. k-3). 1982. 11.95 (*0-688-22097-5*) Morrow Jr Bks.

Isadora, Rachel. City Seen from A to Z. ALC Staff, ed. LC 82-11966. (Illus.). 32p. (gr. k up). 1992. pap. 3.95 (*0-688-12032-6*, Mulberry) Morrow.

Jacobson, Jane. City, Sing, for Me: A Country Child Moves to the City. Rowen, Amy, illus. LC 77-11130. 32p. (gr. 1-5). 1978. 16.95 (*0-87705-358-8*) Human Sci Pr.

Kalman, Maira. Chicken Soup, Boots. Kalman, Maira, illus. 40p. 1993. reinforced bdg. 14.99 (*0-670-85201-5*) Viking Child Bks.

Klass, Sheila S. Kool Ada. (gr. 4-7). 1991. 13.95 (*0-590-43902-2*, Scholastic Hardcover) Scholastic Inc.

La Mann, Angela. Mom Is Going to Stop It. 27p. (gr. k). 1992. pap. text ed. 23.00 big bk. (*1-56843-014-0*); pap. text ed. 4.50 (*1-56843-064-7*) BGR Pub.

Lent, Blair. Bayberry Bluff. Lent, Blair, illus. 32p. (gr. k-3). 1992. pap. 4.80 (*0-395-62984-5*, Sandpiper) HM.

Levine, Arthur A. Pearl Moscowitz's Last Stand. Roth, Rob, illus. LC 91-10652. 32p. (ps up). 1993. 14.00 (*0-688-10753-2*, Tambourine Bks); PLB 13.93 (*0-688-10754-0*, Tambourine Bks) Morrow.

Lewin, Hugh. Jafta: The Town. Kopper, Lisa, illus. LC 84-4950. 24p. (ps-3). 1984. PLB 15.95 (*0-87614-266-8*) Carolrhoda Bks.

Lobel, Anita. On Market Street. 1993. pap. 28.67 (*0-590-71697-2*) Scholastic Inc.

Lorenz, Lee. A Weekend in the City. Lorenz, Lee, illus. 32p. (gr. k-3). 1991. 14.95 (*0-945912-15-3*) Pippin Pr.

Lotz, Karen E. Can't Sit Still. Browning, Colleen, illus. LC 92-28853. 48p. (ps-3). 1993. 13.99 (*0-525-45066-1*, DCB) Dutton Child Bks.

Lundgren, Mary B. We Sing the City. Huerta, Catherine, illus. LC 93-34860. 1994. write for info. (*0-395-68188-X*, Clarion Bks) HM.

McCullough, Mary F. The City: Sights, Sounds, & Smells. McClain, Cindy, ed. (Illus.). 32p. (Orig.). (ps). 1991. pap. text ed. 3.95 (*0-936625-96-1*, New Hope AL) Womans Mission Union.

Martin, Jacqueline M. The Second Street Gardens & the Green Truck Almanac. Gillman, Alec, illus. LC 94-10869. 1995. 15.95 (*0-02-762460-9*, Four Winds) Macmillan Child Grp.

Martin, Melanie. Madison Moves to the Country. Karas, G. Brian, illus. LC 88-1313. 48p. (Orig.). (gr. 1-4). 1989. PLB 10.59 (*0-8167-1345-6*); pap. text ed. 3.50 (*0-8167-1346-4*) Troll Assocs.

Mayer, Mercer. Little Critter's This Is My Town. (ps-3). 1993. pap. 3.50 (*0-307-11567-4*, Golden Pr) Western Pub.

Mazer, Harry. Cave under the City. LC 86-45008. 160p. (gr. 3-7). 1989. pap. 3.95 (*0-06-440303-3*, Trophy) HarpC Child Bks.

Myers, Walter D. The Young Landlords. 208p. (gr. 5-9). 1989. pap. 4.99 (*0-14-034244-3*, Puffin) Puffin Bks.

National Geographic Staff. Around My Town. (ps). 1993. 5.00 (*0-7922-1968-6*) Natl Geog.

Nims, Bonnie L. Where Is the Bear in the City? Mathews, Judith, ed. Gill, Madelaine, illus. LC 92-3390. 24p. (ps-1). 1992. 11.95g (*0-8075-8937-3*) A Whitman.

Nixon, Joan L. Shadowmaker. LC 93-32314. 1994. 14.95 (*0-385-32030-2*) Delacorte.

Olivarez, Anna & Rohmer, Harriet, eds. Mr. Sugar Came to Town Read-Along. LC 88-38781. (SPA & ENG.). (ps-7). 1990. incl. audiocassette 22.95 (*0-89239-062-X*) Childrens Book Pr.

Packard, Edward. Deadwood City. 128p. (gr. 4). 1989. pap. 2.50 (*0-553-26213-0*) Bantam.

Panova, V. On Faraway Street. Gabel, Rya, tr. White, Anne Terry, adapted by. LC 68-12891. (Illus.). 129p. (gr. 3-7). 1968. 3.95 (*0-8076-0445-3*) Braziller.

Poploff, Michelle. Busy O'Brien & the Caterpillar Punch Bunch. (Illus.). 119p. (gr. 2-5). 1992. 13.95 (*0-8027-8151-9*) Walker & Co.

—Busy O'Brien & the Great Bubble Gum Blowout. Carter, Abby, illus. 96p. (gr. 2-5). 1990. 12.95 (*0-8027-6983-7*); lib. bdg. 13.85 (*0-8027-6984-5*) Walker & Co.

Porte, Barbara A. Taxicab Tales. Abolafia, Yossi, illus. LC 90-24609. 56p. 1992. 13.00 (*0-688-09908-4*) Greenwillow.

Priest, Robert. The Town that Got Out of Town. LC 88-46108. (Illus.). 32p. 1989. 14.95 (*0-87923-786-4*) Godine.

Privensen, Alice. Shaker Lane. 1990. pap. 4.95 (*0-14-050713-2*, Puffin) Puffin Bks.

Ransom, Candice. The Big Green Pocketbook. Bond, Felicia, illus. LC 92-29393. 32p. (ps-2). 1993. 14.00 (*0-06-020848-1*); PLB 13.89 (*0-06-020849-X*) HarpC Child Bks.

Repp, Gloria. Noodle Soup. Roberts, John, illus. LC 93-42417. 1994. write for info. (*0-89084-582-4*) Bob Jones Univ Pr.

Rotner, Shelley & Kreisler, Ken. Citybook. Rotner, Shelley, photos by. LC 93-6350. (Illus.). 32p. (ps-1). 1994. 14.95 (*0-531-06837-4*); lib. bdg. 14.99 RLB (*0-531-08687-9*) Orchard Bks Watts.

Rylant, Cynthia. But I'll Be Back Again: An Album. LC 88-17860. (Illus.). 80p. (gr. 5-7). 1989. 12.95 (*0-531-05806-9*); PLB 12.99 (*0-531-08406-X*) Orchard Bks Watts.

—The Everyday Books: Everyday Town. LC 92-40541. (Illus.). 14p. (ps-k). 1993. bds. 4.95 with rounded corners (*0-02-788026-5*, Bradbury Pr) Macmillan Child Grp.
Scarry, Richard. Richard Scarry's Postman Pig & His Busy Neighbors. LC 77-91646. (Illus.). (ps-2). 1978. lib. bdg. 5.99 (*0-394-93898-4*) Random Bks Yng Read.
Schwartz, Amy. A Teeny, Tiny Baby. LC 93-4876. (Illus.). 32p. (ps-1). 1994. 15.95 (*0-531-06818-8*); PLB 15.99 (*0-531-08668-2*) Orchard Bks Watts.
Slawson, Michele B. Apple Picking Time. Ray, Deborah K., illus. LC 92-23400. 32p. (ps-2). 1994. 15.00 (*0-517-58971-0*); PLB 15.99 (*0-517-58976-1*) Crown Bks Yng Read.
Slote, Elizabeth. Nelly's Grannies. Slote, Elizabeth, illus. LC 91-32600. 32p. (ps up). 1993. 14.00 (*0-688-11314-1*, Tambourine Bks); PLB 13.93 (*0-688-11315-X*, Tambourine Bks) Morrow.
Smalls-Hector, Irene. Jonathan & His Mommy. (ps-3). 1992. 14.95 (*0-316-79870-3*) Little.
Spinelli, Eileen. If You Want to Find Golden. Shuett, Stacey, illus. LC 93-12000. (gr. 1-3). 1993. 14.95 (*0-8075-3585-0*) A Whitman.
Stevens, Carla. Anna, Grandpa & the Big Storm. Tomes, Margot, illus. 48p. (gr. 6-9). 1982. 13.95 (*0-89919-066-9*, Clarion Bks) HM.
Wainwright, Richard M. Garden of Dreams. Dvorsack, Carolyn S., illus. LC 93-17974. 1994. 14.00 (*0-9619566-6-6*) Family Life.
Weisman, Joan. The Storyteller. Bradley, David, illus. LC 93-20460. 32p. 1993. 15.95 (*0-8478-1742-3*) Rizzoli Intl.
Willis, Meredith S. The Secret Super Power of Marco. LC 93-14491. 112p. (gr. 3-7). 1994. 14.00 (*0-06-023558-6*); PLB 13.89 (*0-06-023559-4*) HarpC Child Bks.
Wong, Olive. From My Window. Bellerose, Mark, illus. LC 94-20303. 1994. 14.95 (*0-382-24666-7*); PLB 16.95 (*0-382-24665-9*); pap. 6.95 (*0-382-24667-5*) Silver Burdett Pr.
Yektai, Niki. The Secret Room. LC 92-6720. 192p. (gr. 4-7). 1992. 14.95 (*0-531-05456-X*); PLB 14.99 (*0-531-08606-2*) Orchard Bks Watts.
Zimmerman. Applesauce & Cottage Cheese. 1995. 15.00 (*0-06-024277-9*); PLB 14.89 (*0-06-024278-7*) HarpC Child Bks.

CITIES AND TOWNS–HISTORY

Ayoub, Abderrahaman, et al. Umm el Madayan: An Islamic City Through the Ages. Corni, Francesco, illus. LC 93-757. (ENG.). (gr. 5 up). 1994. 16.95 (*0-395-65967-1*) HM.
Comes, Pilar & Hernandez, Xavier. Barmi: A Mediterranean City Through the Ages. Ballonga, Jordi, illus. 64p. (gr. 5 up). 1990. 14.45 (*0-395-54227-8*) HM.
Ewing, Juliana H. Our Field. LC 85-31445. 32p. (gr. 4 up). 1986. PLB 13.95 (*0-88682-074-X*) Creative Ed.
Ganeri, Anita. Benares. LC 93-72036. (Illus.). 48p. (gr. 5 up). 1993. text ed. 13.95 RSBE (*0-87518-573-8*, Dillon) Macmillan Child Grp.
Hernandez, Xavier & Ballonga, Jordi. Lebek: A City of Northern Europe Through the Ages. Leverich, Kathleen, tr. Corni, Francesco, illus. 64p. 1991. 16.45 (*0-395-57442-0*, Sandpiper) HM.
Husain, Shahrukh. Mecca. LC 93-72324. (Illus.). 48p. (gr. 5 up). 1993. text ed. 13.95 RSBE (*0-87518-572-X*, Dillon) Macmillan Child Grp.
Kalman, Bobbie. Visiting a Village. (Illus.). 32p. (gr. 3-4). 1990. PLB 15.95 (*0-86505-487-8*); pap. 7.95 (*0-86505-507-6*) Crabtree Pub Co.
Von Tscharner, Renata & Fleming, Ronald L. New Providence: A Changing Cityscape. Orloff, Denis, illus. 32p. (gr. k-4). 1992. pap. 9.95 (*0-89133-191-3*) Preservation Pr.

CITIES AND TOWNS–PICTURES, ILLUSTRATIONS, ETC.

Rius, Maria & Parramon, J. M. The City. (ps). 1986. 6.95 (*0-8120-5748-1*); pap. 3.95 (*0-8120-3700-6*) Barron.
Soentpiet, Chris K. Around Town. LC 93-23519. (Illus.). 1994. 15.00 (*0-688-04572-3*); PLB 14.93 (*0-688-04573-1*) Lothrop.

CITIES AND TOWNS–PLANNING

see City Planning

CITIES AND TOWNS–POETRY

Adoff, Arnold. Street Music: City Poems. Barbour, Karen, illus. LC 92-28539. 1994. 16.00 (*0-06-021522-4*); PLB 15.89 (*0-06-021523-2*) HarpC Child Bks.
Brooks, Gwendolyn. Bronzeville Boys & Girls. Solbert, Ronni, illus. LC 56-8152. 48p. (gr. 3-6). 1967. PLB 13.89 (*0-06-020651-9*) HarpC Child Bks.
Greenfield, Eloise. Night on Neighborhood Street. (ps-3). 1991. 14.00 (*0-8037-0777-0*); PLB 13.89 (*0-8037-0778-9*) Dial Bks Young.
Grimes, Nikki. Meet Danitra Brown. Cooper, Floyd, illus. LC 92-43707. (gr. 4 up). 1995. 15.00 (*0-688-12073-3*); PLB 14.93 (*0-688-12074-1*) Lothrop.
Kuskin, Karla. City Noise. Flower, Renee, illus. LC 91-44213. 32p. (ps-3). 1994. 15.00 (*0-06-021076-1*); PLB 14.89 (*0-06-021077-X*) HarpC Child Bks.
Merriam, Eve. The Inner City Mother Goose. LC 93-19735. (Illus.). 1996. pap. 15.00 (*0-671-88033-0*, S&S BFYR) S&S Trade.

CITIES AND TOWNS, RUINED, EXTINCT, ETC.

see also Excavations (Archeology)

Stone, Lynn. Ghost Towns. LC 93-143. 1993. 15.93 (*0-86625-449-8*); 11.95s.p. (*0-685-66533-X*) Rourke Pubns.
Tyler, Deborah. The Greeks & Troy. LC 93-18693. (Illus.). 32p. (gr. 6-8). 1993. text ed. 13.95 RSBE (*0-87518-537-1*, Dillon) Macmillan Child Grp.

CITIES AND TOWNS–U. S.

Loewen, Nancy & Stewart, Gail. Great Cities of the U. S, 8 bks, Reading Level 6. (Illus.). 384p. (gr. 5 up). 1989. Set. PLB 127.52 (*0-86592-537-2*); 95.60s.p. (*0-685-58767-3*) Rourke Corp.

CITIES AND TOWNS IN ART

Richardson, Wendy & Richardson, Jack. Cities: Through the Eyes of Artists. LC 90-34277. 48p. (gr. 4 up). 1991. PLB 15.40 (*0-516-09282-0*); pap. 7.95 (*0-516-49282-9*) Childrens.

CITIZENSHIP

see also Patriotism

Branson, Margaret & Coombs, Fred. Civics for Today. (Illus.). (gr. 7-9). 1980. text ed. 36.72 (*0-395-26201-1*); wkbk. 11.28 (*0-395-26203-8*) HM.
Bratman, Fred. Becoming a Citizen: Adopting a New Home. LC 92-24061. (Illus.). 48p. (gr. 5-6). 1992. PLB 21.34 (*0-8114-7354-6*) Raintree Steck-V.
Harik, Elsa M. The Lebanese in America. (Illus.). 96p. (gr. 5 up). 1987. PLB 15.95 (*0-8225-0234-8*); pap. 5.95 (*0-8225-1032-4*) Lerner Pubns.
Kownslar, Allan O. & Smart, Terry L. Civics: Citizens & Society. 2nd ed. (Illus.). 576p. (gr. 7-8). 1983. text ed. 31.88 (*0-07-035433-2*) McGraw.
Petersen, Peter L. The Danes in America. (Illus.). 96p. (gr. 5 up). 1987. PLB 15.95 (*0-8225-0233-X*); pap. 5.95 (*0-8225-1031-6*) Lerner Pubns.
Pincus, Debbie & Ward, Richard J. Citizenship. 112p. (gr. 4-9). 1991. 10.95 (*0-86653-608-6*, GA 1327) Good Apple.
Profiles Corporation Staff. Buckle down! on American Citizenship: Student Text. 2nd ed. (Illus.). 73p. (gr. 7-12). 1992. pap. text ed. 30.00 (*0-7836-1302-4*, ST BD01) Profiles Corp.
Rutledge, Paul. The Vietnamese in America. (Illus.). 64p. (gr. 5 up). 1987. PLB 15.95 (*0-8225-0235-6*); pap. 5.95 (*0-8225-1033-2*) Lerner Pubns.
Shuker-Haines, Frances. Rights & Responsibilities: Using Your Freedom. LC 92-25732. (Illus.). 48p. (gr. 5-6). 1992. PLB 21.34 (*0-8114-7355-4*) Raintree Steck-V.

CITRUS FRUIT

see also names of citrus fruits, e.g. Orange, etc.

Stone, Lynn M. Citrus Country. LC 93-22978. 1993. pap. write for info. (*0-86593-304-9*) Rourke Corp.
Wake, Susan. Citrus Fruits. (Illus.). 32p. (gr. 1-4). 1990. PLB 14.95 (*0-87614-389-3*) Carolrhoda Bks.

CITY LIFE

see Cities and Towns

CITY PLANNING

see also Housing

Bruning, Nancy. Cities Against Nature. LC 91-34604. 128p. (gr. 4-8). 1992. PLB 20.55 (*0-516-05510-0*) Childrens.
Hooper, Rosanne. Living in Towns. LC 93-12514. (gr. 4 up). Date not set. write for info. (*0-531-14266-3*) Watts.

CIVICS

see Citizenship; Political Science; U. S.–Politics and Government

CIVIL DISOBEDIENCE

see Government, Resistance to

CIVIL DISORDERS

see Riots

CIVIL ENGINEERING

see also Bridges; Canals; Dams; Harbors; Masonry; Military Engineering; Mining Engineering; Rivers; Roads; Subways; Surveying; Tunnels; Water Supply

CIVIL GOVERNMENT

see Political Science

CIVIL LIBERTY

see Liberty

CIVIL RIGHTS

see also Free Speech; Freedom of the Press; Liberty; Religious Liberty

also names of groups of people with the subdivision Civil rights, e.g. Blacks–Civil Rights

Amnesty International, Human Rights for Children Committee Staff. Human Rights for Children. Sinetar, Marsha, illus. LC 92-35575. 80p. (Orig.). (ps-6). 1992. spiral bdg. 12.95 (*0-89793-120-3*); pap. 10.95 (*0-89793-121-1*) Hunter Hse.
Bronson, Marsha. Amnesty International. LC 93-26367. 1994. text ed. 13.95 (*0-02-714550-6*, New Discovery Bks) Macmillan Child Grp.
Bullard, Sara. Free At Last: A History of the Civil Rights Movement & Those Who Died in the Struggle. Bond, Julian, intro. by. LC 92-38174. (Illus.). 112p. 1993. PLB 20.00 (*0-19-508381-4*) OUP.
Cavan, Seamus. Thurgood Marshall & Equal Rights. LC 92-12995. (Illus.). 32p. (gr. 2-4). 1993. PLB 12.40 (*1-56294-277-8*); pap. 4.95 (*1-56294-793-1*) Millbrook Pr.
Coil, Suzanne M. The Civil Rights Movement. (Illus.). 64p. (gr. 5-8). 1995. bds. 15.95 (*0-8050-2987-7*) TFC Bks NY.
Cozic, Charles P., ed. Civil Liberties: Opposing Viewpoints. rev. ed. LC 93-16419. 1994. lib. bdg. 17.95 (*1-56510-058-1*); pap. 9.95 (*1-56510-057-3*) Greenhaven.
Fox, Ken. Everything You Need to Know about Your Legal Rights. (gr. 7-12). 1992. PLB 14.95 (*0-8239-1322-8*) Rosen Group.
Frankel, Marvin E. International Human. 1989. pap. 16.95 (*0-440-50145-8*) Dell.
Frankel, Marvin E. & Saideman, Ellen. Out of the Shadows of Night: The Struggle for International Human Rights. (gr. 9 up). 1989. pap. 8.95 (*0-385-29820-X*) Delacorte.
Kronenwetter, Michael. Taking a Stand Against Human Rights Abuses. LC 89-70450. 1990. PLB 14.40 (*0-531-10921-6*) Watts.
Landau, Elaine. Big Brother Is Watching. 1992. 14.95 (*0-8027-8160-8*); lib. bdg. 15.85 (*0-8027-8161-6*) Walker & Co.
Lee. Discrimination. 1991. 12.95s.p. (*0-86593-113-5*) Rourke Corp.
Levine, Ellen. Freedom's Children: Young Civil Rights Activists Tell Their Own Stories. 224p. 1993. 16.95 (*0-399-21893-9*) Putnam Pub Group.
Lowe, William C. Blessings of Liberty: Safeguarding Civil Rights. LC 92-9756. 1992. 22.60 (*0-86593-173-9*); 16.95s.p. (*0-685-59325-8*) Rourke Corp.
Marzollo, Jean. Happy Birthday, Martin Luther King. Pinkney, J. Brian, illus. LC 91-42137. 32p. (ps-3). 1993. 14.95 (*0-590-44065-9*) Scholastic Inc.
Moore, Yvette. Freedom Songs. LC 88-43073. 176p. (gr. 7 up). 1991. 14.95 (*0-531-05812-3*); PLB 14.99 (*0-531-08412-4*) Orchard Bks Watts.
Sherwin, Jane. Human Rights. (Illus.). 48p. (gr. 5 up). 1990. lib. bdg. 18.60 (*0-86592-099-0*); lib. bdg. 13.95s.p. (*0-685-36379-1*) Rourke Corp.
Universal Declaration of Human Rights: An Adaptation for Children. 46p. 1990. 9.95 (*92-1-100424-1*, 89.I.19); pap. 9.95 (*0-685-47757-6*, 90.I.20) UN.
Wilson, Reginald. Our Rights: Civil Liberties in the U. S. rev. ed. 160p. (gr. 7 up). 1993. PLB 15.85 (*0-8027-8127-6*); pap. 9.95 (*0-8027-7371-0*) Walker & Co.
—Think about Our Rights: Civil Liberties & the United States. LC 87-22989. 123p. 1988. 14.85 (*0-8027-6751-6*); pap. 5.95 (*0-8027-6752-4*) Walker & Co.
Zeltmann, Walter F. Human Rights. LC 90-71594. 76p. (Orig.). 1990. 24.90 (*0-9622705-2-0*); pap. 9.90 (*0-9622705-3-9*) Yellow Hook Pr.

CIVIL RIGHTS–BIOGRAPHY

Hughes, Libby. Nelson Mandela: Voice of Freedom. LC 91-31543. (Illus.). 144p. (gr. 5 up). 1992. text ed. 13.95 RSBE (*0-87518-484-7*, Dillon) Macmillan Child Grp.
Jacobs, William J. Great Lives: Human Rights. LC 89-37211. (Illus.). 288p. (gr. 4-6). 1990. SBE 23.00 (*0-684-19036-2*, Scribners Young Read) Macmillan Child Grp.
Jakoubek, Robert E. James Farmer & the Freedom Rides. (Illus.). 32p. (gr. 2-4). 1994. 12.90 (*1-56294-381-2*) Millbrook Pr.
—Walter White & the Power of Organized Protest. (Illus.). 32p. (gr. 2-4). 1994. 12.90 (*1-56294-378-2*) Millbrook Pr.
Johnson, Jacqueline. Stokely Carmichael: The Story of Black Power. Gallin, Richard, ed. Young, Andrew, intro. by. (Illus.). 128p. (gr. 5 up). 1990. lib. bdg. 12.95 (*0-382-09920-6*); pap. 7.95 (*0-382-24056-1*) Silver Burdett Pr.
Kenan, Randall. James Baldwin. (Illus.). 1994. 19.95 (*0-7910-2301-X*, Am Art Analog) Chelsea Hse.
Levine, Ellen. Freedom's Children: Young Civil Rights Activists Tell Their Own Stories. large type ed. LC 93-10388. (Illus.). 1993. 16.95 (*1-56054-744-8*) Thorndike Pr.
Medearis, Angela S. Dare to Dream: Coretta Scott King & the Civil Rights Movement. Rich, Anna, illus. LC 93-33573. 64p. (gr. 3-6). 1994. 13.99 (*0-525-67426-8*, Lodestar Bks) Dutton Child Bks.
Pogrund, Benjamin. Nelson Mandela: Strength & Spirit of a Free South Africa. LC 90-24026. (Illus.). 68p. (gr. 5-6). 1992. PLB 19.93 (*0-8368-0357-4*) Gareth Stevens Inc.
Powledge, Fred. We Shall Overcome: Heroes of the Civil Rights Movement. LC 92-25184. (Illus.). 224p. (gr. 7 up). 1993. SBE 16.95 (*0-684-19362-0*, Scribners Young Read) Macmillan Child Grp.
Rochelle, Belinda. Witnesses to Freedom: Young People Who Fought for Civil Rights. LC 93-16165. (Illus.). 112p. (gr. 3-7). 1993. 15.99 (*0-525-67377-6*, Lodestar Bks) Dutton Child Bks.
Siegel, Beatrice. Murder on the Highway: The Viola Liuzzo Story. Parks, Rosa, intro. by. LC 93-7148. (Illus.). 136p. (gr. 4-7). 1994. SBE 14.95 (*0-02-782632-5*, Four Winds) Macmillan Child Grp.

Walker, Lydia. Challenge & Change: The Story of Civil Rights Activist, C. T. Vivian. Lewis, John. LC 93-60228. (Illus.). 61p. (Orig.). (gr. 5 up). 1993. pap. 8.95 (*1-877852-14-7*) Dreamkeeper Pr.
CHALLENGE & CHANGE is the story of civil rights activist C.T. Vivian. The title of this biography is the essence of the narrative which places in local color the developmental experiences that changed a once bullied six year-old boy from a scrappy aggressor to a peace maker. Challenged from the beginning of first grade when

relocation from his native Missouri to Illinois made him an outsider, C.T.'s eventual & unexpected self-defense had a dramatic effect on his bullying peers. They changed from foes to followers as a newly confident C.T. became their leader & defender of the underdog on the playground & in the alleys of Macomb, Illinois. Defending others remained a life-long habit. Fighting did not. C.T. discovered the disarming power of non-violence at age 9 when a kid would not fight back. Many years later, C.T. could articulate what happened: "He won the fight; it was non-violence in action." "And", continued C.T., "It had a lasting effect on me." Call or write for information to order, Dreamkeeper Press, P.O. Box 4802, Atlanta, GA 30302. 404-696-7416.
Publisher Provided Annotation.

Winner, David. Peter Beneson: Taking a Stand Against Injustice-Amnesty International. LC 90-47877. (Illus.). 68p. (gr. 5-6). 1992. PLB 19.93 (*0-8368-0400-7*) Gareth Stevens Inc.

CIVIL RIGHTS–U. S.

Almonte, Paul & Desmond, Theresa. Police, People & Power. LC 91-46951. (Illus.). 48p. (gr. 5-6). 1992. text ed. 12.95 RSBE (*0-89686-748-X*, Crestwood Hse) Macmillan Child Grp.

Bornstein, Jerry. Police Brutality: A National Debate. LC 92-42146. (Illus.). 112p. (gr. 6 up). 1993. lib. bdg. 17. 95 (*0-89490-430-2*) Enslow Pubs.

Bray, Rosemary L. Martin Luther King. Zeldis, Malcah, illus. LC 93-41002. 48p. (gr. 2 up). 1995. write for info. (*0-688-13131-X*); PLB write for info. (*0-688-13132-8*) Greenwillow.

Bryant, Eric H. Arrest Me Not: The Common Sense Survival Guide for Teens (& Adults) When Stopped by Police. 41p. (gr. 7 up). 1994. pap. 5.95 (*0-9640336-0-7*) Page One Communs.

Cwiklik, Robert. A. Philip Randolph & the Labor Movement. LC 92-32167. (Illus.). 32p. (gr. 2-4). 1993. PLB 12.90 (*1-56294-326-X*); pap. 4.95 (*1-56294-788-5*) Millbrook Pr.

Hess, Debra. Thurgood Marshall: The Fight for Equal Justice. Gallin, Richard, ed. Young, Andrew, intro. by. (Illus.). 128p. (gr. 5 up). 1990. lib. bdg. 12.95 (*0-382-09921-4*); pap. 7.95 (*0-382-24058-8*) Silver Burdett Pr.

Hull, Mary. Rosa Parks: Civil Rights Leader. LC 93-17699. (Illus.). (gr. 5 up). 1994. PLB 18.95 (*0-7910-1881-4*, Am Art Analog); write for info. (*0-7910-1910-1*, Am Art Analog) Chelsea Hse.

Katz, William L. The Great Society to the Reagan Era, 1964-1993. LC 92-43709. (Illus.). 96p. (gr. 7-8). 1993. PLB 22.80 (*0-8114-6282-X*) Raintree Steck-V.

—Minorities Today. LC 92-47438. (Illus.). 96p. (gr. 7-8). 1992. PLB 22.80 (*0-8114-6281-1*) Raintree Steck-V.

Kent, Deborah. The Freedom Riders. LC 92-33424. (Illus.). 32p. (gr. 3-6). 1993. PLB 12.30 (*0-516-06662-5*); pap. 3.95 (*0-516-46662-3*) Childrens.

Levine, Ellen. If You Lived At the Time of Martin Luther King. 1990. pap. 2.95 (*0-590-42582-X*) Scholastic Inc.

Miller, Marilyn. The Bridge at Selma. LC 84-40379. (Illus.). 64p. (gr. 5 up). 1984. PLB 12.95 (*0-382-06826-2*); pap. 7.95 (*0-382-06973-0*) Silver Burdett Pr.

Perseverance. (Illus.). 256p. (gr. 9 up). 1993. write for info. (*0-7835-2250-9*); PLB write for info. (*0-7835-2251-7*) Time-Life.

Rennert, Richard, ed. Civil Rights Leaders. LC 92-37655. (Illus.). 1993. 13.95 (*0-7910-2051-7*, Am Art Analog); pap. 5.95 (*0-7910-2052-5*, Am Art Analog) Chelsea Hse.

Wekesser, Carol & Swisher, Karin, eds. Social Justice: Opposing Viewpoints. LC 90-42855. (Illus.). 240p. (gr. 10 up). 1990. PLB 17.95 (*0-89908-482-6*); pap. text ed. 9.95 (*0-89908-457-5*) Greenhaven.

Yette, Samuel F. & Yette, Frederick W. Washington & Two Marches: 1963 & 1983. (Illus.). 1984. 25.00 (*0-911253-02-5*); pap. 16.95 (*0-911253-03-3*); deluxe ed. 50.00 deluxe ltd. ed (*0-317-11590-1*) Cottage Bks.

CIVIL RIGHTS DEMONSTRATIONS

see Blacks–Civil Rights

CIVIL SERVICE

Here are entered general works on the history and development of public service. Works on public personnel administration, including the duties of civil service employees, their salaries, pensions, etc., are entered under the name of the country, state or city with the subdivision Officials and Employees.

see also names of countries, cities, etc. with the subdivision Officials and Employees, e.g. U. S.–Officials and Employees

CIVIL WAR–ENGLAND

see Great Britain–History–Civil War and Commonwealth, 1642-1660

CIVIL WAR–U. S.

see U. S.–History–Civil War

CIVILIZATION

see also Anthropology; Archeology; Art; Culture; Education; Ethics; Ethnology; Industry; Inventions; Learning and Scholarship; Manners and Customs; Religions; Science and Civilization; Social Problems; Technology and Civilization

also names of countries, states, etc. with the subdivision Civilization, e.g. U. S.–Civilization

Cultures of the World, 6 vols. 128p. (gr. 5-10). 1992. Set. PLB 131.70 (*1-85435-543-0*) Marshall Cavendish.

East - West. (Illus.). (gr. 8 up). 1992. PLB 16.95 (*0-8239-1375-9*); pap. 8.95 (*0-8239-1376-7*) Rosen Group.

Mason, Antony. The Children's Atlas of Civilizations. LC 93-23564. (Illus.). 96p. (gr. 2-6). 1994. PLB 18.90 (*1-56294-494-0*); pap. 12.95 (*1-56294-733-8*) Millbrook Pr.

Merriman, Nick. Early Humans. King, Dave, photos by. LC 88-13431. (Illus.). 64p. (gr. 5 up). 1989. 16.00 (*0-394-82257-9*); lib. bdg. 16.99 (*0-394-92257-3*) Knopf Bks Yng Read.

Monteith, Jay. A Multicultural Activity Workbook: Africa, Asia & the Americas. (Illus.). 72p. (Orig.). (gr. 1 up). 1991. pap. text ed. 7.95 (*0-9627366-1-9*) Arts & Comns NY.

Reardon, Judy A. & Smock, Raymond W. The Western Civilization Slide Collection Master Guide. rev. ed. 253p. (Orig.). (gr. 7 up). 1988. 25.00 (*0-923805-01-X*) Instruc Resc MD.

—The Western Civilization Slide Collection. (Illus.). 253p. (Orig.). (gr. 7 up). 1988. incl. 2100 slides 895.00 (*0-923805-02-8*); pap. 25.00 (*0-685-24654-X*) Instruc Resc MD.

Reid, Struan. Cultures & Civilizations. (Illus.). 48p. (gr. 6 up). 1994. text ed. 15.95 RSBE (*0-02-726315-0*, New Discovery Bks) Macmillan Child Grp.

Tames, Richard. Exploring Other Civilizations. 52p. (gr. 11 up). 1987. pap. 7.95 (*0-685-19629-1*, Pub. by S Thornes UK) Dufour.

CIVILIZATION, ANCIENT

see also Man, Prehistoric

The Atlas of Ancient Worlds. LC 93-27041. 1994. 19.95 (*1-56458-471-2*) Dorling Kindersley.

Buxton, John, illus. Secret Treasures; Animal Acrobats, 2 vols. LC 93-9767. (Illus.). 1993. Set 27.50 (*0-87044-956-7*) Natl Geog.

Cervera, Isabel. The Mughal Empire. LC 94-16115. (Illus.). 36p. (gr. 3 up). 1994. PLB 20.00 (*0-516-08392-9*); pap. 6.95 (*0-516-48392-7*) Childrens.

Chadefaud, Catherine & Coblence, Jean-Michel. The First Empires. Ridett, Anthea, tr. from FRE. Tarride, Michel, illus. 77p. (gr. 7 up). 1988. 12.95 (*0-382-09481-6*); 10.37s.p. (*0-685-18824-8*) Silver Burdett Pr.

Corbishley, Mike. Where People Came From? LC 94-16651. 1995. write for info. (*0-8114-3880-5*) Raintree Steck-V.

Frazee, Charles & Yopp, Hallie Kay. Early People & the First Civilizations. Frazee, Kathleen & Lumba, Eric, illus. (gr. 6). 1990. write for info. Delos Pubns.

Hoobler, Dorothy & Hoobler, Tom. The Fact or Fiction Files: Lost Civilizations. 160p. (gr. 7-10). 1992. 14.95 (*0-8027-8152-7*); lib. bdg. 15.85 (*0-8027-8153-5*) Walker & Co.

Hunter, Erica C. D. First Civilizations. Evans, Gillian, ed. LC 93-41079. (Illus.). 96p. (gr. 5-9). 1994. 17.95 (*0-8160-2976-8*) Facts on File.

Jones, Christopher. Lost Civilizations: An Exploration Kit. LC 93-87364. (Illus.). 64p. (gr. 3 up). 1994. incl. kit 17.95 (*1-56138-388-0*) Running Pr.

Krupp, Robin R. Let's Go Traveling. Krupp, Robin R., illus. LC 91-21845. 40p. (gr. 2 up). 1992. 15.00 (*0-688-08989-5*); PLB 14.93 (*0-688-08990-9*) Morrow Jr Bks.

Odijk, Pamela. The Phoenicians. (Illus.). 48p. (gr. 5-8). 1989. PLB 12.95 (*0-382-09891-9*); 7.95 (*0-382-24266-1*); 4.50 (*0-382-24281-5*) Silver Burdett Pr.

Oliphant, Margaret. The Earliest Civilizations. (Illus.). 80p. (gr. 2-6). 1993. 17.95x (*0-8160-2785-4*) Facts on File.

Pollard, Michael. Empire Builders. Stefoff, Rebecca, ed. LC 91-36501. (Illus.). 48p. (gr. 5-8). 1992. PLB 19.93 (*1-56074-038-8*) Garrett Ed Corp.

Szekely, Edmond B. & Bordeaux, Norma N. Messengers from Ancient Civilizations. (Illus.). 44p. (gr. 5 up). 1974. pap. 3.50 (*0-89564-068-6*) IBS Intl.

The Visual Dictionary of Ancient Civilizations. LC 94-8395. 64p. (gr. 7 up). 1994. 15.95 (*1-56458-701-0*) Dorling Kindersley.

CIVILIZATION–FICTION

Gardam, Jane. The Hollow Land. Rawlings, Janet, illus. LC 81-6620. 160p. (gr. 5-9). 1982. 10.25 (*0-688-00873-9*) Greenwillow.

Mitgutsch, Ali. A Knight's Book. Crawford, Elizabeth D., tr. Mitgutsch, Ali, illus. 40p. (gr. 2-5). 1991. 16.45 (*0-395-58103-6*, Clarion Bks) HM.

CIVILIZATION, GREEK

Clare, John D., ed. Ancient Greece. LC 93-6267. 1994. 16.95 (*0-15-200516-1*, Gulliver Bks) HarBrace.

Dineen, Jacqueline. The Greeks. LC 91-512. (Illus.). 64p. (gr. 6 up). 1992. text ed. 14.95 RSBE (*0-02-730650-X*, New Discovery) Macmillan Child Grp.

Ganeri, Anita. Ancient Greeks. LC 93-11178. (Illus.). (gr. 5 up). 1993. PLB 12.40 (*0-531-17369-0*, Gloucester Pr) Watts.

Nicholson, Robert. Ancient Greece. LC 93-29442. 1994. write for info. (*0-7910-2703-1*); write for info. (*0-7910-2727-9*) Chelsea Hse.

Pearson, Anne. Ancient Greece. Nicholls, Nick, photos by. LC 92-4713. (Illus.). 64p. (gr. 5 up). 1992. 16.00 (*0-679-81682-8*); PLB 16.99 (*0-679-91682-2*) Knopf Bks Yng Read.

—Everyday Life in Ancient Greece. LC 93-37519. 1994. write for info. (*0-531-14310-4*) Watts.

Poulton, Michael. Life in the Time of Pericles & the Ancient Greeks. James, John, illus. LC 92-5817. 63p. (gr. 6-7). 1992. PLB 24.26 (*0-8114-3352-8*) Raintree Steck-V.

Terzi, Marinella. Ancient Greece. LC 92-7508. (Illus.). 36p. (gr. 3 up). 1992. PLB 14.95 (*0-516-08376-7*) Childrens.

CIVILIZATION–HISTORY

Adams, Jean-Pierre. Mediterranean Civilizations. LC 86-426550. (Illus.). 77p. (gr. 7 up). 1987. 12.95 (*0-382-09215-5*) Silver Burdett Pr.

Millard. The First Civilization. (Illus.). (gr. 4-9). 1977. (Usborne-Hayes); PLB 13.96 (*0-88110-107-9*); pap. 6.95 (*0-86020-138-4*) EDC.

Millard, Anne. How People Lived. Sergio, illus. LC 92-54315. 64p. (gr. 3-7). 1993. 12.95 (*1-56458-237-X*) Dorling Kindersley.

Steele, Philip. City Through the Ages. Lapper, Ivan, et al, illus. LC 91-37350. 32p. (gr. 3-6). 1993. PLB 11.89 (*0-8167-2727-9*); pap. text ed. 3.95 (*0-8167-2728-7*) Troll Assocs.

—House Through the Ages. Howett, Andrew & Davidson, Gordon, illus. LC 91-36481. 32p. (gr. 3-6). 1993. PLB 11.89 (*0-8167-2733-3*); pap. text ed. 3.95 (*0-8167-2734-1*) Troll Assocs.

—River Through the Ages. Ingpen, Robert, illus. LC 91-33279. 32p. (gr. 3-6). 1993. PLB 11.89 (*0-8167-2735-X*); pap. text ed. 3.95 (*0-8167-2736-8*) Troll Assocs.

CIVILIZATION, MEDIEVAL

see also Chivalry; Feudalism; Middle Ages

Aliki. A Medieval Feast. LC 82-45923. (Illus.). 32p. (gr. 2-6). 1983. 14.00 (*0-690-04245-0*, Crowell Jr Bks); PLB 13.89 (*0-690-04246-9*, Crowell Jr Bks) HarpC Child Bks.

Cairns, Trevor. Medieval Knights. (Illus.). 64p. (gr. 7 up). 1992. pap. 10.95 (*0-521-38953-4*) Cambridge U Pr.

Caselli, Giovanni. The Renaissance & the New World. Caselli, Giovanni, illus. LC 85-22900. 48p. (gr. 5 up). 1986. 16.95 (*0-87226-050-X*) P Bedrick Bks.

Castle. LC 93-30158. 32p. 1994. 16.95 (*1-56458-467-4*) Dorling Kindersley.

Clare, John D., ed. Knights in Armor. (gr. 4-7). 1992. 16. 95 (*0-15-200508-0*, Gulliver Bks) HarBrace.

Corbishley, Mike. Middle Ages. (Illus.). 96p. 1990. 17.95 (*0-8160-1973-8*) Facts on File.

Dann, Geoff & Gravett, Chris. Knight. LC 92-1590. 64p. (gr. 5 up). 1993. 15.00 (*0-679-83882-1*); PLB 15.99 (*0-679-93882-6*) Knopf Bks Yng Read.

Dawson, Imogen. In the Middle Ages. LC 93-27200. (Illus.). 32p. (gr. 6 up). 1994. text ed. 14.95 RSBE (*0-02-726324-X*, New Discovery Bks) Macmillan Child Grp.

Hunt, Jonathan. Illuminations. Hunt, Jonathan, illus. LC 92-23542. 40p. (ps-12). 1993. pap. 5.95 (*0-689-71700-8*, Aladdin) Macmillan Child Grp.

Jones, Madeline. Knights & Castles. (Illus.). 72p. (gr. 7-11). 1991. 19.95 (*0-7134-6352-X*, Pub. by Batsford UK) Trafalgar.

Macdonald, Fiona. A Medieval Cathedral. James, John, illus. 48p. (gr. 5 up). 1994. 17.95 (*0-87226-350-9*); pap. 8.95 (*0-87226-266-9*) P Bedrick Bks.

Penner, Lucille R. Knights & Castles. Bell, Owain, illus. LC 93-45710. (gr. 4 up). 1994. PLB 2.50 (*0-679-85095-3*) Random.

CIVILIZATION, MODERN

see also History, Modern; Renaissance

Greene, Janice, et al. Our Century: 1900-1910. LC 93-11445. (gr. 4 up). 1993. Repr. of 1989 ed. PLB 21.27 (*0-8368-1032-5*) Gareth Stevens Inc.

CIVILIZATION AND SCIENCE

see Science and Civilization

CIVILIZATION AND TECHNOLOGY

see Technology and Civilization

CLAIRVOYANCE

see also Divination; Extrasensory Perception; Fortune Telling; Hypnotism; Thought Transference

Green, Carl R. & Sanford, William R. Seeing the Unseen. Robinson, Keith, illus. LC 92-44677. 48p. (gr. 4-10). 1993. lib. bdg. 14.95 (*0-89490-454-X*) Enslow Pubs.

CLARK, WILLIAM, 1770-1838

Fitz-Gerald, Christine A. Meriwether Lewis & William Clark: The Northwest Expedition. LC 90-20696. (Illus.). 128p. (gr. 3 up). 1991. PLB 20.55 (*0-516-03061-2*); pap. 9.95 (*0-516-43061-0*) Childrens.

Kroll, Steven. Lewis & Clark: Explorers of the Far West. Williams, Richard, illus. LC 92-40427. 32p. (gr. 3-7). 1994. reinforced bdg. 16.95 (*0-8234-1034-X*) Holiday.

Noonan, Jon. Lewis & Clark. LC 92-9381. (Illus.). 48p. (gr. 5). 1993. text ed. 12.95 RSBE (*0-89686-707-2*, Crestwood Hse) Macmillan Child Grp.

Roop, Peter & Roop, Connie. Off the Map: The Journals of Lewis & Clark. Tanner, Tim, illus. LC 92-18340. 48p. (gr. 3-7). 1993. 14.95 (*0-8027-8207-8*); PLB 15. 85 (*0-8027-8208-6*) Walker & Co.

Stefoff, Rebecca. Lewis & Clark. (Illus.). 80p. (gr. 3-5). 1992. lib. bdg. 12.95 (*0-7910-1750-8*) Chelsea Hse.
Twist, Clint. Lewis & Clark: Exploring North America. LC 93-33624. 1994. PLB 22.80 (*0-8114-7255-8*) Raintree Steck-V.
Zadra, Dan. Explorers of America: Lewis & Clark. rev. ed. (gr. 2-4). 1988. PLB 14.95 (*0-88682-183-5*) Creative Ed.

CLASS CONFLICT
see Social Conflict

CLASS STRUGGLE
see Social Conflict

CLASSES (MATHEMATICS)
see Set Theory

CLASSICAL ANTIQUITIES
see also Archeology; Art, Greek; Mythology, Classical also names of countries, cities, etc. with the subdivision Antiquities, e.g. Greece–Antiquities

CLASSICAL ART
see Art, Greek

CLASSICAL BIOGRAPHY
see Greece–Biography; Rome–Biography

CLASSICAL LANGUAGES
see Latin Language

CLASSICAL MYTHOLOGY
see Mythology, Classical

CLAY, CASSIUS MARCELLUS, 1942-
see Muhammad Ali, 1942-

CLAY, HENRY, 1777-1852
Kelly, Regina Z. Henry Clay. Walker, C., illus. (gr. 4-6). 1960. (Piper); pap. 2.44 (*0-395-01717-3*) HM.
Stone-Peterson, Helen. Henry Clay: Leader in Congress. Dowd, Vic, illus. 80p. (gr. 2-6). 1991. Repr. of 1964 ed. lib. bdg. 12.95 (*0-7910-1457-6*) Chelsea Hse.

CLAY
see also Modeling
Making Models & Games. LC 91-17039. (Illus.). 48p. (gr. 4-8). 1991. PLB 14.95 (*1-85435-409-4*) Marshall Cavendish.
Murphy, Lois. Story Clay. Wilson, Karen, illus. 8p. (gr. 1-8). 1990. pap. write for info. (*0-9620672-0-2*) Dragon Studio.

CLAY INDUSTRIES
see also Pottery
Rickard, Graham. Bricks. LC 93-6833. (Illus.). 32p. (gr. 3-6). 1993. 13.95 (*1-56847-046-0*) Thomson Lrning.

CLAY MODELING
see Modeling

CLEANING
see also House Cleaning; Soap

CLEANLINESS
see Hygiene

CLEMENS, SAMUEL LANGHORNE, 1835-1910
Collins, David R. Mark T-W-A-I-N! A Story about Samuel Clemens. Carey, Vicky, illus. LC 93-15164. 1993. write for info. (*0-87614-801-1*) Carolrhoda Bks.
—Mark T-W-A-I-N! A Story about Samuel Clemens. (gr. 4-7). 1994. pap. 5.95 (*0-87614-640-X*) Carolrhoda Bks.
Cox, Clinton. Mark Twain. LC 94-18624. (gr. 4-7). Date not set. 13.95 (*0-590-45642-3*) Scholastic Inc.
Greene, Carol. Mark Twain: Author of Tom Sawyer. LC 91-40829. (Illus.). 48p. (gr. k-3). 1992. PLB 12.85 (*0-516-04228-9*); pap. 4.95 (*0-516-44228-7*) Childrens.
Hargrove, Jim. Mark Twain: The Story of Samuel Clemens. LC 83-23157. (Illus.). 128p. (gr. 4 up). 1984. PLB 14.40 (*0-516-03204-6*) Childrens.
Lyttle, Richard B. Mark Twain - The Man & His Adventure. LC 93-11247. (gr. 5 up). 1994. 15.95 (*0-689-31712-3*, Atheneum Child Bk) Macmillan Child Grp.
Mason, Miriam E. Mark Twain: Young Writer. Gillette, Henry S., illus. LC 90-23768. 192p. (gr. 3-7). 1991. pap. 4.95 (*0-689-71480-7*, Aladdin) Macmillan Child Grp.
Press, Skip. Mark Twain. LC 93-1827. (gr. 5-8). 1994. 14.95 (*1-56006-043-3*) Lucent Bks.
Quackenbush, Robert. Mark Twain? What Kind of Name is That? A Story of Samuel Langhorn Clemens. LC 83-19086. (Illus.). 40p. (gr. 2-6). 1984. pap. 11.95 (*0-671-66294-5*, S&S BFYR) S&S Trade.
Sabin, Louis. Young Mark Twain. Burns, Ray, illus. LC 89-33982. 48p. (gr. 4-6). 1990. PLB 10.79 (*0-8167-1783-4*); pap. text ed. 3.50 (*0-8167-1784-2*) Troll Assocs.
Wade, L. Hannibal: Mark Twain's Boyhood Home. 1991. 11.95s.p. (*0-86592-466-X*) Rourke Enter.

CLEMENS, SAMUEL LANGHORNE, 1835-1910–FICTION
Quackenbush, Robert. Mark Twain? What Kind of Name is That? A Story of Samuel Langhorne Clemens. (gr. 4). 1990. pap. 3.95 (*0-663-56240-6*) Silver Burdett Pr.

CLEMENTE, ROBERTO, 1934-1972
Bjarkman, Peter C. Roberto Clemente. Murray, Jim, intro. by. (Illus.). 64p. (gr. 3 up). 1991. lib. bdg. 14.95 (*0-7910-1171-2*) Chelsea Hse.
Gilbert, Tom. Roberto Clemente. (gr. 4-7). 1993. pap. 7.95 (*0-7910-1267-0*) Chelsea Hse.
Greene, Carol. Roberto Clemente: Baseball Superstar. LC 91-12664. (Illus.). 48p. (gr. k-3). 1991. PLB 12.85 (*0-516-04222-X*); pap. 4.95 (*0-516-44222-8*) Childrens.
O'Connor, Jim. Story of Roberto Clemente. (gr. 4-7). 1991. pap. 2.95 (*0-440-40425-8*) Dell.
Sabin, Louis. Roberto Clemente: Young Baseball Hero. DeJohn, Marie, illus. LC 91-17851. 48p. (gr. 4-6). 1992. PLB 10.79 (*0-8167-2509-8*); pap. text ed. 3.50 (*0-8167-2510-1*) Troll Assocs.
Walker, Paul R. Pride of Puerto Rico: The Life of Roberto Clemente. 132p. (gr. 3-7). 1988. 11.95 (*0-15-200562-5*, Gulliver Bks) HarBrace.
—Pride of Puerto Rico: The Life of Roberto Clemente. 157p. (gr. 3-7). 1990. pap. 4.95 (*0-15-263420-7*, Odyssey) HarBrace.

CLEOPATRA, QUEEN OF EGYPT, 69-30 B.C.
Hoobler, Dorothy & Hoobler, Thomas. Cleopatra. (Illus.). 112p. (gr. 5 up). 1987. lib. bdg. 17.95x (*0-87754-589-8*) Chelsea Hse.
Nardo, Don. Cleopatra. LC 93-11079. (gr. 5-8). 1994. 14.95 (*1-56006-023-9*) Lucent Bks.
Shakespeare, William. Antony & Cleopatra. Rudvik, O. H., intro. by. (gr. 10 up). 1966. pap. 0.60 (*0-8049-1011-1*, S-11) Airmont.
Shaw, George Bernard. Caesar & Cleopatra. (gr. 11 up). pap. 0.95 (*0-8049-0119-8*, CL-119) Airmont.
Stanley, Diane, illus. Cleopatra. Vennema, Peter. LC 93-27032. (Illus.). (gr. 4 up). 1994. pap. write for info. (*0-688-10413-4*); PLB write for info. (*0-688-10414-2*) Morrow Jr Bks.

CLERGY
Bentley, Judith. Teachers & Preachers. (Illus.). 96p. (gr. 5-8). 1995. bds. 16.95 (*0-8050-2996-6*) TFC Bks NY.
Briscoe, Jill. The Man Who Would Not Hate: Festo Kivengere. 1991. pap. 4.99 (*0-8499-3309-9*) Word Inc.
Franck, Irene M. & Brownstone, David M. Scholars & Priests. (Illus.). 208p. (gr. 7 up). 1988. 17.95x (*0-8160-1449-3*) Facts on File.
Hutchinson, Duane. Grotto Father: Artist-Priest of the West Bend Grotto. LC 89-39029. (Illus.). 64p. 1989. pap. 4.95 (*0-934988-20-X*) Foun Bks.
Lyngheim, Linda, et al. Father Junipero Serra, the Traveling Missionary. Garber, Phyllis, illus. LC 85-82131. 64p. (gr. 3-5). 1986. 12.95 (*0-915369-01-X*) Langtry Pubns.
Parker, Julie F. Careers for Women As Clergy. Rosen, Ruth, ed. (gr. 7-12). 1993. PLB 14.95 (*0-8239-1424-0*); pap. 9.95 (*0-8239-1727-4*) Rosen Group.
Wilson, Jean. Crusader for Christ (Billy Graham) (gr. 6-9). 1979. pap. 3.95 (*0-87508-602-0*) Chr Lit.

CLERGY–FICTION
Barrie, James. Little Minister. (gr. 10 up). 1968. pap. 0.75 (*0-8049-0187-2*, CL-187) Airmont.
Dahl, Roald. The Vicar of Nibbleswicke. Blake, Quentin, illus. 24p. 1992. 12.50 (*0-670-84384-9*) Viking Child Bks.
Goldsmith, Oliver. Vicar of Wakefield. (gr. 10 up). 1964. pap. 1.25 (*0-8049-0052-3*, CL-52) Airmont.
Sheehan, Canon P. My New Curate. LC 89-81657. 340p. (Orig.). (gr. 10-12). 1990. pap. 16.95 (*0-85342-877-8*, Pub. by Mercier Pr Eire) Dufour.
Whelan, Gloria. Time to Keep Silent. (gr. 4-7). 1993. pap. 5.99 (*0-8028-0118-8*) Eerdmans.

CLERGY–VOCATIONAL GUIDANCE
Poling, Nancy W. Most Ministers Wear Sneakers. Ortiz, Gloria C., illus. LC 91-15116. 32p. (gr. 4-8). 1991. 12.95 (*0-8298-0907-4*); pap. 6.95 (*0-8298-0901-5*, P-0901-5) Pilgrim OH.
Tierney, Terence. Should You Become a Priest? 64p. (Orig.). (gr. 9 up). 1975. pap. 3.95 (*0-89243-586-0*, 29530) Liguori Pubns.

CLERICAL WORK–TRAINING
see Business Education

CLERKS (SALESMENSHIP)
see Salesmen and Salesmanship

CLEVELAND, GROVER, PRESIDENT U. S. 1837-1908
Collins, David R. Grover Cleveland: 22nd & 24th President of the United States. Young, Richard G., ed. LC 87-35794. (Illus.). (gr. 5-9). 1988. PLB 17.26 (*0-944483-01-1*) Garrett Ed Corp.
Kent, Zachary. Grover Cleveland. LC 88-10885. (Illus.). 100p. (gr. 3 up). 1988. PLB 14.40 (*0-516-01360-2*) Childrens.

CLEVELAND
Judson, Thomas, illus. Color Me Cleveland: A Cleveland Coloring Book. Johnston, Christopher, text by. (Illus.). 32p. 1993. pap. 4.95 (*0-9631738-2-0*) Gray & Co Pubs.

CLEVELAND–FICTION
Manry, Douglas. The Land the Cleves Built. Sloan, Stephen, ed. Manry, Douglas, illus. 32p. (gr. 2-5). 1989. write for info. (*0-9622316-0-6*) Sloan Manry Pubs.

CLEVELAND INDIANS (BASEBALL TEAM)
Cleveland Indians. (gr. 4-7). 1993. pap. 1.49 (*0-553-56409-9*) Bantam.
Rambeck, Richard. Cleveland Indians. 48p. (gr. 4-10). 1992. PLB 14.95 (*0-88682-439-7*) Creative Ed.

CLIFF DWELLERS AND CLIFF DWELLINGS
see also Mounds and Mound Builders
Arnold, Caroline. The Ancient Cliff Dwellers of Mesa Verde. Hewett, Richard, illus. 64p. (gr. 3-6). 1992. 15.45 (*0-395-56241-4*, Clarion Bks) HM.
Radlauer, Ruth. Mesa Verde National Park. updated ed. Zillmer, Rolf, photos by. LC 76-27350. (Illus.). 48p. (gr. 3 up). 1984. pap. 4.95 (*0-516-47490-1*) Childrens.
Trimble, Stephen. The Village of Blue Stone. Dewey, Jennifer O. & Reade, Deborah, illus. LC 88-34194. 64p. (gr. 3-7). 1990. RSBE 14.95 (*0-02-789501-7*, Macmillan Child Bk) Macmillan Child Grp.

CLIMATE
Here are entered works on climate as it relates to man and to plant and animal life, including the effects of changes of climate. Works limited to the climate of a particular region are entered under the name of the place with the subdivision Climate. Works on the state of the atmosphere at a given time and place with respect to heat and cold, wetness or dryness, calm or storm, are entered under Weather. Scientific works on the atmosphere, especially weather factors, are entered under Meteorology.
see also Meteorology; Rain and Rainfall; Seasons; Weather
Duden, Jane. The Ozone Layer. LC 90-36297. (Illus.). 48p. (gr. 6). 1990. text ed. 12.95 RSBE (*0-89686-546-0*, Crestwood Hse) Macmillan Child Grp.
Facklam, Margery & Facklam, Howard. Changes in the Wind: The Earth's Shifting Climate. Facklam, Paul, illus. LC 85-5475. 128p. (gr. 7 up). 1986. 14.95 (*0-15-216115-5*, HB Juv Bks) HarBrace.
Flint, David. Weather & Climate: Projects with Geography. LC 91-6806. (Illus.). 32p. (gr. 5-8). 1991. PLB 12.40 (*0-531-17321-6*, Gloucester Pr) Watts.
Fowler, Allan. What's the Weather Today? LC 91-3125. 32p. (ps-2). 1991. PLB 10.75 (*0-516-04918-6*); PLB 22.95 big bk. (*0-516-49478-3*); pap. 3.95 (*0-516-44918-4*) Childrens.
Harris, Jack C. The Greenhouse Effect. LC 90-36294. (Illus.). 48p. (gr. 6). 1990. text ed. 12.95 RSBE (*0-89686-543-6*, Crestwood Hse) Macmillan Child Grp.
Johnson, Rebecca L. The Greenhouse Effect: Life on a Warmer Planet. (Illus.). 112p. (gr. 5 up). 1990. PLB 23.95 (*0-8225-1591-1*) Lerner Pubns.
Knapp, Brian. Drought. LC 89-19730. (Illus.). 48p. (gr. 5-9). 1990. PLB 22.80 (*0-8114-2376-X*) Raintree Steck-V.
Mason, John. Weather & Climate. (Illus.). 48p. (gr. 5-8). 1991. PLB 12.95 (*0-382-24225-4*) Silver Burdett Pr.
Merk, Ann & Merk, Jim. The Weather & Us. LC 94-13322. (gr. 3 up). 1994. write for info. (*0-86593-387-1*) Rourke Corp.
Rowe, Julian & Perham, Molly. Weather Watch! LC 94-16944. (Illus.). 32p. (gr. 1-4). 1994. PLB 18.60 (*0-516-08142-X*); pap. 4.95 (*0-516-48142-8*) Childrens.
Simon, Seymour. Weather & Climate. (gr. 4-6). 1969. lib. bdg. 4.99 (*0-394-90804-X*) Random Bks Yng Read.
Stewart, Gail B. Drought. LC 90-36293. (Illus.). 48p. (gr. 6). 1990. text ed. 12.95 RSBE (*0-89686-544-4*, Crestwood Hse) Macmillan Child Grp.
Taylor, Barbara. Weather & Climate: Geography Facts & Experiments. LC 92-28420. 32p. (gr. 1-4). 1993. 10.95 (*1-85697-878-8*, Kingfisher LKC); pap. 5.95 (*1-85697-940-7*) LKC.
Time Life Books Staff. Weather & Climate. 1992. 18.95 (*0-8094-9683-6*) Time-Life.
Torjman, Nathalie. History & Geography of Climates. (gr. 6 up). 1988. 4.95 (*0-8120-3838-X*) Barron.
Watt, F. Weather & Climate. (Illus.). 48p. (gr. 4-11). 1992. PLB 13.96 (*0-88110-511-2*, Usborne); pap. 7.95 (*0-7460-0683-7*, Usborne) EDC.

CLIMATOLOGY
see Climate

CLIPPER SHIPS
McNeese, Tim. Clippers & Whaling Ships. LC 91-27187. (Illus.). 48p. (gr. 5). 1993. text ed. 11.95 RSBE (*0-89686-735-8*, Crestwood Hse) Macmillan Child Grp.

CLOCKS AND WATCHES
see also Sundials
Aust, Siegfried. Clocks! How Time Flies. Poppel, Hans, illus. 32p. (gr. 2-5). 1991. PLB 18.95 (*0-8225-2154-7*) Lerner Pubns.
Brackin, A. J. Clocks: Chronicling Time. LC 91-16713. (Illus.). 96p. (gr. 5-8). 1991. PLB 15.95 (*1-56006-208-8*) Lucent Bks.
Bragg, Ruth G. Colors of the Day. Bragg, Ruth G., illus. LC 92-7790. 40p. 1992. pap. 14.95 (*0-88708-245-9*) Picture Bk Studio.
Branley, Franklyn M. Keeping Time. Van Rynbach, Iris, illus. LC 92-6783. 1993. 13.95 (*0-395-47777-8*) HM.
Breiter, Herta S. Time & Clocks. rev. ed. LC 87-23229. (Illus.). 48p. (gr. 2-6). 1987. PLB 10.95 (*0-8172-3262-1*) Raintree Steck-V.
Dale, Rodney. Timekeeping. LC 92-21661. 1992. 16.00 (*0-19-520968-0*) OUP.
Williams, John. Simple Science Projects with Time. LC 91-50548. (Illus.). 32p. (gr. 2-4). 1992. PLB 17.27 (*0-8368-0770-7*) Gareth Stevens Inc.

CLOCKS AND WATCHES–FICTION
Bellairs, John. The House with a Clock in Its Walls. 192p. (gr. 3 up). 1974. pap. 3.50 (*0-440-43742-3*, YB) Dell.
Best, Elizabeth. Mr. McGillicuddy's Clocks. Culic, Ned, illus. LC 93-26928. 1994. 4.25 (*0-383-03765-4*) SRA Schl Grp.
Brown, Kathryn. Muledred. (Illus.). 32p. (ps-3). 1990. 12.95 (*0-15-256265-6*) HarBrace.
Browne, Eileen. Tick-Tock. Parkins, David, illus. LC 93-927. 32p. (ps up). 1994. 14.95 (*1-56402-300-1*) Candlewick Pr.
Dickinson, Peter. Time & the Clock Mice, Etcetera. Chichester-Clark, Emma, illus. LC 93-11434. 1994. 16.95 (*0-385-32038-8*) Delacorte.
Edens, Cooper. The Wonderful Counting Clock. Kimball, Katherine, illus. LC 93-14404. 1995. 15.00 (*0-671-88334-8*, Green Tiger) S&S Trade.

Fuchshuber, Annegert. The Cuckoo-Clock Cuckoo. 32p. (gr. k-4). 1988. lib. bdg. 18.95 (*0-87614-320-6*) Carolrhoda Bks.
Houghton, Eric. The Backwards Watch. Abel, Simone, illus. LC 91-16951. 32p. (ps-2). 1992. 13.95 (*0-531-05968-5*); PLB 13.99 (*0-531-08568-6*) Orchard Bks Watts.
Hutchins, Pat. Clocks & More Clocks. Hutchins, Pat, illus. LC 93-11208. 32p. (gr. k-3). 1994. pap. 4.95 (*0-689-71769-5*, Aladdin) Macmillan Child Grp.
—Clocks & More Clocks. Hutchins, Pat, illus. LC 93-86027. 32p. (ps-3). 1994. RSBE 13.95 (*0-02-745921-7*, Macmillan Child Bk) Macmillan Child Grp.
Magic Castle Clock Book. (Illus.). 24p. (ps-1). 1992. with movable hands 9.95 (*0-8431-3418-6*) Price Stern.
Mickey Mouse's Telling Time. 24p. 1994. 8.98 (*1-57082-155-0*) Mouse Works.
Molesworth, M. L. The Cuckoo Clock. (Orig.). (gr. k-6). 1987. pap. 4.95 (*0-440-41618-3*, Pub. by Yearling Classics) Dell.
Muller, Robin. Hickory, Dickory, Dock. Duranceau, Suzanne, illus. LC 92-37588. 32p. (ps-6). 1994. 15.95 (*0-590-47278-X*) Scholastic Inc.
Rappoport, Doreen. The Night the Minute Hand Stopped. LC 88-81466. (Illus.). 32p. (Orig.). (ps-2). 1988. pap. 8.95 (*0-937124-16-8*) Kimbo Educ.
Stanley, Diane. Siegfried. (ps-3). 1991. 15.00 (*0-553-07022-3*) Bantam.
Stolz, Mary. Cuckoo Clock. Johnson, Pamela, illus. LC 86-45538. 112p. 1986. 13.95 (*0-87923-653-1*) Godine.
—Cuckoo Clock. 1993. pap. 10.95 (*0-87923-938-7*) Godine.
Time Life Inc. Editors. CB: A Book about Time. Ward, Elizabeth & Kagan, Neil, eds. (Illus.). 30p. (ps-2). 1992. write for info. (*0-8094-9303-9*); lib. bdg. write for info. (*0-8094-9304-7*) Time-Life.
Tompert, Ann. Sue Patch & the Crazy Clocks. LC 88-25720. (Illus.). 48p. (ps-3). 1992. pap. 3.99 (*0-8037-1061-5*, Dial Easy to Read) Puffin Bks.
Vallet, Muriel. Clocks Are Neat. Vallet, Muriel, illus. 10p. (gr. k-3). 1994. pap. 10.95 (*1-895583-69-1*) MAYA Pubs.

CLOCKS AND WATCHES–HISTORY

Dale, Rodney. Timekeeping. LC 92-21661. 1992. 16.00 (*0-19-520968-0*) OUP.

CLOG DANCING

see Folk Dancing

CLOTHIERS

see Clothing Trade

CLOTHING AND DRESS

Here are entered works dealing with clothing from a practical standpoint including the art of dress. Descriptive and historical works on the costume of particular countries or periods are entered under Costume.
see also Buttons; Costume; Costume Design; Fashion; Hats; Shoes and Shoe Industry

Accessories. (Illus.). (gr. 5 up). 1987. lib. bdg. 15.94 (*0-86625-281-9*) Rourke Corp.
Arma, Tom, illus. Dress-up Time! 18p. (ps). 1994. bds. 4.95 (*0-448-40438-9*, G&D) Putnam Pub Group.
Asamoah-Yaw, Ernest. Kente Cloth: Introduction to History. (Illus.). 120p. (Orig.). 1993. pap. 9.95 (*0-9635566-0-6*) Ghanam Text.
Baker, Wendy. The Dressing-up Book. Baker, Wendy, illus. LC 93-36430. 48p. (gr. 3-5). 1994. 16.95 (*1-56847-136-X*) Thomson Lrning.
Ball, Jacqueline. Looking Good, 8 bks, Set 11. (Illus.). 64p. (gr. 5 up). 1990. Set. lib. bdg. 127.52 (*0-86625-287-8*); 95.60 (*0-685-58754-1*) Rourke Corp.
Bantam Staff. Things to Wear. (ps). 1994. 2.99 (*0-685-69322-8*) Bantam.
Blumberg, Rhoda. Bloomers! Morgan, Mary, illus. LC 92-27154. 32p. (gr. k-5). 1993. RSBE 14.95 (*0-02-711684-0*, Bradbury Pr) Macmillan Child Grp.
Brooks, F. Clothes & Fashion. (Illus.). 24p. (gr. 2-4). 1990. PLB 3.95 (*0-7460-0448-6*, Usborne) EDC.
—Clothes & Fashion. (Illus.). 24p. (gr. 2-4). 1990. lib. bdg. 11.96 (*0-88110-400-0*, Usborne) EDC.
Clothes. (Illus.). 16p. (ps-1). 1994. pap. 6.95 (*1-56458-524-7*) Dorling Kindersley.
Clothing. (Illus.). (gr. 5 up). 1987. lib. bdg. 15.94 (*0-86625-277-0*); lib. bdg. 11.95 Rourke Corp.
Cobb, Vicki. Getting Dressed. Hafner, Marylin, illus. LC 87-26097. 32p. (gr. k-3). 1989. (Lipp Jr Bks); PLB 11.89 (*0-397-32143-0*) HarpC Child Bks.
—Snap, Button, Zip: Inventions to Keep Your Clothes On. Hafner, Marylin, illus. LC 87-26097. 32p. (gr. 1-4). 1993. pap. 3.95 (*0-06-446106-8*, Trophy) HarpC Child Bks.
Consumer Clothing. (gr. 7-12). 1989. Package of 10. 15.95 (*1-877844-00-4*, 2121) Meridian Educ.
De Paola, Tomie. Charlie Needs a Cloak. LC 73-16365. (Illus.). 32p. (gr. k-4). 1982. pap. 14.00 (*0-671-66466-2*, S&S BFYR); pap. 5.95 (*0-671-66467-0*, S&S BFYR) S&S Trade.
Everett, F. & Garbera, C. Making Clothes. (Illus.). 48p. (gr. 6 up). 1986. PLB 14.96 (*0-88110-321-7*); pap. 7.95 (*0-86020-981-4*) EDC.
Gibson, R. Decorating T-Shirts. (Illus.). 32p. (gr. 2-6). 1994. PLB 12.96 (*0-88110-710-7*, Usborne); pap. 5.95 (*0-7460-1696-4*, Usborne) EDC.
Giff, Patricia R. If the Shoe Fits. (Orig.). (gr. k-6). 1988. pap. 3.50 (*0-440-40086-4*, YB) Dell.
Govier, Heather. Clothes. Young, Richard, ed. LC 91-20533. (Illus.). 32p. (gr. 3-5). 1991. PLB 15.93 (*1-56074-009-4*) Garrett Ed Corp.
Harrison, Kathryn & Kohn, Valerie. Easy-to-Make Costumes. (Illus.). 80p. (gr. 4 up). 1993. pap. 12.16 (*1-895569-10-9*, Pub. by Tamos Bks CN) Sterling.
Kalman, Bobbie. Eighteenth Century Clothing. DeBiasi, Antoinette, illus. 32p. (Orig.). (gr. 3-6). 1993. PLB 15.95 (*0-86505-492-4*); pap. 7.95 (*0-86505-512-2*) Crabtree Pub Co.
—Nineteenth Century Clothing. DeBiasi, Antoinette, illus. 32p. (Orig.). (gr. 3-6). 1993. PLB 15.95 (*0-86505-493-2*); pap. 7.95 (*0-86505-513-0*) Crabtree Pub Co.
Llewellyn, Claire. First Look at Clothes. LC 91-9425. (Illus.). 32p. (gr. 1-2). 1991. PLB 17.27 (*0-8368-0677-8*) Gareth Stevens Inc.
Lynn, Sara. I Can Make It! Dress Up. (ps-3). 1994. pap. 4.99 (*0-553-37260-2*) Bantam.
M. J. Studios Staff, illus. Dress up Sticker Pad. 32p. (gr. k-6). 1993. pap. 2.95 (*1-879424-17-7*) Nickel Pr.
McCoy, Sharon. Fifty Nifty Ways to Jazz up Your Jeans. Olexiewicz, Charlene, illus. 64p. 1994. pap. 4.95 (*1-56565-168-5*) Lowell Hse Juvenile.
Mitgutsch, Ali. From Cotton to Pants. Mitgutsch, Ali, illus. LC 80-29552. 24p. (ps-3). 1981. PLB 10.95 (*0-87614-150-5*) Carolrhoda Bks.
Morley, Jacqueline. Clothes for Work, Play & Display. LC 92-4852. 1992. 13.95 (*0-531-15249-9*) Watts.
Oliver, Stephen, photos by. Clothes. LC 90-23999. (Illus.). 24p. (ps-k). 1991. 7.00 (*0-679-81806-5*) Random Bks Yng Read.
Oxenbury, Helen. Dressing. Oxenbury, Helen, illus. 14p. (ps-k). 1981. 3.95 (*0-671-42113-1*, Little Simon) S&S Trade.
Pfiffner, George. Earth-Friendly Wearables: How to Make Fabulous Clothes & Accessories from Reusable Objects. Date not set. pap. text ed. 12.95 (*0-471-00823-0*) Wiley.
Ricklen, Neil, illus. My Clothes: Mi Ropa. LC 93-27162. (ENG & SPA.). 14p. (ps-k). 1994. pap. 3.95 (*0-689-71773-3*, Aladdin) Macmillan Child Grp.
Ripley, Robert L. Clothing. Stott, Carol, illus. 48p. (gr. 3-6). Date not set. PLB 12.95 (*1-56065-131-8*) Capstone Pr.
Ruby, Jennifer. The Nineteen Sixties & Nineteen Seventies. (Illus.). 64p. (gr. 6-9). 1989. 24.95 (*0-7134-6074-1*, Pub. by Batsford UK) Trafalgar.
—The Regency. (Illus.). 64p. (gr. 6-9). 1989. 24.95 (*0-7134-5992-1*, Pub. by Batsford UK) Trafalgar.
Saltzberg, Barney. Where, Oh, Where's My Underwear? LC 93-61051. (Illus.). 12p. (ps-3). 1994. 9.95 (*1-56282-694-8*) Hyprn Child.
Solga, Kim. Make Clothes Fun! (Illus.). 48p. (gr. 1-6). 1992. 11.95 (*0-89134-421-7*, 30377) North Light Bks.
Stinson, K. The Dressed up Book. (Illus.). 32p. (ps-8). 1990. PLB 14.95 (*1-55037-103-7*, Pub. by Annick CN); pap. 4.95 (*1-55037-104-5*, Pub. by Annick CN) Firefly Bks Ltd.
Ventura, Pietro. Clothing: Garments, Styles, & Uses. Casalini, Max, et al. LC 93-107. 1993. 16.95 (*0-395-66791-7*) HM.
Worth, Bonnie. I Can Dress Myself. Cooke, Tom, illus. 18p. (ps). 1993. bds. 3.50 (*0-307-12204-2*, 12204, Golden Pr) Western Pub.

CLOTHING AND DRESS–FICTION

Aldridge, Josephine H. The Pocket Book. Moreno, Rene K., illus. LC 93-1699. 1994. pap. 14.00 (*0-671-87128-5*, S&S BFYR) S&S Trade.
Allen, Jonathan. Purple Sock, Pink Sock. Allen, Jonathan, illus. LC 91-43379. 12p. (ps). 1992. 3.95 (*0-688-11782-1*, Tambourine Bks) Morrow.
Anderson, Marilyn. The Haunted Underwear. (Illus.). 128p. (gr. 3-5). 1992. pap. 2.50 (*0-87406-592-5*) Willowisp Pr.
Avery, Kristin. The Crazy Quilt. 16p. (ps-2). 1994. text ed. 3.95 (*0-673-36199-3*) GdYrBks.
Banks, Katherine A. Peter & the Talking Shoes. Rosenthal, Marc, illus. 40p. (ps-3). 1994. 15.00 (*0-394-82723-6*); PLB 15.99 (*0-394-92723-0*) Knopf Bks Yng Read.
Bannah, Max. Bulldog George. LC 93-20807. 1994. 4.25 (*0-383-03739-5*) SRA Schl Grp.
Beskow, Elsa. Pelle's New Suit. Woodburn, Marion L., tr. from SWE. Beskow, Elsa, illus. 32p. Repr. of 1979 ed. 14.95 (*0-86315-092-6*, Pub. by Floris Bks UK) Gryphon Hse.
Blackman, Malorie. A New Dress for Maya. James, Rhian N., illus. LC 91-50337. 32p. (ps-3). 1993. PLB 17.27 (*0-8368-0713-8*) Gareth Stevens Inc.
Boynton, Sandra. Blue Hat Green Hat. 14p. 1984. 3.95 (*0-671-49320-5*, Little Simon) S&S Trade.
Breeze, Lynn. Baby's Clothes. (Illus.). 14p. (ps). 1994. bds. 4.50 fold-outs (*0-8120-6410-0*) Barron.
Buckle, Mariette. All Dressed Up. Strahan, Heather, illus. LC 92-21447. 1993. 3.75 (*0-383-03613-5*) SRA Schl Grp.
Calderwood, Simone. Clothes. Cullo, Ned, illus. LC 92-27086. 1993. 2.50 (*0-383-03560-0*) SRA Schl Grp.
Charnas, Suzy M. The Silver Glove. (gr. 7 up). 1989. pap. 2.95 (*0-318-41646-8*, Starfire) Bantam.
Christiansen, Candace. The Mitten Tree. Greenstein, Elaine, illus. LC 94-8753. 1995. 15.95 (*0-399-22714-8*, Philomel Bks) Putnam Pub Group.
Cleary, Beverly. Socks. 160p. 1990. pap. 3.99 (*0-380-70926-0*, Camelot) Avon.
Collins, David R. Ursi's Amazing Fur Coat. (Illus.). (ps-2). 1987. PLB 6.95 (*0-8136-5186-7*, TK7265); pap. 3.50 (*0-8136-5686-9*, TK7266) Modern Curr.
Cowley, Stewart. Getting Dressed. (ps). 1994. 2.99 (*0-89577-594-8*, Readers Digest Kids) RD Assn.
De Paola, Tomie. The Walking Coat. LC 81-7395. (Illus.). 32p. (gr. k-4). 1981. 4.95 (*0-13-944314-2*) P-H.
Desputeaux, Helene. My Clothes. (Illus.). 26p. (ps). 1993. bds. 2.95 (*2-921198-25-8*, Pub. by Les Edits Herit CN) Adams Inc MA.
Dudko, Mary A. & Larsen, Margie. Where Are My Shoes? Hartley, Linda, ed. Daste, Larry, illus. 24p. (ps-k). 1993. pap. 2.25 (*0-7829-0375-4*) Lyons Group.
—Where Are My Shoes? Hartley, Linda, ed. Daste, Larry, illus. LC 93-77013. 24p. (ps-1). 1993. pap. 2.25 (*1-57064-004-1*) Barney Pub.
Estes, Eleanor. The Hundred Dresses. Slobodkin, Louis, illus. LC 73-12940. 80p. (gr. 1-5). 1974. pap. 4.95 (*0-15-642350-2*, Voyager Bks) HarBrace.
Farjeon, Eleanor. The Glass Slipper. 159p. 1981. Repr. PLB 16.95x (*0-89966-360-5*) Buccaneer Bks.
—The Glass Slipper. 108p. 1981. Repr. PLB 16.95x (*0-89967-034-2*) Harmony Raine.
Gaban, Jesus. Harry Dresses Himself. Colorado, Nani, illus. 16p. (ps-1). 1992. PLB 13.27 (*0-8368-0715-4*) Gareth Stevens Inc.
Gary, Soto. Skirt. (gr. 4-7). 1994. pap. 3.50 (*0-440-40924-1*) Dell.
Gordon, Sharon. Drip Drop. Page, Don, illus. LC 81-5112. 32p. (gr. k-2). 1981. PLB 11.59 (*0-89375-507-9*); pap. 2.95 (*0-89375-508-7*) Troll Assocs.
Gross, Ruth B. The Emperor's New Clothes. Kent, Jack, illus. 32p. (Orig.). (ps-2). 1991. pap. 2.50 (*0-590-43267-2*) Scholastic Inc.
Hanrahan, Brendan. My Sisters Love My Clothes. (Illus.). 32p. (gr. 1-4). 1992. 12.95 (*0-9630181-0-8*) Perry Heights.
Hasan, Khurshid & Warner, Rachel. Rumana's New Clothes. (Illus.). 25p. (gr. 2-4). 1991. 15.95 (*0-237-60160-5*, Pub. by Evans Bros Ltd) Trafalgar.
Hazen, Barbara S. Who Lost a Shoe? 16p. (ps-2). 1992. pap. 14.95 (*1-56784-050-7*) Newbridge Comms.
Hest, Amy. The Purple Coat. Schwartz, Amy, illus. LC 91-38499. 32p. (gr. k-3). 1992. pap. 4.95 (*0-689-71634-6*, Aladdin) Macmillan Child Grp.
Hilton, Nette. The Long Red Scarf. Power, Margaret, illus. 32p. (ps-3). 1990. PLB 18.95 (*0-87614-399-0*) Carolrhoda Bks.
—Long Red Scarf. (ps-3). 1992. pap. 5.95 (*0-87614-561-6*) Carolrhoda Bks.
Hissey, Jane. Little Bear's Trousers. (Illus.). 32p. (ps-3). 1992. PLB 5.95 (*0-399-21761-4*, Philomel Bks) Putnam Pub Group.
Hooks, William H. Moss Gown. Carrick, Donald, illus. (ps-3). 1990. pap. 5.70 (*0-395-54793-8*, Clarion Bks) HM.
Hurwitz, Johanna. New Shoes for Silvia. Pinkney, Jerry, illus. LC 91-40868. 32p. (ps up). 1993. 15.00 (*0-688-05286-X*); PLB 14.93 (*0-688-05287-8*) Morrow Jr Bks.
Johnson, Richard. Look at Me in Funny Clothes! Chatterton, Martin, illus. LC 93-32380. 14p. (ps up). 1994. 4.99 (*1-56402-415-6*) Candlewick Pr.
Johnston, Nikki. Magenta's Tartan Socks. Vane, Mitch, illus. LC 93-18047. 1994. write for info. (*0-383-03700-X*) SRA Schl Grp.
Joseph, Daniel M. All Dressed Up & Nowhere to Go. (ps-3). 1993. 14.95 (*0-395-60196-7*) HM.
Klein, David J. Irwin the Sock. (Illus.). 32p. (gr. 2-4). 1987. incl. audiocassette 29.28 (*0-8172-2473-4*) Raintree Steck-V.
—Irwin the Sock. (ps-3). 1993. pap. 3.95 (*0-8114-5211-5*) Raintree Steck-V.
Komaiko, Leah. Shoe Shine Shirley. Spohn, Franz, illus. LC 92-25816. 1993. 14.95 (*0-385-30526-5*) Doubleday.
Korman, Justine. Stinky Socks. (gr. 4-7). 1994. pap. 2.95 (*0-8167-3413-5*) Troll Assocs.
London, Jonathan. Froggy Gets Dressed. Remkiewicz, Frank, illus. 32p. (ps-1). 1992. 13.00 (*0-670-84249-4*) Viking Child Bks.
Loomis, Christine. At the Laundromat. Poydar, Nancy, illus. LC 93-10884. 1993. 14.95 (*0-590-72830-X*); pap. 4.95 (*0-590-49488-0*) Scholastic Inc.
Mason, Margo C. Winter Coats. 1989. pap. 3.50 (*0-553-34726-8*) Bantam.
Mayer, Marianna. The Little Jewel Box. Torres, Margot, illus. (ps-3). 1990. pap. 3.95 (*0-8037-0737-1*, Puff Pied Piper) Puffin Bks.
Medearis. Poppa's New Pants. 1994. 14.95 (*0-8050-1840-9*) H Holt & Co.
Miller, Margaret. Where Does It Go? LC 91-30160. (Illus.). 40p. (ps-4). 1992. 14.00 (*0-688-10928-4*); PLB 13.93 (*0-688-10929-2*) Greenwillow.
Monsell, Mary E. Underwear! (ps-3). 1993. pap. 4.95 (*0-8075-8309-X*) A Whitman.
Moore, Dessie. Getting Dressed. Moore, Chevelle, illus. 16p. (ps). 1994. 5.95 (*0-694-00590-8*, Festival) HarpC Child Bks.
Myers, Walter D. Fashion by Tasha. 1993. pap. 3.50 (*0-553-29724-4*) Bantam.
Nagel, Karen B. The Three Young Maniacs & the Red Rubber Boots. Gullikson, Sandy, illus. LC 91-30842. 32p. (ps-3). 1993. 15.00 (*0-06-020777-9*); PLB 14.89 (*0-06-020778-7*) HarpC Child Bks.
Neitzel, Shirley. The Dress I'll Wear to the Party. Parker, Nancy W., illus. LC 91-30906. 32p. (ps-4). 1992. 14.00 (*0-688-09959-9*); PLB 13.93 (*0-688-09960-2*) Greenwillow.
—Jacket I Wear in the Snow. LC 88-18767. (Illus.). 32p. (ps up). 1989. 15.00 (*0-688-08028-6*); PLB 13.93 (*0-688-08030-8*) Greenwillow.

—The Jacket I Wear in the Snow. Cohr, Amy, ed. Parker, Nancy W., illus. LC 92-43789. 32p. (ps up). 1994. pap. 4.95 (*0-688-04587-1*, Mulberry) Morrow.

Nielsen, Laura F. Jeremy's Muffler. Desch, Christine, illus. 1995. 16.00 (*0-02-768135-1*, Bradbury Pr) Macmillan Child Grp.

Parton, Dolly. Coat of Many Colors. Sutton, Judith, illus. LC 93-3866. 32p. (gr. 1 up). 1994. 14.00 (*0-06-023413-X*); PLB 13.89 (*0-06-023414-8*) HarpC Child Bks.

Pascal, Francine. The Hand-Me-Down Kid. 176p. (gr. k-6). 1982. pap. 2.95 (*0-440-43449-1*, YB) Dell.

Probasco, Teri. Blue Jean Gum. 35p. (ps-4). Date not set. pap. 5.90 (*0-932970-95-8*) Prinit Pr.

Pulver, Robin. Mrs. Toggle's Zipper. Alley, Robert W., illus. LC 92-39355. 32p. (ps-2). 1993. pap. 3.95 (*0-689-71689-3*, Aladdin) Macmillan Child Grp.

Razvan. Two Little Shoes. Stupple, Deborah, tr. LC 92-40814. (Illus.). 32p. (ps-1). 1993. SBE 14.95 (*0-02-775667-X*, Bradbury Pr) Macmillan Child Grp.

Rice, Eve. Oh, Lewis! Rice, Eve, illus. LC 92-24584. 32p. (ps up). 1993. pap. 4.95 (*0-688-11790-2*, Mulberry) Morrow.

—Peter's Pockets. Parker, Nancy W., illus. LC 87-15640. 32p. (ps up). 1989. 16.95 (*0-688-07241-0*); PLB 14.88 (*0-688-07242-9*) Greenwillow.

Rogers, Mary. The Torn Jacket. 30p. (gr. 1). 1992. pap. text ed. 23.00 big bk. (*1-56843-018-3*); pap. text ed. 4.50 (*1-56843-068-X*) BGR Pub.

Rousseau, May. Everyone Is Dressing Up! (Illus.). 12p. (ps). 1991. bds. 4.95 (*0-916291-38-3*) Kane-Miller Bk.

Roy, Ron. Whose Shoes Are These? Hausherr, Rosmarie, illus. LC 87-24279. 40p. (ps-4). 1991. pap. 5.70 (*0-395-55353-9*, Clarion Bks) HM.

Sanfield, Steve. Bit by Bit. Gaber, Susan, illus. LC 94-8752. 1995. 15.95 (*0-399-22736-9*, Philomel Bks) Putnam Pub Group.

Saylor, Melissa, illus. Mary Wore Her Red Dress Big Book. (ps-2). 1988. pap. text ed. 14.00 (*0-922053-17-0*) N Edge Res.

Sharples, Joseph. The Flyaway Pantaloons. Scullard, Sue, illus. 32p. (ps-4). 1990. PLB 18.95 (*0-87614-408-3*) Carolrhoda Bks.

Sirois, Allen. Dinosaur Dress Up. Street, Janet, illus. LC 91-10583. 32p. (ps-3). 1992. 15.00 (*0-688-10459-2*, Tambourine Bks); PLB 14.93 (*0-688-10460-6*, Tambourine Bks) Morrow.

Soto, Gary. The Shirt. Velasquez, Eric, illus. LC 91-26145. 64p. (gr. 2-5). 1992. 14.95 (*0-385-30665-2*) Delacorte.

Spohn, Kate. Clementine's Winter Wardrobe. LC 89-42531. (Illus.). 32p. (ps-1). 1989. 13.95 (*0-531-05841-7*); PLB 13.99 (*0-531-08441-8*) Orchard Bks Watts.

Steinbaum, Michael & Cohen, Diana. Simon & His Shrinking Socks. Balkovek, James, illus. 64p. (ps-4). 1993. pap. 9.95 (*0-8449-4253-7*); FRE Translation Tool, "Trans-it" 4.95 (*0-8449-4293-6*); CHI Translation Tool, "Trans-it" 4.95 (*0-8449-4295-2*); GER Translation Tool, "Trans-it" 4.95 (*0-8449-4294-4*); SPA Translation Tool, "Trans-it" 4.95 (*0-8449-4292-8*) Good Morn Tchr.

Streatfeild, Noel. Traveling Shoes. 256p. (gr. 4-7). 1984. pap. 2.95 (*0-440-48732-3*, YB) Dell.

Sutcliff, Rosemary. Flame-Colored Taffeta. 144p. (gr. 3 up). 1989. pap. 3.50 (*0-374-42341-5*, Sunburst) FS&G.

Tamar, Erika. High Cheekbones. 240p. (gr. 7 up). 1990. pap. 12.95 (*0-670-82843-2*) Viking Child Bks.

Thomson, Pat & Ross, Tony. The Treasure Sock. (Orig.). (gr. k-6). 1987. pap. 2.50 (*0-440-48814-1*, YB) Dell.

Van der Beek, Deborah. Melinda & the Class Photograph. 28p. (gr. k-4). 1991. PLB 18.95 (*0-87614-694-9*) Carolrhoda Bks.

Viorst, Judith. Earrings! Malone, Nola L., illus. LC 92-42984. 32p. (gr. 1-5). 1993. pap. 4.95 (*0-689-71669-9*, Aladdin) Macmillan Child Grp.

Vulliamy, Clara. Blue Hat, Red Coat. LC 93-22737. (Illus.). 14p. (ps). 1994. 4.95 (*1-56402-353-2*) Candlewick Pr.

Wells, Rosemary. Max's Dragon Shirt. Wells, Rosemary, illus. LC 90-43755. 32p. (ps-2). 1991. 12.00 (*0-8037-0944-7*); lib. bdg. 10.89 (*0-8037-0945-5*) Dial Bks Young.

—Max's New Suit. Wells, Rosemary, illus. LC 79-50747. (ps-k). 1979. bds. 3.95 (*0-8037-6065-5*) Dial Bks Young.

Winthrop, Elizabeth. Shoes Big Book. Joyce, William, illus. LC 85-45841. 24p. (ps-3). 1993. pap. 19.95 (*0-06-443320-X*, Trophy) HarpC Child Bks.

Wolff, Ferida. Woodcutter's Coat. Wilsdorf, Anne, illus. (ps-3). 1992. 15.95 (*0-316-95048-3*, Joy St Bks) Little.

Wood, D. No Clothes. (Illus.). 40p. (ps-8). 1990. pap. 5.95 (*1-55037-089-8*, Pub. by Annick CN) Firefly Bks Ltd.

Woodworth, Viki. Would You Wear a Snake? Woodworth, Viki, illus. (gr. 1-8). 1992. PLB 12.95 (*0-89565-821-6*) Childs World.

Yektai, Niki. Crazy Clothes. Stevenson, Sucie, illus. LC 93-19738. 32p. (gr. k-2). 1994. pap. 4.95 (*0-689-71781-4*, Aladdin) Macmillan Child Grp.

Ziefert, Harriet. Let's Get Dressed. (ps). 1988. 3.95 (*0-671-65539-6*, S&S BFYR) S&S Trade.

—A New Coat for Anna. Lobel, Anita, illus. LC 86-2722. 40p. (ps-3). 1988. pap. 5.99 (*0-394-89861-3*) Knopf Bks Yng Read.

Zokeisha. Things I Like to Wear. Zokeisha, illus. 16p. (ps-k). 1981. pap. 2.95 board (*0-671-44452-2*, Little Simon) S&S Trade.

CLOTHING TRADE

Black, Judy. Fashion. LC 93-4639. (gr. 9 up). 1994. text ed. 14.95 (*0-89686-791-9*, Crestwood Hse) Macmillan Child Grp.

CLOTHING TRADE–FICTION

Cleary, Beverly. Socks. 160p. 1990. pap. 3.99 (*0-380-70926-0*, Camelot) Avon.

Streatfeild, Noel. Family Shoes. 224p. (gr. 5 up). 1985. pap. 3.50 (*0-440-42479-8*, YB) Dell.

Trella, Phyllis. Jodee's Closet. Trella, Phyllis, illus. LC 82-73689. 48p. (gr. 2-6). write for info. (*0-914201-04-2*) Cheeruppet.

CLOUD SEEDING

see Weather Control

CLOUDS

De Paola, Tomie. The Cloud Book. De Paola, Tomie, illus. LC 74-34493. 32p. (ps-3). 1975. reinforced bdg. 15.95 (*0-8234-0259-2*); pap. 5.95 (*0-8234-0531-1*) Holiday.

Fitzgerald, Bridget. Little Dark Cloud. Alston, Virgil, illus. Harman, Sandra L., intro. by. LC 78-189877. (Illus.). 44p. (gr. 1-2). 1973. 2.50 (*0-87884-012-5*) Unicorn Ent.

George, Michael. Clouds. 1992. PLB 18.95 (*0-88682-435-4*) Creative Ed.

Greene, Carol. Hi, Clouds. Sharp, Gene, illus. LC 82-19854. 32p. (ps-2). 1983. PLB 10.25 (*0-516-02036-6*); pap. 2.95 (*0-516-42036-4*) Childrens.

McMillan, Bruce. The Weather Sky. (Illus.). 40p. (gr. 5 up). 1991. 16.95 (*0-374-38261-1*) FS&G.

Markert, Jenny. Clouds. (gr. 4-7). 1993. 15.95 (*1-56846-060-0*) Creat Editions.

Merk, Ann & Merk, Jim. Clouds. LC 94-13324. (gr. 2 up). 1994. write for info. (*0-86593-389-8*) Rourke Corp.

Ostrovsky, Alexsandr. Clouds (Oblaka) Ostrovsky, Alexsandr, illus. (RUS.). 16p. (Orig.). 1984. pap. 14.95 (*0-934393-20-6*) Rector Pr.

Peebles, J. Winston. My Funny Cloud. Beach, Bettye, illus. LC 81-50915. 36p. (ps-3). 1981. 4.95 (*0-938232-00-2*) Winston-Derek.

Wandelmaier, Roy. Clouds. Jones, John, illus. LC 84-8643. 32p. (gr. k-2). 1985. PLB 11.59 (*0-8167-0338-8*); pap. text ed. 2.95 (*0-8167-0441-4*) Troll Assocs.

CLOWNS

Gaskin, Carol. A Day in the Life of a Circus Clown. Klein, John F., illus. LC 87-10954. 32p. (gr. 4-8). 1988. PLB 11.79 (*0-8167-1107-0*); pap. text ed. 2.95 (*0-8167-1108-9*) Troll Assocs.

Stolzenberg, Mark. Be a Clown. LC 89-33783. (Illus.). 160p. (gr. 4-12). 1989. pap. 10.95 (*0-8069-5804-9*) Sterling.

CLOWNS–FICTION

Coco, Eugene. The Magic Clown. Pavia, Cathy, illus. 24p. (ps-2). 1993. pap. text ed. 0.99 (*1-56293-348-5*) McClanahan Bk.

Cole, Joanna. The Clown-Arounds. Smath, Jerry, illus. LC 81-4662. 48p. (ps-3). 1981. 5.95 (*0-8193-1059-X*); PLB 5.95 (*0-8193-1060-3*) Parents.

—The Clown-Arounds. Smath, Jerry, illus. 48p. (ps-2). 1992. pap. 2.95 (*0-448-40321-8*, G&D) Putnam Pub Group.

—The Clown-Arounds Go on Vacation. Smath, Jerry, illus. LC 83-13480. 48p. (ps-3). 1984. 5.95 (*0-8193-1120-0*) Parents.

—The Clown-Arounds Go on Vacation. Smath, Jerry, illus. LC 93-15471. 1993. 13.27 (*0-8368-0966-1*) Gareth Stevens Inc.

—Get Well, Clown-Arounds. (Illus.). 42p. (ps-3). 1993. PLB 13.27 (*0-8368-0895-9*); PLB 13.26 s.p. (*0-685-61526-X*) Gareth Stevens Inc.

—Sweet Dreams, Clown-Arounds. Smath, Jerry, illus. LC 85-6348. 48p. (ps-3). 1985. 5.95 (*0-8193-1138-3*) Parents.

—Sweet Dreams, Clown-Arounds. Smath, Jerry, illus. LC 93-13038. 1994. PLB 13.27 (*0-8368-0976-9*) Gareth Stevens Inc.

Dale, Nora. The Best Trick of All. (Illus.). 32p. (gr. 1-4). 1989. PLB 18.99 (*0-8172-3505-1*); pap. 3.95 (*0-8114-6700-7*) Raintree Steck-V.

De Paola, Tomie. Jingle the Christmas Clown. (Illus.). 40p. (ps-3). 1992. 15.95 (*0-399-22338-X*, Putnam) Putnam Pub Group.

Falwell, Cathryn. Clowning Around. LC 90-29064. (Illus.). 32p. (ps-1). 1991. 13.95 (*0-531-05952-9*); RLB 13.99 (*0-531-08552-X*) Orchard Bks Watts.

Gipson, Morrell & Hansson, Peter. Clumsy Clown Willie. Stefoff, Rebecca, ed. LC 90-13793. (Illus.). 24p. (gr. k-3). 1990. PLB 14.60 (*0-944483-90-9*) Garrett Ed Corp.

Johnson, Lois W. The Runaway Clown. 144p. (Orig.). 1993. pap. 5.99 (*1-55661-240-0*) Bethany Hse.

Johnson, Sharon S. I Want to Be a Clown. Gregorich, Barbara, ed. (Illus.). 16p. (Orig.). (gr. k-2). 1985. pap. 2.25 (*0-88743-014-7*, 06014) Sch Zone Pub Co.

—I Want to Be a Clown. Gregorich, Barbara, ed. (Illus.). 32p. (gr. k-2). 1992. pap. 3.95 (*0-88743-412-6*, 06064) Sch Zone Pub Co.

Long, Kathy. Hallelujah the Clown: A Story of Blessing & Discovery. Boddy, Joe, illus. LC 92-70384. 32p. (ps-k). 1992. pap. 4.99 (*0-8066-2560-0*, 9-2560, Augsburg) Augsburg Fortress.

Parish, Peggy. Clues in the Woods. 160p. (gr. k-6). 1980. pap. 3.50 (*0-440-41461-X*, YB) Dell.

Pennington, Lillian B. Snafu: The Littlest Clown. Gardner, Earle, illus. LC 73-90113. 32p. (gr. 1-6). 1972. PLB 9.95 (*0-913532-00-2*); cassette 7.94x (*0-87783-225-0*) Oddo.

Smith, Matthew V. Clowns Are People Too. Smith, Matthew V., illus. 12p. (gr. 1-3). 1992. pap. 11.95 (*1-56606-010-9*) Bradley Mann.

—Why Do Clowns Smile? Smith, Matthew V., illus. 14p. (gr. k-3). 1992. pap. 14.95 (*1-895583-06-3*) MAYA Pubs.

Van der Meer, Ron & Van der Meer, Atie. Jumping Clowns. (gr. 4 up). 1989. 4.95 (*0-85953-263-1*) Childs Play.

Zeplin, Zeno. Clowns to the Rescue. Brown, Bernice, illus. 48p. (gr. k-3). 1993. 9.95 (*1-877740-12-8*); pap. 5.50 (*1-877740-13-6*) Nel-Mar Pub.

Ziefert, Harriet. Clown Games. Stevens, Larry, illus. 32p. (ps-3). 1993. 9.00 (*0-670-84652-X*) Viking Child Bks.

—Clown Games. Stevens, Larry, illus. 32p. (ps-3). 1993. pap. 3.50 (*0-14-054581-6*) Puffin Bks.

—Where's Bobo? Rader, Laura, illus. LC 92-24495. 24p. (ps up). 1993. 10.95 (*0-688-12327-9*, Tambourine Bks) Morrow.

CLUBS

Erickson, Judith. The Directory of American Youth Organizations, 1992-93 Edition: A Guide to 500 Clubs, Groups, Troops, Teams, Societies, Lodges, & More for Young People. Espeland, Pamela, ed. 184p. (gr. k up). 1992. pap. 18.95 (*0-915793-36-9*) Free Spirit Pub.

Orgel, Doris. Nobodies & Somebodies. 160p. (gr. 3-7). 1993. pap. 3.99 (*0-14-034098-X*, Puffin) Puffin Bks.

CLUBS–FICTION

Alexander, Sue. Seymour the Prince. Hoban, Lillian, illus. LC 78-31406. (gr. 2-4). 1979. 6.95 (*0-685-03943-9*) Pantheon.

Berenstain, Stan & Berenstain, Jan. Los Osos Berenstain, No Se Permiten Ninas. LC 93-29904. (SPA.). 32p. (ps-3). 1994. pap. 2.50 (*0-679-85431-2*) Random Bks Yng Read.

Berenstain, Stan & Berenstain, Janice. The Berenstain Bears: No Girls Allowed. Berenstain, Stan & Berenstain, Janice, illus. LC 85-18246. 32p. (ps-1). 1986. pap. 2.50 (*0-394-87331-9*) Random Bks Yng Read.

Bograd, Larry. The Fourth-Grade Dinosaur Club. Lauter, Richard, illus. LC 88-22876. (gr. 3 up). 1989. 13.95 (*0-440-50128-8*) Delacorte.

Bonsall, Crosby N. The Case of the Double Cross. LC 80-7768. (Illus.). 64p. (gr. k-3). 1980. PLB 13.89 (*0-06-020603-9*) HarpC Child Bks.

—Case of the Scaredy Cats. LC 75-159039. (Illus.). 64p. (gr. k-3). 1971. PLB 13.89 (*0-06-020566-0*) HarpC Child Bks.

Cleary, Beverly. Henry & the Clubhouse. Darling, Louis, illus. LC 62-7161. (gr. 3-7). 1962. 12.95 (*0-688-21381-2*); PLB 12.88 (*0-688-31381-7*, Morrow Jr Bks) Morrow Jr Bks.

Cooper, Ilene. Queen of the Sixth Grade. 160p. (gr. 3 up). 1992. pap. 3.99 (*0-14-036098-0*, Puffin) Puffin Bks.

Craig, Lynn. New Friends in New Places. LC 94-1929. 1994. pap. 4.99 (*0-8407-9239-5*) Nelson.

—Summer of Choices. LC 94-4504. 1994. pap. 4.99 (*0-8407-9241-7*) Nelson.

Griffin, Peni R. The Brick House Burglars. LC 93-22914. 144p. (gr. 4-7). 1994. SBE 14.95 (*0-689-50579-5*, M K McElderry) Macmillan Child Grp.

Haynes, Betsy. The Against Taffy Sinclair Club. 112p. (gr. 3-6). 1984. pap. 2.50 (*0-553-15413-3*) Bantam.

Hines, Anna G. Tell Me Your Best Thing. Ritz, Karen, illus. LC 91-7833. 124p. (gr. 2-4). 1991. 13.95 (*0-525-44734-2*, DCB) Dutton Child Bks.

Kamins, Tamar. The B. Y. Times Kid Sisters: The "I-Can't-Cope-Club, No. 1. 1992. pap. 5.95 (*0-944070-84-1*) Targum Pr.

—The B. Y. Times Kid Sisters: The Treehouse Kids, No. 2. 1992. pap. 5.95 (*0-944070-92-2*) Targum Pr.

Kelleher, D. V. Defenders of the Universe. Brown, Jane C., illus. LC 92-1617. 128p. (gr. 3-5). 1993. 13.45 (*0-395-60515-6*) HM.

Klein, Leah. The B. Y. Times: Here We Go Again, No. 9. 1992. pap. 7.95 (*0-944070-90-6*) Targum Pr.

—The B. Y. Times: Summer Daze, No. 8. pap. 7.95 (*0-944070-83-3*) Targum Pr.

—The B. Y. Times: The New Kids, No. 10. 1992. pap. 7.95 (*0-944070-91-4*) Targum Pr.

Klevin, Jill R. The Turtle Street Trading Co. Edwards, Linda S., illus. LC 82-70312. 144p. (gr. 4-6). 1982. 11.95 (*0-385-29043-8*); PLB 11.95 (*0-685-05625-2*) Delacorte.

Leedy, Loreen. The Monster Money Book. Leedy, Loreen, illus. LC 91-18168. 32p. (ps-3). 1992. reinforced bdg. 14.95 (*0-8234-0922-8*) Holiday.

Levitin, Sonia. Adam's War. LC 93-13833. Date not set. write for info. (*0-8037-1506-4*); PLB write for info. (*0-8037-1507-2*) Dial Bks Young.

McCants, William D. Anything Can Happen in High School: And It Usually Does. LC 92-32982. 1993. write for info. (*0-15-276604-9*); pap. write for info. (*0-15-276605-7*) HarBrace.

Macdonald, Maryann. No Room for Francie. Christelow, Eileen, illus. LC 94-8596. 1995. write for info. (*0-7868-0032-1*); lib. bdg. write for info. (*0-7868-2027-6*) Hyprn Child.

Maifair, Linda. No Girls Allowed. Johnson, Meredith, illus. LC 93-40083. 1993. 3.99 (*0-8066-2688-7*, Augsburg) Augsburg Fortress.

Martin, Ann M. Claudia & the Bad Joke. large type ed. 176p. (gr. 4 up). 1993. PLB 15.93 (*0-8368-1023-6*) Gareth Stevens Inc.
—Dawn & the We Kids Club. (gr. 4-7). 1994. pap. 3.50 (*0-590-47010-8*) Scholastic Inc.
—Kristy & the Snobs. 1993. pap. 3.50 (*0-590-43660-0*) Scholastic Inc.
—Kristy & the Snobs. large type ed. LC 93-15968. 176p. (gr. 4 up). 1993. PLB 15.93 (*0-8368-1015-5*) Gareth Stevens Inc.
—Kristy & the Walking Disaster. large type ed. 176p. (gr. 4 up). 1993. PLB 15.93 (*0-8368-1024-4*) Gareth Stevens Inc.
—Kristy's Great Idea. 1991. collector's ed. 9.95 (*0-590-44816-1*, Scholastic Hardcover) Scholastic Inc.
—Mary Anne's Bad-Luck Mystery. large type ed. LC 93-4346. 176p. (gr. 4 up). 1993. PLB 15.93 (*0-8368-1021-X*) Gareth Stevens Inc.
Myrick, Mildred. Secret Three. Lobel, Arnold, illus. LC 63-13323. 64p. (gr. k-3). 1963. PLB 13.89 (*0-06-024356-2*) HarpC Child Bks.
Naylor, Phyllis R. All but Alice. LC 91-28722. 160p. (gr. 4-8). 1992. SBE 13.95 (*0-689-31773-5*, Atheneum Child Bk) Macmillan Child Grp.
Nesbit, Jeffrey A. A War of Words. LC 92-27663. (Illus.). 1992. pap. 4.99 (*0-89693-076-9*, Victor Books) SP Pubns.
Pearson, Susan. The Green Magician Puzzle. Fiammenghi, Gioia, illus. LC 90-22436. 1991. pap. 11. 95 (*0-671-74054-7*, S&S BFYR); pap. 2.95 (*0-671-74053-9*, S&S BFYR) S&S Trade.
Regan, Dian C. The Initiation. 176p. (Orig.). (gr. 5). 1993. pap. 3.50 (*0-380-76325-7*, Flare) Avon.
Roos, Stephen. Crocodile Christmas: The Pet Lovers Club. Rogers, Jacqueline, illus. LC 91-47079. 128p. (gr. 3-6). 1992. 14.00 (*0-385-30681-4*) Delacorte.
Schulte, Elaine L. Melanie & the Modeling Mess. LC 93-45377. 1994. 4.99 (*1-55661-254-0*) Bethany Hse.
York, Carol B. Ten O'Clock Club. (gr. 4-7). 1994. pap. 2.95 (*0-590-33475-1*) Scholastic Inc.

COACHING (ATHLETICS)

Beatty, Patricia. The Coach That Never Came. LC 85-15213. 176p. (gr. 5-9). 1985. 11.95 (*0-688-05477-3*) Morrow Jr Bks.

COAL MINES AND MINING

see also Mining Engineering

Asimov, Isaac. How Did We Find Out about Coal. 58p. 1992. text ed. 4.64 (*1-56956-114-1*) W A T Braille.
Davey, John. Mining Coal. (Illus.). 64p. (gr. 6 up). 1976. 15.95 (*0-7136-1596-6*) Dufour.
Hansen, Michael C. Coal: How It Is Found & Used. LC 89-34452. (Illus.). 64p. (gr. 6 up). 1990. lib. bdg. 15.95 (*0-89490-286-5*) Enslow Pubs.
Harris, Nathaniel. The Coal Mines. (Illus.). 64p. (gr. 7-12). 1986. 19.95 (*0-7134-5097-5*, Pub. by Batsford UK) Trafalgar.
Hendershot, Judith. In Coal Country. Foster, Frances, ed. Rosenthal, Eileen, designed by. LC 86-15311. (Illus.). 48p. (ps-5). 1987. 16.00 (*0-394-88190-7*) Knopf Bks Yng Read.
Mitgutsch, Ali. From Swamp to Coal. Mitgutsch, Ali, illus. LC 84-17465. 24p. (ps-3). 1985. PLB 10.95 (*0-87614-233-1*) Carolrhoda Bks.
Stewart, Gail. Coal Miners. LC 88-11860. (Illus.). 48p. (gr. 5-6). 1988. text ed. 11.95 RSBE (*0-89686-395-6*, Crestwood Hse) Macmillan Child Grp.
Witt, Matt. In Our Blood: Four Coal Mining Families. Dotter, Earl, photos by. LC 78-71518. (Illus., Orig.). (gr. 10-12). 1979. pap. text ed. 6.95 (*0-9602226-1-8*) Highlander.

COAL MINES AND MINING–FICTION

Aiken, Joan. Is Underground. LC 92-27423. 1993. 15.00 (*0-385-30898-1*) Delacorte.
Bartoletti, Susan C. Silver at Night. Ray, David, illus. 32p. (gr. k-4). 1994. 15.00 (*0-517-59426-9*); PLB 15. 99 (*0-517-59427-7*) Crown Bks Yng Read.
Welch, Catherine A. Danger at the Breaker. Shine, Andrea, illus. 48p. (gr. k-4). 1991. PLB 14.95 (*0-87614-693-0*) Carolrhoda Bks.

COAL OIL

see Petroleum

COASTAL SIGNALS

see Signals and Signaling

COATS OF ARMS

see Heraldry

COBB, TYRUS RAYMOND, 1886-1961

Jacobs, William J. They Shaped the Game. LC 94-14007. (gr. 4-6). 1994. 15.95 (*0-684-19734-0*, Scribner) Macmillan.

COCHISE, APACHE CHIEF, d. 1874

Schwartz, Melissa. Cochise. (Illus.). 112p. (gr. 5 up). 1992. lib. bdg. 17.95 (*0-7910-1706-0*) Chelsea Hse.

COCHRANE, ELIZABETH, 1867-1922

Ehrlich, Elizabeth. Nellie Bly. Horner, Matina S., intro. by. (Illus.). 112p. (gr. 5 up). 1989. 17.95 (*1-55546-643-5*) Chelsea Hse.
Emerson, Karen L. Nellie Bly: Making Headlines: A Biography of Nellie Bly. LC 88-35910. (Illus.). 112p. (gr. 5 up). 1989. text ed. 13.95 RSBE (*0-87518-406-5*, Dillon) Macmillan Child Grp.
Kendall, Martha E. Nellie Bly: Reporter for the World. LC 91-37643. (Illus.). 48p. (gr. 2-4). 1992. PLB 12.90 (*1-56294-061-9*); pap. 4.95 (*1-56294-787-7*) Millbrook Pr.
—Nellie Bly: Reporter for the World. (gr. 4-7). 1992. pap. 4.95 (*0-395-64538-7*) HM.

COCKROACHES

Kerby, Mona. Cockroaches. LC 88-37857. (Illus.). 64p. (gr. 3 up). 1989. PLB 12.90 (*0-531-10689-6*) Watts.

COCKROACHES–FICTION

Porizkova, Paulina & Russell, Joanne. The Adventures of Ralphie the Roach. (Illus.). 48p. (gr. k-4). 1992. 15.00 (*0-385-42402-7*) Doubleday.

COCOA

see also Chocolate

COCOONS

see Butterflies; Caterpillars; Moths; Silkworms

CODE NAMES

see Ciphers

CODY, WILLIAM FREDERICK, 1846-1917

Buntline, Ned. Buffalo Bill: His Adventures in the West. LC 74-15731. (Illus.). 320p. (gr. 7 up). 1974. Repr. of 1886 ed. 23.00x (*0-405-06366-0*) Ayer.
Dadey, Debbie. Buffalo Bill & the Pony Express. Bill Smith Studio Staff, illus. 80p. (gr. 1-4). 1994. pap. 3.50 (*0-7868-4005-6*); PLB 12.89 (*0-7868-5004-3*) Disney Pr.
Harris, Aurand. Buffalo Bill. 1954. 4.50 (*0-87602-110-0*) Anchorage.
Robison, Nancy. Buffalo Bill. LC 90-47221. (Illus.). 64p. (gr. 3-5). 1991. PLB 12.90 (*0-531-20007-8*) Watts.
Stevenson, Augusta. Buffalo Bill: Frontier Daredevil. Dreany, F. Joseph, illus. LC 90-23767. 192p. (gr. 3-7). 1991. pap. 3.95 (*0-689-71479-3*, Aladdin) Macmillan Child Grp.
Zadra, Dan. Frontiersmen in America: Buffalo Bill. rev. ed. (gr. 2-4). 1988. 14.95 (*0-88682-194-0*) Creative Ed.

COFFEE

Focus on Nicotine & Caffeine. (Illus.). 64p. (gr. 3-7). 1990. PLB 15.40 (*0-516-07355-9*) Childrens.

COGNITION

see Knowledge, Theory of

COIN COLLECTING

see Coins

COINAGE

see also Gold; Money; Silver

COINS

see also Numismatics

Coin Collecting. (Illus.). 32p. (gr. 6-12). 1975. pap. 1.85 (*0-8395-3390-X*, 33390) BSA.
Lewis, Brenda R. Coins & Currency. LC 92-46359. (Illus.). 80p. (gr. 5 up). 1993. 13.00 (*0-679-82662-9*); PLB 13.99 (*0-679-92662-3*) Random Bks Yng Read.
Longue, Bob. World's Best Coin Tricks. LC 92-11370. (Illus.). 128p. 1992. 12.95 (*0-8069-8660-3*) Sterling.
Mayhew, Nicholas. Coinage in France from the Dark Ages to Napoleon. (Illus.). 163p. (gr. 10 up). 1988. 39. 95 (*0-900652-87-X*, Pub. by Seaby UK) Trafalgar.

COINS–FICTION

Aliki. Three Gold Pieces. Aliki, illus. 32p. (ps-3). 1994. pap. 5.95 (*0-06-443386-2*, Trophy) HarpC Child Bks.
Gipson, Morrell & Frank, Herta. Tom's Lucky Quarter. Stefoff, Rebecca, ed. LC 90-13796. (Illus.). 24p. (gr. k-3). 1990. PLB 14.60 (*0-944483-89-5*) Garrett Ed Corp.
Martin, Ann M. Karen's Lucky Penny. (gr. 4-7). 1994. pap. 2.95 (*0-590-47048-5*) Scholastic Inc.

COLERIDGE, SAMUEL TAYLOR, 1772-1834

Mayberry, Tom. Coleridge & Wordsworth in the West Country. (Illus.). 224p. (gr. 11-12). 1992. 30.00 (*0-86299-896-4*) A Sutton Pub.

COLLAGE

Boutan, Mila. Collages. (Illus.). (ps-1). 1992. 4.50 (*1-56021-196-2*) W J Fantasy.
Hodge, Anthony. Collage. Hodge, Anthony, illus. LC 91-34408. 32p. (gr. 5-9). 1992. PLB 12.40 (*0-531-17323-2*, Gloucester Pr) Watts.
Steele, Philip. Collage. LC 92-42678. 40p. (gr. 3-7). 1993. 10.95 (*1-85697-921-0*, Kingfisher LKC); pap. 5.95 (*1-85697-920-2*) LKC.
Stocks, Sue. Collage. LC 93-46891. (Illus.). 32p. (gr. 1-4). 1994. 14.95 (*1-56847-161-0*) Thomson Lrning.
Thomson, Ruth. Collage. LC 94-12305. (Illus.). 24p. (ps-3). 1994. PLB 14.40 (*0-516-07988-3*); pap. 4.95 (*0-516-47988-1*) Childrens.

COLLECTING

see Collectors and Collecting

COLLECTIONS OF LITERATURE

see Short Stories;
also names of literatures and literary forms with the subdivision Collections, e.g. English Literature–Collections; Poetry–Collections

COLLECTIVE SETTLEMENTS

Taylor, Allegra. A Kibbutz in Israel. (Illus.). 32p. (gr. 2-5). 1987. 13.50 (*0-8225-1678-0*) Lerner Pubns.

COLLECTIVE SETTLEMENTS–FICTION

Banks, Lynne R. One More River. rev. ed. 256p. (gr. 5 up). 1992. 14.00 (*0-688-10893-8*) Morrow Jr Bks.
Dennison, George. And Then a Harvest Feast. (gr. 4-7). 1992. pap. 4.50 (*0-374-40377-5*) FS&G.
Edwards, Michelle. Chicken Man. (Illus.). (gr. k-3). 1991. 13.95 (*0-688-09708-1*); PLB 13.88 (*0-688-09709-X*) Lothrop.
—Chicken Man. Edwards, Michelle, illus. LC 93-11728. 32p. (ps up). 1994. pap. 4.95 (*0-688-13106-9*, Mulberry) Morrow.

COLLECTIVISM

see Communism

COLLECTORS AND COLLECTING

see also names of natural specimens with the subdivision Collection and Preservation, e.g. Zoological Specimens–Collection and Preservation

Boy Scouts of America Staff. Collections. (Illus.). 48p. (gr. 6-12). 1991. pap. 1.85 (*0-8395-3242-3*, 33242) BSA.
Childress, Casey & McKenzie, Linda. A Beginner's Guide to Baseball Card Collecting: A Step-by-Step Guide for the Young Collector. LC 88-90757. (Illus.). 46p. (Orig.). (gr. 4-8). 1990. Repr. of 1988 ed. vinyl covers 7.95 (*0-9620167-0-5*) C Mack Pub.
DeSimone, James. The Official G. I. Joe Collectors Guide to Completing & Collating Your G. I. Joes & Accessories. 1993. pap. 11.94 (*0-9635956-0-1*) GI Joe Collect.
Garrett, B. J. Who's on What? Basketball Trading Cards Reference Book, 1990-1991. Taylor, David S., illus. 100p. (Orig.). (gr. 3 up). 1993. pap. write for info. (*1-882816-00-5*) Eyes of August.
Kennedy, Trish & Schodorf, Timothy. Baseball Card Crazy. LC 92-14597. 80p. (gr. 4-6). 1993. SBE 11.95 (*0-684-19536-4*, Scribner Young Read) Macmillan Child Grp.
Young, Robert S. Action Figures. LC 92-7697. (Illus.). 64p. (gr. 5 up). 1992. text ed. 13.95 RSBE (*0-87518-516-9*, Dillon) Macmillan Child Grp.

COLLECTORS AND COLLECTING–FICTION

Cole, Shelia. The Dragon in the Cliff: A Novel Based on the Life of Mary Anning. Farrow, T. C., illus. LC 90-40455. (gr. 4-7). 1991. 12.95 (*0-688-10196-8*) Lothrop.
Drew, David. Collections. Davy, Mary, illus. LC 93-16141. 1994. write for info. (*0-383-03683-6*) SRA Schl Grp.
Gilson, Jamie. Harvey, the Beer Can King. Wallner, John, illus. LC 78-1807. 128p. (gr. 4-6). 1983. 13.95 (*0-688-02382-7*) Lothrop.
Krasilovsky, Phyllis. The Woman Who Saved Things. Cymerman, John E., illus. LC 92-5126. 32p. (gr. k up). 1993. 14.00 (*0-688-11162-9*, Tambourine Bks); PLB 13.93 (*0-688-11163-7*, Tambourine Bks) Morrow.
Manushkin, Fran. Buster Loves Buttons! Zimmer, Dirk, illus. LC 84-48332. 64p. (gr. k-3). 1985. HarpC Child Bks.
Poskanzer, Susan C. The Superduper Collector. Harvey, Paul, illus. LC 85-14051. 48p. (Orig.). (gr. 1-3). 1986. PLB 10.59 (*0-8167-0606-9*); pap. text ed. 3.50 (*0-8167-0607-7*) Troll Assocs.
Smyth, Gwenda. Horrie the Hoarder. Power, Margaret, illus. LC 93-20061. 1994. write for info. (*0-383-03696-8*) SRA Schl Grp.
Van Pallandt, Nicolas. The Butterfly Night of Old Brown Bear. (ps-3). 1992. bds. 15.00 jacketed (*0-374-31009-2*) FS&G.

COLLECTS

see Prayers

COLLEGE, CHOICE OF

Blaker, Charles W. The College Matchmaker. New, Dwight, illus. LC 80-67604. 56p. (Orig.). (gr. 11-12). 1980. pap. text ed. 3.50 (*0-9604614-0-X*) Rekalb Pr.
Buckalew, Walker. Coping with Choosing a College. Rosen, Roger, ed. 64p. (gr. 7-12). 1990. PLB 14.95 (*0-8239-1079-2*) Rosen Group.
Fischgrund, Tom, ed. Barron's Top Fifty: An Inside Look at America's Best Colleges. 2nd ed. LC 92-39776. (gr. 9 up). 1993. pap. 13.95 (*0-8120-1447-2*) Barron.
Heron, Helen H. College Countdown: A Planning Guide for High School Students. 155p. (gr. 9-12). 1992. pap. 14.95 (*1-880639-24-6*) Heron Pub CA.
Mooney, Chuck, III. The Recruiting Survival Guide: How to Be a Smart Recruit. Bucheit, Kelly S., ed. Swan, Kyle, illus. 84p. (Orig.). (gr. 11-12). 1991. pap. 9.95 (*0-9630239-0-X*) C Mooney.
Solorzano, Lucia. Best Buys in College Education. 3rd ed. 700p. (gr. 10-12). 1994. pap. 14.95 (*0-8120-1857-5*) Barron.
Weinstein, Miriam. Making a Difference College Guide: Exciting Choices for Students Who Want to Make A Better World. 3rd, rev. ed. 248p. (gr. 11-12). 1994. pap. 12.95 (*0-9634618-2-6*) Sage Pr CA.

COLLEGE ATHLETICS

see Athletics

COLLEGE ENTRANCE REQUIREMENTS

see Colleges and Universities–Entrance Requirements

COLLEGE TEACHERS

see Educators; Teachers

COLLEGES AND UNIVERSITIES

see also Education, Higher; Scholarships, Fellowships, etc.; Students
also headings beginning with the word College and names of individual institutions

Cernea, Ruth F., ed. The Hillel Guide to Jewish Life on Campus: The Most Comprehensive Guide to a Quality College Experience. rev. ed. Dever Designs Staff, illus. Joel, Richard M., intro. by. (Illus.). (gr. 11-12). 1993. pap. 14.95g (*0-9603058-8-2*) B'nai B'rith-Hillel.
Deegan, Paul. Harvard University. LC 88-71725. (Illus.). 48p. (gr. 4 up). 1988. lib. bdg. 10.95 (*0-939179-50-4*) Abdo & Dghtrs.
—Rice University. LC 88-71729. (Illus.). 48p. (gr. 4 up). 1988. lib. bdg. 10.95 (*0-939179-52-0*) Abdo & Dghtrs.
—Stanford University. LC 88-71728. (Illus.). 48p. (gr. 4 up). 1988. lib. bdg. 10.95 (*0-939179-53-9*) Abdo & Dghtrs.
—University of California of Los Angeles. LC 88-71727. (Illus.). 48p. (gr. 4 up). 1988. lib. bdg. 10.95 (*0-939179-48-2*) Abdo & Dghtrs.
—University of Chicago. LC 88-71726. (Illus.). 48p. (gr. 4 up). 1988. lib. bdg. 10.95 (*0-939179-49-0*) Abdo & Dghtrs.

Hutchcraft, Doug & Hutchcraft, Ronald P. Letters from the College Front: Guys' Edition. (Illus.). 80p. (gr. 9-12). 1993. 8.99 (*0-8010-4379-4*) Baker Bk.

Schwartz, Saryl Z. How to Find Money for College: The Disabled Student. (gr. 8 up). 1994. one add-on cassette 21.20 (*0-9629535-4-7*) Path-Coll Afford Prod.

—How to Find Money for College: The Minority Student. (gr. 8 up). 1993. one add-on cassette 21.20 (*0-9629535-3-9*) Path-Coll Afford Prod.

Spargo, Edward. The College Student. 4th ed. 251p. (gr. 12). 1994. pap. 12.00 (*0-89061-757-0*) Jamestown Pubs.

Spethman, Martin J. How to Get into & Graduate from College in Four Years with Good Grades, a Useful Major, a Lot of Knowledge, a Little Debt, Great Friends, Happy Parents, Maximum Party Attendance, Minimal Weight Gain, Decent Habits, Fewer Hassles, a Career Goal, & a Super Attitude All While Remaining Extremely Cool. Cabrera, Ralph, illus. 192p. (Orig.). (gr. 11-12). 1993. pap. 10.95 (*0-9633598-0-0*) Westgate Pub & Ent.

Whitmer, Lisa H. & Hutchcraft, Ronald P. Letters from the College Front: Girls' Edition. 96p. (gr. 9-12). 1993. 8.99 (*0-8010-9722-3*) Baker Bk.

COLLEGES AND UNIVERSITIES–DIRECTORIES

Dilts, Susan & Stokes, Chris, eds. Peterson's Guide to Colleges in New England 1995. 11th, rev. ed. 138p. (gr. 11-12). 1994. pap. 13.95 (*1-56079-359-7*) Petersons Guides.

—Peterson's Guide to Colleges in New York 1995. 11th, rev. ed. 135p. (gr. 11-12). 1994. pap. 13.95 (*1-56079-358-9*) Petersons Guides.

Fischgrund, Tom, ed. Barron's Top Fifty: An Inside Look at America's Best Colleges. 2nd ed. LC 92-39776. (gr. 9 up). 1993. pap. 13.95 (*0-8120-1447-2*) Barron.

Hodge-Wright, Toni, et al, eds. The Handbook of Historically Black Colleges & Universities, Premier Edition 1992-94: Comprehensive Profiles & Photos of Black Colleges & Universities. Evans, Christine, et al, illus. LC 92-71364. 248p. (gr. 10 up). 1992. 19.95 (*0-9632669-0-X*) Jireh & Assocs.

Kraus International Publications. How to Get to the College of Your Choice: By Road, Plane or Train: A Practical Guide to Campus Visits, Central States. (Illus.). 440p. (Orig.). (gr. 9-12). 1993. pap. 17.95 (*0-527-42650-4*) Kraus Intl.

Mitchell, Joyce S. The Best Guide to the Top Colleges: How to Get into the Ivies or Nearly Ivies. LC 90-24012. (Illus.). 111p. (Orig.). (gr. 11-12). 1991. pap. 10.95 (*0-912048-85-9*) Garrett Pk.

Solorzano, Lucia. Best Buys in College Education. 3rd ed. 700p. (gr. 10-12). 1994. pap. 14.95 (*0-8120-1857-5*) Barron.

Weinstein, Miriam. Making a Difference College Guide: Exciting Choices for Students Who Want to Make A Better World. 3rd, rev. ed. 248p. (gr. 11-12). 1994. pap. 12.95 (*0-9634618-2-6*) Sage Pr CA.

Woodrow, James I. The Christian College Advantage: A Student-Parent Guide to Colleges Affiliated with the Churches of Christ. 102p. (gr. 10-12). 1992. 11.95 (*0-9631429-0-9*) Inst Advan PHE.

COLLEGES AND UNIVERSITIES–ENTRANCE REQUIREMENTS

Brownstein, Samuel C., et al. Pass Key to SAT I. 2nd ed. (gr. 10-12). 1994. pap. 6.95 (*0-8120-1884-2*) Barron.

Ehrenhaft, George. Write Your Way into College. 2nd, rev. ed. LC 93-13380. 120p. (gr. 9 up). 1993. pap. 8.95 (*0-8120-1415-4*) Barron.

Mason, Michael. How to Write a Winning College-Application Essay. 250p. (Orig.). (gr. 10 up). 1991. pap. 8.95 (*1-55958-083-6*) Prima Pub.

Mitchell, Joyce S. The Best Guide to the Top Colleges: How to Get into the Ivies or Nearly Ivies. LC 90-24012. (Illus.). 111p. (Orig.). (gr. 11-12). 1991. pap. 10.95 (*0-912048-85-9*) Garrett Pk.

Paul-Matos, Janice. How to Get into College: Step by Step, Vol. 1. 24p. (Orig.). (gr. 9-12). 1985. pap. 5.00 (*0-9615165-0-X*) Coll Acceptance.

Schell, Kent. How to Apply to College Step by Step. 1988. pap. 9.95 (*0-87738-027-9*) Youth Ed.

Shniderman, Jeffrey & Hurwitz, Sue. Applications: A Guide to Filling Out All Kinds of Forms. LC 93-7911. 1993. 13.95 (*0-8239-1609-X*) Rosen Group.

COLLEGES AND UNIVERSITIES–FICTION

Bernard, Robert, ed. All Problems Are Simple & Other Stories: Nineteen Views of the College Years. (gr. 12 up). 1988. 3.50 (*0-318-37398-X*, LF) Dell.

Choi, Sook-Nyul. Gathering of Pearls. LC 94-10868. 1994. 13.95 (*0-395-67437-9*) HM.

Cooney, Linda A. Freshman Feud. 1992. pap. 3.50 (*0-06-106141-7*, Harp PBks) HarpC.

—Freshman Flames. 1991. pap. 3.50 (*0-06-106127-1*, Harp PBks) HarpC.

—Freshman Follies. 1992. pap. 3.50 (*0-06-106142-5*, Harp PBks) HarpC.

—Freshman Heat. (gr. 9-12). 1993. pap. 3.99 (*0-06-106738-5*, Harp PBks) HarpC.

—Freshman Passion. (gr. 9-12). 1993. pap. 3.99 (*0-06-106745-8*, Harp PBks) HarpC.

—Freshman Promises. 1992. pap. 3.99 (*0-06-106134-4*, Harp PBks) HarpC.

—Freshman Summer. 1992. pap. 3.99 (*0-06-106780-6*, Harp PBks) HarpC.

—Freshman Taboo. (gr. 9-12). 1993. pap. 3.99 (*0-06-106741-5*, Harp PBks) HarpC.

—Freshman Wedding. 1992. pap. 3.50 (*0-06-106135-2*, Harp PBks) HarpC.

Cruise, Beth. Exit, Stage Right. LC 94-16981. (gr. 5 up). 1994. pap. 3.95 (*0-02-042792-1*, Collier) Macmillan.

—Mistletoe Magic. 1994. pap. 3.95 (*0-02-042794-8*, Aladdin) Macmillan Child Grp.

Harrell, Janice. Dusty Brannigan. 160p. (Orig.). 1993. pap. 3.50 (*0-380-76113-0*, Flare) Avon.

Newton, Suzanne. Where Are You When I Need You? 1991. 14.00 (*0-670-81702-3*) Viking Child Bks.

—Where Are You When I Need You? LC 92-31360. 208p. (gr. 7 up). 1993. pap. 3.99 (*0-14-034454-3*) Puffin Bks.

Singh, Maria E. Carry on, My Friends. LC 88-71123. 64p. (Orig.). 1989. pap. 5.00 (*0-916383-61-X*) Aegina Pr.

COLOMBIA

DuBois, Jill. Colombia. LC 90-22468. (Illus.). 128p. (gr. 5-9). 1991. PLB 21.95 (*1-85435-384-5*) Marshall Cavendish.

Lerner Publications, Department of Geography Staff, ed. Colombia in Pictures. (Illus.). 64p. (gr. 5 up). 1987. PLB 17.50 (*0-8225-1810-4*) Lerner Pubns.

Morrison, Marion. Colombia. LC 90-36528. (Illus.). 128p. (gr. 5-9). 1990. PLB 20.55 (*0-516-02722-0*) Childrens.

Pearce, Jenny. Colombia: The Drug War. (Illus.). 40p. (gr. 6-8). 1990. PLB 12.90 (*0-531-17237-6*, Gloucester Pr) Watts.

Stewart, Gail B. Colombia. LC 90-47694. (Illus.). 48p. (gr. 6-7). 1991. text ed. 4.95 RSBE (*0-89686-603-3*, Crestwood Hse) Macmillan Child Grp.

COLOMBIA–FICTION

Becerra De Jenkins, Lyll. Celebrating the Hero. (Illus.). 160p. (gr. 7 up). 1993. 15.99 (*0-525-67399-7*, Lodestar Bks) Dutton Child Bks.

Elwood, Roger. Forbidden River. (gr. 3-7). 1991. pap. 4.99 (*0-8499-3304-8*) Word Inc.

Kendall, Sarita. Ransom for a River Dolphin. LC 93-19929. 1993. 18.95 (*0-8225-0735-8*) Lerner Pubns.

COLONIAL HISTORY (U. S.)

see U. S.–History–Colonial Period

COLONIAL LIFE AND CUSTOMS (U. S.)

see U. S.–History–Colonial Period; U. S.–Social Life and Customs–Colonial Period

COLOR

Adoff, Arnold. Greens. Lewin, Betsy, illus. LC 85-16631. (gr. 1-5). 1988. 12.95 (*0-688-04276-7*); lib. bdg. 12.88 (*0-688-04277-5*) Lothrop.

Allington, Richard L. Colors. Spangler, Noel, illus. LC 79-19116. 32p. (gr. k-3). 1985. PLB 9.95 (*0-8172-1280-9*); pap. 3.95 (*0-8114-8240-5*) Raintree Steck-V.

Anderson, L. W. Light & Color. rev. ed. LC 87-23225. (Illus.). 48p. (gr. 2-6). 1987. PLB 10.95 (*0-8172-3257-5*) Raintree Steck-V.

Ardley, Neil. Science Book of Color. 29p. (gr. 2-5). 1991. 9.95 (*0-15-200576-5*) HarBrace.

Arnold, Tedd, illus. Colors. 16p. (ps). 1992. pap. 3.95 (*0-671-77825-0*, Little Simon) S&S Trade.

Bailey, Vanessa. Animal Colors. Stillwell, Stella, illus. 16p. (ps). 1991. 5.95 (*0-8120-6245-0*) Barron.

Balducci, Rita. Walt Disney's Alice in Wonderland: Book of Colors. DiCicco, Sue, illus. 12p. (ps). 1993. bds. 1.95 (*0-307-06079-9*, 6079, Golden Pr) Western Pub.

Barnes-Murphy, Rowan. Colors. 16p. (ps). 1992. bds. 3.95 (*0-8249-8530-3*, Ideals Child) Hambleton-Hill.

Behm, Barbara J., adapted by. Investigating the Color Blue. LC 93-23815. 1993. 17.27 (*0-8368-1028-7*) Gareth Stevens Inc.

Behm, Barbara J., ed. Investigating the Color Green. LC 93-23816. 1993. 17.27 (*0-8368-1029-5*) Gareth Stevens Inc.

Behm, Barbara J., adapted by. Investigating the Color Red. LC 93-23817. 1993. 17.27 (*0-8368-1027-9*) Gareth Stevens Inc.

—Investigating the Color Yellow. LC 93-23814. 1993. 17.27 (*0-8368-1030-9*) Gareth Stevens Inc.

Bell, Jo G. Hide & Seek with Colors. Conahan, Carolyn, illus. 32p. (ps-2). Date not set. 11.95 (*1-56065-158-X*) Capstone Pr.

Benjamin, Alan. What Color? Que Color? (ENG & SPA.). (ps). 1992. pap. 2.95 (*0-671-76930-8*, Little Simon) S&S Trade.

Big Bird's Red Book. 1987. pap. 1.00 (*0-307-01029-5*) Western Pub.

Bishop, Roma. Colors. (ps). 1992. pap. 2.95 (*0-671-79120-6*, Little Simon) S&S Trade.

Bond, Michael. Paddington's Colors. Lobban, John, illus. 32p. (ps-1). 1991. 10.99 (*0-670-84102-1*) Viking Child Bks.

Boyle, Alison. Playdays Colours & Shapes. Johnson, Paul, illus. 32p. (ps-2). 1992. pap. 2.95 (*0-563-20887-2*, BBC-Parkwest) Parkwest Pubns.

Bradbury, Lynne. Shapes & Colors. Grundy, Lynn N., illus. 28p. (ps). 1992. Series 921. 3.50 (*0-7214-1510-5*) Ladybird Bks.

Bradman, Tony. The Bad Babies' Book of Colors. Schulman, Janet, ed. Van der Beek, Deborah, illus. Greenstein, Mina, designed by. LC 86-27860. (Illus.). 32p. (ps-2). 1987. 5.95 (*0-394-89046-9*) Knopf Bks Yng Read.

Bragg, Ruth G. Colors of the Day. Bragg, Ruth G., illus. LC 92-7790. 40p. 1992. pap. 14.95 (*0-88708-245-9*) Picture Bk Studio.

Brenner, Barbara A. The Color Wizard: Level 1. Dillon, Leo D., ed. Dillon, Diane, illus. (ps-3). 1989. 9.99 (*0-553-05825-8*) Bantam.

Brown, Charlene & Davis, Carolyn. Color Fun. Davis, Carolyn, illus. 64p. (Orig.). (gr. k up). 1990. pap. 3.95 (*0-929261-27-5*, BA02) W Foster Pub.

Brown, Kenneth, illus. Dollhouse Book: Color & Counting Concepts. 1994. 12.95 (*1-56743-044-9*) Amistad Pr.

Brown, Margery W. Afro-Bets: Book of Shapes. Blair, Culverson, illus. LC 91-76333. 24p. (Orig.). (ps-1). 1991. pap. 3.95 (*0-940975-29-7*) Just Us Bks.

Bryant-Mole, K. Colors. (Illus.). 24p. (ps up). 1990. pap. 3.50 (*0-7460-0594-6*, Usborne) EDC.

Burningham, John. First Steps: Letters, Numbers, Colors, Opposites. Burningham, John, illus. LC 93-18844. 48p. (ps up). 1994. lib. bdg. 14.95 (*1-56402-205-6*) Candlewick Pr.

Callinan, Karen. Green. Marden, Carol K., illus. 32p. (ps-2). 1992. 11.95 (*1-56065-152-0*) Capstone Pr.

Carle, Eric. My Very First Book of Colors. reissued ed. Carle, Eric, illus. LC 72-83776. 10p. (ps-1). 1985. 4.95 (*0-694-00011-6*, Crowell Jr Bks) HarpC Child Bks.

Carrie, Christopher. Wild about Color. (Illus.). 40p. (gr. k up). 1990. 1.99 (*0-86696-234-4*) Binney & Smith.

Carroll, Jeri. The Complete Color Book. (Illus.). 112p. (ps-3). 1991. 10.95 (*0-86653-585-3*, GP1300) Good Apple.

Carter, David A. Baby Bug Colors. (gr. 3 up). 1993. pap. 4.95 (*0-671-86875-6*, Little Simon) S&S Trade.

Chermayeff, Ivan. Tomato & Other Colors. (ps-3). 1981. 13.55 (*0-13-924753-X*) P-H.

Church, Vivian. Colors Around Me. LC 75-154209. (Illus.). 28p. (gr. k-3). 1971. 4.95 (*0-910030-15-4*) Afro-Am.

Color Scheme, Unit 6. (gr. 2). 1991. 5-pack 21.25 (*0-88106-752-0*) Charlesbridge Pub.

Colors. (Illus.). 24p. (ps). 1994. bds. 2.95 (*1-56458-535-2*) Dorling Kindersley.

Conteh-Morgan, Jane, illus. Colors. 9p. (ps-1). 1993. bds. 4.95 (*0-448-40522-9*, G&D) Putnam Pub Group.

Cony, Sue, illus. Colors. 8p. (ps-k). 1991. bds. 4.95 (*1-56293-148-2*) McClanahan Bk.

Cooke, Tom. Flash Cards Get Ready Colors. (ps). 1986. pap. 2.60 (*0-307-04982-5*, Golden Pr) Western Pub.

Davis, Nancy M., et al. Colors. Davis, Nancy M., illus. (Orig.). (ps-2). 1986. pap. 4.95 (*0-937103-13-6*) DaNa Pubns.

De Bourgoing, Pascale. Colors. Valat, P. M. & Perols, Sylvie, illus. 1991. pap. 10.95 (*0-590-45236-3*, Cartwheel) Scholastic Inc.

De Brunhoff, Laurent. Babar's Book of Color. De Brunhoff, Laurent, illus. LC 84-42737. 36p. (ps-2). 1984. lib. bdg. 10.99 (*0-394-96896-4*) Random Bks Yng Read.

Dewey, Ariane. Naming Colors. LC 93-2635. (gr. 1-8). 1995. 16.00 (*0-06-021291-8*); PLB 15.89 (*0-06-021292-6*) HarpC Child Bks.

Dillion, Leo & Dillion, Diane. What Am I? LC 93-48835. (gr. 1 up). 1994. 13.95 (*0-590-47885-0*, Blue Sky Press) Scholastic Inc.

Disney Babies Name the Colors. LC 85-81572. 12p. (ps). 1988. pap. write for info. (*0-307-06045-4*, Pub. by Golden Bks) Western Pub.

Disney Color Surprises. (gr. 2 up). 1991. pap. 1.97 (*1-56297-120-4*) Lee Pubns KY.

Disney Colorful Characters. (gr. 2 up). 1991. pap. 1.97 (*1-56297-121-2*) Lee Pubns KY.

Disney, Walt, Productions Staff. Goofy's Book of Colors. LC 82-18630. (Illus.). 32p. (ps-1). 1983. lib. bdg. 4.99 (*0-394-95734-2*) Random Bks Yng Read.

Disney's Pop-up Book of Colors. LC 90-85431. (Illus.). 12p. (ps-k). 1991. 6.95 (*1-56282-020-6*) Disney Pr.

Edge, Nellie. I Can Read Colors Big Book. Saylor, Melissa, illus. (ps-2). 1988. pap. text ed. 14.00 (*0-922053-03-0*) N Edge Res.

—Se Leer Colores. Zamora-Pearson, Marissa, tr. from ENG. Saylor, Melissa, illus. (SPA.). (ps-2). 1993. pap. text ed. 15.00 (*0-922053-28-6*) N Edge Res.

Ehlert, Lois. Color Zoo. Ehlert, Lois, illus. LC 87-17065. 32p. (ps-1). 1989. 14.00 (*0-397-32259-3*, Lipp Jr Bks); PLB 13.89 (*0-397-32260-7*) HarpC Child Bks.

Evans, David & Williams, Claudette. Color & Light. LC 92-53480. (Illus.). 24p. (gr. k-3). 1993. 9.95 (*1-56458-207-8*) Dorling Kindersley.

Felix, Monique. Colors. (ps up). 1993. 7.95 (*1-56846-075-9*) Creat Editions.

Flying Colors. (Illus.). (gr. 2 up). 1991. 5.95 (*0-87449-577-6*) Modern Pub NYC.

Frank, Marjorie. I Can Make a Rainbow. LC 76-506. (Illus.). 300p. (gr. k-6). 1976. pap. 16.95 (*0-913916-19-6*, IP 19-6) Incentive Pubns.

Gill, Bob. What Color Is Your World. Gill, Bob, illus. (gr. k-3). 1963. 10.95 (*0-8392-3042-7*) Astor-Honor.

Goennel, Heidi. Colors, Vol. 1. (ps-4). 1990. 15.95 (*0-316-31843-4*) Little.

Gorbaty, Norman, illus. Ducky Colors. 12p. (ps). 1991. pap. 3.95 (*0-671-74435-6*, Little Simon) S&S Trade.

Gregory, Elizabeth. Blinky & the Blends. (Illus.). 1981. 6.95 (*0-933184-11-5*); pap. 4.95 (*0-933184-12-3*) Flame Intl.

Groening, Matt & Groening, Maggie. Maggie Simpson's Book of Colors & Shapes. LC 91-2864. (Illus.). 32p. (ps-1). 1991. HarpC Child Bks.

Hill, Eric. Book of Colors. (ps). 6.95 (*0-317-13663-1*) Determined Prods.

Hoban, Tana. Colors Everywhere. LC 93-24847. (Illus.). 32p. (gr. 3 up). 1995. write for info. (*0-688-12762-2*); PLB write for info. (*0-688-12763-0*) Greenwillow.

—Of Colors & Things. LC 92-43785. (Illus.). 24p. (ps-12). 1989. 15.00 (*0-688-07534-7*); PLB 14.93 (*0-688-07535-5*) Greenwillow.

—Red, Blue, Yellow Shoe. Hoban, Tana, illus. LC 86-3095. 12p. (ps). 1986. bds. 4.95 (*0-688-06563-5*) Greenwillow.

Howard, Katherine. Do You Know Colors? Miller, J. P., illus. LC 78-1133. (ps-1). 1979. lib. bdg. 5.99 (*0-394-93957-3*); 2.25 (*0-394-83957-9*) Random Bks Yng Read.

I Know Colors. (Illus.). 1991. 4.99 (*0-517-05883-9*) Random Hse Value.

Imershein, Betsy. Finding Red Finding Yellow. Imershein, Betsy, photos by. LC 88-35808. (Illus.). 32p. (ps). 1989. 10.95 (*0-15-200453-X*, Gulliver Bks) HarBrace.

Jennings, Terry. Light & Color. LC 88-36220. (Illus.). 32p. (gr. 3-6). 1989. pap. 4.95 (*0-516-48440-0*) Childrens.

Joval, Nomi. Color of Light. Kubinyi, Laszlo, illus. 16p. (ps-4). 1993. PLB 13.95 (*1-879567-19-9*, Valeria Bks) Wonder Well.

—Power of Glass. Kubinyi, Laszlo, illus. 16p. (ps-4). 1993. PLB 13.95 (*1-879567-21-0*, Valeria Bks) Wonder Well.

Kalman, Bobbie. The Colors of Nature. (Illus.). 32p. (Orig.). (gr. 3-6). 1993. PLB 15.95 (*0-86505-557-2*); pap. 7.95 (*0-86505-583-1*) Crabtree Pub Co.

Konigsburg, E. L. Samuel Todd's Book of Great Colors. Konigsburg, E. L., illus. LC 89-6640. 32p. (ps-k). 1990. SBE 13.95 (*0-689-31593-7*, Atheneum Child Bk) Macmillan Child Grp.

Kowalczyk, Carolyn. El Morado es Parte del Arco Iris-Libro Grande: Purple Is Part of a Rainbow-Big Book. 32p. (ps-2). 1988. PLB 22.95 (*0-516-59513-X*) Childrens.

Kropa, Susan. Sky Blue, Grass Green. Kropa, Susan, illus. 128p. (gr. 1-3). 1986. wkbk. 11.95 (*0-86653-355-9*, GA 698) Good Apple.

Lambert, Jonathan, illus. Colors. 18p. (ps-1). 1992. bds. 1.95 (*0-681-41562-2*) Longmeadow Pr.

Lauber, Patricia. What Do You See? Wexler, Jerome & Lessin, Leonard, photos by. LC 93-2388. (Illus.). 48p. (gr. 3-7). 1994. 17.00 (*0-517-59390-4*); PLB 17.99 (*0-517-59391-2*) Crown Bks Yng Read.

Learn with Tom Kitten: Book of Colors. 1993. 2.99 (*0-517-07698-5*) Random Hse Value.

LeGros, Lucy C. Instant Centers - Colors. (Illus.). 40p. (Orig.). (gr. k-2). 1984. pap. 5.95 (*0-937306-03-7*) Creat Res NC.

Lionni, Leo. Little Blue & Little Yellow. (Illus.). (gr. k-1). 1959. 10.95 (*0-8392-3018-4*) Astor-Honor.

Lonergan, Elaine. The Sea's Many Color. Lopez, Paul, illus. 12p. (ps-k). 1994. 5.95 (*1-884506-01-1*) Third Story.

Loveland Comm. Staff. Discover Colors. 1992. 4.49 (*1-55513-916-7*, Chariot Bks) Chariot Family.

Mack, Karen. The Magical Adventures of Sun Beams. Johnson, Tani B., illus. 32p. (ps-4). 1992. pap. 5.95 (*0-9631644-0-6*) Shooting Star.

MacKinnon, Debbie. What Color? Sieveking, Anthea, photos by. (Illus.). 24p. (ps-k). 1994. 10.99 (*0-8037-0909-9*) Dial Bks Young.

McKinnon, Elizabeth S., ed. One-Two-Three Colors: Activities for Introducing Color to Young Children. Warren, Jean, compiled by. Ekberg, Marion H., illus. LC 87-51241. 160p. (Orig.). (ps-1). 1988. pap. 14.95 (*0-911019-17-0*) Warren Pub Hse.

McMillan, Bruce. Growing Colors. McMillan, Bruce, photos by. LC 88-2767. (Illus.). 40p. (ps-2). 1988. 15.00 (*0-688-07844-3*); PLB 14.93 (*0-688-07845-1*) Lothrop.

—Growing Colors. McMillan, Bruce, photos by. LC 93-28804. (Illus.). 32p. (ps up). 1994. pap. 4.95 (*0-688-13112-3*, Mulberry) Morrow.

Marks, Burton. Colors & Numbers. Harvey, Paul, illus. LC 91-17493. 24p. (gr. k-2). 1992. PLB 9.89 (*0-8167-2411-3*); pap. text ed. 2.50 (*0-8167-2412-1*) Troll Assocs.

Meisenheimer, Sharon. Color Days. (gr. k-3). 1988. pap. 8.95 (*0-8224-1641-7*) Fearon Teach Aids.

Miller, J. P. Learn about Colors with Little Rabbit. Miller, J. P., illus. LC 84-6943. (ps-1). 1984. lib. bdg. 4.99 (*0-394-96671-6*) Random Bks Yng Read.

Morgan, Sally & Morgan, Adrian. Colour in Art & Advertising. (Illus.). 48p. (gr. 7-10). 1994. 19.95 (*0-237-51277-7*, Pub. by Ebury Pr UK) Trafalgar.

Morris, Neil. Rummage Sale: A Fun Book of Shapes & Colors. Stevenson, Peter, illus. 32p. (ps-2). 1991. PLB 13.50 (*0-87614-676-0*) Carolrhoda Bks.

Moss, David. Colors. 10p. 1989. 4.99 (*0-517-69421-2*) Random Hse Value.

Murphy, Chuck. My First Book of Colors. (ps). 1991. 5.95 (*0-590-44481-6*) Scholastic Inc.

My Very First Colors, Shapes, Sizes, & Opposites Book. 1993. write for info. (*1-56458-377-5*) Dorling Kindersley.

Oana, Katherine. Learning the Words of Color. Baird, Tate, ed. Wallace, Dorathye B., illus. LC 86-50866. 32p. (Orig.). (ps-1). 1986. pap. 2.65 (*0-914127-79-9*) Univ Class.

Oliver, Stephen, photos by. My First Look at Colors. LC 89-63091. (Illus.). 24p. (ps-k). 1990. 8.00 (*0-679-80535-4*) Random Bks Yng Read.

Ong, Cristina, illus. The Little Engine That Could Colors. 20p. (ps-3). 1994. bds. 2.95 (*0-448-40264-5*, Platt & Munk Pubs) Putnam Pub Group.

—The Little Engine That Could: Little Library, 3 bks. (Set incls. Colors, ABC & Numbers, 20 pgs. ea. bk.). (ps). 1992. Set. bds. 7.95 slipcased (*0-448-40261-0*, Platt & Munk Pubs) Putnam Pub Group.

Ortiz, Simon. Blue & Red. Aragon, Hilda, illus. 14p. (Orig.). (ps-7). 1981. pap. 3.75 (*0-915347-08-3*) Pueblo Acoma Pr.

Parramon, J. M. My First Colors. (Illus.). 32p. (ps). 1991. pap. 5.95 (*0-8120-4725-7*) Barron.

Peppe, Rodney. The Color Catalog. Peppe, Rodney, illus. 24p. (gr. k-2). 1992. 9.95 (*0-87226-472-6*, Bedrick Blackie) P Bedrick Bks.

Picnic Colors. 1990. text ed. 3.95 cased (*0-7214-5270-1*) Ladybird Bks.

Pienkowski, Jan. Colors. Pienkowski, Jan, illus. 14p. (ps). 1989. 2.95 (*0-671-68134-6*, Little Simon) S&S Trade.

Poulet, Virginia. El Libro de Colores de Azulin: Blue Bug's Book of Colors. 32p. (ps-3). 1989. PLB 11.80 (*0-516-33442-5*); pap. 3.95 (*0-516-53442-4*) Childrens.

Reiss, John J. Colors. Reiss, John J., illus. LC 69-13653. 32p. (ps-2). 1982. RSBE 13.95 (*0-02-776130-4*, Bradbury Pr) Macmillan Child Grp.

Ricklen, Neil. First Word Books: Colors. (ps). 1994. pap. 5.95 (*0-671-86726-1*, Little Simon) S&S Trade.

Ricklen, Neil, illus. My Colors: Mis Colores. LC 93-27195. (ENG & SPA.). 14p. (ps-k). 1994. pap. 3.95 (*0-689-71772-5*, Aladdin) Macmillan Child Grp.

Rieck, Sondra & Rutledge, Carol. Move & Match Colors with Busy Bear. 22p. (ps-k). 1990. 9.95 (*0-9634376-0-7*) Woodville Pr.

Ross, Anna. Little Elmo's Book of Colors. Gorbaty, Norman, illus. LC 91-23979. 24p. (ps). 1992. 3.99 (*0-679-82238-0*) Random Bks Yng Read.

Rowe, Julian & Perham, Molly. Colorful Light. LC 93-8217. (Illus.). 32p. (gr. 1-4). 1993. PLB 13.95 (*0-516-08131-4*) Childrens.

Scarry, Richard. Richard Scarry's Color Book. Scarry, Richard, illus. LC 75-36465. 14p. (ps-1). 1976. 3.95 (*0-394-83237-X*) Random Bks Yng Read.

Schwartz, Jeanne. A Handful of Colors. Mansfield, Carol, illus. 32p. 1981. 4.25 (*0-9604538-2-2*) CBH Pub.

Science of Color, 4 titles. 1993. Set. 69.08 (*0-8368-1026-0*) Gareth Stevens Inc.

Siede, George & Preis, Donna, photos by. Colors: Active Minds. Schwager, Istar, contrib. by. (Illus.). 24p. (ps-3). 1992. PLB 9.95 (*1-56674-001-0*) Forest Hse.

Silsbe, Brenda. Just One More Color. Steffler, Shawn, illus. 24p. (ps-3). 1991. PLB 14.95 (*1-55037-133-9*, Pub. by Annick CN); pap. 4.95 (*1-55037-136-3*, Pub. by Annick CN) Firefly Bks Ltd.

Silver, Norman. An Eye for Color. (gr. 8 up). 1993. 14.99 (*0-525-44859-4*, DCB) Dutton Child Bks.

Smith, Matthew V. Time for Learning Colors. Smith, Matthew V., illus. 12p. (gr. k-3). 1993. pap. 10.95 (*1-895583-55-1*) MAYA Pubs.

Sniffen, Caroline & Sniffen, Frances. Coloring Shadows. (Illus.). 80p. 1994. saddle-stitch 5.95 (*0-8059-3536-3*) Dorrance.

Steig, William. Yellow & Pink. Steig, William, illus. LC 84-80503. 32p. (ps up). 1984. 12.00 (*0-374-38670-6*) FS&G.

Sticker Fun with Colors. 32p. 1991. pap. 5.99 (*0-517-03353-4*) Random Hse Value.

Stine, Megan, et al. Hands-On Science: Color & Light. Taback, Simms, illus. LC 92-56889. 1993. PLB 18.60 (*0-8368-0954-8*) Gareth Stevens Inc.

Stroble, Bill. Hello Yellow! My Book of God's Colors. (ps). 1991. bds. 6.99 (*1-55513-731-8*, Chariot Bks) Chariot Family.

Taylor, Barbara. Color & Light. LC 91-9571. (Illus.). 40p. (gr. k-4). 1991. PLB 12.90 (*0-531-19127-3*, Warwick) Watts.

—Over the Rainbow! The Science of Color & Light. Bull, Peter, et al, illus. LC 91-4291. 40p. (Orig.). (gr. 2-5). 1992. pap. 4.95 (*0-679-82041-8*) Random Bks Yng Read.

Theroux, Alexander. The Primary Colors: Three Essays. LC 93-29692. (gr. 3 up). 1994. 17.95 (*0-8050-3105-7*) H Holt & Co.

Thompson, Kim M. & Hilderbrand, Karen M. A Little Rhythm, Rhyme & Read: Colors & Shapes. Kozjak, Goran, illus. 28p. (ps-1). 1993. Wkbk., incl. audio cass. 9.98 (*1-882331-16-8*) Twin Sisters.

Toda, Koshiro. A Tale of Six Colors. (Illus.). 44p. (ps-1). 1992. 11.95 (*1-881267-01-6*) Intercultural.

—What Color Would You Choose? (Illus.). 44p. (gr. k-3). 1992. 11.95 (*1-881267-00-8*) Intercultural.

Tucker, Sian. Colors. (Illus.). 24p. (ps-k). 1992. pap. 2.95 (*0-671-76907-3*, Little Simon) S&S Trade.

University of Mexico City Staff, tr. Colores: Mentes Activas. Siede, George & Preis, Donna, photos by. Schwager, Istar, contrib. by. (SPA., Illus.). 24p. (ps-8). 1992. PLB 11.95 (*1-56674-037-1*) Forest Hse.

Valat, P. M. & Perols, S., illus. Couleur. (FRE.). (ps-1). 1989. 13.95 (*2-07-035706-6*) Schoenhof.

Van Fleet, Matthew. One Yellow Lion: Fold-Out Fun with Numbers, Colors, Animals. LC 91-11972. (Illus.). 24p. (ps up). 1992. 7.95 (*0-8037-1099-2*) Dial Bks Young.

Weiss, Ellen. Baby Kermit's Color Book. (ps). 1993. 3.95 (*0-307-12539-4*, Golden Pr) Western Pub.

Westray, Kathleen, text by. & illus. A Color Sampler. LC 93-19967. 32p. (gr. 1-4). 1993. PLB 14.95 (*0-395-65940-X*) Ticknor & Flds Bks Yng Read.

Williams, John. Simple Science Projects with Color & Light. LC 91-50544. (Illus.). 32p. (gr. 2-4). 1992. PLB 17.27 (*0-8368-0766-9*) Gareth Stevens Inc.

Winograd, Deborah. My Color Is Panda. Winograd, Deborah, illus. LC 92-17423. 32p. (ps-1). 1993. JRT 13.00 (*0-671-79152-4*, Green Tiger) S&S Trade.

Wise, Beth A. Colors, Shapes, & Sizes. Morgado, Richard, illus. 32p. (ps). 1992. wkbk. 1.95 (*1-56293-168-7*) McClanahan Bk.

Wood, J. Moo Moo, Brown Cow. Bonner, R., illus. 1992. 12.95 (*0-15-200533-1*, HB Juv Bks) HarBrace.

Woodworth, Viki. Have You Seen a Green Gorilla? Woodworth, Viki, illus. (ps-2). 1992. PLB 12.95 (*0-89565-825-9*) Childs World.

Wren & Maile. Local Colors. Wren, illus. (ENG & HAW.). 10p. (ps). 1992. bds. 3.95 (*1-880188-02-3*) Bess Pr.

Yenawine, Philip. Colors. (Illus.). (gr. 2-5). 1991. 14.95 (*0-385-30254-1*); PLB 14.99 (*0-385-30314-9*) Delacorte.

COLOR–FICTION

Allen, Jonathan. Purple Sock, Pink Sock. Allen, Jonathan, illus. LC 91-43379. 12p. (ps). 1992. 3.95 (*0-688-11782-1*, Tambourine Bks) Morrow.

Barasch, Lynne, text by. & illus. A Winter Walk. LC 92-39804. 32p. (ps-2). 1993. PLB 13.95 (*0-395-65937-X*) Ticknor & Flds Bks Yng Read.

Barrett, John E., photos by. Big Bird Is Yellow: A Sesame Street Book of Colors. LC 89-63996. (Illus.). 14p. (ps). 1990. bds. 3.95 (*0-679-80752-7*) Random Bks Yng Read.

Bergman, Donna. Timmy Green's Blue Lake. Ohlsson, Ib, illus. LC 91-30232. 32p. (ps up). 1992. 14.00 (*0-688-10747-8*, Tambourine Bks); PLB 13.93 (*0-688-10748-6*, Tambourine Bks) Morrow.

Blueberry Bear. Kaler, Rebecca. 16p. (ps). 1993. 12.95 (*0-9634637-0-5*) Inquir Voices.

Boyd, Lizi. Black Dog Red House. Boyd, Lizi, illus. (ps-2). 1993. 12.95 (*0-316-10443-4*) Little.

Boynton, Sandra. Blue Hat Green Hat. 14p. 1984. 3.95 (*0-671-49320-5*, Little Simon) S&S Trade.

Charles, Donald. Gata Galano Observa los Colores: Calico Cat Looks at Colors. LC 75-12948. (SPA., Illus.). 32p. (ps-3). 1992. PLB 11.80 (*0-516-33437-9*); pap. 3.95 (*0-516-53437-8*) Childrens.

Childs, Phyllis. Color Me. 35p. (ps-k). 1985. wkbk. 2.95 (*0-931749-03-4*) PJC Lrng Mtrls.

Colors. (Illus.). 12p. (gr. k-2). 1982. bds. 3.95 (*0-87449-174-6*) Modern Pub NYC.

Desputeaux, Helene. Lollypop's Colors. (Illus.). 8p. (ps). 1993. bath bk. 4.95 (*2-921198-38-X*, Pub. by Les Edits Herit CN) Adams Inc MA.

Dodds, Dayle A. The Color Box. Laroche, Giles, illus. 32p. (ps-1). 1992. 12.95 (*0-316-18820-4*) Little.

Dudko, Mary A. & Larsen, Margie. Barney's Color Surprise. Hartley, Linda, ed. Full, Dennis, photos by. LC 93-77865. (Illus.). 18p. (ps). 1993. Repr. bds. 3.95 chunky board (*1-57064-007-6*) Barney Pub.

Dykstra, Mary A. The Best Color of All. Chandler, Jean, illus. 24p. (ps-k). 1993. 9.00 (*0-307-74816-2*, 64816, Golden Pr) Western Pub.

Ehlert, Lois. Color Farm. Ehlert, Lois, illus. LC 89-13561. 40p. (ps-k). 1990. 14.00 (*0-397-32440-5*, Lipp Jr Bks); PLB 12.89 (*0-397-32441-3*, Lipp Jr Bks) HarpC Child Bks.

Erickson, Gina & Foster, Kelli C. Pink & Blue. Gifford, Kerri, illus. 24p. (gr. k-8). 1994. pap. 3.50 (*0-8120-1921-0*) Barron.

Falwell, Cathryn. Nicky's Walk. Falwell, Cathryn, illus. 32p. (ps). 1991. 5.70 (*0-395-56914-1*, Clarion Bks) HM.

Felix, Monique. The Colors. 1992. PLB 10.95s.p. (*0-88682-404-4*) Creative Ed.

—Colors: Mouse Books. (Illus.). 32p. (ps). 1993. pap. 2.95 (*1-56189-093-6*) Amer Educ Pub.

Fleming, Denise. Lunch. LC 92-178. (Illus.). 32p. (ps-2). 1992. 14.95 (*0-8050-1636-8*, Bks Young Read) H Holt & Co.

Friend, Catherine. My Head Is Full of Colors. LC 93-5787. (Illus.). 32p. (ps-3). 1994. 14.95 (*1-56282-360-4*); PLB 14.89 (*1-56282-361-2*) Hyprn Child.

Greeley, Valerie. White Is the Moon. Greeley, Valerie, illus. LC 90-40522. 32p. (ps-1). 1991. 13.95 (*0-02-736915-3*, Macmillan Child Bk) Macmillan Child Grp.

Griffith, Neysa & Duarte, Steven. The Magic of Blue. Morse, Deborah, illus. (ps-3). 1994. 5.95 (*1-56844-029-4*) Enchante Pub.

—The Magic of Violet. Morse, Deborah, illus. (ps-3). 1994. 5.95 (*1-56844-031-6*) Enchante Pub.

Gundersheimer, Karen. Colors to Know. Gundersheimer, Karen, illus. LC 85-45390. 32p. (ps-1). 1986. HarpC Child Bks.

Hoban, Tana. Is It Red? Is It Yellow? Is It Blue? LC 78-2549. (Illus.). 32p. (gr. k-3). 1978. 16.00 (*0-688-80171-4*); PLB 15.93 (*0-688-84171-6*) Greenwillow.

Jackson, Ellen. Yellow, Mellow, Green, & Brown. Raymond, Victoria, illus. LC 93-37091. 1995. write for info. (*0-7868-0010-0*); lib. bdg. write for info. (*0-7868-2006-3*) Hyprn Child.

Jenkins, Jessica. Thinking about Colors. LC 91-33460. (Illus.). 32p. (gr. k-5). 1992. 14.00 (*0-525-44908-6*, DCB) Dutton Child Bks.

Kim, Joy. Rainbows & Frogs: A Story about Colors. Harvey, Paul, illus. LC 81-4685. 32p. (gr. k-2). 1981. PLB 11.59 (*0-89375-505-2*); pap. text ed. 2.95 (*0-89375-506-0*) Troll Assocs.

Kleven, Elisa. The Lion & the Little Red Bird. LC 91-36691. (Illus.). 32p. (ps-2). 1992. 13.50 (*0-525-44898-5*, DCB) Dutton Child Bks.

Kowalczyk, Carolyn. Purple Is Part of a Rainbow Big Book. 32p. (ps-2). 1988. PLB 22.95 (*0-516-49513-5*) Childrens.

Kunhardt, Edith. Red Day, Green Day. Hafner, Marylin, illus. LC 90-38490. 32p. (ps up). 1992. 14.00 (*0-688-09399-X*); PLB 13.93 (*0-688-09400-7*) Greenwillow.

Lionni, Leo. Little Blue & Little Yellow. Cohn, Amy, ed. LC 94-7324. (Illus.). 48p. (ps up). 1994. pap. 4.95 (*0-688-13285-5*, Mulberry) Morrow.

Macdonald, Maryann. The Pink Party. LC 93-20989. (Illus.). 40p. (gr. k-3). 1994. 10.95 (*1-56282-620-4*); PLB 10.89 (*1-56282-621-2*) Hyprn Child.

Martin, Bill, Jr. Brown Bear, Brown Bear, What Do You See? 25th Anniversary Edition. Carle, Eric, illus. LC 91-29115. 32p. (ps-k). 1992. 14.95 (*0-8050-1744-5*, Bks Young Read) H Holt & Co.

Mayer, Marianna & McDermott, Gerald. The Brambleberrys Animal Book of Colors. LC 91-70418. (Illus.). 32p. (ps up). 1991. 3.95 (*1-878093-76-2*) Boyds Mills Pr.

Miss Lori. Shapeless & the Magic Box, Bk. 1. White, Lori G., ed. Miss Lori, illus. 18p. (Orig.). (ps-1). 1990. pap. 11.99 (*0-9623368-3-1*) Shapeless Enterprises.

Moncure, Jane B. Magic Monsters Look for Colors. Magnuson, Diana, illus. LC 78-23792. (ps-3). 1979. PLB 14.95 (*0-89565-056-8*) Childs World.

Munsch, Robert. Purple, Green & Yellow. Desputeaux, Helene, illus. 32p. (ps-2). 1992. PLB 14.95 (*1-55037-255-6*, Pub. by Annick Pr); pap. 4.95 (*1-55037-256-4*, Pub. by Annick Pr) Firefly Bks Ltd.

O'Callahan, Jay. Orange Cheeks. Raine, Patricia, illus. LC 92-43509. 40p. (ps-3). 1983. 15.95 (*1-56145-073-1*) Peachtree Pubs.

Peek, Merle. Mary Wore Her Red Dress & Henry Wore His Green Sneakers. Peek, Merle, illus. 1993. Incl. cassette. 7.70 (*0-395-61577-1*, Clarion Bks) HM.

Potter, Beatrix. Benjamin Bunny's Colors. (Illus.). 24p. (ps). 1994. bds. 2.99 (*0-7232-4118-X*) Warne.

—The Tale of Mrs. Tiggy-Winkle & Mr. Jeremy Fisher. (Illus.). 32p. (ps-3). 1994. pap. 4.99 (*0-7232-4149-X*) Warne.

Poulet, Virginia. Blue Bug's Book of Colors. Anderson, Peggy P., illus. LC 80-23229. 32p. (ps-3). 1981. PLB 11.80 (*0-516-03442-1*); pap. 3.95 (*0-516-43442-X*) Childrens.

Reiss, John J. Colors. Reiss, John J., illus. LC 69-13653. 32p. (ps-2). 1982. RSBE 13.95 (*0-02-776130-4*, Bradbury Pr) Macmillan Child Grp.

Richard Scarry's Colors. 24p. (ps-k). 1993. pap. 1.45 (*0-307-11542-9*, 11542, Golden Pr) Western Pub.

Rikys, Bodel. Red Bear. LC 91-9039. (Illus.). 32p. (ps). 1992. 11.00 (*0-8037-1048-8*) Dial Bks Young.

Rogers, Alan. Little Giants, 4 vols. Rogers, Alan, illus. 64p. (ps-1). 1990. Set. PLB 53.08 (*0-8368-0434-1*) Gareth Stevens Inc.

—Yellow Hippo. Rogers, Alan, illus. LC 90-9834. 16p. (ps-1). 1990. PLB 13.27 (*0-8368-0405-8*) Gareth Stevens Inc.

Saylor, Melissa, illus. Mary Wore Her Red Dress Big Book. (ps-2). 1988. pap. text ed. 14.00 (*0-922053-17-0*) N Edge Res.

Schultz, Betty K. Purple Patches. Buffo, Cindy, illus. 32p. (gr. k-3). 1994. PLB write for info. (*0-929568-01-X*) Raspberry IL.

Serfozo, Mary. Who Said Red? Narahashi, Keiko, illus. LC 91-21160. 32p. (ps-1). 1992. pap. 4.95 (*0-689-71592-7*, Aladdin); pap. 18.95 big bk. (*0-689-71651-6*, Aladdin) Macmillan Child Grp.

Sis, Peter. Going Up! A Color Counting Book. LC 87-37203. (Illus.). 24p. (ps up). 1989. 12.95 (*0-688-08125-8*); PLB 12.88 (*0-688-08126-6*) Greenwillow.

Spinelli, Eileen. If You Want to Find Golden. Shuett, Stacey, illus. LC 93-12000. (gr. 1-3). 1993. 14.95 (*0-8075-3585-0*) A Whitman.

Stinson, Kathy. Red Is Best. Lewis, Robin B., illus. (ps-1). 1992. 0.99 (*1-55037-252-1*, Pub. by Annick Pr) Firefly Bks Ltd.

Testa, Fulvio. If You Take a Paintbrush: A Book of Colors. Testa, Fulvio, illus. LC 82-45512. 32p. (ps-2). 1986. pap. 4.95 (*0-8037-0282-5*) Dial Bks Young.

Time Life Inc., Staff. Balderdash the Brilliant: A Hole-in-the-Page Color Book. Kagan, Neil, ed. (Illus.). 56p. (ps-2). 1991. write for info. (*0-8094-9266-0*); lib. bdg. write for info. (*0-8094-9267-9*) Time-Life.

Vulliamy, Clara. Blue Hat, Red Coat. LC 93-22737. (Illus.). 14p. (ps). 1994. 4.95 (*1-56402-353-2*) Candlewick Pr.

Williams, Sue. I Went Walking. Vivas, Julie, illus. 30p. (ps-2). 1990. 13.95 (*0-15-200471-8*, Gulliver Bks) HarBrace.

Yamaka, Sara. The Gift of Driscoll Lipscomb. Kim, Joung U., illus. LC 93-43207. 1995. 16.00 (*0-02-793599-X*, Four Winds) Macmillan Child Grp.

Yardley, Joanna. The Red Ball. Yolen, Jane, ed. Yardley, Joanna, illus. 32p. (ps-3). 1991. 14.95 (*0-15-200894-2*, J Yolen Bks) HarBrace.

Ziefert, Harriet. Bear's Colors. Baum, Susan, illus. 12p. (ps). 1993. 4.50 (*0-694-00454-5*, Festival) HarpC Child Bks.

COLOR–POETRY

Griffith, Neysa & Duarte, Steven. The Magic of Green. Morse, Deborah, illus. LC 93-34811. 1994. 4.95 (*1-56844-028-6*) Enchante Pub.

—The Magic of Orange. Morse, Deborah, illus. LC 93-35439. 1994. 4.95 (*1-56844-026-X*) Enchante Pub.

—The Magic of Red. Morse, Deborah, illus. LC 93-34813. 1994. 4.95 (*1-56844-025-1*) Enchante Pub.

—The Magic of Yellow. Morse, Deborah, illus. LC 93-34812. 1994. 4.95 (*1-56844-027-8*) Enchante Pub.

O'Neill, Mary. Hailstones & Halibut Bones: Adventures in Color. Wallner, John, illus. 1989. 12.95 (*0-385-24484-3*) Doubleday.

Oram, Hiawyn. Out of the Blue: Poems about Color. McKee, David, illus. LC 92-55044. 64p. (gr. 1-5). 1993. 18.95 (*1-56282-469-4*); PLB 18.89 (*1-56282-470-8*) Hyprn Child.

COLOR OF ANIMALS

Green, Robyn & Scarffe, Bronwen. Black & White. Sofilas, Mark, illus. LC 92-21393. (gr. 4 up). 1993. 2.50 (*0-383-03555-4*) SRA Schl Grp.

Kipling, Rudyard. How the Leopard Got His Spots. Loestoeter, Lori, illus. LC 89-31374. (ps up). 1991. pap. 14.95 (*0-88708-111-8*, Rabbit Ears); book & cassette package 19.95 (*0-88708-112-6*, Rabbit Ears) Picture Bk Studio.

McDonnell, Janet. Animal Camouflage. LC 88-36642. (Illus.). 48p. (gr. 2-6). 1989. PLB 14.95 (*0-89565-512-8*) Childs World.

—Animal Camouflage: Hide & Seek Animals. Magnuson, Diana, illus. LC 89-28083. 32p. (ps-2). 1990. PLB 14.95 (*0-89565-562-4*) Childs World.

Powzyk, Joyce. Animal Camouflage: A Closer Look. Powzyk, Joyce, illus. LC 89-9848. 40p. (gr. 2-9). 1990. SBE 15.95 (*0-02-774980-0*, Bradbury Pr) Macmillan Child Grp.

Rosen, Marcia. How the Animals Got Their Colors: Animal Myths from Around the World. Clementson, J., illus. 1992. 14.95 (*0-15-236783-7*, HB Juv Bks) HarBrace.

Wilson, April, illus. Look Again! The Second Ultimate Spot-the-Difference Book. Wood, A. J., notes by. LC 91-31214. (Illus.). 40p. (gr. 1 up). 1992. 13.00 (*0-8037-0958-7*) Dial Bks Young.

COLOR OF MAN

Asimov, Isaac & Dierks, Carrie. Why Do People Come in Different Colors? LC 93-20157. 1993. PLB 15.93 (*0-8368-0808-8*) Gareth Stevens Inc.

Walton, Darwin. What Color Are You? Franklin, Hal A., photos by. (Illus.). 64p. (gr. 5 up). 1973. 10.95 (*0-87485-045-2*) Johnson Chi.

COLOR SENSE

Colors & Shapes. (Illus.). (ps). pap. 1.25 (*0-7214-9555-9*) Ladybird Bks.

Les Couleurs. (FRE., Illus.). 3.50 (*0-7214-1428-1*) Ladybird Bks.

Feraro, Bonita. Colors & Shapes. Robison, Don, illus. 32p. (Orig.). (ps). 1993. wkbk. 1.99 (*1-56189-058-8*) Amer Educ Pub.

My Book of Shapes & Colors. (ps-2). 3.95 (*0-7214-5148-9*) Ladybird Bks.

Szekeres, Cyndy. Cyndy Szekeres' Colors. Szekeres, Cyndy, illus. 24p. (ps-k). 1992. bds. write for info. (*0-307-12167-4*, 12167, Golden Pr) Western Pub.

Taulbee, Annette. Colors. (Illus.). 24p. (ps-k). 1986. 3.98 (*0-86734-060-6*, FS-3052) Schaffer Pubns.

—Shapes & Colors. (Illus.). 24p. (ps-k). 1986. 3.98 (*0-86734-068-1*, FS-3061) Schaffer Pubns.

COLOR SENSE–FICTION

Big Bird's Color Game. 14p. (ps). 1980. write for info. (*0-307-12254-9*, Golden Bks) Western Pub.

Lionni, Leo. A Color of His Own. Lionni, Leo, illus. LC 75-28456. 40p. (ps-k). 1993. 8.99 (*0-679-84197-0*); PLB 9.99 (*0-679-94197-5*) Knopf Bks Yng Read.

Posey, Pam, illus. Thomas the Tank Engine - Colors. Awdry, W., contrib. by. (Illus.). 12p. (ps). 1993. bds. 2.29 (*0-679-81646-1*) Random Bks Yng Read.

COLORADO

Aylesworth, Thomas G. & Aylesworth, Virginia L. The Southwest (Texas, New Mexico, Colorado) (Illus.). 64p. (gr. 3 up). 1992. lib. bdg. 16.95 (*0-7910-1048-1*) Chelsea Hse.

Barker, Jane V. Trappers & Traders. Downing, Sybil, ed. (Illus.). 36p. (gr. k-6). pap. 3.95 (*1-878611-03-8*) Silver Rim Pr.

Barker, Jane V. & Downing, Sybil. Mountain Treasures. (Illus.). 44p. (gr. k-6). pap. 3.95 (*1-878611-01-1*) Silver Rim Pr.

Bledsoe, Sara. Colorado. LC 92-31054. 1993. 17.50 (*0-8225-2750-2*) Lerner Pubns.

Butler, Mike. Colorado - Mile by Mile. 36p. (gr. 3-8). 1991. pap. 6.95 (*1-880372-12-6*) Mile By Mile.

Carole Marsh Colorado Books, 44 bks. 1994. lib. bdg. 1027.80 set (*0-7933-1280-9*); pap. 587.80 set (*0-7933-5132-4*) Gallopade Pub Group.

Carpenter, Allan. Colorado. LC 77-13921. (Illus.). 96p. (gr. 4 up). 1978. PLB 16.95 (*0-516-04106-1*) Childrens.

Eccles, Anne. Colorado Activity & Coloring Book. Eccles, Anne, illus. 32p. (ps-8). 1986. pap. 2.95 (*0-9618555-0-9*) Anne M Eccles.

Fischer, Lee, ed. Colorado Is for Kids! An Activity Book for Kids! Parker, Steve, illus. 32p. (gr. 1-6). 1990. pap. 2.95 (*0-929526-05-8*) Double B Pubns.

Fradin, Dennis. Colorado: In Words & Pictures. Wahl, Richard, illus. LC 80-15778. 48p. (gr. k-4). 1980. pap. 4.95 (*0-516-43906-5*) Childrens.

Fradin, Dennis B. Colorado - From Sea to Shining Sea. LC 93-2648. (Illus.). 64p. (gr. 3-5). 1993. PLB 16.45 (*0-516-03806-0*) Childrens.

Kent, Deborah. Colorado. 187p. 1993. text ed. 15.40 (*1-56956-138-9*) W A T Braille.

Laing, David & Lampiris, Nicholas. Aspen High Country: The Geology, a Pictorial Guide to Roads & Trails. Laing, Jennifer, illus. 144p. (Orig.). (gr. 9-12). 1980. pap. write for info. (*0-9604274-0-6*) Thunder River.

McCabe, Michael. Colorado: Grassroots. (Illus.). 48p. (gr. 4-6). 1984. Repr. of 1983 ed. wkbk. 5.45 (*0-911981-13-6*) Cloud Pub.

McCabe, Michael & Brew, Virginia. Colorado: Grassroots. 20p. (gr. 4-6). 1983. tchr's. ed. 8.95 (*0-911981-14-4*) Cloud Pub.

Marsh, Carole. Avast, Ye Slobs! Colorado Pirate Trivia. (Illus.). (gr. 3-12). 1994. PLB 24.95 (*0-7933-0208-0*); pap. 14.95 (*0-7933-0207-2*); computer disk 29.95 (*0-7933-0209-9*) Gallopade Pub Group.

—The Beast of the Colorado Bed & Breakfast. (Illus.). (gr. 3-12). 1994. PLB 24.95 (*0-7933-1413-5*); pap. 14.95 (*0-7933-1414-3*); computer disk 29.95 (*0-7933-1415-1*) Gallopade Pub Group.

—Bow Wow! Colorado Dogs in History, Mystery, Legend, Lore, Humor & More! (Illus.). (gr. 3-12). 1994. PLB 24.95 (*0-7933-3482-9*); pap. 14.95 (*0-7933-3483-7*); computer disk 29.95 (*0-7933-3484-5*) Gallopade Pub Group.

—Christopher Columbus Comes to Colorado! Includes Reproducible Activities for Kids! (Illus.). (gr. 3-12). 1994. PLB 24.95 (*0-7933-3635-X*); pap. 14.95 (*0-7933-3636-8*); computer disk 29.95 (*0-7933-3637-6*) Gallopade Pub Group.

—Colorado & Other State Greats (Biographies) (Illus.). (gr. 3-12). 1994. PLB 24.95 (*1-55609-534-1*); pap. 14.95 (*1-55609-533-3*); computer disk 29.95 (*0-7933-1421-6*) Gallopade Pub Group.

—Colorado Bandits, Bushwackers, Outlaws, Crooks, Devils, Ghosts, Desperadoes & Other Assorted & Sundry Characters! (Illus.). (gr. 3-12). 1994. PLB 24.95 (*0-7933-0190-4*); pap. 14.95 (*0-7933-0189-0*); computer disk 29.95 (*0-7933-0191-2*) Gallopade Pub Group.

—Colorado Classic Christmas Trivia: Stories, Recipes, Activities, Legends, Lore & More! (Illus.). (gr. 3-12). 1994. PLB 24.95 (*0-7933-0193-9*); pap. 14.95 (*0-7933-0192-0*); computer disk 29.95 (*0-7933-0194-7*) Gallopade Pub Group.

—Colorado Coastales! (Illus.). (gr. 3-12). 1994. PLB 24.95 (*1-55609-530-9*); pap. 14.95 (*1-55609-529-5*); computer disk 29.95 (*0-7933-1417-8*) Gallopade Pub Group.

—Colorado Coastales! 1994. lib. bdg. 24.95 (*0-7933-7270-4*) Gallopade Pub Group.

—Colorado Dingbats! Bk. 1: A Fun Book of Games, Stories, Activities & More about Our State That's All in Code! for You to Decipher. (Illus.). (gr. 3-12). 1994. PLB 24.95 (*0-7933-3788-7*); pap. 14.95 (*0-7933-3789-5*); computer disk 29.95 (*0-7933-3790-9*) Gallopade Pub Group.

—Colorado Festival Fun for Kids! (Illus.). (gr. 3-12). 1994. lib. bdg. 24.95 (*0-7933-3941-3*); pap. 14.95 (*0-7933-3942-1*); disk 29.95 (*0-7933-3943-X*) Gallopade Pub Group.

—The Colorado Hot Air Balloon Mystery. (Illus.). (gr. 2-9). 1994. 24.95 (*0-7933-2363-0*); pap. 14.95 (*0-7933-2364-9*); computer disk 29.95 (*0-7933-2365-7*) Gallopade Pub Group.

—Colorado Jeopardy! Answers & Questions about Our State! (Illus.). (gr. 3-12). 1994. PLB 24.95 (*0-7933-4094-2*); pap. 14.95 (*0-7933-4095-0*); computer disk 29.95 (*0-7933-4096-9*) Gallopade Pub Group.

—Colorado "Jography" A Fun Run Thru Our State! (Illus.). (gr. 3-12). 1994. PLB 24.95 (*1-55609-525-2*); pap. 14.95 (*1-55609-524-4*); computer disk 29.95 (*0-7933-1407-0*) Gallopade Pub Group.

—Colorado Kid's Cookbook: Recipes, How-to, History, Lore & More! (Illus.). (gr. 3-12). 1994. PLB 24.95 (*0-7933-0202-1*); pap. 14.95 (*0-7933-0201-3*); computer disk 29.95 (*0-7933-0203-X*) Gallopade Pub Group.

—Colorado Quiz Bowl Crash Course! (Illus.). (gr. 3-12). 1994. PLB 24.95 (*0-685-45927-6*); pap. 14.95 (*1-55609-531-7*); computer disk 29.95 (*0-7933-1416-X*) Gallopade Pub Group.

—Colorado Rollercoasters! (Illus.). (gr. 3-12). 1994. PLB 24.95 (*0-7933-5239-8*); pap. 14.95 (*0-7933-5240-1*); computer disk 29.95 (*0-7933-5241-X*) Gallopade Pub Group.

—Colorado School Trivia: An Amazing & Fascinating Look at Our State's Teachers, Schools & Students! (Illus.). (gr. 3-12). 1994. PLB 24.95 (*0-7933-0199-8*); pap. 14.95 (*0-7933-0198-X*); computer disk 29.95 (*0-7933-0200-5*) Gallopade Pub Group.

—Colorado Silly Basketball Sportsmysteries, Vol. I. (Illus.). (gr. 3-12). 1994. PLB 24.95 (*0-7933-0196-3*); pap. 14.95 (*0-7933-0195-5*); computer disk 29.95 (*0-7933-0197-1*) Gallopade Pub Group.

—Colorado Silly Basketball Sportsmysteries, Vol. II. (Illus.). (gr. 3-12). 1994. PLB 24.95 (*0-7933-1577-8*); pap. 14.95 (*0-7933-1578-6*); computer disk 29.95 (*0-7933-1579-4*) Gallopade Pub Group.

—Colorado Silly Football Sportsmysteries, Vol. I. (Illus.). (gr. 3-12). 1994. PLB 24.95 (*1-55609-528-7*); pap. 14.95 (*1-55609-527-9*); computer disk 29.95 (*0-7933-1409-7*) Gallopade Pub Group.

—Colorado Silly Football Sportsmysteries, Vol. II. (Illus.). (gr. 3-12). 1994. PLB 24.95 (*0-7933-1410-0*); pap. 14.95 (*0-7933-1411-9*); computer disk 29.95 (*0-7933-1412-7*) Gallopade Pub Group.

—Colorado Silly Trivia! (Illus.). (gr. 3-12). 1994. PLB 24. 95 (*1-55609-523-6*); pap. 14.95 (*1-55609-522-8*); computer disk 29.95 (*0-7933-1406-2*) Gallopade Pub Group.

—Colorado's (Most Devastating!) Disasters & (Most Calamitous!) Catastrophies! (Illus.). (gr. 3-12). 1994. PLB 24.95 (*0-7933-0187-4*); pap. 14.95 (*0-7933-0186-6*); computer disk 29.95 (*0-7933-0188-2*) Gallopade Pub Group.

—The Hard-to-Believe-But-True! Book of Colorado History, Mystery, Trivia, Legend, Lore, Humor & More. (Illus.). (gr. 3-12). 1994. PLB 24.95 (*0-7933-0205-6*); pap. 14.95 (*0-7933-0204-8*); computer disk 29.95 (*0-7933-0206-4*) Gallopade Pub Group.

—If My Colorado Mama Ran the World! (Illus.). (gr. 3-12). 1994. PLB 24.95 (*0-7933-1418-6*); pap. 14.95 (*0-7933-1419-4*); computer disk 29.95 (*0-7933-1420-8*) Gallopade Pub Group.

—Jurassic Ark! Colorado Dinosaurs & Other Prehistoric Creatures. (gr. k-12). 1994. PLB 24.95 (*0-7933-7443-X*); pap. 14.95 (*0-7933-7444-8*); computer disk 29.95 (*0-7933-7445-6*) Gallopade Pub Group.

—Let's Quilt Colorado & Stuff It Topographically! (Illus.). (gr. 3-12). 1994. PLB 24.95 (*1-55609-526-0*); pap. 14.95 (*1-55609-126-5*); computer disk 29.95 (*0-7933-1408-9*) Gallopade Pub Group.

—Let's Quilt Our Colorado County. 1994. lib. bdg. 24.95 (*0-7933-7128-7*); pap. text ed. 14.95 (*0-7933-7129-5*); disk 29.95 (*0-7933-7130-9*) Gallopade Pub Group.

—Let's Quilt Our Colorado Town. 1994. lib. bdg. 24.95 (*0-7933-6978-9*); pap. text ed. 14.95 (*0-7933-6979-7*); disk 29.95 (*0-7933-6980-0*) Gallopade Pub Group.

—Meow! Colorado Cats in History, Mystery, Legend, Lore, Humor & More! (Illus.). (gr. 3-12). 1994. PLB 24.95 (*0-7933-3329-6*); pap. 14.95 (*0-7933-3330-X*); computer disk 29.95 (*0-7933-3331-8*) Gallopade Pub Group.

—Uncle Rebus: Colorado Picture Stories for Computer Kids. (Illus.). (gr. k-3). 1994. PLB 24.95 (*0-7933-4519-7*); pap. 14.95 (*0-7933-4520-0*); disk 29. 95 (*0-7933-4521-9*) Gallopade Pub Group.

Moorhead, Carol A. Colorado's Backyard Wildlife. Moorhead, Carol A., illus. 96p. (Orig.). (gr. 6-8). 1992. pap. 10.95 (*1-879373-08-4*) R Rinehart.

Rankin, William. Come Hibernate with Me. Camphouse, Marylyn J., frwd. by. (Illus.). 214p. (Orig.). (gr. 9 up). 1989. 30.00 (*0-9623948-0-7*) M Camphouse.

Schmidt, Cynthia. Colorado: Grassroots. (Illus.). 64p. (gr. 4-6). 1989. Repr. of 1983 ed. text ed. 11.95 (*0-911981-12-8*) Cloud Pub.

Thomas, Carolyn S. Kenta Comes to Colorado: A Bilingual Educational Activity Book. Holdorf, Kurt, illus. Romer, Roy, intro. by. (ENG & JPN., Illus.). 64p. (gr. k-4). 1990. pap. 6.95 (*0-913730-41-6*) Robinson Pr.

Thompson, Kathleen. Colorado. LC 87-16374. 48p. (gr. 3 up). 1987. 19.97 (*0-86514-463-X*) Raintree Steck-V.

Thumhart, Suzanne. Colorado Wonders. Ayer, Eleanor H., ed. Kline, Jane, illus. 48p. (gr. 4-7). 1986. pap. 6. 95x (*0-939650-16-9*) R H Pub.

COLORADO–FICTION

Barker, Jane V. & Downing, Sybil. Colorado Heritage Series, 10 vols. (Illus.). (ps-8). Set. pap. 39.50 (*1-878611-00-3*) Silver Rim Pr.

Downing, Sybil & Barker, Jane V. Happy Harvest. (Illus.). 43p. pap. text ed. 3.95 (*1-878611-02-X*) Silver Rim Pr.

—Mesas to Mountains. (Illus.). 47p. (ps-8). pap. 3.95 (*1-878611-04-6*) Silver Rim Pr.

Moore, Beverly. Echo's Song. Moore, Beverly, illus. 40p. (gr. k-3). 1993. PLB 13.95g (*0-9637288-7-3*) River Walker Bks.

Myers, Edward. Climb or Die. LC 93-44861. 192p. (gr. 5-9). 1994. 14.95 (*0-7868-0026-7*); PLB 14.89 (*0-7868-2021-7*) Hyprn Child.

Shirley, Gayle. C Is for Colorado. Bergum, Connie, illus. LC 89-83793. 40p. (Orig.). (gr. k-3). 1989. 7.95 (*0-937959-85-5*) Falcon Pr MT.

COLORADO–HISTORY

Ayer, Eleanor H. Hispanic Colorado. Kline, Jane, illus. 48p. (gr. 4-7). 1982. 11.95x (*0-939650-11-8*); pap. 6. 95x (*0-939650-10-X*) R H Pub.

Barker, Jane V. & Downing, Sybil. Adventures in the West. (Illus.). 40p. pap. 5.95 (*1-878611-05-4*) Silver Rim Pr.

Friggens, Myriam. Tales, Trails & Tommyknockers: Stories from Colorado's Past. Coulter, Gene, illus. LC 79-84876. 144p. (gr. 6 up). 1979. pap. 7.95 (*0-933472-01-3*) Johnson Bks.

Fugitt, Douglas & Christensen, Roxane. Our Rocky Mountain Homestead. Thomas, DeVoe M., illus. 208p. (Orig.). 1994. pap. 11.95 (*0-685-71363-6*) Willow Pr.

Kent, Deborah. Colorado. LC 88-11745. (Illus.). 144p. (gr. 4 up). 1988. PLB 20.55 (*0-516-00452-2*) Childrens.

Marsh, Carole. Chill Out: Scary Colorado Tales Based on Frightening Colorado Truths. (Illus.). 1994. lib. bdg. 24.95 (*0-7933-4672-X*); pap. 14.95 (*0-7933-4673-8*); disk 29.95 (*0-7933-4674-6*) Gallopade Pub Group.

—Colorado "Crinkum-Crankum" A Funny Word Book about Our State. (Illus.). 1994. lib. bdg. 24.95 (*0-7933-4825-0*); pap. 14.95 (*0-7933-4826-9*); disk 29. 95 (*0-7933-4827-7*) Gallopade Pub Group.

—The Colorado Mystery Van Takes Off! Book 1: Handicapped Colorado Kids Sneak Off on a Big Adventure. (Illus.). (gr. 3-12). 1994. 24.95 (*0-7933-4979-6*); pap. 14.95 (*0-7933-4980-X*); computer disk 29.95 (*0-7933-4981-8*) Gallopade Pub Group.

—Colorado Timeline: A Chronology of Colorado History, Mystery, Trivia, Legend, Lore & More. (Illus.). (gr. 3-12). 1994. PLB 24.95 (*0-7933-5890-6*); pap. 14.95 (*0-7933-5891-4*); computer disk 29.95 (*0-7933-5892-2*) Gallopade Pub Group.

—Colorado's Unsolved Mysteries (& Their "Solutions") Includes Scientific Information & Other Activities for Students. (Illus.). (gr. 3-12). 1994. PLB 24.95 (*0-7933-5737-3*); pap. 14.95 (*0-7933-5738-1*); computer disk 29.95 (*0-7933-5739-X*) Gallopade Pub Group.

—My First Book about Colorado. (gr. k-4). 1994. PLB 24.95 (*0-7933-5584-2*); pap. 14.95 (*0-7933-5585-0*); computer disk 29.95 (*0-7933-5586-9*) Gallopade Pub Group.

Skolout, Patricia F. Colorado Springs: History A to Z. rev. ed. (Illus.). 69p. (gr. k-6). 1991. pap. text ed. 4.95 (*0-9625712-3-7*) P F Skolout.

—Colorado Springs History A to Z: For Children. Rasmusseu-Frerichs, Cyndy, illus. 37p. (gr. k-6). 1990. Repr. of 1989 ed. activity bk. 3.95 (*0-9625712-0-2*) P F Skolout.

Thumhart, Suzanne, compiled by. Colorado Businesses. Kline, Jane, illus. 48p. (gr. 4-7). 1984. 11.95x (*0-939650-21-5*) R H Pub.

COLORED PEOPLE (U. S.)

see Blacks

COLORING BOOKS

ABCs. (Illus.). 32p. (ps-1). 1992. pap. 2.95 (*1-56144-104-X*, Honey Bear Bks) Modern Pub NYC.

Aladdin Coloring & Activity Books, Bks. 1-4. (Illus., 32 pgs. ea. bk.). (gr. k-3). 1992. Bk. 1. pap. 0.99 (*1-56144-155-4*, Honey Bear Bks) Bk. 2. pap. 0.99 (*1-56144-156-2*); Bk. 3. pap. 0.99 (*1-56144-157-0*); Bk. 4. pap. 0.99 (*1-56144-158-9*) Modern Pub NYC.

Ali, S. Ameer. Color & Learn the Names of the Family of Prophet Muhammad. 32p. (Orig.). (ps). Date not set. pap. 3.50 (*0-934905-13-4*) Kazi Pubns.

Anderson, Kathleen. Old Mission San Luis Obispo de Tolosa: A Miniature Cut-Out & Color Model. Fast, Marti, illus. 8p. (Orig.). (gr. 4). 1990. pap. 3.95 (*0-945092-12-1*) EZ Nature.

Bahlinger, Nanette M. The Jekyll Island Historic District Coloring Book. Bahlinger, Nanette M., illus. 32p. (Orig.). (gr. 5). 1993. wkbk. 4.00 (*0-9638256-1-5*) N M Bahlinger.

Baird, Mary & Larrivee-Cohen, Donna, eds. Painting Our Way to a Better Future: An Art-Coloring Book of Contemporary Career Options for Women. Grigsby, Diane, illus. 56p. (Orig.). (gr. 1-9). 1990. pap. 6.95 (*0-9627833-0-7*) Hard Hatted Women.

Banks, Valerie J. Kwanzaa Coloring Book. 6th ed. (ENG & SWA., Illus.). 46p. (gr. k-8). 1992. pap. 5.95 (*0-9622340-6-0*) Sala Enterp.

Barris, Sara L. & Seltzer, Doryle P. Together Forever: An Adoption Story Coloring Book. Mazer, Susan, illus. 32p. 1992. pap. 3.95 (*0-9632023-0-8*) Shoot Star Pr.

Berkowitz, Henry. Monsters, an Educational Coloring Book. Berkowitz, Henry, illus. 32p. (Orig.). (gr. 1-9). 1994. pap. 2.50 (*0-938059-03-3*) Henart Bks.

Bible Stories to Read & Color. (Illus.). 388p. (ps-4). pap. 9.95 (*1-55748-069-9*) Barbour & Co.

Brower, Bob, illus. Latter-Day Saints Temple Coloring Book. 80p. (Orig.). (gr. 2-6). 1993. pap. 5.95 (*0-910523-22-3*) Grandin Bk Co.

—Presidents of the LDS Church Coloring Book. 50p. (Orig.). (gr. 2-6). 1993. pap. 5.95 (*0-910523-21-5*) Grandin Bk Co.

Brown, Eric. Different Shades of Courage: A Coloring & Activities Book of African American Achievement, Vol. 1. Sheen, Jen, ed. (Illus.). 53p. (Orig.). (gr. 4 up). 1993. pap. 9.95 (*0-9636468-0-X*) Little Tike.

Color & Learn Muslim Names. 32p. (ps). Date not set. pap. 3.50 (*0-933511-03-5*) Kazi Pubns.

Colors of Washington. 16p. (gr. k-6). 1991. 2.50 (*0-9631472-0-X*) Martin Barry Prods.

Conservation Treaty Support Group Staff. Cites Endangered Species Coloring Book. rev. ed. Dollinger, Peter, ed. Silk, Linda, illus. 72p. 1993. pap. 4.95 (*1-56002-281-7*) Aegina Pr.

Dec, Myra & Dec, Sam. Wilderness Tails: A Book to Color, Poetry to Share. 32p. (ps-3). 1993. pap. 3.50 (*0-9638192-0-8*) Quinn Pubng.

Delis-Abrams, Alexandra. ABC Feelings: A Coloring - Learning Book. rev. ed. Follendore, Joan, ed. Gurstein, Shari, illus. 64p. (gr. 3-8). 1991. pap. text ed. 7.95 (*1-879889-00-5*) Adage Pubns.

Dewey, Jennifer. Mammals on the Rise: A Prehistoric Southwest Coloring Book. (ps-3). 1992. pap. 4.95 (*0-89013-238-0*) Museum NM Pr.

DiMino, Frank. Hot Rod Coloring Album. DiMino, Frank, illus. 32p. (Orig.). (gr. 1-6). 1993. pap. 4.50 (*0-8431-3514-X*, Troubador) Price Stern.

Donohue, Julie. Fancy Fish Coloring Book. 22p. (gr. 3-5). 1990. 3.95 (*0-943864-61-5*) Davenport.

Drum & Spear Collective Staff. Children of Africa: A Coloring Book. Drum & Spear Collective Staff, illus. LC 92-63013. 24p. (ps-3). 1993. pap. 5.95 (*0-88378-076-3*) Third World.

Duffy, Karen & Lokenvitz, Judith. Angel, Devils, Mermaids, & Monsters. Katz, Kathleen, illus. 1989. pap. 4.95 (*0-89013-187-2*) Museum NM Pr.

Dulac, Glen. The Color Coded Alphabet: The Best Coloring Book Ever. Fischer, Robert, et al, illus. (gr. k-3). 1991. pap. 5.00 (*0-9628227-4-4*) Desert Bks.

Dunn, Sandra. A Walk Through Biosphere 2: Coloring Book. (Illus.). 16p. (gr. 3 up). 1993. pap. 4.00 (*1-882428-00-5*) Biosphere Pr.

Eccles, Anne M. United States Activity & Coloring Book. Eccles, Anne M., illus. 36p. (ps-8). 1992. activity/coloring bk. 3.95 (*0-9618555-2-5*) Anne M Eccles.

Elwell, Marty. Searching for Treasure: A Guide to Wisdom & Character Development. Rose, Steve, illus. 147p. 1993. pap. text ed. 20.00 (*0-923463-84-4*) Noble Pub Assocs.

—Searching for Treasure Coloring Book. Rose, Steve, illus. 1992. 5.00 (*0-923463-85-2*) Noble Pub Assocs.

Endangered Mammals - Africa: An Educational Coloring Book. (gr. 3 up). pap. 1.75 (*0-86545-213-X*) Spizzirri.

Endangered Mammals - Asia & China: An Educational Coloring Book. (gr. 3 up). pap. 1.75 (*0-86545-214-8*) Spizzirri.

Endangered Mammals - South America: An Educational Coloring Book. pap. 1.75 (*0-86545-215-6*) Spizzirri.

Engelmann, Jeanne. My Body Is My House: A Coloring Book about Alcohol, Drugs & Health. Barton, Patrice, illus. 16p. (gr. k-5). 1990. pap. 1.75 (*0-89486-735-0*, 5100B) Hazelden.

—Wonder What I Feel Today? A Coloring Book about Feelings. Barton, Patrice, illus. 16p. (gr. k-5). 1991. pap. 1.50 (*0-89486-744-X*, 5177B) Hazelden.

Ferguson, Dwayne. Afro-Bets Kids Christmas Fun: An Activity & Coloring Book. Ferguson, Dwayne, illus. LC 92-72003. 48p. (gr. k-3). 1992. pap. 2.95 (*0-940975-41-6*) Just Us Bks.

Goodman, Beth. Fun with the Norfin Trolls: A Coloring & Activity Book. (ps-8). 1992. pap. 1.95 (*0-590-45926-0*) Scholastic Inc.

Guhm, Susan & Guhm, Karl. The Great Sierra Redwood Activity Book. (Illus.). 32p. (gr. 1-6). 1990. write for info. (*0-9627621-0-5*) Froggy Bywater. This is NOT just a coloring book. This activity book contains two WORD SCRAMBLES, two CROSSWORD PUZZLES, two WORD SEARCHES, two DOT-TO-DOTS, one FINISH-THE-PICTURE, one BOARD GAME, one MATH PUZZLE, several COLORING PAGES, plus two answer pages - each & every page about the Sierra Redwood (also called Giant Sequoia, Sequoiadendron giganteum, & Giant Sequoia). Illustrations depict features of the tree in a simple humorous manner - height (as tall as 20 one-story houses or 30 school buses), weight (as heavy as 12 million hamburgers or 120,000 50-pound bags of dog food), their antiquity, their seeds & seedlings, how they grow, tree rings, associated plants & animals in the surrounding forest, etc. THE GREAT SIERRA REDWOOD BOOK is perfect for educators looking for an exciting way to teach their class about redwoods, with a redwood unit or as part of a plants unit in general. Whether visiting a Sierra Redwood forest or not, this activity book is entertaining & educational. For order information call or write: Froggy Bywater Press, P.O. Box 7920, Fresno, CA 93747; 209-251-0243.
Publisher Provided Annotation.

Hablallah, Jeanette. Color a Story: Nuh. 32p. (ps). 1989. pap. 3.50 (*1-56744-251-X*) Kazi Pubns.

Hamza, A. Color & Learn the Names of the Prophets. (Orig.). (ps). Date not set. pap. 3.50 (*0-934905-11-8*) Kazi Pubns.

Haring, Keith. The Keith Haring Coloring Book. Haring, Keith, illus. 20p. (Orig.). (ps-5). 1992. pap. 6.95 (*1-881270-51-3*) FotoFolio.

Harris, Gregg. The Twenty-One Rules of This House. rev. ed. 52p. 1993. pap. text ed. 11.00 (*0-923463-88-7*) Noble Pub Assocs.

Heller, Ruth. Designs for Coloring Seashells. (Illus.). 64p. 1992. pap. 3.95 (*0-448-03144-2*, G&D) Putnam Pub Group.

Hijazi, N. Color & Learn the Names of Animals. (Orig.). (ps). Date not set. pap. 3.50 (*0-934905-12-6*) Kazi Pubns.

Hooban, Louis. Indian Heritage Coloring Book. 50p. 1994. pap. 10.00 (*1-884710-05-0*) Indian Heritage.

Hoofnagle, Keith L. Hawaii Volcanoes Coloring Book. Hoofnagle, Keith L., illus. 32p. (ps-3). 1979. pap. 1.50 coloring book (*0-940295-07-5*) HI Natural Hist.

Jackson, Michael. Moonwalk Coloring Book. (Illus.). 1989. pap. 2.95 (*0-385-26155-1*) Doubleday.

Jemima Puddle-Duck. (Illus.). (ps-2). 1989. 1.95 (*0-7214-5218-3*) Ladybird Bks.

Jones, B. J. Let's Color Korea: Everyday Life in Traditional. 24p. (gr. k-3). 1990. oversized 8.50x (*0-930878-98-1*) Hollym Intl.

Judson, Thomas, illus. Color Me Cleveland: A Cleveland Coloring Book. Johnston, Christopher, text by. (Illus.). 32p. 1993. pap. 4.95 (*0-9631738-2-0*) Gray & Co Pubs.

Kapraun, Francis. Santa's Red Toy Bag: (How It All Began) Archer, Jolynn, illus. 14p. 1994. write for info. (*0-9643313-0-6*) Inspired Ink.
Many years ago, Santa used boxes to deliver toys around the world. SANTA'S RED TOY BAG (How it all began) tells us WHY he is now seen with his famous huge toy bag & WHO sparked the idea for its use. A delightful story children will enjoy & remember. This is a twenty-four page activity book with story pages to color & pages to draw. To order, contact: Inspired Ink Productions by Kapraun, 36745 Hill St., Lower Salem, OH 45745; 614-585-2706.
Publisher Provided Annotation.

Kelly, Susan & Kelly, Thomas. Fishes of Hawaii Coloring Book. Kelly, Susan & Kelly, Thomas, illus. 32p. (ps-2). 1992. pap. 3.95 (*1-880188-32-5*) Bess Pr.

Kelsch, Gregg B. A World of Dinosaurs Series. Kelsch, Gregg B., illus. 1993. write for info. (*1-883736-01-3*) Acorn Pub UT.

Kricher, John C. & Morrison, Gordon. A Field Guide to Tropical Forests Coloring Book. Kricher, John & Morrison, Gordon, illus. 64p. 1991. pap. 4.80 (*0-395-57321-1*) HM.

Lancaster, Derek. Picture America: States & Capitals. Lancaster, Derek, illus. Anderson, Stevens, ed. (Illus.). 136p. (gr. 5). 1991. pap. 4.95 (*1-880184-02-8*) Compact Classics.

Landry, Sarah. Field Guide to Fishes Coloring Book. 1987. pap. 4.80 (*0-395-44095-5*) HM.

Larson, Russell J. Africa by Four: Coloring Book. (Illus.). 14p. (Orig.). (gr. k-6). 1992. pap. text ed. 1.85 (*1-881087-01-8*) Storm Moutain.

—USA Coloring Book. (Illus.). 50p. (Orig.). (gr. k-6). 1992. pap. text ed. 4.95 (*1-881087-00-X*) Storm Moutain.

Lee, Michelle. Estes Park Souvenir Coloring Book. 48p. (ps-8). 1993. 4.50 (*0-9637687-0-0*) Vacation Color.

Lopez, Ruth K. A Child's Garden Diary: Coloring & Activity Book. Lopez, Ruth K., illus. 56p. (Orig.). (gr. k-6). 1992. pap. 5.95 (*0-9627463-4-7*) Gardens Growing People.

McNair, Wallace Y. Black & Beautiful: A Self-Discovery Coloring Book. Caldwell, Herschel V., illus. 26p. (Orig.). (gr. 2 up). 1992. pap. 10.00 (*0-9627600-3-X*) Wstrn Images.

Mason, B. J., Jr. Elliott B. in Birds of a Feather. Moore, Kevin R., illus. Dibler-Mason, Betty J., intro. by. (Illus.). 66p. (Orig.). (gr. 2-4). 1993. Incl. audio cass. pap. 14.95 (*0-9640707-0-7*) Color-Me Storybks.
Most of us are aware that the general makeup of the domestic cat is to watch & chase birds. But did you ever hear of a cat that actually takes care of them? Color-Me Storybooks introduces its first in a series of characters that aid in accelerating learning & reinforcing family values - initially, through a friendly cat named Elliott B. that teaches children about wild birds. In fact, he even owns his own wild bird store! Elliott B. dedicates his life to educating school children & the community about the habits & habitats of wild birds through an exchange of dialogue about our feathery friends. "It cleverly combines visual, auditory & tactile learning," states Professional Educator & President of King Tree Book Company, Deer Park, Washington, Craig Palmer. "...good visual stimulation...bold print," adds Special Education Professor, Denton, Texas, Dr. Claude Cheek. Librarian Marsha Barker, Happy Hill Farm Academy, Granbury, Texas, found her students to be "fascinated & drawn to Elliott B...materials are wonderful... excellent for use in teaching across the curriculum...recommend to any early elementary educator." Sixty-six pages of educational fun that includes coloring, a glossary & sheet music. Schedule storytime & character appearance. Call 214-495-8225.
Publisher Provided Annotation.

Massasati, Ahmad. Islamic Calligraphy Coloring Book. (Illus.). 57p. (Orig.). (gr. 3-6). 1991. pap. 4.95 (*0-89259-120-X*) Am Trust Pubns.

Meyer, Nancy. Endangered Species Coloring-Learning Books Adventure Series. Meyer, George, illus. (ps-3). 1993. write for info. (*1-883408-05-9*) Meyer Pub FL.

Mike, Jan. Chana, An Anasazi Girl: Historical Paperdoll Books to Read, Color & Cut. Lowmiller, Cathy, illus. 32p. (Orig.). (gr. k-4). 1991. pap. 3.95 (*0-918080-61-4*) Treasure Chest.

Mollica, Tony & Northup, Bill. Touring the One Thousand Islands. (Illus.). 28p. 1993. wkbk. 3.95 (*1-883029-03-1*) CHP NY.

Monroe, Betsy. My Visit to My Doctor: A Coloring Book for Kids. Monroe, Betsy, illus. 24p. (Orig.). (gr. k-4). 1989. pap. write for info. (*1-878083-01-5*) Color Me Well.

—My Visit to the Emergency Room: A Coloring Book for Kids. Monroe, Betsy, illus. (SPA.). 32p. (gr. k-4). 1990. pap. write for info. (*1-878083-03-1*) Color Me Well.

—My Visit to the Hospital: A Coloring Book for Kids. Monroe, Betsy, illus. 32p. (Orig.). (gr. k-4). 1986. pap. write for info. (*1-878083-02-3*) Color Me Well.

—My Visit to the Outpatient Department: A Coloring Book for Kids. Monroe, Betsy, illus. 24p. (gr. k-4). 1986. pap. write for info. (*1-878083-04-X*) Color Me Well.

Monteith, Jay. ABCs African Art Coloring Book. Monteith, Jay, illus. 32p. (ps-3). 1992. pap. text ed. 6.95 (*0-9627366-3-5*) Arts & Comns NY.

Newman, Chris. Phillip's Dream World: A Coloring Book. Newman, Chris, illus. 52p. (Orig.). 1992. pap. 5.95 (*0-9635004-3-0*) Flying Heart.

Nichols, V. Dinosaur Coloring Book. M. J. Studios Staff, illus. 32p. (Orig.). (gr. k-6). 1993. pap. 2.95 (*1-879424-50-9*) Nickel Pr.

Opler, Paul. Butterflies East & West: A Book to Color. Strawn, Susan, illus. 96p. (Orig.). (gr. 1-6). 1993. pap. 8.95 (*1-879373-45-9*) R Rinehart.

Orr, Katherine. The Hawaiian Coral Reef Coloring Book. Orr, Katherine, illus. 48p. (Orig.). (gr. 1-6). 1992. pap. 5.95 (*0-88045-122-X*) Stemmer Hse.

Petterson, Jay, illus. Giants, Witches & Dragons Three-D Coloring Book. 32p. (Orig.). 1990. pap. 3.95 (*0-942025-81-4*) Kidsbks.

Pittenger, Shari. Listen, Color, & Learn, Vol. II: A Coloring Book for Family Devotions, Psalm 31-60. 40p. 1990. wkbk. 5.00 (*0-923463-75-5*) Noble Pub Assocs.

—Listen, Color, & Learn, Vol. III: A Coloring Book for Family Devotions, Psalm 61-90. 40p. 1991. wkbk. 5.00 (*0-923463-77-1*) Noble Pub Assocs.

Preschool Color & Learn: I Can Do It Myself. 1992. pap. 1.95 (*0-590-45036-0*) Scholastic Inc.

Preschool Color & Learn: Kindergarten Skills. (ps). 1992. pap. 1.95 (*0-590-45038-7*) Scholastic Inc.

Preschool Color & Learn: Making Friends & Sharing. (ps). 1992. pap. 1.95 (*0-590-45059-X*) Scholastic Inc.

Preschool Color & Learn: Sounds All Around. (ps). 1992. pap. 1.95 (*0-590-45037-9*) Scholastic Inc.

Pysz, Stephen. Team Earth: Advanced ABC Environmental Coloring Book. America, Alexis & Marcil, Beth, illus. 56p. (gr. k-1). 1991. pap. text ed. 4.95 (*0-9630186-7-1*) Team Earth.

Qazi, M. A. Arabic Alphabet Coloring Book. 20p. (ps). 1984. pap. 3.50 (*1-56744-220-X*) Kazi Pubns.

Quincannon, Alan, ed. Lifestyles of Colonial America. Lanawn-Shee Studios Staff, illus. 24p. (Orig.). (gr. k-6). 1992. pap. 3.95 (*1-878452-10-X*) Tory Corner Editions.

—More Soldiers of Colonial America. Lanawn-Shee Studios Staff, illus. 24p. (Orig.). (gr. k-6). 1992. pap. 3.95 (*1-878452-12-6*) Tory Corner Editions.

—People of Colonial America. Lanawn-Shee Studios Staff, illus. 20p. (Orig.). (gr. k-6). 1992. pap. 3.95 (*1-878452-09-6*) Tory Corner Editions.

—Soldiers of Colonial America. Lanawn-Shee Studios Staff, illus. 24p. (Orig.). (gr. k-6). 1992. pap. 3.95 (*1-878452-11-8*) Tory Corner Editions.

Read & Color Black History. (Illus.). 1992. 2.25 (*0-9634154-0-9*) R & C Black Hist.

Read & Color Book Series. (Illus.). Date not set. pap. write for info. (*0-86545-223-7*) Spizzirri.
This series of educational read & color books features realistic illustrations & text. Over 100 titles cover interesting topics about everything from Dinosaurs, Indians & Space to many species of animals. ($1.95 pap.). 48 titles from the series are available on cassette with music & sound effects added. ($5.95). These museum curator approved books are a "must have" for anyone with children or grandchildren & an eye for superior quality at a reasonable price. For the younger child: an entire line of activity & workbooks that help make it fun to learn the ABCs, counting, & reading words. ($2.95 pap.). Many titles are available bilingually in English & Spanish. ($2.95 pap.). All titles 32 p. (Preschool to 5th gr.). For your store call our wholesale division toll free at 1-800-325-9819. Schools & libraries call toll free at 1-800-322-9819.
Publisher Provided Annotation.

Reid, Elizabeth. Moms & Dads - Mamis y Papis: Bilingual Coloring Book. (SPA & ENG., Illus.). 64p. (gr. 1-4). 1992. pap. 1.95 (*0-9627080-5-4*) In One EAR.

Shepherd, Sarah & Shepherd, Thomas. AlphaBuddies Coloring & Reading Book, No. 1. 56p. (gr. 1-2). 1992. wkbk. 4.95 (*0-9634846-0-5*) AlphaBuddies.

Smith, J. C. & McLean, J. Kidworks Series, No. 1. Horine, Billie & Seitz, Connie, illus. (ps-5). 1993. Set. PLB 32.65g (*1-882627-17-2*) KTS Pub.

Smith, Tom & Smith, Diane. Northwest Coast Indian Coloring Book. Smith, Tom, illus. 32p. (Orig.). (gr. 1-6). 1993. pap. 4.50 (*0-8431-3491-7*, Troubador) Price Stern.

Solomakos, Linda. Cosmic Coloring: The Magic Robe. (Illus., Orig.). (gr. 1-5). 1987. pap. 2.95 (*0-9622288-1-8*) Cosmic Color Bks.

Sommers, Maxine S. Learn to Count & Color with Spot the Cat. Kennedy, Suzanne, ed. (Illus.). 10p. (Orig.). (gr. k-1). 1993. pap. 2.50 (*0-685-65603-9*) Pound Sterling Pub.

—Texas Cool Cat Coloring Book. Bircham, Don, illus. 10p. (Orig.). (gr. k-1). 1991. pap. 1.95 size: 8 1/2" x 11" (*0-943991-20-X*) Pound Sterling Pub.

Spizzirri, Peter M. Colonies: An Educational Coloring Book. Spizzirri, Linda, ed. (Illus.). 32p. (gr. 1-8). 1989. pap. 1.75 (*0-86545-137-0*) Spizzirri.

Spizzirri Publishing Co. Staff. Comets: An Educational Coloring Book. Spizzirri, Linda, ed. (Illus.). 32p. (gr. k-5). 1982. pap. 1.75 (*0-86545-071-4*) Spizzirri.

—Fish: An Educational Coloring Book. Spizzirri, Linda, ed. (Illus.). 32p. (gr. k-5). 1982. pap. 1.75 (*0-86545-028-5*) Spizzirri.

Squirrel Nutkin. (Illus.). (ps-2). 1989. 1.95 (*0-7214-5139-X*) Ladybird Bks.

Starbuck, Marnie. The Gladimals Help Save the Earth. (Illus.). 16p. 1990. 0.75 (*1-56456-203-4*, 473) W Gladden Found.

Sternburg, Sharon. Suzie Q. Mouse Adventures: Coloring Book. Coyne, John P., illus. 39p. (Orig.). (ps-1). Date not set. pap. 1.99x (*0-9633513-0-3*) S M Resar Pub.

Stoner, Laura M. Acts - a Story Color Book. Huskey, Freeda, ed. Stoner, Laura M., illus. 80p. (Orig.). (gr. k-6). 1992. wkbk. 5.95 (*0-934426-46-5*) NAPSAC Reprods.

Student Lifeline, Inc., Staff. Police Officer Friendly's Safety Tips Activity & Coloring Book. rev. ed. Milisello, Clif, illus. 32p. (gr. k-3). 1993. pap. text ed. 1.79x (*1-884888-00-3*) Student Lifeline.
POLICE OFFICER FRIENDLY is a 36 page coloring/activity book which illustrates the primary causes of injury sustained by young children here in the U.S.A. Each "color-in" page is a lesson in safety with an "I promise..." text, for which the child is instructed to print its name. These books are great for teaching safety lessons & prove to be significant regarding the "retention value" of each lesson among tots since the child is actively coloring-in & promising. FREE SUPPLIES ARE MADE AVAILABLE VIA AD

Tate, Susan. Blessings of Abraham Coloring Book. Henium, Marian, illus. 12p. (Orig.). (gr. k-3). 1993. pap. 0.39 (*1-884395-06-6*) Clear Blue Sky.

—Faith Coloring Book. Henium, Marian, illus. 12p. (Orig.). (gr. k-3). 1993. pap. 0.39 (*1-884395-04-X*) Clear Blue Sky.

—Ninety First Psalm Coloring Book. Henium, Marian, illus. 12p. (gr. k-3). 1993. pap. 0.39 (*1-884395-05-8*) Clear Blue Sky.

—Petal Pals Coloring Books, 3 bks. Henium, Marian, illus. (gr. k-3). 1993. Set. pap. 1.17 (*1-884395-08-2*) Clear Blue Sky.

Taylor, Donald G. Story Picture Poem & Coloring Book for Children. (Illus.). 30p. (ps-3). 1993. pap. 6.95 (*0-9638002-0-5*) D G Taylor.
The book is in two sections. The first section consists of 10 animals in beautiful color, each accompanied by an original story poem. The second section consists of eight of the same animals in black & white that appear in the first section. The child then attempts to color the animals in the second section as close as possible to the animals in the first section. This makes it interesting & challenging. This book is unique in that the child learns by seeing & comparing while doing. The little story poems enhance the child's reading ability & create an urge to MEMORIZE these cute little stories. This is a very educational little book. The drawings are large & easily discernable & THE PRINT IS LARGE & EASY TO READ. To order, write or call Publisher, Donald G. Taylor, 3651 S. Arville St., Las Vegas, NV 89103. (702) 221-8380. Publisher's price $1.75. Suggested retail price to $6.95. Educational & fun. Great for little budding artists & poets.
Publisher Provided Annotation.

Thomas, M. Angele & Ramey, Mary L. Many Children Coloring Book. (Illus.). 24p. 1988. pap. 1.50 (*0-9619293-1-6*) M A Thomas.

Tom Kitten. (Illus.). (ps-2). 1.95 (*0-7214-5219-1*) Ladybird Bks.

Turner, Herschell. The Black West Coloring Book. 32p. (gr. 4-6). 1992. pap. 3.95 (*1-882205-01-4*) All Media Prods.

Turner, Herschell & Blanchard, G. L. The Buffalo Soldiers Coloring Book. 32p. (gr. 4-6). 1992. pap. 3.95 (*1-882205-02-2*) All Media Prods.

Turner, Teresa R. ABCs from the Book of Life. 32p. (gr. k-2). 1991. pap. 3.95 (*0-9633509-3-5*) T R Turner.

Tyler, J. Dot to Dot on the Farm. (Illus.). 24p. (ps-2). 1991. pap. 3.50 (*0-7460-0595-4*, Usborne) EDC.

Tynes, Rick & Whittemore, Diane. Monster Dots: Connect the Dots & Color. (Illus.). 80p. (gr. 1-6). 1993. pap. 4.95 (*0-8069-8642-5*) Sterling.

Wagenman, Mark A. Aloha Bear ABC: Coloring & Activity Book. Wagenman, Mark A., illus. 24p. (ps-k). 1989. pap. 2.95 (*0-89610-146-0*) Island Heritage.

—Aloha Bear: Color & Activity Book. Wagenman, Mark A., illus. 24p. (ps-k). 1988. pap. 2.95 (*0-89610-023-5*) Island Heritage.

Walton, Richard K. & Morrison, Gordon. A Field Guide to Endangered Wildlife Coloring Book. Walton, Richard K. & Morrison, Gordon, illus. 64p. 1991. pap. 4.80 (*0-395-57324-6*) HM.

Willhoite, Michael. Families: A Coloring Book. Willhoite, Michael, illus. 32p. (Orig.). (ps-1). 1991. pap. 2.95 saddle-stitched (*1-55583-192-3*) Alyson Pubns.

Woofenden, Louise. Rainbow Colors in the Word: An Activity Book with Puzzles & Pictures to Color. Hill, Betty, ed. Woofenden, Louise, illus. 32p. (Orig.). 1992. pap. text ed. 2.50 (*0-917426-08-8*) Am New Church Sunday.

Wren. Flowers of Hawaii Coloring Book. Wren, illus. 32p. (ps-2). 1992. pap. 3.95 (*1-880188-42-2*) Bess Pr.

COLUMBIA RIVER

Baljo, Wallace, Jr. Grand Coulee: A Story of the Columbia River from Molten Lavas & Ice to Grand Coulee Dam. rev. ed. Hemsley, Roberta G., illus. 80p. (gr. 4-6). pap. write for info. (*0-9606084-0-0*) Clipboard.

COLUMBUS, CHRISTOPHER, 1451-1506

Adler, David A. Christopher Columbus: Great Explorer. Miller, Lyle, illus. LC 90-28668. 48p. (gr. 2-5). 1991. reinforced bdg. 14.95 (*0-8234-0895-7*) Holiday.

—Un Libro Ilustrado Sobre Cristobal Colon. Mlawer, Teresa, tr. from ENG. Wallner, John & Wallner, Alexandra, illus. (SPA.). 32p. (ps-3). 1992. reinforced bdg. 14.95 (*0-8234-0981-3*); pap. 5.95 (*0-8234-0990-2*) Holiday.

—A Picture Book of Christopher Columbus. Wallner, John & Wallner, Alexandra, illus. LC 90-39211. 32p. (ps-3). 1991. reinforced bdg. 15.95 (*0-8234-0857-4*) Holiday.

—A Picture Book of Christopher Columbus. Wallner, John & Wallner, Alexandra, illus. (ps-3). pap. 5.95 (*0-8234-0949-X*) Holiday.

Anderson, Joan. Christopher Columbus: From Vision to Voyage. (gr. 4-7). 1991. 14.95 (*0-8037-1041-0*); PLB 14.89 (*0-8037-1042-9*) Dial Bks Young.

Anderson, Scoular. Land Ahoy! The Story of Christopher Columbus. (Illus.). 96p. (gr. 3-7). 1992. pap. 2.99 (*0-14-034617-1*) Puffin Bks.

Asimov, Isaac. Christopher Columbus. LC 90-25836. (Illus.). 64p. (gr. 3-4). 1991. PLB 18.60 (*0-8368-0556-9*) Gareth Stevens Inc.

Bains, Rae. Christopher Columbus. Smolinski, Dick, illus. LC 84-2585. 32p. (gr. 3-6). 1985. lib. bdg. 9.49 (*0-8167-0150-4*); pap. text ed. 2.95 (*0-8167-0151-2*) Troll Assocs.

Brenner, Barbara. If You Were There in 1492. LC 90-24099. (Illus.). 112p. (gr. 3-7). 1991. SBE 13.95 (*0-02-712321-9*, Bradbury Pr) Macmillan Child Grp.

Carpenter, Eric. Young Christopher Columbus: Discoverer of the New Worlds. Himmelman, John, illus. LC 91-24975. 32p. (gr. k-2). 1992. PLB 11.59 (*0-8167-2526-8*); pap. text ed. 2.95 (*0-8167-2527-6*) Troll Assocs.

Cauper, Eunice. The Story of Christopher Columbus & Our October 12th Holiday for Kindergarten Children. Cauper, David, illus. 16p. (Orig.). (gr. k-3). 1985. pap. 3.95 (*0-9617551-0-5*) E Cauper.

Christopher Columbus. (Illus.). 4p. (gr. 2-5). 1991. 8.95 (*0-8167-2566-7*) Troll Assocs.

Clare, John D., ed. Voyages of Christopher Columbus. (gr. 4-7). 1992. 16.95 (*0-15-200507-2*, Gulliver Bks) HarBrace.

Columbus, Christopher. I, Columbus. 49p. 1992. text ed. 3.92 (*1-56956-115-X*) W A T Braille.

—The Log of Christopher Columbus: The First Voyage: Spring, Summer & Fall, 1492. Lowe, Steve, ed. Sabuda, Robert, illus. 32p. (ps-3). 1992. 14.95 (*0-399-22139-5*, Philomel Bks) Putnam Pub Group.

Conrad, Pam. Pedro's Journal: A Voyage with Christopher Columbus. Koeppen, Peter, illus. LC 90-85723. 96p. (gr. 3-7). 1991. 13.95 (*1-878093-17-7*) Boyds Mills Pr.

Cox, Nonie. Christopher Columbus. (Illus.). 48p. (gr. k-1). 1992. pap. 9.95 (*1-55799-240-1*) Evan-Moor Corp.

De Kay, James T. Meet Christopher Columbus. Edens, John, illus. LC 88-19068. 72p. (gr. 2-4). 1989. PLB 6.99 (*0-394-91963-7*); pap. 2.99 (*0-394-81963-2*) Random Bks Yng Read.

DeZinno, Ted. Christopher Columbus: The Dream That Changed the World. (Illus.). 1992. pap. 12.50 (*0-9632182-0-4*) McClain.

Dodge, Steven C. Christopher Columbus & the First Voyages to the New World. Goetzmann, William H., ed. Collins, Michael, intro. by. (Illus.). 112p. (gr. 5 up). 1991. lib. bdg. 18.95 (*0-7910-1299-9*); pap. 9.95 (*0-7910-1522-X*) Chelsea Hse.

Eckhart, Mary L. Columbus' Dictionary. 100p. (Orig.). (gr. 5-10). 1992. pap. 11.95 (*0-8283-1993-6*) Branden Pub Co.

Eidsmoe, John. Columbus & Cortez: Conquerors for Christ. LC 92-81425. 304p. (Orig.). 1992. pap. 9.95 (*0-89221-223-3*) New Leaf.

Fradin, Dennis B. Columbus Day. LC 89-7663. (Illus.). 48p. (gr. 1-4). 1990. lib. bdg. 14.95 (*0-89490-233-4*) Enslow Pubs.

—The Nina, the Pinta, & the Santa Maria. LC 91-4664. (Illus.). 64p. (gr. 5-8). 1991. PLB 12.90 (*0-531-20034-5*) Watts.

Fritz, Jean. Where Do You Think You're Going, Christopher Columbus? Tomes, Margot, illus. 80p. (gr. 3-7). 1981. (Putnam); pap. 7.95 (*0-399-20734-1*, Putnam) Putnam Pub Group.

Gleiter, Jan & Thompson, Kathleen. Christopher Columbus. Whipple, Rick, illus. 32p. (gr. 2-5). 1986. PLB 19.97 (*0-8172-2643-5*); pap. text ed. 9.27 (*0-8172-2647-8*) Raintree Steck-V.

Goodnough, David. Christopher Columbus. new ed. LC 78-18052. (Illus.). 48p. (gr. 4-7). 1979. PLB 10.59 (*0-89375-170-7*); pap. 3.50 (*0-89375-162-6*) Troll Assocs.

Greene, Carol. Christopher Columbus: A Great Explorer. Dobson, Steven, illus. LC 88-37943. 48p. (gr. k-3). 1989. PLB 12.85 (*0-516-04204-1*); pap. 4.95 (*0-516-44204-X*) Childrens.

Haskins, Jim. Christopher Columbus: Admiral of the Ocean Sea. Lasker, Joe, illus. 64p. (gr. 2-5). 1991. pap. 2.95 (*0-590-42396-7*) Scholastic Inc.

Humble, Richard. The Voyages of Columbus. Hook, Richard, illus. LC 90-45889. 32p. (gr. 5-8). 1991. PLB 12.40 (*0-531-14189-6*) Watts.

Italia, Bob. Christopher Columbus. Walner, Rosemary, ed. LC 90-82621. (Illus.). 32p. (gr. 4). 1990. PLB 11.96 (*0-939179-94-6*) Abdo & Dghtrs.

Jones, Mary E., ed. Christopher Columbus & His Legacy: Opposing Viewpoints. LC 92-18160. (Illus.). 240p. (gr. 10 up). 1992. PLB 17.95 (*0-89908-196-7*); pap. text ed. 9.95 (*0-89908-171-1*) Greenhaven.

Kent, Zachary. Christopher Columbus: Expeditions to the New World. LC 91-13863. 128p. (gr. 3 up). 1991. PLB 20.55 (*0-516-03064-7*); pap. 9.95 (*0-516-43064-5*) Childrens.

Knight, David. I Can Read About Christopher Columbus. LC 78-73774. (Illus.). (gr. 2-5). 1979. pap. 2.50 (*0-89375-206-1*) Troll Assocs.

Krensky, Stephen. Christopher Columbus: A Step Two Book. Green, Norma, illus. LC 89-62507. 48p. (Orig.). (gr. 1-3). 1991. lib. bdg. 7.99 (*0-679-90369-0*); pap. 3.50 (*0-679-80369-6*) Random Bks Yng Read.

Las Casas, Bartholomew. The Log of Christopher Columbus' First Voyage to America: In the Year 1492, As Copied Out in Brief by Bartholomew Las Casas. LC 88-32567. (Illus.). 84p. (gr. 3 up). 1989. Repr. of 1938 ed. lib. bdg. 17.00 (*0-208-02247-3*, Pub. by Linnet) Shoe String.

Levinson, Nancy S. Christopher Columbus: Voyager to the Unknown. (Illus.). 128p. (gr. 4-7). 1990. 17.00 (*0-525-67292-3*, Lodestar Bks) Dutton Child Bks.

Lillegard, Dee. My First Columbus Day Book. Raskin, Betty, illus. LC 87-10304. 32p. (ps-2). 1987. PLB 11. 45 (*0-516-02909-6*); pap. 3.95 (*0-516-42909-4*) Childrens.

McGovern, Ann. Christopher Columbus. 1992. 4.95 (*0-590-45765-9*, 051) Scholastic Inc.

Martini, Teri. Christopher Columbus: The Man Who Unlocked the Secrets of the World. LC 91-44755. 96p. (gr. 4-7). 1992. pap. 4.95 (*0-8091-6604-6*) Paulist Pr.

Marx, Robert F. Following Columbus: The Voyage of the Nina II. (Illus.). 80p. 1991. 17.95 (*0-88415-004-6*, 5004) Gulf Pub.

Marzollo, Jean. In Fourteen Ninety-Two. Bjorkman, Steven, illus. 40p. 1991. 14.95 (*0-590-44413-1*, Scholastic Hardcover) Scholastic Inc.

Marzollo, Jean & Bjorkman, Steven. In 1492. 1993. pap. 19.95 (*0-590-72737-0*) Scholastic Inc.

Meltzer, Milton. Columbus & the World Around Him. LC 89-24764. (gr. 9-12). 1990. PLB 15.40 (*0-531-10899-6*) Watts.

—Columbus & the World Around Him. 245p. 1991. text ed. 19.60 (*1-56956-213-X*) W A T Braille.

Morgan, Lee & Solarino, Claudio. Christopher Columbus. (Illus.). 104p. (gr. 5-8). 1990. 9.95 (*0-382-09974-5*); pap. 5.95 (*0-382-24001-4*) Silver Burdett Pr.

Morison, Samuel E. Christopher Columbus, Mariner. (Illus.). 192p. (gr. 9-12). 1983. pap. 9.00 (*0-452-00992-8*, Mer) NAL-Dutton.

Murphy, Carol. Christopher Columbus. Reese, Bob, illus. (gr. k-6). 1991. 11.95 (*0-89868-228-2*) ARO Pub.

—Christopher Columbus. Reese, Bob, illus. (gr. k-6). 1991. pap. 20.00 (*0-89868-229-0*) ARO Pub.

Osborne, Mary P. Christopher Columbus: Admiral of the Sea. (Orig.). (gr. k-6). 1987. pap. 3.50 (*0-440-41275-7*, YB) Dell.

Pelta, Kathy. Discovering Christopher Columbus: How History Is Invented. 112p. (gr. 4-6). 1991. PLB 19.95 (*0-8225-4899-2*) Lerner Pubns.

Postgate, Oliver & Linnell, Naomi. Columbus: The Triumphant Failure. Postgate, Oliver, illus. 44p. (gr. 5-8). 1992. 14.95 (*0-531-15240-5*) Watts.

Rhodes, Bennie. Christopher Columbus. Smith, A. G. & Smith, A. G., illus. LC 76-5788. (gr. 3-6). 1977. pap. 6.95 (*0-915134-26-8*) Mott Media.

Richards, Dorothy F. Christopher Columbus, Who Sailed On! Nelson, John, illus. LC 78-7664. (gr. 1-5). 1978. PLB 13.95 (*0-89565-032-0*) Childs World.

Roop, Peter & Roop, Connie, eds. I, Columbus: My Journal - 1492. Hanson, Peter, illus. 57p. (gr. 4-7). 1990. 13.95 (*0-8027-6977-2*); lib. bdg. 14.85 (*0-8027-6978-0*) Walker & Co.

Scavone, Daniel C. Christopher Columbus. LC 92-29499. (Illus.). 112p. (gr. 5-8). 1992. PLB 14.95 (*1-56006-034-4*) Lucent Bks.

Sis, Peter. Follow the Dream. Sis, Peter, illus. LC 90-5392. 40p. (gr. k-5). 1991. 15.00 (*0-679-80628-8*); lib. bdg. 15.99 (*0-679-90628-2*) Knopf Bks Yng Read.

Soule, Gardner. Christopher Columbus: Green Sea of Darkness. LC 90-48975. (Illus.). 112p. (gr. 6-10). 1991. PLB 13.95 (*1-55905-076-4*) Marshall Cavendish.

Spencer, Eve. Three Ships for Columbus. Sperling, Tom, illus. LC 92-14401. 32p. (gr. 2-5). 1992. PLB 18.51 (*0-8114-7212-4*) Raintree Steck-V.

Stein, R. Conrad. Christopher Columbus. LC 91-34744. (Illus.). 32p. (gr. 3-6). PLB 12.30, Apr. 1992 (*0-516-04851-1*); pap. 3.95, Jul. 1992 (*0-516-44851-X*) Childrens.

Stone, Elaine M. Christopher Columbus. (Illus.). (gr. 3-7). 1991. 12.99 (*0-8423-0468-1*) Tyndale.

Twist, Clint. Christopher Columbus: The Discovery of the Americas. LC 93-19017. 1994. PLB 22.80 (*0-8114-7253-1*) Raintree Steck-V.

Urbide, Fernanado & Engler, Dan. Columbus: Adventures to the Edge of the World. CCC of America Staff, illus. 35p. (Orig.). (ps-7). 1991. incl. video 21.95 (*1-56814-005-3*); pap. text ed. 4.95 book (*0-685-62402-1*) CCC of America.

Ventura, Piero. Fourteen Ninety-Two: The Year of the New World. 96p. 1992. 19.95 (*0-399-22332-0*, Putnam) Putnam Pub Group.

Watermill Press Staff. Columbus Model Book. (gr. 4-7). 1992. pap. 9.95 (*0-8167-2748-1*) Troll Assocs.

Weisman, JoAnne B. & Deitch, Kenneth M. Christopher Columbus & the Great Voyage of Discovery: With a Message from President George Bush. Eldridge, Marion, illus. Bush, George, contrib. by. LC 90-81362. 40p. (gr. k-6). 1990. PLB 14.95 (*1-878668-00-5*); pap. 7.95g (*1-878668-01-3*) Disc Enter Ltd.

West, Delno C. & West, Jean M. Christopher Columbus: The Great Adventure & How We Know about It. LC 90-936. (Illus.). 144p. (gr. 5-9). 1991. SBE 15.95 (*0-689-31433-7*, Atheneum Child Bk) Macmillan Child Grp.

Young, Robert. Christopher Columbus. Brook, Bonnie, ed. Stewart, Arvis, illus. 32p. (gr. k-2). 1990. 4.95 (*0-671-69110-4*); PLB 6.95 (*0-671-69104-X*) Silver Pr.

Yue, Charlotte & Yue, David. Christopher Columbus: How He Did It. Yue, David, illus. 144p. (gr. 3-6). 1992. 14.95 (*0-395-52100-9*) HM.

Zadra, Dan. Explorers of America: Columbus. rev. ed. (gr. 2-4). 1988. PLB 14.95 (*0-88682-184-3*) Creative Ed.

COLUMBUS, CHRISTOPHER, 1451-1506–FICTION

Columbus, Christopher. I, Columbus: My Journal 1492-1493. Roop, Peter & Roop, Connie, eds. 64p. (gr. 5). 1991. pap. 5.99 (*0-380-71545-7*, Camelot) Avon.

D'Aulaire, Ingri & D'Aulaire, Edgar P. Columbus. 64p. (gr. 2-5). 1992. pap. 8.00 (*0-440-40701-X*, YB) Dell.

Dyson, John. Westward with Columbus: A Time Quest Book. 64p. 1991. 15.95 (*0-590-43846-8*, Scholastic Hardcover) Scholastic Inc.

Foreman, Michael. The Boy Who Sailed with Columbus. Foreman, Michael, illus. 80p. (gr. 1-4). 1992. 16.95 (*1-55970-178-1*) Arcade Pub Inc.

Hughes, Alice D. Cajun Columbus. rev. ed. Rice, James, illus. LC 91-16783. 40p. 1991. 12.95 (*0-88289-875-2*) Pelican.

Litowinsky, Olga. The High Voyage: The Final Crossing of Christopher Columbus. McKeveny, Tom, illus. 160p. (gr. 5-9). 1992. pap. 3.50 (*0-440-40703-6*, YB) Dell.

McGee, Marni. Diego Columbus: Adventures on the High Seas. (Illus.). 128p. (Orig.). (gr. 3-7). 1992. pap. 6.99 (*0-8007-5433-6*) Revell.

Mandrell, Louise. Eye of an Eagle: A Story about the Meaning of Columbus Day. (gr. 4-7). 1993. 12.95 (*1-56530-009-2*) Summit TX.

Martin, Susan. I Sailed with Columbus: The Adventures of a Ship's Boy. La Padulla, Tom, illus. 154p. (gr. 5 up). 1991. 17.95 (*0-87951-431-0*) Overlook Pr.

O'Connor, Genevieve A. The Admiral & the Deck Boy: One Boy's Journey with Christopher Columbus. LC 91-17978. (Illus.). 168p. (gr. 5 up). 1991. 12.95 (*1-55870-218-0*, 70002) Shoe Tree Pr.

Schlein, Miriam. I Sailed with Columbus. Newsom, Tom, illus. LC 90-24532. 144p. (gr. 3-6). 1991. 14.00 (*0-06-022513-0*); PLB 13.89 (*0-06-022514-9*) HarpC Child Bks.

—I Sailed with Columbus. Newsom, Tom, illus. LC 90-24532. 144p. (gr. 3-6). 1992. pap. 3.95 (*0-06-440423-4*, Trophy) HarpC Child Bks.

Smith, Barry. The First Voyage of Christopher Columbus. Smith, Barry, illus. 32p. (ps-3). 1992. 12.95 (*0-670-84051-3*) Viking Child Bks.

Smithmark Staff. Where's Columbus? 1992. 4.98 (*0-8317-9284-1*) Smithmark.

Yolen, Jane. Encounter. Shannon, David A., illus. 1992. 14.95 (*0-15-225962-7*, HB Juv Bks) HarBrace.

COLUMBUS DAY

Liestman, Vicki. Columbus Day. (ps-3). 1992. pap. 5.95 (*0-87614-559-4*) Carolrhoda Bks.

Moncure, Jane B. Our Columbus Day Book. Shackelford, Jean, illus. LC 86-6818. 32p. (ps-3). 1986. PLB 13.95 (*0-89565-347-8*) Childs World.

Sandak, Cass. Columbus Day. LC 89-25399. (Illus.). 48p. (gr. 5-6). 1990. text ed. 12.95 RSBE (*0-89686-498-7*, Crestwood Hse) Macmillan Child Grp.

COLUMNISTS

see Journalists

COMAL (COMPUTER PROGRAM LANGUAGE)

Captain Comal's Staff. Cartridge Graphics & Sound. Hejndorf, Frank, illus. 64p. (Orig.). (gr. 6 up). 1984. pap. 6.95 (*0-928411-02-8*) Comal Users.

Skelton, Mindy. Graphics Primer. Schmidt, Wayne, illus. 84p. (Orig.). (gr. 6 up). 1984. pap. 14.95 (*0-928411-04-4*) Comal Users.

COMETS

Asimov, Isaac. Comets & Meteors. (gr. 4-7). 1991. pap. 4.99 (*0-440-40450-9*, YB) Dell.

—How Did We Find Out about Comets? Wool, David, illus. LC 74-78115. 64p. (gr. 5-8). 1975. lib. bdg. 10.85 (*0-8027-6204-2*) Walker & Co.

Bendick, Jeanne. Comets & Meteors: Visitors from Space. (Illus.). 32p. (gr. k-2). 1991. PLB 12.90 (*1-56294-001-5*); pap. 4.95 (*1-878841-55-6*) Millbrook Pr.

Branley, Franklyn M. Comets. rev. ed. Maestro, Giulio, illus. LC 83-46161. 32p. (gr. k-3). 1984. (Crowell Jr Bks); PLB 13.89 (*0-690-04415-1*) HarpC Child Bks.

—Comets. Maestro, Giulio, illus. LC 83-46161. 32p. (ps-3). 1989. 7.95 (*0-694-00199-6*, Trophy); pap. 4.50 (*0-06-445088-0*, Trophy) HarpC Child Bks.

Fradin, Dennis B. Comets, Asteroids, & Meteors. LC 83-23231. (Illus.). 48p. (gr. k-4). 1984. PLB 12.85 (*0-516-01723-3*); pap. 4.95 (*0-516-41723-1*) Childrens.

Krupp, Edwin C. The Comet & You. Krupp, Robin R., illus. LC 84-20152. 48p. (gr. 1-4). 1985. RSBE 13.95 (*0-02-751250-9*, Macmillan Child Bk) Macmillan Child Grp.

Lyon, Charleen C. The Tale of Halley's Comet: An Educational Coloring Book. (Illus.). 32p. (Orig.). (gr. 3-6). 1985. pap. 2.95 (*0-9614973-0-0*) Niota Pr.

Marsh, Carole. Crazy Comet Classroom Gamebook. (Illus., Orig.). (gr. 3-12). 1994. pap. 19.95 (*0-935326-87-1*) Gallopade Pub Group.

Schatz, Dennis & Osawa, Yasu. The Return of the Comet. Osawa, Yasu, illus. 42p. (gr. 4-9). 1985. pap. 7.95 (*0-935051-00-7*) Pacific Sci Ctr.

Simon, Seymour. Comets, Meteors, & Asteroids. LC 93-51251. 1994. write for info. (*0-688-12709-6*); PLB write for info. (*0-688-12710-X*) Morrow Jr Bks.

Sorensen, Lynda. Comets & Meteors. LC 93-15690. (gr. 5 up). 1993. write for info. (*0-86593-277-8*) Rourke Corp.

Spizzirri Publishing Co. Staff. Comets: An Educational Coloring Book. Spizzirri, Linda, ed. (Illus.). 32p. (gr. k-5). 1982. pap. 1.75 (*0-86545-071-4*) Spizzirri.

Winter, Frank H. Comet Watch: The Return of Halley's Comet. (Illus.). 64p. (gr. 4-10). 1986. PLB 13.50 (*0-8225-1579-2*) Lerner Pubns.

COMIC BOOKS, STRIPS, ETC.

see also Cartoons and Caricatures

The Addams Family. 32p. 1991. pap. 2.50 (*0-590-45539-7*) Scholastic Inc.

The Addams Family, Mass Market. 128p. 1991. pap. 2.95 (*0-590-45541-9*) Scholastic Inc.

Avi. City of Light, City of Dark: A Comic Book Novel. Floca, Brian, illus. LC 93-2887. 192p. (gr. 4 up). 1993. 15.95 (*0-531-06800-5*); PLB 15.99 (*0-531-08650-X*) Orchard Bks Watts.

Barks, Carl. Walt Disney's Donald & Gladstone Album. (Illus.). 48p. (Orig.). (ps up). 1988. pap. 5.95 (*0-944599-12-5*) Gladstone Pub.

—Walt Disney's Donald Duck Album. Blum, Geoffrey, intro. by. (Illus.). 48p. (Orig.). 1989. pap. 5.95 (*0-944599-26-5*) Gladstone Pub.

—Walt Disney's Donald Duck Album. Blum, Geoffrey, intro. by. (Illus.). 48p. (Orig.). 1989. pap. 5.95 (*0-944599-23-0*) Gladstone Pub.

—Walt Disney's Donald Duck Family Album. Blum, Geoffrey, intro. by. (Illus.). 48p. (Orig.). 1989. pap. 5.95 (*0-944599-22-2*) Gladstone Pub.

—Walt Disney's Uncle Scrooge Album. Blum, Geoffrey, intro. by. (Illus.). 48p. (Orig.). 1989. pap. 5.95 (*0-944599-24-9*) Gladstone Pub.

—Walt Disney's Uncle Scrooge & Donald Duck Giant Album. Blum, Geoffrey, intro. by. (Illus.). 72p. (Orig.). 1989. pap. 8.95 (*0-944599-27-3*) Gladstone Pub.

—Walt Disney's Uncle Scrooge Comic Album. Barks, Carl, illus. Blum, Geoff, intro. by. (Illus.). 48p. (Orig.). 1989. pap. 5.95 (*0-944599-16-8*) Gladstone Pub.

—Walt Disney's Uncle Scrooge Comic Album. Barks, Carl, illus. Blum, Geoff, intro. by. (Illus.). 48p. (Orig.). 1989. pap. 5.95 (*0-944599-19-2*) Gladstone Pub.

Barks, Carl & Hannah, Jack. Walt Disney's Donald Duck Giant Comic Album. Barks, Carl & Hannah, Jack, illus. Blum, Geoff, intro. by. 72p. (gr. k up). 1989. pap. 8.95 (*0-944599-20-6*) Gladstone Pub.

Barks, Carl & Rosa, Don. Walt Disney's Uncle Scrooge Giant Album. Blum, Geoffrey, intro. by. (Illus.). 96p. (Orig.). 1989. pap. 11.95 (*0-944599-28-1*) Gladstone Pub.

Barks, Carl, illus. Walt Disney's Comics in Color, Vol. 4. rev. ed. 192p. 1990. pap. 19.95 (*0-944599-42-7*) Gladstone Pub.

Barks, Carl & Gollub, Mo, illus. Walt Disney's Comics in Color, Vol. 1. rev. ed. 192p. 1990. pap. 19.95 (*0-944599-39-7*) Gladstone Pub.

Barks, Carl & Gottfredson, Floyd, illus. Walt Disney's Comics in Color. rev. ed. 192p. (ps up). 1990. pap. 19. 95 (*0-944599-35-4*) Gladstone Pub.

—Walt Disney's Comics in Color, Vol. 2. rev. ed. 192p. 1990. pap. 19.95 (*0-944599-40-0*) Gladstone Pub.

—Walt Disney's Comics in Color, Vol. 3. rev. ed. 192p. 1990. pap. 19.95 (*0-944599-41-9*) Gladstone Pub.

—Walt Disney's Comics in Color, Vol. 5. rev. ed. 200p. 1990. pap. 19.95 (*0-944599-38-9*) Gladstone Pub.

—Walt Disney's Comics in Color, Vol. 6. rev. ed. 184p. (ps up). 1990. pap. 19.95 (*0-944599-37-0*) Gladstone Pub.

Barks, Carl & Rosa, Don, illus. Walt Disney's Comics in Color, Vol. 7. rev. ed. 206p. (ps up). 1990. pap. 19.95 (*0-944599-36-2*) Gladstone Pub.

Bond, Michael. Paddington Meets the Queen. Lobban, John, illus. LC 92-24938. 32p. (ps-3). 1993. 3.95 (*0-694-00460-X*, Festival) HarpC Child Bks.

—Paddington Rides On! Lobban, John, illus. LC 92-24937. 32p. (ps-3). 1993. 3.95 (*0-694-00461-8*, Festival) HarpC Child Bks.

Braguet, Anne & Noblet, Martine. India. (Illus.). 76p. (gr. 5 up). 1994. 13.95 (*0-8120-6427-5*); pap. 7.95 (*0-8120-1866-4*) Barron.

Caniff, Milton. The Complete Color Terry & the Pirates, Vol. 1. Marschall, Richard, intros. by. Feiffer, Jules. (Illus.). 96p. (gr. 6 up). 1990. 34.95 (*0-924359-19-6*) Remco Wrldserv Bks.

The Comic Adventures of Felix the Cat. LC 82-74029. (Illus.). 1983. pap. 3.95 (*0-915696-62-2*) Determined Prods.

Cummings, Richard. Make Your Own Comics for Fun & Profit. (gr. 7 up). 1985. 8.95 (*0-679-51208-X*) McKay.

Davis, Jim. La Bonne Vie. (FRE.). 1988. 18.95 (*0-8288-4581-6*) Fr & Eur.

—La Diete, Jamais! (FRE.). 1987. 18.95 (*0-8288-4582-4*) Fr & Eur.

—La Faim Justifie Les Moyens. (FRE.). 1985. 18.95 (*0-8288-4583-2*, F91530) Fr & Eur.

—Faut Pas S'En Faire. (FRE.). 1984. 18.95 (*0-8288-4584-0*, F101551) Fr & Eur.

—Garfield Prend Du Poids. (FRE.). 1984. 18.95 (*0-8288-4586-7*, F101550) Fr & Eur.

—Garfield, Tiens Bon la Rampe. (FRE.). 1989. 18.95 (*0-8288-4585-9*) Fr & Eur.

—Moi, On M'Aime. (FRE.). 1986. 18.95 (*0-8288-4587-5*, M4211) Fr & Eur.

—Qui Dort Dine. (FRE.). 1988. 18.95 (*0-8288-4588-3*) Fr & Eur.

—Tiens Bon la Rampe. (FRE.). 1989. 18.95 (*0-8288-4589-1*) Fr & Eur.

—Les Yeux Plus Gros Que le Ventre. (FRE.). 1985. 18. 95 (*0-8288-4590-5*, F91520) Fr & Eur.

De Bruycker, Daniel & Dauber, Maximilien. Africa. (Illus.). 76p. (gr. 5 up). 1994. 13.95 (*0-8120-6425-9*); pap. 7.95 (*0-8120-1864-8*) Barron.

—China. Walker, Maureen, tr. from FRE. (Illus.). 76p. (gr. 5 up). 1994. 13.95 (*0-8120-6426-7*); pap. 7.95 (*0-8120-1865-6*) Barron.

Disney, Walt. The Rescuers. (ps-3). 1993. 6.98 (*0-453-03010-6*) Mouse Works.

—Snow White. (ps-3). 1993. 6.98 (*0-453-03166-8*) Mouse Works.

Fischer, Steven. There's a Blue Dog under My Bed. Fischer, Thomas, ed. Fischer, Steven, illus. LC 90-84006. 64p. (Orig.). (gr. k-6). 1991. pap. 2.95 (*0-9627367-0-8*) Blue Dog Prodns.

A Flintstones' Family Christmas. (gr. 7 up). 1993. 12.95 (*1-878685-77-5*, Bedrock Press) Turner Pub GA.

The Flintstones' Great Dinosaur Adventure. (Illus.). 32p. (gr. 6-9). 1993. 12.95 (*1-878685-67-8*, Bedrock Press) Turner Pub GA.

Flintstones: the Movie Storybook. 1994. pap. 9.95 (*0-448-40725-6*, Platt & Munk) Putnam Pub Group.

Flintstones: the Novelization. 1994. pap. 3.95 (*0-448-40726-4*, Platt & Munk) Putnam Pub Group.

Fulop, Scott, intro. by. Archie Americana, Vol. 1: The 1940's. King, Stephen, frwd. by. (Illus.). 128p. 1991. pap. 8.95 (*1-879794-00-4*, Archie Comics) Archie Comic.

Gately, George. Heathcliff: The Good Life. 128p. (Orig.). 1992. pap. 3.50 (*0-8125-1745-8*) Tor Bks.

Gottfredson, Floyd. Walt Disney's Mickey Mouse Comic Album. Gottfredson, Floyd, illus. Blum, Geoff, intro. by. (Illus.). 48p. (Orig.). 1989. pap. 5.95 (*0-944599-17-6*) Gladstone Pub.

—Walt Disney's Mickey Mouse Comic Album. Gottfredson, Floyd, illus. Blum, Geoff, intro. by. (Illus.). 48p. (Orig.). 1989. pap. 5.95 (*0-944599-21-4*) Gladstone Pub.

—Walt Disney's Mickey Mouse Giant Album. Blum, Geoffrey, intro. by. (Illus.). 72p. (Orig.). 1989. pap. 8.95 (*0-944599-25-7*) Gladstone Pub.

Gray, Harold. Little Orphan Annie in the Great Depression. Gray, Harold, illus. 58p. (Orig.). (gr. 5 up). 1979. pap. 3.95 (*0-486-23737-0*) Dover.

Have a Scream! with Minnie Mouse. 1993. pap. 6.98 (*0-453-03130-7*) Mouse Works.

Havin' a Ball in Bedrock. (ps-3). 1994. pap. 2.50 (*0-448-40727-2*, Platt & Munk) Putnam Pub Group.

Helfer, Andrew. Batman: Mask of the Phantasm: M-TV. (gr. 4-7). 1994. pap. 3.99 (*0-553-48174-6*, Skylark) Bantam.

Herge. Tintin Games Book, Vol. 1. 1990. pap. 6.95 (*0-316-35858-4*) Little.

Herriman, George. The Komplete Kolor Krazy Kat, Vol. I: 1935-1936. Marschall, Richard, intros. by. Watterson, Bill. (Illus.). 96p. (gr. 6 up). 1990. 34.95 (*0-924359-06-4*) Remco WrldServ Bks.

Hopkins, Andrea. Harald the Ruthless. 1994. write for info. (*0-8050-3176-6*) H Holt & Co.

Horowitz, Jordan. Dennis the Menace. (Illus.). (gr. 4-7). 1993. pap. 3.25 (*0-590-47350-6*) Scholastic Inc.

—Dennis the Menace. (Illus.). (gr. k-2). 1993. pap. 2.95 (*0-590-47349-2*) Scholastic Inc.

The Jetsons Explore Space. (Illus.). 32p. (gr. 6-9). 1993. 12.95 (*1-878685-68-6*, Bedrock Press) Turner Pub GA.

Lander, Michael. Teenage Mutant Ninja Turtle Trivia Quiz Book. (gr. 4-7). 1991. pap. 3.50 (*0-440-40543-2*) Dell.

Lankford, Robert D. Dream Weaver in the Face of Fear, Vol. 1, No. 3. (Illus.). 48p. (gr. 11 up). 1991. pap. 2.75 (*0-9621811-2-9*) Lankford Comics.

Lynde, Stan. Stan Lynde's Pardners, Bk. 1: The Bonding. LC 90-84936. (Illus.). 40p. (Orig.). (gr. 3 up). 1990. pap. 4.95 (*0-9626999-1-8*) Cttnwd Graphics.

McCay, Winsor. The Complete Little Nemo in Slumberland, Vol. III: 1908-1910. Marschall, Richard, intro. by. (Illus.). 96p. (gr. 6 up). 1990. 34.95 (*0-924359-03-X*) Remco Wrldserv Bks.

—The Complete Little Nemo in Slumberland, Vol. IV: 1910-1911. Marschall, Richard, intro. by. (Illus.). 96p. (gr. 6 up). 1990. 34.95 (*0-924359-04-8*) Remco Wrldserv Bks.
McCoy, James C., et al. Comic Tales Anthology, No. 2. 2nd ed. Davenport, May, intro. by. Walker, Timothy, et al, illus. LC 88-70551. 100p. (Orig.). (gr. 7-12). 1988. pap. 6.95x (*0-943864-53-4*) Davenport.
Marvel Staff. Morlock Madness. (gr. 4-7). 1993. pap. 2.50 (*0-679-85710-9*) Random Bks Yng Read.
—Night of the Sentinels, Pt. 1: Meet the X-Men. (gr. 4-7). 1993. pap. 2.50 (*0-679-85707-9*) Random Bks Yng Read.
—Night of the Sentinels, Pt. 2: Wolverine's Vengeance. (gr. 4-7). 1993. pap. 2.50 (*0-679-85708-7*) Random Bks Yng Read.
—To Stop a Juggernaut. (gr. 4-7). 1993. pap. 2.50 (*0-679-85709-5*) Random Bks Yng Read.
Merrison, Tim. Comics & Magazines. Stefoff, Rebecca, ed. LC 90-13985. (Illus.). 32p. (gr. 4-8). 1991. PLB 17.26 (*0-944483-97-6*) Garrett Ed Corp.
Mickey Mouse. (Illus.). 204p. 1991. 17.99 (*0-517-69715-7*) Random Hse Value.
Peeters, Benoit. Tintin & the World of Herge: An Illustrated History. (Illus.). 160p. (gr. 5 up). 1992. 40.00 (*0-316-69752-4*, Joy St Bks) Little.
Riebe, Ernest. Mister Block: IWW Comics. Rosemont, Franklin, ed. (Illus.). 36p. pap. 7.00 (*0-88286-062-3*) C H Kerr.
Salten, Felix. Walt Disney's Bambi Comic Album. Crawford, Mel & Hultgren, Ken, illus. Blum, Geoffrey, intro. by. 48p. (Orig.). (ps up). 1988. pap. 5.95 (*0-944599-09-5*) Gladstone Pub.
Schulz, Charles. Good Grief More Peanuts. (Illus.). 1994. pap. write for info. (*0-8050-3312-2*) H Holt & Co.
—Le Grand Livre des Questions, No. 4: Aux Sujets de Tous les Peuples du Monde et De. (FRE.). 125p. 1992. pap. 10.95 (*0-7859-4569-5*) Fr & Eur.
—Peanuts Sunday. (Illus.). 1994. pap. write for info. (*0-8050-3310-6*) H Holt & Co.
—Unsinkable Charlie Brown. (Illus.). 1994. pap. write for info. (*0-8050-3311-4*) H Holt & Co.
Schulz, Charles M. Al Colegio. (SPA.). 64p. 1971. 4.95 (*0-8288-4506-9*) Fr & Eur.
—Los Amigos de Snoopy. (SPA.). 64p. 1971. 1.50 (*0-8288-4507-7*) Fr & Eur.
—Un Amour de Charlie Brown. (FRE.). 1985. 4.95 (*0-8288-4514-X*) Fr & Eur.
—Apuros Escolares. (SPA.). 64p. 1971. 4.95 (*0-8288-4504-2*) Fr & Eur.
—Le Beagle Est Revenu Sur Terre. (FRE.). 1985. 9.95 (*0-8288-4532-8*) Fr & Eur.
—Un Beagle Qui a Du Chien. (FRE.). 1985. 9.95 (*0-8288-4531-X*) Fr & Eur.
—Belle Mentalite, Snoopy. (FRE.). 1985. 4.95 (*0-8288-4526-3*) Fr & Eur.
—Bienvenue Snoopy. (FRE.). 45p. 1987. 19.95 (*0-8288-4538-7*) Fr & Eur.
—Carlitos y Snoopy. (SPA.). 64p. 1971. 4.95 (*0-8288-4512-3*) Fr & Eur.
—Le Chef des Briquets. (FRE.). 1985. 4.95 (*0-8288-4518-2*) Fr & Eur.
—Deportes de Invierno. (SPA.). 64p. 1971. 4.95 (*0-8288-4508-5*) Fr & Eur.
—Les Dieux du Tennis Etaient Contre Moi. (FRE.). 1985. 9.95 (*0-8288-4528-X*) Fr & Eur.
—Dis Pas de Betises, Charlie Brown. (FRE.). 1985. 4.95 (*0-8288-4520-4*) Fr & Eur.
—Du Calme, Charlie Brown. (FRE.). 1985. 4.95 (*0-8288-4519-0*) Fr & Eur.
—Elementaire Mon Cher Snoopy. (FRE.). 48p. 1988. 18.95 (*0-8288-4539-5*) Fr & Eur.
—Fantastique Snoopy. (FRE.). 47p. 1988. 18.95 (*0-8288-4540-9*) Fr & Eur.
—Feu D'Artifice. (FRE.). 48p. 1989. 19.95 (*0-8288-4541-7*) Fr & Eur.
—Gente Menuda. (SPA.). 64p. 1971. 4.95 (*0-8288-4502-6*) Fr & Eur.
—El Gran Jefe. (SPA.). 64p. 1971. 4.95 (*0-8288-4505-0*) Fr & Eur.
—Le Grand Livre des Questions, No. 4. (FRE.). 160p. 1982. write for info. (*0-7859-4565-2*) Fr & Eur.
—Le Grand Livre Des Questions, No. 5. (FRE.). 158p. 1983. 29.95 (*0-8288-4543-3*) Fr & Eur.
—Home Is on Top of a Doghouse. (Illus.). 1982. 6.95 (*0-915696-52-5*) Determined Prods.
—Inattaquable Snoopy. (FRE.). 123p. 1992. pap. 11.95 (*0-7859-4574-1*) Fr & Eur.
—Incroyable Snoopy. (FRE.). 121p. 1989. pap. 10.95 (*0-7859-4568-7*) Fr & Eur.
—Ineffable Snoopy. (FRE.). 48p. 1985. 18.95 (*0-8288-4547-6*) Fr & Eur.
—Inegalable Snoopy. (FRE.). 124p. 1990. pap. 10.95 (*0-7859-4570-9*) Fr & Eur.
—Inenarrable Snoopy. (FRE.). 48p. 1987. 18.95 (*0-8288-4548-4*) Fr & Eur.
—Inepuisable Snoopy. (FRE.). 48p. 1987. 18.95 (*0-8288-4549-2*) Fr & Eur.
—L' Infaillible Snoopy. (FRE.). 126p. 1990. pap. 10.95 (*0-7859-4571-7*) Fr & Eur.
—Intrepide Snoopy. (FRE.). 48p. 1983. 18.95 (*0-8288-4551-4*) Fr & Eur.
—Invincible Snoopy. (FRE.). 123p. 1991. pap. 11.95 (*0-7859-4573-3*) Fr & Eur.
—Irresistible Snoopy. (FRE.). 124p. 1991. pap. 11.95 (*0-7859-4572-5*) Fr & Eur.
—Je Ne T'Ai Jamais Promis un Verger. (FRE.). 1985. 9.95 (*0-8288-4530-1*) Fr & Eur.
—Joyeuses Paques. (FRE.). 1984. 14.95 (*0-8288-4537-9*) Fr & Eur.
—Meme Mes Critiques Ratent la Cible. (FRE.). 1985. 9.95 (*0-8288-4533-6*) Fr & Eur.
—Mi Pequeno Mundo. (SPA.). 64p. 1971. 4.95 (*0-8288-4501-8*) Fr & Eur.
—Misere! Charlie Brown. (FRE.). 1985. 4.95 (*0-8288-4515-8*) Fr & Eur.
—Ne Me Casse Pas les Oreilles. (FRE.). 1984. 9.95 (*0-8288-4534-4*) Fr & Eur.
—No Me Comprenden. (SPA.). 64p. 1971. 4.95 (*0-8288-4511-5*) Fr & Eur.
—El Pajarito Emilio. (SPA.). 64p. 1971. 4.95 (*0-8288-4510-7*) Fr & Eur.
—Regreso al Colegio. (SPA.). 64p. 1971. 4.95 (*0-8288-4509-3*) Fr & Eur.
—Reviens, Snoopy. (FRE.). 48p. 1982. 10.95 (*0-8288-4554-9*) Fr & Eur.
—Reviens, Snoopy: Presses Pocket. (FRE.). 124p. 1989. 10.95 (*0-8288-4555-7*) Fr & Eur.
—Security Is a Thumb & a Blanket. LC 82-70029. (Illus.). 1982. 6.95 (*0-915696-53-3*) Determined Prods.
—Snoopy Arbitre. (FRE.). 1984. 14.95 (*0-8288-4559-X*) Fr & Eur.
—Snoopy Connait La Musique. (FRE.). 128p. 1974. 9.95 (*0-8288-4561-1*) Fr & Eur.
—Snoopy Delire. (FRE.). 50p. 1983. 14.95 (*0-8288-4562-X*) Fr & Eur.
—Snoopy Detective. (FRE.). 50p. 1983. 14.95 (*0-8288-4563-8*) Fr & Eur.
—Snoopy: Droles D'Oiseau. (FRE.). 128p. 1975. 9.95 (*0-8288-4557-3*) Fr & Eur.
—Snoopy Escritor. (SPA.). 64p. 1971. 4.95 (*0-8288-4503-4*) Fr & Eur.
—Snoopy et Compagnie. (FRE.). 156p. 1987. write for info. (*0-8288-4564-6*) Fr & Eur.
—Snoopy Et la Culture. (FRE.). 1975. 9.95 (*0-8288-4565-4*) Fr & Eur.
—Snoopy et la St-Valentin. (FRE.). 1984. 14.95 (*0-8288-4566-2*) Fr & Eur.
—Snoopy Et Ses Freres. (FRE.). 128p. 1974. 9.95 (*0-8288-4567-0*) Fr & Eur.
—Snoopy Et Son Copain Linus. (FRE.). 128p. 1975. 9.95 (*0-8288-4568-9*) Fr & Eur.
—Snoopy Grand Coeur. (FRE.). 1975. 9.95 (*0-8288-4569-7*) Fr & Eur.
—Snoopy, le Petit Receuil de Pensees. (FRE.). 1985. write for info. (*0-8288-4558-1*) Fr & Eur.
—Snoopy Patineur. (FRE.). 1984. 14.95 (*0-8288-4570-0*) Fr & Eur.
—Snoopy Prestidigitateur. (FRE.). 50p. 1983. 14.95 (*0-8288-4571-9*) Fr & Eur.
—Snoopy S'En Va-T-En Guerre. (FRE.). 128p. 1974. 9.95 (*0-8288-4572-7*) Fr & Eur.
—Snoopy's Love Book. (gr. 1 up). 1994. 6.95 (*0-8050-3146-4*) H Holt & Co.
—Sois Philosophe, Charlie Brown. (FRE.). 1985. 4.95 (*0-8288-4517-4*) Fr & Eur.
—T'As Pas de Veine, Charlie Brown. (FRE.). 1985. 4.95 (*0-8288-4525-5*) Fr & Eur.
—Te Fais Pas de Bile, Charlie Brown. (FRE.). 1985. 4.95 (*0-8288-4523-9*) Fr & Eur.
—T'Es le Meilleur, Charlie Brown. (FRE.). 1985. 4.95 (*0-8288-4521-2*) Fr & Eur.
—Tiens Bon, Charlie Brown. (FRE.). 1985. 4.95 (*0-8288-4527-1*) Fr & Eur.
—Tout Connaitre en S'Amusant: Camions. (FRE.). 32p. 1983. 10.95 (*0-8288-4578-6*) Fr & Eur.
—Tout Connaitre en S'Amusant: La Ferme. (FRE.). 34p. 1982. 10.95 (*0-8288-4573-5*) Fr & Eur.
—Tout Connaitre en S'Amusant: La Nature. (FRE.). 34p. 1983. 10.95 (*0-8288-4574-3*) Fr & Eur.
—Tout Connaitre en S'Amusant: La Plage. (FRE.). 34p. 1982. 10.95 (*0-8288-4575-1*) Fr & Eur.
—Tout Connaitre en S'Amusant: Les Avions. (FRE.). 34p. 1982. 10.95 (*0-8288-4576-X*) Fr & Eur.
—Tout Connaitre en S'Amusant: Maisons. (FRE.). 32p. 1983. 10.95 (*0-8288-4579-4*) Fr & Eur.
—Tout Connaitre en S'Amusant: Saisons. (FRE.). 32p. 1983. 10.95 (*0-8288-4580-8*) Fr & Eur.
—Tu Cours Apres l'Ete, et l'Hiver... (FRE.). 1985. 9.95 (*0-8288-4535-2*) Fr & Eur.
—Tu Te Crois Malin, Charlie Brown. (FRE.). 1985. 4.95 (*0-8288-4522-0*) Fr & Eur.
—Tu Veux Rire, Charlie Brown. (FRE.). 1985. 4.95 (*0-8288-4524-7*) Fr & Eur.
—Une Vie de Chien. (FRE.). 1985. 4.95 (*0-8288-4513-1*) Fr & Eur.
—Vois la Vie en Rose, Snoopy. (FRE.). 1985. 4.95 (*0-8288-4516-6*) Fr & Eur.
—What's Wrong with Being Crabby? 128p. (ps-2). 1992. pap. 6.95 (*0-8050-2400-X*, Owl Bks) H Holt & Co.
—Y'A Qu'Un Woodstock. (FRE.). 1985. 9.95 (*0-8288-4529-8*) Fr & Eur.
Scott, Elaine. Funny Papers: Behind the Scenes of the Comics. Miller, Margaret, photos by. LC 92-46727. (Illus.). 96p. (gr. 3 up). 1993. 15.00 (*0-688-11575-6*); PLB 14.93 (*0-688-11576-4*) Morrow Jr Bks.
Smith, Frank C. I Can Draw Comics & Cartoons. Smith, Frank C., illus. 64p. (Orig.). (gr. 3 up). 1982. pap. 3.95 (*0-671-44490-5*, Little Simon) S&S Trade.
Sterrett, Cliff. The Complete Color Polly & Her Pals, Vol. I: The Surrealist Period, 1926-1927. Marschall, Richard, intros. by. Spiegelman, Art. (Illus.). 96p. 1990. 34.95 (*0-924359-14-5*) Remco Wrldserv Bks.
Walker, Mort. Beetle Bailey: Three's a Crowd. 288p. (Orig.). 1986. pap. 2.95 (*0-8125-6111-2*) Tor Bks.
Walt Disney Staff. Donald & His Friends. 1988. 6.98 (*0-8317-2392-0*) Viking Child Bks.
—Great Mouse Detective. 1988. 6.98 (*0-8317-3993-2*) Viking Child Bks.
—Little Mermaid. 1989. 6.98 (*0-8317-5605-5*) Viking Child Bks.
—Mickey's Christmas Carol. 1988. 6.98 (*0-8317-5929-1*) Viking Child Bks.
—Robin Hood. 1989. 6.98 (*0-8317-7408-8*) Viking Child Bks.
—Sword in the Stone. 1988. 6.98 (*0-8317-8015-0*) Viking Child Bks.
Watterson, Bill. The Essential Calvin & Hobbes: A Calvin & Hobbes Treasury. Watterson, Bill, illus. Schulz, Charles. 256p. 1988. 19.95 (*0-8362-1809-4*); pap. 12.95 (*0-8362-1805-1*) Andrews & McMeel.
Wenk, Richard. Batman & the Doomsday Prophecy. Delbo, Jose, illus. (gr. 3-6). 1989. pap. 2.99 (*0-671-68312-8*, Archway) PB.
Wright, Dan. Way Cool Comic, No. 1, Pt. 1. 27p. 1993. 1.95 (*0-685-70279-0*) Bristol Hse.
—Way Cool Comic, No. 1, Pt. 2. 27p. 1993. 1.95 (*0-917851-64-1*) Bristol Hse.
Yabba Dabba Doo Adventure. (ps-3). 1994. pap. 2.50 (*0-448-40728-0*, Platt) Putnam Pub Group.

COMIC BOOKS, STRIPS, ETC.–MORAL AND RELIGIOUS ASPECTS

Walt Disney Staff. Follow that Squeak with Mickey Mouse. (ps-3). 1993. 6.98 (*0-453-03092-0*) Mouse Works.

COMIC LITERATURE

see Satire

COMIC OPERA

see Opera

COMMANDMENTS, TEN

see Ten Commandments

COMMENTARIES, BIBLICAL

see Bible–Commentaries

COMMERCE

see also Banks and Banking; Business; Geography, Commercial; Merchants; Retail Trade; Statistics; Stock Exchange; Stocks; Trade Routes; Transportation

Across Africa & Arabia. (Illus.). 128p. 1990. 17.95x (*0-8160-1878-2*) Facts on File.
Across Asia by Land. (Illus.). 128p. 1990. 17.95x (*0-8160-1874-X*) Facts on File.
The American Way West. (Illus.). 128p. 1990. 17.95x (*0-8160-1880-4*) Facts on File.
Dudley, William, ed. Trade: Opposing Viewpoints. LC 90-24087. (Illus.). 264p. (gr. 10 up). 1991. PLB 17.95 (*0-89908-176-2*); pap. 9.95 (*0-89908-151-7*) Greenhaven.
Sold! The Origins of Money & Trade. LC 93-37782. 1994. PLB write for info. (*0-8225-3206-9*, Runestone Pr) Lerner Pubns.
The Southern World. (Illus.). 128p. 1990. 17.95x (*0-8160-1881-2*) Facts on File.
Williams, Brian. Trading. Robinson, Bernard, illus. LC 92-27031. 48p. (gr. 5-8). 1993. PLB 21.34 (*0-8114-4787-1*) Raintree Steck-V.

COMMERCIAL ART

see also Costume Design; Posters

COMMERCIAL AVIATION

see Aeronautics, Commercial

COMMERCIAL EDUCATION

see Business Education

COMMERCIAL GEOGRAPHY

see Geography, Commercial

COMMERCIAL PRODUCTS

see also Geography, Commercial; Manufactures; Marine Resources

COMMERCIAL SCHOOLS

see Business Education

COMMERCIAL TRAVELERS

see Salesmen and Salesmanship

COMMODORE 64 (COMPUTER)

Buxton, Robin. Commodore 64, Vol. 1. 50p. (gr. 4-12). 1983. pap. text ed. 11.95 (*0-88193-041-5*) Create Learn.
—Commodore 64, Vol. 2. 58p. (gr. 4-12). 1983. pap. text ed. 11.95 (*0-88193-042-3*) Create Learn.
Buxton, Robin & Buxton, Marilyn. Commodore 64, Vol. 3. 59p. (gr. 5-12). 1983. pap. text ed. 11.95 (*0-88193-043-1*) Create Learn.
—Commodore 64, Vol. 4. 59p. (gr. 5-12). 1983. pap. text ed. 11.95 (*0-88193-044-X*) Create Learn.
Captain Comal's Staff. Cartridge Graphics & Sound. Hejndorf, Frank, illus. 64p. (Orig.). (gr. 6 up). 1984. pap. 6.95 (*0-928411-02-8*) Comal Users.
Skelton, Mindy. Graphics Primer. Schmidt, Wayne, illus. 84p. (Orig.). (gr. 6 up). 1984. pap. 14.95 (*0-928411-04-4*) Comal Users.

COMMON MARKET

see European Economic Community

COMMON SCHOOLS

see Public Schools

COMMONWEALTH, THE

see Political Science

COMMONWEALTH OF ENGLAND

see Great Britain–History–Civil War and Commonwealth, 1642-1660

COMMUNAL LIVING

see Collective Settlements

COMMUNES

see Collective Settlements

COMMUNICABLE DISEASES

see also Bacteriology; Immunity; Vaccination

Diskavich, Laura & Woods, Samuel, Jr. Everything You Need to Know about STD (Sexually Transmitted Diseases) Rosen, Ruth, ed. (gr. 7-12). 1990. PLB 14. 95 (*0-8239-1799-1*) Rosen Group.

Harris. Communicable Diseases. 1993. write for info. (*0-8050-3040-9*) H Holt & Co.

Harris, Jacqueline L. Communicable Diseases. (Illus.). 64p. (gr. 5-8). 1993. PLB 14.95 (*0-8050-2599-5*) TFC Bks NY.

McCauslin, Mark. Sexually Transmitted Diseases. LC 91-18445. (Illus.). 48p. (gr. 5-6). 1992. text ed. 12.95 RSBE (*0-89686-720-X*, Crestwood Hse) Macmillan Child Grp.

Nelson, JoAnne. When I'm Sick. Keith, Doug, illus. LC 93-9348. 1994. 5.95 (*0-935529-61-6*) Comprehen Health Educ.

Nourse, Alan E. Lumps, Bumps, & Rashes: A Look at Kids' Diseases. rev. ed. LC 90-32785. (Illus.). 64p. (gr. 5-8). 1990. PLB 12.90 (*0-531-10865-1*) Watts.

—Sexually Transmitted Diseases. LC 91-21707. (Illus.). 128p. (gr. 9-12). 1992. PLB 14.40 (*0-531-11065-6*) Watts.

COMMUNICATION

see also Books and Reading; Language and Languages; Newspapers; Postal Service; Writing

Barbour, William, ed. The Mass Media: Opposing Viewpoints. LC 93-30960. (Illus.). 264p. (gr. 10 up). 1994. PLB 17.95 (*1-56510-107-3*); pap. text ed. 9.95 (*1-56510-106-5*) Greenhaven.

Barker, Larry L. Communication Skills: Objectives & Criterion Referenced Exercises for Grades 7-12. (Illus.). 321p. (Orig.). 1988. pap. text ed. 84.95 incl. Listening Skills (*0-685-27248-6*) SPECTRA Inc.

Beechick, Ruth. A Strong Start in Language: Grades K-3. 32p. (Orig.). (gr. k-3). 1986. pap. 4.00 (*0-940319-02-0*) Arrow Press.

Bernhard, Gwyn K. Gwyn Karon Bernhard's Kids' Talk: Kids' Talk in the Classroom Workbook, No. 1. 125p. (gr. 5-9). 1989. 85.00 (*1-87-781904-2*) Kids Talk CT.

Berry, Joy. Every Kid's Guide to Being a Communicator. (Illus.). 48p. (gr. 3-7). 1987. 5.95 (*0-516-21418-7*) Childrens.

Borchers, Deena. Communicating with Friends. (Illus.). 48p. (gr. 9-12). 1992. pap. 8.99 (*1-55945-228-5*) Group Pub.

Boy Scouts of America Staff. Cub Scout Academics: Communicating. (Illus.). 112p. 1992. pap. 1.35 (*0-8395-3033-1*, 33033) BSA.

Butterworth, Rod R. & Flodin, Mickey. The Pocket Dictionary of Signing. rev. ed. 224p. (Orig.). 1992. pap. 5.95 (*0-399-51743-X*, Perigee Bks) Berkley Pub.

Dixon, Malcolm. Communications. LC 90-22495. (Illus.). 48p. (gr. 5-8). 1991. 12.90 (*0-531-18411-0*, Pub. by Bookwright Pr) Watts.

Dolan, Edward F. Communications. 1995. PLB write for info. (*0-8050-2861-7*) H Holt & Co.

Educational Assessment Publishing Company Staff. Parent - Child Learning Library: Communication English Big Book. (Illus.). 32p. (gr. k-3). 1991. text ed. 16.95 (*0-942277-75-9*) Am Guidance.

—Parent - Child Learning Library: Communication Spanish Big Book. (SPA., Illus.). 32p. (gr. k-3). 1991. text ed. 16.95 (*0-942277-76-7*) Am Guidance.

—Parent - Child Learning Library: Communication Spanish Edition. (SPA.). 32p. (ps). 1991. text ed. 9.95 (*0-942277-93-7*) Am Guidance.

—Parent - Child Learning Library: Communication. (Illus.). 32p. (ps). 1991. text ed. 9.95 (*0-942277-61-9*) Am Guidance.

Fant, Louie J., Jr. Intermediate Sign Language. LC 78-61003. (Illus.). 225p. (gr. 7 up). 1980. text ed. 24.95 (*0-917002-54-7*) Joyce Media.

Franck, Irene M. & Brownstone, David M. Communicators. (Illus.). 240p. (gr. 7 up). 1986. 17.95x (*0-8160-1443-4*) Facts on File.

Frisch, Carlienne & Balcziak, Bill. Communications, Reading Level 5: Today & Tomorrow, 6 bks. (Illus.). 288p. (gr. 4-8). 1989. Set. PLB 103.60 (*0-685-54148-7*); lib. bdg. 77.70s.p. (*0-86592-055-9*) Rourke Corp.

Gardner, Robert. Communication. (Illus.). 96p. (gr. 5-8). 1994. bds. 16.95 (*0-8050-2854-4*) TFC Bks NY.

Gay, Kathlyn. Getting Your Message Across. LC 92-41820. (Illus.). 128p. (gr. 6 up). 1993. text ed. 13.95 RSBE (*0-02-735815-1*, New Discovery Bks) Macmillan Child Grp.

Geiger, Eve. Two Hundred & Ninety-Two Activities for Literature & Language Arts. (gr. 1-6). 1990. pap. 8.95 (*0-8224-6746-1*) Fearon Teach Aids.

Gilbert, Sara. You Can Speak up in Class. Doty, Roy, illus. 64p. (gr. 3 up). 1991. pap. 6.95 (*0-688-10304-9*, Pub. by Beech Tree Bks) Morrow.

—You Can Speak up in Class. Doty, Roy, illus. LC 90-19268. 64p. (gr. 3 up). 1991. PLB 12.88 (*0-688-09867-3*) Morrow Jr Bks.

Griffer, D. More Hearsay: Interactive Listening & Speaking. 1994. pap. text ed. 12.95 (*0-201-50969-5*); cassette 55.00 (*0-8013-1374-0*, 76357) Longman.

Gross, Ruth B. You Don't Need Words. Ryan, Susannah, illus. 48p. 1991. 13.95 (*0-590-43897-2*, Scholastic Hardcover) Scholastic Inc.

Hamilton, Harley. Grandfather Moose: Children's Sign Language Book with Rhymes, Games & Chants. 32p. 1989. pap. 8.50 (*0-916708-21-7*) Modern Signs.

Hawkes, Nigel. Communications. (Illus.). 32p. (gr. 5-8). PLB 13.95 (*0-8050-3420-X*) TFC Bks NY.

Helgesen, M., et al. Talking Together. 1903. pap. text ed. 9.95 (*0-582-10240-5*); cassette 37.95 (*0-582-10237-5*) Longman.

Huisingh, Rosemary, et al. ACHIEV-Blue (Activities for Children Involving Everyday Vocabulary) (ps-5). 1989. complete pkg. 198.70 (*1-55999-002-3*) LinguiSystems.

—ACHIEV-Blue Books (Activities for Children Involving Everyday Vocabulary) (ps-5). 1986. spiral manual 49. 95 (*1-55999-004-X*) LinguiSystems.

Juntune, Joyce E. Developing Creative Thinking: Fun Book, No. 2. Dougherty, Edie, illus. 26p. (gr. k-4). 1984. pap. 5.00 (*0-912773-08-1*) One Hund Twenty Creat.

Kalman, Bobbie. How We Communicate. (Illus.). 32p. (gr. 2-3). 1986. 15.95 (*0-86505-074-0*) Crabtree Pub Co.

Kerrod, Robin. Communications. Evans, Ted, illus. LC 93-1913. 64p. (gr. 5 up). 1993. PLB write for info. (*1-85435-624-0*) Marshall Cavendish.

Kramer, Patricia. Discovering Self-Expression & Communication. (gr. 7-12). 1991. PLB 14.95 (*0-8239-1276-0*) Rosen Group.

LinguiSystems Staff. ACHIEV-Red Sing-a-Longs Manual (Activities for Children Involving Everyday Vocabulary - Home & Family Vocabulary) (ps-3). 1989. 27.95 (*1-55999-006-6*) LinguiSystems.

Littlefield, Kathy M. & Littlefield, Robert S. Let's Work Together! Stark, Steve, illus. 32p. (Orig.). (gr. 3-6). 1991. pap. text ed. 8.95 (*1-879340-08-9*, K0109) Kidspeak.

—Speak Up! Stark, Steve, illus. 32p. (Orig.). (gr. 3-6). 1989. pap. text ed. 8.95 (*1-879340-00-3*, K0101) Kidspeak.

Littlefield, Robert S. & Ball, Jane A. Who Am I? Who Are They? Stark, Steve, illus. 28p. (Orig.). (gr. 3-6). 1990. pap. text ed. 8.95 (*1-879340-06-2*, K0107) Kidspeak.

McCutcheon, Randall, et al. Communication Matters. LC 93-10452. 1993. text ed. 43.75 (*0-314-01390-3*) West Pub.

Mayo, Patty, et al. Communicate Junior. Madsen, Kris, illus. 60p. (gr. 1-4). 1991. incl. game board 35.00 (*0-930599-68-3*) Thinking Pubns.

Nelson, Nigel. Body Talk. De Saulles, Tony, illus. LC 93-27780. 32p. (gr. k-2). 1993. 12.95 (*1-56847-099-1*) Thomson Lrning.

Orange County Association Staff. Frases Fundamentales para Comunicarse. (gr. k-12). 1975. 5.15 (*0-89075-200-1*) Bilingual Ed Serv.

Palumbo, Thomas. Language Arts Thinking Motivators. 96p. (gr. 2-7). 1988. wkbk. 9.95 (*0-86653-432-6*, GA1050) Good Apple.

Schwartz, Linda. Trivia Trackdown-Communication & Transportation. (Illus.). 32p. (gr. 4-6). 1986. 3.95 (*0-88160-139-X*, LW258) Learning Wks.

Sesame Street Staff. Sesame Street Sign Language Fun. Cooke, Tom, illus. Selkirk, Neil, photos by. LC 79-5570. (Illus.). 72p. (ps-3). 1980. 10.00 (*0-394-84212-X*) Random Bks Yng Read.

Skurzynski, Gloria. Get the Message: Telecommunications in Your High-Tech World. LC 92-14892. (Illus.). 64p. (gr. 4 up). 1993. SBE 16.95 (*0-02-778071-6*, Bradbury Pr) Macmillan Child Grp.

Slier, Debby. A First Book of Sign Language: Animal Signs. 16p. (ps). 1993. 4.95 (*1-56288-385-2*) Checkerboard.

—A First Book of Sign Language: Word Signs. 16p. (ps). 1993. 4.95 (*1-56288-386-0*) Checkerboard.

Swanson, Norma F. Horizons Plus: A Student's Progress Profile. 1988. write for info. Window World NY.

Thurston, Cheryl M. Cottonwood Game Book. 58p. (Orig.). (gr. 5-12). 1986. pap. text ed. 14.95 (*1-877673-01-3*) Cottonwood Pr.

Traxler, Mary A. Elementary Language Arts Flipper, No. I. 39p. (gr. 4 up). 1989. trade edition 6.25 (*1-878383-15-9*) C Lee Pubns.

Weiss, Ann E. Who's to Know? Information, the Media & Public Awareness. 192p. (gr. 5-9). 1990. 14.45 (*0-395-49702-7*) HM.

Wirths, Claudine G. & Bowman-Kruhm, Mary. Your Power with Words. (Illus.). 64p. (gr. 5-8). 1993. PLB 14.95 (*0-8050-2075-6*) TFC Bks NY.

Zachman, Linda, et al. ACHIEV-Red (Activities for Children Involving Everyday Vocabulary) Package. (ps-5). 1989. commplete pkg. 198.70 (*1-55999-001-5*) LinguiSystems.

—ACHIEV-Red Books (Activities for Children Involving Everyday Vocabulary) (ps-5). 1985. spiral manuals 49. 95 (*1-55999-005-8*) LinguiSystems.

COMMUNICATION–FICTION

Everett, Louise. Amigo Means Friend. Radinowitz, Sandy, illus. LC 87-11274. 32p. (gr. k-2). 1988. PLB 7.89 (*0-8167-1000-7*); pap. text ed. 1.95 (*0-8167-1001-5*) Troll Assocs.

Hughes, Shirley. Chatting. LC 93-22747. 24p. (ps up). 1994. 13.95 (*1-56402-340-0*) Candlewick Pr.

Hutchins, Pat. The Surprise Party. Hutchins, Pat, illus. LC 91-10599. 32p. (gr. k-3). 1991. pap. 16.95 big bk. (*0-689-71542-0*, Aladdin); pap. 3.95 (*0-689-71543-9*, Aladdin) Macmillan Child Grp.

Lowry, Lois. Anastasia Krupnik. 128p. 1984. pap. 3.25 (*0-553-15534-2*) Bantam.

Nordstrom, Ursula. Secret Language. LC 60-7701. (Illus.). 192p. (gr. 3-5). 1972. pap. 3.95 (*0-06-440022-0*, Trophy) HarpC Child Bks.

Pfeffer, Susan B. What Do You Do When Your Mouth Won't Open? Tomei, Lorna, illus. LC 80-68731. 160p. (gr. 4-6). 1981. 8.95 (*0-440-09471-2*); pap. 9.89 (*0-385-29140-X*) Delacorte.

Schulman, Janet. The Big Hello. Hoban, Lillian, illus. 32p. (gr. 1-4). 1980. pap. 1.95 (*0-440-40484-3*, YB) Dell.

COMMUNICATION–HISTORY

Ardley, Neil. Language & Communications. LC 89-31561. (Illus.). 40p. (gr. 6-8). 1989. PLB 12.40 (*0-531-17187-6*, Gloucester Pr) Watts.

Ventura, Piero & Casalini, Max. Communication: The Ways & Means of Spreading Information. LC 94-4521. 1994. 16.95 (*0-395-66789-5*) HM.

COMMUNICATION AMONG ANIMALS

see Animal Communication

COMMUNISM

see also Individualism; Social Conflict

Kort, Michael. Marxism in Power: The Rise & Fall of a Doctrine. LC 92-15697. (Illus.). 176p. (gr. 7 up). 1993. PLB 16.90 (*1-56294-241-7*) Millbrook Pr.

Trager, Oliver, ed. Communism: The Final Crisis? 224p. 1990. lib. bdg. 29.95x (*0-8160-2507-X*) Facts on File.

COMMUNISM–FICTION

Huxley, Aldous. Brave New World. abr. ed. 137p. 1973. pap. text ed. 5.95 (*0-582-53033-4*) Longman.

Pride, Mary. The Better Butter Battle. (Illus.). 48p. 1990. 8.95 (*0-943497-93-0*) Wolgemuth & Hyatt.

COMMUNIST CHINA

see China (People's Republic of China)

COMMUNIST COUNTRIES

Trager, Oliver, ed. Communism: The Final Crisis? 224p. 1990. lib. bdg. 29.95x (*0-8160-2507-X*) Facts on File.

COMMUNITY CHESTS

see Fund Raising

COMMUNITY LIFE

see also Cities and Towns

Bogart, Ann, photos by. Thinking Green: My Neighborhood. (Illus.). 24p. (ps-k). 1993. 3.98 (*0-8317-2529-X*) Smithmark.

Kalman, Bobbie. Colonial Crafts. (Illus.). 32p. (gr. k-9). 1992. PLB 15.95 (*0-86505-490-8*); pap. 7.95 (*0-86505-510-6*) Crabtree Pub CO.

—A Colonial Town: Williamsburg. (Illus.). 32p. (gr. k-9). 1992. PLB 15.95 (*0-86505-489-4*); pap. 7.95 (*0-86505-509-2*) Crabtree Pub Co.

—The Gristmill. (Illus.). 32p. (gr. 3-4). 1991. PLB 15.95 (*0-86505-486-X*); pap. 7.95 (*0-86505-506-8*) Crabtree Pub Co.

—Home Crafts. (Illus.). 32p. (gr. 3-4). 1990. PLB 15.95 (*0-86505-485-1*); pap. 7.95 (*0-86505-505-X*) Crabtree Pub Co.

—The Kitchen. (Illus.). 32p. (gr. 3-4). 1990. PLB 15.95 (*0-86505-484-3*); pap. 7.95 (*0-86505-504-1*) Crabtree Pub Co.

—Tools & Gadgets. (Illus.). 32p. (gr. k-9). 1992. PLB 15. 95 (*0-86505-488-6*); pap. 7.95 (*0-86505-508-4*) Crabtree Pub CO.

McKaughan, Larry. Why Are Your Fingers Cold? Keenan, Joy D., illus. LC 92-16549. 32p. (Orig.). (ps-1). 1992. 14.95 (*0-8361-3604-7*) Herald Pr. Childlike questions & reassuring answers are complemented by exquisite illustrations. Several family groupings including African American & Caucasian people appear, as children & adults interact. This delightful picture book helps children to become more sensitive to the needs of others. It fosters a strong sense of extended family & community. For children ages 2 to 6 & the adults that love them. *Publisher Provided Annotation.*

Plattner, Sandra S. Connecting with My Community. (ps-k). 1991. pap. 10.95 (*0-8224-3912-3*) Fearon Teach Aids.

Time Life Editors. Who Named My Street Magnolia? First Questions & Answers about Neighborhoods. Mark, Sara, ed. (Illus.). 48p. (ps-k). 1995. PLB write for info. (*0-7835-0898-0*) Time-Life.

COMMUNITY LIFE–FICTION

Arnold, Tedd. The Simple People. Shachat, Andrew, illus. LC 91-17697. 32p. (ps-3). 1992. 14.00 (*0-8037-1012-7*); PLB 13.89 (*0-8037-1013-5*) Dial Bks Young.

Borntrager, Mary C. Daniel. large type ed. 160p. (gr. 4 up). 1993. pap. 8.95 (*0-8361-3639-X*) Herald Pr.

Carlson, Nancy. Loudmouth George & the New Neighbors. LC 83-7298. (Illus.). 32p. (ps-3). 1983. PLB 13.50 (*0-87614-216-1*) Carolrhoda Bks.

Cooper, Melrose. I Got Community. 1995. write for info. (*0-8050-3179-0*) H Holt & Co.

Cowley, Stewart. From My Window. (ps). 1994. 2.99 (*0-89577-595-6*, Readers Digest Kids) RD Assn.

DiSalvo-Ryan, DyAnne. City Green. LC 93-27117. 1994. write for info. (*0-688-12786-X*); PLB write for info. (*0-688-12787-8*) Morrow Jr Bks.

Faulkner, Keith. My New Neighbors. Lambert, Jonathan, illus. 24p. (ps-2). 1992. 9.95 (*0-694-00426-X*, Festival) HarpC Child Bks.

Gackenbach, Dick. Claude Has a Picnic. Gackenbach, Dick, illus. LC 92-8242. 32p. (ps-1). 1993. 14.95 (*0-395-61161-X*, Clarion Bks) HM.

Ghrist, Julie, illus. Taelly's Counting Adventures: In the Neighborhood. 12p. (ps). 1993. 4.95 (*1-56828-030-0*) Red Jacket Pr.

Henwood, Simon. The Troubled Village. (Illus.). 26p. (ps-3). 1991. 13.95 (*0-374-37780-4*) FS&G.

Heo, Yumi. One Afternoon. LC 93-49394. (Illus.). 32p. (ps-1). 1994. 15.95 (*0-531-06845-5*); lib. bdg. 15.99 (*0-531-08695-X*) Orchard Bks Watts.

Hest, Amy. How to Get Famous in Brooklyn. Sawaya, Linda D., illus. LC 93-35920. 1995. 14.00 (*0-02-743655-1*, Four Winds) Macmillan Child Grp.

Hillert, Margaret. Take a Walk, Johnny. (Illus.). (ps-2). 1981. PLB 6.95 (*0-8136-5111-5*, TK2256); pap. 3.50 (*0-8136-5611-7*, TK2257) Modern Curr.

Hurwitz, Johanna. New Neighbors for Nora. Jeschke, Susan, illus. LC 78-12631. 80p. (gr. k-3). 1979. 11.95 (*0-688-22173-4*) Morrow Jr Bks.

Komaiko, Leah. My Perfect Neighborhood. Westman, Barbara, illus. LC 89-37871. 32p. (ps-3). 1990. HarpC Child Bks.

Levy, Elizabeth. Something Queer Is Going On. Gerstein, Mordicai, illus. 48p. (gr. 1-4). 1982. pap. 3.25 (*0-440-47974-6*, YB) Dell.

Marion, Kenneth P. Volunteer Firefighter. Beyer, Beverly, illus. 32p. (Orig.). (ps-2). 1990. pap. 4.00 (*0-945878-00-1*) JK Pub.
In VOLUNTEER FIREFIGHTER, Brad, a city kid, moves to the suburbs & is faced, for the first time, with an empty firehouse. This puzzling fact is soon understood. A fire down the street from his new house prompts a call to 911, which he recently learned about in school. As the VOLUNTEER FIREFIGHTERS arrive, Brad sees mothers & fathers of his new friends & local storekeepers including the banker that he recognizes. After the fire is extinguished, Brad returns to the firehouse where he learns about volunteering; as the book closes, Brad helps too. VOLUNTEER FIREFIGHTER combines the excitement of a traditional firefighting story with the concept of 911 & the principle of volunteering. "We need more material for young children that they can enjoy & from which they can gain reinforcement of our basic values." --Smithtown News. VOLUNTEER FIREFIGHTER is beautifully illustrated by Beverly Beyer. VOLUNTEER FIREFIGHTER is available from JK Publishing, Box 994, Kings Park, NY 11754-0994 for $4.00. Quantity orders or additional information please call 516-375-7011.
Publisher Provided Annotation.

Plemons, Marti. Michael & the Dark Cross. (Illus.). 128p. (gr. 3-6). 1992. pap. 4.99 (*0-87403-936-3*, 24-03766) Standard Pub.

Robertson, Keith. Henry Reed's Think Tank. LC 86-4070. 176p. (gr. 3-7). 1986. pap. 12.95 (*0-670-80968-3*) Viking Child Bks.

Ross, Anna. Sesame Street Busy Little Neighborhood, 4 bks. Ewers, Joe, illus. (ps). 1991. Set, 12p. ea. bds. 8.00 (*0-679-80252-5*) Random Bks Yng Read.

Soto, Gary. Living up the Street: Narrative Recollections. 1992. pap. 3.99 (*0-440-21170-0*) Dell.

—Neighborhood Odes. 1993. pap. 3.25 (*0-590-47335-2*) Scholastic Inc.

Stevenson, James. The Worst Goes South. LC 94-25354. 1995. write for info. (*0-688-13059-3*); write for info. (*0-688-13060-7*) Greenwillow.

Witmer, Edith. Ray's Adventures with New Neighbors. (gr. 3 up). 1981. 6.85 (*0-686-30774-7*) Rod & Staff.

Wittlinger, Ellen. Lombardo's Law. LC 92-28916. 1993. 13.95 (*0-395-65969-8*) HM.

—Lombardo's Law. Cohn, Amy, ed. 144p. 1995. pap. 4.95 (*0-688-05294-0*, Beech Tree Bks) Morrow.

Yoaker, Harry. The View. LC 91-13353. (Illus.). 32p. (ps-3). 1992. 14.00 (*0-8037-1105-0*) Dial Bks Young.

Young, Karen E. Hello, Mr. Bennett. 23p. (gr. 1). 1992. pap. text ed. 23.00 big bk. (*1-56843-017-5*); pap. text ed. 4.50 (*1-56843-067-1*) BGR Pub.

COMMUNITY SCHOOLS
see Schools

COMMUNITY SONGBOOKS
see Songbooks

COMPARATIVE ANATOMY
see Anatomy, Comparative

COMPARATIVE LINGUISTICS
see Language and Languages

COMPARATIVE RELIGION
see Religions

COMPLEXION
see Beauty, Personal; Cosmetics

COMPOSERS

Brownell, David. Great Composers, Bk. 1. Conkle, Nancy, illus. (gr. 7 up). 1978. pap. 3.95 (*0-88388-058-X*) Bellerophon Bks.

Great Composers, Bks. 1 & 2. (ARA., Illus.). (gr. 5-12). 1987. Bk. 1. 3.95 (*0-685-73349-1*); Bk. 2. 3.95 (*0-685-73350-5*) Intl Bk Ctr.

Greene, Carol. Franz Joseph Haydn: Great Man of Music. LC 93-37522. (Illus.). 48p. (gr. k-3). 1994. PLB 12.85 (*0-516-04260-2*) Childrens.

—Wolfgang Amadeus Mozart: Musical Genius. LC 92-36879. (Illus.). 48p. (gr. k-3). 1993. PLB 12.85 (*0-516-04256-4*); pap. 4.95 (*0-516-44256-2*) Childrens.

Kendall, Catherine W. More Stories of Composers for Young Musicians. large type ed. (Illus.). 340p. (Orig.). (gr. 1-10). 1985. pap. 12.95 (*0-9610878-1-1*) Toadwood Pubs.

—Stories of Composers for Young Musicians. large type ed. LC 83-103936. (Illus.). 192p. (Orig.). (gr. 1-10). 1982. pap. 12.95 (*0-9610878-0-3*) Toadwood Pubs.
Composers, well-known & some not-so-well known, come alive as real & believable people for children ages 6-16. Based on extensive research & study of the composers' lives & their milieu but without use of excessive dates, pedantic factual material or musicological jargon, each story sets the emotional tone of the life of each musician, beginning with early childhood. The books are set in large type & wide margins, with portraits of composers, a birthday calendar, & recorded sources of composers' works. --"delightful & charming introduction to the world of music composition & performance" --"gives a feel for some of the exciting common threads that run through the lives of extraordinarily gifted musicians" --"communicates the essence of a composer's life in a warmly, perceptive, quiet way" --" Vividly fleshed out each life" --"careful research has been done."--Susan Grille, music educator, SAA Journal. "Composers are introduced as children, who, like the young readers, take music lessons, have brothers & sisters, & get excited over special events. It eavesdrops on conversations between the composer as a child & his parents & draws the reader into the setting, the lifestyle, & the attitudes of the day."-- Phyllis Young, Professor of Cello, American String Teachers Journal. Also available "More Stories of Composers for Young Musicians," 1985, ISBN 0-9610878-1-1. To order contact: Shar Inc., P.O. Box 1411, Ann Arbor, MI 48106. 1-800-248-7427.
Publisher Provided Annotation.

—Stories of Women Composers for Young Musicians. large type ed. (Illus.). 212p. (Orig.). (gr. 1-12). 1993. pap. 12.95 (*0-9610878-2-X*) Toadwood Pubs.

Lambert, Lee. Basic Library of the World's Greatest Music. (Illus.). 155p. (gr. 7 up). 1988. pap. text ed. 39. 00 (*0-9621630-1-5*) L Lambert.

Nichols, Janet. American Music Makers. (Illus.). 232p. (gr. 7 up). 1990. 19.95 (*0-8027-6957-8*); lib. bdg. 19.85 (*0-8027-6958-6*) Walker & Co.

Stwertka, Eve. Duke Ellington: A Life of Music. LC 93-21267. (Illus.). (gr. 9-12). 1994. PLB 14.40 (*0-531-13035-5*) Watts.

Tames, Richard. Frederic Chopin. LC 90-38304. 1991. 12.40 (*0-531-14179-9*) Watts.

Tomb, Eric. Early Composers. Conkle, Nancy, illus. 48p. (Orig.). (gr. 7). 1988. pap. 3.95 (*0-88388-124-1*) Bellerophon Bks.

Venezia, Mike. George Gershwin. Venezia, Mike, illus. LC 94-9478. 48p. (gr. 4 up). 1994. PLB 17.20 (*0-516-04536-9*); pap. 4.95 (*0-516-44536-7*) Childrens.

—Peter Tchaikovsky. Venezia, Mike, illus. LC 94-9479. 48p. (gr. 4 up). 1994. PLB 17.20 (*0-516-04537-7*); pap. 4.95 (*0-516-44537-5*) Childrens.

Ventura, Piero. Great Composers. Ventura, Piero, illus. 128p. 1989. 24.95 (*0-399-21746-0*, Putnam) Putnam Pub Group.

COMPOSITION (ART)
see also Painting

COMPOSITION (RHETORIC)
see Rhetoric;
also names of languages with the subdivision Composition and exercises, e.g. English Language–Composition and exercises

COMPULSORY SCHOOL ATTENDANCE
see School Attendance

COMPUTER-ASSISTED INSTRUCTION

Bitter, Gary G. & Camuse, Ruth A. Using a Microcomputer in the Classroom. (gr. k-12). 1983. pap. text ed. 25.00 (*0-8359-8144-4*, Reston) P-H.

Buxton, Marilyn & Buxton, Robin. PET, Vol. 3. 58p. (gr. 5-12). 1983. pap. text ed. 11.95 (*0-88193-023-7*) Create Learn.

—PET, Vol. 4. 54p. (gr. 5-12). 1983. pap. text ed. 11.95 (*0-88193-024-5*) Create Learn.

Buxton, Robin. Commodore 64, Vol. 1. 50p. (gr. 4-12). 1983. pap. text ed. 11.95 (*0-88193-041-5*) Create Learn.

—Commodore 64, Vol. 2. 58p. (gr. 4-12). 1983. pap. text ed. 11.95 (*0-88193-042-3*) Create Learn.

—PET, Vol. 1. 51p. (gr. 4-12). 1983. pap. text ed. 11.95 (*0-88193-021-0*) Create Learn.

—PET, Vol. 2. 51p. (gr. 5-12). 1983. pap. text ed. 11.95 (*0-88193-022-9*) Create Learn.

—PET, Vol. 5. 72p. (gr. 6-12). 1984. pap. text ed. 11.95 (*0-88193-025-3*) Create Learn.

Buxton, Robin & Buxton, Marilyn. Commodore 64, Vol. 3. 59p. (gr. 5-12). 1983. pap. text ed. 11.95 (*0-88193-043-1*) Create Learn.

—Commodore 64, Vol. 4. 59p. (gr. 5-12). 1983. pap. text ed. 11.95 (*0-88193-044-X*) Create Learn.

Levine, Janice R. Microcomputers in Elementary & Secondary Education: A Guide to Resources. 64p. (gr. k-12). 1983. 3.75 (*0-937597-06-6*, IR-65) ERIC Clear.

Muir, Michael. Fantastic Journey Through Minds & Machines. (gr. 9-12). 1990. pap. text ed. 19.95 incl. 2 5.25 inch disks (*0-924667-74-5*) Intl Society Tech Educ.

Pantiel, Mindy & Petersen, Becky. Kids, Teachers, & Computers: A Guide to Computers in the Elementary School. (Illus.). 176p. 1984. pap. text ed. 25.00 (*0-13-515420-0*); pap. text ed. 16.95 (*0-13-515396-4*) P-H.

Taitt, Henry A. Beginning Projects for Adults. 45p. (Prog. Bk.). (gr. 10 up). 1983. pap. text ed. 11.95 (*0-88193-121-7*) Create Learn.

—Beginning Projects for Junior High. 46p. (gr. 7-9). 1983. pap. text ed. 11.95 (*0-88193-111-X*) Create Learn.

Taitt, Jennifer. IBM, Vol. 1. 55p. (gr. 4-12). 1983. pap. text ed. 11.95 (*0-88193-031-8*) Create Learn.

—IBM, Vol. 2. 54p. (gr. 4-12). 1983. pap. text ed. 11.95 (*0-88193-032-6*) Create Learn.

—IBM, Vol. 3. 51p. (gr. 5-12). 1983. pap. text ed. 11.95 (*0-88193-033-4*) Create Learn.

—IBM, Vol. 4. 66p. (gr. 5-12). 1983. pap. text ed. 11.95 (*0-88193-034-2*) Create Learn.

Taitt, Kathy. Apple, Vol. 1. 59p. (gr. 4-12). 1983. pap. text ed. 11.95 (*0-88193-001-6*) Create Learn.

—Apple, Vol. 2. 61p. (gr. 4-12). 1983. pap. text ed. 11.95 (*0-88193-002-4*) Create Learn.

—Apple, Vol. 3. 55p. (gr. 5-12). 1983. pap. text ed. 11.95 (*0-88193-003-2*) Create Learn.

—Apple, Vol. 4. 57p. (gr. 5-12). 1983. pap. text ed. 11.95 (*0-88193-004-0*) Create Learn.

—Apple, Vol. 5. 57p. (gr. 6-12). 1983. pap. text ed. 11.95 (*0-88193-005-9*) Create Learn.

—Apple, Vol. 6. 68p. (gr. 6-12). 1984. pap. text ed. 11.95 (*0-88193-006-7*) Create Learn.

COMPUTER CONTROL
see Automation

COMPUTER CRIMES

Judson, Karen. Computer Crime: Phreaks, Spies, & Salami Slicers. LC 93-41198. (Illus.). 128p. (gr. 6 up). 1994. lib. bdg. 17.95 (*0-89490-491-4*) Enslow Pubs.

COMPUTER GAMES

Addams, Shay, ed. Quest for Clues, No. III. Dee, Jeff, illus. 198p. 1990. pap. 24.99 (*0-929373-02-2*) Origin Syst.

Computer Club: Includes the Editor, Animated Memory, Strudle, Instant Recall. 1993. pap. text ed. 19.95 incl. disk (*0-8306-4249-8*, Windcrest) TAB Bks.

Consumer Guide Staff, ed. Strategies for Nintendo Games. (Illus.). 128p. 1991. spiralbd. 5.99 (*0-517-03208-2*) Random Hse Value.

Consumer Guides Staff. Super Strategies for Nintendo. 1991. 1.99 (*0-517-07330-7*) Random Hse Value.

Schepp, Debra & Schepp, Brad. Mac Club! Ellinger, Debra, illus. LC 93-8520. 1993. 19.60 (*0-8306-4253-6*) TAB Bks.

—Mac Party! Ellinger, Debra, illus. LC 93-8519. 1993. 19.60 (*0-8306-4250-1*) TAB Bks.

—Shareware for Kids: With Ready-to-Run Programs for the IBM for Ages 2 Through 5. LC 92-35447. (ps-k). 1993. write for info. (*0-8306-4248-X*) TAB Bks.

COMPUTER GRAPHICS

Captain Comal's Staff. Cartridge Graphics & Sound. Hejndorf, Frank, illus. 64p. (Orig.). (gr. 6 up). 1984. pap. 6.95 (*0-928411-02-8*) Comal Users.

Delta Drawing Today - Apple Two. (ps-8). 1993. Repr. of 1982 ed. 69.95 (*1-879387-03-4*) Power Indst LP.

Delta Drawing Today - MS DOS. (ps-8). 1993. Repr. of 1982 ed. 39.95 (*1-879387-01-8*) Power Indst LP.

Delta Drawing Today - MS DOS: Spanish Version. (SPA.). (ps-8). 1992. Repr. of 1982 ed. 39.95 (*1-879387-05-0*) Power Indst LP.

Imagination Station - MS DOS. (ps-8). 1993. 49.95 (*1-879387-50-6*) Power Indst LP.

Kettelkamp, Larry. Computer Graphics: How it Works, What it Does. LC 88-38924. (Illus.). 144p. (gr. 7 up). 1989. 12.95 (*0-688-07504-5*) Morrow Jr Bks.

Maran, Richard. In Full Color Windows 3.1 Expanded. 1993. pap. 12.95 (*0-13-458241-1*) P-H.

Riede, Anne M. Coach's Clipboards. (Illus.). 306p. (Orig.). (gr. 5-8). 1986. 10.95 (*0-931983-02-9*, BCLTXT-3) Basic Comp Lit.

Sabato, Olive. An Easy Guide for Creating Computer Graphics in the Elementary Schools, Videocassette - Glenville School Computer Graphics. Tucker, Dorothy, ed. Dunlap, Susan, intro. by. (Illus.). 36p. (gr. 5-6). 1987. pap. 19.95 lesson plan (*0-942475-06-2*); videocassette 39.95, (*0-942475-05-4*) ArtsAmerica.

Schepp, Debra & Schepp, Brad. Shareware for Kids: With Ready-to-Run Programs for the IBM for Ages 2 Through 5. LC 92-35447. (ps-k). 1993. write for info. (*0-8306-4248-X*) TAB Bks.

Skelton, Mindy. Graphics Primer. Schmidt, Wayne, illus. 84p. (Orig.). (gr. 6 up). 1984. pap. 14.95 (*0-928411-04-4*) Comal Users.

Welsh, Patricia A. Art in BASIC: Computer Graphics Using Apple BASIC. 44p. (gr. 3-6). 1984. wkbk. 5.95 (*1-884620-04-3*) PAW Prods.

COMPUTER LITERACY

Here are entered workson the ability to use and understand computers, including their capabilities, applications, and social implications, in order to function in a computer-based society.

Kennedy, Sandra. Introduction to Computing, Bk. 1. Schroeder, Bonnie, ed. Knapp, William & Kennedy, Kara, illus. (gr. 2). 1989. wkbk. 5.95 (*1-56177-101-5*, 491-1) CES Compu-Tech.

Sodano, Dominick, et al. Computer Literacy & Use. (gr. 4-12). 1983. pap. text ed. 3.25 (*0-9611246-0-1*) Ed Activities.

COMPUTER PROGRAMMING

see Programming (Electronic Computers)

COMPUTER SOFTWARE

see Programming (Electronic Computers)

COMPUTERS

Use for works on modern electronic computers developed after 1945. Works on calculating machines and mechanical computers made before 1945 are entered under Calculating Machines.

see also Calculating Machines; Electronic Data Processing; Information Storage and Retrieval Systems

Advantage International, Inc. Staff. My First Computer Book. (Illus.). 18p. 1992. activity bk. 3.00 (*1-56756-002-4*, SAC200) Advant Intl.

Aliaga, Barbara. Keyboarding for Kids. (Illus.). 99p. (Orig.). (gr. 1-6). 1985. pap. 7.95 (*0-88908-606-0*, 9538) Self-Counsel Pr.

Alternate Computers. 128p. (gr. 7 up). 1989. 19.93 (*0-8094-5745-8*); lib. bdg. 25.93 (*0-8094-5746-6*) Time-Life.

Anderson, Jill & Weinman, Susan. Skill Builders: Course Code 392-2. Schroeder, Bonnie & Doheny, Catherine, eds. Anastasia, Karyn & Black, Jean, illus. 90p. (gr. 4). 1989. pap. text ed. 5.95 (*0-917531-88-4*) CES Compu-Tech.

Asimov, Isaac. How Did We Find Out about Computers? Wool, David, illus. LC 83-40401. 64p. (gr. 5 up). 1984. lib. bdg. 11.85 (*0-8027-6533-5*) Walker & Co.

Ault, Rosalie S. BASIC Programming for Kids. LC 83-12773. (Illus.). 192p. (gr. 5 up). 1983. 10.95 (*0-685-06975-3*) HM.

Barger, Amy & Barger, Andrew. MacFroggy Teaches BASIC. (gr. 5-10). 1993. pap. text ed. 12.00 (*0-944838-39-1*) Med Physics Pub.

Bartoletti, Susan & Lisandrelli, Elaine. Easy Writer: Student Worksheets, Level G. Gompper, Gail, illus. 38p. (Orig.). (gr. 7-9). 1986. pap. text ed. 14.95 (*0-913935-37-9*) ERA-CCR.

—Easy Writer: Student Worksheets, Level H. (Illus.). 38p. (Orig.). (gr. 8-10). 1986. pap. text ed. 14.95 (*0-913935-38-7*) ERA-CCR.

Berliner, Larry & Berliner, Susan. ReWriter, Bk. I. Gompper, Gail, illus. 38p. (Orig.). (gr. 5 up). 1985. Bk. I, gr. 5-8 & high school sp. needs. pap. text ed. 17.95 (*0-913935-28-X*) Bk. II, gr. 6-9 & high school sp. needs. pap. text ed. 17.95 (*0-913935-29-8*) ERA-CCR.

Bertrand, Armand L., Jr. How to Start Understanding the Computer. LC 83-90306. (Illus.). 208p. (Orig.). (gr. 7 up). 1986. pap. 12.95 (*0-912447-02-8*) Eclectical.

Bitter, Gary G. & Camuse, Ruth A. Using a Microcomputer in the Classroom. (gr. k-12). 1983. pap. text ed. 25.00 (*0-8359-8144-4*, Reston) P-H.

Bonnet, Robert L. Computers: Forty-Nine Science Fair Projects. (Illus.). 160p. (gr. 4-7). 1990. 16.95 (*0-8306-7524-8*, 3524); pap. 9.95 (*0-8306-3524-6*) TAB Bks.

Borman, Jami L. A Computer Dictionary for Kids...And Their Parents. (Illus.). (gr. 4-6). Date not set. write for info. (*0-8120-9079-9*) Barron.
Are your kids' questions about "graphical user interfaces" driving you berserk? Frustrated with arcane computer manuals? Don't have the time to be bothered? Jami Lynne Borman's fun & exciting new book, A COMPUTER DICTIONARY FOR KIDS...AND THEIR PARENTS, is the perfect solution! Using illustrations & simple, non-technical language, she makes over 600 computer-related terms clear to kids...AND THEIR PARENTS! From Abbreviation to Zip, each entry uses either a game or an example to make learning EASY & FUN! A COMPUTER DICTIONARY FOR KIDS...AND THEIR PARENTS will make kids comfortable with computers & will answer the questions of parents who've wondered "Am I still smarter than my children?" Jami Lynne Borman is a professional computer consultant, the author of four other books on computers & a mother.. .the perfect author for your perfect solution!
Publisher Provided Annotation.

Buxton, Marilyn. Beginning Projects for Children. Harrison, Gaye, illus. 47p. (gr. 4-7). 1983. pap. text ed. 11.95 (*0-88193-101-2*) Create Learn.

—Intermediate Projects for Children. Harrison, Gaye, illus. 60p. (gr. 5-7). 1983. pap. text ed. 11.95 (*0-88193-103-9*) Create Learn.

Buxton, Marilyn & Buxton, Robin. PET, Vol. 3. 58p. (gr. 5-12). 1983. pap. text ed. 11.95 (*0-88193-023-7*) Create Learn.

—PET, Vol. 4. 54p. (gr. 5-12). 1983. pap. text ed. 11.95 (*0-88193-024-5*) Create Learn.

—VIC-20, Vol. 4. 63p. (gr. 5-12). 1983. pap. text ed. 11.95 (*0-88193-064-4*) Create Learn.

Buxton, Marilyn & Buxton, Tammy. TI 99-4A, Vol. 3. 65p. (gr. 5-12). 1983. pap. text ed. 11.95 (*0-88193-053-9*) Create Learn.

—TI 99-4A, Vol. 4. 45p. (gr. 5-12). 1983. pap. text ed. 11.95 (*0-88193-054-7*) Create Learn.

Buxton, Robin. Commodore 64, Vol. 1. 50p. (gr. 4-12). 1983. pap. text ed. 11.95 (*0-88193-041-5*) Create Learn.

—Commodore 64, Vol. 2. 58p. (gr. 4-12). 1983. pap. text ed. 11.95 (*0-88193-042-3*) Create Learn.

—Commodore 64, Vol. 5. 66p. (gr. 6-12). 1984. pap. text ed. 11.95 (*0-88193-045-8*) Create Learn.

—Commodore 64, Vol. 6. 76p. (gr. 6-12). 1984. pap. text ed. 11.95 (*0-88193-046-6*) Create Learn.

—PET, Vol. 1. 51p. (gr. 4-12). 1983. pap. text ed. 11.95 (*0-88193-021-0*) Create Learn.

—PET, Vol. 2. 51p. (gr. 5-12). 1983. pap. text ed. 11.95 (*0-88193-022-9*) Create Learn.

—PET, Vol. 5. 72p. (gr. 6-12). 1984. pap. text ed. 11.95 (*0-88193-025-3*) Create Learn.

—PET, Vol. 6. 56p. (gr. 6-10). 1984. pap. text ed. 11.95 (*0-88193-026-1*) Create Learn.

—VIC-20, Vol. 1. 51p. (gr. 4-12). 1983. pap. text ed. 11.95 (*0-88193-061-X*) Create Learn.

—VIC-20, Vol. 2. 59p. (gr. 4-12). 1983. pap. text ed. 11.95 (*0-88193-062-8*) Create Learn.

—VIC-20, Vol. 3. 59p. (gr. 5-12). 1983. pap. text ed. 11.95 (*0-88193-063-6*) Create Learn.

Buxton, Robin & Buxton, Marilyn. Commodore 64, Vol. 3. 59p. (gr. 5-12). 1983. pap. text ed. 11.95 (*0-88193-043-1*) Create Learn.

—Commodore 64, Vol. 4. 59p. (gr. 5-12). 1983. pap. text ed. 11.95 (*0-88193-044-X*) Create Learn.

Buxton, Tammy. TI 99-4A, Vol. 1. 54p. (gr. 4-12). 1983. pap. text ed. 11.95 (*0-88193-051-2*) Create Learn.

—TI 99-4A, Vol. 2. 53p. (gr. 4-12). 1983. pap. text ed. 11.95 (*0-88193-052-0*) Create Learn.

Captain Comal's Staff. Cartridge Graphics & Sound. Hejndorf, Frank, illus. 64p. (Orig.). (gr. 6 up). 1984. pap. 6.95 (*0-928411-02-8*) Comal Users.

Cassidy, Pat & Close, Jim. Kids, BASIC & the Coleco Adam. (Illus.). 200p. 1984. P-H.

CES Industries, Inc. Staff. Ed-Lab Experiment Manual: CES 6010 Microwave Training System. (Illus., Orig.). (gr. 9-12). 1984. pap. write for info. (*0-86711-083-X*) CES Industries.

—Ed-Lab Experiment Manual: CES 6016 Telephone Modem. (Illus., Orig.). (gr. 9-12). 1984. pap. write for info. (*0-86711-085-6*) CES Industries.

Chaffin, Ken. Computers. Nolte, Larry, illus. 48p. (gr. 3-6). Date not set. PLB 12.95 (*1-56065-115-6*) Capstone Pr.

Computer Age. 1992. 18.95 (*0-8094-9670-4*) Time-Life.

Dunning, Jack. Future Computer Opportunities: Business Ideas into the Year 2000. Lingham, Gretchen & Steward-Shahan, Leah, eds. 200p. (Orig.). 1991. pap. text ed. 8.95 (*0-945776-24-1*) Comptr Pub Enterprises.

—How to Make Money with Computers. Lingham, Gretchen & Shahan, Leah S., eds. 208p. (Orig.). 1991. pap. 8.95 (*0-945776-18-7*) Comptr Pub Enterprises.

Egertson, Eric. Developing Computer Skills: Operating Principles for Apple IIc, IIe & IIgs. 212p. (Orig.). (gr. 7-10). 1989. pap. text ed. 14.95 (*0-8134-2791-6*); 2.95 (*0-8134-2792-4*) Interstate.

Epstein, Lawrence. Exploring Careers in Computer Sales. Rosen, Roger, ed. 64p. (gr. 7-12). 1990. PLB 14.95 (*0-8239-0667-1*) Rosen Group.

Fry, Edward B. Computer Keyboarding for Children. rev. ed. (gr. 3-6). 1984. pap. text ed. 9.95x (*0-8077-2754-7*) Tchrs Coll.

Gardenier, Turkan K. Songs for Computing & Marching: Adapted from Turkish Melodies. LC 89-90942. (Illus.). (gr. 7-12). 1989. 20.00 (*0-685-67706-0*, 0007) Teka Trends.

Graham, Ian. Computers. LC 91-34405. (Illus.). 32p. (gr. 5-8). 1992. PLB 12.40 (*0-531-17330-5*, Gloucester Pr) Watts.

Harbin, Carey E. Fay's New Computer. (Illus.). 30p. (Orig.). (ps-1). 1990. pap. text ed. 2.95 (*0-918995-03-5*) Voc-Offers.

Haugo, John E. Introduction to Microcomputers: Apple Set. (Illus.). 40p. (gr. 4-6). 1982. Set. 71.92 (*0-07-079115-5*) McGraw.

—Introduction to Microcomputers: TRS-80 Model III. (Illus.). 40p. (gr. 4-6). 1982. 71.92 (*0-07-079221-6*) McGraw.

Hill, John. Exploring Information Technology. Hill, John, illus. LC 92-28172. 48p. (gr. 4-8). 1992. PLB 22.80 (*0-8114-2605-X*) Raintree Steck-V.

Hurley, L. ZX-81 TS-1000: Programming for Young Programmers. (Illus.). 96p. (gr. 9up). 1983. pap. text ed. 9.95 (*0-07-031449-7*, BYTE Bks) McGraw.

Kaplan, Andrew. Careers for Computer Buffs. 1992. pap. 4.95 (*0-395-63560-8*) HM.

Kemnitz, T. M. & Mass, Lynne. Kids Working with Computers: Acorn BASIC. (gr. 2-6). 1984. 4.99 (*0-89824-086-7*) Trillium Pr.

—Kids Working with Computers: Commodore LOGO. (gr. 2-6). 1985. 4.99 (*0-89824-093-X*) Trillium Pr.

—Kids Working with Computers: IBM LOGO. (gr. 2-6). 1985. 4.99 (*0-89824-094-8*) Trillium Pr.

Kemnitz, Thomas M. & Mass, Lynne. Kids Working with Computers: An Apple LOGO Manual. Schlendorf, Lori, illus. 58p. (gr. 4-7). 1983. pap. 4.99 (*0-89824-073-5*) Trillium Pr.

—Kids Working with Computers: The Atari BASIC Manual. Schlendorf, Lori, illus. 48p. (gr. 4-7). 1983. pap. 4.99 (*0-89824-062-X*) Trillium Pr.

—Kids Working with Computers: The Commodore BASIC Manual. Schlendorf, Lori, illus. 48p. (gr. 4-7). 1983. pap. 4.99 (*0-89824-060-3*) Trillium Pr.

—Kids Working with Computers: The IBM BASIC Manual. Schlendorf, Lori, illus. 48p. (gr. 4-7). 1983. pap. 4.99 (*0-89824-063-8*) Trillium Pr.

Kemnitz, Thomas M. & Romanowich, Barbara. Buckfang's Primary LOGO Activity Cards: Apple & IBM LOGO. 32p. (gr. k-3). 1985. pap. text ed. 12.99 (*0-89824-117-0*) Trillium Pr.

—Buckfang's Primary LOGO Activity Cards: Commodore & Apple Terrapin. 32p. (gr. k-3). 1985. pap. text ed. 12.99 (*0-89824-118-9*) Trillium Pr.

Kemntz, T. M. & Mass, Lynne. Kids Working with Computers: TRS-80 Color LOGO. 1984. 4.95 (*0-89824-078-6*) Trillium Pr.

Kinkoph, Sherry. Alpha-Bytes Fun with Computers. (ps up). 1992. pap. 16.95 incl. disk (*0-672-30238-1*) Alpha Bks IN.

Kumbaraci, Turkan & Gardenier, George H. Computer Models: Statistical Methods: Games & Songs. Gardenier, Turhan K., illus. LC 89-90944. 19p. (gr. 1-8). 1989. Incl. manipulatives. 20.00 (*0-685-29040-9*, 0004) Teka Trends.

Kuntz, Margy. Kermit Learns How Computers Work. 48p. (Orig.). (gr. 4 up). 1993. 9.95 (*1-55958-367-3*) Prima Pub.

Lear, Peter. Computer Play. Migliore, Ron, illus. 48p. (gr. 1-5). 1985. pap. 4.95 (*0-88625-087-0*) Durkin Hayes Pub.

—Computers. (Illus.). 32p. (gr. 1-5). 1985. pap. 4.95 (*0-88625-083-8*) Durkin Hayes Pub.

LeGros, Lucy C. Square One. 41p. (gr. k-2). 1988. tchr's ed. 4.95 (*0-937306-08-8*); 16.95 (*0-937306-09-6*) Creat Res NC.

Lipson, Shelley. It's BASIC: The ABC's of Computer Programming. Stapleton, Janice, illus. LC 81-20027. 48p. (gr. 4-6). 1982. 8.95 (*0-03-061592-5*, Bks Young Read); pap. 3.95 (*0-685-05626-0*) H Holt & Co.

Mackie, Dean & Mackie, David. BASIC. Migliore, Ron, illus. 48p. (gr. 1-5). 1985. pap. 3.95 (*0-88625-085-4*) Durkin Hayes Pub.

Madama, John. Desktop Publishing: The Art of Communication. (Illus.). 80p. (gr. 5-12). 1993. PLB 19.95 (*0-8225-2303-5*) Lerner Pubns.

Maran, Richard & Feistmantl, Eric. Computers Simplified: MaranGraphics Simplified Computer Guide. LC 93-12260. 160p. 1993. Academic edition. pap. text ed. 10.00 (*0-13-095324-5*) P-H Gen Ref & Trav.

Mass, Lynne. Kids Working with Computers: The Texas Instruments LOGO Manual. Schlendorf, Lori, illus. 64p. (gr. 4-7). 1983. pap. 4.99 (*0-89824-074-3*) Trillium Pr.

Mostoller, Dwight E. & Campbell, Margaret F. Ready-to-Use Computer Literacy Activities Kits, Level I. 64p. (gr. 4-6). 1987. student wkbk. 5.95 (*0-317-66399-2*); tchr's. manual 24.95 (*0-13-762022-5*) P-H.

—Ready-to-Use Computer Literacy Activities Kits Level II. 64p. (gr. 7-10). 1987. student wkbk. 5.95 (*0-317-66401-8*); tchr's. manual 24.95 (*0-13-762048-9*) P-H.

Murphy, Linda. Computer Entrepreneurs: People Who Built Successful Businesses Around Computers. Berke, Tina, ed. Verougstraete, Randy, contrib. by. 128p. (Orig.). 1990. pap. text ed. 7.95 (*0-945776-14-4*) Comptr Pub Enterprises.

Nelson, Bonnie E. Science & Computer Activities for Children 3 to 9 Years Old. 2nd, rev. ed. (Illus.). 146p. (gr. k-3). 1988. 28.00x (*0-931642-21-3*) Lintel.

Orsetti, Marion. The Computer Zone. LC 87-42912. 44p. (ps-2). 1988. 8.95 (*1-55523-111-X*) Winston-Derek.

Pantiel, Mindy & Petersen, Becky. Kids, Teachers, & Computers: A Guide to Computers in the Elementary School. (Illus.). 176p. 1984. pap. text ed. 25.00 (*0-13-515420-0*); pap. text ed. 16.95 (*0-13-515396-4*) P-H.

Pouts-Lajus, Serge. Robots y Ordenadores (Robots & Computers) Villanueva, Marciano, tr. Davot, Francois, illus. (SPA.). 96p. (gr. 4 up). 1992. PLB 15.90 (*1-56294-178-X*) Millbrook Pr.

Quiggle, Kevin. COMAL Library of Functions & Procedures. (Illus.). 71p. (Orig.). (gr. 6 up). 1984. pap. 14.95 (*0-928411-03-6*) Comal Users.

Rajaraman, Dharma. Computer: A Child's Play. 120p. 1989. pap. text ed. 12.95 (*0-9615336-9-2*) Silicon Pr.

Rego, Paul. Computer Encounters...of the First Kind: "What the Beginner Should Know Before Buying a Computer" (Illus.). 54p. (Orig.). (ps up). 1988. pap. 14.95 (*0-945876-00-9*) Insight Data.

—Computer Encounters...of the Fourth Kind: "What the Beginner Should Know When Exploring the Apple II" Rego, Paul, illus. 139p. (Orig.). (ps up). 1988. pap. 29.95 (*0-945876-03-3*) Insight Data.

—Computer Encounters...of the Second Kind: "What the Beginner Should Know After Buying a Computer" (Illus.). 84p. (Orig.). (ps up). 1988. pap. 32.95 (*0-945876-01-7*) Insight Data.

—Computer Encounters...of the Third Kind: "What the Beginner Should Know When Programming the Apple II" (Illus.). 126p. (Orig.). (ps up). 1988. pap. 29.95 (*0-945876-02-5*) Insight Data.

Richman, Ellen. Spotlight on Computer Literacy. (gr. 6-8). 1984. pap. 14.00 (*0-07-480653-X*) McGraw.

Riede, Anne M. Coach's Clipboards. (Illus.). 306p. (Orig.). (gr. 5-8). 1986. 10.95 (*0-931983-02-9*, BCLTXT-3) Basic Comp Lit.

Robinson, Jerry W., et al. Applied Keyboarding. LC 93-7454. 1994. text ed. 21.95 (*0-538-62297-0*); text ed. 26.95 (*0-538-62298-9*) S-W Pub.

Sabin, Francene. Computers. Veno, Joseph, illus. LC 84-2708. 32p. (gr. 3-6). 1985. PLB 9.49 (*0-8167-0314-0*); pap. text ed. 2.95 (*0-8167-0315-9*) Troll Assocs.

Sebranek, Patrick. Computer Folder. (Illus.). (gr. 7-12). 1984. pap. text ed. 0.95x (*0-9605312-9-7*) Write Source.

Shigley, Gordon. COMAL Workbook. Hejndorf, Frank, illus. 69p. (Orig.). (gr. 6 up). 1985. pap. text ed. 6.95 (*0-928411-05-2*) Comal Users.

Simon, Seymour. The BASIC Book. Emberley, Barbara & Emberley, Ed E., illus. LC 85-42736. 32p. (gr. k-4). 1985. pap. 4.50 (*0-06-445015-5*, Trophy) HarpC Child Bks.

Singletary, Helen P. & Glover, Zebrena M. Computers & Children, Bk. I. Thrall, Sidney, illus. 81p. (Orig.). 1994. Set, Bks. I & II. pap. text ed. 40.00; Bk. I. pap. text ed. write for info. (*1-880850-05-2*); Bk. II. pap. text ed. write for info. (*1-880850-06-0*) Comp Trng Clinic.
COMPUTERS & CHILDREN is a series of two books beginning with children in preschool through kindergarten. Book I identifies alphabets, numbers, shapes, directions, easy words & easy math. It gives an excellent foundation, reinforces the basics & prepares the child for Book II. Book II addresses the basic steps to using a computer from turning on the computer system to using the basic commands. COMPUTERS & CHILDREN can be the first step to a new world of learning for your child. A child will recieve a strong basic educational background that gives enjoyment as the learning process takes place. Our specially designed graphics, pictures, & words make learning easy. These books will have been used with hundreds of children in some of our most well-known national learning centers. If the mind of your child is to be focused on worthwhile goals, you must begin now. "The mind is a terrible thing to waste." Book I ISBN 1-880850-05-2, Book II 1-880850-06-0. Plan to purchase a set of these books for your child today. Place your order early & avoid a back order delay. You may place an order by sending a check or money order for $40.00 which covers the set to: Computer Training Clinic, 632 Dupont Road, Charleston, SC 29407.
Publisher Provided Annotation.

—Understanding Colors, Shapes, & Direction. Glover, Zebrena M., illus. 31p. (Orig.). (ps-6). 1991. pap. text ed. 20.00 (*1-880850-02-8*) Comp Trng Clinic.

—Understanding the Alphabets. Matthews, Sam, illus. 59p. (Orig.). (ps-6). 1991. pap. text ed. 20.00 (*1-880850-03-6*) Comp Trng Clinic.

Singletary, Helen P., et al. Understanding Numbers. Butler, Synovia, illus. 47p. (Orig.). (ps-6). 1991. pap. text ed. 20.00 (*1-880850-04-4*) Comp Trng Clinic.

Skelton, Mindy. Graphics Primer. Schmidt, Wayne, illus. 84p. (Orig.). (gr. 6 up). 1984. pap. 14.95 (*0-928411-04-4*) Comal Users.

Snyder, Thomas F. & O'Neill, Martha. Community Search Apple Set. Cullinan, Dorothy K. & Podgorski, Mary E., illus. (gr. 4-12). 1982. Set. 219.76 (*0-07-079006-X*) McGraw.

—Community Searchbook. Cullinan, Dorothy K. & Podgorski, Mary E., illus. 32p. (gr. 4 up). 1982. pap. text ed. 8.08 reorders (*0-07-059463-5*) McGraw.

Spencer, Donald D. Discover Computers. LC 88-6044. 240p. (gr. 6-9). 1988. pap. 14.95 (*0-89218-121-4*, NO. 3083); tchr. resource bk. 19.95 (*0-89218-123-0*, NO. 3084); student wkbk. 6.95 (*0-89218-122-2*, NO. 3085) Camelot Pub.

—Exploring the World of Computers. LC 82-4116. 102p. (gr. 4-6). 1982. 6.95 (*0-89218-055-2*, NO. 1110); pap. 2.95 (*0-89218-054-4*, NO. 1134) Camelot Pub.

—Understanding Computers. 2nd ed. LC 87-27738. 272p. (gr. 7 up). 1988. pap. 16.95 (*0-89218-092-7*, NO. 3025); tchr's. manual 15.95x (*0-89218-118-4*, NO. 3031); student wkbk. 6.95 (*0-89218-119-2*, NO. 3034); test bank 12.95 (*0-89218-120-6*, NO. 3035) Camelot Pub.

—What Computers Can Do. 2nd ed. LC 81-21664. 256p. (gr. 9 up). 1982. 6.95x (*0-89218-043-9*, 1003) Camelot Pub.

Spencer, Jean. Exploring Careers As a Computer Technician. rev. ed. Rosen, Ruth, ed. (gr. 7-12). 1989. PLB 14.95 (*0-8239-0994-8*) Rosen Group.

Stankowich, Mimi. A Child's Guide to Computers, 4 vols. Taylor, Karen & Arkle, Dave, illus. 32p. (ps-3). 1984. Bk. 1. 3.95 (*0-916881-00-8*, ALP701) Bk. 2. 3.95 (*0-916881-01-6*, ALP702); Bk. 3. 3.95 (*0-916881-02-4*, ALP703); Bk. 4. 3.95 (*0-916881-03-2*, ALP704) Advan Learning.

Suid, Murray. The Teacher-Friendly Computer Book. (Illus.). 96p. (gr. 2-6). 1984. pap. 8.95 (*0-912107-19-7*) Monday Morning Bks.

Taitt, Henry A. Advanced Projects for Junior High. 51p. (Prog. Bk.). (gr. 7-9). 1984. pap. text ed. 11.95 (*0-88193-115-2*) Create Learn.

—Beginning Projects for Adults. 45p. (Prog. Bk.). (gr. 10 up). 1983. pap. text ed. 11.95 (*0-88193-121-7*) Create Learn.

—Beginning Projects for Junior High. 46p. (gr. 7-9). 1983. pap. text ed. 11.95 (*0-88193-111-X*) Create Learn.

—Intermediate Projects for Junior High. 46p. (gr. 7-9). 1983. pap. text ed. 11.95 (*0-88193-113-6*) Create Learn.

Taitt, Henry A. & Taitt, Jennifer. Atari, Vol. 3. 47p. (gr. 5-12). 1983. pap. text ed. 11.95 (*0-88193-073-3*) Create Learn.

—Atari, Vol. 4. 51p. (gr. 5-12). 1983. pap. text ed. 11.95 (*0-88193-074-1*) Create Learn.

—TRS-80, Vol. 3. 53p. (gr. 5-12). 1983. pap. text ed. 11.95 (*0-88193-013-X*) Create Learn.

—TRS-80, Vol. 4. 56p. (gr. 5-12). 1983. pap. text ed. 11.95 (*0-88193-014-8*) Create Learn.

—TRS-80, Vol. 5. 57p. (gr. 6-12). 1983. pap. text ed. 11.95 (*0-88193-015-6*) Create Learn.

—TRS-80, Vol. 6. 54p. (gr. 6-12). 1984. pap. text ed. 11.95 (*0-88193-016-4*) Create Learn.

Taitt, Henry A. & Taitt, Kathy. TRS-80, Vol. 1. 53p. (gr. 4-12). 1983. pap. text ed. 11.95 (*0-88193-011-3*) Create Learn.

—TRS-80, Vol. 2. 56p. (gr. 4-12). 1983. pap. text ed. 11.95 (*0-88193-012-1*) Create Learn.

Taitt, Jennifer. IBM, Vol. 5. 53p. (gr. 6-12). 1984. pap. text ed. 11.95 (*0-88193-035-0*) Create Learn.

—IBM, Vol. 6. 65p. (gr. 6-12). 1984. pap. text ed. 11.95 (*0-88193-036-9*) Create Learn.

Taitt, Nancy. Atari, Vol. 1. 55p. (gr. 4-12). 1983. pap. text ed. 11.95 (*0-88193-071-7*) Create Learn.

—Atari, Vol. 2. 64p. (Prog. Bk.). (gr. 4-12). 1984. pap. text ed. 11.95 (*0-88193-072-5*) Create Learn.

Timms, Howard. Measuring & Computing. (Illus.). 40p. (gr. 6-8). 1989. PLB 12.40 (*0-531-17188-4*, Gloucester Pr) Watts.

Tison & Woodside. The Ultimate Collection of Computer Facts & Fun: A Kid's Guide to Computers. (Illus.). 100p. (Orig.). (gr. 3 up). 1991. pap. 12.95 (*0-672-30093-1*) Alpha Bks IN.

Trainor, Timothy N. & Krasnewich, Diane. Computer Concepts & Applications. 2nd ed. LC 86-62012. (Illus.). 350p. (gr. 7-8). 1987. pap. text ed. 26.50 (*0-394-39052-0*) Mitchell Pub.

Walker, M. A-W Kids, Level 3. (Illus.). 144p. 1990. tchr's. ed. 14.50 (*0-201-52130-X*); cassette 17.25 (*0-201-52132-6*) Addison-Wesley.

—A-W Kids, Level 4. (Illus.). 1990. activity bk., 48p. 8.95 (*0-201-52135-0*); tchr's. ed., 128p. avail. (*0-201-52134-2*); cassette 17.25 (*0-201-52136-9*) Addison-Wesley.

—A-W Kids, Level 5. (Illus.). 1990. pap. text ed. 8.25 student ed., 80p. (*0-685-47383-X*); tchr's. ed., 128p. avail.; activity bk., 48p. 2.95 (*0-201-52139-3*); cassette pkg. 17.25 (*0-201-52140-7*) Addison-Wesley.

Walnum, Clayton. DataMania: A Child's Computer Organizer. (Illus., Orig.). (gr. k up). 1992. pap. 19.95 (*0-672-30207-1*) Alpha Bks IN.

Watts, L. & Inglis, L. Computers. (Illus.). 32p. (gr. 3-9). 1993. PLB 13.96 (*0-88110-595-3*); pap. 6.95 (*0-7460-1055-9*) EDC.

Weigle, Janice B. & Rackliffe, Robert E. Uzertoons "Kid, Parent & Teacher" Fun Computer Learning Guide, 2 vols, Vol. 1. Weigle, Charles W., ed. Weigle, Charles W., et al, illus. 48p. (Orig.). (gr. 3 up). 1994. Wkbk. 5.95 (*0-9640569-1-7*) Uzertoons Pubng.
UZERTOONS books contain hundreds of some of the most used computer words & phrases, explained with humorous cartoons & easy-to-read definitions. The UZERTOONS LEARNING GUIDE focuses on computer basics - hardware, software & commands common to beginner computer operation, & is a fun workbook containing puzzles & games to help the reader learn. Highly acclaimed by top educators, the new UZERTOONS is a must for the teacher, young student, parent or "beginner" who wants an easy & fun method for learning about computers. UZERTOONS is family-owned & operated, & accommodates middleman-free discounts for schools, libraries, etc. "The UZERTOONS series is absolutely the best computer learning material I've seen in my 27 years of teaching. When my fellow teachers & I began reading the first sample copies, the UZERTOONS books were hard to set down. Each truly gave a unique, simplified approach to a subject that traditionally has had its complications." - 1987 (Gifted & Talented) Georgia Science Teacher of the Year Lynn Carpenter, Dalton Public School District. Uzertoons Publishing, P.O. Box 5594, Aiken, SC 29804-5594; 1913 Alpine Dr., Aiken, SC 29803; 117 Knollwood Trail, Belvedere, SC 29841.
Publisher Provided Annotation.

Wicks, Keith. Working with Computers. (Illus.). 64p. (gr. 4-7). 15.95x (*0-8160-1071-4*) Facts on File.

Wood, Beverly J. ROM & RAM the Silicon Valley Boys. (Illus.). 40p. 1994. text ed. 13.00 (*0-8059-3538-X*) Dorrance.

COMPUTERS, ELECTRONIC
see Computers

COMPUTERS–FICTION

Anderson, Margaret J. The Ghost Inside the Monitor. LC 89-26848. 128p. (Orig.). (gr. 3-7). 1994. PLB NLD (*0-679-90359-3*); pap. 3.50 (*0-679-80359-9*) Random Bks Yng Read.

Black, J. R. Revenge of the Computer Phantoms. 132p. (gr. 3-5). 1993. pap. 3.50 (*0-679-85407-X*, Bullseye Bks) Random Bks Yng Read.

Byars, Betsy C. The Computer Nut. LC 84-7239. 144p. (gr. 3-7). 1984. pap. 12.95 (*0-670-23548-2*) Viking Child Bks.

—The Computer Nut. Byars, Guy, illus. 144p. (gr. 3-7). 1986. pap. 3.99 (*0-14-032086-5*, Puffin) Puffin Bks.

Chetwin, Grace. Out of the Dark World. 160p. (gr. 6 up). 1985. 11.95 (*0-688-04272-4*) Lothrop.

Computer Park. (Illus.). (ps-2). 1991. PLB 6.95 (*0-8136-5144-1*, TK3395); pap. 3.50 (*0-8136-5644-3*, TK3396) Modern Curr.

The Computer Rules. (Illus.). (ps-2). 1991. PLB 6.95 (*0-8136-5143-3*, TK3401); pap. 3.50 (*0-8136-5643-5*, TK3402) Modern Curr.

Fettig, Art. The Three Robots Discover Their Pos-Abilities: A Lesson in Goal Setting. Carpenter, Joe, illus. LC 84-81461. (gr. k-7). 1984. pap. 3.95 (*0-916927-00-8*) Growth Unltd.

Francis, Dorothy B. Computer Crime. LC 87-4190. 128p. (gr. 7 up). 1987. 12.95 (*0-525-67192-7*, Lodestar Bks) Dutton Child Bks.

Haas, Dorothy. The Secret Life of Dilly McBean. LC 86-8255. 224p. (gr. 5-7). 1986. SBE 14.95 (*0-02-738200-1*, Bradbury Pr) Macmillan Child Grp.

Hoban, Lillian & Hoban, Phoebe. The Laziest Robot in Zone One. Hoban, Lillian, illus. LC 82-48613. 64p. (gr. k-3). 1985. pap. 3.50 (*0-06-444089-3*, Trophy) HarpC Child Bks.

Keagy, Denita. Minicomputer to the Rescue! Sistare, Betty L., illus. LC 87-62051. 36p. (gr. k-5). 1987. PLB 10.95 (*0-944027-01-6*) New Memories.

King, Buzz. Silicon Songs. 1990. 14.95 (*0-385-30087-5*) Doubleday.

Lucas, Leanne C. Addie McCormick & the Computer Pirate. LC 93-32203. (Orig.). (gr. 5 up). 1994. pap. 3.99 (*1-56507-165-4*) Harvest Hse.

Marney, Dean. The Computer That Ate My Brother. 128p. (Orig.). (gr. 6-8). 1987. pap. 2.75 (*0-590-44005-5*) Scholastic Inc.

Mister Tom. The Little Computer. Spivey, Elvera, illus. 32p. (gr. 2-4). 1978. write for info. Oddo.

Modell, Frank. Skeeter & the Computer. LC 84-1585. (Illus.). 24p. (ps-3). 1988. 11.95 (*0-688-03703-8*); lib. bdg. 11.88 (*0-688-03706-2*) Greenwillow.

Papagapitos, Karen. Gemini Code II. Kleinman, Estelle, ed. Middleton, Curt, illus. Nicholson, David, ed. (Illus.). 96p. (Orig.). (gr. 5-9). 1994. pap. 7.95 (*0-9637328-2-X*); pap. 4.95 (*0-9637328-3-8*) Kapa Hse Pr.
THE GEMINI CODE II, the third book in the "JB Series" (JB=Jose's Basket), takes place in the 1990s. Jose & his wife Alicia, a banking executive, have twin ten-year-old sons, Hector & Luis. A favorite hobby of theirs is to play computer games, each trying to outsmart the other with new codes for different games. Alicia & Jose, who are now successful authors, are delighted with this shared interest. When Hector, the first-born twin, lost his hearing at the age of two because of a severe ear infection, the ability to communicate by computer, in addition to sign language, contributed to the closeness of the brothers & their parents. Little does anyone realize just how important this computer knowledge will be. Luis gets trapped on the other side of an arroyo filled with rushing water during a flash flood. Hector, Jose & Alicia are running out of time in their search for him when suddenly a code of Luis' is transmitted on the computer screen. Without waiting to figure out who could have sent the message, Hector breaks the code & Luis is found before it's too late. Distributed by: Baker & Taylor Books, 652 E. Main St., P.O. Box 6920, Bridgewater, NJ 08807-0920; 908-218-0400.
Publisher Provided Annotation.

Rosales, Michael & Sider, Eva. The Adventures of Panchito & Miguel: Panchito's Guide to Computers. Agustini, Michelle, illus. 24p. (Orig.). (gr. 1-4). 1988. pap. text ed. 4.95 (*0-929297-00-8*, 301-158 (005996642)) R & S Books.

Strasser, Todd. Complete Computer Popularity Contest. (gr. 4-7). 1991. pap. 3.25 (*0-440-40436-3*) Dell.

COMPUTERS–PROGRAMMING

see Programming (Electronic Computers)

COMPUTERS–STUDY AND TEACHING (ELEMENTARY)

Kinkoph, Sherry. Alpha-Bytes Count with Computers. (ps up). 1993. pap. 16.95 incl. disk (*1-56761-031-5*) Alpha Bks IN.

COMPUTING MACHINES (ELECTRONIC)

see Computers

CONCENTRATION CAMPS

Auerbacher, Inge. I Am a Star: Child of the Holocaust. Bernbaum, Israel, illus. LC 92-31444. 80p. (gr. 3-7). 1993. pap. 4.99 (*0-14-036401-3*) Puffin Bks.

Leitner, Isabella & Leitner, Irving. The Big Lie: A True Story. 1992. 13.95 (*0-590-45569-9*, 025, Scholastic Hardcover) Scholastic Inc.

CONCENTRATION CAMPS–FICTION

Boyle, Kay. Winter Night. LC 92-44043. 1994. 13.95 (*0-88682-576-8*) Creative Ed.

Uchida, Yoshiko. Journey to Topaz. rev. ed. Carrick, Donald, illus. LC 84-70422. 160p. (gr. 4-12). 1985. pap. 7.95 (*0-916870-85-5*) Creative Arts Bk.

CONCEPTION–PREVENTION

see Birth Control

CONCHOLOGY

see Mollusks; Shells

CONDORS

Arnold, Caroline. On the Brink of Extinction: The California Condor. Wallace, Michael, photos by. LC 92-14914. (Illus.). 1993. write for info. (*0-15-257990-7*) HarBrace.

—On the Brink of Extinction: The California Condor. LC 92-14914. (gr. 4-7). 1993. pap. 8.95 (*0-15-257991-5*) HarBrace.

Peters, Westberg. Condor. LC 89-28270. (Illus.). 48p. (gr. 5). 1990. text ed. 12.95 RSBE (*0-89686-515-0*, Crestwood Hse) Macmillan Child Grp.

Tibbitts, Alison & Roocroft, Alan. California Condor. (Illus.). 32p. (ps-2). 1992. PLB 12.95 (*1-56065-107-5*) Capstone Pr.

CONDUCT OF LIFE

see Behavior

CONDUCTING

Here are entered works on orchestral conducting or a combination of orchestral and choral conducting.

see also Bands (Music); Orchestra

CONDUCTORS (MUSIC)

Greene, Carol. John Philip Sousa: The March King. LC 91-37891. (Illus.). 48p. (gr. k-3). PLB 12.85 (*0-516-04226-2*); pap. 4.95, Jul. 1992 (*0-516-44226-0*) Childrens.

Simon, Charnan. Seiji Ozawa: Symphony Conductor. LC 91-36741. (Illus.). 32p. (gr. 2-5). 1992. PLB 11.80 (*0-516-04182-7*); pap. 3.95 (*0-516-44182-5*) Childrens.

CONFECTIONERY

Barkin, Carol & James, Elizabeth. Happy Valentines Day. LC 87-35812. (Illus.). 96p. (gr. 4-7). 1988. 14.00 (*0-688-06796-4*) Lothrop.

Neimark, Jill. Ice Cream. Milone, Karen, illus. LC 84-10915. (gr. 2-6). 1986. 11.95 (*0-8038-3440-3*); pap. 11. 95 (*0-8038-9290-X*) Hastings.

Rice, Karen. Does Candy Grow on Trees? Cohen, Sharon, illus. LC 83-40407. 32p. (gr. 2-5). 1984. 9.95 (*0-8027-6555-6*) Walker & Co.

Stevenson, James W. If I Owned a Candy Factory. Stevenson, James, illus. LC 87-37581. 32p. (ps up). 1989. 11.95 (*0-688-08106-1*); PLB 11.88 (*0-688-08107-X*) Greenwillow.

CONFEDERATION OF AMERICAN COLONIES

see U. S.–History–1783-1809

CONFLICT, SOCIAL

see Social Conflict

CONFUCIUS AND CONFUCIANISM

Clooney, Francis X. Confucianism. (Illus.). 128p. (gr. 7-12). 1992. bds. 17.95x (*0-8160-2445-6*) Facts on File.

CONGRESS–U. S.

see U. S. Congress

CONJURING

see Magic

CONNECTICUT

Carole Marsh Connecticut Books, 44 bks. 1994. lib. bdg. 1027.80 set (*0-7933-1281-7*); pap. 587.80 set (*0-7933-5134-0*) Gallopade Pub Group.

Fradin, Dennis B. & Fradin, Judith B. Connecticut. LC 93-44696. (Illus.). 64p. (gr. 3-5). 1994. PLB 22.00 (*0-516-03807-9*) Childrens.

Kagan, Myrna. Vision in the Sky: New Haven's Early Years, 1638-1783. LC 89-2762. (Illus.). xiv, 161p. (gr. 4-8). 1989. lib. bdg. 17.50 (*0-208-02246-5*, Linnet) Shoe String.

Kent, Deborah. Connecticut. 184p. 1993. text ed. 15.40 (*1-56956-132-X*) W A T Braille.

Macourek, Milos. Max & Sally & the Phenomenal Phone. Herrmann, Dagmar, tr. from CZE. Born, Adolf, illus. LC 88-33871. 82p. (gr. 2-4). 1989. 16.95 (*0-922984-00-X*) Wellington IL.

Marsh, Carole. Avast, Ye Slobs! Connecticut Pirate Trivia. (Illus.). (gr. 3-12). 1994. PLB 24.95 (*0-7933-0232-3*); pap. 14.95 (*0-7933-0231-5*); computer disk 29.95 (*0-7933-0233-1*) Gallopade Pub Group.

—The Beast of the Connecticut Bed & Breakfast. (Illus.). (gr. 3-12). 1994. PLB 24.95 (*0-7933-1429-1*); pap. 14. 95 (*0-7933-1430-5*); computer disk 29.95 (*0-7933-1431-3*) Gallopade Pub Group.

—Bow Wow! Connecticut Dogs in History, Mystery, Legend, Lore, Humor & More! (Illus.). (gr. 3-12). 1994. PLB 24.95 (*0-7933-3485-3*); pap. 14.95 (*0-7933-3486-1*); computer disk 29.95 (*0-7933-3487-X*) Gallopade Pub Group.

—Christopher Columbus Comes to Connecticut! Includes Reproducible Activities for Kids! (Illus.). (gr. 3-12). 1994. PLB 24.95 (*0-7933-3638-4*); pap. 14.95 (*0-7933-3639-2*); computer disk 29.95 (*0-7933-3640-6*) Gallopade Pub Group.

—Connecticut & Other State Greats (Biographies) (Illus.). (gr. 3-12). 1994. PLB 24.95 (*1-55609-547-3*); pap. 14. 95 (*1-55609-546-5*); computer disk 29.95 (*0-7933-1437-2*) Gallopade Pub Group.

—Connecticut Bandits, Bushwackers, Outlaws, Crooks, Devils, Ghosts, Desperadoes & Other Assorted & Sundry Characters! (Illus.). (gr. 3-12). 1994. PLB 24. 95 (*0-7933-0214-5*); pap. 14.95 (*0-7933-0213-7*); computer disk 29.95 (*0-7933-0215-3*) Gallopade Pub Group.

—Connecticut Classic Christmas Trivia: Stories, Recipes, Activities, Legends, Lore & More! (Illus.). (gr. 3-12). 1994. PLB 24.95 (*0-7933-0217-X*); pap. 14.95 (*0-7933-0216-1*); computer disk 29.95 (*0-7933-0218-8*) Gallopade Pub Group.

—Connecticut Coastales. (Illus.). (gr. 3-12). 1994. PLB 24.95 (*1-55609-543-0*); pap. 14.95 (*1-55609-542-2*); computer disk 29.95 (*0-7933-1433-X*) Gallopade Pub Group.

—Connecticut Coastales! 1994. lib. bdg. 24.95 (*0-7933-7271-2*) Gallopade Pub Group.

—Connecticut Dingbats! Bk. 1: A Fun Book of Games, Stories, Activities & More about Our State That's All in Code! for You to Decipher. (Illus.). (gr. 3-12). 1994. PLB 24.95 (*0-7933-3791-7*); pap. 14.95 (*0-7933-3792-5*); computer disk 29.95 (*0-7933-3793-3*) Gallopade Pub Group.

—Connecticut Festival Fun for Kids! (Illus.). (gr. 3-12). 1994. lib. bdg. 24.95 (*0-7933-3944-8*); pap. 14.95 (*0-7933-3945-6*); disk 29.95 (*0-7933-3946-4*) Gallopade Pub Group.

—The Connecticut Hot Air Balloon Mystery. (Illus.). (gr. 2-9). 1994. 24.95 (*0-7933-2372-X*); pap. 14.95 (*0-7933-2373-8*); computer disk 29.95 (*0-7933-2374-6*) Gallopade Pub Group.

—Connecticut Jeopardy! Answers & Questions about Our State! (Illus.). (gr. 3-12). 1994. PLB 24.95 (*0-7933-4097-7*); pap. 14.95 (*0-7933-4098-5*); computer disk 29.95 (*0-7933-4099-3*) Gallopade Pub Group.

—Connecticut "Jography" A Fun Run Thru Our State! (Illus.). (gr. 3-12). 1994. PLB 24.95 (*1-55609-538-4*); pap. 14.95 (*1-55609-537-6*); computer disk 29.95 (*0-7933-1423-2*) Gallopade Pub Group.

—Connecticut Kid's Cookbook: Recipes, How-to, History, Lore & More! (Illus.). (gr. 3-12). 1994. PLB 24.95 (*0-7933-0226-9*); pap. 14.95 (*0-7933-0225-0*); computer disk 29.95 (*0-7933-0227-7*) Gallopade Pub Group.

—Connecticut Quiz Bowl Crash Course! (Illus.). (gr. 3-12). 1994. PLB 24.95 (*1-55609-545-7*); pap. 14.95 (*1-55609-544-9*); computer disk 29.95 (*0-7933-1432-1*) Gallopade Pub Group.

—Connecticut Rollercoasters! (Illus.). (gr. 3-12). 1994. PLB 24.95 (*0-7933-5242-8*); pap. 14.95 (*0-7933-5243-6*); computer disk 29.95 (*0-7933-5244-4*) Gallopade Pub Group.

—Connecticut School Trivia: An Amazing & Fascinating Look at Our State's Teachers, Schools & Students! (Illus.). (gr. 3-12). 1994. PLB 24.95 (*0-7933-0223-4*); pap. 14.95 (*0-7933-0222-6*); computer disk 29.95 (*0-7933-0224-2*) Gallopade Pub Group.

—Connecticut Silly Basketball Sportsmysteries, Vol. I. (Illus.). (gr. 3-12). 1994. PLB 24.95 (*0-7933-0220-X*); pap. 14.95 (*0-7933-0219-6*); computer disk 29.95 (*0-7933-0221-8*) Gallopade Pub Group.

—Connecticut Silly Basketball Sportsmysteries, Vol. II. (Illus.). (gr. 3-12). 1994. PLB 24.95 (*0-7933-1580-8*); pap. 14.95 (*0-7933-1581-6*); computer disk 29.95 (*0-685-45929-2*) Gallopade Pub Group.

—Connecticut Silly Football Sportsmysteries, Vol. I. (Illus.). (gr. 3-12). 1994. PLB 24.95 (*1-55609-541-4*); pap. 14.95 (*1-55609-540-6*); computer disk 29.95 (*0-7933-1425-9*) Gallopade Pub Group.

—Connecticut Silly Football Sportsmysteries, Vol. II. (Illus.). (gr. 3-12). 1994. PLB 24.95 (*0-7933-1426-7*); pap. 14.95 (*0-7933-1427-5*); computer disk 29.95 (*0-7933-1428-3*) Gallopade Pub Group.

—Connecticut Silly Trivia! (Illus.). (gr. 3-12). 1994. PLB 24.95 (*1-55609-536-8*); pap. 14.95 (*1-55609-535-X*); computer disk 29.95 (*0-7933-1422-4*) Gallopade Pub Group.

—Connecticut's (Most Devastating!) Disasters & (Most Calamitous!) Catastrophies! (Illus.). (gr. 3-12). 1994. PLB 24.95 (*0-7933-0211-0*); pap. 14.95 (*0-7933-0210-2*); computer disk 29.95 (*0-7933-0212-9*) Gallopade Pub Group.

—The Hard-to-Believe-But-True! Book of Connecticut History, Mystery, Trivia, Legend, Lore, Humor & More. (Illus.). (gr. 3-12). 1994. PLB 24.95 (*0-7933-0229-3*); pap. 14.95 (*0-7933-0228-5*); computer disk 29.95 (*0-7933-0230-7*) Gallopade Pub Group.

—If My Connecticut Mama Ran the World! (Illus.). (gr. 3-12). 1994. PLB 24.95 (*0-7933-1434-8*); pap. 14.95 (*0-7933-1435-6*); computer disk 29.95 (*0-7933-1436-4*) Gallopade Pub Group.

—Jurassic Ark! Connecticut Dinosaurs & Other Prehistoric Creatures. (gr. k-12). 1994. PLB 24.95 (*0-7933-7446-4*); pap. 14.95 (*0-7933-7447-2*); computer disk 29.95 (*0-7933-7448-0*) Gallopade Pub Group.

—Let's Quilt Connecticut & Stuff It Topographically! (Illus.). (gr. 3-12). 1994. PLB 24.95 (*1-55609-539-2*); pap. 14.95 (*0-685-45928-4*); computer disk 29.95 (*0-7933-1424-0*) Gallopade Pub Group.

—Let's Quilt Our Connecticut County. 1994. lib. bdg. 24.95 (*0-7933-7131-7*); pap. text ed. 14.95 (*0-7933-7132-5*); disk 29.95 (*0-7933-7133-3*) Gallopade Pub Group.

—Let's Quilt Our Connecticut Town. 1994. lib. bdg. 24.95 (*0-7933-6981-9*); pap. text ed. 14.95 (*0-7933-6982-7*); disk 29.95 (*0-7933-6983-5*) Gallopade Pub Group.

—Meow! Connecticut Cats in History, Mystery, Legend, Lore, Humor & More! (Illus.). (gr. 3-12). 1994. PLB 24.95 (*0-7933-3332-6*); pap. 14.95 (*0-7933-3333-4*); computer disk 29.95 (*0-7933-3334-2*) Gallopade Pub Group.

—Uncle Rebus: Connecticut Picture Stories for Computer Kids. (Illus.). (gr. k-3). 1994. PLB 24.95 (*0-7933-4522-7*); pap. 14.95 (*0-7933-4523-5*); disk 29.95 (*0-7933-4524-3*) Gallopade Pub Group.

Turner Program Services, Inc. Staff & Clark, James I. Connecticut. 48p. (gr. 3 up). 1985. PLB 19.97 (*0-8174-4265-0*); pap. text ed. 9.27 (*0-86514-501-6*) Raintree Steck-V.

Van Rynbach, Iris. Everything from a Nail to a Coffin. LC 90-23035. (Illus.). 48p. (gr. 2-4). 1991. 15.95 (*0-531-05941-3*); RLB 15.99 (*0-531-08541-4*) Orchard Bks Watts.

CONNECTICUT–FICTION

White, Glenn E. Folk Tales of Connecticut, Vol. I. Zangari, Rose M., illus. 61p. (Orig.). (gr. k-12). 1977. pap. 6.50 (*0-9611926-0-7*) GEF White.

—Folk Tales of Connecticut, Vol. II. Zangari, Rose M., illus. 62p. (gr. k-12). 1981. pap. 6.50 (*0-9611926-1-5*) GEF White.

CONNECTICUT–HISTORY

Fradin, Dennis B. The Connecticut Colony. LC 89-29205. (Illus.). 160p. (gr. 4 up). 1990. PLB 17.95 (*0-516-00393-3*) Childrens.

Kagan, Myrna. Vision in the Sky: New Haven's Early Years, 1638-1783. LC 89-2762. (Illus.). xiv, 161p. (gr. 4-8). 1989. lib. bdg. 17.50 (*0-208-02246-5*, Linnet) Shoe String.

Marsh, Carole. Chill Out: Scary Connecticut Tales Based on Frightening Connecticut Truths. (Illus.). 1994. lib. bdg. 24.95 (*0-7933-4675-4*); pap. 14.95 (*0-7933-4676-2*); disk 29.95 (*0-7933-4677-0*) Gallopade Pub Group.

—Connecticut "Crinkum-Crankum" A Funny Word Book about Our State. (Illus.). 1994. lib. bdg. 24.95 (*0-7933-4828-5*); pap. 14.95 (*0-7933-4829-3*); disk 29.95 (*0-7933-4830-7*) Gallopade Pub Group.

—The Connecticut Mystery Van Takes Off! Book 1: Handicapped Connecticut Kids Sneak Off on a Big Adventure. (Illus.). (gr. 3-12). 1994. 24.95 (*0-7933-4982-6*); pap. 14.95 (*0-7933-4983-4*); computer disk 29.95 (*0-7933-4984-2*) Gallopade Pub Group.

—Connecticut Timeline: A Chronology of Connecticut History, Mystery, Trivia, Legend, Lore & More. (Illus.). (gr. 3-12). 1994. PLB 24.95 (*0-7933-5893-0*); pap. 14.95 (*0-7933-5894-9*); computer disk 29.95 (*0-7933-5895-7*) Gallopade Pub Group.

—Connecticut's Unsolved Mysteries (& Their "Solutions") Includes Scientific Information & Other Activities for Students. (Illus.). (gr. 3-12). 1994. PLB 24.95 (*0-7933-5740-3*); pap. 14.95 (*0-7933-5741-1*); computer disk 29.95 (*0-7933-5742-X*) Gallopade Pub Group.

Murphy, Jim. A Young Patriot: The American Revolution As Experienced by One Boy. LC 93-38789. 1995. write for info. (*0-395-60523-7*, Clarion Bks) HM.

CONQUISTADORES

see America–Discovery and Exploration

CONRAD, JOSEPH, 1857-1924

Reilly, Jim. Conrad. (Illus.). 112p. (gr. 7 up). 1990. lib. bdg. 19.94 (*0-86593-021-X*); lib. bdg. 14.95s.p. (*0-685-36351-1*) Rourke Corp.

CONSERVATION OF ENERGY

see Force and Energy

CONSERVATION OF FORESTS

see Forests and Forestry; Natural Resources

CONSERVATION OF NATURAL RESOURCES

see also Natural Resources

Allison, John P. & Allison, Lee A. David, the Trash Cop: A Child's Guide to Recycling. McCulloch, Jerry, illus. 21p. (Orig.). (gr. 1-6). 1992. pap. 6.95 (*0-9632789-2-4*) RMC Pub Grp.

Ancona, George. Riverkeeper. LC 89-36777. (Illus.). 48p. (gr. 3 up). 1990. RSBE 14.95 (*0-02-700911-4*, Macmillan Child Bk) Macmillan Child Grp.

Appelhof, Mary, et al. Worms Eat Our Garbage: Classroom Activities for a Better Environment. Fenton, Mary F. & Kostecke, Nancy, illus. Dindal, Daniel L., pref. by. 232p. (Orig.). (gr. 4 up). 1993. Wkbk. 19.95 (*0-942256-05-0*) Flower Pr.

WORMS EAT OUR GARBAGE integrates earthworms with ecology, composting, natural resources, soil science, conservation, the environment, recycling, & biology in a curriculum guide & workbook designed for grades 4-8. Over 150 activities use the world of worms to help students develop science, language, math, problem-solving, & critical-thinking skills. Whether the book is used at home, in a classroom, outdoor education center, nature center or master composting program, users will find themselves drawn in & captivated by the diversity & scope of information presented. Dr. Dan Dindal, Distinguished Professor of Soil Ecology at SUNY in Syracuse, says in the preface, "Even though this book was prepared as a teaching aid for elementary & middle school grades, its potential use extends far beyond. Anyone who is fascinated & wishes to learn more about earthworms, as well as those whose active quest is to be an exciting & creative educator, will be served well by this book." Barbara Hannaford, teacher of 6-8 grade math & science, says, "The format is appealing to both teachers & students & the content is fantastic." Teacher's guide, 400 illustrations, resources, bibliography, 16 appendices, glossary, & index. See also WORMS EAT MY GARBAGE for how to set up & maintain worm composting systems. To order: Flower Press 616-327-0108.

Publisher Provided Annotation.

Atwood, Margaret. For the Birds. Bianchi, John, illus. 56p. (gr. 8-12). 1991. pap. 9.95 (*0-920668-32-1*) Firefly Bks Ltd.

Bell, David O. Awesome Chesapeake. Ramsey, Marcy D., illus. 48p. (gr. 3-8). 1994. 11.95 (*0-87033-457-3*) Tidewater.

The Chesapeake Bay is certainly an amazing body of water - the largest estuary in North America. This book, the first of its kind, stimulates elementary & middle school children's interest in the Bay by exposing them to the fascinating creatures & plants found in & around the Bay's 2,500 square miles. Concepts like watershed, airshed & food web are explained in concise, understandable terms to promote awareness of the human role in this vast system. Teachers will find this book a valuable resource for their students. How many children, for example, know about a prehistoric creature found in the Bay that help fight cancer? The readers may be surprised to learn that the critter in question is the horseshoe crab. This book is an effective means for children to discover the interesting traits of some of the plants, animals, birds & fish they are likely to find in & around the Bay. Outstanding drawings bring the estuary & its inhabitants to life. At Echo Hill Outdoor School in Worton, Maryland, David Owen Bell teaches Bay ecology to youngsters. Marcy Dunn Ramsey has illustrated more than twenty books. To order please contact Tidewater Publishers 800-638-7641.

Publisher Provided Annotation.

Benson, Laura. This Is Our Earth. (Illus.). 32p. (ps-4). 1994. 14.95 (*0-88106-445-9*); PLB 15.88 (*0-88106-446-7*) Charlesbridge Pub.

Birkby, Robert C. Conservation Handbook. Boy Scouts of America Staff, ed. LC 91-58676. (Illus.). 136p. 1991. pap. 6.00 (*0-8395-3570-8*, 33570) BSA.

Braun, Elisabeth. Profiles in Conservation: Eastern & Southern Africa. (Illus.). 250p. (gr. 9 up). 1994. text ed. 26.50x (*1-55591-914-6*, North Amer Pr) Fulcrum Pub.

Brooks, F. Protecting Our World. (Illus.). 72p. (gr. 2-5). 1992. pap. 10.95 (*0-7460-1082-6*, Usborne) EDC.

Burrill, Richard. Protectors of the Land: An Environmental Journey to Understanding the Conservation Ethic. Macias, Regina, ed. Waters, Robyn & Ipina, David, illus. 300p. (gr. 3-12). 1993. pap. text ed. 22.95 (*1-878464-02-7*); write for info. (*1-878464-03-5*) Anthro Co.

Cherry, Lynne. A River Ran Wild. 1992. 14.95 (*0-15-200542-0*, HB Juv Bks) HarBrace.

Conservation at Home Activity Book. (Illus.). (ps-6). pap. 2.95 (*0-565-01098-0*, Pub. by Natural Hist Mus) Parkwest Pubns.

Cook, Kevin. Disappearing Grasslands. LC 93-1193. 1993. 17.27 (*0-8368-0483-X*) Gareth Stevens Inc.

Cossi, Olga. Water Wars: The Fight to Control & Conserve Nature's Most Precious Resource. LC 92-43968. (Illus.). 128p. (gr. 6-7). 1993. text ed. 13.95 RSBE (*0-02-724595-0*, New Discovery Bks) Macmillan Child Grp.

D'Amato, Janet P. & Carter, Laurel S. How on Earth Do We Recycle Plastic? D'Amato, Janet P., illus. LC 91-22430. 64p. (gr. 4-6). 1992. PLB 13.40 (*1-56294-143-7*) Millbrook Pr.

Denton, Peter. The World Wildlife Fund. LC 94-7491. 1995. text ed. 13.95 (*0-02-726334-7*, New Discovery Bks) Macmillan Child Grp.

DeStefano, Susan. Chico Mendes: Fight for the Forest. Raymond, Larry, illus. 76p. (gr. 4-7). 1992. PLB 14.95 (*0-8050-2887-0*) TFC Bks NY.

Dolan, Edward F. The American Wilderness & Its Future: Conservation Versus Use. LC 91-33440. (Illus.). 160p. (gr. 9-12). 1992. PLB 14.40 (*0-531-11062-1*) Watts.

Earthworks Group Staff. Fifty Simple Things Kids Can Do to Recycle. (gr. 2-12). 1993. pap. 5.95 (*1-879682-00-1*) Earth Works.

Facklam, Margery. And Then There Was One: The Mysteries of Extinction. Johnson, Pamela, illus. 48p. (gr. 3-6). 1993. pap. 5.95 (*0-316-25982-9*) Sierra.

Fischetto, Laura. The Jungle Is My Home. Galli, Letizia, illus. 32p. (ps-3). 1991. 13.95 (*0-670-83550-1*) Viking Child Bks.

Fletcher, Helen J. & Groves, Seli. How on Earth Do We Recycle Paper? Seiden, Art, illus. LC 91-24404. 64p. (gr. 4-6). 1992. PLB 13.40 (*1-56294-140-2*) Millbrook Pr.

Foreman, Michael. One World. Foreman, Michael, illus. 32p. (gr. 2-5). 1991. 14.95 (*1-55970-108-0*) Arcade Pub Inc.

Gates, Richard. Conservation. LC 81-38482. (Illus.). 48p. (gr. k-4). 1982. PLB 12.85 (*0-516-01618-0*) Childrens.

Gay, Kathlyn. Caretakers of the Earth. LC 92-23048. (Illus.). 104p. (gr. 6 up). 1993. lib. bdg. 17.95 (*0-89490-397-7*) Enslow Pubs.

Godman, Arthur. Energy Supply A-Z. LC 90-34909. 144p. (gr. 6 up). 1991. lib. bdg. 18.95 (*0-89490-262-8*) Enslow Pubs.

Golland, Derrick. Pressures on the Countryside. (Illus.). 48p. (gr. 7-12). 1986. 19.95 (*0-85219-625-3*, Pub. by Batsford UK) Trafalgar.

Goodman, Billy. Camelot World: A Kid's Guide to How to Save the Planet. 128p. (Orig.). 1990. pap. 3.50 (*0-380-76041-X*, Camelot) Avon.

Gordon, Jo W. Recycling. LC 92-9788. 1992. 12.40 (*0-531-17332-1*, Gloucester Pr) Watts.

Greene, Carol. Caring for Our People. LC 91-9235. (Illus.). 32p. (gr. k-3). 1991. lib. bdg. 12.95 (*0-89490-355-1*) Enslow Pubs.

Grimaldi, Alicia, ed. Education for the Earth: A Guide to Top Environmental Studies Programs. LC 92-33025. 192p. (Orig.). 1992. pap. 10.95 (*1-56079-164-0*) Petersons Guides.

Haines, Gail B. The Challenge of Supplying Energy. LC 89-28498. (Illus.). 64p. (gr. 6 up). 1991. lib. bdg. 15.95 (*0-89490-269-5*) Enslow Pubs.

Hare, Tony. Habitat Destruction. LC 91-8402. (Illus.). 32p. (gr. 5-8). 1991. PLB 12.40 (*0-531-17307-0*, Gloucester Pr) Watts.

—Recycling. (Illus.). 32p. (gr. k-4). 1991. PLB 11.90 (*0-531-17352-6*, Gloucester Pr) Watts.

Hawkes, Nigel. Toxic Waste & Recycling. LC 91-9888. (Illus.). 32p. (gr. 5-8). 1991. PLB 12.40 (*0-531-17359-3*, Gloucester Pr) Watts.

Hogan, Paula. Dying Oceans. LC 91-10216. (Illus.). 32p. (gr. 3-4). 1991. PLB 17.27 (*0-8368-0476-7*) Gareth Stevens Inc.

—Fragile Mountains. LC 91-2019. (Illus.). 32p. (gr. 3-4). 1991. PLB 17.27 (*0-8368-0475-9*) Gareth Stevens Inc.

Holmes, Anita. I Can Save the Earth: A Kid's Handbook for Keeping Earth Healthy & Green. Neuhaus, David, illus. LC 91-30611. 96p. (gr. 2-5). 1993. PLB 13.98 (*0-671-74544-1*, J Messner); pap. 7.95 (*0-671-74545-X*, J Messner) S&S Trade.

Hooper, Rosanne. Living in Towns. LC 93-12514. (gr. 4 up). Date not set. write for info. (*0-531-14266-3*) Watts.

Hoyt, Erich. Extinction A-Z. LC 90-23701. 128p. (gr. 6 up). 1991. lib. bdg. 17.95 (*0-89490-325-X*) Enslow Pubs.

Ingpen, Robert & Dunkle, Margaret. Conservation: A Thoughtful Way of Explaining Conservation to Children. (Illus.). 40p. (gr. 1-7). 1994. 11.95 (*0-85572-166-9*, Pub. by Hill Content Pubng AT) Seven Hills Bk Dists.

James, Barbara. Conserving the Polar Regions. LC 90-46064. (Illus.). 48p. (gr. 4-9). 1990. PLB 21.34 (*0-8114-2393-X*); pap. 5.95 (*0-8114-3458-3*) Raintree Steck-V.

Javna, John. Fifty Simple Things Kids Can Do to Save the Earth. 156p. (gr. 1-12). 1990. pap. 6.95 (*0-8362-2301-2*) Andrews & McMeel.

Kalman, Bobbie. Buried in Garbage. 32p. (gr. 3-4). 1991. PLB 15.95 (*0-86505-424-X*); pap. 7.95 (*0-86505-454-1*) Crabtree Pub Co.

—Reducing, Reusing, & Recycling. (Illus.). 32p. (gr. 3-4). 1991. PLB 15.95 (*0-86505-426-6*); pap. text ed. 7.95 (*0-86505-456-8*) Crabtree Pub Co.

Kohen, Clarita. El Agua y Tu. Barath, Judith, illus. (SPA.). 16p. (gr. k-5). 1993. PLB 7.50x (*1-56492-101-8*) Laredo.

Krupin, Paul J. Krupin's Toll-Free Environmental Directory. 128p. (Orig.). (gr. 9 up). 1994. pap. 14.95 (*1-885035-02-0*) Direct Contact.
Want to contact Kids For a Clean Enivronment? Trout Unlimited? The Hazardous Materials Advisory Council, U.S. Fish & Wildlife Service, the Earthquake Preparedness Society, or thirty-plus EPA toll-free hotlines? All long distance for free? KRUPIN'S TOLL-FREE ENVIRONMENTAL DIRECTORY lists over 4500 toll-free 800 numbers. Provides access to companies, professional & non-profit organizations & government agencies involved in environmental issues nationwide. Easy-to-use, information-packed. Covers air pollution associations, the "green market", eco-tourism, conservation organizations all across the political spectrum, consulting firms, government agencies, ground water, hazardous waste, laboratories, recycling, health, safety, software, schools & more. Job hunters can research companies & organizations, contact employers & secure internships, jobs & careers. Students, teachers & librarians can request & obtain information for papers, projects & collections. Develop business contacts & uncover new business opportunities. Contact experts in contracting, procurement, diversification & technology transfer. Environmentalists & problem solvers can call government agency & industry hotlines & receive technical guidance & advice solving environmental problems.
Publisher Provided Annotation.

Landau, Elaine. Endangered Plants. Rosoff, Iris, ed. LC 91-34926. (Illus.). 64p. (gr. 3-5). 1992. PLB 12.90 (*0-531-20134-1*) Watts.

Lepthien, Emilie U. & Klabacken, Joan. Wetlands. LC 92-35051. (Illus.). 48p. (gr. k-4). 1993. PLB 12.85 (*0-516-01334-3*); pap. 4.95 (*0-516-41334-1*) Childrens.

Lorbiecki, Marybeth & Lowery, Linda. Earthwise at Play: A Guide to the Care & Feeding of Your Planet. Mataya, David, illus. LC 92-9870. 1993. 19.95 (*0-87614-729-5*) Carolrhoda Bks.

Love, Ann & Drake, Jane. Take Action. LC 92-30412. 1993. pap. 7.95 (*0-688-12465-8*, Pub. by Beech Tree Bks) Morrow.

—Take Action: An Environmental Book for Kids. Cupples, Pat, illus. LC 92-30412. 96p. (gr. 3 up). 1993. Repr. PLB 13.93 (*0-688-12464-X*, Tambourine Bks) Morrow.

Lowery, Linda & Lorbiecki, Marybeth. Earthwise at School: A Guide to the Care & Feeding of Your Planet. LC 92-11221. (ps-3). 1993. lib. bdg. 19.95 (*0-87614-731-7*); pap. write for info. (*0-87614-587-X*) Carolrhoda Bks.

Lucas, Eileen. Naturalists, Conservationists & Environmentalists. (Illus.). 128p. (gr. 4-11). 1994. 16. 95x (*0-8160-2919-9*) Facts on File.

Luthor. Chico Mendes. Date not set. PLB write for info. (*0-8050-2270-8*) H Holt & Co.

Morrison, Ellen E. The Smokey Bear Story. U.S. Forest Service, illus. 64p. (gr. 1 up). 1995. 15.95 (*0-9622537-4-X*) Morielle Pr.
THE SMOKEY BEAR STORY tells young readers how Smokey Bear originated in 1944 as the advertising symbol of the U.S. Forest Service's Cooperative Forest Fire Prevention Program. It also gives a true account of the bear cub who was rescued after being burned in a 1950 forest fire, & later was sent to the National Zoo in Washington, D.C., as the living Smokey Bear, staying there until his death in 1976. Meanwhile, the original advertising symbol continued to campaign actively for forest fire prevention through the years, even when there was a live bear at the Zoo. Smokey Bear celebrated his 50th birthday in 1994, & is one of the most widely-recognized advertising symbols in the world. He receives so much mail that he has his own zip code. His most famous message: "Remember-- only YOU can prevent forest fires!" is well-known to both children & adults. THE SMOKEY BEAR STORY is by the author of the popular adult reference book, GUARDIAN OF THE FOREST: A HISTORY OF THE SMOKEY BEAR PROGRAM. Order from: Morielle Press, P.O. Box 10612, Alexandria, VA 22310-0612. (Tel. 703-960-2638).
Publisher Provided Annotation.

Nardo, Don. Recycling. LC 92-27849. (Illus.). 112p. (gr. 5-8). 1992. PLB 14.95 (*1-56006-135-9*) Lucent Bks.

Patent, Dorothy H. The Challenge of Extinction. LC 90-3288. (Illus.). 64p. (gr. 6 up). 1991. lib. bdg. 15.95 (*0-89490-268-7*) Enslow Pubs.

—Habitats: Saving Wild Places. LC 92-28082. (Illus.). 112p. (gr. 6 up). 1993. lib. bdg. 17.95 (*0-89490-401-9*) Enslow Pubs.

Penny, Malcolm. Pollution & Conservation. Furstinger, Nancy, ed. (Illus.). 48p. (gr. 5-8). 1989. PLB 12.95 (*0-382-09792-0*) Silver Burdett Pr.

Pfiffner, George. Earth-Friendly Toys: How to Make Fabulous Toys & Games from Reusable Objects. (Illus.). 128p. (gr. 3-7). 1994. pap. text ed. 12.95 (*0-471-00822-2*) Wiley.
These days earth-savvy kids know the value of recycling. They're using old scraps of paper cardboard & foil to make their own erector sets. Or setting up a miniature space station for their action figures using old plastic bottles. Or maybe they're flying a sea plane made of discarded styrofoam. These are just a few of the imaginative toys you'll find in the first title of the exciting Earth-Friendly Series. Includes step-by-step instructions for creating 30 toys, including costumes, dolls, musical instruments, & much more. Lists interesting facts about recycling & other things kids can do to help clean up the planet. Illustrated with over 200 line drawings. Other Earth-Friendly Books coming soon! Earth-Friendly Fashion (Fall 1994), Earth-Friendly Outdoor Fun (Spring 1995), & Earth-Friendly Holidays (Fall 1995).
Publisher Provided Annotation.

Pifer, Joanne. EarthWise: Earth's Energy. (Illus.). 48p. (gr. 5-8). 1993. pap. text ed. 7.95 (*0-9633019-3-4*) WP Pr.

Pringle, Laurence. Living Treasure: Saving Earth's Threatened Biodiversity. LC 90-21463. 64p. (gr. 3 up). 1991. 12.95 (*0-688-07709-9*); PLB 12.88 (*0-688-07710-2*, Morrow Jr Bks) Morrow Jr Bks.

Ross, Suzanne. What's in the Rainforest? One Hundred Six Answers from A to Z. Ross, Suzanne, illus. LC 91-72682. 48p. (Orig.). (gr. 1-7). 1991. pap. 5.95 (*0-9629895-0-9*) Enchanted Rain Pr.

Rott, Joanna R. & Groves, Seli. How on Earth Do We Recycle Glass? Seiden, Art, illus. LC 91-24241. 64p. (gr. 4-6). 1992. PLB 13.40 (*1-56294-141-0*) Millbrook Pr.

Santrey, Laurence. Conservation & Pollution. Maccabe, Richard, illus. LC 84-2703. 32p. (gr. 3-6). 1985. PLB 9.49 (*0-8167-0260-8*); pap. text ed. 2.95 (*0-8167-0261-6*) Troll Assocs.

Savan, Beth. Earthwatch: Earthcycles & Ecosystems. Cupples, Pat, illus. 96p. 1992. pap. 9.57 (*0-201-58148-5*) Addison-Wesley.

Schwartz, Linda. Earth Book for Kids: Activities to Help Heal the Environment. Armstrong, Beverly, illus. LC 90-91737. 184p. (Orig.). (gr. 3-6). 1990. pap. 9.95x (*0-88160-195-0*, LW 289) Learning Wks.

Seltzer, Meyer. Here Comes the Recycling Truck! Mathews, Judith, ed. Seltzer, Meyer, photos by. LC 91-37927. (Illus.). 32p. (ps-2). 1992. PLB 13.95 (*0-8075-3235-5*) A Whitman.

Thompson, Sharon E. The Greenhouse Effect. LC 92-27848. (Illus.). 112p. (gr. 5-8). 1992. PLB 14.95 (*1-56006-133-2*) Lucent Bks.

Tompkins, Terence. Ravaged Temperate Forests. LC 93-13048. 1993. 17.27 (*0-8368-0728-6*) Gareth Stevens Inc.

Toussaint, Michael E. The Playland Kids, Featuring Marcus Toussaint, the Recycler. Hamburg, Cary, illus. 24p. (Orig.). (gr. k-6). 1992. pap. 2.95 (*0-9630905-0-X*) Michael T Enter.

Whitman, Sylvia. This Land Is Your Land: The American Conservation Movement. LC 94-3099. (Illus.). 88p. 1994. PLB 17.50 (*0-8225-1729-9*) Lerner Pubns.

Williams, Lawrence. Mountains. LC 89-25349. (Illus.). 48p. (gr. 4-8). 1990. PLB 12.95 (*1-85435-173-7*) Marshall Cavendish.

—Polar Lands. LC 89-25350. (Illus.). 48p. (gr. 4-8). 1990. PLB 12.95 (*1-85435-170-2*) Marshall Cavendish.

Willis, Terri. Land Use & Abuse. LC 92-8842. (Illus.). 128p. (gr. 4-8). 1992. PLB 20.55 (*0-516-05507-0*) Childrens.

Wonders, Allison & Edelheit, Jami. The Global Kidz Handbook, No. 2: Over 100 Self-Esteem & Environmental Hands-on Activities. 118p. (gr. 4 up). 1992. pap. write for info. (*1-881497-01-1*) Global Pr Wks.

—The Global Kidz Handbook: The Internal Self-Esteem & Environmental Program. 138p. (gr. 4 up). 1991. pap. text ed. write for info. (*1-881497-00-3*) Global Pr Wks.

CONSERVATION OF THE SOIL
see Soil Conservation

CONSERVATION OF WATER
see Water Conservation

CONSTELLATIONS
see Astronomy; Stars

CONSTITUTION
see names of countries and states with subhead constitution, e.g. U. S. Constitution–Amendments

CONSTITUTION (FRIGATE)

Richards, Norman. Story of Old Ironsides. Dunnington, Tom, illus. LC 67-20099. 32p. (gr. 3-6). 1967. pap. 3.95 (*0-516-44628-2*) Childrens.

CONSTITUTIONAL AMENDMENTS–U. S.
see U. S. Constitution–Amendments

CONSTITUTIONAL LAW
see also Citizenship; Civil Rights; Democracy; Political Science
also names of countries with the subdivision Constitutional Law, e.g. U. S.–Constitutional Law

CONSTRUCTION
see Architecture; Building; Engineering

CONSTRUCTION OF ROADS
see Roads

CONSULS
see Diplomats

CONSUMER EDUCATION
Here are entered works on the selection and most efficient use of consumer goods and services, including methods of educating the consumer. Works on the economic theory of consumption are entered under Consumption (Economics).
see also Shopping

Boy Scouts of America. Consumer Buying. (Illus.). 64p. (gr. 6-12). 1975. pap. 1.85 (*0-8395-3387-X*, 33387) BSA.

Freebies Magazine Editors Staff. The Official Freebies for Kids: Something for Nothing or Next to Nothing! Leary, Catherine, illus. LC 93-45528. 80p. (gr. 5 up). 1994. pap. 4.95 (*1-56565-135-9*) Lowell Hse Juvenile.

Milios, Rita. Shopping Savvy. Rosen, Ruth, ed. (gr. 7-12). 1992. 13.95 (*0-8239-1455-0*) Rosen Group.

Riekes, Linda. Young Consumers. 2nd ed. Ackerly, Sally M., ed. (Illus.). 124p. (gr. 5-9). 1980. pap. text ed. 20. 50 (*0-8299-1021-2*); tchr's. ed. 20.50 (*0-8299-1022-0*) West Pub.

Schmitt, Lois. Smart Spending: A Consumer's Guide. LC 88-29524. 112p. (gr. 5-9). 1989. SBE 13.95 (*0-684-19035-4*, Scribners Young Read) Macmillan Child Grp.

Yardley, Thompson. Buy Now, Pay Later! Smart Shopping Counts. LC 91-22497. (Illus.). 40p. (gr. 2-6). 1992. PLB 12.90 (*1-56294-149-6*) Millbrook Pr.

CONSUMER GOODS

see Manufactures

CONSUMER PROTECTION

Abramowitz, Jack & Uva, Kenneth. Consumers & the Law. (gr. 7-12). 1987. pap. text ed. 3.50 (*0-89525-871-4*) Ed Activities.

Taylor, Binah B. Buyer Beware: Safeguarding Consumer Rights. LC 92-5493. 1992. 22.60 (*0-86593-172-0*); 16. 95s.p. (*0-685-59286-3*) Rourke Corp.

Walz, Michael K. & Killen, M. Barbara. The Law & Economics: Your Rights As a Consumer. (Illus.). 88p. (gr. 5 up). 1990. PLB 21.50 (*0-8225-1779-5*) Lerner Pubns.

CONSUMERS' GUIDES

see Consumer Education

CONTACT LENSES

see Eyeglasses

CONTAGION AND CONTAGIOUS DISEASES

see Communicable Diseases

CONTAGIOUS DISEASES

see Communicable Diseases

CONTINENTAL DRIFT

Miller, Russell. Continents in Collision. (Illus.). 176p. (gr. 7 up). 1983. 18.60 (*0-8094-4326-0*); lib. bdg. 24.60 (*0-8094-4325-2*) Time-Life.

CONTRACEPTION

see Birth Control

CONTRACTIONS

see Ciphers

CONUNDRUMS

see Riddles

CONVICTS

see Crime and Criminals; Prisons

COOK, JAMES, 1728-1779

Blumberg, Rhoda. The Remarkable Voyages of Captain Cook. LC 91-11219. (Illus.). 160p. (gr. 5 up). 1991. SBE 18.95 (*0-02-711682-4*, Bradbury Pr) Macmillan Child Grp.

Haney, David. Captain James Cook & the Explorers of the Pacific. Goetzmann, William H., ed. Collins, Michael, intro. by. (Illus.). 112p. (gr. 5 up). 1992. lib. bdg. 18.95 (*0-7910-1310-3*) Chelsea Hse.

Harley, Ruth. Captain James Cook. new ed. LC 78-18044. (Illus.). 48p. (gr. 4-7). 1979. PLB 10.59 (*0-89375-177-4*); pap. 3.50 (*0-89375-169-3*) Troll Assocs.

Kent, Zachary. James Cook: Pacific Voyager. LC 91-12571. 128p. (gr. 3 up). 1991. PLB 20.55 (*0-516-03066-3*) Childrens.

Noonan, Jon. Captain Cook. LC 92-8231. (Illus.). 48p. (gr. 5). 1993. text ed. 12.95 RSBE (*0-89686-709-9*, Crestwood Hse) Macmillan Child Grp.

Sylvester, David W. Captain Cook & the Pacific. Reeves, Marjorie, ed. (Illus.). 92p. (gr. 7-12). 1971. pap. text ed. 4.75x (*0-582-20462-3*) Longman.

COOK BOOKS

see Cookery

COOKERY

see also Baking; Bread; Coffee; Confectionery; Desserts; Diet; Food; Outdoor Cookery; Salads; Soups

Aber, Linda W. Stuck on Cooking. 96p. (Orig.). (gr. 4 up). 1991. pap. 6.95 (*0-590-43281-8*) Scholastic Inc.

Akmon, Nancy C. Come to My Tea Party: A Cookbook for Children. Akmon, Roni, illus. 84p. (gr. 3-6). 1993. 9.95 (*0-926684-09-4*) Eclectic Oregon.

Alvarez Del Real, Maria E., ed. Cocina Latino Americana. (SPA., Illus.). 304p. (Orig.). 1988. pap. 4. 50x (*0-944499-44-9*) Editorial Amer.

Amari, Suad. Cooking the Lebanese Way. (Illus.). 48p. (gr. 5 up). 1985. PLB 14.95 (*0-8225-0913-X*) Lerner Pubns.

American Heart Association Staff & Moller, James. American Heart Association Kids' Cookbook. Holub, Joan, illus. LC 92-56800. 128p. (gr. 4 up). 1993. pap. 15.00 (*0-8129-1930-0*, Times Bks) Random.

Bacon, Josephine. Cooking the Israeli Way. Wolfe, Bob, et al, illus. LC 85-18059. 48p. (gr. 5 up). 1986. PLB 14.95 (*0-8225-0912-1*) Lerner Pubns.

Baker, Margaret. Food & Cooking. (Illus.). 64p. (gr. 6 up). 1979. 14.95 (*0-7136-1465-X*) Dufour.

The Baking Storybox. (ps). Date not set. bds. 16.95 activity kit incl. bks. (*1-56828-053-X*) Red Jacket Pr.

Balkwill, Richard. Food & Feasts in Ancient Egypt. LC 94-4706. 1994. text ed. 14.95 (*0-02-726323-1*, New Discovery Bks) Macmillan Child Grp.

Barkan, Joanne. My Cooking Spoon. Wheeler, Jody, illus. 12p. (ps). Date not set. 4.95 (*1-56828-051-3*) Red Jacket Pr.

—My Measuring Cup. Sheeler, Jody, illus. 12p. (ps). Date not set. 4.95 (*1-56828-052-1*) Red Jacket Pr.

Barrett-Dragan, Patricia & Dalton, Rosemary. The Kid's Cookbook. rev. ed. Nelson, Mike, illus. 176p. (gr. 2-8). 1992. pap. 8.95 (*1-55867-043-2*, Nitty Gritty Ckbks) Bristol Pub Ent CA.

Beachy, Mary D. & Wolferman, Kristie. When Peanut Butter Is Not Enough. Flick, Deborah M., illus. 100p. (gr. 2-7). 1986. pap. 7.95 (*0-9616883-0-0*) Petit Appetit.

Belk, C. Joy. Conscious Directional Recipes for the 90s. (Illus.). 50p. (Orig.). 1990. pap. text ed. write for info. (*0-9620258-3-6*) Babe Co.

Bell, Louise P. Kitchen Fun. 1988. 3.99 (*0-517-66927-7*) Random Hse Value.

Bell, Peg, intro. by. Batchin' It Specialties: Cooking for "1 or 2" Can Be Fun. rev. ed. LC 88-92429. 198p. (gr. 8). 1988. plastic comb bdg. 12.95 (*0-9621056-0-0*) P A Bell Enterps.

Better Homes & Gardens Editors. Better Homes & Gardens Step-by-Step Kids' Cook Book. 1984. pap. 9.95 (*0-696-01325-8*) Meredith Bks.

—New Junior Cook Book. rev. ed. (Illus.). 96p. (gr. 3-5). 1989. Repr. of 1979 ed. 9.95 (*0-696-01147-6*) Meredith Bks.

Betty Crocker's New Boys & Girls Cookbook. (Illus.). 144p. 1990. pap. 11.00 comb. bdg. (*0-13-083262-6*, B Crocker Ckbks) P-H Gen Ref & Trav.

Bisignano, Alphonse. Cooking the Italian Way. LC 82-12641. (Illus.). 48p. (gr. 5 up). 1982. PLB 14.95 (*0-8225-0906-7*) Lerner Pubns.

Bissett, Isabel. How to Make Cheese Muffins. Costeloe, Brenda, illus. LC 93-21247. 1994. 4.25 (*0-383-03748-4*) SRA Schl Grp.

Blain, Diane. The Boxcar Children Cookbook. Tucker, Kathy, ed. Deal, L. Kate & Neill, Eileen M., illus. LC 91-15080. 96p. (gr. 2-8). 1991. 13.95g (*0-8075-0859-4*); pap. 9.95g (*0-8075-0856-X*) A Whitman.

Bodily, Jolene & Kreiswirth, Kinny. The Lunch Book & Bag: A Fit Kid's Guide to Making Delicious (& Nutritious) Lunches. Kreiswirth, Kinny, illus. LC 92-2815. 56p. (gr. 2-6). 1992. pap. 12.95 (*0-688-11624-8*, Tambourine Bks) Morrow.

Bourne, Miriam A. A Day in the Life of a Chef. Jann, Gayle, illus. LC 87-13762. 32p. (gr. 4-8). 1988. PLB 11.79 (*0-8167-1115-1*); pap. text ed. 2.95 (*0-8167-1116-X*) Troll Assocs.

Bove, Eugene. Uncle Gene's Breadbook for Kids! Bove, Eugene, illus. 64p. (gr. 5-12). 1986. pap. 11.95 (*0-937395-00-5*) Happibook Pr.

Boys & Girls Cookbook. (Illus.). 64p. 1988. pap. 3.95 (*0-8249-3079-7*) Ideals.

Buckman, Mary. The Animal Cookbook. (Illus.). (gr. k-2). 1982. pap. text ed. 9.95 (*1-879414-01-5*) Mary Bee Creat.

—The Count & Cook Book. (Illus.). (gr. k-2). 1982. pap. text ed. 9.95 (*1-879414-00-7*) Mary Bee Creat.

—The Shape & Cook Book. (Illus.). (gr. k-2). 1982. pap. text ed. 9.95 (*1-879414-02-3*) Mary Bee Creat.

Burstein, Chaya M. A First Jewish Holiday Cookbook. Burstein, Chaya M., illus. (gr. 3-8). 1979. (Bonim Bks); pap. 8.95 (*0-88482-775-5*, Bonim Bks) Hebrew Pub.

Cappelloni, Nancy. Ethnic Cooking the Microwave Way. Wolfe, Robert L. & Wolfe, Diane, photos by. LC 93-29543. (Illus.). 48p. (gr. 4-7). 1994. PLB 14.95 (*0-8225-0929-6*); pap. 5.95 (*0-8225-9660-1*) Lerner Pubns.

Chancellor, Betty. A Child's Christmas Cookbook. Obering, Kay & Nast, Thomas, illus. 40p. (Orig.). (gr. 1-8). 1969. pap. 4.00 (*0-914510-00-2*) Evergreen.

Cherkerzian, Diane. Christmas Fun: Holiday Crafts & Treats. Eitzen, Allen, illus. LC 92-75840. 32p. (ps-5). 1994. 4.95 (*1-56397-277-8*); prepack 14.95 (*1-56397-278-6*) Boyds Mills Pr.

Christian, Rebecca. Cooking the Spanish Way. LC 82-4709. (Illus.). 48p. (gr. 5 up). 1982. PLB 14.95 (*0-8225-0908-3*) Lerner Pubns.

Chung, Okwha & Monroe, Judy. Cooking the Korean Way. (Illus.). 48p. (gr. 5 up). 1988. PLB 14.95 (*0-8225-0921-0*) Lerner Pubns.

Coats, Carolyn. Come Cook with Me! 1994. pap. 9.99 (*0-7852-8051-0*) Nelson.

Cobb, Vicki. More Science Experiments You Can Eat. Maestro, Giulio, illus. LC 78-12732. (gr. 5 up). 1979. 13.00 (*0-397-31828-6*, Lipp Jr Bks); PLB 14.89 (*0-397-31878-2*, Lipp Jr Bks) HarpC Child Bks.

—Science Experiments You Can Eat. rev. ed. Cain, David, illus. LC 93-13679. 160p. (gr. 5-9). 1994. 15.00 (*0-06-023534-9*); PLB 14.89 (*0-06-023551-9*) HarpC Child Bks.

Cobblestone Publishing, Inc Staff. Recipes from Around the World: For Young People 8-14. (Illus.). 36p. (gr. 4-8). 1987. pap. text ed. 4.95 (*0-942389-03-4*) Cobblestone Pub.

Coronado, Rosa. Cooking the Mexican Way. LC 82-254. (Illus.). 48p. (gr. 5 up). 1982. PLB 14.95 (*0-8225-0907-5*) Lerner Pubns.

Corum, Ann K. Easy Cooking: The Island Way. LC 81-19881. (Illus.). 120p. (Orig.). (gr. 8 up). 1982. pap. 6.95 (*0-916630-24-2*) Pr Pacifica.

Corwin, Judith H. Asian Crafts. Rosoff, Iris, ed. LC 91-13500. (Illus.). 48p. (gr. 1-4). 1992. PLB 12.90 (*0-531-11013-3*) Watts.

—Cookie Fun. Corwin, Judith H., illus. 64p. (gr. 3 up). 1985. lib. bdg. 10.98 (*0-671-50797-4*, J Messner); lib. bdg. 5.95 (*0-671-55019-5*); PLB 7.71s.p. (*0-685-47050-4*); pap. 3.71s.p. (*0-685-47051-2*) S&S Trade.

—Halloween Crafts. LC 93-6367. (Illus.). (gr. k-4). Date not set. PLB write for info. (*0-531-11148-2*) Watts.

—Latin American & Caribbean Crafts. Rosoff, Iris, ed. LC 91-13466. (Illus.). 48p. (gr. 1-4). 1992. PLB 12.90 (*0-531-11014-1*) Watts.

—Thanksgiving Crafts. LC 93-6369. (Illus.). (gr. k-4). Date not set. PLB write for info. (*0-531-11147-4*) Watts.

—Valentine Crafts. LC 93-11970. 1994. 12.90 (*0-531-11146-6*) Watts.

Coyle, Rena. My First Cookbook. Joyner, Jerry, illus. LC 84-40683. 128p. (Orig.). (gr. 1-5). 1985. pap. 8.95 (*0-89480-846-X*, 846) Workman Pub.

Creative Cooking - FAST. (gr. 7-12). 1989. Package of 10. 15.95 (*1-877844-01-2*, 2221) Meridian Educ.

Croft, Karen. Good for Me Cookbook. (Illus.). (gr. k-5). 1971. pap. 3.95 (*0-88247-177-5*) R & E Pubs.

Cuyler, Margery. All Around Pumpkin Book. McClintock, Barbara, illus. LC 79-4820. 96p. (ps-2). 1980. 8.95 (*0-03-047101-X*, Bks Young Read) H Holt & Co.

D'Amico, J. & Drummond, Karen E. The Science Chef: One Hundred Fun Food Experiments & Recipes for Kids. Cash-Walsh, Tina, illus. LC 94-9045. 1994. pap. text ed. 12.95 (*0-471-31045-X*) Wiley.

Darling, Abigail. Teddy Bears' Picnic Cookbook. Day, Alexandra, illus. LC 92-28174. 1993. 4.99 (*0-14-054157-8*) Puffin Bks.

Davies, Kay, et al. My Cake. Pragoff, Fiona, photos by. (Illus.). 32p. (gr. 1 up). 1995. PLB 17.27 (*0-8368-1186-0*) Gareth Stevens Inc.

De Mauro, Lisa. Fisher Price Fun with Food Cookbook. 1988. pap. 3.95 (*0-87135-163-3*) Marvel Entmnt.

Denny, Roz. A Taste of India. LC 93-37197. (Illus.). 48p. (gr. 3-5). 1994. 14.95 (*1-56847-164-5*) Thomson Lrning.

Disney Minnie 'N Me: Cooking Together: A Book of Recipes. 48p. (ps). 1992. 5.98 (*0-8317-2348-3*) Viking Child Bks.

Domke, Lonnie. Kids Cook Too! Creative Cookery for Children & Teens. Domke, Tim, ed. LC 90-84362. (Illus.). 100p. (gr. k up). 1991. 12.95 (*0-9627795-2-0*); pap. 10.95 spiral bdg. (*0-9627795-1-2*) Carolina Cnslts Network.

Dooley, Norah. Everybody Cooks Rice. Thornton, Peter, illus. 32p. (ps-3). 1991. PLB 18.95 (*0-87614-412-1*) Carolrhoda Bks.

Drew, David. Make a Salad Face. Robertson, Ian, illus. LC 92-34335. 1993. 2.50 (*0-383-03640-2*) SRA Schl Grp.

Dr. Oetker. Let's Cook. (Illus.). 48p. (gr. 4-10). 1993. pap. 5.95 (*0-8069-8533-X*) Sterling.

Eckstein, Joan & Gleit, Joyce. Fun in the Kitchen. rev. ed. 160p. 1990. pap. 2.95 (*0-380-75919-5*, Camelot) Avon.

Edge, Nellie. Kindergarten Cooks. Leitz, Pierr M., illus. LC 76-48558. 165p. (gr. k-6). 1975. pap. 9.95 (*0-918146-00-3*) Peninsula WA.

Edge, Nellie & Leitz, Pierr M. Kids in the Kitchen. LC 76-48558. (Illus.). 165p. (gr. k-6). 1979. pap. 9.95 (*0-918146-18-6*) Peninsula WA.

Elinsky, Stephen E. Innovations in Cooking. 2nd ed. Summy, Barbara L., illus. 85p. (gr. 7 up). 1988. pap. 17.95 (*0-9620526-0-4*) Elins Laboratories.

Ellinger, Marko. Fun Food to Tickle Your Mood: A Cookbook for Children Who Cherish the Earth. Krone, Mike & Panek, Judy, illus. 96p. (Orig.). (gr. 2-6). 1992. pap. 9.95 (*0-9630147-5-7*) Piccadilly TX.

Elliott, Allison. Humpty Dumpty Was an Egg: A Coloring Cookbook. (Illus.). 64p. (gr. k-6). 1989. 8.95x (*0-941099-03-2*) Tourmaline Pub.

Feig, Barbara K. Now You're Cooking: A Guide to Cooking for Boys & Girls. Haney, Elizabeth M., illus. LC 75-10991. 144p. (gr. 7 up). 1975. pap. 4.95 (*0-916836-01-0*) J B Pal.

Ferguson, David L. Cookbook for Kids: The Kids Can Cook, Too, Cookbook. Ferguson, Jane, ed. Cheney, Glenn L., illus. LC 90-86154. 56p. (Orig.). (gr. 3-6). 1991. cerlox bound 9.95 (*0-9628148-0-6*) Abigail Pubns.

Florian, Douglas. A Chef. LC 91-29545. (Illus.). 32p. (ps-3). 1992. 14.00 (*0-688-11108-4*); PLB 13.93 (*0-688-11109-2*) Greenwillow.

Forte, Imogene. Cookbook: A No Cook & Learn Book. LC 83-80962. (Illus.). 80p. (gr. k-6). 1983. pap. text ed. 3.95 (*0-86530-089-5*, IP-895) Incentive Pubns.

Gattis, L. S., III. Cooking for Pathfinders: A Basic & Advanced Youth Enrichment Skill Honor Packet. (Illus.). 24p. (Orig.). (gr. 5 up). 1989. pap. 5.00 tchr's. ed. (*0-936241-49-7*) Cheetah Pub.

Gillis, Jennifer S. Hearts & Crafts: Over Twenty Projects for Fun-Loving Kids. Steege, Gwen, ed. Delmonte, Patti, illus. LC 93-4841. 64p. (gr. k-4). 1994. pap. 9.95 (*0-88266-844-7*) Storey Comm Inc.

Goldstein, Helen H. Kids' Cuisine. Bolch, Judy, ed. Pittman, Jackie, illus. LC 83-60306. 64p. (Orig.). (gr. k-7). 1983. pap. 5.95 (*0-935400-09-5*) News & Observer.

Green, Caroline. My Cook Book. 1993. 9.99 (*0-307-16751-8*) Western Pub.

Gustafson, Helen. Dinner's Ready, Mom. LC 86-11802. 96p. (Orig.). (gr. k-3). 1986. pap. 8.95 (*0-89087-470-0*) Celestial Arts.

Hargittai, Magdolna. Cooking the Hungarian Way. (Illus.). 48p. (gr. 5 up). 1986. PLB 14.95 (*0-8225-0916-4*) Lerner Pubns.

Harrison, Supenn & Monroe, Judy. Cooking the Thai Way. (Illus.). 48p. (gr. 5 up). 1986. PLB 14.95 (*0-8225-0917-2*) Lerner Pubns.

Hautzig, Esther. Holiday Treats. Yaroslava, illus. LC 83-9347. 96p. (gr. 3 up). 1983. SBE 13.95 (*0-02-743350-1*, Macmillan Child Bk) Macmillan Child Grp.

Hill, Barbara. Cooking the English Way. LC 82-257. (Illus.). 48p. (gr. 5 up). 1982. PLB 14.95 (*0-8225-0903-2*) Lerner Pubns.

Howard, Nina. Classroom Chefs. Rayl, Eleanor, illus. 96p. (gr. 2). 1981. 7.95 (*0-917206-14-2*) Children Learning Ctr.

Huber, Judy. Gardening & Cooking with Children. 60p. (gr. 1-8). 1987. plastic comb. 4.95 (*0-944793-00-2*); pap. 2.95 (*0-944793-01-0*) Prairie Family Pubs.

Hundley, David H. The Southwest. LC 94-9099. 1994. write for info. (*0-86625-512-5*) Rourke Pubns.

Hunt, Linda & Frase, Marianne. Loaves & Fishes. LC 80-12165. (Illus.). 176p. (gr. 2-5). 1980. pap. 9.95 spiral bdg. (*0-8361-1922-3*) Herald Pr.

Hunter, Gerald R. & Hoffmann, Peggy. Bake a Snake: How to Survive by Your Own Cooking. Massingill, Susan, illus. LC 81-10293. 68p. (Orig.). (gr. 1-7). 1981. 9.00 (*0-939710-10-2*); pap. 4.75 (*0-939710-09-9*) Meridional Pubns.

Johnson, Barbara. Cup Cooking: Individual Child-Portion Picture Recipes. 12th ed. (Illus.). (ps up). 1990. pap. 2.95 (*0-317-99815-3*) Early Educators.

Johnson, Evelyne & Santoro, Christopher. A First Cookbook for Children: With Illustrations to Color. (Illus.). 48p. (Orig.). (gr. 4 up). 1983. pap. 2.95 (*0-486-24275-7*) Dover.

Katzen, Mollie & Henderson, Ann. Pretend Soup: And Other Real Recipes. Katzen, Mollie, illus. 96p. (ps). 1993. 14.95 (*1-883672-06-6*) Tricycle Pr.

Kaufman, Cheryl. Cooking the Caribbean Way. (Illus.). 48p. (gr. 5 up). 1988. PLB 14.95 (*0-8225-0920-2*) Lerner Pubns.

Kelly, Karen & Hopkins, Joan. Tilda's Treat: A New Way to Eat. Smith, Richard, illus. LC 74-15232. 128p. (gr. 6-12). 1975. pap. 2.95 (*0-87983-091-3*) Keats.

Kenda, Margaret & Williams, Phyllis S. Cooking Wizardry for Kids. (gr. 4-7). 1990. pap. 13.95 (*0-8120-4409-6*); pap. 19.95 incl. chef's apron & hat (*0-8120-7703-2*) Barron.

Kids at Work. (Illus.). 176p. (gr. k-7). 1993. write for info. (*0-9627729-2-5*) J B Browning.

Kid's Recipes for Success. (Illus.). (gr. 1-6). 1991. write for info. (*0-9629736-0-2*) Riviana Foods.

Leeb, Olli. Von Frueh an Fit Mit Nico's Kinderkueche. 2nd ed. (GER., Illus.). 77p. 1990. 17.25x (*3-921799-87-2*, Pub. by Olli Leeb GW) Lubrecht & Cramer.

Lemley, Virg & Lemley, Jo. Children's Cookery, Naturally. (Illus.). 57p. (gr. 1-10). 1980. pap. 3.75 (*0-931798-05-1*) Wilderness Hse.

Leppard, Lois G. Mandie's Cookbook. 80p. (Orig.). (gr. 3-7). 1991. spiral bdg. 9.99 (*1-55661-224-9*) Bethany Hse.

Lesley, Salley M. Cookbook Index Plus. 96p. 1979. pap. 5.95 (*0-918544-33-5*) Wimmer Bks.

A Little Book for a Little Cook. 32p. 1992. Repr. of 1905 ed. 8.95 (*1-55709-171-4*) Applewood.

Lynch, Patti. Kids' Stuffin's: Good & Healthy Stuff for Kids to Make & Eat. Bale, Melissa, illus. 100p. (Orig.). 1995. Spiral Bound. pap. write for info. (*0-9620469-2-2*) Sweet Inspirations. KIDS' STUFFIN'S is a cookbook filled with recipes FUN & TASTY enough to delight a child's appetite. The recipes are HEALTHY enough to win a parents praise. Children ages 4 to Adult will enjoy these fun to prepare snacks. KIDS' STUFFIN'S is a delightful positive way for children to learn to prepare & eat healthy snacks. Illustrated in FULL COLOR with DELIGHTFUL ANIMATED ANIMAL CHARACTERS. Simple instructions give children a positive hands-on experience in the kitchen. The recipes are LOW FAT & FREE OF REFINED SUGAR. Recipes are appropriate for children with DIET RESTRICTIONS, such as Diabetes. Food Groups/values included. Price not determined. Publisher: Sweet Inspirations, 1420 NW Gilman Blvd. #2258, Issaquah, WA 98027; 206-643-8621.
Publisher Provided Annotation.

Lynn, Sara. I Can Make It! Fun Food. (ps-3). 1994. pap. 4.99 (*0-553-37259-9*) Bantam.

Lynn, Sara & James, Diane. What We Eat. Wright, Joe, illus. LC 93-35627. 32p. (gr. k-2). 1994. 14.95 (*1-56847-141-6*) Thomson Lrning.

McClenahan, Pat & Jaqua, Ida. Cool Cooking for Kids. LC 75-32841. (ps-k). 1976. pap. 9.95 (*0-8224-1614-X*) Fearon Teach Aids.

Macdonald, Kate. The Anne of Green Gables Cookbook. DiLella, Barbara, illus. 48p. 1987. 12.95 (*0-19-540496-3*) OUP.

McKay, D. Jay & Combs, Robert M. Ren & Stimpy's Oh Joy of Cooking! Bates, George, illus. 64p. (gr. 3-7). 1994. pap. 5.95 (*0-448-40548-2*, G&D) Putnam Pub Group.

Madavan, Vijay. Cooking the Indian Way. (Illus.). 52p. (gr. 5 up). 1985. lib. bdg. 14.95 (*0-8225-0911-3*) Lerner Pubns.

Making Gifts. LC 91-17042. (Illus.). 48p. (gr. 4-8). 1991. PLB 14.95 (*1-85435-408-6*) Marshall Cavendish.

Marsh, Carole. The Kitchen House: How Yesterdays Black Women Created Todays American Foods. (gr. 3-12). 1994. PLB 24.95 (*1-55609-309-8*); pap. 14.95 (*1-55609-308-X*); computer disk 29.95 (*1-55609-310-1*) Gallopade Pub Group.

Martel, Jane, ed. Smashed Potatoes: A Kid's Eye View of the Kitchen. LC 74-10947. 96p. (gr. 2 up). 1975. HM.

Meijer, Marie, created by. The Bake-a-Cake Book: Beat the Batter, Measure the Flour, Bake a Cake with the Cakebakers. Ramel, Charlotte, illus. LC 93-40877. (ps-3). 1994. 16.95 (*0-8118-0693-6*) Chronicle Bks.

Mellett, Peter & Rossiter, Jane. Hot & Cold. LC 92-5141. (Illus.). 32p. (gr. 5-8). 1993. PLB 12.40 (*0-531-14236-1*) Watts.

—Liquids in Action. LC 92-7649. (Illus.). 32p. (gr. 5-8). 1993. PLB 12.40 (*0-531-14235-3*) Watts.

Meyer, Annie & Munro, Mary Lynn. A Coloring Cookbook for Children. 64p. (Orig.). (gr. 1-6). 1974. pap. 3.95 (*0-89716-061-4*) Peanut Butter.

Millard, A. Round the World Cookbook. (Illus.). 48p. 1993. pap. 7.95 (*0-7460-0966-6*, Usborne) EDC.

Milne, A. A. Winnie-the-Pooh's Teatime Cookbook. Shepard, Ernest H., illus. LC 92-35650. 64p. 1993. 9.99 (*0-525-45135-8*, DCB) Dutton Child Bks.

Monroe, Lucy. Creepy Cuisine. Burke, Dianne O., illus. LC 92-41654. 80p. (gr. 4-7). 1993. pap. 4.99 (*0-679-84402-3*) Random Bks Yng Read.

Montgomery, Bertha & Nabwire, Constance. Cooking the African Way. (Illus.). 48p. (gr. 5 up). 1988. PLB 14.95 (*0-8225-0919-9*) Lerner Pubns.

Morris, Ting & Morris, Neil. No-Cook Cooking. LC 93-31801. (Illus.). 32p. (gr. 2-4). 1994. PLB 12.40 (*0-685-70145-X*) Watts.

Munsen, Sylvia. Cooking the Norwegian Way. LC 82-259. (Illus.). 48p. (gr. 5 up). 1982. PLB 14.95 (*0-8225-0901-6*) Lerner Pubns.

Murray, Beth. Kitchen Fun: A Hearty Helping of Things to Make, Play, & Eat. Jordan, Charles, illus. LC 93-70872. 32p. (ps-5). 1994. 4.95 (*1-56397-317-0*); prepack 14.85 (*1-56397-398-7*) Boyds Mills Pr.

Murray, Peter. The Perfect Pizza. Dann, Penny, illus. LC 93-4032. (gr. 2-5). 1995. 14.95 (*1-56766-080-0*) Childs World.

Nabwire, Constance. Cooking the African Way. 1990. pap. 5.95 (*0-8225-9564-8*) Lerner Pubns.

Neely, Cynthia H. & Lyerly, Elaine M. Mister Cookie Breakfast Cookbook. Lyerly, Elaine M., illus. LC 86-2386. 32p. (gr. k-4). 1986. pap. 3.25 (*0-88289-493-5*) Pelican.

Nguyen, Chi. Cooking the Vietnamese Way. (gr. 4-7). 1993. pap. 5.95 (*0-8225-9647-4*) Lerner Pubns.

Nguyen, Chi & Monroe, Judy M. Cooking the Vietnamese Way. (Illus.). 48p. (gr. 5 up). 1985. PLB 14.95 (*0-8225-0914-8*) Lerner Pubns.

O'Hare, Jeff. Hanukkah, Happy Hanukkah: Crafts, Recipes, Games, Puzzles, Songs, & More for the Joyous... Friedman, Arthur, illus. LC 93-73302. 32p. (ps-5). 1994. 4.95 (*1-56397-369-3*); 14.85 (*1-56397-396-0*) Boyds Mills Pr.

Olmsted, Cheryl. Alphabet Cooking Cards. (gr. k-1). 1990. pap. 11.95 (*0-8224-0454-0*) Fearon Teach Aids.

Outlet Staff. The Kids' Cookbook. 1993. 7.99 (*0-517-05589-9*) Random Hse Value.

Owen, Barbara. Look, I'm Cooking! Simple Recipes for Preschoolers. Gross, Karen, ed. 64p. (Orig.). (ps). 1993. pap. text ed. 5.95 (*1-56309-079-1*, New Hope) Womans Mission Union.

Palumbo, Nancy. Rainy Days Are for Baking: Les Recettes Preferee de Penelope P'Nutt. Weaver, Judith, illus. 32p. (gr. k-6). 1989. wkbk. 5.95 (*0-927024-01-2*) Crayons Pubns.

Parham, Vanessa R. The African-American Child's Heritage Cookbook. Rolle-Whatley, R., ed. LC 92-60006. (Illus.). 296p. (Orig.). 1992. pap. 19.95 (*0-9627756-2-2*) Sandcastle Pub.

Parnell, Helga. Cooking the South American Way. (Illus.). 48p. (gr. 5 up). 1991. PLB 14.95 (*0-8225-0925-3*) Lerner Pubns.

Paul, Aileen. Kids' Cooking Without a Stove: A Cookbook for Young Children. rev. ed. Inouye, Carol, illus. LC 84-22230. 64p. 1985. pap. 7.95 (*0-86534-060-9*) Sunstone Pr.

Pemberton, Judy. Let's Get Cooking. Anderson, Judith, illus. 103p. (Orig.). (gr. 3-12). 1984. text ed. 7.95 (*0-317-02695-X*) King Fisher Pr.

Penner, Lucille R. Colonial Cookbook. (Illus.). 128p. (gr. 4 up). 1976. 14.95 (*0-8038-1202-7*) Hastings.

—A Native American Feast. LC 94-10336. (Illus.). (gr. 1 up). 1994. 14.95 (*0-02-770902-7*) Macmillan.

Perl, Lila. Hunter's Stew & Hangtown Fry. Cuffari, Richard, illus. LC 77-5366. 176p. (gr. 6 up). 1979. 13.95 (*0-395-28922-X*, Clarion Bks) HM.

Peterseil, Tamar. Zap It! A Microwave Cookbook Just for Kids. (gr. 4-7). 1993. 12.95 (*0-943706-13-0*) Yllw Brick Rd.

Pillsbury Co. Staff. Little Book for a Little Cook. 1992. incl. apron 14.95 (*1-55709-172-2*) Applewood.

Pillsbury Company Editors. The Pillsbury Doughboy's First Cookbook. (Illus.). 72p. (ps-3). 1992. 15.00 (*0-385-23871-1*) Doubleday.

Pinder, Polly. Polly Pinder's Chocolate Cookbook. Pinder, Polly, illus. Search Studios Staff, photos by. (Illus.). 144p. (gr. 7 up). 1988. 24.95 (*0-85532-603-4*, Pub. by Search Pr UK) A Schwartz & Co.

Please Touch Museum Staff. Please Touch Cookbook. Brook, Bonnie, ed. (Illus.). 64p. (ps-2). 1990. pap. 6.95 spiral (*0-671-70558-X*, S&S BYR) S&S Trade.

Plotkin, Gregory & Plotkin, Rita. Cooking the Russian Way. (Illus.). 48p. (gr. 5 up). 1986. PLB 14.95 (*0-8225-0915-6*) Lerner Pubns.

Poe, Margie. The No-Cooking Cookbook for Kids. (Illus.). (gr. k-6). 1985. pap. 4.95 (*0-936985-75-5*, 1096A) Kidsmart.

Poskanzer, Susan C. What's It Like to Be a Chef. Pellaton, Karen E., illus. LC 89-34390. 32p. (gr. k-3). 1990. lib. bdg. 10.89 (*0-8167-1797-4*); pap. text ed. 2.95 (*0-8167-1798-2*) Troll Assocs.

Potter, Beatrix. The Peter Rabbit & Friends Cookbook. (Illus.). 48p. (ps-3). 1994. 6.99 (*0-7232-4146-5*) Warne.

Potter, Betty M. The Just for Kids Cookbook. Linehan, Maxene M., illus. 180p. (Orig.). (gr. 1-6). 1985. pap. 9.95 comb. bdg. (*0-913703-06-0*) Branches.

Potts, Leanna K. & Potts, Evangela. Thyme for Kids. Potts, Leanna K. & Potts, Evangela, illus. 84p. (ps-8). 1990. pap. 7.95 (*0-935069-24-0*) White Oak Pr.

Pulleyn, Micah & Bracken, Sarah. Kids In The Kitchen: Delicious, Fun, & Healthy Recipes to Cook & Bake. LC 93-39111. 112p. (gr. 4 up). 1993. Repr. of 1994 ed. 19.95 (*0-8069-0447-X*, Sterling Pub) Sterling.

Ragland, Teresa B., illus. Cooking in the Kitchen with Santa. 32p. 1992. pap. 4.95 (*0-8249-3096-7*, Ideals Child) Hambleton-Hill.

Ransford, Lynn & Robinson, Phyllis. ABC Crafts & Cooking. (Illus.). 64p. (ps-2). 1987. wkbk. 7.95 (*1-55734-090-0*) Tchr Create Mat.

Redjou, Pat C. No-Gluten Solution: Children's Cookbook. Rader, Marjie, illus. (gr. 4 up). 1991. pap. 22.00 (*0-9626052-2-0*) Rae Pub.

Ridgewell, Jenny. A Taste of Japan. LC 93-14148. (Illus.). 48p. (gr. 3-5). 1993. 14.95 (*1-56847-097-5*) Thomson Lrning.

Ringling Bros. & Barnum & Bailey Combined Shows, Inc. Staff. Circus Days Cookbook. Self, Kathy A., ed. LC 90-62393. (Orig.). 1990. pap. 13.00 (*1-878163-00-0*) Ringling Bros.

Robins, Deri, et al. The Kids Can Do It Book: Fun Things to Make and Do. Stowell, Charlotte, illus. LC 92-43345. 80p. (gr. k-4). 1993. pap. 9.95 (*1-85697-860-5*, Kingfisher LKC) LKC.

Robinson, Heather. The Simply Wonderful Cookbook. (Illus.). 48p. (gr. 4-8). 1992. text ed. 12.95 (*0-7459-2204-X*) Lion USA.

Robson, Denny A. Cooking: Hands-on Projects. LC 91-2738. (Illus.). 32p. (gr. k-4). 1991. PLB 11.90 (*0-531-17344-5*, Gloucester Pr) Watts.

Rosin, Arielle. Eclairs & Brown Bears. Czap, Daniel, photos by. Collomb, Etienne. LC 93-24971. (Illus.). 60p. (gr. 3 up). 1994. 12.95 (*0-395-68380-7*) Ticknor & Flds Bks Yng Read.

—Pizzas & Punk Potatoes. Czap, Daniel, photos by. Collomb, Etienne, contrib. by. LC 93-24970. (Illus.). 60p. (gr. 3 up). 1994. 12.95 (*0-395-68381-5*) Ticknor & Flds Bks Yng Read.

Salaman, Maureen K. Foods That Heal. Scheer, James F., ed. Atkins, Robert, intro. by. 521p. (Orig.). 1989. pap. 19.95 (*0-913087-02-5*) Statford CA.

Scherie, Strom. Stuffin' Muffin: Muffin Pan Cooking for Kids. Konefal, Norma, frwd. by. (Illus.). 100p. (Orig.). (gr. 4-7). 1982. pap. 13.95 (*0-9606964-9-0*) Yng Peoples Pr.

Schrader, Ann. Healthy Yummies for Young Tummies. LC 92-8952. (Illus.). 192p. (Orig.). 1993. pap. 12.95 (*1-55853-174-2*) Rutledge Hill Pr.

Scobey, Joan. The Fannie Farmer Junior Cook Book. rev. ed. Brewster, Patience, illus. LC 92-42632. 1993. 19.95 (*0-316-77624-6*) Little.

Seelig, Tina L. Incredible Edible Science: The Amazing Things That Happen When You Cook. Brunelle, Lynn, illus. LC 93-33480. 1994. text ed. write for info. (*0-7167-6501-2*, Sci Am Yng Rdrs); pap. text ed. write for info. (*0-7167-6507-1*) W H Freeman.

Shalant, Phyllis. Look What We've Brought You from Vietnam: Crafts, Games, Recipes, Stories & Other Cultural Activities from New Americans. LC 87-20276. (Illus.). 48p. (gr. 2-6). 1988. PLB 9.98 (*0-671-63919-6*, J Messner); pap. 4.95 (*0-671-65978-2*) S&S Trade.

Shirk-Heath, Sandra J. Mom's Metric Cookbook. LC 86-90378. 150p. (gr. 1-6). 1986. PLB write for info. (*0-9615104-0-4*) Shirk-Heath.

Sledge, Sharlande. Guess What I Made!?! Recipes for Children from Around the World. Dillard, Karen, illus. 64p. (Orig.). (gr. 1-6). 1988. pap. 4.95 (*0-936625-39-2*, New Hope AL) Womans Mission Union.

Spence, Lora T., et al. There Once Was a Cook. Baker, Gary G., illus. (gr. k up). 1985. pap. 12.95 (*0-9614501-0-X*) Wesley Inst.

Stabell, B. B. Little Chefs Cook Book. 70p. (gr. 7 up). 1982. pap. 4.75 (*0-9610872-0-X*) B B Stabell.

Steele, Philip. Between the Two World Wars. LC 94-10692. (gr. 3 up). 1994. text ed. 14.95 (*0-02-726322-3*, New Discovery Bks) Macmillan Child Grp.

—In Ancient Rome. LC 93-28384. (Illus.). 32p. (gr. 6 up). 1995. text ed. 14.95 RSBE (*0-02-726321-5*, New Discovery Bks) Macmillan Child Grp.

Stewart, J. Kids' Cuisine. (Illus.). 48p. (gr. 2-6). 1988. pap. 5.95 (*0-88625-153-2*) Durkin Hayes Pub.

Stewart, Janet, ed. Kid's Party Cookbook. Rowden, Rick, et al, illus. 32p. (gr. 2-6). 1988. PLB 14.65 (*0-88625-201-6*); pap. 5.95 (*0-88625-200-8*) Durkin Hayes Pub.

Stine, Megan, et al. Hands-On Science: Food & the Kitchen. Taback, Simms, illus. LC 92-56890. 1993. PLB 18.60 (*0-8368-0955-6*) Gareth Stevens Inc.

Story Rhyme Staff. Recipe Story Rhyme Cookbook. Story Rhyme Staff, illus. 60p. (gr. 7-10). 1993. binder 21.95 (*1-56820-103-6*) Story Time.

—Recipe Story Rhyme Greetings to Duplicate & Use. Story Rhyme Staff, illus. 60p. (gr. 7-10). 1993. binder 29.95 (*1-56820-104-4*) Story Time.

Summit Group Staff. Kids on Cooking: Favorite Original Recipes, by Kids for Kids. (ps-3). 1993. pap. 6.95 (*1-56530-099-8*) Summit TX.

Supraner, Robyn. Quick & Easy Cookbook. Barto, Renzo, illus. LC 80-24021. 48p. (gr. 1-5). 1981. PLB 11.89 (*0-89375-438-2*); pap. 3.50 (*0-89375-439-0*) Troll Assocs.

Tabs, Judy & Steinberg, Barbara. Matzah Meals: A Passover Cookbook for Kids. McLean, Chari P., illus. LC 85-40. 72p. (ps up). 1985. pap. 6.95 spiral bd. (*0-930494-44-X*) Kar-Ben.

Takeshita, Jiro. Food in Japan. LC 88-31465. (Illus.). 32p. (gr. 3-6). 1989. lib. bdg. 15.94 (*0-86625-340-8*); 11. 95s.p. (*0-685-58501-8*) Rourke Corp.

Thieme, Jeanne. The American Girls Cookbook: A Peek at Dining in the Past with Meals You Can Cook Today. (Illus.). 64p. (Orig.). (gr. 2-5). 1989. pap. 9.95 (*0-937295-59-0*) Pleasant Co.

Travers, Pamela L. & Moore-Betty, Maurice. Mary Poppins in the Kitchen: A Cookery Book with a Story. Shepard, Mary, illus. LC 75-10131. 128p. (gr. k up). 1975. 6.95 (*0-15-252898-9*, HB Juv Bks) HarBrace.

Van der Linde, Polly & Van der Linde, Tasha. Around the World in Eighty Dishes. Lemke, Horst, illus. LC 71-160447. 88p. (gr. k-7). 10.95 (*0-87592-007-1*) Scroll Pr.

Vaughan, Marcia. How to Cook a Gooseberry Fool: Unusual Recipes from Around the World. Wolfe, Robert & Wolfe, Diane, photos by. LC 93-9117. 1993. 14.95 (*0-8225-0928-8*) Lerner Pubns.

—How to Cook a Gooseberry Fool: Unusual Recipes from Around the World. (gr. 4-7). 1994. pap. 5.95 (*0-8225-9661-X*) Lerner Pubns.

Villios, Lynne W. Cooking the Greek Way. Wolfe, Robert L., et al, illus. 52p. (gr. 5 up). 1984. PLB 14.95 (*0-8225-0910-5*) Lerner Pubns.

Vincent, Richard J. Any Kid Can Cook: A Kid Friendly Cookbook. Tanaka, Rita K. & Brandes, Mary J., eds. Teague, Mark W., illus. LC 93-94116. 160p. (Orig.). (gr. 2-8). Date not set. pap. write for info. (*0-9638354-0-8*) Vision Pr CA.

Waldee, Lynne M. Cooking the French Way. LC 82-258. (Illus.). 48p. (gr. 5 up). 1982. PLB 14.95 (*0-8225-0904-0*) Lerner Pubns.

Walker, Barbara M. Little House Cookbook. LC 76-58733. (Illus.). 256p. (gr. 4 up). 1989. pap. 6.95 (*0-06-446090-8*, Trophy) HarpC Child Bks.

—The Little House Cookbook: Frontier Foods from Laura Ingalls Wilder's Classic Stories. Williams, Garth, illus. LC 76-58733. 256p. (gr. 4 up). 1979. 15.00 (*0-06-026418-7*); PLB 14.89 (*0-06-026419-5*) HarpC Child Bks.

Walker, Lois. Get Growing! Exciting Plant Projects for Kids. 104p. 1991. pap. text ed. 9.95 (*0-471-54488-4*) Wiley.

Waters, Alice L. Fanny at Chez Panisse: A Child's Restaurant Adventure with Forty-Two Recipes. LC 92-52586. (Illus.). 1992. 23.00 (*0-06-016896-X*, HarpT) HarpC.

Watson, N. Cameron. The Little Pigs' First Cookbook. Watson, N. Cameron, illus. 48p. (gr. 1-3). 1987. 12.95 (*0-316-92467-9*) Little.

Weber, Judith E. Melting Pots: Family Stories & Recipes. Bryant, Michael, illus. 64p. (gr. 1-3). 1994. PLB 11.95 (*1-881889-53-X*) Silver Moon.

Wermert, Rosie & McClurg, Marie. Teddy Toast & Twelve Other Yummy Easy Recipes You Can Make Yourself: With a Little Help from a Grownup & a Very Special Cookie Cutter! Weissman, Bari, illus. 24p. (ps-2). 1992. bds. 7.99 plastic comb bdg. (*0-679-80745-4*) Random Bks Yng Read.

Weston, Reiko. Cooking the Japanese Way. LC 81-12656. (Illus.). 48p. (gr. 5 up). 1983. PLB 14.95 (*0-8225-0905-9*) Lerner Pubns.

Wilder. My First Little House Cookbook. Date not set. 12.00 (*0-06-024296-5*); PLB 11.89 (*0-06-024297-3*) HarpC Child Bks.

Wilkes, A. First Cookbook. (Illus.). 24p. (gr. 1-4). 1993. pap. 10.95 (*0-7460-0233-5*, Usborne) EDC.

—Hot Things. (Illus.). 24p. (gr. 1-4). 1993. pap. 4.50 (*0-7460-0229-7*, Usborne) EDC.

—Party Things. (Illus.). 24p. (gr. 1-4). 1993. pap. 4.50 (*0-7460-0231-9*, Usborne) EDC.

Wilkes, Angela. Children's Step-by-Step Cookbook. (gr. 1-7). 1994. 18.95 (*1-56458-474-7*) Dorling Kindersley.

—My First Cookbook. Johnson, David, photos by. LC 88-13798. (Illus.). 48p. (gr. 3-7). 1989. 15.00 (*0-394-80427-9*) Knopf Bks Yng Read.

Williams, Barbara. Cornzapoppin! Popcorn Recipes & Party Ideas for All Occasions. LC 75-28329. (Illus.). 160p. (gr. 6-12). 1979. 5.95 (*0-03-015166-X*, Bks Young Read) H Holt & Co.

Wishik, Cindy. Kids Dish It up...Sugar-Free. LC 82-82188. (Illus.). 160p. (gr. k-3). 1982. pap. 9.95 (*0-918146-22-4*) Peninsula WA.

Wolfe, Bob & Wolfe, Diane, photos by. Holiday Cooking Around the World. Swofford, Jeannette, illus. 52p. (gr. 5 up). 1988. 15.95 (*0-8225-0922-9*) Lerner Pubns.

Wolfe, Robert L. & Wolfe, Diane. Holiday Cooking Around the World. Swofford, Jeannette, illus. 52p. (gr. 5 up). pap. 5.95 (*0-8225-9573-7*) Lerner Pubns.

Wornall, Ruthie. Three Ingredient Cookbook. Classic American Fundraisers Staff, illus. 64p. (gr. 9-12). 1988. pap. 5.95 (*0-685-29002-6*) R Wornall.

Young-Stirs: The Pittsburgh Children's Cookbook. (Illus.). 200p. (Orig.). (ps-12). 1985. pap. 7.95 (*0-9615457-0-4*) Genesis Inc.

Yu, Ling. Cooking the Chinese Way. LC 82-263. (Illus.). 48p. (gr. 5 up). 1982. PLB 14.95 (*0-8225-0902-4*) Lerner Pubns.

Zamojska-Hutchins, Danuta. Cooking the Polish Way. Wolfe, Robert, et al, illus. LC 84-11226. 52p. (gr. 5 up). 1984. PLB 14.95 (*0-8225-0909-1*) Lerner Pubns.

Zweifel, Frances. The Make-Something Club: Fun with Crafts, Food & Gifts. Schweninger, Ann, illus. LC 93-2393. 32p. (ps-3). 1994. 13.99 (*0-670-82361-9*) Viking Child Bks.

COOKERY–BEEF

Taylor, Carol. Burger Time. Culic, Ned, illus. LC 93-9281. 1994. pap. write for info. (*0-383-03678-X*) SRA Schl Grp.

COOKERY–FICTION

Adams, Pam, illus. The Gingerbread Man. LC 90-45757. 24p. (ps-2). 1981. 9.95 (*0-85953-107-4*, Pub. by Child's Play England) Childs Play.

Bastyra, Judy. Busy Little Cook. 1990. 5.99 (*0-517-03602-9*) Random Hse Value.

Blundell, Tony. Beware of Boys. LC 90-24299. (Illus.). 32p. (ps up). 1992. 15.00 (*0-688-10924-1*); PLB 14.93 (*0-688-10925-X*) Greenwillow.

Carle, Eric. Pancakes, Pancakes! Carle, Eric, illus. LC 88-32438. 36p. (gr. k up). 1991. pap. 15.95 (*0-88708-120-7*) Picture Bk Studio.

—Pancakes, Pancakes! Carle, Eric, illus. LC 92-6633. 28p. 1992. pap. 4.95 minibk. (*0-88708-275-0*) Picture Bk Studio.

Cary, Pam. I Can Cook. (ps-3). 1994. pap. 9.95 (*0-89577-599-9*, Readers Digest Kids) RD Assn.

Chandra, Deborah. Miss Mabel's Table. Grover, Max, illus. LC 93-9137. (ps-2). 1994. 14.95 (*0-15-276712-6*, Browndeer Pr) HarBrace.

Cole, Joanna. Who Put the Pepper in the Pot? Alley, Robert W., illus. 42p. (ps-3). 1992. PLB 13.27 (*0-8368-0883-5*) Gareth Stevens Inc.

Conford, Ellen. What's Cooking, Jenny Archer? Palmisciano, Diane, illus. (gr. 2-4). 1989. Little.

Croll, Carolyn. Too Many Babas. newly illus. ed. Croll, Carolyn, illus. LC 92-18779. 64p. (gr. k-3). 1979. 14. 00 (*0-06-021383-3*); PLB 13.89 (*0-06-021384-1*) HarpC Child Bks.

Darling, Benjamin. Valerie & the Silver Pear. Lane, Dan, illus. LC 90-24945. 32p. (gr. k-3). 1992. RSBE 14.95 (*0-02-726100-X*, Four Winds) Macmillan Child Grp.

Drucker, M. Grandma's Latkes. Chwast, E., ed. 1992. write for info. (*0-15-200468-8*, Gulliver Bks) HarBrace.

Ellison, Virginia. The Pooh Cook Book. 1991. pap. 3.50 (*0-440-47300-4*) Dell.

Everitt, B. Mean Soup. 1992. 13.95 (*0-15-253146-7*, HB Juv Bks) HarBrace.

Falwell, Cathryn. Feast for Ten. Falwell, Cathryn, illus. LC 92-35512. 32p. (ps-3). 1993. 14.95 (*0-395-62037-6*, Clarion Bks) HM.

Graeber, Charlotte T. Mustard. Diamond, Donna, illus. 64p. 1988. pap. 2.75 (*0-553-15674-8*, Skylark) Bantam.

Grey, Judith. Mud Pies. Sims, Deborah, illus. LC 81-4042. 32p. (gr. k-2). 1981. PLB 11.59 (*0-89375-541-9*); pap. 2.95 (*0-89375-542-7*) Troll Assocs.

Heath, Amy. Sofie's Role. Hamanaka, Sheila, illus. LC 91-33488. 40p. (gr. k-2). 1992. RSBE 14.95 (*0-02-743505-9*, Four Winds) Macmillan Child Grp.

Hines, Anna G. Daddy Makes the Best Spaghetti. Hines, Anna G., illus. LC 85-13993. 32p. (ps-1). 1988. pap. 5.95 (*0-89919-794-9*, Clarion Bks) HM.

Hoban, Lillian. Arthur's Christmas Cookies. LC 72-76496. (Illus.). 64p. (gr. k-3). 1972. PLB 13.89 (*0-06-022368-5*) HarpC Child Bks.

Hutchins, Pat. The Doorbell Rang. Hutchins, Pat, illus. LC 85-12615. 24p. (ps-3). 1986. 15.00 (*0-688-05251-7*); PLB 14.93 (*0-688-05252-5*) Greenwillow.

Kahl. Duchess Bakes a Cake. 1985. 2.95 (*0-684-16007-2*, Scribner) Macmillan.

Kline, Suzy. Orp & the Chop Suey Burgers. (Illus.). 112p. (gr. 4-8). 1990. 13.95 (*0-399-22185-9*, Putnam) Putnam Pub Group.

Kunhardt, Dorothy. Pudding Is Nice. Kunhardt, Dorothy, illus. LC 75-19948. 64p. (gr. 1 up). 1975. 15.00 (*0-912846-18-6*); pap. 8.00 (*0-912846-12-7*) Bookstore Pr.

Kurtz, Shirley. Applesauce. Benner, Cheryl, illus. LC 92-32017. 32p. (Orig.). (ps-5). 1992. pap. 6.95 (*1-56148-065-7*) Good Bks PA.

Latimer, Jim. James Bear's Pie. Franco-Feeney, Betsy, illus. LC 90-36193. 32p. (ps-2). 1992. SBE 13.95 (*0-684-19226-8*, Scribners Young Read) Macmillan Child Grp.

Light, John. What's Cooking. LC 90-34355. (gr. 4 up). 1991. 3.95 (*0-85953-337-9*) Childs Play.

Lord, John V. & Burroway, Janet. The Giant Jam Sandwich. Lord, John V., illus. LC 72-13578. 32p. (gr. k-3). 1987. 15.45 (*0-395-16033-2*); pap. 4.80 (*0-395-44237-0*) HM.

Phillips, Wanda C. My Mother Doesn't Like to Cook. Claycamp, Micah, illus. 28p. (Orig.). (ps-5). 1993. pap. 6.95 (*0-936981-20-2*) ISHA Enterprises.

Politi, Leo. Three Stalks of Corn. Politi, Leo, illus. LC 93-19737. 32p. (gr. k-3). 1994. pap. 4.95 (*0-689-71782-2*, Aladdin) Macmillan Child Grp.

Rattigan, Jama K. Dumpling Soup. Hsu-Flanders, Lillian, illus. 32p. (gr. 4-8). 1993. 15.95 (*0-316-73445-4*) Little.

Robinson, Fay. Pizza Soup. Iosa, Ann W., illus. LC 92-10756. 32p. (ps-2). 1993. PLB 11.60 (*0-516-02373-X*); pap. 3.95 (*0-516-42373-8*) Childrens.

Rockwell, Thomas. How to Eat Fried Worms. McCully, Emily A., illus. LC 73-4262. (gr. 4-6). 1973. PLB 13. 90 (*0-531-02631-0*) Watts.

Shecter, Ben. The Big Stew. Shecter, Ben, illus. LC 90-46271. 32p. (ps-2). 1991. PLB 14.89 (*0-06-025610-9*) HarpC Child Bks.

Sikirycki, Igor. The Best Cook. Knobbe, Czeslaw, ed. & tr. from POL. Thoenes, Michael, illus. 26p. (gr. 1-6). 1993. text ed. 9.95 (*0-9630328-2-8*) SDPI.

Spirn, Michele. The Know-Nothings. Alley, R. W., illus. LC 93-43533. 1995. 14.00 (*0-06-024499-2*); PLB 13. 89 (*0-06-024500-X*) HarpC Child Bks.

Steadman, Ralph. The Jelly Book. Steadman, Ralph, illus. LC 73-99918. 32p. (ps-3). 7.95 (*0-685-04570-6*) Scroll Pr.

Tobias, Tobi. Pot Luck. Malone, Nola L., illus. LC 92-27678. 32p. (ps-3). 1993. pap. 15.00 (*0-688-09824-X*); PLB 14.93 (*0-688-09825-8*) Lothrop.

Wagner, Karen. Chocolate Chip Cookies. Preiss, Leah P., illus. 32p. (ps-2). 1990. 14.95 (*0-8050-1268-0*, Bks Young Read) H Holt & Co.

Weinberger, Jane. The Little Ones. LC 86-50874. (FRE & ENG., Illus.). 54p. (Orig.). (ps-4). 1987. pap. 5.95 (*0-932433-29-4*) Windswept Hse.

Wellington, Monica. Mr. Cookie Baker. LC 91-43307. (Illus.). 32p. (ps-1). 1992. 12.50 (*0-525-44965-5*, DCB) Dutton Child Bks.

Wild, Jocelyn. Florence & Eric Take the Cake. LC 87-639. (Illus.). 32p. (ps-2). 1987. 11.95 (*0-8037-0305-8*) Dial Bks Young.

COOKERY–NATURAL FOODS

Baker, Elizabeth. The Gourmet Uncook Book. LC 93-72256. (gr. 11 up). 1994. pap. 13.95 (*0-937766-15-1*) Drelwood Comns.

Baxter, Kathleen M. Come & Get It: A Natural Foods Cookbook for Children. rev. ed. LC 81-70782. (Illus.). 128p. (ps-6). 1989. PLB 13.95 (*0-9603696-4-3*); pap. 8.95 spiral bdg. (*0-9603696-3-5*) Children First.

George, Jean C. Acorn Pancakes, Dandelion Salad & Other Wild Dishes. Mirocha, Paul, illus. LC 93-42490. 1995. Repr. of 1982 ed. 15.00 (*0-06-021549-6*); PLB 14.89 (*0-06-021550-X*) HarpC Child Bks.

Green, Karen. Once upon a Recipe: Delicious, Healthy Foods for Kids of all Ages. Heinz, Anna M. & Greene, Karen, illus. LC 92-9666. 96p. 1992. pap. 12. 95 (*0-399-51784-7*, Perigee Bks) Berkley Pub.

Isphording, Julie. Food Fun For Kids: A Recipe Coloring Book. Wolterman, Jan, ed. (Illus.). 48p. (gr. 1-6). 1991. pap. 6.95 spiral bdg. (*0-9629589-0-5*) Kids Kitchen.

COOKERY–POULTRY

Willan, Anne. Chicken Classics. LC 91-58569. (Illus.). 128p. 1992. 19.95 (*1-56458-030-X*) Dorling Kindersley.

COOKERY–VEGETABLES

Salter, Charles A. The Vegetarian Teen. (Illus.). 112p. (gr. 7 up). 1991. PLB 15.90 (*1-56294-048-1*) Millbrook Pr.

Wolfe, Robert L. & Wolfe, Diane, photos by. Vegetarian Cooking Around the World. (Illus.). 52p. (gr. 5-12). 1992. PLB 14.95 (*0-8225-0927-X*) Lerner Pubns.

COOKERY–WILD FOODS

Burns, Diane. Sugaring Season: Making Maple Syrup. Nygren, Tord, illus. 32p. (gr. k-4). 1990. PLB 19.95 (*0-87614-420-2*) Carolrhoda Bks.

COOKERY, AMERICAN

Avis, Jen & Ward, Kathy. Just for Kids. Johnson, Colleen C., illus. 166p. 1990. spiral bdg. 12.95 (*0-9628683-1-0*) Avis & Ward.

Brown, Anne H. The Colonial South. LC 93-49008. 1994. write for info. (*0-86625-509-5*) Rourke Pubns.

Elliott, Allison. The Cowboy Cookbook. LC 88-51042. (Illus.). 120p. (Orig.). (gr. 1-8). 1989. 8.95x (*0-941099-02-4*) Tourmaline Pub.

Garrett, Sandra. The Pacific Northwest Coast. LC 94-9098. 1994. write for info. (*0-86625-513-3*) Rourke Pubns.

Greenberg, Janet. California. LC 94-1038. 1994. write for info. (*0-86625-511-7*) Rourke Pubns.

Harner, Carol. The Three Sisters Cookbook: Recipes & Remembrances. (Illus.). 164p. (Orig.). (gr. 12). 1989. pap. 9.95 (*0-685-26082-8*) Harner Pubns.

Land, Leslie. The New England Epicure: Reading Between the Recipes. 1988. pap. 9.95 (*0-440-50078-8*, Dell Trade Pbks) Dell.

Marsh, Carole. Minnesota Kid's Cookbook: Recipes, How-To, History, Lore & More. (Illus.). (gr. 3 up). 1994. PLB 24.95 (*0-7933-0635-3*); pap. 14.95 (*0-7933-0634-5*); computer disk 29.95 (*0-7933-0636-1*) Gallopade Pub Group.

Penner, Lucille R. Eating the Plates: A Pilgrim Book of Food & Manners. LC 90-5918. (Illus.). 128p. (gr. 1-5). 1991. SBE 14.95 (*0-02-770901-9*, Macmillan Child Bk) Macmillan Child Grp.

Perl, Lila. Hunter's Stew & Hangtown Fry. Cuffari, Richard, illus. LC 77-5366. 176p. (gr. 6 up). 1979. 13.95 (*0-395-28922-X*, Clarion Bks) HM.

Remole, Mary J. Mary Jane's Cookbook: From the Heart of America. (Illus.). 144p. (gr. 9-12). 1986. text ed. 8.95 (*0-317-90470-1*) Mary Janes Cookbook.

Sagan, Miriam. The Middle Atlantic States. LC 93-49007. 1994. write for info. (*0-86625-508-7*) Rourke Pubns.

Swendson, Patsy. The Potluck Adventures of Mrs. Marmalade: A Children's Cookbook. Roberts, Melissa, ed. Little, Debbie, illus. 32p. (gr. k-3). 1989. 10.95 (*0-89015-718-9*, Pub. by Panda Bks) Sunbelt Media.

Williams, Thelma. Our Family Table: Recipes & Food Memories from African-American Life Models. Cellino, Maria E. & Rolfes, Ellen, eds. Jackson, Al, illus. Cosby, Camille O., intro. by. (Illus.). 96p. (gr. 7 up). 1993. 14.95 (*1-879958-14-7*); PLB 14.95 (*1-879958-16-3*) Tradery Hse.

COOKERY, AMERICAN–NEW ENGLAND STYLE

Cahill, Robert E. Olde New England's Sugar & Spice & Everything... America's First Cookbook & Food History. Cahill, Keri M., ed. (Illus.). 63p. (Orig.). 1991. pap. 3.95 (*0-9626162-2-2*) Old Saltbox Pub Hse.

Norris, Joan D. & Forsberg, Barbara. New England. LC 93-49006. 1994. write for info. (*0-86625-510-9*) Rourke Pubns.

COOKERY, CHINESE

Denny, Roz. A Taste of China. LC 94-734. (Illus.). 48p. (gr. 3-5). 1994. 14.95 (*1-56847-183-1*) Thomson Lrning.

Yu, Ling. Cooking the Chinese Way. (gr. 4-7). 1993. pap. 5.95 (*0-8225-9631-8*) Lerner Pubns.

COOKERY, ENGLISH

Denny, Roz. A Taste of Britain. LC 94-2317. (Illus.). 48p. (gr. 3-5). 1994. 14.95 (*1-56847-184-X*) Thomson Lrning.

COOKERY, FRENCH

Denny, Roz. A Taste of France. LC 93-37198. (Illus.). 48p. (gr. 3-5). 1994. 14.95 (*1-56847-163-7*) Thomson Lrning.

Loewen. Food in France. 1991. 11.95s.p. (*0-86625-344-0*) Rourke Pubns.

COOKERY, GERMAN

Loewen. Food in Germany. 1991. 11.95s.p. (*0-86625-347-5*) Rourke Pubns.

Parnell, Helga. Cooking the German Way. (Illus.). 48p. (gr. 5 up). 1988. PLB 14.95 (*0-8225-0918-0*) Lerner Pubns.

COOKERY, GREEK

Loewen. Food in Greece. 1991. 11.95s.p. (*0-86625-348-3*) Rourke Pubns.

Villios, Lynne W. Cooking the Greek Way. Wolfe, Robert L., et al, illus. 52p. (gr. 5 up). 1984. PLB 14.95 (*0-8225-0910-5*) Lerner Pubns.

COOKERY, HUNGARIAN

Hargittai, Magdolna. Cooking the Hungarian Way. (Illus.). 48p. (gr. 5 up). 1986. PLB 14.95 (*0-8225-0916-4*) Lerner Pubns.

COOKERY, ITALIAN

Gaspari, Claudia. Food in Italy. LC 88-33269. (Illus.). 32p. (gr. 3-6). 1989. lib. bdg. 15.94 (*0-86625-342-4*); 11.95s.p. (*0-685-58498-4*) Rourke Corp.

Krensky, Stephen. The Pizza Book. (Illus.). 1992. pap. 2.50 (*0-590-44844-7*, 042, Cartwheel) Scholastic Inc.

Martino, Teresa. Pizza! (Illus.). 32p. (gr. 1-4). 1989. PLB 18.99 (*0-8172-3533-7*); pap. 3.95 (*0-8114-6730-9*) Raintree Steck-V.

Pillar, Marjorie. Pizza Man. Pillar, Marjorie, illus. LC 89-35526. 40p. (gr. k-3). 1990. (Crowell Jr Bks); (Crowell Jr Bks) HarpC Child Bks.

COOKERY, JEWISH

Burstein, Chaya M. A First Jewish Holiday Cookbook. Burstein, Chaya M., illus. (gr. 3-8). 1979. (Bonim Bks); pap. 8.95 (*0-88482-775-5*, Bonim Bks) Hebrew Pub.

Feder, Harriet. What Can You Do with a Bagel? Springer, Sally, illus. LC 91-60591. 12p. (ps). 1992. bds. 4.95 (*0-929371-59-3*) Kar Ben.

Loewen. Food in Israel. 1991. 11.95s.p. (*0-86625-349-1*) Rourke Pubns.

Tabs, Judy & Steinberg, Barbara. Matzah Meals: A Passover Cookbook for Kids. McLean, Chari P., illus. LC 85-40. 72p. (ps up). 1985. pap. 6.95 spiral bd. (*0-930494-44-X*) Kar-Ben.

COOKERY, MEXICAN

Gomez, Paolo. Food in Mexico. LC 88-31529. (Illus.). 32p. (gr. 6-9). 1989. lib. bdg. 15.94 (*0-86625-341-6*); 11.95s.p. (*0-685-58499-2*) Rourke Corp.

Paulsen, Gary. The Tortilla Factory. Paulsen, Ruth, illus. LC 93-48590. 1995. write for info. (*0-15-292876-6*, HB Juv Bks) HarBrace.

COOKERY, POLISH

Zamojska-Hutchins, Danuta. Cooking the Polish Way. Wolfe, Robert, et al, illus. LC 84-11226. 52p. (gr. 5 up). 1984. PLB 14.95 (*0-8225-0909-1*) Lerner Pubns.

COOKERY, RUSSIAN

Andreev, Tania. Food in Russia. LC 88-32179. (Illus.). 32p. (gr. 3-6). 1989. lib. bdg. 15.94 (*0-86625-343-2*); 11.95s.p. (*0-685-58497-6*) Rourke Corp.

Plotkin, Gregory & Plotkin, Rita. Cooking the Russian Way. (Illus.). 48p. (gr. 5 up). 1986. PLB 14.95 (*0-8225-0915-6*) Lerner Pubns.

COOKERY, SCANDINAVIAN

Field Drake, Christin. The Sleepy Baker: A Collection of Stories & Recipes for Children. Eldridge, Alexandra, illus. LC 92-56509. 56p. (gr. k-5). 1993. 12.95 (*0-87358-551-8*) Northland AZ.

COOKERY, THAI

Harrison, Supenn & Monroe, Judy. Cooking the Thai Way. (Illus.). 48p. (gr. 5 up). 1986. PLB 14.95 (*0-8225-0917-2*) Lerner Pubns.

COOKIES

Carlson, Faith. A Cookie Christmas. Carlson, Faith, illus. 28p. (Orig.). (ps-2). 1986. pap. 5.00 (*0-932591-05-1*) Baggeboda Pr.

Corwin, Judith H. Cookie Fun. Corwin, Judith H., illus. 64p. (gr. 3 up). 1985. lib. bdg. 10.98 (*0-671-50797-4*, J Messner); lib. bdg. 5.95 (*0-671-55019-5*); PLB 7.71s.p. (*0-685-47050-4*); pap. 3.71s.p. (*0-685-47051-2*) S&S Trade.

Debnam, Betty. Rookie Cookie Cookbook: Everyday Recipes for Kids. (Illus.). 128p. (Orig.). 1989. pap. 7.95 (*0-8362-4206-8*) Andrews & McMeel.

Jaspersohn, William. Cookies. Jaspersohn, William, illus. LC 91-45023. 48p. (gr. 3-7). 1993. RSBE 14.95 (*0-02-747822-X*, Macmillan Child Bk) Macmillan Child Grp.

Mrs. Beeton's Complete Book of Cakes & Biscuits. (Illus.). 336p. (gr. 10-12). 1992. 27.95 (*0-7063-6806-1*, Pub. by Ward Lock UK) Sterling.

Murray, Peter. World's Greatest Chocolate Chip Cookies. (Illus.). (gr. 2-6). 1992. PLB 14.95 (*0-89565-892-5*) Childs World.

Perry, Josephine. Cookies from Many Lands. 160p. (gr. 6-12). 1972. pap. 4.95 (*0-486-22832-0*) Dover.

St. Pierre, Stephanie & Lovak, Matt. Bunny Bakeshop: Book & Cookie Cutter Set. (gr. k-3). 1989. pap. 3.95 (*0-590-63281-7*) Scholastic Inc.

Storybox Cookie Cookbook. 12p. (ps). Date not set. 1.95 (*1-56828-070-X*) Red Jacket Pr.

COOKING

see Cookery

COOKING, OUTDOOR

see Outdoor Cookery

COOKING UTENSILS

see Household Equipment and Supplies

COOLIDGE, CALVIN, PRESIDENT U. S. 1872-1933

Kent, Zachary. Calvin Coolidge. LC 88-10880. (Illus.). 100p. (gr. 3 up). 1988. PLB 14.40 (*0-516-01362-9*) Childrens.

Stevens, Rita. Calvin Coolidge: Thirtieth President of the United States. Young, Richard G., ed. LC 89-39949. (Illus.). 128p. (gr. 5-9). 1990. PLB 17.26 (*0-944483-57-7*) Garrett Ed Corp.

COPPER

Fodor, R. V. Gold, Copper, Iron: How Metals Are Formed, Found, & Used. LC 87-24464. (Illus.). 96p. (gr. 6 up). 1989. lib. bdg. 16.95 (*0-89490-138-9*) Enslow Pubs.

Lambert, M. Copper. (Illus.). 48p. (gr. 5 up). 1985. PLB 17.27 (*0-86592-270-5*); lib. bdg. 12.95s.p. (*0-685-58324-4*) Rourke Corp.

CORAL REEFS AND ISLANDS

Barrett, Norman S. Coral Reef. LC 90-42931. (Illus.). 32p. (gr. k-4). 1991. PLB 11.90 (*0-531-14110-1*) Watts.

Berger, Melvin. Life in a Coral Reef. 16p. (gr. 2-4). 1994. pap. 14.95 (*1-56784-204-6*) Newbridge Comms.

De Larramendi Ruis, Alberto. Coral Reefs. LC 93-3438. (Illus.). 36p. (gr. 3 up). 1993. PLB 14.95 (*0-516-08384-8*); pap. 6.95 (*0-516-48384-6*) Childrens.

Gentry, Linnea. Inside Biosphere 2: The Ocean & Its Reef. 64p. (gr. 3 up). 1993. pap. 8.95 (*1-882428-02-1*) Biosphere Pr.

George, Michael. Coral Reef. 40p. (gr. 4-7). 1993. 15.95 (*1-56846-059-7*) Creat Editions.

Gutnik, Martin J. & Browne-Gutnik, Natalie. Great Barrier Reef. LC 94-3029. (gr. 4 up). 1994. write for info. (*0-8114-6369-9*) Raintree Steck-V.

Holing, Dwight. Coral Reefs. Leon, Vicki, ed. (Illus.). 40p. (Orig.). (gr. 5 up). 1990. pap. 7.95 (*0-918303-22-2*) Blake Pub.

Johnson, Rebecca L. The Great Barrier Reef: A Living Laboratory. (Illus.). 64p. (gr. 5 up). 1991. PLB 21.50 (*0-8225-1596-2*) Lerner Pubns.

Lampton, Christopher. Coral Reefs in Danger. LC 91-41441. (Illus.). 64p. (gr. 4-8). 1992. PLB 15.40 (*1-56294-091-0*) Millbrook Pr.

Muzik, Katy. Dentro del Arrecife de Coral (At Home in the Coral Reef) (Illus.). 32p. (ps-3). 1993. PLB 15.88 (*0-88106-642-7*); pap. 6.95 (*0-88106-422-X*) Charlesbridge Pub.

Orr, Katherine. The Coral Reef Coloring Book. Orr, Katherine, illus. 48p. (gr. 2 up). 1988. pap. 5.95 (*0-88045-090-8*) Stemmer Hse.

—The Hawaiian Coral Reef Coloring Book. Orr, Katherine, illus. 48p. (Orig.). (gr. 1-6). 1992. pap. 5.95 (*0-88045-122-X*) Stemmer Hse.

Sargent, William. Night Reef: Dusk to Dawn on a Coral Reef. (Illus.). 40p. (gr. 5-8). 1991. 14.95 (*0-531-15219-7*); PLB 14.90 (*0-531-11073-7*) Watts.

Segaloff, Nat & Erickson, Paul. A Reef Comes to Life: Creating an Undersea Exhibit. LC 90-13129. (Illus.). 48p. (gr. 5-7). 1991. PLB 14.90 (*0-531-10994-1*) Watts.

Siy, Alexandra. The Great Astrolabe Reef. LC 91-37267. (Illus.). 80p. (gr. 5 up). 1992. text ed. 14.95 RSBE (*0-87518-499-5*, Dillon) Macmillan Child Grp.

Wells, Sue. Make Your Own Coral Reef: Includes Giant Three-Dimensional Press-Out Model. Tomblin, Gill, illus. Johnston, Damian, designed by. (Illus.). 18p. (gr. 3-7). 1994. 13.99 (*0-525-67461-6*, Lodestar Bks) Dutton Child Bks.

Wells, Sue & Hanna, Nick. The Greenpeace Book of Coral Reefs. LC 92-41504. (Illus.). 160p. (gr. 10-12). 1992. 35.00 (*0-8069-8795-2*) Sterling.

Wood, Jenny. Coral Reefs. (Illus.). 32p. (gr. 3-4). 1991. PLB 17.27 (*0-8368-0630-1*) Gareth Stevens Inc.

CORALS

Cousteau Society Staff. Corals: The Sea's Great Builders. LC 91-34458. (Illus.). 32p. (gr. 1-5). 1992. pap. 12.00 jacketed (*0-671-77068-3*, S&S BFYR) S&S Trade.

De Larramendi Ruis, Alberto. Coral Reefs. LC 93-3438. (Illus.). 36p. (gr. 3 up). 1993. PLB 14.95 (*0-516-08384-8*); pap. 6.95 (*0-516-48384-6*) Childrens.

CORN

Aliki. Corn Is Maize: The Gift of the Indians. Aliki, illus. LC 75-6928. 40p. (gr. k-3). 1976. PLB 14.89 (*0-690-00975-5*, Crowell Jr Bks) HarpC Child Bks.

—Corn Is Maize: The Gift of the Indians. Aliki, illus. LC 75-6928. 40p. (gr. k-3). 1986. pap. 4.95 (*0-06-445026-0*, Trophy) HarpC Child Bks.

Bial, Raymond. Corn Belt Harvest. (Illus.). 48p. (gr. 3-6). 1991. 14.45 (*0-395-56234-1*, Sandpiper) HM.

Fowler, Allan. Corn. LC 94-10471. (Illus.). 32p. (ps-2). 1994. PLB 14.40 (*0-516-06027-9*); pap. 3.95 (*0-516-46027-7*) Childrens.

Kellogg, Cynthia. Corn: What It Is, What It Does. LC 88-18784. (Illus.). 48p. 1989. 11.95 (*0-688-08024-3*); PLB 11.88 (*0-688-08026-X*) Greenwillow.

CORN–FICTION

Ketteman, Helen. The Year of No More Corn. Parker, Robert A., illus. LC 90-29092. 32p. (ps-2). 1993. 14.95 (*0-531-05950-2*); PLB 14.99 (*0-531-08550-3*) Orchard Bks Watts.

Levin, Betty. Starshine & Sunglow. Smith, Joseph A., illus. LC 93-26672. 96p. (gr. 4-7). 1994. PLB 14.00 (*0-688-12806-8*) Greenwillow.

Politi, Leo. Three Stalks of Corn. Politi, Leo, illus. LC 93-19737. 32p. (gr. k-3). 1994. pap. 4.95 (*0-689-71782-2*, Aladdin) Macmillan Child Grp.

CORNWALL–FICTION

Weatherhill, Craig. The Lyonesse Stone: A Novel of West Cornwall. (Illus.). 176p. 1992. pap. 9.95 (*0-907018-85-8*, Pub. by Tabb Hse Pubs UK) Seven Hills Bk Dists.

CORONADO, FRANCISCO VASQUEZ DE, 1510?-1554

Weisberg, Barbara. Coronado's Golden Quest. Eagle, Mike, illus. LC 92-18078. 79p. (gr. 2-5). 1992. PLB 21.34 (*0-8114-7232-9*); pap. 4.95 (*0-8114-8072-0*) Raintree Steck-V.

Zadra, Dan. Explorers of America: Coronado. rev. ed. (gr. 2-4). 1988. PLB 14.95 (*0-88682-182-7*) Creative Ed.

CORONARY HEART DISEASES

see Heart–Diseases

CORPULENCE

see Weight Control

CORRECTIONAL INSTITUTIONS

see Prisons

CORRESPONDENCE

see Letter Writing; Letters

CORRUPTION (IN POLITICS)–FICTION

Tunis, John R. City for Lincoln. 392p. (gr. 3-7). 1989. pap. 3.95 (*0-15-218580-1*, Odyssey) HarBrace.

Westall, Robert. A Place to Hide. 208p. (gr. 7 up). 1994. 13.95 (*0-590-47748-X*, Scholastic Hardcover) Scholastic Inc.

CORSAIRS

see Pirates

CORTES, HERNANDO, 1485-1547

De Castillo, Bernal D. Cortez & the Conquest of Mexico by the Spaniards in 1521. Herzog, B. G., abridged by. LC 88-581. xii, 165p. (gr. 5 up). 1988. Repr. of 1942 ed. 19.50 (*0-208-02221-X*, Linnet) Shoe String.

Jacobs, William J. Cortes: Conquerer of Mexico. LC 93-31177. (Illus.). 64p. (gr. 5-8). 1994. PLB 12.90 (*0-531-20138-4*) Watts.

Larsen, Anita. Montezuma's Missing Treasure. LC 91-19259. (Illus.). 48p. (gr. 5-6). 1992. text ed. 11.95 RSBE (*0-89686-615-7*, Crestwood Hse) Macmillan Child Grp.

Stein, R. Conrad. Hernando Cortes: Conqueror of Mexico. LC 90-20655. (Illus.). 128p. (gr. 3 up). 1991. PLB 20.55 (*0-516-03059-0*) Childrens.

COSBY, WILLIAM HENRY, JR., 1938-

Conord, Bruce W. Bill Cosby. (Illus.). 80p. (gr. 3-5). 1993. PLB 12.95 (*0-7910-1761-3*) Chelsea Hse.

Herbert, Solomon & Hill, George. Bill Cosby. (Illus.). 104p. (gr. 5 up). 1992. lib. bdg. 17.95 (*0-7910-1121-6*) Chelsea Hse.

Martin, Patricia S. Bill Cosby: Superstar. (Illus.). 24p. (gr. 1-4). 1987. PLB 14.60 (*0-86592-169-5*); 10.95s.p. (*0-685-67569-6*) Rourke Corp.

Rosenberg, Robert. Bill Cosby: The Changing Black Image. (Illus.). 96p. (gr. 7 up). 1991. PLB 15.40 (*1-878841-17-3*); pap. 5.95 (*1-56294-828-8*) Millbrook Pr.

—Bill Cosby: The Changing Black Image. 1992. pap. 5.95 (*0-395-63615-9*) HM.

Woods, Harold & Woods, Geraldine. Bill Cosby: Making America Laugh & Learn. LC 82-23497. (Illus.). 48p. (gr. 3 up). 1989. text ed. 13.95 RSBE (*0-87518-240-2*, Dillon) Macmillan Child Grp.

COSMETICS

Cobb, Vicki. The Secret Life of Cosmetics: A Science Experiment Book. Cobb, Theo, illus. LC 85-40097. 128p. (gr. 5-9). 1985. 14.00 (*0-397-32121-X*, Lipp Jr Bks); PLB 13.89 (*0-397-32122-8*, Lipp Jr Bks) HarpC Child Bks.

Everett, F. Make-up. (Illus.). 32p. (gr. 6 up). 1987. PLB 13.96 (*0-88110-242-3*); pap. 5.95 (*0-7460-0075-8*) EDC.

Gunter, Annetta, illus. Kitchen Cosmetics: Using Herbs, Fruits & Eatables in Natural Cosmetics. 2nd, rev. ed. 131p. (gr. 8 up). 1988. pap. 9.95 (*0-9620838-0-1*) Herb Studies.

COSMETICS–FICTION

Stratton-Porter, Gene. Freckles. 254p. 1980. Repr. PLB 21.95 (*0-89966-224-2*) Buccaneer Bks.

COSMOGONY

see Universe

COSMOGONY, BIBLICAL

see Creation

COSMOGRAPHY

see Universe

COSMOLOGY

see Universe

COSMOLOGY, BIBLICAL

see Creation

COSMONAUTS

see Astronauts

COSTA RICA

Cummins, Ronnie & Weber, Valerie. Children of the World: Costa Rica. Welch, Rose, photos by. LC 89-43138. 64p. (gr. 5-6). 1990. PLB 21.26 (*0-8368-0222-5*) Gareth Stevens Inc.

Lerner Publications, Department of Geography Staff. Costa Rica in Pictures. (Illus.). 64p. (gr. 5 up). 1987. PLB 17.50 (*0-8225-1805-8*) Lerner Pubns.

COSTA RICA–FICTION

Franklin, Kristine L. Cuando Regresaron los Monos. Roth, Robert, illus. Zubizarreta, Rosa, tr. from ENG. LC 93-46783. (SPA., Illus.). (gr. k-3). 1994. 14.95 (*0-689-31950-9*, Atheneum) Macmillan.

—When the Monkeys Came Back. Roth, Robert, illus. LC 92-33684. 1994. 14.95 (*0-689-31807-3*, Atheneum) Macmillan.

COSTUME

Here are entered descriptive and historical works on the costume of particular countries or periods and for works on fancy costume. Works dealing with clothing from a practical standpoint, including the art of dress, are entered under Clothing and Dress. Works describing the prevailing mode or style in dress are entered under Fashion.

see also Arms and Armor; Clothing and Dress; Cosmetics; Fashion; Hats; Indians of North America–Costume and Adornment; Jewelry; Make-Up, Theatrical; Uniforms, Military

Baker, Patricia. The Forties. (Illus.). 64p. (gr. 6-10). 1992. lib. bdg. 16.95x (*0-8160-2467-7*) Facts on File.

Blumberg, Rhoda. Bloomers! Morgan, Mary, illus. LC 92-27154. 32p. (gr. k-5). 1993. RSBE 14.95 (*0-02-711684-0*, Bradbury Pr) Macmillan Child Grp.

Chernoff, Goldie T. Easy Costumes You Don't Have to Sew. LC 76-46428. (Illus.). 48p. (gr. 1-3). 1984. RSBE 13.95 (*0-02-718230-4*, Four Winds) Macmillan Child Grp.

Conaway, Judith. Happy Haunting: Halloween Costumes You Can Make. Barto, Renzo, illus. LC 85-28840. 48p. (gr. 1-5). 1986. PLB 11.89 (*0-8167-0666-2*); pap. text ed. 3.50 (*0-8167-0667-0*) Troll Assocs.

—Make Your Own Costumes & Disguises. Barto, Renzo, illus. LC 86-11212. 48p. (gr. 1-5). 1987. PLB 11.89 (*0-8167-0840-1*); pap. text ed. 3.50 (*0-8167-0841-X*) Troll Assocs.

Costantino, Maria. The Thirties. Cumming, Valerie & Feldman, Elane, eds. (Illus.). 64p. (gr. 6-10). 1992. lib. bdg. 16.95x (*0-8160-2466-9*) Facts on File.

Costumes of the Saxons & Vikings. 72p. (gr. 7-11). 1991. 19.95 (*0-7134-5750-3*, Pub. by Batsford UK) Trafalgar.

Dickenson, Gill. Children's Costume. 1993. 12.98 (*1-55521-919-5*) Bk Sales Inc.

Dubuc, Suzanne. Paper Costumes. (Illus.). 32p. (gr. 3-7). 1993. 7.95 (*2-7625-6739-4*, Pub. by Les Edits Herit CN) Adams Inc MA.

Fabian, Erika. Costumes of Splendid China. Limtiaco, Lily C., illus. 12p. (gr. 1-4). 1994. pap. write for info. (*0-9638417-1-8*) Eriako Assocs.

Herald, Jacqueline. The Twenties. Cumming, Valerie & Feldman, Elane, eds. (Illus.). 64p. (gr. 7-12). 1991. 16. 95x (*0-8160-2465-0*) Facts on File.

Kerins, Anthony. Tat Rabbit's Treasure. Kerins, Anthony, illus. LC 92-32600. 32p. (ps-1). 1993. SBE 14.95 (*0-689-50553-1*, M K McElderry) Macmillan Child Grp.

Kingshead Corporation Staff. Cut-Color-&-Create: Make Your Own: Box Magic. Kingshead Corporation Staff, illus. 24p. (ps-1). 1989. pap. 2.97 (*1-55941-039-6*) Kingshead Corp.

—Cut-Color-&-Create: Make Your Own: Box Magic. Kingshead Corporation Staff, illus. 24p. (ps-1). 1989. pap. 2.97 (*1-55941-038-8*) Kingshead Corp.

Lipson, Michelle, et al. The Fantastic Costume Book: Forty Complete Patterns to Amaze & Amuse. LC 92-11365. (Illus.). 128p. (gr. 4 up). 1992. 19.95 (*0-8069-8376-0*) Sterling.

Masters, Nanvy R. The Horrible, Homemade Halloween Costume. Warr, Debra H., illus. 32p. (gr. 2-4). 1993. 14.95 (*0-9623563-3-6*) J R Matthews.

Oldfield, Margaret J. Costumes & Customs of Many Lands. (Illus.). (gr. k-3). 1982. pap. 2.95 (*0-934876-19-3*) Creative Storytime.

Rawson. Disguise & Make-Up. (gr. 2-5). 1979. (Usborne-Hayes); pap. 4.50 (*0-86020-166-X*) EDC.

Ruby, Jennifer. Nineteen Fifties & Nineteen Sixties. (Illus.). 48p. (gr. 6-9). 1994. 19.95 (*0-7134-7217-0*, Pub. by Batsford UK) Trafalgar.

—Nineteen Seventies & Nineteen Eighties. (Illus.). 48p. (gr. 6-9). 1994. 19.95 (*0-7134-7218-9*, Pub. by Batsford UK) Trafalgar.

Shulz, Charles, illus. People & Customs of the World. LC 94-13723. 1994. write for info. (*0-517-11898-X*, Pub. by Derrydale Bks) Random Hse Value.

COSTUME–HISTORY

ABC: Costume & Textiles from the Los Angeles County Museum of Art. (Illus.). 32p. (gr. 2 up). 1988. 12.95 (*0-8109-1877-3*) Abrams.

Carnegie, Vicky. The Eighties. Cumming, Valerie & Feldman, Elane, eds. (Illus.). 64p. 1990. 16.95x (*0-8160-2471-5*) Facts on File.

Connikie, Yvonne. The Sixties. Cumming, Valerie & Feldman, Elane, eds. (Illus.). 1990. 16.95x (*0-8160-2469-3*) Facts on File.

First Ladies Gowns. (Illus.). 32p. (ps-6). 1983. pap. 29.50 per set of 10 (*0-87474-621-3*, FLCBP) Smithsonian.

Greenlaw, M. Jean. Ranch Dressing: The Story of Western Wear. (Illus.). 64p. (gr. 3-7). 1993. 15.99 (*0-525-67432-2*, Lodestar Bks) Dutton Child Bks.

Morley, Jacqueline. Clothes for Work, Play & Display. LC 92-4852. 1992. 13.95 (*0-531-15249-9*) Watts.

Patteson, Nelda. Clara Driscoll: Savior of the Alamo: Her Life Story Presented Through the Clothes She Wore. (Illus.). 32p. (gr. 4-7). 1991. pap. 14.95 (*0-9629001-0-9*) Smiley Originals.

Rowland-Warne, L. Costume. McAulay, Liz, photos by. LC 91-53135. (Illus.). 64p. (gr. 5 up). 1992. 16.00 (*0-679-81680-1*); PLB 16.99 (*0-679-91680-6*) Knopf Bks Yng Read.

Ruby, Jennifer. Costume in Context: Medieval Times. (Illus.). 64p. (gr. 7-11). 1990. 24.95 (*0-7134-6075-X*, Pub. by Batsford UK) Trafalgar.

—Costume in Context: The 1940s & 1950s. (Illus.). 64p. (gr. 7-11). 1990. 24.95 (*0-7134-6016-4*, Pub. by Batsford UK) Trafalgar.

—Costume in Context: The 1980s. (Illus.). 72p. (gr. 7-11). 1991. 24.95 (*0-7134-6539-5*, Pub. by Batsford UK) Trafalgar.

—The Edwardians & the First World War. (Illus.). 72p. (gr. 7-9). 1988. 24.95 (*0-7134-5605-1*, Pub. by Batsford UK) Trafalgar.

—The Nineteen Twenties & Nineteen Thirties. (Illus.). 64p. (gr. 7-9). 1989. 24.95 (*0-7134-5773-2*, Pub. by Batsford UK) Trafalgar.

—The Stuarts. (Illus.). 72p. (gr. 7-9). 1988. 24.95 (*0-7134-5604-3*, Pub. by Batsford UK) Trafalgar.

COSTUME DESIGN

Everett, F. Fashion Design. (Illus.). (gr. 6 up). 1988. PLB 14.96 (*0-88110-307-1*); pap. 8.95 (*0-7460-0187-8*) EDC.

Lipson, Michelle. The Fantastic Costume Book: Forty Complete Patterns to Amaze & Amuse. (Illus.). 128p. (gr. 4 up). 1993. pap. 12.95 (*0-8069-8377-9*, Pub. by Lark Bks) Sterling.

Molyneux, Lynn & Gordner, Brad. Act It Out: Original Plays Plus Crafts for Costumes & Scenery. Marasco, Pam, illus. 192p. (gr. 2-6). 1986. spiral bdg. 12.95 (*0-685-29139-1*) Trellis Bks Inc.

Moss, Miriam. Fashion Designer. LC 90-48323. (Illus.). 32p. (gr. 5-6). 1991. text ed. 13.95 RSBE (*0-89686-610-6*, Crestwood Hse) Macmillan Child Grp.

Oscar De La Renta. (ps-3). 1993. 18.95 (*0-7910-1783-4*) Chelsea Hse.

Riehecky, Janet. Carolina Herrera: International Fashion Designer. LC 90-28886. (Illus.). 32p. (gr. 2-4). 1991. PLB 11.80 (*0-516-04178-9*); pap. 3.95 (*0-516-44178-7*) Childrens.

COSTUME DESIGN–FICTION

Chevance, Audrey. Tutu. Chevance, Audrey, illus. LC 91-3506. 32p. (ps-4). 1991. 13.95 (*0-525-44769-5*, DCB) Dutton Child Bks.

Garelick, May. Just My Size. Pene Du Bois, William, illus. LC 89-34513. 32p. (ps-3). 1990. HarpC Child Bks.

Viorst, Judith. Earrings! Malone, Nola L., illus. LC 89-17846. 32p. (gr. 1-4). 1990. SBE 13.95 (*0-689-31615-1*, Atheneum Child Bk) Macmillan Child Grp.

COSTUMES, MILITARY

see Uniforms, Military

COTTAGES

see Houses

COTTON

see also Fibers

Cotton. (Illus.). (gr. 5 up). 1984. lib. bdg. 17.27 (*0-86592-266-7*); lib. bdg. 12.95s.p. (*0-685-73927-9*) Rourke Corp.

Riquier, Aline. The Cotton in Your T-Shirt. Riquier, Aline, illus. 40p. (gr. k-5). 1993. PLB 9.95 (*1-56674-058-4*, HTS Bks) Forest Hse.

Selsam, Millicent E. Cotton. Wexler, Jerome, illus. LC 82-6496. 48p. (gr. k-3). 1982. 12.95 (*0-688-01499-2*); lib. bdg. 14.88 (*0-688-01500-X*, Morrow Jr Bks) Morrow Jr Bks.

Wonsham, Genevieve. Cotton Carta: To Our City Cousins, Big Town, U. S. A. LC 77-83628. (Illus.). (ps-2). 1978. PLB 5.95 (*0-89508-023-0*) Rainbow Bks.

Worsham, Genevieve. Cotton Carta. LC 77-83627. (Illus.). 32p. (gr. 2-4). 1978. PLB 9.95 (*0-87783-144-0*); pap. 3.94 deluxe ed. (*0-87783-149-1*) Oddo.

COTTON–FICTION

Williams, S. Working Cotton. Byard, C., ed. 1992. 14.95 (*0-15-299624-9*, HB Juv Bks) HarBrace.

COTTON MANUFACTURE AND TRADE

Mitgutsch, Ali. From Cotton to Pants. Mitgutsch, Ali, illus. LC 80-29552. 24p. (ps-3). 1981. PLB 10.95 (*0-87614-150-5*) Carolrhoda Bks.

Riquier, Aline. The Cotton in Your T-Shirt. Bogard, Vicki, tr. from FRE. Riquier, Aline, illus. LC 91-45786. 38p. (gr. k-5). 1992. 5.95 (*0-944589-40-5*) Young Discovery Lib.

Selsam, Millicent E. Cotton. Wexler, Jerome, illus. LC 82-6496. 48p. (gr. k-3). 1982. 12.95 (*0-688-01499-2*); lib. bdg. 14.88 (*0-688-01500-X*, Morrow Jr Bks) Morrow Jr Bks.

Wonsham, Genevieve. Cotton Carta: To Our City Cousins, Big Town, U. S. A. LC 77-83628. (Illus.). (ps-2). 1978. PLB 5.95 (*0-89508-023-0*) Rainbow Bks.

COUNSELING

see also Vocational Guidance

Painter, Carol. Friends Helping Friends: A Manual for Peer Counselors. Sorenson, Don L., ed. 224p. (Orig.). (gr. 9-12). 1989. pap. text ed. 9.95x (*0-932796-28-1*) Ed Media Corp.

Tucker, Jeff & Tucker, Ramona. No Artificial Flavors: One Hundred Per Cent Friendship. LC 88-34710. 110p. (gr. 7 up). 1989. pap. 5.99 (*0-87788-582-6*) Shaw Pubs.

COUNTER-REFORMATION

see Reformation

COUNTERFEITS AND COUNTERFEITING–FICTION

Clifford, Eth. Harvey's Mystifying Raccoon Mix-Up. LC 93-27471. 1994. 13.95 (*0-395-68714-4*) HM.

Wald, Ann. Choice Adventure: Counterfeit Collection. LC 92-36279. 1993. 4.99 (*0-8423-5049-7*) Tyndale.

COUNTING BOOKS

Abby Aldrich Rockefeller Folk Art Center Staff & Watson, Amy. The Folk Art Counting Book: From the Abby Aldrich Rockefeller Folk Art Center. (Illus.). 40p. (ps-k). 1992. 9.95 (*0-87935-084-9*, Co-Pub. by Abrams) Williamsburg.

Ada, Alam F. In the Cow's Backyard - La Hamaca de la Vaca. Escriva, Vivi, illus. (SPA & ENG.). 23p. (gr. k-2). 1991. English ed. 6.95 (*1-56014-275-8*); Spanish ed. 6.95 (*1-56014-219-7*) Santillana.

Aker, Suzanne. What Comes in Twos, Threes & Fours? LC 89-35482. 1990. pap. 13.95 (*0-671-67173-1*, S&S BFYR) S&S Trade.

—What Comes in Twos, Threes, & Fours? LC 89-3548. (ps). 1992. pap. 4.95 (*0-671-79247-4*, S&S BFYR) S&S Trade.

Alexander, Lloyd. The Book of Three. 192p. (gr. k-6). 1978. pap. 3.99 (*0-440-40702-8*, YB) Dell.

Allen, Jonathan. One with a Bun. Allen, Jonathan, illus. LC 91-44055. 12p. (ps). 1992. 3.95 (*0-688-11781-3*, Tambourine Bks) Morrow.

Ambrus, Victor G. Count, Dracula! Ambrus, Victor G., illus. LC 91-40269. 24p. (ps-1). 1992. 3.99 (*0-517-58969-9*) Crown Bks Yng Read.

Anastasio, Dina. Sesame Street Counting Book. 1985. 1.00 (*0-307-02023-1*) Western Pub.
Anholt, Catherine & Anholt, Laurence. One, Two, Three, Count with Me. (Illus.). 32p. (ps-1). 1994. 12.99 (*0-670-85261-9*) Viking Child Bks.
Anno, Mitsumasa. Anno's Counting Book. Anno, Mitsumasa, illus. LC 76-28977. 32p. (ps-3). 1977. 16. 00 (*0-690-01287-X*, Crowell Jr Bks); PLB 15.89 (*0-690-01288-8*) HarpC Child Bks.
—Anno's Counting Book Big Book. LC 65-28977. (Illus.). 32p. (ps-3). 1992. pap. 19.95 (*0-06-443315-3*, Trophy) HarpC Child Bks.
—Anno's Counting House. (Illus.). 48p. (ps-3). 1982. 16. 95 (*0-399-20896-8*, Philomel) Putnam Pub Group.
Argent, Kerry & Trinca, Rod. One Woolly Wombat. Argent, Kerry, illus. 32p. (ps-1). 1987. pap. 6.95 (*0-916291-10-3*) Kane-Miller Bk.
Ashton, Elizabeth A. An Old-Fashined One Two Three Book. Smith, Jessie W., illus. LC 92-21109. 32p. (ps-3). 1993. pap. 4.99 (*0-14-054310-4*) Puffin Bks.
—An Old-Fashioned One Two Three Book. Smith, Jesse W., illus. 32p. (ps-3). 1991. 14.95 (*0-670-83499-8*) Viking Child Bks.
Audry-Iljic, Francoise & Courtin, Thierry. My First Numbers. Herbst, Judith, adapted by. LC 94-1090. (Illus.). 60p. (ps-k). 1994. 12.95 (*0-8120-6314-7*) Barron.
Aylesworth, Jim. One Crow: A Counting Rhyme. Young, Ruth, illus. LC 85-45856. 32p. (ps-1). 1990. pap. 5.95 (*0-06-443242-4*, Trophy) HarpC Child Bks.
Baby's First Counting Book. 12p. (ps). 1978. 3.95 (*0-448-40863-5*, G&D) Putnam Pub Group.
Baker, Keith. Big Fat Hen. LC 93-19160. 1994. 13.95 (*0-15-292869-3*) HarBrace.
Balducci, Rita. Poky Little Puppy's Busy Counting Book. (ps-3). 1994. pap. 1.95 (*0-307-10015-4*, Golden Pr) Western Pub.
Bang, Molly. Ten, Nine, Eight. 1993. pap. 28.67 (*0-590-73313-3*) Scholastic Inc.
Bassett, Lisa. Ten Little Bunnies. Bassett, Jeni, illus. LC 92-37986. (gr. 2 up). 1993. 3.99 (*0-517-08154-7*) Random Hse Value.
Beck, Ian. Five Little Ducks. LC 92-27193. (Illus.). 32p. (ps-2). 1993. 14.95 (*0-8050-2525-1*, Bks Young Read) H Holt & Co.
Becker, John. Seven Little Rabbits. 2nd ed. Cooney, Barbara, tr. (Illus.). 32p. (ps-3). 1994. Repr. of 1974 ed. 5.95 (*0-8027-8311-2*) Walker & Co.
Beeson, Bob. Ten Little Circus Mice. Beeson, Bob, illus. 32p. (ps-1). 1993. 11.95 (*0-8249-8616-4*, Ideals Child) Hambleton-Hill.
Benjamin, Alan. Let's Count, Dracula: A Chubby Board Book. (ps). 1992. pap. 3.95 (*0-671-77008-X*, Little Simon) S&S Trade.
Bertrand, Lynne. One Day, Two Dragons. Street, Janet, illus. LC 91-32743. 32p. (ps-2). 1992. 14.00 (*0-517-58411-5*); PLB 14.99 (*0-517-58413-1*) Crown Bks Yng Read.
Bishop, Roma. Numbers. (Illus.). 14p. (ps-k). 1991. pap. 2.95 (*0-671-74832-7*, Little Simon) S&S Trade.
Bjorke, Drew. The Viking Counting Book. Bjorke, Drew, illus. 12p. (ps). 1993. 4.95 (*1-56828-034-3*) Red Jacket Pr.
Blumenthal, Nancy. Count-A-Saurus. Kaufman, Robert J., illus. LC 91-41250. 24p. (gr. k-3). 1992. pap. 3.95 (*0-689-71633-8*, Aladdin) Macmillan Child Grp.
Borgo, Deborah C., illus. Thomas the Tank Engine Counts to Ten. Awdry, W., contrib. by. (Illus.). 14p. (ps). 1993. bds. 2.50 (*0-679-81644-5*) Random Bks Yng Read.
Breeze, Lynn. Baby's Food. (Illus.). 14p. (ps). 1994. bds. 4.50 fold-outs (*0-8120-6413-5*) Barron.
Brisson, Pat. Benny's Pennies. (gr. 4 up). 1993. pap. 14.95 (*0-385-41602-4*) Doubleday.
Brookes, Diane. Passing the Peace: A Counting Book for Kids. (FRE & ENG., Illus.). 24p. 1990. pap. 8.95 (*0-921254-20-2*, Pub. by Penumbra Pr CN) U of Toronto Pr.
Brown, Kenneth, illus. Dollhouse Book: Color & Counting Concepts. 1994. 12.95 (*1-56743-044-9*) Amistad Pr.
Bryant-Mole, Karen. Dot-to-Dot Space. (Illus.). 24p. (gr. k-1). 1993. pap. 3.50 (*0-7460-1373-6*, Usborne) EDC.
Bursik, Rose. Zoe's Sheep. 1994. 14.95 (*0-8050-2530-8*) H Holt & Co.
Burton, Marilee R. One Little Chickadee. Street, Janet, illus. LC 93-27271. (gr. 2 up). 15.00 (*0-688-12651-0*, Tambourine Bks); PLB 14.93 (*0-688-12652-9*) Morrow.
Can You Count in the Dark? LC 92-30145. 16p. (ps-1). 1993. pap. 4.99 (*0-679-84195-4*) Random Bks Yng Read.
Capdevila, Roser, illus. Let's Count. Ballar, Elisabet, text by. LC 92-2813. 44p. (ps-4). 1992. 13.95 (*1-56566-011-0*) Thomasson-Grant.
Carroll, Kathleen S. One Red Rooster. Barbier, Suzette, illus. 32p. (ps). 1992. 13.45 (*0-395-60195-9*) HM.
Cars, Trucks, Trains, & Planes. (Illus.). 48p. (Orig.). (ps-2). 1989. pap. 2.95 (*0-8431-2727-9*) Price Stern.
Carter, David A. Baby Bug Counting. (Illus.). (ps-6). 1993. pap. 4.95 (*0-671-86876-4*, Little Simon) S&S Trade.
Cartwright, S. One, Two, Three. (Illus.). 32p. 1992. (Usborne); pap. 8.95 (*0-7460-0726-4*, Usborne) EDC.
Challoner, J. The Science Book of Numbers. 1992. 9.95 (*0-15-200623-0*, Gulliver Bks) HarBrace.
Chandra, Deborah. Miss Mabel's Table. Grover, Max, illus. LC 93-9137. (ps-2). 1994. 14.95 (*0-15-276712-6*, Browndeer Pr) HarBrace.
Chariot Staff. Christmas Pop-up Counting Book. (ps). 1993. 9.99 (*0-7814-0127-5*, Chariot Bks) Chariot Family.
Charlip, Remy & Joyner, Jerry. Thirteen. LC 75-8875. (Illus.). 40p. (ps up). 1984. Repr. of 1975 ed. RSBE 14.95 (*0-02-718120-0*, Four Winds) Macmillan Child Grp.
Chwast, Seymour. The Twelve Circus Rings. LC 92-13576. 1993. write for info. (*0-15-200627-3*) HarBrace.
Clements, Andrew. Mother Earth's Counting Book. Johnson, Lonni S., illus. LC 90-7343. 44p. (gr. k up). 1992. pap. 15.95 (*0-88708-138-X*) Picture Bk Studio.
Coats, Lucy. One Hungry Baby: A Bedtime Counting Rhyme. Hellard, Sue, illus. LC 93-42620. 32p. (ps-k). 1994. 9.99 (*0-517-59887-6*) Crown Bks Yng Read.
Cole, Norma. Blast Off! A Space Counting Book. Peck, Marshall, III, illus. LC 93-28794. 32p. (ps-4). 1994. 14.95 (*0-88106-499-8*); PLB 15.88 (*0-88106-493-9*); pap. 6.95 (*0-88106-498-X*) Charlesbridge Pub.
Conran, Sebastian. My First 1-2-3 Book. Conran, Sebastian, illus. LC 88-6275. 64p. (ps-1). 1988. pap. 7.95 POB (*0-689-71267-7*, Aladdin) Macmillan Child Grp.
Cory's Counting Game. 24p. (ps). 1979. 6.95 (*0-8431-0629-8*) Price Stern.
Count on It. (Illus.). (gr. 2 up). 1991. 5.95 (*0-87449-578-4*) Modern Pub NYC.
Count Ten Baby Animals. (Illus.). 6p. (gr. k-2). 1988. bds. 6.95 (*0-87449-452-4*) Modern Pub NYC.
Count Ten Circus Friends. (Illus.). 6p. (gr. k-2). 1988. bds. 6.95 (*0-87449-455-9*) Modern Pub NYC.
Count Ten Fun & Games. (Illus.). 6p. (gr. k-2). 1988. bds. 6.95 (*0-87449-454-0*) Modern Pub NYC.
Count Ten Playtime Toys. (Illus.). 6p. (gr. k-2). 1988. bds. 6.95 (*0-87449-453-2*) Modern Pub NYC.
The Count Your Change Wipe-Off Book. 24p. (ps-3). 1992. pap. 1.95 (*0-590-45694-6*) Scholastic Inc.
Crews, Donald. Ten Black Dots. rev. ed. Crews, Donald, illus. LC 85-14871. 32p. (ps-3). 1986. 15.00 (*0-688-06067-6*); PLB 14.93 (*0-688-06068-4*) Greenwillow.
Crowther, Robert. The Most Amazing Hide & Seek Counting Book. Crowther, Robert, illus. 14p. (ps-3). 1981. pap. 13.95 (*0-670-48997-2*) Viking Child Bks.
Culton, Wilma. Down at the Billabong. Crossett, Warren, illus. LC 92-31951. 1993. 3.75 (*0-383-03565-1*) SRA Schl Grp.
D'Andrea, Deborah. Count with Me 1,2,3. Ayers, Michael B., illus. 12p. (ps-k). 1991. 4.99 (*1-878338-07-2*) Picture Me Bks.
Dee, Ruby. Two Ways to Count to Ten. Meddaugh, Susan, illus. LC 86-33513. 32p. (ps-2). 1990. pap. 5.95 (*0-8050-1314-8*, Owlet BYR) H Holt & Co.
Delcher, Eden, compiled by. Mother Goose Counting Rhymes. 1993. 2.98 (*1-55521-832-6*) Bk Sales Inc.
Disney's Pop-up Book of Numbers. LC 90-85432. (Illus.). 12p. (ps-k). 1991. 6.95 (*1-56282-021-4*) Disney Pr.
Dodds, Dayle Ann. Someone Is Hiding. 1994. PLB 8.95 (*0-671-75542-0*, Little Simon) S&S Trade.
Drew, David. How Many Legs? Stewart, Chantal, illus. LC 92-34268. 1993. 4.25 (*0-383-03631-3*) SRA Schl Grp.
Dudko, Mary A. & Larsen, Margie. Baby Bop's Counting Book. Hartley, Linda, ed. 22p. (ps). 1993. bds. 3.95 (*0-7829-0374-6*) Lyons Group.
—Baby Bop's Counting Book. Hartley, Linda, ed. Full, Dennis, photos by. LC 93-77866. (Illus.). 22p. (ps). 1993. Repr. bds. 3.95 chunky board (*1-57064-006-8*) Barney Pub.
Duerrstein, Richard, illus. One Mickey Mouse: A Disney Book of Numbers. LC 92-52973. 12p. (ps). 1992. 5.95 (*1-56282-251-9*) Disney Pr.
Dunbar, Joyce. Ten Little Mice. 24p. (ps-1). 1990. 13.95 (*0-15-200601-X*) HarBrace.
Dunrea, Olivier. Deep down Underground. Dunrea, Olivier, illus. LC 92-45273. 32p. (gr. k-3). 1993. pap. 4.95 (*0-689-71756-3*, Aladdin) Macmillan Child Grp.
Edens, Cooper. The Wonderful Counting Clock. Kimball, Katherine, illus. LC 93-14404. 1995. 15.00 (*0-671-88334-8*, Green Tiger) S&S Trade.
Edwards, Richard. Ten Tall Oaktrees. Crossland, Caroline, illus. LC 92-41771. 32p. (ps up). 1993. 15.00 (*0-688-04620-7*, Tambourine Bks); PLB 14.93 (*0-688-04621-5*, Tambourine Bks) Morrow.
Ehlert, Lois. Fish Eyes: A Book You Can Count On. LC 89-1535. (ps-3). 1992. pap. 4.95 (*0-15-228051-0*, Voyager Bks) HarBrace.
Eichenberg, Fritz. Dancing in the Moon: Counting Rhymes. Eichenberg, Fritz, illus. LC 75-8514. 25p. (gr. k-1). 1975. pap. 3.95 (*0-15-623811-X*, Voyager Bks) HarBrace.
English, Tracey. Old Macdonald Had a Farm: A Lift & Look Counting Book. (ps-3). 1993. 9.95 (*0-307-17601-0*, Artsts Writrs) Western Pub.
Faber, Roger A. Birds on a Wire. Faber, Roger A., illus. (ps-1). Date not set. pap. write for info. (*1-880122-06-5*) White Stone.
Facklam, Margery & Thomas, Margaret. The Kids' World Almanac of Amazing Facts about Numbers, Math, & Money. (Illus.). 256p. (Orig.). 1992. 14.95 (*0-88687-635-4*); pap. 7.95 (*0-88687-634-6*) Wrld Almnc.
Falwell, Cathryn. Feast for Ten. Falwell, Cathryn, illus. LC 92-35512. 32p. (ps-3). 1993. 14.95 (*0-395-62037-6*, Clarion Bks) HM.
—Nicky, 1-2-3. Briley, Dorothy, ed. Falwell, Cathryn, illus. 24p. (ps). 1991. 5.70 (*0-395-56913-3*, Clarion Bks) HM.
Fancy Dress Party Counting Book. 1993. 3.99 (*0-517-08760-X*) Random Hse Value.
Faulkner, Keith. I Can Count. (ps). 1994. pap. 7.95 (*0-671-88027-6*, Little Simon) S&S Trade.
Feelings, Muriel. Moja Means One: A Swahili Counting Book. LC 76-134856. (Illus.). 32p. (gr. k up). 1976. pap. 4.95 (*0-8037-5711-5*) Dial Bks Young.
Felix, Monique. Numbers: Mouse Books. (Illus.). 32p. (ps). 1993. pap. 2.95 (*1-56189-091-X*) Amer Educ Pub.
Ferarro, Bonita. Numbers & Counting. Robison, Don, illus. 32p. (Orig.). (ps). 1993. wkbk. 1.99 (*1-56189-057-X*) Amer Educ Pub.
Fleming, Denise. Count! Fleming, Denise, illus. LC 91-25686. 32p. (ps-1). 1992. 14.95 (*0-8050-1595-7*, Bks Young Read) H Holt & Co.
Friedman, Aileen. The King's Commissioners. Guevara, Susan, illus. LC 94-11275. 1994. write for info. (*0-590-48989-5*) Scholastic Inc.
Funtime ABC & 123. (Illus.). 24p. (gr. k-2). 1988. 3.95 (*0-87449-498-2*) Modern Pub NYC.
Gabriele. One Two Threes. 1985. pap. 1.95 (*0-911211-66-7*) Penny Lane Pubns.
Gamec, Hazel S. The Magic Pencil Counting Book. Gamec, Hazel S., illus. 12p. 1980. write for info. (*0-938042-00-9*) Printek.
Geisert, Arthur. Pigs from One to Ten. Geisert, Arthur, illus. LC 92-5097. 32p. (gr. k-3). 1992. 14.45 (*0-395-58519-8*) HM.
Ghrist, Julie, illus. Taelly's Counting Adventures. (ps). 1993. Gift box set of 4 bks., 12p. ea. incl. counting flash cards. bds. 14.95 (*1-56828-042-4*) Red Jacket Pr.
—Taelly's Counting Adventures: At Sea. 12p. (ps). 1993. 4.95 (*1-56828-027-0*) Red Jacket Pr.
—Taelly's Counting Adventures: Down on the Farm. 12p. (ps). 1993. 4.95 (*1-56828-029-7*) Red Jacket Pr.
—Taelly's Counting Adventures: In the Neighborhood. 12p. (ps). 1993. 4.95 (*1-56828-030-0*) Red Jacket Pr.
—Taelly's Counting Adventures: On Mars. 12p. (ps). 1993. 4.95 (*1-56828-028-9*) Red Jacket Pr.
Giganti, Paul, Jr. Each Orange Had Eight Slices: A Counting Book. Crews, Donald, illus. LC 90-24167. 24p. (ps up). 1992. 14.00 (*0-688-10428-2*); PLB 13.93 (*0-688-10429-0*) Greenwillow.
—Each Orange Had Eight Slices: Big Book Edition. Crews, Donald, illus. 32p. (ps up). 1994. pap. 18.95 (*0-688-13116-6*, Mulberry) Morrow.
Gisler, David. Addition Annie. Dunnington, Tom, illus. LC 91-17654. 32p. (ps-2). 1991. PLB 10.25 (*0-516-02007-2*); pap. 2.95 (*0-516-42007-0*) Childrens.
Goennel, Heidi. Odds & Evens: A Numbers Book. Goennel, Heidi, illus. LC 93-15420. 32p. 1994. 15.00 (*0-688-12918-8*, Tambourine Bks); PLB 14.93 (*0-688-12919-6*, Tambourine Bks) Morrow.
Gorbaty, Norman, illus. Turtle Count. 12p. (ps). 1991. pap. 3.95 (*0-671-74434-8*, Little Simon) S&S Trade.
Gould, Ellen. The Blue Number Counting Book. Kelly, Cathy, illus. 13p. (ps-2). pap. 6.00 (*0-938017-01-2*) Learn Tools.
Greenfield, Eloise. Aaron & Gayla's Counting Book. Gilchrist, Jan S., illus. 20p. 1992. 9.95 (*0-86316-209-6*) Writers & Readers.
—Aaron & Gayla's Counting Book. (ps). 1993. pap. 6.95 (*0-86316-214-2*) Writers & Readers.
Gregorich, Barbara. Contando del 1 al 10: Counting 1 to 10. Hoffman, Joan, ed. Shepherd-Bartram, tr. from ENG. Pape, Richard, illus. (SPA.). 32p. (Orig.). 1987. wkbk. 1.99 (*0-938256-79-3*) Sch Zone Pub Co.
—Counting Caterpillars. Hoffman, Joan, ed. Alexander, Barbara, et al, illus. 32p. (Orig.). (ps-1). 1986. wkbk. 1.99 (*0-88743-126-7*) Sch Zone Pub Co.
Gretz, Susanna. Teddy Bears 1 to 10. Gretz, Susanna, illus. LC 86-4795. 32p. (ps-k). 1986. RSBE 13.95 (*0-02-738140-4*, Four Winds) Macmillan Child Grp.
Groening, Matt & Groening, Maggie. Maggie Simpson's Counting Book. LC 91-2865. (Illus.). 32p. (ps-1). 1991. HarpC Child Bks.
Grover, Max. Amazing & Incredible Counting Stories. LC 94-17837. 1995. write for info. (*0-15-200090-9*, Browndeer Pr) HarBrace.
Grundy, Lynn A., illus. Let's Count. 28p. (ps). 1992. 3.50 (*0-7214-1509-1*) Ladybird Bks.
Hague, Kathleen. Numbears: Alphabears. Hague, Michael, illus. LC 85-27006. 32p. (ps-2). 1991. pap. 4.95 (*0-8050-1679-1*, Bks Young Read) H Holt & Co.
Halpern, Shari. Moving from One to Ten. Halpern, Shari, illus. LC 92-26992. 32p. (ps-1). 1993. RSBE 13.95 (*0-02-741981-9*, Macmillan Child Bk) Macmillan Child Grp.
Halsey, Megan. Three Pandas Planting: Counting down to Help the Earth. Halsey, Megan, illus. LC 93-22971. 40p. (gr. k-2). 1994. RSBE 14.95 (*0-02-742035-3*, Bradbury Pr) Macmillan Child Grp.
Hammond. Ten Little Ducks. 1993. pap. 28.67 (*0-590-73338-9*) Scholastic Inc.
Hansen, Lee. My Christmas Counting Book. (ps-3). 1993. pap. 4.95 (*0-307-10361-7*, Golden Pr) Western Pub.
Harshman, Marc. Only One. Garrison, Barbara, illus. LC 92-11349. 32p. (ps-3). 1993. 12.99 (*0-525-65116-0*, Cobblehill Bks) Dutton Child Bks.

Hartmann, Wendy. One Sun Rises: An African Wildlife Counting Book. Maritz, Nicolaas, illus. LC 93-49735. 32p. (ps-1). 1994. 13.99 (*0-525-45225-7*, DCB) Dutton Child Bks.

Haskins, Jim. Count Your Way Through Germany. Byers, Helen, illus. 24p. (gr. 1-4). 1990. PLB 17.50 (*0-87614-407-5*) Carolrhoda Bks.

—Count Your Way Through Germany. LC 89-22232. (ps-3). 1991. pap. 5.95 (*0-87614-532-2*) Carolrhoda Bks.

—Count Your Way Through India. (ps-3). 1992. pap. 5.95 (*0-87614-577-2*) Carolrhoda Bks.

—Count Your Way Through Israel. (ps-3). 1992. pap. 5.95 (*0-87614-558-6*) Carolrhoda Bks.

—Count Your Way Through Italy. Wright, Beth, illus. 24p. (gr. 1-4). 1990. PLB 17.50 (*0-87614-406-7*) Carolrhoda Bks.

—Count Your Way Through Italy. LC 89-37455. (ps-3). 1991. pap. 5.95 (*0-87614-533-0*) Carolrhoda Bks.

Hawkins, Colin & Hawkins, Jacqui. The Numberlies: Number Eight. (Illus.). 32p. (ps-k). 1993. 8.95 (*0-370-31513-8*, Pub. by Bodley Head UK) Trafalgar.

—The Numberlies: Number Five. (Illus.). 32p. (ps-2). 1992. 8.95 (*0-370-31510-3*, Pub. by Bodley Head UK) Trafalgar.

—The Numberlies: Number Four. (Illus.). 32p. (ps-2). 1992. 8.95 (*0-370-31509-X*, Pub. by Bodley Head UK) Trafalgar.

—The Numberlies: Number One. (Illus.). 32p. (ps-1). 1992. 8.95 (*0-370-31506-5*, Pub. by Bodley Head UK) Trafalgar.

—The Numberlies: Number Seven. (Illus.). 32p. (ps-k). 1993. 8.95 (*0-370-31512-X*, Pub. by Bodley Head UK) Trafalgar.

—The Numberlies: Number Six. (Illus.). 32p. (ps-k). 1993. 8.95 (*0-370-31511-1*, Pub. by Bodley Head UK) Trafalgar.

—The Numberlies: Number Three. (Illus.). 32p. (ps-2). 1992. 8.95 (*0-370-31508-1*, Pub. by Bodley Head UK) Trafalgar.

—The Numberlies: Number Two. (Illus.). 32p. (ps-2). 1992. 8.95 (*0-370-31507-3*, Pub. by Bodley Head UK) Trafalgar.

—The Numberlies: Zero. (Illus.). 32p. (ps-k). 1993. 8.95 (*0-370-31640-1*, Pub. by Bodley Head UK) Trafalgar.

Hawksley, Gerald. At Home. Hawksley, Gerald, illus. 10p. (ps). 1990. bds. 4.95 (*1-878624-18-0*) McClanahan Bk.

—Farm. Hawksley, Gerald, illus. 10p. (ps). 1990. bds. 4.95 (*1-878624-16-4*) McClanahan Bk.

—Trucks. Hawksley, Gerald, illus. 10p. (ps). 1990. bds. 4.95 (*1-878624-17-2*) McClanahan Bk.

—Zoo. Hawksley, Gerald, illus. 10p. (ps). 1990. bds. 4.95 (*1-878624-19-9*) McClanahan Bk.

Hefter, Richard. Lots of Little Bears. Hefter, Richard, illus. LC 83-2184. 32p. (ps-1). 1983. 5.95 (*0-911787-04-6*) Optimum Res Inc.

Heinst, Marie. My First Number Book. LC 91-58193. (Illus.). 48p. (ps-3). 1992. 12.95 (*1-879431-73-4*); PLB 13.99 (*1-879431-74-2*) Dorling Kindersley.

Hirsch, Lynn A., illus. Count With Me: One, Two, Three. 32p. (ps-k). 1992. 4.99 (*0-517-07395-1*, Pub. by Derrydale Bks) Random Hse Value.

Hoban, Tana. One, Two, Three. Hoban, Tana, illus. LC 84-10306. 12p. (ps). 1985. bds. 4.95 (*0-688-02579-X*) Greenwillow.

—Who Are They? LC 93-33644. (Illus.). 12p. (ps up). 1994. bds. 4.95 (*0-688-12921-8*) Greenwillow.

Holmes, Stephen. Hidden Numbers. LC 89-78486. (Illus.). 20p. (ps-2). 1990. 13.95 (*0-15-200469-6*, Gulliver Bks) HarBrace.

Honey Bear ABC & Counting Book. (gr. 2-4). 1991. 6.95 (*0-87449-782-5*) Modern Pub NYC.

Honey Bear Animals, Birds & Other Creatures. (gr. 2-4). 1991. 6.95 (*0-87449-781-7*) Modern Pub NYC.

Howard, Katherine. I Can Count to One Hundred...Can You? Smollin, Michael J., illus. LC 78-62700. (ps). 1979. pap. 2.25 (*0-394-84090-9*) Random Bks Yng Read.

Hubbard, Woodleigh. Two Is for Dancing: A One, Two, Three of Actions. Hubbard, Woodleigh, illus. 32p. (ps-1). 1991. 13.95 (*0-87701-895-2*) Chronicle Bks.

Hunt, Jonathan & Hunt, Lisa. One is a Mouse: A Counting Book. LC 94-25618. 1995. 13.00 (*0-02-745781-8*) Macmillan Child Grp.

Hutchinson, Joy. Twelve Friends Counting Book about Jesus's Disciples. LC 91-71037. 32p. (gr. 2 up). 1991. pap. 4.99 (*0-8066-2559-7*, 9-2559) Augsburg Fortress.

I Can Count. (ps-k). 3.95 (*0-7214-5053-9*) Ladybird Bks.

Jonas, Ann. Splash! LC 94-4110. 1995. write for info. (*0-688-11051-7*); lib. bdg. write for info. (*0-688-11052-5*) Greenwillow.

Jones, Carol. This Old Man. Jones, Carol, illus. 48p. (gr. k-3). 1990. 13.45 (*0-395-54699-0*) HM.

Jonson, Liz & Silliman, Emery. Counting. Nayer, Judith E., ed. Tomonari, Itsuko, illus. 32p. (gr. k-1). 1991. wkbk. 1.95 (*1-878624-54-7*) McClanahan Bk.

Karin, Nurit. Ten Little Bunnies. Wilhelm, Hans, illus. LC 93-13450. 1994. pap. 14.00 (*0-671-88026-8*, S&S BFYR) S&S Trade.

Kawai'ae'a, Keiki C. Let's Learn to Count in Hawaiian. Tanaka, Cliff, illus. 24p. (ps-k). 1988. 7.95 (*0-89610-076-6*) Island Heritage.

—Let's Learn to Count in Hawaiian. Tanaka, Cliff, illus. 24p. (ps-k). 1988. incl. cassette 11.95 (*0-89610-080-4*) Island Heritage.

Kingsley, Emily P., et al. Sesame Street One, Two, Three Story Book: Stories About the Numbers from One to Ten. (Illus.). (ps-4). 1973. 6.95 (*0-394-82694-9*); lib. bdg. 6.99 (*0-394-92694-3*) Random Bks Yng Read.

Kinin, Claudia. My Christmas Book of Numbers. (ps-3). 1993. 6.95 (*0-307-13721-X*, Golden Pr) Western Pub.

Kitchen, Bert. Animal Numbers. LC 87-5365. (Illus.). 24p. (ps up). 1987. 12.95 (*0-8037-0459-3*) Dial Bks Young.

—Animal Numbers. LC 87-5365. (Illus.). 24p. (gr. k up). 1991. pap. 4.95 (*0-8037-0910-2*, Puff Pied Piper) Puffin Bks.

Kitman, Carol & Hurwitz, Carol. One Mezuzah: A Jewish Counting Book. (Illus.). 48p. (ps-k). 1984. pap. 6.95 (*0-940646-54-4*) Rossel Bks.

Kontoyiannaki, Elizabeth. I Can Count. Kontoyiannaki, Elizabeth, illus. 16p. (gr. k-3). 1992. pap. 12.95 (*1-895583-41-1*) MAYA Pubs.

Kosowsky, Cindy. Wordless Counting Book. (Illus.). 24p. (ps-k). 1992. 10.95 (*1-880851-00-8*) Greene Bark Pr.

The Kuekumber Kids Meet the Numberasaurus. 12.95x (*0-9617199-7-4*) Sutton Pubns.

Kuhn, Dwight R., photos by. Hungry Little Frog. Hirschi, Ron, text by. (Illus.). 32p. (ps-2). 1992. 9.95 (*0-525-65109-8*, Cobblehill Bks) Dutton Child Bks.

Kunin, Claudia. My Hanukkah Book of Numbers. (ps-3). 1993. 6.95 (*0-307-13718-X*, Golden Pr) Western Pub.

Kuskin, Karla. James & the Rain. Cartwright, Reg, illus. LC 93-49345. 1995. 15.00 (*0-671-88808-0*, S&S BFYR) S&S Trade.

Landa, Norbert. Rabbit & Chicken Count Eggs. Turk, Hanne, illus. LC 90-33436. (ps). 1992. bds. 4.95 (*0-688-09971-8*, Tambourine Bks) Morrow.

Learn with Peter Rabbit: Book of Numbers. 1993. 2.99 (*0-517-07697-7*) Random Hse Value.

Levin, Ina M. & Sterling, Mary E. Readiness Manipulatives: Counting. Vasconcelles, Keith, illus. 28p. (Orig.). (ps-1). 1992. wkbk. 7.95 (*1-55734-179-6*) Tchr Create Mat.

Liebler, John. Frog Counts to Ten. LC 93-40116. (Illus.). 32p. (gr. k-3). 1994. 13.90 (*1-56294-436-3*) Millbrook Pr.

Linden, Ann M. One Smiling Grandma: A Caribbean Counting Book. Russell, Lynne, illus. LC 91-30826. 32p. (ps-3). 1992. 15.00 (*0-8037-1132-8*) Dial Bks Young.

Little Bear Counts His Favorite Things. (ps-k). 1991. write for info. (*0-307-12289-1*, Golden Pr) Western Pub.

Loomis, Christine. One Cow Coughs: A Counting Book for the Sick & Miserable. Dypold, Pat, illus. LC 93-1836. 32p. (ps-2). 1994. 14.95g (*0-395-67899-4*) Ticknor & Flds Bks Yng Read.

Loveless, Liz. One, Two, Buckle My Shoe. Loveless, Liz, illus. LC 92-40947. 32p. (ps). 1993. 13.95 (*1-56282-477-5*); PLB 13.89 (*1-56282-478-3*) Hyprn Child.

Luttrell, Ida. The Star Counters. Pretro, Korinna, illus. LC 93-20342. 32p. 1994. 15.00 (*0-688-12149-7*, Tambourine Bks); PLB 14.93 (*0-688-12150-0*, Tambourine Bks) Morrow.

McCarthy, Bobette. Ten Little Hippos: A Counting Book. McCarthy, Bobette, illus. LC 91-17175. 32p. (ps-2). 1992. SBE 13.95 (*0-02-765445-1*, Bradbury Pr) Macmillan Child Grp.

MacCarthy, Patricia. Ocean Parade. 1990. 11.95 (*0-8037-0780-0*) Dial Bks Young.

McGee, Barbara. Counting Sheep. McGee, Barbara, illus. 24p. (gr. k-3). 1991. 12.95 (*1-55037-157-6*, Pub. by Annick CN); pap. 4.95 (*1-55037-160-6*, Pub. by Annick CN) Firefly Bks Ltd.

McGuire, Richard. The Orange Book. (Illus.). 32p. (ps-1). 1993. 12.95 (*0-87663-798-5*) Universe.

McKellar, Shona, selected by. Counting Rhymes. LC 93-12383. (Illus.). 32p. (ps-3). 1993. 12.95 (*1-56458-309-0*) Dorling Kindersley.

MacKinnon, Debbie. How Many? Sieveking, Anthea, photos by. LC 91-46720. (Illus.). 24p. (ps-k). 1993. 10.99 (*0-8037-1253-7*) Dial Bks Young.

McKissack, Patricia & McKissack, Fredrick. Big Bug Book of Counting. Bartholomew, illus. LC 87-61655. 24p. (Orig.). (gr. k-1). 1987. spiral bdg. 14.95 (*0-88335-762-3*); pap. text ed. 4.95 (*0-88335-772-0*) Milliken Pub Co.

McMillan, Bruce. One Two One Pair. LC 90-37410. (ps-3). 1991. 12.95 (*0-590-43767-4*, Scholastic Hardcover) Scholastic Inc.

McOmber, Rachel B., ed. McOmber Phonics Storybooks: Number Fun. rev. ed. (Illus.). write for info. (*0-944991-58-0*) Swift Lrn Res.

Manushkin, Fran. My Christmas Safari. Alley, R. W., illus. LC 92-28643. 32p. (ps-1). 1993. 13.99 (*0-8037-1294-4*); PLB 13.89 (*0-8037-1295-2*) Dial Bks Young.

—Walt Disney-One Hundred One Dalmatas: Un Libro para Contar. Santacruz, Daniel, tr. from ENG. Hicks, Russell, illus. LC 93-70677. (SPA.). 32p. 1994. PLB 13.89 (*1-56282-697-2*); pap. 5.95 (*1-56282-568-2*) Disney Pr.

—Walt Disney's One Hundred One Dalmatians: A Counting Book. Hicks, Russell, illus. LC 90-85426. 32p. (ps-k). 1991. 9.95 (*1-56282-012-5*); PLB 9.89 (*1-56282-032-X*) Disney Pr.

—Walt Disney's One Hundred One Dalmatians: A Counting Book. Hicks, Russell, illus. LC 92-53493. 32p. (ps-k). 1993. pap. 4.95 (*1-56282-324-8*) Disney Pr.

—Walt Disney's One Hundred One Dalmatians Counting Book & Puppy. Hicks, Russell, illus. 32p. (ps-1). 1993. Boxed set incl. plush puppy. 16.95 (*1-56282-572-0*) Disney Pr.

Marks, Burton. Colors & Numbers. Harvey, Paul, illus. LC 91-17493. 24p. (gr. k-2). 1992. PLB 9.89 (*0-8167-2411-3*); pap. text ed. 2.50 (*0-8167-2412-1*) Troll Assocs.

Martin. Knots on a Counting. 1987. 14.95 (*0-8050-1932-4*) H Holt & Co.

Marzollo, Jean. Ten Cats Have Hats. McPhail, David, illus. LC 93-20136. (ps). 1994. 6.95 (*0-590-46968-1*) Scholastic Inc.

Mathieu, Joe. Sesame Street One Two Three: A Counting Book from 1 to 100. Mathieu, Joe, illus. LC 91-1992. 32p. (ps-1). 1991. 10.00 (*0-679-81230-X*) Random Bks Yng Read.

Mayer, Marianna & McDermott, Gerald. The Brambleberrys Animal Book of Counting. LC 91-70419. (Illus.). 32p. (ps up). 1991. 3.95 (*1-878093-75-4*) Boyds Mills Pr.

Mecklenberg, Jan. Counting God's Creatures. Mecklenberg, Jan, illus. LC 93-36019. 1994. 4.99 (*0-7852-8217-3*) Nelson.

Merriam, Eve. Train Leaves the Station. Gottlieb, Dale, illus. LC 91-28009. 32p. (ps-k). 1992. 14.95 (*0-8050-1934-0*, B Martin BYR) H Holt & Co.

—Twelve Ways to Get to Eleven. Karlin, Bernie, illus. LC 92-25810. 40p. (ps-1). 1993. pap. 14.00 JRT (*0-671-75544-7*, S&S BFYR) S&S Trade.

Micklethwait, Lucy, selected by. & created by. I Spy Two Eyes: Numbers in Art. LC 92-35641. (Illus.). 48p. (ps up). 1993. 19.00 (*0-688-12640-5*); PLB 18.93 (*0-688-12642-1*) Greenwillow.

Miller, Jane. Farm Counting Book. Miller, Jane, illus. 24p. (ps-3). 1986. P-H.

—Farm Counting Book. (Illus.). 24p. (ps-4). 1992. pap. 5.00 (*0-671-66552-9*, S&S BFYR) S&S Trade.

Moncure, Jane B. Magic Monsters Count to Ten. Fudala, Rosemary, illus. LC 78-23634. (ps-3). 1979. PLB 14.95 (*0-89565-058-4*) Childs World.

Mora, Pat. Uno, Dos, Tres: One, Two, Three. Lavallee, Barbara, illus. LC 94-15337. (ps-3). Date not set. write for info. (*0-395-67294-5*, Clarion Bks) HM.

Morehead, Ruth J., illus. A Christmas Countdown with Ruth J. Morehead's Holly Babes. LC 90-61905. 22p. (ps). 1991. bds. 2.95 (*0-679-81417-5*) Random Bks Yng Read.

Morozumi, Atsuko. One Gorilla. (ps). 1993. pap. 4.95 (*0-374-45646-1*, Sunburst) FS&G.

—One Gorilla: A Counting Book. Morozumi, Atsuko, illus. 26p. (ps-1). 1990. 15.00 (*0-374-35644-0*) FS&G.

Moss, Lloyd. Zin! Zin! Zin! A Violin. Priceman, Marjorie, illus. LC 93-37902. 1995. 14.00 (*0-671-88239-2*, S&S BFYR) S&S Trade.

Moss, Marissa. Knick Knack Paddywack. Moss, Marissa, illus. 32p. (ps-3). 1992. 13.45 (*0-395-54701-6*) HM.

Muldron, Diane. Walt Disney's Bambi: Count to Five. Langley, Bill & Wakeraw, Diana, illus. (ps-k). 1991. bds. write for info. (*0-307-06114-0*, Golden Pr) Western Pub.

Munsch, Robert. Violet, Vert et Jaune: Purple, Green & Yellow in French. Desputeaux, Helene, illus. 32p. 1992. pap. 5.95 (*1-55037-272-6*, Pub. by Annick Pr) Firefly Bks Ltd.

Murphy, Chuck. My First Book of Counting. (ps). 1991. 5.95 (*0-590-44471-9*) Scholastic Inc.

My Counting Book. (ps-2). 3.95 (*0-7214-5146-2*) Ladybird Bks.

Nayer, Judy. My First Numbers. Cocca-Leffler, Maryann, illus. 32p. (ps). 1991. wkbk. 1.95 (*1-56293-166-0*) McClanahan Bk.

Nayer, Judy, ed. Rhymes to Count On. Bates, Louise, illus. 24p. (ps-2). 1992. pap. 0.99 (*1-56293-104-0*) McClanahan Bk.

Nelson, JoAnne. Count by Twos. Beylon, Cathy, illus. 16p. (Orig.). (gr. k-2). 1990. pap. 3.95 (*1-878624-10-5*) McClanahan Bk.

Nikola-Lisa, W. No Babies Asleep. Palagonia, Peter, illus. LC 93-20589. 32p. (ps-1). 1995. SBE 15.00 (*0-689-31841-3*, Atheneum) Macmillan Child Grp.

—One, Two, Three Thanksgiving! Levine, Abby, ed. Kramer, Robin, illus. LC 90-28638. 32p. (ps-1). 1991. 13.95 (*0-8075-6109-6*) A Whitman.

Novit, Renee Z. Counting by Tens & Fives. Novit, R. Z., Graphic Design Staff, illus. 16p. (ps-k). Date not set. pap. 7.95 (*1-883371-02-3*) Kidz & Katz.

—Counting One to Twenty. Novit, R. Z., Graphic Design Staff, illus. 16p. (ps-k). Date not set. pap. 7.95 (*1-883371-01-5*) Kidz & Katz.

Numbers. (Illus.). 12p. (gr. k-2). 1982. bds. 3.95 (*0-87449-021-9*) Modern Pub NYC.

Odgers, Sally F. Up the Stairs. Hunnam, Lucinda, illus. LC 92-21395. 1993. 4.25 (*0-383-03601-1*) SRA Schl Grp.

O'Keefe, Susan H. One Hungry Monster: A Counting Book in Rhyme. Munsinger, Lynn, illus. 32p. (ps-3). 1992. pap. 4.95 (*0-316-63388-7*, Joy St Bks) Little.

Oliver, Stephen, photos by. Counting. LC 90-8577. (Illus.). 24p. (ps-k). 1991. 7.00 (*0-679-81163-X*) Random Bks Yng Read.

Olyff, Clotilde. One, Two, Three. Olyff, Clotilde, illus. & designed by. LC 94-1238. 22p. (ps). 1994. 13.95 (*0-395-70736-6*, Ticknor & Flds Bks Yng Read) HM.

One to Ten. (ps). 1976. 5.50 (*0-900195-19-3*, Brimax Bks) Borden.

One Two Three. (Illus.). 24p. (ps). 1994. bds. 2.95 (*1-56458-534-4*) Dorling Kindersley.

Ong, Cristina, illus. The Little Engine That Could: Little Library, 3 bks. (Set incls. Colors, ABC & Numbers, 20 pgs. ea. bk.). (ps). 1992. Set. bds. 7.95 slipcased (*0-448-40261-0*, Platt & Munk Pubs) Putnam Pub Group.
—The Little Engine That Could Numbers. 20p. (ps-3). 1994. bds. 2.95 (*0-448-40263-7*, Platt & Munk Pubs) Putnam Pub Group.
Ormerod, Jan. Joe Can Count. LC 92-43781. (Illus.). 24p. (ps up). 1993. pap. 3.95 (*0-688-04588-X*, Mulberry) Morrow.
Outlet Staff. In the Garden: A Book about Numbers. 1992. 2.99 (*0-517-03596-0*) Random Hse Value.
Owens, Mary B. Counting Cranes. (ps-3). 1993. 14.95 (*0-316-67719-1*) Little.
Pacovska, Kveta. One Five Many. (ps-3). 1990. 16.95 (*0-685-54064-2*, Clarion Bks) HM.
—One, Five, Many. Pacovska, Kveta, illus. 30p. (gr. k-3). 1990. 16.45 (*0-395-54997-3*, Clarion Bks) HM.
Pallotta, Jerry. Cuenta los Insectos (The Icky Bug Counting Book) (Illus.). 32p. (ps-3). 1993. PLB 15.88 (*0-88106-639-7*); pap. 6.95 (*0-88106-419-X*) Charlesbridge Pub.
—The Icky Bug Counting Book. (Illus.). 32p. (ps-8). 1991. 14.95 (*0-88106-497-1*); pap. 6.95 (*0-88106-496-3*) Charlesbridge Pub.
Palmer, Glenda. Two Enormous Elephants: God's Wonderful World of Numbers. LC 92-34714. (Illus.). 1993. pap. 4.99 (*0-7814-0709-5*, Chariot Bks) Chariot Family.
Palumbo, Nancy. Lets Color & Count: Colorions et Comptons. Weaver, Judith, illus. 32p. (gr. k-6). 1989. wkbk. 5.95 (*0-927024-09-8*) Crayons Pubns.
Parramon, J. M. My First Numbers. (Illus.). 32p. (ps). 1991. pap. 5.95 (*0-8120-4723-0*) Barron.
Patrick, Lewis. Walt Disney's Snow White & the Seven Dwarfs Counting Book. (ps). 1993. 3.95 (*0-307-12529-7*, Golden Pr) Western Pub.
Peppe, Rodney. The Animal Directory: A First Counting Book. LC 89-18000. (Illus.). 24p. (gr. k-2). 1990. bds. 9.95 (*0-87226-421-1*, Bedrick Blackie) P Bedrick Bks.
Petach, Heidi. One, Two, Buckle My Shoe: A Counting Rhyme. (ps). 1994. 3.95 (*0-307-06146-9*, Golden Pr) Western Pub.
Pienkowski, Jan. One Two Three. Pienkowski, Jan, illus. 14p. (ps). 1989. 2.95 (*0-671-68136-2*) S&S Trade.
Pomerantz, Charlotte. One Duck, Another Duck. Aruego, Jose & Dewey, Ariane, illus. LC 83-20767. 24p. (ps-1). 1984. 10.25 (*0-688-03744-5*); PLB 13.93 (*0-688-03745-3*) Greenwillow.
Pooh's Honey Bee Counting Book. 24p. 1994. 8.98 (*1-57082-149-6*) Mouse Works.
Potter, Beatrix. Jemima Puddle-Duck's Numbers. (Illus.). 24p. (ps). 1994. bds. 2.99 (*0-7232-4091-4*) Warne.
Preston, Hap. Three Seas: A Christopher Columbus Counting Book. LC 92-80784. (Illus.). 44p. (ps-3). 1992. pap. 5.95 (*1-55523-529-8*) Winston-Derek.
Rae, Mary M. Over in the Meadow: A Counting-Out Rhyme. (Illus.). 32p. (ps-k). 1986. pap. 3.95 (*0-685-14199-3*, Penguin Bks) Viking Penguin.
Raffi. Five Little Ducks. Aruego, Jose & Dewey, Ariane, illus. LC 88-3752. 32p. (ps-2). 1992. pap. 3.99 (*0-517-58360-7*) Crown Bks Yng Read.
Randall, Ronne P. One to Ten. Smallman, Steve, illus. 24p. (ps). 1987. pap. 1.25 (*0-7214-9554-0*, S871-10) Ladybird Bks.
Reasoner, Charles. Number Munch! Reasoner, Charles, illus. 36p. (ps). 1993. bds. 9.95 (*0-8431-3674-X*) Price Stern.
Reasoner, Chuck. One Big Number Book. Reasoner, Chuck, illus. (ps). 1993. bds. 9.95 (*0-8431-3551-4*) Price Stern.
Reichmeier, Betty, illus. Sing with Me Play-along & Counting Songs. (ps-1). 1987. incl. cassette 5.95 (*0-394-88810-3*) Random Bks Yng Read.
Reiser, Lynn. Christmas Counting. LC 91-32501. (Illus.). 32p. (ps-4). 1992. 14.00 (*0-688-10676-5*); PLB 13.93 (*0-688-10677-3*) Greenwillow.
Reiss, John J. Numbers. Reiss, John J., illus. LC 76-151313. 32p. (ps-2). 1982. RSBE 13.95 (*0-02-776150-9*, Bradbury Pr) Macmillan Child Grp.
Ricklen, Neil. First Word Books: 1-2-3. (ps). 1994. pap. 5.95 (*0-671-86727-X*, Little Simon) S&S Trade.
Ricklen, Neil, illus. My Numbers: Mis Numeros. LC 93-27165. (ENG & SPA.). 14p. (ps-k). 1994. pap. 3.95 (*0-689-71770-9*, Aladdin) Macmillan Child Grp.
Rocklin, Joanne. Musical Chairs & Dancing Bears. De Matharel, Laure, illus. LC 92-41078. 32p. (ps-2). 1993. write for info. (*0-8050-2374-7*, Bks Young Read) H Holt & Co.
Rockwell, Anne. Willy Can Count. Rockwell, Anne, illus. 32p. (ps). 1989. 13.95 (*1-55970-013-0*) Arcade Pub Inc.
Ruschak, Lynette. The Counting Zoo: A Pop-up Number Book. Rousseau, May, illus. LC 91-42462. 24p. (ps-2). 1992. pap. 13.95 POB (*0-689-71619-2*, Aladdin) Macmillan Child Grp.
Rutman, Shereen G. Numbers. Loh, Carolyn, illus. 16p. (ps). 1992. wkbk. 2.25 (*1-56293-191-1*) McClanahan Bk.
Salt, Jane. My Giant Word & Number Book. Pooley, Sarah, illus. LC 92-31508. 1993. 9.95 (*1-85697-861-3*, Kingfisher LKC) LKC.
Santacruz, Daniel, tr. Un Raton Mickey: Un Libro Disney de Numeros. Duerrstein, Richard, illus. (SPA.). 12p. 1993. 5.95 (*1-56282-460-0*) Disney Pr.
Scarry, Richard. Richard Scarry's Best Counting Book Ever. Scarry, Richard, illus. LC 74-2544. 48p. (ps-2). 1975. PLB 9.99 (*0-394-92924-1*) Random Bks Yng Read.
Schade, Susan. Hello! Hello! Buller, Jon, illus. 32p. (ps). 1993. pap. 2.25 (*0-671-79608-9*, Little Simon) S&S Trade.
Schwager, Istar. Counting. Siede, George & Preis, Donna, photos by. (Illus.). 24p. (ps-3). 1993. PLB 12.95 (*1-56674-067-3*, HTS Bks) Forest Hse.
Schwartz, David M. How Much Is a Million? Kellogg, Steven, illus. LC 93-12589. 40p. (gr. k up). 1993. pap. 4.95 (*0-688-09933-5*, Mulberry) Morrow.
Scott, Ann H. One Good Horse: A Cowpuncher's Counting Book. LC 89-1984. (Illus.). 32p. (ps up). 1990. 12.95 (*0-688-09146-6*); lib. bdg. 12.88 (*0-688-09147-4*) Greenwillow.
Sendak, Maurice. One Was Johnny: A Counting Book. Sendak, Maurice, illus. 32p. (ps-3). 1962. PLB 13.89 (*0-06-025540-4*) HarpC Child Bks.
—One Was Johnny: A Counting Book. Sendak, Maurice, illus. LC 62-13315. 48p. (ps-3). 1991. pap. 3.95 (*0-06-443251-3*, Trophy) HarpC Child Bks.
Serfozo, Mary. Who Wants One? Narahashi, Keiko, illus. LC 92-4341. 32p. (ps-1). 1992. pap. 4.95 (*0-689-71642-7*, Aladdin); pap. 18.95 Big bk. (*0-689-71652-4*, Aladdin) Macmillan Child Grp.
Siede, George & Preis, Donna, photos by. Numbers: Active Minds. Schwager, Istar, contrib. by. (Illus.). 24p. (ps-3). 1992. PLB 9.95 (*1-56674-003-7*) Forest Hse.
Simpson. Gretchen's 123. Date not set. 16.00 (*0-06-024305-8*); PLB 15.89 (*0-06-024306-6*) HarpC Child Bks.
Simpson, Cathy, ed. My Little Book of Counting Rhymes. (Illus.). 28p. 1994. 5.95 (*0-87226-518-8*) P Bedrick Bks.
Sis, Peter. Going Up! A Color Counting Book. LC 87-37203. (Illus.). 24p. (ps up). 1989. 12.95 (*0-688-08125-8*); PLB 12.88 (*0-688-08126-6*) Greenwillow.
Sloat, Teri. From One to One Hundred. Sloat, Teri, illus. LC 91-21948. 32p. 1991. 13.95 (*0-525-44764-4*, DCB) Dutton Child Bks.
Smith, Kaitlin M. Counting with Buster Bear. Smith, Kaitlin M., illus. 15p. (gr. k-3). 1992. pap. 12.95 (*1-895583-15-2*) MAYA Pubs.
Smith, Maggie. Counting Our Way to Maine. LC 94-24874. (gr. 2 up). 1995. write for info. (*0-531-06884-6*); pap. write for info. (*0-531-08734-4*) Orchard Bks Watts.
Smoothey, Marion. Numbers. Evans, Ted, illus. 64p. (gr. 4-8). 1992. text ed. 16.95 (*1-85435-457-4*) Marshall Cavendish.
Sommers, Maxine S. Learn to Count & Color with Spot the Cat. Kennedy, Suzanne, ed. (Illus.). 10p. (Orig.). (gr. k-1). 1993. pap. 2.50 (*0-685-65603-9*) Pound Sterling Pub.
Spencer, Eve. Animal Babies One Two Three. David, Susan, illus. 24p. (ps-2). 1990. PLB 17.10 (*0-8172-3581-7*); pap. 4.95 (*0-8114-6738-4*) Raintree Steck-V.
Sticker Fun with Numbers. (Illus.). 32p. (ps-1). 1991. pap. 5.99 (*0-517-03352-6*) Random Hse Value.
Stoneway Books Staff. How Does Monster Count to Nine? (ps-3). 1990. pap. 5.95 (*1-55923-038-X*) Stoneway Ltd.
Stortz, Diane. A One-Two-Three Christmas. Munger, Nancy, illus. 28p. (ps-k). 1993. 4.99 (*0-7847-0064-8*, 24-03844) Standard Pub.
Su, Lucy. Ten Little Teddies. LC 93-24148. 24p. (ps up). 1994. 3.99 (*1-56402-251-X*) Candlewick Pr.
Sugita, Yutaka. Goodnight, One, Two, Three. Sugita, Yutaka, illus. LC 76-149045. 32p. (ps-2). 9.95 (*0-87592-022-5*) Scroll Pr.
Sullivan, Charles. Numbers at Play: A Counting Book. LC 91-33154. (Illus.). 48p. (ps-2). 1992. 15.95 (*0-8478-1501-3*) Rizzoli Intl.
Tabor, Nancy M. Fifty on the Zebra (Cincuenta en la Cebra) Counting with Animals (Contando Con los Animales) Tabor, Nancy M., illus. 32p. (Orig.). (ps-4). 1994. PLB 15.00 (*0-88106-858-6*); pap. 6.95 (*0-88106-856-X*) Charlesbridge Pub.
Tafuri, Nancy. Who's Counting? Tafuri, Nancy, illus. LC 85-17702. 24p. (ps-1). 1986. 15.00 (*0-688-06130-3*); PLB 14.93 (*0-688-06131-1*) Greenwillow.
—Who's Counting? LC 92-24604. (Illus.). 32p. (ps up). 1993. pap. 4.95 (*0-688-12266-3*, Mulberry) Morrow.
Tallarico, Tony. Preschool Can You Find Counting Picture Book. (Illus.). 12p. (ps). 1992. 3.95 (*0-448-40425-7*, G&D) Putnam Pub Group.
Tallarico, Tony, illus. Finger Counting. 28p. (ps-1). 1984. bds. 2.95 (*0-448-48820-5*, Tuffy) Putnam Pub Group.
Ten in the Bed. (Illus.). 24p. (ps up). 1992. write for info. incl. long-life batteries (*0-307-74812-X*, 64812, Golden Pr) Western Pub.
Theobalds, Prue. Ten Tired Teddies. Theobalds, Prue, illus. 10p. 1992. 5.95 (*0-87226-471-8*, Bedrick Blackie) P Bedrick Bks.
—Wake up, Teddies! A Counting Book. Theobalds, Prue, illus. 10p. 1994. bds. 5.95 (*0-87226-515-3*) P Bedrick Bks.
Thornhill, Jan. Wild Life 123: A Nature Counting Book. LC 89-5970. (ps-3). 1994. pap. 5.95 (*0-671-88613-4*, Half Moon BKs) S&S Trade.
Time-Life Books Editors. How Many Hippos? A Mix-&-Match Counting Book. (Illus.). 40p. (ps-2). 1990. write for info. (*0-8094-9258-X*); lib. bdg. write for info. (*0-8094-9259-8*) Time-Life.
Troll Staff. Christmas Countdown. 10p. (ps). 1991. pap. 3.95 (*0-8167-2183-1*) Troll Assocs.
Tryon, Leslie. One Gaping Wide-Mouthed Hopping Frog. Tryon, Leslie, illus. LC 92-11368. 32p. (ps-1). 1993. SBE 14.95 (*0-689-31785-9*, Atheneum Child Bk) Macmillan Child Grp.
Tudor, Tasha. One Is One. (ps). 1993. pap. 4.95 (*0-689-71743-1*, Atheneum) Macmillan.
Tuer, Judy. Ten Crazy Caterpillars. Forss, Ian, illus. LC 92-30672. 1993. 2.50 (*0-383-03658-5*) SRA Schl Grp.
Tyler, J. & Round, G. Starting to Count. (Illus.). 24p. (ps up). 1987. pap. 3.50 (*0-7460-0216-5*) EDC.
Una, Dos, Tres, Por Bambi. (SPA.). (ps-3). 1993. pap. 4.95 (*0-307-72392-5*, Golden Pr) Western Pub.
University of Mexico City Staff, tr. Numeros: Mentes Activas. Siede, George & Preis, Donna, photos by. Schwager, Istar, contrib. by. (SPA., Illus.). 24p. (ps-8). 1992. PLB 11.95 (*1-56674-039-8*) Forest Hse.
Van Fleet, Matthew. One Yellow Lion: Fold-Out Fun with Numbers, Colors, Animals. LC 91-11972. (Illus.). 24p. (ps up). 1992. 7.95 (*0-8037-1099-2*) Dial Bks Young.
Van Laan, Nancy. Mama Rocks, Papa Sings. Smith, Roberta, illus. LC 93-39225. 40p. (ps-2). 1995. 15.00 (*0-679-84016-8*); PLB 15.99 (*0-679-94016-2*) Knopf Bks Yng Read.
Voce, Louise. Over in the Meadow: A Counting Rhyme. LC 93-21294. (Illus.). 32p. (ps up). 1994. 14.95 (*1-56402-428-8*) Candlewick Pr.
Walsh, Ellen S. Mouse Count. D'Andrade, Diane, ed. Walsh, Ellen S., illus. 32p. (ps-1). 1991. 11.95 (*0-15-256023-8*) HarBrace.
Walton, Rick. How Many, How Many, How Many. Jabar, Cynthia, illus. LC 92-54408. 32p. (ps up). 1993. 14.95 (*1-56402-062-2*) Candlewick Pr.
Warren, Jean. Alphabet & Number Rhymes. Bittinger, Gayle, ed. Walker-Carleson, Cora, illus. 160p. (Orig.). (ps-1). 1989. pap. text ed. 14.95 (*0-911019-27-8*) Warren Pub Hse.
Warren, Vic & Reasoner, Charles. Alpha-Books & Count with Us. Woodman, Nancy, illus. (ps-1). 1991. miniature board books in a tray 19.95 (*1-878624-83-0*) McClanahan Bk.
Weird & Wacky Animals. (Illus.). 48p. (Orig.). (gr. k-2). 1989. pap. 2.95 (*0-8431-2728-7*) Price Stern.
Weiss, Ellen. How Many Are There? (Illus.). 12p. (ps-k). 1994. 6.95 (*1-884506-02-X*) Third Story.
Weiss, Monica. Birthday Cake Candles, Counting. Berlin, Rosemary, illus. LC 91-16033. 24p. (gr. k-2). 1992. PLB 10.59 (*0-8167-2496-2*); pap. text ed. 2.95 (*0-8167-2497-0*) Troll Assocs.
Wells, Rosemary. Max's Toys: A Counting Book. Wells, Rosemary, illus. LC 79-50748. (ps-k). 1979. bds. 4.50 (*0-8037-6068-X*) Dial Bks Young.
West, Colin. One Little Elephant. West, Colin, illus. LC 93-36273. 32p. 1994. 3.99 (*1-56402-375-3*) Candlewick Pr.
—Ten Little Crocodiles. LC 93-44027. 1995. write for info. (*1-56402-463-6*) Candlewick Pr.
Weston, Martha. Bea's Four Bears. Weston, Martha, illus. 32p. (ps-k). 1992. 9.70 (*0-395-57791-8*, Clarion Bks) HM.
Williams, Jennifer. Playtime 123. LC 91-4683. (Illus.). 32p. (ps-1). 1992. 10.95 (*0-8037-1077-1*) Dial Bks Young.
Wing, Natasha. Hippity Hop, Frog on Top. McGraw, DeLoss, illus. LC 93-11473. 1994. 15.00 (*0-671-87045-9*, S&S BFYR) S&S Trade.
Winslow, Phillips. A Number of Things You Can Count On. 16p. (ps-k). 1992. pap. text ed. 23.00 big bk. (*1-56843-007-8*); pap. text ed. 4.50 (*1-56843-057-4*) BGR Pub.
Wise, William. Ten Sly Piranhas: A Counting Story in Reverse (A Tale of Wickedness - & Worse!) Chess, Victoria, illus. LC 91-33704. 32p. (ps-3). 1993. 13.50 (*0-8037-1200-6*); PLB 13.89 (*0-8037-1201-4*) Dial Bks Young.
Wood, J. Moo Moo, Brown Cow. Bonner, R., illus. 1992. 12.95 (*0-15-200533-1*, HB Juv Bks) HarBrace.
Wood, Jakki. One Tortoise, Ten Wallabies. LC 93-23534. (gr. 2 up). 1994. write for info. (Bradbury Pr) Macmillan Child Grp.
Woodard, James & Purdy, Linda. One to Ten Count Again. (Illus.). (ps-k). 1972. PLB 6.89x (*0-914844-07-5*) J Alden.
Wormell, Christopher & Green, Kate. A Number of Animals. LC 93-17134. (Illus.). (ps-3). 1993. PLB 19. 95 (*0-88682-625-X*) Creative Ed.
Wren & Maile. One-Two-Three Counting Locally. Wren, illus. (ENG & HAW.). 10p. (ps). 1992. bds. 3.95 (*1-880188-01-5*) Bess Pr.
Wylie, Joanne & Wylie, David. Cuantos Monstruos?: Un Cuento de Numeros (How Many Monsters? Learning about Counting) LC 85-15136. (SPA., Illus.). 32p. (ps-2). 1988. PLB 11.45 (*0-516-34494-3*); pap. 3.95 (*0-516-54494-2*) Childrens.
Yolen, Jane. Old Dame Counterpane. Councell, Ruth T., illus. LC 93-11528. 40p. (ps-2). 1994. PLB 14.95 (*0-399-22686-9*) Putnam Pub Group.
Zabar, Abbie. Fifty-Five Friends. LC 93-47366. (ps-2). 1994. 13.95 (*0-7868-0021-6*); pap. write for info. (*0-7868-2017-9*) Hyprn Child.

Zeldin, Florence. A Mouse in Our Jewish House. Rauchwerger, Lisa, illus. LC 89-40362. 32p. (ps). 1990. 11.95 (*0-933873-43-3*) Torah Aura.

Ziefert, Harriet. Bear's Numbers. Baum, Susan, illus. 12p. (ps). 1993. 4.50 (*0-694-00455-3*, Festival) HarpC Child Bks.

—A Dozen Dogs: A Read-&-Count Story. Nicklaus, Carol, illus. LC 84-17797. 32p. (ps-1). 1985. 3.50 (*0-394-86935-4*); lib. bdg. 6.99 (*0-394-96935-9*) Random Bks Yng Read.

COUNTRY HOUSES

see Architecture, Domestic

COUNTRY LIFE

Here are entered descriptive, popular and literary works on living in the country. Works dealing with social organization and conditions in rural communities are entered under Sociology, Rural.

see also Farm Life; Outdoor Life

Country Fact Files, 6 vols. (gr. 4-7). 1994. Set. 95.76 (*0-8114-1872-3*) Raintree Steck-V.

Crews, Donald. Bigmama's. Crews, Donald, illus. LC 90-33142. 32p. (ps up). 1991. 15.00 (*0-688-09950-5*); PLB 14.93 (*0-688-09951-3*) Greenwillow.

Jennings, Jay. Moments of Courage. (Illus.). 64p. (gr. 5-7). 1991. PLB 10.95 (*0-382-24108-8*); pap. 5.95 (*0-382-24114-2*) Silver Burdett Pr.

Miller, Shirley J. Billy. Casey, Marjorie, illus. 60p. (Orig.). (gr. 2-6). 1993. pap. 6.95 (*1-878580-92-2*) Asylum Arts.

Morley, Jacqueline & James, John. A Roman Villa: Inside Story. LC 92-15279. (Illus.). 48p. (gr. 5 up). 1992. 17.95 (*0-87226-360-6*) P Bedrick Bks.

North, Sterling. Rascal. (gr. 5 up). 1976. pap. 2.75 (*0-380-01518-8*, Flare) Avon.

Rius, Maria & Parramon, J. M. The Countryside. (ps). 1986. 6.95 (*0-8120-5749-X*); pap. 6.95 (*0-8120-3701-4*) Barron.

Rogers, Paul & Rogera, Emma. Zoe's Tower. Corfield, Robin B., illus. LC 90-48291. 32p. (ps-1). 1991. pap. 13.95 jacketed (*0-671-73811-9*, S&S BFYR) S&S Trade.

COUNTRY LIFE–FICTION

Asch, Frank & Vagin, Vladimir. Dear Brother. 32p. 1992. 13.95 (*0-590-43107-2*, Scholastic Hardcover) Scholastic Inc.

Backus, Mary L. All the Way Around Green Lake. Newman, Sheila, illus. 24p. (Orig.). (ps). 1984. pap. write for info. (*0-9613400-0-2*) Grnwillow End.

Bauer, Joan. Squashed. LC 91-44905. 192p. (gr. 7 up). 1992. 15.95 (*0-385-30793-4*) Delacorte.

Birdseye, Tom. A Regular Flood of Mishap. Loyd, Megan, illus. LC 93-9888. 32p. (ps-3). 1994. reinforced bdg. 15.95 (*0-8234-1070-6*) Holiday.

Borden, Louise. Just in Time for Christmas. Lewin, Ted, illus. LC 93-40082. (ps-3). 1994. 14.95 (*0-590-45355-6*) Scholastic Inc.

Braby, Marie. The Longest Wait. Ward, John, illus. LC 94-24875. 1995. write for info. (*0-531-06871-4*); PLB write for info. (*0-531-08721-2*) Orchard Bks Watts.

Brown, Margaret W. The Summer Noisy Book. new ed. Weisgard, Leonard, illus. LC 92-31435. 40p. (ps-1). 1993. 15.00 (*0-06-020855-4*); PLB 15.89 (*0-06-020856-2*) HarpC Child Bks.

—Walt Disney's the Old Mill. LC 93-74249. (Illus.). 32p. (ps-3). 1994. 12.95 (*1-56282-644-1*); PLB 12.89 (*1-56282-645-X*) Disney Pr.

Burch, Robert. Ida Early Comes Over the Mountain. LC 79-20532. (gr. 5-9). 1980. pap. 14.99 (*0-670-39169-7*) Viking Child Bks.

—Ida Early Comes over the Mountain. (gr. 4 up). 1990. pap. 3.99 (*0-14-034534-5*, Puffin) Puffin Bks.

—Queenie Peavy. 160p. (gr. 3-7). 1987. pap. 3.99 (*0-14-032305-8*, Puffin) Puffin Bks.

Cartwright, Pauline. Home. Tulloch, Coral, illus. LC 93-20062. 1994. write for info. (*0-383-03695-X*) SRA Schl Grp.

Caudill, Rebecca. A Pocketful of Cricket. Ness, Evaline, illus. LC 64-12617. 48p. (gr. k-2). 1989. 7.95 (*0-03-089752-1*, Bks Young Read); pap. 5.95 (*0-8050-1275-3*) H Holt & Co.

Child, Lydia M. Over the River & Through the Wood. Manson, Christopher, illus. LC 93-16614. 32p. (gr. k-3). 1993. 14.95 (*1-55858-210-X*); lib. bdg. 14.88 (*1-55858-211-8*) North-South Bks NYC.

Douglas, Ben. What Is There to Do in the Country? Reed, Mary L., illus. 32p. (ps-3). 1994. write for info. (*1-885483-00-7*) Sontag Pr.
John & Lucas live on a farm deep in the woods. They know they have more fun than anybody, but when Rupert, a city cousin comes to visit he sees things differently. "Golly, this place is boring," he says. "It's Dullsville. What could you ever do here to have any fun?" Rupert discovers the answer when he stays for a week. He learns about farm animals & farm work. He has fun at the swimming hole & at the country store. The week is filled with adventures. When Rupert's mama comes to take him home he makes a surprising request. Children who live in urban areas frequently ask parents & grandparents, "What did you do when you lived on the farm?" They can find out by reading WHAT IS THERE TO DO IN THE COUNTRY? & the forthcoming books in this "life in the country" series. To order: Sontag Press, P.O. Box 1487, Madison, MS 39130. (601) 856-5488.
Publisher Provided Annotation.

Dunlop, Eileen. Finn's Search. LC 93-44880. 128p. (gr. 5-9). 1994. 14.95 (*0-8234-1099-4*) Holiday.

Dupasquier, Philippe. Our House on the Hill. (Illus.). 32p. (ps-3). 1990. pap. 3.95 (*0-14-054227-2*, Puffin) Puffin Bks.

Enright, Elizabeth. Then There Were Five. Enright, Elizabeth, illus. (gr. k-6). 1987. pap. 2.95 (*0-440-48806-0*, YB) Dell.

Evans, Sanford. Naomi's Geese. Chabrian, Deborah, illus. LC 92-44109. (gr. 5 up). 1993. pap. 15.00 (*0-671-75623-0*, S&S BFYR) S&S Trade.

Gipson, Fred. Curly & the Wild Boar. Himler, Ronald, illus. LC 77-25644. 96p. (gr. 5 up). 1979. HarpC Child Bks.

Glines, Edna L. A Turtle on Her Toe. Pierpoint, Marsha W., illus. LC 83-17870. 66p. (ps up). 1984. 9.95 (*0-9612160-0-X*) Tumbleweed Pub Co.

Grahame, Kenneth. Dream Days. Parrish, Maxfield, illus. LC 92-44589. 1993. 18.95 (*0-89815-546-0*) Ten Speed Pr.

—The Golden Age. Parrish, Maxfield, illus. LC 92-44992. 1993. 18.95 (*0-89815-545-2*) Ten Speed Pr.

Griffith, Connie. The Shocking Discovery. 128p. (gr. 6-8). 1994. pap. 5.99 (*0-8010-3866-9*) Baker Bk.

Haas, Jessie. Uncle Daney's Way. LC 93-22192. (gr. 4 up). 1994. 14.00 (*0-688-12794-0*) Greenwillow.

Hall, Lynn. Flying Changes. D'Andrade, Diane, ed. 148p. (gr. 9 up). 1991. 13.95 (*0-15-228790-6*) HarBrace.

Haseley, Dennis. Shadows. Bowman, Leslie, illus. 80p. (gr. 2-6). 1991. 12.95 (*0-374-36761-2*) FS&G.

Heo, Yumi. Father's Rubber Shoes. LC 94-21961. (gr. 1-8). 1995. write for info. (*0-531-06873-0*); PLB write for info. (*0-531-08723-9*) Orchard Bks Watts.

Hirschi, Ron. Harvest Song. Haeffele, Deborah, illus. LC 90-27009. 32p. (ps-3). 1991. 13.95 (*0-525-65067-9*, Cobblehill Bks) Dutton Child Bks.

Hite, Sid. Dither Farm. LC 91-31323. 224p. (gr. 7 up). 1992. 15.95 (*0-8050-1871-9*, Bks Young Read) H Holt & Co.

Holt, S. Marie. Mike Moves to the City. Holt, Shirley, illus. 28p. (gr. k-5). 1992. 21.95x (*0-9613476-5-1*) Shirlee.

Houston, Gloria. Littlejim. Allen, Thomas, illus. 176p. 1990. 14.95 (*0-399-22220-0*, Philomel Bks) Putnam Pub Group.

—Littlejim. Allen, Thomas B., illus. LC 92-43775. 176p. (gr. 5 up). 1993. pap. 4.95 (*0-688-12112-8*, Pub. by Beech Tree Bks) Morrow.

Hurwitz, Johanna. Yellow Blue Jay. Carrick, Donald, illus. LC 92-24597. 128p. (gr. 3 up). 1993. pap. 3.95 (*0-688-12278-7*, Pub. by Beech Tree Bks) Morrow.

Jarrow, Gail. Beyond the Magic Sphere. LC 94-6884. (gr. 3-7). 1994. 15.95 (*0-15-200193-X*) HarBrace.

Kerr, Rita. The Texas Orphans: A Story of the Orphan Trail Children. Kerr, Rita, illus. LC 94-1995. 1994. 10.95 (*0-89015-962-9*) Sunbelt Media.

Levinson, Riki. Country Dawn to Dusk. LC 91-34600. (Illus.). 32p. (ps-2). 1992. 14.00 (*0-525-44957-4*, DCB) Dutton Child Bks.

Lyon, George-Ella. Come a Tide. Gammell, Stephen, illus. LC 89-35650. 32p. (ps-2). 1990. 14.95 (*0-531-05854-9*); PLB 14.99 (*0-531-08454-X*) Orchard Bks Watts.

McGuire, Donald D. The Country Kids' Encounter with Buttsy. 1992. 7.95 (*0-533-10346-0*) Vantage.

MacLachlan, Patricia. All the Places to Love. Wimmer, Mike, illus. LC 92-794. 32p. (gr. 1 up). 1994. 15.00 (*0-06-021098-2*); PLB 14.89 (*0-06-021099-0*) HarpC Child Bks.

Major, Beverly. Over Back. Allen, Thomas B., illus. LC 91-19696. 32p. (gr. k-4). 1993. 15.00 (*0-06-020286-6*); PLB 14.89 (*0-06-020287-4*) HarpC Child Bks.

Martin, Melanie. Madison Moves to the Country. Karas, G. Brian, illus. LC 88-1313. 48p. (Orig.). (gr. 1-4). 1989. PLB 10.59 (*0-8167-1345-6*); pap. text ed. 3.50 (*0-8167-1346-4*) Troll Assocs.

Montgomery, L. M. Anne of Green Gables. Felder, Deborah, adapted by. LC 93-36331. 108p. (Orig.). (gr. 2-6). 1994. pap. 2.99 (*0-679-85467-3*) Random Bks Yng Read.

Montgomery, Lucy M. Anne of Avonlea. 288p. (gr. 5-8). 1976. pap. 2.95 (*0-553-24740-9*) Bantam.

—Anne of Green Gables. 320p. (gr. 7-12). 1976. pap. 2.95 (*0-553-24295-4*) Bantam.

—Anne of Green Gables. Mattern, Joanne, ed. Graef, Renee, illus. LC 92-12703. 48p. (gr. 3-6). 1992. PLB 12.89 (*0-8167-2866-6*); pap. text ed. 3.95 (*0-8167-2867-4*) Troll Assocs.

—Anne of Ingleside, No. 6. 1984. pap. 2.95 (*0-553-21315-6*, Bantam Classics) Bantam.

—Anne of Windy Poplars, No. 4. 1984. pap. 2.95 (*0-553-21316-4*, Bantam Classics) Bantam.

Moore, Lilian. Don't Be Afraid, Amanda. McCord, Kathleen, illus. LC 91-19661. 64p. (gr. 2-5). 1992. SBE 12.95 (*0-689-31725-5*, Atheneum Child Bk) Macmillan Child Grp.

Nesbit, Edith. The Railway Children. Butts, Dennis, intro. by. 224p. 1991. pap. 3.95 (*0-19-282659-X*, 11912) OUP.

—The Railway Children. 1993. 12.95 (*0-679-42534-9*, Everymans Lib) Knopf.

—Railway Children. (gr. 4 up). 1993. pap. 3.25 (*0-553-21415-2*, Bantam Classics) Bantam.

Peck, Robert N. Little Soup's Hayride. (ps-3). 1991. pap. 2.99 (*0-440-40383-9*) Dell.

—Soup's Goat. Robinson, Charles, illus. LC 83-16245. 112p. (gr. 4-6). 1984. lib. bdg. 12.99 (*0-394-96322-9*) Knopf Bks Yng Read.

Radin, Ruth Y. A Winter Place. O'Kelley, Mattie L., illus. LC 82-15349. 32p. (gr. 3 up). 1982. 15.95 (*0-316-73218-4*, Joy St Bks) Little.

Ransom, Candice. The Man on Stilts. Bowman, Leslie, illus. LC 92-39358. 1994. write for info. (*0-399-22537-4*, Philomel Bks) Putnam Pub Group.

Ransom, Candice F. We're Growing Together. Wright-Frierson, Virginia, illus. LC 92-7424. 32p. (ps-2). 1993. RSBE 14.95 (*0-02-775666-1*, Bradbury Pr) Macmillan Child Grp.

Rawls, Wilson. Where the Red Fern Grows. (gr. 7 up). 1992. 16.95 (*0-553-08900-5*, Starfire) Bantam.

Reaver, Chap. Bill. 1994. 14.95 (*0-385-31175-3*) Delacorte.

Rhodes, Judy C. The Hunter's Heart. LC 92-47025. 192p. (gr. 5 up). 1993. SBE 14.95 (*0-02-773935-X*, Bradbury Pr) Macmillan Child Grp.

—The King Boy. LC 91-2159. 160p. (gr. 5-9). 1991. SBE 14.95 (*0-02-776115-0*, Bradbury Pr) Macmillan Child Grp.

Richardson, Arleta. The Grandma's Attic Storybook. LC 92-33823. 1993. pap. 9.99 (*0-7814-0070-8*, Chariot Bks) Chariot Family.

Robinson, Colin. Sunrise. Robinson, Colin, illus. LC 91-40988. 32p. (ps-1). 1992. PLB 12.95 (*0-87226-468-8*, Bedrick Blackie) P Bedrick Bks.

Robinson, Nancy K. The Ghost of Whispering Rock. Eagle, Ellen, illus. LC 92-52856. 64p. (gr. 2-6). 1992. 13.95 (*0-8234-0944-9*) Holiday.

Roessler, Mark. The Last Magician in Blue Haven. Hundgen, Donald, illus. 52p. (Orig.). (gr. 4-8). 1994. pap. 12.95 (*0-9638293-0-0*) Hundelrut Studio.
THE LAST MAGICIAN is an imaginative tale for children & adults, filled with numerous delicate pen drawings by Donald Hundgen. A sophisticated city doctor comes to Blue Haven to serve the rural community but ends up becoming a thorn in their side. The simple villagers love magic. The doctor, Fortunamus Gengeloof, drives off all the magicians by revealing their secrets, until one comes along who is a match for the doctor. For prepublication order & general information: Write: Hundelrut Studio, 10 Hawthorne Street, Plymouth, NH 03264. USA. Phone: 603-536-4396.
Publisher Provided Annotation.

Ryan, Cheryl. Sally Arnold. Farnsworth, Bill, illus. LC 94-6455. 1995. write for info. (*0-525-65176-4*, Cobblehill Bks) Dutton Child Bks.

Rylant, Cynthia. Night in the Country. Szilagyi, Mary, illus. LC 85-70963. 32p. (ps-1). 1986. RSBE 14.95 (*0-02-777210-1*, Bradbury Pr) Macmillan Child Grp.

—Night in the Country. Szilagyi, Mary, illus. LC 90-1043. 32p. (ps-2). 1991. pap. 4.95 (*0-689-71473-4*, Aladdin) Macmillan Child Grp.

—This Year's Garden. Szilagyi, Mary, illus. LC 86-22224. 32p. (ps-3). 1987. pap. 4.95 (*0-689-71122-0*, Aladdin) Macmillan Child Grp.

Schertle, Alice. Down the Road. Date not set. 14.95 (*0-06-020057-X*, HarpT) HarpC.

—Down the Road. Lewis, E. B., illus. LC 94-9901. 1995. write for info. (*0-15-276622-7*, Browndeer Pr) HarBrace.

Slote, Elizabeth. Nelly's Grannies. Slote, Elizabeth, illus. LC 91-32600. 32p. (ps up). 1993. 14.00 (*0-688-11314-1*, Tambourine Bks); PLB 13.93 (*0-688-11315-X*, Tambourine Bks) Morrow.

Sorensen, Virginia. Miracles on Maple Hill. Davis, Lambert, contrib. by. 232p. (gr. 3-7). 1990. pap. 3.95 (*0-15-254561-1*, Odyssey) HarBrace.

Stowe, Cynthia M. Dear Mom, in Ohio for a Year. 1992. 13.95 (*0-590-45060-3*, 024, Scholastic Hardcover) Scholastic Inc.

Thompson, Richard. Maggee & the Lake Minder. Fernandes, Eugenie, illus. 32p. (gr. k-3). 1991. PLB 14.95 (*1-55037-154-1*, Pub. by Annick CN); pap. 4.95 (*1-55037-152-5*, Pub. by Annick CN) Firefly Bks Ltd.

Watson, Harvey. Bob War & Poke. 144p. (gr. 5-9). 1991. 13.45 (*0-395-57038-7*, Sandpiper) HM.
Wiggin, Eric. Maggie: Life at the Elms. LC 93-27054. 1994. pap. 3.99 (*1-56507-133-6*) Harvest Hse.
—Maggie's Homecoming. LC 93-27053. 1994. pap. 3.99 (*1-56507-134-4*) Harvest Hse.
Wilder, Laura Ingalls. Farmer Boy. rev. ed. Williams, Garth, illus. LC 52-7527. 372p. (gr. 3-7). 1961. 15.95 (*0-06-026425-X*); PLB 15.89 (*0-06-026421-7*) HarpC Child Bks.

COUPS D'ETAT
see Revolutions

COURAGE
see also Fear; Heroes

Brady, Janeen. Standin' Tall Courage. Wilson, Grant, illus. 22p. (Orig.). (ps-6). 1982. pap. text ed. 1.50 activity bk. (*0-944803-43-1*); cassette & bk. 9.95 (*0-944803-45-8*) Brite Music.
Dann, Penny, illus. A Little Book of Courage. LC 93-6640. (gr. 1-8). 1993. 12.95 (*1-56766-094-0*) Childs World.
Goley, Elaine. Courage. (Illus.). 32p. (gr. 1-4). 1987. PLB 15.94 (*0-86592-377-9*); lib. bdg. 11.95 (*0-685-67576-9*) Rourke Corp.
Lewis, Barbara A. Kids with Courage: True Stories about Young People Making a Difference. Espeland, Pamela, ed. LC 91-46726. 184p. (gr. 5-12). 1992. pap. 10.95 (*0-915793-39-3*); write for info. tchr's. guide (*0-915793-40-7*) Free Spirit Pub.
Masters, Anthony, compiled by. Heroic Stories. Molan, Chris, illus. LC 93-45413. 256p. (gr. 5-10). 1994. 6.95 (*1-85697-983-0*, Kingfisher LKC) LKC.
Moncure, Jane B. Courage. rev. ed. Endes, Helen, illus. LC 80-39515. (ENG & SPA.). 32p. (ps-2). 1981. PLB 14.95 (*0-89565-202-1*) Childs World.
Sanford, Doris. Help! Fire! Escaping with My Life. Evans, Graci & Evans, Gracie, illus. 32p. 1992. 9.99 (*0-88070-520-5*, Gold & Honey) Questar Pubs.
—My Friend, the Enemy: Surviving a Prison Camp. Evans, Graci, illus. 32p. 1992. 9.99 (*0-88070-518-3*, Gold & Honey) Questar Pubs.
—No Longer Afraid: Living with Cancer. Evans, Graci, illus. 1992. 9.99 (*0-88070-519-1*, Gold & Honey) Questar Pubs.
Saxby, Maurice. The Great Deeds of Heroic Women. Ingpen, Robert, illus. LC 91-11211. 152p. (gr. 4 up). 1992. 18.95 (*0-87226-348-7*) P Bedrick Bks.
Shusterman, Neal. Kid Heroes: True Stories of Rescuers, Survivors & Achievers. 1991. 14.95 (*0-312-85081-6*) Tor Bks.
Sperry, Armstrong. Call It Courage. 2nd ed. LC 89-18456. 96p. (gr. 4-7). 1990. pap. 3.95 (*0-689-71391-6*, Aladdin) Macmillan Child Grp.

COURAGE–FICTION

Baillie, Allan. Rebel. Wu, Di, illus. LC 93-23512. 32p. (ps-2). 1994. reinforced bdg. 13.95 (*0-395-69250-4*) Ticknor & Flds Bks Yng Read.
Bartlett, Jaye. Caterpillar Had a Dream: A Poetic Story about Dreams Coming True. (Illus.). 1991. 8.95 (*1-878064-02-9*) TLC Bks.
—Caterpillar Had a Dream: A Story about Dreams Coming True. Dubina, Alan, illus. 38p. (Orig.). (ps up). 1990. PLB 11.95 incl. cassette (*1-878064-00-2*) New Age CT.
Brightfield, Richard. Master of Martial Arts. 1992. pap. 3.25 (*0-553-29296-X*) Bantam.
Card, Margaret. Angelina Trueheart & the Fox. Vane, Mitch, illus. LC 93-26224. 1994. 4.25 (*0-383-03732-8*) SRA Schl Grp.
Church, Kristine. My Brother John. Niland, Kilmeny, illus. LC 90-25868. 32p. (ps-3). 1991. 12.95 (*0-688-10800-8*, Tambourine Bks); PLB 12.88 (*0-688-10801-6*, Tambourine Bks) Morrow.
Clark, Marnie, et al, eds. Lighting Candles in the Dark. Thomas, Sylvia, illus. 215p. (Orig.). 1992. pap. 9.50 (*0-9620912-3-5*) Friends Genl Conf.
Crofford, Emily. A Matter of Pride. LaMarche, Jim, illus. LC 81-387. 48p. (gr. 2-6). 1981. Repr. of 1981 ed. PLB 17.50 (*0-87614-171-8*, AACR2) Carolrhoda Bks.
Duncan, Jane. Brave Janet Reachfar. Hedderwick, Mairi, illus. LC 74-8693. 32p. (ps-3). 1975. 7.95 (*0-8164-3130-2*, Clarion Bks) HM.
Hall, Kirsten. I'm Not Scared. (Illus.). 28p. (ps-2). 1994. PLB 14.00 (*0-516-05366-3*); pap. 3.95 (*0-516-45366-1*) Childrens.
Hamilton, Kersten. Natalie Jean & the Haints' Parade. 1991. 2.99 (*0-8423-4622-8*) Tyndale.
Henkes, Kevin. Sheila Rae, the Brave. Henkes, Kevin, illus. LC 86-25761. 32p. (gr. k-3). 1987. 15.00 (*0-688-07155-4*); PLB 14.93 (*0-688-07156-2*) Greenwillow.
—Sheila Rae, the Brave. LC 87-62370. (ps-3). 1988. pap. 4.99 (*0-14-050897-X*, Puffin) Puffin Bks.
Herman, Gail. Fievel's Big Showdown: An American Tail. (ps-3). 1992. 9.95 (*0-448-40379-X*, G&D) Putnam Pub Group.
Holland, Lynda. The Snicker-Snees. LC 90-71710. 44p. 1991. 5.95 (*1-55523-403-8*) Winston-Derek.
Kehret, Peg. Night of Fear. LC 93-24051. 144p. (gr. 5 up). 1994. 13.99 (*0-525-65136-5*, Cobblehill Bks) Dutton Child Bks.

Kent, Richard. The Mosquito Test. Weinberger, Jane, ed. 250p. (Orig.). (gr. 8-12). 1994. pap. 8.95 (*1-883650-03-8*) Windswept Hse.
Narrated by the main character, this young adult novel addresses two teenagers' vailiant efforts to overcome the emotional & physical setbacks of cancer & cystic fibrosis. Against the background of tennis courts, high school hallways & hospital wards, these boys discover the meaning of courage & the legacy of friendship. The author was Maine Teacher of the Year in 1993 & winner of the National Educator Award from the Milken Foundation in 1994. Over 20,000 sold to date.
Publisher Provided Annotation.

Koralek, Jenny. The Boy & the Cloth of Dreams. Mayhew, James, illus. LC 93-23091. 32p. (ps up). 1994. 14.95 (*1-56402-349-4*) Candlewick Pr.
Malone, P. M. Out of the Nest. Lewison, Terry, illus. 198p. (Orig.). (gr. 1-8). 1991. pap. text ed. 11.95 (*0-9631957-0-0*) Raspberry Hill.
Mann, Kenny. I Am Not Afraid! Based on a Masai Tale. Leonard, Richard, illus. LC 92-13811. 1993. 9.99 (*0-553-09119-0*, Little Rooster); 3.50 (*0-553-37108-8*, Little Rooster) Bantam.

Marsano, Daniel T. Sun Day, the Not-Quite Knight. Stroschin, J. H., illus. 48p. (gr. k-6). 1994. PLB 15.00 (*1-883960-13-4*) Henry Quill.
SUN DAY THE NOT-QUITE KNIGHT is the second book in this developing series. It has ever been said that the young ask, "Why?" & the old say, "Because!" In this story poem, Sir Day's son, Sun Day, questions the task that he must complete in order to attain knighthood. As he begins his quest, however, he learns that his greatest challenge is in meeting the test on his own terms while preserving who he is & who he wants to be. SIR DAY THE KNIGHT. Daniel T. Marsano. Illus. by Jane H. Stroschin. 48p. (Gr. k-6) 1993. $15.00 (1-883960-11-8). SIR DAY THE KNIGHT is a story of courage. The MICHIGAN READING JOURNAL, Volume 27, No. 3, Spring 1994, gave this review: "This story poem tells of a knight who embarks on a quest to defeat a dragon. He realizes how afraid he is, & finds that his fear is a greater problem than the reality of his quest. When he faces his dragon, he finds some pleasant surprises. Readers will be pleased with the delightful ending to this book by a Michigan author & illustrator." Call or write Henry Quill Press, Jane Stroschin, 7340 Lake Drive, Fremont, MI 49412-9146, (616) 924-3026.
Publisher Provided Annotation.

Massi, Jeri. Courage by Darkness. 157p. (Orig.). 1987. pap. 4.95 (*0-89084-412-7*) Bob Jones Univ Pr.
May, Kara. Big Brave Brother Ben. LC 91-530234. (Illus.). (ps-3). 1992. 14.00 (*0-688-11235-8*); PLB 13. 93 (*0-688-11234-X*) Lothrop.
Mock, Dorothy. Aqua Kid Saves the Day: The Good News Kids Learn about Peace. (Illus.). 32p. (Orig.). (ps-2). 1992. pap. 3.99 (*0-570-04718-8*) Concordia.
Naylor, Phyllis R. One of the Third-Grade Thonkers. Gaffney-Kessell, Walter, illus. LC 88-3130. 144p. (gr. 3-7). 1988. SBE 13.95 (*0-689-31424-8*, Atheneum Child Bk) Macmillan Child Grp.
O'Connor, Jane. Sarah's Incredible Idea. Long, Laurie S., illus. LC 92-36803. 64p. (gr. 1-4). 1993. 7.99g (*0-448-40163-0*, G&D); pap. 3.95 (*0-448-40162-2*, G&D) Putnam Pub Group.
Pepin, Muriel. Brave Little Fox. Jensen, Patricia, adapted by. Fichaux, Catherine, illus. LC 93-4238. 22p. (ps-3). 1993. 5.98 (*0-89577-541-7*, Readers Digest Kids) RD Assn.
Reynolds, Susan L. Strandia. (Illus.). 240p. (gr. 9-12). 1991. 14.95 (*0-374-37274-8*) FS&G.
Sperry, Armstrong. Call It Courage. LC 40-4229. (gr. 5-7). 1973. pap. 3.95 (*0-02-045270-5*, Collier Young Ad) Macmillan Child Grp.
—Call It Courage. large type ed. 1989. Repr. of 1940 ed. 15.95 (*1-55736-147-9*, Crnrstn Bks) BDD LT Grp.
Stridh, Kicki. The Horrible Spookhouse. Eriksson, Eva, illus. LC 93-22076. 1993. write for info. (*0-87614-811-9*) Carolrhoda Bks.
Thompson-Hoffman, Susan. Little Porcupine's Winter Den. Thomas, Peter, narrated by. Haberstock, Jennifer, illus. LC 92-14295. 32p. (ps-3). 1992. 11.95 (*0-924483-64-4*); incl. audiocass. tape 16.95 (*0-924483-63-6*); incl. audiocass. tape & 9" stuffed porcupine toy 39.95 (*0-924483-62-8*); incl. audiocass. tape & 7 inch stuffed porcupine toy 25.95 (*0-924483-71-7*); write for info. audiocass. tape (*0-924483-73-3*) Soundprints.
Thureen, Faythe D. Jenna's Big Jump. Sandeen, Eileen, illus. 112p. (gr. 2-5). 1993. SBE 12.95 (*0-689-31834-0*, Atheneum Child Bk) Macmillan Child Grp.
Vecere, Joel. Story about Courage. (gr. 4-7). 1993. pap. 3.95 (*0-8114-4307-8*) Raintree Steck-V.
Williamson, Denise. Chariots to China: A Story of Eric Liddell. 130p. (gr. 5 up). 1991. pap. 5.95 (*1-56121-058-7*) Wolgemuth & Hyatt.
Wilson, John. Lucky & the Pot of Gold. (Illus.). (gr. 1-3). 1990. PLB 4.95 (*0-9627193-2-3*, 428-983) Wilson Investment.

COURTESY
see also Behavior; Etiquette

Dunlea, Nancy. The Courtesy Book. Saunders, Dorothy, illus. Hubalek, Linda K. & Rex, Margeryintro. by. LC 93-80030. (Illus.). 128p. (gr. 4-8). pap. 7.95 (*1-882420-07-1*) Hearth KS.
Fiday, Beverly & Crowdy, Deborah. Respect. Hutton, Kathryn, illus. LC 87-36981. (SPA & ENG.). 32p. (ps-2). 1988. PLB 14.95 (*0-89565-417-2*) Childs World.
Fletcher, Sarah. Teen Manners--Why Bother: Showing You Care Helps Others to Like you. (Illus.). 64p. (gr. 7-12). 1987. pap. 3.99 (*0-570-04449-9*, 12-3060) Concordia.
Harris, Gregg & Harris, Josh. Uncommon Courtesy for Kids Kit. 56p. 1990. pap. text ed. 13.00 (*0-923463-72-0*) Noble Pub Assocs.
Odor, Ruth S. Thanks. Indereiden, Nancy, illus. LC 79-23926. (ps-2). 1980. PLB 12.95 (*0-89565-113-0*) Childs World.

COURTESY–FICTION

Berenstain, Stan & Berenstain, Janice. The Berenstain Bears Forget Their Manners. Berenstain, Stan & Berenstain, Janice, illus. 32p. (ps-1). 1986. pap. 6.95 with cassette (*0-394-88343-8*) Random Bks Yng Read.
Meyer, Kathleen A. Bear, Your Manners Are Showing. Creative Studios 1, Inc. Staff, illus. 32p. (gr. k-2). 1987. 2.50 (*0-87403-271-7*, 3771) Standard Pub.
Parry, Alan & Parry, Linda. Bruno Says Thanks. Parry, Alan & Parry, Linda, illus. LC 91-70404. 16p. (ps-k). 1991. bds. 1.49 (*0-8066-2531-7*, 9-2531, Augsburg) Augsburg Fortress.

COURTING
see Dating (Social Customs)

COURTS
see also Judges; Jury; Justice, Administration of

Summer, Lila & Woods, Samuel G. The Judiciary: Laws We Live By. LC 92-15199. (Illus.). 48p. (gr. 5-6). 1992. PLB 21.34 (*0-8114-7350-3*) Raintree Steck-V.

COURTS AND COURTIERS–FICTION

Ossorio, Joseph D., et al. The Court of the Lost Woods. (Illus.). 48p. (gr. 3-5). 1994. pap. 6.95 (*1-56721-052-X*) Twenty-Fifth Cent Pr.
—The Little Duke. (Illus.). 48p. (gr. 3-5). 1994. pap. 6.95 (*1-56721-049-X*) Twenty-Fifth Cent Pr.

COURTSHIP
see Dating (Social Customs)

COUSTEAU, JACQUES-YVES, 1910-

Cousteau Society Staff. An Adventure in the Amazon. LC 91-34167. (Illus.). 48p. (gr. 3-7). 1992. pap. 14.00 jacketed (*0-671-77071-3*, S&S BFYR) S&S Trade.
Greene, Carol. Jacques Cousteau: Man of the Oceans. Dobson, Steven, illus. LC 90-2162. 48p. (gr. k-3). 1990. PLB 12.85 (*0-516-04215-7*); pap. 4.95 (*0-516-44215-5*) Childrens.
Luthor. Jacques Cousteau. Date not set. PLB write for info. (*0-8050-2273-2*) H Holt & Co.
Reef, Catherine. Jacques Cousteau: Champion of the Sea. Raymond, Larry, illus. 72p. (gr. 4-7). 1992. PLB 14.95 (*0-8050-2114-0*) TFC Bks NY.
Sinnott, Susan. Jacques-Yves Cousteau: Undersea Adventurer. LC 91-32960. (Illus.). 128p. (gr. 3 up). 1992. PLB 20.55 (*0-516-03069-8*) Childrens.

COVERLETS

Johnston, Tony. The Quilt Story. De Paola, Tomie, illus. LC 84-18212. 32p. (gr. k-2). 1992. 14.95 (*0-399-21009-1*, Putnam); pap. 5.95 (*0-399-22403-3*, Putnam) Putnam Pub Group.
Jonas, Ann. The Quilt. Jonas, Ann, illus. LC 83-25385. 32p. (ps-1). 1984. 16.00 (*0-688-03825-5*); PLB 15.93 (*0-688-03826-3*) Greenwillow.
Lyons, Mary E. Stitching Stars: The Story Quilts of Harriet Powers. LC 92-38561. (Illus.). 48p. (gr. 3-6). 1993. SBE 15.95 (*0-684-19576-3*, Scribners Young Read) Macmillan Child Grp.
Paul, Ann W. Eight Hands Round: A Patchwork Alphabet. Winter, Jeanette, illus. LC 88-745. 32p. (gr. 3 up). 1991. 15.00 (*0-06-024689-8*); PLB 14.89 (*0-06-024704-5*) HarpC Child Bks.

COW
see Cows

COWBOYS
see also Rodeos

Adams, Andy. Log of a Cowboy. (gr. 7 up). 1969. pap. 1.95 (*0-8049-0201-1*, CL-201) Airmont.

Artman, John. Cowboys: An Activity Book. 64p. (gr. 4 up). 1982. 8.95 (*0-86653-068-1*, GA 417) Good Apple.
Brown, William F. True Texas Tales. Mazzu, Kenneth, illus. LC 92-93887. 64p. (Orig.). (gr. 7 up). 1992. pap. 8.75 perfect bdg. (*1-881936-14-7*) WFB Ent.
Christian, Mary B. Hats Are for Watering Horses: Why the Cowboy Dressed That Way. Miller, Lyle, illus. 64p. (gr. 2 up). 1993. 14.95 (*0-937460-89-3*) Hendrick-Long.
Freedman, Russell. Cowboys of the Wild West. LC 85-4200. (Illus.). 128p. (gr. 3-7). 1985. 15.95 (*0-89919-301-3*, Clarion Bks) HM.
—Cowboys of the Wild West. LC 85-4200. (Illus.). 128p. (gr. 3-6). 1990. pap. 7.95 (*0-395-54800-4*, Clarion Bks) HM.
Gintzler, A. S. Rough & Ready Cowboys. 48p. (gr. 4-7). 1994. text ed. 12.95 (*1-56261-152-6*) John Muir.
Gorsline, Marie & Gorsline, Douglas. Cowboys. Gorsline, Douglas, illus. LC 78-1131. 32p. (ps-2). 1980. lib. bdg. 5.99 (*0-394-93935-2*); pap. 2.25 (*0-394-83935-8*) Random Bks Yng Read.
Granfield, Linda. Cowboy: An Album. LC 93-11027. (Illus.). 96p. (gr. 3 up). 1994. 18.95 (*0-395-68430-7*) Ticknor & Flds Bks Yng Read.
Johnson, Neil. Jack Creek Cowboy. Johnson, Neil, photos by. LC 92-921. (Illus.). 32p. (gr. 2-5). 1993. 14.99 (*0-8037-1228-6*); PLB 14.89 (*0-8037-1229-4*) Dial Bks Young.
Landau, Elaine. Cowboys. LC 90-31025. (Illus.). 64p. (gr. 5-8). 1990. PLB 12.90 (*0-531-10866-X*) Watts.
McCafferty, Jim. Holt & the Cowboys. Davis, Florence S., illus. LC 93-16618. 40p. (gr. 4-8). 1993. 12.95 (*0-88289-985-6*) Pelican.
Martini, Teri. Cowboys. LC 81-10049. (Illus.). 48p. (gr. k-4). 1981. PLB 12.85 (*0-516-01611-3*) Childrens.
Matthews, L. Cowboys. (Illus.). 32p. (gr. 3-8). 1989. PLB 18.00 (*0-86625-363-7*); lib. bdg. 13.50s.p. (*0-685-58277-9*) Rourke Corp.
Miller, Robert H. The Story of Nat Love. Bryant, Michael, illus. LC 93-46287. 1994. 10.95 (*0-382-24398-6*); pap. 4.95 (*0-382-24393-5*); PLB 14.95 (*0-382-24389-7*) Silver Burdett Pr.
Murdoch, David H. Cowboy. Brightling, Geoff, illus. LC 93-12768. 64p. (gr. 5 up). 1993. 16.00 (*0-679-84014-1*); PLB 16.99 (*0-679-94014-6*) Knopf Bks Yng Read.

Murray, Fred. God Loves Even Cowboys. Murray, Jody L., ed. (Illus.). 177p. (gr. 4 up). 1994. pap. 11.95 (*0-9642685-4-X*) F Murray Pubng.
GOD LOVES EVEN COWBOYS uses true stories of cowboy life to illustrate positive traditional values of daily living. The main theme is to teach children that they are responsible for their actions. Each story contains an illustrated drawing by the author of the action in the story. The book cover features a portrait of the author & his horse by noted equine artist Kim McGuiness entitled COW PONY which will be featured in the January/ February 1995 issue of EQUINE IMAGES. The picture was on exhibit at the 15th annual American Academy of Equine Art National exhibition in Lexington, Kentucky. Over the last 35 years, author Fred Murray, who is known as the cowboy storyteller, has entertained thousands of children & adults with his frontier stories at churches, schools & civic functions. The stories in this book were the most requested by audiences. The stories come from the author's experiences growing up & working on ranches in Western Colorado. He worked with many old-time cowboys & pioneers who shared their experiences with him which he hopes to pass on to future generations. Address your book requests to Murray Publishing, Box 99A, Firth, NE 68358 or call 402-791-5741.
Publisher Provided Annotation.

O'Rear, Sybil J. Charles Goodnight: Pioneer Cowman. LC 89-48652. (Illus.). 69p. (gr. 5-8). 1990. 10.95 (*0-89015-741-3*) Sunbelt Media.
Rounds, Glen. The Cowboy Trade. (Illus.). 96p. (gr. 5 up). 1994. Repr. of 1972 ed. 15.95 (*0-8234-1075-7*) Holiday.
—The Cowboy Trade. Rounds, Glen, illus. (gr. 5 up). 1994. pap. 6.95 (*0-8234-1083-8*) Holiday.
Sandler, Martin W. Cowboys. Billington, James, illus. LC 93-20386. 96p. (gr. 3 up). 1994. 19.95 (*0-06-023318-4*); PLB 20.89 (*0-06-023319-2*) HarpC Child Bks.
Schlissel. Black Frontiers. 1995. 16.00 (*0-671-73853-4*) S&S Trade.
Scott, Ann H. Cowboy Country. Lewin, Ted, photos by. LC 92-24499. 1993. 14.45 (*0-395-57561-3*, Clarion Bks) HM.
Seidman, Laurence I. Once in the Saddle: The Cowboy's Frontier 1866-1896. (Illus.). 160p. 1990. 16.95x (*0-8160-2373-5*) Facts on File.
Tomb, Ubet. Cowboys. (Illus.). 48p. (gr. 6). 1984. pap. 3.95 (*0-88388-114-4*) Bellerophon Bks.
Williams, Robert L. Cowboy's Caravan. (Illus.). 150p. 1990. 16.95 (*0-9627534-0-8*) Skyspec Pub.

COWBOYS–DICTIONARIES

Brusca, Maria C. My Mama's Little Ranch on the Pampas. LC 93-28113. 1994. 15.95 (*0-8050-2782-3*) H Holt & Co.

COWBOYS–FICTION

Birney, Betty G. Tyrannosaurus Tex. O'Brien, John, illus. LC 93-30727. 1994. 14.95 (*0-395-67648-7*) HM.
Blackmore, Richard D. Lorna Doone. 378p. 1981. Repr. PLB 24.95 (*0-89967-024-5*) Harmony Raine.
Bond, Michael. Paddington Rides On! Lobban, John, illus. LC 92-24937. 32p. (ps-3). 1993. 3.95 (*0-694-00461-8*, Festival) HarpC Child Bks.
Crawford, Diane M. Cowboy Kisses. 1993. pap. 3.50 (*0-553-29984-0*) Bantam.
Downing, Warwick. Kid Curry's Last Ride. 176p. (gr. 5-7). 1992. pap. 3.95 (*0-06-440421-8*, Trophy) HarpC Child Bks.
Erickson, John, tr. Hank el Perro Vaquero, No. 1. (SPA.). 112p. (gr. 3 up). 1992. pap. 6.95 (*0-87719-216-2*) Gulf Pub.
—Hank el Perro Vaquero, No. 2. 116p. 1992. pap. 6.95 (*0-87719-217-0*) Gulf Pub.
Erickson, John R. Cowboys Are Partly Human. Holmes, Gerald L., illus. 110p. (Orig.). (gr. 3 up). 1983. 9.95 (*0-9608612-6-2*); pap. 5.95 (*0-9608612-4-6*) Maverick Bks.
Evans, Max. My Pardner. Bjorklund, Lorence, illus. LC 75-187421. 104p. (gr. 5-9). 1972. 3.95 (*0-395-13725-X*) HM.
Everett, Percival. The One That Got Away. Zimmer, Dirk, illus. (gr. 1-4). 1992. 14.45 (*0-395-56437-9*, Clarion Bks) HM.
Findlay, Lois P. The Enchanted Cowboy. Roberts, Anne F., ed. Williams, Exin R., illus. 99p. (Orig.). (gr. 1 up). 1988. pap. 5.00 (*0-317-89520-6*) Libr Commns Servs.
Fontes, Ron & Korman, Justine. Wild Bill Hickok & the Rebel Raiders. Shaw, Charlie & Bill Smith Studios Staff, illus. LC 92-56159. 80p. (Orig.). (gr. 1-4). 1993. PLB 12.89 (*1-56282-494-5*); pap. 3.50 (*1-56282-493-7*) Disney Pr.
Hafen, Lyman. Over the Joshua Slope. LC 93-30712. 160p. (gr. 4-8). 1994. SBE 14.95 (*0-02-741100-1*, Bradbury Pr) Macmillan Child Grp.
Halvorson, Marilyn. Cowboys Don't Cry. (gr. 6 up). 1986. pap. 3.50 (*0-440-91303-9*, LFL) Dell.
Harper, Jo. Jalapeno Hal. Haris, Jennifer B., illus. LC 92-16921. 40p. (ps-2). 1993. RSBE 14.95 (*0-02-742645-9*, Four Winds) Macmillan Child Grp.
Hillert, Margaret. Little Cowboy & Big... (Illus.). (ps-k). 1981. PLB 6.95 (*0-8136-5076-3*, TK2326); pap. 3.50 (*0-8136-5576-5*, TK2327) Modern Curr.
Hooker, Ruth. Matthew the Cowboy. Tucker, Kathy, ed. Smith, Cat B., illus. LC 89-21456. 32p. (ps-2). 1990. PLB 13.95 (*0-8075-4999-1*) A Whitman.
—Matthew the Cowboy. (ps-3). 1994. pap. 5.95 (*0-8075-4998-3*) A Whitman.
Hutchens, Paul. Sugar Creek Gang & the Battle of the Bees. 128p. (gr. 3-7). 1972. pap. 4.99 (*0-8024-4830-5*) Moody.
Johnston, Tony. The Cowboy & the Blackeyed Pea. Ludwig, Warren, illus. 32p. (ps-3). 1992. 14.95 (*0-399-22330-4*, Putnam) Putnam Pub Group.
Kellogg, Steven. Pecos Bill. Kellogg, Steven, illus. LC 86-784. 32p. (ps up). 1986. 15.95 (*0-688-05871-X*); lib. bdg. 15.88 (*0-688-05872-8*, Morrow Jr Bks) Morrow Jr Bks.
Khalsa, Dayal K. Cowboy Dreams. Khalsa, Dayal K., illus. LC 89-22782. 32p. (gr. k-4). 1990. 16.00 (*0-517-57490-X*, Clarkson Potter); PLB 16.99 (*0-517-57491-8*, Clarkson Potter) Crown Bks Yng Read.
Kimmel, Eric A. Four Dollars & Fifty Cents. Rounds, Glen, illus. LC 89-77515. 32p. (ps-3). 1990. reinforced 14.95 (*0-8234-0817-5*) Holiday.
Lenski, Lois. Cowboy Small. LC 60-12094. (Illus.). (gr. k-3). 1980. 5.25 (*0-8098-1021-2*) McKay.
Lightfoot, D. J. Trail Fever: The Life of a Texas Cowboy. Bobbish, John, illus. LC 92-5458. 1992. 11.00 (*0-688-11537-3*) Lothrop.

Mora, Jo. Budgee Budgee Cottontail. Mitchell, Steve, ed. Mora, Jo, illus. (gr. 3). 1994. 24.95 (*0-922029-23-7*) D Stoecklein Photo.
A wonderful story written in verse & gorgeously illustrated by famous artist, sculptor, & writer, Jo Mora. Written in 1936, eleven years before his death, the book contains a multitude of animal sketches & color illustrations by Mora. He was known as a cowboy & author of classic books on the American West, but Mora began as a Boston cartoonist & children's book author at the turn of the century. After sculpting the Will Rogers Memorial, the Father Serra Sarcophagus at the Carmel, California, mission, & the Don Quixote statue in San Francisco's Golden Gate Park, Mora returned to complete the children's book he always wanted to write - BUDGEE BUDGEE COTTONTAIL!
Publisher Provided Annotation.

Morris, Neil. Longhorn on the Move. LC 89-7153. (Illus.). 32p. (gr. 3-8). 1989. PLB 9.95 (*1-85435-166-4*) Marshall Cavendish.
Reeves, Greg. Judy Ford: World Champion Cowgirl. (Illus.). 46p. (gr. 4-8). 1992. pap. 5.95 (*0-938349-88-0*) State House Pr.
Reid, Ace. Cowpokes Comin' Yore Way. 5th ed. Reid, Ace, illus. 64p. (gr. k up). 1985. pap. 5.95 (*0-917207-05-X*) Reid Ent.
—Cowpokes Cookbook & Cartoons. 12th ed. Reid, Ace, illus. 64p. (gr. 5 up). pap. 5.95 (*0-917207-06-8*) Reid Ent.
—Cowpokes Cow Country Cartoons. 14th ed. Reid, Ace, illus. Barker, S. Omar, intro. by. (Illus.). 56p. (gr. 5 up). pap. 5.95 (*0-917207-00-9*) Reid Ent.
—Cowpokes Rarin' to Go. 2nd ed. Reid, Ace, illus. 74p. (gr. 5 up). pap. 5.95 (*0-917207-09-2*) Reid Ent.
—Cowpokes Ride Again. 4th ed. Reid, Ace, illus. 64p. (gr. k up). 1985. pap. 5.95 (*0-917207-08-4*) Reid Ent.
—Cowpokes Tales & Cartoons. 2nd ed. Reid, Ace, illus. Pickens, Slim, intro. by. (Illus.). 64p. (gr. 5 up). pap. 5.95 (*0-917207-10-6*) Reid Ent.
—Cowpokes Wanted. 12th ed. Reid, Ace, illus. Gipson, Fred, intro. by. (Illus.). 62p. (gr. 5 up). pap. 5.95 (*0-917207-02-5*) Reid Ent.
—Draggin' S Ranch Cowpokes. 14th ed. Reid, Ace, illus. 65p. (gr. 5 up). pap. 5.95 (*0-917207-04-1*) Reid Ent.
—More Cowpokes. 14th ed. Reid, Ace, illus. Robertson, FrankC., intro. by. (Illus.). 60p. (gr. 5 up). pap. 5.95 (*0-917207-01-7*) Reid Ent.
Rounds, Glen. Cowboys. Rounds, Glen, illus. LC 90-46501. 32p. (ps-3). 1991. reinforced 14.95 (*0-8234-0867-1*) Holiday.
—Cowboys. 1993. pap. 5.95 (*0-8234-1061-7*) Holiday.
Sanfield, Steve. The Great Turtle Drive. Zimmer, Dirk, illus. LC 93-43753. 1994. write for info. (*0-679-85834-2*); lib. bdg. write for info. (*0-679-95834-7*) Knopf.
Scieszka, Jon. The Good, the Bad, & the Goofy. Smith, Lane, illus. LC 93-15136. 80p. (gr. 2-5). 1993. pap. 2.99 (*0-14-036170-7*, Puffin) Puffin Bks.
Smith, George S. The Christmas Eve Cattle Drive. Bacon, Eliza, illus. 32p. (gr. 1-4). 1991. pap. 3.95 (*0-89015-820-7*) Sunbelt Media.
Wister, Owen. Virginian. (gr. 8 up). 1964. pap. 2.95 (*0-8049-0046-9*, CL-46) Airmont.

COWBOYS–LEGENDS

Scieszka, Jon. The Good, the Bad, & the Goofy. Smith, Lane, illus. 64p. (gr. 3-7). 1992. 11.00 (*0-670-84380-6*) Viking Child Bks.

COWBOYS–SONGS AND MUSIC

Medearis, Angela S., compiled by. The Zebra-Riding Cowboy: A Folk Song of the Old West. Brusca, Maria C., illus. LC 91-27941. 32p. (ps-2). 1992. 14.95 (*0-8050-1712-7*, Bks Young Read) H Holt & Co.
Moon, Dolly. My Very First Piano Book of Cowboy Songs: Twenty-Two Favorite Songs Easy in Piano Arrangement. (Illus.). 32p. (gr. 2 up). 1983. pap. 3.50 (*0-486-24311-7*) Dover.

COWS

see also Dairying; Milk

Aliki. Milk from Cow to Carton. rev. ed. LC 91-23807. (Illus.). 32p. (gr. k-4). 1992. 14.00 (*0-06-020434-6*); PLB 13.89 (*0-06-020435-4*) HarpC Child Bks.
—Milk from Cow to Carton. rev. ed. LC 91-23807. (Illus.). 32p. (gr. k-4). 1992. pap. 4.50 (*0-06-445111-9*, Trophy) HarpC Child Bks.
Benedict, Kitty. The Cow: My First Nature Books. Felix, Monique, illus. 32p. (gr. k-2). 1993. pap. 2.95 (*1-56189-177-0*) Amer Educ Pub.
Cow. 1989. 3.50 (*1-87865-729-1*) Blue Q.
Fowler, Allan. Gracias a las Vacas: Thanks to Cows. LC 91-35062. (SPA., Illus.). 32p. (ps-2). 1992. PLB 10.75 (*0-516-34924-4*); pap. 3.95 (*0-516-54924-3*); big bk. 22.95 (*0-516-59625-X*) Childrens.
—Thanks to Cows. LC 91-35062. (Illus.). 32p. (ps-2). 1992. PLB 10.75 (*0-516-04924-0*); PLB 22.95 big bk. (*0-516-49625-5*); pap. 3.95 (*0-516-44924-9*) Childrens.
Henderson, Kathy. Dairy Cows. LC 88-11123. 48p. (gr. k-4). 1988. PLB 12.85 (*0-516-01152-9*); pap. 4.95 (*0-516-41152-7*) Childrens.
Herriot, James. Blossom Comes Home. Brown, Ruth, illus. 32p. (gr. 1-8). 1993. pap. 6.95 (*0-312-09131-1*) St Martin.

Ling, Mary. Calf. Clayton, Gordon, photos by. LC 92-53486. (Illus.). 24p. (ps-1). 1993. 7.95 (*1-56458-205-1*) Dorling Kindersley.

Moncure, Jane B. Ice-Cream Cows & Mitten Sheep. Friedman, Joy, illus. LC 87-14603. (SPA & ENG.). 32p. (ps-2). 1987. PLB 14.95 (*0-89565-403-2*) Childs World.

Royston, Angela. Cow. LC 89-22536. (ps-3). 1990. PLB 10.90 (*0-531-19077-3*, Warwick) Watts.

Stone, L. Vacas (Cows) 1991. 8.95s.p. (*0-86592-952-1*) Rourke Enter.

Stone, Lynn. Cows. (Illus.). 24p. (gr. k-5). 1990. lib. bdg. 11.94 (*0-86593-039-2*); lib. bdg. 8.95s.p. (*0-685-36309-0*) Rourke Corp.

COWS–FICTION

Afanasiev, A. N. Ivan Korovavich: The Son of a Cow. Lesch, Christiane, illus. 28p. (gr. k-4). 1990. 14.95 (*0-903540-57-6*, 625, Pub. by Floris Bks UK) Anthroposophic.

Allen, Pamela. Belinda. Allen, Pamela, illus. 32p. (ps-3). 1993. 13.00 (*0-670-84372-5*) Viking Child Bks.

Ayme, Marcel. Vaches. Sabatier, Roland, illus. (FRE.). 72p. (gr. 1-5). 1990. pap. 9.95 (*2-07-031215-1*) Schoenhof.

Babcock, Chris. No Moon, No Milk! Teague, Mark, illus. LC 92-40697. 32p. (ps-2). 1993. 12.00 (*0-517-58779-3*); PLB 12.99 (*0-517-58780-7*) Crown Bks Yng Read.

Brown, Paula. Moon Jump. LC 92-22216. 32p. 1993. 13.50 (*0-670-84237-0*) Viking Child Bks.

Chase, Edith N. New Baby Calf. (Illus.). 32p. (gr. k-3). 1991. pap. 2.95 (*0-590-44776-9*) Scholastic Inc.

Christison, MaryAnn & Bassano, Sharron. Purple Cows & Potato Chips. (Illus.). 120p. (gr. 5-12). 1987. pap. text ed. 19.95 (*0-13-739178-1*) Alemany Pr.

Cole, Ann & Haas, Carolyn. Purple Cow to the Rescue. LC 82-47913. (Illus.). 160p. (gr. 1-5). 1982. 14.95 (*0-316-15104-1*) Little.

Cole, Babette. Supermoo! LC 92-8967. (Illus.). 32p. (ps-3). 1993. 14.95 (*0-399-22422-X*, Putnam) Putnam Pub Group.

Cooper, Susan. The Silver Cow: A Welsh Tale. Hutton, Warwick, illus. LC 82-13928. 32p. (gr. k-4). 1983. SBE 14.95 (*0-689-50236-2*, M K McElderry) Macmillan Child Grp.

Dennis, Wesley. Flip & the Cows. LC 88-39705. (Illus.). 64p. (ps-2). 1989. Repr. of 1942 ed. lib. bdg. 16.00 (*0-208-02240-6*, Linnet) Shoe String.

Dubanevich, Arlene. Calico Cows. (Illus.). 32p. (ps-3). 1993. PLB 13.50 (*0-670-84436-5*) Viking Child Bks.

Edens, Cooper. Santa Cows. Lane, Daniel, illus. LC 91-57. 40p. (gr. 2 up). 1991. jacketed, reinforced bdg. 14.00 (*0-671-74863-7*, Green Tiger) S&S Trade.

Ericsson, Jennifer A. No Milk! Eitan, Ora, illus. LC 92-21806. 32p. (ps up). 1993. 14.00 (*0-688-11306-0*, Tambourine Bks); PLB 13.93 (*0-688-11307-9*, Tambourine Bks) Morrow.

Ernst, Lisa C. When Bluebell Sang. Ernst, Lisa C., illus. LC 91-15552. 40p. (ps-1). 1992. pap. 4.95 (*0-689-71584-6*, Aladdin) Macmillan Child Grp.

Geringer, Laura. The Cow Is Mooing Anyhow. Zimmer, Dirk, illus. LC 85-45251. 40p. (ps-4). 1993. pap. 4.95 (*0-06-443332-3*, Trophy) HarpC Child Bks.

Greenleaf, E. Who Wants to Nap? LC 68-56820. (Illus.). 32p. (gr. 2-3). PLB 9.95 (*0-87783-050-9*) Oddo.

Greenstein, Elaine. Emily & the Crows. Greenstein, Elaine, illus. LC 91-39917. 28p. (gr. k up). 1992. pap. 14.95 (*0-88708-238-6*) Picture Bk Studio.

Harrison, David L. When Cows Come Home. Demarest, Chris L., illus. 32p. (ps-3). 1994. 14.95 (*1-56397-143-7*) Boyds Mills Pr.

Herriot, James. Blossom Comes Home. Brown, Ruth, illus. 1988. 13.00 (*0-312-02169-0*) St Martin.

Hicks, Grace R. The Most Mannerly Cow & the Rude Cowbird. (Illus.). 1992. 11.95 (*0-89015-882-7*) Sunbelt Media.

Hillert, Margaret. The Cow That Got Her Wish. (Illus.). (ps-2). 1981. PLB 6.95 (*0-8136-5121-2*, TK2608); pap. 3.50 (*0-8136-5621-4*, TK2607) Modern Curr.

Horstman, Lisa. Fast Friends: A Tail & Tongue Tale. Horstman, Lisa, illus. LC 93-28630. 40p. (ps-3). 1994. 13.00 (*0-679-85404-5*); PLB 13.99 (*0-679-95404-X*) Knopf Bks Yng Read.

Horvath, Polly. An Occasional Cow. (Illus.). 112p. (gr. 3-7). 1989. 13.95 (*0-374-35559-2*) FS&G.

—An Occasional Cow. (Illus.). 112p. (gr. 3-7). 1991. pap. 3.95 (*0-374-45573-2*, Sunburst) FS&G.

Johnson, Evelyne, retold by. The Cow in the Kitchen. Rao, Anthony, illus. LC 90-85905. 24p. (ps-2). 1991. Repr. 8.95 (*1-878093-45-2*) Boyds Mills Pr.

Johnson, Paul B. The Cow Who Wouldn't Come Down. LC 92-27592. (Illus.). 32p. (ps-1). 1993. 14.95 (*0-531-05481-0*); PLB 14.99 (*0-531-08631-3*) Orchard Bks Watts.

Kanno, Wendy. Holy Moley Cow. Reese, Bob, illus. (gr. k-2). 1984. 7.95 (*0-89868-159-6*); pap. 2.95 (*0-89868-160-X*) ARO Pub.

Keavney, Pamela. The Promise. LC 89-26896. (Illus.). 32p. (ps-3). 1992. 15.00 (*0-06-023019-3*); PLB 14.89 (*0-06-023020-7*) HarpC Child Bks.

Krasilovsky, Phyllis. Cow Who Fell in the Canal. Spier, Peter, illus. LC 56-8236. 38p. (gr. k-1). 1985. pap. 11.95 (*0-385-07585-5*) Doubleday.

—Cow Who Fell in the Canal. (ps-3). 1993. 4.99 (*0-440-40825-3*) Dell.

Obligado, Lilian. The Chocolate Cow. LC 91-27464. (Illus.). 48p. (ps-2). 1993. pap. 14.00 JRT (*0-671-73852-6*, S&S BFYR) S&S Trade.

Oppenheim, Joanne. The Not Now! Said the Cow-Bank Street. (ps-3). 1989. pap. 3.99 (*0-553-34691-1*) Bantam.

—Not Now! Said the Cow: Level 2. Demarest, Chris, illus. 1989. 9.99 (*0-553-05826-6*) Bantam.

Paterson, Katherine. The Smallest Cow in the World. new ed. Brown, Jane C., illus. LC 90-30521. 64p. (gr. k-3). 1991. 14.00 (*0-06-024690-1*); PLB 13.89 (*0-06-024691-X*) HarpC Child Bks.

—Smallest Cow in the World. new ed. Brown, Jane C., illus. LC 90-30521. 64p. (gr. k-3). 1993. pap. 3.50 (*0-06-444164-4*, Trophy) HarpC Child Bks.

Rose, Phoebe E. You & the Cow. Skidmore, Joan L., illus. LC 91-60008. 20p. (Orig.). (gr. k-6). 1991. pap. 8.50 (*0-9630050-0-6*) Oregon Info.

Seymour, Tres. Hunting the White Cow. Halperin, Wendy A., illus. LC 92-43757. 32p. (ps-2). 1993. 15.95 (*0-531-05496-9*); PLB 15.99 (*0-531-08646-1*) Orchard Bks Watts.

Sims, Larry K. Little Spotted Moo. Antolik, Jerry, illus. 24p. (Orig.). 1991. pap. text ed. 3.95 (*1-880706-00-8*) Goldrock Bks.

Speed, Toby. Two Cool Cows. Root, Barry, illus. LC 93-34258. 1995. 14.95 (*0-399-22647-8*, Putnam) Putnam Pub Group.

Swan, Walter. Brenda the Cow & the Little White Hen. Swan, Deloris, ed. Asch, Connie, illus. 16p. (Orig.). (gr. 2-3). 1989. pap. 1.50 (*0-927176-02-5*) Swan Enterp.

Van Laan, Nancy. The Tiny, Tiny Boy & the Big, Big Cow. Priceman, Marjorie, illus. LC 91-33738. 40p. (ps-2). 1993. 8.99 (*0-679-82078-7*); PLB 9.99 (*0-679-92078-1*) Knopf Bks Yng Read.

Whishaw, Iona. Henry & the Cow Problem. McLeod, Chum, illus. (ps-1). 1992. 0.99 (*1-55037-254-8*, Pub. by Annick Pr) Firefly Bks Ltd.

Woodman, Allen & Kirby, David. The Cows Are Going to Paris. Demarest, Chris L., illus. LC 90-85733. 32p. (ps-3). 1991. 15.95 (*1-878093-11-8*) Boyds Mills Pr.

Zidrou. Ms. Blanche, the Spotless Cow. Merveille, David, illus. LC 92-28673. 32p. (ps-k). 1993. 14.95 (*0-8050-2550-2*, Bks Young Read) H Holt & Co.

COYOTES

Ahlstrom, Mark E. The Coyote. LC 85-24290. (Illus.). 48p. (gr. 5). 1985. text ed. 12.95 RSBE (*0-89686-277-1*, Crestwood Hse) Macmillan Child Grp.

Lee, Sandra. Coyotes. (gr. 2-6). 1992. PLB 15.95 (*0-89565-843-7*) Childs World.

Lepthien, Emilie U. Coyotes. LC 92-35050. (Illus.). 48p. (gr. k-4). 1993. PLB 12.85 (*0-516-01331-9*); pap. 4.95 (*0-516-41331-7*) Childrens.

Mendel, Kathleen L. Coyote Solitude: A Wilderness Meditation. Brethauer, Candy K., ed. LC 92-71827. 40p. 1993. pap. 4.00 (*1-878142-32-1*, Blue Earth Pr) Telstar TX.

Samuelson, Mary L. & Schlaepfer, Gloria G. The Coyote. LC 92-44739. (Illus.). 60p. (gr. 5 up). 1993. text ed. 13.95 RSBE (*0-87518-560-6*, Dillon) Macmillan Child Grp.

COYOTES–FICTION

Bierhorst, John, retold by. & tr. Doctor Coyote: A Native American Aesop's Fables. LC 86-8669. (Illus.). 48p. (gr. 2-5). 1987. SBE 15.95 (*0-02-709780-3*, Macmillan Child Bk) Macmillan Child Grp.

Levy. Cleo & Coyote. Date not set. 15.00 (*0-06-024271-X*); PLB 14.89 (*0-06-024272-8*) HarpC Child Bks.

Lowell, Susan. The Three Little Javelinas. Harris, Jim, illus. LC 92-14232. 32p. (ps-2). 1992. 14.95 (*0-87358-542-9*) Northland AZ.

Lund, Jillian. Way Out West Lives a Coyote Named Frank. LC 91-46011. (Illus.). 32p. (ps-2). 1993. 13.95 (*0-525-44982-5*, DCB) Dutton Child Bks.

Nunes, Susan. Coyote Dreams. Himler, Ronald, illus. LC 87-30288. 32p. (ps-3). 1988. SBE 14.95 (*0-689-31398-5*, Atheneum Child Bk) Macmillan Child Grp.

—Coyote Dreams. Himler, Ronald, illus. LC 93-22931. 32p. (gr. k-3). 1994. pap. 4.95 (*0-689-71804-7*, Aladdin) Macmillan Child Grp.

Stinson, Douglas. C Is for Coyote. Goggin, Lewisa, illus. 40p. (gr. 1 up). 1993. 15.95 (*1-879244-04-7*) Windom Bks.

Strauss, Susan. Coyote Stories for Children. Norman, Howard, ed. Lund, Gary, illus. 50p. (gr. 1-6). 1991. 10.95 (*0-941831-61-2*); pap. 6.95 (*0-941831-62-0*) Beyond Words Pub.

CRABS

Bailey, Jill. Life Cycle of a Crab. (ps-3). 1990. PLB 11.90 (*0-531-18317-3*, Pub. by Bookwright Pr) Watts.

Butterworth, Christine & Bailey, Donna. Crabs. LC 90-36168. (Illus.). 32p. (gr. 1-4). 1990. PLB 18.99 (*0-8114-2640-8*) Raintree Steck-V.

Coldrey, Jennifer. The Crab on the Seashore. LC 85-30293. (Illus.). 32p. (gr. 4-6). 1987. PLB 17.27 (*1-55532-060-0*) Gareth Stevens Inc.

—The World of Crabs. LC 85-30294. (Illus.). 32p. (gr. 2-3). 1986. 17.27 (*1-55532-063-5*) Gareth Stevens Inc.

Fichter, George S. Starfish, Seashells, & Crabs. Sandstrom, George, illus. 36p. (gr. k-3). 1993. 4.95 (*0-307-11430-9*, 11430, Golden Pr) Western Pub.

Holling, Holling C. Pagoo. Holling, Lucille W., illus. (gr. 3-9). 1957. 16.45 (*0-395-06826-6*) HM.

Johnson, Sylvia A. Crabs. Sakurai, Atsushi, illus. LC 82-10056. 48p. (gr. 4 up). 1982. PLB 19.95 (*0-8225-1471-0*) Lerner Pubns.

—Hermit Crabs. Kawashima, Kazunari, illus. 48p. (gr. 4 up). 1989. PLB 19.95 (*0-8225-1488-5*) Lerner Pubns.

—Hermit Crabs. LC 89-8221. (gr. 4-7). 1991. pap. 5.95 (*0-8225-9577-X*) Lerner Pubns.

Kite, Patricia. Down in the Sea: The Crab. LC 93-21494. 1994. write for info. (*0-8075-1709-7*) A Whitman.

McDonald, Megan. Is This a House for Hermit Crab? Schindler, Stephen D., illus. LC 89-35653. 32p. (ps-1). 1990. 14.95 (*0-531-05855-7*); PLB 14.99 (*0-531-08455-8*) Orchard Bks Watts.

Pohl, Kathleen. Crabs. (Illus.). 32p. (gr. 3-7). 1986. PLB 10.95 (*0-8172-2716-4*) Raintree Steck-V.

—Hermit Crabs. (Illus.). 32p. (gr. 3-7). 1986. PLB 10.95 (*0-8172-2721-0*) Raintree Steck-V.

Whately, Bruce. Looking for Crabs. (ps-3). 1993. 12.00 (*0-207-17596-9*, Pub. by Angus & Robertson AT) HarpC.

CRABS–FICTION

Beveridge, Barbara. Waves. Costeloe, Brenda, illus. LC 92-31948. 1993. 3.75 (*0-383-03603-8*) SRA Schl Grp.

Childress, Mark. Joshua & the Big Bad Blue Crabs. Brown, Mary B., illus. LC 93-30351. 1995. reinforced bdg. 15.95 (*0-316-14118-6*) Little.

Cummings, Priscilla. Chadwick & the Garplegrungen. Cohen, A. R., illus. LC 87-71087. 32p. (gr. k-4). 1987. 8.95 (*0-87033-377-1*) Tidewater.

—Chadwick the Crab. Cohen, A. R., illus. LC 85-41005. 32p. (gr. k-4). 1986. 8.95 (*0-87033-347-X*) Tidewater.

—Chadwick's Wedding. Cohen, A. R., illus. LC 88-51677. 30p. (gr. k-4). 1989. 8.95 (*0-87033-390-9*) Tidewater.

Harriman, Edward. Leroy the Lobster & Crabby Crab. (Illus.). (ps-1). 1967. pap. 7.95 (*0-89272-000-X*) Down East.

Knutson, Barbara. Why the Crab Has No Head: An African Folktale. (Illus.). 24p. (ps-3). 1987. lib. bdg. 15.95 (*0-87614-322-2*); pap. 4.95 (*0-87614-489-X*) Carolrhoda Bks.

Lewis, Paul O. Grasper: A Young Crab's Discovery out of His Shell. Roehm, Michelle, ed. Lewis, Paul O., illus. 36p. 1993. 14.95 (*0-941831-85-X*) Beyond Words Pub.

McDonald, Megan. Is This a House for Hermit Crab? Schindler, Stephen D., illus. LC 89-35653. 32p. (ps-1). 1993. pap. 5.95 (*0-531-07041-7*) Orchard Bks Watts.

Peet, Bill. Kermit the Hermit. (Illus.). (gr. k-3). 1980. 14.95 (*0-395-15084-1*); pap. 5.95 (*0-395-29607-2*) HM.

Tafuri, Nancy. Follow Me! LC 89-23259. (Illus.). 24p. (ps up). 1990. 13.95 (*0-688-08773-6*); lib. bdg. 13.88 (*0-688-08774-4*) Greenwillow.

Tate, Suzanne. Crabby & Nabby: A Tale of Two Blue Crabs. Melvin, James, illus. LC 88-61096. 28p. (Orig.). (gr. k-3). 1988. pap. 3.95 (*0-9616344-3-X*) Nags Head Art.

—Harry Horseshoe Crab: A Tale of Crawly Creatures. Melvin, James, illus. LC 91-61375. 28p. (Orig.). (gr. k-9). 1991. pap. 3.95 (*1-878405-03-9*) Nags Head Art.

Watkins, Dawn L. The Cranky Blue Crab: A Tale in Verse. Smith, Anne, ed. Davis, Tim, illus. 32p. (Orig.). (gr. k-1). 1990. pap. write for info. (*0-89084-506-9*) Bob Jones Univ Pr.

Whatley, Bruce. Looking for Crabs. (ps-3). 1994. pap. 7.00 (*0-207-17771-6*, Pub. by Angus & Robertson AT) HarpC.

CRADLE SONGS

see Lullabies

CRAFTS

see Arts and Crafts; Handicraft

CRANE, STEPHEN, 1871-1900

Sufrin, Mark. Stephen Crane. LC 91-47896. (Illus.). 160p. (gr. 7 up). 1992. SBE 13.95 (*0-689-31669-0*, Atheneum Child Bk) Macmillan Child Grp.

CRANES (BIRDS)

Byars, Betsy C. The House of Wings. Schwartz, Daniel, illus. 136p. (gr. 3-7). 1982. pap. 3.99 (*0-14-031523-3*, Puffin) Puffin Bks.

Friedman, Judi. Operation Siberian Crane: The Story Behind the International Effort to Save an Amazing Bird. LC 92-13775. (Illus.). 96p. (gr. 5 up). 1992. text ed. 13.95 RSBE (*0-87518-515-0*, Dillon) Macmillan Child Grp.

Horn, Gabriel. The Crane. LC 88-12031. (Illus.). 48p. (gr. 5). 1988. text ed. 12.95 RSBE (*0-89686-393-X*, Crestwood Hse) Macmillan Child Grp.

Patent, Dorothy H. The Whooping Crane: A Comeback Story. Munoz, William, photos by. LC 88-2871. (Illus.). 96p. (gr. 4 up). 1988. 14.95 (*0-89919-455-9*, Clarion Bks) HM.

Roop, Peter & Roop, Connie. Seasons of the Cranes. (Illus.). 32p. (gr. 4-7). 1989. 14.95 (*0-8027-6859-8*); PLB 15.85 (*0-8027-6860-1*) Walker & Co.

Voeller, Edward. The Red-Crowned Crane. LC 89-11718. (Illus.). 60p. (gr. 3 up). 1990. text ed. 13.95 RSBE (*0-87518-417-0*, Dillon) Macmillan Child Grp.

CRAYON DRAWING

see also Pastel Drawing

Rovira, Albert. Wax Crayon. Ballestar, Vincenc & Martinez, Francesc, illus. 48p. 1991. pap. 7.95 (*0-8120-4718-4*) Barron.

CRAYON DRAWING–FICTION

Johnson, Crockett. Harold & the Purple Crayon. Johnson, Crockett, illus. LC 55-7683. 64p. (ps-3). 1981. pap. 3.95 (*0-06-443022-7*, Trophy) HarpC Child Bks.

—Harold's Circus. Johnson, Crockett, illus. LC 59-5318. 64p. (ps-3). 1981. pap. 3.95 (*0-06-443024-3*, Trophy) HarpC Child Bks.

—Harold's Trip to the Sky. Johnson, Crockett, illus. LC 57-9262. 64p. (ps-3). 1981. pap. 3.95 (*0-06-443025-1*, Trophy) HarpC Child Bks.

—Picture for Harold's Room. Johnson, Crockett, illus. LC 60-6372. (gr. k-3). 1960. PLB 13.89 (*0-06-023006-1*) HarpC Child Bks.

CRAZY HORSE, OGLALA INDIAN, 1842?-1877

Benchley, Nathaniel. Only Earth & Sky Last Forever. LC 72-82891. 204p. (gr. 7 up). 1974. pap. 4.95 (*0-06-440049-2*, Trophy) HarpC Child Bks.

Guttmacher, Peter. Crazy Horse, Sioux War Chief. LC 93-38545. 1994. write for info. (*0-7910-1712-5*); pap. write for info. (*0-7910-2045-2*) Chelsea Hse.

St. George, Judith. Crazy Horse. (Illus.). 192p. 1994. 16.95 (*0-399-22667-2*) Putnam Pub Group.

Vinson, Brown. Crazy Horse: Hoka Hey! LC 90-42985. (Illus.). 176p. (gr. 6-10). 1991. PLB 13.95 (*1-55905-077-2*) Marshall Cavendish.

Wheeler, Jill. The Story of Crazy Horse. Deegan, Paul, ed. Dodson, Liz, illus. LC 89-84913. 32p. (gr. 4). 1989. PLB 11.96 (*0-939179-66-0*) Abdo & Dghtrs.

Zadra, Dan. Indians of America: Crazy Horse. rev. ed. (gr. 2-4). 1987. PLB 14.95 (*0-88682-163-0*) Creative Ed.

CREATION

see also Earth; Evolution; Geology; God; Man; Mythology; Theology; Universe

All the Animals. (ps-1). 1990. bds. 6.99 (*0-7459-1838-7*) Lion USA.

Animals Two by Two. (ps-1). 1990. bds. 6.99 (*0-7459-1839-5*) Lion USA.

Aronow, Sara. Seven Days of Creation. Seligson, Judith, illus. 32p. (ps-2). 1985. pap. 4.95 (*0-87203-119-5*) Hermon.

Beaude, Pierre-Marie. The Book of Creation. Clements, Andrew, tr. Lemoine, Georges, illus. LC 90-35418. 56p. (gr. 5 up). 1991. pap. 16.95 (*0-88708-141-X*) Picture Bk Studio.

Bond, Alan & Bond, Jill, eds. Our Planet, His Creation. (Illus.). 112p. (Orig.). (gr. k-12). 1992. pap. 5.00 (*0-9631992-2-6*) Bonding Place.

Caswell, Helen. God Must Like to Laugh. Caswell, Helen, illus. LC 87-1362. (ps-3). 1987. pap. 5.95 (*0-687-15188-0*) Abingdon.

Cowan, James. Kun-Man-Gur: The Rainbow Serpent. Bancroft, Bronwyn, illus. LC 93-32319. 1994. 16.00 (*1-56957-906-7*) Barefoot Bks.

Dakenbing, William F. The Creation Book. Hendrickson, et al, illus. Von Braun, Wehrner. LC 75-39840. 70p. (gr. 3 up). 1976. 5.95 (*0-685-68397-4*); pap. 3.95 (*0-685-68398-2*) Triumph Pub.

Daniel, Rebecca. The Days of Creation. 16p. (ps-3). 1991. 16.95 (*0-86653-633-7*, SS1877, Shining Star Pubns) Good Apple.

Daniel, Rebecca & Hierstein, Judy. God's Animal Alphabet. 48p. (ps-1). 1991. 9.95 (*0-86653-577-2*, Shining Star Pubns) Good Apple.

Davidson, Alice J. Alice in Bibleland Storybooks: Story of Creation. Marshall, Victoria, illus. 32p. (gr. 3 up). 1984. 5.50 (*0-8378-5066-5*) Gibson.

Eberle, Bob. Warm-Up to Creativity. Weber, June Kern, illus. 64p. (gr. 5 up). 1985. wkbk. 7.95 (*0-86653-275-7*, GA 667) Good Apple.

Erickson, Dean. Seven Days to Care for God's World: Rupert Learns What It Means to Take Care of God's Earth. LC 91-8875. 48p. 1991. pap. 6.99 (*0-8066-2533-3*, 9-2533) Augsburg Fortress.

Frank, Penny. In the Beginning. (ps-3). 1988. 3.99 (*0-85648-726-0*) Lion USA.

—In the Beginning. Haysom, John, illus. LC 92-31617. 1992. 6.95 (*0-7459-2608-8*) Lion USA.

Goble, Paul. I Sing for the Animals. Goble, Paul, illus. LC 90-19812. 32p. 1991. SBE 9.95 (*0-02-737725-3*, Bradbury Pr) Macmillan Child Grp.

God's World, Our World. (Illus.). 32p. (ps-2). 1985. 1.95 (*0-225-66389-9*) Harper SF.

Great & Small. 8p. (ps). 1983. bds. 3.99 (*0-7459-1427-6*) Lion USA.

Hamilton, Virginia. In the Beginning: Creation Stories from Around the World. Moser, Barry, illus. 161p. (ps up). 1988. 22.95 (*0-15-238740-4*) HarBrace.

Hershey, Katherine. Beginnings. (Illus.). 51p. (gr. k-6). 1979. pap. text ed. 9.45 (*1-55976-004-4*) CEF Press.

Hilliard, Dick & Valenti-Hilliard, Beverly. Surprises! Collopy, George F., illus. LC 81-52714. 64p. (Orig.). (gr. 1 up). 1981. pap. text ed. 4.95 (*0-89390-031-1*) Resource Pubns.

In the Beginning. 1992. pap. 4.99 (*0-517-06730-7*) Random Hse Value.

Katz, Ellie. The Conception Connection: The Journey into Creation. rev. ed. Neyndorff, Mark, illus. 100p. (gr. k-12). 1991. pap. 12.95 (*1-880806-00-2*) Playology Hlth.

Lashbrook, Marilyn. Someone to Love: The Story of Creation. Britt, Stephanie M., illus. LC 87-60261. 32p. (ps). 1987. 5.95 (*0-86606-426-5*, 841) Roper Pr.

Lavitt, Edward & McDowell, Robert. In the Beginning Creation Stories. new ed. 156p. (gr. 6-12). 1973. 18.95 (*0-89388-096-5*) Okpaku Communications.

McNeil. How Things Began. (gr. 2-5). 1975. (Usborne-Hayes); PLB 13.96 (*0-88110-114-1*); pap. 6.95 (*0-86020-199-6*) EDC.

Medicine, Story. Children of the Morning Light: Wampanoag Tales As Told by Manitonquat. Arquette, Mary F., illus. LC 92-32328. 80p. (gr. 1 up). 1994. SBE 16.95 (*0-02-765905-4*, Macmillan Child Bk) Macmillan Child Grp.

Mitchell, Stephen. Creation. LC 89-39726. (Illus.). 40p. 1990. 15.95 (*0-8037-0617-0*); PLB 15.89 (*0-8037-0618-9*) Dial Bks Young.

Palmer, Glenda. P Is for Pink Polliwogs: God's Wonderful World of Letters. LC 92-34715. (Illus.). 1993. pap. 4.99 (*0-7814-0708-7*, Chariot Bks) Chariot Family.

Pipe, Rhona. When Time Began. Press, Jenny, illus. LC 92-13321. 1993. 7.99 (*0-8407-3419-0*) Nelson.

Ray, Jane, photos by. The Story of the Creation: Words from Genesis. LC 92-20862. (Illus.). 32p. (gr. 1 up). 1993. 16.00 (*0-525-44946-9*, DCB); Spanish ed. 16.00 (*0-525-45055-6*, DCB) Dutton Child Bks.

Richards, Larry. It Couldn't Just Happen. 191p. (gr. 2-7). 1989. write for info. (*0-8499-0715-2*) Word Inc.

Sattgast, L. J. Look What God Made! Smith, Julie, ed. McDonnell, Janet, illus. LC 94-9201. 32p. (ps-2). Date not set. 5.99 (*0-7814-0184-4*, Chariot Bks) Chariot Family.

Snellenberger, Earl & Snellenberger, Bonita. God Created Birds of the World. Snellenberger, Earl & Snellenberger, Bonita, illus. 36p. (Orig.). (ps-6). 1989. pap. 4.95 (*0-89051-152-7*) Master Bks.

—God Created Sea Life of the World. Snellenberger, Earl & Snellenberger, Bonita, illus. 36p. (Orig.). (ps-6). 1989. pap. 4.95 (*0-89051-151-9*) Master Bks.

—God Created the Dinosaurs of the World. Snellenberger, Earl & Snellenberger, Bonita, illus. 36p. (Orig.). (ps-6). 1993. pap. 4.95 (*0-89051-153-5*) Master Bks.

—God Created the World & the Universe. Snellenberger, Earl & Snellenberger, Bonita, illus. 36p. (Orig.). (ps-6). 1989. pap. 4.95 (*0-89051-149-7*) Master Bks.

Swartzentruber. God Made Us in a Wonderful Way. 1976. 2.50 (*0-686-18184-0*) Rod & Staff.

Taylor, Kenneth N. My First Bible for Tots: Creation. (Illus.). 12p. (ps). 1992. bds. 3.99 (*0-8423-1696-5*) Tyndale.

—What High School Students Should Know about Creation. (gr. 9-12). 1983. pap. 2.95 (*0-8423-7872-3*) Tyndale.

Tyndale. Story of Creation. 1992. pap. 12.99 (*0-8423-5923-0*) Tyndale.

Ulmer. Adam's Story. LC 59-1292. 24p. (Orig.). (gr. k-4). 1985. pap. 1.99 (*0-570-06191-1*) Concordia.

Waldman, Sarah. Light: The First Seven Days. LC 92-8767. (ps-3). 1993. 14.95 (*0-15-220870-4*) HarBrace.

Waskow, Arthur, et al. Before There Was a Before. LC 84-11177. (Illus.). 88p. (gr. 1-6). 1984. 8.95 (*0-915361-08-6*) Modan-Adama Bks.

Williamson, Ray A. & Monroe, Jean G. First Houses: Native American Homes & Sacred Structures. Carlson, Susan, illus. LC 92-34900. 160p. 1993. 14.95 (*0-395-51081-3*) HM.

CREATION–POETRY

Alexander, Cecil. All Things Bright & Beautiful. Heyer, Carol, illus. LC 91-28428. 32p. (ps-2). 1992. 11.95 (*0-8249-8544-3*, Ideals Child) Hambleton-Hill.

Johnson, James Weldon. The Creation. Ransome, James, illus. LC 93-3207. 32p. (ps-3). 1994. reinforced bdg. 15.95 (*0-8234-1069-2*) Holiday.

CREATION (LITERARY, ARTISTIC, ETC.)

Bauman, Toni & Zinkgraf, June. Spring Surprises. 240p. (gr. k-6). 1979. 15.95 (*0-916456-54-4*, GA109) Good Apple.

Bean, Vaughan. The ABCs of Meditation & More: How to Maximize Your Child's Innate Intelligence. Miuru, illus. 96p. (Orig.). (gr. 2-6). 1994. pap. 11.95 (*0-9631740-1-0*) Millinnium-Holographic.

Each child born into our world arrives with their own individual & innate brand of intelligence. Before a child grows old enough to stop using his or her active imagination, you can instill positive & beneficial concepts inside them. In the opinion of the author, children who learn the art of meditation will usually & grow into adulthood with an expanded spiritual awareness & will possess the positive psychological tools necessary to help them be successful in adult life. THE ABC'S OF MEDITATION & MORE is designed to help develop a child's innate intelligence by introducing them to elementary concepts of meditation, creative visualization, guardian angels, lucid dreaming, the power of intuition, positive self image, & other beneficial concepts. Meditation can also help to temporarily calm children & reduce their stress level. THE ABC'S OF MEDITATION & MORE is recommended for children between the ages of 7 & 11 & is published by Books That Teach (an imprint of Holographic Books). Illustrations by Sri Lankan Artist Miuru. For additional information, contact: Holographic Books, P.O. Box 101862, Ft. Worth, TX 76185 or call 817-377-3303.

Publisher Provided Annotation.

Berry, Joy W. Teach Me about Pretending. Dickey, Kate, ed. LC 85-45091. (Illus.). 36p. (ps). 1986. 4.98 (*0-685-10731-0*) Grolier Inc.

Cline, Starr. Teaching for Talent. Taylor, Christina, illus. Tannenbaum, A. J., intro. by. (Illus.). 56p. (Orig.). (gr. k-6). 1984. 6.50 (*0-88047-040-2*, 8406) DOK Pubs.

Cote. Fairness, Reading Level 2. (Illus.). 32p. (gr. 1-4). 1989. PLB 15.94 (*0-86592-445-7*); lib. bdg. 11.95s.p. (*0-685-58780-0*) Rourke Corp.

Davis, Duane. My Friends & Me Activity Manual. rev. ed. (ps-k). 1988. pap. text ed. 64.95 (*0-88671-325-0*, 4601) Am Guidance.

Duna, Bill & Duna, Lois. Let's Play & Play & Play... Practice & Assignment Book. (Illus.). 56p. (ps up). 1983. pap. 6.95 (*0-942928-02-4*) Duna Studios.

Espeland, Pamela & Wallner, Rosemary. Making the Most of Today: Daily Readings for Young People on Self-Awareness, Creativity & Self-Esteem. LC 91-14494. 392p. (Orig.). (gr. 5 up). 1991. pap. 8.95 (*0-915793-33-4*) Free Spirit Pub.

Evans, Vicki. Be Like the Sun & Shine. (ENG, FRE & SPA., Illus.). 32p. (ps-5). 1993. pap. 9.00 (*0-9636367-0-7*) V Evans.

Fearn, Leif. The First First I Think. 91p. (gr. 1-3). 1981. 6.95 (*0-940444-14-3*) Kabyn.

Fearn, Leif & Garner, Irene A. The Alpha Cards. 54p. (gr. 2-9). 1982. card pack 14.00 (*0-940444-12-7*) Kabyn.

—Maneras de Divertirme con Mi Mente. (Illus.). 182p. (gr. 3-9). 1982. 6.50 (*0-940444-16-X*) Kabyn.

Fearn, Leif & Goliaz-Benson, Ursula. Forty-Two Ways to Have Fun with My Mind. Curtner, Rondi L., illus. 58p. (ps-6). 1976. 5.00 (*0-940444-00-3*) Kabyn.

Fearn, Leif & Golisz-Benson, Ursula. Fifty-Two Ways to Have Fun with My Mind. Emmet, Mary, illus. 62p. (gr. 1-3). 1975. 5.00 (*0-940444-01-1*) Kabyn.

—Seventy-Two Ways to Have Fun with My Mind. Curtner, Rondi, illus. 80p. (Orig.). (gr. 4-6). 1976. 5.00 (*0-940444-03-8*) Kabyn.

—Sixty-Two Ways to Have Fun with My Mind. (Illus.). 72p. (Orig.). (gr. 3-6). 1982. 5.00 (*0-940444-02-X*) Kabyn.

Forte, Imogene. Box Crafts: Over 50 Things to Make & Do with Boxes of Every Size. LC 86-82933. (Illus.). 80p. (gr. k-6). 1987. pap. text ed. 3.95 (*0-86530-123-9*, IP 942) Incentive Pubns.

—Crayons & Markers: Artistic Creations, One of a Kind & Made By You. LC 86-82934. (Illus.). 80p. (gr. k-6). 1987. pap. text ed. 3.95 (*0-86530-162-X*, IP 943) Incentive Pubns.

—Dinosaurs: Facts Fun, & Fantastic Crafts. LC 86-82932. (Illus.). 80p. (gr. k-6). 1987. pap. text ed. 3.95 (*0-86530-149-2*, IP 944) Incentive Pubns.

—The Kids' Stuff: Book of Patterns, Projects & Plans to Perk Up Early Learning Programs. LC 82-83051. (Illus.). 200p. (ps-1). 1982. pap. text ed. 12.95 (*0-86530-054-2*, IP 54-2) Incentive Pubns.

Frost, Joan. Exceptional Art--Exceptional Children: Fostering Creativity & Developing Independence. (Illus.). 140p. (gr. 1-8). 1985. spiral bdg. 16.95 (*0-938594-07-9*) Spec Lit Pr.

Fun to Make Witches. 1989. pap. 3.99 (*0-517-68793-3*) Random Hse Value.

Galt, Margot F. The Story in History: Writing Your Way into the American Experience. (Illus.). 280p. (Orig.). 1992. 24.95 (*0-915924-38-2*); pap. 15.95 (*0-915924-39-0*) Tchrs & Writers Coll.

Gattis, L. S., III. Trailblazer Fun Honors I: Birds, Buttons, Computers, Dress, Kites & Stamps. (Illus.). 20p. (Orig.). (ps-5). 1986. pap. 5.00 tchr's. ed. (*0-936241-08-X*) Cheetah Pub.

Haas, Carolyn B. Look at Me: Creative Learning Activities for Babies & Toddlers. Phillips, Jane B., illus. LC 87-20288. 230p. (Orig.). 1987. pap. 9.95 (*1-55652-021-2*) Chicago Review.

Helwig, Barbara & Stewart, Susan. Wishful Thinking. rev. ed. (Illus.). 90p. (gr. 2-6). 1992. spiral bdg. 4.95 (*1-881285-06-5*) Arbus Pub.

Herman, Emmi S. Christmas KidDoodles, Bk. 1. Sims, Deborah, illus. 64p. (Orig.). (ps-2). 1991. pap. 0.99 activity pad (*1-56293-153-9*) McClanahan Bk.

—KidDoodles, Bk. 1. Boyd, Patti, illus. 64p. (ps-2). 1991. pap. 0.99 activity pad (*1-878624-50-4*) McClanahan Bk.

Keefe, Betty. Fingerpuppet Tales: Making & Using Puppets with Folk & Fairytales. (Illus.). 148p. (ps-3). 1986. spiral bdg. 17.95 (*0-938594-08-7*) Spec Lit Pr.

Lamping, Ed. The Awareness Book. (Illus.). 40p. (gr. 3-6). 1982. 5.00 (*0-940444-15-1*) Kabyn.

McAllister, Constance. Creative Writing Activities, 2-6. 32p. (gr. 2-6). 1980. pap. 2.95 (*0-87534-176-4*) Highlights.

McGowan, Tom & McGowan, Meredith. Children, Literature & Social Studies: Activities for the Intermediate Grades. (Illus.). 218p. (gr. 4-6). 1986. spiral bdg. 18.95 (*0-938594-06-0*) Spec Lit Pr.

Myers, Garry C. Creative Thinking Activities. Rev. ed. 32p. (gr. 2-6). 1980. pap. 2.95 (*0-87534-113-6*) Highlights.

Nicholas, Robert J. Fifty Creative Exercises, 2 bks. (gr. 7 up). 1991. Set. pap. 24.00 (*1-879777-02-9*); Bk. I. pap. 12.95 (*1-879777-00-2*); Bk. II. pap. 12.95 (*1-879777-01-0*) Leonardos Work.

Outdoor Fun. 32p. (ps-1). 1989. pap. 3.50 (*0-517-68797-6*, Chatham River Pr) Random Hse Value.

Petrucelli. Creativity, Reading Level 2. (Illus.). 32p. (gr. 1-4). 1989. PLB 15.94 (*0-86592-444-9*) Rourke Corp.

Pizzo, Joan E. Little Crumb Fun Book. (Illus.). 32p. (Orig.). (gr. k-6). 1983. pap. 3.95 (*0-939126-04-4*) Back Bay.

Spies & Detectives: Cut & Color Activity Book. 1989. pap. 3.99 (*0-517-68795-X*) Random Hse Value.

Spizman, Robyn. All Aboard with Bulletin Boards. Pesiri, Evelyn, illus. 96p. (gr. k-8). 1983. wkbk. 9.95 (*0-86653-105-X*, GA 467) Good Apple.

—Good Apple & Bulletin Board Bonanzas. 144p. (gr. 3-7). 1981. 12.95 (*0-86653-049-5*, GA 281) Good Apple.

Thomas, Sue & Dinges, Susan. Curtain I: A Guide to Creative Drama for Children 5-8 Years Old. (gr. k-3). 1985. 15.00 (*0-89824-148-0*) Trillium Pr.

Tuchman, Gail. Christmas KidDoodles, Bk. 3. Nethery, Susan, illus. 64p. (Orig.). (ps-2). 1991. pap. 0.99 activity pad (*1-56293-155-5*) McClanahan Bk.

Whaley, Charles E. & Whaley, Helen F. Future Images: Future Studies for Grades 4-12. (gr. 4-12). 1985. 12.99 (*0-89824-149-9*) Trillium Pr.

Wise, Beth A. Christmas KidDoodles, Bk. 2. Hoffman, Judy, illus. 64p. (Orig.). (ps-2). 1991. pap. 0.99 activity pad (*1-56293-154-7*) McClanahan Bk.

—Christmas KidDoodles, Bk. 4. Boyd, Patti, illus. 64p. (Orig.). (ps-2). 1991. pap. 0.99 activity pad (*1-56293-156-3*) McClanahan Bk.

—KidDoodles, Bk. 4. Nethery, Susan, illus. 64p. (Orig.). (ps-2). 1991. pap. 0.99 activity pad (*1-878624-53-9*) McClanahan Bk.

CREATIVENESS

see Creation (Literary, Artistic, etc.)

CREDIBILITY

see Truthfulness and Falsehood

CREDIT

see also Banks and Banking

Ortiz, Lucio. Sus Derechos de Credito en Estados Unidos. Garcia, Santos, intro. by. (SPA., Orig.). (gr. 9-12). 1989. pap. 6.00 (*0-685-28998-2*) Publicaciones Nuevos.

Yardley, Thompson. Buy Now, Pay Later! Smart Shopping Counts. LC 91-22497. (Illus.). 40p. (gr. 2-6). 1992. PLB 12.90 (*1-56294-149-6*) Millbrook Pr.

CRESTS

see Heraldry

CRETE–FICTION

Cheney, David M. Son of Minos. LC 64-25838. (gr. 7). 18.00 (*0-8196-0142-X*) Biblo.

CREWE, SARA

Burnett, Frances H. A Little Princess. 240p. (gr. 5-9). 1975. pap. 3.50 (*0-440-44767-4*, YB) Dell.

CRICKET–FICTION

Ferguson, Alane. Cricket & the Crackerbox Kid. LC 89-39291. 192p. (gr. 3-7). 1990. SBE 14.95 (*0-02-734525-4*, Bradbury Pr) Macmillan Child Grp.

Selden, George. Chester Cricket's New Home. Williams, Garth, illus. 144p. (gr. 3 up). 1984. pap. 3.99 (*0-440-41246-3*, YB) Dell.

CRICKETS

Cole, Joanna. An Insect's Body. Wexler, Jerome & Mendez, Raymond A., photos by. LC 83-22027. (Illus.). 48p. (ps-3). 1984. 13.95 (*0-688-02771-7*); PLB 13.88 (*0-688-02772-5*, Morrow Jr Bks) Morrow Jr Bks.

Hasegawa, Yo. The Cricket. Pohl, Kathy, ed. LC 85-28201. (Illus.). 32p. (gr. 3-7). 1986. text ed. 10.95 (*0-8172-2532-3*) Raintree Steck-V.

Watts, Barrie. Grasshoppers & Crickets. LC 90-45996. (Illus.). 32p. (gr. k-4). 1991. PLB 11.40 (*0-531-14161-6*); pap. 4.95 (*0-531-15618-4*) Watts.

CRICKETS–FICTION

Carle, Eric. The Very Quiet Cricket: A Multi-Sensory Book. LC 89-78317. (Illus.). 32p. (ps-1). 1990. 18.95x (*0-399-21885-8*, Philomel Bks) Putnam Pub Group.

Caudill, Rebecca. A Pocketful of Cricket. Ness, Evaline, illus. LC 64-12617. 48p. (gr. k-2). 1989. 7.95 (*0-03-089752-1*, Bks Young Read); pap. 5.95 (*0-8050-1275-3*) H Holt & Co.

—A Pocketful of Cricket. Ness, Evaline, illus. LC 64-12617. 48p. (ps-2). 1964. Repr. of 1964 ed. 15.95 (*0-8050-1200-1*, Bks Young Read) H Holt & Co.

Hoppy the Cricket Jumps High & Low. LC 93-85486. 20p. (ps-1). 1994. 3.99 (*0-89577-567-0*) RD Assn.

Keats, Ezra J. Maggie & the Pirate. Keats, Ezra J., illus. LC 85-29347. 32p. (gr. k-3). 1987. Repr. of 1979 ed. RSBE 13.95 (*0-02-749710-0*, Four Winds) Macmillan Child Grp.

Maxner, Joyce. Nicholas Cricket. Joyce, William, illus. LC 88-33076. 32p. (gr. k-3). 1989. 14.00 (*0-06-024216-7*); PLB 13.89 (*0-06-024222-1*) HarpC Child Bks.

—Nicholas Cricket. Joyce, William, illus. LC 88-33076. 28p. (gr. k-3). 1991. pap. 4.95 (*0-06-443275-0*, Trophy) HarpC Child Bks.

Oetting, R. Orderly Cricket. Marilue, illus. LC 68-16395. 32p. (gr. 2-3). 1967. PLB 9.95 (*0-87783-028-2*) Oddo.

Porte, Barbara A. Leave That Cricket Be, Alan Lee. Ruff, Donna, illus. LC 92-29401. 32p. (ps up). 1993. 14.00 (*0-688-11793-7*); PLB 13.93 (*0-688-11794-5*) Greenwillow.

Selden, George. Chester Cricket's New Home. Williams, Garth, illus. LC 82-24206. 144p. (gr. 4 up). 1983. 15.00 (*0-374-31240-0*) FS&G.

—Chester Cricket's Pigeon Ride. Williams, Garth, illus. 80p. (gr. 2-6). 1983. pap. 3.50 (*0-440-41389-3*, YB) Dell.

—Cricket in Times Square. Williams, Garth, illus. (gr. 2-7). 1970. pap. 3.99 (*0-440-41563-2*, YB) Dell.

—Cricket in Times Square. (gr. 4-7). 1993. pap. 1.99 (*0-440-21622-2*) Dell.

—Un Grillo En Times Square: The Cricket in Times Square. Longshaw, Robin, tr. Williams, Garth, illus. (SPA.). 160p. (gr. 3-7). 1992. 15.00 (*0-374-32790-4*, Mirasol) FS&G.

—Tucker's Countryside. Williams, Garth, illus. LC 69-14975. 176p. (gr. 3 up). 1969. 16.00 (*0-374-37854-1*) FS&G.

Stilwell, Alison. Chin Ling, the Chinese Cricket. Stilwell, Alison, illus. LC 81-90045. 48p. (gr. 1-4). 1981. Repr. of 1947 ed. 12.95 (*0-9605862-0-2*) Stilwell Studio.

CRIME AND CRIMINALS

see also Capital Punishment; Criminal Law; Detectives; Justice, Administration of; Juvenile Delinquency; Pirates; Police; Prisons; Riots; Robbers and Outlaws; Smuggling; Trials

Abel, Ernest L. America's Twenty-Five Top Killers. LC 90-30768. 144p. (gr. 6 up). 1991. lib. bdg. 18.95 (*0-89490-279-2*) Enslow Pubs.

Barden. Prisons. 1991. 12.95s.p. (*0-86593-110-0*); 17.27 (*0-685-59207-3*) Rourke Corp.

Binford, Shari, et al, eds. Crime: Is It Out of Control? 52p. 1991. pap. text ed. 11.95 (*1-878623-21-4*) Info Plus TX.

Brown, Gene. Violence on America's Streets. 1992. pap. 4.95 (*0-395-62469-X*) HM.

Cohen, Sharron. Mysteries of Research. 128p. (Orig.). (gr. 4-12). 1992. pap. text ed. 15.95 (*0-913853-21-6*, 32532, Alleyside) Highsmith Pr.

Colby-Newton, Katie. Jack the Ripper: Opposing Viewpoints. LC 90-3835. (Illus.). 112p. (gr. 5-8). 1990. PLB 14.95 (*0-89908-081-2*) Greenhaven.

Crary, Elizabeth. Finders, Keepers. Strecker, Rebekah, illus. LC 87-60369. 64p. (Orig.). (gr. 2-6). 1987. PLB 16.95 (*0-943990-39-4*); pap. 5.95 (*0-943990-38-6*) Parenting Pr.

Fine, John C. Racket Squad. LC 92-5199. (Illus.). 144p. (gr. 5 up). 1993. SBE 14.95 (*0-689-31569-4*, Atheneum Child Bk) Macmillan Child Grp.

Freeman, Charles. Terrorists. (Illus.). 72p. (gr. 7-10). 1990. 19.95 (*0-7134-6076-8*, Pub. by Batsford UK) Trafalgar.

Gardner, Robert. Crime Lab 101: Experimenting with Crime Detection. 96p. (Orig.). (gr. 7 up). 1994. pap. 5.95 (*0-8027-7420-2*) Walker & Co.

Goldentyer, Debra. Gangs. LC 93-14227. (Illus.). 80p. (gr. 6-9). 1993. PLB 21.34 (*0-8114-3527-X*) Raintree Steck-V.

Greenberg, Keith. Terrorism: The New Menace. LC 93-23565. (Illus.). 64p. (gr. 5-8). 1994. PLB 15.90 (*1-56294-488-6*) Millbrook Pr.

Hamilton, Sue. Public Enemy No. One: Baby Face Nelson. Hamilton, John, ed. LC 89-84922. (Illus.). 32p. (gr. 4). 1989. PLB 11.96 (*0-939179-61-X*) Abdo & Dghtrs.

—Public Enemy No. One: Bonnie & Clyde. Hamilton, John, ed. LC 89-84921. (Illus.). 32p. (gr. 4). 1989. PLB 11.96 (*0-939179-62-8*) Abdo & Dghtrs.

—Public Enemy No. One: John H. Dillinger. Hamilton, John, ed. LC 89-84920. (Illus.). 32p. (gr. 4). 1989. PLB 11.96 (*0-939179-60-1*) Abdo & Dghtrs.

—Public Enemy No. One: Ma Barker. Hamilton, John, ed. LC 89-84925. (Illus.). 32p. (gr. 4). 1989. PLB 11.96 (*0-939179-65-2*) Abdo & Dghtrs.

—Public Enemy No. One: Machine Gun Kelly. Hamilton, John, ed. LC 89-84924. (Illus.). 32p. (gr. 4). 1989. PLB 11.96 (*0-939179-64-4*) Abdo & Dghtrs.

—Public Enemy No. One: Pretty Boy Floyd. Hamilton, John, ed. LC 89-84923. (Illus.). 32p. (gr. 4). 1989. PLB 11.96 (*0-939179-63-6*) Abdo & Dghtrs.

Larsen, Anita. True Crimes & How They Were Solved. (gr. 4-7). 1993. pap. 2.95 (*0-590-46856-1*) Scholastic Inc.

LeVert, Marianne. Crime in America. Leinwand, Gerald, ed. 160p. (gr. 9-12). 1991. 16.95x (*0-8160-2102-3*) Facts on File.

Moe, Barbara. Coping When You Are a Survivor of a Violent Crime. LC 94-14117. 1994. 14.95 (*0-8239-1882-3*) Rosen Group.

Morgan, Bill. Incredible Captures. (gr. 4-7). 1993. pap. 2.95 (*0-590-47142-2*) Scholastic Inc.

Nelson, Joan E. Kids Who Kill Kids. LC 93-85136. 284p. (Orig.). (gr. 8-12). 1994. pap. 12.95 (*0-9637293-1-4*) Storm Pub.

Osman, Karen. Gangs. LC 92-28009. (Illus.). 112p. (gr. 5-8). 1992. PLB 14.95 (*1-56006-131-6*) Lucent Bks.

Redpath, Ann. What Happens If You Shoplift? (Illus.). 48p. (gr. 3-6). Date not set. PLB 12.95 (*1-56065-137-7*) Capstone Pr.

Robins, Dave. Just Punishment. LC 90-3220. (Illus.). 64p. (gr. 5-8). 1990. PLB 12.40 (*0-531-17252-X*, Gloucester Pr) Watts.

Rohr, Janelle, ed. Violence in America: Opposing Viewpoints. LC 89-29401. (Illus.). 288p. (gr. 10 up). 1990. lib. bdg. 17.95 (*0-89908-449-4*); pap. text ed. 9.95 (*0-89908-424-9*) Greenhaven.

Ryan, Perry T. The Criminal Justice System of Kentucky. (Illus.). 50p. (gr. 9). 1990. pap. 4.95 (*0-9625504-1-8*) P T Ryan.

Schenkerman, Rona D. Growing up with Sexual Abuse. 16p. (gr. 3-8). 1993. 1.95 (*1-56688-117-X*) Bur For At-Risk.

Sobol, David J. Encyclopedia Brown's Book of Strange but True Facts. (gr. 4-7). 1991. 12.95 (*0-590-44147-7*) Scholastic Inc.

Sobol, Donald J. & Sobol, Rose. Encyclopedia Brown's Book of Strange But True Crimes. 128p. 1992. pap. 2.95 (*0-590-44148-5*, Apple Paperbacks) Scholastic Inc.

Stark, Evan. Everything You Need to Know about Street Gangs. (gr. 7-12). 1992. PLB 14.95 (*0-8239-1319-8*) Rosen Group.

Steele, Philip. Kidnapping. LC 91-42691. (Illus.). 48p. (gr. 6 up). 1992. text ed. 12.95 RSBE (*0-02-735403-2*, New Discovery) Macmillan Child Grp.

Terrell, Ruth H. A Kid's Guide to How to Stop the Violence. Genzo, John P., illus. 144p. (Orig.). 1992. pap. 3.99 (*0-380-76652-3*, Camelot) Avon.

Tipp, Stacey. Causes of Crime: Distinguishing Between Fact & Opinion. LC 91-22123. (Illus.). 32p. (gr. 4-7). 1991. PLB 10.95 (*0-89908-615-2*) Greenhaven.

Weiss, Karl, ed. The Prison Experience: An Anthology. LC 75-32920. 352p. (gr. 6 up). 1976. pap. 9.95 (*0-440-06017-6*) Delacorte.

Whiting, Roger. Crime & Punishment: A Study Across Time. LC 87-50949. 220p. (Orig.). (gr. 9-12). 1987. pap. text ed. 16.95 (*0-685-19579-1*, Pub. by S. Thornes) Dufour.

Wilkes, A. Fakes & Forgeries. (Illus.). 64p. (gr. 3-7). 1979. (Usborne); pap. 4.50 (*0-86020-231-3*) EDC.

Winters, Paul A., ed. Crime & Criminals: Opposing Viewpoints. LC 94-4976. (Illus.). 264p. (gr. 10 up). 1995. PLB 17.95 (*1-56510-176-6*); pap. text ed. 9.95 (*1-56510-177-4*) Greenhaven.

CRIME AND CRIMINALS–FICTION

Addy, Sharon. We Didn't Mean to. Blair, Jay, illus. McDermot, Gerald, intro. by. LC 80-24976. (Illus.). 32p. (gr. k-6). 1981. PLB 16.67 (*0-8172-1370-8*) Raintree Steck-V.

Ashley, Bernard. A Kind of Wild Justice. Keeping, Charles, illus. LC 78-10899. (gr. 7 up). 1979. 21.95 (*0-87599-229-3*) S G Phillips.

Benton, John. Lefty. 192p. (Orig.). (gr. 7-12). 1981. pap. 3.50 (*0-8007-8401-4*) J Benton Bks.

Bradford, Ann & Gezi, Kal. The Mystery at the Tree House. McLean, Mina G., illus. LC 80-15654. 32p. (gr. k-4). 1980. PLB 12.95 (*0-89565-148-3*) Childs World.

Carlson, Nancy. Arnie & the Stolen Markers. (Illus.). 32p. (ps-3). 1987. pap. 11.95 (*0-670-81548-9*) Viking Child Bks.

Christelow, Eileen. The Robbery at the Diamond Dog Diner. LC 86-2682. (Illus.). 32p. (ps-3). 1988. 13.95 (*0-89919-425-7*, Clarion Bks); pap. 4.95 (*0-89919-722-1*, Clarion Bks) HM.

Cohn, Janice I. Why Did It Happen? Helping Children Cope in a Violent World. Owens, Gail, illus. LC 93-1573. 32p. (ps up). 1994. 15.00g (*0-688-12312-0*); PLB 14.93 (*0-688-12313-9*) Morrow Jr Bks.

Collier, James L. My Crooked Family. LC 90-27747. 288p. (gr. 5-9). 1991. pap. 15.00 jacketed, 3-pc. bdg. (*0-671-74224-8*, S&S BFYR) S&S Trade.

—My Crooked Family. LC 90-27747. 288p. (gr. 5-9). 1993. pap. 3.95 (*0-671-86693-1*, Half Moon Bks) S&S Trade.

Connell, David D. & Thurman, Jim. Despair in Monterey Bay: A Mathnet Casebook. LC 93-183351. (gr. 4-7). 1993. text ed. write for info. (*0-7167-6505-5*, Sci Am Yng Rdrs); pap. text ed. write for info. (*0-7167-6502-0*) W H Freeman.

Corcoran, Barbara. The Hideaway. 128p. (Orig.). 1989. pap. 2.75 (*0-380-70635-0*, Flare) Avon.

DeClements, Barthe. Five-Finger Discount. (gr. 4-7). 1989. 13.95 (*0-440-50166-0*) Delacorte.

—Five-Finger Discount, Bk. 1. 1990. pap. 3.25 (*0-440-40321-9*, YB) Dell.

Ehrlich, Amy. Lucy's Winter Tale. Howell, Troy, illus. LC 88-25740. 32p. (gr. k). 1992. 14.00 (*0-8037-0659-6*); PLB 13.89 (*0-8037-0661-8*) Dial Bks Young.

Ferguson, Alane. Show Me the Evidence. LC 88-39203. 160p. (gr. 7 up). 1989. SBE 14.95 (*0-02-734521-1*, Bradbury Pr) Macmillan Child Grp.

Frye, Tom. The Kid, the Cop, & the Con. 256p. (Orig.). (gr. 6 up). 1993. pap. 9.95 (*1-881663-18-3*) Advent Mean Pr.

—The Kid, the Cop & the Con. 239p. (gr. 4 up). 1994. 9.95 (*0-685-71641-4*, 788) W Gladden Found.

—Scratchin' on the Eight Ball. 240p. (gr. 6 up). 1993. pap. 9.95 (*1-881663-16-7*) Advent Mean Pr.

Giff, Patricia R. Shark in School. LC 93-39016. (gr. 1 up). 1994. 14.95 (*0-385-32029-9*) Delacorte.

Hall, Roger. Julie Rescues Big Mack. Antonie, Joy, illus. LC 93-26217. 1994. 4.25 (*0-383-03755-7*) SRA Schl Grp.

Hamilton, Dorothy. Amanda Fair. Converse, James, illus. LC 80-25073. 136p. (gr. 5-10). 1981. pap. 3.95 (*0-8361-1943-6*) Herald Pr.

—Eric's Discovery. Wind, Betty, illus. LC 79-18537. 120p. (gr. 4-9). 1979. pap. 3.95 (*0-8361-1903-7*) Herald Pr.

Hoban, Lillian. The Case of the Two Masked Robbers. LC 85-45819. (Illus.). 64p. (gr. k-3). 1986. PLB 13.89 (*0-06-022299-9*) HarpC Child Bks.

Kehret, Peg. Danger at the Fair. LC 94-16873. 1995. write for info. (*0-525-65182-9*, Cobblehill Bks) Dutton Child Bks.

Kelleher, D. V. Defenders of the Universe. Brown, Jane C., illus. LC 92-1617. 128p. (gr. 3-5). 1993. 13.45 (*0-395-60515-6*) HM.

Lexau, Joan M. Trouble Will Find You. Chesworth, Michael, illus. LC 93-6813. (ps-6). 1994. 13.95 (*0-395-64380-5*) HM.

Lloyd, Errol. Sasha & the Bicycle Thieves. (Illus.). 42p. (gr. 2-4). 1989. 3.95 (*0-8120-6141-1*) Barron.

McNamara, Brooks. The Merry Muldoons & the Brighteyes Affair. LC 91-46923. 160p. (gr. 5-12). 1992. 14.95 (*0-531-05454-3*); PLB 14.99 (*0-531-08604-6*) Orchard Bks Watts.

Massey Weddle, Linda. T. J. & the Big Trout River Vandals. LC 91-14678. 94p. (Orig.). (gr. 4-7). 1991. pap. 3.95 (*0-87227-148-X*, RBP5180) Reg Baptist.

Miller, Marvin. You Be the Jury: Courtroom Two. 1992. pap. 2.50 (*0-590-45727-6*) Scholastic Inc.

Nixon, Joan L. Shadowmaker. LC 93-32314. 1994. 14.95 (*0-385-32030-2*) Delacorte.

O. Henry. The Ransom of Red Chief. (Illus.). 40p. (gr. 4 up). 1980. PLB 13.95 (*0-87191-776-9*) Creative Ed.

Petersen, P. J. Would You Settle for Improbable? A Novel. LC 80-69465. 192p. (gr. 5-9). 1981. 8.95 (*0-440-09601-4*); PLB 8.44 (*0-440-09672-3*) Delacorte.

Poe, Edgar Allan. The Cask of Amontillado. Cutts, David E., adapted by. Toulmin-Rothe, Ann, illus. LC 81-15997. 32p. (gr. 5-10). 1982. PLB 10.79 (*0-89375-622-9*); pap. text ed. 2.95 (*0-89375-623-7*) Troll Assocs.

Polonsky, Daniel L. The Letter Bandits. (Illus.). 72p. (gr. 3 up). 1991. 12.95 (*0-931474-41-8*) TBW Bks.

Roberts, Willo D. The Pet-Sitting Peril. LC 82-13757. 192p. (gr. 4-6). 1983. SBE 14.95 (*0-689-30963-5*, Atheneum Child Bk) Macmillan Child Grp.

—What Could Go Wrong? LC 88-27484. 176p. (gr. 3-7). 1989. SBE 13.95 (*0-689-31438-8*, Atheneum Child Bk) Macmillan Child Grp.

Schlee, Ann. The Vandal. LC 81-2859. (Illus.). 192p. (gr. 7 up). 1981. 8.95 (*0-517-54424-5*) Crown Bks Yng Read.

Schwartzman, Lee T. Crippled Detectives or the War of the Red Romer. Mandel, Gerry, ed. (Illus.). (gr. 3-8). 1978. 3.00 (*0-89409-009-7*) Childrens Art.

Sebestyen, Ouida. On Fire. 208p. (gr. 6 up). 1985. 12.45 (*0-87113-010-6*, Joy St Bks) Little.

Smith, Dorothy L. Don't Grow Old Peeking Through a Prison Hole. 1993. 8.95 (*0-8062-4425-9*) Carlton.

Sobel, Barbara. To Catch a Thief! LC 87-81234. (gr. 3-6). 1987. 7.59 (*0-87386-047-0*); bk. & cassette 16.99 (*0-317-55326-7*); pap. 1.95 (*0-87386-046-2*) Jan Prods.

Steiner, Barbara. The Photographer Two: The Dark Room. 176p. (Orig.). 1993. pap. 3.50 (*0-380-77064-4*, Flare) Avon.

Stone, G. H. Rough Stuff. LC 88-11904. 144p. (Orig.). (gr. 5 up). 1989. pap. 2.95 (*0-394-80178-4*) Knopf Bks Yng Read.

Terris, Susan. Baby-Snatcher. 192p. (gr. 5 up). 1985. 14.00 (*0-374-30473-4*) FS&G.

Weiss, Ellen & Friedman, Mel. The Tiny Parents. LC 88-23103. 96p. (Orig.). (gr. 3-7). 1989. pap. 2.95 (*0-394-82418-0*) Knopf Bks Yng Read.

Wilhelm, Doug. Scene of the Crime. (gr. 4-7). 1993. pap. 3.25 (*0-553-56004-2*) Bantam.

CRIME AND CRIMINALS–IDENTIFICATION

Tesar, Jenny. Scientific Crime Investigation. LC 91-16368. (Illus.). 96p. (gr. 9-12). 1991. PLB 12.90 (*0-531-12500-9*) Watts.

CRIMES, POLITICAL

see Political Crimes and Offenses

CRIMINAL INVESTIGATION

see also Crime and Criminals–Identification; Detectives; Police

Cowger, James F. Friction Ridge Skin: Comparison & Identification of Fingerprints. LC 93-24980. (gr. 7 up). 1992. 72.00 (*0-8493-9502-X*) CRC PR.

Gardner, Robert. Crime Lab. 101: Experimenting with Crime Detection. 123p. (gr. 6-9). 1992. 13.95 (*0-8027-8158-6*); lib. bdg. 14.85 (*0-8027-8159-4*) Walker & Co.

Graham, Ian. Crime-Fighting. LC 94-13839. 1995. write for info. (*0-8114-3840-6*) Raintree Steck-V.

CRIMINAL LAW

see also Capital Punishment; Jury; Trials

Biskup, Michael D., ed. Criminal Justice: Opposing Viewpoints. (Illus.). 264p. (gr. 10 up). 1993. PLB 17.95 (*0-89908-624-1*); pap. text ed. 9.95 (*0-89908-623-3*) Greenhaven.

CRIMINALS

see Crime and Criminals

CRIMINOLOGY

see Crime and Criminals

CRIPPLES

see Physically Handicapped

CRITICISM

Insel, Eunice & Edson, Ann. Developing Critical Thinking, Bk. 1. (gr. 3-4). 1983. wkbk. 4.25 (*1-55737-651-4*) Ed Activities.

CROCHETING

see also Beadwork

O'Reilly, Susie. Knitting & Crochet. Mukhida, Zul, photos by. (Illus.). 32p. (gr. 4-6). 1994. 14.95 (*1-56847-221-8*) Thomson Lrning.

CROCKERY

see Pottery

CROCKETT, DAVID, 1785-1836

Crockett, Davy. Davy Crockett's Own Story: A Narrative of the Life of David Crockett of the State of Tennessee. LC 93-34222. (Illus.). 128p. 1993. pap. 12.95 (*1-55709-218-4*) Applewood.

Davy Crockett. (Illus.). (gr. 2-5). 1989. 29.28 (*0-8172-2953-1*) Raintree Steck-V.

Farr, Naunerle C. Davy Crockett-Daniel Boone. Carrillo, Fred & Redondo, Nestor, illus. (gr. 4-12). 1979. pap. text ed. 2.95 (*0-88301-351-7*); wkbk. 1.25 (*0-88301-375-4*) Pendulum Pr.

Moseley, Elizabeth R. Davy Crockett: Hero of the Wild Frontier. Beecham, Thomas, illus. 80p. (gr. 2-6). 1991. Repr. of 1967 ed. lib. bdg. 12.95 (*0-7910-1409-6*) Chelsea Hse.

Parachute Press Staff. The Story of Davey Crockett. (Illus.). 1993. pap. 3.50 (*0-440-40881-4*) Dell.

Parks, Aileen W. Davy Crockett: Young Rifleman. Pearson, Justin, illus. LC 86-10781. 192p. (gr. 2-6). 1986. pap. 3.95 (*0-02-041840-X*, Aladdin) Macmillan Child Grp.

Santrey, Laurence. Davy Crockett: Young Pioneer. Livingston, Francis, illus. LC 82-16040. 48p. (gr. 4-6). 1983. PLB 10.79 (*0-89375-847-7*); pap. text ed. 3.50 (*0-89375-848-5*) Troll Assocs.

Townsend, Tom. Davy Crockett: An American Hero. Eakin, Edwin M., ed. LC 87-16545. (Illus.). 72p. (gr. 4-7). 1987. 10.95 (*0-89015-643-3*); pap. 5.95 (*0-89015-627-1*) Sunbelt Media.

Trotman, Felicity & Greenway, Shirley, eds. Davy Crockett. LC 85-16694. (Illus.). 32p. (gr. 2-5). 1985. PLB 19.97 (*0-8172-2504-8*) Raintree Steck-V.

Wade, Mary D. David Crockett: Sure He Was Right. Finney, Pat, illus. 64p. (gr. 2-3). 1992. 11.95 (*0-89015-854-1*) Sunbelt Media.

Zadra, Dan. Frontiersmen in America: Davy Crocket. rev. ed. (gr. 2-4). 1988. 14.95 (*0-88682-195-9*) Creative Ed.

CROCKETT, DAVID, 1786-1836–FICTION

Cohen, Caron L., retold by. Sally Ann Thunder Ann Whirlwind Crockett. Dewey, Ariane, illus. LC 92-24585. 40p. 1993. pap. 4.95 (*0-688-12331-7*, Mulberry) Morrow.

Cohen, Caron Lee. Sally Ann Thunder Ann Whirlwind Crockett. Dewey, Ariane, illus. LC 84-7978. 40p. (gr. 1-3). 1985. 11.75 (*0-688-04006-3*); PLB 11.88 (*0-688-04007-1*) Greenwillow.

Dewey, Ariane. The Narrow Escapes of Davy Crockett. Dewey, Ariane, illus. LC 88-34902. (gr. 1 up). 1990. 13.95 (*0-688-08914-3*); PLB 13.88 (*0-688-08915-1*) Greenwillow.

—The Narrow Escapes of Davy Crockett. LC 92-24586. (Illus.). 48p. (gr. 1 up). 1993. pap. 4.95 (*0-688-12269-8*, Mulberry) Morrow.

Fontes, Ron & Korman, Justine. Davy Crockett & the Highwaymen. LC 92-52975. (Illus.). 80p. (gr. 1-4). 1992. PLB 12.89 (*1-56282-261-6*); pap. 3.50 (*1-56282-260-8*) Disney Pr.

—Davy Crockett Meets Death Hug. Shaw, Charlie, illus. LC 93-71032. 80p. (gr. 1-4). 1993. PLB 12.89 (*1-56282-496-1*); pap. 3.50 (*1-56282-495-3*) Disney Pr.

CROCODILES

For the American crocodiles use Alligators.

Barrett, Norman S. Cocodrilos y Caimanes. LC 90-71415. (SPA., Illus.). 32p. (gr. k-4). 1991. PLB 11.90 (*0-531-07919-8*) Watts.

—Crocodiles & Alligators. LC 88-51517. (Illus.). 32p. (gr. k-6). 1990. 11.90 (*0-531-10705-1*) Watts.

Bright, Michael. Alligators & Crocodiles. LC 90-3225. (Illus.). 32p. (gr. 5-8). 1990. PLB 12.40 (*0-531-17245-7*, Gloucester Pr) Watts.

Crocodile. 1989. 3.50 (*1-87865-726-7*) Blue Q.

Dow, Lesley. Alligators & Crocodiles. 72p. 1990. 17.95 (*0-8160-2273-9*) Facts on File.

Farre, Marie. Crocodiles & Alligators. Matthews, Sarah, tr. from FRE. Wallis, Diz, illus. LC 87-31804. 38p. (gr. k-5). 1988. 5.95 (*0-944589-01-4*, 014) Young Discovery Lib.

George, Michael. Alligators & Crocodiles. 32p. 1991. 15.95 (*0-89565-720-1*) Childs World.

Hawcock, David. Crocodile. (ps). 1994. 3.95 (*0-307-17301-1*, Artsts Writrs) Western Pub.

Hogan, Paula Z. The Crocodile. Nachreiner, Tom, illus. LC 79-13699. 32p. (gr. 1-4). 1979. PLB 19.97 (*0-8172-1503-4*) Raintree Steck-V.

—The Crocodile. LC 79-13699. (Illus.). 32p. (gr. 1-4). 1981. PLB 29.28 incl. cassette (*0-8172-1842-4*) Raintree Steck-V.

Knight, David. I Can Read About Alligators & Crocodiles. LC 78-73733. (Illus.). (gr. 2-4). 1979. pap. 2.50 (*0-89375-200-2*) Troll Assocs.

Ling, Mary. Amazing Crocodiles & Other Reptiles. Young, Jerry, photos by. LC 90-19239. (Illus.). 32p. (Orig.). (gr. 1-5). 1991. PLB 9.99 (*0-679-90689-4*); pap. 7.99 (*0-679-80689-X*) Knopf Bks Yng Read.

Petty, Kate. Crocodiles & Alligators. Johnson, Karen, illus. 1990. pap. 3.95 (*0-531-15153-0*) Watts.

Serventy, Vincent. Crocodile & Alligator. LC 84-15890. (Illus.). 24p. (gr. k-5). 1985. PLB 9.95 (*0-8172-2404-1*); pap. 3.95 (*0-8114-6873-9*) Raintree Steck-V.

—Crocodile & Alligator. Serventy, Vincent, et al, illus. 24p. (gr. k-3). 1986. pap. 2.50 (*0-590-44722-X*) Scholastic Inc.

Stone, Lynn. Crocodiles. (Illus.). 24p. (gr. k-5). 1990. lib. bdg. 11.94 (*0-86593-060-0*); lib. bdg. 8.95s.p. (*0-685-36369-4*) Rourke Corp.

Stone, Lynn M. Alligators & Crocodiles. LC 89-9985. 48p. (gr. k-4). 1989. PLB 12.85 (*0-516-01170-7*); pap. 4.95 (*0-516-41170-5*) Childrens.

Stoops, Erik D. & Stone, Debbie L. Alligators & Crocodiles. LC 94-15691. (Illus.). 80p. 1994. 14.95 (*0-8069-0422-4*) Sterling.

Storms, John. Cory the Crocodile. Storms, Robert, illus. 24p. (Orig.). (gr. k-4). 1993. pap. 4.95 (*0-89346-530-5*) Heian Intl.

Tibbitts, Alison & Roocroft, Alan. Crocodile. (Illus.). 24p. (ps-2). 1992. PLB 12.95 (*1-56065-102-4*) Capstone Pr.

Wildlife Education, Ltd. Staff. Alligators & Crocodiles. Hoopes, Barbara, illus. 20p. (Orig.). (gr. 5 up). 1984. pap. 2.75 (*0-937934-25-9*) Wildlife Educ.

CROCODILES–FICTION

Aliki. Keep Your Mouth Closed, Dear. Aliki, illus. LC 66-19310. (gr. k-3). 1966. PLB 13.89 (*0-8037-4418-8*) Dial Bks Young.

Aruego, Jose & Dewey, Ariane. Rockabye Crocodile. LC 87-463. (Illus.). 32p. (ps-3). 1988. 14.00 (*0-688-06738-7*); lib. bdg. 13.93 (*0-688-06739-5*) Greenwillow.

—Rockabye Crocodile. LC 92-24587. 32p. (ps up). 1993. pap. 4.95 (*0-688-12333-3*, Mulberry) Morrow.

Carrick, Carol. The Crocodiles Still Wait. Carrick, Donald, illus. LC 79-23519. 32p. (gr. 1-4). 1980. 14.45 (*0-395-29102-X*, Clarion Bks) HM.

Cutchins, Judy & Johnston, Ginny. The Crocodile & the Crane: Surviving in a Crowded World. LC 86-5339. (Illus.). 64p. (gr. 2-5). 1986. 12.95 (*0-688-06304-7*); lib. bdg. 12.88 (*0-688-06305-5*, Morrow Jr Bks) Morrow Jr Bks.

Dahl, Roald. The Enormous Crocodile. 48p. (Orig.). (gr. 1-3). 1984. pap. 2.95 (*0-553-15243-2*, Skylark) Bantam.

—The Enormous Crocodile. reissue ed. Blake, Quentin, illus. LC 77-5081. 32p. (ps-3). 1978. 14.00 (*0-394-83594-8*); lib. bdg. 14.99 (*0-394-93594-2*) Knopf Bks Yng Read.

—The Enormous Crocodile. Blake, Quentin, illus. 32p. (gr. 1-5). 1993. pap. 3.99 (*0-14-036556-7*, Puffin) Puffin Bks.

De Paola, Tomie. Bill & Pete. De Paola, Tomie, illus. LC 78-5330. (gr. k-2). 1978. 14.95 (*0-399-20646-9*, Putnam); (Putnam) Putnam Pub Group.

Dumbleton, Mike. Dial-a-Croc. James, Ann, illus. LC 90-25385. 32p. (ps-2). 1991. 14.95 (*0-531-05945-6*); RLB 14.99 (*0-531-08545-7*) Orchard Bks Watts.

Grindley, Sally. The Big Crocodile Book. (Illus.). 80p. (gr. 2-5). 1993. 19.95 (*0-09-176382-7*, Pub. by Hutchinson UK) Trafalgar.

Hirokazu Miyazaki. Croc & the Baby Tree. Clements, Andrew, adapted by. Hirokazu Miyazaki, illus. LC 91-41719. 28p. (gr. k up). 1993. Repr. of 1990 ed. 14.95 (*0-88708-224-6*) Picture Bk Studio.

Hoban, Russell. Arthur's New Power. Barton, Byron, illus. LC 77-11550. (gr. 1-5). 1978. PLB 12.89 (*0-690-01371-X*, Crowell Jr Bks) HarpC Child Bks.

—Dinner at Alberta's. Marshall, James, illus. LC 73-94796. 40p. (gr. 1-3). 1975. PLB 13.89 (*0-690-23993-9*, Crowell Jr Bks) HarpC Child Bks.

Inkpen, Mick. Crocodile! (Illus.). (gr. 4-7). 1993. 4.99 (*1-878685-73-2*, Bedrock Press) Turner Pub GA.

Jorgensen, Gail. Crocodile Beat. Mullins, Patricia, illus. LC 94-7135. (ps-1). 1994. pap. 4.95 (*0-689-71881-0*, Aladdin) Macmillan.

Knuppel, Helga. Christabel Crocodile's Birthday Egg. Knuppel, Helga, illus. LC 92-24360. 32p. (ps-3). 1993. 13.95 (*1-56656-113-2*, Crocodile Bks) Interlink Pub.

Lehan, Daniel. Crocodile Snaps - Kangaroo Jumps. LC 92-50842. (Illus.). 32p. (ps-k). 1993. 13.95 (*0-531-05484-5*) Orchard Bks Watts.

McOmber, Rachel B., ed. McOmber Phonics Storybooks: The Invisible Crocodiles. rev. ed. (Illus.). write for info. (*0-944991-80-7*) Swift Lrn Res.

—McOmber Phonics Storybooks: Yellow Crocodile. rev. ed. (Illus.). write for info. (*0-944991-76-9*) Swift Lrn Res.

Moncure, Jane B. Smile, Says Little Crocodile. Hohag, Linda, illus. LC 87-13833. 32p. (ps-2). 1987. PLB 14.95 (*0-89565-401-6*) pap. 6.96 (*0-89565-449-0*) Childs World.

Rocard, Ann. Cool Calvin. Rousset, Francoise, illus. (ps-4). 1991. smythe sewn reinforced bdg. 9.95 (*1-56182-030-X*) Atomium Bks.

Roos, Stephen. Crocodile Christmas: The Pet Lovers Club. Rogers, Jacqueline, illus. LC 91-47079. 128p. (gr. 3-6). 1992. 14.00 (*0-385-30681-4*) Delacorte.

Rubel, Nicole. Conga Crocodile. LC 92-31856. 1993. 14.95 (*0-395-58773-5*) HM.

Schotter, Roni. When Crocodiles Clean Up. Wickstrom, Thor, illus. LC 92-10808. 32p. (gr. k-3). 1993. RSBE 14.95 (*0-02-781297-9*, Macmillan Child Bk) Macmillan Child Grp.

Taylor, Carol. Toothless Albert. Moroney, Tracey, illus. LC 93-28937. 1994. 4.25 (*0-383-03780-8*) SRA Schl Grp.

Velthuijs, Max. Crocodile's Masterpiece. (Illus.). 32p. (ps-1). 1992. bds. 14.00 (*0-374-31658-9*) FS&G.

—Elephant & Crocodile. LC 90-55039. 32p. (gr. 4-8). 1990. 14.00 (*0-374-37675-1*) FS&G.

Waber, Bernard. House on East Eighty-Eighth Street. (Illus.). 48p. (gr. k-3). 1973. 14.95 (*0-395-18157-7*) HM.
—The House on East Eighty-Eighth Street. Waber, Bernard, illus. LC 62-8144. 48p. (gr. k-4). 1975. pap. 4.80 (*0-395-19970-0*, Sandpiper) HM.
—Lovable Lyle. LC 69-14728. (Illus.). (gr. k-3). 1977. 14.95 (*0-395-19858-5*); pap. 5.95 (*0-395-25378-0*) HM.
—Lyle & the Birthday Party. (Illus.). (gr. k-3). 1966. 13.45 (*0-395-15080-9*) HM.
—Lyle at the Office. LC 93-49644. 1994. 14.95 (*0-395-70563-0*) HM.
—Lyle, Lyle, Crocodile. (Illus.). (gr. k-3). 1965. 13.45 (*0-395-16995-X*) HM.
—Lyle, Lyle Crocodile. LC 65-19305. (ps-3). 1987. pap. 4.80 (*0-395-13720-9*) HM.
Waddell, Martin. Harriet & the Crocodiles. Burgess, Mark, illus. (gr. 3-7). 1984. 11.95 (*0-316-91622-6*, Joy St Bks) Little.
Wagner, Gerda. Konstantine. Barankova, Vlasta, illus. 28p. (ps-1). 1991. smythe sewn reinforced bdg. 9.95 (*1-56182-023-7*) Atomium Bks.
West, Colin. Ten Little Crocodiles. LC 93-44027. 1995. write for info. (*1-56402-463-6*) Candlewick Pr.
Williams, Michael. Crocodile Burning. 208p. (gr. 7 up). 1994. pap. 3.99 (*0-14-036793-4*) Puffin Bks.

CROMWELL, OLIVER, 1599-1658

Sarage, Jessica. Cromwell. (Illus.). 64p. (gr. 7-10). 1989. 19.95 (*0-7134-6033-4*, Pub. by Batsford UK) Trafalgar.

CROPS

see Farm Produce

CROSS-COUNTRY RUNNING

see Track Athletics

CROSSWORD PUZZLES

Aero Products Research, Inc., Industries Division Staff. Official CB Crossword Puzzles for Big Dummy's. (Illus.). (gr. 8 up). 1977. pap. 1.98 (*0-912682-18-3*) Aero Products.
Anduze, A. L. Caribbean Crosswords. LC 93-70926. (Illus.). 64p. (gr. 5-12). Date not set. pap. 8.95 (*0-932831-10-9*) Eastern Caribbean Inst.
Bell, Irene W. Literature Cross-A-Word Book I: Crossword Learning Experiences with Animal Stories, Modern Fantasy, & Space & Time. Kirby, Keith, illus. 96p. 1982. pap. 14.75 (*0-89774-062-9*) Oryx Pr.
Chirinian, Helene. Crossword Mysteries: Daring Detective Challenge, Private Eye Challenge. Yamamoto, Neal, illus. 96p. 1994. pap. 3.95 (*1-56565-171-5*) Lowell Hse Juvenile.
Cobblestone Publishing Inc. Staff. U. S. History Crosswords: For Young People 8-14. (Illus.). 36p. (gr. 4-8). 1987. pap. text ed. 4.95 (*0-942389-01-8*) Cobblestone Pub.
Cron, Mary. More Phonics Fun. McMahan, Kelly, illus. 48p. (Orig.). (gr. 2 up). 1989. pap. 2.95 incl. chipboard (*0-8431-2358-3*) Price Stern.
Crossword Puzzle Challenges. (Illus.). 64p. (gr. 2-5). 1990. pap. 1.99 (*0-671-72335-9*, Little Simon) S&S Trade.
Crosswords for Kids. 1991. pap. 1.95 (*0-8167-0882-7*) Troll Assocs.
Davis, S. K. Bible Crossword Puzzle Book. (gr. k-3). 1969. pap. 4.99 (*0-8010-2812-4*) Baker Bk.
Everett, Louise. More Fun Crosswords. (ps). 1991. pap. 1.95 (*0-8167-0884-3*) Troll Assocs.
Glicksburg, Joy B. Crosswords for Language Arts. (gr. 1-5). 1985. pap. 9.95 (*0-8224-2353-7*) Fearon Teach Aids.
Hovanec. Double Clued Crossword Puzzles. 1992. pap. 1.95 (*0-590-44726-2*) Scholastic Inc.
Hovanec, Helene. Crazy Crosswords. 48p. (gr. 2 up). 1993. pap. 2.95 incl. chipboard (*0-8431-3492-5*) Price Stern.
Keesing UK Ltd. Staff, ed. Travel Crosswords for Kids. 96p. (Orig.). 1993. pap. 9.95x (*0-572-01786-3*, Pub. by W Foulsham UK) Trans-Atl Phila.
Maleska, Eugene T. Children's Word Games & Crossword Puzzles, Vol. 2. (gr. 2-4). 1988. pap. 7.50 (*0-8129-1692-1*) Random.
—Children's Word Games & Crossword Puzzles, Vol. 3. (gr. 2-4). 1992. pap. 7.00 (*0-8129-1980-7*, Times Bks) Random.
Moore, Rosalind, ed. The Dell Big Book of Crosswords & Pencil Puzzles, No. 7. (Orig.). 1989. pap. 9.99 (*0-440-50161-X*, Dell Trade Pbks) Dell.
Nowlin, Susan S. Holiday Crossword Puzzles. Spence, Paula, illus. 48p. (gr. 2-5). 1988. wkbk. 6.95 (*1-55734-366-7*) Tchr Create Mat.
Quinn, Kaye. Bizarre Bugs. 48p. (Orig.). 1990. pap. 2.95 (*0-8431-2811-9*) Price Stern.
—Freaky Fish. 48p. (Orig.). 1990. pap. 2.95 (*0-8431-2820-8*) Price Stern.
Spivak, Darlene. Crossword Puzzles, Wordsearches & Codes. Spivak, Darlene, illus. 48p. (gr. 2-5). 1986. wkbk. 6.95 (*1-55734-067-6*) Tchr Create Mat.
Spizzirri Publishing Co. Staff. Picture Crosswords: An Educational Activity-Coloring Book. Spizzirr, Linda, ed. (Illus.). 32p. (gr. 1-8). 1986. pap. 1.75 (*0-86545-081-1*) Spizzirri.
Sterling, Mary E. & Nowlin, Susan S. Crossword Puzzles. Spence, Paula & Wright, Terry, illus. 48p. (gr. 2-5). 1988. wkbk. 6.95 (*1-55734-365-9*) Tchr Create Mat.
—Patriotic Wordsearches, Codes & Crossword Puzzles. Spence, Paula, illus. 48p. (gr. 2-5). 1988. wkbk. 5.95 (*1-55734-367-5*) Tchr Create Mat.
Super Crossword Puzzles & Word Games Activity Book. (Illus.). 48p. (gr. k-3). 1988. pap. 2.95 (*0-8431-2270-6*) Price Stern.
Thornton, Christine. Crosswords for Spelling. (gr. 4-6). 1985. pap. 8.95 (*0-8224-2354-5*) Fearon Teach Aids.
Van Ronzelen, George & Oberste, Kenneth, illus. TiL: A Book of Puzzles. LC 88-70805. 264p. (Orig.). (gr. 6 up). 1988. pap. 13.00 (*0-934426-18-X*) NAPSAC Reprods.

CROWS–FICTION

Armstrong, Jennifer. King Crow. LC 93-39261. 1995. write for info. (*0-517-59634-2*); write for info. (*0-517-59635-0*) Crown Pub Group.
Bell, Joseph. Sandy of Laguna. Garrison, Ben, illus. 72p. (Orig.). (gr. k-8). 1992. pap. 9.95 (*1-880812-01-0*) S Ink WA.
Burgess, Thornton. Blacky the Crow. 93p. 1981. Repr. PLB 17.95 (*0-89966-351-6*) Buccaneer Bks.
—Blacky the Crow. 198p. 1981. Repr. PLB 17.95 (*0-89967-025-3*) Harmony Raine.
Burgess, Thornton W. Blacky the Crow. 18.95 (*0-8488-0394-9*) Amereon Ltd.
Damon, Valerie H. Tea with Adella Dine Crow. Damon, Dave, ed. LC 88-92261. (Illus.). 32p. (ps-5). 1990. 9.95 (*0-932356-15-X*) Star Pubns MO.
George, Jean C. The Cry of the Crow. LC 79-2016. 160p. (gr. 5 up). 1982. pap. 3.95 (*0-06-440131-6*, Trophy) HarpC Child Bks.
Greenstein, Elaine. Emily & the Crows. Greenstein, Elaine, illus. LC 91-39917. 28p. (gr. k up). 1992. pap. 14.95 (*0-88708-238-6*) Picture Bk Studio.
Guy, Ginger F. Black Crow, Black Crow. Parker, Nancy W., illus. LC 89-34619. 24p. (ps up). 1991. 13.95 (*0-688-08956-9*); PLB 13.88 (*0-688-08957-7*) Greenwillow.
Houts, Marshall. Cousin Charlie, the Crow. Ryan, Donna, illus. 84p. (Orig.). (gr. 2-8). 1992. pap. 10.95 (*1-880812-00-2*) S Ink WA.
Lionni, Leo. Six Crows. LC 87-3141. (Illus.). 32p. (ps-2). 1988. PLB 13.99 (*0-394-99572-4*) Knopf Bks Yng Read.
Marion, Jeff D. Hello, Crow. Bowman, Leslie W., illus. LC 91-18561. 32p. (ps-2). 1992. 13.95 (*0-531-05975-8*); PLB 13.99 (*0-531-08575-9*) Orchard Bks Watts.
Mason, Margo C. Go Away, Crows. 1989. pap. 8.95 (*0-553-05817-7*, Little Rooster) Bantam.
Sampson, Mary Y. & Bertschmann, Harry. Crow. Bertschmann, Mary, ed. Bertschmann, Harry, illus. 48p. 1989. pap. 8.00x (*0-935505-05-9*) Bank St Pr.
Shankar, Alaka. Sonali's Friend. Joshi, Jagadish, illus. 16p. (Orig.). (gr. k-3). 1980. pap. 2.50 (*0-89744-218-0*, Pub. by Childrens Bk Trust IA) Auromere.

CROWS–POETRY

Hellsing, Lennart. Cantankerous Crow. Stroyer, Paul, illus. (gr. k-3). 1962. 9.95 (*0-8392-3002-8*) Astor-Honor.

CRUELTY TO ANIMALS

see Animals–Treatment

CRUSADES

see also Chivalry

Biel, Timothy L. The Crusades. (Illus.). 128p. (gr. 5-9). 1995. 14.95 (*1-56006-245-2*) Lucent Bks.
Jessop, Joanne. Crusaders. (ps-3). 1990. PLB 10.90 (*0-531-18324-6*, Pub. by Bookwright Pr) Watts.
Kernaghan, Pamela. The Crusades: Cultures in Conflict. LC 93-27297. 1993. pap. 8.95 (*0-521-42846-7*) Cambridge U Pr.
Steffens, Bradley. The Children's Crusade. LC 91-29498. (Illus.). 96p. (gr. 5-8). 1991. PLB 11.95 (*1-56006-019-0*) Lucent Bks.
Williams, Ann. The Crusaders. 2nd ed. Reeves, Marjorie, ed. (Illus.). 95p. (gr. 7-12). 1975. pap. text ed. 8.60 (*0-582-31096-2*, 78069) Longman.

CRYOGENICS

see Low Temperatures

CRYPTOGRAPHY

see also Ciphers

Aaseng, Nathan. Navajo Code Talkers. LC 92-11408. 114p. 1992. 14.95 (*0-8027-8182-9*); PLB 15.85 (*0-8027-8183-7*) Walker & Co.
Barker, Wayne G. Cryptograms, One Hundred Ten Cryptograms to Be Solved. 119p. (gr. 9 up). 1980. lib. bdg. 14.45 (*0-89412-090-5*); pap. 4.95 (*0-89412-043-3*) Aegean Park Pr.
Hovanec, Helene. Doubletalk: Codes, Signs & Symbols. Wimmer, Chuck, illus. (gr. 7-10). 1993. pap. 1.25 (*0-553-37218-1*) Bantam.
Wrixon, Fred B. Codes & Ciphers: An A to Z of Covert Communication, from the Clay Tablet to the Microdot. (Illus.). 288p. 1992. pap. 18.00 (*0-13-277047-4*) P-H Gen Ref & Trav.

CRYSTAL GAZING

see Divination

CRYSTALLINE ROCKS

see Rocks

CRYSTALLIZATION

see Crystallography

CRYSTALLOGRAPHY

see also Mineralogy

Bell, Robert A. Crystals. Lopez, Paul, illus. 24p. (gr. k-5). 1992. pap. write for info. blister pk., incl. 3 crystal specimens & magnifying glass (*0-307-12856-3*, 12856, Golden Pr) Western Pub.
Greene, Leia A. Crystals R for Kids. Greene, Leia A., illus. 40p. (gr. k-12). 1991. wkbk. 4.95 (*1-880737-04-3*) Crystal Jrns.
Singer, Marcia. Crystal Kids: PLAYBook. Rendal, Camille, illus. LC 89-90988. 64p. (Orig.). 1989. pap. 9.95 (*0-9622543-0-4*) PLAY House.
Stang, Jean. Crystals & Crystal Gardens You Can Grow. (Illus.). (ps-3). 1990. PLB 12.90 (*0-531-10889-9*) Watts.

CRYSTALS

see Crystallography

CUB SCOUTS

see Boy Scouts

CUBA

Clinton, Susan M. The Cuban Missile Crisis. LC 93-12689. (Illus.). 32p. (gr. 3-6). 1993. PLB 12.30 (*0-516-06667-6*); pap. 3.95 (*0-516-46667-4*) Childrens.
Crouch, Clifford. Cuba. (Illus.). 112p. (gr. 5 up). 1991. 14.95 (*0-7910-1362-6*) Chelsea Hse.
Cummins, Ronald. Cuba. Lopez, Mercedes, illus. LC 89-43170. 64p. (gr. 5-6). 1991. PLB 21.26 (*0-8368-0219-5*) Gareth Stevens Inc.
Garver, Susan & McGuire, Paula. From Mexico, Cuba, & Puerto Rico. (gr. 7-11). pap. 2.50 (*0-317-13311-X*, LFL) Dell.
Grenquist, Barbara. Cubans. LC 90-12984. (Illus.). 64p. (gr. 5-10). 1991. PLB 13.40 (*0-531-11107-5*) Watts.
Haverstock, Nathan A. Cuba in Pictures. (Illus.). 64p. (gr. 5 up). 1987. PLB 17.50 (*0-8225-1811-2*) Lerner Pubns.
Jacobsen, Karen. Cuba. LC 89-25426. (Illus.). 48p. (gr. k-4). 1990. PLB 12.85 (*0-516-01183-9*); pap. 4.95 (*0-516-41183-7*) Childrens.
Jose Marti. (Illus.). 32p. (gr. 3-6). 1988. PLB 19.97 (*0-8172-2906-X*); pap. 4.95 (*0-8114-6761-9*) Raintree Steck-V.
Morris, Emily. Cuba. LC 90-10354. (Illus.). 96p. (gr. 6-12). 1991. PLB 22.80 (*0-8114-2439-1*) Raintree Steck-V.
Vazquez, Ana & Casas, Rosa. Cuba. LC 87-10235. (Illus.). 128p. (gr. 5-9). 1987. PLB 20.55 (*0-516-02758-1*) Childrens.

CUBA–HISTORY

Jose Marti. (Illus.). 32p. (gr. 3-6). 1988. PLB 19.97 (*0-8172-2906-X*); pap. 4.95 (*0-8114-6761-9*) Raintree Steck-V.
Madden, Paul. Fidel Castro. LC 92-46482. 1993. 19.93 (*0-86625-479-X*); 14.95s.p. (*0-685-67776-1*) Rourke Pubns.
Mendez, Adriana. Cubans in America. LC 93-14339. (Illus.). 72p. (gr. 5 up). 1994. lib. bdg. 17.50 (*0-8225-1953-4*); pap. 5.95 (*0-8225-1039-1*) Lerner Pubns.
Stewart, Gail B. Cuba. LC 91-12352. (Illus.). 48p. (gr. 6-7). 1991. text ed. 4.95 RSBE (*0-89686-658-0*, Crestwood Hse) Macmillan Child Grp.

CULTS AND SECTS

see Sects

CULTURE

see also Civilization; Education; Learning and Scholarship; Self-Culture

Chan, Barbara J. Kid Pix Around the World: A Computer & Activities Book. Chan, Barbara J., illus. LC 92-46141. 1993. pap. 12.95 (*0-201-62226-2*) Addison-Wesley.
Cultures of the World, 6 vols. 128p. (gr. 5-10). 1992. Set. PLB 131.70 (*1-85435-543-0*) Marshall Cavendish.
McSharry, Patra & Rosen, Roger, eds. Coca Cola Culture: Icons of Pop. (gr. 7-12). 1993. 16.95 (*0-8239-1593-X*); pap. 8.95 (*0-8239-1594-8*) Rosen Group.
Moore, Jo E. Stories about Children from Many Lands. Supancich, Jo, illus. 64p. (gr. k-2). 1993. pap. text ed. 11.95 (*1-55799-248-7*) Evan-Moor Corp.
Multi-Culture: Grades 6-8. 1993. PLB write for info. (*0-8050-3076-X*) H Holt & Co.
Multi-Culture: K-2. (ps-2). 1993. PLB write for info. (*0-8050-3075-1*) H Holt & Co.
Roland, Donna. Grandfather's Stories. Oden, Ron, illus. (Orig.). (gr. k-3). 1993. pap. 4.95 (*0-941996-00-X*); Tchr's. ed. 5.50 (*0-685-42442-1*); Flannelboard set. 12.00 (*0-685-73481-1*); Video cass. 32.00 (*0-685-73482-X*); Audio cass., per culture. 5.95 (*0-685-73483-8*) Open My World.
—More of Grandfather's Stories. Oden, Ron, illus. 25p. (Orig.). (gr. k-3). 1993. pap. 4.95 (*0-941996-02-6*); tchr's. ed. 5.50 (*0-941996-13-1*) Open My World.
Tulling, Virginia. Threatened Cultures. (Illus.). 48p. (gr. 5 up). 1990. lib. bdg. 18.60 (*0-86592-096-6*); lib. bdg. 13.95s.p. (*0-685-36381-3*) Rourke Corp.
Your School Report (TM) (Illus.). 51p. (gr. 5-11). 1994. 19.95 (*1-884618-00-6*) Unique Information.

CUMMINGS, EDWARD ESTLIN, 1894-1962

Berry, Skip L. E. E. Cummings. LC 93-743. 1994. PLB 18.95 (*0-88682-611-X*) Creative Ed.

CURATES

see Clergy

CURIE, MARIE (SKLODOWSKA) 1867-1934

Birch, Beverley. Marie Curie: Pioneer in the Study of Radiation. LC 89-77762. (Illus.). 64p. (gr. 3-4). 1990. PLB 19.93 (*0-8368-0388-4*) Gareth Stevens Inc.
—Marie Curie: The Polish Scientist Who Discovered Radium & Its Life-Saving Properties. Sherwood, Rhoda, ed. LC 88-2091. (Illus.). 68p. (gr. 5-6). 1988. PLB 19.93 (*1-55532-818-0*) Gareth Stevens Inc.
Birch, Beverly. Marie Curie. LC 88-2091. (Illus.). 68p. (gr. 5-6). 1990. pap. 7.95 (*0-8192-1522-8*) Morehouse Pub.
Brandt, Keith. Marie Curie: Brave Scientist. Milone, Karen, illus. LC 82-16092. 48p. (gr. 4-6). 1983. PLB 10.79 (*0-89375-855-8*); pap. text ed. 3.50 (*0-89375-856-6*) Troll Assocs.
Bull, Angela. Marie Curie. (Illus.). 64p. (gr. 5-9). 1991. 11.95 (*0-237-60024-2*, Pub. by Evans Bros Ltd) Trafalgar.

Dunn, Andrew. Marie Curie. LC 90-37563. (Illus.). 48p. (gr. 5-8). 1991. PLB 12.40 (*0-531-18375-0*, Pub. by Bookwright Pr) Watts.
Farr, Naunerle. Madame Curie - Albert Einstein. Leonidez, Nestor & Redondo, Nestor, illus. (gr. 4-12). 1979. pap. text ed. 2.95 (*0-88301-356-8*); wkbk. 1.25 (*0-88301-380-0*) Pendulum Pr.
Fisher, Leonard E. Marie Curie. LC 93-40211. (Illus.). (gr. 2-6). 1994. 14.95 (*0-02-735375-3*, Macmillan Child Bk) Macmillan Child Grp.
Grady, Sean M. Marie Curie. LC 92-21031. (Illus.). 112p. (gr. 5-8). 1992. PLB 14.95 (*1-56006-033-6*) Lucent Bks.
Greene, Carol. Marie Curie: Pioneer Physicist. LC 83-26273. (Illus.). 112p. (gr. 4 up). 1984. PLB 14.40 (*0-516-03203-8*) Childrens.
Lepscky, Ibi. Marie Curie. Cardoni, Paolo, illus. 24p. (gr. k-3). 1993. 9.95 (*0-8120-6340-6*); pap. 4.95 (*0-8120-1558-4*) Barron.
Montgomery, Mary & Baraldi, Severino. Marie Curie. (Illus.). 104p. (gr. 5-8). 1990. lib. bdg. 9.95 (*0-382-09981-8*); pap. 5.95 (*0-382-24006-5*) Silver Burdett Pr.
Parker, Steve. Marie Curie & Radium. LC 92-3616. (Illus.). 32p. (gr. 3-7). 1992. 14.00 (*0-06-020847-3*); PLB 13.89 (*0-06-021472-4*) HarpC Child Bks.
—Marie Curie & Radium. Parker, Steve, illus. LC 92-3616. 32p. (gr. 3-7). 1992. pap. 5.95 (*0-06-446143-2*, Trophy) HarpC Child Bks.
Pflaum, Rosalynd. Marie Curie & Her Daughter Irene. LC 92-2453. 1993. 21.50 (*0-8225-4915-8*) Lerner Pubns.
Poynter, Margaret. Marie Curie: Discoverer of Radium. LC 93-21224. (Illus.). 128p. (gr. 4-10). 1994. lib. bdg. 17.95 (*0-89490-477-9*) Enslow Pubs.
Sabin, Louis. Marie Curie. Eitzen, Allan, illus. LC 84-2654. 32p. (gr. 3-6). 1985. PLB 9.49 (*0-8167-0162-8*); pap. text ed. 2.95 (*0-8167-0163-6*) Troll Assocs.
Steinke, Ann. Marie Curie. (Illus.). 144p. (gr. 3-6). 1987. pap. 5.95 (*0-8120-3924-6*) Barron.
Tames, Richard. Marie Curie. LC 89-14794. (Illus.). 32p. (gr. 7-9). 1990. PLB 12.40 (*0-531-10850-3*) Watts.
—Marie Curie. (Illus.). 32p. (gr. 5 up). 1991. pap. 5.95 (*0-531-24612-4*) Watts.

CURIOSITIES AND WONDERS

Adams, Simon. Explore the World of Man-Made Wonders. (gr. 4-7). 1991. 8.95 (*0-307-15603-6*) Western Pub.
Allen, Eugenie. The Best Ever Kids' Book of Lists. 128p. (Orig.). 1991. pap. 2.95 (*0-380-76357-5*, Camelot) Avon.
Arvey, Michael. Miracles: Opposing Viewpoints. LC 90-39156. (Illus.). 112p. (gr. 5-8). 1990. PLB 14.95 (*0-89908-084-7*) Greenhaven.
Asher, Sandy. Teddy Teabury's Fabulous Facts. Jones, Bob, illus. 110p. (Orig.). (gr. 4-5). 1985. pap. 2.50 (*0-440-48576-2*, YB) Dell.
Caselli, Giovanni. Wonders of the World. LC 92-52798. (Illus.). 64p. (gr. 3 up). 1992. 11.95 (*1-56458-145-4*) Dorling Kindersley.
Clark, Judith F. Awesome Facts to Blow Your Mind. Morrow, Skip, illus. 48p. (Orig.). (gr. 2-6). 1993. pap. 4.95 (*0-8431-3577-8*) Price Stern.
—Gross Facts to Blow Your Mind. Morrow, Skip, illus. LC 93-12250. 48p. (Orig.). (gr. 1-6). 1993. pap. 4.95 (*0-8431-3578-6*) Price Stern.
—Scary Facts to Blow Your Mind. Morrow, Skip, illus. 48p. (Orig.). (gr. 1-6). 1993. pap. 4.95 (*0-8431-3580-8*) Price Stern.
—Weird Facts to Blow Your Mind. Morrow, Skip, illus. 48p. (Orig.). (gr. 1-6). 1993. pap. 4.95 (*0-8431-3579-4*) Price Stern.
Cohen, Daniel. The Mummy's Curse: One Hundred One of the World's Strangest Mysteries. LC 94-4378. 224p. (Orig.). 1994. pap. 3.99 (*0-380-77093-8*, Camelot) Avon.
Crawford, Jean, ed. Amazing Facts. LC 93-11599. (Illus.). 88p. (gr. k-3). 1994. write for info. (*0-8094-9458-2*); PLB write for info. (*0-8094-9459-0*) Time-Life.
Creatures. 48p. (gr. 5-6). 1991. PLB 11.95 (*1-56065-061-3*) Capstone Pr.
Crump, Donald J., ed. The Far-Out Fact Book. LC 79-1793. (Illus.). 104p. (gr. 3-8). 1980. 8.95 (*0-87044-319-4*); PLB 12.50 (*0-87044-324-0*) Natl Geog.
—Hidden Worlds. LC 79-3244. (Illus.). 104p. (gr. 3-8). 1981. 8.95 (*0-87044-336-4*); PLB 12.50 (*0-87044-341-0*) Natl Geog.
Doyle, Arthur Conan. The White Company. Wyeth, N. C., illus. Glassman, Peter, afterword by. LC 87-62625. (Illus.). 362p. (ps up). 1988. 17.00 (*0-688-07817-6*) Morrow Jr Bks.
Edens, Cooper. Caretakers of Wonder. Edens, Cooper, illus. LC 91-24035. 40p. (gr. 3 up). 1991. 11.95 (*0-671-75193-X*, Green Tiger) S&S Trade.
—Caretakers of Wonder. 1987. pap. 4.95 (*0-671-97231-6*, Green Tiger) S&S Trade.
Edom, H., et al. Where Things Come From. (Illus.). 72p. (gr. 2-4). 1989. 11.95 (*0-7460-0282-3*, Usborne) EDC.
Emert, Phyllis R. Mysteries of People & Places. 128p. 1992. pap. 2.50 (*0-8125-2056-4*) Tor Bks.
—Mysteries of Space & the Universe, No. 6. 128p. (Orig.). 1994. pap. 2.99 (*0-8125-3631-2*) Tor Bks.
Everyday Things. LC 91-60898. (Illus.). 64p. (gr. 6 up). 1991. 14.95 (*1-879431-17-3*); PLB 15.99 (*1-879431-32-7*) Dorling Kindersley.
Far & Wide. 48p. (gr. 5-6). 1991. PLB 11.95 (*1-56065-066-4*) Capstone Pr.
Ganeri, A. Amazing Feats. (Illus.). 48p. (gr. 3-7). 1992. PLB 12.96 (*0-88110-584-8*); pap. 5.95 (*0-7460-0946-1*) EDC.
Getting There. 48p. (gr. 5-6). 1991. PLB 11.95 (*1-56065-067-2*) Capstone Pr.
Goldman, Phyllis B. Monkeyshines on Strange & Wonderful Facts. Grigni, John, illus. 116p. (Orig.). (ps-8). 1991. pap. 8.95 (*0-9620900-2-6*) NC Learn Inst Fitness.
Hagerman, Paul. It's a Weird World. LC 90-37643. (Illus.). 128p. (Orig.). (gr. 10 up). 1990. pap. 5.95 (*0-8069-7412-5*) Sterling.
Hanson, Amy. The Annual Manual for Girls. 192p. (Orig.). (gr. 3-7). 1993. pap. 4.95 (*1-56565-057-3*) Lowell Hse.
Hicks, Donna E. The Most Fascinating Places on Earth. Hicks, Mark A., illus. LC 92-41777. 128p. 14.95 (*0-8069-8692-1*) Sterling.
Iverson, Carol. Fish Sleep with Their Eyes Open: And Other Facts & Curiosities. (gr. 4-7). 1991. pap. 3.95 (*0-8225-9607-5*) Lerner Pubns.
—Hummingbirds Can Fly Backwards: And Other Facts & Curiosities. (gr. 4-7). 1991. pap. 3.95 (*0-8225-9606-7*) Lerner Pubns.
—I Bet You Didn't Know That Fish Sleep with Their Eyes Open & Other Facts & Curiosities. Lindstrom, Jack, illus. 32p. (gr. 3-6). 1990. PLB 10.95 (*0-8225-2277-2*) Lerner Pubns.
—I Bet You Didn't Know That You Can't Sink in the Dead Sea & Other Facts & Curiosities. Lindstrom, Jack, illus. 32p. (gr. 3-6). 1990. PLB 10.95 (*0-8225-2278-0*) Lerner Pubns.
Kallen, Stuart A. Amazing Animal Records. Wallner, Rosemary, ed. LC 91-73055. 1991. 12.94 (*1-56239-046-5*) Abdo & Dghtrs.
—Amazing Human Feats. Wallner, Rosemary, ed. LC 91-73052. 1991. 12.94 (*1-56239-049-X*) Abdo & Dghtrs.
—Awesome Entertainment Records. LC 91-73054. 32p. 1991. 12.94 (*1-56239-047-3*) Abdo & Dghtrs.
—Human Oddities. LC 91-73057. 202p. 1991. 12.94 (*1-56239-044-9*) Abdo & Dghtrs.
—Super Structures of the World. Wallner, Rosemary, ed. LC 91-73053. 202p. 1991. 12.94 (*1-56239-048-1*) Abdo & Dghtrs.
Keats, Robin. Slime Lives! & Other Weird Facts That Will Amaze You. Erkmann, Chris, illus. LC 94-18503. 80p. (Orig.). 1995. pap. 3.50 (*0-380-77304-X*, Camelot) Avon.
—Why Frogs Go to School & Other Weird Facts You Never Learned. Erkmann, Chris, illus. 96p. (Orig.). 1992. pap. 3.50 (*0-380-76718-X*, Camelot) Avon.
King, Celia. Seven Mysterious Wonders: A Pop-up Book. LC 93-8179. 1993. 9.95 (*0-8118-0361-9*) Chronicle Bks.
Lawless, Joann A. Strange Stories of Life. LC 77-10866. (Illus.). 48p. (gr. 4 up). 1983. PLB 20.70 (*0-8172-1062-8*) Raintree Steck-V.
Little, Jocelyn. World's Strangest Animal Facts. Twinem, Nancy, illus. LC 93-47248. 96p. 1994. 12.95 (*0-8069-8520-8*) Sterling.
McLeish, Kenneth. The Seven Wonders of the World. (Illus.). 1989. pap. 9.95 (*0-521-37911-3*) Cambridge U Pr.
Matthews, Rupert. Record Breakers of the Air. LC 89-5212. (Illus.). 32p. (gr. 2-6). 1990. PLB 9.59 (*0-8167-1921-7*); pap. text ed. 2.50 (*0-8167-1922-5*) Troll Assocs.
—Record Breakers of the Land. LC 89-5202. (Illus.). 32p. (gr. 2-6). 1990. PLB 9.59 (*0-8167-1923-3*); pap. text ed. 2.50 (*0-8167-1924-1*) Troll Assocs.
Miller, C., et al. Mysteries of Unknown (B - U) (Illus.). 96p. (gr. 5 up). 1992. pap. 12.95 (*0-86020-492-8*) EDC.
More Far-Out Facts. LC 80-8798. (Illus.). 104p. (gr. 3-8). 1982. 8.95 (*0-87044-384-4*); lib. bdg. 12.50 (*0-87044-389-5*) Natl Geog.
O'Neill, Catherine. Amazing Mysteries of the World. Crump, Donald J., ed. LC 83-13444. 104p. (gr. 3-8). 1983. PLB 12.50 (*0-87044-502-2*) Natl Geog.
Owl Magazine Editors. Amazing but True. (Illus.). 96p. (gr. 3 up). 1992. pap. 3.95 (*0-920775-69-1*, Pub. by Greey dePencier CN) Firefly Bks Ltd.
—Weird & Wonderful. (Illus.). 96p. (gr. 3 up). 1992. pap. 3.95 (*0-919872-81-6*, Pub. by Greey dePencier CN) Firefly Bks Ltd.
Pearce, Q. L. Quicksand & Other Earthly Wonders. Steltenpohl, Jane, ed. Fraser, Mary A., illus. 64p. (gr. 4-6). 1989. PLB 12.98 (*0-671-68530-9*, J Messner); pap. 5.95 (*0-671-68646-1*) S&S Trade.
The Physical World. 48p. (gr. 5-6). 1991. PLB 11.95 (*1-56065-064-8*) Capstone Pr.
Razzi, Jim. Nightmare Island: And Other Real-Life Mysteries. Palencar, John J., illus. LC 92-32638. 96p. (gr. 3-7). 1993. pap. 3.95 (*0-06-440426-9*, Trophy) HarpC Child Bks.
Reynolds, Patrick M. The Book of Silly Lists. LC 92-38660. 1993. 1.25 (*0-89375-354-8*, Pub. by Watermill Pr) Troll Assocs.
Ripley, Robert L. Amazing Records. Stott, Carol, illus. 48p. (gr. 3-6). 1992. PLB 12.95 (*1-56065-124-5*) Capstone Pr.
—The Psychic & Supernatural. Stott, Carol, illus. 48p. (gr. 3-6). 1992. PLB 12.95 (*1-56065-127-X*) Capstone Pr.
Ripley Staff. Hours, Days & Years. (Illus.). 48p. (gr. 3-6). 1991. 11.95 (*1-56065-065-6*) Capstone Pr.
Schreiber, Brad. Weird Wonders & Bizarre Blunders. LC 89-33911. 88p. 1989. pap. 4.95 (*0-88166-174-0*) Meadowbrook.
Siegel, Alice. Kid Stuff: People, Places, & Things to Know. (gr. 4-7). 1991. pap. 3.99 (*0-553-15914-3*) Bantam.
Sobol, Donald J. Encyclopedia Brown's Record Book of Weird & Wonderful Facts. Murdocca, Sal, illus. LC 78-72857. (gr. 3 up). 1979. PLB 9.89 (*0-440-02330-0*) Delacorte.
—Encyclopedia Brown's Second Record Book of Weird & Wonderful Facts. Degen, Bruce, illus. LC 81-790. 160p. (gr. 4-6). 1981. 10.95 (*0-385-28243-5*); PLB 10.95 (*0-685-01395-2*) Delacorte.
Tallarico, Tony. I Didn't Know That about Strange but True Mysteries. (Illus.). 32p. 1992. 9.95 (*1-56156-117-7*); pap. 2.95 (*1-56156-177-0*) Kidsbks.
Taylor, Paula. The Kids' Whole Future Catalog. LC 82-5279. (Illus.). 256p. (gr. 4-7). 1982. pap. 6.95 (*0-394-85090-4*) Random Bks Yng Read.
Urton, Andrea. Mind Boggles. 64p. 1994. pap. 4.95 (*1-56565-176-6*) Lowell Hse Juvenile.
Visual Encyclopedia of Science: Stars & Planets, Planet Earth, the Living World, Science & Technology, World History, Countries of the World. LC 93-43118. 320p. (gr. 5 up). 1994. 29.95 (*1-85697-998-9*, Kingfisher LKC) LKC.
Warren, William E. The Screaming Skull: True Tales of the Unexplained. Waldman, Neil, illus. LC 87-6909. 144p. (gr. 5 up). 1987. pap. 11.95 jacketed (*0-671-66809-9*, S&S BFYR) S&S Trade.
Wassermann, Selma & Wassermann, Jack. The Book of Hypotheses. Smith, Dennis, illus. LC 89-78082. 32p. (gr. k-3). 1990. PLB 12.85 (*0-8027-6946-2*); pap. 4.95 (*0-8027-9452-1*) Walker & Co.
The Whatever Book, 2 bks. (gr. 3-7). 1981. (Little Simon) S&S Trade.
Winik, J. T. Mysteries. Rowden, Rick, illus. 48p. (gr. 5-9). 1985. pap. 5.95 (*0-88625-094-3*) Durkin Hayes Pub.
Wonders! Classroom Set. (Orig.). (gr. 1-3). 1994. pap. 353.00 set incl. 6 big bks., tchr's. activity bk. & student learning log (*1-56334-099-2*) Hampton-Brown.
Woods, Harold & Woods, Geraldine. The Book of the Unknown. Mathieu, Joe, illus. LC 82-3683. 72p. (gr. 4-7). 1982. lib. bdg. 5.99 (*0-394-95233-2*) Random Bks Yng Read.
Wulffson, Don L. Amazing True Stories. Jones, John R., illus. LC 90-28105. 128p. (gr. 4-9). 1991. 13.95 (*0-525-65070-9*, Cobblehill Bks) Dutton Child Bks.
—Amazing True Stories. (gr. 4-7). 1994. pap. 2.95 (*0-590-45958-9*) Scholastic Inc.

CURRENCY

see Money

CUSTER, GEORGE ARMSTRONG, 1839-1876

Armstrong, Virgil. The Assassination of General George Armstrong Custer: The True Story Behind the Battle of the Little Big Horn. Whitman, Patricia, ed. 300p. (gr. 9-12). 1990. pap. write for info. (*0-925390-22-4*) Armstrong Assocs.
Bachrach, Deborah. Custer's Last Stand: Opposing Viewpoints. LC 90-36967. (Illus.). 112p. (gr. 5-8). 1990. PLB 14.95 (*0-89908-077-4*) Greenhaven.
Razzi, Jim. Custer & Crazy Horse. (gr. 3-7). 1989. pap. 2.95 (*0-590-41836-X*) Scholastic Inc.
Reedstrom, E. Lisle. Custer's Seventh Cavalry: From Fort Riley to the Little Big Horn. LC 92-26524. (Illus.). 176p. (gr. 10-12). 1992. pap. 14.95 (*0-8069-8762-6*) Sterling.

CUSTER, GEORGE ARMSTRONG, 1839-1876–FICTION

Irwin, Hadley. Jim-Dandy. LC 93-22611. 144p. (gr. 5-9). 1994. SBE 14.95 (*0-689-50594-9*, M K McElderry) Macmillan Child Grp.

CUSTOMS,SOCIAL

see Manners and Customs

CYBERNETICS

see also Bionics; Computers

CYCLES, MOTOR

see Motorcycles

CYCLING

see Bicycles and Bicycling; Motorcycles

CYCLOPEDIAS

see Encyclopedias and Dictionaries

CYTOLOGY

see Cells

CZECHOSLOVAK REPUBLIC

Symynkywicz, Jeffrey. Vaclav Havel & the Velvet Revolution. LC 94-2384. (gr. 5 up). 1995. text ed. 13.95 (*0-87518-607-6*, Dillon) Macmillan Child Grp.

CZECHOSLOVAK REPUBLIC–FICTION

Sis, Peter. The Three Golden Keys. LC 94-6743. 1994. 19.95 (*0-385-47292-7*) Doubleday.

CZECHS IN THE U. S.

Sakson-Ford, Stephanie. Czech Americans. Moynihan, Daniel P., intro. by. (Illus.). 112p. (gr. 5 up). 1989. lib. bdg. 17.95 (*0-87754-870-6*) Chelsea Hse.

D

D N A

Asimov, Isaac. How Did We Find Out about DNA? Wool, David, illus. LC 85-15589. 61p. (gr. 9 up). 1985. 9.95 (*0-8027-6596-3*); PLB 10.85 (*0-8027-6604-8*) Walker & Co.

Balkwill, Fran. DNA Is Here to Stay. Rolph, Mic, illus. 32p. (gr. 3-6). 1993. 17.50 (*0-87614-763-5*) Carolrhoda Bks.

Lampton, Christopher. DNA Fingerprinting. LC 91-16533. (Illus.). 112p. (gr. 9-12). 1991. PLB 13.40 (*0-531-13003-7*) Watts.

Wilcox, Frank H. DNA: The Thread of Life. (Illus.). 80p. (gr. 5 up). 1988. PLB 17.50 (*0-8225-1584-9*) Lerner Pubns.

DAHL, ROALD, 1916-

Meeks, Christopher. Roald Dahl. LC 92-42286. (gr. 3-7). 1993. 14.60 (*0-86593-259-X*); 10.95s.p. (*0-685-66357-4*) Rourke Corp.

DAIRIES

see Dairying

DAIRY CATTLE

see Cows

DAIRY PRODUCTS

see also Dairying;
also names of dairy products, e.g. Milk

Illsley, Linda. Cheese. (Illus.). 32p. (gr. 1-4). 1991. PLB 14.95 (*0-87614-654-X*) Carolrhoda Bks.

Peterson, Cris. Extra Cheese, Please! Mozzarella's Journey from Cow to Pizza. Upitis, Alvis, illus. 32p. (ps-3). 1994. 14.95 (*1-56397-177-1*) Boyds Mills Pr.

Wake, Susan. Butter. Yeats, John, illus. 32p. (gr. 1-4). 1990. PLB 14.95 (*0-87614-427-X*) Carolrhoda Bks.

DAIRYING

see also Cattle; Cows; Dairy Products; Milk

Aliki. Milk from Cow to Carton. rev. ed. LC 91-23807. (Illus.). 32p. (gr. k-4). 1992. 14.00 (*0-06-020434-6*); PLB 13.89 (*0-06-020435-4*) HarpC Child Bks.

—Milk from Cow to Carton. rev. ed. LC 91-23807. (Illus.). 32p. (gr. k-4). 1992. pap. 4.50 (*0-06-445111-9*, Trophy) HarpC Child Bks.

Fowler, Allan. Gracias a las Vacas: Thanks to Cows. LC 91-35062. (SPA., Illus.). 32p. (ps-2). 1992. PLB 10.75 (*0-516-34924-4*); pap. 3.95 (*0-516-54924-3*); big bk. 22.95 (*0-516-59625-X*) Childrens.

—Thanks to Cows. LC 91-35062. (Illus.). 32p. (ps-2). 1992. PLB 10.75 (*0-516-04924-0*); PLB 22.95 big bk. (*0-516-49625-5*); pap. 3.95 (*0-516-44924-9*) Childrens.

Mitgutsch, Ali. From Grass to Butter. Mitgutsch, Ali, illus. LC 80-28588. 24p. (ps-3). 1981. PLB 10.95 (*0-87614-156-4*) Carolrhoda Bks.

—From Milk to Ice Cream. Mitgutsch, Ali, illus. LC 81-81. 24p. (ps-3). 1981. PLB 10.95 (*0-87614-158-0*) Carolrhoda Bks.

Morris, Ann. Seven Hundred Kids on Grandpa's Farm. Heyman, Ken, photos by. (Illus.). 32p. (ps-3). 1994. 14.99 (*0-525-45162-5*, DCB) Dutton Child Bks.

National Dairy Council Staff. Uncle Jim's Dairy Farm: A Summer Visit with Aunt Helen & Uncle Jim. (Illus.). 4p. (gr. 3-6). 1980. Set incls. 12 user's guides & 1 tchr's. guide. write for info. (*1-55647-611-6*); write for info. 1/2 inch VHS tape (*1-55647-634-5*) Natl Dairy Coun.

Poskanzer, Susan C. Dairy Farmer. Ulrich, George, illus. LC 88-10040. 32p. (gr. k-3). 1989. PLB 10.89 (*0-8167-1426-6*); pap. text ed. 2.95 (*0-8167-1427-4*) Troll Assocs.

Ross, Catherine S. Amazing Milk Book. 1991. pap. 6.68 (*0-201-57087-4*) Addison-Wesley.

Stone, Lynn M. Dairy Country. LC 93-13503. 1993. write for info. (*0-86593-302-2*) Rourke Corp.

Ziegler, Sandra. A Visit to the Dairy Farm. LC 87-19692. (Illus.). 32p. (ps-3). 1987. PLB 11.45 (*0-516-01496-X*); pap. 3.95 (*0-516-41496-8*) Childrens.

DAIRYING–FICTION

Ericsson, Jennifer A. No Milk! Eitan, Ora, illus. LC 92-21806. 32p. (ps up). 1993. 14.00 (*0-688-11306-0*, Tambourine Bks); PLB 13.93 (*0-688-11307-9*, Tambourine Bks) Morrow.

Gibbons, Gail. The Milk Makers. LC 84-20081. (Illus.). 32p. (gr. k-3). 1985. RSBE 14.95 (*0-02-736640-5*, Macmillan Child Bk) Macmillan Child Grp.

Lindbergh, Anne M. The Hunky-Dory Dairy. Brinckloe, Julie, illus. LC 85-16408. 147p. (gr. 4-6). 1986. 14.95 (*0-15-237449-3*, HB Juv Bks) HarBrace.

Morris, Linda L. Morning Milking. DeRan, David, illus. LC 91-13103. 32p. (gr. k up). 1991. pap. 16.95 (*0-88708-173-8*) Picture Bk Studio.

Shebar, Sharon. Milk. Wasserman, Dan, ed. Reese, Bob, illus. (gr. k-1). 1979. 7.95 (*0-89868-067-0*); pap. 2.95 (*0-89868-078-6*) ARO Pub.

DALLAS

Velvin, Elaine. Discover Dallas: A Child's Guide. rev. ed. (Illus.). 68p. (gr. 2-7). 1987. pap. 5.95 (*0-937460-18-4*) Hendrick-Long.

DALLAS COWBOYS (FOOTBALL TEAM)

Alcorta, Joe H., Sr. La Historia de un Famoso Equipo: Los Dallas Cowboys. (SPA., Illus.). 410p. (gr. 9-12). 1989. 14.95 (*0-685-29025-5*) Hermenejildo Pr.

Dippold, Joel. Troy Aikman, Quick-Draw Quarterback. LC 93-47909. (Illus.). 64p. (gr. 4-9). 1994. PLB 13.50 (*0-8225-2880-0*); pap. 5.95 (*0-8225-9663-6*) Lerner Pubns.

Italia, Bob. The Dallas Cowboys: Nineteen Ninety-Three Super Bowl Champions. LC 93-15260. 1993. 14.96 (*1-56239-238-7*) Abdo & Dghtrs.

DAMIEN, FATHER, 1840-1889

Brown, Pam. Father Damien: Missionary to a Forgotten People. Birch, Beverley, adapted by. LC 89-49751. (Illus.). 64p. (gr. 3-4). 1990. PLB 19.93 (*0-8368-0389-2*) Gareth Stevens Inc.

—Father Damien: The Man Who Lived & Died for the Victims of Leprosy. Sherwood, Rhoda, ed. LC 88-2106. (Illus.). 68p. (gr. 5-6). 1988. PLB 19.93 (*1-55532-815-6*) Gareth Stevens Inc.

DAMS

Ardley, Neil. Dams. Stefoff, Rebecca, ed. LC 90-40360. (Illus.). 48p. (gr. 4-7). 1990. PLB 17.26 (*0-944483-75-5*) Garrett Ed Corp.

Baljo, Wallace, Jr. Grand Coulee: A Story of the Columbia River from Molten Lavas & Ice to Grand Coulee Dam. rev. ed. Hemsley, Roberta G., illus. 80p. (gr. 4-6). pap. write for info. (*0-9606084-0-0*) Clipboard.

Cooper, J. Dams. 1991. 8.95s.p. (*0-86592-627-1*) Rourke Enter.

—Represas (Dams) (SPA.). 1991. 8.95s.p. (*0-86592-924-6*) Rourke Enter.

Dunn, Andrew. Dams. LC 93-6835. 32p. (gr. 5-8). 1993. 13.95 (*1-56847-029-0*) Thomson Lrning.

DANCERS

Anderson, Joan. Twins on Toes: A Ballet Debut. Ancona, George, photos by. LC 92-35104. (Illus.). 32p. (gr. 3-7). 1993. 14.99 (*0-525-67415-2*, Lodestar Bks) Dutton Child Bks.

Arnold, Sandra M. Alicia Alonso: First Lady of the Ballet. LC 93-18098. 104p. (gr. 7 up). 1993. 14.95 (*0-8027-8242-6*); PLB 15.85 (*0-8027-8243-4*) Walker & Co.

Brighton, Catherine. Nijinsky: Scenes from the Childhood of the Great Dancer. (Illus.). 32p. (ps-3). 1989. 13.95 (*0-385-24663-3*, Zephyr-BFYR); PLB 14.99 (*0-385-24926-8*, Zephyr-BFYR) Doubleday.

Butterworth, Emma M. As the Waltz Was Ending. 262p. (gr. 7 up). 1991. pap. 3.25 (*0-590-44440-9*, Point); tchr's. guide 1.25 (*0-590-40665-5*) Scholastic Inc.

Clarke, Mary & Ashton, Frederick, illus. Antoinette Sibley. Ashton, Frederick, intro. by. 128p. (gr. 8-12). 1981. 29.95 (*0-903102-64-1*, Pub. by Dance Bks UK) Princeton Bk Co.

Davis Pinkney, Andrea. Alvin Ailey. Pinkney, Brian, illus. LC 92-54865. 32p. (gr. 1-4). 1993. 13.95 (*1-56282-413-9*); PLB 13.89 (*1-56282-414-7*) Hyprn Child.

Gherman, Beverly. Agnes de Mille: Dancing off the Earth. LC 93-26606. (Illus.). 160p. (gr. 7 up). 1994. pap. 5.95 (*0-02-043240-2*, Collier Young Ad) Macmillan Child Grp.

Haskins, James S. Black Dance in America: A History Through Its People. LC 89-35529. (Illus.). 240p. (gr. 7 up). 1990. 15.00 (*0-690-04657-X*, Crowell Jr Bks); (Crowell Jr Bks) HarpC Child Bks.

Kozodoy, Ruth. Isadora Duncan. Horner, Matina, intro. by. (Illus.). 112p. (gr. 5 up). 1988. lib. bdg. 17.95x (*1-55546-650-8*) Chelsea Hse.

Lewis-Ferguson, Julinda. Alvin Ailey, Jr. A Life in Dance. LC 93-17906. 64p. (gr. 3-8). 1994. 14.95 (*0-8027-8239-6*); PLB 15.85 (*0-8027-8241-8*) Walker & Co.

Linnell, Andrew & Auer, Varvara. The Dance of the Elves. (Illus.). 32p. (Orig.). (ps). 1984. pap. 13.50 (*0-936132-68-X*) Merc Pr NY.

Martin, John H. A Day in the Life of a Ballet Dancer. Jann, Gayle, illus. LC 84-2424. 32p. (gr. 4-8). 1985. PLB 11.79 (*0-8167-0089-3*); pap. text ed. 2.95 (*0-8167-0090-7*) Troll Assocs.

Menning, Viiu. Great Dancers. Conkle, Nancy & Neary, D., illus. (Orig.). (gr. 8). 1978. pap. 3.95 (*0-88388-065-2*) Bellerophon Bks.

O'Connor, Barbara. Barefoot Dancer: The Story of Isadora Duncan. LC 93-14312. (gr. 5 up). 1994. 17.50 (*0-87614-807-0*) Carolrhoda Bks.

Probosz, Kathilyn S. Alvin Ailey, Jr. (gr. 4-7). 1991. pap. 3.50 (*0-553-15930-5*) Bantam.

Stewart, Rachel. Margot Fonteyn. (Illus.). 64p. (gr. 5-9). 1991. 11.95 (*0-237-60033-1*, Pub. by Evans Bros Ltd) Trafalgar.

Townsend, Alecia C. Mikhail Baryshnikov. LC 92-42547. (gr. 1-8). 1993. 19.93 (*0-86625-484-6*); 14.95s.p. (*0-685-66287-X*) Rourke Pubns.

DANCERS–FICTION

Brenner, Summer. Dancers & the Dance. LC 90-30312. 144p. (Orig.). 1990. pap. 9.95 (*0-918273-75-7*) Coffee Hse.

Candors Danced. 1987. pap. 14.95 (*0-440-50233-0*) Dell.

Coombs, Karen M. Samantha Gill, Belly Dancer. 128p. 1989. pap. 2.75 (*0-380-75737-0*, Camelot) Avon.

Estoril, Jean. Drina's Dancing Year, No. 2. 1989. pap. 2.75 (*0-590-42192-1*) Scholastic Inc.

Fox, Paula. The Slave Dancer. (Orig.). (gr. k-6). 1991. pap. 3.99 (*0-440-40402-9*, Pub. by Yearling Classics) Dell.

Gauch, Patricia L. Dance, Tanya. Ichikawa, Satomi, illus. 32p. (ps-3). 1989. 13.95 (*0-399-21521-2*, Philomel Bks) Putnam Pub Group.

Hill, Elizabeth S. The Street Dancers. 192p. (gr. 3-7). 1991. 13.95 (*0-670-83435-1*) Viking Child Bks.

Holabird, Katharine. Angelina Dances. Craig, Helen, illus. LC 92-80524. 6p. (ps-k). 1992. bds. 5.99 (*0-679-83484-2*) Random Bks Yng Read.

King, Sandra. Shannon: An Ojibway Dancer. 48p. (gr. 4-7). 1993. pap. 6.95 (*0-8225-9643-1*) Lerner Pubns.

Mathers, Petra. Sophie & Lou. Mathers, Petra, illus. LC 90-37562. 32p. (ps-3). 1991. 15.00 (*0-06-024071-7*); PLB 14.89 (*0-06-024072-5*) HarpC Child Bks.

Saller, Carol. The Bridge Dancers. Talifero, Gerald, illus. 40p. (gr. 2-4). 1991. PLB 17.50 (*0-87614-653-1*) Carolrhoda Bks.

Sutton, Elizabeth H. The Pony Champions. LC 92-10518. 48p. (gr. 1-4). 1992. 13.95 (*1-56566-019-6*) Thomasson-Grant.

DANCING

see also Ballet; Folk Dancing

Bailey, Donna. Dancing. LC 90-23057. (Illus.). 32p. (gr. 1-4). 1991. PLB 18.99 (*0-8114-2902-4*); pap. 3.95 (*0-8114-4707-3*) Raintree Steck-V.

Berger, Melvin. The World of Dance. LC 78-14498. (Illus.). (gr. 7 up). 1978. 24.95 (*0-87599-221-8*) S G Phillips.

Berk, Fred. Chasidic Dance. (gr. 9 up). 1975. pap. 5.00 (*0-8074-0083-1*, 582050) UAHC.

Bessant, P. & Smith, L. Dance. (Illus.). 48p. (gr. 5 up). 1987. PLB 14.96 (*0-88110-245-8*); pap. 7.95 (*0-7460-0087-1*) EDC.

Bussell, Darcy. The Young Dancer. (Illus.). 72p. (gr. 2-6). 1994. 15.95 (*1-56458-468-2*) Dorling Kindersley.

Caney, Steven. Teach Yourself Tap Dancing. LC 89-40726. (Illus.). 64p. (Orig.). (gr. 2-5). 1991. pap. 12.95 (*0-89480-428-6*, 1428) Workman Pub.

Carter, Eneida & Mikalac, Miriam. Break Dance: The Free & Easy Way! Forman, Jan A., illus. 32p. (gr. 7 up). 1984. pap. 9.95 (*0-916391-00-0*) Free & Easy Pubns.

Haskins, James S. Black Dance in America: A History Through Its People. LC 89-35529. (Illus.). 240p. (gr. 7 up). 1992. pap. 6.95 (*0-06-446121-1*, Trophy) HarpC Child Bks.

Hutchinson Guest, Ann. Primer for Dance, Bk. II. 24p. (ps). 1958. pap. text ed. 6.95 (*0-932582-65-6*) Dance Notation.

Johnston, Edith. Regional Dances of the Mexico. (Illus.). 64p. (gr. 3 up). 1983. pap. 7.95 (*0-8442-7509-3*, Natl Textbk) NTC Pub Grp.

Mitchell, Pratima. Dance of Shiva. (Illus.). 25p. (gr. 2-4). 1991. 12.95 (*0-237-60148-6*, Pub. by Evans Bros Ltd) Trafalgar.

Sanchez, Sharon S. About Ballet Performance. Bower, Adele, illus. 32p. (ps up). 1990. pap. 5.95 (*0-9626651-1-8*) Dance Data.

—About Jazz Dance. Roussan, Irina, illus. 32p. (Orig.). 1991. pap. text ed. 5.95 (*0-9626651-2-6*) Dance Data.

Sanchez, Sharon S., ed. About Ballet Class. Bower, Adele, illus. 32p. (Orig.). (ps up). 1990. pap. 5.95 (*0-9626651-0-X*) Dance Data.

Thomas, A., et al. Ballet & Dance. (Illus.). 96p. (gr. 5 up). 1987. pap. 12.95 (*0-7460-0201-7*) EDC.

DANCING–FICTION

Alpert, Lou. Emma's Turn to Dance. Alpert, Lou, illus. 32p. (ps-3). 1991. smythe sewn reinforced bdg. 12.95 (*1-879085-00-3*) Whsprng Coyote Pr.

Asch, Frank. Moondance. 1994. pap. 3.95 (*0-590-45488-9*) Scholastic Inc.

Berenstain, Stan & Berenstain, Jan. The Berenstain Bears Gotta Dance. Berenstain, Stan & Berenstain, Jan, illus. LC 92-32565. 112p. (Orig.). (gr. 2-6). 1993. PLB 7.99 (*0-679-94032-4*); pap. 3.50 (*0-679-84032-X*) Random Bks Yng Read.

Carter, Alden R. Dancing on Dark Water. 1994. pap. 3.25 (*0-590-45600-8*) Scholastic Inc.

Cone, Molly. Dance Around the Fire. Friedman, Marvin, illus. LC 74-9378. 160p. (gr. 7 up). 1974. 5.95 (*0-395-19490-3*) HM.

Cormier, Larry. The Captain, the Gypsy & the Giant Bird. Bruni, Mary-Ann S., ed. Pressley, Ann, illus. 48p. (gr. k-8). 1986. 12.95 (*0-935857-07-9*); pap. write for info. (*0-935857-08-7*) Texart.

Couture, Susan A. Alfonso's Dream. LC 93-5784. 1996. 14.95 (*0-02-724827-5*, Macmillan Child Bk) Macmillan Child Grp.

Daly, Niki. Papa Lucky's Shadow. Daly, Niki, illus. LC 91-24283. 32p. (gr. k-3). 1992. SBE 14.95 (*0-689-50541-8*, M K McElderry) Macmillan Child Grp.

Delessert, Etienne. Dance! Delessert, Etienne, illus. 32p. (gr. 1-8). 1994. RLB smythe-sewn 16.95 (*0-88682-627-6*, 97938-098) Creative Ed.

De Paola, Tomie. Oliver Button Is a Sissy. De Paola, Tomie, illus. LC 78-12624. 46p. (ps-3). 1979. pap. 4.95 (*0-15-668140-4*, Voyager Bks) HarBrace.

Dinardo, Jeffrey. Henry's Bunny Hop. (ps-3). 1993. pap. 3.25 (*0-440-40769-9*) Dell.

Edwards, Richard. Moles Can Dance. Anstey, Caroline, illus. LC 93-2462. 32p. (ps up). 1994. 13.95 (*1-56402-361-3*) Candlewick Pr.

Giannini, Enzo. Zorina Ballerina. LC 91-21970. (Illus.). 40p. (ps-1). 1993. pap. 14.00 JRT (*0-671-74776-2*, S&S BFYR) S&S Trade.

Guard, Jean & Williamson, Ray A. They Dance in the Sky. Stewart, Edgar, illus. (gr. 6 up). 1987. 14.45 (*0-395-39970-X*) HM.

Hao, Kuang-ts'ai. Dance, Mice, Dance! Tartarotti, Stefano, illus. (ENG & CHI.). 32p. (gr. 2-4). 1994. 14. 95 (*1-57227-000-4*) Pan Asian Pubns.

—Dance, Mice, Dance! Tartarotti, Stefano, illus. (ENG & VIE.). 32p. (gr. 2-4). 1994. 16.95 (*1-57227-002-0*) Pan Asian Pubns.

—Dance, Mice, Dance! Tartarotti, Stefano, illus. (ENG & KOR.). 32p. (gr. 2-4). 1994. 16.95 (*1-57227-003-9*) Pan Asian Pubns.

—Dance, Mice, Dance! Tartarotti, Stefano, illus. (ENG & THA.). 32p. (gr. 2-4). 1994. 16.95 (*1-57227-004-7*) Pan Asian Pubns.

—Dance, Mice, Dance! Tartarotti, Stefano, illus. (ENG & TAG.). 32p. (gr. 2-4). 1994. 16.95 (*1-57227-005-5*) Pan Asian Pubns.

—Dance, Mice, Dance! Tartarotti, Stefano, illus. (ENG & CAM.). 32p. (gr. 2-4). 1994. 16.95 (*1-57227-006-3*) Pan Asian Pubns.
—Dance, Mice, Dance! Tartarotti, Stefano, illus. (ENG & LAO.). 32p. (gr. 2-4). 1994. 16.95 (*1-57227-007-1*) Pan Asian Pubns.
—Dance, Mice, Dance! Tartarotti, Stefano, illus. (ENG & KOR.). 32p. (gr. 2-4). 1994. 16.95 (*1-57227-008-X*) Pan Asian Pubns.
Hazen, Barbara S. Turkey in the Straw. Sneed, Brad, illus. LC 92-27516. 32p. (ps-3). 1993. 13.99 (*0-8037-1298-7*); PLB 13.89 (*0-8037-1299-5*) Dial Bks Young.
Hermes, Patricia. Mama, Let's Dance. (gr. 4-7). 1993. pap. 2.95 (*0-590-46633-X*) Scholastic Inc.
Hoff, Bernard. Duncan the Dancing Duck. LC 93-13058. (Illus.). 32p. (ps-3). 1994. 13.95 (*0-395-67400-X*, Clarion Bks) HM.
Hoffmann, E. T. Cascanueces - Nutcracker. (ps-3). 1994. pap. 2.95 (*0-486-28012-8*) Dover.
Hollinshead, Marilyn. The Nine Days Wonder. Morgan, Pierr, illus. 32p. (ps-3). 1994. 14.95 (*0-399-21967-6*, Philomel) Putnam Pub Group.
Isadora, Rachel. Max. Isadora, Rachel, illus. LC 76-9088. 32p. (gr. k-3). 1976. RSBE 13.95 (*0-02-747450-X*, Macmillan Child Bk) Macmillan Child Grp.
Keremis, Constance A. Hootenanny Night. LC 91-32505. (Illus.). 32p. (gr. k-4). 1992. 12.95 (*0-938349-79-1*); pap. 6.95 (*0-938349-80-5*) State House Pr.
Kllair, Bevan. Elferina & the Christmas Cha Cha. LC 79-91132. (ps-6). 1979. pap. 3.00 (*0-935712-00-3*) B A Scott.
—The Ziggle Dance at the Zoo. LC 79-91133. (ps-6). 1979. pap. 3.00 (*0-935712-01-1*) B A Scott.
Komaiko, Leah. Aunt Elaine Does the Dance from Spain. Mathers, Petra, illus. LC 91-45474. 32p. (ps-3). 1992. 15.00 (*0-385-30674-1*) Doubleday.
—Aunt Elaine Does the Dance from Spain. (ps-3). 1994. pap. 4.99 (*0-440-40975-6*) Dell.
Krementz, Jill. A Very Young Dancer. (gr. 3-6). 1986. pap. 7.95 (*0-440-49212-2*, YB) Dell.
Lantz, Francess. Marissa's Dance. LC 93-43225. (Illus.). 128p. (gr. 3-7). 1994. pap. text ed. 2.95 (*0-8167-3475-5*) Troll Assocs.
Lasky, Kathryn. The Solo. McCarthy, Bobette, illus. LC 92-44456. 32p. (ps-2). 1994. RSBE 14.95 (*0-02-751664-4*, Macmillan Child Bk) Macmillan Child Grp.
Lee, Jeanne. Silent Lotus. (Illus.). 32p. (gr. k-3). 1991. 14.95 (*0-374-36911-9*) FS&G.
Lowery, Linda. Twist with a Burger, Jitter with a Bug. Dypold, Pat, illus. LC 93-38236. 32p. 1994. 14.95g (*0-395-67022-5*) Ticknor & Fields.
Macsolis. Baile de Luna: Dance Moon. Macsolis, illus. (SPA.). 25p. (ps-2). 1991. 12.95 (*84-261-2583-2*) Donars.
Marshall, James. The Cut-ups Carry On. (Illus.). 32p. (ps-2). 1990. pap. 12.95 (*0-670-81645-0*) Viking Child Bks.
—The Cut-ups Carry On. LC 92-40721. (Illus.). 32p. (ps-3). 1993. pap. 4.99 (*0-14-050726-4*, Puffin) Puffin Bks.
Martin, Bill, Jr. & Archambault, John. Barn Dance! Rand, Ted, illus. LC 86-14225. 32p. (ps-2). 1988. 13.95 (*0-8050-0089-5*, Bks Young Read); pap. 4.95 (*0-8050-0799-7*) H Holt & Co.
Medearis, Angela S. Dancing with the Indians. Byrd, Samuel, illus. LC 90-28666. 32p. (ps-3). 1991. reinforced 14.95 (*0-8234-0893-0*) Holiday.
Moers, Hermann. Annie's Dancing Day. Unzner-Fischer, Christa, illus. Lanning, Rosemary, tr. from GER. LC 92-3612. (Illus.). 32p. (gr. k-3). 1992. 14.95 (*1-55858-160-X*); PLB 14.88 (*1-55858-161-8*) North-South Bks NYC.
Nicklaus, Carol. Come Dance with Me. Nicklaus, Carol, illus. 32p. (ps-1). 1991. PLB 5.95 (*0-671-73503-9*); pap. 2.95 (*0-671-73507-1*) Silver Pr.
Norman, Philip R. Dancing Dogs. LC 93-2533. 1995. 14.95 (*0-316-61208-1*) Little.
Oxenbury, Helen. The Dancing Class. (Illus.). 24p. (ps-1). 1993. pap. 3.99 (*0-14-054934-X*, Puff Pied Piper) Puffin Bks.
Patrick, Denise L. Red Dancing Shoes. Ransome, James E., illus. LC 91-32666. 32p. (ps up). 1993. 14.00 (*0-688-10392-8*, Tambourine Bks); PLB 13.93 (*0-688-10393-6*, Tambourine Bks) Morrow.
Rocklin, Joanne. Musical Chairs & Dancing Bears. De Matharel, Laure, illus. LC 92-41078. 32p. (ps-2). 1993. write for info. (*0-8050-2374-7*, Bks Young Read) H Holt & Co.
Rostkowski, Margaret I. After the Dancing Days. LC 85-45810. 224p. (gr. 5-9). 1988. pap. 3.95 (*0-06-440248-7*, Trophy) HarpC Child Bks.
Rotunno, Rocco & Rotunno, Betsy. Tessa Becomes a Ballerina. Rotunno, Betsy, illus. 12p. (gr. 2-6). 1992. Mixed Media Pkg. incls. stamp pad, stamps, box of 4 crayons. 7.00 (*1-881980-01-4*) Noteworthy.
Ryder, Joanne. Earthdance. 1994. write for info. (*0-8050-2678-9*) H Holt & Co.
Rylant, Cynthia. Waiting to Waltz: A Childhood. Gammell, Stephen, illus. LC 84-11030. 48p. (gr. 6-8). 1984. 12.95 (*0-02-778000-7*, Bradbury Pr) Macmillan Child Grp.
Saller, Carol. The Bridge Dancers. Talifero, Gerald, illus. (gr. 2-4). 1993. pap. 5.95 (*0-87614-579-9*) Carolrhoda Bks.
Schaefer, Jackie. Miranda's Day to Dance. Schaefer, Jackie, illus. LC 94-9372. (ps-k). 1994. 14.95 (*0-02-781111-5*) Macmillan.
Schick, Eleanor. I Have Another Language: The Language Is Dance. Schick, Eleanor, illus. LC 91-9485. 32p. (gr. k-6). 1992. RSBE 13.95 (*0-02-781209-X*, Macmillan Child Bk) Macmillan Child Grp.
Schroeder, Alan. Ragtime Tumpie. Fuchs, Bernie, illus. (gr. k-4). 1989. 15.95 (*0-316-77497-9*, Joy St Bks) Little.
Shannon, George. April Showers. Aruego, Jose & Dewey, Ariane, illus. LC 94-6266. 24p. 1995. write for info. (*0-688-13121-2*); PLB write for info. (*0-688-13122-0*) Greenwillow.
—Dance Away! Aruego, Jose & Dewey, Ariane, illus. LC 81-6391. 32p. (gr. k-3). 1982. 13.95 (*0-688-00838-0*); PLB 13.88 (*0-688-00839-9*) Greenwillow.
Simon, Carly. Amy the Dancing Bear. Datz, Margot, illus. (ps-3). 1989. 15.00 (*0-385-26637-5*) Doubleday.
Slater, Teddy. The Bunny Hop. Difiori, Larry, illus. 32p. 1992. pap. 2.95 (*0-590-45354-8*, Cartwheel) Scholastic Inc.
Spinelli, Eileen. Boy, Can He Dance! Yalowitz, Paul, illus. LC 92-12929. 32p. (ps-2). 1993. RSBE 14.95 (*0-02-786350-6*, Four Winds) Macmillan Child Grp.
Spinelli, Jerry. Do the Funky Pickle. 1992. 2.95 (*0-590-45448-X*, Apple Paperbacks) Scholastic Inc.
Stapler, Sarah. Cordellia, Dance! LC 89-39352. (Illus.). 32p. (ps-3). 1990. 10.95 (*0-8037-0792-4*); PLB 10.89 (*0-8037-0793-2*) Dial Bks Young.
Streatfeild, Noel. Dancing Shoes. 288p. (gr. k-6). 1980. pap. 3.25 (*0-440-42289-2*, YB) Dell.
Streatfield, Noel. Ballet Shoes. Goode, Diane, illus. LC 89-24390. 288p. (gr. 4-9). 1993. pap. 3.99 (*0-679-84759-6*, Bullseye Bks) Random Bks Yng Read.
—Dancing Shoes. 276p. (gr. 4-9). 1994. pap. 3.99 (*0-679-85428-2*) Random Bks Yng Read.
Swann, Brian. Tongue Dancing. Dodge, Katherine, illus. 56p. (gr. 7-12). 1984. 12.95g (*0-937672-12-2*) Rowan Tree.
Thesman, Jean. The Last April Dancers. 224p. (gr. 7 up). 1989. pap. 2.75 (*0-380-70614-8*, Flare) Avon.
Uchida, Yoshiko. The Dancing Kettle. LC 86-70457. 184p. (gr. 5 up). 1986. pap. 7.95 (*0-88739-014-5*) Creative Arts Bk.
Ure, Jean. You Win Some, You Lose Some. LC 85-16134. 182p. (gr. 7 up). 1986. pap. 14.95 (*0-385-29434-4*) Delacorte.
Wallace, Ian. Chin Chiang & the Dragon's Dance. LC 83-13442. (Illus.). 32p. (gr. k-4). 1984. SBE 13.95 (*0-689-50299-0*, M K McElderry) Macmillan Child Grp.
Walsh, Ellen S. Hop Jump. LC 92-21037. 1993. 13.95 (*0-15-292871-5*) HarBrace.
Weyn, Suzanne. Pointing Toward Trouble. Iskowitz, Joel, illus. LC 89-34549. 96p. (gr. 3-5). 1990. pap. text ed. 2.95 (*0-8167-1654-4*) Troll Assocs.

DANDELIONS

Hogan, Paula Z. The Dandelion. LC 78-21155. (Illus.). 32p. (gr. 1-4). 1979. PLB 19.97 (*0-8172-1250-7*); pap. 4.95 (*0-8114-8182-4*); pap. 9.95 incl. cassette (*0-8114-8190-5*) Raintree Steck-V.
—The Dandelion. LC 78-21155. (Illus.). 32p. (gr. 1-4). 1984. PLB 29.28 incl. cassette (*0-8172-2227-8*) Raintree Steck-V.
Long, Olivia. The Dandelion Queen. Long, Olivia, illus. 32p. (ps-4). Date not set. 9.95 (*1-880042-08-8*, SL12461) Shelf-Life Bks.
Pohl, Kathleen. Dandelions. (Illus.). 32p. (gr. 3-7). 1986. pap. text ed. 10.95 (*0-8172-2708-3*) Raintree Steck-V.
Watts, Barrie. Dandelion. (Illus.). 25p. (gr. k-4). 1991. 5.95 (*0-382-09442-5*); PLB 7.95 (*0-382-09438-7*); pap. 3.95 (*0-382-24016-2*) Silver Burdett Pr.

DANIEL, THE PROPHET

Caswell, Helen. Daniel & His Friends. LC 93-25305. 24p. 1993. 11.95 (*0-687-10085-2*) Abingdon.
Crowder, Susan, illus. Daniel in the Lions' Den. 36p. (Orig.). 1984. pap. 3.00 (*0-912927-08-9*, X008) St John Kronstadt.
Daniel. (ps-2). 3.95 (*0-7214-5069-5*) Ladybird Bks.
Eynon, Dana. Daniel. (Illus.). 16p. 1992. 8.99 (*9-5032-0570-0*, 14-02240) Standard Pub.
Jenkins, Lee. Daniel: A Melodrama. Jenkins, Todd, illus. Greeno, Ron, frwd. by. (Illus.). 32p. (Orig.). (ps-3). 1993. pap. 6.95 (*1-883952-02-6*) Hse of Steno.
Morgan, Les. Taming the Lions in Your Life. LC 91-58677. 160p. (Orig.). (gr. 8-12). 1992. pap. 6.99 (*0-87509-479-1*) Chr Pubns.
New International Version of the Bible Staff. Daniel & the Lions. (Orig.). 1986. pap. 4.95 (*0-918789-08-7*) FreeMan Prods.
Pipe, Rhona. Daniel & the Lions' Den. Spencely, Annabel, illus. LC 92-12073. 1993. 7.99 (*0-8407-3422-0*) Nelson.
Simon, Mary M. Daniel & the Tattletales: Daniel 6: Daniel in the Lions' Den. Jones, Dennis, illus. LC 92-31887. 32p. (Orig.). (gr. 1-3). 1993. pap. 3.99 (*0-570-04733-1*) Concordia.
Stirrup Associates, Inc. Staff. My Jesus Pocketbook of Daniel in the Lion's Den. Harvey, Bonnie C. & Phillips, Cheryl M., eds. Fulton, Ginger A., illus. LC 84-50916. 32p. (Orig.). (ps-3). 1984. pap. text ed. 0.69 (*0-937420-12-3*) Stirrup Assoc.

DANTE ALIGHIERI, 1265-1321–ADAPTATIONS

Tusiani, Joseph. Dante's Inferno. Pfeiffer, Werner, illus. (gr. 5 up). 1965. 9.95 (*0-8392-3046-X*) Astor-Honor.
—Dante's Paradiso. Dore, Gustav, illus. (gr. 7 up). 1969. 9.95 (*0-685-00563-1*) Astor-Honor.
—Dante's Purgatorio. (Illus.). (gr. 5 up). 1968. 9.95 (*0-8392-3053-2*) Astor-Honor.

DARK AGES

see Middle Ages

DARROW, CLARENCE SEWARD, 1857-1938

Clarence Darrow: Mini-Play. (gr. 5 up). 1978. 6.50 (*0-89550-312-3*) Stevens & Shea.
Driemen, John E. Clarence Darrow. (Illus.). 112p. (gr. 5 up). 1992. lib. bdg. 17.95 (*0-7910-1624-2*) Chelsea Hse.
Kurland, Gerald. Clarence Darrow: Attorney for the Damned. Rahmas, D. Steve, ed. LC 75-190240. 32p. (Orig.). (gr. 7-12). 1972. lib. bdg. 4.95 incl. catalog cards (*0-87157-522-1*) SamHar Pr.

DARWIN, CHARLES ROBERT, 1809-1882

Aaseng, Nathan. Charles Darwin: Revolutionary Biologist. LC 92-45281. 1993. 21.50 (*0-8225-4914-X*) Lerner Pubns.
Anderson, Margaret J. Charles Darwin: Naturalist. LC 93-29839. (Illus.). 128p. (gr. 4-10). 1994. lib. bdg. 17.95 (*0-89490-476-0*) Enslow Pubs.
Clarke, Brenda. Charles Darwin. (Illus.). 32p. (gr. 3-8). 1988. PLB 10.95 (*0-86307-923-7*) Marshall Cavendish.
Hyndley, Kate. The Voyage of the Beagle. Bull, Peter, illus. LC 88-28695. 32p. (gr. 5-9). 1989. PLB 11.90 (*0-531-18272-X*, Pub. by Bookwright Pr) Watts.
Milner, Richard. Charles Darwin. 128p. (gr. 5 up). 1993. PLB 16.95x (*0-8160-2557-6*) Facts on File.
Nardo, Don. Charles Darwin. (Illus.). 112p. (gr. 5 up). 1993. 18.95 (*0-7910-1729-X*, Am Art Analog); pap. write for info. (*0-7910-1730-3*, Am Art Analog) Chelsea Hse.
Parker, Steve. Charles Darwin & Evolution. Parker, Steve, illus. LC 91-30272. 32p. (gr. 3-7). 1992. 14.00 (*0-06-020733-7*) HarpC Child Bks.
Skelton, Renee. Charles Darwin. LC 87-19564. (Illus.). 144p. (gr. 3-6). 1987. pap. 5.95 (*0-8120-3923-8*) Barron.
Twist, Clint. Darwin: On the Trail of Evolution. LC 93-31789. 1994. PLB 22.80 (*0-8114-7256-6*) Raintree Steck-V.

DARWIN, CHARLES ROBERT, 1809-1882–FICTION

Johnson, Vargie. Charles Darwin, the Adventurer. 1992. 10.00 (*0-533-10092-5*) Vantage.

DARWINISM

see Evolution

DATA PROCESSING

see Information Storage and Retrieval Systems

DATA STORAGE AND RETRIEVAL SYSTEMS

see Information Storage and Retrieval Systems

DATE ETIQUETTE

see Dating (Social Customs)

DATING, RADIOCARBON

see Radiocarbon Dating

DATING (SOCIAL CUSTOMS)

see also Love; Marriage

Cassady, David. Dating Decisions. (Illus.). 48p. (gr. 9-12). 1991. pap. 8.99 (*1-55945-215-3*) Group Pub.
DeSpain, Andrew. The Dating Journal. 66p. (gr. 10 up). 1993. 13.95 (*0-9637911-0-9*) A&D Pub.
Diorio, MaryAnn L. Dating Etiquette for Christian Teens. Crescenzo, Phil, illus. 48p. (Orig.). (gr. 6-12). 1984. pap. 3.95 (*0-930037-00-6*) Daystar Comm.
Eager, George B. Dating: What to Do...What Not to Do. Philbrook, Diana, illus. 29p. (Orig.). (gr. 6-12). 1993. pap. 3.00x (*1-879224-09-7*) Mailbox.
—Love & Dating. rev. ed. Philbrook, Diana, illus. LC 93-80760. 96p. (gr. 6-12). 1994. 12.95 (*1-879224-18-6*); pap. 7.95 (*1-879224-11-9*) Mailbox.
—Love, Dating & Sex: What Teens Want to Know. Philbrook, Diana, illus. 208p. (gr. 7-12). 1989. PLB 14.95 (*0-9603752-9-5*); pap. text ed. 9.95 (*0-9603752-8-7*) Mailbox.
Everything You Need to Know about Dating. (Illus.). 1993. 14.95 (*0-8239-1616-2*) Rosen Group.
Hunt, Gary & Hunt, Angela. Now That He's Asked You Out: Straight Talk for Girls. LC 89-30704. 132p. (Orig.). (gr. 7-12). 1989. pap. 7.99 (*0-89840-258-1*) Nelson.
—Now That You've Asked Her Out: Straight Talk for Guys. LC 89-30703. 132p. (Orig.). (gr. 7-12). 1989. pap. 7.99 (*0-8407-4457-9*) Nelson.

want to marry a girl who does. 4. Tries to boss you. 5. Expects the girl to make the first move. Guys: 1. Girls are stuck-up. 2. Wears too much make-up. 3. She reads more into the relationship than is really there. 4. They gossip. 5. They're expensive. Advice is given by youths & Joy Kerley & ranges from humorous to profound. GUYS VS. GALS gives insight that will help youths understand & relate to the opposite sex with more confidence. Joy & her husband Bud are founders & directors of Teen Round-Up Inc., a 40-acre farm turned into a retreat facility for youths. Order from: Joy Kerley, Route One Box 226A, Duncan, OK 73533. Telephone: 405-255-5207. *Publisher Provided Annotation.*

Landau, Elaine. Interracial Dating. LC 92-44814. (gr. 7 up). 1993. lib. bdg. 13.98 (*0-671-75258-8*, J Messner); lib. bdg. 7.95 (*0-671-75261-8*) S&S Trade.

McAllister, Dawson. How to Know If You're Really in Love. LC 93-40906. 1994. 8.99 (*0-8499-3312-9*) Word Pub.

Nash, Renea D. Coping with Interracial Dating. LC 93-6895. 1994. 14.95 (*0-8239-1606-5*) Rosen Group.

Rue, Nancy N. Coping with Dating Violence. Rosen, Ruth, ed. (gr. 7-12). 1989. PLB 14.95 (*0-8239-0997-2*) Rosen Group.

St. Clair, Barry & Jones, Bill. Dating: Going out in Style. 140p. (Orig.). 1993. pap. 5.99 (*1-56476-189-4*, Victor Books) SP Pubns.

—Love: Making It Last. 140p. (Orig.). 1993. pap. 5.99 (*1-56476-188-6*, Victor Books) SP Pubns.

Schneider, Meg F. Romance! Can You Survive It? A Guide to Sticky Dating Situations. 160p. (Orig.). (gr. 7-12). 1984. pap. 2.25 (*0-440-97478-X*, LFL) Dell.

Scott, Timothy. You Can't Hurry Love: (A Guide to Christian Dating) 10p. (Orig.). (gr. 10-12). 1989. pap. write for info. (*1-877784-05-2*) T Scott Pub.

Sharmat, Marjorie W. How to Meet a Gorgeous Girl. 160p. (Orig.). (gr. k up). 1989. pap. 2.95 (*0-440-93808-2*, LFL) Dell.

Silverstein, Herma. Date Abuse. LC 93-25011. (Illus.). 128p. (gr. 6 up). 1994. lib. bdg. 17.95 (*0-89490-474-4*) Enslow Pubs.

DATING (SOCIAL CUSTOMS)–FICTION

Anderson, Mary. Do You Call That a Dream Date? 176p. (gr. 6 up). 1989. pap. 2.95 (*0-440-20350-3*, LFL) Dell.

Byars, Betsy C. The Cybil War. Owens, Gail, illus. LC 80-26912. 144p. (gr. 8-12). 1981. pap. 12.95 (*0-670-25248-4*) Viking Child Bks.

Cruise, Beth. Going, Going, Gone! LC 94-14475. (gr. 3-7). 1994. pap. 3.95 (*0-689-71852-7*, Aladdin Bks) Macmillan Child Grp.

Dickenson, Celia. Too Many Boys. 160p. (Orig.). (gr. 5-6). 1984. pap. 2.50 (*0-553-26615-2*) Bantam.

Hall, Lynn. Dagmar Schultz & the Angel Edna. LC 88-36862. 96p. (gr. 5-8). 1989. SBE 13.95 (*0-684-19097-4*, Scribners Young Read) Macmillan Child Grp.

Hamilton, Linda J. The Saturday Night Bash. LC 94-6646. 1994. 3.95 (*1-56565-143-X*) Lowell Hse Juvenile.

Hoh, Diane. Last Date. 1994. pap. 3.50 (*0-590-48133-9*) Scholastic Inc.

James, Dean. Three's a Crowd. 1993. pap. 3.99 (*0-06-106205-7*, Harp PBks) HarpC.

Landis, James D. Looks Aren't Everything. (gr. 7 up). 1990. 13.95 (*0-553-05847-9*, Starfire) Bantam.

McFann, Jane. Nothing More, Nothing Less. 176p. (Orig.). (gr. 5). 1993. pap. 3.50 (*0-380-76636-1*, Flare) Avon.

Plante, Edmund. Last Date. 176p. (Orig.). (gr. 5). 1993. pap. 3.50 (*0-380-77154-3*, Flare) Avon.

Quin-Harkin, Janet. The Great Boy Chase. 192p. (gr. 7-12). 1985. pap. 2.50 (*0-553-26743-4*) Bantam.

Santori, Helen. The Perfect Couple. (gr. 5 up). 1988. pap. 2.95 (*0-8041-0238-4*) Ivy Books.

Singleton, Linda J. Opposites Attract. 1991. pap. 2.99 (*0-553-29021-5*) Bantam.

—Spring Break. LC 94-4570. (gr. 7 up). 1994. 3.95 (*1-56565-144-8*) Lowell Hse Juvenile.

Smith, Sinclair. Dream Date. 1993. pap. 3.25 (*0-590-46126-5*) Scholastic Inc.

Stine, R. L. Broken Date. MacDonald, Patricia, ed. 224p. 1991. pap. 3.99 (*0-671-69322-0*, Archway) PB.

Weyn, Suzanne. Boy Trouble. LC 90-11142. 128p. (gr. 4-8). 1991. lib. bdg. 9.89 (*0-8167-2011-8*); pap. text ed. 2.95 (*0-8167-2012-6*) Troll Assocs.

Wyeth, Sharon D. Too Cute for Words. (Orig.). (gr. k-6). 1989. pap. 2.95 (*0-440-40225-5*, YB) Dell.

DAVID, KING OF ISRAEL

Amoss, Berthe. David & Goliath. (Illus.). 10p. (ps-7). 1989. pap. 2.95 (*0-922589-12-7*) More Than Card.

David. (ps-2). 3.95 (*0-7214-5068-7*) Ladybird Bks.

Eisler, Colin, compiled by. David's Songs: His Psalms & Their Story. Pinkney, Jerry, illus. Eisler, Bolin, intro. by. LC 90-25459. (Illus.). 64p. 1992. 17.00 (*0-8037-1058-5*); PLB 16.89 (*0-8037-1059-3*) Dial Bks Young.

Fisher, Leonard E., adapted by. & illus. David & Goliath. LC 92-24063. 32p. (ps-3). 1993. reinforced bdg. 15.95 (*0-8234-0997-X*) Holiday.

Hershey, Katherine. David, Vol. I. Butcher, Sam, illus. 52p. (gr. k-6). 1972. pap. text ed. 9.45 (*1-55976-020-6*) CEF Press.

—David, Vol. II. Butcher, Sam, illus. 55p. (gr. k-6). 1973. pap. text ed. 9.45 (*1-55976-021-4*) CEF Press.

Lashbrook, Marilyn. I May be Little: The Story of David's Growth. Britt, Stephanie M., illus. LC 87-60262. 32p. (ps). 1987. 5.95 (*0-86606-429-X*, 843) Roper Pr.

Metaxas, Eric. David & Goliath. Fraser, Douglas, illus. 40p. (gr. k up). 1993. incl. cass. 19.95 (*0-88708-295-5*, Rabbit Ears); 14.95 (*0-88708-294-7*, Rabbit Ears) Picture Bk Studio.

Mills, Peter. David's Adventure with the Giant: (Bible Flap Book) (Illus.). 24p. 1994. 7.95 (*0-687-10278-2*) Abingdon.

New International Version of the Bible Staff. The Giant & the Boy. (Illus., Orig.). 1986. pap. 4.95 (*0-918789-06-0*) FreeMan Prods.

Robbins, Duffy. It's How You Play the Game. 132p. 1991. pap. 4.99 (*0-89693-856-5*) SP Pubns.

Segal, Lore. The Story of King Saul & King David. LC 90-52544. (Illus.). 144p. 1991. 19.50 (*0-8052-4088-8*) Pantheon.

Tangvald, Christine H. Too Little - Too Big, & Other Bible Stories about Faith. Girouard, Patrick, illus. LC 93-42082. (gr. 2 up). 1994. write for info. (*0-7814-0928-4*, Chariot Bks) Chariot Family.

Taylor, Kenneth N. My First Bible for Tots: David & Goliath. (Illus.). 12p. (ps). 1992. bds. 3.99 (*0-8423-1697-3*) Tyndale.

DAVID, KING OF ISRAEL–FICTION

Bearman, Jane. David. Bearman, Jane, illus. LC 65-21753. (gr. 3 up). 1975. 3.95 (*0-8246-0085-1*) Jonathan David.

Paxton, Lenore & Siadi, Phillip. His Name Was David, Around the World: The Story of David & Goliath. Snavely, Linda W., illus. 32p. (ps-4). Date not set. pap. 7.95 coloring bk.-cassette pkg. (*1-880449-07-2*) Wrldkids Pr.

DAVIS, ANGELA Y., 1944-

Finke, Blythe F. Angela Davis: Traitor or Martyr of the Freedom of Expression? Rahmas, D. Steve, ed. LC 77-190246. 32p. (Orig.). (gr. 7-12). 1972. lib. bdg. 4.95 incl. catalog cards (*0-87157-528-0*) SamHar Pr.

DAVIS, JEFFERSON, 1808-1889

Caldeira, Ernesto. Jefferson Davis Coloring Book. Rice, James, illus. 32p. (Orig.). (gr. 1-6). 1982. pap. 2.95 (*0-88289-256-8*) Pelican.

Kent, Zachary. Jefferson Davis. LC 92-36894. (Illus.). 32p. (gr. 3-6). 1993. PLB 12.30 (*0-516-06664-1*); pap. 3.95 (*0-516-46664-X*) Childrens.

King, Perry. Jefferson Davis. (Illus.). 112p. (gr. 5 up). 1990. 17.95 (*1-55546-806-3*) Chelsea Hse.

Potter, Robert R. Jefferson Davis. LC 92-16914. (Illus.). 128p. (gr. 7-10). 1992. PLB 22.80 (*0-8114-2330-1*) Raintree Steck-V.

Varina Howell Davis: Mrs. Jefferson Davis. 106p. (gr. 3 up). 1994. write for info. (*0-9616894-5-5*) RuSK Inc.

DAYAN, MOSHE, 1915-

Amdur, Richard. Moshe Dayan. Schlesinger, Arthur M., intro. by. (Illus.). 112p. (gr. 5 up). 1989. 17.95 (*1-55546-829-2*) Chelsea Hse.

DAYS

see Birthdays; Fasts and Feasts; Holidays

DEAD SEA SCROLLS

Weir, Christy. The Very Best Book. Woodard, Virginia, ed. Brooks, Nan, illus. LC 92-32744. 35p. (ps-2). 1993. 12.99 (*0-8307-1595-9*, 5112262) Regal.

DEAF

Bergman, Thomas. Finding a Common Language: Children Living with Deafness. LC 88-42969. (Illus.). 48p. (gr. 4-5). 1989. PLB 18.60 (*1-55532-916-0*) Gareth Stevens Inc.

Brearley, Sue. Talk to Me. (Illus.). 26p. (gr. 1-4). 10.95 (*0-7136-3192-9*, Pub. by A&C Black UK) Talman.

Burchard, Elizabeth & Higgens-Nelson, Kelley. Sign Language: In a Flash. Soroka, Cynthia, ed. 400p. (gr. 7-12). 1994. pap. 12.95 (*1-881374-18-1*) Flash Blasters.

Charlip, Remy & Miller, Mary B. Handtalk: An ABC of Finger Spelling & Sign Language. Ancona, George, illus. LC 85-3667. 48p. (ps up). 1984. Repr. of 1974 ed. SBE 15.95 (*0-02-718130-8*, Four Winds) Macmillan Child Grp.

Flodin, Mickey. Signing for Kids: The Fun Way for Anyone to Learn American Sign Language. (Illus.). 144p. (gr. 3-9). 1991. pap. 9.95 (*0-399-51672-7*, Perigee Bks) Berkley Pub.

Greene, Laura & Dicker, Eva B. Discovering Sign Language. LC 88-24609. (Illus.). 104p. (gr. 5-12). 1988. pap. 6.95 (*0-930323-48-3*, Kendall Green Pubns) Gallaudet Univ Pr.

—Sign-Me-Fine: Experiencing American Sign Language. Caraway, Caren, illus. LC 90-5148. 120p. (gr. 7-12). 1989. pap. 6.95 (*0-930323-76-9*, Pub. by K Green Pubns) Gallaudet Univ Pr.

Gustason, Gerilee & Zawolkow, Esther. Signing Exact English. Lopez, Lilian, illus. LC 93-86649. 472p. (gr. k-12). 1993. text ed. 39.95 (*0-916708-22-5*); pap. text ed. 29.95 (*0-916708-23-3*) Modern Signs.

Hillebrand, Linda L. & Riekehof, Lottie L. The Joy of Signing Puzzle Book: Have Fun Learning to Sign. (Illus.). 57p. (Orig.). 1989. pap. 2.95 (*0-88243-676-7*, 02-0676) Gospel Pub.

Hunter, Edith F. Child of the Silent Night. Holmes, Bea, illus. LC 94-26217. 1995. pap. write for info. (*0-688-13794-6*) Morrow.

Keller, Helen A. Story of My Life. LC 54-11951. (Illus.). (gr. 7 up). 1954. 15.95 (*0-385-04453-4*) Doubleday.

LaBarre, Alice, et al. Sexual Abuse! What Is It? An Informational Book for the Hearing Impaired. Nelson, Mary F., illus. LC 92-80161. 80p. (gr. 1-6). 1992. pap. 9.00 (*0-9629302-1-0*) Liberty.

LaMore, Gregory S. Now I Understand. Ensing-Keelan, Jan, illus. LC 85-20639. 52p. (gr. 3-6). 1986. 8.95 (*0-930323-13-0*, Kendall Green Pubns) Gallaudet Univ Pr.

Landau, Elaine. Deafness. (Illus.). 64p. (gr. 5-8). 1994. bds. 15.95 (*0-8050-2993-1*) TFC Bks NY.

MacKinnon, Christy. Silent Observer. (Illus.). 48p. 1993. 15.95 (*1-56368-022-X*, Pub. by K Green Pubns) Gallaudet Univ Pr.

Mango, Karin N. Hearing Loss. Perrotta, Mary, ed. LC 90-19746. (Illus.). 144p. (gr. 7-12). 1991. PLB 13.90 (*0-531-12519-X*) Watts.

Miller, Betty. Sign Language House. 32p. 1984. 4.50 (*0-915035-03-0*, 4162) Dawn Sign.

Miller, Mary Beth & Ancona, George. Handtalk School. LC 90-24030. (Illus.). 32p. (gr. k-6). 1991. RSBE 14.95 (*0-02-700912-2*, Four Winds) Macmillan Child Grp.

Miller, Ralph, Sr. Sign Language Clowns. 32p. 1983. 4.50 (*0-915035-00-6*, 4160) Dawn Sign.

One Two Three Sign with Me. (Illus.). 24p. 1987. pap. 3.95 (*0-939849-01-1*, 104P) Sugar Sign Pr.

Paul, Frank A. Sign Language Feelings. 32p. 1985. 4.50 (*0-915035-05-7*, 4165) Dawn Sign.

—Sign Language Fun. 32p. 1984. 4.50 (*0-915035-02-2*, 4163) Dawn Sign.

—Sign Language Opposites. 32p. 1985. 4.50 (*0-915035-04-9*, 4164) Dawn Sign.

Peterson, Jeanne W. I Have a Sister, My Sister Is Deaf. Ray, Deborah K., illus. LC 76-24306. (gr. k-3). 1977. PLB 13.89 (*0-06-024702-9*) HarpC Child Bks.

St. George, Judith. Dear Dr. Bell - Your Friend, Helen Keller. 172p. (gr. 5-9). 1992. 15.95 (*0-399-22337-1*, Putnam) Putnam Pub Group.

—Dear Dr. Bell...Your Friend, Helen Keller. LC 93-9304. 96p. (gr. 6 up). 1993. pap. text ed. 4.95 (*0-688-12814-9*, Pub. by Beech Tree Bks) Morrow.

Shea, George. The Silent Hero. LC 93-5492. 112p. (Orig.). (gr. 2-5). 1994. PLB 9.99 (*0-679-94361-7*); pap. 2.99 (*0-679-84361-2*) Random Bks Yng Read.

Sign with Me Colors. (Illus.). 24p. 1987. pap. 3.95 (*0-939849-02-X*, 105P) Sugar Sign Pr.

Sign with Me Weather. 24p. 1987. pap. 3.95 (*0-939849-03-8*, 106P) Sugar Sign Pr.

Slier, Debby. A First Book of Sign Language: Animal Signs. 16p. (ps). 1993. 4.95 (*1-56288-385-2*) Checkerboard.

—A First Book of Sign Language: Word Signs. 16p. (ps). 1993. 4.95 (*1-56288-386-0*) Checkerboard.

Star, Robin R. We Can, 2 vols. (gr. 4 up). 1980. Set. PLB 4.95 (*0-685-00153-9*) Vol. 1 88 pgs (*0-88200-135-3*, C2670) Vol. 2 98 pgs (*0-88200-136-1*, C2786) Alexander Graham.

Starowitz, Anne M. The Day We Met Cindy. LC 88-8979. (Illus.). 16p. (gr. k-3). 1988. pap. 9.50 (*0-930323-43-2*, Kendall Green Pubns) Gallaudet Univ Pr.

Walker, Lou A. Amy, the Story of a Deaf Child. Abramson, Michael, illus. LC 84-21152. 64p. (gr. 4-6). 1985. 14.95 (*0-525-67145-5*, Lodestar Bks) Dutton Child Bks.

DEAF–EDUCATION

Bornstein, Harry. All by Myself. (Illus.). 16p. (ps). 1975. pap. 3.50 (*0-913580-43-0*, Pub. by K Green Pubns) Gallaudet Univ Pr.

—Be Careful. (Illus.). 32p. (ps-3). 1976. pap. 5.50 (*0-913580-55-4*, Pub. by K Green Pubns) Gallaudet Univ Pr.

—A Book about Me. (Illus.). 16p. (ps). 1973. pap. 3.50 (*0-913580-19-8*, Pub. by K Green Pubns) Gallaudet Univ Pr.

—Circus Time. (Illus.). 16p. (ps). 1976. pap. 3.50 (*0-913580-51-1*, Pub. by K Green Pubns) Gallaudet Univ Pr.

—The Clock Book. (Illus.). 36p. (ps-2). 1975. pap. 5.95 (*0-913580-48-1*, Pub. by K Green Pubns) Gallaudet Univ Pr.

—Count & Color. (Illus.). 16p. (ps). 1973. pap. 3.50 (*0-913580-20-1*, Pub. by K Green Pubns) Gallaudet Univ Pr.

—The Gingerbread Man. (Illus.). 48p. (ps-2). 1976. pap. 5.95 (*0-913580-52-X*, Pub. by K Green Pubns) Gallaudet Univ Pr.

—I Want to Be a Farmer. LC 72-84675. (Illus.). 48p. (ps-2). 1972. pap. 5.95 (*0-913580-14-7*, Kendall Green Pubs) Gallaudet Univ Pr.

—Jack & the Beanstalk. (Illus.). 64p. (ps-3). 1975. pap. 6.50 (*0-913580-47-3*, Pub. by K Green Pubns) Gallaudet Univ Pr.

—Little Poems for Little People. (Illus.). 56p. (ps-3). 1974. pap. 6.50 (*0-913580-31-7*, Pub. by K Green Pubns) Gallaudet Univ Pr.
—Mouse's Christmas Eve. (Illus.). 44p. (ps-3). 1974. pap. 5.95 (*0-913580-28-7*, Pub. by K Green Pubns) Gallaudet Univ Pr.
—My Animal Book. (Illus.). 16p. (ps). 1973. pap. 3.50 (*0-913580-21-X*, Kendall Green Pubs) Gallaudet Univ Pr.
—My Toy Book. (Illus.). 16p. (ps). 1973. pap. 3.50 (*0-913580-22-8*, Pub. by K Green Pubns) Gallaudet Univ Pr.
—Oliver in the City. (Illus.). 56p. (ps-3). 1975. pap. 6.50 (*0-913580-49-X*) Gallaudet Univ Pr.
—The Pet Shop. (Illus.). 16p. (ps). 1976. pap. 3.50 (*0-913580-54-6*, Pub. by K Green Pubns) Gallaudet Univ Pr.
—Police Officer Jones. (Illus.). 16p. (ps). 1976. pap. 3.50 (*0-913580-53-8*, Pub. by K Green Pubns) Gallaudet Univ Pr.
—Questions & More Questions. (Illus.). 52p. (ps-3). 1973. pap. 6.50 (*0-913580-24-4*, Kendall Green Pubs) Gallaudet Univ Pr.
—Songs in Signed English. (Illus.). 44p. (ps-2). 1973. pap. 9.00 incl. record (*0-913580-12-0*, Pub. by K Green Pubns) Gallaudet Univ Pr.
—Spring Is Green. (Illus.). 52p. (ps-2). 1973. pap. 6.50 (*0-913580-17-1*, Kendall Green Pubs) Gallaudet Univ Pr.
—Three Little Kittens. (Illus.). 32p. (ps-2). 1973. pap. 5.50 (*0-913580-16-3*, Kendall Green Pubs) Gallaudet Univ Pr.
—Three Little Pigs. (Illus.). 44p. (ps-3). 1972. pap. 6.50 (*0-913580-09-0*, Pub. by K Green Pubns) Gallaudet Univ Pr.
—The Ugly Duckling. (Illus.). 48p. (ps-2). 1974. pap. 6.50 (*0-913580-29-5*, Pub. by K Green Pubns) Gallaudet Univ Pr.
—We're Going to the Doctor. (Illus.). 28p. (ps-3). 1985. pap. 5.50 (*0-913580-26-0*, Pub. by K Green Pubns) Gallaudet Univ Pr.
—With My Legs. (Illus.). 16p. (ps). 1975. pap. 3.50 (*0-913580-42-2*, Pub. by K Green Pubns) Gallaudet Univ Pr.
Bornstein, Harry & Saulnier, Karen L. The Signed English Starter. Miller, Ralph R., Sr., illus. LC 84-4042. 232p. (ps-6). 1984. pap. text ed. 13.95 (*0-913580-82-1*, Clerc Bks) Gallaudet Univ Pr.
Collins, S. Harold. Caring for Young Children: Signing for Day Care Providers & Sitters. Kifer, Kathy, illus. 32p. (Orig.). (gr. 1-8). 1993. pap. text ed. 2.95 (*0-931993-58-X*, GP-058) Garlic Pr OR.
Dellinger, Annetta. Ann Elizabeth Signs With Love. (ps-2). 1991. 8.99 (*0-570-04192-9*, 56-1651) Concordia.
Johnson, Sue. At Grandma's House: Story Book for Young Children in Sign Language. Herigstad, Joni, illus. 28p. 1985. pap. 4.50 (*0-916708-14-4*) Modern Signs.
Oberkotter, Mildred, et al, eds. The Possible Dream: Mainstream Experiences of Hearing-Impaired Students. 68p. (Orig.). 1990. pap. text ed. 7.95 (*0-88200-171-X*) Alexander Graham.
Rankin, Laura. The Handmade Alphabet. 1991. 14.00 (*0-8037-0974-9*); PLB 13.89 (*0-8037-0975-7*) Dial Bks Young.
Sullivan, Mary B., et al. A Show of Hands: Say It in Sign Language. Bourke, Linda, illus. LC 84-48782. 96p. (gr. 2-6). 1985. pap. 4.95 (*0-06-446007-X*, Trophy) HarpC Child Bks.
Walker, Lou A. Hand, Heart, & Mind: The Story of the Education of America's Deaf People. LC 92-45631. 1994. 14.95t (*0-8037-1225-1*) Dial Bks Young.

DEAF–FICTION

Abbott, Deborah & Kisor, Henry. One TV Blasting & a Pig Outdoors: A Concept Book. Tucker, Kathy, ed. Morrill, Leslie, illus. LC 94-6649. 40p. (gr. 2-6). 1994. PLB 13.95 (*0-8075-6075-8*) A Whitman.
Andrews, Jean F. Hasta Luego, San Diego. LC 90-27125. 104p. (Orig.). (gr. 3-6). 1991. pap. 4.95 (*0-930323-83-1*, Pub. by K Green Pubns) Gallaudet Univ Pr.
Bridges, Christina. The Hero. Batten, Linda, illus. 29p. (gr. k-6). 1981. pap. text ed. 8.95 (*0-917002-39-3*) Joyce Media.
Charlip, Remy & Miller, Mary B. Handtalk Birthday: A Number & Story Book in Sign Language. Ancona, George, illus. LC 86-22755. 48p. (ps up). 1987. SBE 15.95 (*0-02-718080-8*, Four Winds) Macmillan Child Grp.
Conly, Jane L. Crazy Lady! LC 92-18348. 192p. (gr. 5 up). 1993. 13.00 (*0-06-021357-4*); PLB 12.89 (*0-06-021360-4*) HarpC Child Bks.
Fleming, Leanne, illus. The Quiet World. LC 93-111. 1994. write for info. (*0-383-03671-2*) SRA Schl Grp.
Geller, Norman. Talk to God... I'll Get the Message: Black Version. Tomlinson, Albert J., illus. 23p. (gr. 1-4). 1985. pap. 4.95 (*0-915753-08-1*) N Geller Pub.
—Talk to God... I'll Get the Message: Spanish Version. Galway, Bonnie, tr. from ENG. Tomlinson, Albert J., illus. 23p. (gr. 1-4). 1985. pap. 4.95 (*0-915753-07-3*) N Geller Pub.
Hodges, Candri. When I Grow Up. Yoder, Dot, illus. 32p. (gr. k-4). Date not set. PLB 13.95 (*0-944727-27-1*); pap. 6.95 (*0-944727-26-3*) Jason & Nordic Pubs.
Hoffman Levi, Dorothy. A Very Special Sister. Gold, Ethel, illus. LC 88-33410. 32p. (gr. k-3). 1992. 9.95 (*0-930323-96-3*, Pub. by K Green Pubns) Gallaudet Univ Pr.
Johnston, Catherine D. I Hear the Day. Mark, Joseph, illus. (gr. 2-3). 1977. 9.00 (*0-914562-04-5*); wkbk 3.00 (*0-914562-05-3*) Merriam-Eddy.
Kadish, Sharona. Discovering Friendship. Scribner, Joanne, illus. LC 93-34500. 1994. PLB 19.97 (*0-8114-4458-9*) Raintree Steck-V.
Kroll, Virginia. Fireflies, Peach Pies & Lullabies. Cote, Nancy, illus. LC 94-19373. 1995. 15.95 (*0-02-751001-8*, S&S BFYR) S&S Trade.
Lakin, Patricia. Dad & Me in the Morning. Steele, Robert, illus. LC 93-36169. (ps-3). 1994. 14.95 (*0-8075-1419-5*) A Whitman.
Lee, Jeanne. Silent Lotus. (Illus.). 32p. (gr. k-3). 1991. 14. 95 (*0-374-36911-9*) FS&G.
Levene, Nancy S. Crocodile Meatloaf. LC 92-32615. (ps-6). 1993. pap. 4.99 (*0-7814-0000-7*, Chariot Bks) Chariot Family.
Levi, Dorothy. A Very Special Friend. Gold, Ethel, illus. LC 88-33410. 40p. (gr. k-3). 1989. 9.95 (*0-930323-55-6*, Kendall Green Pubns) Gallaudet Univ Pr.
Levi, Dorothy H. A Very Special Friend. Gold, Ethel, illus. 32p. (gr. k-3). 9.95 (*1-878363-24-7*) Forest Hse.
—A Very Special Sister. Gold, Ethel, illus. 36p. (gr. k-3). 1992. PLB 11.95 (*1-56674-033-9*) Forest Hse.
Levine, Edna S. Lisa & Her Soundless World. Kamen, Gloria, illus. (gr. 1-5). 1984. 14.95 (*0-87705-104-6*); pap. 9.95 (*0-89885-204-8*) Human Sci Pr.
Litchfield, Ada B. A Button in Her Ear. Rubin, Caroline, ed. Mill, Eleanor, illus. LC 75-28390. 32p. (gr. 2-4). 1976. PLB 13.95 (*0-8075-0987-6*) A Whitman.
—Words in Our Hands. Tucker, Kathleen, ed. Cogancherry, Helen, illus. LC 79-28402. (gr. 2-4). 1980. PLB 13.95 (*0-8075-9212-9*) A Whitman.
Miller, Mary B. & Charlip, Remy. Handtalk Birthday: A Number & Story Book in Sign Language. Ancona, George, illus. LC 91-1967. 48p. (ps-3). 1991. pap. 4.95 (*0-689-71531-5*, Aladdin) Macmillan Child Grp.
My Brother Sam Is Dead: L-I-T Guide. (gr. 6-9). 1993. 8.95 (*1-56644-952-9*) Educ Impress.
Okimoto, Jean D. A Place for Grace. Keith, Doug, illus. 32p. (gr. 1 up). 1993. 14.95 (*0-912365-73-0*) Sasquatch Bks.
Scott, Virginia M. Belonging. Crowe, Patricia, illus. LC 85-31135. 176p. (gr. 7-12). 1987. pap. 2.95 (*0-930323-33-5*, Kendall Green Pubns) Gallaudet Univ Pr.
Shreve, Susan. The Gift of the Girl Who Couldn't Hear. LC 91-2247. 80p. (gr. 3 up). 1991. 12.95 (*0-688-10318-9*, Tambourine Bks) Morrow.
—The Gift of the Girl Who Couldn't Hear. LC 92-43763. 80p. (gr. 5 up). 1993. pap. 3.95 (*0-688-11694-9*, Pub. by Beech Tree Bks) Morrow.
Taylor, Morris. Top of the Hill. 64p. 1988. pap. 4.95 (*0-87961-183-9*) Naturegraph.
Wakeman, Cheryl A. Johnnie Ollie Carri III & His Friend. Womack, Fred, illus. 32p. (ps-3). 1985. 5.95 (*0-9614819-0-0*) R E Moen.
Watkins, Dawn L. The Spelling Window. Roberts, John, illus. LC 92-47049. 1993. write for info. (*0-89084-677-4*) Bob Jones Univ Pr.
Yates, Elizabeth. Sound Friendships: The Story of Willa & Her Hearing Dog. Leaman, Christine, ed. Roberts, John, illus. O'Brien, Sheila, frwd. by. (Illus.). 113p. (Orig.). (gr. 7-12). 1992. pap. 4.95 (*0-89084-650-2*) Bob Jones Univ Pr.

DEAN, JEROME HERMAN, 1911-

Kavanagh, Jack. Dizzy Dean. Murray, Jim, intro. by. (Illus.). 64p. (gr. 3 up). 1991. PLB 14.95 (*0-7910-1173-9*) Chelsea Hse.

DEATH

Andresen, Roberta. My Daddy Died: When Someone You Love Dies & You Need to Tell a Child. (Illus.). 50p. (ps-5). 1994. PLB 5.98 (*0-9641718-0-5*) Andresen Ent.
This story describes how to explain death effectively to children. It explains the separation between body & soul/spirit in a way that a child can effectively understand & deal with the process. It gives knowledge of the afterlife, of the funeral rites, & a meaningful way to say goodbye which helps accept the finality of death. A total guide in dealing with death & children that has been proven to work completely. This story uses examples that will prevent most of the fear associated with death & describes a way to express love for the deceased that brings peace & happiness to a child. A must for such a vulnerable time. Order from the publisher: Andresen Enterprises, 57 Richmond St., Raynham, MA 02767; 508-822-1053.
Publisher Provided Annotation.

Bisnignano, Judith. Living with Death - Middle School. 64p. (gr. 5-9). 1991. 7.95 (*0-86653-584-5*, GA1317) Good Apple.
Blackburn, Lynn B. Timothy Duck: The Story of the Death of a Friend. Johnson, Joy, ed. Borum, Shari, illus. 24p. (Orig.). (gr. 1-6). 1989. pap. 3.45 (*1-56123-013-8*) Centering Corp.
Boulden, Jim. Saying Goodbye. 2nd ed. (SPA., Illus., Orig.). (gr. 1-7). 1991. pap. 3.95 (*1-878076-02-7*) Boulden Pub.
Bratman, Fred. Everything You Need to Know When a Parent Dies. (gr. 7-12). 1992. PLB 14.95 (*0-8239-1324-4*) Rosen Group.
Breebaart, Joeri & Breebaart, Piet. When I Die, Will I Get Better? Kushner, Harold, intro. by. LC 93-2713. (Illus.). 32p. (gr. k-4). 1993. 11.95 (*0-87226-375-4*) P Bedrick Bks.
Center for Attitudinal Healing Staff. Another Look at the Rainbow. LC 82-12951. (gr. 1-5). 1983. pap. 8.95 (*0-89087-341-0*) Celestial Arts.
Cera, Mary J. Living with Death - Primary. 64p. (gr. 1-4). 1991. 7.95 (*0-86653-588-8*, GA1316) Good Apple.
Cohn, Janice. I Had a Friend Named Peter: Talking to Children about the Death of a Friend. Owens, Gail, illus. LC 86-31150. 32p. (ps-2). 1987. 13.00 (*0-688-06685-2*); lib. bdg. 13.88 (*0-688-06686-0*, Morrow Jr Bks) Morrow Jr Bks.
Connelly, Maureen. All Babies. Sieff, Janet, ed. Vecchio, Loretta, illus. 16p. (ps-3). 1993. pap. 1.50 (*1-56123-063-4*) Centering Corp.
Corley, Elizabeth A. Tell Me about Death, Tell Me about Funerals. Pecoraro, Philip, intro. by. (Illus.). 36p. (Orig.). (gr. 3-6). 1973. pap. text ed. 2.00 (*0-686-02638-1*) Grammatical Sci.
Crouthamel, Thomas G., Sr. It's OK. 2nd ed. Hasty, Patti, illus. LC 86-27694. 36p. (gr. 6 up). 1990. pap. 6.95 (*0-940701-18-9*) Keystone Pr.
Dockrey, Karen. It's Not Fair! Through Grief to Healing. Nelson, Becky, ed. 22p. (Orig.). (gr. 7-12). 1992. pap. text ed. 1.95 (*1-56309-035-X*, Wrld Changers Res) Womans Mission Union.
Fayerweather Street School Staff. The Kids' Book about Death & Dying. Rofes, Eric E., ed. 119p. (gr. 5 up). 1985. 16.95 (*0-316-75390-4*) Little.
Gravelle, Karen & Haskins, Charles. Teenagers Face to Face with Bereavement. Steltenpohl, Jane, ed. 128p. (gr. 7 up). 1989. lib. bdg. 12.98 (*0-671-65856-5*, J Messner); pap. 5.95 (*0-671-65975-8*) S&S Trade.
Greenlee, Sharon. When Someone Dies. Drath, Bill, illus. 40p. (gr. 1-7). 1992. 13.95 (*1-56145-044-8*) Peachtree Pubs.
Grollman, Earl A. Straight Talk about Death for Teenagers: How to Cope with Losing Someone You Love. LC 92-34540. 144p. 1993. 22.50 (*0-8070-2500-3*); pap. 7.95 (*0-8070-2501-1*) Beacon Pr.
Haasl, Beth & Marrocha, Jean. Bereavement Support Group Program for Children: Participant Workbook. 39p. (Orig.). (ps-8). 1990. 6.95 (*1-55959-012-2*) Accel Devel.
Hammond, Janice M. When My Mommy Died: A Child's View of Death. Hammond, Janice M., illus. 27p. (Orig.). (ps-5). 1980. pap. 6.95 (*0-9604690-0-1*) Cranbrook Pub.
Heegaard, Marge E. When Someone Very Special Dies: Children Can Learn to Cope with Grief. (Illus.). 32p. (gr. 1-6). 1988. wkbk. 4.95 (*0-9620502-0-2*) Woodland Pr.
Hermoso, Elizabeth S. The Chair. Hermoso, Elizabeth S., illus. 15p. (Orig.). (gr. k-2). 1991. pap. 3.00x (*971-10-0442-9*, Pub. by New Day Pub PI) Cellar.
Holden, Sue. My Daddy Died & It's All God's Fault. (Illus.). (gr. 4-7). 1991. 8.99 (*0-8499-0879-5*) Word Inc.
Hyde, Margaret O. & Hyde, Lawrence E. Meeting Death. 129p. (gr. 5 up). 1989. 14.95 (*0-8027-6873-3*); PLB 15.85 (*0-8027-6874-1*) Walker & Co.
Johnson, Joy & Johnson, Marvin. Tell Me, Papa: A Family Book for Children's Questions about Death & Funerals. Borum, Shari, illus. 24p. (Orig.). (gr. 2-7). 1978. pap. 3.35 (*1-56123-011-1*) Centering Corp.
Jordan, MaryKate. The Weather Kids. Johnson, Joy, ed. Enbody, Shari B., illus. 34p. (gr. k-5). 1993. pap. 5.25 (*1-56123-065-0*) Centering Corp.
Juneau, Barbara F. Sad, but O.K. - My Daddy Died Today: A Child's View of Death. LC 88-155937. (Illus.). 112p. (Orig.). (gr. 5 up). 1988. pap. 9.95 (*0-931892-19-8*) B Dolphin Pub.
—Sad, but O.K. - My Daddy Died Today: A Child's View of Death. LC 89-7174. 112p. 1989. Repr. of 1988 ed. lib. bdg. 26.00x (*0-8095-6557-9*) Borgo Pr.
Jussim, Daniel. Euthanasia: The "Right to Die" Issue. LC 92-42147. (Illus.). 112p. (gr. 6 up). 1993. lib. bdg. 17. 95 (*0-89490-429-9*) Enslow Pubs.
Knox, Jean. Death & Dying. Koop, C. Everett, intro. by. (Illus.). 112p. (gr. 6-12). 1989. 18.95 (*0-7910-0037-0*) Chelsea Hse.
Landau, Elaine. The Right to Die. (Illus.). 208p. (gr. 7-12). 1993. PLB 13.40 (*0-531-13015-0*) Watts.
LaVelle, Steven. Just Passing Through. (Illus.). 32p. (Orig.). (gr. k-3). 1980. pap. 4.95 (*0-87516-402-1*) DeVorss.

LeShan, Eda. Learning to Say Good-bye: When a Parent Dies. Giovanopoulous, Paul, illus. LC 76-15155. 96p. (gr. 3 up). 1976. SBE 13.95 (0-02-756360-X, Macmillan Child Bk) Macmillan Child Grp.

Lowden, Stephanie G. Emily's Sadhappy Season. Johnson, Joy, ed. McGee, Deborah, illus. 24p. (gr. 2-6). 1993. pap. 4.95 (0-685-72223-6) Centering Corp.

McGuire, Leslie. Death & Illness. (Illus.). 64p. (gr. 7 up). 1990. lib. bdg. 17.27 (0-86593-079-1); lib. bdg. 12. 95s.p. (0-685-46439-3) Rourke Corp.

Norton, Yuri E. Dear Uncle Dave. Waring, Shirley B., photos by. (Illus.). 40p. (Orig.). (gr. 1 up). 1993. PLB 13.95 (0-9622808-4-4) S&T Waring.

Nystrom, Carolyn. What Happens When We Die? 32p. (ps-2). 1981. pap. 4.99 (0-8024-6154-9) Moody.

Osei, G. K. The African Concept of Life & Death. Obaba, Al I., ed. (Illus.). 49p. (Orig.). 1991. pap. text ed. 3.00 (0-916157-64-4) African Islam Miss Pubns.

Powell, E. Sandy. Geranium Morning: A Book about Grief. (ps-3). 1991. pap. 4.95 (0-87614-542-X) Carolrhoda Bks.

Pringle, Laurence. Death Is Natural. LC 90-46402. (Illus.). 64p. (gr. 1 up). 1991. pap. 5.95 (0-688-10528-9, Pub. by Beech Tree Bks) Morrow.

—Death Is Natural. LC 90-46402. (Illus.). 64p. (gr. 1 up). 1991. Repr. of 1977 ed. PLB 12.88 (0-688-10467-3) Morrow Jr Bks.

Raab, Robert A. Coping with Death. rev. ed. Rosen, Ruth, ed. (gr. 7-12). 1989. PLB 14.95 (0-8239-0960-3) Rosen Group.

Rushton, Lucy. Death Customs. LC 92-42150. (Illus.). 32p. (gr. 4-8). 1993. 13.95 (1-56847-031-2) Thomson Lrning.

Schenkerman, Rona D. Growing up When Someone You Love Has Died. 16p. (gr. 3-8). 1993. 1.95 (1-56688-115-3) Bur For At-Risk.

Schlitt, RaRa S. Robert Nathaniel's Tree. Armstrong, Camilla B., illus. 36p. (gr. k up). 1993. 14.95 (0-9630017-3-6) Light-Bearer.

Schouweiler, Thomas. Life after Death: Opposing Viewpoints. LC 90-39092. (Illus.). 112p. (gr. 5-8). 1990. PLB 14.95 (0-89908-082-0) Greenhaven.

Scrivani, Mark. I Heard Your Mommy Died. Johnson, Joy, ed. Aitken, SUsan, illus. 16p. (ps-3). 1994. pap. 3.50 (1-56123-070-7) Centering Corp.

Sinclair-House, Elizabeth & Muir, Alison. Advanced Years. LC 90-28922. (Illus.). 64p. (gr. 5-9). 1991. PLB 11.95 (0-8114-7807-6) Raintree Steck-V.

Stein, Sara B. About Dying. LC 73-15268. (Illus.). 48p. (ps-8). 1984. pap. 8.95 (0-8027-7223-4) Walker & Co.

—About Dying. LC 73-15268. (Illus.). 48p. (gr. 1 up). 1974. 10.95 (0-8027-6172-0) Walker & Co.

Stewart, Gail. Death. LC 89-31257. (Illus.). 48p. (gr. 5-6). 1989. text ed. 12.95 RSBE (0-89686-446-4, Crestwood Hse) Macmillan Child Grp.

Tanner, Laurie. Two Loves for Selena. Johnson, Joy, ed. Avner, Wendy, illus. 24p. (gr. k-5). 1993. pap. 5.25 (1-56123-061-8) Centering Corp.

Tott-Rizzuti, Kim. Mommy, What Does Dying Mean? (Illus., Orig.). (gr. k-4). 1992. pap. 6.95 (0-8059-3292-5) Dorrance.

Traisman, Enid S. A Child Remembers. Sieff, Janet, ed. 16p. (gr. 3-7). 1994. pap. 5.50 (1-56123-069-3) Centering Corp.

Van Den Berg, Marinus. The Three Birds: A Story for Children about the Loss of a Loved One, 3 vols. Ireland, Sandra, illus. (ps up). 1994. PLB 189.86 Set (0-8368-1096-1) Gareth Stevens Inc.

Vogel, Robin H. The Snowman. Johnson, Joy, ed. Enbody, Shari B., illus. 24p. (gr. 2-6). 1994. pap. 3.50 (1-56123-068-5) Centering Corp.

Wilde, Gary. Dealing with Death. (Illus.). 48p. (gr. 6-8). 1991. pap. 8.99 (1-55945-112-2) Group Pub.

Zagdanski, Doris. How Teenagers Cope with Grief: Something I've Never Felt Before. 100p. (Orig.). (gr. 8-12). 1994. pap. 7.95 (0-85572-199-5, Pub. by Hill Content Pubng AT) Seven Hills Bk Dists.

DEATH–FICTION

Adler, C. S. Daddy's Climbing Tree. 144p. (gr. 4-7). 1993. 13.95 (0-395-63032-0, Clarion Bks) HM.

Anderson, Janet. The Key into Winter. Soman, David, illus. LC 93-13017. 1993. write for info. (0-8075-4170-2) A Whitman.

Angell, Judie. Ronnie & Rosey. 192p. (gr. 6-9). 1979. pap. 2.25 (0-440-97491-7, LFL) Dell.

Balter, Lawrence. A Funeral for Whiskers: Understanding Death. Schanzer, Roz, illus. 40p. (ps-3). 1991. 5.95 (0-8120-6153-5) Barron.

Bauer, Marion D. Shelter from the Wind. LC 75-28184. 112p. (gr. 6 up). 1979. 13.95 (0-395-28890-8, Clarion Bks) HM.

Bierce, Ambrose. An Occurrence at Owl Creek Bridge. Neumeier, Marty, illus. 40p. (gr. 6 up). 1980. PLB 13. 95 (0-87191-770-X) Creative Ed.

Block, Francesca L. The Hanged Man. LC 94-720. 128p. (gr. 7 up). 1994. 14.00 (0-06-024536-0); PLB 13.89 (0-06-024537-9) HarpC Child Bks.

Blume, Judy. Tiger Eyes. LC 81-6152. 256p. (gr. 7 up). 1982. SBE 14.95 (0-02-711080-X, Bradbury Pr) Macmillan Child Grp.

—Tiger Eyes. 224p. (gr. 7 up). 1982. 4.50 (0-440-98469-6, LFL) Dell.

Boyd, Candy D. Forever Friends. 192p. (gr. 5-9). 1986. pap. 4.99 (0-14-032077-6, Puffin) Puffin Bks.

Brown, Margaret W. The Dead Bird. Charlip, Remy, illus. LC 84-43124. 48p. (gr. k-3). 1989. Repr. of 1958 ed. PLB 13.89 (0-06-020758-2) HarpC Child Bks.

Bruchac, Joseph. Fox Song. Morin, Paul, illus. LC 92-24815. 32p. (ps). 1993. 14.95 (0-399-22346-0, Philomel Bks) Putnam Pub Group.

Buffie, Margaret. Someone Else's Ghost. LC 93-48015. (gr. 6 up). 1994. write for info. (0-590-46922-3) Scholastic Inc.

Bunting, Eve. A Sudden Silence. 107p. (gr. 7 up). 1988. 14.95 (0-15-282058-2) HarBrace.

Byars, Betsy C. Good-Bye, Chicken Little. LC 78-19829. 112p. (gr. 5 up). 1979. PLB 13.89 (0-06-020911-9) HarpC Child Bks.

Cadnum, Michael. Calling Home. 192p. (gr. 7 up). 1991. 14.95 (0-670-83566-8) Viking Child Bks.

Calvert, Patricia. Writing to Richie. LC 94-14458. (gr. 4-6). 1994. 14.95 (0-684-19764-2, Scribner) Macmillan.

Cameron, Eleanor. Beyond Silence. LC 80-10350. 208p. (gr. 5-9). 1980. 9.95 (0-525-26463-9, DCB) Dutton Child Bks.

Carlstrom, Nancy W. Blow Me a Kiss, Miss Lilly. Schwartz, Amy, illus. LC 89-34505. 32p. (ps-3). 1990. PLB 13.89 (0-06-021013-3) HarpC Child Bks.

Carrick, Carol. The Accident. Carrick, Donald, illus. LC 76-3532. 32p. (ps-3). 1981. (Clarion Bks); pap. 5.95 (0-89919-041-3) HM.

Carson, Jo. You Hold Me & I'll Hold You. Cannon, Annie, illus. LC 91-16370. 32p. (ps-2). 1992. 14.95 (0-531-05895-6); lib. bdg. 14.99 (0-531-08495-7) Orchard Bks Watts.

Clise, Michele D. Stop the Violence Please. Burns, Marsha, photos by. Salvator, Michael, frwd. by. LC 94-9168. 1994. write for info. (0-295-97367-6) U of Wash Pr.

Coerr, Eleanor. Sadako. Young, Ed, illus. LC 92-41483. 48p. (gr. 1-4). 1993. TLB 16.95 (0-399-21771-1, Putnam) Putnam Pub Group.

Cohen, Miriam. Jim's Dog Muffins. Hoban, Lillian, illus. LC 83-14090. 32p. (gr. k-3). 1984. 13.95 (0-688-02564-1); PLB 13.88 (0-688-02565-X) Greenwillow.

Cohn, Janice. Molly's Rosebush: A Concept Book. Tucker, Kathy, ed. Owens, Gail, illus. LC 93-50612. 32p. (ps-2). 1994. PLB 13.95 (0-8075-5213-5) A Whitman.

Coman, Carolyn. Tell Me Everything. 1993. 15.00 (0-374-37390-6) FS&G.

Conley, Bruce H. Butterflies, Grandpa & Me. (Illus.). 25p. (gr. 4 up). 1976. pap. 2.00 (0-685-65885-6) Conley Outreach.

Conrad, Joseph. The Lagoon. 32p. (gr. 6). 1990. PLB 13. 95 (0-88682-309-9) Creative Ed.

Conrad, Pam. My Daniel. LC 88-19850. 144p. (gr. 5 up). 1991. pap. 3.95 (0-06-440309-2, Trophy) HarpC Child Bks.

Cooney, Caroline B. Driver's Ed. LC 94-445. 1994. 15.95 (0-385-32087-6) Delacorte.

Creech, Sharon. Walk Two Moons. LC 93-31277. 288p. (gr. 3-7). 1994. 16.00 (0-06-023334-6); PLB 15.89 (0-06-023337-0) HarpC Child Bks.

Cullen, Ruth V. My Letter from Grandma. Antonucci, Emil, illus. LC 92-34381. 32p. 1993. pap. 4.95 (0-8091-6610-0) Paulist Pr.

Dabcovich, Lydia. Mrs. Huggins & Her Hen Hannah. Dabcovich, Lydia, illus. LC 85-4406. 24p. (ps-2). 1988. 12.95 (0-525-44203-0, DCB); pap. 3.95 (0-525-44368-1, DCB) Dutton Child Bks.

Deaver, Julie R. You Bet Your Life. LC 92-28211. 224p. (gr. 7 up). 1993. 15.00 (0-06-021516-X); PLB 14.89 (0-06-021517-8) HarpC Child Bks.

Deem, James M. Three NBs of Julian Drew. LC 93-39306. 1994. 14.95 (0-395-69453-1) HM.

Devore, Cynthia D. A Week Past Forever. LC 93-7722. 1993. 14.96 (1-56239-246-8) Abdo & Dghtrs.

Dostoyevsky, Fyodor. The Heavenly Christmas Tree. (gr. 5 up). 1992. PLB 13.95 (0-88682-492-3) Creative Ed.

Dragonwagon, Crescent. Winter Holding Spring. Himler, Ronald, illus. LC 88-13747. 32p. (gr. 2-5). 1990. RSBE 12.95 (0-02-733122-9, Macmillan Child Bk) Macmillan Child Grp.

Draper, Sharon. Tears of a Tiger. LC 94-10278. (gr. 7 up). 1994. 14.95 (0-689-31878-2, Atheneum) Macmillan.

Durant, Penny R. When Heroes Die. LC 93-47355. 1995. pap. 3.95 (0-689-71835-7, Aladdin) Macmillan Child Grp.

Ehrlich, Amy. Maggie & Silky & Joe. Blake, Robert, illus. LC 94-9149. 32p. (ps up). 1994. PLB 14.99 (0-670-83387-8) Viking Child Bks.

Eskridge, Ann E. The Sanctuary. 144p. 1994. 13.99 (0-525-65168-3, Cobblehill Bks) Dutton Child Bks.

Fassler, Joan. My Grandpa Died Today. Kranz, Stewart, illus. LC 71-147126. 32p. (ps-3). 1983. 14.95 (0-87705-053-8); pap. 9.95 (0-89885-174-2) Human Sci Pr.

Field, Shirley. Fire! 128p. (gr. 7-10). 1990. pap. 4.99 (0-7459-1851-4) Lion USA.

Forever Friends. LC 91-12471. 144p. 1991. pap. 4.99 (0-8066-2535-X, 9-2535) Augsburg Fortress.

Forward, Toby. Traveling Backward. Cornell, Laura, illus. LC 93-32514. 1994. write for info. RTE (0-688-13076-3, Tambourine Bks) Morrow.

Fox, Mem. Sophie. Robinson, Aminah B. L., illus. LC 94-1976. (ps-3). 1994. 13.95 (0-15-277160-3) HarBrace.

Gibson, Roxie C. Hey God! What Is Death? LC 90-70219. (Illus.). 50p. (gr. k-5). 1990. 4.95 (1-55523-329-5) Winston-Derek.

Giff, Patricia R. The Gift of the Pirate Queen. Rutherford, Jenny, illus. LC 82-70310. 160p. (gr. 4-6). 1982. 11.95 (0-385-28338-5); PLB 11.95 (0-385-28339-3) Delacorte.

—The Gift of the Pirate Queen. Rutherford, Jenny, illus. LC 82-70310. 160p. (gr. 4-8). 1982. 9.95 (0-440-02970-8); PLB 9.89 (0-440-02972-4) Delacorte.

Godreau, Cecile. Call Me Jonathan for Short. Peterson, Mary J., illus. 64p. (gr. 4-5). 1991. pap. 2.95 (0-8198-1463-6) St Paul Bks.

Grant, Cynthia D. Phoenix Rising: or How to Survive Your Life. 160p. (gr. 7 up). 1991. pap. 3.50 (0-06-447060-1, Trophy) HarpC Child Bks.

Green, Martha G. Grampa's in Heaven. LC 90-71356. (Illus.). 44p. (gr. 3-8). 1991. pap. 5.95 (1-55523-399-6) Winston-Derek.

Greene, Constance C. Beat the Turtle Drum. 128p. (gr. 5-8). 1979. pap. 3.25 (0-440-40875-X, YB) Dell.

Gregory, Valiska. Through the Mickle Woods. (ps-3). 1992. 15.95 (0-316-32779-4) Little.

Griffith, Helen V. Dream Meadow. Barnet, Nancy, illus. LC 93-18175. 24p. (ps up). 1994. 14.00 (0-688-12293-0); PLB 13.93 (0-688-12294-9) Greenwillow.

Guy, Rosa. Mirror of Her Own. LC 80-69448. 192p. (gr. 7 up). 1981. 8.95 (0-385-28636-8) Delacorte.

Halam, Ann. King Death's Garden. large type ed. (gr. 1-8). 1991. 16.95 (0-7451-0657-9, Galaxy Child Lrg Print) Chivers N Amer.

Hamley, Dennis. Hare's Choice. Rutherford, Meg, illus. 96p. (gr. 5 up). 1992. pap. 3.25 (0-440-40698-6, YB) Dell.

Hammond, Janice M. When My Dad Died: A Child's View of Death. Hammond, Janice M., illus. 48p. (Orig.). (gr. k-6). 1981. pap. 6.95 (0-9604690-3-6) Cranbrook Pub.

Hathorn, Libby. Grandma's Shoes. Elivia, illus. LC 93-20776. (ps-3). 1994. 14.95 (0-316-35135-0) Little.

Haynes, Dorothy K. The Gay Goshawk. LC 85-32531. 32p. (gr. 4 up). 1986. PLB 13.95 (0-88682-073-1) Creative Ed.

Heckert, Connie. Dribbles. Sayles, Elizabeth, illus. LC 92-24846. 1993. 14.45 (0-395-62336-7, Clarion Bks) HM.

Heide, Florence P. & Pierce, Roxanne H. Tio Armando. LC 93-37434. (Illus.). (gr. 5 up). 1994. 14.00 (0-688-12107-1); 13.93 (0-688-12108-X) Lothrop.

Hesse, Karen. Phoenix Rising. 1994. 15.95 (0-8050-3108-1) H Holt & Co.

Heymans, Annemie & Heymans, Margriet. The Princess in the Kitchen Garden. (Illus.). 48p. (ps-3). 1993. bds. 16.00 (0-374-36122-3) FS&G.

Hill, David. See Ya, Simon. LC 93-39870. 120p. 1994. 14.99 (0-525-45247-8, DCB) Dutton Child Bks.

Hines, Anna G. Remember the Butterflies. Hines, Anna G., illus. LC 90-3536. 32p. (ps-2). 1991. 12.95 (0-525-44679-6, DCB) Dutton Child Bks.

Hirsch, Karen. Ellen Anders on Her Own. LC 93-13350. 96p. (gr. 3-7). 1994. SBE 13.95 (0-02-743975-5, Macmillan Child Bk) Macmillan Child Grp.

Hollingsworth, Mary. Captain, the Countess & Cobbie the Swabby. LC 92-4714. (ps-3). 1992. pap. 8.99 (0-7814-0967-5, Chariot Bks) Chariot Family.

Hosie, Bounar. Life Belts. LC 92-43048. 1993. 14.95 (0-385-31074-9) Delacorte.

Howard, Ellen. Murphy & Kate. Graham, Mark, illus. LC 93-26002. 1995. 15.00 (0-671-79775-1, S&S BFYR) S&S Trade.

—The Tower Room. LC 92-39240. 160p. (gr. 3-7). 1993. SBE 13.95 (0-689-31856-1, Atheneum Child Bk) Macmillan Child Grp.

Jacobs, Dee. Laura's Gift. Karlsson, Kris, illus. 64p. (Orig.). (gr. 6-12). 1980. PLB 15.95 (0-938628-00-3); pap. 9.95 (0-938628-01-1) Oriel Pr.

Jenkins, Catherine. Monday Came. Thomas, Meredith, illus. LC 93-28982. 1994. 4.25 (0-383-03762-X) SRA Schl Grp.

Kelleher, Victor. Del-Del. (gr. 7-10). 1992. 17.95 (0-8027-8154-3) Walker & Co.

King, Buzz. Silicon Songs. 1990. 14.95 (0-385-30087-5) Doubleday.

Klause, Annette C. The Silver Kiss. (gr. 9 up). 1990. 14. 95 (0-385-30160-X) Delacorte.

—The Silver Kiss. 208p. (gr. 7 up). 1992. pap. 3.99 (0-440-21346-0, LFL) Dell.

Kroll, Virginia L. Helen the Fish. Mathews, Judith, ed. Weidner, Teri, illus. LC 91-17230. 32p. (gr. k-3). 1992. PLB 13.95 (0-8075-3194-4) A Whitman.

Lanton, Sandy. Daddy's Chair. Haas, Shelly O., illus. LC 90-44908. 32p. (gr. k-4). 1991. 12.95 (0-929371-51-8) Kar Ben.

Lehne, Judith L. When the Ragman Sings. LC 93-20346. 128p. (gr. 3-7). 1993. 14.00 (0-06-023316-8); PLB 13. 89 (0-06-023317-6) HarpC Child Bks.

L'Engle, Madeleine. A Ring of Endless Light. 336p. (gr. 9 up). 1981. pap. 4.50 (0-440-97232-9, LE) Dell.

Levine, Jennifer. Forever in My Heart: A Story to Help Children Participate in Life As a Parent Dies. Maurer, Jason F., illus. LC 92-50678. 32p. (Orig.). (gr. 1-6). 1992. pap. 6.95 (1-878321-08-0) Rainbow NC.

Limb, Sue. Come Back, Grandma. Munoz, Claudio, illus. LC 92-43534. 32p. (ps-2). 1994. 13.00 (0-679-84720-0) Knopf Bks Yng Read.

Little, Jean. Mama's Going to Buy You a Mockingbird. 208p. (gr. 5-9). 1986. pap. 3.95 (0-14-031737-6, Puffin) Puffin Bks.

Lobel, Arnold. Frog & Toad Are Friends: (Sapo y Sepo Son Amigos) (SPA.). (gr. 1-6). 9.95 (84-204-3043-9) Santillana.

London, Jonathan. Liplap & the Snowbunny. Long, Sylvia, illus. LC 93-31007. 1994. 13.95 (*0-8118-0505-0*) Chronicle Bks.
Lowry, Lois. A Summer to Die. Oliver, Jenni, illus. (gr. 3-7). 1977. 13.45 (*0-395-25338-1*) HM.
McDaniel, Lurlene. Please Don't Die. (gr. 10 up). 1993. pap. 3.50 (*0-553-56262-2*) Bantam.
—She Died Too Young. 1994. pap. 3.50 (*0-553-56263-0*) Bantam.
—Sixteen & Dying. 1992. pap. 3.50 (*0-553-29932-8*) Bantam.
McFarlane, Sheryl. Waiting for the Whales. Lightburn, Ron, illus. LC 92-25117. 32p. (ps-3). 1993. PLB 14.95 (*0-399-22515-3*, Philomel Bks) Putnam Pub Group.
Madler, Trudy. Why Did Grandma Die? Lewis, Gloria, intro. by. LC 79-23892. (Illus.). 32p. (gr. k-6). 1980. PLB 19.97 (*0-8172-1354-6*) Raintree Steck-V.
—Why Did Grandma Die? (ps-3). 1993. pap. 3.95 (*0-8114-7156-X*) Raintree Steck-V.
Manber, David. Zachary of the Wings. 88p. (gr. 9-12). 1993. PLB 10.95 (*1-879567-27-X*) Wonder Well.
Mansfield, Katherine. The Garden Party. (gr. 4-12). 1989. 13.95 (*0-88682-342-0*, 97216-098) Creative Ed.
Marquez, Gabriel G. The Handsomest Drowned Man in the World: A Tale for Children. Rabazza, Gregory, tr. LC 92-44055. 1994. 13.95 (*0-88682-587-3*) Creative Ed.
Maugham, W. Somerset. Appointment. Benjamin, Alan, adapted by. Essley, Roger, illus. LC 92-391. (ps-3). 1993. 16.00 (*0-671-75887-X*, Green Tiger) S&S Trade.
Maynard, Frankie. A Tree! for Me! LC 86-51132. (Illus.). 68p. 15.00 (*0-912783-07-9*) Upton Sons.
Mazer, Norma F. After the Rain. LC 86-33270. 304p. (gr. 7 up). 1987. 12.95 (*0-688-06867-7*) Morrow Jr Bks.
—After the Rain. large type ed. 408p. (gr. 7 up). 1989. 14.95 (*0-8161-4807-4*, Large Print Bks) Hall.
Miles, Betty. The Trouble with Thirteen. LC 78-31678. (gr. 4-7). 1979. PLB 12.99 (*0-394-93930-1*) Knopf Bks Yng Read.
Mills, Joyce C. Gentle Willow: A Story for Children about Dying. Chesworth, Michael, illus. LC 93-22770. 32p. (ps-3). 1993. 16.95 (*0-945354-54-1*); pap. 8.95 (*0-945354-53-3*) Magination Pr.
—Gentle Willow: A Story For Children about Dying. Chesworth, Michael, illus. LC 93-38212. (gr. 2 up). 1994. 17.27 (*0-8368-1070-8*) Gareth Stevens Inc.
Moulton, Deborah. Summer Girl. LC 91-15790. 128p. (gr. 5-9). 1992. 15.00 (*0-8037-1153-0*) Dial Bks Young.
Murphy, Claire R. Gold Star Sister. LC 94-48135. 224p. (gr. 5-9). 1994. 14.99 (*0-525-67492-6*, Lodestar Bks) Dutton Child Bks.
Naughton, Jim. My Brother Stealing Second. LC 88-22035. 288p. (gr. 7 up). 1991. pap. 3.95 (*0-06-447017-2*, Trophy) HarpC Child Bks.
Nesbit, Jeffrey A. All the King's Horses. 192p. (Orig.). (gr. 9-12). 1990. pap. 6.99 (*0-87788-040-9*) Shaw Pubs.
Newman, Leslea. Too Far Away to Touch, Close Enough to See. Stock, Catherine, illus. LC 93-30327. 1995. write for info. (*0-395-68968-6*, Clarion Bks) HM.
Nodar, Carmen M. Abuelita's Paradise. Mathews, Judith, ed. Paterson, Diane, illus. LC 91-42330. 32p. (gr. k-3). 1992. 13.95g (*0-8075-0129-8*) A Whitman.
—El Paraiso de Abuelita. Mathews, Judith, ed. Mlawer, Teresa, tr. Paterson, Diane, illus. LC 92-3767. (SPA.). 32p. (gr. k-3). 1992. 13.95g (*0-8075-6346-3*) A Whitman.
Nystrom, Carolyn. Emma Says Goodbye. (Illus.). 48p. (gr. 4-8). 1990. 7.99 (*0-7459-1826-3*) Lion USA.
O. Henry. The Last Leaf. (Illus.). 32p. (gr. 6 up). 1980. PLB 13.95 (*0-87191-774-2*) Creative Ed.
O'Toole, Donna. Aarvy Aardvark Finds Hope: A Read-Aloud Story for People of All Ages. McWhirter, Mary Lou, illus. 80p. (Orig.). (ps up). 1989. pap. 9.95 (*1-878321-25-0*, Mntn Rainbow); tchr's. guide 6.95 (*1-878321-26-9*, Mntn Rainbow); audio tape 9.95 (*0-685-20985-7*, Mntn Rainbow) Rainbow NC.
Paterson, Katherine. Bridge to Terabithia. Diamond, Donna, illus. LC 77-2221. (gr. 5 up). 1977. 14.00 (*0-690-01359-0*, Crowell Jr Bks) HarpC Child Bks.
—Bridge to Terabithia. large type ed. Diamond, Donna, illus. 155p. (gr. 2-6). 1987. Repr. of 1977 ed. lib. bdg. 14.95 (*1-55736-010-3*, Crnrstn Bks) BDD LT Grp.
—Bridge to Terabithia: (Puente Hasta Terabithia) (SPA.). (gr. 1-6). 8.95 (*84-204-3633-X*) Santillana.
—Flip-Flop Girl. 128p. (gr. 3-7). 1994. 13.99 (*0-525-67480-2*, Lodestar Bks) Dutton Child Bks.
Paulsen, Gary. A Christmas Sonata. Bowman, Leslie W., illus. LC 90-46891. 80p. (gr. 3-7). 1992. 14.95 (*0-385-30441-2*) Delacorte.
Peyton, K. M. A Midsummer's Night Death. 192p. (gr. 7 up). 1982. pap. 1.75 (*0-440-95615-3*, LE) Dell.
Pfeffer, Susan B. About David: A Novel. LC 80-65837. 176p. (gr. 7 up). 1980. 11.95 (*0-385-28013-0*) Delacorte.
Plemons, Marti. Erin & the Special Promise. (Illus.). 128p. (gr. 3-6). 1992. pap. 4.99 (*0-87403-935-5*, 24-03765) Standard Pub.
Polikoff, Barbara. Life's a Funny Proposition, Horatio. LC 91-28010. 144p. (gr. 4-7). 1992. 13.95 (*0-8050-1972-3*, Bks Young Read) H Holt & Co.
Porte, Barbara A. Something Terrible Happened: A Novel. LC 94-6923. 224p. (gr. 6-9). 1994. 16.95 (*0-531-06869-2*); PLB 16.99 (*0-531-08719-0*) Orchard Bks Watts.
Quinlan, Patricia. Tiger Flowers. Wilson, Janet, illus. LC 93-15214. Date not set. write for info. (*0-8037-1407-6*); PLB write for info. (*0-8037-1408-4*) Dial Bks Young.
Rose, Kent & Rose, Alice. Cemetery Quilt. Kaloustian, Rosemary, illus. LC 94-17617. Date not set. write for info. (*0-395-70948-2*) HM.
Rosen, Michael J. Bonesy & Isabel. Ransome, James E., illus. LC 93-7892. 1995. write for info. (*0-15-209813-5*) HarBrace.
Ruckman, Ivy. Who Invited the Undertaker? LC 89-1865. 192p. (gr. 3-7). 1991. pap. 3.95 (*0-06-440352-1*, Trophy) HarpC Child Bks.
Sanford, Doris. It Must Hurt a Lot: A Child's Book about Death. Evans, Graci, illus. LC 86-25009. 24p. (gr. k-6). 1985. 7.99 (*0-88070-131-5*, Gold & Honey) Questar Pubs.
Shott, James. The House Across the Street. LC 87-51498. 30p. (gr. 2-4). 1988. 6.95 (*1-55523-129-2*) Winston-Derek.
Slattery, Kathryn. Grandma, I'll Miss You: A Child's Story about Death & New Life. LC 92-18984. 1993. 14.99 (*0-7814-0937-3*, Chariot Bks) Chariot Family.
Smith, Barbara A. Somewhere Just Beyond. LC 93-14672. 96p. (gr. 3-7). 1993. SBE 12.95 (*0-689-31877-4*, Atheneum Child Bk) Macmillan Child Grp.
Smith, Jane D. Mary by Myself. LC 93-47457. 128p. (gr. 3 up). 1994. 14.00 (*0-06-024517-4*); PLB 13.89 (*0-06-024518-2*) HarpC Child Bks.
Smith, Sinclair. Let Me Tell You How I Died. 1994. pap. 3.50 (*0-590-47786-2*) Scholastic Inc.
Springer, Nancy. The Friendship Song. LC 91-9483. 144p. (gr. 4 up). 1992. SBE 13.95 (*0-689-31727-1*, Atheneum Child Bk) Macmillan Child Grp.
—Toughing It. LC 93-42231. (gr. 7 up). 1994. 10.95 (*0-15-200008-9*); pap. 4.95 (*0-15-200011-9*) Harbrace.
Steel, Danielle. Max & Grandma & Grandpa Winky. (ps-3). 1991. 9.95 (*0-385-30165-0*) Delacorte.
Talbert, Marc. Dead Birds Singing. LC 85-147. 224p. (gr. 6 up). 1985. 13.95 (*0-316-83125-5*) Little.
Temes, Roberta. The Empty Place: A Child's Guide Through Grief. Carlisle, Kim, illus. LC 92-60613. 48p. (Orig.). (gr. k-5). 1992. pap. 6.95 (*0-88282-118-0*) New Horizon NJ.
Thesman, Jean. Nothing Grows Here. LC 93-45739. 208p. (gr. 4 up). 1994. 14.00 (*0-06-024457-7*); PLB 13.89 (*0-06-024458-5*) HarpC Child Bks.
Thompson, Colin. Looking for Atlantis. LC 93-24068. 1994. 16.00 (*0-679-85648-X*) Knopf Bks Yng Read.
Tolstoy, Leo. The Death of Ivan Ilych. 112p. (gr. 6). 1990. PLB 13.95 (*0-88682-298-X*) Creative Ed.
Updike, David. The Sounds of Summer. Parker, Robert A., illus. 40p. (gr. 2-5). 1993. 14.95 (*0-945912-20-X*) Pippin Pr.
Van den Berg, Marinus. The Three Birds: A Story for Children about the Loss of a Loved One. Ireland, Sandra, illus. LC 93-38211. 32p. (ps up). 1994. PLB 17.27 (*0-8368-1072-4*) Gareth Stevens Inc.
Velthuijs, Max. Frog & the Birdsong. (ps-3). 1991. bds. 13.95 jacketed (*0-374-32467-0*) FS&G.
Vigna, Judith. Saying Goodbye to Daddy. Levine, Abby, ed. Vigna, Judith, illus. LC 90-12757. 32p. (gr. k-2). 1991. 13.95 (*0-8075-7253-5*) A Whitman.
Viorst, Judith. The Tenth Good Thing about Barney. Blegvad, Eric, illus. LC 71-154764. 32p. (gr. k-4). 1971. SBE 13.95 (*0-689-20688-7*, Atheneum Child Bk) Macmillan Child Grp.
Warburg, Sandol S. Growing Time. Weisgard, Leonard, illus. LC 69-14729. (gr. k-3). 1975. 13.95 (*0-395-16966-6*) HM.
Weaver, Will. Striking Out. LC 93-565. 288p. (gr. 5 up). 1993. 15.00 (*0-06-023346-X*); PLB 14.89 (*0-06-023347-8*) HarpC Child Bks.
Westall, Robert. The Promise. 208p. (gr. 5 up). 1991. 13.95 (*0-590-43760-7*, Scholastic Hardcover) Scholastic Inc.
—Urn Burial. LC 87-23816. 160p. (gr. 7 up). 1988. 11.95 (*0-688-07595-9*) Greenwillow.
Whelan, Gloria. Time to Keep Silent. (gr. 4-7). 1993. pap. 5.99 (*0-8028-0118-8*) Eerdmans.
Wild, Margaret. Toby. Young, Noela, illus. LC 93-14394. 32p. (ps-3). 1994. reinforced bdg. 13.95 (*0-395-67024-1*) Ticknor & Flds Bks Yng Read.
Williams, Carol L. Kelly & Me. LC 92-20492. 1993. 13.95 (*0-385-30897-3*) Delacorte.
Willner-Pardo, Gina. Hunting Grandma's Treasures. Krudop, Walter L., illus. LC 94-13191. (gr. 4 up). 1994. pap. write for info. (*0-395-68190-1*, Clarion Bks) HM.
Windsor, Patricia. The Summer Before. 176p. (gr. 7 up). 1974. pap. 1.95 (*0-440-98382-7*, LFL) Dell.
Woodruff, Elvira. The Secret Funeral of Slim Jim the Snake. LC 92-54419. 144p. (gr. 3-7). 1993. 13.95 (*0-8234-1014-5*) Holiday.
Wright, Betty R. The Cat Next Door. Owens, Gail, illus. LC 90-29080. 32p. (ps-3). 1991. reinforced 14.95 (*0-8234-0896-5*) Holiday.
Wurmfeld, Hope H. Baby Blues. LC 92-5828. 80p. (gr. 7 up). 1992. 14.00 (*0-670-84151-X*) Viking Child Bks.
Yates, Elizabeth. Hue & Cry. 182p. (gr. 7-12). 1991. pap. 4.95 (*0-89084-536-0*) Bob Jones Univ Pr.
Young, Alida E. Is My Sister Dying? 144p. (Orig.). (gr. 5-8). 1991. pap. 2.99 (*0-87406-541-0*) Willowisp Pr.
Zalben, Jane B. The Fortuneteller in 5B. (Illus.). 144p. (gr. 4-7). 1991. 14.95 (*0-8050-1537-X*, Bks Young Read) H Holt & Co.
Zemach, Margot. Jake & Honeybunch Go to Heaven. LC 82-71752. (Illus.). 40p. (gr. 3 up). 1982. 16.00 (*0-374-33652-0*) FS&G.
Zindel, Paul & Zindel, Bonnie. A Star for the Latecomer. 160p. (gr. 6 up). 1985. pap. 2.50 (*0-553-25578-9*) Bantam.
Zolotow, Charlotte. The Old Dog. rev. ed. Ransome, James, illus. LC 93-41081. 1995. 15.00 (*0-06-024409-7*); PLB 14.89 (*0-06-024412-7*) HarpC.

DEATH PENALTY
see Capital Punishment

DEATH VALLEY, CALIFORNIA
Salts, Bobbi. Death Valley Discovery! Parker, Steve, illus. 32p. (Orig.). (gr. k-6). 1991. pap. 3.95 (*1-878900-19-6*) DVNH Assn.

DEBATES AND DEBATING
see also Parliamentary Practice
Comber, Geoffrey, et al, eds. Touchstones, Vol. 1: Texts for Discussion. 201p. (Orig.). (gr. 9-12). 1985. pap. text ed. 11.00 (*1-878461-01-X*) CZM Pr.
Dunbar, Robert E. How to Debate. 2nd ed. LC 93-11959. 1994. 13.40 (*0-531-11122-9*) Watts.
Hensley, Dana & Prentice, Diana. Mastering Competitive Debate. 4th ed. (gr. 10-12). 1994. text ed. 30.00 (*0-931054-32-X*); pap. text ed. 20.00 (*0-931054-35-4*); tchr's. manual 8.00 (*0-931054-33-8*) Clark Pub.
Littlefield, Kathy M. & Littlefield, Robert S. Let's Debate! Stark, Steve, illus. 36p. (Orig.). (gr. 3-6). 1989. pap. text ed. 8.95 (*1-879340-03-8*, K0104) Kidspeak.
This Is My Opinion About. 32p. (gr. 5 up). 1994. 4.95 (*0-685-71580-9*, 516) W Gladden Found.
Ziegelmueller, George, et al. Advancing in Debate: Skills & Concepts. (gr. 10-12). 1994. 28.00 (*0-931054-37-0*); pap. 20.00 (*0-931054-36-2*); tchr's. manual 8.00 (*0-931054-38-9*) Clark Pub.

DEBUSSY, CLAUDE
Thompson, Wendy. Claude Debussy. (Illus.). 48p. (gr. 5 up). 1993. 17.99 (*0-670-84482-9*) Viking Child Bks.

DECALOGUE
see Ten Commandments

DECISION MAKING
Iozzi, Louis A. Space Encounters. rev. ed. (gr. 6-9). 1991. tchr's. ed. 45.00 (*0-944584-30-6*) Sopris.
Smith, Sandra L. Coping with Decision Making. rev. ed. Rosen, Ruth, ed. (gr. 7 up). 1993. PLB 14.95 (*0-8239-1000-8*) Rosen Group.
Swanson, Steve. Is There Life after High School? Making Decisions about Your Future. LC 90-15499. 112p. (Orig.). (gr. 9 up). 1991. pap. 5.99 (*0-8066-2500-7*, 9-2500, Augsburg) Augsburg Fortress.

DECLARATION OF INDEPENDENCE
see U. S. Declaration of Independence

DECORATION, INTERIOR
see Interior Decoration

DECORATION AND ORNAMENT
see also Art, Decorative; Design; Enamel and Enameling; Flower Arrangement; Furniture; Gems; Illustration of Books; Interior Decoration; Jewelry; Leather Work; Lettering; Metalwork; Mosaics; Pottery; Sculpture; Wood Carving
Perret, Annick. Painting on Porcelain: Traditional & Contemporary Design. (Illus.). 96p. (Orig.). 1994. pap. 22.50 (*0-85532-766-9*, Pub. by Search Pr UK) A Schwartz & Co.
Stine, Megan. Tattoo Mania: The Newest Craze in Wearable Art. (gr. 1-3). 1993. pap. 5.99 (*0-553-48144-4*) Bantam.
Tea, Vic-Kayla & Shine, E. P. The Most Unusual Ornament in the World. Abell, ed. & illus. 50p. (Orig.). (gr. 1-3). 1994. 23.00 (*0-685-71029-7*); pap. 15.00 (*1-56611-086-6*) Jonas.

DECORATION ART
see Art, Decorative

DECORATIONS OF HONOR
see also Heraldry
Sherrard, Raymond & Stumpf, George. Badges of the United States Marshals. Esquivel, Jim & Leaf, Richard, illus. LC 89-61859. (Orig.). 1991. 35.45 (*0-914503-02-2*); pap. 22.45 (*0-914503-03-0*) RHS Ent.

DECORATIVE ARTS
see Art, Decorative; Art Industries and Trade; Arts and Crafts; Decoration and Ornament; Interior Decoration

DECOUPAGE
Boutan, Mila. Decoupage. (Illus.). (ps-1). 1992. 4.50 (*1-56021-194-6*) W J Fantasy.

DEDUCTION LOGIC
see Logic

DEEP-SEA DIVING
see Skin Diving

DEEP SEA TECHNOLOGY
see Oceanography

DEER
see also Reindeer
Ahlstrom, Mark E. The Mule Deer. LC 87-614. (Illus.). 48p. (gr. 5). 1987. text ed. 12.95 RSBE (*0-89686-324-7*, Crestwood Hse) Macmillan Child Grp.
Bailey, Jill. Discovering Deer. LC 87-73167. (Illus.). 48p. (gr. 1-6). 1988. PLB 12.40 (*0-531-18196-0*, Pub. by Bookwright Pr) Watts.
Bare, Colleen S. Never Grab a Deer by the Ear. Bare, Colleen S., photos by. LC 92-7702. (Illus.). 32p. (gr. 1-4). 1993. 13.00 (*0-525-65112-8*, Cobblehill Bks) Dutton Child Bks.

Butterworth, Christine & Bailey, Donna. Deer. LC 90-9960. (Illus.). 32p. (gr. 1-4). 1990. PLB 18.99 (*0-8114-2638-6*) Raintree Steck-V.

Chavez, Juana. Mother Deer & Her Spotted Fawns. Aragon, Hilda, illus. 14p. (Orig.). (ps-7). 1981. pap. 3.75 (*0-915347-10-5*) Pueblo Acoma Pr.

Gamlin, Linda. The Deer in the Forest. Oxford Scientific Film Staff, illus. LC 87-9916. 32p. (gr. 4-6). 1987. PLB 17.27 (*1-55532-273-5*) Gareth Stevens Inc.

George, Jean C. The Moon of the Deer. Catalano, Sal, illus. LC 91-14607. 48p. (gr. 3-7). 1992. 15.00 (*0-06-020261-0*); PLB 14.89 (*0-06-020262-9*) HarpC Child Bks.

Kalbacken, Joan. White-Tailed Deer. LC 91-35277. (Illus.). 48p. (gr. k-4). 1992. PLB 12.85 (*0-516-01138-3*); pap. 4.95 (*0-516-41138-1*) Childrens.

Long, Evelyn. Grandma Tellmie About...Big Deer, Little Deer...Reindeer. Plott, Dave & Longmeyer, Carole M., eds. 46p. 1985. pap. 3.00 (*0-931881-01-3*) Collaborare Pub.

Patent, Dorothy H. Deer & Elk. Munoz, William, illus. LC 93-25894. 1994. 15.95 (*0-395-52003-7*, Clarion Bks) HM.

Ryden, Hope. The Little Deer of the Florida Keys. rev. ed. (Illus.). 64p. (Orig.). (gr. 5 up). 1986. 13.95 (*0-912451-13-0*); pap. 8.95 (*0-912451-14-9*) Florida Classics.

Saintsing, David. The World of Deer. Oxford Scientific Films Staff, illus. LC 87-6539. 32p. (gr. 2-3). 1987. PLB 17.27 (*1-55532-302-2*) Gareth Stevens Inc.

Simon, Serge & Simon, Dominique. The Deer. (Illus.). 28p. (ps-4). 1993. pap. 6.95 (*0-88106-429-7*) Charlesbridge Pub.

Stone, L. Venados (Deer) 1991. 8.95s.p. (*0-86592-831-2*) Rourke Enter.

Stone, Lynn. Deer. (Illus.). 24p. (gr. k-5). 1990. lib. bdg. 11.94 (*0-86593-043-0*); lib. bdg. 8.95s.p. (*0-685-36339-2*) Rourke Corp.

Wolpert, Tom. Whitetail Magic for Kids. Cox, Daniel S., illus. LC 90-50719. 48p. (gr. 2-3). 1991. PLB 18.60 (*0-8368-0661-1*) Gareth Stevens Inc.

DEER–FICTION

Arnosky, Jim. Long Spikes. Arnosky, Jim, illus. 96p. (gr. 3-7). 1992. 12.70 (*0-395-58830-8*, Clarion Bks) HM.

Bambi. (FRE.). (gr. 3-8). 13.95 (*0-7859-0613-4*, S26622) Fr & Eur.

Bambi. (Illus.). 24p. (ps-2). 1991. write for info. (*0-307-74017-X*, Golden Pr) Western Pub.

Boyle, Doe & Thomas, Peter, eds. Caribou Country: From an Original Article Which Appeared in Ranger Rick Magazine, Copyright National Wildlife Federation. Langford, Alton, illus. Luther, Sallie, contrib. by. LC 92-7732. (Illus.). 20p. (gr. k-3). 1992. 6.95 (*0-924483-53-9*); incl. audiocass. tape & 13" toy 35.95 (*0-924483-50-4*); incl. 9" toy 21.95 (*0-924483-51-2*); incl. audiocass. tape 9.95 (*0-924483-52-0*); write for info. audiocass. tape (*0-924483-80-6*) Soundprints.

Burgess, Thornton W. Adventures of Lightfoot the Deer. 19.95 (*0-8488-0393-0*) Amereon Ltd.

Carrick, Donald. Harald & the Great Stag. Carrick, Donald, illus. LC 87-17875. 32p. (gr. k-4). 1988. 14.95 (*0-89919-514-8*, Clarion Bks) HM.

Crozat, Francois. I Am a Little Deer. (Illus.). 28p. (ps-k). 1994. large size 8.95 (*0-8120-6418-6*); miniature size 3.50 (*0-8120-6419-4*) Barron.

Forest, Heather, retold by. The Baker's Dozen: A Colonial American Tale. Gaber, Susan, illus. 28p. (ps-3). 1988. 14.95 (*0-15-200412-2*, Gulliver Bks) HarBrace.

Harbin, Carey E. Bucky Leaves Home. (Illus.). 26p. (Orig.). (ps-1). 1991. pap. 2.95 (*0-918995-02-7*) Voc-Offers.

Holmes, Efner T. Deer in the Hollow. DeChristoper, Marlowe, illus. 32p. (ps-3). 1993. 15.95 (*0-399-21735-5*, Philomel) Putnam Pub Group.

McGee, Charmayne. So Sings the Blue Deer. LC 93-26580. 160p. (gr. 3-7). 1994. SBE 14.95 (*0-689-31888-X*, Atheneum Child Bk) Macmillan Child Grp.

Marvin, Fred, illus. Walt Disney's Bambi: The New Prince. LC 93-71377. 10p. (ps-k). 1994. 4.95 (*1-56282-601-8*) Disney Pr.

Mayfield, Helen, illus. The Enchanted Deer. 77p. (Orig.). (gr. 6 up). Date not set. pap. 4.00 (*1-884993-03-6*) Koldarana.

Miller, A. G. Walt Disney's Bambi Gets Lost. (ps-3). 1973. lib. bdg. 4.99 (*0-394-92520-3*) Random Bks Yng Read.

Monson, A. M. The Deer Stand. Pearson, Susan, ed. LC 91-32122. 160p. (gr. 4 up). 1992. reinforced bdg. 13.00 (*0-688-11057-6*) Lothrop.

Patrick, Denise L., adapted by. Walt Disney's Bambi. Mones, illus. 28p. (ps). 1992. bds. write for info. (*0-307-12535-1*, 12535, Golden Pr) Western Pub.

Paulsen, Gary. Night the White Deer Died. 1991. pap. 3.50 (*0-440-21092-5*, YB) Dell.

Phillips, Joan. Walt Disney's Bambi's Game. Langley, Bill & Wakeman, Diana, illus. (ps-1). 1991. write for info. (*0-307-11599-2*, Golden Pr) Western Pub.

Prusski, Jeffrey. Bring Back the Deer. Waldman, Neil, illus. 32p. (ps-3). 1988. 13.95 (*0-15-200418-1*, Gulliver Bks) HarBrace.

Radcliffe, Theresa. Shadow the Deer. Butler, John, illus. 32p. (ps-1). 1993. 13.99 (*0-670-83852-7*) Viking Child Bks.

Ryder, Joanne, adapted by. Walt Disney's Bambi. LC 92-54875. (Illus.). 64p. (gr. 2-6). 1993. pap. 3.50 (*1-56282-444-9*) Disney Pr.

—Walt Disney's Bambi. Pacheco, David & Clay, Jesse, illus. LC 92-54876. 96p. 1993. 14.95 (*1-56282-442-2*); PLB 14.89 (*1-56282-443-0*) Disney Pr.

Salten, Felix. Bambi. 134p. 1981. Repr. PLB 16.95x (*0-89966-358-3*) Buccaneer Bks.

—Bambi. 112p. 1981. Repr. PLB 16.95x (*0-89967-032-6*) Harmony Raine.

—Bambi. Cooney, Barbara, illus. (ps up). 1988. pap. 3.99 (*0-671-66607-X*, Minstrel Bks) PB.

—Bambi. Woods, Michael J., illus. LC 90-26533. 160p. (ps up). 1992. pap. 18.00 jacketed, three-piece bdg (*0-671-73937-9*, S&S BFYR) S&S Trade.

—Bambi's Children. (Illus.). 316p. 1992. Repr. PLB 21.95x (*0-89966-894-1*) Buccaneer Bks.

Sargent, Dave & Sargent, Pat. Dawn the Deer. 48p. (gr. 2-6). 1992. write for info. Ozark Pub.

Seredy, Kate. The White Stag. (gr. 4-7). 1979. pap. 4.99 (*0-14-031258-7*, Puffin) Puffin Bks.

Sharp, Mary & Niemi, Matt. Bobbi, Father of the Finnish White Tailed Deer. Shappell, Sherry, illus. LC 79-54100. (Orig.). (gr. 4-6). 1979. pap. 5.95 (*0-9603200-0-8*) Bobbi Ent.

Siekkinen, Raija. The Curious Fawn. Taina, Hannu, illus. 32p. (gr. k-4). 1990. PLB 18.95 (*0-87614-379-6*) Carolrhoda Bks.

Smajda, Michael J. A Deer Love Story. (Illus.). 39p. 1988. text ed. 12.95 (*0-533-07680-3*) Vantage.

Storm, Tom. Stormy Finds the New Forest. Powell, Lori, illus. 48p. (Orig.). (gr. 1-6). 1994. pap. 8.95 (*0-9643019-0-3*) T Storm.
Tom Storm has written a mesmerizing children's book which contains endearing characters such as "Stormy," the whitetail fawn, & "Flapjack," the local beaver. Its many characters in bright vivid colors reach out & grasp children's attention from cover to cover. The story features Stormy & many other birds & animals. Because of deer overpopulation in their forest, Stormy & his mother must journey to find a new forest. They encounter many delightful animals & fun-filled experiences along the way. Finally, once settled into their new, abundant, & balanced forest, Stormy meets Joey, the son of a local hunter & soon to be a hunter himself. Joey & Stormy set out on their own adventures. Along the way, Joey gently educates Stormy on how hunting helps to sustain the quality environment for birds & animals by preventing overpopulation & starvation. Tom Storm's intent is to provide the public with a better understanding of the hunters' historic role in conservation & wildlife management of all birds & animals. Tom is able to strike a balanced approach between environmental & pro-hunting viewpoints, &, indeed, will please both sides with this charming story. There has never been anything like this book on the market. STORMY is unique, educational & fascinating - a charming story. Order from Storm Press, Box 2012, Great Falls, MT 59403.
Publisher Provided Annotation.

Vail, Virginia. Oh Deer! 128p. (gr. 3-7). 1990. pap. 2.75 (*0-590-42802-0*) Scholastic Inc.

Walt Disney Staff. Bambi. (ps-3). 1992. 6.98 (*0-453-03019-X*) Viking Penguin.

Walt Disney's Bambi. 24p. (ps-k). 1986. write for info. (*0-307-10380-3*, Pub. by Golden Bks) Western Pub.

Walt Disney's Play with Bambi. (ps-k). 1991. write for info. (*0-307-12002-3*, Golden Pr) Western Pub.

Walt Disney's The Bambi Book. 24p. (gr. 2-5). 1987. pap. write for info. (*0-307-10055-3*, Pub. by Golden Bks) Western Pub.

Wilder, Laura I. The Deer in the Wood. Graef, Renee, illus. LC 94-18684. 1995. 15.00 (*0-06-024881-5*, Festival); PLB 14.89 (*0-06-024882-3*) HarpC Child Bks.

DEERE, JOHN, 1804-1886

Collins, David R. Pioneer Plowmaker: A Story about John Deere. Michaels, Steve, illus. 64p. (gr. 3-6). 1990. PLB 14.95 (*0-87614-424-5*) Carolrhoda Bks.

DEGAS, HILAIRE GERMAIN EDGAR, 1834-1917

Loumaye, Jacqueline. Degas: The Painted Gesture. LC 93-33682. 1994. write for info. (*0-7910-2809-7*) Chelsea Hse.

Meyer, Susan E. Edgar Degas. LC 94-8420. 1994. 19.95 (*0-8109-3220-2*) Abrams.

Muhlberger, Richard, text by. What Makes a Degas a Degas? (Illus.). 48p. (gr. 5 up). 1993. 9.95 (*0-670-85205-8*) Viking Child Bks.

Skira-Venturi, Rosabianca. A Weekend with Degas. LC 91-38364. (Illus.). 64p. (gr. 1-6). 1992. 19.95 (*0-8478-1439-4*) Rizzoli Intl.

DEGREES OF LATITUDE AND LONGITUDE

see Geodesy

DELAWARE

Brown, Dottie. Delaware. LC 92-44845. 1993. PLB 17.50 (*0-8225-2733-2*) Lerner Pubns.

Carole Marsh Delaware Books, 44 bks. 1994. lib. bdg. 1027.80 set (*0-7933-1282-5*); pap. 587.80 set (*0-7933-5136-7*) Gallopade Pub Group.

Cheripko, Jan. Voices of the River: Adventures on the Delaware. (Illus.). 48p. (gr. 7 up). 1994. 15.95 (*1-56397-325-1*) Boyds Mills Pr.

Fradin, Dennis. Delaware: In Words & Pictures. LC 80-5842. (Illus.). 48p. (gr. 2-5). 1980. PLB 12.95 (*0-516-03908-3*) Childrens.

Kent, Deborah. Delaware. LC 90-21116. (Illus.). 144p. (gr. 5-8). 1991. PLB 20.55 (*0-516-00454-9*) Childrens.

—Delaware. 174p. 1993. text ed. 15.40 (*1-56956-137-0*) W A T Braille.

Marsh, Carole. Avast, Ye Slobs! Delaware Pirate Trivia. (Illus.). (gr. 3-12). 1994. PLB 24.95 (*0-7933-0256-0*); pap. 14.95 (*0-7933-0255-2*); computer disk 29.95 (*0-7933-0257-9*) Gallopade Pub Group.

—The Beast of the Delaware Bed & Breakfast. (Illus.). (gr. 3-12). 1994. PLB 24.95 (*0-7933-1447-X*); pap. 14.95 (*0-7933-1448-8*); computer disk 29.95 (*0-7933-1449-6*) Gallopade Pub Group.

—Bow Wow! Delaware Dogs in History, Mystery, Legend, Lore, Humor & More! (Illus.). (gr. 3-12). 1994. PLB 24.95 (*0-7933-3488-8*); pap. 14.95 (*0-7933-3489-6*); computer disk 29.95 (*0-7933-3490-X*) Gallopade Pub Group.

—Christopher Columbus Comes to Delaware! Includes Reproducible Activities for Kids! (Illus.). (gr. 3-12). 1994. PLB 24.95 (*0-7933-3641-4*); pap. 14.95 (*0-7933-3642-2*); computer disk 29.95 (*0-7933-3643-0*) Gallopade Pub Group.

—Delaware & Other State Greats (Biographies) (Illus.). (gr. 3-12). 1994. PLB 24.95 (*1-55609-558-9*); pap. 14.95 (*1-55609-557-0*); computer disk 29.95 (*0-7933-1455-0*) Gallopade Pub Group.

—Delaware Bandits, Bushwackers, Outlaws, Crooks, Devils, Ghosts, Desperadoes & Other Assorted & Sundry Characters! (Illus.). (gr. 3-12). 1994. PLB 24.95 (*0-7933-0238-2*); pap. 14.95 (*0-7933-0237-4*); computer disk 29.95 (*0-7933-0239-0*) Gallopade Pub Group.

—Delaware Classic Christmas Trivia: Stories, Recipes, Activities, Legends, Lore & More! (Illus.). (gr. 3-12). 1994. PLB 24.95 (*0-7933-0241-2*); pap. 14.95 (*0-7933-0240-4*); computer disk 29.95 (*0-7933-0242-0*) Gallopade Pub Group.

—Delaware Coastales. (Illus.). (gr. 3-12). 1994. PLB 24.95 (*1-55609-554-6*); pap. 14.95 (*1-55609-553-8*); computer disk 29.95 (*0-7933-1451-8*) Gallopade Pub Group.

—Delaware Coastales! 1994. lib. bdg. 24.95 (*0-7933-7272-0*) Gallopade Pub Group.

—Delaware Dingbats! Bk. 1: A Fun Book of Games, Stories, Activities & More about Our State That's All in Code! for You to Decipher. (Illus.). (gr. 3-12). 1994. PLB 24.95 (*0-7933-3794-1*); pap. 14.95 (*0-7933-3795-X*); computer disk 29.95 (*0-7933-3796-8*) Gallopade Pub Group.

—Delaware Festival Fun for Kids! (Illus.). (gr. 3-12). 1994. lib. bdg. 24.95 (*0-7933-3947-2*); pap. 14.95 (*0-7933-3948-0*); disk 29.95 (*0-7933-3949-9*) Gallopade Pub Group.

—The Delaware Hot Air Balloon Mystery. (Illus.). (gr. 2-9). 1994. 24.95 (*0-685-37849-7*); pap. 14.95 (*0-7933-2382-7*); computer disk 29.95 (*0-7933-2383-5*) Gallopade Pub Group.

—Delaware "Jography" A Fun Run Thru Our State! (Illus.). (gr. 3-12). 1994. PLB 24.95 (*1-55609-551-1*); pap. 14.95 (*1-55609-550-3*); computer disk 29.95 (*0-7933-1439-9*) Gallopade Pub Group.

—Delaware Kid's Cookbook: Recipes, How-to-, History, Lore & More! (Illus.). (gr. 3-12). 1994. PLB 24.95 (*0-7933-0250-1*); pap. 14.95 (*0-7933-0249-8*); computer disk 29.95 (*0-7933-0251-X*) Gallopade Pub Group.

—Delaware Quiz Bowl Crash Course! (Illus.). (gr. 3-12). 1994. PLB 24.95 (*1-55609-556-2*); pap. 14.95 (*1-55609-555-4*); computer disk 29.95 (*0-7933-1450-X*) Gallopade Pub Group.

—Delaware Rollercoasters! (Illus.). (gr. 3-12). 1994. PLB 24.95 (*0-7933-5245-2*); pap. 14.95 (*0-7933-5246-0*); computer disk 29.95 (*0-7933-5247-9*) Gallopade Pub Group.

—Delaware School Trivia: An Amazing & Fascinating Look at Our State's Teachers, Schools & Students! (Illus.). (gr. 3-12). 1994. PLB 24.95 (*0-7933-0247-1*); pap. 14.95 (*0-7933-0246-3*); computer disk 29.95 (*0-7933-0248-X*) Gallopade Pub Group.
—Delaware Silly Basketball Sportsmysteries, Vol. I. (Illus.). (gr. 3-12). 1994. PLB 24.95 (*0-7933-0244-7*); pap. 14.95 (*0-7933-0243-9*); computer disk 29.95 (*0-7933-0245-5*) Gallopade Pub Group.
—Delaware Silly Basketball Sportsmysteries, Vol. II. (Illus.). (gr. 3-12). 1994. PLB 24.95 (*0-7933-1456-9*); pap. 14.95 (*0-7933-1457-7*); computer disk 29.95 (*0-7933-1458-5*) Gallopade Pub Group.
—Delaware Silly Football Sportsmysteries, Vol. I. (Illus.). (gr. 3-12). 1994. PLB 24.95 (*0-7933-1441-0*); pap. 14.95 (*0-7933-1442-9*); computer disk 29.95 (*0-7933-1443-7*) Gallopade Pub Group.
—Delaware Silly Football Sportsmysteries, Vol. II. (Illus.). (gr. 3-12). 1994. PLB 24.95 (*0-7933-1444-5*); pap. 14.95 (*0-7933-1445-3*); computer disk 29.95 (*0-7933-1446-1*) Gallopade Pub Group.
—Delaware Silly Trivia! (Illus.). (gr. 3-12). 1994. PLB 24.95 (*1-55609-549-X*); pap. 14.95 (*1-55609-548-1*); computer disk 29.95 (*0-7933-1438-0*) Gallopade Pub Group.
—Delaware's (Most Devastating!) Disasters & (Most Calamitous!) Catastrophies! (Illus.). (gr. 3-12). 1994. PLB 24.95 (*0-7933-0235-8*); pap. 14.95 (*0-7933-0234-X*); computer disk 29.95 (*0-7933-0236-6*) Gallopade Pub Group.
—The Hard-to-Believe-But-True! Book of Delaware History, Mystery, Trivia, Legend, Lore, Humor & More. (Illus.). (gr. 3-12). 1994. PLB 24.95 (*0-7933-0253-6*); pap. 14.95 (*0-7933-0252-8*); computer disk 29.95 (*0-7933-0254-4*) Gallopade Pub Group.
—If My Delaware Mama Ran the World! (Illus.). (gr. 3-12). 1994. PLB 24.95 (*0-7933-1452-6*); pap. 14.95 (*0-7933-1453-4*); computer disk 29.95 (*0-7933-1454-2*) Gallopade Pub Group.
—Let's Quilt Delaware & Stuff It Topographically! (Illus.). (gr. 3-12). 1994. PLB 24.95 (*1-55609-552-X*); pap. 14.95 (*1-55609-063-3*); computer disk 29.95 (*0-7933-1440-2*) Gallopade Pub Group.
—Let's Quilt Our Delaware County. 1994. lib. bdg. 24.95 (*0-7933-7134-1*); pap. text ed. 14.95 (*0-7933-7135-X*); disk 29.95 (*0-7933-7136-8*) Gallopade Pub Group.
—Let's Quilt Our Delaware Town. 1994. lib. bdg. 24.95 (*0-7933-6984-3*); pap. text ed. 14.95 (*0-7933-6985-1*); disk 29.95 (*0-7933-6986-X*) Gallopade Pub Group.
—Meow! Delaware Cats in History, Mystery, Legend, Lore, Humor & More! (Illus.). (gr. 3-12). 1994. PLB 24.95 (*0-7933-3335-0*); pap. 14.95 (*0-7933-3336-9*); computer disk 29.95 (*0-7933-3337-7*) Gallopade Pub Group.
—Uncle Rebus: Delaware Picture Stories for Computer Kids. (Illus.). (gr. k-3). 1994. PLB 24.95 (*0-7933-4525-1*); pap. 14.95 (*0-7933-4526-X*); disk 29.95 (*0-7933-4527-8*) Gallopade Pub Group.
Thompson, Kathleen. Delaware. 48p. (gr. 3 up). 1986. PLB 19.97 (*0-8174-4508-0*) Raintree Steck-V.

DELAWARE–HISTORY

Fradin, Dennis B. The Delaware Colony. LC 92-10467. (Illus.). 190p. (gr. 4 up). 1992. PLB 17.95 (*0-516-00398-4*) Childrens.
Hoffecker, Carol E. Delaware, the First State. (Illus.). 256p. (Orig.). 1987. pap. 9.95 (*0-912608-47-1*) Mid Atlantic.
Marsh, Carole. Chill Out: Scary Delaware Tales Based on Frightening Delaware Truths. (Illus.). 1994. lib. bdg. 24.95 (*0-7933-4678-9*); pap. 14.95 (*0-7933-4679-7*); disk 29.95 (*0-7933-4680-0*) Gallopade Pub Group.
—Delaware "Crinkum-Crankum" A Funny Word Book about Our State. (Illus.). 1994. lib. bdg. 24.95 (*0-7933-4831-5*); pap. 14.95 (*0-7933-4832-3*); disk 29.95 (*0-7933-4833-1*) Gallopade Pub Group.
—The Delaware Mystery Van Takes Off! Book 1: Handicapped Delaware Kids Sneak Off on a Big Adventure. (Illus.). (gr. 3-12). 1994. 24.95 (*0-7933-4985-0*); pap. 14.95 (*0-7933-4986-9*); computer disk 29.95 (*0-7933-4987-7*) Gallopade Pub Group.
—Delaware Timeline: A Chronology of Delaware History, Mystery, Trivia, Legend, Lore & More. (Illus.). (gr. 3-12). 1994. PLB 24.95 (*0-7933-5896-5*); pap. 14.95 (*0-7933-5897-3*); computer disk 29.95 (*0-7933-5898-1*) Gallopade Pub Group.
—Delaware's Unsolved Mysteries (& Their "Solutions") Includes Scientific Information & Other Activities for Students. (Illus.). (gr. 3-12). 1994. PLB 24.95 (*0-7933-5743-8*); pap. 14.95 (*0-7933-5744-6*); computer disk 29.95 (*0-7933-5745-4*) Gallopade Pub Group.
—My First Book about Delaware. (gr. k-4). 1994. PLB 24.95 (*0-7933-5590-7*); pap. 14.95 (*0-7933-5591-5*); computer disk 29.95 (*0-7933-5592-3*) Gallopade Pub Group.

DELINQUENCY, JUVENILE
see Juvenile Delinquency

DELIQUENTS
see Crime and Criminals; Juvenile Delinquency

DELUSIONS
see Superstition; Witchcraft

DE MILLE, AGNES, 1908-

Gherman, Beverly. Agnes de Mille: Dancing off the Earth. LC 93-26606. (Illus.). 160p. (gr. 7 up). 1994. pap. 5.95 (*0-02-043240-2*, Collier Young Ad) Macmillan Child Grp.
Speaker-Yuan, Margaret. Agnes De Mille. Horner, Matina, intro. by. (Illus.). 112p. (gr. 5 up). 1990. lib. bdg. 17.95 (*1-55546-648-6*) Chelsea Hse.

DEMOCRACY
see also Liberty

Adams, Henry. Democracy: An American Novel. Andrews, C. A., intro. by. (gr. 9 up). 1968. pap. 1.50 (*0-8049-0164-3*, CL-164) Airmont.
Aten, Jerry. Democracy for Young Americans. 112p. (gr. 4-8). 1989. 10.95 (*0-86653-483-0*, GA1083) Good Apple.
Eannace, Maryrose. The Pizza Problem: Democracy in Action. 70p. (Orig.). (gr. 6-10). 1990. pap. text ed. 8.75x (*0-936826-35-5*) PS Assocs Croton.
Nardo, Don. Democracy. LC 93-4912. (gr. 5-8). 1994. 14.95 (*1-56006-147-2*) Lucent Bks.
Slappey, Mary M. Democracies in Crisis. (Illus.). 150p. 1992. pap. 10.95 (*0-930061-27-6*) Interspace Bks.

DEMONOLOGY–FICTION

Buck, Pearl S. The Old Demon. Higashi, Sandra, illus. 40p. (gr. 4 up). 1982. PLB 13.95 (*0-87191-828-5*) Creative Ed.

DEMONSTRATIONS FOR NEGRO CIVIL RIGHTS
see Blacks–Civil Rights

DENMARK

Hintz, Martin. Denmark. LC 93-35487. (Illus.). 128p. (gr. 5-8). 1994. PLB 20.55 (*0-516-02620-8*) Childrens.
Lerner Geography Dept. Staff, ed. Denmark in Pictures. (Illus.). 64p. (gr. 5 up). 1991. Repr. PLB 17.50 (*0-8225-1880-5*) Lerner Pubns.

DENMARK–FICTION

Reuter, Bjarne. The Boys from St. Petri. 192p. (gr. 6 up). 1994. 14.99 (*0-525-45121-8*, DCB) Dutton Child Bks.

DENOMINATIONS, RELIGIOUS
see Sects

DENTISTRY
see also Teeth

Berry, Joy W. Teach Me about the Baby Sitter. Dickey, Kate, ed. LC 85-45077. (Illus.). 36p. (ps). 1986. 4.98 (*0-685-10722-1*) Grolier Inc.
—Teach Me about the Dentist. Dickey, Kate, ed. LC 85-45084. (Illus.). 36p. (ps). 1986. 4.98 (*0-685-10724-8*) Grolier Inc.
Boy Scouts of America. Dentistry. (Illus.). 32p. (gr. 6-12). 1975. pap. 1.85 (*0-8395-3394-2*, 33394) BSA.
Going to the Dentist. (Illus.). 32p. (ps). 1990. 2.99 (*0-517-69198-1*) Random Hse Value.
Hafford, Jeannette N. Boys & Girls & Doctors & Dentists. 24p. (Orig.). 1986. pap. 7.22 (*0-9616549-0-2*) Tinys Self Help Bks.
Rockwell, Harlow. My Dentist. LC 75-6974. (Illus.). 32p. (ps-3). 1975. 16.00 (*0-688-80011-4*); PLB 15.93 (*0-688-84004-3*) Greenwillow.
Rogers, Fred. Going to the Dentist. Judkis, Jim, photos by. (Illus.). 32p. (Orig.). (ps-2). 1989. (Putnam); pap. 5.95 (*0-399-21634-0*, Putnam) Putnam Pub Group.
Siegel, Dorothy S. Dental Health. Garell, Dale C. & Snyder, Solomon H., eds. (Illus.). 112p. (gr. 5-12). 1994. 19.95 (*0-7910-0014-1*, Am Art Analog) Chelsea Hse.
Silverstein, Alvin & Silverstein, Virginia B. So You're Getting Braces: A Guide to Orthodontics. LC 77-16488. (Illus.). 128p. (gr. 5 up). 1978. (Lipp Jr Bks); pap. 3.95_o.p. (*0-397-31787-5*, Lipp Jr Bks) HarpC Child Bks.
Stamper, Judith. What's It Like to Be a Dentist. Gustafson, Dana, illus. LC 89-34392. 32p. (gr. k-3). 1989. lib. bdg. 10.89 (*0-8167-1799-0*); pap. text ed. 2.95 (*0-8167-1800-8*) Troll Assocs.

DENTISTRY–FICTION

Allen, Julia. My First Dentist Visit. Reese, Bob, illus. (gr. k-3). 1987. 7.95 (*0-89868-185-5*); pap. 2.95 (*0-89868-186-3*) ARO Pub.
Civardi, Anne & Cartwright, Stephen. Going to the Dentist. 16p. (ps up). 1987. pap. 3.95 (*0-7460-1515-1*) EDC.
Devlin, Wende & Delvin, Harry. Cranberry Trip to the Dentist. LC 93-36280. (ps-1). 1994. pap. 2.95 (*0-689-71779-2*) MacMillan Child Grp.
Lewis, Kim. Floss. Lewis, Kim, illus. LC 91-71853. 32p. (ps up). 1994. pap. 4.99 (*1-56402-271-4*) Candlewick Pr.
Luttrell, Ida. Milo's Toothache. Giannini, Enzo, illus. LC 91-24315. 40p. (ps-3). 1992. 11.00 (*0-8037-1034-8*); PLB 10.89 (*0-8037-1035-6*) Dial Bks Young.

McNutt, Timothy E., Sr. Alley Alligator's Awesome Smile. (Illus.). (ps). 1994. pap. text ed. 3.95 (*0-9642475-0-X*) T E McNutt.
Colorfully illustrated, ALLEY ALLIGATOR'S AWESOME SMILE was written to present pediatric preventive oral care in a positive manner. Alfred & Abbey Alligator take little Alley Alligator to visit Dr. Smiley, Pleasant View Pond's favorite dentist. Dr. Smiley explains with non-threatening language the names of his dental instruments, & Alley completes her first dental visit with an awesome smile. This book is ideal for introducing young children to dentistry. Dr. McNutt's specialization in pediatric dentistry caused him to write this book to introduce parents & children to the following concepts: *not all baby teeth must be present to go to the dentist *children can "like" dental visits *the doctor intends to help the child *pain is not required to seek dental care, & *that a healthy oral environment should be promoted to the child at an early age. This book can be a useful educational tool for parents, children & dental care professionals. Dr. McNutt is a member of the American Dental Association & the American Academy of Pediatric Dentistry.
Publisher Provided Annotation.

Rasburry, Kaitlin. A Monster in My Mouth: My Retainer. Rasburry, Keitlin, illus. (gr. 3-6). Date not set. 14.95 (*1-884825-01-X*) Raspberry Pubns.
Thaler, Mike. Fang the Dentist. Lee, Jared, illus. LC 92-18594. 32p. (ps-3). 1993. PLB 9.79 (*0-8167-3020-2*); pap. 2.95 (*0-8167-3021-0*) Troll Assocs.

DENVER

Hawley, Frances, ed. The Children's Pages of Metro Denver - Fall Edition, 1988: A Directory of Products & Services for Children of All Ages & Their Parents. (gr. 7 up). 1988. pap. write for info. (*0-932439-08-X*) Denver Busn Media.
Smith, Barbara A. Historic Denver for Kids. rev. ed. Taylor, Alice, illus. 90p. (Orig.). (gr. k up). 1982. pap. 5.00 (*0-943804-25-6*) U of Denver Teach.
Spies, Karen. Denver. LC 88-20246. (Illus.). 60p. (gr. 3 up). 1988. text ed. 13.95 RSBE (*0-87518-386-7*, Dillon) Macmillan Child Grp.

DEOXYRIBONUCLEIC ACID
see D N A

DEPARTMENT STORES
see also Salesmen and Salesmanship

DEPARTMENT STORES–FICTION

Fitzmaurice, Gabriel. The Moving Stair. Teskey, Donald, illus. 80p. (gr. 1-4). 1994. pap. 6.95 (*1-85371-267-1*, Pub. by Poolbeg Pr ER) Dufour.
Gauthier, Bertrand. Zachary in the Wawabongbong. Sylvestre, Daniel, illus. LC 93-15456. 1993. 15.93 (*0-8368-1011-2*) Gareth Stevens Inc.
Morrison, Rob & Morrison, Penelope. Snorkels for Tadpoles. Morrison, Penelope, illus. LC 93-28967. 1994. 4.25 (*0-383-03775-1*) SRA Schl Grp.
Peck, Richard. Secrets of the Shopping Mall. 192p. (gr. k-6). 1989. pap. 3.99 (*0-440-40270-0*, LFL); pap. 3.99 (*0-440-98099-2*) Dell.
Slater, Teddy. Shopping with Samantha. Hearn, Diane D., illus. 24p. (ps-1). 1991. 4.95 (*0-671-72984-5*); PLB 6.95 (*0-671-72983-7*) Silver Pr.
Wells, Rosemary. Max's Dragon Shirt. Wells, Rosemary, illus. LC 90-43755. 32p. (ps-2). 1991. 12.00 (*0-8037-0944-7*); lib. bdg. 10.89 (*0-8037-0945-5*) Dial Bks Young.

DEPENDENT CHILDREN
see Child Welfare

DEPRESSIONS

Alexander, James E. Depression Kids: Shaping the Character of Our Lives. 260p. (Orig.). 1993. pap. 12.50 (*0-939965-07-0*) Macedon Prod.
Andryszewski, Tricia. The Dust Bowl: Disaster on the Plains. LC 92-15300. (Illus.). 64p. (gr. 4-6). 1993. PLB 15.40 (*1-56294-272-7*); pap. 5.95 (*1-56294-747-8*) Millbrook Pr.
Davies, Nancy M. The Stock Market Crash of Nineteen Twenty-Nine. LC 92-23310. (Illus.). 96p. (gr. 6 up). 1994. text ed. 14.95 RSBE (*0-02-726221-9*, New Discovery Bks) Macmillan Child Grp.
Glassman, Bruce. The Crash of Twenty-Nine & the New Deal. (Illus.). 64p. (gr. 5 up). 1985. PLB 12.95 (*0-382-06831-9*); pap. 7.95 (*0-382-06978-1*) Silver Burdett.
Meltzer, Milton. Brother, Can You Spare a Dime: The Great Depression 1929-1933. (Illus.). 144p. 1990. 16.95x (*0-8160-2372-7*) Facts on File.
Migneco, Ronald & Biel, Timothy L. The Crash of 1929. LC 89-33556. (Illus.). 64p. (gr. 5-8). 1989. PLB 11.95 (*1-56006-007-7*) Lucent Bks.
Norrell, Robert J. We Want Jobs! A Story of the Great Depression. Jones, Jan N., illus. LC 92-18082. 40p. (gr. 2-5). 1992. PLB 21.34 (*0-8114-7229-9*) Raintree Steck-V.
Schraff, Anne E. The Great Depression & the New Deal: America's Economic Collapse & Recovery. (Illus.). 128p. (gr. 9-12). 1990. PLB 13.90 (*0-531-10964-X*) Watts.
Stanley, Jerry. Children of the Dustbowl: The True Story of the School at Weedpatch Camp. LC 92-393. (Illus.). 96p. (gr. 4 up). 1992. 15.00 (*0-517-58781-5*); PLB 15.99 (*0-517-58782-3*) Crown Bks Yng Read.
Stein, Richard C. The Great Depression. LC 93-752. (Illus.). 32p. (gr. 3-6). 1993. PLB 12.30 (*0-516-06668-4*); pap. 3.95 (*0-516-46668-2*) Childrens.

Stewart, Gail B. The New Deal. LC 92-41264. (Illus.). 112p. (gr. 6 up). 1993. text ed. 14.95 RSBE (*0-02-788369-8*, New Discovery Bks) Macmillan Child Grp.

Wormser, Richard L. Growing up in the Great Depression. LC 93-20686. (Illus.). 112p. (gr. 5-9). 1994. SBE 15.95 (*0-689-31711-5*, Atheneum Child Bk) Macmillan Child Grp.

DEPRESSIONS–FICTION

Ames, Mildred. The Dancing Madness: A Novel. LC 80-65831. 144p. (gr. 7 up). 1980. 8.95 (*0-385-28113-7*) Delacorte.

Antle, Nancy. Hard Times: A Story of the Great Depression. Watling, James, illus. 64p. (gr. 2-6). 1993. RB 12.99 (*0-670-84665-1*) Viking Child Bks.

Cannon, Bettie. A Bellsong for Sarah Raines. LC 87-4299. 192p. (gr. 7 up). 1987. 14.95 (*0-684-18839-2*, Scribners Young Read) Macmillan Child Grp.

Caseley, Judith. My Father, the Nutcase. LC 91-46750. 196p. (gr. 7 up). 1992. 15.00 (*0-679-83394-3*); PLB 15.99 (*0-679-93394-8*) Knopf Bks Yng Read.

Crofford, Emily. A Place to Belong. LC 93-9289. 1993. 19.95 (*0-87614-808-9*) Carolrhoda Bks.

Deal, Borden. The Least One. Davis, Sara D., intro. by. 368p. 1992. pap. 19.95t (*0-8173-0673-0*) U of Ala Pr.

Green, Michelle Y. Willie Pearl Series. 1992. write for info. (*0-9627697-6-2*) W Ruth Co.

Koller, Jackie F. Nothing to Fear. Grove, Karen, ed. 279p. (gr. 5 up). 1991. 14.95 (*0-15-200544-7*, Gulliver Bks) HarBrace.

Levinson, Riki. Boys Here - Girls There. Ritz, Karen, illus. LC 92-5321. 1993. 13.00 (*0-525-67374-1*, Lodestar Bks) Dutton Child Bks.

Mills, Claudia. What about Annie? LC 84-20862. 128p. (gr. 5 up). 1985. 9.95 (*0-8027-6573-4*) Walker & Co.

Myers, Anna. Red-Dirt Jessie. 107p. 1992. 13.95 (*0-8027-8172-1*) Walker & Co.

Ransom, Candice. The Man on Stilts. Bowman, Leslie, illus. LC 92-39358. 1994. write for info. (*0-399-22537-4*, Philomel Bks) Putnam Pub Group.

Reasonover, Ila. Lottie Daughter of the Depression. Caroland, Mary, ed. LC 90-71004. 154p. (gr. 4-8). 1991. 7.95 (*1-55523-365-1*) Winston-Derek.

Snyder, Zilpha K. Cat Running. LC 94-447. 1994. 14.95 (*0-385-31056-0*) Delacorte.

—Velvet Room. Raible, Alton, illus. LC 65-10474. 224p. (gr. 3-7). 1972. (Atheneum Childrens Bk); pap. 1.95 (*0-685-00576-3*) Macmillan Child Grp.

Stein, Charlotte M. The Stained Glass Window. Sakurai, Jennifer, ed. Stein, Michele P., illus. LC 88-70883. 150p. (Orig.). 1994. pap. 11.95 incl. wkbk. (*0-916634-12-4*) Double M Pr.

Tolliver, Ruby C. Have Gun - Need Bullets. Washington, Burl, illus. LC 90-49363. 120p. (gr. 4 up). 1991. 15.95 (*0-87565-085-6*); pap. 10.95 (*0-87565-089-9*) Tex Christian.

Turnbull, Ann. Speedwell. LC 91-58757. 128p. (gr. 5-9). 1992. 14.95 (*1-56402-112-2*) Candlewick Pr.

—Speedwell. LC 91-58757. 128p. (gr. 5-9). 1994. pap. 3.99 (*1-56402-281-1*) Candlewick Pr.

Turner, Ann W. Dust for Dinner. 1995. 14.00 (*0-06-023376-1*); PLB 13.89 (*0-06-023377-X*) HarpC Child Bks.

DERMATOLOGY

see Skin–Diseases

DESERT ANIMALS

see also Camels

Arvetis, Chris & Palmer, Carole. Deserts. LC 93-502. (Illus.). 1993. write for info. (*0-528-83574-2*) Rand McNally.

Burton, Robert. Desert. (Illus.). 24p. (gr. k-4). 1991. PLB 10.40 (*1-878137-17-4*) Newington.

Chinery, Michael. Desert Animals. Wright, David, illus. LC 91-53146. 40p. (Orig.). (gr. 2-5). 1992. PLB 8.99 (*0-679-92048-X*); pap. 4.99 (*0-679-82048-5*) Random Bks Yng Read.

Clutterbuck, Mary, illus. Animals & Birds of the Desert. 32p. (gr. 3-5). 1985. 7.95x (*0-86685-445-2*) Intl Bk Ctr.

Deming, Susan. The Desert: A Nature Panorama. Deming, Susan, illus. 7p. (ps-3). 1991. bds. 5.95 (*0-8118-0291-4*) Chronicle Bks.

Gibson, Barbara & Pinkney, Jerry. Creatures of the Desert World & Strange Animals of the Sea, 2 bks. Crump, Donald J., ed. (Illus.). 20p. (gr. 3-8). 1987. Set. 21.95 (*0-87044-688-6*) Natl Geog.

Lerner, Carol. A Desert Year. Lerner, Carol, illus. LC 90-44643. 48p. 1991. 13.95 (*0-688-09382-5*); PLB 13.88 (*0-688-09383-3*) Morrow Jr Bks.

Pallotta, Jerry. The Desert Alphabet Book. Astrella, Mark, illus. LC 93-42651. 32p. (Orig.). (ps-4). 1994. 14.95 (*0-88106-473-4*); PLB 15.88 (*0-88106-687-7*); pap. 6.95 (*0-88106-472-6*) Charlesbridge Pub.

Pearce, Q. L. & Pearce, W. L. In the Desert. Brook, Bonnie, ed. Bettoli, Delana, illus. 24p. (ps-1). 1990. 4.95 (*0-671-68829-4*); PLB 6.95 (*0-671-68825-1*) Silver Pr.

Philabaum, Dabney M. Desert Buddies. Alegret, Nancy L., illus. 40p. (gr. k-4). 1994. pap. 8.95 (*0-9639215-0-9*) Earth Buddies.

An informative & engaging text presenting the look, smell, & feel of the Sonoran Desert & the unusual animals & plants that live there. Curious about roadrunners or rattlesnakes? Wary of tumbleweeds & tarantulas? This book introduces animals you might see during the day, after a rainstorm, at sunset, & at night. How do they spend the day, & which ones are really dangerous? What kind of odd plants live in the desert, & what happens to them when it rains, or when it doesn't? Using the concept of "buddy," this book strives to encourage a sense of familiarity, acceptance, & guardianship toward these inhabitants. The 70# paper is perfect for coloring with crayons, colored pencils, or markers, but this book is much more than a coloring book. Full-page illustrations stand beautifully on their own. A center foldout & a cover flap with Velcro closure set this book apart from others. Great for parents, teachers, environmentalists & anyone concerned with encouraging children to appreciate the desert. DESERT BUDDIES is the first in a series that will focus on inhabitants of unique regions of the Earth. EARTH BUDDIES PUBLISHING, 820 S. 2nd Ave., Tucson, AZ 85701; 602-628-1753. *Publisher Provided Annotation.*

Plantimal Safari. (ps-6). 1986. 3.00 (*0-9605656-3-9*) Desert Botanical.

Twist, Clint. Deserts. LC 91-22471. (Illus.). 48p. (gr. 4-6). 1991. text ed. 13.95 RSBE (*0-87518-490-1*, Dillon) Macmillan Child Grp.

DESERT PLANTS

Almeleh, Fiona, illus. Plants & Flowers of the Desert. 32p. (gr. 3-5). 1985. 7.95x (*0-86685-446-0*) Intl Bk Ctr.

Arvetis, Chris & Palmer, Carole. Deserts. LC 93-502. (Illus.). 1993. write for info. (*0-528-83574-2*) Rand McNally.

Deming, Susan. The Desert: A Nature Panorama. Deming, Susan, illus. 7p. (ps-3). 1991. bds. 5.95 (*0-8118-0291-4*) Chronicle Bks.

Lerner, Carol. A Desert Year. Lerner, Carol, illus. LC 90-44643. 48p. 1991. 13.95 (*0-688-09382-5*); PLB 13.88 (*0-688-09383-3*) Morrow Jr Bks.

Philabaum, Dabney M. Desert Buddies. Alegret, Nancy L., illus. 40p. (gr. k-4). 1994. pap. 8.95 (*0-9639215-0-9*) Earth Buddies.

An informative & engaging text presenting the look, smell, & feel of the Sonoran Desert & the unusual animals & plants that live there. Curious about roadrunners or rattlesnakes? Wary of tumbleweeds & tarantulas? This book introduces animals you might see during the day, after a rainstorm, at sunset, & at night. How do they spend the day, & which ones are really dangerous? What kind of odd plants live in the desert, & what happens to them when it rains, or when it doesn't? Using the concept of "buddy," this book strives to encourage a sense of familiarity, acceptance, & guardianship toward these inhabitants. The 70# paper is perfect for coloring with crayons, colored pencils, or markers, but this book is much more than a coloring book. Full-page illustrations stand beautifully on their own. A center foldout & a cover flap with Velcro closure set this book apart from others. Great for parents, teachers, environmentalists & anyone concerned with encouraging children to appreciate the desert. DESERT BUDDIES is the first in a series that will focus on inhabitants of unique regions of the Earth. EARTH BUDDIES PUBLISHING, 820 S. 2nd Ave., Tucson, AZ 85701; 602-628-1753. *Publisher Provided Annotation.*

Plantimal Safari. (ps-6). 1986. 3.00 (*0-9605656-3-9*) Desert Botanical.

Reading, Susan. Desert Plants. 64p. 1990. 15.95x (*0-8160-2421-9*) Facts on File.

Twist, Clint. Deserts. LC 91-22471. (Illus.). 48p. (gr. 4-6). 1991. text ed. 13.95 RSBE (*0-87518-490-1*, Dillon) Macmillan Child Grp.

DESERTS

see also Desert Animals; Desert Plants

Amsel, Sheri. Deserts. Amsel, Sheri, illus. LC 92-8789. 32p. 1992. 19.24 (*0-8114-6300-1*) Raintree Steck-V.

Arnold, Caroline. A Walk in the Desert. Brook, Bonnie, ed. Tanz, Freya, illus. 32p. (ps-1). 1990. 4.95 (*0-671-68668-2*); lib. bdg. 6.95 (*0-671-68664-X*) Silver Pr.

—Watching Desert Wildlife. Arnold, Arthur, photos by. LC 93-48076. (Illus.). 1994. write for info. (*0-87614-841-0*) Carolrhoda Bks.

Arvetis, Chris & Palmer, Carole. Deserts. LC 93-502. (Illus.). 1993. write for info. (*0-528-83574-2*) Rand McNally.

Baker, Lucy. Life in the Deserts. (gr. 4-7). 1993. pap. 4.95 (*0-590-46129-X*) Scholastic Inc.

Barnard, Alan. Kalahari Bushmen. LC 93-32423. (Illus.). 48p. (gr. 6-10). 1994. 16.95 (*1-56847-160-2*) Thomson Lrning.

Barrett, Norman S. Desiertos. LC 90-71416. (SPA., Illus.). 32p. (gr. k-4). 1991. PLB 11.90 (*0-531-07924-4*) Watts.

Baylor, Byrd. The Desert Is Theirs. Parnall, Peter, illus. LC 74-24417. 32p. (ps-3). 1975. SBE 14.95 (*0-684-14266-X*, Scribners Young Read) Macmillan Child Grp.

—The Desert Is Theirs. Parnall, Peter, illus. LC 86-17323. 32p. (gr. 1-5). 1987. pap. 4.95 (*0-689-71105-0*, Aladdin) Macmillan Child Grp.

Behm, Barbara J. Exploring Deserts: Adapted from Veronica Bonar's Take a Square of Desert. LC 93-37062. 1994. 17.27 (*0-8368-1063-5*) Gareth Stevens Inc.

Brandt, Keith. Deserts. Watling, James, illus. LC 84-8623. 32p. (gr. 3-6). 1985. PLB 9.49 (*0-8167-0262-4*); pap. text ed. 2.95 (*0-8167-0263-2*) Troll Assocs.

Carrie, Christopher. Chase Through the Desert Wilds. (Illus.). 40p. (gr. k up). 1990. 1.59 (*0-86696-244-1*) Binney & Smith.

Catchpole, Clive. Deserts. McIntyre, Brian, illus. LC 83-7757. 32p. (ps-4). 1985. pap. 4.95 (*0-8037-0037-7*, 0481-140) Dial Bks Young.

Chicago Zoological Society Staff, ed. Desert Communities. (Orig.). (gr. 4-6). 1986. pap. text ed. 30.00 (*0-913934-06-2*) Chicago Zoo.

Cobb, Vicki. This Place Is Dry. Lavallee, Barbara, illus. 32p. (Orig.). (gr. 2-5). 1993. pap. 6.95 (*0-8027-7400-8*) Walker & Co.

Dewey, Jennifer O. Night & Day in the Desert, Vol. 1. (ps-3). 1991. 15.95 (*0-316-18210-9*) Little.

Dunphy, Madeleine. Here Is the Southwestern Desert. Coe, Anne, illus. LC 94-9375. 1995. write for info. (*0-7868-0049-6*); lib. bdg. write for info. (*0-7868-2038-1*) Hyprn Child.

George, Michael. Deserts. (gr. 5 up). 1992. PLB 18.95 (*0-88682-434-6*) Creative Ed.

—Deserts. 40p. (gr. 4-7). 1993. 15.95 (*1-56846-054-6*) Creat Editions.

Higginson, Mel. Deserts. LC 94-9403. 1994. write for info. (*0-86593-380-4*) Rourke Corp.

Hogan, Paula. Expanding Deserts. LC 90-27799. (Illus.). 32p. (gr. 3-4). 1991. PLB 17.27 (*0-8368-0474-0*) Gareth Stevens Inc.

Hughes, Jill. Deserts. (Illus.). 32p. (gr. 4-6). 1991. 13.95 (*0-237-60175-3*, Pub. by Evans Bros Ltd) Trafalgar.

Hunt, Joni P. The Desert. Leon, Vicki, ed. (Illus.). 40p. (Orig.). (gr. 5 up). 1991. pap. 7.95 (*0-918303-28-1*) Blake Pub.

Jablonsky, Alice. One Hundred One Questions: Desert Life. Foreman, Ronald J., ed. LC 93-84874. (Illus.). 32p. (Orig.). Date not set. pap. write for info. (*1-877856-32-0*) SW Pks Mnmts.

Knowlton, Jack. Deserts of the World. Barton, Harriett, illus. LC 92-19169. 48p. (gr. 2-5). 1995. 15.00 (*0-06-021309-4*); PLB 14.89 (*0-06-021310-8*) HarpC Child Bks.

Lawler, Howard E. Discover Deserts. (Illus.). 48p. (gr. 3-6). 1992. PLB 14.95 (*1-56674-029-0*, HTS Bks) Forest Hse.

Lye, Keith. Deserts. (Illus.). 48p. (gr. 5-8). 1987. PLB 12.95 (*0-382-09501-4*) Silver Burdett Pr.

McLeish, Ewan. Spread of Deserts. LC 90-10018. (Illus.). 48p. (gr. 4-9). 1990. PLB 21.34 (*0-8114-2390-5*); pap. 5.95 (*0-8114-3456-7*) Raintree Steck-V.

MacQuitty, Miranda. Desert. LC 93-21068. 1994. 16.00 (*0-679-86003-7*); PLB 16.99 (*0-679-96003-1*) Knopf Bks Yng Read.

Marchand, Peter. What Good Is a Cactus? Brown, Craig, illus. LC 94-65088. 32p. (Orig.). (gr. 3-6). 1994. pap. 9.95 (*1-879373-83-1*) R Rinehart.

Mariner, Tom. Deserts. LC 89-17278. (Illus.). 32p. (gr. 3-8). 1990. PLB 9.95 (*1-85435-192-3*) Marshall Cavendish.

Moore, Randy & Vodopich, Darrell S. The Living Desert. LC 90-42243. (Illus.). 64p. (gr. 6 up). 1991. lib. bdg. 15.95 (*0-89490-182-6*) Enslow Pubs.

Nabhan, Gary. Desert Life. 1994. write for info. (*0-8050-3100-6*) H Holt & Co.

National Wildlife Federation Staff. Discovering Deserts. (gr. k-8). 1991. pap. 7.95 (*0-945051-34-4*, 75005) Natl Wildlife.

Norden, Carroll R. Deserts. rev. ed. LC 87-23224. (Illus.). 48p. (gr. 2-6). 1987. PLB 10.95 (*0-8172-3252-4*) Raintree Steck-V.

Olin, George. House in the Sun: A Natural History of the Sonoran Desert. rev. ed. LC 93-86936. 230p. (gr. 8-12). 1994. pap. 12.95 (*1-877856-39-8*) SW Pks Mnmts.

Palmer, Joy. Deserts. LC 92-12406. (Illus.). 32p. (gr. 2-3). 1992. PLB 18.99 (*0-8114-3402-8*) Raintree Steck-V.

Petty, Kate. Deserts. Wood, Jakki, illus. 32p. (gr. 2-4). 1993. pap. 5.95 (*0-8120-1762-5*) Barron.

Philabaum, Dabney M. Desert Buddies. Alegret, Nancy L., illus. 40p. (gr. k-4). 1994. pap. 8.95 (*0-9639215-0-9*) Earth Buddies.
An informative & engaging text presenting the look, smell, & feel of the Sonoran Desert & the unusual animals & plants that live there. Curious about roadrunners or rattlesnakes? Wary of tumbleweeds & tarantulas? This book introduces animals you might see during the day, after a rainstorm, at sunset, & at night. How do they spend the day, & which ones are really dangerous? What kind of odd plants live in the desert, & what happens to them when it rains, or when it doesn't? Using the concept of "buddy," this book strives to encourage a sense of familiarity, acceptance, & guardianship toward these inhabitants. The 70# paper is perfect for coloring with crayons, colored pencils, or markers, but this book is much more than a coloring book. Full-page illustrations stand beautifully on their own. A center foldout & a cover flap with Velcro closure set this book apart from others. Great for parents, teachers, environmentalists & anyone concerned with encouraging children to appreciate the desert. DESERT BUDDIES is the first in a series that will focus on inhabitants of unique regions of the Earth. EARTH BUDDIES PUBLISHING, 820 S. 2nd Ave., Tucson, AZ 85701; 602-628-1753.
Publisher Provided Annotation.

Posell, Elsa. Deserts. LC 81-15548. (Illus.). 48p. (gr. k-4). 1982. PLB 12.85 (*0-516-01613-X*); pap. 4.95 (*0-516-41613-8*) Childrens.

Sabin, Louis. Wonders of the Desert. Baldwin-Ford, Pamela, illus. LC 81-7397. 32p. (gr. 2-4). 1982. PLB 11.59 (*0-89375-574-5*); pap. text ed. 2.95 (*0-89375-575-3*) Troll Assocs.

Salts, Bobbi. Desert Discovery: An Activity Book for Kids. Parker, Steve, illus. 32p. (gr. 1-6). 1989. pap. text ed. 2.95 (*0-929526-01-5*) Double B Pubns.

Sanders, John. All about Deserts. Boyd, Patti, illus. LC 83-4857. 32p. (gr. 3-6). 1984. lib. bdg. 10.59 (*0-89375-965-1*); pap. text ed. 2.95 (*0-89375-966-X*) Troll Assocs.

Sayre, April P. Deserts. (Illus.). 64p. (gr. 5-8). 1994. bds. 15.95 (*0-8050-2825-0*) TFC Bks NY.

Simon, Seymour. Deserts. LC 89-39738. (Illus.). 32p. (gr. k up). 1990. 13.95 (*0-688-07415-4*); PLB 13.88 (*0-688-07416-2*, Morrow Jr Bks) Morrow Jr Bks.

Spencer, Guy. A Living Desert. Fuller, Tim, illus. LC 87-3488. 32p. (gr. 3-6). 1988. PLB 10.79 (*0-8167-1169-0*); pap. text ed. 2.95 (*0-8167-1170-4*) Troll Assocs.

Steele, Philip. Deserts. LC 90-20759. (Illus.). 32p. (gr. 5-6). 1991. text ed. 11.95 RSBE (*0-89686-588-6*, Crestwood Hse) Macmillan Child Grp.

Stewart, G. In the Desert. (Illus.). 32p. (gr. 3-8). 1989. lib. bdg. 15.74 (*0-86592-106-7*); 11.95s.p. (*0-685-58594-8*) Rourke Corp.

Stone, L. Deserts. (Illus.). 48p. (gr. 4-8). 1989. lib. bdg. 15.94 (*0-86592-438-4*); 11.95s.p. (*0-685-67722-2*) Rourke Corp.

Taylor, Barbara. Desert Life. LC 91-58195. (Illus.). 32p. (gr. 1-4). 1992. 9.95 (*1-879431-93-9*) Dorling Kindersley.

Twist, Clint. Deserts. LC 91-22471. (Illus.). 48p. (gr. 4-6). 1991. text ed. 13.95 RSBE (*0-87518-490-1*, Dillon) Macmillan Child Grp.

Watts, Barrie. Twenty-Four Hours in a Desert. LC 90-46322. (Illus.). 48p. (gr. 4-6). 1991. PLB 12.90 (*0-531-14187-X*) Watts.

Wilkes. Deserts. (gr. 4-6). 1980. (Usborne-Hayes); PLB 11.96 (*0-88110-694-1*); pap. 4.50 (*0-7460-0757-4*) EDC.

Williams, Lawrence. Deserts. LC 89-17340. (Illus.). 48p. (gr. 4-8). 1990. PLB 12.95 (*1-85435-169-9*) Marshall Cavendish.

Wolfe, Robert L. & Wolfe, Diane, photos by. Desserts Around the World. (Illus.). 56p. (gr. 5 up). 1991. PLB 14.95 (*0-8225-0926-1*) Lerner Pubns.

DESERTS–FICTION

Albert, Richard E. Alejandro's Gift. Long, Sylvia, illus. LC 93-30199. 1994. 13.95 (*0-8118-0436-4*) Chronicle Bks.

Baylor, Byrd. Desert Voices. Parnall, Peter, illus. LC 80-17061. 32p. (ps-3). 1981. SBE 14.95 (*0-684-16712-3*, Scribners Young Read) Macmillan Child Grp.

—Desert Voices. Parnell, Peter, illus. LC 92-24475. 32p. (gr. 1-5). 1993. pap. 3.95 (*0-689-71691-5*, Aladdin) Macmillan Child Grp.

Blanco, Alberto. Desert Mermaid (La sirena del desierto) LC 92-1105. (Illus.). 32p. (gr. k-5). 1992. 13.95 (*0-89239-106-5*) Childrens Book Pr.

Brown, Hayden & Dickins, Roberts. The Sombrero. Dickins, Robert, illus. LC 93-6633. 1994. write for info. (*0-383-03714-X*) SRA Schl Grp.

Buchanan, Ken & Buchanan, Debby. It Rained on the Desert Today. Tracy, Libba, illus. LC 93-44813. 32p. (ps up). 1994. 14.95 (*0-87358-575-5*) Northland AZ.

Haarhoff, Dorian. Desert December. Vermeulen, Leon, illus. 32p. (ps-3). 1992. 13.95 (*0-395-61300-0*, Clarion Bks) HM.

Johnson, Angela. Toning the Sweep: A Novel. LC 92-34062. 112p. (gr. 6 up). 1993. 13.95 (*0-531-05476-4*); PLB 13.99 (*0-531-08626-7*) Orchard Bks Watts.

L'Engle, Madeleine. Dance in the Desert. Shimin, Symeon, illus. LC 68-29465. 64p. (ps up). 1969. 14.95 (*0-374-31684-8*) FS&G.

Levy. Cleo & Coyote. Date not set. 15.00 (*0-06-024271-X*); PLB 14.89 (*0-06-024272-8*) HarpC Child Bks.

Mora, Francisco X. Juan Tuza & the Magic Pouch. Mora, Francisco X., illus. 32p. (ps-1). 1993. PLB 15.00 (*0-917846-24-9*, 95563) Highsmith Pr.

Nunes, Susan. Coyote Dreams. Himler, Ronald, illus. LC 93-22931. 32p. (gr. k-3). 1994. pap. 4.95 (*0-689-71804-7*, Aladdin) Macmillan Child Grp.

Papagapitos, Karen. Gemini Code II. Kleinman, Estelle, ed. Middleton, Curt, illus. Nicholson, David, ed. (Illus.). 96p. (Orig.). (gr. 5-9). 1994. pap. 7.95 (*0-9637328-2-X*); pap. 4.95 (*0-9637328-3-8*) Kapa Hse Pr.
THE GEMINI CODE II, the third book in the "JB Series" (JB=Jose's Basket), takes place in the 1990s. Jose & his wife Alicia, a banking executive, have twin ten-year-old sons, Hector & Luis. A favorite hobby of theirs is to play computer games, each trying to outsmart the other with new codes for different games. Alicia & Jose, who are now successful authors, are delighted with this shared interest. When Hector, the first-born twin, lost his hearing at the age of two because of a severe ear infection, the ability to communicate by computer, in addition to sign language, contributed to the closeness of the brothers & their parents. Little does anyone realize just how important this computer knowledge will be. Luis gets trapped on the other side of an arroyo filled with rushing water during a flash flood. Hector, Jose & Alicia are running out of time in their search for him when suddenly a code of Luis' is transmitted on the computer screen. Without waiting to figure out who could have sent the message, Hector breaks the code & Luis is found before it's too late. Distributed by: Baker & Taylor Books, 652 E. Main St., P.O. Box 6920, Bridgewater, NJ 08807-0920; 908-218-0400.
Publisher Provided Annotation.

Reid, Mary C. Come to the Desert with Me. LC 91-71036. 32p. 1991. pap. 4.99 (*0-8066-2552-X*, 9-2552) Augsburg Fortress.

Seymour, Tres. Life in the Desert. LC 92-7945. 96p. (gr. 7-12). 1992. 12.95 (*0-531-05458-6*); PLB 12.99 (*0-531-08608-9*) Orchard Bks Watts.

Skurzynski, Gloria. Lost in the Devil's Desert. Scrofani, Joseph M., illus. LC 92-45656. 96p. (gr. 5 up). 1993. pap. 3.95 (*0-688-04593-6*, Pub. by Beech Tree Bks) Morrow.

Woolgar, Jack. Mystery in the Desert. (gr. 6-8). 1967. 7.19 (*0-8313-0107-4*); PLB 7.19 (*0-685-13778-3*) Lantern.

DESIGN

For works on the theory of design.
see also Costume Design

Bullach, Ivan & Chambers, Tony. Design. Maudlsley, Toby & Johnson, James, photos by. Bulloch, Ivan, designed by. LC 93-35626. (Illus.). 48p. (gr. 5-9). 1994. 16.95 (*1-56847-148-3*) Thomson Lrning.

Gerson, Trina. Poetic Shapes. Gerson, Janice, illus. 52p. (ps-7). 1981. pap. text ed. 2.95 (*0-9605878-0-2*) Anirt Pr.

McDermott, Catherine. Design. LC 90-10000. (Illus.). 48p. (gr. 6-11). 1990. PLB 11.95 (*0-8114-2364-6*) Raintree Steck-V.

Malcolm, Dorothea C. Design: Elements & Principles. LC 71-148087. (Illus.). 128p. (gr. 5-12). 1972. 15.95 (*0-87192-039-5*) Davis Mass.

Morton, Lone. My Second Design Book. 24p. (gr. 1-4). 1994. pap. 4.95 (*0-8120-1262-3*) Barron.

Polette, Nancy. Pick a Pattern. 4th, expanded ed. (Illus.). 48p. (gr. k-3). 1992. pap. 5.95 (*1-879287-05-6*) Bk Lures.

DESIGN, DECORATIVE

see also Art, Decorative; Decoration and Ornament; Drawing; Lettering

DESSERTS

Klevin, Jill R. Turtles Together Forever! Edwards, Linda S., illus. LC 82-70313. 160p. (gr. 4-6). 1982. pap. 9.95 (*0-385-29045-4*); pap. 9.89 (*0-385-29046-2*) Delacorte.

Mitgutsch, Ali. From Milk to Ice Cream. Mitgutsch, Ali, illus. LC 81-81. 24p. (ps-3). 1981. PLB 10.95 (*0-87614-158-0*) Carolrhoda Bks.

Rosin, Arielle. Eclairs & Brown Bears. Czap, Daniel, photos by. Collomb, Etienne. LC 93-24971. (Illus.). 60p. (gr. 3 up). 1994. 12.95 (*0-395-68380-7*) Ticknor & Flds Bks Yng Read.

Wilkes, A. Sweet Things. (Illus.). 24p. (gr. 1-4). 1993. pap. 4.50 (*0-7460-0227-0*, Usborne) EDC.

DETECTIVE STORIES

see Mystery and Detective Stories

DETECTIVES

see also Criminal Investigation; Police

Albert, Burton, Jr. Top Secret! Codes to Crack. Levine, Abby, ed. Warshaw, Jerry, illus. LC 87-2146. 32p. (gr. 4-7). 1987. PLB 11.95 (*0-8075-8027-9*) A Whitman.

Civardi, A., et al. Detective's Handbook (B - U) (Illus.). 192p. (gr. 2-6). 1992. pap. 9.95 (*0-86020-278-X*) EDC.

Paige, David. A Day in the Life of a Police Detective. Ruhlin, Roger, photos by. LC 80-54102. (Illus.). 32p. (gr. 4-8). 1981. PLB 11.79 (*0-89375-442-0*) Troll Assocs.

Travis, F., et al. Spy's Guidebook (B - U) (Illus.). 192p. (gr. 2-6). 1993. pap. 9.95 (*0-86020-169-4*) EDC.

Wormser, Richard. Allan Pinkerton: America's First Private Eye. (Illus.). 119p. (gr. 5 up). 1990. 17.95 (*0-8027-6964-0*); lib. bdg. 18.85 (*0-8027-6965-9*) Walker & Co.

DETECTIVES–FICTION

Armstrong, Bev. Dinosaur Detective. Armstrong, Bev, illus. 32p. (gr. k-3). 1979. 3.95 (*0-88160-075-X*, LW 808) Learning Wks.

Avi. The Man Who Was Poe. LC 89-42537. 224p. (gr. 6-8). 1989. 13.95 (*0-531-05833-6*); PLB 13.99 (*0-531-08433-7*) Orchard Bks Watts.

Ehrlich, Amy. Where It Stops, Nobody Knows. LC 88-4095. 192p. (gr. 6 up). 1988. 14.95 (*0-8037-0575-1*) Dial Bks Young.

Johnson, Larry D. & Mills, Jane L. Arnie the Detective. Hebert, Kim T., illus. LC 86-60364. 24p. (ps). 1986. pap. 4.50 (*0-938155-06-7*); pap. 12.00 set of 3 bks. (*0-685-13514-4*) Read A Bol.

Kelso, Mary J. Sierra Summer. Kelso, Mary J., illus. 120p. (Orig.). (gr. 6 up). 1992. pap. 6.95 (*0-9621406-3-5*) Markel Pr.

Kwitz, Mary D. Gumshoe Goose, Private Eye. Ernst, Lisa C., illus. LC 86-29331. 48p. (ps-3). 1988. 9.95 (*0-8037-0423-2*); PLB 9.89 (*0-8037-0424-0*) Dial Bks Young.

Miller, Marvin. Who Dunnnit? How to Be a Detective in Ten Easy Lessons. (gr. 4-7). 1992. pap. 2.75 (*0-590-44717-3*) Scholastic Inc.

Platt, Kin. Big Max. Lopshire, Robert, illus. LC 91-14743. (gr. k-3). 1978. pap. 3.50 (*0-06-444006-0*, Trophy) HarpC Child Bks.

Reed, Joyce G. Take a Whistler's Walk. Reed, J., illus. 77p. (gr. 4-9). 1988. 12.95 (*0-943487-08-0*); pap. 4.95 (*0-943487-07-2*) Sevgo Pr.

Rosenberg, Amye & Mason, Patrice G. Sam the Detective & the Alef Bet Mystery. Rossel, Seymour, ed. Rosenberg, Amye, illus. 64p. (Orig.). (gr. 1-3). 1980. pap. text ed. 4.45 (*0-87441-328-1*) Behrman.

Sobol, Donald J. Encyclopedia Brown & the Case of the Mysterious Handprints, No. 16. 128p. 1986. pap. 3.50 (*0-553-15739-6*, Skylark) Bantam.

—Encyclopedia Brown Lends a Hand. (gr. 4-6). 1993. pap. 3.25 (*0-553-48133-9*) Bantam.
—Encyclopedia Brown's Book of Wacky Animals. 128p. (Orig.). 1985. pap. 2.25 (*0-553-15346-3*, Skylark) Bantam.
—Encyclopedia Brown's Third Record Book of Weird & Wonderful Facts. 144p. 1985. pap. 2.50 (*0-553-15372-2*, Skylark) Bantam.
Vestavia Elementary School Fourth Grade Class & Cockrell, Marcille. The Adventures of a Bubble-Bellied Bloopy Droopy Detective. (Illus.). 32p. (gr. k-5). 1989. pap. 3.95 (*0-943487-22-6*) Sevgo Pr.

DETROIT–FICTION

Burgess, Barbara H. The Fred Field. LC 93-14260. 1994. 14.95 (*0-385-31070-6*) Delacorte.

DETROIT TIGERS (BASEBALL TEAM)

Detroit Tigers. (gr. 4-7). 1993. pap. 1.49 (*0-553-56410-2*) Bantam.
Rambeck, Richard. Detroit Tigers. 48p. (gr. 4-10). 1991. PLB 14.95 (*0-88682-447-8*) Creative Ed.

DEVELOPING COUNTRIES

Rohr, Janelle, ed. The Third World: Opposing Viewpoints. LC 89-36524. (Illus.). 264p. (gr. 10 up). 1989. PLB 17.95 (*0-89908-447-8*); pap. 9.95 (*0-89908-422-2*) Greenhaven.

DEVELOPMENT

see Embryology; Evolution; Growth

DEVICES (HERALDRY)

see Heraldry; Symbolism

DEVIL

Leslie, Elsie. Is Satan Real? Bates, Stephen, illus. (gr. k-6). 1987. pap. 4.25 (*1-55976-153-9*) CEF Press.
Ottens, Allen & Myer, Rick. Coping with Satanism. Rosen, Ruth, ed. (gr. 7-12). 1994. 14.95 (*0-8239-1423-2*) Rosen Group.

DEVIL–FICTION

Avi. Devil's Race. LC 84-47636. 160p. (gr. 7 up). 1984. (Lipp Jr Bks); PLB 15.89 (*0-397-32095-7*, Lipp Jr Bks) HarpC Child Bks.
Babbitt, Natalie. The Devil's Storybook. (Illus.). 102p. (gr. 3-7). 1974. 13.00 (*0-374-31770-4*) FS&G.
Beat the Devil. 118p. (Orig.). (gr. 7-12). 1984. pap. 2.50 (*0-553-26755-8*) Bantam.
Benet, Stephen Vincent. The Devil & Daniel Webster. 48p. (gr. 6). 1990. PLB 13.95s.p. (*0-88682-295-5*) Creative Ed.
Hooks, William H. Mean Jake & the Devils. Zimmer, Dirk, illus. LC 81-65846. 64p. (gr. 3-6). 1981. Dial Bks Young.
Lewis, C. S. The Screwtape Letters. 160p. 1992. pap. text ed. 4.95 (*1-55748-315-9*) Barbour & Co.
Marsh, Carole. The Legend of the Devil's Hoofprints. (Illus., Orig.). (gr. 2 up). 1994. PLB 24.95 (*1-55609-177-X*); pap. 14.95 (*0-935326-57-X*) Gallopade Pub Group.
Reberg, Evelyne. A Devil in the Grog Garage. (Illus.). (gr. 3-8). 1992. PLB 8.95 (*0-89565-893-3*) Childs World.
Smith, David B. Watching the War. LC 93-48994. 1994. write for info. (*0-8280-0790-X*) Review & Herald.
Tate, Joan. Ling & the Little Devils. Otto, Svend, illus. (ps-3). 9.95 (*0-317-61896-2*) Viking Child Bks.
Zemach, Harve. Duffy & the Devil. Zemach, Margot, illus. LC 72-81491. 40p. (ps up). 1973. 17.00 (*0-374-31887-5*); pap. 4.95, 1986 (*0-374-41897-7*, Sunburst) FS&G.

DEVOTION

see Worship

DIABETES

Aiello, Barbara & Shulman, Jeffrey. A Portrait of Me: Featuring Christine Kontos. (Illus.). 48p. (gr. 3-6). 1989. PLB 13.95 (*0-941477-05-3*) TFC Bks NY.
Almonte, Paul & Desmond, Theresa. Diabetes. LC 90-45745. (Illus.). 48p. (gr. 5-6). 1991. text ed. 12.95 RSBE (*0-89686-604-1*, Crestwood Hse) Macmillan Child Grp.
American Diabetes Association Staff. Teddy Ryder Rides Again! 22p. 1990. pap. 1.50 (*0-945448-21-X*, CCHTRRA) Am Diabetes.
Bergman, Thomas. Meeting the Challenge: Children Living with Diabetes. LC 91-50334. (Illus.). 56p. (gr. 3-8). 1992. PLB 18.60 (*0-8368-0738-3*) Gareth Stevens Inc.
Connelly, John P. You're Too Sweet. (gr. 4-9). 1968. 9.95 (*0-8392-1173-2*) Astor-Honor.
Dacquino, V. T. Kiss the Candy Days Good-Bye. LC 82-70324. 160p. (gr. 4-6). 1982. pap. 11.95 (*0-385-28532-9*) Delacorte.

Fennoy, Thelma R. Kristina & Diabetes: How Kristina Faced the Disease. Durant, Charlotte T., illus. 56p. (Orig.). (gr. 2 up). 1993. pap. text ed. 5.00 (*0-9637350-0-4*) T R Fennoy. A tender book that helps kids learn about diabetes, helps kids live better & understand their condition. Fennoy tells the real life story of ten-year old Kristina who has diabetes, a disease without a cure. Kristina is faced with responsibilities for her own body & her life, & has to make adult decisions. For big adjustments, kids need a helping hand. Fennoy's book, a vital guide, provides accurate information. Kristina has to overcome her fear, learn the cause & symptoms of diabetes, & learn how to manage her condition. No small feat for a kid. Fennoy & Durant show exactly how a child can give herself painless shots, can test her own blood sugar level. A compassionate book that helps children with diabetes to live well-adjusted, happy lives. Fennoy Publisher, RR2 Box 173, Jefferson, TX 75657, paper, $5 plus $2 shipping & handling.
Publisher Provided Annotation.

Goodheart, Barbara. Diabetes. LC 90-31328. (Illus.). 128p. (gr. 9-12). 1990. PLB 13.40 (*0-531-10882-1*) Watts.
Gosselin, Kim. Taking Diabetes to School. Freedman, Moss, illus. 24p. (gr. k-6). 1994. pap. 9.95 (*0-9639449-0-8*) JayJo Bks.
Heegaard, Marge. When a Family Gets Diabetes. (Illus.). 50p. (Orig.). (gr. 1-9). 1990. pap. 6.95 (*0-937721-75-1*) Chronimed.
Landau, Elaine. Diabetes. (Illus.). 64p. (gr. 5-8). 1994. bds. 15.95 (*0-8050-2988-5*) TFC Bks NY.
Little, Marjorie. Diabetes. (Illus.). 112p. (gr. 6-12). 1991. 18.95 (*0-7910-0061-3*) Chelsea Hse.
Nemaneic, Allison, et al. Diabetes Care Made Easy: A Simple Step-by-Step Guide for Controlling Your Diabetes. LC 92-11193. 1992. 9.95 (*1-56561-013-X*) Chronimed.
Pirner, Connie. Even Little Kids Get Diabetes. Tucker, Kathy, ed. Westcott, Nadine B., illus. LC 90-12738. 24p. (ps-2). 1991. 10.95 (*0-8075-2158-2*) A Whitman.
—Even Little Kids Get Diabetes. (ps-3). 1994. pap. 4.95 (*0-8075-2159-0*) A Whitman.
Silverstein, Alvin, et al. Diabetes. LC 93-41199. (Illus.). 128p. (gr. 6 up). 1994. PLB 17.95 (*0-89490-464-7*) Enslow Pubs.
Tiger, Steven. Diabetes. Reingold, Michael, illus. LC 86-23498. 72p. (gr. 4-8). 1987. lib. bdg. 13.98 (*0-671-63273-6*, J Messner) S&S Trade.

DIALECTICS

see Logic

DIARIES

see Autobiographies

DICKENS, CHARLES, 1812-1870

Collins, David R. Tales for Hard Times: A Story about Charles Dickens. Mataya, David, illus. 64p. (gr. 3-6). 1990. PLB 14.95 (*0-87614-433-4*) Carolrhoda Bks.
Martin, Christopher. Dickens. (Illus.). 112p. (gr. 7 up). 1990. lib. bdg. 19.94 (*0-86593-016-3*); lib. bdg. 14. 95s.p. (*0-685-36352-X*) Rourke Corp.

DICKINSON, EMILY, 1830-1886

Barth, Edna. I'm Nobody, Who Are You: The Story of Emily Dickinson. Cuffari, Richard, illus. LC 72-129211. 128p. (gr. 3-6). 1979. 15.95 (*0-395-28843-6*, Clarion Bks) HM.
Greene, Carol. Emily Dickinson: American Poet. LC 94-11167. (Illus.). 32p. (gr. 2-4). 1994. PLB 17.20 (*0-516-04263-7*); pap. 4.95 (*0-516-44263-5*) Childrens.
Olsen, Victoria. Emily Dickinson. Horner, Matina S., intro. by. (Illus.). 112p. (gr. 5 up). 1990. 17.95 (*1-55546-649-4*) Chelsea Hse.
Thayer, Bonita E. Emily Dickinson. LC 88-31376. (Illus.). 144p. (gr. 7-12). 1990. 14.40 (*0-531-10658-6*) Watts.

DICTATORS

Blackwood, Alan. Twenty Tyrants. LC 89-23853. (Illus.). 48p. (gr. 3-8). 1990. PLB 12.95 (*1-85435-255-5*) Marshall Cavendish.

DIET

see also Beverages; Cookery; Digestion; Food; Vegetarianism; Weight Control

Kamen, Betty. The Chromium Diet, Supplement & Exercise Strategy: An Easy to Follow Routine for Everyone. Rosenbaum, Michael E., intro. by. (Illus.). 216p. (Orig.). 1990. pap. 9.95 (*0-944501-03-6*) Nutrition Encounter.
Leedy, Loreen. The Edible Pyramid. Leedy, Loreen, illus. LC 94-2122. 32p. 1994. reinforced bdg. 15.95 (*0-8234-1126-5*) Holiday.
Ward, Elizabeth, ed. What Makes Popcorn Pop? First Questions & Answers about Food. (Illus.). 48p. (ps). 1994. write for info. (*0-7835-0862-X*); PLB write for info. (*0-7835-0863-8*) Time-Life.
Wolhart, Dayna. Anorexia & Bulimia. LC 88-21553. (Illus.). 48p. (gr. 5-6). 1988. text ed. 12.95 RSBE (*0-89686-416-2*, Crestwood Hse) Macmillan Child Grp.

DIET IN DISEASE

Lynch, Patti. Kids' Stuffin's: Good & Healthy Stuff for Kids to Make & Eat. Bale, Melissa, illus. 100p. (Orig.). 1995. Spiral Bound. pap. write for info. (*0-9620469-2-2*) Sweet Inspirations. KIDS' STUFFIN'S is a cookbook filled with recipes FUN & TASTY enough to delight a child's appetite. The recipes are HEALTHY enough to win a parents praise. Children ages 4 to Adult will enjoy these fun to prepare snacks. KIDS' STUFFIN'S is a delightful positive way for children to learn to prepare & eat healthy snacks. Illustrated in FULL COLOR with DELIGHTFUL ANIMATED ANIMAL CHARACTERS. Simple instructions give children a positive hands-on experience in the kitchen. The recipes are LOW FAT & FREE OF REFINED SUGAR. Recipes are appropriate for children with DIET RESTRICTIONS, such as Diabetes. Food Groups/values included. Price not determined. Publisher: Sweet Inspirations, 1420 NW Gilman Blvd. #2258, Issaquah, WA 98027; 206-643-8621.
Publisher Provided Annotation.

DIETETICS

see Diet

DIGESTION

see also Diet; Food; Nutrition

All about Our Bodies, Our Digestion. 14p. (gr. k-6). pap. 4.50 (*0-89346-297-7*) Heian Intl.
Avraham, Regina. The Digestive System. (Illus.). 104p. (gr. 6-12). 1989. 18.95 (*0-7910-0015-X*) Chelsea Hse.
Bailey, Donna. All about Digestion. LC 90-41010. (Illus.). 48p. (gr. 2-6). 1990. PLB 20.70 (*0-8114-2781-1*) Raintree Steck-V.
Bryan, Jenny. Digestion: The Digestive System. LC 92-35052. (Illus.). 48p. (gr. 5 up). 1993. text ed. 13.95 RSBE (*0-87518-564-9*, Dillon) Macmillan Child Grp.
Cho, Shinta. The Gas We Pass: The Story of Farts. Stinchecum, Amanda M., tr. from JPN. LC 94-14267. (Illus.). 32p. (ps-k). 1994. 11.95 (*0-916291-52-9*) Kane-Miller Bk.
Erlanger, Ellen. Eating Disorders: A Question & Answer Book about Anorexia Nervosa & Bulimia Nervosa. LC 87-15311. (gr. 6-10). 1988. 15.95 (*0-8225-0038-8*) Lerner Pubns.
Food & Digestion. 48p. (gr. 5-8). 1988. PLB 10.95 (*0-382-09704-1*) (*0-685-24612-4*) Silver Burdett Pr.
Ganeri, Anita. Eating. (Illus.). 32p. (gr. 2-4). 1994. PLB 18.99 (*0-8114-5522-X*) Raintree Steck-V.
Nardo, Don. Eating Disorders. LC 91-15563. (Illus.). 112p. (gr. 5-8). 1991. PLB 14.95 (*1-56006-129-4*) Lucent Bks.
Needham, Kate. Why Do People Eat? (Illus.). 24p. (gr. 1-5). 1993. lib. bdg. 11.96 (*0-88110-638-0*, Usborne); pap. 3.95 (*0-7460-1302-7*, Usborne) EDC.
Parker, Steve. Eating a Meal: How You Eat, Drink & Digest. LC 90-77856. (Illus.). 32p. (gr. k-4). 1991. PLB 11.40 (*0-531-14086-5*) Watts.
—Food & Digestion. rev. ed. (Illus.). 48p. (gr. 5 up). 1991. pap. 6.95 (*0-531-24603-5*) Watts.
Showers, Paul. What Happens to a Hamburger? rev. ed. Rockwell, Anne, illus. LC 84-45343. 32p. (ps-3). 1985. (Crowell Jr Bks); PLB 14.89 (*0-690-04427-5*, Crowell Jr Bks) HarpC Child Bks.
Silverstein, Alvin & Silverstein, Virginia. Digestive System. (Illus.). 96p. (gr. 5-8). 1994. bds. 16.95 (*0-8050-2832-3*) TFC Bks NY.
—Excretory Systems. (Illus.). 96p. (gr. 5-8). 1994. bds. 16.95 (*0-8050-2834-X*) TFC Bks NY.
Zim, Herbert S. Your Stomach & Digestive Tract. Martin, Rene, illus. LC 72-6734. 64p. (gr. 3-7). 1973. PLB 12. 88 (*0-688-31838-X*, Morrow Jr Bks) Morrow Jr Bks.

DI MAGGIO, JOSEPH PAUL, 1914-

Engel, Trudie. Joe DiMaggio, Baseball Star. (gr. 4-7). 1994. pap. 2.95 (*0-590-46067-6*) Scholastic Inc.
Sanford, William R. & Green, Carl R. Joe DiMaggio. LC 91-42180. (Illus.). 48p. (gr. 5). 1993. text ed. 11.95 RSBE (*0-89686-738-2*, Crestwood Hse) Macmillan Child Grp.

DINERS

see Restaurants, Bars, Etc.

DINOSAURS

Alden, Laura. Megalosaurus. Magnuson, Diana, illus. (SPA & ENG.). 32p. (ps-2). 1990. PLB 14.95 (*0-89565-629-9*) Childs World.
—Ornithomimus. Ching, illus. (SPA & ENG.). 32p. (gr. k-4). 1990. PLB 14.95 (*0-89565-630-2*) Childs World.
Aliki. Aliki's Dinosaur Dig: A Book & Card Game. Aliki, illus. 32p. (gr. k-6). 1992. pap. 9.95 incl. cards (*0-694-00286-0*) HarpC Child Bks.
—Digging up Dinosaurs. rev. ed. Aliki, illus. LC 87-29949. 32p. (ps-3). 1988. 15.00i (*0-690-04714-2*, Crowell Jr Bks); PLB 14.89 (*0-690-04716-9*) HarpC Child Bks.
—Digging up Dinosaurs. rev. ed. Aliki, illus. LC 85-42979. 32p. (gr. k-3). 1988. pap. 4.95 (*0-06-445078-3*, Trophy) HarpC Child Bks.
—Digging up Dinosaurs. 32p. (ps-2). 1991. pap. 7.95 (*1-55994-302-5*, Caedmon) HarperAudio.

—Dinosaur Bones. Aliki, illus. 32p. (gr. k-4). 1990. pap. 4.95 (*0-06-445077-5*, Trophy) HarpC Child Bks.
—Dinosaurs Are Different. Aliki, illus. LC 84-45332. 32p. (ps-3). 1985. 14.00 (*0-690-04456-9*, Crowell Jr Bks); PLB 13.89 (*0-690-04458-5*) HarpC Child Bks.
—Dinosaurs Are Different. Aliki, illus. LC 84-45332. 32p. (ps-3). 1988. (Trophy); pap. 4.95 (*0-06-445056-2*, Trophy) HarpC Child Bks.
—My Visit to the Dinosaurs. rev. ed. Aliki, illus. LC 85-47538. 32p. (ps-3). 1985. 14.00 (*0-690-04422-4*, Crowell Jr Bks); PLB 13.89 (*0-690-04423-2*) HarpC Child Bks.
—My Visit to the Dinosaurs. 2nd ed. Aliki, illus. LC 85-42748. 32p. (ps-3). 1987. (Trophy); pap. 4.95 (*0-06-445020-1*, Trophy) HarpC Child Bks.
All about Dinosaurs. (Illus.). 32p. (Orig.). 1994. pap. 8.95 incl. cass. (*0-7935-2379-6*, 00330502) H Leonard.
Amazing Dinosaurs: The Fastest, the Smallest, the Fiercest, & the Tallest. (ps-1). 1991. write for info. (*0-307-15747-4*, Golden Pr) Western Pub.
Amery, Heather. Looking at Velociropator. Gibbons, Tony, illus. LC 93-37064. 1994. 17.27 (*0-8368-1087-2*) Gareth Stevens Inc.
Amery, Heather, et al. Looking at... Brachiosaurus: A Dionsaur from the Jurassic Period. Gibbons, Tony, illus. 24p. (gr. 2 up). 1993. PLB 17.27 (*0-8368-1044-9*) Gareth Stevens Inc.
—Looking at... Iguanodon: A Dinosaur from the Cretaceous Period. Gibbons, Tony, illus. 24p. (gr. 2 up). 1993. PLB 17.27 (*0-8368-1045-7*) Gareth Stevens Inc.
—Looking at... Protoceratops: A Dinosaur from the Cretaceous Period. Gibbons, Tony, illus. LC 93-5536. 24p. (gr. 2 up). 1993. PLB 17.27 (*0-8368-1046-5*) Gareth Stevens Inc.
—Looking at... Stegosaurus: A Dinosaur from the Jurassic Period. Gibbons, Tony, illus. LC 93-5535. 24p. (gr. 2 up). 1993. PLB 17.27 (*0-8368-1047-3*) Gareth Stevens Inc.
—Looking at... Triceratops: A Dinosaur from the Cretaceous Period. Gibbons, Tony, illus. 24p. (gr. 2 up). 1993. PLB 17.27 (*0-8368-1048-1*) Gareth Stevens Inc.
—Looking at... Tyrannosaurus Rex: A Dinosaur from the Cretaceous Period. Gibbons, Tony, illus. 24p. (gr. 2 up). 1993. PLB 17.27 (*0-8368-1049-X*) Gareth Stevens Inc.
Arem, Joel E. Descubre Dinosaurios. University of Mexico City Staff, tr. from SPA. O'Neill, Pablo M. & Robare, Lorie, illus. 48p. (gr. 3-8). 1993. PLB 16.95 (*1-56674-049-5*, HTS Bks) Forest Hse.
Armstrong, B. Dinosaurs. 32p. (gr. 1-7). 1988. 3.95 (*0-88160-160-8*, LW 265) Learning Wks.
Arnold, Caroline. Dinosaurs Down Under: And Other Fossils from Australia. Hewett, Richard, photos by. (Illus.). 48p. (gr. 3-7). 1990. 15.45 (*0-89919-814-7*, Clarion Bks) HM.
Asimov, Isaac. Did Comets Kill the Dinosaurs? 1990. pap. 4.95 (*0-440-40347-2*, YB) Dell.
—How Did We Find Out about Dinosaurs. LC 72-95793. (gr. 5 up). 1981. PLB 11.85 (*0-8027-6134-8*) Walker & Co.
Asimov, Isaac, et al. Death from Space: What Killed the Dinosaurs? rev. & updated ed. (Illus.). (gr. 3 up). 1994. PLB 17.27 (*0-8368-1129-1*) Gareth Stevens Inc.
Barlowe, Dorothea & Barlowe, Sy, illus. Dinosaurs. LC 77-70862. (ps-3). 1977. 8.99 (*0-394-83538-7*) Random Bks Yng Read.
Barner, Bob. Too Many Dinosaurs. LC 93-46523. (gr. 2 up). 1995. 6.95 (*0-553-37566-0*, Little Rooster) Bantam.
Barrett, Judi. Benjamin's Three Hundred Sixty-Five Birthdays. Barrett, Ron, illus. LC 92-2497. 40p. (ps-1). 1992. RSBE 13.95 (*0-689-31791-3*, Atheneum Child Bk) Macmillan Child Grp.
Barton, Byron. Dinosaurs, Dinosaurs. Barton, Byron, illus. LC 88-22938. 40p. (ps-1). 1989. 10.95 (*0-694-00269-0*, Crowell Jr Bks); PLB 13.89 (*0-690-04768-1*) HarpC Child Bks.
—Dinosaurs, Dinosaurs. Barton, Byron, illus. LC 88-22938. 40p. (ps-1). 1991. 21.95 (*0-06-020410-9*) HarpC Child Bks.
Beaufay, Gabriel. Dinosaurs & Other Extinct Animals. (Illus.). 80p. (gr. 7 up). 1987. pap. 4.95 (*0-8120-3836-3*) Barron.
Bennett, S. Christopher. Pterosaurs: The Flying Reptiles. Franczak, Brian, illus. LC 93-29845. Date not set. write for info. (*0-531-11181-4*) Watts.
Benton, Michael. Deinonychus. LC 93-43402. 40p. (gr. 3-7). 1994. pap. 5.95 (*1-85697-991-1*, Kingfisher LKC) LKC.
—Dinosaur & Other Prehistoric Animal Factfinder. Channell, Jim & Maddison, Kevin, illus. LC 92-53119. 256p. (Orig.). (gr. 4-8). 1992. pap. 12.95 (*1-85697-802-8*, Kingfisher LKC) LKC.
—Dinosaurs. LC 94-9362. (Illus.). 128p. (gr. k-4). 1994. pap. 5.95 (*1-85697-524-X*, Kingfisher LKC) LKC.
—Discovering Dinosaurs. LC 93-50178. 1994. write for info. (*1-85697-503-7*, Kingfisher LKC) LKC.
Benton, Michael J. The Dinosaur Encyclopedia. Barish, Wendy, ed. Channell, Jim, et al, illus. 192p. (gr. 3-7). 1984. (S&S BFYR); pap. 7.95 (*0-671-51046-0*, S&S BFYR) S&S Trade.
—Dinosaurs. LC 90-30837. (Illus.). 96p. (gr. 1-5). 1992. (S&S BFYR); pap. 8.00 (*0-671-75999-X*, S&S BFYR) S&S Trade.
—Dinosaurs. (Illus.). 32p. (gr. 5-7). 1993. PLB 12.40 (*0-531-17370-4*, Gloucester Pr) Watts.
—Dinosaurs. LC 93-19072. (Illus.). 1993. 12.95 (*1-56458-382-1*) Dorling Kindersley.
Benton, Mike. Dinosaurs Existed? LC 94-16252. 1995. write for info. (*0-8114-3878-3*) Raintree Steck-V.
Berger, Melvin. Dinosaurs. 128p. 1990. pap. 2.95 (*0-380-76052-5*, Camelot) Avon.
—The World of Dinosaurs. (Illus.). 16p. (ps-2). 1994. pap. text ed. 14.95 (*1-56784-016-7*) Newbridge Comms.
Berkowitz, Henry. The Dinosaurs: An Educational Coloring Book. Berkowitz, Henry, illus. 32p. (Orig.). (gr. 1-9). 1986. pap. 2.50 (*0-938059-00-9*) Henart Bks.
Bishop, Roma. Pop up My First Book of Dinosaurs. 1993. pap. 13.00 (*0-671-86723-7*, S&S BFYR) S&S Trade.
Bixenman, Judy. Dinosaur Jokes. (Illus.). 32p. (gr. 1-4). 1991. 13.95 (*0-89565-728-7*) Childs World.
Bloch, C. Book of Dinosaurs. M. J. Studios Staff, illus. 64p. (Orig.). (gr. k-6). 1993. pap. 3.95 (*1-879424-46-0*) Nickel Pr.
—Dinosaur Sticker Atlas. M. J. Studios Staff, illus. 32p. (gr. k-6). 1993. pap. 3.95 (*1-879424-19-3*) Nickel Pr.
Boney, Lesley, illus. Dinosaurs. 48p. (gr. k-5). 1988. pap. 2.95 (*0-8431-2245-5*) Price Stern.
Branley, Franklyn M. What Happened to the Dinosaurs? Simont, Marc, illus. LC 88-37626. 32p. (gr. k-3). 1989. (Crowell Jr Bks); PLB 14.89 (*0-690-04749-5*, Crowell Jr Bks) HarpC Child Bks.
—What Happened to the Dinosaurs? Simont, Marc, illus. LC 88-37626. 32p. (gr. k-4). 1991. pap. 4.95 (*0-06-445105-4*, Trophy) HarpC Child Bks.
Brenner, Barbara A. Dinosaurium. LC 91-6335. (ps-3). 1993. pap. 9.50 (*0-553-35427-2*) Bantam.
Brown, Mike. Looking at Allosaurus. Gibbons, Tony, illus. LC 93-37056. 1994. 17.27 (*0-8368-1082-1*) Gareth Stevens Inc.
—Looking at Ankylosaurus. Gibbons, Tony, illus. LC 93-37055. 24p. (gr. 2 up). 1994. PLB 17.27 (*0-8368-1083-X*) Gareth Stevens Inc.
—Looking at....Ceratosaurus: A Dinosaur from the -- Period. Gibbons, Tony, illus. Date not set. 17.27 (*0-8368-1138-0*) Gareth Stevens Inc.
—Looking at....Deinonychus: A Dinosaur from the Cretaceous Period. Gibbons, Tony, illus. Date not set. 17.27 (*0-8368-1140-2*) Gareth Stevens Inc.
—Looking at....Dilophosaurus: A Dinosaur from the Jurassic Period. Gibbons, Tony, illus. Date not set. 17. 27 (*0-8368-1141-0*) Gareth Stevens Inc.
Bryant-Mole, Karen. Dot-to-Dot Dinosaurs. (Illus.). 24p. (gr. k-1). 1993. pap. 3.50 (*0-7460-1374-4*, Usborne) EDC.
Burkle, Diane, et al. Big Fearon Book of Dinosaurs. (gr. 1-3). 1989. pap. 12.95 (*0-8224-0698-5*) Fearon Teach Aids.
Buxton, Jane H., ed. Dinosaur Babies, Bk. 1 of 2. (Illus.). (ps-3). 1991. Set. 21.95 (*0-87044-841-2*) Natl Geog.
Carnegie Museum of Natural History, Division of Education Staff. Dippy Diplodocus: Story & Gameboard. Kelley, Patte, illus. 16p. (Orig.). (ps-2). 1988. pap. 4.95 (*0-911239-23-5*) Carnegie Mus.
Cast, C. Vance. Where Did the Dinosaurs Go? Wilkinson, Sue, illus. 40p. (ps-2). 1994. pap. 4.95 (*0-8120-1573-8*) Barron.
Chenel, Pascale. Life & Death of Dinosaurs. (Illus.). 80p. (gr. 7 up). 1987. pap. 4.95 (*0-8120-3840-1*) Barron.
Clark, Mary. Dinosaurios: Dinosaurs. Kratky, Lada, tr. from ENG. (SPA., Illus.). 48p. (gr. k-4). 1984. PLB 12.85 (*0-516-31612-5*); pap. 4.95 (*0-516-51612-4*) Childrens.
Clark, Mary L. Dinosaurs. LC 81-7750. (Illus.). 48p. (gr. k-4). 1981. PLB 12.85 (*0-516-01612-1*); pap. 4.95 (*0-516-41612-X*) Childrens.
Cohen, Daniel & Cohen, Susan. Where to Find Dinosaurs Today. LC 91-32084. (Illus.). 224p. 1992. 15.00 (*0-525-65098-9*, Cobblehill Bks) Dutton Child Bks.
—Where to Find Dinosaurs Today. (Illus.). 224p. (ps up). 1992. pap. 6.99 (*0-14-036154-5*, Puff Unicorn) Puffin Bks.
Cole, Joanna. Dinosaur Story. Kunstler, Mort, illus. LC 74-5931. 32p. (gr. k-3). 1974. PLB 13.88 (*0-688-31826-6*) Morrow Jr Bks.
—The Magic School Bus: In the Time of the Dinosaurs. Degen, Bruce, illus. LC 93-5753. (gr. 1-4). 1994. 14.95 (*0-590-44688-6*) Scholastic Inc.
Coleman, Graham. Looking at Diplodocus. Gibbons, Tony, illus. LC 93-37054. 24p. (gr. 2 up). 1994. PLB 17.27 (*0-8368-1084-8*) Gareth Stevens Inc.
—Looking at Parasaurolophus. Gibbons, Tony, illus. LC 93-37052. 24p. (gr. 2 up). 1994. PLB 17.27 (*0-8368-1086-4*) Gareth Stevens Inc.
—Looking at....Coelophysis: A Dinosaur from the Triassic Period. Gibbons, Tony, illus. Date not set. 17.27 (*0-8368-1139-9*) Gareth Stevens Inc.
Cutts, David. More about Dinosaurs. Wenzel, Gregory C., illus. LC 81-11432. 32p. (gr. k-2). 1982. PLB 11.59 (*0-89375-668-7*); pap. text ed. 2.95 (*0-89375-669-5*) Troll Assocs.
Delafosse, Claude & Prunier, James. Dinosaurs. (Illus.). (gr. 4 up). 1993. 10.95 (*0-590-46358-6*) Scholastic Inc.
Dingus, Lowell. What Color Is That Dinosaur? Questions, Answers, & Mysteries. Quinn, Stephen C., illus. LC 93-10664. 80p. (gr. 4-6). 1994. PLB 16.90 (*1-56294-365-0*) Millbrook Pr.
Dinosaur Activity Book. (Illus.). 64p. (Orig.). (gr. 2-5). 1993. pap. 2.95 (*1-56144-300-X*, Honey Bear Bks) Modern Pub NYC.
Dinosaur Activity Fun Box. (Illus.). (gr. k-3). 1993. 25.41 (*1-56144-306-9*, Honey Bear Bks) Modern Pub NYC.
The Dinosaur Hunter's Kit. 64p. (Orig.). (gr. 2 up). 1990. pap. 17.95 pkg. with bk. (*0-89471-804-5*) Running Pr.
Dinosaurs. (Illus.). 32p. (ps-6). 1983. pap. 29.50 per set of 10 (*0-87474-331-1*, DICBP) Smithsonian.
Dinosaurs. 88p. (ps-3). 1989. 15.93 (*0-8094-4889-0*); lib. bdg. 21.27 (*0-8094-4890-4*) Time-Life.
Dinosaurs. (Illus.). 20p. (gr. k up). 1990. laminated, wipe clean surface 3.95 (*0-88679-821-3*) Educ Insights.
Dinosaurs. (Illus.). 16p. (gr. k up). 1990. laminated, wipe clean surface 9.95 (*0-88679-661-X*) Educ Insights.
Dinosaurs. (gr. 1-4). 1991. pap. 3.95 (*0-7214-5319-8*) Ladybird Bks.
Dinosaurs. LC 91-16121. (Illus.). 24p. (ps-k). 1991. pap. 7.95 POB (*0-689-71518-8*, Aladdin) Macmillan Child Grp.
Dinosaurs - Prehistoric Animals. (gr. k-2). 1991. pap. 1.29 (*0-87449-189-4*) Modern Pub NYC.
Dinosaurs Activity Book. (Illus.). (ps-6). pap. 2.95 (*0-565-01078-6*, Pub. by Natural Hist Mus) Parkwest Pubns.
Dinosaurs & Prehistoric Creatures. (Illus.). 240p. (gr. k-2). 1989. 19.95 (*0-87449-513-X*) Modern Pub NYC.
Dinosaurs & Prehistoric Creatures. (Illus.). 24p. (Orig.). (gr. 2-5). 1993. pap. 2.50 (*1-56144-290-9*, Honey Bear Bks) Modern Pub NYC.
Dinosaurs & Prehistoric Life: A Look at the Animals & Plants of Prehistory. LC 93-85520. (Illus.). 240p. 1994. pap. 5.95 (*1-56138-381-3*) Running Pr.
Dinosaurs Big & Small. (gr. k-2). 1991. pap. 1.29 (*0-87449-186-X*) Modern Pub NYC.
Dinosaurs Big & Small. (Illus.). 24p. (Orig.). (gr. 2-5). 1993. pap. 2.50 (*1-56144-292-5*, Honey Bear Bks) Modern Pub NYC.
Dinosaurs-Coloring Book. 1985. pap. 1.95 (*0-88388-084-9*) Bellerophon Bks.
Dinosaurs Colouring Book. (Illus.). (ps-6). pap. 2.95 (*0-565-00825-0*, Pub. by Natural Hist Mus) Parkwest Pubns.
Dinosaurs of the Land, Sea & Air. (Illus.). 240p. (gr. k-2). 1989. 19.95 (*0-87449-512-1*) Modern Pub NYC.
Dinosaurs of the Land, Sea & Air. (Illus.). 24p. (Orig.). (gr. 2-5). 1993. pap. 2.50 (*1-56144-289-5*, Honey Bear Bks) Modern Pub NYC.
Dinosaurs of the Prehistoric Era. (Illus.). 24p. (Orig.). (gr. 2-5). 1993. pap. 2.50 (*1-56144-291-7*, Honey Bear Bks) Modern Pub NYC.
Dinosaurs: Superdoodles. LC 92-74102. (gr. 3 up). 1993. pap. 4.95 (*0-88160-223-X*, LW301) Learning Wks.
Dinosaurs: Superfacts. 1992. 4.99 (*0-517-07325-0*) Random Hse Value.
Discovering Dinosaurs. (gr. k-2). 1991. pap. 1.29 (*0-87449-187-8*) Modern Pub NYC.
Dixon, Dougal. Be a Dinosaur Detective. Lings, Steve, illus. 36p. (gr. k-4). 1988. 18.95 (*0-8225-0894-X*); pap. 4.95 (*0-8225-9538-9*) Lerner Pubns.
—Dinosaur. (Illus.). (gr. 3-7). 1994. 16.95 (*1-56458-683-9*) Dorling Kindersley.
—The Dinosaur Dynasty, 5 titles. 160p. (gr. k-4). 1994. lib. bdg. 99.65 (*1-884756-00-X*) Davidson Titles.
—Dinosaurs: A Closer Look. 32p. (gr. k-4). 1994. lib. bdg. 19.93 (*1-884756-04-2*) Davidson Titles.
—Dinosaurs: All Shapes & Sizes. 32p. (gr. k-4). 1994. lib. bdg. 19.93 (*1-884756-03-4*) Davidson Titles.
—Dinosaurs: Giants of the Earth. 32p. (gr. k-4). 1994. lib. bdg. 19.93 (*1-884756-01-8*) Davidson Titles.
—Dinosaurs: The Fossil Hunters. 32p. (gr. k-4). 1994. lib. bdg. 19.93 (*1-884756-05-0*) Davidson Titles.
—Dinosaurs: The Real Monsters. 32p. (gr. k-4). 1994. lib. bdg. 19.93 (*1-884756-02-6*) Davidson Titles.
—The First Dinosaurs. Burton, Jane, illus. LC 87-6460. 32p. (gr. 2-3). 1987. PLB 17.27 (*1-55532-258-1*) Gareth Stevens Inc.
—The First Dinosaurs. (Orig.). 1990. pap. 4.95 (*0-440-40373-1*, Pub. by Yearling Classics) Dell.
—Hunting the Dinosaurs. Burton, Jane, illus. LC 87-6461. 32p. (gr. 2-3). 1987. PLB 17.27 (*1-55532-259-X*) Gareth Stevens Inc.
—The Jurassic Dinosaurs. Burton, Jane, illus. LC 87-6462. 32p. (gr. 2-3). 1987. PLB 17.27 (*1-55532-260-3*) Gareth Stevens Inc.
—The Last Dinosaurs. Burton, Jane, illus. LC 87-6463. 32p. (gr. 2-3). 1987. PLB 17.27 (*1-55532-261-1*) Gareth Stevens Inc.
—The Last Dinosaurs. (Orig.). 1990. pap. 4.95 (*0-440-40377-4*, Pub. by Yearling Classics) Dell.
Dixon, Douglas. Hunting the Dinosaurs. (Orig.). 1990. pap. 4.95 (*0-440-40372-3*, Pub. by Yearling Classics) Dell.
—The Jurassic Dinosaurs. (Orig.). 1990. pap. 4.95 (*0-440-40375-8*, Pub. by Yearling Classics) Dell.
—The New Dinosaur Library, 4 vols. Burton, Jene, illus. 128p. (gr. 2-3). 1988. Set. PLB 69.60 (*1-55532-262-X*) Gareth Stevens Inc.
Dodson, Peter. An Alphabet of Dinosaurs. Barlowe, Wayne, illus. LC 94-15522. 1995. 15.95 (*0-590-46486-8*) Scholastic Inc.
—Discover Dinosaurs. (Illus.). 48p. (gr. 3-6). 1992. PLB 14.95 (*1-878363-68-9*, HTS Bks) Forest Hse.
Durrell, Gerald. The Fantastic Dinosaur Adventure. Percy, Graham, illus. LC 89-49099. 96p. (gr. 2-5). 1990. pap. 16.95 (*0-671-70871-6*) S&S Trade.
Earthbooks, Inc. Staff. The National Wildlife Federation's Book of Dinosaurs & Other Pre-Historic Animals. Aaestas, Ken, illus. 64p. (Orig.). (gr. 4). 1991. pap. 5.95 (*1-877731-16-1*) Earthbooks Inc.
Eldridge, David. Flying Dragons, Ancient Reptiles That Ruled the Air. Nodel, Norman, illus. LC 79-87965. 32p. (gr. 3-6). 1980. PLB 10.79 (*0-89375-241-X*); pap. 2.95 (*0-89375-245-2*) Troll Assocs.

—The Giant Dinosaurs, Ancient Reptiles That Ruled the Land. Nodel, Norman, illus. LC 79-87967. 32p. (gr. 3-6). 1980. PLB 10.79 (*0-89375-242-8*); pap. 2.95 (*0-89375-246-0*) Troll Assocs.
—Last of the Dinosaurs, the End of an Age. Nodel, Norman, illus. LC 79-64636. 32p. (gr. 3-6). 1980. PLB 10.79 (*0-89375-243-6*); pap. 2.95 (*0-89375-247-9*) Troll Assocs.
Elting, Mary. The Big Golden Book of Dinosaurs. Santoro, Christopher, illus. LC 87-81784. 64p. (gr. 3-6). pap. text ed. write for info. (*0-307-15567-6*, Golden Pr) Western Pub.
—The Macmillan Book of Dinosaurs & Other Prehistoric Creatures. LC 84-4944. (Illus.). 80p. (gr. 3-7). 1984. pap. 8.95 (*0-02-043000-0*, Aladdin) Macmillan Child Grp.
Emberley, Michael. Dinosaurs! A Drawing Book. Emberley, Michael, illus. 48p. (gr. 3 up). 1985. pap. 5.95 (*0-316-23631-4*) Little.
—Dinosaurs!, Vol. 1: A Drawing Book. 1980. 14.95 (*0-316-23417-6*) Little.
Esslinger, Jessica. Discover Dinosaurs: Activity Book. Belcher, Cynthia, illus. (Illus.). 20p. (gr. 1-6). 1988. wkbk. 2.95 (*0-911239-26-X*) Carnegie Mus.
—Discover Dinosaurs at the Carnegie. (Illus.). 20p. (gr. 1-6). 1988. wkbk. 2.95 (*0-911239-25-1*) Carnegie Mus.
Farlow, James O. On the Tracks of Dinosaurs: A Study of Dinosaur Footprints. Tischler, Doris, illus. LC 90-19432. 64p. (gr. 4-6). 1991. 15.95 (*0-531-15220-0*); PLB 15.90 (*0-531-10991-7*) Watts.
Farlow, James O. & Molnar, Ralph E. The Great Hunters: Meat-Eating Dinosaurs. Franczak, Brian, illus. LC 93-29844. 1994. write for info. (*0-531-11180-6*) Watts.
Fowler, Allan. It Could Still Be a Dinosaur. LC 92-9411. (Illus.). 32p. (ps-2). 1993. lib. bdg. 10.75 (*0-516-06002-3*); pap. 3.95 (*0-516-46002-1*) Childrens.
Freedman, Russell. Dinosaurs & Their Young. Morrill, Leslie, illus. LC 83-6160. 32p. (gr. 1-4). 1983. reinforced bdg. 13.95 (*0-8234-0496-X*) Holiday.
Fuchshuber, Annegert. From Dinosaurs to Fossils. Fuchshuber, Annegert, illus. LC 80-28596. 24p. (ps-3). 1981. PLB 10.95 (*0-87614-152-1*) Carolrhoda Bks.
Gabriele. Last Days of the Dinosaurs. 1984. pap. 1.50 (*0-911211-06-3*) Penny Lane Pubns.
Gabriele, Joseph. The First Days of the Dinosaurs: Text Edition. Hurst, Marageret, illus. 32p. (Orig.). (gr. 1-3). pap. 1.95 (*0-911211-55-1*, Pub. by Know & Show Bks) Penny Lane Pubns.
—The Great Age of the Dinosaurs. Hurst, Margaret, illus. 32p. (Orig.). (gr. 1-3). 1985. pap. text ed. 1.95 (*0-911211-56-X*, Pub. by Know & Show Bks) Penny Lane Pubns.
—The Last Days of the Dinosaurs: Text Editions. Hurst, Maragaret, illus. 32p. (Orig.). (gr. 1-3). 1985. pap. 1.95 (*0-911211-57-8*, Pub. by Know & Show Bks) Penny Lane Pubns.
Gamiello, Elvira. Dinosaurs Trivia Fun Book. (Illus.). 32p. (Orig.). 1989. pap. 1.50 (*0-942025-09-1*) Kidsbks.
—Giant Word Find Dinosaurs Poster Book. (Illus., Orig.). 1988. pap. 1.95 (*0-942025-49-0*) Kidsbks.
Geis, Darlene. Dinosaurs. Shannon, Kenyon, illus. (Orig.). (gr. 4-6). 1960. pap. 2.95 (*0-8431-4250-2*, Wonder-Treas) Price Stern.
Giant Dinosaurs. (gr. k-2). 1991. pap. 1.29 (*0-87449-188-6*) Modern Pub NYC.
Gibbons, Gail. Dinosaurs. Gibbons, Gail, illus. LC 87-364. 32p. (ps-3). 1987. reinforced bdg. 15.95 (*0-8234-0657-1*); pap. 5.95 (*0-8234-0708-X*) Holiday.
Gillette, J. Lynett. The Search for Seismosaurus. Hallett, Mark, photos by. LC 92-28199. (Illus.). 1993. 14.99 (*0-8037-1358-4*) Dial Bks Young.
Gillette, J. Lynette. Search for Seismosaurus: The World's Longest Dinosaur. LC 92-28199. (gr. 4-7). 1994. 14.89 (*0-8037-1359-2*) Dial Bks Young.
Gillette, Lynett. Dinosaur Diary: My Triassic Homeland. Larkin, Catherine, illus. 32p. (gr. 4). 1988. pap. 2.95 (*0-945695-00-4*) Petrified Forest Mus Assn.
Glut, D. F. The Dinosaur Dictionary. Romer, A. S. & Techter, D.intro. by. (Illus.). (gr. 2-6). 1985. pap. 5.98 (*0-517-45589-7*) Random Hse Value.
Glut, Donald F. The Dinosaur Dictionary. Romer, Alfred S., intro. by. (gr. 9 up). 1972. 12.50 (*0-8065-0283-5*, Pub. by Citadel Pr) Carol Pub Group.
Gohier, Francois. Dinosaurs. LC 94-3045. (Illus.). 1994. 9.95 (*0-918303-41-9*) Blake Pub.
Goyallon, Jerome. Drawing Dinosaurs. LC 93-2809. (Illus.). 80p. (gr. 3 up). 1993. 12.95 (*0-8069-8742-1*) Sterling.
Granger, Judith. Amazing World of Dinosaurs. Baldwin-Ford, Pamela, illus. LC 81-7476. 32p. (gr. 2-4). 1982. PLB 11.59 (*0-89375-562-1*); pap. text ed. 2.95 (*0-89375-563-X*) Troll Assocs.
Granowsky, Alvin. Dinosaur Fossils. Herring, Lee, illus. LC 91-23407. 32p. (gr. 1-4). 1992. PLB 18.51 (*0-8114-3253-X*); pap. 3.95 (*0-8114-6228-5*) Raintree Steck-V.
—The Dinosaurs' Last Days. Lopez, Paul, illus. LC 91-23408. 32p. (gr. 1-4). 1992. PLB 18.51 (*0-8114-3250-5*); pap. 3.95 (*0-8114-6225-0*) Raintree Steck-V.
—Dinosaurs of All Sizes. Lopez, Paul, illus. LC 91-22343. 32p. (gr. 1-4). 1992. PLB 18.51 (*0-8114-3251-3*); pap. 3.95 (*0-8114-6229-3*) Raintree Steck-V.
—Hungry Dinosaurs. Inouye, Carol, illus. LC 91-23405. 32p. (gr. 1-4). 1992. PLB 18.51 (*0-8114-3252-1*); pap. 3.95 (*0-8114-6226-9*) Raintree Steck-V.
—Meat-Eating Dinosaurs. Inouye, Carol, illus. LC 91-23406. 32p. (gr. 1-4). 1992. PLB 18.51 (*0-8114-3254-8*); pap. 3.95 (*0-8114-6227-7*) Raintree Steck-V.
Greenberg, Judith E. & Carey, Helen H. Dinosaurs. Birmingham, Lloyd, illus. 32p. (gr. 2-4). 1990. PLB 10.95 (*0-8172-3751-8*) Raintree Steck-V.
Hawcock, David. Archaeopteryx. 1994. 5.95 (*0-8050-3194-4*) H Holt & Co.
—Mini Dinos: Brontosaurus. (Illus.). 10p. (ps-2). 1993. 5.95 (*0-8050-2361-5*) H Holt & Co.
—Mini Dinos: Stegosaurus. (Illus.). 10p. (ps-2). 1993. 5.95 (*0-8050-2362-3*) H Holt & Co.
—Mini Dinos: Triceratops. (Illus.). 10p. (ps-2). 1993. 5.95 (*0-8050-2364-X*) H Holt & Co.
—Mini Dinos: Tyrannosaurus. (Illus.). 10p. (ps-2). 1993. 5.95 (*0-8050-2363-1*) H Holt & Co.
—Plesiosaur-Minibeast. 1994. 5.95 (*0-8050-3196-0*) H Holt & Co.
Haynes, Max. Dinosaur Island. LC 90-48148. (Illus.). 32p. (ps up). 1991. 13.95 (*0-688-10329-4*); PLB 13.88 (*0-688-10330-8*) Lothrop.
Heck, Joseph. Dinosaur Riddles. Barish, Wendy, ed. Hoffman, Sandy, illus. 128p. (gr. 3-7). 1982. 9.29 (*0-685-05613-9*, Little Simon) S&S Trade.
Henderson, Douglas. Dinosaur Tree. LC 93-34204. (gr. 1-7). 1994. 15.95 (*0-02-743547-4*, Bradbury Pr) Macmillan Child Grp.
Highlights for Children Staff. Dinosaurs: A Closer Look. Highlights for Children Staff, illus. 32p. (gr. 3-10). 1992. pap. 3.50 (*0-87534-316-3*) Highlights.
—Dinosaurs: All Shapes & Sizes. Highlights for Children Staff, illus. 32p. (gr. 3-10). 1992. pap. 3.50 (*0-87534-315-5*) Highlights.
—Dinosaurs: Giants of the Earth. Highlights for Children Staff, illus. 32p. (gr. 3-10). 1992. pap. 3.50 (*0-87534-313-9*) Highlights.
—Dinosaurs: the Fossil Hunters. Highlights for Children Staff, illus. 32p. (gr. 3-10). 1992. pap. 3.50 (*0-87534-317-1*) Highlights.
—Dinosaurs: The Real Monsters. Highlights for Children Staff, illus. 32p. (gr. 3-10). 1992. pap. 3.50 (*0-87534-314-7*) Highlights.
Hincks, J. The Rourke Dinosaur Dictionary. (Illus.). 96p. (gr. k-8). 1987. PLB 26.60 (*0-86592-049-4*) Rourke Corp.
Honey Bear Dinosaurs & Prehistoric Animals. (gr. 2-4). 1991. 6.95 (*0-87449-779-5*) Modern Pub NYC.
Hopkins, Lee B. Dinosaurs. Tinkleman, Murray, illus. 47p. (ps-3). 1987. 12.95 (*0-15-223495-0*) HarBrace.
—Dinosaurs. 1990. pap. 4.95 (*0-15-223496-9*, Voyager Bks) HarBrace.
Hopwood, Clive. Dinosaur Fun File. Green, Barry, illus. (gr. 3-6). 1992. pap. 4.95 (*1-56680-508-2*) Mad Hatter Pub.
Horner, Jack & Lessem, Don. Digging up Tyrannosaurus Rex. LC 92-2204. (Illus.). 36p. (gr. 2-6). 1992. 15.00 (*0-517-58783-1*); PLB 14.99 (*0-517-58784-X*) Crown Bks Yng Read.
Howard, John. I Can Read About Dinosaurs. (Illus.). (gr. 2-4). 1972. pap. 2.50 (*0-89375-051-4*) Troll Assocs.
Incredible Dinosaurs. (Illus.). 32p. (Orig.). (gr. 2-5). 1994. pap. 4.95 (*1-56458-551-4*) Dorling Kindersley.
Ingle, Annie. Glow-in-the-Dark Dinosaur Skeletons. Barrett, Peter, illus. LC 92-18176. 16p. (ps-1). 1993. pap. 4.99 (*0-679-84366-3*) Random Bks Yng Read.
Ingoglia, Gina. Let's Look at Dinosaurs. (Illus.). 16p. (ps-1). 1991. bds. 11.95 (*0-448-40086-3*, G&D) Putnam Pub Group.
Johnson, James H., Jr. They Walked the Earth. Johnson, James H., Jr., illus. 112p. (Orig.). (gr. 1-6). 1992. pap. 12.95 (*0-9632717-0-9*) P Q Pubns.
Johnson, Rolf E. & Piggins, Carol A. Dinosaur Hunt! LC 91-50336. (Illus.). 32p. (gr. 2-8). 1993. PLB 15.93 (*0-8368-0740-5*); PLB 17.27 s.p. (*0-685-61502-2*) Gareth Stevens Inc.
Joyce. Dinosaur Bob Gift Edition. Date not set. 40.00 (*0-06-023851-8*, HarpT) HarpC.
Jurassic Park Dinosaur Hunter's Guide: How to Dig up Fossils. (gr. 4-7). 1993. pap. 2.95 (*0-307-02958-1*, Golden Pr) Western Pub.
Kallen, Stuart A. Brontosaurus. Berg, Julie, ed. LC 94-1819. 1994. write for info. (*1-56239-286-7*) Abdo & Dghtrs.
—Monsters, Dinosaurs & Beasts. LC 91-73061. 202p. 1991. 12.94 (*1-56239-040-6*) Abdo & Dghtrs.
—Plesiosaurus. Berg, Julie, ed. LC 94-6356. 1994. write for info. (*1-56239-287-5*) Abdo & Dghtrs.
—Pteranodon. Berg, Julie, ed. LC 94-4534. 1994. write for info. (*1-56239-283-2*) Abdo & Dghtrs.
—Stegosaurus. Berg, Julie, ed. LC 94-4532. 1994. write for info. (*1-56239-285-9*) Abdo & Dghtrs.
—Triceratops. LC 94-7796. (gr. 2 up). 1994. write for info. (*1-56239-288-3*) Abdo & Dghtrs.
—Tyrannosaurus Rex. Berg, Julie, ed. LC 94-4533. 1994. write for info. (*1-56239-284-0*) Abdo & Dghtrs.
Keen, Martin L. Prehistoric Mammals. Hull, John, illus. (gr. 4-6). pap. 2.95 (*0-8431-4255-3*, Wonder-Treas) Price Stern.
Kelsch, Gregg B. A World of Dinosaurs Series. Kelsch, Gregg B., illus. 1993. write for info. (*1-883736-01-3*) Acorn Pub UT.
Knight, David C. The Battle of the Dinosaurs. Ames, Lee J., illus. 96p. (gr. 3-7). 1982. (Pub. by Treehouse); pap. 5.95 (*0-13-069518-1*) P-H.
Kricher, John C. Peterson First Guide to Dinosaurs. Morrison, Gordon, illus. Peterson, Roger T., frwd. by. (Illus.). 128p. 1990. pap. 4.80 (*0-395-52440-7*) HM.
Kurokawa, Mitsuhiro. Dinosaur Valley. Kurokawa, Mitsuhiro, illus. LC 92-10788. 48p. (gr. 1-5). 1992. 14.95 (*0-8118-0257-4*) Chronicle Bks.
—The Great Big Book of Dinosaurs. Kurokawa, Mitsuhiro, illus. Obata, Ikuo, contrib. by. LC 88-24779. (Illus.). 32p. (gr. 4-5). 1989. PLB 21.26 (*0-8368-0000-1*) Gareth Stevens Inc.
—The Great Dinosaur Timescape. Strigens, Jerry, illus. (gr. 4-5). 1989. PLB 22.60 (*0-8368-0001-X*) Gareth Stevens Inc.
Lambert, David. Dinosaurs. LC 89-22542. (ps-3). 1990. PLB 11.40 (*0-531-19070-6*) Watts.
Lambert, David & Wright, Rachel. Dinosaurs. LC 91-21118. (Illus.). 32p. (gr. 4-6). 1992. PLB 11.90 (*0-531-14159-4*) Watts.
Langley, Andrew. Dinosaurs. rev. ed. Franklin Watts Ltd. Staff, ed. (Illus.). 32p. (gr. 2-4). 1985. PLB 10.90 o.s. (*0-531-10449-4*) Watts.
Langley, Glynis. The Age of Dinosaurs. Atkinson, Mike, illus. 64p. (gr. k-5). 1992. pap. 6.95 perfect bdg. (*0-8249-8537-0*, Ideals Child) Hambleton-Hill.
Latta, Rich. Dinosaur Mazes. 48p. (gr. 2 up). 1990. pap. 2.95 incl. chipboard (*0-8431-2822-4*) Price Stern.
Lessem, Don. Ornithomimids, the Fastest Dinosaur. Franczak, Brian, illus. LC 93-10264. 1993. 19.95 (*0-87614-813-5*) Carolrhoda Bks.
—Troodon, the Smartest Dinosaur. Franczak, Brian, illus. LC 92-44689. 1993. 19.95 (*0-87614-798-8*) Carolrhoda Bks.
Lindsay, William. Barosaurus. Norell, Mark, contrib. by. LC 92-52819. (Illus.). 32p. (gr. 3 up). 1993. 12.95 (*1-56458-123-3*) Dorling Kindersley.
—Great Dinosaur Atlas. Fornari, Giuliano, illus. (gr. 3 up). 1991. 16.00 (*0-671-74480-1*, J Messner); (J Messner) S&S Trade.
Little People Big Book About Dinosaurs. 64p. (ps-1). 1989. write for info. (*0-8094-7466-2*); PLB write for info. (*0-8094-7467-0*) Time-Life.
Long, Robert A. & Welles, Samuel P. All New Dinosaurs. (gr. 7 up). 1975. pap. 3.95 (*0-88388-031-8*) Bellerophon Bks.
M. J. Studios Staff, illus. Daffy Dinosaurs Sticker Pad. 32p. (Orig.). (gr. k-6). 1993. pap. 2.95 (*1-879424-48-7*) Nickel Pr.
McCord. Dinosaurs. (Illus.). (gr. 4-6). 1977. (Usborne-Hayes); PLB 13.96 (*0-88110-680-1*); pap. 6.95 (*0-7460-1469-4*) EDC.
McGowan, Christopher. Discover Dinosaurs: Become a Dinosaur Detective. Holdcroft, Tina, illus. LC 92-42627. 96p. (gr. 4-7). 1993. pap. 9.57 (*0-201-62267-X*) Addison-Wesley.
McMullan, Kate. Dinosaur Hunters. Jones, John R., illus. LC 88-30742. 48p. (Orig.). (gr. 2-4). 1989. PLB 7.99 (*0-394-91150-4*); 3.50 (*0-394-81150-X*) Random Bks Yng Read.
Mansell, Dom. Dinosaurs Came to Town. (ps-3). 1991. 13.95 (*0-316-54584-8*) Little.
Mayes, Sue. Dinosaurs. (Illus.). 32p. (gr. k-1). 1993. lib. bdg. 13.96 (*0-88110-641-0*, Usborne); pap. 5.95 (*0-7460-1020-6*, Usborne) EDC.
Maynard, Christopher. Dinosaurs. LC 92-32265. 1993. 3.95 (*1-85697-892-3*, Kingfisher LKC) LKC.
Minelli, Giuseppe. Dinosaurs & Birds. (Illus.). 64p. 1988. 15.95x (*0-8160-1559-7*) Facts on File.
Moncure, Jane B. Dinosaurs: Back in Time. Hohag, Linda, illus. LC 89-38469. 32p. (ps-2). 1990. PLB 14.95 (*0-89565-550-0*) Childs World.
Moody, Richard T. Over Sixty-Five Million Years Ago: Before the Dinosaurs Died. LC 91-44774. (Illus.). 32p. (gr. 6 up). 1992. text ed. 13.95 RSBE (*0-02-767270-0*, New Discovery) Macmillan Child Grp.
Morris, Dean. Dinosaurs & Other First Animals. LC 87-16670. (Illus.). 48p. (gr. 2-6). 1987. PLB 10.95 (*0-8172-3206-0*) Raintree Steck-V.
Morris, John, et al. What Really Happened to the Dinosaurs? (Illus.). 24p. (ps-2). 1990. pap. 9.95 (*0-89051-159-4*) Master Bks.
Morris, Ting & Morris, Neil. Dinosaurs. LC 92-32915. 1993. 12.40 (*0-531-14258-2*) Watts.
Most, Bernard. Dinosaur Cousins? LC 86-18485. (Illus.). 40p. (ps-3). 1987. 13.95 (*0-15-223497-7*, HB Juv Bks) HarBrace.
—A Dinosaur Named after Me. D'Andrade, Diane, ed. Most, Bernard, illus. 32p. (ps-3). 1991. 12.95 (*0-15-223494-2*) HarBrace.
—Happy Holidaysaurus! 1992. 13.95 (*0-15-233386-X*, HB Juv Bks) HarBrace.
—How Big Were the Dinosaurs? LC 93-19152. (Illus.). 1994. 14.95 (*0-15-236800-0*, HB Juv Bks) HarBrace.
—The Littlest Dinosaurs. Most, Bernard, illus. 30p. (ps-3). 1989. 13.95 (*0-15-248125-7*) HarBrace.
—Where to Look for a Dinosaur. LC 92-19443. 1993. 12.95 (*0-15-295616-6*, HB Juv Bks) HarBrace.
Muller, Carrel & Jacques, Ethel M. Dinosaur Discovery. Muller, Carrel, illus. 32p. (gr. 4-6). 1987. wkbk. 3.75 (*0-915785-02-1*) Bonjour Books.
Mullins, Patricia. Dinosaur Encore. Mullins, Patricia, illus. LC 92-19848. 32p. (ps-2). 1993. 15.00 (*0-06-021069-9*) HarpC Child Bks.
Murphy, Jim. Dinosaur for a Day. (Illus.). 1992. 15.95 (*0-590-42866-7*, Scholastic Hardcover) Scholastic Inc.
My Giant Book of Dinosaurs. (Illus.). 24p. 1991. 7.99 (*0-517-05257-1*) Random Hse Value.
Nardo, Don. Dinosaurs. LC 93-4314. (gr. 5 up). 1994. write for info. (*1-56510-154-5*) Lucent Bks.
—Dinosaurs: Unearthing the Secrets of Ancient Beasts. (Illus.). (gr. 5-8). 1994. 15.95 (*1-56006-253-3*) Lucent Bks.

—The Extinction of the Dinosaurs. LC 93-4314. (gr. 3-5). 1994. 14.95 (*1-56006-154-5*) Lucent Bks.

National Wildlife Federation Staff. Digging into Dinosaurs. (gr. k-8). 1991. pap. 7.95 (*0-945051-33-6*, 75002) Natl Wildlife.

Nayer, Judy. Dinosaurs. Goldberg, Grace, illus. 12p. (ps-2). 1993. bds. 6.95 (*1-56293-336-1*) McClanahan Bk.

Neilson, Gena, illus. Dinosaurs. (ps-1). 1986. spiral bdg. 9.95 (*0-937763-00-4*) Lauri Inc.

Nelson, Jeffrey. The Dinosaur Hunt Activity Book. (Orig.). 1994. pap. 2.99 (*0-8125-9439-8*) Tor Bks.

Nemes, Claire. A Picture Book of Dinosaurs. Kinnealy, Janice, illus. LC 89-37331. 24p. (gr. 1-4). 1990. lib. bdg. 9.59 (*0-8167-1900-4*); pap. text ed. 2.50 (*0-8167-1901-2*) Troll Assocs.

The New Dinosaur Collection, 12 vols. (Illus.). 288p. (gr. 2 up). 1994. PLB 207.24 Set (*0-8368-1098-8*) Gareth Stevens Inc.

Nichols, V. Dinosaur Coloring Book. M. J. Studios Staff, illus. 32p. (Orig.). (gr. k-6). 1993. pap. 2.95 (*1-879424-50-9*) Nickel Pr.

—The Incredible Dionsaur Activity Book. M. J. Studios Staff, illus. 128p. (gr. k-6). Date not set. pap. 2.95 (*1-879424-64-9*) Nickel Pr.

Noffs, David & Noffs, Laurie. Day of the Dinosaur. Noffs, Laurie, illus. 24p. (Orig.). (gr. 4-8). 1989. wkbk. 2.50 (*0-929875-12-5*) Noffs Assocs.

Norell, Mark. All You Need to Know about Dinosaurs. LC 91-21701. (Illus.). 96p. (gr. 2-9). 1991. 12.95 (*0-8069-8396-5*) Sterling.

Norman, D. Dinosaurs. (Illus.). 64p. (gr. 10 up). 1993. pap. 4.95 (*0-86020-458-8*) EDC.

Norman, David. When Dinosaurs Ruled the Earth. 1985. 6.98 (*0-671-07522-5*) S&S Trade.

Norman, David & Miller, Angela. Dinosaur. Keates, Colin, illus. LC 88-27167. 64p. (gr. 5 up). 1989. 16.00 (*0-394-82253-6*); PLB 16.99 (*0-394-92253-0*) Knopf Bks Yng Read.

Oliver. Ankylosaurus. (Illus.). 24p. 1984. PLB 14.00 (*0-86592-212-8*) Rourke Enter.

—Archaeopteryx. (Illus.). 24p. 1984. PLB 14.00 (*0-86592-209-8*) Rourke Enter.

—Brachiosaurus. (Illus.). 24p. 1986. PLB 14.00 (*0-86592-219-5*) Rourke Enter.

—Chasmosaurus. (Illus.). 24p. 1986. PLB 14.00 (*0-86592-218-7*) Rourke Enter.

—Deinonychus. (Illus.). 24p. 1984. PLB 14.00 (*0-86592-213-6*) Rourke Enter.

—Dilophosaurus. (Illus.). 24p. 1984. PLB 14.00 (*0-86592-215-2*) Rourke Enter.

—Dimetrodon. (Illus.). 24p. 1984. PLB 14.00 (*0-86592-210-1*) Rourke Enter.

—Dimorphodon. (Illus.). 24p. 1986. PLB 14.00 (*0-86592-217-9*) Rourke Enter.

—Dinosaur Library, 6 bks, Set III. (Illus.). 144p. 1986. Set. PLB write for info. (*0-86592-214-4*) Rourke Enter.

—Mamenchisaurus. (Illus.). 24p. 1986. PLB 14.00 (*0-86592-220-9*) Rourke Enter.

—Plesiosaurus. (Illus.). 24p. 1984. PLB 14.00 (*0-86592-211-X*) Rourke Enter.

—Protoceratops. (Illus.). 24p. 1986. PLB 14.00 (*0-86592-216-0*) Rourke Enter.

Oliver & Wilson. Dinosaur Library, 13 bks, Set II. (Illus.). 312p. 1984. Set. PLB write for info. (*0-86592-200-4*) Rourke Enter.

Oliver, ed. Iguanodon. (Illus.). 24p. 1984. PLB 14.00 (*0-86592-207-1*) Rourke Enter.

—Nothosaurus. (Illus.). 24p. 1984. PLB 14.00 (*0-86592-208-X*) Rourke Enter.

O'Neill, Mary. Dinosaur Mysteries. Bindon, John, illus. LC 89-4789. 32p. (gr. 3-7). 1989. lib. bdg. 12.89 (*0-8167-1635-8*); pap. text ed. 3.95 (*0-8167-1636-6*) Troll Assocs.

—A Family of Dinosaurs. Bindon, John, illus. LC 89-4792. 32p. (gr. 3-7). 1989. lib. bdg. 12.89 (*0-8167-1633-1*); pap. text ed. 3.95 (*0-8167-1634-X*) Troll Assocs.

—Where Are All the Dinosaurs? Bindon, John, illus. LC 89-31165. 32p. (gr. 2-6). 1989. lib. bdg. 12.89 (*0-8167-1637-4*); pap. text ed. 3.95 (*0-8167-1638-2*) Troll Assocs.

Owl Magazine Staff. Dinosaur Question & Answer Book: Everything Kids Want to Know about Dinosaurs, Fossils, And... (gr. 4-7). 1992. 16.95 (*0-316-67736-1*, Joy St Bks) Little.

Packard, Ann & Stafford, Shirley. Time of the Dinosaurs. 92p. (ps-3). 1981. write for info. (*0-9607580-1-1*) S Stafford.

Packard, Mary. Dinosaurs. Santoro, Christopher, illus. 48p. (ps-3). 1981. pap. 9.95 (*0-671-43040-8*, S&S BFYR) S&S Trade.

Pallotta, Jerry. The Dinosaur Alphabet Book. (Illus.). 32p. (Orig.). (ps-4). 1990. 14.95 (*0-88106-467-X*); PLB 15.88 (*0-88106-683-4*); pap. 6.95 (*0-88106-466-1*) Charlesbridge Pub.

Parish, Peggy. Dinosaur Time. Lobel, Arnold, illus. LC 73-14331. 32p. (gr. k-3). 1974. 14.00 (*0-06-024653-7*); PLB 13.89 (*0-06-024654-5*) HarpC Child Bks.

—Dinosaur Time. Lobel, Arnold, illus. LC 73-14331. 32p. (ps-2). 1983. pap. 3.50 (*0-06-444037-0*, Trophy) HarpC Child Bks.

Parker, Steve. Inside Dinosaurs & Other Prehistoric Creatures. Dewan, Ted, illus. LC 93-10045. (gr. 1-8). 1995. 16.95 (*0-385-31143-5*); pap. 10.95 (*0-385-31189-3*) Delacorte.

Pearce, Q. L. All about Dinosaurs. Boney, Leslie, illus. (gr. 2 up). 1989. pap. 7.95 (*0-671-64517-X*, Little Simon) S&S Trade.

—The Dinosaur Almanac. Bild, Linda, illus. 96p. (gr. 1 up). 1994. pap. 4.95 (*1-56565-175-8*) Lowell Hse Juvenile.

—My Favorite Dinosaur: Tyrannosaurus Rex. Fraser, Mary A., illus. 32p. 1993. pap. 12.95 (*1-56565-014-X*) Lowell Hse.

—Tyrannosaurus Rex & Other Dinosaur Wonders. Fraser, Mary A., illus. 64p. (gr. 4-6). 1990. lib. bdg. 12.98 (*0-671-70687-X*, J Messner); pap. 5.95 (*0-671-70688-8*) S&S Trade.

Penner, Lucille R. Dinosaur Babies: A Step One Book. Barrett, Peter, illus. LC 90-36045. 32p. (Orig.). (ps-1). 1991. lib. bdg. 7.99 (*0-679-91207-X*); pap. 3.50 (*0-679-81207-5*) Random Bks Yng Read.

Petersen, David. Apatosaurus. LC 88-37654. (Illus.). 48p. (gr. k-4). 1989. pap. 4.95 (*0-516-41159-4*) Childrens.

—Tyrannosaurus Rex. LC 88-38054. (Illus.). 48p. (gr. k-4). 1989. PLB 12.85 (*0-516-01167-7*); pap. 4.95 (*0-516-41167-5*) Childrens.

Pienkowski, Jan, illus. ABC Dinosaurs: And Other Prehistoric Creatures. 10p. (ps-k). 1993. 18.99 (*0-525-67468-3*, Lodestar Bks) Dutton Child Bks.

Polisar, Barry L. Dinosaurs I Have Known. Stewart, Michael, illus. 48p. (Orig.). (gr. 2-6). 1988. 9.95 (*0-938663-00-3*); pap. 7.95 (*0-938663-05-4*) Rainbow Morn.

Prunier, J. & Galeron, H., illus. Dinosaure. (FRE.). (ps-1). 1991. 17.95 (*2-07-056642-0*) Schoenhof.

Quinn, Kay. Dinosaurs & Prehistoric Animals. Quinn, Kay, illus. 64p. (gr. 2-10). 1990. 4.99 (*0-517-03566-9*) Random Hse Value.

Quinn, Kaye. World of the Dinosaurs. Quinn, Kaye, illus. 40p. (Orig.). (gr. k-4). 1987. pap. 2.95 (*0-8431-1890-3*) Price Stern.

Raham, R. Gary. Sillysaurs: Dinosaurs That Could Have Been. Raham, R. Gary, illus. 16p. (Orig.). (gr. k-4). 1990. write for info. saddle-stitched (*0-9626301-0-1*) Biostration.

Richardson, James. Science Dictionary of Dinosaurs. Quinn, Kaye, illus. LC 91-4110. 48p. (gr. 3-7). 1992. lib. bdg. 11.59 (*0-8167-2522-5*); pap. 3.95 (*0-8167-2441-5*) Troll Assocs.

Riehecky, Janet. Allosaurus. Hunter, Llyn, illus. LC 88-1693. (ENG & SPA.). 32p. (ps-2). 1988. PLB 14.95 (*0-89565-421-0*) Childs World.

—Anatosaurus. Magnuson, Diana, illus. (ENG & SPA.). 32p. (ps-2). 1989. PLB 14.95 (*0-89565-545-4*) Childs World.

—Ankylosaurus. Magnuson, Diana, illus. (ENG & SPA.). 32p. (ps-2). 1990. PLB 14.95 (*0-89565-621-3*) Childs World.

—Apatosaurus. Halverson, Lydia, illus. LC 88-1694. (ENG & SPA.). 32p. (ps-2). 1988. PLB 14.95 (*0-89565-423-7*) Childs World.

—Baryonyx. Conaway, Jim, illus. (ENG & SPA.). 32p. (ps-2). 1990. PLB 14.95 (*0-89565-622-1*) Childs World.

—Brachiosaurus. Conaway, James, illus. LC 89-22069. (ENG & SPA.). 32p. 1989. PLB 21.35 (*0-89565-542-X*); PLB 14.95 (*0-685-74150-8*) Childs World.

—Coelophysis. Halverson, Lydia, illus. (ENG & SPA.). 32p. (ps-2). 1990. PLB 14.95 (*0-89565-623-X*) Childs World.

—Compsognathus. Lexa-Senning, Susan, illus. (ENG & SPA.). 32p. (ps-2). 1990. PLB 14.95 (*0-89565-624-8*) Childs World.

—Deinonychus. Hunter, Llyn, illus. (ENG & SPA.). 32p. (ps-2). 1990. PLB 14.95 (*0-89565-625-6*) Childs World.

—Dinosaur Relatives. Magnuson, Diana, illus. (ENG & SPA.). 32p. (ps-2). 1990. PLB 14.95 (*0-89565-626-4*) Childs World.

—Diplodocus. Conaway, Jim, illus. (ENG & SPA.). 32p. (ps-2). 1990. PLB 14.95 (*0-89565-627-2*) Childs World.

—Discovering Dinosaurs. Endres, Helen, illus. (ENG & SPA.). 32p. (ps-2). 1990. PLB 14.95 (*0-89565-620-5*) Childs World.

—Hypsilophodon. Ching, illus. (SPA & ENG.). 32p. (ps-2). 1990. PLB 14.95 (*0-89565-628-0*) Childs World.

—Iguanodon. Magnuson, Diana, illus. LC 89-15850. (SPA & ENG.). 32p. (ps-2). 1989. PLB 14.95 (*0-89565-544-6*) Childs World.

—Maiasaura. Magnuson, Diana, illus. LC 89-22076. (ENG & SPA.). 32p. (ps-2). 1989. PLB 14.95 (*0-89565-543-8*) Childs World.

—Oviraptor. Magnuson, Diana, illus. (SPA & ENG.). 32p. (ps-2). 1990. PLB 14.95 (*0-89565-631-0*) Childs World.

—Pachycephalosaurus. Hunter, Llyn, illus. (SPA & ENG.). 32p. (ps-2). 1990. PLB 14.95 (*0-89565-632-9*) Childs World.

—Parasaurolophus. LeBlanc, Andre, illus. (SPA & ENG.). 32p. (ps-2). 1990. PLB 14.95 (*0-89565-633-7*) Childs World.

—Protoceratops. Magnuson, Diana, illus. (SPA & ENG.). 32p. (ps-2). 1990. PLB 14.95 (*0-89565-634-5*) Childs World.

—Saltasaurus. Raskin, Betty, illus. (SPA & ENG.). 32p. (ps-2). 1990. PLB 14.95 (*0-89565-635-3*) Childs World.

—Stegosaurus. Magnuson, Diana, illus. LC 88-15347. (SPA & ENG.). 32p. (ps-2). 1988. PLB 14.95 (*0-89565-385-0*) Childs World.

—Triceratops. Magnuson, Diana, illus. LC 88-508. (SPA & ENG.). 32p. (ps-2). 1988. PLB 14.95 (*0-89565-422-9*) Childs World.

—Troodon. Conaway, James, illus. (SPA & ENG.). 32p. (ps-2). 1990. PLB 14.95 (*0-89565-636-1*) Childs World.

—Tyrannosaurus. Magnuson, Diana L., illus. LC 88-1692. (SPA & ENG.). 32p. (ps-2). 1988. PLB 14.95 (*0-89565-424-5*) Childs World.

Riley, T. The Amazing World of Dinosaurs. (Illus.). 80p. (gr. 2-6). 1991. 4.99 (*0-517-63993-9*) Random Hse Value.

Rothaus, Jim. Dinosaurs. 24p. (gr. 3). 1988. PLB 14.95 (*0-88682-223-8*) Creative Ed.

Rowe. Giant Dinosaurs. 1993. pap. 28.67 (*0-590-73275-7*) Scholastic Inc.

Rowe, Erna. Los Dinosaurios Gigantes (Giant Dinosaurs) Palacios, Argentina, tr. Smith, Merle, illus. 32p. (ps-2). pap. 3.95 (*0-590-40647-7*) Scholastic Inc.

—Giant Dinosaurs. Smith, Merle, illus. (gr. k-3). 1975. pap. 2.95 (*0-590-40262-5*) Scholastic Inc.

Running Press Staff. Dinosaurs. LC 93-83583. (Illus.). (gr. 4-7). 1993. 5.95 (*1-56138-319-8*) Running Pr.

Russell, Dale A. & Acorn, John. The Tiny Perfect Dinosaur Book, Bones, Egg & Poster: Presenting Leptoceratops. Kish, Ely, illus. 32p. (Orig.). 1991. pap. 10.95 (*0-8362-4213-0*) Andrews & McMeel.

—The Tiny Perfect Dinosaur Book, Bones, Egg, & Poster: Presenting Tyrannosaurus Rex. Kish, Ely, illus. 32p. 1993. pap. 12.95 incl. poster & toy (*0-8362-4216-5*) Andrews & McMeel.

Russo, Monica. Weird & Wonderful Dinosaur Facts. LC 92-45770. (Illus.). 96p. (gr. 6-12). 1992. 12.95 (*0-8069-8320-5*) Sterling.

—Weird & Wonderful Dinosaur Facts. LC 92-45770. (Illus.). 96p. (gr. 3-9). 1993. pap. 4.95 (*0-8069-8321-3*) Sterling.

Sandell, Elizabeth. Ankylosaurus: The Armored Dinosaur. Oelerich, Marjorie & Hansen, Harlan S., eds. Vista III Design Staff, illus. LC 88-39806. 32p. (gr. k-5). 1989. PLB 12.95 (*0-944280-16-1*); pap. text ed. 5.95 (*0-944280-22-6*) Bancroft-Sage.

—Apatosaurus: The Deceptive Dinosaur. Oelerich, Marjorie & Hansen, Harlan S., eds. Vista III Design Staff, illus. LC 88-39805. 32p. (gr. k-5). 1989. PLB 12.95 (*0-944280-12-9*); pap. text ed. 5.95 (*0-944280-18-8*) Bancroft-Sage.

—Archaeopteryx: The First Bird. Oelerich, Marjorie & Hansen, Harlan S., eds. Vista III Design Staff, illus. LC 88-39803. 32p. (gr. k-5). 1989. PLB 12.95 (*0-944280-13-7*); pap. text ed. 5.95 (*0-944280-19-6*) Bancroft-Sage.

—Compsognathus: The Smallest Dinosaur. Oelerich, Marjorie & Hansen, Harlan S., eds. Vista III Design Staff, illus. LC 88-39801. 32p. (gr. k-5). 1989. PLB 12.95 (*0-944280-14-5*); pap. text ed. 5.95 (*0-944280-20-X*) Bancroft-Sage.

—Dimetrodon: The Sail-Backed Dinosaur. Oelerich, Marjorie & Hansen, Harlan S., eds. Vista III Design Staff, illus. LC 88-39802. 32p. (gr. k-5). 1989. PLB 12.95 (*0-944280-15-3*); pap. text ed. 5.95 (*0-944280-21-8*) Bancroft-Sage.

—Maiasaura: The Good Mother Dinosaur. Oelerich, Marjorie & Hansen, Harlan S., eds. Vista III Design Staff, illus. LC 88-39799. 32p. (gr. k-5). 1989. lib. bdg. 12.95 (*0-944280-17-X*); pap. text ed. 5.95 (*0-944280-23-4*) Bancroft-Sage.

—Plesiosaurus: The Swimming Reptile. Oelerich, Marjorie & Schroeder, Howard, eds. Vista III Design, illus. LC 88-962. 32p. (gr. k-5). 1988. lib. bdg. 12.95 (*0-944280-04-8*); pap. 5.95 (*0-944280-10-2*) Bancroft-Sage.

—Pteranodon: The Flying Reptile. Oelerich, Marjorie & Schroeder, Howard, eds. Vista III Design, illus. LC 88-953. 32p. (gr. k-5). 1988. lib. bdg. 12.95 (*0-944280-05-6*); pap. 5.95 (*0-944280-11-0*) Bancroft-Sage.

—Seisomasaurus: The Longest Dinosaur. Oelerich, Marjorie & Schroeder, Howard, eds. Vista III Design, illus. LC 88-963. 32p. (gr. k-5). 1988. lib. bdg. 12.95 (*0-944280-03-X*); pap. 5.95 (*0-944280-09-9*) Bancroft-Sage.

—Stegosaurus: The Dinosaur with the Smallest Brain. Oelerich, Marjorie & Schroeder, Howard, eds. Vista III Design, illus. LC 88-995. 32p. (gr. k-5). 1988. lib. bdg. 12.95 (*0-944280-02-1*); pap. 5.95 (*0-944280-08-0*) Bancroft-Sage.

—Triceratops: The Last Dinosaur. Oelerich, Marjorie & Schroeder, Howard, eds. Vista III Design, illus. LC 88-952. 32p. (gr. k-5). 1988. lib. bdg. 12.95 (*0-944280-01-3*); pap. 5.95 (*0-944280-07-2*) Bancroft-Sage.

—Tyrannsasaurus Rex: The Fierce Dinosaur. Oelerich, Marjorie & Schroeder, Howard, eds. Vista III Design, illus. LC 88-958. 32p. (gr. k-5). 1988. lib. bdg. 12.95 (*0-944280-00-5*); pap. 5.95 (*0-944280-06-4*) Bancroft-Sage.

Sanders, George. The Mix & Match Book of Dinosaurs. Block, Alex, illus. 10p. (ps-6). 1992. pap. 7.95 (*0-671-76911-1*, Little Simon) S&S Trade.

Sattler, Helen R. Baby Dinosaurs. Zallinger, Jean D., illus. LC 83-25631. 40p. (ps-3). 1984. 12.95 (*0-688-03817-4*); PLB 12.88 (*0-688-03818-2*) Lothrop.

—Dinosaurs of North America. Rao, Anthony, illus. Ostrom, John H., intro. by. LC 80-27411. (Illus.). 160p. (gr. 2 up). 1981. 17.95 (*0-688-51952-0*) Lothrop.
—The New Illustrated Dinosaur Dictionary. Powzyk, Joyce, illus. 1990. 24.95 (*0-688-08462-1*) Lothrop.
—Tyrannosaurus Rex & Its Kin: The Mesozoic Monsters. Powzyk, Joyce, illus. LC 88-1577. 48p. (gr. 3 up). 1989. 15.00 (*0-688-07747-1*); PLB 14.93 (*0-688-07748-X*) Lothrop.
Schlein, Miriam. Discovering Dinosaur Babies. Colbert, Margaret, illus. LC 89-23496. 40p. (gr. 1-5). 1991. RSBE 14.95 (*0-02-778091-0*, Four Winds) Macmillan Child Grp.
—Let's Go Dinosaur Tracking! Duke, Kate, illus. LC 90-39632. 48p. (gr. 2-5). 1991. PLB 14.89 (*0-06-025139-5*) HarpC Child Bks.
Selsam, Millicent E. & Hunt, Joyce. A First Look at Dinosaurs. Springer, Harriett, illus. 32p. (gr. 1-4). 1982. 7.95 (*0-8027-6454-1*); PLB 12.85 (*0-8027-6456-8*) Walker & Co.
Sheehan. Brontosaurus. (Illus.). 24p. 1981. PLB 14.00 (*0-86592-111-3*) Rourke Enter.
—Dinosaur Library, 4 bks, Set I. (Illus.). 96p. 1981. Set. PLB write for info. (*0-86592-110-5*) Rourke Enter.
—Stegosaurus. (Illus.). 24p. 1981. PLB 14.00 (*0-86592-112-1*) Rourke Enter.
—Triceratops. (Illus.). 24p. 1981. PLB 14.00 (*0-86592-113-X*) Rourke Enter.
—Tyrannosaurus. (Illus.). 24p. 1981. PLB 14.00 (*0-86592-114-8*) Rourke Enter.
Shuey, Karen. Dinosaurs. (Illus.). 48p. (gr. k-4). 1987. wkbk. 6.95 (*1-55734-218-0*) Tchr Create Mat.
Silver, Donald & Wynne, Patricia. Dinosaur Life Activity Book. 32p. (gr. 1-3). 1988. pap. 2.50 (*0-486-25809-2*) Dover.
Simon, Seymour. The Largest Dinosaurs. Carroll, Pamela, illus. LC 85-24088. 32p. (gr. k-3). 1986. RSBE 13.95 (*0-02-782910-3*, Macmillan Child Bk) Macmillan Child Grp.
—New Questions & Answers about Dinosaurs. Dewey, Jennifer, illus. LC 88-36226. 48p. (gr. k up). 1990. 13.95 (*0-688-08195-9*); PLB 13.88 (*0-688-08196-7*, Morrow Jr Bks) Morrow Jr Bks.
—New Questions & Answers about Dinosaurs. Dewey, Jennifer, illus. LC 92-25546. 48p. (gr. 2 up). 1993. pap. 4.95 (*0-688-12271-X*, Mulberry) Morrow.
Smith, Kathy B. In Search of Dinosaurs. M. J. Studios Staff, illus. 32p. (Orig.). (gr. k-6). 1993. pap. 3.95 (*1-879424-47-9*) Nickel Pr.
Speregen, Debra N. All about Dinosaurs Activity Book. (ps-3). 1994. pap. 1.95 (*0-590-47589-4*) Scholastic Inc.
Spizzirri, Linda, ed. Prehistoric Mammals: An Educational Coloring Book. (Illus.). 32p. (gr. 1-8). 1981. pap. 1.75 (*0-86545-022-6*) Spizzirri.
Spizzirri Publishing Co. Staff. Dinosaurs: An Educational Coloring Book. Spizzirri, Linda, ed. Kohn, Arnie, illus. 32p. (gr. 1-8). 1981. pap. 1.75 (*0-86545-019-6*) Spizzirri.
—Dinosaurs of Prey: An Educational Coloring Book. Spizzirri, Linda, ed. (Illus.). 32p. (gr. k-5). 1985. pap. 1.75 (*0-86545-063-3*) Spizzirri.
—Dot-to-Dot Dinosaurs: An Educational Activity-Coloring Book. Spizziri, Linda, ed. (Illus.). 32p. (gr. 1-8). 1986. pap. 1.00 (*0-86545-078-1*) Spizzirri.
Stewart, J. Dinosaurs: A New Discovery. (Illus.). 32p. (gr. 1-6). 1989. 10.95 (*0-88625-234-2*) Durkin Hayes Pub.
Sticker Fun with Dinosaur Bones. 12p. (ps-3). 1994. 4.95 (*1-56458-739-8*) Dorling Kindersley.
Sticker Fun with Dinosaurs. 12p. (ps-3). 1994. 4.95 (*1-56458-740-1*) Dorling Kindersley.
Stidworthy, John. The World of Dinosaurs. LC 94-16305. 1994. write for info. (*0-8160-3215-7*) Facts on File.
Storrs, Glenn. Stegosaurus. LC 93-43403. 40p. (gr. 3-7). 1994. pap. 5.95 (*1-85697-992-X*, Kingfisher LKC) LKC.
—Tyrannosaurus. LC 93-45531. 40p. (gr. 3-7). 1994. pap. 5.95 (*1-85697-993-8*, Kingfisher LKC) LKC.
Sullivan, Dianna J. Big & Easy Dinosaurs. Adkins, Lynda, illus. 48p. (ps-2). 1988. wkbk. 5.95 (*1-55734-103-6*) Tchr Create Mat.
Swann. Albertosaurus. (Illus.). 24p. 1984. PLB 14.00 (*0-86592-527-5*) Rourke Enter.
—Oviraptor. (Illus.). 24p. 1984. PLB 14.00 (*0-86592-528-3*) Rourke Enter.
—Struthiomimus. (Illus.). 24p. 1984. PLB 14.00 (*0-86592-525-9*) Rourke Enter.
Swann, F. Corythosaurus. (Illus.). 24p. (gr. 3 up). 1989. PLB 14.60 (*0-86592-521-6*); lib. bdg. 10.95s.p. (*0-685-58283-3*) Rourke Corp.
—Psittacosaurus. (Illus.). 24p. (gr. 3 up). 1989. PLB 14.60 (*0-86592-518-6*); 10.95s.p. (*0-685-58285-X*) Rourke Corp.
Tallarico, Tony. Drawing & Cartooning Dinosaurs: A Step-by-Step Guide for the Aspiring Prehistoric Artist. LC 93-16278. (Illus.). 96p. (Orig.). 1993. pap. 7.95 (*0-399-51814-2*, Perigee Bks) Berkley Pub.
Taylor, Paul S. The Great Dinosaur Mystery & the Bible. LC 89-81581. 63p. (gr. 4-8). 1990. 13.99 (*0-89636-264-7*, AC 215, Chariot Bks) Chariot Family.
Teitelbaum, Michael. Dinosaurs & Prehistoric Creatures. LC 93-50056. 1994. write for info. (*0-86593-355-3*) Rourke Corp.
—Dinosaurs, Big & Small. LC 93-50058. 1994. write for info. (*0-86593-352-9*) Rourke Corp.
—Dinosaurs of the Land, Sea, & Air. LC 93-49614. 1994. write for info. (*0-86593-353-7*) Rourke Corp.
—Dinosaurs of the Prehistoric Era. LC 93-50057. 1994. write for info. (*0-86593-354-5*) Rourke Corp.
—Welcome to Jurassic Park. (ps-3). 1993. pap. 2.25 (*0-307-12796-6*, Golden Pr) Western Pub.
Tewell, Debbie & Shirley, Gayle C. Where Dinosaurs Still Rule: A Guide to Dinosaur Areas of the West. Mooney, David, illus. 48p. (Orig.). 1993. pap. 6.95 (*1-56044-177-1*) Falcon Pr MT.
Thompson, C. E. Dinosaur Bones! Billin-Frye, Paige, illus. 32p. (ps-3). 1992. 6.95 (*0-448-41087-7*, G&D) Putnam Pub Group.
Timeline of Dinosaurs: Tracing the Evolution of the World's Most Incredible Creatures. 1993. 12.98 (*0-88394-974-1*) Promntory Pr.
Tyrannosaurus. LC 92-52820. (Illus.). 32p. (gr. 3 up). 1993. 12.95 (*1-56458-124-1*) Dorling Kindersley.
Unwin, David. Brachiosaurus. LC 93-46612. 1994. pap. 5.95 (*1-85697-990-3*, Kingfisher LKC) LKC.

VanCleave, Janice. Janice VanCleave's Dinosaurs for Every Kid: Easy Activities That Make Science Fun. LC 93-28226. 1994. text ed. 24.95 (*0-471-30813-7*); pap. text ed. 10.95 (*0-471-30812-9*) Wiley.
New in the Science for Every Kid series: They're huge! They're awesome! And kids can't get enough of them! Now everyone's favorite science teacher focuses on children's all time favorite topic: dinosaurs. Through easy-to-do experiments, children reconstruct the lives of legendary beasts that once stalked prehistoric jungles. Following in the best-selling footprints of the Science For Every Kid series, DINOSAURS FOR EVERY KID is packed with intriguing activities that use materials found around the house to teach kids the science of dinosaur biology & behavior. Features easy-to-do activities, like making a dinosaur jigsaw puzzle & building an imaginary dinosaur, called a "cubeosaurous". Examines theories on what dinosaurs ate, whether they were warm or cold blooded, & why they became extinct. Includes dozens of illustrations & fascinating facts about dinosaur names, sizes, eggs, tails, & much more. *Publisher Provided Annotation.*

Vaughan, Jenny. Looking at Maiasaura. Gibbons, Tony, illus. LC 93-37053. 24p. (gr. 2 up). 1994. PLB 17.27 (*0-8368-1085-6*) Gareth Stevens Inc.
Walker, Chris. Dinosaurs: A New Discovery. (gr. 4-7). 1989. pap. 5.95 (*0-88625-235-0*) Durkin Hayes Pub.
Weishampel, David B. Plant-Eating Dinosaurs. LC 91-16264. (Illus.). 64p. (gr. 4-8). 1992. PLB 14.90 (*0-531-11021-4*) Watts.
West, Robin. Dinosaur Discoveries: How to Create Your Own Prehistoric World. Wolfe, Bob & Wolfe, Diane, illus. 72p. (gr. 1-5). 1989. PLB 19.95 (*0-87614-351-6*) Carolrhoda Bks.
Wexo, John B. Dinosaurs. 24p. (gr. 3 up). 1991. PLB 14.95 (*0-88682-393-5*) Creative Ed.
Where Did Dinosaurs Go? 24p. (gr. 1-6). 1992. PLB 11.96 (*0-88110-582-1*); pap. 3.95 (*0-7460-1016-8*) EDC.
Whitcomb, Norma A. Those Mysterious Dinosaurs: A Biblical Approach for Children, Their Parents & Their Teachers. 2nd ed. Job, Heather H., illus. Wyrtzen, Jack, frwd. by. (Illus.). 125p. (gr. 4 up). 1993. Spiral bdg. pap. 7.20x (*0-685-67781-8*); pap. text ed. 11.99 (*0-9635049-0-8*) Whitcomb Minist.
White. Deinosuchus. (Illus.). 24p. 1984. PLB 14.00 (*0-86592-524-0*) Rourke Enter.
—Pachycephalosaurus. (Illus.). 24p. 1984. PLB 14.00 (*0-86592-526-7*) Rourke Enter.
—Parasaurolophus. (Illus.). 24p. 1984. PLB 14.00 (*0-86592-529-1*) Rourke Enter.
White & Swann. Dinosaur Library, 6 bks, Set V. (Illus.). 144p. 1984. Set. PLB write for info. (*0-86592-523-2*) Rourke Enter.
—Dinosaur Library, 6 bks, Set IV. (Illus.). 144p. 1989. Set. PLB write for info. (*0-86592-516-X*) Rourke Enter.
White, D. Anatosaurus. (Illus.). 24p. (gr. 3 up). 1989. PLB 14.60 (*0-86592-520-8*) Rourke Corp.
—Rutiodon. (Illus.). 24p. (gr. 3 up). 1989. PLB 14.60 (*0-86592-522-4*); 10.95s.p. (*0-685-58284-1*) Rourke Corp.
—Scolosaurus. (Illus.). 24p. (gr. 3 up). 1989. PLB 14.60 (*0-86592-519-4*); 10.95 (*0-685-58286-8*) Rourke Corp.
—Spinosaurus. (Illus.). 24p. (gr. 3 up). 1989. PLB 14.60 (*0-86592-517-8*); PLB 10.95s.p. (*0-685-58287-6*) Rourke Corp.
Whitfield, Philip. Macmillan Children's Guide to Dinosaurs & Other Prehistoric Animals. LC 91-45562. (Illus.). 96p. (gr. 2 up). 1992. SBE 16.95 (*0-02-762362-9*, Macmillan Child Bk) Macmillan Child Grp.
Whyte, Malcolm. The Second Dinosaur Action Set. Smith, Dan, illus. 24p. (gr. 1 up). 1994. pap. 5.95 (*0-8431-1951-9*, Troubador) Price Stern.
—Undersea Dinosaur Action Set. Smith, Dan, illus. 24p. (gr. 1 up). 1994. pap. 5.95 (*0-8431-1954-3*, Troubador) Price Stern.
Wildlife Education, Ltd. Staff. Dinosaurs. Hallett, Mark, illus. 20p. (Orig.). (gr. k-12). 1985. pap. 2.75 (*0-937934-34-8*) Wildlife Educ.
Wilkes, Angela. The Big Book of Dinosaurs. LC 94-4675. (Illus.). 32p. (ps). 1994. 12.95 (*1-56458-718-5*) Dorling Kindersley.
Williams, Geoffrey T. Explorers in Dinosaur World. Cremins, Robert, illus. 32p. (gr. 1-6). 1988. pap. 9.95 incl. cass. (*0-8431-2265-X*) Price Stern.
Wilson. Allosaurus. (Illus.). 24p. 1984. PLB 14.00 (*0-86592-206-3*) Rourke Enter.
—Diplodocus. (Illus.). 24p. 1984. PLB 14.00 (*0-86592-202-0*) Rourke Enter.
—Hypsilophodon. (Illus.). 24p. 1984. PLB 14.00 (*0-86592-205-5*) Rourke Enter.
—Pteranodon. (Illus.). 24p. 1984. PLB 14.00 (*0-86592-201-2*) Rourke Enter.
—Woolly Mammoth. (Illus.). 24p. 1984. PLB 14.00 (*0-86592-203-9*) Rourke Enter.
Wilson, ed. Ichthyosaurus. (Illus.). 24p. 1984. PLB 14.00 (*0-86592-204-7*) Rourke Enter.
World Book, Inc. Staff, ed. Dinosaurs! LC 65-25105. (Illus.). 304p. (gr. 3-7). 1987. PLB write for info. (*0-7166-0687-9*) World BK.
Zallinger, Peter. Dinosaurs. Zallinger, Peter, illus. LC 76-24178. (ps-1). 1977. pap. 2.25 (*0-394-83485-2*) Random Bks Yng Read.
Zanini, G. The Dinosaur Book. (Illus.). 72p. (gr. k-6). 1985. 5.98 (*0-517-42525-4*) Random Hse Value.
Zim, Herbert S. Dinosaurs. Irving, James G., illus. LC 54-5080. 64p. (gr. 3-7). 1954. PLB 11.88 (*0-688-31239-X*) Morrow Jr Bks.

DINOSAURS–FICTION

Ahlberg, Allan. Dinosaur Dreams. LC 90-2943. (Illus.). 24p. (ps up). 1991. 12.95 (*0-688-09955-6*); PLB 12.88 (*0-688-09956-4*) Greenwillow.
Akins, Kelly, illus. My Dinosaur Library, 14 bks. (ps-2). 1992. bds. 17.95 (*1-56293-201-2*, Set, mini-board bks. in a tray) McClanahan Bk.
Aliki. My Visit to the Dinosaurs Big Book. Aliki, illus. LC 85-47538. 32p. (gr. k-4). 1994. pap. 19.95 (*0-06-443350-1*, Trophy) HarpC Child Bks.
Arnold, Caroline. Dinosaur Mountain. (gr. 4-7). 1993. pap. 6.95 (*0-395-66503-5*, Clarion Bks) HM.
Attack of the Dinosaurs. 1993. pap. 6.95 (*0-8125-3492-1*) Tor Bks.
Aunt Eeebs. The Dinosaur Debut. rev. ed. Aunt Eeebs, illus. 24p. (ps-2). 1991. pap. write for info. (*1-878908-00-6*) Rivercrest Indus.
Ball, Jacqueline A. A Kitten Named Cuddles. (gr. 4-7). 1991. pap. 2.95 (*0-06-106038-0*, PL) HarpC.
—Revenge of the Terror Dactyls. (gr. 4-7). 1991. pap. 2.95 (*0-06-106081-X*, PL) HarpC.
—Sara's Biggest Valentine. (gr. 4-7). 1991. pap. 2.95 (*0-06-106043-7*, PL) HarpC.
—Sneeze-O-Saurus. (gr. 4-7). 1990. pap. 2.95 (*0-06-106008-9*, PL) HarpC.
—T. Rex's Missing Tooth. (gr. 4-7). 1991. pap. 2.95 (*0-06-106055-0*, Harp PBks) HarpC.
Barney First Fun. 1993. pap. 1.95 (*0-307-03521-2*, Golden Pr) Western Pub.
Barton, Byron. Bones, Bones, Dinosaur Bones. Barton, Byron, illus. LC 89-71306. 32p. (ps-1). 1990. 15.00 (*0-690-04825-4*, Crowell Jr Bks); PLB 14.89 (*0-690-04827-0*, Crowell Jr Bks) HarpC Child Bks.
—Dinosaurs, Dinosaurs. Barton, Byron, illus. LC 88-22938. 40p. (ps-1). 1993. pap. 4.95 (*0-06-443298-X*, Trophy) HarpC Child Bks.
Birchman, David F. Brother Billy Bronto's Bygone Blues Band. O'Brien, John, illus. LC 90-2611. (ps-3). 1992. 14.00 (*0-688-10423-1*); PLB 13.93 (*0-688-10424-X*) Lothrop.
Birney, Betty G. Tyrannosaurus Tex. O'Brien, John, illus. LC 93-30727. 1994. 14.95 (*0-395-67648-7*) HM.
Blackwood, Mary. Derek the Knitting Dinosaur. Argent, Kerry, illus. 32p. (ps-3). 1990. PLB 18.95 (*0-87614-400-8*) Carolrhoda Bks.
—Derek the Knitting Dinosaur: Picture Book. (ps-3). 1991. pap. 5.95 (*0-87614-540-3*) Carolrhoda Bks.

Blake, Doron W. The Adventure of George the Dinosaur (La Adventura de Jorge il Dinosaurio) Lucas, Winafred B., ed. Gremard, Anna, tr. Gremard, David, illus. 32p. (gr. k-3). 1994. English ed. 11.95 (*1-882530-04-7*); Spanish ed. 11.95 (*1-882530-05-5*) Deep Forest Pr.
This book relates the delightful adventure of a small dinosaur named George who wanted to know if spooks were real. When his mother & grandmother would not tell him, he

went out into the forest to find out for himself. His journey took him into unusual situations & won him interesting friends. The story suggests the rewards to a child when he reaches out in expanded states of awareness. Doron Blake, now eleven, typed out the original draft of this story when he was six years old. At ten, he edited it & put it on computer. As the first boy born from the Nobel Prize Sperm Bank, he gives frequent magazine & TV interviews. David Gremard was named one of the top artists in the 1993 high school graduation class in California & drew the illustrations for the book when he was 17. Together, the boys worked on many details of the adventure, each suggesting to the other small embellishments of the original story so that the result is a sparkling fusion of painting & narrative. Available from Deep Forest Press, P.O. Drawer 4, Crest Park, CA 92326 (909-337-1179) or from Bookpeople. ***Publisher Provided Annotation.***

Bliss, Richard B., ed. Dinosaur ABC's Activity Book. rev. ed. Schmitt, Doug, illus. 32p. (gr. k-3). 1986. pap. 3.95 (*0-89051-113-6*) Master Bks.

Booth, Jerry. The Big Beast Book: Dinosaurs & How They Got That Way. Weston, Martha, illus. LC 87-36206. (gr. 3-7). 1988. pap. 10.95 (*0-316-10266-0*) Little.

Boynton, Sandra. Boynton on Board: Oh My Oh My Oh Dinosaurs! Boynton, Sandra, illus. 24p. (ps). 1993. bds. 6.95 (*1-56305-441-8*, 3441) Workman Pub.

Bradman, Tony. Dilly & the Horror Movie. Hellard, Susan, illus. 64p. (gr. 2-5). 1991. pap. 3.95 (*0-14-032799-1*, Puffin) Puffin Bks.

—Dilly the Dinosaur. Hellard, Susan, illus. 64p. (Orig.). (gr. 2-5). 1988. pap. 3.95 (*0-14-032337-6*, Puffin) Puffin Bks.

Brandt, Keith. Case of the Missing Dinosaur. Wallner, John, illus. LC 81-7620. 48p. (gr. 2-4). 1982. PLB 10.89 (*0-89375-586-9*); pap. text ed. 3.50 (*0-89375-587-7*) Troll Assocs.

Brillhart, Julie. The Dino Expert. LC 92-43474. 1993. write for info. (*0-8075-1597-3*) A Whitman.

Brown, Laurene K. Rex & Lilly Family Time. Brown, Marc T., illus. LC 93-24162. 1995. lib. bdg. 12.95 (*0-316-11385-9*) Little.

Brown, Laurie K. Dinosaurs Travel, Vol. 1. (ps-3). 1991. pap. 5.95 (*0-316-11253-4*) Little.

Brown, Marc. Dinosaurs to the Rescue: A Guide to Protecting Our Planet. (ps-3). 1994. 5.95 (*0-316-11397-2*) Little.

Brown, Marc T. & Krensky, Stephen. Dinosaurs, Beware! A Safety Guide. Brown, Marc T. & Krensky, Stephen, illus. LC 82-15207. 32p. (ps-3). 1984. 15.95 (*0-316-11228-3*, Joy St Bks); pap. 6.95 (*0-316-11219-4*, Joy St Bks) Little.

Butler, M. Christine. The Dinosaur Egg Mystery. (ps-3). 1992. 11.95 (*0-8120-6297-3*); pap. 5.95 (*0-8120-1379-4*) Barron.

Calhoun. Bite Makes Right. 128p. Date not set. text ed. write for info. (*0-7167-6542-X*); pap. text ed. write for info. (*0-7167-6550-0*) W H Freeman.

—Out of Place. 128p. 1994. text ed. write for info. (*0-7167-6543-8*); pap. text ed. write for info. (*0-7167-6551-9*) W H Freeman.

Camp, Lindsay. Dinosaurs at the Supermarket. Skilbeck, Clare, illus. LC 92-16936. 32p. (gr. 3-8). 1993. 13.99 (*0-670-84802-6*) Viking Child Bks.

Carmine, Mary. Daniel's Dinosaurs. (gr. 4-7). 1991. 12.95 (*0-590-44638-X*, Scholastic Hardcover) Scholastic Inc.

Carnegie Museum of Natural History, Division of Education Staff. Dippy Diplodocus: Story Only. (Illus.). 16p. (Orig.). (ps-2). 1988. pap. 1.50 (*0-911239-40-5*) Carnegie Mus.

Carr, Barbara. The Planet of the Dinosaurs. Bear, Alice, illus. LC 92-9287. 32p. (gr. k-3). 1992. 12.95 (*0-89334-161-4*, 161-4) Humanics Ltd.

Carrick, Carol. Big Old Bones: A Dinosaur Tale. (ps-3). 1992. pap. 5.70 (*0-395-61582-8*, Clarion Bks) HM.

—What Happened to Patrick's Dinosaurs? Carrick, Donald, illus. LC 85-13989. (gr. k-3). 1988. 14.95 (*0-89919-406-0*, Clarion Bks); pap. 5.95 (*0-89919-797-3*, Clarion Bks) HM.

Cauley, Lorinda B. The Trouble with Tyrannosaurus Rex. Cauley, Lorinda B., illus. 32p. (ps-3). 1988. 14.95 (*0-15-290880-3*) HarBrace.

—The Trouble with Tyrannosaurus Rex. 32p. (ps-3). 1990. pap. 4.95 (*0-15-290881-1*, Voyager Bks) HarBrace.

Child, A. Yabba Dabba Dinosaur. 23p. (gr. k). 1992. pap. text ed. 23.00 big bk. (*1-56843-009-4*); pap. text ed. 4.50 (*1-56843-059-0*) BGR Pub.

Clark, Emma C. The Bouncing Dinosaur. (Illus.). 32p. (ps-3). 1990. 13.95 (*0-374-30912-4*) FS&G.

Cohen, Daniel. Dinosaurs. (ps-3). 1993. pap. 4.99 (*0-440-40784-2*) Dell.

Cohen, Miriam. Lost in the Museum. Hoban, Lillian, illus. (gr. k-3). 1983. pap. 2.95 (*0-440-44780-1*, YB) Dell.

Cole, Betsy. Is Aetosaur a Dinosaur? Spear, Scott, illus. Hager, Michael, contrib. by. (Illus.). 64p. (Orig.). (gr. k-3). 1992. pap. 11.95 (*0-9625801-4-7*) VA Mus Natl Hist.

Coville, Bruce. The Dinosaur That Followed Me Home. Pierard, John, illus. 160p. (Orig.). (gr. 3-6). 1990. pap. 3.50 (*0-671-64750-4*, Minstrel Bks) PB.

Craig, Janet. Little Danny Dinosaur. Harvey, Paul, illus. LC 87-16228. 32p. (gr. k-2). 1988. PLB 7.89 (*0-8167-1229-8*); pap. text ed. 1.95 (*0-8167-1230-1*) Troll Assocs.

Crozat, Francois. I Am a Big Dinosaur. (Illus.). 24p. (ps-k). 1989. 8.95 (*0-8120-6097-0*) Barron.

—I Am a Big Dinosaur-Mini. 24p. (ps). 1990. 3.50 (*0-8120-6193-4*) Barron.

Curran, Eileen. Home for a Dinosaur. Karas, G. Brian, illus. LC 84-8627. 32p. (gr. k-2). 1985. lib. bdg. 11.59 (*0-8167-0351-5*); pap. text ed. 2.95 (*0-8167-0431-7*) Troll Assocs.

Cuyler, Margery. Baby Dot: A Dinosaur Story. Weiss, Ellen, illus. 32p. (ps-1). 1990. 13.45 (*0-395-51934-9*, Clarion Bks) HM.

Day, Marie. Dragon in the Rocks: A Story Based on the Childhood of the Early Paleontologist, Mary Anning. Day, Marie, illus. 32p. (ps up). 1992. 12.95 (*0-920775-76-4*, Pub. by Greey de Pencier CN) Firefly Bks Ltd.

Demi. Demi's Dozen Dinos. (gr. 4 up). 1994. 9.95 (*0-8050-2783-1*) H Holt & Co.

Los Dinosaurios Gigantes. (SPA.). 1993. pap. 28.67 (*0-590-73764-3*) Scholastic Inc.

Dixon, Dougal. Dougal Dixon's Dinosaurs. (Illus.). 160p. (gr. 4-7). 1993. 17.95 (*1-56397-261-1*) Boyds Mills Pr.

Dolby, K. The Incredible Dinosaur Expedition. (Illus.). 48p. (gr. 3-5). 1987. PLB 11.96 (*0-88110-300-4*); pap. 4.95 (*0-7460-0149-5*) EDC.

Donnelly, Liza. Dinosaur Beach. Donnelly, Liza, illus. 32p. (Orig.). (ps-3). 1991. 2.50 (*0-590-42176-X*); pap. 2.50 (*0-685-43744-2*) Scholastic Inc.

—Dinosaur Day. 32p. (ps-3). 1987. pap. 2.50 (*0-590-41800-9*) Scholastic Inc.

—Dinosaur Garden. (Illus.). 32p. (ps-3). 1991. pap. 2.50 (*0-590-43172-2*) Scholastic Inc.

—Dinosaurs' Christmas. 32p. 1991. 12.95 (*0-590-44797-1*, Scholastic Hardcover) Scholastic Inc.

—Dinosaurs' Halloween. (ps-3). 1988. 12.95 (*0-590-41025-3*); pap. 2.50 (*0-590-41006-7*) Scholastic Inc.

Donnely, Marcus. Squeak the Dinosaur. Young, Debby, illus. 32p. (ps-2). 1987. 9.00 (*0-938715-02-X*) Toy Works Pr.

Dubowski, Cathy E. We're Back! The Novelization. (Illus.). 64p. (gr. 2-6). 1993. pap. 3.95 (*0-448-40445-1*, G&D) Putnam Pub Group.

Dudko, Mary A. & Larsen, Margie. Barney's Color Surprise. Hartley, Linda, ed. Full, Dennis, photos by. LC 93-77865. (Illus.). 18p. (ps). 1993. Repr. bds. 3.95 chunky board (*1-57064-007-6*) Barney Pub.

—Barney's Hats. Hartley, Linda, ed. 24p. (ps-k). 1993. pap. 2.25 (*0-7829-0376-2*) Lyons Group.

—Barney's Hats. Hartley, Linda, ed. Full, Dennis, photos by. LC 93-77016. (Illus.). 24p. (ps-1). 1993. pap. 2.25 (*1-57064-005-X*) Barney Pub.

—A Day with Barney. Dowdy, Linda C., ed. Daste, Larry, illus. LC 93-74292. 24p. (ps). 1994. chunky board 3.95 (*1-57064-013-0*) Barney Pub.

Eisberg, Tiffany B., et al. Bronto Lost. (Illus.). 60p. (gr. 3-5). 1994. pap. 6.95 (*1-56721-070-8*) Twnty-Fifth Cent Pr.

Emberley, Michael. Dinosaurs! A Drawing Book. Emberley, Michael, illus. 48p. (gr. 3 up). 1985. pap. 5.95 (*0-316-23631-4*) Little.

Faulkner, Keith. Amble Has a Dream. (Illus.). 20p. (ps-1). 1994. lift-a-flap 3.95 (*0-8431-3653-7*) Price Stern.

—Munch Looks for Lunch. Lambert, Jonathan, illus. 20p. (ps-1). 1994. pap. 3.95 lift-a-flap (*0-8431-3652-9*) Price Stern.

—Rumble Frightens Himself. Lambert, Jonathan, illus. 20p. (ps-1). 1994. lift-a-flap 3.95 (*0-8431-3650-2*) Price Stern.

—Swoop Flies Too High. Lambert, Jonathan, illus. 20p. (ps-1). 1994. lift-a-flap 3.95 (*0-8431-3651-0*) Price Stern.

Fedotousky, Alex. Dingle Dorts vs Dingle Saurs. Fedotousky, Alex, illus. 32p. 1993. pap. text ed. 2.75 (*0-9638756-0-4*) Skylght Studios.

Fleischman, Paul. Time Train. Ewart, Claire, illus. LC 90-27357. 32p. (gr. k-4). 1991. 15.00 (*0-06-021709-X*); PLB 14.89 (*0-06-021710-3*) HarpC Child Bks.

Giff, Patricia R. In the Dinosaur's Paw. Sims, Blanche, illus. 80p. (gr. k-6). 1985. pap. 3.50 (*0-440-44150-1*, YB) Dell.

Gil, Yvonne. Professor Curious & the Mystery of the Hiking Dinosaurs. Timmons, Bonnie, illus. LC 90-42592. 24p. (gr. 1-5). 1991. 13.95 (*0-517-58025-X*, Clarkson Potter) Crown Bks Yng Read.

Gordon, Sharon. Un Dinosauro en Peligro. Havey, Paul, illus. (SPA.). 32p. (gr. k-2). 1981. PLB 7.89 (*0-89375-554-0*); pap. 1.95 (*0-685-42386-7*) Troll Assocs.

Grambling, Lois G. Can I Have a Stegosaurus, Mom? Can I!? Please? Lewis, H. B., illus. LC 93-39178. 32p. (gr. k-3). 1995. PLB 14.95 (*0-8167-3386-4*); pap. text ed. 4.95 (*0-8167-3387-2*) BrdgeWater.

Green, Kate. Between Friends. (Illus.). 32p. (gr. 1-4). 1992. 15.95 (*0-89565-780-5*) Childs World.

—Buddy Rock's Race. (Illus.). 32p. (gr. 1-4). 1992. 15.95 (*0-89565-781-3*) Childs World.

—Everything a Dinosaur Could Want. (Illus.). 32p. 1992. 15.95 (*0-89565-739-2*) Childs World.

—Grumble Day. Mark, Steve, illus. (gr. 1-4). 1992. PLB 15.95 (*0-89565-870-4*) Childs World.

—Just about Perfect. Mark, Steve, illus. (gr. 1-4). 1992. PLB 15.95 (*0-89565-871-2*) Childs World.

—T-Bone's Tent. (Illus.). 32p. (gr. 1-4). 1992. 15.95 (*0-89565-782-1*) Childs World.

Greenberg, Robert B. Tyrannosaurus Tex. Zady, Mary, illus. LC 89-4225. 64p. (gr. k-4). 1989. pap. 6.95 (*0-938349-38-4*) State House Pr.

—Tyrannosaurus Tex: First Grade. LC 90-9749. (Illus.). 64p. (gr. k-4). 1991. pap. 5.95 (*0-938349-56-2*) State House Pr.

Haddon, Mark. Baby Dinosaurs at Home. (ps). 1994. 3.95 (*0-307-17575-8*, Artsts Writrs) Western Pub.

—Baby Dinosaurs at Playgroup. (ps). 1994. 3.95 (*0-307-17576-6*, Artsts Writrs) Western Pub.

—Baby Dinosaurs in the Garden. (ps). 1994. 3.95 (*0-307-17578-2*, Artsts Writrs) Western Pub.

Hearn, Diane D. Dad's Dinosaur Day. LC 92-22549. (Illus.). 32p. (gr. k-3). 1993. RSBE 14.95 (*0-02-743485-0*, Macmillan Child Bk) Macmillan Child Grp.

Hennessy, B. G. The Dinosaur Who Lived in My Backyard. Davis, Susan, illus. 32p. (ps-3). 1990. pap. 3.99 (*0-14-050736-1*, Puffin) Puffin Bks.

Herman, Gail. Time for School, Little Dinosaur. Gorbaty, Norman, illus. LC 89-70331. 24p. (Orig.). (ps-2). 1990. pap. 2.25 (*0-679-80789-6*) Random Bks Yng Read.

Hoban, Lillian. Joe & Betsy the Dinosaur. Hoban, Lillian, photos by. LC 93-44725. (Illus.). (gr. k up). 1995. 14.00 (*0-06-024473-9*) HarpC.

Hoff, Syd. Danielito y el Dinosauria. Mlawer, Teresa, tr. from ENG. Hoff, Syd, illus. 64p. (gr. 5-7). 1991. PLB 11.95 (*0-9625162-2-8*) Lectorum Pubns.

—Danny & the Dinosaur. Hoff, Syd, illus. LC 92-13609. 64p. (gr. k-3). 1958. 14.00 (*0-06-022465-7*); PLB 13.89 (*0-06-022466-5*) HarpC Child Bks.

—Danny & the Dinosaur. Hoff, Syd, illus. LC 58-7754. 64p. (gr. k-3). 1985. incl. cassette 5.98 (*0-694-00017-5*, Trophy); pap. 3.50 (*0-06-444002-8*, Trophy) HarpC Child Bks.

Holcomb, J. Paul & Holcomb, Sue A. Tex R Masaur: The Beginning. Holcomb, Sue A., illus. 32p. (Orig.). (gr. k-3). 1993. pap. 3.95 (*0-9636122-1-2*) Post Oak Hill.

Holcomb, Sue A. Tex R Masaur: Down in the Dump. Holcomb, J. Paul & Holcomb, Sue A., illus. 32p. (Orig.). (gr. k-3). Date not set. pap. 3.95 (*0-9636122-2-0*) Post Oak Hill.

Hooks, William H. Mr. Dinosaur. Meisel, Paul, illus. LC 92-33476. 1994. (Little Rooster); pap. 3.99 (*0-553-37234-3*, Little Rooster) Bantam.

The Horned Dinosaur. (ps-3). 1991. write for info. (*0-307-14174-8*, 14174) Western Pub.

Hughes, Francine, adapted by. Dinosaurs on Parade. (Illus.). (ps-3). 1993. pap. 2.50 (*0-448-40446-X*, G&D); pap. 5.95 incl. tape (*0-448-40448-6*, G&D) Putnam Pub Group.

Inkpen, Mick. The Very Good Dinosaur. (Illus.). 12p. (gr. 4-7). 1993. 4.99 (*1-878685-72-4*, Bedrock Press) Turner Pub GA.

James, Sara. Littlest Dinosaur Finds a Friend. Digregorio, Elizabeth, illus. 24p. (Orig.). 1992. pap. 2.50 (*1-56156-110-X*) Kidsbks.

Johansen, Hanna. Dinosaur with an Attitude. Maccari, Elisabetta, tr. from GER. Johansen, Hanna, illus. 143p. (gr. 4-7). 1994. 12.95 (*1-57143-018-0*, Wetlands) RDR Bks.

Joyce, William. Dinosaur Bob: And His Adventures with the Family Lazardo. Joyce, William, illus. LC 87-30796. 32p. (ps-3). 1988. 15.00 (*0-06-023047-9*); PLB 14.89 (*0-06-023048-7*) HarpC Child Bks.

Kearns, Kimberly & O'Brien, Marie. Barney's Farm Animals. Hartley, Linda, ed. Malzeke-McDonald, Karen, illus. LC 93-77014. 24p. (ps). 1993. bds. 3.95 chunky board (*1-57064-002-5*) Barney Pub.

Kelly, Karla, et al. Tales of Terratopia: The Secret of the Dragonfly & the Daring Dino Rescue. (Illus.). 36p. (gr. 1-6). 1993. 6.95 (*1-883871-00-X*) Nature Co.

King, Ed. All-American Dinosaur Family: Meet the Hoadleys. (Illus.). 24p. (gr. k-12). 1993. 3.95 (*1-56288-387-9*) Checkerboard.

—All-American Dinosaur Family: The Hoadleys in Town. (Illus.). 24p. (ps-12). 1993. 3.95 (*1-56288-390-9*) Checkerboard.

—All-American Dinosaur Family: The Hoadleys on Vacation. (Illus.). 24p. (ps-12). 1993. 3.95 (*1-56288-388-7*) Checkerboard.

—All-American Dinosaur Family: The Hoadleys Travel in Time. (Illus.). 24p. (ps-12). 1993. 3.95 (*1-56288-389-5*) Checkerboard.

Korman, Justine. We're Back! The Illustrated Story. Lazor-Bahr, Beverly, illus. 48p. (ps-3). 1993. 9.95 (*0-448-40444-3*, G&D) Putnam Pub Group.

Kralis, Don D. The Lost Dinosaur of Stone Ridge. Ingram, tr. 1994. pap. 7.95 (*1-56901-276-8*) NW Pub.

Kroll, Steven. The Tyrannosaurus Game. De Paola, Tomie, illus. LC 75-37078. 40p. (ps-3). 1976. reinforced bdg. 14.95 (*0-8234-0275-4*); pap. 5.95 (*0-8234-0620-2*) Holiday.

LaFleur, Tom & Brennan, Gale. Isadore the Dinosaur. Berghauer, Meri H., illus. 16p. (Orig.). (gr. k-6). 1981. pap. 1.25 (*0-685-02456-3*) Brennan Bks.

Lasky, Kathryn. Dinosaur Dig. Knight, Christopher G., photos by. LC 89-13212. (Illus.). 64p. (gr. 3 up). 1990. 13.95 (*0-688-08574-1*); PLB 13.88 (*0-688-08575-X*, Morrow Jr Bks) Morrow Jr Bks.

Longyear, Barry B. The Homecoming. Clark, Alan M., illus. 224p. 1989. 15.95 (*0-8027-6863-6*) Walker & Co.

Lowenstein, Christina. Fair Play. LC 93-37746. 1994. text ed. write for info. (*0-7167-6520-9*); pap. text ed. write for info. (*0-7167-6531-4*) Spr-Verlag.

McGowan, Christopher. Discover Dinosaurs: A Royal Ontario Museum Book. Holdcroft, Tina, illus. (gr. 3-7). 1993. pap. 10.95 (*1-55074-048-2*) Addison-Wesley.

Mannetti, William. Dinosaurs in Your Backyard. Mannetti, William, illus. LC 81-7998. 160p. (gr. 4-7). 1982. SBE 13.95 (*0-689-30906-6*, Atheneum Child Bk) Macmillan Child Grp.

Manning, Linda. Dinosaur Days. Van Kampen, Vlasta, illus. LC 93-28443. 32p. (ps-2). 1993. PLB 12.95 (*0-8167-3315-5*); pap. 3.95 (*0-8167-3316-3*) BrdgeWater.

Manson, Frank A. The Adventures of Prince Albert & the Royal Dinosaurs. Henley, Joan, illus. 144p. (gr. 2-7). 1990. 11.95 (*0-918339-17-0*) Vandamere.

Martin, Linda. When Dinosaurs Go Visiting. LC 93-10207. 1993. 12.95 (*0-8118-0122-5*) Chronicle Bks.

Martin, Rodney. There's a Dinosaur in the Park! Siow, John, illus. LC 86-42811. 31p. (gr. 2-3). 1987. PLB 18.60 (*1-55532-151-8*) Gareth Stevens Inc.

Marzollo, Jean. I'm Tyrannosaurus! A Book of Dinosaur Rhymes. Wilhelm, Hans, illus. 32p. (ps-1). 1993. pap. 2.50 (*0-590-44641-X*, Cartwheel) Scholastic Inc.

Mayhew, James. Katie & the Dinosaurs. Mayhew, James, illus. (ps-3). 1992. 15.00 (*0-553-08129-2*, Little Rooster) Bantam.

Milton, Joyce. Dinosaur Days. Roe, Richard, illus. LC 84-17861. 48p. (gr. k-3). 1985. lib. bdg. 7.99 (*0-394-97023-3*); pap. 3.50 (*0-394-87023-9*) Random Bks Yng Read.

—Dinosaur Days. Roe, Richard, illus. 48p. (gr. k-3). 1988. pap. 6.99 bk. & cassette pkg. (*0-394-89774-9*) Random Bks Yng Read.

Moncure, Jane B. A Wish-for Dinosaur. Gohman, Vera, illus. LC 88-20302. (SPA & ENG.). 32p. (ps-2). 1989. PLB 14.95 (*0-89565-393-1*) Childs World.

—Word Bird's Dinosaur Day. Hohag, Linda, illus. 32p. (ps-2). 1990. PLB 14.95 (*0-89565-617-5*) Childs World.

Morgan, Michaela. Dinostory. Kelley, True, illus. LC 90-44935. 32p. (ps-4). 1991. 13.95 (*0-525-44726-1*, DCB) Dutton Child Bks.

Morss, Martha. When Dinosaurs Ruled the Earth. (Illus.). 32p. (gr. 1-2). 1991. pap. 2.99 (*0-87406-560-7*) Willowisp Pr.

Moser, Cindy & Hummel, Nancy. Dinosaurs Don't Wear Diapers. Parker, Sherry, illus. 16p. (Orig.). (ps). 1990. pap. text ed. 9.95 (*0-9628204-0-7*) Stopher.

Mosley, Francis. The Dinosaur Eggs. (Illus.). 32p. (ps-2). 1992. pap. 5.95 (*0-8120-4959-4*) Barron.

Most, Bernard. Dinosaur Cousins? 32p. (ps-3). 1990. pap. 4.95 (*0-15-223498-5*, Voyager Bks) HarBrace.

—If the Dinosaurs Came Back. Most, Bernard, illus. LC 77-23911. (ps-2). 1978. 13.95 (*0-15-238020-5*, HB Juv Bks) HarBrace.

—If the Dinosaurs Came Back. Most, Bernard, illus. LC 77-23911. 32p. (ps-2). 1984. pap. 4.95 (*0-15-238021-3*, Voyager Bks) HarBrace.

—If the Dinosaurs Came Back. Most, Bernard, illus. 32p. (ps-2). 1991. pap. 19.95 (*0-15-238022-1*) HarBrace.

—Littlest Dinosaurs. LC 88-30063. (ps-3). 1993. pap. 5.95 (*0-15-248126-5*) HarBrace.

—Whatever Happened to the Dinosaurs? Most, Bernard, illus. LC 84-3779. 30p. (ps-3). 1984. 13.95 (*0-15-295295-0*, HB Juv Bks) HarBrace.

Murphy, Jane. My Pet Tyrannosaurus. LC 88-81468. (Illus.). 32p. (Orig.). (ps-3). 1988. pap. 8.95 (*0-937124-17-6*) Kimbo Educ.

Murphy, Jim. The Last Dinosaur. Weatherby, Mark A., illus. 1991. pap. 3.95 (*0-590-44875-7*, Blue Ribbon Bks) Scholastic Inc.

Nelson, Jeffrey. Dinosaur Jokes & Riddles Book. (Illus.). 24p. (gr. 3 up). 1988. pap. 1.95 (*1-56288-341-0*) Checkerboard.

Night of the Dinosaurs. 1990. text ed. 3.95 cased (*0-7214-5265-5*) Ladybird Bks.

Nixon, Joan L. Watch Out for Dinosaurs. (gr. 4-7). 1991. pap. 2.99 (*0-440-40459-2*) Dell.

Nolan, Dennis. Dinosaur Dream. Nolan, Dennis, illus. LC 89-78208. 32p. (ps-2). 1990. RSBE 14.95 (*0-02-768145-9*, Macmillan Child Bk) Macmillan Child Grp.

—Dinosaur Dream. Nolan, Dennis, illus. LC 93-48409. (gr. k-3). 1994. pap. 4.95 (*0-689-71832-2*, Aladdin) Macmillan Child Grp.

Oram, Hiawyn. A Boy Wants a Dinosaur. (ps-3). 1991. bds. 13.95 jacketed (*0-374-30939-6*) FS&G.

Osborne, Mary P. Dinosaurs Before Dark. Murdocca, Sal, illus. LC 91-51106. 80p. (Orig.). (gr. 1-4). 1992. PLB 9.99 (*0-679-92411-6*); pap. 2.99 (*0-679-82411-1*) Random Bks Yng Read.

Otto, Carolyn B. Dinosaur Chase. Hurd, Thacher, illus. LC 90-2021. 32p. (ps-1). 1991. 15.00 (*0-06-021613-1*); PLB 14.89 (*0-06-021614-X*) HarpC Child Bks.

—Dinosaur Chase. Hurd, Thacher, illus. LC 90-2021. 32p. (ps-1). 1993. pap. 4.95 (*0-06-443330-7*, Trophy) HarpC Child Bks.

Packard, Edward. A Day with the Dinosaurs, No. 46. 64p. (Orig.). 1988. pap. 2.99 (*0-553-15612-8*, Skylark) Bantam.

—Dinosaur Island. (gr. 4-7). 1993. pap. 3.50 (*0-553-56007-7*) Bantam.

Packard, Mary. The Pet That I Want. Magino, John, illus. LC 94-16976. 1995. 3.95 (*0-590-48512-1*) Scholastic Inc.

Parish, Peggy & Lobel, Arnold. Dinosaur Time. 32p. (ps-2). 1990. pap. 6.95 (*1-55994-262-2*, Caedmon) HarperAudio.

Park, Y. H. Tae Kwon Do Dinosaurs: How Dinosaurs Train to Get Their Black Belts. Choi, Butto, illus. 32p. 1994. pap. 5.95 (*0-9637151-2-7*) YH Pk Taekwondo.

Patience, John. The Roarasaurus. Patience, John, illus. 12p. (ps up). 1994. 14.95 (*0-8431-3686-3*) Price Stern.

Peel, John. Dinotek: Golden Mini Play Lights. (ps-3). 1993. 14.95 (*0-307-75402-2*, Pub. by Golden Bks) Western Pub.

Penn, Audrey. No Bones about Driftiss. Loving, Judy V., illus. LC 89-13326. viii, 146p. (gr. 2-6). 1989. lib. bdg. 14.95 (*0-939923-11-4*); pap. 7.95 (*0-939923-12-2*) M & W Pub Co.

Polhamus, Jean B. Dinosaur Do's & Don'ts. O'Neill, Steven, illus. LC 75-11743. (gr. 1-3). 1978. (Pub. by Treehouse) P-H.

Polhamus, Jean B. & Funai, M. Dinosaur Funny Bones. 1980. 4.95 (*0-13-214536-7*) P-H.

Pollock, Steve. Dinosaurs. (Illus.). 48p. (gr. 7-9). 1992. 13.95 (*0-563-34753-8*, BBC-Parkwest); pap. 6.95 (*0-563-34607-8*, BBC-Parkwest) Parkwest Pubns.

Preiss, Byron. Last of the Dinosaurs. (Illus.). 144p. (Orig.). (gr. 7-12). 1988. pap. 2.50 (*0-553-27007-9*) Bantam.

Preiss, Byron & Bischoff, David. Search for Dinosaurs. Henderson, Doug & Nino, Alex, illus. 144p. (Orig.). 1984. pap. 2.25 (*0-553-25399-9*) Bantam.

Pulver, Robin. Mrs. Toggle & the Dinosaur. Alley, R. W., illus. LC 90-35771. 32p. (ps-2). 1991. RSBE 13.95 (*0-02-775452-9*, Four Winds) Macmillan Child Grp.

Raney, Ken. It's Probably Good That Dinosaurs Are Extinct. LC 92-33739. 1993. 14.00 (*0-671-86576-5*, Green Tiger) S&S Trade.

Ransom, Candice F. My Sister, the Traitor. 1990. pap. 2.75 (*0-590-41528-X*) Scholastic Inc.

Reese, Bob. Little Dinosaur. Wasserman, Dan, ed. Reese, Bob, illus. (gr. k-1). 1979. 7.95 (*0-89868-070-0*); pap. 2.95 (*0-89868-081-6*) ARO Pub.

Richler, Mordecai. Jacob Two-Two & the Dinosaur. 96p. (gr. 3-7). 1988. pap. 2.95 (*0-553-15589-X*) Bantam.

Ritthaler, Shelly. Dinosaurs Alive! 96p. (Orig.). (gr. 2 up). 1994. pap. 3.50 (*0-380-77323-6*, Camelot Young) Avon.

—Dinosaurs for Lunch. 80p. (Orig.). (gr. 2). 1993. pap. 3.50 (*0-380-76796-1*, Camelot Young) Avon.

—Dinosaurs Wild! 96p. (Orig.). 1994. pap. 3.50 (*0-380-77322-8*, Camelot Young) Avon.

Roberts, Sarah. The Adventures of Big Bird in Dinosaur Days. Mathieu, Joe, illus. LC 83-61891. 32p. (ps-3). 1984. pap. 1.50 (*0-394-85926-X*) Random Bks Yng Read.

Rogers, Jean. Dinosaurs Are Five Hundred Sixty-Eight. (gr. 4-7). 1991. pap. 2.99 (*0-440-40434-7*) Dell.

Rohmann, Eric. Time Flies. LC 93-28200. (Illus.). 32p. (ps-4). 1994. 15.00 (*0-517-59598-2*); lib. bdg. 15.99 (*0-517-59599-0*) Crown Bks Yng Read.

Ross, Katharine. Open the Door, Little Dinosaur. Gorbaty, Norman, illus. LC 92-80950. 14p. (ps-k). 1993. bds. 3.99 (*0-679-83689-6*) Random Bks Yng Read.

Ross, Katharine & Lukas, Noah. Little Dinosaur's Little Sister. Gorbaty, Norman, illus. 24p. (Orig.). (ps-2). 1994. pap. 2.50 (*0-679-86178-5*) Random Bks Yng Read.

Ross, Tom, et al. Itzwibble & the Big Birthday Party. 32p. (Orig.). (ps-3). 1990. pap. 2.50 (*0-590-43861-1*) Scholastic Inc.

Rotunno, Roccy & Rotunno, Betsy. Dennis the Dinosaur Moves to Crystal Pond. Rotunno, Betsy, illus. 12p. (gr. 2-6). 1992. Mixed Media Pkg. incls. stamp pad, stamps & box of 4 crayons. 7.00 (*1-881980-03-0*) Noteworthy.

Sattler, Helen R. Stegosaurs: The Solar-Powered Dinosaurs. Pearson, Susan, ed. MacCombie, Turi, illus. LC 90-49733. 32p. (gr. 1 up). 1992. 15.00 (*0-688-10055-4*); PLB 14.93 (*0-688-10056-2*) Lothrop.

Schatz, Dennis. Dinosaurs - A Journey Through Time: A Children's Activity Book. Quan, Daniel, designed by. 48p. (ps-6). 1987. pap. 9.95 (*0-935051-01-5*) Pacific Sci Ctr.

Schultz, Mark. Cadillacs & Dinosaurs. Schreiner, Davd, ed. Schultz, Mark, illus. Williamson, Al, intro. by. (Illus.). 136p. (gr. 3 up). 1994. pap. 14.95 (*0-87816-261-5*) Kitchen Sink.

Schwartz, Henry. How I Captured a Dinosaur. Schwartz, Amy, illus. LC 88-1482. 32p. (ps-2). 1993. pap. 5.95 (*0-531-07028-X*) Orchard Bks Watts.

Senn, Steve. The Double Disappearance of Walter Fozbek. Senn, Steve, illus. 128p. (gr. 3-5). 1983. pap. 2.50 (*0-380-62737-X*, 60064-1, Camelot) Avon.

Shaine, Frances. If Tiny Little Dinosaurs Played House... Bingham, Edith, illus. 30p. (Orig.). (ps-3). 1993. pap. 4.95 (*1-884217-02-8*) Wellford.

Shrode, Mary. Just Imagine, with Barney. White, Stephen, ed. Eubank, Mary G., illus. 32p. (ps-k). 1992. 7.95g (*0-7829-0137-9*) Lyons Group.

—Just Imagine with Barney. White, Stephen, ed. Eubank, Mary G., illus. 32p. (ps-1). 1992. 7.95 (*1-57064-000-9*) Barney Pub.

Sibbick, John, illus. Creatures of Long Ago: Dinosaurs, Vol. 1. (ps-3). 1993. 16.00 (*0-87044-723-8*) Natl Geog.

Silverman, Maida. Dinosaur Babies. Inouye, Carol, illus. LC 88-4690. 1990. pap. 4.95 (*0-671-69438-3*, Little Simon) S&S Trade.

Sirois, Allen. Dinosaur Dress Up. Street, Janet, illus. LC 91-10583. 32p. (ps-3). 1992. 15.00 (*0-688-10459-2*, Tambourine Bks); PLB 14.93 (*0-688-10460-6*, Tambourine Bks) Morrow.

Steinberg, Sari. And Then There Were Dinosaurs. (ps-3). 1993. 14.95 (*0-943706-19-X*) Yllw Brick Rd.

Steiner, Barbara. Oliver Dibbs & the Dinosaur Cause. 160p. 1988. pap. 2.95 (*0-380-70466-8*, Camelot) Avon.

Stickland, Paul & Stickland, Henrietta. Dinosaur Roar! LC 93-43959. (Illus.). 32p. (ps-1). 1994. 9.99 (*0-525-45276-1*, DCB) Dutton Child Bks.

Sundgaard, Arnold. Jethro's Difficult Dinosaur. Mack, Stan, illus. LC 76-29616. (ps-3). 1977. Pantheon.

Sweat, Lynn & Phillips, Louis. The Smallest Stegosaurus. Sweat, Lynn, illus. 32p. (ps-k). 1993. PLB 13.99 (*0-670-83865-9*) Viking Child Bks.

Talbott, Hudson. Going Hollywood: A Dinosaur's Dream. Talbott, Hudson, illus. LC 89-1190. 32p. (ps-2). 1993. pap. 4.99 (*0-517-58983-4*) Crown Bks Yng Read.

—We're Back! A Dinosaur's Story. Talbott, Hudson, illus. LC 87-5355. 32p. (ps-2). 1993. pap. 4.99 (*0-517-58985-0*) Crown Bks Yng Read.

Telles, Cecilia R. Dinosaurs Galore. (Illus.). 32p. (ps-2). 1993. pap. 3.50 (*0-87406-652-2*) Willowisp Pr.

Thaler, Mike. Colossal Fossil. 64p. 1994. text ed. write for info. (*0-7167-6561-6*); pap. text ed. write for info. (*0-7167-6571-3*) W H Freeman.

Threadgall, Colin. Dinosaur Fright. Threadgall, Colin, illus. LC 91-40049. 32p. (ps up). 1993. 15.00 (*0-688-11733-3*, Tambourine Bks); PLB 14.93 (*0-688-11734-1*, Tambourine Bks) Morrow.

Two Homes for Dainty Dinosaur. (Illus.). (ps-2). 1991. PLB 6.95 (*0-8136-5216-2*, TK7299); pap. 3.50 (*0-8136-5716-4*, TK7300) Modern Curr.

Up & Down, Dainty Dinosaur. (Illus.). (ps-2). 1991. PLB 6.95 (*0-8136-5211-1*, TK7295); pap. 3.50 (*0-8136-5711-3*, TK7296) Modern Curr.

Valat, Pierre-Marie. Dinosaur Faces. (Illus.). 16p. (ps up). 1990. 14.95 (*0-525-44631-1*, DCB) Dutton Child Bks.

Watson, John. We're the Noisy Dinosaurs. Watson, John, illus. LC 91-58764. 32p. (ps up). 1992. 14.95 (*1-56402-089-4*) Candlewick Pr.

Welty, Harry R. Visit to the Attic. Lee, Marlene K., illus. LC 92-90838. 250p. (Orig.). (gr. 6-8). 1992. pap. 6.95 (*0-9632953-0-6*) Welty Pr.

Westell, Kerry. Dinosaur Dreams. Ritchie, Scot, illus. 24p. (Orig.). (ps-2). 1989. pap. 0.99 (*1-55037-049-9*, Pub. by Annick CN) Firefly Bks Ltd.

What Is It, Dainty Dinosaur? (Illus.). (ps-2). 1991. PLB 6.95 (*0-8136-5222-7*, TK7277); pap. 3.50 (*0-8136-5722-9*, TK7278) Modern Curr.

When Will I, Dainty Dinosaur? (Illus.). (ps-2). 1991. PLB 6.95 (*0-8136-5223-5*, TK7289); pap. 3.50 (*0-8136-5723-7*, TK7290) Modern Curr.

Where Is It, Dainty Dinosaur? (Illus.). (ps-2). 1991. PLB 6.95 (*0-8136-5224-3*, TK7285); pap. 3.50 (*0-8136-5724-5*, TK7286) Modern Curr.

White, Stephen. Barney & Baby Bop Follow That Cat! Dowdy, Linda C., ed. Valentine, June, illus. LC 94-71470. 14p. (ps). 1994. 4.95 (*1-57064-017-3*) Barney Pub.

—Barney Says, "Please & Thank You" Dowdy, Linda C., ed. Grayson, Rick, illus. LC 93-74288. 24p. (ps-k). 1994. pap. 2.25 (*1-57064-023-8*) Barney Pub.

Whitman, Candace. If I Met A Dinosaur. LC 94-15120. 1994. 4.99 (*0-517-10150-5*, Pub. by Derrydale Bks) Random Hse Value.

Who Did This, Dainty Dinosaur? (Illus.). (ps-2). 1991. PLB 6.95 (*0-8136-5221-9*, TK7283); pap. 3.50 (*0-8136-5721-0*, TK7284) Modern Curr.

Why, Dainty Dinosaur? (Illus.). (ps-2). 1991. PLB 6.95 (*0-8136-5225-1*, TK7287); pap. 3.50 (*0-8136-5725-3*, TK7288) Modern Curr.

Wiesmuller, Dieter. Pernix: The Adventures of a Small Dinosaur. Weismuller, Dieter, illus. LC 92-39419. 44p. (gr. 3-6). 1993. 14.99 (*0-525-65127-6*, Cobblehill Bks) Dutton Child Bks.

Wild, Margaret. My Dearest Dinosaur. Rawlins, Donna, illus. LC 91-46166. 32p. (ps-2). 1992. 14.95 (*0-531-05453-5*); PLB 14.99 (*0-531-08603-8*) Orchard Bks Watts.

Wilhelm, Hans. Tyrone the Double Dirty Rotten Cheater. Wilhelm, Hans, illus. 32p. (gr. 1-3). 1991. 12.95 (*0-590-44079-9*, Scholastic Hardcover) Scholastic Inc.

Williams, Geoffrey T. Lost in Dinosaur World. Svensson, Borje, illus. 32p. (gr. k-6). 1987. pap. 9.95 bk. & cass. (*0-8431-1878-4*); incl. audiocassette 9.95 (*0-8431-1885-7*) Price Stern.

Wiltshire, Teri. The Tale of Bella Brontosaurus. Archer, Rebecca, illus. LC 92-46250. (ps). 1993. 8.95 (*1-85697-857-5*, Kingfisher LKC) LKC.

You Are Here, Dainty Dinosaur. (Illus.). (ps-2). 1991. PLB 6.95 (*0-8136-5214-6*, TK7281); pap. 3.50 (*0-8136-5714-8*, TK7282) Modern Curr.

You Are What You Are. (Illus.). (ps-2). 1991. PLB 6.95 (*0-8136-5081-X*, TK2390); pap. 3.50 (*0-8136-5581-1*, TK2391) Modern Curr.

You Have a Friend, Dainty Dinosaur. (Illus.). (ps-2). 1991. PLB 6.95 (*0-8136-5212-X*, TK7293); pap. 3.50 (*0-8136-5712-1*, TK7294) Modern Curr.

Zeplin, Zeno. Discovery on Dusty Creek. Jones, Judy, illus. 112p. (gr. 3-6). 1994. 14.95 (*1-877740-23-3*); pap. 7.95 (*1-877740-24-1*) Nel-Mar Pub.

DINOSAURS–POETRY

Beall, Pamela C. & Nipp, Susan H. Wee Sing Dinosaurs. (Illus.). 64p. (ps-2). 1991. pap. 2.95 (*0-8431-3809-2*); pap. 9.95 bk. & cass. (*0-8431-3801-7*) Price Stern.

Faulkner, Keith. David Dreaming of Dinosaurs. Lambert, Jonathan, illus. (ps-3). 1992. 13.00 (*1-56021-182-2*) W J Fantasy.

Schwartz, Henry. Albert Goes Hollywood. Schwartz, Amy, illus. LC 91-18495. 32p. (ps-2). 1992. 14.95 (*0-531-05980-4*); lib. bdg. 14.99 (*0-531-08580-5*) Orchard Bks Watts.

Sierra, Judy. Good Night, Dinosaurs. Chess, Victoria, illus. LC 93-8855. Date not set. write for info. (*0-395-65016-X*, Clarion Bks) HM.

DIPLOMACY

see also Diplomats

DIPLOMATS

Larsen, Anita. Raoul Wallenberg: Missing Diplomat. LC 91-19937. (Illus.). 48p. (gr. 5-6). 1992. text ed. 11.95 RSBE (*0-89686-616-5*, Crestwood Hse) Macmillan Child Grp.

Raoul Wallenberg. LC 91-19712. (Illus.). 68p. (gr. 3-8). PLB 19.93 (*0-8368-0629-8*) Gareth Stevens Inc.

DIPSOMANIA

see Alcoholism

DIPTERA

see Flies; Mosquitoes

DIRECTION, SENSE OF

see Orientation

DIRIGIBLE BALLOONS

see Airships

DISARMAMENT

see also Peace

Smoke, Richard. Think about Nuclear Arms Control: Understanding the Arms Race. (Illus.). 178p. 1988. PLB 14.85 (*0-8027-6761-3*); pap. 5.95 (*0-8027-6762-1*) Walker & Co.

Thro, Ellen. Taking a Stand Against Nuclear War. LC 89-24979. 1990. PLB 14.40 (*0-531-10922-4*) Watts.

Weiss, Ann E. The Nuclear Arms Race-Can We Survive It? 160p. (gr. 5-9). 1983. 10.95 (*0-395-34928-1*) HM.

DISASTERS

see also Earthquakes; Fires; Floods; Shipwrecks; Storms

Arnold, Caroline. Coping with Natural Disasters. (gr. 5 up). 1988. 13.95 (*0-8027-6716-8*); PLB 14.85 (*0-8027-6717-6*) Walker & Co.

Baines, John. Environmental Disasters. LC 93-8526. (Illus.). 48p. (gr. 4-6). 1993. 15.95 (*1-56847-086-X*) Thomson Lrning.

Berry, Joy. About Disasters. (Illus.). 48p. (gr. 3 up). 1990. 12.30 (*0-516-02959-2*); pap. 4.95 (*0-516-42959-0*) Childrens.

Cush, Cathie. Disasters That Shook the World. LC 93-10299. (Illus.). 48p. (gr. 5-7). 1993. PLB 22.80 (*0-8114-4929-7*) Raintree Steck-V.

Diamond, Arthur. The Bhopal Chemical Leak. LC 90-6011. (Illus.). 64p. (gr. 5-8). 1990. PLB 11.95 (*1-56006-009-3*) Lucent Bks.

Engholm, Christopher. The Armenian Earthquake. LC 89-33555. (Illus.). 64p. (gr. 5-8). 1989. PLB 11.95 (*1-56006-004-2*) Lucent Bks.

Jamestown Editorial Group Staff. Calamities. 158p. (gr. 6-8). 1994. pap. 8.75 (*0-89061-748-1*) Jamestown Pubs.

Keller, David. Great Disasters. 112p. 1990. pap. 2.95 (*0-380-76043-6*, Camelot) Avon.

Marsh, Carole. Minnesota's (Most Devastating!) Disasters & (Most Calamitous!) Catastrophies! (Illus.). (gr. 3 up). 1994. PLB 24.95 (*0-7933-0620-5*); pap. 14.95 (*0-7933-0619-1*); computer disk 29.95 (*0-7933-0621-3*) Gallopade Pub Group.

Nardo, Don. Chernobyl. McGovern, Brian, illus. LC 90-33567. 64p. (gr. 5-8). 1990. PLB 11.95 (*1-56006-008-5*) Lucent Bks.

—Krakatoa. McGovern, Brian, illus. LC 90-6003. 64p. (gr. 5-8). 1990. PLB 11.95 (*1-56006-011-5*) Lucent Bks.

Nottridge, Rhoda. Sea Disasters. LC 93-6830. 48p. (gr. 4-6). 1993. 15.95 (*1-56847-084-3*) Thomson Lrning.

Peissel, Michel & Allen, Missy. Dangerous Natural Phenomena. (Illus.). 112p. (gr. 5 up). 1993. PLB 19.95 (*0-7910-1794-X*, Am Art Analog) Chelsea Hse.

Stallone, Linda. The Flood That Came to Grandma's House. Schooley, Joan, illus. LC 91-33955. 21p. (ps-3). 1992. 9.95 (*0-912975-02-4*) Upshur Pr.

Standiford, Natalie. The Bravest Dog Ever: The True Story of Balto. Cook, Donald, tr. LC 89-3465. (Illus.). 47p. (Orig.). (gr. 1-3). 1989. pap. 3.50 (*0-394-89695-5*) Random Bks Yng Read.

Stefoff, Rebecca. Environmental Disasters. Train, Russell E., intro. by. LC 93-8183. 1994. write for info. (*0-7910-1584-X*) Chelsea Hse.

Wood, Tim. Natural Disasters. LC 93-8525. 48p. (gr. 4-6). 1993. 15.95 (*1-56847-085-1*) Thomson Lrning.

DISASTERS–FICTION

Epperley, Mike. The Three Bucketeers: Commander, Thinker, Player. Erb, Sherry, illus. 48p. (Orig.). (gr. k-6). 1994. pap. 6.98 (*1-882183-22-3*) Computer Pr.

Voigt, Cynthia. Izzy, Willy-Nilly. LC 85-22933. 276p. (gr. 7 up). 1986. SBE 15.95 (*0-689-31202-4*, Atheneum Child Bk) Macmillan Child Grp.

DISCIPLINE OF CHILDREN

see Children–Management

DISCOVERERS

see Discoveries (In Geography); Explorers

DISCOVERIES (IN GEOGRAPHY)

see also America–Discovery and Exploration; Antarctic Regions; Arctic Regions; Explorers; Northwest Passage; Scientific Expeditions; Voyages and Travels; also names of countries with the subdivision description and travel, e.g. U. S.–Description and Travel

Adams, Simon. Explore the World of Man-Made Wonders. Biesty, Stephan, illus. (gr. 3-7). 1991. 7.95 (*0-685-54426-5*, Golden Pr) Western Pub.

Chrisp, Peter. The Search for the East. LC 93-12826. (Illus.). 48p. (gr. 4-6). 1993. 14.95 (*1-56847-120-3*) Thomson Lrning.

Discovery & Exploration, 17 vols. LC 89-15723. (Illus.). 2866p. (gr. 7-12). 1990. Set. PLB 399.95x (*1-85435-114-1*) Marshall Cavendish.

Eugene, Toni, ed. Beyond the Horizon: Adventures in Faraway Lands. (Illus.). 1992. 12.95 (*0-87044-831-5*) Natl Geog.

Fritz, Jean. Around the World in a Hundred Years: Henry the Navigator - Magellan. Venti, Anthony B., illus. LC 92-27042. 128p. (gr. 2-6). 1994. 17.95 (*0-399-22527-7*, Putnam) Putnam Pub Group.

Grant, Neil. The Great Atlas of Discovery. Morter, Peter, illus. LC 91-29668. 64p. 1992. 20.00 (*0-679-81660-7*); PLB 21.99 (*0-679-91660-1*) Knopf Bks Yng Read.

Julivert, Maria A. El Fascinante Mundo de los Murcielagos. Studio, Marcel S., illus. 32p. (gr. 3-7). 1994. pap. 7.95 (*0-8120-1954-7*) Barron.

Last Frontiers for Mankind Series, 6 vols. (gr. 4-8). 1990. Set. PLB 77.70 (*1-85435-168-0*) Marshall Cavendish.

Mason, Antony & Lye, Keith. The Children's Atlas of Exploration. LC 92-28856. (Illus.). 96p. (gr. 2-6). 1993. PLB 18.90 (*1-56294-256-5*); pap. 10.95 (*1-56294-711-7*) Millbrook Pr.

National Geographic Society Staff, ed. Books for Young Explorers, 4 vols, Set 15. (gr. k-4). 1988. Set: No. 1, Animals in Summer; No. 2, Animals at Play; No. 3, Busy Beavers; No. 4, Let's Explore a River. 13.95 (*0-87044-737-8*); PLB 16.95 (*0-87044-742-4*) Natl Geog.

Starkey, Dinah. Scholastic Atlas of Exploration. LC 93-41402. 1994. 14.95 (*0-590-27548-8*, Scholastic Reference) Scholastic Inc.

Stefoff, Rebecca. The Accidental Explorers: Surprises & Sidetrips in the History of Discovery. (Illus.). 152p. 1992. PLB 22.00 (*0-19-507685-0*) OUP.

—The Young Oxford Companion to Maps & Mapmaking. (Illus.). 320p. 1994. lib. bdg. 35.00 (*0-19-508042-4*) OUP.

Williams, Brian. Voyages of Discovery. LC 89-26337. (Illus.). 48p. (gr. 4-8). 1990. PLB 22.80 (*0-8114-2756-0*) Raintree Steck-V.

DISCOVERIES (IN SCIENCE)

see Inventions; Science

DISCOVERIES, MARITIME

see Discoveries (In Geography)

DISCRIMINATION

For general works on discrimination by race, religion, sex, age, social status, or other factors.

see also Blacks–Civil Rights; Civil Rights; Minorities; Toleration

Everything You Need to Know about Discrimination. rev. ed. 1993. lib. bdg. 14.95 (*0-8239-1656-1*) Rosen Group.

Gay, Kathlyn. Pollution & the Powerless: The Movement fo Environmental Justice. (Illus.). 160p. (gr. 7-12). 1994. lib. bdg. 13.93 (*0-531-11190-3*) Watts.

Landau, Elaine. Sexual Harassment. LC 92-43748. 128p. (gr. 5 up). 1993. 14.95 (*0-8027-8265-5*); PLB 15.85 (*0-8027-8266-3*) Walker & Co.

Lee. Discrimination. 1991. 12.95s.p. (*0-86593-113-5*) Rourke Corp.

Miller, Maryann. Coping with a Bigoted Parent. (gr. 7-12). 1992. PLB 14.95 (*0-8239-1345-7*) Rosen Group.

Phillips, Angela. Discrimination. LC 92-39446. (Illus.). 48p. (gr. 6 up). 1993. text ed. 12.95 RSBE (*0-02-786881-8*, New Discovery) Macmillan Child Grp.

Querry, Ron. Native American Struggle for Equality. LC 92-7474. 1992. 22.60 (*0-86593-179-8*); 16.95s.p. (*0-685-59320-7*) Rourke Corp.

Stewart, Gail. Discrimination. LC 89-31259. (Illus.). 48p. (gr. 5-6). 1989. text ed. 4.95 RSBE (*0-89686-445-6*, Crestwood Hse) Macmillan Child Grp.

DISCRIMINATION–FICTION

Neufeld, John. Edgar Allan. Dunlap, Loren, illus. LC 68-31175. (gr. 5-8). 1968. 21.95 (*0-87599-149-1*) S G Phillips.

Sanchez, Jose R. El Reino de la Geometria. (SPA., Illus.). 24p. 1993. 16.95x (*1-56492-109-3*) Laredo.

Taylor, Mildred D. Let the Circle Be Unbroken. LC 81-65854. 432p. (gr. 7 up). 1981. 15.95 (*0-8037-4748-9*) Dial Bks Young.

—Roll of Thunder, Hear My Cry. Pinkney, Jerry, illus. LC 76-2287. (gr. 6 up). 1976. 15.00 (*0-8037-7473-7*) Dial Bks Young.

Tunis, John R. Keystone Kids. Brooks, Bruce & Bacom, Paulintro. by. 239p. (gr. 3-7). 1990. pap. 3.95 (*0-15-242388-5*, Odyssey) HarBrace.

DISCRIMINATION IN EDUCATION

see also Segregation in Education

O'Neil, Laurie A. Little Rock: The Desegregation of Central High. LC 93-29057. (Illus.). 64p. (gr. 4-6). 1994. 15.40 (*1-56294-354-5*) Millbrook Pr.

DISCRIMINATION IN EMPLOYMENT

Hanmer, Trudy J. Affirmative Action: Opportunity for All? LC 92-44972. (Illus.). 128p. (gr. 6 up). 1993. lib. bdg. 17.95 (*0-89490-451-5*) Enslow Pubs.

DISCUSSION

see Debates and Debating

DISEASE (PATHOLOGY)

see Pathology

DISEASE GERMS

see Bacteriology

DISEASES

see also names of diseases and groups of diseases e.g. Communicable Diseases; and subjects with the subdivision Diseases, e.g. Children–diseases; Skin–Diseases

Allison, Linda & Ferguson, Tom. The Get-Well-Quick Kit. Allison, Linda & Wells, William S., illus. LC 92-42626. 1993. 14.38 (*0-201-63213-6*) Addison-Wesley.

Alvin, Virginia & Silverstein, Robert. Cystic Fibrosis. LC 93-30045. (Illus.). 128p. (gr. 9-12). 1994. PLB 13.40 (*0-531-12552-1*) Watts.

Asimov, Isaac. How Did We Find Out About Vitamins? Wool, David, illus. LC 73-92453. 64p. (gr. 5-8). 1974. PLB 11.85 (*0-8027-6184-4*) Walker & Co.

Beckelman, Laurie. Alzheimer's Disease. LC 89-25251. (Illus.). 48p. (gr. 5-6). 1990. text ed. 12.95 RSBE (*0-89686-489-8*, Crestwood Hse) Macmillan Child Grp.

Beshore, George, ed. Sickle Cell Anemia. LC 94-15513. (gr. 4 up). 1994. lib. bdg. 13.93 (*0-531-12510-6*) Watts.

Cristall, Barbara. Coping When a Parent Has Multiple Sclerosis. Rosen, Ruth, ed. (gr. 7-12). 1992. 14.95 (*0-8239-1406-2*) Rosen Group.

Eagles, Douglas A. Nutritional Diseases. LC 87-8124. (Illus.). (gr. 4-8). 1987. PLB 10.90 (*0-531-10391-9*) Watts.

Frank, Julia. Alzheimer's Disease: The Silent Epidemic. (Illus.). 80p. (gr. 5 up). 1985. PLB 13.50 (*0-8225-1578-4*) Lerner Pubns.

French, Barbara. Coping with Bulimia. (Illus.). 160p. (Orig.). (gr. 10 up). 1984. pap. 8.95 (*0-7225-1380-1*) Thorsons SF.

Graham, Ian. Fighting Disease. LC 94-19981. Date not set. write for info. (*0-8114-3844-9*) Raintree Steck-V.

Harris. Hereditary Diseases. 1993. write for info. (*0-8050-3042-5*) H Holt & Co.

Hinnefeld, Joyce. Everything You Need to Know When Someone You Love Has Alzheimer's Disease. LC 93-44301. 1994. 14.95 (*0-8239-1688-X*) Rosen Group.

Kerby, Mona. Asthma. LC 89-8905. (Illus.). 128p. (gr. 7-12). 1989. PLB 12.90 (*0-531-10697-7*) Watts.

Lampton, Christopher. Epidemic. LC 91-21413. (Illus.). 64p. (gr. 4-6). 1992. PLB 13.90 (*1-56294-126-7*) Millbrook Pr.

—Epidemic: A Disaster Book. (gr. 4-7). 1992. pap. 5.95 (*0-395-62466-5*) HM.

LeVert, Suzanne. Teens Face to Face with Chronic Illness. LC 92-45819. 1993. lib. bdg. 13.98 (*0-671-74540-9*, J Messner); pap. 7.95 (*0-671-74541-7*, J Messner) S&S Trade.

Matthews, John R. Eating Disorders. (Illus.). 240p. (gr. 9-12). 1990. 21.95x (*0-8160-1911-8*) Facts on File.

Nixon, Joan L. The Specter. LC 82-70322. 160p. (gr. 7 up). 1982. pap. 12.95 (*0-385-28948-0*) Delacorte.

Perry, Susan. A Cold Is Nothing to Sneeze At. Mitchell, Anastasia, illus. (gr. 2-6). 1992. PLB 14.95 (*0-89565-819-4*) Childs World.

Sanford, Doris. Maria's Grandma Gets Mixed Up. Evans, Graci, illus. LC 89-3161. 28p. (gr. k-4). 1989. 6.99 (*0-88070-298-2*, Gold & Honey) Questar Pubs.

Siegel, Dorothy S. & Newton, David E. Leukemia. LC 94-15517. 1994. lib. bdg. 13.93 (*0-531-12509-2*) Watts.

Silverstein, Alvin, et al. Hepatitis. LC 93-48734. (Illus.). 128p. (gr. 6 up). 1994. PLB 17.95 (*0-89490-467-1*) Enslow Pubs.

—Mononucleosis. LC 93-48721. (Illus.). 112p. (gr. 6 up). 1994. PLB 17.95 (*0-89490-466-3*) Enslow Pubs.

—Rabies. LC 93-21417. 128p. (gr. 6 up). 1994. PLB 17.95 (*0-89490-465-5*) Enslow Pubs.

—Tuberculosis. LC 93-4686. (Illus.). 128p. (gr. 6 up). 1994. lib. bdg. 17.95 (*0-89490-462-0*) Enslow Pubs.

Taylor, Margaret & Schuett, Virginia E. You & PKU. (Illus.). 43p. 1988. pap. text ed. 5.00 (*0-299-97065-5*) U of Wis Pr.

Thacker, John & Kranz, Rachel. Straight Talk about Sexually Transmitted Diseases. Ryan, Elizabeth A., ed. 128p. (gr. 9-12). Date not set. 16.95x (*0-8160-2864-8*) Facts on File.

Tiger, Steven. Arthritis. LC 85-8947. (Illus.). 72p. 1986. lib. bdg. 11.98 (*0-671-55566-9*, J Messner) S&S Trade.

Virginia, Alvin & Silverstein, Robert. Common Cold & Flu. LC 93-4685. (Illus.). 128p. (gr. 6 up). 1994. PLB 17.95 (*0-89490-463-9*) Enslow Pubs.

Zinsser, Hans. Rats, Lice & History. (gr. 9 up). 1984. (Pub. by Atlantic Monthly Pr); pap. 12.95 (*0-316-98896-0*) Little.

DISEASES, COMMUNICABLE

see Communicable Diseases

DISEASES, INFECTIONS

see Communicable Diseases

DISEASES, MENTAL

see Mental Illness; Psychology, Pathological

DISEASES AND PESTS
see Fungi; Insects, Injurious and Beneficial; Parasites; see names of individual pests (e.g. Locusts)
DISEASES OF ANIMALS
see Veterinary Medicine
DISEASES OF CHILDREN
see Children–Diseases
DISEASES OF THE BLOOD
see Blood Diseases
DISHES
see Glassware; Porcelain; Pottery
DISNEY, WALTER ELIAS, 1901-1966
Barrett, Katherine & Greene, Richard. The Man Behind the Magic: The Story of Walt Disney. (Illus.). 208p. (gr. 5 up). 1991. 18.00 (*0-670-82259-0*) Viking Child Bks.
Ford, Barbara. Walt Disney: A Biography. (Illus.). 160p. (gr. 4-7). 1989. 15.95 (*0-8027-6864-4*); PLB 16.85 (*0-8027-6865-2*) Walker & Co.
The Story of Walt Disney. (gr. k-6). 1989. pap. 3.50 (*0-440-40240-9*, YB) Dell.
DISPLACED PERSONS
see Refugees
DISPOSAL OF REFUSE
see Refuse and Refuse Disposal
DISSENT
Finke, Blythe F. Angela Davis: Traitor or Martyr of the Freedom of Expression? Rahmas, D. Steve, ed. LC 77-190246. 32p. (Orig.). (gr. 7-12). 1972. lib. bdg. 4.95 incl. catalog cards (*0-87157-528-0*) SamHar Pr.
DISTRIBUTION (ECONOMICS)
see Commerce
DISTRIBUTION OF ANIMALS AND PLANTS
see Geographical Distribution of Animals and Plants
DISTRIBUTION OF WEALTH
see Economics
DISTRICT NURSES
see Nurses and Nursing
DIVIDENDS
see Stocks
DIVINATION
see also Astrology; Clairvoyance; Dreams; Fortune Telling; Occult Sciences; Superstition
Schwartz, Alvin. Telling Fortunes: Love Magic, Dream Signs, & Other Ways to Learn the Future. Cameron, Tracey, illus. LC 85-45174. 128p. (gr. 4 up). 1987. 12.95 (*0-397-32132-5*, Lipp Jr Bks); PLB 12.89 (*0-397-32133-3*, Lipp Jr Bks) HarpC Child Bks.
DIVINE HEALING
see Christian Science
DIVING
American Red Cross Staff. American Red Cross Swimming & Diving. 356p. 1992. pap. 20.00 (*0-8016-6506-X*) Mosby Yr Bk.
Carson, Charles. Make the Team: Swimming & Diving. (gr. 4-7). 1991. pap. 5.95 (*0-316-13028-1*, Spts Illus Kids) Little.
Fischel, E. Swimming & Diving Skills. (Illus.). 48p. (gr. 6-12). 1989. (Usborne); pap. 5.95 (*0-7460-0171-1*) EDC.
Goldberg, Bob. Diving Basics. Seiden, Art, illus. 48p. (gr. 3-7). 1986. 10.95 (*0-13-215963-5*) P-H.
McDonald, Kendall. Divers. Stefoff, Rebecca, ed. LC 91-46577. (Illus.). 32p. (gr. 5-9). 1992. PLB 17.26 (*1-56074-043-4*) Garrett Ed Corp.
DIVING–FICTION
Wojciechowska, Maia. Dreams of the Deep. Karsky, A. K., illus. 52p. 1994. 14.50 (*1-883740-12-6*) Pebble Bch Pr Ltd.
DIVING, SKIN
see Skin Diving
DIVING, SUBMARINE
see Skin Diving
DIVING SUBMARINE
see also Submarines
Conley, Andrea. Window on the Deep: The Adventures of Underwater Explorer Sylvia Earle. LC 91-17792. (Illus.). 40p. (gr. 5-8). 1991. 14.95 (*0-531-15232-4*); PLB 14.90 (*0-531-11119-9*) Watts.
DIVORCE
see also Marriage
Berry, Joy. About Divorce. Bartholomew, illus. 48p. (gr. 3 up). 1990. PLB 12.30 (*0-516-02953-3*) Childrens.
Bolick, Nancy O. How to Survive Your Parents' Divorce. LC 94-15075. 1994. lib. bdg. 13.93 (*0-531-11054-0*) Watts.
Booher, Dianna D. Coping: When Your Family Falls Apart. LC 79-17342. 192p. (gr. 7 up). 1979. lib. bdg. 11.98 (*0-671-33083-7*, J Messner) S&S Trade.
Boulden, Jim & Boulden, Joan. Let's Talk. (Illus., Orig.). (gr. 1-7). 1991. pap. 4.95 wkbk. (*1-878076-05-1*) Boulden Pub.
—My Story. (Orig.). (gr. 1-7). 1991. pap. 4.95 wkbk. (*1-878076-06-X*) Boulden Pub.
Brown, Laurene K. & Brown, Marc T. Dinosaurs Divorce: A Guide for Changing Families. Brown, Marc T., illus. 32p. (ps-3). 1988. 15.95 (*0-316-11248-8*); pap. 5.95 (*0-316-10996-7*) Little.
Cain, Barbara & Benedek, Elissa P. What Would You Do? A Child's Book about Divorce. Cummins, James, illus. 50p. 1976. text ed. 9.00 (*0-88048-300-8*) Am Psychiatric.
Carlson, Linda. Everything You Need to Know about Your Parents' Divorce. rev. ed. Rosen, Ruth, ed. (gr. 7-12). 1992. PLB 14.95 (*0-8239-1510-7*) Rosen Group.
Center for Learning Network. Divorce: Adjusting to Change: Looking at Life. 12p. (gr. 7-12). 1992. pap. text ed. 0.80 (*1-56077-223-9*) Ctr Learning.
Coleman, William L. What Children Need to Know When Parents Get Divorced. LC 83-6006. 91p. (gr. k-5). 1983. pap. 6.99 (*0-87123-612-5*) Bethany Hse.
Craven, Linda. Stepfamilies: New Patterns of Harmony. LC 82-60652. (Illus.). 192p. (gr. 7 up). 1983. (J Messner) S&S Trade.
Crown, Bonnie & Atlas, Susan. D-I-V-O-R-C-E-S Spell Discover: A Kit to Help Children Express Their Feelings about Divorce. (Illus.). 52p. (Orig.). (gr. k-8). 1992. pap. 14.95 spiral bdg. (*0-9633626-0-7*) Courageous Kids.
Field, Mary B. All about Divorce. Forbes, Alex, illus. Shapiro, Lawrence, intro. by. (Illus.). 150p. (Orig.). (gr. k-6). 1992. pap. 16.95 (*1-882732-00-6*) Ctr Applied Psy.
Field, Mary B. & Shore, Hennie. My Life Turned Upside Down but I Turned It Rightside Up. Van Patter, Bruce, illus. (Orig.). (gr. k-6). 1994. pap. 13.50 (*1-882732-06-5*) Ctr Applied Psy.
Gardner, Richard A. Boys & Girls Book about Divorce. LC 84-2815. (Illus.). 160p. (gr. 7 up). 1992. Repr. of 1983 ed. 25.00 (*0-87668-664-1*) Aronson.
—The Boys & Girls Book about Divorce. (Illus.). (gr. 4 up). 1971. pap. 3.50 (*0-553-25310-7*) Bantam.
—Boys & Girls of Divorce. 1985. pap. 4.99 (*0-553-27619-0*) Bantam.
Garigan, Elizabeth & Urbanski, Michael. Living with Divorce - Middle School. 64p. (gr. 5-9). 1991. 7.95 (*0-86653-596-9*, GA1315) Good Apple.
—Living with Divorce - Primary. 64p. (gr. 1-4). 1991. 7.95 (*0-86653-595-0*, GA1314) Good Apple.
Gordon, Jeanie. If My Parents Are Getting Divorced, Why Am I the One Who Hurts? 144p. (gr. 9-12). 1993. pap. 7.99 (*0-310-59311-5*, Pub. by Youth Spec) Zondervan.
Grollman, Earl A. Talking about Divorce & Separation: A Dialogue Between Parent & Child. Cann., Alison, illus. LC 75-5289. (gr. k-4). pap. 9.00 (*0-8070-2375-2*, BP524) Beacon Pr.
Hazen, Barbara S. Two Homes to Live In: A Child's-Eye View of Divorce. Luks, Peggy, illus. LC 77-21849. 32p. (ps-3). 1978. 16.95 (*0-87705-313-8*); pap. 9.95 (*0-89885-173-4*) Human Sci Pr.
Hunt, Angela E. Pulling Yourself Together When Your Parents Are Pulling Apart. LC 94-11147. (gr. 3 up). 1995. write for info. (*0-8423-5104-3*) Tyndale.
Ives, Sally B., et al. The Divorce Workbook: A Guide for Kids & Families. (Illus.). 160p. (Orig.). (ps-7). 1985. plastic comb bdg. 14.95 (*0-914525-04-2*); pap. 12.95 (*0-914525-05-0*) Waterfront Bks.
Kimball, Gayle. How to Survive Your Parents' Divorce: Kids' Advice to Kids. (Illus.). 160p. (Orig.). (gr. 6-12). 1994. pap. 9.95 (*0-938795-22-8*) Equality Pr.
Lazo, Caroline E. Divorce. LC 89-2156. (Illus.). 48p. (gr. 5-6). 1989. text ed. 12.95 RSBE (*0-89686-436-7*, Crestwood Hse) Macmillan Child Grp.
LeShan, Eda. What's Going to Happen to Me? When Parents Separate or Divorce. rev. ed. Cuffari, Richard, illus. LC 86-10769. 144p. (gr. 3-7). 1986. pap. 4.95 (*0-689-71093-3*, Aladdin) Macmillan Child Grp.
McGuire, Paula. Putting It Together: Teenagers Talk about Family Breakup. LC 86-29238. 224p. (gr. 7 up). 1987. pap. 15.95 (*0-385-29564-2*) Delacorte.
Minnick, Molly A. Divorce Illustrated: Workbook. Minnick, Molly A., illus. 60p. (Orig.). (gr. 4). 1990. pap. 5.00 (*1-878526-03-0*) Pineapple MI.
Nickman, Steven L. When Mom & Dad Divorce. De Groat, Diane, illus. 80p. (gr. 3-6). 1986. lib. bdg. 10.98 (*0-671-60153-9*, J Messner) S&S Trade.
Prokop, Michael S. Divorce Happens to the Nicest Kids: A Self-Help Book For Kids (3-15) & Adults. Peters, Robert C., ed. Fogarty, Michelle D., illus. LC 85-72180. 224p. (Orig.). (gr. k up). 1986. 18.95 (*0-933879-25-3*); pap. 6.45 Kids' Divorce Wkbk. (*0-933879-26-1*); kids' Divorce wkbk. 6.45 (*0-933879-27-X*) Alegra Hse Pubs.
Raab, Robert A. Coping with Divorce. rev. ed. (gr. 7-12). 1984. PLB 14.95 (*0-8239-0428-8*) Rosen Group.
Rofes, Eric E., ed. The Kids' Book of Divorce: By, for & about Kids. LC 82-4004. (Illus.). 144p. (gr. 2 up). 1982. pap. 9.00 (*0-394-71018-5*, Vin) Random.
Rogers, Fred. Let's Talk about It. Judkis, Jim, photos by. LC 94-2312. Date not set. write for info. (*0-399-22449-1*); pap. write for info. (*0-399-22800-4*) Putnam Pub Group.
Schenkerman, Rona D. Growing up with Divorce. 16p. (gr. 3-8). 1993. 1.95 (*1-56688-110-2*) Bur For At-Risk.
Schuchman, Joan. Two Places to Sleep. LaMarche, Jim, illus. LC 79-88201. 32p. (gr. 1-4). 1979. PLB 13.50 (*0-87614-108-4*) Carolrhoda Bks.
Snyder, James R. What's (Bad) Good about Divorce? 1977. 1st ed. LC 77-84446. (Illus.). 23p. 1977. 6.95 (*0-9601452-1-4*) FIG Ltd.
Sprague, Gary. My Parents Got a Divorce. LC 91-43023. 1992. pap. 7.99 (*0-7814-0486-X*, Chariot Bks) Chariot Family.
Stein, Sara B. On Divorce. LC 78-15687. (Illus.). 48p. (ps-8). 1984. pap. 4.95 (*0-8027-7226-9*) Walker & Co.
—On Divorce. Stone, Erika, illus. 48p. 1979. 10.95 (*0-8027-6344-8*) Walker & Co.
Steiner, Michael P., Sr. Not a Wicked Stepmother. rev. ed. (Illus.). 42p. (Orig.). (gr. 4 up). 1991. pap. text ed. 12.95 (*1-879417-00-6*) Stern & Stern.
Terkel, Susan N. Understanding Child Custody. LC 90-48268. 128p. (gr. 7-12). 1991. PLB 13.40 (*0-531-12521-1*) Watts.
Tonner, Leslie. My Mom, Your Dad. 128p. 1989. 14.95 (*0-89015-720-0*, Pub. by Panda Bks) Sunbelt Media.
Weyland, Jack. Kimberly. LC 92-730. 151p. (gr. 9-12). 1992. 11.95 (*0-87579-599-4*) Deseret Bk.
DIVORCE–FICTION
Adler, C. S. Tuna Fish Thanksgiving. 160p. (gr. 5-9). 1992. 13.45 (*0-395-58829-4*, Clarion Bks) HM.
Aiello, Barbara & Shulman, Jeffrey. On with the Show! Featuring Brenda Dubrowski. Barr, Loel, illus. 56p. (gr. 3-6). 1989. PLB 13.95 (*0-941477-06-1*) TFC Bks NY.
Angell, Judie. Yours Truly: A Novel. LC 92-29472. 192p. (gr. 7-12). 1993. 14.95 (*0-531-05472-1*); PLB 14.99 (*0-531-08622-4*) Orchard Bks Watts.
Betancourt, Jeanne. The Rainbow Kid. 112p. (Orig.). (gr. 3-7). 1983. pap. 2.50 (*0-380-84665-9*, Camelot) Avon.
Blume, Judy. It's Not the End of the World. LC 70-181739. 176p. (gr. 5-7). 1982. SBE 14.95 (*0-02-711050-8*, Bradbury Pr) Macmillan Child Grp.
Boyd, Candy D. Chevrolet Saturdays. LC 92-32119. 176p. (gr. 3-7). 1993. SBE 14.95 (*0-02-711765-0*, Macmillan Child Bk) Macmillan Child Grp.
Buchanan-Hedman, Pat. Tracy & the Lavender Piece of Paper: A Realistic Story to Help Children Cope with Painful & Bitter Divorces. Koop, Christie, illus. (Orig.). (gr. 1-6). 1991. write for info. (*1-880121-75-1*) Three Cs Ent.
Bunting, Eve. A Part of the Dream. (Illus.). 64p. (gr. 3-8). 1992. 8.95 (*0-89565-771-6*) Childs World.
Burns, Peggy. The Splitting Image of Rosie Brown. 128p. (Orig.). (gr. 7-10). 1990. pap. 4.99 (*0-7459-1831-X*) Lion USA.
Christiansen, C. B. My Mother's House, My Father's House. (ps-3). 1990. pap. 3.95 (*0-14-054210-8*, Puffin) Puffin Bks.
Cleary, Beverly. Dear Mr. Henshaw. Zelinsky, Paul O., illus. 144p. (gr. k-6). 1984. pap. 4.50 (*0-440-41794-5*, YB) Dell.
—Dear Mr. Henshaw. large type ed. Zelinsky, Paul O., illus. 141p. (gr. 2-6). 1987. Repr. of 1983 ed. lib. bdg. 14.95 (*1-55736-001-4*, Crnrstn Bks) BDD LT Grp.
—Strider. Zelinsky, Paul O., illus. LC 90-6608. 192p. (gr. 3 up). 1991. 13.95 (*0-688-09900-9*); PLB 13.88 (*0-688-09901-7*) Morrow Jr Bks.
Danziger, Paula. The Divorce Express. LC 82-70318. 144p. (gr. 7 up). 1982. pap. 14.95 (*0-385-28217-6*) Delacorte.
—The Divorce Express. 160p. (gr. 7 up). 1983. pap. 3.99 (*0-440-92062-0*, LFL) Dell.
—It's an Aardvark-Eat-Turtle World. large type, unabr. ed. 145p. (gr. 4 up). 1989. lib. bdg. 13.95 (*0-8161-4704-3*) G K Hall.
—You Can't Eat Your Chicken Pox, Amber Brown. Ross, Tony, illus. LC 93-37761. (gr. 3 up). 1995. write for info. (*0-399-22702-4*, Putnam) Putnam Pub Group.
De Saint Mars, Dominique. Zoe's Parents Are Getting Divorced. Bloch, Serge, illus. LC 93-19767. (gr. 2-4). Date not set. 8.95 (*1-56766-104-1*) Childs World.
Devore, Cynthia D. Breakfast for Dinner. LC 93-13066. 32p. (gr. 5 up). 1993. 14.96 (*1-56239-245-X*) Abdo & Dghtrs.
Ferris, Jean. Relative Strangers. 1993. 16.00 (*0-374-36243-2*) FS&G.
Fine, Anne. Alias Madame Doubtfire. 1990. pap. 3.99 (*0-553-56615-6*) Bantam.
—Madame Doubtfire. Pena, Flora, tr. (SPA.). 165p. (gr. 5-8). 1992. pap. write for info. (*84-204-4680-7*) Santillana.
Fitzhugh, Louise. Sport. 224p. (gr. 7 up). 1980. pap. 1.75 (*0-440-98350-9*, LFL) Dell.
George, J. Carroll & Eaton, Joi. Divorcing Daddy. 125p. (gr. 7-12). 1992. pap. 5.95 (*1-881223-01-9*) Zulema Ent.
Goff, Beth. Where Is Daddy? The Story of a Divorce. Perl, Susan, illus. LC 69-14608. 32p. (ps-k). 1969. pap. 4.95 (*0-8070-2305-1*, BP 694) Beacon Pr.
Hamm, Diane J. Second Family. LC 91-42968. 128p. (gr. 5-7). 1992. SBE 13.95 (*0-684-19436-8*, Scribners Young Read) Macmillan Child Grp.
Hawkins, Laura. Valentine to a Flying Mouse. (ps-7). 1993. 13.95 (*0-395-61628-X*) HM.
Hillman, Carole D. It's Different Now...a New Beginning. Hillman, Carole D., illus. 10p. (Orig.). 1990. pap. text ed. write for info. (*0-9624257-1-0*) Early Childhood.
Hogan, Paula Z. Will Dad Ever Move Back Home? Leder, Dora, illus. Muir, Martha F., intro. by. LC 79-24058. (Illus.). 32p. (gr. k-6). 1980. PLB 19.97 (*0-8172-1356-2*) Raintree Steck-V.
Jones, Cordelia. Cat Called Camouflage. LC 79-166339. (Illus.). (gr. 7 up). 1971. 21.95 (*0-87599-189-0*) S G Phillips.
Jones, Robin D. The Beginning of Unbelief. LC 92-22907. 160p. (gr. 7 up). 1993. SBE 13.95 (*0-689-31781-6*, Atheneum Child Bk) Macmillan Child Grp.
Klass, Sheila S. Pork Bellies Are Down. LC 94-20235. 1995. 13.95 (*0-590-46686-0*) Scholastic Inc.
Kropp, Paul. Moonkid & Liberty. (gr. 3-6). 1990. 13.95 (*0-316-50485-8*, Joy St Bks) Little.
Lapka, Fay S. The Sea, the Song & the Trumpetfish. 160p. (Orig.). (gr. 7-12). 1991. pap. 6.99 (*0-87788-754-3*) Shaw Pubs.
Lehrman, Robert. Separations. LC 92-26782. 224p. (gr. 5-9). 1993. pap. 3.99 (*0-14-032322-8*) Puffin Bks.
LeMieux, A. C. The TV Guidance Counselor. LC 92-33664. 240p. (gr. 7 up). 1993. 13.00 (*0-688-12402-X*, Tambourine Bks) Morrow.

Levinson, Marilyn. No Boys Allowed. Leer, Rebecca, illus. LC 93-22335. 128p. (gr. 5-8). 1993. PLB 13.95 (*0-8167-3135-7*); pap. 2.95 (*0-8167-3136-5*) BrdgeWater.

Lisle, Janet T. The Gold Dust Letters. LC 93-11806. 128p. (gr. 3-5). 1994. 14.95 (*0-531-06830-7*); lib. bdg. 14.99 RLB (*0-531-08680-1*) Orchard Bks Watts.

Littleton, Mark. Winter Thunder. LC 92-5433. 1993. pap. 3.99 (*1-56507-008-9*) Harvest Hse.

McAfee, A. & Browne, A. Visitors Who Came to Stay. LC 84-40333. 32p. (gr. 4-6). 1985. pap. 11.95 (*0-670-74714-9*) Viking Child Bks.

McEwan, Elaine K. Murphy's Mansion. Norton, LoraBeth, ed. 96p. (gr. 3-6). Date not set. pap. 4.99 (*0-7814-0160-7*, Chariot Bks) Chariot Family.

—Operation Garbage: A Josh McIntire Book. LC 92-43761. 1993. pap. 4.99 (*0-7814-0121-6*, Chariot Bks) Chariot Family.

—Underground Hero. LC 92-27104. (gr. 3-6). 1993. pap. 4.99 (*0-7814-0113-5*, Chariot Bks) Chariot Family.

Marshall, Linda D. What Is a Step? Marshall, Linda D. & Johnson, Daphane, illus. LC 91-67511. 48p. (Orig.). (ps-5). 1992. pap. 8.00 (*1-879289-00-8*) Native Sun Pubs. "If you are looking for a mind-strengthening fun gift to get a special little one..., then we recommend Linda D. Marshall's WHAT IS A STEP? Our children are faced with the reality of such unfortunate words as 'bastard,' 'half-brother,' 'half-sister,' 'separation,' 'divorce,' & the like; & they need a way out of the confusion & sickness produced by the manifestations of those terms. This is especially true for children of Afrikan descent whose LONGER historical & cultural reality preclude such terms. Told with good humor, maternal caring, & a child's splendid wonder, WHAT IS A STEP? is a book useful to all parents who read to & communicate with their young." - THE RICHMOND NEWS LEADER. To be sure, here is a children's book whose integrity is not compromised by both its widespread & its specific appeal: it has mainstream, multicultural, & Afrikan-centered relevance, all genuine as the warm adults & enthusiastic children who will enjoy & learn from this story of Whobee & his family. Indeed, once we open this book's bright seven-color covers, we will learn how Whobee's overhearing his mother on the phone confuses him, the lessons he will learn, & the nature of his summer's special gift to him. A book of life-long value. *Publisher Provided Annotation.*

Mazer, Norma F. E, My Name is Emily. 176p. 1991. 13.95 (*0-590-43653-8*, Scholastic Hardcover) Scholastic Inc.

—Taking Terri Mueller. LC 82-18849. 224p. (gr. 7 up). 1983. 12.95 (*0-688-01732-0*) Morrow Jr Bks.

Orlev, Uri. Lydia: Queen of Palestine. Halkin, Hillel, tr. from HEB. LC 93-12488. 1993. 13.95 (*0-395-65660-5*) HM.

Park, Barbara. Don't Make Me Smile. 132p. (gr. 4-7). 1983. pap. 2.95 (*0-380-61994-6*, Camelot) Avon.

—Don't Make Me Smile. LC 81-4880. 128p. (gr. 3-7). 1990. pap. 3.25 (*0-394-84745-8*) Random Bks Yng Read.

Petersen, P. J. I Want Answers & a Parachute. DiVito, Anna, illus. LC 92-38262. (gr. 6 up). 1993. pap. 13.00 (*0-671-86577-3*, S&S BFYR) S&S Trade.

Pevsner, Stella. A Smart Kid Like You. LC 74-19320. 192p. (gr. 4-8). 1979. 14.45 (*0-395-28876-2*, Clarion Bks) HM.

Ransom, Candice. Third Grade Detectives. LC 93-48920. (Illus.). 128p. (gr. 2-4). 1994. PLB 9.89 (*0-8167-2992-1*); pap. 2.95 (*0-8167-2993-X*) Troll Assocs.

Ransom, Candice F. Who Needs Third Grade? LC 92-30754. 128p. (gr. 2-4). 1992. PLB 9.89 (*0-8167-2988-3*); pap. text ed. 2.95 (*0-8167-2989-1*) Troll Assocs.

Sanford, Doris. Please Come Home: A Child's Book about Divorce. Evans, Graci, illus. LC 86-106753. 24p. (ps-5). 1985. 7.99 (*0-88070-138-2*, Gold & Honey) Questar Pubs.

Sommer, Karen. Satch & the Motormouth. LC 86-24031. (gr. 3-7). 1987. pap. 4.99 (*1-55513-063-1*, Chariot Bks) Chariot Family.

Steiner, Barbara. Tessa. LC 87-31524. 224p. (gr. 7 up). 1988. 12.95 (*0-688-07232-1*) Morrow Jr Bks.

Stinson, Kathy. Mom & Dad Don't Live Together Anymore. Reynolds, Nancy L., illus. 32p. (gr. k-3). 1984. PLB 14.95 (*0-920236-92-8*, Pub. by Annick CN); pap. 4.95 (*0-920236-87-1*, Pub. by Annick CN) Firefly Bks Ltd.

Williams, Vera B. Scooter. LC 90-38489. (Illus.). 160p. (gr. 4-7). 1993. 15.00 (*0-688-09376-0*); PLB 14.93 (*0-688-09377-9*) Greenwillow.

Willner-Pardo, Gina. Jason & the Losers. LC 93-44156. 1996. write for info. (*0-395-70160-0*, Clarion Bks) HM.

—What I'll Remember When I Am a Grownup. Krudop, Walter L., illus. LC 92-42148. (gr. 2-4). 1994. 13.95 (*0-395-63310-9*, Clarion Bks) HM.

Wilson, Nancy H. The Reason for Janey. LC 93-22930. 176p. (gr. 3-7). 1994. SBE 14.95 (*0-02-793127-7*, Macmillan Child Bk) Macmillan Child Grp.

DIX, DOROTHEA LYNDE, 1802-1887

Malone, Mary. Dorothea L. Dix: Hospital Founder. Sampson, Katharine, illus. 80p. (gr. 2-6). 1991. Repr. of 1968 ed. lib. bdg. 12.95 (*0-7910-1436-3*) Chelsea Hse.

Schleichert, Elizabeth. The Life of Dorothea Dix. Castro, Antonio, illus. 80p. (gr. 4-7). 1991. PLB 13.95 (*0-941477-68-1*) TFC Bks NY.

DOBIE, JAMES FRANK, 1888-

Mitchell, Mark. The Mustang Professor: The Story of J. Frank Dobie. Mitchell, Mark, illus. 96p. (gr. 4-7). 1993. 12.95 (*0-89015-823-1*) Sunbelt Media.

DOCKS

see also Harbors

DOCTORS

see Physicians

DOCTRINAL THEOLOGY

see Theology

DOCTRINES

see Theology

DODGSON, CHARLES LUTWIDGE, 1832-1898

Greene, Carol. Lewis Carroll: Author of Alice in Wonderland. LC 91-37821. (Illus.). 48p. (gr. k-3). 1992. PLB 12.85 (*0-516-04227-0*); pap. 4.95 (*0-516-44227-9*) Childrens.

DODO–FICTION

Baender, Margaret W. Tail Waggings of Maggie. Hinkle, Janet W., illus. 64p. (gr. 8-10). 1982. pap. 6.00x (*0-88100-012-4*) Philmar Pub.

DOG

see Dogs

DOG GUIDES

see Guide Dogs

DOG-SHOWS

Miller, Mary A. Junior Showmanship from Hand to Lead: The Complete Handbook for Junior Handlers. LC 94-1099. 1994. write for info. (*0-931866-66-9*) Alpine Pubns.

Vanacore, Connie. New Guide to Junior Showmanship. (Illus.). 160p. 1994. 22.00 (*0-87605-653-2*) Howell Bk.

DOGMATIC THEOLOGY

see Theology

DOGS

see also classes of dog e.g. Guide Dogs; also names of specific breeds

Adamoli, Vida & Howard, Tom. The Love of Dogs. (Illus.). 96p. 1993. 12.98 (*0-8317-2187-1*) Smithmark.

Anderson, J. I. I Can Read About Dogs & Puppies. LC 72-96953. (Illus.). (gr. 2-4). 1973. pap. 2.50 (*0-89375-053-0*) Troll Assocs.

Ashabranner, Brent. Crazy about German Shepherds. Ashabranner, Jennifer, photos by. LC 90-1303. (Illus.). 96p. (gr. 5 up). 1990. 14.95 (*0-525-65032-6*, Cobblehill Bks) Dutton Child Bks.

Aymerich, Angela F. The Three Pups. Billin-Frye, Paige, illus. 16p. (Orig.). (gr. 1-3). 1991. pap. text ed. 29.95 big bk. (*1-56334-049-6*); pap. text ed. 6.00 small bk. (*1-56334-055-0*) Hampton-Brown.

—Los Tres Perritos. Billin-Frye, Paige, illus. (SPA.). 16p. (Orig.). (gr. 1-3). 1991. pap. text ed. 29.95 big bk. (*1-56334-021-6*); pap. text ed. 6.00 small bk. (*1-56334-035-6*) Hampton-Brown.

Barrett, Norman S. Dogs. LC 89-29346. (Illus.). 32p. (gr. k-4). 1990. PLB 11.90 (*0-531-14040-7*) Watts.

Boorer, Wendy. Dogs. Coombs, Roy, illus. LC 88-17653. 24p. (Orig.). (gr. 2-5). 1989. lib. bdg. 5.99 (*0-394-99988-6*) Random Bks Yng Read.

Boy Scouts of America. Dog Care. (Illus.). 48p. (gr. 6-12). 1984. pap. 1.85 (*0-8395-3289-X*, 33289) BSA.

Boyd-Smith, Wendy. The No Barking at the Table Cookbook: Canine Recipes Most Begged For. Saltzberg, Barney, illus. 106p. (Orig.). 1991. pap. text ed. write for info. (*0-9629459-0-0*) Lip Smackers.

Bryant, Donna. My Dog Jessie. Wood, Jakki, illus. 20p. (ps-3). 1991. 8.95 (*0-8120-6212-4*) Barron.

Burton, Jane. Jack the Puppy. LC 89-11422. (Illus.). 32p. (gr. 2-3). 1989. PLB 17.27 (*0-8368-0209-8*) Gareth Stevens Inc.

Burton, Jane, photos by. See How They Grow: Puppy. (Illus.). 24p. (gr. k-3). 1991. 6.95 (*0-525-67342-3*, Lodestar Bks) Dutton Child Bks.

Carpentier, Marcel. Your First Puppy. (Illus.). 34p. (Orig.). (gr. 1-6). 1991. pap. 1.95 (*0-86622-064-X*, YF-119) TFH Pubns.

Casanova, Mary. The Golden Retriever. LC 90-34141. (Illus.). 48p. (gr. 4-5). 1990. text ed. 12.95 RSBE (*0-89686-525-8*, Crestwood Hse) Macmillan Child Grp.

Clutton-Brock, Juliet. Dog. Young, Jerry, photos by. LC 91-10135. (Illus.). 64p. (gr. 5 up). 1991. 16.00 (*0-679-81459-0*); lib. bdg. 16.99 (*0-679-91459-5*) Knopf Bks Yng Read.

Cole, Joanna. A Dog's Body. Wexler, Jerome, illus. LC 85-25885. 48p. (ps-3). 1986. 12.95 (*0-688-04153-1*); lib. bdg. 12.88 (*0-688-04154-X*, Morrow Jr Bks) Morrow Jr Bks.

—My Puppy Is Born. rev. ed. Miller, Margaret, photos by. LC 90-42011. (Illus.). 48p. (ps up). 1991. pap. 4.95 (*0-688-10198-4*, Mulberry) Morrow.

—My Puppy Is Born. rev. ed. Miller, Margaret, photos by. LC 90-42011. (Illus.). 48p. (ps up). 1991. 13.95 (*0-688-09770-7*); PLB 13.88 (*0-688-09771-5*, Morrow Jr Bks) Morrow Jr Bks.

Cole, Joanna & Calmenson, Stephanie, eds. Give a Dog a Bone: Stories, Poems, Jokes, & Riddles about Dogs. Speirs, John, illus. LC 93-2536. 1994. write for info. (*0-590-46374-8*) Scholastic Inc.

Cooper, Michael. Racing Sled Dogs: An Original North American Sport. LC 87-25007. (Illus.). 96p. (gr. 4-7). 1988. 13.95 (*0-89919-499-0*, Clarion Bks) HM.

Cowley, Stewart & Davies, Kate. Hide-&-Seek Puppies. LC 92-60793. (Illus.). (ps). 1992. 6.99 (*0-89577-455-0*, Dist. by Random) RD Assn.

Davidson, Margaret. Five True Dog Stories. 1989. pap. 2.50 (*0-590-42401-7*) Scholastic Inc.

De Zutter, Hank. Who Says a Dog Goes Bow-Wow? LC 92-4232. (ps-3). 1993. pap. 15.00 (*0-385-30659-8*) Doubleday.

Dogs: A Complete Guide to More Than 200 Breeds. LC 93-85521. (Illus.). 240p. 1994. pap. 5.95 (*1-56138-382-1*) Running Pr.

Ebeling, Jean. Waldo, the Goat Dog. Roberts, Melissa, ed. Arlitt, Nancy, illus. 48p. (gr. 4-7). 1987. 8.95 (*0-89015-588-7*, Pub. by Panda Bks) Sunbelt Media.

Eltinge, et al. The Staffordshire Bull Terrier in America. Eltinge, Steve, ed. Epps, Sarah, illus. Eltinge, Steve, intro. by. 140p. (gr. 4 up). 1986. pap. 24.95 (*0-9617204-0-9*) MIP Pub.

Emert, Phyllis R. Hearing-Ear Dogs. LC 85-12841. (Illus.). 48p. (gr. 5-6). 1985. text ed. 11.95 RSBE (*0-89686-283-6*, Crestwood Hse) Macmillan Child Grp.

—Military Dogs. LC 85-17488. (Illus.). 48p. (gr. 5-6). 1985. text ed. 11.95 RSBE (*0-89686-286-0*, Crestwood Hse) Macmillan Child Grp.

—Search & Rescue Dogs. LC 85-18967. (Illus.). 48p. (gr. 5-6). 1985. text ed. 11.95 RSBE (*0-89686-285-2*, Crestwood Hse) Macmillan Child Grp.

—Sled Dogs. LC 85-14967. (Illus.). 48p. (gr. 5-6). 1985. text ed. 11.95 RSBE (*0-89686-288-7*, Crestwood Hse) Macmillan Child Grp.

Evans, Mark. Puppy. LC 92-52828. (Illus.). 48p. (gr. 2 up). 1992. 9.95 (*1-56458-127-6*) Dorling Kindersley.

Fowler, Allan. It Could Still Be a Dog. LC 93-880. (Illus.). 32p. (ps-2). 1993. PLB 10.75 (*0-516-06016-3*); pap. 3.95 (*0-516-46016-1*) Childrens.

Gackenbach, Dick. Claude the Dog. LC 74-3403. 32p. (ps-2). 1979. 13.95 (*0-395-28792-8*, Clarion Bks) HM.

Gambill, Henrietta, ed. Little Puppy. (Illus.). 18p. 1994. 7.99 (*0-7847-0236-5*, 24-03126) Standard Pub.

Goennel, Heidi. My Dog. LC 88-38706. (Illus.). 32p. (ps-1). 1989. 14.95 (*0-531-05834-4*); PLB 14.99 (*0-531-08434-5*) Orchard Bks Watts.

Hains, Harriet. My New Puppy. LC 91-58200. (Illus.). 24p. (ps-3). 1992. 9.95 (*1-879431-77-7*) Dorling Kindersley.

Hall, Lynn. Barry: The Bravest Saint Bernard. Castro, Antonio, illus. LC 92-1228. 48p. (Orig.). (gr. 2-4). 1992. PLB 7.99 (*0-679-93054-X*); pap. 3.50 (*0-679-83054-5*) Random Bks Yng Read.

Hausherr, Rosmarie. My First Puppy. Hausherr, Rosmarie, illus. LC 86-14979. 64p. (gr. 1-4). 1986. RSBE 14.95 (*0-02-743410-9*, Four Winds) Macmillan Child Grp.

Herriot, James. Only One Woof. Barrett, Peter, illus. 32p. (ps up). 1985. 13.00 (*0-312-58583-7*) St Martin.

—Only One Woof. Barrett, Peter, illus. 32p. (gr. 1-8). 1993. pap. 6.95 (*0-312-09129-X*) St Martin.

Hill. Dog & Puppies. Goaman, Karen, ed. Kennan, Elaine & Ward, Fredrick, illus. (gr. 2-5). 1983. pap. 4.50 (*0-86020-646-7*) EDC.

Hill, Eric. Spot Goes to School. Hill, Eric, illus. LC 84-42695. 22p. (ps-2). 1984. 11.95 (*0-399-21073-3*, Putnam) Putnam Pub Group.

Houk, Randy. Bentley & Blueberry. Houk, Randy, illus. 32p. (gr. k-3). 1993. 14.95 (*1-882728-00-9*); read-along cass. 7.95 (*1-882728-03-3*) Benefactory.

Hughes, Dean. Dog Detectives & Other Amazing Canines. LC 93-50851. (gr. 3 up). 1994. 2.99 (*0-679-84818-5*) Random Bks Yng Read.

Jameson, P. Dogs. (Illus.). 32p. (gr. 2-5). 1989. lib. bdg. 15.94 (*0-86625-184-7*); 11.95s.p. (*0-685-58610-3*) Rourke Corp.

Jones, Teri C. Dogs. (Illus.). 64p. (gr. k-4). 1992. PLB 13.75 (*1-878363-83-2*, HTS Bks) Forest Hse.

Jons, John A. Studies of the French Dog Sports "Championship of France" (1982-1988) & the Belgian Shepherd Dog Breeds (Malinois, Teruren Groenendael, Laenenois) in Schutzhund Competition in the U. S. A. (1979-1988) 1989. pap. text ed. 12.50 (*0-685-29411-0*) J Jons LA.

Kappeler, Markus. Dogs Wild & Domestic. LC 91-2682. (Illus.). 32p. (gr. 4-6). 1991. PLB 18.60 (*0-8368-0686-7*) Gareth Stevens Inc.

Khalsa, Dayal K. I Want a Dog. (Illus.). 24p. (ps up). 1988. 15.00 (*0-517-56532-3*, Clarkson Potter) Crown Bks Yng Read.

Lesterson, David. The Regal Beagle. Hoffman, Beverly, et al, eds. Graham, Jennifer, illus. LC 93-70504. 29p. (gr. 3). Date not set. write for info. (*0-9634122-3-X*) Feather Fables.

Ling, Mary. Amazing Wolves, Dogs, & Foxes. Young, Jerry, photos by. LC 91-6514. (Illus.). 32p. (Orig.). (gr. 1-5). 1991. lib. bdg. 9.99 (*0-679-91521-4*); pap. 7.99 (*0-679-81521-X*) Knopf Bks Yng Read.

Lord, Suzanne. The Labrador Retriever. LC 90-34198. (Illus.). 48p. (gr. 4-5). 1990. text ed. 12.95 RSBE (*0-89686-526-6*, Crestwood Hse) Macmillan Child Grp.

McPherson, Mark. Caring for Your Dog. Bernstein, Marianne, illus. LC 84-222. 48p. (gr. 3-7). 1985. PLB 9.89 (*0-8167-0113-X*); pap. 2.95 (*0-8167-0114-8*) Troll Assocs.

Manson, Ainslie. A Dog Came, Too: A True Story. Blades, Ann, illus. LC 91-44891. 32p. (gr. 1-5). 1993. SBE 13.95 (*0-689-50567-1*, M K McElderry) Macmillan Child Grp.

Marquardt, Max. Working Dogs. (Illus.). 32p. (gr. 1-4). 1989. PLB 18.99 (*0-8172-3506-X*); pap. 3.95 (*0-8114-6711-2*) Raintree Steck-V.

Marsh, Carole. Bow Wow! Alabama Dogs in History, Mystery, Legend, Lore, Humor & More! (Illus.). (gr. 3-12). 1994. PLB 24.95 (*0-7933-3467-5*); pap. 14.95 (*0-7933-3468-3*); computer disk 29.95 (*0-7933-3469-1*) Gallopade Pub Group.

—Bow Wow! Alaska Dogs in History, Mystery, Legend, Lore, Humor & More! (Illus.). (gr. 3-12). 1994. PLB 24.95 (*0-7933-3470-5*); pap. 14.95 (*0-7933-3471-3*); computer disk 29.95 (*0-7933-3472-1*) Gallopade Pub Group.

—Bow Wow! Arizona Dogs in History, Mystery, Legend, Lore, Humor & More! (Illus.). (gr. 3-12). 1994. PLB 24.95 (*0-7933-3473-X*); pap. 14.95 (*0-7933-3474-8*); computer disk 29.95 (*0-7933-3475-6*) Gallopade Pub Group.

—Bow Wow! Arkansas Dogs in History, Mystery, Legend, Lore, Humor & More! (Illus.). (gr. 3-12). 1994. PLB 24.95 (*0-7933-3476-4*); pap. 14.95 (*0-7933-3477-2*); computer disk 29.95 (*0-7933-3478-0*) Gallopade Pub Group.

—Bow Wow! California Dogs in History, Mystery, Legend, Lore, Humor & More! (Illus.). (gr. 3-12). 1994. PLB 24.95 (*0-7933-3479-9*); pap. 14.95 (*0-7933-3480-2*); computer disk 29.95 (*0-7933-3481-0*) Gallopade Pub Group.

—Bow Wow! Colorado Dogs in History, Mystery, Legend, Lore, Humor & More! (Illus.). (gr. 3-12). 1994. PLB 24.95 (*0-7933-3482-9*); pap. 14.95 (*0-7933-3483-7*); computer disk 29.95 (*0-7933-3484-5*) Gallopade Pub Group.

—Bow Wow! Connecticut Dogs in History, Mystery, Legend, Lore, Humor & More! (Illus.). (gr. 3-12). 1994. PLB 24.95 (*0-7933-3485-3*); pap. 14.95 (*0-7933-3486-1*); computer disk 29.95 (*0-7933-3487-X*) Gallopade Pub Group.

—Bow Wow! Delaware Dogs in History, Mystery, Legend, Lore, Humor & More! (Illus.). (gr. 3-12). 1994. PLB 24.95 (*0-7933-3488-8*); pap. 14.95 (*0-7933-3489-6*); computer disk 29.95 (*0-7933-3490-X*) Gallopade Pub Group.

—Bow Wow! Florida Dogs in History, Mystery, Legend, Lore, Humor & More! (Illus.). (gr. 3-12). 1994. PLB 24.95 (*0-7933-3494-2*); pap. 14.95 (*0-7933-3495-0*); computer disk 29.95 (*0-7933-3496-9*) Gallopade Pub Group.

—Bow Wow! Georgia Dogs in History, Mystery, Legend, Lore, Humor & More! (Illus.). (gr. 3-12). 1994. PLB 24.95 (*0-7933-3497-7*); pap. 14.95 (*0-7933-3498-5*); computer disk 29.95 (*0-7933-3499-3*) Gallopade Pub Group.

—Bow Wow! Hawaii Dogs in History, Mystery, Legend, Lore, Humor & More! (Illus.). (gr. 3-12). 1994. PLB 24.95 (*0-7933-3500-0*); pap. 14.95 (*0-7933-3501-9*); computer disk 29.95 (*0-7933-3502-7*) Gallopade Pub Group.

—Bow Wow! Idaho Dogs in History, Mystery, Legend, Lore, Humor & More! (Illus.). (gr. 3-12). 1994. PLB 24.95 (*0-7933-3503-5*); pap. 14.95 (*0-7933-3504-3*); computer disk 29.95 (*0-7933-3505-1*) Gallopade Pub Group.

—Bow Wow! Illinois Dogs in History, Mystery, Legend, Lore, Humor & More! (Illus.). (gr. 3-12). 1994. PLB 24.95 (*0-7933-3506-X*); pap. 14.95 (*0-7933-3507-8*); computer disk 29.95 (*0-7933-3508-6*) Gallopade Pub Group.

—Bow Wow! Indiana Dogs in History, Mystery, Legend, Lore, Humor & More! (Illus.). (gr. 3-12). 1994. PLB 24.95 (*0-7933-3509-4*); pap. 14.95 (*0-7933-3510-8*); computer disk 29.95 (*0-7933-3511-6*) Gallopade Pub Group.

—Bow Wow! Iowa Dogs in History, Mystery, Legend, Lore, Humor & More! (Illus.). (gr. 3-12). 1994. PLB 24.95 (*0-7933-3512-4*); pap. 14.95 (*0-7933-3513-2*); computer disk 29.95 (*0-7933-3514-0*) Gallopade Pub Group.

—Bow Wow! Kansas Dogs in History, Mystery, Legend, Lore, Humor & More! (Illus.). (gr. 3-12). 1994. PLB 24.95 (*0-7933-3515-9*); pap. 14.95 (*0-7933-3516-7*); computer disk 29.95 (*0-7933-3517-5*) Gallopade Pub Group.

—Bow Wow! Kentucky Dogs in History, Mystery, Legend, Lore, Humor & More! (Illus.). (gr. 3-12). 1994. PLB 24.95 (*0-7933-3518-3*); pap. 14.95 (*0-7933-3519-1*); computer disk 29.95 (*0-7933-3520-5*) Gallopade Pub Group.

—Bow Wow! Louisiana Dogs in History, Mystery, Legend, Lore, Humor & More! (Illus.). (gr. 3-12). 1994. PLB 24.95 (*0-7933-3521-3*); pap. 14.95 (*0-7933-3522-1*); computer disk 29.95 (*0-7933-3523-X*) Gallopade Pub Group.

—Bow Wow! Maine Dogs in History, Mystery, Legend, Lore, Humor & More! (Illus.). (gr. 3-12). 1994. PLB 24.95 (*0-7933-3524-8*); pap. 14.95 (*0-7933-3525-6*); computer disk 29.95 (*0-7933-3526-4*) Gallopade Pub Group.

—Bow Wow! Maryland Dogs in History, Mystery, Legend, Lore, Humor & More! (Illus.). (gr. 3-12). 1994. PLB 24.95 (*0-7933-3527-2*); pap. 14.95 (*0-7933-3528-0*); computer disk 29.95 (*0-7933-3529-9*) Gallopade Pub Group.

—Bow Wow! Massachusetts Dogs in History, Mystery, Legend, Lore, Humor & More! (Illus.). (gr. 3-12). 1994. PLB 24.95 (*0-7933-3530-2*); pap. 14.95 (*0-7933-3531-0*); computer disk 29.95 (*0-7933-3532-9*) Gallopade Pub Group.

—Bow Wow! Michigan Dogs in History, Mystery, Legend, Lore, Humor & More! (Illus.). (gr. 3-12). 1994. PLB 24.95 (*0-7933-3533-7*); pap. 14.95 (*0-7933-3534-5*); computer disk 29.95 (*0-7933-3535-3*) Gallopade Pub Group.

—Bow Wow! Minnesota Dogs in History, Mystery, Legend, Lore, Humor & More! (Illus.). (gr. 3-12). 1994. PLB 24.95 (*0-7933-3536-1*); pap. 14.95 (*0-7933-3537-X*); computer disk 29.95 (*0-7933-3538-8*) Gallopade Pub Group.

—Bow Wow! Mississippi Dogs in History, Mystery, Legend, Lore, Humor & More! (Illus.). (gr. 3-12). 1994. PLB 24.95 (*0-7933-3539-6*); pap. 14.95 (*0-7933-3540-X*); computer disk 29.95 (*0-7933-3541-8*) Gallopade Pub Group.

—Bow Wow! Missouri Dogs in History, Mystery, Legend, Lore, Humor & More! (Illus.). (gr. 3-12). 1994. PLB 24.95 (*0-7933-3542-6*); pap. 14.95 (*0-7933-3543-4*); computer disk 29.95 (*0-7933-3544-2*) Gallopade Pub Group.

—Bow Wow! Montana Dogs in History, Mystery, Legend, Lore, Humor & More! (Illus.). (gr. 3-12). 1994. PLB 24.95 (*0-7933-3545-0*); pap. 14.95 (*0-7933-3546-9*); computer disk 29.95 (*0-7933-3547-7*) Gallopade Pub Group.

—Bow Wow! Nebraska Dogs in History, Mystery, Legend, Lore, Humor & More! (Illus.). (gr. 3-12). 1994. PLB 24.95 (*0-7933-3548-5*); pap. 14.95 (*0-7933-3549-3*); computer disk 29.95 (*0-7933-3550-7*) Gallopade Pub Group.

—Bow Wow! Nevada Dogs in History, Mystery, Legend, Lore, Humor & More! (Illus.). (gr. 3-12). 1994. PLB 24.95 (*0-7933-3551-5*); pap. 14.95 (*0-7933-3552-3*); computer disk 29.95 (*0-7933-3553-1*) Gallopade Pub Group.

—Bow Wow! New Hampshire Dogs in History, Mystery, Legend, Lore, Humor & More! (Illus.). (gr. 3-12). 1994. PLB 24.95 (*0-7933-3554-X*); pap. 14.95 (*0-7933-3555-8*); computer disk 29.95 (*0-7933-3556-6*) Gallopade Pub Group.

—Bow Wow! New Jersey Dogs in History, Mystery, Legend, Lore, Humor & More! (Illus.). (gr. 3-12). 1994. PLB 24.95 (*0-7933-3557-4*); pap. 14.95 (*0-7933-3558-2*); computer disk 29.95 (*0-7933-3559-0*) Gallopade Pub Group.

—Bow Wow! New Mexico Dogs in History, Mystery, Legend, Lore, Humor & More! (Illus.). (gr. 3-12). 1994. PLB 24.95 (*0-7933-3560-4*); pap. 14.95 (*0-7933-3561-2*); computer disk 29.95 (*0-7933-3562-0*) Gallopade Pub Group.

—Bow Wow! New York Dogs in History, Mystery, Legend, Lore, Humor & More! (Illus.). (gr. 3-12). 1994. PLB 24.95 (*0-7933-3563-9*); pap. 14.95 (*0-7933-3564-7*); computer disk 29.95 (*0-7933-3565-5*) Gallopade Pub Group.

—Bow Wow! North Carolina Dogs in History, Mystery, Legend, Lore, Humor & More! (Illus.). (gr. 3-12). 1994. PLB 24.95 (*0-7933-3566-3*); pap. 14.95 (*0-7933-3567-1*); computer disk 29.95 (*0-7933-3568-X*) Gallopade Pub Group.

—Bow Wow! North Dakota Dogs in History, Mystery, Legend, Lore, Humor & More! (Illus.). (gr. 3-12). 1994. PLB 24.95 (*0-7933-3569-8*); pap. 14.95 (*0-7933-3570-1*); computer disk 29.95 (*0-7933-3571-X*) Gallopade Pub Group.

—Bow Wow! Ohio Dogs in History, Mystery, Legend, Lore, Humor & More! (Illus.). (gr. 3-12). 1994. PLB 24.95 (*0-7933-3572-8*); pap. 14.95 (*0-7933-3573-6*); computer disk 29.95 (*0-7933-3574-4*) Gallopade Pub Group.

—Bow Wow! Oklahoma Dogs in History, Mystery, Legend, Lore, Humor & More! (Illus.). (gr. 3-12). 1994. PLB 24.95 (*0-7933-3575-2*); pap. 14.95 (*0-7933-3576-0*); computer disk 29.95 (*0-7933-3577-9*) Gallopade Pub Group.

—Bow Wow! Oregon Dogs in History, Mystery, Legend, Lore, Humor & More! (Illus.). (gr. 3-12). 1994. PLB 24.95 (*0-7933-3578-7*); pap. 14.95 (*0-7933-3579-5*); computer disk 29.95 (*0-7933-3580-9*) Gallopade Pub Group.

—Bow Wow! Pennsylvania Dogs in History, Mystery, Legend, Lore, Humor & More! (Illus.). (gr. 3-12). 1994. PLB 24.95 (*0-7933-3581-7*); pap. 14.95 (*0-7933-3582-5*); computer disk 29.95 (*0-7933-3583-3*) Gallopade Pub Group.

—Bow Wow! Rhode Island Dogs in History, Mystery, Legend, Lore, Humor & More! (Illus.). (gr. 3-12). 1994. PLB 24.95 (*0-7933-3584-1*); pap. 14.95 (*0-7933-3585-X*); computer disk 29.95 (*0-7933-3586-8*) Gallopade Pub Group.

—Bow Wow! South Carolina Dogs in History, Mystery, Legend, Lore, Humor & More! (Illus.). (gr. 3-12). 1994. PLB 24.95 (*0-7933-3587-6*); pap. 14.95 (*0-7933-3588-4*); computer disk 29.95 (*0-7933-3589-2*) Gallopade Pub Group.

—Bow Wow! South Dakota Dogs in History, Mystery, Legend, Lore, Humor & More! (Illus.). (gr. 3-12). 1994. PLB 24.95 (*0-7933-3590-6*); pap. 14.95 (*0-7933-3591-4*); computer disk 29.95 (*0-7933-3592-2*) Gallopade Pub Group.

—Bow Wow! Tennessee Dogs in History, Mystery, Legend, Lore, Humor & More! (Illus.). (gr. 3-12). 1994. PLB 24.95 (*0-7933-3593-0*); pap. 14.95 (*0-7933-3594-9*); computer disk 29.95 (*0-7933-3595-7*) Gallopade Pub Group.

—Bow Wow! Texas Dogs in History, Mystery, Legend, Lore, Humor & More! (Illus.). (gr. 3-12). 1994. PLB 24.95 (*0-7933-3596-5*); pap. 14.95 (*0-7933-3597-3*); computer disk 29.95 (*0-7933-3598-1*) Gallopade Pub Group.

—Bow Wow! Utah Dogs in History, Mystery, Legend, Lore, Humor & More! (Illus.). (gr. 3-12). 1994. PLB 24.95 (*0-7933-3599-X*); pap. 14.95 (*0-7933-3600-7*); computer disk 29.95 (*0-7933-3601-5*) Gallopade Pub Group.

—Bow Wow! Vermont Dogs in History, Mystery, Legend, Lore, Humor & More! (Illus.). (gr. 3-12). 1994. PLB 24.95 (*0-7933-3602-3*); pap. 14.95 (*0-7933-3603-1*); computer disk 29.95 (*0-7933-3604-X*) Gallopade Pub Group.

—Bow Wow! Virginia Dogs in History, Mystery, Legend, Lore, Humor & More! (Illus.). (gr. 3-12). 1994. PLB 24.95 (*0-7933-3605-8*); pap. 14.95 (*0-7933-3606-6*); computer disk 29.95 (*0-7933-3607-4*) Gallopade Pub Group.

—Bow Wow! Washington D. C. Dogs in History, Mystery, Legend, Lore, Humor & More! (Illus.). (gr. 3-12). 1994. PLB 24.95 (*0-7933-3491-8*); pap. 14.95 (*0-7933-3492-6*); computer disk 29.95 (*0-7933-3493-4*) Gallopade Pub Group.

—Bow Wow! Washington Dogs in History, Mystery, Legend, Lore, Humor & More! (Illus.). (gr. 3-12). 1994. PLB 24.95 (*0-7933-3608-2*); pap. 14.95 (*0-7933-3609-0*); computer disk 29.95 (*0-7933-3610-4*) Gallopade Pub Group.

—Bow Wow! West Virginia Dogs in History, Mystery, Legend, Lore, Humor & More! (Illus.). (gr. 3-12). 1994. PLB 24.95 (*0-7933-3611-2*); pap. 14.95 (*0-7933-3612-0*); computer disk 29.95 (*0-7933-3613-9*) Gallopade Pub Group.

—Bow Wow! Wisconsin Dogs in History, Mystery, Legend, Lore, Humor & More! (Illus.). (gr. 3-12). 1994. PLB 24.95 (*0-7933-3614-7*); pap. 14.95 (*0-7933-3615-5*); computer disk 29.95 (*0-7933-3616-3*) Gallopade Pub Group.

—Bow Wow! Wyoming Dogs in History, Mystery, Legend, Lore, Humor & More! (Illus.). (gr. 3-12). 1994. PLB 24.95 (*0-7933-3617-1*); pap. 14.95 (*0-7933-3618-X*); computer disk 29.95 (*0-7933-3619-8*) Gallopade Pub Group.

Murray, Peter. Dogs. (gr. 2-6). 1992. PLB 15.95 (*0-89565-848-8*) Childs World.

National Geographic Staff. Pile of Puppies. (ps). 1993. 4.50 (*0-7922-1834-5*) Natl Geog.

Newman, Matthew. Watch-Guard Dogs. LC 85-19542. (Illus.). 48p. (gr. 5-6). 1985. text ed. 11.95 RSBE (*0-89686-287-9*, Crestwood Hse) Macmillan Child Grp.

Nicholas, Anna K. The Great Dane. (Illus.). 319p. (gr. 7 up). 1988. 19.95 (*0-86622-122-0*, PS-826) TFH Pubns.

Nordmark, Magdalene L. Moss, a Border Collie. Miller, Robert W., illus. Miller, Janus W., prologue by. (Illus.). 37p. (Orig.). 1988. pap. 7.00 (*0-685-21901-1*) Willow Run UT.

O'Neill, Catherine. Dogs on Duty. LC 88-15933. (Illus.). 104p. (gr. 4 up). 1988. 8.95 (*0-87044-659-2*); lib. bdg. 12.50 (*0-87044-664-9*) Natl Geog.

Owl Magazine Editors, ed. The Kids' Dog Book. (Illus.). 96p. (gr. 3 up). 1992. pap. 9.95 (*0-920775-50-0*, Pub. by Greey de Pencier CN) Firefly Bks Ltd.

Petersen-Fleming, Judy & Fleming, Bill. Kitten Care & Critters, Too! Reingold-Reiss, Debra, photos by. LC 93-24200. (Illus.). 40p. 1994. 15.00 (*0-688-12563-8*, Tambourine Bks); PLB 14.93 (*0-688-12564-6*, Tambourine Bks) Morrow.

Petty, Kate. Baby Animals: Puppies. (Illus.). 24p. (ps-3). 1992. pap. 3.95 (*0-8120-4969-1*) Barron.

—Dogs. (Illus.). 24p. (ps-3). 1993. pap. 3.95 (*0-8120-1484-7*) Barron.

—Perros. Thompson, George, illus. LC 90-71411. (SPA.). 24p. (gr. k-4). 1991. PLB 10.90 (*0-531-07915-5*) Watts.

—Puppies. (Illus.). 24p. (gr. k-4). 1990. PLB 10.90 (*0-531-17232-5*, Gloucester Pr) Watts.

Piers, Helen. Taking Care of Your Dog. (Illus.). 32p. 1992. pap. 4.95 (*0-8120-4874-1*) Barron.

Pinkwater, Jill & Pinkwater, Daniel M. Superpuppy: How to Choose, Raise & Train the Best Possible Dog for You. LC 76-8825. (Illus.). 208p. (gr. 6 up). 1979. (Clarion Bks); pap. 7.95 (*0-89919-084-7*, Clarion) HM.

Posell, Elsa. Dogs. LC 81-7742. (Illus.). 48p. (gr. k-4). 1981. PLB 12.85 (*0-516-01614-8*); pap. 4.95 (*0-516-41614-6*) Childrens.

Rees, Yvonne. Dogs. (Illus.). 64p. 1991. 4.99 (*0-517-05152-4*) Random Hse Value.

Rinard, Judith E. Puppies. Crump, Donald J., ed. LC 82-47857. 32p. (ps-3). 1982. 13.95 (*0-87044-451-4*) Natl Geog.

Ring, Elizabeth. Companion Dogs: More Than Best Friends. (Illus.). 32p. (gr. 2-4). 1994. 13.40 (*1-56294-293-X*) Millbrook Pr.

—Detector Dogs: Hot on the Scent. LC 93-7275. (Illus.). 32p. (gr. 2-4). 1993. PLB 13.40 (*1-56294-289-1*) Millbrook Pr.

—Patrol Dogs: Keeping the Peace. (Illus.). 32p. (gr. 2-4). 1994. 13.40 (*1-56294-291-3*) Millbrook Pr.

—Performing Dogs: Stars of Stage, Screen, & Television. LC 93-41964. (Illus.). 32p. (gr. 2-4). 1994. PLB 13.40 (*1-56294-296-4*) Millbrook Pr.

—Ranch & Farm Dogs: Herders & Guards. LC 93-41529. (Illus.). 32p. (gr. 2-4). 1994. PLB 13.40 (*1-56294-295-6*) Millbrook Pr.

—Search-&-Rescue Dogs: Expert Trackers & Trailers. LC 93-42278. (Illus.). 32p. (gr. 2-4). 1994. PLB 13.40 (*1-56294-294-8*) Millbrook Pr.

—Sled Dogs: Arctic Athletes. (Illus.). 32p. (gr. 2-4). 1994. 13.40 (*1-56294-292-1*) Millbrook Pr.

Roach, Margaret J. I Love You, Charles Henry: Cats & Dogs in My Life. Moore, Susan & Craft, Page, eds. Moore, Susan J., illus. (gr. 1-6). 1994. pap. 13.50 (*1-882666-02-X*) M Roach & Assocs.

Roalf, Peggy. Dogs. LC 93-20585. (Illus.). 48p. (gr. 3-7). 1993. PLB 14.89 (*1-56282-530-5*); pap. 6.95 (*0-685-70878-0*) Hyprn Ppbks.

Rosen, Michael J., ed. Speak! Children's Book Illustrators Brag about Their Favorite Dogs. LC 92-30325. 1993. 16.95 (*0-15-277848-9*) HarBrace.

Ryden, Hope, photos by. Your Dog's Wild Cousins. LC 93-26855. (Illus.). 48p. (gr. 2-5). 1994. 16.99 (*0-525-67482-9*, Lodestar Bks) Dutton Child Bks.

Salladay, Susan. I Want a Puppy! (Illus.). 48p. (gr. 1-3). 1992. pap. 2.99 (*0-8423-1645-0*) Tyndale.

Sanderson, Jeannette. Dog to the Rescue: Seventeen True Tales of Dog Heroism. (gr. 4-7). 1993. pap. 2.95 (*0-590-47112-0*) Scholastic Inc.

Sanford, William & Green, Carl. The Beagle. LC 90-34211. (Illus.). 48p. (gr. 4-5). 1990. text ed. 12.95 RSBE (*0-89686-529-0*, Crestwood Hse) Macmillan Child Grp.

—The Cocker Spaniel. LC 90-34059. (Illus.). 48p. (gr. 4-5). 1990. text ed. 12.95 RSBE (*0-89686-531-2*, Crestwood Hse) Macmillan Child Grp.

—The Dachshund. LC 90-34058. (Illus.). 48p. (gr. 4-5). 1990. text ed. 12.95 RSBE (*0-89686-530-4*, Crestwood Hse) Macmillan Child Grp.

—The German Shepherd. LC 90-34212. (Illus.). 48p. (gr. 4-5). 1990. text ed. 12.95 RSBE (*0-89686-527-4*, Crestwood Hse) Macmillan Child Grp.

—The Poodle. LC 90-34199. (Illus.). 48p. (gr. 4-5). 1990. text ed. 12.95 RSBE (*0-89686-528-2*, Crestwood Hse) Macmillan Child Grp.

Selsam, Millicent E. How Puppies Grow. Johnson, Neil, photos by. (Illus.). 32p. (ps-3). 1990. pap. 2.50 (*0-590-42736-9*) Scholastic Inc.

Selsam, Millicent E. & Hunt, Joyce. A First Look at Dogs. Springer, Harriett, tr. 32p. (gr. 1-4). 1981. 7.95 (*0-8027-6409-6*); lib. bdg. 9.85 (*0-8027-6421-5*) Walker & Co.

Shields, Mary. Can Dogs Talk, Vol. 1. Gates, Donna, illus. 32p. (Orig.). (ps-3). 1991. pap. 10.00 (*0-9618348-1-1*); incl. tape 13.00 (*0-9618348-4-6*); write for info. Pyrola Pub.

—Loving a Happy Dog. Gates, Donna, illus. 32p. 1992. pap. 12.00 (*0-9618348-3-8*) Pyrola Pub.

Silverstein, Alvin & Silverstein, Virginia. Dogs: All about Them. LC 84-29723. (Illus.). 256p. (gr. 6 up). 1986. 12.95 (*0-688-04805-6*) Lothrop.

Spier, Peter. Peter Spier's Dogs. 1984. pap. 2.50 (*0-385-18196-5*) Doubleday.

Spinelli, Eileen. Puppies. (Illus.). 64p. (gr. k-4). 1992. PLB 13.75 (*1-878363-87-5*, HTS Bks) Forest Hse.

Spooner, J. B. The Story of the Little Black Dog. Seeley, Terre L., illus. LC 93-34690. 32p. (ps-3). 1994. 14.95 (*1-55970-239-7*) Arcade Pub Inc.

Squire, Ann. Understanding Man's Best Friend: Why Dogs Look & Act the Way They Do. LC 90-30631. (Illus.). 128p. (gr. 3-7). 1991. SBE 14.95 (*0-02-786590-8*, Macmillan Child Bk) Macmillan Child Grp.

Standiford, Natalie. The Bravest Dog Ever: The True Story of Balto. Cook, Donald, tr. LC 89-3465. (Illus.). 47p. (Orig.). (gr. 1-3). 1989. pap. 3.50 (*0-394-89695-5*) Random Bks Yng Read.

Stone, Lynn. Canids. LC 92-34486. 1993. 12.67 (*0-86625-439-0*); 9.50s.p. (*0-685-66271-3*) Rourke Pubns.

—Dingoes. (Illus.). 24p. (gr. k-5). 1990. lib. bdg. 11.94 (*0-86593-057-0*); lib. bdg. 8.95s.p. (*0-685-36370-8*) Rourke Corp.

Ullman, H. J. & Ullman, E. Spaniels. (Illus.). (gr. k-12). 1982. pap. 5.95 (*0-8120-2424-9*) Barron.

Unkelbach, Kurt. Both Ends of the Leash: Selecting & Training Your Dog. Petie, Haris, illus. (gr. 3-7). 1968. P-H.

Vanacore, Connie. New Guide to Junior Showmanship. (Illus.). 160p. 1994. 22.00 (*0-87605-653-2*) Howell Bk.

Vrbova, Zuza. Puppies. McAulay, Robert, illus. 48p. (gr. 2 up). 1990. PLB 9.95 (*0-86622-552-8*, J-002) TFH Pubns.

Wijngaard, Juan. Dog. Wijngaard, Juan, illus. LC 90-81895. 12p. (ps). 1991. bds. 3.95 (*0-517-58203-1*) Crown Bks Yng Read.

Wild Dog. (Illus.). 24p. (gr. k-5). 1987. PLB 9.95 (*0-8172-2704-0*); pap. 3.95 (*0-8114-6894-1*) Raintree Steck-V.

World Book Staff, ed. Childcraft Supplement, 5 vols. LC 91-65174. (Illus.). (gr. 2-6). 1991. Set. write for info. (*0-7166-0666-6*) Prehistoric Animals, 304p. About Dogs, 304p. The Magic of Words, 304p. The Indian Book, 304p. The Puzzle Book, 304p. World Bk.

Zenk, Heather. The Siberian Husky. LC 90-34315. (Illus.). 48p. (gr. 4-5). 1990. text ed. 12.95 RSBE (*0-89686-535-5*, Crestwood Hse) Macmillan Child Grp.

DOGS–FICTION

Abbott, Jennie. The Most Beautiful Dog in the World. Badenhop, Mary, illus. LC 87-14985. 96p. (gr. 5-8). 1988. PLB 9.89 (*0-8167-1187-9*); pap. text ed. 2.95 (*0-8167-1188-7*) Troll Assocs.

Adler, David A. My Dog & the Birthday Mystery. Gackenbach, Dick, illus. LC 86-14269. 32p. (gr. 1-4). 1987. reinforced bdg. 13.95 (*0-8234-0632-6*); pap. 5.95 (*0-8234-0710-1*) Holiday.

—My Dog & the Green Sock Mystery. Gackenbach, Dick, illus. LC 85-14145. 32p. (gr. 1-4). 1986. reinforced bdg. 13.95 (*0-8234-0590-7*) Holiday.

Adoff, Arnold. Friend Dog. Howell, Troy, illus. LC 80-7773. 48p. (gr. k-5). 1980. PLB 11.89 (*0-685-02080-0*, Lipp Jr Bks) HarpC Child Bks.

Allen, Jonathan. My Dog. Allen, Jonathan, illus. LC 89-30857. 32p. (gr. 1-2). 1989. PLB 18.60 (*0-8368-0095-8*) Gareth Stevens Inc.

Amery, H. Silly Sheepdog. (Illus.). 16p. (ps-3). 1992. pap. 3.95 (*0-7460-1412-0*) EDC.

Ancona, George. Sheep Dog. LC 84-20100. (Illus.). 64p. (gr. 5 up). 1985. 15.00 (*0-688-04118-3*); PLB 14.93 (*0-688-04119-1*) Lothrop.

Anderson, Peggy P. Wendle, What Have You Done? LC 93-11291. 1994. 13.95 (*0-395-64346-5*) HM.

Argueta, Manlio & Ross, Stacey. The Magic Dogs of the Volcanoes (Los perros magicos de los volcanoes) Simmons, Elly, illus. LC 90-2254. (SPA & ENG.). 32p. (gr. k-5). 1990. 13.95 (*0-89239-064-6*) Childrens Book Pr.

Armstrong, Jennifer. Little Salt Lick & the Sun King. Goodell, Jon, illus. LC 93-18673. 32p. (ps-3). 1994. 15.00 (*0-517-59620-2*); 15.99 (*0-517-59621-0*) Crown Bks Yng Read.

Arnosky, Jim. Gray Boy. LC 87-29337. (gr. 4-9). 1988. PLB 14.00 (*0-688-07345-X*) Lothrop.

Atelier Philippe Harchy Staff, illus. Walt Disney's One Hundred & One Dalmatians Puppy Love: Walt Disney's 101 Dalmatians Puppy Love. 10p. (ps-1). 1994. 4.95 (*1-56282-610-7*) Disney Pr.

Auch, Mary J. Bird Dogs Can't Fly. Auch, Mary J., illus. LC 93-2746. (ps-3). 1993. reinforced bdg. 15.95 (*0-8234-1050-1*) Holiday.

—The Latch-Key Dog. Smith, Cat B., illus. LC 93-18604. 1994. 13.95 (*0-316-05916-1*) Little.

Avrett, Robert. Timid Pup. (Illus.). (gr. 1-3). PLB 7.19 (*0-8313-0004-3*) Lantern.

Axworthy, Anni. Along Came Toto. Axworthy, Anni, illus. LC 92-52992. 32p. (ps-3). 1993. 12.95 (*1-56402-172-6*) Candlewick Pr.

Ayme, Marcel. Chien. Sabatier, Roland, illus. (FRE.). 72p. (gr. 1-5). 1990. pap. 10.95 (*2-07-031201-1*) Schoenhof.

Baillie, Marilyn. My Dog. (ps-3). 1994. pap. 6.95 (*0-316-07689-9*) Little.

Baker, Barbara & Winborn, Martha. Digby & Kate Again. (Illus.). (gr. k-3). 1994. pap. 3.25 (*0-14-036665-2*) Puffin Bks.

Balducci, Rita. Poky Little Puppy's Busy Counting Book. (ps-3). 1994. pap. 1.95 (*0-307-10015-4*, Golden Pr) Western Pub.

—Walt Disney's Lady & the Tramp. (ps). 1994. 3.95 (*0-307-12549-1*, Golden Pr) Western Pub.

Ball, Nancy. Boots: The Story of a Saint. Decker, Tim, illus. LC 88-72340. 44p. (Orig.). (gr. 2-5). 1989. pap. 5.00 (*0-916383-72-5*) Aegina Pr.

Ball, Zachary. Bristle Face. LC 93-10394. 208p. (gr. 5 up). 1993. pap. 3.99 (*0-14-036444-7*, Puffin) Puffin Bks.

Baltazzi, Evan S. Dog Gone West: A Western for Dog Lovers. Kyziridis, Gregory, illus. 115p. (Orig.). (gr. 7 up). 1994. pap. 3.95 (*0-918948-05-3*) Evanel. DOG GONE WEST is a western for dog lovers, young & old. It is the story of a farmer & his family migrating from Pennsylvania to California in the middle of the last century, narrated by their dog Buck. The trip, with its few good times & many tribulations, follows a true itinerary, each part of which is seen through the eyes of the dog, who has some unusual comments about his masters, their fellow travellers, the Indians & even the landscapes the wagon train is going through. DOG GONE WEST is overflowing with the love of Buck for his masters & their love for him. He shares with the readers his feelings of puzzlement, wonder & affection as he saves more than once the lives of members of his "family." "'How about it?' Montana took Ann by the hand. That was it! I jumped from behind the bush growling & showing my teeth. My sudden appearance, size & fierce expression took them by surprise & gave Matt a chance to grab his rifle. Pointing it at them, he ordered: 'Better leave! Now!' Figuring the odds, they apologized sheepishly that they meant no harm & left."
Publisher Provided Annotation.

Bannah, Max. Bulldog George. LC 93-20807. 1994. 4.25 (*0-383-03739-5*) SRA Schl Grp.

Barracca, Debra & Barracca, Sal. Maxi, the Hero. Buehner, Mark, illus. (ps-3). 1991. 12.95 (*0-8037-0939-0*); PLB 12.89 (*0-8037-0940-4*) Dial Bks Young.

Barracca, Sal & Barracca, Debra. The Adventures of Taxi Dog. Fogelman, Phyllis J., ed. Buehner, Mark, illus. LC 89-1056. 32p. (ps-3). 1990. 13.00 (*0-8037-0671-5*); PLB 12.89 (*0-8037-0672-3*) Dial Bks Young.

—Maxi, the Star. Ayers, Alan, illus. LC 91-44962. 32p. (ps-3). 1993. 13.99 (*0-8037-1348-7*); PLB 13.89 (*0-8037-1349-5*) Dial Bks Young.

Bayley, Monica & Schulz, Charles M. Snoopy Omnibus. LC 82-71285. (Illus.). 1983. 6.95 (*0-915696-54-1*); pap. 4.95 (*0-915696-81-9*) Determined Prods.

Becker, Jim & Mayer, Andy. Where Does Little Puppy Go? 1992. 4.95 (*0-590-44912-5*, Cartwheel) Scholastic Inc.

Benjamin, Alan. Buck. Morley, Carol, illus. LC 93-31161. 1994. 15.00 (*0-671-88718-1*, S&S BFYR) S&S Trade.

Benjamin, Carol L. The Wicked Stepdog. 128p. (gr. 5 up). 1986. pap. 2.50 (*0-380-70089-1*, Flare) Avon.

Benjamin, Saragail K. My Dog Ate It. LC 93-25218. 128p. (gr. 3-7). 1994. 14.95 (*0-8234-1047-1*) Holiday.

Berkley Staff. Beethoven's Second. 1993. pap. 4.50 (*0-425-13987-5*) Berkley Pub.

Billin-Frye, Paige, illus. The Sleepy Little Puppy. 12p. (ps). 1993. bds. 4.95 (*0-448-40541-5*, G&D) Putnam Pub Group.

Biros, Florence K. Dog Jack. Libb, Melva, ed. (Illus.). 192p. (Orig.). 1988. pap. 6.95 (*0-936369-22-1*) Son-Rise Pubns.

Biros, Florence W. Dog Jack. 2nd ed. (Illus.). (gr. 5 up). 1990. 7.95 (*0-936369-47-7*) Son-Rise Pubns.

Black, Sheila. Lassie. 128p. (gr. 3-7). 1994. pap. 3.50 (*0-14-036802-7*) Puffin Bks.

Blake, Robert J. Dog. Blake, Robert J., illus. LC 92-39313. 32p. (ps-3). 1994. 14.95 (*0-399-22019-4*, Philomel Bks) Putnam Pub Group.

Blaney, Christine. My Dog's Day: A Moving Picture Book. Blaney, Christine, illus. 8p. (ps). 1993. 11.99 (*0-670-85202-3*) Viking Child Bks.

Blau, Judith. Puppy Mitten's Present. Blau, Judith, illus. 7p. (ps). 1992. incl. puppet 5.99 (*0-679-83045-6*) Random Bks Yng Read.

Bly, Stephen. The Dog Who Would Not Smile. 128p. (gr. 4-7). 1992. pap. 4.99 (*0-89107-656-5*) Crossway Bks.

Bogaerts, Rascal & Bogaerts, Gert. Socrates. LC 92-24120. 1993. 14.95 (*0-8118-0314-7*) Chronicle Bks.

Bogart, Jo-Ellen. Daniel's Dog. Wilson, Janet, illus. 1992. pap. 3.95 (*0-590-43401-2*, Blue Ribbon Bks) Scholastic Inc.

Bonsall, Crosby N. Amazing the Incredible Super Dog. LC 85-45811. (Illus.). 32p. (gr. k-3). 1986. PLB 14.89 (*0-06-020591-1*) HarpC Child Bks.

—And I Mean It, Stanley. LC 73-14324. (Illus.). 32p. (gr. k-3). 1974. PLB 13.89 (*0-06-020568-7*) HarpC Child Bks.

Borden, Louise. Just in Time for Christmas. Lewin, Ted, illus. LC 93-40082. (ps-3). 1994. 14.95 (*0-590-45355-6*) Scholastic Inc.

Borovsky, Paul. George. Borovsky, Paul, illus. LC 89-2022. (ps up). 1990. 12.95 (*0-688-09150-4*); PLB 12.88 (*0-688-09151-2*) Greenwillow.

Boughton, Richard. Rent-a-Puppy, Inc. LC 93-41688. 1995. pap. 3.95 (*0-689-71836-5*, Atheneum) Macmillan.

Boyd, Lizi. Black Dog Red House. Boyd, Lizi, illus. (ps-2). 1993. 12.95 (*0-316-10443-4*) Little.

Boynton, Sandra. Doggies. 1984. 3.95 (*0-671-49318-3*, Little Simon) S&S Trade.

Braybrooks, Ann, adapted by. Walt Disney's One Hundred One Dalmatians. LC 90-85424. (Illus.). 96p. 1991. 14.95 (*1-56282-010-9*); PLB 14.89 (*1-56282-011-7*) Disney Pr.

—Walt Disney's One Hundred One Dalmatians. Dicicco, Gil, illus. LC 90-85425. 72p. (Orig.). (gr. 2-6). 1991. pap. 3.50 (*1-56282-013-3*) Disney Pr.

Breslow, Susan. I Really Want a Dog. LC 89-38567. (Illus.). 40p. (ps-3). 1990. 12.95 (*0-525-44589-7*, DCB) Dutton Child Bks.

Breslow, Susan & Blakemore, Sally. I Really Want a Dog. Kelley, True, illus. 40p. (ps-3). 1993. pap. 4.99 (*0-14-054941-2*, Puff Unicorn) Puffin Bks.

Brett, Jan. The First Dog. (Illus.). 28p. (ps-3). 1988. 13.95 (*0-15-227650-5*) HarBrace.

—First Dog. LC 88-222. (ps-3). 1992. pap. 5.95 (*0-15-227651-3*, Voyager Bks) HarBrace.

Bridwell, Norman. Clifford & the Grouchy Neighbors. Bridwell, Norman, illus. 32p. (gr. k-3). 1989. pap. 2.25 (*0-590-44261-9*); pap. 5.95 incl. cass. (*0-590-63437-2*) Scholastic Inc.

—Clifford Gets a Job. Bridwell, Norman, illus. 32p. (gr. k-3). 1985. pap. 2.25 (*0-590-44296-1*) Scholastic Inc.

—Clifford Goes to Hollywood. Bridwell, Norman, illus. 32p. (gr. k-3). 1990. pap. 2.25 (*0-590-44289-9*); pap. 5.95 incl. cass. (*0-590-63435-6*) Scholastic Inc.

—Clifford Grow Chart. 1993. pap. 2.95 (*0-590-63637-5*) Scholastic Inc.

—Clifford Takes a Trip. (ps-3). 1985. pap. 2.25 (*0-590-44260-0*) Scholastic Inc.

—Clifford Takes a Trip. 1991. pap. 5.95 incl. cassette (*0-590-63823-8*) Scholastic Inc.

—Clifford the Big Red Dog. Bridwell, Norman, illus. (ps-3). 1988. 2.25 (*0-590-44297-X*); pap. 5.95 incl. cassette (*0-590-63212-4*) Scholastic Inc.

—Clifford the Big Red Dog. Bridwell, Norman, illus. 32p. (ps-3). 1988. 10.95 (*0-590-40743-0*, Pub. by Scholastic Hardcover) Scholastic Inc.

—Clifford the Small Red Puppy. (ps-2). 1988. 2.25 (*0-590-44294-5*); incl. cassette 5.95 (*0-590-63211-6*) Scholastic Inc.

—Clifford the Small Red Puppy. (ps-3). 1990. 10.95 (*0-590-43496-9*) Scholastic Inc.

—Clifford the Small Red Puppy Follows His Nose. 32p. 1992. bds. 5.95 (*0-590-44345-3*, Scholastic Hardcover) Scholastic Inc.

—Clifford Treasury, No. I: Small Puppy - Big Red - Pals - Grouchy - Neighbors. 1991. pap. 9.00 (*0-590-63953-6*) Scholastic Inc.

—Clifford Treasury, No. II: Birthday - Puppy - Days - Family - Kitten. 1991. pap. 9.00 (*0-590-63952-8*) Scholastic Inc.

—Clifford Va de Viaje. rev. ed. Palacios, Argentina, tr. (SPA., Illus.). 32p. (Orig.). (gr. k-3). 1987. pap. 2.95 (*0-590-40844-5*) Scholastic Inc.

—Clifford Wants a Cookie. (Illus.). 16p. (ps-3). 1988. Book & Cookie Cutter Package. pap. 3.95 (*0-590-63282-5*) Scholastic Inc.

—Clifford, We Love You. (ps-3). 1991. pap. 2.25 (*0-590-43843-3*); pap. 5.95 incls. cass. (*0-590-63604-9*) Scholastic Inc.

—Clifford, We Love You. LC 94-4005. (gr. 2 up). 1994. 10.95 (*0-590-48612-8*) Scholastic Inc.

—Clifford's ABC. (ps-3). 1986. pap. 2.25 (*0-590-44286-4*) Scholastic Inc.

—Clifford's Bathtime. (ps). 1991. 3.95 (*0-590-44735-1*) Scholastic Inc.

—Clifford's Bedtime. (ps). 1991. 3.95 (*0-590-44736-X*) Scholastic Inc.

—Clifford's Big Book of Stories. LC 93-31367. (Illus.). 64p. (ps-3). 1994. 9.95 (*0-590-47925-3*, Cartwheel) Scholastic Inc.

—Clifford's Birthday Party. Bridwell, Norman, illus. 32p. (Orig.). (gr. k-3). 1991. 8.95 (*0-590-44232-5*); pap. 5.95 incl. cassette (*0-590-63237-X*) Scholastic Inc.

—Clifford's Birthday Party. 1993. pap. 19.95 (*0-590-73102-5*) Scholastic Inc.

—Clifford's Christmas. Bridwell, Norman, illus. 32p. (Orig.). (gr. k-3). 1987. 2.25 (*0-590-44288-0*); incl. cassette 5.95 (*0-590-63210-8*) Scholastic Inc.

—Clifford's Family. Bridwell, Norman, illus. 32p. (gr. k-3). 1984. pap. 2.25 (*0-590-44290-2*) Scholastic Inc.

—Clifford's Good Deeds. Bridwell, Norman, illus. 32p. (gr. k-3). 1985. pap. 2.25 (*0-590-44292-9*) Scholastic Inc.

—Clifford's Good Deeds. 1991. pap. 5.95 incl. cassette (*0-590-63824-6*) Scholastic Inc.

—Clifford's Halloween. Bridwell, Norman, illus. 32p. (gr. k-3). 1989. pap. 2.25 (*0-590-44287-2*); pap. 5.95 (*0-590-63436-4*) Scholastic Inc.

—Clifford's Happy Days: A Pop-up Book. Bridwell, Norman, illus. 16p. (Orig.). (gr. k-3). 1990. pap. 12.95 (*0-590-42926-4*) Scholastic Inc.

—Clifford's Kitten. Bridwell, Norman, illus. 32p. (gr. k-3). 1984. pap. 2.25 (*0-590-44280-5*) Scholastic Inc.

—Clifford's Manners. Bridwell, Norman, illus. 32p. (gr. k-3). 1987. pap. 2.25 (*0-590-44285-6*) Scholastic Inc.

—Clifford's Manners. LC 94-4004. 1994. 10.95 (*0-590-48697-7*) Scholastic Inc.

—Clifford's Noisy Day. (Illus.). 1992. bds. 3.95 (*0-590-45737-3*, 036, Cartwheel) Scholastic Inc.

—Clifford's Pals. Bridwell, Norman, illus. 32p. (gr. k-3). 1985. pap. 2.25 (*0-590-44295-3*) Scholastic Inc.

—Clifford's Peekaboo. (ps). 1991. 3.95 (*0-590-44737-8*) Scholastic Inc.

—Clifford's Puppy Days. 1989. pap. 1.95 (*0-590-42189-1*) Scholastic Inc.

—Clifford's Puppy Days. (ps-3). 1988. pap. 2.25 (*0-590-44262-7*) Scholastic Inc.

—Clifford's Puppy Days. LC 93-1802. (Illus.). 32p. (ps-6). 1994. 12.95 (*0-590-43339-3*, Cartwheel) Scholastic Inc.

—Clifford's Riddles. Bridwell, Norman, illus. 32p. (gr. k-3). 1984. pap. 2.25 (*0-590-44282-1*) Scholastic Inc.

—Clifford's Sticker Book. Bridwell, Norman, illus. 24p. (ps-3). 1984. pap. 3.95 (*0-590-33657-6*) Scholastic Inc.

—Clifford's Tricks. Bridwell, Norman, illus. 32p. (gr. k-3). 1986. pap. 2.25 (*0-590-44291-0*) Scholastic Inc.

—Clifford's Word Book. Bridwell, Norman, illus. 32p. (Orig.). (ps-1). 1990. pap. 2.25 (*0-590-43095-5*) Scholastic Inc.

—Clifford's Word Book. LC 94-4003. 1994. 10.95 (*0-590-48696-9*) Scholastic Inc.

—Count on Clifford. (Illus.). 32p. (gr. k-3). 1987. 5.95 (*0-590-33614-2*); pap. 2.25 (*0-590-44284-8*) Scholastic Inc.

—Count on Clifford. (Illus.). 32p. (ps-k). 1987. pap. 2.25 (*0-685-67546-7*) Scholastic Inc.

—La Familia de Clifford. (SPA.). 1993. pap. 28.67 (*0-590-73228-5*) Scholastic Inc.

Brown, Marc T. Arthur's Pet Business. (ps-3). 1990. 14.95 (*0-316-11262-3*, Joy St Bks) Little.

—Arthur's Puppy. LC 92-46342. (gr. 1-8). 1993. 14.95 (*0-316-11355-7*, Joy St Bks) Little.

Brown, Margaret W. The Noisy Book. new ed. Weisgard, Leonard, illus. LC 92-8322. 48p. (ps-1). 1939. 15.00 (*0-06-020830-9*); PLB 14.89 (*0-06-020831-7*) HarpC Child Bks.

—The Noisy Book. new ed. Weisgard, Leonard, illus. LC 92-8322. 48p. (ps-1). 1939. pap. 4.95 (*0-06-443001-4*, Trophy) HarpC Child Bks.

—The Quiet Noisy Book. new ed. Weisgard, Leonard, illus. LC 92-8320. 40p. (ps-1). 1993. 15.00 (*0-06-020845-7*); PLB 14.89 (*0-06-021220-9*) HarpC Child Bks.

—The Quiet Noisy Book. new ed. Weisgard, Leonard, illus. LC 92-8320. 40p. (ps-1). 1993. pap. 4.95 (*0-06-443215-7*, Trophy) HarpC Child Bks.

—The Sailor Dog. reissued ed. Williams, Garth, illus. 24p. (ps-k). 1992. write for info. (*0-307-00143-1*, 312-08, Golden Pr) Western Pub.

—The Seashore Noisy Book. new ed. Weisgard, Leonard, illus. LC 92-31433. 48p. (ps-1). 1993. 15.00 (*0-06-020840-6*); PLB 15.89 (*0-06-020841-4*) HarpC Child Bks.

—The Summer Noisy Book. new ed. Weisgard, Leonard, illus. LC 92-31435. 40p. (ps-1). 1993. 15.00 (*0-06-020855-4*); PLB 15.89 (*0-06-020856-2*) HarpC Child Bks.

Brown, Regina. Little Brother. Bornschlegel, Ruth, illus. (gr. 3-7). 1962. 8.95 (*0-8392-3019-2*) Astor-Honor.

Brown, Ruth. Our Puppy's Vacation. LC 87-5433. (Illus.). 32p. (ps-1). 1991. pap. 3.95 (*0-525-44701-6*, Puffin) Puffin Bks.

Brownell, Rick. Trixie. Shaw, Peter, illus. LC 93-169. 1994. write for info. (*0-383-03670-4*) SRA Schl Grp.

Burgess, Thornton W. Bowser the Hound. 19.95 (*0-8488-0391-4*) Amereon Ltd.

Burke, Timothy. Cocoa Puppy. Burke, Ann & Burke, Ann, illus. LC 89-50890. 32p. (Orig.). (ps-3). 1989. 5.00 (*0-9623227-0-9*) Thunder & Ink.

Burnford, Sheila. The Incredible Journey. 1985. pap. 3.99 (*0-553-15616-0*) Bantam.

—The Incredible Journey. 1984. pap. 3.99 (*0-553-27442-2*) Bantam.

Burningham, John. Cannonball Simp. Burningham, John, illus. LC 93-32369. 32p. (ps up). 1994. 15.95 (*1-56402-338-9*) Candlewick Pr.

—Courtney. LC 93-43508. (Illus.). 32p. (ps-2). 1994. 16.00 (*0-517-59883-3*); PLB 16.99 (*0-517-59884-1*) Crown Bks Yng Read.

—The Dog. 2nd ed. LC 93-10344. 24p. (ps). 1994. 6.95 (*1-56402-326-5*) Candlewick Pr.

Bushey, Jeanne. A Sled Dog for Moshi. (Illus.). 40p. (gr. 3-7). 1994. 14.95 (*1-56282-631-X*); PLB 14.89 (*1-56282-632-8*) Hyprn Child.

Butler, Dale. Blossom. Caffin, Liz, illus. LC 92-34265. 1993. 14.00 (*0-383-03620-8*) SRA Schl Grp.

Byars, Betsy C. Wanted...Mud Blossom. (gr. 4-7). 1991. 14.95 (*0-385-30428-5*) Delacorte.

Cachoritos. (SPA.). (ps-3). 1993. pap. 2.25 (*0-307-70078-X*, Golden Pr) Western Pub.

Caitlin, Stephen. You Dirty Dog. LC 87-19182. (Illus.). (gr. k-2). 1988. PLB 11.59 (*0-8167-1103-8*); pap. 2.95 (*0-8167-1104-6*) Troll Assocs.

The Call of the Wild. (Illus.). (gr. 3-12). 1965. deluxe ed. 12.95 (*0-448-06027-2*, G&D) Putnam Pub Group.

Calvert, Patricia. Bigger. LC 93-14415. 144p. (gr. 4-6). 1994. SBE 14.95 (*0-684-19685-9*, Scribners Young Read) Macmillan Child Grp.

Carlson, Nancy. Harriet & the Roller Coaster. 32p. (gr. k-3). 1984. pap. 3.95 (*0-14-050467-2*, Puffin) Puffin Bks.

—Poor Carl. (Illus.). 32p. (ps-3). 1991. pap. 3.95 (*0-14-050773-6*, Puffin) Puffin Bks.

Carratello, Patty. My Truck & My Pup. Spivak, Darlene, ed. Brostrom, Eileen, illus. 16p. (gr. k-2). 1988. wkbk. 1.95 (*1-55734-390-X*) Tchr Create Mat.

Carrick, Carol. The Foundling. Carrick, Donald, illus. LC 77-1587. 32p. (ps-4). 1979. 14.45 (*0-395-28775-8*, Clarion Bks) HM.

Carris, Joan D. The Greatest Idea Ever. Newsom, Carol, illus. LC 89-34516. 176p. (gr. 3-7). 1990. (Lipp Jr Bks); PLB 13.89 (*0-397-32379-4*, Lipp Jr Bks) HarpC Child Bks.

—Howling for Home. (ps). 1992. 12.95 (*0-316-13017-6*) Little.

Carter, Alden R. Dogwolf. LC 93-43518. (gr. 7 up). 1994. 14.95 (*0-590-46741-7*) Scholastic Inc.

Catalanotto, Peter. Dylan's Day Out. LC 88-36440. (Illus.). 32p. (ps-1). 1989. 14.95 (*0-531-05829-8*); PLB 14.99 (*0-531-08429-9*) Orchard Bks Watts.

—Dylan's Day Out. Catalanotto, Peter, illus. LC 88-36440. 32p. (ps-1). 1993. pap. 5.95 (*0-531-07034-4*) Orchard Bks Watts.

Cavanna, Betty. Going on Sixteen. LC 85-4877. 224p. (gr. 5-9). 1985. Repr. of 1946 ed. 11.95 (*0-688-05892-2*) Morrow Jr Bks.

Chapman, Cheryl. Snow on Snow on Snow. St. James, Synthia, illus. 1994. write for info. (*0-8037-1456-4*); PLB write for info. (*0-8037-1457-2*) Dial Bks Young.

Chenery, Janet. Wolfie. (ps-3). 1991. pap. 2.75 (*0-440-40496-7*) Dell.

Chorao, Kay. Annie & Cousin Precious. LC 93-32611. 1994. write for info. (*0-525-45238-9*, DCB) Dutton Child Bks.

—The Cherry Pie Baby. Chorao, Kay, illus. LC 88-2630. 32p. (ps-3). 1989. 12.95 (*0-525-44435-1*, DCB) Dutton Child Bks.

Christelow, Eileen. The Five-Dog Night. LC 92-36958. 1993. 14.45 (*0-395-62399-5*, Clarion Bks) HM.

Christian, Mary B. Sebastian (Super Sleuth) & the Copycat Crime. McCue, Lisa, illus. LC 93-7038. 64p. (gr. 2-6). 1993. SBE 11.95 (*0-02-718211-8*, Macmillan Child Bk) Macmillan Child Grp.

—Sebastian, Super-Sleuth, & the Flying Elephant. McCue, Lisa, illus. LC 94-14434. (gr. 2-6). 1994. 11.95 (*0-02-718252-5*) Macmillan.

—Sebastian (Super Sleuth) & the Impossible Crime. McCue, Lisa, illus. LC 91-28633. 64p. (gr. 2-6). 1992. SBE 11.95 (*0-02-718435-8*, Macmillan Child Bk) Macmillan Child Grp.

—Sebastian (Super Sleuth) & the Stars-In-His-Eyes Mystery. McCue, Lisa, illus. LC 86-21771. 64p. (gr. 2-5). 1987. RSBE 11.95 (*0-02-718540-0*, Macmillan Child Bk) Macmillan Child Grp.

Christopher, Matt. The Dog That Pitched a No-Hitter. Vasconcellos, Daniel, illus. (gr. 1-3). 1988. 13.95 (*0-316-14057-0*) Little.

—Dog That Pitched a No-Hitter. (ps-3). 1993. pap. 3.95 (*0-316-14103-8*) Little.

—The Dog That Stole Football Plays. Ogden, Bill, illus. 48p. (gr. 3-5). 1980. 14.95 (*0-316-13978-5*) Little.

Clayton, Elaine. Pup in School. Clayton, Elaine, illus. LC 92-18457. 24p. (ps-1). 1993. 12.00 (*0-517-59085-9*); PLB 12.99 (*0-517-59086-7*) Crown Bks Yng Read.

Cleary, Beverly. Henry & Ribsy. Darling, Louis, illus. LC 54-6402. 192p. (gr. 3-7). 1954. 12.95 (*0-688-21382-0*); PLB 12.88 (*0-688-31382-5*, Morrow Jr Bks) Morrow Jr Bks.

—Henry Huggins. Darling, Louis, illus. LC 50-8615. (gr. 3-7). 1950. 13.95 (*0-688-21385-5*); PLB 13.88 (*0-688-31385-X*, Morrow Jr Bks) Morrow Jr Bks.

—Ribsy. Darling, Louis, illus. LC 64-13263. (gr. 3-7). 1964. 15.95 (*0-688-21662-5*); PLB 15.88 (*0-688-31662-X*) Morrow Jr Bks.

—Ribsy. 1923. pap. 2.50 (*0-440-77456-X*) Dell.

—Ribsy. 144p. 1992. pap. 3.99 (*0-380-70955-4*, Camelot) Avon.

—Strider. Zelinsky, Paul O., illus. LC 90-6608. 192p. (gr. 3 up). 1991. 13.95 (*0-688-09900-9*); PLB 13.88 (*0-688-09901-7*) Morrow Jr Bks.

—Strider. 160p. 1992. pap. 3.99 (*0-380-71236-9*, Camelot) Avon.

—Two Dog Biscuits. rev. ed. DeSalvo-Ryan, Dyanne, illus. LC 85-18816. 32p. (ps-1). 1986. 11.95 (*0-688-05847-7*); lib. bdg. 11.88 (*0-688-05848-5*, Morrow Jr Bks) Morrow Jr Bks.

Clough, Fred. Sal T. Dog. Kirehoff, Dan, illus. 48p. (gr. 1-3). 1990. 12.95 (*0-89272-281-9*) Down East.

Coates, Anna. Dog Magic. (gr. 4-7). 1991. pap. 2.99 (*0-553-15910-0*, Skylark) Bantam.

Coffelt, Nancy. The Dog Who Cried Woof. LC 94-5653. 1994. write for info. (*0-15-200201-4*, Gulliver Bks) HarBrace.

—Dogs in Space. (Illus.). 32p. (ps-3). 1993. 14.95 (*0-15-200440-8*) HarBrace.

Cohen, Caron L. Bronco Dogs. Shepherd, Roni, illus. LC 90-47952. 32p. (ps-3). 1991. 12.95 (*0-525-44721-0*, DCB) Dutton Child Bks.

Cole, Joanna & Calmenson, Stephanie, eds. Give a Dog a Bone: Stories, Poems, Jokes, & Riddles about Dogs. Speirs, John, illus. LC 93-2536. 1994. write for info. (*0-590-46374-8*) Scholastic Inc.

Cone, Molly. Mishmash & The Sauerkraut Mystery. Shortall, Leonard, illus. (gr. 4-6). 1974. pap. 0.95 (*0-395-18556-4*) HM.

Coombs, Karen M. Saving Casey. 192p. (Orig.). 1992. pap. 3.50 (*0-380-76634-5*, Camelot) Avon.

Cooper, Margaret C. The Riddle of Changewater Pond. LC 93-15699. 128p. (gr. 4-7). 1993. SBE 13.95 (*0-02-724495-4*, Bradbury Pr) Macmillan Child Grp.

Copeland, Eric. Milton, My Father's Dog. Copeland, Eric, illus. LC 93-61795. 24p. (gr. 1-5). 1994. 14.95 (*0-88776-339-1*) Tundra Bks.

Coplans, Peta. Dottie. Coplans, Peta, illus. LC 92-41955. 1994. write for info. (*0-395-66788-7*) HM.

Corcoran, Barbara. Annie's Monster. LC 89-28121. 192p. (gr. 3-7). 1990. SBE 14.95 (*0-689-31632-1*, Atheneum Child Bk) Macmillan Child Grp.

Cory, Beverly. Dell & His Dot. Balkovek, James, illus. 64p. (Orig.). (ps-4). 1993. pap. 9.95 (0-8449-4252-9); FRE Translation Tool, "Trans-it" 4.95 (0-8449-4281-2); CHI Translation Tool, "Trans-it" 4.95 (0-8449-4283-9); GER Translation Tool, "Trans-it" 4.95 (0-8449-4282-0); SPA Translation Tool, "Trans-it" 4.95 (0-8449-4280-4) Good Morn Tchr.

—Gork & the Mop Tops. Balkovek, James, illus. 64p. (Orig.). (ps-4). 1993. pap. 9.95 (0-8449-4251-0); FRE Translation Tool, "Trans-it" 4.95 (0-8449-4285-5); CHI Translation Tool, "Trans-it" 4.95 (0-8449-4287-1); GER Translation Tool, "Trans-it" 4.95 (0-8449-4286-3); SPA Translation Tool, "Trans-it" 4.95 (0-8449-4284-7) Good Morn Tchr.

Cosgrove, Stephen. Heidi's Rose. Edelson, Wendy, illus. LC 90-71079. 32p. (gr. 3-6). 1991. 14.95 (1-55868-033-0) Gr Arts Ctr Pub.

Cousins, Lucy. Little Dog Laughed. LC 89-34517. (Illus.). 64p. (ps-k). 1990. 14.95 (0-525-44573-0, DCB) Dutton Child Bks.

Cresswell, Helen. Posy Bates, Again! Aldous, Kate, illus. LC 93-5789. 112p. (gr. k-4). 1994. SBE 13.95 (0-02-725372-4, Macmillan Child Bk) Macmillan Child Grp.

Crozat, Francois. I Am a Little Dog. (Illus.). 28p. (ps-k). 1992. 8.95 (0-8120-6276-0); miniature version o.p. 2.95 (0-8120-6286-8) Barron.

Currie, Quinn. Beautiful Joe. rev. & abr. ed. Heinonen, Susan, illus. Amory, Cleveland, intro. by. (Illus.). 72p. (gr. k-8). 1990. pap. 9.95 (0-9623072-1-1) S Ink WA.

Czarnecki, Lois R. The Six Wrinkled Woos. Almada, Laura, illus. 32p. (gr. k-3). 1992. 17.95 (0-9627275-0-4) Ohana Pr.

Dale, Penny. Wake up, Mr. B.! Dale, Penny, illus. LC 91-58763. 32p. (ps up). 1992. 14.95 (1-56402-104-1) Candlewick Pr.

Davis, Dawn S. A Good Dog to Have Around the House. LC 90-90462. (Illus.). 52p. (Orig.). (gr. 1). 1990. pap. 3.95 (1-879318-00-8) Magnolia South Pub.

—Motorcycle Dog. LC 90-72039. (Illus.). 52p. (Orig.). (gr. 2-4). 1990. pap. 3.95 (1-879318-01-6) Magnolia South Pub.

Day, Alexandra. Carl Goes to Daycare. (ps). 1993. 12.95 (0-374-31093-9) FS&G.

—Carlito en el Parque una Tarde: Carl's Afternoon in the Park. (SPA., Illus.). 32p. 1992. bds. 12.95 (0-374-31100-5, Mirasol) FS&G.

—Carl's Afternoon in the Park. (Illus.). 32p. 1991. bds. 12.95 (0-374-31109-9) FS&G.

—Carl's Masquerade. 1992. 12.95 (0-374-31094-7) FS&G.

—Carl's Masquerade. (ps). 1993. 5.95 (0-374-31090-4) FS&G.

—Good Dog, Carl. Day, Alexandra, illus. 36p. (Orig.). (ps up). 1991. (Green Tiger) S&S Trade.

—Paddy's Pay Day. Day, Alexandra, illus. (ps-3). 1989. 14.00 (0-670-82598-0, Puffin) Puffin Bks.

—Paddy's Pay-Day. Day, Alexandra, illus. (ps-3). 1991. pap. 4.00x (0-14-050963-1, Puffin) Puffin Bks.

DeJong, Meindert. Along Came a Dog. Sendak, Maurice, illus. LC 57-9265. 192p. (gr. 3-6). 1958. PLB 15.89 (0-06-021421-X) HarpC Child Bks.

—Along Came a Dog. Sendak, Maurice, illus. LC 57-9265. 192p. (gr. 4-7). 1980. pap. 4.95 (0-06-440114-6, Trophy) HarpC Child Bks.

—Hurry Home, Candy. Sendak, Maurice, illus. LC 53-8536. 224p. (gr. 4-7). 1953. PLB 14.89 (0-06-021486-4) HarpC Child Bks.

—Hurry Home, Candy. LC 53-8536. (Illus.). 244p. (gr. 4-7). 1972. pap. 3.50 (0-06-440025-5, Trophy) HarpC Child Bks.

Devlin, Wende & Devlin, Harry. The Trouble with Henriette. 1995. 15.00 (0-02-729937-6, Four Winds) Macmillan Child Grp.

De Warren, Shaun. The Harris Visits the Garden of Everything. Coupland, Gill, illus. 32p. (ps-3). 1985. cloth 12.95 (0-913299-21-9, Dist. by PGW) Stillpoint.

Dicks, Terrance. Goliath & the Buried Treasure. Littlewood, Valerie, illus. (gr. k-4). 1987. 7.95 (0-8120-5822-4); pap. 2.95 (0-8120-3819-3) Barron.

—Goliath at the Seaside. Littlewood, Valerie, illus. 52p. (gr. 2-4). 1989. pap. 2.95 (0-8120-4209-3) Barron.

—Goliath Goes to Summer School. Littlewood, Valerie, illus. 52p. (gr. 2-4). 1989. pap. 2.95 (0-8120-4210-7) Barron.

—Goliath's Birthday. Littlewood, Valerie, illus. 52p. (gr. 2-5). 1992. pap. 3.50 (0-8120-4821-0) Barron.

—Teacher's Pet. Littlewood, Valerie, illus. 52p. (gr. 2-5). 1992. pap. 3.50 (0-8120-4820-2) Barron.

Disney, Walt. Goofy Family Mix Up: A Mix & Match Book. (ps-3). 1993. 6.98 (0-453-03125-0) Mouse Works.

—Lady & the Tramp. (Illus.). 48p. (ps-6). 1988. 5.99 (0-517-66194-2) Random Hse Value.

—Oliver & Company. 1988. 5.99 (0-517-67004-6) Random Hse Value.

Disney, Walt, Productions Staff. Walt Disney's One Hundred & One Dalmatians. LC 74-10829. (Illus.). 48p. (ps-3). 1975. 6.95 (0-394-82571-3); lib. bdg. 4.99 (0-394-92571-8) Random Bks Yng Read.

Dobson, Danae. Woof & the Big Fire. 32p. 1990. write for info. (0-8499-8362-2) Word Inc.

—Woof, the Seeing-Eye Dog. 32p. 1990. write for info. (0-8499-8363-0) Word Inc.

Dodd, Lynley. Hairy Maclary's Show Business. LC 91-50554. (Illus.). 32p. (gr. 1-2). 1992. PLB 17.27 (0-8368-0763-4) Gareth Stevens Inc.

—Schnitzel Von Krumm's Basketwork. Dodd, Lynley, illus. LC 94-14560. 32p. (gr. 1 up). Date not set. PLB 17.26 (0-8368-1149-6) Gareth Stevens Inc.

A Dog for Keeps (EV, Unit 10. (gr. 3). 1991. 5-pack 21.25 (0-88106-781-4) Charlesbridge Pub.

Dog Walk. (Illus.). (ps-2). 1991. PLB 6.95 (0-8136-5113-1, TK2258); pap. 3.50 (0-8136-5613-3, TK2259) Modern Curr.

The Dog Who Came to Dinner. (Illus.). (ps-2). 1991. PLB 6.95 (0-685-50732-7, TK2294); pap. 3.50 (0-8136-5543-9, TK2295) Modern Curr.

Dogs Have Paws. (Illus.). (ps-2). 1991. PLB 6.95 (0-8136-5122-0, TK2616); pap. 3.50 (0-8136-5622-2, TK2615) Modern Curr.

Drew, David. Jock Jerome. Culio, Ned, illus. LC 92-31133. 1993. 2.50 (0-383-03636-4) SRA Schl Grp.

Duffey, Betsy. A Boy in the Doghouse. Morrill, Leslie, illus. LC 90-47751. 96p. (gr. 2-6). 1993. pap. 2.95 (0-671-86698-2, Half Moon Bks) S&S Trade.

—Lucky Christmas. Morrill, Leslie, illus. LC 93-41092. (gr. 2-5). 1994. pap. 13.00 (0-671-86425-4, S&S BFYR) S&S Trade.

—Lucky in Left Field. LC 91-4579. (ps-3). 1992. pap. 13.00 (0-671-74687-1, S&S BFYR) S&S Trade.

—Lucky on the Loose. Morrill, Leslie, illus. LC 92-21421. 1993. pap. 13.00 (0-671-86424-6, S&S BFYR) S&S Trade.

—Puppy Love. Natti, Susanna, illus. LC 92-12705. 64p. (gr. 2-6). 1992. 13.00 (0-670-84346-6) Viking Child Bks.

Duffy, James. Cleaver of the Good Luck Diner. LC 88-29906. (Illus.). 128p. (gr. 3-6). 1989. SBE 13.95 (0-684-18969-0, Scribners Young Read) Macmillan Child Grp.

Duncan, Lois. Hotel for Dogs. (gr. 4-7). 1991. pap. 3.25 (0-440-40435-5) Dell.

Durrell, Dennis, illus. Walt Disney's Lady & the Tramp: A Pop-up Book. LC 93-71380. 12p. (ps-3). 1994. 11.95 (1-56282-612-3) Disney Pr.

Eastman, P. D. Go, Dog, Go! (ps-1). 1986. pap. 6.95 incl. cassette (0-394-88328-4) Random Bks Yng Read.

—Perro Grande...Perro Pequeno: (Big Dog...Little Dog) De Cuenca, Pilar & Alvarez, Ines, trs. Eastman, P. D., illus. LC 81-12070. (SPA.). 32p. (ps-3). 1982. pap. 2.50 (0-394-85142-0) Random Bks Yng Read.

Eastman, Philip D. Big Dog, Little Dog: A Bedtime Story. (Illus.). (ps-1). 1973. pap. 2.50 (0-394-82669-8) Random Bks Yng Read.

—Go, Dog, Go. LC 61-7069. (Illus.). 72p. (gr. 1-3). 1961. 6.95 (0-394-80020-6); lib. bdg. 7.99 (0-394-90020-0) Random Bks Yng Read.

Ehrlich, Amy. Maggie & Silky & Joe. Blake, Robert, illus. LC 94-9149. 32p. (ps up). 1994. PLB 14.99 (0-670-83387-8) Viking Child Bks.

Enell, Trinka. Roll Over, Rosie. Gackenbach, Dick, illus. 32p. (ps-3). 1992. 13.45 (0-395-59340-9, Clarion Bks) HM.

Erickson, John. The Case of the Missing Cat: Discover the Land of Enchantment. (Illus.). 144p. 1990. 11.95 (0-87719-186-7); pap. 6.95 (0-87719-185-9); 2 cass. 15.95 (0-87719-187-5) Gulf Pub.

Erickson, John, tr. Hank el Perro Vaquero, No. 1. (SPA.). 112p. (gr. 3 up). 1992. pap. 6.95 (0-87719-216-2) Gulf Pub.

—Hank el Perro Vaquero, No. 2. 116p. 1992. pap. 6.95 (0-87719-217-0) Gulf Pub.

Erickson, John R. The Case of the Car-Barkaholic Dog. (Illus.). 118p. 1991. 11.95 (0-87719-198-0, 9198); pap. 6.95 (0-87719-199-9, 9199); incls. 2 cass. 15.95 (0-87719-200-6) Gulf Pub.

—The Further Adventures of Hank the Cowdog. Holmes, Gerald L., illus. 93p. (Orig.). (gr. 3). 1983. 9.95 (0-9608612-7-0); pap. 6.95 (0-9608612-5-4); tape 13.95 (0-916941-02-7) Maverick Bks.

—Hank the Cowdog: It's a Dog's Life. (Illus.). 100p. (Orig.). (gr. 3). 9.95 (0-916941-04-3); pap. 5.95 (0-9608612-9-7); talking book 13.95 (0-916941-03-5) Maverick Bks.

—Hank the Cowdog: Let Sleeping Dogs Lie. Holmes, Gerald, illus. 19p. (gr. 3 up). 1986. 9.95 (0-916941-15-9); pap. 6.95 (0-916941-14-0); talking book 13.95 (0-916941-16-7) Maverick Bks.

—Hank the Cowdog: The Case of the Hooking Bull, No. 18. 118p. 1992. 11.95 (0-87719-213-8); pap. 6.95 (0-87719-212-X); 2 cassettes 15.95 (0-87719-214-6) Gulf Pub.

—Hank the Cowdog, Vol. 19: The Case of the Midnight Rustler. Holmes, Gerald, illus. 116p. (Orig.). (gr. 4-6). 1992. 11.95 (0-87719-219-7); pap. 6.95 (0-87719-218-9); tape 15.95 (0-87719-220-0) Gulf Pub.

—Moonlight Madness. Holmes, Gerald L., illus. LC 94-14263. 118p. (Orig.). (gr. 3-12). 1994. 11.95 (0-87719-252-9); pap. 6.95 (0-87719-251-0); Audio cass. 15.95 (0-87719-253-7) Gulf Pub. BILLBOARD magazine reports that, "in the past twelve years HANK THE COWDOG has sold more than 90,000 audiobooks & more than a million books, starred in 23 titles, won (1994's) Audie Award for outstanding children's audio...& inspired a fan club with 4,000 members." In his latest adventure, #23 MOONLIGHT MADNESS, Hank meets Eddy the Rac, an orphan raccoon & must guard the crafty masked bandit every moment. Hero, philosopher & head of ranch security, HANK THE COWDOG is a "... marvelous situation comedy."-- SCHOOL LIBRARY JOURNAL. Written by real-life cowboy John Erickson, Hank is available in paperback ($6.95), hardcover ($11.95), & word-for-word cassette tapes ($15.95 two, hour-long, song-filled tapes performed by the author). Teacher's Guides: Grades K-2 & 3-6 embrace the whole-language approach. Now in Spanish. HANK EL PERRO VAQUERO paperbacks #1 through #6 are available in Spanish. For a free catalog all about the adventures of Hank the Cowdog: Head of Ranch Security contact -- Gulf Publishing Company, P.O. Box 2608, Houston, TX 77252-2608. 713-520-4444. FAX: 713-525-4647. Available from your favorite wholesaler.

Publisher Provided Annotation.

Ernst, Lisa C. Ginger Jumps. Ernst, Lisa C., illus. LC 89-38706. 32p. (ps-2). 1990. RSBE 14.95 (0-02-733565-8, Bradbury Pr) Macmillan Child Grp.

—Walter's Tail. Ernst, Lisa C., illus. LC 91-19948. 40p. (ps-2). 1992. RSBE 14.95 (0-02-733564-X, Bradbury Pr) Macmillan Child Grp.

Estes, Eleanor. Ginger Pye. Estes, Eleanor, illus. LC 51-10446. (gr. 3-7). 1951. 14.95 (0-15-230930-6, HB Juv Bks) HarBrace.

—Ginger Pye. Schwartz, Amy, contrib. by. 306p. (gr. 3-7). 1990. pap. 3.95 (0-15-230933-0, Odyssey) HarBrace.

Evans, Katie. Hunky Dory Ate It. Stoeke, Janet M., illus. LC 91-13992. 32p. (ps-1). 1992. 13.50 (0-525-44847-0, DCB) Dutton Child Bks.

—Hunky Dory Found It. Stoeke, Janet M., illus. LC 93-15826. 32p. (ps-k). 1994. 13.99 (0-525-45192-7, DCB) Dutton Child Bks.

Evans, Mark. Pepito: The Little Dancing Dog. Cugat, Xavier, illus. LC 78-65354. (gr. k-4). 1979. 6.95 (0-87592-063-2) Scroll Pr.

Farley, Walter. The Great Dane Thor. 192p. (gr. 4-7). 1980. pap. 1.50 (0-440-93095-2, LFL) Dell.

Feldman, Eve B. Dog Crazy. Nones, Eric J., illus. LC 91-11083. 112p. (gr. 2 up). 1992. 13.00 (0-688-10819-9, Tambourine Bks) Morrow.

Fidler, Kathleen. Flash the Sheepdog. (Illus.). 164p. (gr. 5-8). 1989. pap. 6.95 (0-86241-071-1, Pub. by Cnngt Pub Ltd) Trafalgar.

—Turk the Border Collie. 160p. (gr. 5-7). 1989. pap. 6.95 (0-86241-130-0, Pub. by Cnngt Pub Ltd) Trafalgar.

Finnigan, Joan. The Dog Who Wouldn't Be Left Behind. Beinicke, Steve, illus. 32p. (ps-2). 1991. 12.95 (0-88899-057-X, Pub. by Groundwood-Douglas & McIntyre CN) Firefly Bks Ltd.

Flack, Marjorie. Angus & the Cat. 40p. (ps-k). 1989. PLB 13.99 (0-685-01488-6); pap. 12.95 (0-685-01489-4) Doubleday.

Fleischman, Sid. Jim Ugly. Sewall, Marcia, illus. LC 91-14392. 144p. (gr. 3 up). 1992. 14.00 (0-688-10886-5) Greenwillow.

Flynn, Mary J. The Lost & Found Puppy. Flynn, Mary J., illus. 48p. (Orig.). (gr. k-1). 1991. pap. 10.95 (0-9623072-6-2) S Ink WA.

Follow That Puppy. LC 90-33877. 40p. 1991. pap. 12.95 jacketed (0-671-70780-9, Little Simon) S&S Trade.

The Fox & the Hound. 96p. 1988. 6.98 (1-57082-038-4) Mouse Works.

Fox, Paula. The Stone-Faced Boy. Mackay, Donald A., illus. LC 68-9053. 112p. (gr. 4-6). 1982. SBE 13.95 (0-02-735570-5, Bradbury Pr) Macmillan Child Grp.

Franklin, Kristine L. The Wolfhound. LC 94-14595. 1995. write for info. (0-688-13674-5); PLB write for info. (0-688-13675-3) Lothrop.

Fulton, Mary J. Walt Disney's One Hundred One Dalmatins. (ps-3). 1994. pap. 2.25 (0-307-12819-9, Golden Pr) Western Pub.

Gabriel, Howard W., III. Loving Memories from Dog to Dog. House, David J., illus. 32p. (Orig.). (gr. k-6). 1987. pap. 2.95 (0-936997-01-X) M & H Enter.

Gackenbach, Dick. A Bag Full of Pups. LC 80-23230. 32p. (gr. k-3). 1983. pap. 5.95 (0-89919-179-7, Clarion Bks) HM.

—Claude Has a Picnic. Gackenbach, Dick, illus. LC 92-8242. 32p. (ps-1). 1993. 14.95 (0-395-61161-X, Clarion Bks) HM.

—Claude the Dog. Gackenbach, Dick, illus. LC 74-3403. 32p. (ps-2). 1984. pap. 4.95 (0-89919-124-X, Clarion Bks) HM.

—Dog for a Day. Gackenbach, Dick, illus. LC 86-17514. 32p. (ps-1). 1989. (Clarion Bks); pap. 6.95 (*0-89919-851-1*, Clarion Bks) HM.
—What's Claude Doing? LC 83-14983. (Illus.). 32p. (ps-3). 1986. pap. 4.95 (*0-89919-464-8*, Clarion Bks) HM.
Gardiner, John R. Stone Fox. Sewall, Marcia, illus. LC 79-7895. 96p. (gr. 2-6). 1980. 14.00 (*0-690-03983-2*, Crowell Jr Bks); PLB 13.89 (*0-690-03984-0*, Crowell Jr Bks) HarpC Child Bks.
Garside, Alice H. The Dog & the Bone. Meeks, Catherine F., illus. 14p. (Orig.). (gr. k-2). 1990. pap. 2.10 (*1-882063-11-2*) Cottage Pr MA.
—The Dog & the Wolf. Meeks, Catherine F., illus. 20p. (Orig.). (gr. k-2). 1990. pap. 2.10 (*1-882063-08-2*) Cottage Pr MA.
George, Sally. Bad Dog, George! Mancini, Rob, illus. LC 92-34258. 1993. 4.25 (*0-383-03616-X*) SRA Schl Grp.
Geronimi, Clyde. Chips Quips. Geronimi, Clyde, illus. LC 83-72694. 55p. (gr. 4 up). 1983. pap. 3.95 (*0-939126-09-5*) Back Bay.
Gerrard, Roy. Jocasta Carr, Movie Star. LC 92-6751. 1992. 15.00 (*0-374-33654-7*) FS&G.
Gerstein, Mordicai. The New Creatures. LC 90-4128. (Illus.). 32p. (ps-3). 1991. PLB 14.89 (*0-06-022167-4*) HarpC Child Bks.
—Roll Over! LC 83-18884. (Illus.). 32p. (ps-1). 1988. 12.00 (*0-517-55209-4*) Crown Bks Yng Read.
Ghigna, Charles. Good Dogs, Bad Dogs. Catrow, David, illus. LC 92-52985. 32p. 1992. 7.95 (*1-56282-290-X*); PLB 10.89 (*1-56282-291-8*) Hyprn Child.
Gilson, Jamie. Double Dare Dog. Primavera, Elise, illus. LC 87-37855. 126p. (gr. 3-5). 1988. 12.95 (*0-688-07969-5*) Lothrop.
—Double Dog Dare. (Illus.). 1989. pap. 2.75 (*0-671-67898-1*, Minstrel Bks) PB.
Gipson, Fred. Old Yeller. LC 56-8780. (Illus.). (gr. 7-9). 1956. 22.00i (*0-06-011545-9*, HarpT) HarpC.
—Old Yeller. LC 56-8780. 176p. (gr. 5 up). 1990. pap. 3.95 (*0-06-440382-3*, Trophy) HarpC Child Bks.
—Old Yeller. 192p. 1992. Repr. PLB 15.95x (*0-89966-906-9*) Buccaneer Bks.
Girion, Barbara. Misty & Me. LC 90-31675. 144p. (gr. 3-7). 1990. pap. 3.95 (*0-689-71442-4*, Aladdin) Macmillan Child Grp.
Gleeson, Libby. The Great Big Scary Dog. Greder, Armin, illus. LC 93-13398. 32p. (ps up). 1994. 15.00 (*0-688-11293-5*, Tambourine Bks); PLB 14.93 (*0-688-11294-3*, Tambourine Bks) Morrow.
—Walking to School. McClelland, Linda, illus. LC 92-31945. 1993. 2.50 (*0-383-03602-X*) SRA Schl Grp.
Goble, Paul. The Gift of the Sacred Dog. Goble, Paul, illus. LC 80-15843. 32p. (gr. k-2). 1982. Repr. of 1980 ed. SBE 14.95 (*0-02-736560-3*, Bradbury Pr) Macmillan Child Grp.
—Gift of the Sacred Dog. LC 87-14817. (gr. k-3). 1984. pap. 4.95 (*0-02-043280-1*, Aladdin) Macmillan Child Grp.
Godden, Rumer. Fu-Dog. Littlewood, Valerie, illus. 64p. (ps-2). 1990. pap. 14.95 (*0-670-82300-7*) Viking Child Bks.
—Listen to the Nightingale. 192p. (gr. 5 up). 1992. 15.00 (*0-670-84517-5*) Viking Child Bks.
Gondosch, Linda. Brutus the Wonder Poodle. Dann, Penny, illus. LC 89-39377. 64p. (Orig.). (gr. 2-4). 1990. PLB 5.99 (*0-679-90573-1*); pap. 2.99 (*0-679-80573-7*) Random Bks Yng Read.
Gordon, Sharon. Home for a Puppy. Wheeler, Jody, illus. LC 86-30853. 32p. (gr. k-2). 1988. PLB 7.89 (*0-8167-0978-5*); pap. text ed. 1.95 (*0-8167-0979-3*) Troll Assocs.
Gottlieb, Dale. Big Dog. (Illus.). 32p. (ps-3). 1992. pap. 3.99 (*0-14-054431-3*) Puffin Bks.
Graham, Amanda. Always Arthur. Gynell, Donna, illus. LC 89-4474. 32p. (gr. 2-3). 1990. PLB 18.60 (*0-8368-0096-6*) Gareth Stevens Inc.
Graham, Margaret B. Benjy & His Friend Fifi. Graham, Margaret B., illus. LC 87-29374. 32p. (ps-3). 1988. HarpC Child Bks.
Greene, Inez. My Puppy. 8p. (ps-k). 1994. text ed. 3.95 (*0-673-36192-6*) GdYrBks.
Gregorie, Caroline. Patate Horreur (Uglypuss) (ps-2). 1994. 14.95 (*0-8050-3300-9*) H Holt & Co.
Griffith, Helen V. Dream Meadow. Barnet, Nancy, illus. LC 93-18175. 24p. (ps up). 1994. 14.00 (*0-688-12293-0*); PLB 13.93 (*0-688-12294-9*) Greenwillow.
—Foxy. LC 83-16392. 144p. (gr. 5-9). 1984. reinforced 11.95 (*0-688-02567-6*) Greenwillow.
—Plunk's Dreams. LC 88-34905. (Illus.). 32p. (ps up). 1990. 12.95 (*0-688-08812-0*); lib. bdg. 12.88 (*0-688-08813-9*) Greenwillow.
Gross, Lisa. The Half & Half Dog. Gross, Lisa, illus. LC 88-9347. 26p. (gr. k-6). 1988. PLB 14.95 (*0-933849-13-3*) Landmark Edns.
Groutage, Cor. The Dog Walkers. LC 93-32597. (gr. 4 up). 1995. write for info. (*0-679-85439-8*); PLB write for info. (*0-679-95439-2*) Knopf Bks Yng Read.
Guy, Rosa. Paris, Pee Wee & Big Dog. Binch, Caroline, illus. LC 85-1654. 112p. (gr. 4-6). 1985. 13.95 (*0-385-29407-7*) Delacorte.
Gwynne, Fred. Easy to See Why. LC 92-27705. 1993. pap. 14.00 (*0-671-79776-X*, S&S BFYR) S&S Trade.
Haas, Jessie. Busybody Brandy. Abolafia, Yossi, illus. LC 93-29569. 24p. 1994. 14.00 (*0-688-12792-4*); lib. bdg. 13.93 (*0-688-12793-2*) Greenwillow.
Hall, Donald. I Am the Dog, I Am the Cat. Moser, Barry, illus. LC 93-28060. (gr. 1 up). 1994. 15.99 (*0-8037-1504-8*); PLB 15.89 (*0-8037-1505-6*) Dial Bks Young.
Hall, L. The Soul of the Silver Dog. 1992. 16.95 (*0-15-277196-4*, HB Juv Bks) HarBrace.
Hall, Lynn. The Soul of the Silver Dog. 132p. (gr. 5-9). pap. 3.50 (*0-685-71034-3*) Random Bks Yng Read.
—Soul of the Silver Dog. LC 91-11072. (gr. 4-7). 1994. pap. 3.50 (*0-679-84758-8*) Knopf Bks Yng Read.
—Windsong. LC 91-46075. 80p. (gr. 6-8). 1992. SBE 12.95 (*0-684-19439-2*, Scribners Young Read) Macmillan Child Grp.
Hall, Roger. Julie Rescues Big Mack. Antonie, Joy, illus. LC 93-26217. 1994. 4.25 (*0-383-03755-7*) SRA Schl Grp.
Happy, Elizabeth. Bailey's Birthday. Chase, Andra, illus. LC 93-32519. 32p. (gr. 1-4). 1994. 16.95 (*1-55942-059-6*, 7658); video, tchr's. guide & storybook 79.95 (*1-55942-062-6*, 9377) Marshfilm.
Harper, Isabelle. My Dog Rosie. Moser, Barry, illus. LC 93-45380. (ps up). 1994. 13.95 (*0-590-47619-X*, Blue Sky Press) Scholastic Inc.
Harris, Christine. Oliver All Alone. Walters, Catherine, illus. LC 94-20453. 36p. (ps-2). 1994. 12.99 (*0-525-45340-7*, DCB) Dutton Child Bks.
Hasenav, Florence A. Pinkey. (Illus.). (gr. 1-6). 1975. 6.00 (*0-913042-02-1*) Holland Hse Pr.
Hasty, Kathy N. Murphy Wants to Be Famous. Newcomer, Carolyn, illus. 27p. (Orig.). (ps-2). 1991. pap. 3.99 (*0-9631480-0-1*) Story Time Pubns.
Hathorn, Libby. Thunderwith. 1991. 15.95 (*0-316-35034-6*) Little.
Hawkins, Laura. Figment, Your Dog, Speaking. (gr. 3-5). 1991. 160p. 13.45 (*0-395-57032-8*, Sandpiper); (Sandpiper) HM.
Haywood, Carolyn. Eddie's Friend Boodles. Stock, Catherine, illus. LC 91-3212. (gr. 1 up). 1991. 12.95 (*0-688-09028-1*) Morrow Jr Bks.
Hazen, Barbara S. Stay, Fang. LC 89-32359. (Illus.). 32p. (gr. k-3). 1990. SBE 13.95 (*0-689-31599-6*, Atheneum Child Bk) Macmillan Child Grp.
Heller, Nicholas. Happy Birthday, Moe Dog. LC 87-14851. (Illus.). 24p. (gr. k up). 1988. 11.95 (*0-688-07670-X*); lib. bdg. 11.88 (*0-688-07671-8*) Greenwillow.
Henkes, Kevin. Protecting Marie. LC 94-16387. 1995. write for info. (*0-688-13958-2*) Greenwillow.
Henry, Kim. Two Prayers for Patches. Stortz, Diane, ed. LC 94-1122. (Illus.). 28p. (ps-k). 1994. 5.49 (*0-7847-0201-2*) Standard Pub.
Henson, Jim. Dog City: The Big Squeak. (ps-3). 1994. pap. 2.25 (*0-307-12845-8*, Golden Pr) Western Pub.
Herman, Gail. What a Hungry Puppy! Gorbaty, Norman, illus. LC 92-24468. 32p. (ps-1). 1993. lib. bdg. 7.99 (*0-448-40537-7*, G&D); pap. 3.50 (*0-448-40536-9*, G&D) Putnam Pub Group.
Herriot, James. The Market Square Dog. Brown, Ruth, illus. 32p. 1991. pap. 6.95 (*0-312-06567-1*) St Martin.
Herzig, Alison C. The Big Deal. Gladden, Scott, illus. 80p. (gr. 3-7). 1992. 13.50 (*0-670-84251-6*) Viking Child Bks.
Hesse, Karen. Lester's Dog. Carpenter, Nancy, illus. LC 92-27674. 32p. (ps-2). 1993. 13.00 (*0-517-58357-7*); PLB 13.99 (*0-517-58358-5*) Crown Bks Yng Read.
—Sable. 1994. 14.95 (*0-8050-2416-6*) H Holt & Co.
Hewett, Joan. Rosalie. Carrick, Donald, illus. LC 86-7333. 32p. (ps-2). 1987. 13.95 (*0-688-06228-8*); PLB 13.88 (*0-688-06229-6*) Lothrop.
Hill, Eric. Donde Esta Spot? (Where's Spot?) Hill, Eric, illus. (SPA.). 22p. (ps-2). 1983. 12.95 (*0-399-21018-0*, Putnam) Putnam Pub Group.
—La Primera Navidad de Spot. Hill, Eric, illus. (SPA.). (ps-2). 1983. 12.95 (*0-399-21024-5*, Putnam) Putnam Pub Group.
—Spot at Home. (Illus.). 14p. (ps-k). 1991. bds. 3.95 (*0-399-21774-6*, Putnam) Putnam Pub Group.
—Spot at Play. Hill, Eric, illus. LC 84-17848. 14p. (ps-1). 1985. bds. 3.95 (*0-399-21228-0*, Putnam) Putnam Pub Group.
—Spot at the Fair. Hill, Eric, illus. LC 84-17849. 14p. (ps-1). 1985. bds. 3.75 (*0-399-21229-9*, Putnam) Putnam Pub Group.
—Spot Goes Splash! Hill, Eric, illus. 8p. (gr. k-1). 1984. vinyl foam-filled 3.95 (*0-399-21068-7*, Putnam) Putnam Pub Group.
—Spot Goes to a Party. (Illus.). 22p. (ps). 1992. 11.95 (*0-399-22409-2*, Putnam) Putnam Pub Group.
—Spot Goes to School. 22p. (ps-k). 1994. pap. 5.99 (*0-14-055282-0*) Puffin Bks.
—Spot Goes to the Beach. LC 84-18291. (Illus.). 22p. (gr. k). 1985. 11.95 (*0-399-21247-7*, Putnam) Putnam Pub Group.
—Spot Goes to the Circus. 22p. (ps-k). 1994. pap. 5.99 (*0-14-055297-9*) Puffin Bks.
—Spot Goes to the Farm. (Illus.). 22p. (ps-1). 1987. 11.95 (*0-399-21434-8*, Putnam) Putnam Pub Group.
—Spot in the Garden. (Illus.). 14p. (ps-k). 1991. bds. 3.95 (*0-399-21772-X*, Putnam) Putnam Pub Group.
—Spot on the Farm. Hill, Eric, illus. LC 84-17850. 14p. (ps-1). 1985. bds. 3.95 (*0-399-21230-2*, Putnam) Putnam Pub Group.
—Spot Pasea por el Bosque - Spot's Walk in the Woods. Hill, Eric, illus. (SPA.). 14p. (ps-k). 1994. 13.95 (*0-399-22675-3*) Putnam Pub Group.
—Spot Sleeps Over. (Illus.). 22p. (ps-k). 1990. 11.95 (*0-399-21815-7*, Putnam) Putnam Pub Group.
—Spot Sleeps Over: (Se Pasa la Noche) (SPA., Illus.). 22p. (ps-k). 1991. 12.95 (*0-399-21835-1*, Putnam) Putnam Pub Group.
—Spot Va Al Parque. (SPA., Illus.). 22p. (ps-k). 1993. 12.95 (*0-399-22345-2*, Putnam) Putnam Pub Group.
—Spot's Birthday Party. (Illus.). 1991. mini ed. 4.95 (*0-399-21770-3*, Putnam) Putnam Pub Group.
—Spot's First Christmas: Mini Edition. (Illus.). 22p. (ps). 1992. 4.95 (*0-399-22410-6*, Putnam) Putnam Pub Group.
—Spot's First Easter. (Illus.). 22p. (ps-1). 1988. 11.95 (*0-399-21435-6*, Putnam) Putnam Pub Group.
—Spot's First Easter: A Lift-the-Flap Book. (Illus.). 22p. (ps-k). 1993. 4.95 (*0-399-22424-6*, Putnam) Putnam Pub Group.
—Spot's First One-Two-Three Frieze. (ps). 1994. pap. 5.95 (*0-399-22773-3*, Putnam) Putnam Pub Group.
—Spot's First Walk. Hill, Eric, illus. 22p. (ps). 1981. 11.95 (*0-399-20838-0*, Putnam) Putnam Pub Group.
—Spot's First Walk. (Illus.). 16p. (ps-1). 1994. pap. 5.99 (*0-14-050725-6*) Puffin Bks.
—Spot's Friends. Hill, Eric, illus. 8p. (gr. k-1). 1984. vinyl foam-filled 3.95 (*0-399-21066-0*, Putnam) Putnam Pub Group.
—Spot's Toys. Hill, Eric, illus. 8p. (gr. k-1). 1984. 3.95 (*0-399-21067-9*, Putnam) Putnam Pub Group.
—Spot's Walk in the Woods. Hill, Eric, illus. 14p. (ps). 1993. 12.95 (*0-399-22528-5*, Philomel) Putnam Pub Group.
—Sweet Dreams, Spot! Hill, Eric, illus. 8p. (gr. k-1). 1984. 3.95 (*0-399-21069-5*, Putnam) Putnam Pub Group.
—Where's Spot? (Illus.). 16p. (ps-1). 1994. pap. 5.99 (*0-14-050740-X*) Puffin Bks.
Hilleary, Jane K. Fletcher & the Great Big Dog. Brown, Richard, illus. 32p. (gr. k-3). 1992. pap. 4.80 (*0-395-62982-9*, Sandpiper) HM.
Hiser, Constance. Night of the Werepoodle. Fisher, Cynthia, illus. LC 93-25732. 128p. (gr. 2-6). 1994. 14.95 (*0-8234-1116-8*) Holiday.
Hoest, Bunny. Howard Huge Comes to Stay. Reiner, John, illus. LC 91-23629. 32p. (Orig.). (ps-1). 1992. pap. 2.25 (*0-679-82033-7*) Random Bks Yng Read.
Hoff, Syd. Barkley. Hoff, Syd, illus. LC 75-6290. 32p. (gr. k-3). 1975. PLB 13.89 (*0-06-022448-7*) HarpC Child Bks.
Holley, Charles. The Chihuahua That Roared. 32p. 1993. pap. 8.95 (*0-9636754-0-0*) Sequitur Systs.
Homes, Patricia. Muffin's Book, Bk. II. Morehead, Arlene, illus. 40p. Date not set. pap. 8.95 (*0-9618379-6-9*) Parkside Pubns.
Hooks, William H. Dirty Dozen Dizzy Dogs-Bank Street. (ps-3). 1990. PLB 9.99 (*0-553-05892-4*, Little Rooster); pap. 3.50 (*0-553-34923-6*) Bantam.
Houghton, Anne. There Stood Our Dog. Smith, Craig, illus. LC 93-171. 1994. write for info. (*0-383-03719-0*) SRA Schl Grp.
The Housekeeper's Dog. 42p. (ps-3). 1992. PLB 13.27 (*0-8368-0885-1*) Gareth Stevens Inc.
Howard, Ellen. Murphy & Kate. Graham, Mark, illus. LC 93-26002. 1995. 15.00 (*0-671-79775-1*, S&S BFYR) S&S Trade.
Howe, James. Creepy-Crawly Birthday. Morrill, Leslie, illus. LC 90-35370. 48p. (gr. k up). 1991. 13.95 (*0-688-09687-5*); PLB 13.88 (*0-688-09688-3*) Morrow Jr Bks.
—Hot Fudge. Morrill, Leslie, illus. LC 89-13468. 48p. (gr. k up). 1990. 13.95 (*0-688-08237-8*); PLB 13.88 (*0-688-09701-4*, Morrow Jr Bks) Morrow Jr Bks.
—Rabbit Cadabra! Daniel, Alan, illus. LC 91-34656. 48p. (gr. k up). 1993. 15.00 (*0-688-10402-9*); PLB 14.93 (*0-688-10403-7*) Morrow Jr Bks.
—Return to Howliday Inn. Daniels, Alan, illus. LC 91-29505. 176p. (gr. 3-7). 1992. SBE 13.95 (*0-689-31661-5*, Atheneum Child Bk) Macmillan Child Grp.
Hughes, Francine. Beethoven's 2nd: The Movie Storybook. (gr. 5-8). 1993. pap. 6.95 (*0-448-40462-1*, G&D) Putnam Pub Group.
Hughes, Shirley. Dogger. Hughes, Shirley, illus. LC 87-33787. 32p. (ps-2). 1988. 11.95 (*0-688-07980-6*); PLB 11.88 (*0-688-07981-4*) Lothrop.
Hurwitz, Johanna. Aldo Peanut Butter. DeGroat, Diane, illus. 112p. (gr. 3-7). 1992. pap. 3.99 (*0-14-036020-4*) Puffin Bks.
Hutchings, Amy & Hutchings, Richard. Firehouse Dog. Hutchings, Richard, photos by. (Illus.). 32p. (ps-2). 1993. pap. 2.50 (*0-590-46846-4*, Cartwheel) Scholastic Inc.
Impey, Rose. No-Name Dog. LC 90-30143. (Illus.). 64p. (gr. 2-5). 1990. 10.95 (*0-525-44592-7*, DCB) Dutton Child Bks.
—No-Name Dog. Knox, Jolyne, illus. LC 92-18957. 64p. (gr. 2-5). 1992. pap. 3.99 (*0-14-036164-2*) Puffin Bks.
Incredible Journey. 1985. pap. 1.50 (*0-440-82001-4*) Dell.
Ingle, Annie. Free Puppies: My Puppy Loves Me. Barto, Bobbi, illus. 24p. (ps-2). 1994. pap. 2.50 (*0-679-86179-3*) Random Bks Yng Read.
Inkpen, Mick. Kipper. (ps-3). 1992. 14.95 (*0-316-41883-8*) Little.
—Kipper's Birthday. LC 92-28202. 1993. PLB write for info. (*0-15-200503-X*) HarBrace.
—Kipper's Toybox. 1992. write for info. (*0-15-200501-3*, Gulliver Bks) HarBrace.
Jennings, Linda. The Dog Who Found Christmas. Walters, Catherine, illus. 40p. (ps-2). 1993. 11.99 (*0-525-45155-2*, DCB) Dutton Child Bks.

Jensen, Patricia & Pepin, Muriel. Little Puppy Saves the Day. Geneste, Marcelle, illus. LC 91-46499. 24p. (ps-3). 1993. 6.99 (*0-89577-473-9*, Dist. by Random) RD Assn.

Jeram, Anita. The Most Obedient Dog in the World. LC 92-43768. 32p. (gr. 3 up). 1994. pap. 4.99 (*1-56402-264-1*) Candlewick Pr.

Jessel, Camilla. Puppy Book. Jessell, Camilla, photos by. LC 91-71825. (Illus.). 32p. (ps up). 1994. pap. 4.99 (*1-56402-279-X*) Candlewick Pr.

Johnson, Audean. Fuzzy As a Puppy. Johnson, Audean, illus. LC 92-80353. 14p. (ps). 1993. 8.00 (*0-679-83239-4*) Random Bks Yng Read.

Jones, Diana W. Dogsbody. LC 76-28715. 256p. (gr. 5-9). 1988. 11.95 (*0-688-08191-6*) Greenwillow.

—Dogsbody. LC 76-28714. 256p. (gr. 4-9). 1990. pap. 3.50 (*0-394-82031-2*) Random Bks Yng Read.

Jones, Jo. That Hardhead Cinnamon. Vansant, Jo, illus. LC 89-92753. 36p. (Orig.). (gr. 2-5). 1989. pap. 6.95 (*0-9602266-1-3*) Jo-Jo Pubns.

Joseph, Vivienne. New Tricks. Rees, Genevieve, illus. LC 93-9286. 1994. write for info. (*0-383-03704-2*) SRA Schl Grp.

K, Lisa. The Adventures of Frenchy & Joe. 1993. 12.95 (*0-533-10415-7*) Vantage.

Kalman, Maira. Max in Hollywood, Baby. Kalman, Maira, illus. 32p. 1992. 15.00 (*0-670-84479-9*) Viking Child Bks.

—Max Makes a Million. 1990. 15.00 (*0-670-83545-5*) Viking Child Bks.

Keast, Winifred. What Happened to Duchess's Pups? (Illus.). 92p. (Orig.). (gr. 7 up). 1984. pap. 10.00 (*0-9613847-0-0*); PLB 5.00 (*0-9613847-1-9*) W Keast.

Keats, Ezra J. Kitten for a Day. Keats, Ezra J., illus. LC 92-40563. 32p. (ps-1). 1993. pap. 4.95 (*0-689-71737-7*, Aladdin) Macmillan Child Grp.

—Silba por Willie: (Whistle for Willie) (SPA., Illus.). 40p. (ps-1). 1992. 14.00 (*0-670-84395-4*) Viking Child Bks.

—Whistle for Willie. Keats, Ezra J., illus. LC 64-13595. (ps-1). 1977. pap. 4.50 (*0-14-050202-5*, Puffin) Puffin Bks.

—Whistle for Willie. Keats, Ezra J., illus. (ps-1). 1964. pap. 14.00 (*0-670-76240-7*) Viking Child Bks.

Keller, Debra. The Trouble with Mister. McNeill, Shannon, illus. LC 94-4048. 1995. 13.95 (*0-8118-0358-9*) Chronicle Bks.

Keller, Holly. Goodbye, Max. Keller, Holly, illus. LC 86-4680. 32p. (ps-3). 1987. 12.95 (*0-688-06561-9*); PLB 12.88 (*0-688-06562-7*) Greenwillow.

Kellogg, Steven. Pinkerton, Behave! Kellogg, Steven, illus. LC 78-31794. (ps-2). 1979. 13.95 (*0-8037-6573-8*); PLB 13.89 (*0-8037-6575-4*) Dial Bks Young.

—Pinkerton, Behave! Kellogg, Steven, illus. 32p. (gr. k-3). 1982. pap. 4.95 (*0-8037-7250-5*) Dial Bks Young.

—A Rose for Pinkerton. Kellogg, Steven, illus. LC 81-65848. 32p. (ps-3). 1981. 14.00 (*0-8037-7502-4*); PLB 12.89 (*0-8037-7503-2*) Dial Bks Young.

—Tallyho, Pinkerton! Kellogg, Steven, illus. LC 82-70198. 32p. (ps-3). 1983. 14.95 (*0-8037-8731-6*) Dial Bks Young.

Kent, Lisa. Hilde Knows: Someone Cries for the Children. Machlin, Mikki, illus. 48p. (Orig.). (gr. 1-7). 1994. pap. 6.95 (*1-880396-38-6*, JP9638-6) Jalmar Pr. Hilde, a wire-haired dachshund, is kidnapped from her happy home & held for ransom by a cruel man & his wife. In their home, Hilde sees how treacherous humans can be to their own child, Marybelle. Hilde becomes the little girl's only friend & confidant. When they are rescued, Marybelle finds love & happiness in a new home & Hilde is reunited with her family. This story, told by Hilde, helps children look at a scary subject, child abuse, from a safe distance & viewpoint: through the eyes of a dog. This removes the onus of self-identification, allowing easy transference by the young reader or audience. HILDE KNOWS reinforces the safety rules we try to teach our children in a unique way & helps children heal & find safety. It clearly demonstrates the dangers of succumbing to temptation, taking bad advice from a friend, & accepting gifts from a stranger. The book includes pages written by Dr. Stanley D. Machlin, a psychiatrist, outlining how caring adults can use the book with a child. Unshaded drawings invite children to color & draw - an important tool in therapeutic settings. Both problem & solution are presented in this meaningful little book.
Publisher Provided Annotation.

Khalsa, Dayal K. I Want a Dog. Khalsa, Dayal K., illus. 32p. (ps-4). 1994. pap. 5.99 (*0-517-88199-3*, Clarkson Potter) Crown Bks Yng Read.

—Julian. Khalsa, Dayal K., illus. 24p. (gr. k-8). 1989. 17.95 (*0-88776-237-9*) Tundra Bks.

Kim, Joy. Come on Up. Harvey, Paul, illus. LC 81-2356. 32p. (gr. k-2). 1981. PLB 11.59 (*0-89375-511-7*); pap. text ed. 2.95 (*0-89375-512-5*) Troll Assocs.

Kimmelman, Leslie. Frannie's Fruits. Mathers, Petra, illus. LC 88-17637. 32p. (ps-3). 1989. PLB 14.89 (*0-06-023164-5*) HarpC Child Bks.

King-Smith, Dick. The Invisible Dog. Roth, Roger, illus. LC 92-26978. 80p. (gr. 2-5). 1993. 14.00 (*0-517-59424-2*); PLB 14.99 (*0-517-59425-0*) Crown Bks Yng Read.

Kjelgaard, Jim. Big Red. 224p. (gr. 4-7). 1992. pap. 3.99 (*0-553-15434-6*, Skylark) Bantam.

—Big Red. Kuhn, Bob, illus. 254p. (gr. 6 up). 1956. 16.95 (*0-8234-0007-7*) Holiday.

—Desert Dog. LC 56-14250. (gr. 5 up). 1975. pap. 2.75 (*0-553-15491-5*) Bantam.

—Irish Red: Son of Big Red. large type ed. (gr. 4-8). 1984. pap. 3.99 (*0-553-15546-6*) Bantam.

—A Nose for Trouble. 1984. pap. 3.50 (*0-553-15578-4*) Bantam.

—Outlaw Red. (gr. 4-8). 1977. pap. 2.75 (*0-553-15535-0*) Bantam.

—Outlaw Red. 230p. (gr. 6 up). 1953. 15.95 (*0-8234-0084-0*) Holiday.

—Outlaw Red. 1985. pap. 3.99 (*0-553-15686-1*) Bantam.

—Snow Dog. 160p. 1980. pap. 2.95 (*0-553-15365-X*) Bantam.

—Snow Dog. 1983. pap. 3.99 (*0-553-15560-1*) Bantam.

—Snow Dog. (gr. 4-7). 1992. 16.75 (*0-8446-6595-9*) Peter Smith.

—Wild Trek. 1984. pap. 3.99 (*0-553-15687-X*) Bantam.

—Wild Trek. (gr. 4-7). 1992. 16.75 (*0-8446-6594-0*) Peter Smith.

Knight, Eric M. Lassie Come Home. 234p. 1981. Repr. PLB 16.95x (*0-89966-346-X*) Buccaneer Bks.

—Lassie Come Home. (gr. k-6). 1989. pap. 4.95 (*0-440-40136-4*, YB) Dell.

—Lassie Come Home. 224p. 1981. Repr. PLB 12.95x (*0-89967-020-2*) Harmony Raine.

—Lassie Come Home. Kirmse, Marguerite, illus. LC 78-3570. 265p. (gr. 4-6). 1978. 16.95 (*0-8050-0721-0*, Bks Young Read) H Holt & Co.

—Lassie Come Home. (gr. 4-7). 1992. pap. 3.50 (*0-440-40750-8*) Dell.

—Lassie Come Home. 1992. pap. 3.50 (*0-440-40760-5*) Dell.

Komaiko, Leah. Great Aunt Ida & Her Great Dane, Doc. Schindler, Stephen D., illus. LC 92-34196. 1994. 14.95 (*0-385-30682-2*) Doubleday.

Kontoyiannaki, Elizabeth. Bozo Is a Dog. Kontoyiannaki, Elizabeth, illus. 17p. (gr. k-3). 1992. pap. 8.95 (*1-895583-44-6*) MAYA Pubs.

Kopper, Lisa. Daisy Thinks She's a Baby. LC 92-44539. (gr. 1-8). 1994. 10.00 (*0-679-84723-5*); PLB 10.99 (*0-679-94723-X*) Knopf Bks Yng Read.

Korman, Justine. Yellow Dog. (gr. 4-7). 1994. pap. 2.95 (*0-8167-3470-4*) Troll Assocs.

Korschunow, Irina. Piebald Pup. Oberlander, Gerhard, illus. (gr. k-3). 1959. 9.95 (*0-8392-3026-5*) Astor-Honor.

Kreloff, Elliot, illus. My Big Puppy Book. (ps-k). 1993. Set, lg. bk. 12p., small bk. 6p. bds. 4.95 (*1-56293-359-0*) McClanahan Bk.

Kunhardt, Dorothy. Pat the Puppy. (ps). 1993. 6.95 (*0-307-12004-X*, Golden Pr) Western Pub.

Kuskin, Karla. City Dog. Kuskin, Karla, illus. LC 93-8252. (ps-3). 1994. 14.95 (*0-395-66138-2*, Clarion Bks) HM.

Laden, Nina. The Night I Followed the Dog. LC 93-31008. 1994. 13.95 (*0-8118-0647-2*) Chronicle Bks.

LaFleur, Tom & Brennan, Gale. Henry the Hound. Flint, Russ, illus. 16p. (Orig.). (gr. k-6). 1982. pap. 1.25 (*0-685-05556-6*) Brennan Bks.

Laird, Elizabeth. The Day Patch Stood Guard. Reeder, Colin, illus. LC 90-11153. 32p. (gr. k up). 1991. 11.95 (*0-688-10239-5*, Tambourine Bks); PLB 11.88 (*0-688-10240-9*, Tambourine Bks) Morrow.

Langley, Bill & Dias, Ron, illus. Walt Disney's One Hundred One Dalmatians. (ps-2). 1991. write for info. (*0-307-12346-4*, Golden Pr) Western Pub.

Larson, Wendy. Puppy Love. (gr. 4-8). 1993. pap. 2.50 (*0-448-40463-X*, G&D) Putnam Pub Group.

Lauber, Patricia. Living with Dinosaurs. Henderson, Doug, illus. LC 90-43265. 48p. (gr. 1-5). 1991. SBE 16.95 (*0-02-754521-0*, Bradbury Pr) Macmillan Child Grp.

Lawlor, Laurie. Second-Grade Dog. Levine, Abby, ed. Fiammenghi, Gioia, illus. LC 84-22700. 40p. (gr. k-3). 1990. 13.95 (*0-8075-7280-2*) A Whitman.

Leemis, Ralph. Smart Dog. (Illus.). 32p. (ps-3). 1993. 14.95 (*1-56397-109-7*) Boyds Mills Pr.

Leonard, Marcia. Laura Jean the Yard Sale Queen. Brook, Bonnie, ed. Iosa, Ann W., illus. LC 89-70304. 24p. (ps-1). 1990. 4.95 (*0-671-70405-2*); PLB 6.95 (*0-671-70401-X*) Silver Pr.

Lerangis, Peter. Bingo, Movie Tie In. 144p. 1991. pap. 2.95 (*0-590-45277-0*, Point) Scholastic Inc.

Leroe, Ellen. Ghost Dog. Basso, Bill, illus. 64p. (gr. 2-5). 1994. pap. 2.95 (*0-7868-1003-3*) Hyprn Ppbks.

LeRoy, Gen. Taxi Cat & Huey. Ritz, Karen, illus. LC 90-27383. 144p. (gr. 3-7). 1992. 14.00 (*0-06-021768-5*); PLB 13.89 (*0-06-021769-3*) HarpC Child Bks.

Levy. Cleo & Coyote. Date not set. 15.00 (*0-06-024271-X*); PLB 14.89 (*0-06-024272-8*) HarpC Child Bks.

Lewis, J. Patrick. One Dog Day. Ramsey, Marcy, illus. LC 92-24573. 64p. (gr. 2-5). 1993. SBE 12.95 (*0-689-31808-1*, Atheneum Child Bk) Macmillan Child Grp.

Lewis, Thomas P. Call for Mr. Sniff. Woldin, Beth W., illus. LC 79-2679. 64p. (gr. k-3). 1981. HarpC Child Bks.

Lexau, Joan M. Emily & the Klunky Baby & the Next-Door Dog. Alexander, Martha, illus. LC 77-181789. 40p. (ps-3). 1972. 5.95 (*0-8037-2309-1*) Dial Bks Young.

—Trouble Will Find You. Chesworth, Michael, illus. LC 93-6813. (ps-6). 1994. 13.95 (*0-395-64380-5*) HM.

Lindenbaum, Pija. Boodil, My Dog. Charbonnet, Gabrielle, retold by. LC 92-13172. (Illus.). 48p. (ps-2). 1992. 14.95 (*0-8050-2444-1*, Bks Young Read) H Holt & Co.

Lindgren, Barbro. Sam's Cookie. Eriksson, Eva, illus. LC 82-3419. 32p. (gr. k-3). 1982. 6.95 (*0-688-01267-1*) Morrow Jr Bks.

—Sam's Teddy Bear. Eriksson, Eva, illus. LC 82-3418. 32p. (gr. k-3). 1982. 5.95 (*0-688-01270-1*) Morrow Jr Bks.

—The Wild Baby Gets a Puppy: Swedish Edition. Prelutsky, Jack, tr. Eriksson, Eva, illus. LC 87-212. 32p. (ps-3). 1988. Repr. of 1985 ed. 11.95 (*0-688-06711-5*); lib. bdg. 11.88 (*0-688-06712-3*) Greenwillow.

Lindman, Maj. Snipp, Snapp, Snurr & the Seven Dogs. (Illus.). 32p. 1993. Repr. lib. bdg. 14.95x (*1-56849-007-0*) Buccaneer Bks.

Lippert, Donald F. Shag & the Bouncing Ball. Hedden, Randall, illus. 32p. (ps). 1989. write for info. Pastel Pubns.

Little, Jane. Spook. Larsen, Suzanne K., illus. LC 90-31296. 128p. (gr. 2-5). 1990. pap. 3.95 (*0-689-71417-3*, Aladdin) Macmillan Child Grp.

Littleton, Mark. Secrets of Moonlight Mountain. 1993. pap. 3.99 (*1-56507-960-4*) Harvest Hse.

London, Jack. Call of the Wild. (gr. 6 up). 1964. pap. 2.25 (*0-8049-0030-2*, CL-30) Airmont.

—The Call of the Wild. new ed. Platt, Kin, ed. Carrillo, Fred, illus. LC 73-75461. 64p. (Orig.). (gr. 5-10). 1973. pap. 2.95 (*0-88301-095-X*) Pendulum Pr.

—The Call of the Wild. 128p. (gr. 3-7). 1983. pap. 2.99 (*0-14-035000-4*, Puffin) Puffin Bks.

—Call of the Wild. Hitchner, Earle, ed. De John, Marie, illus. LC 89-33890. 48p. (gr. 3-6). 1990. PLB 12.89 (*0-8167-1863-6*); pap. text ed. 3.95 (*0-8167-1864-4*) Troll Assocs.

—Call of the Wild. 128p. (gr. 9-12). 1990. pap. 2.50 (*0-8125-0432-1*) Tor Bks.

—The Call of the Wild. 1991. 12.99 (*0-517-06003-5*) Random Hse Value.

—Call of the Wild. (Illus.). 1991. pap. 2.95 (*1-56156-094-4*) Kidsbks.

—The Call of the Wild. (gr. 8). 1991. pap. write for info. (*0-663-56265-1*) Silver Burdett Pr.

—The Call of the Wild. Moser, Barry, illus. Paulsen, Gary, intro. by. LC 93-18409. (Illus.). (gr. 4 up). 1994. 19.95 (*0-02-759455-6*) Macmillan.

—White Fang. new & abr. ed. Farr, Naunerle, ed. Carrillo, Fred, illus. (gr. 4-12). 1977. pap. text ed. 2.95 (*0-88301-271-5*) Pendulum Pr.

—White Fang. 256p. (gr. 6 up). 1986. pap. 3.25 (*0-590-42591-9*) Scholastic Inc.

—White Fang. 224p. 1989. pap. 2.50 (*0-8125-0512-3*) Tor Bks.

—White Fang: Illustrated Classics. Arneson, D. J., ed. Walker, Karen, illus. 128p. (Orig.). 1990. pap. 2.95 (*0-942025-84-9*) Kidsbks.

London, Jack, et al. The Call of the Wild. (Illus.). 52p. Date not set. pap. 4.95 (*1-57209-010-3*) Classics Int Ent.

Lorenz, Lee. Hugo & the Spacedog. Lorenz, Lee, illus. LC 82-22960. 30p. (ps-3). 1986. P-H.

Lowrey, Janette S. The Poky Little Puppy. Tenggren, Gustaf, illus. 24p. (ps-k). 1992. Repr. of 1942 ed. write for info. (*0-307-10394-3*, 10394, Pub. by Golden Bks) Western Pub.

—The Poky Little Puppy. Hansen, Rosanna, adapted by. Chandler, Jean, illus. 14p. (ps-k). 1992. bds. write for info. (*0-307-12333-2*, 12333, Golden Pr) Western Pub.

McConnell, Nancy P. Dusty D. Dawg Has Feelings, Too! Gress, Jonna, ed. (Illus.). 16p. (ps-3). 1992. pap. text ed. 14.25 (*0-944943-15-2*, CODE 20018-8) Current Inc.

McCue, Lisa, illus. Ten Little Puppy Dogs. LC 86-63577. 28p. (ps). 1987. 2.95 (*0-394-89149-X*) Random Bks Yng Read.

McDonnell, Janet. The Fourth of July. Endres, Helen, illus. LC 94-4827. 32p. (ps-2). 1994. PLB 16.40 (*0-516-00694-0*); pap. 3.95 (*0-516-40694-9*) Childrens.

McElroy, Eugene J. Needle-Nosed Ned. LC 89-50144. (gr. 4-6). 1989. pap. 5.00 (*0-932433-54-5*) Windswept Hse.

McGeorge, Constance W. Boomer's Big Day. Whyte, Mary, illus. LC 93-27273. 1994. 12.95 (*0-8118-0526-3*) Chronicle Bks.

Macht, Philip. Wonderpup. Faust, Jeff, illus. 40p. (gr. 4-6). 1992. 15.00 (*0-930339-03-7*) Maxrom Pr.
McInerney, Judith W. Judge Benjamin: The Superdog Gift. Morrill, Leslie, illus. 128p. (gr. 2-4). 1987. pap. 2.95 (*0-8167-1043-0*) Troll Assocs.
McKinley, Robin. Rowan. Ruff, Donna, illus. LC 91-31809. 24p. (ps-4). 1992. 14.00 (*0-688-10682-X*); PLB 13.93 (*0-688-10683-8*) Greenwillow.
MacLachlan, Patricia. Three Names. Pertzoff, Alexander, illus. LC 90-4444. 32p. (gr. k-4). 1991. 14.95 (*0-06-024035-0*); PLB 14.89 (*0-06-024036-9*) HarpC Child Bks.
McLean, Janet. Hector & Maggie. McLean, Andrew, illus. 32p. (Orig.). (gr. k-2). 1993. 16.95 (*0-04-442162-1*, Pub. by Allen & Unwin Aust Pty AT); pap. 6.95 (*0-04-442245-8*, Pub. by Allen & Unwin Aust Pty AT) IPG Chicago.
—Oh, Kipper! McLean, Andrew, illus. 32p. (Orig.). (gr. k-2). 1993. 16.95 (*1-86373-013-3*, Pub. by Allen & Unwin Aust Pty AT); pap. 6.95 (*1-86373-080-X*, Pub. by Allen & Unwin Aust Pty AT) IPG Chicago.
McMillan, Bruce & McMillan, Brett. Puniddles. McMillan, Bruce, illus. (gr. 2 up). 1982. pap. 4.80 (*0-395-32076-3*) HM.
Maddox, Tony. Fergus's Upside-Down Day. LC 94-16656. 1994. write for info. (*0-8120-6471-2*); pap. write for info. (*0-8120-9074-8*) Barron.
Maddux, Bob, et al. The Dog That Went Too Fast. French, Marty, et al, illus. 26p. (ps up). 1987. 7.95 (*1-55578-104-7*); cass. incl. Worlds Wonder.
Madokoro, Hisako. The Adventures of Buster the Puppy, 6 vols. Kuroi, Ken, illus. 96p. (gr. k-2). 1991. Sct. PLB 95.58 (*0-8368-0488-0*) Gareth Stevens Inc.
—Buster & the Dandelions. Karoi, Ken, illus. LC 90-47926. 24p. (gr. k-2). 1991. PLB 15.93 (*0-8368-0491-0*) Gareth Stevens Inc.
—Buster & the Little Kitten. Kuroi, Ken, illus. LC 90-47947. 24p. (gr. k-2). 1991. PLB 15.93 (*0-8368-0490-2*) Gareth Stevens Inc.
—Buster Catches a Cold. Kuroi, Ken, illus. LC 90-47948. 24p. (gr. k-2). 1991. PLB 15.93 (*0-8368-0489-9*) Gareth Stevens Inc.
—Buster's Blustery Day. Kuroi, Ken, illus. LC 90-47927. 24p. (gr. k-2). 1991. PLB 15.93 (*0-8368-0494-5*) Gareth Stevens Inc.
—Buster's First Snow. Kuroi, Ken, illus. LC 90-47946. 24p. (gr. k-2). 1991. PLB 15.93 (*0-8368-0492-9*) Gareth Stevens Inc.
—Buster's First Thunderstorm. Kuroi, Ken, illus. LC 90-47869. 24p. (gr. k-2). 1991. PLB 15.93 (*0-8368-0493-7*) Gareth Stevens Inc.
Mangas, Brian. Follow that Puppy. (ps-6). 1993. pap. 4.95 (*0-671-87171-4*, S&S BFYR) S&S Trade.
Mantegazza, Giovanna. Dog. (ps). 1993. 6.95 (*1-56397-200-X*) Boyds Mills Pr.
Markoe, Merrill. Bad Dog, Bo! Markoe, Merrill, illus. LC 93-38684. 32p. (gr. k-3). 1994. PLB 13.95 (*0-8167-3462-3*); pap. text ed. 3.95 (*0-8167-3463-1*) BrdgeWater.
Marshak, Samuel. The Pup Grew Up! Pevear, Richard, tr. from RUS. Radunsky, Vladimir, illus. LC 88-28428. 32p. (ps-2). 1989. 13.95 (*0-8050-0952-3*, Bks Young Read) H Holt & Co.
Marshall, James. Old Mother Hubbard & Her Wonderful Dog. (ps-3). 1993. pap. 4.95 (*0-374-45611-9*) FS&G.
Martin, Ann M. Dawn & the Disappearing Dogs. (gr. 4-7). 1993. pap. 3.50 (*0-590-44960-5*) Scholastic Inc.
—Kristy & the Snobs. 1993. pap. 3.50 (*0-590-43660-0*) Scholastic Inc.
—Kristy & the Snobs. large type ed. LC 93-15968. 176p. (gr. 4 up). 1993. PLB 15.93 (*0-8368-1015-5*) Gareth Stevens Inc.
Martin, David. Lizzie & Her Puppy. Gliori, Debi, illus. LC 92-53008. 24p. (ps). 1993. 5.95 (*1-56402-059-2*) Candlewick Pr.
Martin, Kerry, illus. Walt Disney's One Hundred One Dalmatians Play Hide-&-Seek. LC 92-52972. 18p. (ps-1). 1992. 9.95 (*1-56282-270-5*) Disney Pr.
Martinez, Ruth. Mrs. McDockerty's Knitting. O'Neill, Catharine, illus. 32p. (ps-3). 1990. 13.45 (*0-395-51591-2*) HM.
Matthews, Billie L. & Hurlburt, Virginia E. Davy's Dawg. Welch, Karen E., ed. Boyce, Kenneth, illus. LC 88-32832. 64p. (gr. 3-8). 1989. PLB 9.95 (*0-937460-58-3*) Hendrick-Long.
Matthews, Cecily. My Dog Ben. Cullo, Ned, illus. LC 92-31946. 1993. 3.75 (*0-383-03585-6*) SRA Schl Grp.
Mauser, Pat R. Love Is for the Dogs. 1989. pap. 2.50 (*0-380-75723-0*, Flare) Avon.
Maxwell, William. Bun. Stevenson, James, illus. LC 93-42390. 1995. write for info. (*0-679-86053-3*); PLB write for info. (*0-679-96053-8*) Knopf Bks Yng Read.
Mayer, Mercer. A Boy, a Dog & a Frog. LC 67-22254. (Illus.). (ps-3). 1985. 9.95 (*0-8037-0763-0*); PLB 9.89 (*0-8037-0767-3*) Dial Bks Young.
—Boy, a Dog, & a Frog. (ps-3). 1992. pap. 3.50 (*0-14-054611-1*) Viking Child Bks.
—Frog, Where Are You? Mayer, Mercer, illus. LC 72-85544. (ps-3). 1969. 9.95 (*0-8037-2737-2*); PLB 9.89 (*0-8037-2732-1*) Dial Bks Young.
Meddaugh, Susan. Martha Speaks. Meddaugh, Susan, illus. LC 91-48455. 32p. (ps-3). 1992. 13.45 (*0-395-63313-3*) HM.
—The Witches' Supermarket. Meddaugh, Susan, illus. 32p. (gr. k-3). 1991. 13.95 (*0-395-57034-4*, Sandpiper) HM.
Meltabarger, P. J. Livingston: The Pedigreed Pooch of Padre Island. Samuelson, Arnold & Samuelson, Billie, eds. Becher, Ivy, illus. Lynn, E. Russell, intro. by. (Illus.). 150p. (gr. 7-10). 1988. 19.95 (*0-923133-02-X*) JM Pub.
Melton, David. A Boy Called Hopeless. Melton, Todd, illus. LC 86-27557. 232p. (gr. 4 up). 1986. pap. 5.95 (*0-933849-07-9*) Landmark Edns.
—The One & Only Autobiography of Ralph Miller: The Dog Who Knew He Was a Boy. LC 86-27551. (Illus.). 90p. (gr. 2-6). 1987. Repr. of 1979 ed. PLB 13.95 (*0-933849-30-3*) Landmark Edns.
—The One & Only Second Autobiography of Ralph Miller: The Dog Who Knew He Was a Boy. Melton, David, illus. LC 86-27556. 128p. (gr. 2-6). 1986. pap. 5.95 (*0-933849-06-0*) Landmark Edns.
—The One & Only Second Autobiography of Ralph Miller: The Dog Who Knew He Was a Boy. LC 86-27556. (Illus.). 116p. (gr. 2-6). 1986. Repr. of 1983 ed. PLB 13.95 (*0-933849-31-1*) Landmark Edns.
Mendelson, Lee. Rock-a-Bye Snoopy. Hill, Frank, illus. 26p. (ps up). 1986. 12.95 (*1-55578-011-3*) Worlds Wonder.
—Snoopy & the Great Pumpkin. Hill, Frank, illus. 26p. (ps up). 1986. 12.95 (*1-55578-006-7*) Worlds Wonder.
—Snoopy at the Dog Show. Hill, Frank, illus. 26p. (ps up). 1986. 12.95 (*1-55578-008-3*) Worlds Wonder.
—Snoopy Goes Camping. Hill, Frank, illus. 26p. (ps up). 1986. 12.95 (*1-55578-002-4*) Worlds Wonder.
—Snoopy Hits the Beach. Hill, Frank, illus. 26p. (ps up). 1986. 12.95 (*1-55578-004-0*) Worlds Wonder.
—Snoopy, Spike & the Cat Next Door. Hill, Frank, illus. 26p. (ps up). 1986. 12.95 (*1-55578-010-5*) Worlds Wonder.
—Snoopy's America. Hill, Frank, illus. 26p. (ps up). 1986. 12.95 (*1-55578-007-5*) Worlds Wonder.
—Snoopy's Band. Hill, Frank, illus. 26p. (ps up). 1986. 12.95 (*1-55578-009-1*) Worlds Wonder.
—Snoopy's Baseball Game. Hill, Frank, illus. 26p. (ps up). 1986. 12.95 (*1-55578-012-1*) Worlds Wonder.
—Snoopy's Birthday Party. Hill, Frank, illus. 26p. (ps up). 1986. 12.95 (*1-55578-001-6*) Worlds Wonder.
—Snoopy's Land of Make Believe. Hill, Frank, illus. 26p. (ps up). 1986. 12.95 (*1-55578-003-2*) Worlds Wonder.
—Snoopy's Show & Tell. Hill, Frank, illus. 26p. (ps up). 1986. 12.95 (*1-55578-005-9*) Worlds Wonder.
—Snoopy's Talent Show. Hill, Frank, illus. 26p. (ps up). 1986. 12.95 (*1-55578-000-8*) Worlds Wonder.
Metoyer, Patrick G. I'm Rattle-Me-Bones III, Esquire. Manchee, Bruce N., illus. LC 87-90349. 24p. (Orig.). (gr. 1-6). 1988. pap. 3.95 (*0-944523-02-1*) Western Slope Pubns.
—No Bones! No Bones! Manchee, Bruce N., illus. LC 87-90350. 24p. (Orig.). (gr. k-2). 1988. pap. 3.95 (*0-944523-03-X*) Western Slope Pubns.
Milgrin, David. Why Benny Barks: A Step One Book. Milgrin, David, illus. LC 93-47102. 32p. (Orig.). (ps-1). 1994. PLB 7.99 (*0-679-96157-7*); pap. 3.50 (*0-679-86157-2*) Random Bks Yng Read.
Miller, Sara S. Three Stories You Can Read to Your Dog. Kelley, True, illus. LC 93-38856. 1994. write for info. (*0-395-69938-X*) HM.
Milnes, Gerald. Granny Will Your Dog Bite? And Other Mountain Rhymes. Root, Kimberly, illus. Bird, Sonja, contrib. by. LC 88-27350. (Illus.). 48p. 1990. Incl. 40 min. cassette. slipcase 18.95 (*0-394-85363-6*) Knopf Bks Yng Read.
Mishica, Clare. Max's Answer. Stortz, Diane, ed. LC 94-2100. (Illus.). 48p. (Orig.). (ps-3). 1994. pap. 4.49 (*0-7847-0177-6*) Standard Pub.
Mitchell, Tucker. The Crystal Whizzard. Graves, Helen, ed. LC 88-50120. 64p. (gr. 2-5). 1988. 12.00 (*1-55523-146-2*) Winston-Derek.
Moncure, Jane B. Polka-Dot Puppy. Endres, Helen, illus. LC 87-15813. (SPA & ENG.). 32p. (ps-2). 1987. PLB 14.95 (*0-89565-407-5*) Childs World.
—What's So Special about Today? It's My Birthday. Williams, Jenny, illus. LC 87-21907. 32p. (ps-2). 1987. PLB 14.95 (*0-89565-414-8*) Childs World.
Morey, Walt. Kavik, the Wolf Dog. Parnall, Peter, illus. LC 68-24727. (gr. 5-9). 1977. 14.95 (*0-525-33093-3*, DCB); (DCB) Dutton Child Bks.
Mosley, Marilyn C. Dachshund Tails Down the Yukon. Ross, Sueellen, illus. 112p. (Orig.). (gr. 5). 1988. pap. 5.95 (*0-9614850-2-7*) M C Mosley.
—Dachshund Tails North. Mosley, Rob & Lingle, Bea, illus. LC 82-90167. 50p. (Orig.). (gr. 5). 1982. pap. 4.95 (*0-9614850-0-0*) M C Mosley.
—Dashchund Tails up the Inside Passage. LC 84-90672. (Illus.). 95p. (Orig.). (gr. 5). 1984. pap. 4.95 (*0-9614850-1-9*) M C Mosley.
Mowat, Farley. The Dog Who Wouldn't Be. 1984. pap. 3.99 (*0-553-27928-9*) Bantam.
Muchmore, Jo Ann. Johnny Rides Again. LC 94-19466. 1995. write for info. (*0-8234-1156-7*) Holiday.
Myers, Anna. Red-Dirt Jessie. 107p. 1992. 13.95 (*0-8027-8172-1*) Walker & Co.
Naylor, Phyllis R. Shiloh. LC 90-603. 144p. (gr. 3-7). 1991. SBE 13.95 (*0-689-31614-3*, Atheneum Child Bk) Macmillan Child Grp.
—Shiloh. 144p. (gr. 3-7). 1992. pap. 3.99 (*0-440-40752-4*, YB) Dell.
Newman, Al. Grub E. Dog. Doody, Jim, illus. LC 93-77686. 32p. (ps-3). 1993. 13.95 (*0-89334-214-9*); pap. 4.95 (*0-89334-218-1*) Humanics Ltd.
Newman, Nanette. That Dog! Hafner, Marylin, contrib. by. LC 81-43892. (Illus.). 48p. (gr. 1-4). 1992. pap. 3.95 (*0-06-440363-7*, Trophy) HarpC Child Bks.
Newton, Jane. Good Morning Dogs! Edgell, Kyle, illus. 20p. (Orig.). (ps). 1991. pap. text ed. 4.95 (*0-931571-08-1*) Lifetime Pr.
Nicklaus, Carol. Come Dance with Me. Nicklaus, Carol, illus. 32p. (ps-1). 1991. PLB 5.95 (*0-671-73503-9*); pap. 2.95 (*0-671-73507-1*) Silver Pr.
Nodset, Joan L. Go Away, Dog. Bonsall, Crosby H., illus. LC 63-11162. 32p. (ps-3). 1963. PLB 9.89 (*0-06-024556-5*) HarpC Child Bks.
Norman, Philip R. Dancing Dogs. LC 93-2533. 1995. 14.95 (*0-316-61208-1*) Little.
North, Sterling. The Wolfling. Schoenherr, John, illus. 224p. (gr. 5-9). 1992. pap. 3.99 (*0-14-036166-9*, Puffin) Puffin Bks.
Nothing-to-Do Puppy. (ps-k). 1991. write for info. (*0-307-12237-9*, Golden Pr) Western Pub.
Nwabugwu, Frank. Sparo; the Wild & Crazy Pretty Dog. 2nd ed. 26p. (gr. 2-8). 1993. write for info. (*1-881687-08-2*) F Nwabugwu.
Oana, Katy D. The Little Dog Who Wouldn't Be. LC 77-18351. (Illus.). 32p. (gr. 2-4). 1978. PLB 9.95 (*0-87783-150-5*) Oddo.
Odgers, Sally F. Dog Went for a Walk. Shaw, Peter, illus. LC 92-27100. (gr. 3 up). 1993. 2.50 (*0-383-03564-3*) SRA Schl Grp.
Odom, Melissa. A Medal for Murphy. Rice, James, illus. LC 86-25369. 32p. (gr. 1-6). 1987. 12.95 (*0-88289-635-0*) Pelican.
Okimoto, Jean D. A Place for Grace. Keith, Doug, illus. 32p. (gr. 1 up). 1993. 14.95 (*0-912365-73-0*) Sasquatch Bks.
Ollivant, Alfred. Bob, Son of Battle. (Illus.). (gr. 5 up). 1967. pap. 2.50 (*0-8049-0141-4*, CL-141) Airmont.
Olsen, E. A. Adrift on a Raft. Le Blanc, L., illus. LC 68-16397. 48p. (gr. 3 up). 1970. PLB 10.95 (*0-87783-000-2*); pap. 3.94 deluxe ed. (*0-87783-078-9*); cassette 10.60x (*0-87783-176-9*) Oddo.
One Hundred & One Dalmatians. (Illus.). 48p. (gr. 3-7). 1992. pap. 2.95 (*1-56115-271-4*, 21812, Golden Pr) Western Pub.
One Hundred One Dalmatas - 101 Dalmatians. (SPA.). 96p. 1992. 6.98 (*1-57082-057-0*) Mouse Works.
One Hundred One Dalmatians. (Illus.). 24p. (ps-2). 1991. write for info. (*0-307-74012-9*, Golden Pr) Western Pub.
Ormerod, Jan. Come Back, Puppies: A Hide & Seek Book with See-Through Pages. Ormerod, Jan, illus. LC 91-30424. 32p. (ps up). 1992. 13.00 (*0-688-09135-0*) Lothrop.
O'Shea, Pat. The Hounds of the Morrigan. LC 85-16435. 469p. (gr. 4 up). 1986. 15.95 (*0-8234-0595-8*) Holiday.
Osofsky, Audrey. My Buddy. Rand, Ted, illus. LC 92-3028. 32p. (gr. k-3). 1992. 14.95 (*0-8050-1747-X*, Bks Young Read) H Holt & Co.
Ossorio, Nelson A. & Salvadeo, Michele B. Puppy & the Parrot. (Illus.). 60p. (gr. 4-6). 1994. pap. 6.95 (*1-56721-059-7*) Twnty-Fifth Cent Pr.
Ostheeren, Ingrid & Corderoc'h, Jean-Pierre. The New Dog. James, J. Alison, tr. from GER. LC 93-10100. (Illus.). 32p. (gr. k-3). 1993. 14.95 (*1-55858-218-5*); lib. bdg. 14.88 (*1-55858-219-3*) North-South Bks NYC.
Otto, Carolyn. One Dog Twenty Stars. 1994. write for info. (*0-8050-2369-0*) H Holt & Co.
Ouida, pseud. A Dog of Flanders. (Illus.). 80p. 1992. pap. 1.00t (*0-486-27087-4*) Dover.
Oxenbury, Helen. Our Dog. Oxenbury, Helen, illus. 24p. (ps-1). 1994. pap. 3.99 (*0-14-050392-7*, Puff Pied Piper) Puffin Bks.
Paine, Penelope C. & Bingham, Mindy. My Way Sally. Maeno, Itoko, illus. LC 88-2653. 48p. (ps-6). 1988. 14.95 (*0-911655-27-1*) Advocacy Pr.
Paraskevas, Betty. The Strawberry Dog. Paraskevas, Michael, illus. LC 92-18216. (ps-3). 1993. 13.99 (*0-8037-1367-3*); PLB 13.89 (*0-8037-1368-1*) Dial Bks Young.
Parker, Ann N. Home Is Where the Shade Tree Is. Vickery, Diane, illus. 18p. (gr. k-4). 1988. pap. 3.95 (*0-943487-13-7*) Sevgo Pr.
Parnall, Peter. Water Pup. Parnall, Peter, illus. LC 92-40850. 144p. (gr. 3 up). 1993. SBE 13.95 (*0-02-770151-4*, Macmillan Child Bk) Macmillan Child Grp.
Patrick & the Hungry Puppy. (Illus.). 24p. (ps-2). 1985. 6.95 (*0-8431-1084-8*) Price Stern.
Paulsen, Gary. Dogsong. (gr. 5-9). 1987. pap. 4.50 (*0-14-032235-3*, Puffin) Puffin Bks.
Paulsen, Gary & Paulsen, Ruth. Dogteam. 1993. pap. 15.95 (*0-385-30550-8*) Delacorte.
Pearson, Tracey C. The Howling Dog. (Illus.). 32p. (ps up). 1991. 13.95 (*0-374-33502-8*) FS&G.
Peet, Bill. Whingdingdilly. Peet, Bill, illus. LC 71-98521. (gr. k-3). 1977. 14.45 (*0-395-24729-2*); pap. 4.80 (*0-395-31381-3*) HM.
Pellegrini, Nina. Charlie Claus: Santa's Best Friend. LC 93-1495. (Illus.). (ps-6). 1993. 4.99 (*0-517-09309-X*, Pub. by Derrydale Bks) Random Hse Value.
Pellowski, Michael J. Copycat Dog. LC 85-14128. (Illus.). 48p. (Orig.). (gr. 1-3). 1986. PLB 10.59 (*0-8167-0652-2*); pap. text ed. 3.50 (*0-8167-0653-0*) Troll Assocs.
—The Puppy Nobody Wanted. Robison, Bill, illus. 24p. (ps-3). 1988. 1.95 (*0-87406-338-8*) Willowisp Pr.
Perkins, Al. Diggingest Dog. Gurney, Eric, illus. LC 67-21920. 72p. (gr. k-3). 1967. 6.95 (*0-394-80047-8*); lib. bdg. 7.99 (*0-394-90047-2*) Beginner.

El Perro y el Gato (Dog & Cat) (SPA., Illus.). 28p. (ps-2). 1991. PLB 11.55 (*0-516-35353-5*); pap. 3.95 (*0-516-55353-4*) Childrens.
Peters, Emilie. Muffin, a Palm Beach Pooch. 30p. (gr. 3-8). 1992. pap. write for info. (*0-9635568-0-0*) Muffin Pubns.
Peters, Sharon. Maxie the Mutt. Mahan, Ben, illus. LC 87-10914. 32p. (gr. k-2). 1988. PLB 11.59 (*0-8167-1087-2*); pap. text ed. 2.95 (*0-8167-1088-0*) Troll Assocs.
Pfloog, Jan. Asi Son los Perritos! Pfloog, Jan, illus. (SPA.). 32p. (ps-3). 1993. pap. 2.25 (*0-394-85064-5*) Random Bks Yng Read.
Phillips, Joan. My New Boy. Munsinger, Lynn, illus. LC 85-30129. 32p. (ps-1). 1986. lib. bdg. 7.99 (*0-394-98277-0*); 3.50 (*0-394-88277-6*) Random Bks Yng Read.
Pilkey, Dav. Dog Breath! The Horrible Terrible Trouble with Hally Tosis. LC 93-43405. (ps-3). 1994. 14.95 (*0-590-47466-9*, Blue Sky Press) Scholastic Inc.
—Dogzilla. LC 92-37906. (gr. 4 up). 1993. 10.95 (*0-15-223944-8*); pap. 5.95 (*0-15-223945-6*) HarBrace.
Pinkwater, Daniel. Aunt Lulu. Pinkwater, Daniel, illus. LC 88-1736. 32p. (gr. k-3). 1988. RSBE 13.95 (*0-02-774661-5*, Macmillan Child Bk) Macmillan Child Grp.
—Aunt Lulu. Pinkwater, Daniel, illus. LC 90-39981. 32p. (gr. k-3). 1991. pap. 3.95 (*0-689-71413-0*, Aladdin) Macmillan Child Grp.
—Jolly Roger: A Dog of Hoboken. LC 84-12629. (Illus.). 64p. (gr. 4-6). 1984. 14.00 (*0-688-03898-0*) Lothrop.
—The Magic Moscow. LC 92-27150. (Illus.). 64p. (gr. 3-7). 1993. pap. 3.95 (*0-689-71710-5*, Aladdin) Macmillan Child Grp.
Points, Maureen. The Adventures of Pepe the Poodle & Other Stories. Points, Maureen, illus. 1978. pap. 3.50 (*0-9601594-1-X*) Maureen Points.
The Poky Little Puppy. 1990. write for info. (*0-307-02134-3*, Golden Pr) Western Pub.
The Poky Little Puppy. (Illus.). 24p. (ps up). 1992. write for info. incl. long-life batteries (*0-307-74805-7*, 64805, Golden Pr) Western Pub.
Pomerantz, Charlotte. The Outside Dog. Plecas, Jennifer, illus. LC 91-6351. 64p. (gr. k-3). 1993. 14.00 (*0-06-024782-7*); PLB 13.89 (*0-06-024783-5*) HarpC Child Bks.
Porte, Barbara A. Harry's Dog. Abolafia, Yossi, illus. LC 83-14129. 48p. (gr. 1-3). 1983. 13.95 (*0-688-02555-2*); PLB 13.88 (*0-688-02556-0*) Greenwillow.
—The Take-Along Dog. McCully, Emily A., illus. LC 88-18775. 40p. (gr. 1 up). 1989. 11.95 (*0-688-08053-7*); PLB 11.88 (*0-688-08054-5*) Greenwillow.
Pulver, Robin. Homer & the House Next Door. Levin, Arnie, illus. LC 93-4377. 32p. (ps-2). 1994. RSBE 14.95 (*0-02-775457-X*, Four Winds) Macmillan Child Grp.
Puppy Says One, Two, Three. LC 92-62560. 20p. (ps). 1993. 4.99 (*0-89577-485-2*, Dist. by Random) RD Assn.
Quayle, Thomas E., ed. Jose' el Diablo: The World's Most Traveled Dog. Quayle, Greg, illus. 95p. (Orig.). 1985. pap. 3.00 (*0-9623144-0-4*) Vilate Pub.
Rand, Gloria. Salty Sails North. Rand, Ted, illus. LC 89-39063. 32p. (ps-3). 1992. pap. 4.95 (*0-8050-2188-4*, Owlet BYR) H Holt & Co.
—Salty Takes Off. Rand, Ted, illus. LC 90-46371. 32p. (ps-2). 1991. 14.95 (*0-8050-1159-5*, Bks Young Read) H Holt & Co.
Rankin, Louise. Daughter of the Mountains. Wiese, Kurt, illus. LC 92-26793. 192p. (gr. 5 up). 1993. pap. 4.99 (*0-14-036335-1*) Puffin Bks.
Rathmann, Peggy. Officer Buckle & Gloria. LC 93-43887. 1995. write for info. (*0-399-22616-8*, Putnam) Putnam Pub Group.
Rawls, Wilson. Where the Red Fern Grows. 25th anniversary ed. LC 61-9201. 216p. (gr. 5 up). 1961. pap. 11.95 (*0-385-05619-2*) Doubleday.
Razzi, Jim. Sherluck Bones-Mystery Detective Book, No. 1. 48p. (Orig.). 1981. pap. 2.25 (*0-553-15382-X*) Bantam.
Reaver, Chap. Bill. 1994. 14.95 (*0-385-31175-3*) Delacorte.
Reese, Bob. Sunshine. Wasserman, Dan, ed. Reese, Bob, illus. (gr. k-1). 1979. 7.95 (*0-89868-073-5*); pap. 2.95 (*0-89868-084-0*) ARO Pub.
Reiser, Lynn. Dog & Cat. LC 90-3553. (Illus.). 24p. (ps up). 1991. 13.95 (*0-688-09892-4*); PLB 13.88 (*0-688-09893-2*) Greenwillow.
Remkiewicz, Frank. The Bone Stranger. LC 93-25214. (Illus.). 1994. 15.00 (*0-688-12041-5*); lib. bdg. 14.93 (*0-688-12042-3*) Lothrop.
Richler, Mordecai. Jacob Two-Two Meets the Hooded Fang. Wegner, Fritz, illus. 96p. (gr. 2-7). 1994. pap. 3.50 (*0-685-71038-6*) Random Bks Yng Read.
Richmond, Gary. The Forgotten Friend. (gr. 1-5). 1991. text ed. 6.99 (*0-8499-0913-9*) Word Inc.
Riddle, Tohby. A Most Unusual Dog. Riddle, Tohby, illus. LC 93-38184. 32p. (gr. 1 up). 1994. PLB 18.60 (*0-8368-1088-0*) Gareth Stevens Inc.
Roberts, Thom. Summerdog. (Illus.). 128p. (Orig.). (gr. 1 up). 1978. pap. 2.25 (*0-380-01950-7*, Camelot) Avon.
Roberts, Willo D. Eddie & the Fairy Godpuppy. Morrill, Leslie, illus. LC 83-15678. 136p. (gr. 3-5). 1984. SBE 13.95 (*0-689-31021-8*, Atheneum Child Bk) Macmillan Child Grp.
—Eddie & the Fairy Godpuppy. Morrill, Leslie, illus. LC 91-28003. 128p. (gr. 3-7). 1992. pap. 3.95 (*0-689-71602-8*, Aladdin) Macmillan Child Grp.
Robertus, Polly. The Dog Who Had Kittens. Stevens, Janet, illus. LC 90-39174. 32p. (ps-3). 1991. reinforced bdg. 14.95 (*0-8234-0860-4*); pap. 5.95 (*0-8234-0974-0*) Holiday.
Rockwell, Anne. Hugo at the Park. Rockwell, Anne, illus. LC 89-2417. 32p. (ps-k). 1990. RSBE 13.95 (*0-02-777301-9*, Macmillan Child Bk) Macmillan Child Grp.
—When Hugo Went to School. LC 89-13211. (Illus.). 32p. (ps-1). 1991. RSBE 13.95 (*0-02-777305-1*, Macmillan Child Bk) Macmillan Child Grp.
Roddy, Lee. The Mad Dog of Lobo Mountain. 132p. (gr. 8-12). 1986. pap. 4.99 (*0-89693-482-9*, Victor Books) SP Pubns.
Rodowsky, Colby. Dog Days. Howell, Kathleen C., illus. 96p. (gr. 2-6). 1990. 14.00 (*0-374-36342-0*) FS&G.
Roffey, Maureen. Quick, Catch Dan! Roffey, Maureen, illus. 24p. (ps). 1991. 6.70 (*0-395-57583-4*, Sandpiper) HM.
Rogers, Mary. New Puppy. 35p. (gr. k). 1992. pap. text ed. 23.00 big bk. (*1-56843-012-4*); pap. text ed. 4.50 (*1-56843-062-0*) BGR Pub.
Rojany, Lisa. Jake & Jenny on the Town. 18p. (ps-2). 1993. 7.95 (*0-8431-3584-0*) Price Stern.
Rosen, Michael J. Bonesy & Isabel. Ransome, James E., illus. LC 93-7892. 1995. write for info. (*0-15-209813-5*) HarBrace.
Ross, Anna. Peekaboo, Puppy! (ps). 1994. 3.50 (*0-679-85700-1*) Random Bks Yng Read.
Ross, K. K. Peekaboo, Puppy! A My Puppy Loves Me Book. Barto, Bobbi, illus. 22p. (ps-k). 1994. 3.50 (*0-685-71037-8*) Random Bks Yng Read.
Rowe, John. Jack the Dog. Rowe, John, illus. 28p. (gr. k up). 1993. 14.95 (*0-88708-266-1*) Picture Bk Studio.
Rubinstein, Gillian. Dog in, Cat Out. James, Ann, illus. LC 92-39785. 32p. (ps-k). 1993. PLB 13.95 (*0-395-66596-5*) Ticknor & Flds Bks Yng Read.
Rylant, Cynthia. The Blue Hill Meadows & the Much-Loved Dog. Beier, Ellen, illus. LC 93-40538. 1994. write for info. (*0-15-253155-6*) HarBrace.
—Henry & Mudge & the Bedtime Thumps. Stevenson, Sucie, illus. LC 89-49529. 40p. (gr. 1-3). 1991. RSBE 12.95 (*0-02-778006-6*, Bradbury Pr) Macmillan Child Grp.
—Henry & Mudge & the Best Day Ever. Stevenson, Sucie, illus. LC 93-35939. 1995. 14.00 (*0-02-778012-0*, Bradbury Pr) Macmillan Child Grp.
—Henry & Mudge & the Careful Cousin: The Thirteenth Book of Their Adventures. Stevenson, Sucie, illus. LC 92-12851. 48p. (gr. 1-3). 1994. RSBE 13.95 (*0-02-778021-X*, Bradbury Pr) Macmillan Child Grp.
—Henry & Mudge & the Forever Sea: The Sixth Book of Their Adventures. Stevenson, Sucie, illus. LC 92-28646. 48p. (gr. 1-3). 1993. pap. 3.95 (*0-689-71701-6*, Aladdin) Macmillan Child Grp.
—Henry & Mudge & the Happy Cat. Stevenson, Sucie, illus. LC 88-18855. 48p. (gr. 1-3). 1990. RSBE 13.95 (*0-02-778008-2*, Bradbury Pr) Macmillan Child Grp.
—Henry & Mudge & the Happy Cat: The Eighth Book of Their Adventures. Stevenson, Sucie, illus. LC 93-10797. 48p. (gr. 1-3). 1994. pap. 3.95 (*0-689-71791-1*, Aladdin) Macmillan Child Grp.
—Henry & Mudge & the Wild Wind. Stevenson, Sucie, illus. LC 91-12644. 40p. (gr. 1-3). 1993. RSBE 12.95 (*0-02-778014-7*, Bradbury Pr) Macmillan Child Grp.
—Henry & Mudge: Book & Toy. (Illus.). 48p. (ps-3). 1992. pap. 19.95 (*0-689-71648-6*, Aladdin) Macmillan Child Grp.
—Henry & Mudge Get the Cold Shivers: The Seventh Book of Their Adventures. Stevenson, Sucie, illus. LC 93-45588. (gr. 1-3). 1994. pap. 3.95 (*0-689-71849-7*, Aladdin) Macmillan Child Grp.
—Henry & Mudge in the Green Time: The Third Book of Their Adventures. Stevenson, Sucie, illus. LC 91-24942. 48p. (gr. 1-3). 1992. pap. 3.95 (*0-689-71582-X*, Aladdin) Macmillan Child Grp.
—Henry & Mudge in the Sparkle Days: The Fifth Book of Their Adventures. Stevenson, Sucie, illus. LC 92-42535. 48p. (gr. 1-3). 1993. pap. 3.95 (*0-689-71752-0*, Aladdin) Macmillan Child Grp.
—Henry & Mudge Take the Big Test: The Tenth Book of Their Adventures. Stevenson, Sucie, illus. LC 90-35171. 40p. (gr. 1-3). 1991. RSBE 12.95 (*0-02-778009-0*, Bradbury Pr) Macmillan Child Grp.
—Henry & Mudge under the Yellow Moon: The Fourth Book of Their Adventures. Stevenson, Sucie, illus. LC 91-23135. 48p. (gr. 1-3). 1992. pap. 3.95 (*0-689-71580-3*, Aladdin) Macmillan Child Grp.
—Mr. Putter & Tabby Walk the Dog. Howard, Arthur, illus. LC 93-21467. (ps-6). 1994. 10.95 (*0-15-256259-1*) HarBrace.
—Mr. Putter & Tabby Walk the Dog. (ps-3). 1994. pap. 4.95 (*0-15-200891-8*, HB Juv Bks) HarBrace.
—The Old Woman Who Named Things. Brown, Kathryn, illus. LC 93-40537. 1994. write for info. (*0-15-257809-9*) HarBrace.
Sachar, Louis. Marvin Redpost: Alone in His Teacher's House. Sullivan, Barbara, illus. LC 93-19791. 96p. (Orig.). (gr. 1-4). 1994. 2.99 (*0-679-81949-5*); PLB 2.99 (*0-679-91949-X*) Random Bks Yng Read.
Sachs, Betsy. The Boy Who Ate Dog Biscuits. Apple, Margot, illus. LC 89-3905. 64p. (gr. 2-4). 1989. pap. 2.99 (*0-394-84778-4*) Random Bks Yng Read.
Sachs, Marilyn. Underdog. LC 84-24676. 128p. (gr. 4-6). 1985. pap. 11.95 (*0-385-17609-0*) Doubleday.
St. Pierre, Stephanie. Peekaboo Puppies. Regan, Dana, illus. 12p. (ps). 1994. bds. 4.95 (*0-448-40460-5*, G&D) Putnam Pub Group.
Salem, Lynn & Stewart, Josie. Aqui Esta Fido. (Illus.). 8p. (gr. 1). 1993. pap. 3.50 (*1-880612-18-6*) Seedling Pubns.
—En Casa de Abuelita Norma. (Illus.). 16p. (gr. 1). 1993. pap. 3.50 (*1-880612-19-4*) Seedling Pubns.
Scarpino, Jane. Nellie, the Light House Dog. Weinberger, Jane, ed. Ensor, Robert, illus. 40p. (ps-3). 1993. pap. 9.95 (*0-932433-23-5*) Windswept Hse.
Scarry, Patsy. My Puppy. reissued ed. Wilkin, Eloise, illus. 24p. (ps-k). 1992. write for info. (*0-307-00147-4*, 312-11, Golden Pr) Western Pub.
Schneider, Howie. No Dogs Allowed. LC 93-10395. 1994. write for info. (*0-399-22612-5*, Putnam) Putnam Pub Group.
Schories, Pat. He's Your Dog. (ps-3). 1993. 15.00 (*0-374-32906-0*) FS&G.
Schutzer, Dena. Polka & Dot. Schutzer, Dena, illus. LC 93-29935. 1994. 14.00 (*0-679-84192-X*); PLB 14.99 (*0-679-94192-4*) Knopf Bks Yng Read.
Schweninger, Ann. Wintertime. (ps-3). 1990. 11.95 (*0-670-83420-3*) Viking Child Bks.
Searcy, Margaret Z. Wolf Dog of the Woodland Indians. Brough, Hazel, illus. LC 90-26215. 112p. (Orig.). (ps-8). 1991. pap. 6.95 (*0-88289-778-0*) Pelican.
Sebestyen, Ouida. Out of Nowhere. (gr. 5 up). 1994. 14.95 (*0-531-06839-0*); lib. bdg. 14.99 RLB (*0-531-08689-5*) Orchard Bks Watts.
Seeley, Laura L. McSpot's Hidden Spots: A Puppyhood Secret. Seeley, Laura L., illus. 32p. (ps-3). 1993. 16.95 (*1-56145-087-1*) Peachtree Pubs.
Seligson, Susan. Amos: The Story of an Old Dog & His Couch. Schneider, Howie, illus. (ps-3). 1992. pap. 4.95 (*0-316-78034-0*, Joy St Bks) Little.
Sendak, Maurice. Hector Protector. 1965. 16.00 (*0-06-025485-8*); PLB 15.89 (*0-06-025486-6*) HarpC Child Bks.
—Higglety Pigglety Pop: Or, There Must Be More to Life. Sendak, Maurice, illus. LC 67-18553. 80p. (gr. k-3). 1967. 15.00 (*0-06-025487-4*) HarpC Child Bks.
Seymour, Tres. Pole Dog. Soman, David, photos by. LC 92-24174. (Illus.). 32p. (ps-1). 1993. 14.95 (*0-531-05470-5*); PLB 14.99 (*0-531-08620-8*) Orchard Bks Watts.
Shanahan, Danny. Buckledown, the Workhound. LC 92-13433. 1993. 14.95 (*0-316-78276-9*) Little.
Sharmat, Marjorie W. Genghis Khan: A Dog Star Is Born. Rigie, Mitchell, illus. 80p. (Orig.). (gr. 1-4). 1994. PLB 9.99 (*0-679-95406-6*); pap. 2.99 (*0-679-85406-1*) Random Bks Yng Read.
—I'm the Best. Hillenbrand, Will, illus. LC 90-39176. 32p. (ps-3). 1991. reinforced 14.95 (*0-8234-0859-0*) Holiday.
Sharratt, Nick. Monday Run-Day. Sharratt, Nick, illus. LC 91-58745. 24p. (ps up). 1992. 5.95 (*1-56402-092-4*) Candlewick Pr.
Sherlock, Patti. Some Fine Dog. LC 91-856. 160p. (gr. 3-7). 1992. 14.95 (*0-8234-0947-3*) Holiday.

Shields, Mary. The Alaskan Happy Dog Trilogy: Can Dogs Talk?, Loving a Happy Dog, Secret Messages--Training a Happy Dog, 3 vols. Gates, Donna, illus. 32p. (ps-3). 1993. Set. pap. 30.00 (*0-9618348-2-X*) Pyrola Pub.
THE ALASKAN HAPPY DOG TRILOGY, $30.00, ISBN 0-9618348-2-X, CAN DOGS TALK?, $10.00, ISBN 0-9618348-1-1, with audio tape, $13.00, ISBN 0-9618348-4-6, LOVING A HAPPY DOG, $12.00, ISBN 0-9618348-3-8, SECRET MESSAGES--TRAINING A HAPPY DOG, $12.00, ISBN 0-9618348-6-2. In the first volume, CAN DOGS TALK? Rita & Ryan answer their own question with the help of an Alaskan dog musher, a book, a team of friendly huskies & a lost puppy. In volume two, LOVING A HAPPY DOG, the kids learn the responsibilities of loving & caring for a Dog, including the understanding of a dog's life span. A pull-out puzzle is included. The final volume, SECRET MESSAGES--TRAINING A HAPPY DOG, unfolds as Rita, Ryan & Happy discover messages along the trail while hiking to Mary's cabin. The kids learn how to train their dog, & another important lesson--it's okay to ask for help. Each volume stands alone, but the complete trilogy gives the young reader a well-rounded introduction into enjoying the companionship of a dog. The author, Mary Shields, lives in Fairbanks, Alaska, where she raises

sled dogs for companions & wilderness travelers. Mary was the first woman to finish the Iditarod. Donna Gates creates her fine art images of sled dogs & interior Alaskan wildlife at her home near Denali Park, Alaska. Pyrola Publishing, P.O. Box 80961, Fairbanks, AK 99708. 907-455-6469 (Alaskan time please).
Publisher Provided Annotation.

Shine, Deborah. Where's the Puppy? 16p. (ps-2). 1992. pap. 14.95 (*1-56784-052-3*) Newbridge Comms.

Shnitzel Is Lost. LC 90-43325. 1991. pap. 13.95 (*0-671-73306-0*, S&S BFYR) S&S Trade.

Shura, Mary F. Some Kind of Friend. 128p. 1992. pap. 3.50 (*0-380-71181-8*, Camelot) Avon.

Simon, Norma. The Baby House. Samuels, Barbara, illus. LC 94-6637. 1995. 14.00 (*0-671-87044-0*, S&S BFYR) S&S Trade.

Singer, Marilyn. Chester the Out-of-Work Dog. Smith, Cat B., illus. LC 92-1141. 32p. (ps-3). 1992. 14.95 (*0-8050-1828-X*, Bks Young Read) H Holt & Co.

Siracusa, Catherine. Bingo, the Best Dog in the World. Levitt, Sidney, illus. LC 90-4400. 64p. (gr. k-3). 1991. 11.95 (*0-06-025812-8*); PLB 11.89 (*0-06-025813-6*) HarpC Child Bks.

Skoglund, Elizabeth. Harold's Dog Horace Is Scared of the Dark. Bjorkman, Dale, illus. 48p. (gr. 2). 1992. pap. 2.99 (*0-8423-1047-9*) Tyndale.

Slater, Helen. Fuzzy Friends: Pet the Puppy. (Illus.). 10p. 1993. 3.95 (*0-681-41811-7*) Longmeadow Pr.

Slater, Teddy. Looking for Lewis. Alley, Robert, illus. 24p. (ps-1). 1991. 4.95 (*0-671-72988-8*); PLB 6.95 (*0-671-72987-X*) Silver Pr.

Slater, Teddy, adapted by. Walt Disney's Lady & the Tramp. Langley, Bill & Dias, Ron, illus. 24p. (ps-3). 1993. 3.50 (*0-307-12367-7*, 12367, Golden Pr) Western Pub.

Smath, Jerry. The Housekeeper's Dog. Smath, Jerry, illus. LC 80-10580. 48p. (ps-3). 1980. 5.95 (*0-8193-1023-9*); PLB 5.95 (*0-8193-1024-7*) Parents.

Smith, Dodie. The Hundred & One Dalmatians. Grahame-Johnstone, Janet & Grahame-Johnstone, Anne, illus. 208p. (gr. 1 up). 1976. pap. 2.50 (*0-380-00628-6*, Camelot) Avon.

—The Hundred & One Dalmatians. (Illus.). 208p. 1989. pap. 14.95 (*0-670-82660-X*) Viking Child Bks.

—The Hundred & One Dalmatians. Dooling, Michael, illus. (gr. 4 up). 1989. pap. 3.95 (*0-318-41739-1*, Puffin) Puffin Bks.

—The One Hundred & One Dalmatians. Dooling, Michael, illus. (gr. 5-9). 1989. pap. 3.99 (*0-14-034034-3*, Puffin) Puffin Bks.

Smith, Elizabeth S. A Service Dog Goes to School: The Story of a Dog Trained to Help the Disabled. Petruccio, Steven, illus. LC 88-17598. 64p. (gr. 1-4). 1988. 12.95 (*0-688-07648-3*); PLB 12.88 (*0-688-07649-1*, Morrow Jr Bks) Morrow Jr Bks.

Smith, Sally Ann. Candle, a Story of Love & Faith. Luther, Luana, ed. Jung, Mary, illus. LC 91-72745. 32p. (gr. 3-6). 1991. pap. 9.95 (*0-944875-22-X*) Doral Pub.

Smith, Susan M. The Booford Summer. Glass, Andrew, illus. LC 93-27925. 1994. 13.95 (*0-395-66590-6*, Clarion Bks) HM.

Snow, Pegeen. A Pet for Pat. Dunnington, Tom, illus. LC 83-23159. 32p. (ps-2). 1984. PLB 10.25 (*0-516-02049-8*); pap. 2.95 (*0-516-42049-6*) Childrens.

Snyder, Phillip C. Poochie. Mohrman, Janet S., illus. 28p. (Orig.). (ps). 1982. pap. 3.95 (*0-940560-04-6*) Custom Hse.

Sohl, Marcia & Dackerman, Gerald. The Call of the Wild Student Activity Book. (Illus.). 16p. (gr. 4-10). 1976. pap. 1.25 (*0-88301-182-4*) Pendulum Pr.

Spyropulos, Diana. Cornelius & the Dog Star. Williams, Ray, illus. LC 94-32335. 48p. (gr. k-5). 1995. 15.95 (*0-935699-08-2*) Illum Arts. CORNELIUS & THE DOG STAR is the tale of a dignified but grouchy old basset hound named Cornelius. Arriving one evening at the Gates of Heaven, he is dismayed when Saint Bernard says he cannot enter until he has learned to open his heart. Feeling lost & alone, he encounters Sirius, the Dog Star, who guides him on a wondrous adventure of the heart. In the end, Cornelius learns to love even Tucker, a hobo he had treated badly on Earth. Featuring Williams' fantastical illustrations, this story will capture the hearts of young & old. To order call Atrium at 1-800-275-2606. "Adults & children alike will enjoy reading this quirky & fun story...Beautiful, full-color illustrations enhance the fantasy experience." - NAPRA Trade Journal.
Publisher Provided Annotation.

Stabile, Angie C. The Miracle of My Dog King. 1991. 6.95 (*0-533-09038-5*) Vantage.

Stack, Richard L. The Doggonest Christmas. Stack, Charles W., illus. 48p. (gr. k-6). 1989. 16.95 (*0-9605400-6-7*) Four Seas Bk. In THE DOGGONEST CHRISTMAS, Josh is only a mutt, but he dreams of being something better. He lives with Miss Elly, a kind lady who believes in dreams & helps him seek his fortune. The little dog triumphs over pessimism, both for himself & his doubting friends. This endearing story is a classic & is enjoyed by all ages. In the sequel, DOGGONEST VACATION (0-9628262-0-0), Josh travels to Maryland, where he meets Trevor, a Chesapeake Bay Retriever who doesn't want to be a hunting dog. Josh teaches his new friend to believe in himself & to trust others. In DOGGONEST PUPPY LOVE (0-9628262-1-9), Josh falls in love with Millie, the first dog. He & Miss Elly travel to Washington, D.C., where Josh & Millie have an exciting adventure. The story proves the power of faith. Josh, Mr. Stack's real life friend, has followed these titles with his autobiography, JOSH, THE STORY OF THE WONDER DOG (0-9628262-5-1). This is the true story of how Josh wandered into the author's life & changed the course of history. For information about school visits, or to order, call Windmill Press at 1-800-932-6112.
Publisher Provided Annotation.

Stadler, John. Hector the Accordion-Nosed Dog. LC 81-7713. (Illus.). 32p. 1985. pap. 4.50 (*0-02-045250-0*, Aladdin) Macmillan Child Grp.

Standiford, Natalie. Space Dog & Roy. 80p. 1990. pap. 2.95 (*0-380-75953-5*, Camelot) Avon.

—Space Dog & the Pet Show. 80p. 1990. pap. 2.95 (*0-380-75954-3*, Camelot) Avon.

—Space Dog the Hero. 80p. 1991. pap. 2.95 (*0-380-75956-X*, Camelot) Avon.

Stanley, Carol. Dog Walkers Club. (gr. 4 up). 1990. pap. 2.95 (*0-380-75916-0*, Camelot) Avon.

Stanley, Diane. Moe the Dog in Tropical Paradise. Primavera, Elise, illus. 32p. (ps-3). 1992. 14.95 (*0-399-22127-1*, Putnam) Putnam Pub Group.

Steel, Danielle. Martha's New Puppy. 1990. 9.95 (*0-385-30166-9*) Delacorte.

—Max Runs Away. 1990. 9.95 (*0-385-30213-4*) Delacorte.

Steig, William. Caleb & Katie. Steig, William, illus. LC 77-4947. 32p. (ps-3). 1977. 16.00 (*0-374-31016-5*) FS&G.

Steiner, Barbara. Dolby & the Woof-Off. LC 90-21464. (Illus.). 128p. (gr. 2 up). 1991. 12.95 (*0-688-08435-4*) Morrow Jr Bks.

Stobbs, William. Gregory's Dog. (Illus.). 16p. 1987. pap. 2.95 (*0-19-272141-0*) OUP.

Stolz, Mary. Deputy Shep. Johnson, Pamela, illus. LC 90-38664. 96p. (gr. 2-5). 1991. HarpC Child Bks.

—Dog on Barkham Street. Shortall, Leonard, illus. LC 60-5787. 176p. (gr. 3-6). 1960. PLB 14.89 (*0-06-025841-1*) HarpC Child Bks.

—A Dog on Barkham Street. Shortall, Leonard, illus. LC 60-5787. 176p. (gr. 3-7). 1985. pap. 3.95 (*0-06-440160-X*, Trophy) HarpC Child Bks.

—The Weeds & the Weather. Watson, N. Cameron, illus. LC 93-240. 40p. (gr. k up). 1994. 14.00 (*0-688-12289-2*); PLB 13.93 (*0-688-12290-6*) Greenwillow.

Stone, Jon. Lovable Furry Old Grover's Resting Places. Smollin, Michael J., illus. LC 83-21087. 32p. (ps-3). 1984. pap. 2.50 (*0-394-86056-X*) Random Bks Yng Read.

Stott, Dorothy. Puppy & Me. (gr. 3 up). 1993. 9.99 (*0-525-45080-7*, DCB) Dutton Child Bks.

Strasser, Todd, adapted by. Walt Disney's Lady & the Tramp. Mateu, Franc, illus. LC 93-71378. 96p. 1994. 14.95 (*1-56282-613-1*); PLB 14.89 (*1-56282-615-8*) Disney Pr.

—Walt Disney's Lady & the Tramp. LC 93-71379. (Illus.). 64p. (gr. 2-6). 1994. pap. 3.50 (*1-56282-614-X*) Disney Pr.

Strayer, Debbie. Chad & Brad, a Home for Spot: Blend Book, 2 bks, Nos. 1 & 2. Majewski, Joy, illus. 14p. (gr. 1). 1992. Set. pap. 8.00 (*1-880892-11-1*) Fam Lrng Ctr.

Strommen, Judith B. Champ Hobarth. 160p. (gr. 4-6). 1993. 14.95 (*0-8050-2414-X*, Bks Young Read) H Holt & Co.

Strub, Susanne. My Dog, My Sister, & I (Mon Chien, Ma Soeur, et Moi) Strub, Susanne, illus. LC 92-22063. (ENG & FRE.). 32p. (ps up). 1993. 14.00 (*0-688-12010-5*, Tambourine Bks); PLB 13.93 (*0-688-12011-3*, Tambourine Bks) Morrow.

Stuart, Jesse. The Rightful Owner. 2nd ed. Miller, Jim W., et al, eds. Henneberger, Robert, illus. Zornes, Rocky, contrib. by. (Illus.). 95p. (gr. 3-6). 1989. 12.00 (*0-945084-14-5*); pap. 6.00 (*0-945084-15-3*) J Stuart Found.

Superdog Rescue. (Illus.). 1987. pap. 1.25 (*0-440-82167-3*) Dell.

Szekeres, Cyndy. Cyndy Szekeres' I Am a Puppy. (ps). 1994. 3.95 (*0-307-12457-6*, Golden Pr) Western Pub.

—Little Puppy Cleans His Room. (ps-3). 1994. pap. 1.95 (*0-307-11546-1*, Golden Pr) Western Pub.

Tada, Joni E. & Jensen, Steve. Darcy's Dog Dilemma. Norton, LoraBeth, ed. LC 93-36330. 128p. (gr. 4-8). 1994. pap. 4.99 (*0-7814-0167-4*, Chariot Bks) Cook.

Taylor, Livingston & Taylor, Maggie. Can I Be Good? Rand, Ted, illus. LC 92-23193. 1993. 14.95 (*0-15-200436-X*) HarBrace.

Taylor, Theodore. Trouble with Tuck. LC 81-43139. 96p. (gr. 4-6). 1989. 13.95 (*0-385-17774-7*); pap. 10.95 (*0-385-17775-5*) Doubleday.

Tell the Time with Benji. (ps). 1983. bds. 5.50 (*0-904494-49-7*) Borden.

Terhune, Albert P. A Dog Named Chips. 1992. Repr. lib. bdg. 24.95x (*0-89966-985-9*) Buccaneer Bks.

—Further Adventures of Lad. 1992. Repr. lib. bdg. 24.95x (*0-89966-983-2*) Buccaneer Bks.

—Great Dog Stories. 1993. 12.99 (*0-517-09337-5*) Random Hse Value.

—The Heart of a Dog. 1992. Repr. lib. bdg. 24.95x (*0-89966-984-0*) Buccaneer Bks.

—Lad: A Dog. 1981. Repr. PLB 24.95 (*0-89966-348-6*) Buccaneer Bks.

—Lad: A Dog. 189p. 1981. Repr. PLB 24.95 (*0-89967-022-9*) Harmony Raine.

—Lad: A Dog. (gr. 6). 1978. pap. 2.50 (*0-451-14626-3*, AE1036, Sig) NAL-Dutton.

—Lad: A Dog. 256p. 1978. pap. 3.50 (*0-451-16417-2*, Sig) NAL-Dutton.

—Lad: A Dog. Savitt, Sam, illus. LC 93-9365. 288p. (gr. 5 up). 1993. pap. 3.99 (*0-14-036474-9*, Puffin) Puffin Bks.

—Treve. 1992. Repr. lib. bdg. 24.95x (*0-89966-996-4*) Buccaneer Bks.

—The Way of a Dog. 1992. Repr. lib. bdg. 24.95x (*0-89966-986-7*) Buccaneer Bks.

Thayer, Jane. The Puppy Who Wanted a Boy. rev. ed. McCue, Lisa, illus. LC 85-15465. 48p. (ps-1). 1986. 12.95 (*0-688-05944-9*); PLB 12.88 (*0-688-05945-7*, Morrow Jr Bks); pap. 4.95 (*0-685-43017-0*, Mulberry Bks) Morrow Jr Bks.

—The Puppy Who Wanted a Boy. McCue, Lisa, illus. LC 85-15465. 48p. (ps up). 1988. pap. 4.95 (*0-688-08293-9*, Mulberry) Morrow.

Thomas, Abagail. Lily. Low, William, illus. LC 93-14199. (gr. 5 up). 1994. 14.95 (*0-8050-2690-8*) H Holt & Co.

Thomas, Jane R. The Comeback Dog. Howell, Troy, illus. 64p. (gr. 2-6). 1981. 13.45 (*0-395-29432-0*, Clarion Bks) HM.

—Comeback Dog. (ps-7). 1983. pap. 3.25 (*0-553-15521-0*, Skylark) Bantam.

Tilden, Ruth. Dog Tricks. (ps-6). 1993. pap. 7.95 (*0-671-87127-7*, S&S BFYR) S&S Trade.

Tokuda, Wendy & Hall, Richard. Shiro in Love. Sasaki, Karen, illus. 32p. (gr. 1-3). 1989. 11.95 (*0-89346-306-X*) Heian Intl.

Tripp, Valerie. El Perro Cantor (The Singing Dog) Martin, Sandra K., illus. LC 86-14797. (SPA.). 24p. (ps-2). 1990. PLB 9.75 (*0-516-31578-1*); pap. 3.95 (*0-516-51578-0*) Childrens.

Troy, John. Ben at Large. 1990. pap. 12.50 (*1-55971-048-9*) NorthWord.

Tsutakawa, Tom. Return to Seward Park. 1994. 7.95 (*0-533-10721-0*) Vantage.

Two Dogs & Freedom: The Open School in Soweto. 1987. pap. 4.95 (*0-8050-0637-0*, North Star Line) Blue Moon Bks.

Updike, David. The Sounds of Summer. Parker, Robert A., illus. 40p. (gr. 2-5). 1993. 14.95 (*0-945912-20-X*) Pippin Pr.

Uspenski, Eduard. Uncle Fedya, His Dog, & His Cat. Shpitalnik, Vladimir, illus. Heim, Michael, tr. from RUS. LC 92-44491. (Illus.). 144p. (gr. 1-5). 1993. 14.00 (*0-679-82064-7*) Knopf Bks Yng Read.

Van Allsburg, Chris. The Sweetest Fig. Van Allsburg, Chris, illus. LC 93-12692. (gr. 4 up). 1993. 17.95 (*0-395-67346-1*) HM.

Vestavia Elementary School Fourth Grade Class & Cockrell, Marcille. The Adventures of a Bubble-Bellied Bloopy Droopy Detective. (Illus.). 32p. (gr. k-5). 1989. pap. 3.95 (*0-943487-22-6*) Sevgo Pr.

Vivelo, Jackie. Beagle in Trouble: Super Sleuth II. 112p. (gr. 4-7). 1992. pap. 2.95 (*0-8167-1548-3*) Troll Assocs.

Wahl, Jan. Dracula's Cat & Frankenstein's Dog. Chorao, Kay, illus. (ps-2). 1990. pap. 13.95 (*0-671-70820-1*) S&S Trade.

Wallace, Bill. A Dog Called Kitty. LC 80-16293. 160p. (gr. 3-7). 1980. 14.95 (*0-8234-0376-9*) Holiday.

—Dog Called Kitty. (gr. 4-7). 1991. pap. 3.50 (*0-671-74389-9*, Archway) PB.

—Dog Called Kitty. (gr. 4-7). 1992. pap. 3.50 (*0-671-77081-0*, Minstrel Bks) PB.

—Red Dog. LC 86-46202. 192p. (gr. 3-7). 1987. 14.95 (*0-8234-0650-4*) Holiday.

—Red Dog. 176p. (Orig.). (gr. 5-7). 1989. pap. 3.50 (*0-671-70141-X*, Archway) PB.

Walsh, Vivian & Seibold, J. Otto. Mr. Lunch Takes a Plane Ride. Seibold, J. Otto, illus. 40p. (ps-3). 1993. RB 13.99 (*0-670-84775-5*) Viking Child Bks.

Walt Disney Staff. Lady & the Tramp. 1987. 6.98 (*0-8317-5411-7*) Viking Child Bks.

—La Noche de las Narices Frias (One Hundred One Dalmatians) (SPA.). (ps-3). 1992. 6.98 (*0-453-03018-1*) Viking Penguin.

Warburg, Sandol S. Growing Time. Weisgard, Leonard, illus. LC 69-14729. (gr. k-3). 1975. 13.95 (*0-395-16966-6*) HM.

Wayne. Max, the Dog Who Refused to Die. (ps-7). 1987. pap. 2.25 (*0-553-25160-0*) Bantam.

Webster-Seek, Vesta. Old Ruff & Life on the Farm. LC 92-12956. (gr. k-3). 1993. pap. 4.99 (*0-7814-0966-7*, Chariot Bks) Chariot Family.

Weeks, Wilfred H. The White Stone. Schlatter, Becky, illus. LC 85-51932. 37p. (Orig.). (gr. 4-9). 1990. pap. write for info. (*0-9615677-0-8*) Three Riv Ctr.

Weller, Frances W. Riptide. Blake, Robert J., illus. 32p. (ps-3). 1990. 14.95 (*0-399-21675-8*, Philomel Bks) Putnam Pub Group.

—Riptide. Blake, Roberrt J., illus. 32p. (ps-3). 1994. pap. 5.95 (*0-399-22766-0*, Philomel) Putnam Pub Group.

Wells, Rosemary. Lucy Comes to Stay. Graham, Mark, illus. LC 91-15779. 32p. (gr. k-3). 1994. 14.99 (*0-8037-1213-8*); PLB 14.89 (*0-8037-1214-6*) Dial Bks Young.

Wersba, Barbara. The Farewell Kid. LC 89-36401. 160p. (gr. 7 up). 1990. 12.95 (*0-06-026378-4*) HarpC Child Bks.

West, Colin. Shape Up, Monty! West, Colin, illus. LC 91-20316. 64p. (gr. 2-5). 1991. 10.95 (*0-525-44777-6*, DCB) Dutton Child Bks.

Westall, Robert. The Kingdom by the Sea. 176p. (gr. 5 up). 1991. 15.00 (*0-374-34205-9*) FS&G.

Western Publishing Company, Inc. Staff. Poky Little Puppy's Friends. (Illus.). (ps). 1990. pap. write for info. (*0-307-06039-X*, Golden Pr) Western Pub.

Westman, Barbara. Dancing Dogs: Charlotte & Emilio at the Circus. Westman, Barbara, illus. LC 90-23070. 32p. (ps-3). 1991. HarpC Child Bks.

Whayne, Susanne S. Watch the House. Morrill, Leslie, illus. LC 91-28071. 80p. (gr. k-3). 1993. pap. 3.95 (*0-671-86700-8*, Half Moon Bks) S&S Trade.

White, James E. The Triumphs of Trisha & Tripod: Tripod Finds a Home. Senf, Richard L., illus. 22p. 1991. pap. 7.95 (*0-9629102-0-1*) Pyramid TX.

Widerberg, Siv. The Boy & the Dog. Fisher, Richard E., tr. Ahlbom, Jens, illus. 28p. (ps up). 1991. bds. 13.95 (*91-29-59926-1*, Pub. by R & S Bks) FS&G.

Wiggins, VeraLee. Shelby's Best Friend. LC 93-27279. 1994. 8.95 (*0-8163-1189-7*) Pacific Pr Pub Assn.

—Shelby's Big Prayer. LC 93-11939. 1994. 8.95 (*0-8163-1188-9*) Pacific Pr Pub Assn.

—Shelby's Big Scare. LC 93-31363. 1994. 8.95 (*0-8163-1190-0*) Pacific Pr Pub Assn.

Wild, Margaret. Toby. Young, Noela, illus. LC 93-14394. 32p. (ps-3). 1994. reinforced bdg. 13.95 (*0-395-67024-1*) Ticknor & Flds Bks Yng Read.

Wildsmith, Brian. The Hunter & His Dog. Wildsmith, Brian, illus. 32p. (ps-2). 1979. 16.00 (*0-19-279725-5*); pap. 7.50 (*0-19-272147-X*) OUP.

Wilhelm, Hans. I'll Always Love You. Wilhelm, Hans, illus. LC 84-20060. 32p. (ps up). 1988. 15.00 (*0-517-55648-0*); pap. 3.99 (*0-517-57265-6*) Crown Bks Yng Read.

—Schnitzel's First Christmas. (Illus.). 1989. pap. 13.95 jacketed (*0-671-67977-5*, S&S BFYR) S&S Trade.

—Schnitzel's First Christmas. LC 89-5858. (Illus.). 40p. (ps-1). 1991. pap. 5.00 (*0-671-74494-1*, S&S BFYR) S&S Trade.

Wilson. Mother Grumpy's Dog. 1991. 12.95 (*0-8050-1432-2*) H Holt & Co.

Wilson, Towana E. Sam, a Cocker: Sam & His Country Home. Wilson, Towana E., illus. LC 90-87585. (Orig.). (gr. 7 up). 1990. pap. 5.00 (*0-9623607-1-6*) BRAT Pubns.

—Sam, a Cocker: Sam & the Periwinkles. Wilson, Towana E., illus. LC 90-83106. (Orig.). (gr. 7 up). 1990. pap. 5.00 (*0-9623607-2-4*) BRAT Pubns.

—Sam a Cocker: Same Goes Home. Wilson, Towana E., illus. LC 89-92115. 24p. (Orig.). (gr. 5 up). 1989. pap. 5.00 (*0-9623607-0-8*) BRAT Pubns.

Wolff, Ashley. Come with Me. LC 89-34482. (Illus.). 32p. (ps-2). 1990. 12.95 (*0-525-44555-2*, DCB) Dutton Child Bks.

Wolters, Richard A. Home Dog. Hill, Gene, frwd. by. (Illus.). 160p. (gr. 7 up). 1984. 16.95 (*0-525-24232-5*, Dutton) NAL-Dutton.

Wood, Leslie. A Dog Called Mischief. (Illus.). 16p. 1987. pap. 2.95 (*0-19-272155-0*) OUP.

Wright, Betty R. The Ghost of Popcorn Hill. Ritz, Karen, illus. LC 92-16391. 96p. (gr. 3-7). 1993. 14.95 (*0-8234-1009-9*) Holiday.

Wynnejones, Pat. Village Tales, 4 bks. (Illus.). (ps-6). 1991. Set, 24p. ea. 14.95 (*0-7459-1830-1*) Lion USA.

Yeoman, John. Old Mother Hubbard's Dog Dresses Up. Blake, Quentin, illus. LC 89-27026. 24p. (ps-3). 1990. 6.70 (*0-395-53358-9*) HM.

—Old Mother Hubbard's Dog Learns to Play. Blake, Quentin, illus. LC 89-39863. 24p. (ps-3). 1990. 6.95 (*0-395-53360-0*) HM.

—Old Mother Hubbard's Dog Needs a Doctor. Blake, Quentin, illus. LC 89-24448. 24p. (ps-3). 1990. 6.70 (*0-395-53359-7*) HM.

—Old Mother Hubbard's Dog Takes up Sport. Blake, Quentin, illus. LC 89-39942. 24p. (ps-3). 1990. 6.70 (*0-395-53361-9*) HM.

Young, Ed. The Other Bone. Young, Ed, illus. LC 83-47706. 32p. (ps-3). 1984. PLB 14.89 (*0-06-026871-9*) HarpC Child Bks.

Ziefert, Harriet. Harry Gets Ready for School. Smith, Mavis, illus. (ps-2). 1993. pap. 3.25 (*0-14-036539-7*, Puffin) Puffin Bks.

—Harry Goes to Day Camp. Smith, Mavis, illus. (ps-2). 1994. pap. 3.25 (*0-14-037000-5*) Puffin Bks.

—Harry Takes a Bath. Smith, Mavis, illus. LC 93-2718. (ps-2). 1993. pap. 3.25 (*0-14-036537-0*, Puffin) Puffin Bks.

—Later, Rover. (Illus.). 32p. (ps-3). 1992. pap. 3.50 (*0-14-054387-2*) Puffin Bks.

—Sam & Lucy. Schumacher, Claire, illus. LC 90-46963. 36p. (ps-1). 1992. HarpC Child Bks.

—Sleepy Dog: A Step One Book. Gorbaty, Norman, illus. LC 84-4775. (ps-2). 1984. PLB 7.99 (*0-394-96877-8*); pap. 3.50 (*0-394-86877-3*) Random Bks Yng Read.

Ziefert, Harriet & Nicklaus, Carol. Later, Rover. Jacobson, David, illus. 32p. (ps-3). 1992. 8.95 (*0-670-83863-2*) Viking Child Bks.

Ziefert, Harriet & Smith, Mavis. Harry Goes to Fun Land. (Illus.). (ps-2). 1994. pap. 3.25 (*0-14-036885-X*) Puffin Bks.

Zion, Gene. Harry & the Lady Next Door. Graham, Margaret B., illus. LC 60-9452. 64p. (gr. k-3). 1978. pap. 3.50 (*0-06-444008-7*, Trophy) HarpC Child Bks.

—Harry by the Sea. Graham, Margaret B., illus. LC 65-21302. 32p. (gr. k-3). 1965. PLB 14.89 (*0-06-026856-5*) HarpC Child Bks.

—Harry the Dirty Dog. Graham, Margaret B., illus. LC 56-8137. 32p. (gr. k-3). 1956. 15.00 (*0-06-026865-4*); PLB 14.89 (*0-06-026866-2*) HarpC Child Bks.

—Harry the Dirty Dog. Graham, Margaret B., illus. LC 56-8137. 32p. (ps-3). 1976. pap. 4.95 (*0-06-443009-X*, Trophy) HarpC Child Bks.

—No Roses for Harry. Graham, Margaret B., illus. LC 58-7752. (gr. k-3). 1958. 15.00 (*0-06-026890-5*); PLB 14.89 (*0-06-026891-3*) HarpC Child Bks.

Zolotow, Charlotte. The Old Dog. rev. ed. Ransome, James, illus. LC 93-41081. 1995. 15.00 (*0-06-024409-7*); PLB 14.89 (*0-06-024412-7*) HarpC.

DOGS–PICTURES, ILLUSTRATIONS, ETC.

Dogs & Puppies. LC 90-80292. 24p. (ps-2). 1991. pap. 1.95 (*1-56288-075-6*) Checkerboard.

King, Helen B. Sandy. King, Helen B., illus. 18p. (ps-3). 1985. pap. 4.95 (*0-9615366-4-0*) King ME.

Pfloog, Jan. Puppies Are Like That. Pfloog, Jan, illus. LC 74-2542. 32p. (Orig.). (ps-1). 1975. pap. 2.25 (*0-394-82923-9*) Random Bks Yng Read.

Sanford, Bill & Green, Carl. The American Pit Bull Terrier. LC 89-31072. (Illus.). 48p. (gr. 4-5). 1989. text ed. 12.95 (*0-89686-447-2*, Crestwood Hse) Macmillan Child Grp.

—The Dalmatian. LC 89-31107. (Illus.). 48p. (gr. 4-5). 1989. text ed. 12.95 (*0-89686-449-9*, Crestwood Hse) Macmillan Child Grp.

—The Doberman Pinscher. LC 89-31071. (Illus.). 48p. (gr. 4-5). 1989. RSBE 12.95 (*0-89686-454-5*, Crestwood Hse) Macmillan Child Grp.

—The English Springer Spaniel. LC 89-31069. (Illus.). 48p. (gr. 4-5). 1989. text ed. 12.95 (*0-89686-453-7*, Crestwood Hse) Macmillan Child Grp.

—The Greyhound. LC 89-31113. (Illus.). 48p. (gr. 4-5). 1989. text ed. 12.95 (*0-89686-450-2*, Crestwood Hse) Macmillan Child Grp.

—The Old English Sheepdog. LC 89-31073. (Illus.). 48p. (gr. 4-5). 1989. text ed. 12.95 RSBE (*0-89686-452-9*, Crestwood Hse) Macmillan Child Grp.

—The Samoyed. LC 89-31070. (Illus.). 48p. (gr. 4-5). 1989. text ed. 12.95 RSBE (*0-89686-451-0*, Crestwood Hse) Macmillan Child Grp.

—The Shih Tzu. LC 89-31108. (Illus.). 48p. (gr. 4-5). 1989. text ed. 12.95 RSBE (*0-89686-448-0*, Crestwood Hse) Macmillan Child Grp.

Spizzirri Publishing Co. Staff. Dogs: An Educational Coloring Book. Spizzirri, Linda, ed. (Illus.). 32p. (gr. 1-8). 1986. pap. 1.75 (*0-86545-076-5*) Spizzirri.

DOGS–POETRY

Field, Eugene. The Gingham Dog & the Calico Cat. Street, Janet, illus. 32p. (ps up). 1993. pap. 5.95 (*0-399-22517-X*, Philomel Bks) Putnam Pub Group.

Gabriel, Howard W., III. Loving Memories from Dog to Dog. House, David J., illus. 32p. (Orig.). (gr. k-6). 1987. pap. 2.95 (*0-936997-01-X*) M & H Enter.

Lipson, Greta B. A Leash on Love: A Book for All Ages. Rundell, Christopher, illus. LC 93-176359. 32p. 1992. 9.95 (*0-9630637-0-7*) Barclay Bks.

Singer, Marilyn. It's Hard to Read a Map with a Beagle on Your Lap. Oubrerie, Clement, photos by. LC 92-26166. (Illus.). 32p. (gr. 1-4). 1993. 15.95 (*0-8050-2201-5*, Bks Young Read) H Holt & Co.

Yolen, Jane. Raining Cats & Dogs. LC 91-24295. (ps-3). 1993. 14.95 (*0-15-265488-7*, HB Juv Bks) HarBrace.

DOGS–TRAINING

Arnold, Caroline. A Guide Dog Puppy Grows Up. Hewett, Richard, photos by. (Illus.). 43p. (gr. 1 up). 1991. 16.95 (*0-15-232657-X*) HarBrace.

Calmenson, Stephanie. Rosie, a Visiting Dog's Story. Sutcliffe, Justin, photos by. LC 93-21243. (Illus.). (gr. k up). 1994. 15.95 (*0-395-65477-7*, Clarion Bks) HM.

Cherry, Denise. Step by Step Children's Guide to Dog Training. (Illus.). 64p. 1993. pap. 3.95 (*0-86622-518-8*, SK044) TFH Pubns.

Frith, Michael. I'll Teach My Dog One Hundred Words. (Illus.). (ps-1). 1973. 6.95 (*0-394-82692-2*); lib. bdg. 7.99 (*0-394-92692-7*) Random Bks Yng Read.

Jones, Robert F. Jake: A Labrador Puppy at Work & Play. (gr. 4-7). 1992. 15.00 (*0-374-33655-5*) FS&G.

Kotes, F. F. A Puppy to Love: A Child's Guide to Dog Care. LC 91-67328. 40p. (Orig.). (gr. 3-8). 1991. pap. 9.95 (*1-878500-00-7*, Valley Hse Bk) Martin Mgmt.

Meisterfeld, C. W. Psychological Dog Training: Behavior Conditioning with Respect & Trust. (Illus.). 232p. (Orig.). (gr. 6 up). 1991. pap. 18.00 (*0-9601292-6-X*) M R K.

Roach, Margaret J. Mac & His Dog, Sir John. Moore, Susan J., illus. (Orig.). (gr. k-8). 1993. Spanish ed., Mac y Su Perro, Don Juan. pap. 13.50 (*1-882666-01-1*); English ed. pap. 13.50 (*1-882666-00-3*) M Roach & Assocs.

Unkelbach, Kurt. Both Ends of the Leash: Selecting & Training Your Dog: Petie, Haris, illus. (gr. 3-7). 1968. P-H.

DOGS–TREATMENT

Howard-Moineau, Henrietta. Twiggy: The Abandoned, Diabetic Dog. (Illus.). 73p. (Orig.). (gr. 4 up). 1982. pap. 5.00 (*0-318-01113-1*) Hampshire Pr.

DOGS FOR THE BLIND

see Guide Dogs

DOLL

see Dolls

DOLLHOUSES

Ashman, Iain. Make This Model Doll's House. (Illus.). 32p. (gr. 4-7). 1993. pap. 9.95 (*0-7460-1316-7*, Usborne) EDC.

Conaway, Judith. Dollhouse Fun! Furniture You Can Make. Barto, Renzo, illus. LC 86-16133. 48p. (gr. 1-5). 1987. PLB 11.89 (*0-8167-0862-2*); pap. text ed. 3.50 (*0-8167-0863-0*) Troll Assocs.

Lellie, Herman & Bateson, Margaret. A Victorian Dollhouse. (Illus.). 4p. 1991. bds. 19.95 (*0-312-06228-1*) St Martin.

Theiss, Nola. The Complete Guide to Remodeling & Expanding Your Dollhouse. LC 92-44443. (Illus.). 128p. 1993. pap. 12.95 (*0-8069-8369-8*, Pub. by Lark Bks) Sterling.

DOLLHOUSES–FICTION

Godden, Rumer. The Doll's House. LC 62-18693. (ps-3). 1976. pap. 3.99 (*0-14-030942-X*, Puffin) Puffin Bks.

Goffstein, M. B. Goldie the Dollmaker. LC 79-85369. (Illus.). 64p. (ps up). 1985. pap. 3.45 (*0-374-42740-2*) FS&G.

Jacobs, Flora G. The Doll House Mystery. (Illus.). 96p. 1958. 5.95 (*0-686-31594-4*) Wash Dolls Hse.

Karas, Jacqueline. The Dollhouse. Riches, Judith, illus. LC 92-32262. 32p. (ps up). 1993. 15.00 (*0-688-12480-1*, Tambourine Bks); PLB 14.93 (*0-688-12481-X*, Tambourine Bks) Morrow.

Mariana. Miss Flora McFlimsey & the Baby New Year. rev. ed. Mariana & Howe, Caroline W., illus. LC 86-15339. 40p. (ps-2). 1988. 11.95 (*0-688-04533-2*); PLB 11.88 (*0-688-04534-0*) Lothrop.

—Miss Flora McFlimsey's Christmas Eve. rev. ed. Mariana & Howe, Caroline W., illus. LC 86-15259. 40p. (ps-2). 1988. 11.95 (*0-688-04282-1*); PLB 11.88 (*0-688-04283-X*) Lothrop.

Martin, Ann M. Karen's Doll House. (gr. 4-7). 1993. pap. 2.95 (*0-590-45652-0*) Scholastic Inc.

Orgel, Doris. Sarah's Room. LC 63-13675. (Illus.). (gr. k-3). 1963. 11.95 (*0-06-024605-7*) HarpC Child Bks.

Reiss, Kathryn. Time Windows. 260p. (gr. 5 up). 1991. 15.95 (*0-15-288205-7*, HB Juv Bks) HarBrace.

DOLLS

Barbie & the Island Resort. (Illus.). 24p. (ps up). 1992. write for info. (*0-307-74022-6*, 64022, Golden Pr) Western Pub.

Children's Museum Staff. Original Shirley Temple Dolls in Full Color. (Illus.). 32p. (gr. 2 up). 1988. pap. 3.95 (*0-486-25461-5*) Dover.

Doll. (Illus.). 20p. (gr. k-6). 1994. pap. 6.95 (*1-56458-482-8*) Dorling Kindersley.

Hecht, Joan B. Best Things about Dolls. Hecht, Muriel, illus. 16p. (ps-3). 1987. pap. 4.95 (*0-931271-08-8*) Hi Plains Pr.

Hunt, Kathryn M. On My Honor. Ross, Lynette C., illus. 40p. (gr. 2-6). 1994. pap. 8.95 (*0-89672-333-X*) Tex Tech Univ Pr.

The Kachina Doll Book 1. (gr. 1-6). 1972. pap. 3.95 (*0-918858-00-3*) Fun Pub AZ.

The Kachina Doll Book 2. (gr. 1-6). 1973. pap. 3.95 (*0-918858-01-1*) Fun Pub AZ.

Morgan, Mary H. How to Dress an Old-Fashioned Doll. LC 72-93612. (Illus.). 96p. (gr. 5-8). 1973. pap. 2.95 (*0-486-22912-2*) Dover.
Pfeffer, Susan B. Paperdolls. 160p. (Orig.). (gr. 7-12). 1984. pap. 2.25 (*0-440-96777-5*, LFL) Dell.
Reinckens, Sunnhild. Making Dolls. Maclean, Donald, tr. (GER., Illus.). 56p. (ps-3). 1989. pap. 10.95 (*0-86315-093-4*, Pub. by Floris Bks UK) Gryphon Hse.
Sleator, William. Among the Dolls. Hyman, Trina S., illus. (gr. 2-5). 1975. 12.50 (*0-525-25563-X*, DCB) Dutton Child Bks.
Spizzirri Publishing Co. Staff. Dolls: An Educational Coloring Book. Spizzirri, Linda, ed. Goodman, Marlene & Spizzirri, Peter M., illus. 32p. (gr. 1-8). 1981. pap. 1.75 (*0-86545-034-X*) Spizzirri.
Werner, Vivian. Dolls. 144p. 1991. pap. 2.95 (*0-380-76044-4*, Camelot) Avon.
York, Carol B. Christmas Dolls. (gr. 4-7). 1993. pap. 2.75 (*0-590-42435-1*) Scholastic Inc.
Young, Robert S. Dolls. LC 92-3498. (Illus.). 72p. (gr. 5 up). 1992. text ed. 13.95 RSBE (*0-87518-517-7*, Dillon) Macmillan Child Grp.

DOLLS–FICTION

Bailey, Carolyn S. Miss Hickory. Gannett, Ruth, illus. LC 46-7275. (gr. 4-7). 1977. pap. 3.99 (*0-14-030956-X*, Puffin) Puffin Bks.
—Miss Hickory. Gannett, Ruth, illus. (gr. 4-7). 1946. pap. 14.00 (*0-670-47940-3*) Viking Child Bks.
Berger, Barbara H. The Jewel Heart. LC 94-5691. (Illus.). 32p. (ps-3). 1994. PLB 15.95 (*0-399-22681-8*, Philomel Bks) Putnam Pub Group.
Bonners, Susan. Wooden Doll. (Illus.). (ps-3). 1991. 13.95 (*0-688-08280-7*); PLB 13.88 (*0-688-08282-3*) Lothrop.
Brink, Carol R. The Bad Times of Irma Baumlein. 2nd ed. Hyman, Trina S., illus. LC 91-13976. 144p. (gr. 3-7). 1991. pap. 3.95 (*0-689-71513-7*, Aladdin) Macmillan Child Grp.
Buffett, Jimmy & Buffett, Savannah J. Trouble Dolls. Ingber, Bonnie V., intro. by. Davis, Lambert, illus. 32p. (gr. 1 up). 1991. 14.95 (*0-15-290790-4*) HarBrace.
Burnett, Frances H. Racketty-Packetty House: As Told by Queen Crosspatch. Cady, Harrison, illus. 72p. (gr. 3-6). 1992. 4.99 (*0-517-07249-1*, Pub. by Derrydale Bks) Random Hse Value.
Caudill, Rebecca. The Best-Loved Doll. Gilbert, Elliot, illus. LC 92-898. 64p. (ps-2). 1992. 12.95 (*0-8050-2103-5*, Bks Young Read) H Holt & Co.
Conrad, Pam. Doll Face Has a Party! Selznick, Brian, illus. LC 93-33207. 32p. (ps-2). 1994. 15.00 (*0-06-024262-0*); PLB 14.89 (*0-06-024263-9*) HarpC Child Bks.
Dexter, Catherine. The Doll Who Knew the Future. Cohn, Amy, ed. LC 94-82. 208p. (gr. 5 up). 1994. pap. 4.95 (*0-688-13117-4*, Pub. by Beech Tree Bks) Morrow.
—The Oracle Doll. (gr. k-6). 1988. pap. 2.95 (*0-440-40114-3*, YB) Dell.
Dicks, Terrance. Sally Ann & the Mystery Picnic. Sims, Blanche, illus. LC 92-22074. (gr. 1-3). 1993. pap. 14.00 JRT (*0-671-79427-2*, S&S BFYR) S&S Trade.
—Sally Ann & the School Show. LC 91-1541. (ps-3). 1992. pap. 14.00 (*0-671-74513-1*, S&S BFYR) S&S Trade.
—Sally Ann on Her Own. Sims, Blanche, illus. LC 91-15379. 64p. (gr. k-3). 1992. pap. 14.00 jacketed (*0-671-74512-3*, S&S BFYR) S&S Trade.
Dillon, Barbara. The Teddy Bear Tree. MacDonald, Patricia, ed. Rose, David, illus. 80p. (gr. 2-5). 1990. pap. 2.95 (*0-671-68432-9*, Minstrel Bks) PB.
Dolson, Gina, ed. Lisa & the Magic Doll: Russian & Ukrainian Fairy Tales. Mandeville, Jerry & Brodsky, Anna, trs. from RUS & UKR. Mawolski, Stanley M., illus. 56p. (Orig.). (gr. 4-10). 1986. pap. 4.50x (*0-914265-07-5*) New Eng Pub MA.
Dreyer, Ellen, retold by. Raggedy Ann & Andy Second Giant Treasury. Gruelle, Johnny, illus. 80p. 1989. 5.99 (*0-517-66719-3*) Random Hse Value.
Elliott, Dan. My Doll Is Lost! Manthieu, Joe, illus. LC 83-11211. 40p. (ps-3). 1984. 4.95 (*0-394-86251-1*); lib. bdg. 6.99 (*0-394-96251-6*) Random Bks Yng Read.
—My Doll Is Lost! Mathieu, Joe, illus. LC 83-11211. 40p. (ps-3). 1993. pap. 2.99 (*0-679-83953-4*) Random Bks Yng Read.
Field, Rachel. Hitty: Her First Hundred Years. reissue ed. Lathrop, Dorothy P., illus. LC 29-22704. 224p. (gr. 4-6). 1969. SBE 14.95 (*0-02-734840-7*, Macmillan Child Bk) Macmillan Child Grp.
Frank, John. Erin's Voyage. Schutzer, Dena, illus. LC 92-31783. (ps-1). 1994. pap. 15.00 (*0-671-79585-6*, S&S BFYR) S&S Trade.
Gardam, Jane. Through the Dolls' House Door. LC 87-200. (Illus.). 128p. (gr. 5 up). 1987. 10.25 (*0-688-07447-2*) Greenwillow.
—Through the Dolls' House Door. (gr. 4-7). 1991. pap. 3.25 (*0-440-40433-9*) Dell.
Garelick, May. Just My Size. Pene Du Bois, William, illus. LC 89-34513. 32p. (ps-3). 1990. HarpC Child Bks.
George, Linda C. The Hallelujah Corn Cobs. Verreaux, V. Carlin, illus. LC 90-71549. 41p. (Orig.). (gr. k-6). 1991. pap. 4.95 (*1-56002-027-X*) Aegina Pr.
Godden, Rumer. Candy Floss. Hogrogian, Nonny, illus. 64p. (ps-3). 1991. 16.95 (*0-399-21807-6*, Philomel) Putnam Pub Group.
—Four Dolls. Baynes, Pauline, illus. LC 83-14157. 144p. (gr. 4-6). 1984. reinforced 13.00 (*0-688-02801-2*) Greenwillow.
—Four Dolls. (gr. 3-7). 1986. pap. 4.95 (*0-440-42568-9*) Dell.
Greenfield, Eloise. My Doll, Keshia. Gilchrist, Jan S., illus. 12p. (ps-1). 1991. bds. 5.95 (*0-86316-203-7*) Writers & Readers.
Griffith, Helen V. Doll Trouble. Lamb, Susan C., illus. LC 92-31510. 128p. (gr. 3 up). 1993. 13.00 (*0-688-12421-6*) Greenwillow.
Gruelle, Johnny. Original Adventures of Raggedy Ann. LC 88-3684. (Illus.). 64p. 1988. 7.99 (*0-517-66581-6*) Random Hse Value.
—Raggedy Andy Stories. Gruelle, Johnny, illus. 96p. (ps up). 1987. Repr. PLB 25.95x (*0-89966-618-3*) Buccaneer Bks.
—Raggedy Andy Stories. (Illus.). 1976. 24.95 (*0-8488-1353-7*) Amereon Ltd.
—Raggedy Andy Stories: Introducing the Little Rag Brother of Raggedy Ann. reissued ed. Gruelle, Johnny, illus. Gruelle, Kim, afterword by. LC 93-21967. (Illus.). 96p. (gr. k up). 1993. SBE 15.95 (*0-02-737586-2*, Macmillan Child Bk) Macmillan Child Grp.
—Raggedy Ann & Andy & the Camel with the Wrinkled Knees. (gr. 1-4). 1977. pap. 1.95 (*0-440-47390-X*) Dell.
—Raggedy Ann Stories. reissued ed. Gruelle, Johnny, illus. Gruelle, Kim, afterword by. LC 93-630. (Illus.). 96p. (gr. k up). 1993. SBE 15.95 (*0-02-737585-4*, Macmillan Child Bk) Macmillan Child Grp.
—The Raggedy Ann Stories. Facsimile ed. LC 93-8698. 1994. 6.99 (*0-517-10037-1*, Pub. by Derrydale Bks) Random Hse Value.
Gruelle, Johny. Original Adventures of Raggedy Ann & Raggedy Andy. (Illus.). 128p. 1991. 9.99 (*0-517-06631-9*, Pub. by Derrydale Bks) Random Hse Value.
Hahn, Mary D. Doll in the Garden. 144p. 1990. pap. 3.50 (*0-380-70865-5*, Camelot) Avon.
Haley, Gail E. Marguerite. Haley, Gail E., illus. (ps-3). 1993. pap. 16.95 (*0-87460-262-9*) Lion Bks.
Hennings, Jennifer. The Penny Doll. LC 93-34496. 1994. 19.97 (*0-8114-4461-9*) Raintree Steck-V.
Hines, Anna C. Maybe a Band-Aid Will Help. Hines, Anna C., illus. LC 84-1533. 24p. (ps-1). 1984. 8.95 (*0-525-44115-8*, 0869-260, DCB) Dutton Child Bks.
Hiser, Constance. The Missing Doll. Ramsey, Marcy, illus. 72p. (gr. 4-7). 1993. 13.95 (*0-8234-1046-3*) Holiday.
Hoban, Russell & Hoban, Lillian. The Stone Doll of Sister Brute. (Illus.). 32p. (gr. 1-4). 1992. pap. 2.99 (*0-440-40681-1*, YB) Dell.
Horowitz, Jordan. Three's a Crowd. Ong, Cristina, illus. 32p. (ps-3). 1992. pap. 2.50 (*0-590-45459-5*) Scholastic Inc.
Jensen, Patricia. Barbie: Show Time! Duarte, Pamela, illus. 24p. (ps-3). 1992. pap. write for info. (*0-307-12691-9*, 12691, Golden Pr) Western Pub.
Johnson, Phyllis. The Boy Toy. Shiffman, Lena, illus. 32p. (gr. k-3). 1988. pap. 5.95 (*0-914996-26-6*) Lollipop Power.
Karas, Jacqueline. The Dollhouse. Riches, Judith, illus. LC 92-32262. 32p. (ps up). 1993. 15.00 (*0-688-12480-1*, Tambourine Bks); PLB 14.93 (*0-688-12481-X*, Tambourine Bks) Morrow.
Kehret, Peg. Wally Amos Presents Chip & Cookie: The First Adventure. (gr. 4-7). 1991. 14.95 (*0-87491-988-6*) Acropolis.
Kirkpatrick, Patricia. Plowie. Kirkpatrick, Joey, illus. LC 93-13712. (ps-3). 1994. 14.95 (*0-15-262802-9*) HarBrace.
Kuklin, Susan. How a Doll Is Made. LC 93-23332. (Illus.). 32p. (gr. k-4). 1994. 15.95 (*1-56282-666-2*); PLB 15.89 (*1-56282-667-0*) Hyprn Child.
Lamm, C. Drew. Anniranni & Mollymishi the Wild-Haired Doll. Ohi, Ruth, illus. 24p. (ps-2). 1990. 14.95 (*1-55037-105-3*, Pub. by Annick CN); pap. 5.95 (*1-55037-106-1*, Pub. by Annick CN) Firefly Bks Ltd.
Leeka, M. C. The Doll's Tea Party. County Studio Staff, illus. 24p. (ps-2). 1993. pap. text ed. 0.99 (*1-56293-343-4*) McClanahan Bk.
Lippert, Donald F. Mister B. Hedden, Randall, illus. 32p. (ps). 1989. write for info. Pastel Pubns.
Lukic, Marie. Pasquale's Gift. Kretschmar, Sonia, illus. LC 93-29002. 1994. 4.25 (*0-383-03768-9*) SRA Schl Grp.
Lunn, Janet. Double Spell. 144p. (gr. 3-7). 1986. pap. 3.95 (*0-14-031858-5*, Puffin) Puffin Bks.
McGinley, Phyllis. Most Wonderful Doll in the World. 1990. 10.95 (*0-590-43476-4*) Scholastic Inc.
—The Most Wonderful Doll in the World. 1992. 3.95 (*0-590-43477-2*, Blue Ribbon Bks) Scholastic Inc.
McKissack, Patricia C. Nettie Jo's Friends. Cook, Scott, illus. LC 87-14080. 40p. (ps-4). 1989. 16.00 (*0-394-89158-9*); lib. bdg. 15.99 (*0-394-99158-3*) Knopf Bks Yng Read.
McMillan, Bruce. Ghost Doll. (Illus.). 32p. (gr. k-6). 1989. 15.00 (*0-317-93062-1*) Apple Isl Bks.
Martin, Ann M. Karen's Doll. 112p. 1991. pap. 2.95 (*0-590-44832-3*) Scholastic Inc.
Martin, David. Lizzie & Her Dolly. Gliori, Debi, illus. LC 92-54404. 24p. (ps). 1993. 5.95 (*1-56402-060-6*) Candlewick Pr.
Mills, Elaine. The Cottage at the End of the Lane. LC 93-45748. (Illus.). 32p. (ps-4). 1994. 15.00 (*0-517-59703-9*) Crown Bks Yng Read.
Minshull, Evelyn. The Cornhusk Doll. Wallace, Edwin B., illus. LC 86-27125. 72p. (ps). 1987. 14.95 (*0-8361-3431-1*) Herald Pr.
Morgan, Helen. The Witch Doll. (Illus.). 144p. (gr. 3-7). 1992. 14.00 (*0-670-84285-0*) Viking Child Bks.
Nash, Corey. Little Treasury of Raggedy Ann & Andy. Gruelle, Johnny, illus. (ps-1). 1984. 5.99 (*0-517-44730-4*) Random Hse Value.
Nister, Ernest. Little Dolls. Intervisual Staff, illus. 10p. (ps up). 1991. 4.95 (*0-399-22107-7*, Philomel) Putnam Pub Group.
Njoku, Scholastica I. The Miracle of a Christmas Doll. McKay, Suzanne, illus. 29p. (gr. k up). 1986. perfect bdg. 5.95x (*0-9617833-0-3*) S I NJOKU.
Parker. The Norfin Trolls from A to Z. 1993. pap. 2.50 (*0-590-46957-6*) Scholastic Inc.
Pendergraft, Patricia. The Legend of Daisy Flowerdew. 192p. 1990. 14.95 (*0-399-22176-X*, Philomel Bks) Putnam Pub Group.
Polacco, Patricia. Babushka's Doll. LC 89-6122. (Illus.). 40p. (ps-1). 1990. pap. 14.95 jacketed, 3-pc. bdg. (*0-671-68343-8*, S&S BFYR) S&S Trade.
—Babushka's Doll. (gr. 2). 1990. pap. 14.95 (*0-663-56215-5*) Silver Burdett Pr.
Pomerantz, Charlotte. The Chalk Doll. Lessac, Frane, illus. LC 88-872. 32p. (gr. k-3). 1989. 15.00 (*0-397-32318-2*, Lipp Jr Bks); PLB 14.89 (*0-397-32319-0*) HarpC Child Bks.
—Chalk Doll. Lessac, Frane, illus. LC 88-872. 32p. (ps-3). 1993. pap. 4.95 (*0-06-443333-1*, Trophy) HarpC Child Bks.
Regan, Dian C. The Curse of the Trouble Dolls. Chesworth, Michael, illus. LC 91-28572. 64p. (gr. 2-4). 1992. 14.95 (*0-8050-1944-8*, Bks Young Read) H Holt & Co.
Rendal, Justine. A Child of Their Own. 96p. (gr. 3-7). 1992. 13.00 (*0-670-84418-7*) Viking Child Bks.
Rosenberg, Liz. The Scrap Doll. Ballard, Robin, illus. LC 90-35668. 32p. (ps-3). 1991. PLB 13.89 (*0-06-024865-3*) HarpC Child Bks.
Rupert, Rona. Straw Sense. Dooling, Mike, illus. LC 92-8775. 1993. pap. 14.00 (*0-671-77047-0*, S&S BFYR) S&S Trade.
Sandburg, Carl. The Wedding Procession of the Rag Doll & the Broom Handle & Who Was in It. Pincus, Harriet, illus. LC 67-10211. 32p. (ps-3). 1978. pap. 3.95 (*0-15-695487-7*, Voyager Bks) HarBrace.
Schulman, Janet. The Big Hello. Hoban, Lillian, illus. LC 75-33672. (gr. 1-4). 1976. 13.95 (*0-688-80036-X*) Greenwillow.
Shaine, Frances. My Doll Is Just Like Me. Bingham, Edith, illus. 30p. (Orig.). (ps-2). 1993. pap. 4.95 (*1-884217-03-6*) Wellford.
Slate, Barbara, et al. Barbie. 96p. 1992. pap. 8.95 (*0-87135-878-6*) Marvel Entmnt.
Snyder, Margaret, adapted by. The Trolls & the Shoemaker. Kong, Emilie, illus. 24p. (ps-4). 1992. 20.00 (*0-307-74027-7*, 64027, Golden Pr) Western Pub.
Stevenson, James. The Night after Christmas. (Illus.). 32p. (ps up). 1993. pap. 4.95 (*0-688-04590-1*, Mulberry) Morrow.
Stover, Marjorie. When the Dolls Woke. Levine, Abby, ed. Loccisano, Karen, illus. LC 85-3154. 128p. (gr. 3-6). 1985. PLB 10.95 (*0-8075-8882-2*) A Whitman.
Stover, Marjorie F. When the Dolls Woke. 1993. pap. 2.95 (*0-590-44624-X*) Scholastic Inc.
Taylor, E. J. Rag Doll Press. (ps up). 1992. 12.95 (*1-56402-150-5*) Candlewick Pr.
Tews, Susan. Gingerbread Doll. 32p. (ps-3). 1993. 14.95 (*0-395-56438-7*, Clarion Bks) HM.
Tsutsui, Yoriko. Anna's Special Present. Hayashi, Akiko, illus. 32p. (ps-3). 1990. pap. 3.95 (*0-14-054219-1*, Puffin) Puffin Bks.
Udry, Janice M. Thump & Plunk. Schweninger, Ann, illus. LC 80-8443. 32p. (ps-3). 1981. 14.00 (*0-06-026149-8*); PLB 13.89 (*0-06-026150-1*) HarpC Child Bks.
Van Walsum-Quispel, J. Tina's Island Home. Leeflang-Oudenarden, C., illus. LC 71-99920. 36p. (gr. k-5). 7.95 (*0-87592-053-5*) Scroll Pr.
Waddell, Martin. The Toymaker. Milne, Terry A. & Milne, Terry A., illus. LC 91-58762. 32p. (ps up). 1992. 13.95 (*1-56402-103-3*) Candlewick Pr.
Waugh, Sylvia. The Mennyms. LC 93-15901. 216p. (gr. 5 up). 1994. 14.00 (*0-688-13070-4*) Greenwillow.
—Mennyms in the Wilderness. LC 94-6881. 1995. write for info. (*0-688-13820-9*) Greenwillow.
Wilkins, Sarah & Mennella, Roxanna. Dolls. Fisher, Barbara, ed. Wilkins, Sarah & Mennella, Roxanna, illus. 27p. (Orig.). (gr. 4-6). 1984. pap. 2.00 (*0-934830-34-7*) Ten Penny.
Willoughby, Alana. My Dolly. Wasserman, Dan, ed. Reese, Bob, illus. (gr. k-1). 1979. 7.95 (*0-89868-075-1*); pap. 2.95 (*0-89868-086-7*) ARO Pub.
Winthrop, Elizabeth. Katharine's Doll. LC 83-1408. (Illus.). 32p. (gr. k-3). 1991. pap. 3.95 (*0-525-44738-5*, Puffin) Puffin Bks.
Zemach, Harve. Mommy, Buy Me a China Doll. Zemach, Margot, illus. 32p. (ps up). 1989. pap. 4.95 (*0-374-45286-5*, Sunburst) FS&G.
Ziefert, Harriet. Where's Bobo? Rader, Laura, illus. LC 92-24495. 24p. (ps up). 1993. 10.95 (*0-688-12327-9*, Tambourine Bks) Morrow.
Zolotow, Charlotte. William's Doll. Pene Du Bois, William, illus. LC 70-183173. 32p. (ps-3). 1972. 14.00 (*0-06-027047-0*); PLB 13.89 (*0-06-027048-9*) HarpC Child Bks.

DOLPHINS

Anderson, J. I. I Can Read About Whales & Dolphins. LC 72-96955. (Illus.). (gr. 2-4). 1973. pap. 2.50 (*0-89375-052-2*) Troll Assocs.

Bailey, Donna. Los Delfines. LC 91-23779. (SPA., Illus.). 32p. (gr. 1-4). 1992. PLB 18.99 (*0-8114-2656-4*) Raintree Steck-V.

—Dolphins. LC 90-22110. (Illus.). 32p. (gr. 1-4). 1992. PLB 18.99 (*0-8114-2647-5*); pap. 3.95 (*0-8114-4616-6*) Raintree Steck-V.

Bakoske, Sharon & Davidson, Margaret. Dolphins. Courtney, illus. 48p. (Orig.). (gr. 1-3). 1993. PLB 7.99 (*0-679-94437-0*); pap. 3.50 (*0-679-84437-6*) Random Bks Yng Read.

Barrett, Norman S. Delfines. LC 90-71418. (SPA., Illus.). 32p. (gr. k-4). 1991. PLB 11.90 (*0-531-07920-1*) Watts.

—Dolphins. LC 88-51518. (Illus.). 32p. (gr. k-6). 1989. PLB 11.90 o.s. (*0-531-10706-X*) Watts.

Behrens, June. Dolphins! LC 89-33846. 48p. (gr. 1-4). 1989. PLB 12.30 (*0-516-00517-0*); pap. 5.95 (*0-516-40517-9*) Childrens.

Berg, Cami. D Is for Dolphin. Bionoi, Janet, illus. 64p. 1991. 18.95 (*1-879244-01-2*) Windom Bks.

Carwardine, Mark. Whales, Dolphins, & Porpoises. LC 92-7624. (Illus.). 64p. (gr. 3 up). 1992. 11.95 (*1-56458-144-6*) Dorling Kindersley.

Cousteau Society Staff. Dolphins. LC 91-30589. (Illus.). 24p. (ps-1). 1992. pap. 3.95 (*0-671-77062-4*, Little Simon) S&S Trade.

Craig, Janet. Discovering Whales & Dolphins. Johnson, Pamela, illus. LC 89-5004. 32p. (gr. 2-4). 1990. PLB 11.59 (*0-8167-1759-1*); pap. text ed. 2.95 (*0-8167-1760-5*) Troll Assocs.

Crump, Donald J., ed. Dolphins: Our Friends in the Sea. LC 86-18126. (Illus.). 104p. (gr. 4-5). 1986. 8.95 (*0-87044-609-6*) Natl Geog.

Davidson, Margaret. Nine True Dolphin Stories. 64p. (gr. 2-5). 1990. pap. 2.75 (*0-590-42399-1*) Scholastic Inc.

The Dolphin. (Illus.). 28p. (gr. 2-5). 1988. pap. 3.50 (*0-8167-1576-9*) Troll Assocs.

Dolphins. 1991. PLB 14.95 (*0-88682-339-0*) Creative Ed.

Ginsberg, Daniel. Whales & Dolphins: An Educational Coloring Book. Ginsberg, Daniel, illus. 32p. (Orig.). (gr. 1-4). 1989. pap. 2.95 (*0-9623284-0-5*) R Rinehart.

Gordon, Sharon. Dolphins & Porpoises. Goldsborough, June, illus. LC 84-8594. 32p. (gr. k-2). 1985. PLB 11.59 (*0-8167-0340-X*); pap. text ed. 2.95 (*0-8167-0443-0*) Troll Assocs.

Green, Carl R. & Sanford, William R. The Bottlenose Dolphin. LC 87-19420. (Illus.). 48p. (gr. 5). 1987. text ed. 12.95 RSBE (*0-89686-329-8*, Crestwood Hse) Macmillan Child Grp.

Grover, Wayne. Dolphin Adventure: A True Story. Fowler, Jim, illus. LC 92-25545. 48p. (gr. 4 up). 1993. pap. 3.95 (*0-688-12277-9*, Pub. by Beech Tree Bks) Morrow.

Hall, Howard. A Charm of Dolphins. rev. ed. Leon, Vicki, ed. LC 93-9752. (Illus.). 48p. (Orig.). (gr. 5 up). 1993. perfect bdg. 9.95 (*0-918303-33-8*) Blake Pub.

Hatherly, Janelle & Nicholls, Delia. Dolphins & Porpoises. 72p. 1990. 17.95 (*0-8160-2272-0*) Facts on File.

Houghton, Sue. Dolphin. Camm, Martin, illus. LC 91-44819. 32p. (gr. 4-6). 1993. lib. bdg. 11.59 (*0-8167-2767-8*); pap. text ed. 3.95 (*0-8167-2768-6*) Troll Assocs.

Hoyt, Erich. Riding with the Dolphins: The Equinox Guide to Dolphins & Porpoises. Folkens, Pieter, illus. 64p. (gr. 5 up). 1992. PLB 17.95 (*0-921820-55-0*, Pub. by Camden Hse CN); pap. 9.95 (*0-921820-57-7*, Pub. by Camden Hse CN) Firefly Bks Ltd.

Kovacs, Deborah. All about Dolphins. (Illus.). 32p. (Orig.). (gr. 1-8). 1994. pap. 3.95 (*1-884506-09-7*) Third Story.

Leatherwood, Stephen P. & Reeves, Randall R. The Sea World Book of Dolphins. LC 86-46212. 111p. (gr. 4-7). 1987. pap. 9.95 (*0-15-271957-1*, Voyager Bks) HarBrace.

Morris, Robert A. Dolphin. Funai, Mamoru, illus. LC 75-6292. 64p. (gr. k-3). 1983. pap. 3.50 (*0-06-444043-5*, Trophy) Irwin Prof Pubng.

Palmer, S. Delfines (Dolphins) 1991. 8.95s.p. (*0-86592-849-5*) Rourke Enter.

—Dolphins. (Illus.). (gr. k-5). 1989. lib. bdg. 11.94 (*0-86592-363-9*); 8.95s.p. (*0-685-58619-7*) Rourke Corp.

Papastavrou, Vassili. Whales & Dolphins. LC 90-14400. (Illus.). 32p. (gr. k-4). 1991. 12.40 (*0-531-18394-7*, Pub. by Bookwright Pr) Watts.

Parker, Steve. Whales & Dolphins. LC 93-38518. (Illus.). 60p. (gr. 3-6). 1994. 16.95 (*0-87156-465-3*) Sierra.

Patent, Dorothy H. Dolphins & Porpoises. LC 87-45332. (Illus.). 96p. (gr. 4 up). 1987. reinforced bdg. 15.95 (*0-8234-0663-6*) Holiday.

—Looking at Dolphins & Porpoises. LC 88-39985. (Illus.). 48p. (ps-4). 1989. reinforced bdg. 13.95 (*0-8234-0748-9*) Holiday.

Propper. Dolphin, Reading Level 3-4. (Illus.). 28p. (gr. 2-5). 1983. PLB 16.67 (*0-86592-861-4*); 12.50s.p. (*0-685-58815-7*) Rourke Corp.

Raintree Publishers Inc. Staff. Dolphins. LC 87-28717. (Illus.). 64p. (Orig.). (gr. 5-9). 1988. PLB 11.95 (*0-8172-3085-8*) Raintree Steck-V.

Reed, Don C. The Dolphins & Me. Carroll, Pamela & Carroll, Walter, illus. 144p. (gr. 5 up). 1989. Little.

—The Dolphins & Me. 1990. pap. 2.95 (*0-590-43294-X*) Scholastic Inc.

Reiss, Diana. Camelot World: The Secrets of the Dolphins. 144p. (Orig.). (gr. 7). 1991. pap. 2.95 (*0-380-76046-0*, Camelot) Avon.

Sabin, Francene. Whales & Dolphins. Johnson, Pamela, illus. LC 84-2709. 32p. (gr. 3-6). 1985. PLB 9.49 (*0-8167-0286-1*); pap. text ed. 2.95 (*0-8167-0287-X*) Troll Assocs.

Seligson, Marcia. Dolphins at Grassy Key. Ancona, George, illus. LC 88-27143. 48p. (gr. 1 up). 1989. RSBE 15.95 (*0-02-781800-4*, Macmillan Child Bk) Macmillan Child Grp.

Serventy, Vincent. Whale & Dolphin. LC 84-15118. (Illus.). 24p. (gr. k-5). 1985. PLB 9.95 (*0-8172-2401-7*); pap. 3.95 (*0-8114-6892-5*) Raintree Steck-V.

Smith, Roland. Whales, Dolphins, & Porpoises in the Zoo. Munoz, William, photos by. LC 93-35425. (Illus.). 64p. (gr. 3-6). 1994. PLB 14.40 (*1-56294-318-9*) Millbrook Pr.

Spizzirri Publishing Co. Staff. Dolphins: An Educational Coloring Book. Spizzirri, Linda, ed. (Illus.). 32p. (gr. 1-8). 1986. pap. 1.75 (*0-86545-073-0*) Spizzirri.

Stahl, Dean. Dolphins. 32p. (gr. 2-6). 1991. 15.95 (*0-89565-718-X*) Childs World.

Strachan. Whales & Dolphins. (Illus.). 32p. (gr. 4-6). 1991. 13.95 (*0-237-60168-0*, Pub. by Evans Bros Ltd) Trafalgar.

Whales & Dolphins. (Illus.). 32p. 1994. incl. chart 5.95 (*1-56138-470-4*) Running Pr.

Whyte, Malcolm. Dolphins & Whales Model Set. Smith, Daniel, illus. 24p. (gr. 1 up). 1994. pap. 5.95 (*0-8431-2993-X*, Troubador) Price Stern.

DOLPHINS–FICTION

Anastasio, Dina. Dolly Dolphin & the Strange New Something. William Langley Studios Staff, illus. 32p. (gr. k-3). 1994. 5.95 (*1-884506-07-0*) Third Story.

Bailey, Jill. Project Dolphin. Green, John, illus. LC 91-16007. 48p. (gr. 3-7). 1992. PLB 21.34 (*0-8114-2711-0*); pap. 4.95 (*0-8114-6547-0*) Raintree Steck-V.

Benchley, Nathaniel. Several Tricks of Edgar Dolphin. Funai, Mamoru, illus. LC 79-85038. 64p. (gr. k-3). 1970. PLB 13.89 (*0-06-020468-0*) HarpC Child Bks.

Burke, Terrill M. Dolphin Magic: The Ancient Knowledge. 310p. (Orig.). (gr. 6 up). 1993. pap. 12.25 (*1-880485-51-6*) Alpha-Dolphin.

—Dolphin Magic: The First Encounter. 305p. (gr. 6 up). 1993. pap. 12.25 (*1-880485-69-9*) Alpha-Dolphin.

Carris, Joan D. A Ghost of a Chance. Henry, Paul, illus. 160p. (gr. 3-7). 1992. 14.95 (*0-316-13016-8*) Little.

Chottin, Ariane. The Curious Little Dolphin. Raquois, Olivier, illus. LC 91-46500. 22p. (ps-3). 1992. 5.98 (*0-89577-425-9*, Readers Digest Kids) RD Assn.

DeSaix, Frank. The Girl Who Danced with Dolphins. DeSaix, Debbi D., illus. 32p. (gr. k-3). 1991. 14.95 (*0-374-32626-6*) FS&G.

Farris, Diane. In Dolphin Time. Farris, Diane, illus. LC 92-42512. 32p. (ps-12). 1994. RSBE 14.95 (*0-02-734365-0*, Four Winds) Macmillan Child Grp.

Fine, John C. The Boy & the Dolphin. Weinberger, Jane, ed. Kardas, Aleksander, intro. by. LC 90-70094. (Illus.). 34p. (gr. 4-6). 1990. 15.95 (*0-932433-60-X*); pap. 9.95 (*0-932433-79-0*) Windswept Hse.

Fun, J. J. The Partners & the Dolphins Who Moved In. 24p. (gr. k-8). 1992. pap. write for info. (*0-9632622-1-1*) J J Fun.

Hall, Elizabeth & O'Dell, Scott. Venus among the Fishes. LC 94-48133. (gr. 3 up). 1994. write for info. (*0-395-70561-4*) HM.

Heintze, Ty. Valley of the Eels: A Science Fiction Mystery. Heintze, Ty, illus. LC 93-2906. 1993. 14.95 (*0-89015-904-1*) Sunbelt Media.

Kendall, Sarita. Ransom for a River Dolphin. LC 93-19929. 1993. 18.95 (*0-8225-0735-8*) Lerner Pubns.

Lasky, Kathryn. Shadows in the Water: A Starbuck Family Adventure. LC 92-8139. 1992. 16.95 (*0-15-273533-X*, HB Juv Bks); pap. write for info. (*0-15-273534-8*) HarBrace.

L'Engle, Madeleine. A Ring of Endless Light. 336p. (gr. 9 up). 1981. pap. 4.50 (*0-440-97232-9*, LE) Dell.

Mannion, Sean. Ireland's Friendly Dolphin. (Illus.). 128p. (Orig.). (gr. 7-11). 1991. pap. 9.95 (*0-86322-122-X*, Pub. by Brandon Bk Pubs ER) Irish Bks Media.

O'Dell, Scott. Island of the Blue Dolphins. 192p. (gr. k-6). 1987. pap. 4.50 (*0-440-43988-4*, YB) Dell.

Olsen, E. A. Adrift on a Raft. Le Blanc, L., illus. LC 68-16397. 48p. (gr. 3 up). 1970. PLB 10.95 (*0-87783-000-2*); pap. 3.94 deluxe ed. (*0-87783-078-9*); cassette 10.60x (*0-87783-176-9*) Oddo.

Orr, Katherine. Story of a Dolphin. Orr, Katherine, illus. LC 92-28656. 1993. 18.95 (*0-87614-777-5*) Carolrhoda Bks.

Packard, Edward. Secret of the Dolphins. (gr. 4-7). 1993. pap. 3.50 (*0-553-29300-1*) Bantam.

Reynolds, Susan L. Strandia. (Illus.). 240p. (gr. 9-12). 1991. 14.95 (*0-374-37274-8*) FS&G.

Saylor, Florence. Orbit the Dolphin. 1993. 7.95 (*0-8062-4692-8*) Carlton.

Simons, Jamie & Simons, Scott. Why Dolphins Call: A Story of Dionysus. (gr. 3). 1991. 10.95 (*0-663-56230-9*); 8.95 (*0-685-70097-6*) Silver Burdett Pr.

Tate, Suzanne. Danny & Daisy: A Tale of a Dolphin Duo. Melvin, James, illus. LC 92-93915. 28p. (Orig.). (gr. k-3). 1992. pap. 3.95 (*1-878405-07-1*) Nags Head Art.

Vigor, John. Danger, Dolphins, & Ginger Beer. LC 92-26182. (Illus.). 192p. (gr. 3-7). 1993. SBE 14.95 (*0-689-31817-0*, Atheneum Child Bk) Macmillan Child Grp.

Zoehfeld, Kathleen W. Dolphin's First Day: The Story of a Bottlenose Dolphin. Petruccio, Steven J., illus. Thomas, Peter, Jr., contrib. by. LC 93-27270. (Illus.). 32p. (ps-2). 1994. 14.95 (*1-56899-024-3*); incl. audiocassette 19.95 (*1-56899-035-9*); incl. 14" plush toy 26.95 (*1-56899-034-0*); mini-sized bk. 4.50 (*1-56899-025-1*); mini-sized bk., incl. 7" plush toy 9.95 (*1-56899-036-7*); audiocassette avail. (*1-56899-033-2*) Soundprints.

DOMESTIC ANIMALS

For general works on farm animals. Books limited to animals as pets are entered under Pets. Books on stock raising as an industry are entered under Livestock; names of all animals are not included in this list but are to be added as needed.

see also Animals–Treatment; Camels; Cats; Cattle; Cows; Dogs; Hogs; Horses; Livestock; Pets; Reindeer; Sheep

Ask about Farm Animals. 64p. (gr. 4-5). 1987. PLB 11.95 (*0-8172-2881-0*) Raintree Steck-V.

Baby Animals on the Farm. (ps-k). 1989. bds. 3.50 (*0-7214-9534-6*) Ladybird Bks.

Baskin, Leonard. Leonard Baskin's Miniature Natural History. Baskin, Leonard, illus. 28p. (gr. k up). 1993. Repr. 14.95 (*0-88708-265-3*) Picture Bk Studio.

Bradley, Melvin. Mules: Missouri's Long Eared Miners. Gwin, Paul, ed. (Illus.). 116p. (Orig.). 1987. pap. 7.50 (*0-933842-06-6*) Extension Div.

Brown, Craig. My Barn. LC 90-41758. (Illus.). 24p. (ps up). 1991. 13.95 (*0-688-08785-X*); PLB 13.88 (*0-688-08786-8*) Greenwillow.

Conteh-Morgan, Jane. My Farm. LC 94-10589. (Illus.). 1995. write for info. (*0-553-09732-6*, Little Rooster) Bantam.

Cousins, Lucy. Farm Animals. Cousins, Lucy, illus. LC 90-35893. (ps). 1991. bds. 3.95 (*0-688-10071-6*, Tambourine Bks) Morrow.

Druist, Miriam. Wildlife on the Farm. (gr. 2 up). 1977. 6.55 (*0-686-23334-4*) Rod & Staff.

Durrell, Julie, illus. The Pudgy Book of Farm Animals. 16p. (gr. k). 1984. 2.95 (*0-448-10211-0*, G&D) Putnam Pub Group.

Everett, F. Farm Animals. (Illus.). 32p. (gr. k-1). 1993. lib. bdg. 13.96 (*0-88110-648-8*, Usborne); pap. 5.95 (*0-7460-1022-2*, Usborne) EDC.

Farm Animals. 32p. (Orig.). (ps-1). 1984. pap. 1.25 (*0-8431-1513-0*) Price Stern.

Farmyard Families. (ps-k). 1992. 8.50 (*1-56021-024-9*) W J Fantasy.

Hawksley, Gerald. Farm. Hawksley, Gerald, illus. 10p. (ps). 1990. bds. 4.95 (*1-878624-16-4*) McClanahan Bk.

Helweg, Hans. Farm Animals. LC 79-27483. (Illus.). 32p. (ps-3). 1980. pap. 2.25 (*0-394-83733-9*) Random Bks Yng Read.

Jacobsen, Karen. Farm Animals. LC 81-7686. (Illus.). 48p. (gr. k-4). 1981. PLB 12.85 (*0-516-01619-9*); pap. 4.95 (*0-516-41619-7*) Childrens.

Kindersley, Dorling. Farm Animals. LC 90-48332. (Illus.). 24p. (ps-k). 1991. pap. 7.95 POB (*0-689-71403-3*, Aladdin) Macmillan Child Grp.

Losito, Linda, et al. Pets & Farm Animals. (Illus.). 300p. (gr. 4-9). 1990. 17.95x (*0-8160-1969-X*) Facts on File.

My Book of Baby Farm Animals. (ps-2). 3.95 (*0-7214-5152-7*) Ladybird Bks.

Noonan, Diana. Donkeys. Black, Don, illus. LC 93-28998. 1994. 4.25 (*0-383-03741-7*) SRA Schl Grp.

Paladino, Catherine. Our Vanishing Farm Animals: Saving America's Rare Breeds. (ps-3). 1991. 15.95 (*0-316-68891-6*) Little.

Pearce, Q. L. & Pearce, W. J. In the Barnyard. Brook, Bonnie, ed. Bettoli, Delana, illus. 24p. (ps-1). 1990. 4.95 (*0-671-68828-6*); PLB 6.95 (*0-671-68824-3*) Silver Pr.

Rice, Ann. Farm Babies. Ogden, Bettina, illus. LC 93-26192. 32p. (ps-3). 1994. pap. 2.25 (*0-448-40212-2*, G&D) Putnam Pub Group.

Scott, Mary. A Picture Book of Farm Animals. Botto, Lisa, illus. LC 90-44888. 24p. (gr. 1-4). 1991. lib. bdg. 9.59 (*0-8167-2150-5*); pap. text ed. 2.50 (*0-8167-2151-3*) Troll Assocs.

Sears, Nancy, illus. Farm Animals. LC 77-70863. (ps-3). 1977. 8.99 (*0-394-83541-7*) Random Bks Yng Read.

Spinelli, Eileen. Farm Animals. (Illus.). 64p. (gr. k-4). 1992. PLB 13.75 (*1-878363-84-0*, HTS Bks) Forest Hse.

Stone, L. Spanish Language Books, Set 1: Animales de Granja (Farm Animals, 6 bks. 1991. 53.70s.p. (*0-86592-948-3*) Rourke Enter.

Stone, Lynn. Farm Animals Discovery Library, 6 bks. (Illus.). 144p. (gr. k-5). 1990. Set. lib. bdg. 71.64 (*0-86593-033-3*); Set. lib. bdg. 53.70s.p. (*0-685-36307-4*) Rourke Corp.

Sweet, Melissa, adapted by. & illus. Fiddle-I-Fee: A Farmyard Song for the Very Young. 32p. (ps-1). 1992. 15.95 (*0-316-82516-6*, Joy St Bks) Little.

Wells, Donna K. What Animals Give Us: So Many Things. Axeman, Lois, illus. LC 89-23991. 32p. (ps-2). 1990. PLB 14.95 (*0-89565-557-8*) Childs World.

Wormell, Christopher & Green, Kate. A Number of Animals. LC 93-17134. (Illus.). (ps-3). 1993. PLB 19.95 (*0-88682-625-X*) Creative Ed.

DOMESTIC ANIMALS–DISEASES

see Veterinary Medicine

DOMESTIC ANIMALS–FICTION

Los Aimales Domesticos. LC 92-61169. (SPA.). 28p. (ps). 1993. 3.25 (*0-679-84169-5*) Random Bks Yng Read.

Alley, R. W., illus. Old MacDonald Had a Farm. 18p. (ps). 1991. 3.95 (*0-448-40106-1*, G&D) Putnam Pub Group.

Brown, Craig. In the Spring. LC 92-17465. (Illus.). 24p. (ps up). 1994. 14.00 (*0-688-10983-7*); PLB 13.93 (*0-688-10984-5*) Greenwillow.

Carlstrom, Nancy W. Rise & Shine. Catalano, Dominic, illus. LC 92-21696. 32p. (ps-2). 1993. 15.00 (*0-06-021451-1*); PLB 14.89 (*0-06-021452-X*) HarpC Child Bks.

Carroll, Kathleen S. One Red Rooster. Barbier, Suzette, illus. 32p. (ps). 1992. 13.45 (*0-395-60195-9*) HM.

Cazet, Denys. Nothing at All. LC 93-25204. (Illus.). 32p. (ps-1). 1994. 14.95 (*0-531-06822-6*); lib. bdg. 14.99 RLB (*0-531-08672-0*) Orchard Bks Watts.

Clement, Claude. Kitty's Special Job. Raquois, Olivier, illus. LC 91-46233. 22p. (ps-3). 1992. 6.99 (*0-89577-427-5*, Readers Digest Kids) RD Assn.

Donaldson, Julia. A Squash & a Squeeze. Scheffler, Axel, illus. LC 92-16507. 32p. (ps-3). 1993. SBE 14.95 (*0-689-50571-X*, M K McElderry) Macmillan Child Grp.

Ehrlich, Amy. Parents in the Pigpen, Pigs in the Tub. Kellogg, Steven, illus. LC 91-15601. 40p. (ps-3). 1993. 14.99 (*0-8037-0933-1*); lib. bdg. 14.89 (*0-8037-0928-5*) Dial Bks Young.

Farm Animals. Dunn, Phoebe, photos by. LC 83-61244. (Illus.). 28p. (gr. k-1). 1984. 2.95 (*0-394-86254-6*) Random Bks Yng Read.

Fleming, Denise. Barnyard Banter. LC 93-11032. 1994. 15.95 (*0-8050-1957-X*) H Holt & Co.

Four Fierce Kittens. 1992. 13.95 (*0-590-45535-4*, Scholastic Hardcover) Scholastic Inc.

Fox, Mem. Hattie & the Fox. Mullins, Patricia, illus. LC 91-41727. 32p. (ps-2). 1992. pap. 4.95 (*0-689-71611-7*, Aladdin) Macmillan Child Grp.

Haas, Jessie. Busybody Brandy. Abolafia, Yossi, illus. LC 93-29569. 24p. 1994. 14.00 (*0-688-12792-4*); lib. bdg. 13.93 (*0-688-12793-2*) Greenwillow.

Harrison, David. Wake up! Sun! Wilhelm, Hans, illus. LC 85-30053. 32p. (ps-1). 1986. 3.50 (*0-394-88256-3*); lib. bdg. 7.99 (*0-394-98256-8*) Random Bks Yng Read.

Hayes, Sarah. Eat up, Gemma. Ormerod, Jan, illus. LC 87-36205. 32p. (ps-1). 1988. 13.00 (*0-688-08149-5*) Lothrop.

Himmelman, John. A Guest Is a Guest. Himmelman, John, illus. LC 90-43020. 32p. (ps-2). 1991. 13.95 (*0-525-44720-2*, DCB) Dutton Child Bks.

Hutchins, Pat. Little Pink Pig. LC 93-18176. (Illus.). 32p. (ps up). 1994. 14.00 (*0-688-12014-8*); PLB 13.93 (*0-688-12015-6*) Greenwillow.

Iverson, Diane. Where Are the Babies? Iverson, Diane, illus. 48p. (Orig.). (ps). 1992. 14.95 (*0-9623349-1-X*); pap. 8.95 (*0-9623349-2-8*) MS Pub.

Kearns, Kimberly & O'Brien, Marie. Barney's Farm Animals. Hartley, Linda, ed. Malzeke-McDonald, Karen, illus. LC 93-77014. 24p. (ps). 1993. bds. 3.95 chunky board (*1-57064-002-5*) Barney Pub.

Keremis, Constance A. Hootenanny Night. LC 91-32505. (Illus.). 32p. (gr. k-4). 1992. 12.95 (*0-938349-79-1*); pap. 6.95 (*0-938349-80-5*) State House Pr.

Kitchen, Bert. Pig in a Barrow. Kitchen, Bert, illus. LC 90-43413. 32p. (ps-3). 1991. 13.95 (*0-8037-0943-9*) Dial Bks Young.

Lesser, Carolyn. What a Wonderful Day to Be a Cow. Mathis, Melissa B., illus. LC 93-13211. 36p. (ps-2). 1995. 15.00 (*0-679-82430-8*); PLB 15.99 (*0-679-92430-2*) Knopf Bks Yng Read.

Lewison, Wendy C. Going to Sleep on the Farm. Wijngaard, Juan, illus. LC 91-3737. 32p. (ps-2). 1992. 13.00 (*0-8037-1096-8*); PLB 12.89 (*0-8037-1097-6*) Dial Bks Young.

—The Rooster Who Lost His Crow. Wickstrom, Thor, illus. LC 93-28059. 1994. write for info. (*0-8037-1545-5*); PLB write for info. (*0-8037-1546-3*) Dial Bks Young.

Lindbergh, Reeve. There's a Cow in the Road! Pearson, Tracey C., illus. LC 92-34883. 32p. (ps-2). 1993. 13.99 (*0-8037-1335-5*); PLB 13.89 (*0-8037-1336-3*) Dial Bks Young.

Lorenz, Lee. Hugo & the Spacedog. Lorenz, Lee, illus. LC 82-22960. 30p. (ps-3). 1986. P-H.

McDonnell, Flora. I Love Animals. LC 93-2463. 32p. (ps up). 1994. 14.95 (*1-56402-387-7*) Candlewick Pr.

Maddox, Tony. Fergus's Upside-Down Day. LC 94-16656. 1994. write for info. (*0-8120-6471-2*); pap. write for info. (*0-8120-9074-8*) Barron.

Maris, Ron. Ducks Quack. Maris, Ron, illus. LC 91-58726. 14p. (ps). 1992. 4.95 (*1-56402-080-0*) Candlewick Pr.

Martin, C. L. Down Dairy Farm Road. Hearn, Diane D., illus. LC 92-42848. 32p. (gr. k-3). 1994. RSBE 14.95 (*0-02-762450-1*, Macmillan Child Bk) Macmillan Child Grp.

Most, Bernard. The Cow That Went Oink. (Illus.). 32p. (ps-k). 1990. 9.95 (*0-15-220195-5*) HarBrace.

Noble, Trinka H. The Day Jimmy's Boa Ate the Wash. Kellogg, Steven, illus. LC 80-15098. 32p. (ps-3). 1980. 13.95 (*0-8037-1723-7*); PLB 13.89 (*0-8037-1724-5*); pap. 4.95 (*0-8037-0094-6*) Dial Bks Young.

Palatini, Margie. Piggie Pie. Fine, Howard, illus. LC 94-19726. 1995. write for info. (*0-395-71691-8*) HM.

Parkes, Brenda. Farmer Schnuck. Webb, Philip, illus. LC 92-31078. 1993. 4.25 (*0-383-03568-6*) SRA Schl Grp.

Potter, Beatrix. Farmyard Noises. 12p. 1991. bds. 3.50 (*0-7232-3784-0*) Warne.

—The Tale of Jemima Puddle-Duck & Other Farmyard Tales. (Illus.). 80p. (ps-3). 1990. pap. 5.95 (*0-14-050588-1*, Puffin) Puffin Bks.

—The Tale of Jemima Puddle-Duck & Other Farmyard Tales. (Illus.). 80p. (ps-3). 1993. 13.00 (*0-7232-3425-6*) Warne.

Provensen, Alice & Provensen, Martin. Our Animal Friends at Maple Hill Farm. reissue ed. Provensen, Alice & Provensen, Martin, illus. LC 74-828. 64p. (ps-3). 1992. 10.00 (*0-394-82123-8*) Random Bks Yng Read.

Ray, Mary L. Alvah & Arvilla. Root, Barry, illus. LC 93-31874. (gr. k-3). 1994. 14.95 (*0-15-202655-X*) HarBrace.

Ripley, Dorothy. Winter Barn. Schories, Pat, illus. LC 93-32420. 32p. (ps-1). 1995. pap. 2.50 (*0-679-84472-4*) Random Bks Yng Read.

Simmons, Lynn S. Sugar Lump, the Orphan Calf. (gr. 5-8). 1994. 7.95 (*0-9642573-0-0*) Argyle Bks. SUGAR LUMP, THE ORPHAN CALF is about a new-born calf found lying all alone in the pasture. Unable to find his mother, twelve-year-old Marcy takes the full responsibility of raising him. As the white-faced calf with a black ring circling his right eye grows, his behavior becomes quite amusing. Although Marcy knows she can not keep the calf she names Sugar Lump after he is weaned, she still forms a strong attachment to him. The night Sugar Lump is put into the pasture to stay with a herd of cows, Marcy becomes involved in a suspenseful search that leads to an unexpected ending. Although the story is chiefly fiction, the descriptions of the calf's humorous behavior are true. He did suck on the door knob & even the cat's ear. He did hide behind trees waiting to be called to come & get a drink of milk, he did run with the dogs, & he did tease the cat. SUGAR LUMP, THE ORPHAN CALF is a heart-warming story for children of all ages & can be easily read by children from eight to twelve years old. Order from Argyle Books, 710 Old Justin Rd., Argyle, TX 76226; 817-464-3368 or FAX 817-320-1073.
Publisher Provided Annotation.

Sloat, Teri & Westcott, Nadine B. The Thing That Bothered Farmer Brown. LC 94-24873. (gr. 1-8). 1995. write for info. (*0-531-06883-8*); PLB write for info. (*0-531-08733-6*) Orchard Bks Watts.

Slobodkina, Esphyr. The Wonderful Feast. LC 92-23416. (Illus.). 24p. 1993. 14.00 (*0-688-12348-1*); PLB 13.93 (*0-688-12349-X*) Greenwillow.

Small, David. George Washington's Cows. LC 93-39989. 1994. 15.00 (*0-374-32535-9*) FS&G.

Tafuri, Nancy. The Barn Party. LC 94-25356. 1995. write for info. (*0-688-04616-9*); write for info. (*0-688-04617-7*) Greenwillow.

—Early Morning in the Barn. Tafuri, Nancy, illus. LC 83-1436. 24p. (ps-1). 1983. 16.00 (*0-688-02328-2*); PLB 15.93 (*0-688-02329-0*) Greenwillow.

Time-Life Books Editors. Barnyard Babies: Oink, Baa, Moo, Meow, Neigh, Peep. Marshall, Blaine, ed. Time-Life Books Staff, illus. 6p. (ps). 1993. 16.95 (*0-8094-6692-9*) Time-Life.

Waddell, Martin. The Pig in the Pond. Barton, Jill, illus. LC 91-58751. 32p. (ps up). 1992. 14.95 (*1-56402-050-9*) Candlewick Pr.

Wildsmith, Rebecca & Wildsmith, Brian. Wake up, Wake up. LC 92-18704. 1993. 6.95 (*0-15-200685-0*); pap. write for info. (*0-15-200686-9*) HarBrace.

Wiltshire, Teri. The Tale of Pepper the Pony. Archer, Rebecca, illus. LC 92-46249. (ps). 1993. 8.95 (*1-85697-858-3*, Kingfisher LKC) LKC.

Wormell, Mary. Hilda Hen's Happy Birthday. LC 94-21020. 1995. write for info. (*0-15-200299-5*) HarBrace.

Ziefert, Harriet. Farm Friends. Baum, Susan, illus. 8p. (ps). 1993. 4.95 (*0-694-00506-1*, Festival) HarpC Child Bks.

—Oh What a Noisy Farm. Bolum, Emily, illus. LC 94-15171. 1994. write for info. (*0-688-13260-X*, Tambourine Bks); PLB write for info. (*0-688-13261-8*, Tambourine Bks) Morrow.

Zimmerman, Andrea G. & Clemesha, David. The Cow Buzzed. Meisel, Paul, illus. LC 91-31905. 32p. (ps-1). 1993. 15.00 (*0-06-020808-2*); PLB 14.89 (*0-06-020809-0*) HarpC Child Bks.

DOMESTIC ANIMALS–HISTORY

Facklam, Margery. Who Harnessed the Horse? The Story of Animal Domestication. Parton, Steven, illus. 176p. (gr. 2-5). 1992. 15.95 (*0-316-27381-3*) Little.

Ryden, Hope. Domestic Animals & Their Wild Ancestors. LC 94-20763. (Illus.). Date not set. write for info. (*0-525-67485-3*, Lodestar Bks) Dutton Child Bks.

DOMESTIC ANIMALS–PICTURES, ILLUSTRATIONS, ETC.

Baby Farm Animals. (Illus.). (ps). pap. 1.25 (*0-7214-9548-6*) Ladybird Bks.

Brown, Margaret W. Big Red Barn. rev. ed. Bond, Felicia, illus. LC 85-45814. 32p. (ps-1). 1989. 14.00 (*0-06-020748-5*); PLB 13.89 (*0-06-020749-3*) HarpC Child Bks.

McNaught, Harry. Animal Babies. LC 76-24175. (Illus.). (ps-1). 1977. 2.25 (*0-394-83570-0*) Random Bks Yng Read.

DOMESTIC APPLIANCES

see Household Equipment and Supplies

DOMESTIC ARCHITECTURE

see Architecture, Domestic

DOMESTIC ARTS

see Home Economics

DOMESTIC RELATIONS

see also Divorce; Marriage; Parent and Child

Berry, Joy. Every Kid's Guide to Handling Family Arguments. Bartholemew, illus. 48p. (gr. 3-7). 1987. 4.95 (*0-516-21402-0*) Childrens.

Crisfield, Deborah. Dysfunctional Families. LC 91-22088. (Illus.). 48p. (gr. 5-6). 1992. text ed. 12.95 RSBE (*0-89686-722-6*, Crestwood Hse) Macmillan Child Grp.

Deaton, Wendy & Johnson, Kendall. Living with My Family. 32p. (gr. 4-6). 1991. wkbk. 5.95 (*0-89793-084-3*); practitioner packs 15.95 (*0-89793-086-X*) Hunter Hse.

Greenberg, Keith. Family Abuse: Why Do People Hurt Each Other? (Illus.). 64p. (gr. 5-8). 1994. bds. 15.95 (*0-8050-3183-9*) TFC Bks NY.

Kurland, Morton L. Coping with Family Violence. rev. ed. Rosen, R., ed. 141p. (gr. 7-12). 1990. PLB 14.95 (*0-8239-1050-4*) Rosen Group.

Rench, Janice E. Family Violence: Coping with Modern Issues. 64p. (gr. 5 up). 1991. PLB 15.95 (*0-8225-0047-7*) Lerner Pubns.

Schenkerman, Rona D. Growing up with Family Violence. 16p. (gr. 3-8). 1993. 1.95 (*1-56688-111-0*) Bur For At-Risk.

Stark, Evan. Everything You Need to Know about Family Violence. rev. ed. (Illus.). 64p. (gr. 7-12). 1993. 14.95 (*0-8239-1755-X*) Rosen Group.

DOMESTIC RELATIONS–FICTION

Bernstein, Sharon C. A Family That Fights. Levine, Abby, ed. Ritz, Karen, illus. LC 90-29889. 32p. (gr. k-4). 1991. 11.95 (*0-8075-2248-1*) A Whitman.

Fisk, Pauline. Midnight Blue. 220p. (gr. 6-10). 1992. pap. text ed. 4.99 (*0-7459-1925-1*) Lion USA.

—Telling the Sea. 256p. (gr. 6-10). 1992. text ed. 11.95 (*0-7459-2061-6*) Lion USA.

Greenwald, Sheila. All the Way to Wit's End. (gr. k-6). 1987. pap. 2.75 (*0-440-40188-7*, YB) Dell.

Kehret, Peg. Cages. LC 90-21230. 160p. (gr. 5 up). 1991. 14.99 (*0-525-65062-8*, Cobblehill Bks) Dutton Child Bks.

DOMINION OF THE SEA

see Sea Power

DONATIONS

see Gifts

DOOLEY, THOMAS ANTHONY, 1927-1961

Brown, Alice H. Tom Dooley, Jungle Doctor. (Illus.). (gr. 1-3). 1979. pap. 1.95 (*0-03-049441-9*) Harper SF.

DOUBLE STARS

see Stars

DOUBLEDAY, ABNER, 1819-1893

Dunham, Montrew. Abner Doubleday, Young Baseball Pioneer. LC 93-45400. 1995. pap. 4.95 (*0-689-71788-1*, Aladdin) Macmillan Child Grp.

DOUBT

see Belief and Doubt

DOUGLASS, FREDERICK, 1817?-1895

AESOP Enterprises, Inc. Staff & Crenshaw, Gwendolyn J. Frederick Douglass: Adventures in Literacy. 20p. (gr. 3-12). 1991. pap. write for info. incl. cassette (*1-880771-03-9*) AESOP Enter.

Archer, Jules. They Had a Dream: The Civil Rights Struggle from Frederick Douglass to Marcus Garvey to Martin Luther King, Jr., & Malcolm X. (Illus.). 288p. (gr. 5 up). 1993. 15.99 (*0-670-84494-2*) Viking Child Bks.

Banta, Melissa. Frederick Douglass. (Illus.). 80p. (gr. 3-5). 1993. PLB 12.95 (*0-7910-1765-6*) Chelsea Hse.

Davidson, Margaret. Frederick Douglass Fights for Freedom. 80p. (gr. 2-5). 1989. pap. 2.50 (*0-590-42218-9*, Apple Paperbacks) Scholastic Inc.

Douglass, Frederick. Escape from Slavery: The Boyhood of Frederick Douglass in His Own Words. McCurdy, Michael, ed. & illus. King, Coretta S., intro. by. LC 93-19239. 64p. (gr. 4 up). 1994. Repr. of 1845 ed. 15. 00 (*0-679-84652-2*) Knopf Bks Yng Read.

Gibbs, Carrol R. Friends of Frederick Douglass. Williams, Robert M., illus. 23p. (Orig.). (gr. 5-12). 1992. pap. 5.00 (*1-877835-50-1*); pap. text ed. 3.75 (*1-877835-51-X*) TD Pub.

Girard, Linda W. Young Frederick Douglass: The Slave Who Learned to Read. Bootman, Collin, illus. LC 93-28245. 1994. write for info. (*0-8075-9463-6*) A Whitman.

Jackson, Garnet N. Frederick Douglass, Freedom Fighter. Holliday, Keaf, illus. LC 92-28777. 1992. 56.40 (*0-8136-5229-4*); pap. 28.50 (*0-8136-5702-4*) Modern Curr.

Kerby, Mona. Frederick Douglass. LC 94-15. (gr. 4 up). 1994. write for info. (*0-531-20173-2*) Watts.

McKissack, Patricia & McKissack, Fredrick. Frederick Douglass: Leader Against Slavery. Ostendorf, Ned, illus. LC 91-3084. 32p. (gr. 1-4). 1991. lib. bdg. 12.95 (*0-89490-306-3*) Enslow Pubs.

—Frederick Douglass: The Black Lion. LC 86-32695. (Illus.). 136p. (gr. 4 up). 1987. PLB 14.40 (*0-516-03221-6*); pap. 5.95 (*0-516-43221-4*) Childrens.

Miller, Douglas T. Frederick Douglass & the Fight for Freedom. (Illus.). 144p. (gr. 5 up). 1988. 16.95x (*0-8160-1617-8*) Facts on File.

Patterson, Lillie. Frederick Douglass: Freedom Fighter. (Illus.). 80p. (gr. 2-6). 1991. Repr. of 1965 ed. lib. bdg. 12.95 (*0-7910-1410-X*) Chelsea Hse.

Russell, Sharman. Frederick Douglass. King, Coretta Scott, intro. by. (Illus.). 112p. (Orig.). (gr. 5 up). 1988. 17.95 (*1-55546-580-3*); pap. 9.95 (*0-7910-0204-7*) Chelsea Hse.

Santrey, Laurence. Young Frederick Douglass: Fight for Freedom. Dodson, Bert, illus. LC 82-15993. 48p. (gr. 4-6). 1983. PLB 10.79 (*0-89375-857-4*); pap. text ed. 3.50 (*0-89375-858-2*) Troll Assocs.

Weiner, Eric. Story of Frederick Douglass: Voice of Freedom. (ps-3). 1992. pap. 3.25 (*0-440-40560-2*) Dell.

DRAFTING, MECHANICAL

see Mechanical Drawing

DRAG RACING

see Automobile Racing

DRAGONFLIES

Bernhard, Emery. Dragonfly. Bernhard, Durga, illus. LC 92-39930. 32p. (ps-3). 1993. reinforced bdg. 15.95 (*0-8234-1033-1*) Holiday.

Dunkle, Sidney W. Damselflies of Florida, Bermuda, & the Bahamas. (Illus.). 148p. (gr. 9-12). 1990. 19.95 (*0-945417-86-1*); pap. 14.95 (*0-945417-85-3*) Sci Pubs.

Harrison, Virginia. The World of Dragonflies. Oxford Scientific Films Staff, illus. LC 87-42610. 32p. (gr. 2-3). 1988. PLB 17.27 (*1-55532-310-3*) Gareth Stevens Inc.

Losito, Linda. Discovering Damselflies & Dragonflies. Caulkins, Janet, ed. LC 87-71047. (Illus.). 48p. (gr. k-6). 1988. PLB 12.40 (*0-531-18168-5*, Pub. by Bookwright Pr) Watts.

Oda, Hidetomo. Dragonflies. Pohl, Kathy, ed. LC 85-28197. (Illus.). 32p. (gr. 3-7). 1986. text ed. 10.95 (*0-8172-2534-X*) Raintree Steck-V.

O'Toole, Christopher. The Dragonfly over the Water. Oxford Scientific Films, photos by. LC 87-42613. (Illus.). 32p. (gr. 4-6). 1988. PLB 17.27 (*1-55532-306-5*) Gareth Stevens Inc.

Watts, Barrie. Dragonfly. LC 88-18412. (Illus.). 25p. (gr. k-4). 1991. PLB 7.95 (*0-382-09799-8*); pap. 3.95 (*0-382-24342-0*) Silver Burdett Pr.

DRAKE, SIR FRANCIS, 1540?-1596

Bard, Roberta. Francis Drake: First Englishman to Circle the Globe. LC 91-34522. (Illus.). 128p. (gr. 3 up). 1992. PLB 20.55 (*0-516-03067-1*) Childrens.

Gerrard, Roy. Sir Francis Drake: His Daring Deeds. (Illus.). 32p. (gr. 3 up). 1988. 15.00 (*0-374-36962-3*) FS&G.

Goodnough, David. Francis Drake. LC 78-18056. (Illus.). 48p. (gr. 4-7). 1979. PLB 10.59 (*0-89375-173-1*); pap. 3.50 (*0-89375-165-0*) Troll Assocs.

Smith, Alice. Sir Francis Drake & the Struggle for an Ocean Empire. Goetzmann, William H., ed. Collins, Michael, intro. by. (Illus.). 112p. (gr. 6-12). 1993. PLB 19.95 (*0-7910-1302-2*, Am Art Analog); pap. write for info. (*0-7910-1525-4*, Am Art Analog) Chelsea Hse.

DRAMA–COLLECTIONS

Use for collections of plays by several authors.

see also Christmas Plays

Cullen, Alan. The Golden Fleece. 74p. 1971. 4.50 (*0-87602-130-5*) Anchorage.

Fleischhacker, Daniel J. The Merry Pranks of Tyll. 46p. 1961. 4.50 (*0-87602-157-7*) Anchorage.

Foxton, David. Sepia & Song. (Illus.). 96p. (Orig.). 1990. pap. 15.00 (*0-333-40923-X*, McMillan Ed UK) Players Pr.

Gallo, Donald R., ed. Center Stage: One-Act Plays for Teenage Readers & Actors. LC 90-4050. 384p. (gr. 7 up). 1991. pap. 4.95 (*0-06-447078-4*, Trophy) HarpC Child Bks.

Garrett, Dan, ed. Friends & Neighbors. (Illus.). 96p. (Orig.). 1990. pap. 15.00 (*0-333-36054-0*, McMillan Ed UK) Players Pr.

—Girls. (Illus.). 96p. (Orig.). 1990. pap. 15.00 (*0-333-46708-6*, McMillan Ed UK) Players Pr.

—Masks & Faces. (Illus.). 96p. (Orig.). 1990. pap. 15.00 (*0-333-36056-7*, McMillan Ed UK) Players Pr.

—Scapegoats. (Illus.). 96p. (Orig.). 1990. pap. 15.00 (*0-333-36055-9*, McMillan Ed UK) Players Pr.

—Taking Issue. (Illus.). 96p. (Orig.). 1990. pap. 15.00 (*0-333-46709-4*, McMillan Ed UK) Players Pr.

Harris, Aurand. No Dogs Allowed (or Junket) 43p. 1959. 4.50 (*0-87602-164-X*) Anchorage.

Ibsen, Henrik. Four Major Plays. Grube, J. Incl. A Doll's House; The Wild Duck; Hedda Gabler; The Master Builder. (gr. 11up). 1966. pap. 3.50 (*0-8049-0120-1*, CL-120) Airmont.

Jennings, Coleman A. & Harris, Aurand. Plays Children Love, Vol. 2. Channing, Carol, frwd. by. 512p. 1988. 19.95x (*0-312-01490-2*) St Martin.

Jennings, Coleman A. & Berghammer, Gretta, eds. Theatre for Youth: Twelve Plays with Mature Themes. Davis, Jed H., frwd. by. LC 85-26515. 524p. (gr. 8 up). 1986. 30.00 (*0-292-78081-8*); pap. 17.95 (*0-292-78085-0*) U of Tex Pr.

Kamerman, Sylvia E., ed. The Big Book of Comedies. 1989. 18.95 (*0-8238-0289-2*) Plays.

—The Big Book of Holiday Plays. LC 90-7615. 335p. 1990. 18.95 (*0-8238-0291-4*) Plays.

—Plays of Black Americans. LC 87-12207. (Orig.). (gr. 2-9). 1987. pap. 13.95 (*0-8238-0279-5*) Plays.

Lamb, Wendy, ed. Meeting the Winter Bike Rider & Other Winning Plays. (Orig.). (gr. 5 up). 1986. pap. 3.50 (*0-440-95548-3*, LFL) Dell.

Lambert, Alan & Scott-Hughes, Brian. Junior Drama Workshop. (Illus.). 96p. (Orig.). 1990. pap. 15.00 (*0-333-43459-5*, McMillan Ed UK) Players Pr.

MacDonald, Margaret R. The Skit Book: One Hundred & One Skits from Kids. LC 89-29654. 152p. (gr. 1-9). 1990. 25.00 (*0-208-02258-9*, Linnet); pap. 15.00 (*0-208-02283-X*, Linnet) Shoe String.

Miller, Helen L. Everyday Plays for Boys & Girls. LC 86-8884. (Orig.). (gr. 1-6). 1986. pap. 12.00 (*0-8238-0274-4*) Plays.

Miller, Sarah W. Bible Dramas for Older Boys & Girls. LC 75-95409. (gr. 3-6). 1970. pap. 4.99 (*0-8054-7506-0*) Broadman.

Perkins, Useni. The Black Fairy & Other Plays for Children. Hill, Patrick, illus. LC 92-60054. 200p. (Orig.). 1993. pap. 13.95 (*0-88378-077-1*) Third World.

Perry, Shauneille & Jackson, Donald. Mio & Other Plays for Young People. LC 73-92790. (gr. 4 up). 1976. 5.95 (*0-89388-154-6*) Okpaku Communications.

Plays, Inc. Staff. Plays: The Drama Magazine for Young People. 1221p. 1993. text ed. 97.68 (*1-56956-382-9*) W A T Braille.

Scott, Louise. Quiet Times. 66p. (ps). 1986. saddle stitched 9.95 (*0-513-01785-2*) Denison.

Slaight, Craig, ed. New Plays from ACT's Young Conservatory. 256p. (gr. 9 up). 1992. pap. 14.95 (*1-880399-25-3*) Smith & Kraus.

Tripp, Valerie & Thieme, Jeanne. The American Girls Theater: Plays about Kirsten, Samantha, & Molly for You & Your Friends to Perform, 5 bks. Backes, Nick, et al, illus. 336p. (Orig.). (gr. 2-5). 1989. Set. pap. 14.95 (*0-937295-58-2*) Pleasant Co.

Willard, Nancy. East of the Sun & West of the Moon: A Play. Moser, Barry, illus. 64p. (gr. 3 up). 1989. 14.95 (*0-15-224750-5*) HarBrace.

DRAMA–HISTORY AND CRITICISM

Kamerman, Sylvia E. Plays of Great Achievers. 366p. (Orig.). 1992. pap. 16.95 (*0-8238-0297-3*) Plays.

Magill, Frank N., ed. Critical Survey of Drama, 7 vols. rev. ed. 3107p. (gr. 9-12). 1994. Set. PLB 425.00 (*0-89356-851-1*, Magill Bks) Salem Pr.

DRAMA–STUDY AND TEACHING

Olfson, Lewy. Fifty Great Scenes for Student Actors. (gr. 9 up). 1990. pap. 4.95 (*0-553-25520-7*) Bantam.

Tanner, Fran A. Basic Drama Projects. 6th ed. (Illus.). (gr. 9-12). 1994. pap. text ed. 20.00 (*0-931054-31-1*); tchr's. manual 8.00 (*0-931054-34-6*) Clark Pub.

DRAMATIC ART

see Acting

DRAMA–TECHNIQUE

Cassin-Scott, Jack. Amateur Dramatics. (Illus.). 144p. (gr. 10-12). 1992. 24.95 (*0-304-34146-0*, Pub. by Cassell UK) Sterling.

Korty, Carol. Writing Your Own Plays: Creating, Adapting, Improvising. LC 86-21969. 112p. (gr. 6 up). 1986. SBE 13.95 (*0-684-18470-2*, Scribners Young Read) Macmillan Child Grp.

DRAMATIC MUSIC

see Opera

DRAMATISTS

Glassman, Bruce S. Arthur Miller. (Illus.). 128p. (gr. 7-9). 1990. 12.95 (*0-382-09904-4*); pap. 9.95 (*0-382-24032-4*) Silver Burdett Pr.

DRAUGHTS

see Checkers

DRAWING

see also Anatomy, Artistic; Crayon Drawing; Drawings; Geometrical Drawing; Graphic Methods; Illustration of Books; Landscape Drawing; Mechanical Drawing; Pastel Drawing; Shades and Shadows

Albert, Gretchen D. Scribble Art: Kindergarten & Preschool. Albert, Gretchen D., illus. 85p. (ps-3). 1980. pap. text ed. 5.80 (*0-686-28105-5*) GDA Pubns.

Ames, Lee J. Draw Fifty Creepy Crawlies: The Step-by-Step Way to Draw Bugs, Slugs, Spiders, Scorpions. 1992. pap. 8.00 (*0-385-42449-3*) Doubleday.

Arnold, Tedd. My First Drawing Book. (Illus.). (ps-2). 1986. bds. 5.95 6 bds. (*0-89480-350-6*, 1350) Workman Pub.

Arnosky, Jim. Sketching Outdoors in Spring. Arnosky, Jim, illus. LC 86-21308. 48p. (gr. 4 up). 1987. 12.95 (*0-688-06284-9*) Lothrop.

Barish, Wendy, ed. I Can Draw Horses. Speirs, Gill, illus. 64p. (gr. 3-7). 1983. pap. 3.95 (*0-671-46447-7*, Little Simon) S&S Trade.

Baxter, Leon. The Drawing Book. Baxter, Leon, illus. 64p. (ps-4). 1993. pap. 5.95 (*0-8249-8633-4*, Ideals Child) Hambleton-Hill.

Berger, Joan. Hot Cars & Super Trucks Tracing Fun: Tracing Fun Books. (gr. 4-7). 1994. pap. 1.95 (*0-590-48124-X*) Scholastic Inc.

—Wacky Animals Tracing Fun. (ps-3). 1994. pap. 1.95 (*0-590-48125-8*) Scholastic Inc.

Bolognese, Don. Drawing Horses & Foals. (ps-3). 1990. pap. 3.95 (*0-531-15200-6*) Watts.

Bolognese, Don & Raphael, Elaine. Drawing America: The Story of the First Thanksgiving. 32p. 1991. 10.95 (*0-590-44373-9*, Scholastic Hardcover) Scholastic Inc.

—The Way to Draw & Color Dinosaurs. Bolognese, Don & Raphael, Elaine, illus. LC 90-8636. 48p. (Orig.). (gr. 1-7). 1991. lib. bdg. 10.99 (*0-679-90477-8*); pap. 5.99 (*0-679-80477-3*) Random Bks Yng Read.

—The Way to Draw & Color Monsters. Bolognese, Don & Raphael, Elaine, illus. LC 90-8637. 48p. (Orig.). (gr. 1-7). 1991. lib. bdg. 10.99 (*0-679-90478-6*); pap. 5.99 (*0-679-80478-1*) Random Bks Yng Read.

Bowers, Tim. Drawing: Face to Face with Tim Bowers. (Illus.). 24p. (gr. 1-6). 1994. pap. write for info. (*0-9641192-0-X*) Bowers Studio.

Boy Scouts of America. Art. (Illus.). 48p. (gr. 6-12). 1968. pap. 1.85 (*0-8395-3320-9*, 33320) BSA.

Bradley, Susannah. How to Draw Cartoons. Archer, Rebecca, illus. 48p. (gr. 3-6). 1992. pap. 2.95 (*1-56680-003-X*) Mad Hatter Pub.

Brook, Bonnie. Let's Celebrate Easter: A Book of Drawing Fun. Klein, Susan, illus. LC 87-50428. 32p. (gr. 2-6). 1988. PLB 10.65 (*0-8167-1051-1*); pap. text ed. 1.95 (*0-8167-1052-X*) Troll Assocs.

Brown, Charlene & Davis, Carolyn. Drawing Fun. Davis, Carolyn, illus. 64p. (Orig.). (gr. k up). 1988. pap. 3.95 (*0-929261-26-7*, BA01) W Foster Pub.

Butterfield, M. How to Draw Machines. 32p. (gr. 2 up). 1988. PLB 12.96 (*0-88110-316-0*); pap. 4.95 (*0-7460-0175-4*) EDC.

Cats & Dogs. (Illus.). 64p. (Orig.). (gr. 3-8). 1993. pap. 3.95 (*1-56144-310-7*, Honey Bear Bks) Modern Pub NYC.

Chip & Dale. 32p. 1991. 6.95 (*1-56010-097-4*, DS04-H); pap. 5.95 (*1-56010-091-5*, DS04) W Foster Pub.

Claridge, M. How to Draw Buildings. (Illus.). 32p. (gr. 4 up). 1992. PLB 12.96 (*0-88110-539-2*, Usborne); pap. 4.95 (*0-7460-0747-7*, Usborne) EDC.

—How to Draw Dinosaurs. (Illus.). 32p. (gr. 4 up). 1991. lib. bdg. 12.96 (*0-88110-502-3*, Usborne); pap. 4.95 (*0-7460-0673-X*, Usborne) EDC.

Cook, J. How to Draw Robots. (Illus.). 32p. (gr. 4 up). 1993. PLB 12.96 (*0-88110-538-4*, Usborne); pap. 4.95 (*0-7460-0745-0*, Usborne) EDC.

Craig, Diana. How to Draw & Paint Pets. 1991. 12.98 (*1-55521-716-8*) Bk Sales Inc.

Deacon, John. The Drawing Book. (Illus.). 64p. (gr. 4 up). 1989. pap. 5.95 (*0-590-42142-5*) Scholastic Inc.

Dean, Wayne. The Incredible, Spreadable, Magic, Drawing Book. Harryman, Diana L. & Leatherbury, Leven C., eds. Dean, Wayne, illus. 56p. (gr. 3-9). 1983. pap. 9.95 (*0-9616161-0-5*) W Dean Editions.

Der Manuelian, Peter. Hieroglyphs from A to Z: A Rhyming Book with Ancient Egyptian Stencils for Kids. (Illus.). 48p. (gr. 2 up). 1993. 19.95 (*0-8478-1701-6*) Rizzoli Intl.

Dinosaurs. (Illus.). 64p. (Orig.). (gr. 3-8). 1993. pap. 3.95 (*1-56144-308-5*, Honey Bear Bks) Modern Pub NYC.

Donald & Daisy. 32p. 1991. 6.95 (*1-56010-094-X*, DS03-H); pap. 5.95 (*1-56010-088-5*, DS03) W Foster Pub.

DuBosque, Doug. Draw! Cars. (Illus.). 80p. (Orig.). (gr. 3-9). 1993. pap. 8.95 (*0-939217-19-8*) Peel Prod.

—Learn to Draw 3-D. (Illus.). 80p. (gr. 3-9). 1992. pap. 8.95 (*0-939217-17-1*) Peel Prod.

Emberley, Ed. Ed Emberley's Great Thumbprint Drawing Book. (ps-3). 1994. 5.95 (*0-316-23668-3*) Little.

Emberley, Ed E. Ed Emberley's Big Green Drawing Book. Emberley, Ed E., illus. LC 79-16247. (gr. k up). 1979. 15.95 (*0-316-23595-4*); pap. 8.95 (*0-316-23596-2*) Little.

—Ed Emberley's Big Orange Drawing Book. (Illus.). 96p. (gr. 1-5). 1980. 15.95 (*0-316-23418-4*); pap. 8.95 (*0-316-23419-2*) Little.

—Ed Emberley's Big Purple Drawing Book. Emberley, Ed E., illus. (gr. 1 up). 1981. 14.95 (*0-316-23422-2*); pap. 9.95 (*0-316-23423-0*) Little.

—Ed Emberley's Drawing Book: Make a World. (ps-3). 1991. pap. 6.95 (*0-316-23644-6*) Little.

—Ed Emberley's Great Thumbprint Drawing Book. Emberley, Ed E., illus. (gr. 1 up). 1977. lib. bdg. 14.95 (*0-316-23613-6*) Little.

Emberley, Michael. More Dinosaurs! & Other Prehistoric Beasts. Emberley, Michael, illus. 64p. (ps-3). 1992. pap. 5.95 (*0-316-23441-9*) Little.

Endangered Animals. (Illus.). 64p. (Orig.). (gr. 3-8). 1993. pap. 3.95 (*1-56144-309-3*, Honey Bear Bks) Modern Pub NYC.

Facklam, Margery. And Then There Was One, Vol. 1. (gr. 4-7). 1990. 14.95 (*0-316-25984-5*, Joy St Bks) Little.

Filson, Henry J. Little Hands with First Drawing Practice. (Illus.). 28p. (gr. 10 up). 1978. plasctic bdg. 2.75 (*0-918554-01-2*) Old Violin.

Foster, Patience. Drawing. (gr. 2-5). 1981. (Usborne-Hayes); PLB 13.96 (*0-88110-025-0*); pap. 6.95 (*0-86020-540-1*) EDC.
Frame, Paul. Drawing Cats & Kittens. (ps-3). 1990. pap. 3.95 (*0-531-15198-0*) Watts.
—Drawing Dogs & Puppies. (ps-3). 1990. pap. 3.95 (*0-531-15199-9*) Watts.
Gillon, Edmund V. Easy to Make Lighthouse. (gr. 4-7). 1992. pap. 2.95 (*0-486-26943-4*) Dover.
Goofy & Pluto. 32p. 1991. 6.95 (*1-56010-095-8*, DS02-H); pap. 5.95 (*1-56010-089-3*, DS02) W Foster Pub.
Hartophilis, Georgene, illus. How to Draw Dinosaurs. 32p. 1991. 3.98 (*1-56156-022-7*) Kidsbks.
—How to Draw Endangered Animals. 32p. 1991. 3.98 (*1-56156-018-9*) Kidsbks.
—How to Draw Endangered Animals. 32p. 1991. pap. 2.95 (*1-56156-027-8*) Kidsbks.
Hodge, Anthony. Cartooning. Hodge, Anthony, illus. LC 91-34409. 32p. (gr. 5-9). 1992. PLB 12.40 (*0-531-17322-4*, Gloucester Pr) Watts.
—Drawing. Hayward, Ron, illus. 32p. (gr. 5-9). 1991. PLB 12.40 (*0-531-17300-3*, Gloucester Pr) Watts.
Hoff, Syd. Drawing with Letters & Numbers. (gr. 4-7). 1994. pap. 1.95 (*0-590-47030-2*) Scholastic Inc.
Holden, Lorraine & Malcarne, Vanessa. Animal Places & Faces: A Drawing Book for Kids Who Care. Arnstrong, Beverly, illus. 30p. 1983. 3.50 (*0-317-60991-2*) NAHEE.
How to Draw Monsters. 32p. (gr. 2 up). 1987. PLB 12.96 (*0-88110-274-1*); pap. 4.95 (*0-7460-0081-2*) EDC.
I Can Draw Cartoon Animals. 64p. (Orig.). (gr. k up). 1994. pap. 3.95 (*1-56010-173-3*, ICD4) W Foster Pub.
I Can Draw Dinosaurs. 64p. (gr. k up). 1994. pap. 3.95 (*1-56010-171-7*, ICD2) W Foster Pub.
I Can Draw Things That Move. 64p. (Orig.). (gr. k up). 1994. pap. 3.95 (*1-56010-172-5*, ICD3) W Foster Pub.
Jenkins, Patrick. Animation. (gr. 2-7). 1991. pap. 8.61 (*0-201-56757-1*) Addison-Wesley.
Johnson, Pamela. How to Draw the Circus. LC 86-50467. (Illus.). 32p. (gr. 2-6). 1987. PLB 10.65 (*0-8167-0856-8*, Pub. by Watermill Pr); pap. text ed. 1.95 (*0-8167-0857-6*, Pub. by Watermill Pr) Troll Assocs.
Kidd, Nina. Draw Science - Dinosaurs. 64p. (ps-3). 1992. pap. 4.95 (*0-929923-89-8*) Lowell Hse.
—Draw Science - Wild Animals. 64p. (ps-3). 1992. pap. 4.95 (*0-929923-90-1*) Lowell Hse.
—Draw Science: Horses & Ponies. 64p. 1994. pap. 4.95 (*1-56565-174-X*) Lowell Hse Juvenile.
—Gifted & Talented Learn to Draw. 64p. (gr. 1-3). 1994. pap. 4.95 (*1-56565-104-9*) Lowell Hse Juvenile.
Kinnealy, Janice. How to Draw Flowers. LC 86-50468. (Illus.). 32p. (gr. 2-6). 1987. PLB 10.65 (*0-8167-0846-0*, Pub. by Watermill Pr); pap. text ed. 1.95 (*0-8167-0847-9*, Pub. by Watermill Pr) Troll Assocs.
LaPlaca, Michael. How to Draw Boats, Trains, & Planes. Laplaca, Michael, illus. LC 81-52123. 32p. (gr. 2-6). 1982. PLB 10.65 (*0-89375-682-2*); pap. text ed. 1.95 (*0-89375-497-8*) Troll Assocs.
—How to Draw Cars & Trucks. LaPlaca, Michael, illus. LC 81-52122. 32p. (gr. 2-6). 1982. PLB 10.65 (*0-89375-681-4*); pap. text ed. 1.95 (*0-89375-498-6*) Troll Assocs.
—How to Draw Dinosaurs. LaPlaca, Michael, illus. LC 81-52118. 32p. (gr. 2-6). 1982. PLB 10.65 (*0-89375-683-0*); pap. text ed. 1.95 (*0-89375-496-X*) Troll Assocs.
Learning Works Staff. Travel Pack, No. 1: Doodle One. (gr. k-6). 1989. 8.95 (*0-88160-175-6*, LW 290) Learning Wks.
—Travel Pack, No. 2: Doodle Two. (gr. k-6). 1989. 8.95 (*0-88160-176-4*, LW 291) Learning Wks.
—Travel Pack, No. 3: Games. (gr. k-6). 1989. 14.95 (*0-88160-177-2*, LW 292) Learning Wks.
—Travel Pack, No. 4: Dinosaurs. (gr. k-6). 1989. 8.95 (*0-88160-178-0*, LW 293) Learning Wks.
Lightfoot, Marge. Cartooning for Kids. Lightfoot, Marge, illus. 64p. 1993. 16.95 (*1-895688-03-5*, Pub. by Greey dePencier CN); pap. 8.95 (*0-920775-84-5*, Pub. by Greey dePencier CN) Firefly Bks Ltd.
Loh, Carolyn. Let's Celebrate Valentine's Day: A Book of Things to Draw. Loh, Carolyn, illus. LC 87-50429. 32p. (gr. 2-6). 1988. PLB 10.65 (*0-8167-1035-X*); pap. text ed. 1.95 (*0-8167-1036-8*) Troll Assocs.
McKay, Bob. How to Draw Funny People. McKay, Bob, illus. LC 81-69658. 32p. (gr. 2-6). 1981. PLB 10.65 (*0-89375-688-1*); pap. text ed. 1.95 (*0-89375-408-0*) Troll Assocs.
McKee, Karen A., illus. How to Draw Airplanes. 32p. 1991. 3.98 (*1-56156-021-9*) Kidsbks.
—How to Draw Cars. 32p. 1991. 3.98 (*1-56156-017-0*) Kidsbks.
—How to Draw Cars. 32p. 1991. pap. 2.95 (*1-56156-026-X*) Kidsbks.
Martin, Judy. Painting & Drawing. (Illus.). 96p. (gr. 3-6). 1993. PLB 16.90 (*0-685-72619-3*); pap. 9.95 (*1-56294-709-5*) Millbrook Pr.
Meiczinger, John. How to Draw Indian Arts & Crafts. Meiczinger, John, illus. LC 88-50807. 32p. (gr. 2-6). 1989. lib. bdg. 10.65 (*0-8167-1537-8*, Pub. by Watermill Pr); pap. text ed. 1.95 (*0-8167-1515-7*, Pub. by Watermill Pr) Troll Assocs.
Mercadoocasio, Gwen. How to Draw Comics. LC 94-1837. 1994. 5.95 (*0-681-00424-X*) Longmeadow Pr.
Mickey & Minnie. 32p. 1991. 6.95 (*1-56010-093-1*, DS01-H); pap. 5.95 (*1-56010-087-7*, DS01) W Foster Pub.
Murray, Linda. How to Draw Prehistoric Animals. Shi Chen, illus. LC 93-23058. 32p. (gr. k-6). 1993. PLB 10.65 (*0-8167-3287-6*, Pub. by Watermill Pr); pap. text ed. 1.95 (*0-8167-3288-4*) Troll Assocs.
Niederhauser, Hans R. & Frohlich, Margaret. Form Drawing. Niederhauser, Hans R. & Frohlich, Margaret, illus. 57p. (Orig.). 1974. pap. 10.00 (*0-318-41110-5*) Merc Pr NY.
Oldfield, Margaret J. Lots More Tell & Draw Stories. (Illus.). (ps-3). 1973. PLB 11.95 (*0-934876-07-X*); pap. 6.95 (*0-934876-03-7*) Creative Storytime.
—More Tell & Draw Stories. (Illus.). (ps-3). 1969. PLB 11.95 (*0-934876-06-1*); pap. 6.95 (*0-934876-02-9*) Creative Storytime.
Olson, Margaret J. Tell & Draw Stories. (Illus.). (ps-3). 1963. PLB 11.95 (*0-934876-05-3*); pap. 6.95 (*0-934876-01-0*) Creative Storytime.
Palazzo, Tony. Magic Crayon. Palazzo, Tony, illus. (gr. k-2). 1967. PLB 12.95 (*0-87460-089-8*) Lion Bks.
Palmer, Glenda. Sidewalk Squares & Triangle Birds: God's Wonderful World of Shapes. LC 92-34717. (Illus.). 1993. pap. 4.99 (*0-7814-0711-7*, Chariot Bks) Chariot Family.
Pistolesi, Roseanna. Let's Celebrate Halloween: A Book of Drawing Fun. Pistolesi, Roseanna, illus. LC 87-50426. 32p. (gr. 2-6). 1988. PLB 10.65 (*0-8167-1002-3*); pap. text ed. 1.95 (*0-8167-1003-1*) Troll Assocs.
Quinn, Kay. Animals: Sixty Things I Can Draw. 1990. 4.99 (*0-517-03564-2*) Random Hse Value.
—Monsters: Sixty Things I Can Draw. 1990. 4.99 (*0-517-03565-0*) Random Hse Value.
Rancan, Janet. How to Draw Cats. Rancan, Janet, illus. LC 81-52121. 32p. (gr. 2-6). 1982. PLB 10.65 (*0-89375-679-2*); pap. text ed. 1.95 (*0-89375-680-6*) Troll Assocs.
Raphael, Elaine & Bolognese, Don. Ancient Greece. Raphael, Elaine & Bolognese, Don, illus. 32p. (gr. 5-6). 1989. PLB 13.90 (*0-531-10738-8*) Watts.
Reisenauer, Cindy, illus. How to Draw Creepy Creatures. 32p. 1991. 3.98 (*1-56156-019-7*); pap. 2.95 (*1-56156-064-2*) Kidsbks.
Robertson, Bruce & Pinkus, Sue. Let's All Draw Dinosaurs, Pterodactyls & Other Prehistoric Creatures. (Illus.). 144p. (gr. 3-7). 1991. pap. 9.95 (*0-8230-2706-6*, Watson-Guptill Bks) Watson-Guptill.
Robertson, Jane & Pinkus, Sue. Let's All Draw Cats, Dogs & Other Animals. (Illus.). 144p. (gr. 3-7). 1991. pap. 9.95 (*0-8230-2705-8*, Watson-Guptill Bks) Watson-Guptill.
—Let's All Draw Monsters, Ghosts, Ghouls & Demons. (Illus.). 144p. (gr. 3-7). 1991. pap. 9.95 (*0-8230-2707-4*, Watson-Guptill Bks) Watson-Guptill.
Robertson, Sue & Punkus, Sue. Let's All Draw Cars, Trucks & Other Vehicles. (Illus.). 144p. (gr. 3-7). 1991. pap. 9.95 (*0-8230-2704-X*, Watson-Guptill Bks) Watson-Guptill.
Sanhez, Isidro. Colored Pencils. Segu, Jordi & Sabat, Jordi, illus. 48p. 1991. pap. 7.95 (*0-8120-4719-2*) Barron.
Schreiber, Jocelyn. How to Draw Zoo Animals. Schreiber, Jocelyn, illus. LC 87-50427. 32p. (gr. 2-6). 1988. PLB 10.65 (*0-8167-1004-X*, Pub. by Watermill Pr); pap. text ed. 1.95 (*0-8167-1005-8*, Pub. by Watermill Pr) Troll Assocs.
Shackelford, Bud. Draw Animals: Learn From Former Disney Artist Bud Shackelford. Shackelford, Bud, illus. LC 92-96937. 64p. (Orig.). (gr. k-6). 1993. pap. 9.50 (*0-9634693-0-4*) B Shackelford.
Simpson, Anne. How to Draw Wild Animals. Botto, Lisa C., illus. LC 91-26928. 32p. (gr. 2-6). 1991. text ed. 10.65 (*0-8167-2481-4*); pap. text ed. 1.95 (*0-8167-2482-2*) Troll Assocs.
Smith, A. How to Draw People. (Illus.). 32p. (gr. 4 up). 1993. PLB 12.96 (*0-88110-626-7*); pap. 4.95 (*0-7460-0998-4*) EDC.
Smith, Frank C. How to Draw Cats and Kittens. (ps-3). 1988. pap. 1.95 (*0-590-44000-4*) Scholastic Inc.
—How to Draw Dinosaurs. (ps-3). 1989. pap. 1.95 (*0-590-43799-2*) Scholastic Inc.
—How to Draw Horses & Ponies. (ps-3). 1990. pap. 1.95 (*0-590-42462-9*) Scholastic Inc.
—How to Draw Silly Monsters. (Illus.). 32p. (gr. 1-6). 1989. pap. 1.95 (*0-590-43914-6*) Scholastic Inc.
Smith, L. How to Draw Horses. (Illus.). 32p. (gr. 4 up). 1993. PLB 12.96 (*0-88110-631-3*); pap. 4.95 (*0-7460-1000-1*) EDC.
Snyder, Carrie A. How to Draw Dogs. Snyder, Carrrie A., illus. LC 81-52120. 32p. (gr. 2-6). 1982. PLB 10.65 (*0-89375-686-5*); pap. text ed. 1.95 (*0-89375-687-3*) Troll Assocs.
—How to Draw Horses. Snyder, Carrie A., illus. LC 84-51871. 32p. (gr. 2-6). 1985. PLB 10.65 (*0-8167-0381-7*, Pub. by Watermill Pr); pap. text ed. 1.95 (*0-8167-0382-5*) Troll Assocs.
—You Can Draw Funny Animals. Snyder, Carrie A., illus. LC 81-69659. 32p. (gr. 2-6). 1981. PLB 10.65 (*0-89375-689-X*); pap. text ed. 1.95 (*0-89375-409-9*) Troll Assocs.
Soloff-Levy, Barbara. How to Draw Birds. LC 86-50550. (Illus.). 32p. (gr. 2-6). 1987. PLB 10.65 (*0-8167-0876-2*, Pub. by Watermill Pr); pap. text ed. 1.95 (*0-8167-0877-0*, Pub. by Watermill Pr) Troll Assocs.
—How to Draw Fairy-Tale Characters. LC 90-26789. (Illus.). 32p. (gr. 2-6). 1991. lib. bdg. 10.65 (*0-8167-2378-8*); pap. text ed. 1.95 (*0-8167-2379-6*) Troll Assocs.
—How to Draw Farm Animals. LC 84-51872. (Illus.). 32p. (gr. 2-6). 1985. PLB 10.65 (*0-89375-797-7*, Pub. by Watermill Pr); pap. 1.95 (*0-89375-798-5*) Troll Assocs.
—How to Draw Forest Animals. Soloff-Levy, Barbara, illus. LC 84-51873. 32p. (gr. 2-6). 1985. PLB 10.65 (*0-8167-0334-5*, Pub. by Watermill Pr); pap. text ed. 1.95 (*0-8167-0335-3*) Troll Assocs.
—How to Draw Ghosts, Goblins & Witches: And Other Spooky Characters. Soloff-Levy, Barbara, illus. LC 81-52124. 32p. (gr. 2-6). 1982. PLB 10.65 (*0-89375-678-4*); pap. text ed. 1.95 (*0-89375-557-5*) Troll Assocs.
—How to Draw Sea Creatures. LC 86-50469. (Illus.). 32p. (gr. 2-6). 1987. PLB 10.65 (*0-8167-0844-4*, Pub. by Watermill Pr); pap. text ed. 1.95 (*0-8167-0845-2*, Pub. by Watermill Pr) Troll Assocs.
Sonkin, Susan. How to Draw Baby Animals. Sonkin, Susan, illus. LC 81-52119. 32p. (gr. 2-6). 1982. PLB 10.65 (*0-89375-684-9*); pap. text ed. 1.95 (*0-89375-685-7*) Troll Assocs.
Speirs, Gill. I Can Draw Sharks & Whales. 64p. 1986. pap. 3.95 (*0-671-60477-5*, Little Simon) S&S Trade.
Spiers, Gill. I Can Draw Faces. 64p. 1984. pap. 3.95 (*0-671-49664-6*, Little Simon) S&S Trade.
—I Can Draw People. 1985. pap. 3.95 (*0-671-55343-7*, SSJ) S&S Trade.

Sprague, Sydney, ed. I Can Draw Animals. Salzman, Yuri, illus. 40p. (Orig.). (gr. k-6). 1994. Wkbk. 3.95 (*1-56010-170-9*, ICD1) W Foster Pub. With Walter Foster's new "I Can Draw" series, kids will enjoy hours of fun drawing pictures of all their favorite subjects, including cartoons, dinosaurs, animals, creepy creatures, bugs & spaceships - & proud parents will soon run out of space on the fridge. Each book is full of colorful step-by-step illustrations with easy-to-follow instructions that explain how to draw anything by starting with the basic shapes kids already know, such as circles, squares, triangles, & ovals. Additionally, the series uses the "grid" technique which makes it even easier for kids to reproduce the examples & achieve proportion & perspective. Each book contains gridded paper at the back that is perforated for easy removal from the binding edge. Other titles in series are: I CAN DRAW DINOSAURS, I CAN DRAW THINGS THAT MOVE, I CAN DRAW CARTOON ANIMALS, I CAN DRAW CARTOONS, I CAN DRAW CREEPYCREATURES, I CAN DRAW BUGS, & I CAN DRAW.
Publisher Provided Annotation.

Stocks, Sue. Drawing. LC 94-374. (Illus.). 32p. (gr. 1-4). 1994. 14.95 (*1-56847-211-0*) Thomson Lrning.
Swartz, Susan S. Where & Why. Reeder, Bill, illus. 24p. (Orig.). (ps-6). 1987. pap. 4.50 wkbk. (*0-943901-00-6*) Creare Pubns.
Tallarico, Tony. The Giant I Can Draw Everything. Schneider, Meg F., ed. (Illus.). 192p. (Orig.). (gr. 3-7). 1982. pap. 4.95 (*0-671-44459-X*, Little Simon) S&S Trade.
—I Can Draw Animals. 64p. (Orig.). (gr. 3 up). 1980. pap. 3.95 (*0-671-41375-9*, Little Simon) S&S Trade.
—I Can Draw Cars, Trucks, Trains & Other Wheels. Tallarico, Tony, illus. 64p. (Orig.). (gr. 3 up). 1981. pap. 3.95 (*0-671-42535-8*, Little Simon) S&S Trade.
—I Can Draw Christmas. (Illus.). 64p. (gr. 4 up). 1990. pap. 3.95 perfect bdg. (*0-671-70446-X*, Little Simon) S&S Trade.
—I Can Draw Monsters. 69p. (gr. 3 up). 1980. pap. 3.95 (*0-671-41374-0*, Little Simon) S&S Trade.
—I Can Draw Pets. 64p. 1989. pap. 3.95 (*0-671-67803-5*, Little Simon) S&S Trade.
—I Can Draw Sports. (Illus.). 40p. (gr. 4 up). 1990. pap. 3.95 (*0-671-70447-8*, Little Simon) S&S Trade.
Tatchell, J. How to Draw, Vol. I. (Illus.). 32p. (gr. 4 up). 1993. pap. 11.95 (*0-7460-0295-5*) EDC.
—How to Draw Animals. 32p. (gr. 2 up). 1988. PLB 12.96 (*0-88110-315-2*); pap. 4.95 (*0-7460-0177-0*) EDC.
—How to Draw Cartoons & Caricatures. 40p. (gr. 2 up). 1987. PLB 12.96 (*0-88110-273-3*); pap. 4.95 (*0-7460-0067-7*) EDC.

Testa, Fulvio. If You Take a Pencil. (ps-3). 1985. pap. 5.99 (*0-14-054645-6*) Dial Bks Young.
Things That Go. (Illus.). 64p. (Orig.). (gr. 3-8). 1993. pap. 3.95 (*1-56144-311-5*, Honey Bear Bks) Modern Pub NYC.
Thomasson, Merry F. I Can Draw. (ps). 1992. 9.95 (*0-9615407-6-1*) Merrybooks VA.
Thompson, R. Draw - & - Tell. Thompson, Richard, illus. 88p. 1988. 19.95 (*1-55037-032-4*, Pub. by Annick CN) Firefly Bks Ltd.
Timms, Diann. Hare & Bear Draw a Boat. (ps-3). 1993. 3.50 (*0-89577-534-4*, Dist. by Random) RD Assn.
—Hare & Bear Draw a Dinosaur. (ps-3). 1993. 3.50 (*0-89577-533-6*, Dist. by Random) RD Assn.
—Hare & Bear Draw a Horse. (ps-3). 1993. 3.50 (*0-89577-532-8*, Dist. by Random) RD Assn.
—Hare & Bear Draw a Tree. (ps-3). 1993. 3.50 (*0-89577-530-1*, Dist. by Random) RD Assn.
—Hare & Bear Draw an Airplane. (ps-3). 1993. 3.50 (*0-89577-531-X*, Dist. by Random) RD Assn.
Uncle Scrooge & Huey, Dewey & Louie. 32p. 1991. pap. 6.95 (*1-56010-098-2*, DS06-H); pap. 5.95 (*1-56010-092-3*, DS06) W Foster Pub.
Walker, Karen, illus. How to Draw Funny Faces. 32p. 1991. 3.98 (*1-56156-020-0*); pap. 2.95 (*1-56156-065-0*) Kidsbks.
Williams, H. Harland Draws Animals. (Illus.). 32p. (gr. 1-6). 1989. pap. 2.95 (*0-88625-226-1*) Durkin Hayes Pub.
—Harland Draws Cartoons. (Illus.). 32p. (gr. 1-6). 1989. pap. 2.95 (*0-88625-224-5*) Durkin Hayes Pub.
—Harland Draws Wacky & Wierd. (Illus.). 32p. (gr. 1-6). 1989. pap. 2.95 (*0-88625-232-6*) Durkin Hayes Pub.
—Harland Draws 3-D. (Illus.). 32p. (gr. 1-6). 1989. pap. 2.95 (*0-88625-229-6*) Durkin Hayes Pub.
Winnie the Pooh & Tigger. 32p. 1991. pap. 6.95 (*1-56010-096-6*, DS05-H); pap. 5.95 (*1-56010-090-7*, DS05) W Foster Pub.
Witty, Ken. A Day in the Life of an Illustrator. Sanacore, Stephen, photos by. LC 80-54100. (Illus.). 32p. (gr. 4-8). 1981. PLB 11.79 (*0-89375-448-X*); pap. 2.95 (*0-89375-449-8*) Troll Assocs.

DRAWING–FICTION

Engel, Diana. The Shelf-Paper Jungle. Engel, Diana, illus. LC 93-21772. 32p. (gr. k-3). 1994. pap. 14.95 RSBE (*0-02-733464-3*, Macmillan Child Bk) Macmillan Child Grp.
Gackenbach, Dick. Mag the Magnificent. Gackenbach, Dick, illus. LC 85-2645. 32p. (ps-3). 1987. 12.95 (*0-89919-339-0*, Clarion Bks); pap. 4.95 (*0-89919-522-9*, Clarion Bks) HM.
Gould, Marilyn. Graffiti Wipeout. LC 91-90783. 112p. (gr. 5 up). 1992. pap. 6.95 (*0-9632305-0-6*) Allied Crafts.
Hamsa, Bobbie. Federico Lapiz Rapido: Fast Draw Freddie. Hayes, Stephen, illus. LC 83-23931. (SPA.). 32p. (ps-2). 1991. PLB 10.25 (*0-516-32046-7*); pap. 2.95 (*0-516-52046-6*) Childrens.
Harding, William H. Alvin's Famous No-Horse. Chesworth, Michael, illus. LC 92-13834. 64p. (gr. 2-4). 1992. alk. paper 14.95 (*0-8050-2227-9*, Redfeather BYR) H Holt & Co.
Kleven, Elisa. The Paper Princess. LC 93-32612. (Illus.). (ps-3). 1994. 14.99 (*0-525-45231-1*, DCB) Dutton Child Bks.
MacDonald, Elizabeth. John's Picture. (ps-3). 1991. 13.95 (*0-670-83579-X*) Viking Child Bks.
McPhail, David. Moony B. Finch, Fastest Draw in the West. LC 93-37408. 1994. lib. bdg. 12.95 (*0-307-17554-5*, Artsts Writrs) Western Pub.
Nerlove, Miriam. If All the World Were Paper. Tucker, Kathy, ed. Nerlove, Miriam, illus. LC 90-39217. 32p. (gr. k-3). 1991. 13.95 (*0-8075-3535-4*) A Whitman.
Pittman, Helena C. Gerald-Not-Practical. (Illus.). 32p. (gr. k-3). 1990. PLB 18.95 (*0-87614-430-X*) Carolrhoda Bks.
Testa, Fulvio. If You Take a Pencil. LC 82-1505. 32p. (ps-2). 1985. pap. 4.95 (*0-8037-0165-9*) Dial Bks Young.
Ziefert, Harriet. Pete's Chicken. Rader, Laura, illus. LC 93-37314. 1994. 15.00 (*0-688-13256-1*, Tambourine Bks); PLB 14.93 (*0-688-13257-X*, Tambourine Bks) Morrow.

DRAWING–STUDY AND TEACHING

Armstrong, B. Build a Doodle, No. 1. 32p. (gr. k-4). 1985. 2.95 (*0-88160-124-1*, LW 133) Learning Wks.
—Build a Doodle, No. 2. 32p. (gr. k-4). 1985. 2.95 (*0-88160-125-X*, LW 134) Learning Wks.
Barto, Renzo. How to Draw Cartoon Characters. LC 92-23057. (Illus.). 32p. (gr. k-6). 1993. PLB 10.65 (*0-8167-3265-5*, Pub. by Watermill Pr); pap. text ed. 1.95 (*0-8167-3218-3*) Troll Assocs.
—How to Draw Monster, Weirdoes, & Aliens. LC 92-23056. (Illus.). 32p. (gr. k-6). 1993. PLB 10.65 (*0-8167-3245-0*, Pub. by Watermill Pr); pap. text ed. 1.95 (*0-8167-3217-5*) Troll Assocs.
Baxter, Leon. The Drawing Book. Baxter, Leon, illus. LC 90-4476. 64p. (ps-4). 1990. 13.95 (*0-8249-8475-7*, Ideals Child) Hambleton-Hill.
Birker, Stefan. Drawing & Painting with Colored Pencils. LC 92-41349. (Illus.). 128p. (gr. 9-12). 1993. pap. 16.95 (*0-8069-0312-0*) Sterling.
Bonforte, Lisa. I Can Draw Dinosaurs. (Illus.). 64p. (Orig.). (gr. 2-7). 1984. pap. 3.95 (*0-671-52756-8*, Little Simon) S&S Trade.
Drawing: A Young Artist's Guide. (Illus.). 48p. (gr. 3-6). 1994. 14.95 (*1-56458-676-6*) Dorling Kindersley.
Drawing Cats & Dogs. 1989. pap. 1.95 (*0-8167-1667-6*) Troll Assocs.
Dr. Seuss. I Can Draw It Myself: By Me, Myself with a Little Help from My Friend Dr. Seuss. Dr. Seuss, illus. LC 75-117541. 48p. (ps-4). 1970. pap. 9.00 (*0-394-80097-4*) Beginner.
DuBosque, D. C. How Do You Draw Dinosaurs? 64p. (Orig.). (gr. 3-9). 1989. pap. 6.95 (*0-939217-10-4*) Peel Prod.
DuBosque, Doug. Draw! Desert Animals. (Illus.). 64p. (Orig.). (gr. 2-8). 1995. pap. 7.95 (*0-939217-26-0*) Peel Prod.
—Draw! Grassland Animals. (Illus.). 64p. (Orig.). (gr. 2-8). 1995. pap. 7.95 (*0-939217-25-2*) Peel Prod.
—Draw! Ocean Animals. (Illus.). 64p. (Orig.). (gr. 2-8). 1994. pap. 7.95 (*0-939217-24-4*) Peel Prod.
—Draw! Rainforest Animals. (Illus.). 64p. (Orig.). (gr. 2-8). 1994. pap. 7.95 (*0-939217-23-6*) Peel Prod.

Dvorak, Robert R. The Magic of Drawing. (Illus.). 160p. (Orig.). (gr. 5 up). 1993. pap. 16.95 (*0-945625-03-0*) Inkwell Pr.
You can draw! This book reveals the secrets of drawing for children & adults, beginners & artists. This is a complete, easy-to-understand, step-by-step drawing course. Whether you are teaching, traveling, vacationing, dining, or sitting in meetings, your skill will unfold like magic when you follow these suggestions. Handsome drawings & clear text will inspire you for a lifetime of creative drawing pleasure that will nourish your heart & soul. * How to make any subject simple to draw (Page 4). * How to draw without the fear of making a mistake (Pages 11-12). * The secrets to teaching, learning, & motivating students to draw (Pages 20-21, 146). * How to make your lines communicate feelings, tell a story (Pages 38-39, 96-99). * The BIG SECRET to getting the hand to draw what your eye sees (Pages 46-51). * The MAGIC of contour drawing (Pages 54-57). * The MOST POWERFUL WAY to create depth on a flat piece of paper (Pages 52-53). * Perspective simplified (Pages 68-79). * The four basic shapes (Pages 86-91). * The secret to drawing trees (Pages 121-123) * The best sequence for drawing a face (Page 50). FREE The Artist's Drawing Pad, a 160-page sketch book, is included along with the book. Inkwell Press, P.O. Box 370371, Montara, CA 94037; 415-726-1906 or 728-1640.
Publisher Provided Annotation.

Emberley, Ed E. Ed Emberley's Drawing Book: Make a World. Emberley, Ed E., illus. LC 70-154962. (gr. 2 up). 1972. lib. bdg. 14.95 (*0-316-23598-9*) Little.
—Ed Emberley's Thumbprint Drawing Box. 32p. (ps-3). 1992. 14.95 (*0-316-23648-9*) Little.
Evans, Joy. Creative Thinking Through Art, Vol. 2: Drawing. (Illus.). 64p. (gr. 2-5). 1993. pap. text ed. 11.95 (*1-55799-264-9*) Evan-Moor Corp.
—Draw Animals Around the World. Shipman, Gary, illus. 36p. (gr. 2-6). 1992. pap. 7.95 (*1-55799-223-1*) Evan-Moor Corp.
Goyallon, Jerome. Drawing Dinosaurs. LC 93-2809. (Illus.). 80p. (gr. 3 up). 1993. 12.95 (*0-8069-8742-1*) Sterling.
Griffin, Georgene, illus. How to Draw Fantasy Creatures. 48p. 1992. pap. 2.95 (*1-56156-144-4*) Kidsbks.
Hablitzel, Marie & Stitzer, Kim H. Draw - Write - Now, Bk. 1: A Drawing & Handwriting Course for Kids! (Illus.). 64p. (gr. k-5). 1994. pap. 8.95 (*0-9639307-1-0*) Barker Creek.
Hartophilis, Georgene, illus. How to Draw Dinosaurs. 32p. (Orig.). 1990. pap. 2.95 (*0-942025-74-1*) Kidsbks.
How to Draw Cats. (Illus.). 32p. 1992. PLB 12.96 (*0-88110-580-5*); pap. 4.95 (*0-7460-0996-8*) EDC.
Levy, Barbara. How to Draw Clowns. LC 91-17171. (Illus.). 32p. (gr. 2-6). 1991. PLB 10.65 (*0-8167-2477-6*); pap. text ed. 1.95 (*0-8167-2478-4*) Troll Assocs.
McKee, Karen A., illus. How to Draw Airplanes. 32p. (Orig.). 1990. pap. 2.95 (*0-942025-73-3*) Kidsbks.
—How to Draw Trucks. 48p. 1992. pap. 2.95 (*1-56156-145-2*) Kidsbks.
Morgan, Judith. An Art Text-Workbook: Drawing (Introduction) Wallace, Dorathye, ed. (Illus.). 150p. (Orig.). (gr. 8-10). 1990. pap. 13.27 (*0-914127-51-9*); tchr's. ed. avail. Univ Class.
Plant, Andrew. Drawing Is Easy. Plant, Andrew, illus. LC 93-16116. 1994. pap. write for info. (*0-383-03692-5*) SRA Schl Grp.
Savitt, Sam. Draw Horses with Sam Savitt. (Illus.). 96p. 1991. Repr. of 1981 ed. 20.95 (*0-939481-23-5*) Half Halt Pr.
Summit Group Staff. You Can Illustrate Jack & the Beanstalk. (gr. 4-7). 1993. pap. 5.95 (*1-56530-057-2*) Summit TX.
—You Can Illustrate Johnny Appleseed. (gr. 4-7). 1993. pap. 5.95 (*1-56530-055-6*) Summit TX.
—You Can Illustrate Paul Bunyan. (gr. 4-7). 1993. pap. 5.95 (*1-56530-056-4*) Summit TX.
—You Can Illustrate Rumpelstiltskin. (gr. 4-7). 1993. pap. 5.95 (*1-56530-058-0*) Summit TX.
Tallarico, Anthony. Mystery Pictures to Draw. (Illus.). 64p. (Orig.). 1990. pap. 1.95 (*0-942025-19-9*) Kidsbks.
Tallarico, Tony. Drawing & Cartooning Dinosaurs: A Step-by-Step Guide for the Aspiring Prehistoric Artist. LC 93-16278. (Illus.). 96p. (Orig.). 1993. pap. 7.95 (*0-399-51814-2*, Perigee Bks) Berkley Pub.
—Drawing & Cartooning Monsters: A Step-by-Step Guide for the Aspiring Monster-Maker. (Illus.). 128p. (Orig.). 1992. pap. 7.95 (*0-399-51785-5*, Perigee Bks) Berkley Pub.
—I Can Draw Halloween. (ps). 1992. pap. 3.95 (*0-671-78376-9*, Little Simon) S&S Trade.
Thomson, Ruth. Drawing. LC 94-17329. (Illus.). 24p. (ps-3). 1994. PLB 14.40 (*0-516-07989-1*); pap. 4.95 (*0-516-47989-X*) Childrens.
Vaughan, Genevieve & Jackson. Sketching Drawing for Children. 1990. pap. 7.95 (*0-399-51619-0*) Putnam Pub Group.
Watermill Press Staff. Drawing Funny Faces. (gr. 4-7). 1989. pap. 1.95 (*0-8167-1668-4*) Troll Assocs.
—Drawing Monsters. (gr. 4-7). 1989. pap. 1.95 (*0-8167-1666-8*) Troll Assocs.

DRAWING MATERIALS

see Artists' Materials

DRAWINGS

Albers, Maura & Cvikota, Tom, eds. Just Add Color: A Children's Coloring Book with Drawings by Contemporary Artists. Rosenblum, Robert, intros. by. (Illus.). 36p. (Orig.). 1991. pap. text ed. 19.95 (*0-9627744-0-5*) HBP NY.
Burns, Charles. Charles Burns Sketchbook. Vance, Jim, ed. (Illus.). 64p. (gr. 4 up). 1993. pap. 6.95 (*0-87816-250-X*) Kitchen Sink.
Hobbs, Anne S. & Noble, Mary, eds. A Victorian Naturalist: Beatrix Potter's Drawings from the Armitt Collection. (Illus.). 192p. 1992. 40.00 (*0-7232-3990-8*) Warne.
Holland, Alex N. Child Art: A Book of Drawings. Holland, Alex N., illus. Lewis, Glenn A., intro. by. (Illus.). 56p. (gr. 1-12). 1991. pap. text ed. 23.95 (*0-9627882-2-8*) Bradley Mann.
L'Officier, Randy & L'Officier, Jean-Marc, eds. Visions of Arzach. Aragones, Sergio, et al, illus. Ellison, Harlan, frwd. by. 64p. (gr. 6 up). 1993. Repr. of 1992 ed. 14.95 (*0-87816-233-X*) Kitchen Sink.
Schultz, Mark. Cadillacs & Dinosaurs. Schreiner, Dave, ed. Jackson, Jack, et al. (Illus.). 392p. (gr. 3 up). 1993. Boxed set. pap. 39.95 (*0-87816-259-3*) Kitchen Sink.

DREAMS

Bell, Alison. The Dream Scene: How to Interpret Your Dreams. 80p. 1994. pap. 4.95 (*1-56565-160-X*) Lowell Hse Juvenile.
Emert, Phyllis R. Monsters, Strange Dreams, & UFO's. 128p. 1994. pap. 2.50 (*0-8125-9425-8*) Tor Bks.
Green, Carl R. & Sanford, William R. The Mystery of Dreams. LC 93-6539. (Illus.). 48p. (gr. 4-10). 1993. lib. bdg. 14.95 (*0-89490-453-1*) Enslow Pubs.
Hobson, J. Allan. Sleep & Dreams. Head, J. J., ed. Whittington, Julianne S., illus. 16p. (Orig.). (gr. 10 up). 1992. pap. text ed. 2.75 (*0-89278-117-3*, 45-9617) Carolina Biological.
Kincher, Jonni. Dreams Can Help: A Journal Guide to Understanding Your Dreams & Making Them Work for You. Morse, Mary & Espeland, Pamela, eds. Staeck, Roy, illus. LC 88-7630. 96p. (Orig.). (gr. 3-9). 1988. pap. 9.95 (*0-915793-15-6*) Free Spirit Pub.
Mayle, Peter. Sweet Dreams & Monsters: A Beginner's Guide to Dreams & Nightmares & Things That Go Bump under the Bed. Robins, Arthur, illus. (gr. k up). 1986. 9.95 (*0-517-55972-2*, Harmony) Crown Pub Group.
Myers, Jack. How Do We Dream? And Other Questions about Your Body. (Illus.). 64p. (gr. 1-5). 1992. bds. 12.95 (*1-56397-091-0*) Boyds Mills Pr.
Parker, Steve. Dreaming in the Night: How You Rest, Sleep & Dream. (Illus.). 32p. (gr. k-4). 1991. PLB 11.40 (*0-531-14099-7*) Watts.
Stafford, Patricia A. Dreaming & Dreams. LC 91-22898. (Illus.). 64p. (gr. 3-7). 1992. 13.95 (*0-689-31658-5*, Atheneum Child Bk) Macmillan Child Grp.
Uncle Hyggly, pseud. Tad Gonopolis & His Adventures in the Slumberyard, No. 3. Uncle Hyggly, illus. 48p. (gr. 3-6). 1987. pap. 8.95 (*0-935583-03-3*) Wounded Coot.
Understanding Dreams: A Concise Guide to Dream Symbols. 256p. 1994. pap. 5.95 (*1-56138-467-4*) Running Pr.

Wiseman, Ann S. Nightmare Help: A Guide for Adults & Children. Wiseman, Ann S., et al, illus. 137p. (Orig.). (gr. 1-12). 1986. pap. text ed. 9.00 (*0-937369-00-4*) Ansayre Pr.

DREAMS–FICTION

Allgood, Dave & Allgood, Stephanie. Merry Bear Book of Dreams: A Book to Read & Color. 2nd ed. (Illus.). 36p. (ps-3). 1985. pap. 2.95 (*0-933103-00-X*) Merry Bears.

Arnold, Tedd. Green Wilma. Arnold, Tedd, illus. LC 91-31501. 32p. (ps-3). 1993. 13.99 (*0-8037-1313-4*); PLB 13.89 (*0-8037-1314-2*) Dial Bks Young.

Aylesworth, Jim. The Bad Dream. Fay, Ann, ed. LC 85-685. (Illus.). 32p. (ps-2). 1985. 11.95 (*0-8075-0506-4*) A Whitman.

Bartelt, Jeanine, et al. A Fence Too High. French, Marty, et al, illus. 26p. (ps up). 1986. 7.95 (*1-55578-103-9*); cass. incl. Worlds Wonder.

Bengston, Gary. Kelly, Adam's Secret Dream. 40p. 1991. smythe-sewn, casebound 19.95 (*0-9631057-0-1*) Five Corn Danforth.

Berenstain, Stan & Berenstain, Jan. The Berenstain Bears & the Bad Dream. (Illus.). 32p. (ps-1). 1992. incl. cassette 6.95 (*0-679-82761-7*) Random Bks Yng Read.

Berger, Barbara H. The Donkey's Dream. Berger, Barbara H., illus. LC 84-18905. 32p. (ps-5). 1986. 14.95 (*0-399-21233-7*, Philomel) Putnam Pub Group.

Braille International, Inc. Staff & Henry, James, illus. No More Nightmares: Keeper of the Dreams. 17p. (Orig.). (gr. 1). 1992. pap. 10.95 (*1-56956-002-1*) W A T Braille.

Brook, Ruth. Toony & the Midnight Monster. Kondo, Vala, illus. LC 86-30739. 32p. (gr. k-3). 1988. lib. bdg. 11.89 (*0-8167-0910-6*); pap. text ed. 2.95 (*0-8167-0911-4*) Troll Assocs.

Brown, Margaret W. Dream Book. (ps). 1990. 9.95 (*0-929077-12-1*) WaterMark Inc.

Brown, Margaret Wise. The Dream Book. LC 90-81630. (Illus.). 32p. (ps-k). 1992. Repr. 10.95 (*1-56282-211-X*) Hyprn Child.

—The Dream Book: First Comes the Dream. Floethe, Richard, illus. 32p. (gr. 1-3). 1990. Repr. of 1950 ed. 9.95 (*0-685-45149-6*) WaterMark Inc.

Brown, Mary K. Let's Go Camping with Mr. Sillypants. LC 94-15991. 1995. write for info. (*0-517-59773-X*); PLB write for info. (*0-517-59774-8*) Crown Pub Group.

Casler, Leigh. The Boy Who Dreamed of an Acorn. Begay, Shonto, illus. LC 92-44902. 32p. (ps up). 1994. PLB 15.95 (*0-399-22547-1*, Philomel) Putnam Pub Group.

Cazet, Denys. Daydreams. Cazet, Denys, illus. LC 89-48939. 32p. (ps-2). 1990. 14.95 (*0-531-05881-6*); PLB 14.99 (*0-531-08481-7*) Orchard Bks Watts.

Chetwin, Grace. Jason's Seven Magical Night Rides. Chetwin, Grace, illus. LC 93-21125. 128p. (gr. 2-6). 1994. SBE 14.95 (*0-02-718221-5*, Bradbury Pr) Macmillan Child Grp.

Cosgrove, Stephen. The Dream Stealer. Heyer, Carol, illus. LC 89-83843. 48p. (gr. 1-4). 1990. 16.95 (*1-55868-009-8*); pap. 5.95 (*1-55868-021-7*); pap. 12.95 incl. audio (*1-55868-042-X*) Gr Arts Ctr Pub.

Daniells, Trenna. No More Nightmares: Keeper of the Dreams. Braille International, Inc. Staff & Henry, James, illus. (Orig.). (gr. 2). 1992. pap. 10.95 (*1-56956-027-7*) W A T Braille.

Davis, Maggie S. A Garden of Whales. O'Connell, Jennifer B., illus. LC 92-34411. 32p. 1993. 16.95 (*0-944475-36-1*); pap. 6.95 (*0-944475-35-3*) Camden Hse Pub.

Devlin, Wende & Devlin, Harry. Maggie Has a Nightmare. LC 93-45818. (ps-1). 1994. pap. 2.95 (*0-689-71778-4*, Aladdin) Macmillan Child Grp.

Dickinson, Peter. Merlin Dreams. Lee, Alan, illus. LC 88-3985. 160p. (gr. k-12). 1988. 19.95 (*0-440-50067-2*) Delacorte.

Duel, John. Wide Awake in Dreamland. Burton, Bruce, illus. LC 91-66837. 239p. (gr. 4-8). 1992. 15.95 (*0-9630923-0-8*) Stargaze Pub.

Duncan, Lois. Horses of Dreamland. Diamond, Donna, illus. 32p. (ps-3). 1986. 12.95 (*0-316-19554-5*) Little.

Edwards, Elsy. Sandy's Suitcase. Webb, Philip, illus. LC 92-34269. 1993. 14.00 (*0-383-03650-X*) SRA Schl Grp.

Fabian, Stella. A Pocketful of Dreams. (Illus.). (gr. 3-6). 1989. write for info. (*0-922434-37-9*) Brighton & Lloyd.

Farmer, Patti. Bartholomew's Dream. Wummer, Amy, illus. 32p. (ps-2). 1994. 12.95 (*0-8120-6403-8*); pap. 4.95 (*0-8120-1991-1*) Barron.

Foreman, Michael. Grandfather's Pencil & the Room of Stories. Foreman, Michael, illus. LC 93-6266. (ps-3). 1994. 13.95 (*0-15-200061-5*) HarBrace.

Garrison, Christian. The Dream Eater. Goode, Diane, illus. LC 85-26671. 32p. (ps-2). 1986. pap. 4.95 (*0-689-71058-5*, Aladdin) Macmillan Child Grp.

Gay, Kristin. Herschel's Special Dream. Matsumoto, Allen, illus. 60p. (Orig.). 1986. pap. 5.95 (*0-945265-08-5*) Accord Comm.

Gorog, Judith. Three Dreams & a Nightmare. 160p. (gr. 7-9). 1992. pap. 2.50 (*0-8167-1822-9*) Troll Assocs.

Greenfield, Eloise. Daydreamers. Feelings, Tom, illus. (gr. k up). 1981. 13.95 (*0-8037-2137-4*) Dial Bks Young.

Haley, Gail E. Dream Peddler. Haley, Gail E., illus. LC 92-42074. 32p. (ps-3). 1993. 14.99 (*0-525-45153-6*, DCB) Dutton Child Bks.

Heller, Nicholas. Peas. LC 92-29740. 24p. 1993. 14.00 (*0-688-12406-2*); PLB 13.93 (*0-688-12407-0*) Greenwillow.

Hendry, Diana. Camel Called April. (ps-3). 1991. 10.95 (*0-688-10193-3*) Lothrop.

Hill, Susan. Go Away, Bad Dreams. Julian-Ottie, Vanessa, illus. Lerner, Sharon, ed. LC 84-17759. (Illus.). 32p. (ps-2). 1985. pap. 2.25 (*0-394-87222-3*) Random Bks Yng Read.

Hoffman, Joan. Peter's Dream. (Illus.). 32p. (gr. k-2). 1992. pap. 3.95 (*0-88743-425-8*, 06077) Sch Zone Pub Co.

—Peter's Dream. (Illus.). 16p. (gr. k-2). 1992. pap. 2.25 (*0-88743-264-6*, 06031) Sch Zone Pub Co.

Hoppe, Joanne. Dream Spinner. LC 92-5258. 240p. (gr. 7 up). 1992. 14.00 (*0-688-08559-8*) Morrow Jr Bks.

Hucklesly, Hope. In My Head. Forss, Ian, illus. LC 92-34267. 1993. 2.50 (*0-383-03634-8*) SRA Schl Grp.

Ichikawa, Satomi. Nora's Roses. (Illus.). 32p. (ps up). 1993. PLB 14.95 (*0-399-21968-4*, Philomel Bks) Putnam Pub Group.

Jarrell, Randall. Fly by Night. Sendak, Maurice, illus. LC 76-27313. 40p. (ps up). 1985. 14.00 (*0-374-32348-8*); pap. 2.95, 1986 (*0-374-42350-4*) FS&G.

Johnson, Debra A. I Dreamed I Was--a Kitten. LC 94-5655. (gr. k up). 1994. write for info. (*1-56239-302-2*) Abdo & Dghtrs.

—I Dreamed I Was--a Panda. LC 94-5654. (gr. k up). 1994. write for info. (*1-56239-301-4*) Abdo & Dghtrs.

—I Dreamed I Was a Koala Bear. LC 94-6623. (gr. k up). 1994. write for info. (*1-56239-300-6*) Abdo & Dghtrs.

Keats, Ezra J. Dreams. 2nd ed. LC 91-25572. (Illus.). 32p. (gr. 1-3). 1992. pap. 4.95 (*0-689-71599-4*, Aladdin) Macmillan Child Grp.

Koralek, Jenny. The Boy & the Cloth of Dreams. Mayhew, James, illus. LC 93-23091. 32p. (ps up). 1994. 14.95 (*1-56402-349-4*) Candlewick Pr.

Lobby, Ted. Jessica & the Wolf: A Story for Children Who Have Bad Dreams. Dixon, Tennessee, illus. LC 89-29688. 32p. (gr. k-3). 1990. 16.95 (*0-945354-22-3*); pap. 6.95 (*0-945354-21-5*) Magination Pr.

—Jessica & the Wolf: A Story for Children Who Have Bad Dreams. Dixon, Tennessee, illus. LC 92-56872. 1993. PLB 17.27 (*0-8368-0933-5*) Gareth Stevens Inc.

Marcus, Irene W. & Marcus, Paul. Into the Great Forest: A Story for Children Away from Parents for the First Time. LC 91-37636. (Illus.). 32p. (ps-3). 1992. pap. 6.95 (*0-945354-40-1*); 16.95 (*0-945354-39-8*) Magination Pr.

—Into the Great Forest: A Story for Children Away from Parents for the First Time. Jeschke, Susan, illus. LC 92-56871. 1993. PLB 17.27 (*0-8368-0932-7*) Gareth Stevens Inc.

Mayer, Mercer. Mercer Mayer's What a Bad Dream. (Illus.). 24p. (ps-3). 1992. write for info. (*0-307-12685-4*, 12685) Western Pub.

—There's a Nightmare in My Closet. 1992. pap. 4.99 (*0-14-054712-6*, Puffin) Puffin Bks.

Milk & Cookies. (Illus.). 42p. (ps-3). 1992. PLB 13.27 (*0-8368-0878-9*) Gareth Stevens Inc.

Modarressi, Mitra. The Dream Pillow. LC 93-49400. (Illus.). 32p. (ps-2). 1994. 14.95 (*0-531-06855-2*); PLB 14.99 (*0-531-08705-0*) Orchard Bks Watts.

Neasi, Barbara J. Dulces Suenos: Sweet Dreams. Martin, Clovis, illus. LC 87-15083. (SPA.). 32p. (ps-2). 1991. PLB 10.25 (*0-516-32084-X*); pap. 2.95 (*0-516-52084-9*) Childrens.

Nightingale, Sandy. A Giraffe on the Moon. (ps-1). 1992. 13.95 (*0-15-230950-0*, HB Juv Bks) HarBrace.

Nixon, Joan L. Will You Give Me a Dream? Degen, Bruce, illus. LC 91-19581. 40p. (ps-1). 1994. RSBE 14.95 (*0-02-768211-0*, Four Winds) Macmillan Child Grp.

Nolan, Dennis. Dinosaur Dream. Nolan, Dennis, illus. LC 89-78208. 32p. (ps-2). 1990. RSBE 14.95 (*0-02-768145-9*, Macmillan Child Bk) Macmillan Child Grp.

—Dinosaur Dream. Nolan, Dennis, illus. LC 93-48409. (gr. k-3). 1994. pap. 4.95 (*0-689-71832-2*, Aladdin) Macmillan Child Grp.

Nye, Naomi S. Dream Bottle. Yu Cha Pak, illus. LC 93-45675. 1995. 15.00 (*0-02-768467-9*, Four Winds) Macmillan Child Grp.

Orgel, Doris. Sarah's Room. Sendak, Maurice, illus. LC 63-13675. 48p. (ps-3). 1991. pap. 4.95 (*0-06-443238-6*, Trophy) HarpC Child Bks.

—Sarah's Room. reissued ed. Sendak, Maurice, illus. LC 63-13675. 48p. (gr. k-3). 1963. PLB 14.89 (*0-06-024606-5*) HarpC Child Bks.

Osofsky, Audrey. Dreamcatcher. Young, Ed, illus. LC 91-20029. 32p. (ps-2). 1992. 14.95 (*0-531-05988-X*); lib. bdg. 14.99 (*0-531-08588-0*) Orchard Bks Watts.

Paek, Min. Aekyung's Dream. Paek, Min, illus. LC 88-18928. (ENG & KOR.). 24p. (gr. 2-7). 1988. 13.95 (*0-89239-042-5*) Childrens Book Pr.

Paraskevas, Betty. On the Edge of the Sea. Paraskevas, Michael, illus. LC 91-31489. 32p. 1992. 14.00 (*0-8037-1130-1*); PLB 13.89 (*0-8037-1263-4*) Dial Bks Young.

Peck, Richard. Dreamland Lake. 128p. (gr. 7 up). 1990. pap. 3.50 (*0-440-92079-5*, LFL) Dell.

Perricone, Jack. I Like to Dream. (Illus.). 16p. (ps-2). 1993. PLB 10.95 (*1-879567-16-4*, Valeria Bks) Wonder Well.

—Me Gusta Sonar. (Illus.). 16p. (ps-2). 1993. PLB 10.95 (*1-879567-17-2*, Valeria Bks) Wonder Well.

Pilkey, Dav. When Cats Dream. LC 91-31355. (Illus.). 32p. (ps-2). 1992. 14.95 (*0-531-05997-9*); PLB 14.99 (*0-531-08597-X*) Orchard Bks Watts.

Pittau, Francisco. Voyage under the Stars. Gervais, Bernadette, illus. LC 91-26075. 32p. (ps-3). 1992. 13.00 (*0-688-11328-1*); PLB 12.93 (*0-688-11329-X*) Lothrop.

Pittman, Helena C. The Moon's Party. LC 92-40866. 1994. 15.95 (*0-399-22541-2*, Putnam) Putnam Pub Group.

Polacco, Patricia. Appelemando's Dreams. Polacco, Patricia, illus. 32p. (ps-3). 1991. 14.95 (*0-399-21800-9*, Philomel) Putnam Pub Group.

Ray, Mary L. My Carousel Horse. Taxali, Gary, illus. LC 93-45876. 1900. write for info. (*0-15-200023-2*) HarBrace.

Romain, Trevor. The Keeper of the Dreams. Romain, Trevor, illus. 32p. (ps-5). 1992. 13.50 (*1-880092-03-4*, Dist. by Publishers Distribution Service) Bright Bks TX.

Rose, David S. Maynard's Dreams. Rose, David S., illus. LC 92-43146. 32p. (ps-3). 1993. SBE 14.95 (*0-689-31847-2*, Atheneum Child Bk) Macmillan Child Grp.

Roth, Susan L. Princess. Roth, Susan, illus. LC 92-55042. 32p. (ps-3). 1993. 13.95 (*1-56282-465-1*); PLB 13.89 (*1-56282-466-X*) Hyprn Child.

Rowe, John. Jack the Dog. Rowe, John, illus. 28p. (gr. k up). 1993. 14.95 (*0-88708-266-1*) Picture Bk Studio.

Rylant, Cynthia. The Dreamer. Moser, Barry, illus. LC 93-19915. 32p. (ps-6). 1993. 14.95 (*0-590-47341-7*) Scholastic Inc.

Sheldon, Dyan. Under the Moon. Blythe, Gary, illus. LC 93-11711. 32p. (ps-3). 1994. 15.99 (*0-8037-1670-2*) Dial Bks Young.

Singer, Marilyn. Thirteen Dreams. 1994. write for info. (*0-8050-3004-2*) H Holt & Co.

Smee, Nicola. Finish the Story, Dad. LC 90-28602. (Illus.). 32p. (ps-1). 1991. pap. 13.95 jacketed (*0-671-74478-X*, S&S BFYR) S&S Trade.

Smith, Lane. The Big Pets. LC 93-18608. (Illus.). 32p. (ps-3). 1993. pap. 4.99 (*0-14-054265-5*, Puffin) Puffin Bks.

Splendor, Meg. Dream Catcher: A Starlight Journey with Meg Splendor. LC 93-1015. 77p. (Orig.). (ps up). 1993. pap. 12.95 incl. 17 min. audio tape (*1-882979-17-6*) What the Heck.

Stevenson, James. Could Be Worse! Stevenson, James, illus. LC 76-28534. 32p. (gr. k-3). 1977. 13.95 (*0-688-80075-0*); PLB 13.88 (*0-688-84075-2*) Greenwillow.

Supraner, Robyn. Molly's Special Wish. Rocklen, Margot, illus. LC 85-14087. 48p. (Orig.). (gr. 1-3). 1986. PLB 10.59 (*0-8167-0660-3*); pap. text ed. 3.50 (*0-8167-0661-1*) Troll Assocs.

Sweet Dreams Big Book. (Illus.). 32p. (ps-3). 1990. pap. 22.95 (*0-516-49456-2*) Childrens.

Sweetie: A Sugar-Coated Nightmare. 36p. (ps-4). 1985. 8.95 (*0-88684-175-5*); cassette tape avail. Listen USA.

Van Allsburg, Chris. Ben's Dream. (Illus.). 32p. (gr. 2 up). 1982. 14.45 (*0-395-32084-4*) HM.

—The Sweetest Fig. Van Allsburg, Chris, illus. LC 93-12692. (gr. 4 up). 1993. 17.95 (*0-395-67346-1*) HM.

Visions. 1987. pap. 16.95 (*0-440-50230-6*) Dell.

Waller, Wanda W. Unicorns & Dreams. Lopez, Ron, ed. Perrin, Sandra, illus. 39p. (Orig.). (gr. k-6). 1985. pap. 4.95 (*0-930825-00-4*) Lola Library.

Weedn, Flavia. Flavia & the Dream Maker. Weedn, Flavia, illus. 56p. 1988. 14.95 (*0-929632-00-1*) deluxe limited 24.95 (*0-929632-02-8*) Applause Inc.

Wild, Margaret. Going Home. Harris, Wayne, illus. LC 93-22975. 32p. (ps-3). 1994. 14.95 (*0-590-47958-X*) Scholastic Inc.

Wilkins, Joyce R. & Hawkins, Edeltraud. The Animal Market. LC 93-25202. 1993. 8.95 (*1-880373-06-8*) Pictorial Herit.

Wright, Betty R. Out of the Dark. LC 93-48025. (gr. 3-7). 1995. 13.95 (*0-590-43598-1*) Scholastic Inc.

—The Secret Window. LC 82-80816. 160p. (gr. 3-7). 1982. 14.95 (*0-8234-0464-1*) Holiday.

—Why Do I Daydream? Glessner, Marc, illus. Silverman, Manuel S., intro. by. LC 80-25561. (Illus.). 32p. (gr. k-6). 1981. PLB 13.45 (*0-8172-1371-6*) Raintree Steck-V.

Yolen, Jane. Fever Dream. Pinkney, Jerry, illus. LC 93-10070. 32p. (gr. k-3). Date not set. 16.00 (*0-06-021482-1*); PLB 15.89 (*0-06-021483-X*) Harpc Child Bks.

Zemach-Bersin, Kaethe. The Funny Dream. LC 87-18769. (Illus.). 32p. (ps-3). 1988. 11.95 (*0-688-07500-2*); lib. bdg. 11.88 (*0-688-07501-0*) Greenwillow.

DRESS

see Clothing and Dress

DRESSMAKING

see also Sewing

DREW, CHARLES RICHARD, 1904-1950

Talmadge, Katherine S. The Life of Charles Drew. Castro, Antonio, illus. 80p. (gr. 4-7). 1991. PLB 13.95 (*0-941477-65-7*) TFC Bks NY.

DRINKS

see Beverages

DRIVERS, AUTOMOBILE

see Automobile Drivers

DROMEDARIES

see Camels

DROPOUTS

Goldentyer, Debra. Dropping Out of School. LC 93-14251. (Illus.). 80p. (gr. 6-9). 1993. PLB 21.34 (*0-8114-3526-1*) Raintree Steck-V.

Redpath, Ann. What Happens If You Quit School? (Illus.). 48p. (gr. 3-6). Date not set. PLB 12.95 (*1-56065-136-9*) Capstone Pr.

Sheffield, Anne & Frankel, Bruce, eds. When I Was Young I Loved School: Dropping Out & Hanging In. (gr. 7 up). 1989. 9.95 (*0-9621641-2-7*) CEF Inc.

DROPOUTS–FICTION

Angell, Judie. Yours Truly: A Novel. LC 92-29472. 192p. (gr. 7-12). 1993. 14.95 (*0-531-05472-1*); PLB 14.99 (*0-531-08622-4*) Orchard Bks Watts.

Zindel, Paul. I Never Loved Your Mind. 144p. (gr. 9 up). 1984. pap. 3.99 (*0-553-27323-X*) Bantam.

—I Never Loved Your Mind. LC 73-105476. 192p. (gr. 7 up). 1970. PLB 13.89 (*0-06-026822-0*) HarpC Child Bks.

DRUG ADDICTION

see Narcotic Habit

DRUG HABIT

see Narcotic Habit

DRUGS

see also Pharmacy; Poisons

also names of individual drugs, and groups of drugs, e.g. Narcotics

Allen County Police Officers Association Staff, compiled by. Kids Talk to Kids. 75p. (Orig.). (gr. 6-12). 1991. pap. write for info. (*0-9614659-7-2*) Cuchullain Pubns.

Avraham, Regina. The Downside of Drugs. Mendelson, Jack H. & Mello, Nancyintro. by. (Illus.). 112p. (gr. 5 up). 1988. lib. bdg. 19.95 (*1-55546-232-4*) Chelsea Hse.

—Substance Abuse: Prevention & Treatment. Mendelson, Jack H. & Mello, Nancyintro. by. (Illus.). 128p. (gr. 5 up). 1988. lib. bdg. 19.95 (*1-55546-219-7*) Chelsea Hse.

—Substance Abuse: Prevention & Treatment. 1988. pap. 9.95 (*0-7910-0807-X*) Chelsea Hse.

Baldwin, Dorothy. Health & Drugs. (Illus.). 32p. 1987. PLB 17.27 (*0-86592-292-6*); 12.95s.p. (*0-685-67609-9*) Rourke Corp.

Berger, Gilda. Drug Abuse: The Impact on Society. Rakos, Jennie, ed. LC 88-10620. (Illus.). 160p. (gr. 6-12). 1988. PLB 13.90 (*0-531-10579-2*) Watts.

—Making up Your Mind about Drugs. Enik, Ted, illus. LC 88-3609. 80p. (gr. 4-6). 1988. (Lodestar Bks); pap. 4.95 (*0-525-67256-7*, Lodestar Bks) Dutton Child Bks.

Berger, Gilda & Berger, Melvin. Drug Abuse A-Z. LC 89-1512. 144p. (gr. 6 up). 1990. lib. bdg. 18.95 (*0-89490-193-1*) Enslow Pubs.

Check, William A. Drugs & Perception. Mendelson, Jack H. & Mello, Nancyintro. by. (Illus.). 112p. (gr. 5 up). 1988. lib. bdg. 19.95 (*1-55546-214-6*) Chelsea Hse.

Chiles, John. Teenage Depression & Drugs. (Illus.). 32p. (gr. 5 up). 1991. pap. 4.49 (*0-7910-0005-2*) Chelsea Hse.

Clayton, Lawrence. Coping with a Drug Abusing Parent. rev. ed. 176p. (gr. 7-12). 1994. PLB 14.95 (*0-8239-1950-1*) Rosen Group.

Cleveland, David. That's Life, 13 vols. Pascarella, Sam, illus. (gr. k-8). 1986. Each individual grade level; k-12. tchrs ed. 65.00 (*1-56117-028-3*); Eng. wkbk. 3.50 (*1-56117-043-7*); Span. wkbk. 3.95 (*1-56117-044-5*); preschool 35.00 (*1-56117-042-9*); complete k-12 curriculum set 795.00 (*0-685-74176-1*) Telesis CA.

Cocaine. rev. ed. 64p. (gr. 8 up). 1994. PLB 14.95 (*0-8239-2040-2*) Rosen Group.

Condon, Judith. Pressure to Take Drugs. LC 89-70581. 1990. PLB 12.40 (*0-531-10934-8*) Watts.

Davies, Leah G. Drug Abuse Prevention Program Leader Guide. 56p. (ps-3). 1993. pap. write for info. (*0-9621054-5-7*) Kelly Bear Pr.

—Kelly Bear Drug Awareness. Hallett, Joy D., illus. 40p. (ps-3). 1993. pap. 10.95 (*0-9621054-6-5*) Kelly Bear Pr.

Desmond, Theresa & Almonte, Paul. Drug Use & Abuse. LC 94-18180. 1995. text ed. 13.95 (*0-89686-811-7*, Crestwood Hse) Macmillan Child Grp.

DeStefano, Susan. Focus on Medicines. (Illus.). 64p. (gr. 2-4). 1991. PLB 14.95 (*0-941477-94-0*) TFC Bks NY.

—Focus on Opiates. (Illus.). 68p. (gr. 2-4). 1991. PLB 14.95 (*0-941477-91-6*) TFC Bks NY.

Drugs: The Complete Story, 4 bks. (gr. 6). 1992. Set 63.84 (*0-8114-3204-1*) Raintree Steck-V.

Edler, Timothy J. Crawfish-Man's Fifty Ways to Keep Your Kids from Using Drugs. (Illus.). 52p. (gr. k-8). 1982. pap. 6.00 (*0-931108-08-X*) Little Cajun Bks.

Educational Assessment Publishing Company Staff. Parent - Child Learning Library: Drug Information. (Illus.). 32p. (gr. k-3). 1991. text ed. 9.95 (*0-942277-54-6*) Am Guidance.

—Parent - Child Learning Library: Drug Information English Big Book. (Illus.). 32p. (gr. k-3). 1991. text ed. 16.95 (*0-942277-48-1*) Am Guidance.

—Parent - Child Learning Library: Drug Information Spanish Big Book. (SPA., Illus.). 32p. (gr. k-3). 1991. text ed. 16.95 (*0-942277-49-X*) Am Guidance.

—Parent - Child Learning Library: Drug Information Spanish Edition. (SPA., Illus.). 32p. (ps). 1991. text ed. 9.95 (*0-942277-90-2*) Am Guidance.

Edwards, Gabrielle. Drugs on Your Streets. rev. ed. (gr. 7-12). 1993. PLB 14.95 (*0-8239-1682-0*) Rosen Group.

Friedman, David. Focus on Drugs & the Brain. Neuhaus, David, illus. 64p. (gr. 2-4). 1990. PLB 14.95 (*0-941477-95-9*) TFC Bks NY.

Go Ask Alice. 192p. (gr. 7 up). 1976. pap. 3.99 (*0-380-00523-9*, Flare) Avon.

Grauer, Neil. Drugs & the Law. Mendelson, Jack H. & Mello, Nancyintro. by. (Illus.). 120p. (gr. 5 up). 1988. lib. bdg. 19.95 (*1-55546-230-8*) Chelsea Hse.

Gunn, Jeffrey. Pen Pals Series, No. 1. Wolfe, Debra, illus. (Orig.). (gr. 1). 1991. pap. write for info. (*1-879146-00-2*) Knowldg Pub.

—Pen Pals, Vol. 1: The Beginning. Doughty, Virgina, illus. (Orig.). (gr. 3). 1990. pap. write for info. (*1-879146-01-0*) Knowldg Pub.

—Pen Pals, Vol. 2: Facts about Cocaine. Wolfe, Debra, illus. (Orig.). (gr. 3). 1990. pap. write for info. (*1-879146-02-9*) Knowldg Pub.

—Pen Pals, Vol. 3: Facts about Heroin. Wolfe, Debra, illus. (Orig.). (gr. 3). 1990. pap. write for info. (*1-879146-03-7*) Knowldg Pub.

—Pen Pals, Vol. 5: Facts about Dust. Doughty, Virgina, illus. (Orig.). (gr. 3). 1990. pap. write for info. (*1-879146-05-3*) Knowldg Pub.

—Pen Pals, Vol. 6: Facts about Speed. Wolfe, Debra, illus. (Orig.). (gr. 3). 1990. pap. write for info. (*1-879146-06-1*) Knowldg Pub.

—Pen Pals, Vol. 7: Facts about Downers. Wolfe, Debra, illus. (Orig.). (gr. 3). 1990. pap. write for info. (*1-879146-07-X*) Knowldg Pub.

—Pen Pals, Vol. 9: Facts about Crack. Wolfe, Debra, illus. (Orig.). (gr. 3). 1990. pap. write for info. (*1-879146-09-6*) Knowldg Pub.

Harris, Jacqueline L. Drugs & Disease. (Illus.). 64p. (gr. 5-8). 1993. PLB 14.95 (*0-8050-2602-9*) TFC Bks NY.

Hawley, Richard. Drugs & Society. rev. ed. 160p. (gr. 7 up). 1992. PLB 15.85 (*0-8027-8114-4*); pap. 9.95 (*0-8027-7366-4*) Walker & Co.

Hemming, Judith. Why Do People Take Drugs? FS Staff, ed. LC 88-50515. (Illus.). 32p. (gr. 1-3). 1988. PLB 11.40 (*0-531-17113-2*, Gloucester Pr) Watts.

Henningfield, Jack E. & Atar, Nancy A. Barbiturates: Sleeping Potion or Intoxicant. (Illus.). 32p. (gr. 5 up). 1991. pap. 4.49 (*0-7910-0004-4*) Chelsea Hse.

Hoobler, Dorothy & Hoobler, Thomas. Drugs & Crime. Mendelson, Jack H. & Mello, Nancyintro. by. (Illus.). 128p. 1988. lib. bdg. 19.95 (*1-55546-228-6*) Chelsea Hse.

Inaba, Darryl S. & Cohen, William E. Uppers, Downers & All Arounders. (Illus.). 260p. 1989. 28.95 (*0-926544-00-4*) CNS Prods.

Johanson, Chris-Ellyn. Cocaine: A New Epidemic. (Illus.). 32p. (gr. 5 up). 1991. pap. 4.49 (*1-55546-998-1*) Chelsea Hse.

Jussim, Daniel. Drug Tests & Polygraphs: Essential Tools or Violations of Privacy? LC 87-11192. (Illus.). 128p. (gr. 7 up). 1987. PLB 12.98 (*0-671-64438-6*, J Messner); pap. 5.95 (*0-671-65977-4*) S&S Trade.

Kittredge, Mary. Prescription & OTC Drugs. (Illus.). 112p. (gr. 6-12). 1989. 18.95 (*0-7910-0062-1*) Chelsea Hse.

Krayer, Christina, ed. Drug Awareness, 13 titles. (Illus.). (gr. k-6). Date not set. Set. PLB 199.00 (*1-882869-01-X*) Read Advent.

Kusinitz, Marc. Celebrity Drug Use. (Illus.). 32p. (gr. 5 up). 1991. pap. 4.49 (*1-55546-995-7*) Chelsea Hse.

Lukas, Scott. Steroids. LC 93-38524. (Illus.). 112p. (gr. 6 up). 1994. PLB 17.95 (*0-89490-471-X*) Enslow Pubs.

Lukas, Scott E. Amphetamines: Danger in the Fast Lane. (Illus.). 32p. (gr. 5 up). 1991. pap. 4.49 (*0-7910-0003-6*) Chelsea Hse.

—Amphetamines: Danger in the Fast Lane. updated ed. (Illus.). (gr. 5 up). 1992. lib. bdg. 19.95 (*0-685-54573-3*) Chelsea Hse.

Madison, Arnold. Drugs & You. rev. ed. LC 82-3450. (Illus.). 80p. (gr. 4 up). 1982. PLB 9.79 (*0-671-43986-3*, J Messner); pap. 4.95 (*0-671-49477-5*) S&S Trade.

Martin, Jo. Drugs & the Family. Mendelson, Jack H. & Mello, Nancyintro. by. (Illus.). 104p. (gr. 5 up). 1988. lib. bdg. 19.95 (*1-55546-220-0*); pap. 9.95 (*0-7910-0797-9*) Chelsea Hse.

Monroe, Judy. Drug Testing. LC 89-25425. (Illus.). 48p. (gr. 5-6). 1990. text ed. 12.95 RSBE (*0-89686-492-8*, Crestwood Hse) Macmillan Child Grp.

—Stimulants & Hallucinogens. LC 88-20350. (Illus.). 48p. (gr. 5-6). 1988. text ed. 12.95 RSBE (*0-89686-415-4*, Crestwood Hse) Macmillan Child Grp.

Moran, Bill. The Mary Wanna Student Activity Book. Lind, Naomi, illus. Mann, Peggy, intro. by. (Illus.). 23p. (gr. 4-6). 1989. pap. 2.50 (*0-942493-10-9*) Woodmere Press.

Nelson, Elizabeth. Coping with Drugs & Sports. (gr. 7-12). 1992. PLB 14.95 (*0-8239-1342-2*) Rosen Group.

No Drugs! No Alcohol! 16p. 1994. 0.95 (*0-685-71607-4*, 732) W Gladden Found.

Nuwer, Hank. Steroids. LC 90-32757. (Illus.). 144p. (gr. 7-12). 1990. PLB 13.90 (*0-531-10946-1*) Watts.

Perinchief, Robert. Drug-Free Word Spree. 58p. (ps-12). 1993. 19.95 (*1-882809-01-7*) Perry Pubns.

Perry, Robert. Focus on Nicotine & Caffeine. (Illus.). 64p. (gr. 2-4). 1990. PLB 14.95 (*0-8050-2217-1*) TFC Bks NY.

Redpath, Ann. What Happens If You Use Drugs? (Illus.). 48p. (gr. 3-6). Date not set. PLB 12.95 (*1-56065-134-2*) Capstone Pr.

Rodgers, Joann. Drugs & Sexual Behavior. Mendelson, Jack H. & Mello, Nancyintro. by. (Illus.). 96p. (gr. 5 up). 1988. lib. bdg. 19.95 (*1-55546-215-4*) Chelsea Hse.

Rogak, Lisa. Steroids: Dangerous Game. 64p. (gr. 5-10). 1992. PLB 15.95 (*0-8225-0048-5*) Lerner Pubns.

Rubbins, Paul R. Designer Drugs. LC 94-16314. 1995. write for info. (*0-89490-488-4*) Enslow Pubs.

Ryan, Alizabeth A. Straight Talk about Drugs & Alcohol. 144p. (gr. 7 up). 1992. pap. 3.99 (*0-440-21392-4*, LFL) Dell.

Ryan, Elizabeth. Hablemos Francamente de las Drogas y el Alcohol. Terrana, Alma, tr. from ENG. (SPA.). 160p. 1990. 16.95x (*0-8160-2496-0*) Facts on File.

Schwartz, L. Drug Questions & Answers. (gr. 6-9). 1989. 5.95 (*0-88160-171-3*, LW 282) Learning Wks.

Schwerdtfeger, Don. America Does Not Have a Drug Problem. 131p. (Orig.). 1989. pap. 7.95 (*0-9624760-0-5*) Bding Better People.

Seixas, Judith S. Drugs--What They Are, What They Do. Huffman, Tom, illus. LC 86-33624. 48p. (gr. 1-4). 1987. 12.95 (*0-688-07399-9*); lib. bdg. 12.88 (*0-688-07400-6*) Greenwillow.

Shulman, Jeffrey. The Drug-Alert Dictionary & Resource Guide. (Illus.). 91p. (gr. 2-4). 1991. PLB 14.95 (*0-941477-85-1*) TFC Bks NY.

—Focus on Cocaine & Crack. Neuhaus, David, illus. 56p. (gr. 2-4). 1990. PLB 14.95 (*0-941477-98-3*) TFC Bks NY.

—Focus on Hallucinogens. (Illus.). 56p. (gr. 2-4). 1991. PLB 14.95 (*0-941477-92-4*) TFC Bks NY.

Silverstein, Alvin, et al. Steroids: Big Muscles, Big Problems. LC 91-876. (Illus.). 112p. (gr. 6 up). 1992. lib. bdg. 17.95 (*0-89490-318-7*) Enslow Pubs.

Simpson, Carlyon. RX: Reading & Following the Directions for All Kinds of Medications. LC 94-702. 1994. 13.95 (*0-8239-1696-0*) Rosen Group.

Smith, Sandra L. Peyote & Magic Mushrooms. LC 94-2268. 1994. 14.95 (*0-8239-1700-2*) Rosen Group.

Steele, Philip. Smuggling. LC 92-13611. (Illus.). 48p. (gr. 6 up). 1993. text ed. 12.95 RSBE (*0-02-786884-2*, New Discovery) Macmillan Child Grp.

Stevens, Sarah. Steroids. LC 90-48050. (Illus.). 48p. (gr. 5-6). 1991. text ed. 12.95 RSBE (*0-89686-606-8*, Crestwood Hse) Macmillan Child Grp.

Super, Gretchen. Drugs & Our World. 48p. (ps-3). 1990. pap. 3.95 (*0-8167-2365-6*) Troll Assocs.

—What Are Drugs. 48p. (ps-3). 1990. pap. 3.95 (*0-8167-2364-8*) Troll Assocs.

—You Can Say No to Drugs. 48p. (ps-3). 1990. pap. 3.95 (*0-8167-2366-4*) Troll Assocs.

Swisher, Karin, ed. Drug Trafficking. LC 91-22022. 200p. (gr. 10 up). 1991. PLB 16.95 (*0-89908-576-8*); pap. text ed. 9.95 (*0-89908-582-2*) Greenhaven.

Talmadge, Katherine S. Focus on Steroids. (Illus.). 64p. (gr. 2-4). 1991. PLB 14.95 (*0-8050-2216-3*) TFC Bks NY.

Theodore, Alan. Origins & Sources of Drugs. Mendelson, Jack & Mello, Nancyintro. by. (Illus.). 128p. (gr. 5 up). 1988. lib. bdg. 19.95 (*1-55546-234-0*) Chelsea Hse.

Turck, Mary C. Crack & Cocaine. LC 89-25409. (Illus.). 48p. (gr. 5-6). 1990. text ed. 12.95 RSBE (*0-89686-491-X*, Crestwood Hse) Macmillan Child Grp.

Tuttle, Dave. Forever Natural: How to Excel in Sports Drug-Free. (Illus.). 190p. (Orig.). (gr. 9 up). 1990. pap. text ed. 15.95 (*0-9625740-0-7*) Iron Bks.

Wilker, Debbie A. Deadly Drugs: An Informative Coloring Book. Wilker, Debbie A., illus. (Orig.). (ps-3). 1990. pap. 5.95 (*1-878282-10-7*) St Johann Pr.

Woods, Geraldine. Heroin. LC 93-34873. (Illus.). 112p. (gr. 6 up). 1994. PLB 17.95 (*0-89490-473-6*) Enslow Pubs.

Yoslow, Mark. Drugs in the Body: Effects of Abuse. LC 91-39030. (Illus.). 144p. (gr. 9-12). 1992. PLB 14.40 (*0-531-12507-6*) Watts.

Zeller, Paula K. Focus on Marijuana. (Illus.). 56p. (gr. 2-4). 1990. PLB 14.95 (*0-941477-97-5*) TFC Bks NY.

DRUGS–FICTION

Coles, William E., Jr. & Schwandt, Stephen. Funnybone. LC 91-13174. 208p. (gr. 7 up). 1992. SBE 14.95 (*0-689-31666-6*, Atheneum Child Bk) Macmillan Child Grp.

Cupo, Hortense. No Way Out but Through. LC 93-29519. Date not set. 4.95 (*0-8198-5130-2*) St Paul Bks.

Gibson, Sylvia S. Latawnya, the Naughty Horse, Learns to Say "No" to Drugs. 1990. 6.95 (*0-533-09102-0*) Vantage.

Hinton, Susie E. That Was Then, This Is Now. 224p. (gr. k up). 1989. pap. 4.50 (*0-440-98652-4*, LFL) Dell.

Knapp, Paul E. False Positive. LC 89-51296. 167p. 1990. 7.95 (*1-55523-260-4*) Winston-Derek.

Kropp, Paul. Dope Deal. Macpherson, Elaine, illus. LC 81-9766. 96p. (gr. 7-12). 1982. pap. 4.50 (*0-88436-818-1*, 35272); wkbk. 1.20 (*0-88436-927-7*, 35685); read-along cassette 10.00 (*0-88436-951-X*, 35106) EMC.

Mahon, Thomas J. Say, Kids! Always Say No to That Junky Stuff, Drugs! 1992. 7.95 (*0-533-09698-7*) Vantage.

Mann, Peggy. La Historia de Maria Wanna: O Como te Dana la Marihuana. Ramirez, Gloria & Gatti, Maria N., trs. from ENG. Lind, Naomi, illus. (SPA.). 44p. (Orig.). (gr. 1-6). 1990. pap. text ed. 3.95 (*0-942493-15-X*) Woodmere Press.

Masihlall, Kamala. Drug Card. Masihlall, Kamala, illus. 13p. (gr. k-3). 1993. pap. 12.95 (*1-895583-61-6*) MAYA Pubs.

Milam, June M. & Gaston, Kathy. All by Myself. Gilmer, Chris & Wilson, Amy L., eds. McIntosh, Chuck, illus. 24p. (Orig.). (ps-k). 1993. pap. text ed. 42.95 (*1-884307-00-0*); student's ed. 4.95 (*1-884307-01-9*) Dev Res Educ.

Milam, June M., et al. The Drugless Douglas Tales Series, 9 vols. Wilson, Amy L., ed. McIntosh, Chuck, illus. (Orig.). (ps-k). 1994. Set. pap. 431.10 (*1-884307-02-7*) Dev Res Educ.

Milan, June M. Just a Little Lie. Gilwer, Chris, ed. McIntosh, Chuck, illus. 20p. (ps-k). 1993. pap. text ed. 42.95 (*1-884307-03-5*); student's ed. 4.95 (*0-685-70993-0*) Dev Res Educ.

Moran, Bill & Mann, Peggy. The Mary Wanna Student Activity Book: Based Upon: The Sad Story of Mary Wanna Or How Marijuana Harms You. rev. ed. Lind, Naomi, illus. 26p. (gr. 4-6). 1990. pap. text ed. 2.95 (*0-942493-11-7*) Woodmere Press.

Skurzynski, Gloria. Caught in the Moving Mountains. (Illus.). 144p. (gr. 7 up). 1994. pap. 4.95 (*0-688-12945-5*, Pub. by Beech Tree Bks) Morrow.

Strasser, Todd. Angel Dust Blues. 208p. (gr. 9 up). 1981. pap. 2.95 (*0-440-90956-2*, LE); tchr's guide by Lou Stanek 0.50 (*0-685-01408-8*) Dell.

Strong, Bryan & DeVault, Christine. Christy's Chance. Nelson, Mary, ed. Ransom, Robert D., illus. 72p. (gr. 5-8). 1987. pap. text ed. 3.95 (*0-941816-33-8*) ETR Assocs.

Tate, Eleanore E. A Blessing in Disguise. LC 94-13073. 1995. 14.95 (*0-385-32103-1*) Delacorte.

Vigna, Judith. My Big Sister Takes Drugs. Mathews, Judith, ed. Vigna, Judith, illus. LC 89-70736. 32p. (gr. k-3). 1990. PLB 13.95 (*0-8075-5317-4*) A Whitman.

Wenkart, Henny. Why Would Matthew Do Crack? (gr. 3-7). 1990. write for info. (*0-911612-00-9*) Wenkart.

Wert, Debra L. Mac's Choice: A Story about Choice & Drug Use. Anfenson-Vance, Deborah, et al, eds. Wilson, Miriam J., intro. by. (Illus.). 40p. (gr. 1 up). 1989. pap. 7.95 (*0-944576-02-8*) Rocky River Pubs.

Wingate, Rosalee M. I'll Make It Happen Without Drugs. Sapenter, Marcellus, illus. 44p. (Orig.). (gr. 4-8). 1990. pap. 6.00 (*0-9625391-0-4*) R M Wingate.

DRUGS–LAWS AND REGULATIONS

Lord, Suzanne. Drug Enforcement Agents. LC 89-1343. (Illus.). 48p. (gr. 5-6). 1989. text ed. 11.95 RSBE (*0-89686-428-6*, Crestwood Hse) Macmillan Child Grp.

Marshall, Eliot. Legalization: A Debate. Mendelson, Jack & Mello, Nancyintro. by. (Illus.). 128p. (gr. 5 up). 1988. lib. bdg. 19.95 (*1-55546-229-4*) Chelsea Hse.

DRUIDS AND DRUIDISM–FICTION

Pevsner, Stella. Jon, Flora, & the Odd-Eyed Cat. LC 93-41218. 1994. 13.95 (*0-395-67021-7*, Clarion Bks) HM.

Pope, Elizabeth M. The Perilous Gard. Cuffari, Richard, illus. 288p. (gr. 7 up). 1992. pap. 4.99 (*0-14-034912-X*) Puffin Bks.

DRUM

Leanza, Frank. How to Get Started with the Drums. (Illus.). 28p. 1993. pap. 3.95 (*0-934687-18-8*) Crystal Pubs.

Paker, Josephine. Beating the Drum. LC 92-5164. (Illus.). 48p. (gr. 2-6). 1992. PLB 14.40 (*1-56294-093-7*) Millbrook Pr.

DRUM–FICTION

Gregorich, Barbara. The Gum on the Drum. Hoffman, Joan, ed. Sandford, John, illus. 16p. (Orig.). (gr. k-2). 1984. pap. 2.25 (*0-88743-004-X*, 06004) Sch Zone Pub Co.

—The Gum on the Drum. Hoffman, Joan, ed. (Illus.). 32p. (gr. k-2). 1992. pap. 3.95 (*0-88743-402-9*, 06054) Sch Zone Pub Co.

Ossorio, Joseph D., et al. Drums. (Illus.). 48p. (gr. 3-5). 1994. pap. 6.95 (*1-56721-078-3*) Twnty-Fifth Cent Pr.

Pinkney, Brian. Max Found Two Sticks. LC 93-12525. 1994. pap. 15.00 (*0-671-78776-4*, S&S BFYR) S&S Trade.

Rubel, Nicole. Conga Crocodile. LC 92-31856. 1993. 14. 95 (*0-395-58773-5*) HM.

DRUM MAJORS

Wheelus, Doris. Baton Twirling: A Complete Illustrated Guide. Bolle, Frank, illus. 144p. (gr. 5 up). 1975. PLB 13.95 (*0-87460-310-2*); pap. 9.95 (*0-87460-311-0*) Lion Bks.

DRUNKENNESS

see Alcoholism

DRY GOODS

see Textile Industry and Fabrics

DU BOIS, WILLIAM EDWARD BURGHARDT, 1868-1963

Cavan, Seamus. W. E. B. Du Bois & Racial Relations. LC 92-33015. (Illus.). 32p. (gr. 2-4). 1993. PLB 12.90 (*1-56294-288-3*); pap. 4.95 (*1-56294-794-X*) Millbrook Pr.

McKissack, Patricia C. & McKissack, Fredrick, Jr. W. E. B. Dubois. LC 90-37823. (Illus.). 128p. (gr. 7-12). 1990. PLB 14.40 (*0-531-10939-9*) Watts.

Neyland, James. W. E. B. DuBois, Scholar & Activist. Locke, Raymond F., ed. (Illus.). 192p. 1993. pap. 3.95 (*0-87067-588-5*, Melrose Sq) Holloway.

Stafford, Mark. W. E. B. Dubois. King, Coretta Scott, intro. by. LC 89-9705. (Illus.). 128p. (Orig.). (gr. 5 up). 1989. lib. bdg. 17.95 (*1-55546-582-X*); pap. 9.95 (*0-7910-0238-1*) Chelsea Hse.

W. E. B. Du Bois: Mini Play. (gr. 5 up). 1977. 6.50 (*0-89550-362-X*) Stevens & Shea.

DUCKS

Allred, Gordon. Dori the Mallard. Brown, Margery, illus. (gr. 5 up). 1968. 8.95 (*0-8392-3052-4*) Astor-Honor.

Arnosky, Jim. All Night near the Water. Arnosky, Jim, illus. LC 93-31078. 32p. (ps-1). 1994. PLB 15.95 (*0-399-22629-X*, Putnam) Putnam Pub Group.

Blackburn, Lynn B. Timothy Duck: The Story of the Death of a Friend. Johnson, Joy, ed. Borum, Shari, illus. 24p. (Orig.). (gr. 1-6). 1989. pap. 3.45 (*1-56123-013-8*) Centering Corp.

Burton, Jane. Dabble the Duckling. Burton, Jane, photos by. LC 89-11398. (Illus.). 32p. (gr. 2-3). 1989. PLB 17.27 (*0-8368-0205-5*) Gareth Stevens Inc.

Crozat, Francois. I Am a Little Duck. (Illus.). 24p. (ps-k). 1989. 8.95 (*0-8120-5904-2*); Miniature. 3.50 (*0-8120-6192-6*) Barron.

Dabcovich, Lydia. Ducks Fly. LC 89-38716. (Illus.). 32p. (ps). 1990. 13.95 (*0-525-44586-2*, DCB) Dutton Child Bks.

Dalmais. Duck, Reading Level 3-4. (Illus.). 28p. (gr. 2-5). 1983. PLB 16.67 (*0-86592-862-2*); 12.50s.p. (*0-685-58816-5*) Rourke Corp.

Dunn, Opal. Duck Match & Patch Book. (ps). 1992. 4.99 (*0-440-40610-2*) Dell.

Fowler, Allan. Quack & Honk. LC 92-35056. (Illus.). 32p. (ps-2). 1993. big bk. 22.95 (*0-516-49643-3*); PLB 10.75 (*0-516-06012-0*); pap. 3.95 (*0-516-46012-9*) Childrens.

Frisch. Ducks. 1981. 11.95s.p. (*0-86625-192-8*) Rourke Pubns.

Gaw, Robyn. Ducks. Lee, Connell, illus. LC 92-31915. 1993. 4.25 (*0-383-03567-8*) SRA Schl Grp.

Georgiady, Nicholas P. & Romano, Louis G. Trudi La Cane. Thorne, Patrice, tr. from ENG. Wilson, Dagmar W., illus. (FRE.). 27p. (gr. k-4). pap. 5.00 (*0-317-03037-X*) Argee Pubs.

Goldin, Augusta. Ducks Don't Get Wet. rev. ed. Kessler, Leonard, illus. LC 88-18073. 32p. (ps-3). 1989. (Crowell Jr Bks); (Crowell Jr Bks) HarpC Child Bks.

—Ducks Don't Get Wet. rev. ed. Kessler, Leonard, illus. LC 88-18073. 32p. (ps-3). 1989. pap. 4.95 (*0-06-445082-1*, Trophy) HarpC Child Bks.

Hawcock, David. Duck. Bampton, Bob, illus. 5p. (ps). 1994. 3.95 (*0-307-17302-X*, Artsts Writrs) Western Pub.

Little Ducks Don't Fly. (Illus.). 32p. (ps-3). 1992. write for info. (*0-914082-27-2*) Syentek.

McBrier, Page. Oliver & the Lucky Duck. Sims, Blanche, illus. LC 85-8417. 96p. (gr. 3-6). 1986. PLB 9.89 (*0-8167-0541-0*); pap. text ed. 2.95 (*0-8167-0542-9*) Troll Assocs.

McCue, Lisa, illus. Ducklings Love. LC 90-61308. 24p. (ps-1). 1991. 4.95 (*0-679-80386-6*) Random Bks Yng Read.

Molleson, Diane. How Ducklings Grow. Kuhn, Dwight R., photos by. 32p. (ps-2). 1993. pap. 2.50 (*0-590-45201-0*) Scholastic Inc.

Nentl, Jerolyn. The Mallard. LC 83-2087. (Illus.). 48p. (gr. 5). 1983. text ed. 12.95 RSBE (*0-89686-221-6*, Crestwood Hse) Macmillan Child Grp.

Nierman, Lewis G. Lefty's Place. Nierman, Lewis G., illus. 32p. (gr. 1-4). 1994. 18.95g (*0-9636820-0-8*) Kindness Pubns.

Petty, Kate. Ducklings. 24p. (gr. k-3). 1993. pap. 3.95 (*0-8120-1489-8*) Barron.

Pope, Joyce. The Duck. (Illus.). 24p. (gr. 3-6). 1991. 8.95 (*0-237-60249-0*, Pub. by Evans Bros Ltd) Trafalgar.

Rothaus, Jim. Ducks, Geese, & Swans. 24p. (gr. 3). 1988. PLB 14.95 (*0-88682-224-6*) Creative Ed.

Selsam, Millicent E. & Hunt, Joyce. A First Look at Ducks, Geese & Swans. Springer, Harriet, illus. 32p. (gr. 1-4). 1990. 11.95 (*0-8027-6975-6*); lib. bdg. 12.85 (*0-8027-6976-4*) Walker & Co.

Spier, Peter. Peter Spier's Ducks. 1984. pap. 2.50 (*0-385-18199-X*) Doubleday.

Stone, L. Patos (Ducks) 1991. 8.95s.p. (*0-86592-953-X*) Rourke Enter.

Stone, Lynn. Ducks. (Illus.). 24p. (gr. k-5). 1990. lib. bdg. 11.94 (*0-86593-036-8*); lib. bdg. 8.95s.p. (*0-685-36310-4*) Rourke Corp.

Watts, Barrie, photos by. See How They Grow: Duck. (Illus.). 24p. (gr. k-3). 1991. 6.95 (*0-525-67346-6*, Lodestar Bks) Dutton Child Bks.

Wijngaard, Juan. Duck. Wijngaard, Juan, illus. LC 90-81896. 12p. (ps). 1991. bds. 3.95 (*0-517-58204-X*) Crown Bks Yng Read.

Williams, Jane S. Super Duck: A True Story. Pruett, Robert H., ed. Williams, Jane S., illus. 61p. (Orig.). (ps-4). 1990. pap. 9.95 (*0-9627635-0-0*) Brandylane.

DUCKS–FICTION

Abell, J. The Only Duck in the Puddle. Abell, J., illus. 50p. (ps-2). 1994. 25.00 (*1-56611-099-8*); pap. 15.00 (*1-56611-525-6*) Jonas.

Akass, Susan. Number Nine Duckling. Ayliffe, Alex, illus. 32p. (ps-1). 1993. 13.95 (*1-56397-224-7*) Boyds Mills Pr.

Andersen, Hans Christian. The Ugly Duckling. Moore, Lilian, retold by. San Souci, Daniel, illus. 48p. (ps-2). 1988. pap. 3.95 (*0-590-43794-1*); incl. cassette 5.95 (*0-590-63231-0*) Scholastic Inc.

—The Ugly Duckling. (Illus.). 32p. (gr. k-3). 1993. pap. 2.99 (*0-87406-656-5*) Willowisp Pr.

Ayme, Marcel. Canard et la Panthere. Sabatier, C. & Sabatier, R., illus. (FRE.). 63p. (gr. 1-5). 1991. pap. 9.95 (*2-07-031128-7*) Schoenhof.

Balan, Bruce. Jeremy Quacks. Meier, David S., illus. LC 89-31372. 32p. (ps up). 1991. pap. 14.95 (*0-88708-104-5*) Picture Bk Studio.

Barks, Carl. Walt Disney's Donald Duck Adventures Album. Barks, Carl, illus. Blum, Geoffrey, intro. by. (Illus.). 48p. (Orig.). (ps up). 1988. pap. 5.95 (*0-944599-08-7*) Gladstone Pub.

—Walt Disney's Donald Duck Adventures Comic Album. Barks, Carl, illus. Blum, Geoffrey, intro. by. (Illus.). 48p. (Orig.). (ps up). 1988. pap. 5.95 (*0-944599-04-4*) Gladstone Pub.

—Walt Disney's Donald Duck Album. Barks, Carl, illus. Blum, Geoffrey, intro. by. (Illus.). 48p. (Orig.). (ps up). 1988. pap. 5.95 (*0-944599-06-0*) Gladstone Pub.

—Walt Disney's Donald Duck Comic Album. Barks, Carl, illus. Blum, Geoffrey, intro. by. (Illus.). 48p. (Orig.). (ps up). 1987. pap. 5.95 (*0-944599-01-X*) Gladstone Pub.

—Walt Disney's Uncle Scrooge Comic Album. Barks, Carl, illus. Blum, Geoffrey, intro. by. (Illus.). 48p. (ps up). 1987. pap. 5.95 (*0-944599-02-8*) Gladstone Pub.

—Walt Disney's Uncle Scrooge Comic Album. Barks, Carl, illus. Blum, Geoffrey, intro. by. (Illus.). 48p. (ps up). 1988. pap. 5.95 (*0-944599-05-2*) Gladstone Pub.

—Walt Disney's Uncle Scrooge Comic Album. Barks, Carl, illus. Blum, Geoffrey, intro. by. (Illus.). 48p. (Orig.). (ps up). 1987. pap. 5.95 (*0-944599-00-1*) Gladstone Pub.

Barks, Carl, intro. by. Donald Duck. (Illus.). 195p. 1991. 17.99 (*0-517-69714-9*) Random Hse Value.

Barr, Marilynn G. Duck Days. (Illus.). 48p. (ps-1). 1993. pap. 5.95 (*1-878279-53-X*) Monday Morning Bks.

Bebe Daisy Sal a Pasar. (SPA.). (ps-3). 1993. pap. 2.95 (*0-307-96095-1*, Golden Pr) Western Pub.

Bebe Donald en el Parque. (SPA.). (ps-3). 1993. pap. 2.95 (*0-307-96096-X*, Golden Pr) Western Pub.

Bizette, Genevieve. The Mallard. Bizette, Genevieve, illus. 12p. (ps). 1992. 3.95 (*1-56828-012-2*) Red Jacket Pr.

Blocksma, Mary. Donde Esta el Pato? - Where's That Duck? Martin, Sandra K., illus. LC 85-15001. (SPA.). 24p. (ps-2). 1990. pap. 3.95 (*0-516-51587-X*) Childrens.

—Where's That Duck? LC 85-15001. (Illus.). 32p. (ps-2). 1985. pap. 3.95 (*0-516-41587-5*) Childrens.

Brown, Margaret W. Walt Disney's the Ugly Duckling. DiCiccio, Gil, illus. 32p. 1994. 13.95 (*0-7868-3007-7*); PLB 13.89 (*0-7868-5001-9*) Disney Pr.

Bulla, Clyde R. Daniel's Duck. Sandin, Joan, illus. LC 78-22156. 64p. (gr. k-3). 1982. pap. 3.50 (*0-06-444031-1*, Trophy) HarpC Child Bks.

Bunting, Eve. Happy Birthday, Dear Duck. Brett, Jan, illus. LC 87-15694. 32p. (ps-1). 1988. 13.95 (*0-89919-541-5*, Clarion Bks) HM.

—Happy Birthday, Dear Duck. Brett, Jan, illus. LC 87-15694. 32p. (ps). 1990. pap. 4.80 (*0-395-52594-2*, Clarion Bks) HM.

Cartlidge, Michelle. Duck in the Pond. Cartlidge, Michelle, illus. 12p. (ps). 1991. bds. 3.50 (*0-525-44675-3*, DCB) Dutton Child Bks.

Clement, Claude. The Hungry Duckling. Geneste, Marcelle, illus. LC 91-40648. 24p. (ps-3). 1992. 6.99 (*0-89577-418-6*, Dist. by Random) RD Assn.

Cossi, Olga. Think Pink. Clarke, Lea A., illus. LC 93-5556. 1994. 10.95 (*0-88289-995-3*) Pelican.

Cowley, Stewart. Naughty Ducklings. Adams, Susi, illus. LC 92-60791. 20p. (ps). 1992. 6.99 (*0-89577-444-5*, Dist. by Random) RD Assn.

Crump, Fred, Jr. Ebony Duckling. Crump, Fred, Jr., illus. LC 91-75090. 44p. (gr. k-3). 1991. pap. 6.95 (*1-55523-457-7*) Winston-Derek.

Darkwing Duck: Just Us Justice Duck. (Illus.). 48p. (gr. 3-7). 1992. pap. 2.95 (*1-56115-268-4*, 21809, Golden Pr) Western Pub.

Demi. Little Lucky Ducky. Demi, illus. 12p. (ps). 1993. bds. 3.95 (*0-448-40581-4*, G&D) Putnam Pub Group.

Dolan, Ellen M. & Bolinske, Janet L., eds. Drakestail. LC 87-61663. (Illus.). 32p. (Orig.). (gr. 1-3). 1987. text ed. 8.95 (*0-88335-562-0*); pap. text ed. 4.95 (*0-88335-582-5*) Milliken Pub Co.

Downy Duckling. (Illus.). (ps-k). 3.50 (*0-7214-0210-0*) Ladybird Bks.

Ducks Can't Count (EV, Unit 1. (gr. 1). 1991. 5-pack 21. 25 (*0-88106-705-9*) Charlesbridge Pub.

Egan, Tim. Friday Night at Hodges' Cafe. LC 93-11290. 1994. 14.95 (*0-395-68076-X*) HM.

Ellis, Anne L. Dabble Duck. Truesdell, Sue, illus. LC 83-47692. 32p. (ps-2). 1984. PLB 12.89 (*0-06-021818-5*) HarpC Child Bks.

—Dabble Duck. Truesdell, Sue, illus. LC 83-47692. 32p. (ps-3). 1984. pap. 3.95 (*0-06-443153-3*, Trophy) HarpC Child Bks.

Elting, Mary & Folsom, Michael. Q Is for Duck. Kent, Jack, illus. LC 80-13854. 64p. (ps-3). 1980. 13.95 (*0-395-29437-1*, Clarion Bks); pap. 5.70 (*0-395-30062-2*) HM.

Farmer, Patti. What Do You Think I Am... Crazy? Veno, Joe, illus. 32p. (ps-3). 1991. 10.95 (*0-8120-5979-4*) Barron.

Finkelstein, Ruth. Dena the Duckling Has an Appointment. Oberman, Devora, illus. 24p. (Orig.). (ps-3). 1993. pap. 3.95 (*0-9628157-2-1*) R Finkelstein.

Flack, Marjorie. The Story about Ping. Wiese, Kurt, illus. (gr. k-2). 1977. pap. 4.99 (*0-14-050241-6*, Puffin) Puffin Bks.

—Story about Ping. Wiese, Kurt, illus. LC 33-29356. (ps-2). 1933. pap. 14.00 (*0-670-67223-8*) Viking Child Bks.

Flack, Marjorie & Wiese, Kurt. The Story about Ping. (Illus.). 1993. pap. 6.99 incl. cassette (*0-14-095117-2*, Puffin) Puffin Bks.

Friskey, Margaret. Seven Diving Ducks. Morey, Jean, illus. LC 65-20889. 32p. (gr. k-3). 1965. PLB 11.45 (*0-516-03605-X*) Childrens.
Garside, Alice H. The Ant & the Duck. Meeks, Catherine F., illus. 16p. (Orig.). (gr. k-2). 1990. pap. 2.10 (*1-882063-07-4*) Cottage Pr MA.
Georgiady, Nicholas P. & Romano, Louis G. Gertie the Duck: Look! I-Can-Read Book. (Illus.). 32p. (gr. k-4). 1988. pap. 3.00 (*0-695-83363-4*) Argee Pubs.
Georgiou, Constantine. Proserpina, the Duck That Came to School. (gr. 3-6). 1992. pap. write for info. (*0-9637111-0-5*) C Georgiou.
Gerstein, Mordicai. Arnold of the Ducks. Gerstein, Mordicai, illus. LC 82-47735. 64p. (gr. k-3). 1983. PLB 14.89 (*0-06-022003-1*) HarpC Child Bks.
Ginsburg, Mirra. The Chick & the Duckling. Suteyev, V., tr. from RUS. Aruego, Jose & Dewey, Ariane, illus. LC 74-18873. 32p. (ps-1). 1972. RSBE 14.95 (*0-02-735940-9*, Macmillan Child Bk) Macmillan Child Grp.
Gordon, Gaelyn. Duckat. (ps). 1992. 13.95 (*0-590-45455-2*, Scholastic Hardcover) Scholastic Inc.
—Duckat. (ps-3). pap. 19.95 (*0-590-72846-6*) Scholastic Inc.
Gottfredson, Floyd. Walt Disney's Mickey Mouse Comic Album. Gottfredson, Floyd, illus. Blum, Geoffrey, intro. by. (Illus.). 48p. (Orig.). (ps up). 1987. pap. 5.95 (*0-944599-03-6*) Gladstone Pub.
—Walt Disney's Mickey Mouse Comic Album. Gottfredson, Floyd, illus. Blum, Geoffrey, intro. by. (Illus.). 48p. (Orig.). (ps up). 1988. pap. 5.95 (*0-944599-07-9*) Gladstone Pub.
Green, I. Where Is Duckling Three? Le Blanc, L., illus. LC 68-16402. 32p. (gr. 1-2). 1967. PLB 9.95 (*0-87783-048-7*) Oddo.
Gretz, Susanna. Duck Takes Off. Gretz, Susanna, illus. LC 90-3846. 32p. (ps-1). 1991. RSBE 12.95 (*0-02-737472-6*, Four Winds) Macmillan Child Grp.
Hammond. Ten Little Ducks. 1993. pap. 28.67 (*0-590-73338-9*) Scholastic Inc.
Hammond, Franklin. Ten Little Ducks. Hammond, Frank, illus. 24p. (ps). 1992. pap. 4.95 (*0-88899-153-3*, Pub. by Groundwood-Douglas & McIntyre CN) Firefly Bks Ltd.
Hide-&-Seek Duck. (ps-k). 1991. write for info. (*0-307-12235-2*, Golden Pr) Western Pub.
Hillert, Margaret. Little Quack. (Illus.). (ps-2). 1961. PLB 6.95 (*0-8136-5044-5*, TK2330); pap. 3.50 (*0-8136-5544-7*, TK2331) Modern Curr.
Hoff, Bernard. Duncan the Dancing Duck. LC 93-13058. (Illus.). 32p. (ps-3). 1994. 13.95 (*0-395-67400-X*, Clarion Bks) HM.
Horowitz, Jordan, adapted by. D-Two: The Mighty Ducks Are Back! (Illus.). 144p. (gr. 1-6). 1994. pap. 3.95 (*1-56282-692-1*) Disney Pr.
—Mighty Ducks. LC 93-71248. (gr. 4-7). 1993. pap. 3.50 (*1-56282-505-4*) Disney Pr.
Ichikawa, Satomi. Nora's Duck. Ichikawa, Satomi, illus. 40p. (ps-3). 1991. 14.95 (*0-399-21805-X*, Philomel) Putnam Pub Group.
Ingoglia, Gina. The Friendly Duck. (Illus.). 24p. (ps-k). 1989. pap. write for info. (*0-307-10069-3*, Pub. by Golden Bks) Western Pub.
Inkpen, Mick. Gumboot's Chocolatey Day. 1991. pap. 11.95 (*0-385-41489-7*) Doubleday.
Johansen, Hanna. Duck & the Owl. Bhend-Zaugg, Kathi, illus. LC 91-33011. 64p. (gr. 2-5). 1992. 12.95 (*0-525-44828-4*, DCB) Dutton Child Bks.
Joyce, William. Bently & Egg. Joyce, William, illus. LC 91-55499. 32p. (ps-3). 1992. 15.00 (*0-06-020385-4*); PLB 14.89 (*0-06-020386-2*) HarpC Child Bks.
Kanno, Wendy. Waldo Duck. Reese, Bob, illus. (gr. k-2). 1984. 7.95 (*0-89868-157-X*); pap. 2.95 (*0-89868-158-8*) ARO Pub.
Kelty, Jean M. If You Have a Duck... rev. ed. Ford, Elizabeth, illus. LC 82-51120. 104p. (gr. 1-9). 1982. pap. 9.95 (*0-910781-00-1*) G Whittell Mem.
Kennedy, Fiona & Noakes, Polly. The Last Little Duckling. LC 92-21695. (Illus.). 28p. (ps-1). 1993. 12.95 (*0-8120-6326-0*); pap. 4.95 (*0-8120-1355-7*) Barron.
Kienlen, Helen & Sandercock, Lois. Big Boss Charger. Bower, J. R., illus. 16p. (gr. k-4). 1989. pap. text ed. 4.00 (*0-9626864-1-7*) Holistic Learning.
Kwitz, Mary D. Little Chick's Friend Duckling. Degen, Bruce, illus. LC 90-5027. 32p. (ps-2). 1992. 13.00 (*0-06-023638-8*); PLB 13.89 (*0-06-023639-6*) HarpC Child Bks.
Laird, Elizabeth. The Day the Ducks Went Skating. Reeder, Colin, illus. LC 90-25899. 32p. (gr. k up). 1991. 11.95 (*0-688-10246-8*, Tambourine Bks); PLB 11.88 (*0-688-10247-6*, Tambourine Bks) Morrow.
Lanni, Deborah. What's a Duck Like You Doing in a Place Like This? (Illus.). iv, 23p. (Orig.). (gr. 3-6). 1984. pap. 2.00 (*0-942788-12-5*) Iris Visual.
Lawhead, Stephen R. Riverbank Stories: The Tale of Timothy Mallard. 112p. (gr. 4). 1993. pap. 3.50 (*0-380-72199-6*, Camelot) Avon.
Leonard, Marcia. Little Duck Finds a Friend. 32p. (ps). 1984. pap. 2.50 (*0-553-15275-0*) Bantam.
—Little Rabbit's Baby Sister. 32p. (Orig.). (ps). 1984. pap. 2.50 (*0-553-15274-2*) Bantam.
LeSieg, Theo. I Wish That I Had Duck Feet. LC 65-21211. (Illus.). 64p. (ps-2). 1965. 6.95 (*0-394-80040-0*); PLB 7.99 (*0-394-90040-5*) Random Bks Yng Read.
Leverich, Kathleen. The Hungry Fox & the Foxy Duck. Galdone, Paul, illus. LC 78-11215. 48p. (ps-3). 1979. 5.95 (*0-8193-0987-7*); PLB 5.95 (*0-8193-0988-5*) Parents.
Lorenz, Lee. A Weekend in the Country. Lorenz, Lee, illus. 32p. (gr. k-3). 1985. 11.95 (*0-13-947961-9*) P-H.
Lubach, Peter. Harry & the Singing Fish. Lubach, Peter, illus. LC 91-73824. 32p. (gr. k-4). 1992. 12.95 (*1-56282-158-X*); PLB 12.89 (*1-56282-159-8*) Hyprn Child.
Lunn, Janet. Duck Cakes for Sale. LaFave, Kim, illus. 32p. (ps-2). 1991. 13.95 (*0-88899-094-4*, Pub. by Groundwood-Douglas & McIntyre CN); pap. 4.95 (*0-88899-157-6*) Firefly Bks Ltd.
McCloskey, Robert. Make Way for Ducklings. (Illus.). (gr. 1-3). 1976. pap. 4.99 (*0-14-050171-1*, Puffin) Puffin Bks.
—Make Way for Ducklings. McCloskey, Robert, illus. (gr. k-3). 1941. pap. 13.99 (*0-670-45149-5*) Viking Child Bks.
—Make Way for Ducklings. (Illus.). 1993. pap. 6.99 incl. cassette (*0-14-095118-0*, Puffin) Puffin Bks.
—Make Way for Ducklings: A Giant Book. giant ed. (ps-3). 1991. pap. 17.99 (*0-14-054434-8*, Puffin) Puffin Bks.
McCue, Lisa, illus. Ducky's Seasons. (ps-2). 1983. pap. 2.95 (*0-671-45491-9*, Little Simon) S&S Trade.
MacKay-Robinson, Christina. Edd the Astronaut. Ellis, Andy, illus. 32p. (gr. k-3). 1992. pap. 4.95 (*0-563-36062-3*, BBC-Parkwest) Parkwest Pubns.
—Edd's Ghost Story. Johnson, Paul, illus. 32p. (gr. k-3). 1992. pap. 4.95 (*0-563-36063-1*, BBC-Parkwest) Parkwest Pubns.
MacKay-Robinson, Christina & Faulkner, Keith. Edd the Duck in Storyland. Johnson, Paul, illus. 32p. (gr. k-3). 1992. 12.95 (*0-563-36046-1*, BBC-Parkwest) Parkwest Pubns.
Make Way for Ducklings. (ps-3). 1988. pap. 6.95 incl. cassette (*0-14-095069-9*, Puffin) Puffin Bks.
Mamin-Sibiryak, D. N. Grey Neck. Rudolph, Marguerita, adapted by. Kronz, Leslie S., illus. LC 88-2100. 32p. (gr. k-3). 1988. 13.95 (*0-88045-068-1*) Stemmer Hse.
Martin, Ann M. Karen's Ducklings. 96p. 1992. pap. 2.75 (*0-590-44830-7*) Scholastic Inc.
Matthews, Morgan. Chuck, the Unlucky Duck. Harvey, Paul, illus. LC 88-1284. 48p. (Orig.). (gr. 1-4). 1989. PLB 10.59 (*0-8167-1333-2*); pap. text ed. 3.50 (*0-8167-1334-0*) Troll Assocs.
Maxey, Kathi. The Duck That Was a Chicken. 1993. 7.00 (*0-8062-4675-8*) Carlton.
Miller, Edna. Duck Duck. (ps-3). 1981. pap. 3.95 (*0-685-03845-9*) P-H.
Miller, J. P. Little Duckling's Surprise. LC 86-62052. (Illus.). 24p. (ps-1). 1987. bk. & doll pkg. 4.95 (*0-394-88682-8*) Random Bks Yng Read.
Mink, Len. Gospel Duck. Strand, David, illus. 20p. (ps-5). 1988. pap. text ed. write for info. Mink Ministries.
—Gospel Duck Goes to School. Strand, David, illus. 24p. (ps-6). 1988. pap. text ed. write for info. Mink Ministries.
Muller, Gerda, illus. The Ugly Duckling. 48p. (gr. 2-6). 1991. 2.99 (*0-517-02422-5*) Random Hse Value.
Ofek, Uriel. Beware! Ducks Crossing. Kriss, David, tr. from HEB. Elchanan, illus. 24p. (Orig.). (ps). 1992. pap. text ed. 3.00x (*1-56134-145-2*) Dushkin Pub.
Ogden, Betina, illus. The Ugly Duckling. 18p. (ps). 1994. bds. 3.95 (*0-448-40184-3*, G&D) Putnam Pub Group.
Oke, Janette. Ducktails. Mann, Brenda, illus. 131p. (gr. 3 up). 1985. pap. 4.99 (*0-934998-20-5*) Bethel Pub.
Otto, Carolyn B. Ducks, Ducks, Ducks. Coxe, Molly, illus. LC 90-42089. 32p. (ps-1). 1991. HarpC Child Bks.
Owen, Annie. Playtime Duck. Owen, Annie, illus. LC 93-79579. 14p. (ps). 1994. bds. 4.95 (*1-85697-947-4*, Kingfisher LKC) LKC.
Paterson, Katherine. The Tale of the Mandarin Ducks. Dillon, Leo D. & Dillon, Diane, illus. (gr. k-3). 1990. 15.00 (*0-525-67283-4*, Lodestar Bks) Dutton Child Bks.
El Patito Feo: (The Ugly Little Duck) LC 85-31428. (SPA & ENG.). (ps-2). 1989. PLB 10.25 (*0-516-33982-6*); pap. 3.95 (*0-516-53982-5*) Childrens.
Pellowski, Michael J. The Duck Who Loved Puddles. Paterson, Diane, illus. LC 85-14058. 48p. (Orig.). (gr. 1-3). 1986. PLB 10.59 (*0-8167-0578-X*); pap. text ed. 3.50 (*0-8167-0579-8*) Troll Assocs.
Petrie, Mildred M. Duck, Duck: The Different Duck. Errickson, Shirley V., illus. LC 87-80921. 40p. 1987. 12.95 (*0-9618241-0-7*) Enfield Pubs.
Phillips, Eva. Nodley, the Duck Who Paddled Backwards. LC 91-65791. 44p. (gr. k-3). 1991. pap. 6.95 (*1-55523-446-1*) Winston-Derek.
Potter, Beatrix. El Cuento de la Oca Carlota. (SPA., Illus.). 64p. 1988. 5.95 (*0-7232-3557-0*) Warne.
—Jemima Puddleduck. 1988. 2.99 (*0-517-65275-7*) Random Hse Value.
—Jemima Puddleduck: Beatrix Potter Deluxe Pop Up. (Illus.). 1992. 4.99 (*0-517-06999-7*) Random Hse Value.
—The Tale of Jemima Puddle-Duck. 64p. (Orig.). (ps). 1984. pap. 2.25 (*0-553-15251-3*) Bantam.
—The Tale of Jemima Puddle-Duck. (Illus.). 64p. (ps-3). 1987. 3.95 (*0-671-63236-1*, Little Simon) S&S Trade.
—The Tale of Jemima Puddle-Duck. (Illus.). (ps-3). 1987. 5.95 (*0-7232-3468-X*); pap. 2.25 (*0-7232-3493-0*) Warne.
—The Tale of Jemima Puddle-Duck. Potter, Beatrix, illus. 24p. (ps-2). 1991. incl. cassette 5.98 (*1-55886-057-6*) Smarty Pants.
—The Tale of Jemima Puddle-Duck. (Illus.). 32p. (ps-3). 1992. pap. 3.99 (*0-14-054498-4*) Puffin Bks.
—The Tale of Jemima Puddle-Duck & Other Farmyard Tales. (Illus.). 80p. (ps-3). 1990. pap. 5.95 (*0-14-050588-1*, Puffin) Puffin Bks.
—The Tale of Jemima Puddle-Duck & Other Farmyard Tales. (Illus.). 80p. (ps-3). 1993. 13.00 (*0-7232-3425-6*) Warne.
Potter, Beatrix, created by. Jemima Puddle-Duck. Schoonover, Pat & Nelson, Anita, illus. 24p. (gr. 2-4). 1992. PLB 10.95 (*1-56674-018-5*, HTS Bks) Forest Hse.
Quackenbush, Robert. Evil Under the Sea: A Miss Mallard Mystery. Quackenbush, Robert, illus. 32p. (gr. 1-4). 1992. 14.95 (*0-945912-16-1*) Pippin Pr.
—Henry Babysits. LC 93-15472. 1993. PLB 13.27 (*0-8368-0968-8*) Gareth Stevens Inc.
—Henry Goes West. LC 82-7971. (Illus.). 48p. (ps-3). 1982. 5.95 (*0-8193-1089-1*); PLB 5.95 (*0-8193-1090-5*) Parents.
—Henry's Awful Mistake. Quackenbush, Robert, illus. LC 80-20327. 48p. (ps-3). 1981. 5.95 (*0-8193-1039-5*); PLB 5.95 (*0-8193-1040-9*) Parents.
—Lost in the Amazon: A Miss Mallard Mystery. Quackenbush, Robert, illus. 32p. (gr. 1-4). 1990. PLB 14.95 (*0-945912-11-0*) Pippin Pr.
—Stairway to Doom: A Miss Mallard Mystery. LC 82-21484. (Illus.). 48p. (ps-5). 1983. PLB 9.95 (*0-13-804595-X*) P-H.
Quackenbush, Robert M. Henry's Awful Mistake. LC 92-32870. (Illus.). 42p. (ps-3). 1992. PLB 13.27 (*0-8368-0882-7*); PLB 13.26 s.p. (*0-685-61513-8*) Gareth Stevens Inc.
Raffi. Five Little Ducks. 1988. 12.00 (*0-517-56945-0*) Crown Bks Yng Read.
Reiser, Lynn. The Surprise Family. LC 93-16249. (Illus.). 32p. (ps up). 1994. 14.00 (*0-688-11671-X*); PLB 13.93 (*0-688-11672-8*) Greenwillow.
Rogers, Mary. The Ducks. 28p. (ps-k). 1992. pap. text ed. 23.00 big bk. (*1-56843-000-0*); pap. text ed. 4.50 (*1-56843-050-7*) BGR Pub.
Ruth, Eddie. How Do the Ducks Know? (Illus.). 28p. (Orig.). (gr. 1-4). 1981. pap. 2.50 saddle-stitched (*0-911826-18-1*, 5448) Am Atheist.
St. Pierre, Stephanie. Ducky's Rainy Day. Regan, Dana, illus. 12p. (ps). 1994. bds. 4.95 (*0-448-40458-3*, G&D) Putnam Pub Group.
Scamell, Ragnhild. Solo Plus One. Martland, Elizabeth, illus. 32p. (ps-3). 1992. 13.95 (*0-316-77242-9*) Little.
Schott, Carolyn J. & Smith, Phillipa A. The Cracker Crumb Rescue. 40p. (gr. 3-6). 1992. PLB 16.95 (*0-9632461-0-0*) Harbour Duck.
Segnit, Clare & Segnit, Jack. The Ugly Duckling: A Pop-up Classic Storybook. Segnit, Clare & Segnit, Jack, illus. 12p. (ps-3). 1993. pap. 14.95 (*0-689-71722-9*, Aladdin) Macmillan Child Grp.
Sesame Street Staff. One Rubber Duckie. Barrett, John E., photos by. LC 81-86375. (Illus.). (ps). 1982. 3.95 (*0-394-85309-1*) Random Bks Yng Read.
Shannon, George. Laughing All the Way. McLean, Meg, illus. LC 91-41135. 32p. (ps-3). 1992. 13.45 (*0-395-62473-8*) HM.
Silverman, Erica. The Freeze-in-Place Contest. Schindler, S. D., illus. LC 93-8707. (ps-2). 1994. 14.95 (*0-02-782685-6*) Macmillan.
Singer, Muff. Little Duck's Friends. LC 93-85484. (ps). 1994. 4.99 (*0-89577-565-4*) RD Assn.
Slater, Helen. Fuzzy Friends: Hug the Duck. (Illus.). 10p. 1993. 3.95 (*0-681-41810-9*) Longmeadow Pr.
Stehr, Frederic. Quack-Quack. Stehr, Frederic, illus. 28p. (ps up). 1988. pap. 3.95 (*0-374-46141-4*) FS&G.
Stott, Dorothy. Little Duck's Bicycle Ride. Stott, Dorothy, illus. LC 90-19425. 32p. (ps-k). 1991. 10.95 (*0-525-44728-8*, DCB) Dutton Child Bks.
—Too Much. LC 89-12078. (Illus.). 32p. (ps-k). 1990. 10.95 (*0-525-44569-2*, DCB) Dutton Child Bks.
Swan, Walter. Brenda the Cow & the Little White Hen. Swan, Deloris, ed. Asch, Connie, illus. 16p. (Orig.). (gr. 2-3). 1989. pap. 1.50 (*0-927176-02-5*) Swan Enterp.
Tafuri, Nancy. Have You Seen My Duckling? Tafuri, Nancy, illus. LC 83-17196. 24p. (ps-1). 1984. 15.95 (*0-688-02797-0*); PLB 15.88 (*0-688-02798-9*) Greenwillow.
—Have You Seen My Duckling? Tafuri, Nancy, illus. 32p. (ps-k). 1986. pap. 3.95 (*0-14-050532-6*) Viking Child Bks.
Teitlebaum, Michael, retold by. The Fuzzy Duckling. Borgo, Deborah, illus. (ps-2). 1991. 5.25 (*0-307-15700-8*, Golden Pr) Western Pub.
Thiele, Colin. Farmer Schulz's Ducks. Milton, Mary, illus. LC 87-21713. 32p. (gr. k-4). 1988. HarpC Child Bks.
Trezise, Percy. Black Duck & Water Rat. (ps-3). 1994. pap. 7.00 (*0-207-18349-X*, Pub. by Angus & Robertson AT) HarpC.
Tryon, Leslie. Albert's Alphabet. 1st ed. LC 93-48408. (ps-2). 1994. pap. 4.95 (*0-689-71799-7*, Aladdin) Macmillan Child Grp.
—Albert's Field Trip. Tryon, Leslie, illus. LC 92-43686. 32p. (gr. k-3). 1993. SBE 14.95 (*0-689-31821-9*, Atheneum Child Bk) Macmillan Child Grp.
—Albert's Thanksgiving. LC 94-8025. (gr. k-3). 1994. 14.95 (*0-689-31865-0*, Atheneum) Macmillan Child Grp.
Twohill, Maggie. Who Has the Lucky Duck in Class 4-B. (gr. k-6). 1986. pap. 2.50 (*0-440-49533-4*, YB) Dell.

Van Shelton, Ricky. Tales from a Duck Named Quacker: The Story Begins. 24p. 1992. pap. 7.00 (*0-9634257-0-6*) RVS Bks.
Waddell, Martin. Farmer Duck. Oxenbury, Helen & Oxenbury, Helen, illus. LC 91-71855. 40p. (ps up). 1992. 15.95 (*1-56402-009-6*) Candlewick Pr.
Walt Disney's Darkwing Duck's Darkest Night. (Illus.). (ps-3). 1991. write for info. (*0-307-12663-3*, Golden Pr) Western Pub.
Weinberger, Jane. Fanny & Sarah. 2nd ed. MacDonald, Karen, illus. LC 84-51987. 40p. (gr. k-4). 1986. pap. 3.95 (*0-932433-02-2*) Windswept Hse.
Wellington, Monica. All My Little Ducklings. Wellington, Monica, illus. LC 88-22841. 32p. (ps-k). 1989. 11.95 (*0-525-44459-9*, DCB) Dutton Child Bks.
Winthrop, Elizabeth. Bear & Mrs. Duck. Brewster, Patience, illus. LC 87-25129. 32p. (ps-3). 1988. reinforced bdg. 15.95 (*0-8234-0687-3*); pap. 5.95 (*0-8234-0843-4*) Holiday.
—Bear's Christmas Surprise. Brewster, Patience, illus. LC 90-26414. 32p. (ps-3). 1991. reinforced 14.95 (*0-8234-0888-4*) Holiday.
Worth, Bonnie. Full House Same to You Duck. (gr. 4-7). 1990. pap. 2.95 (*0-440-40468-1*) Dell.
Ziegler, J. F. The Duck & the Fox: A Metaphysical Fairy Tale. Butler, Sandra L., ed. Gillard, Dianne & Kirkpatrick, Cindy F., illus. LC 88-32071. 75p. (ps-9). 1988. pap. 9.00 (*0-9621235-0-1*) Hallelujah Pr.

DULLES, JOHN FOSTER, 1888-1959

Finke, Blythe F. John Foster Dulles: Master of Brinksmanship & Diplomacy. Ramas, D. Steve, ed. LC 77-185666. 32p. (Orig.). (gr. 7-12). 1972. lib. bdg. 4.95 incl. catalog cards (*0-87157-510-8*) SamHar Pr.
Shivanandan, Mary. Nasser: Modern Leader of Egypt. Rahmas, D. Steve, ed. LC 73-87627. 32p. (Orig.). (gr. 7-12). 1973. lib. bdg. 4.95 incl. catalog cards (*0-87157-564-7*) SamHar Pr.

DUMB (DEAF MUTES)

see Deaf

DUNANT, JEAN HENRI, 1828-1910

Gray, Charlotte. Henry Dunant: Founder of the Red Cross, the Relief Organization Dedicated to Helping Suffering People All over the World. Sherwood, Rhoda, ed. LC 88-4917. (Illus.). 68p. (gr. 5-6). 1989. PLB 19.93 (*1-55532-824-5*) Gareth Stevens Inc.

DUNBAR, PAUL LAURENCE, 1872-1906

Gentry, Tony. Paul L. Dunbar. King, Coretta Scott, intro. by. (Illus.). 112p. (Orig.). (gr. 5 up). 1989. 17.95 (*1-55546-583-8*); pap. 9.95 (*0-7910-0223-3*) Chelsea Hse.
McKissack, Patricia. Paul Laurence Dunbar: A Poet to Remember. LC 84-7625. (Illus.). 112p. (gr. 4 up). 1984. PLB 14.40 (*0-516-03209-7*); pap. 5.95 (*0-516-43209-5*) Childrens.

DUNES

see Sand Dunes

DUNGEONS

see Prisons

DUNHAM, KATHERINE, 1910-

Greene, Carol. Katherine Dunham: Black Dancer. Dobson, Steven, illus. LC 92-8769. 48p. (gr. k-3). 1992. PLB 12.85 (*0-516-04252-1*) Childrens.
—Katherine Dunham: Black Dancer. Dobson, Steven, illus. LC 92-8769. 48p. (gr. k-3). 1993. pap. 4.95 (*0-516-44252-X*) Childrens.

DURER, ALBRECHT, 1471-1528

Raboff, Ernest. Albrecht Durer. Durer, Albrecht, illus. LC 87-17702. 32p. (gr. 1 up). 1988. pap. 5.95 (*0-06-446071-1*, Trophy) HarpC Child Bks.

DUTCH IN THE U. S.–FICTION

Frost, Marie & Hanson, Bonnie C. Hattie's Cry for Help. (Illus.). 1992. pap. 5.99 (*1-56121-104-4*) Wolgemuth & Hyatt.
Joosse, Barbara M. The Morning Chair. Sewall, Marcia, illus. LC 93-4870. Date not set. write for info. (*0-395-62337-5*, Clarion Bks) HM.

DWARFS

see also Pygmies

Carrick, Carol. Two Very Little Sisters. (ps-3). 1993. 14.95 (*0-395-60927-5*, Clarion Bks) HM.
Giblin, James C., retold by. The Dwarf, the Giant, & the Unicorn: A Tale of King Arthur. Ewart, Claire, illus. LC 92-34031. 1994. write for info. (*0-395-60520-2*, Clarion Bks) HM.
Kuklin, Susan. Thinking Big: The Story of a Young Dwarf. LC 85-10425. (Illus.). 48p. (ps-1). 1986. 15.95 (*0-688-05826-4*) Lothrop.

DWARFS–FICTION

Hugo, Victor. Hunchback of Notre Dame. Canon, R. R., intro. by. (gr. 11 up). 1968. pap. 2.25 (*0-8049-0162-7*, CL-162) Airmont.
Kerr, M. E. Little Little. LC 80-8454. 160p. (gr. 7 up). 1981. PLB 14.89 (*0-06-023185-8*) HarpC Child Bks.
Russo, Marisabina. Alex Is My Friend. LC 90-24643. 32p. 1992. 14.00 (*0-688-10418-5*); PLB 13.93 (*0-688-10419-3*) Greenwillow.
Talkington, Bruce. Walt Disney's Tales from the Cottage: Stories by the Seven Dwarfs. Williams, Don, illus. 96p. (ps-3). 1994. 14.95 (*0-7868-3008-5*); PLB 14.89 (*0-7868-5003-5*) Disney Pr.

DWELLINGS

see Architecture, Domestic; Houses

DYNAMICS

see also Force and Energy; Matter; Motion; Physics; Thermodynamics

Kinetic Model. (gr. 7-12). 1992. pap. 10.50 (*0-941008-84-3*) Tops Learning.

E

E S P

see Extrasensory Perception

EAGLES

Aguilas. LC 92-8454. 1992. 12.67 (*0-86593-196-8*); 9.50s.p. (*0-685-59292-8*) Rourke Corp.
Bright, Michael. Eagles. Kline, Marjory, ed. LC 90-43984. (Illus.). 32p. (gr. 4-8). 1991. PLB 12.40 (*0-531-17262-7*, Gloucester Pr) Watts.
Butterworth, Christine & Bailey, Donna. Las Aguilas. LC 91-22808. (SPA., Illus.). 32p. (gr. 1-4). 1992. PLB 18.99 (*0-8114-2660-2*) Raintree Steck-V.
Cooper, Ann. Eagles: Hunters of the Sky. (Illus., Orig.). (gr. 4-6). 1992. pap. 7.95 (*1-879373-11-4*) R Rinehart.
Craighead, Charles. The Eagle & the River. Mangelsen, Tom, photos by. LC 92-23240. (Illus.). (gr. 1-5). 1994. RSBE 14.95 (*0-02-762265-7*, Macmillan Child Bk) Macmillan Child Grp.
Gieck, Charlene. Bald Eagle Magic for Kids. LC 91-50552. (Illus.). 48p. (gr. 3-4). 1992. PLB 18.60 (*0-8368-0761-8*) Gareth Stevens Inc.
—Eagles for Kids. 48p. 1991. 14.95 (*1-55971-120-5*); pap. 6.95 (*1-55971-133-7*) NorthWord.
Harrison, Virginia & Scott, Jim. The World of Eagles. Shahild, Wendy & Rosinski, Bob, photos by. LC 89-4459. (Illus.). 32p. (gr. 2-3). 1989. PLB 17.27 (*0-8368-0138-5*) Gareth Stevens Inc.
Highlights for Children Editors. Eagles. (Illus.). 32p. (gr. 2-5). 1994. pap. 3.95 (*1-56397-290-5*) Boyds Mills Pr.
Lang, Aubrey. Eagles. (gr. 3-6). 1990. 15.95 (*0-316-51387-3*) Little.
Lee, Sandra. Bald Eagles. 32p. (gr. 2-6). 1991. 15.95 (*0-89565-706-6*) Childs World.
Lepthien, Emilie U. Bald Eagles. LC 88-38055. (Illus.). 45p. (gr. k-2). 1989. PLB 12.85 (*0-516-01160-X*); pap. 4.95 (*0-516-41160-8*) Childrens.
McConoughey, Jana. Bald Eagle. LC 83-5162. (Illus.). 48p. (gr. 5). 1983. text ed. 12.95 RSBE (*0-89686-218-6*, Crestwood Hse) Macmillan Child Grp.
Patent, Dorothy H. Where the Bald Eagles Gather. Munoz, William, illus. LC 83-20852. 64p. (gr. 3-6). 1984. 15.45 (*0-89919-230-0*, Clarion Bks) HM.
Rothaus, Jim. Eagles. 24p. (gr. 3). 1988. PLB 14.95 (*0-88682-225-4*) Creative Ed.
Ryden, Hope. America's Bald Eagle. (Illus.). 64p. 1992. pap. 9.95 (*1-55821-141-1*) Lyons & Burford.
Sattler, Helen R. The Book of Eagles. Zallinger, Jean D., illus. LC 88-38806. 64p. (gr. 3 up). 1989. 14.95 (*0-688-07021-3*); PLB 14.88 (*0-688-07022-1*) Lothrop.
Scott, Jim. The Eagle in the Mountains. Shattil, Wendy & Rozinsky, Bob, photos by. LC 89-4461. (Illus.). 32p. (gr. 4-6). 1989. PLB 17.27 (*0-8368-0113-X*) Gareth Stevens Inc.
Selsam, Millicent E. & Hunt, Joyce. A First Look at Owls, Eagles, & Other Hunters of the Sky. Springer, Harriet, illus. 32p. (gr. 6-9). 1986. 10.95 (*0-8027-6625-0*); PLB 10.85 (*0-8027-6642-0*) Walker & Co.
Sorensen, Lynda. The American Eagle. LC 94-7051. 1994. write for info. (*1-55916-045-4*) Rourke Bk Co.
Spizzirri Publishing Co. Staff. Eagles: An Educational Coloring Book. Spizzirri, Linda, ed. (Illus.). 32p. (gr. k-5). 1985. pap. 1.75 (*0-86545-067-6*) Spizzirri.
Stone, Lynn M. Eagles. LC 88-26427. (Illus.). 24p. (gr. 2-4). 1989. PLB 11.94 (*0-86592-321-3*); 8.95s.p. (*0-685-58505-0*) Rourke Corp.
Two Can Publishing Ltd. Staff. Eagles. (Illus.). 32p. (gr. 2-7). 1991. pap. 3.50 (*0-87534-222-1*) Highlights.
Weinberger, Jane. Mrs. Witherspoon's Eagles. Whitaker, Kate, ed. DeVito, Pam, illus. 56p. (ps-6). 1994. pap. 9.95 (*1-883650-09-7*) Windswept Hse.
Wildlife Education, Ltd. Staff. Eagles. 1983 ed. Boyer, Trevor, illus. 20p. (gr. 5 up). pap. 2.75 (*0-937934-14-3*) Wildlife Educ.

EAGLES–FICTION

Allen, Judy. Eagle. Humphries, Tudor, illus. LC 93-28541. 32p. (ps up). 1994. reinforced bdg. 15.95 (*1-56402-143-2*) Candlewick Pr.
Alvarez, Everett, Jr. & Pitch, Anthony S. Chained Eagle. LC 89-45547. (Illus.). 308p. (gr. 8-12). 1989. 18.95 (*1-55611-167-3*) D I Fine.
Bliss, Ronald G. Eagle Trap. LC 82-71045. (Illus.). 108p. (gr. 3-5). 1990. pap. 3.50x (*0-943864-05-4*) Davenport.
Costello, Gwen. Edna Eagle. Kendzia, Mary C., ed. McCall, Jeff, illus. 32p. (Orig.). 1992. pap. 4.95 (*0-89622-528-3*) Twenty-Third.
Dayrell, Elphinstone. Why the Sun & Moon Live in the Sky. Lent, Blair, illus. 32p. (gr. k-3). 1990. pap. 5.95 (*0-395-53963-3*) HM.
Gothard, Bill. The Eagle Story. LC 81-85536. (Illus.). 64p. (gr. 3-12). 1982. 8.00 (*0-916888-07-X*) Inst Basic Youth.
Jordan, Tina. A Visit to the Eagles' Nest. Jordan, Debra, illus. 20p. (gr. 3-5). 1980. PLB 2.25 (*0-938574-00-0*) Cherubim.
Marshall, James. Yummers Too: The Second Course. Marshall, James, illus. 32p. (gr. k-3). 1990. pap. 4.95 (*0-395-53967-6*) HM.
Mason, Jane. River Day. Sorensen, Henri, illus. LC 93-26573. 32p. (gr. k-3). 1994. RSBE 14.95 (*0-02-762869-8*, Macmillan Child Bk) Macmillan Child Grp.
Melville, Herman. Catskill Eagle. Locker, Thomas, illus. 32p. (ps-3). 1991. 15.95 (*0-399-21857-2*, Philomel) Putnam Pub Group.
Nesbit, Jeff. Mountaintop Rescue. LC 93-49796. (gr. 4 up). 1994. pap. 4.99 (*0-8407-9257-3*) Nelson.
Patent, Dorothy H. Where the Bald Eagles Gather. Munoz, William, photos by. (Illus.). 56p. (gr. 3-7). 1990. pap. 5.95 (*0-395-52598-5*) HM.

EAR

see also Hearing

Mathers, Douglas. Ears. Farmer, Andrew & Green, Robina, illus. LC 90-42176. 32p. (gr. 4-6). 1992. lib. bdg. 11.89 (*0-8167-2092-4*); pap. text ed. 3.95 (*0-8167-2093-2*) Troll Assocs.
Parker, Steve. The Ear & Hearing. rev. ed. Mayron-Parker, Alan, contrib. by. LC 88-51611. (Illus.). 48p. (gr. 5-6). 1989. PLB 12.90 (*0-531-10712-4*) Watts.
—The Ear & Hearing. rev. ed. (Illus.). 48p. (gr. 5 up). 1991. pap. 5.95 (*0-531-24601-9*) Watts.
Perkins, Al. Ear Book. O'Brian, Bill, illus. LC 68-28464. (ps-1). 1968. 6.95 (*0-394-81199-2*); lib. bdg. 7.99 (*0-394-91199-7*) Random Bks Yng Read.
Rauzon, Mark J. Eyes & Ears, Vol. 1. (ps-3). 1994. 13.00 (*0-688-10237-9*) Morrow.
Santa Fe Writers Group. Bizarre & Beautiful Ears. (Illus.). 48p. (gr. 3 up). 1993. 14.95 (*1-56261-122-4*) John Muir.
Showers, Paul. Ears Are for Hearing. Keller, Holly, illus. LC 89-17479. 32p. (gr. k-4). 1993. pap. 4.50 (*0-06-445112-7*, Trophy) HarpC Child Bks.
Wright, Rachel. Eyes, Ears & Noses. (ps-3). 1990. PLB 10.90 o.s. (*0-531-14001-6*) Watts.

EARHART, AMELIA, 1898-1937

Alcott, Sarah. Young Amelia Earhart: A Dream to Fly. Hormann, Toni, illus. LC 91-24974. 32p. (gr. k-2). 1992. text ed. 11.59 (*0-8167-2528-4*); pap. text ed. 2.95 (*0-8167-2529-2*) Troll Assocs.
Blau, Melinda. Whatever Happened to Amelia Earhart? LC 77-22173. (Illus.). 48p. (gr. 4 up). 1983. PLB 20.70 (*0-8172-1057-1*) Raintree Steck-V.
Bursik, Rose. Amelia's Fantastic Flight. LC 91-28809. (ps-3). 1994. pap. 5.95 (*0-8050-3386-6*) H Holt & Co.
Chadwick, Roxane. Amelia Earhart: Aviation Pioneer. (Illus.). 56p. (gr. 4 up). 1987. PLB 13.50 (*0-8225-0484-7*); pap. 4.95 (*0-8225-9515-X*) Lerner Pubns.

Davies, Kath. Amelia Earhart Flies Around the World. LC 93-29954. (Illus.). 32p. (gr. 4 up). 1994. text ed. 13.95 RSBE (*0-87518-531-2*, Dillon) Macmillan Child Grp.

Farr, Naunerle C. & Fago, John N. Amelia Earhart - Charles Lindbergh. Vicatan, illus. (gr. 4-12). 1979. pap. text ed. 2.95 (*0-88301-349-5*); wkbk. 1.25 (*0-88301-373-8*) Pendulum Pr.

Kerby, Mona. Amelia Earhart: Courage in the Sky. (gr. 4-7). 1990. pap. 10.95 (*0-670-83024-0*) Viking Child Bks.

—Amelia Earhart: Courage in the Sky. McKeating, Eileen, illus. LC 92-19520. 64p. (gr. 3-5). 1992. pap. 3.99 (*0-14-034263-X*) Puffin Bks.

Larsen, Anita. Amelia Earhart: Missing, Declared Dead. LC 91-19246. (Illus.). 48p. (gr. 5-6). 1992. text ed. 11. 95 RSBE (*0-89686-613-0*, Crestwood Hse) Macmillan Child Grp.

Lauber, Patricia. Lost Star: The Story of Amelia Earhart. (gr. 4-7). 1990. pap. 2.75 (*0-590-41159-4*) Scholastic Inc.

Leder, Jane. Amelia Earhart: Opposing Viewpoints. LC 89-12028. (Illus.). 112p. (gr. 5-8). 1989. PLB 14.95 (*0-89908-070-7*) Greenhaven.

Morey, Eileen. Amelia Earhart. LC 94-556. (Illus.). 112p. (gr. 5-8). 1994. 14.95 (*1-56006-065-4*) Lucent Bks.

Parlin, John. Amelia Earhart: Pioneer in the Sky. (Illus.). 80p. (gr. 2-6). 1992. Repr. of 1962 ed. lib. bdg. 12.95 (*0-7910-1437-1*) Chelsea Hse.

Quackenbush, Robert. Clear the Cow Pasture: I'm Comin' In. LC 89-6164. 1990. pap. 11.95 (*0-671-68548-1*, S&S BFYR); (S&S BFYR) S&S Trade.

Randolph, Blythe. Amelia Earhart. LC 90-49175. (Illus.). 160p. (gr. 6-10). 1991. PLB 13.95 (*1-55905-078-0*) Marshall Cavendish.

Sabin, Francene. Amelia Earhart: Adventure in the Sky. Milone, Karen, illus. LC 82-15987. 48p. (gr. 4-6). 1983. PLB 10.79 (*0-89375-839-6*); pap. text ed. 3.50 (*0-89375-840-X*) Troll Assocs.

Shore, Nancy. Amelia Earhart. Horner, Matina, intro. by. (Illus.). 112p. (Orig.). (gr. 5 up). 1987. 17.95 (*1-55546-651-6*); pap. 9.95 (*0-7910-0415-5*) Chelsea Hse.

Tames, Richard. Amelia Earhart. (Illus.). 32p. (gr. 5 up). 1991. pap. 5.95 (*0-531-24610-8*) Watts.

Wade, Mary D. Amelia Earhart: Flying for Adventure. LC 91-37645. (Illus.). 48p. (gr. 2-4). 1992. PLB 12.90 (*1-56294-059-7*); pap. 4.95 (*1-56294-763-X*) Millbrook Pr.

—Amelia Earhart: Flying for Adventure. (gr. 4-7). 1992. pap. 4.95 (*0-395-64539-5*) HM.

Zierau, Lillee D. Amelia Earhart: Leading Lady of the Air Age. Rahmas, D. Steve, ed. LC 73-190237. 32p. (gr. 7-12). 1972. lib. bdg. 4.95 incl. catalog cards (*0-87157-519-1*) SamHar Pr.

EARHART, AMELIA, 1898-1937–FICTION

Wehr, Fred. Amelia. LC 93-46451. 1994. 14.95 (*1-87785-333-X*) Nautical & Aviation.

EARP, WYATT BERRY STAPP, 1848-1929

Green, Carl R. & Sanford, William R. Wyatt Earp. LC 91-29855. (Illus.). 48p. (gr. 4-10). 1992. lib. bdg. 14.95 (*0-89490-367-5*) Enslow Pubs.

EARTH

see also Antarctic Regions; Arctic Regions; Atmosphere; Creation; Earthquakes; Geodesy; Geography; Geology; Geophysics; Glacial Epoch; Meteorology; Ocean; Oceanography; Physical Geography; Universe

Allen, Carol. Earth: All about Earthquakes, Volacnoes, Glaciers, Oceans & More. Pearson, David, illus. 32p. 1993. pap. 5.95 (*1-895688-06-X*, Pub. by Greey dePencier CN) Firefly Bks Ltd.

Amdur, Richard. The Fragile Earth. Train, Russell E., intro. by. LC 93-827. 1994. write for info. (*0-7910-1572-6*); pap. write for info. (*0-7910-1597-1*) Chelsea Hse.

Asimov, Isaac. How Did We Find Out the Earth Is Round? Selsam, Millicent E., ed. Kalmenoff, Matthew, illus. LC 72-81378. 64p. (gr. 5-8). 1972. PLB 5.85 (*0-8027-6122-4*) Walker & Co.

Asimov, Isaac, et al. Our Planet Earth. rev. & updated ed. (Illus.). (gr. 3 up). 1995. PLB 17.27 (*0-8368-1194-1*) Gareth Stevens Inc.

Barnes-Svarney, Patricia L. Clocks in the Rocks: Learning about Earth's Past. LC 89-7698. (Illus.). 64p. (gr. 6 up). 1990. lib. bdg. 15.95 (*0-89490-275-X*) Enslow Pubs.

Beautier, Francois. Descubrir la Tierra (Discover the Earth) Calzada, Francisco-Javier, tr. Davot, Francois, illus. (SPA.). 96p. (gr. 4 up). 1992. PLB 15.90 (*1-56294-175-5*) Millbrook Pr.

Behm, Barbara J., ed. Ask about the Earth & the Sky. (Illus.). 64p. (gr. 4-5). 1987. PLB 11.95 (*0-8172-2876-4*) Raintree Steck-V.

Bender, Lionel. Our Planet. LC 91-30843. (Illus.). 96p. (gr. 1-5). 1992. pap. 13.00 (*0-671-75995-7*, S&S BFYR); pap. 8.00 (*0-671-75994-9*, S&S BFYR) S&S Trade.

Benedict, Kitty. Earth: My First Nature Books. Felix, Monique, illus. 32p. (gr. k-2). 1993. pap. 2.95 (*1-56189-168-1*) Amer Educ Pub.

Bennett, David. Earth. Kightley, Rosalinda, illus. 32p. (ps-12). 1988. pap. 3.95 (*0-553-05481-3*) Bantam.

Bramwell, Martyn. The Simon & Schuster Young Readers' Book of Planet Earth. LC 91-38216. (Illus.). 192p. (gr. 4 up). 1992. pap. 13.00 (*0-671-77830-7*, S&S BFYR); pap. 8.00 (*0-671-77831-5*, S&S BFYR) S&S Trade.

Brandt, Keith. Earth. Jones, John, illus. LC 84-8444. 32p. (gr. 3-6). 1985. PLB 9.49 (*0-8167-0250-0*); pap. text ed. 2.95 (*0-8167-0251-9*) Troll Assocs.

Branley, Franklyn M. The Beginning of the Earth. rev. ed. Maestro, Giulio, illus. LC 87-47765. 32p. (ps-3). 1988. (Crowell Jr Bks); PLB 13.89 (*0-690-04654-5*, Crowell Jr Bks) HarpC Child Bks.

—The Beginning of the Earth. rev. ed. Maestro, Giulio, illus. LC 87-45677. 32p. (ps-3). 1988. pap. 4.50 (*0-06-445074-0*, Trophy) HarpC Child Bks.

—What Makes Day & Night? rev. ed. Dorros, Arthur, illus. LC 85-40657. 32p. (gr. k-3). 1986. pap. 4.95 (*0-06-445050-3*, Trophy) HarpC Child Bks.

—What Makes Day & Night? rev. ed. Dorros, Arthur, illus. LC 85-47903. 32p. (ps-3). 1986. PLB 14.89 (*0-690-04524-7*, Crowell Jr Bks) HarpC Child Bks.

Butterfield, Moira. The Earth. LC 92-53101. (Illus.). 48p. (Orig.). (gr. 3-8). 1992. pap. 5.95 (*1-85697-808-7*, Kingfisher LKC) LKC.

Carratello, John & Carratello, Patty. Hands on Science: Our Changing Earth. Wright, Terry, illus. 32p. (gr. 2-5). 1988. wkbk. 5.95 (*1-55734-226-1*) Tchr Create Mat.

Charman, Andrew. Earth. LC 93-31791. 1994. write for info. (*0-8114-5510-6*) Raintree Steck-V.

Chisholm. Our Earth. (gr. 2-5). 1982. (Usborne-Hayes); pap. 3.95 (*0-86020-582-7*) EDC.

Cleeve, Roger. The Earth. Steltenpohl, Jane, ed. (Illus.). 32p. (gr. 3-5). 1990. PLB 10.98 (*0-671-68626-7*, J Messner); pap. 4.95 (*0-671-68629-1*) S&S Trade.

Clements, Andrew. Mother Earth's Counting Book. Johnson, Lonni S., illus. LC 90-7343. 44p. (gr. k up). 1992. pap. 15.95 (*0-88708-138-X*) Picture Bk Studio.

Conway, Lorraine. Earth Science: Tables & Tabulations. Akins, Linda, illus. 64p. (gr. 5 up). 1984. wkbk. 7.95 (*0-86653-154-8*, GA 553) Good Apple.

Curtis, Neil. How Do We Know the Earth Is Round? LC 94-16253. 1995. write for info. (*0-8114-3879-1*) Raintree Steck-V.

Curtis, Neil, et al. Planet Earth. LC 93-20103. (Illus.). 96p. (Orig.). (gr. 5 up). 1993. 15.95 (*1-85697-848-6*, Kingfisher LKC); pap. 9.95 (*1-85697-847-8*) LKC.

Daily, Robert. Earth. LC 93-6102. (Illus.). 64p. (gr. 5-8). 1994. PLB 12.90 (*0-531-20158-9*) Watts.

Darling, David. Could You Ever Dig a Hole to China? (Illus.). 60p. (gr. 5 up). 1991. text ed. 14.95 RSBE (*0-87518-449-9*, Dillon) Macmillan Child Grp.

Dixon, Debra S. & Henry, Susan V. Our Earth: The Water Planet, Vol. 1: An Introduction. Spence, Lundie & San Jose, Christine, eds. (Illus.). 45p. (Orig.). (gr. 3-7). 1992. pap. 14.95 (*0-9609506-2-1*) Prescott Durrell & Co.

The Earth. (Illus.). 80p. (gr. k-6). 1986. per set 199.00 (*0-8172-2585-4*); 14.95 ea. Raintree Steck-V.

The Earth. 112p. (gr. 4-9). 1989. 18.95 (*1-85435-070-6*) Marshall Cavendish.

The Earth. (Illus.). 96p. (ps-4). 1994. write for info. (*1-56458-793-2*) Dorling Kindersley.

Earth Processes Series, 10 bks. (Illus.). (gr. 6 up). Set. lib. bdg. 159.50 (*0-89490-343-8*) Enslow Pubs.

Estalella, Robert. Our Planet: Earth. Socias, Marcel, illus. LC 93-24597. (gr. 4-8). 1994. pap. 6.95 (*0-8120-1741-2*) Barron.

Farndon, John. Dictionary of the Earth. (Illus.). 192p. 1994. write for info. (*1-56458-709-6*) Dorling Kindersley.

—How the Earth Works: One Hundred Ways Parents & Kids Can Share the Secrets of the Earth. LC 91-45004. (Illus.). 192p. (gr. 3 up). 1992. 24.00 (*0-89577-411-9*, Dist. by Random) RD Assn.

Fisher, David E. The Origin & Evolution of Our Own Particular Universe. LC 88-14108. (Illus.). 192p. (gr. 7 up). 1988. SBE 15.95 (*0-689-31368-3*, Atheneum Child Bk) Macmillan Child Grp.

Fradin, Dennis B. Earth. LC 89-9982. 48p. (gr. k-4). 1989. PLB 12.85 (*0-516-01172-3*); pap. 4.95 (*0-516-41172-1*) Childrens.

Ganeri, Anita. I Wonder Why the Wind Blows & Other Questions about Our Planet. LC 93-48559. 32p. (gr. k-3). 1994. 8.95 (*1-85697-996-2*, Kingfisher LKC) LKC.

Gang, Philip S. Our Planet, Our Home: A Gaia Learning Material. 60p. (gr. 1-9). 1989. Incl. card material. tchr's. ed. 30.00 (*0-685-27868-9*); wkbk. 5.00 (*0-685-27869-7*) Dagaz Pr.

George, Jean C. The Talking Earth. LC 82-48850. 160p. (gr. 6 up). 1983. PLB 13.89 (*0-06-021976-9*) HarpC Child Bks.

Greene, Carol. Caring for Our Earth Series, 6 bks. (Illus.). (gr. k-3). Set. lib. bdg. 77.70 (*0-89490-377-2*) Enslow Pubs.

Hehner, B. E. Blue Planet. 1992. write for info. (*0-15-200423-8*, Gulliver Bks) HarBrace.

Heller, Robert, et al. Earth Science. 2nd ed. (Illus.). 1978. text ed. 32.24 (*0-07-028037-1*) McGraw.

Heslewood, Juliet. Earth, Air, Fire & Water. Lydbury, Jane, et al, illus. 182p. (gr. 4-8). 1989. jacketed 15.95 (*0-19-278107-3*) OUP.

Hubley, Faith & Towe, Kenneth M. Enter Life. Hubley, Faith, illus. LC 82-71680. 32p. (gr. 4 up). pap. 9.95 (*0-440-02357-2*, E Friede) Delacorte.

Italia, Bob. Earth Words: Target Earth Ser. LC 93-19062. 1993. 14.96 (*1-56239-212-3*) Abdo & Dghtrs.

Kalman, Bobbie. Our Earth. (Illus.). 32p. (gr. 2-3). 1987. 15.95 (*0-86505-078-3*); pap. 7.95 (*0-86505-100-3*) Crabtree Pub Co.

Kerven, Rosalind. Saving Planet Earth. LC 91-43300. (Illus.). 32p. (gr. 5-8). 1992. PLB 11.90 (*0-531-14199-3*) Watts.

Koenig, Herbert G., et al. Earth Science: A Concise Competency Review. rev. ed. Gamsey, Wayne, ed. Fairbanks, Eugene B., illus. 96p. (gr. 7-12). 1991. pap. text ed. 4.11 (*0-935487-44-1*) N & N Pub Co.

Larson, Wendy. Earth. Curti, Anna, illus. 14p. (ps-1). 1994. bds. 4.95 (*0-448-40570-9*, G&D) Putnam Pub Group.

Lasky, Kathryn. The Librarian Who Measured the Earth. Hawkes, Kevin, illus. LC 92-42656. (gr. 4 up). 1994. 16.95 (*0-316-51526-4*, Joy St Bks) Little.

Lauber, Patricia. How We Learned the Earth Is Round. Lloyd, Megan, illus. LC 89-49650. 32p. (gr. k-4). 1990. 14.00 (*0-690-04860-2*, Crowell Jr Bks); PLB 13. 89 (*0-690-04862-9*, Crowell Jr Bks) HarpC Child Bks.

—How We Learned the Earth Is Round. Lloyd, Megan, illus. LC 89-49650. 32p. (gr. k-4). 1992. pap. 4.50 (*0-06-445109-7*, Trophy) HarpC Child Bks.

Lord, Suzanne. Our World of Mysteries: Fascinating Facts about the Planet Earth. 96p. 1991. pap. 2.75 (*0-590-44595-2*) Scholastic Inc.

Lucas, Hazel & Lucas, Ernest. Our World. (Illus.). 48p. (gr. 4 up). 1986. 13.95 (*0-85648-948-4*) Lion USA.

Lye, Keith. The Earth. (Illus.). 64p. (gr. 4-6). 1991. PLB 15.40 (*1-56294-025-2*) Millbrook Pr.

—Our Planet Earth. LC 92-21675. (Illus.). 128p. (ps-3). 1993. 7.00 (*0-679-83696-9*); PLB 11.99 (*0-679-93696-3*) Random Bks Yng Read.

—Our Planet the Earth. LC 79-2346. (Illus.). (gr. 3-6). 1980. PLB 13.50 (*0-8225-1182-7*, First Ave Edns); pap. 4.95 (*0-8225-9510-9*, First Ave Edns) Lerner Pubns.

McNeil, Mary. Earth Sciences Reference. 709p. (gr. 6 up). 1991. 55.00 (*0-938905-00-7*); pap. 49.00 (*0-938905-01-5*) Flamingo Pr. CHOICE notes that, "There is no other single volume that combines the wealth of knowledge found in this work...Definitions are concise but informative & they are indexed geographically & by subject... Appropriate...especially for those libraries with small earth science collections or tight budgets." October, 1991. LIBRARY JOURNAL: "McNeil's bibliography of books & journal articles published through 1990 is exhaustive. Special emphasis has been given to the Southern Hemisphere since it has often been underrepresented. Appropriate for large public or academic library reference collections...More detailed coverage of earth science than a multi-volume encyclopedia." June 1, 1991. The reference has been found useful for curriculum development from middle school to college level. To order: Flamingo Press, 2956 Roosevelt St., Carlsbad, CA 92008; 619-471-8705 or FAX 619-279-0357.
Publisher Provided Annotation.

Mariner, Tom. Earth in Action Series, 6 vols. (Illus.). (gr. 3-8). 1990. PLB 59.70 (*1-85435-189-3*) Marshall Cavendish.

Mariner, Tom & Ellis, Anyon. The Dillon Press Book of the Earth. LC 94-16855. (gr. 3 up). 1994. text ed. 16. 95 (*0-87518-640-8*, Dillon Pr) Macmillan Child Grp.

Murray, Peter. Earth. LC 92-8412. (gr. 2-6). 1992. PLB 15.95 (*0-89565-854-2*) Childs World.

Norton, Penny. Earth Watch. (Illus.). 48p. (gr. 7-9). 1992. 13.95 (*0-563-34407-5*, BBC-Parkwest); pap. 6.95 (*0-563-34408-3*, BBC-Parkwest) Parkwest Pubns.

Our World Series, 13 Bks. (Illus.). 480p. (gr. 5-8). 1991. Set. PLB 155.40 (*0-382-09599-5*) Silver Burdett Pr.

Parker, Steve. The Earth & How It Works. Gornari, Giuliano & Corbella, Luciano, illus. LC 92-54317. 64p. (gr. 3-7). 1993. 12.95 (*1-56458-235-3*) Dorling Kindersley.

—Our Planet Earth. LC 94-16302. 1994. write for info. (*0-8160-3216-5*) Facts on File.

Parramon, J. M., et al. Earth. 32p. (ps). 1985. pap. 6.95 (*0-8120-3596-8*) Barron.

—La Tierra. (SPA.). 32p. (ps). 1985. pap. 6.95 (*0-8120-3618-2*) Barron.

Pearce, Q. L. The Earth. Mallout, Christine, illus. 48p. (Orig.). (ps-1). 1991. wkbk. 2.95 (*0-8431-2913-1*) Price Stern.

—Strange Science: Planet Earth. 64p. (Orig.). 1993. pap. 3.50 (*0-8125-2365-2*) Tor Bks.

Petty, Kate. The Ground Below Us. (Illus.). 32p. (gr. 2-4). 1993. pap. 5.95 (*0-8120-1232-1*) Barron.

Pifer, Joanne. EarthWise: Environmental Learning Series, Vol. II. (Illus.). 192p. (gr. 5-8). Date not set. Incl., Earth's Atmosphere, Earth's Humans, Earth's Wildlife, Earth's Waste. 24.95 (*0-9633019-6-9*) WP Pr.

Planet Earth. 160p. 1993. 30.00 (*0-19-910144-2*) OUP.

Pomeroy, Johanna P. Content Area Reading Skills Our Earth: Locating Details. (Illus.). (gr. 3). 1989. pap. text ed. 3.25 (*1-55737-688-3*) Ed Activities.

Ride, Sally K. & O'Shaughnessy, Tam. Third Planet. LC 92-40609. (Illus.). 48p. (gr. 3-7). 1994. 15.00 (*0-517-59361-0*); PLB 15.99 (*0-517-59362-9*) Crown Bks Yng Read.

—Third Planet. LC 92-40609. (Illus.). 48p. (gr. 3-7). 1994. 15.00 (*0-517-59361-0*); PLB 15.99 (*0-517-59362-9*) Crown Bks Yng Read.

Robbins. Earth. 1995. write for info. (*0-8050-2294-5*) H Holt & Co.

Schwartz, Linda. My Earth Book: Puzzles, Projects, Facts & Fun. Armstrong, Beverly, illus. LC 91-60123. 64p. (gr. 1-4). 1991. pap. 7.95 (*0-88160-201-9*, LW153) Learning Wks.

Silver, Donald M. Earth: The Ever-Changing Planet. Wynne, Patricia J., illus. LC 88-11331. 96p. (Orig.). (gr. 5 up). 1989. lib. bdg. 12.99 (*0-394-99195-8*) Random Bks Yng Read.

Simon, Seymour. Earth: Our Planet in Space. LC 84-28754. (Illus.). 32p. (gr. k-3). 1984. RSBE 14.95 (*0-02-782830-1*, Four Winds) Macmillan Child Grp.

Smith, Norman F. Millions & Billions of Years Ago: Dating Our Earth & Its Life. LC 92-42744. (Illus.). 128p. (gr. 7-12). 1993. PLB 13.40 (*0-531-12533-5*) Watts.

Sneider, Cary I. Earth, Moon, & Stars. Bergman, Lincoln & Fairwell, Kay, eds. Baker, Lisa H. & Bevilacqua, Carol, illus. Sneider, Cary I., photos by. 50p. (Orig.). (gr. 5-9). 1986. pap. 10.00 (*0-912511-18-4*) Lawrence Science.

Sorensen, Lynda. The Earth. LC 93-17007. 1993. 12.67 (*0-86593-275-1*); 9.50s.p. (*0-685-66579-8*) Rourke Corp.

Stanley, Steven M. Earth & Life Through Time. 2nd ed. LC 88-16454. (Illus.). 704p. 1988. text ed. write for info. (*0-7167-1975-4*) W H Freeman.

Stephenson, Robert & Browne, Roger. Exploring Earth in Space. Hughes, Jenny, illus. LC 91-44198. 48p. (gr. 4-8). 1992. PLB 22.80 (*0-8114-2603-3*) Raintree Steck-V.

Stone, Lynn M. The Changing Earth. LC 93-41103. 1994. write for info. (*1-55916-017-9*) Rourke Bk Co.

Stover, Susan G. & Macdonald, R. Heather. On the Rocks: Earth Science Activities. (Illus.). 204p. (gr. 1-8). 1993. pap. text ed. 9.00 (*1-56576-005-0*) SEPM.

Time Life Books Staff. Planet Earth. 1992. 18.95 (*0-8094-9666-6*) Time-Life.

Vancleave, Janice P. Janice Vancleave's Earth Science for Every Kid: One Hundred & One Experiments That Really Work. (gr. 3-7). 1991. pap. text ed. 10.95 (*0-471-53010-7*) Wiley.

—Janice Vancleave's Earth Science for Every Kid: One Hundred One Easy Experiments That Really Work. (Illus.). 224p. (gr. 3-8). 1991. text ed. 24.95 (*0-471-54389-6*) Wiley.

Van Rose, Susanna. Earth. LC 93-33102. (gr. 3 up). 1994. 15.95 (*1-56458-476-3*) Dorling Kindersley.

Verdet, Jean-Pierre. The Earth & Sky. (Illus.). 1992. bds. 10.95 (*0-590-45268-1*, 040, Cartwheel) Scholastic Inc.

Watson, Nancy, et al. Our Violent Earth. LC 80-8797. (Illus.). 104p. (gr. 3-8). 1982. 8.95 (*0-87044-383-6*); lib. bdg. 12.50 (*0-87044-388-7*) Natl Geog.

Watt, F. Planet Earth. (Illus.). 48p. (gr. 4-11). 1991. PLB 13.96 (*0-88110-510-4*, Usborne); pap. 7.95 (*0-7460-0637-3*, Usborne) EDC.

Watts & Tyler. Earth, The. (gr. 3-6). 1976. pap. 6.95 (*0-86020-062-0*, Usborne-Hayes) EDC.

Wood, Tim. Our Planet Earth. Graham, Alastair, illus. LC 91-26681. 32p. (ps-2). 1992. pap. 5.95 (*0-689-71589-7*, Aladdin) Macmillan Child Grp.

EARTH–DICTIONARIES

Heese. Jugendhandbuch Naturwissen: Saeugetiere, Vol. 3. (GER.). 144p. 1976. pap. 5.95 (*0-7859-0933-8*, M-7488, Pub. by Rowohlt) Fr & Eur.

—Jugendhandbuch Naturwissen, Vol. 4: Erde und Weltall. (GER.). 128p. 1976. pap. 5.95 (*0-7859-0412-3*, M7489) Fr & Eur.

EARTH, EFFECT OF MAN ON

see Man–Influence on Nature

EARTH–ROTATION

Stone, Lynn M. Day & Night. 1994. write for info. (*1-55916-022-5*) Rourke Bk Co.

EARTHQUAKES

see also Volcanoes

Archer, Jules. Earthquake! LC 90-45370. (Illus.). 48p. (gr. 5-6). 1991. text ed. 12.95 RSBE (*0-89686-593-2*, Crestwood Hse) Macmillan Child Grp.

Asimov, Isaac. How Did We Find Out about Earthquakes? Wool, David, illus. LC 77-78984. (gr. 6 up). 1978. PLB 12.85 (*0-8027-6306-5*) Walker & Co.

Bolt, Bruce A. Discover Volcanoes & Earthquakes. (Illus.). 48p. (gr. 3-6). 1992. PLB 14.95 (*1-56674-031-2*, HTS Bks) Forest Hse.

Booth, Basil. Earthquakes & Volcanoes. LC 91-44878. (Illus.). 48p. (gr. 4-6). 1992. text ed. 13.95 RSBE (*0-02-711735-9*, New Discovery) Macmillan Child Grp.

—Volcanoes & Earthquakes. (Illus.). 48p. (gr. 5-8). 1991. PLB 12.95 (*0-382-24227-0*) Silver Burdett Pr.

Borgardt, Marianne. Volcanoes & Earthquakes in Action: An Early Reader Pop-up Book. Harris, Greg, illus. 16p. (Orig.). (ps-3). 1993. pap. 8.95 (*0-689-71720-2*, Aladdin) Macmillan Child Grp.

Branley, Franklyn M. Earthquakes. Rosenblum, Richard, illus. LC 89-35424. 32p. (gr. k-4). 1990. 15.00 (*0-690-04661-8*, Crowell Jr Bks); PLB 14.89 (*0-690-04663-4*, Crowell Jr Bks) HarpC Child Bks.

British Museum, Geological Department Staff. Earthquakes. (Illus.). 36p. (Orig.). (gr. 7 up). 1986. pap. 5.95 (*0-521-32411-4*) Cambridge U Pr.

Challand, Helen. Earthquakes. LC 82-9699. (Illus.). (gr. k-4). 1982. PLB 12.85 (*0-516-01636-9*); pap. 4.95 (*0-516-41636-7*) Childrens.

Chiesa, Pierre. Volcanes y Terremotos (Volcanos & Earthquakes) Cobielles, Antonio, tr. Henroit, Jean-Louis, illus. (SPA.). 96p. (gr. 4 up). 1992. PLB 15.90 (*1-56294-176-3*) Millbrook Pr.

Clark, John O. Earthquakes to Volcanoes: Projects with Geography. LC 91-35076. (Illus.). 32p. (gr. 5-9). 1992. PLB 12.40 (*0-531-17316-X*, Gloucester Pr) Watts.

Conlon, Laura. Earthquakes. LC 92-43124. 1993. 12.67 (*0-86593-247-6*); 9.50s.p. (*0-685-66353-1*) Rourke Corp.

Damon, Laura. Discovering Earthquakes & Volcanoes. Jones, John R., illus. LC 89-4974. 32p. (gr. 2-4). 1990. PLB 11.59 (*0-8167-1757-5*); pap. text ed. 2.95 (*0-8167-1758-3*) Troll Assocs.

Deery, Ruth. Earthquakes & Volcanoes. Miller-Ray, Sue E., illus. 48p. (gr. 4-8). 1985. wkbk. 7.95 (*0-86653-272-2*, GA 630) Good Apple.

Dudman, John. Earthquake. LC 92-41510. 32p. (gr. 3-6). 1993. 14.95 (*1-56847-000-2*) Thomson Lrning.

Elting, Mary. Volcanoes & Earthquakes. Courtney, illus. LC 89-37107. 48p. (gr. 3-7). 1990. pap. 9.95 (*0-671-67217-7*, S&S BFYR) S&S Trade.

Engholm, Christopher. The Armenian Earthquake. LC 89-33555. (Illus.). 64p. (gr. 5-8). 1989. PLB 11.95 (*1-56006-004-2*) Lucent Bks.

Field, Nancy & Schepige, Adele. Discovering Earthquakes. Gillham, Andrew, illus. 40p. (Orig.). (gr. 3-6). 1995. pap. 4.95 (*0-685-69779-7*) Dog Eared Pubns.

George, Michael. Earthquakes. LC 93-46806. 40p. 1994. 18.95 (*0-88682-709-4*) Creative Ed.

Knapp, Brian. Earthquake. LC 89-21574. (Illus.). 48p. (gr. 5-9). 1990. PLB 22.80 (*0-8114-2375-1*) Raintree Steck-V.

Lafferty, Libby & Lafferty, Tina. Be Ready, Be Safe for Earthquakes: A Child's Guide to Preparedness. Lafferty, Tina, illus. 32p. (Orig.). (gr. k-4). 1994. pap. text ed. 3.00 (*0-9641072-0-1*) Lafferty & Assocs.

Lampton, Christopher. Earthquake. (Illus.). 64p. (gr. 4-6). 1991. PLB 13.90 (*1-56294-031-7*); pap. 5.95 (*1-56294-777-X*) Millbrook Pr.

—Earthquake: A Disaster Book. (gr. 4-7). 1992. pap. 5.95 (*0-395-63642-6*) HM.

Lye, Keith. Earthquakes. LC 92-31816. (Illus.). 32p. (gr. 2-3). 1992. PLB 18.99 (*0-8114-3409-5*) Raintree Steck-V.

Merrians, Deborah. I Can Read About Earthquakes & Volcanoes. LC 74-24966. (Illus.). (gr. 2-4). 1975. pap. 2.50 (*0-89375-067-0*) Troll Assocs.

Newton, David E. Earthquakes. LC 92-23291. 1993. 12.90 (*0-531-20054-X*) Watts.

—Earthquakes. (Illus.). 64p. (gr. 5-8). 1993. pap. 5.95 (*0-531-15664-8*) Watts.

Poynter, Margaret. Earthquakes: Looking for Answers. LC 89-36403. (Illus.). 64p. (gr. 6 up). 1990. lib. bdg. 15.95 (*0-89490-274-1*) Enslow Pubs.

Radlauer, Ed & Radlauer, Ruth. Earthquakes. LC 87-13772. (Illus.). 48p. (gr. 3 up). 1987. pap. 4.95 (*0-516-47841-9*) Childrens.

Santrey, Laurence. Earthquakes & Volcanoes. Jones, John, illus. LC 84-2676. 32p. (gr. 3-6). 1985. PLB 9.49 (*0-8167-0212-8*); pap. text ed. 2.95 (*0-8167-0213-6*) Troll Assocs.

Simon, Seymour. Earthquakes. LC 90-19328. (Illus.). 32p. (gr. k up). 1991. 14.95 (*0-688-09633-6*); PLB 14.88 (*0-688-09634-4*) Morrow Jr Bks.

Spies, Karen B. Earthquakes. (Illus.). 64p. (gr. 5-8). 1994. bds. 15.95 (*0-8050-3096-4*) TFC Bks NY.

VanCleave, Janice. Janice VanCleave's Earthquakes. 88p. (Orig.). 1993. pap. text ed. 9.95 (*0-471-57107-5*) Wiley.

Van Rose, Susanna. Volcano & Earthquake. Stevenson, James, photos by. LC 92-4710. (Illus.). 64p. (gr. 5 up). 1992. 15.00 (*0-679-81685-2*); PLB 16.99 (*0-679-91685-7*) Knopf Bks Yng Read.

Walker, Jane. Earthquakes. LC 91-31098. (Illus.). 32p. (gr. 5-9). 1992. PLB 12.40 (*0-531-17360-7*, Gloucester Pr) Watts.

Wilson, Kate. Earthquake! San Francisco, Nineteen Hundred Six. Courtney, Richard, illus. LC 92-18081. 62p. (gr. 2-5). 1992. PLB 19.97 (*0-8114-7216-7*) Raintree Steck-V.

EARTHQUAKES–FICTION

Brandon, Fran. The Day the Woods Went Crazy. LC 89-51294. 44p. (gr. 4-7). 1990. 5.95 (*1-55523-256-6*) Winston-Derek.

Carson, Jo. The Great Shaking: An Account of the Earthquakes of 1811 & 1812. Parker, Robert A., illus. LC 93-4887. 1994. write for info. (*0-531-06809-9*); lib. bdg. write for info. (*0-531-08659-3*) Orchard Bks Watts.

Coache, D. M. Earthquake. 1993. 7.95 (*0-533-10653-2*) Vantage.

Gilligan, Alison. Earthquake! (gr. 4-7). 1992. pap. 3.25 (*0-553-29299-4*) Bantam.

Gregory, K. Earthquake at Dawn. 1992. 15.95 (*0-15-200446-7*, HB Juv Bks) HarBrace.

Gregory, Kristiana. Earthquake at Dawn. LC 92-715. (gr. 4-7). 1994. pap. 3.95 (*0-15-200099-2*, HB Juv Bks) HarBrace.

Kudlinski, Kathleen V. Earthquake! A Story of Old San Francisco. Himler, Ronald, illus. 64p. (gr. 2-6). 1993. RB 12.99 (*0-670-84874-3*) Viking Child Bks.

Levine, Ellen. If You Lived at the Time of the Great San Francisco Earthquake. Williams, Richard, illus. 64p. 1992. pap. 4.95 (*0-590-45157-X*) Scholastic Inc.

Lowell, Susan. I Am Lavina Cumming. Mirocha, Paul, illus. LC 93-24155. 200p. (gr. 2-6). 1993. 14.95 (*0-915943-39-5*); pap. 6.95 (*0-915943-77-8*) Milkweed Ed.

Pascal, Francine. Jessica & the Earthquake. (gr. 4-7). 1994. pap. 3.50 (*0-553-48061-8*) Bantam.

Pridmore, Saxby & McGrath, Mary. Julia, Mungo, & the Earthquake: A Story for Young People about Epilepsy. LC 91-7232. (Illus.). 48p. (gr. 3-6). 1992. pap. 7.95 (*0-945354-31-2*) Magination Pr.

Sage, Kathleen A. Quakey Bear's Amazing Earthquake Adventure. 24p. (ps-3). 1992. pap. write for info. (*0-9630089-5-1*) Quakey Bear.

—Quakey Bear's Earthquake Lessons: A Gentle Earthquake Journey for Children. (ps-3). 1991. pap. write for info. (*0-9630089-0-0*) Quakey Bear.

Skurzynski, Gloria. Caught in the Moving Mountains. (Illus.). 144p. (gr. 7 up). 1994. pap. 4.95 (*0-688-12945-5*, Pub. by Beech Tree Bks) Morrow.

EARTHWORKS (ARCHEOLOGY)

see Excavations (Archeology)

EARTHWORMS

Appelhof, Mary, et al. Worms Eat Our Garbage: Classroom Activities for a Better Environment. Fenton, Mary F. & Kostecke, Nancy, illus. Dindal, Daniel L., pref. by. 232p. (Orig.). (gr. 4 up). 1993. Wkbk. 19.95 (*0-942256-05-0*) Flower Pr.

WORMS EAT OUR GARBAGE integrates earthworms with ecology, composting, natural resources, soil science, conservation, the environment, recycling, & biology in a curriculum guide & workbook designed for grades 4-8. Over 150 activities use the world of worms to help students develop science, language, math, problem-solving, & critical-thinking skills. Whether the book is used at home, in a classroom, outdoor education center, nature center or master composting program, users will find themselves drawn in & captivated by the diversity & scope of information presented. Dr. Dan Dindal, Distinguished Professor of Soil Ecology at SUNY in Syracuse, says in the preface, "Even though this book was prepared as a teaching aid for elementary & middle school grades, its potential use extends far beyond. Anyone who is fascinated & wishes to learn more about earthworms, as well as those whose active quest is to be an exciting & creative educator, will be served well by this book." Barbara Hannaford, teacher of 6-8 grade math & science, says, "The format is appealing to both teachers & students & the content is fantastic." Teacher's guide, 400 illustrations, resources, bibliography, 16 appendices, glossary, & index. See also WORMS EAT MY GARBAGE for how to set up & maintain worm composting systems. To order: Flower Press 616-327-0108. *Publisher Provided Annotation.*

Benedict, Kitty. The Earthworm: My First Nature Books. Felix, Monique, illus. 32p. (gr. k-2). 1993. pap. 2.95 (*1-56189-176-2*) Amer Educ Pub.

Lauber, Patricia. Earthworms: Underground Farmers. LC 93-79784. (ps-3). 1994. 14.95 (*0-8050-1910-3*) H Holt & Co.

Watts, Barrie. Earthworms. 32p. (gr. k-4). 1991. pap. 4.95 (*0-531-15621-4*) Watts.

EAST (FAR EAST)
Lum, Peter. Growth of Civilization in East Asia. LC 73-77311. (Illus.). (gr. 8 up). 1969. 32.95 (*0-87599-144-0*) S G Phillips.
EAST AFRICA
see Africa, East
EAST INDIANS IN THE U. S.
Gordon, Susan. Asian Indians. Daniels, Roger, contrib. by. LC 90-12275. (Illus.). 64p. (gr. 5-8). 1990. PLB 13.40 (*0-531-10976-3*) Watts.
EASTER
Barth, Edna. Lilies, Rabbits, & Painted Eggs: The Story of the Easter Symbols. Arndt, Ursula, illus. LC 74-79033. (gr. 3-6). 1979. (Clarion Bks); pap. 5.95 (*0-395-30550-0*, Clarion Bks) HM.
Bonica, Diane. Biblical Easter & Spring Performances. (Illus.). 96p. (ps-2). 1989. 10.95 (*0-86653-478-4*, SS1869, Shining Star Pubns) Good Apple.
Burgess, Beverly C. Is Easter Just for Bunnies? Titolo, Nancy, illus. 30p. (Orig.). (gr. 1-3). 1985. pap. 1.98 (*0-89274-310-7*) Harrison Hse.
Charette, Beverly. The Story of Easter for Children. Wells, Lorraine, illus. 24p. (Orig.). (ps-2). 1987. pap. 2.95 (*0-8249-8183-9*, Ideals Child) Hambleton-Hill.
Cherkerzian, Diane. Easter Fun. (ps-3). 1993. pap. 3.95 (*1-56397-164-X*) Boyds Mills Pr.
Corwin, Judith H. Easter Crafts. LC 93-21258. 1994. 12.90 (*0-531-11145-8*) Watts.
—Easter Fun. Corwin, Judith H., illus. 64p. (gr. 3 up). 1984. (J Messner); lib. bdg. 5.95 (*0-671-53108-5*); PLB 7.71s.p. (*0-685-47054-7*); pap. 4.46s.p. (*0-685-47055-5*) S&S Trade.
Cosgrove, Stephen. Easter Bunnies. Edelson, Wendy, illus. 32p. (Orig.). (gr. k-4). 1992. pap. 4.95 (*0-8249-8538-9*, Ideals Child) Hambleton-Hill.
Cura, M. J., et al. A Path Through Easter - Pentecost for Children 1994. (Illus.). 48p. (gr. 3-7). 1994. pap. 1.00 (*0-915531-10-0*) OR Catholic.
Currie, Robin. Easter Activity Book. (Illus.). 48p. (gr. 1-5). 1993. pap. 1.49 (*0-7459-2149-3*) Lion USA.
Daniel, Rebecca. The First Easter. (Illus.). 48p. (ps-6). 1992. 7.95 (*0-86653-641-8*, SS1898, Shining Star Pubns) Good Apple.
Daniel, Rebecca & Hierstein, Judy. Easter Week. 16p. (ps-3). 1991. 16.95 (*0-86653-575-6*, SS1883, Shining Star Pubns) Good Apple.
Davis, Nancy M., et al. April & Easter. Davis, Nancy M., illus. 45p. (Orig.). (ps-2). 1986. pap. 5.95 (*0-937103-10-1*) DaNa Pubns.
Dellinger, Annetta E. My First Easter Book. Hohag, Linda, illus. LC 84-21512. 32p. (ps-2). 1985. PLB 11.45 (*0-516-02904-5*); pap. 3.95 (*0-516-42904-3*) Childrens.
Doll, F., et al. Preparing Young Children for Easter 1994. (Illus.). 48p. (ps-2). 1994. pap. 1.00 (*0-915531-07-0*) OR Catholic.
Folmer, A. P. Super Eggs Easter Fun Book. (ps-3). 1992. pap. 2.95 (*0-590-45557-5*) Scholastic Inc.
Fox. Easter, Reading Level 4. (Illus.). 48p. (gr. 3-8). 1989. PLB 15.94 (*0-86592-985-8*); 11.95 (*0-685-58772-X*) Rourke Corp.
Fryar, Jane. The Easter Day Surprise. (Illus.). 24p. (Orig.). (ps-4). 1993. pap. 1.99 (*0-570-09033-4*) Concordia.
Gibbons, Gail. Easter. Gibbons, Gail, illus. LC 88-23292. 32p. (ps-3). 1989. reinforced bdg. 15.95 (*0-8234-0737-3*); pap. 5.95 (*0-8234-0866-3*) Holiday.
Greene, Carol. Kiri & the First Easter. (Illus.). 32p. (ps-4). 1972. pap. 1.99 (*0-570-06064-8*, 59-1182) Concordia.
Group Publishing, Inc. Editors. The Miracle of Easter. (Illus.). 48p. (gr. 6-8). 1993. pap. 8.99 (*1-55945-143-2*) Group Pub.
Hall. The Easter Story. 1992. 7.49 (*0-7814-0020-1*, Chariot Bks) Chariot Family.
Hallinan, P. K. Today Is Easter. Hallinan, P. K., illus. 24p. (ps-3). 1993. PLB 11.45 (*1-878363-94-8*) Forest Hse.
Hartwig, Judy. Easter Bulletin Boards. (Illus.). 96p. (ps-8). 1989. 10.95 (*0-86653-480-6*, SS1829, Shining Star Pubns) Good Apple.
Hayes, Dan, illus. The Easter Activity Book. 24p. (Orig.). (ps-3). 1991. pap. 4.95 (*0-8249-8499-4*, Ideals Child) Hambleton-Hill.
Heyer, Carol. The Easter Story. Heyer, Carol, illus. LC 89-49056. 32p. (ps-1). 1990. 11.95 (*0-8249-8439-0*, Ideals Child) Hambleton-Hill.
Hibbard, Ann. Family Celebrations at Easter. (Illus.). 1994. pap. 10.99 (*0-8007-4390-3*) Revell.
James, Lillie. What is Easter? (Illus.). 16p. (ps-2). 1994. 5.95 (*0-694-00480-4*, Festival) HarpC Child Bks.
Kalman, Bobbie. We Celebrate Easter. (Illus.). 56p. (gr. 3-4). 1985. 15.95 (*0-86505-042-2*); pap. 7.95 (*0-86505-052-X*) Crabtree Pub Co.
Kennedy, Pamela. An Easter Celebration: Traditions & Customs from Around the World. Bachleda, F. Lynn, illus. LC 90-21722. 32p. (gr. 1-5). 1991. 10.95 (*0-8249-8506-0*, Ideals Child) Hambleton-Hill.
Laplaca, Michael. Easter Decorations: Make & Color Your Own. (ps-3). 1989. pap. 1.95 (*0-89375-647-4*) Troll Assocs.
Lindvall, Ella K. My Teacher Jesus. Walles, Dwight, illus. (ps-2). pap. 2.99 (*0-8024-5946-3*) Moody.
Lion Books Staff. First Easter. (ps-3). 1994. pap. 1.99 (*0-7459-1793-3*) Lion USA.
MacDonald, Alan. The Family Easter Book. LC 92-36602. (Illus.). 96p. 1993. 12.95 (*0-7459-2349-6*) Lion USA.
McKissack, Patricia & McKissack, Frederick. Oh, Happy, Happy Day! A Child's Easter in Story, Song, & Prayer. Swisher, Elizabeth, illus. LC 88-83017. 32p. 1989. pap. 5.99 (*0-8066-2394-2*, 10-4733, Augsburg) Augsburg Fortress.
MacMillan, Dianne M. Easter. LC 92-18970. (Illus.). 48p. (gr. 1-4). 1993. lib. bdg. 14.95 (*0-89490-405-1*) Enslow Pubs.
Mattozzi, Patricia R. Eastertime. Mattozzi, Patricia R., illus. 1992. 4.50 (*0-8378-2459-1*) Gibson.
Moncure, Jane B. Our Easter Book. Rev. ed. Endres, Helen, illus. LC 86-29876. 32p. (ps-3). 1987. PLB 13.95 (*0-89565-345-1*) Childs World.
My Easter Basket of Little Books, 4 bks. 24p. 1991. Set. 8.95 (*0-8249-7418-2*, Ideals Child) Hambleton-Hill.
Nerlove, Miriam. Easter. Mathews, Judith, ed. Nerlove, Miriam, illus. LC 89-35394. 24p. (ps-1). 1989. 11.95 (*0-8075-1871-9*); pap. 4.95 (*0-8075-1872-7*) A Whitman.
Nielsen, Shelly. Easter. Wallner, Rosemary, ed. LC 91-73032. 1992. 13.99 (*1-56239-069-4*) Abdo & Dghtrs.
Pipe, Rhona. The Easter Story. Spencely, Annabel, illus. LC 92-13325. 1993. 7.99 (*0-8407-3420-4*) Nelson.
Rathert, Donna R. Lent Is for Remembering. LC 56-1613. 24p. (Orig.). (ps-1). 1987. pap. 2.99 (*0-570-04147-3*, 56-1613) Concordia.
Riley, Kelly. Celebrate Easter. Filkins, Vanessa, illus. 144p. (gr. k-6). 1987. pap. 11.95 (*0-86653-385-0*, SS 842, Shining Star Pubns) Good Apple.
Ross, Bill, illus. Easter Bunnyheads. 12p. (Orig.). (ps-2). 1992. pap. 2.95 (*0-8249-8541-9*, Ideals Child) Hambleton-Hill.
—Easter Eggheads. 12p. (Orig.). (ps-2). 1992. pap. 2.95 (*0-8249-8540-0*, Ideals Child) Hambleton-Hill.
St. John, Patricia. A King Is Risen. Scott, Richard, illus. (gr. 2-7). 8.99 (*0-8024-4576-4*) Moody.
Sandak, Cass. Easter. LC 89-28626. (Illus.). 48p. (gr. 5-6). 1990. text ed. 12.95 RSBE (*0-89686-499-5*, Crestwood Hse) Macmillan Child Grp.
Stamper, Judith. Easter Holiday Grab Bag. Durrell, Julie, illus. LC 92-10132. 48p. (gr. 2-5). 1992. PLB 11.89 (*0-8167-2912-3*); pap. text ed. 3.95 (*0-8167-2913-1*) Troll Assocs.
Stock, Catherine. Easter Surprise. Stock, Catherine, illus. LC 90-1915. 32p. (ps-1). 1991. SBE 11.95 (*0-02-788371-X*, Bradbury Pr) Macmillan Child Grp.
Tangvald, Christine H. The Best Thing about Easter. Couri, Kathy, illus. 28p. (ps). 1993. PLB 4.99 (*0-7847-0035-4*, 24-03825) Standard Pub.
—Easter Is for Me. LC 88-70663. 24p. (ps-1). 1990. 3.99 (*1-55513-741-5*, Chariot Bks) Chariot Family.
Umnik, Sharon D., ed. One Hundred Seventy-Five Easy-to-Do Easter Crafts: Easy-to-Do Projects with Easy-to-Do Things. Cary, C., photos by. (Illus.). 64p. (gr. k-5). 1994. pap. 6.95 (*1-56397-316-2*) Boyds Mills Pr.
Vesey, Susan. Easter Activity Book. (Illus.). 32p. (gr. 1-5). 1993. pap. 5.99 (*0-7459-2371-2*) Lion USA.
Winthrop, Elizabeth, adapted by. He Is Risen: The Easter Story. Mikolaycak, Charles, illus. LC 84-15869. 32p. (gr. 4-6). 1985. reinforced bdg. 15.95 (*0-8234-0547-8*) Holiday.
Wolf, Jill. Story of Easter. (ps up). 1990. pap. 2.50 (*0-89954-392-8*) Antioch Pub Co.
EASTER–FICTION
Adams, Adrienne. The Easter Egg Artists. Adams, Adrienne, illus. LC 75-39301. 32p. (ps-3). 1976. RSBE 13.95 (*0-684-14652-5*, Scribners Young Read) Macmillan Child Grp.
Auch, Mary J. The Easter Egg Farm. Auch, Mary J., illus. LC 91-15681. 32p. (ps-3). 1992. reinforced bdg. 15.95 (*0-8234-0917-1*) Holiday.
—Easter Egg Farm. Auch, Mary J., illus. 1994. pap. 5.95 (*0-8234-1076-5*) Holiday.
Backstein, Karen. Little Chick's Easter Surprise. (ps-3). 1993. pap. 4.95 (*0-590-46263-6*) Scholastic Inc.
Bassett, Lisa. The Bunny's Alphabet Eggs. Bassett, Jeni, illus. LC 92-37987. (gr. 2 up). 1993. 3.99 (*0-517-08153-9*) Random Hse Value.

Bishop, Adela. The Easter Wolf: An Easter Fable. Czapla, Carole, illus. 32p. (ps-5). 1991. 12.95 (*0-9625620-1-7*) DOT Garnet.
Everyone knows the Easter Rabbit; now this highly entertaining story introduces a new character to the Easter scene. Easter Rabbit & White Hen barely have time to complete their preparations for the annual egg hunt when a hungry wolf threatens everyone's fun. But when, after a wild chase, the wolf falls through the ice in the river, it's Easter Rabbit & white Hen who save him - & find a humorous way to feed him an early Easter feast. In return, he helps them with the Easter egg hunt, & earns the name Easter Wolf. Children will love this wise & funny fable about the spirit of Easter. ADELA BISHOP is a writer, storyteller & teacher from Oakland, California. $12.95, ISBN 0-9625620-1-7, 32 pages, 7 1/2" X 9 1/2". 16-full color illustrations, Ages 3 to 8. To order: DOT*GARNET, 2225 Eighth Avenue, Oakland, CA 94606. (510) 834-6063, FAX: 834-7516.
Publisher Provided Annotation.

Black, Sheila. The Story of the Easter Bunny. Officer, Robyn, illus. LC 87-81934. 32p. (ps-1). 1988. write for info. (*0-307-10415-X*, Pub. by Golden Bks) Western Pub.
Bridwell, Norman. Clifford's Happy Easter. (Illus.). 32p. (ps-3). 1994. pap. 2.25 (*0-590-47782-X*, Cartwheel) Scholastic Inc.
Brownrigg, Sheri. My Easter Basket. 1994. 9.98 (*0-8317-6284-5*) Smithmark.
Compton, Kenn & Compton, Joanne. Little Rabbit's Easter Surprise. Compton, Kenn & Compton, Joanne, illus. LC 91-17957. 32p. (ps-3). 1992. reinforced bdg. 14.95 (*0-8234-0920-1*) Holiday.
Curran, Eileen. Easter Parade. Goodman, Joan E., illus. LC 84-8630. 32p. (gr. k-2). 1985. PLB 11.59 (*0-8167-0353-1*); pap. text ed. 2.95 (*0-8167-0433-3*) Troll Assocs.
Dahlin, Kari. The Very First Easter Bunny. 16p. 1995. write for info. (*0-944943-57-8*, 247799) Current Inc.
Davidson, Alice J. Alice in Bibleland Storybooks: Story of Easter. Marshall, Victoria, illus. 32p. (gr. 3 up). 1988. 5.50 (*0-8378-1839-7*) Gibson.
DeJong, Meindert. The Easter Cat. Hoban, Lillian, illus. LC 90-24407. 128p. (gr. 3-7). 1991. pap. 3.95 (*0-689-71468-8*, Aladdin) Macmillan Child Grp.
Delacre, Lulu. Peter Cottontail's Easter Book. Delacre, Lulu, illus. 32p. (ps-1). 1991. 12.95 (*0-590-43338-5*, Scholastic Hardcover) Scholastic Inc.
—Peter Cottontail's Easter Book. 32p. 1992. pap. 2.50 (*0-590-43337-7*) Scholastic Inc.
De Paola, Tomie. My First Easter. (Illus.). 12p. 1991. 5.95 (*0-399-21783-5*, Putnam) Putnam Pub Group.
Devlin, Wende & Devlin, Harry. Cranberry Easter. Devlin, Harry, illus. LC 88-21370. 40p. (gr. k-3). 1990. RSBE 13.95 (*0-02-729935-X*, Four Wind) Macmillan Child Grp.
—Cranberry Easter. Devlin, Harry, illus. LC 92-23537. 40p. (ps-3). 1993. pap. 4.95 (*0-689-71698-2*, Aladdin) Macmillan Child Grp.
Doyle, Tara. Little Bunny's Easter Surprise. (ps-3). 1993. pap. 4.95 (*0-590-46262-8*) Scholastic Inc.
The Easter Bunny's Helper. 1989. text ed. 3.95 cased (*0-7214-5233-7*) Ladybird Bks.
Egan, Louise B., retold by. The Easter Bunny. Dieneman, Debbie, illus. LC 92-32435. 1993. 6.95 (*0-8362-4935-6*) Andrews & McMeel.
Fittro, Charlene C. Hoppy the Easter Bunny. LC 92-71919. (Illus.). 20p. (Orig.). (ps-3). 1992. pap. 7.95 (*0-9633053-4-4*) Child Bks & Mus.
Friedrich, Priscilla & Friedrich, Otto. The Easter Bunny That Overslept. Adams, Adrienne, illus. LC 82-13013. 32p. (ps up). 1987. pap. 4.95 (*0-688-07038-8*, Mulberry) Morrow.
Fulton, Mary J. Too Many Jellybeans! Gleeson, Kate, illus. 24p. (ps-k). 1993. pap. 1.45 (*0-307-11539-9*, 11539, Golden Pr) Western Pub.
Gipson, Morrell & Mann, Marek. Easter with Friends. Steloff, Rebecca, ed. LC 90-13794. (Illus.). 24p. (gr. k-3). 1990. PLB 14.60 (*0-944483-88-7*) Garrett Ed Corp.
Grambling, Lois G. Elephant & Mouse Get Ready for Easter. Maze, Debrah, illus. 32p. (ps-3). 1991. 12.95 (*0-8120-6200-0*) Barron.
Griest, Lisa. Lost at the White House: A 1909 Easter Story. Shine, Andrea, illus. LC 93-7945. 1993. 14.95 (*0-87614-726-0*) Carolrhoda Bks.
—Lost at the White House: A 1909 Easter Story. (ps-3). 1994. pap. 5.95 (*0-87614-632-9*) Carolrhoda Bks.
Hallinan, P. K. Today Is Easter! Hallinan, P. K., illus. 24p. (Orig.). (ps-2). 1993. pap. 4.95 perfect bdg. (*0-8249-8604-0*, Ideals Child) Hambleton-Hill.
Hallinan, Patrick. The Small Town Children's Easter. Hallinan, Patrick, illus. 24p. (ps-3). 1989. pap. 2.95 (*0-8249-8319-X*, Ideals Child) Hambleton-Hill.
Heyward, Du Bose. The Country Bunny & the Little Gold Shoes. Flack, Marjorie, illus. 48p. (gr. k-3). 1974. reinforced bdg. 13.45 (*0-395-15990-3*, Sandpiper); pap. 4.80 (*0-395-18557-2*, Sandpiper) HM.
Hildebrandt, Mary, illus. Story of the Easter Bunny. 48p. (ps). 1993. 5.95 (*0-88101-275-0*) Unicorn Pub.
Hill, Eric. Spot's First Easter: A Lift-the-Flap Book. (Illus.). 22p. (ps-k). 1993. 4.95 (*0-399-22424-6*, Putnam) Putnam Pub Group.
Hoban, Lillian. Silly Tilly & the Easter Bunny. Hoban, Lillian, illus. LC 86-7682. 32p. (ps-3). 1987. PLB 13.89 (*0-06-022393-6*) HarpC Child Bks.
—Silly Tilly & the Easter Bunny. Hoban, Lillian, illus. LC 86-7682. 32p. (ps-2). 1989. pap. 3.50 (*0-06-444127-X*, Trophy) HarpC Child Bks.
Hoban, Tana. Where Is It? LC 73-8573. (Illus.). 32p. (ps-1). 1974. RSBE 13.95 (*0-02-744070-2*, Macmillan Child Bk) Macmillan Child Grp.
Honey Bunny's Easter Surprise. (Illus., Orig.). (ps-1). 1988. pap. 2.95 (*0-671-64824-1*, Little Simon) S&S Trade.
Hopkins, Lee B. Easter Buds Are Springing. (Illus.). (ps-3). 1993. 9.95 (*1-878093-58-4*) Boyds Mills Pr.

Houselander, Caryll. Petook: An Easter Story. De Paola, Tomie, illus. LC 87-21228. 32p. (ps-3). 1988. reinforced bdg. 15.95 (*0-8234-0681-4*) Holiday.

James, Barbara. Easter Basket Book - Easter Egg Hunt. 10p. (ps-3). 1991. pap. 2.95 (*0-8167-2226-9*) Troll Assocs.

—Easter Basket Book - Easter Surprises. 10p. (ps-3). 1991. pap. 2.95 (*0-8167-2079-7*) Troll Assocs.

—Easter Basket Book - Teddy's Easter Basket. 10p. (ps-3). 1991. pap. 2.95 (*0-8167-2027-4*) Troll Assocs.

—Easter Basket Book: Bunny's Beans. 10p. (ps-3). 1991. pap. 2.95 (*0-8167-2073-8*) Troll Assocs.

Jordan, Myra J. & Grant, Roy E. Floppy Rabbit: An Easter Musical. (Illus.). 30p. (Orig.). (ps-1). 1980. pap. 5.00 (*0-914562-09-6*) Merriam-Eddy.

Kraus, Robert. How Spider Saved Easter. (Illus.). 32p. (ps-2). 1988. pap. 2.50 (*0-590-41092-X*) Scholastic Inc.

Kroll, Steven. Big Bunny & the Easter Egg. Stevens, Janet, illus. 32p. (gr. k-3). 1988. pap. 2.95 (*0-590-41660-X*) Scholastic Inc.

—The Big Bunny & the Easter Eggs. LC 81-11613. (Illus.). 32p. (ps-3). 1982. reinforced bdg. 15.95 (*0-8234-0436-6*) Holiday.

Krulik, Nancy E. Little Duck's Easter Surprise. (ps-3). 1993. pap. 4.95 (*0-590-46261-X*) Scholastic Inc.

Kunhardt, Edith I. Danny & the Easter Egg. LC 88-1164. (Illus.). 24p. (ps up). 1989. 11.95 (*0-688-08035-9*); PLB 11.88 (*0-688-08036-7*) Greenwillow.

Lewis, Shari. One-Minute Easter Stories. 1990. 10.00 (*0-385-24960-8*) Doubleday.

—One-Minute Easter Stories. (ps-3). 1993. pap. 3.99 (*0-440-40764-8*) Dell.

Lindgren, Astrid. Lotta's Easter Surprise. Wikland, Ilon, illus. Lucas, Barbara, tr. (Illus.). 32p. (ps up). 1991. bds. 13.95 (*91-29-59862-1*, Pub. by R&S Bks) FS&G.

Little Chick's Easter Treasure. (Illus.). (ps-3). 1991. pap. 4.95 (*0-88101-113-4*) Unicorn Pub.

McDonnell, Janet. The Easter Surprise. Hohag, Linda, illus. LC 93-11004. 32p. (ps-2). 1993. PLB 12.30 (*0-516-00683-5*); pap. 3.95 (*0-516-40683-3*) Childrens.

McQueen, Lucinda. Little Lamb's Easter Surprise. (Illus.). 10p. (ps). 1994. bds. 4.95 (*0-590-47803-6*, Cartwheel) Scholastic Inc.

Mandrell, Louise. Peril in Evans Woods: A Story about the Meaning of Easter. (ps-3). 1993. 12.95 (*1-56530-035-1*) Summit TX.

Maxwell, Cassandre. Yosef's Gift of Many Colors: An Easter Story. Maxwell, Cassandre, illus. LC 92-44189. 32p. (ps-3). 1993. 14.99 (*0-8066-2627-5*, 9-2627) Augsburg Fortress.

Mayer, Mercer. Happy Easter, Little Critter. Mayer, Mercer, illus. LC 87-81759. 24p. (ps-3). 1988. pap. write for info. (*0-307-11723-5*, Pub. by Golden Bks) Western Pub.

Milhous, Katherine. The Egg Tree. Milhous, Katherine, illus. LC 50-6817. 32p. (gr. 1-4). 1971. RSBE 13.95 (*0-684-12716-4*, Scribners Young Read) Macmillan Child Grp.

—The Egg Tree. LC 91-15854. (Illus.). 32p. (gr. k-3). 1992. pap. 4.95 (*0-689-71568-4*, Aladdin) Macmillan Child Grp.

Miller, Edna. Mousekin's Easter Basket. Miller, Edna, illus. LC 86-22511. 32p. (ps-3). 1989. pap. 12.95 jacketed (*0-671-66803-X*, S&S BFYR); pap. 5.95 (*0-671-67439-0*, S&S BFYR) S&S Trade.

Molan, Chris, illus. The First Easter: Retold by Catherine Storr. 32p. (gr. k-4). 1984. 14.65 (*0-8172-1987-0*, Raintree Childrens Books Belitha Press Ltd. - London) Raintree Steck-V.

My Easter Book. (ps-3). 1989. pap. 1.95 (*0-8167-0004-4*) Troll Assocs.

Myra, Harold. Easter Bunny, Are You for Real? LC 78-21268. (Illus.). (gr. 5-8). 1979. 8.99 (*0-8407-5148-6*) Nelson.

Ostheeren, Ingrid. Coriander's Easter Adventure. Corderoc'h, Jean-Pierre, illus. Lanning, Rosemary, tr. from GER. LC 91-26867. (Illus.). 32p. (gr. k-3). 1992. 14.95 (*1-55858-136-7*); lib. bdg. 14.88 (*1-55858-150-2*) North-South Bks NYC.

Peeper & the Giant Easter Egg. (Illus., Orig.). (ps-1). 1988. pap. 2.95 (*0-671-64823-3*, Little Simon) S&S Trade.

Polacco, Patricia. Chicken Sunday. Polacco, Patricia, illus. 32p. (ps-3). 1992. PLB 14.95 (*0-399-22133-6*, Philomel Bks) Putnam Pub Group.

Roloff, Nan & Flynn, Amy. The Bunnies' Easter Bonnet. Flynn, Amy, illus. LC 94-6728. 1994. 2.25 (*0-448-40739-6*, G&D) Putnam Pub Group.

Sabin, Fran & Sabin, Lou. The Great Easter Egg Mystery. Trivas, Irene, illus. LC 81-7610. 48p. (gr. 2-4). 1982. PLB 10.89 (*0-89375-604-0*); pap. text ed. 3.50 (*0-89375-605-9*) Troll Assocs.

St. Pierre, Stephanie. Bunny's Easter Basket. Regan, Dana, illus. 12p. (ps). 1994. bds. 4.95 (*0-448-40461-3*, G&D) Putnam Pub Group.

Siegenthaler, Kathrin & Pfister, Marcus. Hopper's Easter Surprise. Pfister, Marcus, illus. Lanning, Rosemary, tr. from GER. LC 92-29117. (Illus.). 32p. (gr. k-3). 1993. 14.95 (*1-55858-199-5*); PLB 14.88 (*1-55858-200-2*) North-South Bks NYC.

Stevenson, James. The Great Big Especially Beautiful Easter Egg. LC 82-11731. (Illus.). (ps up). 1990. 4.95 (*0-688-09355-8*, Mulberry) Morrow.

Swanson, Harry. Easter Is Not for Bears. Swanson, Harry, illus. 56p. (Orig.). (ps-6). 1989. pap. 5.00 (*1-878200-04-6*) SwanMark Bks.

Tarlow, Nora. An Easter Alphabet. (Illus.). 32p. 1991. 15.95 (*0-399-22194-8*, Putnam) Putnam Pub Group.

Tudor, Tasha. Tale for Easter. Tudor, Tasha, illus. LC 62-8626. (gr. k-3). 1985. 6.95 (*0-8098-1008-5*); pap. 4.95 (*0-8098-1807-8*) McKay.

Watson, Wendy. Happy Easter Day! Watson, Wendy, illus. 32p. (ps-1). 1993. 14.45 (*0-395-53629-4*, Clarion Bks) HM.

Wiese, Kurt. Happy Easter. (Illus.). 32p. (ps-1). 1989. pap. 3.99 (*0-14-050977-1*, Puffin) Puffin Bks.

Wolf, Winfried. The Easter Bunny. Mathieu, Agnes, illus. LC 85-10115. 32p. (ps-3). 1987. 8.95 (*0-8037-0239-6*) Dial Bks Young.

Wolf, Winifried. The Easter Bunny. Mathieu, Agnes, illus. LC 85-10115. 24p. (ps-3). 1991. pap. 3.99 (*0-8037-0912-9*, Puff Pied Piper) Puffin Bks.

EASTER–POETRY

Winfrey, Buford A., illus. An Easter Parade of Verse. 24p. (Orig.). (ps-3). 1991. pap. 3.95 (*0-8249-8504-4*, Ideals Child) Hambleton-Hill.

EASTER ISLAND–ANTIQUITIES

Meyer, Miriam W. The Blind Guards of Easter Island. LC 77-14528. (Illus.). 48p. (gr. 4 up). 1983. PLB 20.70 (*0-8172-1048-2*) Raintree Steck-V.

EASTERN SEABOARD

see Atlantic States

ECCLESIASTICAL ART

see Christian Art and Symbolism

ECCLESIASTICAL BIOGRAPHY

see Christian Biography

ECCLESIASTICAL FASTS AND FEASTS

see Fasts and Feasts

ECCLESIASTICAL HISTORY

see Church History

ECCLESIASTICAL RITES AND CEREMONIES

see Rites and Ceremonies; Funeral Rites and Ceremonies

ECOLOGY

see also Adaptation (Biology); Botany–Ecology; Geographical Distribution of Animals and Plants; Marine Ecology

AIT Staff. Earth, the Environment, & Beyond from Science Source. Grewar, Mindy, ed. 40p. (Orig.). (gr. 7-12). 1992. text ed. 7.95 (*0-7842-0605-8*) Agency Instr Tech.

Aldis, Rodney. Polar Lands. LC 91-34170. (Illus.). 48p. (gr. 5 up). 1992. text ed. 13.95 RSBE (*0-87518-494-4*, Dillon) Macmillan Child Grp.

—Rainforests. LC 91-20595. (Illus.). 48p. (gr. 4-6). 1991. text ed. 13.95 RSBE (*0-87518-495-2*, Dillon) Macmillan Child Grp.

—Towns & Cities. LC 91-35801. (Illus.). 48p. (gr. 5 up). 1992. text ed. 13.95 RSBE (*0-87518-496-0*, Dillon) Macmillan Child Grp.

Amsel, Sheri. A Wetland Walk. Amsel, Sheri, illus. LC 92-5105. 32p. (gr. k-3). 1993. PLB 15.40 (*1-56294-213-1*); pap. 6.95 (*1-56294-719-2*) Millbrook Pr.

Anderson, Margaret J. Food Chains: The Unending Cycle. LC 90-3282. (Illus.). 64p. (gr. 6 up). 1991. lib. bdg. 15.95 (*0-89490-290-3*) Enslow Pubs.

Appelhof, Mary, et al. Worms Eat Our Garbage: Classroom Activities for a Better Environment. Fenton, Mary F. & Kostecke, Nancy, illus. Dindal, Daniel L., pref. by. 232p. (Orig.). (gr. 4 up). 1993. Wkbk. 19.95 (*0-942256-05-0*) Flower Pr.

WORMS EAT OUR GARBAGE integrates earthworms with ecology, composting, natural resources, soil science, conservation, the environment, recycling, & biology in a curriculum guide & workbook designed for grades 4-8. Over 150 activities use the world of worms to help students develop science, language, math, problem-solving, & critical-thinking skills. Whether the book is used at home, in a classroom, outdoor education center, nature center or master composting program, users will find themselves drawn in & captivated by the diversity & scope of information presented. Dr. Dan Dindal, Distinguished Professor of Soil Ecology at SUNY in Syracuse, says in the preface, "Even though this book was prepared as a teaching aid for elementary & middle school grades, its potential use extends far beyond. Anyone who is fascinated & wishes to learn more about earthworms, as well as those whose active quest is to be an exciting & creative educator, will be served well by this book." Barbara Hannaford, teacher of 6-8 grade math & science, says, "The format is appealing to both teachers & students & the content is fantastic." Teacher's guide, 400 illustrations, resources, bibliography, 16 appendices, glossary, & index. See also WORMS EAT MY GARBAGE for how to set up & maintain worm composting systems. To order: Flower Press 616-327-0108. *Publisher Provided Annotation.*

Baines, Chris. The Picnic. Ives, Penny, illus. LC 89-77746. 24p. (ps-3). 1990. 7.95 (*0-940793-54-7*, Crocodile Bks) Interlink Pub.

Baines, John. Exploring Humans & the Environment. Hughes, Jenny, illus. LC 92-24734. 48p. (gr. 4-8). 1992. PLB 22.80 (*0-8114-2604-1*) Raintree Steck-V.

Bash, Barbara. Ancient Ones: The World of the Old-Growth Douglas Fir. Bash, Barbara, illus. 32p. (gr. 1-5). 1994. 16.95 (*0-87156-561-7*) Sierra.

Bates, Robin. Islands. LC 94-3155. 40p. 1994. 18.95 (*0-88682-711-6*) Creative Ed.

Behm, Barbara J. Exploring Deserts: Adapted from Veronica Bonar's Take a Square of Desert. LC 93-37062. 1994. 17.27 (*0-8368-1063-5*) Gareth Stevens Inc.

—Exploring Forests. LC 93-37061. 1994. 17.27 (*0-8368-1064-3*) Gareth Stevens Inc.

—Exploring Lakeshores. LC 93-37060. 1994. 17.27 (*0-8368-1065-1*) Gareth Stevens Inc.

—Exploring Mountains. LC 93-37059. 1994. 17.27 (*0-8368-1066-X*) Gareth Stevens Inc.

—Exploring Seashores. LC 93-37058. 1994. 17.27 (*0-8368-1067-8*) Gareth Stevens Inc.

—Exploring Woodlands. LC 93-37057. 1994. 17.27 (*0-8368-1068-6*) Gareth Stevens Inc.

Behm, Barbara J. & Bonar, Veronica. Eco-Journey Series, 6 vols. (Illus.). 32p. (gr. 1 up). 1994. PLB 103.62 Set (*0-8368-1062-7*) Gareth Stevens Inc.

Bendick, Jeanne. Exploring an Ocean Tide Pool. Telander, Todd, illus. LC 91-34572. 64p. (gr. 2-4). 1992. 14.95 (*0-8050-2043-8*, Bks Young Read) H Holt & Co.

Berry, Joy. Every Kid's Guide to Saving the Earth. LC 92-38724. (Illus.). 64p. (gr. 1-6). 1992. PLB 16.95 (*1-878363-72-7*) Forest Hse.

Better Earth Series, 7 bks. (Illus.). (gr. 6 up). Set. lib. bdg. 125.65 (*0-89490-449-3*) Enslow Pubs.

Bierhorst, John. The Way of the Earth: Native America & the Environment. LC 93-28971. (Illus.). 336p. (gr. 7 up). 1994. 15.00 (*0-688-11560-8*) Morrow Jr Bks.

Blashfield, Jean F. & Black, Wallace B. Global Warming. LC 90-7119. (Illus.). 128p. (gr. 4-8). 1991. PLB 20.55 (*0-516-05501-1*) Childrens.

Blue & Beautiful: Planet Earth, Our Home. 48p. (gr. 1 up). 1990. 9.95 (*92-1-100441-1*, 90.I.15); poster 5.95 (*0-685-39198-1*, 90.I.19) UN.

Bonnet, Robert L. Environmental Science: Forty-Nine Science Fair Projects. (Illus.). 160p. 1990. 17.95 (*0-8306-7369-5*); pap. 9.95 (*0-8306-3369-3*) TAB Bks.

Book of the Earth. (Illus.). 192p. (gr. 5-11). 1993. pap. 18.95 (*0-7460-1454-6*) EDC.

Boy Scouts of America. Environmental Science. (Illus.). 72p. (gr. 6-12). 1983. pap. 1.85 (*0-8395-3363-2*, 33363) BSA.

Bright, Michael. The Greenhouse Effect. LC 90-44676. (Illus.). 32p. (gr. 2-4). 1991. PLB 11.90 (*0-531-17304-6*, Gloucester Pr) Watts.

Brimner, Larry D. Unusual Friendships: Symbiosis in the Animal World. LC 92-24953. (Illus.). 64p. (gr. 5-8). 1993. PLB 12.90 (*0-531-20106-6*) Watts.

—Unusual Friendships: Symbiosis in the Animal World. (Illus.). 64p. (gr. 5-8). 1993. pap. 6.95 (*0-531-15675-3*) Watts.

Bronze, Lewis, et al. The Blue Peter Green Book. (Illus.). 64p. (gr. 7-9). 1992. 9.95 (*0-563-20886-4*, BBC-Parkwest) Parkwest Pubns.

Brumley, Karen. Saving Our Planet. Altop, Tammy, illus. 40p. (gr. 6). 1991. wkbk. 3.95 (*1-561894-06-0*) Amer Educ Pub.

—Saving Our Planet. Altop, Tammy, illus. 40p. (gr. 5). 1991. wkbk. 3.95 (*1-561894-05-2*) Amer Educ Pub.

—Saving Our Planet. Altop, Tammy, illus. 40p. (gr. 4). 1991. wkbk. 3.95 (*1-561894-04-4*) Amer Educ Pub.

Bruning, Nancy. Cities Against Nature. LC 91-34604. 128p. (gr. 4-8). 1992. PLB 20.55 (*0-516-05510-0*) Childrens.

Burrill, Richard. Protectors of the Land: An Environmental Journey to Understanding the Conservation Ethic. Macias, Regina, ed. Waters, Robyn & Ipina, David, illus. 300p. (gr. 3-12). 1993. pap. text ed. 22.95 (*1-878464-02-7*); write for info. (*1-878464-03-5*) Anthro Co.

Capon, Brian. Plant Survival: Adapting to a Hostile World. Capon, Brian, illus. LC 93-43342. 144p. 1994. 24.95 (*0-88192-283-8*); pap. 15.95 (*0-88192-287-0*) Timber.

Challand, Helen J. Disappearing Wetlands. LC 91-38243. 128p. (gr. 4-8). 1992. PLB 20.55 (*0-516-05511-9*) Childrens.

Collinson, Alan. Grasslands. LC 92-4021. (Illus.). 48p. (gr. 5 up). 1992. text ed. 13.95 RSBE (*0-87518-492-8*, Dillon) Macmillan Child Grp.

Collinson, Allan. Mountains. LC 91-34171. (Illus.). 48p. (gr. 5 up). 1992. text ed. 13.95 RSBE (*0-87518-493-6*, Dillon) Macmillan Child Grp.
Costa-Pace, Rosa. The City. LC 93-17918. (Illus.). 1994. 13.95 (*0-7910-2101-7*, Am Art Analog) Chelsea Hse.
Cousteau Society Staff. Corals: The Sea's Great Builders. LC 91-34458. (Illus.). 32p. (gr. 1-5). 1992. pap. 12.00 jacketed (*0-671-77068-3*, S&S BFYR) S&S Trade.
Cowcher, Helen. Whistling Thorns. LC 92-39533. (gr. 6 up). 1993. 14.95 (*0-590-47299-2*) Scholastic Inc.
Dehr, Roma & Bazar, Ronald. Good Planets Are Hard to Find: An Environmental Information Guide for Kids. Johnson, Nola, illus. 40p. (Orig.). (gr. 4 up). 1990. pap. 4.95 (*0-919597-09-2*) Firefly Bks Ltd.
Drutman, Ava & Zuckerman, Susan. Protecting Our Planet (Intermediate) 144p. (gr. 4-8). 1991. 13.95 (*0-86653-589-6*, GA1302) Good Apple.
Drutman, Ava D. Protecting Our Planet - Primary Grades. 144p. (gr. 1-3). 1991. 13.95 (*0-86653-619-1*, GA1338) Good Apple.
Dubin, Stephen. Biospherians, the New Pioneers. 40p. (gr. 2 up). 1994. pap. 7.95 (*1-882428-05-6*) Biosphere Pr.
Duckworth. Environmental Lawyer. Date not set. PLB write for info. (*0-8050-2280-5*) H Holt & Co.
Dudley, William. The Environment: Distinguishing Between Fact & Opinion. LC 90-3819. (Illus.). 32p. (gr. 3-6). 1990. PLB 10.95 (*0-89908-603-9*) Greenhaven.
Duffy, Trent. The Vanishing Wetlands. LC 93-26332. (Illus.). 160p. (gr. 7-12). 1994. PLB 13.40 (*0-531-13034-7*) Watts.
Dunn, Sandra. A Walk Through Biosphere 2: Coloring Book. (Illus.). 16p. (gr. 3 up). 1993. pap. 4.00 (*1-882428-00-5*) Biosphere Pr.
Dunphy, Madeleine. Here Is the Southwestern Desert. Coe, Anne, illus. LC 94-9375. 1995. write for info. (*0-7868-0049-6*); lib. bdg. write for info. (*0-7868-2038-1*) Hyprn Child.
Earth Works Project Staff. Fifty Simple Things You Can Do to Save the Earth. (gr. 9 up). 1990. pap. 4.95 (*0-929634-06-3*) Grnleaf Pubs.
Environment Reference Series, 5 bks. (gr. 6 up). Set. lib. bdg. 90.75 (*0-89490-358-6*) Enslow Pubs.
Environmental Issues Series, 4 bks. (Illus.). (gr. 6 up). Set. lib. bdg. 63.80 (*0-89490-357-8*) Enslow Pubs.
Enz, Judith & Diffenderfer, Susan. Ecology: Learning to Love Our Planet. Tanner, Joey, ed. 120p. (gr. k-8). 1984. 19.95 (*0-913705-01-2*) Zephyr Pr AZ.
Esko, Edward. Healing Planet Earth. 64p. (Orig.). (gr. 8 up). 1992. pap. 5.95 (*0-9628528-5-6*) One Peaceful World.
Ferraro, Bonita. Saving Our Planet. Robinson, Don, illus. 40p. (gr. 3). 1991. wkbk. 3.95 (*1-561894-03-6*) Amer Educ Pub.
—Saving Our Planet. Robinson, Don, illus. 40p. (gr. 2). 1991. wkbk. 3.95 (*1-561894-02-8*) Amer Educ Pub.
—Saving Our Planet. Robinson, Don, illus. 40p. (gr. 1). 1991. wkbk. 3.95 (*1-561894-01-X*) Amer Educ Pub.
Field, Nancy, et al. Nature Discovery Library. Machlis, Sally & Torvik, Sharon, illus. (gr. 3-6). 1990. Set. pap. text ed. 42.50 (*0-941042-15-4*) Dog Eared Pubns.
Finch, Max. The A, B, C of the Biosphere. 32p. 1993. pap. 7.95 (*1-882428-03-X*) Biosphere Pr.
Fischetto, Laura. The Jungle Is My Home. Galli, Letizia, illus. 32p. (ps-3). 1993. pap. 4.99 (*0-14-054324-4*, Puffin) Puffin Bks.
Fleisher, Paul. Ecology A to Z. LC 93-13623. (Illus.). 224p. (gr. 4 up). 1994. text ed. 14.95 RSBE (*0-87518-561-4*, Dillon) Macmillan Child Grp.
Frank-Mosenson, Sandra. Earth Day Lessons from Planet Mars. Carlos, Christina, illus. 72p. (Orig.). (gr. 4 up). 1991. Perfect bdg. 10.95 (*0-9629607-3-X*) Wisdom Pr IL.
Gallant, Roy A. Earth's Vanishing Forests. LC 91-2624. (Illus.). 176p. (gr. 5-9). 1992. SBE 15.95 (*0-02-735774-0*, Macmillan Child Bk) Macmillan Child Grp.
Ganeri, Anita. Giant Book of Animal Worlds. Butler, John, illus. 14p. (gr. 2-5). 1992. 19.95 (*0-525-67369-5*, Lodestar Bks) Dutton Child Bks.
—Ponds & Pond Life. LC 92-6263. (Illus.). 32p. (gr. 5-7). 1993. PLB 11.90 (*0-531-14226-4*) Watts.
—Ponds, Rivers, & Lakes. LC 91-5039. (Illus.). 48p. (gr. 5 up). 1992. text ed. 13.95 RSBE (*0-87518-497-9*, Dillon) Macmillan Child Grp.
Gentry, Linnea. Inside Biosphere 2: The Ocean & Its Reef. 64p. (gr. 3 up). 1993. pap. 8.95 (*1-882428-02-1*) Biosphere Pr.
George, Jean C. The Moon of the Wild Pigs. Mirocha, Paul, illus. LC 91-3495. 48p. (gr. 3-7). 1992. 15.00 (*0-06-020263-7*); PLB 14.89 (*0-06-020264-5*) HarpC Child Bks.
George, Michael. Rain Forest. 1992. PLB 18.95 (*0-88682-483-4*) Creative Ed.
Gibbons, Gail. Nature's Green Umbrella: Tropical Rain Forests. Gibbons, Gail, illus. LC 93-17569. 32p. (gr. 2 up). 1994. 15.00g (*0-688-12353-8*); PLB 14.93 (*0-688-12354-6*) Morrow Jr Bks.
Godkin, Celia. What about Ladybugs? Godkin, Celia, illus. LC 93-4202. 40p. (ps-3). 1995. 14.95 (*0-87156-549-8*) Sierra.
—Wolf Island. (ps-3). 1993. text ed. write for info. (*0-7167-6513-6*) W H Freeman.
Goldstein, Natalie. Rebuilding Prairies & Forests. (Illus.). 96p. (gr. 3-6). 1994. PLB 23.20 (*0-516-05542-9*) Childrens.
Goodman, Billy. The Rain Forest. Goodman, Billy, illus. 96p. (gr. 3-7). 1992. 17.95 (*0-316-32019-6*) Little.
Gore, Sheila. Swamps. Burns, Robert, illus. LC 91-45081. 32p. (gr. 4-6). 1993. PLB 11.59 (*0-8167-2755-4*); pap. text ed. 3.95 (*0-8167-2756-2*) Troll Assocs.
Grant, Lesley. Great Careers for People Concerned About the Environment, 6 vols. LC 93-78077. (Illus.). 48p. (gr. 6-9). 1993. 16.95 (*0-8103-9388-3*, 102106, UXL) Gale.
Greene, Carol. Caring for Our Forests. LC 91-4703. (Illus.). 32p. (gr. k-3). 1991. lib. bdg. 12.95 (*0-89490-353-5*) Enslow Pubs.
—Caring for Our People. LC 91-9235. (Illus.). 32p. (gr. k-3). 1991. lib. bdg. 12.95 (*0-89490-355-1*) Enslow Pubs.
Guiberson, Brenda Z. Salmon Story. Guiberson, Brenda, illus. LC 93-1360. 64p. (gr. 2-4). 1993. 14.95 (*0-8050-2754-8*, Bks Young Read) H Holt & Co.
Gutnik, Martin A. Ecology Projects for Young Scientists. 1989. pap. 6.95 (*0-531-15128-X*) Watts.
Halliburton, Warren J. African Wildlife. LC 91-43514. (Illus.). 48p. (gr. 6). 1992. text ed. 13.95 RSBE (*0-89686-674-2*, Crestwood Hse) Macmillan Child Grp.
Hallinan, P. K. For the Love of Our Earth. Hallinan, P. K., illus. 24p. (gr. k-3). 1992. PLB 11.45 (*1-878363-73-5*) Forest Hse.
Harlow, Rosie & Morgan, Gareth. Energy & Growth. Kuo Kang Chen & Fitzsimmons, Cecilia, illus. 40p. (gr. 5-8). 1991. PLB 12.90 (*0-531-19124-9*, Warwick) Watts.
Herridge, Douglas & Hughes, Susan. The Environmental Detective Kit. LC 90-48247. (Illus.). 80p. (gr. 3 up). 1991. pap. 4.00 (*0-06-107408-X*) HarpC Child Bks.
Hester, Nigel. The Living House. LC 90-32531. (Illus.). 32p. (gr. 3-5). 1991. PLB 12.40 (*0-531-14120-9*) Watts.
—The Living River. LC 90-32526. (Illus.). 32p. (gr. 3-5). 1991. PLB 12.40 (*0-531-14121-7*) Watts.
Hickman, Pamela M. Habitats. English, Sarah J., illus. LC 93-12683. 1993. write for info. (*0-201-62651-9*); pap. 9.57 (*0-201-62618-7*) Addison-Wesley.
Higginson, Mel. Deserts. LC 94-9403. 1994. write for info. (*0-86593-380-4*) Rourke Corp.
—The Forests. LC 94-9405. 1994. write for info. (*0-86593-382-0*) Rourke Corp.
—Grasslands. LC 94-9402. 1994. write for info. (*0-86593-381-2*) Rourke Corp.
Hirschi, Ron. Save Our Wetlands. Bauer, Irwin A. & Bauer, Peggy, photos by. LC 93-4984. (Illus.). 1994. 17.95 (*0-385-31152-4*); pap. 9.95 (*0-385-31197-4*) Delacorte.
Hirschi, Ron & Bauer, Peggy. Save Our Forests. (gr. 4-7). 1993. 17.95 (*0-385-31077-3*) Delacorte.
Hoff, Mary & Roders, Mary M. Our Endangered Planet: Tropical Rain Forests. (Illus.). 64p. (gr. 4-6). 1991. PLB 21.50 (*0-8225-2503-8*) Lerner Pubns.
Hoff, Mary & Rodgers, Mary M. Life on Land. (Illus.). 72p. (gr. 4-6). 1992. PLB 21.50 (*0-8225-2507-0*) Lerner Pubns.
Hogan, Paula. Vanishing Rain Forests. (Illus.). 32p. (gr. 3-4). 1991. PLB 17.27 (*0-8368-0477-5*) Gareth Stevens Inc.
Holstead, Christy & Linder, Pamela. Learn about Growing Friendships with Little Bud. rev. ed. Arlt, Bob, illus. (ps-3). 1992. activity bk. 3.98 (*1-881037-00-2*) McGreen Wisdom.
Inside Biosphere 2: The Marsh, Where Land & Water Meet. 64p. (gr. 3 up). 1994. pap. 8.95 (*1-882428-18-8*) Biosphere Pr.
Jeffers, Susan, illus. Brother Eagle, Sister Sky: A Message from Chief Seattle. LC 90-27713. 32p. 1991. 16.00 (*0-8037-0969-2*); PLB 14.89 (*0-8037-0963-3*) Dial Bks Young.
Jungle. (gr. 5 up). Date not set. 16.00 (*0-679-86168-8*); PLB 17.99 (*0-679-96168-2*) Random.
Kallen, Stuart A. Eco-Arts & Crafts. LC 93-19059. (gr. 3 up). 1993. 14.96 (*1-56239-208-5*) Abdo & Dghtrs.
—Eco-Fairs & Carnivals. LC 93-4156. 1993. 14.96 (*1-56239-205-0*) Abdo & Dghtrs.
Kallen, Stuart A. & Berg, Julie. If the Waters Could Talk. LC 93-18953. 1993. lib. bdg. 14.96 (*1-56239-186-0*) Abdo & Dghtrs.
Knapp, Brian. What Do We Know about Rainforests? LC 92-5187. (Illus.). 40p. (gr. 4-6). PLB 15.95 (*0-87226-358-4*) P Bedrick Bks.
Kopen, Pamela A. & Kopen, Dan F. The Trillium Trail. Kopen, Pamela A., illus. LC 93-28228. 32p. (ps-12). 1993. pap. 9.95 (*0-9628914-3-6*) Padakami Pr.
Lambert, Mark. Farming & the Environment. LC 90-45614. (Illus.). 48p. (gr. 4-9). 1990. PLB 21.34 (*0-8114-2392-1*); pap. 5.95 (*0-8114-3453-2*) Raintree Steck-V.
LaMorte, Kathy & Lewis, Sharen. Ecology Green Pages for Students & Teachers. Keeling, Jan, ed. LaMorte, Kathy, illus. 64p. (Orig.). 1993. pap. text ed. 7.95 (*0-86530-269-3*) Incentive Pubns.
Lauber, Patricia. Who Eats What. Keller, Holly, illus. LC 93-10609. (ps-6). 1995. 15.00 (*0-06-022981-0*); PLB 14.89 (*0-06-022982-9*) HarpC Child Bks.
Lavies, Bianca. Compost Critters. Lavies, Bianca, illus. LC 92-35651. 32p. (gr. 2-6). 1993. 14.99 (*0-525-44763-6*, DCB) Dutton Child Bks.
—Mangrove Wilderness: Nature's Nursery. Lavies, Bianca, photos by. (Illus.). 32p. (gr. 4 up). 1994. 15.99 (*0-525-45186-2*, DCB) Dutton Child Bks.
Leinwand, Gerald. The Environment. 128p. (gr. 7-12). 1990. 16.95x (*0-8160-2099-X*) Facts on File.
Lepthien, Emilie U. & Klabacken, Joan. Wetlands. LC 92-35051. (Illus.). 48p. (gr. k-4). 1993. PLB 12.85 (*0-516-01334-3*); pap. 4.95 (*0-516-41334-1*) Childrens.
Lessard, Richard L. The Circus. 32p. 1993. pap. 4.95 (*1-883656-00-1*) Earth Bound.
Life Cycle - Natural Environment (Fifth A) (gr. k-6). 1992. 25.00 (*1-56638-181-9*) Math Sci Nucleus.
Life Cycle - Natural Environment (Fifth B) (gr. k-6). 1992. 25.00 (*1-56638-183-5*) Math Sci Nucleus.
Life Cycle - Natural Environment (Sixth A) (gr. k-6). 1992. 25.00 (*1-56638-185-1*) Math Sci Nucleus.
Life Cycle - Natural Environment (Sixth B) (gr. k-6). 1992. 25.00 (*1-56638-186-X*) Math Sci Nucleus.
Links, Marty & Linse, Barbara. Love the Earth: An Ecology Resource Book. (Illus.). 1991. 5.95 (*1-878079-01-8*); poster 4.95 (*0-685-59046-1*) Arts Pubns.
Linse, Barbara & Knight, Marilyn. Love the Earth. Dresser, Ginny, ed. Links, Marty & Clark, Cindy, illus. 32p. 1991. pap. write for info. Arts Pubns.
Litteral, Linda L. Boobies, Iguanas, & Other Critters: Nature's Story in the Galapagos. (Illus.). 72p. (gr. 5-9). 1994. 23.00 (*1-883966-01-9*) Am Kestrel Pr.
The Living World Series, 5 bks. (Illus.). (gr. 6 up). Set. lib. bdg. 79.75 (*0-89490-360-8*) Enslow Pubs.
Loewer, Peter. Pond Water Zoo: An Introduction to Microscopic Life. Jenkins, Jean, illus. LC 93-18468. (gr. 1-8). 1995. 13.95 (*0-689-31736-0*, Atheneum Child Bk) Macmillan Child Grp.
Lorbiecki, Marybeth & Lowery, Linda. Earthwise at Play: A Guide to the Care & Feeding of Your Planet. Mataya, David, illus. LC 92-9870. 1993. 19.95 (*0-87614-729-5*) Carolrhoda Bks.
Lowery, Linda. Earth Day. (ps-3). 1992. pap. 5.95 (*0-87614-560-8*) Carolrhoda Bks.
Luenn, Nancy. Squish! A Wetland Walk. Himler, Ronald, illus. LC 93-22628. 1994. 14.95 (*0-689-31842-1*, Atheneum Child Bk) Macmillan Child Grp.
Macdonald, Fiona. Rain Forest. Scrace, Carolyn, illus. LC 93-24449. 1994. PLB 19.97 (*0-8114-9243-5*) Raintree Steck-V.
Mclaughlin, Molly. Earthworms, Dirt & Rotten Leaves: An Exploration in Ecology. Shetterly, Robert, illus. LC 86-3318. 96p. (gr. 3-7). 1986. SBE 13.95 (*0-689-31215-6*, Atheneum Child Bk) Macmillan Child Grp.
McVey, Vicki. The Sierra Club Kid's Guide to Planet Care & Repair. Weston, Martha, illus. LC 91-38307. 96p. (gr. 4-7). 1993. 16.95 (*0-87156-567-6*) Sierra.
—The Sierra Club Wayfinding Book. Weston, Martha, illus. 96p. (gr. 4-7). 1991. 14.95 (*0-316-56340-4*); pap. 7.95 (*0-316-56342-0*) Little.
Markle, Sandra. Weather, Electricity, Environmental Investigations. 112p. (gr. 4-6). 1982. 9.95 (*0-88160-082-2*, LW 902) Learning Wks.
Matthews, Downs. Wetlands. Guravich, Dan, photos by. LC 93-3439. 1994. pap. 15.00 (*0-671-86562-5*, S&S BFYR) S&S Trade.
Merk, Ann & Merk, Jim. Studying Weather. LC 94-13320. (gr. 3 up). 1994. write for info. (*0-86593-385-5*) Rourke Corp.
Middleton, Nick. Atlas of Environmental Issues. (Illus.). 64p. (gr. 6 up). 1989. 16.95x (*0-8160-2023-X*) Facts on File.
Miller, Christina G. & Berry, Louise A. Jungle Rescue: Saving the New World Tropical Rain Forests. LC 90-1150. (Illus.). 128p. (gr. 5-9). 1991. SBE 14.95 (*0-689-31487-6*, Atheneum Child Bk) Macmillan Child Grp.
Morgan, Nina. The Sea. LC 94-9084. (Illus.). 128p. (gr. k-4). 1994. pap. 5.95 (*1-85697-526-6*, Kingfisher LKC) LKC.
Morris, Ting & Morris, Neil. Rain Forest. LC 93-26686. (Illus.). 32p. (gr. 2-4). 1994. PLB 12.40 (*0-531-14281-7*) Watts.
Murray, Peter. Earth. LC 92-8412. (gr. 2-6). 1992. PLB 15.95 (*0-89565-854-2*) Childs World.
Nielsen, Shelly & Berg, Julie. Love Earth: The Beauty Makeover. LC 93-18954. 1993. lib. bdg. 14.96 (*1-56239-198-4*) Abdo & Dghtrs.
Norsgaard, E. Jaediker. Nature's Great Balancing Act: In Our Own Backyard. Norsgaard, Campbell, photos by. LC 89-38589. (Illus.). 64p. (gr. 4 up). 1990. 14.95 (*0-525-65028-8*, Cobblehill Bks) Dutton Child Bks.
Owen, Oliver S. Eco-Solutions: How We Can Make Our Sick Earth Well. LC 93-19132. 1993. 14.96 (*1-56239-203-4*) Abdo & Dghtrs.
Palmer, Joy. Rain Forests. LC 92-10634. (Illus.). 32p. (gr. 2-3). 1992. PLB 18.99 (*0-8114-3400-1*) Raintree Steck-V.
Patent, Dorothy H. Prairie Dogs. Munoz, William, photos by. LC 92-34724. (Illus.). 1993. 15.45 (*0-395-56572-3*, Clarion Bks) HM.
Peacock, Graham & Hudson, Terry. Exploring Habitats. Hughes, Jenny, illus. LC 92-29907. 48p. (gr. 4-8). 1992. PLB 22.80 (*0-8114-2608-4*) Raintree Steck-V.
Pedersen, Anne. The Kid's Environment Book: What's Awry & Why. (Illus.). 192p. (Orig.). (gr. 6 up). 1991. pap. 13.95 (*0-945465-74-2*) John Muir.
Perry, Susan. Ecology. Nolte, Larry, illus. 48p. (gr. 3-6). Date not set. PLB 12.95 (*1-56065-117-2*) Capstone Pr.
The Picture-Perfect Planet. LC 92-20831. 1992. write for info. (*0-8094-9319-5*); PLB write for info. (*0-8094-9320-9*) Time-Life.
Pifer, Joanne. EarthWise: Earth's Oceans. (Illus.). 48p. (gr. 5-8). 1992. pap. text ed. 7.95 (*0-9633019-2-6*) WP Pr.

—EarthWise: Environmental Learning Series, Vol. II. (Illus.). 192p. (gr. 5-8). Date not set. Incl., Earth's Atmosphere, Earth's Humans, Earth's Wildlife, Earth's Waste. 24.95 (0-9633019-6-9) WP Pr.

—EarthWise: Environmental Learning Series, Vol. 1. (Illus.). 216p. (gr. 5-8). 1993. Incl. Earth's Trees, Sunlight, Earth's Oceans, Earth's Energy, Earth's Food. pap. text ed. 24.95 (0-9633019-5-0) WP Pr.

Polette, Nancy. Earthwatch. Dillon, Paul, illus. 48p. (gr. 3-6). 1993. pap. 5.95 (1-879287-26-9) Bk Lures.

Pringle, Laurence. Restoring Our Earth. LC 87-615. (Illus.). 64p. (gr. 6 up). 1985. lib. bdg. 15.95 (0-89490-143-5) Enslow Pubs.

Raintree Steck-Vaughn Staff. Atlas of the Environment. Coote, Roger, ed. LC 92-8196. (Illus.). 96p. (gr. 6-7). 1992. PLB 26.99 (0-8114-7250-7) Raintree Steck-V.

Rand McNally Children's Atlas of the Environment. (Illus.). 80p. (gr. 2-6). PLB 18.95 (1-878363-74-3) Forest Hse.

Reed, Willow. Succession: From Field to Forest. LC 90-3216. (Illus.). 64p. (gr. 6 up). 1991. lib. bdg. 15.95 (0-89490-271-7) Enslow Pubs.

Rosenbaum, Cindy, et al. For the Love of Animals: Six Delightful Songs & a Story about How the Children Save the Animals. Feiza, Anne, illus. 24p. (Orig.). (ps-4). 1992. pap. text ed. 12.95 incl. audio tape (1-881567-00-1) Happy Kids Prods.

Ross, Suzanne. What's in the Rainforest? One Hundred Six Answers from A to Z. Ross, Suzanne, illus. LC 91-72682. 48p. (Orig.). (gr. 1-7). 1991. pap. 5.95 (0-9629895-0-9) Enchanted Rain Pr.

Rothman, Joel. Once There Was a Stream. Roberts, Bruce, photos by. LC 72-90692. (Illus.). 32p. (gr. k-4). 1973. 8.95 (0-87592-038-1) Scroll Pr.

Rybolt, Thomas R. & Mebane, Robert C. Environmental Experiments about Water. LC 92-41235. (Illus.). 96p. (gr. 4-9). 1993. lib. bdg. 16.95 (0-89490-410-8) Enslow Pubs.

—Science Experiments for Young People Series, 5 bks. (Illus.). (gr. 4-9). Set. lib. bdg. 84.75 (0-89490-448-5) Enslow Pubs.

Sabin, Francene. Ecosystems & Food Chains. Cumings, Art, illus. LC 84-2707. 32p. (gr. 3-6). 1985. PLB 9.49 (0-8167-0282-9); pap. text ed. 2.95 (0-8167-0283-7) Troll Assocs.

Sadler, Tony. Forests & Their Environment. LC 93-25643. 1994. pap. 16.95 (0-521-43786-5) Cambridge U Pr.

Savan, Beth. Earthwatch: Earthcycles & Ecosystems. Cupples, Pat, illus. 96p. 1992. pap. 9.57 (0-201-58148-5) Addison-Wesley.

Schmidt, Fran & Friedman, Alice. Come in Spaceship Earth. Heyne, Chris, illus. 61p. (Orig.). (gr. 4-9). 1990. Incl. poster. pap. text ed. 21.95 (1-878227-06-8) Peace Educ.

Schwartz, Linda. Earth Book for Kids: Activities to Help Heal the Environment. Armstrong, Beverly, illus. LC 90-91737. 184p. (Orig.). (gr. 3-6). 1990. pap. 9.95x (0-88160-195-0, LW 289) Learning Wks.

Silver, Donald. Why Save the Rain Forest? Wynne, Patricia, illus. LC 93-22313. 1993. lib. bdg. 12.98 (0-671-86609-5, Messner); pap. 6.95 (0-671-86610-9, Messner) S&S Trade.

Silver, Donald M. One Small Square: Arctic Tundra. Wynne, Patricia J., illus. LC 94-4143. (gr. 5 up). 1994. text ed. write for info. (0-7167-6517-9, Sci Am Yng Rdrs) W H Freeman.

—One Small Square Backyard. Wynne, Patricia J., illus. LC 93-18353. (gr. 4 up). 1993. text ed. write for info. (0-7167-6510-1, Sci Am Yng Rdrs) W H Freeman.

—Seashore. (gr. 7-12). 1993. text ed. write for info. (0-7167-6511-X, Sci Am Yng Rdrs) W H Freeman.

Simon, Seymour. Earth Words: A Dictionary of the Environment. Kaplan, Mark, illus. LC 92-34005. 48p. (gr. 2-5). 1995. 16.00 (0-06-020233-5); PLB 15.89 (0-06-020234-3) HarpC Child Bks.

Singer, Marcia. Love Me, Love My Planet P.L.A.Y. Book: An Environmental Guide. Rendal, Camille, illus. LC 91-91308. 64p. (Orig.). (gr. 1-7). 1991. pap. 7.95 (0-9622543-2-0) PLAY House.

Siy, Alexandra. The Amazon Rainforest. LC 91-37640. (Illus.). 80p. (gr. 5 up). 1992. text ed. 14.95 RSBE (0-87518-470-7, Dillon) Macmillan Child Grp.

—Arctic National Wildlife Refuge. LC 91-3882. (Illus.). 80p. (gr. 5 up). 1991. text ed. 14.95 RSBE (0-87518-468-5, Dillon) Macmillan Child Grp.

—The Great Astrolabe Reef. LC 91-37267. (Illus.). 80p. (gr. 5 up). 1992. text ed. 14.95 RSBE (0-87518-499-5, Dillon) Macmillan Child Grp.

—Hawaiian Islands. LC 91-14185. (Illus.). 80p. (gr. 5 up). 1991. text ed. 14.95 RSBE (0-87518-467-7, Dillon) Macmillan Child Grp.

Staub, Frank. America's Prairies. LC 93-7841. 1993. 19.95 (0-87614-781-3) Carolrhoda Bks.

—America's Wetlands. LC 94-3872. 1994. write for info. (0-87614-827-5) Carolrhoda Bks.

—The Yellowstone Cycle of Fires. LC 92-29631. 1993. 19.95 (0-87614-778-3) Carolrhoda Bks.

Stidworthy, John. Environmentalist. LC 91-34608. (Illus.). 32p. (gr. 4-7). 1992. PLB 12.40 (0-531-17268-6, Gloucester Pr) Watts.

Stone, L. Deserts. (Illus.). 48p. (gr. 4-8). 1989. lib. bdg. 15.94 (0-86592-438-4); 11.95s.p. (0-685-67722-2) Rourke Corp.

—Prairies. (Illus.). 48p. (gr. 4-8). 1989. lib. bdg. 15.94 (0-86592-446-5); 11.95 (0-685-58573-5) Rourke Corp.

—Rain Forests. (Illus.). 48p. (gr. 4-8). 1989. lib. bdg. 15.94 (0-86592-437-6); 11.95s.p. (0-685-67720-6) Rourke Corp.

—Temperate Forests. (Illus.). 48p. (gr. 4-8). 1989. lib. bdg. 15.94 (0-86592-439-2); 11.95 (0-685-58574-3) Rourke Corp.

—Wetlands. (Illus.). 48p. (gr. 4-8). 1989. lib. bdg. 15.94 (0-86592-447-3); 11.95 (0-685-58569-7) Rourke Corp.

Stone, Lynn. Ecozones, 8 bks, Reading Level 6. (Illus.). 384p. (gr. 4-8). 1988. Set. PLB 127.52 (0-86592-434-1); 95.60s.p. (0-685-58766-5) Rourke Corp.

Stone, Lynn M. Marshes & Swamps. LC 82-17861. (Illus.). 48p. (gr. k-4). 1983. PLB 12.85 (0-516-01681-4); pap. 4.95 (0-516-41681-2) Childrens.

Suid, Annalisa. Learn to Recycle. (Illus.). 48p. (ps-6). 1993. pap. 9.95 (1-878279-49-1) Monday Morning Bks.

—Love the Earth. (Illus.). 48p. (gr. 1-3). 1993. pap. 9.95 (1-878279-48-3) Monday Morning Bks.

Sullivan, George. Disaster! The Destruction of Our Planet. (gr. 4-7). 1992. pap. 3.25 (0-590-44331-3) Scholastic Inc.

Szekely, Edmond B. Brother Tree. Matinez, Antonielena C., illus. 32p. 1977. pap. 3.50 (0-89564-074-0) IBS Intl.

Tesar, Jenny. Endangered Habitats. (Illus.). 128p. (gr. 7-12). 1991. lib. bdg. 18.95x (0-8160-2493-6) Facts on File.

Thornhill, Jan. A Tree in a Forest. LC 91-25857. (Illus.). 40p. (ps-3). 1992. pap. 15.00 (0-671-75901-9, S&S BFYR) S&S Trade.

Train, Russell E., intro. by. Earth at Risk, 24 vols. (gr. 5 up). 1991. PLB 478.80 (0-7910-1571-8) Chelsea Hse.

Twist, Clint. Deserts. LC 91-22471. (Illus.). 48p. (gr. 4-6). 1991. text ed. 13.95 RSBE (0-87518-490-1, Dillon) Macmillan Child Grp.

Walker, Jane. Vanishing Habitats & Species. (Illus.). 32p. (gr. 5-7). 1993. PLB 12.40 (0-531-17426-3, Gloucester Pr) Watts.

Ward, Lorraine. Un Paseo Por la Naturaleza: Explorando una Reserva Natural. Jacques, Laura, illus. (SPA.). 32p. (Orig.). (ps-4). 1993. PLB 15.88 (0-88106-645-1); pap. 6.95 (0-88106-812-8) Charlesbridge Pub.

Wheeler, Jill C. Healthy Earth, Healthy Bodies. Kallen, Stuart A., ed. LC 91-73069. 202p. 1991. 12.94 (1-56239-032-5) Abdo & Dghtrs.

Williams, Lawrence. Jungles. LC 89-17322. (Illus.). 48p. (gr. 4-8). 1990. PLB 12.95 (1-85435-171-0) Marshall Cavendish.

Wong, Ovid. Hands-On Ecology. LC 91-12751. (Illus.). 128p. (gr. 5 up). 1991. PLB 13.95 (0-516-00539-1) Childrens.

Wood, Jenny. Rain Forests: Lush Tropical Paradise. (Illus.). 32p. (gr. 3-4). 1991. PLB 17.27 (0-8368-0632-8) Gareth Stevens Inc.

World of the Mountain Gorillas, 3 vols. (Illus.). (gr. 2-3). 1994. Set. PLB 51.80 (0-8368-0441-4) Gareth Stevens Inc.

Wosmek, Frances. ABC of Ecology. 2nd ed. LC 82-70224. (ENG, SPA & FRE., Illus.). 60p. (ps-3). 1990. 3.50 (0-943864-00-3) Davenport.

Wright, Alexander. Can We Be Friends? Nature's Partners. Peck, Marshall, III, illus. LC 93-42652. 1994. 14.95 (0-88106-860-8); PLB 15.00 (0-88106-861-6); pap. 6.95 (0-88106-859-4) Charlesbridge Pub.

Wu, Norbert. Beneath the Waves: Exploring the World of the Kelp Forest. Wu, Norbert, illus. (gr. 3-7). 1992. 12.95 (0-87701-835-9) Chronicle Bks.

Yanda, Bill. Rads, Ergs, & Cheeseburgers: The Kid's Guide to Energy & the Environment. (Illus.). 108p. (Orig.). (gr. 3 up). 1991. pap. 12.95 (0-945465-75-0) John Muir.

Yolen, Jane. Welcome to the Greenhouse. Regan, Laura, illus. 32p. (ps-3). 1993. PLB 14.95 (0-399-22335-5, Putnam) Putnam Pub Group.

ECOLOGY–FICTION

Asch, Frank. Up River. Levin, Ted & Lehmer, Steve, illus. LC 93-38687. 1995. 16.00 (0-671-88703-3, S&S BFYR) S&S Trade.

Baker, Jeannie. Window. LC 90-3922. (Illus.). 32p. (ps up). 1991. 14.00 (0-688-08917-8); PLB 13.93 (0-688-08918-6) Greenwillow.

Bell, D. Morgans. The Adventures of Ecomunk: Mr. Beaver Builds a Dam. 1992. 8.95 (0-533-10212-X) Vantage.

Blackistone, Mick. The Day They Left the Bay. 2nd ed. Boynton, Lee, illus. (gr. 1-6). 1991. Repr. of 1988 ed. PLB 14.95 (0-9627726-3-1) Blue Crab MD.

Bond, Nancy. The Voyage Begun. LC 81-3481. 336p. (gr. 7 up). 1981. SBE 16.95 (0-689-50204-4, M K McElderry) Macmillan Child Grp.

Boyle, Doe & Thomas, Peter, eds. Deputy Scarlett: From an Original Article Which Appeared in Ranger Rick Magazine, copyright National Wildlife Federation. Langford, Alton, illus. Luther, Sallie, contrib. by. LC 92-8024. (Illus.). 20p. (gr. k-3). 1992. 6.95 (0-924483-49-0); incl. audiocass. tape & 11" toy 35.95 (0-924483-46-6); incl. 8" toy 21.95 (0-924483-47-4); incl. audiocass. tape 9.95 (0-924483-48-2); write for info. audiocass. tape (0-924483-79-2) Soundprints.

—Operation Beaver: From an Original Article Which Appeared in Ranger Rick Magazine, Copyright National Wildlife Federation. Beylon, Cathy, illus. Luther, Sallie, contrib. by. LC 92-11869. (Illus.). 20p. (gr. k-3). 1992. 6.95 (0-924483-57-1); incl. audiocass. tape & 13" toy 35.95 (0-924483-54-7); incl. 9" toy 21.95 (0-924483-55-5); incl. audiocass. tape 9.95 (0-924483-56-3); write for info. audiocass. tape (0-924483-81-4) Soundprints.

—Rick's First Adventure: From an Original Article Which Appeared in Ranger Rick Magazine, Copyright National Wildlife Federation. Langford, Alton, illus. Luter, Sallie, contrib. by. LC 92-11868. (Illus.). 20p. (gr. k-3). 1992. 6.95 (0-924483-45-8); incl. audiocass. tape & 13" toy 35.95 (0-924483-42-3); incl. 9" toy 21.95 (0-924483-43-1); incl. audiocass. tape 9.95 (0-924483-44-X); write for info. audiocass. tape (0-924483-78-4) Soundprints.

Brown, Ruth. The World That Jack Built. Brown, Ruth, illus. LC 90-25034. 32p. (ps-1). 1991. 13.95 (0-525-44635-4, DCB) Dutton Child Bks.

Carpenter, Mimi G. Of Lucky Pebbles & Mermaid's Tears. Carpenter, Mimi G., illus. 32p. (ps-5). 1994. pap. 9.95 (*0-9614628-2-5*) Beachcomber Pr. Author/Illustrator Mimi Gregoire Carpenter (What The Sea Left Behind, 1981), presents a rhyming fantasy with an environmental theme for children through fifth grade (Includes a shell identification page). "Mimi Gregoire Carpenter conveys a child-like sense of wonder in her artwork & writing. As revealed in her work, her inspiration comes from the sea & its creatures. Mimi's philosophy, spirituality & love... of the environment are embodied in her beautiful illustrations & storylines."-- New England Science Center, Worcester, Mass. Don't miss this unusual bunch of creatures - Sea Uglies & Sandcreatures, Tidal Pool Trolls & Lagoonies. Learn about the environment, mischief, being different, being creative - about things you can change & about things you cannot & while you're at it - learn about why we call beachglass "Mermaid's Tears" & why pebbles with rings around them are called "Lucky." Shorah, a "non-traditional" mermaid & the story's main character, learns to face the consequences of her actions after she conjures a storm that disrupts the sea world. 8 1/2" X 10 1/2" - detailed opaque watercolors & graphite - durable coated paper - stapled binding - paperback 32pp. $9.95. Write or call Beachcomber "Studio" Press, RR3, Box 2220, Oakland, ME 04963; 207-465-7197.
Publisher Provided Annotation.

Cosgrove, Stephen. Serendipity. (Illus.). 32p. (Orig.). (gr. 1-4). pap. 2.95 (0-8431-0562-3) Price Stern.

Cowcher, Helen. Tigress. (ps-3). 1993. pap. 5.95 (0-374-47781-7) FS&G.

Davis, Rebecca J. A Sunnybrook Garden Tale. Kvarnes, Davette L., illus. LC 92-97014. 32p. (gr. 3-5). 1993. PLB 12.00 (0-9634032-0-6) R J Davis.

Farquhar, Kristin. Voices of the Earth: Florida's Environmental Storybook, Vol. 1: Coastal Creatures. Wright, Betty & Griffin, Kimbra, eds. Farquhar, Kristin, illus. 48p. (Orig.). (gr. 2-3). 1992. pap. 7.95 (0-9632864-0-4) ECO-ALERT Pubns.

Finlay, Alice S. A Victory for Laura Lee. LC 93-3501. 48p. (gr. k-2). 1993. pap. 3.99 (0-310-59851-6, Pub. by Youth Spec) Zondervan.

George, Jean C. The Fire Bug Connection: An Ecological Mystery. LC 92-18005. 160p. (gr. 3-7). 1993. 14.00 (0-06-021490-2); PLB 13.89 (0-06-021491-0) HarpC Child Bks.

—The Missing 'Gator of Gumbo Limbo: An Ecological Mystery. LC 91-20779. 176p. (gr. 3-7). 1992. 14.00 (0-06-020396-X); PLB 13.89 (0-06-020397-8) HarpC Child Bks.

—Who Really Killed Cock Robin? An Ecological Mystery. LC 90-38659. 176p. (gr. 3-7). 1991. 15.00 (0-06-021980-7); PLB 14.89 (0-06-021981-5) HarpC Child Bks.

—Who Really Killed Cock Robin? An Ecological Mystery. LC 90-38659. 192p. (gr. 3-7). 1992. pap. 3.95 (0-06-440405-6, Trophy) HarpC Child Bks.

Greenblat, Rodney A. Slombo the Gross. LC 91-31235. (Illus.). 32p. (ps-3). 1993. 15.00 (*0-06-020775-2*); PLB 14.89 (*0-06-020776-0*) HarpC Child Bks.

Hamilton, Jean. Tropical Rainforests. rev. ed. Leon, Vicki, ed. LC 93-12987. (Illus.). 48p. (Orig.). (gr. 5 up). 1993. perfect bdg. 9.95 (*0-918303-35-4*) Blake Pub.

Hannah, Valerie. Cyril Squirrel & Sheryl: An Ecological Tale. Herrick, George H., ed. Meek, Barbara, illus. 46p. (Orig.). (gr. k-3). 1991. pap. 6.95 (*0-941281-78-7*) V H Pub.

—Sheryl Visits Cyril: An Ecological Tale. Herrick, George, ed. (Illus.). 1992. pap. 6.95x (*0-941281-87-6*) V H Pub.

Harris, Louise. Orange Blobs, Yellow Fluff & Green Spaghetti. Harris, Louise, illus. LC 94-65904. 37p. (Orig.). 1994. pap. 9.95 (*0-9640674-0-4*) New World SC.
This is a picture book about healing the environment. Characters called Wombles who live on another planet have similar environmental problems to those on Earth. They pollute their water & their air, & their world becomes full of orange blobs, yellow fluff & green spaghetti. They must figure out what is causing all this to happen. Their Womble leader calls a world meeting. The Wombles push their way past the blobs, the fluff & the spaghetti to begin their meeting. They decide to break up into small groups & do research on their problems. In the process of doing research, they all become friends & begin to listen & learn from each other. They realize the importance of joining hands & working together to solve their planet's environmental problems. This story is a great way for children to focus in on problems with the Earth's environment while reading about the Wombles' experiences. It would be a good book to supplement & enrich the school curriculum. Here is a fiction story which lends itself to discussing environmental facts. For more information or to order copies of the book, contact A New World Press, 1010 Coatsdale Rd., Columbia, SC 29209, or call 1-803-776-5658.
Publisher Provided Annotation.

Hoban, Russell. Arthur's New Power. Barton, Byron, illus. LC 77-11550. (gr. 1-5). 1978. PLB 12.89 (*0-690-01371-X*, Crowell Jr Bks) HarpC Child Bks.

Hoose, Phillip. It's Our World, Too! (gr. 4-7). 1993. pap. 12.95 (*0-316-37245-5*) Little.

Kempton, Kate. The World Beyond the Waves. Salk, Larry, illus. Trehearn, Carol, created by. (Illus.). 96p. (gr. 4-8). 1995. 19.95 (*0-9641330-1-6*) Portunus Pubng.
Like Dorothy in THE WIZARD OF OZ, Sam, the young heroine of THE WORLD BEYOND THE WAVES, is carried away by the tremendous force of a storm only to wake up in a strange & magical world beneath the sea, a refuge for animals escaping from mankind's abuse of the world's oceans. Helped to recover by these marine creatures & led on a series of adventures, Sam develops a deep awareness of the consequences of mankind's collective behavior towards the oceans from the use of drift nets for fishing to the pollution of the sea by industrial waste, oil & garbage. After her return to the surface, where her aunt & uncle have been leading the search for her, Sam succeeds in preventing an oil-test drilling ship from destroying the magical world which had saved her life, affirming in the process that with love & determination, one person can make a difference. With its skillful combination of a message of environmental awareness with a moving story of initiation into responsibility, THE WORLD BEYOND THE WAVES should prove a favorite for parents, children & teachers alike.
Publisher Provided Annotation.

Lavie, Arlette. Tower. (ps-3). 1990. 11.95 (*0-85953-392-1*); pap. 5.95 (*0-85953-393-X*) Childs Play.

Luenn, Nancy. Mother Earth. Waldman, Neil, illus. LC 90-19134. 32p. (ps-3). 1992. SBE 14.95 (*0-689-31668-2*, Atheneum Child Bk) Macmillan Child Grp.

Makris, Kathryn. The Clean-up Crew. 160p. (Orig.). (gr. 5 up). 1994. pap. 3.50 (*0-380-77050-4*, Camelot Young) Avon.

—The Five Cat Club. 176p. (Orig.). (gr. 5 up). 1994. pap. 3.50 (*0-380-77049-0*, Camelot Young) Avon.

—The Green Team. 160p. (Orig.). (gr. 5 up). 1994. pap. 3.50 (*0-380-77051-2*, Camelot Young) Avon.

Mannino, Marc P. & Mannino, Angelica L. Marjorie's Magical Tail. LC 93-86041. (Illus.). 32p. (Orig.). (ps-5). 1993. pap. 7.95 (*0-9638340-0-2*) Sugar Sand.

Morrison, Maighan. Long Live Earth. (ps-3). 1994. pap. 4.95 (*0-590-48012-X*) Scholastic Inc.

Nehemias, Paulette. Wiggler's Worms: Stories about God's Green Earth. Harris, Jim, illus. LC 92-28486. 128p. (Orig.). (gr. 3-5). 1993. pap. 4.99 (*0-570-04731-5*) Concordia.

Reich, Janet. Gus & the Green Thing. LC 92-33845. 1993. 8.95 (*0-8027-8252-3*); PLB 9.85 (*0-8027-8253-1*) Walker & Co.

Rymer, Alta M. Hobart & Humbert Gruzzy. Rymer, Alta M., illus. LC 85-61860. 56p. (gr. 5-7). 1994. 25.00x (*0-685-70989-2*) Rymer Bks.

Schott, Carolyn J. & Smith, Phillipa A. The Cracker Crumb Rescue. 40p. (gr. 3-6). 1992. PLB 16.95 (*0-9632461-0-0*) Harbour Duck.

Scott, Bob. The Backcountry. Arcade, Greg, illus. 24p. (gr. 4-12). 1989. cardstock cover 5.00 (*0-9621201-0-3*) B Scott Bks.

Starr, Susan B. I Was Good to the Earth Today. Sterling, Terry S., illus. 32p. (ps-k). 1992. PLB 12.95 (*0-9619556-0-0*); pap. 5.95 (*0-9619556-1-9*) Starhse Pub.

Storm, Tom. Stormy Finds the New Forest. Powell, Lori, illus. 48p. (Orig.). (gr. 1-6). 1994. pap. 8.95 (*0-9643019-0-3*) T Storm.
Tom Storm has written a mesmerizing children's book which contains endearing characters such as "Stormy," the whitetail fawn, & "Flapjack," the local beaver. Its many characters in bright vivid colors reach out & grasp children's attention from cover to cover. The story features Stormy & many other birds & animals. Because of deer overpopulation in their forest, Stormy & his mother must journey to find a new forest. They encounter many delightful animals & fun-filled experiences along the way. Finally, once settled into their new, abundant, & balanced forest, Stormy meets Joey, the son of a local hunter & soon to be a hunter himself. Joey & Stormy set out on their own adventures. Along the way, Joey gently educates Stormy on how hunting helps to sustain the quality environment for birds & animals by preventing overpopulation & starvation. Tom Storm's intent is to provide the public with a better understanding of the hunters' historic role in conservation & wildlife management of all birds & animals. Tom is able to strike a balanced approach between environmental & pro-hunting viewpoints, &, indeed, will please both sides with this charming story. There has never been anything like this book on the market. STORMY is unique, educational & fascinating - a charming story. Order from Storm Press, Box 2012, Great Falls, MT 59403.
Publisher Provided Annotation.

Turner, Ann. Heron Street. Desimini, Lisa, illus. LC 87-24948. 32p. (gr. 1-4). 1989. 15.00i (*0-06-026184-6*); PLB 14.89 (*0-06-026185-4*) HarpC Child Bks.

Woe, Jonathan. The Longneck Bird of Longboat Key: One of the Privileged Class. Woe, Jonathan, illus. 32p. 1992. 14.95 (*0-9627946-6-X*) Hawk FL.

—The Wing'ed Whale from Woefully. Constantine, R., ed. Woe, Jonathan, illus. 32p. 1992. 14.95 (*0-9627946-3-5*) Hawk FL.

ECOLOGY, MARINE

see Marine Ecology

ECONOMIC CONDITIONS

see also Economic Policy; Geography, Commercial; Statistics; U. S.–Economic Conditions

Hopper, Hilary L. Around the World Program Series. (gr. 4 up). 1993. Smyth sewn casebound. 17.95 (*0-939923-28-9*); Perfect bdg. 7.95 (*0-939923-27-0*); Family ed. 48.00 (*0-939923-26-2*) M & W Pub Co.

O'Toole, Thomas. Global Economics. (Illus.). 80p. (gr. 5 up). 1991. PLB 21.50 (*0-8225-1782-5*) Lerner Pubns.

ECONOMIC DEPRESSIONS

see Depressions

ECONOMIC DEVELOPMENT

see Economic Conditions

ECONOMIC ENTOMOLOGY

see Insects, Injurious and Beneficial

ECONOMIC GEOGRAPHY

see Geography, Commercial

ECONOMIC HISTORY

see Economic Conditions

ECONOMIC PLANNING

see Economic Policy

ECONOMIC POLICY

For works on the policy of governments towards economic problems.

see also International Economic Relations

also names of countries and states with the subdivision Economic Policy e.g. U. S.–Economic Policy)

Rawcliffe, Michael. Timeline: The Welfare State. (Illus.). 72p. (gr. 7 up). 1990. 19.95 (*0-7134-9806-4*, Pub. by Batsford UK) Trafalgar.

ECONOMIC RELATIONS, FOREIGN

see International Economic Relations

ECONOMICS

see also Business; Commerce; Credit; Depressions; Economic Conditions; Economic Policy; Finance; Industry; Labor and Laboring Classes; Land; Money; Population

Asimov, Isaac. Ask Isaac Asimov, 41 vols. (Illus.). 24p. (gr. 1-8). PLB 570.01 subscription set (*0-8368-0789-8*); PLB 14.60 ea., standing order (*0-8368-0788-X*) Gareth Stevens Inc.

Banks, Ann. It's My Money: A Kid's Guide to the Green Stuff. Natti, Susanna, illus. 32p. (gr. 2-6). 1993. pap. 3.99 (*0-14-036086-7*, Puffin) Puffin Bks.

Clawson, Elmer. Activities & Investigations in Economics. 1994. pap. text ed. 9.95 (*0-201-49005-6*) Addison-Wesley.

—Activities & Investigations in Economics. 1993. pap. 12.95 tchr's. ed. (*0-201-49006-4*) Addison-Wesley.

Economics Study Aid. 1987. pap. 3.25 (*0-87738-045-7*) Youth Ed.

Hess, Karl. Capitalism for Kids: Growing Up to be Your Own Boss. (gr. 5 up). 1992. 12.95 (*0-942103-03-3*, 5615-34, Enter-Dearbrn); pap. 8.95 (*0-942103-06-8*, 5615-35, Enter-Dearbrn) Dearborn Finan.

Jones, Vada L. Kids Can Make Money Too! How Young People Can Succeed Financially...Over 200 Ways to Earn Money & How to Make It Grow. LC 87-71607. (Illus., Orig.). (gr. 3-12). 1988. pap. 9.95 (*0-944104-00-2*) Calico Paws.

Marsh, Carole. The Teddy Bear Company: Economics for Kids. (Illus.). (gr. 4-8). 1994. 14.95 (*0-935326-16-2*); tchr's. ed. o.p. 6.00 (*0-935326-90-1*) Gallopade Pub Group.

—Teddy Bear's Annual Report. (Illus.). (gr. 4-8). 1994. 14.95 (*0-935326-26-X*) Gallopade Pub Group.

O'Neill, Terry & Swisher, Karin, eds. Economics in America: Opposing Viewpoints. LC 91-42802. (Illus.). 264p. (gr. 10 up). 1992. PLB 17.95 (*0-89908-187-8*); pap. text ed. 9.95 (*0-89908-162-2*) Greenhaven.

Pool, John C. & Stamos, Stephen C., Jr. Exploring the Global Economy. (Illus.). 125p. (Orig.). (gr. 9-12). 1994. pap. text ed. 9.95 (*1-882505-03-4*) Durell Inst MSASU.

Uncle Eric, pseud. Whatever Happened to Penny Candy? A Fast, Clear, & Fun Explanation of the Economics You Need for Success in Your Career, Business, & Investments. 3rd, rev. & enl. ed. Bixler, Nancy, illus. LC 92-36378. (gr. 5 up). 1993. 8.95 (*0-942617-15-0*) Blstckng Pr.

Wyatt, Elaine & Hinden, Stan. The Money Book & Bank. LC 91-13237. (Illus.). 64p. (gr. 2 up). 1991. pap. 11.95 (*0-688-10365-0*, Tambourine Bks) Morrow.

ECONOMICS–DICTIONARIES

Guenter, H. Jugendlexikon Wirtschaft. (GER.). 192p. 1976. 12.95 (*0-8288-5715-6*, M7492, Pub. by Rowohlt) Fr & Eur.

ECONOMISTS

Victor, R. F. John Maynard Keynes: Father of Modern Economics. Rahmas, D. Steve, ed. 32p. (Orig.). (gr. 7-12). 1972. lib. bdg. 4.95 incl. catalog cards (*0-87157-517-5*) SamHar Pr.

ECUADOR

Lepthien, Emilie U. Ecuador. LC 85-26967. (Illus.). 128p. (gr. 5-9). 1986. PLB 20.55 (*0-516-02760-3*) Childrens.

Lerner Publications, Department of Geography Staff. Ecuador in Pictures. (Illus.). 64p. (gr. 5 up). 1987. PLB 17.50 (*0-8225-1813-9*) Lerner Pubns.

Peck, Robert M. Headhunters & Hummingbirds: An Expedition into Ecuador. LC 86-15908. (Illus.). 128p. (gr. 11 up). 1987. 14.95 (*0-8027-6645-5*); PLB 14.85 (*0-8027-6646-3*) Walker & Co.

Siy, Alexandra. The Waorani: People of the Ecuadoran Rain Forest. LC 92-36985. (Illus.). 80p. (gr. 5 up). 1993. text ed. 14.95 RSBE (*0-87518-550-9*, Dillon) Macmillan Child Grp.

ECUMENICAL MOVEMENT

see Christian Unity

EDDY, MARY (BAKER) 1821-1910

Sass, Karin. Mary Baker Eddy, a Special Friend. Kieffer, Christa, illus. LC 83-72002. 32p. (gr. k-3). 1983. 8.95 (*0-87510-165-8*) Christian Sci.

Smith, Louise. Mary Baker Eddy. Horner, Matina S., intro. by. 112p. (gr. 5 up). 1991. 17.95 (*1-55546-652-4*) Chelsea Hse.

EDIBLE PLANTS

see Plants, Edible

EDISON, THOMAS ALVA, 1847-1931

Adler, David A. Thomas Alva Edison: Great Inventor. Miller, Lyle, illus. LC 89-77507. 48p. (gr. 2-5). 1990. reinforced bdg. 14.95 (*0-8234-0820-5*) Holiday.

AESOP Enterprises, Inc. Staff & Crenshaw, Gwendolyn J. Thomas Alva Edison: Persistent Dreamer & Doer. 14p. (gr. 3-12). 1991. pap. write for info. incl. cassette (*1-880771-13-6*) AESOP Enter.

Anderson, Kelly C. Thomas Edison. LC 93-14156. (gr. 5-8). 1994. 14.95 (*1-56006-041-7*) Lucent Bks.

Cousins, Margaret. The Story of Thomas Alva Edison. LC 81-805. (Illus.). 160p. (gr. 5-9). 1981. pap. 4.99 (*0-394-84883-7*) Random Bks Yng Read.

Davidson, Margaret. Story of Thomas Alva Edison: The Wizard of Menlo Park. 1990. pap. 2.75 (*0-590-42403-3*) Scholastic Inc.

Egan, Louise. Thomas A. Edison. (Illus.). 144p. (gr. 3-6). 1987. pap. 5.95 (*0-8120-3922-X*) Barron.

Farr, Naunerle C. Thomas Edison - Alexander Graham Bell. Taloac, Gerry & Trinidad, Angel, illus. (gr. 4-12). 1979. pap. text ed. 2.95 (*0-88301-357-6*); wkbk. 1.25 (*0-88301-381-9*) Pendulum Pr.

Greene, Carol. Thomas Alva Edison: Bringer of Light. LC 84-23247. (Illus.). 128p. (gr. 4 up). 1985. PLB 14.40 (*0-516-03213-5*) Childrens.

Guthridge, Sue. Thomas A. Edison: Young Inventor. Wook, Wallace, illus. LC 86-10862. 192p. (gr. 2-6). 1986. pap. 3.95 (*0-02-041850-7*, Aladdin) Macmillan Child Grp.

Keller, Jack. Tom Edison's Bright Idea. (Illus.). 32p. (gr. 1-4). 1989. PLB 18.99 (*0-8172-3532-9*); pap. 3.95 (*0-8114-6733-3*) Raintree Steck-V.

Lampton, Christopher. Thomas Alva Edison. LC 90-49178. (Illus.). 88p. (gr. 6-10). 1991. PLB 13.95 (*1-55905-079-9*) Marshall Cavendish.

Lowitz, Sadyebeth & Lowitz, Anson. Tom Edison Finds Out. 1979. pap. 0.95 (*0-440-48384-0*, YB) Dell.

Morgan, Nina. Thomas Edison. LC 90-27784. (Illus.). 48p. (gr. 5-8). 1991. RLB 12.40 (*0-531-18406-4*, Pub. by Bookwright Pr) Watts.

Nirgiotis, Nicholas. Thomas Edison. LC 93-37028. (Illus.). 32p. (gr. 3-6). 1994. PLB 12.30 (*0-516-06676-5*) Childrens.

Parker, Steve. Thomas Edison & Electricity. LC 92-6805. (Illus.). 32p. (gr. 3-7). 1992. 14.00 (*0-06-020859-7*); PLB 13.89 (*0-06-021473-2*) HarpC Child Bks.

—Thomas Edison & Electricity. Parker, Steve, illus. LC 92-6805. 32p. (gr. 3-7). 1992. pap. 5.95 (*0-06-446144-0*, Trophy) HarpC Child Bks.

Rowland-Entwistle, Theodore. Thomas Edison. (Illus.). 32p. (gr. 3-8). 1988. PLB 10.95 (*0-86307-928-8*) Marshall Cavendish.

Sabin, Louis. Thomas Alva Edison: Young Inventor. Ulrich, George, illus. LC 82-15889. 48p. (gr. 4-6). 1983. PLB 10.79 (*0-89375-841-8*); pap. text ed. 3.50 (*0-89375-842-6*) Troll Assocs.

Tames, Richard. Thomas Edison. LC 89-29279. (Illus.). 32p. (gr. 4-6). 1990. PLB 12.40 (*0-531-14004-0*) Watts.

Weinberg, Michael. Thomas Edison. Ford, George, illus. 48p. (gr. 2-4). 1988. pap. 2.50 (*0-681-40687-9*) Longmeadow Pr.

Wizard of Sound: A Story about Thomas Edison. (gr. 4-7). 1992. pap. 5.95 (*0-87614-563-2*) Carolrhoda Bks.

EDISON, THOMAS ALVA, 1847-1931–FICTION

Calmenson, Stephanie, adapted by. Race to Danger. LC 92-56396. 136p. (Orig.). (gr. 4-8). 1993. pap. 3.50 (*0-679-84388-4*) Random Bks Yng Read.

EDITORS AND EDITING

see Journalism; Journalists; Publishers and Publishing

EDMUNDSON, SARAH EMMA, 1841-1898

Stevens, Bryna. Frank Thompson: Her Civil War Story. LC 91-45382. (Illus.). 144p. (gr. 5-9). 1992. SBE 13.95 (*0-02-788185-7*, Macmillan Child Bk) Macmillan Child Grp.

EDUCATION

see also Audio-Visual Education; Books and Reading; Business Education; Character Education; Child Study; Colleges and Universities; Culture; Educators; Learning and Scholarship; Libraries; Military Education; Physical Education and Training; Religious Education; Scholarships, Fellowships, Etc.; Schools; Self-Culture; Study, Method of; Teachers; Teaching

also names of classes of people and social and ethnic groups with the subdivision Education, (e.g. Blacks–Education); subjects with the subdivision Study and Teaching (e.g. Science–Study and Teaching); and headings beginning with the words Education and Educational

Ames, Louise B. Why Am I So Noisy? Why Is She So Shy? 48p. (Orig.). (ps-8). 1991. pap. text ed. 7.95 (*0-935493-45-X*) Modern Learn Pr.

Berry, Joy. Every Kid's Guide to Laws That Relate to School & Work. Bartholomew, illus. 48p. (gr. 3-7). 1987. 4.95 (*0-516-21412-8*) Childrens.

Binford, Shari, et al, eds. Education: Is It Improving or Declining. 48p. 1991. pap. text ed. 11.95 (*1-878623-20-6*) Info Plus TX.

Borba, Michele. Esteem Builders: A Self-Esteem Curriculum for Improving Student Achievement, Behavior & School-Home Climate. Taylor-McMillan, Birah, ed. Highpoint Type & Graphics Staff, illus. LC 88-80769. 444p. (Orig.). (gr. k-8). 1989. pap. 49.95 spiral bdg. (*0-915190-53-2*, JP9053-2) Jalmar Pr.

Bosch, Carl W. Making the Grade. Strecker, Rebekah, illus. LC 90-62674. 64p. (Orig.). (gr. 3). 1991. lib. bdg. 16.95 (*0-943990-49-1*); pap. 5.95 (*0-943990-48-3*) Parenting Pr.

Burke, Amy M. & Wallace, Roger. Not Just Schoolwork. LC 76-9524. 201p. (Orig.). (gr. 3-12). 1990. pap. 29.95 (*0-8290-0354-1*) NL Assocs.

Caballero, Jane A. & Whordley, Derek. Children Around the World. rev. ed. LC 82-81892. 176p. (Orig.). (ps-4). 1991. pap. 16.95 (*0-89334-112-6*) Humanics Ltd.

Carroll, Jeri. Learning Centers for Little Kids. Foster, Tom, illus. 64p. (ps-2). 1983. wkbk. 8.95 (*0-86653-103-3*, GA 458) Good Apple.

Colbert, Cynthia & Taunton, Martha. Discover Art - Kindergarten. (gr. k). 1989. kit 199.50 (*0-87192-219-3*, 219-3) Davis Mass.

Cummings, Rhoda & Fisher, Gary. The Survival Guide for Teenagers with LD. 200p. 1994. 11.95 (*0-685-71626-0*, 758); 2 audio cass. 160 min. 19.95 (*0-685-71627-9*, 758A) W Gladden Found.

Delisle, James R. Gifted Kids Speak Out: Hundreds of Kids Ages 6-13 Talk about School, Friends, Their Families & the Future. Espeland, Pamela, ed. Urbanovic, Jackie, illus. LC 87-25139. 120p. (Orig.). (gr. 2-7). 1987. pap. 9.95 (*0-915793-10-5*) Free Spirit Pub.

Dixon, Dougal. Dino Dots. LC 88-28583. 96p. 1988. pap. 4.95 (*0-88166-122-8*) Meadowbrook.

Dolan, Edward F. & Scariano, Margaret M. Illiteracy in America. LC 93-29528. Date not set. write for info. (*0-531-11178-4*) Watts.

Dunn, Kathryn B. & Dunn, Allison B. Trouble with School: A Family Story about Learning Disabilities. Stromoski, Rick, illus. 32p. (Orig.). (gr. 1-5). 1993. 9.95 (*0-933149-57-3*) Woodbine House.

Embry, Lynn. Rx for the Classroom Blahs. Filkins, Vanessa, illus. 64p. (gr. 4-8). 1983. wkbk. 8.95 (*0-86653-104-1*, GA 462) Good Apple.

Enns, Peter. Street Smarts! The Rewards of a Good Education. Wolverton, Lock, illus. 40p. (Orig.). (ps-6). 1992. pap. 5.98 incl. cassette (*0-943593-75-1*) Kids Intl Inc.

Fisher, Gary & Cummings, Rhoda. The Survival Guide for Kids with LD. 97p. (gr. 3 up). 1994. 9.95 (*0-685-71624-4*, 757); 96 min. audio cass. 10.00 (*0-685-71625-2*, 757A) W Gladden Found.

Forte, Imogene. Think about It! Middle Grades. (Illus.). 80p. (gr. 4-6). 1981. pap. text ed. 7.95 (*0-913916-98-6*, IP 98-6) Incentive Pubn.

—Think about It! Primary. (Illus.). 80p. (gr. 1-3). 1981. pap. text ed. 7.95 (*0-913916-97-8*, IP 97-8) Incentive Pubn.

Foster, Elizabeth S. Tutoring: Learning by Helping: A Student Handbook for Training Peer & Cross Age Tutors. rev. ed. McKee, Mary M., illus. LC 92-71011. 140p. (gr. 8-12). 1992. pap. text ed. 12.95x (*0-932796-44-3*) Ed Media Corp.

Galbraith, Judy. The Gifted Kids Survival Guide (For Ages 10 & Under) LC 83-83015. (Illus.). 72p. (Orig.). (gr. k-5). 1984. pap. 7.95 (*0-915793-00-8*) Free Spirit Pub.

Hazouri, Sandra P. & Smith, Miriam F. Peer Listing in the Middle School: Training Activities for Students. Brown, Christine M., illus. LC 91-75586. 134p. (Orig.). (gr. 6-8). 1991. pap. text ed. 8.95x (*0-932796-34-6*) Ed Media Corp.

Kizer, Kathryn. Two Hundred Plus Games & Fun Activities for Teaching Preschoolers. (Illus.). 72p. (Orig.). (ps). 1989. pap. text ed. 4.95 (*0-936625-70-8*, New Hope AL) Womans Mission Union.

Kleman, Mary L. & Kleman, James. Listening Comprehension Training Program: Manuals A-E. 40p. (gr. 4-8). 1982. manual 5.00 (*0-938464-01-9*) JML Enter MD.

Learning Exchange Staff. Seasonal Learning Activities. 112p. (gr. 2-6). 1988. wkbk. 10.95 (*0-86653-435-0*, GA1045) Good Apple.

LeGros, Lucy C. Activities & Games. rev. ed. (Illus.). 75p. (Orig.). (gr. k-2). 1989. pap. 7.95 (*0-318-41419-8*) Creat Res NC.

Leuning, Kevin. Archie Givens Sr. Collection Curriculum Guide. x, 30p. (ps-12). 1988. pap. text ed. write for info. (*0-9632976-0-0*) A Givens Sr Collect.

Liebermann, M. Coloring Books on Events of the Jewish Months: Tishrei, Cheshvan. (ps-2). 1987. 2.50 (*0-914131-84-2*, D710) Torah Umesorah.

Loeper, John J. Going to School in 1776. LC 72-86940. (Illus.). 112p. (gr. 4-7). 1973. SBE 14.95 (*0-689-30089-1*, Atheneum) Macmillan Child Grp.

McDonough, Kathleen L. School Survival Skills: Student Syllabus. (Illus.). 64p. (gr. 8 up). 1985. pap. 7.95 (*0-89420-246-4*, 340025) Natl Book.

McInnes, Celia. Projects for Summer & Holiday Activities. Young, Richard G., ed. Wheele, Stephen, illus. LC 89-11791. 32p. (gr. 3-5). 1989. PLB 15.93 (*0-944483-39-9*) Garrett Ed Corp.

McKinley, Nancy L. & Schwartz, Linda. Make-It-Yourself Barrier Activities. 210p. (gr. k-12). 1987. pap. 33.00 (*0-930599-16-0*) Thinking Pubns.

Mainwaring, S. & Shouse, C. Learning Through Construction. 43p. (gr. k-3). 1983. pap. 8.00 (*0-685-51017-4*) High-Scope.

Molyneux, Lynn. Get It Together: Group Projects for Creative Bulletin Boards. Bucur, Mike, illus. 160p. (gr. k-4). 1983. perfect bdg. 9.95 (*0-685-29141-3*) Trellis Bks Inc.

Myrick, Robert D. & Sorenson, Don L. Helping Skills for Middle School Students. Mitchell, Hetty, illus. LC 92-70820. 160p. (Orig.). (gr. 6-8). 1992. pap. text ed. 7.95x (*0-932796-40-0*) Ed Media Corp.

Neufeld, Evelyn. Homework! 64p. (ps-2). 1987. pap. text ed. 8.50 (*0-914040-56-1*) Cuisenaire.

Patacsil, Priscila M. Actividades Educativas para Preescolares. 172p. (ps). 1988. pap. 6.25 (*0-311-11049-5*) Casa Bautista.

Petreshene, Susan S. More Mind Joggers! One Hundred Two Ready-to-Use Activities That Make Kids Think. 288p. (gr. 1-6). 1988. pap. 27.95x (*0-87628-584-1*) Ctr Appl Res.

Sorenson, Don L. Conflict Resolution & Mediation for Peer Helpers. Sorenson, Reid, illus. LC 92-70818. 128p. (Orig.). (gr. 8-12). 1992. pap. text ed. 8.95x (*0-932796-42-7*) Ed Media Corp.

Steinmetz, Shirley A. Silly Scribbles: A Complete Readiness Program for Young Children. 272p. (ps-k). 1988. pap. 24.95x (*0-87628-776-3*) Ctr Appl Res.

Stoppleman, Monica. School Day. (Illus.). 32p. (gr. 3-6). 1992. 12.95 (*0-7136-3185-6*, Pub. by A&C Black UK) Talman.

Stull, Elizabeth C. Children's Books Activities Kit. 256p. (gr. 1-3). 1988. pap. 24.95x (*0-87628-014-9*) Ctr Appl Res.

Thurston, Cheryl M. Extra Book, Level One. Blackstone, Ann, illus. 46p. (Orig.). (gr. 5-12). 1988. pap. text ed. 12.95 (*1-877673-05-6*) Cottonwood Pr.

Welch, Joyce. The Illustrated I Hate School Workbook. Gustafson, Dru, illus. 88p. (Orig.). (gr. 7-9). 1979. pap. 6.95 (*0-935996-00-1*) Wibat Pubns.

Westridge Young Writers Workshop Staff. Kids Explore the Gifts of Children with Special Needs. 112p. (gr. 4-7). 1994. pap. 8.95 (*1-56261-156-9*) John Muir.

Winston, Barbara F. The Hardest Thing about Going to School. Wilson, James P., illus. (Orig.). (gr. k-5). 1987. pap. text ed. 3.95 (*0-9622810-0-X*) B Winston.

EDUCATION–AIMS AND OBJECTIVES

Adams, Pam, illus. Day Dreams. LC 90-45583. 32p. (Orig.). (ps-2). 1978. 11.95 (*0-85953-105-8*, Pub. by Child's Play England); pap. 5.95 (*0-85953-082-5*) Childs Play.

Cozic, Charles P., ed. Education in America: Opposing Viewpoints. LC 91-42495. (Illus.). 264p. (gr. 10 up). 1992. PLB 17.95 (*0-89908-188-6*); pap. text ed. 9.95 (*0-89908-163-0*) Greenhaven.

Sherrow, Victoria. Challenges in Education. 1990. lib. bdg. 13.98 (*0-671-70556-3*, J Messner) S&S Trade.

EDUCATION–DATA PROCESSING

Fry, Edward B. Computer Keyboarding for Children. rev. ed. (gr. 3-6). 1984. pap. text ed. 9.95x (*0-8077-2754-7*) Tchrs Coll.

Levine, Janice R. Microcomputers in Elementary & Secondary Education: A Guide to Resources. 64p. (gr. k-12). 1983. 3.75 (*0-937597-06-6*, IR-65) ERIC Clear.

EDUCATION, BUSINESS

see Business Education

EDUCATION, CHARACTER

see Character Education

EDUCATION, CHRISTIAN

see Religious Education

EDUCATION, DISCRIMINATION IN

see Discrimination in Education

EDUCATION, ELEMENTARY

Armstrong, Bev. Who's Following Directions? Armstrong, Bev, illus. 32p. (gr. 4-7). 1979. wkbk. 3.95 (*0-88160-072-5*, LW 805) Learning Wks.

Armstrong, Beverly. Awards Galore. 48p. (gr. 1-6). 1981. 5.95 (*0-88160-040-7*, LW 225) Learning Wks.

Clarke, Joy A. Multicultural Social Studies Unit: Who Am I? Blocker, Kearn, illus. 150p. (gr. 3-8). 1991. 3-ring binder 79.95 (*0-9626984-1-5*); pap. 69.95 (*0-685-62443-9*) Clarke Enterprise.

Cummings, Rhoda & Fisher, Gary. The School Survival Guide for Kids with LD (Learning Differences) Ways to Make Learning Easier & More Fun. LC 91-14489. (Illus.). 176p. (gr. 2 up). 1991. pap. 10.95 (*0-915793-32-6*) Free Spirit Pub.

Galbraith, Judy. The Gifted Kids Survival Guides. 72p. (ps-5). 1994. 7.95 (0-685-71628-7, 759) W Gladden Found.
Greanias, Francis. More Pasting Penguins. 24p. (gr. k-3). 1980. 3.95 (0-88160-060-1, LW 608) Learning Wks.
—Pasting Penguin. 24p. (gr. k-3). 1980. 3.95 (0-88160-059-8, LW 607) Learning Wks.
Levin, Rita. Punctuation Partners. 48p. (gr. 2-4). 1983. 6.95 (0-88160-098-9, LW 121) Learning Wks.
Mors, A. & Williams, J. Americans at School. 1991. pap. text ed. 5.25 (0-582-01714-9) Longman.
Polon, Linda. Paragraph Production. 48p. (gr. 4-6). 1981. 5.95 (0-88160-039-3, LW 224) Learning Wks.
Roets, Lois. Student Projects: Ideas & Plans. 272p. (gr. 3 up). 1987. pap. text ed. 30.00 (0-911943-11-0) Leadership Pub.
Roets, Lois F. Outline Wizard. 48p. (gr. 4-6). 1980. 5.95 (0-88160-034-2, LW 219) Learning Wks.
Schwartz, Linda. The Center Solution. 74p. (gr. 4-6). 1977. 7.95 (0-88160-025-3, LW 210) Learning Wks.
Snowball, Marilyn. Preschool Packrat. 112p. (ps). 1982. 9.95 (0-88160-011-3, LW 113) Learning Wks.
—Preschool Pelican. 112p. (ps). 1982. 9.95 (0-88160-085-7, LW 114) Learning Wks.
Tyler, Sydney B. Young Think Program Two. 90p. (Orig.). (gr. k-1). 1988. pap. text ed. 25.00 report cover (0-912781-13-0) Thomas Geale.

EDUCATION, ETHICAL
see Character Education; Religious Education

EDUCATION–FICTION
Bond, Michael. Paddington Takes the Test. (Illus.). (gr. 3-6). 1980. 13.45 (0-395-29519-X) HM.
Cosgrove, Stephen. Leo the Lop: Tail Three. James, Robin, illus. 32p. (Orig.). (gr. 1-4). 1978. pap. 2.95 (0-8431-0577-1) Price Stern.
Duey, Kathleen. Mr. Stumpguss Is a Third Grader. Fiammenghi, Gioia, illus. 80p. (Orig.). 1992. pap. 3.50 (0-380-76939-5, Camelot Young) Avon.
Fitzpatrick, Blanche. Getting A Living, Getting A Life: After the Senior Prom. LC 94-66196. 110p. (Orig.). 1994. pap. 9.95 (0-9627397-2-3) Pemberton Pubs.
Hamilton, Dorothy. Jason. LC 73-14813. 120p. (gr. 10-12). 1974. pap. 3.95 (0-8361-1728-X) Herald Pr.
Harry Stottlemeier's Discovery. 92p. (gr. 1-5). 6.50 (0-686-74918-9); tchr's. manual 30.00 (0-686-74919-7) ADL.
Kaminski, Gerald. Good Questions. Cooper, Ryan M., illus. 32p. (Orig.). (gr. k-3). 1980. pap. 5.95 (0-931896-00-2) Cove View.
Korman, Gordon. Don't Care High. 256p. (gr. 7 up). 1986. pap. 2.50 (0-590-40251-X, Point) Scholastic Inc.
—Don't Care High. 1986. pap. 3.25 (0-590-43129-3) Scholastic Inc.

Mire, Betty. T-Pierre Frog & T-Felix Frog Go to School. Mire, Betty, illus. LC 93-74275. 32p. (Orig.). (gr. 1-3). 1994. PLB 6.95 (0-9639378-0-4) Cajun Bay Pr.
T-PIERRE FROG & T-FELIX FROG GO TO SCHOOL focuses on the importance of education & reading. This unique book is incorporated with the CAJUN FRENCH language (approximately one CAJUN FRENCH sentence on every page of text). And for every CAJUN FRENCH sentence there is a cute cartoon picture associated with it. It's a book that parents will enjoy reading to their children. The story begins with the first day of school on the Louisiana bayous. T-PIERRE FROG likes going to school & he loves to read. He tells his friend T-FELIX FROG that he wants to learn all he can, because he wants to one day become an astronaut. But T-FELIX FROG doesn't like school. And he tells T-PIERRE that he doesn't have to learn, because his only wish is to become a lazy hobo taking it easy in the shade. Sometimes wishes come true. T-FELIX finds that out, but not without woes. Although T-FELIX FROG is soon enlightened on the importance of an education through a dream or rather a nightmare. T-PIERRE FROG & T-FELIX FROG GO TO SCHOOL is simultaneously entertaining & educational. The book is complete with pronunciation guide. *Publisher Provided Annotation.*

Mr. Cuckoo's Clock Shop. 24p. (ps-2). 1981. 5.95 (0-8431-0634-4) Price Stern.
Ritchie, Jo-An. Jonie Graduates. LC 78-27431. (gr. 6-12). 1979. pap. 4.50 (0-8127-0201-8) Review & Herald.
Sobol, Donald J. Encyclopedia Brown Tracks Them Down, No. 8. 96p. (gr. 3-6). 1982. pap. 2.50 (0-553-15525-3) Bantam.
Squiggly Wiggly's Surprise. 24p. (ps-2). 1980. 6.95 (0-8431-0632-8) Price Stern.

EDUCATION, HIGHER
Blair, Alison. Higher Education. (gr. 10 up). 1988. pap. 2.95 (0-8041-0070-5) Ivy Books.
Carr, Roberta, ed. Directory of Pre-College Programs. 75p. (Orig.). (gr. 9-12). 1992. pap. text ed. 25.00x (1-880468-05-0) Col Connect.
Mors, A. & Williams, J. Americans at School. 1991. pap. text ed. 5.25 (0-582-01714-9) Longman.

EDUCATION–HISTORY
Sherrow, Victoria. Challenges in Education. 1990. lib. bdg. 13.98 (0-671-70556-3, J Messner) S&S Trade.

EDUCATION, INTERCULTURAL
see Intercultural Education

EDUCATION, MILITARY
see Military Education

EDUCATION, MORAL
see Character Education

EDUCATION, MUSICAL
see Music–Study and Teaching

EDUCATION, PHYSICAL
see Physical Education and Training

EDUCATION, PRESCHOOL
see Nursery Schools

EDUCATION, PRIMARY
see Education, Elementary

EDUCATION, RELIGIOUS
see Religious Education

EDUCATION, SCIENTIFIC
see Science–Study and Teaching

EDUCATION, SECONDARY
Galbraith, Judy. The Gifted Kids Survival Guide. 144p. (gr. 6-12). 1994. 8.95 (0-685-71629-5, 780) W Gladden Found.

EDUCATION, SEGREGATION IN
see Segregation in Education

EDUCATION–STUDY AND TEACHING
see also Teachers–Training

EDUCATION, THEOLOGICAL
see Religious Education

EDUCATION AND STATE
see also Scholarships, Fellowships, Etc.

EDUCATION OF CHILDREN
see Education, Elementary

EDUCATION OF THE BLIND
see Blind–Education

EDUCATION OF THE DEAF
see Deaf–Education

EDUCATIONAL ADMINISTRATION
see School Administration and Organization

EDUCATIONAL MEASUREMENTS
see Educational Tests and Measurements

EDUCATIONAL PSYCHOLOGY
see also Child Study; Imagination; Perception; Psychology, Applied; Thought and Thinking

EDUCATIONAL TESTS AND MEASUREMENTS
Abresch, Richard T. & Kern, Roger G. The Test Taking Advantage Strategy Manual. (Illus.). 181p. (gr. 10-12). 1990. pap. text ed. 35.50 (0-9627360-0-7) Test Taking Advan.
Barton, Charles D. What Happened to SAT Scores, No. 1. rev. ed. Barton, David, illus. 52p. 1988. pap. 3.00 (0-317-93056-7) Wallbuilders.
Brownstein, Samuel C., et al. Pass Key to SAT I. 2nd ed. (gr. 10-12). 1994. pap. 6.95 (0-8120-1884-2) Barron.
—PSAT - NMSQT: How to Prepare for the Preliminary Scholastic Aptitude Test - National Merit Scholarship Qualifying Test. 8th ed. LC 93-21849. 380p. (gr. 9 up). 1993. pap. 10.95 (0-8120-1414-6) Barron.
Campbell, John P. Campbell's Middle School Quiz Book, No. 2. 332p. (Orig.). (gr. 5-8). 1986. pap. 14.95x (0-9609412-6-6) Patricks Pr.
Carris, Joan D., et al. SAT Success. 3rd ed. LC 91-19039. 600p. (gr. 10-12). 1991. pap. 11.95 (1-56079-049-0) Petersons Guides.
Carter, Philip J. & Russell, Ken A. Beat the IQ Challenge. (Illus.). 128p. (gr. 10-12). 1993. pap. 4.95 (0-7063-7128-3, Pub. by Ward Lock UK) Sterling.
Eder, James M. How to Prepare for the Advanced Placement Examination: AP European History. LC 93-21094. (gr. 9-12). 1994. pap. 11.95 (0-8120-1623-8) Barron.
Fredericks & Lipner. Barron's How to Prepare for the Regents Competency Examination: Reading. (gr. 11-12). 1982. pap. 12.95 (0-8120-2287-4) Barron.
Gruber, Gary R. Dr. Gary Gruber's Essential Guide to Test Taking for Kids. LC 86-8655. 120p. (Orig.). (gr. 3-5). 1986. pap. text ed. 7.95 (0-688-06350-0, Quill) Morrow.
—Gruber's Complete Preparation for the SAT - Featuring Critical Thinking Skills. (Orig.). (gr. 10-12). 1992. pap. 12.95 (0-935475-00-1) Critical Book.
Kendris, Christopher. How to Prepare for SAT II: Spanish. 7th ed. LC 93-20714. 1994. pap. 11.95 incl. 60-min. cass. (0-8120-1764-1) Barron.
Lawrence, Marcia. How to Take the SAT. 336p. (gr. 9-12). 1979. pap. 10.00 (0-452-26296-8, Plume) NAL-Dutton.
Lewis, Rosemary, et al. Reviewbooks for the GED Test. (Illus.). 1992. pap. text ed. 83.65 (1-56030-089-2) Comex Systs.
Peters, Max & Shostak, Jerome. How to Prepare for Catholic High School Entrance Examinations - COOP & HSPT. 576p. 1992. pap. 11.95 (0-8120-4955-1) Barron.
Random House Staff. How to Get Better Test Scores on Elementary School Standarized Tests. (Illus.). 152p. (Orig.). (gr. 3-4). 1991. pap. 9.00 (0-679-82108-2) Random Bks Yng Read.
—How to Get Better Test Scores on Elementary School Standardized Tests. (Illus.). 152p. (Orig.). (gr. 5-6). 1991. pap. 9.00 (0-679-82109-0) Random Bks Yng Read.
—How to Get Better Test Scores on Elementary School Standardized Tests. (Illus.). 152p. (Orig.). (gr. 7-8). 1991. pap. 9.00 (0-679-82110-4) Random Bks Yng Read.
Sennet, Carole L. & Sennet, Edith. Power Words SAT Cartoon Flashcards. Monse, Keith, illus. (gr. 7 up). 1991. 301 2-sided cards plus thesaurus 21.95 (1-879871-01-7) Sennet & Sarnoff.
Sommerfield, Elissa B. A Beginner's Guide to the SATs. 85p. (Orig.). (gr. 7-10). 1987. pap. text ed. 10.95 (0-9604058-2-8) Ed Skills Dallas.
—Junior SAT Exercises: SAT Exercises for the Ninth & Tenth Grades. 94p. (Orig.). (gr. 9-10). 1987. pap. text ed. 10.95 (0-9604058-1-X) Ed Skills Dallas.

EDUCATORS
see also Teachers
Poole, Bernice A. Mary McLeod Bethune: (Educator) (Illus.). 208p. (Orig.). 1994. pap. 3.95 (0-87067-783-7, Melrose Sq) Holloway.
Unger, Harlow G. Teachers & Educators. LC 94-8628. 1994. write for info. (0-8160-2990-3) Facts on File.

EDWARD 6TH, KING OF ENGLAND, 1537-1553–FICTION
Twain, Mark. Prince & the Pauper. (gr. 5 up). 1964. pap. 2.50 (0-8049-0032-9, 32) Airmont.
—The Prince & the Pauper. James, Raymond, ed. Couri, Kathryn A., illus. LC 89-33892. 48p. (gr. 3-6). 1990. lib. bdg. 12.89 (0-8167-1873-3); pap. text ed. 3.95 (0-8167-1874-1) Troll Assocs.

EGGS
see also Birds–Eggs and Nests
Benedict, Kitty. The Egg: My First Nature Books. Felix, Monique, illus. 32p. (gr. k-2). 1993. pap. 2.95 (1-56189-175-4) Amer Educ Pub.
Binato, Leonardo. What Hatches from an Egg? Turn & Learn. 12p. (ps-3). 1992. 4.95 (1-56566-007-2) Thomasson-Grant.
Burton, Robert. The Egg Book. Burton, Jane & Taylor, Kim, photos by. LC 93-28365. (Illus.). 48p. (ps-3). 1994. 13.95 (1-56458-460-7) Dorling Kindersley.
De Bourgoing, Pascale. Egg. Valat, P. M. & Perols, Sylvie, illus. 24p. 1992. pap. 10.95 (0-590-45266-5, Cartwheel) Scholastic Inc.
Fowler, Allan. The Chicken or the Egg? LC 92-35054. (Illus.). 32p. (ps-2). 1993. PLB 10.75 (0-516-06008-2); pap. 3.95 (0-516-46008-0); big bk. 22.95 (0-516-49639-5) Childrens.
Hariton, Anca. Egg Story. LC 91-34588. (Illus.). 24p. (gr. k-2). 1992. 12.00 (0-525-44861-6, DCB) Dutton Child Bks.
Heller, Ruth. Chickens Aren't the Only Ones. Heller, Ruth, illus. LC 80-85257. 48p. (ps-1). 1981. 10.95 (0-448-01872-1, G&D) Putnam Pub Group.
Johnson, Sylvia A. Inside an Egg. LC 81-17235. (Illus.). 48p. (gr. 4 up). 1982. PLB 19.95 (0-8225-1472-9); pap. 5.95 (0-8225-9522-2) Lerner Pubns.
Moss, Miriam. Eggs. Stefoff, Rebecca, ed. Pickett, Robert, photos by. LC 91-18186. (Illus.). 32p. (gr. 3-5). 1991. PLB 15.93 (1-56074-005-1) Garrett Ed Corp.
Roddie, Shen. Hatch, Egg, Hatch: Touch & Feel Action Flap Book. (ps). 1991. 14.95 (0-316-75345-9) Little.
Selsam, Millicent E. Egg to Chick. rev. ed. Wolff, Barbara, illus. LC 74-85034. 64p. (ps-3). 1970. PLB 13.89 (0-06-025290-1) HarpC Child Bks.
Turner, Dorothy. Eggs. Yates, John, illus. 32p. (gr. 1-4). 1989. PLB 14.95 (0-87614-360-5) Carolrhoda Bks.
Wood, A. J. Egg! A Dozen Eggs, What Will They Be? Unfold Each Page & You Will See! Stillwell, Stella, illus. LC 92-17930. 1993. 12.95 (0-316-81616-7) Little.

EGGS–FICTION
Aliki. The Eggs. Aliki, illus. 32p. (ps-3). 1994. pap. 5.95 (0-06-443385-4, Trophy) HarpC Child Bks.
Anderson, Sherwood. The Egg. LC 92-44057. 1994. 13.95 (0-88682-573-3) Creative Ed.
Auch, Mary J. The Easter Egg Farm. Auch, Mary J., illus. LC 91-15681. 32p. (ps-3). 1992. reinforced bdg. 15.95 (0-8234-0917-1) Holiday.
Barber, Antonia. Gemma & the Baby Chick. Littlewood, Karin, illus. 32p. (ps-3). 1993. 14.95 (0-590-45479-X) Scholastic Inc.
Bowring, Ian. Exploding Egg. (gr. 4-7). 1994. pap. 3.95 (0-207-17392-3, Pub. by Angus & Robertson AT) HarpC.
Brown, Margaret W. The Golden Egg Book. Wisegard, Leonard, illus. 32p. (ps-1). 1976. write for info. (0-307-12045-7, Golden Pr); PLB 9.15 (0-685-05367-9) Western Pub.
Butterworth, Oliver. The Enormous Egg. (gr. k-6). 1987. pap. 3.50 (0-440-42337-6, YB) Dell.
—Enormous Egg; You Won't Believe Your Eyes! (gr. 4-7). 1993. pap. 3.95 (0-316-11920-2) Little.
Demi. Demi's Dozen Good Eggs, 12 bks. (Illus.). (ps-2). 1993. Set, 12p. per bk. boxed 9.95 (0-8050-2552-9) H Holt & Co.

Ernst, Lisa C. Zinnia & Dot. (Illus.). 32p. (ps-3). 1992. 14.00 (*0-670-83091-7*) Viking Child Bks.

Harrell, Janice. The Great Egg Bust. Ashby, Ruth, ed. Montgomery, Lucy, illus. 112p. (Orig.). 1993. pap. 2.99 (*0-671-72861-X*, Minstrel Bks) PB.

Heine, Helme. The Most Wonderful Egg in the World. Heine, Helme, illus. LC 82-49350. 32p. (ps-3). 1983. SBE 14.95 (*0-689-50280-X*, M K McElderry) Macmillan Child Grp.

Jenkins. Nest Full of Eggs. 1995. 15.00 (*0-06-023441-5*); PLB 14.89 (*0-06-023442-3*) HarpC Child Bks.

Joyce, William. Bently & Egg. Joyce, William, illus. LC 91-55499. 32p. (ps-3). 1992. 15.00 (*0-06-020385-4*); PLB 14.89 (*0-06-020386-2*) HarpC Child Bks.

Kenah, Katharine. Eggs over Easy. Chambliss, Maxie, illus. 96p. (gr. 2-5). 1993. 13.99 (*0-525-45071-8*, DCB) Dutton Child Bks.

Kneen, Maggie, illus. The Great Egg Hunt. LC 93-27272. 1993. 13.95 (*0-8118-0552-2*) Chronicle Bks.

Levitin, Sonia. A Single Speckled Egg. Larrecq, John M., illus. LC 75-4189. 40p. (ps-3). 1976. 6.95 (*0-87466-074-2*, Pub. by Parnassus) HM.

McDonnell, Janet. Spring: New Life Everywhere. Hohag, Linda, illus. LC 93-10309. 32p. (gr. 2 up). 1993. PLB 12.30 (*0-516-00677-0*) Childrens.

Maxwell, Cassandre. Yosef's Gift of Many Colors: An Easter Story. Maxwell, Cassandre, illus. LC 92-44189. 32p. (ps-3). 1993. 14.99 (*0-8066-2627-5*, 9-2627) Augsburg Fortress.

Morgan, Michaela & Kemp, Moira. Helpful Betty Solves a Mystery. LC 93-39050. (gr. 3 up). 1994. 18.95 (*0-87614-832-1*) Carolrhoda Bks.

Nicklaus, Carol, illus. Eggs-O-Poppin' LC 91-68547. 48p. (Orig.). (ps up). 1993. pap. 2.50 (*0-679-83448-6*) Random Bks Yng Read.

Olson, Michelle. The Adventures of Eggbert Egghead. Van Treese, James B., ed. Ingram, tr. (Illus.). 1992. 9.95 (*1-880416-27-1*) NW Pub.

Peet, Bill. Pinkish, Purplish, Bluish Egg. (Illus.). (gr. k-3). 1984. 13.45 (*0-395-18472-X*); pap. 5.95 (*0-395-36172-9*) HM.

Polacco, Patricia. Chicken Sunday. Polacco, Patricia, illus. 32p. (ps-3). 1992. PLB 14.95 (*0-399-22133-6*, Philomel Bks) Putnam Pub Group.

Ross, Tom. Eggbert, the Slightly Cracked Egg. Barran, Rex, illus. 32p. (ps-3). 1994. 14.95 (*0-399-22416-5*) Putnam Pub Group.

San Souci, Robert D. The Talking Eggs. Pinkney, Jerry, illus. (ps-3). 1989. 15.00 (*0-8037-0619-7*) Dial Bks Young.

Schertle, Alice. Down the Road. Lewis, E. B., illus. LC 94-9901. 1995. write for info. (*0-15-276622-7*, Browndeer Pr) HarBrace.

Sherlock Chick & the Giant Egg Mystery. (Illus.). 42p. (ps-3). 1993. PLB 13.27 (*0-8368-0897-5*) Gareth Stevens Inc.

Smith, Janice L. The Baby Blues: An Adam Joshua Story. Gackenbach, Dick, illus. LC 93-14492. 96p. (gr. 1-4). 1994. 12.00 (*0-06-023642-6*, HarpT); PLB 11.89 (*0-06-023643-4*, HarpT) HarpC.

Stevenson, James. The Great Big Especially Beautiful Easter Egg. Stevenson, James, illus. LC 82-11731. 32p. (gr. k-3). 1983. 15.88 (*0-688-01789-4*); PLB 13.88 (*0-688-01791-6*) Greenwillow.

Vyner, Sue. The Stolen Egg. Vyner, Tim, illus. 32p. (ps-3). 1992. 14.00 (*0-670-84460-8*) Viking Child Bks.

EGYPT

Allen. Pharaohs & Pyramids. (gr. 4-9). 1977. (Usborne-Hayes); PLB 13.96 (*0-88110-103-6*); pap. 6.95 (*0-86020-084-1*) EDC.

Bennet, Olivia. A Family in Egypt. LC 84-19468. (Illus.). 32p. (gr. 2-5). 1985. PLB 13.50 (*0-8225-1652-7*) Lerner Pubns.

Browder, Atlantis T. & Browder, Anthony T. My First Trip to Africa. Browder, Anne, ed. Aaron, Malcolm, illus. LC 91-70328. 38p. (Orig.). 1991. 16.95 (*0-924944-02-1*); pap. 8.95 (*0-924944-01-3*) Inst Karmic.

Caselli, Giovanni. An Egyptian Craftsman. Caselli, Giovanni, illus. LC 85-30685. 32p. (gr. 3-6). 1991. lib. bdg. 12.95 (*0-87226-100-X*) P Bedrick Bks.

Cross, Wilbur. Egypt. LC 82-9465. (Illus.). (gr. 5-9). 1982. PLB 20.55 (*0-516-02762-X*) Childrens.

David, Rosalie. Growing up in Ancient Egypt. McBride, Angus, illus. LC 91-40264. 32p. (gr. 3-5). 1993. PLB 11.89 (*0-8167-2717-1*); pap. text ed. 3.95 (*0-8167-2718-X*) Troll Assocs.

Department of Geography, Lerner Publications. Egypt in Pictures. (Illus.). 64p. (gr. 5 up). 1988. PLB 17.50 (*0-8225-1840-6*) Lerner Pubns.

Diamond, Arthur. Egypt: Land of Mysteries. LC 91-43105. (Illus.). 128p. (gr. 4 up). 1992. text ed. 14.95 RSBE (*0-87518-511-8*, Dillon) Macmillan Child Grp.

Flint, David. Egypt. LC 93-10995. (Illus.). 32p. (gr. 3-4). 1993. PLB 19.24 (*0-8114-3420-6*) Raintree Steck-V.

Great Civilisations: Egypt. (ARA., Illus.). (gr. 5-12). 1987. 3.95x (*0-86685-253-0*) Intl Bk Ctr.

Harkonen, Reijo. The Children of Egypt. Pitkanen, Matti A., photos by. (Illus.). 40p. (gr. 3-6). 1991. PLB 19.95 (*0-87614-396-6*) Carolrhoda Bks.

Harrison, Steve & Harrison, Patricia. Egypt. (Illus.). 48p. (gr. 7-9). 1992. 13.95 (*0-563-34754-6*, BBC-Parkwest); pap. 6.95 (*0-563-34589-6*, BBC-Parkwest) Parkwest Pubns.

Jacobsen, Karen. Egypt. LC 89-25347. (Illus.). 48p. (gr. k-4). 1990. PLB 12.85 (*0-516-01184-7*); pap. 4.95 (*0-516-41184-5*) Childrens.

Manniche, Lise. The Ancient Egyptians. (Illus.). (gr. 2-6). pap. 3.95 (*0-7141-0941-X*, Pub. by Brit Mus UK) Parkwest Pubns.

Morrison, Ian A. Egypt. LC 91-7791. (Illus.). 96p. (gr. 6-12). 1991. PLB 22.80 (*0-8114-2445-6*) Raintree Steck-V.

Newman, Pamela, et al. Egyptian Peaks. (Illus.). 60p. (Orig.). (gr. 4-12). 1988. pap. 24.95 (*0-943804-66-3*) U of Denver Teach.

Odijk, Pamela. The Egyptians. (Illus.). 48p. (gr. 5-8). 1989. PLB 12.95 (*0-382-09886-2*) Silver Burdett Pr.

Parker, Lewis K. Dropping in on Egypt. LC 93-47098. 1994. write for info. (*1-55916-004-7*) Rourke Bk Co.

Pateman, Robert. Egypt. LC 92-10209. 1992. 21.95 (*1-85435-535-X*) Marshall Cavendish.

Zimmerman, Julie & Torumasu, Kimiaki. Wishing on Daruma. LC 91-76745. (Illus.). 112p. (Orig.). (gr. 5 up). 1992. pap. 9.95 (*1-879418-05-3*) Biddle Pub.

EGYPT–ANTIQUITIES

Bendick, Jeanne. Egyptians Tombs. LC 88-27918. (Illus.). 64p. (gr. 3-5). 1989. PLB 12.90 (*0-531-10462-1*) Watts.

Clare, John D., ed. Pyramids of Ancient Egypt. (gr. 4-7). 1992. 16.95 (*0-15-200509-9*, Gulliver Bks) HarBrace.

Clarke, Sue. The Tomb of the Pharaohs: A Three-Dimensional Discovery. (Illus.). 10p. 1994. 16.95 (*1-56282-485-6*) Hyprn Child.

Delany, Martin R. Origin of Races & Color: With an Archeological Compendium of Ethiopian & Egyptian Civilization. LC 90-82685. 100p. 1991. 19.95 (*0-933121-51-2*); pap. 8.95 (*0-933121-50-4*) Black Classic.

Gold, Susan D. The Pharaohs' Curse. LC 89-25424. (Illus.). 48p. (gr. 5-6). 1990. text ed. 11.95 RSBE (*0-89686-511-8*, Crestwood Hse) Macmillan Child Grp.

Harrast, Tracy & Craft, Louise. Discover Ancient Egypt: Activity Book. Girdler, Netta & Belcher, Cynthia, illus. 24p. (gr. 3-7). 1990. wkbk. 2.95 (*0-911239-28-6*) Carnegie Mus.

—Discover Ancient Egypt at the Carnegie. (Illus.). 24p. (gr. 3-7). 1990. wkbk. 2.95 (*0-911239-27-8*) Carnegie Mus.

Macaulay, David. Pyramid. Macaulay, David, illus. 80p. (gr. 7 up). 1975. 14.95 (*0-395-21407-6*) HM.

Morley, Jacqueline. An Egyptian Pyramid. Bergin, Mark & James, John, illus. 48p. (gr. 5 up). 1993. pap. 8.95 (*0-87226-255-3*) P Bedrick Bks.

Reeves, Nicholas. Into the Mummy's Tomb: The Real-Life Discovery of Tutankhamun's Treasures. 1992. 16.95 (*0-590-45752-7*, Scholastic Hardcover) Scholastic Inc.

Reiff, Stephanie A. Secrets of Tut's Tomb & the Pyramids. LC 77-22770. (Illus.). (gr. 4 up). 1983. PLB 20.70 (*0-8172-1051-2*) Raintree Steck-V.

Santrey, Laurence. Ancient Egypt. Frenck, Hal, illus. LC 84-2728. 32p. (gr. 3-6). 1985. PLB 9.49 (*0-8167-0248-9*); pap. text ed. 2.95 (*0-8167-0249-7*) Troll Assocs.

Smith, Tony, illus. The Great Pyramids & the Sphinx. 48p. (gr. 3-5). 1987. 7.95x (*0-86685-454-1*) Intl Bk Ctr.

Steele, Philip. The Egyptians & the Valley of the Kings. (Illus.). 32p. (gr. 4 up). 1994. text ed. 13.95 RSBE (*0-87518-539-8*, Dillon) Macmillan Child Grp.

Terzi, Marinella. The Land of the Pharaohs. LC 92-7510. (Illus.). 36p. (gr. 3 up). 1992. PLB 14.95 (*0-516-08378-3*) Childrens.

—Land of the Pharaohs. LC 92-7510. 36p. (gr. 3 up). 1993. pap. 6.95 (*0-516-48378-1*) Childrens.

EGYPT–CIVILIZATION

Coote, Roger. The Egyptians. LC 93-8466. (Illus.). 32p. (gr. 4-6). 1993. 14.95 (*1-56847-061-4*) Thomson Lrning.

Courtalon, Corinne. On the Banks of the Pharaoh's Nile. Broutin, Christian, illus. LC 87-37195. 38p. (gr. k-5). 1988. 5.95 (*0-944589-07-3*, 073) Young Discovery Lib.

Defrates, Joanna. What Do We Know about the Egyptians? LC 91-25175. (Illus.). 40p. (gr. 3-7). 1992. PLB 16.95 (*0-87226-353-3*) P Bedrick Bks.

Donnelly, Judy. Tut's Mummy: Lost & Found. Watling, James, illus. LC 87-20790. (Orig.). (gr. 2-3). 1988. lib. bdg. 7.99 (*0-394-99189-3*); pap. 3.50 (*0-394-89189-9*) Random Bks Yng Read.

Fleming, Stuart. The Egyptians. LC 91-41198. (Illus.). 64p. (gr. 6 up). 1992. text ed. 14.95 RSBE (*0-02-730654-2*, New Discovery) Macmillan Child Grp.

Ganeri, Anita. Ancient Egyptians. (Illus.). 32p. (gr. 5-7). 1993. PLB 12.40 (*0-531-17373-9*, Gloucester Pr) Watts.

Harris, Geraldine. Gods & Pharaohs from Egyptian Mythology. O'Connor, David & Sibbick, John, illus. LC 90-23455. 132p. (gr. 6 up). 1992. 22.50 (*0-87226-907-8*) P Bedrick Bks.

Hart, George. Ancient Egypt. Biesty, Stephen, illus. LC 88-30065. 64p. (gr. 3-7). 1989. 14.95 (*0-15-200449-1*) HarBrace.

Koenig, Viviane. The Ancient Egyptians: Life in the Nile Valley. LaRose, Mary K., tr. from FRE. Ageorges, Veronique, illus. LC 91-25772. 64p. (gr. 4-6). 1992. PLB 15.40 (*1-56294-161-5*) Millbrook Pr.

MacDonald, Fiona. Ancient Egyptians. (Illus.). 60p. (gr. 4 up). 1993. 15.95 (*0-8120-6378-3*) Barron.

Morley, Jacqueline. How Would You Survive As an Ancient Egyptian? James, John, illus. Salariya, David. LC 94-26157. (gr. 3-7). 1995. lib. bdg. write for info. (*0-531-14345-7*) Watts.

Pearson, Anne. Everyday Life in Ancient Egypt. LC 93-37520. 1994. write for info. (*0-531-14309-0*) Watts.

Steele, Philip. The Egyptians & the Valley of the Kings. (Illus.). 32p. (gr. 4 up). 1994. text ed. 13.95 RSBE (*0-87518-539-8*, Dillon) Macmillan Child Grp.

Terzi, Marinella. The Land of the Pharaohs. LC 92-7510. (Illus.). 36p. (gr. 3 up). 1992. PLB 14.95 (*0-516-08378-3*) Childrens.

—Land of the Pharaohs. LC 92-7510. 36p. (gr. 3 up). 1993. pap. 6.95 (*0-516-48378-1*) Childrens.

Wright, Rachel. Egyptians. LC 92-7840. (Illus.). 32p. (gr. 4-6). 1993. PLB 11.90 (*0-531-14209-4*) Watts.

EGYPT–FICTION

Adinolfi, JoAnn. The Egyptian Polar Bear. Adinolfi, JoAnn, illus. 1994. 14.95 (*0-395-68074-3*) HM.

Bradshaw, Gillian. The Dragon & the Thief. LC 90-48259. (Illus.). (gr. 5 up). 1991. 13.95 (*0-688-10575-0*) Greenwillow.

Carter, Dorothy S. His Majesty, Queen Hatshepsut. Chessare, Michele, illus. LC 85-45855. 256p. (gr. 5 up). 1987. (Lipp Jr Bks); PLB 13.89 (*0-397-32179-1*, Lipp Jr Bks) HarpC Child Bks.

Dexter, Catherine. The Gilded Cat. 208p. (gr. 4 up). 1992. 14.00 (*0-688-09425-2*) Morrow Jr Bks.

Ellerby, Leona. King Tut's Game Board. LC 79-91279. 120p. (gr. 4 up). 1980. 13.50 (*0-8225-0765-X*) Lerner Pubns.

Kalman, Maira. Hey Willy, See the Pyramids. (ps-3). 1988. pap. 14.95 (*0-670-82163-2*) Viking Child Bks.

Lattimore, Deborah N. The Winged Cat: A Tale of Ancient Egypt. Lattimore, Deborah N., illus. LC 90-38441. 40p. (gr. 2-5). 1992. 15.00 (*0-06-023635-3*); PLB 14.89 (*0-06-023636-1*) HarpC Child Bks.

Lepon, Shoshana. The Ten Plagues of Egypt. Goldstein-Alpern, Neva, ed. Forst, Siegmund, illus. 32p. (gr. k-4). 1988. 11.95 (*0-910818-77-0*); pap. 8.95 (*0-910818-76-2*) Judaica Pr.

Macaulay, David. Pyramid PA. Macaulay, David, illus. (gr. 5 up). 1982. pap. 7.70 (*0-395-32121-2*) HM.

McGraw, Eloise J. Mara, Daughter of the Nile. LC 85-567. 280p. (gr. 5-9). 1985. pap. 4.50 (*0-14-031929-8*, Puffin) Puffin Bks.

Smith, Parker. The Young Indiana Jones Chronicles: The Mummy's Curse. Mones, illus. 24p. (ps-3). 1992. pap. write for info. (*0-307-12689-7*, 12689, Golden Pr) Western Pub.

Snyder, Zilpha K. The Egypt Game. LC 67-2717. (gr. 4-6). 1986. pap. 4.50 (*0-440-42225-6*, YB) Dell.

Somper, J. Pyramid Plot. (Illus.). 48p. (gr. 3-8). 1993. PLB 11.96 (*0-88110-403-5*); pap. 4.95 (*0-7460-0506-7*) EDC.

Stine, Megan & Stine, H. William, eds. The Mummy's Curse. LC 91-53167. (Illus.). 136p. (Orig.). (gr. 4-8). 1992. PLB cancelled (*0-679-92774-3*); pap. 3.50 (*0-679-82774-9*) Random Bks Yng Read.

Walsh, Jill P. Pepi & the Secret Names. French, Fiona, illus. LC 93-48620. 1994. 15.00 (*0-688-13428-9*) Lothrop.

Wynne-Jones, Tim. Zoom Upstream. Beddows, Eric, illus. LC 93-22162. 32p. (ps-2). 1994. 15.00 (*0-06-022977-2*, HarpT); PLB 14.89 (*0-06-022978-0*, HarpT) HarpC.

EGYPT–HISTORY

Ancient Egypt. (Illus.). 50p. (gr. k-6). 1994. pap. 6.95 (*1-56458-560-3*) Dorling Kindersley.

Ancient Egypt-Coloring Book. 1985. pap. 3.95 (*0-88388-005-9*) Bellerophon Bks.

Balkwill, Richard. Food & Feasts in Ancient Egypt. LC 94-4706. 1994. text ed. 14.95 (*0-02-726323-1*, New Discovery Bks) Macmillan Child Grp.

Boyd, Anne. Ancient Egyptians. 1981. pap. 5.95 (*0-521-28233-0*) Cambridge U Pr.

Burland, Cottie A. Ancient Egypt. (Illus.). (gr. 4-8). 1974. Repr. of 1957 ed. 10.95 (*0-7175-0014-4*) Dufour.

Conway, Lorraine. Ancient Egypt. Akins, Linda, illus. 64p. (gr. 4-8). 1987. pap. 8.95 (*0-86653-399-0*, GA 1021) Good Apple.

Crosher, Judith. Ancient Egypt. (Illus.). 48p. (gr. 3-7). 1993. 14.99 (*0-670-84755-0*) Viking Child Bks.

Ganeri, Anita. Ancient Egyptians. (Illus.). 32p. (gr. 5-7). 1993. PLB 12.40 (*0-531-17373-9*, Gloucester Pr) Watts.

Giblin, James C. The Riddle of the Rosetta Stone: Key to Ancient Egypt. LC 89-29289. (Illus.). 96p. (gr. 3-7). 1990. 15.00 (*0-690-04797-5*, Crowell Jr Bks); PLB 14.89 (*0-690-04799-1*, Crowell Jr Bks) HarpC Child Bks.

Harper, et al. Flashpoints, 7 bks, Set I, Reading Level 8. (Illus.). 560p. (gr. 7 up). 1988. Set. PLB 130.20 (*0-86592-025-7*); 97.65s.p. (*0-685-58792-4*) Rourke Corp.

Harrast, Tracy & Craft, Louise. Discover Ancient Egypt at the Carnegie. (Illus.). 24p. (gr. 3-7). 1990. wkbk. 2.95 (*0-911239-27-8*) Carnegie Mus.

Harris, Geraldine. Ancient Egypt. (Illus.). 96p. 1990. 17.95 (*0-8160-1971-1*) Facts on File.

Hart, George. Ancient Egypt: Three Thousand Years of Mystery to Unlock & Discover. (Illus.). 64p. 1994. incl. kit 19.95 (*1-56138-462-3*) Running Pr.

Jenkins, Earnestine. A Glorious Past: Ancient Egypt, Ethiopia, & Nubia. LC 94-10713. 1994. write for info. (*0-7910-2258-7*); pap. write for info. (*0-7910-2684-1*) Chelsea Hse.

Kerr, James L. Egyptian Farmers. LC 90-35696. (Illus.). 24p. (gr. 2-5). 1991. PLB 10.90 (*0-531-18374-2*, Pub. by Bookwright Pr) Watts.

Lumpkin, Beatrice. Senefer: A Young Genius in Old Egypt. Nickens, Linda, illus. LC 92-71026. 32p. (gr. 2-5). 1992. 16.95 (*0-86543-244-9*); pap. 8.95 (*0-86543-245-7*) Africa World.

MacDonald, Fiona. Ancient Egyptians. (Illus.). 60p. (gr. 4 up). 1993. 15.95 (*0-8120-6378-3*) Barron.

Morley, Jacqueline. An Egyptian Pyramid: Inside Story. Bergin, Mark & James, John, illus. 48p. (gr. 5 up). 1991. 17.95 (*0-87226-346-0*) P Bedrick Bks.

Nicholson, Robert & Watts, Claire. El Antiguo Egipto: Hechos - Histoias - Actividades. Araluce, Jose R., tr. (SPA., Illus.). 32p. (gr. 6-10). 1993. 14.95x (*1-56492-094-1*) Laredo.

Payne, Elizabeth. The Pharaohs of Ancient Egypt. LC 80-21392. (Illus.). 192p. (gr. 5-9). 1981. 4.95 (*0-394-84699-0*) Knopf Bks Yng Read.

Pearson, Anne. Everyday Life in Ancient Egypt. LC 93-37520. 1994. write for info. (*0-531-14309-0*) Watts.

Sauvain, Philip. Over Three Thousand Years Ago: In Ancient Egypt. (Illus.). 32p. (gr. 6 up). 1993. text ed. 13.95 RSBE (*0-02-781084-4*, New Discovery) Macmillan Child Grp.

Stewart, Gail B. Egypt. LC 91-33485. (Illus.). 48p. (gr. 6-7). 1992. text ed. 4.95 RSBE (*0-89686-744-7*, Crestwood Hse) Macmillan Child Grp.

Woods, Geraldine. Science in Ancient Egypt. LC 87-23746. (Illus.). 96p. (gr. 5-8). 1988. PLB 10.90 (*0-531-10486-9*) Watts.

EGYPT–KINGS AND RULERS

AESOP Enterprises, Inc. Staff & Crenshaw, Gwendolyn J. Akhenaton: Torchbearer of Light. 14p. (gr. 3-12). 1991. pap. write for info. incl. cassette (*1-880771-12-8*) AESOP Enter.

—Imhotep: Developing Your Talents. 14p. (gr. 3-12). 1991. pap. write for info. incl. cassette (*1-880771-07-1*) AESOP Enter.

—Queen Hatshepsut: Glorifying the Past for the Present & Future. 14p. (gr. 3-12). 1991. pap. write for info. incl. cassette (*1-880771-11-X*) AESOP Enter.

Diamond, Arthur. Anwar Sadat. LC 93-17096. (gr. 5-8). 1994. 14.95 (*1-56006-020-4*) Lucent Bks.

Payne, Elizabeth. The Pharaohs of Ancient Egypt. LC 80-21392. (Illus.). 192p. (gr. 5-9). 1981. 4.95 (*0-394-84699-0*) Knopf Bks Yng Read.

Sullivan, George. Sadat: The Man Who Changed Mid-East History. LC 81-50739. (Illus.). 99p. (gr. 6 up). 1981. reinforced bdg 9.85 (*0-8027-6435-5*) Walker & Co.

EGYPTOLOGY

see Egypt–Antiquities

EIGHTEENTH CENTURY

Ruby, Jennifer. The Eighteenth Century. (gr. 7 up). 1989. 24.95 (*0-7134-5772-4*, Pub. by Batsford UK) Trafalgar.

EINSTEIN, ALBERT, 1879-1955

AESOP Enterprises, Inc. Staff & Crenshaw, Gwendolyn J. Albert Einstein: Physicist & Peace Seeker. 12p. (gr. 3-12). 1991. pap. write for info. incl. cassette (*1-880771-10-1*) AESOP Enter.

Cwiklik, Robert. Albert Einstein. (Illus.). 144p. (gr. 3-6). 1987. pap. 5.95 (*0-8120-3921-1*) Barron.

Einstein, Albert. Albert Einstein. Redpath, Ann, ed. Delessert, Etienne, illus. 32p. (gr. 9 up). 1986. PLB 12.95 (*0-88682-011-1*) Creative Ed.

Farr, Naunerle. Madame Curie - Albert Einstein. Leonidez, Nestor & Redondo, Nestor, illus. (gr. 4-12). 1979. pap. text ed. 2.95 (*0-88301-356-8*); wkbk. 1.25 (*0-88301-380-0*) Pendulum Pr.

Goldenstern, Joyce. Albert Einstein: Physicist & Genius. LC 94-860. (Illus.). 128p. (gr. 4-10). 1994. lib. bdg. 17. 95 (*0-89490-480-9*) Enslow Pubs.

Hammontree, Marie. Albert Einstein: Young Thinker. Doremus, Robert, illus. LC 86-10730. 192p. (gr. 2-6). 1986. pap. 3.95 (*0-02-041860-4*, Aladdin) Macmillan Child Grp.

Ireland, Karin. Albert Einstein. (Illus.). 144p. (gr. 5-9). 1989. PLB 10.95 (*0-382-09523-5*) Silver Burdett Pr.

Lafferty, Peter. Albert Einstein. LC 91-15774. (Illus.). 48p. (gr. 5-7). 1992. PLB 12.40 (*0-531-18458-7*, Pub. by Bookwright Pr) Watts.

Lepscky, Ibi. Albert Einstein. Cardoni, Paolo, illus. 24p. (gr. k-3). 1992. pap. 4.95 (*0-8120-1452-9*) Barron.

Reef, Catherine. Albert Einstein. LC 91-7560. (Illus.). 64p. (gr. 3 up). 1991. text ed. 13.95 RSBE (*0-87518-462-6*, Dillon) Macmillan Child Grp.

Santrey, Laurence. Young Albert Einstein. Beier, Ellen, illus. LC 89-33940. 48p. (gr. 4-6). 1990. PLB 10.79 (*0-8167-1777-X*); pap. text ed. 3.50 (*0-8167-1778-8*) Troll Assocs.

Smith, Kathie B. Albert Einstein. Steltenpohl, Jane, ed. Seward, James, illus. 24p. (gr. 4-6). 1989. lib. bdg. 7.98 (*0-671-67514-1*, J Messner); PLB 5.99s.p. (*0-685-25426-7*) S&S Trade.

Smith, Kathie B. & Bradbury, Pamela Z. Albert Einstein. (Illus.). 24p. (ps up). 1989. pap. 2.25 (*0-671-64767-9*, Little Simon) S&S Trade.

Swisher, Clarice. Albert Einstein. LC 93-17280. (gr. 5-8). 1994. 14.95 (*1-56006-042-5*) Lucent Bks.

EISENHOWER, DWIGHT DAVID, PRESIDENT U. S. 1890-1969

Cannon, Marian G. Dwight David Eisenhower: War Hero & President. LC 89-24791. (gr. 4-7). 1990. PLB 14.40 (*0-531-10915-1*) Watts.

Darby, Jean. Dwight D. Eisenhower. (Illus.). 112p. (gr. 5 up). 1989. 21.50 (*0-8225-4900-X*) Lerner Pubns.

Deitch, Kenneth M. & Weisman, JoAnne B. Dwight D. Eisenhower: Man of Many Hats; With a Message from John S. D. Eisenhower. Connolly, Jay, illus. Eisenhower, John S., intro. by. LC 90-82588. (Illus.). 48p. (gr. 5-12). 1990. PLB 14.95 (*1-878668-02-1*) Disc Enter Ltd.

Dwight David Eisenhower: President. 128p. (gr. 5 up). 1987. 12.95 (*0-8027-6670-6*); PLB 13.85 (*0-8027-6671-4*) Walker & Co.

Ellis, Rafaela. Dwight D. Eisenhower: Thirty-Fourth President of the United States. Young, Richard G., ed. LC 88-24538. (Illus.). (gr. 5-9). 1989. PLB 17.26 (*0-944483-13-5*) Garrett Ed Corp.

Hargrove, Jim. Dwight D. Eisenhower. LC 86-29918. (Illus.). 100p. (gr. 3 up). 1987. PLB 14.40 (*0-516-01389-0*) Childrens.

Hudson, Wilma J. Dwight D. Eisenhower: Young Military Leader. LC 92-8377. (Illus.). 192p. (gr. 3-7). 1992. pap. 3.95 (*0-689-71656-7*, Aladdin) Macmillan Child Grp.

Sandak, Cass R. The Eisenhowers. (Illus.). 48p. (gr. 5). 1993. text ed. 12.95 RSBE (*0-89686-653-X*, Crestwood Hse) Macmillan Child Grp.

Sandberg, Peter L. Dwight D. Eisenhower. Schlesinger, Arthur M., Jr., intro. by. (Illus.). 112p. (gr. 5 up). 1986. lib. bdg. 16.95 (*0-87754-521-9*); pap. 9.95 (*0-7910-0566-6*) Chelsea Hse.

EL ALAMEIN, BATTLE OF, 1942

Sauvain, Philip. El Alamein. LC 91-28378. (Illus.). 32p. (gr. 6 up). 1992. text ed. 13.95 RSBE (*0-02-781081-X*, New Discovery) Macmillan Child Grp.

EL SALVADOR

see Salvador

ELECTIONEERING

see Politics, Practical

ELECTIONS

see also Presidents–U. S.–Election

Ballots & Bandwagons Series, 3 vols. (gr. 5 up). 1991. Set, 128p. ea. lib. bdg. 32.85 (*0-382-24313-7*); Set, 128p. ea. pap. 23.85 (*0-382-24318-8*) Silver Burdett Pr.

Bernards, Neal. Elections: Locating the Author's Main Idea. LC 92-21793. (Illus.). 32p. (gr. 4-7). 1992. PLB 10.95 (*1-56510-022-0*) Greenhaven.

Dunnahoo, Terry. How to Win a School Election. Rosenbloom, Richard, illus. LC 88-30341. 96p. (gr. 7-12). 1990. 12.90 (*0-531-10695-0*) Watts.

Fradin, Dennis B. Voting & Elections. LC 85-7715. (Illus.). 45p. (gr. k-4). 1985. PLB 12.85 (*0-516-01274-6*); pap. 4.95 (*0-516-41274-4*) Childrens.

Greenberg, Judith & Carey, Helen. Election Special. (gr. 7-12). 1988. Set incl. 10 texts & 1 tchr's. guide (updated annually) pap. text ed. 24.95 (*0-941342-18-2*) Entry Pub.

Rayburn, Richard. Elections. Buhler, Cheryl, et al, illus. 96p. (Orig.). (gr. 4-8). 1992. wkbk. 10.95 (*1-55734-069-2*) Tchr Create Mat.

Scher, Linda. The Vote: Making Your Voice Heard. LC 92-14474. (Illus.). 48p. (gr. 5-6). 1992. PLB 21.34 (*0-8114-7357-0*) Raintree Steck-V.

Strasheim, Lorraine A. Oro Vos Faciatis... an Election Unit. 7p. (gr. 9-12). 1991. spiral bdg. 1.00 (*0-939507-32-3*, B11) Amer Classical.

Sullivan, George. Campaigns & Elections. (Illus.). 128p. (gr. 5 up). 1991. PLB 10.95 (*0-382-24315-3*); pap. 7.95 (*0-382-24321-8*) Silver Burdett Pr.

—Choosing the Candidates. (Illus.). 128p. (gr. 5 up). 1991. PLB 10.95 (*0-382-24314-5*); pap. 7.95 (*0-382-24319-6*) Silver Burdett Pr.

ELECTIONS–FICTION

Hughes, Dean. Nutty for President. 128p. 1986. pap. 2.50 (*0-553-15376-5*, Skylark) Bantam.

Mills, Claudia. Dinah for President. LC 93-44668. (gr. 3-7). 1994. pap. 3.95 (*0-689-71854-3*, Aladdin) Macmillan Child Grp.

ELECTORAL COLLEGE

see Presidents–U. S.–Election

ELECTRIC APPLIANCES

see Electric Apparatus and Appliances

ELECTRIC APPARATUS AND APPLIANCES

see also Electric Batteries

Asimov, Isaac. How Did We Find Out about Microwaves? Kors, Erika, illus. 64p. (gr. 1-4). 1989. 11.95 (*0-8027-6837-7*); PLB 12.85 (*0-8027-6838-5*) Walker & Co.

Wilkins, Mary-Jane. Everyday Things & How They Work. Bull, Peter, illus. LC 90-12999. 40p. (gr. 4-6). 1991. PLB 12.40 (*0-531-19109-5*, Warwick) Watts.

ELECTRIC BATTERIES

Challoner, Jack. My First Batteries & Magnets. LC 92-52825. (Illus.). 48p. (gr. k-4). 1992. 12.95 (*1-56458-133-0*) Dorling Kindersley.

ELECTRIC ENGINEERING

see also Electric Apparatus and Appliances; Radio; Telephone

ELECTRIC POWER

Berger, Melvin. Switch On, Switch Off. Croll, Carolyn, illus. LC 88-17638. 32p. (gr. k-3). 1989. (Crowell Jr Bks); PLB 14.89 (*0-690-04786-X*, Crowell Jr. Bks) HarpC Child Bks.

ELECTRIC WIRING

see also Telephone

ELECTRICAL

see headings beginning with the word Electric

ELECTRICITY

see also Lightning; Magnetism; Radioactivity; Telephone; X Rays

Amery, H. & Littler, A. Batteries & Magnets. (Illus.). 32p. (gr. 3-6). 1977. pap. 6.95 (*0-86020-008-6*) EDC.

Ardley, Neil. Electricity. LC 91-4963. (Illus.). 48p. (gr. 8-9). 1992. text ed. 13.95 RSBE (*0-02-705665-1*, New Discovery) Macmillan Child Grp.

—Science Book of Electricity. 29p. (gr. 2-5). 1991. 9.95 (*0-15-200583-8*, HB Juv Bks) HarBrace.

Asimov, Isaac. How Did We Find Out About Electricity? Selsam, Millicent E., ed. Kalmenoff, Matthew, illus. LC 72-81380. 64p. (gr. 5-8). 1973. PLB 10.85 (*0-8027-6124-0*) Walker & Co.

Bailey, Mark W. Electricity. rev. ed. LC 87-20796. (Illus.). 48p. (gr. 2-6). 1988. PLB 10.95 (*0-8172-3253-2*); pap. 4.50 (*0-8114-8218-9*) Raintree Steck-V.

Bains, Rae. Discovering Electricity. Snyder, Joel, illus. LC 81-3339. 32p. (gr. 2-4). 1982. PLB 11.59 (*0-89375-564-8*); pap. text ed. 2.95 (*0-89375-565-6*) Troll Assocs.

Baker, Wendy & Haslam, Andrew. Electricity: A Creative Hands-on Approach to Science. LC 92-24566. (Illus.). 48p. (gr. 2-5). 1993. pap. 12.95 POB (*0-689-71663-X*, Aladdin) Macmillan Child Grp.

Berger, Melvin. Switch On, Switch Off. Croll, Carolyn, illus. LC 88-17638. 32p. (gr. k-3). 1989. (Crowell Jr Bks); PLB 14.89 (*0-690-04786-X*, Crowell Jr. Bks) HarpC Child Bks.

—Switch on, Switch Off. Croll, Carolyn, illus. LC 88-17638. 32p. (gr. k-3). 1990. pap. 4.95 (*0-06-445097-X*, Trophy) HarpC Child Bks.

Bortz, Alfred B. Superstuff! Materials That Have Changed Our Lives. LC 90-12565. (Illus.). 128p. (gr. 9-12). 1990. PLB 13.40 (*0-531-10887-2*) Watts.

Boy Scouts of America Staff. Electricity. (Illus.). 56p. (gr. 6-12). 1991. pap. 1.85 (*0-8395-3236-9*, 33236) BSA.

Brandt, Keith. Electricity. Harriton, Chuck, illus. LC 84-2705. 32p. (gr. 3-6). 1985. PLB 9.49 (*0-8167-0198-9*); pap. text ed. 2.95 (*0-8167-0199-7*) Troll Assocs.

Brill, Ethel C. Copper Country Adventure. LC 87-31485. 213p. (gr. 4 up). 1988. 8.50 (*0-933249-05-5*) Mid-Peninsula Lib.

Buban, Peter, Sr. & Schmitt, Marshall L. Understanding Electricity & Electronics. 3rd ed. 1974. text ed. 28.32 (*0-07-008675-3*, W) McGraw.

Cast, C. Vance. Where Does Electricity Come From? Wilkinson, Sue, illus. 40p. (ps-2). 1992. pap. 5.95 (*0-8120-4835-0*) Barron.

Challand, Helen. Experiments with Electricity. LC 85-30887. (Illus.). 48p. (gr. k-4). 1986. PLB 12.85 (*0-516-01276-2*); pap. 4.95 (*0-516-41276-0*) Childrens.

Chapman, Phil. Electricity. (gr. 5-9). 1976. (Usborne-Hayes); PLB 13.96 (*0-88110-006-4*); pap. 6.95 (*0-86020-078-7*) EDC.

Clemence, John. Electricity. Young, Richard, ed. LC 91-20534. (Illus.). 32p. (gr. 3-5). 1991. PLB 15.93 (*1-56074-008-6*) Garrett Ed Corp.

Cosner, Shaaron. The Light Bulb: Inventions That Changed Our Lives. LC 83-40398. 64p. (gr. 5 up). 1984. PLB 10.85 (*0-8027-6527-0*) Walker & Co.

Davis, Kay & Oldsfield, Wendy. Electricity & Magnetism. LC 91-30069. (Illus.). 32p. (gr. 2-5). 1991. PLB 19.97 (*0-8114-3004-9*); pap. 4.95 (*0-8114-1532-5*) Raintree Steck-V.

Dolan, Edward F. Electricity. (gr. 4 up). 1995. PLB write for info. (*0-8050-2862-5*) H Holt & Co.

Dunn, Andrew. It's Electric. LC 93-7520. (Illus.). 32p. (gr. 3-6). 1993. 13.95 (*1-56847-019-3*) Thomson Lrning.

Electricity. (gr. 7-12). 1990. pap. 15.70 (*0-941008-89-4*) Tops Learning.

Gardner, Robert. Electricity. LC 92-34075. (gr. 4 up). 1993. lib. bdg. 14.98 (*0-671-69039-6*, J Messner); pap. 9.95 (*0-671-69044-2*, J Messner) S&S Trade.

—Electricity & Magnetism. (Illus.). 96p. (gr. 5-8). 1994. bds. 16.95 (*0-8050-2850-1*) TFC Bks NY.

—Science Projects about Electricity & Magnets. LC 93-45252. (Illus.). 128p. (gr. 6 up). 1994. lib. bdg. 17.95 (*0-89490-530-9*) Enslow Pubs.

Glover, David. Batteries, Bulbs & Wires. LC 92-40215. 32p. (gr. 1-4). 1993. 10.95 (*1-85697-837-0*, Kingfisher LKC); pap. 5.95 (*1-85697-933-4*) LKC.

Heese. Jugendhandbuch Naturwissen, Vol. 5: Energie. (GER.). 128p. 1976. pap. 5.95 (*0-7859-0413-1*, M7490) Fr & Eur.

—Jugendhandbuch Naturwissen, Vol. 6: Elektrizitaet und Elektronic. (GER.). 144p. 1976. pap. 5.95 (*0-7859-0414-X*, M7491) Fr & Eur.

Henderson, Harry. Electricity. (Illus.). (gr. 5-8). Date not set. 15.95 (*1-56006-252-5*) Lucent Bks.

Hooper, Tony. Electricity. LC 93-17023. (Illus.). 48p. (gr. 5-8). 1993. PLB 22.80 (*0-8114-2334-4*) Raintree Steck-V.

Jennings, Terry. Electricity & Magnetism. LC 88-36215. (Illus.). 32p. (gr. 3-6). 1989. pap. 4.95 (*0-516-48437-0*) Childrens.

Johnston, Tom. Electricity Turns the World On! Pooley, Sarah, illus. LC 87-42655. 32p. (gr. 4-6). 1987. PLB 17.27 (*1-55532-410-X*) Gareth Stevens Inc.

Kerrod, Robin. Electricity & Magnetism. Evans, Ted, illus. LC 93-46013. 1994. 16.95 (*1-85435-626-7*) Marshall Cavendish.

Mackie, Dan. Electricity. Goshorn, Bill, ed. Bastien, Charles, illus. 32p. (gr. 4). 1986. PLB 14.65 (*0-88625-133-8*); pap. 5.95 (*0-685-30764-6*) Durkin Hayes Pub.

Magnets, Bulbs, Batteries. (ARA., Illus.). (gr. 5-12). 1987. 3.95x (*0-86685-206-9*) Intl Bk Ctr.

Markle, Sandra. Weather, Electricity, Environmental Investigations. 112p. (gr. 4-6). 1982. 9.95 (*0-88160-082-2*, LW 902) Learning Wks.

Math, Irwin. More Wires & Watts: Understanding & Using Electricity. Keith, Hal, illus. LC 88-15767. 96p. (gr. 7 up). 1988. SBE 14.95 (*0-684-18914-3*, Scribners Young Read) Macmillan Child Grp.

—Wires & Watts: Understanding & Using Electricity. Keith, Hal, illus. LC 88-15767. 96p. (gr. 7 up). 1981. RSBE 15.95 (*0-684-16854-5*, Scribners Young Read) Macmillan Child Grp.

—Wires & Watts: Using & Understanding Electricity. Math, Irwin, illus. LC 81-2255. 96p. (gr. 7 up). 1989. pap. 4.95 (*0-689-71298-7*, Aladdin) Macmillan Child Grp.

Mayes, S. Where Does Electricity Come From? (Illus.). 24p. (gr. 1-4). 1989. (Usborne); pap. 3.95 (*0-7460-0358-7*, Usborne) EDC.

Neal, Philip. Energy, Power Sources & Electricity. (Illus.). 48p. (gr. 6-9). 1989. 19.95 (*0-85219-776-4*, Pub. by Batsford UK) Trafalgar.

Parker, Steve. Thomas Edison & Electricity. LC 92-6805. (Illus.). 32p. (gr. 3-7). 1992. 14.00 (*0-06-020859-7*); PLB 13.89 (*0-06-021473-2*) HarpC Child Bks.

—Thomas Edison & Electricity. Parker, Steve, illus. LC 92-6805. 32p. (gr. 3-7). 1992. pap. 5.95 (*0-06-446144-0*, Trophy) HarpC Child Bks.

Peacock, Graham. Electricity. LC 93-3347. 32p. (gr. 3-6). 1993. 13.95 (*1-56847-048-7*) Thomson Lrning.

—Electricity. LC 93-33258. (Illus.). 32p. (gr. 2-4). 1994. 14.95 (*1-56847-078-9*) Thomson Lrning.

Pomeroy, Johanna P. Content Area Reading Skills Electricity & Magnetism. (Illus.). (gr. 4). 1987. pap. text ed. 3.25 (*0-89525-859-5*) Ed Activities.

Reuben, Gabriel. Electricity Experiments for Children. (Illus.). 88p. (gr. 5-9). pap. 2.95 (*0-486-22030-3*) Dover.

Robson, Pam. Electricity. LC 92-37099. (Illus.). 32p. (gr. 5-8). 1993. PLB 12.40 (*0-531-17398-4*, Gloucester Pr) Watts.

Snedden, Robert. The History of Electricity. LC 93-33258. (Illus.). 48p. (gr. 6-9). 1995. 15.95 (*1-56847-250-1*) Thomson Lrning.

Sneider, Cary I., et al. The Magic of Electricity. Bergman, Lincoln & Fairwell, Kay, eds. Sneider, Cary I. & Baker, Lisa H., illus. Sneider, Cary I., photos by. 50p. (Orig.). (gr. 3-6). 1985. pap. 15.00 (*0-912511-52-4*) Lawrence Science.

Stwertka, Albert. Superconductors: The Irresistible Future. LC 90-19309. (Illus.). 96p. (gr. 7-9). 1991. PLB 12.90 (*0-531-12526-2*) Watts.

Taylor, Barbara. Batteries & Magnets. LC 91-2558. (Illus.). 40p. (gr. k-4). 1991. PLB 12.90 (*0-531-19130-3*, Warwick) Watts.

—Electricity & Magnets. LC 90-31021. (Illus.). 32p. (gr. 5-8). 1990. PLB 12.40 (*0-531-14083-0*) Watts.

—More Power to You! The Science of Batteries & Magnets. Bull, Peter, et al, illus. LC 91-4293. 40p. (Orig.). (gr. 2-5). 1992. pap. 4.95 (*0-679-82040-X*) Random Bks Yng Read.

VanCleave, Janice. Janice VanCleave's Electricity: Mind-Boggling Experiments You Can Turn into Science Fair Projects. LC 93-40913. 1994. pap. text ed. 9.95 (*0-471-31010-7*) Wiley.

Ward, Alan. Experimenting with Batteries, Bulbs, & Wires. Flax, Zena, illus. 48p. (gr. 2-7). 1991. lib. bdg. 12.95 (*0-7910-1516-5*) Chelsea Hse.

Whalley, Margaret. Experiment with Magnets & Electricity. LC 92-41109. 1993. 17.50 (*0-8225-2457-0*) Lerner Pubns.

Williams, John. Simple Science Projects with Electricity. LC 91-50545. (Illus.). 32p. (gr. 2-4). 1992. PLB 17.27 (*0-8368-0767-7*) Gareth Stevens Inc.

Wong, Ovid K. Experimenting with Electricity & Magnetism. LC 92-37672. (gr. 7-12). 1993. 13.40 (*0-531-12547-5*) Watts.

—Experimenting with Electricity & Magnetism. (Illus.). 128p. (gr. 7-12). 1993. pap. 6.95 (*0-531-15681-8*) Watts.

Zubrowski, Bernie. Blinkers & Buzzers: Building & Experimenting with Electricity & Magnetism. Doty, Roy, illus. LC 90-44519. 112p. (gr. 3 up). 1991. pap. 6.95 (*0-688-09965-3*, Pub. by Beech Tree Bks) Morrow.

—Blinkers & Buzzers: Building & Experimenting with Electricity & Magnetism. Doty, Roy, illus. LC 90-44519. 112p. (gr. 3 up). 1991. PLB 12.88 (*0-688-09966-1*) Morrow Jr Bks.

ELECTRICITY–FICTION

Sanchez, Jesus A. Max Science & the Burned Out Bulb. Sanchez, Brenda L., ed. Sanchez, Jesus A., illus. 24p. (gr. k-5). 1990. pap. 3.95 (*1-879350-00-9*) Max Sci Pub.

Wheeler, Bernelda. The Bannock. Bekkering, Herman, illus. LC 92-34255. 1993. 4.25 (*0-383-03617-8*) SRA Schl Grp.

ELECTROCHEMISTRY

see also Electric Batteries

ELECTROMAGNETISM

Parramon Staff. Electromagnets in Action. (Illus.). 48p. (gr. 5 up). 1994. 12.95 (*0-8120-6437-2*) Barron.

ELECTRONIC COMPUTERS

see Computers

ELECTRONIC DATA PROCESSING

Zink, Richard M. Computer Jobs Worldwide: The Employment Manual. (Illus.). 50p. (Orig.). (gr. 9 up). 1993. pap. text ed. 14.95x (*0-939469-32-4*) Zinks Career Guide.

ELECTRONIC SPREADSHEETS

Luehrmann, Arthur & Peckham, Herbert. Appleworks Spreadsheets: A Hands-On Guide. (Illus.). 160p. (Orig.). (gr. 7-12). 1987. pap. text ed. 11.95 (*0-941681-05-X*); tchr's. set 24.95 (*0-941681-12-2*); tchr's. guide 14.95 (*0-685-67549-1*); 5.25 inch disk 19.95 (*0-685-67550-5*) Computer Lit Pr.

—Hands-on Appleworks: A Guide to Word Processing, Data Bases & Spreadsheets, 3 bks. LC 87-836. (Illus.). 478p. (Orig.). (gr. 7-12). 1987. Set. pap. text ed. 21.95 (*0-941681-07-6*); Set. tchr's. ed. 34.95 (*0-941681-13-0*); tchr's. guide 14.95 (*0-685-58103-9*); 5.25 inch disk 19.95 (*0-685-67553-X*) Computer Lit Pr.

MaranGraphics Development Group Staff. MaranGraphics Learn at First Sight Lotus 1-2-3 for Windows Release 4. LC 93-34098. 1994. write for info. (*0-13-458233-0*) P-H.

ELECTRONICS

see also Microelectronics; Transistors

Beasant, Pam & Findly, Ian. Electronics. Newton, Martin & Andrews, Jane, illus. 48p. (gr. 5-8). 1985. (Pub. by Usborne); pap. 6.95 (*0-86020-809-5*) EDC.

The Boy Mechanic, Bk. 1. 470p. (gr. 5 up). 29.95 (*0-917914-89-9*); pap. 17.95 (*0-917914-88-0*) Lindsay Pubns.

Boy Scouts of America. Electronics. (Illus.). 72p. (gr. 6-12). 1977. pap. 1.85 (*0-8395-3279-2*, 33279) BSA.

Buban, Peter, Sr. & Schmitt, Marshall L. Understanding Electricity & Electronics. 3rd ed. 1974. text ed. 28.32 (*0-07-008675-3*, W) McGraw.

Heese. Jugendhandbuch Naturwissen, Vol. 6: Elektrizitaet und Elektronic. (GER.). 144p. 1976. pap. 5.95 (*0-7859-0414-X*, M7491) Fr & Eur.

How Things Work. 88p. (ps-3). 1989. 15.93 (*0-8094-4873-4*); lib. bdg. 21.27 (*0-8094-4874-2*) Time-Life.

Jugendhandbuch Naturwissen: Bausteine des Lebens, 6 vols, Vol. 1. (GER.). 144p. pap. 750.00 (*3-499-16203-2*, M-7486, Pub. by Rowohlt) Fr & Eur.

Leon, George D. Electronics Projects for Young Scientists. LC 91-17823. (Illus.). 128p. (gr. 9-12). 1991. PLB 13.90 (*0-531-11071-0*) Watts.

McPherson, J. G. Fun with Electronics. 64p. (gr. 3-6). 1983. pap. 4.95 (*0-86020-525-8*); lib. bdg. 11.96 (*0-88110-160-5*) EDC.

ELECTRONICS–VOCATIONAL GUIDANCE

Groneman, Chris H. & Feirer, John L. Getting Started in Electricity & Electronics. LC 78-19120. (Illus.). (gr. 7-9). 1979. text ed. 9.52 (*0-07-024999-7*) McGraw.

ELEMENTARY EDUCATION

see Education, Elementary

ELEMENTS, CHEMICAL

see Chemical Elements

ELEPHANTS

Aliki. Wild & Woolly Mammoths. LC 76-18082. (Illus.). 40p. (ps-3). 1983. pap. 4.50 (*0-06-445005-8*, Trophy) HarpC Child Bks.

Arnold, Caroline. Elephant. Hewett, Richard, photos by. LC 92-31095. (Illus.). 48p. (gr. 2 up). 1993. 15.00 (*0-688-11342-7*); PLB 14.93 (*0-688-11343-5*) Morrow Jr Bks.

Barkhausen, Annette & Geiser, Franz. Elephants. LC 93-13049. (gr. 3 up). 1994. 18.60 (*0-8368-1001-5*) Gareth Stevens Inc.

Barrett, Norman S. Elephants. FS Staff, ed. LC 87-50848. (Illus.). 32p. (gr. 1-6). 1988. PLB 11.90 (*0-531-10528-8*) Watts.

Blakeman, Sarah. Elephant. Field, James, illus. LC 91-44728. 32p. (gr. 4-6). 1993. PLB 11.59 (*0-8167-2769-4*); pap. text ed. 3.95 (*0-8167-2770-8*) Troll Assocs.

Blumberg, Rhoda. Jumbo. Hunt, Jonathan, illus. LC 91-34789. 48p. (gr. k-5). 1992. RSBE 15.95 (*0-02-711683-2*, Bradbury Pr) Macmillan Child Grp.

Bowden, Joan. A World Without Elephants. Cremins, Bob, illus. Moseley, Keith, contrib. by. LC 92-18889. (Illus.). (ps-3). 1993. 7.99 (*0-8037-1382-7*) Dial Bks Young.

Bright, Michael. Elephants. (gr. 4-6). 1990. PLB 12.40 (*0-531-17215-5*, Gloucester Pr) Watts.

Brody, Jean. Elephants. Leon, Vicki, ed. LC 93-12668. (Illus.). 48p. (Orig.). (gr. 5 up). 1993. pap. 9.95 perfect bdg. (*0-918303-32-X*) Blake Pub.

Cartlidge, Michelle. Elephant in the Jungle. Cartlidge, Michelle, illus. 12p. (ps). 1991. bds. 3.50 (*0-525-44676-1*, DCB) Dutton Child Bks.

Denis-Huot, Christine & Denis-Huot, Michel. The Elephant. (Illus.). 28p. (gr. 3-8). 1992. pap. 6.95 (*0-88106-427-0*) Charlesbridge Pub.

Dorros, Arthur. Elephant Families. Dorros, Arthur, illus. LC 92-38972. 32p. (gr. k-4). 1994. 15.00 (*0-06-022948-9*); PLB 14.89 (*0-06-022949-7*) HarpC Child Bks.

Elephant. 1989. 3.50 (*1-87865-728-3*) Blue Q.

Goodall, Jane. Jane Goodall's Animal World: Elephants. LC 89-78128. (Illus.). 32p. (gr. 3-7). 1990. pap. 3.95 (*0-689-71395-9*, Aladdin) Macmillan Child Grp.

Green, Carl R. & Sanford, William R. Asiatic Elephant. LC 87-20200. (Illus.). 48p. (gr. 5). 1987. text ed. 12.95 RSBE (*0-89686-333-6*, Crestwood Hse) Macmillan Child Grp.

Harrison, Virginia. The World of Elephants. Oxford Scientific Films Staff, photos by. LC 89-11547. (Illus.). 32p. (gr. 2-3). 1989. PLB 17.27 (*0-8368-0141-5*) Gareth Stevens Inc.

Highlights for Children Editors. Elephants. (Illus.). 32p. (gr. 2-5). 1994. pap. 3.95 (*1-56397-289-1*) Boyds Mills Pr.

Hoffman, Mary. Elephant. LC 84-15119. (Illus.). 24p. (gr. k-5). 1985. PLB 9.95 (*0-8172-2408-4*); pap. 3.95 (*0-8114-6874-7*) Raintree Steck-V.

Hogan, Paula Z. The Elephant. Craft, Kinuko Y., illus. LC 79-13307. (gr. 1-4). 1979. PLB 29.28 incl. cassette (*0-8172-1844-0*); PLB 19.97 (*0-8172-1505-0*); pap. 4.95 (*0-8114-8177-8*); pap. 9.95 incl. cassette (*0-8114-8185-9*) Raintree Steck-V.

Kim, Melissa. The African Elephant. Strugnell, Ann, illus. LC 94-10159. 32p. (gr. 1-5). 1994. lib. bdg. 12.00 (*1-57102-025-X*, Ideals Child); pap. 5.95 (*1-57102-009-8*, Ideals Child) Hambleton-Hill.

McClung, Robert M. America's First Elephant. Janovitz, Marilyn, illus. LC 89-13764. 40p. (gr. k up). 1991. 14.95 (*0-688-08358-7*); PLB 14.88 (*0-688-08359-5*) Morrow Jr Bks.

MacMillan, Dianne M. Elephants: Our Last Land Giants. LC 92-35268. 1993. 19.95 (*0-87614-770-8*) Carolrhoda Bks.

Markert, Jenny. Elephants. 32p. 1991. 15.95 (*0-89565-724-4*) Childs World.

Martin, L. Elephants. (Illus.). 24p. (gr. k-5). 1988. PLB 11.94 (*0-86592-998-X*); 8.95s.p. (*0-685-58306-6*) Rourke Corp.

Naden, C. J. I Can Read About Elephants. LC 78-65834. (Illus.). (gr. 2-5). 1979. pap. 2.50 (*0-89375-208-8*) Troll Assocs.

Overbeck, Cynthia. Elephants. LC 80-27550. (Illus.). 48p. (gr. 4-10). 1981. PLB 19.95 (*0-8225-1452-4*) Lerner Pubns.

Payne, Katharine. Elephants Calling. Payne, Katharine, photos by. LC 91-34547. (Illus.). 36p. (gr. 2-6). 1992. 14.00 (*0-517-58175-2*); PLB 14.99 (*0-517-58176-0*) Crown Bks Yng Read.

Petty, Kate. Baby Animals: Elephants. (Illus.). 24p. (ps-3). 1992. pap. 3.95 (*0-8120-4966-7*) Barron.

—Elephants. LC 89-26037. (ps-3). 1990. PLB 10.90 (*0-531-17194-9*, Gloucester Pr) Watts.

Pfeffer, Pierre. Elephants: Big, Strong & Wise. Matthews, Sarah, tr. from FRE. Mettler, Rene, illus. LC 87-33995. 38p. (gr. k-5). 1988. 5.95 (*0-944589-04-9*, 049) Young Discovery Lib.

Posell, Elsa. Elephants. LC 81-38470. (Illus.). 48p. (gr. k-4). 1982. PLB 12.85 (*0-516-01621-0*) Childrens.

Redmond, Ian. Elephant. LC 92-20855. 64p. (gr. 5 up). 1993. 16.00 (*0-679-83880-5*); PLB 16.99 (*0-679-93880-X*) Knopf Bks Yng Read.

—The Elephant in the Bush. Oxford Scientific Films Staff, photos by. LC 89-11297. (Illus.). 32p. (gr. 4-6). 1989. PLB 17.27 (*0-8368-0116-4*) Gareth Stevens Inc.

Rothaus, Jim. Elephants. 24p. (gr. 3). 1988. PLB 14.95s.p. (*0-88682-226-2*); PLB 14.95 (*0-685-74012-9*) Creative Ed.

Schlein, Miriam. Jane Goodall's Animal World: Elephants. LC 89-38551. (Illus.). 32p. (gr. 3-7). 1990. SBE 12.95 (*0-689-31468-X*, Atheneum Child Bk) Macmillan Child Grp.

Schmidt, Jeremy. In the Village of the Elephants. Wood, Ted, photos by. LC 93-8545. (Illus.). 32p. (gr. 2-5). 1994. 15.95 (*0-8027-8226-4*); PLB 16.85 (*0-8027-8227-2*) Walker & Co.

Sobol, Richard. One More Elephant: The Fight to Save Wildlife in Uganda. Sobol, Richard, photos by. LC 93-45663. 1995. PLB write for info. (*0-525-65179-9*, Cobblehill Bks) Dutton Child Bks.

Taylor, Dave. The Elephant & the Scrub Forest. (Illus.). 32p. (gr. 3-4). 1990. PLB 15.95 (*0-86505-365-0*); pap. 7.95 (*0-86505-395-2*) Crabtree Pub Co.

Tibbitts, Alison & Roocroft, Alan. African Elephant. (Illus.). 32p. (ps-2). 1992. PLB 12.95 (*1-56065-100-8*) Capstone Pr.

Two Can Publishing Ltd. Staff. Elephants. (Illus.). 32p. (gr. 2-7). 1991. pap. 3.50 (*0-87534-217-5*) Highlights.

Wildlife Education, Ltd. Staff. Elephants. Hoopes, Barbara, et al, illus. 20p. (Orig.). (gr. 5 up). 1980. pap. 2.75 (*0-937934-00-3*) Wildlife Educ.

ELEPHANTS–FICTION

Allen, Judy. Elephant. Humphries, Tudor, illus. LC 92-54407. 32p. (ps up). 1993. 14.95 (*1-56402-069-X*) Candlewick Pr.

Appelt, Kathi. Elephants Aloft. LC 92-4231. (ps-3). 1993. 13.95 (*0-15-225384-X*, HB Juv Bks) HarBrace.

Aren't You Forgetting Something, Fiona? 1994. 13.27 (*0-8368-0981-5*) Gareth Stevens Inc.

Avery, Gillian. The Elephant War. (gr. k-6). 1988. pap. 4.95 (*0-440-40040-6*, Pub by Yearning Classics) Dell.

Awdry, W. Henry & the Elephant: Based on the Railway Series. Bell, Owain, illus. LC 89-62528. 32p. (Orig.). (ps-3). 1990. pap. 1.50 (*0-679-80408-0*) Random Bks Yng Read.

Babar Compeur. 4.95 (*0-685-33973-4*) Fr & Eur.

Babar et la Vieille Dame. (gr. 2-3). pap. 15.95 (*0-7859-0614-2*, FC254) Fr & Eur.

Bailey, Jill. Operation Elephant. Green, John, illus. LC 90-46056. 48p. (gr. 3-7). 1991. PLB 21.34 (*0-8114-2706-4*); pap. 4.95 (*0-8114-6554-3*) Raintree Steck-V.

Barnes, Jill & Teramura, Terua. Elephant Rescue. Rubin, Caroline, ed. Japan Foreign Rights Centre Staff, tr. from JPN. Murakami, Tsutomu, illus. LC 90-37750. 40p. (gr. k-3). 1990. PLB 15.93 (*0-944483-85-2*) Garrett Ed Corp.

Bartlett, Jaye. Freddy the Elephant: The Story of a Sensitive Leader. Dubina, Alan, illus. 45p. (Orig.). (ps up). 1991. pap. 11.95 incl. cassette (*1-878064-01-0*) New Age CT.

Beames, Margaret. Juno Loves Barney. Campbell, Caroline, illus. LC 93-20030. 1994. pap. write for info. (*0-383-03698-4*) SRA Schl Grp.

Beittel, Kenneth R. & Beittel, Joan N. Ralph & Deno in Vermont. Beittel, Kenneth R., illus. LC 90-86028. 32p. (Orig.). (gr. 5 up). 1990. pap. 6.00 (*0-9628511-0-8*) HVHA.

Berry. Don't Leave an Elephant. Date not set. 15.00 (*0-06-023509-8*); PLB 14.89 (*0-06-023510-1*) HarpC Child Bks.

The Biggest Shadow in the Zoo. (Illus.). 42p. (ps-3). 1992. PLB 13.26 (*0-8368-0874-6*); PLB 13.27 s.p. (*0-685-61511-1*) Gareth Stevens Inc.

Bos, Burny. Olli, der Kleine Elefant. De Beer, Hans, illus. (GER.). 32p. (gr. k-3). 1992. 13.95 (*3-85825-328-6*) North-South Bks NYC.

—Olli, le Petit Elephant. De Beer, Hans, illus. (FRE.). 32p. (gr. k-3). 1992. 13.95 (*3-85539-659-0*) North-South Bks NYC.

—Ollie the Elephant. De Beer, Hans, illus. LC 89-42608. 32p. (gr. k-3). 1989. 13.95 (*1-55858-012-3*) North-South Bks NYC.

—Ollie the Elephant. De Beer, Hans, illus. 32p. (gr. k-3). 1991. pap. 2.95 (*1-55858-110-3*) North-South Bks NYC.

Broker, Loretta. Ellie the Elephant. Meyer, Jacque S., illus. 28p. (Orig.). (ps-k). 1990. pap. 2.95 (*0-916109-09-7*) Summers Pub.

Brown, Ken. Nellie's Knot. LC 92-27910. (Illus.). 32p. (ps-1). 1993. SBE 13.95 (*0-02-714930-7*, Four Winds) Macmillan Child Grp.

Brunhoff, Jean de. Babar au Cirque. (Illus.). 16p. 1974. 4.95 (*0-686-54121-9*, FC241) Fr & Eur.

—Babar en Famille. 26p. 1975. 15.95 (*0-7859-0672-X*, FC589) Fr & Eur.

—Babar et le Crocodile. 16p. 1975. 4.95 (*0-7859-0673-8*, FC242) Fr & Eur.

—Babar et le Pere Noel. 29p. 1975. 15.95 (*0-7859-0674-6*, FC582) Fr & Eur.

—Le Couronnement de Babar. 16p. 1975. 4.95 (*0-7859-0930-3*, FC251) Fr & Eur.

—L' Enfance de Babar. 16p. 1975. 4.95 (*0-686-54127-8*) Fr & Eur.

—Histoire de Babar, le Petite Elephant. (Illus.). 32p. 18.95 (*0-686-54129-4*, FC593) Fr & Eur.

—Vive le Roi Babar. 20p. 1976. 4.95 (*0-7859-0675-4*, FC253) Fr & Eur.

—Le Voyage de Babar. 27p. 1975. 15.95 (*0-7859-0676-2*, FC581) Fr & Eur.

Brunhoff, Laurent de. L' Anniversaire de Babar. 28p. 1975. 17.95 (*0-7859-0677-0*, M11806) Fr & Eur.

—Les Aventures de Babar. 18p. 1977. 15.95 (*0-686-54134-0*) Fr & Eur.

—Babar a Celesteville. 16p. 1974. 4.95 (*0-7859-0678-9*, F12062) Fr & Eur.

—Babar aux Sports d'Hiver. (Illus.). 20p. 1976. 4.95 (*0-7859-0679-7*, FC250) Fr & Eur.

—Babar Aviateur. 16p. 1974. 4.95 (*0-7859-0680-0*, M5989) Fr & Eur.

—Babar Campeur. 16p. 1974. 4.95 (*0-686-54138-3*) Fr & Eur.

—Babar dans l'Ile aux Oiseaux. 29p. 15.95 (*0-7859-0681-9*, F2002) Fr & Eur.

—Babar en Amerique. 23p. 1975. 15.95 (*0-686-54140-5*) Fr & Eur.

—Babar et le Docteur. 16p. 1975. 4.95 (*0-686-54141-3*) Fr & Eur.

—Babar et le Wouly-Wouly. 26p. 15.95 (*0-7859-0682-7*, M11805) Fr & Eur.

—Babar et Sa Famille. 26p. 1976. 4.95 (*0-686-54143-X*) Fr & Eur.

—Babar Patissier. 16p. 1975. 4.95 (*0-686-54144-8*) Fr & Eur.

But No Elephants. (Illus.). 42p. (ps-3). 1992. PLB 13.26 (*0-8368-0875-4*); PLB 13.26 s.p. (*0-685-61510-3*) Gareth Stevens Inc.

Carpenter, Humphrey. Elephants Don't Bounce. write for info. HM.

Carrick, Carol. The Elephant. Carrick, Donald, illus. write for info. (Clarion Bks) HM.

—The Elephant in the Dark. Carrick, Donald, photos by. write for info. (Clarion Bks) HM.

—The Elephant in the Dark. Carrick, Donald, illus. LC 88-2591. 144p. (gr. 3-7). 1988. 13.95 (*0-89919-757-4*, Clarion Bks) HM.

—Elephant in the Dark. (gr. 4-7). 1990. pap. 2.95 (*0-590-42995-7*) Scholastic Inc.

Chase, Alyssa. Jomo & Mata. Chase, Andra, illus. LC 93-25206. 32p. (gr. 1-4). 1993. 16.95 (*1-55942-051-0*, 7656); video, tchr's. guide & storybook 79.95 (*1-55942-054-5*, 9375) Marshfilm.

Cole, Joanna. Aren't You Forgetting Something, Fiona? Delaney, Ned, illus. LC 83-13457. 48p. (ps-3). 1984. 5.95 (*0-8193-1121-9*) Parents.

Collins, David R. Probo's Amazing Trunk. (Illus.). (ps-2). 1987. PLB 6.95 (*0-8136-5184-0*, TK7267); pap. 3.50 (*0-8136-5684-2*, TK7268) Modern Curr.

Cristaldi, Kathryn. Babar in the Jungle. Fritz, Ronald, illus. LC 88-63342. 32p. (Orig.). (ps-3). 1989. pap. 1.50 (*0-679-80215-0*) Random Bks Yng Read.

Cross, Gillian. The Great American Elephant Chase. LC 92-54492. 160p. (gr. 4-7). 1993. 14.95 (*0-8234-1016-1*) Holiday.

—The Great American Elephant Chase. 208p. (gr. 5 up). 1994. pap. 3.99 (*0-14-037014-5*) Puffin Bks.

Davidar, E. R. & Joshi, Jagadish. The Runaway Elephant Calf. (Illus.). 24p. (Orig.). (gr. k-3). 1980. pap. 2.75 (*0-89744-216-4*, Pub. by Childrens Bk Trust IA) Auromere.

Day, Alexandra. Frank & Ernest on the Road. (Illus.). 48p. (ps-3). 1994. 14.95 (*0-590-45048-4*, Scholastic Hardcover) Scholastic Inc.

—Frank & Ernest Play Ball. Day, Alexandra, illus. LC 89-10312. (gr. k-3). 1990. 12.95 (*0-590-42548-X*) Scholastic Inc.

De Brunhoff, Jean. Babar & Father Christmas. De Brunhoff, Jean, illus. LC 90-61863. 48p. 1991. 4.95 (*0-679-81483-3*) Random Bks Yng Read.

—Babar & His Children. Haas, Merle, tr. (Illus.). (ps). 1969. 11.00 (*0-394-80577-1*); lib. bdg. 11.99 (*0-394-90577-6*) Random Bks Yng Read.

Debrunhoff, Jean. Babar the King. 1937. 11.00 (*0-394-80580-1*); lib. bdg. 11.99 (*0-394-90580-6*) Random Bks Yng Read.

De Brunhoff, Jean. Babar the King: (El Rey Babar) (SPA.). 11.50 (*84-204-3038-2*) Santillana.

—Meet Babar & His Family. (Illus.). (ps-1). 1973. pap. 2.25 (*0-394-82682-5*) Random Bks Yng Read.

—The Story of Babar. (Illus.). (ps). 1937. 9.95 (*0-394-80575-5*); PLB 10.99 (*0-394-90575-X*) Random Bks Yng Read.

—The Story of Babar. De Brunhoff, Jean, illus. 48p. (ps-1). 1984. Oversized Facsimile ed. 19.00 (*0-394-86823-4*) Random Bks Yng Read.

—The Story of Babar. De Brunhoff, Jean, illus. LC 84-3308. 48p. (ps up). 1989. pap. 5.99 (*0-394-82940-9*) Knopf Bks Yng Read.

—Travels of Babar. (Illus.). (ps). 1967. 11.00 (*0-394-80576-3*); lib. bdg. 11.99 (*0-394-90576-8*) Random Bks Yng Read.

—The Travels of Babar. De Brunhoff, Jean, illus. LC 85-2236. 48p. (ps up). 1985. 18.95 (*0-394-87453-6*) Random Bks Yng Read.

—Le Voyage de Babar. (FRE & SPA., Illus.). bds. 15.95 (*0-685-11626-3*) Fr & Eur.

De Brunhoff, Laurent. Babar a la Mer. (FRE.). (gr. 2-3). 15.95 (*0-685-11023-0*) Fr & Eur.

—Babar a New York. (FRE., Illus.). (gr. 4-6). 1975. bds. 15.95 (*0-7859-5281-0*, 2010025520) Fr & Eur.

—Babar & the Ghost: An Easy-to-Read Version: A Step Two Book. De Brunhoff, Laurent, illus. LC 85-11841. 48p. (gr. 1-3). 1986. pap. 3.50 (*0-394-87908-2*) Random Bks Yng Read.

—Babar Artiste Peintre. (FRE.). (gr. 2-3). 1991. 15.95 (*0-7859-5285-3*, 209201417X) Fr & Eur.

—Babar au Cirque. (gr. 2-3). pap. 15.95 (*0-685-33966-1*, FC241) Fr & Eur.

—Babar Chez le Docteur. (FRE.). (gr. 2-3). 15.95 (*0-685-28425-5*) Fr & Eur.

—Babar en Ballon. (FRE.). (gr. 2-3). 15.95 (*0-685-28422-0*) Fr & Eur.

—Babar en Promenade. (FRE.). (gr. 2-3). 15.95 (*0-685-11026-5*) Fr & Eur.

—Babar et ce coquin d'Arthur. (FRE., Illus.). (gr. 4-6). bds. 15.95 (*0-685-11027-3*) Fr & Eur.

—Babar et le Prof. Grifaton. (FRE.). (gr. 2-4). 15.95 (*0-685-28434-4*) Fr & Eur.

—Babar et ses Enfants. (FRE.). (gr. 2-3). 15.95 (*0-685-28436-0*) Fr & Eur.

—Babar Fait Du Ski. (FRE.). (gr. 2-3). 14.95 (*0-685-11029-X*) Fr & Eur.

—Babar Jardinier. (FRE.). (gr. 2-3). 15.95 (*0-685-11030-3*) Fr & Eur.

—Babar Loses His Crown. De Brunhoff, Laurent, illus. LC 67-21918. 72p. (gr. k-3). 1967. Beginner.

—Babar Saves the Day. LC 76-11684. (Illus.). (gr. 3-6). 1976. 2.25 (*0-394-83341-4*) Random Bks Yng Read.

—Babar's Bath Book. De Brunhoff, Laurent, illus. 10p. (ps). 1992. vinyl bdg. 3.95 (*0-679-83434-6*) Random Bks Yng Read.

—Babar's Battle. De Brunhoff, Laurent, illus. LC 91-53169. 36p. (ps-3). 1992. 10.00 (*0-679-81068-4*); PLB 10.99 (*0-679-91068-9*) Random Bks Yng Read.

—Babar's Birthday Surprise. LC 74-123071. (Illus.). 36p. (ps-2). 1970. Repr. of 1970 ed. 12.00 (*0-394-80591-7*) Random Bks Yng Read.

—Babar's Busy Year: a Book about Seasons: Just Right for 2's & 3's. De Brunhoff, Laurent, illus. LC 88-35726. 24p. (ps). 1989. 6.00 (*0-394-82882-8*) Random Bks Yng Read.

—Babar's Car. De Brunhoff, Laurent, illus. 14p. (ps-k). 1992. bds. 3.99 (*0-679-83242-4*) Random Bks Yng Read.

—Babar's Castle. Haas, Merle, tr. De Brunhoff, Laurent, illus. (ps). 1994. 4.95 (*0-394-80586-0*); lib. bdg. 5.99 (*0-394-90586-5*) Random Bks Yng Read.

—Babar's Family Album: Five Favorite Stories. De Brunhoff, Laurent, illus. LC 90-8748. 112p. (ps-3). 1991. 17.00 (*0-679-81167-2*); lib. bdg. 17.99 (*0-679-91167-7*) Random Bks Yng Read.

—Babar's French Lessons. (Illus.). (ps). 1963. 11.00 (*0-394-80587-9*); lib. bdg. 5.99 (*0-394-90587-3*) Random Bks Yng Read.

—Babar's Little Circus Star. De Brunhoff, Laurent, illus. LC 87-14149. 32p. (Orig.). (ps-1). 1988. lib. bdg. 7.99 (*0-394-98959-7*); pap. 3.50 (*0-394-88959-2*) Random Bks Yng Read.

—Babar's Peekaboo Fair. De Brunhoff, Laurent, illus. LC 92-64269. 14p. (ps). 1993. bds. 3.99 (*0-679-83935-6*) Random Bks Yng Read.

—Babar's Picnic. De Brunhoff, Laurent, illus. LC 90-61349. 24p. (Orig.). (ps-2). 1991. pap. 2.25 (*0-679-81245-8*) Random Bks Yng Read.

—Chateau du Roi Babar. (FRE.). (gr. 3-8). 15.95 (*0-685-11078-8*) Fr & Eur.

—Le Couronnement de Babar. (FRE.). (gr. 2-3). 4.95 (*0-685-28420-4*) Fr & Eur.

—Enfance de Babar. (FRE.). (gr. 2-3). 4.95 (*0-685-28421-2*) Fr & Eur.

—Hello, Babar! De Brunhoff, Laurent, illus. 12p. (ps). 1991. foam filling 4.99 (*0-679-81073-0*) Random Bks Yng Read.

—Histoire de Babar. (FRE.). (gr. 2-4). 15.95 (*0-685-28435-2*) Fr & Eur.

—Isabelle's New Friend: A Babar Book. De Brunhoff, Laurent, illus. LC 89-3727. 32p. (ps-1). 1990. PLB 5.99 (*0-394-92880-6*); pap. 2.25 (*0-394-82880-1*) Random Bks Yng Read.

—Je Parle Allemand avec Babar. (FRE., Illus.). (gr. 4-6). 15.95 (*0-685-11271-3*) Fr & Eur.

—Je Parle Anglais avec Babar. (FRE., Illus.). (gr. 4-6). 15.95 (*0-685-11272-1*) Fr & Eur.

—Je Parle Espagnol avec Babar. (FRE., Illus.). (gr. 4-6). 15.95 (*0-685-11273-X*) Fr & Eur.

—Je Parle Italien avec Babar. (FRE.). (gr. 4-6). 7.95 (*0-685-11274-8*) Fr & Eur.

—Meet Babar & His Family. De Brunhoff, Laurent, illus. 32p. (ps-1). 1985. pap. 5.95 incl. cassette (*0-394-87653-9*) Random Bks Yng Read.

—The Rescue of Babar. De Brunhoff, Laurent, illus. LC 92-50958. 36p. (ps-3). 1993. 20.00 (*0-679-83897-X*) Random Bks Yng Read.

—Roi Babar. (FRE.). (gr. 4-6). 1975. 15.95 (*0-685-11533-X*) Fr & Eur.

—Vive le Roi Babar. (FRE.). (gr. 2-3). 4.95 (*0-685-28423-9*) Fr & Eur.

Delacre, Lulu. Time for School for, Nathan! 1989. pap. 12.95 (*0-590-41942-0*) Scholastic Inc.

Disney, Walt. Dumbo. 1988. 5.99 (*0-517-66197-7*) Random Hse Value.

DiVito, Anna. Elephants on Ice. LC 90-22392. (Illus.). 32p. (ps-4). 1991. 12.95 (*0-8037-0797-5*); PLB 12.89 (*0-8037-0798-3*) Dial Bks Young.

Don't Forget, Dumbo! 18p. 1994. 6.98 (*1-57082-099-6*) Mouse Works.

Dr. Seuss. Horton Hatches the Egg. reissued ed. Crystal, Billy, read by. Dr. Seuss, illus. LC 40-27753. 64p. (ps up). 1991. pap. 10.95 incls. cassette (*0-394-82956-5*) Random Bks Yng Read.

—Horton Hears a Who! Hoffman, Dustin, narrated by. LC 54-7012. (Illus.). 72p. (ps-1). 1990. pap. 13.00 incl. cassette (*0-679-80003-4*) Random Bks Yng Read.

Dumbo's Circus. 1985. 4.95 (*0-553-05403-1*) Bantam.

Elephant's Child. 24p. (ps-3). 1989. 2.25 (*1-56288-164-7*) Checkerboard.

Els. Silver Elephant, No. 2. 1987. 4.95 (*0-02-970370-0*) Macmillan.

Everett, Louise. Skating on Thin Ice. Kolding, Richard M., illus. LC 86-30857. 32p. (gr. k-2). 1988. PLB 7.89 (*0-8167-0992-0*); pap. text ed. 1.95 (*0-8167-0993-9*) Troll Assocs.

Faulkner, Keith. Elephant & the Rainbow. Lambert, Jonathan, illus. 22p. (gr. 1-3). 1990. 5.95 (*0-681-40977-0*) Longmeadow Pr.

Ford, Miela. Little Elephant. Hoban, Tana, photos by. LC 93-25208. (Illus.). 24p. 1994. 14.00 (*0-688-13140-9*); PLB 13.93 (*0-688-13141-7*) Greenwillow.

Geraghty, Paul. The Hunter. LC 93-22730. (Illus.). 32p. (ps-3). 1994. 15.00 (*0-517-59692-X*); PLB 15.99 (*0-517-59693-8*) Crown Bks Yng Read.

Giannini, Enzo. Zorina Ballerina. LC 91-21970. (Illus.). 40p. (ps-1). 1993. pap. 14.00 JRT (*0-671-74776-2*, S&S BFYR) S&S Trade.

Grambling, Lois. Elephant & Mouse Celebrate Halloween. Maze, Deborah, illus. (ps-1). 1991. 12.95 (*0-8120-6186-1*); pap. 5.95 (*0-8120-4761-3*) Barron.

Grambling, Lois G. Elephant & Mouse Get Ready for Christmas. Maze, Deborah, illus. 32p. 1990. with dust jacket 12.95 (*0-8120-6185-3*) Barron.

Greenberg, Kenneth R. The Adventures of Tusky & His Friends: A Christmas Mystery. Pearson, Allison K., illus. 63p. (gr. k-3). 1991. PLB 14.95 (*1-879100-01-0*) Tusky Enterprises.

—The Adventures of Tusky & His Friends, Bk. 1: A Jungle Adventure. Pearson, Allison K., illus. 51p. (gr. k-3). 1991. 13.95 (*1-879100-00-2*) Tusky Enterprises.

—The Adventures of Tusky & His Friends, Bk. 3: Tusky Gets Mad at Tusky. Pearson, Allison K., illus. 52p. (gr. k-4). 1992. 15.50 (*1-879100-02-9*) Tusky Enterprises.

—The Adventures of Tusky & His Friends, Vol. 2: Tusky Meets the Green-Eyed Monster. Pearson, Allison K., illus. 66p. (gr. k-4). 1992. 15.95 (*1-879100-03-7*) Tusky Enterprises.

Greenburg, Dan. Jumbo the Boy & Arnold the Elephant. Perl, Susan, illus. LC 87-24931. 48p. (gr. 2-4). 1989. Repr. of 1969 ed. HarpC Child Bks.

Greene, Carol. The Insignificant Elephant. Gantner, Susan, illus. LC 84-1531. 32p. (ps-3). 1985. 13.95 (*0-15-238730-7*, HB Juv Bks) HarBrace.

Gregorich, Barbara. Elephant & Envelope. Hoffman, Joan, ed. (Illus.). 16p. (Orig.). (gr. k-2). 1985. pap. 2.25 (*0-88743-017-1*, 06017) Sch Zone Pub Co.

Griffin, Sandi Z. Lumpa Lou Elephant, Vol. I: Tails with a Moral. Griffin, Sandi Z., illus. 28p. (ps-2). 1993. write for info. S Z Griffin.

Harvey, Dean. The Secret Elephant of Harlan Kooter. Richardson, Mark, illus. LC 91-45955. 160p. (gr. 2-5). 1992. 13.95 (*0-395-62523-8*) HM.

Herman, Gail. Babar the Boy King. Prebenna, David, illus. LC 88-63343. 32p. (Orig.). (ps-3). 1989. pap. text ed. 1.50 (*0-394-84533-1*) Random Bks Yng Read.

Hiccups for Elephant. LC 94-15585. 2.95 (*0-590-48588-1*) Scholastic Inc.

Hoff, Syd. Oliver. Hoff, Syd, illus. LC 60-5779. 64p. (gr. k-3). 1960. PLB 13.89 (*0-06-022516-5*) HarpC Child Bks.

—Oliver. Hoff, Syd, illus. LC 60-5779. 64p. (gr. k-3). 1986. pap. 3.50 (*0-06-444097-4*, Trophy) HarpC Child Bks.

Hurd, Edith T. Stop Stop. Hurd, Clement, illus. LC 61-12095. 64p. (gr. k-3). 1961. PLB 13.89 (*0-06-022746-X*) HarpC Child Bks.

Johnson, Doug. Never Ride Elephants. 1994. write for info. (*0-8050-2880-3*) H Holt & Co.

Joyce, Susan. Peel, the Extraordinary Elephant. DuBosque, D. C., illus. LC 86-61990. 48p. (ps up). 1988. pap. 7.95 sewn bdg. (*0-939217-01-5*) Peel Prod.

—Pilon, el Extraordinario Elefanton. Marcuse, Aida, tr. from ENG. DuBosque, D. C., illus. LC 92-35437. (SPA.). 48p. (Orig.). (gr. 1-6). 1993. pap. 8.95 (*0-939217-05-8*) Peel Prod.

Kennaway, Adrienne. Little Elephant's Walk. Kennaway, Adrienne, illus. LC 91-19727. 32p. (ps-2). 1992. 13.95 (*0-06-020377-3*) HarpC Child Bks.

Kessler, Ethel & Kessler, Leonard. Is There an Elephant in Your Kitchen? (Illus.). 32p. (ps-k). 1986. 4.95 (*0-671-62065-7*, Little Simon) S&S Trade.

Kimberling, Bryce, illus. One Elephant Went Out to Play Big Book. (ps-2). 1988. pap. text ed. 14.00 (*0-922053-16-2*) N Edge Res.

Kipling, Rudyard. The Elephant's Child. Cauley, Lorinda B., illus. LC 85-9098. 48p. (ps-3). 1988. pap. 4.95 (*0-15-225386-6*, HB Juv Bks) HarBrace.

—The Elephant's Child. Cauley, Lorinda B., illus. 44p. (ps-3). 1983. 14.95 (*0-15-225385-8*, Voyager Bks) HarBrace.

—The Elephant's Child. Mogensen, Jan, illus. LC 89-7787. 48p. 1989. 13.95 (*0-940793-41-5*, Pub. by Crocodile Bks) Interlink Pub.

—The Elephant's Child. Mogensen, Jan, illus. LC 89-7787. 48p. 1991. pap. 6.95 (*0-940793-77-6*, Crocodile Bks) Interlink Pub.

—The Elephant's Child. Bolam, Emily, illus. LC 91-19378. 24p. (gr. k up). 1992. 13.95 (*0-525-44862-4*, DCB) Dutton Child Bks.

—El Hijo del Elefante: The Elephant's Child. Martinez, Lourdes, tr. from GER. Mogensen, Jan, illus. (SPA.). 42p. (gr. k-4). 1990. 13.95 (*87-14-18825-2*) Hispanic Bk Dist.

Lemaitre, Pascal. Zelda's Secret. Lemaitre, Pascal, illus. LC 93-28448. (ps-3). 1993. PLB 13.95 (*0-8167-3309-0*); pap. 3.95t (*0-8167-3310-4*) BrdgeWater.

Le Tord, Bijou. Elephant Moon. LC 92-28234. 1993. 14.95 (*0-385-30623-7*) Doubleday.

Lobel, Arnold. Uncle Elephant. LC 80-8944. (Illus.). 64p. (gr. k-3). 1986. pap. 3.50 (*0-06-444104-0*, Trophy) HarpC Child Bks.

McKee, David. Elmer Again. Pearson, Susan, ed. LC 91-38901. (Illus.). 32p. (ps up). 1992. reinforced bdg. 14.00 (*0-688-11596-9*) Lothrop.

McNulty, Faith. The Elephant Who Couldn't Forget. Reissue. ed. Simont, Marc, illus. LC 79-2741. 64p. (gr. k-3). 1980. PLB 13.89 (*0-06-024146-2*) HarpC Child Bks.

—The Elephant Who Couldn't Forget. Simont, Marc, illus. LC 79-2741. 64p. (gr. k-3). 1989. pap. 3.50 (*0-06-444128-8*, Trophy) HarpC Child Bks.

Mahy, Margaret. Seventeen Kings & Forty-Two Elephants. Fogelman, Phyllis J., ed. MacCarthy, Patricia, illus. LC 87-5311. 32p. (ps-3). 1990. pap. 4.95 (*0-8037-0781-9*) Dial Bks Young.

Mayer, Mercer. Ah-Choo. (Illus.). (gr. k-2). 1977. PLB 4.58 (*0-8037-4895-7*) Dial Bks Young.

Mills, Joyce C. & Crowley, Richard J. Sammy the Elephant & Mr. Camel: A Story to Help Children Overcome Bedwetting While Discovering Self-Appreciation. Cook, Germaine, illus. LC 88-13581. 48p. (gr. 1 up). 1988. PLB 16.95 (*0-945354-09-6*); pap. 6.95 (*0-945354-08-8*) Magination Pr.

Miranda, Anne. The Elephant at the Waldorf. Vanderbeek, Don, illus. LC 93-33804. 32p. (gr. k-3). 1995. PLB 14.95 (*0-8167-3452-6*); pap. text ed. 3.95 (*0-8167-3453-4*) BrdgeWater.

Mok, Esther. Sumo, the Wrestling Elephant. LC 92-82936. (Illus.). 24p. (gr. 2-5). 1994. write for info.; pap. 4.95 (*0-943864-68-2*) Davenport.

Morton, Lone. I'm Too Big (Je Suis Trop Gros) Weatherill, Steve, illus. Helie, Ide M., tr. from FRE. McCourt, Ella, concept by. LC 94-561. (ENG & FRE., Illus.). 28p. (ps up). 1994. 6.95 (*0-8120-6454-2*) Barron.

—I'm Too Big (Soy Demasiado Grande) Weatherill, Steve, illus. McCourt, Ella, concept by. LC 94-563. (ENG & SPA., Illus.). 28p. (ps up). 1994. 6.95 (*0-8120-6451-8*) Barron.

Moser, Erwin. Wilma the Elephant. Agee, Joel, tr. LC 86-1145. (gr. 3-8). 1986. 9.95 (*0-915361-45-0*) Modan-Adama Bks.

Muldrow, Diane. Walt Disney's Dumbo the Circus Baby. (ps). 1993. 4.95 (*0-307-12397-9*, Golden Pr) Western Pub.

Murphy, Jill. A Quiet Night In. Murphy, Jill, illus. LC 93-875. (ps up). 1994. 12.95 (*1-56402-248-X*) Candlewick Pr.

Noble, Kate. The Blue Elephant. Bass, Rachel, illus. 32p. (ps-4). 1994. 14.95 (*0-9631798-3-7*) Silver Seahorse. Sassi is a young African elephant. She loves living in the zoo & she likes to see the children who come to play. Her efforts to get what she dreams of produce some startling results. Witty full-color paintings show the big-city zoo. Besides all the fun, there's lots of information on animal behavior. Kate Nobel is author of BUBBLE GUM & OH LOOK, IT'S A NOSSERUS in the AFRICA STORIES Series. She's a former teacher & a zoo volunteer. Rachel Bass is an artist & an art therapist who works with children. They both know a good deal about early childhood development. Silver Seahorse Press, 2568 N. Clark Street, Suite 320, Chicago, IL 60614. 312-871-1772. FAX: 312 327-8978. Distributed by: Lifetime Books, Inc., 2131 Hollywood Boulevard, Hollywood, FL 33020-6750. 1-800-771-3355. Fax number for orders: 1-800-931-7411. *Publisher Provided Annotation.*

Norman, Jane & Beazley, Frank. The Mystery of the Flying Elephants. 24p. (ps-3). 1993. pap. write for info. (*1-883585-02-3*) Pixanne Ent.

O'Donnell, Peter. Dizzy. (Illus.). (ps up). 1992. 14.95 (*0-590-45475-7*, 021, Scholastic Hardcover) Scholastic Inc.

Oetting, Rae. Timmy Tiger & the Elephant. LC 73-108730. (Illus.). 32p. (ps-2). 1970. PLB 9.95 (*0-87783-041-X*); pap. 3.94 deluxe ed (*0-87783-111-4*); cassette 7.94x (*0-87783-277-3*) Oddo.

Offen, Hilda. Elephant Pie. Offen, Hilda, illus. 32p. (ps-2). 1993. 13.99 (*0-525-45123-4*, DCB) Dutton Child Bks.

Oliviero, Jamie. Som See & the Magic Elephant. Kelly, Jo'Anne, illus. LC 94-1164. 32p. 1995. write for info. (*0-7868-0025-9*); deluxe ed. write for info. Hyprn Child.

Ostrovsky, Alexsandr & Ostrovsky, Alexsandr. Besely Clon (Merry Elephant) (RUS., Illus.). 32p. (Orig.). 1991. pap. 14.95 (*0-934393-22-2*) Rector Pr.

Pearce, Philippa. Emily's Own Elephant. Lawrence, John, illus. LC 87-14039. 32p. (gr. k-3). 1988. 11.95 (*0-688-07678-5*); lib. bdg. 11.88 (*0-688-07679-3*) Greenwillow.

Peek, Merle. The Balancing Act. LC 86-17547. 32p. (ps-1). 1987. 12.95 (*0-89919-458-3*, Clarion Bks) HM.

Percy, Graham. Max and the Orange Door. LC 92-45563. (Illus.). (ps-3). 1993. 15.95 (*1-56766-076-2*) Childs World.

—Max & the Very Rare Bird. (Illus.). 32p. 1991. 15.95 (*0-89565-786-4*) Childs World.

—Meg & Her Circus Tricks. (Illus.). 32p. 1991. 15.95 (*0-89565-785-6*) Childs World.

—Meg & the Great Race. Percy, Graham, illus. LC 92-44851. (ps-3). 1993. 15.95 (*1-56766-077-0*) Childs World.

Perkins, Al. Tubby & the Lantern. LC 70-158390. (Illus.). (gr. k-2). 1971. lib. bdg. 4.99 (*0-394-92297-2*) Beginner.

Petersham, Maud & Petersham, Miska. Circus Baby. Petersham, Maud & Petersham, Miska, illus. LC 50-9295. 32p. (ps-1). 1968. RSBE 13.95 (*0-02-771670-8*, Macmillan Child Bk) Macmillan Child Grp.

Platt, Kin. Big Max. Lopshire, Robert, illus. LC 91-14742. 64p. (gr. k-3). 1965. 13.00 (*0-06-024750-9*); PLB 12.89 (*0-06-024751-7*) HarpC Child Bks.

Poltarness, Weller. Martin & Tommy. Krestjanoff, illus. LC 93-13609. (gr. 4 up). 1994. 14.00 (*0-671-88067-5*, Green Tiger Pr) S&S Trade.

Resch, Barbara. A Place for Everyone. Resch, Barbara, illus. 28p. (ps-3). 1991. smythe sewn reinforced bdg. 9.95 (*1-56182-022-9*) Atomium Bks.

Richardson, Judith B. The Way Home. Mavor, Salley, illus. LC 93-25729. 32p. (gr. k-3). 1994. pap. 3.95 (*0-689-71790-3*, Aladdin) Macmillan Child Grp.

Riddell, Chris. The Trouble with Elephants. Riddell, Chris, illus. LC 87-24963. 32p. (ps-2). 1990. pap. 5.95 (*0-06-443170-3*, Trophy) HarpC Child Bks.

Rispin, Karen. Ambush at Amboseli. LC 93-37801. 1994. 4.99 (*0-8423-1295-1*) Tyndale.

Romain, Trevor. How to Go to Bed with an Elephant in Your Head. Romain, Trevor, illus. 32p. (ps-5). 1994. 13.95 (*1-880092-10-7*) Bright Bks TX.

Roth, Susan L. We'll Ride Elephants Through Brooklyn. (ps up). 1989. 13.95 (*0-374-38258-1*) FS&G.

Sadler, Marilyn & Bollen, Roger. Alistair's Elephant. LC 82-23091. (Illus.). 48p. (gr. k-4). 1991. pap. 14.00 jacketed (*0-671-66680-0*, S&S BFYR); pap. 5.95 (*0-671-66681-9*) S&S Trade.

Scarry, Richard. Mr. Frumble: Richard Scarry's Smallest Pop-up Book Ever! (Illus.). 10p. (ps-3). 1992. write for info. (*0-307-12463-0*, 12463, Golden Pr) Western Pub.

Sellers, Naomi. The Little Elephant Who Liked to Play. Mitsuhashi, Yoko, illus. LC 94-20299. 1994. write for info. (*0-382-24682-9*) Silver Burdett Pr.

Setterlund, Donna J. Elephant, Please Go Back to the Zoo. Setterlund, Donna J., illus. 30p. 1990. write for info. (*0-9624342-3-X*) Carriage Hse Studio Pubns.

Sheppard, Jeff. The Right Number of Elephants Big Book. Bond, Felicia, illus. LC 90-4148. 32p. (ps-3). 1993. pap. 19.95 (*0-06-443338-2*, Trophy) HarpC Child Bks.

Slightly Off-Center Writers Group, Ltd. Staff. The Last Elephant's Journey. (Illus.). 60p. (gr. 4-6). 1994. pap. 6.95 (*1-56721-063-5*) Twnty-Fifth Cent Pr.

Smath, Jerry. But No Elephants. Smath, Jerry, illus. LC 79-16136. 48p. (ps-3). 1979. 5.95 (*0-8193-1007-7*); PLB 5.95 (*0-8193-1008-5*) Parents.

—Elephant Goes to School. Smath, Jerry, illus. LC 83-23823. 48p. (ps-3). 1984. 5.95 (*0-8193-1126-X*) Parents.

—Elephant Goes to School. LC 93-7769. 1993. PLB 13.27 (*0-8368-0967-X*) Gareth Stevens Inc.

Smee, Nicola. The Tusk Fairy. Smee, Nicola, illus. LC 93-28444. 32p. (ps-2). 1993. PLB 14.95 (*0-8167-3311-2*); pap. 3.95 (*0-8167-3312-0*) BrdgeWater.

Smucker, Barbara. Incredible Jumbo. 1991. 12.95 (*0-670-82970-6*) Viking Child Bks.

Stinga, Frank, illus. The Carousel Elephant. 12p. (ps). Date not set. 4.95 (*1-56828-066-1*) Red Jacket Pr.

Talbot, John. Pins & Needles. LC 91-13317. (Illus.). 32p. (ps-2). 1992. 12.00 (*0-8037-0942-0*) Dial Bks Young.

Tarr, Judith. His Majesty's Elephant. 1993. 16.95 (*0-15-200737-7*, HB Juv Bks) HarBrace.

Thaler, Mike. Never Mail an Elephant. Smath, Jerry, illus. LC 93-14395. 32p. (ps-3). 1993. PLB 9.89 (*0-8167-3018-0*); pap. text ed. 2.50 (*0-8167-3019-9*) Troll Assocs.

Tompert, Ann. Just a Little Bit. Munsinger, Lynn, illus. LC 92-31857. 1993. 14.95 (*0-395-51527-0*) HM.

Tryon, Thomas. The Adventures of Opal & Cupid. (Illus.). 224p. 1992. 14.00 (*0-670-82239-6*) Viking Child Bks.

Van Loon, Paul. Agarrar la Luna. Akkerman, Dinie, illus. LC 92-43067. 1993. 5.95 (*0-8120-1676-9*) Barron.

Velthuijs, Max. Crocodile's Masterpiece. (Illus.). 32p. (ps-1). 1992. bds. 14.00 (*0-374-31658-9*) FS&G.

—Elephant & Crocodile. LC 90-55039. 32p. (gr. 4-8). 1990. 14.00 (*0-374-37675-1*) FS&G.

Wahl, Jan. Little Gray One. Lessac, Frane, illus. LC 92-33776. 32p. (ps up). 1993. 15.00 (*0-688-12037-7*, Tambourine Bks); PLB 14.93 (*0-688-12038-5*, Tambourine Bks) Morrow.

West, Colin. One Little Elephant. West, Colin, illus. LC 93-36273. 32p. 1994. 3.99 (*1-56402-375-3*) Candlewick Pr.

Yushij, Nima. When the Elephants Came. Evans, Mariam & Batmanglij, M., eds. Evans, Mariam, tr. from PER. Fanta, illus. LC 87-31690. 32p. (gr. 4 up). 1988. 18.50 (*0-934211-15-9*); English-Persian Version. 18.50 (*0-934211-09-4*) Mage Pubs Inc.

ELEPHANTS–POETRY

Dr. Seuss. Horton Hatches the Egg. Dr. Seuss, illus. (gr. k-3). 1940. 14.00 (*0-394-80077-X*); lib. bdg. 13.99 (*0-394-90077-4*) Random Bks Yng Read.

Peet, Bill. Ella. (Illus.). 48p. (gr. k-3). 1964. 13.45 (*0-395-17577-1*) HM.

ELEVATORS

Ford, Barbara. The Elevator. LC 82-70440. (Illus.). 64p. (gr. 4-6). 1982. 7.95 (*0-8027-6450-9*); PLB 8.85 (*0-8027-6451-7*) Walker & Co.

ELIJAH, THE PROPHET

Colburn, Rhonda. The Story of Elijah. Pickett, Stacy, illus. 24p. (ps-3). 1990. pap. 3.95 (*0-8249-8419-6*, Ideals Child) Hambleton-Hill.

Frank, Penny. Elijah Asks for Bread. Morris, Tony, et al, illus. 24p. (ps-3). 3.99 (*0-85648-746-5*) Lion USA.

Kolbrek, Loyal. The Day God Made It Rain. (gr. k-2). 1977. pap. 1.99 (*0-570-06108-3*, 59-1226) Concordia.

Lashbrook, Marilyn. God, Please Send Fire: Elijah & the Prophets of Baal. Sharp, Chris, illus. LC 90-60458. 32p. (gr. k-3). 1990. 5.95 (*0-86606-440-0*, 871) Roper Pr.

Miller, Susan M. Elijah. (Illus.). (gr. 3 up). pap. 2.50 perfect bdg. (*1-55748-189-X*) Barbour & Co.

Overholtzer, Ruth. Elijah. Butcher, Sam, illus. 36p. (gr. k-6). 1967. pap. text ed. 9.45 (*1-55976-009-5*) CEF Press.

Singer, Isaac Bashevis. Elijah the Slave. Frasconi, Antonio, illus. LC 70-124146. 32p. (ps-3). 1970. 16.00 (*0-374-32084-5*) FS&G.

ELIOT, THOMAS STEARNS, 1888-1965

Reilly, Jim. Eliot. (Illus.). 112p. (gr. 7 up). 1990. lib. bdg. 19.94 (*0-86593-022-8*); lib. bdg. 14.95s.p. (*0-685-36353-8*) Rourke Corp.

ELIZABETH 1ST, QUEEN OF ENGLAND, 1533-1603

Frost, Abigail. Elizabeth I. (Illus.). 32p. (gr. 3-8). 1989. PLB 10.95 (*1-85435-113-3*) Marshall Cavendish.

Greene, Carol. Elizabeth the First: Queen of England. Dobson, Steven, illus. LC 90-2204. 48p. (gr. k-3). 1990. PLB 12.85 (*0-516-04214-9*); pap. 4.95 (*0-516-44214-7*) Childrens.

Palmer, Michael. Elizabeth I. (Illus.). 64p. (gr. 6-9). 1989. 19.95 (*0-7134-5660-4*, Pub. by Batsford UK) Trafalgar.
Stanley, Diane & Vennema, Peter. Good Queen Bess: The Story of Queen Elizabeth I of England. Stanley, Diane, illus. LC 88-37501. 40p. (gr. 1-4). 1990. RSBE 16.95 (*0-02-786810-9*, Four Winds) Macmillan Child Grp.

ELIZABETH 2ND, QUEEN OF GREAT BRITAIN, 1926-

Auerbach, Susan. Queen Elizabeth II. LC 92-46478. 1993. 19.93 (*0-86625-481-1*); 14.95s.p. (*0-685-67777-X*) Rourke Pubns.
Sabin, Francene. Young Queen Elizabeth. Lawn, John, illus. LC 89-33941. 48p. (gr. 4-6). 1990. PLB 10.79 (*0-8167-1785-0*); pap. text ed. 3.50 (*0-8167-1786-9*) Troll Assocs.

ELK

Ahlstrom, Mark E. The Elk. LC 85-11667. (Illus.). 48p. (gr. 5). 1985. text ed. 12.95 RSBE (*0-89686-278-X*, Crestwood Hse) Macmillan Child Grp.
Arnold, Caroline. Tule Elk. Hewett, Richard R., photos by. (Illus.). 48p. (gr. 2-5). 1989. 19.95 (*0-87614-343-5*) Carolrhoda Bks.
Lepthien, Emilie U. Elk. LC 94-10469. (Illus.). 48p. (gr. k-4). 1994. PLB 17.20 (*0-516-01063-8*); pap. 4.95 (*0-516-41063-6*) Childrens.
Patent, Dorothy H. Deer & Elk. Munoz, William, illus. LC 93-25894. 1994. 15.95 (*0-395-52003-7*, Clarion Bks) HM.

ELK–FICTION

Benander, Carl D. Little Elk's Miracle. Teasley, Jamie, ed. Beyer, Paul, illus. LC 89-51758. 45p. (gr. k-3). 1991. 7.95 (*0-685-31291-7*) Winston-Derek.
London, Jonathon. Master Elk & the Mountain Lion. McLoughlin, Wayne, illus. LC 94-1754. 1995. write for info. (*0-517-59917-1*, Crown); deluxe ed. write for info. (*0-517-59918-X*) Crown Pub Group.

ELLINGTON, DUKE, 1899-1974

Brown, Gene. Duke Ellington. Easton, Emily, ed. (Illus.). 128p. (gr. 7-9). 1990. lib. bdg. 12.95 (*0-382-09906-0*); pap. 9.95 (*0-382-24034-0*) Silver Burdett Pr.
Collier, James L. Duke Ellington. LC 90-26303. 144p. (gr. 5-9). 1991. SBE 13.95 (*0-02-722985-8*, Macmillan Child Bk) Macmillan Child Grp.
—Duke Ellington. LC 92-39793. 144p. (gr. 7 up). 1994. pap. 5.95 (*0-02-042675-5*, Aladdin) Macmillan Child Grp.
Frankl, Ron. Duke Ellington. King, Coretta Scott, intro. by. (Illus.). 112p. (Orig.). (gr. 5 up). 1988. 17.95 (*1-55546-584-6*); pap. 9.95 (*0-7910-0208-X*) Chelsea Hse.
King, Coretta Scott, intro. by. Duke Ellington: Bandleader & Composer. (Illus.). 112p. (gr. 7-12). PLB 16.95 (*0-685-21875-9*, 200417) Know Unltd.
Stwertka, Eve. Duke Ellington: A Life of Music. LC 93-21267. (Illus.). (gr. 9-12). 1994. PLB 14.40 (*0-531-13035-5*) Watts.

ELLIS ISLAND

Fisher, Leonard E. Ellis Island: Gateway to the New World. Fisher, Leonard E., illus. LC 86-2286. 64p. (gr. 3-7). 1986. reinforced bdg. 14.95 (*0-8234-0612-1*) Holiday.
Goodman, Roger B. The Statue of Liberty & Ellis Island. (Illus.). 74p. (Orig.). (gr. 9 up). 1990. pap. 6.50 (*0-9632191-0-3*); pap. text ed. 6.50 (*0-9632191-1-1*); tchr's. ed. 6.50 (*0-9632191-2-X*); wkbk. 3.00 (*0-685-57051-7*) Pulitzer-Goodman.
Jacobs, William J. Ellis Island: New Hope in a New Land. LC 89-38075. (Illus.). 40p. (gr. 2-5). 1990. RSBE 14.95 (*0-684-19171-7*, Scribners Young Read) Macmillan Child Grp.
Levine, Ellen. If Your Name Was Changed at Ellis Island. Parmenter, Wayne, illus. LC 92-27940. 80p. (gr. 2-5). 1993. 15.95 (*0-590-46134-6*) Scholastic Inc.
Reef, Catherine. Ellis Island. LC 91-18755. (Illus.). 72p. (gr. 4-6). 1991. text ed. 14.95 RSBE (*0-87518-473-1*, Dillon) Macmillan Child Grp.
Rosenblum, Richard. Journey to the Golden Land. Rosenblum, Richard, illus. LC 91-44941. 32p. (gr. k-4). 1992. 14.95 (*0-8276-0405-X*) JPS Phila.
Stein, R. Conrad. Ellis Island. 2nd ed. LC 91-33222. (Illus.). 32p. (gr. 3-6). PLB 12.30, Apr. 1992 (*0-516-06653-6*); pap. 3.95, Jul. 1992 (*0-516-46653-4*) Childrens.

ELOCUTION

see Public Speaking

ELVES

see Fairies

EMANCIPATION OF SLAVES

see Slavery in the U. S.

EMANCIPATION PROCLAMATION

Barrett, Anna P. Juneteenth. rev. ed. Goodman, Frances B., ed. Costner, Howard, illus. 64p. (gr. k-8). 1993. pap. 9.95 (*0-89896-111-4*) Larksdale.
Young, Robert. The Emancipation Proclamation: Why Lincoln Really Freed the Slaves. LC 94-9361. 1994. text ed. 14.95 (*0-87518-613-0*, Dillon) Macmillan Child Grp.

EMBLEMS

see Heraldry; Symbolism

EMBROIDERY

see also Beadwork

Cherry, Winky. My First Embroidery Book. Cherry, Winky, illus. 40p. (ps-6). 1990. pap. 12.00 (*0-317-93838-X*) ITS Pub.
Hodges, Jean. Smocking Design. 1989. pap. 10.95 (*0-486-26036-4*) Dover.
Newhouse, Sue. Creative Hand Embroidery. (Illus.). 64p. (Orig.). 1993. pap. 14.95 (*0-85532-727-8*, Pub. by Search Pr UK) A Schwartz & Co.
Thomas, M. Embroidery Book. 320p. (gr. 5-8). 32.50 (*0-87559-110-8*) Shalom.

EMBRYOLOGY

see also Cells; Reproduction

Conway, Lorraine. Heredity & Embryology. (gr. 5 up). 1980. 7.95 (*0-916456-90-0*, GA 179) Good Apple.
Taylor, Nicole. Baby. LC 92-41338. 1993. 18.95 (*0-88682-595-4*) Creative Ed.

EMIGRATION

see Immigration and Emigration

EMOTIONALLY DISTURBED CHILDREN

see Problem Children

EMOTIONS

see also Attitude (Psychology); Belief and Doubt; Fear; Love; Prejudices and Antipathies

Alexander, Debra W. All My Dreams. 16p. (gr. 6-12). 1993. 3.95 (*1-56688-067-X*) Bur For At-Risk.
—All My Feelings. 23p. (gr. k-5). 1992. 3.95 (*1-56688-055-6*) Bur For At-Risk.
—In This House Called Home. 24p. (gr. 6-12). 1993. 3.95 (*1-56688-065-3*) Bur For At-Risk.
—It Happened in Autumn. 24p. (gr. 6-12). 1993. 3.95 (*1-56688-069-6*) Bur For At-Risk.
—It's My Life. 24p. (gr. 6-12). 1993. 3.95 (*1-56688-066-1*) Bur For At-Risk.
—The Way I Feel. 16p. (gr. 6-12). 1993. 3.95 (*1-56688-064-5*) Bur For At-Risk.
—When I Remember. 24p. (gr. 6-12). 1993. 3.95 (*1-56688-068-8*) Bur For At-Risk.
Aliki. Feelings. Aliki, illus. LC 84-4098. 32p. (gr. k-3). 1984. 15.00 (*0-688-03831-X*); PLB 14.93 (*0-688-03832-8*) Greenwillow.
Allington, Richard L. & Krull, Kathleen. Feelings. Cody, Brian, illus. LC 79-27549. 32p. (ps-2). 1985. pap. text ed. 3.95 (*0-8114-8236-7*) Raintree Steck-V.
Amos, Janine. Afraid. LC 90-46540. (Illus.). 32p. (ps-3). 1991. 19.97 (*0-8172-3775-5*); pap. 4.95 (*0-8114-6908-5*) Raintree Steck-V.
—Angry. LC 90-46540. (Illus.). 32p. (ps-3). 1991. 19.97 (*0-8172-3776-3*); pap. 4.95 (*0-8114-6909-3*) Raintree Steck-V.
—Feelings, 10 vols. (gr. 4-7). 1994. Set. 139.80 (*0-8114-9275-3*) Raintree Steck-V.
—Feelings: Brave. (gr. 4-7). 1994. 19.97 (*0-8114-9228-1*) Raintree Steck-V.
—Feelings: Confident. (gr. 4-7). 1994. 19.97 (*0-8114-9229-X*) Raintree Steck-V.
—Hurt. LC 90-46540. (Illus.). 32p. (ps-3). 1991. 19.97 (*0-8172-3777-1*); pap. 4.95 (*0-8114-6910-7*) Raintree Steck-V.
—Jealous. LC 90-46540. (Illus.). 32p. (ps-3). 1991. 19.97 (*0-8172-3778-X*); pap. 4.95 (*0-8114-6911-5*) Raintree Steck-V.
—Lonely. LC 90-46540. (Illus.). 32p. (ps-3). 1991. 19.97 (*0-8172-3779-8*); pap. 4.95 (*0-8114-6912-3*) Raintree Steck-V.
—Sad. LC 90-46540. (Illus.). 32p. (ps-3). 1991. 19.97 (*0-8172-3780-1*); pap. 4.95 (*0-8114-6913-1*) Raintree Steck-V.
Anderson, Penny S. Feeling Frustrated. Siculan, Dan, illus. LC 82-19910. 32p. (ps-2). 1983. PLB 14.95 (*0-89565-245-5*) Childs World.
Barsuhn, Rochelle N. Feeling Angry. Hutton, Kathryn, illus. LC 82-19911. 32p. (ps-2). 1983. PLB 14.95 (*0-89565-244-7*) Childs World.
Beckelman, Laurie. Anger. LC 93-40641. 1994. text ed. 13.95 (*0-89686-841-9*, Crestwood Hse) Macmillan Child Grp.
Berger, Terry. I Have Feelings. Spivak, I. Howard, photos by. LC 70-147123. (Illus.). 32p. (ps-3). 1971. 14.95 (*0-87705-021-X*); pap. 9.95 (*0-89885-342-7*) Human Sci Pr.
—I Have Feelings Too. LC 79-15863. 32p. (ps-3). 1979. 16.95 (*0-87705-441-X*) Human Sci Pr.
Berry, Joy. Every Kid's Guide to Handling Feelings. Bartholemew, illus. 48p. (gr. 3-7). 1987. 4.95 (*0-516-21403-9*) Childrens.
Boddy, Marlys. ABC Book of Feelings. (Illus.). 32p. (ps-3). 1991. 8.99 (*0-570-04190-2*, 56-1649) Concordia.
Boulden, Jim. Feelings & Faces: Feelings Activity Book. Winter, Peter, illus. 32p. (Orig.). (gr. 1-7). 1993. pap. 4.95 (*1-878076-20-5*) Boulden Pub.
—How I Feel: Feelings Activity Book. Vecchio, Tony, illus. 32p. (Orig.). (gr. 1-7). Date not set. pap. 4.95 (*1-878076-21-3*) Boulden Pub.
Cain, Barbara S. Double-Dip Feelings: Stories to Help Children Understand Emotions. Patterson, Anne, illus. LC 92-56870. 1993. Repr. of 1990 ed. PLB 17.27 (*0-8368-0931-9*) Gareth Stevens Inc.
Campbell, James A. The Secret Places: The Story of a Child's Adventure with Grief. McConnell, Mary, illus. 45p. (Orig.). (gr. 4-9). 1992. pap. 5.25 (*1-56123-051-0*) Centering Corp.
Carpenter, Karen & Howard, Susie. Something Happened in My House: A Journey of Children's Grief. (Illus.). 36p. (Orig.). (gr. 3-8). 1993. pap. 9.95 (*1-883613-01-9*) Byte Size.
Crary, Elizabeth. I'm Excited. Whitney, Jean, illus. LC 93-85378. 32p. (ps-4). 1994. lib. bdg. 16.95 (*0-943990-92-0*); pap. 5.95 (*0-943990-91-2*) Parenting Pr.
—I'm Furious. Whitney, Jean, illus. LC 93-79529. 32p. (ps-4). 1994. lib. bdg. 16.95 (*0-943990-94-7*); pap. 5.95 (*0-943990-93-9*) Parenting Pr.
—I'm Scared. Whitney, Jean, illus. LC 93-85377. 32p. (Orig.). (ps-4). 1994. lib. bdg. 16.95 (*0-943990-90-4*); pap. 5.95 (*0-943990-89-0*) Parenting Pr.
Cush, Cathie. Depression. LC 93-14252. (Illus.). (gr. 6-9). 1993. PLB 21.34 (*0-8114-3529-6*) Raintree Steck-V.
Davies, Leah. Kelly Bear Beginnings, 5 bks. Hallett, Leah, illus. 176p. (ps-5). 1991. Set incl. Kelly Bear Feelings; Kelly Bear Behavior; Kelly Bear Health; Kelly Bear Activities; Kelly Bear Drug Awareness. pap. 29.95 (*0-9621054-7-3*) Kelly Bear Pr.
Dlugokinski, Eric. The Boys' & Girls' Book of Dealing with Feelings. 31p. (gr. k-6). 1988. pap. 10.95 (*1-882801-02-4*) Feelings Factory.
Dockrey, Karen. Will I Ever Feel Good Again? When You're Overwhelmed by Grief & Loss. LC 93-31249. 160p. (Orig.). 1993. pap. 7.99 (*0-8007-5475-1*) Revell.
Dombrower, Jan. Getting to Know Your Feelings. Stricklin, Patricia, illus. Johnson, Debbie, ed. 32p. (Orig.). (ps-3). 1990. pap. text ed. 5.95 (*0-9626348-0-8*) Heartwise Pr.
Draper, Kathy. Sunny or Stormy? The Kid's Guide to Mastering the Stress Mess. 83p. (gr. 2-6). 1993. pap. 10.95 (*1-883771-00-5*) Except Educ.
Duerrstein, Richard, illus. Mickey Is Happy: A Disney Book of Feelings. LC 92-52974. 12p. (ps). 1992. bds. 5.95 (*1-56282-267-5*) Disney Pr.
Elchoness, Monte. Why Do Kids Need Feelings? A Guide to Healthy Emotions. (Illus.). 96p. (Orig.). 1992. pap. 9.95 (*0-936781-07-6*) Monroe Pr.
Everything You Need to Know about Grieving. (Illus.). 1993. lib. bdg. 14.95 (*0-8239-1617-0*) Rosen Group.
Farrington, Liz & Sawaf, Ayman. Exploring Anger. Cash, Tina, illus. (ps-3). 1994. pap. 3.95 (*1-56844-051-0*) Enchante Pub.
—Exploring Fear. Cash, Tina, illus. (ps-3). 1994. pap. 3.95 (*1-56844-053-7*) Enchante Pub.
—Exploring Grief. Cash, Tina, illus. (ps-3). 1994. pap. 3.95 (*1-56844-050-2*) Enchante Pub.
—Exploring Guilt. Cash, Tina, illus. (ps-3). 1994. pap. 3.95 (*1-56844-055-3*) Enchante Pub.
—Exploring Jealousy. Cash, Tina, illus. (ps-3). 1994. pap. 3.95 (*1-56844-052-9*) Enchante Pub.
—Exploring Loneliness. Cash, Tina, illus. (ps-3). 1994. pap. 3.95 (*1-56844-054-5*) Enchante Pub.
Feelings, 6 bks. (gr. 2-5). 1991. lib. bdg. 19.97 (*0-685-58968-4*) Raintree Steck-V.
Ferguson, Dorothy. A Bunch of Balloons: A Book - Workbook for Grieving Children. Enbody, Shari B., illus. (Orig.). (gr. 1-6). 1992. pap. 5.95 (*1-56123-054-5*) Centering Corp.
Gebhart, Leslie, et al. Have You Ever Been a Child? (Hints for Helping When Life Seems Complicated) LC 93-60305. (Illus.). 1993. pap. 10.00 (*0-9636399-8-6*) Trinehrt Pubs.
Gillespie, Mike. Feelings: Frazzled, Frenzied & Frantic. Clark, Brian, ed. Day, Bruce, illus. 96p. (gr. 4 up). 1994. pap. 12.99 (*0-87403-766-2*) Standard Pub.
Goldman, Margaret F. My A, B, C, D, E Thinking, Feeling & Doing Book. Era, Diane, illus. Ellis, Albert, intro. by. LC 83-90397. (Illus.). 48p. (ps up). 11.95 (*0-914237-00-4*) L & M Bks.
Gross, Cheryl & Werz, Ed. The Sock Club: Angry Feelings - Smart Choices. 16p. (gr. k-4). 1992. 0.95 (*1-56688-053-X*) Bur For At-Risk.
—The Sock Club: Real & Fake. 16p. (gr. k-4). 1992. 0.95 (*1-56688-049-1*) Bur For At-Risk.
Hislop, Julia. Coping with Rejection. LC 90-29123. 107p. (gr. 7-12). 1991. PLB 14.95 (*0-8239-1183-7*) Rosen Group.
Kempler, Susan, et al. A Man Can Be... Dian, Russell, photos by. (Illus.). (ps-3). 1984. 16.95 (*0-89885-046-0*); pap. 9.95 (*0-89885-208-0*) Human Sci Pr.
Kerr, Robert. Positively! Learning to Manage Negative Emotions. Meyers, Steven, illus. 81p. (gr. 6-10). 1994. 15.95 (*0-685-71635-X*, 786) W Gladden Found.

---

listeners to think about their own funny feelings & can open the way for discussion with parents, teachers, counselors, church groups, & friends. Paperback, $7.95. Call or write for information to order, Green Timber Publications, P.O. Box 3884, Portland, ME 04104, 207-797-4180.
Publisher Provided Annotation.

Kolf, June C. Teenagers Talk about Grief. 64p. (Orig.). 1990. pap. 4.99 (*0-8010-5292-0*) Baker Bk.
Lamb, Jane M. Sharing with Thumpy: My Story of Love & Grief. Dodge, Nancy C., illus. 48p. (gr. k-12). 1985. pap. 8.95 workbook (*0-918533-10-4*) Prairie Lark.
Leonard, Marcia. Angry. 1988. pap. 3.95 (*0-553-05482-1*) Bantam.
—Happy. 1988. pap. 3.95 (*0-553-05483-X*) Bantam.
—Scared. 1988. pap. 3.95 (*0-553-05484-8*) Bantam.
—Silly. 1988. pap. 3.95 (*0-553-05485-6*) Bantam.
McElmurry, Mary A. Appreciating. Herrick, Elizabeth T., illus. 64p. (gr. 2-8). 1983. wkbk. 8.95 (*0-9607366-1-1*, GA 493) Good Apple.
—Belonging. Herrick, Elizabeth T., illus. 64p. (gr. 2-8). 1983. wkbk. 8.95 (*0-9607366-0-3*, GA 492) Good Apple.
—Caring. 64p. (gr. 4-8). 1981. 8.95 (*0-86653-052-5*, GA275) Good Apple.
McElmurry, Mary Anne. Feelings. 80p. (gr. 3-8). 1981. 9.95 (*0-86653-027-4*, GA 276) Good Apple.
Murphy, J. Feelings. (Illus.). 24p. (ps-8). 1985. pap. 4.95 (*0-88753-129-6*, Pub. by Black Moss Pr CN) Firefly Bks Ltd.
Murphy, Mary. The Way We Feel Inside: With the Song "How I'm Made" Freitag, Jim, illus. 48p. (ps-3). 1990. pap. 9.00 incl. 17 min. audiocassette (*0-89486-618-4*) Hazelden.
My Own Book of Feelings. 32p. (gr. 2-6). 1994. 4.95 (*0-685-71576-0*, 512) W Gladden Found.
Nelson, JoAnne. How Do You Feel? Vance, R. Scott, illus. LC 91-36336. 24p. (Orig.). (gr. k-2). 1993. pap. write for info. (*0-935529-15-2*) Comprehen Health Educ.
Norton, Yuri E. Dear Uncle Dave. Waring, Shirley B., photos by. (Illus.). 40p. (Orig.). (gr. 1 up). 1993. PLB 13.95 (*0-9622808-4-4*) S&T Waring.
Odor, Ruth S. Moods & Emotions. Bolt, John, illus. LC 81-17008. 112p. (gr. 2-6). 1980. PLB 14.95 (*0-89565-210-2*) Childs World.
O'Toole, Donna. Healing & Growing Through Grief. (Illus.). 20p. 1986. pap. 3.25 (*0-685-31273-9*, HG-02-4) Rainbow NC.
Palmer, Patricia. Liking Myself. Shank, Will, illus. LC 77-88185. 80p. (gr. k-4). 1977. pap. 6.95 (*0-915166-41-0*) Impact Pubs Cal.
—The Mouse, the Monster & Me. Shank, Will, illus. LC 77-88186. 80p. (Orig.). (gr. 3-6). 1977. pap. 6.95 (*0-915166-43-7*) Impact Pubs Cal.
Path Works Staff. Feelings: Having Them, Sharing Them. Nelson, Coleen, illus. 20p. (gr. 3-5). 1993. incl. tchr's. guide 1.95 (*0-685-71925-1*, 740) W Gladden Found.
Pincus, Debbie. Sharing. Lasky, Mark, illus. 80p. (gr. 4-8). 1983. wkbk. 9.95 (*0-86653-117-3*, GA 468) Good Apple.
Polland, Barbara K. Feelings: Inside You & Outloud Too. LC 74-25835. (Illus.). 64p. (ps-3). 1984. pap. 6.95 (*0-89087-006-3*) Celestial Arts.
Richards, Joanne & Standley, Marianne V. Dealing with Feelings. 72p. (gr. 3-7). 1982. 7.95 (*0-88160-015-6*, LW 118) Learning Wks.
Riley, Sue. Angry. LC 77-16791. (Illus.). (ps-2). 1978. PLB 12.95 (*0-89565-014-2*) Childs World.
—Sorry. LC 77-16811. (Illus.). (ps-2). 1978. PLB 12.95 (*0-89565-013-4*) Childs World.
Santacruz, Daniel, tr. Mickey Esta Feliz: Un Libro Disney de Emociones. Duerrstein, Richard, illus. (SPA.). 12p. 1993. 5.95 (*1-56282-459-7*) Disney Pr.
Schenkerman, Rona D. Growing up with Angry Feelings. 16p. (gr. 3-8). 1993. 1.95 (*1-56688-113-7*) Bur For At-Risk.
Schwartz, Amy & Schwartz, Henry. Make a Face: A Book with a Mirror. (Illus.). 28p. (gr. 2 up). 1994. 9.95 (*0-590-46301-2*, Cartwheel) Scholastic Inc.
Sciacca, Fran & Sciacca, Jill. Does Anyone Else Feel This Way? Conquering Loneliness & Depression. 64p. 1992. pap. 3.99 saddle stitch bdg. (*0-310-48021-3*) Zondervan.
Sheehan, Cilla. The Colors That I Am. Elliot, Glen, photos by. LC 80-25351. (Illus.). 32p. (ps-5). 1981. 16.95 (*0-89885-047-9*) Human Sci Pr.
Simon, Norma. How Do I Feel? Lasker, Joe, illus. LC 77-126430. (ps-2). 1970. PLB 13.95 (*0-8075-3414-5*) A Whitman.
Sodeika, Zita. Caged-In. Kezys, Algimantas, photos by. 94p. (Orig.). 1992. pap. 15.00 (*0-685-59569-2*) Galerija.
Walter, Nancy L. Inside of Me. Walter, Nancy L., photos by. (Illus.). 48p. (ps-3). 1993. pap. 19.95 (*0-9635127-9-X*) Naturally by Nan.
—Inside of Me I Feel... 48p. (ps-3). 1993. pap. 10.95 (*0-9635127-3-0*) Naturally By Nan.
—Inside of Me There's a Storm a Brewing. 48p. (ps-3). 1995. pap. 10.95 (*0-9635127-7-3*) Naturally By Nan.
Walter, Nancy T. Inside of Me I Have Feelings. 48p. (ps-3). 1992. pap. 10.95 (*0-9635127-0-6*) Naturally by Nan.
Ward, Elaine M. Being Human: Learning Through Feelings. 57p. (Orig.). (gr. 1-6). 1988. pap. 9.95 (*0-940754-63-0*) Ed Ministries.
Waring, Shirley B. What Happened to Benjamin: A True Story. Bergstrom, Lucy, illus. LC 92-83949. 38p. (Orig.). (gr. k-6). 1993. PLB 13.95g (*0-9622808-2-8*); Audio cass. 9.98 (*0-9622808-3-6*) S&T Waring.
Wilkinson, Beth. Coping with Jealousy. Rosen, Ruth, ed. (gr. 7-12). 1992. 14.95 (*0-8239-1516-6*) Rosen Group.

EMOTIONS–FICTION

Alpert, Lou. Max & the Great Blueness. Alpert, Lou, illus. LC 92-23313. 32p. (ps-3). 1993. smythe sewn reinforced 13.95 (*1-879085-38-0*) Whsprng Coyote Pr.
Atkins, Kirsten. How Long Is a Piece of String? Posey, Pam, illus. LC 93-18062. 1994. write for info. (*0-383-03672-0*) SRA Schl Grp.
Balter, Lawrence. What's the Matter with A. J? Understanding Jealousy. Schanzer, Roz, illus. 40p. (ps-2). 1989. 5.95 (*0-8120-6119-5*) Barron.
Bobbi. T-Neck. 63p. 1992. pap. 5.95 (*0-9626608-4-1*) Magik NY.
Brownmiller, Arlan J. Nixie's Wild Zoo. 1992. pap. 11.95 (*0-533-10308-8*) Vantage.
Cain, Barbara S. Double-Dip Feelings: A Book to Help Children Understand Emotions. O'Brien, Ann S., illus. LC 89-49382. 32p. 1990. 16.95 (*0-945354-23-1*); pap. 8.95 (*0-945354-20-7*) Magination Pr.
Chartrand, Micheline. Lollypop Is Angry. (Illus.). 12p. (ps). 1993. bds. 3.95 (*2-921198-09-6*, Pub. by Les Edits Herit CN) Adams Inc MA.
Conlin, Susan & Friedman, Susan L. Ellie's Day. Smith, M. Kathryn, illus. Illsley-Clarke, Jean, intro. by. LC 89-60334. (Illus.). 32p. (Orig.). (ps-2). 1989. PLB 16.95 (*0-943990-45-9*); pap. 5.95 (*0-943990-44-0*) Parenting Pr.

Curtis, Chara M. All I See Is Part of Me. rev. ed. Aldrich, Cynthia, illus. 48p. 1994. 15.95 (*0-935699-07-4*) Illum Arts.
In ALL I SEE IS PART OF ME a child discovers his universal connection with all of life. Illuminating answers to life's questions are discovered on an enchanting journey of awakening. The conclusion brings reassurance & comfort from knowing that for each of us, "there can be no end." "This warm, gentle, tender, trusting book is just what the world needs." - Gerald G. Jampolsky, M.D., author. "You will be warmed by its love - as I have - over & over." - NAPRA Trade News. "The child in this world shines forth with vibrancy & warmth," - Montessori Life. To order, call Atrium 1-800-275-2606.
Publisher Provided Annotation.

—Fun Is a Feeling. Aldrich, Cynthia, illus. 32p. (gr. k-5). 1992. 14.95 (*0-935699-04-X*) Illum Arts.
FUN IS A FEELING playfully embraces the development of positive attitudes & feelings. Ageless truths are powerfully presented through the inspiring verse & delightful illustrations. The child's imagination is challenged to view everyday events (including chores) in a creative, magical way. In the end, each reader is left with a secret smile - knowing "fun can be found wherever you go." "The artwork is fantastic. The message of treasuring our feelings is outstanding & uplifting. This book is a 'must' for children." - Gerald G. Jampolsky, M.D., author. "This vibrant text delights in the challenge of making fun the 'path' in life rather than the destination." - NAPRA Trade Journal. "Here's a book about new ways to have fun. Fun likes to hide, so look for it everywhere." - The Seattle Times. To order, call Atrium 1-800-275-2606.
Publisher Provided Annotation.

Dijs, Carla. A Giraffe Needs to Laugh: A Pop-up Book about Feelings. Dijs, Carla, illus. 10p. (gr. k-2). 1993. 7.95 (*0-8431-3480-1*) Price Stern.
Disney Happy Pictures. (gr. 3 up). 1991. pap. 1.97 (*1-56297-123-9*) Lee Pubns KY.
Duffy, James. The Graveyard Gang. LC 92-30990. 192p. (gr. 5-7). 1993. SBE 14.95 (*0-684-19449-X*, Scribners Young Read) Macmillan Child Grp.
Edens, Cooper. Nineteen Hats, Ten Teacups, an Empty Birdcage, & the Art of Longing. LC 91-25277. (Illus.). 40p. 1992. signed & numbered 20.00 (*0-671-75592-7*, Green Tiger); pap. 8.00 (*0-671-74968-4*, Green Tiger) S&S Trade.
Everitt, B. Mean Soup. 1992. 13.95 (*0-15-253146-7*, HB Juv Bks) HarBrace.
Faber, Adele & Mazlish, Elaine. Bobby & the Brockles. Morehouse, Hank, illus. LC 93-42283. 64p. (Orig.). 1994. pap. 15.00 (*0-380-77067-9*) Avon.
Giff, Patricia R. Today Was a Terrible Day. Natti, Suzanna, illus. (gr. k-3). 1984. incl. cassette 19.95 (*0-941078-50-7*); pap. 12.95 incl. cassette (*0-941078-48-5*); pap. 27.95 4 bks, cassette, & guide (*0-941078-49-3*); sound fimlstrip 22.95 (*0-941078-47-7*) Live Oak Media.
—Today Was a Terrible Day. Natti, Susanna, illus. 32p. (ps-k). 1984. pap. 4.99 (*0-14-050453-2*) Viking Child Bks.
—Today Was a Terrible Day. Natti, Susanna, illus. 32p. (ps-k). 1984. pap. 3.95 incl. cassette (*0-685-54175-4*, Penguin Bks) Viking Penguin.
Grifalconi, Ann. Kinda Blue. Grifalconi, Ann, illus. 32p. (ps-3). 1993. 15.95 (*0-316-32869-3*) Little.
Haugen, Tormod. The Night Birds. La Farge, Sheila, tr. from NOR. LC 82-70311. 160p. (gr. 4-6). 1982. 11.95 (*0-385-28735-6*, Sey Lawr); pap. 9.89 (*0-385-28736-4*) Delacorte.
Hines, Anna G. Maybe a Band-Aid Will Help. LC 84-1533. (Illus.). 24p. (ps-1). 1990. pap. 3.95 (*0-525-44561-7*, DCB) Dutton Child Bks.
Hogan, Paula Z. Sometimes I Get So Mad. Shapiro, Karen, illus. Silverman, Manuel S., intro. by. LC 79-24057. (Illus.). 32p. (gr. k-6). 1980. PLB 19.97 (*0-8172-1359-7*) Raintree Steck-V.
—Sometimes I Get So Mad. (ps-3). 1993. pap. 3.95 (*0-8114-5207-7*) Raintree Steck-V.
Jahn-Clough, Lisa. Alicia Has a Bad Day. LC 94-4520. 1994. 13.95 (*0-395-69454-X*) HM.
Johnson, Lee & Johnson, Sue K. If I Ran the Family. Espeland, Pamela, ed. Collier-Morales, Roberta, illus. LC 92-948. 32p. (ps-3). 1992. 13.95 (*0-915793-41-5*) Free Spirit Pub.
King-Smith, Dick. Harry's Mad. large type ed. 136p. (gr. 2-7). 1990. lib. bdg. 15.95x (*0-7451-1101-7*, Lythway Large Print) Hall.
Klein, Norma. Learning How to Fall. 1989. 14.95 (*0-553-05809-6*, Starfire) Bantam.
Lamb, Jane M. Sharing with Thumpy: My Story of Love & Grief. Dodge, Nancy C., illus. 48p. (gr. k-12). 1985. pap. 8.95 workbook (*0-918533-10-4*) Prairie Lark.
Lester, Alison. I'm Green & I'm Grumpy. 16p. (ps-1). 1993. pap. 4.99 (*0-14-054478-X*, Puffin) Puffin Bks.
Levoy, Myron. Pictures of Adam. LC 92-24598. 224p. (gr. 7 up). 1993. pap. 4.95 (*0-688-11941-7*, Pub. by Beech Tree Bks) Morrow.
Littleton, Mark. Winter Thunder. LC 92-5433. 1993. pap. 3.99 (*1-56507-008-9*) Harvest Hse.
Lobel, Arnold. Great Blueness & Other Predicaments. Lobel, Arnold, illus. LC 68-24323. 32p. (ps-3). 1994. pap. 5.95 (*0-06-443316-1*, Trophy) HarpC Child Bks.
McDonald, Megan. The Bridge to Nowhere. LC 92-50844. 160p. (gr. 6 up). 1993. 14.95 (*0-531-05478-0*); PLB 14.99 (*0-531-08628-3*) Orchard Bks Watts.
Marcus, Irene W. & Marcus, Paul. Scary Night Visitors: A Story for Children with Bedtime Fears. Jeschke, Susan, illus. LC 92-56874. 1993. PLB 17.27 (*0-8368-0935-1*) Gareth Stevens Inc.

Mazzola, Toni & Guten, Mimi. Wally Koala & the Little Green Peach. Cohen, Keri, ed. McCoy, William M., illus. LC 93-94002. 22p. (ps-3). 1993. saddlestitch bdg. incl. cassette 9.95 (*1-883747-01-5*) WK Prods.
WALLY KOALA'S SLOGAN: "I'M WONDERFUL & SO ARE YOU." Books lovingly narrated by CHARLOTTE RAE (TV'S FACTS OF LIFE) who also sings original songs. IN WALLY KOALA & THE LITTLE GREEN PEACH, Farmer Jim picks all other peaches, leaving lonely little green peach at the top of the tree. Through the story of Mr. Big Peach Tree, Wally comforts Little Green Peach & previews all the changes he can expect during metamorphosis from green peach to glorious blossoming tree. (Vernon Woolf) "Magical journey into patience, trust in self, nature & process of life. A must for those who

feel they're not blossoming as fast as their peers or their expectations." IN WALLY KOALA & FRIENDS, Wally travels from Australia to America with friends Sadie Kangaroo & Timmy Kookaburra. This book introduces the loveable characters. Self-esteem subtly emphasized. WALLY helps to make children aware that we all make mistakes, as he & Sadie did by sneaking Timmy on the plane. Mistakes are OK. We learn from them. (Vernon Woolf) "WALLY & FRIENDS teaches trust in the world of adult authority in an easy-going, delightful style." (BUSINESS STARTUPS mag) "Loveable koala from 'down under,' winning the hearts of North American children..." To order contact: W.K. Productions, P.O. Box 801504, Dallas, TX 75380-1504. Distributors: Baker & Taylor, Brodart Co., 717-326-2461, Hervey's Booklink, 214-480-9987, Ingram.
Publisher Provided Annotation.

Miles, Miska. Gertrude's Pocket. McCully, Emily, illus. (gr. 2-5). 1984. 15.25 (*0-8446-6164-3*) Peter Smith.
Modesitt, Jeanne. Sometimes I Feel Like a Mouse. (Illus.). 1992. 14.95 (*0-590-44835-8*, Scholastic Hardcover) Scholastic Inc.
—The Story of Z. Johnson, Lonnie S., illus. LC 89-3923. 28p. (ps up). 1991. pap. 14.95 (*0-88708-105-3*) Picture Bk Studio.
Moncure, Jane B. Joy. (SPA & ENG., Illus.). 32p. (ps-2). 1980. PLB 14.95 (*0-89565-224-2*) Childs World.
Nixon, Joan L. The Specter. LC 82-70322. 160p. (gr. 7 up). 1982. pap. 12.95 (*0-385-28948-0*) Delacorte.
Odor, Ruth S. Glad. Indereiden, Nancy, illus. LC 79-26076. (ps-2). 1980. PLB 12.95 (*0-89565-114-9*) Childs World.
Paley, Nina, illus. Inside-Out Feelings. LC 93-8953. 1993. write for info. (*1-56071-315-1*) ETR Assocs.
Pendergast, Kathleen. Say Another One about How I Feel. Tindal, Pauline, illus. LC 81-90678. 54p. (Orig.). (gr. k-6). 1982. pap. 6.95 (*0-942178-00-9*) Madison Park Pr.
Plum, Carol T. Peter's Angry Toys: I Am Special Childrens Story Books. 32p. (ps-3). 1989. lib. bdg. 9.95 (*0-87973-015-3*, 15); pap. text ed. 5.95 (*0-87973-012-9*, 12) Our Sunday Visitor.
Rowe, William. Viu's Night Book. (Illus.). 55p. (gr. 3-6). 1995. pap. 7.95 (*0-9641330-0-8*) Portunus Pubng.
Rozman, Deborah. The Crystal Lady. Royall, Sandy, illus. 72p. (gr. 1 up). 1991. 19.95 (*1-879052-01-6*, Planet Pubns) Planetary Pubns.
Sachs, Marilyn. What My Sister Remembered. LC 91-32263. 120p. (gr. 5-9). 1992. 15.00 (*0-525-44953-1*, DCB) Dutton Child Bks.
Selway, Martina. Don't Forget to Write. Selway, Martina, illus. LC 91-28430. 32p. (ps-2). 1992. 12.95 (*0-8249-8543-5*, Ideals Child) Hambleton-Hill.
Sherwood, Jonathan & Farrington, Liz. Tanya & the Green-Eyed Monster. Thornton, Jeremy, illus. 40p. (gr. k-4). 1993. 14.95 (*1-56844-002-2*) Enchante Pub.

Shles, Larry. The Adventure of the Squib Owl: Squib Ser. Shles, Larry, illus. 1988. pap. 7.95 (*0-915190-85-0*) Jalmar Pr.
Squib the Owl series, written & whimsically illustrated by Larry Shles, teaches self-esteem & personal & social responsibility as it entertains. The author uses the name Squib to personify the small vulnerable part of us all that struggles & at times feels helpless in an enormous world filled with emotions. This Series, five volumes, traces the adventures of this tiny owl as he struggles with his feelings searching at least for understanding. Each of the five titles explores a different vulnerability. MOTHS & MOTHERS, FEATHERS & FATHERS (explores feelings); HOOTS & TOOTS & HAIRY BRUTES (explores disabilities); ALIENS IN MY NEST (explores adolescent behavior); HUGS & SHRUGS (explores inner peace). The latest volume DO I HAVE TO GO TO SCHOOL TODAY? is great for the young reader who needs encouragement from teachers who accept him "just as he is". Brilliantly simple, yet realistically complex, Squib personifies each & every one of us. He is a reflection of what we are, & what we can become. Every reader who has struggled with life's limitations will recognize his own struggles & triumphs in the microcosm of Squib's forest world - in Squib we find a parable for all ages from 8-80.
Publisher Provided Annotation.

Simon, Norma. I Was So Mad! LC 73-22425. (Illus.). 40p. (gr. k-2). 1974. PLB 11.95 (*0-8075-3520-6*); pap. 4.95 (*0-8075-3519-2*) A Whitman.
Starbuck, Marnie. The Gladimals Talk about Feelings. 16p. (ps-3). 1991. pap. text ed. 0.75 (*1-56456-225-5*) W Gladden Found.
Tester, Sylvia R. Frustrated. Indereiden, Nancy, illus. LC 79-23804. (ps-2). 1980. PLB 12.95 (*0-89565-110-6*) Childs World.
—Jealous. Indereiden, Nancy, illus. LC 79-24042. (ps-2). 1980. PLB 12.95 (*0-89565-111-4*) Childs World.
—Sad. Indereiden, Nancy, illus. LC 79-26252. (ps-2). 1980. PLB 12.95 (*0-89565-112-2*) Childs World.
Walsh, Ellen S. Brunus & the New Bear. LC 92-29060. 1993. pap. 4.95 (*0-15-212675-9*) HarBrace.
Warren, Peggy. Where Love Starts. LC 91-77291. (Illus.). 36p. (gr. k-3). 1992. 5.95 (*0-9628710-4-4*) Art After Five.
Waters, Virginia. Color Us Rational. Lee, Penny, illus. LC 78-71011. (ps-3). 1979. pap. 3.00 (*0-917476-15-8*) Inst Rational-Emotive.
Winston-Hiller, Randy. Some Secrets Are For Sharing. Cleaveland, C. A. & McCreary, Jane, illus. 33p. (Orig.). (gr. 4 up). 1986. pap. 5.95 (*0-910223-08-4*) MAC Pub.

EMPERORS
see Kings and Rulers;
see and names of emperors

EMPLOYEES AND OFFICIALS
see and names of countries, cities, etc. and organizations with the subdivision officials and employees, e.g. U. S. –Officials and Employees

EMPLOYMENT DISCRIMINATION
see Discrimination in Employment

EMPRESSES
see Queens

ENAMEL AND ENAMELING
Hawkins, Leslie V. Art Metal & Enameling. 234p. (gr. 9-12). 1974. text ed. 17.60 (*0-02-662240-8*) Bennett IL.
Zechlin, Katharina. Creative Enameling & Jewelry-Making. Kuttner, Paul, tr. LC 65-20877. (gr. 10 up). 1965. 6.95 (*0-8069-5062-5*); PLB 6.69 (*0-8069-5063-3*) Sterling.

ENCYCLOPEDIAS AND DICTIONARIES
Auriga. Enciclopedia Juvenil Auriga: Inventos Que Conmovieron el Mundo, Descubrimientos e Inventos, Armas Que Conmovieron el Mundo, Historia Ilustrada de los Barcos, Artistas Que Conmovieron el Mundo. (SPA.). 360p. 1977. leatherette 42.00 (*84-201-0202-4*, French & Eur) Fr & Eur.
Bailey, Kenneth. Enciclopedia Infantil Molino. (SPA.). 234p. 1973. 95.00 (*0-8288-6277-X*, S22860) Fr & Eur.
Barnhart, Clarence L. & Barnhart, Robert K. The World Book Dictionary. World Book Editors, ed. LC 93-60574. (Illus.). 2430p. 1993. PLB write for info. (*0-7166-0294-6*) World Bk.
Barron's New Student's Concise Encyclopedia. 2nd ed. 1300p. 1993. 29.95 (*0-8120-6329-5*) Barron.
Beal, George. The Julian Messner Young Reader's Thesaurus. 1984. pap. 6.95 (*0-685-09676-9*) S&S Trade.
—Simon & Schuster Young Readers' Thesaurus. (Illus.). 192p. 1984. pap. 7.95 (*0-671-50816-4*, S&S BFYR) S&S Trade.
Calder, S. J. First Facts, 12 bks. Van Wright, Cornelius, illus. (ps-1). 1989. Set, 32p. ea. write for info. (*0-671-94108-9*, J Messner); Set, 32p. ea. lib. bdg. write for info. (*0-671-94107-0*) S&S Trade.
Carrogio. Enciclopedia Infantil, 10 vols. (SPA.). 2400p. 1974. Set. leather 495.00 (*0-8288-6033-5*, S50480) Fr & Eur.
Children's Britannica, 20 vols. (ps-8). 1992. Set. 299.00 (*0-85229-229-5*) Ency Brit Ed.
Children's Dictionary. 832p. (gr. 8-12). 1988. 13.95 (*0-673-12491-6*) Scott F.
Children's First Dictionary. (Illus.). 192p. 1991. 7.99 (*0-517-64469-X*) Random Hse Value.
Child's First Library of Learning, 17 bks. (ps-3). 1990. Set, 88p. ea. 270.81 (*0-8094-4825-4*); Set, 88p. ea. lib. bdg. 361.59 (*0-8094-4826-2*) Time-Life.
Compton's Encyclopedia, 26 vols. (gr. 5-10). 1992. Set. 569.00 (*0-85229-554-5*) Ency Brit Ed.
Compton's Precyclopaedia, 16 vols. (gr. 1-4). 1988. Set. 269.00 (*0-85229-479-4*) Ency Brit Ed.
Dempsey, Walter. Children's First Encyclopedia. 1985. 6.98 (*0-671-07744-9*) S&S Trade.
Diccionario Enciclopedico, 15 vols. (gr. 7 up). Set. 199.00 (*0-8347-5189-5*) Ency Brit Ed.
The Dorling Kindersley Big Book of Knowledge. LC 93-31723. (Illus.). 480p. (gr. k-5). 1994. 29.95 (*1-56458-518-2*) Dorling Kindersley.
Dupre, Jean-Paul. The Barron's Junior Fact-Finder: An Illustrated Encyclopedia for Children. (Illus.). 296p. (gr. 2-6). 1989. 19.95 (*0-8120-6072-5*) Barron.
Eastman, Philip D. Cat in the Hat Beginner Book Dictionary. LC 64-1157. (Illus.). 144p. (gr. k-6). 1964. 10.00 (*0-394-81009-0*); lib. bdg. 9.99 (*0-394-91009-5*) Random Bks Yng Read.
—Cat in the Hat Beginner Book Dictionary in Spanish & English. LC 66-10688. (SPA & ENG., Illus.). 144p. (gr. k-3). 1966. 16.00 (*0-394-81542-4*) Beginner.
Elliot, J. Children's Encyclopedia. King, Colin, illus. 128p. (gr. 3-6). 1987. PLB 16.96 (*0-88110-265-2*); pap. 16.96 (*0-7460-0000-6*) EDC.
Encyclopaedia Britannica, 32 vols. 1992. Set. 1199.00 (*0-85229-553-7*) Ency Brit Ed.
Fact Finders, 4 vols. 128p. (gr. 4-5). 1989. Set. PLB 69.08 (*0-8368-0131-8*) Gareth Stevens Inc.
First Picture Dictionary. (Illus.). (ps-2). 3.50 (*0-7214-0617-3*) Ladybird Bks.
Fun Facts & Records. (Illus.). 128p. (gr. 2-6). 1990. 7.99 (*0-517-69601-0*) Random Hse Value.
Gaynor, Brigid. Alpha Box & Dictionary. (Illus.). 28p. (ps). Date not set. incl. alphabet blocks 14.95 (*0-685-70747-4*) Red Jacket Pr.
Greisman, Joan. First Dictionary. (ps-3). 1990. pap. write for info. (*0-307-15853-5*) Western Pub.
Hubbard, L. Ron, concept by. How to Use a Dictionary Picture Book for Children. 260p. (gr. 3-7). 1992. 34.99 (*0-88404-747-4*) Bridge Pubns Inc.
The Kingfisher Young World Encyclopedia. LC 93-50796. 1995. write for info. (*1-85697-519-3*, Kingfisher LKC) LKC.
Let's Discover, 16 vols. (Illus.). (gr. k-6). 1981. Set. PLB 199.00 per set (*0-8172-1782-7*) Raintree Steck-V.
Levey, Judith, ed. The Macmillan Dictionary for Children. rev. ed. LC 89-60916. (Illus.). 896p. (gr. 3-7). 1989. SBE 14.95 (*0-02-761561-8*, Macmillan Child Bk) Macmillan Child Grp.
Macmillan Dictionary for Children: Multimedia Edition. (Illus.). 1992. 59.95 (*1-56574-000-9*, Maxwell Elects) Macmlln New Media.
Mi Primer Diccionario Escolar. 4th ed. (SPA.). 480p. 1975. pap. 5.95 (*0-7859-0890-0*, S-27087) Fr & Eur.
My First Dictionary. 1989. 11.95 (*0-673-28497-2*) Scott F.
My First Picture Dictionary. (Illus.). 64p. (ps-1). 1985. 4.99 (*0-517-48000-X*) Random Hse Value.
My First Picture Dictionary. (ps-1). 1985. 5.98 (*0-517-44379-1*) Random Hse Value.
Nauta Staff. Mi Primera Enciclopedia, 2 vols. 7th ed. (SPA.). 420p. 1978. Set. 65.00 (*0-8288-5254-5*, S26910) Fr & Eur.
The New Book of Knowledge. LC 92-22145. 1993. Set. write for info. (*0-7172-0524-X*) Grolier Inc.
The New Book of Knowledge. LC 93-35438. 1994. Set. write for info. (*0-7172-0525-8*) Grolier Inc.
Paton, John, ed. Doubleday Children's Encyclopedia. 1990. PLB 149.99 (*0-385-41211-8*) Doubleday.
Pef. Dictionnaires des Mots Tordus. (FRE.). 79p. (gr. 1-5). 1989. pap. 10.95 (*2-07-031192-9*) Schoenhof.
The Random House Children's Encyclopedia. rev. ed. LC 90-253234. (Illus.). 644p. (gr. 2-7). 1993. 50.00 (*0-679-85093-7*) Random Bks Yng Read.
Renyi Bilingual Picture Dictionary. (CHI & ENG.). 192p. (ps-12). 19.95 (*1-878363-39-5*) Forest Hse.
Renyi Bilingual Picture Dictionary. (ENG.). 192p. (ps-12). 19.95 (*1-878363-40-9*) Forest Hse.
Renyi Bilingual Picture Dictionary. (EST & ENG.). 192p. (ps-12). 19.95 (*1-878363-41-7*) Forest Hse.
Renyi Bilingual Picture Dictionary. (FRE & ENG.). 192p. (ps-12). 19.95 (*1-878363-42-5*) Forest Hse.
Renyi Bilingual Picture Dictionary. (GER & ENG.). 192p. (ps-12). 19.95 (*1-878363-43-3*) Forest Hse.
Renyi Bilingual Picture Dictionary. (GRE & ENG.). 192p. (ps-12). 18.95 (*1-878363-44-1*) Forest Hse.
Renyi Bilingual Picture Dictionary. (HEB & ENG.). 192p. (ps-12). 18.95 (*1-878363-45-X*) Forest Hse.
Renyi Bilingual Picture Dictionary. (ITA & ENG.). 192p. (ps-12). 18.95 (*1-878363-46-8*) Forest Hse.
Renyi Bilingual Picture Dictionary. (JPN & ENG.). 278p. (ps-12). 24.95 (*1-878363-47-6*) Forest Hse.
Renyi Bilingual Picture Dictionary. (LAV & ENG.). 192p. (ps-12). 19.95 (*1-878363-48-4*) Forest Hse.
Renyi Bilingual Picture Dictionary. (LIT & ENG.). 192p. (ps-12). 19.95 (*1-878363-49-2*) Forest Hse.
Renyi Bilingual Picture Dictionary. (MAC & ENG.). 192p. (ps-12). 19.95 (*1-878363-50-6*) Forest Hse.
Renyi Bilingual Picture Dictionary. (POL & ENG.). 192p. (ps-12). 19.95 (*1-878363-51-4*) Forest Hse.
Renyi Bilingual Picture Dictionary. (POR & ENG.). 192p. (ps-12). 19.95 (*1-878363-52-2*) Forest Hse.
Renyi Bilingual Picture Dictionary. (RUS & ENG.). 192p. (ps-12). 19.95 (*1-878363-53-0*) Forest Hse.
Renyi Bilingual Picture Dictionary. (SPA & ENG.). 192p. (ps-12). 19.95 (*1-878363-54-9*) Forest Hse.
Renyi Bilingual Picture Dictionary. (UKR & ENG.). 192p. (ps-12). 19.95 (*1-878363-55-7*) Forest Hse.
Renyi Bilingual Picture Dictionary. (ARM & ENG.). 192p. (ps-12). 19.95 (*1-878363-56-5*) Forest Hse.
Reynolds, Jean, ed. New Book of Knowledge. (gr. 3-8). 1989. write for info (*0-7172-0520-7*) Grolier Inc.

Scarry, Richard. Mi Diccionario Infantil. 3rd ed. (SPA.). 96p. 1974. pap. 14.95 (*0-8288-6073-4*, S-27628) Fr & Eur.
—Mi Primer Gran Diccionario Infantil. 4th ed. (SPA.). 90p. 1978. 13.95 (*0-8288-5253-7*, S26637) Fr & Eur.
Second Picture Dictionary. (Illus.). (ps-2). 3.50 (*0-7214-0618-1*) Ladybird Bks.
Shapiro, William E., ed. The Kingfisher Young People's Encyclopedia of the United States. LC 93-42501. 808p. (gr. 4-10). 1994. 39.95 (*1-85697-521-5*, Kingfisher LKC) LKC.
Snow, Alan. My First Encyclopedia. 1991. 5.98 (*0-8317-0227-3*) Smithmark.
—My First Encyclopedia. Snow, Alan, illus. LC 91-24320. 32p. (gr. k-3). 1992. PLB 12.79 (*0-8167-2519-5*); pap. 4.95 (*0-8167-2520-9*) Troll Assocs.
Standard Educational Corporation Staff. New Standard Encyclopedia, 20 vols. Downey, Douglas W., et al, eds. LC 92-5529. (gr. 6-12). 1993. Set. write for info. (*0-87392-198-4*) Standard Ed.
—New Standard Encyclopedia. Downey, Douglas W., et al, eds. LC 93-7724. (Illus.). (gr. 6-12). 1994. Set. write for info. (*0-87392-199-2*) Standard Ed.
Stockley, C. & Colvin, L. Living World Encyclopedia. (Illus.). 128p. (gr. 5-7). 1992. PLB 16.96 (*0-88110-434-5*, Usborne); pap. 14.95 (*0-7460-0766-3*, Usborne) EDC.
Vitale, Miralla. Enciclopedia de la Nina. 3rd ed. (SPA.). 64p. 1979. 29.95 (*0-8288-4738-X*, S50471) Fr & Eur.
Watermill Press Staff. Webster's English-French - Francais-Anglais Dictionary. 224p. (gr. 4-7). 1992. pap. 2.95 (*0-8167-2919-0*, Pub. by Watermill Pr) Troll Assocs.
—Webster's English-Spanish - Espanol-Ingles Dictionary. 224p. (gr. 4-7). 1992. pap. 2.95 (*0-8167-2918-2*, Pub. by Watermill Pr) Troll Assocs.
Watson, Carol. My First Encyclopedia. LC 92-53477. (Illus.). 80p. (gr. k-3). 1993. 16.95 (*1-56458-214-0*) Dorling Kindersley.
The Webster's II New Riverside Children's Dictionary. 800p. 1985. pap. 9.70 (*0-395-37884-2*) HM.
Webster's Scholastic Dictionary. (gr. 9 up). pap. 2.95 (*0-8049-2001-X*, D1) Airmont.
Welch, R. C. The Very Scary Dictionary: Who's Who in Fright. Warburton, Bartt, illus. 64p. 1993. pap. 4.95 (*1-56565-072-7*) Lowell Hse.
Williams, Brian & Williams, Brenda. The Random House Library of Knowledge First Encyclopedia. LC 91-32817. (Illus.). 192p. (gr. 2-6). 1992. 18.00 (*0-679-83059-6*) Random Bks Yng Read.
Wittels, Harriet & Greisman, Joan. The Clear & Simple Thesaurus Dictionary. (Illus.). (gr. 3 up). 1976. pap. 8.95 (*0-448-12198-0*, G&D) Putnam Pub Group.
World Book Editors. The World Book Encyclopedia, 1994, 22 vols. rev. ed. LC 93-60768. (Illus.). 14000p. (gr. 4 up). 1993. PLB write for info. Set (*0-7166-0094-3*) World Bk.
World Book Editors, ed. The World Book Encyclopedia of People & Places, 6 vols. rev. ed. LC 93-60511. (Illus.). 1630p. 1993. Set. PLB write for info. (*0-7166-3793-6*) World Bk.
—The World Book Year Book. LC 62-4818. 576p. (gr. 6-12). 1994. PLB write for info. (*0-7166-0494-9*) World Bk.
World Book Staff, ed. Childcraft Dictionary (1993) rev. ed. LC 92-64303. (Illus.). 900p. (gr. 3-6). 1993. PLB write for info. (*0-7166-1493-6*) World Bk.
—Childcraft Supplement: Prehistoric Animals, About Dogs, The Magic of Words, The Indian Book, The Puzzle Book, 5 vols. (Illus.). 1520p. (gr. 2-6). 1989. PLB write for info. (*0-7166-0669-0*) World Bk SW.
—The World Book Student Information Finder, 2 vols. LC 90-71009. (Illus.). 590p. (gr. 7-12). 1993. Set. PLB write for info. (*0-7166-3247-0*) Vol. 1: Language Arts & Social Studies. Vol. 2: Math & Science. World Bk.
—The World Book Year Book - 1993. LC 62-4818. (Illus.). 576p. (gr. 6-12). 1993. PLB write for info. (*0-7166-0493-0*) World Bk.
—The World Book Year Book, 1992. LC 62-4818. (Illus.). 576p. (gr. 6-12). 1992. write for info. (*0-7166-0492-2*) World Bk.
Worrall, Mary, ed. Oxford's Children Encyclopedia, 7 vols. upd. ed. (Illus.). 1648p. (gr. 3-8). 1994. Set. bds. 200.00 (*0-19-910151-5*) OUP.

END OF THE WORLD
Cohen, Daniel. Prophets of Doom. LC 91-34509. (Illus.). 144p. (gr. 7 up). 1992. PLB 15.90 (*1-56294-068-6*) Millbrook Pr.

ENDURANCE, PHYSICAL
see Physical Fitness

ENERGY
see Force and Energy

ENGINEERING
see also specific forms of engineering, e.g. Chemical Engineering
Boring, Mel. Incredible Constructions & the People Who Built Them. LC 84-19522. 96p. (gr. 4 up). 1985. PLB 13.85 (*0-8027-6560-2*) Walker & Co.
Boy Scouts of America. Engineering. (Illus.). 48p. (gr. 6-12). 1978. pap. 1.85 (*0-8395-3376-4*, 33376) BSA.
Clarke, Donald & Dartford, Mark, eds. The New Illustrated Science & Invention Encyclopedia: How It Works. LC 93-3331. (Illus.). 1994. Set. 349.95 (*0-86307-491-X*) Marshall Cavendish.
Dixon, Malcolm. Structures. LC 90-38122. (Illus.). 48p. (gr. 3-7). 1991. PLB 12.90 (*0-531-18379-3*, Pub. by Bookwright Pr) Watts.
Gay, Kathlyn. Ergonomics: Making Products & Places Fit People. LC 85-20634. (Illus.). 128p. (gr. 6 up). 1986. lib. bdg. 17.95 (*0-89490-118-4*) Enslow Pubs.
Goodwin, Peter. Engineering Projects for Young Scientists. LC 86-32528. 1989. PLB 13.90 (*0-531-10339-0*); pap. 6.95 (*0-531-15130-1*) Watts.
Morgan, Sally & Morgan, Adrian. Structures. LC 93-20164. 1993. write for info. (*0-8160-2983-0*) Facts on File.
Nash, Paul. Colossal Constructions. Young, Richard G., ed. LC 89-11714. (Illus.). 32p. (gr. 3-5). 1989. PLB 13.26 (*0-944483-35-6*) Garrett Ed Corp.
Wood, Robert W. Science for Kids: Thirty-nine Easy Engineering Experiments. (gr. 3-8). 1991. 16.95 (*0-8306-1946-1*); pap. 9.95 (*0-8306-1943-7*) TAB Bks.

ENGINEERING–HISTORY
Crump, Donald J., ed. Builders of the Ancient World: Marvels of Engineering. LC 86-5278. (Illus.). (gr. 8 up). 1986. 12.95 (*0-87044-585-5*) Natl Geog.

ENGINEERING–VOCATIONAL GUIDANCE
Cohen, Judith L. Tu Puedes Ser una Ingeniera. Yanez, Juan, tr. from ENG. Katz, David A., illus. (SPA.). 40p. (Orig.). (gr. 4-7). 1992. pap. 6.00 (*1-880599-03-1*) Cascade Pass.
Salvadori, Mario. The Art of Construction: Projects & Principles for Beginning Engineers & Architects. 3rd ed. Hooker, Saralinda & Ragus, Christopher, illus. LC 89-49406. 144p. (gr. 5 up). 1990. pap. 9.95 (*1-55652-080-8*) Chicago Review.

ENGINEERING DRAWING
see Mechanical Drawing

ENGINEERING MATERIALS
see Materials

ENGINEERS
Taylor, Barbara. Charles Ginsburg. LC 93-494. (gr. 7-8). 1993. 15.93 (*0-86592-159-8*); 11.95s.p. (*0-685-66582-8*) Rourke Enter.
Williams, Brian. Karl Benz. LC 90-21744. (Illus.). 48p. (gr. 5-8). 1991. RLB 12.40 (*0-531-18404-8*, Pub. by Bookwright Pr) Watts.

ENGINES
see also Automobiles–Engines; Fire Engines; Fuel; Steam Engines
Cole, Joanna. Cars & How They Go. Gibbons, Gail, illus. LC 82-45575. 32p. (gr. 2-6). 1983. (Crowell Jr Bks); PLB 13.89 (*0-690-04262-0*, Crowell Jr Bks) HarpC Child Bks.

ENGLAND
Greene, Carol. England. LC 82-4471. (Illus.). (gr. 5-9). 1982. PLB 20.55 (*0-516-02763-8*) Childrens.
Herriot, James. The Christmas Day Kitten. (Illus.). 32p. (gr. 3 up). 1993. pap. 6.95 (*0-312-09767-0*) St Martin.
—Oscar, Cat-about-Town. Brown, Ruth, illus. 32p. (gr. 1-3). 1993. pap. 6.95 (*0-312-09130-3*) St Martin.
Parker, Lewis K. England. LC 94-5471. 1994. write for info. (*1-55916-006-3*) Rourke Corp.

ENGLAND–FICTION
Aiken, Joan. Is Underground. LC 92-27423. 1993. 15.00 (*0-385-30898-1*) Delacorte.
—Return to Harken House. (gr. 5-9). 1990. 13.95 (*0-385-29975-3*) Delacorte.
Anderson, Rachel. The Bus People. LC 92-1506. 96p. (gr. 5 up). 1992. 13.95 (*0-8050-2297-X*, Bks Young Read) H Holt & Co.
Austen, Jane. Pride & Prejudice. LC 92-50183. 368p. 1992. 5.98 (*1-56138-171-3*) Courage Bks.
Avery, Gillian. A Likely Lad. LC 92-43911. 1994. pap. 16.00 (*0-671-79867-7*, S&S BFYR) S&S Trade.
—Maria Escapes. Snow, Scott, illus. LC 91-36730. 272p. (gr. 4-8). 1992. pap. 15.00 jacketed, 3-pc. bdg. (*0-671-77074-8*, S&S BFYR) S&S Trade.
Bellairs, John. The Secret of the Underground Room. LC 92-17304. 128p. (gr. 5 up). 1992. pap. 3.99 (*0-14-034932-4*, Puffin) Puffin Bks.
Berry, Liz. Mel. LC 93-7484. 224p. (gr. 7 up). 1993. pap. 3.99 (*0-14-036534-6*, Puffin) Puffin Bks.
Bond, Michael. Paddington Takes the Test. 128p. (gr. k-6). 1982. pap. 1.95 (*0-440-47021-8*, YB) Dell.
Boston, Lucy M. River at Green Knowe. 161p. (gr. 3-7). 1989. pap. 3.95 (*0-15-267450-0*, Odyssey) HarBrace.
Bronte, Charlotte. Jane Eyre. 448p. (gr. 5 up). 1992. pap. 2.95 (*0-14-035131-0*, Puffin) Puffin Bks.
Bronte, Emily. Wuthering Heights. 224p. 1989. pap. 2.50 (*0-8125-0516-6*) Tor Bks.
—Wuthering Heights. 1992. 3.50 (*0-590-46030-7*, Apple Classics) Scholastic Inc.
Bronte, Emily & Geary, Rick. Wuthering Heights. (Illus.). 52p. Date not set. pap. 4.95 (*1-57209-011-1*) Classics Int Ent.
Burgess, Melvin. Burning Issy. LC 93-32430. (gr. 5 up). 1994. 15.00 (*0-671-89003-4*, S&S BFYR) S&S Trade.
Burnett, Frances H. Little Lord Fauntleroy. Butts, Dennis, intro. by. LC 92-13794. 208p. 1993. pap. 7.95 (*0-19-282961-0*) OUP.
—Little Lord Fauntleroy. 19.95 (*0-8488-0792-8*) Amereon Ltd.
—A Little Princess. 1990. pap. 3.50 (*0-440-40386-3*, Pub. by Yearling Classics) Dell.
—The Secret Garden. 1979. pap. 3.25 (*0-440-77706-2*) Dell.
—The Secret Garden. 288p. (gr. 5-8). 1991. pap. 2.99 (*0-87406-575-5*) Willowisp Pr.
—The Secret Garden. 1993. 14.95 (*0-679-42309-5*, Everymans Lib) Knopf.
—The Secret Garden. Howe, James, adapted by. Allen, Thomas B., illus. LC 93-18509. 128p. (Orig.). (gr. 2-6). 1993. pap. 3.50 (*0-679-84751-0*, Bullseye Bks) Random Bks Yng Read.
—The Secret Garden. Bishop, Michael, illus. 200p. 1993. 25.00 (*0-88363-202-0*) H L Levin.
—The Secret Garden. Bauman, Jill, illus. LC 94-17836. 1994. 10.95 (*0-681-00646-3*) Longmeadow Pr.
Burnett, Frances Hodgson. The Secret Garden. (Illus.). 96p. (Orig.). (gr. 4-7). 1994. pap. 1.00 (*0-486-28024-1*) Dover.
Chapin, Kim. The Road to Wembley. LC 93-50815. (gr. 4-7). 1994. 15.00 (*0-374-34849-9*) FS&G.
Chaucer, Geoffrey. The Canterbury Tales. Stewart, Diana, adapted by. Hubrich, Dan, illus. LC 80-22141. 48p. (gr. 4 up). 1983. PLB 20.70 (*0-8172-1666-9*) Raintree Steck-V.
Clark, Walter V. The Ox-Bow Incident. 224p. (gr. 9-12). 1943. pap. 4.50 (*0-451-52386-5*, CE1497, Sig Classics) NAL-Dutton.
Cobb, Vicki. Lots of Rot. Schatell, Brian, illus. LC 80-8726. 40p. (gr. 1-3). 1981. (Lipp Jr Bks); PLB 15.89 (*0-397-31939-8*) HarpC Child Bks.
Copping, Harold. Children's Stories from Dickens. Copping, Harold, illus. LC 92-37666. 1993. 8.99 (*0-517-08485-6*, Pub. by Derrydale Bks) Random Hse Value.
Cushman, Karen. Catherine, Called Birdy. 224p. (gr. 7 up). 1994. 14.95 (*0-395-68186-3*, Clarion Bks) HM.
Dhondy, Farrukh. Black Swan. LC 92-30425. 208p. (gr. 6 up). 1993. 14.95 (*0-395-66076-9*) HM.
Dickens, Charles. The Baron of Grogzwig. Greenway, Shirley, ed. Barnes-Murphy, Rowan, illus. LC 93-18627. (gr. 2-7). 1993. write for info. (*1-879085-81-X*) Whsprng Coyote Pr.
—A Christmas Carol. Innocenti, Roberto, illus. 152p. (gr. 1-12). 1990. lib. bdg. 25.00 RLB smythe-sewn (*0-88682-327-7*, 97200-098) Creative Ed.
—Great Expectations. 464p. (gr. 5 up). 1992. pap. 3.50 (*0-14-035130-2*, Puffin) Puffin Bks.
—Great Expectations. LC 92-50184. 536p. 1992. 5.98 (*1-56138-170-5*) Courage Bks.
—Oliver Twist. abr. ed. 137p. 1962. pap. text ed. 5.95 (*0-582-53014-8*) Longman.
Doherty, Berlie. Granny Was a Buffer Girl. LC 92-24594. (Illus.). 144p. (gr. 8 up). 1993. pap. 3.95 (*0-688-11863-1*, Pub. by Beech Tree Bks) Morrow.
Doherty, Bertie. White Peak Farm. LC 92-43778. 112p. (gr. 8 up). 1993. pap. 3.95 (*0-688-11864-X*, Pub. by Beech Tree Bks) Morrow.
Doyle, Arthur Conan. Mysteries of Sherlock Holmes. reissued ed. Conaway, Judith, adapted by. Miller, Lyle, illus. 96p. (gr. 2-6). 1994. pap. 3.50 (*0-679-85086-4*, Bullseye Bks) Random Bks Yng Read.
Dubowski, Cathy E. Scrooge: Adapted from Charles Dickens' "A Christmas Carol" Dubowski, Mark, illus. LC 94-661. 48p. (gr. 1-3). 1994. PLB 7.99 (*0-448-40222-X*, G&D); pap. 3.50 (*0-448-40221-1*, G&D) Putnam Pub Group.
Farmer, Penelope. Thicker Than Water. LC 92-53133. 32p. (gr. 6-10). 1993. 14.95 (*1-56402-178-5*) Candlewick Pr.
Geras, Adele. Pictures of the Night. LC 92-27425. 1993. write for info. (*0-15-261588-1*) HarBrace.
Gleitzman, Morris. Misery Guts. LC 92-22570. 1993. 12.95 (*0-15-254768-1*) HarBrace.
Godden, Rumer. Listen to the Nightingale. 192p. (gr. 5 up). 1992. 15.00 (*0-670-84517-5*) Viking Child Bks.
Grahame, Kenneth. Dream Days. Parrish, Maxfield, illus. LC 92-44589. 1993. 18.95 (*0-89815-546-0*) Ten Speed Pr.
—The Golden Age. Parrish, Maxfield, illus. LC 92-44992. 1993. 18.95 (*0-89815-545-2*) Ten Speed Pr.
Haley, Gail E. Dream Peddler. Haley, Gail E., illus. LC 92-42074. 32p. (ps-3). 1993. 14.99 (*0-525-45153-6*, DCB) Dutton Child Bks.
Hayes, Sheila. Zoe's Gift. LC 93-42621. 144p. 1994. 14.99 (*0-525-67484-5*, Lodestar Bks) Dutton Child Bks.
Hendry, Diana. Double Vision. LC 92-52996. 272p. (gr. 7-11). 1993. 14.95 (*1-56402-125-4*) Candlewick Pr.
Hollinshead, Marilyn. The Nine Days Wonder. Morgan, Pierr, illus. 32p. (ps-3). 1994. 14.95 (*0-399-21967-6*, Philomel) Putnam Pub Group.
Hughes, Shirley. An Evening at Alfie's. Hughes, Shirley, illus. LC 84-11297. 32p. (ps-1). 1985. 14.95 (*0-688-04122-1*); PLB 14.88 (*0-688-04123-X*) Lothrop.
Lewis, J. Patrick. The Christmas of the Reddle Moon. Kelley, Gary, illus. LC 93-28049. (gr. 3 up). 1994. 15.99 (*0-8037-1566-8*); PLB 15.89 (*0-8037-1567-6*) Dial Bks Young.
McCully, Emily A. Little Kit, or, the Industrious Flea Circus Girl. LC 93-40658. 1995. write for info. (*0-8037-1671-0*); PLB write for info. (*0-8037-1674-5*) Dial Bks Young.
McKay, Hilary. The Exiles at Home. LC 94-14225. (gr. 4-7). 1994. 15.95 (*0-689-50610-4*, M K McElderry) Macmillan Child Grp.
Magorian, Michelle. Not a Swan. LC 91-19507. 416p. (gr. 7 up). 1992. 18.00 (*0-06-024214-0*); PLB 17.89 (*0-06-024215-9*) HarpC Child Bks.
Nesbit, Edith. The Railway Children. Butts, Dennis, intro. by. 224p. 1991. pap. 3.95 (*0-19-282659-X*, 11912) OUP.
—Railway Children. (gr. 4-7). 1992. pap. 3.50 (*0-440-40602-1*) Dell.
—The Railway Children. 1993. 12.95 (*0-679-42534-9*, Everymans Lib) Knopf.
—Railway Children. (gr. 4 up). 1993. pap. 3.25 (*0-553-21415-2*, Bantam Classics) Bantam.

Norton, Mary. The Borrowers. Krush, Beth & Krush, Joe, illus. 200p. (gr. 3-7). 1989. pap. 4.95 (0-15-209990-5, Odyssey) HarBrace.
Paton Walsh, Jill. Grace. 256p. (gr. 7 up). 1992. 16.00 (0-374-32758-0) FS&G.
Phillips, Ann. A Haunted Year. Flavin, Teresa, illus. LC 92-45638. 176p. (gr. 4-8). 1994. SBE 14.95 (0-02-774605-4, Macmillan Child Bk) Macmillan Child Grp.
—The Peace Child. (Illus.). 160p. (gr. 5 up). 1988. 15.00 (0-19-271560-7) OUP.
Shulman, Dee. Roaring Billy. (Illus.). 32p. (ps-k). 1992. 15.95 (0-370-31585-5, Pub. by Bodley Head UK) Trafalgar.
Slater, Teddy, adapted by. Disney's the Prince & the Pauper. Wilson, Phil, illus. LC 92-56165. 48p. 1993. 12.95 (1-56282-511-9); PLB 12.89 (1-56282-512-7) Disney Pr.
Steiber, Ellen. Fangs of Evil. LC 93-44043. 108p. (Orig.). (gr. 2-6). 1994. pap. 2.99 (0-679-85466-5, Bullseye Bks) Random Bks Yng Read.
Streatfield, Noel. Dancing Shoes. 276p. (gr. 4-9). 1994. pap. 3.99 (0-679-85428-2) Random Bks Yng Read.
Tale of Two Cities. 1993. pap. text ed. 6.50 (0-582-08466-0, 79830) Longman.
Travers, Pamela L. Mary Poppins & the House Next Door. Shepard, Mary, illus. 96p. (gr. 4-7). 1992. pap. 3.50 (0-440-40656-0, YB) Dell.
—Mary Poppins in Cherry Tree Lane. (gr. 3-7). 1992. 3.50 (0-440-40637-4, YB) Dell.
Traynor, Shauwn. Little Man in England. 112p. 1989. pap. 5.95 (1-85371-032-6, Pub. by Poolbeg Press Ltd Eire) Dufour.
Turnbull, Ann. Speedwell. LC 91-58757. 128p. (gr. 5-9). 1994. pap. 3.99 (1-56402-281-1) Candlewick Pr.
Twain, Mark. The Prince & the Pauper. James, Raymond, ed. Couri, Kathryn A., illus. LC 89-33892. 48p. (gr. 3-6). 1990. lib. bdg. 12.89 (0-8167-1873-3); pap. text ed. 3.95 (0-8167-1874-1) Troll Assocs.
Waugh, Sylvia. The Mennyms. LC 93-15901. 216p. (gr. 5 up). 1994. 14.00 (0-688-13070-4) Greenwillow.
—Mennyms in the Wilderness. LC 94-6881. 1995. write for info. (0-688-13820-9) Greenwillow.
Weatherhill, Craig. The Lyonesse Stone: A Novel of West Cornwall. (Illus.). 176p. 1992. pap. 9.95 (0-907018-85-8, Pub. by Tabb Hse Pubs UK) Seven Hills Bk Dists.
Westall, Robert. A Place to Hide. 208p. (gr. 7 up). 1994. 13.95 (0-590-47748-X, Scholastic Hardcover) Scholastic Inc.
—Stormsearch. (gr. 4-7). 1992. 14.00 (0-374-37272-1) FS&G.
Wu, William F. Time Tours No. 1: Robin Hood Ambush. 1990. pap. 3.50 (0-06-106003-8, Harp PBks) HarpC.
Wuthering Heights. 1993. pap. text ed. 6.50 (0-582-09672-3, 79835) Longman.

ENGLAND–HISTORY
see Great Britain–History

ENGLISH AUTHORS
see Authors, English

ENGLISH COMPOSITION
see English Language–Composition and Exercises

ENGLISH DRAMA
see also Mysteries and Miracle Plays

Ayckbourn, Alan. Confusions. (Illus.). 63p. 1988. pap. 9.95 (0-413-53270-4, A0063, Pub. by Methuen UK) Heinemann.
Birch, Beverly, retold by. Shakespeare's Stories: Tragedies. Kerins, Tony, illus. LC 88-18112. 126p. (gr. 7-12). 1988. 12.95 (0-87226-193-X) P Bedrick Bks.
Hamlet. (Illus.). 48p. (gr. 4 up). 1988. PLB 20.70 (0-8172-2764-4) Raintree Steck-V.
Johnson, Meredith, illus. The Children's Macbeth. (gr. 5-9). 1994. pap. 3.95 (0-88388-186-1) Bellerophon Bks.
Miles, Bernard. Well-Loved Tales from Shakespeare. Ambrus, Victor G., illus. LC 85-63829. 128p. (gr. 2 up). 1986. 12.95 (0-528-82758-8) Checkerboard.
More Tales from Shakespeare. 1993. pap. text ed. 6.50 (0-582-09675-8, 79821) Longman.
Shakespeare, William. All's Well That Ends Well. Rowland, Beryl, intro. by. LC 85-4167. (gr. 9 up). 1968. pap. 0.60 (0-8049-1022-7, S22) Airmont.
—Antony & Cleopatra. Rudvik, O. H., intro. by. (gr. 10 up). 1966. pap. 0.60 (0-8049-1011-1, S-11) Airmont.
—As You Like It. Pitt, David G., intro. by. (gr. 10 up). 1965. pap. 1.25 (0-8049-1006-5, S-6) Airmont.
—Comedy of Errors. Rudzik, O. H., intro. by. (gr. 9 up). 1968. pap. 0.60 (0-8049-1023-5, S-23) Airmont.
—Coriolanus. Rowland, Beryl, intro. by. (gr. 10 up). 1968. pap. 0.60 (0-8049-1021-9, S-21) Airmont.
—Hamlet. Mattea, Gino, intro. by. (gr. 11 up). pap. 1.95 (0-8049-1001-4, S1) Airmont.
—Hamlet. Davidson, Diane, ed. LC 83-12310. (Illus.). 154p. (gr. 8-12). 1983. pap. 5.95 (0-934048-12-6) Swan Books.
—Henry IV, Pts. 1 & 2. Young, Archibald, intro. by. (gr. 10 up). pap. Pt. 1. pap. 1.25 (0-8049-1018-9, S18); Pt. 2. pap. 1.25 (0-685-00150-4, S19) Airmont.
—Julius Caesar. Rudzik, O. H., intro. by. (Illus.). (gr. 9 up). 1965. pap. 1.95 (0-8049-1004-9, S4) Airmont.
—Julius Caesar. Davidson, Diane, ed. LC 83-12307. (Illus.). 121p. (gr. 8-12). 1983. pap. 5.95 (0-934048-04-5) Swan Books.
—King John. Rowland, Beryl, intro. by. (gr. 9 up). 1968. pap. 1.95 (0-8049-1024-3, S24) Airmont.
—King Lear. Girling, H. K., intro. by. (gr. 11 up). 1966. pap. 1.75 (0-8049-1012-X, S12) Airmont.
—Macbeth. Duffy, John D., intro. by. (gr. 11 up). 1965. pap. 1.75 (0-8049-1002-2, S2) Airmont.
—Macbeth. Davidson, Diane, ed. LC 83-12312. (Illus.). 111p. (gr. 8-12). 1983. pap. 5.95 (0-934048-02-9) Swan Books.
—Merchant of Venice. Redekop, Ernest, intro. by. (gr. 9 up). 1965. pap. 1.25 (0-8049-1003-0, S3) Airmont.
—Merchant of Venice. Davidson, Diane, ed. LC 83-12308. (Illus.). 112p. (gr. 8-12). 1983. pap. 5.95 (0-934048-08-8) Swan Books.
—Midsummer Night's Dream. Pitt, David G., intro. by. (gr. 10 up). 1965. pap. 1.95 (0-8049-1005-7, S5) Airmont.
—Midsummer Night's Dream. Davidson, Diane, ed. LC 83-12311. (Illus.). 99p. (gr. 8-12). 1983. pap. 5.95 (0-934048-10-X) Swan Books.
—Much Ado about Nothing. Rowland, Beryl, intro. by. (gr. 10 up). 1967. pap. 0.60 (0-8049-1020-0, S20) Airmont.
—Othello. Rudvik, O. H., intro. by. (gr. 10 up). 1966. pap. 1.75 (0-8049-1013-8, S13) Airmont.
—Richard Second. Young, Archibald M., intro. by. (gr. 9 up). 1966. pap. 0.60 (0-8049-1014-6, S14) Airmont.
—Richard Third. Willoughby, John, intro. by. (gr. 9 up). 1966. pap. 0.60 (0-8049-1015-4, S15) Airmont.
—Romeo & Juliet. Thomas, Clara, intro. by. (gr. 8 up). 1966. pap. 1.75 (0-8049-1009-X, S9) Airmont.
—Romeo & Juliet. rev. ed. Gill, Roma, ed. (Illus.). 168p. (gr. 9-11). 1993. pap. 7.50 (0-19-831972-X) OUP.
—Taming of the Shrew. Girling, Z. N., intro. by. (gr. 10 up). 1966. pap. 1.75 (0-8049-1010-3, S10) Airmont.
—The Taming of the Shrew. rev. ed. Gill, Roma, ed. (Illus.). 144p. (gr. 9-11). 1993. pap. 7.50 (0-19-831976-2) OUP.
—Tempest. Pitt, D. G., intro. by. (gr. 11 up). pap. 1.25 (0-8049-1007-3, S7) Airmont.
—Twelfth Night. Pitt, David G., intro. by. (gr. 10 up). 1965. pap. 1.75 (0-8049-1008-1, S8) Airmont.
Shaw, George Bernard. Caesar & Cleopatra. (gr. 11 up). pap. 0.95 (0-8049-0119-8, CL-119) Airmont.
—Man & Superman. Teitel, N. R., intro. by. (gr. 11 up). pap. 0.95 (0-8049-0096-5, CL-96) Airmont.
Tales from Shakespeare. 1993. pap. text ed. 6.50 (0-582-08481-4, 79832) Longman.
Wilde, Oscar. Five Major Plays. Incl. Lady Windermere's Fan; Importance of Being Earnest; Salome; Woman of No Importance; Ideal Husband. (gr. 10 up). 1970. pap. 2.75 (0-8049-0208-9, CL-208) Airmont.

ENGLISH FOR FOREIGNERS
see English Language–Textbooks for Foreigners

ENGLISH GRAMMAR
see English Language–Grammar

ENGLISH HISTORY
see Great Britain–History

ENGLISH LANGUAGE

Aderholdt, Kristel. Boredom Rx. (Illus.). 144p. (gr. 1-8). 1991. 27.95 (0-937857-19-X, 1583) Speech Bin.
Bachman, Barbara. Frisky Phonics Fun I. Bachman, Barbara, illus. 152p. (gr. 1-3). 1984. wkbk. 12.95 (0-86653-195-5, GA 548) Good Apple.
—Frisky Phonics Fun II. Bachman, Barbara, illus. 152p. (gr. 1-3). 1984. wkbk. 12.95 (0-86653-212-9, GA 549) Good Apple.
Barrier, Jean & Kennedy, Alice. English Is Fun Books. McCombs, Toni, illus. 192p. (gr. k-8). 1991. pap. text ed. 12.00 (0-911743-07-3) Barrier & Kennedy.
Beechick, Ruth. A Strong Start in Language: Grades K-3. 32p. (Orig.). (gr. k-3). 1986. pap. 4.00 (0-940319-02-0) Arrow Press.
Carlson, Lori. English con Salsa. 1994. 14.95 (0-8050-3135-9) H Holt & Co.
Cera, Mary J. & Else, JoAnn. Trivial Pursuit - Language Arts (Intermediate) (Illus.). 64p. (gr. 4-6). 1992. 12.95 (0-86653-648-5, GA1383) Good Apple.
—Trivial Pursuit - Language Arts (Primary) (Illus.). 64p. (gr. 1-3). 1992. 12.95 (0-86653-646-9, GA1382) Good Apple.
Civardi, Anne. Word Finders in English. 48p. (gr. k-3). 1984. 8.95 (0-7460-0392-7) EDC.
Cooke, Tom. Flash Cards Get Ready Words. (ps). 1986. pap. 5.25 (0-307-04983-3, Golden Pr) Western Pub.
De Brunhoff, Laurent. Je Parle Anglais avec Babar. (FRE., Illus.). (gr. 4-6). 15.95 (0-685-11272-1) Fr & Eur.
Gerber, Carole, ed. English. 2nd ed. Robison, Don, illus. 40p. (gr. 2). 1992. wkbk. 1.99 (1-56189-082-0) Amer Educ Pub.
—English. Robison, Don, illus. 40p. (gr. 3). 1992. wkbk. 1.99 (1-56189-083-9) Amer Educ Pub.
—English & Phonics. Robison, Don, illus. 32p. (gr. k). 1992. wkbk. 1.99 (1-56189-080-4) Amer Educ Pub.
—English & Phonics. Robison, Don, illus. 40p. (gr. 1). 1992. wkbk. 1.99 (1-56189-081-2) Amer Educ Pub.
Gregory, Elizabeth. The Short & Long. (Illus.). 1981. 6.95 (0-933184-09-3); pap. 4.95 (0-933184-10-7) Flame Intl.
Harlan, Judith. Bilingualism in the United States: Conflict & Controversy. LC 91-18518. (Illus.). 128p. (gr. 9-12). 1991. PLB 12.90 (0-531-13001-0) Watts.
Harrison, Susan. AlphaZoo Christmas. Harrison, Susan, illus. LC 93-20351. 40p. (ps-2). 1993. 13.95 (0-8249-8623-7, Ideals Child); PLB 14.00 (0-8249-8632-6) Hambleton-Hill.
Hopkins, Lee B. Let Them Be Themselves. 3rd ed. LC 91-19119. 224p. 1992. pap. 10.95 (0-06-446126-2, Trophy) HarpC Child Bks.
Jenkins, Betty. Vowel Fun. Brown, Virginia, illus. 96p. (gr. 1-3). 1983. wkbk. 10.95 (0-86653-107-6, GA 465) Good Apple.
Kindergarten Vocabulary. (Illus.). 24p. (ps-k). 1986. 3.98 (0-86734-069-X, FS-3059) Schaffer Pubns.
Learn with Benjamin Bunny: Book of Words. 1993. 2.99 (0-517-07700-0) Random Hse Value.
McElmurray, Mary A. Trivial Pursuit - Language Arts (Jr. High) (Illus.). 64p. (gr. 7-9). 1992. 12.95 (0-86653-650-7, GA1384) Good Apple.
McMillan, Bruce. Super, Super, Superwords. McMillan, Bruce, illus. LC 88-9342. 32p. (ps-2). 1989. 14.00 (0-688-08098-7); PLB 13.93 (0-688-08099-5) Lothrop.
Maestro, Betsy. All Aboard Overnight: A Book of Compound Words. Maestro, Giulio, illus. 32p. (ps-2). 1992. 14.45 (0-395-51120-8, Clarion Bks) HM.
Moncure, Jane. My "a" Sound Box. Beltier, Pam, illus. 32p. (gr. k-2). 1993. pap. text ed. 5.95 (1-56189-384-6) Amer Educ Pub.
—My "e" Sound Box. Gohman, Vera, illus. 32p. (gr. k-2). 1993. pap. text ed. 5.95 (1-56189-385-4) Amer Educ Pub.
—My "i" Sound Box. Gohman, Vera, illus. 32p. (gr. k-2). 1993. pap. text ed. 5.95 (1-56189-386-2) Amer Educ Pub.
—My "o" Sound Box. Gohman, Vera, illus. 32p. (gr. k-2). 1993. pap. text ed. 5.95 (1-56189-387-0) Amer Educ Pub.
—My Sound Parade. Sommers, Linda, illus. 32p. (gr. k-2). 1993. pap. text ed. 5.95 (1-56189-389-7) Amer Educ Pub.
—My "u" Sound Box. Beltier, Pam, illus. 32p. (gr. k-2). 1993. pap. text ed. 5.95 (1-56189-388-9) Amer Educ Pub.
Moretti, Stephanie. The An Book. (Illus.). 16p. (ps-1). 1993. large format easle bk. 18.95 (1-879567-09-1) Wonder Well.
Mulford, Philippa G. Making Room for Katherine. LC 93-32268. 160p. (gr. 5-9). 1994. SBE 14.95 (0-02-767652-8, Macmillan Child Bk) Macmillan Child Grp.
Nielsen, Shelly. Fun with A - a. LC 92-16038. 1992. 13.99 (1-56239-134-8) Abdo & Dghtrs.
—Fun with E - e. LC 92-16041. 1992. 13.99 (1-56239-135-6) Abdo & Dghtrs.
—Fun with I - i. LC 92-16040. 1992. 13.99 (1-56239-136-4) Abdo & Dghtrs.
—Fun with O - o. LC 92-16039. 1992. 13.99 (1-56239-137-2) Abdo & Dghtrs.
—Fun with U - u. LC 92-16042. 1992. 13.99 (1-56239-138-0) Abdo & Dghtrs.
Singer, Marilyn. Sky Words. Ray, Deborah K., illus. LC 92-3765. 32p. (gr. k-3). 1994. RSBE 14.95 (0-02-782882-4, Macmillan Child Bk) Macmillan Child Grp.
Terban, Marvin. It Figures! Fun Figures of Speech. Maestro, Guilio, illus. LC 92-35529. 1993. 13.95 (0-395-61584-4, Clarion Bks) HM.
Terdy, Dennis. Content Area ESL: Social Studies. Mrowicki, Linda, ed. (Illus.). 169p. (gr. 5-12). 1986. pap. 8.95 (0-916591-06-9) Linmore Pub.
Thurston, Cheryl M. Cottonwood Game Book. 58p. (Orig.). (gr. 5-12). 1986. pap. text ed. 14.95 (1-877673-01-3) Cottonwood Pr.
—What's in a Name? rev. ed. Blackstone, Ann, illus. 24p. (Orig.). (gr. 5-12). 1993. pap. text ed. 8.95 (1-877673-04-8) Cottonwood Pr.
Winitz, Harris. Text for the Learnables, American English, Bk. 1. 36p. (gr. 3 up). 1990. pap. text ed. 6.50 (0-939990-69-5) Intl Linguistics.

ENGLISH LANGUAGE–AMERICANISMS
see Americanisms

ENGLISH LANGUAGE–BUSINESS ENGLISH

Merriss, William E. & Griswold, David H. A Composition Handbook. 3rd ed. 1985. tchr's. guide 10.84 (0-8013-0074-6, 75738); pap. text ed. 17.28 (0-88334-186-7, 76152) Longman.

ENGLISH LANGUAGE–COMPOSITION AND EXERCISES

Artman, John H. The Write Stuff! Filkins, Vanessa, illus. 64p. (gr. 4-8). 1985. wkbk. 8.95 (0-86653-273-0, GA 681) Good Apple.
Bernstein, Bonnie. Writing Crafts Workshop. LC 81-85351. (gr. 3-8). 1982. pap. 10.95 (0-8224-9785-9) Fearon Teach Aids.
Black, Ann N. & Smith, Jo R. Ten Tools of Language-Written. 2nd ed. (Illus.). 166p. (gr. 11-12). 1982. pap. text ed. 12.60x (0-910513-00-7) Mayfield Printing.
Buchter, Carol & Quigley, Elaine. Developing Basic Writing Skills, Bk. 1. (gr. 3-4). 1983. wkbk. 4.95 (0-89525-391-7) Ed Activities.
—Developing Basic Writing Skills, Bk. 2. (gr. 5-6). 1983. wkbk. 4.95 (0-89525-392-5) Ed Activities.
Buschemeyer, Robin Q. Word Pal. Launching Pad Studio, Inc. Staff, illus. 40p. (Orig.). (ps-3). 1986. pap. 2.99 (0-935609-00-8) Eduplay.
Cahill, Robert B. & Hrebic, Herbert J. Cut the Deck. rev. ed. Barry, Jimi, ed. (gr. 8-9). 1985. text ed. 9.10 (0-933282-16-8); pap. text ed. 6.00 (0-933282-15-X) Stack the Deck.
Cassedy, Sylvia. In Your Own Words: A Beginner's Guide to Writing. rev. ed. LC 89-78079. 240p. (gr. 5 up). 1990. (Crowell Jr Bks); (Crowell Jr Bks) HarpC Child Bks.
—In Your Own Words: A Beginner's Guide to Writing. rev. ed. LC 89-78079. 240p. (gr. 5 up). 1990. pap. 7.95 (0-06-446102-5, Trophy) HarpC Child Bks.

Christensen, J. A. Young Writer. LC 74-88375. (Illus.). xii, 364p. (gr. 8-12). 1970. text ed. 18.95x (0-87015-180-0) Pacific Bks.

Daniel, Becky. Writing Brainstorms. 80p. (gr. 1-4). 1990. 9.95 (0-86653-569-1, GA1172) Good Apple.

—Writing Thinker Sheets. 64p. (gr. 4-8). 1989. 7.95 (0-86653-490-3, GA1098) Good Apple.

Donovan, Melissa. Teaching Creative Writing. 144p. (gr. 3-8). 1990. 12.95 (0-86653-559-4, GA1156) Good Apple.

Dubrovin, Vivian. Storytelling for the Fun of It: A Handbook for Children. LC 93-93694. 160p. (gr. 4-7). 1994. pap. 14.95 (0-9638339-0-1) Storycraft Pub.

Ehrenhaft, George. How to Prepare for SAT II: Writing. 288p. (Orig.). (gr. 7 up). 1994. pap. 11.95 (0-8120-1477-4) Barron.

English Composition Study Aid. 1978. pap. 1.95 (0-87738-029-5) Youth Ed.

Fleisher, Paul. Write Now! 80p. (gr. 5-8). 1989. 8.95 (0-86653-493-8, GA1088) Good Apple.

Forte, Imogene. Write about It Series, 3 vols. Incl. Beginning Writers. (gr. k-1). 1983. pap. text ed. 7.95 (0-86530-044-5, IP 44-5); Primary. (gr. 2-4). 1983. pap. text ed. 7.95 (0-86530-045-3, IP 45-3); Middle Grades. (gr. 4-6). 1983. pap. text ed. 7.95 (0-86530-046-1, IP 46-1). (Illus., 80 pgs. ea. volume). (gr. k-6). 1983. pap. text ed. 23.50 (0-685-06165-5, IP 43-7) Incentive Pubns.

Glover, Susanne & Grewe, Georgeann. Bone up on Book Reports. 64p. (gr. 3-8). 1981. 7.95 (0-86653-001-0, GA 228) Good Apple.

Grimm, Gary & Mitchell, Don. Good Apple Creative Writing Book. 112p. (gr. 3-8). 1976. 10.95 (0-916456-04-8, GA61) Good Apple.

Harvey, Thomas. Harvey's Elementary Grammar & Composition. (Illus.). (gr. 4-6). 1986. 10.95 (0-88062-041-2) Mott Media.

—Harvey's Revised English Grammar. (Illus.). (gr. 7-11). 1986. 13.95 (0-88062-042-0) Mott Media.

Hutson-Nechkash, Peg. Storybuilding: A Guide to Structuring Oral Narratives. 128p. (Orig.). (gr. 3-8). 1990. pap. text ed. 24.00x (0-930599-63-2) Thinking Pubns.

James, Elizabeth & Barkin, Carol. How to Write a Great School Report. Greenlaw, M. Jean, intro. by. LC 83-764. (Illus.). 167p. (gr. 3-5). 1983. PLB 11.93 (0-688-02283-9) Lothrop.

—How to Write a Great School Report. Greenlaw, M. Jean, intro. by. LC 83-764. (Illus.). 80p. (gr. 3 up). 1993. pap. 6.95 (0-688-02278-2, Pub. by Beech Tree Bks) Morrow.

—How to Write a Term Paper. Jacobs, Leland B., intro. by. LC 80-13734. 96p. (gr. 7 up). 1980. 11.88 (0-688-00682-5) Lothrop.

—How to Write a Term Paper. Jacobs, Leland B., intro. by. LC 80-13734. (Illus.). 96p. (gr. 5 up). 1980. pap. 3.95 (0-688-45025-3, Pub. by Beech Tree Bks) Morrow.

—How to Write Your Best Book Report. Doty, Roy, illus. LC 86-8597. 80p. (gr. 3-7). 1986. 14.93 (0-688-05744-6) Lothrop.

—How to Write Your Best Book Report. Doty, Roy, illus. LC 86-8597. 80p. (gr. 3 up). 1986. pap. 6.00 (0-688-05743-8, Pub. by Beech Tree Bks) Morrow.

Johnson, Eric. You Are the Editor: Sixty-One Editing Lessons That Improve Writing Skills. (gr. 5 up). 1981. pap. 12.95 (0-8224-7696-7); wkbk. o.p. 4.95 (0-8224-7697-5) Fearon Teach Aids.

Kadra, Sheila & Smith, Patricia. Painting with Words. 1987. pap. text ed. 12.90 (0-88334-195-6, 76160) Longman.

Kimeldorf, Martin. Exciting Writing, Successful Speaking: Activities to Make Language Come Alive. Espeland, Pamela, ed. LC 93-30613. 216p. (Orig.). (gr. 5 up). 1994. pap. 14.95 (0-915793-65-2) Free Spirit Pub.

Klawitter, P. Bookworks. 64p. (gr. 4-8). 1993. 8.95 (0-88160-212-4, LW204) Learning Wks.

Lester, James D., Sr. & Lester, James D., Jr. Writing: Style & Grammar. 400p. (Orig.). (gr. 6-10). 1994. pap. 14.95 spiralbound (0-673-36128-4) GdYrBks.

McAllister, Constance. Creative Writing for Beginners. 32p. (Orig.). (gr. 1-3). 1976. pap. 2.95 (0-87534-165-9) Highlights.

McBaine, Robert. Student Workbook for Sentence Combining with Exercises & Key. 135p. (Orig.). (gr. 8 up). 1984. pap. 8.90 (0-89420-244-8, 261000) Natl Book.

Maid, Amy. Write, from the Beginning. (Illus.). 92p. (Orig.). (gr. 2-4). 1982. pap. 11.95x (0-8290-0993-0) Irvington.

Mammen, Lori. TEAMS Vocabulary Plus: Learning & Using TEAMS Vocabulary Words, 3 vols. (Illus.). 120p. 1988. Grade 3. pap. text ed. 7.95 (0-944459-00-5) Grade 5. pap. text ed. 7.95 (0-944459-01-3); Grade 7. pap. text ed. 7.95 (0-944459-02-1) ECS Lrn Systs.

—Writing Prompts Plus: Preparing Students for the TEAMS Composition Test, 4 vols. (Illus.). 160p. 1988. Grade 3. pap. text ed. 7.95 (0-944459-03-X) Grade 5. pap. text ed. 7.95 (0-944459-04-8); Grade 7. pap. text ed. 7.95 (0-944459-05-6); Grade 9. pap. text ed. 7.95 (0-944459-06-4) ECS Lrn Systs.

—Writing Warm-Ups. 80p. (gr. 7-12). 1989. pap. text ed. 9.95 (0-944459-08-0) ECS Lrn Systs.

Marsh, Carole. A-Plus Very Good! Secrets of Good Writing for Students. (Orig.). (gr. 4-12). 1994. 24.95 (1-55609-272-5); pap. text ed. 14.95 (0-935326-63-4) Gallopade Pub Group.

Moore, Jo E., et al. Write Every Day. (Illus.). 48p. (gr. 1-6). 1988. pap. 4.95 (1-55799-128-6) Evan-Moor Corp.

Nelson, Nigel. Writing & Numbers. De Saulles, Tony, illus. LC 93-40963. 32p. (gr. k-2). 1994. 12.95 (1-56847-158-0) Thomson Lrning.

O'Brien-Palmer, Michelle. Read & Write: Fun Literature & Writing Connections for Kids. (gr. 4-7). 1994. pap. 16.95 (1-879235-04-8) MicNik Pubns.

Olshtain, Elite, et al. The Junior Files, File 1: English for Today & Tomorrow. rev. ed. Berman, Aaron & Chapman, Charles, eds. (Illus.). 270p. (gr. 6-10). 1991. pap. write for info. (1-878598-02-3) Alta Bk Co Pubs.

Richards, Joanne & Standley, Marianne. One for the Books. (Illus.). 128p. (gr. 4-6). 1984. pap. text ed. 8.95 (0-86530-023-2, IP 23-2) Incentive Pubns.

Rico, Armando B. School Adventures: Aventuras Escolares. 27p. (Orig.). 1989. pap. text ed. 4.95 (1-879219-04-2) Veracruz Pubs.

Ronnholm, Ursula O. & Ronnholm, Paul F. My Book of Words, Songs & Sentences. Enrique, Miguel M., illus. 91p. (gr. k-3). 1986. pap. text ed. 7.00 (0-941911-03-9) Two Way Bilingual.

Rothstein, Evelyn & Gess, Diane. EarlyWriter. Gompper, Gail, illus. 80p. (gr. k-1). 1989. pap. text ed. 7.95 (0-913935-44-1) ERA-CCR.

Ryan, Elizabeth. How to Be a Better Writer. LC 91-3135. 96p. (gr. 5-9). 1992. lib. bdg. 9.89 (0-8167-2462-8); pap. text ed. 3.95 (0-8167-2463-6) Troll Assocs.

—How to Write Better Book Reports. LC 91-3134. 80p. (gr. 5-9). 1992. lib. bdg. 9.89 (0-8167-2458-X); pap. text ed. 3.95 (0-8167-2459-8) Troll Assocs.

Schwartz, L. Pick a Picture. 40p. (gr. 3-6). 1993. 6.95 (0-88160-258-2, LW242) Learning Wks.

—Pick a Picture - Kit. 40p. (gr. 3-6). 1989. 9.95 (0-88160-179-9, LW 285) Learning Wks.

—Select a Story. 40p. (gr. 3-6). 1989. 9.95 (0-88160-182-9, LW 286) Learning Wks.

—Select a Story. 40p. (gr. 3-6). 1993. 6.95 (0-88160-259-0, LW249) Learning Wks.

—Sharpen Your Senses. (gr. 1-6). 1978. 3.95 (0-88160-056-3, LW 604) Learning Wks.

Segan, Eleanor. How to Write Right, No. 1: From Lists to Letters. (Illus.). 96p. (gr. 7-12). 1986. pap. 5.75 (0-941342-15-8, 2115) Entry Pub.

—How to Write Right, No. 2: Forms & More. (Illus.). 64p. (gr. 7-12). 1986. pap. 4.40 (0-941342-16-6, 2116) Entry Pub.

Smith, Mary D. & Smith, Brad. Creative Writing Patterns. Tom, Tiana, illus. 48p. (gr. k-4). 1983. wkbk. 6.95 (1-55734-130-3) Tchr Create Mat.

Stanish, Bob. Creativity for Kids Through Writing. (Illus.). 64p. (gr. 1 up). 1983. wkbk. 7.95 (0-86653-118-1, GA 486) Good Apple.

Suid, Murray. For the Love of Sentences. 64p. (gr. 4-6). 1986. 6.95 (0-912107-51-0) Monday Morning Bks.

Suid, Murray & Lincoln, Wanda. Ten-Minute Language Warm-ups. (Illus.). 128p. (gr. 2-6). 1992. pap. 11.95 (1-878279-38-6) Monday Morning Bks.

—Ten-Minute Thinking Tie-Ins. (Illus.). 128p. (gr. 2-6). 1992. pap. 11.95 (1-878279-39-4) Monday Morning Bks.

Tchudi, Susan & Tchudi, Stephen. The Young Writer's Handbook: A Practical Guide for the Beginner Who Is Serious about Writing. LC 87-1463. (Illus.). 176p. (gr. 7 up). 1987. pap. 5.95 (0-689-71170-0, Aladdin) Macmillan Child Grp.

Terban, Marvin. Your Foot's on My Feet. 34p. 1992. text ed. 2.72 (1-56956-124-9) W A T Braille.

—Your Foot's on My Feet: And Other Tricky Nouns. Maestro, Giulio, illus. LC 85-19561. (gr. 2-5). 1986. pap. 11.95 (0-89919-411-7, Clarion Bks); pap. 4.95 (0-89919-413-3, Clarion Bks) HM.

Thurston, Cheryl M. Cottonwood Composition Book. 62p. (Orig.). (gr. 5-12). 1986. pap. text ed. 14.95 (1-877673-00-5) Cottonwood Pr.

Tilkin, Sheldon. Paragraph & Topic Sentence. Pape, Richard, illus. 24p. (gr. 3-4). 1980. wkbk. 2.95 (0-89403-606-8) EDC.

Tyler, J. & Round, G. Ready for Writing. (Illus.). 24p. (ps up). 1989. pap. 3.50 (0-7460-0218-1, Usborne) EDC.

Weiner, Mitchel & Green, Sharon W. Verbal Workbook for SAT I. 8th ed. 320p. (gr. 10-12). 1994. pap. 10.95 (0-8120-1850-8) Barron.

Weisberg, Valerie H. Students' Discourse: Comprehensive Examples & Explanations of All Expository Modes & Argument, Precis, Narrative, Examination Writing & MLA Reccomendations for Research Paper Documentation Writing Exposition. 2nd ed. 126p. 1990. pap. 9.95 (0-685-49571-X) V H Pub.

Whiteside, Sandra & Whiteside, Rita G. Primary Writing Fun. Whiteside, Saundra & Whiteside, Rita, illus. 80p. (gr. 1-3). 1983. wkbk. 8.95 (0-86653-101-7, GA 461) Good Apple.

Winitz, Harris. Basic Structures - American English, Bk. 1: A Textbook for the Learnables. Baker, Syd, illus. 100p. (gr. 7 up). 1990. pap. text ed. 45.00 incl. 4 cass. tapes (0-939990-60-1) Intl Linguistics.

World Book Editors, ed. Ready to Write, 2 vols. LC 93-60512. (Illus.). 120p. (gr. 4-7). 1993. Set. PLB write for info. (0-7166-2993-3) World Bk.

ENGLISH LANGUAGE–CONVERSATION AND PHRASE BOOKS

see English Language–Textbooks for Foreigners; see use subdivision conversation and phrase books for languages other than english

ENGLISH LANGUAGE–DICTIONARIES

Abbs, Brian. Longman Picture Wordbook. (Illus.). (ps-2). 1988. 18.95 (0-582-02239-8, 70444) Longman.

The American Heritage Children's Dictionary. (Illus.). 864p. (gr. 3-5). 1994. 14.95 (0-395-69191-5) HM.

The American Heritage First Dictionary. 368p. (gr. 1-2). 1994. 13.95 (0-395-67289-9) HM.

The American Heritage Picture Dictionary. (Illus.). 144p. (gr. k-1). 1994. 10.95 (0-395-69585-6) HM.

The American Heritage Student Dictionary. LC 93-32433. (Illus.). 1994. 16.95 (0-395-55857-3, AHD & Ref) HM.

Amery & Mila. First Thousand Words in English. (Illus.). (gr. 1-9). 1979. 11.95 (0-86020-266-6, Usborne-Hayes) English ed. EDC.

Beal, George. The Kingfisher Book of Words: A-Z Guide to Quotations, Proverbs, Origins, Usage, & Idioms. Stevenson, Peter, illus. LC 92-53105. 192p. (gr. 4 up). 1992. 10.95 (1-85697-805-2, Kingfisher LKC) LKC.

—The Simon & Schuster Young Readers' Thesaurus. Barish, Wendy, ed. (Illus.). 192p. (gr. 3-7). 1984. pap. 6.95 (0-685-09127-9, Little Simon) S&S Trade.

Beebe, Brooke M. & Rosenblatt, Ruth Y. The Dictionary. Maas, Mieke, illus. LC 77-730283. (gr. 3-5). 1977. pap. text ed. 165.00 4 filmstrips, 4 cass., 24 skill sheets, Guide (0-89290-121-7, A151-SATC) Soc for Visual.

Beginner's Irish Dictionary. (ENG & IRI., Illus.). 128p. (Orig.). (gr. 1-8). 1990. pap. 11.95 (0-7171-1763-4, Pub. by Gill & Macmillan ER) Irish Bks Media.

Byrd, Elizabeth L. A Fonalfubet Pronunciation Dictionary of American English Words. (Orig.). (gr. k up). 1986. pap. text ed. 20.00 (0-9615393-2-1) U Assocs.

Coogan, John W. A Workbook of Words. 1987. pap. text ed. 16.20 (0-8013-0116-5, 75780) Longman.

Cooke, Tom, illus. Open Sesame Picture Dictionary. Malecki, Ed, designed by. (ENG & JPN.). 1987. pap. 7.75 (0-19-434170-4) OUP.

Eastman, Philip D. Cat in the Hat Beginner Book Dictionary. LC 64-1157. (Illus.). 144p. (gr. k-6). 1964. 10.00 (0-394-81009-0); lib. bdg. 9.99 (0-394-91009-5) Random Bks Yng Read.

Foust, Sylvia J. Dictionary Skills. Foust, Sylvia J., illus. 48p. (gr. 2-6). 1986. wkbk. 6.95 (1-55734-339-X) Tchr Create Mat.

Gikow, Louise, et al. My First Muppet Dictionary. Cooke, Tom, illus. 112p. (ps-2). 1992. 9.95 (0-307-15610-9, 15610, Golden Pr) Western Pub.

Gregorich, Barbara. Dictionary Skills. Pape, Richard, illus. 24p. (gr. 3-4). 1980. wkbk. 2.95 (0-89403-605-X) EDC.

Grisewood, John, et al, eds. The Kingfisher Illustrated Children's Dictionary. LC 93-45414. 480p. (gr. 5 up). 1994. 25.00 (1-85697-841-9, Kingfisher LKC) LKC.

The Harcourt Brace Student Dictionary. (gr. 4-7). 1994. 17.95 (0-15-200187-5, HB Juv Bks) HarBrace.

Harvey, Jane. Marvin & Max Big Word Book. (Illus.). 64p. (ps-1). 1991. 6.99 (0-517-05391-8) Random Hse Value.

Hillerich, Robert L. The American Heritage Picture Dictionary. Swanson, Maggie, illus. 144p. (gr. k-1). 1986. 10.95 (0-395-42531-X) HM.

Hollander, Cass. My Phonics Word Book. Morgado, Richard, illus. 64p. 1993. pap. 5.95 (1-56293-321-3) McClanahan Bk.

Honey Bear Picture Word Book. (gr. 2-4). 1991. 6.95 (0-87449-777-9) Modern Pub NYC.

Houghton Mifflin Company Staff, ed. The American Heritage Children's Dictionary. Webber, Howard, contrib. by. LC 86-7349. (Illus.). 864p. (gr. 3-6). 1986. 14.95 (0-395-42529-8) HM.

Houghton Mifflin Company Staff, ed. & contrib. by. The American Heritage Student's Dictionary. rev. ed. LC 86-7337. (Illus.). 1024p. (gr. 6-9). 1986. 12.95 (0-395-40417-7) HM.

Houghton Mifflin Company Staff, ed. Children's Dictionary. Rev. ed. LC 78-27760. (Illus.). 864p. (gr. 3-6). 1979. 12.70 (0-395-27512-1) HM.

—First Dictionary. Ulrich, George, illus. LC 78-27760. 864p. (gr. 3-6). 1979. text ed. 11.95 (0-685-07955-4) HM.

Houghton Mifflin Primary Dictionary & Workbook-Primary. 1986. 18.40 (0-395-38393-5) HM.

Koh, Frances M., ed. English-Korean Picture Dictionary. Vignes, Denise S., illus. LC 87-83309. 49p. (Orig.). (ps up). 1987. pap. 9.95 (0-9606090-3-2) EastWest Pr.

Krensky, Stephen, ed. The American Heritage First Dictionary. Ulrich, George, illus. LC 86-7363. (Illus.). (gr. 1-2). 1986. 12.70 (0-395-42530-1) HM.

Langenscheidt Staff. Langenscheidt Picture Dictionary. (gr. 4-7). 1993. English. 19.95 (0-88729-850-8) FRE-ENG. 19.95 (0-88729-851-6); GER-ENG. 19.95 (0-88729-852-4); ITA-ENG. 19.95 (0-88729-853-2); SPA-ENG. 19.95 (0-88729-854-0); JPN-ENG. 24.95 (0-88729-855-9); GRE-ENG. 19.95 (0-88729-862-1); HEB-ENG. 19.95 (0-88729-863-X) Langenscheidt.

—Langenscheidt Picture Dictionary. (gr. 4-7). 1993. ENG. pap. 14.95 (0-88729-856-7) FRE-ENG. pap. 14.95 (0-88729-857-5); GER-ENG. pap. 14.95 (0-88729-858-3); ITA-ENG. pap. 14.95 (0-88729-859-1); SPA-ENG. pap. 14.95 (0-88729-860-5); JPN-ENG. pap. 17.95 (0-88729-861-3) Langenscheidt.

—Langenscheidt Picture Dictionary. (gr. 4-7). 1993. 19.95 (0-88729-864-8) POL-ENG. POR-ENG. 19.95 (0-88729-865-6); RUS-ENG. 19.95 (0-88729-866-4); CHI-ENG. 19.95 (0-88729-867-2) Langenscheidt.

Law, Felicia. Doubleday Children's Picture Dictionary. Holmes, Carol, illus. LC 86-16216. 192p. (gr. k-6). 1987. pap. 16.00 (*0-385-23711-1*) Doubleday.

Levey, Judith, ed. The Macmillan First Dictionary. rev. & expanded ed. LC 90-6062. (Illus.). 416p. (gr. k-4). 1990. SBE 12.95 (*0-02-761731-9*, Macmillan Child Bk) Macmillan Child Grp.

Longman Staff. Longman Dictionary of English Idioms. 1979. pap. text ed. 25.95 (*0-582-05863-5*) Longman.

—Longman Handy Learner's Dictionary. (gr. 9-12). 1988. pap. text ed. 11.95 (*0-582-96413-X*, 78324) Longman.

Longmeyer, Carole M. What Did You Sayeth? Rhodes, Priscilla, illus. (Orig.). (gr. 4 up). 1994. pap. 14.95 (*0-935326-45-6*) Gallopade Pub Group.

Macmillan Publishing Company Staff. Macmillan Dictionary for Students. LC 84-3880. (Illus.). 1216p. (gr. 6-12). 1984. SBE 16.95 (*0-02-761560-X*, Macmillan Child Bk) Macmillan Child Grp.

Merriam-Webster Editorial Staff. Merriam-Webster's Elementary Dictionary. (Illus.). 608p. (gr. 1-6). 1986. 14.95 (*0-87779-575-4*) Merriam-Webster Inc.

Murray, William. Picture Dictionary. Matthews, Anne, illus. 28p. (ps-2). 1991. 3.50 (*0-7214-1416-8*, 9112-1) Ladybird Bks.

My Big Dictionary. LC 93-33756. (gr. 4 up). 1994. 24.95 (*0-395-66377-6*) HM.

My First Sticker Book of Words. (Illus.). 12p. (ps-2). 1994. 6.95 (*1-56458-715-0*) Dorling Kindersley.

My First Words Picture Dictionary. (ps-2). 1993. 9.95 (*0-943706-17-3*) Yllw Brick Rd.

Nayer, Judy. My First Picture Dictionary. Schanzer, Roz, illus. 24p. (ps-2). 1992. pap. 0.99 (*1-56293-110-5*) McClanahan Bk.

The New Scholastic Dictionary of American English. 1024p. (gr. 4-7). 1986. pap. 6.95 (*0-590-40415-6*) Scholastic Inc.

Passport Books Staff, ed. Let's Learn English: Picture Dictionary. Goodman, Marlene, illus. 72p. 1991. 9.95 (*0-8442-5453-3*, Natl Textbk) NTC Pub Grp.

Pesiri, Evelyn & Cheney, Martha. Gifted & Talented Dictionary: A Reference Workbook for Ages 4-6. 80p. (ps-1). 1994. pap. 3.95 (*1-56565-183-9*) Lowell Hse Juvenile.

Pheby, John A., ed. The Oxford-Duden Pictorial English Dictionary. (Illus.). 824p. (gr. 9 up). 1984. pap. 15.95 (*0-19-864155-9*) OUP.

Ridout, Ronald. Activity Picture Dictionary. Wingham, Peter, illus. 48p. (gr. 1 up). 1987. 9.95 (*0-8120-5844-5*) Barron.

Root, Betty. Dictionary. LC 91-26178. (Illus.). 96p. (gr. 1-5). 1992. pap. 13.00 (*0-671-76002-5*, S&S BFYR); pap. 8.00 (*0-671-76003-3*, S&S BFYR) S&S Trade.

Scarry, Huck, illus. My First Picture Dictionary. LC 76-24174. (ps-2). 1978. lib. bdg. 5.99 (*0-394-93486-5*); pap. 2.25 (*0-394-83486-0*) Random Bks Yng Read.

Scarry, Richard. Richard Scarry's Busytown Word Book. (ps-3). 1994. pap. 2.25 (*0-307-12846-6*, Golden Pr) Western Pub.

Schimpff, Jill W. Open Sesame Picture Dictionary: Featuring Jim Henson's Sesame Street Muppets, Children's Television Workshop. Cooke, Tom, illus. (gr. k-6). 1982. 12.75x (*0-19-503201-2*); pap. 7.75x (*0-19-503035-4*); activity book 4.95 (*0-19-434253-0*); Picture Dictionary, English-Chinese. 7.75 (*0-19-583744-4*) OUP.

Sesame Street Staff & Hayward, Linda. The Sesame Street Dictionary. Mathieu, Joe, illus. LC 80-11644. 256p. (ps-3). 1980. bds. 17.00 (*0-394-84007-0*); PLB 17.99 (*0-394-94007-5*) Random Bks Yng Read.

Shaw, John R. & Shaw, Janet. The New Horizon Ladder Dictionary of the English Language. rev. & updated ed. 686p. (gr. 9-12). 1970. pap. 4.95 (*0-451-16804-6*, Sig) NAL-Dutton.

Sheheen, Dennis, illus. Children's Picture Dictionary: English-Chinese, (gr. k up). 9.95 (*0-685-18873-6*) Modan-Adama Bks.

—A Child's Picture English-Arabic Dictionary. LC 85-15658. (gr. k-2). 1985. 9.95 (*0-915361-30-2*) Modan-Adama Bks.

—A Child's Picture English-Italian Dictionary. LC 86-14052. (gr. k-2). 1986. 9.95 (*0-915361-57-4*) Modan-Adama Bks.

—A Child's Picture English-Yiddish Dictionary. LC 85-15659. (gr. k-2). 1985. 9.95 (*0-915361-29-9*) Modan-Adama Bks.

The Simon & Schuster Young Readers' Illustrated Dictionary. (gr. 3 up). 1985. pap. 7.95 (*0-671-50821-0*) S&S Trade.

Smith, David & Newton, Derek. Troll Young People's Dictionary. Goldsmith, Evelyn, rev. by. Bayly, Clifford, illus. LC 89-27331. 128p. (gr. 1-4). 1991. PLB 14.89 (*0-8167-2255-2*); pap. 9.95 (*0-8167-2256-0*) Troll Assocs.

Snow, Alan. My First Dictionary. Snow, Alan, illus. LC 91-23485. 32p. (gr. k-3). 1992. PLB 12.79 (*0-8167-2515-2*); pap. text ed. 4.95 (*0-8167-2516-0*) Troll Assocs.

Southworth, Mary C. Wordworks. 1986. pap. text ed. 13.50 (*0-88334-192-1*, 76157) Longman.

Terban, Marvin. Time to Rhyme: A Rhyming Dictionary. Demarest, Chris, illus. LC 93-60242. 96p. (gr. 2-4). 1994. 15.95 (*1-56397-128-3*) Boyds Mills Pr.

Watermill Press Staff. Webster's Dictionary. (gr. 4-7). 1992. pap. 4.95 (*0-8167-2917-4*) Troll Assocs.

Webster's Intermediate Dictionary. LC 86-5428. 960p. 1986. 14.95 (*0-87779-379-4*) Merriam-Webster Inc.

Webster's New World Dictionaries Staff. Webster's New World Children's Dictionary. Neufeldt, Victoria & De Mello Vianna, Fernando, eds. (Illus.). 912p. 1991. 16.00 (*0-13-945726-7*, Webster New Wrld) P-H Gen Ref & Trav.

Webster's New World Dictionary for Young Adults. (Illus.). 1056p. (gr. 6-10). 1992. pap. 18.00 (*0-13-945734-8*, Webster New Wrld) P-H Gen Ref & Trav.

Weston, John & Spooner, Alan, eds. The Oxford Children's Dictionary. 3rd ed. Le Fever, Bill, et al, illus. LC 93-17585. 1993. 7.99 (*0-19-861297-4*) OUP.

Williams, Bill. The New Webster's Comprehensive Dictionary of the English Language. 2nd, rev. ed. Cayne, Bernard S. & Lechner, Doris E., eds. (Illus.). 1930p. (gr. 3 up). 1992. deluxe ed. 99.99 (*0-9623476-0-4*); lib. bdg. 99.99 (*0-685-28124-8*) Amer Intl Pr.

World Book Staff, ed. The World Book Student Dictionary (1993) rev. ed. LC 92-64304. (Illus.). 900p. (gr. 3-6). 1993. write for info. (*0-7166-1593-2*) World Bk.

ENGLISH LANGUAGE–DICTIONARIES–FRENCH

Berlitz. Berlitz Jr. French Dictionary. LC 91-40123. (Illus.). 144p. (ps-2). 1992. pap. 11.95 POB (*0-689-71539-0*, Aladdin) Macmillan Child Grp.

Eastman, Philip D. The Cat in the Hat Beginner Book Dictionary in French & English. LC 65-22650. (Illus.). 144p. (gr. 2-3). 1965. 15.95 (*0-394-81063-5*) Beginner.

Mon Grand Dictionnaire Francais-Anglais. (FRE & ENG.). 23.50 (*0-685-11402-3*) Fr & Eur.

Objets Familiers - Everyday Things. (ENG & FRE.). 63p. 1991. 19.95 (*2-07-057513-6*) Schoenhof.

ENGLISH LANGUAGE–DICTIONARIES–GERMAN

Sheheen, Dennis, illus. A Child's Picture English-German Dictionary. LC 86-13987. (gr. k-2). 1986. 9.95 (*0-915361-41-8*) Modan-Adama Bks.

ENGLISH LANGUAGE–DICTIONARIES–SPANISH

Berlitz. Berlitz Jr. Spanish Dictionary. LC 91-43927. (Illus.). 144p. (ps-2). 1992. pap. 11.95 POB (*0-689-71538-2*, Aladdin) Macmillan Child Grp.

Eastman, Philip D. Cat in the Hat Beginner Book Dictionary in Spanish & English. LC 66-10688. (SPA & ENG., Illus.). 144p. (gr. k-3). 1966. 16.00 (*0-394-81542-4*) Beginner.

Madrigal, Margarita. Open Door to Spanish, Bk. 2. 222p. (gr. 7-12). 1981. pap. text ed. 5.25 (*0-88345-427-0*, 18470); cassettes 45.00 (*0-686-77684-4*, 58472); ans. key Bk 1, 2 1.50 (*0-88345-487-4*, 18474) Prentice ESL.

ENGLISH LANGUAGE–ETYMOLOGY

Asimov, Isaac. Words from the Myths. Barss, William, illus. 224p. (gr. 5-10). 1961. 14.95 (*0-395-06568-2*) HM.

Dewey, Ariane. Naming Colors. LC 93-2635. (gr. 1-8). 1995. 16.00 (*0-06-021291-8*); PLB 15.89 (*0-06-021292-6*) HarpC Child Bks.

Graham-Barber, Lynda. Doodle Dandy! The Complete Book of Independence Day Words. Lewin, Betsy, illus. LC 91-19409. 128p. (gr. 4-10). 1992. SBE 13.95 (*0-02-736675-8*, Bradbury Pr) Macmillan Child Grp.

—Mushy! The Complete Book of Valentine Words. Lewin, Betsy, illus. LC 90-33047. 128p. (gr. 4-10). 1991. 13.95 (*0-02-736941-2*, Bradbury Pr) Macmillan Child Grp.

McNamara, Rita. Fourteen Basic Roots & the Key to 100,000 English Words. 52p. (gr. 9-12). 1991. spiral 3.95 (*0-939507-18-8*, B117) Amer Classical.

Steckler, Arthur. One Hundred & One Words & How They Began. LC 78-1012. (Illus.). 96p. 1979. pap. 6.95 (*0-385-14074-6*) Doubleday.

Tracy, Kristin. English Words Grow from Latin & Greek Roots. 27p. (Orig.). (gr. 1-4). 1992. spiral bdg. 3.80 (*0-939507-40-4*, B120) Amer Classical.

ENGLISH LANGUAGE–GRAMMAR

Adams, Pam, illus. Letters & Words. 16p. (Orig.). (ps-2). 1975. pap. 3.95 (*0-85953-046-9*, Pub. by Child's Play England) Childs Play.

Bonner, Margaret. Step into Writing: A Basic Writing Text. LC 93-34652. 1994. pap. text ed. write for info. (*0-201-59265-7*) Longman.

Chapman, John. Welcome to English: Let's Begin. (Illus.). 48p. (gr. 1 up). 1980. pap. 3.25 (*0-88345-422-X*, 18480); tchr's manual 4.50 (*0-88345-423-8*, 18493); tchr's. manual 4-5 7.50 (*0-88345-368-1*, 18499) Prentice ESL.

Collins, Gretchen. English Grammar Flipper: A Guide to Correct English Usage. 49p. (gr. 5 up). 1989. Repr. of 1977 ed. trade edition 5.95 (*1-878383-01-9*) C Lee Pubns.

Coon, Pam. The Vowel Van. 72p. (gr. k-3). 1980. 7.95 (*0-88160-010-5*, LW 112) Learning Wks.

Criscuolo, Nicholas P. & Herman, Barry. Fun With Words. (gr. 2-5). 1988. pap. 8.95 (*0-8224-3172-6*) Fearon Teach Aids.

Crystal, David. Rediscover Grammar. 1987. pap. text ed. 15.08 (*0-582-00258-3*, 78071) Longman.

English Grammar Study Aid. 1978. pap. 1.95 (*0-87738-028-7*) Youth Ed.

Forte, Imogene. I'm Ready to Learn about Beginning Consonants. (Illus.). 64p. (ps-1). 1987. pap. text ed. 1.95 (*0-86530-155-7*, IP 111-4) Incentive Pubns.

—Private "I" LC 84-62933. (Illus.). 80p. (gr. k-6). 1985. wkbk 3.95 (*0-86530-096-8*, IP 91-0) Incentive Pubns.

Gregorich, Barbara. Adjectives & Adverbs. Pape, Richard, illus. 24p. (gr. 3-4). 1980. wkbk. 2.95 (*0-89403-596-7*) EDC.

—Figures of Speech. Pape, Richard, illus. 24p. (gr. 3-4). 1980. wkbk. 2.95 (*0-89403-601-7*) EDC.

—Prefixes, Bases, & Suffixes. Pape, Richard, illus. 24p. (gr. 3-4). 1980. wkbk. 2.95 (*0-89403-600-9*) EDC.

—Prepositions & Conjunctions. Pape, Richard, illus. 24p. (gr. 3-4). 1980. wkbk. 2.95 (*0-89403-597-5*) EDC.

Grubbs, Joan, et al. Possessive Pronouns. rev. ed. Abell, ed. Grubbs, Joan, illus. 50p. (gr. 3-6). 1993. 23.00 (*0-685-65773-6*); PLB 25.00 (*1-56611-026-2*); pap. 15.00 (*1-56611-999-5*) Jonas.

Harvey, Thomas. Harvey's Elementary Grammar & Composition. (Illus.). (gr. 4-6). 1986. 10.95 (*0-88062-041-2*) Mott Media.

—Harvey's Revised English Grammar. (Illus.). (gr. 7-11). 1986. 13.95 (*0-88062-042-0*) Mott Media.

Heller, Ruth. A Cache of Jewels & Other Collective Nouns. (ps-3). 1989. 13.95 (*0-448-19211-X*, G&D) Putnam Pub Group.

—Kites Sail High: A Book about Verbs. LC 87-82718. (Illus.). 48p. (ps-3). 1988. PLB 13.95 (*0-448-10480-6*, Sandcastle Bks.); pap. 6.95 (*0-448-40452-4*, Sandcastle Bks.) Putnam Pub Group.

—Merry-Go-Round: A Book about Nouns. (Illus.). 48p. (gr. 1 up). 1990. 13.95 (*0-448-40085-5*, G&D) Putnam Pub Group.

—Up, up & Away: A Book about Adverbs. Heller, Ruth, illus. 48p. (gr. 1 up). 1993. pap. 6.95 (*0-448-40159-2*, Sandcastle Bks.) Putnam Pub Group.

Hoban, Tana. All about Where. LC 90-30849. (Illus.). 32p. (ps up). 1991. 13.95 (*0-688-09697-2*); PLB 13.88 (*0-688-09698-0*) Greenwillow.

Hubbard, L. Ron, concept by. Grammar & Communication for Children. 468p. (gr. 3-7). 1992. 49.99 (*0-88404-746-6*) Bridge Pubns Inc.

Koch, Michelle. Just One More. LC 88-17736. (Illus.). 32p. (ps up). 1989. 11.95 (*0-688-08127-4*); PLB 11.88 (*0-688-08128-2*) Greenwillow.

LeGros, Lucy C. Instant Centers - Letters. (Illus.). 46p. (Orig.). (gr. k-2). 1984. pap. 5.95 (*0-937306-04-5*) Creat Res NC.

Lester, James D., Sr. & Lester, James D., Jr. Writing: Style & Grammar. 400p. (Orig.). (gr. 6-10). 1994. pap. 14.95 spiralbound (*0-673-36128-4*) GdYrBks.

Lutgendorf, Philip & James, Shirley M. The Parts of Speech. Reichmann, Naczinski & Associates, illus. LC 77-730079. (gr. 7-9). 1976. pap. text ed. 219.00 6 filmstrips, 6 cass., 30 skill sheets, Guide (*0-89290-118-7*, A134-SATC) Soc for Visual.

Phillips, Wanda C. Easy Grammar: Adverbs. (gr. 4-12). 1987. pap. text ed. 11.50 (*0-936981-04-0*) ISHA Enterprises.

—Easy Grammar: Direct Objects & Indirect Objects. 33p. (gr. 4-12). 1986. pap. text ed. 5.50 (*0-936981-02-4*) ISHA Enterprises.

—Easy Grammar: Verbs. 130p. (gr. 4-12). 1986. pap. text ed. 12.50 (*0-936981-03-2*) ISHA Enterprises.

Robinson, Joan. WordBuilding. (gr. 4-8). 1989. pap. 9.95 (*0-8224-7450-6*) Fearon Teach Aids.

—WordStrength. (gr. 4-8). 1989. pap. 9.95 (*0-8224-7451-4*) Fearon Teach Aids.

—WordWise. (gr. 4-8). 1989. pap. 9.95 (*0-8224-7452-2*) Fearon Teach Aids.

Rowh, Mark. How to Improve Your Grammar & Usage. LC 93-31276. (Illus.). 128p. (gr. 9-12). 1994. PLB 13.40 (*0-531-11177-6*) Watts.

Ryan, Elizabeth. How to Make Grammar Fun - & Easy! LC 91-12525. 112p. (gr. 5-9). 1992. lib. bdg. 9.89 (*0-8167-2456-3*); pap. text ed. 3.95 (*0-8167-2457-1*) Troll Assocs.

Schoehberg, I., et al. Focus on Grammar: A Basic Course for Reference & Practice. (Illus.). 1994. pap. text ed. 20.00 (*0-685-71530-2*, 78512); wkbk. 14.00 (*0-685-71531-0*, 65683); tchr's. manual 23.00 (*0-685-71532-9*, 65682); cassette 38.00 (*0-685-71533-7*, 65684) Longman.

—Focus on Grammar: A Hi-Intermediate Course for Reference & Practice. (Illus.). 1994. pap. text ed. 20.00 (*0-685-71496-9*, 79644); tchr's. manual 23.00 (*0-685-71497-7*, 65690); wkbk. 14.00 (*0-685-71498-5*, 65691); cassette 38.00 (*0-685-71499-3*, 65692) Longman.

Schuster, Slade. The Slade Short Course. 2nd ed. 1982. pap. text ed. 8.25 (*0-88334-161-1*, 76128) Longman.

Schwartz, Linda. Gumball Grammar. 32p. (gr. 4-7). 1979. 3.95 (*0-88160-068-7*, LW 801) Learning Wks.

—Long Vowel Voyage. 20p. (gr. 1-3). 1980. 3.95 (*0-88160-058-X*, LW 606) Learning Wks.

—Short Vowel Voyage. 20p. (gr. 1-3). 1980. 3.95 (*0-88160-057-1*, LW 605) Learning Wks.

Shorto, Russell & Cwiklik, Robert. The Secret History of Grammar: An Epic Fantasy. Faulkner, Matt, illus. 160p. (gr. 5 up). 1988. Kipling Pr.

Smith, Carl B. Grammar Handbook for Home & School. Reade, Eugene W., ed. LC 92-19371. 96p. (Orig.). (gr. 5 up). 1992. pap. 8.95 (*0-9628556-7-7*) Grayson Bernard Pubs.

—Intermediate Grammar: A Student's Resource Book. Reade, Eugene, ed. LC 92-3659. 320p. (Orig.). (gr. 5 up). 1992. pap. 16.95 (*0-9628556-3-4*) Grayson Bernard Pubs.

Southworth, Mary C. Wordworks. 1986. pap. text ed. 13.50 (*0-88334-192-1*, 76157) Longman.

Terban, Marvin. I Think I Thought & Other Tricky Verbs. Maestro, Giulio, illus. LC 83-19034. 64p. (Orig.). (ps-4). 1984. (Clarion Bks); pap. 5.70 (*0-89919-290-4*, Clarion Bks) HM.

Tilkin, Sheldon. Verbs. Pape, Richard, illus. 24p. (gr. 3-4). 1980. wkbk. 2.95 (*0-89403-598-3*) EDC.

Tilkin, Sheldon L. Nouns & Pronouns. Pape, Richard, illus. 24p. (gr. 3-4). 1980. wkbk. 2.95 (*0-89403-599-1*) EDC.

Trisler, Alana & Cardiel, Patrice H. My Word Book. (Illus.). 56p. (Orig.). 1994. pap. text ed. 2.50 (*1-56762-055-8*) Modern Learn Pr.

World Book Editors, ed. The World Book of Word Power Activities 1. LC 93-61408. (Illus.). 64p. (gr. k-2). 1994. PLB write for info. (*0-7166-3994-7*) World Bk.

—The World Book of Word Power Activities 2. LC 93-61457. (Illus.). 64p. (gr. 3-5). 1994. PLB write for info. (*0-7166-3995-5*) World Bk.

ENGLISH LANGUAGE–HISTORY

Groff, Richard L., Jr. Ic Spraece Angel-Seax: A Beginning Anglo-Saxon Grammar for Children. Groff, Richard L., illus. LC 91-67263. 36p. (Orig.). (gr. 2-6). 1991. pap. 10.98 incl. audio tape (*0-9630718-1-5*) New Dawn NY.

Klausner, Janet. Talk about English: How Words Travel & Change. Doniger, Nancy, illus. LC 89-49116. 208p. (gr. 5 up). 1990. 14.95 (*0-690-04831-9*, Crowell Jr Bks); (Crowell Jr Bks) HarpC Child Bks.

ENGLISH LANGUAGE–HOMONYMS

Gwynne, Fred. A Chocolate Moose for Dinner. Gwynne, Fred, illus. LC 80-14150. (gr. 1-6). 1988. pap. 13.00 jacketed (*0-671-66685-1*, S&S BFYR); pap. 5.95 (*0-671-66741-6*, S&S BFYR) S&S Trade.

—The King Who Rained. Gwynne, Fred, illus. LC 80-12939. (gr. 1-6). 1988. pap. 14.00 jacketed (*0-671-66363-1*, S&S BFYR); pap. 5.95 (*0-671-66744-0*, S&S BFYR) S&S Trade.

Newhouse, Dora. The Encyclopedia of Homonyms-Sound Alikes: Condensed & Abridged Edition. LC 76-50944. (Illus.). (gr. 6-12). 1978. pap. 6.95 (*0-918050-00-6*) Newhouse Pr.

Newhouse, Dora, illus. Homonyms Plus. (gr. 6-12). 1979. wkbk 6.95 (*0-918050-42-1*); tchr's guide 6.95 (*0-918050-41-3*); activity cards 4.95 (*0-918050-44-8*) Newhouse Pr.

ENGLISH LANGUAGE–IDIOMS

Artell, Mike & Armstrong, Beverly. Fun with Expressions. LC 91-77126. (Illus.). 40p. (gr. 2-6). 1992. 5.95 (*0-88160-209-4*, LW 299) Learning Wks.

Cox, James A. Put Your Foot in Your Mouth & Other Silly Sayings. Weissman, Sam Q., illus. LC 80-12877. 72p. (gr. 2-5). 1980. bds. 3.95 (*0-394-84503-X*) Random Bks Yng Read.

Longman Staff. Longman Dictionary of English Idioms. 1979. pap. text ed. 25.95 (*0-582-05863-5*) Longman.

Terban, Marvin. Mad As a Wet Hen & Other Funny Idioms. Maestro, Giulio, illus. LC 86-17575. (gr. 3-6). 1987. (Clarion Bks); pap. 4.95 (*0-89919-479-6*, Clarion Bks) HM.

—Punching the Clock: Funny Action Idioms. Huffman, Tom, illus. 64p. (gr. 3-7). 1990. pap. 4.80 (*0-89919-865-1*) HM.

ENGLISH LANGUAGE–ORTHOGRAPHY

see English Language–Spelling

ENGLISH LANGUAGE–PHRASES AND TERMS

see English Language–Terms and Phrases

ENGLISH LANGUAGE–PUNCTUATION

see Punctuation

ENGLISH LANGUAGE–READERS

see Readers;

also subdivision readers for languages other than English, e.g. French Language–Readers

ENGLISH LANGUAGE–RHETORIC

see Rhetoric

ENGLISH LANGUAGE–RIME

Hughes, Joleen. Things! LC 93-44877. 1994. 4.99 (*0-517-10151-3*, Pub. by Derrydale Bks) Random Hse Value.

Kalish, Muriel & Kalish, Lionel. Bears on Stairs: A Beginner's Book of Rhymes. LC 92-10144. (Illus.). 12p. (ps-1). 1993. 7.95 (*0-590-44918-4*) Scholastic Inc.

McMillan, Bruce. Play Day: A Book of Terse Verse. McMillan, Bruce, illus. LC 90-29077. 32p. (ps-3). 1991. reinforced 14.95 (*0-8234-0894-9*) Holiday.

Noll, Sally. Jiggle, Wiggle, Prance. LC 92-25332. 1993. pap. 3.99 (*0-14-054883-1*) Puffin Bks.

Rutman, Shereen G. Rhyming Words. Morgado, Richard, illus. 32p. (ps). 1992. wkbk. 1.95 (*1-56293-170-9*) McClanahan Bk.

Young, Sue K. The Scholastic Rhyming Dictionary. (Illus.). 224p. (gr. 3 up). 1994. 14.95 (*0-590-49460-0*, Scholastic Ref) Scholastic Inc.

ENGLISH LANGUAGE–SPELLING

Baggiani, J. M. & Tewell, V. M. Phonics; a Tool for Better Reading & Spelling, Bk. I. Birt, Jane L., illus. (gr. 1-2). 1982. pap. 9.50 student's copy (*0-934329-00-1*); tchr's. manual 10.75 (*0-934329-01-X*) Baggiani-Tewell.

—Phonics: A Tool for Better Reading & Spelling, Bk. II. Jacobson, Mary M., illus. (gr. 3-6). 1967. pap. 3.50 (*0-934329-02-8*); wkbk. 2.00 (*0-934329-03-6*) Baggiani-Tewell.

—Phonics: A Tool for Better Reading & Spelling, Bk. III. Jacobson, Mary M. & Davis, Mary I., illus. (gr. 5-12). 1984. pap. 5.75 (*0-934329-04-4*); wkbk. 4.00 (*0-934329-05-2*) Baggiani-Tewell.

Brown, Frances. My First Book of Words. LC 78-58344. 144p. (gr. k-6). 1979. Walker Educ.

Brown, Rick. What Rhymes with Snake? A Word & Picture Flap Book. Brown, Rick, illus. LC 92-37870. 24p. 1994. 11.95 (*0-688-12328-7*, Tambourine Bks) Morrow.

Daniel, Becky. Spelling Thinker Sheets. 64p. (gr. 4-8). 1988. wkbk. 8.95 (*0-86653-423-7*, GA1035) Good Apple.

Daniel, Charlie & Daniel, Becky. Super Spelling Fun. 64p. (gr. 2-6). 1978. 8.95 (*0-916456-31-5*, GA82) Good Apple.

Downey, Tiffany. Spelling Fitness: One Thousand One of the Most Frequently Misspelled Words. Downey, Cynthia, ed. 102p. (Orig.). (gr. 7-12). 1988. 29.95 (*0-685-22519-4*) Infini Educ.

Gordon, Sharon. The Spelling Bee. Garcia, Tom, illus. LC 81-4648. 32p. (gr. k-2). 1981. PLB 11.59 (*0-89375-535-4*); pap. 2.95 (*0-89375-536-2*) Troll Assocs.

Gresko, Bernetta. How Do You Spell...? English Only. Gresko, Bernetta, illus. 44p. (gr. 2-8). 1987. pap. 4.95 (*0-939755-11-4*); wkbk. act sheets 4.95 (*0-939755-14-9*); wkbk. crossword puzzles 4.95 (*0-939755-06-8*) Sunset Prods.

Henry, Marcia K. Words. (gr. 3-9). 1990. write for info. (*1-878653-00-8*) Lex Pr.

Huelsberg, Enid L. Crossword Puzzle Mastery, Level 1. 32p. (gr. 1-3). 1975. wkbk. 5.00 (*0-87879-783-1*, Ann Arbor Div) Acad Therapy.

—Crossword Puzzle Mastery: Level 2. 32p. (gr. 4-6). 1975. wkbk. 3.00 (*0-87879-784-X*, Ann Arbor Div) Acad Therapy.

—Michigan Programmed Spelling Series, Basic Word List Level 1: Reusable Edition. (gr. 1). 1974. wkbk. 10.00 (*0-87879-772-6*, Ann Arbor Div) Acad Therapy.

—Michigan Programmed Spelling Series, Basic Word List, Level 3: Reusable Edition. (gr. 3). 1974. wkbk. 10.00 (*0-87879-774-2*, Ann Arbor Div) Acad Therapy.

—Michigan Programmed Spelling Series, Basic Word List, Level 2: Reusable Edition. (gr. 2). 1974. 10.00 (*0-87879-773-4*, Ann Arbor Div) Acad Therapy.

—Michigan Programmed Spelling Series, Use Frequency Based Words, Level 4: Reusable Edition. (gr. 4). 1975. wkbk. 10.00 (*0-87879-778-5*, Ann Arbor Div) Acad Therapy.

—Michigan Programmed Spelling Series, Use Frequency Based Words, Level 5: Reusable Edition. (gr. 5). 1975. wkbk. 10.00 (*0-87879-779-3*, Ann Arbor Div) Acad Therapy.

—Michigan Programmed Spelling Series, Use Frequency Based Words, Level 6: Reusable Edition. (gr. 6). 1975. wkbk. 10.00 (*0-87879-780-7*, Ann Arbor Div) Acad Therapy.

Johnson, Eric W. Improve Your Own Spelling. (gr. 6-9). 1977. pap. text ed. 4.95 (*0-88334-093-3*) Longman.

Laurita, Raymond E. Building Word Power Through Spelling Mastery: Questions & Answers about Words & Their Origins. 64p. (Orig.). (gr. 6-12). 1991. pap. text ed. 9.50 (*0-914051-25-3*) Leonardo Pr.

—The Spelling Doctor Says...,Pt. 1: (Roots 1-10) 87p. (Orig.). 1991. pap. text ed. 11.00 (*0-914051-20-2*) Leonardo Pr.

—Spelling Keys to One Thousand One Words from Ten Greek Based Roots. 80p. (Orig.). (gr. 8-12). 1991. pap. text ed. 11.50 (*0-914051-26-1*) Leonardo Pr.

Learning About Letters. 1986. pap. 9.95 (*0-394-88319-5*) Random Bks Yng Read.

LeGros, Lucy C. Instant Centers - Holidays. (Illus.). 45p. (Orig.). (gr. k-2). 1985. 5.95 (*0-937306-06-1*) Creat Res NC.

Loomer, Bradley M. & Strege, Maxine G. Useful Spelling: Levels 2-8. (gr. 2-8). 1990. write for info. (*1-878712-03-9*) Useful Lrn.

McCulloch, Myrna & Madsen, Sharon, eds. Spelling & Usage Vocabulary Builder. large type ed. (Illus.). 478p. (gr. k-2). 1993. Repr. of 1991 ed. 26.50 (*0-924277-04-1*, Dist. by Riggs Institute Pr) K & M Pub.
This picture/word book's 4832 words have been edited with the mnemonic marketing system for precise speech & correct spelling used in Romalda Spalding's WRITING ROAD TO READING (WRTR), Wm. Morrow, N.Y., also distributed through the Riggs Institute. A truly usable, primary-level reference text; covers word explanations, grammar helps (verb forms including tenses, nouns, formation of plurals, adjectives, adverbs), extensive composition "models" with correct usage & word(s) substitutions (homonyms & antonyms), connected writing models, manuscript printing, syllabication, alphabetization practice & 1200 descriptive pictures. Large (14 point) print, 478 pages (4 to 5 words per page). Editing includes a 7-page Introduction for teachers which describes the WRTR system of teaching, the entire phonetic system for correct spelling, the mnemonic marking system, 28 spelling rules & tips for using multi-sensory, direct instruction. Order from: The Riggs Institute, 4185 SW 102nd Ave., Beaverton, OR 97005; 503-646-9459, FAX 503-644-5191. *Publisher Provided Annotation.*

Most, Bernard. Hippopotamus Hunt. LC 93-39988. (ps-3). 1994. 14.95 (*0-15-234520-5*) HarBrace.

Pen Notes Staff. Learning to Print. (ps up). 1984. 10.95 (*0-939564-01-7*) Pen Notes.

Schwartz, L. Spelling Works. 48p. (gr. 3-8). 1993. 6.95 (*0-88160-257-4*, LW288) Learning Wks.

Trisler, Alana & Cardiel, Patrice H. Words I Use When I Write. Trisler, Alana & Cardiel, Patrice H., illus. 36p. (Orig.). (gr. k-3). 1989. pap. text ed. 2.50 (*0-935493-33-6*) Programs Educ.

Tyler, J. & Gee, R. Spelling Puzzles. (Illus.). 32p. (gr. 2-5). 1992. pap. 4.95 (*0-7460-1053-2*) EDC.

Wittles, Harriet & Greisman, Joan. How to Spell It: A Dictionary of Commonly Misspelled Words. Wittles, Harriet & Greisman, Joan, illus. 336p. (gr. 1 up). 1982. pap. 10.95 (*0-448-14756-4*, G&D) Putnam Pub Group.

ENGLISH LANGUAGE–STUDY AND TEACHING

Claire, Elizabeth. ESL Wonder Workbook, No. 1: This Is Me. Flamm, Jackie, ed. Frazier, J. D., illus. 104p. (Orig.). (gr. 1-6). 1990. pap. 7.65 (*1-878598-00-7*) Alta Bk Co Pubs.

—ESL Wonder Workbook, No. 2: All Around Me. Chapman, Charles, ed. Frazier, J. D., illus. 104p. (Orig.). (gr. 1-6). 1991. pap. write for info. (*1-878598-01-5*) Alta Bk Co Pubs.

Clark, Raymond C. Money: Exploring the Ways We Use It. (Illus.). 96p. (gr. 7 up). 1989. 10.50x (*0-86647-029-8*) Pro Lingua.

—Story Cards: The Tales of Nasreddin Hodja - Pairwork Conversation Activities. (Illus.). 44p. (gr. 6 up). 1991. 14.50x (*0-86647-044-1*) Pro Lingua.

Clark, Raymond C. & Duncan, Janie L. Getting a Fix on Vocabulary, Using Words in the News: The System of Affixation & Compounding in English. (Illus.). 96p. (gr. 7 up). 1991. 11.00x (*0-86647-038-7*) Pro Lingua.

Clark, Raymond C., ed. Max in America, Pt. 1: Communcating in the Culture. (Illus.). 128p. (gr. 8 up). 1987. 5.00x (*0-86647-024-7*) Pro Lingua.

—Max in America, Pt. 2: Communcating in the Culture. (Illus.). 128p. (gr. 8 up). 1987. 5.00x (*0-86647-025-5*) Pro Lingua.

Cook, Marcy. Numbers & Words: A Problem Per Day. Formaro, Rita, illus. 64p. (gr. 3-8). 1987. pap. text ed. 8.50 (*0-914040-52-9*) Cuisenaire.

Costigan, Shirleyann. Just One Seed. Remkiewicz, Frank, illus. 16p. (Orig.). (ps-1). 1992. pap. text ed. 29.95 big bk. (*1-56334-180-8*) Hampton-Brown.

Cousins, Michael. English Matters, Vol. 3. (gr. 8-10). 1985. pap. 8.95 (*0-7175-1201-0*) Dufour.

Geoffrion, Sondra. Power Study to up Your Grades in English. LC 88-61276. 60p. (Orig.). 1989. pap. text ed. 3.95 (*0-88247-784-6*) R & E Pubs.

Henry, Marcia K. Words. (gr. 3-9). 1990. write for info. (*1-878653-00-8*) Lex Pr.

Howard, Lati, et al. Learning English Book: A TV-Video Standard Program. McLaughlin, Michael & Schneider, Amy, eds. Murphy, Marty, illus. 240p. (Orig.). 1992. pap. text ed. 10.95 (*0-937354-76-7*) Delta Systems.

Joy, Flora. Word Wizardry, Level II. Harroll, Pat, illus. 112p. (gr. 4-12). 1987. pap. 11.95 (*0-86653-404-0*, GA 1017) Good Apple.

—Word Wizardry, Level I. Harroll, Pat, illus. 112p. (gr. 2-8). 1987. pap. 11.95 (*0-86653-403-2*, GA 1016) Good Apple.

Kiebanow, Barbara & Fischer, Sara. American Holidays: Exploring Traditions, Customs, & Backgrounds. (Illus.). 128p. (gr. 5 up). 1986. 10.50x (*0-86647-018-2*) Pro Lingua.

Kleman, James A. Short Shots..A Drill a Day: The Easy Way to Language Literacy. 2nd ed. 44p. (gr. 4-8). 1982. manual 5.00 (*0-938464-09-4*) JML Enter MD.

Long, Sheron. The Goat in the Chile Patch. Remkiewicz, Frank, illus. 16p. (Orig.). (gr. k-3). 1992. pap. text ed. 29.95 big bk. (*1-56334-181-6*) Hampton-Brown.

Mahoney, Judy, compiled by. Sing with Me in English: A Teach Me Tapes Songbook. Thiede, Carla R., contrib. by. (Illus.). 26p. (Orig.). (ps-6). 1994. pap. 7.95 (*0-934633-90-8*) Teach Me.

Michener, Dorothy & Muschlitz, Beverly. Bulletin Board Bonanza. (Illus.). 96p. (gr. 2-6). 1981. pap. 7.95 (*0-86530-028-3*, IP-283) Incentive Pubns.

Mylet, Trish. Children, Today's Joy & Tomorrow's Hope, 8 bks, Set 2. Sheffield, Antoinette, illus. 224p. (ps-3). 1991. Set. pap. text ed. 16.00 (*0-945590-62-8*) Pals 1, Pals 2, Pals 3, Pals 4, Pals 5, Pals 6, Pals 7, Pals 8. Sizzy Bks.

—Fun with Phonics, 19 bks. Sheffield, Antoinette, illus. 448p. (ps-3). 1991. Set 1 & 2. pap. text ed. 39.95 (*1-881754-70-7*) Set 1: Jan & Pam, The Van, Rex & Tex, The Bed, Siz & Liz, The Pit, Dod & Bob, The Box, Hun & Sun, The Hut, Pals. Set 2: Pals 1, Pals

2, Pals, 3, Pals 4, Pals 5, Pals, 6, Pals 7, Pals 8. Dolphin Lrning.
FUN WITH PHONICS: Set 1 & Set 2, 19 books. This SERIES consists of two Sets of books. Set 1 contains 11 beginning reader & activity books. Set 2 contains 8 books of short stories & activity books. The CHILDREN SERIES consists of positive global readers incorporating geography (the fifty United States & the District of Columbia), phonics (short & long vowels, blends, diagraphs), number recognition & self expression & explores the areas of zoology, botany, history & global unity. Each pair of books in Set 1 & each story in Set 2 contain a state reference page with a dot-to-dot exercise in the shape of that state's outline. The first sixteen books include sentence completion exercises & that story's word list. In Set 2 at least one story in each book has an O. Henry-type ending in which the child decides how the story ends. The SERIES includes a Reference Guide. Building on Set 1's themes of fun & fantasy, Set 2 expands & concludes with joy, fact & hope. This warmly written & illustrated series has been well received worldwide by Early Education, Special Education & English as a Second Language teachers, parents & most importantly, children. $39.95. Trish Mylet, author. Antoinette Sheffield, illustrator. Dolphin Publishing Group, Box 2570, Fair Oaks, CA 95628. ISBN 1-881754-70-7 Write for brochure.
Publisher Provided Annotation.

Polette, Keith. Read, Write, Now! Dillon, Paul, illus. 44p. (gr. 5-9). 1993. pap. text ed. 5.95 (*1-879287-20-X*) Bk Lures.

Roberts, John & Roberts, Nedra P. Excellence in English. 1987. pap. text ed. 12.00 (*0-8013-0134-3*, 75798) Longman.

Sather, Edgar, et al. People at Work: Listening & Communicative Skills, Vocabulary Building. (Illus.). 112p. (gr. 8 up). 1990. student wkbk. only 14.00x (*0-86647-037-9*) Pro Lingua.

—People at Work: Student's Package. (Illus.). 112p. (gr. 8 up). 1990. incl. wkbk. & 3 cassettes 25.00 (*0-86647-033-6*) Pro Lingua.

Segal, Bertha E. We Learn English Through Action. 106p. (gr. 3-12). 1987. 12.99 (*0-938395-11-4*) B Segal.

Thurston, Cheryl M. Ideas That Really Work! The Best of the Cottonwood Monthly, 1987-1991. (Illus.). 158p. (Orig.). (gr. 6-9). 1991. pap. text ed. 21.95 (*1-877673-13-7*) Cottonwood Pr.

Zeman, Anne & Kelly, Kate. Everything You Need to Know about English Homework. LC 93-46358. 1995. 19.95 (*0-590-49360-4*) Scholastic Inc.

ENGLISH LANGUAGE–SYNONYMS AND ANTONYMS

Allen, Jonathan. Big Owl, Little Towel. Allen, Jonathan, illus. LC 91-39349. 12p. (ps). 1992. 3.95 (*0-688-11783-X*, Tambourine Bks) Morrow.

—Up the Steps, Down the Slide. Allen, Jonathan, illus. LC 91-44534. 12p. (ps). 1992. 3.95 (*0-688-11784-8*, Tambourine Bks) Morrow.

The American Heritage Student Thesaurus. LC 93-33755. 1994. pap. 6.95 (*0-395-68177-4*) HM.

Arnold, Tedd, illus. Opposites. 16p. (ps). 1992. pap. 3.95 (*0-671-77823-4*, Little Simon) S&S Trade.

Asch, Frank. Little Fish, Big Fish. (Illus.). (ps). 1992. bds. 8.95 (*0-590-44492-1*, 027, Cartwheel) Scholastic Inc.

—Short Train, Long Train. (Illus.). (ps). 1992. bds. 8.95 (*0-590-44493-X*, 028, Cartwheel) Scholastic Inc.

Bailey, Vanessa. Animal Opposites. (ps). 1991. 5.95 (*0-8120-6244-2*) Barron.

Balducci, Rita. Walt Disney's Bambi: Thumper's Book of Opposites. Pacheco, David & Wakeman, Diana, illus. 12p. (ps). 1993. bds. 1.95 (*0-307-06124-8*, 6124, Golden Pr) Western Pub.

Barnes-Murphy, Rowan. Opposites. Barnes-Murphy, Rowan, illus. 16p. (ps). 1993. bds. 3.95 (*0-8249-8611-3*, Ideals Child) Hambleton-Hill.

Beal, George. The Kingfisher Illustrated Thesaurus. Rees, Gary, illus. LC 93-50709. 144p. (gr. 6 up). 1994. write for info. (*1-85697-520-7*, Kingfisher LKC) LKC.

Beal, George & Chatterton, Martin. The Kingfisher First Thesaurus. LC 92-45572. (Illus.). 144p. (gr. 2-6). 1993. 14.95 (*1-85697-914-8*, Kingfisher LKC) LKC.

Bellamy, John. Doubleday Children's Thesaurus. Stevenson, Peter, illus. LC 86-16217. 192p. (gr. k-6). 1987. 15.00 (*0-385-23833-9*) Doubleday.

Bishop, Roma. Opposites. (ps). 1992. pap. 2.95 (*0-671-79128-1*, Little Simon) S&S Trade.

Carter, David A. Baby Bug In & Out. (gr. 3 up). 1993. pap. 4.95 (*0-671-86630-3*, Little Simon) S&S Trade.

—Baby Bug Opposites. (Illus.). (ps-6). 1993. pap. 4.95 (*0-671-86877-2*, Little Simon) S&S Trade.

Cony, Sue, illus. Opposites. 8p. (ps-k). 1991. bds. 4.95 (*1-56293-150-4*) McClanahan Bk.

Disney's Pop-up Book of Opposites. LC 90-85429. (Illus.). 12p. (ps-k). 1991. 6.95 (*1-56282-018-4*) Disney Pr.

Dudko, Mary A. & Larsen, Margie. Barney's Book of Opposites. Full, Dennis, photos by. LC 94-72000. (Illus.). 20p. (ps-k). 1994. bds. 3.95 (*1-57064-016-5*) Barney Pub.

Duerrstein, Richard, illus. In - Out: A Disney Book of Opposites. LC 91-58979. 12p. (ps). 1992. bds. 5.95 (*1-56282-266-7*) Disney Pr.

Edge, Nellie, adapted by. La Cancion De Opuestos. Zamora-Pearson, Marissa, tr. from ENG. Nichols, Barry & Nicholas, Barry, illus. (SPA.). (ps-2). 1993. pap. text ed. 15.00 (*0-922053-25-1*) N Edge Res.

—Opposite Song Big Book. Nichols, Barry, illus. (ps-2). 1988. pap. text ed. 14.00 (*0-922053-06-5*) N Edge Res.

Felix, Monique. Opposites: Mouse Books. (Illus.). 32p. (ps). 1993. pap. 2.95 (*1-56189-092-8*) Amer Educ Pub.

The Harcourt Brace Student Thesaurus. (gr. 4-7). 1994. 14.95 (*0-15-200186-7*, HB Juv Bks) HarBrace.

Harvey, Jane. Marvin the Mouse Opposites Book. (Illus.). 64p. (ps-1). 1991. 6.99 (*0-517-05390-X*) Random Hse Value.

Hellweg, Paul. The Facts on File Student's Thesaurus. 304p. 1991. 24.95 (*0-8160-1634-8*) Facts on File.

—Macmillan Children's Thesaurus. LC 93-21773. (gr. 1-8). 1995. 14.95 (*0-02-743525-3*) Macmillan Child Grp.

Hoban, Tana. Exactly the Opposite. LC 89-27227. (Illus.). 32p. (ps up). 1990. 15.00 (*0-688-08861-9*); PLB 14.93 (*0-688-08862-7*) Greenwillow.

—Push, Pull, Empty, Full: A Book of Opposites. LC 72-90410. (Illus.). 32p. (ps-2). 1972. RSBE 13.95 (*0-02-744810-X*, Macmillan Child Bk) Macmillan Child Grp.

In the Park, a Book about Opposites. (gr. 3 up). 1992. pap. 2.99 (*0-517-03597-9*) Random Hse Value.

Koch, Michelle. By the Sea. LC 89-23344. (Illus.). 24p. (ps up). 1991. 13.95 (*0-688-09549-6*); PLB 13.88 (*0-688-09550-X*) Greenwillow.

Laird, Charlton G. Webster's New World Thesaurus. 854p. (gr. 9-12). 1987. pap. 12.00 (*0-13-948126-5*) P-H.

Lambert, Jonathan, illus. Opposites. 18p. (ps-1). 1992. bds. 1.95 (*0-681-41565-7*) Longmeadow Pr.

Lenssen, Ann. A Rainbow Balloon: A Book of Concepts. LC 91-31830. (Illus.). 32p. (ps-3). 1992. 13.50 (*0-525-65093-8*, Cobblehill Bks) Dutton Child Bks.

Lunn, Carolyn. A Whisper Is Quiet. Martin, Clovis, illus. LC 88-11968. 32p. (ps-2). 1988. PLB 10.25 (*0-516-02087-0*); pap. 2.95 (*0-516-42087-9*) Childrens.

McLenighan, Valjean. Stop-Go, Fast-Slow. Fiddle, Margrit, illus. LC 81-17080. 32p. (ps-2). 1982. PLB 10.25 (*0-516-03617-3*); pap. text ed. 2.95 (*0-516-43617-1*) Childrens.

My Book of Opposites. (ps-2). 3.95 (*0-7214-5147-0*) Ladybird Bks.

My Very First Colors, Shapes, Sizes, & Opposites Book. 1993. write for info. (*1-56458-377-5*) Dorling Kindersley.

Oliver, Stephen, photos by. Opposites. LC 89-63093. (Illus.). 24p. (ps-k). 1990. 7.00 (*0-679-80620-2*) Random Bks Yng Read.

Posey, Pam, illus. Thomas the Tank Engine: Coming & Going -- A Book of Opposites. Awdry, W., contrib. by. (Illus.). 14p. (ps). 1993. pap. 57.48 (*0-679-81645-3*) McKay.

Push 'n' Pull: Book of Togethers. 12p. 1992. pap. 8.95 (*0-590-45089-1*) Scholastic Inc.

Randall, Ronne P. Opposites. Smallman, Steve, illus. 24p. (ps). 1987. pap. 1.25 (*0-7214-9556-7*, S871) Ladybird Bks.

Rutman, Shereen G. My Book of Opposites. Loh, Carolyn, illus. 32p. (ps). 1992. wkbk. 1.95 (*1-56293-171-7*) McClanahan Bk.

Siede, George & Preis, Donna, photos by. Opposites: Active Minds. Schwager, Istar, contrib. by. (Illus.). 24p. (ps-3). 1992. PLB 9.95 (*1-56674-004-5*) Forest Hse.

The Thesaurus for Kids. 144p. (gr. 3-7). 1993. pap. 7.95 (*1-56293-355-8*) McClanahan Bk.

Tilkin, Sheldon. Synonyms, Antonyms, Homonyms. Pape, Richard, illus. 24p. (gr. 3-4). 1980. wkbk. 2.95 (*0-89403-603-3*) EDC.

Turner, Gwenda. Opposites. Turner, Gwenda, illus. 24p. (ps-k). 1993. 9.99 (*0-670-84813-1*) Viking Child Bks.

Windridge, C. A Student's First Thesaurus. LC 92-45115. 144p. 1993. pap. 3.95 (*0-681-45226-9*) Longmeadow Pr.

Wittels, Harriet & Greisman, Joan. A First Thesaurus. Block, Alex, illus. 144p. (gr. 2-4). 1985. pap. write for info. (*0-307-15835-7*, Pub. by Golden Bks) Western Pub.

ENGLISH LANGUAGE–TERMS AND PHRASES

Artman, John. Slanguage. 80p. (gr. 4 up). 1980. 8.95 (*0-916456-60-9*, GA 175) Good Apple.

Asimov, Isaac. Words from the Myths. (Illus.). 144p. (gr. 6). 1969. pap. 2.50 (*0-451-14097-4*, Sig) NAL-Dutton.

DeWitt, Jim. Means Something Else--"The Doubles" Figures of Speech Writing Book, No. 2. Gleissner, Alex & Nordgren, Steve, illus. 64p. (Orig.). (gr. 6-12). 1987. wkbk. 6.00 (*0-915199-51-3*) Pen-Dec.

Fakih, Kimberly O. Off the Clock: A Lexicon of Time Words & Expressions. LC 94-2082. (Illus.). 144p. (gr. 5 up). 1994. 15.95g (*0-395-66374-1*) Ticknor & Flds Bks Yng Read.

MacCarthy, Patricia. Herds of Words. MacCarthy, Patricia, illus. LC 90-31537. 32p. (ps-3). 1991. 11.95 (*0-8037-0892-0*) Dial Bks Young.

Terban, Marvin. In a Pickle & Other Funny Idioms. Maestro, Giulio, illus. LC 82-9585. 64p. (gr. 1-4). 1983. (Clarion Bks); pap. 4.95 (*0-89919-164-9*, Clarion Bks) HM.

Thomas, Robert. How to Talk Midwestern. Carlson, Bruce, ed. Thomas, Tony & Carlson, Bruce, illus. 109p. (Orig.). (gr. 9 up). 1990. pap. 7.95 (*1-878488-21-X*) Quixote Pr IA.

Wehrli, Kitty. Thought Tracking Level 1: Simple Phrases. (gr. 2). 1976. wkbk. 10.00 (*0-87879-739-4*, Ann Arbor Div) Acad Therapy.

—Thought Tracking Level 2: Sequential Phrases. (gr. 2). wkbk. 10.00 (*0-87879-740-8*, Ann Arbor Div) Acad Therapy.

ENGLISH LANGUAGE–TEXTBOOKS FOR FOREIGNERS

Barrier, Jean & Kennedy, Alice. English Is Fun Books. McCombs, Toni, illus. 192p. (gr. k-8). 1991. pap. text ed. 12.00 (*0-911743-07-3*) Barrier & Kennedy.

Christison, Mary Ann. English Through Poetry. Peterson, Kathleen, illus. 130p. (gr. 3-6). 1982. pap. text ed. 8.95 (*0-88084-002-1*) Alemany Pr.

Costingan, Shirleyann. The Little Ant. Boyd, Patti, illus. (gr. k-3). 1993. complete set 99.50 (*1-56334-317-7*); audio cassette 10.50 (*1-56334-315-0*); 35.00 (*1-56334-316-9*) Hampton-Brown.

Graham, Carolyn. The Electric Elephant & Other Stories. (Illus., Orig.). (gr. 7-12). 1982. pap. text ed. 7.95x (*0-19-503229-2*) OUP.

Hazzan, Anne-Francoise. Let's Learn English Coloring Book. (Illus.). 64p. 1988. pap. 3.95 (*0-8442-5451-7*, Passport Bks) NTC Pub Grp.

Keyes, Joan R. Now You're Talking. (Illus.). (gr. 4-9). 1988. wkbk. 5.95 (*1-55737-067-2*) Ed Activities.

McCallum, George P. Visitor from Another Planet & Other Plays. (gr. 4-6). 1982. student's ed. 7.95x (*0-19-502743-4*) OUP.

Viney, Peter, et al. Main Street Student Book. LC 92-22748. 1992. 7.95 (*0-19-434485-1*) OUP.

ENGLISH LANGUAGE–TEXTBOOKS FOR FOREIGNERS–SPANISH

Kahn, Michele. Mi Libro de Palabras Usadas Cada Dia En Ingles. (gr. k-6). 1982. pap. 13.95 (*0-8120-5431-8*) Barron.

Schott, Darlyne F. The Apple Tree, Vol. 9: Pasitos English Language Development Books. 16p. (gr. k-1). 1990. pap. text ed. 11.00 (*1-56537-068-6*) D F Schott Educ.

—Bono Goes to School, Vol. 6: Pasitos English Language Development Books. 25p. (gr. k-1). 1990. pap. text ed. 11.00 (*1-56537-065-1*) D F Schott Educ.

—Four Pretty Presents, Vol. 2: Pasitos English Language Development Books. 31p. (gr. k-1). 1990. pap. text ed. 11.00 (*1-56537-061-9*) D F Schott Educ.

—It's Snowing!, Vol. 10: Pasitos English Language Development Books. 18p. (gr. k-1). 1991. pap. text ed. 11.00 (*1-56537-069-4*) D F Schott Educ.

—Mr. Opposite Pumpkin, Vol. 5: Pasitos English Language Development Books. 15p. (gr. k-1). 1990. pap. text ed. 11.00 (*1-56537-064-3*) D F Schott Educ.

—My Little Red Kite, Vol. 8: Pasitos English Language Development Books. 11p. (gr. k-1). 1990. pap. text ed. 11.00 (*1-56537-067-8*) D F Schott Educ.

—Pasitos English Language Development Books, 10 vols. (gr. k-1). 1991. Set. pap. text ed. 105.00 (*1-56537-091-0*) D F Schott Educ.

—Pretty Valentine, Vol. 7: Pasitos English Language Development Books. 19p. (gr. k-1). 1990. pap. text ed. 11.00 (*1-56537-066-X*) D F Schott Educ.

—The Rare Pig, Vol. 1: Pasitos English Language Development Books. 15p. (gr. k-1). 1990. pap. text ed. 11.00 (*1-56537-060-0*) D F Schott Educ.

—Three Bears, Three Sizes, Vol. 4: Pasitos English Language Development Books. 24p. (gr. k-1). 1990. pap. text ed. 11.00 (*1-56537-063-5*) D F Schott Educ.

—Where Are You Mrs. Caterpillar?, Vol. 3: Pasitos English Language Development Books. 14p. (gr. k-1). 1990. pap. text ed. 11.00 (*1-56537-062-7*) D F Schott Educ.

Weisberg, Valerie H. English Verbs: Every Irregular Conjugation. Herrick, George H., intro. by. Bartz, Susie, illus. (SPA & ENG.). 168p. 1991. pap. 9.95x (*0-941281-76-0*); English verb wkbk. 3.95 (*0-941281-52-3*); with Spanish 15.50 (*0-9610912-6-6*) V H Pub.

White, Judith. Phrase-a-Day English for Hispanic Children. Macbain, Carol, illus. 100p. (gr. k-6). 1993. 7.95 (*0-88432-500-8*); incl. 2 audiocassettes 19.95 (*0-88432-498-2*) Audio-Forum. Spanish-speaking children ages 5-11 will have fun while learning the English

language. The program consists of an activity book that can be used in conjunction with audio cassettes. Young users can imitate the voices of the native speaking children & adults while following along with coloring & drawing activities. Seasons of the year are used as the framework within which are organized illustrations, vocabulary, & activities. Progress is natural because the words, phrases, & expressions are easy to say & are taken from the child's daily life. Numbers & counting, days of the week, foods & mealtime, articles of clothing, family members, & colors are an example of the practical vocabulary that is taught. The cassettes include music & sound effects. Effectiveness is enhanced because children are most likely to be interested & motivated when learning is self-directed. It is suggested that an adult teach the child to follow along with the book & to operate the cassette player. Words & phrases that are learned can then be used at home, at school, or at play. The book & two (62 min. tl.) cassette combination are $19.95, ISBN 0-88432-498-2. Book only, $7.95, ISBN 0-88432-500-8. Order from Audio-Forum, 96 Broad St., Guilford, CT 06437. 1-800-243-1234.
Publisher Provided Annotation.

ENGLISH LITERATURE
see also Authors, English; English Drama; English Poetry; English Wit and Humor; Short Stories
Carroll, Lewis. The Alice in Wonderland Pop-up. Thorne, Jenny, illus. LC 80-7615. 12p. (gr. k-4). 1980. pap. 6.95 (*0-385-28038-6*) Delacorte.
Dickens, Charles. A Christmas Carol. abr. ed. Wendt, Michael & Pizar, Kathleen, eds. Sturrock, Walt, illus. 80p. (gr. 2-5). 1988. 5.95 (*0-88101-087-1*) Unicorn Pub.
Wells, H. G. Island of Dr. Moreau. Lowndes, R. A., intro. by. (gr. 7 up). 1966. pap. 1.75 (*0-8049-0110-4*, CL-110) Airmont.
Wilde, Oscar. Picture of Dorian Gray. (gr. 9 up). 1964. pap. 2.50 (*0-8049-0039-6*, CL-39) Airmont.
ENGLISH LITERATURE–BIOGRAPHY
see Authors, English
ENGLISH LITERATURE–COLLECTIONS
Rook, Lizzie J. & Goodfellow, E. J. Tiny Tot's Speaker. facsimile ed. LC 73-160907. (gr. 7 up). Repr. of 1895 ed. 14.00 (*0-8369-6271-0*) Ayer.
ENGLISH LITERATURE–CRITICISM
see English Literature–History and Criticism
ENGLISH LITERATURE–HISTORY AND CRITICISM
Lyon, Sue, ed. Great Writers of the English Language, 14 vols. LC 88-21077. (Illus.). 1450p. 1991. PLB 449.95 (*1-85435-000-5*) Marshall Cavendish.
ENGLISH POETRY
Belloc, Hilaire. Matilda: Who Told Such Dreadful Lies. Simmonds, Posy, illus. LC 91-15852. 32p. 1992. 15.00 (*0-679-82658-0*) Knopf Bks Yng Read.
Blake, Quentin. All Join In. (ps-3). 1991. 14.95 (*0-316-09934-1*) Little.
Blake, William. The Tyger. Waldman, Neil, illus. LC 92-23378. 1993. 15.95 (*0-15-292375-6*) HarBrace.
British Hedgehog Society Staff. Prickly Poems. (Illus.). 64p. (gr. 3-5). 1993. 18.95 (*0-09-176379-7*, Pub. by Hutchinson UK) Trafalgar.
Browning, Robert. The Pied Piper of Hamelin. 1993. 12.95 (*0-679-42812-7*, Everymans Lib) Knopf.
Carroll, Lewis. Lewis Carroll's Jabberwocky. reissue ed. Zalben, Jane B., illus. Humpty Dumpty, annotations by. (Illus.). 32p. 1992. PLB 14.95 (*1-56397-080-5*) Boyds Mills Pr.
Chaucer, Geoffrey. The Canterbury Tales. 496p. (ps-8). 1990. Repr. lib. bdg. 29.95x (*0-89966-671-X*) Buccaneer Bks.
Coleridge, Samuel Taylor. Portable Coleridge. Richards, Ivor A., ed. (gr. 10 up). 1977. pap. 11.00 (*0-14-015048-X*, P48, Penguin Bks) Viking Penguin.
—The Rime of the Ancient Mariner. Young, Ed, illus. LC 90-20403. 64p. (ps up). 1992. SBE 16.95 (*0-689-31613-5*, Atheneum Child Bk) Macmillan Child Grp.
Crossley-Holland, Kevin. Beowulf. Keeping, Charles, illus. 48p. (gr. 5 up). 1988. 16.00 (*0-19-279770-0*); pap. 7.50 (*0-19-272184-4*) OUP.
Farjeon, Eleanor. Between the Earth & Sun. Date not set. 15.00 (*0-06-020795-7*, HarpT) HarpC.
Jennings, Elizabeth. Secret Brother & Other Poems. Stevens, Meg, illus. LC 69-14765. (gr. 1-5). 1966. 13.95 (*0-8023-1194-6*) Dufour.
King-Smith, Dick. Alphabeasts. Blake, Quentin, illus. LC 91-38435. 64p. (gr. 1 up). 1992. SBE 14.95 (*0-02-750720-3*, Macmillan Child Bk) Macmillan Child Grp.
Lear, Edward. A Book of Nonsense. Lear, Edward, illus. LC 92-53176. 240p. 1992. 12.95 (*0-679-41798-2*, Evrymans Lib Childs Class) Knopf.

—How Pleasant to Know Mr. Lear: Nonsense Poems. Butenko, Bohdan, illus. LC 94-4389. 76p. (gr. 1 up). 1994. 16.95 (*0-88045-126-2*) Stemmer Hse. For the first time, Edward Lear's great nonsense verse is presented for very young readers, who will relate to the charming chalkboard-style illustrations on bright-colored pages more readily than to the elaborate paintings of earlier volumes. Included are four favorite poems: "How Pleasant to Know Mr. Lear," "The Jumblies," "The Dong with a Luminous Nose" & "The Scroobious Pip." The book is square, 9" x 9", enjoyably easy to hold. Short accounts about author & artist are included, & with the title poem, make it easy to introduce biography, as well as poetry & fantasy. Other books in this series of great poetry for young people are I'M NOBODY! WHO ARE YOU?, Emily Dickinson (ISBN 0-916144-21-6, hardbound $21.95; 0-96144-22-4, paper $14.95), A SWINGER OF BIRCHES, Robert Frost (0-919144-92-5, hardbound $21.95; 0-916144-93-3, paper $14.95) & UNDER THE GREENWOOD TREE, William Shakespeare (0-88045-028-2, hardbound $21.95; 0-88045-029-0, paper $14.95). "This irresistible book is its own reason for being." - SLJ. To order, contact Stemmer House Publishers, Inc., 2627 Caves Rd., Owings Mills, MD 21117; tel. 800-676-7511; fax 800-645-6958.
Publisher Provided Annotation.

—Nonsense Poems. LC 93-39193. (Illus.). 96p. (Orig.). 1994. pap. 1.00 (*0-486-28031-4*) Dover.
—The Table & the Chair. Powers, Tom, illus. LC 91-45538. 32p. (ps-3). 1993. 15.00 (*0-06-020804-X*); PLB 14.89 (*0-06-020805-8*) HarpC Child Bks.
—There Was an Old Man: A Gallery of Nonsense Rhythms, a Selection of Limericks. Lemieux, Michele, illus. LC 93-46492. 1994. write for info. (*0-688-10788-5*); PLB write for info. (*0-688-10789-3*) Morrow Jr Bks.
Marsh, James. From the Heart: Light-Hearted Verse. LC 92-17912. (Illus.). 32p. 1993. 6.99 (*0-8037-1449-1*) Dial Bks Young.
Marshall, James. Old Mother Hubbard & Her Wonderful Dog. (ps-3). 1991. 13.95 (*0-374-35621-1*) FS&G.
Milne, A. A. Now We Are Six. (Illus.). 112p. (ps-6). 1992. full-color gift ed. 17.50 (*0-525-44960-4*, DCB) Dutton Child Bks.
—Now We Are Six. Shepard, Ernest H., illus. 112p. 1992. pap. 3.99 (*0-14-036124-3*, Puffin) Puffin Bks.
—When We Were Very Young. (Illus.). 112p. (ps-6). 1992. full-color gift ed. 17.50 (*0-525-44961-2*, DCB) Dutton Child Bks.
—When We Were Very Young. Shepard, Ernest H., illus. 112p. 1992. pap. 3.99 (*0-14-036123-5*, Puffin) Puffin Bks.
Milton, John. Paradise Lost. new ed. Tromley, F., intro. by. Bd. with Paradise Regained. (gr. 11up). 1968. pap. 2.50 (*0-8049-0173-2*, CL-173) Airmont.
Moon, Pat. Earth Lines: Poems for the Green Age. LC 92-27570. 64p. (gr. 5 up). 1993. 14.00 (*0-688-11853-4*) Greenwillow.
Moses, Brian. Hippopotamus Dancing & Other Poems. LC 93-43968. 1994. pap. 14.95 (*0-521-44141-2*); 7.95 (*0-521-44684-8*) Cambridge U Pr.
—Knock Down Ginger & Other Poems. LC 93-43969. 1994. write for info. (*0-521-44140-4*); pap. 7.95 (*0-521-44683-X*) Cambridge U Pr.
Opie, Iona & Opie, Peter, eds. The Oxford Book of Children's Verse. 448p. 1995. pap. text ed. 14.95 (*0-19-282349-3*) OUP.
Potter, Beatrix. Little Treasury of Beatrix Potter Nursery Rhymes. LC 93-8697. (Illus.). 1994. 5.99 (*0-517-10030-4*, Pub. by Derrydale Bks) Random Hse Value.
Rossetti, Christina G. Color. Teichman, Mary, illus. LC 90-25588. 40p. (ps-1). 1992. 15.00 (*0-06-022626-9*); PLB 14.89 (*0-06-022650-1*) HarpC Child Bks.
Scott, Walter. Lady of the Lake & Other Poems. Bennet, C. L., intro. by. (gr. 9 up). 1967. pap. 1.75 (*0-8049-0137-6*, CL-137) Airmont.
Shakespeare, William. Complete Sonnets & Poems. Fisher, Neil H., intro. by. (gr. 9 up). 1966. pap. 0.60 (*0-8049-1016-2*, S-16) Airmont.
Stevenson, Robert Louis. Block City. Wolff, Ashley, illus. 32p. (ps-2). 1992. pap. 3.99 (*0-14-054551-4*, Puff Unicorn) Puffin Bks.
—A Child's Garden of Verses. Gregori, Lee, illus. LC 85-12766. (gr. 3 up). 1969. pap. 2.25 (*0-8049-0195-3*, CL-195) Airmont.
—Child's Garden of Verses. Messenger, Jannat, illus. 12p. (ps-6). 1992. 13.95 (*0-525-44997-3*, DCB) Dutton Child Bks.
—A Child's Garden of Verses. unabr. ed. Kliros, Thea, illus. LC 92-25818. 96p. 1992. pap. 1.00 (*0-486-27301-6*) Dover.
—A Child's Garden of Verses. Dorr, Mary A., illus. 24p. (ps-2). 1993. pap. text ed. 0.99 (*1-56293-351-5*) McClanahan Bk.
Taylor, Jane. Twinkle, Twinkle, Little Star. 1992. 10.95 (*0-590-45566-4*, Cartwheel) Scholastic Inc.
Tennyson, Alfred. The Brook. Micucci, Charles, illus. LC 93-46404. 32p. (ps-2). 1994. 14.95 (*0-531-06854-4*); pap. 14.99 (*0-531-08704-2*) Orchard Bks Watts.
Weil, Zaro. Mud, Moon & Me. Burroughes, Jo, illus. 80p. (gr. 2-5). 1992. 13.45 (*0-395-58038-2*) HM.
Wines, James, illus. Edward Lear's Nonsense. LC 93-20461. 32p. 1994. 12.95 (*0-8478-1682-6*) Rizzoli Intl.
ENGLISH POETRY–COLLECTIONS
Daniel, Mark, compiled by. A Child's Treasury of Seaside Verse. LC 90-2819. (Illus.). 144p. (ps up). 1991. 16.95 (*0-8037-0889-0*) Dial Bks Young.
Eccleshare, Julia, compiled by. First Poems. Young, Selina, illus. LC 93-40894. 64p. 1994. 14.95 (*0-87226-373-8*) P Bedrick Bks.
Elledge, Scott, ed. Wider Than the Sky: Poems to Grow up With. LC 90-4135. 368p. (gr. 5 up). 1990. 20.00 (*0-06-021786-3*); PLB 19.89 (*0-06-021787-1*) HarpC Child Bks.
Family Treasury of One Thousand Poems. LC 93-18994. 1993. 9.99 (*0-517-09333-2*, Pub. by Wings Bks) Random Hse Value.
Heaney, Seamus & Hughes, Ted, eds. The Rattle Bag: An Anthology of Poetry. 498p. (gr. 3 up). 1985. pap. 15.95 (*0-571-11976-X*) Faber & Faber.
Hieatt, Constance B., ed. Beowulf & Other Old English Poems. 2nd, rev. & enl. ed. Hieatt, A. Kent, intro. by. 192p. (gr. 9-12). 1988. pap. 3.50 (*0-553-21347-4*) Bantam.
Hopkins, Lee B., compiled by. Flit, Flutter, Fly! Poems about Bugs & Other Crawly Creatures. Palagonia, Peter, illus. LC 91-12441. 32p. (gr. k-4). 1992. pap. 14.00 (*0-385-41468-4*) Doubleday.
—Weather. Hall, Melanie, photos by. LC 92-14913. (Illus.). 64p. (gr. k-3). 1994. 14.00 (*0-06-021463-5*); PLB 13.89 (*0-06-021462-7*) HarpC Child Bks.
Lear, Edward & Carroll, Lewis. Owls & Pussycats: Nonsense Verse. Palin, Nicki, illus. LC 93-2714. 64p. (gr. 3 up). 1993. 16.95 (*0-87226-366-5*) P Bedrick Bks.
Marcus, Leonard S., selected by. Lifelines: A Poetry Anthology Patterned on the Stages of Life. LC 93-26413. 112p. (gr. 6 up). 1994. 16.99 (*0-525-45164-1*, DCB) Dutton Child Bks.
Nister, Ernest. Ernest Nister's Book of Christmas. Intervisual Staff, illus. 12p. 1991. 12.95 (*0-399-21799-1*, Philomel) Putnam Pub Group.
—Hide-&-Seek. (Illus.). 20p. (ps-8). 1992. 14.95 (*0-399-21810-6*, Philomel Bks) Putnam Pub Group.
Palgrave, Francis T. & Press, John, eds. Golden Treasury of the Best Songs & Lyrical Poems in the English Language: From Shakespeare to Larkin. 5th ed. (gr. 5-9). 1987. pap. 10.95 (*0-19-282035-4*) OUP.
Prelutsky, Jack. A Nonny Mouse Writes Again! Priceman, Marjorie, illus. LC 92-5214. 40p. (ps-5). 1993. 13.00 (*0-679-83715-9*); PLB 13.99 (*0-679-93715-3*) Knopf Bks Yng Read.
Richardson, Polly. Animal Poems. (ps-3). 1992. 12.95 (*0-8120-6283-3*) Barron.
Rogasky, Barbara, selected by. Winter Poems. Hyman, Trina S., illus. 40p. (gr. 2 up). 1994. 15.95 (*0-590-42872-1*, Scholastic Hardcover) Scholastic Inc.
Shakespeare, William. Under the Greenwood Tree. Holdridge, Barbara, ed. DeWitt, Robin & DeWitt, Pat, illus. Rowse, A. L., pref. by. 80p. (gr. 4 up). 1986. 21.95 (*0-88045-028-2*); pap. 14.95 (*0-88045-029-0*); cass. & bk. 23.90 (*0-88045-103-3*); cassette only 8.95 (*0-88045-100-9*) Stemmer Hse.
Time-Life Inc. Editors. On Top of Spaghetti: A Lift-the-Flap Poetry Book. (Illus.). 20p. (ps-2). 1992. write for info. (*0-8094-9291-1*); PLB write for info. (*0-8094-9292-X*) Time-Life.
Westcott, Nadine B., ed. & illus. Never Take a Pig to Lunch: And Other Poems about the Fun of Eating. LC 93-11801. 64p. 1994. 16.95 (*0-531-06834-X*); lib. bdg. 16.99 RLB (*0-531-08684-4*) Orchard Bks Watts.
Williams, Oscar, ed. The Mentor Book of Major British Poets. 576p. (gr. 9-12). 1985. pap. 5.99 (*0-451-62637-0*, Ment) NAL-Dutton.
ENGLISH SHORT STORIES
see Short Stories

ENGLISH WIT AND HUMOR

Jerome, Jerome K. Diary of a Pilgrimage. (Illus.). 176p. (gr. 6-9). 1990. pap. 8.00 (*0-86299-010-6*) A Sutton Pub.

ENGRAVING

see also Gems; Wood Engraving

ENSEMBLES (MATHEMATICS)

see Set Theory

ENSIGNS

see Flags

ENTERTAINERS

see also Actors and Actresses; Clowns; Dancers

Eichhorn, Dennis P. Hammer. (Illus.). 96p. (Orig.). (gr. 8-12). 1993. pap. 3.25 (*0-89872-219-5*, 217) Turman Pub.

Fox, Fiona. How to Reach Your Favorite Star, No. 2. (gr. 4-7). 1993. pap. 2.95 (*0-307-22550-X*, Golden Pr) Western Pub.

Gikow, Louise. Meet Jim Henson. LC 92-30225. 80p. (Orig.). (gr. 2-6). 1993. pap. 2.99 (*0-679-84642-5*, Bullseye Bks) Random Bks Yng Read.

Hirsch, Linda. You're Going Out There a Kid, but You're Coming Back a Star. Wallner, John, illus. 128p. (Orig.). (gr. 3-7). 1984. pap. 2.25 (*0-553-15272-6*, Skylark) Bantam.

Krohn, Katherine E. Lucille Ball: Pioneer of Comedy. (Illus.). 64p. (gr. 4-7). 1992. PLB 13.50 (*0-8225-0543-6*); pap. 4.95 (*0-8225-9603-2*) Lerner Pubns.

Nickell, Joe. Wonderworkers! How They Perform the Impossible. Nickell, Joe, illus. 80p. (Orig.). 1991. pap. 12.95 (*0-87975-688-8*) Prometheus Bks.

Oleksy, Walter. Entertainers. (Illus.). 128p. (gr. 3-6). Date not set. 19.95 (*1-56065-120-2*) Capstone Pr.

Petrucelli. Jim Henson, Reading Level 2. (Illus.). 24p. (gr. 1-4). 1989. PLB 14.60 (*0-86592-426-0*); 10.95s.p. (*0-685-58800-9*) Rourke Corp.

Rich, Jason. Celebrity Teen Talk: Exclusive Celebrity Interviews, Video Game Tips & Reviews. (Illus.). 224p. (Orig.). (gr. 4-12). 1991. pap. 6.95 (*0-9625057-5-7*) DMS ID.

Richardson, Wendy & Richardson, Jack. Entertainers: Through the Eyes of Artists. LC 90-34278. 48p. (gr. 4 up). 1991. PLB 15.40 (*0-516-09283-9*); pap. 7.95 (*0-516-49283-7*) Childrens.

Schroeder, Alan. Josephine Baker. King, Coretta Scott, intro. by. (Illus.). 128p. (gr. 5 up). 1991. lib. bdg. 17.95 (*0-7910-1116-X*) Chelsea Hse.

Sonneborn, Liz. Performers. LC 94-25587. 1995. write for info. (*0-8160-3045-6*) Facts on File.

Wilbourn, Debrah. Eddie Murphy. King, Coretta Scott, intro. by. (Illus.). 112p. (gr. 5 up). 1993. PLB 17.95 (*0-7910-1879-2*); pap. write for info. (*0-7910-1908-X*) Chelsea Hse.

ENTERTAINING

see also Amusements; Etiquette; Games

Ball, Jacqueline. Let's Party. (Illus.). 32p. (gr. 5 up). 1990. lib. bdg. 15.94 (*0-86625-418-8*); lib. bdg. 11.95s.p. (*0-685-36382-1*) Rourke Corp.

Basow, Lynn. The Room Parent's Party Planner: How to Host Great Parties in Your Child's Classroom. Marsh, Chuck, ed. Wallace, Dan, illus. 56p. (Orig.). 1993. pap. 9.95 (*0-9638975-0-0*) Inverness Pr.

Boteler, Alison. Disney Party Handbook. LC 91-58610. (Illus.). 176p. 1992. PLB 13.89 (*1-56282-200-4*); pap. 9.95 (*1-56282-173-3*) Disney Pr.

Ellison, Virginia. Pooh Party Book. 1991. pap. 3.50 (*0-440-47299-7*) Dell.

Fulk, Penny. Children's Parties Made Easy. Durdee, Becky, illus. 142p. (Orig.). pap. 6.00 (*0-941951-00-6*) JJJ Pubs.

Jackson, Sonia. Eeeeaaassy Party Planning. Negrini, Wendy, illus. 80p. 1988. pap. 6.95 (*0-9619056-0-3*) Entrtnmnt Enter.

James, Diane. The Party Book. Tofts, Hannah, illus. LC 93-21219. 48p. (gr. 3-5). 1994. 16.95 (*1-56847-135-1*) Thomson Lrning.

Jenny, Gerri. Birthday Parties for Children: Activities, Games, Cakes & Fun for Children from 4-10. Macdonald, Roland B. & Gray, Dan, illus. 128p. (gr. k-5). 1991. pap. 9.95 (*1-878767-15-1*) Murdoch Bks.

Reinhard, Dale W. Simply Celebrating Children: Parties As Unique & Special As a Child. 140p. 1991. 12.95 (*0-9628888-0-X*) Pressed Duck.

Robson, Denny A. Having a Party. LC 92-9552. 1992. 11.90 (*0-531-17340-2*, Gloucester Pr) Watts.

Rosen, C. Party Fun. (Illus.). 14p. (gr. 2-6). 1986. pap. 4.50 (*0-7460-0124-X*) EDC.

Wallach, Susan. Great Parties, How to Plan Them. Magnuson, Diana, illus. LC 90-46879. 128p. (gr. 5-9). 1991. PLB 10.89 (*0-8167-2291-9*); pap. text ed. 2.95 (*0-8167-2292-7*) Troll Assocs.

Wilkes, Angela. My First Party Book. LC 90-40331. (Illus.). 48p. (gr. 1-5). 1991. 13.00 (*0-679-80909-0*) Knopf Bks Yng Read.

ENTERTAINING–FICTION

Allard, Harry. The Stupids Have a Ball. Marshall, James, illus. LC 77-27660. (gr. k-3). 1984. 13.45 (*0-395-26497-9*); pap. 4.80 (*0-395-36169-9*) HM.

Bunnikin's Picnic Party. (Illus.). (ps-k). pap. 3.50 (*0-7214-0206-2*, Plume) Ladybird Bks.

Carlson, Nancy. The Talent Show. Carlson, Nancy, illus. LC 85-4122. 32p. (ps-3). 1985. PLB 13.50 (*0-87614-284-6*) Carolrhoda Bks.

Dewey, Ariane. The Tea Squall. Dewey, Ariane, illus. LC 93-11725. 40p. (gr. 1 up). 1994. pap. 4.95 (*0-688-04582-0*, Mulberry) Morrow.

Dubanevich, Arlene. Pig William. LC 85-5776. (Illus.). 32p. (gr. k-3). 1990. pap. 3.95 (*0-689-71372-X*, Aladdin) Macmillan Child Grp.

Hill, Elizabeth S. Broadway Chances. 160p. (gr. 3-7). 1992. RB 14.00 (*0-670-84197-8*) Viking Child Bks.

Johnson, Stacie. The Party. 1992. pap. 3.50 (*0-553-29720-1*) Bantam.

Johnston, Annie F. The Little Colonel's House Party. (gr. 5 up). 13.95 (*0-89201-039-8*) Zenger Pub.

Keats, Ezra J. Hi, Cat! (gr. k-3). 1990. incl. cass. 19.95 (*0-87499-180-3*); pap. 12.95 incl. cass. (*0-87499-179-X*); Set; incl. 4 bks., cass., & guide. pap. 27.95 (*0-685-38540-X*) Live Oak Media.

Kozikowski, Renate. Teddy Bears' Picnic. (Illus.). 32p. (ps-2). 1990. pap. 10.95 POB (*0-689-71362-2*, Aladdin) Macmillan Child Grp.

Krupinski. Blue Water Journal. Date not set. 15.00 (*0-06-023436-9*); PLB 14.89 (*0-06-023437-7*) HarpC Child Bks.

Shreve, Susan R. The Masquerade. 160p. (gr. 7 up). 1981. pap. 1.95 (*0-440-95396-0*, LE) Dell.

Stine, R. L. The Surprise Party. large type ed. (gr. 6 up). Date not set. PLB 14.60 (*0-8368-1161-5*) Gareth Stevens Inc.

Storybook Heirlooms Staff. You're Invited to a Storybook Tea Party. (Illus.). 14p. (ps-6). 1994. 9.00 (*0-9638614-1-7*) Strybook Heirlooms.

Willhoite, Michael. The Entertainer. (Illus.). 32p. (ps-1). 1992. pamphlet 3.95 (*1-55583-202-4*, Alyson Wonderland) Alyson Pubns.

ENTERTAINMENTS

see Amusements

ENTOMOLOGY

see Insects

ENTOMOLOGY, ECONOMIC

see Insects, Injurious and Beneficial

ENTOZOA

see Parasites

ENTRANCE REQUIREMENTS FOR COLLEGE AND UNIVERSITIES

see Colleges and Universities–Entrance Requirements

ENVIRONMENT

see Adaptation (Biology); Anthropogeography; Ecology; Man–Influence of Environment; Man–Influence on Nature

ENVIRONMENT AND PESTICIDES

see Pesticides and the Environment

ENVIRONMENTAL PROTECTION

see also Conservation of Natural Resources

Aaseng, Nathan. Jobs vs. the Environment: Can We Save Both? LC 94-37. (Illus.). 128p. (gr. 6 up). 1994. lib. bdg. 17.95 (*0-89490-574-0*) Enslow Pubs.

Amdur, Richard. Toxic Materials. (Illus.). 112p. (gr. 5 up). 1993. PLB 19.95 (*0-7910-1574-2*) Chelsea Hse.

Ancona, George, photos by. Earth Keepers. Anderson, Joan, text by. LC 92-38627. (Illus.). 1993. 17.95 (*0-15-242199-8*) HarBrace.

Arneson, D. J. Toxic Cops. LC 90-13102. (Illus.). 128p. (gr. 7-12). 1991. PLB 13.40 (*0-531-12525-4*) Watts.

Atwood, Margaret. For the Birds. Bianchi, John, illus. 56p. (gr. 8-12). 1991. pap. 9.95 (*0-920668-32-1*) Firefly Bks Ltd.

Aylesworth, Thomas G. Government & the Environment: Tracking the Record. LC 92-24515. (Illus.). 104p. (gr. 6 up). 1993. lib. bdg. 17.95 (*0-89490-398-5*) Enslow Pubs.

Bailey, Donna. What We Can Do about Protecting Nature. Kline, Marjory, ed. LC 91-11534. (Illus.). 32p. (gr. 3-5). 1992. PLB 11.40 (*0-531-11080-X*) Watts.

—What We Can Do about Recycling Garbage. (Illus.). 32p. (gr. k-4). 1991. PLB 11.40 (*0-531-11017-6*) Watts.

Baines, John. Exploring Humans & the Environment. Hughes, Jenny, illus. LC 92-24734. 48p. (gr. 4-8). 1992. PLB 22.80 (*0-8114-2604-1*) Raintree Steck-V.

Bellamy, David. How Green Are You? Dann, Penny, illus. LC 90-19453. 32p. (gr. 1-4). 1991. 14.95 (*0-517-58429-8*, Clarkson Potter); PLB 15.99 (*0-517-58447-6*, C N Potter Bks) Crown Bks Yng Read.

Bender, Lionel. Our Planet. LC 91-30843. (Illus.). 96p. (gr. 1-5). 1992. pap. 13.00 (*0-671-75995-7*, S&S BFYR); pap. 8.00 (*0-671-75994-9*, S&S BFYR) S&S Trade.

Benson, Laura. This Is Our Earth. (Illus.). 32p. (ps-4). 1994. 14.95 (*0-88106-445-9*); PLB 15.88 (*0-88106-446-7*) Charlesbridge Pub.

Berger, Melvin. Can Kids Save the Earth? 16p. (gr. 2-4). 1994. pap. 14.95 (*1-56784-209-7*) Newbridge Comms.

—Hazardous Substances: A Reference. LC 86-8806. 128p. (gr. 6 up). 1986. lib. bdg. 17.95 (*0-89490-116-8*) Enslow Pubs.

—Where Does All the Garbage Go? Student Edition. (Illus.). 16p. (ps-2). 1993. pap. text ed. 14.95 (*1-56784-027-2*) Newbridge Comms.

Bernards, Neal, ed. The Environmental Crisis: Opposing Viewpoints. LC 90-24086. (Illus.). 264p. (gr. 10 up). 1991. PLB 17.95 (*0-89908-175-4*); pap. 9.95 (*0-89908-150-9*) Greenhaven.

Berry, Joy. Every Kid's Guide to Saving the Earth. (Illus.). 64p. (gr. 1-5). 1993. pap. 6.95 (*0-8249-8554-0*, Ideals Child) Hambleton-Hill.

Blashfield, Jean F. & Black, Wallace B. Recycling. LC 90-400. (Illus.). 128p. (gr. 4-8). 1991. PLB 20.55 (*0-516-05502-X*) Childrens.

Blue, Rose & Naden, Corinne. Andes Mountains. LC 94-3028. (Illus.). 64p. (gr. 5-8). 1994. PLB write for info. (*0-8114-6363-X*) Raintree Steck-V.

Bogart, Ann, photos by. Thinking Green: My Home. (Illus.). 24p. (ps-k). 1993. 3.98 (*0-8317-2530-3*) Smithmark.

—Thinking Green: My Neighborhood. (Illus.). 24p. (ps-k). 1993. 3.98 (*0-8317-2529-X*) Smithmark.

Bosse, Malcolm. Deep Dream of the Rain Forest. LC 92-55095. 1993. 15.00 (*0-374-31757-7*) FS&G.

Bright, Michael. The Ozone Layer. LC 90-45648. 32p. (gr. 2-4). 1991. PLB 11.90 (*0-531-17302-X*, Gloucester Pr) Watts.

Brody, Ed, et al, eds. Spinning Tales, Weaving Hope: Stories, Storytelling & Activities for Peace, Justice, & the Environment. Bond, Lahki, illus. 288p. (Orig.). 1992. lib. bdg. 49.95 (*0-86571-228-X*); pap. 22.95 (*0-86571-229-8*) New Soc Pubs.

Brown, Laurene K. & Brown, Marc T. Dinosaurs to the Rescue: A Guide to Protecting Our Planet. Brown, Marc T., illus. (ps-3). 1992. 14.95 (*0-316-11087-6*, Joy St Bks) Little.

Brown, Paul. Greenpeace. LC 94-7476. 1995. text ed. 13.95 (*0-02-726336-3*) Macmillan.

Chevat, Richard. Ready, Set, Recycle! (ps-3). 1993. pap. 1.95 (*0-307-10554-7*, Golden Pr) Western Pub.

Cone, Molly. Come Back, Salmon: How a Group of Dedicated Kids Adopted a Stream & Brought It Back to Life. Wheelwright, Sidnee, photos by. (Illus.). 48p. (gr. 2-6). 1992. 16.95 (*0-87156-572-2*) Sierra.

—Come Back, Salmon: How a Group of Dedicated Kids Adopted Pigeon Creek & Brought It Back to Life. Wheelwright, Sidnee, photos by. LC 91-29023. (Illus.). 48p. (gr. 2-6). 1994. pap. 6.95 (*0-87156-489-0*) Sierra.

Crawford, Jearn, ed. Ecology. LC 93-28657. (Illus.). 88p. (gr. k-3). 1994. write for info. (*0-8094-9466-3*); PLB write for info. (*0-8094-9467-1*) Time-Life.

Denton, Peter. The World Wildlife Fund. LC 94-7491. 1995. text ed. 13.95 (*0-02-726334-7*, New Discovery Bks) Macmillan Child Grp.

Doney, Meryl. The Green Activity Book. (Illus.). 32p. (Orig.). (ps-8). 1991. pap. 4.99 (*0-7459-1901-4*) Lion USA.

Drutman, Ave D. & Deutsch, Evelyn. Protecting Our Planet (Early Childhood Version) (Illus.). 128p. (ps-1). 1992. 12.95 (*0-86653-665-5*, GA1400) Good Apple.

Duggleby, John. Pesticides. LC 90-35496. (Illus.). 48p. (gr. 6). 1990. text ed. 12.95 RSBE (*0-89686-540-1*, Crestwood Hse) Macmillan Child Grp.

Durell, Ann, et al, eds. The Big Book for Our Planet. LC 92-33433. 144p. (gr. k-12). 1993. 17.99 (*0-525-45119-6*, DCB) Dutton Child Bks.

Earthworks Group Staff. Kid Heroes of the Environment: Simple Things Real Kids Are Doing To Save the Earth. (gr. 3-12). 1991. pap. 4.95 (*1-879682-12-5*) Earth Works.

Elkington, John, et al. Going Green: A Kid's Handbook to Saving the Planet. Ross, Tony, illus. 96p. (gr. 3 up). 1990. 16.00 (*0-670-83611-7*) Viking Child Bks.

—Going Green: A Kid's Handbook to Saving the Planet. (Illus.). 96p. (gr. 3 up). 1990. pap. 9.99 (*0-14-034597-3*, Puffin) Puffin Bks.

Enns, Peter. The Pollution Solution: Keeping Earth a Beautiful Place. Wolverton, Lock, illus. 40p. (Orig.). (ps-6). 1992. pap. 5.98 incl. cassette (*0-943593-76-X*) Kids Intl Inc.

Environment Alert, 29 vols. (Illus.). (gr. 3-8). Standing Order. PLB 15.93 ea. (*0-8368-0786-3*); Subscription Order. PLB 17.27 ea. (*0-8368-0787-1*) Gareth Stevens Inc.

The Environment: Protecting Our Home. 68p. (gr. 6-9). 1992. pap. text ed. 12.95 (*1-878623-42-7*) Info Plus TX.

Gardner, Robert. Celebrating Earth Day: A Sourcebook of Activities & Experiments. LC 91-38297. (Illus.). 96p. (gr. 5 up). 1992. PLB 15.90 (*1-56294-070-8*) Millbrook Pr.

Gartner, Robert. Working Together Against the Destruction of the Environment: Library of Social Activism. LC 94-2278. 1994. 14.95 (*0-8239-1774-6*) Rosen Group.

Gay, Kathlyn. Caretakers of the Earth. LC 92-23048. (Illus.). 104p. (gr. 6 up). 1993. lib. bdg. 17.95 (*0-89490-397-7*) Enslow Pubs.

—Pollution & the Powerless: The Movement fo Environmental Justice. (Illus.). 160p. (gr. 7-12). 1994. lib. bdg. 13.93 (*0-531-11190-3*) Watts.

Goldberg, Jake. Economics & the Environment. (Illus.). 112p. (gr. 5 up). 1993. PLB 19.95 (*0-7910-1594-7*); pap. write for info. (*0-7910-1619-6*) Chelsea Hse.

Greene, Carol. Caring for Our Air. LC 91-9236. (Illus.). 32p. (gr. k-3). 1991. lib. bdg. 12.95 (*0-89490-351-9*) Enslow Pubs.

—Caring for Our Land. LC 91-10613. (Illus.). 32p. (gr. k-3). 1991. lib. bdg. 12.95 (*0-89490-354-3*) Enslow Pubs.

—Friends in Danger Series, 6 bks. (Illus.). (gr. k-3). Set. lib. bdg. 83.70 (*0-89490-447-7*) Enslow Pubs.

Grimaldi, Alicia, ed. Education for the Earth: A Guide to Top Environmental Studies Programs. LC 92-33025. 192p. (Orig.). 1992. pap. 10.95 (*1-56079-164-0*) Petersons Guides.

Gutnik, Martin J. The Energy Question: Thinking about Tomorrow. LC 92-31315. (Illus.). 104p. (gr. 6 up). 1993. lib. bdg. 17.95 (*0-89490-400-0*) Enslow Pubs.

—Recycling: Learning the Four R's: Reduce, Reuse, Recycle, Recover. LC 92-24330. (Illus.). 104p. (gr. 6 up). 1993. lib. bdg. 17.95 (*0-89490-399-3*) Enslow Pubs.

Hallinan, P. K. For the Love of Our Earth. (Illus.). 24p. (ps-2). 1992. pap. 4.95 perfect bdg. (*0-8249-8539-7*, Ideals Child) Hambleton-Hill.

Halsey, Megan. Three Pandas Planting: Counting down to Help the Earth. Halsey, Megan, illus. LC 93-22971. 40p. (gr. k-2). 1994. RSBE 14.95 (*0-02-742035-3*, Bradbury Pr) Macmillan Child Grp.

Hamilton, John. ECO-Careers: A Guide to Jobs in the Environental Field. LC 93-7601. 1993. 14.96 (*1-56239-209-3*) Abdo & Dghtrs.

—Eco-Disasters. LC 93-10259. 1993. 14.96 (*1-56239-200-X*) Abdo & Dghtrs.

Hare, Tony. Toxic Waste. LC 91-8666. (Illus.). 32p. (gr. 5-8). 1991. PLB 12.40 (*0-531-17308-9*, Gloucester Pr) Watts.

—Vanishing Habitats. LC 91-11578. (Illus.). 32p. (gr. k-4). 1991. PLB 11.90 (*0-531-17350-X*, Gloucester Pr) Watts.

Harris, Colin. Protecting the Planet. LC 93-18936. (Illus.). 32p. (gr. 4-6). 1993. 14.95 (*1-56847-055-X*) Thomson Lrning.

Herriott, Joy A. & Herrin, Betty G. Summer Opportunities in Marine & Environmental Science: A Students' Guide to Jobs, Internships & Study, Camp, & Travel Programs. 2nd ed. LC 94-96000. (Illus.). 60p. (gr. 9-12). 1994. pap. 14.95 (*0-9640176-0-1*) White Pond.

Hirschi, Ron & Bauer, Peggy. Save Our Forests. (gr. 4-7). 1993. 17.95 (*0-385-31077-3*) Delacorte.

Holmes, Anita. I Can Save the Earth: A Kid's Handbook for Keeping Earth Healthy & Green. Neuhaus, David, illus. LC 91-30611. 96p. (gr. 2-5). 1993. PLB 13.98 (*0-671-74544-1*, J Messner); pap. 7.95 (*0-671-74545-X*, J Messner) S&S Trade.

Jakobson, Cathryn. Think About: The Environment. 160p. (gr. 7 up). 1992. PLB 15.85 (*0-8027-8105-5*); pap. 9.95 (*0-8027-7357-5*) Walker & Co.

Jeffers, Susan, illus. Brother Eagle, Sister Sky: A Message from Chief Seattle. LC 90-27713. 32p. 1991. 16.00 (*0-8037-0969-2*); PLB 14.89 (*0-8037-0963-3*) Dial Bks Young.

Jenkins. Toxic Waste. 1991. 12.95s.p. (*0-86593-111-9*) Rourke Corp.

Johnson, Rebecca L. The Greenhouse Effect: Life on a Warmer Planet. LC 93-17178. 1993. PLB 23.95 (*0-8225-1572-5*); pap. 9.95 (*0-8225-9652-0*) Lerner Pubns.

Kallen, Stuart A. Earth Keepers. LC 93-15329. (gr. 4 up). 1993. 14.96 (*1-56239-211-5*) Abdo & Dghtrs.

—Eco-Games. LC 93-7750. 1993. 14.96 (*1-56239-201-8*) Abdo & Dghtrs.

Kalman, Bobbie. Buried in Garbage. 32p. (gr. 3-4). 1991. PLB 15.95 (*0-86505-424-X*); pap. 7.95 (*0-86505-454-1*) Crabtree Pub Co.

—Reducing, Reusing, & Recycling. (Illus.). 32p. (gr. 3-4). 1991. PLB 15.95 (*0-86505-426-6*); pap. text ed. 7.95 (*0-86505-456-8*) Crabtree Pub Co.

Kerrod, Robin. The Environment. (Illus.). 64p. (gr. 5 up). 1993. PLB 15.95g (*1-85435-625-9*) Marshall Cavendish.

Koral, April. Our Global Greenhouse. (Illus.). 64p. (gr. 3 up). 1991. pap. 5.95 (*0-531-15601-X*) Watts.

Krensky, Stephen. Four Against the Odds: The Struggle to Save Our Environment. 1992. pap. 2.95 (*0-590-44743-2*) Scholastic Inc.

Krull, Kathleen. It's My Earth Too: How I Can Help the Earth Stay Alive. Greenberg, Melanie H., illus. (ps-2). 1992. 13.50 (*0-385-42088-9*) Doubleday.

Krupin, Paul J. Krupin's Toll-Free Environmental Directory. 128p. (Orig.). (gr. 9 up). 1994. pap. 14.95 (*1-885035-02-0*) Direct Contact. Want to contact Kids For a Clean Enivronment? Trout Unlimited? The Hazardous Materials Advisory Council, U.S. Fish & Wildlife Service, the Earthquake Preparedness Society, or thirty-plus EPA toll-free hotlines? All long distance for free? KRUPIN'S TOLL-FREE ENVIRONMENTAL DIRECTORY lists over 4500 toll-free 800 numbers. Provides access to companies, professional & non-profit organizations & government agencies involved in environmental issues nationwide. Easy-to-use, information-packed. Covers air pollution associations, the "green market", eco-tourism, conservation organizations all across the political spectrum, consulting firms, government agencies, ground water, hazardous waste, laboratories, recycling, health, safety, software, schools & more. Job hunters can research companies & organizations, contact employers & secure internships, jobs & careers. Students, teachers & librarians can request & obtain information for papers, projects & collections. Develop business contacts & uncover new business opportunities. Contact experts in contracting, procurement, diversification & technology transfer. Environmentalists & problem solvers can call government agency & industry hotlines & receive technical guidance & advice solving environmental problems. *Publisher Provided Annotation.*

Lachecki, Marina & Kasperson, James. More Teaching Kids to Love the Earth. Holman, Karyln, illus. 192p. (Orig.). 1994. pap. 14.95 (*1-57025-040-5*) Pfeifer-Hamilton.

Landau, Elaine. Environmental Groups: The Earth Savers. LC 92-23679. (Illus.). 112p. (gr. 6 up). 1993. lib. bdg. 17.95 (*0-89490-396-9*) Enslow Pubs.

Langone, John J. Our Endangered Earth: Our Fragile Environment & What We Can Do to Save It. (gr. 6 up). 1992. 16.95 (*0-316-51415-2*) Little.

Levine, Shar & Grafton, Allison. Projects for a Healthy Planet: Simple Environmental Experiments for Kids. 1992. pap. text ed. 10.95 (*0-471-55484-7*) Wiley.

Lorbiecki, Marybeth & Lowery, Linda. Earthwise at Play: A Guide to the Care & Feeding of Your Planet. Mataya, David, illus. LC 92-9870. 1993. 19.95 (*0-87614-729-5*) Carolrhoda Bks.

Love, Ann & Drake, Jane. Take Action. LC 92-30412. 1993. pap. 7.95 (*0-688-12465-8*, Pub. by Beech Tree Bks) Morrow.

—Take Action: An Environmental Book for Kids. Cupples, Pat, illus. LC 92-30412. 96p. (gr. 3 up). 1993. Repr. PLB 13.93 (*0-688-12464-X*, Tambourine Bks) Morrow.

Lowery, Linda. Earthwise at Home. (ps-3). 1992. 19.95 (*0-87614-730-9*) Carolrhoda Bks.

—Earthwise at Home: A Guide to the Care & Feeding of Your Planet. (ps-3). 1992. pap. 7.95 (*0-87614-585-3*) Carolrhoda Bks.

Lowery, Linda & Lorbiecki, Marybeth. Earthwise at School: A Guide to the Care & Feeding of Your Planet. LC 92-11221. (ps-3). 1993. lib. bdg. 19.95 (*0-87614-731-7*); pap. write for info. (*0-87614-587-X*) Carolrhoda Bks.

McCormick, Anita L. Vanishing Wetlands. (Illus.). (gr. 5-8). 1995. 14.95 (*1-56006-162-6*) Lucent Bks.

McQueen, Kelly & Fassler, David. Let's Talk Trash: The Kids' Book about Recycling. LC 90-21400. (Illus.). 168p. (ps-6). 1991. pap. 14.95g (*0-914525-19-0*); plastic comb 18.95 (*0-914525-20-4*) Waterfront Bks.

McVey, Vicki. The Sierra Club Kid's Guide to Planet Care & Repair. Weston, Martha, illus. LC 91-38307. 96p. (gr. 4-7). 1993. 16.95 (*0-87156-567-6*) Sierra.

Managing Toxic Wastes. (Illus.). 128p. (gr. 7-10). 1989. 11.96 (*0-382-09577-4*, J Messner) S&S Trade.

Mandel, Linda & Mandel, Heidi. The Treasure of Trash: A Recycling Story. Codor, Dick, illus. LC 92-41222. 48p. (gr. 4 up). 1993. pap. 12.95 (*0-89529-575-X*) Avery Pub.

Markham, Adam. The Environment. (Illus.). 48p. (gr. 5 up). 1988. PLB 18.60 (*0-86592-286-1*); 13.95 (*0-685-58320-1*) Rourke Corp.

Markle, Sandra. The Kids' Earth Handbook. Markle, Sandra, illus. LC 90-27478. 48p. (gr. 3-7). 1991. SBE 13.95 (*0-689-31707-7*, Atheneum Child Bk) Macmillan Child Grp.

Meyer, Nancy. Endangered Species Coloring-Learning Books Adventure Series. Meyer, George, illus. (ps-3). 1993. write for info. (*1-883408-05-9*) Meyer Pub FL.

Miles, Betty. Save the Earth: An Action Handbook for Kids. Davis, Nelle, illus. LC 90-46514. 128p. (Orig.). (gr. 5 up). 1991. pap. 6.95 (*0-679-81731-X*) Knopf Bks Yng Read.

Morris, Scott, ed. The Endangered World. De Blij, Harm J., intro. by. LC 92-22289. (Illus.). 1993. 15.95 (*0-7910-1806-7*, Am Art Analog); pap. write for info. (*0-7910-1819-9*, Am Art Analog) Chelsea Hse.

Neal, Philip. The Ozone Layer: Conservation 2000. (Illus.). 64p. (gr. 7-10). 1994. 24.95 (*0-7134-6713-4*, Pub. by Batsford UK) Trafalgar.

Nelson, JoAnne. Our Friend, the Earth. Thomsen, Ernie, illus. LC 92-37716. 1994. pap. 5.95 (*0-935529-59-4*) Comprehen Health Educ.

Peissel, Michel & Allen, Missy. Dangerous Environments. (Illus.). 112p. (gr. 5 up). 1993. PLB 19.95 (*0-7910-1793-1*, Am Art Analog) Chelsea Hse.

Polesetsky, Matthew, et al, eds. Global Resources: Opposing Viewpoints. LC 90-24088. (Illus.). 264p. (gr. 10 up). 1991. PLB 17.95 (*0-89908-177-0*); pap. 9.95 (*0-89908-152-5*) Greenhaven.

Postcard Power! You Can Do Something for the Environment. (Illus.). 16p. (gr. 3-8). 1992. pap. 3.95 (*0-671-74476-3*, Little Simon) S&S Trade.

Pringle, Laurence. Global Warming: Assessing the Greenhouse Threat. 48p. (gr. 4-7). 1990. 15.95 (*1-55970-012-2*) Arcade Pub Inc.

Pysz, Stephen. Team Earth: Advanced ABC Environmental Coloring Book. America, Alexis & Marcil, Beth, illus. 56p. (gr. k-1). 1991. pap. text ed. 4.95 (*0-9630186-7-1*) Team Earth.

—Team Earth: Show You Care. Patton, Sarah, ed. America, Alexis, illus. 32p. (gr. 2-5). 1992. pap. text ed. 4.95 wkbk. (*0-9630186-1-2*) Team Earth.

Raintree Steck-Vaughn Staff. Atlas of the Environment. Coote, Roger, ed. LC 92-8196. (Illus.). 96p. (gr. 6-7). 1992. PLB 26.99 (*0-8114-7250-7*) Raintree Steck-V.

Rosenberg, Harvey. Joey's Cabbage Patch. 32p. (gr. k-3). 1991. write for info. (*0-9629587-0-0*) Go Jolly Pubns.

Rozens, Aleksandrs. Environmental Destruction. LC 93-41213. (Illus.). 64p. (gr. 5-8). 1994. PLB 15.95 (*0-8050-3098-0*) TFC Bks NY.

Rybolt, Thomas R. & Mebane, Robert C. Environmental Experiments about Land. LC 93-15581. (Illus.). 96p. (gr. 4-9). 1993. lib. bdg. 16.95 (*0-89490-411-6*) Enslow Pubs.

—Environmental Experiments about Life. LC 93-15582. (Illus.). 96p. (gr. 4-9). 1993. lib. bdg. 16.95 (*0-89490-412-4*) Enslow Pubs.

Sailer, John. A Vogt for the Environment. LC 93-15313. (Illus.). (gr. 7-12). 1993. 6.95 (*0-913990-34-5*) Book Pub Co.

Savage, Candace. Get Growing: How the Earth Feeds Us. Clement, Gary, illus. 56p. (gr. 3-7). 1991. pap. 9.95 (*0-920668-95-X*) Firefly Bks Ltd.

—Trash Attack: Garbage, & What We Can Do about It. Beinicke, Steve, illus. 56p. (gr. 3-7). 1991. pap. 9.95 (*0-920668-73-9*) Firefly Bks Ltd.

Schwartz, Meryl. The Environment & the Law. (Illus.). 112p. (gr. 5 up). 1993. PLB 19.95 (*0-7910-1595-5*) Chelsea Hse.

—The Environment & the Law. Train, Russell E., intro. by. LC 92-25542. 1993. write for info. (*0-7910-1596-3*); write for info. (*0-7910-1620-X*) Chelsea Hse.

Stamper, Judith B. Save the Everglades! Davis, Allen, illus. LC 92-18085. 56p. (gr. 2-5). 1992. PLB 19.97 (*0-8114-7219-1*) Raintree Steck-V.

Starbuck, Marnie. The Gladimals Help Save the Earth. (Illus.). 16p. 1990. 0.75 (*1-56456-203-4*, 473) W Gladden Found.

Stefoff, Rebecca. Environmental Disasters. Train, Russell E., intro. by. LC 93-8183. 1994. write for info. (*0-7910-1584-X*) Chelsea Hse.

Steinberg, Michael. Our Wilderness: How the People of New York Found, Changed, & Preserved the Adirondacks. Burdick, Neal S., ed. LC 91-16550. (Illus.). 112p. (gr. 5 up). 1994. 18.95 (*0-935272-56-9*); pap. 9.95 (*0-935272-57-7*) ADK Mtn Club. A history of the 6-million-acre Adirondack Park of New York State, which includes towns & farms, businesses & timberlands as well as 1.2 million acres of wilderness. Written for ages 10 & up (Gr. 4 plus). Described by KIRKUS REVIEWS as "a cultural history full of charming, quirky people, plus both funny & sobering anecdotes... Gracefully written with lessons that go far beyond regional interest." APPALACHIA noted that "there is probably no other book available that can provide as thorough an introduction to Adirondack history, particularly with anything close to the brevity & efficiency of this book." Author received award from Adirondack Park Centennial Committee for his contribution to education via OUR WILDERNESS. Historic photographs by Stoddard & Apperson. Publication coincided with the 1992 Centennial of the Adirondack Park. Book carries conservationist message. "The entertaining & informative 'young people's history'... contains plenty of interest the mature mind."--New York's Rochester DEMOCRAT & CHRONICLE. *Publisher Provided Annotation.*

Stewart, Gail. Acid Rain. LC 90-5854. (Illus.). 112p. (gr. 5-8). 1990. PLB 14.95 (*1-56006-111-1*) Lucent Bks.

Stidworthy, John. Environmentalist. LC 91-34608. (Illus.). 32p. (gr. 4-7). 1992. PLB 12.40 (*0-531-17268-6*, Gloucester Pr) Watts.

Suzuki, David. Looking at the Environment. (Illus.). 96p. 1992. text ed. 22.95 (*0-471-54749-2*); pap. text ed. 9.95 (*0-471-54051-X*) Wiley.

Tanaka, Shelly. The Heat Is On: Facing Our Energy Problem. Beinicke, Steve, illus. 56p. (gr. 3-7). 1991. pap. 9.95 (*0-920668-94-1*) Firefly Bks Ltd.

Temple, Lannis, ed. Dear World: How Children Around the World Feel about Our Environment. LC 92-29929. (Illus.). 152p. (gr. k up). 1993. pap. 15.00 (*0-679-84403-1*) Random Bks Yng Read.
Tesar, Jenny E. Global Warming. (Illus.). 128p. (gr. 7-12). 1991. 18.95x (*0-8160-2490-1*) Facts on File.
—Waste Crisis. (Illus.). 128p. (gr. 9-12). 1991. 18.95x (*0-8160-2491-X*) Facts on File.
The Toxic Waste Time Bomb. LC 91-50342. (Illus.). 32p. (gr. 3-8). 1993. PLB 17.27 (*0-8368-0699-9*) Gareth Stevens Inc.
Wald, Mike. What You Can Do for the Environment. (Illus.). 112p. (gr. 5 up). 1993. PLB 19.95 (*0-7910-1587-4*); pap. write for info. (*0-7910-1612-9*) Chelsea Hse.
Westrup, Hugh. Maurice Strong: Working for Planet Earth. LC 93-41528. (Illus.). 48p. (gr. 2-4). 1994. PLB 12.90 (*1-56294-414-2*) Millbrook Pr.
Wheeler, Jill. Earth Kids. LC 93-15330. (gr. 3 up). 1993. 14.96 (*1-56239-199-2*) Abdo & Dghtrs.
Wheeler, Jill C. Earth Day Every Day. LC 91-73070. 1991. 12.94 (*1-56239-031-7*) Abdo & Dghtrs.
—The Food We Eat. Kallen, Stuart A., ed. LC 91-73068. 202p. 1991. 17.95 (*1-56239-033-3*) Abdo & Dghtrs.
—The Throw-Away Generation. Kallen, Stuart A., ed. LC 91-73071. 202p. 1991. 12.94 (*1-56239-030-9*) Abdo & Dghtrs.
Whitman, Sylvia. This Land Is Your Land: The American Conservation Movement. LC 94-3099. (Illus.). 88p. 1994. PLB 17.50 (*0-8225-1729-9*) Lerner Pubns.
Wilkes, Angela. My First Green Book. LC 91-4371. (Illus.). 48p. (gr. 2-5). 1991. 12.00 (*0-679-81780-8*) Knopf Bks Yng Read.
Willis, Terri. Healing the Land. LC 94-18024. (Illus.). 96p. (gr. 3-6). 1994. PLB 23.20 (*0-516-05541-0*) Childrens.
Wonders, Allison & Edelheit, Jami. The Global Kidz Handbook, No. 2: Over 100 Self-Esteem & Environmental Hands-on Activities. 118p. (gr. 4 up). 1992. pap. write for info. (*1-881497-01-1*) Global Pr Wks.
—The Global Kidz Handbook: The Internal Self-Esteem & Environmental Program. 138p. (gr. 4 up). 1991. pap. text ed. write for info. (*1-881497-00-3*) Global Pr Wks.
Wong, Ovid. Hands-On Ecology. LC 91-12751. (Illus.). 128p. (gr. 5 up). 1991. PLB 13.95 (*0-516-00539-1*) Childrens.
Zeff, Robin L. Environmental Action Groups. (Illus.). 112p. (gr. 5 up). 1993. PLB 19.95 (*0-7910-1593-9*) Chelsea Hse.

ENZYMES

Breslow, Ronald. Enzymes: The Machines of Life. Head, J. J., ed. Steffen, Ann T., illus. LC 84-45828. 16p. (Orig.). (gr. 10 up). 1986. pap. text ed. 2.75 (*0-89278-155-6*, 45-9755) Carolina Biological.

EOLITHIC PERIOD

see Stone Age

EPIGRAMS

see also Proverbs; Quotations

Christiansen, Helen E. Trinkets & Treasures: A Collection of Favorite Bits of Wisdom. 130p. (Orig.). (gr. 7 up). 1988. pap. 8.50 (*0-9621419-0-9*) H Christiansen.

EPILEPSY

Bergman, Thomas. Moments That Disappear: Children Living with Epilepsy. LC 91-50335. (Illus.). 56p. (gr. 3-8). 1992. PLB 18.60 (*0-8368-0739-1*) Gareth Stevens Inc.
Buckel, Marian C. & Buckel, Tiffany. Mom, I Have a Staring Problem: A True Story of Petit Mal Seizures & the Hidden Problem It Can Cause: Learning Disability. LC 92-90113. (Illus.). 1992. pap. 3.95 saddle stitch (*0-317-04291-2*) M C Buckel.
Kornfield, Elizabeth. Dreams Come True. Kornfield, Lee, ed. (Illus.). 32p. (gr. 3-6). 1986. pap. 5.95 (*0-940611-00-7*) Rocky Mntn Child.
Landau, Elaine. Epilepsy. (Illus.). 64p. (gr. 5-8). 1994. bds. 15.95 (*0-8050-2991-5*) TFC Bks NY.

EPISTEMOLOGY

see Knowledge, Theory of

EPIZOA

see Parasites

EQUALITY

see also Democracy

EQUESTRIANISM

see Horsemanship

ERIE CANAL

Harness, Cheryl. The Amazing Impossible Ditch. LC 94-11114. 1995. 16.00 (*0-02-742641-6*, Bradbury Pr) Macmillan Child Grp.
Nirgiotis, Nicholas. Erie Canal: Gateway to the West. LC 92-24547. (Illus.). 64p. (gr. 5-8). 1993. PLB 12.90 (*0-531-20146-5*) Watts.
Spier, Peter. The Erie Canal. Spier, Peter, illus. LC 70-102055. 36p. (gr. 1-3). 1990. pap. 10.95 (*0-385-06777-1*); pap. 5.95 (*0-385-05234-0*) Doubleday.
Stein, R. Conrad. The Story of the Erie Canal. Neely, Keith, illus. LC 84-28525. 32p. (gr. 3-6). 1985. pap. 3.95 (*0-516-44682-7*) Childrens.

EROSION

see also Soil Conservation

Stille, Darlene. Soil Erosion & Pollution. LC 89-25360. (Illus.). 48p. (gr. k-4). 1990. 12.85 (*0-516-01188-X*); pap. 4.95 (*0-516-41188-8*) Childrens.

ERUPTIONS

see Volcanoes

ERVING, JULIUS

Bell, Marty. The Legend of Dr. J. The Story of Julius Erving. updated & expanded ed. (Illus.). 192p. (gr. 9-12). 1976. pap. 4.95 (*0-451-15464-9*, Sig) NAL-Dutton.

ESCAPES

Stewart, J. & Hamilton, N. Great Escapes. (Illus.). 48p. (gr. 5-9). 1988. PLB 14.97 (*0-88625-208-3*); pap. 5.95 (*0-88625-207-5*) Durkin Hayes Pub.

ESCAPES–FICTION

Holman, Felice. Slake's Limbo. LC 74-11675. 126p. (gr. 4-8). 1974. RSBE 14.95 (*0-684-13926-X*, Scribners Young Read) Macmillan Child Grp.
McInerney, Judith W. Judge Benjamin: The Superdog Rescue. Morrill, Leslie, illus. (gr. 4-6). pap. 2.75 (*0-317-66178-7*, Minstrel Bks) PB.

ESKIMOS

Aigner, Jean S. The Eskimo. (Illus.). (gr. 5 up). 1989. 17.95 (*1-55546-705-9*) Chelsea Hse.
Alexander, Bryan & Alexander, Cherry. An Eskimo Family. (Illus.). 32p. (gr. 2-5). 1985. PLB 13.50 (*0-8225-1656-X*) Lerner Pubns.
—Inuit. LC 92-9894. (Illus.). 48p. (gr. 5-6). 1992. PLB 22.80 (*0-8114-2301-8*) Raintree Steck-V.
Armitage, Peter. The Innu. (Illus.). 112p. (gr. 5 up). 1991. lib. bdg. 17.95 (*0-685-47584-0*) Chelsea Hse.
Carter, Marilyn. Peluk, an Eskimo Boy. (Illus.). 44p. (gr. 3 up). pap. text ed. 5.95 (*0-944677-04-5*) Aladdin Pub.
Davis, Nancy M. Eskimos. Davis, Nancy M., illus. 32p. (Orig.). (ps-5). 1986. pap. 4.95 (*0-937103-06-3*) DaNa Pubns.
De Coccola, Raymond & King, Paul. The Incredible Eskimo. Cameron, J., ed. Houston, James, illus. 435p. (Orig.). (gr. 9). 1986. pap. 16.95 (*0-88839-189-7*) Hancock House.
Ekoomiak, Normee. Arctic Memories. LC 89-39194. (Illus.). 32p. (gr. 3 up). 1990. 15.95 (*0-8050-1254-0*, Bks Young Read) H Holt & Co.
Hahn, Elizabeth. Inuit. (Illus.). 32p. (gr. 5-8). 1990. lib. bdg. 15.74 (*0-86625-386-6*); lib. bdg. 11.95s.p. (*0-685-46459-8*) Rourke Corp.
Kendall, Russell. Eskimo Boy. 32p. 1992. 13.95 (*0-590-43695-3*, Scholastic Hardcover) Scholastic Inc.
Newman, Shirlee P. The Inuits. LC 93-18370. (Illus.). 64p. (gr. 4-6). 1993. PLB 12.90 (*0-531-20073-6*) Watts.
—The Inuits. (Illus.). 64p. (gr. 5-8). 1994. pap. 5.95 (*0-531-15702-4*) Watts.
—Inuits. (gr. 4-7). 1994. pap. 5.95 (*0-531-15701-6*) Watts.
Osinski, Alice. The Eskimo: Inuit & Yupik. LC 85-9691. (Illus.). 45p. (gr. 2-3). 1985. PLB 12.85 (*0-516-01267-3*); pap. 4.95 (*0-516-41267-1*) Childrens.
Planche, Bernard. Living with the Eskimos. Matthews, Sarah, tr. from FRE. Grant, Donald, illus. LC 87-31805. 38p. (gr. k-5). 1988. 5.95 (*0-944589-12-X*, 12X) Young Discovery Lib.
Reynolds, Jan. Frozen Land: Vanishing Cultures. LC 92-30324. 1993. write for info. (*0-15-238787-0*); pap. write for info. (*0-15-238788-9*) HarBrace.
Schultz, Ellen. I Can Read About Eskimos. LC 78-73735. (gr. 2-4). 1979. pap. 2.50 (*0-89375-219-3*) Troll Assocs.
Senungetuk, Vivian & Tiulana, Paul. Place for Winter: Paul Tiulana's Story, (A) (Illus.). 120p. (gr. 10-12). 1989. Repr. of 1987 ed. 17.95 (*0-938227-02-5*) CIRI Found.
Siska, Heather S. People of the Ice: How the Inuit Lived. Bateson, Ian, illus. 48p. (gr. 4-7). 1992. pap. 7.95 (*0-88894-404-7*, Pub. by Groundwood-Douglas & McIntyre CN) Firefly Bks Ltd.
Vickery, Eugene L. The Ramiluk Stories: Adventures of an Eskimo Family in the Prehistoric Arctic. Tolpo, Lily, illus. 124p. (Orig.). (gr. 5 up). 1989. 16.00 (*0-937775-11-8*); pap. 10.95 (*0-937775-10-X*) Stonehaven Pubs.
Younkin, Paula. Indians of the Arctic & Subarctic. (Illus.). 96p. (gr. 5-8). 1991. lib. bdg. 18.95x (*0-8160-2391-3*) Facts on File.
Yue, Charlotte & Yue, David. The Igloo. 128p. (gr. 3-7). 1992. pap. 4.80 (*0-395-62986-1*, Sandpiper) HM.

ESKIMOS–ART

Morgan, Lael. Art & Eskimo Power: The Life & Times of Alaskan Howard Rock. Sims, Virginia, ed. LC 88-24408. (Illus.). 260p. (Orig.). (gr. 9-12). 1988. 24.95 (*0-945397-02-X*); pap. 16.95 (*0-945397-03-8*) Epicenter Pr.

ESKIMOS–FICTION

Biggar, Joan R. Danger at Half-Moon Lake. (Illus.). 128p. (gr. 5-8). 1991. pap. 3.99 (*0-570-04194-5*) Concordia.
Craighead-George, Jean. Julie & the Wolves: (Julie y los Lobos) (SPA.). (gr. 1-6). 9.95 (*84-204-3206-7*) Santillana.
George, Jean C. Julie of the Wolves. Schoenherr, John, illus. LC 72-76509. 180p. (gr. 7 up). 1974. 15.00i (*0-06-021943-2*); PLB 14.89 (*0-06-021944-0*); pap. 3.95 (*0-06-440058-1*) HarpC Child Bks.
—Julie of the Wolves. Minor, Wendell, illus. LC 93-27738. 240p. (gr. 5 up). 1994. 15.00 (*0-06-023528-4*); PLB 14.89 (*0-06-023529-2*) HarpC Child Bks.
—Water Sky. George, Jean C., illus. LC 86-45496. 224p. (gr. 5 up). 1989. pap. 3.95 (*0-06-440202-9*, Trophy) HarpC Child Bks.
George, Jean G. Julie of the Wolves. 190p. 1992. text ed. 15.20 (*1-56956-117-6*) W A T Braille.
Hill, Kirkpatrick. Winter Camp. LC 92-41200. (Illus.). 192p. (gr. 3-7). 1993. SBE 14.95 (*0-689-50588-4*, M K McElderry) Macmillan Child Grp.
Houston, James. Drifting Snow: An Arctic Search. Houston, James, illus. LC 91-42674. 160p. (gr. 5 up). 1992. SBE 13.95 (*0-689-50563-9*, M K McElderry) Macmillan Child Grp.
Houston, James R. Akavak. 80p. (gr. 5 up). 1990. pap. 8.95 (*0-15-201731-3*) HarBrace.
—Long Claws: An Arctic Adventure. (Illus.). 32p. (ps-3). 1992. pap. 4.99 (*0-14-054522-0*, Puffin) Puffin Bks.
Jenness, Aylette & Rivers, Alice. In Two Worlds: A Yup'ik Eskimo Family. Jenness, Aylette, illus. (gr. 6 up). 1989. 13.45 (*0-395-42797-5*) HM.
Kortum, Jeanie. Ghost Vision. Stermer, Dugald, illus. LC 83-4706. 160p. (gr. 5-9). 1983. 10.95 (*0-394-86190-6*, Pant Bks Young) Pantheon.
Kortum, Jeanie & Stermer, Dugald. Ghost Vision. LC 82-19410. (Illus.). 144p. (gr. 5-9). o.s.i 10.95 (*0-685-42976-8*); PLB 10.99 (*0-685-42977-6*) Sierra.
Kroll, Virginia. The Seasons & Someone. Kiuchi, Tatsuro, illus. LC 93-11123. (ps-3). 1994. write for info. (*0-15-271233-X*) HarBrace.
Luenn, Nancy. Nessa's Story (El Cuento de Nessa) Ada, Alma F., tr. Waldman, Neil, illus. LC 93-34814. (ENG & SPA.). 32p. (ps-3). 1994. SBE, English ed. 14.95 (*0-689-31782-4*, Atheneum Child Bk); SBE, Spanish ed. 14.95 (*0-689-31919-3*, Atheneum Child Bk) Macmillan Child Grp.
Paulsen, Gary. Dogsong. LC 84-20443. 192p. (gr. 7 up). 1985. SBE 14.95 (*0-02-770180-8*, Bradbury Pr) Macmillan Child Grp.
Rocard, Ann. Kouk & the Ice Bear. Morgan, illus. 38p. (ps-1). 1991. smythe sewn reinforced bdg. 9.95 (*1-56182-029-6*) Atomium Bks.
Rogers, Jean. Goodbye, My Island. Munoz, Rie, illus. LC 82-15816. 96p. (gr. 5-7). 1983. 12.95 (*0-688-01964-1*); PLB 12.88 (*0-688-01965-X*) Greenwillow.
Scott, Ann H. On Mother's Lap. Coalson, Glo, illus. 32p. (ps-k). 1992. 14.45 (*0-395-58920-7*, Clarion Bks); pap. 5.70 (*0-395-62976-4*, Clarion Bks) HM.
Sis, Peter. A Small, Tall Tale from the Far, Far North. Sis, Peter, illus. LC 92-75906. 40p. (gr. k-5). 1993. 15.00 (*0-679-84345-0*); PLB 15.99 (*0-679-94345-5*) Knopf Bks Yng Read.

ESKIMOS–LEGENDS

Bernhard, Emery, retold by. How Snowshoe Hare Rescued the Sun: A Yuit Folktale. Bernhard, Durga, illus. LC 92-47124. (ps-3). 1993. reinforced bdg. 15.95 (*0-8234-1043-9*) Holiday.
Cohlene, Terri. Ka-Ha-Si & the Loon. (Illus.). 48p. (gr. 4-8). 1990. lib. bdg. 19.93 (*0-86593-002-3*); lib. bdg. 14.95s.p. (*0-685-46448-2*) Rourke Corp.
—Ka-Ha-Si & the Loon: An Eskimo Legend. 48p. (gr. 4-7). 1990. pap. 3.95 (*0-8167-2359-1*) Troll Assocs.
DeArmond, Dale. The Seal Oil Lamp. DeArmond, Dale, illus. 48p. (gr. k-4). 1988. 14.95 (*0-316-17786-5*) Little.
Houston, James R. The Falcon Bow: An Arctic Legend. (Illus.). 96p. (gr. 5 up). 1992. pap. 3.99 (*0-14-036078-6*, Puffin) Puffin Bks.
—Tikta'liktak. 63p. (gr. 5 up). 1990. pap. 8.95 (*0-15-287748-7*) HarBrace.
—The White Archer: An Eskimo Legend. LC 79-14458. (Illus.). 95p. (gr. 5 up). 1990. pap. 8.95 (*0-15-696224-1*, Voyager Bks) HarBrace.
Jessell, Tim. Amorak. LC 93-48622. 32p. 1994. 14.95 (*0-88682-662-4*) Creative Ed.
Sloat, Teri, retold by. & illus. The Eye of the Needle: Based on a Yupik Tale Told by Betty Huffman. LC 89-49476. 32p. (ps-3). 1990. 13.95 (*0-525-44623-0*, DCB) Dutton Child Bks.

ESQUIMAUX

see Eskimos

ESTATE PLANNING

see also Insurance; Investments

ESTHER, QUEEN OF PERSIA–FICTION

Pingry, Patricia. The Story of Esther. Harrison, Susan, illus. 24p. (ps-3). 1990. pap. 3.95 (*0-8249-8420-X*, Ideals Child) Hambleton-Hill.

ETHICAL EDUCATION

see Religious Education

ETHICS

Almonte, Paul & Desmond, Theresa. Medical Ethics. (Illus.). 48p. (gr. 5-6). 1991. text ed. 12.95 RSBE (*0-89686-662-9*, Crestwood Hse) Macmillan Child Grp.
Baker, Eugene. What's Right? A Handbook about Values. 112p. (gr. 2-6). 1980. PLB 14.95 (*0-89565-208-0*) Childs World.
Barker, Dan. Maybe Right, Maybe Wrong: A Guide for Young Thinkers. Strassburg, Brian, illus. 76p. 1992. pap. 13.95 (*0-87975-731-0*) Prometheus Bks.
Bernards, Neal, ed. Euthanasia: Opposing Viewpoints. LC 89-2181. (Illus.). 235p. (gr. 10 up). 1989. PLB 17.95 (*0-89908-442-7*); pap. 9.95 (*0-89908-417-6*) Greenhaven.
Berry, Joy. Casey's Revenge Activity Guide: A Story about Fighting & Disagreements. Vertuca, Cathy, ed. Sharp, Chris, illus. 20p. (Orig.). (gr. k-6). 1991. pap. 12.99 (*0-923790-32-2*) Kids Media Group.
—The Fair Weather Friend Activity Guide: A Story about Making Friends. Vertuca, Cathy, ed. Sharp, Chris, illus. 20p. (Orig.). (gr. k-6). 1991. pap. 12.99 (*0-923790-33-0*) Kids Media Group.
—A High Price to Pay Activity Guide: A Story about Earning Money. Vertuca, Cathy, ed. Sharp, Chris, illus. 20p. (Orig.). (gr. k-6). 1991. pap. 12.99 (*0-923790-34-9*) Kids Media Group.

—The Lean Mean Machine Activity Guide: A Story about Handling Emotions. Vertuca, Cathy, ed. Sharp, Chris, illus. 20p. (Orig.). (gr. k-6). 1991. pap. 12.99 (*0-923790-31-4*) Kids Media Group.

—The Letter on Light Blue Stationery Activity Guide: A Story about Self-Esteem. Vertuca, Cathy, ed. Sharp, Chris, illus. 20p. (Orig.). (gr. k-6). 1991. pap. 12.99 (*0-923790-35-7*) Kids Media Group.

—The Unforgettable Pen Pal Activity Guide: A Story about Prejudice & Discrimination. Vertuca, Cathy, ed. Sharp, Chris, illus. 20p. (Orig.). (gr. k-6). 1991. pap. 12.99 (*0-923790-30-6*) Kids Media Group.

Burstein, Chaya M. The UAHC Kids Catalog of Jewish Living. Burstein, Chaya M., illus. LC 91-42815. (gr. 4-6). 1992. pap. 8.95 (*0-8074-0464-0*, 123934) UAHC.

Cooperation. (gr. 7-12). 1991. PLB 14.95 (*0-8239-1232-9*) Rosen Group.

Fine, Helen. At Camp Kee Tov: Ethics for Jewish Juniors. (Illus.). (gr. 4-6). Date not set. 6.95 (*0-8074-0128-5*, 121711) UAHC.

Garnett, Paul D. Investigating Morals & Values in Today's Society. 160p. (gr. 5-10). 1988. wkbk. 12.95 (*0-86653-443-1*, GA1053) Good Apple.

Grosshandler, Janet. The Value of Generosity. (gr. 7-12). 1991. PLB 15.95 (*0-8239-1287-6*) Rosen Group.

Hashim, A. S. Islamic Ethics. pap. 5.95 (*1-56744-095-9*) Kazi Pubns.

Justice. (gr. 7-12). 1991. PLB 14.95 (*0-8239-1231-0*) Rosen Group.

Mabie, Margot C. Bioethics & the New Medical Technology. LC 92-22642. 176p. (gr. 7 up). 1993. SBE 14.95 (*0-689-31637-2*, Atheneum Child Bk) Macmillan Child Grp.

Marsh, Carole. What the Heck Are Ethics? (gr. 4-9). 1994. 24.95 (*1-55609-342-X*); pap. 14.95 (*0-318-37388-2*) Gallopade Pub Group.

Morality. (gr. 7-12). 1991. PLB 14.95 (*0-8239-1230-2*) Rosen Group.

Pennock, Michael. Choosing: Cases in Moral Decision Making. LC 90-85155. 160p. (Orig.). (gr. 9-12). 1991. spiral bdg. 7.95 (*0-87793-446-0*) Ave Maria.

Rue, Nancy. The Value of Compassion. (gr. 7-12). 1991. PLB 15.95 (*0-8239-1240-X*) Rosen Group.

Schwartz, L. What Do You Think? LC 92-74103. 184p. (gr. 3-7). 1993. 9.95 (*0-88160-224-8*, LW221) Learning Wks.

Shibles, Warren. Good & Bad Are Funny Things: Ethics in Rhyme for Children. LC 77-93808. (gr. k up). 1978. pap. 6.50 (*0-912386-14-2*) Language Pr.

Sioles, Anna M. An Ethics Primer for Children, Honesty - Kindness - Respect: A Catalyst to Discussion. Sioles, Anna M. & Boethner, Sandra, illus. 83p. (Orig.). (gr. 1-7). 1989. pap. text ed. 9.95 (*0-9620893-0-3*) Agatha Pub Co.

It's TIME TO TEACH our children RIGHT from WRONG. If America is to be saved, we need a forthcoming generation strong in Ethics: Honesty, Kindness & Respect. AN ETHICS PRIMER provides just that! A NO GLITZ, black & white book with cartoon-like illustrations. This book is intended to serve as an Ethical primer for children - to nurture honesty, kindness & respect. THE THOUGHT-PROVOKING SITUATIONS ARE TO BE USED AS A BASIS FOR DISCUSSION BETWEEN PARENT & CHILD OR TEACHER & STUDENT. The inherent beauty of this book is that it will enable the parent or teacher to also impart his or her own philosophical wisdom & experience to the child according to each situation. These ideals are fundamental to the survival of the universe & the dignity of man. To order: send $9.95 plus postage to Agatha Publishing, 83 Michael Rd., Stamford, CT 06903; 203-329-1790.
Publisher Provided Annotation.

Terkel, Susan N. Ethics. 144p. (gr. 5 up). 1992. 15.00 (*0-525-67371-7*, Lodestar Bks) Dutton Child Bks.

Von Harrison, Grant. Is Kissing Sinful? 16p. 1985. pap. text ed. 2.95 (*0-929985-27-3*) Jackman Pubng.

Weiss, Ann E. Bioethics: Dilemmas in Modern Medicine. LC 85-11608. 128p. (gr. 6 up). 1985. lib. bdg. 17.95 (*0-89490-113-3*) Enslow Pubs.

Wilson, Etta. The Value of Excellence. (gr. 7-12). 1991. PLB 15.95 (*0-8239-1289-2*) Rosen Group.

ETHICS, CHRISTIAN
see Christian Ethics

ETHICS, SEXUAL
see Sexual Ethics

ETHIOPIA

Delany, Martin R. Origin of Races & Color: With an Archeological Compendium of Ethiopian & Egyptian Civilization. LC 90-82685. 100p. 1991. 19.95 (*0-933121-51-2*); pap. 8.95 (*0-933121-50-4*) Black Classic.

Department of Geography, Lerner Publications. Ethiopia in Pictures. (Illus.). 64p. (gr. 5 up). 1988. PLB 17.50 (*0-8225-1836-8*) Lerner Pubns.

Fradin, Dennis B. Ethiopia. LC 88-10882. (Illus.). 128p. (gr. 5-9). 1988. PLB 20.55 (*0-516-02706-9*) Childrens.

Gilkes, Patrick. Conflict in Somalia & Ethiopia. (Illus.). 48p. (gr. 6 up). 1994. text ed. 13.95 RSBE (*0-02-792528-5*, New Discovery Bks) Macmillan Child Grp.

Jenkins, Earnestine. A Glorious Past: Ancient Egypt, Ethiopia, & Nubia. LC 94-10713. 1994. write for info. (*0-7910-2258-7*); pap. write for info. (*0-7910-2684-1*) Chelsea Hse.

Kurtz, Jane. Ethiopia: The Roof of Africa. LC 91-18660. (Illus.). 128p. (gr. 4-6). 1991. text ed. 14.95 RSBE (*0-87518-483-9*, Dillon) Macmillan Child Grp.

Stewart, Gail B. Ethiopia. LC 90-49795. (Illus.). 48p. (gr. 6-7). 1991. text ed. 4.95 RSBE (*0-89686-601-7*, Crestwood Hse) Macmillan Child Grp.

ETHIOPIA–FICTION

Kendall, Jonathan. My Name Is Rachamim. (Illus.). (gr. 2-3). 1987. 7.95 (*0-8074-0321-0*, 123925) UAHC.

Kurtz, Jane. Pulling the Lion's Tail. Cooper, Floyd, illus. LC 93-22836. 1995. pap. 15.00 (*0-671-88183-3*, S&S BFYR) S&S Trade.

Schur, Maxine R. Day of Delight: A Jewish Sabbath in Ethiopia. Pinkney, Brian, illus. LC 93-31451. (gr. 3 up). 1994. 15.99 (*0-8037-1413-0*); PLB 15.89 (*0-8037-1414-9*) Dial Bks Young.

ETHNIC GROUPS
see Minorities

ETHNOGRAPHY
see Ethnology

ETHNOLOGY
see also Anthropogeography; Anthropology; Archeology; Civilization; Color of Man; Costume; Folklore; Language and Languages; Man, Prehistoric; Manners and Customs; Race; Race Problems; Totems and Totemism

Butterfield, Moira. People & Places. Forsey, Chris, illus. LC 91-214. 40p. (Orig.). (gr. 2-5). 1991. pap. 3.99 (*0-679-80868-X*) Random Bks Yng Read.

Cardwell, Rosemary. Skin Deep. (Illus.). 32p. 1994. saddlestitch 12.95 (*0-8059-3552-5*) Dorrance.

Cherryholmes, C. & Manson, G. Studying Cultures. (Illus.). (gr. 4). 1979. text ed. 24.64 (*0-07-011984-8*) McGraw.

Delany, Martin R. Origin of Races & Color: With an Archeological Compendium of Ethiopian & Egyptian Civilization. LC 90-82685. 100p. 1991. 19.95 (*0-933121-51-2*); pap. 8.95 (*0-933121-50-4*) Black Classic.

Golden, Michael. Celebrating Cultural Diversity: A Study Guide. (gr. 5-8). 1991. pap. text ed. 19.95 (*0-88122-689-0*) LRN Links.

Grande Tabor, Nancy M. Are We Different? Somos Diferentes? Grande Tabor, Nancy M., illus. 32p. (ps-4). 1995. PLB 15.88 (*0-88106-814-4*); pap. 6.95 (*0-88106-813-6*) Charlesbridge Pub.

Herda, D. J. Ethnic America: The North Central States. (Illus.). 64p. (gr. 5-8). 1991. PLB 15.40 (*1-56294-016-3*) Millbrook Pr.

—Ethnic America: The Northeastern States. (Illus.). 64p. (gr. 5-8). 1991. PLB 15.40 (*1-56294-014-7*) Millbrook Pr.

—Ethnic America: The Northwestern States. (Illus.). 64p. (gr. 5-8). 1991. PLB 15.40 (*1-56294-018-X*) Millbrook Pr.

—Ethnic America: The South Central States. (Illus.). 64p. (gr. 5-8). 1991. PLB 15.40 (*1-56294-017-1*) Millbrook Pr.

—Ethnic America: The Southeastern States. (Illus.). 64p. (gr. 5-8). 1991. PLB 15.40 (*1-56294-015-5*) Millbrook Pr.

—Ethnic America: The Southwestern States. (Illus.). 64p. (gr. 5-8). 1991. PLB 15.40 (*1-56294-019-8*) Millbrook Pr.

Lands & Peoples, 6 vols, Vols. 1-6. LC 92-17742. 1993. Set. write for info. (*0-7172-8016-0*) Grolier Inc.

Langley, Andrew & Butterfield, Maira. People. Young, Norman, illus. LC 89-42986. 48p. (gr. 5-6). 1989. PLB 17.27 (*0-8368-0132-6*) Gareth Stevens Inc.

Lewin, Ted. The Reindeer People. Lewin, Ted, illus. LC 93-19252. (gr. 1-4). 1994. 14.95 (*0-02-757390-7*) Macmillan Child Grp.

Lipson, Greta & Romatowski, Jane. Ethnic Pride. Simmons, Sheri, illus. 152p. (gr. 4-9). 1983. wkbk. 12. 95 (*0-86653-121-1*, GA 464) Good Apple.

Liptak, Karen. Endangered Peoples. LC 92-41391. 1993. 13.40 (*0-531-10987-9*) Watts.

MacQuitty, Miranda. Desert. LC 93-21068. 1994. 16.00 (*0-679-86003-7*); PLB 16.99 (*0-679-96003-1*) Knopf Bks Yng Read.

Margolies, Barbara A. Warriors, Wigmen, & Crocodile People: Journeys in Papua New Guinea. Margolies, Barbara, illus. LC 92-27475. 40p. (gr. 1-5). 1993. RSBE 14.95 (*0-02-762283-5*, Four Winds) Macmillan Child Grp.

Nile, Richard. Australian Aborigines. LC 92-17044. (Illus.). 48p. (gr. 5-6). 1992. PLB 22.80 (*0-8114-2303-4*) Raintree Steck-V.

People & Customs. (Illus.). 80p. (gr. k-6). 1986. per set 199.00 (*0-8172-2583-8*) Raintree Steck-V.

Shulz, Charles, illus. People & Customs of the World. LC 94-13723. 1994. write for info. (*0-517-11898-X*, Pub. by Derrydale Bks) Random Hse Value.

Siy, Alexandra. The Penan: People of the Borneo Jungle. LC 93-10007. (Illus.). 72p. (gr. 5 up). 1993. text ed. 14.95 RSBE (*0-87518-552-5*, Dillon) Macmillan Child Grp.

—The Waorani: People of the Ecuadoran Rain Forest. LC 92-36985. (Illus.). 80p. (gr. 5 up). 1993. text ed. 14.95 RSBE (*0-87518-550-9*, Dillon) Macmillan Child Grp.

Vilsoni, Patricia H. South Pacific Islanders. (Illus.). 48p. (gr. 4-8). 1987. PLB 16.67 (*0-86625-259-2*); 12.50 (*0-685-67606-4*) Rourke Corp.

Waybill, Marjorie. Chinese Eyes. Cutrell, Pauline, illus. LC 74-5751. 32p. (gr. k-2). 1974. 14.95 (*0-8361-1738-7*) Herald Pr.

Williams, Brenda & Williams, Brian. People & Places. Forsey, Chris, illus. LC 90-12982. 40p. (gr. 4-6). 1991. PLB 12.40 (*0-531-19111-7*) Watts.

Winter, Frank H. The Filipinos in America. (Illus.). 80p. (gr. 5 up). 1988. 15.95 (*0-8225-0237-2*); pap. 5.95 (*0-8225-1035-9*) Lerner Pubns.

ETIQUETTE
see also Courtesy; Dancing; Dating (Social Customs); Entertaining; Letter Writing; Manners and Customs; also names of countries with the subdivision Social life and customs

Adachi, Kelly. The Kids' Handbook. (Illus.). 112p. (gr. 1 up). 1985. 7.95 (*0-8184-0365-9*); pap. 4.95 (*0-8184-0368-3*) Carol Pub Group.

Alden, Laura. Saying I'm Sorry. Siculan, Dan, illus. LC 82-19945. 32p. (ps-2). 1983. PLB 14.95 (*0-89565-247-1*) Childs World.

Aliki. Manners. LC 92-43788. Date not set. write for info. (*0-688-04579-0*, Mulberry) Morrow.

Beyer, Kay. The Value of Good Manners. (gr. 7-12). 1992. PLB 15.95 (*0-8239-1353-8*) Rosen Group.

Brainard, Beth & Behr, Sheila. Soup Should Be Seen, Not Heard! The Kids' Etiquette Book. (Illus.). 107p. (Orig.). (ps-7). 1988. pap. 10.00 (*0-9621908-0-2*) Good Idea Kids.

Brooks, Courtaney. How to Teach Children Kindness & Manners with Puppets: Including Stories, Plays, Puppets & Props. Brooks, Courtaney & Runyan, Merrilee, illus. 100p. (Orig.). 1994. pap. 14.95 (*0-941274-06-3*) Belnice Bks.

HOW TO TEACH CHILDREN KINDNESS & MANNERS WITH PUPPETS shows parents & teachers how to help children be kind & mannerly, by using puppet characters in stories, plays & exercises. Through puppets, children can experience the way characters feel & act. Everything in the book enables children to suggest & use their own ways of expressing kindness & manners. Part I explains & shows through illustrations & patterns: 1) how to make simple hand or glove puppets, sock & stick puppets; 2) how to find or make simple props: a sausage, a basket of cookies; 3) how to get acquainted with your puppet as he walks, talks, picks up a spoon. Part II presents the stories & plays with puppet patterns & props. The plays & stories are short, usually two pages each, with many animal characters. You can prepare & present them easily, change the characters, add characters, have children change parts. You do not need a puppet stage; just the puppets, props & children. For more information or to order, write or call: Courtaney Brooks, Belnice Books, 337 8th St., Manhattan Beach, CA 90266; (310) 379-5405.
Publisher Provided Annotation.

Buehner, Caralyn & Buehner, Mark. The Courtesy Quiz Book. LC 93-36293. (gr. 5 up). 1994. write for info. (*0-8037-1494-7*); PLB write for info. (*0-8037-1495-5*) Dial Bks Young.

Clise, Michele D. No Bad Bears: Ophelia's Book of Manners. (Illus.). 32p. 1992. 14.00 (*0-670-83883-7*) Viking Child Bks.

Coats, Carolyn & Smith, Pamela. Come Cook with Me! A Cookbook for Kids. Coats, Carolyn, illus. 133p. 1989. pap. 10.00 spiral bound (*1-878722-06-9*) C Coats Bestsellers.

David, Jo. Finishing Touches, Manners with Style. Richey, Donald, illus. LC 90-10888. 128p. (gr. 5-9). 1991. lib. bdg. 10.89 (*0-8167-2179-3*); pap. text ed. 2.95 (*0-8167-2180-7*) Troll Assocs.

Dellinger, Annetta E. Good Manners for God's Children. (ps-k). 1984. pap. 4.99 (*0-570-04093-0*, 56-1461) Concordia.

Donahue, Bob & Donahue, Marilyn. The Right Way to Eat Spaghetti. (Illus.). 128p. (Orig.). (gr. 9-12). 1988. pap. 4.95 (*0-8423-5597-9*) Tyndale.

Educational Assessment Publishing Company Staff. Parent - Child Learning Library: Courtesy English Big Book. (Illus.). 32p. (gr. k-3). 1991. text ed. 16.95 (*0-942277-77-5*) Am Guidance.

—Parent - Child Learning Library: Courtesy Spanish Big Book. (SPA., Illus.). 32p. (gr. k-3). 1991. text ed. 16. 95 (*0-942277-78-3*) Am Guidance.

—Parent - Child Learning Library: Courtesy Spanish Edition. (SPA.). 32p. 1991. text ed. 9.95 (*0-942277-94-5*) Am Guidance.

—Parent - Child Learning Library: Courtesy. (Illus.). 32p. (ps). 1991. text ed. 9.95 (*0-942277-62-7*) Am Guidance.

Everding, Maria P. Pretty As a Picture: A Guide to Manners, Poise & Appearance. 138p. (Orig.). (gr. 4-7). 1986. pap. 14.95 (*0-9617665-0-6*) GME Pub Co.

Frost, Erica. I Can Read about Good Manners. LC 74-24878. (Illus.). (gr. 1-2). 1975. pap. 2.50 (*0-89375-059-X*) Troll Assocs.

Fulton, Ginger A. Good Manners & Me. (Illus.). (ps-2). pap. 3.25 (*0-8024-3083-X*) Moody.

Gardner, Richard A. The Girls & Boys Book about Good & Bad Behavior. Lowenheim, Al, illus. LC 90-31241. 221p. (gr. 2-6). 1990. 17.00 (*0-933812-21-3*) Creative Therapeutics.

Goffe, Toni. Charm School. LC 91-32061. 1992. 7.95 (*0-85953-367-0*); pap. 3.95 (*0-85953-357-3*) Childs Play.

Goley. Manners, Reading Level 2. (Illus.). 32p. (gr. 1-4). 1989. PLB 15.94 (*0-86592-395-7*); 11.95 (*0-685-58787-8*) Rourke Corp.

Hammond, Elizabeth. A Pocket Book of Manners for Young People. Oppenheimer, Jennie, illus. LC 90-90325. 96p. (Orig.). (gr. 4-8). 1990. pap. 5.95 (*0-9627061-0-8*) Trotwood Press.

Hamoy, Carol. What's Wrong? What's Wrong? Hamoy, Carol, illus. (gr. k-3). 1965. 8.95 (*0-685-00564-X*) Astor-Honor.

Hartley, Fred. Teenage Book of Manners Please. 1991. pap. 9.95 (*1-55748-246-2*) Barbour & Co.

—The Teenage Book of Manners...Please! 14.95 (*1-55748-245-4*) Barbour & Co.

Hazen, Barbara. Hello Gnu, How Do You Do? (ps-3). 1990. 14.95 (*0-385-26449-6*) Doubleday.

Hillings, Phyllis. A Web of Good Manners: Grown-up Manners for Young People. Tegtmeyer, John, illus. LC 92-85125. 96p. (gr. 3 up). 1993. 14.95 (*0-9634642-1-3*) Manhattan Pr.

Joslin, Sesyle. What Do You Say, Dear? Sendak, Maurice, illus. LC 84-43140. 48p. 1958. 14.00 (*0-201-09391-X*); PLB 13.89 (*0-06-023074-6*) HarpC Child Bks.

Klare, Judy. Manners. (Illus.). 32p. (gr. 5 up). 1990. PLB 15.94 (*0-86625-419-6*); PLB 11.95s.p. (*0-685-36384-8*) Rourke Corp.

Leaf, Munro. Four-&-Twenty Watchbirds. LC 89-49742. (Illus.). 32p. (ps-3). 1990. lib. bdg. 15.00 (*0-208-02208-2*, Pub. by Linnet) Shoe String.

Learning Forum Staff. Communications & Motivation Personal Growth Set. (gr. 8-12). 1988. 45.00 (*0-945525-14-1*) Supercamp.

Mehew, Randall & Mehew, Karen. The Best Manners Book Ever. Bales, Marcia, illus. 68p. 1990. pap. text ed. 5.95 (*0-929985-55-9*) Jackman Pubng.

Meltzer, Maxine. Pups Speak Up. Schmidt, Karen L., illus. LC 92-33687. 32p. (ps-3). 1994. RSBE 14.95 (*0-02-766710-3*, Bradbury Pr) Macmillan Child Grp.

Milios, Rita. Mean Words. Lemeiux, Margo, illus. LC 92-10837. 32p. (ps-2). Date not set. 11.95 (*1-56065-163-6*) Capstone Pr.

Moncure, Jane B. Please? Thanks! I'm Sorry. Axeman, Lois, illus. LC 85-11664. (SPA & ENG.). 32p. (gr. k-2). 1985. PLB 14.95 (*0-89565-331-1*) Childs World.

—Saying Please. Inderieden, Nancy, illus. LC 82-19927. 32p. (ps-2). 1983. PLB 14.95 (*0-89565-248-X*) Childs World.

Nehlsen, Nancy & Stewart, Marjabelle Y. Princess Marjabelle Visits Lollygag Lake: Marjabelle Stewart's Introduction to Manners. Carlson, Sandra, illus. 32p. (ps). 1994. 14.95 (*0-88331-214-X*) Luce.

Nielsen, Shelly. Manners. Wallner, Rosemary, ed. LC 91-73042. 1992. 13.99 (*1-56239-066-X*) Abdo & Dghtrs.

Noffs, David & Noffs, Laurie. The Daily Harold, Bk. 6. Lynch, Reg, illus. 24p. (Orig.). (gr. 6). 1987. wkbk. 2.50 (*0-929875-07-9*) Noffs Assocs.

—The Daily Harold, Bk. 7. (Illus.). 24p. (Orig.). (gr. 7). 1988. wkbk. 2.50 (*0-929875-08-7*) Noffs Assocs.

—The Daily Harold, Bk. 8. Noffs, Lauri, illus. 24p. (Orig.). (gr. 8). 1991. wkbk. 2.50 (*0-929875-09-5*) Noffs Assocs.

—Harold, Bk. 3: You Are Special. Hilliard, Kristin, illus. 24p. (Orig.). (gr. 3). 1987. wkbk. 2.50 (*0-929875-04-4*) Noffs Assocs.

Nystrom, Carolyn. Why Do I Do Things Wrong? 32p. (ps-2). 1994. 5.99 (*0-8024-7862-X*) Moody.

Parish, Peggy. Mind Your Manners. Hafner, Marylin, illus. LC 77-19096. 56p. (gr. 1-3). 1978. PLB 13.88 (*0-688-84157-0*) Greenwillow.

—Mind Your Manners. Hafner, Marilyn, illus. LC 93-11732. 56p. (gr. 1 up). 1994. pap. 4.95 (*0-688-13109-3*, Mulberry) Morrow.

Polisar, Barry L. Don't Do That: A Child's Guide to Bad Manners, Ridiculous Rules & Inadequate Etiquette. Young, Debby, illus. 64p. (Orig.). (gr. 3-6). 1989. 9.95 (*0-938663-01-1*); pap. 7.95 (*0-938663-10-0*) Rainbow Morn.

Post, Elizabeth L. Emily Post Talks with Teens about Manners & Etiquette. 1991. pap. 9.00 (*0-06-273163-7*, Harp PBks) HarpC.

Reece, Colleen L. Saying Thank You. Connelly, Gwen, illus. LC 82-21992. 32p. (ps-2). 1983. PLB 14.95 (*0-89565-249-8*) Childs World.

Riehecky, Janet. May I? Connelly, Gwen, illus. LC 88-16838. 32p. (ps-2). 1989. PLB 12.95 (*0-89565-388-5*) Childs World.

—Thank-You. Connelly, Gwen, illus. LC 88-16840. 32p. (ps-2). 1989. PLB 12.95 (*0-89565-387-7*) Childs World.

Scarry, Richard. Richard Scarry's Please & Thank You Book. LC 73-2441. (ps-2). 1973. 2.50 (*0-394-82681-7*); lib. bdg. 5.99 (*0-394-92681-1*) Random Bks Yng Read.

—Richard Scarry's Please & Thank You Book. LC 73-2441. (Illus.). 32p. (ps-1). 1990. pap. 6.95 incl. cassette (*0-679-80799-3*) Random Bks Yng Read.

Schmidt, Melinda. The Courtesy Workbook. Saunders, Dorothy, illus. 52p. (Orig.). (gr. 1-6). 1994. pap. 4.95 (*1-882420-18-7*) Hearth KS.

Sibbald, Linda, pref. by. The Polite Academy, Vol. 2: London, Seventeen Sixty-Five. 3rd ed. (Illus.). 181p. 1973. Repr. leather bdg. 55.80 (*0-685-48091-7*) P Lang Pubs.

Smith, Barry. A Child's Guide to Bad Behavior. Smith, Barry, illus. 32p. (ps). 1991. 9.70 (*0-395-57435-8*, Sandpiper) HM.

Snell, Nigel. What Do You Say? A Child's Guide to Manners. (Illus.). 25p. (gr. k-2). 1991. 13.95 (*0-237-60294-6*, Pub. by Evans Bros Ltd) Trafalgar.

Stewart, Marjabelle Y. & Buchwald, Ann. Stand Up, Shake Hands, Say "How Do You Do" What Boys Need to Know about Today's Manners News. rev. ed. LC 77-8159. (gr. 7 up). 1988. 12.95 (*0-88331-100-3*) Luce.

Strazzabosco, Gina & Reynolds, Moira. The Telephone: Uses & Abuses. LC 93-25717. (gr. 5 up). 1993. 13.95 (*0-8239-1608-1*) Rosen Group.

Thiry, Joan. How to Cope with an Artichoke & other Mannerly Mishaps. Walsh, Karen J., illus. 40p. (gr. 7-12). 1982. pap. 4.95 (*0-935046-04-6*) Chateau Thierry.

—How to Entertain a Gnu & Not Disturb Your Family. Walsh, Karen J., illus. 40p. (gr. k-3). 1982. pap. 4.95 (*0-935046-02-X*) Chateau Thierry.

—How to Make a Courtesy Butter Sandwich & Serve it Properly. Walsh, Karen J., illus. 40p. (Orig.). (gr. 4-6). 1982. pap. 4.95 (*0-935046-03-8*) Chateau Thierry.

Uhrich, Ethel. Manners in God's House. Hayes, Theresa, ed. Posey, Pam, illus. 16p. (gr. 3-6). 1992. wkbk. 7.99 (*0-87403-929-0*, 14-03501) Standard Pub.

World Book, Inc. Staff, ed. Put Your Best Foot Forward with the Alphabet Pals: Right Time for Rosie. LC 89-50457. (Illus.). 20p. (ps). 1989. lib. bdg. write for info. (*0-7166-1902-4*) World Bk.

Young, Marjabelle Y. & Buchwald, Ann. White Gloves & Party Manners. LC 65-25830. (gr. 7 up). 1988. 12.95 (*0-88331-054-6*) Luce.

Ziegler, Sandra. Manners. Hutton, Kathryn, illus. LC 88-15013. (ENG & SPA.). 32p. (ps-2). 1986. PLB 14.95 (*0-89565-377-X*) Childs World.

ETIQUETTE–FICTION

American Etiquette Institute Staff. Eddycat & Buddy Entertain a Guest, Bk. 5. (Illus.). 32p. (gr. k-3). 1991. 13.95 (*1-879322-14-5*) Amer Etiquette Inst.

—Eddycat & Gabby Gorilla Babysit, Bk. 9. (Illus.). 32p. (gr. k-3). 1991. 13.95 (*1-879322-18-8*) Amer Etiquette Inst.

—Eddycat Attends Sunshine's Birthday Party, Bk. 3. (Illus.). 32p. (gr. k-3). 1991. 13.95 (*1-879322-12-9*) Amer Etiquette Inst.

—Eddycat Brings Soccer to Mannersville, Bk. 8. (Illus.). 32p. (gr. k-3). 1991. 13.95 (*1-879322-17-X*) Amer Etiquette Inst.

—Eddycat Goes on Vacation with the Ducks, Bk. 11. (Illus.). 32p. (gr. k-3). 1991. 13.95 (*1-879322-20-X*) Amer Etiquette Inst.

—Eddycat Goes Shopping with Becky Bunny, Bk. 6. (Illus.). 32p. (gr. k-3). 1991. 13.95 (*1-879322-15-3*) Amer Etiquette Inst.

—Eddycat Helps Sunshine Plan Her Party, Bk. 2. (Illus.). 32p. (gr. k-3). 1991. 13.95 (*1-879322-11-0*) Amer Etiquette Inst.

—Eddycat Introduces Leonardo Lion, Bk. 12. (Illus.). 32p. (gr. k-3). 1991. 13.95 (*1-879322-21-8*) Amer Etiquette Inst.

—Eddycat Introduces Mannersville, USA, Bk. 1. (Illus.). 32p. (gr. k-3). 1991. 13.95 (*1-879322-10-2*) Amer Etiquette Inst.

—Eddycat Serves Grandma's Birthday Brunch, Bk. 10. (Illus.). 32p. (gr. k-3). 1991. 13.95 (*1-879322-19-6*) Amer Etiquette Inst.

—Eddycat Teaches Telephone Skills, Bk. 4. (Illus.). 32p. (gr. k-3). 1991. 13.95 (*1-879322-13-7*) Amer Etiquette Inst.

—Eddycat Visits Wright Street School, Bk. 7. (Illus.). 32p. (gr. k-3). 1991. 13.95 (*1-879322-16-1*) Amer Etiquette Inst.

Barnett, Ada, et al. Eddycat & Buddy Entertain a Guest. Hoffmann, Mark, illus. LC 92-56883. 32p. (gr. 1 up). 1993. Repr. of 1991 ed. PLB 17.27 incl. tchr's. guide (*0-8368-0946-7*) Gareth Stevens Inc.

—Eddycat Attends Sunshine's Birthday Party. Hoffmann, Mark, illus. LC 92-56881. 1993. PLB 17.27 (*0-8368-0943-2*) Gareth Stevens Inc.

—Eddycat Goes Shopping with Becky Bunny. Hoffmann, Mark, illus. LC 93-56884. 32p. (gr. 1 up). 1993. Repr. of 1991 ed. PLB 17.27 incl. tchr's. guide (*0-8368-0947-5*) Gareth Stevens Inc.

—Eddycat Helps Sunshine Plan Her Party. Hoffmann, Mark, illus. LC 92-56880. 1993. PLB 17.27 (*0-8368-0942-4*) Gareth Stevens Inc.

—Eddycat Introduces Mannersville. Hoffmann, Mark, illus. LC 92-56877. 1993. PLB 17.27 (*0-8368-0939-4*) Gareth Stevens Inc.

—Eddycat Teaches Telephone Skills. Hoffmann, Mark, illus. LC 92-56882. 1993. PLB 17.27 (*0-8368-0944-0*) Gareth Stevens Inc.

Bridwell, Norman. Clifford's Manners. LC 94-4004. 1994. 10.95 (*0-590-48697-7*) Scholastic Inc.

Chapman, Cheryl. Pass the Fritters, Critters. Roth, Susan L., illus. LC 91-45055. 40p. (ps-k). 1993. RSBE 14.95 (*0-02-717975-3*, Four Winds) Macmillan Child Grp.

Gabriel, Howard W., III. Growing up with Character: Character Building Stories for Children, Vol. 1. Hasting, Christine Q., illus. 112p. (Orig.). (gr. k-8). 1986. pap. 7.95 (*0-936997-00-1*, 038601) M & H Enter.

Hartman, Bob. Aunt Mabel's Table. Stortz, Diane, ed. LC 94-2766. (Illus.). 48p. (Orig.). (ps-3). 1994. pap. 4.49 (*0-7847-0178-4*) Standard Pub.

Herr, Selma & Piequet, Miriam. Manners Matter. Anyone Can Read Staff, ed. 150p. (Orig.). (gr. 3-7). 1987. pap. 10.50 (*0-914275-12-7*) Anyone Can Read Bks.

Hoban, Russell. Dinner at Alberta's. Marshall, James, illus. LC 73-94796. 40p. (gr. 1-3). 1975. PLB 13.89 (*0-690-23993-9*, Crowell Jr Bks) HarpC Child Bks.

Miller, Virginia. On Your Potty! LC 90-49221. (Illus.). 32p. (ps up). 1991. 13.95 (*0-688-10617-X*); PLB 13.88 (*0-688-10618-8*) Greenwillow.

Riehecky, Janet. I'm Sorry. (ps-2). 1989. PLB 12.95 (*0-89565-389-3*) Childs World.

Ross, Sandra. The Nicelies at Home: A Lil'l Charmers Book. (Illus.). 76p. (Orig.). (ps-2). 1993. pap. 5.95 (*1-881235-01-7*) Creat Opport.

Smith, Kaitlin M. Big Monster Learns about Manners. Smith, Kaitlin M., illus. 18p. (gr. 1-5). 1992. pap. 10. 95 (*1-56606-006-0*) Bradley Mann.

Stewart, Harris. Grungy George & Sloppy Sally: A How-Not-to Manners Book for Mature Children & Adults. 1993. 7.95 (*0-533-10432-7*) Vantage.

Thomas, Charlotte E. Our Little Flower Girl: A Child Has Her First Experience Participating in a Wedding. Jonsson, Deborah, illus. LC 92-72538. 32p. (ps-3). 1992. PLB 16.95 singer-sewn (*0-9633607-0-1*) Golden Rings. Finally, a delightful story written specifically to help little girls selected to take part in a wedding ceremony. While informing them of what their role will entail, it also entertains them with a charming story. The tale begins with her invitation to join the bridal party & proceeds through the many preparations & customs leading up to THE BIG DAY. Her finery is chosen & she discovers it must be ordered, which is a new experience for her. She solicits her friends & their toys to help her practice for her exciting role. The meanings of rehearsal & reception are also made known. An apprehensive child in the beginning ends up eagerly anticipating becoming a bride herself someday. This must have book is beautifully illustrated in full color & contains a page for her photo & one for signatures of the wedding party & special friends. This KEEPSAKE book is available for $19.95 incl. S&H. Please send check or money order payable to: Golden Rings Publishing Co., 6173 Doe Haven Dr., Farmington, NY 14425 or call 1-800-433-6173 for MC/VISA orders.
Publisher Provided Annotation.

—The Ring Bearer's Big Day: A Child Has His First Experience Participating

in a Wedding. Jonsson, Deborah, illus. LC 94-79366. 1994. 19.95 (*0-9633607-1-X*) Golden Rings.
Finally, a delightful storybook written specifically to help little boys selected to take part in a wedding ceremony. While informing them of what their role will entail, it also entertains them with a charming story about a little boy who is in love with his old sneakers & climbing trees. The tale begins with his invitation to join the bridal party & proceeds through the many preparations & customs leading up to THE BIG DAY. He tries on his tuxedo & tries to convince the salesman he could wear his sneaks, as they are black. His worries are greatly reduced when he finds a kindly neighbor who gives him some insight into the joys of joining the wedding party. In finality, he has a great time & is really proud to have been chosen. This must have book is beautifully illustrated in full color & contains a page for his photo & one for signatures of the wedding party & special friends. This KEEPSAKE BOOK IS AVAILABLE FOR $19.95 incl. S&H. Please send check or money order payable to: Golden Rings Publishing Co., 6173 Doe Haven Dr., Farmington, NY 14425 or call 1-800-433-6173 for MC/VISA orders.
Publisher Provided Annotation.

White, Stephen. Barney Says, "Please & Thank You" Dowdy, Linda C., ed. Grayson, Rick, illus. LC 93-74288. 24p. (ps-k). 1994. pap. 2.25 (*1-57064-023-8*) Barney Pub.

Wylie, Joanne & Wylie, David. Has Abrazado Hoy a Tu Monstruo? Un Cuento de los Modales: Have You Hugged Your Monster Today? Learning about Manners. LC 86-21624. (Illus.). 32p. (ps-2). 1986. pap. 3.95 (*0-516-54493-4*) Childrens.

Yee, Wong H. Big Black Bear. Yee, Wong H., illus. LC 92-40862. 1993. 14.95 (*0-395-66359-8*) HM.

ETIQUETTE–POETRY

Burgess, Gelett. Goops & How to Be Them: A Manual of Manners for Polite Infants. Burgess, Gelett, illus. LC 68-55630. 96p. (ps-4). 1968. pap. 3.95 (*0-486-22233-0*) Dover.

—More Goops & How Not to Be Them: A Manual of Manners for Impolite Infants. Burgess, Gelett, illus. LC 68-55531. 96p. (ps-4). 1968. pap. 3.95 (*0-486-22234-9*) Dover.

ETRURIANS

Sebesta, Judith L. The Etruscans. (Illus.). 94p. (Orig.). (gr. 9-12). 1992. pap. 13.20 spiral bdg. (*0-939507-37-4*, B422) Amer Classical.

ETYMOLOGY

see names of languages with the subdivision Etymology, e.g. English Language–Etymology, etc.

EUROPE

Bains, Rae. Europe. Eitzen, Allan, illus. LC 84-8598. 32p. (gr. 3-6). 1985. PLB 9.49 (*0-8167-0304-3*); pap. text ed. 2.95 (*0-8167-0305-1*) Troll Assocs.

Cultures of the World: Europe, 6 vols. (Illus.). (gr. 5-9). Set. PLB 131.70 (*1-85435-448-5*) Marshall Cavendish.

Durbin, Chris. The European Community. LC 93-12513. (Illus.). 32p. (gr. 5-8). 1994. PLB 12.40 (*0-531-14261-2*) Watts.

Flint, David C. The Baltic States. LC 92-2240. (Illus.). 32p. (gr. 4-6). 1992. PLB 14.40 (*1-56294-310-3*) Millbrook Pr.

EUROPE–CIVILIZATION–HISTORY

Biel, Timothy L. The Age of Feudalism. LC 93-19290. (gr. 6-9). 1994. 14.95 (*1-56006-232-0*) Lucent Bks.

EUROPE–DESCRIPTION AND TRAVEL

Georges, D. V. Europe. LC 86-9585. (Illus.). 48p. (gr. k-4). 1986. PLB 12.85 (*0-516-01292-4*); pap. 4.95 (*0-516-41292-2*) Childrens.

Twain, Mark. Innocents Abroad. Gemme, F. R., intro. by. (gr. 9 up). 1967. pap. 2.95 (*0-8049-0151-1*, CL-151) Airmont.

EUROPE, EASTERN

Ashabranner, Brent. A New Frontier: The Peace Corps in Eastern Europe. Conklin, Paul, photos by. LC 93-38535. (Illus.). 112p. (gr. 5 up). 1994. 13.99 (*0-525-65155-1*, Cobblehill Bks) Dutton Child Bks.

Bradley, John F. Eastern Europe: The Road to Democracy. rev. ed. LC 93-11186. (Illus.). 40p. (gr. 6-8). 1993. PLB 12.90 (*0-531-17430-1*, Gloucester Pr) Watts.

Eastern Europe. (gr. 7-12). 1992. 22.95 (*0-7134-6769-X*, Pub. by Batsford UK) Trafalgar.

Geography Department Staff, Lerner Publications Company, ed. Albania--In Pictures. LC 94-10616. (gr. 5 up). 1995. lib. bdg. write for info. (*0-8225-1902-X*) Lerner Pubns.

Harbor, Bernard. Conflict in Eastern Europe. LC 93-3035. (Illus.). 48p. (gr. 6 up). 1993. text ed. 13.95 RSBE (*0-02-742626-2*, New Discovery Bks) Macmillan Child Grp.

Holm, Anne. North to Freedom. (gr. 5-9). 1984. 17.25 (*0-8446-6156-2*) Peter Smith.

Kronenwetter, Michael. The New Eastern Europe. LC 91-18512. (Illus.). 192p. (gr. 9-12). 1991. PLB 14.40 (*0-531-11066-4*) Watts.

Mayberry, Jodine. Eastern Europeans. Cullerton, P., ed. LC 90-12995. (Illus.). 64p. (gr. 5-8). 1991. PLB 13.40 (*0-531-11109-1*) Watts.

Riordan, James. Eastern Europe. (Illus.). 48p. (gr. 5 up). 1987. PLB 12.95 (*0-382-09468-9*) Silver Burdett Pr.

Rohr, Janelle, ed. Eastern Europe: Opposing Viewpoints. LC 90-44330. (Illus.). 240p. (gr. 10 up). 1990. PLB 17.95 (*0-89908-480-X*); pap. text ed. 9.95 (*0-89908-455-9*) Greenhaven.

EUROPE–FICTION

Hughes, Virginia E. Anna: The Little Peasant Girl. LC 92-91117. (Illus.). 64p. (gr. 4 up). 1994. pap. 8.00 (*1-56002-264-7*, Univ Edtns) Aegina Pr.

James, Henry. Portrait of a Lady. Fisher, N. H., intro. by. (gr. 11 up). 1966. pap. 2.50 (*0-8049-0098-1*, CL-98) Airmont.

Mullin, Penn. Postcards from Europe Series, 5 bks. Kratoville, B. L., ed. Rarey, D., illus. 48p. (gr. 6-10). 1994. pap. text ed. 15.00 (*0-87879-976-1*) High Noon Bks.
Four multi-cultural junior high students & their teacher are treated to a trip to Europe by an anonymous benefactor. The four young travelers never stop learning as facts about the historical & cultural treasures of each country are woven into these fast-paced, exciting stories. THE LONDON CONNECTION: The kids climb on board a double-decker bus to see the sights: Buckingham Palace, Westminster Abbey, the Tower of London, & more. PASSPORT TO PARIS: The history of the Arc de Triomphe & the Eiffel Tower, fine art at the Louvre, & folklore & facts about Notre Dame are all part of this whirlwind tour. RIDDLES IN ROME: The kids roam through the ruins at the Forum & the Coliseum, marvel at Michelangelo's Pieta & Sistine Chapel at Vatican City, & enjoy gelato. THE CLUES TO MADRID: In Madrid, the kids are dazzled by the Prado Museum, Picasso's Guernica, & the Plaza Mayor, & end up at the bullfights. SECRETS OF THE MATTERHORN: A fondue dinner & a hike to a Swiss hut on the slopes of the Matterhorn are only a part of this entertaining excursion.
Publisher Provided Annotation.

Standish, Burt L. Frank Merriwell in Europe. Rudman, Jack, ed. (gr. 9 up). Date not set. 9.95 (*0-8373-9308-6*); pap. 3.95 (*0-8373-9008-7*) F Merriwell.

EUROPE–HISTORY

Cairns, Trevor. Power for the People. LC 76-30607. (Illus.). 96p. (gr. 7 up). 1978. pap. 13.95 (*0-521-20902-1*) Cambridge U Pr.

Clare, John D., ed. Industrial Revolution. LC 93-2554. 1994. 16.95 (*0-15-200514-5*) HarBrace.

Guthrie, Kari H. National Anthems: Western & Middle Europe, 4 bks. (Illus.). 163p. (Orig.). (gr. 4-9). 1993. Set. pap. 24.95 (*0-9631333-4-9*) Hi I Que Pub.
NATIONAL ANTHEMS--WESTERN & MIDDLE EUROPE is an integrated learning book series. Each anthem includes a map of the individual country & surrounding countries, form of government, language spoken, capital, currency, & national holidays. The cover displays the flags of the included countries in vibrant color. Also included are the words in the original language & English translations. Music is in piano score, arranged for easy to intermediate abilities. This book is suitable for all ages, but is specifically formatted to appeal to grades 4-9. These books provide a wonderful aspect of cultural, historical & heritage information. Ideal reference for schools, teachers, & libraries; also as gifts to young students of history or music. Since these anthems are not easily accessible it is important to note that college age students studying culture, history, music or language may be interested in this series. NATIONAL ANTHEMS (WESTERN & MIDDLE EUROPE) is a series of 4 books. Book 1 (0-9631333-0-6) includes France, Iceland, Ireland, Portugal, Spain. Book 2 (0-9631333-1-4), Andorra, Belgium, Denmark, Germany, Lichtenstein, Luxembourg, Monaco, Netherlands, Norway, Switzerland. Book 3 (0-9631333-2-2), Albania, Austria, Czechoslovakia (1918-1993), Hungary, Italy, Malta, San Marino, Sweden. Book 4 (0-9631333-0-0), Bulgaria, Finland, Greece, Poland, Romania, the former U.S.S.R., Yugoslavia. Each book also available separately at $6.95 each. Order directly from: Hi. I. Que Publishing, P.O. Box 508, Claremont, CA 91711-0508. (909) 622-7501, or your local distributor.
Publisher Provided Annotation.

Hernandez, Xavier & Ballonga, Jordi. Lebek: A City of Northern Europe Through the Ages. Leverich, Kathleen, tr. Corni, Francesco, illus. 64p. 1991. 16.45 (*0-395-57442-0*, Sandpiper) HM.

Martin, Ana. Prehistoric Stone Monuments. LC 93-756. (ENG & SPA., Illus.). 36p. (gr. 3 up). 1993. PLB 14.95 (*0-516-08386-4*); pap. 6.95 (*0-516-48386-2*) Childrens.

Roberts, Elizabeth. The New Europe: Maastricht & Beyond - Update. LC 93-11187. (Illus.). 40p. (gr. 6-8). 1993. PLB 12.90 (*0-531-17429-8*, Gloucester Pr) Watts.

Treays, R. Book of Europe. (Illus.). 64p. (gr. 5 up). 1994. PLB 13.96 (*0-88110-677-1*, Usborne); pap. 8.95 (*0-7460-1024-9*, Usborne) EDC.

EUROPE–HISTORY–FICTION

Cosman, Madeleine P. The Medieval Baker's Daughter: A Bilingual Adventure in Medieval Life with Costumes, Banners, Music, Food, & a Mystery Play. LC 84-71590. (ENG & SPA., Illus.). 112p. (gr. 3-12). 1984. pap. 7.95 (*0-916491-18-8*) Bard Hall Pr.

Dickinson, Peter. Shadow of a Hero. LC 94-8667. 1994. 15.95 (*0-385-32110-4*) Delacorte.

Treece, Henry. Men of the Hills. Price, Christine, illus. LC 58-5448. (gr. 6-9). 1958. 21.95 (*0-87599-115-7*) S G Phillips.

—Ride into Danger. Price, Christine, illus. LC 59-12203. (gr. 7-10). 1959. 21.95 (*0-87599-113-0*) S G Phillips.

EUROPE–HISTORY–TO 476

Europe at the Time of Greece & Rome. (Illus.). 80p. (gr. 4 up). 1988. PLB 25.67 (*0-8172-3305-9*) Raintree Steck-V.

Frazee, Charles & Yopp, Hallie K. Ancient Europe. Frazee, Kathleen & Lumba, Eric, illus. (gr. 6). 1990. pap. text ed. write for info. Delos Pubns.

—Medieval & Early Modern Europe. Frazee, Kathleen & Lumba, Eric, illus. (gr. 7). 1990. pap. text ed. 5.50 wkbk. (*0-685-44932-7*) Delos Pubns.

Prehistoric & Ancient Europe. (Illus.). 80p. (gr. 4 up). 1988. PLB 25.67 (*0-8172-3304-0*) Raintree Steck-V.

EUROPE–HISTORY–476-1492

see also Hundred Years' War, 1339-1453

Dambrosio, Monica & Barbieri, Roberto. The Birth of Modern Europe. Di Ianni, Mary, tr. Berselli, Remo, illus. LC 92-22076. (ITA & ENG.). 72p. (gr. 5-6). 1992. PLB 25.67 (*0-8114-3325-0*) Raintree Steck-V.

EUROPE–HISTORY–1492-1789

Dambrosio, Monica & Barbieri, Roberto. The Birth of Modern Europe. Di Ianni, Mary, tr. Berselli, Remo, illus. LC 92-22076. (ITA & ENG.). 72p. (gr. 5-6). 1992. PLB 25.67 (*0-8114-3325-0*) Raintree Steck-V.

EUROPE–HISTORY–1789-1900

Fix, Philippe. Not So Very Long Ago: Life in a Small Country Village. Fix, Philippe, illus. LC 93-8428. 40p. (gr. 2 up). 1994. 16.99 (*0-525-44594-3*, DCB) Dutton Child Bks.

EUROPE–HISTORY–20TH CENTURY

Lerner Geography Department Staff, ed. Estonia. (Illus.). 64p. (gr. 5-12). 1992. PLB 19.95 (*0-8225-2803-7*) Lerner Pubns.

—Latvia. LC 92-7260. (Illus.). 64p. (gr. 5-12). 1992. PLB 19.95 (*0-8225-2802-9*) Lerner Pubns.

—Lithuania. LC 92-9698. (Illus.). 64p. (gr. 5-12). 1992. PLB 19.95 (*0-8225-2804-5*) Lerner Pubns.

EUROPE–HISTORY–1914-1945

see also World War, 1939-1945

EUROPE–POLITICS–20TH CENTURY

Dunnan, Nancy. One Europe. LC 91-30083. (Illus.). 64p. (gr. 5-8). 1992. PLB 15.90 (*1-56294-105-4*) Millbrook Pr.

—One Europe. 1992. pap. 4.95 (*0-395-62470-3*) HM.

Wekesser, Carol & Biskup, Michael D., eds. Europe. LC 92-23066. 200p. (gr. 10 up). 1992. PLB 16.95 (*1-56510-024-7*); pap. text ed. 9.95 (*1-56510-023-9*) Greenhaven.

EUROPEAN COMMON MARKET

see European Economic Community

EUROPEAN ECONOMIC COMMUNITY

Ashabranner, Brent. A New Frontier: The Peace Corps in Eastern Europe. Conklin, Paul, photos by. LC 93-38535. (Illus.). 112p. (gr. 5 up). 1994. 13.99 (*0-525-65155-1*, Cobblehill Bks) Dutton Child Bks.

EUROPEAN FEDERATION

Dunnan, Nancy. One Europe. LC 91-30083. (Illus.). 64p. (gr. 5-8). 1992. PLB 15.90 (*1-56294-105-4*) Millbrook Pr.

—One Europe. 1992. pap. 4.95 (*0-395-62470-3*) HM.

Roberts, Elizabeth. The New Europe: Maastricht & Beyond - Update. LC 93-11187. (Illus.). 40p. (gr. 6-8). 1993. PLB 12.90 (*0-531-17429-8*, Gloucester Pr) Watts.

EUROPEAN WAR, 1939-1945

see World War, 1939-1945

EVALUATION OF LITERATURE

see Books and Reading–Best Books; Criticism; Literature–History and Criticism

EVANGELISTIC WORK–HISTORY

Gilroy, Mark. Sharing My Faith: A Teen's Guide to Evangelism. (Illus.). 104p. 1991. pap. 5.95 (*0-8341-1384-8*) Beacon Hill.

EVANGELISTS–FICTION

Whalen, Terry. When I Grow up, I Can Go Anywhere for Jesus. LC 92-6768. (ps-3). 1992. pap. 8.99 (*1-55513-488-2*, Chariot Bks) Chariot Family.

EVEREST, MOUNT

Davidson, Bob. Hillary & Tenzing Climb Everest. (Illus.). 32p. (gr. 5 up). 1993. text ed. 13.95 RSBE (*0-87518-534-7*, Dillon) Macmillan Child Grp.

Fraser, Mary A. On Top of the World: The Conquest of Mount Everest. Fraser, Mary A., illus. LC 90-48988. 40p. (gr. 2-5). 1991. 14.95 (*0-8050-1578-7*, Bks Young Read) H Holt & Co.

Montgomery, R. A. Everest Attempt. 1994. pap. 3.50 (*0-553-56005-0*) Bantam.

Rosen, Mike. Conquest of Everest. LC 89-9688. (gr. 4-6). 1990. PLB 11.90 (*0-531-18319-X*, Pub. by Bookwright Pr) Watts.

EVERGLADES, FLORIDA–FICTION

Buffett, Jimmy & Buffett, Savannah J. Trouble Dolls. Ingber, Bonnie V., intro. by. Davis, Lambert, illus. 32p. (gr. 1 up). 1991. 14.95 (*0-15-290790-4*) HarBrace.

Hall, Nancy & Packard, Mary. Spike & Mike. McCue, Lisa, illus. LC 93-13684. 40p. (ps-4). 1993. PLB 11.80 (*0-516-00830-7*) Childrens.

Packard, Mary. Fairest of All. McCue, Lisa, illus. LC 93-11056. 40p. (ps-4). 1993. PLB 11.80 (*0-516-00826-9*) Childrens.

—Playing by the Rules. McCue, Lisa, illus. LC 93-4423. 40p. (ps-4). 1993. PLB 11.80 (*0-516-00827-7*) Childrens.

—Safe & Sound. McCue, Lisa, illus. LC 93-11058. 40p. (ps-4). 1993. PLB 11.80 (*0-516-00828-5*) Childrens.

—Save the Swamp. McCue, Lisa, illus. LC 93-11059. 40p. (ps-4). 1993. PLB 11.80 (*0-516-00829-3*) Childrens.

—Spike & Mike & the Treasure Hunt. McCue, Lisa, illus. LC 92-50295. 1993. write for info. (*0-679-93936-9*); lib. bdg. write for info. (*0-679-83936-4*) Random Bks Yng Read.

—Starting Over. McCue, Lisa & Scribner, Toni, illus. LC 93-11060. 40p. (ps-4). 1993. PLB 11.80 (*0-516-00831-5*) Childrens.

EVERGLADES NATIONAL PARK

Andryszewski, Tricia. Marjory Stoneman Douglas, Friend of the Everglades. LC 93-26731. (Illus.). 48p. (gr. 2-4). 1994. PLB 12.90 (*1-56294-384-7*) Millbrook Pr.

Bryant, Jennifer. Marjory Stoneman Douglas: Voice of the Everglades. Raymond, Larry, illus. 72p. (gr. 4-7). 1992. PLB 14.95 (*0-8050-2113-2*) TFC Bks NY.

George, Jean C. The Everglades. Minor, Wendell, illus. LC 92-9517. Date not set. 15.00 (*0-06-021228-4*); PLB 14.89 (*0-06-021229-2*) HarpC Child Bks.

Linn, Christopher. The Everglades: Exploring the Unknown. LC 75-23414. (Illus.). 32p. (gr. 5-10). 1976. PLB 10.79 (*0-89375-006-9*) Troll Assocs.

Rom, Christine S. Everglades. LC 88-18644. (Illus.). (gr. 4-5). 1988. text ed. 13.95 RSBE (*0-89686-404-9*, Crestwood Hse) Macmillan Child Grp.

EVOLUTION

see also Adaptation (Biology); Anatomy, Comparative; Biology; Color of Animals; Color of Man; Creation; Embryology; Man–Influence of Environment; Man–Origin and Antiquity; Religion and Science; Social Change

Bailey, Marilyn. Evolution: Opposing Viewpoints. LC 90-3837. (Illus.). 112p. (gr. 5-8). 1990. PLB 14.95 (*0-89908-078-2*) Greenhaven.

Baylor, Byrd. If You Are a Hunter of Fossils. Parnall, Peter, illus. LC 79-17926. 32p. (ps-3). 1980. SBE 14.95 (*0-684-16419-1*, Scribners Young Read) Macmillan Child Grp.

Childers, Norman H. The Great Monkey Debate. Childers, Norman H., illus. 44p. (gr. k-5). 1988. 14.95g (*0-940561-12-3*) White Rose Pr.

Cole, Joanna. Evolution. Aliki, illus. LC 87-638. 32p. (gr. k-3). 1987. (Crowell Jr Bks); PLB 13.89 (*0-690-04598-0*, Crowell Jr Bks) HarpC Child Bks.

—Evolution. Aliki, illus. LC 87-638. 32p. (ps-3). 1989. pap. 4.50 (*0-06-445086-4*, Trophy) HarpC Child Bks.

Dal Sasso, Cristiano. Animals: Origin & Evolution. Serini, Rocco, tr. from ITA. LC 94-2541. (Illus.). 48p. (gr. 6-8). 1994. PLB write for info. (*0-8114-3333-1*) Raintree Steck-V.

Evolution of Life. LC 92-8227. 1992. write for info. (*0-8094-9695-X*); pap. write for info. (*0-8094-9696-8*) Time-Life.

Facchini, Fiorenzo. Humans: Origins & Evolution. Serini, Rocco, tr. from ITA. LC 94-7911. (Illus.). 48p. (gr. 6-8). 1994. PLB write for info. (*0-8114-3336-6*) Raintree Steck-V.

Fisher, David E. The Origin & Evolution of Our Own Particular Universe. LC 88-14108. (Illus.). 192p. (gr. 7 up). 1988. SBE 15.95 (*0-689-31368-3*, Atheneum Child Bk) Macmillan Child Grp.

Gallant, Roy A. Before the Sun Dies: The Story of Evolution. LC 88-8284. (Illus.). 224p. (gr. 5 up). 1989. SBE 15.95 (*0-02-735771-6*, Macmillan Child Bk) Macmillan Child Grp.

Gamlin, Linda. Evolution. LC 92-54478. (Illus.). 64p. (gr. 7 up). 1993. 15.95 (*1-56458-233-7*) Dorling Kindersley.

Garassino, Alessandro. Life: Origins & Evolution. Serini, Rocco, tr. from ITA. Gonano, Maria E. & Moriggia, Rosalba, illus. LC 94-8582. 48p. (gr. 6-8). 1994. PLB write for info. (*0-8114-3335-8*) Raintree Steck-V.

—Plants: Origin & Evolution. LC 94-3838. 1994. write for info. (*0-8114-3332-3*) Raintree Steck-V.

Jackson, Ellen. The Tree of Life: The Wonders of Evolution. Winter, Judeanne, illus. 40p. (gr. k-3). 1993. 14.95 (*0-87975-819-8*) Prometheus Bks.

Lewin, Roger. The Origin of Modern Humans: A Scientific American Library Volume. LC 93-17647. 1993. text ed. write for info. (*0-7167-5039-2*, Sci Am Yng Rdrs) W H Freeman.

Lindsay, William. Prehistoric Life. LC 93-32076. (gr. 5 up). 1994. 16.00 (*0-679-86001-0*); PLB 16.99 (*0-679-96001-5*) Knopf Bks Yng Read.

Litteral, Linda L. Boobies, Iguanas, & Other Critters: Nature's Story in the Galapagos. (Illus.). 72p. (gr. 5-9). 1994. 23.00 (*1-883966-01-9*) Am Kestrel Pr.

McGowen, Tom. The Great Monkey Trial: Science Versus Fundamentalism in America. Gould, Stephen J., frwd. by. LC 90-33610. (Illus.). 128p. (gr. 9-12). 1990. PLB 13.90 (*0-531-10965-8*) Watts.

Norman, David. Prehistoric Life. 1994. 30.00 (*0-671-79940-1*) P-H.

Parker, Steve. Charles Darwin & Evolution. Parker, Steve, illus. LC 91-30272. 32p. (gr. 3-7). 1992. 14.00 (*0-06-020733-7*) HarpC Child Bks.

Peters, David. From the Beginning: The Story of Human Evolution. LC 90-19187. (Illus.). 128p. (gr. 3 up). 1991. 13.95 (*0-688-09476-7*) Morrow Jr Bks.

Peters, Lisa W. Evolution Book. 1994. write for info. (*0-8050-2418-2*) H Holt & Co.

Richards, Larry. It Couldn't Just Happen. 191p. (gr. 2-7). 1989. write for info. (*0-8499-0715-2*) Word Inc.

Stein, Sara. The Evolution Book. Stein, Sara, illus. LC 84-40682. 400p. (Orig.). (gr. 5-9). 1986. pap. 12.95 (*0-89480-927-X*, 927) Workman Pub.

Taylor, Kenneth N. What High School Students Should Know about Evolution. 70p. (gr. 9-12). 1983. pap. 3.99 (*0-8423-7873-1*) Tyndale.

Twist, Clint. Darwin: On the Trail of Evolution. LC 93-31789. 1994. PLB 22.80 (*0-8114-7256-6*) Raintree Steck-V.

Wexo, John B. Out of the Water. 24p. (gr. 3 up). 1991. PLB 14.95 (*0-88682-391-9*) Creative Ed.

—Plants & Animals. 24p. (gr. 3 up). 1991. PLB 14.95 (*0-88682-389-7*) Creative Ed.

Wexo, John G. Life Expands. 24p. (gr. 3 up). 1991. PLB 14.95 (*0-88682-388-9*) Creative Ed.

EXCAVATION–FICTION

Sargent, Dave & Sargent, Pat. Tunnel King. Sapaugh, Blaine, illus. 48p. (Orig.). (gr. k-8). 1993. text ed. 11.95 (*1-56763-032-4*); pap. text ed. 5.95 (*1-56763-033-2*) Ozark Pub.

EXCAVATIONS (ARCHEOLOGY)

see also Mounds and Mound Builders

Lessem, Don. The Iceman. LC 93-31534. (Illus.). 32p. (gr. 2-6). 1994. 14.00 (*0-517-59596-6*); lib. bdg. 14.99 (*0-517-59597-4*) Crown Bks Yng Read.

Martell, Hazel M. The Vikings & Jorvik. LC 92-25215. (Illus.). 32p. (gr. 5 up). 1993. text ed. 13.95 RSBE (*0-87518-541-X*, Dillon) Macmillan Child Grp.

Tyler, Deborah. The Greeks & Troy. LC 93-18693. (Illus.). 32p. (gr. 6-8). 1993. text ed. 13.95 RSBE (*0-87518-537-1*, Dillon) Macmillan Child Grp.

EXECUTIONS

see Capital Punishment

EXERCISE

see also Gymnastics; Physical Education and Training; Physical Fitness;

also names of special kinds of exercises, e.g. Rowing, etc.

Baldwin, Dorothy. Health & Exercise. (Illus.). 32p. (gr. 3-8). 1987. PLB 17.27 (*0-86592-293-4*); 12.95s.p. (*0-685-67611-0*) Rourke Corp.

Crelinsten, J. To the Limit. 1992. write for info. (*0-15-200616-8*, Gulliver Bks) HarBrace.

Duyff, Roberta L. Big Bug Book of Exercise. McKissack, Patricia & McKissack, Fredrick, eds. Bartholomew, illus. LC 87-61656. 24p. (Orig.). (gr. k-1). 1987. spiral bdg. 14.95 (*0-88335-761-5*); pap. text ed. 4.95 (*0-88335-771-2*) Milliken Pub Co.

Goldstein, Rebecca. The Mind-Body Problem. 304p. (gr. 5 up). 1985. pap. 4.95 (*0-440-35651-2*, LE) Dell.

Isenberg, Barbara & Jaffe, Marjorie. Albert the Running Bear's Exercise Book. De Groat, Diane, illus. LC 84-7064. 64p. (Orig.). (ps-4). 1984. (Clarion Bks) HM.

Jones, Lucile. Hop, Skip, & Jump. Van Dolson, Bobbie J., ed. 32p. (gr. k up). 1981. pap. 3.95 (*0-8280-0038-7*) Review & Herald.

Kamen, Betty. The Chromium Diet, Supplement & Exercise Strategy: An Easy to Follow Routine for Everyone. Rosenbaum, Michael E., intro. by. (Illus.). 216p. (Orig.). 1990. pap. 9.95 (*0-944501-03-6*) Nutrition Encounter.

Moncure, Jane B. Healthkins Exercise! Endres, Helen, illus. LC 82-14712. 32p. (ps-2). 1982. PLB 13.95 (*0-89565-241-2*) Childs World.

Nardo, Don. Exercise. (Illus.). 112p. (gr. 6-12). 1992. 18.95 (*0-7910-0017-6*) Chelsea Hse.

Nelson, JoAnne. Feeling Fit, That's It! McKinnell, Michael, illus. LC 92-37719. 1994. pap. 5.95 (*0-935529-58-6*) Comprehen Health Educ.

Perry, Susan. Getting in Step. (Illus.). (gr. 2-6). 1992. PLB 14.95 (*0-89565-872-0*) Childs World.

Reef, Catherine. Stay Fit: Build a Strong Body. LC 93-19349. 64p. (gr. 4-7). 1993. 15.95 (*0-8050-2441-7*) TFC Bks NY.

Reiss, Elayne & Friedman, Rita. Exercise Expert. (gr. k-1). 12.50 (*0-89796-866-2*) New Dimens Educ.

Savage, Jeff. Aerobics. LC 93-37296. 1995. text ed. 13.95 (*0-89686-853-2*, Crestwood Hse) Macmillan Child Grp.

Schwarzenegger, Arnold & Gaines, Charles. Arnold's Fitness for Kids: A Guide to Health, Exercise, & Nutrition. LC 92-28577. (gr. 1-5). 1993. 15.00 (*0-385-42267-9*) Doubleday.

—Arnold's Fitness for Kids Ages Birth to Five: A Guide to Health, Exercise, & Nutrition. LC 92-26209. (ps-k). 1993. 15.00 (*0-385-42266-0*) Doubleday.

—Arnold's Fitness for Kids Ages Eleven to Fourteen: A Guide to Health, Exercise, & Nutrition. LC 92-26786. (gr. 6-8). 1993. 15.00 (*0-385-42268-7*) Doubleday.

Silkwood, Chris & Levicki, Nancy. Awesome Teen. Schwarzenegger, Arnold, frwd. by. (Illus.). 140p. (Orig.). (gr. 8-12). 1991. pap. 11.95 (*0-9631318-0-X*) NJL Interests.
The topic on a recent TV show was obese children. The startling statistic, 1 out of 5 children are obese children, was over-shadowed by the alarming increase in obese children (54% over the last ten years). AWESOME TEEN is a fitness guide that teenagers can read & use to make positive changes in their life style. Arnold Schwarzenegger wrote the foreword for this book for boys & girls ages 12-18. Arnold has this to say: "This book is an excellent example of the grassroots effort & support that is so needed in this country if we are to reverse the decline in youth fitness." AWESOME TEEN is candidly written in teen vernacular. The authors' use of photographs of teens exercising along with charts the readers can use to plan their fitness routine make this book "user friendly." A section on food choices includes "smart choice" recipes, simple in preparation & written so the teen can prepare the recipes. Linda Johnson, a high school teacher in the Houston Independent School District, has this to say about AWESOME TEEN: "I've taught nutrition & exercise to students & had to obtain information from

several sources. Now I have it all in one book! The point system is a great motivator." To order, please contact NJL Interests 713-780-1268.
Publisher Provided Annotation.

EXHIBITIONS
Fowler, Allan. World's Fairs & Expos. LC 91-8891. 48p. (gr. k-4). 1991. PLB 12.85 (*0-516-01130-8*); pap. 4.95 (*0-516-41130-6*) Childrens.
Marsh, Carole. World's Fair Fun Trivia Book. Marsh, Carole, illus. (Orig.). (gr. 4 up). 1994. pap. 4.95 (*0-935326-06-5*) Gallopade Pub Group.
EXILES
see Refugees
EXISTENTIALISM
State of Being Staff. Some States of Being. State of Being Staff, illus. 22p. (Orig.). (gr. 7 up). 1988. pap. 2.00 (*0-929611-03-9*) Plutonium Pr.
EXORCISM
see Witchcraft
EXPEDITIONS, ANTARCTIC AND ARCTIC
see Arctic Regions; Antarctic Regions
EXPEDITIONS, SCIENTIFIC
see Scientific Expeditions
EXPERIMENTS, SCIENTIFIC
see Science–Experiments
EXPLORATION, SUBMARINE
see Underwater Exploration
EXPLORATION, UNDERWATER
see Underwater Exploration
EXPLORATIONS
see America–Discovery and Exploration; Discoveries (In Geography); Explorers
EXPLORERS
see also America–Discovery and Exploration; Discoveries (In Geography); Voyages and Travels
also names of countries with the subdivision Description and Travel and Exploring Expeditions, e.g. U. S. –Description and Travel; U. S.–Exploring Expeditions, etc.; and names of individual explorers
Alper, Ann. Forgotten Voyager: The Story of Amerigo Vespucci. (Illus.). 80p. (gr. 3-6). 1991. PLB 17.50 (*0-87614-442-3*) Carolrhoda Bks.
Anderson, Dale. Explorers Who Found New Worlds. LC 93-19016. (Illus.). 48p. (gr. 5-7). 1993. PLB 22.80 (*0-8114-4931-9*) Raintree Steck-V.
Artman, John. Explorers. Hyndman, Kathryn, illus. 64p. (gr. 4 up). 1986. 8.95 (*0-86653-340-0*, GA 796) Good Apple.
Asimov, Isaac. Isaac Asimov's Pioneers of Science & Exploration, 3 vols. (Illus.). 64p. (gr. 3-4). 1991. Set. PLB 55.80 (*0-8368-0754-5*) Gareth Stevens Inc.
Baker, Susan. Explorers of North America. LC 89-26364. (Illus.). 48p. (gr. 4-8). 1990. PLB 11.95 (*0-8114-2752-8*) Raintree Steck-V.
Bentley, Judith. Explorers, Guides & Trappers. (Illus.). 96p. (gr. 5-8). 1994. bds. 16.95 (*0-8050-2995-8*) TFC Bks NY.
Brice, Donald & Dandola, John. Explorers Before Columbus. (Illus., Orig.). (gr. k up). 1991. pap. write for info. (*1-878452-07-X*) Tory Corner Editions.
Chrisp, Peter. The Search for the East. LC 93-12826. (Illus.). 48p. (gr. 4-6). 1993. 14.95 (*1-56847-120-3*) Thomson Lrning.
Clare, John D., ed. Voyages of Christopher Columbus. (gr. 4-7). 1992. 16.95 (*0-15-200507-2*, Gulliver Bks) HarBrace.
Darling, Benjamin. Tips for Teens: Telephone Tactics, Petting Practices, & Other Milestones on the Road to Popularity. LC 93-35815. 60p. (gr. 7-12). 1994. 9.95 (*0-8118-0520-4*) Chronicle Bks.
Discovery & Exploration, 17 vols. LC 89-15723. (Illus.). 2866p. (gr. 7-12). 1990. Set. PLB 399.95x (*1-85435-114-1*) Marshall Cavendish.
Everett, F. Explorers. (Illus.). 48p. (gr. 4 up). 1991. PLB 14.96 (*0-88110-504-X*, Usborne); pap. 7.95 (*0-7460-0514-8*) EDC.
Faber, Harold. The Discoverers of America. LC 91-17001. (Illus.). 304p. (gr. 9 up). 1992. SBE 17.95 (*0-684-19217-9*, Scribners Young Read) Macmillan Child Grp.
Ferris, Jeri. Arctic Explorer: The Story of Matthew Henson. (Illus.). 80p. (gr. 3-6). 1989. PLB 17.50 (*0-87614-370-2*); pap. 5.95 (*0-87614-507-1*) Carolrhoda Bks.
Fradin, Dennis. Explorers. LC 84-7077. (Illus.). 48p. (gr. k-4). 1984. PLB 12.85 (*0-516-01926-0*) Childrens.
Fritz, Jean. Around the World in a Hundred Years: Henry the Navigator - Magellan. Venti, Anthony B., illus. LC 92-27042. 128p. (gr. 2-6). 1994. 17.95 (*0-399-22527-7*, Putnam) Putnam Pub Group.
—Where Do You Think You're Going, Christopher Columbus? Tomes, Margot, illus. 80p. (gr. 3-7). 1981. (Putnam); pap. 7.95 (*0-399-20734-1*, Putnam) Putnam Pub Group.
Gaines, Ann. Herodotus & the Explorers of the Classical Age. Goetzmann, William H., ed. Collins, Michael, intro. by. (Illus.). 112p. (gr. 6-12). 1993. PLB 19.95 (*0-7910-1293-X*, Am Art Analog) Chelsea Hse.
Gaines, Richard. The Explorers of the Undersea World. Goetzmann, William H., ed. Collins, Michael, intro. by. (Illus.). 112p. (gr. 6-12). 1994. PLB 19.95 (*0-7910-1323-5*, Am Art Analog); pap. write for info. (*0-7910-1547-5*, Am Art Analog) Chelsea Hse.
Goetzmann, William H., ed. World Explorers Series, 32 vols. Collins, Michael, intro. by. (Illus.). 3696p. (gr. 5 up). 1993. Set. lib. bdg. 625.35 (*0-7910-1290-5*, Am Art Analog) Chelsea Hse.
Grant, Neil. Explorers & Discoverers. (Illus.). 48p. (Orig.). (gr. 4 up). 1992. pap. 6.95 (*0-563-34791-0*, BBC-Parkwest) Parkwest Pubns.
Grosseck, Joyce & Atwood, Elizabeth, eds. Great Explorers. rev. ed. LC 87-81354. (Illus.). 160p. (gr. 4 up). 1988. 14.95 (*0-934291-22-5*); 11.95 (*0-317-91140-6*) Gateway Pr MI.
Hargrove, Jim. Ferdinand Magellan: First Around the World. LC 89-15781. (Illus.). 128p. (gr. 3 up). 1990. PLB 20.55 (*0-516-03051-5*) Childrens.
—Rene-Robert Cavelier, Sieur De La Salle: Explorer of the Mississippi River. LC 89-25442. (Illus.). 128p. (gr. 3 up). 1990. 20.55 (*0-516-03054-X*) Childrens.
Haskins, Jim. Against All Opposition: Black Explorers in America. 128p. 1992. 13.95 (*0-8027-8137-5*); PLB 14.85 (*0-8027-8138-1*) Walker & Co.
Hernando de Soto. (Illus.). 32p. (gr. 3-5). 1988. PLB 19.97 (*0-8172-2903-5*) Raintree Steck-V.
Italia, Bob. Robert Ballard. Walner, Rosemary, ed. LC 90-82623. (Illus.). 32p. (gr. 4). 1990. PLB 11.96 (*0-939179-95-4*) Abdo & Dghtrs.
—Will Steger. Walner, Rosemary, ed. LC 90-82624. (Illus.). 32p. (gr. 4). 1990. PLB 11.96 (*0-939179-97-0*) Abdo & Dghtrs.
Jacobs, William J. Champlain: A Life of Courage. LC 93-31176. (Illus.). 64p. (gr. 5-8). 1994. PLB 12.90 (*0-531-20112-0*) Watts.
—Cortes: Conquerer of Mexico. LC 93-31177. (Illus.). 64p. (gr. 5-8). 1994. PLB 12.90 (*0-531-20138-4*) Watts.
—La Salle: A Life of Boundless Adventure. LC 93-29699. (Illus.). 64p. (gr. 5-8). 1994. PLB 12.90 (*0-531-20141-4*) Watts.
Langley, Andrew. Twenty Explorers. LC 89-23852. (Illus.). 48p. (gr. 3-8). 1990. PLB 12.95 (*1-85435-252-0*) Marshall Cavendish.
Lillegard, Dee. My First Columbus Day Book. Raskin, Betty, illus. LC 87-10304. 32p. (ps-2). 1987. PLB 11.45 (*0-516-02909-6*); pap. 3.95 (*0-516-42909-4*) Childrens.
Lindsley, Margaret. Andrew Henry: Mine & Mountain Major. (Illus.). 370p. 1990. 19.95 (*0-936204-79-6*); pap. 15.95 (*0-936204-78-8*) Jelm Mtn.
Lomask, Milton. Great Lives: Exploration. LC 88-15744. (Illus.). 288p. (gr. 4-6). 1988. SBE 23.00 (*0-684-18511-3*, Scribners Young Read) Macmillan Child Grp.
Martini, Teri. Christopher Columbus: The Man Who Unlocked the Secrets of the World. LC 91-44755. 96p. (gr. 4-7). 1992. pap. 4.95 (*0-8091-6604-6*) Paulist Pr.
Mason, Antony & Lye, Keith. The Children's Atlas of Exploration. LC 92-28856. (Illus.). 96p. (gr. 2-6). 1993. PLB 18.90 (*1-56294-256-5*); pap. 10.95 (*1-56294-711-7*) Millbrook Pr.
Matthews, Rupert. Explorer. Stevenson, Jim, illus. LC 91-8428. 64p. (gr. 5 up). 1991. 16.00 (*0-679-81460-4*); lib. bdg. 16.99 (*0-679-91460-9*) Knopf Bks Yng Read.
Morrison, Dorothy N. Under a Strong Wind: The Adventures of Jessie Benton Fremont. LC 83-6356. (Illus.). 224p. (gr. 5-9). 1983. SBE 14.95 (*0-689-31004-8*, Atheneum Child Bk) Macmillan Child Grp.
Mumford, Donald & Mumford, Esther. From Africa to the Arctic: Five Explorers. Lee, Nancy, illus. 48p. (gr. 1-3). 1992. 9.95 (*0-9605670-6-2*) Ananse Pr.
Richards, Dorothy F. Christopher Columbus, Who Sailed On! Nelson, John, illus. LC 78-7664. (gr. 1-5). 1978. PLB 13.95 (*0-89565-032-0*) Childs World.
Ryan, Peter. Explorers & Mapmakers. Molan, Chris, illus. LC 89-31824. 48p. (gr. 4-7). 1990. 14.95 (*0-525-67285-0*, Lodestar Bks) Dutton Child Bks.
Scheller, William. The World's Greatest Explorers. LC 92-18418. (Illus.). 160p. (gr. 5-12). 1992. PLB 14.95 (*1-881508-03-X*) Oliver Pr MN.
Simon, Charnan. Explorers of the Ancient World. LC 89-25431. (Illus.). 128p. (gr. 3 up). 1990. PLB 20.55 (*0-516-03053-1*) Childrens.
—Henry the Navigator: Master Teacher of Explorers. LC 92-37048. (Illus.). 128p. (gr. 3 up). 1993. PLB 20.55 (*0-516-03071-X*) Childrens.
—Leif Eriksson & the Vikings: The Norse Discovery of America. LC 90-20804. (Illus.). 128p. (gr. 3 up). 1991. PLB 20.55 (*0-516-03060-4*) Childrens.
—Richard Burton: Explorer of Arabia & Africa. LC 90-20814. (Illus.). 128p. (gr. 3 up). 1991. PLB 20.55 (*0-516-03062-0*) Childrens.
Stefoff, Rebecca. The Accidental Explorers: Surprises & Sidetrips in the History of Discovery. (Illus.). 152p. 1992. PLB 22.00 (*0-19-507685-0*) OUP.
—Scientific Explorers. (Illus.). 144p. 1992. PLB 22.00 (*0-19-507689-3*) OUP.
—Vasco da Gama & the Portuguese Explorers. Goetzmann, William H., ed. Collins, Michael, intro. by. (Illus.). 112p. (gr. 6-12). 1993. PLB 18.95 (*0-7910-1303-0*); pap. write for info. (*0-7910-1526-2*) Chelsea Hse.
—The Viking Explorers. Goetzmann, William H., ed. Collins, Michael, intro. by. (Illus.). 112p. (gr. 6-12). 1993. PLB 19.95 (*0-7910-1295-6*, Am Art Analog); pap. write for info. (*0-7910-1520-3*, Am Art Analog) Chelsea Hse.
—Women of the World. (Illus.). 144p. 1992. PLB 22.00 (*0-19-507687-7*) OUP.
—The Young Oxford Companion to Maps & Mapmaking. (Illus.). 320p. 1994. lib. bdg. 35.00 (*0-19-508042-4*) OUP.
Stein, R. Conrad. Hernando Cortes: Conquerer of Mexico. LC 90-20655. (Illus.). 128p. (gr. 3 up). 1991. PLB 20.55 (*0-516-03059-0*) Childrens.
Warren, Betsy. Explorers in Early Texas. Long, Joann M., ed. (Illus.). 128p. (gr. 4 up). 1992. 14.95 (*0-937460-74-5*) Hendrick-Long.
Waterlow, Julia. The Explorer Through History. LC 93-5656. (Illus.). 48p. (gr. 5-8). 1994. 15.95 (*1-56847-101-7*) Thomson Lrning.
West, Delno C. & West, Jean M. Christopher Columbus: The Great Adventure & How We Know about It. LC 90-936. (Illus.). 144p. (gr. 5-9). 1991. SBE 15.95 (*0-689-31433-7*, Atheneum Child Bk) Macmillan Child Grp.
Wilkie, Katherine. Ferdinand Magellan: Noble Captain. Coyle, P., illus. (gr. 4-6). 1963. pap. 2.44 (*0-395-01751-3*, Piper) HM.
Zadra, Dan. Explorers of America: DeSoto. rev. ed. (gr. 2-4). 1988. PLB 14.95 (*0-88682-185-1*) Creative Ed.
EXPLORERS–FICTION
Christian, Mary B. Who'd Believe John Colter? Kubinyi, Laszlo, illus. LC 92-33822. 64p. (gr. 2-6). 1993. SBE 13.95 (*0-02-718477-3*, Macmillan Child Bk) Macmillan Child Grp.
Ellis, Terry. Explorers from Willow Wood Springs. LC 85-63827. (Illus.). 180p. (Orig.). (gr. 4 up). 1989. pap. 4.75 (*0-915677-31-8*) Roundtable Pub.
Emert, Phyllis R. Ghosts, Hauntings, & Mysterious Happenings. 1992. pap. 4.99 (*0-8125-2038-6*) Tor Bks.
Lee, Rebecca L. Kori & the Island of Enchantment. LC 89-49376. 80p. (Orig.). (gr. 8 up). 1990. pap. 6.95 (*0-931832-46-2*) Fithian Pr.
Moerbeek, Kees. Six Brave Explorers. (Illus.). 12p. (ps up). 1992. 4.95 (*0-8431-3449-6*) Price Stern.
Moses, Amy. I Am an Explorer. Hackney, Richard, illus. LC 90-38374. 32p. (ps-2). 1990. PLB 10.25 (*0-516-02059-5*); pap. 2.95 (*0-516-42059-3*) Childrens.
—I Am an Explorer Big Book. (Illus.). 32p. (ps-2). 1991. PLB 22.95 (*0-516-49517-8*) Childrens.
Pepper Bird Staff. Frozen Fury: Adventures of Matthew Henson. Rose, Ann C., illus. 48p. (Orig.). (gr. 4-7). 1993. pap. 4.95 (*1-56817-001-7*) Pepper Bird.
Primavera, Elise. Ralph's Frozen Tale. LC 90-35521. 32p. 1991. 14.95 (*0-399-22252-9*, Putnam) Putnam Pub Group.
Sheldon, Dyan. Harry the Explorer. Heap, Sue, illus. LC 91-58734. 80p. (gr. 3-6). 1994. pap. 3.99 (*1-56402-393-1*) Candlewick Pr.
EXPLORING EXPEDITIONS
see names of countries with the subdivision Exploring Expeditions (e.g. U. S.–Exploring Expeditions; etc.) and names of Expeditions, e.g. Lewis and Clark Expedition; etc.
EXPLOSIVES
Grady, Sean M. Explosives: Devices of Controlled Destruction. (Illus.). (gr. 5-8). 1994. 15.95 (*1-56006-250-9*) Lucent Bks.
EXTINCT ANIMALS
see also names of extinct animals, e.g. Mastodon, etc.
Aliki. Wild & Woolly Mammoths. Aliki, illus. LC 76-18082. 40p. (gr. k-3). 1977. PLB 13.89 (*0-690-01276-4*, Crowell Jr Bks) HarpC Child Bks.
Benton, Michael. Prehistoric Animals: An A-Z Guide. (Illus.). 176p. 1989. 7.99 (*0-517-69190-6*) Random Hse Value.
Cox, Barry. Prehistoric Animals. (Illus.). (gr. 5 up). 1971. pap. 3.95 (*0-553-23610-5*) Bantam.
Crofford, Emily. The Great Auk. LC 89-31576. (Illus.). 48p. (gr. 5-6). 1989. text ed. 12.95 RSBE (*0-89686-459-6*, Crestwood Hse) Macmillan Child Grp.
Dewey, Jennifer & Lyon, Lucy. Prehistoric Swimmers & Flyers of the Southwest. (Illus.). 32p. (gr. 4 up). 1990. pap. text ed. 4.95 (*0-89013-195-3*) Museum NM Pr.
Duggleby, John. Saber-Tooth Cat. LC 89-31574. (Illus.). 48p. (gr. 5-6). 1989. text ed. 12.95 RSBE (*0-89686-462-6*, Crestwood Hse) Macmillan Child Grp.
Earthbooks, Inc. Staff. The National Wildlife Federation's Book of Dinosaurs & Other Pre-Historic Animals. Aaestas, Ken, illus. 64p. (Orig.). (gr. 4). 1991. pap. 5.95 (*1-877731-16-1*) Earthbooks Inc.
Eastman, David. I Can Read About Prehistoric Animals. Nodel, Norman, illus. LC 76-54492. (gr. 2-4). 1977. pap. 2.50 (*0-89375-039-5*) Troll Assocs.
Goyallon, Jerome. Drawing Dinosaurs. LC 93-2809. (Illus.). 80p. (gr. 3 up). 1993. 12.95 (*0-8069-8742-1*) Sterling.
Hecht, Jeff. Vanishing Life: The Mystery of Mass Extinctions. LC 92-41713. (Illus.). 160p. (gr. 7 up). 1993. SBE 15.95 (*0-684-19331-0*, Scribners Young Read) Macmillan Child Grp.
Horn, Gabriel. The Steller's Sea Cow. LC 89-7702. (Illus.). 48p. (gr. 5-6). 1989. text ed. 12.95 (*0-89686-460-X*, Crestwood Hse) Macmillan Child Grp.
Hornblow, Leonora & Hornblow, Arthur. Prehistoric Monsters Did the Strangest Things. abr. ed. Barlowe, Sy, illus. LC 88-30212. 64p. (gr. 2-4). 1990. Repr. lib. bdg. 6.99 (*0-394-94307-4*); 4.99 (*0-394-84307-X*) Random Bks Yng Read.
Patent, Dorothy H. The Challenge of Extinction. LC 90-3288. (Illus.). 64p. (gr. 6 up). 1991. lib. bdg. 15.95 (*0-89490-268-7*) Enslow Pubs.

Pearce, Q. L. Saber-Toothed Cats - Prehistoric Worlds. (Illus.). 64p. (gr. 4-6). 1991. lib. bdg. 12.98 (*0-671-70691-8*, J Messner); pap. 5.95 (*0-671-70692-6*) S&S Trade.
Raintree Publishers Inc. Staff. Prehistoric Animals. (Illus.). 64p. (Orig.). (gr. 5-9). 1988. PLB 11.95 (*0-8172-3082-3*) Raintree Steck-V.
Robertson, Bruce & Pinkus, Sue. Let's All Draw Dinosaurs, Pterodactyls & Other Prehistoric Creatures. (Illus.). 144p. (gr. 3-7). 1991. pap. 9.95 (*0-8230-2706-6*, Watson-Guptill Bks) Watson-Guptill.
Sanford, Bill & Green, Carl. Woolly Mammoth. LC 89-31575. (Illus.). 48p. (gr. 5-6). 1989. text ed. 12.95 RSBE (*0-89686-456-1*, Crestwood Hse) Macmillan Child Grp.
Silver, Donald. Extinction Is Forever. Wynne, Patricia J., illus. LC 93-32567. 1995. 12.00 (*0-671-86769-5*, J Messner); pap. 6.95 (*0-671-86770-9*, J Messner) S&S Trade.
Silverstein, Alvin, et al. Saving Endangered Animals. LC 92-1765. (Illus.). 128p. (gr. 6 up). 1993. lib. bdg. 17.95 (*0-89490-402-7*) Enslow Pubs.
Steele, Philip. Extinct Amphibians: And Those in Danger of Extinction. Kline, Marjory, ed. LC 91-9886. (Illus.). 32p. (gr. 4-7). 1992. PLB 11.90 (*0-531-11031-1*) Watts.
—Extinct Birds: And Those in Danger of Extinction. Kline, Marjory, ed. (Illus.). 32p. (gr. 5-8). 1991. PLB 11.90 (*0-531-11027-3*) Watts.
—Extinct Insects: And Those in Danger of Extinction. Kline, Marjory, ed. (Illus.). 32p. (gr. 4-7). 1992. PLB 11.90 (*0-531-11032-X*) Watts.
—Extinct Land Mammals: And Those in Danger of Extinction. Kline, Marjory, ed. (Illus.). 32p. (gr. 4-7). 1992. PLB 11.90 (*0-531-11028-1*) Watts.
—Extinct Reptiles: And Those in Danger of Extinction. Kline, Marjory, ed. (Illus.). 32p. (gr. 5-8). 1991. PLB 11.90 (*0-531-11030-3*) Watts.
World Book Staff, ed. Childcraft Supplement, 5 vols. LC 91-65174. (Illus.). (gr. 2-6). 1991. Set. write for info. (*0-7166-0666-6*) Prehistoric Animals, 304p. About Dogs, 304p. The Magic of Words, 304p. The Indian Book, 304p. The Puzzle Book, 304p. World Bk.
Zallinger, Peter. Prehistoric Animals. Zallinger, Peter, illus. 32p. (ps-3). 1981. 2.25 (*0-394-83737-1*) Random Bks Yng Read.

EXTINCT CITIES
see Cities and Towns, Ruined, Extinct, etc.

EXTINCT PLANTS
see Plants, Fossil

EXTACURRICULAR ACTIVITIES
see Student Activities

EXTRASENSORY PERCEPTION
Arvey, Michael. ESP: Opposing Viewpoints. LC 88-24316. (Illus.). 112p. (gr. 5-8). 1989. PLB 14.95 (*0-89908-057-X*) Greenhaven.
Green, Carl R. & Sanford, William R. Out-of-Body Experiences. LC 93-9172. (Illus.). 48p. (gr. 4-10). 1993. lib. bdg. 14.95 (*0-89490-457-4*) Enslow Pubs.
Larsen, Anita. Psychic Sleuths: How Psychic Information Is Used to Solve Crimes. LC 93-40593. 1994. text ed. 14.95 (*0-02-751645-8*, New Discovery Bks) Macmillan Child Grp.
Nash, Bruce & Zullo, Allan. Spooky Kids: Strange but True Tales. LC 93-44029. (Illus.). 128p. (gr. 1-6). 1994. pap. 2.95 (*0-8167-3447-X*, Pub. by Watermill Pr) Troll Assocs.
Petschek, Joyce. Silver Dreams: A Myth of the Sixth Sense. LC 90-82143. (Illus.). 208p. (gr. 8-12). 1990. 29.95 (*0-89087-619-3*); pap. 19.95 (*0-89087-620-7*) Celestial Arts.
Razzi, Jim. Nightmare Island: And Other Real-Life Mysteries. Palencar, John J., illus. LC 92-32638. 96p. (gr. 3-7). 1993. pap. 3.95 (*0-06-440426-9*, Trophy) HarpC Child Bks.

EXTRASENSORY PERCEPTION–FICTION
Alexander, Lloyd. Fortune Tellers. LC 91-30684. (Illus.). 32p. (gr. k-3). 1992. 15.00 (*0-525-44849-7*, DCB) Dutton Child Bks.
Bunting, Eve. The Mask. (Illus.). 64p. (gr. 3-8). 1992. 8.95 (*0-89565-769-4*) Childs World.
Christopher, Matt. The Dog That Stole Football Plays. Ogden, Bill, illus. 48p. (gr. 3-5). 1980. 14.95 (*0-316-13978-5*) Little.
Duncan, Lois. The Third Eye. (gr. 7up). 1984. 15.95 (*0-316-19553-7*) Little.
—The Third Eye. 224p. (gr. 6-12). 1991. pap. 3.99 (*0-440-98720-2*, LFL) Dell.
Grant, Charles L. Fire Mask. (gr. 7 up). 1991. 14.95 (*0-553-07167-X*, Starfire) Bantam.
Harris, Jesse. The Vampire's Kiss. LC 92-9019. 1992. 9.99 (*0-679-93669-6*) Knopf.
Hayes, Sheila. Zoe's Gift. LC 93-42621. 144p. 1994. 14.99 (*0-525-67484-5*, Lodestar Bks) Dutton Child Bks.
Jordan, Sherryl. Juniper Game. 1991. 13.95 (*0-590-44728-9*, Scholastic Hardcover) Scholastic Inc.
Kehret, Peg. Danger at the Fair. LC 94-16873. 1995. write for info. (*0-525-65182-9*, Cobblehill Bks) Dutton Child Bks.
Lasky, Kathryn. Shadows in the Water: A Starbuck Family Adventure. LC 92-8139. 1992. 16.95 (*0-15-273533-X*, HB Juv Bks); pap. write for info. (*0-15-273534-8*) HarBrace.
—Voice in the Wind: A Starbuck Family Adventure. (gr. 4-7). 1993. 16.95 (*0-15-294102-9*, HB Juv Bks); pap. 6.95 (*0-15-294103-7*) HarBrace.
Pinkwater, Jill. Mister Fred. 160p. (gr. 5-8). 1994. 15.99 (*0-525-44778-4*) Dutton Child Bks.
Sleator, William. Into the Dream. Sanderson, Ruth, illus. LC 78-11825. 144p. (gr. 4-7). 1979. 13.95 (*0-525-32583-2*, DCB) Dutton Child Bks.
Spicer, Dorothy. Humming Top. LC 68-31176. (gr. 7-11). 1968. 21.95 (*0-87599-147-5*) S G Phillips.
Sweeney, Joyce. Shadow: A Novel. LC 93-32215. 1994. 15.95 (*0-385-32051-5*) Delacorte.
Towne, Mary. Paul's Game. LC 82-72750. 192p. (gr. 7 up). 1983. 13.95 (*0-385-29248-1*) Delacorte.
Vinge, Joan D. Psion. LC 82-70323. 256p. (gr. 7 up). 1982. pap. 12.95 (*0-385-28780-1*) Delacorte.
Wright, Betty R. The Secret Window. LC 82-80816. 160p. (gr. 3-7). 1982. 14.95 (*0-8234-0464-1*) Holiday.

EXTRATERRESTRIAL LIFE
see Life on Other Planets

EYE
see also Optometry; Vision
Amstutz, Beverly. The Fly Has Lots of Eyes. (Illus.). 34p. (gr. k-9). 1981. pap. 2.50x (*0-937836-04-4*) Precious Res.
Chernus-Mansfield, Nancy & Horn, Marilyn. My Fake Eye: The Story of My Prosthesis. LC 91-73190. 24p. (ps-9). 1991. pap. write for info. (*0-9630118-0-4*) Inst Fam Blind Child.
Fowler, Allan. Lo Que Ves - Libro Grande: (Seeing Things Big Book) LC 90-22527. (SPA., Illus.). 32p. (ps-2). 1993. 22.95 (*0-516-59470-2*) Childrens.
—Seeing Things. LC 90-22527. (Illus.). 32p. (ps-2). 1991. PLB 10.75 (*0-516-04910-0*); pap. 3.95 (*0-516-44910-9*) Childrens.
Jedrosz, Aleksander. Eyes. Farmer, Andrew & Green, Robina, illus. LC 90-42177. 32p. (gr. 4-6). 1992. lib. bdg. 11.89 (*0-8167-2094-0*); pap. text ed. 3.95 (*0-8167-2095-9*) Troll Assocs.
Le Sieg, Theodore. Eye Book. McKie, Roy, illus. (ps-1). 1968. 6.95 (*0-394-81094-5*, BE2); lib. bdg. 7.99 (*0-394-91094-X*, BE2) Random Bks Yng Read.
Parker, Steve. Eye & Seeing. LC 88-51606. 1989. PLB 12.90 (*0-531-10654-3*) Watts.
Rauzon, Mark J. Eyes & Ears, Vol. 1. (ps-3). 1994. 13.00 (*0-688-10237-9*) Morrow.
Santa Fe Writers Group. Bizarre & Beautiful Eyes. (Illus.). 48p. (gr. 3 up). 1993. 14.95 (*1-56261-121-6*) John Muir.
Showers, Paul. Look at Your Eyes. rev. ed. Kelley, True, illus. LC 91-10167. 32p. (ps-1). 1992. 14.00 (*0-06-020188-6*); PLB 13.89 (*0-06-020189-4*) HarpC Child Bks.
Smith, Kathie B. & Crenson, Victoria. Seeing. Storms, Robert S., illus. LC 87-5862. 24p. (gr. k-3). 1988. PLB 10.59 (*0-8167-1008-2*); pap. text ed. 2.50 (*0-8167-1009-0*) Troll Assocs.
Thomson, Ruth. Eyes. FS Staff, ed. Galletly, Mike, illus. LC 87-51710. 32p. (gr. 1-3). 1988. PLB 10.90 (*0-531-10549-0*) Watts.
Tytla, Milan & Crystal, Nancy. You Won't Believe Your Eyes. Eldridge, Susan, illus. 88p. (gr. 2-8). 1992. pap. 9.95 (*1-55037-218-1*, Pub. by Annick CN) Firefly Bks Ltd.
Wright, Rachel. Eyes, Ears & Noses. (ps-3). 1990. PLB 10.90 o.s. (*0-531-14001-6*) Watts.

EYEGLASSES
see also Lenses
Asimov, Isaac & Dierks, Carrie. Why Do Some People Need Glasses? LC 93-20156. 1993. PLB 15.93 (*0-8368-0809-6*) Gareth Stevens Inc.
Joval, Nomi. La Lupa Maravillosa. Kubinyi, Laszlo, illus. (SPA.). 24p. (ps-4). 1993. PLB 13.95 (*1-879567-22-9*, Valeria Bks) Wonder Well.
Stuart, Sandra L. Why Do I Have to Wear Glasses? Robins, Arthur, illus. 48p. 1989. 12.00 (*0-8184-0477-9*) Carol Pub Group.
Wolff, Angelika. Mom, I Need Glasses. Hill, Dorothy, illus. Saltzman, S. L., intro. by. LC 74-112648. (Illus.). (gr. k-3). 1971. PLB 12.95 (*0-87460-139-8*) Lion Bks.

EYEGLASSES–FICTION
Adams, Pam. Mrs Honey's Glasses. LC 93-12368. (Illus.). (ps-3). 1993. 7.95 (*0-85953-757-9*); pap. 3.95 (*0-85953-758-7*) Childs Play.
Bogaerts, Rascal & Bogaerts, Gert. Socrates. LC 92-24120. 1993. 14.95 (*0-8118-0314-7*) Chronicle Bks.
Brown, Marc T. Arthur's Eyes. Brown, Marc T., illus. LC 79-11734. (ps-3). 1979. lib. bdg. 14.95 (*0-316-11063-9*, Joy St Bks) Little.
Cousins, Lucy. What Can Rabbit See? LC 90-21213. (Illus.). 16p. (ps up). 1991. 12.95 (*0-688-10454-1*, Tambourine Bks) Morrow.
Giff, Patricia R. Watch Out, Ronald Morgan. Natti, Susanna, illus. LC 84-19623. 24p. (gr. k-3). 1985. pap. 10.95 (*0-670-80433-9*) Viking Child Bks.
Koeleman, Paul. Dr. Paul's Amazing Eyewear. 10p. (Orig.). (ps-3). 1993. pap. 12.95 (*1-55550-883-9*) Universe.
Leggett, Linda R. & Andrews, Linda G. The Rose-Colored Glasses: Melanie Adjusts to Poor Vision. Hartman, Laura, illus. LC 79-12501. 32p. (gr. 3 up). 1979. 16.95 (*0-87705-408-8*) Human Sci Pr.
Little, Jean. From Anna. Sandin, Joan, illus. LC 72-76505. 208p. (gr. 4-6). 1972. PLB 14.89 (*0-06-023912-3*) HarpC Child Bks.
Pape, D. L. Liz Dearly's Silly Glasses. LC 68-56824. (Illus.). 48p. (gr. 2-5). 1968. PLB 10.95 (*0-87783-023-1*) Oddo.
Reese, Bob. Glasses. Reese, Bob, illus. LC 92-12185. 24p. (ps-2). 1992. PLB 9.75 (*0-516-05580-1*) Childrens.
Rogers, Mary & Rosario, Bernada D. New Glasses. 28p. (gr. 1). 1992. pap. text ed. 23.00 big bk. (*1-56843-021-3*); pap. text ed. 4.50 (*1-56843-071-X*) BGR Pub.
Shusterman, Neal. The Eyes of Kid Midas. LC 92-17897. 1992. 15.95 (*0-316-77542-8*) Little.
Smith, Lane. Glasses: Who Needs 'em? (ps-3). 1991. 13.95 (*0-670-84160-9*) Viking Child Bks.
Turin, Adela & Bosnia, Nella. The Real Story of the Bonobos Who Wore Spectacles. (Illus.). 32p. (gr. 3-6). 1980. 6.95 (*0-904613-18-6*) Writers & Readers.
Whitney's New Glasses. (Illus.). 40p. (gr. k-5). 1994. pap. 4.95 (*0-685-71582-5*) W Gladden Found.
Wild, Margaret. All the Better to See You With. Tucker, Kathy, ed. Reynolds, Pat, illus. LC 92-39127. 32p. (gr. 1-3). 1993. PLB 13.95 (*0-8075-0284-7*) A Whitman.
Wilson, Johnniece M. Poor Girl, Rich Girl. 176p. 1992. 13.95 (*0-590-44732-7*, Scholastic Hardcover) Scholastic Inc.
Wolff, Angelika. Mom, I Need Glasses. Hill, Dorothy, illus. Saltzman, S. L., intro. by. LC 74-112648. (Illus.). (gr. k-3). 1971. PLB 12.95 (*0-87460-139-8*) Lion Bks.

F

FABLES
see also Animals–Fiction; Folklore; Parables
Aesop. The Aesop for Children. large type ed. Clauss, J., intro. by. Winter, Nilo, illus. (gr. 1-12). 1976. lib. bdg. 23.95x (*0-88411-991-2*, Pub. by Aeonian Pr) Amereon Ltd.
—Aesop for Children. Winter, Milo, illus. LC 86-73175. 96p. (gr. 2 up). 1984. Repr. of 1919 ed. 12.95 (*1-56288-039-X*) Checkerboard.
—Aesop for Children. (ps). 1994. pap. 4.95 (*0-590-47977-6*) Scholastic Inc.
—Aesop's Fables. Winder, Blanche, ed. LC 33-31662. (Illus.). (gr. 4 up). 1965. pap. 1.95 (*0-8049-0081-7*, CL-81) Airmont.
—Aesop's Fables. Kredel, Fritz, illus. LC 33-31662. (gr. 4-6). 1963. (G&D); deluxe ed. 12.95 (*0-448-06003-5*); Companion Library. companion lib. o.p. 2.95 (*0-448-05453-1*); pap. ed (IJL) o.p. 4.95 (*0-686-76870-1*) Putnam Pub Group.
—Aesop's Fables. Paxton, Tom, retold by. Rayevsky, Robert, illus. LC 88-1652. 40p. (ps-2). 1988. 13.95 (*0-688-07360-3*); PLB 13.88 (*0-688-07361-1*, Morrow Jr Bks) Morrow Jr Bks.
—Aesop's Fables. LC 89-62860. 80p. (ps up). 1990. 4.95 (*0-89471-795-2*) Running Pr.
—Aesop's Fables. Hejduk, John, illus. LC 90-26710. 32p. 1991. 17.95 (*0-8478-1364-9*) Rizzoli Intl.
—Aesop's Fables. LC 91-2414. (ps-3). 1992. write for info. (*0-15-200350-9*, HB Juv Bks) HarBrace.
—Aesop's Fables. (Illus.). 96p. (Orig.). (ps-3). 1994. pap. 1.00 (*0-486-28020-9*) Dover.
—Fables. Gooden, Stephen, illus. L'Estrange, Roger, tr. LC 92-53179. (Illus.). 224p. 1992. 12.95 (*0-679-41790-7*, Evrymans Lib Childs Class) Knopf.
—The Tortoise & the Hare. Alchemy II, Inc. Staff, illus. 26p. 1988. incl. cassette 9.95 (*1-55578-902-1*) Worlds Wonder.
—The Wind & the Sun. Watts, Bernadette, illus. LC 92-2653. 32p. (gr. k-3). 1992. 14.95 (*1-55858-162-6*); PLB 14.88 (*1-55858-163-4*) North-South Bks NYC.
Aesop & Holder, Heidi. Aesop's Fables. LC 33-31662. (Illus.). 1981. pap. 16.00 (*0-670-10643-7*) Viking Child Bks.
Aesop's Fables. 1989. 12.99 (*0-517-67901-9*) Random Hse Value.
Andersen, Hans Christian. Emperor's New Clothes. Ford, Pamela B., illus. LC 78-18063. 32p. (gr. k-4). 1979. PLB 9.79 (*0-89375-132-4*); pap. 1.95 (*0-89375-110-3*) Troll Assocs.
Anno, Mitsumasa, retold by. & illus. Anno's Aesop: A Book of Fables by Aesop & Mr. Fox. LC 88-60087. 64p. (ps-2). 1989. 18.95 (*0-531-05774-7*); PLB 18.99 (*0-531-08374-8*) Orchard Bks Watts.
Ash, Russell & Higton, Bernard, eds. Aesop's Fables: A Classic Illustrated Edition. (Illus.). 1990. 15.95 (*0-87701-780-8*) Chronicle Bks.
Avi. The Bird, the Frog, & the Light: A Fable. Henry, Matthew, illus. LC 93-4886. 1994. write for info. (*0-531-06808-0*); PLB write for info. (*0-531-08658-5*) Orchard Bks Watts.
Backstein, Karen. The Blind Men & the Elephant, Level 3. 1992. 2.95 (*0-590-45813-2*) Scholastic Inc.
Bader, Barbara, retold by. Aesop & Company: With Scenes from His Legendary Life. Geisert, Arthur, illus. 64p. 1991. 16.45 (*0-395-50597-6*, Sandpiper) HM.
Barnes-Murphy, Frances, retold by. Aesop's Fables. LC 93-48462. (Illus.). 1994. 19.95 (*0-688-07051-5*) Lothrop.
Barnett, Carol. Boy Who Cried Wolf. (ps-3). 1990. 7.95 (*0-8442-9419-5*, Natl Textbk) NTC Pub Grp.
—Lion & the Mouse. (ps-3). 1990. 7.95 (*0-8442-9420-9*, Natl Textbk) NTC Pub Grp.
—Milkmaid & Her Pail. (ps-3). 1990. 7.95 (*0-8442-9421-7*, Natl Textbk) NTC Pub Grp.
Bird, E. J. Ten Tall Tales. LC 84-12086. (Illus.). 56p. (gr. 2-6). 1984. PLB 14.95 (*0-87614-267-6*) Carolrhoda Bks.
Black, Fiona. Aesop's Fables. (ps-3). 1991. 6.95 (*0-8362-4914-3*) Andrews & McMeel.

Brett, Jan. Town Mouse, Country Mouse. Brett, Jan, illus. LC 93-41227. 32p. (ps-3). 1994. PLB 15.95 (*0-399-22622-2*, Putnam) Putnam Pub Group.

Calder, Alexander. Fables of Aesop According to Sir Roger L'Estrange. (Illus.). 124p. (gr. k-6). pap. 3.95 (*0-486-21780-9*) Dover.

Calmenson, Stephanie, retold by. The Children's Aesop: Selected Fables. Byrd, Robert, illus. LC 91-73884. 64p. (ps-3). 1992. 14.95 (*1-56397-041-4*) Boyds Mills Pr.

Chaikin, Miriam. Three Aesop Fox Fables. (gr. 4-7). 1992. pap. 7.70 (*0-395-61580-1*, Clarion Bks) HM.

Ching. The Baboon's Umbrella. LC 91-7952. (Illus.). 24p. (ps-3). 1991. PLB 12.85 (*0-516-05131-8*); pap. 4.95 (*0-516-45131-6*) Childrens.

Clark, Margaret G. Best of Aesop's Fables. (ps-4). 1990. 16.95 (*0-316-14499-1*, Joy St Bks) Little.

Clauss, J., ed. Timeless Children's Tales from Around the World. (Illus.). (gr. 5-6). 1976. lib. bdg. 21.95x (*0-88411-992-0*, Pub. by Aeonian Pr) Amereon Ltd.

Cole, Judith. Another Tortoise & a Different Hare. Van Dun, Anke, illus. 32p. (gr. k-6). 1993. 12.95 (*0-918080-31-2*) Treasure Chest.

Collodi. Le Avventure di Pinocchio. (gr. 7-12). pap. 6.95 (*0-88436-050-4*, 55254) EMC.

Constantopoulos, E. Aesop's Fables. (GRE., Illus.). 160p. (gr. 2-3). 4.00 (*0-686-79630-6*); wkbk. 2.50 (*0-686-79631-4*) Divry.

Craig, Helen, retold by. & illus. The Town Mouse & the Country Mouse. LC 91-58761. 32p. (ps up). 1992. 13. 95 (*1-56402-102-5*) Candlewick Pr.

Culbertson, Roger & Zorn, Steven, eds. Aesop's Fables. Yerkes, Lane, illus. 12p. 1994. pop-up bk. with audiocassette 12.95 (*1-56138-365-1*) Running Pr.

Deibert, Alvin N. B. J. & the Language of the Woodland. Joy, Carol, illus. LC 82-24422. 48p. (Orig.). (gr. 2-6). 1983. pap. 7.50 (*0-87743-701-7*, 353-019, Pub. by Bellwood Pr) Bahai.

De Paola, Tomie. The Wind & the Sun. LC 94-20301. (Illus.). 1994. pap. 3.95 (*0-382-24657-8*) Silver Burdett Pr.

Desnos, Robert. Chantefables. Annen, Sharon, tr. from FRE. Annen, Charles, illus. LC 84-61257. 60p. (gr. 1-6). 1988. 17.95 (*0-9613938-0-7*) Penstemon Pr.

Fahy, Mary. The Tree That Survived the Winter. Antonucci, Emil, illus. 64p. (gr. 8-12). 1989. pap. 8.95 (*0-8091-0432-6*) Paulist Pr.

Farnagle, A. E. & Smith, W. Hovey. Farnagle's Fables for Children & Adults. Crawford, Kimberly Ann, illus. 64p. (Orig.). (gr. 1-5). 1984. pap. 4.25 (*0-916565-04-1*) Whitehall Pr.

Fisher, Lucretia. Two Monsters: A Fable. Jardine, Thomas, illus. LC 76-21684. 48p. (ps up). 1976. pap. 3.95 (*0-916144-08-9*) Stemmer Hse.

Flett, Douglas & Fletcher, Guy. The Goose That Laid the Golden Egg. 38p. (gr. 3-6). 1991. pap. 69.95 (*1-56516-003-7*) Houston IN.

—The Hare & the Tortoise. 38p. (gr. 3-6). 1991. pap. 69. 95 (*1-56516-004-5*) Houston IN.

Galdone, Paul. Monkey & The Crocodile. Galdone, Paul, illus. LC 78-79939. 32p. (ps-3). 1987. 13.45 (*0-395-28806-1*, Pub. by Clarion); pap. 4.80 (*0-89919-524-5*, Pub. by Clarion) HM.

—Three Aesop Fox Fables. Galdone, Paul, illus. LC 79-133061. 32p. (ps-2). 1979. 13.45 (*0-395-28810-X*, Clarion Bks) HM.

Garside, Alice H. The Garside Readers, 6 vols. Meeks, Catherine F., illus. 1990. Set. pap. 6.25 (*1-882063-18-X*) Cottage Pr MA.

Ginsburg, Mirra. Merry-Go-Round: Four Stories. Aruego, Jose & Dewey, Ariane, illus. LC 90-30439. 48p. 1992. 15.00 (*0-688-09256-X*); PLB 14.93 (*0-688-09257-8*) Greenwillow.

Goffin, Josse. Who Is the Boss? Goffin, Josse, illus. 32p. (gr. k-3). 1992. 13.45 (*0-395-61192-X*, Clarion Bks) HM.

Grimm, Jacob & Grimm, Wilhelm K. Little Red Cap. Crawford, Elizabeth D., tr. from GER. Zwerger, Lisbeth, illus. LC 82-14211. 24p. (ps-3). 1983. PLB 11.88 (*0-688-01716-9*) Morrow Jr Bks.

Hare & the Tortoise. 24p. (ps-3). 1989. 2.25 (*1-56288-160-4*) Checkerboard.

The Hare & the Tortoise; The Travelers & the Bear, 2 bks. in 1. (Illus.). 24p. (Orig.). (gr. 1-4). 1993. pap. 2.50 (*1-56144-305-0*, Honey Bear Bks) Modern Pub NYC.

Hegeman, Kathryn T., ed. Aesop's Fables, 4 vols. (gr. 1-4). 1984. Set. 16.00 (*0-89824-050-6*); Vol. I. 5.00 (*0-89824-051-4*); Vol. II. 5.00 (*0-89824-052-2*); Vol. III. 5.00 (*0-89824-053-0*); Vol. IV. 5.00 (*0-89824-054-9*) Trillium Pr.

Heins, Ethel L., retold by. The Cat & the Cook & Other Fables of Krylov. Lobel, Anita, illus. 32p. (gr. 1 up). Date not set. write for info. (*0-688-12310-4*); PLB write for info. (*0-688-12311-2*) Greenwillow.

Holder, Heidi, illus. Aesop's Fables. 32p. (ps-3). 1993. pap. 4.99 (*0-14-054872-6*) Puffin Bks.

Hwa-I Publishing Co., Staff. Chinese Children's Stories, Vol. 16: How to Build a Nest, Moving the Mountain. Ching, Emily, et al, eds. Wonder Kids Publications Staff, tr. from CHI. (Illus.). 28p. (gr. 3-6). 1991. Repr. of 1988 ed. 7.95 (*1-56162-016-5*) Wonder Kids.

Jacobs, Joseph, ed. The Fables of Aesop. LC 66-29408. (Illus.). (gr. k up). 1966. pap. 8.95 (*0-8052-0138-6*) Schocken.

James, Henry G. Limericks, Fables & Poems. (Orig.). (gr. 12). 1987. 12.00 (*0-942951-00-X*); PLB 12.00 (*0-942951-01-8*); pap. 12.00 (*0-942951-02-6*) Universal Res LA.

Kavanaugh, James. A Village Called Harmony - A Fable. 2nd ed. Biamonte, Daniel, illus. LC 90-62063. 70p. 1990. pap. 7.95 (*1-878995-06-5*) S J Nash Pub.

Kraus, Robert. Fables Aesop Never Wrote. Kraus, Robert, illus. 32p. (gr. k up). 1994. PLB 14.99 (*0-670-85630-4*) Viking Child Bks.

Krill, Richard M. Forty Fabulous Fables of Aesop. Grant, Peggy, illus. 90p. (gr. 3-6). 1982. 7.95 (*0-942624-00-9*) Promethean Arts.

La Fontaine. The Hare & the Tortoise. Wildsmith, Brian, illus. 32p. 1987. 16.00 (*0-19-279625-9*); pap. 7.50 (*0-19-272126-7*) OUP.

La Fontaine, Jean de. A Hundred Fables of La Fontaine. Billinghurst, P. J., illus. 208p. (gr. 2-6). 2.98 (*0-517-40206-8*) Random Hse Value.

Lang, Jenny, adapted by. The Tortoise & the Hare. Baker, Darrell, illus. 24p. (ps-k). 1993. 9.00 (*0-307-74814-6*, 64814, Golden Pr) Western Pub.

Lanhei Kim Park. The Heavenly Pomegranate. 76p. (gr. 5-7). 1973. pap. text ed. 3.00 (*0-686-05501-2*) Simpson Pub.

Leonard, Robert J. Stupid Stories: Nonstop Nonsense for Children of All Ages. Green, Herb, illus. 108p. (Orig.). (gr. 5-10). 1989. pap. 5.95 (*0-930753-05-4*, Pub. by Spectacle Ln Pr) Spect Ln Pr.

Levine, David, selected by. The Fables of Aesop. Gregory, Patrick & Gregory, Justina, trs. Levine, David, illus. LC 84-12894. 108p. (gr. 8). 1984. 13.95 (*0-87645-074-5*, Pub. by Gambit); pap. 8.95 (*0-87645-116-4*) Harvard Common Pr.

Lewis, Shari. The Boat Contest: The Lion & the Mouse. Marshall, Blaine, ed. (Illus.). 32p. (ps-3). 1993. 9.95 (*0-8094-7446-8*) Time-Life.

—Lamb Chop's Fables: The Lamb Who Could Featuring Aesop's The Tortoise & the Hare. Doyle, Robert A., ed. Campana, Manny & Pidgeon, Jean, illus. 32p. Date not set. write for info. (*0-8094-7804-8*) Time-Life.

The Lion & the Mouse; The Wind & the Sun, 2 bks. in 1. (Illus.). 24p. (Orig.). (gr. 1-4). 1993. pap. 2.50 (*1-56144-302-6*, Honey Bear Bks) Modern Pub NYC.

Lionni, Leo. Frederick's Fables: A Leo Lionni Treasury of Favorite Stories. reissued ed. Lionni, Leo, illus. Bettelheim, Bruno, intro. by. LC 85-5186. (Illus.). 144p. (ps-3). 1993. 20.00 (*0-394-87710-1*) Knopf Bks Yng Read.

Lobel, Arnold. Fables. LC 79-2004. (Illus.). 48p. (gr. 1-4). 1983. pap. 5.95 (*0-06-443046-4*, Trophy) HarpC Child Bks.

—Fables: (Fabulas) (SPA.). (gr. 1-6). 21.95 (*84-204-4552-5*) Santillana.

MacDonald, George. The Light Princess. rev. ed. Sendak, Maurice, illus. LC 69-14981. 120p. (gr. 1 up). 1969. 15.00 (*0-374-34455-8*); pap. 4.95, 1984 (*0-374-44458-7*) FS&G.

McFarland, John. The Exploding Frog: & Other Fables from Aesop. Marshall, James, illus. (gr. 3 up). 1981. pap. 8.70i (*0-685-03085-7*, Pub. by Atlantic Pr) (*0-316-55577-0*) Little.

McGovern, Ann, retold by. Aesop's Fables. 80p. (gr. 4-7). 1990. pap. 2.75 (*0-590-43880-8*) Scholastic Inc.

McKissack, Patricia & McKissack, Fredrick. El Ratoncito del Campo y el Ratoncito de la Ciudad: Country Mouse & City Mouse. LC 86-21565. 32p. (ps-2). 1986. pap. 3.95 (*0-516-52362-7*) Childrens.

Magorian, James. The Bonkly Dribblefink Fables. LC 87-70706. (Illus.). 16p. (gr. 1-4). 1987. pap. 3.00 (*0-930674-24-3*) Black Oak.

Martell, Ralph. Aesop's Fables in Song. Martell, Ralph, illus. 21p. (gr. k-5). 1987. bk. & cassette 9.95 (*0-941977-00-5*, RTB-1) Ralmar Enter.

The Miller & His Donkey; The Greedy Dog, 2 bks. in 1. (Illus.). 24p. (Orig.). (gr. 1-4). 1993. pap. 2.50 (*1-56144-304-2*, Honey Bear Bks) Modern Pub NYC.

Miller, Edna. Mousekin's Fables. Miller, Edna, illus. 28p. (ps-3). 1982. 11.95 (*0-13-604165-5*) P-H.

Mooy, John & Stroschin, Jane. Sidney: The Story of a Kingfisher. Stroschin, Jane, illus. 32p. (gr. k-6). 1991. text ed. 15.00 (*1-883960-08-8*); pap. 7.00 (*1-883960-09-6*) Henry Quill.

Morse, Robert E. Fabulae Latinae. (LAT.). 36p. (Orig.). (gr. 9-12). 1992. pap. 2.50 spiral bdg. (*0-939507-42-0*, B729) Amer Classical.

Nister, Ernest. Golden Tales from Long Ago, 3 vols. Nister, Ernest, illus. LC 80-7614. (24p. ea.). 1980. Set. 6.95 (*0-440-03015-3*) Delacorte.

Oana, Katherine. Kippy Koala. Cooper, William, ed. Butrick, Lyn M., illus. LC 85-51823. 16p. (Orig.). (ps up). 1985. pap. text ed. 3.72 (*0-914127-21-7*) Univ Class.

El Palito Feo. (SPA.). (ps-3). 1993. pap. 4.95 (*0-307-72106-X*, Golden Pr) Western Pub.

Parry, Marian, illus. City Mouse - Country Mouse & Two More Mouse Tales from Aesop. (gr. 2-3). 1989. big bk. 28.67 (*0-590-65228-1*) Scholastic Inc.

Paxton, Tom. Belling the Cat: And Other Aesop's Fables. Rayevsky, Robert, illus. LC 89-39851. 40p. (ps up). 1990. 13.95 (*0-688-08158-4*); PLB 13.88 (*0-688-08159-2*, Morrow Jr Bks) Morrow Jr Bks.

—Birds of a Feather: And Other Aesop's Fables. Payevsky, Robert, illus. LC 92-2909. 40p. (ps up). 1993. 15.00 (*0-688-10400-2*); PLB 14.93 (*0-688-10401-0*) Morrow Jr Bks.

Paxton, Tom, retold by. Androcles & the Lion: And Other Aesop's Fables. Rayevsky, Robert, illus. LC 90-19173. 40p. (ps up). 1991. 13.95 (*0-688-09682-4*); PLB 13.88 (*0-688-09683-2*) Morrow Jr Bks.

Peck, M. Scott. The Friendly Snowflake: A Fable of Faith, Love & Family. Peck, Christopher S., illus. 40p. (gr. 3 up). 14.95 (*1-878685-28-7*) Turner Pub GA.

Percy, Graham. City Mouse & Country Mouse, Heron & the Fish, Crow & the Fox, Lion & the Mouse, 4 bks. Percy, Graham, illus. 32p. (ps-2). 1993. Set. 12.95 (*0-8050-2563-4*, Bks Young Read) H Holt & Co.

—Favorite Fable Special. 1993. write for info. (*0-8050-3083-2*) H Holt & Co.

Percy, Graham, retold by. & illus. The Tortoise & the Hare: And Other Favorite Fables, 4 bks. (ps-2). 1993. Set, 32p. eac. bk. boxed 12.95 (*0-8050-2556-1*) H Holt & Co.

Phillips, Gina, ed. Three Minute Aesop's Fables. Persico, F. S., illus. 24p. 1991. 2.98 (*1-56156-088-X*) Kidsbks.

Plante, Patricia & Bergman, David. The Turtle & the Two Ducks: Animal Fables Retold from La Fontaine. Rockwell, Anne, illus. LC 81-47409. 32p. (ps-2). 1981. (Crowell Jr Bks) HarpC Child Bks.

Polette, Nancy. Exploring Themes with Aesop's Fables & Picture Books. (Illus.). 48p. (gr. 2-6). 1992. pap. 5.95 (*1-879287-12-9*) Bk Lures.

Poskanzer, Susan C., retold by. Aesop's Fables. Bettoli, Delana, illus. 64p. (gr. 2 up). 1992. 10.95 (*0-671-74116-0*); lib. bdg. 12.95 (*0-671-74117-9*) Silver Pr.

Pride, Mary. Too Many Chickens: Old Wise Tales. 64p. (ps-3). 1990. 8.95 (*1-56121-010-2*) Wolgemuth & Hyatt.

Rackham, Arthur, illus. Aesop's Fables. (gr. 2-9). 1992. 7.99 (*0-517-17198-8*) Random Hse Value.

Reiser, Lynn. Two Mice in Three Fables. LC 93-35935. 32p. 1995. write for info. (*0-688-13389-4*); PLB write for info. (*0-688-13390-8*) Greenwillow.

Resnick, Jane P. The Ant & the Dove. Lindy, Heidi, illus. 1992. bds. 3.25 (*0-8378-2523-7*) Gibson.

—The Fox & the Crow. Lindy, Heidi, illus. 1992. bds. 3.25 (*0-8378-2525-3*) Gibson.

—The Lion & the Mouse. Lindy, Heidi, illus. 1992. bds. 3.25 (*0-8378-2526-1*) Gibson.

—The Tortoise & the Hare. Lindy, Heidi, illus. 1992. bds. 3.25 (*0-8378-2524-5*) Gibson.

Rice, Eve, adapted by. & illus. Once in a Wood: Ten Tales from Aesop. LC 92-24605. 64p. (gr. 1 up). 1993. pap. 4.95 (*0-688-12268-X*, Mulberry) Morrow.

Sanchez, Sonia. Adventures of Small Head, Square Head & Fat Head. new ed. Taiwo, illus. 32p. (gr. 2-6). 1973. 11.95 (*0-89388-094-9*) Okpaku Communications.

Schecter, Ellen. The Boy Who Cried Wolf. (ps-3). 1994. pap. 3.99 (*0-553-37232-7*) Bantam.

Schecter, Ellen, retold by. The Boy Who Cried Wolf! Chalk, Gary, illus. (gr. 4 up). 1994. 10.95 (*0-553-09043-7*) Bantam.

Shulevitz, Uri. El Tesoro: The Treasure. Negroni, Maria, tr. (SPA., Illus.). 32p. (ps-3). 1992. 16.00 (*0-374-37422-8*, Mirasol) FS&G.

Solomon, L. Ursa. The Rotten Chicken: A Modern Fable. rev., 2nd ed. Cummings, B. Martin, illus. Lewis, Benjamin G., frwd. by. (Illus.). 34p. 1989. Repr. of 1984 ed. wire 7.95 (*0-9615756-3-8*) Henchanted Bks.

Steffens, J. & Carr, J. Myths & Fables. (gr. 7-12). 1984. 9.95 (*0-88160-113-6*, LW 1008) Learning Wks.

Stevens, Janet. The Tortoise & the Hare: An Aesop Fable. Steven, Janet, illus. LC 83-18668. 32p. (ps-3). 1984. reinforced bdg. 14.95 (*0-8234-0510-9*); pap. 5.95 (*0-8234-0564-8*) Holiday.

Sturrock, Walt, illus. Aesop's Fables. 48p. (ps-3). 1992. 5.95 (*0-88101-262-9*) Unicorn Pub.

Tell, Paul. Fun with Aesop, Vol. I. Ross, Connie, illus. 32p. (gr. 2-6). 1991. pap. 2.25 (*1-878893-06-8*) Telcraft Bks.

—Fun with Aesop, Vol. II. Ross, Connie, illus. 32p. (gr. 2-6). 1991. pap. 2.25 (*1-878893-07-6*) Telcraft Bks.

—Fun with Aesop, Vol. III. Ross, Connie, illus. 32p. (gr. 2-6). 1991. pap. 2.25 (*1-878893-08-4*) Telcraft Bks.

—Fun with Aesop, 3 vols. Ross, Connie, illus. 32p. (gr. 2-6). 1991. Set. pap. 6.75 (*1-878893-09-2*) Telcraft Bks.

—Fun with Aesop Reader. Ross, Connie, illus. LC 91-90956. 96p. (gr. 2-6). 1991. 9.95 (*1-878893-05-X*); lib. bdg. 14.95 (*1-878893-10-6*); pap. 5.95 (*1-878893-04-1*) Telcraft Bks.

Testa, Fulvio, illus. Aesop's Fables. 48p. (gr. 2 up). 1989. incl. dust jacket 12.95 (*0-8120-5958-1*) Barron.

Thomas, Vernon. Aesop's Fables. Bhushan, Reboti, illus. 135p. (gr. 1-7). 1981. 7.50 (*0-89744-231-8*, Pub. by Hemkunt IA) Auromere.

The Town Mouse & the Country Mouse; The Boy Who Cried Wolf, 2 bks. in 1. (Illus.). 24p. (Orig.). (gr. 1-4). 1993. pap. 2.50 (*1-56144-303-4*, Honey Bear Bks) Modern Pub NYC.

Vincent, Eric. Aesop's Fables. (Illus.). 52p. Date not set. pap. 4.95 (*1-57209-026-X*) Classics Int Ent.

Warburg, Sandol S. Free. Oliver, Jenni, illus. LC 75-40013. 48p. (gr. 1 up). 1976. PLB 5.95 (*0-395-24210-X*) HM.

Watkins, Dawn L. Pocket Change: Five Small Fables. Habegger, Christa & Sidwell, Mark, eds. Davis, Tim, illus. 34p. (Orig.). (gr. 2-6). 1992. pap. 4.95 (*0-89084-645-6*) Bob Jones Univ Pr.

Wildsmith, Brian & LaFontaine, Jean de. The Rich Man & the Shoe-Maker. (Illus.). (ps-3). 1965. pap. 7.50 (*0-19-272104-6*) OUP.

Williams, Jay & Williams, Victoria. The Water of Life. McQueen, Lucinda, illus. 40p. (gr. k-12). 1980. 15.00 (*0-89486-721-0*, T5129) Hazelden.
Wonder Kids Publications Group Staff (USA) & Hwa-I Publishing Co., Staff. Fables: Chinese Children's Stories, Vols. 16-20. Ching, Emily & Ching, Ko-Shee, eds. Wonder Kids Publications Staff, tr. from CHI. Hwa-I Publishing Co., Staff, illus. LC 90-60794. (gr. 3-6). 1991. Repr. of 1988 ed. Five vol. set, 28p. ea. bk. 39.75 (*0-685-58703-7*) Wonder Kids.
Young, Ed. Seven Blind Mice. Young, Ed, illus. 40p. (ps-6). 1992. PLB 16.95 (*0-399-22261-8*, Philomel Bks) Putnam Pub Group.
Zwerger, Lisbeth, illus. Aesop's Fables. (ps up). 1991. pap. 15.95 (*0-88708-108-8*); pap. 4.95 (*0-88708-179-7*) Picture Bk Studio.

FABRIC PICTURES
see Collage

FABRICS
see Textile Industry and Fabrics

FACETIAE
see Wit and Humor

FACTORIES

Steele, Philip. Factory Through the Ages. Lapper, Ivan, et al, illus. LC 91-33262. 32p. (gr. 3-6). 1993. PLB 11.89 (*0-8167-2729-5*); pap. text ed. 3.95 (*0-8167-2730-9*) Troll Assocs.
Sundvall, Viveca. Mimi & the Biscuit Factory. Eriksson, Eva, illus. Bibb, Eric, tr. (Illus.). 32p. (ps up). 1989. 12.95 (*91-29-59142-2*, Pub. by R & S Bks) FS&G.
Weisman, Joanne B. Lowell Mill Girls: Life in the Factory. 48p. (gr. 5-12). 1991. pap. 4.95 (*1-878668-06-4*) Disc Enter Ltd.

FACULTY (EDUCATION)
see Educators; Teachers

FAIENCE
see Pottery

FAIR EMPLOYMENT PRACTICE
see Discrimination in Employment

FAIRIES
see also Fairy Tales

Alexander, Sue. More Witch, Goblin & Ghost Stories. Winter, Jeanette, illus. LC 78-3280. (gr. 1-4). 1978. 6.95 (*0-394-83933-1*) Pantheon.
Andersdatter, Karla M. Marissa the Tooth Fairy. write for info. In Between.
Banks, Lynne R. The Fairy Rebel. Geldart, William M., illus. LC 87-28740. 128p. (gr. 5 up). 1988. 12.95 (*0-385-24483-5*) Doubleday.
Barker, Cicely M. Fairy Magic: Pop-up Book. (Illus.). 5p. (ps-3). 1993. 7.95 (*0-7232-4038-8*) Warne.
—The Fairy Necklaces. (Illus.). 64p. 1992. 6.95 (*0-7232-4000-0*) Warne.
—Fairy Places: Pop-up Book. (Illus.). 5p. (ps-3). 1993. 7.95 (*0-7232-4039-6*) Warne.
—The Flower Fairies Activity Book. (Illus.). 24p. (gr. 3 up). 1992. pap. 5.95 (*0-7232-3994-0*) Warne.
—The Flower Fairies Poster Activity Book. (Illus.). 24p. 1993. 6.95 (*0-7232-4037-X*) Warne.
—Four Seasons of the Flower Fairies: A Flower Fairies Gift Set, 4 bks. (Illus.). 1992. Boxed Set. 24.00 (*0-7232-5181-9*) Warne.
—A Treasury of Flower Fairies. (Illus.). 128p. 1992. deluxe ed. 19.95 (*0-7232-3796-4*, Warne) Viking Child Bks.
—A World of Flower Fairies. (Illus.). 128p. 1993. 20.00 (*0-7232-4002-7*) Warne.
Barker, Cicely M., illus. A Flower Fairies Postcard Book. 30p. (ps up). 1991. pap. 7.95 (*0-7232-3710-7*) Warne.
Barrie, J. M. Peter Pan in Kensington Gardens. 16.95 (*0-8488-0427-9*) Amereon Ltd.
Barrie, James M. Peter Pan in Kensington Gardens & Peter & Wendy. Hollindale, Peter, intro. by. (Illus.). 288p. 1991. pap. 5.95 (*0-19-282593-3*) OUP.
Baum, L. Frank. The Sea Fairies. Neill, John R., illus. 240p. 1987. 19.95 (*0-929605-03-9*); pap. 11.95 (*0-929605-00-4*) Books Wonder.
Blyton, Enid. The Yellow Fairy Book. Edwards, Gunvor, illus. 196p. (ps-1). 1994. pap. 6.95 (*0-09-999730-4*, Pub. by Hutchinson UK) Trafalgar.
Brett, Jan. The Trouble with Trolls. (Illus.). 32p. (ps-3). 1992. 14.95 (*0-399-22336-3*, Putnam) Putnam Pub Group.
Briggs, Katherine M. An Encyclopedia of Fairies: Hobgoblins, Brownies, Bogies, & Other Supernatural Creatures. LC 76-12939. (Illus.). (gr. 4 up). 1978. 12.95 (*0-394-40918-3*); pap. 19.00 (*0-394-73467-X*) Pantheon.
Burnett, Frances H. The Spring Cleaning: As Told by Queen Crosspatch. Cady, Harrison, illus. 56p. (gr. 3-6). 1992. 4.99 (*0-517-07248-3*, Pub. by Derrydale Bks) Random Hse Value.
—The Troubles of Queen Silver-Bell: As Told by Queen Crosspatch. Cady, Harrison, illus. 56p. (gr. 3-6). 1992. 4.99 (*0-517-07247-5*, Pub. by Derrydale Bks) Random Hse Value.
Cole, Joanna. Mixed-Up Magic. Donnelly, Judy, ed. Kelley, True, illus. LC 87-14965. 32p. (gr. k-3). 1987. 8.95 (*0-8038-9298-5*) Hastings.
Cosgrove, Stephen. Gnome from Nome. James, Robin, illus. 32p. (Orig.). (gr. 1-4). 1974. pap. 2.95 (*0-8431-0555-0*) Price Stern.
Cox, Palmer. The Brownies' Merry Adventures. Cox, Palmer, illus. LC 93-563. 224p. 1993. 6.00 (*1-56957-901-6*) Shambhala Pubns.
D'Aulaire, Ingri. D'Aulaire's Trolls. (ps-3). 1993. pap. 8.00 (*0-440-40779-6*) Dell.
Denan, Corinne. Goblin Tales. LC 79-66326. (Illus.). 48p. (gr. 3-6). 1980. lib. bdg. 9.89 (*0-89375-320-3*); pap. 2.95 (*0-89375-319-X*) Troll Assocs.
Ellis, Carol. There's a Troll in My Closet. 1994. pap. 2.99 (*0-671-87161-7*, Minstrel Bks) PB.
—There's a Troll in My Popcorn. 1994. pap. 3.50 (*0-671-87162-5*, Minstrel Bks) PB.
Enright, Elizabeth. Zeee. LC 92-29611. (ps-3). 1993. 15.95 (*0-15-299958-2*) HarBrace.
Fitzgerald, Jean. The Golden Gate Bridge Troll. Donovan, Karen, illus. 48p. (Orig.). (gr. k-2). 1978. pap. 6.95x (*0-9618225-0-3*) Bridge Troll Pr.
Forest, Heather. The Woman Who Flummoxed the Fairies. Gaber, Susan, illus. 28p. (ps-3). 1990. 14.95 (*0-15-299150-6*) HarBrace.
Gilligan, Shannon. The Fairy Kidnap. 64p. (Orig.). (gr. 2 up). 1985. pap. 2.25 (*0-553-15488-5*) Bantam.
Hart, Tom. Fairies & Friends. Pearson-Cooper, Michelle, illus. 120p. 1981. 8.95 (*0-685-01043-0*, Pub. by Quartet England) Charles River Bks.
Inkpen, Mick. This Troll That Troll. (Illus.). (gr. 4-7). 1993. 4.99 (*1-878685-70-8*, Bedrock Press) Turner Pub GA.
Jewell. Two Silly Trolls, No. 2. Date not set. 14.00 (*0-06-024292-2*); PLB 13.89 (*0-06-024293-0*) HarpC Child Bks.
Jewell, Nancy. Two Silly Trolls. Thiesing, Lisa, illus. LC 90-4387. 64p. (gr. k-3). 1992. 14.00 (*0-06-022829-6*); PLB 13.89 (*0-06-022830-X*) HarpC Child Bks.
—Two Silly Trolls. Thiesing, Lisa, illus. LC 90-4387. 64p. (ps-3). 1994. pap. 3.50 (*0-06-444173-3*, Trophy) HarpC Child Bks.
Kimmel, Eric A. Hershel & the Hanukkah Goblins. Hyman, Trina S., illus. LC 89-1954. 32p. (ps-3). 1989. reinforced bdg. 15.95 (*0-8234-0769-1*); pap. 6.95 (*0-8234-1131-1*) Holiday.
Koski, Mary. The Stowaway Fairy in Hawaii. (Illus.). 36p. (gr. k-5). 1991. 9.95 (*0-89610-225-4*) Island Heritage.
Kovacs, Deborah. The Tooth Fairy Book. Lydecker, Laura, illus. LC 92-53679. 32p. 1992. 9.95 (*1-56138-147-0*) Running Pr.
Lagerlof, Selma. The Changeling. Stevens, Susanna, tr. from SWE. Winter, Jeanette, illus. LC 90-45277. 48p. (gr. k-5). 1992. 15.00 (*0-679-81035-8*); PLB 15.99 (*0-679-91035-2*) Knopf Bks Yng Read.
Leedy, Loreen. The Potato Party & Other Troll Tales. Leedy, Loreen, illus. LC 89-1746. 32p. (ps-3). 1989. reinforced 14.95 (*0-8234-0761-6*) Holiday.
Lemoine, Charles A. Louisiana's Cypress Bayou Elves: Pontain the Trapper. Lemoine, Charles A., illus. 40p. (Orig.). (gr. 1-12). 1986. pap. 5.00 (*0-941327-01-9*) Charles A Lemoine.
Linnell, Andrew & Auer, Varvara. The Dance of the Elves. (Illus.). 32p. (Orig.). (ps). 1984. pap. 13.50 (*0-936132-68-X*) Merc Pr NY.
Lisle, Janet T. Afternoon of the Elves. (gr. 4-7). 1991. pap. 2.75 (*0-590-43944-8*, Apple Paperbacks) Scholastic Inc.
McAllister, Frank & McAllister, Fran. The Tooth Fairy Legend. LC 76-9595. (gr. k-4). 1976. 9.95 (*0-916864-01-4*) Block.
Maeterlinck, Maurice. The Blue Bird. Goscinsky, Michael, illus. Poesnecker, Gerald E. & Poesnecker, Gerald E.intro. by. Bd. with The Betrothal. 304p. (gr. 1 up). 1985. 16.95 (*0-932785-02-6*); pap. 10.95 (*0-932785-01-8*) Philos Pub.
Marshall, Edward. Troll Country. Marshall, James, illus. LC 79-19324. 56p. (ps-3). 1980. pap. 4.95 (*0-8037-6210-0*) Dial Bks Young.
Mennella, Roxanna, et al. Fairies, Elves & Gnomes. (Illus.). 32p. (Orig.). (gr. 3-8). 1985. pap. 2.00x (*0-934830-38-X*, Dist. by Waterways Project) Ten Penny.
Myers, Bernice. Sidney Rella & the Glass Sneaker. Myers, Bernice, illus. LC 85-3044. 32p. (gr. k-3). 1985. RSBE 14.95 (*0-02-767790-7*, Macmillan Child Bk) Macmillan Child Grp.
Peters, Sharon. The Tooth Fairy. Sims, Deborah, illus. LC 81-5100. 32p. (gr. k-2). 1981. PLB 11.59 (*0-89375-519-2*); pap. 2.95 (*0-89375-520-6*) Troll Assocs.
Pini, Wendy & Pini, Richard. Elfquest: Captives of Blue Mountain. rev. ed. (Illus.). 192p. (gr. 4 up). 1988. pap. 17.95 (*0-936861-08-8*, Father Tree Pr) Warp Graphics.
Pope, Elizabeth M. The Perilous Gard. Cuffari, Richard, illus. LC 73-21648. 272p. (gr. 6 up). 1974. 16.95 (*0-395-18512-2*) HM.
Reader, Carl. The Twelfth Elf of Kindness. 53p. (gr. 4-6). 1990. pap. 7.00 (*0-9630560-0-X*) Reader.
Scheidl, Gerda M. Loretta & the Little Fairy. Unzner-Fischer, Christa, illus. James, J. Alison, tr. from GER. LC 92-33832. (Illus.). 32p. (gr. 2-3). 1993. 13.95 (*1-55858-185-5*); PLB 13.88 (*1-55858-186-3*) North-South Bks NYC.
Ullrich, Annie. Fairy Tea. Rawley-Whitaker, Jena, illus. 52p. (ps up). 1992. 16.95g (*1-879244-35-7*) Windom Bks.
Van Sickle, Carol S. With Love, the Fairies. LC 89-51346. 44p. (gr. k-4). 1990. 5.95 (*1-55523-240-X*) Winston-Derek.
Wangerin, Walter. Elisabeth & the Water-Troll. Healy, Deborah, illus. LC 90-4359. 64p. (gr. 3-7). 1991. HarpC Child Bks.
Wells, Rosemary. Fritz & the Mess Fairy. LC 90-26671. (Illus.). 32p. (ps-2). 1991. 14.00 (*0-8037-0981-1*); PLB 13.89 (*0-8037-0983-8*) Dial Bks Young.
Wood, Audrey. Tooth Fairy. LC 90-46911. 1989. 7.95 (*0-85953-237-2*); pap. 3.95 (*0-85953-238-0*) Childs Play.

FAIRS
see also Exhibitions

Bial, Raymond. County Fair. Bial, Raymond, illus. 40p. (gr. 3-6). 1992. 14.45 (*0-395-57644-X*) HM.
Gibbons, Gail. Country Fair. LC 93-30289. (ps-3). 1994. 14.95 (*0-316-30951-6*) Little.
Harshman, Marc. Only One. Garrison, Barbara, illus. LC 92-11349. 32p. (ps-3). 1993. 12.99 (*0-525-65116-0*, Cobblehill Bks) Dutton Child Bks.

FAIRS–FICTION

Brook, Ruth. Good for You, Lolly. Kondo, Vala, illus. LC 86-30733. 32p. (gr. k-3). 1988. PLB 11.89 (*0-8167-0914-9*); pap. text ed. 2.95 (*0-8167-0915-7*) Troll Assocs.
Casad, Mary B. Bluebonnet at the State Fair. Binder, Pat, illus. 40p. (gr. 2-4). 1985. 11.95 (*0-89015-530-5*) Sunbelt Media.
Froehlich, Margaret W. That Kookoory! Frazee, Marla, illus. LC 93-41833. 1995. write for info. (*0-15-277650-8*, Browndeer Pr) HarBrace.
Godden, Rumer. Candy Floss. Hogrogian, Nonny, illus. 64p. (ps-3). 1991. 16.95 (*0-399-21807-6*, Philomel) Putnam Pub Group.
Greenstein, Elaine. Mrs. Rose's Garden. Greenstein, Elaine, illus. 28p. (gr. k up). 1993. 14.95 (*0-88708-264-5*) Picture Bk Studio.
Kehret, Peg. Danger at the Fair. LC 94-16873. 1995. write for info. (*0-525-65182-9*, Cobblehill Bks) Dutton Child Bks.
Kiser, SuAnn. The Hog Call to End All! Gurney, John S., illus. LC 93-49392. 32p. (ps-2). 1994. 14.95 (*0-531-06826-9*); PLB 14.99 (*0-531-08676-3*) Orchard Bks Watts.
Lamb, Nancy & Singer, Muff. The World's Greatest Toe Show. Sims, Blanche, illus. LC 93-28440. 64p. (gr. 2-5). 1993. PLB 13.95 (*0-8167-3322-8*); pap. 3.95 (*0-8167-3323-6*) BrdgeWater.
Larke, Joe. Dopie Dope Goes to the Fair. Larke, Karol, illus. 49p. (gr. k-5). 1992. 13.95 (*0-9620112-7-4*) Grin A Bit.
Lawson, Robert. The Great Wheel. Lawson, Robert, illus. 180p. 1993. pap. 7.95 (*0-8027-7392-3*) Walker & Co.
Lord, Wendy. Gorilla on the Midway. LC 93-1051. 1994. pap. 4.99 (*0-7814-0892-X*, Chariot Bks) Chariot Family.
McOmber, Rachel B., ed. McOmber Phonics Storybooks: At the Fair. rev. ed. (Illus.). write for info. (*0-944991-60-2*) Swift Lrn Res.
Marsh, Carole. Mystery of the World's Fair. Marsh, Carol, illus. (Orig.). (gr. 3-9). 1994. pap. 14.95 (*0-935326-04-9*) Gallopade Pub Group.
Muntean, Michaela. The Very Bumpy Bus Ride. Wiseman, Bernard, illus. LC 81-16905. 48p. (ps-3). 1982. 5.95 (*0-8193-1079-4*); 5.95 (*0-8193-1080-8*) Parents.
—The Very Bumpy Bus Ride. Wiseman, Bernard, illus. LC 93-13042. 1993. PLB 13.27 (*0-8368-0980-7*) Gareth Stevens Inc.
National Geographic Staff. Fun at the Fair. (ps). 1993. 4.50 (*0-7922-1919-8*) Natl Geog.
Odgers, Sally F. Mrs. Honey's List. Cooper-Brown, Jean, illus. LC 93-6572. 1994. write for info. (*0-383-03703-4*) SRA Schl Grp.
Razvan. Two Little Shoes. Stupple, Deborah, tr. LC 92-40814. (Illus.). 32p. (ps-1). 1993. SBE 14.95 (*0-02-775667-X*, Bradbury Pr) Macmillan Child Grp.
Reese, Bob. Field Trip. Reese, Bob, illus. LC 92-12186. 24p. (ps-2). 1992. PLB 9.75 (*0-516-05579-8*) Childrens.
Stolz, Mary. Bartholomew Fair. LC 89-27230. 160p. (gr. 6 up). 1992. pap. 3.95 (*0-688-11501-2*, Pub. by Beech Tree Bks) Morrow.
Turner, Margret & Scott, Alyson. Come on Everybody! Let's Go to the Fair. 32p. (ps-k). 1991. pap. write for info. (*0-9630453-0-X*) Lifeworks.
Wild, Margaret. But Granny Did! Forss, Ian, illus. LC 92-31906. 1993. 3.75 (*0-383-03559-7*) SRA Schl Grp.

FAIRY PLAYS

Barrie, James Matthew. Peter Pan & Wendy. 1988. 7.99 (*0-517-66189-6*) Random Hse Value.
Shakespeare, William. Midsummer Night's Dream. Pitt, David G., intro. by. (gr. 10 up). 1965. pap. 1.95 (*0-8049-1005-7*, S5) Airmont.

FAIRY TALES
see also Folklore

Absolon, Karel B. The Tale of the Bad Macocha & the Fable of the Underground Punkva River. Absolon, K. B., ed. & illus. 40p. (Orig.). (gr. 4). 1984. pap. text ed. 12.00 (*0-930329-02-3*) KABEL Pubs.
Adams, Michael, illus. Andersen's Classic Fairy Tales. 48p. (gr. k-5). 1993. 5.95 (*0-88101-276-9*) Unicorn Pub.
—Andersen's Fables & Fairy Tales. 48p. (gr. k-5). 1993. 5.95 (*0-685-63134-6*) Unicorn Pub.
Aesop. Little Red Riding Hood. Dyer, Jane, illus. LC 85-70289. 18p. (ps). 1985. 3.95 (*0-448-10227-7*, G&D) Putnam Pub Group.
—Town Mouse & the Country Mouse. new ed. LC 78-18062. (Illus.). 32p. (gr. k-3). 1979. PLB 9.79 (*0-89375-131-6*); pap. 1.95 (*0-89375-109-X*) Troll Assocs.
Ahlberg, Allan. Ten in a Bed. Amstutz, Andre, illus. 112p. (gr. 2-6). 1991. pap. 3.99 (*0-14-032531-X*, Puffin) Puffin Bks.

Aiken, Joan. The Shoemaker's Boy. Ambrus, Victor G., illus. LC 93-6613. (ps-6). 1994. pap. 14.00 (*0-671-86647-8*, S&S BFYR) S&S Trade.
—The Stolen Lake: A Novel. LC 81-5015. 256p. (gr. 7 up). 1981. 10.95 (*0-385-28982-0*) Delacorte.
Aladdin. (ARA., Illus.). (gr. 5-12). 1987. 3.95x (*0-86685-182-8*) Intl Bk Ctr.
Aladdin & Other Tales from the Arabian Nights. LC 93-55071. 1993. 12.95 (*0-679-42533-0*) Knopf.
Aladdin & the Magic Lamp. 24p. (gr. k-3). 1992. pap. 2.50 (*1-56144-169-4*, Honey Bear Bks) Modern Pub NYC.
Alchemy II, Inc. Staff, illus. Goldilocks & the Three Bears. 26p. 1988. incl. cassette 9.95 (*1-55578-906-4*) Worlds Wonder.
—Jack & the Beanstalk. 26p. (ps). 1988. incl. cassette 9.95 (*1-55578-907-2*) Worlds Wonder.
Alexander, Lloyd. Black Cauldron. LC 65-13868. (gr. 4-6). 1965. 16.95 (*0-8050-0992-2*, Bks Young Read) H Holt & Co.
—Book of Three. LC 64-18250. 224p. (gr. 4-6). 1964. 16. 95 (*0-8050-0874-8*, Bks Young Read) H Holt & Co.
—Castle of Llyr. LC 66-13461. 204p. (gr. 4-6). 1966. 16. 95 (*0-8050-1115-3*, Bks Young Read) H Holt & Co.
—King's Fountain. Keats, Ezra J., illus. LC 72-13310. 32p. (ps-3). 1989. (DCB); pap. 4.95 (*0-525-44537-4*, DCB) Dutton Child Bks.
—Taran Wanderer. 272p. (gr. k-6). 1969. pap. 3.99 (*0-440-48483-9*, YB) Dell.
—Taran Wanderer. LC 67-10230. 256p. (gr. 4-6). 1967. 16.95 (*0-8050-1113-7*, Bks Young Read) H Holt & Co.
Ali Baba: In Arabic. (Illus.). (gr. 4-12). 1987. 3.95x (*0-86685-184-4*) Intl Bk Ctr.
Ali Baba the Forty Thieves & Other Stories. 1993. 8.99 (*0-517-10178-5*) Random Hse Value.
Alice in Wonderland. (Illus.). (ps). 1985. bds. 1.98 (*0-517-48141-3*) Random Hse Value.
Alice in Wonderland. 1989. 5.99 (*0-517-67008-9*) Random Hse Value.
Allan, Nicholas. The Hefty Fairy. (Illus.). 32p. (gr. 1-3). 1990. 13.95 (*0-09-173751-6*, Pub. by Hutchinson UK) Trafalgar.
Alonso, Fernando. Little Red Hen - La Gallina Paulina. Gimeno, J. M., illus. (SPA & ENG.). 26p. (gr. k-2). 1989. Spanish ed. 5.25 (*0-88272-467-3*); English ed. 5.25 (*0-88272-468-1*) Santillana.
Amery, H. Cinderella. (gr. 1 up). 1989. 6.96 (*0-88110-339-X*); 3.95 (*0-7460-0250-5*) EDC.
Amoss, Berthe. Cinderella. Amoss, Berthe, illus. 10p. (ps-7). 1989. pap. 2.95 (*0-922589-04-6*) More Than Card.
—Little Red Riding Hood. (Illus.). 10p. (ps-7). 1989. pap. 2.95 (*0-922589-11-9*) More Than Card.
Andersen, Hans Christian. Andersen's Fairy Tales. LC 58-6191. (Illus.). 352p. (gr. 3-9). 1981. (G&D); deluxe ed 13.95 (*0-448-06005-1*) Putnam Pub Group.
—Andersen's Fairy Tales. 1991. lib. bdg. 250.00 (*0-8490-4569-X*) Gordon Pr.
—Complete Hans Christian Andersen Fairy Tales. 1987. 11.99 (*0-517-45375-4*) Random Hse Value.
—Dulac's the Snow Queen: And Other Stories. Haugaard, Erik C., tr. Dulac, Edmund, illus. LC 76-7308. 144p. (ps up). 1976. 9.95 (*0-385-11678-0*) Doubleday.
—Emperor & the Nightingale. Watling, James, illus. LC 78-18065. 32p. (gr. k-4). 1979. PLB 9.79 (*0-89375-134-0*); pap. 1.95 (*0-89375-112-X*) Troll Assocs.
—The Emperor's New Clothes. Burton, Virginia L., illus. LC 83-19610. 48p. (gr. k-3). 1979. pap. 5.70 (*0-395-28594-1*) HM.
—The Emperor's New Clothes. Westcott, Nadine B., illus. (ps-3). 1984. pap. 5.95 (*0-316-93124-1*) Little.
—The Emperor's New Clothes. Duntze, Dorothee, illus. LC 86-2509. 32p. (gr. k-3). 1986. 14.95 (*1-55858-036-0*) North-South Bks NYC.
—The Emperor's New Clothes. Alchemy II, Inc. Staff, illus. 26p. (ps). 1988. incl. cassette 9.95 (*1-55578-901-3*) Worlds Wonder.
—The Emperor's New Clothes. Levinson, Riki, retold by. Byrd, Robert, illus. LC 89-23820. 40p. (ps-2). 1991. 14.95 (*0-525-44611-7*, DCB) Dutton Child Bks.
—The Emperor's New Clothes. Easton, Samantha, retold by. Walz, Richard, illus. 1991. 6.95 (*0-8362-4928-3*) Andrews & McMeel.
—The Emperor's New Clothes. 1991. PLB 13.95 (*0-88682-479-6*) Creative Ed.
—Fairy Tales. Thomas, Charles & Robinson, W. Heath, illus. Spink, Reginald, tr. LC 92-53178. 416p. 1992. 14.95 (*0-679-41791-5*, Evrymans Lib Childs Class) Knopf.
—Fairy Tales from Hans Christian Andersen. Ash, Russell & Higton, Bernard, eds. (Illus.). 128p. 1992. 16.95 (*0-8118-0230-2*) Chronicle Bks.
—The Fir Tree. Imsand, Marcel & Marshall, Rita, illus. 40p. (gr. 6 up). 1983. PLB 13.95 (*0-87191-949-4*) Creative Ed.
—Hans Andersen: His Classic Fairy Tales. Haugaard, Erik C., tr. Foreman, Michael, illus. LC 77-74792. 196p. (gr. 1 up). 1978. 15.95 (*0-385-13364-2*) Doubleday.
—Hans Andersen's Fairy Tales. Kingsland, L. W., tr. Birkett, Rachel, illus. 268p. (ps-6). 1987. 18.95 (*0-19-274532-8*) OUP.
—Hans Andersen's Fairy Tales: A Selection. Frolich, Lorenz & Pedersen, Vilhelm, illus. Kingsland, L. W., tr. from DAN. Lewis, Naomi, intro. by. LC 84-7120. 1985. pap. 4.95 (*0-19-281699-3*) OUP.
—Hans Christian Andersen Fairy Tales. Zwerger, Lisbeth, selected by. Bell, Anthea, tr. from DAN. Zwerger, Lisbeth, illus. LC 91-13132. 68p. (ps up). 1992. 19.95 (*0-88708-182-7*) Picture Bk Studio.
—Hans Christian Andersen's Fairy Tales. Gotlieb, Jules, illus. LC 58-6191. (gr. 3 up). 1958. pap. 1.95 (*0-8049-0169-4*, CL-169) Airmont.
—Little Match Girl. Lent, Blair, illus. LC 68-28050. (gr. k-3). 1975. pap. 1.95 (*0-685-02294-3*) HM.
—Little Mermaid. pap. 2.95 (*0-88388-039-3*) Bellerophon Bks.
—The Little Mermaid. Hague, Michael, illus. LC 92-29807. 1994. 16.95 (*0-8050-1010-6*, Bks Young Read) H Holt & Co.
—The Little Mermaid: A Step Three Book. Hautzig, Deborah, adapted by. May, Darcy, illus. LC 91-6632. 48p. (Orig.). (gr. 2-3). 1991. lib. bdg. 7.99 (*0-679-92241-5*); pap. 3.50 (*0-679-82241-0*) Random Bks Yng Read.
—The Little Mermaid & Other Fairy Tales. Kliros, Thea, illus. LC 93-14418. 96p. 1993. pap. 1.00 (*0-486-27816-6*) Dover.
—The Little Mermaid: The Original Story. Santore, Charles, illus. LC 93-20375. 1993. 14.00 (*0-517-06495-2*) Random Hse Value.
—Michael Hague's Favourite Hans Christian Andersen Fairy Tales. Hague, Michael, illus. LC 81-47455. 168p. (ps-2). 1981. 19.95 (*0-8050-0659-1*, Bks Young Read) H Holt & Co.
—Die Nachtigall. Palecek, Josef, illus. (GER.). 40p. (gr. k-3). 1992. 13.95 (*3-314-00521-0*) North-South Bks NYC.
—Nightingale. Le Gallienne, Eva, tr. Burkert, Nancy E., illus. LC 64-18574. 48p. (gr. 3 up). 1965. PLB 14.89 (*0-06-023781-3*) HarpC Child Bks.
—The Nightingale. Demi, illus. 32p. (ps-3). 1988. pap. 3.95 (*0-15-257428-X*, Voyager Bks) HarBrace.
—The Nightingale. Darke, Alison C., illus. 32p. (ps-3). 1989. 13.95 (*0-385-26081-4*, Zephyr-BFYR); (Zephyr-BFYR) Doubleday.
—The Nightingale. Bell, Anthea, tr. from DAN. Zwerger, Lisbeth, illus. LC 92-6632. 28p. (gr. 4 up). 1993. Repr. Mini-bk. 4.95 (*0-88708-269-6*) Picture Bk Studio.
—The Princess & the Pea. Galdone, Paul, illus. LC 77-12707. (ps-2). 1979. 14.45 (*0-395-28807-X*, Clarion Bks) HM.
—The Princess & the Pea. Stevens, Janet, adapted by. LC 81-13395. (Illus.). 32p. (ps-3). 1982. reinforced bdg. 14.95 (*0-8234-0442-0*); pap. 5.95 (*0-8234-0753-5*) Holiday.
—The Princess & the Pea. Duntze, Dorothee, illus. LC 85-7199. 32p. (gr. k-2). 1985. 14.95 (*1-55858-034-4*) North-South Bks NYC.
—The Princess & the Pea. Alchemy II, Inc. Staff, illus. 26p. (ps). 1988. incl. cassette 9.95 (*1-55578-909-9*) Worlds Wonder.
—The Red Shoes. (gr. 7-12). 1983. pap. 3.25x (*0-19-421741-8*) OUP.
—La Reine Des Neiges. Watts, Bernadette, illus. (FRE.). 32p. (gr. k-3). 1992. 14.95 (*3-85539-629-9*) North-South Bks NYC.
—Le Rossignol. Palecek, Josef, illus. (FRE.). 40p. (gr. k-3). 1992. 13.95 (*3-314-20707-7*) North-South Bks NYC.
—Rossignol de l'Empereur de Chine. Lemoine, Georges, illus. (FRE.). 56p. (gr. 3-7). 1990. pap. 8.95 (*2-07-031179-1*) Schoenhof.
—Die Schneekonigin. Watts, Bernadette, illus. (GER.). 32p. (gr. k-3). 1992. 14.95 (*3-85825-292-1*) North-South Bks NYC.
—Seven Tales by H. C. Andersen. Le Gallienne, Eva, retold by. Sendak, Maurice, illus. LC 59-16151. 144p. (gr. k up). 1991. pap. 7.95 (*0-06-443172-X*, Trophy) HarpC Child Bks.
—Seven Tales by Hans Christian Andersen. reissued ed. Le Gallienne, Eva, tr. from DAN. Sendak, Maurice, illus. LC 59-16151. 144p. (gr. 3 up). 1959. 13.95 (*0-06-023790-2*); PLB 13.89 (*0-06-023791-0*) HarpC Child Bks.
—The Snow Queen. Lewis, Naomi, adapted by. Bogdanovic, Toma, illus. LC 68-17218. 32p. (ps-5). 9.95 (*0-87592-048-9*) Scroll Pr.
—The Snow Queen. Jeffers, Susan, illus. LC 82-70199. 40p. (gr. k up). 1982. 15.95 (*0-8037-8011-7*); PLB 12. 89 (*0-8037-8029-X*); pap. 4.95 (*0-8037-0692-8*) Dial Bks Young.
—The Snow Queen. Hess, Dick & Eidrigewcius, Stasys, illus. LC 83-71172. 48p. (gr. 6 up). 1984. PLB 13.95 (*0-87191-950-8*) Creative Ed.
—The Snow Queen. Lewis, Naomi, retold by. Barrett, Angela, illus. LC 92-54412. 48p. (ps up). 1993. 16.95 (*1-56402-215-3*) Candlewick Pr.
—The Snow Queen. Peachey, Caroline, retold by. Lynch, P. J., illus. LC 93-42711. (gr. 1-5). 1994. write for info. (*0-15-200874-8*, Gulliver Bks) HarBrace.
—The Steadfast Tin Soldier. Lemoine, Georges, illus. 32p. 1983. PLB 13.95 (*0-87191-948-6*) Creative Ed.
—The Steadfast Tin Soldier. Easton, Samantha, retold by. Montgomery, Michael, illus. 1991. 6.95 (*0-8362-4929-1*) Andrews & McMeel.
—The Steadfast Tin Soldier. Lynch, Patrick J., ed. 1992. write for info. (*0-15-200599-4*, Gulliver Bks) HarBrace.
—The Steadfast Tin Soldier. Seidler, Tor, retold by. Marcellino, Fred, illus. LC 92-52690. 32p. (ps-3). 1992. 15.00 (*0-06-205000-1*); PLB 14.89 (*0-06-205001-X*) HarpC Child Bks.
—Thumbelina. Jeffers, Susan, illus. LC 79-50146. (ps-3). 1979. PLB 14.89 (*0-8037-8814-2*) Dial Bks Young.
—Thumbelina. Nigoghossian, Christine W., illus. LC 78-18080. 32p. (gr. k-4). 1979. PLB 9.79 (*0-89375-141-3*); pap. 1.95 (*0-89375-119-7*) Troll Assocs.
—Thumbelina. Jeffers, Susan, illus. LC 79-50146. 32p. (ps-3). 1985. pap. 5.95 (*0-8037-0232-9*) Dial Bks Young.
—Thumbelina. Officer, Robyn, illus. 32p. (ps-3). 1992. 6.95 (*0-8362-4926-7*) Andrews & McMeel.
—Thumbelina. 32p. 1992. pap. 2.99 (*0-8125-2318-0*) Tor Bks.
—Thumbelina. Johnson, David, illus. 64p. 1992. Repr. of 1989 ed. Mini-bk. incl. cass. 9.95 (*0-88708-256-4*, Rabbit Ears) Picture Bk Studio.
—Thumbelina & Other Stories. LC 88-43554. 96p. 1989. 4.95 (*0-89471-722-7*) Running Pr.
—Thumbeline. Zwerger, Lisbeth, illus. LC 85-12062. 28p. (gr. 1 up). 1991. pap. 14.95 (*0-88708-006-5*) Picture Bk Studio.
—The Tin Soldier. (gr. k-6). 1983. pap. 3.25x (*0-19-421742-6*) OUP.
—The Top & the Ball. Nyman, Elisabeth, illus. LC 92-83. 32p. (gr. k-3). 1992. 14.95 (*0-8249-8547-8*, Ideals Child); PLB 15.00 (*0-8249-8583-4*) Hambleton-Hill.
—Twelve Tales. Blegvad, Erik, tr. & illus. LC 93-6927. 96p. (gr. 3-7). 1994. SBE 18.95 (*0-689-50584-1*, M K McElderry) Macmillan Child Grp.
—The Ugly Duckling. Bogdanovic, Toma, illus. LC 75-145207. 32p. (ps-3). 9.95 (*0-87592-055-1*) Scroll Pr.
—Ugly Duckling. Williams, Jennie, illus. LC 78-18059. 32p. (gr. k-2). 1979. PLB 9.79 (*0-89375-128-6*); pap. 1.95 (*0-89375-106-5*) Troll Assocs.
—The Ugly Duckling. (gr. k-6). 1983. pap. 3.25x (*0-19-421704-3*) OUP.
—The Ugly Duckling. Mayer, Marianna, retold by. Locker, Thomas, illus. LC 85-23869. 40p. (ps up). 1987. RSBE 16.95 (*0-02-765130-4*, Macmillan Child Bk) Macmillan Child Grp.
—The Ugly Duckling. Howell, Troy, retold by. & illus. 40p. 1990. 15.95 (*0-399-22158-1*, Putnam) Putnam Pub Group.
—The Ugly Duckling. (Illus.). 24p. (ps up). 1990. write for info. (*0-307-12106-2*, Pub. by Golden Bks) Western Pub.
—The Ugly Duckling. (Illus.). 32p. (gr. k-3). 1993. pap. 2.99 (*0-87406-656-5*) Willowisp Pr.
—The Ugly Duckling: A Classic Tale. Jose, Eduard, adapted by. McDonnell, Janet, tr. Asensio, Augusti, illus. LC 88-36795. 32p. (gr. k-3). 1988. PLB 13.95 (*0-89565-474-1*) Childs World.
—The Ugly Duckling & Other Fairy Tales. (Illus.). 96p. (Orig.). 1992. pap. 1.00t (*0-486-27081-5*) Dover.
—The Wild Swans. Milone, Karen, illus. LC 80-27685. 32p. (gr. k-4). 1981. PLB 9.79 (*0-89375-480-3*); pap. text ed. 1.95 (*0-89375-481-1*) Troll Assocs.
—The Wild Swans. Hautzig, Deborah, adapted by. Kaila, Kaarina, illus. LC 91-47879. 32p. (gr. k-3). 1992. 12. 00 (*0-679-83446-X*); PLB 12.99 (*0-679-93446-4*) Knopf Bks Yng Read.
Angelina & the Princess. Holabird, Katharine. Craig, Helen, illus. LC 84-6818. 24p. (ps-2). 1988. 15.00 (*0-517-55273-6*, Clarkson Potter) Crown Bks Yng Read.
Annable, Toni & Kaspar, Maria H. The Runaway Match: La Cerilla Fugitiva. Viola, Amy, tr. 24p. (Orig.). (gr. 3 up). 1992. pap. 4.95 (*1-882828-04-6*) Kasan Imprints.
—The Runaway Match: L'Allumette Fugitive. 24p. (Orig.). (gr. 3 up). 1992. pap. 4.95 (*1-882828-05-4*) Kasan Imprints.
Appleby. The Three Billy-Goats Gruff. 1993. pap. 19.95 (*0-590-71393-0*) Scholastic Inc.
Ariel Books Staff. Beauty & the Beast - Gift Book. (ps-3). 1993. 4.95 (*0-8362-3036-1*) Andrews & McMeel.
—Cinderella. (ps-3). 1993. 4.95 (*0-8362-3034-5*) Andrews & McMeel.
—Jack & the Beanstalk. (ps-3). 1993. 4.95 (*0-8362-3035-3*) Andrews & McMeel.
Arnold, Tim, retold by. & illus. The Three Billy Goats Gruff. LC 92-23992. 32p. (ps-3). 1993. SBE 14.95 (*0-689-50575-2*, M K McElderry) Macmillan Child Grp.
Arpi, Erik. A Troll Wedding: The Troll Children's Search for the Magic Wedding Flower. Engen, Kari & Gracey, Kirsten, trs. from SWE. Lidberg, Rolf, illus. LC 92-60297. 30p. (ps-5). 1992. 12.95 (*1-881278-00-X*) M S Pr.
Atkinson, Allen. Old King Cole & Other Favorites. (Illus.). 64p. (Orig.). 1986. pap. 2.50 (*0-553-15355-2*) Bantam.
Attinella, Lauren. Muppet Babies Big Book of Nursery Rhymes & Fairy Tales. 1993. 9.99 (*0-307-16752-6*) Western Pub.
Ayres, Becky H. Matreshka. Natchev, Alexi, illus. LC 91-36359. 32p. (gr. k-3). 1992. pap. 15.00 (*0-385-30657-1*) Doubleday.
—Per & the Dala Horse. Gilbert, Yvonne, illus. LC 93-38596. 1995. write for info. (*0-385-32075-2*) Doubleday.
Babbitt, Natalie. Kneeknock Rise. Babbitt, Natalie, illus. LC 79-105622. 96p. (gr. 3 up). 1970. 15.00 (*0-374-34257-1*); pap. 3.95, 1984 (*0-374-44260-6*, Sunburst) FS&G.
—The Search for Delicious. Babbitt, Natalie, illus. LC 69-20374. 176p. (gr. 3 up). 1969. 15.00 (*0-374-36534-2*) FS&G.

Bacon, Ron. The Bone Tree. Wilson, Mark, illus. LC 93-20806. 1994. 4.25 (*0-383-03738-7*) SRA Schl Grp.
Balducci, Rita, retold by. Little Red Riding Hood. Eubank, Mary G., illus. (ps-k). 1991. pap. 1.25 (*0-307-11511-9*, Golden Pr) Western Pub.
Balducci, Rita, adapted by. Walt Disney's Cinderella. Mones, illus. 28p. (ps). 1992. bds. write for info. (*0-307-12530-0*, 12530, Golden Pr) Western Pub.
—Walt Disney's Snow White & the Seven Dwarfs. Williams, Don, illus. 24p. (ps-k). 1992. pap. write for info. laminated covers (*0-307-10037-5*, 10037, Golden Pr) Western Pub.
Banks, Lynne R. The Adventures of King Midas. 160p. (gr. 4). 1993. pap. 3.99 (*0-380-71564-3*, Camelot) Avon.
—The Fairy Rebel. 128p. (gr. 4). 1989. pap. 3.99 (*0-380-70650-4*, Camelot) Avon.
Barker, Cicely M. The Flower Fairies Changing Seasons: A Sliding Picture Book. (Illus.). 140p. 1992. 9.95 (*0-7232-4001-9*) Warne.
Barnett, Carol. Goldilocks & the Three Bears. (ps-3). 1990. 7.95 (*0-8442-9416-0*, Natl Textbk) NTC Pub Grp.
—Little Red Hen. (ps-3). 1990. 7.95 (*0-8442-9418-7*, Natl Textbk) NTC Pub Grp.
Barrie, J. M. Peter Pan. (Illus.). (ps). 1985. bds. 1.00 (*0-517-48144-8*) Random Hse Value.
—Peter Pan. Hildebrandt, Greg, illus. 160p. 1987. 14.95 (*0-88101-270-X*) Unicorn Pub.
—Peter Pan in Kensington Gardens. 175p. 1981. Repr. PLB 16.95x (*0-89966-328-1*) Buccaneer Bks.
—Peter Pan: Return to Never-Never Land. Forten, Ron, adapted by. (Illus.). 56p. 1991. pap. 5.95 (*1-56398-016-9*) Malibu Graphics.
Barrie, James M. Peter Pan. LC 80-14510. (Illus.). 192p. (gr. k up). 1980. SBE 19.95 (*0-684-16611-9*, Scribners Young Read) Macmillan Child Grp.
—Peter Pan. 1986. pap. 2.95 (*0-14-035066-7*, Puffin) Puffin Bks.
—Peter Pan. Lurie, Alison, afterword by. 208p. 1987. pap. 3.50 (*0-451-52088-2*, Sig Classics) NAL-Dutton.
—Peter Pan. Hague, Michael, illus. LC 87-403. 144p. (gr. 4-6). 1987. 19.95 (*0-8050-0276-6*, Bks Young Read) H Holt & Co.
Barton, Byron, retold by. & illus. The Three Bears. LC 90-43151. 32p. (ps-1). 1991. 15.00 (*0-06-020423-0*); PLB 14.89 (*0-06-020424-9*) HarpC Child Bks.
—Three Bears Big Book. LC 91-34151. 32p. (ps-1). 1994. pap. 19.95 (*0-06-443380-3*, Trophy) HarpC Child Bks.
Bartos-Hoppner, Barbara. The Pied Piper of Hamelin. Fuchshuber, Annegert, illus. LC 87-45150. 32p. (gr. k-3). 1987. (Lipp Jr Bks) HarpC Child Bks.
Baum, Arline & Baum, Joseph. Opt: An Illusionary Tale. LC 86-28130. (ps-3). 1987. pap. 11.95 (*0-670-80870-9*) Viking Child Bks.
Baum, L. Frank. Dorothy & the Wizard in Oz. (gr. 4 up). 18.75 (*0-8446-6141-4*) Peter Smith.
—Land of Oz. (Illus.). (gr. 4 up). 1968. pap. 1.25 (*0-8049-0181-3*, CL-181) Airmont.
—Marvelous Land of Oz. Neill, John R., illus. Gardner, M., intro. by. (Illus.). xvii, 287p. (gr. 4-6). 1969. pap. 5.95 (*0-486-20692-0*) Dover.
—Ozma of Oz. (gr. 5 up). 18.75 (*0-8446-6180-5*) Peter Smith.
—Queen Zixi of Ix: Or, the Story of the Magic Cloak. Richardson, Frederick, illus. Gardner, M., intro. by. (Illus.). 231p. (gr. 1-3). 1971. pap. 4.95 (*0-486-22691-3*) Dover.
—The Road to Oz. LC 79-88480. 1986. pap. 4.95 (*0-345-33467-1*, Del Rey) Ballantine.
—The Road to Oz. 160p. (gr. 5 up). 1993. pap. 2.99 (*0-14-035121-3*, Puffin) Puffin Bks.
—Surprising Adventures of the Magical Monarch of Mo & His People. Ver Beck, Frank, illus. (ps-4). 1968. pap. 6.95 (*0-486-21892-9*) Dover.
—Wizard of Oz. Copelman, Evelyn, et al, illus. (gr. 4-6). 1956. il. jr. lib. o.p. 5.95 (*0-448-05826-X*, G&D); deluxe ed. 12.95 (*0-448-06026-4*) Putnam Pub Group.
—The Wizard of Oz. Hague, Michael, illus. LC 82-1109. 232p. (gr. 4-6). 1982. 19.95 (*0-8050-0221-9*, Bks Young Read) H Holt & Co.
—The Wizard of Oz. (gr. 3-7). 1983. pap. 2.99 (*0-14-035001-2*, Puffin) Puffin Bks.
—The Wizard of Oz. Smith, Jos A., illus. Hautzig, Deborah, adapted by. LC 83-13792. (Illus.). 64p. (ps-3). 1984. lib. bdg. 8.99 (*0-394-95331-2*) Random Bks Yng Read.
—Wizard of Oz. Hildebrandt, Greg, illus. 160p. 1985. 14.95 (*0-88101-273-4*) Unicorn Pub.
—The Wonderful Wizard of Oz. Krenkel, Roy, illus. (gr. 4 up). 1965. pap. 1.75 (*0-8049-0069-8*, CL-69) Airmont.
—The Wonderful Wizard of Oz. 139p. 1981. Repr. PLB 15.95x (*0-89966-347-8*) Buccaneer Bks.
—Wonderful Wizard of Oz. Denslow, W. W., illus. Gardner, Martin, intro. by. (Illus.). vii, 268p. (gr. k-6). 1960. pap. 7.95 (*0-486-20691-2*) Dover.
—The Wonderful Wizard of Oz. Leach, William R., ed. 188p. 1991. pap. 16.95 (*0-534-14736-4*) Wadsworth Pub.
Baumann, Kurt. The Hungry One. Eidrigevicius, Stasys, illus. Lewis, Naomi, tr. from GER. LC 92-31030. (Illus.). 32p. (gr. k-3). 1993. 14.95 (*1-55858-121-9*); PLB 14.88 (*1-55858-196-0*) North-South Bks NYC.
Beauty & the Beast. (Illus.). (gr. 2-4). 3.50 (*0-7214-0642-4*) Ladybird Bks.
Beauty & the Beast: Tale of Enchantment. (Illus.). 48p. (gr. 3-7). 1992. pap. 2.95 (*1-56115-267-6*, 21808, Golden Pr) Western Pub.
Bedard, Michael. The Nightingale. Ricci, Regolo, illus. (gr. k-4). 1992. 14.95 (*0-395-60735-3*, Clarion Bks) HM.
Belfiore, Sammantha. Little, Little Fairy Tales. 1993. 7.95 (*0-533-10203-0*) Vantage.
Bender, Robert. The Three Billy Goats Gruff. Bender, Robert, illus. LC 92-41077. 32p. (ps-2). 1993. 14.95 (*0-8050-2529-4*, Bks Young Read) H Holt & Co.
Bender, Robert, retold by. & illus. Toads & Diamonds. LC 93-46602. 1995. write for info. (*0-525-67509-4*, Lodestar Bks) Dutton Child Bks.
Berenzy, A. Puss in Boots. 1994. 14.95 (*0-8050-1284-2*) H Holt & Co.
Berger, Thomas. The Little Troll. Lawson, Polly, tr. Heuninck, Ronald, illus. (GER.). 32p. (gr. k-3). 1992. 14.95 (*0-86315-112-4*, Pub. by Floris Bks UK) Gryphon Hse.
Bert y la Lampara Magica. (SPA.). (ps-3). 1993. pap. 4.95 (*0-307-52073-0*, Golden Pr) Western Pub.
Birch Lane Press Staff. Jack & the Beanstalk. (ps). 1990. 12.95 (*1-55972-048-4*, Birch Ln Pr) Carol Pub Group.
Birney, Betty. Disney's Beauty & the Beast. (ps). 1993. 3.95 (*0-307-12536-X*, Golden Pr) Western Pub.
—Walt Disney's Sleeping Beauty. (ps). 1993. 3.95 (*0-307-12528-9*, Golden Pr) Western Pub.
Birney, Betty, adapted by. Disney's The Little Mermaid. Martin, Kerry & Marvin, Fred, illus. 28p. (ps). 1992. bds. write for info. (*0-307-12534-3*, 12534, Golden Pr) Western Pub.
Bishop, Dorothy S. Habia Una Vez. (SPA., Illus.). 96p. 1991. pap. 9.95 incl. 60-min. cassette (*0-8442-7349-X*, Natl Textbk) NTC Pub Grp.
Black, Sheila. Hansel & Gretel: The Witch's Story. Klemushin, Arlene, illus. LC 93-42780. 1994. pap. 8.95 (*0-8065-1520-1*, Citadel Pr) Carol Pub Group.
Black, Sheila, ed. Andersen's Fairy Tales. LC 90-55649. (Illus.). 56p. (gr. 1-4). 1991. 9.98 (*0-89471-981-5*) Courage Bks.
Black, Shelia. Hansel & Gretel & the Witch's Story. (ps-3). 1991. 13.95 (*1-55972-080-8*, Birch Ln Pr) Carol Pub Group.
Blanca Nieves. (SPA.). (ps-3). 1993. pap. 4.95 (*0-307-72323-2*, Golden Pr) Western Pub.
Book of Classic Fairy Tales. (ps). 1978. 6.95 (*0-904494-88-8*) Borden.
Bornstein, Harry & Saulnier, Karen. Little Red Riding Hood. Pomeroy, Bradley O., illus. 48p. (gr. 1-6). 1990. PLB 15.95 (*1-878363-26-3*) Forest Hse.
Bos, Burny. Valentino Frosch und das Himbeerrote Cabrio. De Beer, Hans, illus. (GER.). 32p. (gr. k-3). 1992. 13.95 (*3-85825-346-4*) North-South Bks NYC.
Boston, Gypsy D. The Rainbow Fairies. Adair, Laura, illus. 1991. 12.95 (*0-9631503-0-8*); pap. 4.95 (*0-9631503-1-6*) Gypsy Damaris.
Boston, Lucy M. Sea Egg. Boston, Peter, illus. LC 67-10200. (gr. 2-6). 1967. 8.95 (*0-15-271050-7*, HB Juv Bks) HarBrace.

Bradford, Betsy A. Princess Patty in Peace on Earth. Bradford, Betsy A., illus. 56p. (gr. k-4). 1995. 16.95 (*0-9633846-3-5*) Scope Pub.
A jealous witch casts an evil spell on a princess, making everything she touches grow very large. Their town, Peace on Earth, becomes anything but peaceful. Patty's hair grows unnaturally long, her bed grows up to the ceiling, her mother grows three times her size, her father gets stuck in a tree & his castle climbs high in the sky. The witch is happy, but the royal family is overwhelmed by out-of-control growth & feelings of sadness. Learn how a wizard & "The Good Fairy Moonmother" help restore peace to Peace on Earth. "A dynamic fairy tale with a clever prescription for peace. 50 watercolors bring alive eleven colorful characters: a king, queen, princess, two guardian fairies, witch, spider, bat, prince, wizard & a Good Fairy Moonmother. An incredible piece of work!"--BILL CARLSON, WCCO TV, Minneapolis, Minnesota. "Bigotry, jealousy & family problems go big-time in this book. All can identify with this story. Highly entertaining!"--MAGGIE LEE, NORTHFIELD NEWS, Northfield, Minnesota. Order from Scope Publishing, 936 Pleasant View Ct., Northfield, MN 55057.
Publisher Provided Annotation.

Bramos, Helen. My Red Storybook. Bramos, Ann S., tr. from GRE & FRE. & illus. 77p. (Orig.). (ps-7). 1993. pap. 8.00 (*0-9635333-1-2*) A S Bramos.
Brett, Jan. Beauty & the Beast. (ps-3). 1990. pap. 5.95 (*0-395-55702-X*, Clarion Bks) HM.
—Christmas Trolls. Brett, Jan, illus. LC 93-10106. 32p. (ps-3). 1993. PLB 15.95 (*0-399-22507-2*, Putnam) Putnam Pub Group.
Briggs, Raymond. The Fairy Tale Treasury. Haviland, Virginia, ed. (gr. k up). 1986. pap. 8.95 (*0-440-42556-5*, YB) Dell.
—The Mother Goose Treasury. Briggs, Raymond, illus. 1986. pap. 8.95 (*0-440-46408-0*, YB) Dell.
Brinsmead, Hesba. Bianca & Roja. Brooks, Ron, illus. 112p. (Orig.). (gr. 2-6). 1993. pap. 7.95 (*1-86373-082-6*, Pub. by Allen & Unwin Aust Pty AT) IPG Chicago.
Brooke, L. Leslie. Golden Goose Book. Brooke, L. Leslie, illus. 96p. (ps-3). 1992. 16.45 (*0-395-61303-5*, Clarion Bks) HM.
Brooke, William J. Teller of Tales. LC 93-43421. 128p. (gr. 5 up). 1994. 15.00 (*0-06-023399-0*); PLB 14.89 (*0-06-023400-8*) HarpC Child Bks.
—A Telling of the Tales: Five Stories. Egielski, Richard, illus. LC 89-36588. 144p. (gr. 3-7). 1993. pap. 5.95 (*0-06-440467-6*, Trophy) HarpC Child Bks.
—Untold Tales. LC 91-4179. 160p. (gr. 5 up). 1992. 15.00 (*0-06-020271-8*); PLB 14.89 (*0-06-020272-6*) HarpC Child Bks.
—Untold Tales. LC 91-4179. 176p. (gr. 5 up). 1993. pap. 5.95 (*0-06-440483-8*, Trophy) HarpC Child Bks.
Bros. Grimm. King of the Golden Mountain. Cutts, David, ed. Watling, James, illus. LC 87-11262. 32p. (gr. 2-4). 1988. PLB 9.79 (*0-8167-1055-4*); pap. text ed. 1.95 (*0-8167-1056-2*) Troll Assocs.
Brown, Beth, compiled by. Fairy Tales of Birds & Beasts, Vol. 1. (Illus.). 128p. (gr. 3-7). 1994. PLB 15.95 (*0-87460-375-7*) Lion Bks.
Brown, Marcia & Perrault, Charles. Cinderella. (Illus.). 32p. (gr. 3). 1971. RSBE 13.95 (*0-684-12676-1*, Scribners Young Read) Macmillan Child Grp.
Brown-Cathers, Barbara. Bobio: A Fairy Tale for All Ages. Shelley, Evelyn, illus. 36p. (Orig.). (gr. 5). 1994. pap. 7.95 (*0-9640122-0-0*) Pen & Pr Unltd.
Bull, Emma. The Princess & the Lord of Night. Gaber, Susan, illus. LC 93-19151. 1994. 14.95 (*0-15-263543-2*, J Yolen Bks) HarBrace.
Burgess, Beverly C. Jack & the Beanstalk. (gr. k-6). 1985. pap. 3.98 (*0-89274-384-0*) Harrison Hse.
Butterworth, Nick & Inkpen, Mich. Jasper's Beanstalk. Inkpen, Mick, illus. LC 92-14886. 32p. (ps-1). 1993. SBE 13.95 (*0-02-716231-1*, Bradbury Pr) Macmillan Child Grp.
Byrnes, Lynne, illus. The Three Little Pigs. 24p. (ps-1). 1991. pap. 1.25 (*0-7214-5305-8*, S9016-6 SER.) Ladybird Bks.
—The Ugly Duckling. 24p. (ps-1). 1991. pap. 1.25 (*0-7214-5304-X*, S9016-5) Ladybird Bks.
Calhoun, Mary. Hungry Leprechaun. Duvoisin, Roger, illus. LC 62-7214. 32p. (gr. k-3). 1962. PLB 12.88 (*0-688-31713-8*) Morrow Jr Bks.
Campbell, Ann. Once upon a Princess & a Pea. Young, Kathy O., illus. LC 92-30526. 32p. 1993. 13.95 (*1-55670-289-2*) Stewart Tabori & Chang.
Campbell, Janet, adapted by. Walt Disney's Three Little Pigs. DiCicco, Gil, illus. LC 92-53443. 32p. 1993. 12.95 (*1-56282-381-7*); PLB 12.89 (*1-56282-382-5*) Disney Pr.
Caperucita Roja. (SPA.). (ps-3). 1993. pap. 2.25 (*0-307-70098-4*, Golden Pr) Western Pub.
Carroll, Lewis. Alice au Pays de Merveilles. (FRE.). (gr. 3-8). 7.95 (*0-8288-6095-5*, M5497) Fr & Eur.
—Alice in Wonderland. 215p. 1981. Repr. PLB 15.95x (*0-89966-345-1*) Buccaneer Bks.
—Alice in Wonderland. Tenniel, John, illus. 160p. (gr. 3-6). 1988. pap. 2.95 (*0-590-42035-6*, Apple Classics) Scholastic Inc.
—Alice in Wonderland: A Classic Tale. Jose, Eduard, adapted by. Riehecky, Janet, tr. from SPA. Rovira, Francesc, illus. LC 88-35309. 32p. (gr. 1-4). 1988. PLB 13.95 (*0-89565-467-9*) Childs World.
—Alice in Wonderland & Through the Looking Glass. Tenniel, John, illus. (gr. 4-6). 1963. 13.95 (*0-448-06004-3*, G&D) Putnam Pub Group.
—Alice's Adventures in Wonderland. Tenniel, John, illus. Bd. with Through the Looking Glass. LC 82-242973. (gr. 5 up). 1965. pap. 1.95 (*0-8049-0079-5*, CL-79) Airmont.
—Alice's Adventures in Wonderland. Hague, Michael, illus. LC 85-856. 128p. (gr. 4-6). 1985. 19.95 (*0-8050-0212-X*, Bks Young Read) H Holt & Co.
—Alice's Adventures in Wonderland & Through the Looking Glass. (gr. 4). 1960. pap. 2.75 (*0-451-52320-2*, Sig Classics) NAL-Dutton.
—Alice's Adventures in Wonderland & Through the Looking Glass. Tenniel, John, illus. Cohen, Morton N., intro. by. (Illus.). 256p. 1984. pap. 2.95 (*0-553-21345-8*, Bantam Classics Spectra) Bantam.
—Alice's Adventures in Wonderland: The Ultimate Illustrated Edition. Edens, Cooper, compiled by. (ps up). 1989. 22.50 (*0-553-05385-X*) Bantam.
—Alice's Adventures Underground. Carroll, Lewis, illus. Gardner, Martin. (Illus.). 128p. (gr. 4-9). 1965. pap. 2.95 (*0-486-21482-6*) Dover.
—Aventures D'Alice au Pays des Merveilles. Bue, Henri, tr. from ENG. Tenniel, John, illus. Cohen, Morton N., intro. by. (FRE., Illus.). 196p. (gr. 4-8). 1972. pap. 4.95 (*0-486-22836-3*) Dover.

—The Little Alice Editions: Alice's Adventures in Wonderland; Through the Looking-Glass. Tenniel, John, illus. 416p. (ps up). 1988. slipcased set 12.95 (*0-8037-0589-1*) Dial Bks Young.

—Reader's Digest Best Loved Books for Young Readers: Alice's Adventures in Wonderland & Through the Looking Glass. Ogburn, Jackie, ed. Tenniel, John, illus. 192p. (gr. 4-12). 1989. 3.99 (*0-945260-21-0*) Choice Pub NY.

Carroll, Lewis & Tenniel, Sir John. Alice's Adventures in Wonderland. LC 82-242973. (Illus.). (gr. 5 up). 1977. 14.95 (*0-312-01821-5*) St Martin.

Carruth, Jane. My Giant Treasury of Fairy Tales. 1988. 9.98 (*0-671-09118-2*) S&S Trade.

Carter, Margaret, retold by. Beauty & the Beast & Other Stories. Offen, Hilda, illus. LC 93-5772. 1994. 3.95 (*1-85697-967-9*, Kingfisher LKC) LKC.

—Cinderella & Other Stories. Offen, Hilda, illus. LC 93-5770. 1994. 3.95 (*1-85697-968-7*, Kingfisher LKC) LKC.

—Goldilocks & Other Stories. Offen, HIlda, illus. LC 93-5771. 1994. 3.95 (*1-85697-969-5*, Kingfisher LKC) LKC.

—Little Red Riding Hood & Other Stories. Offen, Hilda, illus. LC 93-5768. 32p. (ps-k). 1994. 3.95 (*1-85697-970-9*, Kingfisher LKC) LKC.

—Sleeping Beauty & Other Stories. Offen, Hilda, illus. LC 93-5769. 1994. 3.95 (*1-85697-971-7*, Kingfisher LKC) LKC.

—Snow White & Other Stories. Offen, HIlda, illus. LC 93-5767. 1994. 3.95 (*1-85697-972-5*, Kingfisher LKC) LKC.

—The Ugly Duckling & Other Stories. Offen, Hilda, illus. LC 93-5766. 1994. 3.95 (*1-85697-974-1*, Kingfisher LKC) LKC.

Cartwright, Pauline. The Troll in the Hole. Culic, Ned, illus. LC 93-9282. 1994. pap. write for info. (*0-383-03722-0*) SRA Schl Grp.

Cauley, Lorinda B. The Ugly Duckling. Canley, Lorinda B., illus. LC 79-12340. 40p. (gr. k-3). 1979. pap. 4.95 (*0-15-692528-1*, Voyager Bks) HarBrace.

Cavanaugh, Kate. I Can't Sleep with Those Elves Watching Me. Kiner, K. C., illus. 24p. (ps-8). 1990. pap. text ed. 4.95 (*0-9622353-1-8*) KAC.

Chapman, Kim W. The Magic Hat. 2nd ed. LC 76-20842. (Illus.). 46p. (gr. k up). 1976. 5.00 (*0-914996-10-X*) Lollipop Power.

Chardiet, Bernice. Rapunzel. 1990. pap. 2.50 (*0-590-42281-2*) Scholastic Inc.

Charles, Veronika M. The Crane Girl. LC 92-50843. (Illus.). 32p. (ps-1). 1993. 14.95 (*0-531-05485-3*) Orchard Bks Watts.

Chase, Richard. Jack Tales. (Illus.). 202p. (gr. 4-6). 1943. 13.45 (*0-395-06694-8*) HM.

Chestnutt, David, illus. Beauty & the Beast. LC 78-54959. 32p. (Orig.). (gr. k-4). 1991. pap. 2.25 (*0-394-83954-4*) Random Bks Yng Read.

Chicken Licken. (Illus.). 28p. (ps up). 1987. 3.95 (*0-7214-5029-6*) Ladybird Bks.

Chorao, Kay. Child's Fairy Tale Book. LC 89-49480. (Illus.). 64p. (ps-3). 1990. 14.95 (*0-525-44630-3*, DCB) Dutton Child Bks.

Chorpenning, Charlotte B. Little Red Riding Hood. 47p. (Orig.). 1946. 4.50 (*0-87602-149-6*) Anchorage.

—The Three Bears. 50p. (Orig.). 1949. 4.50 (*0-87602-208-5*) Anchorage.

Chwast, Seymour, illus. Bushy Bride: Norwegian Fairy Tale. LC 83-71174. 32p. (gr. 6 up). 1983. PLB 13.95 (*0-87191-952-4*) Creative Ed.

Cincerelli, Carol J. The Tales of Hans Christian Andersen. 144p. (gr. 1-6). 1990. 11.95 (*0-86653-544-6*, GA1159) Good Apple.

—The Tales of the Brothers Grimm. 144p. (gr. 1-6). 1990. 11.95 (*0-86653-562-4*, GA1160) Good Apple.

Cinderella. (ARA., Illus.). (gr. 2-5). 1987. 3.95x (*0-86685-193-3*) Intl Bk Ctr.

Cinderella. (Illus.). (ps-3). 1985. 1.98 (*0-517-28807-9*) Random Hse Value.

Cinderella. (Illus.). (ps-1). 1.98 (*0-517-39461-8*) Random Hse Value.

Cinderella. (Illus.). 48p. 1989. 5.99 (*0-517-67010-0*) Random Hse Value.

Cinderella. (ps-1). 1989. 2.99 (*0-517-69215-5*) Random Hse Value.

Cinderella. (ps-2). 3.95 (*0-7214-5058-X*) Ladybird Bks.

Cinderella. 16p. 1991. write for info. incl. cassette (*1-880459-03-5*) Arrow Trad.

Cinderella. 24p. 1992. pap. 2.50 (*1-56144-088-4*) Modern Pub NYC.

Cinderella. (Illus.). 24p. (gr. 2-5). 1993. pap. 3.95 (*1-56144-359-X*, Honey Bear Bks) Modern Pub NYC.

Cinderella: Treasures from the Library of Congress. 20p. 1992. Repr. of 1870 ed. saddle wired 3.95 (*1-55709-166-8*) Applewood.

Cinderella's Magic. 1985. 4.95 (*0-553-05404-X*) Bantam.

Claverie, Jean. Die Drei Kleinen Schweinchen. Claverie, Jean, illus. (GER.). 32p. (gr. k-3). 1992. 13.95 (*3-85825-330-8*) North-South Bks NYC.

—Les Trois Petits Cochons. Claverie, Jean, illus. (FRE.). 32p. (gr. k-3). 1992. 13.95 (*3-314-20655-0*) North-South Bks NYC.

Coady, Christopher, retold by. & illus. Red Riding Hood. LC 91-25567. 32p. (ps-6). 1992. 15.00 (*0-525-44896-9*, DCB) Dutton Child Bks.

Coatsworth, Elizabeth. The Cat Who Went to Heaven. Ward, Lynd, illus. LC 58-10917. 72p. (gr. 4-6). 1967. RSBE 15.00 (*0-02-719710-7*, Macmillan Child Bk) Macmillan Child Grp.

Cocca-Leffler, Maryann, illus. The Elves & the Shoemaker. 18p. (ps). 1993. bds. 3.95 (*0-448-40177-0*, G&D) Putnam Pub Group.

Cohen, Lynn. Fairy Tale World. 64p. (ps-k). 1986. 6.95 (*0-912107-48-0*) Monday Morning Bks.

Collodi, Carlo. Adventures of Pinocchio. Kredel, Fritz, illus. (gr. 4-6). 1982. 12.95 (*0-448-06001-9*, G&D) Putnam Pub Group.

—The Adventures of Pinocchio. Kassirer, Sue, adapted by. Haverfield, Mary, illus. LC 92-2503. 32p. (Orig.). (ps-2). 1992. pap. 2.25 (*0-679-83466-4*) Random Bks Yng Read.

—Pinocchio. (FRE., Illus.). (gr. 3-8). 5.95 (*0-685-11495-3*, S16273) Fr & Eur.

—Pinocchio. LC 87-15789. 1988. 10.99 (*0-517-61815-X*) Random Hse Value.

—Pinocchio. Hildebrandt, Greg, illus. 160p. 1986. 14.95 (*0-88101-271-8*) Unicorn Pub.

—Pinocchio. Mattotti, Lorenzo, illus. LC 92-44161. (ENG.). (gr. 2 up). 1993. 15.00 (*0-688-12450-X*); lib. bdg. 14.93 (*0-688-12451-8*) Lothrop.

—Pinocchio: A Classic Tale. Jose, Eduard, adapted by. Moncure, Jane B., tr. from SPA. Asensio, Augusti, illus. LC 88-35308. 32p. (gr. k-2). 1988. PLB 13.95 (*0-89565-458-X*) Childs World.

The Complete Brothers Grimm Fairy Tales. (gr. 2-6). 6.98 (*0-517-33631-6*) Random Hse Value.

The Complete Hans Christian Andersen Fairy Tales. (gr. 2-6). 6.98 (*0-517-33632-4*) Random Hse Value.

Compton, Joanne. Ashpet: An Appalachian Tale. Compton, Kenn, illus. LC 93-16034. 40p. (ps-3). 1994. reinforced bdg. 15.95 (*0-8234-1106-0*) Holiday.

Conover, Chris. Mother Goose & the Sly Fox. (Illus.). (ps-3). 1991. pap. 4.95 (*0-374-45397-7*) FS&G.

Cooney, Barbara. Snow White & Rose Red. (ps-3). 1991. pap. 13.95 (*0-685-54227-0*) Delacorte.

—Snow White & Rose Red. LC 89-78013. (ps-3). 1991. 13.95 (*0-385-30175-8*) Delacorte.

Cooper, Susan, retold by. Tam Lin. Hutton, Warwick, illus. LC 90-5571. 32p. (gr. k-4). 1991. SBE 14.95 (*0-689-50505-1*, M K McElderry) Macmillan Child Grp.

Corpening, Gene S. I Love to Hear the Cold Wind Howl. James, Linda & Corpening, Gene S., illus. 40p. (Orig.). (gr. 2 up). 1993. pap. 7.95g (*0-9636775-9-4*) Alice Pub.

Corrin, Sara & Corrin, Stephen, eds. More Stories for Under-Fives. Julian-Ottie, Vanessa, illus. 116p. (ps). 1990. pap. 9.95 (*0-571-12921-8*) Faber & Faber.

Cosgrove, Stephen. Button Breaker. Bonin, Diana R., illus. 32p. (gr. k-5). 1993. PLB 12.95 (*1-56674-043-6*, HTS Bks) Forest Hse.

—Snicker Doodle. Bonin, Diana R., illus. 32p. (gr. k-5). 1993. PLB 12.95 (*1-56674-044-4*, HTS Bks) Forest Hse.

—Tinkling. Bonin, Diana R., illus. 32p. (gr. k-5). 1993. PLB 12.95 (*1-56674-045-2*, HTS Bks) Forest Hse.

—Tizzy. Bonin, Diana R., illus. 32p. (gr. k-5). 1993. PLB 12.95 (*1-56674-046-0*, HTS Bks) Forest Hse.

Courson, Diana. Let's Learn about Fairy Tales & Nursery Rhymes. 64p. (ps-2). 1988. wkbk. 7.95 (*0-86653-437-7*, GA1040) Good Apple.

Coville, Bruce. The Dragonslayers. MacDonald, Pat, ed. Coville, Katherine, illus. LC 93-40194. 128p. (gr. 7 up). 1994. 14.00 (*0-671-89036-0*, Minstrel Bks) PB.

Cox, Palmer. The Brownies' Merry Adventures. Cox, Palmer, illus. LC 93-563. 224p. 1993. 6.00 (*1-56957-901-6*) Shambhala Pubns.

Craig, M. Jean. The Three Wishes. Salzman, Yuri, illus. 48p. (Orig.). (gr. k-3). 1986. pap. 2.50 (*0-590-41744-4*) Scholastic Inc.

Cresswell, Helen. Classic Fairy Tales. (ps-3). 1994. 12.95 (*0-307-17503-0*, Artsts Writrs) Western Pub.

Croll, Carolyn, adapted by. & illus. The Little Snowgirl. 32p. (ps-k). 1989. 14.95 (*0-399-21691-X*, Putnam) Putnam Pub Group.

Crump, Fred. Afrotina & the Three Bears: (A Retold Story) Crump, Fred, illus. LC 88-51222. 44p. (gr. k-2). 1991. pap. 6.95 (*1-55523-195-0*) Winston-Derek.

—Little Red Riding Hood: (A Retold Story) Crump, Fred, illus. LC 88-51219. 44p. (gr. k-2). 1989. pap. 6.95 (*1-55523-193-4*) Winston-Derek.

—Mother Goose: A Retold Story. Crump, Fred, illus. LC 88-51224. 44p. (gr. k-2). 1989. pap. 6.95 (*1-55523-194-2*) Winston-Derek.

—Thumbelina: A Retold Story. Crump, Fred, illus. LC 88-51223. 44p. (gr. k-2). 1989. pap. 6.95 (*1-55523-191-8*) Winston-Derek.

Crump, Fred, Jr. Beauty & the Beast. Crump, Fred, Jr., illus. 44p. (gr. k-2). 1991. pap. 6.95 (*1-55523-379-1*) Winston-Derek.

—Jamako & the Beanstalk. Crump, Fred, illus. 44p. (gr. k-3). 1992. pap. 8.95 incl. cass. (*1-55523-481-X*) Winston-Derek.

—MGambo & the Tiger. Crump, Fred, Jr., illus. 44p. (gr. k-2). 1991. pap. 6.95 (*1-55523-410-0*) Winston-Derek.

—Rapunzel. Crump, Fred, Jr., illus. 272p. (gr. k-2). 1991. pap. 6.95 (*1-55523-408-9*) Winston-Derek.

—Rapunzel. Crump, Fred, Jr., illus. LC 91-67499. 44p. (gr. k-3). 1992. pap. 8.95 incl. cass. (*1-55523-482-8*) Winston-Derek.

—Rumpelstiltskin. Crump, Fred, illus. 44p. (gr. k-2). 1991. pap. 6.95 (*1-55523-409-7*) Winston-Derek.

—Winston-Derek's Traditional Fairy Tales, 2 vols, Vols. I-II. (Illus.). (gr. k-3). 1992. PLB 39.95 (*1-55523-490-9*) Vol. I, 224p (*1-55523-491-7*) Vol. II, 224p. Winston-Derek.

Culbertson, Roger, ed. Cinderella. Wenzel, David, illus. 12p. 1994. 12.95 (*0-685-72753-X*) Running Pr.

Culbertson, Roger, retold by. Jack & the Beanstalk. Yerkes, Lane, illus. 12p. 1994. pop-up bk. with audiocassette 12.95 (*1-56138-366-X*) Running Pr.

Cummings, E. E. Fairy Tales. Eaton, John, illus. LC 65-18727. 39p. (gr. k up). 1975. pap. 4.95 (*0-15-629895-3*, Voyager Bks) HarBrace.

Cummings, Pat. The Blue Lake. LC 92-24354. (Illus.). 64p. (gr. 1-5). Date not set. 18.00 (*0-06-021535-6*); PLB 17.89 (*0-06-021536-4*) HarpC Child Bks.

Cutburth, Ronald W. Love from the Sea. Naumann, Cynthia E., ed. Percels, Beth, illus. 27p. (Orig.). (gr. 4-7). 1990. pap. 3.50 (*1-878291-01-7*) Love From Sea.

Cutts, David, retold by. Gingerbread Boy. Goodman, Joan E., illus. LC 78-18069. 32p. (gr. k-2). 1979. PLB 9.79 (*0-89375-122-7*); pap. 1.95 (*0-89375-100-6*) Troll Assocs.

Dahl, Roald. James & the Giant Peach. Burkert, Nancy E., illus. (gr. 3 up). 1961. 16.00 (*0-394-81282-4*); PLB 16.99 (*0-394-91282-9*) Knopf Bks Yng Read.

—Magic Finger. Pene Du Bois, William, illus. LC 66-18657. 46p. (gr. 3-6). 1966. 15.00 (*0-06-021381-7*); PLB 14.89 (*0-06-021382-5*) HarpC Child Bks.

Damjan, Mischa. Das Eichhorn und das Nashornchen. De Beer, Hans, illus. (GER.). 32p. (gr. k-3). 1992. 14.95 (*3-314-00538-5*) North-South Bks NYC.

—La Foret Aux Milles Ombres. De Beer, Hans, illus. (FRE.). 32p. (gr. k-3). 1992. 14.95 (*3-314-20740-9*) North-South Bks NYC.

Daniels, Patricia. Aladdin & the Magic Lamp. LC 79-27304. (Illus.). 24p. (gr. k-5). 1980. PLB 9.95 (*0-8393-0257-6*) Raintree Steck-V.

—Aladdin & the Magic Lamp. LC 79-27304. (Illus.). 24p. (gr. k-5). 1981. PLB 29.28 (*0-8393-1832-4*) Raintree Steck-V.

—Ali Baba & the Forty Thieves. LC 79-27042. (Illus.). 24p. (gr. k-5). 1981. PLB 29.28 (*0-8393-1837-5*); PLB 9.95 incl. cassette (*0-8393-0255-X*); cassette 14.00 (*0-685-42782-X*) Raintree Steck-V.

—Beauty & the Beast. Large, Annabel, illus. LC 79-28433. 24p. (gr. k-5). 1980. PLB 9.95 (*0-8393-0258-4*) Raintree Steck-V.

—Beauty & the Beast. LC 79-28433. (Illus.). 24p. (gr. k-5). 1981. PLB 29.28 incl. cassette (*0-8172-1833-5*); cassette 14.00 (*0-685-09554-1*) Raintree Steck-V.

—Cinderella. Read, Maggie, illus. LC 79-28526. 24p. (gr. k-5). 1980. PLB 29.28 incl. cassette (*0-8393-1834-0*); PLB 14.64 (*0-8393-0253-3*) Raintree Steck-V.

—Rumpelstiltskin. Nightingale, Sandy, illus. LC 79-27140. 24p. (gr. k-5). 1980. PLB 9.95 (*0-8393-0252-5*) Raintree Steck-V.

—Rumpelstiltskin. LC 79-27140. (Illus.). 24p. (gr. k-5). 1981. PLB 29.28 incl. cassette (*0-8393-1831-6*); cassette 14.00 (*0-685-09555-X*) Raintree Steck-V.

—Sinbad the Sailor. Webb, Roger, illus. LC 79-28588. 24p. (gr. k-5). 1980. PLB 9.95 (*0-8393-0256-8*) Raintree Steck-V.

—Sinbad the Sailor. LC 79-28588. (Illus.). 24p. (gr. k-5). 1980. PLB 29.28 incl. cassette (*0-8393-1835-9*) Raintree Steck-V.

—Sleeping Beauty. Tarrant, Carol, illus. LC 79-26974. 24p. (gr. k-5). 1980. PLB 9.95 (*0-8393-0254-1*) Raintree Steck-V.

—Sleeping Beauty. LC 79-26974. (Illus.). 24p. (gr. k-5). 1980. PLB 29.28 incl. cassette (*0-8393-1838-3*) Raintree Steck-V.

—Snow White & the Dwarfs. LC 79-28431. (Illus.). 24p. (gr. k-5). 1980. PLB 29.28 (*0-8393-1836-7*); cassette 14.00 (*0-685-09557-6*) Raintree Steck-V.

—Snow White & the Seven Dwarfs. Spalding, Tony, illus. LC 79-28431. 24p. (gr. k-5). 1980. PLB 9.95 (*0-8393-0251-7*) Raintree Steck-V.

Dasent, George W. East o' the Sun & West o' the Moon. LC 70-97214. (Illus.). xv, 418p. (gr. 1 up). 1970. pap. 8.95 (*0-486-22521-6*) Dover.

Dasent, George W., tr. East o' the Sun & West o' the Moon. Lynch, P. J., illus. LC 91-58727. 48p. (ps up). 1992. 15.95 (*1-56402-049-5*) Candlewick Pr.

Davenport, Tom & Carden, Gary. From the Brothers Grimm: A Contemporary Retelling of American Folktales & Classic Stories. LC 92-30828. (Illus.). 105p. (gr. 2-12). 1993. pap. 12.95 (*0-917846-20-6*, 95526) Highsmith Pr.

David, Alfred & Meek, Mary E. The Twelve Dancing Princesses & Other Fairy Tales. LC 73-16517. (Illus.). 320p. (gr. 1-6). 1974. pap. 12.95 (*0-253-20173-X*, MB-173) Ind U Pr.

Davis, Rebecca J. A Sunnybrook Garden Tale. Kvarnes, Davette L., illus. LC 92-97014. 32p. (gr. 3-5). 1993. PLB 12.00 (*0-9634032-0-6*) R J Davis.

Dawood, N. J. Aladdin: And Other Tales from the Arabian Nights. 176p. (gr. 4 up). 1990. pap. 2.99 (*0-14-035105-1*, Puffin) Puffin Bks.

De Beer, Hans. Plume en Bateau. De Beer, Hans, illus. (FRE.). 32p. (gr. k-3). 1992. 13.95 (*3-85539-647-7*) North-South Bks NYC.

De Castiglione, Silvia. Mini Treasury of Fairy Tales, Vol. 1. 1994. 4.99 (*0-517-10340-0*) Random Hse Value.

—Mini Treasury of Fairy Tales, Vol. 2. 1994. 4.99 (*0-517-10351-6*) Random Hse Value.

Delamare, David. Cinderella. LC 92-25126. 1993. 15.00 (*0-671-76944-8*, S&S BFYR) S&S Trade.

Delamare, David, illus. Steadfast Tin Soldier. 48p. (ps-3). 1992. 4.95 (*0-88101-245-9*) Unicorn Pub.

De La Mare, Walter. The Turnip. Hawkes, Kevin, illus. LC 92-6191. 1992. 18.95 (*0-87923-934-4*) Godine.

De Leprince de Beaumont. Belle et la Bete. Glaseur, Willi, illus. (FRE.). 87p. (gr. 1-5). 1989. pap. 11.95 (2-07-031188-0) Schoenhof.

Delval, Marie-Helene. The Seven Witches. (Illus.). (gr. 3-8). 1992. PLB 8.95 (0-89565-897-6) Childs World.

Demi, retold by. & illus. The Magic Tapestry: A Chinese Folktale. LC 93-11426. 1994. 17.95 (0-8050-2810-2) H Holt & Co.

De Paola, Tomie. Helga's Dowry. De Paola, Tomie, illus. LC 76-54953. 32p. (gr. k-3). 1977. pap. 4.95 (0-15-640010-3, Voyager Bks) HarBrace.

DePaola, Tomie, illus. Tomie dePaola's Mother Goose. LC 84-26314. 127p. (ps-2). 1985. 18.95 (0-399-21258-2, Putnam) Putnam Pub Group.

De Regniers, Beatrice S. Jack & the Beanstalk: Retold in Verse for Boys & Girls to Read Themselves. Wilsdorf, Anne, illus. LC 89-18663. 48p. (ps-2). 1990. pap. 4.95 (0-689-71421-1, Aladdin) Macmillan Child Grp.

—Red Riding Hood: Retold in Verse for Boys & Girls to Read Themselves. 2nd ed. LC 89-38024. (Illus.). 48p. (gr. k-3). 1990. pap. 4.95 (0-689-71373-8, Aladdin) Macmillan Child Grp.

De Saint-Exupery, Antoine. Little Prince. Woods, Katherine, tr. De Saint-Exupery, Antoine, illus. LC 67-1144. 91p. (gr. 3-7). 1943. 13.95 (0-15-246503-0, HB Juv Bks) HarBrace.

—The Little Prince. Woods, Katherine, tr. LC 92-37907. (gr. 4 up). 1993. 50.00 (0-15-243820-3) HarBrace.

Diamantes, Kitty, illus. Favorite Tales from Grimm. 96p. (gr. 3 up). 1988. 9.95 (0-02-689060-7) Checkerboard.

Dick Whittington. (ARA., Illus.). (gr. 4-12). 1987. 3.95x (0-86685-196-8) Intl Bk Ctr.

Disney Little Libraries: Yellow. 5p. (Incls. Alice in Wonderland, Dumbo at the Airport, Winnie the Pooh is Hungry & Lady at the Pond). 1992. bds. 5.98 (0-8317-2377-7) Viking Child Bks.

Disney Staff. Disney's Beauty & the Beast. 1991. 6.98 (0-8317-2434-X) Viking Child Bks.

—Prince & the Pauper. 1990. 6.98 (0-8317-2433-1) Viking Child Bks.

—Walt Disney Fairy Tale Treasury: Blue. 1991. 9.98 (0-8317-9291-4) Viking Child Bks.

—Walt Disney Fairy Tale Treasury: Red. 1991. 9.98 (0-8317-9292-2) Viking Child Bks.

Disney, Walt. Cinderella. (ps-3). 1993. 6.98 (0-453-03167-6) Mouse Works.

—Sleeping Beauty. (ps-3). 1993. 6.98 (0-453-03168-4) Mouse Works.

—Snow White & Seven Dwarfs. (Illus.). 1988. 5.99 (0-517-66196-9) Random Hse Value.

Disney, Walt, Productions Staff. Walt Disney's Cinderella. LC 74-22325. (Illus.). 48p. (ps-3). 1974. 6.95 (0-394-82552-7); lib. bdg. 4.99 (0-394-92552-1) Random Bks Yng Read.

—Walt Disney's Snow White & the Seven Dwarfs. (Illus.). (ps-3). 1973. 6.95 (0-394-82625-6); lib. bdg. 5.99 (0-394-92625-0) Random Bks Yng Read.

Disney's Beauty & the Beast. (Illus.). 24p. (ps up). 1992. deluxe ed. write for info. incl. long-life batteries (0-307-74024-2, 64024, Golden Pr) Western Pub.

Disney's Beauty & the Beast. LC 92-50805. (Illus.). 128p. 1993. 5.95 (1-56138-252-3) Running Pr.

Disney's Little Mermaid. (Illus.). 128p. 1992. 5.95 (1-56138-154-3) Running Pr.

Dixon, Doris N. Rumpelstiltskin. Fox, Neal, illus. 24p. (ps-2). 1993. pap. 9.95 (1-882171-01-2) Confetti Ent.

Dixon, Peter W., intro. by. Great Tales of Old. LC 87-83338. (Illus.). 312p. (gr. k-3). 1988. text ed. 15.95 (0-945161-01-8); pap. 9.95 (0-945161-00-X) Lantern Bks.

Dr. Mac: The Tooth Fairy Legend. 50p. (gr. k-3). 1994. 12.95 (0-9638033-8-7) Storybk Pub.
Ever wondered or been asked, "What is the story of the Tooth Fairy?" Years ago Dr. Mac, a Dentist & Teacher, was asked this question from children. Not knowing the answer, he decided to find it. He discovered that the origin of the Tooth Fairy was one of the least known & documented stories in our heritage, & that no tale of the Tooth Fairy, based on history & culture, had ever been told. So he wrote THE TOOTH FAIRY LEGEND to give her a place in Western literature. Written to entertain children, the story can enlighten for its basic content is from historical information, folklore, superstitions & customs of the past & present relating to teeth from international sources. His endearing classic, long a favorite of children & adults alike, in this new full-color edition, beautifully illustrated in a classical manner & praised by some of America's leading artists, is still the standard work on this beloved character. For every parent who has ever watched a child place a baby tooth under a pillow, & for every child who has done so in eager anticipation, THE TOOTH FAIRY LEGEND will be an enlightening & fascinating reading. Storybook Publishing, P.O. Box 3218, Manhattan Beach, CA 90266-5133. 310-372-2950.
Publisher Provided Annotation.

Dodge, Mary M. Hans Brinker. (gr. k-6). 1985. pap. 4.95 (0-440-43446-7, Pub. by Yearling Classics) Dell.

Dodson, Bert, illus. Lazy Jack. LC 78-18070. 32p. (gr. k-4). 1979. PLB 9.79 (0-89375-123-5); pap. 1.95 (0-89375-101-4) Troll Assocs.

Dolan, Ellen M. & Bolinske, Janet L., eds. Aladdin & the Magic Lamp. Lie, Eula, illus. LC 87-61661. 32p. (Orig.). (gr. 1-3). 1987. text ed. 8.95 (0-88335-564-7); pap. text ed. 4.95 (0-88335-584-1) Milliken Pub Co.

Dreizler, Loch A. Princess Pickle Head. Mallord, Lauri, illus. LC 88-80123. 42p. (Orig.). (ps-4). 1988. pap. 2.95 (0-9620053-0-4) LAD Redondo Beach.

Duchak, Kathleen D. The Three Bears. Lang, Anne D., illus. 28p. (ps). Date not set. 15.00 (0-9640865-0-6) Family Pubng.

Duffield, Francesca, illus. A Bedtime Story. LC 92-75613. 10p. 1993. 5.95 (1-85697-915-6, Kingfisher LKC) LKC.

Dulac, Edmund. Fairy Tales of the World. Cott, Jonathan, ed. Dulac, Edmund, illus. LC 93-24486. 200p. 1994. 6.00 (1-56957-914-8) Barefoot Bks.

Dunlap, Hope. The Little Lame Prince. Dunlap, Hope, illus. LC 92-37665. 1993. 8.99 (0-517-08484-8, Pub. by Derrydale Bks) Random Hse Value.

Dunn, Patricia. Children's Book of Irish Fairy Tales. 1988. pap. 9.95 (0-85342-843-3) Dufour.

Dunster, Mark. Marsh King. 10p. (Orig.). 1990. pap. 4.00 (0-89642-184-8) Linden Pubs.

—Zond. 45p. (Orig.). 1989. pap. 5.00 (0-89642-168-6) Linden Pubs.

Eastman, David. Peter & the Wolf. Atkinson, Allen, illus. LC 87-11275. 32p. (gr. k-3). 1988. PLB 9.79 (0-8167-1057-0); pap. text ed. 1.95 (0-8167-1058-9) Troll Assocs.

Edelman, Heinz, illus. Prince Ring: Icelandic Fairy Tale. 32p. (gr. 6 up). 1983. PLB 13.95 (0-87191-951-6) Creative Ed.

Edens, Cooper. Jack & the Beanstalk. (Illus.). 48p. (gr. 9-12). 1991. 14.95 (0-88138-139-X, Green Tiger) S&S Trade.

—Three Princesses: The Ultimate Illustrated Edition. (Illus.). (ps-3). 1991. 22.50 (0-553-07368-0) Bantam.

Edens, Cooper, ed. & intro. by. Beauty & the Beast. abr. ed. LC 88-81988. (Illus.). 48p. (gr. 9-12). 1991. 14.95 (0-88138-115-2, Green Tiger) S&S Trade.

Edens, Cooper & Darling, Harold, eds. Favorite Fairy Tales: A Classic Illustrated Edition. Rackham, Arthur, et al, illus. 128p. (ps up). 1991. 16.95 (0-87701-848-0) Chronicle Bks.

Edwards, Gunvor, illus. Tales from Fairyland. 80p. (gr. 3-5). 1994. pap. 5.95 (0-685-70752-0, Pub. by Hutchinson UK) Trafalgar.

Ehrlich, Amy. Rapunzel. Waldherr, Kris, illus. LC 88-25918. 32p. (ps-3). 1989. 12.95 (0-8037-0654-5); PLB 12.89 (0-8037-0655-3) Dial Bks Young.

Ehrlich, Amy, adapted by. The Random House Book of Fairy Tales. Goode, Diane, illus. LC 83-13833. 224p. (gr. k-4). 1985. bds. 17.00 (0-394-85693-7); lib. bdg. 17.99 (0-394-95693-1) Random Bks Yng Read.

Ehrlich, Susanne. Es War Einmal. (GER., Illus.). 96p. 1991. pap. 9.95 incl. 60-min. cassette (0-8442-2426-X, Natl Textbk); pap. 6.95 bk. only (0-8442-2433-2, Natl Textbk) NTC Pub Grp.

Eimon, Mina H. Why Cats Chase Mice: A Story of the 12 Zodiac Signs. Eimon, Mina H., illus. 32p. (gr. k-6). 1993. 11.95 (0-89346-533-X) Heian Intl.

Eisberg, Tiffany B. & Salvadeo, Michele B. Why Did Cinderella Thank Her Ugly Sisters? (Illus.). 48p. (gr. 3-5). 1994. pap. 6.95 (1-56721-023-6) Twnty-Fifth Cent Pr.

Elves & the Shoemaker. (ARA., Illus.). (gr. 3-5). 1978. 3.95x (0-86685-199-2); incl. cassette 14.95x (0-685-02571-3) Intl Bk Ctr.

Emberley, Rebecca. Three Cool Kids. LC 93-40113. 1995. 14.95 (0-316-23666-7) Little.

The Emperor's New Suit. (Illus.). 24p. (Orig.). (gr. k-3). 1993. pap. 2.50 (1-56144-295-X, Honey Bear Bks) Modern Pub NYC.

The Enormous Turnip. (ARA., Illus.). (gr. 3-5). 1987. 3.95x (0-86685-200-X) Intl Bk Ctr.

Enright, Elizabeth. Tatsinda. Johnston, Allyn, ed. Treherne, Katie T., illus. 65p. (gr. k-5). 1991. 16.95 (0-15-284280-2) HarBrace.

Erben, Karel J. Listen, Kids... Czech Fairy Tales. Ciuffreda, Lillian, ed. Kalnoky, Julius, tr. Jelinek, Otakar, illus. LC 87-83652. 65p. (gr. 3-8). 1988. 13.95 (0-9619982-0-2) Kalnoky Pr.

Evans, C. S. Cinderella. 1993. 12.95 (0-679-42313-3, Everymans Lib) Knopf.

—Sleeping Beauty. 1993. 12.95 (0-679-42814-3, Everymans Lib) Knopf.

Evans, Eugene. Bremen Town Musicians. Boddy, Joe & Boddy, Joe, illus. LC 90-10974. 48p. (gr. 1-5). 1990. 5.95 (0-88101-102-9) Unicorn Pub.

Everett, Mimi, illus. Cinderella. 24p. 1991. pap. 1.25 (0-7214-5300-7, S9016-1 SER.) Ladybird Bks.

—Snow White & the Seven Dwarfs. 24p. (ps-1). 1991. pap. 1.25 (0-7214-5306-6, S9016-7) Ladybird Bks.

Fairy Tales Clippers. (Illus.). (gr. k-5). 1989. Complete Package: 8 clippers. PLB 223.92 (0-8172-1830-0); PLB write for info. (0-8393-0250-9) Raintree Steck-V.

Fairy Tales from Many Lands. (Illus.). 288p. 1989. 10.99 (0-517-67951-5) Random Hse Value.

Faulkner, Keith. Fairy Tales. Galvani, Maureen, illus. 24p. (ps-1). 1994. 7.95 (0-8431-3720-7) Price Stern.

Faulkner, Matt. Jack & the Beanstalk. (Illus.). 48p. (Orig.). (gr. k-3). 1986. pap. 2.50 (0-590-40164-5) Scholastic Inc.

Favorite Tales of Hans Christian Andersen. 96p. (gr. 2 up). 1988. 9.95 (1-56288-253-8) Checkerboard.

Ferris, Lynn B., retold by. & illus. Goldilocks & the Three Bears. LC 86-46154. 24p. (gr. k up). 1987. 9.95 (0-394-55882-0) Knopf Bks Yng Read.

Field, Eugene. Wynken, Blynken & Nod. 1989. pap. 2.95 (0-590-42422-X) Scholastic Inc.

Finger, Charles J. Tales from Silver Lands. Honore, Paul, illus. 225p. (gr. 7 up). 1965. 16.95 (0-685-01496-7) Doubleday.

El Flautista De Hamelin. (SPA.). (gr. 2). 1990. casebound 3.50 (0-7214-1413-3) Ladybird Bks.

Fleischman, Susan. Boy Who Looked for Spring. LC 90-36819. (gr. 4-7). 1993. 15.95 (0-15-210699-5) HarBrace.

Foreman, Michael, ed. & illus. Michael Foreman's World of Fairy Tales. 144p. (gr. 1 up). 1991. 18.95 (1-55970-164-1) Arcade Pub Inc.

Fowler, Richard. Ted & Dolly Fairytale Flight. (Illus.). 24p. (ps-3). 1984. 9.95 (0-88110-190-7) EDC.

—Ted & Dolly's Magic Carpet Ride. 24p. (ps-1). 1984. 9.95 (0-88110-155-9) EDC.

The Fox & the Hound. (Illus.). 48p. (ps-6). 1989. 5.99 (0-517-67007-0) Random Hse Value.

Fox, Naomi. Hansel & Gretel. Fox, Neal, illus. 24p. (ps-1). 1992. Incl. cassette. pap. 9.95 (1-882179-12-9) Confetti Ent.

—Little Red Riding Hood. Fox, Neal, illus. 24p. (ps-1). 1993. Incl. cassette. pap. 9.95 (1-882179-14-5) Confetti Ent.

—The Shoemaker & the Elves. Fox, Neal, illus. 24p. (ps-1). 1993. Incl. cassette. pap. 9.95 (1-882179-15-3) Confetti Ent.

—Sleeping Beauty. Fox, Neal, illus. 24p. (ps-1). 1992. Incl. cassette. pap. 9.95 (1-882179-13-7) Confetti Ent.

Frank-Mosenson, Sandra. Earth Day Lessons from Planet Mars. Carlos, Christina, illus. 72p. (Orig.). (gr. 4 up). 1991. Perfect bdg. 10.95 (0-9629607-3-X) Wisdom Pr IL.

French, Fiona. Little Inchkin. LC 93-23904. 1994. write for info. (0-8037-1478-5) Dial Bks Young.

French, Vivian. Once upon a Time. Prater, John, illus. LC 92-53139. 32p. (ps up). 1993. 14.95 (1-56402-177-7) Candlewick Pr.

—Under the Moon. Fisher, Chris, illus. LC 93-877. 96p. (gr. 3-6). 1994. 14.95 (1-56402-330-3) Candlewick Pr.

The Frog Prince. (Illus.). 20p. (ps up). 1992. write for info. incl. long-life batteries (0-307-74709-3, 64709, Golden Pr) Western Pub.

Fuentes, Vilma M. The Fairy of Masara. Inis, Ninabeth R., illus. 24p. (Orig.). (gr. k-3). 1984. pap. 3.50 (971-10-0211-6, Pub by New Day Philippines) Cellar.

Gal, Laszlo. East of the Sun & West of the Moon. 1993. 16.95 (1-895565-29-4) Firefly Bks Ltd.

Galdone, Paul. Henny Penny. Galdone, Paul, illus. LC 68-24735. 32p. (ps-3). 1979. 13.45 (0-395-28800-2, Clarion Bks) HM.

—Rumpelstiltskin. Galdone, Paul, illus. LC 84-12741. 32p. (ps-3). 1985. 14.95 (0-89919-266-1, Clarion Bks) HM.

Galdone, Paul, retold by. & illus. The Monster & the Tailor. LC 82-1246. 32p. (ps-1). 1988. pap. 5.70 (0-89919-795-7, Clarion Bks) HM.

Galdone, Paul, illus. Little Red Riding Hood. LC 74-6426. 32p. (gr. k-3). 1974. text ed. 14.95 (0-07-022732-2) McGraw.

La Gallinita Roja. (SPA.). (ps-3). 1993. pap. 2.25 (0-307-70097-6, Golden Pr) Western Pub.

Gardner, Richard A. Dr. Gardner's Fairy Tales for Today's Children. Lowenheim, Alfred, illus. LC 80-16187. 96p. (gr. 1-6). 1978. Repr. of 1974 ed. PLB 14.95 (0-933812-02-7) Creative Therapeutics.

—Dr. Gardner's Modern Fairy Tales. Lowenheim, Al, illus. LC 83-40149. 106p. (gr. 2-6). Repr. 14.95 (0-933812-09-4) Creative Therapeutics.

Garner, Alan. Jack & the Beanstalk. Heller, Julek, illus. LC 91-36717. 32p. (gr. k-3). 1992. 14.00 (0-385-30693-8) Doubleday.

El Gato Con Botas. (SPA.). (ps-3). 1993. pap. 4.95 (0-307-72197-3, Golden Pr) Western Pub.

Geis, Darlene, ed. Walt Disney's Treasury of Children's Classics. (Illus.). (gr. 5 up). 1978. 29.95 (0-8109-0812-3) Abrams.

German Craftsmen Staff, illus. King Winter: Treasures from the Library of Congress. 16p. 1992. Repr. of 1859 ed. saddle wired 3.95 (1-55709-168-4) Applewood.

Gerson, Mary-Joan, retold by. How Night Came from the Sea: A Story from Brazil. Golembe, Carla, illus. LC 93-20054. (ps-3). 1994. 15.95 (0-316-30855-2, Joy St Bks) Little.

Gerstein, Mordicai, retold by. & illus. Beauty & the Beast. 48p. (ps-2). 1989. (DCB); bk. & cassette 17.95 (*0-525-44511-0*) Dutton Child Bks.
Gilchrist, Cherry, retold by. Prince Ivan & the Firebird. Troshkov, Andrei, illus. LC 93-38136. 1994. 16.00 (*1-56957-920-2*) Barefoot Bks.
The Gingerbread Man. (Illus.). 28p. (ps up). 1987. 3.95 (*0-7214-5030-X*) Ladybird Bks.
Gipson, Morrell. Rip Van Winkle. San Souci, Daniel, illus. LC 83-20624. 32p. (gr. k-3). 1987. pap. 4.95 (*0-385-23965-3*, Pub. by Zephyr-BFYR) Doubleday.
Goble, Paul. The Girl Who Loved Wild Horses. Goble, Paul, illus. LC 92-29560. 32p. (ps-3). 1993. pap. 4.95 (*0-689-71696-6*, Aladdin) Macmillan Child Grp.
Goldberg, Moses. Rumpelstiltskin: A Participation Play. (gr. k-3). 1987. pap. 4.50 playscript (*0-87602-269-7*) Anchorage.
Golden Foot. (Illus.). 32p. (gr. 1-6). 1993. pap. 7.95 (*0-89800-252-4*) Dharma Pub.
Goldilocks. (Illus.). (ps-3). 1985. 2.98 (*0-517-28808-7*) Random Hse Value.
Goldilocks. (Illus.). (ps-1). 2.49 (*0-517-39462-6*) Random Hse Value.
Goldilocks & the Three Bears. (Illus.). 44p. (ps-2). 1987. pap. 5.50 (*0-913580-06-6*, Pub. by K Green Pubns) Gallaudet Univ Pr.
Goldilocks & the Three Bears. (ARA., Illus.). (gr. 1-5). 1987. 3.95x (*0-685-82827-1*) Intl Bk Ctr.
Goldilocks & the Three Bears. (Illus.). (ps-1). 1989. 2.98 (*0-517-69217-1*) Random Hse Value.
Goldilocks & the Three Bears. (ps-2). 3.95 (*0-7214-5060-1*) Ladybird Bks.
Goldilocks & the Three Bears. (ps-1). 1991. 2.99 (*0-517-47825-0*) Random Hse Value.
Goldilocks & the Three Bears. 1991. pap. 2.99 (*0-517-05216-4*) Random Hse Value.
Goldilocks & the Three Bears. 32p. 1992. 4.95 (*0-8362-3025-6*) Andrews & McMeel.
Gooc, Van. Goldilocks & the Three Bears. (Illus.). 48p. (ps-1). 1989. 5.99 (*0-517-69318-6*) Random Hse Value.
Goodall, John S. Puss in Boots. Goodall, John S., illus. LC 90-38606. 56p. (ps-3). 1990. SBE 14.95 (*0-689-50521-3*, M K McElderry) Macmillan Child Grp.

Goodridge, R. Keith. Discovery of the Little Yodel People. (Illus.). 24p. (gr. k-3). 1994. pap. 3.95 (*1-885945-10-8*) Goodreeder Pubns.
DISCOVERY OF THE LITTLE YODEL PEOPLE is a refreshing new children's book with beautifully illustrated pictures. The story begins with two children taking a walk in the country with their grandfather. As they admire the view, their grandfather begins to tell a story. The reader is transported back to when the grandfather was an eight-year-old boy embarking on an adventure in the forest. As the small boy continues, he encounters a group of tiny green elf-like characters called the Little Yodel People. He finds out that these people are responsible for supplying echoes. This book is the first in a series & is a sure hit with the children that will be cherished forever. Book two: CARING & SHARING WITH THE LITTLE YODEL PEOPLE, ISBN: 1-885945-12-4, takes the reader on a journey into their village showing them at work & play. The compassion of these tiny people is evident when one of them encounters an enemy in pain & puts his fear aside to help (Spring 1995). All of the Little Yodel People books convey the importance of family & cooperation. These books are timeless & will sell for years. To order contact: GOODREEDER PUBLICATIONS, INC., P.O. Box 53819, Cincinnati, OH 45253-0819. 513-741-2722.
Publisher Provided Annotation.

Gool, Van. The Emperor's New Clothes. (Illus.). 48p. 1989. 5.99 (*0-517-69316-X*) Random Hse Value.
—Puss in Boots. (Illus.). 48p. (ps-1). 1989. 5.99 (*0-517-69319-4*) Random Hse Value.
Grahame, Kenneth. Reluctant Dragon. Shepard, Ernest H., illus. LC 89-1658. 58p. (gr. 3-6). 1938. 12.95 (*0-8234-0093-X*); pap. 4.95 (*0-8234-0755-1*) Holiday.
—Wind in the Willows. (gr. 4 up). 1966. pap. 2.75 (*0-8049-0105-8*, CL-105) Airmont.
—Wind in the Willows. 234p. 1981. Repr. lib. bdg. 17.95 (*0-89966-305-2*) Buccaneer Bks.
—The Wind in the Willows. Green, Peter, ed. (gr. 5 up). 1983. pap. 2.95 (*0-19-281640-3*) OUP.
—Wind in the Willows, Vol. 1. 272p. (gr. 8 up). 1972. RSBE 13.95 (*0-684-12819-5*, Scribners Young Read) Macmillan Child Grp.
Grauer, Rita & Grauer, Rita. Vasalisa & Her Magic Doll. (Illus.). 32p. (ps-3). 1994. 14.95 (*0-399-21986-2*, Philomel) Putnam Pub Group.
Graves, Carolyn. Skip-a-Star: The Legend of the Christmas Snow. 2nd ed. (Illus.). 32p. (gr. 2-4). 1993. Set, audio cass. & bk. 9.95 (*1-882716-03-5*); Bk. pap. text ed. 4.95 (*1-882716-05-1*); write for info. audio cassette (*1-882716-04-3*) PAVE.
Greaves, Margaret. Tattercoats. Chamberlain, Margaret, illus. LC 90-6919. 32p. (ps-2). 1990. 13.95 (*0-517-58026-8*) Crown Bks Yng Read.
Greene, Ellin, retold by. Billy Beg & His Bull: An Irish Tale. Root, Kimberly B., illus. LC 93-7730. 32p. (ps-3). 1994. reinforced bdg. 15.95 (*0-8234-1100-1*) Holiday.
Greenway, Jennifer, retold by. Jack & the Beanstalk. Bernal, Richard, illus. 1991. 6.95 (*0-8362-4903-8*) Andrews & McMeel.
—The Three Billy Goats Gruff. Lustig, Loretta, illus. 1991. 6.95 (*0-8362-4913-5*) Andrews & McMeel.
Greer, Blanche. The Black Swan & the Green See Saw. Sarnoff, Arthur, illus. LC 75-261399. (gr. 5 up). 1977. 4.50 (*0-930422-07-4*) Dennis-Landman.
Gregory, Philippa. Florizella & the Wolves. Aggs, Patrice, illus. LC 92-52998. 80p. (gr. 3-6). 1993. 13.95 (*1-56402-126-2*) Candlewick Pr.
Gregory, Valiska. Through the Mickle Woods. (ps-3). 1992. 15.95 (*0-316-32779-4*) Little.
Greinke, Pamylle & King, Lise. Jacqueline & the Beanstalk. LC 83-63250. (Illus.). 64p. (ps-7). 1984. pap. 5.95 (*0-932966-52-7*) Permanent Pr.
Griffin, Peni R. Hobkin. LC 93-7758. 208p. (gr. 3-7). 1993. pap. 3.99 (*0-14-036356-4*, Puffin) Puffin Bks.
Griffith, Linda. Sleeping Beauty: Perform Your Very Own Ballet with Cassette, Tiara, Book, & Poster. (Illus.). 36p. 1993. incl. 40-min. audiotape 16.95 (*0-8362-4215-7*) Andrews & McMeel.
Grimes, Nikki, retold by. Walt Disney's Cinderella. Williams, Don & Story, Jim, illus. 24p. (ps-3). 1993. pap. 1.95 (*0-307-12684-6*, 12684, Golden Pr) Western Pub.
Grimm. Grimm's Fairy Tales. 1994. write for info. (*0-8050-3127-8*) H Holt & Co.
Grimm, Jacob & Grimm, Wilhelm K. About Wise Men & Simpletons: Twelve Tales from Grimm. Shub, Elizabeth, tr. Hogrogian, Nonny, illus. LC 85-15330. 128p. (gr. 4-6). 1986. SBE 14.95 (*0-02-737450-5*, Macmillan Child Bk) Macmillan Child Grp.
—Anno's Twice Told Tales: The Fisherman & His Wife & The Four Clever Brothers. Anno, Mitsumasa, retold by. & illus. LC 92-25307. 64p. (ps up). 1993. PLB 17.95 (*0-399-22005-4*, Philomel Bks) Putnam Pub Group.
—The Bear & the Bird King. Byrd, Robert, retold by. & illus. LC 93-15741. 32p. (ps-3). 1994. 14.99 (*0-525-45118-8*, DCB) Dutton Child Bks.
—Brave Little Tailor. Corcoran, Mark, illus. LC 78-18075. 32p. (gr. 1-4). 1979. PLB 9.79 (*0-89375-137-5*); pap. 1.95 (*0-89375-115-4*) Troll Assocs.
—Bremen Town Musicians. Ford, Pamela B., illus. LC 78-18064. 32p. (gr. k-3). 1979. PLB 9.79 (*0-89375-133-2*); pap. 1.95 (*0-89375-111-1*) Troll Assocs.
—The Bremen Town Musicians. Easton, Samantha, retold by. Corcoran, Mark, illus. 1991. 6.95 (*0-8362-4925-9*) Andrews & McMeel.
—The Bremen Town Musicians. Watts, Bernadette, illus. Bell, Anthea, tr. from GER. LC 91-30375. (Illus.). 32p. (gr. k-3). 1992. 14.95 (*1-55858-140-5*); lib. bdg. 14.88 (*1-55858-148-0*) North-South Bks NYC.
—Children's Classics: Grimm's Fairy Tales. 1989. 5.98 (*0-671-08756-8*) S&S Trade.
—The Classic Grimm's Fairy Tales. Egan, L. Betts, ed. LC 89-43005. (Illus.). 56p. (gr. 1-8). 1989. 9.98 (*0-89471-768-5*) Courage Bks.
—Complete Brothers Grimm Fairy Tale. 1986. 9.99 (*0-517-45374-6*) Random Hse Value.
—The Complete Grimm's Fairy Tales. Scharl, Josef, illus. Stern, James, ed. LC 44-40373. (Illus.). 1976. 17.00 (*0-394-49415-6*); pap. 16.00 (*0-394-70930-6*) Pantheon.
—The Devil with the Three Golden Hairs. Hogrogian, Nonny, illus. LC 82-12735. 40p. (gr. k-3). 1983. PLB 10.99 (*0-394-95560-9*) Knopf Bks Yng Read.
—The Elves & the Shoemaker. LC 80-27634. (Illus.). 32p. (gr. k-3). 1981. PLB 9.79 (*0-89375-472-2*); pap. text ed. 1.95 (*0-89375-473-0*) Troll Assocs.
—Fairy Tales. Rackham, Arthur, illus. LC 92-53180. 224p. 1992. 12.95 (*0-679-41796-6*, Evrymans Lib Childs Class) Knopf.
—The Fisherman & His Wife. Howe, John, illus. 32p. (gr. 6 up). 1983. PLB 13.95 (*0-87191-937-0*) Creative Ed.
—The Fisherman & His Wife. Jarrell, Randall, tr. from GER. Zemach, Margot, illus. 32p. (ps up). 1987. pap. 4.95 (*0-374-42326-1*) FS&G.
—The Fisherman & His Wife. Richardson, I. M., ed. Lippincott, Gary, illus. LC 87-10902. 32p. (gr. k-4). 1988. PLB 9.79 (*0-8167-1075-9*); pap. text ed. 1.95 (*0-8167-1076-7*) Troll Assocs.
—Fitcher's Bird. Arisman, Marshall, illus. 32p. (gr. 9 up). 1983. PLB 13.95 (*0-87191-942-7*) Creative Ed.
—The Frog King & Other Tales of the Brothers Grimm. 315p. (ps-8). 1989. pap. 2.95 (*0-451-52379-2*, Sig Classics) NAL-Dutton.
—Frog Prince. Baxter, Robert, illus. LC 78-18073. 32p. (gr. k-4). 1979. PLB 9.79 (*0-89375-126-X*); pap. 1.95 (*0-89375-104-9*) Troll Assocs.
—The Frog Prince. Alchemy II, Inc. Staff, illus. 26p. (ps). 1988. incl. cassette 9.95 (*1-55578-900-5*) Worlds Wonder.
—The Frog Prince. Lewis, Naomi, tr. from GER. Schroeder, Binette, illus. LC 89-42613. (GER.). 32p. (gr. k-3). 1989. 15.95 (*1-55858-015-8*) North-South Bks NYC.
—The Frog Prince. Black, Fiona, retold by. Parmenter, Wayne, illus. 1991. 6.95 (*0-8362-4920-8*) Andrews & McMeel.
—Der Froschkonig. Schroeder, Binette, illus. (GER.). 32p. (gr. k-3). 1992. 15.95 (*3-314-00336-6*) North-South Bks NYC.
—The Golden Goose. Paterson, Diane, illus. LC 80-29207. 32p. (gr. k-3). 1981. PLB 9.79 (*0-89375-476-5*); pap. 1.95 (*0-89375-477-3*) Troll Assocs.
—The Goose Girl. Perret, Paul, illus. 32p. (gr. 4 up). 1984. PLB 13.95 (*0-87191-934-6*) Creative Ed.
—The Goose Maiden. Archipowa, Anastassija, illus. 24p. 1990. 5.99 (*0-517-05388-8*) Random Hse Value.
—Grimms' Fairy Tales. Gotlieb, Jules, illus. (gr. 3 up). 1968. pap. 2.50 (*0-8049-0168-6*, CL-168) Airmont.
—Grimms' Fairy Tales. (Illus.). 1981. (G&D); deluxe ed. 13.95 (*0-448-06009-4*, G&D) Putnam Pub Group.
—Grimm's Fairy Tales. Carter, Peter, ed. & tr. Richardson, Peter, illus. 238p. (ps-6). 1987. 18.95 (*0-19-274529-8*) OUP.
—Grimm's Tales for Young & Old: The Complete Stories. Manheim, Ralph, tr. LC 76-56318. 648p. (gr. k-12). 1983. 14.95 (*0-385-11005-7*); pap. 15.95 (*0-385-18950-8*) Doubleday.
—Hansel & Gretel. Jeffers, Susan, illus. LC 80-15079. 32p. (gr. k up). 1980. 16.00 (*0-8037-3492-1*); PLB 14.89 (*0-8037-3491-3*) Dial Bks Young.
—Hansel & Gretel. Felix, Monique, illus. 32p. (gr. 6 up). 1983. PLB 13.95 (*0-87191-935-4*) Creative Ed.
—Hansel & Gretel. Zwerger, Lisbeth, illus. 32p. (ps-2). 1991. pap. 3.95 (*0-590-44459-X*, Blue Ribbon Bks) Scholastic Inc.
—Hansel & Gretel. Black, Fiona, retold by. Gurney, John, illus. 1991. 6.95 (*0-8362-4912-7*) Andrews & McMeel.
—Hansel & Gretel. 2nd, abr. ed. Crawford, Elizabeth D., tr. LC 91-40656. (Illus.). 28p. (gr. k up). 1992. pap. 4.95 (*0-88708-225-4*) Picture Bk Studio.
—Household Stories of the Brothers Grimm. Crane, Lucy, tr. Crane, Walter, illus. x, 269p. (gr. 3-9). 1886. pap. 4.95 (*0-486-21080-4*) Dover.
—Iron Hans. Heyer, Marilee, illus. LC 93-14662. 32p. 1993. 14.99 (*0-670-81741-4*) Viking Child Bks.
—Jack in Luck. Bell, Anthea, tr. Tharlet, Eve, illus. LC 92-7102. 28p. (ps up). 1992. pap. 14.95 (*0-88708-249-1*) Picture Bk Studio.
—Jorinda & Joringel. Cutts, David, ed. Rickman, David, illus. LC 87-10937. 32p. (gr. k-4). 1988. PLB 9.79 (*0-8167-1065-1*); pap. text ed. 1.95 (*0-8167-1066-X*) Troll Assocs.
—King Grisly-Beard. Sendak, Maurice, illus. Taylor, Edgar, tr. from GER. LC 73-77911. (Illus.). (ps-3). 1973. 14.00 (*0-374-34133-8*) FS&G.
—Little Red Riding Hood. Mahan, Benton, illus. LC 80-27684. 32p. (gr. k-3). 1981. PLB 9.79 (*0-89375-488-9*); pap. 1.95 (*0-89375-489-7*) Troll Assocs.
—Little Red Riding Hood. Hyman, Trina S., retold by. & illus. LC 82-7700. 32p. (ps-3). 1983. reinforced bdg. 15.95 (*0-8234-0470-6*); pap. 5.95 (*0-8234-0653-9*) Holiday.
—Little Red Riding Hood. Alchemy II, Inc. Staff, illus. 26p. (ps). 1988. incl. cassette 9.95 (*1-55578-903-X*) Worlds Wonder.
—Les Nains. Watts, Bernadette, illus. (FRE.). 32p. (gr. k-3). 1992. 14.95 (*3-85539-581-0*) North-South Bks NYC.
—Le Prince Grenouille. Schroeder, Binette, illus. (FRE.). 32p. (gr. k-3). 1992. 15.95 (*3-314-20666-6*) North-South Bks NYC.
—The Queen Bee. Dumas, Phillipe, illus. 32p. (gr. 4 up). 1984. PLB 13.95 (*0-87191-939-7*) Creative Ed.
—Ragamuffins. Watts, Bernadette, illus. LC 89-42609. 32p. (gr. k-3). 1989. 13.95 (*1-55858-014-X*) North-South Bks NYC.
—Rapunzel. Dodson, Bert, illus. LC 78-18066. 32p. (gr. k-3). 1979. PLB 9.79 (*0-89375-135-9*); pap. 1.95 (*0-89375-113-8*) Troll Assocs.
—Rapunzel. Rogasky, Barbara, retold by. Hyman, Trina S., illus. LC 81-6419. 32p. (ps-3). 1982. reinforced bdg. 15.95 (*0-8234-0454-4*); pap. 5.95 (*0-8234-0652-0*) Holiday.
—Rapunzel. Hague, Michael, illus. 32p. (gr. 6 up). 1986. PLB 13.95 (*0-87191-936-2*) Creative Ed.
—Rapunzel. Heyer, Carol, illus. LC 92-6712. 32p. (gr. k-3). 1992. 14.95 (*0-8249-8558-3*, Ideals Child); PLB 15.00 (*0-8249-8585-0*) Hambleton-Hill.
—Rapunzel, & The Seven Ravens. Archipowa, Anastassija, illus. 24p. 1990. 3.99 (*0-517-05386-1*) Random Hse Value.

—Rumpelstiltskin. Hockerman, Dennis, illus. LC 78-18079. 32p. (gr. k-3). 1979. PLB 9.79 (*0-89375-140-5*); pap. 1.95 (*0-89375-118-9*) Troll Assocs.

—Rumpelstiltskin. Zelinsky, Paul O., retold by. & illus. LC 86-4482. 40p. (gr. k up). 1986. 14.00 (*0-525-44265-0*, DCB) Dutton Child Bks.

—Rumpelstiltskin. Alchemy II, Inc. Staff, illus. 26p. 1988. incl. cassette 9.95 (*1-55578-910-2*) Worlds Wonder.

—Rumpelstiltskin. Sage, Alison, retold by. Spirin, Gennady, illus. 32p. (ps-3). 1991. 12.95 (*0-8037-0908-0*) Dial Bks Young.

—Rumpelstiltskin. (Illus.). 20p. (ps up). 1992. write for info. incl. long-life batteries (*0-307-74711-5*, 64711, Golden Pr) Western Pub.

—Rumpelstiltskin: A Fairy Tale. Watts, Bernadette, illus. Bell, Anthea, tr. LC 92-31331. (Illus.). 32p. (gr. k-3). 1993. 14.95 (*1-55858-188-X*); PLB 14.88 (*1-55858-189-8*) North-South Bks NYC.

—The Seven Ravens. adpt. ed. Geringer, Laura, adapted by. Gazsi, Edward S., illus. LC 93-8161. 32p. (gr. k-4). 1994. 16.00 (*0-06-023552-7*); PLB 15.89 (*0-06-023553-5*) HarpC Child Bks.

—The Sleeping Beauty. Alchemy II, Inc. Staff, illus. 26p. (ps). 1988. incl. cassette 9.95 (*1-55578-908-0*) Worlds Wonder.

—Sleeping Beauty & Other Fairy Tales. (Illus.). 96p. (Orig.). 1992. pap. 1.00t (*0-486-27084-X*) Dover.

—Sleeping Beauty, & The Frog Prince. Archipowa, Anastassija, illus. 24p. 1990. 5.99 (*0-517-05385-3*) Random Hse Value.

—Snow White. Greenway, Jennifer, retold by. Augestine, Erin, illus. 1991. 6.95 (*0-8362-4906-2*) Andrews & McMeel.

—Snow White. Poole, Josephine, ed. LC 91-18411. (Illus.). 32p. 1991. 15.00 (*0-679-82656-4*) Knopf Bks Yng Read.

—Snow White & Rose Red. Weren, James, illus. LC 78-18074. 32p. (gr. k-3). 1979. PLB 9.79 (*0-89375-136-7*); pap. 1.95 (*0-89375-114-6*) Troll Assocs.

—Snow White & Rose Red. Topor, Roland, illus. 32p. (gr. 6 up). 1984. PLB 13.95 (*0-87191-938-9*) Creative Ed.

—Snow White & Rose Red. Watts, Bernadette, illus. LC 87-72036. 32p. (gr. k-3). 1988. 14.95 (*1-55858-054-9*) North-South Bks NYC.

—Snow White & Rose Red. Spirin, Gennady, illus. 32p. (ps up). 1992. 14.95 (*0-399-21873-4*, Philomel Bks) Putnam Pub Group.

—Snow White & the Seven Dwarfs. (FRE., Illus.). (gr. 3-8). 8.95 (*0-685-11566-6*) Fr & Eur.

—Snow-White & the Seven Dwarfs. Jarrell, Randall, tr. from GER. Burkert, Nancy E., illus. LC 28-1489. 32p. (ps up). 1972. 17.00 (*0-374-37099-0*) FS&G.

—Snow White & the Seven Dwarfs. Iwasaki, Chihiro, illus. LC 85-12158. 40p. (gr. 1 up). 1991. pap. 15.95 (*0-88708-012-X*) Picture Bk Studio.

—Snow-White & the Seven Dwarfs. Jarrell, Randall, tr. from GER. Burkert, Nancy E., illus. 32p. (ps up). 1987. pap. 5.95 (*0-374-46868-0*, Sunburst) FS&G.

—The Table, the Donkey & the Stick. Galdone, Paul, illus. (ps-3). 1976. PLB 7.95 (*0-07-022701-2*) McGraw.

—Tales from the Brothers Grimm. 1987. 1.98 (*0-671-08490-9*) S&S Trade.

—Three Feathers. Schmid, Eleanor, illus. 32p. (gr. 4 up). 1984. PLB 13.95 (*0-87191-941-9*) Creative Ed.

—Three Languages. Chermayeff, Ivan, illus. 32p. (gr. 4 up). 1984. PLB 13.95 (*0-87191-940-0*) Creative Ed.

—Twelve Dancing Princesses. Hockerman, Dennis, illus. LC 78-18077. 32p. (gr. k-4). 1979. PLB 9.79 (*0-89375-139-1*); pap. 1.95 (*0-89375-117-0*) Troll Assocs.

—The Twelve Dancing Princesses. Carter, Anne, retold by. Dalton, Anne, illus. LC 88-13794. 32p. (ps-4). 1989. (Lipp Jr Bks); (Lipp Jr Bks) HarpC Child Bks.

—Die Wichtelmanner. Watts, Bernadette, illus. (GER.). 32p. (gr. k-3). 1992. 14.95 (*3-85825-256-5*) North-South Bks NYC.

—Wolf & the Seven Kids. new ed. Craft, Kinuko Y., illus. LC 78-18076. 32p. (gr. 1-4). 1979. PLB 9.79 (*0-89375-138-3*); pap. 1.95 (*0-89375-116-2*) Troll Assocs.

Gross, Ruth B. The Bremen-Town Musicians. Kent, Jack, illus. 32p. (Orig.). (ps-2). 1985. pap. 2.50 (*0-590-42364-9*) Scholastic Inc.

Gruelle, Johnny. Raggedy Ann & Andy Giant Treasury: Four Adventures Plus 12 Short Stories. Golden, N., retold by. Nash, C., frwd. by. (Illus.). 96p. (ps-1). 1985. 5.99 (*0-517-45594-3*) Random Hse Value.

Grundtvig, Sven. Danish Fairy Tales. Cramer, J. Grant, tr. from DAN. Van Heusen, Drew, illus. vii, 115p. (gr. k-5). 1972. pap. 4.95 (*0-486-22891-6*) Dover.

Hader, Berta & Hader, Elmer, illus. The Story of Hansel & Gretel. LC 94-1297. 1994. write for info. (*0-486-28299-6*) Dover.

—The Story of the Ugly Duckling. LC 94-1298. (gr. 1 up). 1994. pap. write for info. (*0-486-28300-3*) Dover.

Hague, Michael, illus. The Fairy Tales of Oscar Wilde. LC 92-14305. 192p. 1993. 19.95 (*0-8050-1009-2*, Bks Young Read) H Holt & Co.

—Mother Goose: A Collection of Classic Nursery Rhymes. LC 83-22559. 80p. (ps-2). 1984. 15.95 (*0-8050-0214-6*, Bks Young Read) H Holt & Co.

Haley, Gail E. Sea Tale. Haley, Gale E., illus. LC 89-34453. 32p. (ps-2). 1990. 13.95 (*0-525-44567-6*, DCB) Dutton Child Bks.

Haley, Gail E., retold by. & illus. Puss in Boots. LC 90-20629. 32p. (ps-3). 1991. 13.95 (*0-525-44740-7*, DCB) Dutton Child Bks.

Haley, Gail E., illus. Jack & the Bean Tree. 48p. (gr. k-3). 1986. 13.95 (*0-517-55717-7*) Crown Bks Yng Read.

Hall, Kirsten. The Tooth Fairy. (Illus.). 64p. (ps-2). 1994. PLB 14.00 (*0-516-05368-X*) Childrens.

Han, Oki S. & Plunkett, Stephanie H., eds. Kongi & Potgi: A Cinderella Story from Korea. Han, Oki S., illus. LC 93-28426. 1994. write for info. (*0-8037-1571-4*); PLB write for info. (*0-8037-1572-2*) Dial Bks Young.

Hansel & Gretel. (Illus.). (ps). 1985. bds. 1.00 (*0-517-48142-1*) Random Hse Value.

Hansel & Gretel. (Illus.). (ps-3). 1985. 2.98 (*0-517-28803-6*) Random Hse Value.

Hansel & Gretel. (Illus.). (ps-1). 2.98 (*0-517-45985-X*) Random Hse Value.

Hansel & Gretel. (Illus.). (ps-k). 2.98 (*0-517-41274-8*) Random Hse Value.

Hansel & Gretel. (ps-2). 3.95 (*0-7214-5101-2*) Ladybird Bks.

Hansel & Gretel. 24p. 1992. pap. 2.50 (*1-56144-089-2*) Modern Pub NYC.

Hanshaw, Carol A., retold by. Cinderella: The Fairy Tale. 16p. (ps-2). 1993. write for info. (*1-883366-19-4*) YES Ent.

—The Sleeping Beauty. 16p. (ps-2). 1993. write for info. (*1-883366-20-8*) YES Ent.

Harbour, Jennie, illus. My Book of Favorite Fairy Tales. LC 92-37669. 1993. 8.99 (*0-517-09125-9*, Pub. by Derrydale Bks) Random Hse Value.

Harness, Cheryl. The Queen with Bees in Her Hair. Harness, Cheryl, illus. LC 92-14409. 32p. (ps-3). 1993. 14.95 (*0-8050-1715-1*, Bks Young Read) H Holt & Co.

Harper, Wilhelmina, ed. Gunniwolf. Wiesner, William, illus. LC 67-22387. 32p. (ps-3). 1970. 13.00 (*0-525-31139-4*, DCB) Dutton Child Bks.

Hastings, Selina. The Firebird. Cartwright, Reg, illus. LC 92-52997. 40p. (ps up). 1993. 15.95 (*1-56402-096-7*) Candlewick Pr.

Hautzig, Deborah, retold by. Beauty & the Beast. LC 93-34694. 1995. write for info. (*0-679-85296-4*); PLB write for info. (*0-679-95296-9*) Random Bks Yng Read.

—The Nutcracker Ballet. Ewing, Carolyn, illus. LC 92-3320. 48p. (Orig.). (gr. 1-3). 1992. PLB 7.99 (*0-679-92385-3*); pap. 3.50 (*0-679-82385-9*) Random Bks Yng Read.

Haviland, Virginia. Favorite Fairy Tales Told in India. Cohn, Amy, ed. Rosenberry, Vera, illus. LC 94-83. 96p. (gr. 2 up). 1994. pap. 4.95 (*0-688-12600-6*, Pub. by Beech Tree Bks) Morrow.

—Favorite Fairy Tales Told in Ireland. Cohn, Amy, ed. O'Neill, Catharine, illus. LC 94-84. 96p. (gr. 2 up). 1994. pap. 4.95 (*0-688-12598-0*, Pub. by Beech Tree Bks) Morrow.

—Favorite Fairy Tales Told in Russia. Cohn, Amy, ed. Howard, Kim, illus. (gr. 3 up). 1995. pap. 4.95 (*0-688-12603-0*, Beech Tree Bks) Morrow.

—Favorite Fairy Tales Told in Sweden. Cohn, Amy, ed. Van Rynbach, Iris, illus. LC 94-85. 72p. (gr. 2 up). 1994. pap. 4.95 (*0-688-12606-5*, Pub. by Beech Tree Bks) Morrow.

Haviland, Virginia, selected by. Favorite Fairy Tales Told Around the World. Schindler, Stephen D., illus. (ps-6). 1985. 26.95 (*0-316-35044-3*) Little.

Haviland, Virginia, compiled by. Favorite Fairy Tales Told in England. Chambliss, Maxie, illus. LC 93-29707. 96p. (gr. 3 up). 1994. pap. 4.95 (*0-688-12595-6*, Pub. by Beech Tree Bks) Morrow.

—Favorite Fairy Tales Told in France. Ambrus, Victor, illus. LC 93-29665. 96p. (gr. 3 up). 1994. pap. 4.95 (*0-688-12596-4*, Pub. by Beech Tree Bks) Morrow.

Haviland, Virginia, ed. Favorite Fairy Tales Told in Germany. Paterson, Diane, illus. LC 93-29706. 96p. (gr. 3 up). 1994. pap. 4.95 (*0-688-12592-1*, Beech Tree Bks) Morrow.

Haviland, Virginia, retold by. Favorite Fairy Tales Told in Japan. LC 94-3079. 1994. pap. write for info. (*0-688-12601-4*, Pub. by Beech Tree Bks) Morrow.

Haviland, Virginia & Cohn, Amy, eds. Favorite Fairy Tales Told in Spain. Passicot, Monique, illus. LC 94-1499. (gr. 3 up). 1995. pap. 4.95 (*0-688-12605-7*, Beech Tree Bks) Morrow.

Havill, Juanita. Kentucky Troll. LC 90-27850. (Illus.). (ps-3). 1993. 13.00 (*0-688-10457-6*); PLB 12.93 (*0-688-10458-4*) Lothrop.

Hawkes, Kevin. Then the Troll Heard the Squeak. LC 92-12528. (gr. 4 up). 1992. 4.50 (*0-14-054469-0*) Puffin Bks.

Hawthorn, P. Usborne Book of Fairy Tales. (ps-3). 1994. pap. 10.95 (*0-7460-1819-3*, Usborne) EDC.

Hayes, Sarah. Blancanieves y los Siete Enanitos (Snow White & the Seven Dwarfs) Puncel, Maria, tr. from ENG. Anestey, Caroline, illus. (SPA.). 32p. (gr. 2-4). 1990. Incl. cass. 11.95 (*84-372-8053-2*) Santillana.

—Cenicienta (Cinderella) Puncel, Maria, tr. from ENG. Tomblin, Gill, illus. (SPA.). 32p. (gr. 2-4). 1990. Incl. cass. 11.95 (*84-372-8055-9*) Santillana.

Hayes, Sarah, ed. The Candlewick Book of Fairy Tales. Lawrence, John & Lynch, P. J., illus. LC 92-54961. 96p. (ps up). 1993. 16.95 (*1-56402-260-9*) Candlewick Pr.

Heide, Florence P. The Shrinking of Treehorn. Gorey, Edward, illus. LC 78-151753. 64p. (gr. 3-6). 1971. reinforced bdg. 13.95 (*0-8234-0189-8*); pap. 4.95 (*0-8234-0975-9*) Holiday.

Heidi. (Illus.). 336p. (gr. 3-7). 1981. deluxe ed. 13.95 (*0-448-06012-4*, G&D); (G&D) Putnam Pub Group.

Helldorfer, M. C. The Mapmaker's Daughter. Hunt, Jonathan, illus. LC 89-39330. 40p. (ps-3). 1991. RSBE 15.95 (*0-02-743515-6*, Bradbury Pr) Macmillan Child Grp.

Henny Penny, The Gingerbread Boy, Three Billy Goats Gruff, The Ugly Duckling. (Illus.). 24p. 1987. (Honey Bear Bks); Henny Penny. text ed. 3.95 (*0-87449-071-5*, Honey Bear Bks); Gingerbread Boy. text ed. 3.95 (*0-87449-109-6*, Honey Bear Bks); Three Billy Goats Gruff. text ed. 3.95 (*0-87449-110-X*, Honey Bear Bks); Ugly Duckling. text ed. 3.95 (*0-87449-111-8*, Honey Bear Bks) Modern Pub NYC.

Herrick, Amy. Kimbo's Marble. Gazsi, Edward S., illus. LC 91-18988. 48p. (gr. 1-5). 1993. 16.00 (*0-06-020373-0*); PLB 15.89 (*0-06-020374-9*) HarpC Child Bks.

Heyer, Carol, illus. Beauty & the Beast. 32p. (gr. k-3). 1992. pap. 4.95 perfect bdg. (*0-8249-8579-6*, Ideals Child) Hambleton-Hill.

High, Jackie L. The Rise & Fall of Ilsa: (The Female Lady Giant) Hillen, Rodolfo, ed. Campbell, Dwayne, illus. 26p. (ps-3). 1991. laminated 8.95x (*1-880605-00-7*) J Laverne Mus.

Hildebrandt, Greg, illus. Aladdin & the Magic Lamp. 48p. (ps-2). 1992. 5.95 (*0-88101-266-1*) Unicorn Pub.

—Alice in Wonderland. 48p. (gr. 2-5). 1991. 6.95 (*0-88101-109-6*) Unicorn Pub.

—Favorite Fairy Tales. 160p. (ps-7). 1985. 14.95 (*0-88101-268-8*) Unicorn Pub.

—Peter Pan. 48p. (gr. 2-5). 1991. 6.95 (*0-88101-111-8*) Unicorn Pub.

—Pinocchio. 48p. (gr. 2-5). 1992. 6.95 (*0-88101-267-X*) Unicorn Pub.

—Wizard of Oz. 48p. (gr. 2-5). 1992. 6.95 (*0-88101-217-3*) Unicorn Pub.

Hildebrandt, Tim & Laurence, Jim, eds. Shoemaker & the Christmas Elves. Hildebrandt, Tim, illus. 1993. 6.99 (*0-517-08488-0*) Random Hse Value.

Hillert, Margaret. Cinderella at the Ball. (Illus.). (ps-k). 1970. PLB 6.95 (*0-8136-5032-1*, TK2282); pap. 3.50 (*0-8136-5532-3*, TK2283) Modern Curr.

—The Golden Goose. (Illus.). (ps-k). 1978. PLB 6.95 (*0-8136-5051-8*, TK2306); pap. 3.50 (*0-8136-5551-X*, TK2307) Modern Curr.

Hjelm, J. Thaddeus Jones & the Dragon. LC 68-56830. (Illus.). 64p. (gr. 2-5). 1968. PLB 10.95 (*0-87783-039-8*); pap. 3.94 deluxe ed. (*0-87783-110-6*) Oddo.

Hodgson-Burnett, Frances. The Land of the Blue Flower. Griffith, Judith A., illus. LC 93-19968. 48p. (ps-5). 1993. Repr. of 1938 ed. 15.95 (*0-915811-46-4*) H J Kramer Inc.

Hoffman, E. T. Nutcracker. Black, Fiona, retold by. Gustafson, Scott, illus. 40p. 1991. 6.95 (*0-8362-4934-8*) Andrews & McMeel.

Hoffmann, E. T. The Nutcracker. Bell, Anthea, adapted by. Zwerger, Lisbeth, illus. LC 87-15249. (gr. 1 up). 1991. pap. 14.95 (*0-88708-051-0*) Picture Bk Studio.

—The Nutcracker. 2nd, abr. ed. Bell, Anthea, tr. Zwerger, Lisbeth, illus. LC 87-15249. 28p. (gr. k up). 1991. pap. 4.95 (*0-88708-156-8*) Picture Bk Studio.

—The Nutcracker. Delamare, David, illus. LC 91-2167. 48p. (gr. 1-5). 1991. 9.95 (*0-88101-115-0*) Unicorn Pub.

—The Nutcracker. Manheim, Ralph, tr. Sendak, Maurice, illus. 120p. 1991. pap. 16.00 (*0-517-58659-2*, Crown) Crown Pub Group.

Hol, Coby. La Ferme Des Tournesols. Hol, Coby, illus. (FRE.). 32p. (gr. k-3). 1992. 13.95 (*3-85539-660-4*) North-South Bks NYC.

Holmes, Sally, illus. The Complete Fairy Tales of Charles Perrault. Philip, Neil & Simborowski, Nicoletta, trs. Philip, Neil & Philip, Neilintro. by. LC 92-17781. (Illus.). 1993. 18.45 (*0-395-57002-6*, Clarion Bks) HM.

Hooks, William A. Gruff Brothers. 1990. 9.99 (*0-553-05855-X*) Bantam.

Hooks, William H. Moss Gown. Carrick, Donald, illus. (gr. k-4). 1987. 13.95 (*0-89919-460-5*, Clarion Bks) HM.

—Snowbear Whittington. Lisi, Victoria, illus. LC 93-8691. (gr. 1-5). 1994. 15.95 (*0-02-744355-8*) Macmillan.

Horio, Seishi. The Monkey & the Crab. Ooka, D. T., tr. from JPN. Murakami, Tsutomu, illus. 32p. 1985. 11.95 (*0-89346-246-2*) Heian Intl.

Horowitz, Jordan. Aladdin & the Magic Lamp. (ps-3). 1993. pap. 2.50 (*0-590-46417-5*) Scholastic Inc.

Howard, Pylen. The Swan Maiden. Green, Ellin. Sauder, Robert, illus. LC 93-34605. 32p. (ps-3). 1994. reinforced bdg. 15.95 (*0-8234-1088-9*) Holiday.

Howe, John. Jack & the Beanstalk, Vol. 1. 1989. 15.95 (*0-316-37579-9*) Little.

Huck, Charlotte. Princess Furball. Lobel, Anita, illus. LC 93-11729. 40p. (ps up). 1994. pap. 4.95 (*0-688-13107-7*, Mulberry) Morrow.

Hughes, Margaret A. The Sleeping Beauty. Forsse, Ken & Becker, Mary, eds. Hicks, Russell, et al, illus. 26p. (ps). 1986. 9.95 (*0-934323-27-5*) Alchemy Comms.

Hughes, Margaret A. & Forsse, Ken, eds. Peter & the Wolf. Hicks, Russell, et al, illus. 26p. (ps). 1986. packaged with preprogrammed audio cass. tape 9.95 (*0-934323-33-X*) Alchemy Comms.

Hunter, Mollie. A Stranger Came Ashore. LC 75-10814. (gr. 4-8). 1977. pap. 3.95 (*0-06-440082-4*, Trophy) HarpC Child Bks.
Hutchins, Pat. Changes, Changes. Hutchins, Pat, illus. LC 70-123133. 32p. (ps-k). 1973. RSBE 14.95 (*0-02-745870-9*, Macmillan Child Bk) Macmillan Child Grp.
Hutchinson, Duane. The Gunny Wolf & Other Fairy Tales. LC 92-43623. (Illus.). 96p. (Orig.). (gr. k-6). 1992. pap. 6.95 (*0-934988-29-3*) Foun Bks.
Hutton, Warwick. Beauty & the Beast. Hutton, Warwick, illus. LC 84-48441. 32p. 1985. SBE 14.95 (*0-689-50316-4*, M K McElderry) Macmillan Child Grp.
Hwa-I Publishing Co., Staff. Chinese Children's Stories, Vol. 46: Ma-Gu's Cock-a-Doodle-Doo, The Crippled God. Ching, Emily, et al, eds. Wonder Kids Publications Staff, tr. from CHI. (Illus.). 28p. (gr. 3-6). 1991. Repr. of 1988 ed. 7.95 (*1-56162-046-7*) Wonder Kids.
Hyman, Trina S., ed. & illus. The Sleeping Beauty. LC 75-43769. (gr. 1 up). 1983. 15.95 (*0-316-38702-9*); pap. 6.95 (*0-316-38708-8*) Little.
Impey, Rose, as told by. Read Me a Fairy Tale: A Child's Book of Classic Fairy Tales. Beck, Ian, illus. LC 92-41949. (gr. k up). 1993. 14.95 (*0-590-49431-7*) Scholastic Inc.
Irving, Washington. Rip Van Winkle. Wyeth, N. C., illus. Glassman, Peter, afterword by. LC 87-60720. (Illus.). 110p. (ps up). 1987. 15.00 (*0-688-07459-6*) Morrow Jr Bks.
—Rip Van Winkle. Kelley, Gary, illus. 64p. (gr. 6 up). 1993. 21.95 (*1-56846-082-1*) Creat Editions.
Isadora, Rachel. Firebird. Isadora, Rachel, illus. 32p. (ps-3). 1994. PLB 15.95 (*0-399-22510-2*) Putnam Pub Group.
—The Princess & the Frog. LC 88-61. (Illus.). 32p. (ps up). 1989. 12.95 (*0-688-06373-X*); PLB 12.88 (*0-688-06374-8*) Greenwillow.
—Swan Lake. LC 88-29843. (Illus.). 32p. 1991. 14.95 (*0-399-21730-4*, Putnam) Putnam Pub Group.
J. Sainsbury's Pure Tea Staff. Cinderella: Full Color Picture Book. (Illus.). 12p. (Orig.). 1993. pap. text ed. 1.00t (*0-486-27799-2*) Dover.
—Goldilocks & the Three Bears: Full-Color Picture Book. LC 92-38398. 1993. write for info. (*0-486-27503-5*) Dover.
—Jack & the Beanstalk: Full-Color Picture Book. LC 92-35299. 1993. pap. 1.00 (*0-486-27504-3*) Dover.
—Puss-in-Boots. (Illus.). 12p. (Orig.). 1993. pap. text ed. 1.00t (*0-486-27800-X*) Dover.
Jack & the Beanstalk. (ARA., Illus.). (gr. 2-5). 1987. Set. incl. cass. 14.95 (*0-685-02572-1*) Intl Bk Ctr.
Jack & the Beanstalk. 24p. (gr. k-3). 1992. pap. 2.50 (*1-56144-170-8*, Honey Bear Bks) Modern Pub NYC.
Jack & the Beanstalk. (Illus.). 24p. (gr. 2-5). 1993. pap. 3.95 (*1-56144-360-3*, Honey Bear Bks) Modern Pub NYC.
Jack & the Beanstalk: Favorite Hse Fairy Tales. 1989. 5.99 (*0-517-69320-8*) Random Hse Value.
Jackson, Ellen. Cinder Edna. O'Malley, Kevin, illus. LC 92-44160. (gr. 3 up). 1994. 15.00 (*0-688-12322-8*); lib. bdg. 14.93 (*0-688-12323-6*) Lothrop.
Jacob, Max. The Story of King Kabul the First & Gawain the Kitchen-Boy: Histoire du Roi Kaboul Ier et du Marmiton Gauwain; Followed by Vulcan's Crown, la Couronne de Vulcan. Black, Moishe & Green, Maria, trs. Blachon, Roger, illus. LC 93-5362. viii, 79p. 1994. 20.00 (*0-8032-2577-6*) U of Nebr Pr.
Jacobs, Joseph, ed. Celtic Fairy Tales. Batten, John D., illus. LC 67-24223. xvi, 267p. (ps-6). 1968. pap. 5.95 (*0-486-21826-0*) Dover.
—English Fairy Tales. Batten, John D., illus. LC 67-19703. xv, 261p. (gr. 3-6). 1898. pap. 5.95 (*0-486-21818-X*) Dover.
—English Fairy Tales. 1993. 13.95 (*0-679-42809-7*, Everymans Lib) Knopf.
—Indian Fairy Tales. Batten, John D., illus. xvi, 255p. (ps-4). 1969. pap. 6.95 (*0-486-21828-7*) Dover.
—More Celtic Fairy Tales. Batten, John D., illus. LC 67-24224. x, 234p. (ps-6). 1968. pap. 5.95 (*0-486-21827-9*) Dover.
Jagen, Edward J. The Good Knights' Quest to Rescue the Flower Faeries. (Illus.). 44p. (gr. k-6). 1991. pap. text ed. 14.95 (*0-9625641-3-3*) White Feather & Co.
Janssen, James S. The Elves of Bellaire Drive. Dietrich, Helen R., ed. Hunn, Diane, illus. Roniger, Mary S., frwd. by. (Illus.). 66p. (Orig.). 1989. pap. 5.95 (*0-944784-02-X*) Habersham.
—Further Adventures of the Elves of Bellaire Drive. Hunn, Diane, illus. Roiniger, Mary Sue, intro. by. (Illus.). (ps-5). 1991. pap. 5.95 (*0-9619160-1-X*) W S Nelson & Co.
—More Fun with the Elves of Bellaire Drive. Hunn, Diane, illus. Roniger, Mary S., intro. by. (Illus.). 66p. (gr. 2-10). 1992. pap. text ed. 5.95 (*0-9619160-2-8*) W S Nelson & Co.
Jensen, Karen. Goldilocks & the Three Bears. Rigg, Lucy, illus. 32p. (ps up). 1987. 9.95 (*0-910079-05-6*) Lucy & Co.
Jerrard, Jane, adapted by. Beauty & the Beast. Nilles, Burgandy & Thiewes, Sam, illus. 24p. 1993. PLB 10.95 (*1-56674-061-4*, HTS Bks) Forest Hse.
—Cinderella. Spellman, Susan & Thiewes, Sam, illus. 24p. (gr. k-4). 1993. PLB 10.95 (*1-56674-062-2*, HTS Bks) Forest Hse.
—Goldilocks & the Three Bears. Nilles, Burgandy & Thiewes, Sam, illus. 24p. (gr. k-4). 1993. PLB 10.95 (*1-56674-063-0*, HTS Bks) Forest Hse.
—Jack & the Beanstalk. Spellman, Susan & Thiewes, Sam, illus. 24p. (gr. k-4). 1993. PLB 10.95 (*1-56674-064-9*, HTS Bks) Forest Hse.
—Little Red Riding Hood. Spellman, Susan & Thiewes, Sam, illus. 24p. (gr. k-4). 1993. PLB 10.95 (*1-56674-065-7*, HTS Bks) Forest Hse.
—The Ugly Duckling. Spellman, Susan & Thiewes, Sam, illus. 24p. (gr. k-4). 1993. PLB 10.95 (*1-56674-066-5*, HTS Bks) Forest Hse.
Johnson, Crockett. Harold's Fairy Tale. Johnson, Crockett, illus. LC 56-8147. 64p. (ps-1). 1994. pap. 4.95 (*0-06-443347-1*, Trophy) HarpC Child Bks.
Johnston, Tony. The Cowboy & the Blackeyed Pea. Ludwig, Warren, illus. 32p. (ps-3). 1992. 14.95 (*0-399-22330-4*, Putnam) Putnam Pub Group.
Jones, Terry. The Beast with a Thousand Teeth. Foreman, Michael, illus. LC 93-30994. 32p. 1994. 9.95 (*0-87226-374-6*) P Bedrick Bks.
—The Fly-by-Night. Foreman, Michael, illus. LC 94-7539. 32p. (gr. k up). 1994. 9.95 (*0-87226-379-7*) P Bedrick Bks.
—The Sea Tiger. Foreman, Michael, illus. LC 94-7546. 32p. (gr. k up). 1994. 9.95 (*0-87226-378-9*) P Bedrick Bks.
—Terry Jones' Fairy Tales. Foreman, Michael, illus. 128p. (ps up). 1986. pap. 8.95 (*0-14-031642-6*, Puffin) Puffin Bks.
—Terry Jones Fairy Tales. Foreman, Michael, illus. 160p. (gr. 3-7). 1993. pap. 3.99 (*0-14-032262-0*, Puffin) Puffin Bks.
Jose, Eduard, adapted by. Aladdin's Lamp: A Classic Tale. Suire, Diane D., tr. from SPA. Lavarello, Jose M., illus. LC 88-35312. 32p. (gr. 1-4). 1988. PLB 13.95 (*0-89565-481-4*) Childs World.
—Fearless John: A Classic Tale. Moncure, Jane B., tr. Lavarello, Jose M., illus. LC 88-35215. 32p. (gr. 1-4). 1988. PLB 13.95 (*0-89565-470-9*) Childs World.
—The Old Sandman: A Classic Tale. Riehecky, Janet, tr. Asensio, Augusti, illus. LC 88-36793. 32p. (gr. 1-4). 1988. PLB 13.95 (*0-89565-461-X*) Childs World.
The Jungle Book. (Illus.). 48p. (ps-6). 1989. 5.99 (*0-517-67006-2*) Random Hse Value.
Karlin, Barbara, retold by. Cinderella. Marshall, James, illus. 32p. (ps-3). 1992. pap. 4.95 (*0-316-48303-6*) Little.
Kase-Baker, Judith. Snow White & the Seven Dwarfs. (ps-6). 1984. pap. 4.50 (*0-87602-256-5*) Anchorage.
Kassirer, Sue. The Gingerbread Boy. Williams, Jennie, illus. 24p. (Orig.). (ps-k). 1993. pap. 1.50 (*0-679-84795-2*) Random Bks Yng Read.
—The Three Billy Goats Gruff. Fritz, Ron, illus. 24p. (Orig.). (ps-k). pap. 1.50 (*0-679-84796-0*) Random Bks Yng Read.
Katherine, Sharon. Sugar Princess. Wood, Paul, ed. Tolley, Lynn & Olds, Tom, illus. 31p. 1989. pap. 8.95 (*0-685-68779-1*) Jungle Pr.
Keith, Adrienne. Fairies from A to Z: A Fairy Box Book. Malinow, Wendy W., illus. 48p. 1994. 14.95 (*1-883672-10-4*) Tricycle Pr.
Kellogg, Steven, retold by. & illus. Jack & the Beanstalk. LC 90-45990. 48p. 1991. 14.95 (*0-688-10250-6*); PLB 14.88 (*0-688-10251-4*) Morrow Jr Bks.
Kendall, Carol. Whisper of Glocken. Gobbato, Imero & Garcia, Manuel, illus. LC 85-17634. 256p. (Orig.). (gr. 3-7). 1986. pap. 4.95 (*0-15-295699-9*, Voyager Bks) HarBrace.
Ketterer, E. Michele. The Lazy King: A Ballet & Fairy Tale. 1994. 7.95 (*0-533-10842-X*) Vantage.
Kidd, Ronald, adapted by. Goldilocks & the Three Bears. (Illus.). 24p. (ps up). 1992. write for info. (*0-307-74803-0*, 64803, Golden Pr) Western Pub.
—Jack & the Beanstalk. 20p. (ps up). 1992. write for info. (*0-307-74701-8*, 64701) Western Pub.
—Snow White & the Seven Dwarfs. Mateu, illus. 24p. (ps up). 1991. write for info. (*0-307-74018-8*, 64018) Western Pub.
Kimmel, Eric A. Asher & the Capmakers: A Hanukkah Story. Hillenbrand, Will, illus. LC 92-37978. 32p. (ps-3). 1993. reinforced bdg. 15.95 (*0-8234-1031-5*) Holiday.
—Bernal & Florinda: A Spanish Tale. Rayevsky, Robert, illus. LC 93-37917. 32p. (ps-3). 1994. reinforced bdg. 15.95 (*0-8234-1089-7*) Holiday.
Kimmel, Eric A., retold by. Baba Yaga: A Russian Folktale. Lloyd, Megan, illus. LC 90-39215. 32p. (ps-3). 1991. reinforced bdg. 14.95 (*0-8234-0854-X*) Holiday.
Kimmel, Eric A., ed. The Four Gallant Sisters. Yuditskaya, Tatyana, illus. LC 91-28231. 32p. (gr. 1-4). 1992. 15.95 (*0-8050-1901-4*, Bks Young Read) H Holt & Co.
Kimmel, Eric A., retold by. The Gingerbread Man. Lloyd, Megan, illus. 32p. (ps-3). 1993. reinforced bdg. 15.95 (*0-8234-0824-8*); pap. 5.95 (*0-8234-1137-0*) Holiday.
—The Goose Girl: A Story from the Brothers Grimm. Sauber, Robert, illus. LC 93-13138. 1995. write for info. (*0-8234-1074-9*) Holiday.
Kimmel, Eric A., adapted by. I-Know-Not-What, I-Know-Not-Where: A Russian Tale. Sauber, Robert, illus. LC 92-32692. 64p. (gr. 1-5). 1994. reinforced bdg. 16.95 (*0-8234-1020-X*) Holiday.
—Iron John: A Tale from the Brothers Grimm. Hyman, Trina S., illus. LC 93-7534. 32p. (ps-3). 1994. reinforced bdg. 15.95 (*0-8234-1073-0*) Holiday.
—Rimonah of the Flashing Sword: A North African Tale. Rayyan, Omar, illus. LC 93-40091. 1995. write for info. (*0-8234-1093-5*) Holiday.
Kimmel, Eric A., retold by. The Three Princes: A Middle Eastern Tale. Fisher, Leonard E., illus. LC 93-25862. 32p. (ps-3). 1994. reinforced bdg. 15.95 (*0-8234-1115-X*) Holiday.
Kimmel, Eric A., adapted by. Three Sacks of Truth: A Story from France. Rayevsky, Robert, illus. 32p. (ps-3). 1993. reinforced bdg. 15.95 (*0-8234-0921-X*) Holiday.
Kindle, Patricia & Finney, Susan. Fantasy & Fairy Tales. McKay, Ardis, illus. 64p. (gr. 4-8). 1985. wkbk. 8.95 (*0-86653-317-6*, GA 669) Good Apple.
Kingsley, Charles. The Water Babies. Smith, Jessie W., illus. LC 94-15218. (gr. 3 up). 1994. 10.95 (*0-681-00647-1*) Longmeadow Pr.
Kipling, Rudyard. The Elephant's Child. (ps-2). 1988. 4.95 (*0-7232-3449-3*) Warne.
—Just So Stories. Foreman, Michael, illus. (ps up). 1987. 15.00 (*0-670-80242-5*) Viking Child Bks.
Kirstein, Lincoln, retold by. Puss in Boots. Vaes, Alain, illus. 32p. (ps-3). 1992. 15.95 (*0-316-89506-7*) Little.
Kreider, Karen. Disney's Aladdin: The Genie's Tale. Marderosian, Mark & Kurtz, John, illus. 24p. (ps). 1993. pap. 1.95 (*0-307-10019-7*, 10019, Golden Pr) Western Pub.
Kroll, Steven. Princess Abigail & the Wonderful Hat. Brewster, Patience, illus. LC 90-39213. 32p. (ps-3). 1991. reinforced 14.95 (*0-8234-0853-1*) Holiday.
Lagerlof, Selma. The Changeling. Stevens, Susanna, tr. from SWE. Winter, Jeanette, illus. LC 90-45277. 48p. (gr. k-5). 1992. 15.00 (*0-679-81035-8*); PLB 15.99 (*0-679-91035-2*) Knopf Bks Yng Read.
Landes, William-Alan. Aladdin n' His Magic Lamp: Music & Lyrics. rev. ed. (gr. 3-12). 1985. pap. text ed. 15.00 (*0-88734-002-4*) Players Pr.
—Rumpelstiltskin. rev. ed. LC 89-43683. 52p. (gr. 3-12). 1985. pap. 6.00 play script (*0-88734-104-7*); tchr's. ed. 30.00 (*0-88734-005-9*) Players Pr.
Landes, William-Alan & Lasky, Mark A. Grandpa's Bedtime Story. rev. ed. LC 89-63868. (gr. 3-12). 1985. pap. 6.00 play script (*0-88734-505-0*) Players Pr.
Landes, William-Alan & Rizzo, Jeff. Rumpelstiltskin: Music & Lyrics. rev. ed. (gr. 3-12). 1985. pap. text ed. 15.00 (*0-88734-004-0*) Players Pr.
Lang, Andrew. The Crimson Fairy Book. Ford, H. J., illus. LC 67-17988. (gr. 4-8). 19.25 (*0-8446-0753-3*) Peter Smith.
—Green Fairy Book. LC 34-28314. (Illus.). (gr. 4 up). 1969. pap. 2.95 (*0-8049-0197-X*, CL-197) Airmont.
—The Olive Fairy Book. Ford, H. J., illus. (gr. 2 up). 17.00 (*0-8446-0754-1*) Peter Smith.
—Pink Fairy Book. Ford, Henry J., illus. 360p. (gr. 4-6). 1966. pap. 6.95 (*0-486-21792-2*) Dover.
—The Pink Fairy Book. Ford, H. J., illus. (gr. 2 up). 19.25 (*0-8446-0755-X*) Peter Smith.
—The Rainbow Fairy Book. Hague, Michael, illus. Glassman, Peter, intro. by. LC 92-33449. (Illus.). 288p. 1993. 20.00 (*0-688-10878-4*) Morrow Jr Bks.
—The Red Fairy Book. Ford, H. J & Speed, illus. (gr. 2 up). 19.25 (*0-8446-0756-8*) Peter Smith.
—The Violet Fairy Book. Ford, H. J., illus. (gr. 2 up). 19.25 (*0-8446-0757-6*) Peter Smith.
—The Yellow Fairy Book. Ford, H. J., illus. (gr. 2 up). 19.25 (*0-8446-0758-4*) Peter Smith.
Lang, Andrew, ed. Arabian Nights Entertainments. Ford, H. J., illus. LC 69-17098. xv, 424p. (gr. k-6). 1969. pap. 6.95 (*0-486-22289-6*) Dover.
—Blue Fairy Book. LC 34-28315. (Illus.). (gr. 4 up). 1969. pap. 2.95 (*0-8049-0196-1*, CL-196) Airmont.
—Blue Fairy Book. Ford, Henry J. & Hood, G. P., illus. LC 34-28315. 390p. (gr. 1-6). 1965. pap. 6.95 (*0-486-21437-0*) Dover.
—Brown Fairy Book. Ford, Henry J., illus. (gr. 1-6). pap. 6.95 (*0-486-21438-9*) Dover.
—Crimson Fairy Book. Ford, Henry J., illus. LC 67-17988. 371p. (gr. 4-6). 1966. pap. 6.95 (*0-486-21799-X*) Dover.
—Green Fairy Book. Ford, Henry J., illus. LC 34-28314. 366p. (gr. 4-6). 1965. pap. 6.95 (*0-486-21439-7*) Dover.
—Grey Fairy Book. Ford, Henry J., illus. LC 67-17983. 387p. (gr. 4-6). 1900. pap. 6.95 (*0-486-21791-4*) Dover.
—Lilac Fairy Book. Ford, H. J., illus. 367p. (ps-4). 1968. pap. 6.95 (*0-486-21907-0*) Dover.
—Olive Fairy Book. Ford, H. J., illus. 330p. (gr. 4-6). 1966. pap. 5.95 (*0-486-21908-9*) Dover.
—Orange Fairy Book. Ford, H. J., illus. 358p. (gr. 1-6). 1968. pap. 6.95 (*0-486-21909-7*) Dover.
—Red Fairy Book. Ford, Henry J. & Speed, Lancelot, illus. 367p. (gr. 4-6). pap. 6.95 (*0-486-21673-X*) Dover.
—Violet Fairy Book. Ford, Henry J. & Lang, H. J., illus. (gr. 4-6). pap. 6.95 (*0-486-21675-6*) Dover.
Lang, Andrew, compiled by. A World of Fairy Tales. Ford, Henry J., illus. Philip, Neil, intro. by. LC 92-46245. 256p. 1993. 20.00 (*0-8037-1250-2*) Dial Bks Young.
Lang, Andrew, ed. Yellow Fairy Book. Ford, Henry J., illus. 321p. (gr. 4-6). pap. 6.95 (*0-486-21674-8*) Dover.
Langley, Jonathan. Goldilocks & the Three Bears. Langley, Jonathan, illus. LC 91-33155. 32p. (gr. k-3). 1993. 11.00 (*0-06-020814-7*); PLB 10.89 (*0-06-020815-5*) HarpC Child Bks.

—The Three Billy Goats Gruff. Langley, Jonathan, illus. LC 92-4842. 32p. (ps-3). Date not set. 15.00 (*0-06-021224-1*); PLB 14.89 (*0-06-021474-0*) HarpC Child Bks.

Larned, W. T. American Indian Fairy Tales. Rae, John, illus. LC 93-46940. 1994. 8.99 (*0-517-10177-7*, Pub. by Derrydale Bks) Random Hse Value.

Latino, Frank. The Legend of Holly Boy: The Holly Boy. Hood, Jack, illus. 38p. (Orig.). (gr. 9-12). 1994. 15.95 (*0-9640474-0-3*); pap. 7.95 (*0-9640474-1-1*) F Latino Pub Co.

Lattimore, Deborah N., as told by. & illus. Three Tales from The Arabian Nights. LC 94-9828. 1995. 18.00 (*0-06-024585-9*); PLB 17.89 (*0-06-024734-7*) HarpC.

Lawson, Julie. The Dragon's Pearl. Morin, Paul, illus. 32p. (gr. k-3). 1993. 15.45 (*0-395-63623-X*, Clarion Bks) HM.

Leamy, Edmund. Fairy Minstrel of Glenmalure & Other Stories for Children. Casseau, Vera, illus. LC 76-9901. (gr. 4-6). 1976. Repr. of 1913 ed. 15.00x (*0-8486-0210-2*) Roth Pub Inc.

—Golden Spears & Other Fairy Tales. Turner, Corinne, illus. LC 76-9902. (gr. 4-6). 1976. Repr. of 1928 ed. 15.00x (*0-8486-0211-0*) Roth Pub Inc.

—Irish Fairy Stories for Children. (Illus.). 86p. (gr. 2 up). 1992. pap. 9.95 (*1-85635-008-8*, Pub. by Mercier Pr Eire) Dufour.

Lee, Sharon. Jack & the Beanstalk. Williams, Jennie, illus. 24p. (Orig.). (ps-k). 1993. pap. 1.50 (*0-679-84794-4*) Random Bks Yng Read.

Leeds, Barbara. Fairy Tale Rap: "Jack & the Beanstalk" & Other Stories. Hamilton, Craig, illus. 32p. (Orig.). (gr. k-8). 1990. pap. 5.95 (*0-9624932-0-1*); pap. 12.95 incl. cass. (*0-9624932-2-8*); cassette 8.95 (*0-9624932-1-X*) Miramonte Pr.

Le Guin, Ursula K. A Ride on the Red Mare's Back. Downing, Julie, illus. LC 91-21677. 48p. (gr. 1-4). 1992. 15.95 (*0-531-05991-X*); PLB 15.99 (*0-531-08591-0*) Orchard Bks Watts.

—The Tombs of Atuan. Garraty, Gail, illus. LC 70-154753. 176p. (gr. 6-9). 1990. SBE 16.95 (*0-689-31684-4*, Atheneum Child Bk) Macmillan Child Grp.

Leprince De Beaumont, Marie. Beauty & the Beast. Howard, Richard, tr. Knight, Hilary, illus. Cocteau, Jean. (Illus.). 48p. (gr. 1-5). 1990. pap. 14.95 jacketed (*0-671-70720-5*, S&S BFYR) S&S Trade.

Leprince De Beaumont, Marie & Perrault, Charles. Beauty & the Beast & Other Fairy Tales. (Illus.). 96p. (Orig.). (ps-3). 1994. pap. 1.00 (*0-486-28032-2*) Dover.

Lesser, Rika, retold by. Hansel & Gretel. Zelinsky, Paul O., illus. 48p. (ps-3). 1989. pap. 6.95 (*0-399-21725-8*, Sandcastle Bks) Putnam Pub Group.

Levine, Arthur A. The Boardwalk Princess. Guevara, Susan, illus. LC 92-8081. 32p. (ps up). 1993. 14.00 (*0-688-10306-5*, Tambourine Bks); PLB 13.93 (*0-688-10307-3*, Tambourine Bks) Morrow.

Lewis, Naomi. Hans Andersen's Fairy Tales. 1988. pap. 2.99 (*0-14-035085-3*, Puffin) Puffin Bks.

Lewis, Patrick, retold by. The Frog Princess: A Russian Folktale. Spirin, Gennady, illus. LC 93-10827. (gr. 2 up). 1994. 15.99 (*0-8037-1623-0*); lib. bdg. 15.89 (*0-8037-1624-9*) Dial Bks Young.

Lewis, Shari. One-Minute Favorite Fairy Tales. (ps). 1991. pap. 3.99 (*0-440-40625-0*, YB) Dell.

Lily Toy Hong. Two of Everything. Mathews, Judith, ed. Hong, Lily T., illus. LC 92-29880. 32p. (gr. k-3). 1993. PLB 14.95 (*0-8075-8157-7*) A Whitman.

Lindgren, Astrid. The Tomten. Wiberg, Harald, illus. LC 61-10658. (gr. 1-3). 1979. 14.95 (*0-698-20147-7*, Coward); (Coward) Putnam Pub Group.

Lipton, Alfred. Cinderella, Vol. 512. rev. ed. Caban, Janice, ed. & illus. 10p. (gr. k). 1989. pap. 2.00 (*1-878501-01-1*) Ntrl Science Indus.

—Goldilox & the Three Bears, Vol. 514. rev. ed. Caban, Janice, ed. & illus. 10p. (gr. k). 1989. pap. 2.00 (*1-878501-02-X*) Ntrl Science Indus.

—Jack & the Beanstalk, Vol. 510. rev. ed. Caban, Janice, ed. & illus. 10p. (gr. k). 1989. pap. 2.00 (*1-878501-00-3*) Ntrl Science Indus.

—Little Red Riding Hood, Vol. 520. rev. ed. Caban, Janice, ed. & illus. 10p. (gr. k). 1989. pap. 2.00 (*1-878501-05-4*) Ntrl Science Indus.

—Pinocchio, Vol. 516. rev. ed. Caban, Janice, ed. & illus. 10p. (gr. k). 1989. pap. 2.00 (*1-878501-03-8*) Ntrl Science Indus.

—Sleeping Beauty, Vol. 518. rev. ed. Caban, Janice, ed. & illus. 10p. (gr. k). 1989. pap. 2.00 (*1-878501-04-6*) Ntrl Science Indus.

Little, Jean & De Vries, Maggie. Once upon a Golden Apple. Gilman, Phoebe, illus. 32p. (ps-3). 1994. pap. 4.99 (*0-14-054164-0*) Puffin Bks.

Little Mermaid. (Illus.). 24p. (ps-2). 1991. write for info. (*0-307-74014-5*, Golden Pr) Western Pub.

The Little Mermaid. 24p. 1992. pap. 2.50 (*1-56144-093-0*) Modern Pub NYC.

Little People Big Book about Magical Worlds. 64p. (ps-1). 1990. write for info. (*0-8094-7495-6*); PLB write for info. (*0-8094-7496-4*) Time-Life.

The Little Red Hen. (Illus.). 28p. (ps up). 1987. 3.95 (*0-7214-5028-8*) Ladybird Bks.

Little Red Riding Hood. (ARA., Illus.). (gr. 3-5). 1987. 3.95x (*0-86685-204-2*) Intl Bk Ctr.

Little Red Riding Hood. 1989. 5.99 (*0-517-69317-8*) Random Hse Value.

Little Red Riding Hood. 24p. (gr. k-3). 1992. pap. 2.50 (*1-56144-171-6*, Honey Bear Bks) Modern Pub NYC.

Little Red Riding Hood. (Illus.). 24p. (ps up). 1992. write for info. incl. long-life batteries (*0-307-74810-3*, 64810, Golden Pr) Western Pub.

Littledale, Freya. The Elves & the Shoemaker. 32p. 1991. pap. 3.95 (*0-590-44855-2*, Blue Ribbon Bks) Scholastic Inc.

Lobel, Anita. The Dwarf Giant. Lobel, Anita, illus. LC 90-39214. 32p. (ps-3). 1991. reinforced 14.95 (*0-8234-0852-3*) Holiday.

Lobel, Arnold. Giant John. Lobel, Arnold, illus. LC 64-16639. 32p. (gr. k-3). 1964. PLB 14.89 (*0-06-022946-2*) HarpC Child Bks.

—Prince Bertram the Bad. Lobel, Arnold, illus. LC 63-8741. 32p. (gr. k-3). 1963. PLB 13.89 (*0-06-023976-X*) HarpC Child Bks.

Lodge, Bernard, retold by. & illus. Prince Ivan & the Firebird: A Russian Folk Tale. LC 93-12343. (ps-5). 1993. smythe sewn reinforced 14.95 (*1-879085-86-0*) Whsprng Coyote Pr.

Lomsky, Gerry. The Beanstalk Bandit: The Giant's Version of "Jack & the Beanstalk" Krug, Ken, illus. 30p. (gr. 2-7). 1993. pap. 4.95 (*1-883499-00-3*); Story cass. 6.95 (*1-883499-01-1*) Princess NJ.

Lopez, N. C. King Pancho & the First Clock. Gutierrez, M., illus. LC 63-16396. 32p. (gr. 2-7). 1967. PLB 9.95 (*0-87783-020-7*); pap. 3.94 deluxe ed. (*0-87783-098-3*); cassette 7.94x (*0-685-03701-0*) Oddo.

Lopez, Norbert. Cuento Del Rey Pancho y el Primer Reloj. LC 70-108730. (Illus.). 32p. (gr. 2-7). 1970. PLB 9.95 (*0-87783-010-X*); pap. 3.94 deluxe ed. (*0-87783-104-1*); cassette 7.94x (*0-685-03700-2*) Oddo.

Lubin, Leonard, adapted by. Aladdin & His Wonderful Lamp. Burton, Richard F., tr. from ARA. Lubin, Leonard, illus. LC 82-70308. 48p. (gr. 1-4). 1982. 10.95 (*0-440-00302-4*); PLB 10.89 (*0-440-00304-0*) Delacorte.

Lundbergh, Holger, tr. from SWE. Great Swedish Fairy Tales. Bauer, John, illus. LC 73-132364. 224p. (gr. 4-6). 1973. (Sey Lawr); pap. 10.95 (*0-440-03041-2*) Delacorte.

McAllister, Frank. Tooth Fairy Legend. McAllister, Stephen, illus. LC 90-28136. 40p. (gr. k-6). 1992. 12.95 (*0-915677-54-7*) Roundtable Pub.

McCarthy, Ralph F., et al, eds. The Inch-High Samurai. Kasamatsu, Shiro, illus. LC 93-16310. 48p. 1993. 13.00 (*4-7700-1758-8*) Kodansha.

McCaughrean, Geraldine. One Thousand & One Arabian Nights. Lavis, Stephen, illus. 260p. 1987. 18.95 (*0-19-274530-1*) OUP.

McCoy, Karen K. A Tale of Two Tengu. Fossey, Koen, illus. LC 93-2. (gr. 1-3). 1993. 14.95 (*0-8075-7748-0*) A Whitman.

McDermott, Gerald. Tim O'Toole & the Wee Folk. McDermott, Gerald, illus. 32p. (ps-3). 1992. pap. 3.99 (*0-14-050675-6*) Puffin Bks.

Macdonald, George. At the Back of the North Wind. Thomas, A. M., intro. by. LC 64-21758. (Illus.). (gr. 5 up). 1966. pap. 1.50 (*0-8049-0100-7*, CL-100) Airmont.

—At the Back of the North Wind. Hughes, Arthur, illus. 378p. 1992. Repr. of 1886 ed. 16.00 (*1-881084-07-8*) Johannesen.

—The Complete Fairy Tales of George MacDonald. Hughes, Arthur, illus. Green, Roger L., intro. by. LC 77-80272. (Illus.). (gr. 3-9). 1987. PLB 10.95 (*0-8052-3700-3*) Schocken.

—George MacDonald Original Works, 5 vols, Series III. (gr. 5 up). 1993. Repr. Set. 74.00 (*1-881084-18-3*); Per volume, first 3 volumes with color plates. 20.00 (*1-881084-20-5*); Per volume, last 2 volumes with B&W illus. 16.00 (*1-881084-21-3*) Johannesen.

—The Light Princess. Hughes, Arthur, illus. LC 93-561. 160p. 1993. 6.00 (*1-56957-903-2*) Shambhala Pubns.

—Princess & the Goblin. Hogan, A. H., intro. by. (gr. 3 up). 1967. pap. 1.50 (*0-8049-0156-2*, CL-156) Airmont.

—Princess & the Goblin. (gr. 1-4). 1984. pap. 2.25 (*0-14-035029-2*, Puffin) Puffin Bks.

—The Princess & the Goblin. (gr. 4-7). 1991. pap. 2.95 (*0-590-44025-X*) Scholastic Inc.

—The Princess & the Goblin. LC 93-11264. (gr. 2 up). 1993. 12.95 (*0-679-42810-0*, Everymans Lib Childs) Knopf.

McEwan, Chris. Pinocchio. 1990. pap. 13.95 (*0-385-41327-0*) Doubleday.

MacGill-Callahan, Sheila. The Children of Lir. Spirin, Gennady, illus. LC 91-2712. 32p. (ps-3). 1993. 14.99 (*0-8037-1121-2*); PLB 14.99 (*0-8037-1122-0*) Dial Bks Young.

—The Seal Prince. Shi, Jihong, illus. LC 93-16248. 1995. 13.99 (*0-8037-1486-6*); PLB 13.89 (*0-8037-1487-4*) Dial Bks Young.

McGovern, Ann. Stone Soup. Pels, Winslow P., illus. 32p. (Orig.). (gr. k-2). 1986. pap. 2.50 (*0-590-41602-2*) Scholastic Inc.

McGraw, Robert. The Rogue & the Horse. McGraw, J. Darrin, illus. 32p. (Orig.). (ps-3). 1993. pap. 5.95 (*0-9633385-0-1*) Imagin Pr.

McKinley, Robin. Beauty: A Retelling of the Story of Beauty & the Beast. LC 77-25636. 256p. (gr. 7-9). 1978. 16.00 (*0-06-024149-7*); PLB 15.89 (*0-06-024150-0*) HarpC Child Bks.

—The Door in the Hedge. LC 80-21903. 224p. (gr. 7 up). 1981. reinforced bdg. 11.75 (*0-688-00312-5*) Greenwillow.

McKissack, Patricia & McKissack, Fredrick. Cinderella. Dunnington, Tom, illus. LC 85-12764. (gr. 1-2). 1985. PLB 10.25 (*0-516-02361-6*); pap. 3.95 (*0-516-42361-4*) Childrens.

MacManus, Seumas, ed. Donegal Fairy Stories. Verbeck, Frank, illus. xii, 256p. (gr. 4-6). 1968. pap. 5.95 (*0-486-21971-2*) Dover.

McPhail, David. Goldilocks & the Three Bears. McPhail, David, illus. LC 93-43992. 1995. write for info. (*0-590-48117-7*) Scholastic Inc.

—Little Red Riding Hood. McPhail, David, illus. LC 93-43990. 1995. write for info. (*0-590-48116-9*) Scholastic Inc.

—The Three Little Pigs. McPhail, David, illus. LC 93-43991. 1995. write for info. (*0-590-48118-5*) Scholastic Inc.

Madame d'Aulnoy's Collection Staff. Jack & the Beanstalk. Francois, Andre, illus. 32p. (gr. 4 up). 1983. PLB 13.95 (*0-87191-947-8*) Creative Ed.

Madame de Villeneuve. Beauty & the Beast. Delessert, Etienne, illus. 48p. (gr. 4 up). 1984. PLB 13.95 (*0-87191-946-X*) Creative Ed.

Madinaveitia, Horacio. Sir Robert's Little Outing. Madinaveitia, Horacio, illus. 32p. (gr. k-4). 1991. PLB 13.95 (*1-879567-01-6*, Valeria Bks); pap. text ed. 7.95 (*1-879567-00-8*) Wonder Well.

The Magic Porridge Pot. (ARA., Illus.). (gr. 3-5). 1987. 3.95x (*0-86685-205-0*) Intl Bk Ctr.

Magorian, James. The Tooth Fairy. LC 93-73338. (Illus.). 22p. (Orig.). (gr. 1-3). 1993. pap. 3.00 (*0-930674-38-3*) Black Oak.

Mandelstein, Paul. Nightingale & the Wind. Silin-Palmer, Pamela, illus. LC 93-31056. 32p. (gr. 4 up). 1994. 17.95 (*0-8478-1787-3*) Rizzoli Intl.

Marcuse, Aida E. Caperucita Roja y la Luna de Papel. Torrecilla, Pablo, illus. (SPA.). 24p. (Orig.). (gr. k-6). 1993. PLB 7.50x (*1-56492-103-4*) Laredo.

Margulies, Teddy S. Walt Disney's Snow White & the Seven Dwarfs. Guell, illus. 24p. (ps-3). 1993. pap. 1.95 (*0-307-12686-2*, 12686, Golden Pr) Western Pub.

Marshall, James. Hansel & Gretel. LC 89-26011. (Illus.). 32p. (ps-3). 1990. 12.95 (*0-8037-0827-0*); PLB 12.89 (*0-8037-0828-9*) Dial Bks Young.

—Red Riding Hood. (ps-3). 1991. pap. 4.95 (*0-8037-1054-2*, Puff Pied Piper) Puffin Bks.

Martin, Claire, retold by. Boots & the Glass Mountain. Spirin, Gennady, illus. LC 91-9724. 32p. (ps-3). 1992. 15.00 (*0-8037-1110-7*); PLB 14.89 (*0-8037-1111-5*) Dial Bks Young.

Martin, Kerry, illus. Disney's The Little Mermaid: On Stage. LC 92-53439. 10p. (ps-k). 1993. 4.95 (*1-56282-375-2*) Disney Pr.

Marvin, Fred, illus. Disney's Beauty & the Beast: The Friendship. LC 92-53440. 10p. (ps-k). 1993. 4.95 (*1-56282-376-0*) Disney Pr.

Mathias, Robert. Beauty & the Beast. 1991. 4.99 (*0-517-66693-9*) Random Hse Value.

Matthews, Andrew, retold by. Stories from Hans Christian Andersen. Snow, Alan, illus. LC 92-45627. 96p. (gr. 2-5). 1993. 18.95 (*0-531-05463-2*) Orchard Bks Watts.

Matthews, Morgan. Squeaky Shoes. Karas, Brian, illus. LC 85-14014. 48p. (Orig.). (gr. 1-3). 1986. PLB 10.59 (*0-8167-0642-5*); pap. text ed. 3.50 (*0-8167-0643-3*) Troll Assocs.

—Tricky Alex. Mahan, Ben, illus. LC 85-14018. 48p. (Orig.). (gr. 1-3). 1986. PLB 10.59 (*0-8167-0598-4*); pap. text ed. 3.50 (*0-8167-0599-2*) Troll Assocs.

Mayer, Marianna. Baba Yaga & Vasilisa the Brave. Craft, Kinuko Y., illus. LC 90-38514. 40p. (ps-3). 1994. 16.00g (*0-688-08500-8*); 15.93 (*0-688-08501-6*) Morrow Jr Bks.

—Beauty & the Beast. Mayer, Marianna, illus. LC 78-54679. 48p. (gr. k up). 1984. SBE 15.95 (*0-02-765270-X*, Four Winds) Macmillan Child Grp.

—Beauty & the Beast. Mayer, Mercer, illus. LC 87-1095. 48p. (ps up). 1987. pap. 5.95 (*0-689-71151-4*, Aladdin) Macmillan Child Grp.

—My First Book of Nursery Tales: Five Favorite Bedtime Tales. reissue ed. Joyce, William, illus. Mayer, Marianna, retold by. LC 82-20452. (Illus.). 48p. (ps-1). 1992. text ed. 10.00 (*0-394-85396-2*) Random Bks Yng Read.

—The Prince & the Princess: A Bohemian Fairy Tale. Rogers, Jacqueline, illus. 64p. (gr. 3 up). 1989. 13.95 (*0-553-05843-6*) Bantam.

—The Sorcerer's Apprentice: A Greek Fable. Wiesner, David, illus. (gr. 3 up). 1989. 13.95 (*0-553-05844-4*) Bantam.

—Turandot. Pels, Winslow, illus. LC 93-27033. Date not set. write for info. (*0-688-09073-7*); lib. bdg. write for info. (*0-688-09074-5*) Morrow.

Mayer, Mercer. East of the Sun & West of the Moon. Mayer, Mercer, illus. LC 80-11496. 48p. (gr. k up). 1984. SBE 15.95 (*0-02-765190-8*, Four Winds) Macmillan Child Grp.

—Terrible Troll. Mayer, Mercer, illus. LC 68-28730. (gr. k-3). 1968. Dial Bks Young.

Mayhew, James. Koshka's Tales: Stories from Russia. LC 92-41185. (Illus.). 80p. (gr. k up). 1993. 16.95 (*1-85697-943-1*, Kingfisher LKC) LKC.

Mayo, Margaret, retold by. Magical Tales from Many Lands. Ray, Jane, illus. LC 93-12164. 128p. 1993. 19.99 (*0-525-45017-3*, DCB) Dutton Child Bks.

Merriam, Eve, retold by. That Noodlehead Epaminondas. (Illus.). 1992. pap. 8.95x (*0-89966-962-X*) Buccaneer Bks.

Metaxas, Eric. The Fool & the Flying Ship. Drescher, Henrik, illus. LC 91-40669. 40p. (gr. k up). 1992. pap. 14.95 (*0-88708-228-9*, Rabbit Ears); incl. cass. 19.95 (*0-88708-229-7*, Rabbit Ears) Picture Bk Studio.
—Jack & the Beanstalk. Sorel, Ed, illus. LC 91-14176. 40p. (gr. k up). 1991. pap. 14.95 (*0-88708-188-6*, Rabbit Ears); incls. cassette 19.95 (*0-88708-189-4*, Rabbit Ears) Picture Bk Studio.
—Puss in Boots. Le-Tan, Pierre, illus. LC 92-7789. 40p. 1992. pap. 14.95 (*0-88708-285-8*, Rabbit Ears); pap. 19.95 incl. cass. (*0-88708-286-6*, Rabbit Ears) Picture Bk Studio.
Micocci, Harriet. Captain Orkle's Treasure. Dora, illus. (gr. 3-7). 1961. 10.95 (*0-8392-3003-6*) Astor-Honor.
Mills, Lauren. Fairy Wings. LC 92-37168. 1995. 15.95 (*0-316-57397-3*) Little.
Mills, Lauren, retold by. Tatterhood & the Hobgoblins: A Norwegian Folktale, Vol. 1. (Illus.). (ps-3). 1993. 15. 95 (*0-316-57406-6*) Little.
Milne, A. A. House at Pooh Corner. Shepard, Ernest H., illus. (gr. k up). 1985. 9.95 (*0-525-32302-3*, Dutton) NAL-Dutton.
—The Pooh Story Book. Shepard, Ernest H., illus. LC 65-19580. 80p. (gr. k-4). 1965. 13.00 (*0-525-37546-5*, DCB) Dutton Child Bks.
—Prince Rabbit. 1991. PLB 13.95 (*0-88682-480-X*) Creative Ed.
—Winnie-the-Pooh. Shepard, Ernest H., illus. (gr. 1-5). 1961. 9.95 (*0-525-43035-0*, Dutton) NAL-Dutton.
—Winnie-the-Pooh. Shepard, Ernest H., illus. 176p. (ps up). 1988. 9.95 (*0-525-44443-2*, DCB) Dutton Child Bks.
Milone, Karen, illus. Beauty & the Beast. LC 81-612. 32p. (gr. k-4). 1981. PLB 9.79 (*0-89375-464-1*); pap. text ed. 1.95 (*0-89375-465-X*) Troll Assocs.
Minard, Rosemary, ed. Womenfolk & Fairy Tales. LC 74-26555. (Illus.). 176p. (gr. 2-5). 1975. 16.95 (*0-395-20276-0*) HM.
Minters, Frances. Cinder-Elly. Karas, G. Brian, illus. LC 93-14533. 32p. (ps-3). 1994. PLB 13.99 (*0-670-84417-9*) Viking Child Bks.
Moats, Lillian S. The Gate of Dreams. 116p. 1993. 21.95 (*0-9636492-0-5*) Cranbrook Educ.
Moncure, Jane. Peter Pan: A Classic Tale. (Illus.). 32p. (gr. k-2). 1988. PLB 13.95 (*0-89565-469-5*) Childs World.
Moore, Charles. Beauty & the Beast. LC 90-26307. (Illus.). 32p. 1991. 17.95 (*0-8478-1368-1*) Rizzoli Intl.
Mora, Emma. Snow White & the Seven Dwarfs. (Illus.). 30p. (ps-1). 1986. 3.95 (*0-8120-5726-0*) Barron.
Morley, Carol. A Spider & a Pig. LC 92-53215. 1993. 14. 95 (*0-316-58405-3*) Little.
Mother Goose Staff. Little Red Riding Hood. Facsimile ed. LC 86-11772. (Illus.). 56p. (gr. k-5). 1986. Repr. of 1924 ed. 11.95 (*0-916410-35-8*) A D Bragdon.
Motomora, Mitchell. Lazy Jack & the Silent Princess. (Illus.). 32p. (gr. 1-4). 1989. PLB 18.99 (*0-8172-3529-9*); pap. 3.95 (*0-8114-6726-0*) Raintree Steck-V.
Mountain, Lee, et al. The Gingerbread Man. (Illus.). 20p. (gr. k-1). 1993. pap. 14.75 (*0-89061-740-6*) Jamestown Pubs.
—The Little Red Hen. (Illus.). 12p. (gr. k-1). 1993. pap. 14.75 (*0-89061-738-4*) Jamestown Pubs.
—The Gingerbread Man. (Illus.). 20p. (gr. k-1). 1991. pap. 18.75 (*0-89061-943-3*) Jamestown Pubs.
—Goldilocks & the Three Bears. (Illus.). 16p. (gr. k-1). 1991. pap. 18.75 (*0-89061-942-5*) Jamestown Pubs.
Murphy, S. Wind Child. 1995. 15.00 (*0-06-024351-1*); PLB 14.89 (*0-06-024352-X*) HarpC Child Bks.
Murphy, Shirley R. Wind Child. Dillon, Leo & Dillon, Diane, illus. LC 94-13861. 1995. 15.00 (*0-06-024903-X*); PLB 14.89 (*0-06-024904-8*) HarpC.
My Big Book of Fairy Tales: A Treasury of Favorite Stories for Children. 1987. 8.98 (*0-671-08503-4*) S&S Trade.
Myers, Walter D. The Dragon Takes a Wife. French, Fiona, illus. LC 93-26877. 1994. 14.95 (*0-590-46693-3*) Scholastic Inc.
Naava. The Golden Goose. LC 93-11681. Date not set. write for info. (*0-688-11302-8*, Tambourine Bks); PLB write for info. (*0-688-11303-6*, Tambourine Bks) Morrow.
Napoli, Donna J. The Magic Circle. LC 92-27008. 112p. (gr. 7 up). 1993. 14.99 (*0-525-45127-7*, DCB) Dutton Child Bks.
Nash, Corey. Little Treasury of Fairy Tales, 6 vols. in 1. 1988. boxed 5.99 (*0-517-43616-7*) Random Hse Value.
Nesbit, E. Five Children & It. Kemp, Sandra, ed. (Illus.). 224p. 1994. pap. 7.95 (*0-19-283163-1*) OUP.
Neubacher, G. Little Red Riding Hood. (Illus.). 32p. (gr. 1-4). 1989. PLB 6.95 (*0-88625-214-8*) Durkin Hayes Pub.
Newby, Robert. Sleeping Beauty. Steiner, Pat & Cozzolino, Sandra, illus. 64p. (gr. k-3). 1992. PLB 15. 95 (*1-56674-035-5*) Forest Hse.
—Sleeping Beauty: With Selected Sentences in American Sign Language. Steiner, Pat & Cozzolino, Sandra, illus. LC 91-29729. 64p. (gr. 1-7). 1992. 14.95 (*0-930323-97-1*, Pub. by K Green Pubns); incl. video 38.20 (*1-56368-009-2*, Pub. by K Green Pubns); video 29.00 (*0-930323-98-X*, Pub. by K Green Pubns) Gallaudet Univ Pr.
Newell, Peter S. Topsys & Turvys. (Illus.). 76p. (gr. 3-7). pap. 3.50 (*0-486-21231-9*) Dover.
Nichols, Nick. The Comfort Fairy Story. 24p. (gr. k-4). 1990. 19.95 (*0-9632531-0-7*) N Squared Ent.
Nimmo, Jenny, retold by. The Starlight Cloak. Todd, Justin, photos by. LC 92-26186. (Illus.). (ps-3). 1993. 14.99 (*0-8037-1508-0*) Dial Bks Young.
Noel, Christopher. Rumpelstiltskin. Sis, Peter, illus. LC 92-4592. 40p. (gr. k up). 1993. incl. cass. 19.95 (*0-88708-280-7*, Rabbit Ears); 14.95 (*0-88708-279-3*, Rabbit Ears) Picture Bk Studio.
Nones, Eric J. Canary Prince. (ps up). 1991. 14.95 (*0-374-31029-7*) FS&G.
North, Carol. Hansel & Gretel. 1990. pap. write for info. (*0-307-10033-2*, Golden Pr) Western Pub.
Norton, Mary. Are All the Giants Dead? Froud, Brian, illus. LC 78-6622. 123p. (gr. 3-7). 1978. pap. 9.95 (*0-15-607888-0*, Voyager Bks) HarBrace.
—Borrowers. Krush, Beth & Krush, Joe, illus. LC 53-7870. 180p. (gr. 3 up). 1953. 13.95 (*0-15-209987-5*, HB Juv Bks) HarBrace.
—Borrowers Afield. Krush, Beth & Krush, Joe, illus. LC 55-11011. 215p. (gr. 3 up). 1955. 13.95 (*0-15-210166-7*, HB Juv Bks) HarBrace.
—Borrowers Afloat. Krush, Beth & Krush, Joe, illus. LC 59-5630. 191p. (gr. 3 up). 1959. 12.95 (*0-15-210345-7*, HB Juv Bks) HarBrace.
—Borrowers Aloft. Krush, Beth & Krush, Joe, illus. LC 61-11751. 192p. (gr. 3 up). 1961. 12.95 (*0-15-210524-7*, HB Juv Bks) HarBrace.
Nuebacher, G. The Frog Prince. (Illus.). 32p. (gr. 1-4). 1989. 6.95 (*0-88625-216-4*) Durkin Hayes Pub.
—Pinocchio. (Illus.). 32p. (gr. 1-4). 1989. 6.95 (*0-88625-218-0*) Durkin Hayes Pub.
—Sleeping Beauty. (Illus.). 32p. (gr. 1-4). 1989. 6.95 (*0-88625-220-2*) Durkin Hayes Pub.
Ogawa & Katayama, eds. Cinderella. (Illus.). 32p. 1994. pap. 7.00 (*4-7700-1796-0*) Kodansha.
—The Story of Snow White. (Illus.). 32p. 1994. pap. 7.00 (*4-7700-1795-2*) Kodansha.
Okawa, Essei. The Adventures of the One Inch Boy. Ooka, D. T., tr. from JPN. Endo, Teruyo, illus. 32p. (gr. k-6). 1985. 11.95 (*0-89346-258-6*) Heian Intl.
—The Fisherman & the Grateful Turtle. Ooka, D. T., tr. from JPN. Murakami, Koichi, illus. 32p. (gr. k-6). 1985. PLB 11.95 (*0-89346-257-8*) Heian Intl.
Olu Easmon, Carol. Bisi & the Golden Disc. LC 89-77347. (Illus.). 32p. 1990. 13.95 (*0-940793-56-3*, Pub. by Crocodile Bks) Interlink Pub.
Olujic, Grozdana. Rose of Mother-of-Pearl. Kessler, Jascha, tr. Jacobi, Kathy, illus. LC 83-18254. (SER & CRO.). 19p. (Orig.). (gr. 4 up). 1983. pap. 6.00 (*0-915124-90-4*, Pub. by Toothpaste) Coffee Hse.
Omnibus of Fairy Tales. (ps). 1983. pap. 9.95 (*0-86112-024-8*, Brimax Bks) Borden.
Osborne, Mary P., retold by. Beauty & the Beast. Pels, Winslow P., illus. 40p. (gr. 1-4). 1988. pap. 3.95 (*0-590-40166-1*) Scholastic Inc.
Otfinoski, Steven. The Truth about Three Billy Goats Gruff. Barnes-Murphy, Rowan, illus. LC 93-42391. 32p. (gr. k-3). 1994. pap. text ed. 2.95 (*0-8167-3013-X*) Troll Assocs.
Outlet Staff. Beauty & the Beast. 1992. 3.99 (*0-517-08665-4*) Random Hse Value.
—Cinderella. 1993. 12.99 (*0-517-03707-6*) Random Hse Value.
—Little Red Riding Hood. 1992. 3.99 (*0-517-08664-6*) Random Hse Value.
—Pinocchio. 1992. 3.99 (*0-517-08666-2*) Random Hse Value.
—Puss-n-Boots. 1992. 3.99 (*0-517-08667-0*) Random Hse Value.
Ozaki, Yei T., compiled by. The Japanese Fairy Book. LC 70-109415. (Illus.). 320p. (gr. 3-8). 1970. pap. 12.95 (*0-8048-0885-6*) C E Tuttle.
Pacovska, Kveta. The Little Flower King. Bell, Anthea, tr. from GER. LC 92-6046. (Illus.). 36p. 1992. pap. 15.95 (*0-88708-221-1*) Picture Bk Studio.
Page, P. K., retold by. The Traveling Musicians of Bremen. Denton, Kady M., illus. 32p. (ps-3). 1992. 13. 95 (*0-316-68836-3*, Joy St Bks) Little.
Pape, D. L. King Robert, the Resting Ruler. LC 68-56823. (Illus.). 48p. (gr. 2-5). 1968. PLB 10.95 (*0-87783-021-5*) Oddo.
—Three Thinkers of Thay-Lee. LC 68-56828. (Illus.). 48p. (gr. 2-5). 1968. PLB 10.95 (*0-87783-040-1*) Oddo.
Parker, Ed, illus. Three Billy Goats Gruff. LC 78-18068. 32p. (gr. k-3). 1979. PLB 9.79 (*0-89375-121-9*); pap. 1.95 (*0-89375-099-9*); cassette 9.95 (*0-685-04953-1*) Troll Assocs.
Paterson, Katherine. The King's Equal. Vagin, Vladimir, illus. LC 90-30527. 64p. (gr. 2-5). 1992. 17.00 (*0-06-022496-7*); PLB 16.89 (*0-06-022497-5*) HarpC Child Bks.
El Patito Feo. (SPA.). (gr. 1). 1990. casebound 3.50 (*0-7214-1407-9*) Ladybird Bks.
Patrick, Denise L., adapted by. Walt Disney's Snow White & the Seven Dwarfs. Mones, illus. 28p. (ps). 1992. bds. write for info. (*0-307-12531-9*, 12531, Golden Pr) Western Pub.
Patrick, Lewis. Walt Disney's Snow White & the Seven Dwarfs Counting Book. (ps). 1993. 3.95 (*0-307-12529-7*, Golden Pr) Western Pub.
Paulson, Tim. The Beanstalk Incident. Corcoran, Mark, illus. 1992. pap. 8.95 (*0-8065-1313-6*, Citadel Pr) Carol Pub Group.
Pearson, Susan, retold by. Jack & the Beanstalk. Warhola, James, illus. (ps-3). 1989. pap. 13.95 (*0-671-67196-0*, S&S BFYR) S&S Trade.
Perrault, Charles. Cinderella. (FRE.). 55p. (Fr.). (gr. 3-8). 1990. pap. 10.95 (*0-7859-1354-8*, 2070312224) Fr & Eur.
—Cinderella. new ed. Smith, Phil, illus. LC 78-18067. 32p. (gr. k-3). 1979. PLB 9.79 (*0-89375-120-0*); pap. 1.95 (*0-89375-098-0*) Troll Assocs.
—Cinderella. Innocenti, Roberto, illus. 32p. (gr. 4 up). 1983. 10.95s.p. (*0-87191-945-1*) Creative Ed.
—Cinderella. Jeffers, Susan, illus. Ehrlich, Amy, retold by. LC 85-1685. (Illus.). 32p. (ps-3). 1985. 14.00 (*0-8037-0205-1*); PLB 12.89 (*0-8037-0206-X*) Dial Bks Young.
—Cinderella. Goode, Diane, tr. from FRE. & illus. Lange, Jessica, contrib. by. LC 87-16886. 48p. (ps up). 1989. incl. cassette 15.95 (*0-394-89600-9*) Knopf Bks Yng Read.
—Cinderella. Alchemy II, Inc. Staff, illus. 26p. (ps). 1988. incl. cassette 9.95 (*1-55578-911-0*) Worlds Wonder.
—Cinderella. 2nd ed. Brown, Marcia, tr. from FRE. & illus. LC 87-34920. 32p. (ps-3). 1988. pap. 4.95 (*0-689-71261-8*, Aladdin) Macmillan Child Grp.
—Cinderella. (ps-3). 1990. pap. 4.95 (*0-8037-0830-0*, Puff Pied Piper) Puffin Bks.
—Cinderella. (ps-3). 1990. pap. 5.99 (*0-14-054618-9*, Puff Pied Piper) Puffin Bks.
—Cinderella: And Other Tales from Perrault. Hague, Michael, illus. 78p. (ps-2). 1989. 18.95 (*0-8050-1004-1*, Bks Young Read) H Holt & Co.
—Cinderella & the Prince: A Colorful Pictorial Recount of the Cinderella Story. Nyborg, Randy, illus. 27p. (gr. k-10). 1992. 12.95 (*1-87776-766-2*); PLB 19.95 (*1-87776-767-0*) Regal Pubns.
—Cinderella; or, The Little Glass Slipper. Le Cain, Errol, illus. (gr. 1 up). 1977. pap. 3.95 (*0-14-050137-1*, Puffin) Puffin Bks.
—Little Red Riding Hood. Moon, Sarah, photos by. (Illus.). 32p. (gr. 9 up). 1983. PLB 13.95 (*0-87191-943-5*) Creative Ed.
—Perrault's Fairy Tales. Dore, Gustave, illus. LC 72-79522. viii, 117p. (gr. 4-6). 1969. pap. 5.95 (*0-486-22311-6*) Dover.
—Puss in Boots. (Illus.). 20p. (ps up). 1992. write for info. incl. long-life batteries (*0-307-74705-0*, 64705, Golden Pr) Western Pub.
—Puss in Boots: A Fairy Tale. Lewis, Naomi, tr. from FRE. Eidrigevicius, Stasys, illus. LC 93-39758. 32p. (gr. k-3). 1994. 14.95 (*1-55858-099-9*); PLB 14.88 (*1-55858-120-0*) North-South Bks NYC.
—Ricky the Tuft: A Classic Tale. Jose, Eduard, adapted by. Moncure, Jane B., tr. from SPA. Lavarello, Jose M., illus. LC 88-36792. 32p. (gr. k-3). 1988. PLB 13. 95 (*0-89565-473-3*) Childs World.
—Sleeping Beauty & Other Classic French Fairy Tales. 1991. 12.99 (*0-517-03706-8*) Random Hse Value.
—Sleeping Beauty & Other Stories. LC 88-43558. 96p. 1989. 4.95 (*0-89471-721-9*) Running Pr.
—The Sleeping Beauty in the Woods. Collier, John, illus. 32p. (gr. 6 up). 1984. PLB 13.95 (*0-87191-944-3*) Creative Ed.
—Three Wishes. Lightbown, Meredith, illus. LC 78-18060. 32p. (gr. k-3). 1979. PLB 9.79 (*0-89375-129-4*); pap. 1.95 (*0-89375-107-3*) Troll Assocs.
Peter Pan. 48p. (ps-6). 1989. 5.99 (*0-517-68647-3*) Random Hse Value.
Peter Pan. (Illus.). 24p. (ps-2). 1991. write for info. (Golden Pr) Western Pub.
Peter Pan. 24p. 1992. pap. 2.50 (*1-56144-090-6*) Modern Pub NYC.
Peter Rabbit. (gr. k-3). 1987. 4.95 (*0-932715-05-2*) Evans FL.
Peterson, Julienne, retold by. Caterina the Clever Farm Girl: A Tuscan Tale. Giannini, Enzo, illus. LC 93-15161. 1994. write for info. (*0-8037-1181-6*); PLB write for info. (*0-8037-1182-4*) Dial Bks Young.
Philip, Neil, as told by. The Arabian Nights. Moxley, Sheila, illus. LC 94-9137. 160p. (gr. 5 up). 1994. 19.95 (*0-531-06868-4*) Orchard Bks Watts.
Philip, Neil, compiled by. Fairy Tales from Eastern Europe. Wilkes, Larry, illus. Philip, Neil, retold by. (Illus.). 160p. (gr. 4 up). 1991. 19.45 (*0-395-57456-0*, Clarion Bks) HM.
Picard, Barbara L. French Legends, Tales & Fairy Stories. Kiddell-Monroe, Joan, illus. 216p. (gr. 4 up). 1992. pap. 10.95 (*0-19-274149-7*) OUP.
Pinocchio. (FRE.). 6.25 (*0-685-33974-2*) Fr & Eur.
Pinocchio. 24p. (gr. 3 up). 1992. incl. recorder 9.95 (*0-7935-1659-5*, 00710363) H Leonard.
Pinocchio. (Illus.). 24p. (gr. 2-5). 1993. pap. 3.95 (*1-56144-361-1*, Honey Bear Bks) Modern Pub NYC.
Ploetz & Lebitritt. Kooken. (gr. 3 up). 1992. 14.95 (*0-8050-2163-9*) H Holt & Co.
Plume, Ilse. Shoemaker & the Elves. 32p. (ps-3). 1991. 14.95 (*0-15-274050-3*, HB Juv Bks) HarBrace.
Pogorelsky, Antony. The Black Hen: or The Underground Inhabitants. Hamilton, Morse, retold by. Yuditskaya, Tatyana, illus. LC 92-28599. 32p. (gr. 2-5). 1994. 14. 99 (*0-525-65133-0*, Cobblehill Bks) Dutton Child Bks.
Porazinska, Janina. The Enchanted Book: A Tale from Krakow. Smith, Bozena, tr. Brett, Jan, photos by. LC 86-22918. 32p. (gr. k-4). 1987. 13.95 (*0-15-225950-3*) HarBrace.
Postma, Lidia. The Stolen Mirror. Postma, Lidia, illus. LC 75-43888. 32p. (ps-3). 1976. McGraw.
Potter, Beatrix. The Complete Tales of Beatrix Potter. Potter, Beatrix, illus. 384p. (ps-6). 1989. 35.00 (*0-7232-3618-6*) Viking Child Bks.

—The Tale of Benjamin Bunny. Stewart, Pat, illus. LC 74-78812. 59p. (gr. 2 up). 1974. pap. 1.75 (*0-486-21102-9*) Dover.
—The Tale of Timmy Tiptoes. (Illus.). 64p. (gr. 3 up). 1987. pap. 1.75 (*0-486-25541-7*) Dover.
—A Treasury of Peter Rabbit & Other Stories. (Illus.). (gr. k up). 1985. 5.98 (*0-517-23948-5*) Random Hse Value.
Potter, Beatrix, created by. Miss Moppet. Schoonover, Pat & Nelson, Anita, illus. 24p. (gr. 2-4). 1992. PLB 10.95 (*1-56674-020-7*, HTS Bks) Forest Hse.
Poucette. (FRE., Illus.). (gr. 1). 3.50 (*0-7214-1274-2*) Ladybird Bks.
Price, Susan, retold by. The Three Bears & Other Stories. Maclean, Moira & Maclean, Colin, illus. LC 92-26450. 24p. (ps-1). 1993. 4.95 (*1-85697-906-7*, Kingfisher LKC) LKC.
La Princesa y el Sapo. (SPA.). (gr. 3). 1990. casebound 3.50 (*0-7214-1410-9*) Ladybird Bks.
The Princess & the Frog. (ARA., Illus.). (gr. 4-6). 1987. 3.95x (*0-86685-217-4*); incl. cassette 12.00x (*0-685-42206-2*) Intl Bk Ctr.
Princess & the Pea. (ARA., Illus.). (gr. 4-6). 1989. 3.95x (*0-86685-218-2*); incl. cassette 12.00x (*0-685-02577-2*) Intl Bk Ctr.
El Principe Feliz. (SPA.). 1990. casebound 3.50 (*0-7214-1400-1*) Ladybird Bks.
Prokofieff, Sergei. Peter & the Wolf. Alchemy II, Inc. Staff, illus. 26p. (ps). 1988. incl. cassette 9.95 (*0-317-89541-9*) Worlds Wonder.
Prokofiev, Sergei. Peter & the Wolf. Crampton, Patricia, tr. LC 91-40185. (Illus.). 28p. (gr. k up). 1992. pap. 4.95 (*0-88708-226-2*) Picture Bk Studio.
Pushkin, Aleksandr. Golden Cockerel & Other Fairy Tales. Wood, Jessie, tr. Zvorykin, Boris, illus. Nureyev, Rudolf, intro. by. 1990. 24.95 (*0-385-26252-3*) Doubleday.
—The Snow Storm. Redpath, Ann, ed. 40p. (gr. 6 up). 1983. PLB 13.95 (*0-87191-923-0*) Creative Ed.
Puss in Boots. (ARA., Illus.). (gr. 2-6). 1987. 3.95x (*0-86685-220-4*) Intl Bk Ctr.
Puss in Boots. (ps-1). 1.79 (*0-517-46234-6*) Random Hse Value.
Puss in Boots. (Illus.). (ps-1). 1.98 (*0-517-39464-2*) Random Hse Value.
Puss in Boots. (ps-1). 1991. 2.99 (*0-517-63340-X*) Random Hse Value.
Puss in Boots. (Illus.). 24p. (Orig.). (gr. k-3). 1993. pap. 2.50 (*1-56144-297-6*, Honey Bear Bks) Modern Pub NYC.
Pyle, Howard. The Wonder Clock or, Four & Twenty Marvelous Tales, Being One for Each Hour of the Day. (Illus.). xiv, 319p. (gr. 3-6). pap. 7.95 (*0-486-21446-X*) Dover.
Rackham, Arthur. Sleeping Beauty. Rackham, Arthur, illus. 110p. (gr. k-4). 1920. pap. 3.95 (*0-486-22756-1*) Dover.
Rackham, Arthur, illus. The Arthur Rackham Fairy Book. 271p. (gr. 2-10). 1991. 3.99 (*0-517-24213-3*) Random Hse Value.
Rader, Laura, illus. Goldilocks & the Three Bears. LC 94-4986. 1995. write for info. (*0-688-13258-8*, Tambourine Bks) Morrow.
—The Three Billy Goats Gruff. LC 94-4987. 1995. write for info. (*0-688-13259-6*, Tambourine Bks) Morrow.
Rael, Elsa O. Marushka's Egg. Wezyk, Joanna, illus. LC 92-303. 40p. (gr. k-4). 1993. RSBE 14.95 (*0-02-775655-6*, Four Winds) Macmillan Child Grp.
Ransome, Arthur. The Fool of the World & the Flying Ship. Shulevitz, Uri, illus. LC 68-54105. 48p. (ps-3). 1968. 16.00 (*0-374-32442-5*) FS&G.
Rapunzel. (Illus.). 32p. (gr. 3-7). 1993. 10.95 (*1-878685-74-0*, Bedrock Press) Turner Pub GA.
Rapunzel in Arabic. (Illus.). (gr. 4-6). 1987. 3.95x (*0-86685-264-6*) Intl Bk Ctr.
Razzi, Jim. Pinocchio's Adventure. 1985. 4.95 (*0-553-05402-3*) Bantam.
Razzi, Jim, adapted by. Walt Disney's Snow White & the Seven Dwarfs. Marvin, Fred, illus. LC 92-53430. 96p. 1993. 14.95 (*1-56282-362-0*); PLB 14.89 (*1-56282-363-9*); pap. 5.95 (*0-7868-4020-X*) Disney Pr.
—Walt Disney's Snow White & the Seven Dwarfs. LC 92-53431. (Illus.). 64p. (gr. 2-6). 1993. pap. 3.50 (*1-56282-364-7*) Disney Pr.
Red Riding Hood. (Illus.). (ps-1). 1.29 (*0-517-47346-1*) Random Hse Value.
Red Riding Hood. (ps-2). 3.95 (*0-7214-5103-9*) Ladybird Bks.
Resnick, Jane. Goldilocks & the Three Bears. 1986. 14.98 (*0-88705-151-0*) Joshua Morris.
—Original Fairy Tales from Brothers Grimm. 1991. 12.99 (*0-517-06577-0*) Random Hse Value.
Reynolds-Strauss, Karen & Gligor, Adrian. Romanian Fairy Tales. Reynolds-Strauss, Karen, illus. 85p. (Orig.). (ps-6). 1992. pap. text ed. 11.95 (*0-9634797-0-9*) K Strauss & A Gligor.
Richardson, Frederick, illus. Mother Goose: The Original Volland Edition. 128p. (gr. k up). 1985. 8.99 (*0-517-43619-1*) Random Hse Value.
Richardson, Jean. The Sleeping Beauty. Crespi, Francesca, illus. 32p. (ps-1). 1991. 14.95 (*1-55970-142-0*) Arcade Pub Inc.
Richardson, Lee & Holt, Shirley, eds. Little Red Riding Hood. (Illus.). 28p. (gr. 3-8). 1985. 16.95 (*0-9613476-1-9*) Shirlee.
Richitos De Oro y los Tres Osos. (SPA.). (gr. 1). 1990. casebound 3.50 (*0-7214-1406-0*) Ladybird Bks.
Riordan, James, retold by. Peter & the Wolf. Ambrus, Victor G., illus. 24p. (ps-6). 1987. 15.00 (*0-19-279824-3*) OUP.
Rip Van Winkle. (Illus.). (ps-3). 1985. 1.98 (*0-517-28806-0*) Random Hse Value.
Ritchie, Rita, adapted by. The Emperor's New Clothes. 20p. (ps up). 1992. write for info. (*0-307-74704-2*) Western Pub.
—The Princess & the Pea. 20p. (ps up). 1992. write for info. (*0-307-74702-6*, 64702) Western Pub.
Robbie, Dorothy & Hand, Desmond. Alice in Wonderland. (gr. k up). 1970. pap. 1.50x (*0-912262-19-2*) Proscenium.
Roberts, Jo-Anna. Alligator & the Toothfairy. Kinnell, Shannon, illus. 56p. (ps-2). 1991. 11.50g (*1-879212-00-5*) Desert Star Intl.
Roberts, Tom. Goldilocks. Kubinyi, Laszlo, illus. LC 93-6679. (ps-6). 1993. Incl. cassette. 9.95 (*0-88708-322-6*, Dist. by S&S Trade) Picture Bk Studio.
—Goldilocks & the Three Bears. Kubinyi, Laszlo, illus. 32p. (gr. k up). 1991. pap. 14.95 (*0-88708-146-0*, Rabbit Ears); pap. 19.95 incl. cass. (*0-88708-147-9*, Rabbit Ears) Picture Bk Studio.
—Red Riding Hood. Kubinyi, Laszlo, illus. LC 93-12152. (ps-6). 1993. Incl. cassette. 9.95 (*0-88708-320-X*, Rabbit Ears) Picture Bk Studio.
—The Three Billy Goats Gruff. Jorgensen, David, illus. LC 93-6678. (ps-6). 1993. 9.95 (*0-88708-319-6*, Dist. by S&S Trade) Picture Bk Studio.
Roberts, Tom & Hunter, Holly, eds. The Three Billy Goats Gruff. Jorgensen, David, illus. Lande, Art, contrib. by. (Illus.). 32p. (ps up). 1993. pap. write for info. slipcase pkg., incl. cassette (*0-307-14329-5*, 14329, Golden Pr) Western Pub.
Rogasky, Barbara, retold by. The Water of Life. Hyman, Trina S., illus. LC 84-19226. 40p. (gr. k-3). 1986. reinforced bdg. 15.95 (*0-8234-0552-4*); pap. 5.95 (*0-8234-0907-4*) Holiday.
Rojankovsky, Feodor. Tall Book of Nursery Tales. Rojankovsky, Feodor, illus. LC 44-3881. 120p. (ps-3). 1944. 9.95 (*0-06-025065-8*) HarpC Child Bks.
Rose, Joan E. The Princess on the Glass Mountain. (gr. k). 1993. 7.95 (*0-8062-4609-X*) Carlton.
Ross, Tony. Hansel & Gretel. LC 93-31047. (Illus.). 32p. (ps-3). 1994. 13.95 (*0-87951-535-X*) Overlook Pr.
—Mrs. Goat & Her Seven Little Kids. Ross, Tony, illus. LC 89-17933. 32p. (gr. 1-3). 1990. SBE 13.95 (*0-689-31624-0*, Atheneum Child Bk) Macmillan Child Grp.
Ross, Tony, retold by. & illus. Goldilocks & the Three Bears. 26p. (ps-3). 1992. 13.95 (*0-87951-453-1*) Overlook Pr.
Rothaus, Jim. Fairy Tale Jokes. Woodworth, Viki, illus. (gr. 1-4). 1992. PLB 13.95 (*0-89565-862-3*) Childs World.
Rounds, Glen, retold by. & illus. The Three Billy Goats Gruff. LC 92-23951. 32p. (ps-3). 1993. reinforced bdg. 15.95 (*0-8234-1015-3*); pap. 5.95 (*0-8234-1136-2*) Holiday.
Rowland, Della. Little Red Riding Hood & the Wolf's Tale. (ps-3). 1991. 13.95 (*1-55972-072-7*, Birch Ln Pr) Carol Pub Group.
—Little Red Riding Hood: The Wolf's Tale. Montgomery, Michael, illus. LC 93-42781. 1994. pap. 8.95 (*0-8065-1526-0*, Citadel Pr) Carol Pub Group.
Royds, Caroline, selected by. The Dragon, Giant & Monster Treasury. Spenceley, Annabel, illus. 96p. 1988. 13.95 (*0-399-21587-5*, Putnam) Putnam Pub Group.
Rumpelstiltskin. (ARA., Illus.). (gr. 4-6). 1987. 3.95x (*0-86685-265-4*) Intl Bk Ctr.
Running Press Staff, ed. Miniature Mother Goose. Wright, Blanche F., illus. LC 91-50783. 128p. 1992. 4.95 (*1-56138-105-5*) Running Pr.
—Original Mother Goose. Wright, Blanche F., illus. LC 91-51057. 136p. 1992. 14.95 (*1-56138-113-6*) Running Pr.
Russell, P. Craig. Fairy Tales of Oscar Wilde, Vol. 1. (Illus.). 48p. (gr. 3-7). 1992. 15.95x (*1-56163-056-X*) NBM.
Rymer, Alta M. Up from Uzam. Rymer, Alta M., illus. 28p. (Orig.). (gr. 2-4). 1987. pap. 11.50 (*0-9600792-8-9*) Rymer Bks.
Sage, Jacqueline I., illus. Many Furs: A Grimm's Fairy Tale. LC 81-947. 32p. (gr. 1-4). 1990. 9.95 (*0-89742-041-1*) Celestial Arts.
Sakade, Florence. Japanese Children's Favorite Stories. Kurosaki, Yoshio, illus. LC 58-11620. 120p. (gr. 2-6). 1958. bds. 16.95 (*0-8048-0284-X*) C E Tuttle.
Salter-Mathieson, Nigel. Little Chief Mischief. Gruen, Chuck, illus. (gr. 2-7). 1962. 10.95 (*0-8392-3020-6*) Astor-Honor.
Sandburg, Carl. Rootabaga Stories. Cott, Jonathan, ed. Petersham, Maud & Petersham, Miska, illus. LC 93-41102. (ps). 1994. pap. 7.50 (*1-56957-925-3*) Barefoot Bks.
Sanderson, Ruth. The Enchanted Wood. (Illus.). (ps-3). 1991. 15.95 (*0-316-77018-3*) Little.
Sanderson, Ruth, retold by. & illus. Sir Gatto: An Italian Fairy Tale. LC 94-16725. 1995. 14.95 (*0-316-77073-6*) Little.
SanSouci, Robert. The Tsar's Promise. Mills, Lauren, illus. 32p. (ps up). 1992. 14.95 (*0-399-21581-6*, Philomel Bks) Putnam Pub Group.
San Souci, Robert D. Donkey Ears. Vanden Broeck, Fabricio, illus. LC 93-36333. 1994. 14.95 (*0-399-22694-X*, Philomel Bks) Putnam Pub Group.
—The Hobyahs. Natchev, Alexi, illus. LC 92-28655. 1994. 14.95 (*0-385-30934-1*) Doubleday.
Saponaro, Sabina. The Ugly Duckling. (Illus.). 30p. (ps-1). 1986. 3.95 (*0-8120-5725-2*) Barron.
Savigny, Francois. Il Etait Une Fois. (FRE., Illus.). 96p. 1991. pap. 9.95 incl. 60-min. cassette (*0-8442-1440-X*, Natl Textbk); (Natl Textbk) NTC Pub Grp.
Scarry, Richard. Richard Scarry's Little Red Riding Hood. (Illus.). 28p. (ps). 1993. bds. 3.25 (*0-307-12522-X*, 12522, Golden Pr) Western Pub.
—Richard Scarry's The Little Red Hen. (Illus.). 28p. (ps). 1993. bds. 3.25 (*0-307-12523-8*, 12523, Golden Pr) Western Pub.
—Richard Scarry's The Three Bears. (Illus.). 28p. (ps). 1993. bds. 3.25 (*0-307-12524-6*, 12524, Golden Pr) Western Pub.
Schecter, Ellen. Diamonds & Toads: A Classic Fairy Tale. Blackshear, Ami, illus. LC 93-14096. 1994. 10.95 (*0-553-09046-1*); pap. 3.99 (*0-553-37339-0*) Bantam.
Schenk De Regniers, Beatrice. Little Sister & the Month Brothers. Cohn, Amy, ed. Tomes, Margot, illus. LC 93-44053. 48p. (ps up). 1994. lib. bdg. write for info. (*0-688-05293-2*, Mulberry); pap. 4.95 (*0-688-13633-8*, Mulberry) Morrow.
Schroeder, Alan. Lily & the Wooden Bowl. (ps-3). 1994. 14.95 (*0-385-30792-6*) Doubleday.
Schroeder, Alan, adapted by. Lily & the Wooden Bowl: A Japanese Folktale. Ito, Yoriko, illus. LC 93-17900. 1994. 15.95 (*0-385-31073-0*) Dial Bks Young.
Schwartz, Carol. Nutcracker (Pop Ups) 1991. 3.95 (*0-8037-1014-3*) Dial Bks Young.
Scieszka, Jon. The Frog Prince, Continued. Johnson, Steve, illus. 32p. (ps-3). 1991. 14.95 (*0-670-83421-1*) Viking Child Bks.
—The Stinky Cheese Man: And Other Fairly Stupid Tales. Smith, Lane, illus. 56p. (gr. 1). 1992. 16.00 (*0-670-84487-X*) Viking Child Bks.
Scott, Michael. Irish Fairytales. Gervin, Joseph, illus. LC 89-50977. 142p. (gr. 2-5). 1989. pap. 11.95 (*0-85342-866-2*, Pub. by Mercier Press Ltd Eire) Dufour.
Seltzer, Richard W., Jr. The Lizard of Oz. Couture, Christin, illus. LC 74-20172. 128p. (Orig.). (gr. 7 up). 1974. pap. 4.50 (*0-915232-01-4*) B & R Samizdat.
—Now & Then & Other Tales from Ome. Seltzer, Richard W., Jr., illus. LC 76-12138. (gr. 5). 1976. 4.50 (*0-915232-03-0*); pap. 1.95 (*0-915232-02-2*) B & R Samizdat.
Severance, Charles L. Tales of the Thumb. 2nd ed. LC 72-86863. (Illus.). (gr. 3-6). 1972. pap. 4.75 (*0-932411-00-2*) Pub Div JCS.
Shealy, Daniel, ed. Louisa May Alcott's Fairy Tales & Fantasy Stories. LC 91-43144. (Illus.). 432p. (Orig.). 1992. text ed. 37.95x (*0-87049-752-9*); pap. 24.95 (*0-87049-758-8*) U of Tenn Pr.
Shearer, Marilyn J. Sleeping Beauty. Walker, Larry, illus. 16p. (ps-6). 1989. 19.95 (*0-685-30099-4*); pap. 10.95 (*0-685-30100-1*) L Ashley & Joshua.
Shepard, Aaron, retold by. The Enchanted Storks: A Tale of the Middle East. Dianov, Alisher, illus. LC 93-41540. 1995. write for info. (*0-395-65377-0*, Clarion Bks) HM.
Shibano, Tamizo. The Old Man Who Made the Trees Bloom. Ooka, D. T., tr. from JPN. Iguchi, Bunshu, illus. 32p. 1985. 11.95 (*0-89346-247-0*) Heian Intl.
Shorto, Russell. The Untold Story of Cinderella. Lewis, T., illus. 1992. pap. 8.95 (*0-8065-1298-9*, Citadel Pr) Carol Pub Group.
Shulevitz, Uri. One Monday Morning. Shulevitz, Uri, illus. LC 66-24483. 48p. (ps-4). 1974. SBE 14.95 (*0-684-13195-1*, Scribners Young Read) Macmillan Child Grp.
Singer, A. L., adapted by. Walt Disney's Sleeping Beauty. Gonzalez, Ric & Durrell, Dennis, illus. LC 92-56158. 96p. 1993. 14.95 (*1-56282-366-3*); PLB 14.89 (*1-56282-367-1*) Disney Pr.
—Walt Disney's Sleeping Beauty. LC 92-56157. (Illus.). 80p. (gr. 2-6). 1993. pap. 3.50 (*1-56282-368-X*) Disney Pr.
Singer, Marilyn. The Golden Heart of Winter. Rayevsky, Robert, illus. LC 90-35346. 40p. (gr. 1 up). 1991. 13.95 (*0-688-07717-X*); PLB 13.88 (*0-688-07718-8*) Morrow Jr Bks.
—The Painted Fan. Ma, Wenhai, illus. LC 92-29796. 40p. 1994. 15.00g (*0-688-11742-2*); lib. bdg. 14.93 (*0-688-11743-0*) Morrow Jr Bks.
Singer, S. B. Naftali the Storyteller & His Horse, Sus. (gr. 4 up). 1979. pap. 1.50 (*0-440-46642-3*) Dell.
Sis, Peter. The Three Golden Keys. LC 94-6743. 1994. 19.95 (*0-385-47292-7*) Doubleday.
Slater, Teddy, adapted by. Walt Disney's Mickey & the Beanstalk. Wilson, Phil, illus. LC 92-53445. 48p. 1993. 12.95 (*1-56282-385-X*); PLB 12.89 (*1-56282-386-8*) Disney Pr.
Sleeping Beauty. (SPA & FRE.). (gr. k-3). Span. ed. 6.25 (*0-685-28438-7*); Fr. ed. 9.95 (*0-685-28439-5*) Fr & Eur.
Sleeping Beauty. (Illus.). (ps-3). 1985. 1.98 (*0-517-28811-7*) Random Hse Value.
Sleeping Beauty. (Illus.). (ps-1). 1.29 (*0-517-47347-X*) Random Hse Value.
Sleeping Beauty. (Illus.). 48p. (ps-6). 1989. 5.99 (*0-517-67009-7*) Random Hse Value.
Sleeping Beauty. (ps-2). 3.95 (*0-7214-5100-4*) Ladybird Bks.
Sleeping Beauty. 1985. 4.95 (*0-553-05406-6*) Bantam.
Sleeping Beauty. 24p. (gr. k-3). 1992. pap. 2.50 (*1-56144-172-4*, Honey Bear Bks) Modern Pub NYC.

Sleeping Beauty. (Illus.). 24p. (gr. 2-5). 1993. pap. 3.95 (*1-56144-362-X*, Honey Bear Bks) Modern Pub NYC.
Smith, Philip, ed. Aladdin & Other Favorite Arabian Nights Stories. Kliros, Thea, illus. LC 93-22073. 96p. (gr. 3 up). 1993. pap. 1.00 (*0-486-27571-X*) Dover.
—Irish Fairy Tales. Kliros, Thea, illus. LC 93-243. 96p. 1993. pap. 1.00 (*0-486-27572-8*) Dover.
—Japanese Fairy Tales. Fujiyama, Kakuzo, illus. LC 92-17648. 96p. 1992. pap. 1.00 (*0-486-27300-8*) Dover.
Snow White. (Illus.). (ps-1). 1.98 (*0-517-39465-0*) Random Hse Value.
Snow White. (Illus.). (ps-1). 1.29 (*0-318-12084-4*) Random Hse Value.
Snow White. 1985. 4.95 (*0-553-05401-5*) Bantam.
Snow White & Rose Red. (ARA., Illus.). (gr. 4-6). 1987. 3.95x (*0-86685-225-5*) Intl Bk Ctr.
Snow White & the Seven Dwarfs. (ARA., Illus.). (gr. 1-12). 1987. pap. 3.95x (*0-86685-268-9*); incl. cassette 12.00x (*0-685-42207-0*) Intl Bk Ctr.
Snow White & the Seven Dwarfs. (ps-2). 3.95 (*0-7214-5062-8*) Ladybird Bks.
Snow White & the Seven Dwarfs. 24p. 1992. pap. 2.50 (*1-56144-092-2*) Modern Pub NYC.
Snow White's Escape. 20p. 1994. 9.98 (*1-57082-153-4*) Mouse Works.
Spier, Peter. London Bridge Is Falling Down. Spier, Peter, illus. LC 67-17695. (ps). 1985. pap. 10.95 (*0-385-08717-9*) Doubleday.
Stamm, Claus & Mizumura, Kazue. Three Strong Women. Tseng, Jean & Tseng, Mou-sien, illus. LC 92-25331. 1993. pap. 4.99 (*0-14-054530-1*) Puffin Bks.
Stanley, Diane. Fortune. Stanley, Diane, illus. LC 88-13204. 32p. (ps-4). 1990. 12.95 (*0-688-07210-0*); PLB 12.88 (*0-688-07211-9*, Morrow Jr Bks) Morrow Jr Bks.
Stanley, Diane, retold by. Petrosinella: A Neopolitan Rapunzel. LC 94-17456. (Illus.). (gr. 7-10). Date not set. write for info. (*0-8037-1712-1*); PLB write for info. (*0-8037-1749-0*) Dial Bks Young.
Steel, Flora A. & Messina, Christine, eds. Goldilocks & the Three Bears & Other Classic English Fairy Tales. LC 93-44688. 1994. 12.99 (*0-517-10176-9*) Random Hse Value.
Steig, William. Caleb & Katie. Steig, William, illus. LC 77-4947. 32p. (ps-3). 1977. 16.00 (*0-374-31016-5*) FS&G.
Stevens, Janet, retold by. Goldilocks & the Three Bears. LC 85-27312. (Illus.). 32p. (ps-3). 1986. reinforced bdg. 14.95 (*0-8234-0608-3*) Holiday.
Stevens, Janet, illus. The Emperor's New Clothes: Adapted from Hans Christian Andersen. LC 85-728. 32p. (ps-3). 1985. reinforced bdg. 15.95 (*0-8234-0566-4*) Holiday.
Stockton, Frank. The Bee-Man of Orn. Delessert, Etienne, illus. LC 85-23272. 40p. (gr. 4 up). 1986. PLB 13.95 (*0-88682-055-3*) Creative Ed.
—Old Pipes & the Dryad. 1991. PLB 13.95 (*0-88682-473-7*) Creative Ed.
Storer, Ronald, ed. Sleeping Beauty & Bluebeard. (gr. k-6). 1972. pap. 3.25x (*0-19-421746-9*) OUP.
Sucie, Stevenson. Princess & the Pea. (ps-3). 1994. pap. 4.99 (*0-440-40964-0*) Dell.
Swift, Jonathan. Gulliver's Travels. LC 47-31082. (gr. 8 up). 1964. pap. 2.95 (*0-8049-0015-9*, CL-15) Airmont.
—Gulliver's Travels. Rackham, Arthur, illus. LC 47-31082. 3.98 (*0-517-46611-2*) Random Hse Value.
Tales from Around the World. 1987. 5.98 (*0-671-08502-6*) S&S Trade.
Tarcov, Edith H., retold by. The Frog Prince. Marshall, James, illus. 32p. (Orig.). (ps-2). 1987. pap. 2.50 (*0-590-43132-3*) Scholastic Inc.
—The Frog Prince. Marshall, James, illus. LC 92-25167. 32p. (ps-2). 1993. pap. 2.95 (*0-590-46571-6*) Scholastic Inc.
Tardi, Jacques, illus. The Enchanted Pig: Rumanian Fairy Tale. 32p. (gr. 6 up). 1984. PLB 13.95 (*0-87191-953-2*) Creative Ed.
Tarrant. Nursery Rhymes & Fairy Tales. 1984. 5.98 (*0-671-06535-1*) S&S Trade.
Terrell, Sandy. Journey to Fairy Tale Castle. (Illus.). 224p. (gr. k-3). 1992. 16.95 (*0-86653-657-4*, GA1346) Good Apple.
Thaler, Mike. The Bully Brothers Trick the Tooth Fairy. Lee, Jared, illus. LC 92-72834. 32p. (ps-3). 1993. pap. 2.25 (*0-448-40519-9*, G&D) Putnam Pub Group.
Thomas, Vernon. Stories from the Arabian Nights. Basu, R. K., illus. (gr. 8-12). 1979. 7.50 (*0-89744-142-7*) Auromere.
Thomas, Vernon, ed. Fairy Tales from India. (Illus.). (gr. 1-9). 1979. 7.50 (*0-89744-137-0*) Auromere.
Thomson, Peggy, retold by. The Brave Little Tailor. Warhola, James, illus. LC 91-20982. 48p. (ps-3). 1992. pap. 15.00 jacketed, 3-pc. bdg. (*0-671-73736-8*, S&S BFYR) S&S Trade.
The Three Bears. 32p. (ps-1). 1985. 2.49 (*0-517-46239-7*) Random Hse Value.
The Three Bears. 24p. (ps-3). 1988. 2.25 (*1-56288-150-7*) Checkerboard.
Three Billy-Goats Gruff. (ARA., Illus.). (gr. 5-8). 1987. 3.95x (*0-86685-239-5*) Intl Bk Ctr.
The Three Billy-Goats-Gruff. (Illus.). 32p. (ps-1). 1985. 2.49 (*0-517-46241-9*) Random Hse Value.
The Three Billy Goats Gruff. (Illus.). 28p. (ps up). 1987. 3.95 (*0-7214-5031-8*) Ladybird Bks.
Three Dwarfs. (ps-1). cancelled (*0-517-48306-8*); pap. 2.49 (*0-517-46823-9*) Random Hse Value.
The Three Little Pigs. (Illus.). (ps-1). 1.98 (*0-517-39466-9*) Random Hse Value.
The Three Little Pigs. (gr. k-3). 1987. 4.95 (*0-932715-03-6*) Evans FL.
The Three Little Pigs. 16p. 1991. write for info. incl. cassette (*1-880459-02-7*) Arrow Trad.
The Three Little Pigs. 24p. (gr. k-3). 1992. pap. 2.50 (*1-56144-173-2*, Honey Bear Bks) Modern Pub NYC.
Thumbelina. 1991. pap. 14.95 (*0-385-41403-X*) Doubleday.
Thumbelina. (Illus.). 24p. (Orig.). (gr. k-3). 1993. pap. 2.50 (*1-56144-298-4*, Honey Bear Bks) Modern Pub NYC.
Thurber, James. The Great Quillow. LC 91-20586. (gr. 1 up). 1994. 16.95 (*0-15-232544-1*) HarBrace.
—Many Moons. Slobodkin, Louis, illus. LC 43-51250. (gr. 3-7). 1943. 14.95 (*0-15-251873-8*, HB Juv Bks) HarBrace.
—Thirteen Clocks. (gr. 4-7). 1992. pap. 3.50 (*0-440-40582-3*, YB) Dell.
Tinder Box. LC 89-48014. 1991. pap. 14.95 (*0-671-70546-6*, S&S BFYR) S&S Trade.
Tom Thumb. (FRE.). (gr. k-3). 3.50 (*0-685-28452-2*) Fr & Eur.
Tom Thumb. (Illus.). (ps-1). 1.79 (*0-517-46236-2*) Random Hse Value.
The Tortoise Fair. 22p. (ps-1). 1985. 1.98 (*0-517-45797-0*) Random Hse Value.
Travers, Pamela L. Mary Poppins from A to Z. Shepard, Mary, illus. LC 62-15629. (gr. 1-4). 1962. 10.95 (*0-15-252590-4*, HB Juv Bks) HarBrace.
Los Tres Cerditos. (SPA.). (gr. 1). 1990. casebound 3.50 (*0-7214-1408-7*) Ladybird Bks.
Los Tres Cochinitos. (SPA.). (ps-3). 1993. pap. 2.25 (*0-307-70099-2*, Golden Pr) Western Pub.
Los Tres Cochinitos. (SPA.). (ps-3). 1993. pap. 5.95 (*0-307-91598-0*, Golden Pr) Western Pub.
Los Tres Osos. (SPA.). (ps-3). 1993. pap. 2.25 (*0-307-70050-X*, Golden Pr) Western Pub.
Trivizas, Eugene. The Three Little Wolves & the Big Bad Pig. Oxenbury, Helen, illus. LC 92-24829. 32p. (gr. k-5). 1993. SBE 15.95 (*0-689-50569-8*, M K McElderry) Macmillan Child Grp.
Tseng, Grace. The Brocade. Tseng, Jean & Tseng, Mou-sien, illus. LC 94-9757. 1994. write for info. (*0-688-12515-8*); lib. bdg. write for info. (*0-688-12516-6*) Lothrop.
Tunnell, Michael O. Beauty & the Beastly Children. Cymerman, John E., illus. LC 92-36757. 32p. (gr. k up). 1993. 15.00 (*0-688-12181-0*, Tambourine Bks); PLB 14.93 (*0-688-12182-9*, Tambourine Bks) Morrow.
Turkle, Brinton. Deep in the Forest. LC 76-21691. (Illus.). 32p. (ps-1). 1976. 12.95 (*0-525-28617-9*, DCB); pap. 3.95 (*0-525-44322-3*, DCB) Dutton Child Bks.
Turnbull, Ann. The Tapestry Cats. Morley, Carol, illus. 1992. 14.95 (*0-316-85626-6*) Little.
Turner, Gwenda. Once Upon a Time. (ps). 1990. 9.95 (*0-670-82551-4*) Viking Child Bks.
Twain, Mark. Arabian Nights. Goodenow, Earle, illus. (gr. 4-9). 1981. (G&D); deluxe ed. 13.95 (*0-448-06006-X*) Putnam Pub Group.
Uchida, Yoshiko. The Magic Purse. Narahashi, Keiko, illus. LC 92-30132. 32p. (gr. 1-4). 1993. SBE 15.95 (*0-689-50559-0*, M K McElderry) Macmillan Child Grp.
The Ugly Duckling. (Illus.). (ps-1). 1985. 1.98 (*0-517-47900-1*) Random Hse Value.
The Ugly Duckling. (Illus.). 28p. (ps up). 1987. text ed. 3.95 cased (*0-7214-5032-6*) Ladybird Bks.
Ugly Duckling. 1989. 5.99 (*0-517-69315-1*) Random Hse Value.
The Ugly Duckling. 1988. write for info. (*0-671-10038-6*) S&S Trade.
The Ugly Duckling. (ps-2). 3.95 (*0-7214-5099-7*) Ladybird Bks.
Ugly Duckling. (ps-3). 1991. 5.95 (*0-88101-117-7*) Unicorn Pub.
The Ugly Duckling. (Illus.). 24p. (Orig.). (gr. k-3). 1993. pap. 2.50 (*1-56144-299-2*, Honey Bear Bks) Modern Pub NYC.
The Ugly Duckling. (Illus.). 32p. (gr. 3-7). 1993. 10.95 (*1-878685-75-9*, Bedrock Press) Turner Pub GA.
Uh Oh, Dopey. 18p. 1994. 6.98 (*1-57082-139-9*) Mouse Works.
Under the Fairy Tale Tree. (gr. 1-2). 1993. 12.95 (*1-56644-957-X*) Educ Impress.
Underhill, Zoe D., ed. The Dwarf's Tailor, & Other Fairy Tales. LC 78-74521. (gr. 4-5). 1979. Repr. of 1896 ed. 21.75x (*0-8486-0224-2*) Roth Pub Inc.
Ustinov. Fairytales. 1987. 12.95 (*0-385-24096-1*) Doubleday.
Vaccaro Associates Staff & Vaccaro, Garparo, illus. Disney's Aladdin: The Magic Carpet Ride. LC 92-54878. 10p. (ps-k). 1993. 4.95 (*1-56282-396-5*) Disney Pr.
Vance, Eleanor G. Tall Book of Fairy Tales. reissued ed. Sharp, William, illus. 128p. (ps-3). 1947. 9.95 (*0-06-025545-5*) HarpC Child Bks.
Van Der Meer, Ron. The Fantastic Fairy Tale Pop-up Book. Thatcher, Fran & Williamson, Tracey, illus. LC 92-80742. 10p. (ps-3). 1993. 16.00 (*0-679-83869-4*) Random Bks Yng Read.
Vard, Colin. Princess Finola: The Battle for Moytura. Kew, Tony, illus. 67p. (Orig.). (gr. 3-6). 1993. pap. 11.95 (*0-685-72575-8*, Pub. by Celtpress ER) Irish Bks Media.
Verne, Jules. The Adventures of the Rat Family. Copeland, Evelyn, tr. Taves, Brian, afterword by. LC 92-36983. 72p. 1993. 14.95 (*0-19-508114-5*) OUP.
Very, Lydia. Goody Two Shoes: Treasures from the Library of Congress. (Illus.). 16p. 1992. Repr. of 1865 ed. saddle wired 3.95 (*1-55709-169-2*) Applewood.
Very, Lydia L. Little Red Riding Hood: Treasures from the Library of Congress. (Illus.). 20p. 1992. Repr. of 1863 ed. saddle wired 3.95 (*1-55709-167-6*) Applewood.
Vittorini, Domenico. The Thread of Life: Twelve Old Italian Tales. Grandpre, Mary, illus. LC 93-29497. 1995. write for info. (*0-517-59594-X*, Crown); lib. bdg. write for info. (*0-517-59595-8*, Crown) Crown Pub Group.
Voake, Charlotte, retold by. & illus. The Three Little Pigs & Other Favorite Nursery Stories. LC 91-58759. 96p. (ps up). 1992. 18.95 (*1-56402-118-1*) Candlewick Pr.
Volkov, Alexander. Tales of Magic Land, No. 1. viii, 344p. 1991. pap. 11.95 (*0-685-49966-9*) Red Branch Pr.
Vozar, David. Yo, Hungry Wolf! A Nursery Rap. Lewin, Betsy, illus. LC 91-46264. (gr. 1-4). 1993. 15.95 (*0-385-30452-8*) Doubleday.
Vuong, Lynette D. The Golden Carp, & Other Tales of Vietnam. Saito, Manabu, illus. LC 92-38208. 128p. (gr. k-5). 1993. 15.00 (*0-688-12514-X*) Lothrop.
—Sky Legends of Vietnam. Vo-Dinh Mai, illus. LC 92-38345. 128p. (gr. 4 up). 1993. 14.00 (*0-06-023000-2*); PLB 13.89 (*0-06-023001-0*) HarpC Child Bks.
Wade, Gini, retold by. & illus. The Wonderful Bag: An Arabian Tale from the "Thousand & One Nights" LC 92-43615. 32p. (gr. k-3). 1993. 14.95 (*0-87226-508-0*) P Bedrick Bks.
Waldman, David K. Crystal Moonlight. 48p. (gr. k-2). 1990. pap. 7.95 (*0-945522-01-0*) Rebecca Hse.
Wallenhorst, Ralph. Ralf's Stories - Princes, Monsters & Magic. Bennett, Gail, et al, illus. LC 89-38025. 128p. (Orig.). (gr. 3-6). 1989. 12.00x (*0-9622905-0-5*); pap. 6.00x (*0-9622905-1-3*) Dragon Tale.
Wallner, S. J. Hans & the Golden Stirrup. LC 68-56815. (Illus.). 48p. (gr. 2-3). PLB 10.95 (*0-87783-016-9*); pap. 3.94 deluxe ed. (*0-87783-093-2*) Oddo.
Walt Disney Company Staff. Disney's Fantasyland. (Illus.). (ps-1). 1989. Contains "Mickey & the Beanstalk", "The Three Little Pigs," & "Mother Goose" write for info. (*0-307-15753-9*, Golden Pr) Western Pub.
Walt Disney Staff. Aladdin. (ps-3). 1992. 6.98 (*0-453-03058-0*) Mouse Works.
—Aladdin Bath Book. (ps-3). 1992. 5.98 (*0-453-03060-2*) Mouse Works.
—Aladdin Little Library. (ps-3). 1992. 5.98 (*0-453-03059-9*) Mouse Works.
—La Bella y la Bestia (Beauty & the Beast) (SPA.). (ps-3). 1992. 6.98 (*0-453-03016-5*) Viking Penguin.
—Cinderella. 1987. 6.98 (*0-8317-1309-7*) Viking Child Bks.
—Disney's Princess Treasury Collection: Snow White & the Seven Dwarfs, Cinderella, Sleeping Beauty. (ps-3). 1993. 6.98 (*0-453-03100-5*) NAL-Dutton.
—Dumbo. 1987. 6.98 (*0-8317-2463-3*) Viking Child Bks.
—Peter Pan. (ps-3). 1992. 6.98 (*0-453-03053-X*) Viking Child Bks.
—Pinocchio. (ps-3). 1992. 6.98 (*0-453-03026-2*) Viking-Penguin.
—Pinocchio Bath Book. (ps). 1992. 5.98 (*0-453-03028-9*) Viking-Penguin.
—Pinocchio Little Library. (ps-3). 1992. 5.98 (*0-453-03027-0*) Viking-Penguin.
—La Sirenita (The Little Mermaid) (SPA.). (ps-3). 1992. 6.98 (*0-453-03017-3*) Viking-Penguin.
—Sleeping Beauty. 1987. 6.98 (*0-8317-7863-6*) Viking Child Bks.
—Snow White & the Seven Dwarfs. 1987. 6.98 (*0-8317-7885-7*) Viking Child Bks.
—Snow White & the Seven Dwarfs Little Library. (ps). 1993. 5.98 (*0-453-03105-6*) NAL-Dutton.
—Sorcerer's Apprentice. (ps-3). 1992. 5.98 (*0-453-03025-4*) Viking-Penguin.
Walt Disney's Beauty & the Beast. (Illus.). (ps-3). 1991. write for info. (*0-307-12645-5*, Golden Pr) Western Pub.
Walt Disney's Beauty & the Beast. (ps-3). 1991. write for info. (*0-307-12343-X*, Golden Pr) Western Pub.
Walt Disney's Cinderella. 24p. (ps-k). 1986. write for info. (*0-307-10200-9*, Pub. by Golden Bks.) Western Pub.
Walt Disney's Feature Animation Dept. Staff. Disney's Aladdin: An Animated Flip Book. (Illus.). 96p. 1992. pap. 3.95 (*1-56282-889-4*) Hyperion.
—Disney's Beauty & the Beast: An Animated Flip Book. 96p. 1992. pap. 3.95 (*1-56282-888-6*) Hyperion.
Walt Disney's Feature Animation Dept. Animators Staff. Walt Disney's Snow White: An Animated Flip Book. (Illus.). 96p. 1994. pap. 3.95 (*1-56282-838-X*) Hyperion.
Walt Disney's Pinocchio. (ps-3). 1990. write for info. (*0-307-12109-7*) Western Pub.
Walt Disney's Sleeping Beauty. 24p. (ps-1). 1986. write for info. (*0-307-10408-7*, Pub. by Golden Bks) Western Pub.
Walt Disney's Snow White & the Seven Dwarfs. 24p. (ps-k). 1986. write for info. (*0-307-10205-X*, Pub. by Golden Bks.) Western Pub.
Walt Disney's Snow White & the Seven Dwarfs. 128p. 1993. 5.95 (*1-56138-282-5*) Running Pr.
Walt Disney's Story Land. (ps-3). 1991. write for info. (Golden Pr) Western Pub.

Ward, Helen. The Golden Pear. Ward, Helen, illus. LC 91-9102. 40p. (ps-3). 1991. 14.95 (*0-8249-8471-4*, Ideals Child) Hambleton-Hill.
Watson, Richard J. Tom Thumb. (Illus.). 20p. (ps-3). 1989. 12.95 (*0-15-289280-X*) HarBrace.
Watts, Bernadette. Goldilocks & the Three Bears. Watts, Bernadette, illus. LC 85-7192. (gr. k-3). 1985. 13.95 (*1-55858-039-5*); pap. 3.95 (*1-55858-040-9*) North-South Bks NYC.
Weber, Ane, et al. Is It Soup Yet? French, Marty & Iwai, Noel, illus. 26p. (ps up). 1988. incl. cassette 7.95 (*1-55578-914-5*) Worlds Wonder.
Weeks, Wilfred H. The White Stone. Schlatter, Becky, illus. LC 85-51932. 37p. (Orig.). (gr. 4-9). 1990. pap. write for info. (*0-9615677-0-8*) Three Riv Ctr.
Wegman, William. Cinderella. Wegman, William, illus. LC 92-72028. 40p. 1993. 16.95 (*1-56282-348-5*); PLB 16.89 (*1-56282-349-3*) Hyprn Child.
—Little Red Riding Hood. Wegman, William, illus. LC 92-54874. 40p. 1993. 16.95 (*1-56282-416-3*); PLB 16.89 (*1-56282-417-1*) Hyprn Child.
Wells, Rosemary. Little Lame Prince. LC 89-23482. 32p. (ps-3). 1990. 12.95 (*0-8037-0788-6*); PLB 12.89 (*0-8037-0789-4*) Dial Bks Young.
Wheeler, Post. Vasilissa the Beautiful. (gr. 4-12). 1989. 13.95 (*0-88682-354-4*, 97226-098) Creative Ed.
Wheeler, Thomas G. Loose Chippings. LC 69-11990. (Illus.). (gr. 10 up). 1969. 21.95 (*0-87599-152-1*) S G Phillips.
Whitehead, Pat. The Nutcracker. Rich, Beverly, illus. LC 87-10916. 32p. (gr. k-4). 1988. PLB 9.79 (*0-8167-1063-5*); pap. text ed. 1.95 (*0-8167-1064-3*) Troll Assocs.
Wiggin, Kate D. & Smith, Nora A., eds. The Arabian Nights: Their Best-Known Tales. Parrish, Maxfield, illus. LC 92-38552. 368p. 1993. (Scribners Young Read); SBE 25.00 (*0-684-19589-5*, Scribners Young Read) Macmillan Child Grp.
Wilde, Oscar. Complete Fairy Tales of Oscar Wilde. Zipes, Jack D., afterword by. 224p. 1990. pap. 3.95 (*0-451-52435-7*, Sig Classics) NAL-Dutton.
—The Happy Prince. 32p. (gr. 6 up). 1983. PLB 13.95 (*0-87191-924-9*) Creative Ed.
—The Happy Prince. Young, Ed, illus. LC 88-29694. (gr. 1-3). 1992. (S&S BFYR); pap. 5.95 (*0-671-77819-6*, S&S BFYR) S&S Trade.
—The Happy Prince & Other Stories. Robinson, Charles, illus. Glassman, Peter, afterword by. LC 90-48353. (Illus.). 144p. 1991. Repr. of 1913 ed. 16.95 (*0-688-10390-1*) Morrow Jr Bks.
—The Happy Prince: From the Fairy Tale. 1st ed. Ray, Jane, illus. LC 94-25888. (gr. k up). 1995. write for info. (*0-525-45367-9*) Dutton Child Bks.
—The Selfish Giant. Gallagher, Saelig, illus. LC 93-10393. 1994. 15.95 (*0-399-22448-3*) Putnam Pub Group.
—Stories for Children. Lynch, P. J., illus. LC 90-38854. 96p. (gr. 3 up). 1991. 14.95 (*0-02-792765-2*, Macmillan Child Bk) Macmillan Child Grp.
Wilhelm, Hans. The Bremen Town Musicians. 32p. 1992. 13.95 (*0-590-44795-5*, Scholastic Hardcover) Scholastic Inc.
Wilkon, Piotr. Trois Chatons Intrepides. Wilkon, Jozef, illus. (FRE.). 32p. (gr. k-3). 1992. 14.95 (*3-314-20735-2*) North-South Bks NYC.
Willard, Nancy. Beauty & the Beast. Moser, B., illus. 1992. 19.95 (*0-15-206052-9*, HB Juv Bks) HarBrace.
Williams, Arlene. Fairy Tales for the New Age. 160p. (gr. 4 up). 1992. pap. 12.95 (*0-9605444-1-0*) Waking Light Pr.
Williams, Don & Bailey, Kathy, illus. Disney's Beauty & the Beast: Belle Explores the Castle. LC 92-52971. 18p. (ps-1). 1992. 9.95 (*1-56282-271-3*) Disney Pr.
Williams, Margery. Velveteen Rabbit. Nicholson, William, illus. 47p. (gr. 3-5). 1958. PLB (*0-385-07748-3*); pap. 9.95 (*0-385-07725-4*); pap. 15.95 slipcased (*0-385-00913-5*) Doubleday.
Williams, Ursula M. Bogwoppit. large type ed. 288p. (ps-5). 1990. lib. bdg. 16.95x (*0-7451-1155-6*, Lythway Large Print) Hall.
Wilsdorf, Anne. Princess: Based on Hans Christian Andersen's "The Princess & the Pea" LC 92-20636. (Illus.). 32p. (ps up). 1993. 14.00 (*0-688-11541-1*); PLB 13.93 (*0-688-11542-X*) Greenwillow.
Wilson, Barbara K. Wishbones: A Folk Tale from China. So, Meilo, illus. LC 92-26993. 32p. (ps-2). 1993. SBE 14.95 (*0-02-793125-0*, Bradbury Pr) Macmillan Child Grp.
Wilson, Karle B. The Reindeer's Shoe & Other Stories. Montgomery, Charlotte B., illus. & intro. by. LC 88-2292. 112p. (ps-12). 1988. casebound 17.95 (*0-936650-07-9*) E C Temple.
Winhdam, Sophie. Read Me a Story: A Child's Book of Favorite Tales. (Illus.). 96p. 1991. 16.95 (*0-590-44950-8*, Scholastic Hardcover) Scholastic Inc.
Winnie the Pooh. (Illus.). 48p. (ps-6). 1989. 5.99 (*0-517-67005-4*) Random Hse Value.
Winthrop, Elizabeth. Vasilissa the Beautiful. Koshkin, Alexander, illus. LC 89-26903. 40p. (gr. 1-5). 1994. pap. 5.95 (*0-06-443345-5*, Trophy) HarpC Child Bks.
Winthrop, Elizabeth, adapted by. Vasilissa the Beautiful: A Russian Folktale. Koshkin, Alexander, illus. LC 89-26903. 40p. (gr. 1-5). 1991. PLB 15.89 (*0-06-021663-8*) HarpC Child Bks.
Wisniewski, David. The Warrior & the Wise Man. Wisniewski, David, illus. LC 88-21678. 32p. (gr. k-3). 1989. 15.00 (*0-688-07889-3*); PLB 14.93 (*0-688-07890-7*) Lothrop.
—The Wave of the Sea-Wolf. LC 93-18265. 1994. 16.95 (*0-395-66478-0*, Clarion Bks) HM.

Wixom, Tedi T. A Princess, Dragon & Baker. Hale, Leon & May, Mike, illus. 40p. (ps-8). 1994. Saddlestitch bdg. 6.95 (*1-885227-33-7*) TNT Bks.
A PRINCESS, DRAGON & BAKER by Tedi Tuttle Wixom (Author of "To Heal A Heart", adult non-fiction, by Northwest Pub. Inc.). Illustrated by Leon Hale & Mike May; TNT Books. A fast-paced NEW fairy tale set high in a mystical kingdom in Europe! Princess Catherine, a vivacious young girl with an attitude, wants to have everything her way. The people of the town realize she has no friends, except for 10 white rabbits. A blue dragon, who is flying around looking for adventure, crashes through the palace window when he smells his favorite food, carrots, inside the castle walls. His crash landing terrifies Princess Catherine & her maid. The rotund village baker, upon hearing her screaming, sprints to the castle to save Princess Catherine from a watery grave when she falls into the shark infested moat. Herein lies action & adventure no child will want to miss. This will be the future classic fairy tale your children will want to tell & retell to their children & grandchildren. 40 pages. 8 1/2 X 11. Exquisite illustrations by experts. Artists utilize magnificent perspectives done in watercolor washes/four-color. $6.95 saddlestitched. ISBN 1-885227-33-7.
Publisher Provided Annotation.

The Wizard of Oz. (Illus.). 20p. (ps up). 1992. write for info. incl. long-life batteries (*0-307-74706-9*, 64706, Golden Pr) Western Pub.
Wolfer, J. The Dog Who Cried Wolf: Based on Old Fairy Tale. Abell, ed. & illus. 50p. (Orig.). (gr. 1-3). 1993. 25.00 (*1-56611-058-0*); pap. text ed. 15.00 (*1-56611-061-0*) Jonas.
Wolkstein, Diane. Oom Razoom or Go I Know Not Where, Bring Back I Know Not What. McDermott, Dennis, illus. LC 91-6308. 32p. (gr. k up). 1991. 14.95 (*0-688-09416-3*); PLB 14.88 (*0-688-09417-1*) Morrow Jr Bks.
Wonder Kids Publications Group Staff (USA) & Hwa-I Publishing Co., Staff. Fairy Tales: Chinese Children's Stories, Vols. 46-50. Ching, Emily, et al, eds. Wonder Kids Publications Staff, tr. from CHI. Hwa-I Publishing Co., Staff, illus. LC 90-60801. (gr. 3-6). 1991. Repr. of 1988 ed. Five vol. set, 28p. ea. bk. 39.75 (*0-685-58709-6*) Wonder Kids.
The Wonderful Wizard of Oz. 24p. (gr. k-3). 1992. pap. 2.50 (*1-56144-174-0*, Honey Bear Bks) Modern Pub NYC.
Wood, Audrey. Princess & the Dragon. (ps-3). 1989. pap. 3.95 (*0-85953-305-0*) Childs Play.
Wood, David. Pop-up Theater Cinderella. Fowler, Richard, illus. LC 93-81274. 24p. (gr. 3-7). 1994. 17.95 (*1-85697-989-X*, Kingfisher LKC) LKC.
Woyiwada, Allison, ed. The Little Fir Tree: A Musical for Primary Children Based on a Story by Hans Christian Andersen. LC 93-50820. 1994. write for info. (*0-88734-428-3*) Players Pr.
Wray, Kit, retold by. & illus. Hidden Picture Fairy Tales: Rapunzel. LC 90-85901. 32p. (gr. k-5). 1991. 7.95 (*1-878093-25-8*) Boyds Mills Pr.
—Hidden Picture Fairy Tales: Snow White. LC 90-85902. 32p. (gr. k-5). 1991. 7.95 (*1-878093-26-6*) Boyds Mills Pr.
Wrede, Patricia C. Calling on Dragons. LC 92-35469. 1993. write for info. (*0-15-200950-7*, J Yolen Bks) HarBrace.
—Talking to Dragons. LC 92-40719. 1993. 16.95 (*0-15-284247-0*, J Yolen Bks) HarBrace.
Yashima, Taro. One-Inch Fellow. LC 93-10824. (ps-6). 1995. write for info. (*0-15-276897-1*, Browndeer Pr) HarBrace.
Yeats, William Butler. Fairy Tales of Ireland. Philip, Neil, selected by. Lynch, Patrick J., illus. Philip, Neil & Philip, Neilintro. by. (Illus.). 1990. 16.95 (*0-385-30249-5*) Delacorte.
Yep, Laurence. The Ghost Fox. Tseng, Jean & Tseng, Mou-Sien, illus. LC 92-21558. 64p. (gr. 3-6). 1994. 13.95 (*0-590-47204-6*, Scholastic Hardcover) Scholastic Inc.
Yep, Laurence, retold by. The Shell Woman & the King: A Chinese Folktale. Ming-Yi, Yang, illus. LC 92-9583. 32p. (gr. k-3). 1993. 13.99 (*0-8037-1394-0*); PLB 13.89 (*0-8037-1395-9*) Dial Bks Young.
Yolen, Jane. The Girl in the Golden Bower. Dyer, Jane, illus. LC 92-37284. (gr. 5 up). 1994. 15.95 (*0-316-96894-3*) Little.
—The Girl Who Loved the Wind. Young, Ed, illus. LC 71-171012. 32p. (ps-3). 1982. (Crowell Jr Bks); PLB 14.89 (*0-690-33101-0*, Crowell Jr Bks) HarpC Child Bks.
—Here There Be Dragons. Wilgus, David, illus. LC 92-23194. 1993. 16.95 (*0-15-209888-7*) HarBrace.
—Sleeping Ugly. (gr. 1-4). 1981. (Coward); pap. 6.95 (*0-698-20617-7*) Putnam Pub Group.
—Tam Lin. Mikolaycak, Charles, illus. LC 88-2280. 24p. (gr. 1-7). 1990. 14.95 (*0-15-284261-6*) HarBrace.
—Touch Magic. 96p. (ps-8). 1992. pap. 10.95 (*0-399-21897-1*, Philomel Bks) Putnam Pub Group.
Yolen, Jane, retold by. The Musicians of Bremen. Segal, John, illus. LC 92-18695. 32p. (ps-2). 1995. 10.00 (*0-06-021498-8*); PLB 9.89 (*0-06-021499-6*) HarpC Child Bks.
Zavrel, Stepan. Vodnik. Zavrel, Stepan, illus. LC 72-121796. 32p. (ps-3). 8.95 (*0-87592-058-6*) Scroll Pr.
Zegers, Lucille D. Another Auntie La La Children's Story: The Clumsy Tooth Fairy. Pusaterg, Michalino, illus. LC 92-91121. 64p. 1994. pap. 8.00 (*1-56002-260-4*) Aegina Pr.
Zemach, Harve. A Penny a Look: An Old Story. Zemach, Margot, illus. LC 71-161373. 48p. (ps-3). 1971. 16.00 (*0-374-35793-5*) FS&G.
Zemach, Harve & Zemach, Kaethe. The Princess & Froggie. Zemach, Margot, illus. (ps-3). 1992. pap. 4.95 (*0-374-46011-6*, Sunburst) FS&G.
Zemach, Margot. Little Red Hen: An Old Story. (ps-3). 1993. pap. 4.95 (*0-374-44511-7*, Sunburst) FS&G.
—Los Tres Deseos; un Viejo Cuento: The Three Wishes; an Old Story. (ps-3). 1993. pap. 16.00 (*0-374-34662-3*) FS&G.
Ziegler, Judy. Judy Ziegler's Zany Fairytales: Hense, Toostel & Elepunzel. 1992. 1.99 (*0-517-06686-6*) Random Hse Value.
—Rhinorella & Rumplecatskin. 1992. pap. 1.99 (*0-517-06685-8*) Random Hse Value.
Zipes, Jack, ed. & tr. from GER. Fairy Tales & Fables from Weimar Days. LC 89-40357. (Illus.). 221p. 1989. 30.00x (*0-87451-501-7*) U Pr of New Eng.

FAIRY TALES–INDEXES

Seros, Kathleen, adapted by. Sun & Moon: Fairy Tales from Korea. Sibley, Norman & Krause, Robert, illus. LC 82-82510. 61p. (gr. 3-9). 1982. PLB 16.50x (*0-930878-25-6*) Hollym Intl.

FAITH

Anderson, Lynn. If I Really Believe, Why Do I Have These Doubts? 224p. (Orig.). 1992. pap. 7.99 (*1-55661-182-X*) Bethany Hse.
Bauer, Marion D. A Question of Trust. 128p. (gr. 4-7). 1994. 13.95 (*0-590-47915-6*, Scholastic Hardcover) Scholastic Inc.
Burgess, Beverly C. God Are You Really Real? Titolo, Nancy, illus. 30p. (Orig.). (gr. 1-3). 1985. pap. 1.98 (*0-89274-309-3*) Harrison Hse.
Cassady, David. Faith for Tough Times. (Illus.). 48p. (gr. 9-12). 1991. pap. 8.99 (*1-55945-216-1*) Group Pub.
DeMoor, Robert. Quest of Faith. 149p. (Orig.). (gr. 9 up). 1989. pap. text ed. 5.75 (*0-930265-74-2*) CRC Pubns.
Father Robert J. Fox. The Day the Sun Danced: The True Story of Fatima. CCC of America Staff, illus. 60p. (Orig.). (gr. k-6). 1989. incl. video 21.95 (*1-56814-001-0*); book 4.95 (*0-685-62401-3*) CCC of America.
Gilroy, Mark. Sharing My Faith: A Teen's Guide to Evangelism. (Illus.). 104p. 1991. pap. 5.95 (*0-8341-1384-8*) Beacon Hill.
Goley. Faith, Reading Level 2. (Illus.). 32p. (gr. 1-4). 1989. PLB 15.94 (*0-86592-386-8*); lib. bdg. 11.95s.p. (*0-685-58781-9*) Rourke Corp.
Herbst, Helen. God's Children Share Their Faith with You. Connor, Genevieve, illus. 48p. (gr. 1-4). 1988. coloring bk. 2.50 (*0-913382-55-8*, 103-20) Prow Bks-Franciscan.
Johnson, Lois W. You Are Wonderfully Made! Peck, Virginia, illus. LC 88-60474. 192p. (Orig.). 1988. pap. 7.00 (*0-89109-235-8*) NavPress.
—You're Worth More Than You Think! Peck, Virginia, illus. LC 88-60476. 180p. (Orig.). 1988. pap. 7.00 (*0-89109-233-1*) NavPress.
Keith, Gretchen L. The Life to Come: Stories for Children about the Spiritual World. Cook, Richard J., illus. 89p. (Orig.). (gr. 3-7). 1990. pap. 5.00 (*0-945003-03-X*) General Church.
O'Collins, Gerald. Friends in Faith. 112p. (gr. 10-12). 1989. pap. 4.95 (*0-8091-3086-6*) Paulist Pr.
O'Connor, Francine M. & Boswell, Kathryn. The ABCs of Faith: God & You. (gr. 1-4). 1979. Bk. 1. pap. 2.95 (*0-89243-113-X*) Liguori Pubns.
Odor, Harold & Odor, Ruth. Sharing Your Faith. Greene, Tom, illus. 16p. (gr. 3-7). 1985. 0.75 (*0-87239-902-8*, 3302) Standard Pub.
Payne, Mary A. Russell's Journal: Trust. (Illus.). 48p. (gr. k-4). 1993. 7.95 (*0-8059-3334-4*) Dorrance.
Shaw, Judy. Little Faith Builders. 30p. (Orig.). (gr. 1-3). 1983. pap. 0.98 (*0-89274-290-9*) Harrison Hse.
Teller, Hanoch. Once upon a Soul. 2nd ed. 224p. (gr. 12). 1988. Repr. of 1984 ed. 9.95 (*0-9614772-3-7*) NYC Pub Co.

Turrentine, Jan. Acteens from A to Z. 24p. (Orig.). (gr. 7-12). 1988. pap. text ed. 1.50 (*0-936625-47-3*) Womans Mission Union.
Vos Wezeman, Phyllis & Wiessner, Colleen A. Fabric of Faith. Chase, Judith, illus. 47p. (Orig.). (gr. 4-8). 1990. pap. 7.50 (*1-877871-04-4*) Ed Ministries.
—Lydia: Filling the Fibers with Faith. 24p. (Orig.). (gr. 1-6). 1989. pap. 5.95 (*0-940754-71-1*) Ed Ministries.
Wells, Tom. Faith the Gift of God. 156p. (gr. 5 up). 1983. pap. 6.95 (*0-85151-361-1*) Banner of Truth.
Wilson, Ginger. Questions! Questions! Questions!!! Sytsma, Cheryle, ed. LC 90-63620. (Illus.). 30p. (Orig.). (gr. k-5). 1991. pap. write for info. (*1-879068-04-4*) Ray-Ma Natsal.

FAITH CURE–FICTION

Robinson, Barbara. My Brother Louis Measures Worms: and Other Louis Stories. LC 87-45302. 160p. (gr. 5 up). 1990. pap. 3.95 (*0-06-440362-9*, Trophy) HarpC Child Bks.

FALCONS

Arnold, Caroline. Saving the Peregrine Falcon. Hewett, Richard R., photos by. LC 84-15576. (Illus.). 48p. (gr. 2-5). 1985. PLB 19.95 (*0-87614-225-0*); pap. 6.95 (*0-87614-523-3*) Carolrhoda Bks.
Birkhead, Mike. The Falcon over the Town. Oxford Scientific Films, photos by. LC 87-42615. (Illus.). 32p. (gr. 4-6). 1988. PLB 17.27 (*1-55532-304-9*) Gareth Stevens Inc.
Funston, Sylvia. Peregrine Falcon. Owl Magazine Staff, ed. Kassian, Olena, illus. 32p. (gr. 1 up). 1992. 4.95 (*0-920775-99-3*, Pub. by Greey de Pencier CN) Firefly Bks Ltd.
Green, Carl R. & Sanford, William R. The Peregrine Falcon. LC 86-2670. (Illus.). 48p. (gr. 5). 1986. text ed. 12.95 RSBE (*0-89686-271-2*, Crestwood Hse) Macmillan Child Grp.
Greene, Carol. Reading about the Peregrine Falcon. LC 92-26804. (Illus.). 32p. (gr. k-3). 1993. lib. bdg. 13.95 (*0-89490-422-1*) Enslow Pubs.
Harrison, Virginia. The World of a Falcon. Oxford Scientific Films Staff, photos by. LC 87-42611. (Illus.). 32p. (gr. 2-3). 1988. PLB 17.27 (*1-55532-308-1*) Gareth Stevens Inc.
Jenkins, Priscilla B. The Falcons Return. Lloyd, Megan, illus. 1996. 15.00 (*0-06-021104-0*, HarpT); PLB 14.89 (*0-06-021105-9*, HarpT) HarpC.
Olsen, Penny. Falcons & Hawks. LC 92-11986. (Illus.). 72p. (gr. 5 up). 1992. PLB 17.95 (*0-8160-2843-5*) Facts on File.

FALCONS–FICTION

Buchanan, Dawna L. The Falcon's Wing. 128p. (gr. 4). 1993. pap. 3.50 (*0-380-72102-3*, Camelot) Avon.
Deliz, Wenceslao S. Adios Falcon. Marichal, Poli, illus. LC 85-1116. (SPA.). 15p. (ps-3). 1985. pap. 2.00 (*0-8477-3530-3*) U of PR Pr.
George, Jean C. On the Far Side of the Mountain. LC 89-25988. 176p. (gr. 3-7). 1990. 15.00 (*0-525-44563-3*, DCB) Dutton Child Bks.
—The Summer of the Falcon. George, Jean C., illus. LC 62-16543. 153p. (gr. 5 up). 1979. pap. 3.95 (*0-06-440095-6*, Trophy) HarpC Child Bks.
Girzone, Joseph F. Kara: The Lonely Falcon. Molloy, Eideen, illus. LC 78-63393. 52p. (gr. 2 up). 1985. Repr. of 1979 ed. 8.95 (*0-911519-05-X*) Richelieu Court.
Mandelstein, Paul. Nightingale & the Wind. Silin-Palmer, Pamela, illus. LC 93-31056. 32p. (gr. 4 up). 1994. 17.95 (*0-8478-1787-3*) Rizzoli Intl.

FALL

see Autumn

FALLACIES

see Logic

FALLING STARS

see Meteors

FALSEHOOD

see Truthfulness and Falsehood

FAMILY

see also Divorce; Domestic Relations; Marriage; Parent and Child
also names of members of the family, e.g., Fathers; Mothers; etc.

Amstutz, Beverly. I Love My Foster Grandparents. (Illus.). 24p. (gr. k-7). 1981. pap. 2.50x (*0-937836-06-0*) Precious Res.
Barmat, Jeanne. Foster Families. LC 90-46834. (Illus.). 48p. (gr. 5-6). 1991. text ed. 4.95 RSBE (*0-89686-605-X*, Crestwood Hse) Macmillan Child Grp.
Bell, Jo G. Sometimes I Wish I Were Big. Conahan, Carolyn, illus. 32p. (ps-2). Date not set. 11.95 (*1-56065-159-8*) Capstone Pr.
Bennett, Marian & Stortz, Diane. My Family & Friends. Oliviera, Gerry, illus. 12p. (ps). 1992. deluxe ed. 4.99 (*0-87403-994-0*, 24-03114) Standard Pub.
Berman, Claire. What Am I Doing in a Stepfamily? Wilson, Dick, illus. (gr. k-7). 1992. pap. 8.95 (*0-8184-0563-5*, L Stuart) Carol Pub Group.
Berry, Joy. About Step Families. Bartholomew, illus. 48p. (gr. 3 up). 1990. 12.30 (*0-516-02955-X*) Childrens.
Bornemann Spies, Karen. The American Family: Can It Survive? (Illus.). 64p. (gr. 5-8). 1993. PLB 14.95 (*0-8050-2568-5*) TFC Bks NY.
Center for Learning Network. Stepfamilies: Personal Adjustment: Looking at Life. 12p. (gr. 7-12). 1992. pap. text ed. 0.80 (*1-56077-224-7*) Ctr Learning.
Cline, Ruth K. J. Focus on Families: A Reference Handbook. 230p. (gr. 9-12). 1989. lib. bdg. 39.50 (*0-87436-508-2*) ABC-CLIO.
Coleman, William. Just 'Cuz You Married My Mom Doesn't Mean You're My Dad: A Survival Guide for Teenagers with Step Parents. 132p. (gr. 7 up). 1993. 9.95 (*0-89638-285-0*) Hazelden.
Cooney, Caroline B. Family Reunion. (gr. 7 up). 1989. 14.95 (*0-553-05836-3*, Starfire) Bantam.
Crisfield, Deborah. Dysfunctional Families. LC 91-22088. (Illus.). 48p. (gr. 5-6). 1992. text ed. 12.95 RSBE (*0-89686-722-6*, Crestwood Hse) Macmillan Child Grp.
Families & Friends. (Illus.). 32p. (ps-2). 1985. 1.95 (*0-225-66390-2*) Harper SF.
Families Theme Pack: Level 1 English. (Orig.). (gr. 1-3). 1992. pap. 129.95 set incl. 2 big bks., 12 small bks. tchr's. guide (*1-56334-077-1*) Hampton-Brown.
Fisher, Leonard E. The Tanners. Fisher, Leonard E., illus. LC 66-10136. 48p. (gr. 3 up). 1986. pap. 5.95 (*0-87923-609-4*) Godine.
Giovanni, Nikki. Grand Mothers. 1994. write for info. (*0-8050-2766-1*) H Holt & Co.
Glassman, Bruce. Everything You Need to Know about Stepfamilies. rev. ed. (Illus.). 64p. (gr. 7-12). 1993. 14.95 (*0-8239-1798-3*) Rosen Group.
Hazen, Barbara S. If It Weren't for Benjamin: (I'd Always Get to Lick the Icing Spoon) Hartman, Laura, illus. LC 78-26403. 32p. (ps-3). 1979. 16.95 (*0-87705-384-7*); pap. 9.95 (*0-89885-172-6*) Human Sci Pr.
Heegaard, Marge. When a Parent Marries Again. (ps-3). 1993. pap. 6.95 (*0-9620502-6-1*) Woodland Pr.
Hill, Margaret. Coping with Family Expectations. Rosen, Ruth, ed. (gr. 7-12). 1990. PLB 14.95 (*0-8239-1159-4*) Rosen Group.
Jamiolkowski, Raymond M. Coping in a Dysfunctional Family. LC 93-13665. 1993. 14.95 (*0-8239-1660-X*) Rosen Group.
Jenness, Aylette. Families: A Celebration of Diversity, Commitment & Love. (Illus.). 48p. (gr. 3-5). 1990. 13.45 (*0-395-47038-2*) HM.
—Families: A Celebration of Diversity, Commitment, & Love. (gr. 4-7). 1993. pap. 4.95 (*0-395-66952-9*) HM.
Kalman, Bobbie. People in My Family. (Illus.). 32p. (gr. k-2). 1985. 15.95 (*0-86505-061-9*); pap. 7.95 (*0-86505-085-6*) Crabtree Pub Co.
Keffer, Lois. Getting along with Your Family. (Illus.). 48p. (gr. 9-12). 1992. pap. 8.99 (*1-55945-233-1*) Group Pub.
Koftan, Jenelle & Koftan, Kenneth. Long-Distance Grandparenting. (Illus.). 96p. (Orig.). (ps-k). 1988. pap. 12.95 (*0-945184-00-X*) Spring Creek Pubns.
—Long-Distance Grandparenting. (Illus.). 96p. (Orig.). (gr. k-2). 1988. pap. 12.95 (*0-945184-01-8*) Spring Creek Pubns.
—Long-Distance Grandparenting. (Illus.). 112p. (Orig.). (gr. 3-5). 1988. pap. 12.95 (*0-945184-02-6*) Spring Creek Pubns.
Kratky, Lada J. La Familia Villarreal. Lovell, Craig, photos by. (SPA., Illus.). 24p. (Orig.). (gr. 1-3). 1991. pap. text ed. 29.95 big bk. (*1-56334-022-4*); pap. text ed. 6.00 small bk. (*1-56334-036-4*) Hampton-Brown.
Lanton, Sandy. The Girl Who Wouldn't See. Noll, Cheryl K., illus. 32p. (ps-2). Date not set. 11.95 (*1-56065-140-7*) Capstone Pr.
—That's Not the Way Mommy Does It. Noll, Cheryl K., illus. 32p. (ps-2). Date not set. 11.95 (*1-56065-142-3*) Capstone Pr.
Lawrence, Kenneth. Kodar's Travels: The Saga of an Israelite Family. Hill, James D. & Sauls, Daleintro. by. (Illus.). 256p. (Orig.). 1993. pap. 20.95 (*0-910653-20-8*, Red River Pr) Archival Servs.
Londner, Renee. Morgan's Whistle. Noll, Cheryl K., illus. LC 92-14390. 32p. (ps-2). Date not set. 11.95 (*1-56065-162-8*) Capstone Pr.
Lucas, Sally. Twin Monkeys. Lucas, Margeaux, illus. 32p. (ps-2). Date not set. 11.95 (*1-56065-156-3*) Capstone Pr.
McFarland, Rhoda. Drugs & Your Brothers & Sisters. rev. ed. (gr. 7-12). 1993. PLB 14.95 (*0-8239-1754-1*) Rosen Group.
Maloof, Karen. For My Child: An Album of Family Memories from Parent to Child. (Illus.). 48p. 1994. 17.95 (*0-8249-8659-8*, Ideals Child) Hambleton-Hill.
Nelson, JoAnne. We Are Family. Woolf, Marie W., illus. LC 93-12176. 1994. 5.95 (*0-935529-60-8*) Comprehen Health Educ.
Packard, Gwen K. Coping in an Interfaith Family. LC 92-39454. 1993. 14.95 (*0-8239-1452-6*) Rosen Group.
Parramon, J. M., et al. Children. 32p. (gr. 3-5). 1987. pap. 6.95 (*0-685-73872-8*); Eng. ed. pap. 6.95 (*0-8120-3850-9*); Span. ed.: Los Ninos. pap. 6.95 (*0-8120-3854-1*) Barron.
—Grandparents. 32p. (gr. 3-5). 1987. Eng. ed. pap. 6.95 Eng. ed. (*0-8120-3853-3*); Span. ed.: Los Abuelos. pap. 6.95 (*0-8120-3857-6*) Barron.
Pendergast, Kathleen. Say Another One about My Family. Tindal, Pauline, illus. LC 82-61139. 54p. (gr. k-6). 1982. pap. 6.95 (*0-942178-01-7*) Madison Park Pr.
Regan, Mary. A Family in France. LC 84-19392. (Illus.). 32p. (gr. 2-5). 1985. PLB 13.50 (*0-8225-1651-9*) Lerner Pubns.
Ricklen, Neil, illus. My Family: Mi Familia. LC 93-30661. (ENG & SPA.). 14p. (ps-k). 1994. pap. 3.95 (*0-689-71771-7*, Aladdin) Macmillan Child Grp.
Schaffer, Patricia. How Babies & Family Are Made-There Is More Than One Way! Corbett, Susanne, illus. LC 86-23087. 64p. (gr. k-4). 1988. pap. 6.95 (*0-935079-17-3*) Tabor Sarah Bks.
Schenkerman, Rona D. Growing up in a Stepfamily. 16p. (gr. 3-8). 1993. 1.95 (*1-56688-112-9*) Bur For At-Risk.
Sciacca, Fran & Sciacca, Jill. Are Families Forever? Understanding Your Family. 64p. 1992. pap. 3.99 saddle stitch bdg. (*0-310-48071-X*) Zondervan.
Shannon, Robert L. Grandpap Remembers from the Book of Life. (Illus.). 40p. 1994. pap. 7.95 (*0-8059-3476-6*) Dorrance.
Simon, Norma. All Kinds of Families. Rubin, Caroline, ed. Lasker, Joe, illus. LC 75-42283. 40p. (gr. k-2). 1976. PLB 13.95 (*0-8075-0282-0*) A Whitman.
Stein, Sara B. That New Baby. LC 73-15271. (Illus.). 48p. (gr. 1 up). 1974. 12.95 (*0-8027-6175-5*) Walker & Co.
Steiner, Michael P., Sr. Not a Wicked Stepmother. rev. ed. (Illus.). 42p. (Orig.). (gr. 4 up). 1991. pap. text ed. 12.95 (*1-879417-00-6*) Stern & Stern.
Tigwell, Tony. A Family in India. LC 84-19446. (Illus.). 32p. (gr. 2-5). 1985. PLB 13.50 (*0-8225-1654-3*) Lerner Pubns.
Time-Life Inc. Editors. Do Mommies Have Mommies? First Questions & Answers about Families. Fallow, Allan, ed. (Illus.). 48p. (ps-k). 1994. write for info. (*0-7835-0874-3*); PLB write for info. (*0-7835-0875-1*) Time-Life.
Tsuchiyama, Steve. Family Problems. LC 93-40415. 1994. 14.95 (*1-85435-618-6*) Marshall Cavendish.
Wagner, Viqi & Swisher, Karin L., eds. The Family in America: Opposing Viewpoints. LC 92-8150. (Illus.). 240p. (gr. 10 up). 1992. PLB 17.95 (*0-89908-194-0*); pap. text ed. 9.95 (*0-89908-169-X*) Greenhaven.
Wagonseller, Bill, et al. Coping in a Single-Parent Home. rev. ed. Rosen, Ruth, ed. (gr. 7-12). 1994. PLB 14.95 (*0-8239-1952-8*) Rosen Group.
Wheeler, Jill C. The People We Live With. Kallen, Stuart A., ed. LC 91-73067. 1991. 12.94 (*1-56239-034-1*) Abdo & Dghtrs.

FAMILY–FICTION

Ackerman, Karen. The Leaves in October. LC 90-550. 128p. (gr. 3-7). 1991. SBE 13.95 (*0-689-31583-X*, Atheneum Child Bk) Macmillan Child Grp.
Adams, Pam. Ups & Downs. (gr. 4 up). 1985. 4.95 (*0-85953-257-7*) Childs Play.
Allan, Jay. Blocks. (Illus.). (ps). 1993. pap. 5.95 (*0-9631798-1-0*) Silver Seahorse.
Ancona, George. Helping Out. (ps-3). 1991. pap. 127.60 (*0-395-55774-7*, Clarion Bks) HM.
Angell, Judie. Don't Rent My Room. 1991. pap. 3.50 (*0-553-29142-4*) Bantam.
Auch, Mary J. The Latch-Key Dog. Smith, Cat B., illus. LC 93-18604. 1994. 13.95 (*0-316-05916-1*) Little.
Avi. Blue Heron. LC 91-4308. 192p. (gr. 5-9). 1992. SBE 14.95 (*0-02-707751-9*, Bradbury Pr) Macmillan Child Grp.
Baillie, Allan. Little Brother. 144p. (gr. 3-7). 1992. 14.00 (*0-670-84381-4*) Viking Child Bks.
Bechard, Margaret. Tory & Me & the Spirit of True Love. LC 92-5821. 156p. (gr. 3-7). 1992. 14.00 (*0-670-84688-0*) Viking Child Bks.
Bennett, Cherie. The Fall of the the Perfect Girl. 224p. (gr. 7 up). 1993. pap. 3.50 (*0-14-036319-X*, Puffin) Puffin Bks.
Bloom, Hanya. Vampire Cousins. (gr. 4-7). 1990. pap. 2.95 (*0-06-106025-9*, PL) HarpC.
Boyd, Lizi. Sam Is My Half Brother. (Illus.). 32p. (ps-3). 1992. pap. 3.99 (*0-14-054190-X*, Puffin) Puffin Bks.
Brandenberg, Franz. Aunt Nina & Her Nephews & Nieces. Aliki, illus. LC 82-12004. 32p. (gr. k-3). 1983. PLB 14.93 (*0-688-01870-X*); 15.00 (*0-688-01869-6*) Greenwillow.
—Aunt Nina, Good Night. Aliki, illus. LC 88-18777. 32p. (ps up). 1989. 12.95 (*0-688-07463-4*); PLB 12.88 (*0-688-07464-2*) Greenwillow.
Bunn, Scott. Just Hold On. LC 82-70316. 160p. (gr. 7 up). 1982. pap. 9.95 (*0-385-28490-X*) Delacorte.
Carney, Mary L. Too Tough to Hurt. 128p. 1991. pap. 6.99 (*0-310-28621-2*, Youth Bks) Zondervan.
Carr, Jan. Dark Day, Light Night. Ransome, James, illus. LC 93-45932. 1995. write for info. (*0-7868-0018-6*); PLB write for info. (*0-7868-2014-4*) Hyprn Child.
Carris, Joan D. Aunt Morbelia & the Screaming Skulls. Cushman, Doug, illus. (gr. 3-7). 1990. 14.95 (*0-316-12945-3*) Little.
Casson, Lee. My Uncle Max. Desputeaux, Helene, illus. 24p. (Orig.). (ps-2). 1990. pap. 0.99 (*1-55037-130-4*, Pub. by Annick CN) Firefly Bks Ltd.
Christopher, Matt. The Fox Steals Home. Johnson, Larry, illus. LC 78-17526. (gr. 4-6). 1985. 14.95 (*0-316-13976-9*); pap. 3.95 (*0-316-13986-6*) Little.
Clark, Emma C. Lunch with Aunt Augusta. LC 91-11969. (Illus.). 32p. (ps-3). 1992. 14.00 (*0-8037-1104-2*) Dial Bks Young.
Cochrane, Shirley G. & Townsend, Betsy B. The Jones Family. Robey, Adele, illus. 50p. (Orig.). 1992. pap. 10.00 (*0-9609062-2-3*) WA Expatriates Pr.
Colman, Hila. Diary of a Frantic Kid Sister. (gr. 4-6). 1985. pap. 2.95 (*0-671-61926-8*, Archway) PB.
Cooney, Caroline B. Family Reunion. 1990. pap. 2.95 (*0-553-28573-4*) Bantam.
Cooper, Melrose. I Got a Family. Gottlieb, Dale, photos by. LC 92-1689. (Illus.). 32p. (ps-2). 1993. 14.95 (*0-8050-1965-0*, Bks Young Read) H Holt & Co.
Cormier, Robert. Eight Plus One. 1991. pap. 3.99 (*0-440-20838-6*, LFL) Dell.
Cunningham, Carolyn. All Kinds of Separation. Mortenson, Bob, illus. 24p. (gr. k-6). 1988. wkbk. 3.95 (*0-685-20040-X*, 0494) Kidsrights.

Curry, Jane L. The Big Smith Snatch. LC 89-8036. 192p. (gr. 4-7). 1989. SBE 14.95 (0-689-50478-0, M K McElderry) Macmillan Child Grp.

Delavan, Elizabeth. Peter & George & Uncle Henry. (Illus.). 48p. (gr. 3-4). 1988. pap. 2.95 (1-55787-020-9, NY75041) Heart of the Lakes.

DiSalvo-Ryan, Dyanne. Uncle Willie & the Soup Kitchen. DiSalvo-Ryan, Dyanne, illus. LC 90-6375. 32p. (gr. 1 up). 1991. 13.95 (0-688-09165-2); PLB 13.88 (0-688-09166-0, Morrow Jr Bks) Morrow Jr Bks.

Drescher, Joan. The Birth-Order Blues. Drescher, Joan, illus. 32p. (ps-3). 1993. RB 13.99 (0-670-83621-4) Viking Child Bks.

Durant, Penny R. When Heroes Die. LC 91-48267. 144p. (gr. 5 up). 1992. SBE 13.95 (0-689-31764-6, Atheneum Child Bk) Macmillan Child Grp.

Ellis, Sarah. A Family Project. LC 87-22818. 144p. (gr. 4-7). 1988. SBE 13.95 (0-689-50444-6, M K McElderry) Macmillan Child Grp.

—A Family Project. (Orig.). (gr. k-6). 1991. pap. 3.25 (0-440-40397-9, Pub. by Yearling Classics) Dell.

Enright, Elizabeth. Then There Were Five. Enright, Elizabeth, illus. (gr. k-6). 1987. pap. 2.95 (0-440-48806-0, YB) Dell.

Estes, Eleanor. The Moffat Museum. Estes, Eleanor, illus. LC 83-8427. 262p. (gr. 3-7). 1983. 10.95 (0-15-255086-0, HB Juv Bks) HarBrace.

Fassler, Joan. All Alone with Daddy: A Young Girl Plays the Role of Mother. Gregory, Dorothy L., illus. LC 76-80120. 32p. (ps-3). 1975. 16.95 (0-87705-009-0) Human Sci Pr.

—One Little Girl. Smyth, M. Jane, illus. LC 76-80120. 32p. (ps-3). 1969. 16.95 (0-87705-008-2) Human Sci Pr.

Fitzhugh, Louise. Nobody's Family Is Going to Change. (Illus.). 221p. (gr. 5-9). 1986. pap. 4.95 (0-374-45523-6) FS&G.

Flournoy, Valerie. Tanya's Reunion. Pinkey, Jerry, illus. LC 94-13067. 1995. write for info. (0-8037-1604-4); PLB write for info. (0-8037-1605-2) Dial Bks Young.

Froissart, Benedicte. Uncle Henry's Dinner Guests. Pratt, Pierre, illus. 32p. (ps-2). 1990. 14.95 (1-55037-141-X, Pub. by Annick CN); pap. 4.95 (1-55037-140-1, Pub. by Annick CN) Firefly Bks Ltd.

Gauch, Patricia L. C. K. & the Time She Quit the Family. Primavera, Elise, illus. 32p. (ps-3). 1992. pap. 5.95 (0-399-22405-X, Putnam) Putnam Pub Group.

Geras, Adele. Watching the Roses. LC 92-8160. 1992. write for info. (0-15-294816-3, HB Juv Bks) HarBrace.

Gerrard, Roy. The Favershams. Gerrard, Roy, illus. 32p. (gr. 1-9). 1983. 15.00 (0-374-32292-9) FS&G.

Giff, Patricia R. The Winter Worm Business. Morrill, Leslie, illus. (gr. 4-6). 1981. pap. 8.95 (0-385-29152-3); pap. 8.89 (0-385-29154-X) Delacorte.

Gipson, Morrell & Mangold, Paul. Walkers Go Hiking. LC 90-13797. (Illus.). 24p. (gr. k-3). 1990. PLB 14.60 (0-944483-91-7) Garrett Ed Corp.

Gordon, Shirley. The Boy Who Wanted a Family. 96p. (gr. 1-4). 1982. pap. 2.95 (0-440-40786-9, YB) Dell.

Grant, Cynthia D. Uncle Vampire. LC 92-44455. 160p. (gr. 8 up). 1993. SBE 13.95 (0-689-31852-9, Atheneum Child Bk) Macmillan Child Grp.

Green, Connie J. Emmy. Croft, bob, illus. LC 92-1513. 160p. (gr. 5-9). 1992. SBE 13.95 (0-689-50556-6, M K McElderry) Macmillan Child Grp.

Greenfield, Eloise. Sister. Barnett, Moneta, illus. LC 73-22182. 96p. (gr. 5-12). 1974. 15.00 (0-690-00497-4, Crowell Jr Bks) HarpC Child Bks.

—Talk about a Family. LC 77-16423. (Illus.). 64p. (gr. 2-5). 1993. pap. 3.95 (0-06-440444-7, Trophy) HarpC Child Bks.

Greenwald, Sheila. Move Over, Columbus, Rosy Cole Discovers America! LC 92-12480. 1992. 13.95 (0-316-32721-2, Joy St Bks) Little.

Haas, Jessie. Keeping Barney. LC 81-7029. 160p. (gr. 5-9). 1982. reinforced bdg. 11.75 (0-688-00859-3) Greenwillow.

Hahn, Mary D. Time for Andrew: A Ghost Story. LC 93-2877. 1994. 13.95 (0-395-66556-6, Clarion Bks) HM.

Hamilton, Dorothy. The Gift of a Home. LC 73-13989. 120p. (gr. 9-11). 1974. pap. 3.95 (0-8361-1727-1) Herald Pr.

—Ken's Bright Room. Converse, James L., photos by. LC 82-23351. (Illus.). 88p. (Orig.). (gr. 7-10). 1982. pap. 3.95 (0-8361-3328-5) Herald Pr.

Hamilton, Virginia. Cousins. (gr. 4-7). 1993. pap. 2.95 (0-590-45436-6) Scholastic Inc.

—Primos - Cousins. (SPA.). (gr. 5-8). Date not set. pap. write for info. (84-204-4747-1) Santillana.

Hartling, Peter. Old John. Crawford, Elizabeth D., tr. from GER. LC 89-12976. 128p. (gr. 4-9). 1990. 11.95 (0-688-08734-5) Lothrop.

Hausman, Karen. My Uncle Mike. 1994. 7.95 (0-8062-4849-1) Carlton.

Havill, Juanita. Treasure Nap. Savadier, Elivia, illus. 32p. (gr. k-3). 1992. 14.95 (0-395-57817-5) HM.

Hayashi, Nancy. Cosmic Cousin. Hayashi, Nancy, illus. (gr. 2-5). 1990. pap. 2.95 (0-553-15841-4, Skylark) Bantam.

Henkes, Kevin. Chester's Way. Henkes, Kevin, illus. 32p. (ps-3). 1989. pap. 3.99 (0-14-054053-9, Puffin) Puffin Bks.

—Two under Par. Henkes, Kevin, illus. LC 86-7556. 128p. (gr. 2-6). 1987. 10.25 (0-688-06708-5) Greenwillow.

Hest, Amy. Pete & Lily. LC 92-42319. 128p. (gr. 6 up). 1993. pap. 4.95 (0-688-12490-9, Pub. by Beech Tree Bks) Morrow.

Hippely, Hilary H. The Crimson Ribbon. McAllister-Stammen, Joellen, illus. LC 92-43066. 32p. (ps-3). 1994. PLB 15.95 (0-399-22542-0, Putnam) Putnam Pub Group.

Hoguet, Susan R. I Unpacked My Grandmother's Trunk. Houget, Susan R., illus. LC 83-1701. 58p. (ps-3). 1983. 13.95 (0-525-44069-0, DCB) Dutton Child Bks.

Holland, Audrey E. How Many More to Go, Mom? Holland, Audrey E., illus. 15p. (gr. k-3). 1992. pap. 13.95 (1-895583-13-6) MAYA Pubs.

—When Is It My Turn. Holland, Audrey E., illus. 15p. (gr. k-3). 1992. pap. 15.95 (1-895583-11-X) MAYA Pubs.

—When We Start Having Fun. Holland, Audrey E., illus. 13p. (gr. k-3). 1992. pap. 10.95 (1-895583-12-8) MAYA Pubs.

Howard, Elizabeth F. What's in Aunt Mary's Room? Lucas, Cedric, illus. LC 94-4985. Date not set. write for info. (0-395-69845-6, Clarion Bks) HM.

Howard, Norman B. Uncle Philip's Fickle Formula. LC 94-60125. (Illus.). 44p. (gr. 1-4). 1994. pap. 5.95 (1-55523-682-0) Winston-Derek.

Hudson, Wade. I Love My Family. Massey, Cal, illus. 32p. (ps-2). 1993. 10.95 (0-590-45763-2) Scholastic Inc.

Hughes, Shirley. An Evening at Alfie's. Hughes, Shirley, illus. LC 84-11297. 32p. (ps-1). 1985. 14.95 (0-688-04122-1); PLB 14.88 (0-688-04123-X) Lothrop.

Hunt, Angela E. Cassie Perkins: A Dream to Cherish. 176p. (gr. 4-8). 1992. pap. 4.99 (0-8423-1064-9) Tyndale.

—Cassie Perkins: Much Adored Shore. 176p. (gr. 4-8). 1992. pap. 4.99 (0-8423-1065-7) Tyndale.

Hunt, Nan. Families Are Funny. Niland, Deborah, illus. LC 91-15628. 32p. (ps-1). 1992. 13.95 (0-531-05969-3); lib. bdg. 13.99 (0-531-08569-4) Orchard Bks Watts.

Irwin, Hadley. The Original Freddie Ackerman. Hosten, James, illus. LC 91-43145. 192p. (gr. 5 up). 1992. SBE 14.95 (0-689-50562-0, M K McElderry) Macmillan Child Grp.

Javernick, Ellen. Where's Brooke? Hackney, Richard, illus. LC 92-11097. 32p. (ps-2). 1993. pap. 2.95 (0-516-42012-7) Childrens.

Jewell, Nancy. The Family under the Moon. Kessler, Leonard, illus. LC 76-2344. (ps-3). 1976. PLB 14.89i (0-06-022827-X) HarpC Child Bks.

Johnson, Lee & Johnson, Sue K. If I Ran the Family. Collier-Morales, Roberta, illus. 32p. (ps-4). 1994. 13.95 (0-685-71595-7, 725) W Gladden Found.

Jones, Diana W. Aunt Maria. LC 90-24742. (Illus.). (gr. 7 up). 1991. 13.95 (0-688-10611-0) Greenwillow.

Katz, Illana. Uncle Jimmy. Schwartz, Stanley, epilogue by. Borowitz, Franz, illus. 40p. (gr. k-6). 1994. PLB 16.95 Smythe Sewn (1-882388-03-8) Real Life Strybks.

—Uncle Jimmy: AIDS. (ps-3). 1994. pap. 9.95 (1-882388-09-7) Real Life Strybks.

Keller, Beverly. Desdemona Moves On. LC 92-7127. 176p. (gr. 3-7). 1992. SBE 13.95 (0-02-749751-8, Bradbury Pr) Macmillan Child Grp.

Keller, Holly. Cromwell's Glasses. Keller, Holly, illus. LC 81-6644. 32p. (gr. k-3). 1982. 14.95 (0-688-00834-8) Greenwillow.

Kirkland, Dianna K. I Have a Stepfamily but... Orlowski, Dennis, illus. 40p. (Orig.). (ps-5). 1981. pap. 6.50 (0-685-00148-2); counseling activity guide-stepfamilies 6.50 (0-686-96649-X) Aid-U Pub.

Klein, Don, et al. Meet the Alpha-Soruses. Klein, Kathy, illus. 15p. (ps-1). 1994. pap. 6.95 (0-685-71457-8) Outside Wrld.

Kleitsch, Christel. Cousin Markie & Other Disasters. LC 91-34641. (Illus.). 96p. (gr. 2-4). 1992. 13.00 (0-525-44891-8, DCB) Dutton Child Bks.

Kobaine, Chayale. A House Full of Guests. (gr. 4-5). 1991. 16.95 (1-56062-103-6); pap. 8.95 (1-56062-104-4) CIS Comm.

Komaiko, Leah. Just My Dad & Me. Greene, Jeffrey, illus. LC 94-18688. 1995. 15.00 (0-06-024573-5, Festival); PLB 14.89 (0-06-024574-3) HarpC Child Bks.

Kontoyiannaki, Kosta. Time. Kontoyiannaki, Kosta, illus. 12p. (gr. k-3). 1992. pap. 10.95 (1-895583-22-5) MAYA Pubs.

Korman, Gordon. Who Is Bugs Potter? 1991. pap. 2.95 (0-590-44207-4) Scholastic Inc.

Kubler, Annie. Where Do We Live? 1985. 4.95 (0-85953-256-9) Childs Play.

Kuchler, Lena. My Hundred Children. (Orig.). (gr. k-12). 1987. pap. 3.50 (0-440-95263-8, LFL) Dell.

Lakin, Patricia. The Palace of Stars. Root, Kimberly B., illus. LC 92-36796. 32p. (ps up). 1993. 14.00 (0-688-11176-9, Tambourine Bks); PLB 13.93 (0-688-11177-7, Tambourine Bks) Morrow.

Lasky, Kathryn. I Have an Aunt on Marlborough Street. Guevara, Susan, illus. LC 91-279. 32p. (gr. k-3). 1992. RSBE 13.95 (0-02-751701-2, Macmillan Child Bk) Macmillan Child Grp.

Lawlor, Laurie. Addie's Long Summer. Tucker, Kathleen, ed. Gowing, Toby, illus. LC 91-34877. 176p. (gr. 3-6). 1992. PLB 11.95 (0-8075-0167-0) A Whitman.

Lindsay, Jeanne W. Yo Tengo Papa? Do I Have a Daddy? Un Cuento Sobre Un Nino de Madre Soltera, A Story about a Single-Parent Child. Palacios, Argentina, tr. Boeller, Cheryl, illus. (SPA.). 48p. (Orig.). (ps-3). 1994. 12.95 (0-930934-83-0); pap. 5.95 (0-930934-82-2) Morning Glory.

Lockwood, Gayle R. Libbie Sims, Worry Wart. 144p. (gr. 3-7). 1993. 13.99 (0-670-84863-8) Viking Child Bks.

Loredo, Betsy. Faraway Families. Gubala, Scott, illus. 64p. (gr. 1-3). 1994. PLB 11.95 (1-881889-61-0) Silver Moon.

McCloskey, Robert. One Morning in Maine. McCloskey, Robert, illus. (gr. k-3). 1952. pap. 14.00 (0-670-52627-4) Viking Child Bks.

McKenna, Colleen O. Cousins: Not Quite Sisters. (gr. 4-7). 1993. pap. 2.95 (0-590-49428-7) Scholastic Inc.

—Cousins: Stuck in the Middle. (gr. 4-7). 1993. pap. 2.95 (0-590-49429-5) Scholastic Inc.

MacLachlan, Patricia. Arthur, for the Very First Time. Bloom, Lloyd, illus. LC 79-2007. 128p. (gr. 4-7). 1980. PLB 13.89 (0-06-024047-4) HarpC Child Bks.

Mahy, Margaret. Aliens in the Family. LC 86-3908. 192p. (gr. 7 up). 1986. pap. 12.95 (0-590-40320-6, Scholastic Hardcover) Scholastic Inc.

—Aliens in the Family. (gr. 4-7). 1991. pap. 2.95 (0-590-44898-6, Apple Paperbacks) Scholastic Inc.

—A Fortunate Name. Young, Marion, illus. LC 93-560. 1993. 13.95 (0-385-31135-4) Delacorte.

—The Good Fortunes Gang, Bk. 1: Cousins Quartet. large type ed. (Illus.). (gr. 1-8). 1994. 15.95 (0-7451-2222-1, Galaxy etc.) Chivers N Amer.

Malot, Hector. En Famille, Tome 1. Lanot, H., illus. (FRE.). 220p. (gr. 5-10). 1980. pap. 9.95 (2-07-033131-8) Schoenhof.

—En Famille, Tome 2. Lanos, H., illus. (FRE.). 221p. (gr. 5-10). 1980. pap. 9.95 (2-07-033132-6) Schoenhof.

—Sans Famille, Tome 1. Bayard, E., illus. (FRE.). 351p. (gr. 5-10). 1990. pap. 10.95 (2-07-033612-3) Schoenhof.

—Sans Famille, Tome 2. Bayard, E., illus. (FRE.). 417p. (gr. 5-10). 1991. pap. 10.95 (2-07-033617-4) Schoenhof.

Martin, Ann M. Dawn's Family Feud. (gr. 4-7). 1993. pap. 3.50 (0-590-45666-0) Scholastic Inc.

—Karen's Two Families. (gr. 4-7). 1994. pap. 2.95 (0-590-47046-9) Scholastic Inc.

Mason, Jane. A Family Affair. (gr. 4-8). 1993. pap. 2.50 (0-448-40464-8, G&D) Putnam Pub Group.

Mathis, Quincy D. Brudder & the Babe. Mathis, Danny E., compiled by. LC 93-60735. 92p. (gr. 1-4). 1994. 8.95 (1-55523-636-7) Winston-Derek.

Moore, Yvette. Freedom Songs. LC 92-20289. 176p. (gr. 7 up). 1992. pap. 3.99 (0-14-036017-4) Puffin Bks.

Mora, Pat. A Birthday Basket for Tia. Lang, Cecily, illus. LC 91-15753. 32p. (ps-1). 1992. RSBE 13.95 (0-02-767400-2, Macmillan Child Bk) Macmillan Child Grp.

Morris-Vann, Artie M. My Dad Is Unemployed... But. Orlowski, Dennis, illus. 40p. (Orig.). (ps-5). 1981. pap. 6.50 (0-940370-01-8); counseling activity guide-unemployed families 6.50 (0-685-00149-0) Aid-U Pub.

Munsil, Janet. Dinner at Auntie Rose's. Ritchie, Scot, illus. 24p. (Orig.). (ps-2). 1989. pap. 0.99 (1-55037-047-2, Pub. by Annick CN) Firefly Bks Ltd.

Murail, Marie-Aude. Uncle Giorgio. (Illus.). 48p. (gr. 3-8). 1990. 8.95 (0-89565-809-7) Childs World.

Murphy, Barbara B. Eagles in Their Flight. LC 93-11438. 1994. 14.95 (0-385-32035-3) Delacorte.

Murphy, Shirley R. Silver Woven in My Hair. Tiegreen, Alan, illus. LC 91-23144. 128p. (gr. 3-7). 1992. pap. 3.95 (0-689-71525-0, Aladdin) Macmillan Child Grp.

Myers, Walter D. The Glory Field. LC 93-43520. (gr. 5 up). 1994. 14.95 (0-590-45897-3) Scholastic Inc.

Newberger-Speregen, Devra. Stephanie: Phone Call from a Flamingo. 128p. (Orig.). (gr. 5 up). 1993. pap. 3.50 (0-671-88004-7, Minstrel Bks) PB.

Norris, Carolyn. In Our House: Story for Young Children in Sign Language. Norris, Carolyn, illus. 32p. (Orig.). (ps-3). 1984. 4.95 (0-916708-11-X) Modern Signs.

Nostlinger, Christine. The Cucumber King. Bell, Anthea, tr. 126p. (gr. 3-7). 1984. 9.95 (0-930267-01-X) Bergh Pub.

Parish, Peggy. Amelia Bedelia's Family Album. Sweat, Lynn, illus. LC 87-15641. 48p. (gr. 3-9). 1988. 13.95 (0-688-07676-9); lib. bdg. 11.88 (0-688-07677-7) Greenwillow.

—Amelia Bedelia's Family Album. 48p. 1994. pap. 3.99 (0-380-71698-4, Camelot) Avon.

Peck, Robert N. Soup's Uncle. Robinson, Charles, illus. LC 87-37538. 112p. (gr. 4-7). 1988. 13.95 (0-440-50062-1) Delacorte.

Pellegrini, Nina. Families Are Different. Pellegrini, Nina, illus. LC 90-22876. 32p. (ps-3). 1991. reinforced bdg. 15.95 (0-8234-0887-6) Holiday.

Perrault, Charles. Contes de Ma Mere l'Oye. Dore, Gustave, illus. (FRE.). 223p. (gr. 5-10). 1988. pap. 8.95 (2-07-033443-0) Schoenhof.

Peterson, John. Littles & the Lost Children. (gr. 4-7). 1991. pap. 2.75 (0-590-43026-2) Scholastic Inc.

Pevsner, Stella. Sister of the Quints. LC 86-17565. 192p. (gr. 5-9). 1987. 13.95 (0-89919-498-2, Clarion Bks) HM.

Pfeffer, Susan B. Claire at Sixteen. 1989. 13.95 (0-553-05819-3, Starfire) Bantam.

—Family of Strangers. 1994. pap. 3.99 (0-440-21895-0) Dell.

Plemons, Marti. Josh & the Guinea Pig. (Illus.). 128p. (gr. 3-6). 1992. pap. 4.99 (0-87403-686-0, 24-03726) Standard Pub.

Polonsky, Stanford I. The Truth about Tubby & Slim. LC 92-60812. 50p. (gr. k-3). 1993. 7.95 (1-55523-543-3) Winston-Derek.

Quattlebaum, Mary. Jackson Jones & the Puddle of Thorns. Rosales, Melodye, illus. LC 93-11433. (gr. 4-7). 1994. 13.95 (*0-385-31165-6*) Delacorte.

Ratera, Rosario K. A Gift. (Illus.). (gr. 1-3). 1972. 3.00 (*0-686-09524-3*, Pub. by New Day Pub Pl) Cellar.

Rattigan, Jama K. Truman's Aunt Farm. Karas, G. Brian, illus. LC 93-4860. 1994. 13.95 (*0-395-65661-3*) HM.

Rawls, Wilson. Where the Red Fern Grows. 1984. pap. 4.50 (*0-553-27429-5*) Bantam.

Richardson, Judith B. The Way Home. Mavor, Sally, illus. (gr. k). 13.95 (*0-685-41406-X*) Macmillan.

Riley, Dorothy W. & Riley, Tiaudra. Dorothy Mae's Cornbread. 25p. 1992. pap. write for info. (*1-880234-05-X*) Winbush Pub.

Rispin, Karen. Anika's Mountain. LC 93-31345. (Illus.). 1994. pap. 4.99 (*0-8423-1219-6*) Tyndale.

Roos, Stephen. Dear Santa, Make Me a Star. Premo, Steve, illus. 96p. (gr. 2-6). 1991. pap. 3.50 perfect bdg. (*0-89486-764-4*, 5174A) Hazelden.

—Leave It to Augie. Premo, Steve, illus. 96p. (gr. 2-6). 1991. pap. 3.50 perfect bdg. (*0-89486-774-1*, T5172) Hazelden.

—My Blue Tongue. Premo, Steve, illus. 96p. (gr. 2-6). 1991. pap. 3.50 perfect bdg. (*0-89486-784-9*, T5173) Hazelden.

—Silver Secrets: Maple Street Kids Ser. Premo, Steve, illus. 96p. (gr. 2-6). 1991. pap. 3.50 perfect bdg. (*0-89486-777-6*, T5171) Hazelden.

Rosofsky, Iris. My Aunt Ruth. LC 90-4940. 224p. (gr. 7 up). 1991. HarpC Child Bks.

Ross, Christine. The Whirlys & the West Wind. LC 92-39011. 1993. 13.95 (*0-395-65379-7*) HM.

Ruiz, Art, illus. The Weirdest Fun Book, Ever! 1992. 7.95 (*0-448-40503-2*, G&D) Putnam Pub Group.

Rundle, Vesta M. Snow Calf. Larison, Arlene, illus. 36p. (Orig.). (gr. 2-8). 1993. pap. 4.50 (*1-882672-01-1*) V M Rundle.
When a fictional family find themselves stranded in their farm home in Western Oklahoma during a record-breaking snow storm it is bad enough; when the calf that Seth is raising to enter in the fair turns up missing it is even worse & a surprise helicopter visit adds to the drama. The magic & the agony of winter are beautifully described as the family survives for nine days without power, telephone service, utilities, or transportation. Readers love the surprise ending about the survival of the calf. A story about pride, disappointment, & hope, the book is arranged in eight very short chapters & could be a first chapter book. There are lovely black & white full-page illustrations & a four-color illustrated cover by California artist Arlene Larison. Response to this book has been enthusiastic from children, teachers, parents, & grandparents. One child: "...my favorite Christmas present." A teacher: "All the fourth grade classes in our school read this story & loved it." A father: "Our family enjoyed this as a bedtime story over several evenings." A junior high reader: "...an animal story I'll always remember." A librarian: "This story could become a classic." Available from: For the Kids Press, 2251 Fourth St., Charleston, IL 61920; Phone (217) 345-2560 or The Distributors, 702 S. Michigan, South Bend, IN 46618.
Publisher Provided Annotation.

Rush, Alison. The Last of Danu's Children. LC 82-2981. (gr. 7 up). 1982. HM.

Ryan, Pam M. One Hundred Is a Family. (Illus.). 32p. (gr. 4 up). 1994. 13.95 (*1-56282-672-7*); PLB 13.89 (*1-56282-673-5*) Hyprn Child.

Rylant, Cynthia. Henry & Mudge & the Careful Cousin: The Thirteenth Book of Their Adventures. Stevenson, Sucie, illus. LC 92-12851. 48p. (gr. 1-3). 1994. RSBE 13.95 (*0-02-778021-X*, Bradbury Pr) Macmillan Child Grp.

Sachs, Marilyn. What My Sister Remembered. LC 91-32263. 120p. (gr. 5-9). 1992. 15.00 (*0-525-44953-1*, DCB) Dutton Child Bks.

Saylor, Melissa, illus. My Aunt Came Back Big Book. (ps-2). 1988. pap. text ed. 14.00 (*0-922053-12-X*) N Edge Res.

Schwartz, Alvin. There Is a Carrot in My Ear & Other Noodle Tales. Weinhaus, Karen A., illus. LC 80-8442. 64p. (gr. k-3). 1982. PLB 13.89 (*0-06-025234-0*) HarpC Child Bks.

Sebestyen, Ouida. Far from Home. 192p. (gr. 7 up). 1980. 15.95 (*0-316-77932-6*, Joy St Bks) Little.

Serres, Alain. Du Commerce de la Souris. Lapointe, Claudine, illus. (FRE.). 55p. (gr. 1-5). 1989. pap. 8.95 (*2-07-031195-3*) Schoenhof.

Sidney, Margaret. The Five Little Peppers & How They Grew. 302p. 1981. Repr. PLB 25.95x (*0-89966-340-0*) Buccaneer Bks.

—Five Little Peppers & How They Grew. 1989. pap. 2.95 (*0-590-42520-X*) Scholastic Inc.

—Five Little Peppers Grown up. 334p. 1981. Repr. lib. bdg. 25.95x (*0-89966-341-9*) Buccaneer Bks.

Silver, Norman. Python Dance. 192p. (gr. 8 up). 1993. 14.99 (*0-525-45161-7*, DCB) Dutton Child Bks.

Simpson, Lesley. The Hug. Simpson, Lesley, illus. 24p. (ps-1). 1987. pap. 0.99 (*0-920303-23-4*, Pub. by Annick CN) Firefly Bks Ltd.

Skurzynski, Gloria. Trapped in Slickrock Canyon. Soucie, Daniel S., illus. LC 83-14988. 128p. (gr. 4-6). 1984. 14.00 (*0-688-02688-5*) Lothrop.

Smith, Doris B. The First Hard Times. 144p. (gr. 5-9). 1984. pap. 2.50 (*0-440-42532-8*, YB) Dell.

Stolz, Mary. What Time of Night Is It? LC 80-7917. 224p. (gr. 6 up). 1993. pap. 3.95 (*0-06-447093-8*, Trophy) HarpC Child Bks.

Tafuri, Nancy. All Year Long. Tafuri, Nancy, illus. LC 82-9275. 32p. (gr. k-2). 1983. PLB 13.88 (*0-688-01416-X*) Greenwillow.

Taylor, Sydney. All-of-a-Kind Family Uptown. 166p. 1992. text ed. 13.28 (*1-56956-106-0*) W A T Braille.

—Ella All-of-a-Kind Family. 174p. 1992. text ed. 13.92 (*1-56956-111-7*) W A T Braille.

—More All-of-a-Kind Family. 166p. 1992. text ed. 13.28 (*1-56956-120-6*) W A T Braille.

Thacker, Nola. Till's Christmas. 144p. 1991. 13.95 (*0-590-43542-6*, Scholastic Hardcover) Scholastic Inc.

Thesman, Jean. The Whitney Cousins: Amelia. 144p. (gr. 4-5). 1990. pap. 2.95 (*0-380-75874-1*, Flare) Avon.

—The Whitney Cousins: Triple Trouble. 160p. (Orig.). 1992. pap. 3.50 (*0-380-76464-4*, Flare) Avon.

Thomson, Pat. Beware of the Aunts! Clark, Emma C., illus. LC 90-28928. 32p. (gr. k-3). 1992. SBE 14.95 (*0-689-50538-8*, M K McElderry) Macmillan Child Grp.

Vallet, Cedric. Almost Finished. Vallet, Cedric, illus. 18p. (gr. k-3). 1992. pap. 11.95 (*1-895583-28-4*) MAYA Pubs.

—Now Is the Time. Vallet, Cedric, illus. 16p. (gr. k-3). 1992. pap. 14.95 (*1-895583-25-X*) MAYA Pubs.

—Where Is Here? Vallet, Cedric, illus. 19p. (gr. k-3). 1992. pap. 12.95 (*1-895583-29-2*) MAYA Pubs.

Van Steenwyk, Elizabeth. Three Dog Winter. (gr. 4-9). 1987. 13.95 (*0-8027-6718-4*) Walker & Co.

Vertreace, Martha. Kelly in the Mirror. Speidel, Sandra, illus. LC 92-22655. 1993. 13.95 (*0-8075-4152-4*) A Whitman.

Walter, Mildred P. Mariah Keeps Cool. LC 89-23981. 144p. (gr. 3-7). 1990. SBE 13.95 (*0-02-792295-2*, Bradbury Pr) Macmillan Child Grp.

Warner, Gertrude C., created by. The Mystery of the Singing Ghost. (Illus.). 192p. (gr. 2-7). 1992. 10.95g (*0-8075-5397-2*); pap. 3.50 (*0-8075-5398-0*) A Whitman.

Weyn, Suzanne. Make Room for Patti. (gr. 4-7). 1991. pap. 2.75 (*0-590-43559-0*) Scholastic Inc.

Widman, Christine. The Lemon Drop Jar. Kieffer, Christa, illus. LC 91-11209. 32p. (gr. k-3). 1992. RSBE 14.95 (*0-02-792759-8*, Macmillan Child Bk) Macmillan Child Grp.

Wiggin, Kate D. Rebecca of Sunnybrook Farm. Grose, Helen M., illus. Glassman, Peter, afterword by. LC 94-9899. (Illus.). 1994. write for info. (*0-688-13481-5*) Morrow.

Wiggins, VeraLee. Shelby's Best Friend. LC 93-27279. 1994. 8.95 (*0-8163-1189-7*) Pacific Pr Pub Assn.

—Shelby's Big Prayer. LC 93-11939. 1994. 8.95 (*0-8163-1188-9*) Pacific Pr Pub Assn.

—Shelby's Big Scare. LC 93-31363. 1994. 8.95 (*0-8163-1190-0*) Pacific Pr Pub Assn.

Willard, Nancy. Uncle Terrible: More Adventures of Anatole. McPhail, David, illus. LC 82-47940. 120p. (gr. 5 up). 1985. pap. 5.95 (*0-15-292794-8*, HB Juv Bks) HarBrace.

Wooldridge, Rhoda. Johnny Tread Water. 1983. pap. 8.00 (*0-8309-0354-2*) Ind Pr MO.

Yardley, Joanna. The Red Ball. Yolen, Jane, ed. Yardley, Joanna, illus. 32p. (ps-3). 1991. 14.95 (*0-15-200894-2*, J Yolen Bks) HarBrace.

Yost, Carolyn K. The Robins Knew. Gardner, Katherine W., illus. 32p. (gr. k-2). 1991. pasted 2.50 (*0-87403-817-0*, 24-03917) Standard Pub.

Zolotow, Charlotte. The Quarreling Book. Lobel, Arnold, illus. LC 63-14445. 32p. (gr. k-3). 1963. PLB 12.89 (*0-06-026976-6*) HarpC Child Bks.

—The Sky Was Blue. Williams, Garth, illus. LC 62-13328. (gr. k-3). 1963. PLB 14.89 (*0-06-027001-2*) HarpC Child Bks.

FAMILY LIFE

Ackley, Meredith, et al, eds. Nicaragua. Birmingham, Lucy, et al, photos by. LC 89-43174. (Illus.). (gr. 3-8). PLB 21.26 (*0-8368-0221-7*) Gareth Stevens Inc.

Amstutz, Beverly. Sprouts: A Diary for the Foster Child. Amstutz, Beverly, illus. 38p. (Orig.). (gr. k-7). 1982. pap. 2.50x (*0-937836-07-9*) Precious Res.

Anglund, Joan W. All about My Family. Anglund, Joan W., illus. 48p. (ps up). 1987. pap. 6.95 (*0-590-40828-3*) Scholastic Inc.

Arnstein, Helene S. Billy & Our New Baby. Smyth, M. Jane, illus. LC 73-7951. 32p. (ps-3). 1973. 16.95x (*0-87705-093-7*) Human Sci Pr.

Bailey, Marilyn. Stepfamilies. LC 89-25325. (Illus.). 48p. (gr. 5-6). 1990. text ed. 12.95 RSBE (*0-89686-495-2*, Crestwood Hse) Macmillan Child Grp.

Bennett, Gay. A Family in Sri Lanka. LC 85-6891. (Illus.). 32p. (gr. 2-5). 1985. PLB 13.50 (*0-8225-1661-6*) Lerner Pubns.

Bennett, Olivia. A Family in Brazil. (Illus.). 32p. (gr. 2-5). 1986. lib. bdg. 13.50 (*0-8225-1665-9*) Lerner Pubns.

Berry, Joy W. Teach Me about Brothers & Sisters. Dickey, Kate, ed. LC 85-45079. (Illus.). 36p. (ps). 1986. 4.98 (*0-685-10718-3*) Grolier Inc.

—Teach Me about Relatives. Dickey, Kate, ed. LC 85-45080. (Illus.). 36p. (ps). 1986. 4.98 (*0-685-10719-1*) Grolier Inc.

Blomquist, Geraldine M. Coping As a Foster Child. (gr. 7-12). 1992. PLB 14.95 (*0-8239-1346-5*) Rosen Group.

Booher, Dianna D. Coping: When Your Family Falls Apart. LC 79-17342. 192p. (gr. 7 up). 1979. lib. bdg. 11.98 (*0-671-33083-7*, J Messner) S&S Trade.

Boy Scouts of America Staff. Family Life. (Illus.). 40p. (gr. 6-12). 1991. pap. 1.85 (*0-8395-3243-1*, 33243) BSA.

Buchman, Dian D. Family Fill-in Book. (gr. 4-7). 1994. pap. 2.95 (*0-590-46412-4*) Scholastic Inc.

Clifton, Lucille, et al. Everett Anderson's Goodbye. Grifalconi, Ann, illus. LC 82-23426. 32p. (ps-2). 1983. 14.95 (*0-8050-0235-9*, Bks Young Read) H Holt & Co.

Coleman, William L. What You Should Know about Getting along with a New Parent. LC 92-18335. 96p. (Orig.). (gr. 3-8). 1992. pap. 5.99 (*0-8066-2611-9*, 9-2611, Augsburg) Augsburg Fortress.

—What You Should Know about Living with One Parent. LC 93-31851. 1993. 5.99 (*0-8066-2636-4*) Augsburg Fortress.

Cosby, Clair G. Lord, Help Me Love My Sister. LC 86-4831. 80p. (Orig.). (gr. 3-10). 1986. pap. 4.95 (*0-8361-3413-3*) Herald Pr.

Crary, Elizabeth. Mommy Don't Go. Megale, Marina, illus. LC 85-63759. 32p. (Orig.). (ps-2). 1986. lib. bdg. 15.95 (*0-943990-27-0*); pap. 4.95 (*0-943990-26-2*) Parenting Pr.

Crews, Donald. Bigmama's. Crews, Donald, illus. LC 90-33142. 32p. (ps up). 1991. 15.00 (*0-688-09950-5*); PLB 14.93 (*0-688-09951-3*) Greenwillow.

Davis, Diane. Something Is Wrong at My House. Megale, Marina, illus. LC 84-62129. 40p. (Orig.). (ps-6). 1985. PLB 15.95 (*0-943990-11-4*); pap. 4.95 (*0-943990-10-6*) Parenting Pr.

Dellinger, A. & Fletcher, S. Family Devotions. (ps-3). 1983. pap. 0.69 (*0-570-08313-3*, 56HH1445) Concordia.

Family Ties Series. (Illus.). (gr. 1-3). 1993. PLB 21.95 (*1-881889-46-7*) Silver Moon.

Fast, Suellen M. Celebrations of Daughterhood. 2nd, rev. ed. Serman, Gina L., ed. 70p. (gr. k up). 1988. pap. 8.00 (*0-317-57532-5*) Daughter Cult.

Getzoff, Ann & McClenahan, Carolyn. Stepkids: A Survival Guide for Teenagers in Stepfamilies...& for Stepparents Doubtful of Their Own Survival. 171p. (gr. 5 up). 1985. pap. 9.95 (*0-8027-7236-6*) Walker & Co.

Gilbreth, Frank B., Jr. & Carey, Ernestine G. Cheaper by the Dozen. (gr. 6 up). 1984. pap. 3.50 (*0-553-25018-3*) Bantam.

Glotzbach, Gerri, et al. The Family, 6 bks. (Illus.). 384p. (gr. 7 up). 1990. Set. lib. bdg. 103.62 (*0-86593-075-9*); lib. bdg. 77.70s.p. (*0-685-58753-3*) Rourke Corp.

Gooden, Kimberly W. Coping with Family Stress. Rosen, Ruth, ed. (gr. 7-12). 1989. PLB 14.95 (*0-8239-0980-8*) Rosen Group.

Goodsmith, Lauren. The Children of Mauritania: Days in the Desert and At the River Shore. LC 92-46145. 56p. (gr. 3 up). 1993. 19.95 (*0-87614-782-1*) Carolrhoda bks.

Goom, Bridget. A Family in Singapore. (Illus.). 32p. (gr. 2-5). 1986. lib. bdg. 13.50 (*0-8225-1663-2*) Lerner Pubns.

Graff, Nancy P. The Call of the Running Tide: A Portrait of an Island Family. Howard, Richard, illus. (gr. 3-7). 1991. 16.95 (*0-316-32278-4*) Little.

Greenblat, Rodney A. Aunt Ippy's Museum of Junk. Greenblat, Rodney A., illus. LC 90-44939. 32p. (gr. k-4). 1991. 14.95 (*0-06-022511-4*); PLB 14.89 (*0-06-022512-2*) HarpC Child Bks.

Grunsell, Angela. Stepfamilies. (Illus.). 32p. (gr. 2-5). 1990. PLB 11.40 (*0-531-17244-9*, Gloucester Pr) Watts.

Hautzig, Esther. Endless Steppe: Growing up in Siberia. LC 68-13582. 256p. (gr. 7 up). 1992. 15.00 (*0-690-26371-6*, Crowell Jr Bks); PLB 14.89 (*0-690-04919-6*, Crowell Jr Bks) HarpC Child Bks.

Herbert, Stefon. I Miss My Foster Parents. (Illus.). 36p. 1991. 12.95 (*0-87868-476-X*, 4760) Child Welfare.

Ireland. LC 89-43187. (Illus.). 64p. (gr. 3-8). 1992. PLB 21.26 (*0-8368-0246-2*) Gareth Stevens Inc.

Ireland Is My Home. 48p. (gr. 2-8). 1992. PLB 18.60 (*0-8368-0902-5*) Gareth Stevens Inc.

Jester, Harold D. Pulling Together: Crisis Prevention for Teens & Their Parents. LC 91-41371. 155p. (Orig.). 1992. pap. 9.95 (*0-938179-30-6*) Mills Sanderson.

Kaplan, Leslie S. Coping with Stepfamilies. rev. ed. (gr. 7-12). 1991. PLB 14.95 (*0-8239-1371-6*) Rosen Group.

Kuklin, Susan. How My Family Lives in America. Kuklin, Susan, illus. LC 91-22949. 40p. (ps-3). 1992. RSBE 13.95 (*0-02-751239-8*, Bradbury Pr) Macmillan Child Grp.

Lee, Valerie. Dysfunctional Families. (Illus.). 64p. (gr. 7 up). 1990. lib. bdg. 15.93 (*0-86593-077-5*); lib. bdg. 12. 95s.p. (*0-685-36296-5*) Rourke Corp.

Little People Big Book about Families. 64p. (ps-1). 1990. write for info. (*0-8094-7491-3*); PLB write for info. (*0-8094-7492-1*) Time-Life.

Loveland Comm. Staff. Discover Families. 1992. 4.49 (*1-55513-911-6*, Chariot Bks) Chariot Family.

Lowry, Lois. Anastasia Again! De Groat, Diane, illus. 160p. (gr. 3-6). 1981. 14.45 (*0-395-31147-0*) HM.

McKaughan, Larry. Why Are Your Fingers Cold? Keenan, Joy D., illus. LC 92-16549. 32p. (Orig.). (ps-1). 1992. 14.95 (*0-8361-3604-7*) Herald Pr. Childlike questions & reassuring answers are complemented by exquisite illustrations. Several family groupings including African American & Caucasian people appear, as children & adults interact. This delightful picture book helps children to become more sensitive to the needs of others. It fosters a strong sense of extended family & community. For children ages 2 to 6 & the adults that love them. *Publisher Provided Annotation.*

Mancini, Richard. Everything You Need to Know about Living with a Single Parent. (gr. 7-12). 1992. PLB 14. 95 (*0-8239-1323-6*) Rosen Group.

Margolies, Barbara A. Warriors, Wigmen, & Crocodile People: Journeys in Papua New Guinea. Margolies, Barbara, illus. LC 92-27475. 40p. (gr. 1-5). 1993. RSBE 14.95 (*0-02-762283-5*, Four Winds) Macmillan Child Grp.

Moran, Tom. A Family in Ireland. (Illus.). 32p. (gr. 2-5). 1986. lib. bdg. 13.50 (*0-8225-1668-3*) Lerner Pubns.

Nicoll, Helen & Pienkowski, Jan. Mog's Mumps. (Illus.). 32p. (ps-1). 1983. 15.95 (*0-434-95640-6*, Pub. by W Heinemann Ltd) Trafalgar.

Paris, Susan. Mommy & Daddy Are Fighting: A Book for Children about Family Violence. Labinski, Gail, illus. LC 85-22193. 24p. (Orig.). (ps-4). 1986. pap. 8.95 (*0-931188-33-4*) Seal Pr Feminist.

Patrick, Diane. Family Celebrations. Bryant, Michael, illus. LC 93-18456. 64p. (ps-4). 1993. PLB 11.95 (*1-881889-04-1*) Silver Moon.

Peru. LC 89-43183. (Illus.). 64p. (gr. 3-8). 1992. PLB 21. 26 (*0-8368-0235-7*) Gareth Stevens Inc.

Peru Is My Home. 48p. (gr. 2-8). 1992. PLB 18.60 (*0-8368-0903-3*) Gareth Stevens Inc.

Poland Is My Home. 48p. (gr. 2-8). 1992. PLB 18.60 (*0-8368-0904-1*) Gareth Stevens Inc.

Robson, John, ed. Me & You. (Illus.). 48p. (Orig.). (gr. 6-9). 1982. pap. 2.50 (*0-936098-33-3*) Intl Marriage.

—You & Your Family. (Illus.). 30p. (Orig.). (gr. 2-4). 1981. pap. 2.50 (*0-936098-30-9*) Intl Marriage.

Rosenberg, Maxine B. Finding a Way: Living with Exceptional Brothers & Sisters. Ancona, George, photos by. LC 88-6776. 48p. (gr. 1-4). 1988. 12.95 (*0-688-06873-1*); PLB 12.88 (*0-688-06874-X*) Lothrop.

St. John, Jetty. A Family in Chile. (Illus.). 32p. (gr. 2-5). 1986. lib. bdg. 13.50 (*0-8225-1667-5*) Lerner Pubns.

Siegel, Eli. Children's Guide to Parents & Other Matters: Little Essays for Children & Others. Koppelman, Dorothy, illus. LC 78-171393. 77p. (gr. 1-6). 1971. text ed. 7.50 (*0-910492-16-6*) Definition.

Snyder, Dianne. George & the Dragon Word. Lies, Brian, illus. 56p. (gr. 2-4). 1991. 13.45 (*0-395-55129-3*, Sandpiper) HM.

Soaries, Buster. My Family Is Driving Me Crazy. 132p. 1991. pap. 4.99 (*0-89693-939-1*) SP Pubns.

Stewart, Judy. A Family in Morocco. (Illus.). 32p. (gr. 2-5). 1986. lib. bdg. 13.50 (*0-8225-1664-0*) Lerner Pubns.

—A Family in Sudan. (Illus.). 32p. (gr. 2-5). 1988. lib. bdg. 13.50 (*0-8225-1682-9*) Lerner Pubns.

Super, Gretchen. Family Traditions. De Kiefte, Kees, illus. 48p. (gr. k-3). 1992. PLB 15.95 (*0-8050-2218-X*) TFC Bks NY.

Switzer, Ellen. Anyplace but Here: Young, Alone & Homeless: What to Do. LC 92-15. 176p. (gr. 5 up). 1992. SBE 14.95 (*0-689-31694-1*, Atheneum Child Bk) Macmillan Child Grp.

Velez, Jose S. Cuando en Casa No Nos Comprenden - When We Are Not Understood at Home. (SPA.). 112p. (Orig.). (gr. 9 up). 1991. pap. 4.90 (*0-311-46263-4*) Casa Bautista.

Vietnam Is My Home. 48p. (gr. 2-8). 1992. PLB 18.60 (*0-8368-0905-X*) Gareth Stevens Inc.

Waring, Shirley B. What Happened to Benjamin: A True Story. Bergstrom, Lucy, illus. LC 92-83949. 38p. (Orig.). (gr. k-6). 1993. PLB 13.95g (*0-9622808-2-8*); Audio cass. 9.98 (*0-9622808-3-6*) S&T Waring.

Webb, Margot. Coping with Parents Who Are Activists. Rosen, Ruth, ed. (gr. 7-12). 1992. 14.95 (*0-8239-1416-X*) Rosen Group.

Wilkins, Frances. Family Life from Nineteen Thirty to the Nineteen Eighties. (Illus.). 72p. (gr. 7-12). 1986. 19.95 (*0-7134-4818-0*, Pub. by Batsford UK) Trafalgar.

Williams, Thelma. Our Family Table: Recipes & Food Memories from African-American Life Models. Cellino, Maria E. & Rolfes, Ellen, eds. Jackson, Al, illus. Cosby, Camille O., intro. by. (Illus.). 96p. (gr. 7 up). 1993. 14.95 (*1-879958-14-7*); PLB 14.95 (*1-879958-16-3*) Tradery Hse.

Yu, Ling. A Family in Taiwan. (Illus.). 32p. (gr. 2-5). 1990. PLB 13.50 (*0-8225-1685-3*) Lerner Pubns.

Zambia Is My Home. 48p. (gr. 2-8). 1992. PLB 21.26 (*0-8368-0906-8*) Gareth Stevens Inc.

FAMILY LIFE–FICTION

Ackerman, Karen. In the Park with Dad. Crockett-Blassingame, Linda, illus. 32p. (ps-2). 1994. 6.95 (*0-8198-3669-9*) St Paul Bks.

Adams, Jeanie. Going for Oysters. (ps-3). 1993. 14.95 (*0-8075-2978-8*) A Whitman.

Adler, C. S. In Our House Scott Is My Brother. LC 79-20693. 144p. (gr. 5-9). 1980. SBE 13.95 (*0-02-700140-7*, Macmillan Child Bk) Macmillan Child Grp.

—One Sister Too Many. LC 91-15530. 176p. (gr. 3-7). 1991. pap. 3.95 (*0-689-71521-8*, Aladdin) Macmillan Child Grp.

—One Sister Too Many (A Sequel to Split Sisters) LC 88-13144. 176p. (gr. 4-8). 1989. SBE 13.95 (*0-02-700271-3*, Macmillan Child Bk) Macmillan Child Grp.

—Split Sisters. LC 89-18308. 176p. (gr. 4-7). 1990. pap. 3.95 (*0-689-71369-X*, Aladdin) Macmillan Child Grp.

—Tuna Fish Thanksgiving. 160p. (gr. 5-9). 1992. 13.45 (*0-395-58829-4*, Clarion Bks) HM.

Adshead, Paul. Incredible Reversing Peppermints. (ps-3). 1993. 7.95 (*0-85953-514-2*) Childs Play.

Agee, James. Death in the Family. 320p. (gr. 10 up). 1971. pap. 3.95 (*0-553-23392-0*) Bantam.

Agell, Charlotte. Mud Makes Me Dance in the Spring. Agell, Charlotte, illus. LC 93-33610. 32p. (ps up). 1994. 7.95 (*0-88448-112-3*) Tilbury Hse.

Alborough, Jez. Cuddly Dudley. Alborough, Jez, illus. LC 92-52994. 32p. (ps up). 1993. 14.95 (*1-56402-095-9*) Candlewick Pr.

Alcott, Louisa May. Eight Cousins. (gr. k-6). 1986. pap. 3.50 (*0-440-42231-0*, Pub. by Yearling Classics) Dell.

—Eight Cousins or the Aunt Hill. 272p. (gr. 5 up). 1989. pap. 3.50 (*0-14-035112-4*, Puffin) Puffin Bks.

—Jo's Boys. 1988. 21.95 (*0-8488-0411-2*) Amereon Ltd.

—Jo's Boys. 1989. Repr. of 1886 ed. lib. bdg. 79.00 (*0-7812-1642-7*) Rprt Serv.

—Little Men. (Illus.). (gr. 4-6). 1947. (G&D); 13.95 (*0-448-06018-3*, G&D) Putnam Pub Group.

—Little Men. 1989. Repr. of 1861 ed. lib. bdg. 79.00 (*0-7812-1629-X*) Rprt Serv.

—Little Women. (Illus.). (gr. 6 up). 1966. pap. 2.95 (*0-8049-0106-6*, CL-106) Airmont.

—Little Women. Magagna, Anna M. & Jambor, Louis, illus. (gr. 4-6). 1981. (G&D); deluxe ed. 15.95 (*0-448-06019-1*) Putnam Pub Group.

—Little Women. (gr. 6 up). 1974. 250.00 (*0-8490-0547-7*) Gordon Pr.

—Little Women. Smith, Jessie W., illus. (gr. 7 up). 1968. 19.95 (*0-316-03095-3*) Little.

—Little Women. 320p. (gr. 3-7). 1983. pap. 2.25 (*0-14-035008-X*, Puffin) Puffin Bks.

—Little Women. (gr. 5 up). 1963. 37.50 (*0-685-20188-0*, 144-7) Saphrograph.

—Little Women. (gr. 6 up). 1983. Repr. lib. bdg. 18.95x (*0-89966-408-3*) Buccaneer Bks.

—Little Women. Douglas, Ann, intro. by. 480p. (gr. 3 up). 1983. pap. 3.95 (*0-451-52341-5*, Sig Classic) NAL-Dutton.

—Little Women. Edwards, Gunvor, illus. Gliberry, Lysbeth, retold by. (Illus.). 48p. (gr. 7-12). 1975. pap. text ed. 3.25x (*0-19-421804-X*) OUP.

—Little Women. LC 62-20197. (gr. 4 up). 1986. pap. 5.00 (*0-02-041240-1*, Collier Young Ad) Macmillan Child Grp.

—Little Women. Smith, Jessie W. & Merrill, Frank, illus. 400p. (gr. 2 up). 1988. 12.99 (*0-517-63489-9*) Random Hse Value.

—Little Women. (Orig.). (gr. k-6). 1987. pap. 6.95 (*0-440-44768-2*, Pub. by Yearling Classics) Dell.

—Little Women. Showalter, Elaine, intro. by. 608p. 1989. pap. 5.95 (*0-14-039069-3*, Penguin Classics) Viking Penguin.

—Little Women. 1989. Repr. of 1867 ed. lib. bdg. 79.00 (*0-7812-1627-3*) Rprt Serv.

—Little Women. Auerbach, Nina, afterword by. 480p. 1983. pap. 3.95 (*0-553-21275-3*, Bantam Classics Spectra) Bantam.

—Little Women. large type ed. 336p. 1987. 15.95 (*0-7089-8384-7*, Charnwood) Ulverscroft.

—Little Women. 1986. pap. 3.25 (*0-590-43797-6*, Apple Paperbacks) Scholastic Inc.

—Little Women. 1988. 2.98 (*0-671-09222-7*) S&S Trade.

—Little Women. Kulling, Monica, adapted by. LC 93-38237. 108p. (gr. 2-6). 1994. pap. 3.50 (*0-679-86175-0*, Bullseye Bks) Random Bks Yng Read.

—Little Women. LC 94-5865. 1994. 15.95 (*0-679-43642-1*, Evrymans Lib Childs) Knopf.

—Little Women, or, Meg, Jo, Beth, & Amy. Hague, Michael, illus. LC 93-18943. 308p. (gr. 4-8). 1993. 15. 95 (*0-8050-2767-X*, Bks Young Read) H Holt & Co.

—Little Women, Vol. 1: Four Funny Sisters. Lindskoog, Kathryn, ed. (Illus.). (gr. 3-7). 1991. pap. 4.99 (*0-88070-437-3*, Gold & Honey) Questar Pubs.

—A Modern Mephistopheles. 1988. 17.95 (*0-8488-0412-0*) Amereon Ltd.

—An Old Fashioned Thanksgiving. Wheeler, Jody, illus. LC 93-20352. 40p. (ps-3). 1993. 13.95 (*0-8249-8620-2*, Ideals Child); PLB 14.00 (*0-8249-8630-X*) Hambleton-Hill.

—Reader's Digest Best Loved Books for Young Readers: Little Women. Ogburn, Jackie, ed. English, Mark, illus. 176p. (gr. 4-12). 1989. 3.99 (*0-945260-25-3*) Choice Pub NY.

—Works of Louisa May Alcott. (gr. 5-6). 38.95 (*0-88411-173-3*, Pub. by Aeonian Pr) Amereon Ltd.

Aldridge, Ruth. I Remember When. Wilkin, Mike, illus. LC 93-26926. 1994. 4.25 (*0-383-03750-6*) SRA Schl Grp.

Alexander, Martha. Nobody Asked Me If I Wanted a Baby Sister. Alexander, Martha, illus. LC 78-153731. (ps-2). 1971. 10.95 (*0-8037-6401-4*); PLB 10.89 (*0-8037-6402-2*) Dial Bks Young.

Allard, Harry. The Stupids Have a Ball. Marshall, James, illus. LC 77-27660. (gr. k-3). 1984. 13.45 (*0-395-26497-9*); pap. 4.80 (*0-395-36169-9*) HM.

—The Stupids Step Out. Marshall, James, illus. LC 73-21698. 32p. (gr. k-3). 1974. 14.95 (*0-395-18513-0*); pap. 4.80 (*0-395-25377-2*) HM.

Anderson, Peggy K. Safe at Home! LC 90-19133. 128p. (gr. 3-7). 1992. SBE 13.95 (*0-689-31686-0*, Atheneum Child Bk) Macmillan Child Grp.

Arter, Jim. Gruel & Unusual. 1993. pap. 3.50 (*0-440-40891-1*) Dell.

Ashley, Bernard. All My Men. LC 78-12683. (gr. 6 up). 1978. 21.95 (*0-87599-228-5*) S G Phillips.

Auch, Mary J. Cry Uncle! LC 87-45330. 224p. (gr. 4-7). 1987. 14.95 (*0-8234-0660-1*) Holiday.

Auster, Benjamin. I Like It When... Winborn, Marsha, illus. 24p. (ps-2). 1990. PLB 14.60 (*0-8172-3578-7*); PLB 17.10 pkg. of 3 (*0-8114-2933-4*) Raintree Steck-V.

Avery, Gillian. A Likely Lad. LC 92-43911. 1994. pap. 16.00 (*0-671-79867-7*, S&S BFYR) S&S Trade.

Baer, Judy. Special Kind of Love. 1993. pap. 3.99 (*1-55661-367-9*) Bethany Hse.

Bailey, Anne. Burn Up. 144p. (gr. 7 up). 1992. pap. 4.95 (*0-571-16504-4*) Faber & Faber.

Baker, Barbara. Oh, Emma. Stock, Catherine, illus. LC 91-2578. 96p. (gr. 2-5). 1991. 12.95 (*0-525-44771-7*, DCB) Dutton Child Bks.

—Oh, Emma. Stock, Catherine, illus. LC 93-7767. 144p. (gr. 2-5). 1993. pap. 3.99 (*0-14-036357-2*, Puffin) Puffin Bks.

—One Saturday Morning. Duke, Kate, illus. LC 93-43957. 48p. (ps-2). 1994. 12.99 (*0-525-45262-1*, DCB) Dutton Child Bks.

Baker, Carin G. Karate Club, No. 5: Out of Control. LC 92-19941. 144p. (gr. 3-7). 1992. pap. 3.50 (*0-14-036264-9*) Puffin Bks.

Banks, Lynne R. The Mystery of the Cupboard. Newsom, Tom, illus. LC 92-39295. 256p. (gr. 5 up). 1993. 13.95 (*0-688-12138-1*); PLB 13.88 (*0-688-12635-9*) Morrow Jr Bks.

Barbour, Karen. Mr. Bow Tie. (ps-3). 1991. 13.95 (*0-15-256165-X*, HB Juv Bks) HarBrace.

Barnes, Joyce A. The Baby Grand, the Moon in July, & Me. LC 93-17984. Date not set. write for info. (*0-8037-1586-2*); PLB write for info. (*0-8037-1600-1*) Dial Bks Young.

Barrett, Joyce D. Willie's Not the Hugging Kind. Cummings, Pat, illus. LC 89-1868. 32p. (gr. k-3). 1991. pap. 4.95 (*0-06-443264-5*, Trophy) HarpC Child Bks.

Barrington, Margaret. My Cousin Justin. 288p. (Orig.). (gr. 10-12). 1990. pap. 11.95 (*0-85640-456-X*, Pub. by Blackstaff Pr Belfast) Dufour.

Bat-Ami, Miriam. When the Frost Is Gone. Ramsey, Marcy D., illus. LC 92-26181. 80p. (gr. 5 up). 1994. SBE 13.95 (*0-02-708497-3*, Macmillan Child Bk) Macmillan Child Grp.

Baylor, Byrd. The Table Where Rich People Sit. Parnall, Peter, illus. LC 93-1251. 1994. 14.95 (*0-684-19653-0*, Scribners Young Read) Macmillan Child Grp.

Beatty, Patricia. Eight Mules from Monterey. LC 92-24596. 224p. (gr. 6 up). 1993. pap. 4.95 (*0-688-12281-7*, Pub. by Beech Tree Bks) Morrow.

—The Nickel-Plated Beauty. LC 92-23318. 272p. (gr. 5 up). 1993. 14.00 (*0-688-12360-0*); pap. 3.95 (*0-685-61089-6*) Morrow Jr Bks.

Belden, Wilanne S. Frankie! LC 86-33507. (Illus.). 163p. (gr. 3-7). 1987. 14.95 (*0-15-229380-9*) HarBrace.

Beni, Ruth. The Family Next Door. (Illus.). 48p. (gr. 2-4). 1990. pap. 6.95 (*0-233-98383-X*, Pub. by A Deutsch UK) Trafalgar.

Birdseye, Tom. A Regular Flood of Mishap. Loyd, Megan, illus. LC 93-9888. 32p. (ps-3). 1994. reinforced bdg. 15.95 (*0-8234-1070-6*) Holiday.

Blacker, Terence. Homebird. LC 92-23536. 144p. (gr. 7 up). 1993. SBE 13.95 (*0-02-710685-3*, Bradbury Pr) Macmillan Child Grp.

Blaine, Marge. The Terrible Thing That Happened at Our House. Wallner, John, illus. LC 86-4827. 40p. (ps-3). 1984. Repr. of 1975 ed. RSBE 13.95 (*0-02-710720-5*, Four Winds) Macmillan Child Grp.

Blos, Joan W. Brooklyn Doesn't Rhyme. Birling, Paul, illus. LC 93-31589. 96p. (gr. 3-6). 1994. SBE 12.95 (*0-684-19694-8*, Scribners Young Read) Macmillan Child Grp.
Blume, Judy. Fudge-A-Mania. LC 90-39627. 128p. (gr. 3-7). 1990. 12.95 (*0-525-44672-9*, DCB) Dutton Child Bks.
—Here's to You, Rachel Robinson. LC 93-9631. 208p. (gr. 5 up). 1993. 14.95 (*0-531-06801-3*); PLB 14.99 (*0-531-08651-8*) Orchard Bks Watts.
—Just as Long as We're Together. LC 87-7980. 304p. (gr. 5-8). 1987. 12.95 (*0-531-05729-1*); PLB 12.99 (*0-531-08329-2*) Orchard Bks Watts.
—Starring Sally J. Freedman As Herself. LC 76-57805. 296p. (gr. 4-7). 1982. SBE 15.95 (*0-02-711070-2*, Bradbury Pr) Macmillan Child Grp.
—Superfudge. 176p. (gr. 2-6). 1981. pap. 3.99 (*0-440-48433-2*, YB) Dell.
—Superfudge. LC 80-10439. 176p. (gr. 3-6). 1980. 13.00 (*0-525-40522-4*, DCB) Dutton Child Bks.
—Superfudge. large type ed. 239p. (gr. 2-6). 1987. Repr. of 1980 ed. lib. bdg. 14.95 (*1-55736-014-6*, Crnrstn Bks) BDD LT Grp.
—Then Again, Maybe I Won't. LC 77-156548. 176p. (gr. 5-7). 1982. SBE 14.95 (*0-02-711090-7*, Bradbury Pr) Macmillan Child Grp.
Bond, Michael. Paddington at Large. Fortnum, Peggy, illus. 128p. (gr. 3-7). 1970. pap. 2.95 (*0-440-46801-9*, YB) Dell.
—Paddington at Work. 128p. (gr. k-8). 1971. pap. 2.95 (*0-440-40797-4*, YB) Dell.
Bonsall, Crosby N. And I Mean It, Stanley. 32p. (ps-2). 1990. pap. 6.95 (*1-55994-265-7*, Caedmon) HarperAudio.
—The Day I Had to Play with My Sister. Bonsall, Crosby N., illus. LC 72-76507. 32p. (ps-2). 1972. PLB 13.89 (*0-06-020576-8*) HarpC Child Bks.
Bontemps, Arna W. & Hughes, Langston. Popo & Fifina. Campbell, E. Simms, illus. Rampersad, Arnold & Rampersad, Arnoldintro. by. (Illus.). 120p. 1993. jacketed 14.95 (*0-19-508765-8*) OUP.
Borden, Louise. Just in Time for Christmas. Lewin, Ted, illus. LC 93-40082. (ps-3). 1994. 14.95 (*0-590-45355-6*) Scholastic Inc.
Bosworth, Michael. My Own Place. Wilkin, Mike, illus. LC 93-27058. 1994. 4.25 (*0-383-03766-2*) SRA Schl Grp.
Bradfield, Carl. Getting in Shape with Wendell & Myrtle: The Wendells Family, at It Again. (Illus.). 216p. (Orig.). (gr. 8-12). Date not set. pap. write for info. (*0-9632319-4-4*) ASDA Pub.
—Hawaii Calls Wendell & Myrtle: The Wendells Family Make It to the Big Island. (Illus.). 196p. (Orig.). (gr. 8-12). Date not set. pap. write for info. (*0-9632319-5-2*) ASDA Pub.
Breckler, Rosemary K. Hoang Breaks the Lucky Teapot. Frankel, Adrian, illus. 32p. (gr. k-3). 1992. 13.45 (*0-395-57031-X*) HM.
Brooks, Martha. Two Moons in August. (gr. 7 up). 1992. 15.95 (*0-316-10979-7*) Little.
Brown, Faye. Chinch Bugs, Chinky Pins, & Chinie-Berry Beads. Brown, Trillie, illus. 191p. (Orig.). 1990. pap. 9.95 (*0-943487-24-2*) Sevgo Pr.
Brown, Jane Clark, illus. George Washington's Ghost. LC 93-39194. 1994. 13.95 (*0-395-69452-3*, HM) HM.
Brown, Marc T. Arthur's Family Vacation. LC 92-26650. 1993. 15.95 (*0-316-11312-3*) Little.
Brown, Margaret W. My World. LC 94-25755. 1995. 13.00 (*0-06-024798-3*, Festival); PLB 12.89 (*0-06-024799-1*) HarpC Child Bks.
Buchanan, Dawna L. The Falcon's Wing. LC 91-22545. 144p. (gr. 5 up). 1992. 13.95 (*0-531-05986-3*); lib. bdg. 13.99 (*0-531-08586-4*) Orchard Bks Watts.
Buchanan-Hedman, Pat. Stepmothers & Moonkisses. Koop, Christie, illus. 23p. (Orig.). (ps-5). 1991. 8.95 (*1-880121-00-X*) Three Cs Ent.
Buchanan-Hedman, Pat & Kingsbury, Kenneth. A Stepfather Named Buddy. Koop, Christie, illus. (Orig.). (ps-5). 1991. write for info. (*1-880121-25-5*) Three Cs Ent.
Burch, Robert. D. J.'s Worst Enemy: A Novel by Robert Burch. Weiss, Emil, illus. LC 92-44783. 144p. (gr. 4-6). 1993. Repr. of 1965 ed. 19.95 (*0-8203-1554-0*) U of Ga Pr.
Burningham, John. Courtney. LC 93-43508. (Illus.). 32p. (ps-2). 1994. 16.00 (*0-517-59883-3*); PLB 16.99 (*0-517-59884-1*) Crown Bks Yng Read.
Butterworth, Oliver. Visitng the Big House. Cohn, Amy, ed. Avishai, Susan, illus. LC 94-20844. 48p. 1995. pap. 3.95 (*0-688-13303-7*, Pub. by Beech Tree Bks) Morrow.
Byars, Betsy. The Not-Just-Anybody Family. 176p. 1993. text ed. 14.08 (*1-56956-380-2*) W A T Braille.
Byars, Betsy C. The Cartoonist. Cuffari, Richard, illus. LC 77-12782. 128p. (gr. 3-7). 1978. pap. 13.95 (*0-670-20556-7*) Viking Child Bks.
—The Glory Girl. (ps-3). 1985. pap. 3.95 (*0-14-031785-6*, Puffin) Puffin Bks.
—Good-Bye, Chicken Little. LC 78-19829. 112p. (gr. 5 up). 1979. PLB 13.89 (*0-06-020911-9*) HarpC Child Bks.
—The Night Swimmers. Howell, Troy, illus. LC 79-53597. 160p. (gr. 4-6). 1980. 9.95 (*0-685-01397-9*); pap. 11.95 (*0-385-28709-7*) Delacorte.
—The Not-Just-Anybody Family. (gr. k-6). 1987. pap. 3.50 (*0-440-45951-6*, YB) Dell.
—Summer of the Swans. CoConis, Ted, illus. (gr. 7 up). 1970. pap. 14.00 (*0-670-68190-3*) Viking Child Bks.
—Wanted...Mud Blossom. (gr. 4-7). 1991. 14.95 (*0-385-30428-5*) Delacorte.
Caines, Jeannette. Window Wishing. LC 79-2698. (Illus.). 32p. (gr. k-3). 1980. PLB 13.89 (*0-06-020934-8*) HarpC Child Bks.
Cameron, Ann. Julian, Dream Doctor. Strugnell, Ann, illus. LC 89-37562. 64p. (Orig.). (gr. 2-4). 1993. PLB 7.99 (*0-679-90524-3*); pap. 2.99 (*0-679-80524-9*) Random Bks Yng Read.
—Julian, Dream Doctor. 46p. 1992. text ed. 3.68 (*1-56956-116-8*) W A T Braille.
—More Stories Julian Tells. Strugnell, Ann, illus. LC 84-10095. 96p. (gr. k-4). 1986. PLB 13.99 (*0-394-96969-3*) Knopf Bks Yng Read.
—The Stories Huey Tells. LC 94-6221. (gr. 2 up). 1995. write for info. (*0-679-86732-5*); PLB write for info. (*0-679-96732-X*) Knopf Bks Yng Read.
Cameron, Eleanor. Julia & the Hand of God. Owens, Gail, illus. LC 77-4507. (gr. 4-7). 1977. 12.95 (*0-525-32910-2*, DCB) Dutton Child Bks.
—Julia's Magic. Owens, Gail, illus. LC 84-8118. 144p. (gr. 2-5). 1984. 13.95 (*0-525-44114-X*, DCB) Dutton Child Bks.
—The Private World of Julia Redfern. 224p. (gr. 5 up). 1990. pap. 4.95 (*0-14-034043-2*, Puffin) Puffin Bks.
—A Room Made of Windows. (gr. 7 up). 1971. 15.95 (*0-316-12523-7*, Joy St Bks) Little.
—That Julia Redfern. Owens, Gail, illus. LC 82-2405. 144p. (gr. 2-5). 1982. 12.95 (*0-525-44015-1*, DCB) Dutton Child Bks.
Carlson, Nancy. The Perfect Family. Carlson, Nancy, illus. LC 85-4123. 32p. (ps-3). 1985. PLB 13.50 (*0-87614-280-3*) Carolrhoda Bks.
—Take Time to Relax. (ps-3). 1991. 14.00 (*0-670-83287-1*) Viking Child Bks.
—Take Time to Relax! LC 92-26584. 1993. pap. 4.99 (*0-14-054242-6*, Puffin) Puffin Bks.
Carrick, Carol. Left Behind. Carrick, Donald, illus. 32p. (ps-3). 1991. pap. 4.80 (*0-395-54380-0*, Clarion Bks) HM.
Cartwright, Pauline. Taking Our Photo. Strahan, Heather, illus. LC 92-31950. 1993. 3.75 (*0-383-03595-3*) SRA Schl Grp.
Caseley, Judith. Harry & Arney. LC 93-20787. 1994. write for info. (*0-688-12140-3*) Greenwillow.
—Hurricane Harry. LC 90-13809. (Illus.). 128p. (gr. 1 up). 1991. 13.95 (*0-688-10027-9*) Greenwillow.
—Hurricane Harry. Caseley, Judith, illus. LC 93-6991. 112p. (gr. 3 up). 1994. pap. 4.95 (*0-688-12549-2*, Pub. by Beech Tree Bks) Morrow.
—My Father, the Nutcase. LC 91-46750. 196p. (gr. 7 up). 1992. 15.00 (*0-679-83394-3*); PLB 15.99 (*0-679-93394-8*) Knopf Bks Yng Read.
—Starring Dorothy Kane. LC 90-24172. (gr. 1 up). 1992. 13.00 (*0-688-10182-8*) Greenwillow.
—Starring Dorothy Kane. Caseley, Judith, illus. LC 93-6992. 160p. (gr. 3 up). 1994. pap. 4.95 (*0-688-12548-4*, Pub. by Beech Tree Bks) Morrow.
Casey, Barbara W. Leilani Zan. LC 90-71707. 113p. (gr. 9-12). 1992. 7.95 (*1-55523-405-4*) Winston-Derek.
Caudill, Rebecca. Happy Little Family. (gr. k-6). 1989. pap. 2.75 (*0-440-40164-X*, YB) Dell.
—Saturday Cousins. (gr. k-6). 1989. pap. 2.75 (*0-440-40208-5*, YB) Dell.
Chang, Margaret & Chang, Raymond. In the Eye of War. LC 89-38027. 208p. (gr. 4-7). 1990. SBE 14.95 (*0-689-50503-5*, M K McElderry) Macmillan Child Grp.
Christiansen, C. B. A Small Pleasure. LC 87-19313. 144p. (gr. 7 up). 1988. SBE 13.95 (*0-689-31369-1*, Atheneum Child Bk) Macmillan Child Grp.
Christopher, Matt. Tight End. 128p. (gr. 3 up). 1981. 15.95 (*0-316-14017-1*) Little.
Cleary, Beverly. Dear Mr. Henshaw. Zelinsky, Paul O., illus. LC 83-5372. 144p. (gr. 3-7). 1983. 12.95 (*0-688-02405-X*); PLB 12.88 (*0-688-02406-8*, Morrow Jr Bks) Morrow Jr Bks.
—The Growing-Up Feet. DiSalvo-Ryan, DyAnne, illus. LC 86-12585. 32p. (ps-1). 1987. 11.95 (*0-688-06619-4*); lib. bdg. 11.88 (*0-688-06620-8*) Morrow Jr Bks.
—Mitch & Amy. Porter, George, illus. LC 67-10041. 224p. (gr. 3-7). 1967. 15.95 (*0-688-21688-9*); PLB 15.88 (*0-688-31688-3*, Morrow Jr Bks) Morrow Jr Bks.
—Ramona & Her Father. Tiegreen, Alan, illus. LC 77-1614. 192p. (gr. 3-7). 1977. 13.95 (*0-688-22114-9*); PLB 13.88 (*0-688-32114-3*) Morrow Jr Bks.
—Ramona, Forever. 192p. (gr. k-6). 1985. pap. 4.50 (*0-440-47210-5*, YB) Dell.
—Ramona Quimby, Age 8. large type ed. Tiegreen, Alan, illus. 142p. (gr. 2-6). 1987. Repr. of 1981 ed. lib. bdg. 14.95 (*1-55736-000-6*, Crnrstn Bks) BDD LT Grp.
—Sister of the Bride. Krush, Beth & Krush, Joe, illus. LC 63-8802. 256p. (gr. 7 up). 1963. PLB 13.88 (*0-688-31742-1*) Morrow Jr Bks.
Cleaver, Vera. Sweetly Sings the Donkey. LC 85-40098. 160p. (gr. 5-9). 1985. (Lipp Jr Bks); (Lipp Jr Bks) HarpC Child Bks.
Cleaver, Vera & Cleaver, Bill. Delpha Green & Company. LC 79-172141. 144p. (gr. 6 up). 1972. (Junior Bks); pap. 2.95 (*0-397-31344-6*, LSC-8) HarpC.
Clifton, Lucille. Everett Anderson's Year. rev. ed. Grifalconi, Ann, illus. LC 92-4683. 32p. (ps-2). 1992. 14.95 (*0-8050-2247-3*, Bks Young Read) H Holt & Co.
—Everett Anderson's 1-2-3. Grifalconi, Ann, illus. LC 92-8031. 32p. (ps-2). 1992. 14.95 (*0-8050-2310-0*, Bks Young Read) H Holt & Co.
Climo, Shirley. Month of Seven Days. 192p. (gr. 2-9). 1989. pap. 2.95 (*0-8167-1476-2*) Troll Assocs.
Clough, Brenda W. An Impossumble Summer. 160p. (gr. 3-6). 1992. 14.95 (*0-8027-8150-0*) Walker & Co.
The Clubhouse Collection. (gr. 4-7). 1993. pap. 4.99 (*1-56179-161-X*) Focus Family.
Cohen, Barbara. People Like Us. 1987. 13.95 (*0-553-05441-4*) Bantam.
Cole, Babette. Winni Allfours. Cole, Babette, illus. LC 93-28447. (gr. k-4). 1993. PLB 13.95 (*0-8167-3308-2*); pap. 3.95t (*0-8167-3307-4*) BrdgeWater.
Cole, Joanna. Who Put the Pepper in the Pot? Alley, Robert W., illus. 42p. (ps-3). 1992. PLB 13.27 (*0-8368-0883-5*) Gareth Stevens Inc.
Colman, Hila. Suddenly. LC 86-28460. 160p. (gr. 7 up). 1987. 12.95 (*0-688-05865-5*) Morrow Jr Bks.
Condra, Estelle. See the Ocean. Crockett-Blassingame, Linda, illus. LC 94-4234. 1994. reinforced bdg. 14.95 (*1-57102-005-5*, Ideas Child) Hambleton-Hill.
Conrad, Pam. Prairie Visions: The Life & Times of Solomon Butcher. Zudeck, Darryl S., illus. LC 90-38658. 96p. (gr. 5 up). 1991. 17.00 (*0-06-021373-6*); PLB 16.89 (*0-06-021375-2*) HarpC Child Bks.
Conteh-Morgan, Jane. My Family: My First Books Ser. LC 94-15279. 1995. write for info. (*0-553-09730-X*) Bantam.
Cooney, Caroline B. Family Reunion. 1990. pap. 2.95 (*0-553-28573-4*) Bantam.
Corcoran, Barbara. Family Secrets. LC 91-13104. 176p. (gr. 3-7). 1992. SBE 13.95 (*0-689-31744-1*, Atheneum Child Bk) Macmillan Child Grp.
Coulter, Hope N. Uncle Chuck's Truck. Brown, Rick, illus. LC 91-42638. 32p. (ps-1). 1993. RSBE 13.95 (*0-02-724825-9*, Bradbury Pr) Macmillan Child Grp.
Creech, Sharon. Walk Two Moons. LC 93-31277. 288p. (gr. 3-7). 1994. 16.00 (*0-06-023334-6*); PLB 15.89 (*0-06-023337-0*) HarpC Child Bks.
Cresswell, Helen. Ordinary Jack: Being the First Part of the Bagthorpe Saga. LC 77-5146. 192p. (gr. 5 up). 1977. SBE 14.95 (*0-02-725540-9*, Macmillan Child Bk) Macmillan Child Grp.
—Posy Bates, Again! Aldous, Kate, illus. LC 93-5789. 112p. (gr. k-4). 1994. SBE 13.95 (*0-02-725372-4*, Macmillan Child Bk) Macmillan Child Grp.
Crew, Linda. Nekomah Creek. LC 90-49119. 192p. (gr. 4-5). 1991. 14.00 (*0-385-30442-0*) Delacorte.
—Nekomah Creek Christmas. Robinson, Charles, illus. LC 94-478. 1994. 14.95 (*0-385-32047-7*) Delacorte.
Crews, Donald. Bigmama's. Crews, Donald, illus. (gr. k-4). 1993. text ed. 3.95 (*0-685-64817-6*); audio cass. 11.00 (*1-882869-75-3*) Read Advent.
Cutler, Jane. Family Dinner. Caswell, Philip, illus. 112p. (gr. 3 up). 1992. 14.00 (*0-374-32267-8*) FS&G.
Cuyler, Margery. Daisy's Crazy Thanksgiving. Kramer, Robin, illus. LC 90-4323. 32p. (ps-2). 1990. 14.95 (*0-8050-0559-5*, Owlet BYR) H Holt & Co.
Dana, Barbara. Necessary Parties. 320p. 1987. pap. 3.50 (*0-553-26984-4*, Starfire) Bantam.
Daniel, Alan. Good Families Don't. (ps-3). 1991. pap. 3.99 (*0-440-40565-3*) Dell.
Danziger, Paula. Can You Sue Your Parents for Malpractice? LC 78-72856. 266p. (gr. 7 up). 1979. 14.95 (*0-385-28112-9*) Delacorte.
—Everyone Else's Parents Said Yes. (gr. 3-7). 1989. 13.95 (*0-385-29805-6*) Delacorte.
Davis, Deborah. My Brother Has AIDS. (gr. 4-8). 1994. 14.95 (*0-689-31922-3*, Atheneum) Macmillan.
Davis, Jenny. Good-bye & Keep Cold. LC 87-5794. 224p. (gr. 7 up). 1987. 12.95 (*0-531-05715-1*); PLB 12.99 (*0-531-08315-2*) Orchard Bks Watts.
De Lint, Charles. The Dreaming Place. Froud, Brian, illus. LC 90-488. 144p. (gr. 7 up). 1990. SBE 14.95 (*0-689-31571-6*, Atheneum Child Bk) Macmillan Child Grp.
Derby, Pat. Grams, Her Boyfriend, My Family, & Me. 256p. (gr. 12 up). 1994. 16.00 (*0-374-38131-3*) FS&G.
De Saint Mars, Dominique. Lily Fights with Max. LC 92-18000. (gr. 2-4). 1992. PLB 8.95 (*0-89565-980-8*) Childs World.
De Vries, David. Home at Last. (gr. 4-7). 1992. pap. 3.25 (*0-440-40621-8*) Dell.
Dionetti, Michelle. Coal Mine Peaches. Riggio, Anita, illus. LC 90-28693. 32p. (ps-2). 1991. 14.95 (*0-531-05948-0*); RLB 14.99 (*0-531-08548-1*) Orchard Bks Watts.
Duffy, James. Cleaver & Company. LC 91-9932. 144p. (gr. 4-6). 1991. SBE 13.95 (*0-684-19371-X*, Scribners Young Read) Macmillan Child Grp.
Eastern, Anne G. The Picolinis. 160p. (Orig.). (gr. 2-5). 1988. pap. 2.75 (*0-553-15566-0*, Skylark) Bantam.
Ehrlich, Amy. Zeek Silver Moon. Parker, Robert A., illus. LC 70-181787. 32p. (ps-3). 1972. Dial Bks Young.
Eisenberg, Lisa. Lexie on Her Own. 128p. (gr. 3-7). 1992. 13.00 (*0-670-84489-6*) Viking Child Bks.
Ellis, Carol. Stepdaughter. 1993. pap. 3.25 (*0-590-46044-7*) Scholastic Inc.
Ellis, Jana. The Best of Everything. LC 88-12380. 160p. (gr. 7 up). 1988. pap. text ed. 2.50 (*0-8167-1356-1*) Troll Assocs.
—Two for One. LC 88-12384. 160p. (gr. 7 up). 1988. pap. text ed. 2.50 (*0-8167-1354-5*) Troll Assocs.
Endersby, Frank. The Nuisance. (gr. 4 up). 1981. 3.95 (*0-85953-233-X*) Childs Play.
—What about Me? (gr. 4 up). 1981. 3.95 (*0-85953-232-1*) Childs Play.

Epperley, Mike. Buckethead Bunch: Bossy, Loser, Show-off & Angry. Erb, Sherry, illus. LC 92-85592. 40p. (Orig.). (gr. k-6). 1992. pap. 5.98x (*1-882183-24-X*) Computer Pr.

—The Buckethead Families: Givers & Takers. rev. ed. Erb, Sherry, illus. LC 92-85597. 32p. (gr. k-6). 1992. pap. 5.98 (*1-882183-23-1*) Computer Pr.

Estes, Eleanor. Middle Moffat. 1989. pap. 3.25 (*0-440-70028-0*) Dell.

—The Middle Moffats. (gr. k-6). 1989. pap. 3.25 (*0-440-40180-1*, YB) Dell.

—Moffat Museum. 1989. pap. 3.25 (*0-440-70029-9*) Dell.

—Moffats. Slobodkin, Louis, illus. LC 41-51893. 32p. (gr. 3-7). 1941. 14.95 (*0-15-255095-X*, HB Juv Bks) HarBrace.

—The Moffats. 1989. pap. 3.25 (*0-440-70026-4*) Dell.

—Rufus M. Slobodkin, Louis, illus. LC 43-51239. (gr. 3-7). 1943. 15.95 (*0-15-269415-3*, HB Juv Bks) HarBrace.

—Rufus M. 1989. pap. 3.25 (*0-440-70027-2*) Dell.

ETR Associates Staff. A Family That Fits. Paley, Nina, illus. LC 92-8361. 1992. write for info. (*1-56071-103-5*) ETR Assocs.

Everett, Gwen. Lil Sis & Uncle Willie. (Illus.). 32p. (ps-3). 1994. pap. 4.95 (*1-56282-593-3*) Hyprn Ppbks.

Fakih, Kimberly O. High on the Hog. LC 93-34214. 1994. 16.00 (*0-374-33209-6*) FS&G.

Falwell, Cathryn. Feast for Ten. Falwell, Cathryn, illus. LC 92-35512. 32p. (ps-3). 1993. 14.95 (*0-395-62037-6*, Clarion Bks) HM.

FamilyVision Press Staff. Dino Mites Declare War! LC 93-71624. (Illus.). 80p. 1993. pap. 8.95 (*1-56969-100-2*) FamilyVision.

Farmer, Nancy. Do You Know Me. Jackson, Shelley, illus. LC 92-34068. 112p. (gr. 3-5). 1993. 15.95 (*0-531-05474-8*); PLB 15.99 (*0-531-08624-0*) Orchard Bks Watts.

—Do You Know Me. Jackson, Shelley, illus. 112p. (gr. 3-7). 1994. pap. 3.99 (*0-14-036946-5*) Puffin Bks.

Fine, Anne. The Book of the Banshee. LC 91-23715. (gr. 7 up). 1992. 13.95 (*0-316-28315-0*) Little.

Finn, Felicity. Jeremy & the Aunties. 156p. (Orig.). (gr. 5-7). 1992. pap. 6.95 (*0-929005-40-6*, Pub. by Second Story Pr CN) InBook.

Fitzhugh, Louise. Nobody's Family Is Going to Change. 224p. (gr. 3-7). 1975. pap. 1.75 (*0-440-46454-4*, YB) Dell.

Flynn, Mary. Cornelius in Charge. Myler, Terry, illus. (Orig.). (gr. 1-6). 1990. 10.95 (*0-947962-53-0*, Pub. by Anvil Bks Ltd Ireland); pap. 7.95 (*0-947962-54-9*, Pub. by Anvil Bks Ltd Ireland) Irish Bks Media.

Fosburgh, Liza. Wrong Way Home. 1990. 14.95 (*0-553-05883-5*) Bantam.

Fowler, Susi G. Fog. Fowler, Jim, illus. LC 91-28509. 32p. (ps-8). 1992. 14.00 (*0-688-10593-9*); PLB 13.93 (*0-688-10594-7*) Greenwillow.

Fox, Paula. Maurice's Room. reissued ed. Fetz, Ingrid, illus. LC 85-7200. 64p. (gr. 2-6). 1985. SBE 13.95 (*0-02-735490-3*, Macmillan Child Bk) Macmillan Child Grp.

Frost, Marie & Hanson, Bonnie C. Hattie's Cry for Help. (Illus.). 1992. pap. 5.99 (*1-56121-104-4*) Wolgemuth & Hyatt.

Gackenbach, Dick. Where Are Momma, Poppa, & Sister June. LC 93-40809. 1994. 13.95 (*0-395-67323-2*, Clarion Bks) HM.

Gantos, Jack. Heads or Tails: Stories from the Sixth Grade. LC 93-43117. 1994. 16.00 (*0-374-32909-5*) FS&G.

Gardner, Richard A. The Boys & Girls Book about Stepfamilies. Lowenheim, Alfred, illus. 180p. (gr. 3-10). 1985. pap. 4.99 (*0-933812-13-2*) Creative Therapeutics.

Gates, Doris. Blue Willow. Lantz, Paul, illus. LC 40-32435. (gr. 4-6). 1976. pap. 3.99 (*0-14-030924-1*, VS30, Puffin) Puffin Bks.

Gehret, Jeanne. I'm Somebody Too. 159p. (gr. 4-7). 1992. text ed. 16.00 (*0-9625136-7-9*); pap. 12.00 (*0-9625136-6-0*) Verbal Images Pr. "This juvenile fiction...held my interest throughout. It is the story of sibling rivalry exacerbated by the younger sib Ben's condition known as attention deficit disorder or ADD. His older sister Emily represses her own needs & resentments as a people-pleaser & tries to keep conflict to a minimum...This is a fictionalized account of their struggles as a family, the growing crisis & the final resolution as the family seeks treatment...The therapy sessions are very well done by someone who knows what therapy is all about... engaging fiction...invaluable to the general public...a valuable addition to bibliotherapy programs involving professionals in schools & public libraries. Many parents as well as children will benefit from reading the book."--Small Press. "In addition to a good story, Gehret offers a few pages on how siblings can deal with frustration."--School Library Journal. A companion to Jeanne Gehret's bestselling picture book EAGLE EYES: A CHILD'S GUIDE TO PAYING ATTENTION (1991), which introduced the same family through the tale of scatterbrained Ben. I'M SOMEBODY TOO. 159 pages. Ages 9 to 12. Paperback $12.00 (ISBN 0-9625136-6-0); Hardcover $16.00 (ISBN 0-9625136-7-9). Verbal Images Press, 19 Fox Hill Dr., Fairport, NY 14450. *Publisher Provided Annotation.*

George, Jean C. The Cry of the Crow. LC 79-2016. 160p. (gr. 5 up). 1980. PLB 12.89 (*0-06-021957-2*) HarpC Child Bks.

Gerson, Corinne. Tread Softly. LC 78-72199. (gr. 4-7). 1979. Dial Bks Young.

Gewing, Lisa. Mama, Daddy, Baby & Me. Larimer, Donna, illus. 30p. (ps). 1989. 12.95 (*0-944296-04-1*) Spirit Pr.

Gibbons, Alan. The Jaws of the Dragon. LC 94-47126. 156p. (gr. 5 up). 1994. PLB 18.95 (*0-8225-0737-4*) Lerner Pubns.

Gilbreth, Frank B., Jr. & Carey, Ernestine G. Cheaper by the Dozen. (gr. 6 up). 1984. pap. 3.99 (*0-553-27250-0*, Starfire) Bantam.

Gleeson, Libby. Hurry Up! Vane, Mitch, illus. LC 92-21448. 1993. 3.75 (*0-383-03632-1*) SRA Schl Grp.

Godden, Rumer. Thursday's Children. (gr. k-12). 1987. pap. 3.25 (*0-440-98790-3*, LFL) Dell.

Gondosch, Linda. Camp Kickapoo. Lincoln, Patricia H., illus. LC 92-28060. 128p. (gr. 4-6). 1993. 13.99 (*0-525-67373-3*, Lodestar Bks) Dutton Child Bks.

Gorman, Carol. Brian's Footsteps. Koehler, Ed, illus. LC 93-38322. 96p. (Orig.). (gr. 4-7). 1994. pap. 3.99 (*0-570-04629-7*) Concordia.

Gracious Plenty. LC 91-6485. 40p. 1991. pap. 13.95 jacketed (*0-671-73566-7*, Little Simon) S&S Trade.

Green, Kate. Everything a Dinosaur Could Want. (Illus.). 32p. 1992. 15.95 (*0-89565-739-2*) Childs World.

Greenfield, Eloise. Talk about a Family. reissued ed. Calvin, James, illus. LC 77-16423. 64p. (gr. 2-5). 1991. PLB 12.89 (*0-397-32504-5*, Lipp Jr Bks) HarpC Child Bks.

Griffin, Peni R. A Dig in Time. LC 90-47388. 192p. (gr. 4-7). 1991. SBE 14.95 (*0-689-50525-6*, M K McElderry) Macmillan Child Grp.

—A Dig in Time. LC 92-18958. 160p. (gr. 3-7). 1992. pap. 3.99 (*0-14-036001-8*) Puffin Bks.

Griffith, Connie. Mysterious Rescuer. LC 93-8421. 128p. (Orig.). 1994. pap. 4.99 (*0-8010-3865-0*) Baker Bk.

—Secret Behind Locked Doors. LC 93-8420. 128p. (gr. 5-8). 1994. pap. 5.99 (*0-8010-3864-2*) Baker Bk.

Haas, Jessie. Skipping School. LC 91-37642. (gr. 6-12). 1992. 14.00 (*0-688-10179-8*) Greenwillow.

Hall, Barbara. Dixie Storms. 197p. (gr. 7 up). 1990. 15.95 (*0-15-223825-5*) HarBrace.

Hall, Lynn. Windsong. LC 91-46075. 80p. (gr. 6-8). 1992. SBE 12.95 (*0-684-19439-2*, Scribners Young Read) Macmillan Child Grp.

Hamilton, Dorothy. Rosalie. Unada, illus. LC 76-39961. 128p. (gr. 3-10). 1977. pap. text ed. 3.95 (*0-8361-1807-3*) Herald Pr.

Hamilton, Gail. Family Rivalry. (gr. 4-6). 1993. pap. 3.99 (*0-553-48042-1*) Bantam.

Hamilton, Virginia. Cousins. 128p. (gr. 5 up). 1990. 14.95 (*0-399-22164-6*, Philomel Bks) Putnam Pub Group.

—M. C. Higgins, the Great. 2nd ed. LC 92-27919. 288p. (gr. 3-7). 1993. pap. 3.95 (*0-689-71694-X*, Aladdin) Macmillan Child Grp.

—Sweet Whispers, Brother Rush. 224p. (gr. 7 up). 1982. 15.95 (*0-399-20894-1*, Philomel) Putnam Pub Group.

Hamm, Diane J. Second Family. LC 91-42968. 128p. (gr. 5-7). 1992. SBE 13.95 (*0-684-19436-8*, Scribners Young Read) Macmillan Child Grp.

Harris, Mark J. Come the Morning. LC 88-24213. 176p. (gr. 5-9). 1989. SBE 14.95 (*0-02-742750-1*, Bradbury Pr) Macmillan Child Grp.

Hart, Jan S. The Many Adventures of Minnie. Wilson, Kay, illus. LC 92-17740. 96p. (gr. 4-7). 1992. 12.95 (*0-89015-859-2*) Sunbelt Media.

Haven, Susan. Maybe I'll Move to the Lost & Found. 160p. (gr. 5 up). 1988. 14.95 (*0-399-21509-3*, Putnam) Putnam Pub Group.

Hazen, Barbara S. Tiempos Duros: Tight Times. Hyman, Trina S., illus. 32p. (ps-3). 1993. PLB 12.99 (*0-670-84841-7*) Viking Child Bks.

Hazen, Nancy. Grownups Cry Too: Los Adultos Tambien Lloran-English-Spanish Text. 2nd ed. Cotera, Martha P., tr. LC 78-71542. (Illus.). 25p. (ps-1). 1978. pap. 5.00 (*0-914996-19-3*) Lollipop Power.

Head, Ann. Mr. & Mrs. Bo Jo Jones. (Illus.). 192p. (gr. 9-12). 1968. pap. 3.99 (*0-451-16319-2*, Sig) NAL-Dutton.

Heath, Amy. Sofie's Role. Hamanaka, Sheila, illus. LC 91-33488. 40p. (gr. k-2). 1992. RSBE 14.95 (*0-02-743505-9*, Four Winds) Macmillan Child Grp.

HeBo. Clean up Your Act! Dirty, Dingy, Daryl. LC 93-48306. 1994. pap. 4.95 (*0-939700-29-8*) I D I C P.

Heide, Florence P. Time Flies! 112p. 1985. pap. 2.50 (*0-553-15370-6*, Skylark) Bantam.

Heide, Florence P. & Gilliland, Judith H. Sami & the Time of the Troubles. Lewin, Ted, illus. 32p. (gr. k-4). 1992. 13.45 (*0-395-55964-2*, Clarion Bks) HM.

Heide, Florence P. & Pierce, Roxanne H. Tio Armando. LC 93-37434. (Illus.). (gr. 5 up). 1994. 14.00 (*0-688-12107-1*); 13.93 (*0-688-12108-X*) Lothrop.

Heitz, True. Mommy Moon & the Rainbow Children. Mattos, D., illus. 13p. (Orig.). (ps-2). 1982. pap. 3.00 (*0-686-37664-1*) True Heitz.

Helldorfer, M. C. Harmonica Night. Natchev, Alexi, illus. LC 93-40669. 1995. 16.95 (*0-02-743518-0*, Bradbury Pr) Macmillan Child Grp.

Henderson, Kathy. Bumpety Bump. Thompson, Carol, illus. LC 93-3541. 24p. (ps). 1994. 9.95 (*1-56402-312-5*) Candlewick Pr.

Hendry, Diana. Double Vision. LC 92-52996. 272p. (gr. 7-11). 1993. 14.95 (*1-56402-125-4*) Candlewick Pr.

Henkes, Kevin. Grandpa & Bo. Henkes, Kevin, illus. LC 85-14869. 32p. (ps-3). 1986. 14.88 (*0-688-04956-7*); PLB 14.95 (*0-688-04957-5*) Greenwillow.

Hennessy, B. G. When You Were Just a Little Girl. (ps-3). 1991. 12.95 (*0-670-82998-6*) Viking Child Bks.

Hermes, Patricia. Take Care of My Girl: A Novel. LC 92-9819. 1992. 14.95 (*0-316-35913-0*) Little.

Hest, Amy. Fancy Aunt Jess. LC 88-34370. (ps-3). 1990. 12.95 (*0-688-08096-0*) Morrow Jr Bks.

Heyer, Georgette. Sylvester (Or the Wicked Uncle) 1991. pap. 3.99 (*0-06-100257-7*, Harp PBks) HarpC.

Heymans, Annemie & Heymans, Margriet. The Princess in the Kitchen Garden. (Illus.). 48p. (ps-3). 1993. bds. 16.00 (*0-374-36122-3*) FS&G.

Hickman, Janet. Jericho. LC 93-37309. 1994. write for info. (*0-688-13398-3*) Greenwillow.

Hill, Elizabeth S. Broadway Chances. 160p. (gr. 3-7). 1992. RB 14.00 (*0-670-84197-8*) Viking Child Bks.

—Evan's Corner. (ps-3). 1991. 13.00 (*0-670-82830-0*) Viking Child Bks.

—Evan's Corner. Speidel, Sandra, illus. LC 92-25334. 1993. pap. 4.99 (*0-14-054406-2*) Puffin Bks.

—The Street Dancers. 176p. (gr. 3-7). 1993. pap. 3.99 (*0-14-034491-8*, Puffin) Puffin Bks.

Himmelman, John. The Day-Off Machine. Brook, Bonnie, ed. Himmelman, John, illus. 48p. (ps-3). 1990. PLB 5.95 (*0-671-69635-1*); pap. 2.95 (*0-671-69639-4*) Silver Pr.

—Fix-It Family Series, 4 vols. Himmelman, John, illus. 192p. (ps-3). 1991. Set. PLB 23.80 (*0-671-31232-4*); Set. pap. 11.80 (*0-671-31233-2*) Silver Pr.

—The Great Leaf Blast-Off. Brook, Bonnie, ed. Himmelman, John, illus. 48p. (ps-3). 1990. PLB 5.95 (*0-671-69634-3*); pap. 2.95 (*0-671-69638-6*) Silver Pr.

Hines, Anna G. Moon's Wish. Hines, Anna G., illus. 32p. (ps-1). 1992. 14.45 (*0-395-58114-1*, Clarion Bks) HM.

Hines, Gary. The Day of the High Climber. Hines, Anna G., illus. LC 93-12254. 32p. (ps up). 1994. 14.00 (*0-688-11494-6*); PLB 13.93 (*0-688-11495-4*) Greenwillow.

Hiser, Constance. No Bean Sprouts, Please! MacDonald, Patricia, ed. Ewing, Carolyn S., illus. 64p. 1991. pap. 2.99 (*0-671-72325-1*, Minstrel Bks) PB.

Hite, Sid. Dither Farm. LC 91-31323. 224p. (gr. 7 up). 1992. 15.95 (*0-8050-1871-9*, Bks Young Read) H Holt & Co.

Hoban, Russell. Bread & Jam for Frances: Big Book. Hoban, Lillian, illus. LC 92-13622. 32p. (ps-3). 1993. pap. 19.95 (*0-06-443336-6*, Trophy) HarpC Child Bks.

Hobbs, Will. Changes in Latitudes. LC 87-17462. 176p. (gr. 7 up). 1988. SBE 14.95 (*0-689-31385-3*, Atheneum Child Bk) Macmillan Child Grp.

Hoberman, Mary A. Mr. & Mrs. Muddle. Hoberman, Mary Ann, illus. LC 87-27320. 32p. (gr. k-4). 1988. 13.95 (*0-316-36735-4*, Joy St Bks) Little.

Hodge, Merle. For the Life of Laetitia. 1993. 15.00 (*0-374-32447-6*) FS&G.

Hoehne, Marcia. A Place of My Own. LC 92-44336. 128p. (Orig.). (gr. 4-7). 1993. pap. 4.99 (*0-89107-718-9*) Crossway Bks.

Honeycutt, Natalie. Ask Me Something Easy. LC 90-7765. 160p. (gr. 6-9). 1991. 13.95 (*0-531-05894-8*); PLB 13.99 (*0-531-08494-9*) Orchard Bks Watts.

Hoobler, Dorothy & Hoobler, Thomas. And Now a Word from Our Sponsor. Leer, Rebecca, illus. 64p. (gr. 4-6). 1992. 5.95 (*0-382-24153-3*); PLB 7.95 (*0-382-24146-0*); pap. 3.95 (*0-382-24350-1*) Silver Burdett Pr.

Houston, Gloria. Littlejim's Gift: An Appalachian Christmas Story. Allen, Thomas B., illus. LC 93-41736. 32p. (gr. 1-5). 1994. PLB 15.95 (*0-399-22696-6*, Philomel Bks) Putnam Pub Group.

Howard, Ellen. Sister. LC 90-196. 160p. (gr. 3-7). 1990. SBE 13.95 (*0-689-31653-4*, Atheneum Child Bk) Macmillan Child Grp.

Hughes, Shirley. The Big Alfie Out of Doors Storybook. LC 91-28635. (Illus.). 64p. (ps up). 1992. reinforced bdg. 16.00 (*0-688-11428-8*) Lothrop.

Hunt, Irene. Up a Road Slowly. LC 92-47118. 192p. 1993. 12.95 (*0-382-24366-8*) Silver Burdett Pr.

Hurst, James. The Scarlet Ibis: A Classic Story of Brotherhood. (Illus.). (gr. 4 up). 1987. PLB 13.95 (*0-88682-000-6*) Creative Ed.

Hurwitz, Johanna. Aldo Peanut Butter. DeGroat, Diane, illus. 112p. (gr. 3-7). 1992. pap. 3.99 (*0-14-036020-4*) Puffin Bks.
—E is for Elisa. Hoban, Lillian, illus. LC 91-159. 80p. (ps up). 1991. 12.95 (*0-688-10439-8*); PLB 12.88 (*0-688-10440-1*) Morrow Jr Bks.
—E Is for Elisa. Hoban, Lillian, illus. LC 92-26796. 96p. (gr. 2-5). 1993. pap. 3.99 (*0-14-036033-6*) Puffin Bks.
—The Rabbi's Girls. Johnson, Pamela, illus. LC 82-2102. 192p. (gr. 4-6). 1982. 11.95 (*0-688-01089-X*) Morrow Jr Bks.
—Roz & Ozzie. McKeating, Eileen, illus. LC 91-42338. 128p. (gr. 2 up). 1992. 13.00 (*0-688-10945-4*) Morrow Jr Bks.
—Tough-Luck Karen. De Groat, Diane, illus. LC 82-6443. 160p. (gr. 4-6). 1982. 12.95 (*0-688-01485-2*) Morrow Jr Bks.
Hutchins, Pat. Titch. Hutchins, Pat, illus. LC 77-146622. 32p. (ps-1). 1971. RSBE 14.95 (*0-02-745880-6*, Macmillan Child Bk) Macmillan Child Grp.
Ireland, Shep. Wesley & Wendell: At Home. Ireland, Shep, illus. 40p. (gr. 1). 1991. lib. bdg. 4.75 (*0-8378-0330-6*) Gibson.
Irwin, Hadley. Abby, My Love. LC 84-24571. 168p. (gr. 7 up). 1985. SBE 13.95 (*0-689-50323-7*, M K McElderry) Macmillan Child Grp.
Ish-Kishor, Sulamith. Our Eddie. reissued ed. LC 92-7719. 192p. (gr. 2-5). 1992. 15.00 (*0-394-81455-X*) Knopf Bks Yng Read.
Jackson, Isaac. Somebody's New Pajamas. Soman, David, photos by. LC 93-32213. 1995. write for info. (*0-8037-1570-6*); lib. bdg. write for info. (*0-8037-1549-8*) Dial Bks Young.
James, Simon. The Day Jake Vacuumed. (ps-3). 1989. pap. 7.95 (*0-553-05840-1*) Bantam.
Johnson, Angela. One of Three. Soman, David, illus. LC 90-29316. 32p. (ps-1). 1991. 14.95 (*0-531-05955-3*); RLB 14.99 (*0-531-08555-4*) Orchard Bks Watts.
—Toning the Sweep: A Novel. LC 92-34062. 112p. (gr. 6 up). 1993. 13.95 (*0-531-05476-4*); PLB 13.99 (*0-531-08626-7*) Orchard Bks Watts.
Johnson, Emily R. A House Full of Strangers. 160p. (gr. 5 up). 1992. 14.00 (*0-525-65091-1*, Cobblehill Bks) Dutton Child Bks.
Johnson, Lee & Johnson, Sue K. If I Ran the Family. Espeland, Pamela, ed. Collier-Morales, Roberta, illus. LC 92-948. 32p. (ps-3). 1992. 13.95 (*0-915793-41-5*) Free Spirit Pub.
Johnston, Norma. Glory in the Flower. 200p. (gr. 4 up). 1990. pap. 3.95 (*0-14-034292-3*, Puffin) Puffin Bks.
—The Keeping Days. 240p. (gr. 4 up). 1990. pap. 3.95 (*0-14-034291-5*, Puffin) Puffin Bks.
Jones, Diana W. The Ogre Downstairs. LC 89-11741. 192p. (gr. 5 up). 1990. 12.95 (*0-688-09195-4*) Greenwillow.
Joosse, Barbara M. Snow Day! Plecas, Jennifer, illus. LC 94-17012. (gr. 1-8). Date not set. write for info. (*0-395-66588-4*, Clarion Bks) HM.
Kabeto, Rita T. The Bradburys. 70p. (gr. 3-7). 1993. pap. write for info. (*0-9635416-0-9*) Buchonia Pub.
Kantenwein, Louise. Tiny Tina, Messy Maggie, & Perfect Pal. 1992. 7.95 (*0-533-10174-3*) Vantage.
Katz, Illana & Ritvo, Edward. Joey & Sam: A Heartwarming Storybook about Autism, a Family, & a Brother's Love. Borowitz, Franz, illus. LC 92-38812. 40p. (gr. k-6). 1993. smythe sewn 16.95 (*1-882388-00-3*) Real Life Strybks.
Kaye, Marilyn. Home's a Nice Place to Visit, But I Wouldn't Want to Live There. (gr. 4-7). 1990. pap. 3.50 (*0-06-106023-2*, PL) HarpC.
Keating, August. Uncle Wooley. LC 87-82084. 55p. (Orig.). (gr. 9 up). 1988. pap. 5.00 (*0-916383-47-4*) Aegina Pr.
Keats, Ezra J. Louie's Search. Keats, Ezra J., illus. LC 80-10176. 40p. (gr. k-3). 1984. RSBE 13.95 (*0-02-749700-3*, Four Winds) Macmillan Child Grp.
—Peter's Chair. Keats, Ezra J., illus. LC 67-4816. (gr. k-3). 1967. 15.00i (*0-06-023111-4*); PLB 14.89 (*0-06-023112-2*) HarpC Child Bks.
Kelleher, Victor. Del-Del. (gr. 7-10). 1992. 17.95 (*0-8027-8154-3*) Walker & Co.
Kerr, M. E. Night Kites. LC 85-45386. 192p. (gr. 7 up). 1986. PLB 14.89 (*0-06-023254-4*) HarpC Child Bks.
Killilea, Marie. Wren. Riger, Robert, illus. (gr. 3-7). 1981. pap. 0.95 (*0-440-49704-3*, YB) Dell.
Kingman, Lee. The Best Christmas. Cooney, Barbara, illus. LC 92-21152. 96p. (gr. 5 up). 1993. pap. 4.95 (*0-688-11838-0*, Pub. by Beech Tree Bks) Morrow.
Kinsey-Warnock, Natalie. When Spring Comes. Schuett, Stacey, illus. LC 92-14066. (ps-3). 1993. 14.99 (*0-525-45008-4*, DCB) Dutton Child Bks.
Kirby, Susan E. Shadow Boy. LC 90-7687. 160p. (gr. 7 up). 1991. 13.95 (*0-531-05869-7*); PLB 13.99 (*0-531-08469-8*) Orchard Bks Watts.
Kiser, SuAnn. The Catspring Somersault Flying One-Handed Flip-Flop. Catalanotto, Peter, illus. LC 92-44519. 32p. (ps-2). 1993. 14.95 (*0-531-05493-4*); PLB 14.99 (*0-531-08643-7*) Orchard Bks Watts.
Klass, Sheila S. Pork Bellies Are Down. LC 94-20235. 1995. 13.95 (*0-590-46686-0*) Scholastic Inc.
Kleitsch, Christel. Cousin Markie & Other Disasters. LC 91-34641. (Illus.). 96p. (gr. 2-4). 1992. 13.00 (*0-525-44891-8*, DCB) Dutton Child Bks.
Kleitsch, Christel & Kelley, True. It Happened at Pickle Lake. (Illus.). 64p. (gr. 2-5). 1993. 11.99 (*0-525-45058-0*, DCB) Dutton Child Bks.
Knight, Joan. Opal in the Closet. Estrada, Pau, illus. LC 91-659. 28p. (gr. k up). 1992. pap. 14.95 (*0-88708-174-6*) Picture Bk Studio.
Koehler, Phoebe. Making Room. Koehler, Phoebe, illus. LC 91-41356. 48p. (ps-3). 1993. SBE 14.95 (*0-02-750875-7*, Bradbury Pr) Macmillan Child Grp.
Koller, Jackie F. Nothing to Fear. Grove, Karen, ed. 279p. (gr. 5 up). 1991. 14.95 (*0-15-200544-7*, Gulliver Bks) HarBrace.
Konigsburg, E. L. Father's Arcane Daughter. LC 76-5495. 128p. (gr. 4-8). 1976. SBE 13.95 (*0-689-30524-9*, Atheneum Child Bk) Macmillan Child Grp.
Kroll, Virginia L. Beginnings: How Families Came to Be. Schuett, Stacey, illus. LC 93-29594. 1994. write for info. (*0-8075-0602-8*) A Whitman.
—A Carp for Kimiko. Roundtree, Katherine, illus. LC 93-6940. 32p. 1993. 14.95 (*0-88106-412-2*); PLB 15.88 (*0-88106-413-0*) Charlesbridge Pub.
Kuskin, Karla. Something Sleeping in the Hall. Kuskin, Karla, illus. LC 82-47721. 64p. (gr. k-3). 1985. PLB 13.89 (*0-06-023634-5*) HarpC Child Bks.
Lansing, Karen E. Time to Fly. LC 91-14393. 104p. (Orig.). (gr. 4-8). 1991. pap. 5.95 (*0-8361-3560-1*) Herald Pr.
L'Engle, Madeleine. Meet the Austins. 192p. (gr. 5-9). 1981. pap. 3.99 (*0-440-95777-X*, LE) Dell.
Lester, Alison. Bumping & Bouncing. (Illus.). 16p. (ps-k). 1989. pap. 3.50 (*0-670-81991-3*) Viking Child Bks.
Levene, Nancy S. Chocolate Chips & Trumpet Tricks. Reck, Sue, ed. LC 93-36195. 192p. (gr. 3-6). 1994. pap. 5.99 (*0-7814-0103-8*, Chariot Bks) Cook.
Levin, Betty. Mercy's Mill. LC 91-31483. (gr. 7 up). 1992. 14.00 (*0-688-11122-X*) Greenwillow.
—The Trouble With Gramary. LC 87-22702. 192p. (gr. 5up). 1988. 13.95 (*0-688-07372-7*) Greenwillow.
Levinson, Marilyn. No Boys Allowed. Leer, Rebecca, illus. LC 93-22335. 128p. (gr. 5-8). 1993. PLB 13.95 (*0-8167-3135-7*); pap. 2.95 (*0-8167-3136-5*) BrdgeWater.
Levinson, Riki. Boys Here - Girls There. Ritz, Karen, illus. LC 92-5321. 1993. 13.00 (*0-525-67374-1*, Lodestar Bks) Dutton Child Bks.
Levit, Rose. With Secrets to Keep. LC 90-20947. 160p. (gr. 7 up). 1991. 12.95 (*1-55870-197-4*, 70119) Shoe Tree Pr.
Levitin, Sonia. The Golem & the Dragon Girl. LC 92-27665. 176p. (gr. 3-7). 1993. 14.99 (*0-8037-1280-4*); PLB 14.89 (*0-8037-1281-2*) Dial Bks Young.
—Silver Days. LC 88-27491. 192p. (gr. 5 up). 1989. SBE 14.95 (*0-689-31563-5*, Atheneum Child Bk) Macmillan Child Grp.
Light, John. Beachcombers. LC 91-38130. (gr. 4 up). 1991. 2.95 (*0-85953-502-9*) Childs Play.
—It's Great Outdoors. LC 90-34353. (gr. 5 up). 1991. 3.95 (*0-85953-338-7*) Childs Play.
—Race Ace Roger. LC 91-33417. (gr. 4 up). 1991. 3.95 (*0-85953-501-0*) Childs Play.
—Snap Happy. LC 91-36610. (gr. 4 up). 1991. 3.95 (*0-85953-504-5*) Childs Play.
—What's Cooking. LC 90-34355. (gr. 4 up). 1991. 3.95 (*0-85953-337-9*) Childs Play.
Lindbergh, Anne M. Bailey's Window. 144p. 1991. pap. 3.50 (*0-380-70767-5*, Camelot) Avon.
Lisle, Janet T. Afternoon of the Elves. LC 88-35099. 128p. (gr. 4-6). 1989. 13.95 (*0-531-05837-9*); PLB 13.99 (*0-531-08437-X*) Orchard Bks Watts.
Litchfield, Ada B. Making Room for Uncle Joe. Tucker, Kathleen, ed. LC 83-17036. (Illus.). 32p. (gr. 3-5). 1984. PLB 11.95 (*0-8075-4952-5*) A Whitman.
Little, Jean. Home from Far. Lazare, Jerry, illus. (gr. 5 up). 1965. 14.95 (*0-316-52792-0*) Little.
—Look Through My Window. Sandin, Joan, illus. LC 71-105470. 270p. (gr. 4-7). 1970. PLB 14.89 (*0-06-023924-7*) HarpC Child Bks.
—Revenge of the Small Small. Wilson, Janet, illus. 32p. (ps-3). 1993. 14.00 (*0-670-84471-3*) Viking Child Bks.
Lomas Garza, Carmen. Family Pictures: Cuadros de familia. (SPA & ENG., Illus.). 32p. (gr. 1-7). 1993. pap. 5.95 (*0-89239-108-1*) Childrens Book Pr.
Lord, Wendy. Pickle Stew. LC 93-19018. 1994. pap. 4.49 (*0-7814-0886-5*, Chariot Bks) Chariot Family.
Lothrop, Harriet M. The Five Little Peppers & How They Grew. (Orig.). (gr. k-6). 1985. pap. 4.95 (*0-440-42505-0*, Pub. by Yearling Classics) Dell.
Lotz, Karen E. Can't Sit Still. Browning, Colleen, illus. LC 92-28853. 48p. (ps-3). 1993. 13.99 (*0-525-45066-1*, DCB) Dutton Child Bks.
Lowry, Lois. Anastasia on Her Own. LC 84-22432. 131p. (gr. 5-7). 1985. 13.45 (*0-395-38133-9*) HM.
—Attaboy, Sam! De Groat, Diane, illus. 128p. (gr. 2-6). 1992. 13.45 (*0-395-61588-7*) HM.
—A Summer to Die. Oliver, Jenni, illus. (gr. 3-7). 1977. 13.45 (*0-395-25338-1*) HM.
Lunn, Janet. One Hundred Shining Candles. Grater, Lindsay, illus. LC 90-8892. 32p. (gr. 2-4). 1991. SBE 13.95 (*0-684-19280-2*, Scribners Young Read) Macmillan Child Grp.
Luttrell, Chuck, illus. Everything's Going Wrong. 74p. (Orig.). (gr. 3-6). 1986. pap. 6.95 (*0-9617609-0-7*) Shade Tree NV.
Lynch, Chris. Gypsy Davey. 160p. (gr. 7 up). 1994. 14.00 (*0-06-023586-1*); PLB 13.89 (*0-06-023587-X*) HarpC Child Bks.
Macdonald, Maryann. No Room for Francie. Christelow, Eileen, illus. LC 94-8596. 1995. write for info. (*0-7868-0032-1*); lib. bdg. write for info. (*0-7868-2027-6*) Hyprn Child.
McDonald, Megan. Insects Are My Life. Johnson, Paul B., illus. LC 94-21960. (gr. 1-8). 1995. write for info. (*0-531-06874-9*); pap. write for info. (*0-531-08724-7*) Orchard Bks Watts.
McEwan, Ian. The Daydreamer. Browne, Anthony, illus. LC 93-44476. 128p. (gr. 5 up). 1994. 14.00 (*0-06-024426-7*); PLB 13.89 (*0-06-024427-5*) HarpC Child Bks.
McKay, Hilary. The Exiles at Home. LC 94-14225. (gr. 4-7). 1994. 15.95 (*0-689-50610-4*, M K McElderry) Macmillan Child Grp.
McKean, Thomas. Secret of the Seven Willows. LC 91-4447. 160p. 1991. pap. 12.95 3-pc. bdg. (*0-671-72997-7*) S&S Trade.
McKenna, Colleen O. Mother Murphy. 160p. (gr. 4-7). 1993. 13.95 (*0-590-44820-X*, Scholastic Hardcover); pap. 3.25 (*0-590-44856-0*, Scholastic Hardcover) Scholastic Inc.
—Too Many Murphys. 144p. (gr. 3-7). 1988. pap. 13.95 (*0-590-41731-2*, Pub. by Scholastic Hardcover) Scholastic Inc.
McKissack. One Family's Story. 1993. 19.95 (*0-8050-1671-6*) H Holt & Co.
MacLachlan, Patricia. Sarah, Plain & Tall. LC 83-49481. 64p. (gr. 3-5). 1985. 12.00 (*0-06-024101-2*); PLB 11.89 (*0-06-024102-0*) HarpC Child Bks.
—Seven Kisses in a Row. Marella, Maria P., illus. LC 82-47718. 64p. (gr. 2-5). 1983. PLB 12.89 (*0-06-024084-9*) HarpC Child Bks.
McPhail, David. Fix-It. (Illus.). 24p. (ps-k). 1993. pap. 17.99 (*0-14-054931-5*, Puff Unicorn) Puffin Bks.
—Sisters. LC 84-3775. (Illus.). 32p. (ps-3). 1984. 12.95 (*0-15-275319-2*, HB Juv Bks) HarBrace.
Marino, Jan. Eighty-Eight Steps to September. 160p. (gr. 3-7). 1991. pap. 2.95 (*0-380-71001-3*, Camelot) Avon.
Markus, Julia. Uncle. 1987. pap. 3.95 (*0-440-39187-3*, LE) Dell.
Marron, Carol A. Just One of the Family. (ps-3). 1993. pap. 4.95 (*0-8114-8404-1*) Raintree Steck-V.
Marshall, James. George & Martha. LC 74-184250. (Illus.). 48p. (gr. k-3). 1974. pap. 4.80 (*0-395-19972-7*, Sandpiper) HM.
—George & Martha Back in Town. Marshall, James, illus. LC 83-22842. 32p. (gr. k-3). 1984. 14.45 (*0-395-35386-6*, 5-90939); pap. 3.95 (*0-685-07886-8*) HM.

Marshall, Linda D. What Is a Step? Marshall, Linda D. & Johnson, Daphane, illus. LC 91-67511. 48p. (Orig.). (ps-5). 1992. pap. 8.00 (*1-879289-00-8*) Native Sun Pubs. "If you are looking for a mind-strengthening fun gift to get a special little one..., then we recommend Linda D. Marshall's WHAT IS A STEP? Our children are faced with the reality of such unfortunate words as 'bastard,' 'half-brother,' 'half-sister,' 'separation,' 'divorce,' & the like; & they need a way out of the confusion & sickness produced by the manifestations of those terms. This is especially true for children of Afrikan descent whose LONGER historical & cultural reality preclude such terms. Told with good humor, maternal caring, & a child's splendid wonder, WHAT IS A STEP? is a book useful to all parents who read to & communicate with their young." - THE RICHMOND NEWS LEADER. To be sure, here is a children's book whose integrity is not compromised by both its widespread & its specific appeal: it has mainstream, multicultural, & Afrikan-centered relevance, all genuine as the warm adults & enthusiastic children who will enjoy & learn from this story of Whobee & his family. Indeed, once we open this book's bright seven-color covers, we will learn how Whobee's overhearing his mother on the phone confuses him, the lessons he will learn, & the nature of his summer's special gift to him. A book of life-long value. *Publisher Provided Annotation.*

Martin, Ann M. Eleven Kids, One Summer. LC 91-55025. 160p. (gr. 3-7). 1991. 14.95 (*0-8234-0912-0*) Holiday.
—Kristy & the Walking Disaster. large type ed. 176p. (gr. 4 up). 1993. PLB 15.93 (*0-8368-1024-4*) Gareth Stevens Inc.

—Little Miss Stoneybrook-- & Dawn. large type ed. LC 93-8100. 176p. (gr. 4 up). 1993. PLB 15.93 (*0-8368-1019-8*) Gareth Stevens Inc.

—Me & Katie (the Pest) Sims, Blanche, illus. LC 85-5558. 160p. (gr. 4-7). 1985. 13.95 (*0-8234-0580-X*) Holiday.

—Me & Katie the Pest. 1990. pap. 2.95 (*0-590-43618-X*) Scholastic Inc.

—Ten Kids, No Pets. LC 87-25206. 184p. (gr. 3-7). 1988. 14.95 (*0-8234-0691-1*) Holiday.

Marvin, Isabel R. Josefina & the Hanging Tree. LC 91-34501. 128p. (gr. 6-9). 1992. pap. 9.95 (*0-87565-103-8*) Tex Christian.

Marx, Trish. Hanna's Cold Winter. Knutson, Barbara, illus. LC 92-27143. 1993. 18.95 (*0-87614-772-4*) Carolrhoda Bks.

Marzollo, Jean. Uproar on Holler Cat Hill. Kellogg, Steven, illus. LC 79-22201. (ps-2). 1981. Dial Bks Young.

Masterton, David S. Get Out of My Face. LC 90-24096. 160p. (gr. 5-9). 1991. SBE 13.95 (*0-689-31675-5*, Atheneum Child Bk) Macmillan Child Grp.

Mathis, Sharon B. The Hundred-Penny Box. Dillon, Leo D., ed. Dillon, Diane, illus. 48p. (gr. k-3). 1975. pap. 15.00 (*0-670-38787-8*) Viking Child Bks.

Maury, Inez. My Mother & I Are Growing Strong. (SPA & ENG., Illus.). (ps-4). 1978. 6.95 (*0-938678-06-X*) New Seed.

Mayer, Gina & Mayer, Mercer. This Is My Family. (Illus.). 24p. (ps-k). 1992. write for info. (*0-307-00137-7*, 312-02, Golden Pr) Western Pub.

Mearian, Judy F. Two Ways About It. LC 79-10029. (gr. 5 up). 1985. Dial Bks Young.

Meddaugh, Susan. Beast Pa. (ps-3). 1985. pap. 5.95 (*0-395-38366-8*) HM.

Metzger, Lois. Barry's Sister. LC 93-7760. 240p. (gr. 5 up). 1993. pap. 4.50 (*0-14-036484-6*, Puffin) Puffin Bks.

Meyer, Carolyn. Killing the Kudu. LC 90-6089. 208p. (gr. 9 up). 1990. SBE 14.95 (*0-689-50508-6*, M K McElderry) Macmillan Child Grp.

Miklowitz, Gloria D. Suddenly Super Rich. (gr. 7 up). 1989. 13.95 (*0-553-05845-2*, Starfire) Bantam.

Miller, Mary J. Upside Down. 128p. (gr. 3-7). 1992. 13.00 (*0-670-83648-6*) Viking Child Bks.

Miller, Mary Jane. Me & My Name. (gr. 4-7). 1990. 11.95 (*0-670-83196-4*) Viking Child Bks.

Milstein, Linda B. Miami-Nanny Stories. Han, Oki, illus. LC 93-28680. 1994. 16.00 (*0-688-11151-3*, Tambourine Bks); PLB 15.93 (*0-688-11152-1*, Tambourine Bks) Morrow.

Mitchell, Greg. Simply Sam. Ridgeway, Jo A., illus. LC 92-21452. 1993. 3.75 (*0-383-03652-6*) SRA Schl Grp.

Mohr, Nicholasa. Felita. Cruz, Ray, illus. LC 79-50149. (gr. 3-6). 1979. Dial Bks Young.

—Going Home. (gr. 4-7). 1989. pap. 3.99 (*0-553-15699-3*, Skylark) Bantam.

Moncure, Jane B. I Never Say I'm Thankful, But I Am. Hook, Frances, illus. LC 78-21577. (ps-2). 1979. PLB 14.95 (*0-89565-023-1*) Childs World.

Montgomery, Lucy M., text by. The Avonlea Album. (Illus.). 72p. 1991. PLB 16.95 (*0-920668-96-8*); pap. 9.95 (*0-920668-97-6*) Firefly Bks Ltd.

Moore, Peggy S. The Case of the Missing Bike & Other Things. 2nd, rev. ed. Adome, Afua, illus. 40p. (Orig.). (gr. 4-6). 1992. pap. 5.95 (*0-9613078-1-1*) Detroit Black.

Morgan, Mary, illus. Guess Who I Love? 18p. (ps). 1992. bds. 2.95 (*0-448-40313-7*) Putnam Pub Group.

Muchmore, Jo Ann. Johnny Rides Again. LC 94-19466. 1995. write for info. (*0-8234-1156-7*) Holiday.

Munsil, Ritchie. Dinner at Auntie Rose's. (Illus.). 24p. (ps-8). 1984. 12.95 (*0-920236-66-9*, Pub. by Annick CN); pap. 4.95 (*0-920236-63-4*, Pub. by Annick CN) Firefly Bks Ltd.

Murrow, Liza K. Allergic to My Family. LC 91-31529. (Illus.). 160p. (gr. 2-6). 1992. 13.95 (*0-8234-0959-7*) Holiday.

Napoli, Donna J. When the Water Closes over My Head. Poydar, Nancy, illus. LC 93-14486. 60p. (gr. 2-5). 1994. 13.99 (*0-525-45083-1*) Dutton Child Bks.

Naylor, Phyllis R. Alice in April. LC 92-17016. 176p. (gr. 4-8). 1993. SBE 14.95 (*0-689-31805-7*, Atheneum Child Bk) Macmillan Child Grp.

—Alice In-Between. LC 93-8167. 160p. (gr. 5-9). 1994. SBE 14.95 (*0-689-31890-1*, Atheneum Child Bk) Macmillan Child Grp.

—Send No Blessings. LC 89-28024. 240p. (gr. 7 up). 1990. SBE 14.95 (*0-689-31582-1*, Atheneum Child Bk) Macmillan Child Grp.

—Send No Blessings. 240p. (gr. 5 up). 1992. pap. 3.99 (*0-14-034859-X*) Puffin Bks.

Nesbit, Edith. The Five Children & It. (gr. 4-6). 1986. pap. 3.50 (*0-440-42586-7*, Pub. by Yearling Classics) Dell.

—The Railway Children. 1993. 12.95 (*0-679-42534-9*, Everymans Lib) Knopf.

—Railway Children. (gr. 4 up). 1993. pap. 3.25 (*0-553-21415-2*, Bantam Classics) Bantam.

Nesbit, Jeffrey A. The Reluctant Runaway. 120p. 1991. pap. 4.99 (*0-89693-131-5*) SP Pubns.

Newberger, Devra. Full House Family Scrapbook. (gr. 4-7). 1992. pap. 3.95 (*0-590-45706-3*) Scholastic Inc.

Newton, Jill. Don't Sit There! LC 93-23538. (Illus.). 1994. 15.00 (*0-688-13309-6*) Lothrop.

Nicholson, Peggy & Warner, John F. The Case of the Squeaky Thief. 120p. (gr. 4-7). 1994. RTB 14.95 (*0-8225-0711-0*) Lerner Pubns.

Nielsen, Shelly. Take a Bow, Victoria. LC 86-8818. 130p. (gr. 3-7). 1986. pap. 4.99 (*0-89191-470-6*, Chariot Bks) Chariot Family.

Novak, Matt. Mouse TV. LC 93-49399. (Illus.). 32p. (ps-1). 1994. 14.95 (*0-531-06856-0*); PLB 14.99 (*0-531-08706-9*) Orchard Bks Watts.

Nystrom, Carolyn. Mike's Lonely Summer. Baum, Ann, illus. 48p. (gr. 1-6). 1986. 7.99 (*0-7459-1016-5*) Lion USA.

Oden, Fay G. Where Is Calvin? (Illus.). 48p. (Orig.). (gr. 2-6). 1994. pap. text ed. 6.95 (*0-9638946-0-9*) Tennedo Pubs. Fay Giles Oden is a retired elementary school teacher, fiction writer, editor, illustrator & poet. Her recently published short fiction (child's book) is WHERE IS CALVIN? (Tennedo, $6. 95). Mrs. Oden received motivation for the story WHERE IS CALVIN? after visiting the zoo. (Summer 1993). The story deals with respect for family life & a child's infatuation with animals. It is a simple story of friendship & entrancement with the animals that somehow caused the boys to become separated. The suspense of the boys' day at the zoo overwhelms you as the animals have been intentionally personified to talk to the boys. They become boys with a mission to find their friend Calvin. The plot is simple. The characters are believable. The narrative techniques of the story skillfully blends literature with poetry. The suspenseful, vivid & colorful story will delight young readers. In short, WHERE IS CALVIN? is a charming story with sympathetic characters. Children will love the humor of it all. You'll be surprised to find out what really happened to Calvin. The book lends itself to a READ-ME-A-STORY book. Child care centers have expressed an interest in the book. WHERE IS CALVIN? can be ordered from the following distributors: Baker & Taylor, 501 South Gladiolus Street, Momence, IL 60954-1799; Tennedo Publishers, 6315 Elwynne Drive, Cincinnati, OH 45236, 1-513-791-3277. Fay Oden is also the author of: CALVIN & HIS VIDEO CAMERA. *Publisher Provided Annotation.*

Osofsky, Audrey. Dreamcatcher. Young, Ed, illus. LC 91-20029. 32p. (ps-2). 1992. 14.95 (*0-531-05988-X*); lib. bdg. 14.99 (*0-531-08588-0*) Orchard Bks Watts.

Palangi, Paula. Last Straw. LC 91-44346. (ps-3). 1992. pap. 9.99 (*0-7814-0562-9*, Chariot Bks) Chariot Family.

Paley, Nina, illus. What about Me? LC 93-8955. 1993. write for info. (*1-56071-314-3*) ETR Assocs.

Papagapitos, Karen. Jose's Basket. 1993. 6.95 (*0-9637328-1-1*) Kapa Hse Pr. JOSE'S BASKET is a touching portrayal of a family forced to be always on the move. Luis & Socorro Vasquez are migrant farm workers, who follow whatever crops need to be harvested. This continuous change of surrounding is very difficult on their four children. The parents try to make the transitions easier by anticipating all the new & exciting things that are sure to be waiting for them at the next stop. At one particular town, in Arizona, eight-year-old Jose (an excellent student & gifted writer) finds a school he never wants to leave. Of course, there does come a time when he must leave this new place & his wonderful teacher, Mrs. Ortega. By learning to piece together his adventures in every new place, much like his mother weaves reeds & grasses from the desert into her special basket (the grasses come from each place in which they pick crops), Jose is able to find the courage he needs to move on & stay in school. JOSE'S BASKET has been placed in the U.S. Department of Education's Library. Distributed by Baker & Taylor Books, 652 East Main St./P.O. Box 6920, Bridgewater, NJ 08807-0920. *Publisher Provided Annotation.*

—Socorro, Daughter of the Desert. Kleinman, Estelle, ed. Collete, Rondi, illus. 64p. (gr. 1-4). 1993. 6.95 (*0-9637328-0-3*) Kapa Hse Pr. SOCORRO, DAUGHTER OF THE DESERT is the story of a young girl who knows the answer to a mystery that nobody else seems to see. It is through the eyes of Socorro Hernandez that we find out who the mysterious phantom of the desert road is & why he wants to warn people of any danger that might lie in their path. Socorro's family is going through a difficult period at the same time, & through this young girl's hard work & perseverance, they manage to weather the father's bout with malaria. This book profiles the resourcefulness, courage, & hope women historically have exhibited in trying times. Young readers should enjoy the several appearances of the mysterious phantom & still come away from the conclusion with a strong respect for women & their strength in an often unsettled world. Distributed by Baker & Taylor Books, 652 E. Main St., P.O. Box 6920, Bridgewater, NJ 08807-0920; 908-218-0400. *Publisher Provided Annotation.*

Parish, Peggy. Amelia Bedelia's Family Album. 48p. 1989. pap. 5.95 (*0-380-70760-8*, Camelot) Avon.

Park, Barbara. My Mother Got Married: (And Other Disasters) LC 88-27257. 128p. (gr. 3-7). 1989. lib. bdg. 13.99 (*0-394-92149-6*) Knopf Bks Yng Read.

Pascal, Francine. Cousin Kelly's Family Secret. (ps-3). 1991. pap. 2.99 (*0-553-15920-8*) Bantam.

—The Parent Plot. 1990. pap. 3.50 (*0-553-28611-0*) Bantam.

Paton Walsh, Jill. Goldengrove. LC 72-81484. 130p. (gr. 6 up). 1985. pap. 3.50 (*0-374-42587-6*, Sunburst) FS&G.

Pearce, Philippa. Here Comes Tod! Gon, Adriano, illus. LC 93-20026. 96p. (gr. k-3). 1994. 14.95 (*1-56402-328-1*) Candlewick Pr.

Pearson, Gayle. The Fog Doggies & Me. LC 92-41069. 128p. (gr. 4-8). 1993. SBE 13.95 (*0-689-31845-6*, Atheneum Child Bk) Macmillan Child Grp.

—One Potato, Tu: Seven Stories. LC 91-22307. 128p. (gr. 5-9). 1992. SBE 13.95 (*0-689-31706-9*, Atheneum Child Bk) Macmillan Child Grp.

Peck, Richard. The Last Safe Place on Earth. LC 94-446. 1995. 15.95 (*0-385-32052-3*) Delacorte.

Perkins, Mitali. The Sunita Experiment. LC 92-37267. 144p. (gr. 1-6). 1993. 14.95 (*0-316-69943-8*, Joy St Bks) Little.

—The Sunita Experiment. LC 93-28525. 192p. (gr. 5-9). 1994. pap. 4.50 (*1-56282-671-9*) Hyprn Ppbks.

Peterson, P. J. Some Days, Other Days. LC 93-3871. (gr. k-2). 1994. 14.95 (*0-684-19595-X*, Scribner) Macmillan.

Peyton, K. M. Darkling. 1990. 14.95 (*0-385-30086-7*) Doubleday.

Pfeffer, Susan B. Family of Strangers. 1992. 16.00 (*0-553-08364-3*) Bantam.

—Twice Taken. LC 93-39010. 1994. 14.95 (*0-385-32033-7*) Delacorte.

—Twin Troubles. Carter, Abby, illus. LC 92-5773. 1992. 14.95 (*0-8050-2146-9*, Redfeather BYR) H Holt & Co.

Platt, Kin. Crocker. LC 82-48456. 128p. (gr. 7 up). 1983. (Lipp Jr Bks) HarpC Child Bks.

Porte, Barbara A. I Only Made up the Roses. LC 86-18307. 128p. (gr. 7 up). 1987. reinforced 14.00 (*0-688-05216-9*) Greenwillow.

—Taxicab Tales. Abolafia, Yossi, illus. LC 90-24609. 56p. 1992. 13.00 (*0-688-09908-4*) Greenwillow.

—When Aunt Lucy Rode A Mule & Other Stories. Chambliss, Maxie, illus. LC 93-4874. 32p. (gr. k-2). 1994. 15.95 (*0-531-06816-1*); PLB 15.99 (*0-531-08666-6*) Orchard Bks Watts.

—When Grandma Almost Fell off the Mountain & Other Stories. Chambliss, Maxie, illus. LC 91-41174. 32p. (ps-2). 1993. 14.95 (*0-531-05965-0*); PLB 14.99 (*0-531-08565-1*) Orchard Bks Watts.

Pryor, Bonnie. Horses in the Garage. LC 92-7287. 160p. (gr. 4 up). 1992. 14.00 (*0-688-10567-X*) Morrow Jr Bks.

—Jumping Jenny. Riggio, Anita, illus. 192p. (gr. 2 up). 1992. 14.00 (*0-688-09684-0*) Morrow Jr Bks.

—The Plum Tree War. Leder, Dora, illus. LC 88-32426. 128p. (gr. 3-6). 1989. 11.95 (*0-688-08142-8*) Morrow Jr Bks.

—Poison Ivy & Eyebrow Wigs. Owens, Gail, illus. LC 92-38881. 176p. (gr. 3 up). 1993. 14.00 (*0-688-11200-5*) Morrow Jr Bks.

—Vinegar Pancakes & Vanishing Cream. Owens, Gail, illus. LC 86-31085. 128p. (gr. 2-5). 1987. 12.95 (*0-688-06728-X*) Morrow Jr Bks.

Pullman, Philip. The Broken Bridge. LC 91-15893. 256p. (gr. 7 up). 1992. 15.00 (*0-679-81972-X*); PLB 15.99 (*0-679-91972-4*) Knopf Bks Yng Read.

Qualey, Marsha. Revolutions of the Heart. LC 92-24528. 192p. (gr. 6 up). 1993. 13.45 (*0-395-64168-3*) HM.

Quindlen, Anna. The Tree That Came to Stay. Carpenter, Nancy, illus. LC 91-31957. 32p. (ps-4). 1992. 14.00 (*0-517-58145-0*) Crown Bks Yng Read.

Ransom, Candice. Third Grade Detectives. LC 93-48920. (Illus.). 128p. (gr. 2-4). 1994. PLB 9.89 (*0-8167-2992-1*); pap. 2.95 (*0-8167-2993-X*) Troll Assocs.

Ransom, Candice F. We're Growing Together. Wright-Frierson, Virginia, illus. LC 92-7424. 32p. (ps-2). 1993. RSBE 14.95 (*0-02-775666-1*, Bradbury Pr) Macmillan Child Grp.

—Why Are Boys So Weird? LC 93-6222. (Illus.). 128p. (gr. 2-6). 1994. PLB 9.89 (*0-8167-2990-5*); pap. text ed. 2.95 (*0-8167-2991-3*) Troll Assocs.

Raskin, Ellen. Figgs & Phantoms. Raskin, Ellen, illus. LC 73-17309. 160p. (gr. 4 up). 1977. pap. 15.95 (*0-525-29680-8*, 01063-320, DCB); (DCB) Dutton Child Bks.

Rattigan, Jama K. Dumpling Soup. Hsu-Flanders, Lillian, illus. 32p. (gr. 4-8). 1993. 15.95 (*0-316-73445-4*) Little.

Rayner, Mary. Garth Pig Steals the Show. Rayner, Mary, illus. LC 92-24508. (ps-3). 1993. 13.99 (*0-525-45023-8*, DCB) Dutton Child Bks.

Reiss, Kathryn. The Glass House People. 1992. 16.95 (*0-15-231040-1*, HB Juv Bks) HarBrace.

Repp, Gloria. The Stolen Years. 152p. (Orig.). (gr. 9-12). 1989. pap. 4.95 (*0-89084-481-X*) Bob Jones Univ Pr.

Reynolds, Phyllis. The Keeper. 192p. (gr. 6 up). 1987. pap. 2.95 (*0-553-26882-1*, Starfire) Bantam.

Riecken, Nancy. Andrew's Own Place. Aubrey, Meg K., illus. LC 92-22953. 1993. 14.95 (*0-395-64723-1*) HM.

Riley, Jocelyn. Only My Mouth Is Smiling. LC 81-18688. 224p. (gr. 7-9). 1982. 12.95 (*0-688-01087-3*) Morrow Jr Bks.

Rinaldi, Ann. A Stitch in Time. 304p. (gr. 7 up). 1994. 13.95 (*0-590-46055-2*, Scholastic Hardcover) Scholastic Inc.

—A Stitch in Time. LC 93-8964. 1994. 13.95 (*0-590-46056-0*) Scholastic Inc.

Ringgold, Faith. Dinner at Aunt Connie's House. Ringgold, Faith, illus. LC 92-54871. 32p. (gr. 1-4). 1993. 14.95 (*1-56282-425-2*); PLB 14.89 (*1-56282-426-0*) Hyprn Child.

Roberts, Willo D. Megan's Island. LC 87-17505. 192p. (gr. 3-7). 1988. SBE 14.95 (*0-689-31397-7*, Atheneum Child Bk) Macmillan Child Grp.

—Megan's Island. LC 89-18457. 192p. (gr. 4-7). 1990. pap. 3.95 (*0-689-71387-8*, Aladdin) Macmillan Child Grp.

Robinson, Barbara. My Brother Louis Measures Worms: And Other Louis Stories. LC 87-45302. 160p. (gr. 3-7). 1988. PLB 13.89 (*0-06-025083-6*) HarpC Child Bks.

Robinson, Nancy K. Angela & the Broken Heart. 1991. 12.95 (*0-590-43212-5*, Scholastic Hardcover) Scholastic Inc.

—Angela & the Broken Heart. 144p. 1992. pap. 2.95 (*0-590-43211-7*, Apple Paperbacks) Scholastic Inc.

—Angela, Private Citizen. LC 89-5918. 146p. (gr. 3-6). 1989. pap. 10.95 (*0-590-41726-6*) Scholastic Inc.

—Just Plain Cat. LC 82-18258. 128p. (gr. 3-6). 1984. SBE 13.95 (*0-02-777350-7*, Four Winds) Macmillan Child Grp.

Rodriguez, Gina M. Green Corn Tamales - Tamales de Elote. (SPA & ENG., Illus.). 40p. 1994. 14.95 (*0-938243-00-4*) Hispanic Bk Dist.

Rogers, Paul & Rogers, Emma. Our House. Lamont, Priscilla, illus. LC 92-53015. 40p. (ps up). 1993. 14.95 (*1-56402-134-3*) Candlewick Pr.

Rylant, Cynthia. A Blue-Eyed Daisy. LC 84-21554. 112p. (gr. 5-7). 1985. SBE 13.95 (*0-02-777960-2*, Bradbury Pr) Macmillan Child Grp.

—The Relatives Came. Gammell, Stephen, illus. LC 85-10929. 32p. (ps-2). 1985. RSBE 14.95 (*0-02-777220-9*, Bradbury Pr) Macmillan Child Grp.

—The Relatives Came. Gammell, Stephen, illus. LC 92-41394. 32p. (ps-2). 1993. pap. 4.95 (*0-689-71738-5*, Aladdin) Macmillan Child Grp.

Sachs, Marilyn. Baby Sister. 160p. 1987. pap. 3.50 (*0-380-70358-0*, Flare) Avon.

St. John, Patricia. Where the River Begins. LC 80-12304. 128p. (Orig.). (gr. 5-8). pap. 4.50 (*0-8024-8124-8*) Moody.

Salem, Lynn & Stewart, Josie. Notes from Mom. (Illus.). 16p. (ps-2). 1992. pap. 3.50 (*1-880612-01-1*) Seedling Pubns.
This book is part of the SEEDLINGS SERIES, designed by primary educators to meet the needs of young readers who are beyond board books, but not quite ready for independent readers or early chapter books. Other delightful titles include: WHAT'S FOR DINNER?, THE CAT WHO LOVED RED, MY PET, STAYING WITH GRANDMA NORMA, & WHAT A SCHOOL. These 8, 12 & 16 page books range from 14 to 164 words. For preschoolers, just starting to explore print, to young readers needing many opportunities to practice, these books are the perfect building blocks. This series includes a beautifully illustrated display with 56 books (4 copies of 14 different titles). The floor model display stands 20" high & has cubbies holding multiple copies of each title. Identical unit also available in a tabletop version. "...early readers find them fun & luring. Children are sure to enjoy the easy text & superb drawings. "--Children's Librarian. Display unit (table-top or floor) & 56 books...$229. 00, plus 8% shipping. Add-on packs (5 additional titles, 4 copies/each) $70.00, plus shipping. ISBN 1-880612-33-X (floor display/series), ISBN 1-880612-34-8 (table top display/series) Seedling Publications, Inc., 4097 Overlook Drive East, Columbus, OH 43214-2931. Phone & FAX 614-451-2412. *Publisher Provided Annotation.*

Sandin, Joan. The Long Way to a New Land. Sandin, Joan, illus. LC 80-8942. 64p. (gr. k-3). 1986. pap. 3.50 (*0-06-444100-8*, Trophy) HarpC Child Bks.

Saunders, Susan. Stephanie's Family Secret. 1989. pap. 2.50 (*0-590-41845-9*) Scholastic Inc.

Savage, Cindy. The Popularity Secret. 112p. (gr. 5-8). 1988. 2.75 (*0-87406-315-9*, 37-16478-9) Willowisp Pr.

Schneider, Rex. That's Not All! Gregorich, Barbara, ed. (Illus.). 16p. (Orig.). (gr. k-2). 1985. pap. 2.25 (*0-88743-019-8*, 06019) Sch Zone Pub Co.

Schultz, Betty K. Morn of Mystery. (Illus., Orig.). (gr. 3-5). 1991. pap. write for info. (*0-929568-02-8*) Raspberry IL.

Segal, Lore. Tell Me a Mitzi. Pincus, Harriet, illus. LC 69-14980. 40p. (ps-3). 1982. 17.00 (*0-374-37392-2*) FS&G.

—Tell Me a Trudy. Wells, Rosemary, illus. LC 77-24123. 40p. (ps-3). 1977. 15.00 (*0-374-37395-7*) FS&G.

Seredy, Kate. The Good Master. (Illus.). 196p. (gr. 5-9). 1986. pap. 4.95 (*0-14-030133-X*, Puffin) Puffin Bks.

Sharmat, Marjorie W. Get Rich Mitch! 96p. (gr. 3-7). 1986. pap. 2.50 (*0-380-70170-7*, Camelot) Avon.

—Mitchell Is Moving. Aruego, Jose & Dewey, Ariane, illus. LC 78-6816. 48p. (gr. 1-4). 1978. RSBE 11.95 (*0-02-782410-1*, Macmillan Child Bk) Macmillan Child Grp.

Shevrin, Aliza, selected by. & tr. from YID. Around the Table: Family Stories of Sholom Aleichem. Gowing, Toby, illus. LC 90-49273. 96p. (gr. 5-8). 1991. SBE 12.95 (*0-684-19237-3*, Scribners Young Read) Macmillan Child Grp.

Shreve, Susan. Wait for Me. De Groat, Diane, illus. LC 91-30233. 112p. (gr. 3 up). 1992. 13.00 (*0-688-11120-3*, Tambourine Bks) Morrow.

Shreve, Susan R. The Bad Dreams of a Good Girl. DeGroat, Diane, illus. LC 92-24593. 96p. (gr. 4 up). 1993. pap. 3.95 (*0-688-12113-6*, Pub. by Beech Tree Bks) Morrow.

Silverman, Maida. The Glass Menorah & Other Stories for Jewish Holidays. Levine, Marge, illus. LC 91-13890. 64p. (gr. 1-4). 1992. RSBE 14.95 (*0-02-782682-1*, Four Winds) Macmillan Child Grp.

Simon, Shirley. Get Lost, Becka! Gregorich, Barbara, ed. (Illus.). 16p. (Orig.). (gr. k-2). 1985. pap. 2.25 (*0-88743-013-9*, 06013) Sch Zone Pub Co.

Sleator, William. Oddballs. LC 92-27666. (gr. 7 up). 1993. 14.99 (*0-525-45057-2*, DCB) Dutton Child Bks.

Smalls-Hector, Irene. Dawn & the Round-to-It. Geter, Tyrone, illus. LC 93-19731. 1994. pap. 15.00 (*0-671-87166-8*, S&S BFYR) S&S Trade.

Smath, Jerry. Pretzel & Pop's Closetful of Stories. Smath, Jerry, illus. 64p. (gr. 1-3). 1991. 5.95 (*0-671-72232-8*); PLB 7.95 (*0-671-72231-X*) Silver Pr.

Smith, Barbara A. Somewhere Just Beyond. LC 93-14672. 96p. (gr. 3-7). 1993. SBE 12.95 (*0-689-31877-4*, Atheneum Child Bk) Macmillan Child Grp.

Smith, Doris B. The First Hard Times. (gr. 4 up). 1990. pap. 3.95 (*0-14-034538-8*, Puffin) Puffin Bks.

Smith, Jane D. And Baby & Kitty & Mommy & Daddy. (ps). 1994. 9.95 (*1-56305-668-2*) Workman Pub.

Smith, Lane. The Happy Hocky Family. Smith, Lane, illus. 64p. (ps-3). 1993. reinforced bdg. 13.99 (*0-670-85206-6*) Viking Child Bks.

Smith, Robert K. The War with Grandpa. Lauter, Richard, illus. LC 83-14366. 128p. (gr. 4-8). 1984. pap. 12.95 (*0-385-29314-3*) Delacorte.

Smothers, Ethel F. Down in the Piney Woods. LC 91-328. 144p. (gr. 5-9). 1992. 14.00 (*0-679-80360-2*); PLB 14.99 (*0-679-90360-7*) Knopf Bks Yng Read.

Smothers, Thelma W. Sweet Savannah. Pitt, Jo J. & Lumpkins, Debbie B., eds. 219p. (gr. 8 up). 1994. PLB 20.00 (*1-882188-06-3*) Magnolia Mktg.

Snyder, Carol. Dear Mom & Dad, Don't Worry. 1993. pap. 3.50 (*0-553-29646-9*) Bantam.

Snyder, Zilpha K. Cat Running. LC 94-447. 1994. 14.95 (*0-385-31056-0*) Delacorte.

Soto, Gary. The Pool Party. Casilla, Robert, illus. LC 92-34407. 1993. 13.95 (*0-385-30890-6*) Delacorte.

Speregen, Devra. Blossom's Family Album. (gr. 4-7). 1993. pap. 4.95 (*0-590-47234-8*) Scholastic Inc.

Spinelli, Jerry. Who Put That Hair in My Toothbrush? LC 83-20716. (gr. 5-9). 1984. 15.95 (*0-316-80712-5*) Little.

—Who Put That Hair in My Toothbrush? (gr. 5-9). 1986. pap. 3.50 (*0-440-99485-3*, LFL) Dell.

Springer, Nancy. Not on a White Horse. LC 87-3477. 192p. (gr. 5 up). 1988. SBE 14.95 (*0-689-31366-7*, Atheneum Child Bk) Macmillan Child Grp.

Stahl, Hilda. Daisy Punkin: Meet Daisy Punkin. 128p. (gr. 2-5). 1991. pap. 4.99 (*0-89107-617-4*) Crossway Bks.

—Elizabeth Gail & the Secret of the Gold Charm, No. 21. (gr. 4-7). 1992. pap. 4.99 (*0-8423-0817-2*) Tyndale.

—Sadie Rose & the Double Secret. LC 89-25423. 124p. (gr. 4-7). 1990. pap. 4.99 (*0-89107-546-1*) Crossway Bks.

Stanek, Muriel. I Won't Go Without a Father. Mill, Eleanor, illus. LC 78-188435. 32p. (gr. 1-3). 1972. PLB 11.95 (*0-8075-3524-9*) A Whitman.

Starkman, Neal. The Quitters. Combs, Jonathan, illus. LC 91-16797. 28p. (Orig.). (gr. 4). 1991. pap. 7.00 (*0-935529-26-8*) Comprehen Health Educ.

Stevenson, James. When I Was Nine. Stevenson, James, illus. LC 85-9777. 32p. (gr. k-3). 1986. 14.00 (*0-688-05942-2*); PLB 13.93 (*0-688-05943-0*) Greenwillow.

Stevenson, Ralph L., Jr. Sam's Stamp Store. Wolgamott, Elizabeth, illus. O'Neil, Greg, intro. by. (Illus.). 28p. (Orig.). (ps-2). 1983. pap. 3.50 (*0-9610762-0-8*) Sirius Leag.

Stevenson, Robert Louis. Reader's Digest Best Loved Books for Young Re`ders: Kidnapped - The Adventures of David Balfour. Ogburn, Jackie, ed. Wyeth, N. C., illus. 136p. (gr. 4-12). 1989. 3.99 (*0-945260-32-6*) Choice Pub NY.

Stolz, Mary. Go & Catch a Flying Fish. LC 78-21785. 224p. (gr. 5 up). 1992. pap. 3.95 (*0-06-447090-3*, Trophy) HarpC Child Bks.

Strasser, Todd. Turn It Up! (gr. 6-12). 1985. pap. 2.50 (*0-440-99059-9*, LFL) Dell.

Sumiko. My Summer Vacation. Sumiko, illus. LC 89-43164. 32p. (Orig.). (ps-1). 1993. pap. 2.25 (*0-679-80525-7*) Random Bks Yng Read.

Sutton, Elizabeth H. Racing for Keeneland. LC 93-43385. (gr. 5-12). 1994. 14.95 (*1-56566-051-X*) Thomasson-Grant.

Sweeney, Joyce. The Dream Collector. (gr. 7 up). 1989. 14.95 (*0-385-29813-7*) Delacorte.

—The Tiger Orchard. 1993. 15.00 (*0-385-30841-8*) Doubleday.

Tate, Eleanore E. A Blessing in Disguise. LC 94-13073. 1995. 14.95 (*0-385-32103-1*) Delacorte.

Taylor, Sydney. All-of-a-Kind Family. John, Helen, illus. 192p. (gr. k-6). 1980. pap. 3.99 (*0-440-40059-7*, YB) Dell.

—All-of-a-Kind Family. John, Helen, illus. 189p. (gr. 3-6). 1988. Repr. of 1951 ed. 11.95 (*0-929093-00-3*) Taylor Prodns.

—All-of-a-Kind Family Downtown. 188p. (gr. k-6). 1973. pap. 3.50 (*0-440-42032-6*, YB) Dell.

—All-of-a-Kind Family Downtown. Krush, Beth & Krush, Joe, illus. 187p. 1988. Repr. of 1972 ed. 11.95 (*0-929093-01-1*) Taylor Prodns.

—All-of-a-Kind Family Uptown. Stevens, Mary, illus. 160p. 1988. Repr. of 1958 ed. 11.95 (*0-929093-03-8*) Taylor Prodns.

—Ella of All-of-a-Kind Family. Rosner, Meryl, illus. 133p. (gr. 4-8). 1988. Repr. of 1978 ed. 11.95 (*0-929093-04-6*) Taylor Prodns.

—More All-of-a-Kind Family. Stevens, Mary, illus. 160p. (gr. 3-6). 1988. Repr. of 1954 ed. 11.95 (*0-929093-02-X*) Taylor Prodns.

Taylor, William. Knitwits. 1992. 13.95 (*0-590-45778-0*, 022, Scholastic Hardcover) Scholastic Inc.

Terris, Susan. The Latchkey Kids. 167p. (gr. 5 up). 1986. 15.00 (*0-374-34363-2*) FS&G.
—No Scarlet Ribbons. LC 80-28501. 154p. (gr. 5 up). 1981. 14.00 (*0-374-35532-0*) FS&G.
Tester, Sylvia R. A Day of Surprises. Hook, Frances, illus. LC 78-23263. (ps-2). 1979. PLB 14.95 (*0-89565-022-3*) Childs World.
Thoene, Bodie. In My Father's House. 400p. (Orig.). 1992. pap. 11.99 (*1-55661-189-7*) Bethany Hse.
Thomas, Jane R. Lights on the River. Dooling, Michael, illus. LC 93-33636. 32p. (ps-3). 1994. 15.95 (*0-7868-0004-6*); PLB 15.89 (*0-7868-2003-9*) Hyprn Child.
Towne, Mary. Dive Through the Wave. LC 93-40999. (Illus.). 128p. (gr. 3-6). 1994. PLB 13.95 (*0-8167-3478-X*); pap. text ed. 2.95 (*0-8167-3479-8*) BrdgeWater.
The Trail on Which They Wept: The Story of a Cherokee Girl. 64p. (gr. 4-6). 1992. incl. jacket 5.95 (*0-382-24333-1*); lib. bdg. 7.95 (*0-382-24331-5*); pap. 3.95 (*0-382-24353-6*) Silver Burdett Pr.
Turner, Ann W. Dust for Dinner. 1995. 14.00 (*0-06-023376-1*); PLB 13.89 (*0-06-023377-X*) HarpC Child Bks.
Tusa, Tricia. The Family Reunion. 32p. 1993. 15.00 (*0-374-32268-6*) FS&G.
Uchida, Yoshiko. A Jar of Dreams. 2nd ed. LC 92-18803. 144p. (gr. 4-7). 1993. pap. 3.95 (*0-689-71672-9*, Aladdin) Macmillan Child Grp.
Ure, Jean. If It Weren't For Sebastian. LC 84-15568. 192p. (gr. 7 up). 1985. 14.95 (*0-385-29380-1*) Delacorte.
—If It Weren't for Sebastian. (gr. k-12). 1987. pap. 2.95 (*0-440-93996-8*, LFL) Dell.
Van Laan, Nancy. Possum Come A-Knocking. Booth, George, illus. LC 88-12751. 32p. (ps-3). 1990. PLB 14.99 (*0-394-92206-9*) Knopf Bks Yng Read.
Van Leeuwen, Jean. Going West. LC 90-20694. (Illus.). 48p. (ps-4). 1992. 15.00 (*0-8037-1027-5*); PLB 14.89 (*0-8037-1028-3*) Dial Bks Young.
—Oliver & Amanda & the Big Snow. Schweninger, Ann, illus. LC 93-48598. 1995. write for info. (*0-8037-1762-8*); lib. bdg. write for info. (*0-8037-1763-6*) Dial Bks Young.
—Tales of Amanda Pig. Schweninger, Ann, illus. LC 93-25615. (gr. k-3). 1994. pap. 3.25 (*0-14-036840-X*, Puffin) Puffin Bks.
Voigt, Cynthia. Homecoming. LC 80-36723. 320p. (gr. 5 up). 1981. SBE 15.95 (*0-689-30833-7*, Atheneum Child Bk) Macmillan Child Grp.
Waber, Bernard. Funny, Funny Lyle. Waber, Bernard, illus. LC 86-27772. 40p. (gr. k-3). 1987. 13.45 (*0-395-43619-2*) HM.
Waddell, Martin. Little Obie & the Kidnap. Lennox, Elsie, illus. LC 93-45959. 80p. (gr. 3-6). 1994. 14.95 (*1-56402-352-4*) Candlewick Pr.
Walker, Barbara M., ed. The Little House Diary. LC 84-48754. (Illus.). 160p. (ps up). 1985. pap. 9.95 (*0-06-446006-1*) HarpC Child Bks.
Wallace, Bill. True Friends. LC 94-6449. 160p. (gr. 4-6). 1994. 14.95 (*0-8234-1141-9*) Holiday.
Ward. I Am Eyes Ni Macho. 1993. pap. 28.67 (*0-590-71935-1*) Scholastic Inc.
Warner, Gertrude C. The Boxcar Children. (Illus.). 158p. 1992. Repr. PLB 14.95x (*0-89966-902-6*) Buccaneer Bks.
Watson, Wendy. Thanksgiving at Our House. Watson, Wendy, illus. 32p. (ps-1). 1991. 14.45 (*0-395-53626-X*, Clarion Bks) HM.
Watts, Margaret. Trouble with Hairgrow. Smith, Craig, illus. LC 93-26298. 1994. 4.25 (*0-383-03782-4*) SRA Schl Grp.
Waugh, Sylvia. The Mennyms. LC 93-15901. 216p. (gr. 5 up). 1994. 14.00 (*0-688-13070-4*) Greenwillow.
—Mennyms in the Wilderness. LC 94-6881. 1995. write for info. (*0-688-13820-9*) Greenwillow.
Wayland, April H. It's Not My Turn to Look for Grandma. Booth, George, illus. LC 93-7018. 1994. 15.00 (*0-679-84491-0*); lib. bdg. 15.99 (*0-679-94491-5*) Knopf.
Weiss, Monica. Birthday Cake Candles, Counting. Berlin, Rosemary, illus. LC 91-16033. 24p. (gr. k-2). 1992. PLB 10.59 (*0-8167-2496-2*); pap. text ed. 2.95 (*0-8167-2497-0*) Troll Assocs.
—Mmmm---Cookies! Simple Subtraction. Berlin, Rosemary, illus. LC 91-18648. 24p. (gr. k-2). 1992. PLB 10.59 (*0-8167-2486-5*); pap. text ed. 2.95 (*0-8167-2487-3*) Troll Assocs.
Wells, Rosemary. Unfortunately Harriet. Wells, Rosemary, illus. LC 76-181786. 32p. (ps-3). 1972. Dial Bks Young.
Werlin, Nancy. Are You Alone on Purpose? 1994. 14.95 (*0-395-67350-X*) HM.
Wesley, Mary. Haphazard House. LC 92-24590. 150p. (gr. 7 up). 1993. 22.80 (*0-87951-470-1*) Overlook Pr.
White, Timothy. Nearest Faraway Place. 1994. 22.50 (*0-8050-2266-X*) H Holt & Co.
Wickstrom, Lois. Oliver: A Story about Adoption. (Illus.). 32p. 1991. 14.95 (*0-9611872-5-5*) Our Child Pr.
Wiggin, Eric. Maggie's Homecoming. LC 93-27053. 1994. pap. 3.99 (*1-56507-134-4*) Harvest Hse.
Wiggin, Eric & Wiggin, Kate D. Rebecca of Sunnybrook Farm: The Girl. 256p. (gr. 4-7). 1990. 9.95 (*1-56121-004-8*) Wolgemuth & Hyatt.
Wilder, Laura I. The Deer in the Wood. Graef, Renee, illus. LC 94-18684. 1995. 15.00 (*0-06-024881-5*, Festival); PLB 14.89 (*0-06-024882-3*) HarpC Child Bks.
—Going to Town. Graef, Renee, illus. LC 92-46722. (gr. k-3). Date not set. 15.00 (*0-06-023012-6*); PLB 14.89 (*0-06-023013-4*) HarpC Child Bks.
Wilder, Laura Ingalls. Dance at Grandpa's. Graef, Renee, illus. LC 93-24535. 40p. (ps-3). 1994. 12.00 (*0-06-023878-X*); PLB 11.89 (*0-06-023879-8*) HarpC Child Bks.
—A Little House Christmas: Holiday Stories from the Little House Books. Williams, Garth, illus. LC 93-24537. 96p. (gr. 3-7). 1994. 18.95 (*0-06-024269-8*); PLB 18.89 (*0-06-024270-1*) HarpC Child Bks.
—Winter Days in the Big Woods. Graef, Renee, illus. LC 92-45883. 40p. (ps-3). 1994. 12.00 (*0-06-023014-2*); PLB 11.89 (*0-06-023022-3*) HarpC Child Bks.
Wilder, Laura Ingalls, adapted by. Christmas in the Big Woods. Graef, Renee, illus. LC 94-14478. 1995. 12.00 (*0-06-024752-5*, HarpT); PLB 11.89 (*0-06-024753-3*) HarpC Child Bks.
Willard, Barbara. The Eldest Son. (gr. k-12). 1989. pap. 3.25 (*0-440-20412-7*, LFL) Dell.
Willhoite, Michael. Uncle What-Is-It Is Coming to Visit!!! (Illus.). 32p. (ps-5). 1993. 12.95 (*1-55583-205-9*) Alyson Pubns.
Williams, Carol L. Kelly & Me. LC 92-20492. 1993. 13.95 (*0-385-30897-3*) Delacorte.
Williams, Vera B. A Chair for My Mother. Williams, Vera B., illus. LC 81-7010. 32p. (gr. k-3). 1982. 15.00 (*0-688-00914-X*); PLB 14.93 (*0-688-00915-8*) Greenwillow.
—Music, Music for Everyone. Williams, Vera B., illus. LC 83-14196. 32p. (gr. k-3). 1984. 14.95 (*0-688-02603-6*); PLB 14.93 (*0-688-02604-4*) Greenwillow.
—Something Special for Me. Williams, Vera B., illus. LC 82-11884. 32p. (gr. k-3). 1983. 16.00 (*0-688-01806-8*); PLB 15.93 (*0-688-01807-6*) Greenwillow.
Willis, Jeanne. Relativity, As Explained by Professor Xargle. Ross, Tony, illus. LC 93-32606. (gr. 5 up). 1994. write for info. (*0-525-45245-1*, DCB) Dutton Child Bks.
Wilson, Nancy H. The Reason for Janey. LC 93-22930. 176p. (gr. 3-7). 1994. SBE 14.95 (*0-02-793127-7*, Macmillan Child Bk) Macmillan Child Grp.
Wilson, Trevor. Let's Go Fishing. Miesen, Christine, illus. LC 93-26220. 1994. 4.25 (*0-383-03758-1*) SRA Schl Grp.
Winter, Jeanette. Klara's New World. Winter, Jeanette, illus. LC 91-30212. 48p. (gr. 2-7). 1992. 15.00 (*0-679-80626-1*); PLB 15.99 (*0-679-90626-6*) Knopf Bks Yng Read.
Winthrop, Elizabeth. I'm the Boss! Morgan, Mary, illus. LC 93-9029. 32p. (ps-3). 1994. reinforced bdg. 15.95 (*0-8234-1113-3*) Holiday.
—Squashed in the Middle. Hoban, Lillian, illus. LC 93-46834. 1994. 13.95 (*0-06-024489-5*); PLB 13.89 (*0-06-024490-9*) HarpC.
Wojciechowski, Susan. Don't Call Me Beanhead. Nash, Susanna, illus. LC 93-45958. 80p. (gr. k-4). 1994. 14.95 (*1-56402-319-2*) Candlewick Pr.
Wolff, Barbara M. Mi Abuelito y Yo. Wolff, Barbara M., illus. (SPA.). 16p. (ps-1). 1992. PLB 13.95 (*1-879567-12-1*, Valeria Bks) Wonder Well.
—My Family & Me. Wolff, Barbara M., illus. 16p. (ps-1). 1993. PLB 13.95 (*0-685-59697-4*, Valeria Bks) Wonder Well.
—Pappa & Me. Wolff, Barbara M., illus. 16p. (ps-1). 1991. PLB 13.95 (*1-879567-11-3*, Valeria Bks) Wonder Well.
Wolitzer, Hilma. Toby Lived Here. (gr. 5-11). 1986. pap. 3.45 (*0-374-47924-0*, Sunburst) FS&G.
Woodrell, Daniel. Give Us a Kiss. (gr. 5 up). 1994. 22.95 (*0-8050-2298-8*) H Holt & Co.
Wosmek, Frances. A Brown Bird Singing. Lewin, Ted, illus. LC 92-43784. 128p. (gr. 5 up). 1993. pap. 4.95 (*0-688-04596-0*, Pub. by Beech Tree Bks) Morrow.
Wright, Betty R. I Like Being Alone. (ps-3). 1993. pap. 3.95 (*0-8114-5208-5*) Raintree Steck-V.
Wyss, Johann. Swiss Family Robinson. (gr. 5 up). 1964. pap. 1.95 (*0-8049-0013-2*, CL-13) Airmont.
—The Swiss Family Robinson. James, Raymond, ed. Beier, Ellen, illus. LC 89-33888. 48p. (gr. 3-6). 1990. lib. bdg. 12.89 (*0-8167-1875-X*); pap. text ed. 3.95 (*0-8167-1876-8*) Troll Assocs.
—Swiss Family Robinson. 1993. 12.99 (*0-517-06022-1*) Random Hse Value.
Wyss, Johann D. The Swiss Family Robinson. (gr. 4-6). 1986. pap. 2.95 (*0-14-035044-6*, Puffin) Puffin Bks.
—The Swiss Family Robinson. 1990. pap. 2.95 (*0-451-52481-0*, Sig Classics) NAL-Dutton.
—The Swiss Family Robinson. LC 94-5858. 1994. 13.95 (*0-679-43640-5*, Evrymans Lib Childs) Knopf.
Yektai, Niki. The Secret Room. LC 92-6720. 192p. (gr. 4-7). 1992. 14.95 (*0-531-05456-X*); PLB 14.99 (*0-531-08606-2*) Orchard Bks Watts.
Young, Ronder Y. Learning by Heart. LC 92-46887. 1993. 13.95 (*0-395-65369-X*) HM.
Zable, Rona S. Landing on Marvin Gardens. (gr. 7 up). 1989. 13.95 (*0-553-05839-8*, Starfire) Bantam.
Zindel, Paul. Effect of Gamma Rays on Man-in-the-Moon Marigolds. Kingman, Dong, illus. (gr. 9 up). 1984. pap. 4.99 (*0-553-28028-7*) Bantam.
Zolotow, Charlotte. May I Visit? Reissue. ed. Blegvad, Erik, illus. LC 75-25405. 32p. (gr. k-3). 1976. PLB 12.89 (*0-06-026933-2*) HarpC Child Bks.
Zucker, David. Uncle Carmello. Miller, Lyle, illus. LC 91-15258. 32p. (gr. k-4). 1993. RSBE 14.95 (*0-02-793760-7*, Macmillan Child Bk) Macmillan Child Grp.

FAMILY LIFE EDUCATION

Matiella, Ana C. Cultural Pride Student Workbook. Salinas, Ron, illus. 96p. (Orig.). (gr. 5-8). 1988. pap. 7.95 (*0-941816-68-0*) ETR Assocs.
—La Familia Student Workbook. Salinas, Ron, illus. 96p. (Orig.). (gr. 5-8). 1988. pap. 7.95 (*0-941816-70-2*) ETR Assocs.

FAMILY PLANNING

see Birth Control

FAMILY RELATIONS

see Domestic Relations

FAMINE

Clinton, Susan. Live Aid. LC 92-33423. (Illus.). 32p. (gr. 3-6). 1993. PLB 12.30 (*0-516-06665-X*); pap. 3.95 (*0-516-46665-8*) Childrens.
Cohen, Marc J. & Hoehn, Richard A., eds. Hunger 1992: Second Annual Report on the State of World Hunger - Ideas That Work. (Illus.). (gr. 11 up). 1991. pap. 12.95 (*0-9628058-3-1*); study aid 3.00 (*0-9628058-4-X*) Bread for the World.
Lampton, Christopher. Famine. LC 93-9428. (Illus.). 48p. (gr. 4-6). 1994. PLB 13.90 (*1-56294-317-0*) Millbrook Pr.
Ricciuti, Edward R. Somalia: A Crisis of Famine & War. LC 93-15094. (Illus.). 64p. (gr. 5-8). 1993. PLB 15.90 (*1-56294-376-6*); pap. 6.95 (*1-56294-751-6*) Millbrook Pr.
Williams, Lawrence. Famine & Hunger. LC 92-16903. (Illus.). 48p. (gr. 6 up). 1992. text ed. 13.95 RSBE (*0-02-793025-4*, New Discovery) Macmillan Child Grp.

FANTASTIC FICTION

see also Ghost Stories; Science Fiction

Aba, Adam. The Secret of the Doo Dah House. Nagle, I., illus. LC 91-89270. 192p. (gr. 4-7). 1992. pap. 16.95 (*1-878756-51-6*) YCP Pubns.
Abbott, Donald. How the Wizard Came to Oz. Abbott, Donald, illus. (gr. 3 up). 1991. 19.95 (*0-929605-24-1*); pap. 9.95 (*0-929605-15-2*) Books Wonder.
—The Magic Chest of Oz. Abbott, Donald, illus. (gr. 3 up). 1993. 34.95 (*0-929605-21-7*); pap. 9.95 (*0-929605-20-9*) Books Wonder.
Adler, C. S. Eddie's Blue-Winged Dragon. 144p. 1990. pap. 3.50 (*0-380-70768-3*, Camelot) Avon.
Ahlberg, Janet & Ahlberg, Allan. Jeremiah in the Dark Woods. (Illus.). 48p. (ps-3). 1990. pap. 4.95 (*0-14-032811-4*, Puffin) Puffin Bks.
Aiken, Joan. The Erl King's Daughter. Warren, Paul, illus. 42p. (gr. 2-4). 1989. 3.95 (*0-8120-6137-3*) Barron.
Aladdin. (Illus.). 64p. 1993. pap. 16.95 (*0-7935-1782-6*, 00312480) H Leonard.
Aladdin: The Genie Gets Wet. 4p. 1993. 5.98 (*1-57082-011-2*) Mouse Works.
Alexander, Margaret. Rachel & the Pink & Green Dragon. (Illus.). 44p. (gr. k-3). 1992. 6.95 (*1-55523-518-2*) Winston-Derek.
Alice in Wonderland. (Illus.). (gr. 3-5). 3.50 (*0-7214-0967-9*) Ladybird Bks.
Alice in Wonderland. (Illus.). 24p. (Orig.). (gr. k-3). 1993. pap. 2.50 (*1-56144-294-1*, Honey Bear Bks) Modern Pub NYC.
Allred, Michael. Madman: The Oddity Odyssey. (Illus.). 144p. (gr. 4 up). 1993. pap. 12.95 (*0-87816-247-X*) Kitchen Sink.
Alpert, Lou. Dancing with the Shadows in My Room. Alpert, Lou, illus. 32p. (ps-3). 1991. 12.95 (*1-879085-06-2*) Whsprng Coyote Pr.
—Emma & the Magic Dance. Alpert, Lou, illus. 32p. (ps-3). 1991. smythe sewn reinforced bdg. 12.95 (*1-879085-01-1*) Whsprng Coyote Pr.
—Emma Lights up the Sky. Alpert, Lou, illus. 32p. (ps-3). 1991. smythe sewn reinforced bdg. 12.95 (*1-879085-03-8*) Whsprng Coyote Pr.
—Emma Swings. Alpert, Lou, illus. 32p. (ps-3). 1991. smythe sewn reinforced bdg. 12.95 (*1-879085-04-6*) Whsprng Coyote Pr.
—The Man in the Moon & His Flying Balloon. Alpert, Lou, illus. 32p. (ps-8). 1991. smythe sewn reinforced bdg. 12.95 (*1-879085-05-4*) Whsprng Coyote Pr.
Amthor, Terry K. Teeth of Mordor. Fenlon, Peter C., Jr., ed. Martin, David & Martin, Elissa, illus. 32p. (gr. 10-12). 1988. pap. 6.00 (*0-915795-96-5*, 8202) Iron Crown Ent Inc.
Anderson, Wayne. Dragon. LC 91-4790. (ps-3). 1992. 15.00 (*0-671-78397-1*, Green Tiger) S&S Trade.
AScott, Michael. October Moon. 129p. (gr. 8 up). 1993. pap. 9.95 (*0-86278-300-3*, Pub. by OBrien Pr IE) Dufour.
Ashby, Ruth. Beetlejuice for President. 96p. (Orig.). 1992. pap. 2.99 (*0-671-75552-8*) PB.
—Lydia's Scream Date. 96p. (Orig.). 1992. pap. 2.99 (*0-671-75553-6*) PB.
Asher, Sandy. Missing Pieces. (gr. 6 up). 1986. pap. 2.50 (*0-440-95716-8*, LFL) Dell.
Asimov, Isaac & Greenberg, Martin H., eds. Visions of Fantasy. Elmore, Larry, illus. 192p. (gr. 5 up). 1989. 14.95 (*0-385-26359-7*, Zephyr-BFYR) Doubleday.
Asimov, Janet & Asimov, Isaac. Norby & the Invaders. LC 85-13635. 138p. (gr. 3-5). 1985. 10.95 (*0-8027-6599-8*); PLB 10.85 (*0-8027-6607-2*) Walker & Co.
—Norby & the Oldest Dragon. (gr. 4-9). 1990. 14.95 (*0-8027-6909-8*); PLB 15.85 (*0-8027-6910-1*) Walker & Co.
Askounis, Christina. The Dream of the Stone. large type ed. LC 93-42092. 1994. 15.95 (*0-7862-0147-9*) Thorndike Pr.

Avi. City of Light, City of Dark: A Comic Book Novel. Floca, Brian, illus. LC 93-2887. 192p. (gr. 4 up). 1993. 15.95 (*0-531-06800-5*); PLB 15.99 (*0-531-08650-X*) Orchard Bks Watts.
—Who Stole the Wizard of Oz? James, Derek, illus. LC 81-884. 128p. (gr. 3-6). 1990. Repr. of 1981 ed. 3.99 (*0-394-84992-2*) Random Bks Yng Read.
Babar, 7 Families. (Illus.). (ps-1). 1990. 6.00 (*1-56021-034-6*) W J Fantasy.
Babbitt, Lucy C. Where the Truth Lies: A Novel. LC 92-34061. 208p. (gr. 7 up). 1993. 15.95 (*0-531-05473-X*); PLB 15.99 (*0-531-08623-2*) Orchard Bks Watts.
Babbitt, Natalie. Tuck Everlasting. LC 75-33306. 160p. (gr. 3 up). 1975. 15.00 (*0-374-37848-7*) FS&G.
—Tuck Para Siempre: Tuck Everlasting. Fradera, Narcis, tr. (SPA.). 158p. (gr. 5 up). 1991. 15.00 (*0-374-37849-5*) FS&G.
—Tuck Para Siempre: Tuck Everlasting. (gr. 4-7). 1993. pap. 3.95 (*0-374-48011-7*) FS&G.
Baillie, Allan. Drac & the Gremlin. Tanner, Jane, illus. LC 88-20275. 32p. (ps-3). 1992. pap. 4.99 (*0-14-054542-5*, Puff Pied Piper) Puffin Bks.
Bakken, Harald. The Fields & the Hills: The Journey, Once Begun, Book I. 240p. (gr. 5 up). 1992. 15.45 (*0-395-59397-2*, Clarion Bks) HM.
Balan, Bruce. Pie in the Sky. Skilbeck, Clare, illus. 32p. (ps-3). 1993. 13.99 (*0-670-85150-7*) Viking Child Bks.
Balian, Lorna. Bah! Humbug? Balian, Lorna, illus. 32p. (ps-3). 1988. Repr. of 1978 ed. 7.50 (*0-687-37107-4*) Humbug Bks.
—Leprechauns Never Lie. Balian, Lorna, illus. 32p. (ps-3). 1988. Repr. of 1981 ed. 7.50 (*0-687-37110-4*) Humbug Bks.
—The Sweet Touch. Balian, Lorna, illus. 52p. (ps-6). 1994. Repr. PLB 12.95 (*1-881772-26-8*) Humbug Bks.
Baltz, Terry & Baltz, Wayne. The Invisible Kid & Dr. Poof's Magic Soap. LC 93-87287. 136p. (gr. 3-6). 1993. pap. 5.95 (*1-884610-11-0*) Prairie Divide.
Bang, Molly G. Tye May & the Magic Brush. LC 80-16488. (Illus.). 56p. (gr. 1 up). 1992. pap. 4.95 (*0-688-11504-7*, Mulberry) Morrow.
Banks, Lynne R. The Fairy Rebel. large type ed. (Illus.). 227p. 1989. lib. bdg. 15.95 (*1-55736-124-X*, Crnrstn Bks) BDD LT Grp.
—Farthest-Away Mountain. (gr. 4-7). 1991. pap. 14.95 (*0-385-41534-6*) Doubleday.
Barber, Antonia. The Ghosts. Ashby, Ruth, ed. 224p. (gr. 6-9). 1989. pap. 3.50 (*0-671-70714-0*, Archway) PB.
Barker, Clive. The Thief of Always: A Fable. LC 92-53428. 1992. 20.00 (*0-06-017724-1*, HarpT) HarpC.
Barklem, Jill. The Four Seasons of Brambly Hedge. (Illus.). 144p. (gr. 3 up). 1990. 25.95 (*0-399-21869-6*, Philomel Bks) Putnam Pub Group.
Barnes, Maryke. Setting Wonder Free. Marton, Jirina, illus. 24p. 1993. lib. bdg. 14.95 (*1-55037-241-6*, Pub. by Annick CN); pap. 4.95 (*1-55037-238-6*, Pub. by Annick CN) Firefly Bks Ltd.
Barr, Mike W. Batman: In the Darkest Knight. Dooley, Kevin, ed. Bingham, Jerry, illus. 48p. (Orig.). 1993. pap. 4.95 (*1-56389-112-3*) DC Comics.
Barrie, J. M. Peter Pan. Arneson, D. J., retold by. Clift, Eva, illus. 128p. 1991. pap. 2.95 (*1-56156-029-4*) Kidsbks.
—Peter Pan & Wendy. Foreman, Michael, illus. 160p. (gr. 3-6). 1992. (Pub. by Pavilion UK); pap. 17.95 (*1-85145-449-7*, Pub. by Pavilion UK) Trafalgar.
—Peter Pan in Kensington Gardens. 150p. 1980. Repr. PLB 16.95x (*0-89967-006-7*) Harmony Raine.
—Peter Pan: Return to Never-Never Land. Forten, Ron, adapted by. (Illus.). 56p. 1991. pap. 5.95 (*1-56398-016-9*) Malibu Graphics.
Barrie, James. Peter Pan. White, Flora & Bedford, F. D., illus. 304p. (gr. k-5). 1988. Repr. of 1911 ed. 12.99 (*0-517-63222-5*) Random Hse Value.
Barrie, James M. Peter Pan. reissue ed. Dubowski, Cathy E., adapted by. Zallinger, Jean, illus. LC 90-23077. 96p. (gr. 2-6). 1991. lib. bdg. 5.99 (*0-679-91044-1*, Bullseye Bks); pap. 3.50 (*0-679-81044-7*, Bullseye Bks) Random Bks Yng Read.
—Peter Pan. 176p. 1992. 9.49 (*0-8167-2554-3*); pap. 2.95 (*0-8167-2555-1*) Troll Assocs.
—Peter Pan. 1985. pap. 2.95 (*0-553-21178-1*, Bantam Classics) Bantam.
—Peter Pan. Bedford, F. D., illus. LC 92-53172. 224p. 1992. 12.95 (*0-679-41792-3*, Evrymans Lib Childs Class) Knopf.
—Peter Pan. Oremerod, Jan, illus. (FRE.). 239p. (gr. 5-10). 1988. pap. 9.95 (*2-07-033411-2*) Schoenhof.
—Peter Pan. Ormerod, Jan, illus. 208p. (gr. 5 up). 1993. pap. 3.99 (*0-14-032007-5*) Puffin Bks.
—Peter Pan. (gr. 4-7). 1993. pap. 3.25 (*0-590-46735-2*) Scholastic Inc.
—Peter Pan: A Changing Picture & Lift-the-Flap Book. abr. ed. Caswell, Edmund, illus. 32p. (ps-3). 1992. 15.95 (*0-670-83608-7*) Viking Child Bks.
—The Study of Peter Pan. unabr., slightly altered ed. O'Connor, Daniel, adapted by. Woodward, Alice B., illus. Kliros, Thea, contrib. by. LC 92-18641. (Illus.). 96p. 1992. Repr. 1.00 (*0-486-27294-X*) Dover.
Bates, A. Dead Game. 1993. pap. 3.25 (*0-590-45829-9*) Scholastic Inc.
Batman Returns: You Write the Script. (ps-3). 1992. pap. 2.95 (*0-307-02944-1*, Golden Pr) Western Pub.
Baum, L. Frank. Adventures in Oz: Ozma of Oz & Marvelous Land of Oz, The Original Editions Complete & Unabridged. 575p. (gr. 2 up). 1985. pap. 11.90 (*0-486-24880-1*) Dover.
—The Emerald City of Oz. Neill, John R., illus. Glassman, Peter, afterword by. LC 92-61765. (Illus.). 304p. 1993. 20.00 (*0-688-11558-6*) Morrow Jr Bks.
—Glinda of Oz. 224p. 1985. pap. 3.95 (*0-345-33394-2*, Del Rey) Ballantine.
—Little Wizard Stories of Oz. (Illus.). 96p. 1988. pap. 2.95 (*0-553-15617-9*, Skylark) Bantam.
—Little Wizard Stories of Oz. Neill, John R., illus. Glassman, Peter, intro. by. LC 93-77316. (Illus.). 176p. (gr. 4-7). 1994. 20.00g (*0-688-12126-8*) Morrow Jr Bks.
—Marvelous Land of Oz. McKee, David, illus. 192p. (gr. 4-6). 1985. pap. 2.25 (*0-14-035041-1*, Puffin) Puffin Bks.
—The Marvelous Land of Oz. Neill, John R., illus. LC 85-4856. 288p. (gr. 4-6). 1985. 15.00 (*0-688-05439-0*) Morrow Jr Bks.
—Ozma of Oz. 272p. (gr. 2 up). 1985. pap. 5.95 (*0-486-24779-1*) Dover.
—Ozma of Oz. Neill, John R., illus. LC 88-63291. 288p. 1989. 19.95 (*0-688-06632-1*) Morrow Jr Bks.
—Ozma of Oz. 160p. (gr. 5 up). 1992. pap. 2.95 (*0-14-035119-1*) Puffin Bks.
—Patchwork Girl of Oz. 1990. pap. 6.95 (*0-486-26514-5*) Dover.
—Rinkitink in Oz. (Illus.). 336p. (gr. 4 up). 1993. pap. text ed. 7.95t (*0-486-27756-9*) Dover.
—The Road to Oz. Neill, John R., illus. Glassman, Peter, afterword by. LC 90-48349. (Illus.). 272p. 1991. Repr. of 1909 ed. 16.95 (*0-688-09997-1*) Morrow Jr Bks.
—Tik Tok of Oz. (Illus.). 192p. (gr. 5 up). 1991. pap. 2.25 (*0-14-035124-8*, Puffin) Puffin Bks.
—Tik-Tok of Oz. LC 93-37906. (Illus.). 304p. pap. 6.95 (*0-486-28002-0*) Dover.
—The Wizard of Oz. Santore, Charles, illus. Hearn, Michael P., intro. by. (Illus.). 96p. 1991. 15.00 (*0-517-69506-5*, Pub. by Jellybean Pr); lib. bdg. 20.00 (*0-517-06655-6*, Pub. by Jellybean Pr) Random Hse Value.
—Wizard of Oz. 1993. pap. 2.95 (*0-590-44089-6*) Scholastic Inc.
—The Wizard of Oz. Denslow, W. W., illus. LC 93-24491. 272p. Repr. of 1900 ed. 6.00 (*1-56957-911-3*) Barefoot Bks.
—The Wizard of Oz. Denslow, W. W., ed. Copelman, Evelyn, illus. LC 93-50738. 1994. write for info. (*0-448-40561-X*, G&D) Putnam Pub Group.
—The Wizard of Oz: (El Mago de Oz) (SPA.). 9.95 (*84-204-3509-0*) Santillana.
—The Wizard of Oz Waddle Book. Denslow, W. W., illus. LC 93-10069. 1993. 24.95 (*1-55709-205-2*); ltd. collector's ed. 85.00 (*1-55709-203-6*) Applewood.
—The Wonderful Wizard of Oz. 193p. 1981. Repr. PLB 11.95x (*0-89967-021-0*) Harmony Raine.
—The Wonderful Wizard of Oz. (gr. 5-6). 20.95 (*0-88411-772-3*, Pub. by Aeonian Pr) Amereon Ltd.
—The Wonderful Wizard of Oz. large type ed. Denslow, W. W., illus. 188p. (gr. 2-6). 1987. lib. bdg. 13.95 (*1-55736-013-8*, Crnrstn Bks) BDD LT Grp.
—Wonderful Wizard of Oz. 176p. 1992. 9.49 (*0-8167-2564-0*); pap. 2.95 (*0-8167-2565-9*) Troll Assocs.
—The Wonderful Wizard of Oz. Mabie, Grace, ed. Newsom, Tom, illus. LC 92-12704. 48p. (gr. 3-6). 1992. PLB 12.89 (*0-8167-2864-X*); pap. text ed. 3.95 (*0-8167-2865-8*) Troll Assocs.
—The Wonderful Wizard of Oz. Denslow, W. W., illus. LC 92-53173. 192p. 1992. 12.95 (*0-679-41794-X*, Evrymans Lib Childs Class) Knopf.
Baum, Roger S. Dorothy of Oz. Miles, Elizabeth, illus. LC 89-6918. 176p. 1989. 14.95 (*0-688-07848-6*) Morrow Jr Bks.
—The SillyOZbul of OZ & the Magic Merry-Go-Round. 32p. 1992. 15.95 (*0-9630101-2-3*) Yellow Brick Rd.
—The SillyOZbul of OZ & Toto. Mertins, Lisa, illus. 1992. 15.95 (*0-9630101-1-5*) Yellow Brick Rd.
—The SillyOZbul Trilogy, 3 vols. Date not set. slipcased 47.85 (*0-9630101-3-1*) Yellow Brick Rd.
—The SillyOZbuls of OZ. Mertins, Lisa, illus. LC 91-66003. 1991. 15.95 (*0-9630101-0-7*) Yellow Brick Rd.
Baumgart, Klaus. Anna & the Little Green Dragon. Baumgart, Klaus, illus. LC 91-26639. 32p. (ps-3). 1992. 12.95 (*1-56282-166-0*); PLB 12.89 (*1-56282-167-9*) Hyprn Child.
—The Little Green Dragon Steps Out. Baumgart, Klaus, illus. LC 92-5120. 32p. (ps-3). 1992. 12.95 (*1-56282-254-3*); PLB 12.89 (*1-56282-255-1*) Hyprn Child.
—Where Are You, Little Green Dragon? Baumgart, Klaus, illus. LC 92-72026. 32p. (ps-3). 1993. 12.95 (*1-56282-344-2*); PLB 12.89 (*1-56282-345-0*) Hyprn Child.
Beatty, Patricia. Charley Skedaddle. LC 87-12270. 192p. (gr. 5-9). 1987. 12.95 (*0-688-06687-9*) Morrow Jr Bks.
Bedard, Michael. Painted Devil. LC 92-35637. 224p. (gr. 5-9). 1994. SBE 15.95 (*0-689-31827-8*, Atheneum Child Bk) Macmillan Child Grp.
Bell, Clare. Clan Ground. (gr. k-12). 1987. pap. 2.95 (*0-440-91287-3*, LFL) Dell.
Bellairs, John. The Mansion in the Mist. 176p. (gr. 5 up). 1993. pap. 3.99 (*0-14-034933-2*, Puffin) Puffin Bks.
Bennett, Denise. The Color Tree. LC 93-77606. 32p. (gr. 4-5). 1993. 12.95 (*1-880851-07-5*) Greene Bark Pr.

Bennett, Helen S. Jack's Amazing Magic Bed. Hone, Michael J., illus. 32p. (gr. k-3). 1994. pap. 9.95 (*0-9638747-0-5*) Tomac Pubng.
What kid hasn't fantasized about driving around like magic? In JACK'S AMAZING MAGIC BED, Jack has to have a funny-looking hospital bed in his room at home for a little while & starts fooling around - pushing the buttons. Suddenly, the bed moves! "WOW! A magic bed." So he drives on the big, scary highway & goes to see the wonderful sights of New York City. When he gets tired, a helicopter pilot picks Jack up & flies above skyscrapers & Yankee Stadium & so close to the Statue of Liberty Jack can look right in her eyes. From up in the air, New York looks like a gigantic jigsaw puzzle: all the pieces tight together. Awesome! Full & double-page illustrations are fresh, imaginative pen & ink drawings with watercolor, whimsical details tucked in everywhere. First Prize: (Nat'l League Am Pen Women Biennial), Selection (New York Magazine). "Absolutely loved it...a fun trip to New York!" Joan Hambug (WOR-NY). To Order: Baker & Taylor distributor or Tomac Publishing, Box 247, Old Greenwich, CT 06870; 800-829-6133.
Publisher Provided Annotation.

Benson, Robert B. The Wizard of Bergen. 125p. (Orig.). (gr. 7-12). 1987. pap. 7.50 (*0-9616327-1-2*) Brandt Bks.
Berger, Barbara H. Gwinna. (Illus.). 128p. 1990. 18.95 (*0-399-21738-X*, Philomel Bks) Putnam Pub Group.
Bhaktipada, Swami. Lila in the Land of Illusion: A Re-Telling of Lewis Carroll's Alice in Wonderland. New Vrindaban Community Artists, illus. LC 87-18626. 127p. (gr. 3-8). 1987. 12.95 (*0-932215-22-X*); pap. text ed. 7.95 (*0-932215-19-X*) Palace Pub.
Bibee, John. Bicycle Hills: How One Halloween Almost Got out of Hand. LC 89-15316. (Illus.). 204p. (Orig.). (gr. 7-8). 1989. pap. 6.99 (*0-8308-1203-2*, 1203) InterVarsity.
—The Last Christmas. LC 90-4870. (Illus.). 204p. (Orig.). (gr. 3-8). 1990. pap. 6.99 (*0-8308-1204-0*, 1204) InterVarsity.
—The Runaway Parents: A Parable of Problem Parents. Turnbaugh, Paul, illus. LC 91-22762. 204p. (gr. 3-8). 1991. pap. 6.99 (*0-8308-1205-9*, 1205) InterVarsity.
Bicknell, Treld, compiled by. Seven Is Heaven. LC 86-45415. (Illus.). 64p. (gr. 2). 1986. 8.95 (*0-15-200580-3*, Gulliver Bks) HarBrace.
Birch, David. The King's Chessboard. Grebu, Devis, illus. 32p. (gr. k up). 1993. pap. 4.99 (*0-14-054880-7*, Puff Pied Piper) Puffin Bks.
Bissett, Isabel. Wheels. Wood, Bill, illus. LC 92-21399. 1993. 3.75 (*0-383-03605-4*) SRA Schl Grp.
The Black Cauldron. 1990. 6.98 (*0-8317-5795-7*) Viking Child Bks.
Blaebst, Werner. Maxi's Bed Magicians. Blaebst, Werner, illus. 28p. (ps-k). 1991. smythe sewn reinforced bdg. 9.95 (*1-56182-020-2*) Atomium Bks.
Blume, Judy. Otherwise Known As Sheila the Great. (gr. 3-6). 1972. 13.99 (*0-525-36455-2*, DCB) Dutton Child Bks.
—Superfudge. LC 80-10439. 176p. (gr. 3-6). 1980. 13.00 (*0-525-40522-4*, DCB) Dutton Child Bks.
Bochak, John. The Gamemaster. Bochak, Grayce, photos by. LC 94-14182. 1995. 14.00 (*0-02-710961-5*, Four Winds) Macmillan Child Grp.
Bohlke, Dorothee. Cokolina & the Wild Island. Max, Jill & Bradford, Elizabeth, eds. Verlag, Mangold, tr. Bohlke, Dorothee, illus. LC 91-24337. 24p. (gr. k-3). 1991. PLB 14.60 (*1-56074-032-9*) Garrett Ed Corp.
Bomans, Godfried. Eric in the Land of the Insects. Kornblith, Regina L., tr. from DUT. LC 93-24071. 1994. 14.95 (*0-395-65231-6*) HM.
Bond, Nancy. A String in the Harp. LC 75-28181. 384p. (gr. 4-8). 1976. SBE 16.95 (*0-689-50036-X*, M K McElderry) Macmillan Child Grp.

Borelli, George. The Great Wizard of Imp. Hippard, Peter, illus. 28p. (Orig.). (gr. k-4). 1994. Set, incl. tape. PLB 12.95 (*1-885792-01-8*); Tape. pap. 5.95 (*1-885792-04-2*) Gemini Pubng.
THE GREAT WIZARD OF IMP is a heart-warming & whimsical adventure story about a little boy named Zack who is lost in the forest. He is looking for his family, who have been captured

by the persnickety scalawags. Zack meets & enlists the aid of the Great Wizard of Imp whose magic (self-confidence) helps Zack rescue his family from the Castle of Dystopia. Zack develops his own magic through self-reliance & the support of the Wizard. Their charming relationship dispels prejudice, fears & explores the differences between people in an accepting & sensitive manner that promises to inspire the imaginations of young readers. The story is narrated on tape by Dr. Borelli, a family psychologist for over 40 years, with original music by Scott Borelli, for youngsters who delight in following along & turning the pages of this powerfully illustrated fantasy of psychological truths. This is the first in a series of five Wizard adventures. Order from Gemini Publishing, 25 East Weber Rd., Columbus, OH 43202. (614) 262-1649.
Publisher Provided Annotation.

Bowen, Sally. Down by the Enchanted Stream. Wasmer, Kristina, illus. 38p. 1992. pap. 10.95 (*0-9633546-1-2*, Dist. by BookWorld Services, Inc.) Bowen & Assocs.
Bradbury, Ray. The Halloween Tree. 192p. (gr. 7 up). 1984. pap. 4.99 (*0-553-25823-0*) Bantam.
Brett, Jan. Beauty & the Beast. Brett, Jan, illus. LC 88-16965. 48p. (gr. 1-7). 1989. 14.95 (*0-89919-497-4*, Clarion Bks) HM.
Brightfield, Richard. Escape from the Kingdom of Frome, No. 4: The Battle of Astar. 128p. (Orig.). 1987. pap. 2.50 (*0-553-26290-4*, Starfire) Bantam.
—The Forest of the King. 128p. (Orig.). (gr. 7-12). 1986. pap. 2.50 (*0-553-26155-X*) Bantam.
—Star System Tenopia, No. 4. 144p. (Orig.). 1986. pap. 2.50 (*0-553-25637-8*) Bantam.
—Terror on Kabran. 144p. (Orig.). 1986. pap. 2.50 (*0-553-25636-X*) Bantam.
—Trapped in the Sea Kingdom. 128p. 1986. pap. 2.50 (*0-553-25473-1*) Bantam.
Brims, Bernagh, ed. Five Potato, Six Potato. (Illus.). 80p. (Orig.). (gr. 1-6). 1992. pap. 5.95 (*0-86281-344-1*, Pub. by Appletree Pr ER) Irish Bks Media.
Brittain, Bill. Wings. LC 90-19785. 128p. (gr. 4-7). 1991. HarpC Child Bks.
Brockway, Warren H. Gnomes I Have Known. 1992. pap. 10.00 (*0-533-10223-5*) Vantage.
Broger, Achim. The Red Armchair. Schluter, Manfred, illus. 28p. (ps-2). 1991. smythe sewn reinforced bdg. 9.95 (*1-56182-034-2*) Atomium Bks.
—The Wonderful Bedmobile. Kalow, Gisela, illus. 28p. (ps-2). 1991. smythe sewn reinforced bdg. 9.95 (*1-56182-033-4*) Atomium Bks.
Brouwer, Sigmund. A City of Dreams. 132p. (Orig.). (gr. 4-8). 1993. pap. 4.99 (*1-56476-048-0*, Victor Books) SP Pubns.
—Merlin's Destiny. 132p. (Orig.). (gr. 4-8). 1993. pap. 4.99 (*1-56476-049-9*, Victor Books) SP Pubns.
Brouwer, Sigmund & Davidson, Wayne. Dr. Drabble's Amazing Invisibility Mirror. 24p. 1992. 5.99 (*0-89693-970-7*) SP Pubns.
—Dr. Drabble's Spectacular Shrinker-Enlarger. 24p. 1992. 5.99 (*0-89693-969-3*) SP Pubns.
Brown, Beverly. The Story of the Traveling Pillow. Ott, Margot J., illus. LC 94-75990. 32p. (ps-2). 1994. 12.95 (*1-880851-12-1*) Greene Bark Pr.
Brown, John R. Living Legends. LC 89-50186. 124p. (Orig.). 1990. pap. 5.95 (*0-916383-89-X*) Aegina Pr.
Brown, Mirella. In the Land of la Fustera. 32p. 1993. pap. 9.95 (*0-8059-3348-4*) Dorrance.
Browne, Anthony. Through the Magic Mirror. LC 90-23166. 32p. (ps up). 1992. 14.00 (*0-688-10725-7*) Greenwillow.
Browne, Jane. The Little One. (Illus.). 24p. (ps). 1993. 14.95 (*1-85681-102-6*, Pub. by J MacRae UK) Trafalgar.
Brunn, Robert. The Initiation. 160p. (gr. 5 up). 1992. pap. 3.50 (*0-440-94047-8*, LFL) Dell.
Bumpus, Jerry. Dawn of the Flying Pigs. (Illus.). 144p. (Orig.). 1992. pap. 12.50x (*0-914140-16-7*) Carpenter Pr.
Bunting, Eve. Dream Dancer. (Illus.). 64p. 1992. 8.95 (*0-89565-779-1*) Childs World.
—The Followers. (Illus.). 64p. (gr. 3-8). 1992. 8.95 (*0-89565-764-3*) Childs World.
—The Girl in the Painting. (Illus.). 64p. (gr. 3-8). 1992. 8.95 (*0-89565-770-8*) Childs World.
—The Island of One. (Illus.). 64p. 1992. 8.95 (*0-89565-768-6*) Childs World.
—Lady's Girl. (Illus.). 64p. (gr. 3-8). 1992. 8.95 (*0-89565-777-5*) Childs World.
—Ride When You're Ready. (Illus.). 64p. (gr. 3-8). 1992. 8.95 (*0-89565-776-7*) Childs World.
—Two Different Girls. (Illus.). 64p. (gr. 3-8). 1992. 8.95 (*0-89565-772-4*) Childs World.
—The Undersea People. (Illus.). 64p. (gr. 3-8). 1992. 8.95 (*0-89565-766-X*) Childs World.
Burgess, Gelett. Goop Tales. LC 72-93766. (Illus.). 128p. (gr. 1-6). 1973. pap. 3.95 (*0-486-22914-9*) Dover.
Burgess, Thornton W. Mother West Wind's Children. Cady, Harrison, illus. 156p. (ps-3). 1985. pap. 8.95 (*0-316-11657-2*) Little.
—Tommy & the Wishing Stone. 19.95 (*0-8488-0932-7*) Amereon Ltd.
—Tommy's Change of Heart. 19.95 (*0-8488-1418-5*) Amereon Ltd.
—Tommy's Wishes Come True. 19.95 (*0-8488-1419-3*) Amereon Ltd.
—While Story-Log Burns. 18.95 (*0-8488-0401-5*) Amereon Ltd.
Burnside, Julian. Matilda & the Dragon. Guthridge, Bettina, illus. 32p. (Orig.). (gr. k-2). 1993. 14.95 (*1-86373-127-X*, Pub. by Allen & Unwin Aust Pty AT); pap. 7.95 (*1-86373-144-X*, Pub. by Allen & Unwin Aust Pty AT) IPG Chicago.
—Matilda & the Dragon. (ps-3). 1993. pap. 7.95 (*1-86373-179-2*, Pub. by Allen & Unwin Aust Pty AT) IPG Chicago.
Burton, Tim. Tim Burton's Nightmare Before Christmas Pop-Up. (ps-3). 1993. 14.98 (*0-453-03132-3*) Mouse Works.
Bush, Max. The Troll & the Elephant Prince. (gr. 4 up). 1985. pap. 4.50 (*0-87602-254-9*) Anchorage.
Busiek, Kurt. The Wizard's Tale, Bk. 1. Yronwode, Catherine & Adair, Lynn, eds. Wenzel, David, illus. 42p. (Orig.). (gr. 1-4). 1993. pap. 4.95t (*1-56060-206-6*) Eclipse Bks.
—The Wizard's Tale, Bk. 2. Yronwode, Catherine & Adair, Lynn, eds. Wenzel, David, illus. 42p. (Orig.). (gr. 1-4). 1993. pap. 4.95t (*1-56060-207-4*) Eclipse Bks.
—The Wizard's Tale, Bk. 3. Yronwode, Catherine & Adair, Lynn, eds. Wenzel, David, illus. 42p. (Orig.). (gr. 1-4). 1994. pap. 4.95t (*1-56060-208-2*) Eclipse Bks.
—The Wizard's Tale, Collection, 3 bks. Yronwode, Catherine & Adair, Lynn, eds. Wenzel, David, illus. 42p. (Orig.). (gr. 1-4). Date not set. write for info. (*1-56060-210-4*); pap. write for info. (*1-56060-209-0*) Eclipse Bks.
Butler, Dorothy. A Happy Tale. Hurford, John, illus. LC 90-34500. 32p. (ps-5). 1990. 11.95 (*0-940793-61-X*, Crocodile Bks) Interlink Pub.
Butterworth, Nick. Rescue Party, Vol. 1. (ps-3). 1993. 14.95 (*0-316-11923-7*) Little.
Byars, Betsy C. The Blossoms & the Green Phantom. Rogers, Jacqueline, illus. 160p. (gr. 4-6). 1987. pap. 14.95 (*0-385-29533-2*) Delacorte.
—The Two-Thousand Pound Goldfish. large type ed. 160p. 1989. Repr. of 1982 ed. lib. bdg. 15.95 (*1-55736-131-2*, Crnrstn Bks) BDD LT Grp.
Carabis, Anne. The Magic Rocking Chair. Carabis, Anne, illus. 28p. (Orig.). (ps-3). 1980. pap. 3.50 (*0-9605802-0-4*) Carabis.
Carlin, Mike, ed. Superman: Panic in the Sky. (Illus.). 192p. (Orig.). 1993. pap. text ed. 9.95 (*1-56389-094-1*) DC Comics.
Carlson, Karyl & Gjovaag, Eric. Queen Ann in Oz. (Illus.). 117p. (gr. 2 up). 1993. 34.95 (*0-929605-26-8*); pap. 9.95 (*0-929605-25-X*) Books Wonder.
Carmichael, Jack B. Black Knight. 89p. (Orig.). (gr. 12). 1991. pap. 9.95 (*0-9626948-1-9*) Dynamics MI.
Carpenter, Humphrey. Mr. Majeika. large type ed. Rodgers, Frank, illus. 96p. (gr. 1-8). 1992. 16.95 (*0-7451-1582-9*, Galaxy Child Lrg Print) Chivers N Amer.
Carr, Jan. Wizard of Oz. (ps-3). 1993. pap. 3.25 (*0-590-46993-2*) Scholastic Inc.
Carrick, Donald. Aladdin & the Wonderful Lamp. 1993. pap. 4.95 (*0-590-41680-4*) Scholastic Inc.
Carroll, Lewis. Alice au Pays des Merveilles. Tenniel, John, illus. (FRE.). 223p. (gr. 5-10). 1987. pap. 9.95 (*2-07-033437-6*) Schoenhof.
—Alice in Wonderland. 299p. 1981. Repr. PLB 12.95x (*0-89967-019-9*) Harmony Raine.
—Alice's Adventures in Wonderland. Tenniel, John, illus. Glassman, Peter, intro. by. LC 91-31482. (Illus.). 208p. 1992. 15.00 (*0-688-11087-8*) Morrow Jr Bks.
—Alice's Adventures in Wonderland. LC 92-50804. (Illus.). 192p. 1993. 4.95 (*1-56138-246-9*) Running Pr.
—Alice's Adventures in Wonderland. Tenniel, John, illus. LC 93-571. 240p. 1993. Repr. of 1866 ed. 6.00 (*1-56957-900-8*) Shambhala Pubns.
—Alice's Adventures in Wonderland. Ross, Tony, illus. LC 93-72323. 96p. (gr. 2 up). 1994. SBE 16.95 (*0-689-31864-2*, Atheneum Child Bk) Macmillan Child Grp.
—Alice's Adventures in Wonderland & Through the Looking Glass: And What Alice Found There. Tenniel, John, illus. 416p. 1992. pap. 3.99 (*0-440-40743-5*, Pub. by Yearling Classics) Dell.
—Alice's Adventures in Wonderland & Through the Looking Glass. Tenniel, John, illus. LC 92-53181. 336p. 1992. 12.95 (*0-679-41795-8*, Evrymans Lib Childs Class) Knopf.
—Alice's Adventures in Wonderland & Through the Looking-Glass, 2 bks. Tenniel, John, illus. 1993. Boxed Set. 29.95 (*0-688-12050-4*) Morrow Jr Bks.
—Best of Lewis Carroll. 1992. 7.98 (*0-89009-700-3*) Bk Sales Inc.
—Jabberwocky. LC 91-58968. (Illus.). 1992. 13.95 (*1-56282-245-4*); PLB 13.89 (*1-56282-246-2*) Disney Pr.
—Through the Looking Glass. 176p. (gr. 7 up). 1985. pap. 2.99 (*0-14-035039-X*, Puffin) Puffin Bks.
—Through the Looking Glass. Tenniel, John, illus. 224p. 1977. Repr. 14.95 (*0-312-80374-5*) St Martin.
—Through the Looking-Glass. abr. ed. Ross, Tony, illus. 128p. (gr. 2 up). 1993. Repr. of 1993 ed. SBE 16.95 (*0-689-31863-4*, Atheneum Child Bk) Macmillan Child Grp.
—Through the Looking Glass, & What Alice Found There. Tenniel, John, illus. LC 84-60960. 184p. (gr. 2 up). 1984. Repr. of 1941 ed. 6.95 (*0-88088-991-8*, 889918) Peter Pauper.
—Through the Looking Glass & What Alice Found There. 1990. 12.99 (*0-517-03346-1*) Random Hse Value.
—Through the Looking Glass & What Alice Found There. (Illus.). 127p. 1991. 7.99 (*0-517-00233-7*) Random Hse Value.
—Through the Looking Glass & What Alice Found There. Tenniel, John, illus. LC 92-20642. 240p. (gr. 1 up). 1993. 15.00 (*0-688-12049-0*) Morrow Jr Bks.
Carroll, Lewis & Baker, Kyle. Through the Looking-Glass. (Illus.). 52p. Date not set. pap. 4.95 (*1-57209-002-2*) Classics Int Ent.
Carruth, Jane. Little Treasury of Alice in Wonderland. 1992. 5.99 (*0-517-06720-X*) Random Hse Value.
—Little Treasury of Peter Pan. 1992. 5.99 (*0-517-06718-8*) Random Hse Value.
Castle, Caroline. Herbert Binns & the Flying Tricycle. 1990. pap. 3.95 (*0-8037-0739-8*, Puff Pied Piper) Puffin Bks.
Chapman, Carol. Barney Bipple's Magic Dandelions. Kellogg, Steven, illus. LC 77-14852. 32p. (ps-3). 1992. pap. 3.99 (*0-14-054540-9*, Puff Unicorn) Puffin Bks.
Charnas, Suzy M. The Kingdom of Kevin Malone. LC 92-40720. 1993. 16.95 (*0-15-200756-3*, J Yolen Bks) HarBrace.
Chaykin, H. & Moore, J. F. Batman & Houdini: The Devil's Workshop. O'Neil, Dennis, ed. Chiarello, M., illus. 64p. (Orig.). 1993. pap. 5.95 (*1-56389-113-1*) DC Comics.
Cheetham, Ann. The Pit. LC 89-26868. 160p. (gr. 4-6). 1990. 14.95 (*0-8050-1142-0*, Bks Young Read) H Holt & Co.
Cheever, John. The Enormous Radio. 32p. (gr. 6 up). 1983. PLB 13.95 (*0-87191-959-1*) Creative Ed.
Chetwin, Grace. The Chimes of Alyafaleyn. LC 92-44156. 240p. (gr. 5-9). 1993. SBE 15.95 (*0-02-718222-3*, Bradbury Pr) Macmillan Child Grp.
—On All Hallows' Eve. LC 91-46440. 160p. (gr. 3-7). 1992. pap. 3.95 (*0-689-71617-6*, Aladdin) Macmillan Child Grp.
Chislett, Gail. Whump. Krykorka, Vladyana, illus. (ps-1). 1992. 0.99 (*1-55037-253-X*, Pub. by Annick Pr) Firefly Bks Ltd.
Chouinard, Marika. Brave Little Toaster Goes to Mars. 1988. pap. 11.95 (*0-385-24162-3*) Doubleday.
Christiana, David. Drawer in a Drawer. 32p. (ps-3). 1992. pap. 4.95 (*0-374-41881-0*, Sunburst) FS&G.
Christopher, Matt. The Kid Who Only Hit Homers. Kidder, Harvey, illus. (gr. 4-6). 1972. lib. bdg. 14.95 (*0-316-13918-1*) Little.
Cissom, Joan. The Enchanted Unicorn. Transue, David, illus. 20p. (Orig.). 1989. pap. 3.95 (*0-929560-01-9*) Southern Rose Prodns.
Clement, Claude. The Voice of the Wood. Clement, Frederic, illus. 32p. (gr. k-8). 1993. pap. 5.99 (*0-14-054594-8*) Puffin Bks.
Cohen, Daniel. Real Vampires. LC 94-22028. (gr. 1-8). 1995. write for info. (*0-525-65189-6*, Cobblehill Bks) Dutton Child Bks.
Cole, Brock. Alfa y el Bebe Sucio: Alpha & the Dirty Baby. Gottlieb, T., tr. (SPA., Illus.). 32p. (ps-3). 1991. 14.95 (*0-374-30242-1*) FS&G.
Cole, Joanna. The Magic School Bus in the Solar System. (ps-3). 1994. pap. 5.95 (*0-590-46429-9*) Scholastic Inc.
—The Magic School Bus Inside the Earth. Degen, Bruce, illus. LC 87-4563. 48p. (gr. k-3). 1987. 14.95 (*0-590-40759-7*, Scholastic Hardcover) Scholastic Inc.
—Magic School Bus on the Ocean Floor. (ps-3). 1994. pap. 4.95 (*0-590-41431-3*) Scholastic Inc.
Collins, David R. & Witter, Evelyn. The Golden Circle. 2nd ed. Nolte, Larry, illus. LC 91-67503. 105p. (gr. 4-8). 1992. pap. 6.95 (*1-55523-492-5*) Winston-Derek.
Collodi, Carlo. Pinocchio. Chiostri, Carlo, illus. (FRE.). 235p. (gr. 5-10). 1985. pap. 10.95 (*2-07-033283-7*) Schoenhof.
Coman, Carolyn. Losing Things at Mr. Mudd's. Hidy, Lance, illus. 32p. (ps-3). 1992. 14.00 (*0-374-34657-7*) FS&G.
Company, Merce. Don Gil y el Paraguas Magico: Sir Gil & the Magic Umbrella. Serra, Aurora M., tr. from GER. Asensio, Agusti, illus. (SPA.). 26p. (gr. 1-4). 1990. 13.95 (*968-6465-03-0*) Hispanic Bk Dist.
Coombs, Patricia. Dorrie & the Dreamyard Monsters. Coombs, Patricia, illus. 48p. (gr. k-6). 1982. pap. 2.25 (*0-440-40896-2*, YB) Dell.
Cooper, Louise. The Sleep of Stone. LC 91-4268. (Illus.). 144p. (gr. 7 up). 1991. SBE 14.95 (*0-689-31572-4*, Atheneum Child Bk) Macmillan Child Grp.
Cooper, Susan. The Dark Is Rising. Cober, Alan, illus. LC 72-85916. 232p. (gr. 5 up). 1973. SBE 15.95 (*0-689-30317-3*, M K McElderry) Macmillan Child Grp.
—The Grey King. Heslop, Michael, illus. LC 75-8526. 224p. (gr. 4-8). 1975. SBE 14.95 (*0-689-50029-7*, M K McElderry) Macmillan Child Grp.

Cooper, Susan L. Matthew's Dragon. Smith, Joseph A., illus. LC 93-26574. 32p. (gr. k-3). 1994. pap. 4.95 (*0-689-71794-6*, Aladdin) Macmillan Child Grp.

Corbin, Linda & Dys, Pat. Jesus Helps Me Grow. Fieser, Stephen, illus. 28p. (Orig.). (gr. 1-6). 1986. pap. 4.99 (*0-87509-374-4*) Chr Pubns.

Corddry, Thomas. Kibby & the Red Elephant. Kock, Carl, illus. LC 72-13771. (gr. 3-6). 1973. 6.95 (*0-87955-106-2*) O'Hara.

Cosgrove, Stephen. Balderdash. Gedrose, E. D., illus. 32p. (gr. 3-6). 1991. 14.95 (*1-55868-045-4*) Gr Arts Ctr Pub.

—Dragolin. James, Robin, illus. LC 85-14400. 32p. (Orig.). (gr. 1-4). 1978. pap. 3.95 (*0-8431-1165-8*) Price Stern.

—The Dream Stealer. Heyer, Carol, illus. LC 89-83843. 48p. (gr. 1-4). 1990. 16.95 (*1-55868-009-8*); pap. 5.95 (*1-55868-021-7*); pap. 12.95 incl. audio (*1-55868-042-X*) Gr Arts Ctr Pub.

—Flutterby Fly. James, Robin, illus. LC 85-14353. 32p. (Orig.). (gr. 1-4). 1984. pap. 2.95 (*0-8431-1162-3*) Price Stern.

Cosgrove, Stephen E. Gigglesnitcher. James, Robin, illus. 48p. (gr. k-9). 1991. 12.95 (*1-55868-034-9*) Gr Arts Ctr Pub.

Costello, Melina P. Tutti-Frutti Town: Blinky Blueberry Finds a Friend. Costello, Melina P., illus. 32p. (Orig.). (gr. k-3). 1991. pap. 6.50 (*1-878130-01-3*) Bang A Drum.

Cover, Arthur B. Blade of the Guillotine. 144p. (Orig.). (gr. 7-12). 1986. pap. 2.50 (*0-553-26038-3*) Bantam.

Coville, Bruce. The Dragonslayers. MacDonald, Pat, ed. Coville, Katherine, illus. 128p. (Orig.). (gr. 7 up). 1994. pap. 3.50 (*0-671-79832-4*, Minstrel Bks) PB.

—Into the Land of the Unicorns. LC 94-16892. (gr. 3-7). 1994. 12.95 (*0-590-45955-4*) Scholastic Inc.

Cresswell, Helen. The Secret World of Polly Flint. Felts, Shirley, illus. LC 91-15531. 176p. (gr. 3-7). 1991. pap. 3.95 (*0-689-71532-3*, Aladdin) Macmillan Child Grp.

Crutchfield, Charlie. Assassins of Dol Amroth. Fenlon, Peter C., Jr., ed. McBride, Angus, illus. (Orig.). (gr. 10-12). 1987. pap. 6.00 (*0-915795-98-1*, 8106) Iron Crown Ent Inc.

Cunningham, Julia. Dorp Dead. LC 87-3735. 96p. (Orig.). (gr. 3-7). 1993. pap. 2.99 (*0-679-84718-9*) Random Bks Yng Read.

Curtis, Chara M. Fun Is a Feeling. Aldrich, Cynthia, illus. 32p. (gr. k-5). 1992. 14.95 (*0-935699-04-X*) Illum Arts.

FUN IS A FEELING playfully embraces the development of positive attitudes & feelings. Ageless truths are powerfully presented through the inspiring verse & delightful illustrations. The child's imagination is challenged to view everyday events (including chores) in a creative, magical way. In the end, each reader is left with a secret smile - knowing "fun can be found wherever you go." "The artwork is fantastic. The message of treasuring our feelings is outstanding & uplifting. This book is a 'must' for children." - Gerald G. Jampolsky, M.D., author. "This vibrant text delights in the challenge of making fun the 'path' in life rather than the destination." - NAPRA Trade Journal. "Here's a book about new ways to have fun. Fun likes to hide, so look for it everywhere." - The Seattle Times. To order, call Atrium 1-800-275-2606. ***Publisher Provided Annotation.***

Cusick, Richie T. Vampire. MacDonald, Patricia, ed. 224p. (Orig.). 1991. pap. 3.99 (*0-671-70956-9*, Archway) PB.

Czernecki, Stefan & Rhodes, Timothy. The Sleeping Bread. LC 91-75422. (Illus.). 40p. (gr. k-4). 1992. 14.95 (*1-56282-183-0*); PLB 14.89 (*1-56282-207-1*) Hyprn Child.

Dadey, Debbie. Genies Don't Ride Bicycles. (ps-3). 1994. pap. 2.75 (*0-590-47297-6*) Scholastic Inc.

Dahl, Roald. Charlie & the Chocolate Factory. 1984. pap. 2.75 (*0-553-15454-0*) Bantam.

—Charlie & the Chocolate Factory. (Illus.). 174p. 1992. Repr. PLB 14.95x (*0-89966-904-2*) Buccaneer Bks.

—Charlie & the Great Glass Elevator. 1984. pap. 2.75 (*0-553-15455-9*) Bantam.

—Charlie et la Chocolaterie. Simeon, Michel, illus. (FRE.). 190p. (gr. 5-10). 1987. pap. 9.95 (*2-07-033446-5*) Schoenhof.

—Charlie et le Grand Ascenseur de Verre. Jacques, Faith, illus. (FRE.). 151p. (gr. 5-10). 1978. pap. 7.95 (*2-07-033065-6*) Schoenhof.

—Fantastique Maitre Renard. Ross, Tony, illus. (FRE.). 119p. (gr. 3-7). 1989. pap. 12.95 (*2-07-031174-0*) Schoenhof.

—James & the Giant Peach. 1984. pap. 2.95 (*0-553-15317-X*) Bantam.

—James et la Grosse Peche. Simeon, Michel, illus. (FRE.). 174p. (gr. 5-10). 1988. pap. 9.95 (*2-07-033517-8*) Schoenhof.

—My Year. Blake, Quentin, illus. 64p. (gr. 4-7). 1994. 14.99 (*0-670-85397-6*) Viking Child Bks.

—Potion Magique de Georges Bouillon. Blake, Quentin, illus. (FRE.). 148p. (gr. 5-10). 1990. pap. 8.95 (*2-07-033463-5*) Schoenhof.

—Three More from Roald Dahl: Includes The Witches, James & the Giant Peach, & Danny the Champion of the World. (gr. 3-7). 1991. 11.95 (*0-14-095381-7*) Puffin Bks.

Dashney, John. The Adventures of Walter the Weremouse. Somerville, Sheila, illus. 164p. (Orig.). (gr. 4-8). 1992. pap. 6.50x (*0-9633236-0-1*) J Dashney.

D'Aulaire, Ingri & D'Aulaire, Edgar P. D'Aulaire's Norse Gods & Giants. LC 86-11677. (Illus.). 168p. (ps up). 1986. pap. 16.95 (*0-385-23692-1*, Pub. by Zephyr-BFYR) Doubleday.

Davids, Paul. The Fountain of Youth. Davids, Paul, photos by. (Illus.). 56p. (Orig.). (gr. 5-9). pap. text ed. 9.95 (*0-939031-01-9*) Pictorial Legends.

Degen, Bruce. Jamberry. Degen, Bruce, illus. LC 82-47708. 32p. (ps-1). 1983. 14.00 (*0-06-021416-3*) HarpC Child Bks.

—Jamberry. (ps-3). 1983. PLB 13.89 (*0-06-021417-1*) HarpC Child Bks.

DeGross, Momalisa. Donovan's Word Jar. Hanna, Cheryl, illus. LC 91-2470. 80p. (gr. 2-5). 1994. 14.00 (*0-06-020190-8*, HarpT); PLB 13.89 (*0-06-020191-6*, HarpT) HarpC.

DeLeeuw, Adele. The Boy with Wings. LC 74-15860. (gr. 1-6). 1971. 8.95 (*0-87874-001-5*, Nautilus) Galloway.

DeMatteis, J. M. Superman: Speeding Bullets. Carlin, Mike, ed. Barreto, illus. 48p. (Orig.). 1993. pap. 4.95 (*1-56389-117-4*) DC Comics.

De Paola, Tomie. The Knight & the Dragon. (ps-k). 1992. pap. 6.95 (*0-399-22401-7*, Sandcastle Bks) Putnam Pub Group.

De Veaux, Alexis. An Enchanted Hair Tale. Hanna, Cheryl, illus. LC 85-45824. 48p. (gr. k-3). 1991. pap. 4.95 (*0-06-443271-8*, Trophy) HarpC Child Bks.

Dexter, Catherine. Mazemaker. Ingraham, Erick, illus. LC 88-32349. 224p. (gr. 5-9). 1989. 11.95 (*0-688-07383-2*) Morrow Jr Bks.

Dickey, James. Bronwen, the Traw, & the Shape-Shifter. Watson, Richard J., illus. LC 85-27082. 32p. (gr. k-3). 1986. 13.95 (*0-15-212580-9*, HB Juv Bks) HarBrace.

Dickinson, Peter. A Box of Nothing. LC 87-25660. 128p. (gr. 3-6). 1988. pap. 14.95 (*0-385-29664-9*) Delacorte.

—The Weathermonger. (gr. k-12). 1988. pap. 2.95 (*0-440-20003-2*) Dell.

Disch, Thomas. Brave Little Toaster. 1986. pap. 12.95 (*0-385-23050-8*) Doubleday.

Disney, Walt. Aladdin: Little Library. (ps). 1993. 5.98 (*0-453-03170-6*) Mouse Works.

Door in the Wall. 1986. pap. 5.25 (*0-440-80356-X*) Dell.

Downer, Ann. The Books of the Keepers. LC 92-30131. 256p. (gr. 7 up). 1993. SBE 15.95 (*0-689-31519-8*, Atheneum Child Bk) Macmillan Child Grp.

Downing, Peggy. Brill of Exitorn. LC 93-50904. 1994. write for info. (*0-89084-736-3*) Bob Jones Univ Pr.

Doyle, Arthur Conan. The Lost World. (Illus.). 272p. (gr. 5 up). 1991. pap. 2.95 (*0-14-035013-6*, Puffin) Puffin Bks.

Doyle, Debra & Macdonald, James. The City by the Sea. Mitchell, Judy, illus. LC 89-5213. 144p. (gr. 5-9). 1990. PLB 9.89 (*0-8167-1830-X*); pap. text ed. 2.95 (*0-8167-1831-8*) Troll Assocs.

—School of Wizardry. Mitchell, Judy, illus. LC 89-33882. 144p. (gr. 5-9). 1990. PLB 9.89 (*0-8167-1826-1*); pap. text ed. 2.95 (*0-8167-1827-X*) Troll Assocs.

—Tournament & Tower. Mitchell, Judy, illus. LC 89-33881. 144p. (gr. 5-9). 1990. PLB 9.89 (*0-8167-1828-8*); pap. text ed. 2.95 (*0-8167-1829-6*) Troll Assocs.

Dr. Seuss. Great Day for Up! Blake, Quentin, illus. LC 74-5517. 36p. (ps-1). 1974. 6.95 (*0-394-82913-1*); lib. bdg. 7.99 (*0-394-92913-6*) Random Bks Yng Read.

—Huevos Verdes Con Jamon. Marcuse, Aida, tr. (Illus.). 62p. (gr. 2-3). 1992. 8.95 (*1-880507-01-3*) Lectorum Pubns.

—Hunches in Bunches. Dr. Seuss, illus. 48p. (gr. 1-5). 1982. lib. bdg. 10.99 (*0-394-95502-1*); pap. 10.95 (*0-394-85502-7*) Random Bks Yng Read.

—I Had Trouble in Getting to Solla Sollew. Dr. Seuss, illus. LC 65-23994. 64p. (gr. 1-4). 1992. 13.00 (*0-394-80092-3*) Random Bks Yng Read.

—The Lorax. Danson, Ted, narrated by. Dr. Seuss, illus. 64p. (ps up). 1992. incl. cassette 13.00 (*0-679-82273-9*) Random Bks Yng Read.

—Fl Lorax. Marcuse, Aida E., tr. (Illus.). 64p. (gr. 3-6). 1993. 13.95 (*1-880507-04-8*) Lectorum Pubns.

—Oh, Cuan Lejos Llegaras. Marcuse, Aida, tr. (Illus.). (gr. 4-6). 1993. 13.95 (*1-880507-05-6*) Lectorum Pubns.

—Oh, the Places You'll Go. 11p. 1991. Braille. 0.88 (*1-56956-292-X*) W A T Braille.

—Scrambled Eggs Super! Dr. Seuss, illus. LC 53-5013. 64p. (gr. 1-4). 1992. 13.00 (*0-394-80085-0*) Random Bks Yng Read.

Dr. Suess. Green Eggs & Ham. Date not set. pap. write for info. (*0-679-85630-7*) Random Bks Yng Read.

Duane, Diane E. Deep Wizardry. 288p. (gr. 4-7). 1992. pap. 3.50 (*0-440-40658-7*, YB) Dell.

Duey, Kathleen. Double-Yuck Magic. 144p. (Orig.). 1991. pap. 2.99 (*0-380-76116-5*, Camelot) Avon.

Dugin, Andrej & Dugina, Olga. Dragon Feathers. LC 93-8700. (Illus.). 24p. 1993. 14.95 (*1-56566-047-1*) Thomasson-Grant.

Duncan, Lois. Locked in Time. (gr. 6 up). 1986. pap. 3.99 (*0-440-94942-4*, LFL) Dell.

—Stranger with My Face. 176p. (gr. 7 up). 1990. pap. 3.99 (*0-440-98356-8*, LFL) Dell.

Dunham, Katharine. Kasamance: A Fantasy. LC 73-92612. (gr. 7 up). 1974. 25.00 (*0-89388-128-7*) Okpaku Communications.

Duran, Gloria. Malinche: Slave Princess of Cortez. LC 92-31776. (Illus.). 248p. (gr. 6-12). 1992. PLB 17.50 (*0-208-02343-7*, Pub. by Linnet) Shoe String.

Eager, Edward. Half Magic. Bodecker, N. M., illus. LC 54-5153. 217p. (gr. 3-7). 1954. 14.95 (*0-15-233078-X*, HB Juv Bks) HarBrace.

—Half Magic. Treherne, Katie T. & Bodecker, N. M., illus. 192p. (gr. 3-7). 1989. pap. 4.95 (*0-15-233081-X*, Odyssey) HarBrace.

—Knight's Castle. Bodecker, N. M., illus. (gr. 4-6). 17.00 (*0-8446-6232-1*) Peter Smith.

—Knight's Castle. Treherne, Katie T. & Bodecker, N. M., illus. 198p. (gr. 3-7). 1989. pap. 3.95 (*0-15-243105-5*, Odyssey) HarBrace.

—Magic by the Lake. Treherne, Katie T. & Bodecker, N. M., illus. 190p. (gr. 3-7). 1989. pap. 3.95 (*0-15-250444-3*, Odyssey) HarBrace.

—Magic or Not? Bodecker, N. M., illus. (gr. 4-6). 1984. 17.00 (*0-8446-6154-6*) Peter Smith.

—Magic or Not? Treherne, Katie T. & Bodecker, N. M., illus. 197p. (gr. 3-7). 1989. pap. 3.95 (*0-15-251160-1*, Odyssey) HarBrace.

—Seven-Day Magic. (gr. 4-6). 17.25 (*0-8446-6381-6*) Peter Smith.

—Seven-Day Magic. Treherne, Katie T. & Bodecker, N. M., illus. 190p. (gr. 3-7). 1989. pap. 4.95 (*0-15-272916-X*, Odyssey) HarBrace.

—The Time Garden. Bodecker, N. M., illus. (gr. 4-6). 17.50 (*0-8446-6233-X*) Peter Smith.

—The Time Garden. Treherne, Katie T. & Bodecker, N. M., illus. 193p. (gr. 3-7). 1990. pap. 4.95 (*0-15-288193-X*, Odyssey) HarBrace.

—The Well-Wishers. (gr. 3-7). 17.50 (*0-8446-6382-4*) Peter Smith.

—The Well Wishers. Treherne, Katie T. & Bodecker, N. M., illus. 220p. (gr. 3-7). 1990. pap. 4.95 (*0-15-294994-1*, Odyssey) HarBrace.

Edens, Cooper. Little World. Edens, Cooper, illus. 32p. 1994. 10.95 (*1-883211-02-6*, Laugh Elephant) Blue Lantern Studio.

Edmiston, Jim. Huff Puff & Ruffly. Burgess, Mark, illus. 96p. (gr. 2-4). 1993. 18.95 (*0-460-88123-X*, Pub. by J M Dent & Sons) Trafalgar.

Ehrlich, Amy. Pome & Peel. Gal, Laszlo, illus. 32p. (ps-3). 1993. pap. 4.99 (*0-14-054587-5*) Puffin Bks.

Ellis, Anne L. The Dragon of Middlethorpe. (Illus.). 192p. (gr. 4-7). 1991. 14.95 (*0-8050-1713-5*, Bks Young Read) H Holt & Co.

Elzbieta. Flon Flon & Musette. (ps-2). 1994. 12.95 (*0-8050-3299-1*) H Holt & Co.

Ende, Michael. The Night of Wishes. Schwarzbauer, Heike & Takvorian, Rick, trs. Kehn, Regina, illus. 244p. (gr. 5 up). 1992. 16.00 (*0-374-19594-3*) FS&G.

Enderle, Judith R. & Tessler, Stephanie G. The Good-for-Something Dragon. Gray, Les, illus. 32p. (ps-3). 1993. pap. 14.95 (*1-56397-214-X*) Boyds Mills Pr.

Engdahl, Sylvia. Enchantress from the Stars. (gr. 6-10). 1991. 16.75 (*0-8446-6448-0*) Peter Smith.

Enik, Ted, illus. Walt Disney's Peter Pan: Where Are Wendy's Brothers? LC 93-73811. (ps). 1994. 9.95 (*1-56282-625-5*) Disney Pr.

Esbensen, Barbara J. The Star Maiden: An Ojibway Tale. Davie, Helen K., illus. (ps-3). 1988. 14.95 (*0-316-24951-3*) Little.

Evans, D. R. Palindor. LC 93-20220. (Illus.). 1993. pap. 7.99 (*0-7814-0117-8*, Chariot Bks) Chariot Family.

Evslin, Bernard. Jason & the Argonauts. Dodson, Bert, illus. LC 86-32114. 176p. (gr. 5 up). 1986. 13.00 (*0-688-06245-8*) Morrow Jr Bks.

Exony's Excursion. (Illus.). 56p. (gr. 5-7). 25.00 (*0-9600792-7-0*) Rymer Bks.

Fager, Charles. The Magic Quilts. Lewis, Charlotte, illus. 100p. (gr. 3-6). 1990. pap. 12.95 (*0-945177-03-8*) Kimo Pr.

Farrington, Liz & Sherwood, Jonathan. Painting the Fire. Moran, J. Douglas, illus. Farrington, Liz, created by. LC 92-76022. (Illus.). 40p. (gr. k-4). 1993. 14.95 (*1-56844-001-4*) Enchante Pub.

Faulkner, Matt. The Moon Clock. Faulkner, Matt, illus. 56p. 1991. 14.95 (*0-590-41593-X*, Scholastic Hardcover) Scholastic Inc.

Favors, Jean. Waters Dark & Deep. 1993. pap. 3.50 (*0-06-106736-9*, Harp PBks) HarpC.

Feltman, John P. Toga & the Kingdom of Croone: Frogs, Turtles, Dragon Snakes, Whales, & Magic Mushrooms. Giannola, Kirk, illus. Feltman, John P., pref. by. LC 93-87067. (Illus.). 120p. (gr. k-8). 1994. 17.95x (*0-9639277-0-1*) Samantha Bks.

The story of Croone is the story of the first frog kingdom. A classical kingdom in that it is ruled by a king & queen. Croone's society is made up of frogs & turtles who live together in a compatible way to survive the perils of nature. The dragon snake is Croone's greatest enemy. King Lor, ruler of Croone, devises a system to defend his kingdom against the snakes that include an army of flying frogs who bravely & skillfully defend their kingdom. Croone is a very beautiful & happy kingdom where frog children, who are called leechins, go to school, play together & create their own excitement when the opportunities exist. Family togetherness is the most important characteristic of Croone's society. It is filled with love, caring & respect for each other. The frogs are also skillful in their abilities to plan & build things like a floating school-log & an amusement park. "This fantasy-type story could appeal to young primary children to adult: in conclusion, I found this fascinating narrative to be well written & capable of being exceptionally literate."--Martin W. Olander, International Reading Association. To order: Samantha Books, P.O. Box 2729, No. Babylon, NY 11703.
Publisher Provided Annotation.

Ferguson, Alane. Stardust. LC 92-33011. 160p. (gr. 3-7). 1993. SBE 13.95 (*0-02-734527-0*, Bradbury Pr) Macmillan Child Grp.

Ferguson, Virginia & Durkin, Peter. Tiptoe Round the Corner. Shaw, Peter, illus. LC 93-168. 1994. write for info. (*0-383-03720-4*) SRA Schl Grp.

Fischer, Sharon G. Lucy & the Leprechaun's Rainbow. 1991. 7.95 (*0-533-09513-1*) Vantage.

Fleming, Ian. Chitty Chitty Bang Bang. reissued ed. Burningham, John, illus. 112p. (gr. 3-7). 1993. pap. 2.99 (*0-679-81948-7*, Bullseye Bks) Random Bks Yng Read.

Fletcher, Susan. Dragon's Milk. LC 91-31358. 256p. (gr. 3-7). 1992. pap. 3.95 (*0-689-71623-0*, Aladdin) Macmillan Child Grp.

—Flight of the Dragon Kyn. LC 92-44787. 224p. (gr. 5-9). 1993. SBE 15.95 (*0-689-31880-4*, Atheneum Child Bk) Macmillan Child Grp.

Foley, Pat. Edge. (Illus.). 19p. (Orig.). (gr. k-1). 1989. pap. 5.00 (*0-9624315-0-8*) Pajari Pr.

Fox. Justice League of America Archives, Vol. 2. Kahan, Bob, ed. Sekowsky, et al, illus. 224p. 1993. text ed. 39.95 collected ed. (*1-56389-119-0*) DC Comics.

Frankel, B. Tertius & Pliny. Clark, E., ed. 1992. 13.95 (*0-15-200604-4*, Gulliver Bks) HarBrace.

Freeman, Don. The Paper Party. (Illus.). (gr. 1 up). 1977. pap. 3.95 (*0-14-050212-2*, Puffin) Puffin Bks.

Friesner, Esther M. Wishing Season. Freas, Frank K., illus. LC 93-71527. 144p. (gr. 7 up). 1993. SBE 14.95 (*0-689-31574-0*, Atheneum Child Bk) Macmillan Child Grp.

Frye, Tom. The Jewel Folk. Hammond, Lee, illus. (Orig.). 1993. pap. 8.95 (*1-881663-17-5*) Advent Mean Pr.

Gackenbach, Dick. Harry y el Terrible Quiensabeque. (ps-3). pap. 2.95 (*0-590-41820-3*) Scholastic Inc.

Gannett, Ruth S. The Dragons of Blueland. Gannett, Ruth C., illus. LC 86-27480. 96p. (gr. 2-5). 1963. 3.99 (*0-394-89050-7*) Knopf Bks Yng Read.

—Elmer & the Dragon. Gannett, Ruth C., illus. LC 86-27479. 96p. (gr. 2-5). 1987. PLB 3.99 (*0-394-89049-3*) Knopf Bks Yng Read.

—My Father's Dragon. Gannett, Ruth C., illus. LC 86-27635. 96p. (gr. 2-5). 1987. pap. 3.99 (*0-394-89048-5*) Knopf Bks Yng Read.

Ganz, Yaffa. Savta Simcha & the Cinnamon Tree. Gewirtz, Bina & Poppins, Jewish M., illus. (gr. 6-10). 11.95 (*0-87306-354-6*) Feldheim.

Garland, Sherry. Shadow of the Dragon. 1993. 10.95 (*0-15-273530-5*, HB Juv Bks); pap. 3.95 (*0-15-273532-1*) HarBrace.

Gaskin, Carol. The Forbidden Towers. Price, T. Alexander, illus. LC 84-16219. 128p. (gr. 3-7). 1985. lib. bdg. 9.49 (*0-8167-0324-8*) Troll Assocs.

—Legend of Hiawatha, No. 2. 80p. (Orig.). 1986. pap. 2.50 (*0-553-15450-8*) Bantam.

—The Magician's Ring. Price, T. Alexander, illus. LC 84-8499. 128p. (gr. 3-7). 1985. PLB 9.49 (*0-8167-0320-5*); pap. text ed. 2.95 (*0-8167-0321-3*) Troll Assocs.

—Master of Mazes. Price, T. Alexander, illus. LC 84-24015. 128p. (gr. 3-7). 1985. PLB 9.49 (*0-8167-0322-1*) Troll Assocs.

Gatt, Elizabeth. In Sea Star Ocean. (ps-3). 1994. 3.99 (*0-89577-573-5*, Readers Digest Kids) RD Assn.

Gibbons, Dave. Batman Versus Predator: The Collected Edition. Kahan, Bob, ed. O'Neil, Dennis, intros. by. (Illus.). 128p. (Orig.). 1992. pap. 5.95 (*1-56389-092-5*) DC Comics.

Gibson, Andrew. Ellis & the Hummick. Riddell, Chris, illus. 132p. (gr. 3-6). 1990. pap. 3.95 (*0-571-14412-8*) Faber & Faber.

Gilden, Mel. Monster Mashers. 96p. (Orig.). (gr. 5 up). 1989. pap. 2.75 (*0-380-75785-0*, Camelot) Avon.

Gilman, Phoebe. Grandma & the Pirates. 1992. pap. 3.95 (*0-590-43425-X*) Scholastic Inc.

Gilson, Jamie. Thirteen Ways to Sink a Sub. Edwards, Linda S., illus. (gr. 3-7). 1982. 13.00 (*0-688-01304-X*) Lothrop.

Gipe, George. Gremlins. (Illus.). 77p. (gr. 3-7). 1984. pap. 2.95 (*0-380-89003-8*, Camelot) Avon.

Glatzer, Nahum N. Quest for the Cities of Gold, No. 16. 144p. (Orig.). (ps-6). 1987. pap. 2.50 (*0-553-26295-5*) Bantam.

Gogol, Nikolai. The Nose. Cowan, Catherine, retold by. Hawkes, Kevin, illus. LC 93-4975. 1995. 15.00 (*0-688-10464-9*); PLB 14.93 (*0-688-10465-7*) Lothrop.

Goldsboro, Bobby. Bobby Goldsboro's The Boy Who Became a Frog. 16p. (ps-2). 1993. write for info. (*1-883366-12-7*) YES Ent.

Gorman, Carol. Chelsea & the Green-Haired Kid. Ashby, Ruth, ed. 128p. (gr. 7 up). 1992. pap. 2.99 (*0-671-78713-6*, Archway) PB.

Gormley, Beatrice. Wanted: UFO. 128p. 1992. pap. 2.99 (*0-380-71313-6*, Camelot) Avon.

Gorog, Judith. Three Dreams & a Nightmare: And Other Tales of the Dark. 160p. (gr. 4 up). 1988. 14.95 (*0-399-21578-6*, Philomel Bks) Putnam Pub Group.

Gouge, Elizabeth. Linnets & Valerians. (gr. 4-7). 1992. pap. 3.50 (*0-440-40590-4*, YB) Dell.

Grahame, Kenneth. The Reluctant Dragon. Hague, Michael, illus. LC 83-209. 48p. (gr. 2-4). 1988. pap. 5.95 (*0-8050-0802-0*, Bks Young Read) H Holt & Co.

Gramatky, Hardie & Gramatky, Dorothea C. Little Toot & the Loch Ness Monster. Gramatky, Hardie, illus. 48p. (ps-3). 1989. 13.95 (*0-399-21684-7*, Putnam) Putnam Pub Group.

Graves, Robert. Big Green Book. (Illus.). 64p. (gr. 1-4). 1990. pap. 4.95 (*0-689-71402-5*, Aladdin) Macmillan Child Grp.

Greaves, Margaret. The Lost Ones. De Lacey, Honey, illus. 96p. (gr. 4-6). 1993. 16.95 (*0-460-88053-5*, Pub. by J M Dent & Sons) Trafalgar.

Green, Phyllis. Eating Ice Cream with a Werewolf. (gr. 4-6). 1985. pap. 2.95 (*0-440-42182-9*, YB) Dell.

Greenberg, David. Your Dog Might Be a Werewolf, Your Toes Could All Explode. (ps-3). 1992. pap. 2.99 (*0-553-15909-7*) Bantam.

Gregorich, Barbara. The Raccoon on the Moon. Hoffman, Joan, ed. (Illus.). 16p. (Orig.). (gr. k-2). 1991. pap. 2.25 (*0-88743-024-4*, 06024) Sch Zone Pub Co.

Griffith, Helen V. Emily & the Enchanted Frog. Lamb, Susan C., illus. LC 88-16511. 32p. (gr. 1 up). 1989. 12.95 (*0-688-08483-4*); PLB 12.88 (*0-688-08484-2*) Greenwillow.

Gripari, Pierre. Gentil Petit Diable et Autres Contes de la Rue Broca. Rosado, Puig, illus. (FRE.). 157p. (gr. 5-10). 1988. pap. 7.95 (*2-07-033451-1*) Schoenhof.

Guderjahn, Ernie L. A Children's Trilogy: Ali's Flying Rug, the Shadow Workers, & the Magic Cricket. (Orig.). (gr. 3 up). 1984. pap. 6.00 play script (*0-88734-504-2*) Players Pr.

Gulliver's Travels. (Illus.). 48p. (gr. 4 up). 1988. PLB 20.70 (*0-8172-2763-6*) Raintree Steck-V.

Gunsher, Cheryl. Danny the Dizzy Draydl. Webb, Sandra, ed. Gunsher, Cheryl, illus. 24p. (ps). 1992. 6.00 (*1-881602-00-1*) Prism NJ.

Gutierrez, Douglas. The Night of the Stars. Dearden, Carmen D., tr. from SPA. Oliver, Maria F., illus. 24p. (ps-1). 1988. 9.95 (*0-916291-17-0*) Kane-Miller Bk.

Haas, Dorothy. Burton's Zoom Zoom Va-room Machine. MacDonald, Pat, ed. 144p. (gr. 4-7). 1993. pap. 2.99 (*0-671-74702-9*, Minstrel Bks) PB.

Hall, Willis. Dragon Days. large type ed. 200p. (gr. 3-7). 1991. 29.00x (*0-7451-1294-3*, Galaxy Child Lrg Print) Chivers N Amer.

Hamilton, E. & Siegel. The Legion of Super-Heroes Archives, Vol. 3. Kahan, Bob, ed. Swon, et al, illus. 224p. 1993. text ed. 39.95 collected ed. (*1-56389-102-6*) DC Comics.

Hamilton, Virginia. Dustland. 224p. (gr. 7 up). 1989. pap. 3.95 (*0-15-224315-1*, Odyssey) HarBrace.

—The Gathering. 214p. (gr. 7 up). 1989. pap. 3.95 (*0-15-230592-0*, Odyssey) HarBrace.

—Justice & Her Brother. 282p. (gr. 7 up). 1989. pap. 3.95 (*0-15-241640-4*, Odyssey) HarBrace.

—The Mystery of Drear House: The Conclusion of the Dies Drear Chronicle. LC 88-2887. 224p. (gr. 7 up). 1988. pap. 3.95 (*0-02-043480-4*, Collier Young Ad) Macmillan Child Grp.

Hamley, Dennis. Pageants of Despair. LC 74-10841. 180p. (gr. 7-10). 1974. 21.95 (*0-87599-205-6*) S G Phillips.

Harris, Geraldine. The Dead Kingdom. (gr. k-12). 1987. pap. 2.50 (*0-440-91810-3*, LFL) Dell.

Haskins, Lori, adapted by. Alice in Wonderland. Goode, Diane, illus. LC 93-40523. 1994. write for info. (*0-679-85468-1*) Random Bks Yng Read.

Hasler, Eveline. En Suenos Puedo Volar: In His Dreams He Could Fly. Krohn, Hildegard M., tr. from GER. Bhend, Kathi, illus. (SPA.). 26p. (ps-5). 1990. 13.95 (*968-6465-05-7*) Hispanic Bk Dist.

Hautzig, Deborah. Aladdin & the Magic Lamp. Mitchell, Kathy, illus. LC 92-1608. 48p. (Orig.). (gr. 2-3). 1993. PLB 7.99 (*0-679-93241-0*); pap. 3.50 (*0-679-83241-6*) Random Bks Yng Read.

Hayes, Sarah. Crumbling Castle. Craig, Helen & Craig, Helen, illus. LC 91-58723. 80p. (gr. 3-6). 1992. 13.95 (*1-56402-108-4*) Candlewick Pr.

Haynes, Betsy. The Power. (Orig.). (gr. 5 up). 1982. pap. 1.95 (*0-440-97164-0*, LFL) Dell.

Haynes, James. Voices in the Dark. (Orig.). (gr. 5 up). 1982. pap. 1.95 (*0-440-99317-2*, LFL) Dell.

Helfer, Andrew. Batman: The House of Horrors. (ps-3). 1993. pap. 3.50 (*0-307-11471-6*, Golden Pr) Western Pub.

Heller, Nicholas. A Troll Story. LC 88-34906. (Illus.). 24p. (ps up). 1990. 12.95 (*0-688-08970-4*); PLB 14.88 (*0-688-08971-2*) Greenwillow.

Herge. The Secret of the Unicorn. (Illus.). 64p. 1992. 12.95 (*0-316-35902-5*, Joy St Bks) Little.

Herman, Gail. Wizard of Oz. (ps-3). 1993. pap. 2.95 (*0-590-46994-0*) Scholastic Inc.

Hermoso, Elizabeth S. The Smartians. Hermoso, Elizabeth S., illus. 15p. 1991. pap. 3.00x (*971-10-0443-7*, Pub. by New Day Pub PI) Cellar.

Herron, John. The Land of Numm. Hallock, Michelle, illus. 14p. 1992. pap. 9.95 (*1-881617-07-6*) Teapot Tales.

Herzig, Alison C. & Mali, Jane L. Sam & the Moon Queen. 176p. (gr. 4-8). 1990. 13.45 (*0-395-53342-2*, Clarion Bks) HM.

Hess, Debra. Three Little Witches & the Blue-Eyed Frog. (gr. 1-6). 1991. pap. 2.99 (*0-06-106114-X*, Harp PBks) HarpC.

—Three Little Witches & the Christmas Ghost. (gr. 1-6). 1991. pap. 2.99 (*0-06-106116-6*, Harp PBks) HarpC.

—Three Little Witches & the Shrinking House. (gr. 1-6). 1991. pap. 2.99 (*0-06-106057-7*, Harp PBks) HarpC.

—Three Little Witches & the Two-Day Spell. (gr. 1-6). 1991. pap. 2.99 (*0-06-106115-8*, Harp PBks) HarpC.

Heyer, Marilee. The Forbidden Door. (Illus.). 32p. (ps-3). 1992. pap. 4.99 (*0-14-050752-3*, Puffin) Puffin Bks.

Hildick, E. W. The Case of the Weeping Witch: A McGurk Fantasy. LC 91-38231. 160p. (gr. 3-7). 1992. SBE 13.95 (*0-02-743785-X*, Macmillan Child Bk) Macmillan Child Grp.

Hilgartner, Beth. The Feast of the Trickster. 240p. (gr. 5-9). 1991. 14.45 (*0-395-55008-4*, Sandpiper) HM.

Hill, Douglas. Goblin Party. Demeyer, Paul, illus. 44p. (gr. 3-5). 1990. 13.95 (*0-575-04338-5*, Pub. by Gollancz England) Trafalgar.

Hill, Fred D. Rescue of the Royal Dream Maker. Hill, Gloria A., ed. Foster, Demetrius, illus. LC 92-73364. 45p. (gr. 1-6). 1994. 15.95 (*1-883519-00-4*) Charill Pubs.

Hillert, Margaret. Come to School, Dear Dragon. (Illus.). (ps-k). 1985. PLB 6.95 (*0-8136-5133-6*, TK2966); pap. 3.50 (*0-8136-5633-8*) Modern Curr.

—Friend for Dear Dragon. (Illus.). (ps-k). 1985. PLB 6.95 (*0-8136-5136-0*, TK2972); pap. 3.50 (*0-8136-5636-2*, TK2973) Modern Curr.

—Go to Sleep Dear Dragon. (Illus.). (ps-k). 1985. PLB 6.95 (*0-8136-5135-2*, TK2970); pap. 3.50 (*0-8136-5635-4*, TK2971) Modern Curr.

—Happy Birthday, Dear Dragon. (Illus.). (ps-k). 1977. PLB 6.95 (*0-8136-5021-6*, TK2308); pap. 3.50 (*0-8136-5521-8*, TK2309) Modern Curr.

—Happy Easter, Dear Dragon. (Illus.). (ps-k). 1981. PLB 6.95 (*0-8136-5022-4*, TK2310); pap. 3.50 (*0-8136-5522-6*, TK2311) Modern Curr.

—Help for Dear Dragon. (Illus.). (ps-k). 1981. PLB 6.95 (*0-8136-5131-X*, TK2962); pap. 3.50 (*0-8136-5631-1*, TK2963) Modern Curr.

—I Love You, Dear Dragon. (Illus.). (ps-k). 1981. PLB 6.95 (*0-8136-5023-2*); pap. 3.50 (*0-8136-5523-4*) Modern Curr.

—I Need You, Dear Dragon. (Illus.). (ps-k). 1985. PLB 6.95 (*0-8136-5134-4*, TK2968); pap. 3.50 (*0-8136-5634-6*, TK2969) Modern Curr.

—It's Circus Time, Dear Dragon. (Illus.). (ps-k). 1985. PLB 6.95 (*0-8136-5132-8*, TK2964); pap. 3.50 (*0-8136-5632-X*, TK2965) Modern Curr.

—It's Halloween Time, Dear Dragon. (Illus.). (ps-k). 1981. PLB 6.95 (*0-8136-5024-0*, TK2318); pap. 3.50 (*0-8136-5524-2*, TK2319) Modern Curr.

—Let's Go Dear Dragon. (Illus.). (ps-k). 1981. PLB 6.95 (*0-8136-5025-9*, TK2322); pap. 3.50 (*0-8136-5525-0*, TK2323) Modern Curr.

—The Magic Nutcracker. (Illus.). (ps-k). 1981. PLB 6.95 (*0-8136-5074-7*, TK2340); pap. 3.50 (*0-8136-5574-9*, TK2341) Modern Curr.

—Merry Christmas, Dear Dragon. (Illus.). (ps-k). 1981. PLB 6.95 (*0-8136-5026-7*, TK2344); pap. 3.50 (*0-8136-5526-9*, TK2345) Modern Curr.

—Run to the Rainbow. (Illus.). (ps-k). 1981. PLB 6.95 (*0-8136-5065-8*, TK2361); pap. 3.50 (*0-8136-5565-X*, TK2362) Modern Curr.

—Up, up & Away. (Illus.). (ps-2). 1982. PLB 6.95 (*0-8136-5096-8*, TK2176); pap. 3.50 (*0-8136-5596-X*, TK2177) Modern Curr.

Hindley, J., et al. Time Traveller's Omnibus. (Illus.). 32p. 1977. text ed. 17.95 (*0-86020-222-4*) EDC.

Hissey, Jane. Jolly Tall. (Illus.). 32p. (ps-3). 1990. 14.95 (*0-399-21827-0*, Philomel Bks) Putnam Pub Group.

Hodges, Margaret, retold by. Gulliver in Lilliput. Root, Kimberly B., illus. LC 94-15037. (gr. 4 up). 1995. write for info. (*0-8234-1147-8*) Holiday.

Hodges, Margaret, adapted by. St. George & the Dragon. Hyman, Trina S., illus. LC 83-19980. (gr. 6-8). 1984. 16.95 (*0-316-36789-3*) Little.

Hodgman, Ann. My Babysitter Flies at Night. Ashby, Ruth, ed. Pierard, John, illus. 144p. (Orig.). 1994. pap. 3.50 (*0-671-88450-6*, Minstrel Bks) PB.

—My Babysitter Is a Vampire. Ashby, Ruth, ed. Pierard, John, illus. (Orig.). 1991. pap. 3.50 (*0-671-64751-2*, Minstrel Bks) PB.

Hoffman, Mary. Dracula's Daughter. Riddell, Chris, illus. 42p. (gr. 2-4). 1989. 3.95 (*0-8120-6135-7*) Barron.

Hoffmann, E. T. The Nutcracker. Manheim, Ralph, tr. Sendak, Maurice, illus. 120p. 1991. pap. 16.00 (*0-517-58659-2*, Crown) Crown Pub Group.

Holabird, Katharine. Alexander & the Magic Boat. Craig, Helen, illus. 24p. (ps-2). 1990. 11.95 (*0-517-58142-6*); PLB 12.99 (*0-517-58149-3*) Crown Bks Yng Read.

Holl, Kristi D. Footprints up My Back. (gr. 3-6). 1986. pap. 2.95 (*0-440-42649-9*, YB) Dell.

Holland, Alex N. Skip. Holland, Alex N., illus. 12p. (gr. 1-3). 1992. pap. 6.95 (*1-895583-02-0*) MAYA Pubs.

Hollenbeck, Patricia. The Adventures of Peela & Keela: Visit to Woodland. (Illus.). 64p. 1994. pap. 9.95 (*0-685-72014-4*) Dorrance.

Holling, Holling C. Pagoo. Holling, Lucille W., illus. 96p. (gr. 4-6). 1990. pap. 7.70 (*0-395-53964-1*) HM.

Hooker, Russell K. A Friend for Dunsworth. Hogelucht, Terry, illus. 40p. (ps-6). 1993. pap. 4.95 (*1-884534-00-7*) Duzall Toys.

—A Pet for Dunsworth. Hogelucht, Terry, illus. 36p. (ps-6). 1993. pap. 4.95 (*1-884534-01-5*) Duzall Toys.

—A Visit from Ellsworth. Hogelucht, Terry, illus. 34p. (ps-6). 1993. pap. 4.95 (*1-884534-02-3*) Duzall Toys.

Huddy, Delia. Puffin Ashore. Heap, Sue, illus. 32p. (ps-1). 1993. 13.95 (*1-85681-171-9*, Pub. by J MacRae UK) Trafalgar.

Hughes, Francine. Thumbelina & the Prince. 24p. (ps-3). 1993. pap. 2.50 (*0-448-40506-7*, G&D) Putnam Pub Group.

—Thumbelina Finds Her Way. 24p. (ps-3). 1993. pap. 2.50 (*0-448-40507-5*, G&D) Putnam Pub Group.

Hughes, Monica. The Promise. LC 91-21674. 208p. (gr. 5-9). 1992. pap. 13.00 jacketed, 3-pc. bdg. (*0-671-75033-X*, S&S BFYR) S&S Trade.

Hunter, Dan. The Magic Blue Giant. LC 90-70450. (Illus.). 80p. (Orig.). (gr. 3-6). 1991. pap. 7.00 (*1-56002-107-1*) Aegina Pr.

Hutchins, Hazel. The Three & Many Wishes of Jason Reid. Tennent, Julie, illus. 96p. (gr. 1-4). 1990. pap. 3.95 (*0-14-032178-0*, Puffin) Puffin Bks.

Igor the Terrible. LC 93-87391. 12p. (gr. k-2). 1994. 11. 95 (*0-89577-590-5*) RD Assn.

Ingle, Annie. The Smallest Elf's Big Surprise. Smath, Jerry, illus. LC 91-67670. 22p. (ps). 1992. bds. 2.95 (*0-679-83380-3*) Random Bks Yng Read.

Ingoglia, Gina, adapted by. Walt Disney's Pinocchio. LC 91-73974. (Illus.). 64p. (Orig.). (gr. 2-6). 1992. pap. 3.50 (*1-56282-033-8*) Disney Pr.

Irving, Washington & Busch, Jeffrey. Rip Van Winkle. (Illus.). 52p. Date not set. pap. 4.95 (*1-57209-009-X*) Classics Int Ent.

Jackson, Steve & Livingstone, Ian. Appointment with F. E.A.R. (Orig.). (gr. 5 up). 1986. pap. 2.50 (*0-440-90258-4*, LFL) Dell.

—Demons of the Deep. (Orig.). (gr. k-12). 1987. pap. 2.50 (*0-440-91843-X*, LFL) Dell.

Jacobs, Joseph. Adventures of Tom Thumb. Cutts, David, adapted by. Fuka, illus. LC 87-10980. 32p. (gr. k-3). 1988. PLB 9.79 (*0-8167-1071-6*); pap. text ed. 1.95 (*0-8167-1072-4*) Troll Assocs.

Jacques, Brian. Mariel of Redwall. 400p. (gr. 5-9). 1992. 17.95 (*0-399-22144-1*, Philomel Bks) Putnam Pub Group.

—Salamandastron: A Tale from Red Wall. Chalk, Gary, illus. 400p. (gr. 5 up). 1993. 17.95 (*0-399-21992-7*, Philomel Bks) Putnam Pub Group.

James, Betsy. Dark Heart. LC 91-45319. 180p. (gr. 7 up). 1992. 14.00 (*0-525-44951-5*, DCB) Dutton Child Bks.

—Long Night Dance. LC 88-38837. 176p. (gr. 7 up). 1989. 13.95 (*0-525-44485-8*, DCB) Dutton Child Bks.

James, Mary. The Shuteyes. LC 92-16170. 176p. (gr. 3-7). 1993. 13.95 (*0-590-45069-7*) Scholastic Inc.

James, Robin. Butterwings. James, Robin, illus. 32p. (Orig.). (gr. 1-4). 1993. pap. 2.95 (*0-8431-3494-1*) Price Stern.

—Maynard's Mermaid. James, Robin, illus. 32p. (Orig.). (gr. 1-4). 1993. pap. 2.95 (*0-8431-3495-X*) Price Stern.

Janoski, Elizabeth. What's Wrong with Eddie? 92p. (Orig.). (gr. 5-8). 1994. PLB 15.00 (*0-88092-041-6*); pap. 5.00 (*0-88092-040-8*) Royal Fireworks.

Jansson, Tove. Comet in Moominland. Portch, Elizabeth, tr. (Illus.). 192p. (gr. 2-5). 1990. 13.95 (*0-374-31526-4*) FS&G.

—Comet in Moominland. Portch, Elizabeth, tr. (Illus.). 192p. (gr. 2-5). 1991. pap. 3.95 (*0-374-41331-2*, Sunburst) FS&G.

—Moominland Midwinter. (gr. 4-7). 1992. 14.00 (*0-374-35041-8*) FS&G.

—Moominland Midwinter. (gr. 4-7). 1992. pap. 4.50 (*0-374-45303-9*) FS&G.

—Moominpappa at Sea. Hart, Kingsley, tr. from FIN. LC 93-1434. 1993. 17.00 (*0-374-35044-2*); pap. 4.95 (*0-374-45306-3*) FS&G.

—Moominpappa's Memoirs. Warburton, Thomas, tr. LC 94-50954. (gr. 2-7). 1994. 17.00 (*0-374-35045-0*) FS&G.

—Moominsummer Madness. (gr. 4-7). 1991. 13.95 (*0-374-35039-6*) FS&G.

—Moominsummer Madness. Warburton, Thomas, tr. (Illus.). 144p. (gr. 2-5). 1992. pap. 4.50 (*0-374-45310-1*, Sunburst) FS&G.

Jarrell, Randall. Fly by Night. Sendak, Maurice, illus. LC 76-27313. 40p. (ps up). 1985. 14.00 (*0-374-32348-8*); pap. 2.95, 1986 (*0-374-42350-4*) FS&G.

Jeffrey, Graham. The Little Man. (Illus.). 32p. (ps-k). 1993. 14.95 (*0-460-88068-3*, Pub. by J M Dent & Sons) Trafalgar.

Jenkins, Gerald & Bear, Magdalen. The Compound of the Five Cubes. (Illus.). 24p. (Orig.). (gr. 5-9). 1986. pap. 4.95 (*0-906212-47-2*, Pub. by Tarquin UK) Parkwest Pubns.

—The Final Stellation of the Icosahedron. (Illus.). 24p. (Orig.). (gr. 5-9). 1986. pap. 4.95 (*0-906212-48-0*, Pub. by Tarquin UK) Parkwest Pubns.

Jennings, Paul. Uncanny! Even More Surprising Stories. 144p. (gr. 5 up). 1993. pap. 3.99 (*0-14-034909-X*, Puffin) Puffin Bks.

Johnson, Gillian. Sahara-Sara: Saranohair. Johnson, Gillian, illus. (FRE.). 56p. 1992. 12.95 (*1-55037-258-0*, Pub. by Annick Pr) Firefly Bks Ltd.

Johnson, Gillian K. Saranohair. Johnson, Gillian K., illus. 56p. 1992. 12.95 (*1-55037-211-4*, Pub. by Annick Pr) Firefly Bks Ltd.

Johnson, Philip R. Chase of the Sorceress. LC 89-50958. 152p. (gr. 7-12). 1989. pap. 8.25x (*0-943864-58-5*) Davenport.

Johnston, Deanna. What Dreams Are Made Of. 1993. 7.95 (*0-533-09736-3*) Vantage.

Jones, Diana W. Cart & Cwidder. Cohn, Amy, ed. LC 94-1512. 1995. write for info. RTE (*0-688-13360-6*, Beech Tree Bks); pap. 4.95 (*0-688-13399-1*, Beech Tree Bks) Morrow.

—Castle in the Air. LC 90-30266. (Illus.). 208p. (gr. 6 up). 1991. 13.95 (*0-688-09686-7*) Greenwillow.

—The Crown of Dalemark. LC 94-17936. 1995. write for info. (*0-688-13363-0*); pap. write for info. (*0-688-13402-5*) Greenwillow.

—Drowned Ammet. Cohn, Amy, ed. LC 94-1513. 1995. write for info. RTE (*0-688-13361-4*, Beech Tree Bks); pap. 4.95 (*0-688-13400-9*, Beech Tree Bks) Morrow.

—Fire & Hemlock. LC 84-4084. 352p. (gr. 7 up). 1984. reinforced bdg. 13.00 (*0-688-03942-1*) Greenwillow.

—Hidden Turnings. LC 89-11742. (gr. 7 up). 1990. 12.95 (*0-688-09163-6*) Greenwillow.

—Howl's Moving Castle. LC 85-21981. 224p. (gr. 7 up). 1986. reinforced bdg. 13.00 (*0-688-06233-4*) Greenwillow.

—The Spellcoats. Cohn, Amy, ed. LC 94-1507. 1995. write for info. RTE (*0-688-13362-2*, Beech Tree Bks); pap. 4.95 (*0-688-13401-7*, Beech Tree Bks) Morrow.

—A Tale of Time City. LC 86-33304. (Illus.). 288p. (gr. 7 up). 1987. 11.75 (*0-688-07315-8*) Greenwillow.

Jones, Ron. The Acorn People. 1990. pap. 3.99 (*0-553-27385-X*) Bantam.

Jones, Terry. Fantastic Stories. large type ed. Foreman, Michael, illus. 1993. 16.95 (*0-7451-1908-5*, Galaxy Child Lrg Print) Chivers N Amer.

—Nicobobinus. Foreman, Michael, illus. LC 85-28630. 176p. (gr. k-6). 1986. 16.95 (*0-87226-065-8*) P Bedrick Bks.

—Nicobobinus. large type ed. 224p. (gr. 3-7). 1991. lib. bdg. 17.95x (*0-7451-1319-2*, Lythway Large Print) Hall.

—Terry Jones' Fantastic Stories. Foreman, Michael, illus. 128p. 1993. 16.99 (*0-670-84899-9*) Viking Child Bks.

Jordan, Sherryl. Wednesday Wizard. (gr. 4-7). 1993. pap. 2.95 (*0-590-46759-X*) Scholastic Inc.

Joyce, William. A Day with Wilbur Robinson. Joyce, William, illus. LC 90-4066. 32p. (ps-3). 1993. pap. 5.95 (*0-06-443339-0*, Trophy) HarpC Child Bks.

Juster, Norton. The Phantom Tollbooth. Feiffer, Jules, illus. LC 61-13202. 256p. (gr. 3-7). 1993. Repr. of 1961 ed. 3.95 (*0-394-82037-1*) Knopf Bks Yng Read.

—The Phantom Tollbooth. large type ed. 320p. (gr. 3-7). 1989. 14.95 (*0-8161-4801-5*, Large Print Bks) Hall.

Kahan, B., ed. Batman: Collected Legends of the Dark Knight. (Illus.). 160p. 1994. pap. 12.95 collected ed. (*1-56389-147-6*) DC Comics.

Kahan, Bob, ed. The Death of Superman. (Illus.). 168p. (Orig.). 1992. pap. 4.95 (*1-56389-097-6*) DC Comics.

—Superman: The Return of Superman. (Illus.). 480p. 1993. pap. 14.95 collected ed. (*1-56389-149-2*) DC Comics.

Kane, Bob & Finger, Bill. Batman Archives, Vol. 3. Kahan, Bob, ed. Kane, Bob, et al, illus. 224p. 1993. text ed. 39.95 (*1-56389-099-2*) DC Comics.

Kaplan, Shelley. Chameleon. Warshaw, Johanna, illus. LC 92-70212. 24p. 1992. 15.00 (*0-9631833-0-3*) Kaplan IL.

Karl, Jean E. Search for the Ten-Winged Dragon. (ps-3). 1990. PLB 14.95 (*0-385-26493-3*) Doubleday.

—Strange Tomorrow. LC 84-28609. 144p. (gr. 4-7). 1985. 12.95 (*0-525-44162-X*, DCB) Dutton Child Bks.

Katz, Welwyn W. Come Like Shadows. (Illus.). 304p. (gr. 7 up). 1993. 13.99 (*0-670-84861-1*) Viking Child Bks.

Kelleher, Victor. Brother Night. LC 90-19743. 160p. (gr. 7 up). 1991. 16.95 (*0-8027-8100-4*) Walker & Co.

Keller, Beverly. A Small, Elderly Dragon. Malone, Nola L., illus. LC 83-13632. 144p. (gr. 5 up). 1984. 12.95 (*0-688-02553-6*) Lothrop.

Kellogg, Steven. Island of the Skog. (ps-3). 1993. pap. 4.99 (*0-14-054649-9*, Puffin) Puffin Bks.

Kempton, Kate. The World Beyond the Waves. Salk, Larry, illus. Trehearn, Carol, created by. (Illus.). 96p. (gr. 4-8). 1995. 19.95 (*0-9641330-1-6*) Portunus Pubng.
Like Dorothy in THE WIZARD OF OZ, Sam, the young heroine of THE WORLD BEYOND THE WAVES, is carried away by the tremendous force of a storm only to wake up in a strange & magical world beneath the sea, a refuge for animals escaping from mankind's abuse of the world's oceans. Helped to recover by these marine creatures & led on a series of adventures, Sam develops a deep awareness of the consequences of mankind's collective behavior towards the oceans from the use of drift nets for fishing to the pollution of the sea by industrial waste, oil & garbage. After her return to the surface, where her aunt & uncle have been leading the search for her, Sam succeeds in preventing an oil-test drilling ship from destroying the magical world which had saved her life, affirming in the process that with love & determination, one person can make a difference. With its skillful combination of a message of environmental awareness with a moving story of initiation into responsibility, THE WORLD BEYOND THE WAVES should prove a favorite for parents, children & teachers alike.
Publisher Provided Annotation.

Kendall, Carol. The Gammage Cup. Garcia, Manuel, contrib. by. 283p. (gr. 4-7). 1990. pap. 3.95 (*0-15-230575-0*, Odyssey) HarBrace.

Kesel, B. K. Hawk & Dove. Kahan, Bob, ed. Liefeld & Kesel, illus. 128p. 1993. pap. 9.95 collected ed. (*1-56389-120-4*) DC Comics.

Key, Alexander. The Forgotten Door. 144p. (gr. 3-7). 1986. pap. 2.95 (*0-590-43130-7*) Scholastic Inc.

Khanna & Ridley. RoleMaster Companion II. Velez, Walter, illus. 112p. (Orig.). (gr. 10-12). 1987. pap. 12. 00 (*0-915795-97-3*, 1600) Iron Crown Ent Inc.

Kilian, Crawford. Wonders, Inc. Larrecq, John M., illus. (gr. 1 up). 1968. 6.95 (*0-87466-058-0*, Pub. by Parnassus) HM.

Kindle, Patricia & Finney, Susan. Fantasy & Fairy Tales. McKay, Ardis, illus. 64p. (gr. 4-8). 1985. wkbk. 8.95 (*0-86653-317-6*, GA 669) Good Apple.

King, Jill. Penelope the Fairy. 1993. 7.95 (*0-533-10362-2*) Vantage.

King, Stephen. The Eyes of the Dragon. Palladini, David, illus. 336p. 1987. pap. 21.95 (*0-670-81458-X*) Viking Child Bks.

Kirby, Susan. Too Good to Be True. 1991. pap. 2.99 (*0-553-29213-7*) Bantam.

Kirwan-Vogel, Anna. The Jewel of Life. Yolen, Jane, ed. 118p. (gr. 5-9). 1991. 15.95 (*0-15-200750-4*, J Yolen Bks) HarBrace.

Kittredge, Elaine. Twelve. Riley, Cyd, illus. 84p. 1989. pap. 9.95 (*0-9611266-1-2*); audiotape, 80 mins. 9.95 (*0-9611266-2-0*) Optext.

Kjelgaard, Jim. Wild Trek. 272p. 1981. pap. 2.75 (*0-553-15466-4*) Bantam.

Klein, Robin. Came Back to Show You I Could Fly. 196p. (gr. 4 up). 1990. pap. 11.95 (*0-670-82901-3*) Viking Child Bks.

Kline, Suzy. Orp. 96p. 1990. pap. 3.50 (*0-380-71038-2*, Camelot) Avon.

Klipper, Ilse. Magic Journey. Osborne, Gretchen, illus. 83p. (Orig.). (gr. k-5). 1983. pap. 5.95 (*0-9605022-1-1*) Pathways Pr CA.

Koller, Jackie F. A Dragon in the Family. Mitchell, Judith, illus. LC 93-7028. 1993. 12.95 (*0-316-50151-4*) Little.

—Dragonling. LC 89-27145. (ps-4). 1990. 10.95 (*0-316-50148-4*) Little.

Konwicki, Tadeusz. Anthropos-Specter-Beast. Korwin-Rodziszewski, George & Korwin-Rodziszewski, Audrey, trs. from POL. LC 77-13500. 320p. (gr. 9 up). 1977. 21.95 (*0-87599-218-8*) S G Phillips.

Korman, Justine, adapted by. Thumbelina: The Novelization. adpt. ed. (Illus.). 64p. (gr. 2-6). 1994. pap. 3.95 (*0-448-40508-3*, G&D) Putnam Pub Group.

Kornblatt, Marc. Flame of the Inquisition, No. 15. 144p. 1986. pap. 2.50 (*0-553-26160-6*) Bantam.

Kraus, Robert. Jack Galaxy, Space Cop. (ps-3). 1990. pap. 2.75 (*0-553-15777-9*, Skylark) Bantam.
Kubler, Annie. Daphne Dragon. 1985. 4.95 (*0-85953-260-7*) Childs Play.
LaCroix, John W. Troggs & Doogles in Thistledom. 1992. 7.95 (*0-533-10129-8*) Vantage.
Lambert, Stephen. The Snowmaiden. Riordan, James, retold by. (Illus.). 32p. (gr. 1-3). 1992. 15.95 (*0-09-173861-X*, Pub. by Hutchinson UK) Trafalgar.
Lanagan, Margo. Wildgame. 160p. (Orig.). (gr. 4-8). 1993. pap. 7.95 (*1-86373-069-9*, Pub. by Allen & Unwin Aust Pty AT) IPG Chicago.
Landes, William-Alan. Alice n' Wonderland. LC 89-63870. (Orig.). (gr. 3 up). 1984. pap. 6.00 play script (*0-88734-112-8*) Players Pr.
La Pierre, Keith C. That Strange Little Man, Bk. 1. (Illus.). 32p. (gr. 2 up). 1991. lib. bdg. 14.95 (*0-9631513-0-4*) Lee Pub NY.
Larocque, Jean-Paul. Wille Wacka Land. Larocque, Jean-Paul, illus. 12p. (gr. 1-3). 1992. pap. 6.95 (*1-895583-04-7*) MAYA Pubs.
Lattimore, Deborah N. Dragon's Robe. Lattimore, Deborah N., illus. LC 89-34512. 32p. (gr. 1-5). 1993. pap. 4.95 (*0-06-443321-8*, Trophy) HarpC Child Bks.
Lawson, Jack. Andro, This Is Crazy. 96p. (Orig.). 1991. pap. 2.95 (*0-380-76234-X*, Camelot) Avon.
Lee, Jeanne M. Legend of the Milky Way. Lee, Jeanne M., illus. LC 81-6906. 32p. (ps-2). 1990. pap. 5.95 (*0-8050-1361-X*, Owlet BYR) H Holt & Co.
Leeson, Robert. The Demon Bike Rider. large type ed. (Illus.). (gr. 1-8). 1994. 15.95 (*0-7451-2226-4*, Galaxy etc.) Chivers N Amer.
Le Guin, Ursula K. The Farthest Shore. rev. ed. Garraty, Gail, illus. LC 72-75273. 240p. (gr. 6 up). 1990. SBE 16.95 (*0-689-31683-6*, Atheneum Child Bk) Macmillan Child Grp.
Leguin, Ursula K. The Visionary, 2 vols. in 1. Bd. with Wonders Hidden. Sanders, Scott R. 7.50 (*0-685-10479-6*) McGraw.
Lehr, Lauralee. The Princess & the Dragon. (Illus.). 32p. 1994. saddlestitched 5.95 (*0-8059-3565-7*) Dorrance.
Leibold, Jay. The Antimatter Formula. 128p. (Orig.). (gr. 4). 1986. pap. 2.25 (*0-553-25741-2*) Bantam.
—The Search for Aladdin's Lamp. 1991. pap. 3.25 (*0-553-29185-8*) Bantam.
L'Engle, Madeleine. A Wind in the Door. LC 73-75176. 224p. (gr. 7 up). 1973. 17.00 (*0-374-38443-6*) FS&G.
Lennox, E. R. The Wizard's Dressing-Gown. (Illus.). 32p. (gr. 2-4). 1991. 14.95 (*0-237-51100-2*, Pub. by Evans Bros Ltd) Trafalgar.
Leroux, Gaston. Phantom of the Opera. Hildebrandt, Greg, illus. 208p. (gr. 7 up). 1988. 9.95 (*0-88101-121-5*) Unicorn Pub.
Leske, Steven. Sir Richard & the Dragon. 14p. (gr. k-6). 1992. pap. text ed. 5.99 (*1-881617-01-7*) Teapot Tales.
—A Two Headed Tale. 16p. (gr. k-6). 1992. pap. text ed. 5.99 (*1-881617-02-5*) Teapot Tales.
Lester, Helen. The Wizard, the Fairy, & the Magic Chicken. (ps-3). 1983. 10.95 (*0-395-33885-9*) HM.
Lev, M. The Day the Sky Split. Levin, Debra K., illus. LC 91-71188. 32p. (gr. 1-3). 1991. 12.95 (*1-877-65607-0*) Antroll Pub.
—The Magic Faucet. Kahn, Katherine J., illus. LC 90-85473. 32p. (gr. 1-3). 1991. 12.95 (*1-877-65604-6*) Antroll Pub.
Levy, Robert. Clan of the Shape-Changers. LC 92-36010. 1994. write for info. (*0-395-66602-3*) HM.
—Clan of the Shape-Changers. (gr. 4-7). 1994. 13.95 (*0-395-66612-0*) HM.
—Escape from Exile. LC 92-20443. 176p. (gr. 5-9). 1993. 13.95 (*0-395-64379-1*) HM.
—Lost Magic. LC 93-1575. (gr. 10). 1995. write for info. (*0-395-68077-8*) HM.
Lewin, Hugh. Picture That Came Alive. (ps-3). 1992. pap. 2.95 (*0-7910-2912-3*) Chelsea Hse.
Lewis, C. S. Chronicles of Narnia, 7 vols. Baynes, Pauline, illus. (gr. 3 up). 1994. pap. 27.65 boxed set racked (*0-06-447119-5*, Trophy) HarpC Child Bks.
—Chronicles of Narnia, 7 vols. Baynes, Pauline, illus. (gr. 3 up). 1994. pap. 41.65 boxed set digest (*0-06-440537-0*, Trophy) HarpC Child Bks.
—The Horse & His Boy. Baynes, Pauline, illus. LC 93-14300. 196p. (gr. 3 up). 1994. 15.00 (*0-06-023488-1*); PLB 14.89 (*0-06-023489-X*) HarpC Child Bks.
—The Horse & His Boy. Baynes, Pauline, illus. LC 93-14300. 192p. (gr. 3 up). 1994. pap. 3.95 (*0-06-447106-3*, Harper Keypoint) HarpC Child Bks.
—The Horse & His Boy: Chronicles of Narnia. Baynes, Pauline, illus. LC 93-14300. 192p. (gr. 3 up). 1994. pap. 5.95 (*0-06-440501-X*, Trophy) HarpC Child Bks.
—The Last Battle. Baynes, Pauline, illus. LC 93-14302. 176p. (gr. 3 up). 1994. 15.00 (*0-06-023493-8*); PLB 14.89 (*0-06-023494-6*) HarpC Child Bks.
—The Last Battle. Baynes, Pauline, illus. 176p. (gr. 3 up). 1994. pap. 5.95 (*0-06-440503-6*) HarpC Child Bks.
—The Last Battle. Baynes, Pauline, illus. LC 93-14302. 176p. (gr. 3 up). 1994. pap. 3.95 (*0-06-447108-X*, Trophy) HarpC Child Bks.
—The Lion, the Witch, & the Wardrobe. Baynes, Pauline, illus. LC 93-8889. 160p. (gr. 3 up). 1994. 15.00 (*0-06-023481-4*); PLB 14.89 (*0-06-023482-2*) HarpC Child Bks.
—The Lion, the Witch & the Wardrobe. Baynes, Pauline, illus. LC 93-8889. 160p. (gr. 3 up). 1994. pap. 5.95 (*0-06-440499-4*) HarpC Child Bks.
—The Lion, the Witch & the Wardrobe. Baynes, Pauline, illus. LC 93-8889. 160p. (gr. 3 up). 1994. pap. 3.95 (*0-06-447104-7*, Trophy) HarpC Child Bks.
—Lion, Witch, & Wardrobe, Bk. I. 1976. 18.95 (*0-8488-0823-1*) Amereon Ltd.
—The Magician's Nephew. Baynes, Pauline, illus. LC 93-14301. 176p. (gr. 3 up). 1994. pap. 5.95 (*0-06-440505-2*, Trophy) HarpC Child Bks.
—The Magician's Nephew: Chronicles of Narnia. Baynes, Pauline, illus. LC 93-14301. 176p. (gr. 3 up). 1994. pap. 3.95 (*0-06-447110-1*, Trophy) HarpC Child Bks.
—Prince Caspian: The Return to Narnia. Baynes, Pauline, illus. LC 93-11514. 192p. (gr. 3 up). 1994. 15.00 (*0-06-023483-0*); PLB 14.89 (*0-06-023484-9*) HarpC Child Bks.
—Prince Caspian: The Return to Narnia. Baynes, Pauline, illus. LC 93-11514. 192p. (gr. 3 up). 1994. pap. 5.95 (*0-06-440500-1*, Trophy) HarpC Child Bks.
—Prince Caspian: The Return to Narnia. Baynes, Pauline, illus. LC 93-11514. 192p. (gr. 3 up). 1994. pap. 3.95 (*0-06-447105-5*, Harper Keypoint) HarpC Child Bks.
—The Silver Chair. Baynes, Pauline, illus. LC 93-14299. 208p. (gr. 3 up). 1994. 15.00 (*0-06-023495-4*); PLB 14.89 (*0-06-023496-2*) HarpC Child Bks.
—The Silver Chair. Baynes, Pauline, illus. LC 93-14299. 208p. (gr. 3 up). 1994. pap. 3.95 (*0-06-447109-8*, Harper Keypoint) HarpC Child Bks.
—The Silver Chair. Baynes, Pauline, illus. LC 93-14299. 208p. (gr. 3 up). 1994. pap. 5.95 (*0-06-440504-4*, Trophy) HarpC Child Bks.
—The Voyage of the Dawn Treader. Baynes, Pauline, illus. LC 93-11515. 208p. (gr. 3 up). 1994. 15.00 (*0-06-023486-5*); PLB 14.89 (*0-06-023487-3*) HarpC Child Bks.
—The Voyage of the Dawn Treader. Baynes, Pauline, illus. 208p. (gr. 3 up). 1994. pap. 3.95 (*0-06-447107-1*, Harper Keypoint) HarpC Child Bks.
—The Voyage of the Dawn Treader: Chronicles of Narnia. Baynes, Pauline, illus. LC 93-11515. 208p. (gr. 3 up). 1994. pap. 5.95 (*0-06-440502-8*, Trophy) HarpC Child Bks.
Lewis, C. S. & Baynes, Pauline. The Magician's Nephew. Van Allsburg, Chris, illus. LC 93-14301. 176p. (gr. 3 up). 1994. 15.00 (*0-06-023497-0*); PLB 14.89 (*0-06-023498-9*) HarpC Child Bks.
Lewis, Dallas & Lewis, Lisa M. The Last Book. (Illus.). 32p. (gr. 1-2). 1992. 16.00 (*0-9634087-0-4*) Silly Billys Bks.
Lightwood, Donald. Alf's Secret War. 180p. (gr. 5-8). 1994. pap. 6.95 (*0-86241-383-4*, Pub. by Cnngt UK) Trafalgar.
Lillington, Kenneth. Jonah's Mirror. 160p. (gr. 7 up). 1992. pap. 6.95 (*0-571-16736-5*) Faber & Faber.
Lindbergh, Anne M. Bailey's Window. Craft, Kinuko Y., illus. LC 83-18360. 115p. (gr. 3-7). 1984. 14.95 (*0-15-205642-4*, HB Juv Bks) HarBrace.
Lindsay, A. Brook, III. The Cygnus Conspiracy. Amthor, Terry, ed. Roberts, Tony, illus. 32p. (Orig.). (gr. 10-12). 1987. pap. 12.00 (*0-915795-92-2*, 9102) Iron Crown Ent Inc.
Lionni, Leo. Cornelius. Lionni, Leo, illus. LC 82-6442. (ps-2). 1994. pap. 4.99 (*0-679-86040-1*) Knopf Bks Yng Read.
Lipskerov, M. F. Samy Malenky Gnom (a Very Small Gnome) Kostrina, Irina, illus. (RUS.). 18p. (Orig.). 1991. pap. 14.95 (*0-934393-23-0*) Rector Pr.
Lively, Penelope. Dragon Trouble. Lively, Penelope, illus. 42p. (gr. 2-4). 1989. 3.95 (*0-8120-6136-5*) Barron.
Lobel, Arnold. Treeful of Pigs. LC 78-1810. (Illus.). 32p. (gr. k-3). 1979. 16.00 (*0-688-80177-3*); PLB 15.93 (*0-688-84177-5*) Greenwillow.
Loeb, Joseph. Batman: Legends of the Dark Knight Halloween Special. Goodwin, Archie, ed. Sale, Tim, illus. 80p. (Orig.). 1993. pap. 6.95 (*1-56389-130-1*) DC Comics.
Lofting, Hugh. Gub-Gub's Book. LC 91-4672. (gr. 4-7). 1992. pap. 15.00 (*0-671-78355-6*, S&S BFYR) S&S Trade.
—Story of Dr. Dolittle. (gr. 4-7). 1969. pap. 3.99 (*0-440-48307-7*) Dell.
Lowry, Lois. Anastasia Again! 160p. (gr. 4-7). 1982. pap. 3.50 (*0-440-40009-0*, YB) Dell.
Lubin, Leonard. Aladdin & His Wonderful Lamp. Burton, Richard T., tr. from ARA. Lubin, Leonard, illus. LC 82-70308. 48p. (ps-3). 1982. 12.95 (*0-385-28033-5*) Delacorte.
Luenn, Nancy. Goldclimbers. LC 90-589. 192p. (gr. 7 up). 1991. SBE 14.95 (*0-689-31585-6*, Atheneum Child Bk) Macmillan Child Grp.
Lukacs, E. & Laha, R. G. Applications of Charateristics Functions. 1964. 17.95 (*0-85264-086-2*) Lubrecht & Cramer.
Lyon, George-Ella. Father Time & the Day Boxes. Parker, Robert A., illus. LC 93-25201. 32p. (gr. k-3). 1994. pap. 4.95 (*0-689-71792-X*, Aladdin) Macmillan Child Grp.
McAllister, Angela. Enchanted Flute. 1991. 14.95 (*0-385-30326-2*) Delacorte.
McArthur, Nancy. The Escape of the Plant that Ate Dirty Socks. 128p. (Orig.). 1992. pap. 3.50 (*0-380-76756-2*, Camelot) Avon.
—The Return of the Plant That Ate Dirty Socks. 128p. (Orig.). (gr. 5-6). 1990. pap. 3.50 (*0-380-75873-3*, Camelot) Avon.
—The Secret of the Plant That Ate Dirty Socks. 128p. (Orig.). 1993. pap. 3.50 (*0-380-76757-0*, Camelot) Avon.
McCaffrey, Anne. Dragonsinger. LC 76-40988. 276p. (gr. 5-9). 1977. SBE 16.95 (*0-689-30570-2*, Atheneum Child Bk) Macmillan Child Grp.
MacDonald, Betty. Mrs. Piggle-Wiggle's Magic. 1976. 15. 95 (*0-8488-1087-2*) Amereon Ltd.
MacDonald, George. At the Back of the North Wind. LC 64-21758. 336p. (gr. 4-6). 1985. pap. 2.25 (*0-14-035030-6*, Puffin) Puffin Bks.
—At the Back of the North Wind. Smith, Jessie W., illus. LC 88-63292. 352p. (gr. 5 up). 1989. 17.95 (*0-688-07808-7*) Morrow Jr Bks.
—George MacDonald Original Works, 5 vols, Series III. (gr. 5 up). 1993. Repr. Set. 74.00 (*1-881084-18-3*); Per volume, first 3 volumes with color plates. 20.00 (*1-881084-20-5*); Per volume, last 2 volumes with B&W illus. 16.00 (*1-881084-21-3*) Johannesen.
—The Princess & the Goblin. 208p. (gr. 5-8). 1990. pap. 7.95 (*0-86241-274-9*, Pub. by Cnngt Pub Ltd) Trafalgar.
McDowell, Mildred. The Little People. Whitaker, Arleen, illus. Harman, Sandra L., intro. by. LC 72-133255. (Illus.). 44p. (gr. 1-2). 1971. 2.50 (*0-87884-002-8*) Unicorn Ent.
McGinnis, Lila S. The Twenty-Four Hour Genie. Sours, Michael, illus. LC 89-77786. 80p. (gr. 2-4). 1990. 12. 95 (*0-8050-1303-2*, Redfeather BYR) H Holt & Co.
McGowen, Tom. The Magical Fellowship. LC 90-45576. 160p. (gr. 5-9). 1991. 14.95 (*0-525-67339-3*, Lodestar Bks) Dutton Child Bks.
—A Question of Magic. 160p. (gr. 5-9). 1993. 14.99 (*0-525-67380-6*, Lodestar Bks) Dutton Child Bks.
—A Trial of Magic. 144p. (gr. 5-9). 1992. 15.00 (*0-525-67376-8*, Lodestar Bks) Dutton Child Bks.
McKeage, Jeff. The Lost Realm of Cardolan. Fenlon, Peter C., Jr., ed. 64p. (Orig.). (gr. 10-12). 1987. pap. 12.00 (*0-915795-95-7*, 3700) Iron Crown Ent Inc.
McKeage, Jeff & Fenlon, Peter C., Jr. Woses of the Black Wood. McBride, Angus, illus. 32p. (gr. 10-12). 1987. pap. 6.00 (*0-915795-99-X*, 8107) Iron Crown Ent Inc.
McKelvy, Charles. Kids in the Woods. Sova, Mike & Sova, Mike, illus. LC 89-50591. 24p. (gr. 1-4). 1993. 14.95x (*0-944771-03-3*) Dunery Pr.
McKenzie, Ellen K. Taash & the Jesters. LC 92-12378. 245p. (gr. 5 up). 1992. 15.95 (*0-8050-2381-X*, Bks Young Read) H Holt & Co.
McKiernan, Dennis L. Trek to Kraagen-Cor. (gr. 9-12). 1989. pap. 3.95 (*0-451-15563-7*, Sig) NAL-Dutton.
McKinley, Robin. The Hero & the Crown. 1987. pap. 4.99 (*0-441-32809-1*) Ace Bks.
—Imaginary Lands. LC 85-21867. 160p. (gr. 7 up). 1986. reinforced bdg. 11.75 (*0-688-05213-4*) Greenwillow.
McOmber, Rachel B., ed. McOmber Phonics Storybooks: Robin Hood's Cook. rev. ed. (Illus.). write for info. (*0-944991-64-5*) Swift Lrn Res.
—McOmber Phonics Storybooks: Under the Rainbow. rev. ed. (Illus.). write for info. (*0-944991-81-5*) Swift Lrn Res.
McQuinn, Anna. Kingdom of Giants. Jones, Bany, illus. LC 93-85640. 16p. (gr. 3-7). 1994. 9.95 (*0-89577-571-9*) RD Assn.
Mahy, Margaret. Door in the Air. (gr. 4-7). 1993. pap. 3.50 (*0-440-40774-5*) Dell.
—The Dragon of an Ordinary Family. LC 91-2513. (Illus.). 48p. (ps-3). 1992. 14.00 (*0-8037-1062-3*) Dial Bks Young.
—The Girl with the Green Ear: Stories about Magic in Nature. Hughes, Shirley, illus. LC 91-14992. 112p. (gr. 3-7). 1993. pap. 3.25 (*0-679-84000-1*, Bullseye Bks) Knopf Bks Yng Read.
Manning, Rosemary. Green Smoke. large type ed. 224p. (gr. 3-7). 1991. 16.95 (*0-7451-1318-4*, Galaxy Child Lrg Print) Chivers N Amer.
Mannino, Marc P. & Mannino, Angelica L. La Cola Magica de Marjorie. Norman-Grumbley, Patricia, tr. from ENG. Mannino, Angelica L., illus. LC 93-86116. (SPA.). 32p. (Orig.). (gr. k-3). 1993. pap. 7.95 (*0-9638340-1-0*) Sugar Sand.
Marino, Tony. Ratchet Hood. LC 92-12841. 1992. 13.99 (*1-56239-152-6*) Abdo & Dghtrs.
—Scraboolee Jubilee. LC 92-12840. 1992. 13.99 (*1-56239-153-4*) Abdo & Dghtrs.
Martin, Ann M. Ma & Pa Dracula. Zimmer, Dirk, illus. LC 89-2081. 128p. (gr. 3-7). 1989. 14.95 (*0-8234-0781-0*) Holiday.
Martin, Bill, Jr. The Wizard. Schaefer, Alex, illus. LC 93-15521. (ps-3). 1994. 14.95 (*0-15-298926-9*) HarBrace.
Marzollo, Jean. Close Your Eyes. Jeffers, Susan, illus. (ps-k). 1981. 4.95 (*0-8037-1617-6*) Dial Bks Young.
—Jed & the Space Bandits. 1989. pap. 4.95 (*0-8037-0682-0*, Puff Pied Piper) Puffin Bks.
Matens, Margaret H. Mandy & the Kookalocka. Matens, Margaret H., illus. LC 93-77130. 32p. (gr. k-5). 1993. 14.95 (*1-882959-53-1*) Foxglove TN.
Mayer, Marianna. Unicorn & the Lake. giant ed. (ps-3). 1990. 17.99 (*0-8037-0844-0*) Dial Bks Young.
—Unicorn & the Lake. LC 81-5469. (Illus.). 32p. (gr. k up). 1987. pap. 4.95 (*0-8037-0436-4*) Dial Bks Young.
Medema, K. Gorgles. Vreeman, J., ed. (Orig.). 1985. pap. 3.95 (*0-918789-05-2*) FreeMan Prods.
—Rennis the Nam. Vreeman, J., ed. (Illus.). 16p. (Orig.). 1985. pap. 3.95 (*0-918789-04-4*) FreeMan Prods.
Messing, Margaret S. Adelma Goes Herbing. Bastiaanse, Nicole, illus. LC 93-94108. 64p. (Orig.). 1994. pap. 6.00 (*1-56002-383-X*, Univ Edtns) Aegina Pr.
Meyers, Odette. The Enchanted Umbrella: With a Short History of the Umbrella. Zemach, Margot, illus. 28p. (ps-3). 1988. 13.95 (*0-15-200448-3*, Gulliver Bks) HarBrace.

Middleton, Gayle. Glim the Glorious or How the Little Folk Bested the Gubgoblins. Pangrazio, Micheal, illus. LC 86-2978. 64p. (gr. k-5). 1987. 12.95 (*0-394-88081-1*) Knopf Bks Yng Read.
Miller, Albert G. More Captain Whopper Tales. Komisarow, Don, illus. (gr. 3-7). 1968. 10.95 (*0-8392-3060-5*) Astor-Honor.
Minar, Barbra. Lamper's Meadow. 160p. (gr. 4-7). 1992. pap. 6.99 (*0-89107-663-8*) Crossway Bks.
Mitchell, Tucker. You're Not Alone When You're Alone. LC 92-70981. (Illus.). 130p. 1992. 12.95 (*1-55523-522-0*) Winston-Derek.
Moench, D. & Dixon, C. Batman: Knightfall, Pt. 1: Broken Bat. Kahan, Bob, ed. (Illus.). 288p. 1993. pap. 12.95 collected ed. (*1-56389-142-5*) DC Comics.
—Batman: Knightfall, Pt. 2: Who Rules the Night. Kahan, Bob, ed. (Illus.). 296p. 1993. pap. 12.95 collected ed. (*1-56389-148-4*) DC Comics.
Mogwe, Gaele. Magic Pool. (ps-3). 1992. pap. 2.95 (*0-7910-2910-7*) Chelsea Hse.

Monroy, Elizabeth. The Magical Mist. LC 93-91857. 52p. (ps-6). 1994. 15.95 (*0-9639760-0-1*) Going Home.
THE MAGICAL MIST is a delightful story that teaches us all, large & small, the value of imagination. THE MAGICAL MIST is a beautifully illustrated fairy tale designed to empower the creative imagination of children. The story is about a young girl who loses a most precious & powerful part of herself in the process of growing & rediscovers it through her young daughter. Synopsis: Lauren's rag doll, Mirabelle, becomes magically alive & takes Lauren on a magical adventure to the World of Imagination, where she learns of the terrible peril facing her world. A cloud of disbelief has descended on the planet Earth & grows thicker every day. If nothing is done to stop it all the people of Earth will be consumed by despair. Lauren is presented with the Key to the World of Imagination. This magical key could free her world from the chains of disbelief. But forces are working against Lauren. Mrs. Grundy, Lauren's school teacher, sees Lauren's vivid imagination as nothing more than a disruption to the discipline & order of her classroom. To order contact: GOING HOME BOOKS, P.O. Box 688, Parker, AZ 85344. 1-800-410-1999, FAX: 619-665-5565.
Publisher Provided Annotation.

Moore, John F. Superman: "Under a Yellow Sun" A Novel by Clark Kent. Carlin, Mike, ed. Gammill, et al, illus. 64p. (Orig.). 1994. pap. 5.95 (*1-56389-109-3*) DC Comics.
Mooser, Stephen. The Hitchhiking Vampire. (gr. 5 up). 1989. 13.95 (*0-385-29725-4*) Delacorte.
—The Man Who Ate a Car. (ps-3). 1991. pap. 2.99 (*0-440-40460-6*) Dell.
Morgan, Allen. Matthew & the Midnight Money Van. Martchenko, Michael, illus. 24p. (ps-2). 1991. pap. 0.99 (*1-55037-194-0*, Pub. by Annick CN) Firefly Bks Ltd.
—Matthew & the Midnight Tow Truck. Martchenko, Michael, illus. 24p. (ps-2). 1991. pap. 0.99 (*1-55037-192-4*, Pub. by Annick CN) Firefly Bks Ltd.
—Matthew & the Midnight Turkeys. Martchenko, Michael, illus. 24p. (ps-2). 1991. pap. 0.99 (*1-55037-193-2*, Pub. by Annick CN) Firefly Bks Ltd.
Morris, Dave. Red Herrings. (gr. 4 up). 1990. pap. 2.95 (*0-440-40390-1*) Dell.
—Six Guns & Shurikens. (gr. 4-7). 1990. pap. 2.95 (*0-440-40392-8*) Dell.
—Sky High. (gr. 4 up). 1990. pap. 2.95 (*0-440-40389-8*) Dell.

Morrissey, Dean. Ship of Dreams. Morrissey, Dean, illus. 37p. 1994. 17. 95 (*0-8109-3848-0*) Abrams.
Dean Morrissey's charming story follows Joey on his journey through the star-filled night to meet the Sandman, a voyage filled with excitement & delight. Joey sails off in his specially adapted wagon, the Redd Rocket, on a flight of discovery followed step-by-step in Morrissey's magically vivid realistic paintings. The boy's adventure, his exhilarating fall through the sky & heart-stopping rescue, his discovery of the Sandman's amazing ship & the secrets contained aboard it, all add up to a bedtime experience that children of all ages will cherish again & again. An accomplished realist painter & illustrator, Dean Morrissey has developed a considerable following among collectors of limited edition prints worldwide. Long interested in connecting painting with storytelling, Morrissey has created this body of work especially to trace the imaginings of his boy hero, Joey & the magical wagon that Joey calls "The Redd Rocket." This, his first book, will surely whet the appetites of readers & lovers of fine illustrated books for more Redd Rocket adventures. Order from: Harry N. Abrams, Inc., 100 Fifth Avenue, New York, NY 10011; 212-206-7715, FAX: 212-645-8437.
Publisher Provided Annotation.

Mosel, Arlene. The Funny Little Woman. Lent, Blair, illus. LC 75-179046. 40p. (ps-4). 1972. 16.00 (*0-525-30265-4*, 01258-370, DCB); pap. 4.95 (*0-525-45036-X*, DCB) Dutton Child Bks.
Moulton, Dwayne. The Mystery of the Pink Waterfall. Headley, Adriane M., illus. LC 80-84116. 192p. (gr. 3-8). 1980. 14.95 (*0-9605236-0-X*) Pandoras Treasures.
Muller, Robin. The Magic Paintbrush. LC 89-51265. (Illus.). 32p. 1990. pap. 13.95 (*0-670-83167-0*) Viking Child Bks.
Munsch, Robert. Murmel, Murmel, Murmel. Martchenko, Michael, illus. 24p. (Orig.). (ps-2). 1989. pap. 0.99 (*1-55037-012-X*, Pub. by Annick CN) Firefly Bks Ltd.
—Murmel Murmel Murmel. (CHI., Illus.). 32p. 1993. pap. 5.95 (*1-55037-303-X*, Pub. by Annick CN) Firefly Bks Ltd.
Murphy, Shirley R. The Dragonbards. LC 87-45295. 256p. (gr. 7 up). 1988. HarpC Child Bks.
—Nightpool. LC 85-42626. 256p. (gr. 7 up). 1987. pap. 2.95 (*0-06-447041-5*, Trophy) HarpC Child Bks.
Murphy, Stephen. Raphael, Big Trouble in Chinatown. (ps-3). 1993. pap. 3.50 (*0-440-40863-6*) Dell.
Murphy, Steven. Leonardo, the Wilderness Adventure. (ps-3). 1993. pap. 3.50 (*0-440-40866-0*) Dell.
—Michelangelo, the Haunted Mansion. (ps-3). 1993. pap. 3.50 (*0-440-40869-5*) Dell.
Murray, Terry & Anderson, Jeff. Cutting Edge, Legends of Larian, Bk. 1. (Illus.). 48p. (Orig.). (gr. 9 up). 1992. pap. 5.99 (*0-7459-2369-0*) Lion USA.
Myers, Bernice. The Flying Shoes. LC 91-335. (ps up). 1992. 15.00 (*0-688-10695-1*); PLB 14.93 (*0-688-10696-X*) Lothrop.
Myers, Bill. The Whirlwind. 160p. (Orig.). (gr. 4-8). 1992. pap. 5.99 (*1-55661-258-3*) Bethany Hse.
Namoika, Lensey. April & the Dragon Lady. LC 93-27958. 1994. pap. write for info. (*0-15-200886-1*) HarBrace.
Neill, John R. Lucky Bucky in Oz. (Illus.). (gr. 3 up). 1992. 24.95 (*0-929605-17-9*) Books Wonder.
—The Scalawagons in Oz. Neill, John R., illus. 309p. (gr. 3 up). 1991. 24.95 (*0-929605-12-8*) Books Wonder.
—The Wonder City of Oz. Neill, John R., illus. 318p. (gr. 2 up). 1990. text ed. 24.95 (*0-929605-07-1*) Books Wonder.
Nesbit, Edith. Five Children & It. Millar, H. R., illus. 224p. (gr. 4-6). 1985. pap. 2.95 (*0-14-035061-6*, Puffin) Puffin Bks.
—The Magic World. (gr. 4 up). 1989. pap. 2.95 (*0-14-035094-2*, Puffin) Puffin Bks.
—Phoenix & the Carpet. Millar, H. R., illus. (gr. 4-6). 1985. pap. 2.25 (*0-14-035062-4*, Puffin) Puffin Bks.
Nickerson, Sara. Martin the Cavebine. Weller, Don, illus. LC 88-71369. 28p. (Orig.). (gr. 1-4). 1989. pap. 8.00 (*0-935529-06-3*) Comprehen Health Educ.
Nickl, Peter. The Wonderful Travels & Adventures of Baron Munchhausen: As Told by Himself in the Company of His Friends & Washed down by Many a Good Bottle of Wine - The Adventures on Land. Schroeder, Binette, illus. Taylor, Elizabeth B., tr. from GER. LC 91-16510. (Illus.). 32p. (gr. 5 up). 1992. 17. 95 (*1-55858-134-0*) North-South Bks NYC.
Nicky at the Magic House. 14.95 (*1-55037-273-4*, Pub. by Annick CN); pap. 6.95 (*1-55037-271-8*, Pub. by Annick CN) Firefly Bks Ltd.
Nimmo, Jenny. The Chestnut Soldier. large type ed. 312p. (gr. 3-7). 1991. lib. bdg. 18.50x (*0-7451-1178-5*, Lythway Large Print) Hall.
—Ultramarine. large type ed. 296p. 1992. 16.95 (*0-7451-1554-3*, Galaxy Child Lrg Print) Chivers N Amer.
Nodelman, Perry. The Same Place but Different. LC 93-29514. Date not set. 15.00 (*0-06-024258-2*); PLB 14. 89 (*0-06-024259-0*) HarpC Child Bks.
Norman, Jane & Beazley, Frank. The Search for the Peanut Butter King. 24p. (ps-3). 1993. pap. write for info. (*1-883585-00-7*) Pixanne Ent.
Norton, Mary. The Borrowers. Krush, Beth & Krush, Joe, illus. 200p. (gr. 3-7). 1989. pap. 4.95 (*0-15-209990-5*, Odyssey) HarBrace.
—Borrowers. (gr. 4-7). 1993. pap. 4.95 (*0-15-200086-0*) HarBrace.
—The Borrowers Afield. Krush, Beth, contrib. by. 238p. (gr. 5-7). 1990. pap. 4.95 (*0-15-210535-2*, Odyssey) HarBrace.
—The Borrowers Afloat. Krush, Beth, contrib. by. 205p. (gr. 3-7). 1990. pap. 3.95 (*0-15-210534-4*, Odyssey) HarBrace.
—The Borrowers Aloft. Krush, Beth & Krush, Joe, illus. 196p. (gr. 3-7). 1990. pap. 4.95 (*0-15-210533-6*, Odyssey) HarBrace.
—The Borrowers Avenged. 365p. (gr. 3-7). 1990. pap. 4.95 (*0-15-210532-8*, Odyssey) HarBrace.
Norton, Mary & Hague, M. The Borrowers. 177p. (ps up). 1991. 22.95 (*0-15-209991-3*, HB Juv Bks) HarBrace.
Nunn, Abigail. The Land of Tuppitry. (Illus.). 96p. (gr. 3-4). 1991. pap. 4.95 (*0-9620765-3-8*) Victory Press.
O'Connor, Edwin. Benjy: A Ferocious Fairy Tale. O'Neill, Catherine, illus. LC 88-46131. 128p. (gr. 4-7). 1995. pap. 10.95 (*0-87923-795-3*) Godine.
O'Dell, Scott. Sing Down the Moon. 144p. (gr. 5 up). 1992. pap. 3.99 (*0-440-40673-0*, YB) Dell.
Oliver, M. The Intergalactic Bus Trip. (Illus.). 48p. (gr. 3-5). 1988. PLB 11.96 (*0-88110-301-2*); pap. 4.95 (*0-7460-0151-7*) EDC.
O'Neil, Dennis. Batman: Venom. Kahan, Bob, ed. Von Eeden, et al, illus. 136p. 1993. pap. 9.95 collected ed. (*1-56389-101-8*) DC Comics.
Orr, Wendy. Pegasus & Ooloo-Moo-loo. Ohi, Ruth, illus. 32p. 1993. lib. bdg. 14.95 (*1-55037-278-5*, Pub. by Annick CN); pap. 4.95 (*1-55037-279-3*, Pub. by Annick CN) Firefly Bks Ltd.
Osborne, Victor. Moondream. LC 88-13654. 128p. (gr. 3-7). 1989. 11.95 (*0-688-08778-7*) Lothrop.
Osborne, Will & Osborne, Mary P. The Deadly Power of Medusa. 96p. (gr. 3-7). 1992. pap. 2.75 (*0-590-45580-X*, Apple Paperbacks) Scholastic Inc.
Ostrander, John. The Spectre: Crimes & Punishments. Kahan, Bob, ed. Mandrake, illus. 104p. 1993. pap. 9.95 collected ed. (*1-56389-127-1*) DC Comics.
Otey, Mimi. Blue Moon Soup Spoon. (ps-3). 1993. 15.00 (*0-374-30851-9*) FS&G.
Packard, Edward. Vampire Invaders. (gr. 4-7). 1991. pap. 3.50 (*0-553-29212-9*) Bantam.
Papa, Ethyl R. A Very Special Family: A Story Book to Color & Teach Your Child to Read. (Illus.). 32p. (ps-2). 1983. saddle stitch, double stapled binding 9.95 (*0-915925-00-1*) Innovative Educ Pub.
Park, Margaret. Crab-Bags & Other Bean-Beings. Bluestone, Sara, illus. (gr. 5 up). 1979. pap. 2.95 (*0-915556-05-7*) Great Ocean.
Parker, George C. The Night the Day Was Stolen. 1991. 7.95 (*0-533-09461-5*) Vantage.
Parkison, Ralph F. Yodeling. Withrow, Marion O., ed. Bush, William, illus. 71p. (Orig.). (gr. 2-8). 1988. pap. write for info. Little Wood Bks.
Patron, Susan. Bobbin Dustdobbin. Shemom, Mike, illus. LC 92-25099. 32p. (ps-2). 1993. 14.95 (*0-531-05468-3*); PLB 14.99 (*0-531-08618-6*) Orchard Bks Watts.
Pattison, Darcy. The River Dragon. Tseng, Jean & Tseng, Mou-Sien, illus. LC 90-49931. 32p. (gr. k up). 1991. 13.95 (*0-688-10426-6*); PLB 13.88 (*0-688-10427-4*) Lothrop.
Pattou, E. Hero's Song. (gr. 3-7). 1991. 16.95 (*0-15-233807-1*, HB Juv Bks) HarBrace.
Pearce, Philippa. Tom's Midnight Garden. reissued ed. LC 69-12008. 240p. (gr. 5-9). 1992. PLB 13.89 (*0-397-30477-3*, Lipp Jr Bks) HarpC Child Bks.
Pearson, Kit. A Handful of Time. (Illus.). 192p. (gr. 3-7). 1991. pap. 3.95 (*0-14-032268-X*, Puffin) Puffin Bks.
Peet, Bill. The Wump World. Peet, Bill, illus. 1991. incl. cass. 7.70 (*0-395-58412-4*) HM.
Peretti, Frank E. Escape from the Island of Aquarius. (gr. 4-7). 1990. pap. 4.99 (*0-89107-592-5*) Crossway Bks.
Perrault, Charles. Sleeping Beauty & The Soldier & the Six Giants. (Illus.). 48p. (ps-3). 1985. 5.95 (*0-88110-255-5*) EDC.
Peter & the Lost Boys. (Illus.). (ps-3). 1991. pap. 1.50 (*0-679-82702-1*) Random Bks Yng Read.
Peterson, John. Littles. (gr. 4-7). 1993. pap. 2.75 (*0-590-46225-3*) Scholastic Inc.
—The Littles & the Terrible Tiny Kid. (gr. 4-7). 1993. pap. 2.75 (*0-590-45578-8*) Scholastic Inc.
—Littles & the Trash Tinies. (gr. 4-7). 1993. pap. 2.75 (*0-590-46595-3*) Scholastic Inc.
—The Littles Give a Party. (gr. 4-7). 1993. pap. 2.75 (*0-590-46597-X*) Scholastic Inc.
—The Littles Take a Trip. 96p. (gr. 2-5). 1986. pap. 2.50 (*0-590-42713-X*) Scholastic Inc.
—The Littles to the Rescue. (gr. 4-7). 1993. pap. 2.75 (*0-590-46223-7*) Scholastic Inc.
Peyton, K. M. Darkling. 1992. pap. 3.50 (*0-440-21211-1*) Dell.

Pierce, Meredith A. Dark Moon. 256p. (gr. 7 up). 1992. 15.95 (*0-685-59346-0*, Joy St Bks) Little.
—Dark Moon, Vol. II: Firebringer Trilogy. (Illus.). (gr. 7 up). 1992. 16.95 (*0-316-70744-9*, Joy St Bks) Little.
—A Gathering of Gargoyles. 272p. 1985. pap. 2.95 (*0-8125-4902-3*) Tor Bks.
Pierce, Tamora. Lioness Rampant: Song of the Lioness, Bk. Four. LC 88-6213. 336p. (gr. 6 up). 1988. SBE 16. 95 (*0-689-31116-8*, Atheneum Child Bk) Macmillan Child Grp.
—Wild Magic: The Immortals. LC 91-43909. 272p. (gr. 5 up). 1992. SBE 16.95 (*0-689-31761-1*, Atheneum Child Bk) Macmillan Child Grp.
—Wolf-Speaker. LC 93-21909. 192p. (gr. 4-8). 1994. SBE 14.95 (*0-689-31833-2*, Atheneum Child Bk) Macmillan Child Grp.
Pilkey, Dav. Dragon Gets By. LC 90-46027. (Illus.). 48p. (gr. 1-3). 1991. 12.95 (*0-531-05935-9*); PLB 12.99 (*0-531-08535-X*) Orchard Bks Watts.
Pilurs, David B. Sun & Storm: The Terminus. Caruso, Lenore R., ed. (Illus.). 16p. (gr. 7 up). 1993. 8.95 (*0-9636551-2-4*, 26635) Storm Pr.
Pini, Wendy & Pini, Richard. Elfquest: Fire & Flight. rev. ed. (Illus.). 192p. (gr. 4 up). 1993. 19.95 (*0-936861-16-9*, Father Tree Pr) Warp Graphics.
—Elfquest: The Cry from Beyond. (Illus.). 160p. (Orig.). (gr. 4 up). 1993. 19.95 (*0-936861-17-7*, Father Tree Pr) Warp Graphics.
Ploss, Douglas A. The Tweens at Deep Lake: An Original American Fantasy. Ploss, Douglas A., illus. LC 79-90996. 88p. (gr. 3 up). 1979. PLB 13.50 (*0-9603632-0-3*); pap. 8.50 (*0-9603632-1-1*) OPC.
Poe, Edgar Allan. Reader's Digest Best Loved Books for Young Readers: Tales of Poe. Ogburn, Jackie, ed. Liebman, Oscar, illus. 152p. (gr. 4-12). 1989. 3.99 (*0-945260-24-5*) Choice Pub NY.
Polcovar, Jane. The Charming. 160p. (Orig.). (gr. 7-12). 1984. pap. 2.50 (*0-553-26691-8*) Bantam.
Porter-Lane, Esther. St. George & the Dragon. (Orig.). (gr. 4 up). 1985. pap. 4.50 (*0-87602-249-2*) Anchorage.
Potter, Beatrix. The Tale of Mrs. Tiggy-winkle. (Illus.). 57p. (gr. k-6). 1973. pap. 1.75 (*0-486-20546-0*) Dover.
Pratchett, Terry. Wings. large type ed. Kirby, C. Josh, contrib. by. 1993. 16.95 (*0-7451-1805-4*, Galaxy Child Lrg Print) Chivers N Amer.
Prater, John. The Gift. Prater, John, illus. 32p. (ps-3). 1986. pap. 9.95 (*0-670-80952-7*) Viking Child Bks.
Price, Susan. Ghost Song. 1992. 15.00 (*0-374-32544-8*) FS&G.
Priest, James D. Kirins: The Flight of the Ain. Ranno, Jim & Johnson, Marc, illus. LC 91-91110. 336p. (Orig.). (gr. 6-12). 1992. pap. 11.95 (*0-9626225-5-9*) Yellow Pr MN.
—Kirins: The Spell of No'an. Round, Jim & Johnson, Marc, illus. LC 90-90174. 470p. (Orig.). 1990. pap. 11. 95 (*0-9626225-4-0*) Yellow Pr MN.
Princess & the Goblin. (ps-3). 1993. pap. 2.95 (*0-8167-3201-9*) Troll Assocs.
Pringle, Froncine R. Tiny Bops: Wee Bop out Alone. 1995. 7.95 (*0-8062-4974-9*) Carlton.
Puckett. Batman: Mask of the Phantasm: The Animated Movie. Peterson, Scott, ed. Parobeck, et al, illus. 64p. (Orig.). Date not set. pap. 4.95 (*1-56389-122-0*) DC Comics.
Puckett, Kelly & Pasko. Batman: The Collected Adventures, Vol. 1. Kahan, Bob, ed. Templeton, et al, illus. 144p. 1993. pap. 5.95 collected ed. (*1-56389-098-4*) DC Comics.
Purtill, Richard. Enchantment at Delphi. LC 85-30556. (gr. 7 up). 1986. 14.95 (*0-15-200447-5*, Gulliver Bks) HarBrace.
Pyle, Howard. The Garden Behind the Moon: The Real Story of the Moon Angel. (Illus.). 176p. (gr. 6-8). 1991. pap. 10.95 (*0-930407-22-9*) Parabola Bks.
Rand, Gloria. The Cabin Key. Rand, Ted, illus. LC 93-10398. (ps-3). 1994. 14.95 (*0-15-213884-6*) HarBrace.
Randall, E. T. Cosmic Kidnappers. Rogers, Jacqueline, illus. LC 84-8579. 128p. (gr. 3-7). 1985. PLB 9.49 (*0-8167-0328-0*); pap. text ed. 2.95 (*0-8167-0329-9*) Troll Assocs.
—Target: Earth. Rogers, Jacqueline, illus. LC 84-2740. 128p. (gr. 3-7). 1985. PLB 9.49 (*0-8167-0326-4*); pap. text ed. 2.95 (*0-8167-0327-2*) Troll Assocs.
—Thieves from Space. Rogers, Jacqueline, illus. LC 84-8538. 128p. (gr. 3-7). 1985. PLB 9.49 (*0-8167-0330-2*); pap. text ed. 2.95 (*0-8167-0331-0*) Troll Assocs.
—Town in Terror. Rogers, Jacqueline, illus. LC 84-5617. 128p. (gr. 3-7). 1985. PLB 9.49 (*0-8167-0332-9*); pap. 2.95 (*0-8167-0333-7*) Troll Assocs.
Ransome, Arthur. Tontimundo y el Barco Volador. Shulevitz, Uri, illus. Negroni, Maria, tr. (SPA., Illus.). 48p. (ps-3). 1991. 15.95 (*0-374-32443-3*) FS&G.
Raskin, Ellen. Figgs & Phantoms. Raskin, Ellen, illus. LC 73-17309. 160p. (gr. 4 up). 1977. pap. 15.95 (*0-525-29680-8*, 01063-320, DCB); (DCB) Dutton Child Bks.
Raven, James. Empty Hand, No. 6. 1993. pap. 3.25 (*0-553-56301-7*) Bantam.
Rayburn, Cherie. Elizabeth's Castle Adventure: A Just Suppose(TM) Story. Gress, Jonna, ed. Beck, Connie & O'Toole, Tim, illus. 4p. (gr. 1-7). 1992. 18.80 (*0-944943-07-1*, CODE 18899-9) Current Inc.
Records, Pam. Once upon a Rhyme: A Wizard's Wacky Story Time. Records, Pam, illus. 21p. (ps). 1993. pap. 10.95 (*0-9639839-0-3*) MP Records.
Red, Carmine. The Magic Binoculars: An Odyssey to Infinity. Red, Carmine, illus. LC 94-82025. 60p. (gr. 3-6). 1994. 12.95 (*0-9640506-7-6*) Rock-It Pr.
Reed, Louis. The Wicks & the Wacks. LC 85-70443. (ps-2). 1985. pap. 5.00 (*0-916383-00-8*, Univ Edtns) Aegina Pr.
Reichert, Mickey Z. Godslayer. (gr. 9-12). 1990. pap. 2.95 (*0-88677-207-9*) DAW Bks.
Reiss, Kathryn. Time Windows. (gr. 4-7). 1994. pap. 3.50 (*0-590-46536-8*) Scholastic Inc.
Reit, Seymour V. & Navaroo, Jose G. Voyage with Columbus. 96p. (Orig.). 1986. pap. 2.50 (*0-553-15431-1*) Bantam.
Renauld, Christiane. Journey in a Shell. (Illus.). 32p. (gr. 3-5). 1991. 12.95 (*0-89565-752-X*) Childs World.
—The Magic Shoes. (Illus.). 32p. (gr. 3-5). 1991. 12.95 (*0-89565-753-8*) Childs World.
Reynolds, Alfred. Kiteman. 208p. (gr. 6 up). 1986. pap. 2.75 (*0-553-26036-7*, Spectra) Bantam.
Rhind, Mary. The Dark Shadow. (Illus.). 128p. (gr. 5-9). 1990. pap. 6.95 (*0-86241-253-6*, Pub. by Cnngt Pub Ltd) Trafalgar.
Rice, James. Lyn & the Fuzzy. Rice, James, illus. LC 75-19096. 40p. (gr. 2-6). 1975. 12.95 (*0-88289-087-5*) Pelican.
Rigby, Rodney. The Night the Moon Fell Asleep. Rigby, Rodney, illus. LC 92-45928. 32p. (ps-3). 1993. 13.95 (*1-56282-334-5*); PLB 13.89 (*1-56282-335-3*) Hyprn Child.
Robinson, W. Heath. Adventures of Uncle Lubin. (ps-3). 1992. 15.95 (*0-87923-884-4*) Godine.
Rocard, Ann. Hobee Scrogneenee. Degano, Marino, illus. 28p. (ps-4). 1991. smythe sewn reinforced bdg. 9.95 (*1-56182-000-8*) Atomium Bks.
—Hobee Scrogneenee at Joey's School. Degano, Marino, illus. 28p. (ps-4). 1991. smythe sewn reinforced bdg. 9.95 (*1-56182-001-6*) Atomium Bks.
Rockwell, Thomas. How to Eat Fried Worms. McCully, Emily A., illus. LC 73-4262. (gr. 4-6). 1973. PLB 13. 90 (*0-531-02631-0*) Watts.
Roe, Elaine C. Circle of Light. LC 87-45855. 256p. (gr. 5 up). 1989. HarpC Child Bks.
Rojany, Lisa, adapted by. Walt Disney's Alice in Wonderland down the Rabbit Hole: A Lift-the-Flap Rebus Book. Cuddy, Robbin, illus. 16p. (ps-3). 1994. 12.95 (*0-7868-3000-X*) Disney Pr.
Rose, Gerald. Grumps. (Illus.). 32p. (gr. k-2). 1993. 17.95 (*0-370-31575-8*, Pub. by Bodley Head UK) Trafalgar.
Ross, Pat. M & M & the Super Child Afternoon. 21p. 1992. Braille. 1.68 (*1-56956-277-6*) W A T Braille.
Rowe, W. W. Amy & Gully in Rainbowland. Chow, Adam, illus. LC 92-9075. 84p. (Orig.). (gr. k-4). 1992. pap. 5.95 (*1-55939-003-4*) Snow Lion.
Rubinstein, Gillian. Skymaze. MacDonald, Pat, ed. 240p. (gr. 7 up). 1993. pap. 2.99 (*0-671-76988-X*, Archway) PB.
Rusack, Caroline M. Topsy-Turvy Town. 1994. 7.95 (*0-533-10688-5*) Vantage.
Russell, David A. Superbike. 180p. (gr. 4-7). 1993. 3.95 (*1-883174-00-7*) High Octane.
Ryder, Joanne. Where Butterflies Grow. Cherry, Lynne, illus. LC 88-37989. 32p. (ps-3). 1989. 14.00 (*0-525-67284-2*, Lodestar Bks) Dutton Child Bks.
Sadler, Marilyn. Alistair's Time Machine. Bollen, Roger, illus. 40p. (ps up). 1992. pap. 13.95 jacketed (*0-671-66679-7*, S&S BFYR); pap. 5.95 (*0-671-68493-0*, S&S BFYR) S&S Trade.
Salsitz, Rhondi V. The Twilight Gate. Clark, Alan M., illus. LC 92-22040. 192p. (gr. 7 up). 1993. 16.95 (*0-8027-8213-2*) Walker & Co.
Sampson, Fay. Chris & the Dragon. Bennett, Jill, illus. 96p. (gr. 4-6). 1987. 14.95 (*0-575-03661-3*, Pub. by Gollancz England) Trafalgar.
Sampson, Mary Y. The Golden Falcon. Bertschmann, Mary, ed. Bertschmann, Harry, illus. 120p. (Orig.). 1993. pap. 25.00 fine print, letter press ed. (*0-935505-08-3*) Bank St Pr.
Sandburg, Carl. Rootabaga Stories, Pt. 1. Hague, Michael, contrib. by. 85p. (gr. 3-7). 1990. pap. 4.95 (*0-15-269065-4*, Odyssey) HarBrace.
—Rootabaga Stories, Pt. 2. Hague, Michael, illus. 179p. (gr. 3-7). 1989. 19.95 (*0-15-269062-X*) HarBrace.
—Rootabaga Stories, Pt. 2. Hague, Michael, contrib. by. 158p. (gr. 3-7). 1990. pap. 4.95 (*0-15-269063-8*, Odyssey) HarBrace.
Sandford. N. Lous Do Pb, Vol. 1. (ps-3). 1993. 9.95 (*0-316-77080-9*) Little.
San Souci, Robert D. Enchaned Tapestry. (ps-3). 1990. pap. 4.99 (*0-14-054626-X*) Viking Penguin.
—The Enchanted Tapestry. Gal, Laszlo, illus. LC 85-29283. 32p. (ps-3). 1987. 11.95 (*0-8037-0304-X*); PLB 11.89 (*0-8037-0306-6*) Dial Bks Young.
—The Enchanted Tapestry. Fogelman, Phyllis J., ed. Gal, Laszlo, illus. LC 85-29283. 32p. (ps-3). 1990. pap. 4.95 (*0-8037-0862-9*) Dial Bks Young.
Sant, Thomas. Amazing Adventures of Albert & His Flying Machine. (gr. 4-7). 1993. pap. 3.50 (*0-440-40814-8*) Dell.
Sapaugh, Micah. Marlusk the Warrior. Sapaugh, Micah, illus. Sargent, Dave, intro. by. (Illus.). 48p. (Orig.). (gr. k-8). 1993. text ed. 11.95 (*1-56763-092-8*); pap. text ed. 5.95 (*1-56763-093-6*) Ozark Pub.
Schertle, Alice. Down the Road. Date not set. 14.95 (*0-06-020057-X*, HarpT) HarpC.
Schields, Gretchen. The Water Shell. LC 94-15606. Date not set. write for info. (*0-15-200404-1*, Gulliver Bks) HarBrace.
Schlein, Miriam. Secret Land of the Past. (gr. 4-7). 1992. pap. 2.75 (*0-590-45701-2*) Scholastic Inc.
Schotter, Roni. Captain Snap & the Children of Vinegar Lane. Sewall, Marcia, illus. LC 88-22489. 32p. (ps-3). 1993. pap. 5.95 (*0-531-07038-7*) Orchard Bks Watts.
Schubert, Ingrid & Schubert, Dieter. The Magic Bubble Trip. LC 84-25071. (Illus.). 32p. (ps-3). 1985. 9.95 (*0-916291-02-2*); pap. 6.95 (*0-916291-03-0*) Kane Miller Bk.
Schwalbe, Donna. The Little Box. Miller, Byron, ed. Burlingame, Burt, illus. LC 94-75226. 24p. (Orig.). 1994. pap. 5.95 (*0-9636637-2-0*) Impatience Pubns.
Scieszka, Jon. The Knights of the Kitchen Table. Smith, Lane, illus. 64p. (gr. 2-6). 1993. pap. 2.99 (*0-14-034603-1*, Puffin) Puffin Bks.
—The Not-So-Jolly Roger. Smith, Lane, illus. 64p. (gr. 2-6). 1993. pap. 2.99 (*0-14-034684-8*, Puffin) Puffin Bks.
Scott, Hugh. The Plant That Ate the World: A Novel of the Near Future. 106p. (gr. 3-6). 1991. 14.95 (*0-571-15440-9*) Faber & Faber.
Scott, Michael, ed. Earthlord: Second of the De Danann Tales. (Illus.). 176p. (gr. 5-8). 1993. pap. 9.95 (*0-86327-343-2*, Pub. by Wolfhound Pr EIRE) Dufour.
Seidler, Tor. The Tar Pit. LC 87-74338. 160p. 1987. 14. 00 (*0-374-37383-3*) FS&G.
Seitz, Leah M. Prince Golden Lashes. 1993. 7.95 (*0-533-10651-6*) Vantage.
Sendak, Maurice. Bernard. 1994. 10.95 (*0-694-00612-2*, Festival) HarpC Child Bks.
—Maurice Sendak Book & Poster Package: Where the Wild Things Are. Sendak, Maurice, illus. LC 63-21253. 48p. (gr. k-3). 1991. incl. poster 21.95 (*0-06-025966-3*) HarpC Child Bks.
—Max. 1994. 10.95 (*0-694-00613-0*, Festival) HarpC Child Bks.
—Moishe. 1994. 10.95 (*0-694-00614-9*, Festival) HarpC Child Bks.
—Outside Over There. Sendak, Maurice, illus. LC 79-2682. 40p. (gr. k up). 1981. 20.00 (*0-06-025523-4*); PLB 19.89 (*0-06-025524-2*) HarpC Child Bks.
—Tsippi. 1994. 10.95 (*0-694-00615-7*, Festival) HarpC Child Bks.
—Where the Wild Things Are. LC 91-45366. (Illus.). 48p. (gr. k up). 1992. incl. mini Bernard doll 16.95 (*0-694-00432-4*, Festival); incl. mini Max doll 16.95 (*0-694-00431-6*, Festival) HarpC Child Bks.
Service, Pamela F. Stinker from Space. LC 87-25266. 96p. (gr. 3-5). 1988. SBE 13.95 (*0-684-18910-0*, Scribners Young Read) Macmillan Child Grp.
Shanower, Eric. Blue Witch of Oz. (Illus.). 72p. (Orig.). 1993. pap. 9.95 (*1-878574-44-2*) Dark Horse Comics.
—The Enchanted Apples of Oz. Oliver, Rick, ed. Ellison, Harlan, intro. by. (Illus.). 48p. (Orig.). 1986. pap. 7.95 (*0-915419-04-1*) First Pub IL.
—Enchanted Apples of Oz. (Illus.). 72p. (Orig.). 1993. pap. 7.95 (*1-878574-66-3*) Dark Horse Comics.
—The Forgotten Forest of Oz. Oliver, Rick, ed. Shanower, Eric, illus. 48p. (Orig.). 1991. pap. 8.95 (*0-915419-44-0*) First Pub IL.
—Forgotten Forest of Oz. (Illus.). 72p. (Orig.). 1993. pap. 8.95 (*1-878574-64-7*) Dark Horse Comics.
—The Giant Garden of Oz. Shunower, Eric, illus. (gr. 3 up). 1993. 39.95 (*0-929605-23-3*); pap. 11.95 (*0-929605-22-5*) Books Wonder.
—The Ice King of Oz. Oliver, Rick, ed. Shanower, Eric, illus. 48p. (Orig.). 1987. pap. 7.95 (*0-915419-25-4*) First Pub IL.
—Ice King of Oz. (Illus.). 72p. (Orig.). 1993. pap. 8.95 (*1-878574-65-5*) Dark Horse Comics.
—The Secret Island of Oz. Oliver, Rick, ed. Shanower, Eric, illus. 48p. (Orig.). 1988. pap. 7.95 (*0-915419-08-4*) First Pub IL.
—Secret Island of Oz. (Illus.). 72p. (Orig.). 1993. pap. 8.95 (*1-878574-67-1*) Dark Horse Comics.
Shaver, Beth. The Little Lost Friggle... Who Can Help? 21p. 1992. Personalized. text ed. 12.95 (*1-883842-05-0*); text ed. 7.95 (*1-883842-04-2*) Kids at Heart.
Shealy, Daniel, ed. Louisa May Alcott's Fairy Tales & Fantasy Stories. LC 91-43144. (Illus.). 432p. (Orig.). 1992. text ed. 37.95x (*0-87049-752-9*); pap. 24.95 (*0-87049-758-8*) U of Tenn Pr.
Sheldon, Dyan. Harry the Explorer. Heap, Sue & Heap, Sue, illus. LC 91-58734. 80p. (gr. 3-6). 1992. 13.95 (*1-56402-109-2*) Candlewick Pr.
Sherman, Josepha. Child of Faerie, Child of Earth. 144p. (gr. 7 up). 1992. 15.95 (*0-8027-8112-8*) Walker & Co.
—Gleaming Bright. LC 93-24156. 168p. (gr. 7-9). 1994. 16.95 (*0-8027-8296-5*) Walker & Co.
Shetterly, Will. Nevernever. LC 93-238. 1993. 16.95 (*0-15-257022-5*, J Yolen Bks) HarBrace.
Shusterman, Neal. The Eyes of Kid Midas. 1994. pap. 3.99 (*0-8125-3460-3*) Tor Bks.
Sidney, Margaret. Five Little Peppers Midway. (Orig.). (gr. k-6). 1987. pap. 4.95 (*0-440-42589-1*, Pub. by Yearling Classics) Dell.
Siegel, et al. The Legion of Super-Heroes Archives, Vol. 4. Kahan, Bob, ed. (Illus.). 224p. 1993. text ed. 39.95 collected ed. (*1-56389-123-9*) DC Comics.
Sikes, Johnie. From Feathers to a King. 40p. 1992. pap. text ed. 3.95 (*0-9633262-0-1*) Vitamemoria.
Sikes, Johnie B. BackWhen Ben Again. 40p. 1992. pap. text ed. 3.95 (*0-9633262-3-6*) Vitamemoria.
—Tales of BackWhen Ben. 40p. 1992. pap. text ed. 3.95 (*0-9633262-2-8*) Vitamemoria.
Singer, A. L. Surf Ninjas. (gr. 4-7). 1993. pap. 3.50 (*0-553-56361-0*) Bantam.

Skinner, Daphne, adapted by. Tim Burton's Nightmare Before Christmas. LC 93-78835. (Illus.). 80p. (gr. 2-6). 1993. pap. 2.95 (*1-56282-592-5*) Hyprn Ppbks.
Skurzynski, Gloria. What Happened in Hamelin. LC 79-12814. (Illus.). 192p. (Orig.). (gr. 5-9). 1993. pap. 3.99 (*0-679-83645-4*, Bullseye Bks) Random Bks Yng Read.
Slater, Teddy. Sooo Big! (ps-3). 1994. pap. 2.25 (*0-307-06034-9*, Golden Pr) Western Pub.
Slater, Teddy, adapted by. Walt Disney's Alice in Wonderland. Maten, Franc, illus. (ps-2). 1991. write for info. (*0-307-12341-3*, Golden Pr) Western Pub.
Sleator, William. Others See Us. (Illus.). 144p. (gr. 5-11). 1993. 14.99 (*0-525-45104-8*, DCB) Dutton Child Bks.
—Singularity. LC 84-26075. 192p. (gr. 7 up). 1985. 12.95 (*0-525-44161-1*, DCB) Dutton Child Bks.
Slote, Alfred. My Trip to Alpha I. Berson, Harold, illus. LC 85-45394. 96p. (gr. 2-5). 1986. pap. 3.95 (*0-06-440166-9*, Trophy) HarpC Child Bks.
Smith, Agnes. An Edge of the Forest. Sharkey, J. Thomas, illus. 207p. (gr. 7 up). 1974. 9.00 (*0-87012-171-5*) Westwind Pr.
Smith, L. J. The Awakening. 1991. pap. 3.99 (*0-06-106097-6*, Harp PBks) HarpC.
—The Fury. 1991. pap. 3.99 (*0-06-106099-2*, Harp PBks) HarpC.
—The Struggle. 1991. pap. 3.99 (*0-06-106098-4*, Harp PBks) HarpC.
Smith, Sherwood. Wren to the Rescue. 216p. (gr. 7 up). 1990. 15.95 (*0-15-200975-2*, J Yolen Bks) HarBrace.
—Wren's Quest. LC 92-18988. 1993. write for info. (*0-15-200976-0*, J Yolen Bks) HarBrace.
Snyder, Dianne. George & the Dragon Word. 1994. pap. 2.99 (*0-671-79393-4*, Minstrel Bks) PB.
Snyder, Zilpha K. And All Between. 224p. (gr. 5 up). 1992. pap. 3.50 (*0-440-21265-0*, LFL) Dell.
—Until the Celebration. 208p. (gr. 5 up). 1992. pap. 3.50 (*0-440-21348-7*, LFL) Dell.
Sochard, Ruth. Weathertop, the Tower of the Wind. Fenlon, Peter C., Jr., ed. Martin, David & Martin, Elissa, illus. 32p. (Orig.). (gr. 10-12). 1987. pap. 6.00 (*0-915795-89-2*, 8201) Iron Crown Ent Inc.
Specter, B. J. Beetlejuice, No. 6: Trial by Ghost. Ashby, Ruth, ed. 96p. (Orig.). 1992. pap. 2.99 (*0-671-75561-7*, Minstrel Bks) PB.
Sprague, Gilbert M. Patchwork Bride of Oz. (Illus.). 40p. (gr. 1 up). 1993. 19.95 (*0-929605-28-4*); pap. 6.95 (*0-929605-27-6*) Books Wonder.
Spremich, Andrew. Flight of the Dragon. Kratoville, Betty L., ed. (Illus.). 64p. (gr. 3-9). 1989. PLB 4.95 (*0-87879-619-3*) High Noon Bks.
Springer, Nancy. The Red Wizard. LC 88-29376. 144p. (gr. 4 up). 1990. SBE 13.95 (*0-689-31485-X*, Atheneum Child Bk) Macmillan Child Grp.
Spurr, Elizabeth. Mrs. Minetta's Car Pool. Sims, Blanche, illus. LC 90-35. 32p. (gr. k-3). 1990. pap. 3.95 (*0-689-71430-0*, Aladdin) Macmillan Child Grp.
Stafford, Greg. Runequest: Deluxe. Peterson, Sandy, ed. (Illus.). 96p. (gr. 8 up). 1989. 29.95 (*0-911605-51-7*) Avalon Hill.
Stanley, Diane. Captain Whiz-Bang. Stanley, Diane, illus. LC 86-16432. 32p. (ps-2). 1987. 12.95 (*0-688-06226-1*); lib. bdg. 12.88 (*0-688-06227-X*, Morrow Jr Bks) Morrow Jr Bks.
Staplehurst, Graham. Minas Tirith. Fenlon, Peter C., Jr., ed. McBride, Angus, illus. 192p. (gr. 10-12). 1988. 18.00 (*1-55806-001-4*, 8301) Iron Crown Ent Inc.
—The Phantom of the Northern Marches. Fenlon, Peter, ed. Horne, Daniel, illus. 32p. (Orig.). (gr. 10-12). 1986. pap. 6.00 (*0-915795-47-7*, 8102) Iron Crown Ent Inc.
Stearns, Michael, ed. A Wizard's Dozen. LC 93-22150. 1993. 16.95 (*0-15-200965-5*, J Yolen Bks); pap. write for info. (*0-15-200966-3*, J Yolen Bks) HarBrace.
Steele, Mary Q. Journey Outside. (gr. 5-9). 1984. 17.25 (*0-8446-6169-4*) Peter Smith.
Steig, William. The Amazing Bone. Steig, William, illus. LC 76-26479. 32p. (ps-3). 1983. 17.00 (*0-374-30248-0*) FS&G.
Steiner, Barbara. Phantom. 1993. pap. 3.50 (*0-590-46425-6*) Scholastic Inc.
Steiner, Claude. The Original Warm Fuzzy Tale. Dick, Joann, illus. Freed, Alvyn M., intro. by. LC 77-77981. (Illus.). 48p. (Orig.). (gr. k up). 1977. 8.95 (*0-915190-08-7*, JP9008-7) Jalmar Pr.
Stephens, Michael. Titans. (ps-3). 1993. pap. 6.95 (*1-86373-133-4*, Pub. by Allen & Unwin Aust Pty AT) IPG Chicago.
Stevenson, Laura C. The Island & the Ring. 304p. (gr. 5-9). 1991. 15.45 (*0-395-56401-8*, Sandpiper) HM.
Strange Case of Dr. Jekyll & Mr. Hyde. (gr. 4-7). 1993. pap. 2.95 (*0-89375-357-2*) Troll Assocs.
Strasser, Todd. Walt Disney's Peter Pan: Illustrated Classic. Cardona, Jose & Marvin, Fred, illus. 96p. 1994. 14.95 (*1-56282-638-7*) Disney Pr.
—Walt Disney's Peter Pan: Junior Novelization. (Illus.). 64p. (gr. 2-6). 1994. pap. 3.50 (*1-56282-640-9*) Disney Pr.
Strasser, Todd, adapted by. Honey, I Blew up the Kid. LC 91-58789. (Illus.). 224p. (gr. 6 up). 1992. pap. 3.50 (*1-56282-204-7*) Disney Pr.
Sullivan, Jem & Dixon, Jim. Flooty Hobbs & the Giggling Jolly Gollywobber. Sullivan, Jem, illus. 36p. (gr. k-2). 1991. 12.95 (*1-880453-00-2*) J Hefty Pub.
Sutton, Scott E. The Family of Ree. Sutton, Scott E., illus. 45p. (gr. 2-4). 1986. 13.95x (*0-9617199-1-5*) Sutton Pubns.
—The Legend of Snow Pookas. Sutton, Scott E., illus. (gr. 2-4). 13.95x (*0-9617199-6-6*) Sutton Pubns.
—More Altitude, Quick! (Illus.). 51p. (gr. 2-4). 1988. 13.95x (*0-9617199-4-X*) Sutton Pubns.
Swift, Jonathan. Gulliver's Adventures in Lilliput. Beneduce, Ann K., retold by. Spirin, Gennady, illus. LC 92-26200. 32p. (ps). 1993. 15.95 (*0-399-22021-6*, Philomel Bks) Putnam Pub Group.
—Gulliver's Travels. Arneson, D. J., retold by. Clift, Eva, illus. 128p. 1992. pap. 2.95 (*1-56156-143-6*) Kidsbks.
Swindells, Robert. Room Thirteen. 192p. 1991. text ed. 15.95 (*0-7451-1371-0*, Pub. by Chivers Pr UK) Hall.
Szernecki, Stefan & Rhodes, Timothy. Time Before Dreams. (Illus.). 80p. (gr. 6-10). 1990. 14.95 (*0-920534-49-X*, Pub. by Hyperion Pr Ltd CN) Sterling.
Tallarico, Beatrice & Stone, S. Callis. The Weeuns Journey of Two Cousins. Stone, S. Callis, illus. 39p. (gr. 2-8). 1984. 12.95 (*0-936191-13-9*) Tallstone Pub.
Tallis, Robyn. Night of Two New Moons. (gr. 6 up). 1989. pap. 2.95 (*0-8041-0209-0*) Ivy Books.
—Visions from the Sea. (gr. 6 up). 1989. pap. 2.95 (*0-8041-0206-6*) Ivy Books.
—Zero-Sum Games. (gr. 6 up). 1989. pap. 2.95 (*0-8041-0207-4*) Ivy Books.
Teitelbaum, Michael, adapted by. Honey, I Blew up the Kid. LC 91-58788. (Illus.). 32p. (ps-3). 1992. pap. 2.95 (*1-56282-203-9*) Disney Pr.
Tenaille, Marie. The Day the Dragon Came to School. 9p. 1992. text ed. 0.72 (*1-56956-109-5*) W A T Braille.
Thaler, Mike. Principal from the Black Lagoon. (ps-3). 1993. pap. 2.50 (*0-590-45782-9*) Scholastic Inc.
Thomas Nelson Publishing Staff. In His Steps: Marvel Comics. (gr. 4-7). 1994. pap. 9.99 (*0-8407-6283-6*) Nelson.
Thompson, Julian. Gypsyworld. LC 93-15451. 240p. (gr. 7 up). 1993. pap. 3.99 (*0-14-036531-1*, Puffin) Puffin Bks.
Thompson, R. I Have to See This! (Illus.). 24p. (ps-8). 1988. 12.95 (*1-55037-015-4*, Pub. by Annick CN); pap. 4.95 (*1-55037-014-6*, Pub. by Annick CN) Firefly Bks Ltd.
Thurber, James. Wonderful O. (gr. 4-7). 1992. pap. 3.50 (*0-440-40579-3*, Pub. by Yearling Classics) Dell.
Tidy, Bill. Incredible Bed. (Illus.). 32p. (ps-1). 1991. 13.95 (*0-86264-268-X*, Pub. by Andersen Pr UK) Trafalgar.
Tinkerbell's Challenge. (Illus.). (ps-3). 1991. pap. 1.50 (*0-679-82701-3*) Random Bks Yng Read.
Titchenell, Elsa-Brita. Once Round the Sun. Gruelle, Justin C. & Russell, Elizabeth A., illus. LC 81-52615. iv, 57p. (gr. 1 up). 1981. Repr. of 1950 ed. 9.50 (*0-911500-61-8*) Theos U Pr.
Tokuma Publishing Staff. Three D Wonderland. (gr. 4-7). 1993. pap. 15.95 (*4-19-086977-5*) Tokuma Pub.
Tolkien, J. R. R. The Hobbit. Hague, Michael, illus. 300p. (ps up). 1989. pap. 16.45 (*0-395-52021-5*, Sandpiper) HM.
Tomkins, Jasper. The Sky Jumps Into Your Shoes at Night. (Illus.). 60p. 1991. pap. 7.95 (*0-671-74971-4*, Green Tiger) S&S Trade.
Toybner, Yenny. Collection of Sonnets. 88p. 1994. pap. 9.95 (*0-8059-3535-5*) Dorrance.
Travers, Pamela L. Mary Poppins & the House Next Door. Shepard, Mary, illus. 96p. (gr. 4-7). 1992. pap. 3.50 (*0-440-40656-0*, YB) Dell.
—Mary Poppins in the Kitchen. (gr. 4-7). 1991. pap. 3.50 (*0-440-40527-0*, YB) Dell.
Trimble, Marshall. It Always Rains after a Dry Spell. Graham, Jack, illus. 288p. (Orig.). (gr. 6 up). 1992. pap. 12.95 (*0-918080-67-3*) Treasure Chest.
Tripp, Wallace. A Great Big Ugly Man Came up & Tied His Horse to Me: A Book of Nonsense Verse. (Illus.). 48p. (gr. k-12). 1974. lib. bdg. 14.95 (*0-316-85280-5*) Little.
Troll. Wizard of Oz Activity Book. 64p. (ps-3). 1991. pap. 1.95 (*0-8167-2283-8*) Troll Assocs.
Turner, Ann. Rosemary's Witch. LC 90-39779. 176p. (gr. 6 up). 1991. 14.00 (*0-06-026127-7*); PLB 13.89 (*0-06-026128-5*) HarpC Child Bks.
Updike, David. Seven Times Eight. Lorenz, Lee, illus. 40p. (gr. 2-5). 1990. PLB 14.95 (*0-945912-10-2*) Pippin Pr.
Ure, Jean. Wizard in the Woods. Anstey, David & Anstey, David, illus. LC 91-58770. 176p. (gr. 3-6). 1992. 14.95 (*1-56402-110-6*) Candlewick Pr.
—The Wizard in Wonderland. Anstey, David, illus. LC 92-53020. 176p. (gr. 3-6). 1993. 14.95 (*1-56402-138-6*) Candlewick Pr.
Uspenski, Eduard. The Little Warranty People. Ignatowicz, Nina, tr. from RUS. LC 93-25259. 1994. 15.00 (*0-679-82063-9*) Knopf Bks Yng Read.
Uttley, Alison. Lavender Shoes: Eight Tales of Enchantment. Ede, Janina, illus. 84p. (gr. k-2). 1991. pap. 3.95 (*0-571-15344-5*) Faber & Faber.
Valentine, Johnny. The Day They Put a Tax on Rainbows. Schmidt, Lynette, illus. 32p. (gr. k-5). 1992. 12.95 (*1-55583-201-6*, Alyson Wonderland) Alyson Pubns.
Van Allsburg, Chris. The Garden of Abdul Gasazi. (Illus.). 32p. (gr. 1-12). 1979. 17.95 (*0-395-27804-X*) HM.
Vandersteen, Willy. An Island Called Hoboken. Lahey, Nicholas, tr. from FLE. LC 75-8496. (Illus.). 56p. (Orig.). (gr. 3 up). 1976. pap. 2.50 (*0-915560-01-1*, 1) Hiddigeigei.
—The Merry Musketeers. Lahey, Nicholas J., tr. from FLE. LC 75-8495. (Illus.). 56p. (Orig.). (gr. 3 up). 1976. pap. 2.50 (*0-915560-18-6*, 18) Hiddigeigei.
VanRynbach, Iris. The Soup Stone. LC 86-31830. (Illus.). 32p. (ps-3). 1988. 11.95 (*0-688-07254-2*); lib. bdg. 11.88 (*0-688-07255-0*) Greenwillow.
Velde, Vande. Dragon's Bait. 1992. write for info. (*0-15-200726-1*, J Yolen Bks) HarBrace.
Verne, Jules. A Journey to the Center of the Earth. 272p. (Orig.). 1992. pap. 2.50 (*0-8125-0471-2*) Tor Bks.
—Twenty Thousand Leagues under the Sea. James, Raymond, ed. Geehan, Wayne, illus. LC 89-34248. 48p. (gr. 3-6). 1990. PLB 12.89 (*0-8167-1879-2*); pap. text ed. 3.95 (*0-8167-1880-6*) Troll Assocs.
Los Viajes De Gulliver. (SPA.). 1990. casebound 3.50 (*0-7214-1403-6*) Ladybird Bks.
Vick, Helen H. Walker of Time. LC 92-46740. 206p. (Orig.). (gr. 6-12). 1993. pap. 9.95 (*0-943173-80-9*) Harbinger AZ.
Viorst, Judith. My Mama Says There Aren't Any Zombies, Ghosts, Vampires, Creatures, Demons, Monsters, Fiends, Goblins, or Things. Chorao, Kay, illus. LC 73-76331. 48p. (gr. k-4). 1973. SBE 13.95 (*0-689-30102-2*, Atheneum Child Bk) Macmillan Child Grp.
Vogt, Esther. The Shiny Dragon. Converse, James, illus. LC 83-12981. 104p. (Orig.). (gr. 5-8). 1983. pap. 3.95 (*0-8361-3348-X*) Herald Pr.
Volkov, Alexander. The Wizard of Emerald City & Urfin Jus & His Wooden Soldiers. Blystone, Peter L., tr. from RUS. LC 90-62416. (gr. 4 up). 1991. pap. 11.95 (*1-878941-16-X*) Red Branch Pr.
Volkov, Alexander M. The Seven Underground Kings; & The Fiery God of the Marrans. Blystone, Peter L., tr. from RUS. & afterword by. LC 90-83409. 384p. (Orig.). (gr. 4 up). 1993. pap. 13.95 (*1-878941-18-6*) Red Branch Pr.
Vrooman, Christine W. Willowby's World of Fluffits. Sidaras, Nanci, illus. 56p. (Orig.). (gr. 2-6). 1984. pap. 8.95 with stickers incl. (*0-910349-02-9*) Cloud Ten.
Wade, Alan. I'm Flying. Mathers, Petra, illus. LC 88-31360. 40p. (ps-2). 1994. pap. 4.99 (*0-679-86019-3*) Knopf Bks Yng Read.
Wagner & Grant. Batman - Judge Dredd: Vendetta in Gotham. O'Neil, Dennis, ed. Kennedy, C., illus. 48p. 1993. pap. 4.95 (*1-56389-121-2*) DC Comics.
Wahl, Jahn. Mooga Mega Mekki. Krahn, Fernando, illus. LC 73-16818. 48p. (gr. 2-4). 1974. 7.95 (*0-87955-111-9*) O'Hara.
Walker, Kate. Dragon of Mith. (Illus.). 128p. (Orig.). (gr. 1-5). 1993. pap. 7.95 (*0-04-928064-3*, Pub. by Allen & Unwin Aust Pty AT) IPG Chicago.
Walt Disney Staff. Black Cauldron. (ps-3). 1993. 6.98 (*0-453-03154-4*) Viking Child Bks.
—Peter Pan. 1987. 6.98 (*0-8317-6799-5*) Viking Child Bks.
Walton, Robert M. Joel in Tananar. (Illus.). (gr. 4-9). 1982. 8.95 (*0-914598-05-8*) Pr MacDonald & Reinecke.
Waltz, Marjorie. The Dragon, the Winds & the Witches. Waltz, Catherine, illus. LC 86-72867. 64p. (Orig.). (gr. k-2). 1987. pap. 5.00 (*0-916383-14-8*) Aegina Pr.
Wang, Rosalind. The Magical Starfruit Tree. Livingston, Julie, ed. Shao Wei Liu, illus. 32p. (gr. k-2). 1994. 13.95 (*0-941831-89-2*) Beyond Words Pub.
Wangerin, Walter, Jr. The Crying for a Vision. LC 93-48589. (gr. 7 up). 1994. 16.00 (*0-671-79911-8*, S&S BFYR) S&S Trade.
Ward, Jane S. Tajar Tales. Drucklieb, Herman L. & Kerry, Jill, illus. LC 93-71385. 48p. (ps-4). 1993. Repr. of 1924 ed. Colorized pictures, music & song added. lib. bdg. 14.95 (*1-883338-01-8*) Classic Wrks.
Waterton, Kulyn. Orff, Twenty-Seven Dragons & a Snarkel. (Illus.). 24p. (ps-8). 1984. 12.95 (*0-920303-02-1*, Pub. by Annick CN); pap. 4.95 (*0-920303-03-X*, Pub. by Annick CN) Firefly Bks Ltd.
Watson, Beverly H. The Angel's Bride. Barrett, Kay L., ed. Hyder, Cynthia M., illus. 50p. (Orig.). (gr. 4-7). 1993. pap. 4.95 (*0-9623647-3-8*) B H Watson.
Watson, Richard J. Tom Thumb. LC 87-12045. (ps-3). 1993. pap. 5.95 (*0-15-289281-8*, HB Juv Bks) HarBrace.
Weiser, Jacob. The Lost Dutchman. (Illus.). 140p. (gr. 3-6). 1989. pap. 9.95 (*0-944770-02-9*) Discovery GA.
Weiss, Ellen & Friedman, Mel. The Poof Point. LC 91-34765. 168p. (gr. 3-7). 1993. pap. 3.99 (*0-679-82272-0*, Bullseye Bks) Random Bks Yng Read.
Wells, H. G. The Invisible Man. 192p. 1992. pap. 2.50 (*0-8125-0467-4*) Tor Bks.
—The Time Machine. Powell, Ivan, illus. Wright, Betty R., adapted by. LC 81-4097. (Illus.). 48p. (gr. 4 up). 1983. PLB 20.70 (*0-8172-1675-8*) Raintree Steck-V.
West, Mark I., ed. Before Oz: Juvenile Fantasy Stories from Nineteenth-Century America. LC 89-35643. (Illus.). 229p. 1989. lib. bdg. 29.50 (*0-208-02234-1*, Archon Bks) Shoe String.
Westall, Robert. Stones of Muncaster Cathedral. (gr. 4-7). 1994. pap. 3.95 (*0-374-47119-3*, Sunburst) FS&G.
Weyn, Suzanne. Collette's Magic Star. 96p. 1991. pap. 2.75 (*0-590-43562-0*) Scholastic Inc.
White, Celeste. The Legend of the Flying Hotdog. (Illus.). 32p. 1991. 11.95 (*0-88138-131-4*, Green Tiger) S&S Trade.
White, John. Gaal the Conqueror. Stockman, Jack, illus. LC 89-19821. 320p. (Orig.). (gr. 7-9). 1989. pap. 10.99 (*0-87784-591-3*, 591) InterVarsity.

—The Iron Sceptre. LC 80-36727. (Illus.). 408p. (Orig.). (gr. 4-7). 1981. pap. 10.99 (0-87784-589-1, 589) InterVarsity.

Whiteley, Keith. Kagiso's Mad Uncle. (ps-3). 1992. pap. 2.95 (0-7910-2909-3) Chelsea Hse.

Wicke, Ed. The Screeps. LC 92-12259. (Illus.). 180p. 1992. pap. 5.99 (0-8308-1352-7, 1352) InterVarsity.

Williams, Jennifer. Stringbean's Trip to Shining Sea. 1990. pap. 4.95 (0-590-44851-X) Scholastic Inc.

Williams, Leslie. A Bear in the Air. Vendrell, Carme S., illus. LC 80-10290. 28p. (gr. k up). 1980. 7.95 (0-916144-54-2) Stemmer Hse.

Williams, Tad & Hoffman, Nina K. Child of an Ancient City. LC 92-16802. (Illus.). 144p. (gr. 7 up). 1992. SBE 14.95 (0-689-31577-5, Atheneum Child Bk) Macmillan Child Grp.

Williams-Ellis, Anabel. Tales from the Enchanted World. Kemp, Moira, illus. (gr. 3-7). 1988. 17.95 (0-316-94133-6) Little.

Williamson, Louis. The Year Christmas Was Almost Spoiled. Galinat, William, illus. (gr. k-3). 1990. pap. 5.95 (0-533-08481-4) Vantage.

Willis, Jeanne. Earth Hounds, As Explained by Professor Xargle. LC 89-23696. (Illus.). 32p. (ps-2). 1990. 12.95 (0-525-44600-1, DCB) Dutton Child Bks.

Wilson, David C. Blackberry Organ. LC 91-67985. 48p. (gr. 3-7). 1992. pap. write for info. (0-9632765-6-5) Spirit Light.

Winterfeld, Henry. Castaways in Lilliput. Lattimore, Deborah N. & Hutchinson, William M., illus. 220p. (gr. 3-7). 1990. pap. 4.95 (0-15-214822-1, Odyssey) HarBrace.

Wisniewski, David. Elfwyn's Saga. 32p. 1990. 13.95 (0-688-09589-5); PLB 13.88 (0-688-09590-9) Lothrop.

Wood, Audrey. Moonflute. Wood, Don, illus. LC 86-4666. 25p. (ps-3). 1986. 14.95 (0-15-255337-1) HarBrace.

Woodcock, John. Trouble in Space. 64p. (Orig.). (gr. 6 up). 1984. pap. 2.25 (0-553-15501-6) Bantam.

Woodruff, Elvira. Awfully Short for the Fourth Grade. Hillenbrand, Will, illus. LC 89-2082. 112p. (gr. 3-6). 1989. 14.95 (0-8234-0785-3) Holiday.

Wrede, Patricia C. Dealing with Dragons. 212p. (gr. 7 up). 1990. 15.95 (0-15-222900-0, J Yolen Bks) HarBrace.

—Dealing with Dragons. 1992. pap. 3.25 (0-590-45722-5, Point) Scholastic Inc.

—Searching for Dragons. 1992. 3.25 (0-590-45721-7, 071, Point) Scholastic Inc.

Yep, Laurence. Dragon Cauldron. LC 90-39584. (Illus.). 320p. (gr. 7 up). 1991. PLB 16.89 (0-06-026754-2) HarpC Child Bks.

—Dragon of the Lost Sea. LC 81-48644. 224p. (gr. 6 up). 1988. pap. 4.95 (0-06-440227-4, Trophy) HarpC Child Bks.

—Dragon Steel. LC 84-48338. 288p. (gr. 7 up). 1985. PLB 12.89 (0-06-026751-8) HarpC Child Bks.

—Dragon Steel. LC 84-48338. 288p. (gr. 7 up). 1993. pap. 4.95 (0-06-440486-2, Trophy) HarpC Child Bks.

Yolen, Jane. All Those Secrets of the World. (ps-3). 1993. pap. 4.95 (0-316-96895-1) Little.

—Dove Isabeau. Nolan, Dennis, illus. 32p. (gr. 3-7). 1989. 13.95 (0-15-224131-0) HarBrace.

—Heart's Blood. LC 83-14978. 224p. (gr. 7 up). 1984. 14. 95 (0-385-29316-X) Delacorte.

—Here There Be Dragons. Wilgus, David, illus. LC 92-23194. 1993. 16.95 (0-15-209888-7) HarBrace.

—Wizard's Hall. (gr. 4-7). 1993. pap. 2.95 (0-590-45811-6) Scholastic Inc.

Yorinks, Arthur. Hey, Al. Egielski, Richard, illus. (ps up). 1989. pap. 4.95 (0-374-42985-5, Sunburst) FS&G.

—Ugh. (ps-3). 1993. pap. 4.95 (0-374-48050-8) FS&G.

Zemoch, Margot. Three Wishes: An Old Story. (ps-3). 1993. pap. 4.95 (0-374-47728-0) FS&G.

Ziefert, Harriet. Good Luck - Bad Luck. (Illus.). 32p. (ps-3). 1992. pap. 3.50 (0-14-054461-5) Puffin Bks.

Zion, Gene. All Falling Down. Graham, Margaret B., illus. LC 51-12571. 32p. (ps-1). 1951. PLB 13.89 (0-06-026831-X) HarpC Child Bks.

Zolna, Ed. Fran an' Maabl: Rel. (Illus.). 64p. (Orig.). (gr. 9-12). 1988. pap. 2.50 (0-945975-00-7) E Zolna Inc.

FAR EAST

see East (Far East)

FARADAY, MICHAEL, 1791-1867

Brophy, Michael. Michael Faraday. LC 90-33893. (Illus.). 48p. (gr. 4-8). 1991. PLB 12.40 (0-531-18376-9, Pub. by Bookwright Pr) Watts.

FARM ANIMALS

see Domestic Animals; Livestock

FARM CROPS

see Farm Produce

FARM IMPLEMENTS

see Agricultural Machinery

FARM LABORERS

see Agricultural Laborers

FARM LIFE

see also Country Life; Ranch Life

Anderson, George. American Family Farm. (gr. 3 up). 1989. 18.95 (0-15-203025-5) HarBrace.

Bentley, Judith. Farmers & Ranchers. (Illus.). 96p. (gr. 5-8). 1994. bds. 16.95 (0-8050-2999-0) TFC Bks NY.

Bolton, Jane. My Grandmother's Patchwork Quilt: A Book & Portfolio of Patchwork Pieces. LC 93-17279. 1994. 17.95 (0-385-31155-9) Doubleday.

Chrisp, Peter. The Farmer Through History. Smith, Tony, illus. LC 92-38485. 48p. (gr. 5-8). 1993. 15.95 (1-56847-011-8) Thomson Lrning.

Fass, Bernie, et al. Old MacDonald Had a Farm. 32p. (gr. k-4). 1981. pap. 14.95 (0-86704-007-6) Clarus Music.

Foster, Janet. The Wilds of Whip-Poor-Will-Farm. Kassian, Olena, illus. 112p. (gr. 3 up). 1992. pap. 7.95 (0-919872-79-4, Pub. by Greey de Pencier CN) Firefly Bks Ltd.

Fun at the Farm. (Illus.). (ps-5). 3.50 (0-7214-0478-2); Ser. S705-4. wkbk. 1.95 (0-317-04010-3); o.p. (0-317-04012-X) Ladybird Bks.

Gildemeister, Jerry. Around the Cat's Back. Gildemeister, Jerry, illus. 128p. (gr. 4-12). 1989. 32.50 (0-936376-06-6) Bear Wallow Pub.

Goodall, John S. The Story of a Farm. Goodall, John S., illus. LC 88-3398. (gr. 4 up). 1989. RSBE 14.95 (0-689-50479-9, M K McElderry) Macmillan Child Grp.

Hellen, Nancy. On the Farm: Match It Up. 1989. 3.99 (0-517-68250-8) Random Hse Value.

Henderson, Kathy. I Can Be a Farmer. LC 88-37716. (Illus.). 32p. (gr. k-3). 1989. pap. 3.95 (0-516-41923-4) Childrens.

Lenski, Lois. Little Farm. Lenski, Lois, illus. LC 58-12902. (gr. k-3). 1980. 5.25 (0-8098-1009-3) McKay.

Lester, Alison. My Farm. LC 93-30894. 1994. 14.95 (0-395-68193-6) HM.

McGregor, Merideth. Cowgirl. 32p. 1992. 14.95 (0-8027-8170-5); PLB 15.85 (0-8027-8171-3) Walker & Co.

Matthews, Morgan. What's It Like to Be a Farmer. Kennedy, Anne, illus. LC 89-34386. 32p. (gr. k-3). 1990. lib. bdg. 10.89 (0-8167-1803-2); pap. text ed. 2.95 (0-8167-1804-0) Troll Assocs.

Provensen, Alice & Provensen, Martin. Town & Country. LC 93-44749. (gr. k-3). 1994. 16.95 (0-15-200182-4, Browndeer Pr) HarBrace.

—The Year at Maple Hill Farm. LC 77-18518. (Illus.). (ps-2). 1981. (Atheneum Child Bk) Macmillan Child Grp.

—The Year at Maple Hill Farm. Provensen, Alice & Provensen, Martin, illus. LC 88-10367. 32p. (ps-2). 1988. pap. 4.95 (0-689-71270-7, Aladdin) Macmillan Child Grp.

Williams, Brian. Farming. Green, Gwen, illus. LC 92-29905. 48p. (gr. 5-8). 1993. PLB 21.34 (0-8114-4786-3) Raintree Steck-V.

Woods, Tom & Schutz, Mary E. The Kelley Farm Activity Book. 32p. (ps up). 1985. pap. 3.50 (0-87351-183-2) Minn Hist.

FARM LIFE–FICTION

Adams, Pam, illus. Old MacDonald Had a Farm. LC 90-46923. (Orig.). (ps-2). 1975. pap. 5.95 (0-85953-053-1, Pub. by Child's Play England) Childs Play.

Addison-Wesley Staff. The Farmer & the Beet Little Book. (Illus.). 16p. (gr. k-3). 1989. pap. text ed. 4.50 (0-201-19053-2) Addison-Wesley.

Allen, Thomas B. On Grandaddy's Farm. Allen, Thomas B., illus. LC 88-23374. 48p. (ps-3). 1989. 13.95 (0-394-89613-0); lib. bdg. 14.99 (0-394-99613-5) Knopf Bks Yng Read.

Amery, H. Barn on Fire. (Illus.). 16p. (ps). 1989. 3.95 (0-7460-0260-2, Usborne); lib. bdg. 7.96 (0-88110-375-6, Usborne) EDC.

—Even More Farmyard Tales. (Illus.). 64p. (ps up). 1993. 9.95 (0-7460-1416-3) EDC.

—Farmyard Tales. (Illus.). 64p. (ps). 1989. 9.95 (0-7460-0263-7, Usborne) EDC.

—Grumpy Goat. (Illus.). 64p. (ps up). 1993. pap. 3.95 (0-7460-1413-9) EDC.

—More Farmyard Tales. (Illus.). 64p. (ps-2). 1992. 9.95 (0-7460-0592-X) EDC.

—New Pony. (Illus.). 64p. (ps up). 1993. pap. 3.95 (0-7460-1414-7) EDC.

Andrews, Jan. The Auction. Reczuch, Karen, illus. LC 90-41378. 32p. (ps-3). 1991. RSBE 13.95 (0-02-705535-3, Macmillan Child Bk) Macmillan Child Grp.

Avi. The Barn. LC 94-6920. 112p. (gr. 4-6). 1994. 13.95 (0-531-06861-7); PLB 13.99 (0-531-08711-5) Orchard Bks Watts.

Awdry, W. Thomas the Tank Engine Visits a Farm. Bell, Owain, illus. 10p. (ps). 1991. vinyl 3.95 (0-679-81580-5) Random Bks Yng Read.

Aylesworth, Jim. My Son John. Frampton, David, illus. LC 92-27192. 1994. 15.95 (0-8050-1725-9, Bks Young Read) H Holt & Co.

Ayme, Marcel. The Wonderful Farm. Sendak, Maurice, illus. LC 51-13662. 192p. (gr. 2-5). 1994. pap. 4.95 (0-06-440556-7, Trophy) HarpC Child Bks.

Barber, Antonia. Gemma & the Baby Chick. Littlewood, Karin, illus. 32p. (ps-3). 1993. 14.95 (0-590-45479-X) Scholastic Inc.

Barton, Byron. Buzz, Buzz, Buzz. 1st ed. LC 93-46931. 1995. pap. 4.95 (0-689-71873-X, Aladdin) Macmillan Child Grp.

Bax, Martin. Edmond Went Far Away. Foreman, Michael, illus. 32p. (ps-3). 1989. 12.95 (0-15-225105-7, HB Juv Bks) HarBrace.

Berst, Barbara. We Are Farmers. Berst, Barbara, illus. 24p. (Orig.). (ps-2). 1990. acid-free cotton paper 25. 00, (0-9614126-3-1); pap. 9.95 (0-9614126-2-3) Natl Lilac Pub.

Blair, Susan M. Unexpected Company. Blair, Susan M., illus. 56p. (ps-7). 1992. 19.95 (0-9631956-0-3) Pendant Pr.

Bright, Velma. The Story of the Little Round Barn. Schultz, Patty, illus. LC 81-65540. 48p. (Orig.). (gr. 2-3). 1981. 10.00x (0-9605968-2-8); pap. 5.00 (0-9605968-3-6) Bright Bks.

Brown. Big Red Barn. 1998. write for info. (0-694-00159-7, HarpT) HarpC Child Bks.

Brown, Craig. My Barn. LC 90-41758. (Illus.). 24p. (ps up). 1991. 13.95 (0-688-08785-X); PLB 13.88 (0-688-08786-8) Greenwillow.

—Patchwork Farmer. LC 88-29229. 24p. (ps up). 1989. 12.95 (0-688-07735-8); PLB 12.88 (0-688-07736-6) Greenwillow.

Brown, Irene B. Before the Lark. Milam, Larry, illus. 180p. (gr. 4 up). 1992. pap. 7.95 (0-936085-22-3) Blue Heron OR.

Brown, Margaret W. Big Red Barn. Bond, Felicia, illus. LC 85-45814. 32p. (ps-1). 1991. 19.95 (0-06-020750-7) HarpC Child Bks.

—Big Red Barn. Bond, Felicia, illus. 32p. (ps-1). Date not set. pap. 5.95 (0-06-443349-8, Trophy) HarpC Child Bks.

Brown, Ruth. The Big Sneeze. LC 84-23385. (Illus.). 32p. (ps-1). 1985. 13.95 (0-688-04665-7); lib. bdg. 12.88 (0-688-04666-5) Lothrop.

Buchanan, Dawna L. The Falcon's Wing. LC 91-22545. 144p. (gr. 5 up). 1992. 13.95 (0-531-05986-3); lib. bdg. 13.99 (0-531-08586-4) Orchard Bks Watts.

Bunting, Eve. The Big Red Barn. Knotts, Howard, illus. LC 78-12186. 32p. (gr. k-3). 1979. pap. 6.95 (0-15-611938-2, Voyager Bks) HarBrace.

Burch, Robert. D. J.'s Worst Enemy: A Novel by Robert Burch. Weiss, Emil, illus. LC 92-44783. 144p. (gr. 4-6). 1993. Repr. of 1965 ed. 19.95 (0-8203-1554-0) U of Ga Pr.

—Tyler, Wilkin & Skee. LC 89-28245. 160p. (gr. 4-6). 1990. Repr. of 1963 ed. 19.95 (0-8203-1194-4) U of Ga Pr.

Burke. Red Acre Farm. 1993. 14.95 (0-8050-2047-0) H Holt & Co.

Byars, Betsy C. The Midnight Fox. Grifalconi, Ann, illus. (gr. 3-7). 1981. pap. 3.99 (0-14-031450-4, Puffin) Puffin Bks.

—The Midnight Fox. Grifalconi, Ann, illus. LC 68-27566. (gr. 3-7). 1968. pap. 13.95 (0-670-47473-8) Viking Child Bks.

Campbell, Joanna. Star of Shadowbrook Farm. 1992. pap. 3.50 (0-06-106783-0, Harp PBks) HarpC.

Campbell, Rod. Oh Dear! Campbell, Rod, illus. LC 84-3993. 20p. (ps-1). 1986. pap. 9.95 (0-02-716430-6, Four Winds) Macmillan Child Grp.

Carrick, Carol. In the Moonlight, Waiting. Carrick, Donald, illus. 32p. (ps-1). 1990. 13.95 (0-89919-867-8) Clarion Pr.

Carrie, Christopher. Mixed up Farm. (Illus.). 32p. (Orig.). (ps-k). 1990. 1.99 (0-86696-236-0) Binney & Smith.

Cather, Willa. Neighbor Rosicky. LC 85-46058. 88p. (gr. 6 up). 1986. PLB 13.95 (0-88682-065-0) Creative Ed.

Christiansen, Candace. Calico & Tin Horns. Locker, Thomas, illus. LC 91-3706. 32p. 1992. 16.00 (0-8037-1179-4); PLB 15.89 (0-8037-1180-8) Dial Bks Young.

Cleary, Beverly. Emily's Runaway Imagination. Krush, Joe & Krush, Beth, illus. LC 61-10939. 224p. (gr. 3-7). 1961. 12.95 (0-688-21267-0); PLB 12.88 (0-688-31267-5, Morrow Jr Bks) Morrow Jr Bks.

Coil, Suzanne M. Mabel. Mayfield, Shannon, illus. Gilbert, Peaches, created by. LC 94-9791. (Illus.). 32p. (gr. 4-7). 1994. 15.95 (0-87905-602-9) Gibbs Smith Pub.

Copeland, Colene. Mystery in the Farrowing Barn. Harrison, Edith, illus. LC 91-62326. 150p. (Orig.). (gr. 3-7). 1991. 9.95 (0-939810-13-1); pap. 3.95 (0-939810-14-X) Jordan Valley.

Cosgrove, Stephen. The Fine Family Farm. Steelhammer, Ilona, illus. 24p. (gr. k-2). 1990. PLB 11.95 (1-878363-19-0) Forest Hse.

Crowther, Robert. How Many Babies on the Farm? (Illus.). 10p. (ps-k). 1991. pap. 5.95 (0-671-73157-2, Little Simon) S&S Trade.

Crozat, Francois. I Am a Little Pig. (Illus.). (ps-3). 1991. large 8.95 (0-8120-6201-9); miniature 2.95 (0-8120-6222-1) Barron.

Dahl, Roald. The Wonderful Story of Henry Sugar & Six More. LC 77-5354. 32p. (gr. 5 up). 1977. 17.00 (0-394-83604-9) Knopf Bks Yng Read.

Day, Betsy. Stefan & Olga. Day, Betsy, illus. LC 89-23647. 32p. (ps-3). 1991. 12.95 (0-8037-0816-5); PLB 12.89 (0-8037-0817-3) Dial Bks Young.

De Armond, Dale. Berry Woman's Children. De Armond, Dale, illus. LC 84-29760. 40p. (gr. 1 up). 1985. 15.00 (0-688-05814-0); lib. bdg. 14.93 (0-688-05815-9) Greenwillow.

DeFelice, Cynthia. Mule Eggs. Shenon, Mike, illus. LC 93-49395. 32p. (ps-2). 1994. 15.95 (0-531-06843-9); lib. bdg. 15.99 (0-531-08693-3) Orchard Bks Watts.

DeJong, Meindert. Along Came a Dog. Sendak, Maurice, illus. LC 57-9265. 192p. (gr. 3-6). 1958. PLB 15.89 (0-06-021421-X) HarpC Child Bks.

De Marolles, Chantal. The Farmer's Three Sons. (Illus.). 48p. (gr. 3-8). 1990. 8.95 (0-89565-816-X) Childs World.

Demuth, Patricia B. Ornery Morning. Brown, Craig M., illus. LC 90-40188. 24p. (ps-1). 1991. 13.95 (0-525-44688-5, DCB) Dutton Child Bks.

Doherty, Berlie. White Peak Farm. LC 89-23060. 128p. (gr. 5 up). 1990. 13.95 (0-531-05867-0); PLB 13.99 (0-531-08467-1) Orchard Bks Watts.

Doherty, Bertie. White Peak Farm. LC 92-43778. 112p. (gr. 8 up). 1993. pap. 3.95 (0-688-11864-X, Pub. by Beech Tree Bks) Morrow.

Domanska, Janina. Busy Monday Morning. Domanska, Janina, illus. LC 83-25362. 32p. (ps-1). 1985. 13.00 (*0-688-03833-6*); PLB 14.93 (*0-688-03834-4*) Greenwillow.

Douglas, Ben. What Is There to Do in the Country? Reed, Mary L., illus. 32p. (ps-3). 1994. write for info. (*1-885483-00-7*) Sontag Pr.
John & Lucas live on a farm deep in the woods. They know they have more fun than anybody, but when Rupert, a city cousin comes to visit he sees things differently. "Golly, this place is boring," he says. "It's Dullsville. What could you ever do here to have any fun?" Rupert discovers the answer when he stays for a week. He learns about farm animals & farm work. He has fun at the swimming hole & at the country store. The week is filled with adventures. When Rupert's mama comes to take him home he makes a surprising request. Children who live in urban areas frequently ask parents & grandparents, "What did you do when you lived on the farm?" They can find out by reading WHAT IS THERE TO DO IN THE COUNTRY? & the forthcoming books in this "life in the country" series. To order: Sontag Press, P.O. Box 1487, Madison, MS 39130. (601) 856-5488.
Publisher Provided Annotation.

Dunrea, Olivier. Eppie M. Says... Dunrea, Olivier, illus. LC 89-8134. 32p. (ps-2). 1990. RSBE 14.95 (*0-02-733205-5*, Macmillan Child Bk) Macmillan Child Grp.
Ehrlich, Amy. Maggie & Silky & Joe. Blake, Robert, illus. LC 94-9149. 32p. (ps up). 1994. PLB 14.99 (*0-670-83387-8*) Viking Child Bks.
—Parents in the Pigpen, Pigs in the Tub. Kellogg, Steven, illus. LC 91-15601. 40p. (ps-3). 1993. 14.99 (*0-8037-0933-1*); lib. bdg. 14.89 (*0-8037-0928-5*) Dial Bks Young.
Engebrecht, P. A. Under the Haystack. (gr. 5-12). 1991. 19.75 (*0-8446-6473-1*) Peter Smith.
Enright, Elizabeth. Thimble Summer. (gr. k-6). 1987. pap. 3.50 (*0-440-48681-5*, YB) Dell.
—Thimble Summer. Enright, Elizabeth, illus. LC 38-27586. 124p. (gr. 6 up). 1938. 16.95 (*0-8050-0306-1*, Bks Young Read) H Holt & Co.
Fakih, Kimberly O. High on the Hog. LC 93-34214. 1994. 16.00 (*0-374-33209-6*) FS&G.
Farm. (Illus.). 48p. (Orig.). (gr. k-4). 1987. pap. 2.95 (*0-8431-1880-6*) Price Stern.
Fiday, Beverly & Fiday, David J. Time to Go. Allen, Thomas B., illus. 30p. (ps-3). 1990. 14.95 (*0-15-200608-7*) HarBrace.
Fleischman, Sid. Here Comes McBroom. Blake, Quentin, illus. LC 91-32689. 80p. (gr. 1 up). 1992. 14.00 (*0-688-11160-2*) Greenwillow.
—McBroom's Wonderful One-Acre Farm. Blake, Quentin, illus. LC 91-31906. 64p. (gr. 1 up). 1992. 14. 00 (*0-688-11159-9*) Greenwillow.
—The Scarebird. Sis, Peter, illus. LC 93-11726. 32p. (ps up). 1994. pap. 4.95 (*0-688-13105-0*, Mulberry) Morrow.
Florian, Douglas. A Year in the Country. LC 88-16026. (Illus.). 32p. (ps up). 1989. 12.95 (*0-688-08186-X*); lib. bdg. 12.88 (*0-688-08187-8*) Greenwillow.
Flournoy, Valerie. Tanya's Reunion. Pinkey, Jerry, illus. LC 94-13067. 1995. write for info. (*0-8037-1604-4*); PLB write for info. (*0-8037-1605-2*) Dial Bks Young.
Forgetful Farmer Fred. (Illus.). (ps-2). 1991. PLB 6.95 (*0-8136-5166-2*, TK3837); pap. 3.50 (*0-8136-5666-4*, TK3838) Modern Curr.
Frances, Marian. Mr. Mac-A-Doodle. (Illus.). (gr. 1). 1972. pap. 1.95 (*0-89375-045-X*) Troll Assocs.
Frascino, Edward. Nanny Noony & the Dust Queen. Frascino, Edward, illus. 32p. (gr. k-3). 1990. PLB 14. 95 (*0-945912-09-9*) Pippin Pr.
Freeman, Mary E. The Revolt of Mother. (gr. 5 up). 1992. PLB 13.95 (*0-88682-495-8*) Creative Ed.
Gaeddert, LouAnn. Breaking Free. LC 93-22600. 144p. (gr. 3-7). 1994. SBE 14.95 (*0-689-31883-9*, Atheneum Child Bk) Macmillan Child Grp.
Gage, Wilson. My Stars, It's Mrs. Gaddy! Hafner, Marylin, illus. LC 90-478577. 96p. (gr. 1 up). 1991. 15.95 (*0-688-10514-9*) Greenwillow.
Galdone, Paul. Cat Goes Fiddle-I-Fee. LC 85-2686. (Illus.). (ps-1). 1988. pap. 5.95 (*0-89919-705-1*, Clarion Bks) HM.
Gammell, Stephen. Once upon Macdonald's Farm. LC 89-17792. (Illus.). 32p. (gr. k-3). 1990. pap. 4.95 (*0-689-71379-7*, Aladdin) Macmillan Child Grp.
Gehman, Mary W. Abdi & the Elephants. 104p. (Orig.). (gr. 6-8). 1995. pap. 5.95 (*0-8361-3699-3*) Herald Pr.
Ghrist, Julie, illus. Taelly's Counting Adventures: Down on the Farm. 12p. (ps). 1993. 4.95 (*1-56828-029-7*) Red Jacket Pr.
Graeber, Charlotte. The Fluff Puff Farm. French, Marty & Lamb, Jim, illus. 26p. (ps up). 1988. incl. cassette 7.95 (*1-55578-917-X*) Worlds Wonder.
—In, Out, & about Catfish Pond. Stockman, Jack, illus. 60p. (gr. 2). 1984. pap. 6.00 (*1-880892-93-6*) Fam Lrng Ctr.
—Up, down, & Around the Raintree. Stockman, Jack, illus. 60p. (gr. 2). 1984. pap. 6.00 (*1-880892-94-4*) Fam Lrng Ctr.
Graeker, Charlotte. The Fluff Puff Farm. French, Marty, et al, illus. 26p. (ps up). 1986. Book & Cassette. 7.95 (*1-55578-110-1*) Worlds Wonder.
Grove, Vicki. Rimwalkers. LC 92-36091. 224p. (gr. 5 up). 1993. 14.95 (*0-399-22430-0*, Putnam) Putnam Pub Group.
Haas, Jessie. Mowing. Smith, Joseph A., photos by. LC 93-12240. 32p. (ps up). 1994. 14.00 (*0-688-11680-9*); lib. bdg. 13.93 (*0-688-11681-7*) Greenwillow.
Hall, Barbara. Dixie Storms. 197p. (gr. 7 up). 1990. 15.95 (*0-15-223825-5*) HarBrace.
Hall, Donald. Lucy's Summer. McCurdy, Michael, illus. LC 93-17130. 1995. write for info. (*0-15-276873-4*, HB Juv Bks) HarBrace.
—Summer of 1944. Moser, Barry, illus. LC 92-38613. 32p. (gr. 1-5). 1994. 15.99 (*0-8037-1501-3*); PLB 15. 89 (*0-8037-1502-1*) Dial Bks Young.
Hamilton, V. Drylongso. Pinkney, J., illus. 1992. write for info. (*0-15-224241-4*, HB Juv Bks) HarBrace.
Hamilton, Virginia. Zeely. Shimin, Symeon, illus. LC 67-10266. 128p. (gr. 5-7). 1968. SBE 13.95 (*0-02-742470-7*, Macmillan Child Bk) Macmillan Child Grp.
Hampton's Happy Farms. 1990. 5.98 (*1-55521-691-9*) Bk Sales Inc.
Harshman, Marc. The Storm. Mohr, Mark, illus. LC 94-4894. 1995. write for info. (*0-525-65150-0*, Cobblehill Bks) Dutton Child Bks.
Hawkins, Colin & Hawkins, Jacqui. Old MacDonald Had a Farm. (Illus.). (ps-2). 1991. 9.95 (*0-8431-2884-4*) Price Stern.
Hazen, Barbara S. Turkey in the Straw. Sneed, Brad, illus. LC 92-27516. 32p. (ps-3). 1993. 13.99 (*0-8037-1298-7*); PLB 13.89 (*0-8037-1299-5*) Dial Bks Young.
Himmelman, John. A Guest Is a Guest. Himmelman, John, illus. LC 90-43020. 32p. (ps-2). 1991. 13.95 (*0-525-44720-2*, DCB) Dutton Child Bks.
Hol, Coby. A Visit to the Farm. Hol, Coby, illus. LC 88-25366. 32p. (gr. k-3). 1989. 13.95 (*1-55858-000-X*) North-South Bks NYC.
Hoppe, Joanne. Pretty Penny Farm. 224p. (gr. 7 up). 1989. pap. 2.50 (*0-8167-1326-X*) Troll Assocs.
Howard, Ellen. The Cellar. Mulvihill, Patricia, illus. LC 90-23190. 64p. (gr. 2-4). 1992. SBE 12.95 (*0-689-31724-7*, Atheneum Child Bk) Macmillan Child Grp.
—Edith Herself. LC 93-28061. (Illus.). 144p. (gr. 3-7). 1994. pap. 3.95 (*0-689-71795-4*, Aladdin) Macmillan Child Grp.
—Sister. LC 90-196. 160p. (gr. 3-7). 1990. SBE 13.95 (*0-689-31653-4*, Atheneum Child Bk) Macmillan Child Grp.
Hunt, Irene. Across Five Aprils. LC 92-46736. 212p. (gr. 4 up). 1993. PLB 10.95 (*0-382-24358-7*); 8.95 (*0-382-24367-6*) Silver Burdett Pr.
Iverson, Diane. Where Are the Babies? Iverson, Diane, illus. 48p. (Orig.). (ps). 1992. 14.95 (*0-9623349-1-X*); pap. 8.95 (*0-9623349-2-8*) MS Pub.
Jackson, Ellen. Yellow, Mellow, Green, & Brown. Raymond, Victoria, illus. LC 93-37091. 1995. write for info. (*0-7868-0010-0*); lib. bdg. write for info. (*0-7868-2006-3*) Hyprn Child.
Jakubowsky, Frank. Frank on a Farm. 60p. (Orig.). 1988. pap. 4.95 (*0-932588-11-5*) Jesus Bks.
Johnson, Allen, Jr. Picker McClikker. Hanson, Stephen, illus. (gr. k-3). 1993. 16.95 (*1-878561-20-0*) Seacoast AL.
Johnson, John E., illus. Here Comes the Farmer. 14p. (ps-3). 1985. 4.99 (*0-394-87552-4*) Random Bks Yng Read.
Kanno, Wendy. The Funny Farm House. Reese, Bob, illus. (gr. k-2). 1984. 7.95 (*0-89868-155-3*); pap. 2.95 (*0-89868-156-1*) ARO Pub.
—Twenty Word Funny Farm Series, 6 bks. Reese, Bob, illus. (gr. k-2). 1984. Set. 47.70 (*0-685-50866-8*); Set. pap. 29.50 (*0-89868-154-5*) ARO Pub.
Karim, Roberta. Mandy Sue Day. Ritz, Karen, illus. LC 93-34671. 1994. 14.95 (*0-395-66155-2*, Clarion Bks) HM.
Kaufman, John. Milk Rock. (gr. k-2). 1994. 14.95 (*0-8050-2814-5*) H Holt & Co.
Keavney, Pamela. The Promise. LC 89-26896. (Illus.). 32p. (ps-3). 1992. 15.00 (*0-06-023019-3*); PLB 14.89 (*0-06-023020-7*) HarpC Child Bks.
Kindergarten, Henry O. The Farmer's Huge Carrot. (Illus.). 24p. (Orig.). (gr. k-3). 1990. pap. text ed. 2.95 (*0-87406-437-6*) Willowisp Pr.
King-Smith, David. Cuckoobush Farm. Kazuko, illus. LC 87-14871. 32p. (ps-1). 1988. 11.95 (*0-688-07680-7*); lib. bdg. 11.88 (*0-688-07681-5*) Greenwillow.
King-Smith, Dick. Pigs Might Fly. (gr. 4 up). 1990. pap. 3.95 (*0-14-034537-X*, Puffin) Puffin Bks.
Kinsey-Warnock, Natalie. The Canada Geese Quilt. Bowman, Leslie W., illus. LC 88-32661. 64p. (gr. 4 up). 1989. 13.00 (*0-525-65004-0*, Cobblehill Bks) Dutton Child Bks.
—The Night the Bells Rang. Bowman, Leslie W., illus. LC 91-3053. 80p. (gr. 4 up). 1991. 12.95 (*0-525-65074-1*, Cobblehill Bks) Dutton Child Bks.
—When Spring Comes. Schuett, Stacey, illus. LC 92-14066. (ps-3). 1993. 14.99 (*0-525-45008-4*, DCB) Dutton Child Bks.
Kirkpatrick, Patricia. Plowie. Kirkpatrick, Joey, illus. LC 93-13712. (ps-3). 1994. 14.95 (*0-15-262802-9*) HarBrace.
Kiser, SuAnn. The Catspring Somersault Flying One-Handed Flip-Flop. Catalanotto, Peter, illus. LC 92-44519. 32p. (ps-2). 1993. 14.95 (*0-531-05493-4*); PLB 14.99 (*0-531-08643-7*) Orchard Bks Watts.
Kubler, Annie. Panic Farm. 1985. 4.95 (*0-85953-258-5*) Childs Play.
Kunhardt, Edith. Which Pig Would You Choose? LC 88-35588. (Illus.). (ps up). 1990. 12.95 (*0-688-08981-X*); lib. bdg. 12.88 (*0-688-08982-8*) Greenwillow.
Kwitz, Mary D. Little Chick's Friend Duckling. Degen, Bruce, illus. LC 90-5027. 32p. (ps-2). 1992. 13.00 (*0-06-023638-8*); PLB 13.89 (*0-06-023639-6*) HarpC Child Bks.
Laird, Elizabeth. The Day Patch Stood Guard. Reeder, Colin, illus. LC 90-11153. 32p. (gr. k up). 1991. 11.95 (*0-688-10239-5*, Tambourine Bks); PLB 11.88 (*0-688-10240-9*, Tambourine Bks) Morrow.
—The Day Sidney Ran Off. Reeder, Colin, illus. LC 90-11154. 32p. (gr. k up). 1991. 11.95 (*0-688-10241-7*, Tambourine Bks); PLB 11.88 (*0-688-10242-5*, Tambourine Bks) Morrow.
—The Day Veronica Was Nosy. Reeder, Colin, illus. LC 90-24063. 32p. (gr. k up). 1991. 11.95 (*0-688-10248-4*, Tambourine Bks); PLB 11.88 (*0-688-10249-2*, Tambourine Bks) Morrow.
Landis, Mary M. The Coon Tree Summer: Merry Brook Farm Story. (gr. 5 up). 1978. 9.05 (*0-686-22987-8*) Rod & Staff.
Lenski, Lois. Strawberry Girl. Lenski, Lois, illus. 208p. (gr. k-6). 1987. pap. 3.50 (*0-440-48347-6*, YB) Dell.
Leslie, Herman & Bateson, Margaret. A Victorian Farm House. 1993. 19.95 (*0-312-08931-7*) St Martin.
Levin, Betty. Starshine & Sunglow. Smith, Joseph A., illus. LC 93-26672. 96p. (gr. 4-7). 1994. PLB 14.00 (*0-688-12806-8*) Greenwillow.
Lillie, Patricia. When the Rooster Crowed. Parker, Nancy W., illus. LC 90-30783. 32p. (ps up). 1991. 13.95 (*0-688-09378-7*); PLB 13.88 (*0-688-09379-5*) Greenwillow.
Lindbergh, Reeve. Benjamin's Barn. Jeffers, Susan, illus. 32p. (ps-3). 1990. 13.95 (*0-8037-0613-8*); PLB 13.89 (*0-8037-0614-6*) Dial Bks Young.
—The Midnight Farm. Jeffers, Susan, illus. LC 86-1722. 32p. (ps-2). 1987. 14.95 (*0-8037-0331-7*); PLB 14.89 (*0-8037-0333-3*) Dial Bks Young.
Lindman, Maj. Snipp, Snapp, Snurr & the Big Farm. (Illus.). 32p. 1993. Repr. lib. bdg. 14.95x (*1-56849-004-6*) Buccaneer Bks.
Lipskerov, M. F. Volk u Telonok: Wolf & Calf. Kostrina, I. D., illus. (RUS.). 18p. (Orig.). 1989. pap. 14.95 (*0-934393-15-X*) Rector Pr.
The Little Red Hen. 24p. (ps-3). 1988. pap. 2.25 (*1-56288-152-3*) Checkerboard.
Littledale, Freya. The Farmer in the Soup. Delaney, Molly, illus. 32p. (Orig.). (gr. k-3). 1987. pap. 2.50 (*0-590-42535-8*) Scholastic Inc.
Locker, Thomas. Family Farm. (Illus.). 32p. 1994. pap. 5.99 (*0-14-050351-X*, Puff Pied Piper) Puffin Bks.
London, Jonathan. Like Butter on Pancakes. Karas, G. Brian, illus. LC 94-9154. 1995. write for info. (*0-670-85130-2*, Viking) Viking Penguin.
MacBride, Roger L. Little Farm in the Ozarks. Gilleece, David, illus. 256p. (ps-2). 1994. pap. 3.95 (*0-06-440510-9*, Trophy) HarpC Child Bks.
McColley, Kevin. Pecking Order. LC 93-17768. 224p. (gr. 7 up). 1994. 16.00 (*0-06-023554-3*); PLB 15.89 (*0-06-023555-1*) HarpC Child Bks.
McConnachie, Brian. Elmer & the Chickens vs. the Big League. Stevenson, Harvey, illus. LC 91-2914. 32p. (ps-2). 1992. 14.00 (*0-517-57616-3*) Crown Bks Yng Read.
McCormick, Maxine. Pretty As You Please. LC 92-39310. 1994. 15.95 (*0-399-22536-6*, Philomel Bks) Putnam Pub Group.
MacDonald, Betty. Hello, Mrs. Piggle-Wiggle. Knight, Hilary, illus. LC 57-5613. (gr. k-3). 1957. 14.00 (*0-397-31715-8*, Lipp Jr Bks) HarpC Child Bks.
—Mrs. Piggle-Wiggle. rev. ed. Knight, Hilary, illus. LC 47-1876. (gr. k-3). 1957. 14.00 (*0-397-31712-3*, Lipp Jr Bks) HarpC Child Bks.
—Mrs. Piggle-Wiggle's Farm. Sendak, Maurice, illus. LC 54-7299. (gr. k-3). 1954. 14.00 (*0-397-31713-1*, Lipp Jr Bks) HarpC Child Bks.
—Mrs. Piggle-Wiggle's Magic. new ed. Knight, Hilary, illus. LC 49-11124. (gr. k-3). 1957. 14.00 (*0-397-31714-X*, Lipp Jr Bks) HarpC Child Bks.
McGee, Marni. The Quiet Farmer. Dennis, Lynne, illus. LC 90-37930. 32p. (ps-1). 1991. SBE 13.95 (*0-689-31678-X*, Atheneum Child Bk) Macmillan Child Grp.
McGuire, Leslie. This Farm Is a Mess. McGuire, Leslie, illus. LC 80-25811. 48p. (ps-3). 1981. 5.95 (*0-8193-1045-X*); PLB 5.95 (*0-8193-1046-8*) Parents.

MacLachlan, Patricia. All the Places to Love. Wimmer, Mike, illus. LC 92-794. 32p. (gr. 1 up). 1994. 15.00 (*0-06-021098-2*); PLB 14.89 (*0-06-021099-0*) HarpC Child Bks.

McOmber, Rachel B., ed. McOmber Phonics Storybooks: In the Dell. rev. ed. (Illus.). write for info. (*0-944991-32-7*) Swift Lrn Res.

McPhail, David. Farm Morning. D'Andrade, Diane, ed. (Illus.). 32p. (Orig.). (ps-3). 1991. pap. 3.95 (*0-15-227300-X*, HB Juv Bks) HarBrace.

Maddox, Tony. Fergus's Upside-Down Day. LC 94-16656. 1994. write for info. (*0-8120-6471-2*); pap. write for info. (*0-8120-9074-8*) Barron.

Mantinband, Gerda B. Blabbermouths. LC 91-3006. (ps-3). 1992. 14.00 (*0-688-10602-1*); PLB 13.93 (*0-688-10604-8*) Greenwillow.

Marsoli, Lisa A. & Strong, Stacie. Jake & Jenny on the Farm. (Illus.). 18p. (ps-2). 1990. 7.95 (*0-8431-2853-4*) Price Stern.

Martin, C. L. Down Dairy Farm Road. Hearn, Diane D., illus. LC 92-42848. 32p. (gr. k-3). 1994. RSBE 14.95 (*0-02-762450-1*, Macmillan Child Bk) Macmillan Child Grp.

Miller, Rose. The Old Barn. Enik, Ted, illus. LC 92-35283. 32p. (gr. 2-6). 1992. PLB 19.97 (*0-8114-3581-4*) Raintree Steck-V.

Mills, Patricia. Until the Cows Come Home. Mills, Patricia, illus. LC 92-31049. 32p. (gr. k-3). 1993. 14.95 (*1-55858-190-1*); PLB 14.88 (*1-55858-191-X*) North-South Bks NYC.

Mishica, Clare. Fraidy Cat Finds a Friend. Stortz, Diane, ed. (Illus.). 28p. (ps-k). 1994. 5.49 (*0-7847-0202-0*) Standard Pub.

Montgomery, Lucy M. Anne of Green Gables. 1987. Boxed set. pap. 8.95 (*0-553-33306-2*) Bantam.

Morris, Linda L. Morning Milking. DeRan, David, illus. LC 91-13103. 32p. (gr. k up). 1991. pap. 16.95 (*0-88708-173-8*) Picture Bk Studio.

Munson, Sammye. Goodbye, Sweden, Hello Texas. LC 93-38928. 1994. 14.95 (*0-89015-948-3*) Sunbelt Media.

Nilsson, Ulf. If You Didn't Have Me. Eriksson, Eva, illus. Blecher, Lone T. & Blecher, George, trs. LC 86-21327. (Illus.). 128p. (gr. 2-5). 1987. SBE 13.95 (*0-689-50406-3*, M K McElderry) Macmillan Child Grp.

Nister, Ernest. Our Farmyard: A Pop-up Book with Punch-out Play Figures. Nister, Ernest, illus. 12p. (ps-3). 1991. 13.95 (*0-525-44689-3*, DCB) Dutton Child Bks.

Noble, Trinka H. Apple Tree Christmas. Noble, Trinka H., illus. LC 84-1901. 32p. (ps-2). 1988. 13.50 (*0-8037-0102-0*); PLB 12.89 (*0-8037-0103-9*) Dial Bks Young.

—The Day Jimmy's Boa Ate the Wash. Kellogg, Steven, illus. 32p. (ps-3). 1993. pap. 4.99 (*0-14-054623-5*, Puff Pied Piper) Puffin Bks.

Nolen, Jerdine. Harvey Potter's Balloon Farm. LC 91-38129. (ps-3). 1994. 15.00 (*0-688-07887-7*); 14.93 (*0-688-07888-5*) Lothrop.

Oxford, Mariesa. Going to Grandma's. (Illus.). (gr. 2-6). 1992. PLB 19.97 (*0-8114-3575-X*) Raintree Steck-V.

Papagapitos, Karen. Jose's Basket. 1993. 6.95 (*0-9637328-1-1*) Kapa Hse Pr.
JOSE'S BASKET is a touching portrayal of a family forced to be always on the move. Luis & Socorro Vasquez are migrant farm workers, who follow whatever crops need to be harvested. This continuous change of surrounding is very difficult on their four children. The parents try to make the transitions easier by anticipating all the new & exciting things that are sure to be waiting for them at the next stop. At one particular town, in Arizona, eight-year-old Jose (an excellent student & gifted writer) finds a school he never wants to leave. Of course, there does come a time when he must leave this new place & his wonderful teacher, Mrs. Ortega. By learning to piece together his adventures in every new place, much like his mother weaves reeds & grasses from the desert into her special basket (the grasses come from each place in which they pick crops), Jose is able to find the courage he needs to move on & stay in school. JOSE'S BASKET has been placed in the U.S. Department of Education's Library. Distributed by Baker & Taylor Books, 652 East Main St./P.O. Box 6920, Bridgewater, NJ 08807-0920.
Publisher Provided Annotation.

Paris, Pat. Old MacDonald Had a Farm. (Illus.). 12p. (ps-1). 1989. text ed. 11.95 (*0-8120-6107-1*) Barron.

Paterson, Katherine. The Smallest Cow in the World. new ed. Brown, Jane C., illus. LC 90-30521. 64p. (gr. k-3). 1991. 14.00 (*0-06-024690-1*); PLB 13.89 (*0-06-024691-X*) HarpC Child Bks.

Paulsen, Gary. Haymeadow. (gr. 4-7). 1994. pap. 3.99 (*0-440-40923-3*) Dell.

Pearson, Susan. Well, I Never! Warhola, James, illus. LC 89-48016. 40p. (ps-1). 1990. pap. 13.95 (*0-671-69199-6*, S&S BFYR) S&S Trade.

Peck, Robert N. Trig. 64p. (gr. 4-6). 1979. pap. 1.25 (*0-440-49098-7*, YB) Dell.

Percy, Graham. The Farm. (Illus.). 16p. (gr. 1-5). 1989. write for info. (*1-881469-27-1*) Safari Ltd.

Peters, Lisa W. The Hayloft. Plum, K. D., illus. LC 93-18718. Date not set. write for info. (*0-8037-1490-4*); lib. bdg. write for info. (*0-8037-1491-2*) Dial Bks Young.

Pienkowski, Jan. Ferme. (FRE.). 5.95 (*2-07-056307-3*) Schoenhof.

Pigs in the House. (Illus.). 42p. (ps-3). 1992. PLB 13.27 (*0-8368-0879-7*) Gareth Stevens Inc.

Pinkney, Gloria J. Back Home. Pinkney, Jerry, illus. LC 91-22610. 40p. (gr. k-4). 1992. 15.00 (*0-8037-1168-9*); PLB 14.89 (*0-8037-1169-7*) Dial Bks Young.

Provensen, Alice & Provensen, Martin. An Owl & Three Pussycats. LC 93-44747. (gr. k-3). 1994. 16.95 (*0-15-200183-2*, Browndeer Pr) HarBrace.

Richardson, Arleta. Eighteen & on Her Own. LC 85-29050. 173p. (gr. 3-7). 1986. pap. 3.99 (*0-89191-512-5*, Chariot Bks) Chariot Family.

Ripley, Dorothy. Winter Barn. Schories, Pat, illus. LC 93-32420. 32p. (ps-1). 1995. pap. 2.50 (*0-679-84472-4*) Random Bks Yng Read.

Rose, Phoebe E. You & the Cow. Skidmore, Joan L., illus. LC 91-60008. 20p. (Orig.). (gr. k-6). 1991. pap. 8.50 (*0-9630050-0-6*) Oregon Info.

Rundle, Vesta M. Snow Calf. Larison, Arlene, illus. 36p. (Orig.). (gr. 2-8). 1993. pap. 4.50 (*1-882672-01-1*) V M Rundle.
When a fictional family find themselves stranded in their farm home in Western Oklahoma during a record-breaking snow storm it is bad enough; when the calf that Seth is raising to enter in the fair turns up missing it is even worse & a surprise helicopter visit adds to the drama. The magic & the agony of winter are beautifully described as the family survives for nine days without power, telephone service, utilities, or transportation. Readers love the surprise ending about the survival of the calf. A story about pride, disappointment, & hope, the book is arranged in eight very short chapters & could be a first chapter book. There are lovely black & white full-page illustrations & a four-color illustrated cover by California artist Arlene Larison. Response to this book has been enthusiastic from children, teachers, parents, & grandparents. One child: "...my favorite Christmas present." A teacher: "All the fourth grade classes in our school read this story & loved it." A father: "Our family enjoyed this as a bedtime story over several evenings." A junior high reader: "...an animal story I'll always remember." A librarian: "This story could become a classic." Available from: For the Kids Press, 2251 Fourth St., Charleston, IL 61920; Phone (217) 345-2560 or The Distributors, 702 S. Michigan, South Bend, IN 46618.
Publisher Provided Annotation.

Saban, Vera. Jennie Barnes: Right Now Forever. Mills, Janie, illus. LC 90-39763. 130p. (Orig.). (gr. 4-6). 1990. pap. 6.95 (*0-914565-34-6*, Timbertrails) Capstan Pubns.

Santoro, Chris, illus. Open the Barn Door, Find a Cow. LC 91-62579. 22p. (ps-k). 1993. 3.50 (*0-679-80901-5*) Random Bks Yng Read.

Schatell, Brian. Farmer Goff & His Turkey Sam. Schatell, Brian, illus. LC 81-47756. 32p. (gr. 1-3). 1982. PLB 13.89 (*0-397-31983-5*, Lipp Jr Bks) HarpC Child Bks.

Schnur, Steven. The Shadow Children. LC 94-5098. 1994. write for info. (*0-688-13281-2*); PLB write for info. (*0-688-13831-4*) Morrow Jr Bks.

Schultz, Elva. Two Story Farmhouse. Tepley, Marilyn, illus. (ps-3). 1986. write for info. (*0-9616431-0-2*) E Schultz.

Selway, Martina. Don't Forget to Write. Selway, Martina, illus. LC 91-28430. 32p. (ps-2). 1992. 12.95 (*0-8249-8543-5*, Ideals Child) Hambleton-Hill.

Seredy, Kate. Singing Tree. (gr. 4 up). 1990. pap. 4.95 (*0-14-034543-4*, Puffin) Puffin Bks.

Sesame Street Staff. Big Bird's Farm. Barrett, John E., photos by. LC 81-50537. (Illus.). 14p. (ps). 1981. bds. 3.95 (*0-394-84812-8*) Random Bks Yng Read.

Shannon, Monica. Dobry. Katchamakoff, Atanas, illus. LC 92-31442. 176p. (gr. 5 up). 1993. pap. 4.99 (*0-14-036334-3*) Puffin Bks.

Sharpe, Susan. Chicken Bucks. LC 92-5049. 144p. (gr. 5-8). 1992. SBE 13.95 (*0-02-782353-9*, Bradbury Pr) Macmillan Child Grp.

Sherlock Chick & the Giant Egg Mystery. (Illus.). 42p. (ps-3). 1993. PLB 13.27 (*0-8368-0897-5*) Gareth Stevens Inc.

Shriver, Jean A. Mayflower Man. 1991. 14.95 (*0-385-30295-9*) Delacorte.

Simmons, Lynn S. Sugar Lump, the Orphan Calf. (gr. 5-8). 1994. 7.95 (*0-9642573-0-0*) Argyle Bks.
SUGAR LUMP, THE ORPHAN CALF is about a new-born calf found lying all alone in the pasture. Unable to find his mother, twelve-year-old Marcy takes the full responsibility of raising him. As the white-faced calf with a black ring circling his right eye grows, his behavior becomes quite amusing. Although Marcy knows she can not keep the calf she names Sugar Lump after he is weaned, she still forms a strong attachment to him. The night Sugar Lump is put into the pasture to stay with a herd of cows, Marcy becomes involved in a suspenseful search that leads to an unexpected ending. Although the story is chiefly fiction, the descriptions of the calf's humorous behavior are true. He did suck on the door knob & even the cat's ear. He did hide behind trees waiting to be called to come & get a drink of milk, he did run with the dogs, & he did tease the cat. SUGAR LUMP, THE ORPHAN CALF is a heart-warming story for children of all ages & can be easily read by children from eight to twelve years old. Order from Argyle Books, 710 Old Justin Rd., Argyle, TX 76226; 817-464-3368 or FAX 817-320-1073.
Publisher Provided Annotation.

Simpson, Juwairiah J. The Four Daughters of Yusuf the Dairy Farmer. Middendorf, Nancy, illus. 40p. (Orig.). (gr. 1-4). 1894. pap. 3.75 (*0-89259-056-4*) Am Trust Pubns.

Smith, E. Boyd. The Farm Book. Smith, E. Boyd, illus. 64p. (gr. 3-5). 1982. 15.45 (*0-395-32951-5*) HM.

—The Farm Book. Smith, E. Boyd, illus. 64p. (ps up). 1990. pap. 6.70 (*0-395-54951-5*) HM.

Sneed, Brad. Lucky Russell. (Illus.). 32p. (ps-3). 1992. 14.95 (*0-399-22329-0*, Putnam) Putnam Pub Group.

Stauffer, Patricia I. Farming Is OK. Mattingly, Jennie, ed. Taylor, Neil, illus. LC 87-50262. 44p. (gr. 1-3). 1987. 6.95 (*1-55523-077-6*) Winston-Derek.

Steig, William. Farmer Palmer's Wagon Ride. (gr. k-5). 1992. pap. 4.95 (*0-374-42268-0*, Sunburst) FS&G.

Stimson, Joan. Farmyard: Stories for under Fives. Archer, Rebecca, illus. 44p. (ps-k). 1992. 3.50 (*0-7214-1506-7*) Ladybird Bks.

Stratton-Porter, Gene. The Harvester. 560p. 1977. PLB 24.95 (*0-89966-225-0*) Buccaneer Bks.

Swan, Walter. The Little Green Tractor. Swan, Deloris, ed. Asch, Connie, illus. 16p. (Orig.). (gr. 2-4). 1989. pap. 1.50 (*0-927176-04-1*) Swan Enterp.

Tafuri, Nancy. Early Morning in the Barn. ALC Staff, ed. LC 83-1436. (Illus.). 24p. (ps up). 1992. pap. 3.95 (*0-688-11710-4*, Mulberry) Morrow.

—This Is the Farmer. LC 92-30082. (Illus.). 24p. (ps up). 1994. 14.00 (*0-688-09468-6*); PLB 13.93 (*0-688-09469-4*) Greenwillow.

Tedrow, T. L. Days of Laura Ingalls Wilder, Vol. 2: Children of Promise. LC 92-1041. 1992. pap. 4.99 (*0-8407-3398-4*) Nelson.
—Days of Laura Ingalls Wilder, Vol. 3: Good Neighbors. 1992. pap. 4.99 (*0-8407-3399-2*) Nelson.
—Days of Laura Ingalls Wilder, Vol. 4: Home to the Prairie. 1992. pap. 4.99 (*0-8407-3401-8*) Nelson.
Thompson, Mae. Janet of Olde Mill Farm. LC 94-60784. 300p. (Orig.). (gr. 8-12). 1994. pap. write for info. (*0-9641583-0-2*) Zionhse Pubng.
Tolliver, Ruby C. Blind Bess, Buddy, & ME. Welch, Karen, ed. Miller, Lyle L., illus. 104p. (gr. 4 up). 1990. lib. bdg. 12.95 (*0-937460-63-X*) Hendrick-Long.
Tresselt, Alvin. Sun Up. (ps-3). 1991. 14.95 (*0-688-08656-X*); PLB 14.88 (*0-688-08657-8*) Lothrop.
—Wake up, Farm! Ewing, Carolyn, illus. LC 90-33646. 32p. (ps up). 1991. 14.95 (*0-688-08654-3*); PLB 14.88 (*0-688-08655-1*) Lothrop.
Tripp, Nathaniel. Thunderstorm! Wijngaard, Juan, illus. LC 93-4612. Date not set. write for info. (*0-8037-1365-7*); PLB write for info. (*0-8037-1366-5*) Dial Bks Young.
Turner, Ann. Apple Valley Year. Resnick, Sandi W., illus. LC 90-37733. 32p. (gr. k-3). 1993. RSBE 14.95 (*0-02-789281-6*, Macmillan Child Bk) Macmillan Child Grp.
Turner, Ann W. Dust for Dinner. 1995. 14.00 (*0-06-023376-1*); PLB 13.89 (*0-06-023377-X*) HarpC Child Bks.
Van Kirk, Eileen. Promise to Keep. 160p. (gr. 7 up). 1990. 14.95 (*0-525-67319-9*, Lodestar Bks) Dutton Child Bks.
Waechter, Friederich K. The Farmers in the Well. Dobak, Annelies, tr. LC 85-1240. (Illus.). (gr. k-3). 1985. 9.95 (*0-915361-16-7*) Modan-Adama Bks.
Wallace, Karen. Why Count Sheep? a Bedtime Book. Aggs, Patrice, illus. LC 92-56140. 32p. (ps-1). 1993. 13.95 (*1-56282-528-3*); PLB 13.89 (*1-56282-529-1*) Hyprn Child.
Wallace-Brodeur, Ruth. The Godmother Tree. LC 91-17951. 128p. (gr. 3-7). 1992. PLB 12.89 (*0-06-022458-4*) HarpC Child Bks.
Warner, Gertrude C. The Mystery Horse. (Illus.). 128p. (gr. 2-7). 1993. PLB 10.95 (*0-8075-5338-7*); pap. 3.50 (*0-8075-5339-5*) A Whitman.
Watkins, Dawn L. Pulling Together. Cooper, Carolyn, ed. Pflug, Kathy, illus. 135p. (Orig.). (gr. 2-4). 1992. pap. 4.95 (*0-89084-609-X*) Bob Jones Univ Pr.
Weaver, Will. Striking Out. LC 93-565. 288p. (gr. 5 up). 1993. 15.00 (*0-06-023346-X*); PLB 14.89 (*0-06-023347-8*) HarpC Child Bks.
Webster-Seek, Vesta. Old Ruff & Life on the Farm. LC 92-12956. (gr. k-3). 1993. pap. 4.99 (*0-7814-0966-7*, Chariot Bks) Chariot Family.
Wells, Rosemary. Waiting for the Evening Star. Jeffers, Susan, illus. LC 92-30492. 40p. (gr. k-3). 1993. 15.00 (*0-8037-1398-3*); PLB 14.89 (*0-8037-1399-1*) Dial Bks Young.
Westcott, Nadine B. There's a Hole in the Bucket. Westcott, Nadine B., illus. LC 89-34538. 32p. (ps-2). 1993. pap. 4.95 (*0-06-443195-9*, Trophy) HarpC Child Bks.
Westcott, Nadine B., adapted by. & illus. Skip to My Lou. 32p. (ps-3). 1992. pap. 4.95 (*0-316-93140-3*, Joy St Bks) Little.
Wiggen, Kate D. Rebecca of Sunnybrook Farm. Bixler, Phyllis, afterword by. 1991. pap. 2.95 (*0-451-52483-7*, Sig Classics) NAL-Dutton.
Wiggin, Kate D. Rebecca of Sunnybrook Farm. 259p. 1981. Repr. PLB 21.95 (*0-89967-028-8*) Harmony Raine.
—Rebecca of Sunnybrook Farm. 288p. (gr. 4-6). 1988. pap. 3.25 (*0-590-41343-0*) Scholastic Inc.
—Rebecca of Sunnybrook Farm. 279p. (gr. 5 up). 1986. pap. 2.95 (*0-14-035046-2*, Puffin) Puffin Bks.
—Rebecca of Sunnybrook Farm. 288p. (gr. 5-8). 1993. pap. 2.99 (*0-87406-655-7*) Willowisp Pr.
Wild, Margaret. The Very Best of Friends. Vivas, Julie, illus. 30p. (ps-3). 1990. 13.95 (*0-15-200625-7*, Gulliver Bks) HarBrace.
Wilder, Laura Ingalls. Farmer Boy. rev. ed. Williams, Garth, illus. LC 52-7527. 372p. (gr. 3-7). 1961. 15.95 (*0-06-026425-X*); PLB 15.89 (*0-06-026421-7*) HarpC Child Bks.
Wildsmith, Rebecca & Wildsmith, Brian. Wake up, Wake up. LC 92-18704. 1993. 6.95 (*0-15-200685-0*); pap. write for info. (*0-15-200686-9*) HarBrace.
Willard, Barbara. Harrow & Harvest. 1989. pap. 3.25 (*0-440-20480-1*, LFL) Dell.
Willis, Patricia. Out of the Storm. LC 94-2133. Date not set. write for info. (*0-395-68708-X*, Clarion Bks) HM.
Wolff, Ferida. Seven Loaves of Bread. Keller, Katie, illus. LC 92-34313. 32p. (ps up). 1993. 14.00 (*0-688-11101-7*, Tambourine Bks); PLB 13.93 (*0-688-11112-2*, Tambourine Bks) Morrow.
Wormell, Mary. Hilda Hen's Happy Birthday. LC 94-21020. 1995. write for info. (*0-15-200299-5*) HarBrace.
Yates, Elizabeth. Mountain Born. Unwin, Nora S., illus. LC 92-40545. 128p. (gr. 3-7). 1993. pap. 6.95 (*0-8027-7402-4*) Walker & Co.
Yolen, Jane. Honkers. Baker, Leslie, illus. LC 92-24302. 1993. 14.95 (*0-316-96893-5*) Little.
York, Carol B. Febold Feboldson, the Fix It Farmer. LC 79-66321. (Illus.). 48p. (gr. 3-6). 1980. lib. bdg. 9.89 (*0-89375-312-2*); pap. 2.95 (*0-89375-311-4*) Troll Assocs.
Ziefert, Harriet. Noisy Barn! Taback, Simms, illus. 16p. (ps-1). 1991. pap. 4.95 (*0-06-107405-5*) HarpC Child Bks.
—Oh What a Noisy Farm. Bolum, Emily, illus. LC 94-15171. 1994. write for info. (*0-688-13260-X*, Tambourine Bks); PLB write for info. (*0-688-13261-8*, Tambourine Bks) Morrow.
Zokeisha. Farm House. Klimo, Kate, ed. (Illus.). 16p. 1983. pap. 3.50 (*0-671-46130-3*, Little Simon) S&S Trade.

FARM LIFE–POETRY

Christiansen, Candace. Calico & Tin Horns. Locker, Thomas, illus. LC 91-3706. 32p. 1992. 16.00 (*0-8037-1179-4*); PLB 15.89 (*0-8037-1180-8*) Dial Bks Young.
Hopkins, Lee B. On the Farm: Poems. Molk, Laurel, illus. (ps-3). 1991. 14.95 (*0-316-37274-9*) Little.

FARM MACHINERY

see Agricultural Machinery

FARM MECHANICS

see Agricultural Machinery

FARM PRODUCE

Cochrane, Jennifer. Food Plants. LC 90-37226. (Illus.). 48p. (gr. 5-9). 1990. PLB 21.34 (*0-8114-2733-1*) Raintree Steck-V.

FARMING

see Agriculture

FARMS

Bennett, Olivia. A Farm in the City. (Illus.). 29p. (gr. 2-4). 1991. 12.95 (*0-237-60121-4*, Pub. by Evans Bros Ltd) Trafalgar.
Bushey, Jerry. Farming the Land: Modern Farmers & Their Machines. Bushey, Jerry, photos by. (Illus.). 40p. (gr. k-4). 1987. PLB 13.50 (*0-87614-314-1*) Carolrhoda Bks.
Damon, Laura. Hide-&-Seek on the Farm. Kramer, Robin, illus. LC 87-13737. 32p. (gr. k-2). 1988. PLB 7.89 (*0-8167-1231-X*); pap. text ed. 1.95 (*0-8167-1232-8*) Troll Assocs.
Dibble, Lisa. Food & Farming. LC 93-19073. (gr. 4 up). 1993. write for info. (*1-56458-387-2*) Dorling Kindersley.
Epstein, Sam & Epstein, Beryl. You Call That a Farm? Raising Leeches, Alligators, Weeds, & Other Unusual Things. (Illus.). 64p. (gr. 2-5). 1991. 13.95 (*0-374-38705-2*) FS&G.
Fitzgerald, Janet. Autumn on the Farm. (Illus.). 32p. (gr. 1-3). 1991. 15.95 (*0-237-60222-9*, Pub. by Evans Bros Ltd) Trafalgar.
—Summer on the Farm. (Illus.). 32p. (gr. 1-3). 1991. 15.95 (*0-237-60221-0*, Pub. by Evans Bros Ltd) Trafalgar.
—Winter on the Farm. (Illus.). 32p. (gr. 1-3). 1991. 15.95 (*0-237-60219-9*, Pub. by Evans Bros Ltd) Trafalgar.
Fitzgerald, Julie. Spring on the Farm. (Illus.). 32p. (gr. 1-3). 1991. 15.95 (*0-237-60220-2*, Pub. by Evans Bros Ltd) Trafalgar.
Fowler, Allan. If It Weren't for Farmers. LC 92-35055. (Illus.). 32p. (ps-2). 1993. PLB 10.75 (*0-516-06009-0*); pap. 3.95 (*0-516-46009-9*) Childrens.
Madrigal, Sylvia. Farms. (Illus.). 24p. (Orig.). (gr. 1-3). 1992. pap. text ed. 29.95 big bk. (*1-56334-063-1*); pap. text ed. 6.00 small bk. (*1-56334-069-0*) Hampton-Brown.
On the Farm. 32p. (ps-3). 1994. 4.95 (*1-56458-734-7*) Dorling Kindersley.
Parramon, J. M. Mi primera Visita a La Granja. 1990. pap. 5.95 (*0-8120-4400-2*) Barron.
—My First Visit to a Farm. 1990. pap. 5.95 (*0-8120-4305-7*) Barron.
Sanchez, Isidro & Peris, Carme. The Farm. (Illus.). 32p. (ps). 1991. pap. 5.95 (*0-8120-4711-7*) Barron.
Spizzirri, Peter M. Farm Maze: Educational Activity-Coloring Book. Spizzirri, Linda, ed. (Illus.). 32p. (gr. k-3). 1992. pap. 1.00 (*0-86545-205-9*) Spizzirri.
Sticker Fun with Farmyard Animals. 12p. (ps-3). 1994. 4.95 (*1-56458-741-X*) Dorling Kindersley.
Taylor, Jody, selected by. On the Farm Hidden Pictures. LC 93-73304. (Illus.). 32p. (ps-5). 1994. 4.95 (*1-56397-356-1*); prepack 14.85 (*1-56397-357-X*) Boyds Mills Pr.

FARRAGUT, DAVID GLASGOW, 1801-1870

Foster, Leila M. David Glasgow Farragut: Courageous Naval Officer. LC 91-8031. (Illus.). 152p. (gr. 4 up). 1991. PLB 14.40 (*0-516-03273-9*); pap. 5.95 (*0-516-43273-7*) Childrens.
Latham, Jean L. David Glasgow Farragut: Our First Admiral. Frame, Paul, illus. 80p. (gr. 2-6). 1991. Repr. of 1967 ed. lib. bdg. 12.95 (*0-7910-1438-X*) Chelsea Hse.
Shorto, Russell. David Farragut & the Great Naval Blockade. (Illus.). 160p. (gr. 5 up). 1990. lib. bdg. 12.95 (*0-382-09941-9*); pap. 7.95 (*0-382-24050-2*) Silver Burdett Pr.

FARRELL, JEFF

Henning, Jean M. Six Days to Swim-Jeff Farrell: A Story of Olympic Courage. Daland, P., intro. by. LC 71-103031. (Illus.). (gr. 6-12). 1970. 3.50 (*0-911822-02-X*) Swimming.

FASCISM–GERMANY

see National Socialism

FASHION

For works describing the prevailing mode or style in dress. Historical works on styles of particular countries or periods are entered under Costume.
see also Clothing and Dress; Costume

Baker, Patricia. The Fifties. Cumming, Valerie & Feldman, Elane, eds. (Illus.). 64p. (gr. 7-12). 1991. 16.95x (*0-8160-2468-5*) Facts on File.
—The Forties. (Illus.). 64p. (gr. 6-10). 1992. lib. bdg. 16.95x (*0-8160-2467-7*) Facts on File.
Baker, Wendy. Fashion. Baker, Wendy, illus. LC 93-21215. 48p. (gr. 5-9). 1994. 16.95 (*1-56847-145-9*) Thomson Lrning.
Black, Judy. Fashion. LC 93-4639. (gr. 9 up). 1994. text ed. 14.95 (*0-89686-791-9*, Crestwood Hse) Macmillan Child Grp.
Carnegie, Vicky. The Eighties. Cumming, Valerie & Feldman, Elane, eds. (Illus.). 64p. 1990. 16.95x (*0-8160-2471-5*) Facts on File.
Connikie, Yvonne. The Sixties. Cumming, Valerie & Feldman, Elane, eds. (Illus.). 1990. 16.95x (*0-8160-2469-3*) Facts on File.
Costantino, Maria. The Thirties. Cumming, Valerie & Feldman, Elane, eds. (Illus.). 64p. (gr. 6-10). 1992. lib. bdg. 16.95x (*0-8160-2466-9*) Facts on File.
Feldman, Elane. The Nineties. Cumming, Valerie, ed. (Illus.). 64p. (gr. 7-12). 1992. bds. 16.95x (*0-8160-2472-3*) Facts on File.
Herald, Jacqueline. The Twenties. Cumming, Valerie & Feldman, Elane, eds. (Illus.). 64p. (gr. 7-12). 1991. 16.95x (*0-8160-2465-0*) Facts on File.
Hodgman, Ann. A Day in the Life of a Fashion Designer. Jann, Gayle, illus. LC 87-13394. 32p. (gr. 4-8). 1988. PLB 11.79 (*0-8167-1119-4*); pap. text ed. 2.95 (*0-8167-1120-8*) Troll Assocs.
Kalman, Bobbie. Eighteenth Century Clothing. DeBiasi, Antoinette, illus. 32p. (Orig.). (gr. 3-6). 1993. PLB 15.95 (*0-86505-492-4*); pap. 7.95 (*0-86505-512-2*) Crabtree Pub Co.
—Nineteenth Century Clothing. DeBiasi, Antoinette, illus. 32p. (Orig.). (gr. 3-6). 1993. PLB 15.95 (*0-86505-493-2*); pap. 7.95 (*0-86505-513-0*) Crabtree Pub Co.
Moss, Miriam. Street Fashion. LC 90-48913. (Illus.). 32p. (gr. 5-6). 1991. text ed. 13.95 RSBE (*0-89686-611-4*, Crestwood Hse) Macmillan Child Grp.
Rowland-Warne, L. Costume. McAulay, Liz, photos by. LC 91-53135. (Illus.). 64p. (gr. 5 up). 1992. 16.00 (*0-679-81680-1*); PLB 16.99 (*0-679-91680-6*) Knopf Bks Yng Read.
Ruby, Jennifer. Costume in Context: The 1980s. (Illus.). 72p. (gr. 7-11). 1991. 24.95 (*0-7134-6539-5*, Pub. by Batsford UK) Trafalgar.

FASHION–FICTION

Cruise, Beth. Saved by the Bell: California Scheming. LC 92-2739. 144p. (Orig.). (gr. 5 up). 1992. pap. 2.95 (*0-02-042776-X*, Collier Young Ad) Macmillan Child Grp.
Wojciechowska, Maia. Dreams of Fashions. Karsky, A. K., illus. 52p. 1994. 14.50 (*1-883740-05-3*) Pebble Bch Pr Ltd.

FASTS AND FEASTS

see also Christmas; Easter; Holidays

Barz, Brigitte. Festivals with Children. 1988. pap. 10.50 (*0-86315-055-1*, 20241) Gryphon Hse.
Burke, Deidre. Food & Fasting. LC 93-537. 32p. (gr. 4-8). 1993. 13.95 (*1-56847-034-7*) Thomson Lrning.
Deshpande, Chris & Macleod-Brudenell, Iain. Festival Crafts. Mukhida, Zul, photos by. (Illus.). 32p. Date not set. lib. bdg. 18.60 (*0-8368-1153-4*) Gareth Stevens Inc.
Everix, Nancy. Ethnic Celebrations Around the World. 160p. (gr. 3-8). 1991. 12.95 (*0-86653-607-8*, GA1326) Good Apple.
Hoyt-Goldsmith, Diane. Day of the Dead: A Mexican-American Celebration. Migdale, Lawrence, photos by. LC 93-42106. (Illus.). 32p. (gr. 3-7). 1994. reinforced bdg. 15.95 (*0-8234-1094-3*) Holiday.
Kapoor. Sikh Festivals, Reading Level 4. (Illus.). 48p. (gr. 3-8). 1989. PLB 15.94 (*0-86592-984-X*); 11.95 (*0-685-58774-6*) Rourke Corp.
MacMillan, Dianne M. Ramadan & Id al-Fitr. LC 93-46185. (Illus.). 48p. (gr. 1-4). 1994. lib. bdg. 14.95 (*0-89490-502-3*) Enslow Pubs.
Saypol, Judyth R. & Wikler, Madeline. My Very Own Sukkot Book. Wikler, Madeline, illus. LC 83-26738. 40p. (gr. k-5). 1980. pap. 3.95 (*0-930494-09-1*) Kar Ben.

FASTS AND FEASTS–FICTION

Cohen, Barbara. Yussel's Prayer. Deraney, Michael J., illus. LC 80-25377. 32p. (gr. k-4). 1981. PLB 14.93 (*0-688-00461-X*) Lothrop.
Cohen, Barbara, retold by. Yussel's Prayer: A Yom Kippur Story. Deraney, Michael J., illus. LC 92-44551. 32p. (ps up). 1993. pap. 4.95 (*0-688-04581-2*, Mulberry) Morrow.
Dorros, Arthur. Por Fin Es Carnaval. Dorros, Sandra M., tr. Club de Madres Virgen del Carmen Staff, illus. LC 90-36222. (SPA.). 32p. (ps-3). 1991. 13.95 (*0-525-44690-7*, DCB) Dutton Child Bks.
Goldin, Barbara D. Cakes & Miracles: A Purim Tale. Weihs, Erika, illus. LC 92-25848. 1993. pap. 4.99 (*0-14-054871-8*) Puffin Bks.
—The Magician's Visit: A Passover Tale. Parker, Robert A., illus. LC 92-22903. 34p. 1993. 14.99 (*0-670-84840-9*) Viking Child Bks.
Hwa-I Publishing Co., Staff. Chinese Children's Stories, Vol. 26: Celebrating New York, Miss Yuan-Tsau. Ching, Emily, et al, eds. Wonder Kids Publications Staff, tr. from CHI. (Illus.). 28p. (gr. 3-6). 1991. Repr. of 1988 ed. 7.95 (*1-56162-026-2*) Wonder Kids.
Krulik, Nancy E. Penny & the Four Questions. Young, Marian, illus. 32p. (gr. 1-3). 1993. pap. 2.50 (*0-590-46339-X*) Scholastic Inc.

Lepon, Shoshana. Hillel Builds a House. Barr, Marilyn, illus. LC 92-39383. 1993. cancelled (*0-929371-41-0*); pap. 5.95 (*0-929371-42-9*) Kar Ben.

Manushkin, Fran. This Is the Matzoh that Papa Brought Home. Bittenger, Ned, illus. LC 94-9952. (gr. 4-7). 1995. 15.95 (*0-590-47146-5*) Scholastic Inc.

My Kwanzaa Book. 48p. (gr. 1-7). 1991. 5.95 (*1-877610-06-2*) Sea Island.

Polacco, Patricia. Tikvah Means Hope. (ps-3). 1994. 15. 95 (*0-385-32059-0*) Doubleday.

Portnoy, Mindy A. Matzah Ball. Kahn, Katherine J., illus. LC 93-39402. 1994. 13.95 (*0-929371-68-2*); pap. 5.95 (*0-929371-69-0*) Kar Ben.

Schotter, Roni. Passover Magic. Hafner, Marylin, illus. LC 93-20053. (gr. 1-8). 1995. 14.95 (*0-316-77468-5*) Little.

Silverman, Maida. The Glass Menorah & Other Stories for Jewish Holidays. Levine, Marge, illus. LC 91-13890. 64p. (gr. 1-4). 1992. RSBE 14.95 (*0-02-782682-1*, Four Winds) Macmillan Child Grp.

Topek, Susan Remick. A Taste for Noah. Springer, Sally, illus. LC 92-39384. (gr. k up). 1993. 12.95 (*0-929371-39-9*); pap. 4.95 (*0-929371-40-2*) Kar Ben.

Waters, Kate. Lion Dancer: Ernie Wan's Chinese New Year. (ps-3). 1991. pap. 3.95 (*0-590-43047-5*) Scholastic Inc.

Zalben, Jane B. Happy New Year, Beni. Zalben, Jane B., photos by. LC 92-25013. (Illus.). 32p. (gr. k-3). 1993. 13.95 (*0-8050-1961-8*, Bks Young Read) H Holt & Co.

Zapater, Beatriz M. Fiesta! Ortega, Jose, illus. 32p. (gr. 2-5). 1993. pap. 4.95 (*0-671-79842-1*, S&S BYR) S&S Trade.

FASTS AND FEASTS–JUDAISM

see also names of individual fasts and feasts, e.g. Yom Kippur, etc.

Adler, David. Jewish Holiday Fun. 64p. (Orig.). (gr. 2-6). 1987. pap. 3.95 (*0-930494-72-5*) Kar Ben.

Adler, David A. A Picture Book of Jewish Holidays. Heller, Linda, illus. LC 81-2765. 32p. (ps-3). 1981. reinforced bdg. 14.95 (*0-8234-0396-3*); pap. 5.95 (*0-8234-0756-X*) Holiday.

Brinn, Ruth Esrig. Jewish Holiday Crafts for Little Hands. Kahn, Katherine Janus, illus. LC 92-39638. (gr. k up). 1993. pap. 10.95 (*0-929371-47-X*) Kar Ben.

Burstein, Chaya M. A First Jewish Holiday Cookbook. Burstein, Chaya M., illus. (gr. 3-8). 1979. (Bonim Bks); pap. 8.95 (*0-88482-775-5*, Bonim Bks) Hebrew Pub.

Cashman, Greer F. & Frankel, Alona. Jewish Days & Holidays. LC 86-70789. (Illus.). 64p. (ps up). 1986. 11.95 (*0-915361-58-2*) Modan-Adama Bks.

Chaikin, Miriam. Shake a Palm Branch: The Story & Meaning of Sukkot. Friedman, Marvin, illus. LC 84-5022. 96p. (gr. 3-6). 1986. 12.95 (*0-89919-254-8*, Clarion Bks); pap. 4.95 (*0-89919-428-1*, Clarion Bks) HM.

Cohen, Barbara. First Fast. (Illus.). 32p. (gr. 4-6). 1987. 7.95 (*0-8074-0354-7*, 101066); tchr's. guide 5.00 (*0-8074-0411-X*, 201445) UAHC.

Corwin, Judith H. Jewish Holiday Fun. Corwin, Judith H., illus. LC 86-16201. 64p. (gr. 3 up). 1987. (J Messner); lib. bdg. 5.95 (*0-671-60127-X*); PLB 7.71s.p. (*0-685-47058-X*); pap. 4.46s.p. (*0-685-47059-8*) S&S Trade.

Dougherty, Karla. The Willowisp Book of Jewish Holidays. (Illus.). 32p. (gr. 3 up). 1992. pap. 3.50 (*0-87406-639-5*) Willowisp Pr.

Drucker, M. A Jewish Holiday ABC. Pocock, Rita, illus. 1992. 13.95 (*0-15-200482-3*, HB Juv Bks) HarBrace.

Drucker, Malka. The Family Treasury of Jewish Holidays. Patz, Nancy, illus. LC 93-7549. (ps up). 1994. 21.95 (*0-316-19343-7*) Little.

Elias, Miriam L. Special Days Are Wonderful: A Guessing Game Book. Leff, Tova, illus. 32p. (ps). 1993. English ed. 9.95 (*0-922613-46-X*); Russian ed. 9.95 (*0-922613-49-4*) Hachai Pubns.

Emerman, Ellen. Is It Shabbos Yet? Vegh, Toby, illus. 32p. (ps-1). 1990. 8.95 (*0-922613-21-4*); pap. 6.95 (*0-922613-22-2*) Hachai Pubns.

Fine, Helen. G'Dees Book of Holiday Fun. (Illus.). 98p. (gr. 4-6). 1970. pap. 3.00 (*0-8074-0243-5*, 121701) UAHC.

Geller, Norman. Color Me Happy: It's Rosh Hashannah & Yom Kippur. Cruchow, Jane C., illus. 36p. (gr. k-4). 1986. pap. 2.95 (*0-915753-10-3*) N Geller Pub.

Gellman, Ellie. It's Rosh-Hashanah. Kahn, Katherine J., illus. LC 85-80783. 12p. (ps). 1985. bds. 4.95 (*0-930494-50-4*) Kar Ben.

Goldin, Barbara D. The Passover Journey: A Seder Companion. Waldman, Neil, illus. LC 93-5133. 64p. 1994. 15.99 (*0-670-82421-6*) Viking Child Bks.

Gold-Vukson, Marji & Gold-Vukson, Micheal. Can You Imagine? Creative Drawing Adventures for the Jewish Holidays. LC 91-42842. 48p. (ps-5). pap. 3.95 (*0-929371-31-3*) Kar Ben.

Greenberg, Melanie H. Celebrations: Our Jewish Holidays. Greenberg, Melanie H., illus. LC 91-12744. 32p. (ps-3). 1991. 14.95 (*0-8276-0396-7*); pap. 9.95 (*0-8276-0505-6*) JPS Phila.

Grishaver, Joel L. Building Jewish Life: High Holy Days. LC 87-13949. (Illus.). 48p. (gr. k-3). 1988. pap. text ed. 4.95 (*0-933873-17-4*) Torah Aura.

—Building Jewish Life Passover Haggadah. (HEB & ENG., Illus.). 48p. (Orig.). (gr. 4-8). 1989. pap. 2.95 (*0-933873-41-7*) Torah Aura.

—Building Jewish Life: Sukkot & Simhat Torah. (Illus.). 48p. 1988. pap. text ed. 4.95 (*0-933873-13-1*) Torah Aura.

Gross, Judith. Celebrate: A Book of Jewish Holidays. Weissman, Bari, illus. 32p. (gr. k-3). 1992. PLB 7.99 (*0-448-40303-X*, Platt & Munk Pubs); pap. 2.25 (*0-448-40302-1*, Platt & Munk Pubs) Putnam Pub Group.

Gunsher, Cheryl. Lev the Lucky Lulav. (Illus.). 24p. (ps-k). 1993. 10.00 (*1-881602-01-X*) Prism NJ.

Jaffe, Nina. The Uninvited Guest & Other Jewish Holiday Tales. Savadier, Elivia, illus. LC 92-36308. 1993. write for info. (*0-590-44653-3*) Scholastic Inc.

Katz, Bobbi. The Family Book of Jewish Holidays. Herzfeld, Caryl, illus. LC 93-27375. 1994. 10.00 (*0-679-85820-2*) Random Bks Yng Read.

Kimmel, Eric A. Days of Awe: Stories for Rosh Hashanah & Yom Kippur. Weihs, Erika, illus. LC 93-583. 48p. (gr. 3-7). pap. 4.99 (*0-14-050271-8*, Puffin) Puffin Bks.

Kleinbard, Gitel. Oh, Zalmy! Or, Tales of Two Esthers, Bk. 3. Vorhand, Rachel, illus. (gr. 1-4). 1979. pap. 3.95 (*0-917274-05-9*) Mah Tov Pubns.

Kolatch, A. J. The Jewish Child's First Book of Why. LC 91-25352. 32p. 1992. 14.95 (*0-8246-0354-0*) Jonathan David.

Kozodoy, Ruth. The Book of Jewish Holidays. Rossel, Seymour, ed. Suba, Suzanne, illus. 192p. (Orig.). (gr. 4-5). 1981. pap. text ed. 7.95x (*0-87441-334-6*); tchr's. guide with duplicating masters by Moshe Ben-Aharon 12.50x (*0-87441-367-2*); By Morris J. Sugarman. student's activity bk. 4.25 (*0-87441-338-9*) Behrman.

Lemelman, Martin, illus. Jewish Holiday Book. 10p. 1989. bds. 4.95 (*0-8074-0431-4*, 102004) UAHC.

Mack, Grace C. My Special Book of Jewish Celebrations. (Illus.). 36p. (Orig.). (ps-2). 1984. pap. 8.95 (*0-9602338-4-9*) Rockdale Ridge.

MacMillan, Dianne M. Jewish Holidays in the Fall. LC 92-30952. (Illus.). 48p. (gr. 1-4). 1993. lib. bdg. 14.95 (*0-89490-406-X*) Enslow Pubs.

—Jewish Holidays in the Spring. LC 93-38637. (Illus.). 48p. (gr. 1-4). 1994. lib. bdg. 14.95 (*0-89490-503-1*) Enslow Pubs.

Marcus, Audrey F. & Zwerin, Raymond A. Shabbat Can Be. Saltzman, Yuri, illus. Syme, Daniel B., ed. (Illus.). (gr. k-3). 1979. 10.95 (*0-8074-0023-8*) UAHC.

Pliskin, Jacqueline. The Jewish Holiday Game & Workbook. (Illus.). (gr. 8-12). 1989. pap. 5.95 (*0-933503-85-7*) Shapolsky Pubs.

—My Very Own Animated Jewish Holiday Activity Book. (Illus.). 96p. (gr. 4-8). 1987. pap. 5.95 (*0-933503-16-4*) Shapolsky Pubs.

Rouss, Sylvia A. Fun with Jewish Holiday Rhymes. Steinberg, Lisa, illus. LC 91-40931. (ps). 1992. 10.95 (*0-8074-0463-2*, 101981) UAHC.

Schaffer, Patricia. Chag Sameach! A Jewish Holiday Book for Children. (Illus.). 28p. (Orig.). (ps-4). 1985. pap. 5.95 (*0-935079-16-5*) Tabor Sarah Bks.

Schlein, Miriam. Our Holidays. Kahn, Katherine, illus. 128p. (gr. k-3). 1983. pap. text ed. 7.95x (*0-87441-382-6*) Behrman.

Sidon, Ephraim. The Animated Megillah. 54p. (gr. 1-5). 1987. 14.95 (*0-8246-0324-9*) Jonathan David.

Silverman, Maida. My First Book of Jewish Holidays. Garrison, Barbara, illus. LC 93-20370. (ps-8). 1994. 14.99 (*0-8037-1427-0*); lib. bdg. 14.89 (*0-8037-1428-9*) Dial Bks Young.

Simon, Norma. Tu Bishvat. Weiss, Harvey, illus. (ps-k). 1961. plastic cover 4.50 (*0-8381-0709-5*) United Syn Bk.

Sokoloff, David. The New Jewish Holiday Activity & Coloring Book. 96p. (ps-8). 1990. pap. 5.95 (*0-944007-92-9*) Shapolsky Pubs.

Springer, Sally, illus. High Holiday Fun for Little Hands. 32p. (ps). 1993. wkbk. 3.95 (*0-929371-76-3*) Kar Ben.

—Sukkot & Simchat Torah Fun for Little Hands. 32p. (ps). 1993. wkbk. 3.95 (*0-929371-77-1*) Kar Ben.

Turck, Mary. Jewish Holidays. LC 89-25398. (Illus.). 48p. (gr. 5-6). 1990. text ed. 12.95 RSBE (*0-89686-502-9*, Crestwood Hse) Macmillan Child Grp.

Turner. Jewish Festivals, Reading Level 4. (Illus.). 48p. (gr. 3-8). 1987. Set. PLB 15.74 (*0-86592-977-7*); 11. 95s.p. (*0-685-58771-1*) Rourke Corp.

Wark, Mary A. We Tell It to Our Children: The Story of Passover: A Haggadah for Seders with Young Children. 2nd ed. Oskow, Craig, illus. Lerner, Leigh D., frwd. by. LC 88-92282. (Illus.). 126p. (Orig.). (ps-6). 1988. pap. 5.95 wire bdg. (*0-9619880-8-8*) Mensch Makers Pr.

Wark, MaryAnn B. We Tell It to Our Children: The Story of Passover: A Haggadah for Seders with Young Children. Oskow, Craig, illus. Lerner, Leigh D., frwd. by. LC 87-63604. (Illus.). 150p. (Orig.). (ps-6). 1988. Leader's Edition with Puppets. pap. 11. 95 wire-o bdg. (*0-9619880-9-6*) Mensch Makers Pr.

Children's active participatory Haggadah makes the Passover story into an engaging drama of the Exodus story. A complete guide, including multi-national recipes, for putting on the traditional Seder meal for Passover. Text is a musical puppet show with Judaically-meaningful lyrics set to simple American folk tunes. Everyone participates in singing throughout the service. This Leader's edition has 9 cut-out puppets who are the "guests" from the past, who in a "you-are-there" style tell the story of the Exodus. Parts for non-readers & early readers. Guest edition - no puppets with full text also available. Endorsed by rabbis, religious educators (Jewish & Christian), children's book store owners, preschool teachers, parents & grandparents nationwide. For home or model seders. Authentically Jewish; easy for non-Jews. Developmentally appropriate for children. Downright fun for adults. Other unique features include the Passover food symbols, like matzoh, explained at the appropriate time in the story; special sections to personalize & teach about world Jewry. Difficult concepts like slavery are taught through action, songs, & pictures. Lyrics respond to children's thinking while tackling complicated issues surrounding freedom. Plentiful, detailed drawings emphasize immediacy of ideas & illustrate every idea & ceremonial symbol.

Publisher Provided Annotation.

Youdovin, Susan S. Why Does It Always Rain on Sukkot? Levine, Abby, ed. Nerlove, Miriam, illus. LC 90-11923. 32p. (ps-3). 1990. PLB 13.95 (*0-8075-9079-7*) A Whitman.

Zeldin, Florence. A Mouse in Our Jewish House. Rauchwerger, Lisa, illus. LC 89-40362. 32p. (ps). 1990. 11.95 (*0-933873-43-3*) Torah Aura.

Zwebner, Janet. UH! OH! Jewish Holidays. (gr. 3-7). 1993. 12.95 (*0-943706-14-9*) Yllw Brick Rd.

FATHER FLANAGAN'S BOYS HOME, BOYS TOWN, NEBRASKA

Marko, Katherine M. Hang Out the Flag. LC 92-349. 144p. (gr. 3-7). 1992. SBE 13.95 (*0-02-762320-3*, Macmillan Child Bk) Macmillan Child Grp.

FATHERS

Ayer, Eleanor. Everything You Need to Know about Teen Fatherhood. Rosen, Ruth, ed. (gr. 7-12). 1993. PLB 14.95 (*0-8239-1532-8*) Rosen Group.

Byers, Ken. The Father & Son Survival Kit: A Journey into the Wilderness of Relationships. (gr. 9 up). 1988. 19.95 (*0-9619040-1-1*); pap. 12.95 (*0-9619040-0-3*); wkbk. 12.95 (*0-9619040-2-X*) Journeys Together.

Driscoll, Jack. Skylight. LC 91-10593. 192p. (gr. 7 up). 1991. 14.95 (*0-531-05961-8*); RLB 14.99 (*0-531-08561-9*) Orchard Bks Watts.

Greenspun, Adele A. Daddies. Greenspun, Adele A., illus. 48p. 1991. 15.95 (*0-399-22259-6*, Philomel Bks) Putnam Pub Group.

Merriam, Eve. Daddies at Work. Fernandes, Eugenie, illus. 32p. (ps-2). 1991. pap. 2.50 (*0-671-73276-5*, Little Simon) S&S Trade.

Nelson, Theresa. The Twenty-Five Cent Miracle. LC 89-6822. 224p. (gr. 4-7). 1989. pap. 3.95 (*0-689-71326-6*, Aladdin) Macmillan Child Grp.

Simon, Norma. I Wish I Had My Father. Tucker, Kathleen, ed. LC 83-1287. (Illus.). 32p. (gr. 1-4). 1983. PLB 11.95 (*0-8075-3522-2*) A Whitman.

Solomon, Joan. News from Dad. (Illus.). 25p. (gr. 2-4). 1991. 12.95 (*0-237-60115-X*, Pub. by Evans Bros Ltd) Trafalgar.

Watanabe, Shigeo. Where's My Daddy? (Illus.). 32p. 1991. (Philomel Bks); pap. 5.95 (*0-399-21851-3*, Philomel Bks) Putnam Pub Group.

FATHERS–FICTION

Abbott, Deborah & Kisor, Henry. One TV Blasting & a Pig Outdoors: A Concept Book. Tucker, Kathy, ed. Morrill, Leslie, illus. LC 94-6649. 40p. (gr. 2-6). 1994. PLB 13.95 (*0-8075-6075-8*) A Whitman.

Aiken, Joan. Dido & Pa. LC 86-2061. 256p. (gr. 7 up). 1986. 14.95 (*0-385-29480-8*) Delacorte.

Asch, Frank. Just Like Daddy. (Illus.). 32p. (gr. k-4). 1984. pap. 12.95 jacketed (*0-671-66456-5*, S&S BFYR); pap. 4.95 (*0-671-66457-3*, S&S BFYR) S&S Trade.

Bauer, Marion D. Face to Face. 192p. (gr. 5-9). 1991. 13. 45 (*0-395-55440-3*, Clarion Bks) HM.

Bawden, Nina. The Robbers. LC 79-4152. (Illus.). 160p. (gr. 4-7). 1989. Repr. of 1979 ed. 12.95 (*0-688-41902-X*) Lothrop.

Baynton, Martin. Why Do You Love Me? LC 89-1861. (Illus.). 32p. (ps up). 1990. 15.00 (*0-688-09156-3*); PLB 14.93 (*0-688-09157-1*) Greenwillow.
Berry, James. Ajeemah & His Son. LC 92-6615. 96p. (gr. 7 up). 1992. 13.00 (*0-06-021043-5*); PLB 12.89 (*0-06-021044-3*) HarpC Child Bks.
—Ajeemah & His Son. LC 92-6615. 96p. (gr. 7 up). 1994. pap. 3.95 (*0-06-440523-0*, Trophy) HarpC Child Bks.
Black, Claudia. My Dad Loves Me, My Dad Has a Disease. LC 59-776. (Illus.). 88p. (Orig.). (gr. k-9). 1982. pap. 9.95 (*0-9607940-2-6*) MAC Pub.
Blair, L. E. Problem Dad. 128p. (gr. 4-7). 1992. 2.95 (*0-307-22022-2*, 22022) Western Pub.
Blake, Robert J. The Perfect Spot. Blake, Robert J., illus. 32p. (ps-8). 1992. PLB 14.95 (*0-399-22132-8*, Philomel Bks) Putnam Pub Group.
Browne, Anthony. The Big Baby. LC 93-20210. (Illus.). (gr. 1-3). 1994. 13.00 (*0-679-84737-5*) Knopf Bks Yng Read.
Bunting, Eve. A Perfect Father's Day. Giblin, James C., ed. Meddaugh, Susan, illus. 32p. (ps-1). 1991. 13.95 (*0-395-52590-X*, Clarion Bks) HM.
—A Perfect Father's Day. Meddaugh, Susan, illus. 32p. (gr. k-3). 1993. pap. 5.70 (*0-395-66416-0*, Clarion Bks) HM.
Butterworth, Oliver. Visitng the Big House. Cohn, Amy, ed. Avishai, Susan, illus. LC 94-20844. 48p. 1995. pap. 3.95 (*0-688-13303-7*, Pub. by Beech Tree Bks) Morrow.
Cannon, Bettie. A Bellsong for Sarah Raines. LC 87-4299. 192p. (gr. 7 up). 1987. 14.95 (*0-684-18839-2*, Scribners Young Read) Macmillan Child Grp.
Cartwright, Pauline. Jimmy Parker's New Job. Hunnam, Lucinda, illus. LC 93-20029. 1994. pap. write for info. (*0-383-03679-8*) SRA Schl Grp.
Caseley, Judith. My Father, the Nutcase. LC 91-46750. 196p. (gr. 7 up). 1992. 15.00 (*0-679-83394-3*); PLB 15.99 (*0-679-93394-8*) Knopf Bks Yng Read.
Cazet, Denys. I'm Not Sleepy. Cazet, Denys, illus. LC 91-15958. 32p. (ps-1). 1992. 14.95 (*0-531-05898-0*); lib. bdg. 14.99 (*0-531-08498-1*) Orchard Bks Watts.
Cleaver, Vera. Sugar Blue. (gr. 3-6). 1986. pap. 2.95 (*0-440-48422-7*, YB) Dell.
Cole, Babette. Trouble with Dad. (ps-3). 1993. pap. 5.95 (*0-399-22534-X*, Sandcastle Bks) Putnam Pub Group.
Conway, Celeste. Where Is Papa Now? (Illus.). 32p. (ps-1). 1994. 14.95 (*1-56397-130-5*) Boyds Mills Pr.
DeJong, Meindert. The House of Sixty Fathers. Sendak, Maurice, illus. LC 56-8148. 192p. (gr. 5-8). 1987. pap. 3.95 (*0-06-440200-2*, Trophy) HarpC Child Bks.
Delton, Judy. All Dads on Deck. (ps-3). 1994. pap. 3.25 (*0-440-40943-8*) Dell.
Dickens, Charles. Dombey & Son. (ps-8). 1990. Repr. lib. bdg. 29.95x (*0-89966-678-7*) Buccaneer Bks.
Dillon, Barbara. My Stepfather Shrank! LC 91-23901. (Illus.). 128p. (gr. 3-7). 1992. 13.00 (*0-06-021574-7*); PLB 12.89 (*0-06-021581-X*) HarpC Child Bks.
Donovan, Mary L. Papa's Bedtime Story. Root, Kimberly B., illus. LC 91-27792. 40p. (ps-3). 1993. 15.00 (*0-679-81790-5*); PLB 15.99 (*0-679-91790-X*) Knopf Bks Yng Read.
Ernst, Lisa C. Squirrel Park. Ernst, Lisa C., illus. LC 92-27920. 40p. (ps-2). 1993. RSBE 15.95 (*0-02-733562-3*, Bradbury Pr) Macmillan Child Grp.
Fassler, Joan. All Alone with Daddy: A Young Girl Plays the Role of Mother. Gregory, Dorothy L., illus. LC 76-80120. 32p. (ps-3). 1975. 16.95 (*0-87705-009-0*) Human Sci Pr.
Faucher, Elizabeth. Getting Even with Dad. 1994. pap. 3.50 (*0-590-48263-7*) Scholastic Inc.
Ferris, Jean. Relative Strangers. 1993. 16.00 (*0-374-36243-2*) FS&G.
Fleischman, Paul. Rear-View Mirrors. LC 85-45387. 128p. (gr. 7 up). 1986. 12.95 (*0-06-021866-5*); PLB 12.89 (*0-06-021867-3*) HarpC Child Bks.
Fox, Paula. Portrait of Ivan. reissue ed. Lambert, Saul, illus. LC 74-93085. 144p. (gr. 5-7). 1985. SBE 13.95 (*0-02-735510-1*, Bradbury Pr) Macmillan Child Grp.
Friend, David. Baseball, Football, Daddy & Me. Brown, Richard, illus. 32p. (ps-3). 1990. 12.95 (*0-670-82420-8*) Viking Child Bks.
Gauthier, Bertrand. Just Me & My Dad, 6 titles. Sylvestre, Daniel, illus. (gr. 2 up). 1993. Set. PLB 95.60 (*0-8368-1006-6*) Gareth Stevens Inc.
—Zachary in I'm Zachary! Sylvestre, Daniel, illus. LC 93-1168. 1993. 15.93 (*0-8368-1007-4*) Gareth Stevens Inc.
—Zachary in the Championship. Sylvestre, Daniel, illus. LC 93-1169. 1993. 15.93 (*0-8368-1008-2*) Gareth Stevens Inc.
—Zachary in the Present. Sylvestre, Daniel, illus. LC 93-7719. 1993. 15.93 (*0-8368-1010-4*) Gareth Stevens Inc.
—Zachary in the Wawabongbong. Sylvestre, Daniel, illus. LC 93-15456. 1993. 15.93 (*0-8368-1011-2*) Gareth Stevens Inc.
—Zachary in the Winner. Sylvestre, Daniel, illus. LC 93-7718. 1993. 15.93 (*0-8368-1009-0*) Gareth Stevens Inc.
Geringer, Laura. Silverpoint. LC 91-6648. 160p. (gr. 5 up). 1991. 13.95 (*0-06-023849-6*) HarpC Child Bks.
Gifaldi, David. One Thing for Sure. LC 86-2677. 160p. (gr. 4-7). 1986. 13.95 (*0-89919-462-1*, Clarion Bks) HM.
Grant, Cynthia D. Keep Laughing. LC 91-6816. 192p. (gr. 7 up). 1991. SBE 14.95 (*0-689-31514-7*, Atheneum Child Bk) Macmillan Child Grp.
Grant, Robin R., Sr. RobinSays Try Manhood Before Fatherhood. 16p. 1993. pap. 2.25 (*0-9638384-1-5*) RobinSays.
Greenfield, Eloise. My Daddy & I. Gilchrist, Jan S., illus. 12p. 1991. bds. 4.95 (*0-86316-206-1*) Writers & Readers.
Grindley, Sally. Wake up, Dad! 1989. 12.95 (*0-385-26017-2*) Doubleday.
Halecroft, David. Breaking Loose. LC 92-12084. 128p. (gr. 3-7). 1992. 13.00 (*0-670-84697-X*) Viking Child Bks.
Hallinan, P. K. We're Very Good Friends, My Father & I. Hallinan, P. K., illus. (ps-2). 1990. pap. 4.95 perfect bdg. (*0-8249-8520-6*, Ideals Child) Hambleton-Hill.
—We're Very Good Friends, My Mother & I. Hallinan, P. K., illus. 24p. (ps-2). 1990. pap. 4.95 perfect bdg. (*0-8249-8519-2*, Ideals Child) Hambleton-Hill.
Hamm, Diane J. Bunkhouse Journal. LC 90-8062. 96p. (gr. 7 up). 1990. SBE 13.95 (*0-684-19206-3*, Scribners Young Read) Macmillan Child Grp.
Hampton, Janie. Come Home Soon, Baba. Brent, Jenny, illus. 32p. (gr. 4 up). 1993. 12.95 (*0-87226-511-0*, Bedrick Blackie) P Bedrick Bks.
Hawks, Robert. This Stranger, My Father. LC 87-26245. 228p. (gr. 5-9). 1988. 13.45 (*0-395-44089-0*) HM.
—This Stranger, My Father. 240p. (gr. 4). 1990. pap. 2.95 (*0-380-70739-X*, Flare) Avon.
Hearn, Diane D. Dad's Dinosaur Day. LC 92-22549. (Illus.). 32p. (gr. k-3). 1993. RSBE 14.95 (*0-02-743485-0*, Macmillan Child Bk) Macmillan Child Grp.
Hess, Donna L. A Father's Promise. (Illus.). 268p. (Orig.). (gr. 6). 1987. pap. 6.94 (*0-89084-379-1*) Bob Jones Univ Pr.
Hesse, Karen. Sable. 1994. 14.95 (*0-8050-2416-6*) H Holt & Co.
Hickman, Martha W. When Andy's Father Went to Prison. rev. ed. Levine, Abby, ed. Raymond, Larry, illus. LC 89-77318. 40p. (gr. 2-5). 1990. PLB 11.95 (*0-8075-8874-1*) A Whitman.
Hines, Anna G. Daddy Makes the Best Spaghetti. Hines, Anna G., illus. LC 85-13993. (ps-1). 1986. 13.95 (*0-89919-388-9*, Clarion Bks) HM.
—Daddy Makes the Best Spaghetti. Hines, Anna G., illus. LC 85-13993. 32p. (ps-1). 1988. pap. 5.95 (*0-89919-794-9*, Clarion Bks) HM.
Hogan, Paula Z. Will Dad Ever Move Back Home? (ps-3). 1993. pap. 3.95 (*0-8114-7160-8*) Raintree Steck-V.
Horowitz, Jordan. Getting Even with Dad. (gr. 4-7). 1994. pap. 3.50 (*0-590-48262-9*) Scholastic Inc.
Hughes, Dean. Lucky's Cool Club. LC 93-28534. 141p. (gr. 3-7). 1993. pap. 4.95 (*0-87579-786-5*) Deseret Bk.
Hunt, Irene. The Everlasting Hills. LC 85-2449. 192p. (gr. 6-8). 1985. SBE 14.95 (*0-684-18340-4*, Scribners Young Read) Macmillan Child Grp.
Isadora, Rachel. At the Crossroads. LC 90-30751. (Illus.). 32p. (ps up). 1991. 15.00 (*0-688-05270-3*); PLB 14.93 (*0-688-05271-1*) Greenwillow.
—At the Crossroads. Isadora, Rachel, illus. 32p. (ps up). 1994. pap. 4.95 (*0-688-13103-4*, Mulberry) Morrow.
Jaffe, Steve. Who Were Fathers? 1995. write for info. (*0-8050-3102-2*) H Holt & Co.
Joyce, James. Eveline. 32p. (gr. 6). 1990. PLB 13.95 (*0-88682-308-0*) Creative Ed.
Kidd, Nina. June Mountain Secret. Kidd, Nina, illus. LC 90-31574. 32p. (gr. k-3). 1991. PLB 14.89 (*0-06-023168-8*) HarpC Child Bks.
Koertge, Ron. Harmony Arms. 1992. 15.95 (*0-316-50104-2*, Joy St Bks) Little.
Konigsburg, E. L. Father's Arcane Daughter. (gr. 5-8). 1986. pap. 3.99 (*0-440-42496-8*, YB) Dell.
Kroll, Steven. Happy Father's Day. Hafner, Marylin, illus. LC 87-7559. 32p. (ps-3). 1988. reinforced bdg. 14.95 (*0-8234-0671-7*) Holiday.
Krulik, Nancy E. Getting Even with Dad. (gr. 4-7). 1994. pap. 2.95 (*0-590-48261-0*) Scholastic Inc.
Laufer, Judy E. Where Did Papa Go: Looking at Death from a Young Child's Perspective. Wingfield, Ken, Jr., illus. 32p. (Orig.). (ps-2). 1991. pap. 9.95 (*1-881669-00-9*) Little Egg Pub.
Le Saux, Alain. Daddy Sleeps. (Illus.). 28p. (ps). 1992. pap. 6.95 (*0-8050-2196-5*, Bks Young Read) H Holt & Co.
Light, John. Odd Jobs. LC 90-34354. (gr. 4 up). 1991. 3.95 (*0-85953-339-5*) Childs Play.
Lindbergh, Reeve. If I'd Known Then What I Know Now. Root, Kimberly B., illus. LC 93-24058. 1994. 14.99 (*0-670-85351-8*) Viking Child Bks.
Lindenbaum, Pija. Else-Marie & Her Seven Little Daddies. LC 91-9077. (Illus.). 32p. (ps-2). 1991. 14.95 (*0-8050-1752-6*, Bks Young Read) H Holt & Co.
Littleton, Mark. Secrets of Moonlight Mountain. 1993. pap. 3.99 (*1-56507-960-4*) Harvest Hse.
Locker, Thomas. Miranda's Smile. LC 93-28050. (gr. 2 up). 1994. 15.99 (*0-8037-1688-5*); PLB 15.89 (*0-8037-1689-3*) Dial Bks Young.
London, Johnathan. Old Salt, Young Salt. LC 94-14593. 1995. write for info. (*0-688-12975-7*); PLB write for info. (*0-688-12976-5*) Lothrop.
Lowery, Linda. Laurie Tells. Karpinski, John E., illus. LC 93-9786. (gr. 4 up). 1994. 18.95 (*0-87614-790-2*) Carolrhoda Bks.
McGraw, Sheila & Cline, Paul. My Father's Hands. McGraw, Sheila, illus. 32p. 1992. 6.95 (*0-9625261-6-9*, Green Tiger) S&S Trade.
McKinley, Robin. My Father Is in the Navy. Gourbault, Martine, illus. LC 91-12566. 24p. (ps up). 1992. 14.00 (*0-688-10639-0*); PLB 13.93 (*0-688-10640-4*) Greenwillow.
Malone, James H. No-Job Dad. LC 92-15873. (Illus.). 30p. (gr. 1-2). 1992. 13.95 (*1-878217-06-2*) Victory Press.
Malouf, Marcellene & DeLeon, David. From Daddy with Love. Kincaid, Shannon, illus. 34p. 1993. 16.95 (*0-9639680-0-9*) Malouf-Christopherson.
Mandelbaum, Pili. You Be Me, I'll Be You. (Illus.). 40p. (ps-3). 1990. 13.95 (*0-916291-27-8*) Kane-Miller Bk.
Mandrell, Louise. Best Man for the Job: A Story about the Meaning of Father's Day. (ps-3). 1993. 12.95 (*1-56530-039-4*) Summit TX.
Mayer, Mercer. Just Me & My Dad. (Illus.). 24p. (ps-3). 1977. pap. write for info. (*0-307-11839-8*, Golden Bks) Western Pub.
Me & My Dad. 32p. 1994. 6.98 (*1-57082-154-2*) Mouse Works.
Mi Papa: My Dad. (SPA.). 14p. (ps). 1992. bds. 4.95 (*1-55037-265-3*, Pub. by Annick Pr) Firefly Bks Ltd.
Miller, Mary J. Me & My Name. LC 92-20302. 128p. (gr. 5 up). 1992. pap. 3.99 (*0-14-034374-1*) Puffin Bks.
Mon Papa: My Dad. (FRE.). 14p. (ps). 1992. 4.95 (*1-55037-266-1*, Pub. by Annick Pr) Firefly Bks Ltd.
Monfried, Lucia. The Daddies Boat. Chessare, Michele, illus. 32p. (ps-3). 1993. pap. 4.99 (*0-14-054938-2*, Puff Unicorn) Puffin Bks.
Morgan, A. Daddy-Care. (Illus.). 24p. (ps-8). 1986. 12.95 (*0-920303-58-7*, Pub. by Annick CN); pap. 4.95 (*0-920303-59-5*, Pub. by Annick CN) Firefly Bks Ltd.
Moulton, Deborah. Summer Girl. LC 91-15790. 128p. (gr. 5-9). 1992. 15.00 (*0-8037-1153-0*) Dial Bks Young.
Munsch, Robert. David's Father. Martchenko, Michael, illus. 32p. (gr. k-3). 1983. PLB 14.95 (*0-920236-62-6*, Pub. by Annick CN); pap. 4.95 (*0-920236-64-2*, Pub. by Annick CN) Firefly Bks Ltd.
—David's Father. Martchenko, Michael, illus. 24p. (Orig.). (ps-2). 1989. pap. 0.99 (*1-55037-011-1*, Pub. by Annick CN) Firefly Bks Ltd.
—David's Father. (CHI., Illus.). 32p. 1993. pap. 5.95 (*1-55037-297-1*, Pub. by Annick CN) Firefly Bks Ltd.
—El Papa de David: David's Father. Martchenko, Michael, illus. (SPA.). 32p. (ps-2). 1991. pap. 5.95 (*1-55037-096-0*, Pub. by Annick CN) Firefly Bks Ltd.
Myers, Anna. Red-Dirt Jessie. 107p. 1992. 13.95 (*0-8027-8172-1*) Walker & Co.
Naylor, Phyllis R. The Keeper. LC 85-20029. 228p. (gr. 5 up). 1986. SBE 14.95 (*0-689-31204-0*, Atheneum Child Bk) Macmillan Child Grp.
Ormerod, Jan. Dad's Back. LC 84-12614. (Illus.). 24p. (ps). 1985. 4.95 (*0-688-04126-4*) Lothrop.
—Reading. LC 84-12628. (Illus.). 24p. (ps). 1985. 4.95 (*0-688-04127-2*) Lothrop.
Otey, Mimi. Daddy Has a Pair of Striped Shorts. LC 90-55289. (Illus.). 32p. (ps-3). 1990. 13.95 (*0-374-31675-9*) FS&G.
Oxenbury, Helen. Tom & Pippo Read a Story. Oxenbury, Helen, illus. LC 87-37438. 14p. (ps-k). 1988. pap. 5.95 (*0-689-71252-9*, Aladdin) Macmillan Child Grp.
Parker, Kristy. My Dad the Magnificent. Hoban, Lillian, illus. LC 86-24077. 32p. (ps-2). 1987. 10.95 (*0-525-44314-2*, DCB) Dutton Child Bks.
—My Dad the Magnificent. Hoban, Lillian, illus. LC 86-24077. 32p. (ps-2). 1990. pap. 3.95 (*0-525-44607-9*, DCB) Dutton Child Bks.
Patron, Susan. Dark Cloud Strong Breeze. Catalanotto, Peter, illus. LC 93-4873. (gr. 5 up). 1994. write for info. (*0-531-06815-3*); PLB write for info. (*0-531-08665-8*) Orchard Bks Watts.
Peck, Richard. Father Figure. (gr. k-12). 1988. pap. 3.99 (*0-440-20069-5*, LFL) Dell.
Pellowski, Michael J. My Father, the Enemy, No. 8. LC 91-58615. (Illus.). 128p. (gr. 4-8). 1992. pap. 2.99 (*1-56282-189-X*) Hyprn Child.
Petersen, P. J. I Want Answers & a Parachute. DiVito, Anna, illus. LC 92-38262. (gr. 6 up). 1993. pap. 13.00 (*0-671-86577-3*, S&S BFYR) S&S Trade.
Pfeffer, Susan B. Dear Dad, Love Laurie. (gr. 4-6). 1990. pap. 2.75 (*0-590-41682-0*) Scholastic Inc.
Porter, Bruce. The Parable of Pa Diggle's Son. Porter, Bruce, illus. 40p. (Orig.). (gr. 3 up). 1987. pap. 3.95 (*0-939925-11-7*) R C Law & Co.
Porter-Gaylord, Laurel. I Love My Daddy Because... Wolff, Ashley, illus. LC 90-2865. 24p. (ps). 1991. 5.95 (*0-525-44624-9*, DCB) Dutton Child Bks.
Quinlan, Patricia. My Dad Takes Care of Me. Van Kampen, Vlasta, illus. 24p. (ps-3). 1987. PLB 14.95 (*0-920303-79-X*, Pub. by Annick CN); pap. 4.95 (*0-920303-76-5*, Pub. by Annick CN) Firefly Bks Ltd.
Random, Candice F. Jimmy Crack Corn. Haas, Shelly O., illus. LC 93-16657. 1993. 7.00 (*0-87614-786-4*) Carolrhoda Bks.
Ray, Deborah K. My Daddy Was a Soldier: A World War Two Story. Ray, Deborah K., illus. LC 89-20056. 40p. (ps-4). 1990. reinforced bdg. 12.95 (*0-8234-0795-0*) Holiday.
Reynolds, Marilyn. Too Soon for Jeff. 224p. (Orig.). (gr. 7 up). 1994. 15.95 (*0-930934-90-3*); pap. 8.95 (*0-930934-91-1*) Morning Glory.
Riddell, Ruth. Ice Warrior. LC 91-29506. 144p. (gr. 4-7). 1992. SBE 13.95 (*0-689-31710-7*, Atheneum Child Bk) Macmillan Child Grp.
Roberts, Bethany. The Two O'Clock Secret. Grant, Christy, ed. Kramer, Robin, illus. LC 92-6405. 32p. (ps-2). 1993. 13.95g (*0-8075-8159-3*) A Whitman.

—Waiting-for-Papa Stories. Stapler, Sarah, illus. LC 89-36589. 32p. (ps-3). 1990. HarpC Child Bks.
Roop, Peter & Roop, Connie. Ahyoka & the Talking Leaves. Miyake, Yoshi, illus. LC 91-3036. (gr. 1 up). 1992. text ed. 12.00 (*0-688-10697-8*) Lothrop.
Rosen, David. Henry's Tower. Feldman, Lynne, illus. LC 84-61581. 36p. (gr. k-5). 1984. 10.95 (*0-930905-01-6*); pap. 4.95 (*0-930905-00-8*) Platypus Bks.
Ryder, Joanne. My Father's Hands. Graham, Mark, illus. LC 93-27116. 1994. write for info. (*0-688-09189-X*); PLB write for info. (*0-688-09190-3*) Morrow Jr Bks.
Sachar, Louis. Monkey Soup. Smith, Cat B., illus. LC 91-15858. 32p. (ps-3). 1992. 12.00 (*0-679-80297-5*); PLB 13.99 (*0-679-90297-X*) Knopf Bks Yng Read.
Seeger, Pete. Abiyoyo: Based on a South African Lullaby & Folk Story. Hays, Michael, illus. LC 85-15341. 48p. (ps-4). 1986. RSBE 15.95 (*0-02-781490-4*, Macmillan Child Bk) Macmillan Child Grp.
Shaw, Richard C. My Dad Sells Insurance. Snyder, Dan, illus. 40p. (ps-5). 1988. PLB write for info. (*0-944900-00-3*) Shaw & Co.
Shusterman, Neal. What Daddy Did. 1991. pap. 15.95 (*0-316-78906-2*) Little.
Simpson, Juwairiah J. The Four Daughters of Yusuf the Dairy Farmer. Middendorf, Nancy, illus. 40p. (Orig.). (gr. 1-4). 1894. pap. 3.75 (*0-89259-056-4*) Am Trust Pubns.
—A Wicked Wazir. Sakkal, Ma'moun, illus. 48p. (Orig.). (gr. 3-6). 1990. pap. 6.50 (*0-89259-084-X*) Am Trust Pubns.
Smath, Jerry. Pretzel & Pop's Closetful of Stories. Smath, Jerry, illus. 64p. (gr. 1-3). 1991. 5.95 (*0-671-72232-8*); PLB 7.95 (*0-671-72231-X*) Silver Pr.
Smith, Eddie. A Lullaby for Daddy. Anderson, Susan, illus. LC 94-9773. 32p. (ps-k). 1994. 16.95 (*0-86543-403-4*); pap. 8.95 (*0-86543-404-2*) Africa World.
Smith, Kaitlin M. It's Time, Dad. Smith, Kaitlin M., illus. 15p. (gr. k-3). 1992. pap. 15.95 (*1-895583-16-0*) MAYA Pubs.
Spinelli, Eileen. Boy, Can He Dance! Yalowitz, Paul, illus. LC 92-12929. 32p. (ps-2). 1993. RSBE 14.95 (*0-02-786350-6*, Four Winds) Macmillan Child Grp.
Spohn, David. Home Field. LC 92-5459. 1993. 10.00 (*0-688-11172-6*); lib. bdg. 9.93 (*0-688-11173-4*) Lothrop.
Stafford, Kim R. We Got Here Together. Frasier, Debra, illus. LC 93-9814. (gr. 5 up). 1994. 13.95 (*0-15-294891-0*) HarBrace.
Steel, Danielle. Martha's New Daddy. Rogers, Jacqueline, illus. (ps-2). 1989. 8.95 (*0-385-29799-8*) Delacorte.
Steptoe, John L. Daddy Is a Monster...Sometimes. Steptoe, John L., illus. LC 77-4464. 32p. (gr. k-3). 1980. PLB 13.89 (*0-397-31893-6*, Lipp Jr Bks) HarpC Child Bks.
—Daddy Is a Monster...Sometimes. LC 77-4464. (Illus.). 32p. (gr. k-3). 1983. pap. 6.95 (*0-06-443042-1*, Trophy) HarpC Child Bks.
Talbert, Marc. The Purple Heart. LC 91-23084. 144p. (gr. 4-8). 1992. 14.00 (*0-06-020428-1*); PLB 13.89 (*0-06-020429-X*) HarpC Child Bks.
Taylor, Sydney. A Papa Like Everyone Else. (gr. k-6). 1989. pap. 2.95 (*0-440-40129-1*, YB) Dell.
Tedrow, T. L. Days of Laura Ingalls Wilder, Vol. 4: Home to the Prairie. 1992. pap. 4.99 (*0-8407-3401-8*) Nelson.
Todd, Leonard. Squaring Off. (gr. 7 up). 1990. 13.95 (*0-670-83377-0*) Viking Child Bks.
Valentine, Johnny. The Daddy Machine. Schmidt, Lynette, illus. 48p. (Orig.). (gr. k-4). 1992. pap. 6.95 (*1-55583-107-9*, Alyson Wonderland) Alyson Pubns.
—One Dad, Two Dads, Brown Dad, Blue Dads. Sarecky, Melody, illus. 32p. (ps-1). 1994. 10.95 (*1-55583-253-9*, Alyson Wonderland) Alyson Pubns.
Voigt, Cynthia. Sons from Afar. LC 87-1857. 224p. (gr. 7 up). 1987. SBE 15.95 (*0-689-31349-7*, Atheneum Child Bk) Macmillan Child Grp.
Wadsworth, Ginger. Tomorrow Is Daddy's Birthday. Chambliss, Maxie, illus. LC 92-71870. 32p. (ps-1). 1994. 14.95 (*1-56397-042-2*) Boyds Mills Pr.
Watanabe, Shigeo. Where's My Daddy? (ps-3). 1996. pap. 5.95 (*0-399-22427-0*, Philomel Bks) Putnam Pub Group.
Welty, Harry R. Visit to the Attic. Lee, Marlene K., illus. LC 92-90838. 250p. (Orig.). (gr. 6-8). 1992. pap. 6.95 (*0-9632953-0-6*) Welty Pr.
Wyeth, Sharon D. Always My Dad. Colon, Raoul, illus. LC 93-43755. 40p. (ps-3). 1995. 15.00 (*0-679-83447-8*, Apple Soup Bks); PLB 15.99 (*0-679-93447-2*, Apple Soup Bks) Knopf Bks Yng Read.
Yolen, Jane. All Those Secrets of the World. (ps-3). 1991. 14.95 (*0-316-96891-9*) Little.
Young, David C. A Father's Love. Whitaker, Angela, illus. 24p. 1993. 14.00 (*0-9638833-0-5*) Yng & Yng Prods.
Ziefert, Harriet. When Daddy Had the Chicken Pox. Kalish, Lionel, illus. LC 90-43559. 32p. (ps-3). 1991. HarpC Child Bks.

FAUNA

see Animals; Zoology

FEAR

see also Courage

Barsuhn, Rochelle N. Feeling Afraid. Connelly, Gwen, illus. LC 82-19946. (ps-2). 1983. PLB 14.95 (*0-89565-246-3*) Childs World.
Frandsen, Karen G. I'd Rather Get a Spanking Than Go to the Doctor. Frandsen, Karen G., illus. LC 86-11735. 32p. (ps-3). 1987. pap. 3.95 (*0-516-43498-5*) Childrens.
Gackenbach, Dick. Harry & the Terrible Whatzit. Gackenbach, Dick, illus. LC 76-40205. 32p. (ps-3). 1979. 14.45 (*0-395-28795-2*, Clarion Bks) HM.
Greene, Leia A. Who's Afraid of the Dark? Greene, Leia A., illus. 32p. (gr. k-12). 1992. pap. text ed. 4.95 (*1-880737-09-4*) Crystal Jrns.
Hipp, Earl. Fighting Invisible Tigers: A Stress Management Guide for Teens. Galbraith, Judy, intro. by. LC 85-80632. (Illus.). 120p. (Orig.). (gr. 6-12). 1985. pap. 9.95 (*0-915793-04-0*) Free Spirit Pub.
Jones, Rebecca C. I Am Not Afraid. (Illus.). (ps). 1987. pap. 2.50 (*0-570-09113-6*, 56-1588) Concordia.
Koplow, Lesley. Tanya & the Tobo Man: A Story for Children Entering Therapy. LC 91-85. (SPA & ENG., Illus.). 32p. (ps-4). 1991. 16.95 (*0-945354-34-7*); pap. 6.95 (*0-945354-33-9*) Magination Pr.
—Tanya & the Tobo Man: A Story for Children Entering Therapy. Velasquez, Eric, illus. LC 92-56875. 1993. PLB 17.27 (*0-8368-0936-X*) Gareth Stevens Inc.
Maloney, Michael. Straight Talk about Anxiety & Depression. 1993. pap. 3.99 (*0-440-21472-6*) Dell.
Nardo, Don. Anxiety & Phobias. (Illus.). 112p. (gr. 6-12). 1992. 18.95 (*0-7910-0041-9*) Chelsea Hse.
Newman, Susan. Dont Be S. A. D. A Teenage Guide to Handling Stress, Anxiety & Depression. 1991. lib. bdg. 12.98 (*0-671-72610-2*, J Messner); lib. bdg. 7.95 (*0-671-72611-0*, J Messner) S&S Trade.
Stein, Sara B. About Phobias. LC 78-65615. (Illus.). 48p. (ps-8). 1984. pap. text ed. 8.95 (*0-8027-7219-6*) Walker & Co.
—About Phobias. Stone, Erika, illus. (ps-8). 1979. 10.95 (*0-8027-6348-0*) Walker & Co.

FEAR–FICTION

Arrington, Frances. Stella's Bull. Arrington, Aileen, illus. LC 93-29068. 1994. 14.95 (*0-395-67345-3*) HM.
Auch, Mary J. Monster Brother. LC 93-41746. (Illus.). 32p. (ps-3). 1994. reinforced bdg. 15.95 (*0-8234-1095-1*) Holiday.
Ball, Karen. The Overnight Ordeal. LC 93-40182. 1994. 4.99 (*0-8423-5134-5*) Tyndale.
Balter, Lawrence. Linda Saves the Day: Understanding Fear. Schanzer, Roz, illus. 40p. (ps-2). 1989. 5.95 (*0-8120-6117-9*) Barron.
Bannah, Max. Bulldog George. LC 93-20807. 1994. 4.25 (*0-383-03739-5*) SRA Schl Grp.
Bauer, Marion D. Face to Face. 192p. (gr. 5-9). 1991. 13.45 (*0-395-55440-3*, Clarion Bks) HM.
Benson, Rita. What Angela Needs. McClelland, Linda, illus. LC 92-34266. 1993. 14.00 (*0-383-03666-6*) SRA Schl Grp.
Berenstain, Stan & Berenstain, Jan. The Berenstain Bears & the Galloping Ghost. Berenstain, Stan & Berenstain, Jan, illus. 112p. (Orig.). (gr. 2-6). 1994. 7.99 (*0-679-95815-0*); pap. 2.99 (*0-679-85815-6*) Random Bks Yng Read.
—The Berenstain Bears & Too Much Pressure. Berenstain, Stan & Berenstain, Jan, illus. LC 92-6544. 32p. (Orig.). (ps-1). 1992. PLB 5.99 (*0-679-93671-8*); pap. 2.50 (*0-679-83671-3*) Random Bks Yng Read.
—Los Osos Berenstain en la Oscuridad. Guibert, Rita, tr. from ENG. Berenstain, Stan & Berenstain, Jan, illus. LC 91-51092. (SPA.). 32p. (ps-3). 1992. pap. 2.25 (*0-679-83471-0*) Random Bks Yng Read.
Berenstain, Stan & Berenstain, Janice. The Berenstain Bears Get Stage Fright. Berenstain, Stan & Berenstain, Janice, illus. LC 85-25716. 32p. (gr. 3-6). 1986. lib. bdg. 5.99 (*0-394-97337-2*); pap. 2.25 (*0-394-87337-8*) Random Bks Yng Read.
Bond, Felicia. Poinsettia & the Firefighters. LC 83-46169. (Illus.). 32p. (ps-3). 1984. PLB 15.89 (*0-690-04401-1*, Crowell Jr Bks) HarpC Child Bks.
Bonsall, Crosby N. Who's Afraid of the Dark? LC 79-2700. (Illus.). 32p. (ps-3). 1980. PLB 13.89 (*0-06-020599-7*) HarpC Child Bks.
Bourgeois, Paulette. Franklin Is Lost. (ps-3). 1993. pap. 3.95 (*0-590-46255-5*) Scholastic Inc.
Browne, Anthony. Changes. Browne, Anthony, illus. LC 90-4283. 32p. (ps-3). 1991. 14.95 (*0-679-81029-3*); PLB 15.99 (*0-679-91029-8*) Knopf Bks Yng Read.
—The Tunnel. Browne, Anthony, illus. (gr. 4-8). 1990. 14.00 (*0-394-84582-X*); lib. bdg. 12.99 (*0-394-94582-4*) Random Bks Yng Read.
Buck, Nola. The Basement Stairs. Lambert, Jonathan, illus. 16p. (ps-2). 1994. 4.95 (*0-694-00649-1*, Festival) HarpC Child Bks.
Bunting, Eve. The Undersea People. (Illus.). 64p. (gr. 3-8). 1992. 8.95 (*0-89565-766-X*) Childs World.
Carlson, Nancy. What If It Never Stops Raining? Carlson, Nancy, illus. 32p. (ps-3). 1992. 14.00 (*0-670-81775-9*) Viking Child Bks.
Carlsruh, Dan K. The Cannibals of Sunset Drive. LC 92-40568. 144p. (gr. 3-7). 1993. SBE 13.95 (*0-02-717110-8*, Macmillan Child Bk) Macmillan Child Grp.
Christelow, Eileen. Henry & the Dragon. Christelow, Eileen, illus. LC 83-14405. 32p. (ps-2). 1984. 13.45 (*0-89919-220-3*, Clarion Bks) HM.
Church, Kristine. My Brother John. Niland, Kilmeny, illus. LC 90-25868. 32p. (ps-3). 1991. 12.95 (*0-688-10800-8*, Tambourine Bks); PLB 12.88 (*0-688-10801-6*, Tambourine Bks) Morrow.
Colman, Penny. Dark Closets & Noises in the Night. 1991. pap. 3.95 (*0-8091-6600-3*) Paulist Pr.
Cooper, Helen. The Bear under the Stairs. Cooper, Helen, illus. LC 92-23840. (ps-2). 1993. 12.99 (*0-8037-1279-0*) Dial Bks Young.
Dalgliesh, Alice. The Courage of Sarah Noble. Weisgard, Leonard, illus. LC 54-5922. 64p. (gr. 1-5). 1987. Repr. of 1954 ed. SBE 13.95 (*0-684-18830-9*, Scribners Young Read) Macmillan Child Grp.
Daniel, Kate. Running Scared. 1993. pap. 3.50 (*0-06-106728-8*, Harp PBks) HarpC.
Derby, Sally. King Kendrick's Splinter. Gore, Leonid, illus. LC 94-4360. 1994. write for info. (*0-8027-8322-8*); Reinforced. write for info. (*0-8027-8323-6*) Walker & Co.
Devlin, Wende & Devlin, Harry. Maggie Has a Nightmare. LC 93-45818. (ps-1). 1994. pap. 2.95 (*0-689-71778-4*, Aladdin) Macmillan Child Grp.
Dutro, Jack. Night Light: A Story for Children Afraid of the Dark. Boyle, Kenneth, illus. LC 91-19612. 32p. (ps-4). 1991. 16.95 (*0-945354-37-1*); pap. 6.95 (*0-945354-38-X*) Magination Pr.
Elsant, Martin. Bar Mitzvah Lessons. LC 93-628. 1993. write for info. (*1-88128-301-1*) Alef Design.
Emberley, Ed. Go Away, Big Green Monster! (ps-3). 1993. 12.95 (*0-316-23653-5*) Little.
Escudie, Rene. Little John's Fears. (Illus.). (gr. 3-8). 1992. PLB 8.95 (*0-89565-886-0*) Childs World.
Freschet, Bernice. Furlie Cat. Lewin, Betsy, illus. LC 85-11656. 32p. (ps-3). 1986. 12.95 (*0-688-05917-1*) Lothrop.
Gleeson, Libby. The Great Big Scary Dog. Greder, Armin, illus. LC 93-13398. 32p. (ps up). 1994. 15.00 (*0-688-11293-5*, Tambourine Bks); PLB 14.93 (*0-688-11294-3*, Tambourine Bks) Morrow.
Gottlieb, Dale. Big Dog. (Illus.). 32p. (ps-3). 1992. pap. 3.99 (*0-14-054431-3*) Puffin Bks.
Grambling, Lois. Elephant & Mouse Celebrate Halloween. Maze, Deborah, illus. (ps-1). 1991. 12.95 (*0-8120-6186-1*); pap. 5.95 (*0-8120-4761-3*) Barron.
Gruber, Suzanne. Monster under My Bed. Britt, Stephanie, illus. LC 84-45687. 32p. (gr. k-2). 1985. PLB 10.89 (*0-8167-0456-2*); pap. text ed. 2.95 (*0-8167-0457-0*) Troll Assocs.
Hall, Kirsten. I'm Not Scared. (Illus.). 28p. (ps-2). 1994. PLB 14.00 (*0-516-05366-3*); pap. 3.95 (*0-516-45366-1*) Childrens.
Harrison, Joanna. Dear Bear. LC 93-44730. 1994. 18.95 (*0-87614-839-9*) Carolrhoda Bks.
Hazen, Barbara S. Alone at Home. Trivas, Irene, illus. LC 91-15878. 64p. (gr. 2-4). 1992. SBE 13.95 (*0-689-31691-7*, Atheneum Child Bk) Macmillan Child Grp.
—The Knight Who Was Afraid to Fight. Goffe, Toni, photos by. LC 93-4608. 1994. write for info. (*0-8037-1591-9*); lib. bdg. write for info. (*0-8037-1592-7*) Dial Bks Young.
Henkes, Kevin. Words of Stone. LC 91-28543. (gr. 5-12). 1992. 13.00 (*0-688-11356-7*) Greenwillow.
—Words of Stone. LC 93-7488. 160p. (gr. 4-7). 1993. pap. 3.99 (*0-14-036601-6*, Puffin) Puffin Bks.
Hesse, Karen. Lester's Dog. Carpenter, Nancy, illus. LC 92-27674. 32p. (ps-2). 1993. 13.00 (*0-517-58357-7*); PLB 13.99 (*0-517-58358-5*) Crown Bks Yng Read.
Hest, Amy. A Sort-of Sailor. Rockwell, Lizzie, illus. LC 89-38252. 32p. (gr. k-3). 1990. RSBE 13.95 (*0-02-743641-1*, Four Winds) Macmillan Child Grp.
Himmelman, John. Lights Out! LC 93-33811. (Illus.). 32p. (gr. k-3). 1995. PLB 14.95 (*0-8167-3450-X*); pap. text ed. 4.95 (*0-8167-3451-8*) BrdgeWater.
Honeycutt, Natalie. Whistle Home. Cannon, Annie, illus. LC 92-47052. 32p. (ps-1). 1993. 14.95 (*0-531-05490-X*); PLB 14.99 (*0-531-08640-2*) Orchard Bks Watts.
Howe, James. Pinky & Rex Go to Camp. Sweet, Melissa, illus. LC 91-16123. 48p. (ps-3). 1992. SBE 12.95 (*0-689-31718-2*, Atheneum Child Bk) Macmillan Child Grp.
Hurwitz, Johanna. The Up & Down Spring. Owens, Gail, illus. LC 92-21337. 112p. (gr. 3 up). 1993. 14.00 (*0-688-11922-0*) Morrow Jr Bks.
Inkpen, Mick. Penguin Small. (ps-3). 1993. pap. 14.95 (*0-15-200567-6*) HarBrace.
Jannson, Tove. The Fillyjonk Who Believed in Disasters. 32p. (gr. 6). 1990. PLB 13.95 (*0-88682-299-8*) Creative Ed.

Johnson, Nancy E. The Magic Blanket That Made All Dreams Happy! Johnson, Nancy E., illus. 42p. (ps-1). 1994. Set incl. blanket, stars 29.95 (*0-9642307-0-4*) TotTales.
THE MAGIC BLANKET THAT MADE ALL DREAMS HAPPY!, first in a series of TotTale(tm) books, is designed not only for enjoyment, but to address fears common to many young children. The lighthearted verse in THE MAGIC BLANKET tells the story of a young prince afraid to go to bed because of frightening dreams. Accompanied by au naturel pictures, a 45" X 60" 100% Polyester OWENS Toddler Blanket, & 20 1/2" glow-in-

the-dark gold stars, (& with a little "reader" help!), the story, the magic blanket & the brightly glowing stars offer a warm solution to those youngsters with vivid nocturnal imaginations. The set comes in a sturdy, bright white box with a see-through lid, making it an ideal gift. THE MAGIC BLANKET THAT MADE ALL DREAMS HAPPY! is available through the Tattered Cover Book Store in Denver, Colorado, (303-322-7727). The set is also being made available to child care centers through the distributor, TotTales(tm) (303-797-8722). Nancy E. Johnson is also the author of the popular dog obedience book, EVERYDAY DOG.
Publisher Provided Annotation.

Klein, Norma. Visiting Pamela. Chorao, Kay, illus. LC 78-72203. (ps-3). 1979. Dial Bks Young.
Koralek, Jenny. The Boy & the Cloth of Dreams. Mayhew, James, illus. LC 93-23091. 32p. (ps up). 1994. 14.95 (*1-56402-349-4*) Candlewick Pr.
Krakauer, Hoong Y. Rabbit Mooncakes. LC 92-23409. 1994. 15.95 (*0-316-50327-4*, Joy St Bks) Little.
Krensky, Stephen. Fraidy Cats. Lewin, Betsy, illus. LC 92-35360. (gr. 3 up). 1993. 2.95 (*0-590-46438-8*) Scholastic Inc.
Lankton, Stephen R. The Blammo-Surprise! Book: A Story to Help Children Overcome Fears. LC 88-13566. (Illus.). 48p. (gr. 1 up). 1988. PLB 16.95 (*0-945354-11-8*); pap. 6.95 (*0-945354-10-X*) Magination Pr.
Leonard, Alain. Barnaby & the Big Gorilla. LC 91-25414. (Illus.). 32p. (ps-3). 1992. 15.00 (*0-688-11291-9*, Tambourine Bks); PLB 14.93 (*0-688-11292-7*, Tambourine Bks) Morrow.
LeRoy, Gen. Cold Feet. 192p. (gr. 7 up). 1986. pap. 1.75 (*0-440-91336-5*, LE) Dell.
Leverich, Kathleen. Brigid, Bewitched. Andreasen, Dan, illus. LC 93-43221. 80p. (Orig.). (gr. 1-4). 1994. PLB 9.99 (*0-679-95433-3*); pap. 2.99 (*0-679-85433-9*) Random Bks Yng Read.
Littke, Lael. There's a Snake at Girls' Camp. LC 94-751. (Orig.). (gr. 3-7). 1994. pap. 4.95 (*0-87579-845-4*) Deseret Bk.
McCully, Emily A. Mirette on the Highwire. (Illus.). 32p. (ps-3). 1992. 14.95 (*0-399-22130-1*, Putnam) Putnam Pub Group.
Marcus, Irene W. & Marcus, Paul. Scary Night Visitors: A Story for Children with Bedtime Fears. Jeschke, Susan, illus. LC 90-41919. 32p. (ps-2). 1990. 16.95 (*0-945354-26-6*); pap. 6.95 (*0-945354-25-8*) Magination Pr.
—Scary Night Visitors: A Story for Children with Bedtime Fears. Jeschke, Susan, illus. LC 92-56874. 1993. PLB 17.27 (*0-8368-0935-1*) Gareth Stevens Inc.
Melton, David. A Boy Called Hopeless. Melton, Todd, illus. LC 86-27557. 231p. (gr. 4-8). 1986. Repr. of 1976 ed. PLB 13.95 (*0-933849-32-X*) Landmark Edns.
Michelson, Richard. Did You Say Ghosts? Baskin, Leonard, illus. LC 92-30134. 32p. (ps up). 1993. RSBE 14.95 (*0-02-766915-7*, Macmillan Child Bk) Macmillan Child Grp.
Morris, Winifred. What If the Shark Wears Tennis Shoes? Lewin, Betsy, illus. LC 89-38150. 32p. (gr. k-3). 1990. SBE 13.95 (*0-689-31587-2*, Atheneum Child Bk) Macmillan Child Grp.
Napoli, Donna J. When the Water Closes over My Head. Poydar, Nancy, illus. LC 93-14486. 60p. (gr. 2-5). 1994. 13.99 (*0-525-45083-1*) Dutton Child Bks.
Naylor, Phyllis R. The Fear Place. LC 93-38891. (gr. 3-7). 1994. 14.95 (*0-689-31866-9*, Atheneum Child Bk) Macmillan Child Grp.
The Night Light. (Illus.). (ps-2). 1991. PLB 6.95 (*0-8136-5112-3*, TK2254); pap. 3.50 (*0-8136-5612-5*, TK2255) Modern Curr.
O'Donnell, Peter. Moonlit Journey. (ps-3). 1991. 13.95 (*0-590-44655-X*) Scholastic Inc.
Olofsdotter, Marie. Sofia & the Heartmender. Olofsdotter, Marie, illus. LC 92-46200. 32p. (gr. k up). 1993. 14.95 (*0-915793-50-4*) Free Spirit Pub.
Pittman, Helena C. Once When I Was Scared. Rand, Ted, illus. LC 88-3598. 32p. (gr. k-3). 1988. 14.00 (*0-525-44407-6*, DCB) Dutton Child Bks.
—Once When I Was Scared. Rand, Ted, illus. 36p. (ps-3). 1993. pap. 4.99 (*0-14-054932-3*, Puff Unicorn) Puffin Bks.
Ploetz, Craig T. Milo's Friends in the Dark. Koslowski, Richard K., illus. 32p. (ps-4). 1992. PLB 11.95 (*1-882172-00-0*) Milo Prods.
Rae, Judy. Bye, Bye Boogieman. Rev. ed. Lalo, illus. Timm, Stephen A., intro. by. LC 83-70412. (Illus.). 42p. (Orig.). (ps-3). 1984. pap. 3.95 (*0-939728-09-5*) Steppingstone Ent.
Riley, Sue. Afraid. LC 77-15627. (Illus.). (ps-2). 1978. PLB 12.95 (*0-89565-011-8*) Childs World.
Rodgers, Frank. Who's Afraid of the Ghost Train? Rodgers, Frank, illus. 23p. (ps-1). 1989. 12.95 (*0-15-200642-7*, Gulliver Bks) HarBrace.
Rosenblatt, Lily. Fire Diary. Grant, Christy, ed. Friedman, Judith, illus. LC 93-45917. 32p. (gr. 2-5). 1994. PLB 13.95 (*0-8075-2439-5*) A Whitman.
Sarai. The Apple Tree That Would Not Let Go of Its Apples. Kozjak, Goran, illus. McNulty, Linda, intro. by. (Illus.). 28p. (Orig.). 1993. pap. 11.50 (*0-938837-13-3*) Behav Sci Ctr Pubs.
—Frieda the Goodnight Fairy. Kozjak, Goran, illus. McNulty, Linda, intro. by. (Illus.). 28p. (Orig.). 1993. pap. 11.50 (*0-938837-12-5*) Behav Sci Ctr Pubs.
Shaw, Charles. What's in the Dark? (Illus.). 32p. (gr. k-4). 1991. 11.95 (*0-938349-66-X*); pap. 5.95 (*0-938349-67-8*) State House Pr.
Shaw, Diana. Lessons in Fear. 176p. (gr. 7 up). 1988. pap. 2.50 (*0-8167-1315-4*) Troll Assocs.
Skoglund, Elizabeth. Harold's Dog Horace Is Scared of the Dark. Bjorkman, Dale, illus. 48p. (gr. 2). 1992. pap. 2.99 (*0-8423-1047-9*) Tyndale.
Skoglund, Elizabeth R. Alfred MacDuff Is Afraid of War. Johnson, Meredith, illus. 48p. (ps-2). 1991. pap. 3.99 (*0-8423-0032-5*) Tyndale.
Snyder, Zilpha K. Fool's Gold. (gr. 4-7). 1994. pap. 3.50 (*0-440-40952-7*) Dell.
Taylor, Maureen. Without Warning. LC 91-12470. 144p. 1991. pap. 4.99 (*0-8066-2538-4*, 9-2538) Augsburg Fortress.
Teague, Mark. The Field Beyond the Outfield. 32p. 1992. 14.95 (*0-590-45173-1*, Scholastic Hardcover) Scholastic Inc.
Tester, Sylvia R. Sometimes I'm Afraid. Hook, Frances, illus. LC 78-23262. (ps-3). 1979. PLB 14.95 (*0-89565-021-5*) Childs World.
Thaler, Mike. The Schmo Must Go On. Lee, Jared, illus. LC 93-4317. 32p. (gr. k-3). 1994. lib. bdg. 9.89 (*0-8167-3519-0*); pap. 2.95 (*0-8167-3520-4*) Troll Assocs.
Trent, John T. There's a Duck in My Closet. Love, Judy, illus. LC 93-15707. (gr. k-5). 1993. 12.99 (*0-8499-1037-4*) Word Pub.
Waddell, Martin. Let's Go Home, Little Bear. Firth, Barbara, illus. LC 92-53003. 32p. (ps up). 1993. 14.95 (*1-56402-131-9*) Candlewick Pr.
Walsh, Ellen S. Pip's Magic. (ps-3). 1994. 13.95 (*0-15-292850-2*) HarBrace.
Wardlaw, Lee. The Eye & I. Stouffer, Deborah, illus. LC 88-15664. 75p. (Orig.). (gr. 3-6). 1988. pap. 3.50 (*0-931093-10-4*) Red Hen Pr.
Weston, Martha. Tuck in the Pool. LC 94-7408. 1995. write for info. (*0-395-65479-3*, Clarion Bks) HM.
Wittmann, Patricia. Scrabble Creek. Poydar, Nancy, illus. LC 92-10810. 32p. (gr. k-3). 1993. RSBE 14.95 (*0-02-793225-7*, Macmillan Child Bk) Macmillan Child Grp.
Wolff, Mia. Catcher. LC 93-33802. (ps-2). 1994. 15.00 (*0-374-31227-3*) FS&G.
Wood, Audrey. Scaredy Cats. Wood, Audrey, illus. LC 90-46913. 32p. (ps-2). 1989. 7.95 (*0-85953-110-4*); pap. 3.95 (*0-85953-323-9*) Childs Play.

FEASTS
see Fasts and Feasts
FEDERATION, INTERNATIONAL
see International Organization
FEDERATION OF EUROPE
see European Federation
FEEBLE MINDED
see Mentally Handicapped
FEELING
see Perception; Touch
FEELINGS
see Emotions
FEET
see Foot
FELLOWSHIPS
see Scholarships, Fellowships, Etc.
FELONY
see Crime and Criminals
FEMINISM
see also Women'S Rights

Carabillo, Toni & Meuli, Judith. The Feminization of Power. Smeal, Eleanor, intro. by. (Illus.). 166p. (Orig.). (gr. 8-12). 1988. pap. 8.95 (*0-929037-02-2*) Fund Feminist Majority.
Chafe, William. The Road to Equality: American Women Since 1962. (Illus.). 144p. 1994. lib. bdg. 20.00 (*0-19-508325-3*) OUP.
Ellis, Patty. Girl Power: Making Choices & Taking Control. 200p. (Orig.). (gr. 6-11). 1994. pap. 9.95 (*1-879094-25-8*) Momentum Bks.
Hanmer, Trudy J. Taking a Stand Against Sexism & Sex Discrimination. LC 90-12567. (Illus.). 144p. (gr. 9-12). 1990. PLB 14.40 (*0-531-10962-3*) Watts.
Henry, Sondra & Taitz, Emily. Betty Friedan: Fighter for Women's Rights. LC 89-23582. (Illus.). 128p. (gr. 6 up). 1990. lib. bdg. 17.95 (*0-89490-292-X*) Enslow Pubs.
Hinding, Andrea, ed. Feminism: Opposing Viewpoints. LC 86-3096. (Illus.). 250p. (Orig.). (gr. 9 up). 1986. PLB 17.95 (*0-89908-388-9*); pap. 9.95 (*0-89908-363-3*) Greenhaven.
Hoff, Mark. Gloria Steinem: The Women's Movement. 1992. pap. 5.95 (*0-395-63567-5*) HM.
Taylor-Boyd, Susan. Betty Friedan. LC 90-9691. (Illus.). 64p. (gr. 5-6). 1990. PLB 19.93 (*0-8368-0104-0*) Gareth Stevens Inc.
Wagner, Shirley A. Equality Now: Safeguarding Women's Rights. LC 92-9746. 1992. PLB 22.60 (*0-86593-177-1*); 16.95s.p. (*0-685-59280-4*) Rourke Corp.
Wekesser, Carol, ed. Feminism: Opposing Viewpoints. LC 94-4974. (Illus.). 264p. (gr. 10 up). 1995. PLB 17.95 (*1-56510-178-2*); pap. text ed. 9.95 (*1-56510-179-0*) Greenhaven.

FERMENTATION
see also Bacteriology
FERMI, ENRICO, 1901-1954

Gottfried, Ted. Enrico Fermi. (Illus.). 128p. (gr. 5 up). 1992. PLB 16.95x (*0-8160-2623-8*) Facts on File.

FERNS

Greenway, Theresa. Ferns. LC 91-14935. (Illus.). 48p. (gr. 5-9). 1992. PLB 21.34 (*0-8114-2735-8*) Raintree Steck-V.

FERRIES

Conrad, Pam. Taking the Ferry Home. LC 87-45856. 224p. (gr. 7 up). 1990. pap. 3.95 (*0-06-447011-3*, Trophy) HarpC Child Bks.

FERRIES–FICTION

Maestro, Betsy. Ferryboat. Maestro, Giulio, illus. LC 85-47887. 32p. (ps-3). 1986. (Crowell Jr Bks); PLB 14.89 (*0-690-04520-4*) HarpC Child Bks.

FESTIVALS
see also Fasts and Feasts; Holidays; Pageants

Burden-Patmon, Denise & Jones, Kathryn D. Carnival. Ruffins, Reynold, illus. 32p. (gr. 2-5). 1993. pap. 4.95 (*0-671-79840-5*, S&S BYR) S&S Trade.
Carbotti, Richard. Summer Festivals. 8p. (gr. k-2). 1993. pap. write for info. (*1-882563-09-3*) Lamont Bks.
Crews, Donald. Carousel. Crews, Donald, illus. LC 82-3062. 32p. (ps-1). 1982. PLB 13.88 (*0-688-00909-3*) Greenwillow.
Geronimo Pack. 32p. (gr. k-2). 1993. pap. 8.95 (*1-882563-05-0*) Lamont Bks.
Li Shufen, ed. Legends of Ten Chinese Traditional Festivals. Zhan, Tong, illus. 54p. (gr. 1-3). 1992. pap. 8.95 (*0-8351-2560-2*) China Bks.
Oni, Sauda. What Kwanzaa Means to Me. Brother Theo, illus. 36p. (gr. k-3). Date not set. pap. 3.95 (*0-912444-38-X*) DARE Bks.
Riehecky, Janet. Japanese Boys' Festival. Stasiak, Krystyna, illus. LC 93-47639. (Illus.). 32p. (ps-2). 1994. PLB 16.40 (*0-516-00695-9*); pap. 3.95 (*0-516-40695-7*) Childrens.
Weilerstein, Sadie R. What the Moon Brought. (Illus.). 159p. (gr. 1-3). 1942. pap. 7.95 (*0-8276-0265-0*) JPS Phila.
Wersba, Barbara. The Carnival in My Mind. LC 81-48640. 224p. (gr. 7 up). 1982. PLB 12.89 (*0-06-026410-1*) HarpC Child Bks.

FESTIVALS–FICTION

Abler, David A. & Natti, Susanna. Cam Jansen & Mystery Carnival Prize. LC 84-3617. (Illus.). 64p. (gr. 2-5). 1984. pap. 10.95 (*0-670-20034-4*) Viking Child Bks.
Ballard, Robin. Carnival! LC 94-6267. (Illus.). 24p. 1995. write for info. (*0-688-13237-5*); PLB write for info. (*0-688-13238-3*) Greenwillow.
Dorros, Arthur. Tonight Is Carnaval. Club De Madres Virgen Del Carmen Staff, illus. LC 90-32391. 32p. (gr. k-3). 1991. 13.95 (*0-525-44641-9*, DCB) Dutton Child Bks.
Hall, Lynn. A Killing Freeze. LC 88-5143. 128p. (gr. 7 up). 1988. 12.95 (*0-688-07867-2*) Morrow Jr Bks.
Ingle, Annie. The Rabbits' Carnival. Bratun, Katy, illus. LC 92-29930. 24p. (Orig.). (ps-3). 1995. pap. 2.50 (*0-679-85337-5*) Random Bks Yng Read.
Kroll, Virginia L. A Carp for Kimiko. Roundtree, Katherine, illus. LC 93-6940. 32p. 1993. 14.95 (*0-88106-412-2*); PLB 15.88 (*0-88106-413-0*) Charlesbridge Pub.
Potter, Beatrix. The Tale of Jemima Puddle-duck. (Illus.). 64p. 1984. pap. 1.75 (*0-486-24634-5*) Dover.
Ross, Katharine. Bunnies' Ball. Bratun, Katy, illus. LC 92-29930. 1994. 2.50 (*0-679-83503-2*); lib. bdg. cancelled (*0-679-93503-7*) Random Bks Yng Read.

FESTIVALS–JEWS
see Fasts and Feasts–Judaism
FEUDALISM
see also Chivalry; Middle Ages

Biel, Timothy L. The Age of Feudalism. LC 93-19290. (gr. 6-9). 1994. 14.95 (*1-56006-232-0*) Lucent Bks.
Jones, Madeline. Knights & Castles. (Illus.). 72p. (gr. 7-11). 1991. 19.95 (*0-7134-6352-X*, Pub. by Batsford UK) Trafalgar.

FEVER
see also names of fevers, e.g. malaria, etc.
FIAT MONEY
see Paper Money
FIBERS
see also Cotton; Paper; Silk

Keeler, Patricia A. & McCall, Francis X., Jr. Unraveling Fibers. LC 93-13906. 1995. 16.00 (*0-689-31777-8*, Atheneum) Macmillan.

FICTION–HISTORY AND CRITICISM

Fabian, William M. Fiction Finder Manual. (gr. 4-12). 1984. 6.95 (*0-916625-08-7*) Computer Assis.
Greenwald, Sheila. It All Began with Jane Eyre: Or, the Secret Life of Franny Dillman. 128p. (gr. 5 up). 1981. pap. 1.75 (*0-440-94136-9*, LE) Dell.

FICTION–TECHNIQUE

Asher, Sandy. Where Do You Get Your Ideas? Hellard, Susan, illus. 96p. (gr. 5 up). 1987. 12.95 (*0-8027-6690-0*); PLB 13.85 (*0-8027-6691-9*) Walker & Co.

Bauer, Marion D. What's Your Story? A Young Person's Guide to Writing Fiction. 144p. (gr. 5 up). 1992. 13.45 (*0-395-57781-0*, Clarion Bks); pap. 6.70 (*0-395-57780-2*, Clarion Bks) HM.
Cameron, Eleanor. The Seed & the Vision: On the Writing & Appreciation of Children's Books. 400p. (gr. 10 up). 1993. 22.99 (*0-525-44949-3*, DCB) Dutton Child Bks.

FICTITIOUS ANIMALS
see Animals, Mythical

FIEFS
see Feudalism

FIELD, EUGENE, 1850-1895
Greene, Carol. Eugene Field: The Children's Poet. LC 93-42863. (Illus.). 48p. (gr. k-3). 1994. PLB 12.85 (*0-516-04259-9*) Childrens.

FIELD ATHLETICS
see Track Athletics

FIELD SPORTS
see Hunting; Sports

FIESTAS
see Fasts and Feasts

FIGHTER PLANES
Dahl, Roald. Going Solo. 224p. (gr. 7 up). 1993. pap. 4.99 (*0-14-032528-X*, Puffin) Puffin Bks.
Emert, Phyllis R. Fighter Planes. (Illus.). 64p. (gr. 5-9). 1990. PLB 12.98 (*0-671-68959-2*, J Messner); pap. 5.95 (*0-671-68964-9*) S&S Trade.
Lowe, Malcolm V. Fighters. Sarson, Peter, et al, illus. LC 84-7941. 48p. (gr. 5 up). 1985. PLB 13.50 (*0-8225-1376-5*, First Ave Edns); pap. 4.95 (*0-8225-9506-0*, First Ave Edns) Lerner Pubns.
Sullivan, George. Modern Fighter Planes. 128p. (gr. 6-10). 1991. lib. bdg. 17.95x (*0-8160-2352-2*) Facts on File.

FIGHTING
see Battles; Boxing; Bullfights; Self-Defense; War

FIGURE SKATING
see Skating

FIJI ISLANDS
Ball, John & Fairclough, Chris. Fiji. (Illus.). 96p. (gr. 5 up). 1988. 14.95 (*0-222-00984-5*) Chelsea Hse.

FINANCE
see also Banks and Banking; Commerce; Credit; Finance, Personal; Insurance; Investments; Money; Paper Money; Stock Exchange
Buhay, Debra. Black & White of Finance. 30p. (gr. 12). 1990. pap. 2.00 (*1-878056-02-6*) D Hockenberry.

FINANCE, PERSONAL
see also Insurance; Investments
Banks, Ann. It's My Money: A Kid's Guide to the Green Stuff. Natti, Susanna, illus. LC 93-12618. (gr. 3-7). 1993. 3.99 (*0-670-36086-4*) Puffin Bks.
Berry, Joy. Every Kid's Guide to Making & Managing Money. Bartholemew, illus. 48p. (gr. 3-7). 1986. 4.95 (*0-516-21405-5*) Childrens.
Burgeson, Nancy. The Money Book for Kids. LC 91-15108. (Illus.). 32p. (gr. 5-9). 1991. pap. text ed. 1.95 (*0-8167-2465-2*) Troll Assocs.
Drew, Bonnie J. & Drew, O. Noel. Fast Cash for Kids. (Illus.). 168p. (Orig.). (gr. 4-9). 1987. pap. 9.95 (*0-939445-01-8*) Homeland Pubns.
Financial Fitness. (gr. 7-12). 1989. Package of 10. 15.95 (*1-877844-03-9*, 2721) Meridian Educ.
Hechler, Ellen. Simulated Real Life Experiences Using Classified Ads in the Classroom. (Illus.). 54p. (Orig.). (gr. 6-10). 1991. pap. 10.00 (*0-9638483-3-X*) Midmath.
Hegeman, William R. & Whinnery, Alice J. Teen Talk: Money: How To Get It...Keep It...Avoid Getting Ripped Off! (Illus.). 160p. (Orig.). (gr. 8-12). 1994. pap. 14.95 (*0-9638808-0-2*) Finan Visions.
Jill, Jodi. Childrens Money Making Jobs. 32p. 1993. pap. 6.95 (*1-883438-04-7*) J J Features.
Jones, Vada L. Kids Can Make Money Too! How Young People Can Succeed Financially...Over 200 Ways to Earn Money & How to Make It Grow. LC 87-71607. (Illus., Orig.). (gr. 3-12). 1988. pap. 9.95 (*0-944104-00-2*) Calico Paws.
King, Chester. Common Cents Credit: Two Hundred Thirty Sense Wits to Keep You Out of the Red. 128p. 1993. text ed. 14.95 (*0-9639263-0-6*); pap. text ed. 9.95 (*0-9639263-1-4*) Che-King Pubng.
Long, J., ed. Budgeting Know-How. 48p. (gr. 4-5). 1988. pap. text ed. write for info. (*0-8428-7172-1*) Cambridge Bk.
Marsh, Carole. A Kid's Book of Smarts: How to Think, Make Decisions, Figure Things Out, Budget Your Time, Money, Plan Your Day, Week, Life & Other Things Adults Wish They'd Learned When They Were Kids! (Illus.). 68p. (gr. 4-12). 1994. PLB 24.95 (*1-55609-173-7*); pap. 14.95 (*0-935326-18-9*) Gallopade Pub Group.
Milios, Rita. Shopping Savvy. Rosen, Ruth, ed. (gr. 7-12). 1992. 13.95 (*0-8239-1455-0*) Rosen Group.
Olden, Diana J. & Smith, Vicki. Pendleton Pennywise Presents the Money Book - Just for You: A Budget Book for Children. 44p. (gr. 3-5). 1991. wirebound 11.95 (*0-9630463-0-6*) S & D.
Rendon, Marion B. & Kranz, Rachel. Straight Talk about Money. Ryan, Elizabeth A., ed. 128p. (gr. 7-12). 1992. lib. bdg. 16.95x (*0-8160-2612-2*) Facts on File.
Santamaria, Peggy. Money Smarts. Rosen, Ruth, ed. (gr. 7-12). 1992. 13.95 (*0-8239-1470-4*) Rosen Group.
Sullivan, Mick. Spare Time Cash: Every Student's Guide to Making Money on the Side. Moe, Mary, ed. 114p. (Orig.). (gr. 10 up). 1989. pap. 12.95 (*1-878330-00-4*) Sullivan MT.
Weathers, Lavern R. Start Smart: The Young Adult's Guide to Independent Living. Davis, Patty, ed. (Illus.). 70p. (Orig.). (gr. 9-12). 1994. pap. 8.95 (*0-9638608-0-1*) Strt Smart.
Wilkinson, Elizabeth. Making Cents: Every Kid's Guide to Money, Vol. 1. 1989. pap. 8.95 (*0-316-94102-6*) Little.

FINANCIERS
see Capitalists and Financiers

FINGER PLAY
Un Arana Encantadora - Spider Magic. LC 90-62626. (Illus.). 12p. 1991. bds. 5.95 incl. finger puppet (*1-877779-21-0*) Schneider Educational.
Brown, Marc T. Finger Rhymes. LC 80-10173. (Illus.). 32p. (ps-2). 1980. 12.95 (*0-525-29732-4*, DCB) Dutton Child Bks.
—Hand Rhymes. Brown, Marc T., illus. 32p. (ps-1). 1993. pap. 4.99 (*0-14-054939-0*, Puff Unicorn) Puffin Bks.
Cahill, Chris. Un Conejito Encantador - Bunny Magic. LC 90-62627. (Illus.). 12p. 1991. bds. 5.95 incl. finger puppet (*1-877779-20-2*) Schneider Educational.
—Un Osito Encantador - Bear Magic. LC 90-62628. (Illus.). 12p. 1991. bds. 5.95 incl. finger puppet (*1-877779-19-9*) Schneider Educational.
Cole, Joanna & Calmenson, Stephanie. Pat-a-Cake & Other Play Rhymes. ALC Staff, ed. Tiegreen, illus. LC 91-32264. 48p. (ps up). 1992. pap. 6.95 (*0-688-11533-0*, Mulberry) Morrow.
Cope, Wendy. Twiddling Your Thumbs: Hand Rhymes by Wendy Cope. 32p. (ps-3). 1992. pap. 6.95 (*0-571-16537-0*) Faber & Faber.

Finger Fun-ics: A Collection of Finger Plays, Action Verses & Songs. (Illus.). 1995. pap. text ed. 9.95 (*0-9635535-1-8*) Kinder Kollege.
FINGER FUN-ICS is a delightful series of fingerplays, action verses, & songs designed to encourage participatory learning & to develop language skills. FINGER FUN-ICS is an invaluable teaching tool for teachers & parents of preschoolers. The daily use of FINGER FUN-ICS strengthens a child's memory & attention span. Through happy play, children learn to follow directions cheerfully while having fun. FINGER FUN-ICS opens up exciting worlds to young children in simple language & catchy rhythms.
Publisher Provided Annotation.

Grayson, Marion. Let's Do Fingerplays. Weyl, Nancy, illus. LC 62-10217. (ps-3). 1962. 12.95 (*0-88331-003-1*) Luce.
Leslie, Amanda. Play Kitten Play: Ten Animal Fingerwiggles. Leslie, Amanda, illus. LC 91-58752. 10p. (ps up). 1992. 6.95 (*1-56402-088-6*) Candlewick Pr.
—Play Puppy Play: Ten Animal Fingerwiggles. Leslie, Amanda, illus. LC 91-58753. 10p. (ps up). 1992. 6.95 (*1-56402-087-8*) Candlewick Pr.
Lindsay, Vachel. Una Tortuga Encantadora - Turtle Magic. LC 90-62625. (Illus.). 12p. 1991. bds. 5.95 incl. finger puppet (*1-877779-22-9*) Schneider Educational.
Rosen, Michael J. Little Rabbit Foo Foo. Robins, Arthur, illus. LC 90-9598. 32p. (ps-1). 1993. pap. 4.95 (*0-671-79604-6*, Little Simon) S&S Trade.
Sclavi, Tiziano. Wiggle Your Fingers. Michelini, Carlo A., illus. 10p. (ps). 1994. bds. 4.95 (*1-56397-341-3*) Boyds Mills Pr.
Self, Margaret, compiled by. Two Hundred Two Things to Do. LC 68-16267. (Illus., Orig.). (gr. k-2). 1968. pap. 4.99 (*0-8307-0026-9*, 5001102) Regal.
Somerville, Sheila, illus. Five Little Pumpkins Big Book. (ps-2). 1988. pap. text ed. 14.00 (*0-922053-18-9*) N Edge Res.
Somerville, Sheila & Muren, Nancy L., illus. Finger Plays & Action Rhymes Big Book. (ps-2). 1988. pap. text ed. 15.00 (*0-922053-01-4*) N Edge Res.
Sutherland, Bob & Sutherland, Mary. Fun with Fingerplays. 50p. 1992. pap. 9.95 (*0-938293-03-6*) Fun Pub OH.
Weimer, Tonja E. Fingerplays & Action Chants: Animals, Vol. 1. Kozlina, Yvonne, illus. 42p. (Orig.). (gr. k-1). 1986. pap. text ed. 8.95 (*0-936823-00-3*); cassette 8.95 (*0-936823-01-1*) Pearce Evetts.
—Fingerplays & Action Chants: Family & Friends, Vol. 2. Kozlina, Yvonne, illus. 44p. (Orig.). (ps-1). 1986. pap. text ed. 8.95 (*0-936823-02-X*); cassette 8.95 (*0-936823-03-8*) Pearce Evetts.

FINGERPRINTS
Ahouse, Jeremy J. Fingerprinting. Bergman, Lincoln & Fairwell, Kay, eds. Klofkorn, Lisa, illus. Hoyt, Richard, photos by. (Illus.). 38p. (Orig.). (gr. 4-8). 1987. pap. 8.50 (*0-912511-21-4*) Lawrence Science.
Fingerprinting. 36p. (gr. 6-12). 1983. pap. 1.85 (*0-8395-3287-3*, 33287) BSA.

FINK, MIKE
Cohen, Caron L., retold by. Sally Ann Thunder Ann Whirlwind Crockett. Dewey, Ariane, illus. LC 92-24585. 40p. 1993. pap. 4.95 (*0-688-12331-7*, Mulberry) Morrow.

FINLAND
Hintz, Martin. Finland. LC 82-17856. (Illus.). 128p. (gr. 5-9). 1983. PLB 20.55 (*0-516-02764-6*) Childrens.
Lander, Patricia S. & Charbonneau, Claudette. The Land & People of Finland. LC 88-27144. (Illus.). 224p. (gr. 6 up). 1990. 18.00 (*0-397-32357-3*, Lipp Jr Bks); PLB 17.89 (*0-397-32358-1*, Lipp Jr Bks) HarpC Child Bks.

FINLAND–FICTION
Sharp, Mary & Niemi, Matt. Bobbi, Father of the Finnish White Tailed Deer. Shappell, Sherry, illus. LC 79-54100. (Orig.). (gr. 4-6). 1979. pap. 5.95 (*0-9603200-0-8*) Bobbi Ent.

FINNS IN THE U. S.–FICTION
Kingman, Lee. The Best Christmas. Cooney, Barbara, illus. LC 92-21152. 96p. (gr. 5 up). 1993. pap. 4.95 (*0-688-11838-0*, Pub. by Beech Tree Bks) Morrow.
Marvin, Isabel R. A Bride for Anna's Papa. LC 93-41175. (Illus.). 144p. 1994. pap. 6.95 (*0-915943-93-X*) Milkweed Ed.

FIR
Fischer-Nagel, Heiderose & Fischer-Nagel, Andreas. Fir Trees. Fischer-Nagel, Heidrose & Fischer-Nagel, Andreas, photos by. (Illus.). 48p. (gr. 2-5). 1989. 19.95 (*0-87614-340-0*) Carolrhoda Bks.

FIRE
see also Fires; Fuel; Heat
Ahbe, Dottie & Pluta, Terry. Safety Always Matters. Saba Designs, Inc. Staff & Ahbe, S., illus. 16p. (gr. 1-3). 1992. wkbk. 0.59 (*0-9620584-1-6*) Safety Always Matters.
—Safety Always Matters. Saba Designs, Inc. Staff & Ahbe, S., illus. 16p. (ps-k). 1992. wkbk. 0.59 (*0-9620584-0-8*) Safety Always Matters.
—Safety Always Matters. Saba Designs, Inc. Staff & Ahbe, S., illus. 16p. (gr. 4-6). 1992. wkbk. 0.59 (*0-9620584-2-4*) Safety Always Matters.
—Safety Always Matters. Saba Designs, Inc. Staff & Ahbe, S., illus. 32p. (ps-k). 1991. wkbk. 2.00 (*0-9620584-3-2*) Safety Always Matters.
—Safety Always Matters. Saba Designs, Inc. Staff & Ahbe, S., illus. 32p. (gr. 1-3). 1988. wkbk. 2.00 (*0-9620584-4-0*) Safety Always Matters.
—Safety Always Matters. Saba Designs, Inc. Staff & Ahbe, S., illus. 32p. (gr. 4-6). 1988. wkbk. 2.00 (*0-9620584-5-9*) Safety Always Matters.
Benedict, Kitty. Fire: My First Nature Books. Felix, Monique, illus. 32p. (gr. k-2). 1993. pap. 2.95 (*1-56189-173-8*) Amer Educ Pub.
Charman, Andrew. Fire. LC 93-20873. 1994. PLB 18.99 (*0-8114-5511-4*) Raintree Steck-V.
Fire. (Illus.). 48p. (gr. 2-6). 1987. PLB 10.95 (*0-8172-3254-0*) Raintree Steck-V.
Knapp, Brian. Fire. LC 89-11423. (Illus.). 48p. (gr. 5-9). 1990. PLB 22.80 (*0-8114-2377-8*) Raintree Steck-V.
Lambert, David. Fires & Floods. LC 92-8687. (Illus.). 48p. (gr. 6 up). 1992. text ed. 13.95 RSBE (*0-02-751350-5*, New Discovery) Macmillan Child Grp.
London, Jonathan & Pinola, Lanny. Fire Race: A Karuk Coyote Tale about How Fire Came to the People. Long, Sylvia, illus. Lang, Julian, afterword by. LC 92-32352. (Illus.). 1993. 13.95 (*0-8118-0241-8*) Chronicle Bks.
Parramon, J. M. & Vendrell, C. S. El Fuego. (SPA.). 32p. (ps). 1985. pap. 6.95 (*0-8120-3619-0*) Barron.
Petty, Kate. Fire. (Illus.). 32p. (gr. k-4). 1990. PLB 11.90 (*0-531-14060-1*) Watts.
Pringle, Laurence. Fire in the Forest. Marstall, Bob, illus. LC 92-32257. 32p. (gr. 2 up). 1994. 15.95 (*0-02-775215-1*, Macmillan Child Bk) Macmillan Child Grp.
Robbins. Fire. 1995. write for info. (*0-8050-2293-7*) H Holt & Co.
Taming Fire. 48p. (gr. 3 up). 1994. 19.95 (*0-590-47637-8*) Scholastic Inc.
Van Laan, Nancy. Rainbow Crow. Vidal, Beatriz, illus. LC 88-12967. 40p. (ps-3). 1989. PLB 13.99 (*0-394-99577-5*) Knopf Bks Yng Read.

FIRE–FICTION
Bauer, Marion D. Rain of Fire. LC 83-2065. 160p. (gr. 4-8). 1983. 14.45 (*0-89919-190-8*, Clarion Bks) HM.
Brown, Lynn. Fire & Firecrackers. 3rd ed. Walker, Granville, Jr., ed. Jackson, Gregory A., illus. 14p. (Orig.). (ps-6). 1982. pap. 2.97x (*0-9608466-1-1*) Fun Reading.
Burgess. Burning Issy. Date not set. 15.00 (*0-06-023511-X*); PLB 14.89 (*0-06-023512-8*) HarpC Child Bks.
Grant, Charles L. Fire Mask. (gr. 7 up). 1992. pap. 3.99 (*0-553-29673-6*, Starfire) Bantam.
Hooks, William H. Circle of Fire. LC 82-3982. 144p. (gr. 5-9). 1982. SBE 13.95 (*0-689-50241-9*, M K McElderry) Macmillan Child Grp.
Stine, R. L. The Fire Game. large type ed. (gr. 6 up). Date not set. PLB 14.60 (*0-8368-1166-6*) Gareth Stevens Inc.
Vogiel, Eva. One Tiny Spark. Hinlicky, Gregg, contrib. by. 176p. (gr. 8-12). 1989. 11.95 (*0-935063-83-8*); pap. 8.95 (*0-935063-84-6*) CIS Comm.

FIRE BALLS
see Meteors

FIRE DEPARTMENTS

Winkleman, Katherine K. Fire House. Winkleman, John S., illus. LC 94-7238. 1994. write for info. (*0-8027-8316-3*) Walker & Co.

FIRE DEPARTMENTS–FICTION

Munsch, Robert. La Estacion de Bomberos: The Fire Station. Martchenko, Michael, illus. (SPA.). 32p. (ps-1). 1992. pap. 5.95 (*1-55037-268-8*, Pub. by Annick CN) Firefly Bks Ltd.

—The Fire Station. Martchenko, Michael, illus. 24p. (Orig.). (gr. k-3). 1991. PLB 14.95 (*1-55037-170-3*, Pub. by Annick CN); pap. 4.95 (*1-55037-171-1*, Pub. by Annick CN) Firefly Bks Ltd.

—The Fire Station. Martchenko, Michael, illus. 24p. (ps-1). 1986. pap. 0.99 (*0-920236-77-4*, Pub. by Annick CN) Firefly Bks Ltd.

FIRE ENGINES

Barrett, Norman S. Picture World of Fire Engines. LC 90-31035. (Illus.). 32p. (gr. k-4). 1991. PLB 12.40 (*0-531-14091-1*) Watts.

Boucher, Jerry. Fire Truck Nuts & Bolts. LC 92-37476. 1993. 19.95 (*0-87614-783-X*) Carolrhoda Bks.

Bracken, Carolyn, illus. Fast Rolling Fire Trucks. (ps). 1984. 6.95 (*0-448-09876-8*, G&D) Putnam Pub Group.

Rockwell, Anne. Fire Engines. Rockwell, Anne, illus. LC 86-4464. 24p. (ps-1). 1986. 12.95 (*0-525-44259-6*, DCB) Dutton Child Bks.

Slater, Teddy. All Aboard Fire Trucks. (Illus.). 32p. (ps-2). 1991. pap. 1.95 (*0-448-34360-6*, G&D) Putnam Pub Group.

FIRE ENGINES–FICTION

Greydanus, Rose. Un Carro De Bomberos Grande y Rojo. Harvey, Paul, illus. (SPA.). 32p. (gr. k-2). 1981. PLB 7.89 (*0-89375-555-9*); pap. 1.95 (*0-685-04944-2*) Troll Assocs.

Haywood, Carolyn. Eddie & the Fire Engine. Haywood, Carolyn, illus. LC 49-9873. 192p. (gr. 1-5). 1949. PLB 12.88 (*0-688-31252-7*) Morrow Jr Bks.

—Eddie & the Fire Engine. ALC Staff, ed. Lewin, Betsy, illus. 192p. (gr. 2 up). 1992. pap. 4.95 (*0-688-11498-9*, Pub. by Beech Tree Bks) Morrow.

McLean, Janet. Fire-Engine Lil. McLean, Andrew, illus. 32p. (Orig.). (gr. k-2). 1993. pap. 6.95 (*0-04-928067-8*, Pub. by Allen & Unwin Aust Pty AT) IPG Chicago.

Rockwell, Anne. Fire Engines. (Illus.). 24p. (ps-1). 1993. pap. 4.50 (*0-14-055250-2*, Puff Unicorn) Puffin Bks.

Smith, Dennis. Little Fire Engine That Saved the City. 1990. 9.95 (*0-385-26257-4*) Doubleday.

Sparky the Fire Truck. 1994. 3.99 (*0-517-10278-1*) Random Hse Value.

FIRE EXTINCTION

see also Fire Engines

Broekel, Ray. Fire Fighters. LC 81-7655. (Illus.). 48p. (gr. k-4). 1981. PLB 12.85 (*0-516-01620-2*); pap. 4.95 (*0-516-41620-0*) Childrens.

Chlad, Dorothy. Cuando Hay un Incendio Sal Para Afuera (When There Is a Fire...Go Outside) Kratky, Lada, tr. from ENG. Halverson, Lydia, illus. LC 85-9636. (SPA.). 32p. (ps-2). 1984. PLB 11.45 (*0-516-31986-8*); pap. 3.95 (*0-516-51986-7*) Childrens.

Gibbons, Gail. Fire! Fire! LC 83-46162. (Illus.). 40p. (gr. k-4). 1984. (Crowell Jr Bks); PLB 14.89 (*0-690-04416-X*) HarpC Child Bks.

Hannum, Dotti. A Visit to the Fire Station. Holmes, Dave & Markson, Sue, illus. LC 84-12155. 32p. (gr. k-3). 1985. PLB 11.45 (*0-516-01491-9*); pap. 3.95 (*0-516-41491-7*) Childrens.

Kuklin, Susan. Fighting Fires. LC 92-38678. (Illus.). 32p. (ps-2). 1993. RSBE 14.95 (*0-02-751238-X*, Bradbury Pr) Macmillan Child Grp.

McGuire, Leslie. Busy Firefighter. Mathieu, Joe, illus. LC 94-1402. (gr. 4 up). 1995. 2.50 (*0-679-85438-X*) Random.

Simon, Norma. Fire Fighters. Paparone, Pam, illus. LC 93-4439. 1995. pap. 14.00 (*0-671-87282-6*) S&S Trade.

FIRE ISLAND–FICTION

Estes, Eleanor. Pinky Pye. Ardizzone, Edward, illus. LC 58-5708. (gr. 3-7). 1958. 12.95 (*0-15-262076-1*, HB Juv Bks) HarBrace.

FIRE PREVENTION

see also Fire Extinction;

also names of cities with the subdivision Fires and Fire Prevention, e.g. Chicago–Fires and Fire Prevention, etc.

Chlad, Dorothy. Cuando Hay un Incendio Sal Para Afuera (When There Is a Fire...Go Outside) Kratky, Lada, tr. from ENG. Halverson, Lydia, illus. LC 85-9636. (SPA.). 32p. (ps-2). 1984. PLB 11.45 (*0-516-31986-8*); pap. 3.95 (*0-516-51986-7*) Childrens.

Conlon, Laura. Fire. LC 92-43123. 1993. 12.67 (*0-86593-246-8*); 9.50s.p. (*0-685-66352-3*) Rourke Corp.

Firemanship. (Illus.). 72p. (gr. 6-12). 1987. pap. 1.85 (*0-8395-3317-9*, 33317) BSA.

Franklin, Herb. Fireman Fred's, Fire Safety Coloring Book. Miller, Jackie, illus. 8p. (gr. 1-5). 1990. pap. 0.50 (*0-945145-02-0*) Miller Family Pubns.

Maas, Robert. Fire Fighters. Maas, Robert, photos by. (Illus.). 32p. (gr. k-3). 1989. pap. 12.95 (*0-590-41459-3*) Scholastic Inc.

Morrison, Ellen E. Guardian of the Forest: A History of the Smokey Bear Program. 2nd, rev. ed. LC 89-60719. (Illus.). 144p. (gr. 6). 1989. 12.95 (*0-9622537-3-1*) Morielle Pr.

Starbuck, Marnie. The Gladimals Fire Safety Book. (Illus.). 16p. 1990. 0.75 (*1-56456-206-9*, 476) W Gladden Found.

FIRE PREVENTION–FICTION

Cox, Mike, et al. Fire Drill. Wasserman, Dan, ed. Reese, Bob, illus. (gr. k-1). 1979. 7.95 (*0-89868-071-9*); pap. 2.95 (*0-89868-082-4*) ARO Pub.

Leonard, Marcia. Jeffrey Lee, Future Fireman. Brook, Bonnie, ed. Chambliss, Maxie & Iosa, Ann W., illus. LC 90-31299. 24p. (ps-1). 1990. 4.95 (*0-671-70407-9*); lib. bdg. 6.95 (*0-671-70403-6*) Silver Pr.

Munsch, Robert. The Fire Station. Martchenko, Michael, illus. 24p. (Orig.). (gr. k-3). 1991. PLB 14.95 (*1-55037-170-3*, Pub. by Annick CN); pap. 4.95 (*1-55037-171-1*, Pub. by Annick CN) Firefly Bks Ltd.

FIREARMS

see also Ordnance

Bernards, Neal. Gun Control. LC 91-15561. (Illus.). 112p. (gr. 5-8). 1991. PLB 14.95 (*1-56006-127-8*) Lucent Bks.

Gottfried, Ted. Gun Control: Public Safety & the Right to Bear Arms. LC 92-32775. (Illus.). 128p. (gr. 7 up). 1993. PLB 15.90 (*1-56294-342-1*) Millbrook Pr.

Harris, Jack C. Gun Control. (Illus.). 48p. (gr. 5-6). 1990. text ed. 4.95 (*0-89686-493-6*, Crestwood Hse) Macmillan Child Grp.

Hitzeroth, Deborah. Guns: Tools of Destructive Force. LC 93-19130. (gr. 5-8). 1994. 15.95 (*1-56006-228-2*) Lucent Bks.

Hook, Donald D. Gun Control: The Continuing Debate. LC 92-28902. 1992. pap. 9.95 (*0-936783-09-5*) Merril Pr.

Horton, et al. Amazing Fact Book of Weapons. (Illus.). 32p. 1987. PLB 14.95 (*0-88682-170-3*) Creative Ed.

Landau, Elaine. Armed America. (Illus.). 128p. (gr. 6 up). 1990. lib. bdg. 12.98 (*0-671-72386-3*, J Messner); pap. 5.95 (*0-671-72387-1*) S&S Trade.

Miller, Maryann. Coping with Weapons & Violence in School & on Your Streets. Rosen, Ruth, ed. (gr. 7-12). 1993. 14.95 (*0-8239-1435-6*) Rosen Group.

—Working Together Against Gun Violence. LC 94-1021. 1994. 14.95 (*0-8239-1779-7*) Rosen Group.

Newton, David E. Gun Control: An Issue for the Nineties. LC 91-23352. (Illus.). 128p. (gr. 6 up). 1992. lib. bdg. 17.95 (*0-89490-296-2*) Enslow Pubs.

O'Sullivan, Carol. Gun Control: Distinguishing Between Fact & Opinion. LC 89-2226. (Illus.). 32p. (gr. 3-6). 1990. PLB 10.95 (*0-89908-638-1*) Greenhaven.

Otfinoski, Steve. Gun Control: Is It a Right or a Danger to Bear Arms? (Illus.). 64p. (gr. 5-8). 1993. PLB 14.95 (*0-8050-2570-7*) TFC Bks NY.

Schleifer, Jay. Everything You Need to Know about Weapons in School & at Home. Rosen, Ruth, ed. (gr. 7-12). 1993. PLB 14.95 (*0-8239-1531-X*) Rosen Group.

Siegel, Mark, et al, eds. Gun Control: An American Issue. 52p. 1991. pap. text ed. 11.95 (*1-878623-17-6*) Info Plus TX.

Strahinich, Helen. Guns in America. 160p. (gr. 7 up). 1992. PLB 15.85 (*0-8027-8104-7*); pap. 9.95 (*0-8027-7356-7*) Walker & Co.

Weksesser, Carol & Cozic, Charles P., eds. Gun Control. LC 92-91875. 200p. (gr. 10 up). 1992. PLB 16.95 (*1-56510-015-8*); pap. text ed. 9.95 (*1-56510-014-X*) Greenhaven.

FIREFLIES

Arnold, Caroline. Fireflies. Johnson, Pamela, illus. LC 93-30439. 1994. write for info. (*0-590-46944-4*) Scholastic Inc.

Brinckloe, Julie. Fireflies! Brinckloe, Julie, illus. LC 84-20158. 32p. (gr. k-2). 1985. RSBE 13.95 (*0-02-713310-9*, Macmillan Child Bk) Macmillan Child Grp.

Edwards, Roger. Max Science & the Glowing Firefly. Sanchez, Brenda L., ed. Beard, Derrick, illus. 26p. (gr. k-5). 1991. pap. 3.95 (*1-879350-01-7*) Max Sci Pub.

Hawes, Judith. Fireflies in the Night. rev. ed. Alexander, Ellen, illus. LC 90-1587. 32p. (ps-1). 1991. PLB 13.89 (*0-06-022485-1*) HarpC Child Bks.

—Fireflies in the Night. rev. ed. Alexander, Ellen, illus. LC 90-4255. 32p. (ps-1). 1991. pap. 4.95 (*0-06-445101-1*, Trophy) HarpC Child Bks.

Hawes, Judy. Fireflies in the Night. LC 63-15088. (Illus.). (gr. k-3). 1963. pap. 4.95 (*0-690-01259-4*, Crowell Jr Bks) HarpC Child Bks.

Johnson, Sylvia A. Fireflies. Kuribayashi, Satoshi, illus. 48p. (gr. 4 up). 1986. PLB 19.95 (*0-8225-1485-0*) Lerner Pubns.

Yajima, Minoru. The Firefly. Pohl, Kathy, ed. LC 85-28193. (Illus.). 32p. (gr. 3-7). 1986. pap. text ed. 10.95 (*0-8172-2535-8*) Raintree Steck-V.

FIREFLIES–FICTION

Oppenheim, Shulamith L. Fireflies for Nathan. Ward, John, illus. LC 93-29568. 1994. 15.00 (*0-688-12147-0*, Tambourine Bks); lib. bdg. 14.93 (*0-688-12148-9*, Tambourine Bks) Morrow.

Swartzentruber. God Made the Firefly. 1976. 2.50 (*0-686-18186-7*) Rod & Staff.

FIREMEN

Bornstein, Harry. Fire Fighter Brown. Tom, Linda C., illus. 16p. (ps). 1976. pap. 3.50 (*0-913580-50-3*, Pub. by K Green Pubns) Gallaudet Univ Pr.

Elliott, Dan. A Visit to the Sesame Street Firehouse. Mathieu, Joe, illus. LC 83-4606. 32p. (ps-3). 1983. lib. bdg. 5.99 (*0-394-96029-7*); pap. 2.25 (*0-394-86029-2*) Random Bks Yng Read.

Hankin, Rebecca. I Can Be a Fire Fighter. LC 84-29282. (Illus.). 32p. (gr. k-3). 1985. PLB 11.80 (*0-516-01847-7*); pap. 3.95 (*0-516-41847-5*) Childrens.

—Puedo Ser Bombero: (I Can Be a Firefighter) LC 84-29282. (SPA & ENG.). 32p. (gr. k-3). 1989. PLB 11.80 (*0-516-31847-0*); pap. 3.95 (*0-516-51847-X*) Childrens.

Here Come the Firemen, 2 vols. in 1. (ps-1). 1990. 3.99 (*0-517-69585-5*) Random Hse Value.

Johnson, Jean. Firefighters: A to Z. Johnson, Jean, photos by. LC 85-5348. (Illus.). 39p. (gr. 1-3). 1985. 11.95 (*0-8027-6589-0*); PLB 11.85 (*0-8027-6590-4*) Walker & Co.

Lee, Mary P. & Lee, Richard S. Careers in Firefighting. Rosen, Ruth, ed. (gr. 7-12). 1993. PLB 14.95 (*0-8239-1515-8*); pap. 9.95 (*0-8239-1724-X*) Rosen Group.

Maass, Robert. Fire Fighters. (Illus.). 1992. 3.95 (*0-590-41460-7*) Scholastic Inc.

McGuire, Leslie. Busy Firefighter. Mathieu, Joe, illus. LC 94-1402. (gr. 4 up). 1995. 2.50 (*0-679-85438-X*) Random.

Pellowski, Michael J. Fire Fighter. Lawn, John, illus. LC 88-10353. 32p. (gr. 1-3). 1989. PLB 10.89 (*0-8167-1428-2*); pap. text ed. 2.95 (*0-8167-1429-0*) Troll Assocs.

Seymour, Peter. Fire Fighters. Ingersoll, Norm, illus. 12p. (gr. k-3). 1990. 12.95 (*0-525-67295-8*, Lodestar Bks) Dutton Child Bks.

Simon, Norma. Fire Fighters. Paparone, Pam, illus. LC 93-4439. 1995. pap. 14.00 (*0-671-87282-6*) S&S Trade.

Smith, Betsy. A Day in the Life of a Firefighter. Noren, Catherine, photos by. LC 80-54099. (Illus.). 32p. (gr. 4-8). 1981. PLB 11.79 (*0-89375-444-7*) Troll Assocs.

Wallington, Neil. Firefighters. Stefoff, Rebecca, ed. LC 91-41210. (Illus.). 32p. (gr. 5-9). 1992. PLB 17.26 (*1-56074-044-2*) Garrett Ed Corp.

FIREMEN–FICTION

Brown, Margaret W. The Little Fireman. Slobodkina, Esphyr, illus. LC 84-43127. 40p. 1952. 11.95 (*0-201-09261-1*) HarpC Child Bks.

—The Little Fireman. new ed. Slobodkina, Esphyr, illus. LC 92-17571. 40p. (ps-3). 1993. 12.00 (*0-06-021476-7*); PLB 11.89 (*0-06-021477-5*) HarpC Child Bks.

Godfrey, Martyn. Fire! Fire! 96p. (gr. 7-12). 1986. pap. text ed. 4.50 (*0-8219-0233-4*, 35360); 1.20 (*0-8219-0234-2*, 35719) EMC.

Horowitz, Jordan. Working Hard with the Busy Fire Truck. (ps-3). 1993. pap. 2.50 (*0-590-46602-X*) Scholastic Inc.

I Want to Be a Fire Fighter. (Illus.). (ps-k). 1991. write for info. (*0-307-12626-9*, Golden Pr) Western Pub.

Lippman, Peter. Firehouse Co., No. 1: Mini House Book. (ps). 1994. 9.95 (*1-56305-663-1*) Workman Pub.

Ten Men on a Ladder. PLB 14.95 (*1-55037-341-2*, Pub. by Annick CN); pap. 4.95 (*1-55037-340-4*, Pub. by Annick CN) Firefly Bks Ltd.

Yee, Wong H. Fireman Small. Yee, Wong H., illus. LC 93-31518. 1994. 13.95 (*0-395-68987-2*) HM.

Zokeisha. Firehouse. Klimo, Kate, ed. Zokeisha, illus. 16p. (ps-k). 1983. pap. 3.50 (*0-671-46128-1*, Little Simon) S&S Trade.

FIRES

see also Fire Extinction; Fire Prevention; Forest Fires

Chlad, Dorothy. When There Is a Fire Go Outside. LC 81-18018. (Illus.). (gr. k-3). 1982. pap. 3.95 (*0-516-41986-2*) Childrens.

Conlon, Laura. Fire. LC 92-43123. 1993. 12.67 (*0-86593-246-8*); 9.50s.p. (*0-685-66352-3*) Rourke Corp.

Gibbons, Gail. Fire! Fire! Gibbons, Gail, illus. LC 83-46162. 40p. (gr. k-4). 1987. pap. 5.95 (*0-06-446058-4*, Trophy) HarpC Child Bks.

Kent, Zachary. The Story of the Triangle Factory Fire. LC 88-36223. (Illus.). 32p. (gr. 3-6). 1989. pap. 3.95 (*0-516-44742-4*) Childrens.

Murphy, Jim. The Great Fire. LC 94-9963. 1995. 15.95 (*0-590-47267-4*) Scholastic Inc.

Wood, Leigh. Fires. LC 93-38268. (Illus.). 64p. (gr. 5-8). 1994. PLB 15.95 (*0-8050-3094-8*) TFC Bks NY.

FIRES–FICTION

Anderson, C. W. Blaze & the Forest Fire: Billy & Blaze Spread the Alarm. 2nd ed. LC 91-26586. (Illus.). 56p. (gr. k-3). 1992. pap. 3.95 (*0-689-71605-2*, Aladdin) Macmillan Child Grp.

Good, Merle. Reuben & the Fire. Moss, P. Buckley, illus. LC 93-1798. 32p. (ps-3). 1993. PLB 14.95 (*1-56148-091-6*) Good Bks Pa.

Jam, Teddy. The Year of Fire. Wallace, Ian, illus. LC 92-2882. 48p. (gr. 1-5). 1993. SBE 14.95 (*0-689-50566-3*, M K McElderry) Macmillan Child Grp.

Laster, Jim. The Birthday Gift That Beeped. Knight, George, ed. Erwin, Julie, illus. LC 83-176266. 56p. (gr. k-4). 1983. 10.95 (*0-9612780-0-5*) J Laster Pub Co.

Polacco, Patricia. Tikvah Means Hope. (ps-3). 1994. 15.95 (*0-385-32059-0*) Doubleday.

Robinet, Harriette G. Children of the Fire. LC 91-9484. 144p. (gr. 3-7). 1991. SBE 13.95 (*0-689-31655-0*, Atheneum Child Bk) Macmillan Child Grp.

Rosenblatt, Lily. Fire Diary. Grant, Christy, ed. Friedman, Judith, illus. LC 93-45917. 32p. (gr. 2-5). 1994. PLB 13.95 (*0-8075-2439-5*) A Whitman.

FIREWORKS–FICTION

Brown, Lynn. Fire & Firecrackers. 3rd ed. Walker, Granville, Jr., ed. Jackson, Gregory A., illus. 14p. (Orig.). (ps-6). 1982. pap. 2.97x (*0-9608466-1-1*) Fun Reading.

Buchanan, Heather S. George & Matilda Mouse & the Moon Rocket. LC 91-24318. (Illus.). 40p. (ps-3). 1992. pap. 14.00 jacketed (*0-671-75864-0*, S&S BFYR) S&S Trade.

Flora, James. The Fabulous Firework Family. Flora, James, illus. LC 93-11472. 32p. (gr. k-4). 1994. SBE 14.95 (*0-689-50596-5*, M K McElderry) Macmillan Child Grp.

FIRST AID

Berger, Melvin. Ouch! A Book about Cuts, Scratches, & Scrapes. Stewart, Pat, illus. 32p. (gr. k-3). 1991. 12.95 (*0-525-67323-7*, Lodestar Bks) Dutton Child Bks.

Boelts, Maribeth & Boelts, Darwin. Kids to the Rescue! First-Aid Techniques for Kids. Megale, Marina, illus. LC 91-50666. 80p. (Orig.). (ps-6). 1992. PLB 17.95 (*0-943990-83-1*); pap. 7.95 (*0-943990-82-3*) Parenting Pr.

Boy Scouts of America. First Aid. (Illus.). 96p. (gr. 6-12). 1988. pap. 1.85 (*0-8395-3276-8*, 33276) BSA.

Carter, Sharon, et al. Coping with Medical Emergencies. rev. ed. 121p. (gr. 7-12). 1988. PLB 14.95 (*0-8239-0782-1*) Rosen Group.

Cole, Joanna. Cuts, Breaks, Bruises, & Burns: How Your Body Heals. Kelley, True, illus. LC 84-45335. 48p. (gr. 2-6). 1985. (Crowell Jr Bks); PLB 13.89 (*0-690-04438-0*) HarpC Child Bks.

Greeley, Sheila. S.T.A.R. Junior First Aid. Strong, Susan, illus. 32p. (gr. k-5). 1989. write for info. spiral bdg. FAFCTPC.

Kittredge, Mary. Emergency Medicine. 112p. (gr. 6-12). 1991. lib. bdg. 18.95 (*0-7910-0063-X*) Chelsea Hse.

Snyder, Carol. Dear Mom & Dad, Don't Worry. (gr. 7 up). 1989. 13.95 (*0-553-05801-0*, Starfire) Bantam.

Tilton, Buck & Griffin, Steve. First-Aid for Youths. 64p. (Orig.). 1994. pap. 6.99 (*1-57034-001-3*) ICS Bks.

FISH

see Fishes

FISH CULTURE

Cone, Molly. Come Back, Salmon: How a Group of Dedicated Kids Adopted a Stream & Brought It Back to Life. Wheelwright, Sidnee, photos by. (Illus.). 48p. (gr. 2-6). 1992. 16.95 (*0-87156-572-2*) Sierra.

Selsam, Millicent E. & Hunt, Joyce. A First Look at Fish. Springer, Harriet, illus. LC 72-81377. 32p. (gr. 2-4). 1972. 5.50 (*0-8027-6119-4*); PLB 9.85 (*0-8027-6120-8*) Walker & Co.

FISH HATCHERIES

see also Fish Culture

FISHERIES

Here are entered works on the fishing industry.

see also Fishes

Klein, John F. & Gaskin, Carol. A Day in the Life of a Commercial Fisherman. Klein, John F., illus. LC 87-10949. 32p. (gr. 4-8). 1988. PLB 11.79 (*0-8167-1109-7*); pap. text ed. 2.95 (*0-8167-1110-0*) Troll Assocs.

Lionni, Leo. Fish Is Fish. LC 78-117452. (Illus.). 32p. (ps-6). 1974. pap. 4.99 (*0-394-82799-6*) Knopf Bks Yng Read.

Rogers, Daniel. Food from the Sea. LC 90-21591. (Illus.). 32p. (gr. 5-8). 1991. 12.40 (*0-531-18388-2*, Pub. by Bookwright Pr) Watts.

Russell, William. Fishermen. LC 93-42483. 1994. write for info. Rourke Pr.

FISHERIES–FICTION

Sharmat, Marjorie W. Nate the Great & the Fishy Prize. (gr. k-6). 1988. pap. 3.50 (*0-440-40039-2*, YB) Dell.

Story Rhyme Staff. Fish Convention Plus Twenty-Five Stories, Story Rhyme Coloring & Activity Book. rev. ed. Doyle, A. C., illus. 22p. (Orig.). (gr. 4-8). 1993. notebk. 19.95 (*0-913597-48-1*, Pub. by Alpha Pyramis) Prosperity & Profits.

Whittle, Emily. The Fisherman's Tale. Burdick, Jeri, illus. LC 91-17386. 32p. 1998. 10.95 (*0-671-74760-6*, Green Tiger) S&S Trade.

FISHES

see also Aquariums; Fish Culture; Fisheries; Fishing; Tropical Fish;

also names of fishes, e.g. Salmon, etc.

Adams, Georgie. Fish Fish Fish. Willgoss, Brigitte, illus. LC 91-43748. 32p. (ps-2). 1993. 13.00 (*0-8037-1208-1*) Dial Bks Young.

Animals, Birds & Fish. (Illus.). (ps-5). 3.50 (*0-7214-8003-9*); Ser. S50. wkbk. B 1.95 (*0-317-04633-0*) Ladybird Bks.

Armstrong, B. Fishes. 32p. (gr. 1-6). 1988. 3.95 (*0-88160-163-2*, LW 268) Learning Wks.

Arnosky, Jim. Crinkleroot's 25 Fish Every Child Should Know. Arnosky, Jim, illus. LC 92-39381. 32p. (gr. k-3). 1993. RSBE 12.95 (*0-02-705844-1*, Bradbury Pr) Macmillan Child Grp.

Bender, Lionel. Fish to Reptiles. Khan, Aziz, illus. LC 89-81607. 40p. (gr. 6-8). 1988. PLB 12.40 (*0-531-17093-4*, Gloucester Pr) Watts.

Broekel, Ray. Dangerous Fish. LC 82-4464. (gr. k-4). 1982. 12.85 (*0-516-01635-0*); pap. 4.95 (*0-516-41635-9*) Childrens.

Chermayeff, Ivan. Fishy Facts. LC 93-31091. 1994. 10.95 (*0-15-228175-4*, Gulliver Bks) HarBrace.

Cole, Joanna. A Fish Hatches. LC 78-13445. (Illus.). 40p. (gr. k-3). 1978. PLB 12.88 (*0-688-32153-4*, Morrow Jr Bks) Morrow Jr Bks.

Compass Productions Staff. Freaky Fish Facts. Mirocha, Paul, illus. 10p. (gr. k-4). 1992. 5.95 (*0-694-00411-1*, Festival) HarpC Child Bks.

Cross, Frank B. & Collins, Joseph T. Illustrated Guide to Fishes in Kansas. Robertson, Jeanne L., illus. 14p. (gr. 4-6). 1976. pap. 1.00 (*0-89338-000-8*) U of KS Mus Nat Hist.

Eastman, David. What Is a Fish? Sweat, Lynn, illus. LC 81-11373. 32p. (gr. k-2). 1982. lib. bdg. 11.59 (*0-89375-660-1*); pap. text ed. 2.95 (*0-89375-661-X*) Troll Assocs.

Evans, Mark. Fish. Caras, Roger, intro. by. LC 92-53476. (Illus.). 48p. (gr. 3-7). 1993. 9.95 (*1-56458-222-1*) Dorling Kindersley.

Fish. (Illus.). 20p. (gr. k up). 1990. laminated, wipe clean surface 3.95 (*0-88679-820-5*) Educ Insights.

Fowler, Allan. It Could Still Be a Fish. LC 90-2203. (Illus.). 32p. (ps-2). 1990. PLB 10.75 (*0-516-04902-X*); pap. 22.95 big bk. (*0-516-49462-7*); pap. 3.95 (*0-516-44902-8*) Childrens.

—Podria Ser un Pez: It Could Still Be a Fish. LC 90-2203. (SPA.). 32p. (ps-2). 1991. PLB 10.75 (*0-516-34902-3*); pap. 3.95 (*0-516-54902-2*) Childrens.

George, Michael. Fish. 32p. 1991. 15.95 (*0-89565-701-5*) Childs World.

Grossman, Susan. Piranhas. LC 93-1772. (Illus.). 60p. (gr. 5 up). 1994. text ed. 13.95 RSBE (*0-87518-593-2*, Dillon) Macmillan Child Grp.

Halton, Cheryl M. Those Amazing Eels. LC 89-25613. (Illus.). 96p. (gr. 4 up). 1990. text ed. 13.95 RSBE (*0-87518-431-6*, Dillon) Macmillan Child Grp.

Harris, Jack C. A Step-by-Step Book about Guppies. (Illus.). 64p. (gr. 9-12). 1988. pap. 3.95 (*0-86622-464-5*, SK-035) TFH Pubns.

Hornblow, Leonora & Hornblow, Arthur. Fish Do the Strangest Things. Eggert, John F., illus. LC 88-30202. 64p. (gr. 2-4). 1990. Repr. lib. bdg. 6.99 (*0-394-94309-0*); 4.99 (*0-394-84309-6*) Random Bks Yng Read.

Horton, et al. Amazing Fact Book of Fish. (Illus.). 32p. 1987. PLB 14.95 (*0-87191-844-7*) Creative Ed.

Illustrated Encyclopedia of Wildlife, Vol. 10: The Fishes. 304p. (gr. 7 up). 1990. lib. bdg. write for info. (*1-55905-046-2*) Grey Castle.

Joseph, James, et al. Tuna & Billfish: Fish Without a Country. 2nd ed. Mattson, George, illus. Revelle, Roger, intro. by. LC 80-81889. (Illus.). 53p. (Orig.). (gr. 7-12). 1980. pap. 7.95 (*0-9603078-1-8*) Inter-Am Tropical.

Keller, Gunter. A Step-by-Step Book about Discus. (Illus.). 64p. (gr. 9-12). 1988. pap. 3.95 (*0-86622-465-3*, SK-008) TFH Pubns.

Kelly, Susan & Kelly, Thomas. Fishes of Hawaii Coloring Book. Kelly, Susan & Kelly, Thomas, illus. 32p. (ps-2). 1992. pap. 3.95 (*1-880188-32-5*) Bess Pr.

Landry, Sarah. Field Guide to Fishes Coloring Book. 1987. pap. 4.80 (*0-395-44095-5*) HM.

Lane, Margaret. The Fish: The Story of the Stickleback. Butler, John, illus. 32p. (gr. k-4). 1994. pap. 4.99 (*0-14-055276-6*, Puff Pied Piper) Puffin Bks.

Ling, Mary. Amazing Fish. Young, Jerry, photos by. LC 90-49651. (Illus.). 32p. (Orig.). (gr. 1-5). 1991. PLB 9.99 (*0-679-91516-8*); pap. 7.99 (*0-679-81516-3*) Knopf Bks Yng Read.

Losito, Linda, et al. Fish. (Illus.). 96p. 1989. 17.95x (*0-8160-1966-5*) Facts on File.

Lovett, Sarah. Extremely Weird Fish. (Illus.). 48p. (Orig.). (gr. 3 up). 1992. pap. 9.95 (*1-56261-041-4*) John Muir.

McPherson, Mark. Caring for Your Fish. Bernstein, Marianne, illus. LC 84-8563. 48p. (gr. 3-7). 1985. PLB 9.89 (*0-8167-0109-1*); pap. text ed. 2.95 (*0-8167-0110-5*) Troll Assocs.

Milkins, Colin S. Fish. LC 91-6726. (Illus.). 32p. (gr. 2-6). 1993. 14.95g (*1-56847-008-8*) Thomson Lrning.

Mitchell, Victor. Fish. Mitchell, Victor, illus. 16p. (gr. k up). 1988. pap. 1.99 (*0-7459-1468-3*) Lion USA.

New England Aquarium Staff & Kaufman, Les. Do Fishes Get Thirsty? Questions Answered by the New England Aquarium. (Illus.). 40p. (gr. 5 up). 1991. PLB 14.90 (*0-531-10992-5*) Watts.

Parker, Steve. Fearsome Fish. Savage, Ann, illus. LC 93-28905. 1993. 19.97 (*0-8114-2346-8*) Raintree Steck-V.

—Fish. King, Dave & Keates, Colin, photos by. LC 89-36445. (Illus.). 64p. (gr. 5 up). 1990. 16.00 (*0-679-80439-0*); PLB 16.99 (*0-679-90439-5*) Random Bks Yng Read.

Pfeffer, Wendy. What Is a Fish? Keller, Holly, illus. LC 94-6543. 1996. 15.00 (*0-06-024428-3*, HarpT); PLB 14.89 (*0-06-024429-1*) HarpC.

Pohl, Kathleen. Killifish. (Illus.). 32p. (gr. 3-7). 1986. PLB 10.95 (*0-8172-2720-2*) Raintree Steck-V.

—Stickleback Fish. (Illus.). 32p. (gr. 3-7). 1986. PLB 10.95 (*0-8172-2722-9*) Raintree Steck-V.

Quinn, John R. The Kid's Fish Book: How to Catch, Keep, & Observe Your Own Native Fish. LC 93-31691. 1994. pap. text ed. 10.95 (*0-471-58601-3*) Wiley.

Quinn, Kaye. Look at Fish. Quinn, Kaye, illus. 40p. (gr. k-5). 1986. pap. 2.95 (*0-8431-1891-1*) Price Stern.

Resnick, Jane. Eyes on Nature: Fish. (Illus.). 32p. 1992. pap. 4.95 (*1-56156-150-9*) Kidsbks.

Ricciuti, Edward. Fish. (Illus.). 64p. (gr. 4-8). 1993. PLB 16.95 (*1-56711-041-X*) Blackbirch.

—Fish. Simpson, Bill, illus. 64p. (gr. 4-8). 1993. jacketed 14.95 (*1-56711-056-8*) Blackbirch.

Richardson, Joy. Fish. LC 92-32914. 1993. 11.40 (*0-531-14255-8*) Watts.

Sabin, Louis. Fish. Helmer, Jean C., illus. LC 84-2624. 32p. (gr. 3-6). 1985. PLB 9.49 (*0-8167-0178-4*); pap. text ed. 2.95 (*0-8167-0179-2*) Troll Assocs.

Seafood. (Illus.). (gr. 5 up). 1984. lib. bdg. 17.27 (*0-86592-265-9*); 12.95s.p. (*0-685-58240-X*) Rourke Corp.

Segaloff, Nat & Erickson, Paul. Fish Tales. LC 89-26279. (Illus.). 32p. 1990. 12.95 (*0-8069-7322-6*); PLB 15.69 (*0-8069-7323-4*) Sterling.

Snedden, Robert. What Is a Fish? Lascom, Adrian, illus. Oxford Scientific Films Staff, photos by. LC 93-6495. (Illus.). 32p. (gr. 2-5). 1993. 13.95 (*0-87156-545-5*) Sierra.

Spizzirri, Linda, ed. Prehistoric Fish: Educational Coloring Book. (Illus.). 32p. (gr. 1-8). 1981. pap. 1.75 (*0-86545-021-8*) Spizzirri.

Spizzirri, Peter M. Fish Dot to Dot: Educational Activity-Coloring Book. Spizzirri, Linda, ed. (Illus.). 32p. (gr. k-3). 1992. pap. 1.25 (*0-86545-206-7*) Spizzirri.

Spizzirri Publishing Co. Staff. Fish: An Educational Coloring Book. Spizzirri, Linda, ed. (Illus.). 32p. (gr. k-5). 1982. pap. 1.75 (*0-86545-028-5*) Spizzirri.

Spizzirri Publishing Co. Staff & Spizzirri, Linda. Deep-Sea Fish: An Educational Coloring Book. (Illus.). 32p. (gr. k-5). 1985. pap. 1.75 (*0-86545-064-1*) Spizzirri.

Steele, Philip. Fish. (gr. 4-7). 1991. lib. bdg. 4.95 (*0-671-72240-9*, J Messner) S&S Trade.

Stratton, Barbara R. What Is a Fish? (Illus.). 32p. (gr. k-4). 1991. PLB 12.90 (*0-531-11020-6*) Watts.

Takeuchi, Hiroshi. The World of Fishes. Pohl, Kathy, ed. LC 85-28212. (Illus.). 32p. (gr. 3-7). 1986. PLB 10.95 (*0-8172-2548-X*) Raintree Steck-V.

Tate, Suzanne. Billy Bluefish: A Tale of Big Blues. Melvin, James, illus. LC 88-92517. 28p. (Orig.). (gr. k-3). 1988. pap. 3.95 (*0-9616344-4-8*) Nags Head Art.

Wildsmith, Brian. Fishes. (Illus.). 32p. 1987. 16.00 (*0-19-279639-9*); pap. 7.50 (*0-19-272151-8*) OUP.

Wood, Jenny. Under the Sea. Livingstone, Malcolm, illus. LC 91-7484. 32p. (gr. k-3). 1991. pap. 5.95 (*0-689-71488-2*, Aladdin) Macmillan Child Grp.

Wu, Norbert. Fish Faces. LC 92-27343. (Illus.). 32p. (ps-2). 1993. 15.95 (*0-8050-1668-6*, Bks Young Read) H Holt & Co.

FISHES–FICTION

Behrangi, Samad. The Tale of the Little Black Fish: Mahi Siah Kuchulu. Amuzegar, Hooshang, tr. Javan, Yousef J., illus. LC 91-73480. (PER & ENG.). 72p. (Orig.). 1992. pap. 6.95 (*0-936347-20-1*) Iran Bks.

Borovsky, Paul. The Fish That Wasn't. LC 93-11680. (Illus.). 32p. (ps-2). 1994. 13.95 (*1-56282-581-X*); PLB 13.89 (*1-56282-582-8*) Hyprn Child.

Brouillard, Anne. Three Cats. LC 91-34180. (Illus.). 32p. 1992. 6.98 (*0-934738-97-1*) Thomasson-Grant.

Brown, Margaret W. The Fish with a Deep Sea Smile. (gr. 5 up). 1993. pap. 8.95 (*0-385-31112-5*) Dell.

—The Fish with the Deep Sea Smile: Stories & Poems for Reading to Young Children. LC 87-26227. (Illus.). 128p. (ps-3). 1988. Repr. of 1938 ed. PLB 18.00 (*0-208-02193-0*, Linnet) Shoe String.

Bush, John. The Fish Who Could Wish. Paul, Korky, illus. 32p. (ps-3). 1991. 13.95 (*0-916291-35-9*) Kane-Miller Bk.

—The Fish Who Could Wish. Paul, Korky, illus. 32p. 1994. pap. 6.95 (*0-916291-48-0*) Kane-Miller Bk.

Byars, Betsy C. The Two-Thousand-Pound Goldfish. 160p. (gr. 3-7). 1991. pap. 2.95 (*0-590-42368-1*) Scholastic Inc.

Carlstrom, Nancy W. Fish & Flamingo. Desimini, Lisa, illus. (ps-3). 1993. 14.95 (*0-316-12859-7*) Little.

Cazet, Denys. A Fish in His Pocket. Cazet, Denys, illus. LC 87-5462. 32p. (ps-2). 1987. 13.95 (*0-531-05713-5*); PLB 13.99 (*0-531-08313-6*) Orchard Bks Watts.

Cech, John. The Southernmost Cat. Osborn, Kathy, illus. LC 93-40671. 1995. 14.00 (*0-02-717885-4*) Macmillan Child Grp.

Clements, Andrew. Big Al. 2nd ed. Yoshi, illus. LC 88-15129. 32p. (gr. k up). 1991. pap. 4.95 (*0-88708-154-1*) Picture Bk Studio.

Coffelt, Nancy. Tom's Fish. LC 92-44114. 1994. 13.95 (*0-15-200587-0*, Gulliver Bks) HarBrace.

Cohen, Barbara. The Carp in the Bathtub. Halpern, Joan, illus. 48p. (gr. 1-5). 1972. PLB 13.88 (*0-688-51627-0*) Lothrop.

Cook. The Little Fish That Got Away. 1993. pap. 2.50 (*0-590-41989-7*) Scholastic Inc.

Cowley, Stewart. Green Fish Blue Fish. (ps). 1994. 2.99 (*0-89577-597-2*, Readers Digest Kids) RD Assn.

Delton, Judy. Fishey Wishes. (ps-3). 1993. pap. 3.25 (*0-440-40850-4*) Dell.

Dijs, Carla. Who Sees You? At the Pond. (Illus.). 12p. (ps-k). 1992. 5.95 (*0-448-40309-9*, G&D) Putnam Pub Group.

Dr. Seuss. One Fish Two Fish Red Fish Blue Fish. Dr. Seuss, illus. 64p. (ps-1). 1987. pap. 7.95 incl. cassette (*0-394-89224-0*) Random Bks Yng Read.

Ehlert, Lois. Fish Eyes: A Book You Can Count On. Ehlert, Lois, illus. 32p. (ps-1). 1990. 14.95 (*0-15-228050-2*) HarBrace.

Erickson, Gina C. & Foster, Kelli C. Sometimes I Wish. Russell, Kerri G., illus. 24p. (ps-2). 1991. pap. 3.50 (*0-8120-4681-1*) Barron.

Farrington, S. Kip. Tony the Tuna. (gr. 4-5). 1976. 6.95 (*0-911660-25-9*) Yankee Peddler.

Faulkner, Keith. A Fish Story. Lambert, Jonathan, illus. 16p. (ps-1). 1994. pap. 11.95 lift-the-flap (*0-8431-3646-4*) Price Stern.

Faville, Barry. Stanley's Aquarium. 160p. (gr. 7 up). 1990. jacketed 15.00 (*0-19-558197-0*) OUP.

Fontenot, Mary A. Clovis Crawfish & His Friends. rev. ed. Graves, Keith, illus. LC 85-16994. 32p. (ps-3). 1985. 12.95 (*0-88289-479-X*) Pelican.

Gomi, Taro. Where's the Fish? Gomi, Taro, illus. LC 85-15282. 32p. (ps-k). 1986. 11.95 (*0-688-06241-5*); lib. bdg. 11.88 (*0-688-06242-3*, Morrow Jr Bks) Morrow Jr Bks.

Hamsa, Bobbie. Lucio el Sucio (Dirty Larry) LC 83-10079. (SPA., Illus.). 32p. (ps-2). 1991. pap. 2.95 (*0-516-52040-7*) Childrens.

Hayward, Linda. The Stupid Fish. LC 93-47278. 1994. 7.99 (*0-679-93948-2*); PLB write for info. Random.

Hearn, Diana D. Who Lives in the Lake? (ps). 1992. 4.95 (*0-87483-247-0*) August Hse.

Huan Ching & the Golden Fish. (Illus.). 32p. (gr. 2-4). 1988. PLB 29.28 incl. audiocassette (*0-8172-2466-1*) Raintree Steck-V.

Jonas, Ann. Splash! LC 94-4110. 1995. write for info. (*0-688-11051-7*); lib. bdg. write for info. (*0-688-11052-5*) Greenwillow.

Jones, Terry. A Fish of the World. Foreman, Michael, illus. LC 93-30995. 32p. 1994. 9.95 (*0-87226-376-2*) P Bedrick Bks.

Kalan, Robert. Blue Sea. Crews, Donald, illus. LC 78-18396. 24p. (gr. k-3). 1979. 14.95 (*0-688-80184-6*); PLB 14.88 (*0-688-84184-8*) Greenwillow.

Komaiko, Leah. Just My Dad & Me. Greene, Jeffrey, illus. LC 94-18688. 1995. 15.00 (*0-06-024573-5*, Festival); PLB 14.89 (*0-06-024574-3*) HarpC Child Bks.

Kroll, Virginia L. Helen the Fish. Mathews, Judith, ed. Weidner, Teri, illus. LC 91-17230. 32p. (gr. k-3). 1992. PLB 13.95 (*0-8075-3194-4*) A Whitman.

Lionni, Leo. Fish Is Fish. Lionni, Leo, illus. LC 78-117452. (gr. k-3). 1970. lib. bdg. 13.99 (*0-394-90440-0*) Pantheon.

—Swimmy. reissued ed. Lionni, Leo, illus. LC 63-8504. 40p. (ps-2). 1963. 14.95 (*0-394-81713-3*); lib. bdg. 15.99 (*0-394-91713-8*) Knopf Bks Yng Read.

Littledale, Freya. The Magic Fish. Pels, Winslow P., illus. 32p. (Orig.). (gr. k-3). 1986. pap. 2.50 (*0-590-41100-4*) Scholastic Inc.

Lovejoy, Pamela. Fish On a Dish. Lovejoy, Pamela, illus. 11p. (Orig.). (ps-2). 1994. pap. write for info. (*1-880038-17-X*) Learn-Abouts.

Luenn, Nancy. Nessa's Fish. Waldman, Neil, illus. LC 89-10548. 32p. (gr. k-3). 1990. SBE 14.95 (*0-689-31477-9*, Atheneum Child Bk) Macmillan Child Grp.

—Nessa's Fish. Waldman, Neil, illus. (gr. k-4). 1993. 13.95 (*0-685-64812-5*); audio cass. 11.00 (*1-882869-81-8*) Read Advent.

McOmber, Rachel B., ed. McOmber Phonics Storybooks: Starfish of Norway. rev. ed. (Illus.). write for info. (*0-944991-72-6*) Swift Lrn Res.

Maddern, Eric. Curious Clownfish. (ps-3). 1990. 14.95 (*0-316-48894-1*, Joy St Bks) Little.

Murph & the School of Fish. (Illus.). (ps-2). 1991. PLB 6.95 (*0-8136-5174-3*, TK3875); pap. 3.50 (*0-8136-5674-5*, TK3876) Modern Curr.

Niedergeses, Catherine. Peter the Ship Eater. LC 88-51703. (Illus.). 44p. (gr. k-3). 1988. pap. 5.95 (*1-55523-210-8*) Winston-Derek.

One Fish, Two Fish. Date not set. write for info. (*0-679-86347-8*) Random Bks Yng Read.

Palmer, Helen. A Fish Out of Water. LC 61-9579. (Illus.). 72p. (ps-3). 1961. 6.95 (*0-394-80023-0*); lib. bdg. 7.99 (*0-394-90023-5*) Beginner.

Pfister, Marcus. Rainbow Fish. Pfister, Marcus, illus. James, J. Alison, tr. from GER. LC 91-42158. (Illus.). 32p. (gr. k-3). 1992. 16.95 (*1-55858-009-3*); PLB 16.88 (*1-55858-010-7*) North-South Bks NYC.

Reese, Bob. Ocean Fish School. LC 82-23572. (Illus.). 24p. (ps-2). 1983. pap. 2.95 (*0-516-42314-2*) Childrens.

—Oola Oyster. LC 82-23609. (Illus.). 24p. (ps-2). 1983. pap. 2.95 (*0-516-42311-8*) Childrens.

—Spongee Sponge. LC 82-23608. (Illus.). 24p. (ps-2). 1983. pap. 2.95 (*0-516-42315-0*) Childrens.

Reeser, Michael. Huan Ching & the Golden Fish. Sakahara, Dick, illus. 32p. (gr. 2-4). 1988. PLB 19.97 (*0-8172-2751-2*); pap. 4.95 (*0-8114-5213-1*) Raintree Steck-V.

Rutman, Shereen. Snap the Clam. DeMarco, Susanne, illus. 16p. (ps). 1993. wkbk. 2.25 (*1-56293-326-4*) McClanahan Bk.

Stowell, Gordon. Ana. Lerin, S. D., tr. from ENG. (Illus.). 24p. (gr. 1). 1981. pap. 0.75 (*0-311-38512-5*, Edit Mundo) Casa Bautista.

Tate, Suzanne. Flossie Flounder: A Tale of Flat Fish. Melvin, James, illus. LC 88-92679. 28p. (Orig.). (gr. k-3). 1989. pap. 3.95 (*0-9616344-5-6*) Nags Head Art.

—Flossie Flounder: Un Cuento Del Pez Chato. LC 90-61962. (Illus.). 28p. (Orig.). (gr. k-3). 1990. pap. 4.95 (*1-878405-01-2*) Nags Head Art.

—Lucky Lookdown: A Tale of a Funny Fish. Melvin, James, illus. LC 89-92221. 28p. (Orig.). (gr. k-3). 1989. pap. 3.95 (*0-9616344-8-0*) Nags Head Art.

—Old Reddy Drum: A Tale of Redfish. Melvin, James, illus. LC 93-83435. 28p. (Orig.). (gr. k-3). 1993. pap. 3.95 (*1-878405-08-X*) Nags Head Art.

—Sammy Shrimp: A Tale of a Little Shrimp. Melvin, James, illus. LC 90-61002. 28p. (Orig.). (gr. k-3). 1990. pap. 3.95 (*1-878405-00-4*) Nags Head Art.

—Spunky Spot: A Tale of One Smart Fish. Melvin, James, illus. LC 88-63784. 28p. (Orig.). (gr. k-3). 1989. pap. 3.95 (*0-9616344-6-4*) Nags Head Art.

—Spunky Spot: Un Cuento De Un Pez Inteligente. LC 90-61966. (Illus.). 28p. (Orig.). (gr. k-3). 1990. pap. 4.95 (*1-878405-02-0*) Nags Head Art.

Tubby, I. M., pseud. I'm a Little Fish. (Illus.). 10p. (ps up). 1982. pap. 2.95 vinyl (*0-671-44435-2*, Little Simon) S&S Trade.

Vaughan, Marcia K. Dorobo the Dangerous. Stone, Kazuko G., illus. LC 93-47891. 1994. 10.95 (*0-382-24076-6*); lib. bdg. 14.95 (*0-382-24070-7*); pap. 4.95 (*0-382-24453-2*) Silver Burdett Pr.

Wakeland, Marcia A. The Big Fish: An Alaskan Fairy Tale. Sagan, Alexander, illus. 32p. (ps-4). 1993. 14.95 (*0-9635083-1-8*) Misty Mtn.

Weiss, Monica. Scoop! Fishbowl Fun, Simple Addition. Berlin, Rosemary, illus. LC 91-18657. 24p. (gr. k-2). 1992. PLB 10.59 (*0-8167-2484-9*); pap. text ed. 2.95 (*0-8167-2485-7*) Troll Assocs.

Wilcox, Cathy, text by. & illus. Enzo the Wonderfish. LC 93-11021. 32p. (ps-2). 1994. PLB 12.95 (*0-395-68382-3*) Ticknor & Flds Bks Yng Read.

Wise, William. Ten Sly Piranhas: A Counting Story in Reverse (A Tale of Wickedness - & Worse!) Chess, Victoria, illus. LC 91-33704. 32p. (ps-3). 1993. 13.50 (*0-8037-1200-6*); PLB 13.89 (*0-8037-1201-4*) Dial Bks Young.

Wylie, J. & Wylie, D. A Big Fish Story Big Book. (Illus.). 32p. (ps-2). 1987. PLB 22.95 (*0-516-49502-X*) Childrens.

Wylie, Joanne. Un Cuento Curioso de Colores. Kratky, Lada, tr. from ENG. Wylie, David, illus. LC 83-7448. (SPA.). 32p. (ps-2). 1984. pap. 3.95 (*0-516-52983-8*) Childrens.

—Un Cuento de un Pez Grande (A Big Fish Story) Kratky, Lada, tr. from ENG. Wylie, David, illus. LC 83-7449. (SPA.). 32p. (ps-2). 1984. pap. 3.95 (*0-516-52982-X*) Childrens.

Wylie, Joanne & Wylie, David. A Big Fish Story. LC 83-7449. (Illus.). 32p. (ps-2). 1983. pap. 3.95 (*0-516-42982-5*) Childrens.

—A Fishy Alphabet Story. LC 83-7510. (Illus.). 32p. (ps-2). 1983. pap. 3.95 (*0-516-42981-7*) Childrens.

—A Fishy Color Story. LC 83-7448. (Illus.). 32p. (ps-2). 1983. pap. 3.95 (*0-516-42983-3*) Childrens.

—A Fishy Color Story Big Book. (Illus.). 32p. (ps-2). 1989. PLB 22.95 (*0-516-49511-9*) Childrens.

—A Fishy Shape Story. Wylie, David, illus. LC 83-25222. 32p. (ps-2). 1984. pap. 3.95 (*0-516-42985-X*) Childrens.

—A Funny Fish Story. Wylie, David, illus. LC 83-24058. 32p. (ps-2). 1984. pap. 3.95 (*0-516-42986-8*) Childrens.

Yee-Nishio, Dolly. A Fishy Tale. Lovejoy, Pamela, illus. 16p. (Orig.). (ps-2). 1994. pap. text ed. write for info. (*1-880038-16-1*) Learn-Abouts.

Yorinks, Arthur. Louis the Fish. Egielski, Richard, illus. LC 80-16855. 32p. (ps up). 1980. 13.95 (*0-374-34658-5*) FS&G.

—Louis the Fish. Egielshi, Richard, illus. 32p. (ps up). 1986. pap. 4.95 (*0-374-44598-2*, Sunburst) FS&G.

FISHING

Arnosky, Jim. Fish in a Flash! A Personal Guide to Spin-Fishing. LC 90-45832. (Illus.). 64p. (gr. 4-9). 1991. SBE 14.95 (*0-02-705854-9*, Bradbury Pr) Macmillan Child Grp.

—Freshwater Fish & Fishing. LC 81-12520. (Illus.). 64p. (gr. 3-7). 1984. SBE 13.95 (*0-02-705850-6*, Four Winds) Macmillan Child Grp.

Bailey, Donna. Fishing. LC 90-9958. (Illus.). 32p. (gr. 1-4). 1990. PLB 18.99 (*0-8114-2851-6*); pap. 3.95 (*0-8114-4713-8*) Raintree Steck-V.

Bennett, Paul. Catching a Meal. (Illus.). 32p. (gr. 2-4). 1994. 14.95 (*1-56847-207-2*) Thomson Lrning.

Broughton, Bruno. Fishing. LC 91-4391. (Illus.). 32p. (gr. k-4). 1991. 11.90 (*0-531-18432-3*, Pub. by Bookwright Pr) Watts.

Civardi, Anne & Rashbrook, F. Fishing. (Illus.). 32p. (gr. 3-6). 1977. pap. 6.95 (*0-86020-032-9*) EDC.

Craig, Janet. Fisherman. Eitzen, Allan, illus. LC 88-10045. 32p. (gr. 1-3). 1989. PLB 10.89 (*0-8167-1438-X*); pap. text ed. 2.95 (*0-8167-1439-8*) Troll Assocs.

Fishing. (Illus.). 80p. (gr. 6-12). 1988. pap. 1.85 (*0-8395-3295-4*, 33295) BSA.

Florian, Douglas. A Fisher. LC 93-26515. 32p. 1994. 15.00 (*0-688-13129-8*); PLB 14.93 (*0-688-13130-1*) Greenwillow.

Fly Fishermans Gold, 24 bks. (gr. 10 up). Set. leather bound & numbered 1029.60 (*1-56416-112-9*); 42.90 ea. Derrydale Pr.

Gibbons, Gail. Surrounded by Sea: Life on a New England Fishing Island. (ps-3). 1991. 14.95 (*0-316-30961-3*) Little.

Graff, Nancy P. The Call of the Running Tide: A Portrait of an Island Family. Howard, Richard, illus. (gr. 3-7). 1991. 16.95 (*0-316-32278-4*) Little.

Grosvenor, Rick. Fishing in Narragansett Bay. 8p. (gr. k-2). 1993. pap. write for info. (*1-882563-04-2*) Lamont Bks.

Haker, Loren F. The Li'l Rascals: Tale of a Fish. Haker, Loren F., illus. 66p. (gr. 1-8). 1984. 7.95 (*0-9609964-2-7*); pap. 4.95 (*0-9609964-3-5*) Haker Books.

Hausherr, Rosmarie. The City Girl Who Went to Sea. Hausherr, Rosmarie, illus. LC 89-27236. 80p. (gr. 3-6). 1990. SBE 14.95 (0-02-743421-4, Four Winds) Macmillan Child Grp.

Herbert, Henry W. Fish & Fishing: Fish & Fishing of the United States & British Provinces of North America. (Illus.). 438p. (gr. 10 up). 1993. Repr. of 1855 ed. 42.90 (1-56416-114-5) Derrydale Pr.

Holden, George P. Ildy of the Split Bamboo. Van Dyke, Henry, intro. by. (Illus.). 278p. (gr. 10 up). 1993. Repr. of 1920 ed. 42.90 (1-56416-113-7) Derrydale Pr.

Morey, Shaun. Incredible Fishing Stories for Kids. Martin, Rick, illus. LC 93-77082. 96p. (Orig.). 1993. pap. 11.95 (0-9633691-1-3) Incrdble Fish.

Quinn, Tom, ed. Fish Tales: A Collection of Angling Stories. (Illus.). 189p. (gr. 8-12). 1992. 28.00 (0-7509-0091-1) A Sutton Pub.

Russell, Ching Y. A Day on a Shrimp Boat. Littlejohn, Beth, ed. Russell, Phillip K., illus. 57p. (gr. 3-6). 1993. 13.95 (0-87844-120-4) Sandlapper Pub Co.

Russell, William. Fishermen. LC 93-42483. 1994. write for info. Rourke Pr.

Sargeant, Frank. The Trout Book: A Complete Angler's Guide. LC 92-71318. (Illus.). 160p. (Orig.). 1992. pap. 9.95 (0-936513-21-7) Larsens Outdoor.

Sobol, Donald J. Encyclopedia Brown's Book of the Wacky Outdoors. (Orig.). (gr. 5 up). 1988. pap. 2.50 (0-553-15598-9) Bantam.

Whieldon, Tony. Fishing. Ashby, David, illus. LC 93-22781. 80p. (gr. 5 up). 1994. 15.00 (0-679-83442-7); lib. bdg. 13.99 (0-679-93442-1) Random Bks Yng Read.

Williams, Brian. Fishing. Robinson, Bernard, illus. LC 92-21389. 48p. (gr. 5-8). 1992. PLB 21.34 (0-8114-4788-X) Raintree Steck-V.

FISHING–FICTION

Abolafia, Yossi. A Fish for Mrs. Gardenia. LC 87-17907. (Illus.). 32p. (gr. k-3). 1988. 11.95 (0-688-07467-7); lib. bdg. 11.88 (0-688-07468-5) Greenwillow.

Adams, Jeanie. Going for Oysters. (ps-3). 1993. 14.95 (0-8075-2978-8) A Whitman.

Alexander, Sally H. Maggie's Whopper. Ray, Deborah K., illus. LC 91-7726. 32p. (gr. k-3). 1992. RSBE 14.95 (0-02-700201-2, Macmillan Child Bk) Macmillan Child Grp.

Belanger, Mark. Old Slippery. (Illus.). (gr. 2-6). 1992. PLB 19.97 (0-8114-3576-8) Raintree Steck-V.

Bozanich, Tony L. Captain Flounder, His Sole Brothers & Friends. Isaksen, Lisa A., ed. Isaksen, Patricia, illus. 16p. (ps-4). 1984. pap. 4.95 (0-930655-00-1) Antarctic Pr.

Brady, Kimberley S. Keeper for the Sea. LC 94-18506. 1995. 15.95 (0-02-711851-7) Macmillan Child Grp.

Carlson, Nancy. Loudmouth George & the Fishing Trip. LC 82-22159. (Illus.). 32p. (ps-3). 1983. PLB 13.50 (0-87614-213-7) Carolrhoda Bks.

—Loudmouth George & the Fishing Trip. LC 84-18119. (Illus.). 32p. (ps-3). 1985. pap. 3.95 (0-14-050508-3, Puffin) Puffin Bks.

—Loudmouth George & the Fishing Trip. Carlson, Nancy, illus. (gr. k-3). 1986. pap. 12.95 incl. cassette (0-87499-017-3); PLB incl. cassette 19.95 (0-87499-019-X); write for info. incl. cassette, 4 paperbacks guide (0-87499-018-1) Live Oak Media.

Carlstrom, Nancy W. Wishing at Dawn in Summer. Allison, Diane W., illus. (ps-2). 1993. 14.95 (0-316-12854-6) Little.

Clark, Billy C. Song of the River. rev. ed. Gifford, James M., et al, eds. LC 92-31483. (Illus.). 176p. (gr. 7 up). 1993. Repr. of 1957 ed. 15.00 (0-945084-35-8) J Stuart Found.

Delacre, Lulu. Nathan's Fishing Trip. (ps-2). 1989. pap. 2.50 (0-590-41282-5) Scholastic Inc.

Dobkin, Bonnie. I Love Fishing. Dunnington, Tom, illus. LC 92-38506. 32p. (ps-2). 1993. PLB 10.25 (0-516-02013-7); pap. 2.95 (0-516-42013-5) Childrens.

Friend, Catherine. Sawfin Stickleback. (Illus.). 32p. (ps-3). 1994. 13.95 (1-56282-473-2); PLB 13.89 (1-56282-474-0) Hyprn Child.

George, Jean C. Pescar un Pez, Conquistar una Montana - Hook a Fish, Catch a Mountain. Fernandez, Joaquin, tr. (SPA.). 141p. (gr. 9-12). 1989. pap. write for info. (84-204-4642-4) Santillana.

George, William T. & George, Lindsay B. Fishing at Long Pond. LC 89-77514. (Illus.). 24p. (ps up). 1991. 13.95 (0-688-09401-5); PLB 13.88 (0-688-09402-3) Greenwillow.

Gilmartin, Thelma. What Happens to Me When I Fish the Sea & a Fish Catches Me. Barton, Kent, illus. LC 76-12929. 36p. (Orig.). (gr. 1-3). 1976. pap. 3.50 (0-89317-009-7) Windward Pub.

Gilson, Jamie. You Cheat! Chambliss, Maxie, illus. LC 91-13886. 64p. (gr. 1-4). 1992. SBE 13.95 (0-02-735993-X, Bradbury Pr) Macmillan Child Grp.

Goffstein, M. Brooke. Fish for Supper. LC 75-27598. (Illus.). 32p. (gr. k-2). 1976. PLB 9.89 (0-8037-2572-8) Dial Bks Young.

—Fish for Supper. Goffstein, M. B., illus. LC 75-27598. 32p. (ps-2). 1986. pap. 3.95 (0-8037-0284-1) Dial Bks Young.

Hager, Betty. Marcie & the Shrimp Boat Adventure. LC 93-44488. 112p. (gr. 3-7). 1994. pap. 4.99 (0-310-38421-4) Zondervan.

Heller, Nicholas. Fish Stories. Heller, Nicholas, illus. LC 86-14906. 24p. (gr. k-3). 1987. 11.75 (0-688-06931-2); PLB 11.88 (0-688-06932-0) Greenwillow.

Hest, Amy. Rosie's Fishing Expedition. Howard, Paul, illus. LC 93-28543. 32p. (ps up). 1994. 13.95 (1-56402-296-X) Candlewick Pr.

Ketteman, Helen. One Baby Boy. Flynn-Stanton, Maggie, illus. LC 93-23044. 1994. pap. 15.00 (0-671-87278-8, S&S BFYR) S&S Trade.

Kherdian, David. The Great Fishing Contest. (Illus.). 48p. (ps-3). 1991. 14.95 (0-399-22263-4, Philomel Bks) Putnam Pub Group.

Kidd, Nina. June Mountain Secret. Kidd, Nina, illus. LC 90-31574. 32p. (gr. k-3). 1991. PLB 14.89 (0-06-023168-8) HarpC Child Bks.

Kipling, Rudyard. Captains Courageous. (gr. 6 up). 1964. pap. 1.75 (0-8049-0027-2, CL-27) Airmont.

Kovacs, Deborah. Moonlight on the River. Shattuck, William, illus. LC 92-28377. (ps-3). 1993. 13.99 (0-670-84463-2) Viking Child Bks.

Lisle, Janet T. The Lampfish of Twill. Halperin, Wendy A., illus. LC 91-8279. 176p. (gr. 5 up). 1991. 15.95 (0-531-05963-4); RLB 15.99 (0-531-08563-5) Orchard Bks Watts.

London, Johnathan. Old Salt, Young Salt. LC 94-14593. 1995. write for info. (0-688-12975-7); PLB write for info. (0-688-12976-5) Lothrop.

Long, Earlene R. Gone Fishing. Brown, Richard, illus. LC 83-22558. 32p. (ps-3). 1984. 15.95 (0-395-35570-2, 5-90090); pap. 4.80 (0-395-44236-2) HM.

McCloskey, Robert. Burt Dow: Deep-Water Man. McCloskey, Robert, illus. LC 68-364. 64p. (gr. 4-6). 1963. pap. 15.95 (0-670-19748-3) Viking Child Bks.

—Burt Dow, Deep-Water Man. (Illus.). 64p. (ps-3). 1989. pap. 4.99 (0-14-050978-X, Puffin) Puffin Bks.

McKissack, Patricia C. A Million Fish...More or Less. Schutzer, Dena, illus. LC 90-34322. 40p. (ps-3). 1992. 14.00 (0-679-80692-X); PLB 14.99 (0-679-90692-4) Knopf Bks Yng Read.

Maris, Ron. Bernard's Boring Day. 1990. 12.95 (0-385-29948-6) Doubleday.

Mitchell, Greg. Going Fishing. Ridgeway, Jo A., illus. LC 92-14449. 1993. 3.75 (0-383-03625-9) SRA Schl Grp.

Mosse, Richard. Bun-Bun's Brook Trout. Sonstegard, Jeff, ed. Mosse, Richard, illus. 32p. (gr. 6-10). 1992. 9.95 (0-9630328-1-X) SDPI.

Pickering, H. G. The Pickering Collection: Neighbors Have My Ducks, Merry Xmas, Mr. Williams Dog Days on Trout Waters & Angling of the Test. Timmins, Harry L. & Gardner, Donald, illus. 189p. (gr. 10 up). 1993. Repr. of 1933 ed. 40.00 (1-56416-047-5) Derrydale Pr.

Real, Rory. The Fishing Derby. (Illus.). 32p. (ps-3). 1990. pap. 3.95 (0-8120-4394-4) Barron.

Robinson, Jacky. Saltwater Adventure in the Florida Keys: An Introduction to Fishing for Kids. Milliner, Paul, illus. LC 94-60394. 104p. (gr. 3-7). 1994. PLB 19.95g (0-9641228-0-4) White Heron.

The experts say the FIRST "how-to" fishing story: "SALTWATER ADVENTURE IN THE FLORIDA KEYS blends the technical accuracies of fishing & the Florida outdoor experience into an interesting & fast moving story."--MARK SOSIN, author, ESPN Producer/Host SALTWATER JOURNAL. "Unlocked my hate-to-read students' capabilities... so well written, so educationally sound. ..an asset to anyone's library, young & old."--DEBBIE BRANDNER GROVE, Teacher, Key Largo Elementary School. "Good reading for youngsters.. .a fine teaching manual about America's most popular outdoor activity."--LEFTY KREH, angler/ author. "Takes me back to my adventures in the Florida Keys when innocent dreams came true."--FLIP PALLOT, Host ESPN's WALKER'S CAY CHRONICLES. "Delightful story...strong environmental message."--SANDY MORET, Director, Florida Keys Fly Fishing School. "Informative, educational & well researched."--PERK PERKINS, President, ORVIS. "Entertaining & educational. A primer not just for kids!"--AL PFLUEGER, JR., Hall of Fame Angler. Order from: White Heron Press, P.O. Box 468, Islamorada, FL 33036, FAX: 305-664-8108.

Publisher Provided Annotation.

Roe, JoAnn. Marco the Manx Series, 3 bks. Runestrand, Meredith & Mayo, Steve, illus. (gr. k-5). Set. write for info. (0-931551-06-4); Fisherman Cat, 1988. PLB 10.95 (0-931551-02-1); Alaska Cat. PLB 10.95 (0-931551-05-6); Castaway Cat. pap. 5.95 (0-931551-03-X); Fisherman Cat, 1988. pap. 6.95 (0-931551-01-3); Alaska Cat. pap. 6.95 (0-931551-04-8) Montevista Pr.

Rowinski, Kate. Ellie Bear & the Fly-Away Fly. Peterson, Dawn, illus. LC 93-25260. 32p. (gr. 1-4). 1993. 14.95 (0-89272-335-1) Down East.

Sharp, N. L. Today I'm Going Fishing with My Dad. Demarest, Chris L., illus. 32p. (ps-3). 1993. 14.95 (1-56397-107-0) Boyds Mills Pr.

Smith, Duncan. Fred Goes Fishing. (Illus.). 25p. (gr. k-2). 1991. 11.95 (0-237-51126-6, Pub. by Evans Bros Ltd) Trafalgar.

Stewig, John W., retold by. The Fisherman & His Wife. Tomes, Margot, illus. LC 88-1698. 32p. (ps-3). 1988. reinforced bdg. 13.95 (0-8234-0714-4) Holiday.

Stock, Catherine. Armien's Fishing Trip. Stock, Catherine & Stock, Catherine, illus. LC 89-3266. 40p. (gr. 1 up). 1990. 13.95 (0-688-08395-1); PLB 13.88 (0-688-08396-X, Morrow Jr Bks) Morrow Jr Bks.

Stolz, Mary. Go Fish. Cummings, Pat, illus. LC 90-4860. 80p. (gr. 2-6). 1991. 13.00 (0-06-025820-9); PLB 12.89 (0-06-025822-5) HarpC Child Bks.

Temple, Charles. On the Riverbank. Hall, Melanie, illus. LC 91-43942. 32p. (ps-3). 1992. 14.45 (0-395-61591-7) HM.

Ward, Sally G. Punky Goes Fishing. LC 90-35538. (Illus.). 32p. (ps-1). 1991. 11.95 (0-525-44681-8, DCB) Dutton Child Bks.

Wichman, Juliet R. Moki Learns to Fish. 1981. pap. 4.75 (0-686-86236-8) Kauai Museum.

Wilson, Trevor. Let's Go Fishing. Miesen, Christine, illus. LC 93-26220. 1994. 4.25 (0-383-03758-1) SRA Schl Grp.

Wylie, Joanne & Wylie, David. A More or Less Fish Story. Wylie, David, illus. LC 83-25223. 32p. (ps-2). 1984. pap. 3.95 (0-516-42984-1) Childrens.

FISHING INDUSTRY

see Fisheries

FITZGERALD, F. SCOTT, 1896-1940

Sufrin, Mark. F. Scott Fitzgerald. LC 93-17767. (Illus.). 160p. (gr. 6 up). 1994. SBE 14.95 (0-689-31810-3, Atheneum Child Bk) Macmillan Child Grp.

FLAGS

see also Signals and Signaling

Armbruster, Ann. The American Flag. (Illus.). 64p. (gr. 5-8). 1991. PLB 12.90 (0-531-20045-0) Watts.

Ayer, Eleanor. Our Flag. LC 91-38892. (Illus.). 48p. (gr. 2-4). 1992. PLB 13.40 (1-56294-107-0); pap. 5.95 (1-878841-86-6) Millbrook Pr.

Blair, Grandpa. Vexillophily: A Capsule History of the Stars & Stripes. 2nd, rev. ed. (Illus.). 46p. (gr. 11 up). 1992. 9.95 (0-930366-74-3) Northcountry Pub.

Brandt, Sue R. State Flags: Including the Commonwealth of Puerto Rico. LC 92-8948. 1992. 13.90 (0-531-20001-9) Watts.

Caudill, Rebecca. Did You Carry the Flag Today, Charley? Grossman, Nancy, illus. LC 66-11422. 96p. (gr. 2-4). 1971. reinforced bdg. 15.95 (0-8050-1201-X, Bks Young Read); 3.95 (0-03-086620-0) H Holt & Co.

Crampton, William. Flag. Plomer, Martin & Shone, Karl, illus. LC 88-27174. 64p. (gr. 5 up). 1989. 16.00 (0-394-82255-2); PLB 16.99 (0-394-92255-7) Knopf Bks Yng Read.

Fisher, Leonard E. Stars & Stripes. LC 93-20176. (Illus.). (ps-3). 1993. reinforced bdg. 15.95 (0-8234-1053-6) Holiday.

Flags: A Guide to More Than Two Hundred Flags of the World. LC 93-85523. (Illus.). 240p. (Orig.). 1994. pap. 5.95 (1-56138-384-8) Running Pr.

Fradin, Dennis B. The Flag of the United States. LC 88-15436. (Illus.). 48p. (gr. k-4). 1988. PLB 12.85 (0-516-01158-8); pap. 4.95 (0-516-41158-6) Childrens.

Gilbert, Charles E., Jr. Flags of Texas. Rice, James, illus. LC 88-34511. 96p. (gr. 6 up). 1989. 14.95 (0-88289-721-7) Pelican.

Miller, Natalie. Story of the Star-Spangled Banner. Wilde, G., illus. LC 65-1221. (gr. 2-5). 1965. pap. 3.95 (0-516-44636-3) Childrens.

Nichols, V. Flags of the World Sticker Atlas. M. J. Studios Staff, illus. 32p. (Orig.). (gr. k-6). 1992. pap. 3.95 (1-879424-22-3) Nickel Pr.

Radlauer, Ruth S. Honor the Flag: A Guide to Its Care & Display. Smith-Moore, J. J., illus. 48p. (gr. 2 up). 1992. PLB 12.95 (1-878363-61-1, JC346) Forest Hse.

Russomanno, Diane. The Story of the American Flag. 32p. 1991. pap. text ed. write for info. (1-880501-01-5) Know Booster.

Sorensen, Lynda. The American Flag. LC 94-7050. 1994. write for info. (1-55916-048-9) Rourke Bk Co.

Spencer, Eve. A Flag for Our Country. Eagle, Mike, illus. LC 92-14414. 32p. (gr. 2-5). 1992. PLB 18.51 (0-8114-7211-6) Raintree Steck-V.

Steele, Philip. Flags. LC 94-2578. 1994. 3.95 (1-85697-505-3, Kingfisher LKC) LKC.

Swanson, June. I Pledge Allegiance. Hanson, Rick, illus. 40p. (gr. k-4). 1990. PLB 14.95 (0-87614-393-1) Carolrhoda Bks.

Veazey, Steve & Porter, John D., Jr. Flags in the History of Texas. McPeek, Ellen, illus. 40p. (gr. 4 up). 1991. pap. 6.95 (0-937460-73-7) Hendrick-Long.

Wallner, Alexandra. Betsy Ross. Wallner, Alexandra, illus. LC 93-3559. 32p. (ps-3). 1994. reinforced bdg. 15.95 (0-8234-1071-4) Holiday.

Williams, Earl P., Jr. What You Should Know about the American Flag. rev. ed. Prosser, Les, illus. Sheads, Scott S., frwd. by. (Illus.). 68p. (gr. 4-6). 1989. pap. text ed. 4.95 (*0-939631-10-5*) Thomas Publications.

FLEAS–FICTION

Lionni, Leo. A Flea Story. Date not set. write for info. (*0-679-86203-X*) Random Bks Yng Read.

—A Flea Story: I Want to Stay Here! I Want to Go There! Lionni, Leo, illus. LC 77-4322. (ps-2). 1977. 15.00 (*0-394-83498-4*); lib. bdg. 15.99 (*0-394-93498-9*) Pantheon.

McCully, Emily A. Little Kit, or, the Industrious Flea Circus Girl. LC 93-40658. 1995. write for info. (*0-8037-1671-0*); PLB write for info. (*0-8037-1674-5*) Dial Bks Young.

Mortensen, Carl M. Flea & Gang & the Tube Dogs. 1993. 6.95 (*0-8062-4437-2*) Carlton.

Pellowski, Michael J. No Fleas, Please! Jones, John, illus. LC 85-14066. 48p. (Orig.). (gr. 1-3). 1986. PLB 10.59 (*0-8167-0608-5*); pap. text ed. 3.50 (*0-8167-0609-3*) Troll Assocs.

Wood, Audrey. The Napping House. Wood, Don, illus. LC 83-13035. 32p. (ps-3). 1984. 13.95 (*0-15-256708-9*, HB Juv Bks) HarBrace.

FLEMING, ALEXANDER, SIR, 1881-1955

Kaye, Judith. The Life of Alexander Fleming. (Illus.). 80p. (gr. 4-7). 1993. PLB 13.95 (*0-8050-2300-3*) TFC Bks NY.

Ross, Josephine. Alexander Fleming. (Illus.). 64p. (gr. 5-9). 1991. 11.95 (*0-237-60013-7*, Pub. by Evans Bros Ltd) Trafalgar.

Tames, Richard. Alexander Fleming. LC 89-70492. (Illus.). 32p. (gr. 5-8). 1990. PLB 12.40 (*0-531-14005-9*) Watts.

FLIES

Fischer-Nagel, Heiderose & Fischer-Nagel, Andreas. The Housefly. Fischer-Nagel, Heiderose & Fischer-Nagel, Andreas, illus. 48p. (gr. 2-6). 1990. PLB 19.95 (*0-87614-374-5*) Carolrhoda Bks.

McClintock, Mike. Fly Went By. LC 58-9018. (Illus.). (gr. 1-3). 1958. 6.95 (*0-394-80003-6*); lib. bdg. 7.99 (*0-394-90003-0*) Beginner.

Wilkinson, Valerie. Flies Are Fascinating. LC 93-38593. (Illus.). 32p. (ps-2). 1994. PLB 10.75 (*0-516-06020-1*) Childrens.

FLIGHT

see also Aeronautics

Ardley, Neil. Science Book of Air. 29p. (gr. 2-5). 1991. 9.95 (*0-15-200578-1*) HarBrace.

Asimov, Isaac. How Do Airplanes Fly? (Illus.). 24p. (gr. 1-8). 1992. PLB 15.93 (*0-8368-0800-2*); PLB 15.93 s.p. (*0-685-61486-7*) Gareth Stevens Inc.

Aust, Siegfried. Flight! Free As a Bird. Poppel, Hans, illus. 32p. (gr. 2-5). 1991. PLB 18.95 (*0-8225-2150-4*) Lerner Pubns.

Balibar, Francoise & Maury, Jean-Pierre. How Things Fly. 80p. (gr. 8 up). 1989. pap. 4.95 (*0-8120-4215-8*) Barron.

Booth, Eugene. In the Air. LC 77-7984. (Illus.). 24p. (gr. k-3). 1977. PLB 13.32 (*0-8393-0105-7*) Raintree Steck-V.

Coombs, Charles I. Ultralights: The Flying Featherweights. LC 83-17411. (Illus.). 160p. (gr. 5 up). 1984. 12.95 (*0-688-02775-X*) Morrow Jr Bks.

Crews, Donald. Flying. Crews, Donald, illus. LC 85-27022. 32p. (ps-3). 1986. 14.95 (*0-688-04318-6*); PLB 14.88 (*0-688-04319-4*) Greenwillow.

—Flying. LC 85-27022. (Illus.). 32p. (ps up). 1989. pap. 4.95 (*0-688-09235-7*, Mulberry) Morrow.

Devonshire, Hilary. Flight. LC 92-6077. (Illus.). 32p. (gr. 5-8). 1993. PLB 12.40 (*0-531-14234-5*) Watts.

Dixon, Malcolm. Flight. LC 90-38122. (Illus.). 48p. (gr. 3-7). 1991. PLB 12.90 (*0-531-18380-7*, Pub. by Bookwright Pr) Watts.

Flying. 80p. (gr. k-3). 1983. pap. 199.00 per set (*0-685-57846-1*) Raintree Steck-V.

Jefferis, David. Flight: Fliers & Flying Machines. (Illus.). 48p. (gr. 5-8). 1994. pap. 7.95 (*0-531-15712-1*) Watts.

Kerrod, Robin. Amazing Flying Machines. Dunning, Mike, photos by. LC 91-53137. (Illus.). 32p. (Orig.). (gr. 1-5). 1992. PLB 9.99 (*0-679-92765-4*); pap. 6.95 (*0-679-82765-X*) Knopf Bks Yng Read.

Lantier-Sampon, Patricia. Wings, 4 vols. (Illus.). 24p. (ps-2). 1994. PLB 63.72 Set (*0-8368-0755-3*) Gareth Stevens Inc.

Let's Discover Flying. (Illus.). 80p. (gr. k-6). 1986. per set 199.00 (*0-8172-2594-3*); 14.95 ea. Raintree Steck-V.

Livingston, Myra C. Up in the Air. Fisher, Leonard E., illus. LC 88-23293. 32p. (ps-3). 1989. reinforced bdg. 14.95 (*0-8234-0736-5*) Holiday.

Llewellyn, Claire. First Look in the Air. (Illus.). 32p. (gr. 1-2). 1991. PLB 17.27 (*0-8368-0701-4*) Gareth Stevens Inc.

Mayes, S. How Does a Bird Fly? (Illus.). 24p. (gr. 1 up). 1991. PLB 11.96 (*0-88110-546-5*, Usborne); pap. 3.95 (*0-7460-0694-2*, Usborne) EDC.

Moore, Kathryn C. My First Flight. rev. ed. Hutson, Ronald, ed. Grant, Leslie, illus. (ps-4). 1991. PLB 3.95 (*0-9633295-0-2*) K Cs Bks N Stuff.

Moser, Barry. Fly! A Brief History of Flight Illustrated. Moser, Barry, illus. LC 92-30960. 56p. (gr. 1 up). 1993. 16.00 (*0-06-022893-8*); PLB 15.89 (*0-06-022894-6*) HarpC Child Bks.

Pearl, Lizzy. The Story of Flight. Bergin, Mark, illus. LC 91-33412. 32p. (gr. 1-4). 1993. PLB 11.89 (*0-8167-2709-0*); pap. text ed. 3.95 (*0-8167-2710-4*) Troll Assocs.

Pluckrose, Henry A. In the Air. LC 93-45662. (Illus.). 32p. (ps-3). 1994. PLB 11.95 (*0-516-08118-7*) Childrens.

Rowe, Julian & Perham, Molly. Flying High. LC 94-12244. (Illus.). 32p. (gr. 1-4). 1994. PLB 18.60 (*0-516-08139-X*); pap. 4.95 (*0-516-48139-8*) Childrens.

Taylor, Barbara. Air & Flight. (Illus.). 40p. (gr. k-4). 1991. PLB 12.90 (*0-531-19129-X*, Warwick) Watts.

—Air & Flying. LC 90-46261. (Illus.). 32p. (gr. 4-6). 1991. PLB 12.40 (*0-531-14183-7*) Watts.

—Up, Up & Away! The Science of Flight. Bull, Peter, et al, illus. LC 91-4292. 40p. (Orig.). (gr. 2-5). 1992. pap. 4.95 (*0-679-82039-6*) Random Bks Yng Read.

Ward, Alan. Flight & Floating. King, Colin, illus. 64p. (gr. 3-6). 1983. pap. 4.95 (*0-86020-529-0*); lib. bdg. 11.96 (*0-88110-162-1*) EDC.

Weiss, Harvey. Strange & Wonderful Aircraft. LC 94-3788. 1995. write for info. (*0-395-68716-0*) HM.

Williams, John. Simple Science Projects with Flight. LC 91-50546. (Illus.). 32p. (gr. 2-4). 1992. PLB 17.27 (*0-8368-0768-5*) Gareth Stevens Inc.

FLIGHT–FICTION

Barrie, James M. Peter Pan. Frank, Josette, adapted by. Goode, Diane, illus. LC 82-13288. 72p. (ps-4). 1983. lib. bdg. 8.99 (*0-394-95717-2*); pap. 8.95 (*0-394-85717-8*) Random Bks Yng Read.

Barron, Judy. I Want to Learn to Fly. Moore, Cyd, illus. LC 93-46696. 1994. write for info. (*0-590-49634-4*); write for info. (*0-590-72915-2*) Scholastic Inc.

Brock, Betty. No Flying in the House. Tripp, Wallace, illus. LC 79-104755. 144p. (gr. 2-5). 1982. pap. 3.95 (*0-06-440130-8*, Trophy) HarpC Child Bks.

Buckingham, Simon. Alec & His Flying Bed. LC 90-52939. (Illus.). 32p. (gr. k up). 1991. 14.95 (*0-688-10555-6*); PLB 14.88 (*0-688-10556-4*) Lothrop.

Chesworth, Michael. Rainy Day Dream. (ps-3). 1992. 14. 00 (*0-374-36177-0*) FS&G.

Collicott, Sharleen. Seeing Stars. Collicott, Sharleen, illus. LC 93-49846. 1994. 14.99 (*0-8037-1522-6*); write for info. (*0-8037-1523-4*) Dial Bks Young.

Dorros, Arthur. Abuela. Kleven, Elisa, illus. LC 90-21459. 40p. (ps-2). 1991. 14.00 (*0-525-44750-4*, DCB) Dutton Child Bks.

Eastman, Elizabeth. Fly Beyond the Mountain. Large, Hazel, illus. ii, 18p. (Orig.). (gr. k-4). 1985. pap. 1.49 (*0-9615959-0-6*) JAARS Inc.

Erickson, Gina C. & Foster, Kelli C. What a Day for Flying! Russell, Kerri G., illus. LC 92-42078. 32p. (ps-2). 1993. pap. 3.95 (*0-8120-1557-6*) Barron.

Gelman, Rita G. Why Can't I Fly? 1993. pap. 28.67 (*0-590-71580-1*) Scholastic Inc.

Gildemeister, Jerry. Avian Dreamers. Gildemeister, Jerry & Larson, Tim, illus. LC 90-85397. (gr. 9-12). 1991. 45.00 (*0-936376-07-4*) Bear Wallow Pub.

Hughes, Shirley. Up & Up. LC 85-24166. (Illus.). 32p. (gr. k-2). 1986. Repr. of 1979 ed. 15.00 (*0-688-06261-X*) Lothrop.

Johnson, Paul B. The Cow Who Wouldn't Come Down. LC 92-27592. (Illus.). 32p. (ps-1). 1993. 14.95 (*0-531-05481-0*); PLB 14.99 (*0-531-08631-3*) Orchard Bks Watts.

Jones, J. David. The Adventures of Little Red. Krull, Kathleen, ed. Sieck, Judythe, illus. 64p. 1993. write for info. (*1-883088-01-1*) Source CA.

Kveton, Steven P. If I Could Fly. 14p. (Orig.). (ps-6). 1987. pap. text ed. 0.75 (*0-9616799-1-3*) Water St Missouri.

Lindbergh, Reeve. View from the Air: Charles Lindbergh's Earth & Sky. Brown, Richard, photos by. (Illus.). 32p. 1992. 15.00 (*0-670-84660-0*) Viking Child Bks.

McPhail, David. First Flight. McPhail, David, illus. LC 86-28804. (ps-3). 1987. 14.95i (*0-316-56323-4*, Joy St Bks) Little.

Maris, Ron. I Wish I Could Fly. 1993. pap. 28.67 (*0-590-72461-4*) Scholastic Inc.

Martin, Ann M. Karen's Plane Trip. 144p. (gr. 2-4). 1991. pap. 3.25 (*0-590-44834-X*) Scholastic Inc.

Murphy, Shirley R. Tattie's River Journey. De Paola, Tomie, illus. LC 82-45508. 32p. (ps-3). 1983. 11.95 (*0-8037-8767-7*) Dial Bks Young.

Pomerantz, Charlotte. Flap Your Wings & Try. LC 88-18766. (Illus.). 24p. (ps up). 1989. 12.95 (*0-688-08019-7*); PLB 12.88 (*0-688-08020-0*) Greenwillow.

Provensen, Alice & Provensen, Martin. The Glorious Flight. (gr. 4-6). 1987. pap. 4.99 (*0-14-050729-9*, Puffin) Puffin Bks.

—The Glorious Flight. (gr. 3-5). 1987. incl. bk. & cassette 19.95 (*0-87499-062-9*); pap. 27.95 incl. 4 bks. & cassette (*0-87499-063-7*); pap. 12.95 incl. bk. & cassette (*0-87499-061-0*) Live Oak Media.

Richmond, Gary. The Early Bird. 32p. 1992. 7.99 (*0-8499-0924-4*) Word Inc.

Savage, Deborah. The Flight of the Albatross. (gr. 7 up). 1989. 14.45 (*0-395-45711-4*) HM.

Schneegans, Nicole. The Bird Fisherman. (Illus.). (gr. 3-8). 1992. PLB 8.95 (*0-89565-896-8*) Childs World.

Semel, Nava. Flying Lessons. Halkin, Hillel, tr. LC 93-10811. 96p. (gr. 7 up). Date not set. 14.00 (*0-06-021470-8*); PLB 13.89 (*0-06-021471-6*) HarpC Child Bks.

Snyder, Zilpha K. Black & Blue Magic. Holtan, Gene, illus. LC 94-791. (gr. 3-7). 1994. pap. 3.95 (*0-689-71848-9*, Aladdin) Macmillan.

Woodruff, Elvira. The Wing Shop. Gammell, Stephen, illus. LC 90-55094. 32p. (ps-3). 1991. reinforced bdg. 15.95 (*0-8234-0825-6*) Holiday.

Wunderli, Stephen. The Blue Between the Clouds. LC 91-28010. 80p. (gr. 5 up). 1992. 13.95 (*0-8050-1772-0*, Bks Young Read) H Holt & Co.

FLIGHT TO THE MOON

see Space Flight to the Moon

FLIGHT TRAINING

see Airplanes–Piloting

FLIGHTS AROUND THE WORLD

see Aeronautics–Flights

FLOODS–FICTION

Dahlstedt, Marden A. The Terrible Wave: Memorial Edition. Robinson, Charles, illus. LC 72-76687. 125p. (gr. 7 up). 1988. pap. 5.00 (*0-9621827-0-2*) R R Dahlstedt.

Hughes, Dean. Lucky's Mud Festival. LC 91-34494. 141p. (Orig.). (gr. 3-6). 1991. pap. text ed. 4.95 (*0-87579-566-8*) Deseret Bk.

Mangas, Brian. Sshaboom! Bratun, Katy, illus. LC 91-24764. 40p. (ps-1). 1993. pap. 14.00 JRT (*0-671-75538-2*, S&S BFYR) S&S Trade.

Ruckman, Ivy. No Way Out. LC 87-47817. 224p. (gr. 6 up). 1988. (Crowell Jr Bks); PLB 12.89 (*0-690-04671-5*, Crowell Jr Bks) HarpC Child Bks.

Samton, Sheila W. Oh No! A Naptime Adventure. Samton, Sheila W., illus. 32p. (ps-1). 1993. RB 13.99 (*0-670-84250-8*) Viking Child Bks.

Stuart, Chad. The Ballymara Flood: A Tale from Old Ireland. Booth, George, illus. LC 94-15162. 1995. write for info. (*0-15-205698-X*) HarBrace.

FLOODS

see also Rivers

Badt, Karin L. The Mississippi Flood of 1993. LC 94-9493. (Illus.). 32p. (gr. 3-6). 1994. PLB 16.40 (*0-516-06680-3*) Childrens.

Conlon, Laura. Floods. LC 92-43122. 1993. 12.67 (*0-86593-245-X*); 9.50s.p. (*0-685-66355-8*) Rourke Corp.

Erlbach, Arlene. Floods. LC 94-14374. (Illus.). 48p. (gr. k-4). 1994. PLB 17.20 (*0-516-01067-0*); pap. 4.95 (*0-516-41067-9*) Childrens.

Knapp, Brian. Flood. LC 89-11437. (Illus.). 48p. (gr. 5-9). 1990. PLB 22.80 (*0-8114-2374-3*) Raintree Steck-V.

Micallef, Mary. Floods & Droughts. Micallef, Mary, illus. 48p. (gr. 4-8). 1985. wkbk. 7.95 (*0-86653-323-0*, GA 632) Good Apple.

Rozens, Aleksandrs. Floods. (Illus.). 64p. (gr. 5-8). 1994. bds. 15.95 (*0-8050-3097-2*) TFC Bks NY.

Stallone, Linda. The Flood That Came to Grandma's House. Schooley, Joan, illus. LC 91-33955. 21p. (ps-3). 1992. 9.95 (*0-912975-02-4*) Upshur Pr.

Walker, Jane. Tidal Waves & Flooding. LC 91-31099. (Illus.). 32p. (gr. 5-9). 1992. PLB 12.40 (*0-531-17361-5*, Gloucester Pr) Watts.

Walker, Paul R. Head for the Hills! The Amazing True Story of the Johnstown Flood. 96p. (gr. 2-5). 1993. PLB 9.99 (*0-679-94761-2*) Random Bks Yng Read.

Waterlow, Julia. Flood. LC 92-43946. (Illus.). 32p. (gr. 3-6). 1993. PLB 14.95t (*1-56847-003-7*) Thomson Lrning.

Waters, John. Flood! LC 90-45371. (Illus.). 48p. (gr. 5-6). 1991. text ed. 12.95 RSBE (*0-89686-596-7*, Crestwood Hse) Macmillan Child Grp.

FLORA

see Botany; Plants

FLORAL DECORATION

see Flower Arrangement

FLORENCE

Caselli, Giovanni. The Everyday Life of a Florentine Merchant. Caselli, Giovanni, illus. LC 86-4365. 32p. (gr. 3-6). 1991. PLB 12.95 (*0-87226-107-7*) P Bedrick Bks.

FLORIDA

Bertsch, Aida C. & Bertsch, Werner J. Florida: Educational & Historical Coloring Book. (Illus.). 24p. (Orig.). (gr. 1-6). 1989. pap. 2.99 (*1-877833-01-0*) Pro Pub Inc.

Carole Marsh Florida Books, 46 bks. 1994. lib. bdg. 1077. 70 set (*0-7933-1284-1*); pap. 617.70 set (*0-7933-5140-5*) Gallopade Pub Group.

Carpenter, Allan. Florida. LC 78-8108. (Illus.). 96p. (gr. 4 up). 1979. PLB 16.95 (*0-516-04109-6*) Childrens.

Childs, Valerie. Walt Disney World & Epcot Center. 1990. 7.99 (*0-517-48085-9*) Random Hse Value.

Davis, T. Frederick. History of Jacksonville, Florida & Vicinity 1513 to 1924. 3rd ed. (Illus.). 513p. (gr. 8 up). 1990. Repr. of 1925 ed. 22.50 (*0-935259-06-6*) San Marco Bk.

Fichter, George S. Floridians All. Cardin, George, illus. LC 91-9858. 96p. (ps-8). 1991. 11.95 (*0-88289-804-3*) Pelican.

Fischer, Marsha. Miami. LC 89-25694. (Illus.). 60p. (gr. 3 up). 1990. text ed. 13.95 RSBE (*0-87518-428-6*, Dillon) Macmillan Child Grp.

Fradin, Dennis. Florida: In Words & Pictures. Wahl, Richard, illus. LC 80-16681. 48p. (gr. 2-5). 1980. PLB 12.95 (*0-516-03909-1*) Childrens.

Fradin, Dennis B. Florida. LC 91-32918. (Illus.). 64p. (gr. 3-5). 1992. PLB 16.45 (*0-516-03809-5*) Childrens.

—Florida - De Mar A Mar: Florida - from Sea to Shining Sea. LC 91-32918. (SPA., Illus.). 64p. (gr. 3-5). Date not set. PLB 21.27 (*0-516-33809-9*) Childrens.

A Kid's Guide to Florida. 152p. (gr. 1 up). 1989. pap. 6.95 (*0-15-200461-0*, Gulliver Bks) HarBrace.

Marsh, Carole. Avast, Ye Slobs! Florida Pirate Trivia. (Illus.). (gr. 3-12). 1994. PLB 24.95 (*0-7933-0304-4*); pap. 14.95 (*0-7933-0303-6*); computer disk 29.95 (*0-7933-0305-2*) Gallopade Pub Group.

—The Beast of the Florida Bed & Breakfast. (Illus.). (gr. 3-12). 1994. PLB 24.95 (*0-7933-1493-3*); pap. 14.95 (*0-7933-1494-1*); computer disk 29.95 (*0-7933-1495-X*) Gallopade Pub Group.

—Bow Wow! Florida Dogs in History, Mystery, Legend, Lore, Humor & More! (Illus.). (gr. 3-12). 1994. PLB 24.95 (*0-7933-3494-2*); pap. 14.95 (*0-7933-3495-0*); computer disk 29.95 (*0-7933-3496-9*) Gallopade Pub Group.

—Chill Out: Scary Florida Tales Based on Frightening Florida Truths. (Illus.). 1994. lib. bdg. 24.95 (*0-7933-4681-9*); pap. 14.95 (*0-7933-4682-7*); disk 29.95 (*0-7933-4683-5*) Gallopade Pub Group.

—Christopher Columbus Comes to Florida! Includes Reproducible Activities for Kids! (Illus.). (gr. 3-12). 1994. PLB 24.95 (*0-7933-3647-3*); pap. 14.95 (*0-7933-3648-1*); computer disk 29.95 (*0-7933-3649-X*) Gallopade Pub Group.

—Florida & Other State Greats (Biographies) Florida Bks. (Illus.). (gr. 3-12). 1994. PLB 24.95 (*1-55609-426-4*); pap. 14.95 (*1-55609-425-6*); computer disk 29.95 (*0-7933-1501-8*) Gallopade Pub Group.

—Florida Bandits, Bushwackers, Outlaws, Crooks, Devils, Ghosts, Desperadoes & Other Assorted & Sundry Characters! (Illus.). (gr. 3-12). 1994. PLB 24.95 (*0-7933-0286-2*); pap. 14.95 (*0-7933-0285-4*); computer disk 29.95 (*0-7933-0287-0*) Gallopade Pub Group.

—Florida Classic Christmas Trivia: Stories, Recipes, Activities, Legends, Lore & More! (Illus.). (gr. 3-12). 1994. PLB 24.95 (*0-7933-0289-7*); pap. 14.95 (*0-7933-0288-9*); computer disk 29.95 (*0-7933-0290-0*) Gallopade Pub Group.

—Florida Coastales. (Illus.). (gr. 3-12). 1994. PLB 24.95 (*1-55609-422-1*); pap. 14.95 (*1-55609-118-4*); computer disk 29.95 (*0-7933-1497-6*) Gallopade Pub Group.

—Florida Coastales! 1994. lib. bdg. 24.95 (*0-7933-7274-7*) Gallopade Pub Group.

—Florida "Crinkum-Crankum" A Funny Word Book about Our State. (Illus.). 1994. lib. bdg. 24.95 (*0-7933-4834-X*); pap. 14.95 (*0-7933-4835-8*); disk 29.95 (*0-7933-4836-6*) Gallopade Pub Group.

—Florida Dingbats! Bk. 1: A Fun Book of Games, Stories, Activities & More about Our State That's All in Code! for You to Decipher. (Illus.). (gr. 3-12). 1994. PLB 24.95 (*0-7933-3800-X*); pap. 14.95 (*0-7933-3801-8*); computer disk 29.95 (*0-7933-3802-6*) Gallopade Pub Group.

—Florida Festival Fun for Kids! (Illus.). (gr. 3-12). 1994. lib. bdg. 24.95 (*0-7933-3953-7*); pap. 14.95 (*0-7933-3954-5*); disk 29.95 (*0-7933-3955-3*) Gallopade Pub Group.

—The Florida Hot Air Balloon Mystery. (Illus.). (gr. 2-9). 1994. 24.95 (*0-7933-2399-1*); pap. 14.95 (*0-7933-2400-9*); computer disk 29.95 (*0-7933-2401-7*) Gallopade Pub Group.

—Florida Jeopardy! Answers & Questions about Our State! (Illus.). (gr. 3-12). 1994. PLB 24.95 (*0-7933-4106-X*); pap. 14.95 (*0-7933-4107-8*); computer disk 29.95 (*0-7933-4108-6*) Gallopade Pub Group.

—Florida "Jography" A Fun Run Thru Our State! (Illus.). (gr. 3-12). 1994. PLB 24.95 (*1-55609-418-3*); pap. 14.95 (*1-55609-048-X*); computer disk 29.95 (*0-7933-1487-9*) Gallopade Pub Group.

—Florida Kid's Cookbook: Recipes, How-To, History, Lore & More! (Illus.). (gr. 3-12). 1994. PLB 24.95 (*0-7933-0298-6*); pap. 14.95 (*0-7933-0297-8*); computer disk 29.95 (*0-7933-0299-4*) Gallopade Pub Group.

—The Florida Mystery Van Takes Off! Book 1: Handicapped Florida Kids Sneak Off on a Big Adventure. (Illus.). (gr. 3-12). 1994. 24.95 (*0-7933-4988-5*); pap. 14.95 (*0-7933-4989-3*); computer disk 29.95 (*0-7933-4990-7*) Gallopade Pub Group.

—Florida Quiz Bowl Crash Course! (Illus.). (gr. 3-12). 1994. PLB 24.95 (*1-55609-424-8*); pap. 14.95 (*1-55609-423-X*); computer disk 29.95 (*0-7933-1496-8*) Gallopade Pub Group.

—Florida Rollercoasters! (Illus.). (gr. 3-12). 1994. PLB 24.95 (*0-7933-5251-7*); pap. 14.95 (*0-7933-5252-5*); computer disk 29.95 (*0-7933-5253-3*) Gallopade Pub Group.

—Florida School Trivia: An Amazing & Fascinating Look at Our State's Teachers, Schools & Students! (Illus.). (gr. 3-12). 1994. PLB 24.95 (*0-7933-0295-1*); pap. 14.95 (*0-7933-0294-3*); computer disk 29.95 (*0-7933-0296-X*) Gallopade Pub Group.

—Florida Silly Basketball Sportsmysteries, Vol. I. (Illus.). (gr. 3-12). 1994. PLB 24.95 (*0-7933-0292-7*); pap. 14.95 (*0-7933-0291-9*); computer disk 29.95 (*0-7933-0293-5*) Gallopade Pub Group.

—Florida Silly Basketball Sportsmysteries, Vol. II. (Illus.). (gr. 3-12). 1994. PLB 24.95 (*0-7933-1502-6*); pap. 14.95 (*0-7933-1503-4*); computer disk 29.95 (*0-7933-1504-2*) Gallopade Pub Group.

—Florida Silly Football Sportsmysteries, Vol. I. (Illus.). (gr. 3-12). 1994. PLB 24.95 (*1-55609-421-3*); pap. 14.95 (*1-55609-420-5*); computer disk 29.95 (*0-7933-1489-5*) Gallopade Pub Group.

—Florida Silly Football Sportsmysteries, Vol. II. (Illus.). (gr. 3-12). 1994. PLB 24.95 (*0-7933-1490-9*); pap. 14.95 (*0-7933-1491-7*); computer disk 29.95 (*0-7933-1492-5*) Gallopade Pub Group.

—Florida Silly Trivia! (Illus.). (gr. 3-12). 1994. PLB 24.95 (*1-55609-417-5*); pap. 14.95 (*1-55609-037-4*); computer disk 29.95 (*0-7933-1486-0*) Gallopade Pub Group.

—Florida Timeline: A Chronology of Florida History, Mystery, Trivia, Legend, Lore & More. (Illus.). (gr. 3-12). 1994. PLB 24.95 (*0-7933-5902-3*); pap. 14.95 (*0-7933-5903-1*); computer disk 29.95 (*0-7933-5904-X*) Gallopade Pub Group.

—Florida's (Most Devastating!) Disasters & (Most Calamitous!) Catastrophies! (Illus.). (gr. 3-12). 1994. PLB 24.95 (*0-7933-0283-8*); pap. 14.95 (*0-7933-0282-X*); computer disk 29.95 (*0-7933-0284-6*) Gallopade Pub Group.

—Florida's Unsolved Mysteries (& Their "Solutions") Includes Scientific Information & Other Activities for Students. (Illus.). (gr. 3-12). 1994. PLB 24.95 (*0-7933-5749-7*); pap. 14.95 (*0-7933-5750-0*); computer disk 29.95 (*0-7933-5751-9*) Gallopade Pub Group.

—Gold Shines Forever! The Discovery & Recovery of the Spanish Treasure Ship Atocha. 1994. lib. bdg. 24.95 (*0-7933-7586-X*); pap. 14.95 (*0-7933-7319-0*) Gallopade Pub Group.

—The Hard-to-Believe-But-True! Book of Florida History, Mystery, Trivia, Legend, Lore, Humor & More. (Illus.). (gr. 3-12). 1994. PLB 24.95 (*0-7933-0301-X*); pap. 14.95 (*0-7933-0300-1*); computer disk 29.95 (*0-7933-0302-8*) Gallopade Pub Group.

—If My Florida Mama Ran the World! (Illus.). (gr. 3-12). 1994. PLB 24.95 (*0-7933-1498-4*); pap. 14.95 (*0-7933-1499-2*); computer disk 29.95 (*0-7933-1500-X*) Gallopade Pub Group.

—Jurassic Ark! Florida Dinosaurs & Other Prehistoric Creatures. (gr. k-12). 1994. PLB 24.95 (*0-7933-7455-3*); pap. 14.95 (*0-7933-7456-1*); computer disk 29.95 (*0-7933-7457-X*) Gallopade Pub Group.

—Let's Quilt Florida & Stuff It Topographically! (Illus.). (gr. 3-12). 1994. PLB 24.95 (*1-55609-419-1*); pap. 14.95 (*1-55609-055-2*); computer disk 29.95 (*0-7933-1488-7*) Gallopade Pub Group.

—Let's Quilt Our Florida County. 1994. lib. bdg. 24.95 (*0-7933-7140-6*); pap. text ed. 14.95 (*0-7933-7141-4*); disk 29.95 (*0-7933-7142-2*) Gallopade Pub Group.

—Let's Quilt Our Florida Town. 1994. lib. bdg. 24.95 (*0-7933-6990-8*); pap. text ed. 14.95 (*0-7933-6991-6*); disk 29.95 (*0-7933-6992-4*) Gallopade Pub Group.

—Meow! Florida Cats in History, Mystery, Legend, Lore, Humor & More! (Illus.). (gr. 3-12). 1994. PLB 24.95 (*0-7933-3341-5*); pap. 14.95 (*0-7933-3342-3*); computer disk 29.95 (*0-7933-3343-1*) Gallopade Pub Group.

—My First Book about Florida. (gr. k-4). 1994. PLB 24.95 (*0-7933-5596-6*); pap. 14.95 (*0-7933-5597-4*); computer disk 29.95 (*0-7933-5598-2*) Gallopade Pub Group.

—Uncle Rebus: Florida Picture Stories for Computer Kids. (Illus.). (gr. k-3). 1994. PLB 24.95 (*0-7933-4528-6*); pap. 14.95 (*0-7933-4529-4*); disk 29.95 (*0-7933-4530-8*) Gallopade Pub Group.

Morgan, Cheryl K. The Everglades. Morgan, Cheryl K., illus. LC 89-5175. 32p. (gr. 3-6). 1990. PLB 10.79 (*0-8167-1733-8*); pap. text ed. 2.95 (*0-8167-1734-6*) Troll Assocs.

Page, Andrea C. Student Success Tutor Directory: Sarasota & Manatee County Edition, 1991-92. (Illus.). 64p. (gr. k-12). 1991. pap. write for info. Computer Pr.

Perry, John & Perry, Jane G. The Nature of Florida. Arnett, Ross H., Jr., ed. LC 94-3146. (Illus.). 246p. (Orig.). (gr. 6-12). 1994. pap. 15.95 (*1-877743-20-8*) Sandhill Crane.

Shore, Carol. The Official Florida Natives: A Friendly Introduction. LC 84-91492. (Illus.). 56p. (ps-7). 1985. pap. 2.98 (*0-9612136-2-0*) C Shore Pr.

Sirvaitis, Karen. Florida. LC 93-25402. (Illus.). 72p. (gr. 3-6). 1994. lib. bdg. 17.50 (*0-8225-2728-6*) Lerner Pubns.

Stone, Lynn M. Citrus Country. LC 93-22978. 1993. pap. write for info. (*0-86593-304-9*) Rourke Corp.

—Florida. LC 87-9391. (Illus.). 144p. (gr. 4 up). 1987. PLB 20.55 (*0-516-00455-7*) Childrens.

—Florida. 216p. 1993. text ed. 15.40 (*1-56956-153-2*) W A T Braille.

Sullivan, George. Slave Ship: The Story of the Henrietta Marie. LC 93-47653. (Illus.). 80p. (gr. 5 up). 1994. 14.99 (*0-525-65174-8*, Cobblehill Bks) Dutton Child Bks.

Turner Program Services, Inc. Staff & Clark, James I. Florida. 48p. (gr. 3 up). 1985. pap. text ed. 19.97 (*0-8174-4273-1*) Raintree Steck-V.

Wade, L. St. Augustine: America's Oldest City. 1991. 11.95s.p. (*0-86592-468-6*) Rourke Enter.

FLORIDA–FICTION

Brink, Carol R. The Pink Motel. Greenwald, Sheila, illus. LC 92-17953. 224p. (gr. 3-7). 1993. pap. 3.95 (*0-689-71677-X*, Aladdin) Macmillan Child Grp.

Carlson, Nancy. A Visit to Grandma's. LC 93-18607. (Illus.). 32p. (ps-3). 1993. pap. 4.99 (*0-14-054243-4*, Puffin) Puffin Bks.

Cavanagh, Helen. Panther Glade. LC 92-23406. 160p. (gr. 5-9). 1993. pap. 15.00 JR3 (*0-671-75617-6*, S&S BFYR) S&S Trade.

George, Jean C. The Missing 'Gator of Gumbo Limbo: An Ecological Mystery. LC 91-20779. 176p. (gr. 3-7). 1992. 14.00 (*0-06-020396-X*); PLB 13.89 (*0-06-020397-8*) HarpC Child Bks.

Griffith, Helen V. Foxy. LC 83-16392. 144p. (gr. 5-9). 1984. reinforced 11.95 (*0-688-02567-6*) Greenwillow.

Harvey, Dean. The Secret Elephant of Harlan Kooter. Richardson, Mark, illus. LC 91-45955. 160p. (gr. 2-5). 1992. 13.95 (*0-395-62523-8*) HM.

Joseph, Daniel M. All Dressed Up & Nowhere to Go. (ps-3). 1993. 14.95 (*0-395-60196-7*) HM.

Kennedy, Barbara. The Boy Who Loved Alligators. LC 93-15982. 144p. (gr. 3-7). 1994. SBE 14.95 (*0-689-31876-6*, Atheneum Child Bk) Macmillan Child Grp.

Konigsburg, E. L. T-Backs, T-Shirts, Coat, & Suit. LC 93-18427. 176p. (gr. 4-8). 1993. SBE 14.00 (*0-689-31855-3*, Atheneum Child Bk) Macmillan Child Grp.

—T-Backs, T-Shirts, Coat & Suit. LC 94-27288. (gr. 1-8). 1995. pap. write for info. (*0-7868-1027-0*) Hyprn Child.

Lasky, Kathryn. Shadows in the Water: A Starbuck Family Adventure. LC 92-8139. 1992. 16.95 (*0-15-273533-X*, HB Juv Bks); pap. write for info. (*0-15-273534-8*) HarBrace.

Peck, Robert N. Arly. 160p. (gr. 5 up). 1989. 16.95 (*0-8027-6856-3*) Walker & Co.

—Arly's Run. 160p. (gr. 5-9). 1991. 16.95 (*0-8027-8120-9*) Walker & Co.

Pilius, Nancy A. A Manatee Recovers. 1994. 7.95 (*0-533-10835-7*) Vantage.

Prather, Ray. Fish & Bones. LC 91-44227. 272p. (gr. 5-9). 1992. 14.00 (*0-06-025121-2*); PLB 14.89 (*0-06-025122-0*) HarpC Child Bks.

Robinson, Jacky. Saltwater Adventure in the Florida Keys: An Introduction to Fishing for Kids. Milliner, Paul, illus. LC 94-60394. 104p. (gr. 3-7). 1994. PLB 19.95g (*0-9641228-0-4*) White Heron.
The experts say the FIRST "how-to" fishing story: "SALTWATER ADVENTURE IN THE FLORIDA KEYS blends the technical accuracies of fishing & the Florida outdoor experience into an interesting & fast moving story."--MARK SOSIN, author, ESPN Producer/Host SALTWATER JOURNAL. "Unlocked my hate-to-read students' capabilities... so well written, so educationally sound. ..an asset to anyone's library, young & old."--DEBBIE BRANDNER GROVE, Teacher, Key Largo Elementary School. "Good reading for youngsters.. .a fine teaching manual about America's most popular outdoor activity."--LEFTY KREH, angler/ author. "Takes me back to my adventures in the Florida Keys when innocent dreams came true."--FLIP PALLOT, Host ESPN's WALKER'S CAY CHRONICLES. "Delightful story...strong environmental message."--SANDY MORET, Director, Florida Keys Fly Fishing School. "Informative, educational & well researched."--PERK PERKINS, President, ORVIS. "Entertaining & educational. A primer not just for kids!"--AL PFLUEGER, JR., Hall of Fame Angler. Order from: White Heron Press, P.O. Box 468, Islamorada, FL 33036, FAX: 305-664-8108.
Publisher Provided Annotation.

Stevenson, James. The Worst Goes South. LC 94-25354. 1995. write for info. (*0-688-13059-3*); write for info. (*0-688-13060-7*) Greenwillow.

Stolz, Mary. Coco Grimes. LC 93-34153. 128p. (gr. 3-6). 1994. 14.00 (*0-06-024232-9*); PLB 13.89 (*0-06-024233-7*) HarpC Child Bks.

—Stealing Home. LC 92-5226. 160p. (gr. 3-6). 1992. 14.00 (*0-06-021154-7*); PLB 13.89 (*0-06-021157-1*) HarpC Child Bks.

Whittaker, Dorothy. Angels of the Swamp. 160p. (gr. 6-9). 1992. 17.95 (*0-8027-8129-2*) Walker & Co.

Williams, Carol L. Kelly & Me. LC 92-20492. 1993. 13.95 (*0-385-30897-3*) Delacorte.

FLORISTS DESIGNS

see Flower Arrangement

FLOWER ARRANGEMENT

Bauzen, Peter & Bauzen, Susanne. Flower Pressing. Kuttner, Paul, tr. from GER. LC 77-167661. (gr. 7 up). 1982. pap. 4.95 (*0-8069-7674-8*) Sterling.

FLOWER GARDENING
Here are entered works on the cultivation of flowering plants for either commercial or private purposes.
see also Flowers; House Plants
FLOWER PAINTING AND ILLUSTRATION
Crowell, Robert L. The Lore & Legends of Flowers. Dowden, Anne O., illus. LC 79-7829. 88p. (gr. 7 up). 1982. (Crowell Jr Bks); (Crowell Jr Bks) HarpC Child Bks.
FLOWERS
see also Flower Arrangement; Flower Painting and Illustration; Plants; State Flowers; Wild Flowers
Anatta, Ivan. Flowers. LC 92-35065. (gr. 2-6). 1993. 15. 95 (*1-56766-005-3*) Childs World.
Barker, Cicely M. Flower Fairies of the Spring. Barker, Cicely M., illus. (ps up). 1991. 5.95 (*0-7232-3753-0*) Warne.
—Flower Fairies of the Summer. Barker, Cicely M., illus. (ps up). 1991. 5.95 (*0-7232-3754-9*) Warne.
—Flower Fairies of the Trees. Barker, Cicely M., illus. (ps up). 1991. 5.95 (*0-7232-3760-3*) Warne.
Bennett, Paul. Pollinating a Flower. (Illus.). 32p. (gr. 2-4). 1994. 14.95 (*1-56847-206-4*) Thomson Lrning.
Broughton, Jacqueline P. Garden Flowers to Color. (Illus.). 32p. (ps-2). 1972. pap. 1.25 (*0-913456-51-9*) Interbk Inc.
Butterfield, Moira. Flower. Johnson, Paul, illus. 24p. (ps-1). 1992. pap. 3.95 (*0-671-75891-8*, Little Simon) S&S Trade.
Cooper, J. Flores (Flowers) 1991. 8.95s.p. (*0-86592-497-X*) Rourke Enter.
—Flowers. 1991. 8.95s.p. (*0-86592-620-4*) Rourke Enter.
Dowden, Anne O. The Clover & the Bee: A Book of Pollination. Dowden, Anne O., illus. LC 87-30116. 96p. (gr. 5 up). 1990. 18.00 (*0-690-04677-4*, Crowell Jr Bks); PLB 17.89 (*0-690-04679-0*, Crowell Jr Bks) HarpC Child Bks.
—State Flowers. Reissue. ed. Dowden, Anne O., illus. LC 78-41927. 96p. (gr. 5 up). 1978. PLB 14.89 (*0-690-03884-4*, Crowell Jr Bks) HarpC Child Bks.
Dowden, Anne O., text by. & illus. From Flower to Fruit. LC 93-24972. 64p. (gr. 3 up). 1994. 15.95 (*0-395-68376-9*); pap. 8.95 (*0-395-68944-9*) Ticknor & Flds Bks Yng Read.
Flowers & Trees. 88p. (ps-3). 1989. 15.93 (*0-8094-4857-2*); lib. bdg. 21.27 (*0-8094-4858-0*) Time-Life.
Fowler, Allan. Cual es Tu Flor Favorita? - What's Your Favorite Flower? LC 92-7404. (SPA., Illus.). 32p. (ps-2). 1993. big bk. 22.95 (*0-516-59634-9*); PLB 10. 75 (*0-516-36007-8*); pap. 3.95 (*0-516-56007-7*) Childrens.
—What's Your Favorite Flower? LC 92-7404. (Illus.). 32p. (ps-2). 1992. PLB 10.75 (*0-516-06007-4*); big bk. 22.95 (*0-516-49634-4*) Childrens.
—What's Your Favorite Flower? LC 92-7404. (Illus.). 32p. (ps-2). 1993. pap. 3.95 (*0-516-46007-2*) Childrens.
Grace, Theresa. A Picture Book of Flowers. Pistolesi, Roseanna, illus. LC 92-8716. 24p. (gr. 1-4). 1992. PLB 9.59 (*0-8167-2836-4*); pap. text ed. 2.50 (*0-8167-2837-2*) Troll Assocs.
Grillis, Carla. Flowers of the Seasons. (Illus.). 12p. (ps). 1990. bds. 5.95 (*0-86315-088-8*, 1362, Pub. by Floris Bks UK) Anthroposophic.
Hildebrand, June. A Book of Flowers. (Illus.). 72p. (Orig.). 1982. write for info. Claremount Pr.
Holmes, Anita. Flowers for You: Blooms for Every Month. Wright-Frierson, Virginia, illus. LC 91-9482. 48p. (gr. 2-5). 1993. SBE 16.95 (*0-02-744280-2*, Bradbury Pr) Macmillan Child Grp.
Ichikawa, Satomi & Laird, Elizabeth. Rosy's Garden: A Child's Keepsake of Flowers. (Illus.). 48p. 1990. 16.95 (*0-399-21881-5*, Philomel Bks) Putnam Pub Group.
Jennings, Terry. Flowers. LC 88-37553. (Illus.). 32p. (gr. 3-6). 1989. pap. 4.95 (*0-516-48439-7*) Childrens.
Johnson, Sylvia A. Morning Glories. Sato, Yuko, illus. 48p. (gr. 4-10). 1985. PLB 19.95 (*0-8225-1462-1*) Lerner Pubns.
—Roses Red, Violets Blue: Why Flowers Have Colors. (Illus.). 64p. (gr. 5 up). 1991. PLB 19.95 (*0-8225-1594-6*) Lerner Pubns.
King, Elizabeth. Backyard Sunflower. King, Elizabeth, photos by. LC 92-31002. (Illus.). (ps-3). 1993. 13.99 (*0-525-45082-3*, DCB) Dutton Child Bks.
Kirkpatrick, Rena K. Look at Flowers. rev. ed. Milne, Annabel & Stebbing, Peter, illus. LC 84-26227. 32p. (gr. 2-4). 1985. PLB 10.95 (*0-8172-2352-5*); pap. 4.95 (*0-8114-6898-4*) Raintree Steck-V.
Lucht, Irmgard. The Red Poppy. Jacoby-Nelson, Frank, tr. LC 94-15057. 1995. 14.95 (*0-7868-0055-0*); lib. bdg. 14.89 (*0-7868-2043-8*) Hyprn Child.
Mayes, S. What Makes a Flower Grow? (Illus.). 24p. (gr. 1-4). 1989. lib. bdg. 11.96 (*0-88110-381-0*, Usborne); pap. 3.95 (*0-7460-0275-0*, Usborne) EDC.
Mineau, Charles. The Flowers. (Illus.). 24p. (ps-8). 1988. pap. 4.95 (*0-88753-171-7*, Pub. by Black Moss Pr CN) Firefly Bks Ltd.
Mitchell, Victor. Flowers. Mitchell, Victor, illus. 16p. (gr. k up). 1988. pap. 1.99 (*0-7459-1470-5*) Lion USA.
Patent, Dorothy H. Flowers for Everyone. Munoz, William, photos by. LC 89-23937. (Illus.). 64p. (gr. 5 up). 1990. 14.95 (*0-525-65025-3*, Cobblehill Bks) Dutton Child Bks.
Pluckrose, Henry A. Flowers. LC 93-45661. (Illus.). 32p. (ps-3). 1994. PLB 11.95 (*0-516-08117-9*) Childrens.
Pohl, Kathleen. Morning Glories. (Illus.). 32p. (gr. 3-7). 1986. PLB 10.95 (*0-8172-2711-3*) Raintree Steck-V.
—Sunflowers. (Illus.). 32p. (gr. 3-7). 1986. PLB 10.95 (*0-8172-2710-5*) Raintree Steck-V.
—Tulips. (Illus.). 32p. (gr. 3-7). 1986. PLB 10.95 (*0-8172-2709-1*) Raintree Steck-V.
Richardson, Joy. Flowers. LC 93-18653. (Illus.). 32p. (gr. 2-4). 1993. PLB 11.40 (*0-531-14274-4*) Watts.
Sabin, Louis. Plants, Seeds & Flowers. Moylan, Holly, illus. LC 84-2720. 32p. (gr. 3-6). 1985. PLB 9.49 (*0-8167-0226-8*); pap. text ed. 2.95 (*0-8167-0227-6*) Troll Assocs.
Wren. Flowers of Hawaii Coloring Book. Wren, illus. 32p. (ps-2). 1992. pap. 3.95 (*1-880188-42-2*) Bess Pr.
FLOWERS–ARRANGEMENT
see Flower Arrangement
FLOWERS–FICTION
Barker, Cicely M. Four Seasons of the Flower Fairies: A Flower Fairies Gift Set, 4 bks. (Illus.). 1992. Boxed Set. 24.00 (*0-7232-5181-9*) Warne.
Beskow, Elsa. The Flowers' Festival. Beskow, Elsa, illus. 32p. (gr. k-4). 1991. Repr. of 1914 ed. 14.95g (*0-86315-120-5*, Pub. by Floris Bks UK) Gryphon Hse.
Birchman, David F. A Tale of Tulips, a Tale of Onions. Hunt, Jonathan, illus. LC 92-31240. 40p. (gr. 1-4). 1994. RSBE 15.95 (*0-02-710112-6*, Four Winds) Macmillan Child Grp.
Cernobous, Wayne J. Millie Milkweed Seed Meets the Genny Geranium Gang. Wyman, Helen B., illus. 46p. (Orig.). (gr. k-5). 1984. pap. 5.95 (*0-9615065-0-4*) Kinnickinnic Pr.
Cox, Mike & Cox, Kris. Flowers. Wasserman, Dan, ed. Reese, Bob, illus. 1979. 7.95 (*0-89868-076-X*); pap. 2.95 (*0-89868-087-5*) ARO Pub.
Cox, Willis F. & Cox, Rosemary C. Phillip's Daffodil. (Orig.). (gr. k-8). 1987. pap. 2.95 (*0-9610758-4-8*) W F Cox.
De La Tour, Shatoiya. The Herbalist of Yarrow: A Fairy Tale of Plant Wisdom. 80p. 1994. 15.95 (*0-929999-04-5*) Tzedakah Pubns.
De Paola, Tomie. The Legend of the Indian Paintbrush. (Illus.). 32p. (ps-3). 1991. pap. 5.95 (*0-399-21777-0*, Sandcastle Bks) Putnam Pub Group.
Dieckmann, Marliese. The Sunflower. Rosenfeld, Christel, illus. LC 94-65094. 24p. (gr. 3-6). 1994. 12.95 (*1-879373-75-0*) R Rinehart.
Dr. Seuss. Daisy-Head Mayzie. Dr. Seuss, illus. LC 94-11349. 1995. 15.00 (*0-679-86712-0*) Random.
Ehlert, Lois. Planting a Rainbow. (ps-3). 1992. pap. 19.95 (*0-15-262611-5*); pap. 4.95 (*0-15-262610-7*) HarBrace.
Ford, Miela. Sunflower. Noll, Sally, illus. 24p. 1995. write for info. (*0-688-13301-0*); PLB write for info. (*0-688-13302-9*) Greenwillow.
Freeman, Don. Dandelion. Freeman, Don, illus. (gr. k-3). 1982. incl. cassette 19.95 (*0-941078-11-6*); pap. 12.95 incl. cassette (*0-941078-09-4*); user's guide incl. 4 pbs. & cassette 27.95 (*0-941078-10-8*) Live Oak Media.
Garfield, Leon. The December Rose. 208p. (gr. 5-9). 1988. pap. 3.99 (*0-14-032070-9*, Puffin) Puffin Bks.
Gaynor, Brigid. The Flower Garden. Rollins, Nancy O., illus. 12p. (ps). 1992. 4.95 (*1-56828-014-9*) Red Jacket Pr.
Hayes, Joe. Mariposa, Mariposa. Jelinek, Lucy, illus. (SPA & ENG.). 32p. (Orig.). (gr. k-5). 1988. pap. 3.95 (*0-939729-08-3*); Bk. & cass. pkg. 7.95 (*0-939729-09-1*) Trails West Pub.
Hendry, Diana. The Rainbow Watchers. Wickstrom, Thor, illus. LC 91-52853. 48p. (gr. 1 up). 1991. text ed. 10.95 (*0-688-10305-7*) Lothrop.
Hutchins, Pat. Titch. Hutchins, Pat, illus. LC 77-146622. 32p. (ps-1). 1971. RSBE 14.95 (*0-02-745880-6*, Macmillan Child Bk) Macmillan Child Grp.
Killien, Christi. Daffodils. (gr. 4-7). 1993. pap. 2.95 (*0-590-44242-2*) Scholastic Inc.
Lobel, Arnold. The Rose in My Garden. Lobel, Anita, illus. LC 83-14097. 40p. (gr. k-3). 1984. 16.00 (*0-688-02586-2*); PLB 15.93 (*0-688-02587-0*) Greenwillow.
—The Rose in My Garden. Lobel, Anita, illus. LC 92-24588. 40p. (ps up). 1993. pap. 4.95 (*0-688-12265-5*, Mulberry) Morrow.
Nicolai, D. Miles. The Summer the Flowers Had No Scent. 3rd ed. Poyser, Victoria, illus. 28p. (gr. 3-5). 1977. pap. 2.75 (*0-933992-19-X*) Coffee Break.
O'Callahan, Jay. Tulips. Santini, Debrah, illus. LC 91-41704. 28p. (gr. k up). 1992. pap. 14.95 (*0-88708-223-8*) Picture Bk Studio.
Powell, E. Sandy. Daisy. Thornton, Peter, illus. 40p. (gr. 1-4). 1991. PLB 13.50 (*0-87614-449-0*) Carolrhoda Bks.
—Geranium Morning. Graef, Renee, illus. 40p. (gr. 1-4). 1990. PLB 13.50 (*0-87614-380-X*) Carolrhoda Bks.
Prieto. Pablo's Petunias. LC 72-190269. (Illus.). 32p. (gr. 3-5). 1972. PLB 9.95 (*0-87783-058-4*); pap. 3.94 deluxe ed. (*0-87783-102-5*) Oddo.
Robbins, Ken. A Flower Grows. Robbins, Ken, illus. (gr. k up). 1990. 12.95 (*0-8037-0764-9*); PLB 12.89 (*0-8037-0765-7*) Dial Bks Young.
Sisson, Joan. Marigold. Sisson, Joan, illus. 24p. (Orig.). (ps-5). 1988. pap. 4.00 (*0-317-93622-0*) J Sisson.
Turner, Ann. Rainflowers. Blake, Robert J., illus. LC 90-39629. 32p. (gr. k-3). 1992. 14.00 (*0-06-026041-6*); PLB 13.89 (*0-06-026042-4*) HarpC Child Bks.
White, Ruth. Weeping Willow. 1994. pap. 3.95 (*0-374-48280-2*) FS&G.
FLOWERS, STATE
see State Flowers
FLOWERS, WILD
see Wild Flowers
FLOWERS IN ART
see Flower Painting and Illustration
FLOWERS IN LITERATURE
Jangl, Alda M. & Jangl, James F. Ancient Legends of the Twelve Birthflowers. Jangl, Alda M., illus. 40p. (gr. 9-12). 1987. pap. 3.95 (*0-942647-01-7*) Prisma Pr.
FLY
see Flies
FLY-CASTING
Wylie, Joanne & Wylie, David. Un Cuento de Peces, Mas o Menos (A More or Less Fish Story) LC 83-25223. (SPA., Illus.). 32p. (ps-2). 1987. pap. 3.95 (*0-516-52984-6*) Childrens.
FLYING
see Flight
FLYING BOMBS
see Guided Missiles
FLYING SAUCERS
Arvey, Michael. UFOs: Opposing Viewpoints. LC 89-11645. (Illus.). 111p. (gr. 5-8). 1989. PLB 14.95 (*0-89908-060-X*) Greenhaven.
Asimov, Isaac. Unidentified Flying Objects. 1990. pap. 4.95 (*0-440-40349-9*, YB) Dell.
Asimov, Isaac, et al. UFO's: Mysteries in Space. rev. & updated ed. (Illus.). (gr. 3 up). 1995. PLB 17.27 (*0-8368-1198-4*) Gareth Stevens Inc.
Bernards, Neal. UFO Abductions. LC 94-2123. 1995. 14. 95 (*1-56006-161-8*) Lucent Bks.
Butts, Donna R. & Corder, S. Scott. UFO Contact, the Four. Stevens, Wendelle C., ed. Butts, Donna R., illus. Caulfield, William, intro. by. (Illus.). 240p. (gr. 9-12). 1989. PLB 17.95 (*0-934269-18-1*) UFO Photo.
Collins, Jim. Unidentified Flying Objects. LC 77-13040. (Illus.). 48p. (gr. 4 up). 1983. PLB 20.70 (*0-8172-1065-2*) Raintree Steck-V.
Emert, Phyllis R. Monsters, Strange Dreams, & UFO's. 128p. 1994. pap. 2.50 (*0-8125-9425-8*) Tor Bks.
Gilligan, Shannon. Project U. F. O, No. 143. 1994. pap. 3.50 (*0-553-56003-4*) Bantam.
If UFOs Are Real. 48p. (gr. 5-6). 1991. PLB 11.95 (*1-56065-094-X*) Capstone Pr.
Kitamura, Satoshi. UFO Diary. (ps up). 1989. 14.00 (*0-374-38026-0*) FS&G.
—UFO Diary. (ps up). 1991. pap. 4.95 (*0-374-48041-9*) FS&G.
Koss, Larry. Could UFOs Be Real? (Illus.). 48p. (gr. 3-6). 1991. 11.95 (*1-56065-093-1*) Capstone Pr.
Kroll, Steven. The Magic Rocket. Hillenbrand, Will, illus. LC 91-10114. 32p. (ps-3). 1992. reinforced bdg. 14.95 (*0-8234-0916-3*) Holiday.
McMurtry, Ken. A History Mystery: The Mystery of the Roswell UFO. 96p. (Orig.). 1992. pap. 3.50 (*0-380-76843-7*, Camelot) Avon.
Rasmussen, Richard M. The UFO Challenge. LC 90-32962. (Illus.). 96p. (gr. 5-8). 1990. PLB 14.95 (*1-56006-122-7*) Lucent Bks.
Riehecky, Janet. UFOs. Siculan, Dan, illus. LC 88-25730. 100p. (gr. 3-7). 1989. PLB 14.95 (*0-89565-453-9*) Childs World.
Spellman, Linda. Monsters, Mysteries, UFOs. 112p. (gr. 4-6). 1984. 9.95 (*0-88160-095-4*, LW 903) Learning Wks.
Stevens, Wendelle C. UFO...Contact from Reticulum, Update. Stevens, Wendelle C., et al, illus. 444p. (gr. 9-12). 1989. PLB 18.95 (*0-934269-15-7*) UFO Photo.
—UFO...Contact from the Pleiades: A Supplementary Investigation Report. Stevens, Wendelle C., illus. 552p. (gr. 9-12). 1989. PLB 29.95 (*0-9608558-4-X*) UFO Photo.
Wilding-White. UFO's. 32p. (gr. k-6). 1977. pap. 5.95 (*0-86020-150-3*) EDC.
FOG–FICTION
Alexander, Frances. Mother Goose on the Rio Grande. (Illus.). 96p. (gr. 4 up). 1983. pap. 6.95 (*0-8442-7641-3*, Natl Textbk) NTC Pub Grp.
Bacheller, Irving. Lost in the Fog. Krupinski, Loretta, adapted by. & illus. LC 88-25923. (gr. k-3). 1990. 14. 95 (*0-316-07462-4*) Little.
Cooney. The Fog. 1993. pap. 3.25 (*0-590-43806-9*) Scholastic Inc.
Flieger, Pat. The Fog's Net. Gamper, Ruth, illus. LC 93-31512. 1994. 14.95 (*0-395-68194-4*) HM.
Fowler, Susi G. Fog. Fowler, Jim, illus. LC 91-28509. 32p. (ps-8). 1992. 14.00 (*0-688-10593-9*); PLB 13.93 (*0-688-10594-7*) Greenwillow.
Tresselt, Alvin R. Hide & Seek Fog. Duvoisin, Roger, illus. LC 65-14087. 32p. (gr. k-2). PLB 14.88 (*0-688-51169-4*) Lothrop.
FOG SIGNALS
see Signals and Signaling
FOLIAGE
see Leaves
FOLK ART
Here are entered general and historical works on peasant and popular art in the fields of decorative arts, music, dancing, theater, etc.
see also Art, Primitive; Art Industries and Trade; Arts and Crafts
Abby Aldrich Rockefeller Folk Art Center Staff & Watson, Amy. The Folk Art Counting Book: From the Abby Aldrich Rockefeller Folk Art Center. (Illus.). 40p. (ps-k). 1992. 9.95 (*0-87935-084-9*, Co-Pub. by Abrams) Williamsburg.
Abernethy, Jane F. & Tune, Suelyn C. Made in Hawaii. Williams, Julie S., illus. LC 83-4895. 140p. (gr. 3-12). 1983. pap. 7.95 (*0-8248-0870-3*) UH Pr.

Esterman, M. M. A Fish That's a Box: Folk Art from the National Museum of American Art, Smithsonian Institution. LC 90-3802. (Illus.). 32p. (gr. k-5). 1990. 12.95 (*0-915556-21-9*) Great Ocean.

Rochester Folk Art Guild Staff. Little Shooter of Birds & the Great Sun. (ps-7). 1981. 9.50 (*0-686-33125-7*) Rochester Folk Art.

Stanislaw, Mary Anne. Kalagas: The Wall Hangings of Southeast Asia. Stedman, Robert, photos by. 64p. (Orig.). (gr. 7 up). 1987. pap. 12.50 (*0-9618445-0-7*) Ainslies.

FOLK DANCING

Cone, Molly. Dance Around the Fire. Friedman, Marvin, illus. LC 74-9378. 160p. (gr. 7 up). 1974. 5.95 (*0-395-19490-3*) HM.

Duke, Jerry. Clog Dance in the Appalachians. (Illus.). 96p. (Orig.). 1984. pap. 7.95 (*0-9613727-0-2*) Duke Pub Co.

Hansen, Carol, et al. Shilpa: Folk Dances, Music, Crafts & Puppetry of India. rev. ed. LC 90-12985. (Illus.). 205p. 1990. tchr. looseleaf 44.95 (*0-930141-38-5*) World Eagle.

FOLK LORE

see Folklore

FOLK MUSIC

see Folk Songs

FOLK SONGS

see also Ballads; Carols; Folklore; National Songs

Adams, Pam. There Was an Old Lady Who Swallowed a Fly. LC 90-46921. (ps-3). 1972. 11.95 (*0-85953-021-3*) Childs Play.

Aliki. Hush Little Baby. Aliki, illus. (ps-1). 1972. (Pub. by Treehouse) P-H.

Beall, Pamela C. & Nipp, Susan H. Wee Sing Fun 'n' Folk. (Illus.). 64p. (Orig.). (ps-2). pap. 2.95 (*0-8431-3810-6*); pap. 9.95 bk. & cass. (*0-8431-3802-5*) Price Stern.

Berger, Melvin. The Story of Folk Music. LC 76-18159. (Illus.). (gr. 6 up). 1976. PLB 24.95 (*0-87599-215-3*) S G Phillips.

Chusid, Nancy. Favorite Folk Songs. Chusid, Nancy, illus. 32p. (Orig.). (gr. 2-6). 1990. pap. 6.95 incl. cassette (*1-878624-07-5*) McClanahan Bk.

Durell, Ann, compiled by. The Diane Goode Book of American Folk Tales & Songs. Goode, Diane, illus. LC 89-1097. 64p. (ps-5). 1989. 14.95 (*0-525-44458-0*, DCB) Dutton Child Bks.

Guthrie, Woody. Woody's Twenty Grow Big Songs. Guthrie, Woody, illus. LC 91-753710. 48p. (ps up). 1992. 16.00 (*0-06-020282-3*); incl. cassette 24.95 (*0-06-021033-8*); PLB 15.89 (*0-06-020283-1*) HarpC Child Bks.

Ochs, Bill. The Clarke Learn to Play Tin Whistle Set. (Illus.). 80p. (Orig.). (gr. 3 up). 1988. pap. 6.95 (*0-9623456-0-1*); pap. 14.95 incl. cassette (*0-9623456-5-2*); Incl. tin whistle & cassette in blister package. pap. 24.95 (*0-9623456-2-8*) Pnnywhstlrs Pr.

Rochester Folk Art Guild Staff. Sunlight in the Morning: Songs from the Farm. (Illus.). 40p. (gr. k-6). 1983. 13.00 (*0-686-40298-7*); cassette tape 6.00 (*0-317-00393-3*) Rochester Folk Art.

Seeger, Ruth C. Animal Folk Songs for Children. Cooney, Barbara, illus. LC 92-767692. 90p. (gr. 1-6). 1992. PLB 22.50 (*0-208-02364-X*, Pub. by Linnet); pap. 13.95 (*0-208-02365-8*, Pub. by Linnet) Shoe String.

Teutsch, Betsy. One Little Goat: Had Gadya. LC 89-18298. (Illus.). 32p. 1990. 20.00 (*0-87668-824-5*) Aronson.

Watson, Wendy. Frog Went A-Courting. Watson, Wendy, illus. LC 89-63022. 32p. (ps-2). 1990. 13.95 (*0-688-06539-2*) Lothrop.

Westcott, Nadine B. There's a Hole in the Bucket. Westcott, Nadine B., illus. LC 89-34538. 32p. (ps-2). 1990. PLB 13.89 (*0-06-026423-3*) HarpC Child Bks.

FOLK SONGS, AFRICAN

Goss, Linda & Goss, Clay. The Baby Leopard: An African Folktale. Bailey-Jones, Suzanne & Jones, Michael R., illus. 32p. (ps-3). 1989. audiocassette 7.95 (*0-318-41503-8*) Bantam.

FOLK SONGS, AMERICAN

see Folk Songs–U. S.

FOLK SONGS, ENGLISH

Cauley, Lorinda B., illus. Old MacDonald Had a Farm. 32p. (ps-3). 1989. 14.95 (*0-399-21628-6*, Putnam) Putnam Pub Group.

Chamberlain, Sarah, illus. Friendly Beasts: A Traditional Christmas Carol. LC 91-2115. 24p. (ps-2). 1991. 13.95 (*0-525-44773-3*, DCB) Dutton Child Bks.

Karas, G. Brian. I Know an Old Lady. LC 93-30420. 1994. 14.95 (*0-590-46575-9*) Scholastic Inc.

Langstaff, John. Oh, A-Hunting We Will Go. Parker, Nancy W., illus. LC 91-1987. 32p. (gr. k-3). 1991. pap. 4.95 (*0-689-71503-X*, Aladdin) Macmillan Child Grp.

Mallett, David. Garden Song. Eitan, Ora, photos by. 1995. 15.00 (*0-06-024303-1*); PLB 14.89 (*0-06-024304-X*) HarpC Child Bks.

Moss, Marissa. Knick Knack Paddywack. Moss, Marissa, illus. 32p. (ps-3). 1992. 13.45 (*0-395-54701-6*) HM.

Rounds, Glen, illus. I Know an Old Lady Who Swallowed a Fly. LC 89-46244. 32p. (ps-3). 1990. reinforced bdg. 15.95 (*0-8234-0814-0*) Holiday.

FOLK SONGS, FRENCH

Shulevitz, Uri. One Monday Morning. LC 85-28583. (Illus.). 32p. (ps-3). 1986. pap. 4.95 (*0-689-71062-3*, Aladdin) Macmillan Child Grp.

FOLK SONGS, SPANISH

West, Patricia M. Hispanic Folk Songs of the Southwest: For Bilingual Programs (Part II) 33p. (gr. k-12). 1982. 5.00 (*0-685-42610-6*) U of Denver Teach.

West, Patricia M. & Otero, George G. Hispanic Folk Songs of the Southwest: An Introduction (Part I) updated ed. 33p. (Orig.). (gr. k-12). 1982. pap. 5.00 (*0-943804-11-6*) U of Denver Teach.

FOLK SONGS–U. S.

Clarke, Gus, illus. E I E I O: The Story of Old MacDonald, Who Had a Farm. LC 92-53462. (gr. 3 up). 1993. write for info. (*0-688-12215-9*) Lothrop.

Emberley, Barbara, adapted by. One Wide River to Cross. Emberley, Ed E., illus. 32p. (ps-3). 1992. pap. 4.95 (*0-316-23445-1*) Little.

Kidd, Ronald. On Top of Old Smoky: A Collection of Songs & Stories from Appalachia. Anderson, Linda, illus. LC 92-14437. 40p. 1992. 13.95 (*0-8249-8569-9*, Ideals Child); PLB 14.00 (*0-8249-8586-9*); incl. 60-min. cassette 17.95 (*0-8249-7513-8*) Hambleton-Hill.

Ledbetter, H. & Lomax, John A. Buenas Noches, Irene. Pike, Raffi & Pike, D., eds. Pichardo, Hector, tr. from ENG. Ferguson, Kay, illus. (SPA.). (ps-2). 1993. pap. text ed. 15.00 (*0-922053-27-8*) N Edge Res.

—Goodnight Irene Big Book. Pike, Raffi & Pike, D., eds. Ferguson, Kay, illus. (ps-2). 1988. pap. text ed. 14.00 (*0-922053-08-1*) N Edge Res.

Medearis, Angela S., compiled by. The Zebra-Riding Cowboy: A Folk Song of the Old West. Brusca, Maria C., illus. LC 91-27941. 32p. (ps-2). 1992. 14.95 (*0-8050-1712-7*, Bks Young Read) H Holt & Co.

Pearson, Tracey C., illus. Old MacDonald Had a Farm. LC 83-18815. 32p. (ps-2). 1984. 11.95 (*0-8037-0068-7*) Dial Bks Young.

Rounds, Glen. Old MacDonald Had a Farm. Rounds, Glen, illus. LC 88-24640. 32p. (ps-3). 1989. reinforced bdg. 15.95 (*0-8234-0739-X*); pap. 5.95 (*0-8234-0846-9*) Holiday.

Seeger, Ruth C. American Folk Songs for Children. Cooney, Barbara, illus. 192p. (gr. k-12). 1980. pap. 12.00 (*0-385-15788-6*, Zephyr-BFYR) Doubleday.

Sweet, Melissa, adapted by. & illus. Fiddle-I-Fee: A Farmyard Song for the Very Young. 32p. (ps-1). 1992. 15.95 (*0-316-82516-6*, Joy St Bks) Little.

Theobalds, Prue. Old MacDonald Had a Farm. Theobalds, Prue, illus. 32p. (ps-3). 1991. PLB 14.95 (*0-87226-452-1*, Bedrick Blackie) P Bedrick Bks.

Tolman, Newton F. Quick Tunes & Good Times. (gr. 7 up). 1972. 10.95 (*0-87233-018-4*) Bauhan.

Watson, Wendy. Fox Went Out on a Chilly Night. LC 92-44157. (Illus.). (gr. k-4). 1993. 16.00 (*0-688-10765-6*); PLB 15.93 (*0-688-10766-4*) Lothrop.

Westcott, Nadine B., illus. I've Been Working for the Railroad. LC 94-14466. 1995. write for info. (*0-7868-0053-4*); PLB write for info. (*0-7868-2041-1*) Hyprn Child.

FOLK TALES

see Folklore

FOLKLORE

see also Devil; Folk Songs; Ghosts; Grail; Halloween; Proverbs; Superstition; Witchcraft

Aesop. The Miller, His Son & Their Donkey. Sopko, Eugen, illus. LC 85-7198. 32p. (gr. k-3). 1988. 14.95 (*1-55858-067-0*) North-South Bks NYC.

Amoss, Berthe. Cinderella. Amoss, Berthe, illus. 10p. (ps-7). 1989. pap. 2.95 (*0-922589-04-6*) More Than Card.

—Little Red Riding Hood. (Illus.). 10p. (ps-7). 1989. pap. 2.95 (*0-922589-11-9*) More Than Card.

Asian Cultural Center for UNESCO Staff. Folk Tales from Asia for Children Everywhere, Bk. 4. 60p. (gr. 3-6). 1986. pap. 6.50 (*0-8348-1035-2*) Weatherhill.

Baden, Robert. And Sunday Makes Seven. Mathews, Judith, ed. Edwards, Michelle, illus. LC 89-37823. 40p. (ps-3). 1990. 13.95 (*0-8075-0356-8*) A Whitman.

Bailey, Carolyn S., ed. The Three Billy Goats Gruff & Other Read-Aloud Stories. LC 93-33492. (Illus.). 96p. (Orig.). 1994. pap. 1.00 (*0-685-75328-X*) Dover.

Barnett, Carol. Boy & the Donkey. (ps-3). 1990. 7.95 (*0-8442-9417-9*, Natl Textbk) NTC Pub Grp.

Barton, Byron. Little Red Hen. Barton, Byron, illus. LC 91-4051. 32p. (ps-1). 1993. 15.00 (*0-06-021675-1*); PLB 14.89 (*0-06-021676-X*) HarpC Child Bks.

Barton, Byron, retold by. & illus. Little Red Hen Big Book. LC 91-4051. 32p. (ps-1). 1994. pap. 19.95 (*0-06-443379-X*, Trophy) HarpC Child Bks.

Baumgartener, Barbara. Crocodile! Crocodile! Stories Told Around the World. Moffatt, Judith, illus. LC 93-28027. 48p. (gr. k-3). 1994. 13.95 (*1-56458-463-1*) Dorling Kindersley.

Bellingham, David, et al. Goddesses, Heroes, & Shamans: The Young People's Guide to World Mythology. LC 94-13174. (Illus.). 160p. (gr. 5 up). 1994. 19.95 (*1-85697-999-7*, Kingfisher LKC) LKC.

Birch Lane Press Staff. Cinderella. (ps-3). 1990. 12.95 (*1-55972-054-9*, Birch Ln Pr) Carol Pub Group.

Bishop, Dorothy S. The City Mouse & the Country Mouse. (FRE & ENG., Illus.). 72p. 1989. pap. 4.95 (*0-8442-1086-2*, Natl Textbk) NTC Pub Grp.

—The Lion & the Mouse. (FRE & ENG., Illus.). 72p. 1989. pap. 4.95 (*0-8442-1084-6*, Natl Textbk) NTC Pub Grp.

Bodie, Idella. Ghost Tales for Retelling. Stone, Barbara, ed. (Illus.). 78p. (Orig.). (gr. 6). 1994. pap. 6.95 (*0-87844-125-5*) Sandlapper Pub Co.

To encourage young readers in the art - & pleasure - of storytelling, author Idella Bodie has pulled together twenty-seven tall tales she & her friends told around their backyard campfires when she was a girl. Older ghost story lovers will recognize old favorites like THE GOLDEN ARM. Ms. Bodie has organized these scary stories into five categories: flesh-tingling stories, spirits returning, supernatural stories, haunted places, & shapes & shadows. To assist the young storytellers, she has included a list of "Hints for Effective Storytelling." A retired English teacher, Ms. Bodie has previously written nine books for young readers: seven novels & two biographies. Call 1-800-849-7263 to order copies or request additional information.

Publisher Provided Annotation.

Brett, Jan. The Mitten: A Ukrainian Folktale. Brett, Jan, illus. 32p. (ps-3). 1990. 15.95 (*0-399-21920-X*, Putnam) Putnam Pub Group.

Brooke, L. Leslie. Golden Goose Book. Brooke, L. Leslie, illus. 96p. (ps-3). 1992. 16.45 (*0-395-61303-5*, Clarion Bks) HM.

Brooke, William J. A Telling of the Tales: Five Stories. Egielski, Richard, illus. LC 89-36588. 144p. (gr. 3-7). 1993. pap. 5.95 (*0-06-440467-6*, Trophy) HarpC Child Bks.

Brown, Jerome C. Folk Tale PaperCrafts. (gr. k-5). 1989. pap. 8.95 (*0-8224-3156-4*) Fearon Teach Aids.

Bruchac, Joseph & Ross, Gayle. The Story of the Milky Way: A Cherokee Tale. Stroud, Virginia A., illus. LC 94-20926. 1995. write for info. (*0-8037-1733-4*); PLB write for info. (*0-8037-1738-5*) Dial Bks Young.

Bryan, Ashley. Beat the Story-Drum, Pum-Pum. Bryan, Ashley, illus. LC 86-20598. 80p. (gr. 4-6). 1987. pap. 8.95 (*0-689-71107-7*, Aladdin) Macmillan Child Grp.

Byer, Carol, illus. Henny Penny. LC 80-28146. 32p. (gr. k-3). 1981. PLB 9.79 (*0-89375-490-0*); pap. text ed. 1.95 (*0-89375-491-9*) Troll Assocs.

Calamaro, Emanuel. Les Trois Ours: The Three Bears. rev. ed. Nofziger, Edward, illus. (FRE.). 22p. (gr. k-12). 1990. pap. 2.95 (*0-922852-07-3*) AIMS Intl.

Carter, Margaret, retold by. Beauty & the Beast & Other Stories. Offen, Hilda, illus. LC 93-5772. 1994. 3.95 (*1-85697-967-9*, Kingfisher LKC) LKC.

—Cinderella & Other Stories. Offen, Hilda, illus. LC 93-5770. 1994. 3.95 (*1-85697-968-7*, Kingfisher LKC) LKC.

—Goldilocks & Other Stories. Offen, HIlda, illus. LC 93-5771. 1994. 3.95 (*1-85697-969-5*, Kingfisher LKC) LKC.

—Little Red Riding Hood & Other Stories. Offen, Hilda, illus. LC 93-5768. 32p. (ps-k). 1994. 3.95 (*1-85697-970-9*, Kingfisher LKC) LKC.

—Sleeping Beauty & Other Stories. Offen, Hilda, illus. LC 93-5769. 1994. 3.95 (*1-85697-971-7*, Kingfisher LKC) LKC.

—Snow White & Other Stories. Offen, HIlda, illus. LC 93-5767. 1994. 3.95 (*1-85697-972-5*, Kingfisher LKC) LKC.

—The Ugly Duckling & Other Stories. Offen, Hilda, illus. LC 93-5766. 1994. 3.95 (*1-85697-974-1*, Kingfisher LKC) LKC.

Cauley, Lorinda B., retold by. & illus. Goldilocks & the Three Bears. (ps-3). 1992. pap. 5.95 (*0-399-22326-6*, Sandcastle Bks) Putnam Pub Group.

Chicken Little. (Illus.). 24p. (ps up). 1992. write for info. incl. long-life batteries (*0-307-74809-X*, 64809, Golden Pr) Western Pub.

Clarke, Nora, compiled by. A Treasury of Bedtime Stories. Spenceley, Annabel, illus. LC 92-43152. 160p. (gr. k-4). 1993. pap. 5.95 (*1-85697-931-8*, Kingfisher LKC) LKC.

Climo, Shirley. The Egyptian Cinderella. Heller, Ruth, illus. LC 88-37547. 32p. (gr. k-3). 1989. 15.00 (*0-690-04822-X*, Crowell Jr Bks); PLB 14.89 (*0-690-04824-6*, Crowell Jr Bks) HarpC Child Bks.

Coady, Christopher, retold by. & illus. Red Riding Hood. LC 91-25567. 32p. (ps-6). 1992. 15.00 (*0-525-44896-9*, DCB) Dutton Child Bks.

Cohen, Daniel. Southern Fried Rat & Other Gruesome Tales. Brier, Peggy, illus. LC 82-25120. 128p. (gr. 7 up). 1982. 9.95 (*0-87131-400-2*) M Evans.

Cook, Joel. Rat's Daughter: From an Old Tale. 32p. (ps-3). 1993. 14.95 (*1-56397-140-2*) Boyds Mills Pr.

Cothran, Jean, ed. Whang Doodle: Folk Tales from the Carolinas. LC 72-86904. (Illus.). (gr. 3-7). 1972. Repr. of 1989 ed. 2.95 (*0-87844-052-6*) Sandlapper Pub Co.

Denan, Corinne. Once upon a Time Tales. LC 79-66337. (Illus.). 48p. (gr. 2-6). 1980. lib. bdg. 9.89 (*0-89375-340-8*); pap. 2.95 (*0-89375-339-4*) Troll Assocs.

—Troll Tales. new ed. LC 79-66327. (Illus.). 48p. (gr. 3-6). 1980. lib. bdg. 9.89 (*0-89375-322-X*); pap. 2.95 (*0-89375-321-1*) Troll Assocs.

De Paola, Tomie. Helga's Dowry. De Paola, Tomie, illus. LC 76-54953. 32p. (gr. k-3). 1977. 15.95 (*0-15-233701-6*, HB Juv Bks) HarBrace.

Dyer, Jane, illus. The Random House Book of Bedtime Stories. LC 94-2631. 160p. (gr. 1 up). 1994. 18.00 (*0-679-80832-9*); PLB 18.99 (*0-679-90832-3*) Random.

Edens, Cooper. Three Princesses: The Ultimate Illustrated Edition. (Illus.). (ps-3). 1991. 22.50 (*0-553-07368-0*) Bantam.

Edens, Cooper & Darling, Harold, eds. Favorite Fairy Tales: A Classic Illustrated Edition. Rackham, Arthur, et al, illus. 128p. (ps up). 1991. 16.95 (*0-87701-848-0*) Chronicle Bks.

Edwards, Roberta. Cinco Pescadores Tontos. Wickstrom, Sylvie, illus. Saunders, Paola B., tr. LC 93-48933. (Illus.). 1994. write for info. (*0-679-86543-8*) Random.

Emberley, Rebecca. Three Cool Kids. LC 93-40113. 1995. 14.95 (*0-316-23666-7*) Little.

Fairy Tales from Many Lands. (Illus.). 288p. 1989. 10.99 (*0-517-67951-5*) Random Hse Value.

Foley, Tom, illus. Sakshi Gopal: A Witness for the Wedding. Greene, Joshua, retold by. (Illus.). 16p. (gr. 1-4). 1981. pap. 2.00 (*0-89647-036-9*) Bala Bks.

French, Vivian, retold by. Why the Sea Is Salt. Aggs, Patrice, illus. LC 92-53138. 32p. (ps up). 1993. 14.95 (*1-56402-183-1*) Candlewick Pr.

Friedman, Amy, adapted by. Tell Me a Story. Gilliland, Jillian H., illus. LC 94-600. (gr. k up). 1994. 14.95 (*0-8362-4228-9*) Andrews & McMeel.

Frost, Abigail. The Wolf. LC 89-17445. (Illus.). 48p. (gr. 4-8). 1990. PLB 13.95 (*1-85435-237-7*) Marshall Cavendish.

Gag, Wanda. The Funny Thing. (Illus.). 32p. (ps-3). 1991. pap. 4.95 (*0-698-20676-2*, Sandcastle) Putnam Pub Group.

Galdone, Paul. Little Tuppen. Galdone, Paul, illus. LC 67-10364. 32p. (ps-3). 1979. 14.45 (*0-395-28804-5*, Clarion Bks) HM.

—Little Tuppen: An Old Tale. Galdone, Paul, illus. 32p. (ps-2). 1991. pap. 5.70 (*0-395-58104-4*, Clarion Bks) HM.

—The Magic Porridge Pot. Galdone, Paul, illus. LC 76-3531. 32p. (ps-3). 1979. 13.45 (*0-395-28805-3*, Clarion Bks) HM.

—Three Little Pigs. Galdone, Paul, illus. LC 75-123456. (ps-3). 1979. 13.45 (*0-395-28813-4*, Clarion Bks) HM.

Galdone, Paul, retold by. & illus. The Monster & the Tailor. LC 82-1246. 32p. (ps-1). 1988. pap. 5.70 (*0-89919-795-7*, Clarion Bks) HM.

Gars, Lissa, ed. The Tree Elf & Other Folktales: Illustrated Tales for Children. (Illus.). 60p. (gr. 2-6). 1993. pap. 9.95 (*1-882427-01-7*) Aspasia Pubns.

Geis, Darlene, ed. Walt Disney's Treasury of Children's Classics. (Illus.). (gr. 5 up). 1978. 29.95 (*0-8109-0812-3*) Abrams.

The Gingerbread Boy. 24p. (ps). 1988. pap. write for info. (*1-56288-153-1*) Checkerboard.

Goode, Diane. Diane Goode's Book of Silly Stories & Songs. LC 91-38192. (Illus.). 64p. (ps-6). 1992. 15.00 (*0-525-44967-1*, DCB) Dutton Child Bks.

Goode, Diane, illus. Diane Goode's Book of Scary Stories & Songs. LC 93-32610. 64p. (gr. 3 up). 1994. 15.99 (*0-525-45175-7*, DCB) Dutton Child Bks.

Greene, Joshua, retold by. Krishna, Master of All Mystics. Amendola, Dominique, illus. 16p. (gr. 1-4). 1981. pap. 4.00 (*0-89647-035-0*) Bala Bks.

Greenway, Jennifer, retold by. Goldilocks & the Three Bears. Miles, Elizabeth, illus. 1991. 6.95 (*0-8362-4900-3*) Andrews & McMeel.

—The Three Little Pigs. Dieneman, Debbie, illus. 1991. 6.95 (*0-8362-4904-6*) Andrews & McMeel.

Greer, David. White Horses & Shooting Stars: A Book of Wishes. McLeod, Chum, illus. 160p. (Orig.). (gr. 3 up). 1994. pap. 9.95 (*0-943233-74-7*) Conari Press.

Grimm, Jacob & Grimm, Wilhelm K. The Falling Stars. Sopko, Eugen, illus. LC 85-7193. (gr. k-3). 1988. 14. 95 (*1-55858-041-7*) North-South Bks NYC.

Hader, Berta & Hader, Elmer. Chicken Little & Little Half Chick. LC 93-38611. (Illus.). 1994. pap. write for info. (*0-486-27979-0*) Dover.

Hader, Berta & Hader, Elmer, illus. The Little Red Hen. LC 93-33702. (gr. 2 up). 1994. pap. write for info. (*0-486-27977-4*) Dover.

Hamilton, Virginia. The Dark Way: Stories from the Spirit World. Davis, Lambert, illus. 154p. (gr. 3 up). 1990. 19.95 (*0-15-222340-1*); Numbered, signed & Ltd. ed. 100.00 (*0-15-222341-X*) HarBrace.

Harbour, Jennie, illus. My Book of Favorite Fairy Tales. LC 92-37669. 1993. 8.99 (*0-517-09125-9*, Pub. by Derrydale Bks) Random Hse Value.

Hausman, Gerald. Beth: The Little Girl of Pine Knoll. Totten, Bob, illus. LC 74-82228. 32p. (gr. 6 up). 1974. 15.00 (*0-912846-08-9*) Bookstore Pr.

Hawthorne, Nathaniel. Twice Told Tales. Gemme, F. R., intro. by. (gr. 9 up). 1965. pap. 2.50 (*0-8049-0066-3*, CL-66) Airmont.

Henny Penny, The Gingerbread Boy, Three Billy Goats Gruff, The Ugly Duckling. (Illus.). 24p. 1987. (Honey Bear Bks); Henny Penny. text ed. 3.95 (*0-87449-071-5*, Honey Bear Bks); Gingerbread Boy. text ed. 3.95 (*0-87449-109-6*, Honey Bear Bks); Three Billy Goats Gruff. text ed. 3.95 (*0-87449-110-X*, Honey Bear Bks); Ugly Duckling. text ed. 3.95 (*0-87449-111-8*, Honey Bear Bks) Modern Pub NYC.

Hillert, Margaret. Little Red Riding Hood. (Illus.). (ps-k). 1982. PLB 6.95 (*0-8136-5095-X*, TK2170); pap. 3.50 (*0-8136-5595-1*, TK2171) Modern Curr.

Hodges, Margaret, retold by. Hauntings: Ghosts & Ghouls from Around the World. Wenzel, David, illus. (gr. 3-7). 1991. 16.95 (*0-316-36796-6*) Little.

Hutchinson, Hanna. Chuyen Ba Con Gau: The Three Bears. Vu, Christine, tr. from ENG. Nofziger, Edward, illus. (VIE.). 22p. (Orig.). (gr. k-12). 1990. pap. 2.95 (*0-922852-10-3*) AIMS Intl.

—Drei Baren: The Three Bears. Proffitt, Bettina, tr. from ENG. Nofziger, Edward, illus. (GER.). 22p. (Orig.). (gr. k-12). 1990. pap. 2.95 (*0-922852-08-1*) AIMS Intl.

—I Tre Orsi: The Three Bears. Amico, Victoria, tr. from ENG. Nofziger, Edward, illus. (ITA.). 22p. (Orig.). (gr. k-12). 1990. pap. 2.95 (*0-922852-09-X*) AIMS Intl.

—Los Tres Osos: The Three Bears. Nofsiger, Edward, illus. (SPA.). 22p. (gr. k-12). 1990. pap. 2.95 (*0-922852-06-5*) AIMS Intl.

Impey, Rose, as told by. Read Me a Fairy Tale: A Child's Book of Classic Fairy Tales. Beck, Ian, illus. LC 92-41949. (gr. k up). 1993. 14.95 (*0-590-49431-7*) Scholastic Inc.

J. Sainsbury's Pure Tea Staff. Goldilocks & the Three Bears: Full-Color Picture Book. LC 92-38398. 1993. write for info. (*0-486-27503-5*) Dover.

Jeffries, David. Multicultural Folk Tales: A Thematic Unit. Fullam, Sue & Vasconcelles, Keith, illus. 80p. (gr. 3-5). 1992. wkbk. 8.95 (*1-55734-230-X*) Tchr Create Mat.

Jenkins, Steve, text by. & illus. Duck Breath & Mouse Pie: A Collection of Animal Superstitions. LC 94-2499. 32p. (gr. k-3). 1994. 14.95g (*0-395-69688-7*) Ticknor & Flds Bks Yng Read.

Jennings, Linda, compiled by. A Treasury of Stories from Around the World. Ambrus, Victor, illus. LC 92-43153. 160p. (gr. k-4). 1993. pap. 5.95 (*1-85697-932-6*, Kingfisher LKC) LKC.

Jose, Eduard, adapted by. The Three Little Pigs: A Classic Tale. McDonnell, Janet, tr. Asensio, Augusti, illus. LC 88-35314. 32p. (gr. k-3). 1988. PLB 13.95 (*0-89565-459-8*) Childs World.

Joyce, Susan. Naro, the Ancient Spider. DuBosque, D. C., illus. (gr. 4). 1990. 12.00 (*0-939217-04-X*) Peel Prod.

Kamerman, Sylvia E., ed. The Big Book of Folktale Plays. 336p. (gr. 3-7). 1991. 18.95 (*0-8238-0294-9*) Plays.

Kerven, Rosalind. King Leopard's Gift: And Other Legends of the Animal World. Waldman, Bryna, illus. 32p. 1990. 15.95 (*0-521-36180-X*) Cambridge U Pr.

—Legends of the Animal World. (Illus.). 32p. (gr. 3-7). 1986. 14.95 (*0-521-30576-4*) Cambridge U Pr.

Kimmel, Eric A., retold by. The Gingerbread Man. Lloyd, Megan, illus. 32p. (ps-3). 1993. reinforced bdg. 15.95 (*0-8234-0824-8*); pap. 5.95 (*0-8234-1137-0*) Holiday.

Lang, Andrew. Pink Fairy Book. Ford, Henry J., illus. 360p. (gr. 4-6). 1966. pap. 6.95 (*0-486-21792-2*) Dover.

—The Rainbow Fairy Book. Hague, Michael, illus. Glassman, Peter, intro. by. LC 92-33449. (Illus.). 288p. 1993. 20.00 (*0-688-10878-4*) Morrow Jr Bks.

Lang, Andrew, ed. Blue Fairy Book. Ford, Henry J. & Hood, G. P., illus. LC 34-28315. 390p. (gr. 1-6). 1965. pap. 6.95 (*0-486-21437-0*) Dover.

—Brown Fairy Book. Ford, Henry J., illus. (gr. 1-6). pap. 6.95 (*0-486-21438-9*) Dover.

—Crimson Fairy Book. Ford, Henry J., illus. LC 67-17988. 371p. (gr. 4-6). 1966. pap. 6.95 (*0-486-21799-X*) Dover.

—Green Fairy Book. Ford, Henry J., illus. LC 34-28314. 366p. (gr. 4-6). 1965. pap. 6.95 (*0-486-21439-7*) Dover.

—Grey Fairy Book. Ford, Henry J., illus. LC 67-17983. 387p. (gr. 4-6). 1900. pap. 6.95 (*0-486-21791-4*) Dover.

—Lilac Fairy Book. Ford, H. J., illus. 367p. (ps-4). 1968. pap. 6.95 (*0-486-21907-0*) Dover.

—Olive Fairy Book. Ford, H. J., illus. 330p. (gr. 4-6). 1966. pap. 5.95 (*0-486-21908-9*) Dover.

—Orange Fairy Book. Ford, H. J., illus. 358p. (gr. 1-6). 1968. pap. 6.95 (*0-486-21909-7*) Dover.

—Red Fairy Book. Ford, Henry J. & Speed, Lancelot, illus. 367p. (gr. 4-6). pap. 6.95 (*0-486-21673-X*) Dover.

—Violet Fairy Book. Ford, Henry J. & Lang, H. J., illus. (gr. 4-6). pap. 6.95 (*0-486-21675-6*) Dover.

Lang, Andrew, compiled by. A World of Fairy Tales. Ford, Henry J., illus. Philip, Neil, intro. by. LC 92-46245. 256p. 1993. 20.00 (*0-8037-1250-2*) Dial Bks Young.

Lang, Andrew, ed. Yellow Fairy Book. Ford, Henry J., illus. 321p. (gr. 4-6). pap. 6.95 (*0-486-21674-8*) Dover.

Langley, Jonathan. Goldilocks & the Three Bears. Langley, Jonathan, illus. LC 91-33155. 32p. (gr. k-3). 1993. 11.00 (*0-06-020814-7*); PLB 10.89 (*0-06-020815-5*) HarpC Child Bks.

Lester, Julius. The Knee-High Man & Other Tales. Pinto, Ralph, illus. LC 72-181785. 32p. (ps-3). 1985. 12.95 (*0-8037-4593-1*) Dial Bks Young.

Lester, Julius, as told by. The Last Tales of Uncle Remus. Pinkney, Jerry, illus. LC 93-7531. (ps-4). 1994. 16.99 (*0-8037-1303-7*); PLB 16.89 (*0-8037-1304-5*) Dial Bks Young.

Lipson, Greta. Fact, Fantasy, Folklore. 160p. (gr. 3-12). 1977. 12.95 (*0-916456-11-0*, GA71) Good Apple.

—Famous Fables for Little Troupers. Kropa, Susan, illus. 168p. (gr. k-6). 1984. 13.95 (*0-86653-202-1*, GA 554) Good Apple.

Little People Big Book about Magical Worlds. 64p. (ps-1). 1990. write for info. (*0-8094-7495-6*); PLB write for info. (*0-8094-7496-4*) Time-Life.

Little Red Riding Hood. (Illus.). 24p. (ps up). 1992. write for info. incl. long-life batteries (*0-307-74810-3*, 64810, Golden Pr) Western Pub.

Lottridge, Celia B. Ten Small Tales. Fitzgerald, Joanne, illus. LC 92-2878. 64p. (gr. k-4). 1994. SBE 15.95 (*0-689-50568-X*, M K McElderry) Macmillan Child Grp.

Low, Alice, ed. Spooky Stories for a Dark & Stormy Night. Wilson, Gahan, illus. LC 93-33638. 128p. (gr. 3 up). 1994. 19.95 (*0-7868-0012-7*); PLB 19.89 (*0-7868-2008-X*) Hyprn Child.

Lurie, Alison. Clever Gretchen & Other Forgotten Folktales. Tomes, Margot, illus. LC 78-22512. 128p. (gr. 4-6). 1980. PLB 12.89 (*0-690-03944-1*, Crowell Jr Bks) HarpC Child Bks.

McCloskey, Robert. Centerburg Tales. McCloskey, Robert, illus. LC 51-10675. 192p. (gr. 4-6). 1951. pap. 14.95 (*0-670-20977-5*) Viking Child Bks.

MacDonald, Margaret R. Peace Tales: World Folktales to Talk About. LC 92-8994. (gr. 1-6). 1992. PLB 22.50 (*0-208-02328-3*, Linnet); pap. text ed. 13.95 (*0-208-02329-1*, Linnet) Shoe String.

Mace, Jean. Home Fairy Tales. Booth, Mary L., tr. from FRE. LC 78-74517. (Illus.). (gr. 4-5). 1979. Repr. of 1867 ed. 24.75x (*0-8486-0220-X*) Roth Pub Inc.

McPhail, David. Goldilocks & the Three Bears. McPhail, David, illus. LC 93-43992. 1995. write for info. (*0-590-48117-7*) Scholastic Inc.

—The Three Little Pigs. McPhail, David, illus. LC 93-43991. 1995. write for info. (*0-590-48118-5*) Scholastic Inc.

McQueen, Lucinda. La Gallinita Roja. (SPA.). 1993. pap. 28.67 (*0-590-71879-7*) Scholastic Inc.

McQueen, Lucinda, illus. The Little Red Hen. 32p. (Orig.). (gr. k-2). 1985. Big book. 19.95 (*0-590-71718-9*); pap. 2.50 (*0-590-41145-4*) Scholastic Inc.

Maggi, Tolstoy M. Fables & Folk Tales. (Illus.). 30p. (ps-1). 1986. 3.95 (*0-8120-5727-9*) Barron.

Mahan, Benton, illus. Goldilocks & the Three Bears. LC 80-27631. 32p. (gr. k-2). 1981. PLB 9.79 (*0-89375-470-6*); pap. text ed. 1.95 (*0-89375-471-4*) Troll Assocs.

Marcuse, Aida E. Caperucita Roja y la Luna de Papel. Torrecilla, Pablo, illus. (SPA.). 24p. (Orig.). (gr. k-6). 1993. PLB 7.50x (*1-56492-103-4*) Laredo.

Mayer, Marianna. The Golden Swan. Sauber, Robert, illus. (gr. 3 up). 1990. 14.95 (*0-553-07054-1*, Skylark) Bantam.

—Noble-Hearted Kate. Pels, Winslow, illus. (gr. 3 up). 1990. 14.95 (*0-553-07049-5*, Skylark) Bantam.

Mayo, Margaret, retold by. Magical Tales from Many Lands. Ray, Jane, illus. LC 93-12164. 128p. 1993. 19. 99 (*0-525-45017-3*, DCB) Dutton Child Bks.

Medearis, Angela S., adapted by. The Christmas Riddle. Ward, John, illus. LC 93-10713. (gr. 2 up). 1994. write for info. (*0-525-67469-1*, Lodestar Bks) Dutton Child Bks.

Merk, Ann & Merk, Jim. Weather Signs. LC 94-13323. (gr. 3 up). 1994. write for info. (*0-86593-388-X*) Rourke Corp.

Minters, Frances. Cinder-Elly. Karas, G. Brian, illus. LC 93-14533. 32p. (ps-3). 1994. PLB 13.99 (*0-670-84417-9*) Viking Child Bks.

Muhaiyaddeen, M. R. Treasures of the Heart: Sufi Stories for Young Children. Steele, Christine, ed. Balamore, Usha, tr. Deis, Ishaq, et al, illus. 110p. (ps). 1993. 10. 00 (*0-914390-33-3*) Fellowship Pr PA.

Ormerod, Jan. The Story of Chicken Licken. Ormerod, Jan, illus. LC 85-7911. 32p. (ps-1). 1986. 13.00 (*0-688-06058-7*) Lothrop.

Pagnucci, Susan & Pagnucci, Franco. I Can! Folktales: Stories from Around the World for Young Children. Pagnucci, Susan, illus. 64p. (Orig.). (ps-3). Date not set. pap. 8.95 (*0-929326-10-5*) Bur Oak Pr Inc.

Pasamanick, Judith & Thoms, Judith J. Folk Tales Told Around the World. Hudson, Carol, illus. LC 92-47128. 48p. (gr. 4-6). 1993. PLB 12.95 (*0-382-24363-3*); 10. 95 (*0-382-24372-2*) Silver Burdett Pr.

Passes, David. Dragons: Truth, Myth, & Legend. Anderson, Wayne, illus. LC 92-44745. (gr. 7 up). 1993. 14.95 (*0-307-17500-6*, Artsts & Writers Guild) Western Pub.

Pearson, Susan. Jack & the Beanstalk. (ps-6). 1993. pap. 5.95 (*0-671-87172-2*, S&S BFYR) S&S Trade.

Pellowski, Anne, ed. A World of Children's Stories. Ortiz, Gloria, illus. LC 93-13509. 192p. (Orig.). (gr. 3-6). 1993. pap. 19.95 (*0-377-00259-3*) Friendship Pr.

Phelps, Ethel J. The Maid of the North: Feminist Folk Tales from Around the World. Bloom, Lloyd, illus. LC 80-21500. 196p. (gr. 4-6). 1982. 10.95 (*0-03-056893-5*, Bks Young Read); pap. 9.95 (*0-8050-0679-6*) H Holt & Co.

Pinocchio. 1991. 1.00 (*1-880459-06-X*) Arrow Trad.

Pizzo, Joan E. Amy Avocet. Geronimi, Clyde, illus. LC 83-70739. (gr. k-6). 1983. 8.95 (*0-939126-06-0*) Back Bay.

Polette, Nancy. Reading the World with Folktales. Dillon, Paul, illus. 124p. (Orig.). (gr. 2-4). 1993. pap. 12.95 (*1-879287-19-6*) Bk Lures.

Pomerantz, Charlotte. Whiff, Sniff, Nibble, & Chew: The Gingerbread Boy Retold. Incisa, Monica, illus. LC 83-14179. 24p. (gr. k-3). 1984. PLB 8.59 (*0-688-02552-8*) Greenwillow.

Price, Susan, retold by. The Three Bears & Other Stories. Maclean, Moira & Maclean, Colin, illus. LC 92-26450. 24p. (ps-1). 1993. 4.95 (*1-85697-906-7*, Kingfisher LKC) LKC.

Rader, Laura, illus. Goldilocks & the Three Bears. LC 94-4986. 1995. write for info. (*0-688-13258-8*, Tambourine Bks) Morrow.

Ragache, Gilles. Dragons. LC 90-25902. (Illus.). 48p. (gr. 4-8). 1991. PLB 13.95 (*1-85435-265-2*) Marshall Cavendish.

Rappaport, Doreen, adapted by. The New King: A Madagascan Legend. Lewis, Earl B., illus. LC 93-28561. 1995. write for info. (*0-8037-1460-2*); PLB write for info. (*0-8037-1461-0*) Dial Bks Young.

Reiff, Tana, retold by. Tales of Wonder: Reading Level 2-3. Dobbs, Holly J., illus. LC 93-16083. 1993. 4.25 (*0-88336-459-X*); read-along tape 10.50 (*0-88336-524-3*) New Readers.

Riordan, James & Lewis, Brenda R. An Illustrated Treasury of Myths & Legends. Ambrus, Victor, illus. 152p. (gr. 7 up). 1991. 12.95 (*0-87226-349-5*) P Bedrick Bks.

Roberts, Tom. Goldilocks. Kubinyi, Laszlo, illus. LC 93-6679. (ps-6). 1993. Incl. cassette. 9.95 (*0-88708-322-6*, Dist. by S&S Trade) Picture Bk Studio.

—Red Riding Hood. Kubinyi, Laszlo, illus. LC 93-12152. (ps-6). 1993. Incl. cassette. 9.95 (*0-88708-320-X*, Rabbit Ears) Picture Bk Studio.

—The Three Little Pigs. Jorgensen, David, illus. 64p. 1993. Repr. of 1990 ed. incl. cass. 9.95 (*0-88708-299-8*, Rabbit Ears) Picture Bk Studio.

Roberts, Tom, adapted by. The Three Little Pigs. Jorgensen, David, illus. LC 92-36277. 1993. 4.95 (*0-88708-298-X*, Rabbit Ears) Picture Bk Studio.

Rohmer, Harriet & Olivarez, Anna, eds. How We Came to the Fifth World Read-Along. (SPA & ENG.). (gr. 2-7). 1987. incl. audiocassette 22.95 (*0-89239-038-7*) Childrens Book Pr.

Rojankovsky, Feodor. Tall Book of Nursery Tales. Rojankovsky, Feodor, illus. LC 44-3881. 120p. (ps-3). 1944. 9.95 (*0-06-025065-8*) HarpC Child Bks.

Roland, Donna. Grandfather's Stories. Oden, Ron, illus. (Orig.). (gr. k-3). 1993. pap. 4.95 (*0-941996-00-X*); Tchr's. ed. 5.50 (*0-685-42442-1*); Flannelboard set. 12.00 (*0-685-73481-1*); Video cass. 32.00 (*0-685-73482-X*); Audio cass., per culture. 5.95 (*0-685-73483-8*) Open My World.

—More of Grandfather's Stories. Oden, Ron, illus. 25p. (Orig.). (gr. k-3). 1993. pap. 4.95 (*0-941996-02-6*); tchr's. ed. 5.50 (*0-941996-13-1*) Open My World.

Rosen, Marcia. How the Animals Got Their Colors: Animal Myths from Around the World. Clementson, J., illus. 1992. 14.95 (*0-15-236783-7*, HB Juv Bks) HarBrace.

Ross, Tony, retold by. & illus. Goldilocks & the Three Bears. 26p. (ps-3). 1992. 13.95 (*0-87951-453-1*) Overlook Pr.

Rounds, Glen, retold by. & illus. Three Little Pigs & the Big Bad Wolf. LC 91-18173. 32p. (ps-3). 1992. reinforced bdg. 14.95 (*0-8234-0923-6*) Holiday.

Rowe, W. W. The Buddha's Question. LC 93-13993. 1994. 9.95 (*1-55939-020-4*) Snow Lion.

Sanfield, Steve. The Feather Merchants: & Other Tales of the Fools of Chelm. Magaril, Mikhail, illus. LC 90-29273. 112p. (gr. 3 up). 1991. 15.95 (*0-531-05958-8*); RLB 15.99 (*0-531-08558-9*) Orchard Bks Watts.

Schwartz, Alvin. All of Our Noses Are Here & Other Noodle Tales. Weinhaus, Karen A., illus. LC 84-48330. 64p. (gr. k-3). 1985. PLB 13.89 (*0-06-025288-X*) HarpC Child Bks.

—Ghosts! Ghostly Tales from Folklore. Chess, Victoria, illus. LC 90-21746. 64p. (gr. k-3). 1991. 14.00 (*0-06-021796-0*); PLB 13.89 (*0-06-021797-9*) HarpC Child Bks.

—Stories to Tell a Cat. Huerta, Catherine, illus. LC 91-37257. 80p. (gr. 4 up). 1992. 15.00 (*0-06-020850-3*); PLB 14.89 (*0-06-020851-1*) HarpC Child Bks.

—Tales of Trickery from the Land of Spoof. Christiana, David, illus. 88p. (gr. 3 up). 1988. pap. 3.50 (*0-374-47426-5*) FS&G.

Shannon, George. More Stories to Solve. Sis, Peter, illus. LC 93-11719. 64p. (gr. 4 up). 1994. pap. 4.95 (*0-688-12947-1*, Pub. by Beech Tree Bks) Morrow.

—More Stories to Solve: Fifteen Folktales from Around the World. Sis, Peter, illus. LC 89-7413. 64p. (gr. k up). 1991. 12.95 (*0-688-09161-X*) Greenwillow.

Shearer, Marilyn J. The Crown of Fools: Based on: The Tortoise & the Hare. 16p. (ps-6). 1989. 19.95 (*0-685-30101-X*); pap. 10.95 (*0-685-30102-8*) L Ashley & Joshua.

Sherman, Josepha. Toldtales: Eight Folktales from Around the World. (Illus.). 96p. (gr. 4-6). 1994. PLB 12.95 (*1-881889-64-5*) Silver Moon.

Shulevitz, Uri. One Monday Morning. LC 85-28583. (Illus.). 32p. (ps-3). 1986. pap. 4.95 (*0-689-71062-3*, Aladdin) Macmillan Child Grp.

Sierra, Judy, ed. Nursery Tales Around the World. Vitale, Stefano, illus. LC 93-2068. Date not set. write for info. (*0-395-67894-3*, Clarion Bks) HM.

Slator, Lana. Giants & Gnomes Coloring Album. (Illus.). 32p. (gr. k-6). 1978. pap. 4.50 (*0-8431-1763-X*, 94-9, Troubador) Price Stern.

Souci, Robert D. S., ed. More Short & Shivery: Thirty Terrifying Tales. LC 94-479. 1994. 13.95 (*0-385-32102-3*) Delacorte.

Stake, Fran. The Animals Talk to One Another: A Christmas Folktale Retold & Illustrated by Fran Stake. STake, Fran, illus. 20p. (ps). 1993. Set with painting. 1100.00 (*0-9619075-0-9*) Stake Studio.

Stevenson, Peter. Play Mask Book - Cinderella. 12p. (ps-3). 1991. pap. 5.95 (*0-8167-2371-0*) Troll Assocs.

Stroyer, Paul. Second Treasure Chest of Tales. (Illus.). (gr. 3 up). 1960. 12.95 (*0-8392-3032-X*) Astor-Honor.

Tales of the Heart. LC 89-11509. 80p. (gr. 3-9). 1990. PLB 19.97 (*0-8114-2408-1*) Raintree Steck-V.

Thompson, Stith, ed. One Hundred Favorite Folktales. LC 68-27355. (Illus.). 456p. 1968. 29.95 (*0-253-15940-7*); pap. 12.95x (*0-253-20172-1*, MB-172) Ind U Pr.

Thornhill, Jan, retold by. & illus. Animal Legends. LC 93-20205. (gr. 1-3). 1993. pap. 15.00 (*0-671-87428-4*, S&S BFYR) S&S Trade.

Three Little Pigs. (Illus.). (ps-1). 1985. 1.98 (*0-517-47899-4*) Random Hse Value.

The Three Little Pigs. 32p. (ps-1). 1985. 2.49 (*0-517-46242-7*) Random Hse Value.

The Three Little Pigs. (Illus.). 24p. (ps up). 1992. write for info. incl. long-life batteries (*0-307-74807-3*, 64807, Golden Pr) Western Pub.

Varnai, Gyorgy. The Mouse & the Lion. Mark, Steve, illus. LC 92-43693. (gr. 1-5). 1995. 15.95 (*1-56766-091-6*) Childs World.

Vornholt, John. Break a Leg! Famous Curses & Superstitions. LC 94-5119. 96p. (Orig.). 1994. pap. 3.50 (*0-380-76858-5*, Camelot) Avon.

Vozar, David. Yo, Hungry Wolf! A Nursery Rap. Lewin, Betsy, illus. LC 91-46264. (gr. 1-4). 1993. 15.95 (*0-385-30452-8*) Doubleday.

Vreeman, J. The Three Bears - Little Red Riding Hood. (Illus.). 16p. (Orig.). 1985. pap. 3.95 (*0-918789-03-6*) FreeMan Prods.

Wahl, Jan. Little Eight John. Clay, Wil, illus. 32p. (gr. k-3). 1992. 14.00 (*0-525-67367-9*, Lodestar Bks) Dutton Child Bks.

Wallner, John. City Mouse - Country Mouse & Two More Tales from Aesop. Wallner, John, illus. 32p. (Orig.). (gr. k-3). 1987. pap. 2.50 (*0-590-41155-1*) Scholastic Inc.

Yeoman, John. The Singing Tortoise: And Other Animal Folktales. Blake, Quentin, illus. LC 93-31208. 96p. (gr. 1 up). 1994. 18.00 (*0-688-13366-5*, Tambourine Bks) Morrow.

Yolen, Jane. The Girl Who Cried Flowers & Other Tales. Palladini, David, illus. LC 73-8903. 64p. (gr. 3-6). 1974. (Crowell Jr Bks); (Crowell Jr Bks) HarpC Child Bks.

FOLKLORE–AFRICA

Aardema, Verna. Bimwili & the Zimwi. Meddaugh, Susan, illus. LC 85-4449. 32p. (ps-3). 1985. 14.99 (*0-8037-0212-4*); PLB 12.89 (*0-8037-0213-2*) Dial Bks Young.

—Bringing the Rain to Kapiti Plain: A Nandi Tale. Vidal, Beatriz, illus. (ps-3). 1993. pap. 6.99 incl. cassette (*0-14-095052-4*, Puffin) Puffin Bks.

Aardema, Verna & Clouse, Nancy. Sebugugugu the Glutton: A Bantu Tale from Ruanda, Africa. (Illus.). 32p. (gr. 2-4). 1993. 14.95 (*0-86543-377-1*) Africa World.

Aardema, Verna, compiled by. Misoso: Once Upon a Time Tales from Africa. Ruffins, Reynold, illus. LC 92-43288. 96p. (gr. k-5). 1994. 18.00 (*0-679-83430-3*, Apple Soup Bks); lib. bdg. 18.99 (*0-679-93430-8*, Apple Soup Bks) Knopf Bks Yng Read.

Aardema, Verna, retold by. Rabbit Makes a Monkey of Lion: A Swahili Tale. Pinkney, Jerry, illus. 32p. (ps-3). 1993. pap. 4.99 (*0-14-054593-X*) Puffin Bks.

—This for That: A Tonga Tale. Chess, Victoria, illus. LC 93-32309. 1995. write for info. (*0-8037-1553-6*); PLB write for info. (*0-8037-1554-4*) Dial Bks Young.

—Traveling to Tondo: A Tale of the Nkundo of Zaire. Hillenbrand, Will, illus. LC 90-39419. 40p. (gr. k-4). 1991. PLB 14.99 (*0-679-90081-0*) Knopf Bks Yng Read.

—Traveling to Tondo: A Tale of the Nkundo of Zaire. Hillenbrand, Will, illus. LC 90-39419. 40p. (ps-3). 1994. pap. 5.99 (*0-679-85309-X*) Knopf Bks Yng Read.

Anderson, David A. & Sankofa. The Rebellion of Humans. Wilson, Kathleen A., illus. 32p. 1994. 18.95 (*0-9629978-6-2*) Sights Prods.

Appiah, Peggy. Tales of an Ashanti Father. Dickson, Mona, illus. LC 88-19059. 160p. (gr. 2-6). 1989. lib. bdg. 12.95x (*0-8070-8312-7*); pap. 6.95 (*0-8070-8313-5*, NL4) Beacon Pr.

Arnott, Kathleen. African Myths & Legends. Kiddell-Monroe, Joan, illus. 224p. (gr. 4 up). 1990. pap. 10.95 (*0-19-274143-8*) OUP.

Barbosa, Rogerio A. African Animal Tales. Guthrie, Feliz, tr. from POR. Fittipaldi, Cica, illus. LC 92-42378. 60p. (gr. 1-3). 1993. 17.95 (*0-912078-96-0*) Volcano Pr.

Bettison, Joan. Baba Nangko. Fleming, Leanne, illus. LC 93-26225. 1994. 4.25 (*0-383-03733-6*) SRA Schl Grp.

Blakely, Nora B. Shani on the Hill. Gilchrist, Jan S., illus. (gr. 1). 1988. pap. 3.95 (*0-88378-123-9*) Third World.

Bryan, Ashley. Lion & the Ostrich Chicks & Other African Folk Tales. Ashley, Bryan, illus. LC 86-3349. 96p. (gr. 2-6). 1986. SBE 14.95 (*0-689-31311-X*, Atheneum Child Bk) Macmillan Child Grp.

—The Ox of the Wonderful Horns: And Other African Folktales. reissue ed. Bryan, Ashley, illus. LC 75-154749. 48p. (ps-4). 1993. RSBE 14.95 (*0-689-31799-9*, Atheneum Child Bk) Macmillan Child Grp.

Cabral, Len. Anansi's Narrow Waist. 16p. (ps-2). 1994. text ed. 3.95 (*0-673-36200-0*) GdYrBks.

Ching. The Baboon's Umbrella. LC 91-7952. (Illus.). 24p. (ps-3). 1991. PLB 12.85 (*0-516-05131-8*); pap. 4.95 (*0-516-45131-6*) Childrens.

Chocolate, Deborah M. Imani in the Belly. Boies, Alex, illus. LC 93-33803. 32p. (gr. k-3). 1994. PLB 14.95 (*0-8167-3466-6*); pap. text ed. 3.95 (*0-8167-3467-4*) BrdgeWater.

Claire, Elizabeth. The Sun, the Wind & Tashira: A Hottentot Tale from Africa. Mills, Elise, illus. 24p. (Orig.). (gr. k-4). 1994. big bk. 19.95 (*1-879531-08-9*); PLB 9.95 (*1-879531-41-0*); pap. 4.95 (*1-879531-20-8*) Mondo Pubng.

Climo, Shirley. Why Monkeys Live in Trees. Date not set. 15.00 (*0-06-020773-6*, HarpT); PLB 14.89 (*0-06-020774-4*, HarpT) HarpC.

Dee, Ruby. Tower to Heaven. Bent, Jennifer, illus. LC 90-34131. 32p. (ps-2). 1991. 14.95 (*0-8050-1460-8*, Bks Young Read) H Holt & Co.

Fairman, Tony. Bury My Bones But Keep My Words: African Tales for Retelling. Asare, Meshack, illus. 192p. 1992. 15.95 (*0-8050-2333-X*, Bks Young Read) H Holt & Co.

Fairman, Tony, retold by. Bury My Bones but Keep My Words: African Tales for Retelling. Asare, Meshack, illus. 192p. (gr. 5 up). 1994. pap. 4.99 (*0-14-036889-2*) Puffin Bks.

Ford, Bernette, adapted by. The Hunter Who Was King & Other African Tales. Ford, George, illus. LC 93-10278. 24p. (ps-3). 1994. 14.95 (*1-56282-585-2*) Hyprn Child.

Gleeson, Brian. Koi & the Kola Nuts. Ruffins, Reynold, illus. LC 92-7094. 40p. 1992. pap. 14.95 (*0-88708-281-5*, Rabbit Ears); pap. 19.95 incl. cass. (*0-88708-282-3*, Rabbit Ears) Picture Bk Studio.

Greaves, Nick. When Hippo Was Hairy & Other Tales from Africa. Clement, Rod, illus. 144p. (gr. 3-12). 1988. 12.95 (*0-8120-4131-3*) Barron.

—When Hippo Was Hairy & Other Tales from Africa. Clement, Rod, illus. 144p. (gr. k up). 1991. pap. 8.95 (*0-8120-4548-3*) Barron.

—When Lion Could Fly: And Other Tales from Africa. Clement, Rod, illus. LC 93-21841. 144p. (gr. 3 up). 1993. 13.95 (*0-8120-6344-9*); pap. 8.95 (*0-8120-1625-4*) Barron.

Haley, Gail E. A Story, A Story. Haley, Gail E., illus. LC 69-18961. 36p. (ps-3). 1970. SBE 15.95 (*0-689-20511-2*, Atheneum Child Bk) Macmillan Child Grp.

Hull, Robert. African Stories. Kettle, Peter, illus. LC 92-40632. 48p. (gr. 5-9). 1993. 15.95 (*1-56847-004-5*) Thomson Lrning.

Hunter, Bobbie D. The Legend of the African Bao-Bab Tree. Hunter, Bobbie D., illus. 32p. (gr. 3-6). 1994. 16.95 (*0-86543-421-2*); pap. 8.95 (*0-86543-422-0*) Africa World.

Katz, William L. & Franklin, Paula A. Proudly Red & Black: Tales of Native & African Americans. LC 92-36119. 1993. 13.95 (*0-684-31801-6*, Atheneum Child Bk) Macmillan Child Grp.

Kimmel, Eric A., retold by. Anansi & the Talking Melon. LC 3-4239. (Illus.). 32p. (ps-3). 1994. reinforced bdg. 15.95 (*0-8234-1104-4*) Holiday.

—Anansi Goes Fishing. Stevens, Janet, illus. LC 91-17813. 32p. (ps-3). 1992. reinforced bdg. 15.95 (*0-8234-0918-X*) Holiday.

—Anansi Goes Fishing. Stevens, Janet, illus. (ps-3). 1993. pap. 5.95 (*0-8234-1022-6*) Holiday.

Knutson, Barbara. How the Guinea Fowl Got Her Spots: A Swahili Tale of Friendship. Knutson, Barbara, illus. 24p. (ps-4). 1990. PLB 18.95 (*0-87614-416-4*) Carolrhoda Bks.

—Why the Crab Has No Head: An African Folktale. (Illus.). 24p. (ps-3). 1987. lib. bdg. 15.95 (*0-87614-322-2*); pap. 4.95 (*0-87614-489-X*) Carolrhoda Bks.

Knutson, Barbara, retold by. & illus. Sungura & Leopard: A Swahili TricksterTale. LC 92-31905. 1993. 15.95 (*0-316-50010-0*) Little.

Kroll, Virginia. Jaha & Jamil Went down the Hill: An African Mother Goose. (Illus.). 32p. (ps-4). 1994. 14.95 (*0-88106-866-7*); PLB 15.00 (*0-88106-867-5*); pap. 6.95 (*0-88106-865-9*) Charlesbridge Pub.

Lester, Julius. The Man Who Knew Too Much: A Moral Tale from the Baila of Zambia. Jenkins, Leonard, illus. LC 94-40810. (gr. 4 up). 1994. 14.95 (*0-395-60521-0*, Clarion Bks) HM.

Lottridge, Celia B., retold by. The Name of the Tree: A Bantu Folktale. Wallace, Ian, illus. LC 89-2430. 36p. (gr. 1-5). 1990. SBE 14.95 (*0-689-50490-X*, M K McElderry) Macmillan Child Grp.

McDermorr, Gerald. The Magic Tree. 1994. 15.95 (*0-8050-3080-8*) H Holt & Co.

Mann, Kenny. I Am Not Afraid! Based on a Masai Tale. Leonard, Richard, illus. LC 92-13811. 1993. 9.99 (*0-553-09119-0*, Little Rooster); 3.50 (*0-553-37108-8*, Little Rooster) Bantam.

Norman, Floyd. Afro-Classic Folk Tales, Bk. 4: High John. Stewart, lyn, ed. Sullivan, Leo, illus. & intro. by. 28p. (Orig.). (gr. 4-7). 1992. pap. 9.95 (*1-881368-21-1*) Vignette.

Norman, Floyd & Sullivan, Leo. Afro-Classic Folk Tales, Bk. 6: Work-Let-Me-See. Stewart, Lyn, ed. Sullivan, Leo, illus. 28p. (Orig.). (gr. 4-7). 1992. pap. 9.95 (*1-881368-23-8*) Vignette.

Onyefulu, Obi, retold by. Chinye: A West African Folk Tale. Safarewicz, Evie, illus. 32p. (gr. k up). 1994. 14.99 (*0-670-85115-9*) Viking Child Bks.

Pitcher, Diana. The Mischief Maker. Dove, Sally, illus. 64p. 1990. pap. 5.95 (*0-86486-106-0*, Pub. by D Philip South Africa) Interlink Pub.

—Tokoloshi: African Folktales Retold. Rutherford, Meg, illus. 64p. (gr. 5 up). 1993. pap. 8.95 (*1-883672-03-1*) Tricycle Pr.

Poland, Marguerite. The Wood-Ash Stars. Altshuler, Shanne, illus. 64p. 1990. pap. 5.95 (*0-86486-089-7*, Pub. by D Philip South Africa) Interlink Pub.

Rohmer, Harriet & Olivarez, Anna, eds. Brother Anansi & the Cattle Ranch Read-Along. (SPA & ENG.). (ps-7). 1989. incl. audiocassette 22.95 (*0-89239-063-8*) Childrens Book Pr.

Roth, Susan L. Fire Came to the Earth People: A Dahomean Folktale. (ps-3). 1994. pap. 4.99 (*0-440-40844-X*) Dell.

Sandlain-Buchanan, Deborah. The Chocolate Tree: An African Folktale. Sandlain-Buchanan, Deborah, illus. 16p. (Orig.). (gr. k-3). 1993. write for info. (*0-9639057-2-4*); lib. bdg. write for info. (*0-9639057-3-2*); pap. 3.99 (*0-9639057-0-8*); 5.00 (*0-9639057-1-6*) Chocolate Tree.

Steptoe, John. Mufaro's Beautiful Daughters: Big Book Edition. 32p. (ps up). 1993. pap. 18.95 (*0-688-12935-8*, Mulberry) Morrow.

Sullivan, Leo. Afro-Classic Folk Tales, Bk. 2: Anancy & the Tiger. Stewart, Lyn, ed. Norman, Floyd, illus. 28p. (Orig.). (gr. 4-7). 1992. pap. 9.95 (*1-881368-19-X*) Vignette.

Sullivan, Leo & Norman, Floyd. Afro-Classic Folk Tales, Bk. 3: Bro Rabbit. Stewart, Lyn, ed. Sullivan, Leo, illus. 28p. (Orig.). (gr. 4-7). 1992. pap. 9.95 (*1-881368-20-3*) Vignette.

—Afro-Classic Folk Tales, Bk. 5: Anancy's Riding Horse. Stewart, Lyn, ed. Sullivan, Leo, illus. 28p. (Orig.). (gr. 4-7). 1992. pap. 9.95 (*1-881368-22-X*) Vignette.

Tadjo, Veronique. Lord of the Dance: An African Retelling. Tadjo, Veronique, illus. LC 89-2785. 32p. (gr. 1-4). 1989. (Lipp Jr Bks); PLB 12.89 (*0-397-32352-2*, Lipp Jr Bks) HarpC Child Bks.

Troughton, Joanna, retold by. Tortoise's Dream: An African Folk Tale. Troughton, Joannna, illus. LC 85-15065. 28p. (ps-2). 1986. PLB 14.95 (*0-87226-039-9*, Bedrick Blackie) P Bedrick Bks.

White, Carolyn. The Children Who Lived in a Tree. Kromer, Christiane, illus. LC 92-46428. 1994. pap. 15.00 (*0-671-79818-9*, S&S BFYR) S&S Trade.

Whiting, Helen A. Negro Folk Tales. Jones, Lois M., illus. (gr. 1). 1990. 4.25 (*0-87498-006-2*) Assoc Pubs DC.

Williams, Sheron. And in the Beginning... Roth, Robert, illus. LC 90-43094. 40p. (gr. 1-5). 1992. SBE 13.95 (*0-689-31650-X*, Atheneum Child Bk) Macmillan Child Grp.

Winther, Barbara. Plays from African Tales. (Orig.). 1992. pap. 13.95 (*0-8238-0296-5*) Plays.

FOLKLORE–AFRICA, CENTRAL

Aardema, Verna. Sebgugugu the Glutton. Clouse, Nancy, illus. 40p. (gr. k-4). 1993. text ed. 14.99 (*0-8028-5073-1*) Eerdmans.

Grifalconi, Ann. Village of Round & Square Houses. Grifalconi, Ann, illus. 32p. (gr. k-3). 1986. lib. bdg. 15.95 (*0-316-32862-6*) Little.

Strong, Polly. African Tales: Folklore of the Central African Republic. Strong, Polly, tr. from SAG. Wimer, Rodney, illus. LC 91-66693. 96p. (gr. 2 up). 1992. 10.95 (*1-878893-15-7*); pap. 6.95 (*1-878893-14-9*) Telcraft Bks.

FOLKLORE–AFRICA, EAST

Mollel, Tololwa M. Rhinos for Lunch & Elephants for Supper! Spurll, Barbara, illus. 32p. (ps-3). 1992. 15.95 (*0-395-60734-5*, Clarion Bks) HM.

Mollel, Tololwa M., retold by. The Princess Who Lost Her Hair: An Akamba Legend. Reasoner, Charles, illus. LC 92-13273. 32p. (gr. 2-5). 1992. lib. bdg. 11.89 (*0-8167-2815-1*); pap. 3.95 (*0-8167-2816-X*) Troll Assocs.

Rosen, Michael J., retold by. How Giraffe Got Such a Long Neck--& Why Rhino Is So Grumpy: A Tale from East Africa. Clementson, John, illus. LC 92-46662. 32p. (ps-3). 1993. 13.99 (*0-8037-1621-4*) Dial Bks Young.

FOLKLORE–AFRICA, SOUTH

Aardema, Verna. Jackal's Flying Lesson. Gottlieb, Dale, illus. LC 93-44129. (gr. 4 up). 1995. write for info. (*0-679-85813-X*); PLB write for info. (*0-679-95813-4*) Knopf Bks Yng Read.

Kerven, Rosalind. The Rain Forest Storybook. (Illus.). 80p. 1994. 17.95 (*0-521-43502-1*); pap. 9.95 (*0-521-43533-1*) Cambridge U Pr.

Ogle, Teresa R. The Great Snake Doctor: A Tswana Folktale from Southern Africa. Ankobra, Kofi, illus. LC 94-14317. 1995. write for info. (*0-688-13274-X*); PLB write for info. (*0-688-13275-8*) Lothrop.

FOLKLORE–AFRICA, WEST

Aardema, Verna. Anansi Finds a Fool. Waldman, Bryna, illus. LC 91-21127. 32p. (ps-3). 1992. 14.00 (*0-8037-1164-6*); PLB 13.89 (*0-8037-1165-4*) Dial Bks Young.

—Why Mosquitoes Buzz in People's Ears: A West African Tale. Dillon, Leo D., ed. Dillon, Diane, illus. LC 77-71514. (ps-3). 1978. pap. 4.95 (*0-8037-6088-4*, Puff Pied Piper) Puffin Bks.

—Why Mosquitoes Buzz in People's Ears: A West African Tale. Dillon, Leo D. & Dillon, Diane, illus. LC 74-2886. 32p. (ps-3). 1975. 15.00 (*0-8037-6089-2*); PLB 14.89 (*0-8037-6087-6*) Dial Bks Young.

Aardema, Verna, retold by. Why Mosquitoes Buzz in People's Ears: A West African Tale. Dillon, Leo D. & Dillon, Diane, illus. 32p. (ps-3). 1995. pap. 4.99 (*0-14-054905-6*) Puffin Bks.

Aardema, Verna & Dillon, Leo D., eds. Why Mosquitoes Buzz in People's Ears: A West African Tale. Dillon, Diane, illus. 32p. (ps-3). 1993. pap. 17.99 (*0-14-054589-1*) Puffin Bks.

—Why Mosquitoes Buzz in People's Ears Read-Aloud Set. Dillon, Diane, illus. (ps-3). 1993. Set incls. 1 Giant copy, 6 paperbacks, giant-sized bookmark & tchr's. guide in a free- standing easel. pap. 47.93 (*0-14-778979-6*) Puffin Bks.

Anderson, David A. The Origin of Life on Earth: An African Creation Myth. Wilson, Kathleen A., illus. 32p. 1991. PLB 18.95 (*0-9629978-5-4*) Sights Prods.

Arkhurst, Joyce C., retold by. The Adventures of Spider: West African Folk Tales. Pinkney, Jerry, illus. LC 92-444. 1992. 6.95 (*0-316-05107-1*) Little.

Bryan, Ashley. The Story of Lightning & Thunder. Bryan, Ashley, illus. LC 92-40509. 32p. (ps-3). 1993. SBE 14.95 (*0-689-31836-7*, Atheneum Child Bk) Macmillan Child Grp.

Chocolate, Deborah M. Talk, Talk: An Ashanti Legend. Albers, Dave, illus. LC 92-13278. 32p. (gr. 2-5). 1992. PLB 11.89 (*0-8167-2817-8*); pap. text ed. 3.95 (*0-8167-2818-6*) Troll Assocs.

Courlander, Harold & Herzog, George. The Cow-Tail Switch & Other West African Stories. Chastain, Madye L., illus. LC 47-30108. 160p. (gr. 2-4). 1988. 13.95 (*0-8050-0288-X*, Bks Young Read) H Holt & Co.

Dupre, Rick. Agassu: Legend of the Leopard King. Dupre, Rick, illus. 40p. (gr. 1-4). 1993. 18.95 (*0-87614-764-3*) Carolrhoda Bks.

Ellis, Veronica F. Land of the Four Winds. Walker, Sylvia, illus. LC 92-72001. 32p. (gr. 1-4). 1993. 14.95 (*0-940975-38-6*); pap. 6.95 (*0-940975-39-4*) Just Us Bks.

McDermott, Gerald. Zomo the Rabbit. 1992. 14.95 (*0-15-299967-1*, HB Juv Bks) HarBrace.

Maddern, Eric, retold by. The Fire Children: A West African Creation Tale. Lessac, Frane, illus. LC 92-34685. (ps-3). 1993. 14.50 (*0-8037-1477-7*) Dial Bks Young.

Medearis, Angela S., adapted by. The Singing Man: A West African Folktale. Shaffer, Terea, illus. LC 93-4219. 32p. 1994. reinforced bdg. 15.95 (*0-8234-1103-6*) Holiday.

Roddy, Patricia. Api & the Boy Stranger: A Village Creation Tale. Russell, Lynne, illus. LC 93-8359. Date not set. 14.99 (*0-8037-1221-9*); PLB 14.89 (*0-8037-1222-7*) Dial Bks Young.

Skivington, Janice. How Anansi Obtained the Sky God's Stories. Livington, Janice, illus. LC 91-7581. 48p. (ps-3). 1991. PLB 15.40 (*0-516-05134-2*); pap. 6.95 (*0-516-45134-0*) Childrens.

FOLKLORE–ALASKA

Wakeland, Marcia A. Big Fish: An Alaskan Fairy Tale. (Illus.). 32p. (ps-4). 1993. pap. 7.95 (*0-9635083-2-6*) Misty Mtn.

Welsh-Smith, Susan. Andy: An Alaskan Tale. Munoz, Rie, illus. 24p. 1988. 14.95 (*0-521-35535-4*) Cambridge U Pr.

FOLKLORE–ARABIA

Aladdin. (ARA., Illus.). (gr. 5-12). 1987. 3.95x (*0-86685-182-8*) Intl Bk Ctr.

Aladdin & Other Tales from the Arabian Nights. LC 93-55071. 1993. 12.95 (*0-679-42533-0*) Knopf.

Ali Baba: In Arabic. (Illus.). (gr. 4-12). 1987. 3.95x (*0-86685-184-4*) Intl Bk Ctr.

Ali Baba the Forty Thieves & Other Stories. 1993. 8.99 (*0-517-10178-5*) Random Hse Value.

Braybrooks, Ann. Disney's Aladdin. Ortiz, Phil & Michaels, Serge, illus. 24p. (ps-3). 1992. pap. write for info. (*0-307-12692-7*, 12692, Golden Pr) Western Pub.

Bull, Rene. The Arabian Knights. (gr. 2-6). 1986. 8.98 (*0-685-16864-6*, 619342) Random Hse Value.

Cohen, Barbara & Lovejoy, Bahija. Seven Daughters & Seven Sons. Cohn, Amy, ed. LC 94-80. 128p. (gr. 7 up). 1994. pap. 4.95 (*0-688-13563-3*, Pub. by Beech Tree Bks) Morrow.

Disney Staff. Squeak Abu: Aladdin. (Illus.). (ps). 1994. 6.98 (*0-453-03243-5*) NAL-Dutton.

Disney's Aladdin. LC 92-50803. (Illus.). 128p. 1993. 5.95 (*1-56138-251-5*) Running Pr.

Eastman, David, adapted by. Aladdin & the Wonderful Lamp. Waldman, Bryna, illus. LC 87-13756. 32p. (gr. 1-4). 1988. PLB 9.79 (*0-8167-1073-2*); pap. text ed. 1.95 (*0-8167-1074-0*) Troll Assocs.

Humphrey, L. Spencer. Aladdin. 32p. 1994. pap. 2.95 (*0-8125-2319-9*) Tor Bks.

Jose, Éduard, adapted by. Aladdin's Lamp: A Classic Tale. Suire, Diane D., tr. from SPA. Lavarello, Jose M., illus. LC 88-35312. 32p. (gr. 1-4). 1988. PLB 13.95 (*0-89565-481-4*) Childs World.

—Ali Baba & the Forty Thieves: A Classic Tale. Riehecky, Janet, tr. from SPA. Rovira, Francesc, illus. LC 88-36871. 32p. (gr. 1-4). 1988. PLB 13.95 (*0-89565-485-7*) Childs World.

—Sinbad the Sailor: A Classic Tale. Riehecky, Janet, tr. from SPA. Rovira, Francesc, illus. LC 88-36872. 32p. (gr. k-3). 1988. PLB 19.95 (*0-89565-472-5*); PLB 13.95 (*0-685-56048-1*) Childs World.

Kidd, Ronald, adapted by. Disney's Aladdin. Mateu, illus. 24p. (ps-4). 1992. 20.00 (*0-307-74026-9*, 64026, Golden Pr) Western Pub.

Kimmel, Eric A., retold by. The Three Princes: A Middle Eastern Tale. Fisher, Leonard E., illus. LC 93-25862. 32p. (ps-3). 1994. reinforced bdg. 15.95 (*0-8234-1115-X*) Holiday.

Kreider, Karen. Disney's Aladdin. Baker, Darrell, illus. 24p. (ps-3). 1992. write for info. (*0-307-12348-0*, 12348, Golden Pr) Western Pub.

Lang, Andrew, ed. Arabian Nights Entertainments. Ford, H. J., illus. LC 69-17098. xv, 424p. (gr. k-6). 1969. pap. 6.95 (*0-486-22289-6*) Dover.

Lattimore, Deborah N., as told by. & illus. Three Tales from The Arabian Nights. LC 94-9828. 1995. 18.00 (*0-06-024585-9*); PLB 17.89 (*0-06-024734-7*) HarpC.

Philip, Neil, as told by. The Arabian Nights. Moxley, Sheila, illus. LC 94-9137. 160p. (gr. 5 up). 1994. 19.95 (*0-531-06868-4*) Orchard Bks Watts.

Riordan, James. Tales from the Arabian Nights. Ambrus, Victor G., illus. LC 84-62456. 128p. (gr. 4 up). 1985. 14.95 (*1-56288-258-9*) Checkerboard.

Smith, Philip, ed. Aladdin & Other Favorite Arabian Nights Stories. Kliros, Thea, illus. LC 93-22073. 96p. (gr. 3 up). 1993. pap. 1.00 (*0-486-27571-X*) Dover.

Thomas, Vernon. Stories from the Arabian Nights. Basu, R. K., illus. (gr. 8-12). 1979. 7.50 (*0-89744-142-7*) Auromere.

Twain, Mark. Arabian Nights. Goodenow, Earle, illus. (gr. 4-9). 1981. (G&D); deluxe ed. 13.95 (*0-448-06006-X*) Putnam Pub Group.

Wade, Gini, retold by. & illus. The Wonderful Bag: An Arabian Tale from the "Thousand & One Nights" LC 92-43615. 32p. (gr. k-3). 1993. 14.95 (*0-87226-508-0*) P Bedrick Bks.

Wiggin, Kate D. & Smith, Nora A., eds. The Arabian Nights: Their Best-Known Tales. Parrish, Maxfield, illus. LC 92-38552. 368p. 1993. (Scribners Young Read); SBE 25.00 (*0-684-19589-5*, Scribners Young Read) Macmillan Child Grp.

FOLKLORE–ARMENIA

Bider, Djemma. A Drop of Honey. Kojoyian, Armen, illus. (ps-4). 1989. pap. 14.95 jacketed (*0-671-66265-1*, S&S BFYR) S&S Trade.

Hogrogian, Nonny. The Contest. LC 75-40389. (Illus.). 32p. (gr. k-3). 1976. 16.00 (*0-688-80042-4*); PLB 15.93 (*0-688-84042-6*) Greenwillow.

FOLKLORE–ASIA

Asian Cultural Center for UNESCO. Folk Tales from Asia for Children Everywhere, Bk. 1. LC 74-82605. (Illus.). 60p. (gr. 1-4). 1975. 6.50 (*0-8348-1032-8*) Weatherhill.

—Folk Tales from Asia for Children Everywhere, Bk. 2. LC 74-82605. (Illus.). 60p. (gr. 3-6). 1975. 6.50 (*0-8348-1033-6*) Weatherhill.

—Folk Tales from Asia for Children Everywhere, Bk. 5. LC 74-82605. (Illus.). 60p. (gr. 3-6). 1977. 6.50 (*0-8348-1036-0*) Weatherhill.

—Folk Tales from Asia for Children Everywhere, Bk. 6. LC 74-82605. (Illus.). 60p. (gr. 3-6). 1978. 6.50 (*0-8348-1037-9*) Weatherhill.

Asian Cultural Center for UNESCO, ed. Folk Tales from Asia for Children Everywhere, Bk. 3. LC 74-82605. (Illus.). 60p. (gr. 3-6). 1976. 6.50 (*0-8348-1034-4*) Weatherhill.

Conger, David, retold by. Many Lands, Many Stories: Asian Folk Tales for Children. Ra, Ruth, illus. LC 87-50167. 94p. 1987. 12.95 (*0-8048-1527-5*) C E Tuttle.

Davison, Katherine. Moon Magic: Stories from Asia. Rosborough, Thomas A., illus. LC 92-44504. 1993. 18.95 (*0-87614-751-1*) Carolrhoda Bks.

Gerstein, Mordicai. The Shadow of a Flying Bird: A Folktale from Kurdistan. Gerstein, Mordicai, illus. 32p. (gr. 1 up). 1994. 15.95 (*0-7868-0016-X*); PLB 15.89 (*0-7868-2012-8*) Hyprn Child.

Harris, Edward N., compiled by. The Rice Fairy: Karen Stories from Southeast Asia. LC 89-21946. (Illus.). 105p. (gr. 4-6). 1989. Repr. of 1987 ed. lib. bdg. 20.00 (*0-929225-33-3*) Simplicity Pr.

Hodges, Margaret, retold by. The Golden Deer. San Souci, Daniel, illus. LC 90-42873. 32p. (gr. 1-3). 1992. SBE 14.95 (*0-684-19218-7*, Scribners Young Read) Macmillan Child Grp.

Long, Hua. The Moon Maiden & Other Asian Folktales. (Illus.). 32p. 1993. 12.95 (*0-8351-2494-0*); pap. 8.95 (*0-8351-2493-2*) China Bks.

Revich, S. J. The Camel Boy. Hinlicky, Gregg, illus. 158p. (gr. 5-8). 1987. 9.95 (*0-935063-44-7*); pap. 7.95 (*0-935063-45-5*) CIS Comm.

—The Poet & the Thief. Hinlicky, Gregg, illus. 158p. (gr. 5-7). 1989. 10.95 (*0-935063-71-4*); pap. 7.95 (*0-935063-72-2*) CIS Comm.

Troughton, Joanna, retold by. & illus. The Quail's Egg: A Folk Tale from Sri Lanka. LC 87-33376. 32p. (gr. k-3). 1988. PLB 14.95 (*0-87226-185-9*, Bedrick Blackie) P Bedrick Bks.

FOLKLORE–ASIA, SOUTHEASTERN

Kerven, Rosalind. The Rain Forest Storybook. (Illus.). 80p. 1994. 17.95 (*0-521-43502-1*); pap. 9.95 (*0-521-43533-1*) Cambridge U Pr.

Xiong, Blia & Spagnoli, Cathy, eds. Nine-in-One Grr! Grr! LC 89-9891. (Illus.). 32p. (ps-5). 1989. 13.95 (*0-89239-048-4*) Childrens Book Pr.

FOLKLORE–AUSTRALIA

Cowan, James. Kun-Man-Gur: The Rainbow Serpent. Bancroft, Bronwyn, illus. LC 93-32319. 1994. 16.00 (*1-56957-906-7*) Barefoot Bks.

Morgan, Sally. The Flying Emu & Other Australian Stories. Morgan, Sally, illus. LC 92-37880. 128p. (gr. k-7). 1993. 18.00 (*0-679-84705-7*) Knopf Bks Yng Read.

Troughton, Joanna, retold by. & illus. Whale's Canoe: A Folk Tale from Australia. LC 92-43616. 32p. (gr. k-3). 1993. 14.95 (*0-87226-509-9*) P Bedrick Bks.

—What Made Tiddalik Laugh: An Australian Aborigine Folk Tale. LC 86-1234. 32p. (gr. k-3). 1986. PLB 14. 95 (*0-87226-081-X*, Bedrick Blackie) P Bedrick Bks.

FOLKLORE–AUSTRIA

Sawyer, Ruth. The Remarkable Christmas of the Cobbler's Sons. Cooney, Barbara, illus. 32p. (ps-3). 1994. PLB 14.99 (*0-670-84922-7*) Viking Child Bks.

FOLKLORE, BLACK

see Black Folklore

FOLKLORE–BOHEMIA

Vopata, Emil. Bohemian Mobility Tales. Bitney, Greg, illus. 80p. (Orig.). (gr. 3-12). 1994. pap. 9.95 (*0-9638668-0-X*) AV Mobility.
BOHEMIAN MOBILITY TALES are stories from the great kingdom of old Bohemia, retold here with an emphasis on the visual & mobility aspects of their colorful characters. The ten tales selected for BOHEMIAN MOBILITY TALES have aspects that can be appreciated at all age levels, but are likely to be most appealing when read by or to children. For instance, in "The Knight Who Came to Kralovice," we read the intriguing tale of the gallant knight, Wolfgang, who overcomes the forces of evil witches to provide a satisfying, surprise ending in the village of the king. Then "Johnny & the Yezinkas" match their wits, with many difficult to predict developments, until the witch maidens finally give Johnny what he is determined to get for his father. In "Marsushka" we have the good daughter struggling to survive her evil step-sister until she receives powerful support from a great force on the mountain. A related tale, "Lenka & Dorla," also includes the good daughter/evil step-sister conflict, but the plot unfolds in a quite different, but just as engrossing, series of events. BOHEMIAN MOBILITY TALES concludes its ten stories with the pungent tale of what happens when chickens choose a skunk to lead them. Order from: AV Mobility Press, 1631 South Conyer, Visalia, CA 93277; 408-998-3072.
Publisher Provided Annotation.

FOLKLORE–BRAZIL

Lippert, Margaret H. La Hija de la Serpiente Marina - the Sea Serpent's Daughter: Una Leyenda Brasilena. LC 92-21438. (gr. 4-7). 1993. PLB 11.89 (*0-8167-3124-1*); pap. 3.95 (*0-8167-3074-1*) Troll Assocs.

—The Sea Serpent's Daughter: A Brazilian Legend. Davalos, Felipe, illus. LC 92-21438. 32p. (gr. 2-5). 1993. lib. bdg. 11.89 (*0-8167-3053-9*); pap. text ed. 3.95 (*0-8167-3054-7*) Troll Assocs.

FOLKLORE–BURMA

Troughton, Joanna. Make-Believe Tales: A Folk Tale from Burma. Troughton, Joanna, illus. LC 90-48962. 32p. (gr. k-3). 1991. PLB 14.95 (*0-87226-451-3*, Bedrick Blackie) P Bedrick Bks.

FOLKLORE–CANADA

Ardizzone, Edward. Tim in Danger. (Illus.). 48p. (ps-3). 1987. pap. 6.95 (*0-19-272106-2*) OUP.

Jessell, Tim. Amorak. LC 93-48622. 32p. 1994. 14.95 (*0-88682-662-4*) Creative Ed.

FOLKLORE–CARIBBEAN AREA

Gershator, Phyllis, retold by. Tukama Tootles the Flute: A Tale from St. Thomas. Saint James, Synthia, illus. LC 93-2253. 1994. write for info. (*0-531-06811-0*); lib. bdg. write for info. (*0-531-08661-5*) Orchard Bks Watts.

Gonzalez, Lucia M., retold by. The Bossy Gallito: A Traditional Cuban Folk Tale. Delacre, Lulu, illus. LC 93-15541. 32p. (ps-2). 1994. 14.95 (*0-590-46843-X*) Scholastic Inc.

Hull, Robert. Caribbean Stories. (Illus.). 48p. (gr. 5-9). 1994. 15.95 (*1-56847-190-4*) Thomson Lrning.

Joseph, Lynn. The Mermaid's Twin Sister: More Stories from Trinidad. Perrone, Donna, illus. LC 93-28436. (gr. 3-7). 1994. 13.95 (*0-395-64365-1*, Clarion Bks) HM.

Lewis, Theresa. Caribbean Folk Legends. LC 89-81981. 90p. (gr. 6-12). 1990. 19.95 (*0-86543-158-2*); pap. 7.95 (*0-86543-159-0*) Africa World.

Makhanlall, David. Brer Anansi & the Boat Race: A Folk Tale from the Caribbean. Rosato, Amelio, illus. LC 88-925. 32p. (gr. k-3). 1988. PLB 14.95 (*0-87226-184-0*, Bedrick Blackie) P Bedrick Bks.

Petersen, Arona. Food & Folklore of the Virgin Islands. 300p. (Orig.). (gr. 9-12). 1990. 20.00 (*0-9626577-0-0*) A Petersen.

San Souci, Robert D. The House in the Sky. Clay, Wil, photos by. LC 92-39958. (Illus.). 1995. 13.99 (*0-8037-1284-7*); PLB 13.89 (*0-8037-1285-5*) Dial Bks Young.

FOLKLORE, CELTIC

Delaney, Frank. Legends of the Celts. (Illus.). 272p. (gr. 10-12). 1992. pap. 14.95 (*0-8069-8351-5*) Sterling.

Guard, David. Deirdre: A Celtic Legend. Guard, Gretchen, illus. LC 80-69774. 120p. (gr. 4-9). 1993. pap. 8.95 (*1-883672-05-8*) Tricycle Pr.

Jacobs, Joseph, ed. Celtic Fairy Tales. Batten, John D., illus. LC 67-24223. xvi, 267p. (ps-6). 1968. pap. 5.95 (*0-486-21826-0*) Dover.

—More Celtic Fairy Tales. Batten, John D., illus. LC 67-24224. x, 234p. (ps-6). 1968. pap. 5.95 (*0-486-21827-9*) Dover.

MacUistin, Liam. Celtic Magic Tales. Negrin, Maria A., illus. 94p. (gr. 3-7). 1994. pap. 7.95 (*0-86278-341-0*, Pub. by OBrien Pr ER) Dufour.

FOLKLORE–CHINA

Birdseye, Tom. A Song of Stars. Ju-Hong Chen, illus. LC 89-20066. 32p. (gr. 4-8). 1990. reinforced bdg. 14.95 (*0-8234-0790-X*) Holiday.

Carpenter, Frances. Tales of a Chinese Grandmother. Hasselriie, Malthe, illus. LC 72-77514. 302p. (gr. 3-8). 1972. pap. 8.95 (*0-8048-1042-7*) C E Tuttle.

Carpenter, Francis. Tales of a Chinese Grandmother. 293p. (gr. 5-6). Repr. of 1937 ed. lib. bdg. 22.95x (*0-89190-481-6*, Pub. by River City Pr) Amereon Ltd.

Chang, Cindy. The Seventh Sister. Reasoner, Charles, illus. LC 92-43179. 32p. (gr. 2-5). 1994. PLB 11.89 (*0-8167-3411-9*); pap. text ed. 3.95 (*0-8167-3412-7*) Troll Assocs.

Chang, Margaret & Chang, Raymond. The Cricket Warrior. Hutton, Warwick, illus. LC 93-35395. (gr. k-4). 1994. 14.95 (*0-689-50605-8*, Atheneum Child Bk) MacMillan.

Chang, Monica. The Mouse Bride: A Chinese Folktale. Lin, Lesley, illus. LC 91-44296. 32p. (gr. k-4). 1992. 14.95 (*0-87358-533-X*) Northland AZ.

—The Mouse Bride: La Novia Raton. Zeller, Beatriz, tr. from CHI. Liu, Lesley, illus. (SPA & ENG.). 32p. (gr. 2-4). 1994. 16.95 (*957-32-2150-0*) Pan Asian Pubns.
After a village cat terrorizes the tiny mice's community, the mouse leader searches for a mighty husband that will protect his daughter. Although he first seeks the Sun, the Cloud, the Wind, & the Wall to wed his mouse daughter, the husband that eventually wins her hand is a touching choice that provides the perfect ending to this ancient Taiwanese folktale. This charming story is accompanied by detailed, award-winning illustrations that show the life, traditions & costumes of rural Taiwan. This book is a guaranteed classic. Also available in English/ Chinese, Vietnamese, Korean, Thai, Tagalog, Khmer, Lao & Hmong. For grades 2-4. Please specify the language when ordering. Available exclusively from: Pan Asian Publications (USA) Inc., 29564 Union City Blvd., Union City, CA 94587. Order toll free: 1-800-853-ASIA, FAX: (510) 475-1489.
Publisher Provided Annotation.

—Story of the Chinese Zodiac: El Zodiaco Chino. Zeller, Beatriz, tr. from CHI. Lee, Arthur, illus. (ENG & SPA.). 32p. (gr. 2-4). 1994. 16.95 (*957-32-2143-8*) Pan Asian Pubns.
How were the twelve animals chosen for the Chinese Zodiac? And why is the rat the first one on the list? These questions, & others, are answered in this hilarious version of the ancient Chinese Zodiac legend. The breathtaking, colorful, "paper cut-out" illustrations that accompany this story will enrapture the young readers as the rollicking story will appear to leap out before their very eyes! STORY OF THE CHINESE ZODIAC is guaranteed to be a popular choice. Also available in English/Chinese, Vietnamese, Korean, Thai, Tagalog, Khmer, Lao & Hmong. For grades 2-4. Please specify the languages when ordering. Available exclusively from: Pan Asian Publications (USA) Inc., 29564 Union City Blvd., Union City, CA 94587. Order toll free: 1-800-853-ASIA, FAX: (510) 475-1489.
Publisher Provided Annotation.

Chin, Charlie. China's Bravest Girl: The Legend of Hua Mu Lan. LC 93-15255. (Illus.). 32p. (gr. 6-12). 1993. 13.95 (*0-89239-120-0*) Childrens Book Pr.

Chin, Yin-lien C., intros. by. Traditional Chinese Folktales. Center, Y. LC 88-31129. (Illus.). 192p. (gr. 8-12). 1989. 30.00 (*0-87332-507-9*) M E Sharpe.

Demi. The Empty Pot. Demi, illus. LC 89-39062. 32p. (ps-2). 1990. 15.95 (*0-8050-1217-6*, Bks Young Read) H Holt & Co.

—The Magic Boat. Demi, illus. LC 90-4425. 32p. (ps-2). 1989. 15.95 (*0-8050-1141-2*, Bks Young Read) H Holt & Co.

Demi, retold by. & illus. The Magic Tapestry: A Chinese Folktale. LC 93-11426. 1994. 17.95 (*0-8050-2810-2*) H Holt & Co.

Demi, Hitz. The Stonecutter. LC 93-42413. 1995. write for info. (*0-517-59864-7*, Crown); lib. bdg. write for info. (*0-517-59865-5*, Crown) Crown Pub Group.

Denman, Cherry. The Little Peacock's Gift: A Folk Tale from China. Denman, Cherry, illus. LC 87-17504. 32p. (gr. k-3). 1988. PLB 14.95 (*0-87226-175-1*, Bedrick Blackie) P Bedrick Bks.

Drummond, Allan. The Willow Pattern Story. Drummond, Allan, illus. LC 91-46239. 32p. (gr. k-3). 1992. 14.95 (*1-55858-171-5*); PLB 14.88 (*1-55858-172-3*) North-South Bks NYC.

Hamada, Cheryl, retold by. The Fourth Question: A Chinese Folktale. Skivington, Janice, illus. LC 93-18237. 32p. (ps-3). 1993. PLB 13.85 (*0-516-05144-X*); pap. 12.95 (*0-516-07091-6*) Childrens.

Hao, Kuang-ts'ai. Seven Magic Brothers: Siete Hermanos Magicos. Zeller, Beatriz, tr. from CHI. Wang, Eva, illus. (ENG & SPA.). 32p. (gr. 2-4). 1994. 16.95 (*957-32-2165-9*) Pan Asian Pubns.
SEVEN MAGIC BROTHERS is a tale about the adventures of seven superpowered brothers who triumph through their cooperation. This tale illustrates the strength of brotherhood & loyalty. Young readers are guaranteed to be inspired by the message of unity & delighted by the brothers' exciting adventures. Young readers are sure to be delighted by the rich & detailed illustrations that accompany this exciting tale. Also available in English/Chinese, Vietnamese, Korean, Thai, Tagalog, Khmer, Lao & Hmong. For grades 2-4. Please specify the language when ordering. Available exclusively from: Pan Asian Publications (USA) Inc., 29564 Union City Blvd., Union City, CA 94587. Order toll free 1-800-853-ASIA, FAX: (510) 475-1489.
Publisher Provided Annotation.

Heyer, Marilee. The Weaving of a Dream. Heyer, Marilee, illus. 32p. (ps-3). 1989. pap. 4.99 (*0-14-050528-8*, Puffin) Puffin Bks.

—The Weaving of a Dream: A Chinese Folktale. Heyer, Marilee, illus. LC 85-20187. 32p. (gr. k-6). 1986. pap. 15.99 (*0-670-80555-6*) Viking Child Bks.

Hong, Lily T. How the Ox Star Fell from Heaven. Fay, Ann, ed. Hong, Lily T., illus. LC 90-38978. 32p. (gr. k-3). 1991. 14.95 (*0-8075-3428-5*) A Whitman.

Hume, Lotta C. Favorite Children's Stories from China & Tibet. Lo-Koon-Chiu, illus. LC 61-6219. 120p. (gr. 1-4). 1962. pap. 14.95 (*0-8048-1605-0*) C E Tuttle.

Hwa-I Publishing Co., Staff. Chinese Children's Stories, Vol. 1: Two Bushels of Grain, Forget the Turnips! Ching, Emily, et al, eds. Wonder Kids Publications Staff, tr. from CHI. (Illus.). 28p. (gr. 3-6). 1991. Repr. of 1988 ed. 7.95 (*1-56162-001-7*) Wonder Kids.

—Chinese Children's Stories, Vol. 16: How to Build a Nest, Moving the Mountain. Ching, Emily, et al, eds. Wonder Kids Publications Staff, tr. from CHI. (Illus.). 28p. (gr. 3-6). 1991. Repr. of 1988 ed. 7.95 (*1-56162-016-5*) Wonder Kids.

—Chinese Children's Stories, Vol. 2: The Blind Man & the Cripple, Orchard Village. Ching, Emily, et al, eds. Wonder Kids Publications Staff, tr. (Illus.). 28p. (gr. 3-6). 1991. Repr. of 1988 ed. 7.95 (*1-56162-002-5*) Wonder Kids.

—Chinese Children's Stories, Vol. 21: Seamless Clothing, The Big Clam & the Snipe. Ching, Emily, et al, eds. Wonder Kids Publications Staff, tr. from CHI. (Illus.). 28p. (gr. 3-6). 1991. Repr. of 1988 ed. 7.95 (*1-56162-021-1*) Wonder Kids.

—Chinese Children's Stories, Vol. 3: The Redbud Tree, Lazy Bones & the Magical Bowl. Ching, Emily, et al, eds. Wonder Kids Publications Staff, tr. from CHI. (Illus.). 28p. (gr. 3-6). 1991. Repr. of 1988 ed. 7.95 (*1-56162-003-3*) Wonder Kids.

—Chinese Children's Stories, Vol. 31: The Refugee Empress, Chi Jiguang Cookies. Ching, Emily, et al, eds. Wonder Kids Publications Staff, tr. from CHI. (Illus.). 28p. (gr. 3-6). 1991. Repr. of 1988 ed. 7.95 (*1-56162-031-9*) Wonder Kids.

—Chinese Children's Stories, Vol. 36: Lu Ban & Old Sir Lee, Umbrellas. Ching, Emily, et al, eds. Wonder Kids Publications Staff, tr. from CHI. (Illus.). 28p. (gr. 3-6). 1991. Repr. of 1988 ed. 7.95 (*1-56162-036-X*) Wonder Kids.

—Chinese Children's Stories, Vol. 4: Golden Needles, Three Treasures. Ching, Emily, et al, eds. Wonder Kids Publications Staff, tr. from CHI. (Illus.). 28p. (gr. 3-6). 1991. Repr. of 1988 ed. 7.95 (*1-56162-004-1*) Wonder Kids.

—Chinese Children's Stories, Vol. 41: Brother Cat & Brother Rat, The Rooster's Antlers. Ching, Emily, et al, eds. Wonder Kids Publications Staff, tr. from CHI. (Illus.). 28p. (gr. 3-6). 1991. Repr. of 1988 ed. 7.95 (*1-56162-041-6*) Wonder Kids.

—Chinese Children's Stories, Vol. 46: Ma-Gu's Cock-a-Doodle-Doo, The Crippled God. Ching, Emily, et al, eds. Wonder Kids Publications Staff, tr. from CHI. (Illus.). 28p. (gr. 3-6). 1991. Repr. of 1988 ed. 7.95 (*1-56162-046-7*) Wonder Kids.

—Chinese Children's Stories, Vol. 61: Pan Koo Creates the World, A Hole in the Sky. Ching, Emily, et al, eds. Wonder Kids Publications Staff, tr. from CHI. (Illus.). 28p. (gr. 3-6). 1991. Repr. of 1988 ed. 7.95 (*1-56162-061-0*) Wonder Kids.

—Chinese Children's Stories, Vol. 76: The Stinky Emperor, The Hero Who Crawled. Ching, Emily, et al, eds. Wonder Kids Publications Staff, tr. from CHI. (Illus.). 28p. (gr. 3-6). 1991. Repr. of 1988 ed. 7.95 (*1-56162-076-9*) Wonder Kids.

—Chinese Children's Stories, Vol. 96: Tsi, the Cheat, The Mill in the Sea. Ching, Emily, et al, eds. Wonder Kids Publications Staff, tr. from CHI. (Illus.). 28p. (gr. 3-6). 1991. Repr. of 1988 ed. 7.95 (*1-56162-096-3*) Wonder Kids.

Jiang, Wei & Jiang, Cheng A. The Legend of Mulan - A Heroine of Ancient China: (Hu Mulan de Gushi - Zhong Guo Gudai Nu Yingxiong) (CHI & ENG., Illus.). 32p. (gr. 1 up). 1992. 13.95 (*1-878217-00-3*) Victory Press.

—The Legend of Mulan - A Heroine of Ancient China: (Hoa Moc Lan - Truyen Ve Nu Anh Hung Co Dai Trung Quoc) (VIE & ENG., Illus.). 32p. (gr. 1 up). 1992. 13.95 (*1-878217-02-X*) Victory Press.

—The Legend of Mulan - A Heroine of Ancient China: (La Heroina Hua Mulan - Una Leyenda de la Antigua China) (SPA & ENG., Illus.). 32p. (gr. 1 up). 1992. 13.95 (*1-878217-01-1*) Victory Press.

—The Legend of Mulan - A Heroine of Ancient China: (La Legende de Mulan, Heroine de la Chine Antique) (FRE & ENG., Illus.). 32p. (gr. 1 up). 1992. 13.95 (*1-878217-04-6*) Victory Press.

—The Legend of Mulan - A Heroine of Ancient China. (CAM & ENG., Illus.). 32p. (gr. 1 up). 1992. 13.95 (*1-878217-03-8*) Victory Press.

Kendall, Carol. The Wedding of the Rat Family. Watts, James, illus. LC 88-2197. 32p. (gr. 2-5). 1988. SBE 13.95 (*0-689-50450-0*, M K McElderry) Macmillan Child Grp.

Kerven, Rosalind. In the Court of the Jade Emperor: Stories from Old China. 80p. 1993. 18.95 (*0-521-43489-0*); pap. 8.95 (*0-521-43538-2*) Cambridge U Pr.

Li, Xiao M., tr. from CHI. The Mending of the Sky & Other Chinese Myths. Wu, Shan M., illus. Buckley, Cicely, intro. by. (Illus.). 54p. (Orig.). (gr. 5 up). 1989. pap. 9.00 (*0-9617481-3-3*) Oyster River Pr.

Lily Toy Hong. Two of Everything. Mathews, Judith, ed. Hong, Lily T., illus. LC 92-29880. 32p. (gr. k-3). 1993. PLB 14.95 (*0-8075-8157-7*) A Whitman.

Ludwig, Lyndell. The Little White Dragon. Ludwig, Lyndell, illus. 23p. (gr. 5 up). 1989. pap. 4.95 (*0-9621782-0-9*) Star Dust Bks. THE LITTLE WHITE DRAGON - This timeless, well-loved tale from ancient China takes you into the world of a wonderful little dragon intent on exploring everything both inside & outside of his realm. At one point he even changes himself into a little fish so he can dive into the waters of the deep sea. However, after numerous adventures, including a miraculous escape, he decides that, after all, it is much better just to be the dragon he really is, with untold worlds yet to discover. The third in a series of authentic Chinese tales in picture book form, delightfully told & illustrated by the author who is well qualified both as an illustrator & in her knowledge of the Chinese language. ("Like the tales of Rudyard Kipling, 'these stories' transport children to another time & a different, fascinating world."--Creative Arts). Children are important! As the world changes cultures are blending. And stories from distant lands such as China are enormously valuable in broadening the scope for growth & understanding. They are also fun to read. TS'AO CHUNG WEIGHS AN ELEPHANT ("...splendid, vibrantly colored paintings..."--Publishers Weekly) & THE SHOEMAKER'S GIFT are also available from Star Dust Books at $4.95 each.
Publisher Provided Annotation.

Mooney, Margaret. Outwitting the Tiger: A Chinese Legend. Forss, Ian, illus. LC 93-26261. 1994. 4.25 (*0-383-03776-X*) SRA Schl Grp.

Morris, Winifred. The Future of Yen-tzu. Henstra, Friso, illus. LC 90-26989. 32p. (ps-3). 1992. SBE 13.95 (*0-689-31501-5*, Atheneum Child Bk) Macmillan Child Grp.

Mosel, Arlene. Tikki Tikki Tembo. Lent, Blair, illus. LC 68-11839. 32p. (ps-2). 1968. 14.95 (*0-8050-0662-1*, Bks Young Read) H Holt & Co.

—Tikki Tikki Tembo: Big Book. Lent, Blair, illus. LC 68-11839. 32p. (ps-2). 1992. pap. 18.95 (*0-8050-2345-3*, Bks Young Read) H Holt & Co.

Rappaport, Doreen. Journey of Meng. (ps-3). 1991. 13.95 (*0-8037-0895-5*); PLB 13.89 (*0-8037-0896-3*) Dial Bks Young.

Rappaport, Doreen, retold by. The Long-Haired Girl: A Chinese Legend. Yang Ming-Yi, illus. LC 93-28626. 1995. write for info. (*0-8037-1411-4*); PLB write for info. (*0-8037-1412-2*) Dial Bks Young.

Sakurai, Gail. Peach Boy. Nagano, Makiko, illus. LC 93-43178. 32p. (gr. 2-5). 1994. PLB 11.89 (*0-8167-3409-7*); pap. text ed. 3.95 (*0-8167-3410-0*) Troll Assocs.

Wang, Rosalind C., retold by. The Fourth Question: A Chinese Folktale. Ju-Hong Chen, illus. LC 90-43536. 32p. (ps-3). 1991. reinforced 14.95 (*0-8234-0855-8*) Holiday.

Wei Jiang & Cheng An Jiang. La Heroina Hua Mulan--The Legend of Mu Lan: Una Leyenda De la Antigua China--A Heroine of Ancient China. (SPA & ENG., Illus.). 32p. (gr. 1 up). 1992. pap. 6.95 (*1-878217-15-1*) Victory Press.

—Hua Mu Lan De Gushi--The Legend of Mu Lan: Zhong Guo Gudai Nu Yingxiong--A Heroine of Ancient China. (CHI & ENG., Illus.). 32p. (gr. 1 up). 1992. pap. 6.95 (*1-878217-14-3*) Victory Press.

Wilkins, Verna & McLean, Gill, eds. Just a Pile of Rice: A Story from China. Wilkinson, Barry, illus. LC 93-6645. 1993. 3.95 (*1-870516-06-0*) Childs Play.

Williams, Jay. Everyone Knows What a Dragon Looks Like. Mayer, Mercer, illus. LC 84-29589. 32p. (gr. k-3). 1984. RSBE 14.95 (*0-02-793090-4*, Four Winds) Macmillan Child Grp.

Wilson, Barbara K. Wishbones: A Folk Tale from China. So, Meilo, illus. LC 92-26993. 32p. (ps-2). 1993. SBE 14.95 (*0-02-793125-0*, Bradbury Pr) Macmillan Child Grp.

Wonder Kids Publications Group Staff. The Blind Man & the Cripple - Orchard Village: Folklore: English - Spanish Version. Ching, Emily, et al, eds. Wonder Kids Publications Staff, tr. from CHI. Hwa-I Publishing Co., Staff, illus. 28p. (gr. 3-6). 1992. Repr. of 1988 ed. 12.95 (*1-56162-126-9*) Wonder Kids.

—The Blind Man & the Cripple - Orchard Village: Folklore: English - Cambodian Version. Ching, Emily, et al, eds. Wonder Kids Publications Staff, tr. from CHI. Hwa-I Publishing Co., Staff, illus. 28p. (gr. 3-6). 1992. Repr. of 1988 ed. 12.95 (*1-56162-128-5*) Wonder Kids.

—The Blind Man & the Cripple - Orchard Village: Folklore: English - Vietnamese Version. Ching, Emily, et al, eds. Wonder Kids Publications Staff, tr. from CHI. Hwa-I Publishing Co., Staff, illus. 28p. (gr. 3-6). 1992. Repr. of 1988 ed. 12.95 (*1-56162-127-7*) Wonder Kids.

—Brother Cat & Brother Rat - The Rooster's Antlers: Twelve Beasts & the Years: English - Spanish Version. Ching, Emily, et al, eds. Wonder Kids Publications Staff, tr. from CHI. Hwa-I Publishing Co., Staff, illus. 28p. (gr. 3-6). 1992. Repr. of 1988 ed. 12.95 (*1-56162-121-8*) Wonder Kids.

—Brother Cat & Brother Rat - The Rooster's Antlers: Twelve Beasts & the Years: English - Vietnamese Version. Ching, Emily, et al, eds. Wonder Kids Publications Staff, tr. from CHI. Hwa-I Publishing Co., Staff, illus. 28p. (gr. 3-6). 1992. Repr. of 1988 ed. 12.95 (*1-56162-122-6*) Wonder Kids.

—Celebrating New Year - Miss Yuan-Shiau: Festivals: English - Cambodian Version. Ching, Emily, et al, eds. Wonder Kids Publications Staff, tr. from CHI. Hwa-I Publishing Co., Staff, illus. 28p. (gr. 3-6). 1992. Repr. of 1988 ed. 12.95 (*1-56162-133-1*) Wonder Kids.

—Celebrating New Year - Miss Yuan-Shiau: Festivals: English - Spanish Version. Ching, Emily, et al, eds. Wonder Kids Publications Staff, tr. from CHI. Hwa-I Publishing Co., Staff, illus. 28p. (gr. 3-6). 1992. Repr. of 1988 ed. 12.95 (*1-56162-131-5*) Wonder Kids.

—Celebrating New Year - Miss Yuan-Shiau: Festivals: English - Vietnamese Version. Ching, Emily, et al, eds. Wonder Kids Publications Staff, tr. from CHI. Hwa-I Publishing Co., Staff, illus. 28p. (gr. 3-6). 1992. Repr. of 1988 ed. 12.95 (*1-56162-132-3*) Wonder Kids.

Wonder Kids Publications Group Staff (USA) & Hwa-I Publishing Co., Staff. Fables: Chinese Children's Stories, Vols. 16-20. Ching, Emily & Ching, Ko-Shee, eds. Wonder Kids Publications Staff, tr. from CHI. Hwa-I Publishing Co., Staff, illus. LC 90-60794. (gr. 3-6). 1991. Repr. of 1988 ed. Five vol. set, 28p. ea. bk. 39.75 (*0-685-58703-7*) Wonder Kids.

—Fairy Tales: Chinese Children's Stories, Vols. 46-50. Ching, Emily, et al, eds. Wonder Kids Publications Staff, tr. from CHI. Hwa-I Publishing Co., Staff, illus. LC 90-60801. (gr. 3-6). 1991. Repr. of 1988 ed. Five vol. set, 28p. ea. bk. 39.75 (*0-685-58709-6*) Wonder Kids.

—Folklore: Chinese Children's Stories, Vols. 1-5. Ching, Emily, et al, eds. Wonder Kids Publications Staff, tr. from CHI. Hwa-I Publishing Co., Staff, illus. LC 90-60791. 28p. (gr. 3-6). 1991. Repr. of 1988 ed. Five vol. set, 28p. ea. bk. 39.75 (*0-685-58701-0*); Set (100 vols.) 795.00 (*1-56162-120-X*) Wonder Kids.

—Taiwanese Folklore: Chinese Children's Stories, Vols. 96-100. Ching, Emily, et al, eds. Wonder Kids Publication Staff, tr. from CHI. Hwa-I Publishing Co., Staff, illus. LC 90-60811. (gr. 3-6). 1991. Repr. of 1988 ed. Five vol. set, 28p. ea. bk. 39.75 (*0-685-58719-3*) Wonder Kids.

Wriggins, Sally. White Monkey King: A Chinese Fable. Solbert, Ronni, illus. LC 76-44281. (gr. 1-5). 1977. 5.95 (*0-394-83450-X*) Pantheon.

Yacowitz, Caryn. The Jade Stone: A Chinese Folktale. Chen, Ju-Hong, illus. LC 91-17934. 32p. (ps-3). 1992. reinforced bdg. 14.95 (*0-8234-0919-8*) Holiday.

Yang, Jwing-Ming. YMAA Children's Book Series: Volume One, Stories One & Two. 32p. (Orig.). (gr. 4 up). 1989. pap. 3.95 (*0-940871-09-2*) Yangs Martial Arts.

Yep, Laurence. The Man Who Tricked a Ghost. Seltzer, Isadore, illus. LC 93-22202. 32p. (gr. k-4). 1993. PLB 15.95 (*0-8167-3030-X*); pap. text ed. write for info. (*0-8167-3031-8*) BrdgeWater.

—The Rainbow People. Wiesner, David, illus. LC 88-21203. 208p. (gr. 3-7). 1989. 16.00 (*0-06-026760-7*); PLB 15.89 (*0-06-026761-5*) HarpC Child Bks.

—The Rainbow People. Wiesner, David, illus. LC 89-21203. 208p. (gr. 3-7). 1992. pap. 3.95 (*0-06-440441-2*, Trophy) HarpC Child Bks.

—Tiger Woman. Roth, Robert, illus. LC 93-38685. 32p. (gr. k-3). 1995. PLB 14.95 (*0-8167-3464-X*); pap. text ed. 4.95 (*0-8167-3465-8*) BrdgeWater.

—Tongues of Jade. Wiesner, David, illus. LC 91-2119. 208p. (gr. 3-7). 1991. 14.95 (*0-06-022470-3*); PLB 14.89 (*0-06-022471-1*) HarpC Child Bks.

Yep, Laurence, retold by. The Shell Woman & the King: A Chinese Folktale. Ming-Yi, Yang, illus. LC 92-9583. 32p. (gr. k-3). 1993. 13.99 (*0-8037-1394-0*); PLB 13.89 (*0-8037-1395-9*) Dial Bks Young.

Yep, Laurence, et al. The Boy Who Swallowed Snakes. Tseng, Jean & Tseng, Mou-Sien, illus. LC 93-21822. 32p. (gr. 5 up). 1994. 14.95 (*0-590-46168-0*) Scholastic Inc.

Young, Ed. Little Plum. LC 93-11526. (Illus.). 32p. (ps-3). 1994. PLB 15.95 (*0-399-22683-4*) Putnam Pub Group.

—Red Thread. (Illus.). 32p. (ps-3). 1993. PLB 14.95 (*0-399-21969-2*, Philomel Bks) Putnam Pub Group.

Young, Ed, tr. from CHI. & illus. Lon Po Po: A Red Riding Hood Story from China. 32p. (gr. k-4). 1989. 14.95 (*0-399-21619-7*, Philomel Bks) Putnam Pub Group.

Yuan Hsi Kuo & Louise Hsi Kuo. Chinese Folk Tales. LC 75-9082. (gr. 7 up). 1976. pap. 5.95 (*0-89087-074-8*) Celestial Arts.

FOLKLORE–CZECHOSLOVAK REPUBLIC

Gabler, Mirko, retold by. Tall, Wide, & Sharp-Eye: A Czech Folktale. LC 93-8967. 1994. 14.95 (*0-8050-2784-X*) H Holt & Co.

FOLKLORE–CZECHOSLOVAKIA

Nemcova, B. Fairy Tales from Czechoslovakia, Vol. I. Velinsky, L., tr. Kabel Pub Staff, illus. Absolon, Karel B., intro. by. (CZE., Illus.). 305p. (Orig.). (gr. 4 up). 1987. pap. 39.50 (*0-685-19314-4*) KABEL Pubs.

FOLKLORE–DENMARK

Andersen, Hans Christian. The Emperor's Nightingale: A Classic Tale. Jose, Eduard, adapted by. Moncure, Jane B., tr. from SPA. Lavarello, Jose M., illus. LC 88-35209. 32p. (gr. 1-4). 1988. PLB 13.95 (*0-89565-484-9*) Childs World.

—The Little Match Girl: A Classic Tale. Jose, Eduard, adapted by. Suire, Diane D., tr. Rovira, Francesc, illus. LC 88-36868. 32p. (gr. 1-4). 1988. PLB 13.95 (*0-89565-476-8*) Childs World.

—The Little Mermaid: A Classic Tale. Jose, Eduard, adapted by. Moncure, Jane B., tr. Lavarello, Jose M., illus. LC 88-36869. 32p. (gr. 1-4). 1988. PLB 13.95 (*0-89565-477-6*) Childs World.

—The Princess & the Pea: A Classic Tale. Jose, Eduard, adapted by. Riehecky, Janet, tr. Rovira, Francesc, illus. LC 88-35206. 32p. (gr. k-2). 1988. PLB 13.95 (*0-89565-486-5*) Childs World.

—The Steadfast Tin Soldier: A Classic Tale. Jose, Eduard, adapted by. Moncure, Jane B., tr. Asensio, Augusti, illus. LC 88-35207. 32p. (gr. k-3). 1988. PLB 13.95 (*0-89565-468-7*) Childs World.

—Thumbelina: A Classic Tale. Jose, Eduard, adapted by. Riehecky, Janet, tr. Rovira, Francesc, illus. LC 88-35307. 32p. (gr. k-3). 1988. PLB 13.95 (*0-89565-466-0*) Childs World.

Seidelin, Anna S. Danish Fairy Tales & Rhymes for Children & Adults: Folke Eventyr Og Remse. Zucker, William V., tr. from DAN. Brande, Marlie, illus. 147p. (Orig.). 1992. pap. 15.00 (*0-9634440-1-8*) Lester St Pub.

FOLKLORE–EGYPT

Green, Roger L. Tales of Ancient Egypt. (gr. k-3). 1990. pap. 3.50 (*0-14-035101-9*, Puffin) Puffin Bks.

Hull, Robert. Egyptian Stories. Loftus, Barbara & Bateman, Noel, illus. LC 93-35684. 48p. (gr. 5-9). 1994. 15.95 (*1-56847-155-6*) Thomson Lrning.

Kimmel, Eric A., adapted by. Rimonah of the Flashing Sword: A North African Tale. Rayyan, Omar, illus. LC 93-40091. 1995. write for info. (*0-8234-1093-5*) Holiday.

Mike, Jan M. Gift of the Nile: An Ancient Egyptian Legend. Reasoner, Charles, illus. LC 92-5826. 32p. (gr. 2-5). 1992. PLB 11.89 (*0-8167-2813-5*); pap. text ed. 3.95 (*0-8167-2814-3*) Troll Assocs.

FOLKLORE–ENGLAND

Amoss, Berthe. Jack & the Beanstalk. Amoss, Berthe, illus. 10p. (ps-7). 1989. pap. 2.95 (*0-922589-00-3*) More Than Card.

Crawford, Tom. The Story of King Arthur. Green, John, illus. LC 94-3363. (gr. 4 up). 1994. pap. write for info. (*0-486-28347-X*) Dover.

Creswick, Paul. Robin Hood. Wyeth, N. C., illus. LC 92-50796. 376p. (gr. 6 up). 1993. 16.95 (*1-56138-265-5*) Running Pr.

Crossley-Holland, Kevin. British Folk Tales: A Selection. large type ed. (gr. 1-8). 1993. 16.95 (*0-7451-1911-5*, Galaxy Child Lrg Print) Chivers N Amer.

De La Mare, Walter. The Three Sillies. 1991. PLB 13.95 (*0-88682-467-2*) Creative Ed.

Esterl, Arnica. The Fine Round Cake. Hejl, Pauline, tr. from GER. Dugin, Andrej & Dugina, Olga, illus. LC 91-6411. 24p. (ps-2). 1991. SBE 14.95 (*0-02-733568-2*, Four Winds) Macmillan Child Grp.

Frost, Abigail. The Age of Chivalry. LC 89-17396. (Illus.). 48p. (gr. 4-8). 1990. PLB 13.95 (*1-85435-235-0*) Marshall Cavendish.

Galdone, Paul. The Teeny Tiny Woman. Galdone, Paul, illus. LC 84-4311. 32p. (ps-3). 1984. 14.95 (*0-89919-270-X*, Pub. by Clarion); pap. 4.95 (*0-89919-463-X*, Pub. by Clarion) HM.

Garner, Alan. Jack & the Beanstalk. Heller, Julek, illus. LC 91-36717. 32p. (gr. k-3). 1992. 14.00 (*0-385-30693-8*) Doubleday.

Giblin, James C., retold by. The Dwarf, the Giant, & the Unicorn: A Tale of King Arthur. Ewart, Claire, illus. LC 92-34031. 1994. write for info. (*0-395-60520-2*, Clarion Bks) HM.

Green, Roger L., retold by. The Adventures of Robin Hood. LC 94-5862. 1994. 13.95 (*0-679-43636-7*, Evrymans Lib Childs) Knopf.

Greenburg, Joanne. Jack in the Beanstalk. Walsh, Michael S., illus. 48p. (gr. 3 up). 1980. 19.00 (*0-8299-1033-6*) West Pub.

Greenway, Jennifer, retold by. Jack & the Beanstalk. Bernal, Richard, illus. 1991. 6.95 (*0-8362-4903-8*) Andrews & McMeel.

Haviland, Virginia, compiled by. Favorite Fairy Tales Told in England. Chambliss, Maxie, illus. LC 93-29707. 96p. (gr. 3 up). 1994. pap. 4.95 (*0-688-12595-6*, Pub. by Beech Tree Bks) Morrow.

Heyer, Carol. Excalibur. Heyer, Carol, illus. LC 91-9100. 32p. (gr. k-4). 1991. 14.95 (*0-8249-8487-0*, Ideals Child) Hambleton-Hill.

Heyer, Carol, retold by. & illus. Robin Hood. LC 93-18591. 32p. (ps-3). 1993. 14.95 (*0-8249-8634-2*, Ideals Child); PLB 15.00 (*0-8249-8648-2*) Hambleton-Hill.

Howe, John, retold by. & illus. The Knight with the Lion: The Story of Yvain. LC 92-25940. 1995. 14.95 (*0-316-37583-7*) Little.

Huck, Charlotte. Princess Furball. Lobel, Anita, illus. LC 93-11729. 40p. (ps up). 1994. pap. 4.95 (*0-688-13107-7*, Mulberry) Morrow.

J. Sainsbury's Pure Tea Staff. Jack & the Beanstalk: Full-Color Picture Book. LC 92-35299. 1993. pap. 1.00 (*0-486-27504-3*) Dover.

Jack & the Beanstalk. (Illus.). (ps-3). 1985. 2.98 (*0-517-28804-4*) Random Hse Value.

Jack & the Beanstalk. 24p. (ps-3). 1989. 2.25 (*1-56288-165-5*) Checkerboard.

Jacobs, Joseph, ed. English Fairy Tales. Batten, John D., illus. LC 67-19703. xv, 261p. (gr. 3-6). 1898. pap. 5.95 (*0-486-21818-X*) Dover.

—English Fairy Tales. 1993. 13.95 (*0-679-42809-7*, Everymans Lib) Knopf.

Litzinger, Rosanne. The Old Woman & Her Pig: An Old English Tale. LC 91-38227. (ps). 1993. 13.95 (*0-15-257802-1*) HarBrace.

Metaxas, Eric. Jack & the Beanstalk. Sorel, Ed, illus. LC 91-14176. 40p. (gr. k up). 1991. pap. 14.95 (*0-88708-188-6*, Rabbit Ears); incls. cassette 19.95 (*0-88708-189-4*, Rabbit Ears) Picture Bk Studio.

Mockler, Anthony. King Arthur & His Knights. Harris, Nick, illus. 308p. 1987. jacketed 18.95 (*0-19-274531-X*) OUP.

O'Connor, Jane, retold by. The Teeny Tiny Woman. Alley, R. W., illus. LC 86-485. 32p. (ps-1). 1986. lib. bdg. 7.99 (*0-394-98320-3*); pap. 3.50 (*0-394-88320-9*, Random Juv) Random Bks Yng Read.

Parker, Ed, illus. Jack & the Beanstalk. LC 78-18072. 32p. (gr. k-4). 1979. PLB 9.79 (*0-89375-125-1*); pap. 1.95 (*0-89375-103-0*) Troll Assocs.

Pyle, Howard. King Arthur & the Magic Sword. LC 89-27793. 21p. (gr. 2-7). 1990. 13.95 (*0-8037-0824-6*) Dial Bks Young.

—The Merry Adventures of Robin Hood. Mattern, Joanne, ed. Sauber, Robert, illus. LC 92-12702. 48p. (gr. 3-6). 1992. PLB 12.89 (*0-8167-2858-5*); pap. text ed. 3.95 (*0-8167-2859-3*) Troll Assocs.

—The Story of the Grail & the Passing of Arthur. unabr. ed. LC 92-29058. (Illus.). 272p. 1992. pap. text ed. 7.95 (*0-486-27361-X*) Dover.

Ross, Tony. Stone Soup. (ps-3). 1990. pap. 3.95 (*0-8037-0890-4*, Puff Pied Piper) Puffin Bks.

San Souci, Robert D. The Hobyahs. Natchev, Alexi, illus. LC 92-28655. 1994. 14.95 (*0-385-30934-1*) Doubleday.

Schmidt, Karen L., illus. The Gingerbread Man. 32p. (gr. k-2). 1985. pap. 2.50 (*0-590-41056-3*) Scholastic Inc.

Shannon, Mark. Gawain & the Green Knight. Shannon, David, illus. LC 93-13037. 32p. (ps-3). 1994. PLB 15.95 (*0-399-22446-7*, Putnam) Putnam Pub Group.

Steel, Flora A. & Messina, Christine, eds. Goldilocks & the Three Bears & Other Classic English Fairy Tales. LC 93-44688. 1994. 12.99 (*0-517-10176-9*) Random Hse Value.

White, Terence H. The Sword in the Stone. Nolan, Dennis, illus. LC 92-24808. 256p. 1993. 18.95 (*0-399-22502-1*, Philomel Bks) Putnam Pub Group.

FOLKLORE–EUROPE

Brodmann, Aliana. Such a Noise! Fillingham, David, tr. from GER. Poppel, Hans, illus. 32p. (gr. k-3). 1989. 11.95 (*0-916291-25-1*) Kane-Miller Bk.

Hillert, Margaret. Tom Thumb. (Illus.). (ps-k). 1982. PLB 6.95 (*0-8136-5091-7*, TK2174); pap. 3.50 (*0-8136-5591-9*, TK2175) Modern Curr.

Moroney, Lynn, adapted by. Elinda Who Danced in the Sky: An Eastern European Folktale from Estonia. Reisberg, Veg, illus. LC 99-2247. 32p. (gr. 1-7). 1990. 13.95 (*0-89239-066-2*) Childrens Book Pr.

Philip, Neil, compiled by. Fairy Tales from Eastern Europe. Wilkes, Larry, illus. Philip, Neil, retold by. (Illus.). 160p. (gr. 4 up). 1991. 19.45 (*0-395-57456-0*, Clarion Bks) HM.

FOLKLORE–FINLAND

Troughton, Joanna, retold by. & illus. The Magic Mill: A Finnish Folk Tale from the Kalevala. LC 88-24170. 32p. 1989. PLB 14.95 (*0-87226-405-X*, Bedrick Blackie) P Bedrick Bks.

FOLKLORE–FRANCE

Beauty & the Beast. (Illus.). (gr. 2-4). 3.50 (*0-7214-0642-4*) Ladybird Bks.

Beauty & the Beast. 24p. (gr. 3 up). 1992. Incl. songbk. & recorder. 9.95 (*0-7935-1501-7*, 00710359) H Leonard.

Beauty & the Beast. 16p. (gr. 3 up). 1992. Incl. xylotone. 14.95 (*0-7935-1502-5*, 00824005) H Leonard.

Bender, Robert, retold by. & illus. Toads & Diamonds. LC 93-46602. 1995. write for info. (*0-525-67509-4*, Lodestar Bks) Dutton Child Bks.

Brown, Marcia. Stone Soup. Brown, Marcia, illus. LC 47-11630. 48p. (ps-4). 1979. RSBE 13.95 (*0-684-92296-7*, Scribners Young Read); (Scribner) Macmillan Child Grp.

Disney's Beauty & the Beast. (Illus.). 24p. (ps up). 1992. deluxe ed. write for info. incl. long-life batteries (*0-307-74024-2*, 64024, Golden Pr) Western Pub.

Evans, C. S. Cinderella. 1993. 12.95 (*0-679-42313-3*, Everymans Lib) Knopf.

Haley, Gail E., retold by. & illus. Puss in Boots. LC 90-20629. 32p. (ps-3). 1991. 13.95 (*0-525-44740-7*, DCB) Dutton Child Bks.

Hautzig, Deborah, retold by. Beauty & the Beast. LC 93-34694. 1995. write for info. (*0-679-85296-4*); PLB write for info. (*0-679-95296-9*) Random Bks Yng Read.

Haviland, Virginia, compiled by. Favorite Fairy Tales Told in France. Ambrus, Victor, illus. LC 93-29665. 96p. (gr. 3 up). 1994. pap. 4.95 (*0-688-12596-4*, Pub. by Beech Tree Bks) Morrow.

Heyer, Carol, retold by. & illus. Beauty & the Beast. LC 89-7624. 32p. (ps-3). 1989. 13.95 (*0-8249-8359-9*, Ideals Child) Hambleton-Hill.

Kimmel, Eric A., adapted by. Three Sacks of Truth: A Story from France. Rayevsky, Robert, illus. 32p. (ps-3). 1993. reinforced bdg. 15.95 (*0-8234-0921-X*) Holiday.

Kirstein, Lincoln, retold by. Puss in Boots. Vaes, Alain, illus. 32p. (ps-3). 1992. 15.95 (*0-316-89506-7*) Little.

Leprince De Beaumont, Marie & Perrault, Charles. Beauty & the Beast & Other Fairy Tales. (Illus.). 96p. (Orig.). (ps-3). 1994. pap. 1.00 (*0-486-28032-2*) Dover.

Mayer, Marianna. Beauty & the Beast. Mayer, Mercer, illus. LC 87-1095. 48p. (ps up). 1987. pap. 5.95 (*0-689-71151-4*, Aladdin) Macmillan Child Grp.

Metaxas, Eric. Puss in Boots. Le-Tan, Pierre, illus. LC 92-7789. 40p. 1992. pap. 14.95 (*0-88708-285-8*, Rabbit Ears); pap. 19.95 incl. cass. (*0-88708-286-6*, Rabbit Ears) Picture Bk Studio.

Milone, Karen, illus. Beauty & the Beast. LC 81-612. 32p. (gr. k-4). 1981. PLB 9.79 (*0-89375-464-1*); pap. text ed. 1.95 (*0-89375-465-X*) Troll Assocs.

Orgel, Doris. Button Soup. Estrada, Pau, illus. LC 93-14087. 1994. 10.95 (*0-553-09045-3*); pap. 3.99 (*0-553-37341-2*) Bantam.

Pagnol. Le Chateau de Ma Mere. (gr. 7-12). pap. 6.95 (*0-88436-045-8*, 40278) EMC.

Paterson, Diane, illus. Stone Soup. LC 80-27947. 32p. (gr. 1-4). 1981. PLB 9.79 (*0-89375-478-1*); pap. text ed. 1.95 (*0-89375-479-X*) Troll Assocs.

Patron, Susan. Burgoo Stew. Shenon, Mike, illus. LC 90-43791. 32p. (ps-1). 1991. 13.95 (*0-531-05916-2*); RLB 13.99 (*0-531-08516-3*) Orchard Bks Watts.

Perrault, Charles. El Gato Con Botas: (Puss in Boots) Marcellino, Fred, illus. Marcuse, Aida, tr. (SPA., Illus.). 32p. 1991. 16.00 (*0-374-36158-4*) FS&G.

—Perrault's Fairy Tales. Dore, Gustave, illus. LC 72-79522. viii, 117p. (gr. 4-6). 1969. pap. 5.95 (*0-486-22311-6*) Dover.

—Puss in Boots. new ed. Da Riff, Andrea, illus. LC 78-18061. 32p. (gr. k-3). 1979. PLB 9.79 (*0-89375-130-8*); pap. 1.95 (*0-89375-108-1*) Troll Assocs.

—Puss in Boots. (Illus.). 20p. (ps up). 1992. write for info. incl. long-life batteries (*0-307-74705-0*, 64705, Golden Pr) Western Pub.

—Puss in Boots: A Classic Tale. Jose, Eduard, adapted by. Suire, Diane D., tr. Asensio, Augusti, illus. LC 88-35316. 32p. (gr. k-2). 1988. PLB 13.95 (*0-89565-482-2*) Childs World.

—Sleeping Beauty & Other Classic French Fairy Tales. 1991. 12.99 (*0-517-03706-8*) Random Hse Value.

Picard, Barbara L. French Legends, Tales & Fairy Stories. Kiddell-Monroe, Joan, illus. 216p. (gr. 4 up). 1992. pap. 10.95 (*0-19-274149-7*) OUP.

Radiguet, Raymond. Le Diable au Corps. (gr. 7-12). pap. 6.95 (*0-88436-059-8*, 40273) EMC.

Saunders, Susan. Puss in Boots. 1989. pap. 2.50 (*0-590-41888-2*) Scholastic Inc.

Schecter, Ellen. Diamonds & Toads: A Classic Fairy Tale. Blackshear, Ami, illus. LC 93-14096. 1994. 10.95 (*0-553-09046-1*); pap. 3.99 (*0-553-37339-0*) Bantam.

Schwartz, Carol. Little Juggler (Pop-Up) 1991. 3.95 (*0-8037-1020-8*) Dial Bks Young.

Stone Soup. 24p. (ps-3). 1989. 2.25 (*1-56288-159-0*) Checkerboard.

Wallis, Diz. Something Nasty in the Cabbages. Wallis, Diz, illus. LC 90-84007. 32p. 1991. 15.95 (*1-878093-10-X*) Boyds Mills Pr.

Willard, Nancy. Beauty & the Beast. Moser, B., illus. 1992. 19.95 (*0-15-206052-9*, HB Juv Bks) HarBrace.

FOLKLORE–GERMANY

Amoss, Berthe. Hansel & Gretel. Amoss, Berthe, illus. 10p. (ps-7). 1989. pap. 2.95 (*0-922589-05-4*) More Than Card.

—Rumpelstiltskin. Amoss, Berthe, illus. 10p. (ps-7). 1989. pap. 2.95 (*0-922589-03-8*) More Than Card.

—Snow White & the Seven Dwarfs. Amoss, Berthe, illus. 10p. (ps-7). 1989. pap. 2.95 (*0-922589-01-1*) More Than Card.

Andersen, Hans Christian. Thumbeline. Zwerger, Lisbeth, illus. LC 85-12062. 28p. (gr. 1 up). 1991. pap. 14.95 (*0-88708-006-5*) Picture Bk Studio.

Anglund, Joan W. Nibble Nibble Mousekin: A Tale of Hansel & Gretel. Anglund, Joan W., illus. LC 62-14422. 32p. (gr. k-3). 1962. 10.95 (*0-15-257400-X*, HB Juv Bks) HarBrace.

Balducci, Rita, adapted by. Walt Disney's Snow White & the Seven Dwarfs. Williams, Don, illus. 24p. (ps-k). 1992. pap. write for info. laminated covers (*0-307-10037-5*, 10037, Golden Pr) Western Pub.

Berenzy, A. Rapunzel. 1992. 14.95 (*0-8050-1283-4*) H Holt & Co.

Black, Sheila. Hansel & Gretel: The Witch's Story. Klemushin, Arlene, illus. LC 93-42780. 1994. pap. 8.95 (*0-8065-1520-1*, Citadel Pr) Carol Pub Group.

Boll. Die Erzahlungen. (gr. 7-12). pap. 6.95 (*0-88436-108-X*, 45275) EMC.

Bornstein, Harry & Saulnier, Karen L. Little Red Riding Hood: Told in Signed English. Pomeroy, Bradley U., illus. LC 90-3477. 48p. (ps-2). 1990. 14.95 (*0-930323-63-7*, Pub. by K Green Pubns) Gallaudet Univ Pr.
The Brementown Musicians. 24p. (ps-3). 1993. 2.25 (*1-56288-166-3*) Checkerboard.
Browning, Robert. The Pied Piper of Hamelin. rev. ed. Small, Terry, illus. 47p. (gr. 1 up). 1988. 10.95 (*0-15-200566-8*, Gulliver Bks) HarBrace.
—The Pied Piper of Hamelin. Greenaway, Kate, illus. LC 93-767. 1993. 5.99 (*0-517-09347-2*, Pub. by Derrydale Bks) Random Hse Value.
—The Pied Piper of Hamelin. 1993. 12.95 (*0-679-42812-7*, Everymans Lib) Knopf.
Carr, Jan. Beauty & the Beast. Bratun, Katy, illus. 32p. (ps-3). 1993. pap. 2.50 (*0-590-46451-5*, Cartwheel) Scholastic Inc.
Chmielarz, Sharon, adapted by. The Pied Piper of Hamelin. DeWitt, Pat & DeWitt, Robin, illus. 40p. (gr. k-6). 1990. 14.95 (*0-88045-115-7*) Stemmer Hse.
Collodi, Carlo. The Adventures of Pinocchio. Innocenti, Roberto, illus. 144p. (gr. 1-12). 1988. lib. bdg. 19.95 RLB smythe-sewn (*0-8211-0394-6*, 97080-098) Creative Ed.
Cooney, Barbara. Snow White & Rose Red. (ps-3). 1991. pap. 13.95 (*0-685-54227-0*) Delacorte.
—Snow White & Rose Red. LC 89-78013. (ps-3). 1991. 13.95 (*0-385-30175-8*) Delacorte.
Croll, Carolyn, adapted by. & illus. The Three Brothers: A German Folktale. (ps-3). 1991. 14.95 (*0-399-22195-6*, Whitebird Bks) Putnam Pub Group.
Crump, Fred, Jr. Sleeping Beauty: A Retold Story. Crump, Fred, Jr., illus. LC 89-51788. 44p. (gr. k-2). 1991. pap. 6.95 (*1-55523-300-7*) Winston-Derek.
Cuddy, Robbin, illus. Walt Disney's Cinderella: The Fairy Godmother's Magic. LC 93-73820. 1994. 9.95 (*1-56282-624-7*) Disney Pr.
De La Mare, Walter. The Turnip. Hawkes, Kevin, illus. LC 92-6191. 1992. 18.95 (*0-87923-934-4*) Godine.
Dolan, Ellen M. & Bolinske, Janet L., eds. Hansel & Gretel. Nichol, Bee, illus. LC 87-61670. 32p. (Orig.). (gr. 1-3). 1987. text ed. 8.95 (*0-88335-555-8*); 4.95 (*0-88335-545-0*); pap. text ed. 3.95 (*0-88335-575-2*) Milliken Pub Co.
Eden, Cooper, intro. by. Goldilocks. abr. ed. (Illus.). 48p. (gr. 9-12). 1991. 14.95 (*0-88138-135-7*, Green Tiger) S&S Trade.
Evans, C. S. Sleeping Beauty. 1993. 12.95 (*0-679-42814-3*, Everymans Lib) Knopf.
The Frog Prince. (Illus.). 20p. (ps up). 1992. write for info. incl. long-life batteries (*0-307-74709-3*, 64709, Golden Pr) Western Pub.
Galdone, Paul. The Elves & the Shoemaker. Galdone, Paul, illus. LC 83-14979. 32p. (ps-3). 1986. 13.95 (*0-89919-226-2*, Clarion Bks); pap. 4.95 (*0-89919-422-2*, Clarion Bks) HM.
Goes. Das Brandopfer. (gr. 7-12). pap. 6.95 (*0-88436-057-1*, 45274) EMC.
Grimm, Jacob & Grimm, Wilhelm K. Anno's Twice Told Tales: The Fisherman & His Wife & The Four Clever Brothers. Anno, Mitsumasa, retold by. & illus. LC 92-25307. 64p. (ps up). 1993. PLB 17.95 (*0-399-22005-4*, Philomel Bks) Putnam Pub Group.
—The Bear & the Bird King. Byrd, Robert, retold by. & illus. LC 93-15741. 32p. (ps-3). 1994. 14.99 (*0-525-45118-8*, DCB) Dutton Child Bks.
—The Bremen Town Musicians. Easton, Samantha, retold by. Corcoran, Mark, illus. 1991. 6.95 (*0-8362-4925-9*) Andrews & McMeel.
—The Bremen Town Musicians. Watts, Bernadette, illus. Bell, Anthea, tr. from GER. LC 91-30375. (Illus.). 32p. (gr. k-3). 1992. 14.95 (*1-55858-140-5*); lib. bdg. 14.88 (*1-55858-148-0*) North-South Bks NYC.
—Cinderella: A Classic Tale. Jose, Eduard, adapted by. Moncure, Jane B., tr. Asensio, Augusti, illus. LC 88-35317. 32p. (gr. 1-4). 1988. PLB 13.95 (*0-89565-483-0*) Childs World.
—Fairy Tales. Rackham, Arthur, illus. LC 92-53180. 224p. 1992. 12.95 (*0-679-41796-6*, Evrymans Lib Childs Class) Knopf.
—The Fisherman & His Wife. Jarrell, Randall, tr. from GER. Zemach, Margot, illus. 32p. (ps up). 1987. pap. 4.95 (*0-374-42326-1*) FS&G.
—The Frog Prince. Black, Fiona, retold by. Parmenter, Wayne, illus. 1991. 6.95 (*0-8362-4920-8*) Andrews & McMeel.
—Grimm's Fairy Tales. Crikshank, G., tr. (Illus.). (gr. 7 up). 1985. pap. 3.50 (*0-14-035070-5*, Puffin) Puffin Bks.
—Hansel & Gretel. Jeffers, Susan, illus. LC 80-15079. 32p. (gr. k up). 1980. 16.00 (*0-8037-3492-1*); PLB 14.89 (*0-8037-3491-3*) Dial Bks Young.
—Hansel & Gretel. Black, Fiona, retold by. Gurney, John, illus. 1991. 6.95 (*0-8362-4912-7*) Andrews & McMeel.
—Hansel & Gretel. 2nd, abr. ed. Crawford, Elizabeth D., tr. LC 91-40656. (Illus.). 28p. (gr. k up). 1992. pap. 4.95 (*0-88708-225-4*) Picture Bk Studio.
—Hansel & Gretel: A Classic Tale. Jose, Eduard, adapted by. Riehecky, Janet, tr. Asensio, Augusti, illus. LC 88-35212. 32p. (gr. 1-4). 1988. PLB 13.95 (*0-89565-480-6*) Childs World.
—Household Stories of the Brothers Grimm. Crane, Lucy, tr. Crane, Walter, illus. x, 269p. (gr. 3-9). 1886. pap. 4.95 (*0-486-21080-4*) Dover.
—Iron Hans. Heyer, Marilee, illus. LC 93-14662. 32p. 1993. 14.99 (*0-670-81741-4*) Viking Child Bks.
—Jack in Luck. Bell, Anthea, tr. Tharlet, Eve, illus. LC 92-7102. 28p. (ps up). 1992. pap. 14.95 (*0-88708-249-1*) Picture Bk Studio.
—Rapunzel. Heyer, Carol, illus. LC 92-6712. 32p. (gr. k-3). 1992. 14.95 (*0-8249-8558-3*, Ideals Child); PLB 15.00 (*0-8249-8585-0*) Hambleton-Hill.
—Rumpelstiltskin. Sage, Alison, retold by. Spirin, Gennady, illus. 32p. (ps-3). 1991. 12.95 (*0-8037-0908-0*) Dial Bks Young.
—Rumpelstiltskin. (Illus.). 20p. (ps up). 1992. write for info. incl. long-life batteries (*0-307-74711-5*, 64711, Golden Pr) Western Pub.
—Rumpelstiltskin: A Classic Tale. Moncure, Jane B., tr. from SPA. Asensio, Augusti, illus. LC 88-35315. 32p. (gr. k-3). 1988. PLB 13.95 (*0-89565-463-6*) Childs World.
—The Seven Ravens. Zwerger, Lisbeth, illus. Bell, Anthea, tr. LC 93-20122. (Illus.). (ps-8). 1993. 4.95 (*0-88708-326-9*) Picture Bk Studio.
—The Seven Ravens. adpt. ed. Geringer, Laura, adapted by. Gazsi, Edward S., illus. LC 93-8161. 32p. (gr. k-4). 1994. 16.00 (*0-06-023552-7*); PLB 15.89 (*0-06-023553-5*) HarpC Child Bks.
—Sleeping Beauty & Other Fairy Tales. (Illus.). 96p. (Orig.). 1992. pap. 1.00t (*0-486-27084-X*) Dover.
—Snow White. Greenway, Jennifer, retold by. Augestine, Erin, illus. 1991. 6.95 (*0-8362-4906-2*) Andrews & McMeel.
—Snow White. Poole, Josephine, ed. LC 91-18411. (Illus.). 32p. 1991. 15.00 (*0-679-82656-4*) Knopf Bks Yng Read.
—Snow White & Rose Red. Spirin, Gennady, illus. 32p. (ps up). 1992. 14.95 (*0-399-21873-4*, Philomel Bks) Putnam Pub Group.
—Snow White & the Seven Dwarfs. Iwasaki, Chihiro, illus. LC 85-12158. 40p. (gr. 1 up). 1991. pap. 15.95 (*0-88708-012-X*) Picture Bk Studio.
—Snow White & the Seven Dwarfs. Kassier, Sue, retold by. May, Darcy, illus. LC 92-44516. (ps-2). 1993. pap. 2.50 (*0-679-84347-7*) Random Bks Yng Read.
Grimm, Jakob. Hansel & Gretel. (ps-3). 1986. pap. 5.99 (*0-14-054636-7*) Dial Bks Young.
Gross, Ruth B. The Bremen-Town Musicians. Kent, Jack, illus. 32p. (Orig.). (ps-2). 1985. pap. 2.50 (*0-590-42364-9*) Scholastic Inc.
Hader, Berta & Hader, Elmer, illus. The Story of Hansel & Gretel. LC 94-1297. 1994. write for info. (*0-486-28299-6*) Dover.
Hansel y Gretel. (SPA.). (ps-3). 1993. pap. 2.25 (*0-307-70033-X*, Golden Pr) Western Pub.
Hastings, Selina. Peter & the Wolf. Cartwright, Reg, illus. LC 86-27004. 32p. (ps-2). 1990. pap. 5.95 (*0-8050-1362-8*, Bks Young Read) H Holt & Co.
Hautzig, Deborah, retold by. The Pied Piper of Hamelin: A Step 2 Book. Schindler, S. D., illus. LC 89-3968. 48p. (Orig.). (gr. 1-3). 1989. lib. bdg. 7.99 (*0-394-96579-5*); pap. 3.50 (*0-394-86579-0*) Random Bks Yng Read.
Hildebrandt, Tim & Laurence, Jim, eds. Shoemaker & the Christmas Elves. Hildebrandt, Tim, illus. 1993. 6.99 (*0-517-08488-0*) Random Hse Value.
Hillert, Margaret. Little Red Riding Hood. (Illus.). (ps-k). 1982. PLB 6.95 (*0-8136-5095-X*, TK2170); pap. 3.50 (*0-8136-5595-1*, TK2171) Modern Curr.
Hodges, Margaret. Hero of Bremen. LC 91-22357. (Illus.). 32p. (ps-3). 1993. reinforced bdg. 15.95 (*0-8234-0934-1*) Holiday.
Hyman, Trina S., ed. & illus. The Sleeping Beauty. LC 75-43769. (gr. 1 up). 1983. 15.95 (*0-316-38702-9*); pap. 6.95 (*0-316-38708-8*) Little.
Janisch, Heinz. Till Eulenspiegel's Merry Pranks. Bell, Anthea, tr. from GER. Zwerger, Lisbeth, illus. LC 90-7168. 32p. (gr. 3 up). 1991. pap. 15.95 (*0-88708-150-9*) Picture Bk Studio.
Jose, Eduard, adapted by. Goldilocks & the Three Bears: A Classic Tale. McDonnell, Janet, tr. Lavarello, Jose M., illus. LC 88-36870. 32p. (gr. 1-4). 1988. PLB 13.95 (*0-89565-465-2*) Childs World.
—Snow White & the Seven Dwarfs: A Classic Tale. McDonnell, Janet, tr. Asensio, Augusti, illus. LC 88-35210. 32p. (gr. k-3). 1988. PLB 13.95 (*0-89565-479-2*) Childs World.
—Till Eulenspiegel's Merry Pranks: A Classic Tale. Riehecky, Janet, tr. Rovira, Francesc, illus. LC 88-36794. 32p. (gr. k-3). 1988. PLB 13.95 (*0-89565-475-X*) Childs World.
Kastner. Drei Manner Im Schnee. (gr. 7-12). pap. 6.95 (*0-88436-038-5*, 45271) EMC.
Kimmel, Eric A. Nanny Goat & the Seven Little Kids. Stevens, Janet, illus. LC 89-20058. 32p. (ps-3). 1990. reinforced bdg. 15.95 (*0-8234-0789-6*); pap. 5.95 (*0-8234-0953-8*) Holiday.
Kimmel, Eric A., ed. The Four Gallant Sisters. Yuditskaya, Tatyana, illus. LC 91-28231. 32p. (gr. 1-4). 1992. 15.95 (*0-8050-1901-4*, Bks Young Read) H Holt & Co.
Kimmel, Eric A., retold by. The Goose Girl: A Story from the Brothers Grimm. Sauber, Robert, illus. LC 93-13138. 1995. write for info. (*0-8234-1074-9*) Holiday.
Kimmel, Eric A., adapted by. Iron John: A Tale from the Brothers Grimm. Hyman, Trina S., illus. LC 93-7534. 32p. (ps-3). 1994. reinforced bdg. 15.95 (*0-8234-1073-0*) Holiday.
Latimer, Jim. The Irish Piper. O'Brien, John, illus. LC 90-34550. 32p. (gr. 1-3). 1991. SBE 13.95 (*0-684-19130-X*, Scribners Young Read) Macmillan Child Grp.
Lemieux, Michele. The Pied Piper of Hamelin. Lemieux, Michele, illus. LC 92-21338. 32p. 1993. 15.00 (*0-688-09848-7*); PLB 14.93 (*0-688-09849-5*) Morrow Jr Bks.
Levine, Arthur A. The Boardwalk Princess. Guevara, Susan, illus. LC 92-8081. 32p. (ps up). 1993. 14.00 (*0-688-10306-5*, Tambourine Bks); PLB 13.93 (*0-688-10307-3*, Tambourine Bks) Morrow.
Little Red Riding Hood. 32p. (ps-1). 1985. 2.49 (*0-517-46240-0*); bds. 1.00 (*0-517-48143-X*) Random Hse Value.
McPhail, David. Little Red Riding Hood. McPhail, David, illus. LC 93-43990. 1995. write for info. (*0-590-48116-9*) Scholastic Inc.
Marshall, James. Red Riding Hood. (Illus.). 32p. (ps-3). 1993. pap. 17.99 (*0-14-054976-5*, Puff Pied Piper) Puffin Bks.
Morris, Neil & Morris, Ting. Heidi. (Illus.). 48p. (gr. 2-5). 1991. 13.95 (*0-237-50935-0*, Pub. by Evans Bros Ltd) Trafalgar.
Naava. The Golden Goose. LC 93-11681. Date not set. write for info. (*0-688-11302-8*, Tambourine Bks); PLB write for info. (*0-688-11303-6*, Tambourine Bks) Morrow.
Noel, Christopher. Rumpelstiltskin. Sis, Peter, illus. LC 92-4592. 40p. (gr. k up). 1993. incl. cass. 19.95 (*0-88708-280-7*, Rabbit Ears); 14.95 (*0-88708-279-3*, Rabbit Ears) Picture Bk Studio.
Ormerod, Jan & LLoyd, David. The Frog Prince. Omerod, Jan, illus. LC 89-12977. 32p. (ps-3). 1990. 12.95 (*0-688-09568-2*); lib. bdg. 12.88 (*0-688-09569-0*) Lothrop.
Page, P. K., retold by. The Traveling Musicians of Bremen. Denton, Kady M., illus. 32p. (ps-3). 1992. 13.95 (*0-316-68836-3*, Joy St Bks) Little.
Patrick, Denise L., adapted by. Walt Disney's Snow White & the Seven Dwarfs. Mones, illus. 28p. (ps). 1992. bds. write for info. (*0-307-12531-9*, 12531, Golden Pr) Western Pub.
Perrault, Charles. Little Red Riding Hood: A Classic Tale. Jose, Eduard, ed. Moncure, Jane B., tr. Lavarello, Jose M., illus. LC 88-37088. 32p. (gr. 1-4). 1988. PLB 13.95 (*0-89565-457-1*) Childs World.
—Sleeping Beauty: A Classic Tale. Jose, Eduard, adapted by. Moncure, Jane B., tr. from SPA. Asensio, Agusti, illus. LC 88-35212. 32p. (gr. k-3). 1988. PLB 13.95 (*0-89565-478-4*) Childs World.
—Tom Thumb: A Classic Tale. Jose, Eduard, adapted by. Riehecky, Janet, tr. from SPA. Rovira, Francesc, illus. LC 88-35211. 32p. (gr. k-3). 1988. PLB 13.95 (*0-89565-462-8*) Childs World.
Plume, Ilse. Shoemaker & the Elves. 32p. (ps-3). 1991. 14.95 (*0-15-274050-3*, HB Juv Bks) HarBrace.
Red Riding Hood. (Illus.). (ps-3). 1985. 2.98 (*0-517-28810-9*) Random Hse Value.
Roberts, Tom & Hunter, Holly, eds. The Three Billy Goats Gruff. Jorgensen, David, illus. Lande, Art, contrib. by. (Illus.). 32p. (ps up). 1993. pap. write for info. slipcase pkg., incl. cassette (*0-307-14329-5*, 14329, Golden Pr) Western Pub.
Rogasky, Barbara, retold by. The Water of Life. Hyman, Trina S., illus. LC 84-19226. 40p. (gr. k-3). 1986. reinforced bdg. 15.95 (*0-8234-0552-4*); pap. 5.95 (*0-8234-0907-4*) Holiday.
Ross, Tony. Hansel & Gretel. (Illus.). 32p. (gr. k-3). 1990. 15.95 (*0-86264-210-8*, Pub. by Anderson Pr UK) Trafalgar.
—Hansel & Gretel. LC 93-31047. (Illus.). 32p. (ps-3). 1994. 13.95 (*0-87951-535-X*) Overlook Pr.
—Mrs. Goat & Her Seven Little Kids. Ross, Tony, illus. LC 89-17933. 32p. (gr. 1-3). 1990. SBE 13.95 (*0-689-31624-0*, Atheneum Child Bk) Macmillan Child Grp.
Rowland, Della. Little Red Riding Hood: The Wolf's Tale. Montgomery, Michael, illus. LC 93-42781. 1994. pap. 8.95 (*0-8065-1526-0*, Citadel Pr) Carol Pub Group.
Sanderson, Ruth, retold by. The Twelve Dancing Princesses. (gr. 2-4). 1990. 15.95 (*0-316-77017-5*) Little.
Snow White & the Seven Dwarfs. (Illus.). (ps-3). 1985. 2.98 (*0-517-28812-5*) Random Hse Value.
Snow White & the Seven Dwarfs. 24p. 1992. incl. songbk., recorder 9.95 (*0-7935-1500-9*, 00710358) H Leonard.
Spri, Johanna. Heidi. (gr. 3 up). 1994. 4.98 (*0-8317-1647-9*) Smithmark.
Storr, Catherine. Pied Piper of Hamelin. (ps-3). 1993. pap. 4.95 (*0-8114-8353-3*) Raintree Steck-V.
Tarcov, Edith H., retold by. The Frog Prince. Marshall, James, illus. LC 92-25167. 32p. (ps-2). 1993. pap. 2.95 (*0-590-46571-6*) Scholastic Inc.
Thomson, Peggy, retold by. The Brave Little Tailor. Warhola, James, illus. LC 91-20982. 48p. (ps-3). 1992. pap. 15.00 jacketed, 3-pc. bdg. (*0-671-73736-8*, S&S BFYR) S&S Trade.
Walt Disney Staff. Pinocchio. 1987. 6.98 (*0-8317-6889-4*) Viking Child Bks.
Yolen, Jane, retold by. The Musicians of Bremen. Segal, John, illus. LC 92-18695. 32p. (ps-2). 1995. 10.00 (*0-06-021498-8*); PLB 9.89 (*0-06-021499-6*) HarpC Child Bks.

FOLKLORE–GHANA

Addo, Peter E. How the Spider Became Bald: Folk Tales & Legends from West Africa. 96p. (gr. 6 up). 1993. cancelled (*1-883846-00-5*); pap. 8.95 (*1-883846-01-3*) M Reynolds.

Chocolate, Deborah M. Spider & the Sky God: An Akan Legend. Albers, Dave, illus. LC 92-13277. 32p. (gr. 2-5). 1992. PLB 11.89 (*0-8167-2811-9*); pap. text ed. 3.95 (*0-8167-2812-7*) Troll Assocs.

FOLKLORE–GREAT BRITAIN

Galdone, Paul. Henny Penny. Galdone, Paul, illus. LC 68-24735. 32p. (ps-3). 1979. 13.45 (*0-395-28800-2*, Clarion Bks) HM.

Hildebrandt, Greg, illus. Robin Hood. 48p. (gr. 2-5). 1991. 6.95 (*0-88101-110-X*) Unicorn Pub.

Hull, Robert. Stories from the British Isles. Ryley, Chris & Robinson, Claire, illus. LC 93-48467. 48p. (gr. 5-9). 1994. 15.95 (*1-56847-182-3*) Thomson Lrning.

Kellogg, Steven, retold by. & illus. Jack & the Beanstalk. LC 90-45990. 48p. 1991. 14.95 (*0-688-10250-6*); PLB 14.88 (*0-688-10251-4*) Morrow Jr Bks.

McSpadden, J. Walker. Robin Hood. Hildebrandt, Greg, illus. 160p. 1991. 14.95 (*0-88101-272-6*) Unicorn Pub.

San Souci, Robert D. Young Guinevere. LC 91-12499. (ps-3). 1993. 16.00 (*0-385-41623-7*) Doubleday.

Stinnet, N. R. Robin Hood. 1994. 4.98 (*0-8317-1648-7*) Smithmark.

FOLKLORE–GREECE

Hull, Robert. Greek Stories. Stower, Adam & Robinson, Claire, illus. LC 93-36496. 48p. (gr. 5-9). 1994. 15.95 (*1-56847-106-8*) Thomson Lrning.

Lines, Kathleen, ed. The Faber Book of Greek Legends. Jacques, Faith, illus. 268p. (gr. 4 up). 1986. pap. 11.95 (*0-571-13920-5*) Faber & Faber.

FOLKLORE, GYPSY

Miller, Joseph. Wandering Gypsies. LC 72-87908. (Illus.). (gr. 6-12). 1969. text ed. 10.00 (*0-912472-08-1*) Miller Bks.

FOLKLORE–HAITI

Johnson, Gyneth. How the Donkeys Came to Haiti & Other Folk Tales. Di Benedetto, Angelo, illus. 124p. (gr. 4-9). 12.95 (*0-8159-5706-8*) Devin.

Turenne Des Pres, Francois & California Afro-American Museum Foundation, Los Angeles Staff. Children of Yayoute: Folk Tales of Haiti. 96p. 1994. 19.95 (*0-87663-791-8*) Universe.

Wolkstein, Diane, ed. The Magic Orange Tree: And Other Haitian Folktales. Henriquez, Elsa, illus. LC 79-22787. (gr. 10 up). 1987. pap. 16.00 (*0-8052-0650-7*) Schocken.

FOLKLORE–HAWAII

Aguiar, Elithe. Legends of Hawaii As Told By Lani Goose. Aguiar, Elithe & Sakamoto, Dean, illus. 20p. (gr. k up). 1986. pap. 8.95 incl. audio cassette (*0-944264-00-X*) Lani Goose Pubns.

Brown, Marcia. Backbone of the King. (Illus.). 180p. (gr. 4-8). 1984. Repr. of 1966 ed. 12.95 (*0-8248-0963-7*) UH Pr.

Guard, David. Hale-mano: A Legend of Hawai'i. Sumile, Caridad, illus. & intro. by. LC 80-60773. 96p. 1993. pap. 8.95 (*1-883672-04-X*) Tricycle Pr.

Kahn, Elithe M. Legends of Maui As Told by Lani Goose. Shiu, Tom, illus. 20p. (gr. k-6). 1989. pap. 8.95 incl. audiocassette (*0-944264-04-2*) Lani Goose Pubns.

Kalakaua, David. The Legends & Myths of Hawaii: The Fables & Folk-Lore of a Strange People. Daggett, R. M., ed. & illus. LC 72-77519. 530p. (gr. 9 up). 1972. pap. 12.95 (*0-8048-1032-X*) C E Tuttle.

Thompson, Vivian L. Hawaiian Myths of Earth, Sea, & Sky. Kahalewai, Marilyn, illus. LC 88-1325. 88p. (gr. 3-8). 1988. pap. 8.50 (*0-8248-1171-2*, Kolowalu Bk) UH Pr.

—Kawelo, Roving Chief. Wozniak, Patricia A., illus. LC 91-13651. 96p. (gr. 4-6). 1991. 14.95 (*0-8248-1339-1*, Kolowalu Bk) UH Pr.

Tune, Suelyn C. How Maui Slowed the Sun. Burningham, Robin Y., illus. LC 88-4548. 32p. (gr. k up). 1988. 8.95 (*0-8248-1083-X*) UH Pr.

—Maui & the Secret of Fire. Burningham, Robin Y., illus. LC 90-27175. 32p. (ps-4). 1991. 9.95 (*0-8248-1391-X*, Kolowalu Bk) UH Pr.

Wardlaw, Lee, adapted by. Punia & the King of Sharks: A Hawaiian Folktale. LC 93-43955. 1995. write for info. (*0-8037-1682-6*); lib. bdg. write for info. (*0-8037-1683-4*) Dial Bks Young.

Williams, Julie S. Maui Goes Fishing. Burningham, Robin Y., illus. LC 90-27176. 32p. (ps-4). 1991. 9.95 (*0-8248-1390-1*, Kolowalu Bk) UH Pr.

FOLKLORE–HUNGARY

Biro, Val. Tobias & the Dragon: A Hungarian Folk Tale. Biro, Val, illus. LC 89-18492. 32p. (gr. k-3). 1990. PLB 12.95 (*0-87226-427-0*, Bedrick Blackie) P Bedrick Bks.

Biro, Val, retold by. & illus. Hungarian Folk-Tales. 192p. (gr. 4 up). 1992. pap. 10.95 (*0-19-274148-9*) OUP.

Bodnar, Judit. The Rooster & the Two Gold Coins: A Hungarian Folk Tale. Bodnar, Judit, tr. LC 94-14827. 1995. write for info. (*0-688-11439-3*); PLB write for info. (*0-688-11440-7*) Lothrop.

Ginsburg, Mirra. Two Greedy Bears: Adapted from a Hungarian Folktale. Aruego, Jose & Dewey, Ariane, illus. LC 76-8819. 32p. (ps-2). 1976. RSBE 13.95 (*0-02-736450-X*, Macmillan Child Bk) Macmillan Child Grp.

FOLKLORE–ICELAND

Helgadottir, Gudrun. Flumbra: An Icelandic Folktale. Sanders, Christopher, tr. from ICE. Pilkington, Brian, illus. LC 86-6173. 32p. (gr. 1-6). 1986. lib. bdg. 18.95 (*0-87614-243-9*) Carolrhoda Bks.

FOLKLORE–INDIA

Backstein, Karen. The Blind Men & the Elephant, Level 3. 1992. 2.95 (*0-590-45813-2*) Scholastic Inc.

Beven, Annette. The Spade Sage. Hall, Diane, illus. 24p. (gr. 1-3). 1976. pap. 7.95 (*0-913546-71-2*) Dharma Pub.

Brown, Marcia. Once a Mouse. Brown, Marcia, illus. LC 61-14769. 32p. (ps-3). 1972. SBE 14.95 (*0-684-12662-1*, Scribners Young Read) Macmillan Child Grp.

Carlson, Jeanne, et al, illus. A King, a Hunter & a Golden Goose. Tulku, Tarthang, intro. by. LC 86-24154. 32p. (gr. 1-4). 1987. PLB 14.95 (*0-89800-155-2*) Dharma Pub.

Chatterjee, Debjani. The Elephant-Headed God & Other Hindu Tales. LC 92-20454. 1992. 13.00 (*0-19-508112-9*) OUP.

Choudhary, Bani. Story of Mahabharata. (ps up). 1988. 7.50 (*0-318-37379-3*) Auromere.

Choudhary, Bani R. Stories from Panchatantra. Bhushan, Reboti, illus. (gr. 3-10). 1979. 7.25 (*0-89744-136-2*) Auromere.

Claire, Elizabeth. The Little Brown Jay: A Tale from India. Katin, Miriam, illus. 24p. (Orig.). (gr. k-4). 1994. big bk. 21.95 (*1-879531-17-8*); PLB 9.95 (*1-879531-44-5*); pap. 4.95 (*1-879531-23-2*) Mondo Pubng.

Clemmons, Bradley & Witwer, Julia, illus. The Fish King's Power of Truth. Tulku, Tarthang, intro. by. LC 86-24159. 32p. (gr. k-4). 1987. PLB 14.95 (*0-89800-158-7*); pap. 7.95 (*0-89800-144-7*) Dharma Pub.

Cook, Elizabeth, adapted by. Rabbit Who Overcame Fear: A Jataka Tale. Meller, Eric, illus. Tulku, Tarthang, intro. by. (Illus.). 32p. (Orig.). (gr. k-4). 1991. 14.95 (*0-89800-212-5*); pap. 7.95 (*0-89800-211-7*) Dharma Pub.

Dalal-Clayton, Diksha. The Adventures of Young Krishna: The Blue God of India. Heeger, Marilyn, illus. LC 92-19072. 128p. 1992. 13.00 (*0-19-508113-7*) OUP.

Gleeson, Brian. The Tiger & the Brahmin. Vargo, Kurt, illus. 40p. (gr. k up). 1992. pap. 14.95 (*0-88708-232-7*, Rabbit Ears); incl. cass. 19.95 (*0-88708-233-5*, Rabbit Ears) Picture Bk Studio.

Haviland, Virginia. Favorite Fairy Tales Told in India. Cohn, Amy, ed. Rosenberry, Vera, illus. LC 94-83. 96p. (gr. 2 up). 1994. pap. 4.95 (*0-688-12600-6*, Pub. by Beech Tree Bks) Morrow.

Hodges, Margaret, retold by. Hidden in Sand. LC 92-41746. (Illus.). 32p. (ps-2). 1994. SBE 15.95 (*0-684-19559-3*, Scribners Young Read) Macmillan Child Grp.

Jacobs, Joseph, ed. Indian Fairy Tales. Batten, John D., illus. xvi, 255p. (ps-4). 1969. pap. 6.95 (*0-486-21828-7*) Dover.

Jaffrey, Madhur. Seasons of Splendour: Tales, Myths & Legends of India. Foreman, Michael, illus. 128p. (gr. 4 up). 1992. pap. 16.95 (*1-85145-933-2*, Pub. by Pavilion UK) Trafalgar.

McSweeney, Terry, illus. Great Gift & the Wish-Fulfilling Gem. Tulku, Tarthang, intro. by. LC 86-19767. (Illus.). 32p. (gr. k-5). 1987. PLB 14.95 (*0-89800-157-9*); pap. 7.95 (*0-89800-143-9*) Dharma Pub.

Newton, Pam, retold by. & illus. The Stonecutter: An Indian Folktale. 32p. (ps-3). 1990. 14.95 (*0-399-22187-5*, Putnam-Whitebird) Putnam Pub Group.

Panday, Daulat. The Tales of India, Vol. 2. 126p. (gr. 3-8). 1985. pap. 5.95 (*0-89071-331-6*, Pub. by Sri Aurobindo Ashram IA) Aurobindo Assn.

The Parrot & the Fig Tree. Harmon, Michael, illus. Tulku, Tarthang, intro. by. LC 86-24159. (Illus.). 32p. (Orig.). (gr. k-4). 1987. PLB 14.95 (*0-89800-156-0*); pap. 7.95 (*0-89800-142-0*) Dharma Pub.

Ram, Govinder. Rama & Sita: A Folk Tale from India. Ram, Govinder, illus. LC 87-14333. 32p. (gr. k-3). 1988. PLB 14.95 (*0-87226-171-9*, Bedrick Blackie) P Bedrick Bks.

Savitri. Tales from Indian Classics, Bk. I. Biswas, Pulak, illus. (gr. 3-9). 1979. 4.50 (*0-89744-167-2*); pap. 3.00 (*0-685-57665-5*) Auromere.

—Tales from Indian Classics, Bk. II. Biswas, Pulak, illus. (gr. 3-9). 1979. 4.50 (*0-89744-168-0*); pap. 3.00 (*0-685-57666-3*) Auromere.

—Tales from Indian Classics, Bk. III. Chatterjee, Sukumar, illus. (gr. 3-9). 1979. 4.50 (*0-89744-169-9*); pap. 3.00 (*0-685-57667-1*) Auromere.

Shankar. Treasury of Indian Tales: Book I. Mukerji, Debrabrata, illus. (gr. 8-12). 1979. 4.95 (*0-89744-170-2*) Auromere.

—Treasury of Indian Tales: Book II. Vyas, Anil, illus. (gr. 8-12). 1979. 4.95 (*0-89744-171-0*) Auromere.

Shanta. Nala Damayanti. Sonkaria, Gyan, illus. (gr. 1-9). 1979. pap. 3.00 (*0-89744-158-3*) Auromere.

Sharma, Rashmi. The Blue Jackal. (Illus.). 32p. (gr. 2 up). 1992. 14.95 (*1-878099-50-7*); pap. 6.95 (*1-878099-51-5*) Vidya Bks.

Stamler, Suzanne. Three Wise Birds. Nolan, Gary, illus. (gr. 1-6). 1976. pap. 7.95 (*0-913546-68-2*) Dharma Pub.

Tagore, Rabindranath. The Cheese Doll. Mukherjee, Meenakshi, tr. from BEN. (Illus.). (gr. 3-11). 1979. 6.25 (*0-89744-143-5*) Auromere.

Thomas, Vernon, ed. Folk Tales from India. Ghosh, R. B., illus. (gr. 3-10). 1979. 7.95 (*0-89744-141-9*) Auromere.

Troughton, Joanna. The Wizard Punchkin: A Folk Tale from India. Troughton, Joanna, illus. LC 87-11517. 32p. (gr. k-3). 1988. PLB 14.95 (*0-87226-162-X*, Bedrick Blackie) P Bedrick Bks.

The Value of Friends. LC 86-24164. 32p. (Orig.). (gr. k-4). 1986. PLB 14.95 (*0-89800-154-4*); pap. 7.95 (*0-89800-140-4*) Dharma Pub.

Wilson, Karen. Agha: The Terrible Demon. 2nd ed. Greene, Joshua, ed. Prubhupada, A. C., tr. from SAN. Dubois, Marie T., illus. 32p. (gr. 1-4). 1989. pap. 6.95 (*0-89647-023-7*) Bala Bks.

Young, Ed. Seven Blind Mice. Young, Ed, illus. 40p. (ps-6). 1992. PLB 16.95 (*0-399-22261-8*, Philomel Bks) Putnam Pub Group.

FOLKLORE, INDIAN

see also Indians of North America–Legends

Bell, Rosemary. Yurok Tales. Webb, Kathy, illus. 90p. (Orig.). (gr. 4-8). 1992. pap. 9.95 (*1-880922-01-0*) Bell Bks CA.

Browne, Vee. Monster Birds: A Navajo Folktale. Whitethorne, Baje, illus. LC 92-82139. 32p. (gr. 2 up). 1993. 14.95 (*0-87358-558-5*) Northland AZ.

Clark, Ann N. Little Boy with Three Names: Stories of Taos Pueblo. reformatted ed. Lujan, Tonita, illus. LC 89-81747. 50p. (gr. 3 up). 1990. pap. 8.95 (*0-941270-59-9*) Ancient City Pr.

Connolly, James E., ed. Why the Possum's Tail Is Bare: And Other North American Indian Nature Tales. Adams, Andrea, illus. LC 84-26871. 64p. (gr. 4-8). 1992. 15.95 (*0-88045-069-X*); pap. 7.95 (*0-88045-107-6*) Stemmer Hse.

Crespo, George. How the Sea Began: A Taino Myth. Crespo, George, illus. 32p. (gr. k-3). 1993. 14.95 (*0-395-63033-9*, Clarion Bks) HM.

Crofts, Trudy & Childers, Peggy, illus. The Hunter & the Quail. 32p. (gr. 1-6). 1993. pap. 7.95 (*0-89800-250-8*) Dharma Pub.

De Angulo, Jaime. Indian Tales. De Angulo, Jaime, illus. 256p. (gr. 5 up). 1984. 10.95 (*0-374-52163-8*, Am Century) FS&G.

Esbensen, Barbara J., retold by. The Great Buffalo Race: How the Buffalo Got His Hump: a Seneca Tale. David, Helen K., illus. LC 92-23410. (gr. k-4). 1994. 14.95 (*0-316-24982-3*) Little.

Gilliland, Hap. How the Dogs Saved the Cheyenne. 32p. 1972. 4.95 (*0-89992-017-9*) Coun India Ed.

Goble, Paul, retold by. & illus. Iktomi & the Ducks: A Plains Indian Story. LC 89-71025. 32p. (ps-1). 1990. 14.95 (*0-531-05883-2*); PLB 14.99 (*0-531-08483-3*) Orchard Bks Watts.

—Iktomi & the Ducks: A Plains Indians Story. LC 89-71025. 32p. (ps-1). 1994. pap. 5.95 (*0-531-07044-1*) Orchard Bks Watts.

Greison, Betty, et al. Black Hawk & Jim Thorp: Super Heroes; Sauk Indian Stories for Children. (gr. 5-12). 1983. pap. 4.95 (*0-89992-085-3*) Coun India Ed.

Gupta, Rupa. Tales from Indian Classics. Basu, R. K., illus. 136p. (gr. 1-9). 1981. 7.50 (*0-89744-233-4*, Pub. by Hemkunt India) Auromere.

Hausman, Gerald. Ghost Walk: Native American Tales of the Spirit. Hausman, Sid, illus. 128p. (Orig.). 1991. pap. 9.95 (*0-933553-07-2*) Mariposa Print Pub.

Hayes, Joe. Soft Child. Sather, Kay, illus. LC 93-1641. 32p. (Orig.). (ps-3). 1993. pap. 8.95 (*0-943173-89-2*) Harbinger AZ.

Holsinger, Rosemary. Karuk Tales. Piemme, P. I., illus. 70p. (gr. 4-8). 1992. pap. 7.95 (*1-880922-00-2*) Bell Bks CA.

How Rabbit Tricked Otter & Other Cherokee Animal Stories. 1992. 11.00 (*1-55994-542-7*) HarperAudio.

Hull, Robert, retold by. Native North American Stories. LC 92-39440. (Illus.). 48p. (gr. 5-9). 1993. 15.95 (*1-56847-005-3*) Thomson Lrning.

Katz, William L. & Franklin, Paula A. Proudly Red & Black: Tales of Native & African Americans. LC 92-36119. 1993. 13.95 (*0-684-31801-6*, Atheneum Child Bk) Macmillan Child Grp.

Lacapa, Michael. Antelope Woman: An Apache Folktale. Lacapa, Michael, illus. LC 92-4198. 48p. (gr. 3 up). 1992. 14.95 (*0-87358-543-7*) Northland AZ.

—The Flute Player: An Apache Folktale. Lacapa, Michael, illus. LC 89-63749. 48p. (gr. 1-3). 1990. 14.95 (*0-87358-500-3*) Northland AZ.

Larry, Charles. Peboan & Seegwun. 32p. (ps-3). 1993. 16.00 (*0-374-35773-0*) FS&G.

Law, Katheryn. Salish Folk Tales. (gr. 2-8). 1972. 1.50 (*0-89992-028-4*) Coun India Ed.

Lewis, Richard. All of You Was Singing. Young, Ed, illus. LC 93-44589. (gr. k-3). 1994. pap. 4.95 (*0-689-71853-5*, Alladin) Macmillan Child Grp.

McDermott, Gerald. Arrow to the Sun: A Pueblo Indian Tale. McDermott, Gerald, illus. (gr. 1 up). 1977. pap. 4.99 (*0-14-050211-4*, Puffin) Puffin Bks.

Dakota storyteller, Pamela Greenhill Kaizen & are accompanied by twelve full-color illustrations by South Dakota artist & educator Mark W. McGinnis. Leonard R. Bruguier, a descendant of the Yankton chiefs War Eagle & Struck by the Ree, presents the introduction. The stories use animal characters to deal with the themes of compassion, greed, generosity, protection, survival, hard work, laziness, bravery, foolishness, trickery, & others. They range from simple humor as in THE FROG & THE TURTLE BROTHERS, where two close friends decide to jump in the lake rather than catch colds by getting wet in the rain, to the rich & complex story of THE CRANE, which weaves a tale of compassion & caring for one's neighbors. The animal characters give insightful guidance on human morals & ethics, & give a glimpse into the wonderful wit & wisdom of the Lakota & Dakota people. Mark McGinnis' paintings interpret a critical instant from each story, translating the oral moment to a visual expression of color, texture & shapes. This book is well suited to be read to younger children, to be read by older children, or for adults who enjoy new perspectives into Native American culture. Available for $11.98 plus $3.00 S/H from Tipi Press, St. Joseph's Indian School, Chamberlain, SD 57326; 605-734-3300.
Publisher Provided Annotation.

Mayo, Gretchen W. Earthmaker's Tales: North American Indian Stories about Earth Happenings. Mayo, Gretchen W., illus. LC 88-20515. 96p. (gr. 5 up). 1989. 12.95 (*0-8027-6839-3*); PLB 13.85 (*0-8027-6840-7*) Walker & Co.
—North American Indian Stories: Earthmaker's Tales. Mayo, Gretchen W., illus. 48p. (gr. 5 up). 1990. pap. 5.95 (*0-8027-7343-5*) Walker & Co.
—North American Indian Stories: More Earthmaker's Tales. Mayo, Gretchen W., illus. 48p. (gr. 5 up). 1990. pap. 5.95 (*0-8027-7344-3*) Walker & Co.
—North American Indian Stories: More Star Tales. Mayo, Gretchen W., illus. 48p. (gr. 5 up). 1990. pap. 5.95 (*0-8027-7347-8*) Walker & Co.
—North American Indian Stories: Star Tales. Mayo, Gretchen W., illus. 48p. (gr. 5 up). 1990. pap. 5.95 (*0-8027-7345-1*) Walker & Co.
—Star Tales: North American Indian Stories about the Stars. 96p. (gr. 5 up). 1987. 12.95 (*0-8027-6672-2*); PLB 13.85 (*0-8027-6673-0*) Walker & Co.
Norman, Howard. How Glooskap Outwits the Ice Giants: And Other Tales of the Maritime Indians, Vol. 1. 1989. 14.95 (*0-316-61181-6*, Joy St Bks) Little.
Oliviero, Jamie. The Day Sun Was Stolen. Hitchcock, Sharon, illus. LC 94-19374. 1995. write for info. (*0-7868-0031-3*); PLB write for info. (*0-7868-2026-8*) Hyprn Child.

Parker, Arthur C. Skunny Wundy: Seneca Indian Tales. Armstrong, George, illus. Bruchac, Joseph, intro. by. (Illus.). 224p. 1994. pap. 12.95 (*0-8156-0292-8*) Syracuse U Pr.
This is an enchanting book of children's tales handed down by Native American storytellers & collected by a noted Seneca anthropologist. "The tales are for boys & girls. It is a shame to hide them away." - Arthur C. Parker. "I wish I could have read it as a child. But the next best thing to that is being able to recommend it to the children of another generation - Native & non-Native children alike. Like the storyteller holding out his bag & asking a child to reach in & pull out the next tale to be told, it is my privilege to offer this book to you & to urge you, as Parker did so well over a century ago, to listen. Listen well." - Joseph Bruchac. Here children will meet the clever fox & raccoon, the rabbit who is often easily duped, courageous but not very bright bears, & the villainous wolf. Here, too, is the turtle, with a special place in Seneca mythology, & many other animal characters: the mink & eagle, buffalo, weasel & the old snowy owl.This is the first paperback printing of SKUNNY WUNDY.
Publisher Provided Annotation.

Powell, Mary, ed. Wolf Tales: Native American Children's Stories. LC 92-29690. (Illus.). 70p. (Orig.). (gr. 3 up). 1993. pap. 8.95 (*0-941270-73-4*) Ancient City Pr.
Reed, Evelyn D. Coyote Tales from the Indian Pueblos. Strock, Glen, illus. LC 86-14544. 96p. (gr. 4 up). 1988. pap. 8.95 (*0-86534-094-3*) Sunstone Pr.
Rosen, Michael, retold by. Crow & Hawk: A Traditional Pueblo Indian Story. Clementson, John, illus. LC 94-15176. 1995. write for info. (*0-15-200257-X*) HarBrace.
Ross, Gayle, retold by. How Turtle's Back Was Cracked: A Traditional Cherokee Tale. Jacob, Murv, illus. LC 93-40657. 1995. write for info. (*0-8037-1728-8*); lib. bdg. write for info. (*0-8037-1729-6*) Dial Bks Young.
Strelkoff, Tatiana. The Changer. (Illus.). 96p. (gr. 4-6). 1994. pap. 8.95 (*0-945522-03-7*) Rebecca Hse.
Tanaka, Beatrice. The Chase: A Kutenai Indian Tale. Gay, Michael, illus. LC 91-10790. 32p. (ps-2). 1991. lib. bdg. 14.99 (*0-517-58624-X*) Crown Bks Yng Read.
Taylor, C. J. How We Saw the World: Nine Native Stories of Beginnings. Taylor, C. J., illus. 32p. (gr. 1-5). 1993. 17.95 (*0-88776-302-2*) Tundra Bks.
Tehanetorens. Sacred Song of the Hermit Thrush. Hutchens, Jerry L., illus. LC 93-945. 64p. (gr. 3 up). 1992. pap. 5.95 (*0-913990-36-1*) Book Pub Co.
Troughton, Joanna, retold by. & illus. Who Will Be the Sun? A North American Indian Folk Tale. LC 85-15074. 32p. (gr. k-3). 1986. PLB 14.95 (*0-87226-038-0*, Bedrick Blackie) P Bedrick Bks.
Walley, Deborah. Grandfather's Good Medicine. Thorne, Kate & Callou, Nadia, eds. Thompson, Tommy, illus. 72p. (Orig.). (gr. k up). 1993. pap. 9.95 (*0-9628329-6-0*) Thorne Enterprises.
Walters, Anna L., retold by. The Two-Legged Creature: An Otoe Story. Bowles, Carol, illus. LC 92-56510. 32p. 1993. 14.95 (*0-87358-553-4*) Northland AZ.
Whitethorne, Baje. Sunpainters: Eclipse of the Navajo Sun. Whitethorne, Baje, illus. LC 94-11146. 32p. (gr. k up). 1994. 14.95 (*0-87358-587-9*) Northland AZ.

FOLKLORE–INDONESIA

Terada, Alice M., retold by. The Magic Crocodile & Other Folktales from Indonesia. Smoyer, Charlene K., illus. LC 94-10876. 144p. (gr. 5-9). 1994. 16.95 (*0-8248-1654-4*, Kolowalu Bk) UH Pr.

FOLKLORE–IRAQ

Shepard, Aaron, retold by. The Enchanted Storks: A Tale of the Middle East. Dianov, Alisher, illus. LC 93-41540. 1995. write for info. (*0-395-65377-0*, Clarion Bks) HM.

FOLKLORE–IRELAND

Croker, T. Crofton. Irish Folk Stories for Children. 1991. pap. 10.95 (*0-85342-919-7*) Dufour.
Danaher, Kevin. Children's Book of Irish Folktales. Berson, Harold, illus. 108p. 1987. pap. 11.95 (*0-85342-718-6*, Pub. by Mercier Press Ltd Eire) Dufour.
De Paola, Tomie. Jamie O'Rourke & the Big Potato: An Irish Folktale. 32p. (ps-3). 1992. 14.95 (*0-399-22257-X*, Whitebird Bks) Putnam Pub Group.
Dillon, Eilis. Lost Island. 204p. 1987. pap. 8.95 (*0-86278-118-3*, Pub. by O'Brien Press Ltd Eire) Dufour.
Dunlop, Eileen. Tales of St. Columba. 136p. (gr. 4 up). 1992. pap. 6.95 (*1-85371-134-9*, Pub. by Poolbeg Pr ER) Dufour.
Dunn, Patricia. Children's Book of Irish Fairy Tales. 1988. pap. 9.95 (*0-85342-843-3*) Dufour.
Fine, Anne. Book of the Banshee. (gr. 4-7). 1994. pap. 2.95 (*0-590-46926-6*) Scholastic Inc.
Fritz, Jean. Brendan the Navigator. Arno, Enrico, illus. LC 78-13247. (gr. 2-5). 1979. 14.95 (*0-698-20473-5*, Coward) Putnam Pub Group.
Gleeson, Brian. Finn McCoul. De Seve, Peter, illus. 40p. (gr. k up). 1993. incl. cass. 19.95 (*0-88708-272-6*, Rabbit Ears); 14.95 (*0-88708-271-8*, Rabbit Ears) Picture Bk Studio.
Greene, Ellin, retold by. Billy Beg & His Bull: An Irish Tale. Root, Kimberly B., illus. LC 93-7730. 32p. (ps-3). 1994. reinforced bdg. 15.95 (*0-8234-1100-1*) Holiday.
Gregory, Isabella A. Irish Legends for Children. (Illus.). 90p. (ps-8). 1983. pap. 5.95 (*0-85342-691-0*, Pub. by Mercier Press Ltd Eire) Dufour.
—Irish Legends for Children. 1991. pap. 10.95 (*0-85342-920-0*) Dufour.
Haviland, Virginia. Favorite Fairy Tales Told in Ireland. Cohn, Amy, ed. O'Neill, Catharine, illus. LC 94-84. 96p. (gr. 2 up). 1994. pap. 4.95 (*0-688-12598-0*, Pub. by Beech Tree Bks) Morrow.
Hodges, Margaret. Saint Patrick & the Peddler. Johnson, Paul B., illus. LC 92-44522. 40p. (gr. k-3). 1993. 15.95 (*0-531-05489-6*); PLB 15.99 (*0-531-08639-9*) Orchard Bks Watts.
Leamy, Edmund. Irish Fairy Stories for Children. (Illus.). 86p. (gr. 2 up). 1992. pap. 9.95 (*1-85635-008-8*, Pub. by Mercier Pr Eire) Dufour.
Lenihan, Edmund. Strange Irish Tales for Children. Gervin, Joseph, illus. 128p. (ps-8). 1992. pap. 9.95 (*0-85342-833-6*, Pub. by Mercier Pr Eire) Dufour.
Lynch, Patricia. Tales of Irish Enchantment. (Illus.). 108p. 1986. pap. 8.95 (*0-85342-790-9*, Pub. by Mercier Press Ltd Eire) Dufour.
McDermott, Gerald. Daniel O'Rourke: An Irish Tale. 1988. pap. 4.99 (*0-14-050673-X*, Puffin) Puffin Bks.
MacGill-Callahan, Sheila. The Children of Lir. Spirin, Gennady, illus. LC 91-2712. 32p. (ps-3). 1993. 14.99 (*0-8037-1121-2*); PLB 14.99 (*0-8037-1122-0*) Dial Bks Young.
—Finn Mac Cool & the Salmon of Knowledge. LC 93-43953. 1995. write for info. (*0-8037-1537-4*); PLB write for info. (*0-8037-1538-2*) Dial Bks Young.
Mullins, Tom, ed. Irish Stories for Children. 111p. (gr. 5 up). 1993. pap. 11.95 (*1-85635-027-4*, Pub. by Mercier Pr Eire) Dufour.
Scott, Michael. The Last of the Fianna: An Irish Legend. (Illus.). 109p. (gr. 3-7). 1993. pap. 9.95 (*0-86278-308-9*, Pub. by OBrien Pr IE) Dufour.
—WindLord: First of the De Dannan Tales. (Orig.). (gr. 3-9). 1991. pap. 8.95 (*0-86327-296-7*, Pub. by Wolfhound Pr EIRE) Dufour.
Smith, Philip, ed. Irish Fairy Tales. Kliros, Thea, illus. LC 93-243. 96p. 1993. pap. 1.00 (*0-486-27572-8*) Dover.
Sutcliff, Rosemary. Tristan & Iseult. 150p. (gr. 5 up). 1991. pap. 3.95 (*0-374-47982-8*, Sunburst) FS&G.

FOLKLORE–ISLANDS OF THE PACIFIC

Hashimoto, Yasuko & Edades, Jean. Tales of a Japanese Grandmother, 5 Vols. Kubota, Kenji, illus. (Orig.). (gr. k-3). 1982. Set. pap. 12.50 (*0-686-37564-5*, Pub. by New Day Pub PI) Cellar.

FOLKLORE–ITALY

Cossi, Olga. Orlanda & the Contest of Thieves. Sarmo, Tom, illus. LC 89-15107. 32p. (gr. 1-6). 1989. 14.95 (*0-917665-32-5*) Pelican.
De Paola, Tomie. The Clown of God. De Paola, Tomie, illus. LC 78-3845. (gr. k up). 1978. 13.95 (*0-15-219175-5*, HB Juv Bks) HarBrace.
—The Legend of Old Befana. De Paola, Tomie, illus. LC 80-12293. 32p. (gr. 1-5). 1980. 14.95 (*0-15-243816-5*, HB Juv Bks) HarBrace.
—The Legend of Old Befana. De Paola, Tomie, illus. LC 80-12293. 32p. (gr. 1-5). 1980. pap. 3.95 (*0-15-243817-3*, Voyager Bks) HarBrace.
—Strega Nona. LC 75-11565. (Illus.). 32p. (ps-4). 1979. pap. 15.00 (*0-671-66283-X*, S&S BFYR); pap. 6.95 (*0-671-66606-1*, S&S BFYR) S&S Trade.
—Tony's Bread. De Paola, Tomie, illus. 32p. (ps-3). 1989. 14.95 (*0-399-21693-6*, Whitebird Bks) Putnam Pub Group.
Fox, Paula. Amzat & His Brothers: Three Italian Folktales. McCully, Emily A., illus. LC 92-19494. 80p. (gr. 3-5). 1993. 15.95 (*0-531-05462-4*); PLB 15.99 (*0-531-08612-7*) Orchard Bks Watts.
Nones, Eric J. Canary Prince. (ps up). 1991. 14.95 (*0-374-31029-7*) FS&G.
Peterson, Julienne, retold by. Caterina the Clever Farm Girl: A Tuscan Tale. Giannini, Enzo, illus. LC 93-15161. 1994. write for info. (*0-8037-1181-6*); PLB write for info. (*0-8037-1182-4*) Dial Bks Young.
Sanderson, Ruth, retold by. & illus. Sir Gatto: An Italian Fairy Tale. LC 94-16725. 1995. 14.95 (*0-316-77073-6*) Little.
Stanley, Diane, retold by. Petrosinella: A Neopolitan Rapunzel. LC 94-17456. (Illus.). (gr. 7-10). Date not set. write for info. (*0-8037-1712-1*); PLB write for info. (*0-8037-1749-0*) Dial Bks Young.
Vittorini, Domenico. The Thread of Life: Twelve Old Italian Tales. Grandpre, Mary, illus. LC 93-29497. 1995. write for info. (*0-517-59594-X*, Crown); lib. bdg. write for info. (*0-517-59595-8*, Crown) Crown Pub Group.

FOLKLORE–JAMAICA

Gleeson, Brian. Anansi. Guarnaccia, Steven, illus. LC 91-40671. 36p. (gr. k up). 1992. pap. 14.95 (*0-88708-230-0*, Rabbit Ears); incl. cass. 19.95 (*0-88708-231-9*, Rabbit Ears) Picture Bk Studio.
Hausman, Gerald, as told by. Duppy Talk: West Indian Tales of Mystery & Magic. LC 93-40586. (gr. 4 up). 1994. 14.00 (*0-671-89000-X*, S&S BFYR) S&S Trade.
Temple, Francis, illus. Tiger Soup: An Anansi Story from Jamaica. LC 93-48834. (ps-2). 1994. 15.95 (*0-531-06859-5*); PLB 15.99 (*0-531-08709-3*) Orchard Bks Watts.

FOLKLORE–JAPAN

Compton, Patricia A. Terrible Eek. LC 91-6421. (Illus.). 40p. (gr. 4-8). 1991. pap. 14.95 jacketed (*0-671-73737-6*, S&S BFYR) S&S Trade.
Edmonds, I. G. Ooka the Wise: Tales of Old Japan. Yamazaki, Sanae, illus. 96p. (gr. 3 up). 1994. Repr. of 1961 ed. PLB 14.95 (*0-208-02379-8*, Pub. by Linnet) Shoe String.
French, Fiona. Little Inchkin. LC 93-23904. 1994. write for info. (*0-8037-1478-5*) Dial Bks Young.

Hamada, Cheryl, retold by. The White Hare of Inaba: A Japanese Folktale. Halverson, Lydia, illus. LC 93-6772. 32p. (ps-3). 1993. PLB 13.85 (*0-516-05147-4*) Childrens.

Hamanaka, Sheila, retold by. & illus. Screen of Frogs: An Old Tale. LC 92-24172. 32p. (ps-2). 1993. 15.95 (*0-531-05464-0*); PLB 15.99 (*0-531-08614-3*) Orchard Bks Watts.

Haugaard, Erik & Haugaard, Masako. The Story of Yuriwaka. (Illus.). 42p. (gr. 3-6). 1991. 12.95 (*1-879373-02-5*) R Rinehart.

Haviland, Virginia, retold by. Favorite Fairy Tales Told in Japan. LC 94-3079. 1994. pap. write for info. (*0-688-12601-4*, Pub. by Beech Tree Bks) Morrow.

Hodges, Margaret. Wave. Lent, Blair, illus. (gr. k-3). 1964. 3.50 (*0-395-06817-7*) HM.

Hooks, William H. Peach Boy. (ps-3). 1992. 9.99 (*0-553-07621-3*) Bantam.

—Peach Boy. Otani, June, illus. (ps-3). 1992. pap. 3.50 (*0-553-35429-9*, Little Rooster) Bantam.

Ikeda, Daisaku. The Snow Country Prince. McCaughrean, Geraldine, tr. Wildsmith, Brian, illus. LC 90-24908. 32p. (ps-3). 1991. 15.00 (*0-679-81965-7*) Knopf Bks Yng Read.

Johnson, David. The Boy Who Drew Cats. Johnson, David, illus. 40p. (gr. k up). 1991. pap. 14.95 (*0-88708-194-0*, Rabbit Ears); incls. cassette 19.95 (*0-88708-195-9*, Rabbit Ears) Picture Bk Studio.

Johnston, Tony. The Badger & the Magic Fan: A Japanese Folktale. De Paola, Tomie, illus. 32p. (ps-3). 1990. 13.95 (*0-399-21945-5*, Putnam) Putnam Pub Group.

Kendall, Carol, retold by. Haunting Tales from Japan. LC 85-50684. (Illus.). 40p. (Orig.). (gr. 6-9). 1985. pap. 6.00 (*0-913689-22-X*) Spencer Muse Art.

Kimmel, Eric A., retold by. The Greatest of All: A Japanese Folktale. Carmi, Giora, illus. LC 90-23658. 32p. (ps-3). 1991. reinforced 14.95 (*0-8234-0885-X*) Holiday.

Levine, Arthur A. The Boy Who Drew Cats: A Japanese Folktale. LC 91-46232. (ps-3). 1994. 16.00 (*0-8037-1172-7*); 15.89 (*0-8037-1173-5*) Dial Bks Young.

Mcalpine, Helen & Mcalpine, William, eds. Japanese Tales & Legends. (Illus.). 218p. 1989. pap. 10.95 (*0-19-274140-3*) OUP.

McCarthy, Ralph F. The Adventures of Momotaro, the Peach Boy. Ogawa & Pockell, eds. Saito, Ioe, illus. LC 93-18501. 48p. 1994. 13.00 (*4-7700-1755-3*) Kodansha.

—Click-Clack Mountain. Ogawa, ed. (Illus.). 48p. 1994. 14.95 (*4-7700-1850-9*, Pub. by Kodansha Ltd JP) Bks Nippan.

—The Monkey & the Crab. Ogawa, ed. (Illus.). 48p. 1994. 14.95 (*4-7700-1844-4*, Pub. by Kodansha Ltd JP) Bks Nippan.

—The Sparrow's Inn. Ogawa, ed. (Illus.). 48p. 1994. 14.95 (*4-7700-1849-5*, Pub. by Kodansha Ltd JP) Bks Nippan.

—Urashima & the Kingdom Beneath the Sea. Ogawa & Pockell, eds. Kasamatsu, Shiro, illus. LC 93-18500. 48p. 1994. 13.00 (*4-7700-1757-X*) Kodansha.

McCarthy, Ralph F., et al, eds. Grandfather Cherry Blossom. Kasamatsu, Shiro, illus. LC 93-18301. 48p. 1993. 13.00 (*4-7700-1759-6*) Kodansha.

—The Inch-High Samurai. Kasamatsu, Shiro, illus. LC 93-16310. 48p. 1993. 13.00 (*4-7700-1758-8*) Kodansha.

—The Moon Princess. Kasamatsu, Shiro & Oda, Kancho, illus. LC 93-18300. 48p. 1993. 13.00 (*4-7700-1756-1*) Kodansha.

McCoy, Karen K. A Tale of Two Tengu. Fossey, Koen, illus. LC 93-2. (gr. 1-3). 1993. 14.95 (*0-8075-7748-0*) A Whitman.

Motomora, Mitchell. Peach Boy. (Illus.). 32p. (gr. 1-3). 1989. PLB 12.33 (*0-8172-3513-2*) Raintree Steck-V.

Muramaru, N. Japanese Folktales. (Illus.). 160p. (gr. 4-9). 1993. pap. 11.95 (*4-89684-228-6*, Pub. by Yohan Pubns JP) Weatherhill.

Ozaki, Yei T., compiled by. The Japanese Fairy Book. LC 70-109415. (Illus.). 320p. (gr. 3-8). 1970. pap. 12.95 (*0-8048-0885-6*) C E Tuttle.

Quackenbuch, Hiroko C. The Runaway Riceball. Ogawa & Tazawa, eds. (Illus.). 32p. 1993. pap. 7.00 (*4-77001-762-6*) Kodansha.

Quackenbush, Hiroko C. The Grateful Crane. Ogawa & Tazawa, eds. (Illus.). 32p. 1993. pap. 7.00 (*4-77001-761-8*) Kodansha.

—Momotaro, the Peach Boy. Ogawa & Tazawa, eds. (Illus.). 32p. 1993. pap. 7.00 (*4-77001-760-X*) Kodansha.

Rampo, Edogawa. Japanese Tales of Mystery & Imagination. Harris, James B., tr. LC 56-6804. (Illus.). 232p. (gr. 9 up). 1956. pap. 12.95 (*0-8048-0319-6*) C E Tuttle.

Richard, Francoise. On Cat Mountain. Levine, Arthur A., adapted by. Buguet, Anne, illus. LC 93-11408. 40p. (ps-4). 1994. 15.95 (*0-399-22608-7*, Putnam) Putnam Pub Group.

Sakade, Florence. Japanese Children's Favorite Stories. Kurosaki, Yoshio, illus. LC 58-11620. 120p. (gr. 2-6). 1958. bds. 16.95 (*0-8048-0284-X*) C E Tuttle.

—Little One-Inch & Other Japanese Children's Favorite Stories. (Illus.). 60p. (gr. 1-5). 1958. pap. 8.95 (*0-8048-0384-6*) C E Tuttle.

—Peach Boy & Other Japanese Children's Favorite Stories. Kurosaki, Yoshisuke, illus. 58p. (gr. 1-5). 1958. pap. 8.95 (*0-8048-0469-9*) C E Tuttle.

Sakade, Florence, ed. Urashima Taro & Other Japanese Children's Stories. (Illus.). 58p. (gr. 1-6). 1958. pap. 8.95 (*0-8048-0609-8*) C E Tuttle.

San Souci, Robert D. The Samurai's Daughter. Johnson, Stephen T., illus. LC 91-15585. 32p. (ps-3). 1992. 15.00 (*0-8037-1135-2*); PLB 14.89 (*0-8037-1136-0*) Dial Bks Young.

San Souci, Robert D., retold by. The Snow Wife. Johnson, Stephen T., illus. LC 92-28966. 32p. (ps-3). 1993. 14.99 (*0-8037-1409-2*); PLB 14.89 (*0-8037-1410-6*) Dial Bks Young.

Schroeder, Alan. Lily & the Wooden Bowl. (ps-3). 1994. 14.95 (*0-385-30792-6*) Doubleday.

Schroeder, Alan, adapted by. Lily & the Wooden Bowl: A Japanese Folktale. Ito, Yoriko, illus. LC 93-17900. 1994. 15.95 (*0-385-31073-0*) Dial Bks Young.

Smith, Philip, ed. Japanese Fairy Tales. Fujiyama, Kakuzo, illus. LC 92-17648. 96p. 1992. pap. 1.00 (*0-486-27300-8*) Dover.

Stamm, Claus. Three Strong Women. Tseng, Jean & Tseng, Mou-sien, illus. 32p. (gr. 2-5). 1990. pap. 12.95 (*0-670-83323-1*) Viking Child Bks.

Stamm, Claus & Mizumura, Kazue. Three Strong Women. Tseng, Jean & Tseng, Mou-sien, illus. LC 92-25331. 1993. pap. 4.99 (*0-14-054530-1*) Puffin Bks.

Tompert, Ann. Bamboo Hats & a Rice Cake: A Tale Adapted from Japanese Folklore. Demi, illus. LC 92-26849. 32p. (ps-3). 1993. 13.00 (*0-517-59272-X*); PLB 13.99 (*0-517-59273-8*) Crown Bks Yng Read.

Uchida, Yoshiko. The Magic Purse. Narahashi, Keiko, illus. LC 92-30132. 32p. (gr. 1-4). 1993. SBE 15.95 (*0-689-50559-0*, M K McElderry) Macmillan Child Grp.

Uchida, Yoshiko, retold by. The Wise Old Woman. Springett, Martin, illus. LC 92-46048. (gr. k-4). 1994. 14.95 (*0-689-50582-5*, M K McElderry) Macmillan Child Grp.

Watkins, Yoko K. Tales from the Bamboo Grove. Tseng, Jean & Mou-sien Tseng, illus. LC 91-38218. 64p. (gr. 4-11). 1992. SBE 14.95 (*0-02-792525-0*, Bradbury Pr) Macmillan Child Grp.

Wells, Ruth, retold by. The Poor God: A Japanese Folktale. Yoshi, illus. LC 93-18236. 1993. 15.95 (*0-88708-330-7*) Picture Bk Studio.

Williams, Carol. Tsubu, the Little Snail. Kiuchi, Tatsuro, illus. LC 93-49344. 1995. 15.00 (*0-671-87167-6*, S&S BFYR) S&S Trade.

Yagawa, Sumiko. The Crane Wife. (ps-3). 1992. 17.75 (*0-8446-6589-4*) Peter Smith.

Yamaguchi, Marianne. The Sea of Gold & Other Tales from Japan. LC 87-72797. (Illus.). 144p. (gr. 7-12). 1988. pap. 7.95 (*0-88739-056-0*) Creative Arts Bk.

Yashima, Taro. One-Inch Fellow. LC 93-10824. (ps-6). 1995. write for info. (*0-15-276897-1*, Browndeer Pr) HarBrace.

FOLKLORE, JEWISH

Alder, David A. The Children of Chelm. Friedman, Arthur, illus. (gr. 1-5). 1979. (Bonim Bks); pap. 4.50 (*0-88482-773-9*, Bonim Bks) Hebrew Pub.

Chaikin, Miriam. Hinkl & Other Shlemiel Stories. Posner, Marcia, illus. LC 86-29755. 96p. (Orig.). (gr. 7 up). 1987. pap. 6.95 (*0-933503-37-7*) Shapolsky Pubs.

Channen, Don. Tallis Ends & Other Tales. 184p. 1992. pap. 14.95 (*965-229-053-X*, Pub. by Gefen Pub Hse IS) Gefen Bks.

Freehof, Lillian S. Bible Legends: An Introduction to Midrash, Vol. 1: Genesis. Schwartz, Howard, ed. (gr. 4-6). 1987. pap. text ed. 6.95 (*0-8074-0357-1*, 123050) UAHC.

Freeman, Florence B. It Happened in Chelm: A Story of the Legendary Town of Fools. Krevitsky, Nik, illus. 64p. (gr. 3-8). 1990. pap. text ed. 9.95 (*0-933503-22-9*) Shapolsky Pubs.

Ganz, Yaffa. Tali's Slippers, Tova's Shoes. Ariel, Liat B., illus. 32p. (gr. k-6). 1989. 6.95 (*0-89906-502-3*) Mesorah Pubns.

Gauz, Yaffa. Savta Simcha & the Seven Splendid Gifts. Gewirtz, Bina, illus. LC 87-3643. (gr. 4-7). 1987. 12.95 (*0-87306-437-2*) Feldheim.

Geras, Adele. My Grandmother's Stories: A Collection of Jewish Folk Tales. Jordan, Jael, illus. LC 90-4309. 96p. (gr. 3-7). 1990. PLB 18.99 (*0-679-90910-9*) Knopf Bks Yng Read.

Gilman, Phoebe, adapted by. Something from Nothing. LC 92-37587. 1993. write for info. (*0-590-47280-1*) Scholastic Inc.

Gordon, Ruth. Feathers. Dabcovich, Lydia, illus. LC 92-26164. 32p. (gr. k-3). 1993. RSBE 14.95 (*0-02-736511-5*, Macmillan Child Bk) Macmillan Child Grp.

Greene, Jacqueline D. What His Father Did. O'Brien, John, illus. 32p. (gr. k-3). 1992. 13.45 (*0-395-55042-4*) HM.

Jaffe, Nina. The Uninvited Guest & Other Jewish Holiday Tales. Savadier, Elivia, illus. LC 92-36308. 1993. write for info. (*0-590-44653-3*) Scholastic Inc.

Kimmel, Eric A. Days of Awe: Stories for Rosh Hashanah & Yom Kippur. Weihs, Erika, illus. LC 93-583. 48p. (gr. 3-7). pap. 4.99 (*0-14-050271-8*, Puffin) Puffin Bks.

Kleinbard, Gitel. Oh, Zalmy! Or, the Tale of the Porcelain Pony, Bk. 1. (Illus.). (gr. k-3). 1976. 5.95 (*0-917274-04-0*); pap. 3.95 (*0-917274-01-6*) Mah Tov Pubns.

Ludwig, Warren. Old Noah's Elephants. LC 90-35379. (Illus.). 32p. (ps-3). 1991. 14.95 (*0-399-22256-1*, Putnam) Putnam Pub Group.

MacGill-Callahan, Sheila. When Solomon Was King. Johnson, Stephen T., illus. LC 93-28058. 1995. write for info. (*0-8037-1589-7*); PLB write for info. (*0-8037-1590-0*) Dial Bks Young.

Omer, Devorah. Once There Was a Hassid. Shvo, Aaron, illus. 28p. (gr. 4 up). 1987. 9.95 (*0-915361-73-6*) Modan-Adama Bks.

Orgel, Doris & Schecter, Ellen. The Flower of Sheba. Kelly, Laura, illus. LC 92-33477. 1994. pap. 3.50 (*0-553-37235-1*, Little Rooster, Little Rooster) Bantam.

Podwal, Mark. The Book of Tens. LC 93-43871. (Illus.). 24p. 1994. 15.00 (*0-688-12994-3*); PLB 14.93 (*0-688-12995-1*) Greenwillow.

Renberg, Dalia H. King Solomon & the Bee. Heller, Ruth, illus. LC 92-30411. 32p. (ps-3). 1994. 15.00 (*0-06-022899-7*); PLB 14.89 (*0-06-022902-0*) HarpC Child Bks.

Rosenfeld, Dina. Why the Moon Only Glows. Holtzman, Yehudit, illus. 32p. (ps-1). 1992. 8.95 (*0-922613-00-1*); pap. 6.95 (*0-922613-01-X*) Hachai Pubns.

Sanfield, Steve. The Feather Merchants & Other Tales of the Fools of Chelm. Magaril, Mikhail, illus. LC 92-43767. 128p. (gr. 5 up). 1993. pap. 4.95 (*0-688-12568-9*, Pub. by Beech Tree Bks) Morrow.

Schwartz, Barry L. Honi the Circlemaker: Eco-Fables from Ancient Israel. LC 92-33715. 1992. pap. 8.95 (*0-377-00251-8*) Friendship Pr.

Schwartz, Howard & Rush, Barbara, eds. Sabbath Lion: A Jewish Folktale from Algeria. LC 91-35766. (Illus.). 32p. (gr. k-4). 1992. 14.00 (*0-06-020853-8*); PLB 13.89 (*0-06-020854-6*) HarpC Child Bks.

Sherman, Josepha. Rachel the Clever: And Other Jewish Folktales. 171p. 1993. 18.95 (*0-87483-306-X*); pap. 9.95 (*0-87483-307-8*) August Hse.

Shulevitz, Uri. El Tesoro: The Treasure. Negroni, Maria, tr. (SPA., Illus.). 32p. (ps-3). 1992. 16.00 (*0-374-37422-8*, Mirasol) FS&G.

—The Treasure. Shulvitz, Uri, illus. LC 78-12952. 32p. (ps-3). 1979. 16.00 (*0-374-37740-5*) FS&G.

Simon, Solomon. Adventures of Simple Shmerel. Fischel, Lillian, illus. (gr. 3-7). 1942. 4.95 (*0-87441-127-0*) Behrman.

—Wise Men of Helm. (gr. 3-7). 1942. pap. 6.50 (*0-87441-125-4*) Behrman.

Singer, Isaac Bashevis. Elijah the Slave. Frasconi, Antonio, illus. 32p. (ps up). 1988. pap. 4.95 (*0-374-42047-5*) FS&G.

—Power of Light. 1990. pap. 7.95 (*0-374-45984-3*, Sunburst) FS&G.

—When Shlemiel Went to Warsaw & Other Stories. Zemach, Margot, illus. 161p. (gr. 3-7). 1986. pap. 4.95 (*0-374-48365-5*) FS&G.

Sofer, G. A Story a Day, Vol. I: Tishrei-Cheshvan. Weinbach, Shaindel, tr. from HEB. Bardugo, Miriam, illus. 206p. (gr. 7-12). 1989. 12.95 (*0-89906-950-9*); pap. 9.95 (*0-89906-951-7*) Mesorah Pubns.

—A Story a Day, Vol. II: Kislev-Teves. Weinbach, Shaindel, tr. from HEB. Bardugo, Miriam, illus. 232p. (gr. 7-12). 1988. 14.95 (*0-89906-952-5*); pap. 10.95 (*0-89906-953-3*) Mesorah Pubns.

—A Story a Day, Vol. III: Shevat-Adar. Weinbach, Shaindel, tr. from HEB. Bardugo, Miriam, illus. 224p. (gr. 7-12). 1989. 14.95 (*0-89906-954-1*); pap. 10.95 (*0-89906-955-X*) Mesorah Pubns.

—A Story a Day, Vol. IV: Nissan-Iyar. Weinbach, Shaindel, tr. from HEB. Bardugo, Miriam, illus. 210p. (gr. 7-12). 1989. 14.95 (*0-89906-956-8*); pap. 10.95 (*0-89906-957-6*) Mesorah Pubns.

—A Story a Day, Vol. V: Sivan-Tammuz. Weinbach, Shaindel, tr. from HEB. Bardugo, Miriam, illus. 210p. (gr. 7-12). 1989. 14.95 (*0-89906-958-4*); pap. 10.95 (*0-89906-959-2*) Mesorah Pubns.

—A Story a Day, Vol. VI: Ev-Elul. Weinbach, Shaindel, tr. from HEB. Bardugo, Miriam, illus. 210p. (gr. 7-12). 1989. 14.95 (*0-89906-960-6*); pap. 10.95 (*0-89906-961-4*) Mesorah Pubns.

Weinstock, Y. Tales from the Gemara, Vol. II: Shabbos. Weinstock, Shaindel, tr. from HEB. (Illus.). 160p. (gr. 5-12). 1989. 13.95 (*0-89906-814-6*); pap. 10.95 (*0-89906-815-4*) Mesorah Pubns.

FOLKLORE–KENYA

Gershator, Phyllis, retold by. The Iroko-Man: A Yoruba Folktale. Kim, Holly C., illus. LC 93-4888. 32p. (ps-2). 1994. 14.95 (*0-531-06810-2*); PLB 14.99 (*0-531-08660-7*) Orchard Bks Watts.

FOLKLORE–KOREA

Adams, Edward B., ed. Blindman's Daughter. Choi, Dong Ho, illus. 32p. (gr. 3). 1981. 8.95 (*0-8048-1472-4*, Pub. by Seoul Intl Tourist SK) C E Tuttle.

—Korean Cinderella. Choi, Dong Ho, illus. 32p. (gr. 3). 1982. 8.95 (*0-8048-1473-2*, Pub. by Seoul Intl Tourist SK) C E Tuttle.

Carpenter, Frances. Tales of a Korean Grandmother. LC 72-77515. (Illus.). 320p. (gr. 3-8). 1972. pap. 8.95 (*0-8048-1043-5*) C E Tuttle.

Climo, Shirley. The Korean Cinderella. Heller, Ruth, illus. LC 93-23268. 48p. (gr. k-3). 1993. 15.00 (*0-06-020432-X*); PLB 14.89 (*0-06-020433-8*) HarpC Child Bks.

Ginsburg, Mirra, ed. The Chinese Mirror. Zemach, Margot, illus. LC 86-22940. 26p. (ps-3). 1988. 15.95 (*0-15-200420-3*, Gulliver Bks) HarBrace.

Han, Oki S. & Plunkett, Stephanie H., eds. Kongi & Potgi: A Cinderella Story from Korea. Han, Oki S., illus. LC 93-28426. 1994. write for info. (*0-8037-1571-4*); PLB write for info. (*0-8037-1572-2*) Dial Bks Young.

—Sir Whong & the Golden Pig. Han, Oki S., illus. LC 91-43389. 32p. (ps-3). 1993. 13.99 (*0-8037-1344-4*); PLB 13.89 (*0-8037-1345-2*) Dial Bks Young.

Han, Suzanne C. The Rabbit's Judgment. Heo, Yumi, illus. LC 93-11031. (ENG & KOR.). 1994. 15.95 (*0-8050-2674-6*) H Holt & Co.

Hyun, Peter, ed. Korea's Favorite Tales & Lyrics. Park, Dong-Il, illus. 124p. 1986. 12.95 (*0-00-000086-8*, Pub. by Seoul Intl Tourist SK) C E Tuttle.

Kim, Yong-Kol. Brave Hong Kil-Dong: The Man Who Bought the Shade of a Tree. Kang, Mi-Sun & Kim, Yong-Kyong, illus. 46p. (gr. 2-5). 1990. PLB 9.95x (*0-930878-91-4*) Hollym Intl.

Korean Folk Tales for Children, 10 vols. (Illus.). (gr. 2-5). 1990. Set. PLB 90.00x (*0-930878-05-1*) Hollym Intl.

Reasoner, Charles. The Magic Amber. Reasoner, Charles, illus. LC 93-43180. 32p. (gr. 2-5). 1994. PLB 11.89 (*0-8167-3407-0*); pap. text ed. 3.95 (*0-8167-3408-9*) Troll Assocs.

Rhee, Nami. Magic Spring. (Illus.). 32p. (ps-3). 1993. PLB 14.95 (*0-399-22420-3*, Putnam) Putnam Pub Group.

Schecter, Ellen. Sim Chung & the River Dragon, Level Three: A Folktale from Korea. LC 92-7652. (ps-3). 1993. 9.99 (*0-553-09117-4*) Bantam.

Vorhees, Duance & Mueller, Mark. The Faithful Daughter Shim Ch'ong: The Little Frog Who Never Listened. Kang, Mi-Sun & Kim, Yon-Kyong, illus. 46p. (gr. 2-5). 1990. PLB 9.95x (*0-930878-92-2*) Hollym Intl.

—The Greedy Princess: The Rabbit & the Tiger. Pak, Mi-Son & Kim, Yon-Kyong, illus. 46p. (gr. 2-5). 1990. PLB 9.95x (*0-930878-90-6*) Hollym Intl.

—The Lazy Man. Kang, Mi-Suk, illus. 46p. (gr. 2-5). 1991. PLB 9.95x (*0-930878-73-6*) Hollym Intl.

—The Ogres' Magic Clubs. Kim, Yon-Kyong, illus. 46p. (gr. 2-5). 1991. PLB 9.95x (*0-930878-88-4*) Hollym Intl.

—The Seven Brothers & the Big Dipper. Pak, Mi-Son, illus. 46p. (gr. 2-5). 1991. PLB 9.95x (*0-930878-74-4*) Hollym Intl.

—The Snail Lady: The Magic Vase. Kang, Mi-Sun, illus. 46p. (gr. 2-5). 1990. PLB 9.95x (*0-930878-89-2*) Hollym Intl.

—The Son of the Cinnamon Tree: The Donkey's Egg. Kim, Yon-Kyong & Kang, Mi-Sun, illus. 46p. (gr. 2-5). 1990. PLB 9.95x (*0-930878-93-0*) Hollym Intl.

Vorhees, Duance & Mueller, Mark, eds. Mr. Moon & Miss Sun. Kim, Yon-Kyong, illus. 45p. (gr. 2-5). 1990. PLB 9.95x (*0-930878-72-8*) Hollym Intl.

—The Woodcutter & the Heavenly Maiden. Kim, Yon-Kyong, illus. 45p. (gr. 2-5). 1990. PLB 9.95x (*0-930878-71-X*) Hollym Intl.

Yoo, Grace S. Two Korean Brothers: The Story of Hungbu & Nolbu. LC 73-18023. (gr. k-3). 1970. 6.95 (*0-912580-01-1*) Far Eastern Res.

FOLKLORE–LATIN AMERICA

Baden, Robert. Y Domingo, Siete. Mathews, Judith, ed. Ada, Alma F., tr. Edwards, Michelle, illus. LC 89-37823. (SPA.). 40p. (ps-3). 1990. 13.95 (*0-8075-9355-9*) A Whitman.

Delacre, Lulu. Arroz Con Leche: Popular Songs & Rhymes from Latin America. (Illus.). (ps-3). 1989. pap. 13.95 (*0-590-41887-4*) Scholastic Inc.

Green, Belva. How the Robin Got Its Red Breast. Beitler, Stanley, ed. White, Monica, illus. LC 90-80399. 32p. (ps-3). 1990. 12.95 (*0-945740-01-8*) Indp Pubs.

Hull, Robert. Pre-Columbian Stories. Cleall, Vanessa & Robinson, Claire, illus. LC 93-48468. 48p. (gr. 5-9). 1994. 15.95 (*1-56847-181-5*) Thomson Lrning.

Palacios, Argentina. The Hummingbird King: A Guatemalan Legend. Davalos, Felipe, illus. LC 92-21437. 32p. (gr. 2-5). 1993. lib. bdg. 11.89 (*0-8167-3051-2*); pap. text ed. 3.95 (*0-8167-3052-0*) Troll Assocs.

—Llama's Secret: A Peruvian Legend. Reasoner, Charles, illus. LC 92-21436. 32p. (gr. 2-5). 1993. lib. bdg. 11.89 (*0-8167-3049-0*); pap. text ed. 3.95 (*0-8167-3050-4*) Troll Assocs.

—El Rey Colibri - the Hummingbird King: Una Leyenda Guatemalteca. (gr. 4-7). 1993. PLB 11.89 (*0-8167-3122-5*); pap. 3.95 (*0-8167-3071-7*) Troll Assocs.

FOLKLORE, MAORI

Kiri, Te Kanawa. Land of the Long White Cloud: Maori Myths, Tales, & Legends. Foreman, Michael, illus. (gr. 3 up). 1990. 16.95 (*1-55970-046-7*) Arcade Pub Inc.

FOLKLORE–MEXICO

Aardema, Verna. Pedro & the Padre. Henstra, Friso, illus. LC 87-24476. 32p. (ps-3). 1991. 12.95 (*0-8037-0522-0*); PLB 12.89 (*0-8037-0523-9*) Dial Bks Young.

Aardema, Verna, retold by. & tr. Borreguita & the Coyote: A Tale from Ayutla, Mexico. Mathers, Peter, illus. LC 90-39419. 40p. (ps-3). 1991. 15.00 (*0-679-80921-X*); lib. bdg. 15.99 (*0-679-90921-4*) Knopf Bks Yng Read.

Ada, Alma F. Mediopollito: Half-Chicken: A New Version of a Traditional Story. Zubizarreta, Rosalma, tr. Howard, Kim, illus. LC 93-41088. (ENG & SPA.). 1995. write for info. (*0-385-32044-2*) Doubleday.

Brenner, Anita. The Boy Who Could Do Anything: And Other Mexican Folktales. Charlot, Jean, illus. LC 92-3903. 128p. (gr. 3-7). 1992. Repr. of 1942 ed. lib. bdg. 17.50 (*0-208-02353-4*, Pub. by Linnet) Shoe String.

De Paola, Tomie. The Lady of Guadalupe. De Paola, Tomie, illus. LC 79-19610. 48p. (ps-4). 1980. reinforced bdg. 16.95 (*0-8234-0373-4*); pap. 6.95 (*0-8234-0403-X*) Holiday.

Hayes, Joe. Monday, Tuesday, Wednesday, Oh! Lunes, Martes, Miercoles, O! Jelinek, Lucy, illus. 32p. (Orig.). (gr. 2-5). 1987. pap. 3.95 (*0-939729-04-0*); bk. & cassette 7.95, (*0-939729-05-9*) Trails West Pub.

—The Terrible Tragadabas: El Terrible Tragadabas. Jelinek, Lucy, illus. 32p. (Orig.). (ps-4). 1987. pap. 3.95 (*0-939729-02-4*); bk. & cassette 7.95, (*0-939729-03-2*) Trails West Pub.

Kimmel, Eric A. The Witch's Face: A Mexican Tale. Vanden Broeck, Fabricio, illus. LC 92-44380. 32p. (ps-3). 1993. reinforced bdg. 15.95 (*0-8234-1038-2*) Holiday.

Kohen, Clarita. El Conejo y el Coyote. Menicucci, Gina, illus. (SPA.). 16p. (Orig.). (gr. k-5). 1993. PLB 7.50x (*1-56492-100-X*) Laredo.

Mike, Jan M. Opossum & the Great Firemaker: A Mexican Legend. Reasoner, Charles, illus. LC 92-36459. 32p. (gr. 2-5). 1993. lib. bdg. 11.89 (*0-8167-3055-5*); tchr's. ed. 3.95 (*0-8167-3056-3*) Troll Assocs.

Montejo, Victor. The Bird Who Cleans the World: And Other Mayan Fables. Perera, Victor & Kaufman, Wallace, trs. from SPA. LC 90-52757. (Illus.). 128p. (Orig.). 1991. 22.95 (*0-915306-93-X*); pap. 13.95 (*1-880684-03-9*) Curbstone.

Mora, Francisco X. The Coyote Rings the Wrong Bell. LC 91-13163. (Illus.). 24p. (ps-3). 1991. PLB 12.85 (*0-516-05136-9*); pap. 4.95 (*0-516-45136-7*) Childrens.

—The Legend of the Two Moons. Mora, Francisco X., illus. LC 92-31552. 32p. (ps-k). 1993. PLB 15.00 (*0-917846-15-X*, 95517) Highsmith Pr.

Parapan, S. M. A Mexican Legend: Quetzalcoat! The Bird-Serpent. Castillo, L., illus. 24p. (Orig.). (gr. k-3). 1989. pap. text ed. write for info.; write for info. tchr's. activity guide Parapan.

Rohmer, Harriet & Anchondo, Mary. How We Came to the Fifth World (Como Vinimos al Quinto Mundo) Lopez, Graciela C., illus. LC 76-7240. (ENG & SPA.). 24p. (gr. 2-6). 1988. 13.95 (*0-89239-024-7*) Childrens Book Pr.

Roland, Donna. More of Grandfather's Stories from Mexico. (gr. 1-3). 1986. pap. 4.95 (*0-941996-10-7*); tchr's. ed. 5.50 (*0-685-55812-6*) Open My World.

Ryder, Virginia P. Three Monkey Saves the Day. Kilgore, Julia, illus. 21p. (Orig.). (gr. k-12). 1991. pap. 8.95 (*0-935098-04-6*) Amigo Pr.

Van Rhijn, Patricia. El Nino Maicero: The Corn Boy. Suarez, Maribel, illus. (SPA.). 35p. (gr. k-4). 1990. 7.95 (*968-494-042-4*) Donars.

FOLKLORE–MIDDLE EAST

Azam, Hina, ed. Good Neighbors & Other Moral Stories. Busool, Assad N., tr. from ARA. Gabriel, George, illus. 49p. (Orig.). Date not set. text ed. write for info. (*1-56316-312-8*) Iqra Intl Ed Fdtn.

DePaola, Tomie. The Legend of the Persian Carpet. Ewart, Claire, illus. 32p. (ps-3). 1993. 14.95 (*0-399-22415-7*, Putnam-Whitebird) Putnam Pub Group.

FOLKLORE–MONGOLIA

Khurelblat, B. & Narain, Aditya. Folk Tales of Mongolia. 85p. 1992. pap. 5.95 (*81-207-1341-9*, Pub. by Sterling Pubs IA) Apt Bks.

FOLKLORE–MOROCCO

Chimenti, Elisa. Tales & Legends of Morocco. Benamy, Arnon, tr. (Illus.). (gr. 5 up). 1965. 10.95 (*0-8392-3049-4*) Astor-Honor.

FOLKLORE–NEAR EAST

Gold, Sharlya & Caspi, Mishael M. The Answered Prayer: And Other Yemenite Folktales. Wunsch, Marjory, illus. 80p. (gr. 3-5). 1990. 13.95 (*0-8276-0354-1*) JPS Phila.

Hashim, A. S. Al-Khulafe al-Rashidoon. pap. 5.95 (*0-935782-29-X*) Kazi Pubns.

Yushij, Nima. When the Elephants Came. Evans, Mariam & Batmanglij, M., eds. Evans, Mariam, tr. from PER. Fanta, illus. LC 87-31690. 32p. (gr. 4 up). 1988. 18.50 (*0-934211-15-9*); English-Persian Version. 18.50 (*0-934211-09-4*) Mage Pubs Inc.

FOLKLORE, NEGRO

see Black Folklore

FOLKLORE–NETHERLANDS

Fisher, Leonard E. Kinderdike. Fisher, Leonard E., illus. LC 93-8140. 32p. (gr. k-3). 1994. 15.95 (*0-02-735365-6*, Macmillan Child Bk) Macmillan Child Grp.

FOLKLORE–NIGERIA

Daly, Niki. Why the Sun & Moon Live in the Sky. LC 93-47304. (Illus.). 1994. 15.00 (*0-688-13331-2*); lib. bdg. 14.93 (*0-688-13332-0*) Lothrop.

Gerson, Mary-Joan. Why the Sky Is Far Away: A Nigerian Folktale. (ps-3). 1992. 15.95 (*0-316-30852-8*, Joy St Bks) Little.

Mollel, Tololwa M., retold by. The Flying Tortoise: An Igbo Tale. Spurll, Barbara, illus. LC 93-14349. 1994. 14.95 (*0-395-68845-0*) HM.

FOLKLORE–NORWAY

Appleby. The Three Billy-Goats Gruff. 1993. pap. 19.95 (*0-590-71393-0*) Scholastic Inc.

Appleby, Ellen. The Three Billy-Goats Gruff. (Illus.). 32p. (gr. k-2). 1985. pap. 2.50 (*0-590-41121-7*) Scholastic Inc.

Arnold, Tim, retold by. & illus. The Three Billy Goats Gruff. LC 92-23992. 32p. (ps-3). 1993. SBE 14.95 (*0-689-50575-2*, M K McElderry) Macmillan Child Grp.

Asbjornsen, P. C. & Moe, J. E. The Man Who Kept House. S, Svend O., illus. LC 91-37599. 32p. (gr. k-3). 1992. SBE 13.95 (*0-689-50560-4*, M K McElderry) Macmillan Child Grp.

Atwell, David L. The Day Hans Got His Way. Atwell, Debby, illus. LC 91-43945. 32p. (ps-3). 1992. 14.45 (*0-395-58772-7*) HM.

Bender, Robert. The Three Billy Goats Gruff. Bender, Robert, illus. LC 92-41077. 32p. (ps-2). 1993. 14.95 (*0-8050-2529-4*, Bks Young Read) H Holt & Co.

Dasent, George W. East o' the Sun & West o' the Moon. LC 70-97214. (Illus.). xv, 418p. (gr. 1 up). 1970. pap. 8.95 (*0-486-22521-6*) Dover.

Feldman, Eve. The Squire Takes a Wife. Weissman, Barry, illus. 24p. (ps-2). 1990. PLB 17.10 (*0-8172-3580-9*); PLB 10.95 pkg. of 3 (*0-685-58551-4*) Raintree Steck-V.

Greenway, Jennifer, retold by. The Three Billy Goats Gruff. Lustig, Loretta, illus. 1991. 6.95 (*0-8362-4913-5*) Andrews & McMeel.

Kassirer, Sue. The Three Billy Goats Gruff. Fritz, Ron, illus. 24p. (Orig.). (ps-k). pap. 1.50 (*0-679-84796-0*) Random Bks Yng Read.

Kimmel, Eric A., retold by. Boots & His Brothers: A Tale from Norway. Root, Kimberly B., illus. LC 90-23659. 32p. (ps-3). 1992. reinforced bdg. 14.95 (*0-8234-0886-8*) Holiday.

Langley, Jonathan. The Three Billy Goats Gruff. Langley, Jonathan, illus. LC 92-4842. 32p. (ps-3). Date not set. 15.00 (*0-06-021224-1*); PLB 14.89 (*0-06-021474-0*) HarpC Child Bks.

Martin, Claire, retold by. Boots & the Glass Mountain. Spirin, Gennady, illus. LC 91-9724. 32p. (ps-3). 1992. 15.00 (*0-8037-1110-7*); PLB 14.89 (*0-8037-1111-5*) Dial Bks Young.

Mills, Lauren, retold by. Tatterhood & the Hobgoblins: A Norwegian Folktale, Vol. 1. (Illus.). (ps-3). 1993. 15. 95 (*0-316-57406-6*) Little.

Rader, Laura, illus. The Three Billy Goats Gruff. LC 94-4987. 1995. write for info. (*0-688-13259-6*, Tambourine Bks) Morrow.

Roberts, Tom. The Three Billy Goats Gruff. Jorgensen, David, illus. LC 93-6678. (ps-6). 1993. 9.95 (*0-88708-319-6*, Dist. by S&S Trade) Picture Bk Studio.

Rounds, Glen, retold by. & illus. The Three Billy Goats Gruff. LC 92-23951. 32p. (ps-3). 1993. reinforced bdg. 15.95 (*0-8234-1015-3*); pap. 5.95 (*0-8234-1136-2*) Holiday.

FOLKLORE, ORIENTAL

Piequet, Miriam. Ting-Li's Tales Told on the Devil's Mountain. Anyone Can Read Staff, ed. Yin-Chwang, Wang Tsen-Zan. (Illus.). 60p. (Orig.). (gr. 3-7). 1987. pap. write for info. (*0-914275-13-5*) Anyone Can Read Bks.

FOLKLORE–PHILIPPINE ISLANDS

De La Paz, Myrna J. Abadeha: The Philippine Cinderella. De Leon, Romeo, illus. 28p. (gr. k-7). 1991. 13.95 (*0-9629255-0-0*) Pazific Queen.

Fuentes, Vilma M. Manggob & His Golden Top. Inis, Ninabeth R., illus. 48p. (Orig.). (gr. k-3). 1985. pap. 4.00 (*971-10-0218-3*, Pub. by New Day Pub PI) Cellar.

Grandfather's Stories from the Philippines. (gr. k-3). 1986. 4.95 (*0-941996-07-7*); tchr's. ed. 5.50 (*0-685-62737-3*) Open My World.

Montero, Jaime A. Gatan & Talaw. (Illus., Orig.). (gr. 1-3). 1984. pap. 3.50 (*971-10-0164-0*, Pub. by New Day Pub PI) Cellar.

FOLKLORE–PUERTO RICO

Bernier-Grand, Carmen, retold by. Juan Bobo: Four Folktales from Puerto Rico. Nieves, Ernesto R., illus. LC 93-12936. 64p. (gr. k-3). 1994. 14.00 (*0-06-023389-3*); PLB 13.89 (*0-06-023390-7*) HarpC.

Jaffe, Nina, adapted by. & tr. The Golden Flower: A Taino Myth from Puerto Rico. Moiles, Holly B., illus. LC 92-42364. 32p. (ps-3). 1995. RSBE 15.95 (*0-02-747585-9*, Macmillan Child Bk) Macmillan Child Grp.

Mora, Francisco X. The Tiger & the Rabbit: A Puerto Rican Folk Tale. Mora, Francisco X., illus. LC 91-3500. 32p. (ps-3). 1991. PLB 13.85 (*0-516-05137-7*); pap. 5.95 (*0-516-45137-5*) Childrens.

Pitre, Felix, retold by. Juan Bobo & the Pig: A Puerto Rican Folktale. Hale, Christy, illus. LC 92-28063. 32p. (gr. k-3). 1993. 13.99 (*0-525-67429-2*, Lodestar Bks) Dutton Child Bks.

Rohmer, Harriet & Guerrero Rea, Jesus. Atariba & Niguayona. Castillo, Consuelo M., illus. LC 76-17495. (ENG & SPA.). 24p. (gr. 2-6). 1988. 13.95 (*0-89239-026-3*) Childrens Book Pr.

FOLKLORE–RUMANIA

Ambrus, Victor, retold by. & illus. Never Laugh at Bears: A Folk Tale from Transylvania. LC 91-40372. 32p. (gr. k-3). 1992. PLB 14.95 (*0-87226-465-3*, Bedrick Blackie) P Bedrick Bks.

Olson, Arielle N. Noah's Cats & the Devil's Fire. Moser, Barry, illus. LC 91-17408. 32p. (ps-2). 1992. 14.95 (*0-531-05984-7*); lib. bdg. 14.99 (*0-531-08584-8*) Orchard Bks Watts.

Reynolds-Strauss, Karen & Gligor, Adrian. Romanian Fairy Tales. Reynolds-Strauss, Karen, illus. 85p. (Orig.). (ps-6). 1992. pap. text ed. 11.95 (*0-9634797-0-9*) K Strauss & A Gligor.

Spariosu, Mihai & Benedek, Dezso, eds. Ghosts, Vampires, & Werewolves: EErie Tales from Transylvania. Kubinyi, Laszlo, illus. LC 93-48837. 112p. (gr. 5 up). 1994. 16.95 (*0-531-06860-9*); PLB 16.99 (*0-531-08710-7*) ORchard Bks Watts.

FOLKLORE–SCANDINAVIA

Hague, Kathleen & Hague, Michael. East of the Sun & West of the Moon. LC 80-13499. (Illus.). 32p. (gr. 3 up). 1989. pap. 4.95 (*0-15-224703-3*, Voyager Bks) HarBrace.

Jones, Gwyn, retold by. Scandinavian Legends & Folk-Tales. Kiddell-Monroe, Joan, illus. 192p. (gr. 4 up). 1992. pap. 10.95 (*0-19-274150-0*) OUP.

Synge, Ursula. Weland: Smith of the Gods. Keeping, Charles, illus. LC 73-5945. 94p. (gr. 7 up). 1973. 22.95 (*0-87599-200-5*) S G Phillips.

FOLKLORE–SCOTLAND

Cooper, Susan. The Selkie Girl. Hutton, Warwick, illus. LC 90-39982. 32p. 1991. pap. 4.95 (*0-689-71467-X*, Aladdin) Macmillan Child Grp.

MacGill-Callahan, Sheila. The Seal Prince. Shi, Jihong, illus. LC 93-16248. 1995. 13.99 (*0-8037-1486-6*); PLB 13.89 (*0-8037-1487-4*) Dial Bks Young.

Nimmo, Jenny, retold by. The Witches & the Singing Mice: A Celtic Tale. Barrett, Angela, illus. LC 92-37642. 32p. (gr. 1 up). 1993. 14.99 (*0-8037-1509-9*) Dial Bks Young.

Robertson, Joanne. Sea Witches. (ps-3). 1991. 14.95 (*0-8037-1070-4*) Dial Bks Young.

Wilkins, Verna & McLean, Gill, eds. The Snowball Rent: A Story from Scotland. Wilkinson, Barry, illus. LC 93-16156. 1993. 3.95 (*1-870516-09-5*) Childs Play.

Wilson, Barbara K. Scottish Folk-Tales & Legends. Kiddell-Monroe, Joan, illus. 224p. (ps-7). 1990. pap. 10.95 (*0-19-274141-1*) OUP.

FOLKLORE–SERBIA

Gaidar. Cyk i Gek. (gr. 7-12). pap. 6.95 (*0-88436-051-2*, 65250) EMC.

FOLKLORE, SLAVIC

De Regniers, Beatrice S. Little Sister & the Month Brothers. Tomes, Margot, illus. LC 75-4594. 48p. (ps-3). 1976. 8.95 (*0-8164-3147-7*, Clarion Bks) HM.

Schenk De Regniers, Beatrice. Little Sister & the Month Brothers. Cohn, Amy, ed. Tomes, Margot, illus. LC 93-44053. 48p. (ps up). 1994. lib. bdg. write for info. (*0-688-05293-2*, Mulberry); pap. 4.95 (*0-688-13633-8*, Mulberry) Morrow.

FOLKLORE–SOUTH AMERICA

Alexander, Ellen. Llama & the Great Flood: A Folktale from Peru. Alexander, Ellen, illus. LC 88-1194. 40p. (gr. k-4). 1989. (Crowell Jr Bks); PLB 13.89 (*0-690-04729-0*) HarpC Child Bks.

Bierhorst, John. The Mythology of South America. LC 87-26237. (Illus.). 256p. (gr. 7 up). 1988. 15.95 (*0-688-06722-0*) Morrow Jr Bks.

Brusca, Maria C. & Wilson, Tona. The Blacksmith & the Devils. Brusca, Maria C., illus. LC 92-176. 40p. (gr. 1-4). 1992. 15.95 (*0-8050-1954-5*, Bks Young Read) H Holt & Co.

—The Cook & the King. Brusca, Maria C., illus. LC 92-25812. 40p. (gr. 1-4). 1993. 14.95 (*0-8050-2355-0*, Bks Young Read) H Holt & Co.

Ehlert, Lois. Moon Rope: Un Lazo a la Luna. 1992. 14.95 (*0-15-255343-6*, HB Juv Bks) HarBrace.

Finger, Charles J. Tales from Silver Lands. Honore, Paul, illus. 225p. (gr. 7 up). 1965. 16.95 (*0-685-01496-7*) Doubleday.

El Herrero y el Diablo. (SPA.). 40p. (gr. 1-4). 1992. 15.95 (*0-8050-2411-5*, Bks Young Read) H Holt & Co.

Kerven, Rosalind. The Rain Forest Storybook. (Illus.). 80p. 1994. 17.95 (*0-521-43502-1*); pap. 9.95 (*0-521-43533-1*) Cambridge U Pr.

Loverseed, Amanda. The Thunder King: A Peruvian Tale. Loverseed, Amanda, illus. 32p. (gr. k-3). 1991. PLB 14.95 (*0-87226-450-5*, Bedrick Blackie) P Bedrick Bks.

Seeger, Pete. Abiyoyo. Hays, Michael, illus. LC 93-25730. 48p. 1994. pap. 4.95 (*0-689-71810-1*, Aladdin) Macmillan Child Grp.

Skivington, Janice, illus. The Girl from the Sky: An Inca Folktale from South America. LC 91-42163. 24p. (ps-3). 1992. PLB 13.85 (*0-516-05138-5*); pap. 5.95 (*0-516-45138-3*) Childrens.

Troughton, Joanna, retold by. & illus. How Night Came: A Folk Tale from the Amazon. LC 86-10917. 32p. (gr. k-3). 1986. PLB 14.95 (*0-87226-093-3*, Bedrick Blackie) P Bedrick Bks.

—How the Birds Changed Their Feathers: A South American Folk Tale. LC 86-1251. 32p. (gr. k-3). 1986. PLB 14.95 (*0-87226-080-1*, Bedrick Blackie) P Bedrick Bks.

FOLKLORE–SOVIET UNION

Afanasyev, Alexander. Fool & the Fish: A Tale from Russia. Hort, Lenny, retold by. Spirin, Gennady, illus. 32p. (ps-3). 1990. 12.95 (*0-8037-0861-0*) Dial Bks Young.

Arnold, Katya, retold by. & illus. Baba Yaga: A Russian Folktale. LC 92-38199. 32p. (gr. k-3). 1993. 14.95 (*1-55858-208-8*); PLB 14.88 (*1-55858-209-6*) North-South Bks NYC.

Ayres, Becky H. Matreshka. Natchev, Alexi, illus. LC 91-36359. 32p. (gr. k-3). 1992. pap. 15.00 (*0-385-30657-1*) Doubleday.

Bernhard, Emery. The Girl Who Wanted to Hunt: A Siberian Tale. LC 93-48024. (Illus.). (ps-3). 1994. reinforced bdg. 15.95 (*0-8234-1125-7*) Holiday.

Carick, Valery. Picture Folk-Tales. (Illus.). 96p. 1992. pap. 1.00t (*0-486-27083-1*) Dover.

Cech, John. First Snow, Magic Snow. McGinley-Nally, Sharon, illus. LC 91-42988. 40p. (gr. k-2). 1992. RSBE 14.95 (*0-02-717971-0*, Four Winds) Macmillan Child Grp.

Cincerelli, Carol J. A Russian Folktale - My Mother Is the Most Beautiful Woman in the World. 96p. (gr. 1-6). 1990. 10.95 (*0-86653-539-X*, GA1162) Good Apple.

Croll, Carolyn, adapted by. & illus. The Little Snowgirl. 32p. (ps-k). 1989. 14.95 (*0-399-21691-X*, Putnam) Putnam Pub Group.

Demi. The Firebird: A Russian Folktale. (gr. 1-5). 1994. 16.95 (*0-8050-3244-4*) H Holt & Co.

Denise, Christopher & Denise, Christopher. The Fool of the World & the Flying Ship. (Illus.). 32p. (ps-3). 1994. 14.95 (*0-399-21972-2*, Philomel) Putnam Pub Group.

Downing, Charles. Russian Tales & Legends. Kiddell-Monroe, Joan, illus. 224p. (gr. 4 up). 1990. pap. 10.95 (*0-19-274144-6*) OUP.

Gilchrist, Cherry, retold by. Prince Ivan & the Firebird. Troshkov, Andrei, illus. LC 93-38136. 1994. 16.00 (*1-56957-920-2*) Barefoot Bks.

Ginsburg, Mirra. Clay Boy. Henwood, Simon, illus. 32p. (ps-3). 1993. PLB 14.95 (*0-399-21988-9*, Philomel Bks) Putnam Pub Group.

Grauer, Rita & Grauer, Rita. Vasalisa & Her Magic Doll. (Illus.). 32p. (ps-3). 1994. 14.95 (*0-399-21986-2*, Philomel) Putnam Pub Group.

Gray, Patricia. The Wolf & the Old Woman. Maya, illus. LC 93-172. 1994. write for info. (*0-383-03728-X*) SRA Schl Grp.

Hastings, Selina. The Firebird. Cartwright, Reg, illus. LC 92-52997. 40p. (ps up). 1993. 15.95 (*1-56402-096-7*) Candlewick Pr.

Haviland, Virginia. Favorite Fairy Tales Told in Russia. Cohn, Amy, ed. Howard, Kim, illus. (gr. 3 up). 1995. pap. 4.95 (*0-688-12603-0*, Beech Tree Bks) Morrow.

Isadora, Rachel. Firebird. Isadora, Rachel, illus. 32p. (ps-3). 1994. PLB 15.95 (*0-399-22510-2*) Putnam Pub Group.

Kimmel, Eric A. Baba Yaga: A Russian Folktale. Lloyd, Megan, illus. 1993. pap. 5.95 (*0-8234-1060-9*) Holiday.

Kimmel, Eric A., adapted by. Bearhead: A Russian Folktale. Mikolaycak, Charles, illus. LC 91-55026. 32p. (ps-3). 1991. reinforced 15.95 (*0-8234-0902-3*) Holiday.

—I-Know-Not-What, I-Know-Not-Where: A Russian Tale. Sauber, Robert, illus. LC 92-32692. 64p. (gr. 1-5). 1994. reinforced bdg. 16.95 (*0-8234-1020-X*) Holiday.

Langton, Jane, retold by. Salt: A Russian Folktale. Plume, Alice, tr. from RUS. Plume, Ilse, illus. LC 91-74007. 40p. (gr. k-3). 1992. 14.95 (*1-56282-178-4*); PLB 14.89 (*1-56282-179-2*) Hyprn Child.

Lewis, Patrick, retold by. The Frog Princess: A Russian Folktale. Spirin, Gennady, illus. LC 93-10827. (gr. 2 up). 1994. 15.99 (*0-8037-1623-0*); lib. bdg. 15.89 (*0-8037-1624-9*) Dial Bks Young.

Lodge, Bernard, retold by. & illus. Prince Ivan & the Firebird: A Russian Folk Tale. LC 93-12343. (ps-5). 1993. smythe sewn reinforced 14.95 (*1-879085-86-0*) Whsprng Coyote Pr.

Malkovych, Ivan. The Cat & the Rooster. Onyschuk, Motria, tr. from RUS. Lavro, Kost, illus. LC 94-14505. (ENG.). (gr. 2 up). 1995. write for info. (*0-679-86964-6*); pap. write for info. (*0-679-96964-0*) Knopf.

Mayer, Marianna. Baba Yaga & Vasilisa the Brave. Craft, Kinuko Y., illus. LC 90-38514. 40p. (ps-3). 1994. 16.00g (*0-688-08500-8*); 15.93 (*0-688-08501-6*) Morrow Jr Bks.

Mayhew, James. Koshka's Tales: Stories from Russia. LC 92-41185. (Illus.). 80p. (gr. k up). 1993. 16.95 (*1-85697-943-1*, Kingfisher LKC) LKC.

Metaxas, Eric. The Fool & the Flying Ship. Drescher, Henrik, illus. LC 91-40669. 40p. (gr. k up). 1992. pap. 14.95 (*0-88708-228-9*, Rabbit Ears); incl. cass. 19.95 (*0-88708-229-7*, Rabbit Ears) Picture Bk Studio.

Mikolaycak, Charles. Babushka: An Old Russian Folktale. Mikolaycak, Charles, illus. LC 84-500. 32p. (ps-3). 1984. reinforced bdg. 15.95 (*0-8234-0520-6*); pap. 5.95 (*0-8234-0712-8*) Holiday.

Milhous, Katherine & Dalgiesh, Alice. The Turnip: An Old Russian Folktale. Morgan, Pierr, illus. 32p. (ps-3). 1990. 14.95 (*0-399-22229-4*, Philomel Bks) Putnam Pub Group.

Philip, Neil, compiled by. Fairy Tales from Eastern Europe. Wilkes, Larry, illus. Philip, Neil, retold by. (Illus.). 160p. (gr. 4 up). 1991. 19.45 (*0-395-57456-0*, Clarion Bks) HM.

Prokofiev, Sergei. Peter & the Wolf. Crampton, Patricia, tr. LC 91-40185. (Illus.). 28p. (gr. k up). 1992. pap. 4.95 (*0-88708-226-2*) Picture Bk Studio.

Ransome, Arthur. The Fool of the World & the Flying Ship: A Russian Tale. Shulevitz, Uri, illus. (ps up). 1987. pap. 5.95 (*0-374-42438-1*) FS&G.

—The Fool of the World & the Flying Ship. Shulevitz, Uri, illus. LC 68-54105. 48p. (ps-3). 1968. 16.00 (*0-374-32442-5*) FS&G.

—Old Peter's Russian Tales. Jaques, Faith, illus. 256p. (gr. 5-9). 1975. pap. 3.50 (*0-14-030696-X*) Viking Child Bks.

Reyher, Becky. My Mother Is the Most Beautiful Woman in the World. Gannett, Ruth, illus. 40p. (gr. k-3). 1945. PLB 14.93 (*0-688-51251-8*) Lothrop.

Robbins, Ruth. Baboushka & the Three Kings. Sidjakov, Nicholas, illus. LC 60-15036. (ps up). 1960. 13.45 (*0-395-27673-X*, Pub. by Parnassus) HM.

SanSouci, Robert. The Tsar's Promise. Mills, Lauren, illus. 32p. (ps up). 1992. 14.95 (*0-399-21581-6*, Philomel Bks) Putnam Pub Group.

San Souci, Robert D. The Firebird. LC 91-574. (Illus.). 32p. (ps-3). 1992. 14.00 (*0-8037-0799-1*); PLB 13.89 (*0-8037-0800-9*) Dial Bks Young.

Schleifer, Jay. Firebird. LC 92-15069. (Illus.). 48p. (gr. 5). 1993. text ed. 13.95 RSBE (*0-89686-702-1*, Crestwood Hse) Macmillan Child Grp.

Tate, Carole. Pancakes & Pies: A Russian Folk Tale. LC 88-38111. 32p. (gr. k-3). 1989. PLB 14.95 (*0-87226-407-6*, Bedrick Blackie) P Bedrick Bks.

Tolstoy, Leo. Chozjain I Rabotnik. (gr. 7-12). pap. 6.95 (*0-88436-054-7*, 65252) EMC.

Tresselt, Alvin. The Mitten. Mills, Yaroslava, illus. LC 64-14436. 30p. (ps up). 1989. pap. 4.95 (*0-688-09238-1*, Mulberry) Morrow.

Weinerman, Eli, tr. The Black Swans (a Russian Folktale) Parker, Robert A., illus. Weinerman, Eli, retold by. (Illus.). 32p. (gr. k-3). 1994. 14.95 (*0-945912-19-6*) Pippin Pr.

Werner, Vivian, retold by. Petrouchka. Collier, John, illus. 32p. (gr. 5 up). 1992. 16.00 (*0-670-83607-9*) Viking Child Bks.

Winthrop, Elizabeth, adapted by. Vasilissa the Beautiful: A Russian Folktale. Koshkin, Alexander, illus. LC 89-26903. 40p. (gr. 1-5). 1991. PLB 15.89 (*0-06-021663-8*) HarpC Child Bks.

Wolkstein, Diane. Oom Razoom or Go I Know Not Where, Bring Back I Know Not What. McDermott, Dennis, illus. LC 91-6308. 32p. (gr. k up). 1991. 14.95 (*0-688-09416-3*); PLB 14.88 (*0-688-09417-1*) Morrow Jr Bks.

FOLKLORE–SPAIN

Araujo, Frank P. Nekane, the Lamina & the Bear: A Tale of the Basque Pyrenees. Xiao Jun Li, illus. LC 93-84620. 32p. 1993. 16.95 (*1-877810-01-0*) Rayve Prodns.

Caperucita Roja. (SPA.). (gr. 2). 1990. casebound 3.50 (*0-7214-1409-5*) Ladybird Bks.

La Cenicienta. (SPA.). (gr. 3). 1990. casebound 3.50 (*0-7214-1405-2*) Ladybird Bks.

Los Duendes y el Zapatero. (SPA.). (gr. 1). 1990. casebound 3.50 (*0-7214-1411-7*) Ladybird Bks.

Guareschi. Don Camillo. (gr. 7-12). 1972. pap. 6.95 (*0-88436-121-7*, 55255) EMC.

Haviland, Virginia & Cohn, Amy, eds. Favorite Fairy Tales Told in Spain. Passicot, Monique, illus. LC 94-1499. (gr. 3 up). 1995. pap. 4.95 (*0-688-12605-7*, Beech Tree Bks) Morrow.

Irving, Washington. Spanish Papers. Irving, Pierre, ed. LC 78-74516. (gr. 7 up). 1979. Repr. of 1868 ed. 42.50x (*0-8486-0219-6*) Roth Pub Inc.

FOLKLORE–SWEDEN

Haviland, Virginia. Favorite Fairy Tales Told in Sweden. Cohn, Amy, ed. Van Rynbach, Iris, illus. LC 94-85. 72p. (gr. 2 up). 1994. pap. 4.95 (*0-688-12606-5*, Pub. by Beech Tree Bks) Morrow.

Langton, Jane. The Queen's Necklace: A Swedish Folktale. Plume, Ilse, illus. 40p. (gr. k-3). 1994. 15.95 (*0-7868-0011-9*); PLB 15.89 (*0-7868-2007-1*) Hyprn Child.

Schaefer, Carole L. Under the Midsummer Sky. Geddes, Pat, illus. 32p. (ps-3). 1994. 14.95 (*0-399-21858-0*, Whitebird Bks) Putnam Pub Group.

FOLKLORE–THAILAND

Hamada, Cheryl, retold by. Kao & the Golden Fish: A Folktale from Thailand. Liu, Monica, illus. LC 93-298. 32p. (ps-3). 1993. PLB 13.85 (*0-516-05145-8*); pap. 12.95 (*0-516-07093-2*) Childrens.

FOLKLORE–TIBET

Cook, Elizabeth, adapted by. Rabbit Who Overcame Fear: A Jataka Tale. Meller, Eric, illus. Tulku, Tarthang, intro. by. (Illus.). 32p. (Orig.). (gr. k-4). 1991. 14.95 (*0-89800-212-5*); pap. 7.95 (*0-89800-211-7*) Dharma Pub.

Gretchen, Sylvia, ed. & tr. from TIB. Hero of the Land of Snow. Witwer, Julia, illus. LC 89-25603. vi, 32p. (gr. 5-8). 1990. 14.95 (*0-89800-201-X*); pap. 7.95 (*0-89800-202-8*) Dharma Pub.

Hume, Lotta C. Favorite Children's Stories from China & Tibet. Lo-Koon-Chiu, illus. LC 61-6219. 120p. (gr. 1-4). 1962. pap. 14.95 (*0-8048-1605-0*) C E Tuttle.

Schroeder, Alan. The Stone Lion. Doney, Todd L., illus. LC 92-38257. 32p. (gr. 1-3). 1994. SBE 14.95 (*0-684-19578-X*, Scribners Young Read) Macmillan Child Grp.

Tulku, Chagdud. The Kind King & the Magnanimous Mice: A Tibetan Folktale. 1993. pap. 9.95 (*1-881847-03-9*) Chagdud Gonpa-Padma.

FOLKLORE–TURKEY

Walker, Barbara K. A Treasury of Turkish Folktales for Children. LC 88-6859. xii, 155p. (gr. 3 up). 1988. lib. bdg. 18.50 (*0-208-02206-6*, Linnet) Shoe String.

—Watermelons, Walnuts & the Wisdom of Allah: And Other Tales of the Hoca. Berson, Harold, illus. 72p. 1991. Repr. of 1967 ed. 17.50 (*0-89672-254-6*) Tex Tech Univ Pr.

Yolen, Jane, retold by. Little Mouse & Elephant: A Tale from Turkey. Segal, John, illus. LC 92-21748. 1994. 10.00 (*0-06-021502-X*, HarpT); PLB 9.89 (*0-06-021503-8*, HarpT) HarpC.

FOLKLORE–UKRAINE

Tresselt, Alvin R. Mitten. Mills, Yaroslava, illus. LC 64-14436. 30p. (gr. k-3). 1964. lib. bdg. 14.93 (*0-688-51053-1*) Lothrop.

FOLKLORE–U. S.

Ainsworth, Catherine H., ed. Folktales of America, Volume IV. 152p. (Orig.). (gr. 12). 1994. pap. 12.00 (*0-933190-16-6*) Clyde Pr.
Buffalo, New York - The Clyde Press announces the publication of FOLKTALES OF AMERICA, VOLUME IV, edited by Catherine Harris Ainsworth. During the 1960s & 1970s, Mrs. Ainsworth collected hundreds of folktales primarily from young adults in Michigan & western New York state. This volume contains 217 folktales that are organized into nine chapters: camp stories; coal mine tales; etiological or origin stories; campus, initiation, & pajama party stories; babysitting stories; ghosts, haunted houses, & witchcraft stories; tales of unexpected wind, noises, motions, & figures; premonition stories; & personal recollections. "The entire population of the United States is now exposed to books, television, & other forms of mass media, but the stories presented in FOLKTALES OF AMERICA, VOLUME IV, show that this country maintains a strong oral tradition," observes Mrs. Ainsworth. "The contributors heard these folktales from their friends & relatives, & they have so kindly passed them on to me. The stories are set in eighteen states & six foreign countries." FOLKTALES OF AMERICA, VOLUME IV, is now available. It is the latest volume in a series of American folktale publications. Volume IV: 152 pages; ISBN 0-933190-16-6; 5 1/2" x 8 1/2"; $12.00. 40% discount for two or more books. The Clyde Press currently offers fourteen books on American folklore subjects. Write for catalogue/ price list.
Publisher Provided Annotation.

Allen, Linda & Snider, Chrystle L., eds. Washington Songs & Lore. Green, Donald A., illus. 200p. (gr. 1-12). 1988. pap. 15.95 (*0-9616441-3-3*); Abridged ed., 72 pg. comb bdg. 8.95 (*0-9616441-4-1*) Melior Dist.

Anderson, J. I. I Can Read About Johnny Appleseed. Krasnoborski, William, illus. LC 76-54445. (gr. 2-5). 1977. pap. 2.50 (*0-89375-037-9*) Troll Assocs.

Bang, Molly G. Wiley & the Hairy Man: Adapted from an American Folk Tale. Bang, Molly G., illus. LC 87-2540. 64p. (gr. 1-4). 1987. pap. 3.95 (*0-689-71162-X*, Aladdin) Macmillan Child Grp.

Bierhorst, John, ed. The Naked Bear: Folktales of the Iroquois. Zimmer, Dirk, illus. LC 86-21836. 144p. (gr. 3 up). 1987. 14.95 (*0-688-06422-1*) Morrow Jr Bks.

Cech, John. Django. McGinley-Nally, Sharon, illus. LC 93-46782. (ps-3). 1994. 15.95 (*0-02-765705-1*, Four Winds) Macmillan Child Grp.

Chase, Richard. Grandfather Tales. (Illus.). 240p. (gr. 4-6). 1973. 17.45 (*0-395-06692-1*) HM.

—Grandfather Tales. (gr. 4-7). 1990. pap. 5.95 (*0-395-56150-7*) HM.

—Jack Tales. (Illus.). 202p. (gr. 4-6). 1943. 13.45 (*0-395-06694-8*) HM.

—Jack Tales. (gr. 4-7). 1993. pap. 4.95 (*0-395-66951-0*) HM.

Chisum, Elizabeth. Lizard Tales. (Illus.). 64p. (Orig.). 1993. pap. 8.95 (*0-86534-201-6*) Sunstone Pr.

Coleman, Larry G. Up from the Eagles' Nest. (Illus.). 44p. Date not set. 12.95 (*0-9629978-8-9*) Sights Prods.

Compton, Joanne. Ashpet: An Appalachian Tale. Compton, Kenn, illus. LC 93-16034. 40p. (ps-3). 1994. reinforced bdg. 15.95 (*0-8234-1106-0*) Holiday.

Compton, Kenn & Compton, Joanne. Jack the Giant Chaser: An Appalachian Tale. LC 92-15911. (Illus.). 32p. (ps-3). 1993. reinforced bdg. 14.95 (*0-8234-0998-8*) Holiday.

Davenport, Tom & Carden, Gary. From the Brothers Grimm: A Contemporary Retelling of American Folktales & Classic Stories. LC 92-30828. (Illus.). 105p. (gr. 2-12). 1993. pap. 12.95 (*0-917846-20-6*, 95526) Highsmith Pr.

Davidson, Sol M. Wild Jake Hiccup: The History of America's First Frontiersman. Davidson, Penny, illus. LC 91-19499. 160p. (Orig.). (gr. 2-9). 1992. 16.95 (*1-56412-003-1*); pap. 9.95 (*1-56412-004-X*); audio cassette 6.95 (*1-56412-001-5*) Hse Nine Muses.
"The story of our tallest unknown folk hero, from his early days in colonial western "Pennsylvanny" to his epic battle with the young Paul Bunyan. Jacob grew up to play no small role in history: he is credited with single-handedly driving the French from Fort Duquesne; suggesting a design for the U.S. flag based on George Washington's pajamas; making Mike Fink the victim of the first April Fool's joke; urging Audubon to add a few birds to his paintings; & inspiring John Chapman, later known as Johnny Peachfuzz - no, Johnny Peanutshell... Johnny Apricotpit something like that. The tale is told in "countrified" prose, illustrated with small, simple line drawings. Readers can absorb a fair dose of history while enjoying the droll adventures of this animal-loving, generally peaceable giant."--KIRKUS REVIEWS, Aug. 1, 1992. "DELICIOUS!"--Mrs. M. Cunningham, 3rd grade teacher, Wash., D.C. "DELIGHTFUL!"--R. Messineo, Administrator, Passaic, N.J. Schools. "CHARMING!"--Mr. J. Wodden, Curriculum Dir., Des Moines, IA, Public Schools. "This book is funny & full of historical information. Overall, this book is very good & on a scale of one to ten, I would give it an eight & a half."--Megan Melamed, Age 12, The Gifted Child Today Magazine (GCT). Also ENJOYING AMERICAN HISTORY: Teacher's Guide to the Mining the Rich Vein of Ideas in Wild Jake Hiccup. Over 200 stimulating projects to make learning American History FUN! 80 pages. Illustrated. ISBN 1-56412-002-3. (softcover.) $5.95. For librarians, parents, grandparents to use with youngsters. Also THE BALLAD OF WILD JAKE HICCUP, audio cassette. Approx. 40 mins. Original words & music composed by John Deltenre & his Pioneer Band. $6. 95. ISBN 1-56412-001-5.
Publisher Provided Annotation.

Davis, Donald. Jack Always Seeks His Fortune: Authentic Appalachian Jack Tales. Sodol, Joseph, intro. by. 176p. 1992. 21.95 (*0-87483-281-0*); pap. 11.95 (*0-87483-280-2*) August Hse.

DeSpain, Pleasant. Twenty-Two Splendid Tales, Vol. I. 128p. 1993. 12.95 (*0-87483-340-X*) August Hse.

—Twenty-Two Splendid Tales, Vol. II. 128p. 1994. 12.95 (*0-87483-341-8*) August Hse.

Durell, Ann, compiled by. The Diane Goode Book of American Folk Tales & Songs. Goode, Diane, illus. LC 89-1097. 64p. (ps-5). 1989. 14.95 (*0-525-44458-0*, DCB) Dutton Child Bks.

Edler, Timothy J. T-Boy in Mossland. (Illus.). 48p. (gr. k-8). 1978. pap. 6.00 (*0-931108-03-9*) Little Cajun Bks.

—T-Boy the Little Cajun. Judice, Van, illus. 36p. (gr. k-8). 1978. pap. 6.00 (*0-931108-01-2*) Little Cajun Bks.

Emberley, Barbara. The Story of Paul Bunyan. Emberley, Ed E., illus. LC 93-11791. 1994. pap. 14.00 (*0-671-88557-X*, S&S BFYR) S&S Trade.

—The Story of Paul Bunyan. Emberley, Ed, illus. LC 93-11791. 1994. pap. 5.95 (*0-671-88647-9*, Half Moon Bks) S&S Trade.

Faulkner, William J. Brer Tiger & the Big Wind. Wilson, Roberta, illus. LC 94-15408. 1995. write for info. (*0-688-12985-4*); PLB write for info. (*0-688-12986-2*) Morrow Jr Bks.

Ferguson, Joe. The Deathless White Stallion & Other Tales. Sky Rivers & Eakin, Edwin M., eds. Morris, Aaron, illus. 64p. (gr. 4-6). 1989. 10.95 (*0-89015-702-2*, Pub. by Panda Bks); pap. 3.95 (*0-89015-712-X*) Sunbelt Media.

Forest, Heather. Baker's Dozen: A Colonial American Tale. (ps-3). 1993. pap. 4.95 (*0-15-205687-4*, HB Juv Bks) HarBrace.

Fowke, Edith, ed. Paul Bunyan: Superhero of the Lumberjacks. (Illus.). 112p. (Orig.). Date not set. pap. 6.95 (*0-919601-63-4*, Pub. by NC Press CN) U of Toronto Pr.

Galbreath, Bob. Tennessee Red Berry Tales. Garrett, Deborah G., ed. 97p. (Orig.). (gr. 3 up). 1986. pap. 7.95 (*0-9616918-0-8*) Whites Creek Pr.

Gianni, Gary, retold by. & illus. John Henry. 32p. (gr. 6 up). 1989. 9.95 (*0-943718-18-X*) Kipling Pr.

Gleeson, Brian. Paul Bunyan. Meyerowitz, Rick, illus. 64p. 1993. Repr. of 1990 ed. incl. cass. 9.95 (*0-88708-303-X*, Rabbit Ears); 5.95 (*0-88708-302-1*, Rabbit Ears) Picture Bk Studio.

Gleiter, Jan & Thompson, Kathleen. Casey Jones. Balistreri, Francis, illus. 32p. (gr. 2-5). 1987. PLB 19.97 (*0-8172-2653-2*) Raintree Steck-V.

Haley, Gail E., illus. Mountain Jack Tales. 144p. (gr. 3-8). 1992. 15.99 (*0-525-44974-4*, DCB) Dutton Child Bks.

Hamilton, Virginia. The People Could Fly. Dillon, Leo & Dillon, Diane, illus. LC 84-25020. 192p. (ps-12). 1985. 18.00 (*0-394-86925-7*); lib. bdg. 18.99 (*0-394-96925-1*) Knopf Bks Yng Read.

Harper, Wilhelmina, ed. Gunniwolf. Wiesner, William, illus. LC 67-22387. 32p. (ps-3). 1970. 13.00 (*0-525-31139-4*, DCB) Dutton Child Bks.

Harris, Joel C. Brer Rabbit & the Wonderful Tar Baby. Drescher, Henrik, illus. 64p. 1992. Repr. of 1990 ed. Mini-bk. incl. cass. 9.95 (*0-88708-250-5*, Rabbit Ears) Picture Bk Studio.

—Uncle Remus & Br'er Rabbit. 1986. Repr. lib. bdg. 17.95x (*0-89966-540-3*) Buccaneer Bks.

Harris, Joel C. & Metaxas, Eric, eds. Brer Rabbit & the Wonderful Tar Baby. Drescher, Henrik, illus. LC 90-7166. 32p. (gr. k up). 1991. pap. 14.95 (*0-88708-144-4*, Rabbit Ears); pap. 19.95 incl. cass. (*0-88708-145-2*, Rabbit Ears) Picture Bk Studio.

Haskins, James. The Headless Haunt & Other African-American Ghost Stories. Otera, Ben, illus. LC 93-26223. 128p. (gr. 3-7). 1994. 14.00 (*0-06-022994-2*); PLB 13.89 (*0-06-022997-7*) HarpC Child Bks.

Hayes, Joe. La Llorona. Treog-Hill, Vicki, illus. 32p. (Orig.). (gr. 1-9). 1986. pap. 4.95 (*0-938317-02-4*) Cinco Puntos.

—That's Not Fair! Earth Friendly Tales. (Illus.). 32p. (Orig.). (gr. k-6). 1991. pap. 5.95 (*0-939729-21-0*) Trails West Pub.

High, Linda R. & Kindt, Carol L. Once upon a Folk Tale: Eight Classic Stories with Easy Songs & Stick Puppet Drawings. Bennett, Michael D., ed. (Illus.). 60p. (Orig.). (gr. 1-4). 1994. pap. text ed. 11.95 (*0-934017-20-4*) Memphis Musicraft.

Hooks, William H. Snowbear Whittington. Lisi, Victoria, illus. LC 93-8691. (gr. 1-5). 1994. 15.95 (*0-02-744355-8*) Macmillan.

Hunter, C. W. The Green Gourd: A North Carolina Folktale. Griego, Tony, illus. 32p. (ps-3). 1992. PLB 14.95 (*0-399-22278-2*, Whitebird Bks) Putnam Pub Group.

Jaquith, Priscilla, as told by. Bo Rabbit Smart for True: Tall Tales from the Gullah. LC 93-50596. 1994. 17.95 (*0-399-22668-0*, Philomel Bks) Putnam Pub Group.

Jensen, Patricia A. John Henry & His Mighty Hammer. Litzinger, Roseanne, illus. LC 93-4810. 32p. (gr. k-2). 1993. PLB 11.59 (*0-8167-3156-X*); pap. text ed. 2.95 (*0-8167-3157-8*) Troll Assocs.

—Paul Bunyan & His Blue Ox. Pidgeon, Jean L., illus. LC 93-24802. 32p. (gr. k-2). 1993. PLB 11.59 (*0-8167-3162-4*); pap. text ed. 2.95 (*0-8167-3163-2*) Troll Assocs.

—Pecos Bill, the Roughest, Toughest Best. Mahan, Benton, illus. LC 93-2217. 32p. (gr. k-2). 1993. PLB 11.59 (*0-8167-3165-9*); pap. text ed. 2.95 (*0-8167-3166-7*) Troll Assocs.

Johnson, Frances. Coyote Tales: How the Sandbur Came to West Texas. Zweiger, Jackie, illus. 32p. (gr. 1-3). 1992. 11.95 (*0-89015-866-5*) Sunbelt Media.

Kellogg, Steven. Paul Bunyan. Marcuse, Aida, tr. from ENG. Kellogg, Steven, illus. (SPA.). 48p. (gr. k up). 1994. pap. 5.95 (*0-688-13202-2*, Mulberry) Morrow.

—Pecos Bill. ALC Staff, ed. LC 86-784. (Illus.). 32p. (gr. k up). 1992. pap. 4.95 (*0-688-09924-6*, Mulberry) Morrow.

Kidd, Ronald. On Top of Old Smoky: A Collection of Songs & Stories from Appalachia. Anderson, Linda, illus. LC 92-14437. 40p. 1992. 13.95 (*0-8249-8569-9*, Ideals Child); PLB 14.00 (*0-8249-8586-9*); incl. 60-min. cassette 17.95 (*0-8249-7513-8*) Hambleton-Hill.

Krauss, Ruth. A Very Special House. Sendak, Maurice, illus. LC 53-7115. 32p. (ps-1). 1990. pap. 4.95 (*0-06-443228-9*, Trophy) HarpC Child Bks.

Lester, Julius. John Henry. Pinkney, Jerry, illus. LC 93-34583. 40p. (ps-3). 1994. 16.99 (*0-8037-1606-0*); PLB 16.89 (*0-8037-1607-9*) Dial Bks Young.

Lester, Julius & Fogelman, Phyllis J., eds. Further Tales of Uncle Remus: The Misadventures of Brer Rabbit, Brer Fox, Brer Wolf, the Doodang, & All the Other Creatures. Pinkney, Jerry, illus. LC 88-20223. 160p. (ps up). 1990. 15.00 (*0-8037-0610-3*); PLB 14.89 (*0-8037-0611-1*) Dial Bks Young.

Littledale, Freya. Rip Van Winkle. Dooling, Mike, illus. 40p. 1991. pap. 3.95 (*0-590-43113-7*) Scholastic Inc.

Lobel, Arnold. Fables. Lobel, Arnold, illus. LC 79-2004. 48p. (gr. 1-4). 1980. 15.00 (*0-06-023973-5*); PLB 14. 89 (*0-06-023974-3*) HarpC Child Bks.

Ludwig, Warren. Good Morning, Granny Rose: An Arkansas Folktale. (Illus.). 32p. (ps-3). 1990. 13.95 (*0-399-21950-1*, Putnam) Putnam Pub Group.

Lyman, Nanci A. Paul Bunyan. new ed. LC 79-66320. (Illus.). 48p. (gr. 3-6). 1980. lib. bdg. 9.89 (*0-89375-310-6*); pap. 2.95 (*0-89375-309-2*) Troll Assocs.

—Pecos Bill. LC 79-66319. (Illus.). 48p. (gr. 3-6). 1980. lib. bdg. 9.89 (*0-89375-308-4*); pap. 2.95 (*0-89375-307-6*) Troll Assocs.

Lyons, Mary. The Butter Tree. 1995. write for info. (*0-8050-2673-8*) H Holt & Co.

McGrath, Patrick, retold by. Johnny Appleseed. Riccio, Frank, illus. 32p. (gr. 1 up). 1989. Kipling Pr.

—Pecos Bill. Lewis, T., illus. 32p. (gr. 1 up). 1989. Kipling Pr.

McKissack, Patricia C. A Million Fish...More or Less. Schutzer, Dena, illus. LC 90-34322. 40p. (ps-3). 1992. 14.00 (*0-679-80692-X*); PLB 14.99 (*0-679-90692-4*) Knopf Bks Yng Read.

Milord, Susan. Tales Alive! Ten Multicultural Folk Tales, with Art, Craft & Creative Experiences. Donato, Michael, illus. 128p. (Orig.). (gr. k-6). 1994. pap. 15. 95 (*0-913589-79-9*) Williamson Pub Co.

Moore, Mary S. Fireside Tales. Clay, Cliff, illus. 21p. (Orig.). (gr. 5-12). 1990. pap. 7.95 (*0-913678-18-X*); paper & audiocassette 10.00 (*0-913678-19-8*) New Day Pr.

Naden, C. J. John Henry, the Steeldriving Man. new ed. LC 79-66317. (Illus.). 48p. (gr. 3-6). 1980. lib. bdg. 9.89 (*0-89375-304-1*); pap. 2.95 (*0-89375-303-3*) Troll Assocs.

Nunis & Knill, Harry. Tales of Mexican California. (gr. 1-9). 1994. pap. 8.95 (*0-88388-161-6*) Bellerophon Bks.

Osborne, Mary P. American Tall Tales. McCurdy, Michael, illus. LC 89-37235. 128p. (gr. 1 up). 1991. 18.00 (*0-679-80089-1*); lib. bdg. 18.99 (*0-679-90089-6*) Knopf Bks Yng Read.

Pagnucci, Susan & Pagnucci, Franco. Do Me! Stories. (Illus.). 64p. (Orig.). (gr. k-3). Date not set. pap. 8.95 (*0-929326-07-5*) Bur Oak Pr Inc.

Paul Bunyan. (Illus.). 20p. (ps up). 1992. write for info. incl. long-life batteries (*0-307-74712-3*, 64712, Golden Pr) Western Pub.

Petersham, Maud & Petersham, Miska. The Rooster Crows: A Book of American Rhymes & Jingles. Petersham, Maud & Petersham, Miska, illus. LC 46-446. 64p. (ps-2). 1969. RSBE 14.95 (*0-02-773100-6*, Macmillan Child Bk) Macmillan Child Grp.

Rees, Ennis. Brer Rabbit & His Tricks. Gorey, Edward, illus. LC 93-32674. 48p. (ps-4). 1994. pap. 5.95 (*1-56282-577-1*) Hyprn Ppbks.

—More of Brer Rabbit's Tricks. Gorey, Edward, illus. LC 93-32676. 48p. (ps-4). 1994. pap. 5.95 (*1-56282-578-X*) Hyprn Ppbks.

Reneaux, J. J. Cajun Folktales. 176p. (gr. 5 up). 1992. 19. 95 (*0-87483-283-7*); pap. 9.95 (*0-87483-282-9*) August Hse.

Robertson, Brian. Brian Robertson's Favorite Texas Tales. Wilson, J. Kay, illus. LC 92-17115. 112p. (gr. 4-7). 1992. 12.95 (*0-89015-862-2*) Sunbelt Media.

Sanfield, Steve. The Adventures of High John the Conqueror. Ward, John, illus. LC 88-17946. 128p. (gr. 3 up). 1989. 12.95 (*0-531-05807-7*); PLB 12.99 (*0-531-08407-8*) Orchard Bks Watts.

—A Natural Man: The True Story of John Henry. Thornton, Peter, illus. LC 85-45965. 32p. (gr. 2-6). 1990. pap. 9.95 (*0-87923-844-5*) Godine.

San Souci, Robert. Cut from the Same Cloth: American Women of Myth, Legend & Tall Tale. Pinkney, Brian, illus. 144p. (gr. 5 up). 1993. 16.95 (*0-399-21987-0*, Philomel Bks) Putnam Pub Group.

San Souci, Robert D. Donkey Ears. Vanden Broeck, Fabricio, illus. LC 93-36333. 1994. 14.95 (*0-399-22694-X*, Philomel Bks) Putnam Pub Group.

—The Hired Hand. Pinkney, Jerry, photos by. LC 93-36285. (Illus.). 1994. write for info. (*0-8037-1296-0*); lib. bdg. write for info. (*0-8037-1297-9*) Dial Bks Young.

—Legend of Sleepy Hollow. San Souci, Daniel, illus. LC 86-2064. 32p. (ps-3). 1986. 11.95 (*0-385-23396-5*, Zephyr-BFYR); PLB 11.95 (*0-385-23397-3*, Zephyr-BFYR) Doubleday.

—Talking Eggs. 1989. PLB 14.89 (*0-8037-0620-0*) Dial Bks Young.

San Souci, Robert D., retold by. Two White Pebbles. LC 93-43952. 1995. write for info. (*0-8037-1640-0*); PLB write for info. (*0-8037-1641-9*) Dial Bks Young.

Schwartz, Alvin. Flapdoodle: Pure Nonsense from American Folklore. O'Brien, John, illus. LC 79-9618. 128p. (gr. 5 up). 1980. PLB 13.89 (*0-397-31920-7*, Lipp Jr Bks) HarpC Child Bks.

Schwartz, Alvin, ed. Whoppers: Tall Tales & Other Lies Collected from American Folklore. Rounds, Glen, illus. LC 74-32024. 128p. (gr. 4 up). 1990. pap. 3.95 (*0-06-446091-6*, Trophy) HarpC Child Bks.

Shay, Kevin J. The Lone Writer & Blazing Bonzo: Tall Universal Tales. LC 93-93626. (Illus.). 52p. (gr. 6-10). 1993. pap. 2.95 (*1-881365-71-9*) Shay Pubns.

Shepard, Aaron. The Baker's Dozen: A St. Nicholas Tale. Edelson, Wendy, photos by. LC 92-38261. (gr. 1-8). 1995. 15.00 (*0-684-19577-1*, Scribners Young Read) Macmillan Child Grp.

Shepard, Aaron, retold by. The Legend of Slappy Hooper. LC 92-18153. (Illus.). 32p. (gr. 1-3). 1993. SBE 14.95 (*0-684-19535-6*, Scribners Young Read) Macmillan Child Grp.

Shephard, Esther. Paul Bunyan. LC 85-5448. (Illus.). 233p. (gr. 7 up). 1985. pap. 6.95 (*0-15-259755-7*, Voyager Bks) HarBrace.

Stevens, Janet, adapted by. & illus. Tops & Bottoms. LC 93-19154. (ps-6). 1994. write for info. (*0-15-292851-0*) HarBrace.

The Storytelling - Folklore Series. rev. ed. 1992. pap. write for info. (*0-938756-99-0*) Yellow Moon.

Varney, Sharon. Cranberry Ridge Tales. 72p. (Orig.). (gr. 7 up). 1986. pap. 7.95 (*0-685-17323-2*) S Varney.

Wahl, Jan. Tailypo! Clay, Wil, illus. LC 90-39491. 32p. (ps-2). 1991. 14.95 (*0-8050-0687-7*, Bks Young Read) H Holt & Co.

Walker, Paul R. Big Men, Big Country: A Collection of American Tall Tales. LC 91-45128. (gr. 4-7). 1993. 16. 95 (*0-15-207136-9*) HarBrace.

Whedbee, Charles H. Legends of the Outer Banks & Tar Heel Tidewater. LC 66-23049. (Illus.). 165p. (gr. 5 up). 1979. 9.95 (*0-910244-41-3*) Blair.

York, Carol B. Casey Jones. new ed. LC 79-66313. (Illus.). 48p. (gr. 3-6). 1980. PLB 9.89 (*0-89375-298-3*); pap. 2.95 (*0-89375-297-5*) Troll Assocs.

—Johnny Appleseed. LC 79-66312. (Illus.). 48p. (gr. 3-6). 1980. lib. bdg. 9.89 (*0-89375-296-7*); pap. 2.95 (*0-89375-295-9*) Troll Assocs.

—Mike Fink. LC 79-66315. (Illus.). 48p. (gr. 3-6). 1980. lib. bdg. 9.89 (*0-89375-302-5*); pap. 2.95 (*0-89375-301-7*) Troll Assocs.

—Old Stormalong: The Seafaring Sailor. LC 79-66322. (Illus.). 48p. (gr. 3-6). 1980. lib. bdg. 9.89 (*0-89375-314-9*); pap. 2.95 (*0-89375-313-0*) Troll Assocs.

—Sam Patch, the Big Time Jumper. new ed. LC 79-66318. (Illus.). 48p. (gr. 3-6). 1980. lib. bdg. 9.89 (*0-89375-306-8*); pap. 2.95 (*0-89375-305-X*) Troll Assocs.

Zorn, Steven. Classic American Folk Tales. LC 91-58125. (Illus.). 56p. 1992. 9.98 (*1-56138-062-8*) Courage Bks.

FOLKLORE–VIETNAM

Garland, Sherry. Why Ducks Sleep on One Leg. Tseng, Jean & Tseng, Mou-sien, illus. LC 92-9709. 32p. (ps-3). 1993. 14.95 (*0-590-45697-0*) Scholastic Inc.

Graham, Gail B. The Beggar in the Blanket. Bryan, Brigitte, illus. LC 77-85548. 96p. (gr. 1-5). 1988. PLB 12.89 (*0-8037-0663-4*) Dial Bks Young.

Hamada, Cheryl, retold by. The Farmer, the Buffalo, & the Tiger: A Folktale from Vietnam. Regan, Rick, illus. LC 93-21725. 32p. (ps-3). 1993. PLB 12.85 (*0-516-05143-1*) Childrens.

Lum, Darrell. The Golden Slipper: A Vietnamese Legend. Nagano, Makiko, illus. LC 93-33588. 32p. (gr. 2-5). 1994. PLB 11.89 (*0-8167-3405-4*); pap. text ed. 3.95 (*0-8167-3406-2*) Troll Assocs.

Vuong, Lynette D. The Brocaded Slipper & Other Vietnamese Tales. Vo, Dinh M., illus. LC 84-40746. 96p. (gr. 3-7). 1992. PLB 13.89 (*0-397-32508-8*, Lipp Jr Bks) HarpC Child Bks.

—The Brocaded Slipper & Other Vietnamese Tales. Vo-Dinh Mai, illus. LC 81-19139. 128p. (gr. 2-5). 1992. pap. 3.95 (*0-06-440440-4*, Trophy) HarpC Child Bks.

—The Golden Carp, & Other Tales of Vietnam. Saito, Manabu, illus. LC 92-38208. 128p. (gr. k-5). 1993. 15. 00 (*0-688-12514-X*) Lothrop.

—Sky Legends of Vietnam. Vo-Dinh Mai, illus. LC 92-38345. 128p. (gr. 4 up). 1993. 14.00 (*0-06-023000-2*); PLB 13.89 (*0-06-023001-0*) HarpC Child Bks.

FOLKLORE–WALES

Cooper, Susan. The Silver Cow: A Welsh Tale. Hutton, Warwick, illus. LC 91-234. 32p. (gr. k-3). 1991. pap. 4.95 (*0-689-71512-9*, Aladdin) Macmillan Child Grp.

Jones, T. Llew. One Moonlit Night. Clarke, Gillian, tr. 108p. 1991. 70.00x (*0-86383-627-5*, Pub. by Gomer Pr UK) St Mut.

Kerven, Rosalind, retold by. The Woman Who Went to Fairyland: A Welsh Folk Tale. De Lacey, Honey, illus. LC 91-40382. 32p. (gr. k-3). 1992. PLB 14.95 (*0-87226-466-1*, Bedrick Blackie) P Bedrick Bks.

FOLKLORE–WEST INDIES

Berry, James. Spiderman Anancy. Olubo, Joseph, illus. LC 89-33418. 148p. (gr. 4-6). 1989. 13.95 (*0-8050-1207-9*, Bks Young Read) H Holt & Co.

Bryan, Ashley, retold by. & illus. Turtle Knows Your Name. LC 92-33553. 32p. (ps-3). 1993. pap. 4.95 (*0-689-71728-8*, Aladdin) Macmillan Child Grp.

De Sauza, James, as told by. Brother Anansi & the Cattle Ranch: (El Hermano Anansi y el Rancho) Zubizarreta, Rosalma, tr. Rohmer, Harriet, adapted by. Von Mason, Stephen, illus. LC 88-37091. (SPA & ENG.). 32p. (ps-7). 1989. 13.95 (*0-89239-044-1*) Childrens Book Pr.

San Souci, Robert D. The Faithful Friend. 1st ed. Pinkney, Brian, illus. LC 93-40672. 1995. 16.00 (*0-02-786131-7*, Four Winds) Macmillan Child Grp.

Sherlock, Philip M. West Indian Folk Tales. Kiddell-Monroe, Joan, illus. 151p. (gr. 3 up). 1988. pap. 10.95 (*0-19-274127-6*) OUP.

FOLKWAYS

see Manners and Customs

FOOD

see also Beverages; Cookery; Diet; Farm Produce; Fruit; Nutrition; Nuts; Poultry; Vegetables; Vegetarianism; Vitamins

also names of foods, e.g. Bread, etc.

Anderson, Margaret J. Food Chains: The Unending Cycle. LC 90-3282. (Illus.). 64p. (gr. 6 up). 1991. lib. bdg. 15.95 (*0-89490-290-3*) Enslow Pubs.

Ask about the World of Food. (Illus.). 64p. (gr. 4-5). 1987. PLB 11.95 (*0-8172-2885-3*) Raintree Steck-V.

Badt, Karin L. Good Morning, Let's Eat. LC 94-12645. (Illus.). 32p. (gr. 3-7). 1994. PLB 17.20 (*0-516-08190-X*); pap. 5.95 (*0-516-48190-8*) Childrens.

Baldwin, Dorothy. Health & Food. (Illus.). 32p. (gr. 3-8). 1987. PLB 17.27 (*0-86592-294-2*); 12.95s.p. (*0-685-67608-0*) Rourke Corp.

Berger, Melvin. From Peanuts to Peanut Butter: Student Edition. (Illus.). 16p. (ps-2). 1993. pap. text ed. 14.95 (*1-56784-026-4*) Newbridge Comms.

—Growing Pumpkins. (Illus.). 16p. (ps-2). 1994. pap. text ed. 14.95 (*1-56784-018-3*) Newbridge Comms.

—Make Mine Ice Cream: Student Edition. (Illus.). 16p. (ps-2). 1993. pap. text ed. 14.95 (*1-56784-032-9*) Newbridge Comms.

—Pasta, Please! (Illus.). 16p. (ps-2). 1994. pap. text ed. 14.95 (*1-56784-021-3*) Newbridge Comms.

—You Are What You Eat. (Illus.). 16p. (ps-2). 1994. pap. text ed. 14.95 (*1-56784-014-0*) Newbridge Comms.

Bonar, Veronica & Daniel, Jamie, eds. Coping with - Food Trash. Kenyon, Tony, illus. LC 93-32478. 1994. 17.27 (*0-8368-1056-2*) Gareth Stevens Inc.

Brooks, F. Food & Eating. (Illus.). 24p. (gr. 2-4). 1989. lib. bdg. 11.96 (*0-88110-399-3*, Usborne); pap. 3.95 (*0-7460-0452-4*, Usborne) EDC.

Burns, Diane. Sugaring Season: Making Maple Syrup. (ps-3). 1992. pap. 5.95 (*0-87614-554-3*) Carolrhoda Bks.

Burns, Marilyn. Good for Me! All about Food in 32 Bites. Clifford, Sandy, illus. LC 78-6727. (gr. 5 up). 1978. pap. 9.95 (*0-316-11747-1*) Little.

Cahill, Robert E. Olde New England's Sugar & Spice & Everything... America's First Cookbook & Food History. Cahill, Keri M., ed. (Illus.). 63p. (Orig.). 1991. pap. 3.95 (*0-9626162-2-2*) Old Saltbox Pub Hse.

Carle, Eric. Today Is Monday. Carle, Eric, illus. 32p. (ps-3). 1993. 14.95 (*0-399-21966-8*, Philomel Bks) Putnam Pub Group.

Carratello, Patricia. Food & Nutrition. Carratello, Patricia, illus. 40p. (gr. 1-4). 1980. wkbk. 6.95 (*1-55734-212-1*) Tchr Create Mat.

Clark, Elizabeth. Fish. (Illus.). 32p. (gr. 1-4). 1990. PLB 14.95 (*0-87614-376-1*) Carolrhoda Bks.

—Meat. (Illus.). 32p. (gr. 1-4). 1990. PLB 14.95 (*0-87614-375-3*) Carolrhoda Bks.

Clark, Raymond C. Potluck: Exploring American Foods & Meals. rev. ed. (Illus.). 128p. (gr. 5 up). 1994. text ed. 10.50x (*0-86647-084-0*) Pro Lingua.

Corey, Melinda. Let's Visit a Spaghetti Factory. Emmerich, Donald, illus. LC 89-5110. 32p. (gr. 2-4). 1990. PLB 10.79 (*0-8167-1741-9*); pap. text ed. 2.95 (*0-8167-1742-7*) Troll Assocs.

D'Amico, J. & Drummond, Karen E. The Science Chef: One Hundred Fun Food Experiments & Recipes for Kids. Cash-Walsh, Tina, illus. LC 94-9045. 1994. pap. text ed. 12.95 (*0-471-31045-X*) Wiley.

Davenport, Zoe. Mealtimes. LC 94-20820. (ps). 1995. 4.95 (*0-395-71536-9*) Ticknor & Flds Bks Yng Read.

Davis, Kay & Oldsfield, Wendy. Food. LC 91-30068. (Illus.). 32p. (gr. 2-5). 1991. PLB 19.97 (*0-8114-3005-7*); pap. 4.95 (*0-8114-1533-3*) Raintree Steck-V.

De Paola, Tomie. The Popcorn Book. LC 77-21456. (Illus.). 32p. (ps-3). 1978. reinforced bdg. 15.95 (*0-8234-0314-9*); pap. 5.95 (*0-8234-0533-8*) Holiday.

Dibble, Lisa. Food & Farming. LC 93-19073. (gr. 4 up). 1993. write for info. (*1-56458-387-2*) Dorling Kindersley.

Dineen, Jacqueline. Chocolate. (Illus.). 32p. (gr. 1-4). 1991. PLB 14.95 (*0-87614-657-4*) Carolrhoda Bks.

Eating. 1988. pap. 3.95 (*0-553-05463-5*) Bantam.

Food: Feasts, Cooks, & Kitchens. (Illus.). 48p. (gr. 5-8). 1994. PLB 13.90 (*0-531-14312-0*) Watts.

Fowler, Allan. If It Weren't for Farmers. LC 92-35055. (Illus.). 32p. (ps-2). 1993. PLB 10.75 (*0-516-06009-0*); pap. 3.95 (*0-516-46009-9*) Childrens.

Geraghty, Paul. Over the Steamy Swamp. Geraghty, Paul, illus. 28p. (ps-1). 1989. 13.95 (*0-15-200561-7*, Gulliver Bks) HarBrace.

Goodwin, Mary T. & Pollen, Gerry. Creative Food Experiences for Children. 2nd rev. ed. Versel, Lauren, illus. 256p. (gr. k-6). 1980. pap. 7.95 (*0-89329-027-0*) Ctr Sci Public.

Hausherr, Rosmarie. What Food is This? LC 93-17328. (Illus.). 40p. (ps-3). 1994. 14.95 (*0-590-46583-X*) Scholastic Inc.

Haycock, Kate. Pasta. (Illus.). 32p. (gr. 1-4). 1991. PLB 13.50 (*0-87614-656-6*) Carolrhoda Bks.

Hemsley, William. Feeding to Digestion: Projects with Biology. LC 91-35075. (Illus.). 32p. (gr. 5-9). 1992. PLB 12.40 (*0-531-17327-5*, Gloucester Pr) Watts.

Hopkins, Lee B., ed. Munching: Poems about Eating. Davis, Nelle, illus. 48p. (gr. 3-6). 1985. 14.95 (*0-316-37269-2*) Little.

Horwitz, Joshua. Night Markets: Bringing Food to a City. Horwitz, Joshua, illus. LC 85-45401. 96p. (gr. 2-6). 1986. pap. 6.95 (*0-06-446046-0*, Trophy) HarpC Child Bks.
Illsley, Linda. Cheese. (Illus.). 32p. (gr. 1-4). 1991. PLB 14.95 (*0-87614-654-X*) Carolrhoda Bks.
Jennings, Terry. Food. LC 88-22866. (Illus.). 32p. (gr. 3-6). 1989. pap. 4.95 (*0-516-48402-8*) Childrens.
Johnson, Sylvia A. Potatoes. Suzuki, Masaharu, illus. 48p. (gr. 4 up). 1984. lib. bdg. 19.95 (*0-8225-1459-1*) Lerner Pubns.
Jones, Norma, et al, eds. Food: What Do We Eat & Where Does It Come From? 52p. (gr. 6-9). 1992. pap. text ed. 11.95 (*1-878623-43-5*) Info Plus TX.
Kalman, Bobbie. The Food We Eat. (Illus.). 32p. (gr. 2-3). 1986. 15.95 (*0-86505-073-2*); pap. 7.95 (*0-86505-095-3*) Crabtree Pub Co.
Kelley, True. Let's Eat. Kelley, True, illus. LC 88-25699. 32p. (ps-1). 1989. 11.95 (*0-525-44482-3*, DCB) Dutton Child Bks.
Kerrod, Robin. Food Resources. LC 93-34612. (Illus.). 32p. (gr. 4-7). 1994. 14.95 (*1-56847-108-4*) Thomson Lrning.
Killeen, Leah R. Rainbow Fruit Salad. Killeen, Leah R., illus. 32p. (ps-2). Date not set. 11.95 (*1-56065-155-5*) Capstone Pr.
Kolodny, Nancy J. When Food's a Foe: How to Confront & Conquer Eating Disorders. rev. ed. 192p. (gr. 7 up). 1992. pap. 7.95 (*0-316-50181-6*) Little.
Kowtaluk, Helen. Discovering Food. (gr. 7-9). 1982. 14. 00 (*0-02-663350-7*) Bennett IL.
Lambert, Mark. Food Technology. LC 91-7982. (Illus.). 48p. (gr. 5-7). 1992. PLB 12.90 (*0-531-18400-5*, Pub. by Bookwright Pr) Watts.
Lambourne, Mike. Down the Hatch! Find Out about Your Food. LC 91-22686. (Illus.). 40p. (gr. 2-6). 1992. PLB 13.40 (*1-56294-150-X*) Millbrook Pr.
Lanton, Sandy. Baby's Dinner. Clark, Linda F., illus. 32p. (ps-2). Date not set. 11.95 (*1-56065-145-8*) Capstone Pr.
Lauber, Patricia. Who Eats What. Keller, Holly, illus. LC 93-10609. (ps-6). 1995. 15.00 (*0-06-022981-0*); PLB 14.89 (*0-06-022982-9*) HarpC Child Bks.
Llewellyn, Claire. First Look at Growing Food. LC 91-9424. (Illus.). 32p. (gr. 1-2). 1991. PLB 17.27 (*0-8368-0678-6*) Gareth Stevens Inc.
Loewen. International Food Library, 6 bks, Set II. 1991. 71.70s.p. (*0-86625-324-6*) Rourke Pubns.
Lynn, Sara & James, Diane. What We Eat. Wright, Joe, illus. LC 93-35627. 32p. (gr. k-2). 1994. 14.95 (*1-56847-141-6*) Thomson Lrning.
McCoy, J. J. How Safe Is Our Food Supply? LC 90-35043. (Illus.). 144p. (gr. 7-12). 1990. PLB 13.90 (*0-531-10935-6*) Watts.
Machotka, Hana. Pasta Factory. Machotka, Hana, illus. LC 92-4333. 32p. (ps-3). 1992. 14.45 (*0-395-60197-5*) HM.
Marshall, David. Food. Young, Richard, ed. LC 91-20535. (Illus.). 32p. (gr. 3-5). 1991. PLB 15.93 (*1-56074-011-6*) Garrett Ed Corp.
Miller, Susanna. Beans & Peas. Yeats, John, illus. 32p. (gr. 1-4). 1990. PLB 14.95 (*0-87614-428-8*) Carolrhoda Bks.
Mumaw, Catherine & Voran, Marilyn. The Whole Thing. 24p. (gr. 6-11). 1981. pap. 1.50 (*0-8361-1962-2*) Herald Pr.
Nottridge, Rhoda. Apples. (Illus.). 32p. (gr. 1-4). 1991. PLB 14.95 (*0-87614-655-8*) Carolrhoda Bks.
Ontario Science Center Staff. Foodworks: Over One Hundred Science Activities & Fascinating Facts That Explore the Magic of Food. LC 87-1796. 96p. (gr. 7-12). 1987. pap. 8.61 (*0-201-11470-4*) Addison-Wesley.
Parker, Steve. Food & Digestion. rev. ed. (Illus.). 48p. (gr. 5 up). 1991. pap. 6.95 (*0-531-24603-5*) Watts.
Patent, Dorothy H. Where Food Comes From. Munoz, William, illus. LC 90-49833. 40p. (gr. 3-7). 1991. reinforced 14.95 (*0-8234-0877-9*) Holiday.
Perl, Lila. Junk Food, Fast Food, Health Food: What America Eats & Why. 192p. (gr. 5 up). 1980. 14.45 (*0-395-29108-9*, Clarion Bks) HM.
—Slumps, Grunts, & Snickerdoodles: What Colonial America Ate & Why. Cuffari, Richard, illus. LC 75-4894. 128p. (gr. 6 up). 1979. 14.95 (*0-395-28923-8*, Clarion Bks) HM.
Pienkowski, Jan. Food. Pienkowski, Jan, illus. 24p. (ps-k). 1991. pap. 2.95 (*0-671-72845-8*, Little Simon) S&S Trade.
Pifer, Joanne. EarthWise: Environmental Learning Series, Vol. 1. (Illus.). 216p. (gr. 5-8). 1993. Incl. Earth's Trees, Sunlight, Earth's Oceans, Earth's Energy, Earth's Food. pap. text ed. 24.95 (*0-9633019-5-0*) WP Pr.
Reece, Colleen L. What Was It Before It Was Ice Cream? Axeman, Lois, illus. LC 85-13262. 32p. (ps-2). 1985. PLB 14.95 (*0-89565-325-7*) Childs World.
Rothman, Cynthia. Bread Around the World. 16p. (ps-2). 1994. pap. 14.95 (*1-56784-301-8*) Newbridge Comms.
Sanders, Peter A., Jr. Food & Hygiene. LC 90-3246. (Illus.). 32p. (gr. 2-5). 1990. PLB 11.40 (*0-531-17243-0*, Gloucester Pr) Watts.
Seelig, Tina L. Incredible Edible Science: The Amazing Things That Happen When You Cook. Brunelle, Lynn, illus. LC 93-33480. 1994. text ed. write for info. (*0-7167-6501-2*, Sci Am Yng Rdrs); pap. text ed. write for info. (*0-7167-6507-1*) W H Freeman.
Seixas, Judith S. Junk Food--What It Is, What It Does. Huffman, Tom, illus. LC 83-14135. 48p. (gr. 1-3). 1984. 12.95 (*0-688-02559-5*); PLB 12.88 (*0-688-02560-9*) Greenwillow.
Shone, Venice. My Lunch Box. Shone, Venice, illus. LC 93-3287. 20p. (ps). 1993. 2.99 (*0-525-67451-9*, Lodestar Bks) Dutton Child Bks.
Shott, Stephen, photos by. Mealtime. LC 91-2600. (Illus.). 12p. (ps). 1991. bds. 4.95 (*0-525-44756-3*, DCB) Dutton Child Bks.
Silverstein, Alvin, et al. Carbohydrates. Green, Anne C., illus. LC 91-41245. 48p. (gr. 3-6). 1992. PLB 14.40 (*1-56294-207-7*) Millbrook Pr.
—Fats. Green, Anne C., illus. LC 91-41169. 48p. (gr. 3-6). 1992. PLB 14.40 (*1-56294-208-5*) Millbrook Pr.
—Proteins. Green, Anne C., illus. LC 91-41230. 48p. (gr. 3-6). 1992. PLB 14.40 (*1-56294-209-3*) Millbrook Pr.
Smalley, Guy, illus. My Very Own Book of What's for Lunch. 24p. (ps-2). 1989. 9.95 (*0-929793-05-6*) Camex Bks Inc.
Solomon, Joan. Chopsticks & Chips. (Illus.). 25p. (gr. 2-4). 1991. 12.95 (*0-237-60142-7*, Pub. by Evans Bros Ltd) Trafalgar.
Sproule, Anna. Food for the World. (Illus.). 48p. (gr. 1-4). 1987. 12.95x (*0-8160-1783-2*) Facts on File.
Steele, Philip. In Ancient Rome. LC 93-28384. (Illus.). 32p. (gr. 6 up). 1995. text ed. 14.95 RSBE (*0-02-726321-5*, New Discovery Bks) Macmillan Child Grp.
Stine, Megan, et al. Hands-On Science: Food & the Kitchen. Taback, Simms, illus. LC 92-56890. 1993. PLB 18.60 (*0-8368-0955-6*) Gareth Stevens Inc.
Tames, Richard. Food: Feasts, Cooks & Kitchens. (Illus.). (gr. 5-8). 1994. pap. 7.95 (*0-531-15711-3*) Watts.
Tan, Jennifer, et al. International Foods, 6 bks, Reading Level 4. (Illus.). 192p. (gr. 3-6). 1989. Set. PLB 95.64 (*0-86625-337-8*); 71.70 (*0-685-58769-X*) Rourke Corp.
Tesar, Jenny. Food & Water: Threats, Shortages & Solutions. (Illus.). 128p. (gr. 7-12). 1992. lib. bdg. 18. 95x (*0-8160-2495-2*) Facts on File.
Ventra, Piero. Food: Its Evolution Through the Ages. LC 94-14419. (gr. 3 up). 1994. 16.95 (*0-395-66790-9*) HM.
Wade, Mary D. Milk, Meat Biscuits & The Terraqueous Machine: The Story of Gail Borden. Roberts, Melissa, ed. (Illus.). 64p. (gr. 4-7). 1987. 9.95 (*0-89015-605-0*) Sunbelt Media.
Wake, Susan. Butter. Yeats, John, illus. 32p. (gr. 1-4). 1990. PLB 14.95 (*0-87614-427-X*) Carolrhoda Bks.
Ward, Elizabeth, ed. What Makes Popcorn Pop? First Questions & Answers about Food. (Illus.). 48p. (ps). 1994. write for info. (*0-7835-0862-X*); PLB write for info. (*0-7835-0863-8*) Time-Life.
Warren, Jean. Super Snacks. Mulvey, Glen, illus. 48p. 1992. 6.95 (*0-911019-49-9*, WPH 1601) Warren Pub Hse.
Wheeler, Jill C. The Food We Eat. Kallen, Stuart A., ed. LC 91-73068. 202p. 1991. 17.95 (*1-56239-033-3*) Abdo & Dghtrs.

FOOD, CANNED

see Canning and Preserving

FOOD–FICTION

Adoff, Arnold. Eats. ALC Staff, ed. Russo, Susan, illus. LC 79-11300. 48p. (gr. 2 up). 1992. pap. 3.95 (*0-688-11695-7*, Mulberry) Morrow.
The Adventures of Rowena & the Wonderful Jam & Jelly Factory. 40p. 1987. 16.95 (*0-944345-11-5*) S C Toof.
American Diabetes Association Staff. Grilled Cheese at Four O'Clock in the Morning. Turner, Jeanne, illus. 90p. (gr. 3-7). 1988. pap. 5.95 (*0-945448-02-3*, CCHGC) Am Diabetes.
Anastasio. Pass the Peas Please, Vol. 1. (gr. 3 up). 1992. pap. 5.95 (*0-316-03833-4*) Little.
Anderheggen, George C. Willie the Weenie Whiner. (Illus.). 20p. (Orig.). (gr. 5 up). 1983. 3.95 (*0-910717-01-X*) Bookling Pubs.
Asch, Frank. Milk & Cookies. (Illus.). 48p. (ps-2). 1991. pap. 2.95 (*0-448-40103-7*, G&D) Putnam Pub Group.
—Sand Cake. LC 93-15452. 1993. PLB 13.27 (*0-8368-0973-4*) Gareth Stevens Inc.
Atkinson, Kathie. What's For Dinner? (ps-3). 1993. pap. 3.95 (*1-86373-375-2*, Pub. by Allen & Unwin Aust Pty AT) IPG Chicago.
Aycock, Theresa. The Banana Pie That Changed the World. (Illus.). 24p. (gr. k-3). 1993. pap. 2.50 (*0-87406-611-5*) Willowisp Pr.
Baker, Bonnie J. A Pear by Itself. LC 82-4430. 32p. (ps-2). 1982. 10.25 (*0-516-02032-3*); pap. 2.95 (*0-516-42032-1*) Childrens.
Balian, Lorna. The Sweet Touch. Balian, Lorna, illus. 52p. (ps-6). 1994. Repr. PLB 12.95 (*1-881772-26-8*) Humbug Bks.
Barbie: A Picnic Surprise. 24p. (ps-3). 1991. write for info. (*0-307-14172-1*, 14172) Western Pub.
Barrett, Judi. Cloudy with a Chance of Meatballs. Barrett, Ron, illus. LC 78-2945. 32p. (ps-3). 1978. RSBE 14.95 (*0-689-30647-4*, Atheneum Child Bk) Macmillan Child Grp.
Barton, Chris & Shulman, Dee. Cream Cake. (Illus.). 32p. (ps-2). 1993. 16.95 (*0-370-31766-1*, Pub. by Bodley Head UK) Trafalgar.
Beames, Margaret. The Lunch That Mom Made. Curtis, Neil, illus. LC 92-21454. 1993. 4.25 (*0-383-03639-9*) SRA Schl Grp.
Bender, Robert. A Most Unsual Lunch. LC 93-34068. (gr. 3 up). 1994. pap. 14.99 (*0-8037-1710-5*); PLB 14. 89 (*0-8037-1711-3*) Dial Bks Young.
Benjamin, Alan. Let's Eat: Vamos a Comer. (SPA & ENG.). (ps). 1992. pap. 2.95 (*0-671-76927-8*, Little Simon) S&S Trade.
Benson, Rita. Alligator Mouse & Other Disasters. Cooper-Brown, Jean, illus. LC 93-18052. 1994. write for info. (*0-383-03674-7*) SRA Schl Grp.
Berg, Eric. Try It, You'll Like It! LC 93-8907. 1993. write for info. (*1-56071-325-9*) ETR Assocs.
Bjork, Christina. Elliot's Extraordinary Cookbook. Sandin, Joan, tr. Anderson, Lena, illus. 60p. 1991. 12. 95 (*91-29-59658-0*, Pub. by R & S Bks) FS&G.
Blair, Cynthia. The Lollipop Plot. 144p. (Orig.). (gr. 4 up). 1990. pap. 3.95 (*0-449-70377-0*, Juniper) Fawcett.
Blume, Judy. Fudge-a-Mania. 1991. pap. 3.50 (*0-440-70695-5*) Dell.
—Fudge-a-Mania. (gr. 4-7). 1992. pap. 1.99 (*0-440-21369-X*) Dell.
Bond, Reed. Betsy's Butter. Bond, Reed, illus. 16p. (Orig.). (gr. 1-3). 1992. pap. 4.50 (*0-9631992-1-8*) Bonding Place.
Borden, Margie. Mincemeat Pie. Graves, Helen, ed. 54p. (gr. 4-8). 1987. 5.95 (*1-55523-048-2*) Winston-Derek.
Breeze, Lynn. Baby's Food. (Illus.). 14p. (ps). 1994. bds. 4.50 fold-outs (*0-8120-6413-5*) Barron.
Brenner, Barbara. Beef Stew. Siracusa, Catherine, illus. LC 89-36769. 32p. (Orig.). (ps-1). 1990. lib. bdg. 7.99 (*0-394-95046-1*); pap. 3.50 (*0-394-85046-7*) Random Bks Yng Read.
Brown, Marcia. Sopa de Piedras. Mlawer, Teresa, tr. from ENG. Brown, Marcia, illus. (gr. 5-7). 1991. PLB 12.95 (*0-9625162-1-X*) Lectorum Pubns.
Bruvelaitis, Lisa. Nearly Noodles. Bruvelaitis, Lisa, illus. 24p. (Orig.). (ps-2). 1990. pap. 0.99 (*1-55037-128-2*, Pub. by Annick CN) Firefly Bks Ltd.
Buchanan, D. H. The Gob-Gob-Goblin's Feast. Balkovek, James, illus. 64p. (ps-4). 1993. pap. 9.95 (*0-8449-4275-8*); FRE Translation Tool, "Trans-it" 4.95 (*0-8449-4289-8*); CHI Translation Tool, "Trans-it" 4.95 (*0-8449-4291-X*); GER Translation Tool, "Trans-it" 4.95 (*0-8449-4290-1*); SPA Translation Tool, "Trans-it" 4.95 (*0-8449-4288-X*) Good Morn Tchr.
Buchanan, J. Nothing Else but Yams for Supper. (Illus.). 24p. (ps-8). 1988. pap. 4.95 (*0-88753-182-2*, Pub. by Black Moss Pr CN) Firefly Bks Ltd.
Buckman, Mary. Wiggle Worm. LC 89-63502. (Illus., Orig.). (gr. k-2). 1989. pap. text ed. 12.95 (*1-879414-06-6*) Mary Bee Creat.
Carle, Eric. Pancakes, Pancakes. 1992. 5.95 (*0-590-44453-0*, Blue Ribbon Bks) Scholastic Inc.
Carlson, Anna L. The Candy Cruncher. 2nd. ed. LC 80-83738. (Illus.). 24p. (gr. k-4). 1983. pap. 1.95 (*0-939938-03-0*) Karwyn Ent.
—The Cookie Looker. 2nd. ed. LC 80-82182. (Illus.). (gr. k-4). 1983. pap. 1.95 (*0-939938-01-4*) Karwyn Ent.
Carlson, Rick. Bubba's Berry Picking Expedition Value: Obedience. 32p. 1992. pap. 1.95 saddle stitched (*0-310-58181-8*, Youth Bks) Zondervan.
Catling, Patrick S. The Chocolate Touch. 1984. pap. 3.50 (*0-553-15639-X*) Bantam.
Chadwick, Tim. Cabbage Moon. Harper, Piers, illus. LC 93-28952. 1994. 14.95 (*0-531-06827-7*); lib. bdg. write for info. (*0-531-08677-1*) Orchard Bks Watts.
Chicken Salad Soup. (Illus.). (ps-2). 1991. PLB 6.95 (*0-8136-5146-8*, TK3393); pap. 3.50 (*0-8136-5646-X*, TK3394) Modern Curr.
Clark, Emma C. Lunch with Aunt Augusta. LC 91-11969. (Illus.). 32p. (ps-3). 1992. 14.00 (*0-8037-1104-2*) Dial Bks Young.
Cocca-Leffler, Maryann. Wednesday Is Spaghetti Day. (ps-3). 1992. pap. 2.50 (*0-590-42895-0*) Scholastic Inc.
Coco, Eugene. The Boy Who Wouldn't Eat Breakfast. Iosa, Ann, illus. 24p. (ps-2). 1993. pap. text ed. 0.99 (*1-56293-349-3*) McClanahan Bk.
Cohen, Peter. Olson's Meat Pies. Landstrom, Olof, illus. Fisher, Richard E., tr. (Illus.). (gr. k-4). 1989. 12.95 (*91-29-59180-5*, Pub. by R & S Bks) FS&G.
Conrad, Pam. Molly & the Strawberry Day. 32p. (ps-2). 1994. 15.00 (*0-06-021369-8*, HarpT); PLB 14.89 (*0-06-021370-1*, HarpT) HarpC.
Coplans, Peta. Spaghetti for Suzy. Coplans, Peta, illus. LC 92-21611. 32p. (gr. k-3). 1993. 13.95 (*0-395-65232-4*) HM.
Cormier, Robert. Beyond the Chocolate War. (gr. 6 up). 1986. pap. 3.99 (*0-440-90580-X*, LFL) Dell.
Cushman, Doug. Possum Stew. LC 89-34481. (Illus.). 32p. (ps-1). 1990. 12.95 (*0-525-44566-8*, DCB) Dutton Child Bks.
Czernecki, Stefan & Rhodes, Timothy. The Sleeping Bread. Czernecki, Stefan, illus. LC 91-75422. 40p. (gr. k-4). 1993. pap. 4.95 (*1-56282-519-4*) Hyprn Ppbks.
Dana, Barbara. Zucchini. 1984. pap. 3.50 (*0-553-15608-X*) Bantam.
Danziger, Paula. The Pistachio Prescription. (gr. k-12). 1988. pap. 2.95 (*0-317-67249-5*) Dell.
Davidson, Martine. Kevin & the School Nurse. Hafner, Marylin, illus. LC 91-30194. 32p. (Orig.). (ps-2). 1992. PLB 5.99 (*0-679-91821-3*); pap. 2.25 (*0-679-81821-9*) Random Bks Yng Read.
Davoll, Barbara. The Potluck Supper. Hockerman, Dennis, illus. 24p. 1988. 6.99 (*0-89693-406-3*, Victor Books); cassette 9.99 (*0-89693-617-1*) SP Pubns.
Degen, Bruce. Jamberry. LC 82-47708. (ps-3). 1985. pap. 3.95 (*0-06-443068-5*, HarpT) HarpC Child Bks.
—Jamberry: Big Book. Degen, Bruce, illus. LC 82-47708. 32p. (ps-3). 1992. pap. 19.95 (*0-06-443311-0*, Trophy) HarpC Child Bks.

Delton, Judy. Cookies & Crutches. 80p. (Orig.). (gr. k-6). 1988. pap. 3.25 (*0-440-40010-4*, YB) Dell.
Demarest, Chris L. No Peas for Nellie. Demarest, Chris L., illus. LC 90-39986. 32p. (gr. k-3). 1991. pap. 3.95 (*0-689-71474-2*, Aladdin) Macmillan Child Grp.
De Paola, Tomie. Pancakes for Breakfast. De Paola, Tomie, illus. LC 77-15523. 32p. (ps-2). 1978. pap. 4.95 (*0-15-670768-3*, Voyager Bks) HarBrace.
Deschaine, Scott. Popcorn! Donovan, Bob, illus. 68p. 1993. pap. 4.95 (*1-878181-06-8*) Discovery Comics.
Desputeaux, Helene. My Food. (Illus.). 26p. (ps). 1993. bds. 2.95 (*2-921198-27-4*, Pub. by Les Edits Herit CN) Adams Inc MA.
Doyle, Charlotte. Freddie's Spaghetti. Reilly, Nicholas, illus. LC 90-61003. 24p. (Orig.). (ps-2). 1991. pap. 2.25 (*0-679-81160-5*) Random Bks Yng Read.
Drescher, Henrik. The Little Boy Who Ate Around. LC 93-40848. (Illus.). 40p. (ps-3). 1994. 14.95 (*0-7868-0014-3*); 14.89 (*0-7868-2011-X*) Hyprn Child.
Dr. Seuss. Green Eggs & Ham. Dr. Seuss, illus. 64p. (ps-1). 1987. pap. 7.95 incl. cassette (*0-394-89220-8*) Random Bks Yng Read.
Dudko, Mary A. & Larsen, Margie. Baby Bop's Foods. Dowdy, Linda C., ed. Full, Dennis, photos by. LC 93-74291. (Illus.). 24p. (ps). 1994. bds. 3.95 chunky board (*1-57064-014-9*) Barney Pub.
Duyff, Roberta L. The Bread That Grew. McKissack, Patricia & McKissack, Fredrick, eds. Dorenkamp, Michelle, illus. LC 87-61646. 32p. (Orig.). (gr. 1-3). 1987. text ed. 8.95 (*0-88335-725-9*); pap. text ed. 4.95 (*0-88335-745-3*) Milliken Pub Co.
Edge, Nellie, adapted by. Peanut Butter & Jelly Big Book. Draper, Tani, illus. (ps-2). 1988. pap. text ed. 14.00 (*0-922053-10-3*) N Edge Res.
Ehlert, Lois. Feathers for Lunch. 33p. (ps-3). 1990. 13.95 (*0-15-230550-5*) HarBrace.
—Feathers for Lunch. LC 89-29459. (ps-3). 1993. pap. 19.95 (*0-15-230551-3*) HarBrace.
Elish, Dan. Worldwide Dessert Contest. (gr. 4 up). 1990. pap. 3.50 (*0-553-15820-1*) Bantam.
Evans, Katie. Hunky Dory Ate It. Stoeke, Janet M., illus. LC 91-13992. 32p. (ps-1). 1992. 13.50 (*0-525-44847-0*, DCB) Dutton Child Bks.
Fleming, Denise. Lunch. LC 92-178. (Illus.). 32p. (ps-2). 1992. 14.95 (*0-8050-1636-8*, Bks Young Read) H Holt & Co.
Gaban, Jesus. Harry's Mealtime Mess. Colorado, Nani, illus. 16p. (ps-1). 1992. PLB 13.27 (*0-8368-0717-0*) Gareth Stevens Inc.
Gelman, Rita G. More Spaghetti, I Say. (ps-3). 1993. pap. 19.95 (*0-590-71439-2*) Scholastic Inc.
Goffstein, M. Brooke. Fish for Supper. Goffstein, M. B., illus. LC 75-27598. 32p. (ps-2). 1986. pap. 3.95 (*0-8037-0284-1*) Dial Bks Young.
Goldthwaite, Howard. Lunch for a Bunch. (Illus.). 6p. 1994. pop-up bk. 3.99 (*1-56476-172-X*, Victor Books) SP Pubns.
Gomi, Taro. Who Ate It? (ps). 1992. pap. 4.80 (*0-395-65834-9*) HM.
Greene, Michael. Where's the Green Pea? Ringston, Ray, illus. LC 91-91536. 32p. (ps-1). 1992. PLB 19.95 incl. audiocassette (*1-881134-00-8*) Tues Child.
Grey, Judith. Yummy, Yummy. Goodman, Joan E., illus. LC 81-2360. 32p. (gr. k-2). 1981. PLB 11.59 (*0-89375-543-5*); pap. 2.95 (*0-89375-544-3*) Troll Assocs.
Haddon, Mark. Toni & the Tomato Soup. Haddon, Mark, illus. 21p. (ps-1). 1989. 12.95 (*0-15-200610-9*, Gulliver Bks) HarBrace.
Harman, Betty & Meador, Nancy, eds. Seven Ears of Corn. Tieman, Peggy, illus. 149p. (gr. 5-9). 1991. pap. 6.00 (*0-9630661-0-2*) Harman & Meador.
Harrison, D. James. Saturn Storm's Broccoli Adventure. LC 89-51459. (Illus.). 44p. (gr. k-3). 1989. 5.95 (*1-55523-278-7*) Winston-Derek.
Hartman, Bob. Aunt Mabel's Table. Stortz, Diane, ed. LC 94-2766. (Illus.). 48p. (Orig.). (ps-3). 1994. pap. 4.49 (*0-7847-0178-4*) Standard Pub.
Hayes, Daniel. The Trouble with Lemons. LC 89-46192. 128p. (gr. 6 up). 1991. 16.95 (*0-87923-825-9*) Godine.
—The Trouble with Lemons. 1992. pap. 3.99 (*0-449-70416-5*, Juniper) Fawcett.
Hayes, Frederick & Hayes, Jean. The Chile Pot. 1988. 6.95 (*0-925605-00-X*) Pinto Pub.
Heide, Florence P. Banana Blitz. 128p. (gr. 3-7). 1984. pap. 2.50 (*0-553-15258-0*, Skylark) Bantam.
Heller, Nicholas. Peas. LC 92-29740. 24p. 1993. 14.00 (*0-688-12406-2*); PLB 13.93 (*0-688-12407-0*) Greenwillow.
Heller, Ruth. Many Luscious Lollipops. (Illus.). 48p. (ps-3). 1992. pap. 6.95 (*0-448-40316-1*, G&D) Putnam Pub Group.
Hennessy, B. G. Jake Baked the Cake. Morgan, Mary, illus. 32p. (ps-3). 1990. pap. 12.95 (*0-670-82237-X*) Viking Child Bks.
Hest, Amy. The Midnight Eaters. LC 94-480. (gr. k-3). 1994. pap. 3.95 (*0-689-71846-2*, Aladdin) Macmillan Child Grp.
Hillert, Margaret. Cookie House. (Illus.). (ps-k). 1978. PLB 6.95 (*0-8136-5012-7*, TK2290); pap. 3.50 (*0-8136-5512-9*, TK2291) Modern Curr.
—The Little Cookie. (Illus.). (ps-k). 1981. PLB 6.95 (*0-8136-5062-3*, TK2324); pap. 3.50 (*0-8136-5562-5*, TK2325) Modern Curr.
Hoban, Russell. Bread & Jam for Frances: Big Book. Hoban, Lillian, illus. LC 92-13622. 32p. (ps-3). 1993. pap. 19.95 (*0-06-443336-6*, Trophy) HarpC Child Bks.
—Dinner at Alberta's. Marshall, James, illus. 48p. (gr. k-6). 1980. pap. 2.95 (*0-440-41864-X*, YB) Dell.
—Jim Hedgehog's Supernatural Christmas. Lewin, Betsy, illus. 48p. (gr. 2-5). 1992. 12.70 (*0-395-56240-6*, Clarion Bks) HM.
Hoffman, Mary. Leon's Lucky Lunch-Break. Noakes, Polly, illus. 32p. (ps-k). 1993. 14.95 (*0-460-88021-7*, Pub. by J M Dent & Sons) Trafalgar.
Holroyd, Angela. Pumpkin Pie. 1991. 4.98 (*0-8317-7161-5*) Smithmark.
Hoopes, Lyn L. The Unbeatable Bread. Sneed, Brad, photos by. LC 94-17043. (Illus.). Date not set. write for info. (*0-8037-1611-7*); PLB write for info. (*0-8037-1612-5*) Dial Bks Young.
Horvath, Polly. No More Cornflakes. (gr. 4-7). 1993. pap. 4.50 (*0-374-45516-3*, Sunburst) FS&G.
Howard, Jane. When I'm Hungry. (Illus.). 24p. (ps-k). 1992. 12.50 (*0-525-44983-3*, DCB) Dutton Child Bks.
Howe, James. Hot Fudge. Morrill, Leslie, illus. LC 89-13468. 48p. (gr. k up). 1990. 13.95 (*0-688-08237-8*); PLB 13.88 (*0-688-09701-4*, Morrow Jr Bks) Morrow Jr Bks.
Hurlbut, Phillip R., Jr. Jeraboam & the Amazing Spaghetti Mountain. Renfroe, Dan, illus. LC 79-90933. 123p. (Orig.). (gr. 3 up). 1979. pap. 2.95 (*0-936086-00-9*) Entertainment Factory.
Hurwitz, Johanna. Much Ado about Aldo. Wallner, John, illus. LC 78-5434. 96p. (gr. 4-6). 1978. PLB 13.88 (*0-688-32160-7*) Morrow Jr Bks.
Hutchins, Pat. Don't Forget the Bacon: Big Book Edition. (Illus.). 32p. (ps up). 1994. pap. 18.95 (*0-688-13102-6*, Mulberry) Morrow.
—The Doorbell Rang: Big Book Edition. (Illus.). 24p. (ps up). 1994. pap. 18.95 (*0-688-13101-8*, Mulberry) Morrow.
Hwa-I Publishing Co., Staff. Chinese Children's Stories, Vol. 31: The Refugee Empress, Chi Jiguang Cookies. Ching, Emily, et al, eds. Wonder Kids Publications Staff, tr. from CHI. (Illus.). 28p. (gr. 3-6). 1991. Repr. of 1988 ed. 7.95 (*1-56162-031-9*) Wonder Kids.
Johnston, Tony. Soup Bone. LC 89-1990. (ps-3). 1992. pap. 4.95 (*0-15-277256-1*, HB Juv Bks) HarBrace.
Jukes, Mavis. Blackberries in the Dark. Allen, Thomas B., illus. LC 85-4259. 48p. (gr. 2-6). 1993. 15.00 (*0-394-87599-0*) Knopf Bks Yng Read.
Kaslow, Florence R. T-Bend Bagelmaker. Leigh, Avra, ed. 24p. (Orig.). (gr. k-5). 1993. pap. 4.95 (*0-9628321-1-1*) Pumpkin Patch Pubs.
Kehret, Peg. Wally Amos Presents Chip & Cookie: The First Adventure. (gr. 4-7). 1991. 14.95 (*0-87491-988-6*) Acropolis.
Kent, Jack. Socks for Supper. Kent, Jack, illus. LC 78-6224. 40p. (ps-3). 1978. 5.95 (*0-8193-0964-8*); PLB 5.95 (*0-8193-0965-6*) Parents.
Khalsa, Dayal K. How Pizza Came to Our Town. Khalsa, Dayal K., illus. 32p. (gr. k-8). 1989. 14.95 (*0-88776-231-X*) Tundra Bks.
—How Pizza Came to Queens. Khalsa, Dayal K., illus. (gr. 1 up). 1989. PLB 15.00 (*0-517-57126-9*, Clarkson Potter) Crown Bks Yng Read.
The Killer Brussel Sprouts. (Illus.). 32p. 1990. incl. cass. 12.95 (*0-938971-45-X*) JTG Nashville.
King, Christopher L. The Vegetables Go to Bed. GrandPre, Mary, illus. LC 92-27650. 24p. (ps-1). 1994. 12.00 (*0-517-59125-1*); PLB 12.99 (*0-517-59126-X*) Crown Bks Yng Read.
King, Virginia. Breakfast. Fleming, Leanne, illus. LC 92-21391. 1993. 2.50 (*0-383-03556-2*) SRA Schl Grp.
Kingston, Arlene. The Bagels Are Coming. Kingston, Arlene, illus. 40p. (ps up). 1988. pap. 5.95 (*0-929934-00-8*) Child Time Pubs.
Korte, Gene J. Green Pickle Pie. Caroland, Mary, ed. LC 90-71141. (Illus.). 44p. 1991. 6.95 (*1-55523-369-4*) Winston-Derek.
Latterman, Terry. The Watermelon Treat. Hawkins, Mary E., ed. Lattermen, Terry, illus. LC 85-63266. 48p. (gr. 1-4). 1987. 8.95 (*0-934739-03-X*); pap. 5.95 (*0-934739-04-8*) Pussywillow Pub.
Lexau, Joan M. Striped Ice Cream. reissued ed. 1992. 2.75 (*0-590-45729-2*, Little Apple) Scholastic Inc.
Lindman, Maj. Snipp, Snapp, Snurr & the Buttered Bread. (Illus.). 32p. 1993. Repr. lib. bdg. 14.95x (*1-56849-002-X*) Buccaneer Bks.
Lofting, Hugh. Gub-Gub's Book. LC 91-4672. (gr. 4-7). 1992. pap. 15.00 (*0-671-78355-6*, S&S BFYR) S&S Trade.
Lord, John V. & Burroway, Janet. The Giant Jam Sandwich. (Illus.). 1990. 7.70 (*0-395-53966-8*) HM.
Lyon, David. The Crumbly Coast. LC 93-41083. 1995. write for info. (*0-385-32079-5*) Doubleday.
Maccarone, Grace. Pizza Party. LC 93-19732. (Illus.). 48p. (ps-4). 1994. pap. 2.95 (*0-590-47563-0*, Cartwheel) Scholastic Inc.
McLean, Bill. The Best Peanut Butter Sandwich in the Whole World. Helmer, Katherine, illus. 28p. (ps-2). 1990. pap. 4.95 (*0-88753-207-1*, Pub. by Black Moss Pr CN) Firefly Bks Ltd.
McLenighan, Valjean. One Whole Doughnut...One Doughnut Hole. LC 82-12838. (Illus.). 32p. (ps-2). 1982. PLB 10.25 (*0-516-02031-5*); pap. 2.95 (*0-516-42031-3*) Childrens.
McOmber, Rachel B., ed. McOmber Phonics Storybooks: A Night to Celebrate. rev. ed. (Illus.). write for info. (*0-944991-71-8*) Swift Lrn Res.
—McOmber Phonics Storybooks: Fizz in the Pit. rev. ed. (Illus.). write for info. (*0-944991-12-2*) Swift Lrn Res.
—McOmber Phonics Storybooks: Fizz Mix. rev. ed. (Illus.). write for info. (*0-944991-11-4*) Swift Lrn Res.
—McOmber Phonics Storybooks: Fizz Mud. rev. ed. (Illus.). write for info. (*0-944991-21-1*) Swift Lrn Res.
Manes, Stephen. Chocolate-Covered Ants. (gr. 4-7). 1993. pap. 2.95 (*0-590-40961-1*) Scholastic Inc.
Marcuse, Aida, tr. from ENG. Lizard's Song. Aruego, Jose & Dewey, Ariane, illus. (SPA.). 32p. (ps up). 1994. pap. 4.95 (*0-688-13201-4*, Mulberry) Morrow.
Martin, JeanRead & Marx, Patricia. Now I Will Never Leave the Dinner Table. Chast, Roz, illus. LC 94-3209. (gr. 4 up). Date not set. 15.00 (*0-06-024794-0*); PLB 14.89 (*0-06-024795-9*) HarpC.

Mayfield, Barbara J. The Kid's Club Cubs & the Search for the Treasures of the Pyramid. Gold, Ethel, illus. 40p. (Orig.). (ps-2). 1994. Incl. audiocassette & puzzle. pap. 24.95 (*1-883983-15-0*) Noteworthy Creat.
Barbara Mayfield, Registered Dietician & nutrition educator, author of KID'S CLUB: NUTRITION LEARNING ACTIVITIES FOR YOUNG CHILDREN, & NUTRITION NOTES: MUSICAL NUTRITION EDUCATION TO SING & COLOR, has written a delightful adventure story to teach young children about the new Food Guide Pyramid. The beautiful color illustrations show the Kid's Club Cubs & their friend Picky Piggy in their search for the treasures of the Pyramid, learning the difference between healthy & less-healthy foods, food groups, & the nutrient treasures they provide. The book invites participation from the reader & comes with a puzzle for the child to build their own Food Guide Pyramid & a cassette tape of the story & 11 original songs. Activity ideas for parents are included in the book as well as lyrics to the 11 songs & camera-ready artwork of the Food Guide Pyramid. The book-puzzle-tape may be ordered directly from the publisher.
Noteworthy Creations, Inc., P.O. Box 335, 107 W. Franklin St., Delphi, IN 46923; phone 317-564-4167 or 800-305-4167.
Publisher Provided Annotation.

Miller, Virginia. Eat Your Dinner! LC 91-58728. 32p. (ps up). 1994. pap. 5.99 (*1-56402-368-0*) Candlewick Pr.
Modell, Frank. Ice Cream Soup. LC 87-21097. (Illus.). 24p. (ps-3). 1988. 11.95 (*0-688-07770-6*); lib. bdg. 11.88 (*0-688-07771-4*) Greenwillow.
Modesitt, Jeanne. Lunch with Milly. Spowart, Robin, illus. LC 93-33808. 32p. (gr. k-3). 1995. PLB 14.95 (*0-8167-3388-0*); pap. text ed. 4.95 (*0-8167-3389-9*) BrdgeWater.
—Vegetable Soup. Spowart, Robin, illus. LC 91-247. 32p. (ps-3). 1991. pap. 4.50 (*0-689-71523-4*, Aladdin) Macmillan Child Grp.
Mouth Won't Open. 1923. pap. 2.25 (*0-440-79320-3*) Dell.
Myers, Edward. Forri the Baker. Natchev, Alexi, photos by. LC 93-2468. 1994. write for info. (*0-8037-1396-7*, MR-291-AF); PLB write for info. (*0-8037-1397-5*) Dial Bks Young.
Myers, Lynne B. & Myers, Christopher A. Turnip Soup. (Illus.). 32p. (ps-2). 1994. 13.95 (*1-56282-445-7*); PLB 13.89 (*1-56282-446-5*) Hyprn Child.
Nordqvist, Sven. Pancake Pie. Wilhelm, Hans, illus. LC 84-16640. 32p. (ps-3). 1985. 11.95 (*0-688-04141-8*); PLB 11.88 (*0-688-04142-6*, Morrow Jr Bks) Morrow Jr Bks.
Norman, Jane & Beazley, Frank. It's Raining Vegetables! 24p. (ps-3). 1993. pap. write for info. (*1-883585-08-2*) Pixanne Ent.
Olaleve, Isaac. Bitter Bananas. Young, Ed, illus. LC 93-73306. 32p. (ps-3). 1994. 14.95 (*1-56397-039-2*) Boyds Mills Pr.
Olsen, Alfa-Betty & Efron, Marshall. Gabby the Shrew. Chast, Roz, illus. LC 92-31902. 1994. lib. bdg. write for info. (*0-679-94467-2*) Random.
Patron, Susan. Burgoo Stew. Shenon, Mike, illus. LC 90-43791. 32p. (ps-1). 1991. 13.95 (*0-531-05916-2*); RLB 13.99 (*0-531-08516-3*) Orchard Bks Watts.
Peck, Robert N. Soup on Fire. Robinson, Charles, illus. LC 87-5261. 112p. (gr. 4-7). 1987. pap. 13.95 (*0-385-29580-4*) Delacorte.
—Soup on Ice. Robinson, Charles, illus. LC 85-218. 128p. (gr. 3-7). 1985. PLB 10.99 (*0-394-97613-4*) Knopf Bks Yng Read.

—Soup on Wheels. (gr. 3-7). 1986. pap. 3.25 (0-440-48190-2, YB) Dell.

—Soup's Drum. (gr. k-6). 1988. pap. 2.95 (0-440-40003-1) Dell.

Peifer, Jane. The Biggest Popcorn Party Ever in Center County. Nolt, Marilyn P., illus. LC 86-27063. 32p. (Orig.). (ps-1). 1987. pap. 4.95 (0-8361-3435-4) Herald Pr.

Pelham, David. Sam's Sandwich. Pelham, David, illus. 22p. (ps-4). 1991. 8.99 (0-525-44751-2, DCB) Dutton Child Bks.

Peters, Lisa W. Purple Delicious Blackberry Jam. McGregor, Barbara, illus. 32p. (ps-3). 1992. 14.95 (1-55970-167-6) Arcade Pub Inc.

Pienkowski, Jan. Dinnertime. (Illus.). 10p. (ps up). 1991. 4.95 (0-8431-2963-8); pap. 9.95 (0-8431-0961-0) Price Stern.

Pittman, Helena C. A Grain of Rice. 1992. pap. 3.50 (0-553-15986-0) Bantam.

Politi, Leo. Three Stalks of Corn. reissue ed. Politi, Leo, illus. LC 75-35009. 32p. (gr. k-3). 1993. RSBE 14.95 (0-684-19538-0, Scribners Young Read) Macmillan Child Grp.

Potter, Beatrix. The Roly-Poly Pudding. 64p. (Orig.). 1984. pap. 2.25 (0-553-15249-1) Bantam.

Power, T. W. The Price of an Apple. 249p. (Orig.). 1992. PLB write for info. (0-9634105-0-4) A J Pub CA.

Priceman, Marjorie. How to Make an Apple Pie & See The World. Priceman, Marjorie, illus. LC 93-12341. 40p. (ps-3). 1994. 15.00 (0-679-83705-1); lib. bdg. 15.99 (0-679-93705-6) Knopf Bks Yng Read.

Pryor, Bonnie. Vinegar Pancakes & Vanishing Cream. 128p. (gr. k-6). 1989. pap. 3.50 (0-440-40173-9, YB) Dell.

Redhead. The Big Block of Chocolate. 1993. pap. 28.67 (0-590-50157-7) Scholastic Inc.

Reese, Bob. Sack Lunch. Reese, Bob, illus. LC 92-12183. 24p. (ps-2). 1992. PLB 9.75 (0-516-05582-8) Childrens.

Regan, Dian C. Liver Cookies. (gr. 4-7). 1991. pap. 2.75 (0-590-44337-2) Scholastic Inc.

Rifas, Leonard. Food First Comic. Goldenman, Gretta, ed. 24p. (Orig.). (gr. 7-12). 1982. pap. 1.00 (0-935028-11-0) Inst Food & Develop.

Riggio, Anita. Beware the Brindlebeast. Riggio, Anita, illus. LC 93-70875. 32p. (ps-1). 1994. 14.95 (1-56397-133-X) Boyds Mills Pr.

Riley, Martin. Boggart's Sandwich. (Illus.). 95p. (gr. 7-9). 1992. pap. 3.95 (0-563-20871-6, BBC-Parkwest) Parkwest Pubns.

Roald Dahl's Charlie & the Chocolate Factory, 4 vols. 1988. Boxed Set. pap. 8.70 (0-685-42774-9) Bantam.

Robart, Rose. The Cake That Mack Ate. Kovalski, Maryann, illus. LC 86-47709. (ps-3). 1987. 14.95 (0-316-74890-0) Little.

Rockwell, Anne. Apples & Pumpkins. Rockwell, Lizzy, photos by. LC 94-629. (ps-1). 1994. pap. 3.95 (0-689-71861-6, Aladdin) MacMillan Child Grp.

Rohmer, Harriet & Gomez, Cruz, eds. Mr. Sugar Came to Town (La visita del Senor Azucar) Zubizarreta, Rosalma, tr. Chagoya, Enrique, illus. (SPA & ENG.). 32p. (ps-5). 1989. 13.95 (0-89239-045-X) Childrens Book Pr.

Romain, Trevor. The Big Cheese. (Illus.). 32p. (Orig.). (ps-3). 1992. pap. 5.25 (1-880092-00-X) Bright Bks TX.

Rosenfeld, Dina. Peanut Butter & Jelly for Shabbos. (Illus.). 32p. (ps-1). 1994. 8.95 (0-922613-69-9); pap. 6.95 (0-922613-70-2) Hachai Pubns.

Ross, Katharine. The Little Pumpkin Book. Bratun, Katy, illus. LC 91-67669. 22p. (ps). 1992. bds. 2.95 (0-679-83384-6) Random Bks Yng Read.

Russell, Ching Y. First Apple. Zhang, Christopher, illus. LC 93-74360. 128p. (gr. 2-5). 1994. 13.95 (1-56397-206-9) Boyds Mills Pr.

Rylant, Cynthia. Mr. Putter & Tabby Bake the Cake. Howard, Arthur, illus. LC 94-9557. (gr. 1-5). 1994. 10.95 (0-15-200205-7); pap. 4.95 (0-15-200214-6) HarBrace.

Salem, Lynn & Stewart, Josie. What's for Dinner? McDill, Layl, illus. 12p. (gr. 1). 1992. pap. 3.50 (1-880612-09-7) Seedling Pubns.

Schiller, Alexandra. The Raisin Eater. Martin, John J. & Schiller, Alexandra, eds. Schiller, Alexandra, illus. 44p. (gr. 3-4). 1984. 5.00 (0-9618682-0-1) A Schiller.

Schindel, John. What's for Lunch? O'Malley, Kevin, illus. LC 93-48621. 1993. 15.00 (0-688-13598-6); PLB 14.93 (0-688-13599-4) Lothrop.

Schotter, Roni. A Fruit & Vegetable Man. Winter, Jeanette, photos by. LC 92-17555. (Illus.). 1993. 15.95 (0-316-77467-7, Joy St Bks) Little.

Schwartz, Alvin. There Is a Carrot in My Ear & Other Noodle Tales. Weinhaus, Karen A., illus. LC 80-8442. 64p. (gr. k-3). 1986. pap. 3.50 (0-06-444103-2, Trophy) HarpC Child Bks.

Sendak, Maurice. The Night Kitchen: (La Cocina de Noche) Sendak, Maurice, illus. (SPA.). (gr. 1-6). 14.95 (84-204-4570-3) Santillana.

Shafner, R. L. & Weisberg, Eric J. Belly's Deli. LC 92-44636. 1993. 13.50 (0-8225-2101-6) Lerner Pubns.

Sherman, Eileen B. The Odd Potato. Kahn, Katherine J., illus. LC 84-17186. 32p. (gr. k-5). 1984. pap. 4.95 (0-930494-37-7) Kar Ben.

Shiefman, Vicky. Sunday Potatoes, Monday Potatoes. August, Louise, illus. LC 92-46112. (gr. 3 up). 1994. pap. 15.00 (0-671-86596-X, S&S BFYR) S&S Trade.

Sikirycki, Igor. The Best Cook. Knobbe, Czeslaw, ed. & tr. from POL. Thoenes, Michael, illus. 26p. (gr. 1-6). 1993. text ed. 9.95 (0-9630328-2-8) SDPI.

Simons-Ailes, Sandra, illus. Mrs. Ortiz Makes Fry Bread. 30p. (Orig.). (ps-7). 1979. pap. 3.00 (0-915347-06-7) Pueblo Acoma Pr.

Siracusa, Catherine. The Banana Split from Outer Space. LC 94-6917. 1995. 12.95 (0-7868-0040-2); 12.89 (0-7868-2033-0) Hyprn Child.

Slater, Teddy. Dining with Prunella. Hearn, Diane D., illus. 24p. (ps-1). 1991. 4.95 (0-671-72982-9); PLB 6.95 (0-671-72981-0) Silver Pr.

Slepian, Jan. The Broccoli Tapes. (gr. 4-7). 1990. pap. 2.95 (0-590-43473-X) Scholastic Inc.

—Hungry Thing Goes to a Restaurant. (ps-3). 1993. pap. 4.95 (0-590-45525-7) Scholastic Inc.

Slepian, Jan & Seidler, Ann. The Hungry Thing Returns. Martin, Richard E., illus. LC 89-6350. (ps-3). 1990. pap. 11.95 (0-590-42890-X) Scholastic Inc.

Sloat, Teri, as told by. & illus. The Eye of the Needle. 32p. (ps-3). 1993. pap. 4.99 (0-14-054933-1, Puff Unicorn) Puffin Bks.

Smith, Doris B. A Taste of Blackberries. Wimmer, Mike, illus. LC 88-45077. 64p. (gr. 3-6). 1988. pap. 3.95 (0-06-440238-X, Trophy) HarpC Child Bks.

Smith, Josephine A. Hickle the Pickle. rev. ed. Dowley, May, illus. LC 92-96864. 40p. 1992. pap. 2.99 (1-881958-00-0, TX2-116-470) Hickle Pickle.

—Off the Vine, Doin' Fine. Dowley, May, illus. LC 92-96865. 48p. (Orig.). 1992. pap. 2.99 (1-881958-01-9, TXU328879) Hickle Pickle.

Smith, Robert K. Chocolate Fever. (gr. 4-7). 1992. pap. 1.99 (0-440-21371-1) Dell.

Smouse, Phil A. Pete, Feet, & Fish to Eat. (Illus.). 32p. (gr. 4-7). 1992. pap. 5.99 (1-56121-082-X) Wolgemuth & Hyatt.

Sopa de Galleta. (SPA.). (ps-3). 1993. pap. 7.00 (0-307-52114-1, Golden Pr) Western Pub.

Speed, Toby. Hattie Baked a Wedding Cake. Hepworth, Cathy, illus. 32p. (ps-3). 1994. PLB 15.95 (0-399-22342-8) Putnam Pub Group.

Stevenson, James. Yuck! LC 83-25421. (Illus.). 32p. (ps up). 1986. 3.95 (0-688-06524-4, Mulberry) Morrow.

Stutchner, Joan B. A Peanut Butter Waltz. Durrand, Diana, illus. 24p. (Orig.). (ps-2). 1990. pap. 0.99 (1-55037-126-6, Pub. by Annick CN) Firefly Bks Ltd.

Sun, Chyng F. On a White Pebble Hill. Chen, Chih-Sien, illus. LC 93-14495. 1994. 14.95 (0-395-68395-5) HM.

Superfudge. 1923. pap. 2.95 (0-440-78433-6) Dell.

Swan, Walter. Teeny Weeny. Swan, Deloris, ed. Asch, Connie, illus. 16p. (Orig.). (ps). 1989. pap. 1.50 (0-927176-01-7) Swan Enterp.

Sweeney, John. A Vegetable Catch Story. 32p. 1984. pap. write for info. (0-9607946-2-X) Bks of Our Times.

Taha, Karen T. Marshmallow Muscles, Banana Brainstorms. (gr. 5-7). 1990. pap. 2.75 (0-590-43394-6) Scholastic Inc.

Tanis, Joel E. & Grooters, Jeff. The Dragon Pack Snack Attack. Tanis, Joel E., illus. LC 92-18933. 32p. (ps-2). 1993. RSBE 14.95 (0-02-788840-1, Four Winds) Macmillan Child Grp.

Tapley, Joyce. Where the Liver Gets Behind Your Teeth. 1995. 8.95 (0-8062-5002-X) Carlton.

Theriot, David. Les Trois Petits Amis et la Decouverte du Gumbo. Easterling, Mae L., illus. (FRE.). 41p. (gr. 3). 1979. pap. 1.25 (0-911409-04-1) Natl Mat Dev.

Thill, Larry. The Adventures of Alice in Nutritionland: A Nutritional Storybook for Children. Thill, Michael, illus. 31p. (Orig.). (gr. k-6). 1989. pap. 8.00 (0-317-93500-3) Impressive Pubns.

Thompson, Julian F. Herb Seasoning. (gr. 7 up). 1990. pap. 3.25 (0-590-43024-6) Scholastic Inc.

Trussell-Cullen. I've Been Eating Blackberries. 1993. pap. 28.67 (0-590-50151-8) Scholastic Inc.

Vesey, Amanda. Duncan & the Bird. LC 92-37335. 1993. 18.95 (0-87614-785-6) Carolrhoda Bks.

Vinje, Marie. I Don't Like Peas. Hoffman, Joan, ed. (Illus.). 32p. (gr. k-2). 1992. pap. 3.95 (0-88743-430-4, 06082) Sch Zone Pub Co.

—I Don't Like Peas. Hoffman, Joan, ed. (Illus.). 16p. (gr. k-2). 1992. pap. 2.25 (0-88743-269-7, 06036) Sch Zone Pub Co.

Wallace, Barbara B. Peppermints in the Parlor. 2nd ed. LC 92-33031. 208p. (gr. 3-7). 1993. pap. 3.95 (0-689-71680-X, Aladdin) Macmillan Child Grp.

Wateron, Betty. Plain Noodles. Fitzgerald, Joanne, illus. 32p. 1993. pap. 4.95 (0-88899-132-0, Pub. by Groundwood-Douglas & McIntyre CN) Firefly Bks Ltd.

Weiss, Monica. Mmmm---Cookies! Simple Subtraction. Berlin, Rosemary, illus. LC 91-18648. 24p. (gr. k-2). 1992. PLB 10.59 (0-8167-2486-5); pap. text ed. 2.95 (0-8167-2487-3) Troll Assocs.

Wells, Rosemary. Max & Ruby's Midas: Another Greek Myth. LC 94-11181. Date not set. write for info. (0-8037-1782-2); PLB write for info. (0-8037-1783-0) Dial Bks Young.

—Max's Breakfast. Wells, Rosemary, illus. LC 84-14968. 12p. (ps-k). 1985. bds. 3.95 (0-8037-0161-6) Dial Bks Young.

Williams, Vera B. Cherries & Cherry Pits. LC 85-17156. (Illus.). 40p. (ps up). 1991. Repr. 3.95 (0-688-10478-9, Mulberry) Morrow.

Wilson, Sarah. Muskrat, Muskrat, Eat Your Peas! Wilson, Sarah, illus. LC 88-29742. (ps). 1992. pap. 13.95 jacketed (0-671-67515-X, S&S BFYR); pap. 3.95 (0-671-77822-6, S&S BFYR) S&S Trade.

Wonder Kids Publications Group Staff (USA) & Hwa-I Publishing Co., Staff. Tales about Food: Chinese Children's Stories, Vols. 31-35. Ching, Emily, et al, eds. Wonder Kids Publications Staff, tr. from CHI. Hwa-I Publishing Co., Staff, illus. LC 90-60798. (gr. 3-6). 1991. Repr. of 1988 ed. Five vol. set, 28p. ea. bk. 39.75 (0-685-58706-1) Wonder Kids.

Yamate, Sandra S. Char Siu Bao Boy. (Illus.). 32p. (gr. k-4). 1991. 12.95 (1-879965-00-3) Polychrome Pub.

Ziefert, Harriet. Dinner's Ready, Jessie! Smith, Mavis, illus. LC 90-55149. 32p. (ps-1). 1991. pap. 4.95 (0-06-107402-0) HarpC Child Bks.

Zimmerman. Applesauce & Cottage Cheese. 1995. 15.00 (0-06-024277-9); PLB 14.89 (0-06-024278-7) HarpC Child Bks.

Zokeisha. Things I Like to Eat. Zokeisha, illus. 16p. (ps-k). 1981. pap. 2.95 (0-671-44449-2, Little Simon) S&S Trade.

FOOD–PRESERVATION

see also Canning and Preserving

FOOD CONTROL

see Food Supply

FOOD PLANTS

see Plants, Edible

FOOD POISONING

Lobstein, Tim. Poisoned Food? LC 89-81603. 1990. PLB 12.40 (0-531-17208-2, Gloucester Pr) Watts.

FOOD SUPPLY

Aaseng, Nathan. Ending World Hunger. LC 90-46207. (Illus.). 144p. (gr. 9-12). 1991. PLB 13.90 (0-531-11007-9) Watts.

Amos, Janine. Feeding the World. LC 92-16337. (Illus.). 32p. (gr. 2-3). 1992. PLB 18.99 (0-8114-3407-9) Raintree Steck-V.

Cohen, Marc J. & Hoehn, Richard A., eds. Hunger 1992: Second Annual Report on the State of World Hunger - Ideas That Work. (Illus.). (gr. 11 up). 1991. pap. 12.95 (0-9628058-3-1); study aid 3.00 (0-9628058-4-X) Bread for the World.

Dando, William A. & Dando, Caroline Z. A Reference Guide to World Hunger. LC 91-10733. 112p. (gr. 6 up). 1991. lib. bdg. 17.95 (0-89490-326-8) Enslow Pubs.

Gibb, Christopher. Food or Famine. (Illus.). 48p. (gr. 5 up). 1987. PLB 18.60 (0-86592-279-9); 13.95 (0-685-67571-8) Rourke Corp.

Smith, David. The Food Cycle. LC 93-24391. (Illus.). 32p. (gr. 2-5). 1993. 12.95 (1-56847-093-2) Thomson Lrning.

Spencer, William. The Challenge of World Hunger. LC 90-49430. (Illus.). 64p. (gr. 6 up). 1991. lib. bdg. 15.95 (0-89490-283-0) Enslow Pubs.

Swallow, Su. Food for the World. LC 90-44954. (Illus.). 48p. (gr. 5-8). 1991. PLB 22.80 (0-8114-2800-1) Raintree Steck-V.

Versfield, Ruth. Why Are People Hungry? Franklin Watts Ltd., ed. LC 87-82886. (Illus.). 32p. (gr. k-3). 1988. 11.40 (0-531-17082-9, Gloucester Pr) Watts.

FOOLS AND JESTERS

Fradon, Dana. The King's Fool: A Book about Medieval & Renaissance Fools. Fradon, Dana, illus. LC 92-43836. 40p. (gr. 3-7). 1993. 14.99 (0-525-45074-2, DCB) Dutton Child Bks.

FOOLS AND JESTERS–FICTION

Sand, George. Histoire du Veritable Gribouille. Sand, Maurice, illus. (FRE.). 122p. (gr. 5-10). 1978. pap. 7.95 (2-07-033043-5) Schoenhof.

FOOT

Aliki. My Feet. Aliki, illus. LC 89-49357. 32p. (ps-1). 1990. 14.00 (0-690-04813-0, Crowell Jr Bks); PLB 13.89 (0-690-04815-7, Crowell Jr Bks) HarpC Child Bks.

—My Feet. Aliki, illus. LC 89-49357. 32p. (ps-1). 1992. pap. 4.50 (0-06-445106-2, Trophy) HarpC Child Bks.

Damon, Laura. Funny Fingers, Funny Toes. Kennedy, Anne, illus. LC 87-10915. 32p. (gr. k-2). 1988. PLB 11.59 (0-8167-1089-9); pap. text ed. 2.95 (0-8167-1090-2) Troll Assocs.

Drew, David. Toenails. Fleming, Leanne, illus. LC 92-31135. 1993. 2.50 (0-383-03661-5) SRA Schl Grp.

Dr. Seuss. Foot Book. Dr. Seuss, illus. LC 68-28462. (ps-1). 1968. 6.95 (0-394-80937-8); lib. bdg. 7.99 (0-394-90937-2) Random Bks Yng Read.

Greene, Leia A. Happy Feet: A Child's Guide to Foot Reflexology. Greene, Leia A., illus. 38p. (gr. k-12). 1992. wkbk. 4.95 (1-880737-10-8) Crystal Jrns.

Hughes, Shirley. Alfie's Feet. Hughes, Shirley, illus. LC 82-13012. 32p. (ps-1). 1983. 14.95 (0-688-01658-8); PLB 14.88 (0-688-01660-X) Lothrop.

Lemoine, Georges, illus. Pied. (FRE.). (ps-1). 1989. 12.95 (2-07-035701-5) Schoenhof.

Machotka, Hana. What Neat Feet! Machotka, Hana, photos by. LC 90-40886. (Illus.). 32p. (gr. k up). 1991. 13.95 (0-688-09474-0); PLB 13.88 (0-688-09475-9, Morrow Jr Bks) Morrow Jr Bks.

Markham-David, Sally. Hands & Feet. Fleming, Leanne, illus. LC 93-28978. 1994. 4.25 (0-383-03746-8) SRA Schl Grp.

Parnall, Peter. Feet! Parnall, Peter, illus. LC 88-5272. 32p. (ps-1). 1988. RSBE 14.95 (0-02-770110-7, Macmillan Child Bk) Macmillan Child Grp.

Reiss, Elayne & Friedman, Rita. Fantastic Funny Feet. (gr. k-1). 12.50 (0-89796-867-0) New Dimens Educ.

Rourke, Arlene C. Los Manos y los Pies. LC 92-5661. (ENG & SPA.). 1992. 15.94 (0-86625-290-8); 11.95s.p. (0-685-59319-3) Rourke Pubns.

Watson, Elaine. Busy Feet. Loman, Roberta K., illus. 28p. (ps). 1992. 2.50 (0-87403-952-5, 24-03592) Standard Pub.

FOOTBALL

see also Soccer

Aaseng, Nathan. You Are the Coach: College Football. (gr. 6-12). 1985. pap. 2.25 (*0-440-99840-9*, LFL) Dell.

—You Are the Coach: Football. 112p. (gr. 5 up). 1983. pap. 2.50 (*0-440-99136-6*, LFL) Dell.

Aylesworth, Thomas G. The Kids' Almanac of Professional Football. LC 92-16483. (Illus.). 176p. 1992. pap. 8.95 (*1-55870-266-0*, 70150) Shoe Tree Pr.

Blinn, William. Brian's Song. (Illus.). 128p. (Orig.). (gr. 6 up). 1983. pap. 3.99 (*0-553-26618-7*) Bantam.

Bloom, Marc. Know Your Game: Football. (gr. 4-7). 1990. pap. 2.95 (*0-590-43312-1*) Scholastic Inc.

Boulais, Sue. Learning How: Football. James, Jody, ed. Concept of Design Staff, illus. 48p. (gr. 4-7). 1992. lib. bdg. 14.95 (*0-944280-37-4*); pap. 5.95 (*0-944280-43-9*) Bancroft-Sage.

Brenner, Richard J. The Complete Super Bowl Story: Games I-XXIII. (Illus.). 112p. (gr. 5 up). 1989. PLB 15.95 (*0-8225-1503-2*) Lerner Pubns.

Broekel, Ray. Football. LC 81-15484. (Illus.). 48p. (gr. k-4). 1982. PLB 12.85 (*0-516-01629-6*); pap. 4.95 (*0-516-41629-4*) Childrens.

Dan Marino Sports Shots. (ps-3). 1992. pap. 1.25 (*0-590-45845-0*) Scholastic Inc.

Duden, Jane. The Super Bowl. LC 91-24692. (Illus.). 48p. (gr. 5). 1992. text ed. 11.95 RSBE (*0-89686-725-0*, Crestwood Hse) Macmillan Child Grp.

Duden, Jane & Osberg, Susan. Football. LC 90-26338. (Illus.). 48p. (gr. 5). 1991. text ed. 11.95 RSBE (*0-89686-626-2*, Crestwood Hse) Macmillan Child Grp.

Duroska, Lud & Schiffer, Don. Football Rules in Pictures. rev. ed. (Illus.). 80p. 1991. pap. 7.95 (*0-399-51689-1*, Perigee Bks) Berkley Pub.

Etheredge, Warren. The All-New Ultimate Football Quiz Book. 176p. (Orig.). 1993. pap. 3.99 (*0-451-17616-2*, Sig) NAL-Dutton.

Ferrell, John M. Playing Flag Football. 32p. (gr. 1-6). 1983. pap. 3.00 (*0-88035-052-0*, 3029, Pub. by YMCA USA) Human Kinetics.

Football Basics Study Aid. 1975. pap. 2.50 (*0-87738-048-1*) Youth Ed.

Football: Superstars & Superstats. (gr. 4-7). 1991. pap. 3.25 (*0-307-22372-8*) Western Pub.

Football You Call the Play. (gr. 4-7). 1991. pap. 3.25 (*0-307-22371-X*) Western Pub.

Greene, Carol. I Can Be a Football Player. LC 84-9609. (Illus.). 32p. (gr. k-3). 1984. PLB 11.80 (*0-516-01839-6*); pap. 3.95 (*0-516-41839-4*) Childrens.

Gutman, Bill. Football. LC 89-7585. (Illus.). 64p. (gr. 3-8). 1990. PLB 14.95 (*0-942545-85-0*) Marshall Cavendish.

—Gamebreakers of the NFL. (Illus.). (gr. 5 up). 1973. lib. bdg. 3.69 (*0-394-92501-7*) Random Bks Yng Read.

Hamilton, Jacklyn & Hamilton, Alfred T. ABCs of Football. Tank-Richard, James, illus. 320p. (Orig.). 1992. pap. 12.00 (*0-9635876-0-9*) J&A Bks.

Harris, Richard. I Can Read About Football. Milligan, John, illus. LC 76-54398. (gr. 2-5). 1977. pap. 2.50 (*0-89375-033-6*) Troll Assocs.

Hawkes, Bob. Playbook: Football, No. 2. (gr. 4-7). 1991. pap. 4.95 (*0-316-34349-8*, Spts Illus Kids) Little.

Hawkes, Robert. Play Book, No. 3: Football. (Illus.). (gr. 3-7). 1999. pap. 4.95 (*0-316-34353-6*, Spts Illus Kids) Little.

Italia, Bob. Football's Finest. LC 93-2285. 1993. 14.96 (*1-56239-242-5*) Abdo & Dghtrs.

Kessler, Leonard. Kick, Pass, & Run. Kessler, Leonard, illus. LC 66-18656. 64p. (ps-3). 1966. PLB 13.89 (*0-06-023160-2*) HarpC Child Bks.

Korch, Rick. The Official Pro Football Hall of Fame Playbook. (Illus.). 64p. (gr. 3 up). 1990. S&S Trade.

Lace, William W. Top Ten Football Quarterbacks. LC 93-40469. (Illus.). 48p. (gr. 4-10). 1994. lib. bdg. 14.95 (*0-89490-518-X*) Enslow Pubs.

—Top Ten Football Rushers. LC 93-40470. (Illus.). 48p. (gr. 4-10). 1994. lib. bdg. 14.95 (*0-89490-519-8*) Enslow Pubs.

Liss, Howard. Making of a Rookie. (Illus.). (gr. 5-9). 1968. lib. bdg. 3.69 (*0-394-90199-1*) Random Bks Yng Read.

—Playoff: Professional Football's Great Championship Games. LC 66-10675. (Illus.). (gr. 7 up). 1966. pap. 4.50 (*0-440-06939-4*) Delacorte.

Nash, Bruce & Zullo, Allan. The Football Hall of Shame Two: Young Fans' Edition. Clancy, Lisa, ed. 160p. (Orig.). (gr. 3-6). 1991. pap. 2.99 (*0-671-73534-9*, Archway) PB.

—The Football Hall of Shame: Young Fans' Edition. (Illus.). 144p. (gr. 5 up). 1990. pap. 2.95 (*0-671-72922-5*, Archway) PB.

Nelson, Colin. American Football. rev. ed. (Illus.). 80p. (gr. 10-12). 1993. pap. 7.95 (*0-7137-2414-5*, Pub. by Blandford Pr UK) Sterling.

Potts, Steve. Buffalo Bills. (gr. 4 up). 1991. PLB 14.95 (*0-88682-360-9*) Creative Ed.

—Denver Broncos. (gr. 4 up). 1991. PLB 14.95 (*0-88682-365-X*) Creative Ed.

Rambeck, Richard. Detroit Lions. 48p. (gr. 4 up). 1991. PLB 14.95 (*0-88682-366-8*) Creative Ed.

Ruffo, Dave. Football. LC 93-23274. 1993. PLB 21.34 (*0-8114-5780-X*) Raintree Steck-V.

Scheffel, Vernon L. Flag Football: How to Play It. LC 87-51055. (Illus.). 90p. (gr. 7-12). 1987. pap. 6.95 (*0-944450-00-8*) La Sierra U Pr.

Smith, Alias & Pelkowski, Robert. Football: Frankie Fumble in Football Friends. 32p. (ps-3). 1989. pap. 3.95 (*0-8120-4242-5*) Barron.

Stanley, Jerry W. The Football Player's Training Diary. 120p. (gr. 7-12). 1988. plastic bdg. 7.95 (*0-685-24024-X*) Sports Diary Pub.

Sullivan, George. All about Football. (Illus.). 128p. (gr. 3-7). 1990. (Putnam); pap. 7.95 (*0-399-21907-2*, Putnam) Putnam Pub Group.

—Football Kids. LC 90-33096. (Illus.). (gr. 4-7). 1990. 13.95 (*0-525-65040-7*, Cobblehill Bks) Dutton Child Bks.

Taylor, Valerie. Til Death Did Us Part. 67p. (gr. 12). 1985. pap. 6.95 (*0-917117-01-8*) Creat Concern.

Teitelbaum, Michael. Playbook! Football: You're the Quarterback, You Call the Shots. (gr. 9-12). 1990. pap. 4.95 (*0-316-83623-0*, Spts Illus Kids) Little.

Walton, Rick & Walton, Ann. Take a Hike: Riddles about Football. Burke, Susan S., illus. LC 92-27011. 1993. 11.95 (*0-8225-2340-X*) Lerner Pubns.

Webb, Equilla B. An Amateur's Guide to Football & Recruiting. 192p. (Orig.). (gr. 9-12). 1990. pap. text ed. 45.00 (*0-9624771-1-7*) Equilla Enterprises.

Weber, Bruce. Bruce Weber's Inside Pro Football, 1991. (gr. 4-7). 1991. pap. 2.50 (*0-590-44707-6*) Scholastic Inc.

—Bruce Weber's Inside Pro Football 1992. 1992. 2.50 (*0-590-45626-1*, 065) Scholastic Inc.

FOOTBALL–BIOGRAPHY

Aaseng, Nathan. Jerry Rice: Touchdown Talent. LC 93-10010. 1993. 13.50 (*0-8225-0521-5*) Lerner Pubns.

Appleman, Marc. Joe Montana. (Illus.). (gr. 3-7). 1991. pap. 4.95 (*0-316-04870-4*, Spts Illus Kids) Little.

Balzar, Howard. Football Super Stars. Allison, B., intro. by. (Illus.). 23p. (Orig.). (gr. 1-8). 1990. pap. 2.50 (*0-943409-13-6*) Marketcom.

—Quarterbacks of the NFL. Allison, B., intro. by. (Illus.). 23p. (Orig.). (gr. 1-8). 1990. pap. 2.50 (*0-943409-12-8*) Marketcom.

Balzer, Howard. Football All Pro Defense. Allison, B., intro. by. Focus on Sports-New York Staff, illus. 28p. (Orig.). 1989. pap. 2.50 (*0-943409-10-1*) Marketcom.

—Football All Pro Offense. Allison, B., intro. by. Focus On Sports-New York Staff, illus. (Orig.). 1989. pap. 2.50 (*0-943409-09-8*) Marketcom.

—Football All Pro Super Stars. Allison, B., ed. Focus On Sports-New York Staff, illus. 28p. (Orig.). 1989. pap. 2.50 (*0-943409-11-X*) Marketcom.

Barry Sanders. 1992. 1.25 (*0-590-46251-2*) Scholastic Inc.

Benagh, Jim. Sports Great Herschel Walker. LC 89-28385. (Illus.). 64p. (gr. 4-10). 1990. lib. bdg. 15.95 (*0-89490-207-5*) Enslow Pubs.

Bo Jackson. 48p. 1991. pap. 1.25 (*0-590-45194-4*) Scholastic Inc.

Cox, Ted. Emmitt Smith: Finding Daylight. LC 93-43837. (Illus.). 48p. (gr. 2-8). 1994. PLB 11.95 (*0-516-04383-8*) Childrens.

Devaney, John. Bo Jackson: A Star for All Seasons. 132p. 1992. 14.95 (*0-8027-8178-0*); PLB 15.85 (*0-8027-8179-9*) Walker & Co.

—Winners of the Heisman Trophy. 2nd ed. (Illus.). (gr. 5 up). 1990. 14.95 (*0-8027-6906-3*); lib. bdg. 15.85 (*0-8027-6907-1*) Walker & Co.

Dickey, Glenn. Sports Great Jerry Rice. LC 93-19997. (Illus.). 64p. (gr. 4-10). 1993. lib. bdg. 15.95 (*0-89490-419-1*) Enslow Pubs.

Dippold, Joel. Troy Aikman, Quick-Draw Quarterback. LC 93-47909. (Illus.). 64p. (gr. 4-9). 1994. PLB 13.50 (*0-8225-2880-0*); pap. 5.95 (*0-8225-9663-6*) Lerner Pubns.

Evans, J. Edward. Jerry Rice: Touchdown Talent. (gr. 4-7). 1993. pap. 4.95 (*0-8225-9634-2*) Lerner Pubns.

Fox, Larry. Sports Great John Elway. LC 89-28465. (Illus.). 64p. (gr. 4-10). 1990. lib. bdg. 15.95 (*0-685-59059-3*) Enslow Pubs.

Frankl, Ron. Terry Bradshaw. LC 94-5780. 1994. 14.95 (*0-7910-2451-2*) Chelsea Hse.

Goodman, Michael E. Lawrence Taylor. LC 87-29023. (Illus.). 48p. (gr. 5-6). 1988. RSBE 11.95 (*0-89686-365-4*, Crestwood Hse) Macmillan Child Grp.

Green, Carl R. Troy Aikman. LC 93-17480. (Illus.). 48p. (gr. 5-6). 1994. text ed. 13.95 RSBE (*0-89686-833-8*, Crestwood Hse) Macmillan Child Grp.

Green, Carl R. & Ford, M. Roxanne. Deion Sanders. LC 93-951. (Illus.). 48p. (gr. 5-6). 1994. text ed. 13.95 RSBE (*0-89686-840-0*, Crestwood Hse) Macmillan Child Grp.

Gutman, Bill. Great Quarterbacks of the N. F. L. Clancy, Lisa, ed. (Illus.). 144p. (Orig.). (gr. 5 up). 1993. pap. 2.99 (*0-671-79244-X*, Archway) PB.

—Reggie White: Star Defensive Lineman. LC 93-38960. (Illus.). 48p. (gr. 3-6). 1994. 13.40 (*1-56294-461-4*) Millbrook Pr.

Hays, Scott R. Hall of Famers. LC 92-5638. 1992. PLB 17.26 (*0-86593-155-0*); 12.95s.p. (*0-685-59287-1*) Rourke Corp.

Jim Kelly. 1992. 1.25 (*0-590-46250-4*) Scholastic Inc.

Joe Montana. 48p. 1991. pap. 1.25 (*0-590-45195-2*) Scholastic Inc.

Kavanagh, Jack. Barry Sanders: Rocket Running Back. (gr. 4-7). 1994. pap. 4.95 (*0-8225-9635-0*) Lerner Pubns.

—Sports Great Joe Montana. LC 91-41527. (Illus.). 64p. (gr. 4-10). 1992. lib. bdg. 15.95 (*0-89490-371-3*) Enslow Pubs.

Knapp, Ron. Sports Great Barry Sanders. LC 92-38432. (Illus.). 64p. (gr. 4-10). 1993. lib. bdg. 15.95 (*0-89490-418-3*) Enslow Pubs.

Koslow, Philip. Walter Payton. LC 94-1352. 1994. 14.95 (*0-7910-2455-5*) Chelsea Hse.

Leder, Jane M. Marcus Allen. LC 84-11375. (Illus.). 48p. (gr. 5-6). 1985. text ed. 11.95 RSBE (*0-89686-251-8*, Crestwood Hse) Macmillan Child Grp.

Liss, Howard. Making of a Rookie. (Illus.). (gr. 5-9). 1968. lib. bdg. 3.69 (*0-394-90199-1*) Random Bks Yng Read.

Marx, Doug. Running Backs. LC 92-8764. 1992. 17.26 (*0-86593-151-8*); lib. bdg. 12.95s.p. (*0-685-59321-5*) Rourke Corp.

Monroe, Judy. John Elway. LC 87-27430. (Illus.). 48p. (gr. 5-6). 1988. text ed. 11.95 RSBE (*0-89686-367-0*, Crestwood Hse) Macmillan Child Grp.

Nadan, Corinne J. & Blue, Rose. Jerry Rice. LC 94-4596. 1994. 14.95 (*0-7910-2456-3*) Chelsea Hse.

Prentzas, Scott. Jim Brown. LC 94-1349. 1994. 14.95 (*0-7910-2452-0*) Chelsea Hse.

Raber, Thomas R. Joe Montana: Comeback Quarterback. 1990. pap. 4.95 (*0-8225-9572-9*) Lerner Pubns.

Raber, Tom. Joe Montana: Comeback Quarterback. (Illus.). 64p. (gr. 4-9). 1989. PLB 13.50 (*0-8225-0486-3*) Lerner Pubns.

Reiser, Howard. Barry Sanders: Lion with a Quiet Roar. LC 93-19780. (Illus.). 48p. (gr. 2-8). 1993. PLB 11.95 (*0-516-04377-3*); pap. 3.95 (*0-516-44377-1*) Childrens.

Rogers, Hal. Generals. LC 92-9478. 1992. PLB 17.26 (*0-86593-154-2*); 12.95s.p. (*0-685-59323-1*) Rourke Corp.

Rolfe, John. Bo Jackson. (gr. 4-7). 1991. pap. 4.95 (*0-316-75457-9*, Spts Illus Kids) Little.

—Bo Jackson. (Illus.). 124p. (gr. 3-6). 1991. PLB 19.95 (*0-8225-3109-7*) Lerner Pubns.

—Jerry Rice. McGarry, Steve, illus. 1993. pap. 3.99 (*0-553-48157-6*) Bantam.

Roth, Leo. Jim Kelly: Star Quarterback. LC 93-38637. 104p. (gr. 4-10). 1994. PLB 17.95 (*0-89490-446-9*) Enslow Pubs.

Rothaus, James R. Barry Sanders. 32p. (gr. 2-6). 1991. 14.95 (*0-89565-737-6*) Childs World.

—Bo Jackson. 32p. (gr. 2-6). 1991. 14.95 (*0-89565-731-7*) Childs World.

—Joe Montana. 32p. 1991. 14.95 (*0-89565-736-8*) Childs World.

Rubin, Bob. Dan Marino: Wonder Boy Quarterback. LC 85-9724. (Illus.). 48p. (gr. 2-8). 1985. pap. 3.95 (*0-516-44347-X*) Childrens.

Sanford, William R. & Green, Carl R. Joe Namath. LC 92-26324. (Illus.). 48p. (gr. 5). 1993. text ed. 11.95 RSBE (*0-89686-782-X*, Crestwood Hse) Macmillan Child Grp.

Savage, Jeff. Thurman Thomas: Star Running Back. LC 93-2557. (Illus.). 104p. (gr. 4-10). 1994. lib. bdg. 17.95 (*0-89490-445-0*) Enslow Pubs.

Stein, Conrad R. Walter Payton: Record-Breaking Runner. LC 87-13241. (Illus.). 48p. (gr. 2-8). 1987. pap. 3.95 (*0-516-44363-1*) Childrens.

Stein, R. Conrad. Don Shula: Football's Winningest Coach. LC 94-9915. (Illus.). 48p. (gr. 2-8). 1994. PLB 15.80 (*0-516-04385-4*); pap. 3.95 (*0-516-44385-2*) Childrens.

Sufrin, Mark. Payton. LC 88-15751. (Illus.). 160p. (gr. 7 up). 1988. SBE 13.95 (*0-684-18940-2*, Scribners Young Read) Macmillan Child Grp.

Thornley, Stew. Deion Sanders: Prime Time Player. LC 92-45686. 1993. 13.50 (*0-8225-0523-1*) Lerner Pubns.

Weber, Bruce. Pro Football Megastars, 1993. (gr. 4-7). 1993. pap. 3.95 (*0-590-47433-2*) Scholastic Inc.

FOOTBALL–DICTIONARIES

Gutman, Bill. The Kids' World Almanac of Football. 1994. 14.95 (*0-88687-765-2*); pap. 7.95 (*0-88687-764-4*) Wrld Almnc.

FOOTBALL–FICTION

Aaseng, Nathan. At Left Linebacker, Chip Demory. LC 87-30905. (gr. 3-7). 1988. pap. 4.49 (*1-55513-921-3*, Chariot Bks) Chariot Family.

—Football: It's Your Team. (gr. k-12). 1987. pap. 2.50 (*0-440-92648-3*, LFL) Dell.

Baczewski, Paul C. Just for Kicks. LC 90-30528. 192p. (gr. 7 up). 1992. pap. 3.95 (*0-06-447074-1*, Trophy) HarpC Child Bks.

Berenstain, Stan & Berenstain, Jan. The Berenstain Bears & the Female Fullback. Berenstain, Stan & Berenstain, Jan, illus. 112p. (Orig.). (gr. 2-6). 1993. PLB 7.99 (*0-679-93611-4*); pap. 3.50 (*0-679-83611-X*) Random Bks Yng Read.

Bernstein, Joanne E. & Cohen, Paul. Touchdown Riddles. Levine, Abby, ed. Signorino, Slug, illus. LC 88-21761. 32p. (gr. 1-5). 1989. 8.95g (*0-8075-8036-8*) A Whitman.

Christopher, Matt. Catch That Pass, Vol. 1. Kidder, Harvey, illus. LC 77-77442. (gr. 4-6). 1989. lib. bdg. 15.95 (*0-316-13932-7*); pap. 3.95 (*0-316-13924-6*) Little.

—The Counterfeit Tackle. (gr. 4-7). 1990. pap. 3.95 (*0-316-14243-3*) Little.

—Football Fugitive. Johnson, Larry, illus. 128p. (gr. 4-6). 1988. 14.95 (*0-316-13971-8*); pap. 3.95 (*0-316-14064-3*) Little.

—The Great Quarterback Switch. Jones, Eric, illus. LC 83-25628. (gr. 4-6). 1984. Little.

—Tackle Without a Team. Sanfilippo, Margaret, illus. LC 88-22644. 128p. (gr. 3-7). 1989. 14.95 (*0-316-14067-8*) Little.

—Tackle Without a Team. (gr. 4-7). 1993. pap. 3.95 (*0-316-14268-9*) Little.

—Touchdown for Tommy. Caddell, Foster, illus. 145p. (gr. 4-6). 1985. pap. 3.95 (*0-316-13982-3*) Little.

—Tough to Tackle. Kidder, Harvey, illus. 152p. (gr. 4-6). 1987. pap. 3.95 (*0-316-14058-9*) Little.
—Undercover Tailback. LC 92-19770. (Illus.). 1992. 15. 95 (*0-316-14251-4*) Little.
D'Andrea, Joseph C. If I Were a Buffalo Bill. Wilson, Bill, illus. 24p. (Orig.). (ps-5). 1993. pap. 5.95 (*1-878338-51-X*) Picture Me Bks.
—If I Were a Carolina Panther. Wilson, Bill, illus. 24p. (Orig.). (gr. k-5). 1994. pap. 5.99 (*1-57151-001-X*) Picture Me Bks.
—If I Were a Denver Bronco. Wilson, Bill, illus. 24p. (Orig.). (gr. k-5). 1994. pap. 5.99 (*1-878338-67-6*) Picture Me Bks.
—If I Were a Jacksonville Jaguar. Wilson, Bill, illus. 24p. (Orig.). (gr. k-5). 1994. pap. 5.99 (*1-57151-006-0*) Picture Me Bks.
—If I Were a Kansas City Chief. Wilson, Bill, illus. 24p. (Orig.). (ps-5). 1993. pap. 5.95 (*1-878338-52-8*) Picture Me Bks.
—If I Were an Atlanta Falcon. Wilson, Bill, illus. 24p. (Orig.). (gr. k-5). 1994. pap. 5.99 (*1-57151-000-1*) Picture Me Bks.
Dygard, Thomas J. Backfield Package. LC 93-7721. 208p. (gr. 5 up). 1993. pap. 3.99 (*0-14-036348-3*, Puffin) Puffin Bks.
—Forward Pass. LC 89-33427. (Illus.). 192p. (gr. 7 up). 1989. 11.95 (*0-688-07961-X*) Morrow Jr Bks.
—Forward Pass. (gr. 4 up). 1990. pap. 3.99 (*0-14-034562-0*, Puffin) Puffin Bks.
—Game Plan. LC 92-47252. 224p. (gr. 7 up). 1993. 14.00 (*0-688-12007-5*) Morrow Jr Bks.
—Halfback Tough. LC 85-25987. 224p. (gr. 7 up). 1986. 12.95 (*0-688-05925-2*) Morrow Jr Bks.
—Halfback Tough. 224p. (gr. 5 up). 1989. pap. 3.99 (*0-14-034113-7*, Puffin) Puffin Bks.
—Quarterback Walk-On. LC 81-18715. 224p. (gr. 7-9). 1982. 13.65 (*0-688-01065-2*) Morrow Jr Bks.
—Quaterback Walk-On. 224p. (gr. 5 up). 1989. pap. 3.99 (*0-14-034115-3*, Puffin) Puffin Bks.
—Running Scared. 192p. (gr. 5 up). 1992. pap. 3.99 (*0-14-034914-6*, Puffin) Puffin Bks.
—Winning Kicker. 192p. (gr. 4 up). 1990. pap. 3.99 (*0-14-034117-X*, Puffin) Puffin Bks.
Eller, Scott. The Johnson Boys: The Football Wars. 1992. pap. 2.95 (*0-590-42828-4*, 060, Apple Paperbacks) Scholastic Inc.
Foley, Louise M. Tackle Twenty-Two. Heinly, John, illus. 48p. (ps-3). 1981. pap. 1.75 (*0-440-48484-7*, YB) Dell.
Halecroft, David. Breaking Loose. (gr. 4 up). 1990. pap. 2.95 (*0-14-034546-9*, Puffin) Puffin Bks.
—Breaking Loose. LC 92-12084. 128p. (gr. 3-7). 1992. 13.00 (*0-670-84697-X*) Viking Child Bks.
Hallowell, Tommy. Last Chance Quarterback. 112p. (gr. 3 up). 1990. pap. 3.50 (*0-14-032909-9*, Puffin) Puffin Bks.
—Last Chance Quarterback. (gr. 4-7). 1991. 12.95 (*0-670-83731-8*) Viking Child Bks.
Hermes, Patricia. What If They Knew? 128p. (gr. k-6). 1989. pap. 2.95 (*0-440-49515-6*, YB) Dell.
Hughes, Dean. Quarterback Hero. Stroud, Steve, illus. LC 93-8039. 112p. (Orig.). 1994. pap. 3.99 (*0-679-84360-4*, Bullseye Bks) Random Bks Yng Read.
Jenkins, Jerry. The Mysterious Football Team. (Orig.). (gr. 7-12). 1986. pap. text ed. 4.99 (*0-8024-8234-1*) Moody.
Kessler, Leonard. Kick, Pass & Run. Kessler, Leonard, illus. LC 66-18656. (gr. k-3). 1978. pap. 3.50 (*0-06-444012-5*, Trophy) HarpC Child Bks.
—Super Bowl. LC 80-10171. (Illus.). 56p. (gr. 1-4). 1980. PLB 12.88 (*0-688-84270-4*) Greenwillow.
—Super Bowl. (gr. k-6). 1991. pap. 2.95 (*0-440-40403-7*, Pub. by Yearling Classics) Dell.
Korman, Gordon. The Zucchini Warriors. 208p. (gr. 4-7). 1988. pap. 10.95 (*0-590-41335-X*, Pub. by Scholastic Hardcover) Scholastic Inc.
Kuskin, Karla. The Dallas Titans Get Ready for Bed. Simont, Marc, illus. LC 83-49470. 48p. (gr. k-3). 1986. PLB 11.89 (*0-06-023563-2*) HarpC Child Bks.
Leggat, Bonnie-Alise. Punt, Pass & Point! Thatch, Nancy R., ed. Leggat, Bonnie-Alise, illus. Melton, David, intro. by. LC 92-17598. (Illus.). 26p. (gr. 3-5). 1992. PLB 14.95 (*0-933849-39-7*) Landmark Edns.
Malmgren, Dallin. The Whole Nine Yards. (gr. 7 up). 1987. pap. 2.95 (*0-440-99575-2*, LFL) Dell.
Marsh, Carole. Minnesota Silly Football Sportsmysteries, Vol. II. (Illus.). (gr. 3 up). 1994. PLB 24.95 (*1-55609-651-8*); pap. 14.95 (*1-55609-652-6*); computer disk 29.95 (*1-55609-653-4*) Gallopade Pub Group.
—Missouri Silly Football Sportsmysteries, Vol. I. (Illus.). (gr. 3 up). 1994. PLB 24.95 (*1-55609-736-0*); pap. 14. 95 (*1-55609-737-9*); computer disk 29.95 (*0-685-45945-4*) Gallopade Pub Group.
—North Dakota Silly Football Sportsmysteries, Vol. 1. (Illus.). 1994. PLB 24.95 (*1-55609-948-7*); pap. 14.95 (*1-55609-949-5*); computer disk 29.95 (*0-685-45971-3*) Gallopade Pub Group.
Miklowitz, Gloria D. Anything to Win. 1989. pap. 14.95 (*0-440-50142-3*) Dell.
Mooser, Stephen. The Snow Bowl. Ulrich, George, illus. 80p. (gr. 2-5). 1992. pap. 3.25 (*0-440-40563-7*, YB) Dell.
Myers, Bernice. Sidney Rella & the Glass Sneaker. Myers, Bernice, illus. LC 85-3044. 32p. (gr. k-3). 1985. RSBE 14.95 (*0-02-767790-7*, Macmillan Child Bk) Macmillan Child Grp.
Nichols, Paul. Blitz: Rookie Quarterback, No. 1. (gr. 3 up). 1988. pap. 3.99 (*0-345-35108-8*) Ballantine.
—Tough Tackle. 1988. pap. 2.95 (*0-345-35109-6*) Ballantine.
Salem, Lynn & Stewart, Josie. Dia de Futbol. (Illus.). 8p. (gr. 1). 1993. pap. 3.50 (*1-880612-27-5*) Seedling Pubns.
Scholz, Jackson V. The Football Rebels. LC 92-43376. 224p. (gr. 6 up). 1993. pap. 4.95 (*0-688-12643-X*, Pub. by Beech Tree Bks) Morrow.
—Rookie Quarterback. LC 92-43375. 224p. (gr. 6 up). 1993. pap. 4.95 (*0-688-12644-8*) Morrow Jr Bks.
Sherman, Harold M. Interference, & Other Football Stories. facsimile ed. LC 70-178460. (gr. 7 up). Repr. of 1932 ed. 18.00 (*0-8369-4061-X*) Ayer.
Shiver, Lee A. Going to the Gator Game! 32p. (gr. k-5). 1992. 19.95 (*1-882466-00-4*) Our Mascot.
Steel, Richard. Touchdown. Parker, Liz, ed. Taylor, Marjorie, illus. 45p. (Orig.). (gr. 6-12). 1992. pap. text ed. 2.95 (*1-56254-054-8*) Saddleback Pubns.
Sullivan, Ann. Molly Maguire: Wide Receiver. 112p. (Orig.). 1992. pap. 2.99 (*0-380-76114-9*, Camelot) Avon.
Tunis, John R. All-American. 261p. (gr. 3-7). 1989. pap. 3.95 (*0-15-202292-9*, Odyssey) HarBrace.
Van Leeuwen, Jean. Benjy the Football Hero. Owens, Gail, illus. LC 84-21459. 192p. (gr. 2-6). 1985. PLB 11.89 (*0-8037-0190-X*) Dial Bks Young.
Wojciechowska, Maia. Dreams of the Super Bowl. Karsky, A. K., illus. 52p. 1994. pap. 5.50 (*1-883740-03-7*) Pebble Bch Pr Ltd.
—Dreams of the Super Bowl. Karsky, A. K., illus. 52p. Date not set. 14.50 (*1-883740-20-7*) Pebble Bch Pr Ltd.

FOOTBALL–HISTORY

Aaseng, Nathan. A Decade of Champions: Super Bowls XVI-XXIV. (Illus.). 64p. (gr. 5 up). 1991. PLB 15.95 (*0-8225-1504-0*) Lerner Pubns.
Calmera, Brenda. Dallas Cowboys. (gr. 4 up). 1991. PLB 14.95 (*0-88682-364-1*) Creative Ed.
Duden, Jane & Osberg, Susan. Football. LC 90-26338. (Illus.). 48p. (gr. 5). 1991. text ed. 11.95 RSBE (*0-89686-626-2*, Crestwood Hse) Macmillan Child Grp.
Good Days, Bad Days: An NFL Book. (Illus.). 128p. (gr. 3-9). 1992. 15.00 (*0-670-84686-4*) Viking Child Bks.
Gutman, Bill. Football Super Teams. (Illus.). 160p. (gr. 5 up). 1991. pap. 2.99 (*0-671-74098-9*, Archway) PB.
—Pro Football Record Breakers. (Illus.). 128p. (gr. 5 up). 1989. pap. 2.99 (*0-671-68623-2*, Archway) PB.
Hays, Scott R. Hall of Famers. LC 92-5638. 1992. PLB 17.26 (*0-86593-155-0*); 12.95s.p. (*0-685-59287-1*) Rourke Corp.
Jarrett, William. Timetables of Sports History: Football. (Illus.). 96p. (gr. 6 up). 1989. 17.95 (*0-8160-1919-3*) Facts on File.
King, Gary. An Autumn Remembered: Reflections of College Football's Greatest Team. King, Charlyce, ed. LC 87-73386. 300p. (Orig.). (gr. 9 up). 1988. pap. 12. 95 (*0-9619712-0-7*) Red Earth OK.
Marx, Doug. Running Backs. LC 92-8764. 1992. 17.26 (*0-86593-151-8*); lib. bdg. 12.95s.p. (*0-685-59321-5*) Rourke Corp.
Potts, Steve. Houston Oilers. (gr. 4 up). 1991. PLB 14.95 (*0-88682-368-4*) Creative Ed.
—Minnesota Vikings. (gr. 4 up). 1991. PLB 14.95 (*0-88682-374-9*) Creative Ed.
—New Orleans Saints. (gr. 4 up). 1991. PLB 14.95 (*0-88682-376-5*) Creative Ed.
—San Francisco Forty Niners. (gr. 4 up). 1991. PLB 14. 95 (*0-88682-383-8*) Creative Ed.
Rambeck, Richard. Atlanta Falcons. (Illus.). 48p. (gr. 4 up). 1991. PLB 14.95 (*0-88682-359-5*) Creative Ed.
—Cincinnati Bengals. (gr. 4 up). 1991. PLB 14.95 (*0-88682-362-5*) Creative Ed.
—Cleveland Browns. 48p. (gr. 4 up). 1991. PLB 14.95 (*0-88682-363-3*) Creative Ed.
—Kansas City Chiefs. (gr. 4 up). 1991. PLB 14.95 (*0-88682-370-6*) Creative Ed.
—Los Angeles Rams. (gr. 4 up). 1991. PLB 14.95 (*0-88682-372-2*) Creative Ed.
—New England Patriots. 48p. (gr. 4 up). 1991. PLB 14. 95 (*0-88682-375-7*) Creative Ed.
—Philadelphia Eagles. 48p. (gr. 4 up). 1991. PLB 14.95 (*0-88682-379-X*) Creative Ed.
—San Diego Chargers. (gr. 4 up). 1991. PLB 14.95 (*0-88682-382-X*) Creative Ed.
—Seattle Seahawks. (gr. 4 up). 1991. PLB 14.95 (*0-88682-384-6*) Creative Ed.
—Tampa Bay Buccaneers. (Illus.). 48p. (gr. 4-12). 1991. PLB 14.95 (*0-88682-385-4*) Creative Ed.
—Washington Redskins. (gr. 4 up). 1991. PLB 14.95 (*0-88682-386-2*) Creative Ed.
Rockwell, Bart. The World's Strangest Football Stories. LC 92-10121. (Illus.). 96p. (gr. 3-7). 1992. PLB 9.89 (*0-8167-2934-4*); pap. text ed. 2.95 (*0-8167-2851-8*) Troll Assocs.
Rogers, Hal. Generals. LC 92-9478. 1992. PLB 17.26 (*0-86593-154-2*); 12.95s.p. (*0-685-59323-1*) Rourke Corp.
Ryan, Pat. Chicago Bears. 48p. (gr. 4 up). 1991. 14.95 (*0-88682-361-7*) Creative Ed.
—Green Bay Packers. (gr. 4 up). 1991. PLB 14.95 (*0-88682-367-6*) Creative Ed.
—Los Angeles Raiders. (gr. 4 up). 1991. PLB 14.95 (*0-88682-371-4*) Creative Ed.
—New York Giants. (gr. 4 up). 1991. PLB 14.95 (*0-88682-377-3*) Creative Ed.
—New York Jets. (gr. 4 up). 1991. PLB 14.95 (*0-88682-378-1*) Creative Ed.
Silverstein, Herma & Dunnahoo, Terry J. Pro Football: The Halls of Fame. LC 93-954. (Illus.). 48p. (gr. 5-6). 1994. text ed. 13.95 RSBE (*0-89686-851-6*, Crestwood Hse) Macmillan Child Grp.
Snypp, Wilbur & Hunter, Bob. Buckeyes: Ohio State Football. (Illus.). 352p. (gr. 6-12). 1988. 16.95 (*0-87397-307-0*) Strode.
Stevenson, Amy. The Super Bowl. 32p. (gr. 4). 1990. PLB 14.95 (*0-88682-315-3*) Creative Ed.
Uhland, Vicki. Miami Dolphins. (gr. 4-8). 1991. PLB 14. 95 (*0-88682-373-0*) Creative Ed.

FOOTBALL–YEARBOOKS

Hollander, Zander. The Complete Handbook of Pro Football, 1993. 19th ed. 368p. (Orig.). 1993. pap. 5.99 (*0-451-17765-7*, Sig) NAL-Dutton.

FOOTBALL CLUBS

Rambeck, Richard. The Indianapolis Colts. (gr. 4 up). 1991. PLB 14.95 (*0-88682-369-2*) Creative Ed.
—Phoenix Cardinals. 48p. (gr. 4 up). 1991. PLB 14.95 (*0-88682-381-1*) Creative Ed.
Ryan, Pat. Pittsburgh Steelers. 1991. PLB 14.95 (*0-88682-380-3*) Creative Ed.

FORAGE PLANTS

see also Grasses

FORCE AND ENERGY

see also Dynamics; Mechanics; Motion

Adler, David. Wonders of Energy. Johnson, Lewis, illus. LC 82-20042. 32p. (gr. 3-6). 1983. PLB 10.59 (*0-89375-884-1*); pap. text ed. 2.95 (*0-89375-885-X*) Troll Assocs.
Althea. What Makes Things Move? Green, Robina, illus. LC 90-10924. 32p. (gr. k-3). 1991. PLB 11.59 (*0-8167-2124-6*); pap. text ed. 3.95 (*0-8167-2125-4*) Troll Assocs.
Bailey, Donna. What We Can Do about Conserving Energy. LC 91-12315. (Illus.). 32p. (gr. 3-5). 1992. PLB 11.40 (*0-531-11079-6*) Watts.
Bardon, Keith. Exploring Forces & Structures. Clay, Marilyn, illus. LC 91-38318. 48p. (gr. 4-8). 1992. PLB 22.80 (*0-8114-2602-5*) Raintree Steck-V.
Breitter, Herta S. Fuel & Energy. rev. ed. LC 87-20804. (Illus.). 48p. (gr. 2-6). 1987. PLB 10.95 (*0-8172-3255-9*); pap. 4.49 (*0-8114-8223-5*) Raintree Steck-V.
Catherall, Ed. Exploring Uses of Energy. LC 90-46703. (Illus.). 48p. (gr. 4-8). 1990. PLB 22.80 (*0-8114-2598-3*) Raintree Steck-V.
Charman, Andrew. Energy. LC 92-6079. (Illus.). 32p. (gr. 5-8). 1993. PLB 12.40 (*0-531-14233-7*) Watts.
Cobb, Vicki. Why Doesn't the Earth Fall Up? And Other Not Such Dumb Questions about Motion. Enik, Ted, illus. LC 88-11108. 40p. (gr. 2-5). 1989. 13.00 (*0-525-67253-2*, Lodestar Bks) Dutton Child Bks.
—Why Doesn't the Sun Burn Out? Enik, Ted, illus. 40p. (gr. 2-5). 1990. 13.95 (*0-525-67301-6*, Lodestar Bks) Dutton Child Bks.
Cohen, Lynn. Energy & Machines. 64p. (ps-2). 1988. 6.95 (*0-912107-78-2*, MM982) Monday Morning Bks.
Conway, Lorraine. Energy. Akins, Linda, illus. 64p. (gr. 5 up). 1985. wkbk. 7.95 (*0-86653-267-6*, GA 639) Good Apple.
Devonshire, Hilary. Movement. LC 92-7837. (Illus.). 32p. (gr. 5-8). 1993. PLB 12.40 (*0-531-14229-9*) Watts.
Dunn, Andrew. The Power of Pressure. LC 92-41512. 32p. (gr. 3-6). 1993. 13.95 (*1-56847-015-0*) Thomson Lrning.
Evans, David & Williams, Claudette. Make It Go. LC 92-52816. (Illus.). 32p. (gr. k-3). 1992. 9.95 (*1-56458-120-9*) Dorling Kindersley.
Gardner, Robert. Forces & Machines. (Illus.). 136p. (gr. 7 up). 1991. lib. bdg. 14.98 (*0-671-69041-8*, J Messner); pap. 9.95 (*0-671-69046-9*) S&S Trade.
Goldin, Augusta. Small Energy Sources: Choices That Work. LC 87-167. (Illus.). 178p. (gr. 7 up). 1988. 17. 95 (*0-15-276215-9*, HB Juv Bks) HarBrace.
Gutnik, Martin J. & Browne-Gutnik, Natalie. Projects That Explore Energy. LC 93-7787. (Illus.). 72p. (gr. 5-8). 1994. PLB 14.40 (*1-56294-334-0*) Millbrook Pr.
Heese. Jugendhandbuch Naturwissen, Vol. 5: Energie. (GER.). 128p. 1976. pap. 5.95 (*0-7859-0413-1*, M7490) Fr & Eur.
Jennings, Terry. Energy Exists? LC 94-20027. 1995. write for info. (*0-8114-3881-3*) Raintree Steck-V.
Johnston, Tom. Energy: Making It Work. Pooley, Sarah, illus. LC 87-42751. 32p. (gr. 4-6). 1987. PLB 17.27 (*1-55532-405-3*) Gareth Stevens Inc.
—The Forces with You! Pooley, Sarah, illus. LC 87-42753. 32p. (gr. 4-6). 1987. PLB 17.27 (*1-55532-408-8*) Gareth Stevens Inc.
Kerrod, Robin. Force & Motion. Evans, Ted, illus. LC 93-4550. 64p. (gr. 5 up). 1993. Set. write for info.; PLB 15.95 (*1-85435-622-4*) Marshall Cavendish.
Lafferty, Peter. Energy & Light. LC 88-83110. (Illus.). 40p. (gr. 7-9). 1990. 12.40 (*0-531-17144-2*, Gloucester Pr) Watts.
Morgan, Sally & Morgan, Adrian. Using Energy. LC 93-20407. (gr. 4 up). 1993. write for info. (*0-8160-2984-9*) Facts on File.
Murphy, Bryan. Experiment with Movement. 32p. (gr. 2-5). 1991. PLB 17.50 (*0-8225-2451-1*) Lerner Pubns.
Neal, Philip. Energy, Power Sources & Electricity. (Illus.). 48p. (gr. 6-9). 1989. 19.95 (*0-85219-776-4*, Pub. by Batsford UK) Trafalgar.
Peacock, Graham. Forces. (Illus.). 32p. (gr. 2-4). 1994. 14.95 (*1-56847-192-0*) Thomson Lrning.

Raintree Publishers Inc. Staff. Energy. LC 87-28699. (Illus.). 64p. (Orig.). (gr. 5-9). 1988. PLB 11.95 (*0-8172-3076-9*) Raintree Steck-V.

Rickard, Graham. Bioenergy. LC 91-9259. (Illus.). 32p. (gr. 4-6). 1991. PLB 17.27 (*0-8368-0707-3*) Gareth Stevens Inc.

Rowe, Julian & Perham, Molly. Make It Move! LC 93-13737. (Illus.). 32p. (gr. 1-4). 1993. PLB 13.95 (*0-516-08135-7*) Childrens.

Sauvain, Philip. Motion. LC 91-24480. (Illus.). 48p. (gr. 6 up). 1992. text ed. 13.95 RSBE (*0-02-781077-1*, New Discovery) Macmillan Child Grp.

Spurgeon, R. Energy & Power. (Illus.). 48p. 1990. PLB 13.96 (*0-88110-418-3*); pap. 7.95 (*0-7460-0422-2*) EDC.

Taylor, Barbara. Force & Movement. LC 89-21505. (Illus.). 32p. (gr. 5-8). 1990. PLB 12.40 (*0-531-14081-4*) Watts.

—Get It in Gear! The Science of Movement. Bull, Peter, et al, illus. LC 90-42617. (Illus.). 40p. (gr. 2-5). 1991. pap. 4.95 (*0-679-80812-4*) Random Bks Yng Read.

Vita-Finzi, Claudio. The Power Pop-up Book: Our Planet's Energy Resources: Production, Consumption, Conservation, & Innovation. Jacobs, Philip, illus. Wilgress, Paul, contrib. by. (Illus.). 10p. (gr. 3 up). 1991. pap. 13.95 casebound pop-up (*0-671-73535-7*, S&S BFYR) S&S Trade.

Ward, Alan. Experimenting with Energy. Flax, Zena, illus. 48p. (gr. 2-7). 1991. lib. bdg. 12.95 (*0-7910-1510-6*) Chelsea Hse.

FORD, GERALD, PRES. U. S., 1913-

Collins, David R. Gerald R. Ford: Thirty-Eighth President of the United States. Young, Richard G., ed. LC 89-39945. (Illus.). 128p. (gr. 5-9). 1990. PLB 17.26 (*0-944483-65-8*) Garrett Ed Corp.

Randolph, Sallie. Gerald R. Ford: President. LC 86-16333. 128p. (gr. 5 up). 1987. 12.95 (*0-8027-6666-8*); PLB 13.85 (*0-8027-6667-6*) Walker & Co.

FORD, HENRY, 1863-1947

Aird, Hazel B. & Ruddiman, Catherine. Henry Ford: Young Man with Ideas. Wood, Wallace, illus. LC 86-10756. 192p. (gr. 2-6). 1986. pap. 3.95 (*0-02-041910-4*, Aladdin) Macmillan Child Grp.

Kent, Zachary. The Story of Henry Ford & the Automobile. LC 90-2163. (Illus.). 32p. (gr. 3-6). 1990. PLB 12.30 (*0-516-04751-5*); pap. 3.95 (*0-516-44751-3*) Childrens.

Mitchell, Barbara. We'll Race You, Henry: A Story about Henry Ford. Haubrich, Kathy, illus. 64p. (gr. 3-6). 1986. PLB 14.95 (*0-87614-291-9*) Carolrhoda Bks.

Sipiera, Paul. Gerald Ford. LC 89-33745. 100p. (gr. 3 up). 1989. PLB 14.40 (*0-516-01371-8*) Childrens.

FORD AUTOMOBILE

Simonds, Christopher. The Model T Ford. (Illus.). 64p. (gr. 5 up). 1991. PLB 12.95 (*0-382-24122-3*); pap. 7.95 (*0-382-24117-7*) Silver Burdett Pr.

FORECASTING WEATHER

see Weather Forecasting

FOREIGN ECONOMIC RELATIONS

see International Economic Relations

FOREIGN MISSIONS

see Missions

FOREIGN POLICY

see names of countries with the subdivision. foreign relations, e. g. U. S.–Foreign Relations; etc.

FOREIGN POPULATION

see Immigration and Emigration

FOREIGN RELATIONS

see International Relations;

see names of countries with subdivision Foreign Relations

FOREIGNERS

see Citizenship

FOREST CONSERVATION

see Forests and Forestry

FOREST FIRES

Guth, A. Richard & Cohen, Stan B. Red Skies of Eighty-Eight: The 1988 Forest Fire Season in the Northern Rockies, the Northern Great Plains & the Greater Yellowstone Area. LC 89-50399. (Illus.). 136p. (Orig.). 1989. pap. text ed. 12.95 (*0-929521-17-X*) Pictorial Hist.

Hines, Gary. Flying Firefighters. Hines, Anna G., illus. LC 92-35500. 1993. 14.95 (*0-395-61197-0*, Clarion Bks) HM.

Lampton, Christopher. Forest Fire. (Illus.). 64p. (gr. 4-6). 1991. PLB 13.90 (*1-56294-033-3*); pap. 5.95 (*1-56294-779-6*) Millbrook Pr.

—Forest Fire: A Disaster Book. (gr. 4-7). 1992. pap. 5.95 (*0-395-63646-9*) HM.

Lauber, Patricia. Summer of Fire: Yellowstone 1988. LC 90-23032. (Illus.). 64p. (gr. 4 up). 1991. 17.95 (*0-531-05943-X*); RLB 17.99 (*0-531-08543-0*) Orchard Bks Watts.

Morrison, Ellen E. Guardian of the Forest: A History of the Smokey Bear Program. 2nd, rev. ed. LC 89-60719. (Illus.). 144p. (gr. 6). 1989. 12.95 (*0-9622537-3-1*) Morielle Pr.

Vogel, Carole G. & Goldner, Kathryn A. The Great Yellowstone Fire, Vol. 1. (Illus.). (gr. 2-6). 1990. 15.95 (*0-316-90522-4*) Little.

FOREST FIRES–FICTION

Carter, Alden R. Dogwolf. LC 93-43518. (gr. 7 up). 1994. 14.95 (*0-590-46741-7*) Scholastic Inc.

FOREST PRODUCTS

see also Lumber and Lumbering; Rubber; Wood

FORESTRY

see Forests and Forestry

FORESTS AND FORESTRY

see also Lumber and Lumbering; Trees; Wood

Aldis, Rodney. Rainforests. LC 91-20595. (Illus.). 48p. (gr. 4-6). 1991. text ed. 13.95 RSBE (*0-87518-495-2*, Dillon) Macmillan Child Grp.

Alexander, Liza. Sesame Street Rainforest Adventure. 24p. (ps up). 1992. write for info. (*0-307-74021-8*, 64021) Western Pub.

Anderson, David & Holland, I. I., eds. Forests & Forestry. 4th ed. (gr. 10-12). 1990. 38.60 (*0-8134-2854-8*); text ed. 28.95 (*0-8134-2855-6*); tchr's. manual 6.95 (*0-685-45077-5*) Interstate.

Anderson, Margaret, et al. Ancient Forests. Torvik, Sharon, illus. 40p. (Orig.). (gr. 3-6). 1994. pap. 4.95 (*0-941042-14-6*) Dog Eared Pubns.

Anderson, Robert. Forests: Identifying Propaganda Techniques. LC 92-28185. (Illus.). 32p. (gr. 4-7). 1992. PLB 10.95 (*0-89908-099-5*) Greenhaven.

Arnold, Caroline. A Walk in the Woods. Brook, Bonnie, ed. Tanz, Freya, illus. 32p. (ps-1). 1990. 4.95 (*0-671-68665-8*); lib. bdg. 6.95 (*0-671-68661-5*) Silver Pr.

Arnosky, Jim. In the Forest. Arnosky, Jim, illus. LC 89-2341. 32p. (gr. 4 up). 1989. PLB 13.88 (*0-688-09138-5*) Lothrop.

Arvetis, Chris & Palmer, Carole. Forests. LC 93-500. (Illus.). 1993. write for info. (*0-528-83573-4*) Rand McNally.

Asimov, Isaac. Why Are the Rain Forests Vanishing? LC 92-5348. 1992. PLB 15.93 (*0-8368-0797-9*) Gareth Stevens Inc.

Bains, Rae. Forests & Jungles. Snyder, Joel, illus. LC 84-8641. 32p. (gr. 3-6). 1985. PLB 9.49 (*0-8167-0312-4*); pap. text ed. 2.95 (*0-8167-0313-2*) Troll Assocs.

Bash, Barbara. Ancient Ones: The World of the Old-Growth Douglas Fir. Bash, Barbara, illus. 32p. (gr. 1-5). 1994. 16.95 (*0-87156-561-7*) Sierra.

Behm, Barbara J. Exploring Forests. LC 93-37061. 1994. 17.27 (*0-8368-1064-3*) Gareth Stevens Inc.

—Exploring Woodlands. LC 93-37057. 1994. 17.27 (*0-8368-1068-6*) Gareth Stevens Inc.

Bellamy, David. Our Changing World: The Forest. Dow, Jill, illus. 24p. (gr. 1-4). 1988. bds. 12.00 (*0-517-56800-4*, Clarkson Potter) Crown Bks Yng Read.

Berger, Melvin. Life in the Rainforest. 16p. (gr. 2-4). 1993. pap. 14.95 (*1-56784-200-3*) Newbridge Comms.

Berger, Melvin & Berger, Gilda. Life in the Rainforest: Plants, Animals, & People. Brittingham, Geoffrey H., illus. LC 94-6006. 1994. lib. bdg. 12.00 (*1-57102-023-3*, Ideals Child); pap. 4.50 (*1-57102-007-1*, Ideals Child) Hambleton-Hill.

Block, Richard. Discover Rain Forests. (Illus.). 48p. (gr. 3-6). 1992. PLB 14.95 (*1-56674-030-4*, HTS Bks) Forest Hse.

Booth, Basil. Temperate Forests. Furstinger, Nancy, ed. (Illus.). 48p. (gr. 5-8). 1989. PLB 12.95 (*0-382-09791-2*) Silver Burdett Pr.

Bosse, Malcolm. Deep Dream of the Rain Forest. LC 92-55095. 1993. 15.00 (*0-374-31757-7*) FS&G.

Bright, Michael. Tropical Rainforest. LC 90-44680. (Illus.). 32p. (gr. 2-4). 1991. PLB 11.90 (*0-531-17301-1*, Gloucester Pr) Watts.

Brooks, F. Protecting Trees & Forests. (Illus.). 24p. (gr. 2-5). 1991. PLB 11.96 (*0-88110-528-7*, Usborne); pap. 4.50 (*0-7460-0656-X*, Usborne) EDC.

Brown, Peter. Brunei Rainforest Adventure. (Illus.). 64p. Date not set. 11.95 (*0-563-36756-3*, BBC-Parkwest) Parkwest Pubns.

Butler, Daphne. First Look in the Forest. LC 90-10240. (Illus.). 32p. (gr. 1-2). 1991. PLB 17.27 (*0-8368-0506-2*) Gareth Stevens Inc.

Butterfield, Moira. Amazon Rainforest. Johnson, Paul, illus. 16p. (gr. k-5). 1992. pap. 7.95 (*0-8249-8566-4*, Ideals Child) Hambleton-Hill.

Calkins-Bascom, Willow. Islands & Rainforests: Living in the Tropics with the Kuna People. (gr. 3). 1994. 4.95 (*0-9640956-0-2*) Willow Wrks.

Challand, Helen J. Vanishing Forests. LC 91-25863. 128p. (gr. 4-8). 1991. PLB 20.55 (*0-516-05505-4*) Childrens.

Chinery, Michael. Rainforest Animals. Holmes, David & Robinson, Bernard, illus. LC 91-53143. 40p. (Orig.). (gr. 2-5). 1992. PLB 8.99 (*0-679-92047-1*); pap. 4.99 (*0-679-82047-7*) Random Bks Yng Read.

Costa-Pace, Rosa. Protecting Our Forests. (Illus.). 1994. 13.95 (*0-7910-2104-1*, Am Art Analog) Chelsea Hse.

Cowcher, Helen. Rain Forest. (Illus.). 32p. (ps up). 1988. 15.00 (*0-374-36167-3*) FS&G.

—Rain Forest. Grammer, Red, narrated by. (Illus.). 32p. (gr. k-3). 1989. incl. audiocassette 19.95 (*0-924483-20-2*) Soundprints.

Craig, Janet. Wonders of the Rain Forest. Schindler, S. D., illus. LC 89-5001. 32p. (gr. 2-4). 1990. PLB 11.59 (*0-8167-1763-X*); pap. text ed. 2.95 (*0-8167-1764-8*) Troll Assocs.

Crump, Donald J., ed. The Emerald Realm: Earth's Precious Rain Forests. (Illus.). 1990. 12.95 (*0-87044-790-4*) Natl Geog.

—Explore a Tropical Forest, No. 1. (Illus.). (ps-3). 1989. 21.95 (*0-87044-757-2*) Natl Geog.

Curran, Eileen. Life in the Forest. Harvey, Paul, illus. LC 84-16455. 32p. (gr. k-2). 1985. PLB 11.59 (*0-8167-0446-5*); pap. text ed. 2.95 (*0-8167-0447-3*) Troll Assocs.

DePauw, Debbie. In the Rainforest. (Illus.). 48p. (gr. k-1). 1993. pap. text ed. 9.95 incl. poster (*1-55799-255-X*) Evan-Moor Corp.

Dixon, Dougal. Jungles. (Illus.). 32p. (gr. 4-6). 1991. 13.95 (*0-237-60161-3*, Pub. by Evans Bros Ltd) Trafalgar.

Dorros, Arthur. Rainforest Secrets. 1990. 14.95 (*0-590-43369-5*, Scholastic Hardcover) Scholastic Inc.

Dowden, Anne O., text by. & illus. The Blossom on the Bough: A Book of Trees. LC 93-22726. 80p. (gr. 3 up). 1994. 16.95 (*0-395-68375-0*); pap. 9.95 (*0-395-68943-0*) Ticknor & Flds Bks Yng Read.

Dunphy, Madeleine. Here Is the Tropical Rainforest. Rothman, Michael, illus. LC 93-24850. 32p. (ps-3). 1994. 14.95 (*1-56282-636-0*); PLB 14.89 (*1-56282-637-9*) Hyprn Child.

Ekey, Robert. Fire! in Yellowstone. Mayer, Larry, illus. LC 89-43156. 32p. (gr. 2-4). 1989. PLB 17.27 (*0-8368-0226-8*) Gareth Stevens Inc.

Fischetto, Laura. The Jungle Is My Home. Galli, Letizia, illus. 32p. (ps-3). 1991. 13.95 (*0-670-83550-1*) Viking Child Bks.

Fitzgerald, Janet. Autumn in the Wood. (Illus.). 32p. (gr. 1-3). 1991. 15.95 (*0-237-60216-4*, Pub. by Evans Bros Ltd) Trafalgar.

—Spring in the Wood. (Illus.). 32p. (gr. 1-3). 1991. 15.95 (*0-237-60218-0*, Pub. by Evans Bros Ltd) Trafalgar.

—Summer in the Wood. (Illus.). 32p. (gr. 1-3). 1991. 15.95 (*0-237-60217-2*, Pub. by Evans Bros Ltd) Trafalgar.

—Winter in the Wood. (Illus.). 32p. (gr. 1-3). 1991. 15.95 (*0-237-60215-6*, Pub. by Evans Bros Ltd) Trafalgar.

Forestry. (Illus.). 80p. (gr. 6-12). 1984. pap. 1.85 (*0-8395-3302-0*, 33302) BSA.

Forsyth, Adrian. Journey Through a Tropical Jungle. LC 88-14683. (gr. 3-7). 1989. pap. 15.95 jacketed (*0-671-66262-7*, S&S BFYR) S&S Trade.

Gallant, Roy A. Earth's Vanishing Forests. LC 91-2624. (Illus.). 176p. (gr. 5-9). 1992. SBE 15.95 (*0-02-735774-0*, Macmillan Child Bk) Macmillan Child Grp.

Ganeri, Anita. Explore the World of Exotic Rainforests. Morton, Robert, illus. 48p. (gr. 3-7). 1992. write for info. (*0-307-15606-0*, 15606, Golden Pr) Western Pub.

George, Jean C. One Day in the Tropical Rain Forest. Allen, Gary, illus. LC 89-36583. 64p. (gr. 4-7). 1990. 14.00 (*0-690-04767-3*, Crowell Jr Bks); PLB 13.89 (*0-690-04769-X*, Crowell Jr Bks) HarpC Child Bks.

George, Michael. Rain Forest. 1992. PLB 18.95 (*0-88682-483-4*) Creative Ed.

—Rain Forest. 40p. (gr. 4-7). 1993. 15.95 (*1-56846-062-7*) Creat Editions.

Gibbons, Gail. Nature's Green Umbrella: Tropical Rain Forests. Gibbons, Gail, illus. LC 93-17569. 32p. (gr. 2 up). 1994. 15.00g (*0-688-12353-8*); PLB 14.93 (*0-688-12354-6*) Morrow Jr Bks.

Gile, John. Footsteps in the Forest. (gr. 3 up). 1992. 14.95 (*0-910941-03-3*) J Gile Comm.

Goldstein, Natalie. Rebuilding Prairies & Forests. (Illus.). 96p. (gr. 3-6). 1994. PLB 23.20 (*0-516-05542-9*) Childrens.

Goodman, Billy. The Rain Forest. Goodman, Billy, illus. 96p. (gr. 3-7). 1992. 17.95 (*0-316-32019-6*) Little.

Gordon, Sharon. Trees. Trivas, Irene, illus. LC 82-20291. 32p. (gr. k-2). 1983. lib. bdg. 11.59 (*0-89375-901-5*); pap. text ed. 2.95 (*0-8167-0879-7*) Troll Assocs.

Greenaway, Theresa. Fir Trees. LC 90-9640. (Illus.). 48p. (gr. 5-9). 1990. PLB 21.34 (*0-8114-2727-7*) Raintree Steck-V.

—Tree Life. Taylor, Kim, photos by. LC 92-52824. (Illus.). 32p. (gr. 2-5). 1992. 9.95 (*1-56458-132-2*) Dorling Kindersley.

Greenberg, Judith E. & Carey, Helen H. The Rain Forest. Masheris, Bob, illus. 32p. (gr. 2-4). 1990. PLB 10.95 (*0-8172-3753-4*) Raintree Steck-V.

Greene, Carol. Caring for Our Forests. LC 91-4703. (Illus.). 32p. (gr. k-3). 1991. lib. bdg. 12.95 (*0-89490-353-5*) Enslow Pubs.

Hamilton, Jean. Tropical Rainforests. rev. ed. Leon, Vicki, ed. LC 93-12987. (Illus.). 48p. (Orig.). (gr. 5 up). 1993. perfect bdg. 9.95 (*0-918303-35-4*) Blake Pub.

Hare, Tony. Rainforest Destruction. LC 91-145801. (Illus.). 32p. (gr. 5-8). 1990. PLB 12.40 (*0-531-17248-1*, Gloucester Pr) Watts.

Higginson, Mel. The Forests. LC 94-9405. 1994. write for info. (*0-86593-382-0*) Rourke Corp.

Hirschi, E. & Bauer, Erwin A. Save Our Forests. 1993. pap. 9.95 (*0-385-31127-3*) Dell.

Hirschi, Ron. Save Our Forests. Bauer, Irwin A. & Bauer, Peggy, photos by. LC 92-37385. (Illus.). 1992. write for info. (*0-553-09521-8*); pap. write for info. (*0-553-37239-4*) Bantam.

—Save Our Forests. (gr. 4-7). 1993. 17.95 (*0-385-31076-5*) Delacorte.

Hirschi, Ron & Bauer, Peggy. Save Our Forests. (gr. 4-7). 1993. 17.95 (*0-385-31077-3*) Delacorte.

Hogan, Paula. Vanishing Rain Forests. (Illus.). 32p. (gr. 3-4). 1991. PLB 17.27 (*0-8368-0477-5*) Gareth Stevens Inc.

Hora, Bayard, ed. Trees & Forests of the World, 2 vols. LC 90-36009. (Illus.). 290p. 1990. PLB 79.95 (*1-85435-330-6*) Marshall Cavendish.

Jaspersohn, William. How the Forest Grew. Eckart, Chuck, illus. LC 79-16286. 56p. (gr. k up). 1992. pap. 4.95 (*0-688-11508-X*, Mulberry) Morrow.

Johnson, Jinny. Rain Forest Wildlife. (Illus.). (gr. 2-7). 1993. 9.95 (*0-89577-537-9*, Dist. by Random) RD Assn.

Knapp, Brian. What Do We Know about Rainforests? LC 92-5187. (Illus.). 40p. (gr. 4-6). PLB 15.95 (*0-87226-358-4*) P Bedrick Bks.

Kricher, John C. & Morrison, Gordon. A Field Guide to Tropical Forests Coloring Book. Kricher, John & Morrison, Gordon, illus. 64p. 1991. pap. 4.80 (*0-395-57321-1*) HM.

Lambert, Jonathan. Giant Jungle Pop-up Book: Animals of the Endangered Rain Forest. Lambert, Jonathan, illus. (ps-3). 1992. 28.00 (*1-56021-183-0*) W J Fantasy.

Landau, Elaine. Tropical Rain Forests Around the World. (Illus.). 64p. (gr. 5-8). 1991. pap. 5.95 (*0-531-15600-1*) Watts.

Lauber, Patricia. Summer of Fire: Yellowstone 1988. LC 90-23032. (Illus.). 64p. (gr. 4 up). 1991. 17.95 (*0-531-05943-X*); RLB 17.99 (*0-531-08543-0*) Orchard Bks Watts.

Lawlor, Elizabeth P. Discover Nature Close to Home: Things to Know & Things to Do. Archer, Pat, illus. 224p. (Orig.). (gr. 8 up). 1993. pap. 14.95 (*0-8117-3077-8*) Stackpole.

Leggett, Jeremy. Dying Forests. LC 90-46574. (Illus.). 48p. (gr. 5-9). 1991. PLB 12.95 (*1-85435-276-8*) Marshall Cavendish.

Lepthien, Emilie U. Tropical Rainforests. LC 93-3408. (Illus.). 48p. (gr. k-4). 1993. PLB 12.85 (*0-516-01198-7*); pap. 4.95 (*0-516-41198-5*) Childrens.

Liptak, Karen. Inside Biosphere 2: The Rainforest. 64p. (gr. 3 up). 1993. pap. text ed. 8.95 (*1-882428-06-4*) Biosphere Pr.

Mason, Helen. Life in a Forest. Rodgers, Gregg, illus. 32p. (Orig.). (gr. 3-6). 1992. pap. 3.50 (*0-88625-260-1*) Durkin Hayes Pub.

Mettler, Rene. The Rain Forest. (Illus.). 24p. (ps-2). 1994. 11.95 (*0-590-47728-5*, Cartwheel) Scholastic Inc.

Miller, Christina G. & Berry, Louise A. Jungle Rescue: Saving the New World Tropical Rain Forests. LC 90-1150. (Illus.). 128p. (gr. 5-9). 1991. SBE 14.95 (*0-689-31487-6*, Atheneum Child Bk) Macmillan Child Grp.

Mitchell, Victor. Woodlands. Mitchell, Victor, illus. 16p. (gr. k up). 1988. pap. 1.99 (*0-7459-1472-1*) Lion USA.

Morris, E. & Sadler, T. Our Rainforests & the Issues. (Illus.). 54p. (gr. 6-11). 1992. pap. 14.95x (*0-643-05141-4*, Pub. by CSIRO) Intl Spec Bk.

Morris, Ting & Morris, Neil. Rain Forest. LC 93-26686. (Illus.). 32p. (gr. 2-4). 1994. PLB 12.40 (*0-531-14281-7*) Watts.

Morrison, Marion. The Amazon Rain Forest & Its People. LC 93-20410. 48p. (gr. 5-8). 1993. 15.95 (*1-56847-087-8*) Thomson Lrning.

Mutel, Cornelia F. Tropical Rain Forests: Our Endangered Planet. (gr. 4-7). 1993. pap. 8.95 (*0-8225-9629-6*) Lerner Pubns.

National Wildlife Federation Staff. Rain Forests: Tropical Treasures. (gr. k-8). 1991. pap. 7.95 (*0-945051-41-7*, 75044) Natl Wildlife.

Newton, James R. Rain Shadow. Bonners, Susan, illus. LC 82-45927. 32p. (gr. 2-6). 1983. (Crowell Jr Bks); (Crowell Jr Bks) HarpC Child Bks.

Paige, David. A Day in the Life of a Forest Ranger. Mauney, Michael, photos by. LC 78-68809. (Illus.). 32p. (gr. 4-8). 1980. PLB 11.79 (*0-89375-227-4*); pap. 2.95 (*0-89375-231-2*) Troll Assocs.

Palmer, Joy. Rain Forests. LC 92-10634. (Illus.). 32p. (gr. 2-3). 1992. PLB 18.99 (*0-8114-3400-1*) Raintree Steck-V.

—Rain Forests. (ps-3). 1993. pap. 4.95 (*0-8114-4911-4*) Raintree Steck-V.

Parkin, Tom. Green Giants: Rainforests of the Pacific Northwest. (Illus.). 48p. (Orig.). (gr. 8-12). 1992. pap. 7.95 (*1-895565-07-3*) Firefly Bks Ltd.

Pearce, Q. L. Piranhas & Other Wonders of the Jungle. Fraser, Mary A., illus. 64p. (gr. 4-6). 1990. lib. bdg. 12.98 (*0-671-70689-6*, J Messner); pap. 5.95 (*0-671-70690-X*) S&S Trade.

Pearce, Q. L. & Pearce, W. L. In the Forest. Brook, Bonnie, ed. Bettoli, Delana, illus. 24p. (ps-1). 1990. 4.95 (*0-671-68830-8*); PLB 6.95 (*0-671-68826-X*) Silver Pr.

Pellowski, Michael J. Forest Ranger. Ulrich, George, illus. LC 88-10355. 32p. (gr. 1-3). 1989. PLB 10.89 (*0-8167-1422-3*); pap. text ed. 2.95 (*0-8167-1423-1*) Troll Assocs.

Perez, Ed. A Look Around Rain Forests. (Illus.). 32p. (gr. 1-3). 1993. pap. 2.99 (*0-87406-643-3*) Willowisp Pr.

Petty, Kate. Rainforests. Wood, Jakki, illus. 32p. (gr. 2-4). 1993. pap. 5.95 (*0-8120-1760-9*) Barron.

Pope, Joyce. Plants of the Tropics. 64p. 1990. 15.95x (*0-8160-2423-5*) Facts on File.

Pratt, Kristen J. Walk in the Rainforest. (Illus.). 32p. 1992. 14.95 (*1-878265-99-7*); pap. 6.95 (*1-878265-53-9*) Dawn CA.

Prosser, Robert. Disappearing Rainforest. (gr. 6 up). 1988. 19.95 (*0-7134-9719-X*, Pub. by Batsford UK) Trafalgar.

Rain Forest: Superdoodles. LC 92-74101. (gr. 1-6). 1993. pap. 4.95 (*0-88160-218-3*, LW302) Learning Wks.

The Rainforests. (gr. 7-12). 1992. 24.95 (*0-7134-6573-5*, Pub. by Batsford UK) Trafalgar.

Ross, Suzanne. What's in the Rainforest? One Hundred Six Answers from A to Z. Ross, Suzanne, illus. LC 91-72682. 48p. (Orig.). (gr. 1-7). 1991. pap. 5.95 (*0-9629895-0-9*) Enchanted Rain Pr.

Sabin, Francene. Wonders of the Forest. Willard, Michael, illus. LC 81-7401. 32p. (gr. 2-4). 1982. PLB 11.59 (*0-89375-572-9*); pap. text ed. 2.95 (*0-89375-573-7*) Troll Assocs.

Sadler, Tony. Forests & Their Environment. LC 93-25643. 1994. pap. 16.95 (*0-521-43786-5*) Cambridge U Pr.

Sanchez, Isidro & Peris, Carme. The Forest. (Illus.). 32p. (ps). 1991. pap. 5.95 (*0-8120-4709-5*) Barron.

Sayre, April P. Temperate Deciduous Forest. (Illus.). 64p. (gr. 5-8). 1994. bds. 15.95 (*0-8050-2828-5*) TFC Bks NY.

—Tropical Rain Forest. (Illus.). 64p. (gr. 5-8). 1994. bds. 15.95 (*0-8050-2826-9*) TFC Bks NY.

Schoonmaker, Peter K. The Living Forest. LC 89-33603. (Illus.). 64p. (gr. 6 up). 1990. lib. bdg. 15.95 (*0-89490-270-9*) Enslow Pubs.

Schwartz, Linda. Rain Forest Kit. 8p. (gr. 2-6). 1991. bklt., incl. poster 4.95 (*0-88160-165-9*, LW270) Learning Wks.

Seymour, Peter. What's in the Prehistoric Forest? Carter, David A., illus. LC 90-80885. 18p. (ps-2). 1990. 10.95 (*0-8050-1450-0*, Bks Young Read) H Holt & Co.

Siy, Alexandra. The Amazon Rainforest. LC 91-37640. (Illus.). 80p. (gr. 5 up). 1992. text ed. 14.95 RSBE (*0-87518-470-7*, Dillon) Macmillan Child Grp.

—Ancient Forests. LC 91-15422. (Illus.). 72p. (gr. 5 up). 1991. text ed. 14.95 RSBE (*0-87518-466-9*, Dillon) Macmillan Child Grp.

Spencer, Guy. An Ancient Forest. Staub, Frank J., illus. LC 87-3487. 32p. (gr. 3-6). 1988. PLB 10.79 (*0-8167-1167-4*); pap. text ed. 2.95 (*0-8167-1168-2*) Troll Assocs.

Starry, Paul & Cleave, Andrew. Rain Forest. LC 92-60796. (Illus.). 32p. (gr. 4-7). 1992. 14.00 (*0-89577-448-8*, Dist. by Random) RD Assn.

Stone, L. Rain Forests. (Illus.). 48p. (gr. 4-8). 1989. lib. bdg. 15.94 (*0-86592-437-6*); 11.95s.p. (*0-685-67720-6*) Rourke Corp.

—Temperate Forests. (Illus.). 48p. (gr. 4-8). 1989. lib. bdg. 15.94 (*0-86592-439-2*); 11.95 (*0-685-58574-3*) Rourke Corp.

Stone, Lynn M. Timber Country. LC 93-4522. (Illus.). 1993. write for info. (*0-86593-305-7*) Rourke Corp.

Tangley, Laura. The Rainforest. (Illus.). (gr. 5 up). 1992. lib. bdg. 19.95 (*0-7910-1579-3*) Chelsea Hse.

Taylor, Barbara. Forest Life. Taylor, Kim, photos by. LC 92-53488. (Illus.). 32p. (gr. 2-5). 1993. 9.95 (*1-56458-210-8*) Dorling Kindersley.

—Rain Forest. LC 91-58197. (Illus.). 32p. (gr. 1-4). 1992. 9.95 (*1-879431-91-2*) Dorling Kindersley.

Terborgh, John. Tropical Deforestation. Head, J. J., ed. (Illus.). 16p. (Orig.). (gr. 10 up). 1992. pap. text ed. 2.75 (*0-89278-161-0*, 45-9761) Carolina Biological.

Tesar, Jenny E. Shrinking Forests. (Illus.). 128p. (gr. 7-12). 1991. 18.95x (*0-8160-2492-8*) Facts on File.

Thomas, Heather S. A Week in the Woods. Woolsey, Raymond H., ed. 64p. (gr. 2-4). 1988. pap. 4.95 (*0-8280-0435-8*) Review & Herald.

Thornhill, Jan. A Tree in a Forest. LC 91-25857. (Illus.). 40p. (ps-3). 1992. pap. 15.00 (*0-671-75901-9*, S&S BFYR) S&S Trade.

Tomblin, Gill, illus. Make Your Own Rain Forest. Johnston, Damian, concept by. & contrib. by. (Illus.). 18p. (gr. 3-7). 1993. incl. kit 12.95 (*0-525-67409-8*, Lodestar Bks) Dutton Child Bks.

Tompkins, Terence. Ravaged Temperate Forests. LC 93-13048. 1993. 17.27 (*0-8368-0728-6*) Gareth Stevens Inc.

Tresselt, Alvin. Gift of the Tree. LC 90-2084. (ps-3). 1992. 14.00 (*0-688-10684-6*); PLB 13.93 (*0-688-10685-4*) Lothrop.

Twist, Clint. Jungles & Forests: Projects with Geography. LC 92-33916. 1993. 12.40 (*0-531-17397-6*, Gloucester Pr) Watts.

Warburton, Lois. Rainforests. LC 90-46278. (Illus.). 96p. (gr. 5-8). 1991. PLB 14.95 (*1-56006-150-2*) Lucent Bks.

Watts, Barrie. Twenty-Four Hours in a Forest. (Illus.). 48p. (gr. 4-6). 1990. PLB 12.90 (*0-531-14036-9*) Watts.

Wilderness Society Staff. Color the Ancient Forest. (Illus.). 48p. (Orig.). (ps-3). 1991. saddle-stitched 4.95 (*1-879326-07-8*) Living Planet Pr.

Williams, Lawrence. Jungles. LC 89-17322. (Illus.). 48p. (gr. 4-8). 1990. PLB 12.95 (*1-85435-171-0*) Marshall Cavendish.

Willow, Diane. At Home in the Rainforest. (Illus.). 32p. (ps-3). 1992. 14.95 (*0-88106-485-8*); PLB 15.88 (*0-88106-688-5*); pap. 6.95 (*0-88106-484-X*) Charlesbridge Pub.

—Dentro de la Selva Tropical (At Home in the Rain Forest) (Illus.). 32p. (ps-3). 1993. PLB 15.88 (*0-88106-641-9*); pap. 6.95 (*0-88106-421-1*) Charlesbridge Pub.

Yolen, Jane. Welcome to the Greenhouse. Regan, Laura, illus. 32p. (ps-3). 1993. PLB 14.95 (*0-399-22335-5*, Putnam) Putnam Pub Group.

Zak, Monica. Save My Rainforest. Runnerstrom, Bengt-Arne, illus. LC 91-40179. 29p. 1992. 14.95 (*0-912078-94-4*) Volcano Pr.

Zuckerman, Seth. Saving Our Ancient Forests. (Illus.). 128p. (Orig.). 1991. pap. 5.95 (*0-9626072-9-0*) Living Planet Pr.

FORESTS AND FORESTRY–FICTION

Abrams, Jodell. Enchanted Forest. (Illus.). 32p. (Orig.). (gr. 1-6). 1981. pap. 4.50 (*0-8431-1712-5*, Troubador) Price Stern.

Anholt, Laurence. The Forgotten Forest. Anholt, Laurence, illus. 32p. (ps-3). 1992. 14.95 (*0-87156-569-2*) Sierra.

Baker, Jeannie. Where the Forest Meets The Sea. LC 87-7551. (Illus.). 32p. (ps-3). 1988. 15.00 (*0-688-06363-2*); lib. bdg. 14.93 (*0-688-06364-0*) Greenwillow.

Cherry, Lynne. Great Kapok Tree: A Tale of the Amazon Rain Forest. 33p. (ps-3). 1990. 14.95 (*0-15-200520-X*) HarBrace.

Coran, Pierre. The Ranger Smokes Too Much. (Illus.). 32p. (gr. k-2). 1991. 12.95 (*0-89565-748-1*) Childs World.

Cristini, Ermanno & Puricelli, Luigi. In the Woods. Cristini, Ermanno & Puricelli, Luigi, illus. LC 83-8153. 28p. (ps up). 1991. pap. 12.95 (*0-907234-31-3*) Picture Bk Studio.

Dobson, Danae. Forest Friends Help Each Other. Morales, Cuitlahuac, illus. 32p. (ps-k). 1993. 7.99 (*0-8499-0986-4*) Word Inc.

Eldrid, Brenda. Teddy's Day in the Forest. Bates, Louise, illus. 24p. (ps-2). 1993. pap. text ed. 0.99 (*1-56293-341-8*) McClanahan Bk.

Evans, Olive. Secrets of the Forest. (gr. 3-12). 1985. pap. 6.00 play script (*0-88734-502-6*) Players Pr.

Frieders, Robert. American Elves - the Yankoos, Bk. 1: The Yankoos & the Oak-Hickory Forest Ecology. LC 93-61530. (Illus.). 64p. (gr. 3). 1993. pap. 7.95 (*0-9639284-0-6*) Yankoo Pubng.

—American Elves - the Yankoos: The Yankoos & the Oak-Hickory Forest, Bk. Two. (Illus.). 96p. (gr. 3). 1994. pap. 7.95 (*0-9639284-1-4*) Yankoo Pubng.

Gile, John. The First Forest. Heflin, Tom, illus. LC 89-91458. 40p. (gr. k up). 1989. 13.95 (*0-910941-01-7*) J Gile Comm.

Goldsborough, June. What's in the Woods? LC 76-10271. (Illus.). 32p. 1981. P-H.

Grange, Wallace B. Those of the Forest. Petrie, Chuck, ed. Murie, Olaus J., illus. Johnson, Dan, intro. by. (Illus.). 336p. (gr. 6 up). 1989. Repr. of 1953 ed. 19.50 (*0-932558-49-6*) Willow Creek Pr.

Grosvenor, Carol. Once upon a Forest. (ps-3). 1993. 12.95 (*1-878685-87-2*) Turner Pub GA.

Hanson, Fred E. Simon. Hanson, Ann R., illus. 54p. (gr. 3-5). 1990. pap. 7.95 (*0-9624292-1-X*) Black Willow Pr.

Hasenau, James. Fuzzy Bear. LC 82-81828. (Illus.). (gr. k-4). 1985. 6.00 (*0-913042-15-3*) Holland Hse Pr.

Hollingsworth, Mary. Polka Dots, Stripes, Humps 'n Hatracks: How God Created Happy Forest. (Illus.). (ps-2). 1990. 6.99 (*1-877719-00-5*) Brownlow Pub Co.

—Twizzler, the Unlikely Hero. (Illus.). (ps-2). 1990. 6.99 (*1-877719-01-3*) Brownlow Pub Co.

In Dragonfly Forest. (ps-k). 1993. 3.99 (*0-89577-479-8*, Dist. by Random) RD Assn.

Johnson, Emily R. A House Full of Strangers. 160p. (gr. 5 up). 1992. 14.00 (*0-525-65091-1*, Cobblehill Bks) Dutton Child Bks.

Jordan, Tanis & Jordan, Martin. Jungle Days, Jungle Nights. LC 92-40366. (Illus.). 40p. (gr. k-4). 1993. 14. 95 (*1-85697-885-0*, Kingfisher LKC) LKC.

Lasky, Kathryn. Sugaring Time. Knight, Christopher G., illus. & photos by LC 82-23928. 64p. (gr. 3-7). 1983. RSBE 13.95 (*0-02-751680-6*, Macmillan Child Bk) Macmillan Child Grp.

Lisle, Janet T. Forest. LC 93-9630. 160p. (gr. 5 up). 1993. 15.95 (*0-531-06803-X*); PLB 15.99 (*0-531-08653-4*) Orchard Bks Watts.

Love, Douglas. Holiday in the Rain Forest. Zimmerman, Robert, illus. 64p. (gr. 3 up). 1994. pap. 3.50 (*0-694-00657-2*, Festival) HarpC Child Bks.

Luenn, Nancy. Song for the Ancient Forest. Kastner, Jill, illus. LC 91-17187. 32p. (gr. k-3). 1993. SBE 14.95 (*0-689-31719-0*, Atheneum Child Bk) Macmillan Child Grp.

McGee, Marni. The Forest Child. Banfill, A. Scott, illus. LC 92-37148. (ps-2). 1994. 15.00 (*0-671-86608-7*, Green Tiger) S&S Trade.

Malone, P. M. Out of the Nest. Lewison, Terry, illus. 198p. (Orig.). (gr. 1-8). 1991. pap. text ed. 11.95 (*0-9631957-0-0*) Raspberry Hill.

—To Find a Way Home. Lewison, Terry, illus. 200p. (Orig.). (gr. 1-8). 1993. pap. text ed. 11.95 (*0-9631957-2-7*) Raspberry Hill.

Miller, Edna. Mousekin's Lost Woodland. LC 91-4201. (Illus.). 40p. (ps-3). 1992. pap. 13.00 jacketed (*0-671-74938-2*, S&S BFYR) S&S Trade.

Morreale, Vin, Jr. The Day the Woods Were One. (Orig.). (gr. 3 up). 1985. pap. 6.00 play script (*0-88734-507-7*) Players Pr.

Muller, Gerda. Around the Oak. LC 93-32310. (gr. 3 up). 1994. write for info. (*0-525-45239-7*, DCB) Dutton Child Bks.

Noonan, Diana. The Shepherd Who Planted a Forest. Campbell, Caroline, illus. LC 93-11828. 1994. write for info. (*0-383-03774-3*) SRA Schl Grp.

Ossorio, Joseph D., et al. The Court of the Lost Woods. (Illus.). 48p. (gr. 3-5). 1994. pap. 6.95 (*1-56721-052-X*) Twnty-Fifth Cent Pr.

Porter, Gene S. Freckles. 272p. (gr. 5 up). 1992. pap. 2.99 (*0-14-035144-2*) Puffin Bks.

—Girl of the Limberlost. (Illus.). 496p. 1992. 8.99 (*0-517-07235-1*, Pub. by Gramercy) Random Hse Value.

—A Girl of the Limberlost. 432p. (gr. 5 up). 1992. pap. 3.99 (*0-14-035143-4*) Puffin Bks.

Pratt, Kristin. Un Paseo Por el Bosque Lluvioso: A Walk in the Rainforest. Pratt, Kristin J., illus. (SPA & ENG.). 32p. (ps-5). 1993. pap. 6.95 (*1-883220-02-5*) Dawn CA.

Ray, Stephen & Murdoch, Kathleen. In the Forest. Ruth, Trevor, illus. LC 92-27266. 1993. 3.75 (*0-383-03635-6*) SRA Schl Grp.

Rhea, Celeste. The Acorn Sprout & His Forest Friends. (Illus.). 23p. (Orig.). (gr. 1-4). 1978. pap. 1.00 (*0-89323-010-3*, 025) Bible Memory.

Rice, Eve. Once in a Wood. LC 78-16294. (Illus.). 64p. 1979. PLB 13.93 (*0-688-84191-0*) Greenwillow.

Richter, Conrad. Light in the Forest. 1994. pap. 3.99 (*0-449-70437-8*) FS&G.

Ryder, Joanne. Walt Disney's Bambi's Forest: A Year in the Life of the Forest. LC 93-72551. (Illus.). 32p. (ps-3). 1994. 11.95 (*1-56282-643-3*); PLB 11.89 (*1-56282-698-0*) Disney Pr.

—When the Woods Hum. LC 90-37879. (Illus.). 32p. (gr. 1 up). 1991. 13.95 (*0-688-07057-4*); PLB 13.88 (*0-688-07058-2*, Morrow Jr Bks) Morrow Jr Bks.

Siegenthaler, Kathrin. Santa Claus & the Woodcutter. Crawford, Elizabeth, tr. from GER. Pfister, Marcus, illus. 32p. (gr. k-3). 1989. pap. 2.95 (*1-55858-032-8*) North-South Bks NYC.

Spohn, David. Winter Wood. LC 90-49944. (Illus.). 32p. (gr. k up). 1991. 13.95 (*0-688-10093-7*); PLB 13.88 (*0-688-10094-5*) Lothrop.

Spring in the Enchanted Forest. (Illus.). (ps-1). 1985. 2.98 (*0-517-46980-4*) Random Hse Value.

Springer, Jean. The Great Forest. Peterson, Pete, ed. French, Ed, illus. 169p. (gr. 3-6). 1986. pap. 3.99 (*0-934998-25-6*) Bethel Pub.

Taylor, Mildred D. Song of the Trees. Pinkney, Jeny, illus. LC 74-18598. 56p. (gr. 2-5). 1975. 13.50 (*0-8037-5452-3*); PLB 11.89 (*0-8037-5453-1*) Dial Bks Young.

Tibo, Gilles. Simon & the Boxes. Tibo, Gilles, illus. LC 92-80416. 24p. (gr. k-4). 1992. PLB 10.95 (*0-88776-287-5*) Tundra Bks.

Vallet, Muriel. Pinky Saves the Forest. Vallet, Muriel, illus. 12p. (gr. 1-3). 1992. pap. 6.95 (*1-895583-01-2*) MAYA Pubs.

Wadlow, Elizabeth. Little Gittamus. 1994. 10.75 (*0-8062-4805-X*) Carlton.

Wells, Rosemary. Forest of Dreams. LC 88-3826. (Illus.). 24p. (ps-3). 1992. pap. 4.99 (*0-8037-1140-9*, Puff Pied Piper) Puffin Bks.

Willard, John A. Ember & His Friends in the Forest. Elliot, Stephen C., illus. 20p. (Orig.). (gr. 2-5). 1991. pap. 3.95 (*0-9612398-4-0*) J A Willard.
Ember, a cuddly but self-sufficient kitten who lives with a young couple deep in Montana's high mountain forest, tells all about his animal & bird friends who live among the firs, pines & larches. His friends include Soft Eyes, the white-tailed deer; Bugler, the huge bull elk from Yellowstone Park country; Jumpy, the Rocky Mountain mule deer; Harry, the snowshoe hare; Splash, the no-nonsense beaver; Ottie, the fun-loving otter; Ruffy, the ruffed grouse; & even Woody, the tiny white-footed wood mouse. Each animal & bird is pictured in a line drawing by Stephen C. Elliott, a Colorado artist who has shown in the prestigious Leigh Yawkey Woodson birds-in-art show & has published a naturalist history for Denver Natural History Museum. John Willard is a veteran western outdoor columnist & writer & is Montana's first & oldest member of the Outdoor Writers of America. Ember easily & quickly teaches children about their wild animal & bird friends. Text is simple & fully readable at first or second grade level. Adapts easily to classroom or home use to acquaint children with wildlife in their western mountains & forest - a striking combination of word & picture. Call or write for information or to order: John A. Willard, 3119 Country Club Circle, Billings, MT 59102; 406-259-1966. *Publisher Provided Annotation.*

Young, Diana. Ferngully: The Last Rainforest Digest. 112p. 1992. pap. 2.95 (*0-590-45433-1*) Scholastic Inc.

Zebra, A. A Rumble in the Jungle. LC 89-82286. (Illus.). 96p. (Orig.). (gr. 2-6). 1990. pap. 7.95 (*0-86327-240-1*, Pub. by Wolfhound Pr EIRE) Dufour.

Ziefert, Harriet. On Our Way to the Forest! Taback, Simms, illus. 16p. (ps-1). 1993. pap. 4.95 (*0-694-00458-8*, Festival) HarpC Child Bks.

FORESTS AND FORESTRY–VOCATIONAL GUIDANCE

Greene, Carol. I Can Be a Forest Ranger. LC 88-37717. (Illus.). 32p. (gr. k-3). 1989. PLB 11.80 (*0-516-01924-4*); pap. 3.95 (*0-516-41924-2*) Childrens.

Paige, David. A Day in the Life of a Forest Ranger. Mauney, Michael, photos by. LC 78-68809. (Illus.). 32p. (gr. 4-8). 1980. PLB 11.79 (*0-89375-227-4*); pap. 2.95 (*0-89375-231-2*) Troll Assocs.

Wille, Christopher M. Opportunities in Forestry Careers. (Illus.). 160p. 1992. 13.95 (*0-8442-8571-4*, VGM Career Bks); pap. 10.95 (*0-8442-8572-2*, VGM Career Bks) NTC Pub Grp.

FORGERY OF WORKS OF ART

Wilkes, A. Fakes & Forgeries. (Illus.). 64p. (gr. 3-7). 1979. (Usborne); pap. 4.50 (*0-86020-231-3*) EDC.

FORM, MUSICAL

see Musical Form

FORMOSA

Cromie, Alice. Taiwan. LC 94-6120. (Illus.). 128p. (gr. 5-9). 1994. PLB 27.40 (*0-516-02627-5*) Childrens.

Lerner Publications, Department of Geography Staff, ed. Taiwan in Pictures. (Illus.). 64p. (gr. 5 up). 1989. PLB 17.50 (*0-8225-1865-1*) Lerner Pubns.

Russell, William. Taiwan. LC 93-48341. 1994. write for info. (*1-55916-033-0*) Rourke Bk Co.

Wee, Jerrie. Taiwan. (Illus.). 96p. (gr. 5 up). 1988. 14.95 (*1-55546-180-8*) Chelsea Hse.

FORMOSA–FICTION

Hwa-I Publishing Co., Staff. Chinese Children's Stories, Vol. 91: A Little City, Beating the Devil. Ching, Emily, et al, eds. Wonder Kids Publications Staff, tr. from CHI. (Illus.). 28p. (gr. 3-6). 1991. Repr. of 1988 ed. 7.95 (*1-56162-091-2*) Wonder Kids.

FORTIFICATION

see also Military Engineering;
also names of countries with the subdivision Defenses, e.g. U. S.–Defenses, etc.

Birdseye, Tom. A Kids' Guide to Building Forts. Klein, Bill, illus. LC 92-45908. 64p. (Orig.). (gr. 3-9). 1993. pap. 9.95 (*0-943173-69-8*) Harbinger AZ.

Gravett, Christopher. Castle. LC 93-32594. (Illus.). 1994. 16.00 (*0-679-86000-2*); PLB 16.99 (*0-679-96000-7*) Knopf Bks Yng Read.

Kalman, Bobbie & Schimky, Dave. Fort Life. (Illus.). 32p. (Orig.). (gr. k-9). 1994. PLB 15.95 (*0-86505-496-7*); pap. 7.95 (*0-86505-516-5*) Crabtree Pub Co.

Macdonald, Fiona. A Roman Fort. Wood, Gerald, illus. LC 93-16397. 48p. (gr. 5 up). 1993. 17.95 (*0-87226-370-3*); pap. 8.95 sewn (*0-87226-259-6*) P Bedrick Bks.

Moss, Miriam. Forts & Castles. Forsey, Chris, illus. LC 93-11167. 32p. (gr. 4-6). 1993. PLB 19.97 (*0-8114-6157-2*) Raintree Steck-V.

Mulvihill, Margaret. Roman Forts. LC 89-28778. 1990. PLB 12.40 (*0-531-17201-5*, Gloucester Pr) Watts.

Steedman, Scott. A Frontier Fort on the Oregon Trail. Bergin, Mark, illus. 48p. 1994. 17.95 (*0-87226-371-1*); pap. 8.95 (*0-87226-264-2*) P Bedrick Bks.

Stone, Lynn. Forts. LC 93-142. 1993. write for info. (*0-86625-447-1*) Rourke Pubns.

FORTS

see Fortification

FORTUNE

see Probabilities; Success

FORTUNE, AMOS, 1709?-1801

Yates, Elizabeth. Amos Fortune, Free Man. Unwin, Nora S., illus. (gr. 7 up). 1967. 15.00 (*0-525-25570-2*, DCB) Dutton Child Bks.

—Amos Fortune, Free Man. Unwin, Nora S., illus. 192p. (gr. 3-7). 1989. pap. 3.99 (*0-14-034158-7*, Puffin) Puffin Bks.

FORTUNE TELLING

see also Astrology; Cards; Clairvoyance; Dreams

Gibson, Litzkah R. How to Read Palms. Adelman, Sherri, ed. (Illus.). 184p. (gr. 10-12). 1989. pap. 8.95 (*0-8119-0033-9*) Lifetime.

Green, Carl R. & Sanford, William R. Fortune Telling. Robinson, Keith, illus. LC 93-12029. 48p. (gr. 4-10). 1993. lib. bdg. 14.95 (*0-89490-456-6*) Enslow Pubs.

—The Mystery of Dreams. LC 93-6539. (Illus.). 48p. (gr. 4-10). 1993. lib. bdg. 14.95 (*0-89490-453-1*) Enslow Pubs.

Schwartz, Alvin. Telling Fortunes: Love Magic, Dream Signs, & Other Ways to Learn the Future. Cameron, Tracey, illus. LC 85-45174. 128p. (gr. 4 up). 1987. 12. 95 (*0-397-32132-5*, Lipp Jr Bks); PLB 12.89 (*0-397-32133-3*, Lipp Jr Bks) HarpC Child Bks.

—Telling Fortunes: Love Magic, Dream Signs, & Other Ways to Learn the Future. Cameron, Tracey, illus. LC 85-45174. 128p. (gr. 4 up). 1990. pap. 4.95 (*0-06-446094-0*, Trophy) HarpC Child Bks.

Shimano, Jimmei. Oriental Fortune Telling. LC 65-18960. (Illus.). 170p. (gr. 9 up). 1965. pap. 9.95 (*0-8048-0448-6*) C E Tuttle.

FOSSIL MAMMALS

see Mammals, Fossil

FOSSIL PLANTS

see Plants, Fossil

FOSSILS

see also Extinct Animals; Mammals, Fossil; Plants, Fossil; Reptiles, Fossil

Aliki. Fossils Tell of Long Ago. Aliki, illus. LC 78-170999. 40p. (gr. k-3). 1972. PLB 12.89 (*0-690-31379-9*, Crowell Jr Bks) HarpC Child Bks.

—Fossils Tell of Long Ago. rev. ed. Aliki, illus. LC 89-17247. 32p. (gr. k-4). 1990. 14.00 (*0-690-04844-0*, Crowell Jr Bks); PLB 13.89 (*0-690-04829-7*, Crowell Jr Bks) HarpC Child Bks.

—Fossils Tell of Long Ago. rev. ed. Aliki, illus. LC 89-15468. 32p. (gr. k-4). 1990. pap. 4.95 (*0-06-445093-7*, JS093, Trophy) HarpC Child Bks.

Arnold, Caroline. Dinosaurs down Under: And Other Fossils from Australia. (gr. 4-7). 1994. pap. 6.95 (*0-395-69119-2*, Clarion Bks) HM.

—Trapped in Tar: Fossils from the Ice Age. LC 86-17614. (Illus.). 64p. (gr. 3-6). 1987. (Clarion Bks); pap. 5.95 (*0-395-54783-0*, Clarion Bks) HM.

Bains, Rae. Prehistoric Animals. Acosta, Andres, illus. LC 84-2735. 32p. (gr. 3-6). 1985. PLB 9.49 (*0-8167-0296-9*); pap. text ed. 2.95 (*0-8167-0297-7*) Troll Assocs.

Barnes-Svarney, Patricia L. Fossils: Stories from Bones & Stones. LC 90-19408. (Illus.). 64p. (gr. 6 up). 1991. lib. bdg. 15.95 (*0-89490-294-6*) Enslow Pubs.

Barrett, Judi. Benjamin's Three Hundred Sixty-Five Birthdays. Barrett, Ron, illus. LC 92-2497. 40p. (ps-1). 1992. RSBE 13.95 (*0-689-31791-3*, Atheneum Child Bk) Macmillan Child Grp.

Baylor, Byrd. If You Are a Hunter of Fossils. Parnall, Peter, illus. LC 79-17926. 32p. (gr. 3-6). 1984. pap. 4.95 (*0-689-70773-8*, Aladdin) Macmillan Child Grp.

Bell, Robert A. Fossils. Spence, James, illus. 24p. (gr. k-5). 1992. pap. write for info. blister pk., incl. 4 fossil specimens (*0-307-12855-5*, 12855, Golden Pr) Western Pub.

Benanti, Carol. Real Fossils. Frank, Michael, ed. Dickens, Earl, illus. 32p. (Orig.). (gr. 3-8). Date not set. pap. 6.95 (*1-880592-06-1*) Pace Prods.

Benton, Michael. Prehistoric Animals: An A-Z Guide. (Illus.). 176p. 1989. 7.99 (*0-517-69190-6*) Random Hse Value.

Berger, Melvin. Monsters. 128p. 1991. pap. 2.95 (*0-380-76053-3*, Camelot) Avon.

Bernanti, Carol. Fossils. (Illus.). 32p. (gr. 3 up). 1994. pap. 10.00 (*0-679-85073-2*) Random Bks Yng Read.

Bliss, Richard, et al. Fossils: Key to the Present. (gr. 6-12). 1990. pap. 4.95 (*0-89051-058-X*) Master Bks.

Burton, Virginia L. Life Story. (Illus.). (gr. k-3). 1989. 15. 45 (*0-395-16030-8*); pap. 6.70 (*0-395-52017-7*) HM.

Cohen, Daniel. Prehistoric Animals. Johnson, Pamela F., illus. LC 86-19666. 48p. (gr. k-3). 1988. 9.95 (*0-385-23416-3*) Doubleday.

—Prehistoric Animals. (ps-3). 1993. pap. 4.99 (*0-440-40787-7*) Dell.

Cork, B. & Bramwell, M. Rocks & Fossils. Jackson, I. & Suttie, A., illus. 32p. (gr. 5-8). 1983. PLB 13.96 (*0-88110-159-1*); pap. 6.95 (*0-86020-765-X*) EDC.

Craig, Janet. Discovering Prehistoric Animals. Watling, James, illus. LC 89-4973. 32p. (gr. 2-4). 1990. PLB 11. 59 (*0-8167-1755-9*); pap. text ed. 2.95 (*0-8167-1756-7*) Troll Assocs.

Dixon, Dougal. Hunting the Dinosaurs. Burton, Jane, illus. LC 87-6461. 32p. (gr. 2-3). 1987. PLB 17.27 (*1-55532-259-X*) Gareth Stevens Inc.
Dixon, Douglas. Be a Fossil Detective. 40p. (gr. 2 up). 1989. 3.99 (*0-517-68022-X*) Random Hse Value.
Fuchshuber, Annegert. From Dinosaurs to Fossils. Fuchshuber, Annegert, illus. LC 80-28596. 24p. (ps-3). 1981. PLB 10.95 (*0-87614-152-1*) Carolrhoda Bks.
Gabriel, Diane & Cohen, Judith. To Puedes Ser una Paleontologa. Yanez, Juan, tr. from ENG. Katz, David, illus. (SPA.). 40p. (gr. 3-7). 1993. pap. text ed. 6.00 (*1-880599-13-9*) Cascade Pass.
—You Can Be a Woman Paleontologist. Katz, David, illus. LC 93-21349. 40p. (gr. 3-6). 1993. pap. 6.00 (*1-880599-12-0*) Cascade Pass.
Gattis, L. S., III. Fossil Collecting for Pathfinders: A Basic Youth Enrichment Skill Honor Packet. (Illus.). 20p. (Orig.). (gr. 5 up). 1987. pap. 5.00 tchr's. ed. (*0-936241-16-0*) Cheetah Pub.
Gillette, J. Lynett. The Search for Seismosaurus. Hallett, Mark, photos by. LC 92-28199. (Illus.). 1993. 14.99 (*0-8037-1358-4*) Dial Bks Young.
Goldish, Meish. What is a Fossil? (Illus.). 32p. (gr. 1-4). 1989. PLB 18.99 (*0-8172-3535-3*); pap. 4.95 (*0-8114-6734-1*) Raintree Steck-V.
Granowsky, Alvin. Dinosaur Fossils. Herring, Lee, illus. LC 91-23407. 32p. (gr. 1-4). 1992. PLB 18.51 (*0-8114-3253-X*); pap. 3.95 (*0-8114-6228-5*) Raintree Steck-V.
Hawcock, David. Sabre Toothed Tiger. 1994. 5.95 (*0-8050-3193-6*) H Holt & Co.
Higginson, Mel. Scientists Who Study Fossils. LC 94-6995. 1994. write for info. (*0-86593-375-8*) Rourke Corp.
Hornblow, Leonora & Hornblow, Arthur. Prehistoric Monsters Did the Strangest Things. abr. ed. Barlowe, Sy, illus. LC 88-30212. 64p. (gr. 2-4). 1990. Repr. lib. bdg. 6.99 (*0-394-94307-4*); 4.99 (*0-394-84307-X*) Random Bks Yng Read.
Horner, Jack & Lessem, Don. Digging up Tyrannosaurus Rex. LC 92-2204. (Illus.). 36p. (gr. 2-6). 1992. 15.00 (*0-517-58783-1*); PLB 14.99 (*0-517-58784-X*) Crown Bks Yng Read.
Howard, John. I Can Read About Fossils. Nodel, Norman, illus. LC 76-54446. (gr. 2-5). 1977. pap. 2.50 (*0-89375-038-7*) Troll Assocs.
Johnson, Rolf E. & Piggins, Carol A. Dinosaur Hunt! LC 91-50336. (Illus.). 32p. (gr. 2-8). 1993. PLB 15.93 (*0-8368-0740-5*); PLB 17.27 s.p. (*0-685-61502-2*) Gareth Stevens Inc.
Lauber, Pat. Dinosaurs Walked Here & Other Stories Fossils Tell. LC 91-40739. (Illus.). 64p. (gr. 2-5). 1992. pap. 5.95 (*0-689-71603-6*, Aladdin) Macmillan Child Grp.
Lauber, Patricia. Dinosaurs Walked Here & Other Stories Fossils Tell. LC 86-8239. (Illus.). 64p. (gr. 2-4). 1987. SBE 16.95 (*0-02-754510-5*, Bradbury Pr) Macmillan Child Grp.
Lessem, Don. Ornithomimids, the Fastest Dinosaur. Franczak, Brian, illus. LC 93-10264. 1993. 19.95 (*0-87614-813-5*) Carolrhoda Bks.
—Troodon, the Smartest Dinosaur. Franczak, Brian, illus. LC 92-44689. 1993. 19.95 (*0-87614-798-8*) Carolrhoda Bks.
Lindsay, William. Prehistoric Life. LC 93-32076. (gr. 5 up). 1994. 16.00 (*0-679-86001-0*); PLB 16.99 (*0-679-96001-5*) Knopf Bks Yng Read.
Looking for Fossils. 64p. 1991. 7.99 (*0-517-03399-2*) Random Hse Value.
Lye, Keith. Rocks, Minerals & Fossils. (Illus.). 48p. (gr. 5-8). 1991. PLB 12.95 (*0-382-24226-2*) Silver Burdett Pr.
McGowan, Christopher. Discover Dinosaurs: Become a Dinosaur Detective. Holdcroft, Tina, illus. LC 92-42627. 96p. (gr. 4-7). 1993. pap. 9.57 (*0-201-62267-X*) Addison-Wesley.
Norman, David. Prehistoric Life. 1994. 30.00 (*0-671-79940-1*) P-H.
Oliver, Ray. Rocks & Fossils. LC 92-44791. (Illus.). 80p. (gr. 5 up). 1993. 13.00 (*0-679-82661-0*); PLB 13.99 (*0-679-92661-5*) Random Bks Yng Read.
Parker, Gary. Dry Bones & Other Fossils. Chong, Jonathon, illus. LC 79-51174. (gr. 2-4). 1979. pap. 5.95 (*0-89051-118-7*) Master Bks.
Parker, Steve. Inside Dinosaurs & Other Prehistoric Creatures. Dewan, Ted, illus. LC 93-10045. (gr. 1-8). 1995. 16.95 (*0-385-31143-5*); pap. 10.95 (*0-385-31189-3*) Delacorte.
Phillips, Gina. First Facts about Prehistoric Animals. Persico, F. S., illus. 24p. 1991. 2.98 (*1-56156-083-9*) Kidsbks.
—First Facts about Prehistoric Animals. Persico, F. S., illus. 24p. 1992. pap. 2.50 (*1-56156-157-6*) Kidsbks.
Pope, Joyce. Fossil Detective. Forsey, Chris, illus. LC 91-45170. 32p. (gr. 3-6). 1993. PLB 11.59 (*0-8167-2781-3*); pap. text ed. 3.95 (*0-8167-2782-1*) Troll Assocs.
Rhodes, Frank H., et al. Fossils. Perlman, Raymond, illus. (gr. 6 up). 1962. PLB write for info. (*0-307-63515-5*); pap. write for info. (*0-307-24411-3*, Golden Pr) Western Pub.
Roberts, Allan. Fossils. LC 82-23521. (Illus.). 48p. (gr. k-4). 1983. PLB 12.85 (*0-516-01678-4*); pap. 4.95 (*0-516-41678-2*) Childrens.
Russell, William. Fossils. LC 94-2402. (gr. 3 up). 1994. write for info. (*0-86593-358-8*) Rourke Corp.
Rydell, Wendy. Discovering Fossils. Burns, Ray, illus. LC 83-4832. 32p. (gr. 3-6). 1984. lib. bdg. 10.59 (*0-89375-973-2*); pap. text ed. 2.95 (*0-89375-974-0*) Troll Assocs.
Sabin, Louis. Fossils. Maccabe, Richard, illus. LC 84-2716. 32p. (gr. 3-6). 1985. PLB 9.49 (*0-8167-0228-4*); pap. text ed. 2.95 (*0-8167-0229-2*) Troll Assocs.
Sandberg, Phillip. Stereogram Book of Fossils. (gr. 7 up). plastic comb bdg. 9.90 (*0-8331-1702-5*) Hubbard Sci.
Schlein, Miriam. Before the Dinosaurs. Franczak, Brian, illus. LC 93-25781. 1994. 14.95 (*0-590-47910-5*) Scholastic Inc.
—Let's Go Dinosaur Tracking! Duke, Kate, illus. LC 90-39632. 48p. (gr. 2-5). 1991. PLB 14.89 (*0-06-025139-5*) HarpC Child Bks.
Skeem, Kenneth A. Genesis Fossil Booklet. Skeem, Jeanette, illus. (gr. 3-12). 1992. pap. text ed. 2.00 (*0-9606782-1-2*) Behemoth Pub.
Steele, Philip. Prehistoric Animals. (gr. 4-7). 1991. lib. bdg. 4.95 (*0-671-72242-5*, J Messner) S&S Trade.
Taylor, Paul. Fossil. Keates, Colin, photos by. LC 89-36444. (Illus.). 64p. (gr. 5 up). 1990. 16.00 (*0-679-80440-4*); PLB 16.99 (*0-679-90440-9*) Random Bks Yng Read.
Thompson, Sharon E. Death Trap: The Story of the La Brea Tar Pits. LC 93-39583. (Illus.). 72p. (gr. 5 up). 1994. PLB 21.50 (*0-8225-2851-7*) Lerner Pubns.
Wexo, John B. Mammals, Pt. II. 24p. (gr. 3 up). 1991. PLB 14.95 (*0-88682-396-X*) Creative Ed.
—Swimmers. 24p. (gr. 3 up). 1991. PLB 14.95 (*0-88682-390-0*) Creative Ed.
Whitfield, Philip. Macmillan Children's Guide to Dinosaurs & Other Prehistoric Animals. LC 91-45562. (Illus.). 96p. (gr. 2 up). 1992. SBE 16.95 (*0-02-762362-9*, Macmillan Child Bk) Macmillan Child Grp.
Zim, Herbert S. Dinosaurs. Irving, James G., illus. LC 54-5080. 64p. (gr. 3-7). 1954. PLB 11.88 (*0-688-31239-X*) Morrow Jr Bks.

FOSTER HOME CARE–FICTION

Amstutz, Beverly. That Boy, That Girl. LC 80-80372. (Illus.). 24p. (gr. k-7). 1979. pap. 2.50x (*0-937836-01-X*) Precious Res.
—Touch Me Not! (Illus.). 20p. (ps-7). 1983. pap. 2.50x (*0-937836-09-5*) Precious Res.
Bennett, James. Dakota Dream. LC 93-17854. 144p. (gr. 7 up). 1994. 14.95 (*0-590-46680-1*) Scholastic Inc.
Blomquist, Geraldine M. & Blomquist, Paul B. Zachary's New Home: A Story for Foster & Adopted Children. Lemieux, Margo, illus. LC 92-56876. 1993. PLB 17.27 (*0-8368-0937-8*) Gareth Stevens Inc.
Byars, Betsy C. The Pinballs. LC 76-41518. 144p. (gr. 5 up). 1977. 15.00 (*0-06-020917-8*); PLB 14.89 (*0-06-020918-6*) HarpC Child Bks.
Calvert, Patricia. Writing to Richie. LC 94-14458. (gr. 4-6). 1994. 14.95 (*0-684-19764-2*, Scribner) Macmillan.
Grifalconi, Ann. Not Home: Somehow, Somewhere, There Must Be Love: A Novel. LC 94-16708. 1995. 14.95 (*0-316-32905-3*) Little.
Hermes, Patricia. Heads, I Win. Newsome, Carol, illus. LC 87-19249. 132p. (gr. 3-7). 1988. 12.95 (*0-15-233659-1*, HB Juv Bks) HarBrace.
Hoehne, Marcia. A Place of My Own. LC 92-44336. 128p. (Orig.). (gr. 4-7). 1993. pap. 4.99 (*0-89107-718-9*) Crossway Bks.
Johnston, Julie. Adam & Eve & Pinch-Me. LC 93-21023. 1994. 14.95 (*0-316-46990-4*) Little.
Kerr, Rita. The Texas Orphans: A Story of the Orphan Trail Children. Kerr, Rita, illus. LC 94-1995. 1994. 10. 95 (*0-89015-962-9*) Sunbelt Media.
Kidd, Diana. Onion Tears. Montgomery, Lucy, illus. LC 90-43011. 72p. (gr. 2-5). 1991. 12.95 (*0-531-05870-0*); PLB 12.99 (*0-531-08470-1*) Orchard Bks Watts.
—Onion Tears. Montgomery, Lucy, illus. LC 94-46601. 80p. (gr. 5 up). 1993. pap. 3.95 (*0-688-11862-3*, Pub. by Beech Tree Bks) Morrow.
Levin, Betty. Mercy's Mill. LC 91-31483. (gr. 7 up). 1992. 14.00 (*0-688-11122-X*) Greenwillow.
MacLachlan, Patricia. Mama One, Mama Two. Bornstein, Ruth L., illus. LC 81-47795. 32p. (gr. 1-3). 1982. 13. 00 (*0-06-024081-4*); PLB 13.89 (*0-06-024082-2*) HarpC Child Bks.
Mora, Pat. Pablo's Tree. Mora, Francisco X., illus. LC 92-27145. 32p. (ps-1). 1994. RSBE 14.95 (*0-02-767401-0*, Macmillan Child Bk) Macmillan Child Grp.
Paterson, Katherine. The Great Gilly Hopkins. LC 77-27075. (gr. 5 up). 1978. 14.00i (*0-690-03837-2*, Crowell Jr Bks); PLB 13.89 (*0-690-03838-0*, Crowell Jr Bks) HarpC Child Bks.
—The Great Gilly Hopkins. large type ed. 170p. (gr. 2-6). 1987. Repr. of 1978 ed. lib. bdg. 14.95 (*1-55736-011-1*, Crnrstn Bks) BDD LT Grp.
—The Great Gilly Hopkins: (La Gran Gilly Hopkins) (SPA.). (gr. 1-6). 8.95 (*84-204-3222-9*) Santillana.
Radley, Gail. The Golden Days. LC 90-46935. 144p. (gr. 3-7). 1991. SBE 13.95 (*0-02-775652-1*) Macmillan Child Grp.
St. John, Patricia. Where the River Begins. LC 80-12304. 128p. (Orig.). (gr. 5-8). pap. 4.50 (*0-8024-8124-8*) Moody.
Sebestyen, Ouida. Out of Nowhere. (gr. 5 up). 1994. 14. 95 (*0-531-06839-0*); lib. bdg. 14.99 RLB (*0-531-08689-5*) Orchard Bks Watts.
Stahl, Hilda. Elizabeth Gail & the Mystery of the Hidden Key, No. 20. (gr. 4-7). 1992. pap. 4.99 (*0-8423-0816-4*) Tyndale.
—Elizabeth Gail & the Secret of the Gold Charm, No. 21. (gr. 4-7). 1992. pap. 4.99 (*0-8423-0817-2*) Tyndale.
Thesman, Jean. When the Road Ends. 192p. (gr. 5-9). 1992. 13.45 (*0-395-59507-X*) HM.
Williams, S. P. Ginger Goes on a Diet. Garafano, Marie, illus. LC 92-28950. 1993. 13.95 (*0-395-66077-7*) HM.
Wood, Phyllis A. The Revolving Door Stops Here. Garrick, Jacqueline, illus. LC 89-23891. 192p. (gr. 6 up). 1990. 14.95 (*0-525-65022-9*, Cobblehill Bks) Dutton Child Bks.

FOUR-H CLUBS–FICTION

Kosman, Miriam. Family for a While. LC 93-72272. 176p. (gr. 6-10). 1993. write for info. (*1-56062-202-4*); pap. write for info. (*1-56062-203-2*) CIS Comm.

FOURTH OF JULY

Anderson, Joan. The Glorious Fourth at Prairietown. Ancona, George, photos by. LC 85-28417. (Illus.). 48p. (gr. 2-6). 1986. 11.95 (*0-688-06246-6*); lib. bdg. 11.88 (*0-688-06247-4*, Morrow Jr Bks) Morrow Jr Bks.
Dalgliesh, Alice. Fourth of July Story. Nonnast, Marie, illus. LC 56-6138. 32p. (ps-3). 1972. RSBE 13.95 (*0-684-13164-1*, Scribners Young Read); (Scribner) Macmillan Child Grp.
Giblin, James C. Fireworks, Picnics, & Flags: The Story of the Fourth of July Symbols. Arndt, Ursula, illus. LC 82-9612. 96p. (gr. 3-6). 1983. 14.95 (*0-89919-146-0*, Clarion Bks); pap. 4.95 (*0-89919-174-6*, Clarion Bks) HM.
Gore, Willma W. Independence Day. LC 92-18946. (Illus.). 48p. (gr. 1-4). 1993. lib. bdg. 14.95 (*0-89490-403-5*) Enslow Pubs.
Graham-Barber, Lynda. Doodle Dandy! The Complete Book of Independence Day Words. Lewin, Betsy, illus. LC 91-19409. 128p. (gr. 4-10). 1992. SBE 13.95 (*0-02-736675-8*, Bradbury Pr) Macmillan Child Grp.
McDonnell, Janet. The Fourth of July. Endres, Helen, illus. LC 94-4827. 32p. (ps-2). 1994. PLB 16.40 (*0-516-00694-0*); pap. 3.95 (*0-516-40694-9*) Childrens.
Nielsen, Shelly. Independence Day. Wallner, Rosemary, ed. LC 91-73030. 1992. 13.99 (*1-56239-071-6*) Abdo & Dghtrs.
Schultz, Ellen. I Can Read About July Fourth, Seventeen Seventy-Six. LC 78-68470. (Illus.). (gr. 3-5). 1979. pap. 2.50 (*0-89375-211-8*) Troll Assocs.

FOURTH OF JULY–FICTION

Houck, Eric L., Jr. Rabbit Surprise. Catalano, Dominic, illus. LC 92-1318. 32p. (ps-2). 1993. 14.00 (*0-517-58777-7*); PLB 14.99 (*0-517-58778-5*) Crown Bks Yng Read.
Lasky, Kathryn. Fourth of July Bear. Cogancherry, Helen, illus. LC 90-37422. 40p. (gr. k up). 1991. 13.95 (*0-688-08287-4*); PLB 13.88 (*0-688-08288-2*, Morrow Jr Bks) Morrow Jr Bks.
Watson, Wendy. Hurray for the Fourth of July. Watson, Wendy, illus. 32p. (ps-1). 1992. 14.45 (*0-395-53627-8*, Clarion Bks) HM.

FOXES

Ahlstrom, Mark. The Foxes. LC 83-5324. (Illus.). 48p. (gr. 5). 1983. text ed. 12.95 RSBE (*0-89686-220-8*, Crestwood Hse) Macmillan Child Grp.
Burton, Jane. Trill the Fox Cub. LC 89-11370. (Illus.). 32p. (gr. 2-3). 1989. PLB 17.27 (*0-8368-0212-8*) Gareth Stevens Inc.
Butterworth, Christine & Bailey, Donna. Foxes. LC 90-36169. (Illus.). 32p. (gr. 1-4). 1990. PLB 18.99 (*0-8114-2641-6*) Raintree Steck-V.
George, Jean C. The Moon of the Fox Pups. new ed. Adams, Norman, illus. LC 90-22386. 48p. (gr. 3-7). 1992. 15.00 (*0-06-022859-8*); PLB 14.89 (*0-06-022860-1*) HarpC Child Bks.
LaBonte, Gail. The Arctic Fox. LC 88-18967. (Illus.). 60p. (gr. 3 up). 1988. RSBE 13.95 (*0-87518-390-5*, Dillon) Macmillan Child Grp.
Lepthien, Emilie U. & Kalbacken, Joan. Foxes. LC 93-3409. (Illus.). 48p. (gr. k-4). 1993. PLB 12.85 (*0-516-01191-X*); pap. 4.95 (*0-516-41191-8*) Childrens.
Ling, Mary. Amazing Wolves, Dogs, & Foxes. Young, Jerry, photos by. LC 91-6514. (Illus.). 32p. (Orig.). (gr. 1-5). 1991. lib. bdg. 9.99 (*0-679-91521-4*); pap. 7.99 (*0-679-81521-X*) Knopf Bks Yng Read.
—Fox. LC 92-52810. (Illus.). 24p. (ps-1). 1992. 7.95 (*1-56458-114-4*) Dorling Kindersley.
MacQuitty, Miranda. Discovering Foxes. LC 87-73166. (Illus.). 48p. (gr. 1-6). 1988. PLB 12.40 (*0-531-18197-9*, Pub. by Bookwright Pr) Watts.
Markert, Jenny. Arctic Foxes. 32p. (gr. 2-6). 1991. 15.95 (*0-89565-710-4*) Childs World.
Mason, Cherie. Wild Fox: A True Story. Stammen, JoEllen M., illus. LC 92-74622. 32p. (gr. 2-5). 1993. 15.95 (*0-89272-319-X*) Down East.
Matthews, Downs. Arctic Foxes. Guravich, Dan & Ovsianikov, Nikita, photos by. LC 94-6012. (gr. 5 up). 1995. 16.00 (*0-671-86563-3*, S&S BFYR) S&S Trade.
Schnieper, Claudia. On the Trail of the Fox. Scherer, Elise, tr. (GER., Illus.). 48p. (gr. 2-5). 1986. lib. bdg. 19.95 (*0-87614-287-0*) Carolrhoda Bks.
—On the Trail of the Fox. (Illus.). 48p. (gr. 1-5). 1987. pap. 6.95 (*0-87614-480-6*, First Ave Edns) Lerner Pubns.
Wallace, Karen. Red Fox. Melnyczuk, Peter, illus. LC 93-32381. 32p. (ps up). 1994. 14.95 (*1-56402-422-9*) Candlewick Pr.

FOXES–FICTION

Abolafia, Yossi. Fox Tale. LC 89-77501. (Illus.). 32p. (ps up). 1991. 13.95 (*0-688-09541-0*); PLB 13.88 (*0-688-09542-9*) Greenwillow.
—Fox Tale. (ps-3). 1992. 3.99 (*0-440-40667-6*, YB) Dell.

Anderson, Rachel & Bradby, David. Reynard the Fox. (Illus.). 80p. (gr. 5-8). 1987. 20.00 (*0-19-274129-2*) OUP.
Arnosky, Jim. Watching Foxes. LC 84-20157. (Illus.). 24p. (ps-3). 1984. 12.95 (*0-688-04259-7*); PLB 12.88 (*0-688-04260-0*) Lothrop.
Berrill, Margaret. Chanticleer. Bottomley, Jane, illus. LC 86-6746. 32p. (gr. 2-5). PLB 19.97 (*0-8172-2626-5*) Raintree Steck-V.
Boyle, Doe & Thomas, Peter, eds. Deputy Scarlett: From an Original Article Which Appeared in Ranger Rick Magazine, copyright National Wildlife Federation. Langford, Alton, illus. Luther, Sallie, contrib. by. LC 92-8024. (Illus.). 20p. (gr. k-3). 1992. 6.95 (*0-924483-49-0*); incl. audiocass. tape & 11" toy 35.95 (*0-924483-46-6*); incl. 8" toy 21.95 (*0-924483-47-4*); incl. audiocass. tape 9.95 (*0-924483-48-2*); write for info. audiocass. tape (*0-924483-79-2*) Soundprints.
Brutschy, Jennifer. The Winter Fox. Garns, Allen, illus. LC 92-33467. 40p. (ps-3). 1993. 15.00 (*0-679-81524-4*); PLB 15.99 (*0-679-91524-9*) Knopf Bks Yng Read.
Bryant, Bonnie. Fox Hunt. (gr. 4-7). 1992. pap. 3.50 (*0-553-15990-9*) Bantam.
Bunting, Eve. Red Fox Running. (ps-3). 1993. 15.95 (*0-395-58919-3*, Clarion Bks) HM.
Burgess, Thornton. The Adventures of Reddy Fox. 1992. Repr. lib. bdg. 17.95x (*0-89966-990-5*) Buccaneer Bks.
Burgess, Thornton W. The Adventures of Reddy Fox. large type ed. 96p. 1992. pap. 1.00 (*0-486-26930-2*) Dover.
—Adventures of Reddy Fox. 18.95 (*0-8488-0380-9*) Amereon Ltd.
—Old Granny Fox. 18.95 (*0-8488-0392-2*) Amereon Ltd.
Byars, Betsy C. The Midnight Fox. Grifalconi, Ann, illus. LC 68-27566. (gr. 3-7). 1968. pap. 13.95 (*0-670-47473-8*) Viking Child Bks.
Caple, Kathy. Fox & Bear. Caple, Kathy, illus. 40p. (gr. k-3). 1992. 13.45 (*0-395-55634-1*) HM.
Chase, Alyssa. Tessa on Her Own. Maeno, Itoko, illus. 32p. (gr. 1-4). 1994. 16.95 (*1-55942-064-2*, 7656) Marshfilm.
Chaucer, Geoffrey. Chanticleer & the Fox. Cooney, Barbara, illus. LC 58-10449. 40p. (ps-3). 1982. 14.00 (*0-690-18561-8*, Crowell Jr Bks); PLB 13.89 (*0-690-18562-6*); pap. 3.95 (*0-690-04318-X*) HarpC Child Bks.
—Chanticleer & the Fox. Cooney, Barbara, illus. LC 58-10449. 32p. (gr. k-3). 1982. pap. 5.95 (*0-06-443087-1*, Trophy) HarpC Child Bks.
Christopher, Matt. The Fox Steals Home. Johnson, Larry, illus. LC 78-17526. (gr. 4-6). 1985. 14.95 (*0-316-13976-9*); pap. 3.95 (*0-316-13986-6*) Little.
Clifford, Eth. Flatfoot Fox & the Case of the Bashful Beaver. Lies, Brian, illus. LC 94-14761. 1995. write for info. (*0-395-70560-6*) HM.
—Flatfoot Fox & the Case of the Missing Eye. Lies, Brian, illus. 48p. (gr. 2-5). 1990. 12.70 (*0-395-51945-4*) HM.
—Flatfoot Fox & the Case of the Missing Whoooo. Lies, Brian, illus. LC 92-21903. 1993. 13.95 (*0-395-65364-9*) HM.
—Flatfoot Fox & the Case of the Missing Eye. (gr. 4-7). 1992. pap. 2.95 (*0-590-45812-4*) Scholastic Inc.
—Flatfoot Fox & the Case of the Nosy Otter. Lies, Brian, illus. LC 91-26930. 48p. (gr. 2-5). 1992. 13.45 (*0-395-60289-0*) HM.
Dahl, Roald. Fantastic Mr. Fox. (gr. 4-8). 1978. pap. 2.50 (*0-553-15390-0*, Skylark) Bantam.
—Fantastic Mr. Fox. Chaffin, Donald, illus. LC 74-118704. 72p. (gr. 3-6). 1986. 14.95 (*0-394-80497-X*) Knopf Bks Yng Read.
—El Superzorro - Fantastic Mr. Fox. Buckley, Ramon, tr. Elena, Horacio, illus. (SPA.). 153p. (gr. 2-4). 1992. pap. write for info. (*84-204-0013-0*) Santillana.
—The Vicar of Nibbleswicke. Blake, Quentin, illus. 48p. (gr. 5 up). 1994. pap. 3.99 (*0-14-036837-X*) Puffin Bks.
Daves, Prentiss V. The Strawberry Fox. Quintahlen, Patrique, ed. James, Nancy D., illus. LC 91-62065. 54p. (Orig.). 1992. pap. 3.95 (*0-9615560-9-9*) Jordan Enterprises.
Dr. Seuss. Fox in Socks. (ps-1). 1986. pap. 6.95 incl. cassette (*0-394-88322-5*) Random Bks Yng Read.
Espinassous, Louis. Little Lost Fox Cub, on the Trail of Little Fox. Routiaux, Claudine, illus. LC 92-27116. 1993. PLB 18.60 (*0-8368-0927-0*) Gareth Stevens Inc.
Firmin, Peter. Hungry Mr. Fox. (gr. k-6). 1990. pap. 2.95 (*0-440-40340-5*, YB) Dell.
The Fox & the Hound. 96p. 1988. 6.98 (*1-57082-038-4*) Mouse Works.
Fox, Mem. Hattie & the Fox. Mullins, Patricia, illus. LC 91-41727. 32p. (ps-2). 1992. pap. 4.95 (*0-689-71611-7*, Aladdin) Macmillan Child Grp.
The Fox with Cold Feet. 42p. (ps-3). 1993. PLB 13.26 (*0-8368-0890-8*); PLB 13.27 s.p. (*0-685-61522-7*) Gareth Stevens Inc.
Galdone, Paul. What's in Fox's Sack. Galdone, Paul, illus. 32p. (ps-1). 1982. 13.95 (*0-89919-062-6*, Clarion Bks) HM.
—What's in Fox's Sack? LC 81-10251. (Illus.). (gr. 1-3). 1987. pap. 6.95 (*0-89919-491-5*, Clarion Bks) HM.
Gardiner, John R. Stone Fox. Sewall, Marcia, illus. LC 79-7895. 96p. (gr. 2-6). 1983. pap. 3.95 (*0-06-440132-4*, Trophy) HarpC Child Bks.
Garside, Alice H. The Fox & the Stork. Meeks, Catherine F., illus. 24p. (Orig.). (gr. k-2). 1990. pap. 2.10 (*1-882063-10-4*) Cottage Pr MA.
—The Fox & the Thrush. Meeks, Catherine F., illus. 20p. (Orig.). (gr. k-2). 1990. pap. 2.10 (*1-882063-09-0*) Cottage Pr MA.
Giffard, Hannah. Red Fox. Giffard, Hannah, illus. LC 90-2807. 36p. (ps-3). 1991. 12.95 (*0-8037-0869-6*) Dial Bks Young.
—Red Fox on the Move. Giffard, Hannah, illus. LC 90-25646. 36p. (ps-3). 1992. 14.00 (*0-8037-1057-7*) Dial Bks Young.
Gregorich, Barbara. The Fox on the Box. Hoffman, Joan, ed. Masheris, Robert, illus. 16p. (Orig.). (gr. k-2). 1984. pap. 2.25 (*0-88743-005-8*, 06005) Sch Zone Pub Co.
—The Fox on the Box. Hoffman, Joan, ed. (Illus.). 32p. (gr. k-2). 1992. pap. 3.95 (*0-88743-403-7*, 06055) Sch Zone Pub Co.
Hastings, Selina, retold by. Reynard the Fox. Percy, Graham, illus. LC 90-11105. 80p. (gr. 2-4). 1991. 16.95 (*0-688-09949-1*, Tambourine Bks); PLB 16.88 (*0-688-10156-9*, Tambourine Bks) Morrow.
Hunter, Mollie. Gilly Martin the Fox. LC 93-24112. (Illus.). 40p. (gr. k-4). 1994. 15.95 (*1-56282-517-8*); PLB 15.89 (*1-56282-518-6*) Hyprn Child.
Kent, Jack. Silly Goose. Kent, Jack, illus. LC 82-21441. 32p. (ps-3). 1986. 5.95 (*0-13-810177-9*) P-H.
King-Smith, Dick. The Fox Busters. Miller, Jon, illus. LC 87-37409. 128p. (gr. 4-7). 1988. 13.95 (*0-440-50064-8*) Delacorte.
Kjelgaard, Jim. Haunt Fox. 160p. 1981. pap. 2.50 (*0-553-15547-4*) Bantam.
—Haunt Fox. 1981. pap. 3.99 (*0-553-15743-4*) Bantam.
—Haunt Fox. (gr. 4-7). 1992. 17.00 (*0-8446-6593-2*) Peter Smith.
Korschunow, Irina. The Foundling Fox. Skofield, James, tr. from GER. Michl, Reinhard, illus. LC 84-47631. 48p. (gr. k-3). 1984. HarpC Child Bks.
Lane, Margaret. The Fox. Lilly, Kenneth, illus. 32p. (gr. k-4). 1994. pap. 4.99 (*0-14-050337-4*, Puff Pied Piper) Puffin Bks.
Lindgren, Astrid. The Tomten & the Fox. Wiberg, Harald, illus. 32p. (ps-3). 1989. pap. 5.95 (*0-698-20644-4*, Sandcastle Bks) Putnam Pub Group.
McKissack, Patricia C. Flossie & the Fox. Isadora, Rachel, illus. LC 86-2024. 32p. (ps-3). 1986. 14.00 (*0-8037-0250-7*); PLB 13.89 (*0-8037-0251-5*) Dial Bks Young.
Marshall, Edward. Fox All Week. Marshall, James, illus. LC 84-1708. (ps-3). 1984. 10.95 (*0-8037-0062-8*) Dial Bks Young.
—Fox All Week. Marshall, James, illus. LC 84-1708. 48p. (ps-3). 1987. pap. 4.95 (*0-8037-0008-3*) Dial Bks Young.
—Fox & His Friends. Marshall, James, illus. LC 81-68769. 56p. (ps-3). 1982. PLB 10.89 (*0-8037-2669-4*); pap. 4.95 (*0-8037-2668-6*) Dial Bks Young.
—Fox & His Friends. (ps-3). 1993. pap. 4.99 (*0-14-036188-X*) Puffin Bks.
—Fox & His Friends. Marshall, James, illus. (gr. 1-4). 1994. pap. 3.25 (*0-14-037007-2*) Puffin Bks.
—Fox at School. Marshall, James, illus. LC 82-45506. 48p. (ps-3). 1983. PLB 9.89 (*0-8037-2675-9*); pap. 4.95 (*0-8037-2674-0*) Dial Bks Young.
—Fox at School. Marshall, James, illus. LC 93-2721. (gr. 1-4). 1993. pap. 3.25 (*0-14-036544-3*, Puffin) Puffin Bks.
—Fox in Love. Marshall, James, illus. LC 82-70190. 56p. (ps-3). 1982. PLB 10.89 (*0-8037-2433-0*) Dial Bks Young.
—Fox on Wheels. Marshall, James, illus. LC 83-5254. 48p. (ps-3). 1983. PLB 10.89 (*0-8037-0002-4*) Dial Bks Young.
—Fox on Wheels. Marshall, James, illus. (gr. 1-4). 1993. pap. 3.25 (*0-14-036541-9*, Puffin) Puffin Bks.
Marshall, James. Fox Be Nimble. Fogelman, Phyllis J., ed. Marshall, James, illus. LC 89-7933. 48p. (ps-3). 1990. 10.95 (*0-8037-0760-6*); PLB 10.89 (*0-8037-0761-4*) Dial Bks Young.
—Fox Be Nimble. (Illus.). (gr. 1-4). 1994. pap. 3.25 (*0-14-036842-6*) Puffin Bks.
—Fox in Love. (Illus.). (gr. 1-4). 1994. pap. 3.25 (*0-14-036843-4*) Puffin Bks.
—Fox on Stage. Marshall, James, illus. LC 91-46740. 48p. (ps-3). 1993. 10.99 (*0-8037-1356-8*); PLB 10.89 (*0-8037-1357-6*) Dial Bks Young.
—Fox on the Job. 1990. pap. 4.99 (*0-8037-0746-0*, Dial Easy to Read) Puffin Bks.
—Fox Outfoxed. Marshall, James, illus. LC 91-21815. 48p. (ps-3). 1992. 11.00 (*0-8037-1036-4*); PLB 10.89 (*0-8037-1037-2*) Dial Bks Young.

Metzler, Rosemary M. Snooty the Fox. 23p. 1993. 5.95 (*0-9637381-0-0*) Snooty Prods.
Rosemary Mezler's irresistable read-aloud children's adventure story, SNOOTY THE FOX, the snootiest, snootiest fox of the Foxville Clan will cast a spell over its readers. This exciting story is for the millions of boys & girls who fall asleep dreaming of being in the saddle during a cattle drive. In this first SNOOTY THE FOX adventure series, Snooty the Fox, the snootiest, snootiest fox, Foxville, England, is invited to his Auntie Margaret Foxville's Colorado cattle ranch to help with the big cattle drive. On the morning of the cattle drive Snooty the Fox dressed in his elegant plaid riding jacket, white breeches & black top hat wants to prove himself to be worthwhile--a true Foxville! Rosemary Metzler has written a page turning story filled with breathtaking escapades.
Publisher Provided Annotation.

Michaels, Ski. Felix, the Funny Fox. Mahan, Ben, illus. LC 85-14097. 48p. (Orig.). (gr. 1-3). 1986. PLB 10.59 (*0-8167-0590-9*); pap. text ed. 3.50 (*0-8167-0591-7*) Troll Assocs.
Morton, Leith D. The Fox. Murakami, Yukuo, illus. LC 91-43003. (ENG & JPN.). 32p. (ps-6). 1992. 14.95 (*0-87358-534-8*) Northland AZ.
Nordqvist, Sven. The Fox Hunt. Nordqvist, Sven, illus. LC 87-28197. 32p. (ps-2). 1988. 12.95 (*0-688-06881-2*); PLB 12.88 (*0-688-06882-0*, Morrow Jr Bks) Morrow Jr Bks.
Pepin, Muriel. Brave Little Fox. Jensen, Patricia, adapted by. Fichaux, Catherine, illus. LC 93-4238. 22p. (ps-3). 1993. 5.98 (*0-89577-541-7*, Readers Digest Kids) RD Assn.
Sargent, Dave & Sargent, Pat. Redi Fox. 64p. (gr. 2-6). 1992. pap. write for info. (*1-56763-010-3*) Ozark Pub.
Scheffler, Ursel. The Return of Rinaldo the Sly Fox. Gider, Iskender, illus. James, J. Alison, tr. from GER. LC 93-17677. (Illus.). 64p. (gr. 2-4). 1993. 12.95 (*1-55858-227-4*); lib. bdg. 12.88 (*1-55858-228-2*) North-South Bks NYC.
—Rinaldo, the Sly Fox. Gider, Iskender, illus. James, J. Alison, tr. from GER. LC 92-2376. (Illus.). 32p. (gr. 2-3). 1992. 13.95 (*1-55858-181-2*); PLB 13.88 (*1-55858-182-0*) North-South Bks NYC.
Scotti, Linda. Mr. Peek-a-Boo. 1993. 7.95 (*0-533-10353-3*) Vantage.
Shepherd, C. A., et al. The Sly Fox. (Orig.). (gr. 3-12). 1985. pap. 8.00 play script (*0-88734-503-4*) Players Pr.
Singer, Bill. The Fox with Cold Feet. Kendrick, Dennis, illus. LC 80-10288. 48p. (ps-3). 1980. 5.95 (*0-8193-1021-2*); PLB 5.95 (*0-8193-1022-0*) Parents.
Spier, Peter. Fox Went Out on a Chilly Night. LC 60-7139. (Illus.). (gr. 1-3). 1989. pap. 5.95 (*0-385-01065-6*, Zephyr) Doubleday.
—Fox Went Out On a Chilly Night: An Old Song. (ps-3). 1993. 4.99 (*0-440-40829-6*) Dell.
Steiber, Ellen. Shadow of the Fox. LC 94-1295. 108p. (gr. 2-6). 1994. pap. 3.50 (*0-679-86667-1*, Bullseye Bks) Random Bks Yng Read.
Tejima, Keizaburo. Fox's Dream. Tejima, Keizaburo, illus. 48p. (ps-1). 1990. 14.95 (*0-399-21455-0*, Sandcastle Bks); pap. 6.95 (*0-399-22017-8*, Sandcastle Bks) Putnam Pub Group.
Thomas, Jane R. Fox in a Trap. Howell, Troy, illus. LC 86-17412. 96p. (gr. 2-5). 1990. pap. 3.95 (*0-395-54426-2*, Clarion Bks) HM.
Threadgall, Colin. Proud Rooster & the Fox. LC 91-15004. (Illus.). 32p. (ps-3). 1992. 14.00 (*0-688-11123-8*, Tambourine Bks); PLB 13.93 (*0-688-11124-6*, Tambourine Bks) Morrow.
Tompert, Ann. Grandfather Tang's Story. Parker, Robert A., illus. LC 89-22205. 32p. (ps-2). 1990. 16.00 (*0-517-57487-X*); PLB 16.99 (*0-517-57272-9*) Crown Bks Yng Read.
Turner, Louise. It's a Great Day: The Story of Rusty, the Gunston Hall Fox. Sonnett, Barbie, illus. 45p. (Orig.). 1983. pap. 6.95 (*1-884085-04-0*) Bd Regents.
Vaughan, Marcia K. Dorobo the Dangerous. Stone, Kazuko G., illus. LC 93-47891. 1994. 10.95 (*0-382-24076-6*); lib. bdg. 14.95 (*0-382-24070-7*); pap. 4.95 (*0-382-24453-2*) Silver Burdett Pr.
Violette's Daring Adventure. (Illus.). 32p. (gr. k-3). 1992. PLB 17.27 (*0-8368-0912-2*) Gareth Stevens Inc.
Voss-Bark, Doris L. Philip the Fox & Other Stories. Brown, Denise, illus. LC 66-10511. (gr. 3-6). 1967. 13.95 (*0-8023-1105-9*) Dufour.
Walsh, Ellen S. You Silly Goose. 1992. 13.95 (*0-15-299865-9*, HB Juv Bks) HarBrace.
Walt Disney Staff. Fox & the Hound. 1988. 6.98 (*0-8317-3472-8*) Viking Child Bks.
Watson, Clyde. Tom Fox & the Apple Pie. Watson, Wendy, illus. LC 74-171010. (ps-3). 1972. (Crowell Jr Bks) HarpC Child Bks.
Wyllie, Stephen. Dinner with Fox. LC 89-25899. (Illus.). 24p. (ps-3). 1990. 12.95 (*0-8037-0796-7*) Dial Bks Young.
Young, Selina. Whistling in the Woods. Young, Selina, illus. LC 93-23765. 32p. 1994. 14.00 (*0-688-13073-9*, Tambourine Bks) Morrow.

FOXES–SONGS AND MUSIC

Spier, Peter. Fox Went Out on a Chilly Night. Spier, Peter, illus. LC 60-7139. 42p. (gr. k-3). 1961. pap. 11.95 (*0-385-07990-7*) Doubleday.

FRACTIONS

Bradford, John. Everything's Coming up Fractions: With Cuisenaire Rods. 64p. (gr. 3-6). 1981. pap. text ed. 8.50 (*0-914040-91-X*) Cuisenaire.

Daniel, Becky. Hooray for Fraction Facts! 80p. (gr. 2-5). 1990. 9.95 (*0-86653-568-3*, GA1165) Good Apple.
Daniel, Charlie & Daniel, Becky. Freaky Fractions. 48p. (gr. 1-5). 1978. 7.95 (*0-916456-19-6*, GA77) Good Apple.
Dennis, J. Richard. Fractions Are Parts of Things. LC 73-127603. (Illus.). 40p. (gr. 2-4). 1972. PLB 12.89 (*0-690-31521-X*, Crowell Jr Bks) HarpC Child Bks.
Leedy, Loreen. Fraction Action. Leedy, Loreen, illus. LC 93-22800. 32p. (ps-3). 1994. reinforced bdg. 15.95 (*0-8234-1109-5*) Holiday.
McMillan, Bruce. Eating Fractions. (ps-3). 1991. 14.95 (*0-590-43770-4*, Scholastic Hardcover) Scholastic Inc.
Ockenga, Earl & Rucker, Walt. Place Value to One Hundred. Dawson, Dave, illus. 16p. (gr. 1). 1990. pap. text ed. 1.25 (*1-56281-115-0*, M115) Extra Eds.
Shepherd, Glenn. Fractions. Bell-Jarrett, Kaytee, illus. 93p. (gr. 6-12). 1994. pap. text ed. 5.75 (*1-885120-02-8*) F E Braswell.
Smart, Margaret & Tuel, Patricia. Focus on Fractions, 3 vols. Laycock, Mary, intro. by. (Illus.). (gr. 6-9). 1977. Set. 16.50 (*0-918932-69-6*); Vol. 1. 7.50 (*0-918932-14-9*); Vol. 2. 7.50 (*0-918932-15-7*); Vol. 3. 7.50 (*0-918932-16-5*) Activity Resources.

FRACTURES–FICTION

Wolff, Angelika. Mom, I Broke My Arm. Glueckselig, Leo, illus. LC 69-18646. (gr. k-3). 1969. PLB 12.95 (*0-87460-121-5*) Lion Bks.

FRANCE

Axworthy, Anni. Anni's Diary of France. LC 93-27278. (Illus.). 32p. (gr. 1-5). 1994. smythe sewn 14.95 (*1-879085-58-5*) Whsprng Coyote Pr.
Bailey, Donna & Sproule, Anna. France. LC 90-9647. (Illus.). 32p. (gr. 1-4). 1990. PLB 18.99 (*0-8114-2561-4*) Raintree Steck-V.
Bender, Lionel. France. (Illus.). 48p. (gr. 4-8). 1987. PLB 14.98 (*0-382-09505-7*) Silver Burdett Pr.
Buckland, Simon. Guide to France. Price-Thomas, Brian, illus. LC 93-39008. 32p. (gr. 1-4). 1994. 3.95 (*1-85697-958-X*, Kingfisher LKC) LKC.
Butler, Daphne. France. LC 92-16648. (Illus.). 32p. (gr. 3-4). 1992. PLB 19.24 (*0-8114-3675-6*) Raintree Steck-V.
France in Pictures. 64p. (gr. 5 up). 1991. PLB 17.50 (*0-8225-1891-0*) Lerner Pubns.
Gamgee, John, ed. Journey Through France. Forsey, Chris, illus. LC 91-46175. 32p. (gr. 3-5). 1993. PLB 11.89 (*0-8167-2759-7*); pap. text ed. 3.95 (*0-8167-2760-0*) Troll Assocs.
Ganeri, Anita. France & the French. (Illus.). 32p. (gr. 5-8). 1993. PLB 12.40 (*0-531-17401-8*, Gloucester Pr) Watts.
Ganeri, Anita & Wright, Rachel. France. LC 92-27136. 1993. 11.90 (*0-531-14256-6*) Watts.
Getting to Know France. 48p. 1990. 7.95 (*0-8442-1410-8*, Natl Textbk) NTC Pub Grp.
Goldstein, Frances. Children's Treasure Hunt Travel to Belgium & France. Goldstein, Frances, illus. LC 80-85012. 230p. (Orig.). (gr. k-12). 1981. pap. 6.95 (*0-933334-02-8*, Dist. by Hippocrene) Paper Tiger Pap.
Moss, Peter & Palmer, Thelma. France. LC 86-9628. (Illus.). 128p. (gr. 5-9). 1986. PLB 20.55 (*0-516-02761-1*) Childrens.
Norbrook, Dominique. Passport to France. rev. ed. LC 93-21188. (Illus.). 48p. (gr. 5-8). 1994. PLB 13.90 (*0-531-14293-0*) Watts.
Somerville, L. First Book of France. (Illus.). 32p. 1989. PLB 13.96 (*0-88110-391-8*); pap. 6.95 (*0-7460-0322-6*) EDC.
Sturges, Jo. France. LC 92-35182. (Illus.). 32p. (gr. 4 up). 1993. text ed. 13.95 RSBE (*0-89686-778-1*, Crestwood Hse) Macmillan Child Grp.
Wright, David & Wright, Jill. France. (Illus.). 32p. (gr. 4-6). 1991. 17.95 (*0-237-60184-2*, Pub. by Evans Bros Ltd) Trafalgar.

FRANCE–FICTION

Albert, Gilbert. Les Champs et Les Forets. Ganim, Barbara, illus. (FRE.). 28p. (gr. 6-8). 1986. pap. text ed. 3.95 (*0-911409-46-7*) Natl Mat Dev.
Anholt, Laurence. Camille & the Sunflowers. (Illus.). 32p. (ps-2). 1994. 13.95 (*0-8120-6409-7*) Barron.
Banks, Lynne R. Melusine: A Mystery. LC 88-32798. 224p. (gr. 7 up). 1991. pap. 3.95 (*0-06-447054-7*, Trophy) HarpC Child Bks.
Bemelmans, Ludwig. Madeline. (Illus.). 32p. (ps-3). 1993. pap. 17.99 (*0-14-054845-9*, Puffin) Puffin Bks.
—Madeline. Grosman, Ernesto L., tr. (SPA., Illus.). 64p. (ps-3). 1993. 14.99 (*0-670-85154-X*) Viking Child Bks.
Carter, Peter. The Hunted. 1994. 17.00 (*0-374-33520-6*) FS&G.
De Balzac, Honore. Le Pere Goriot. (gr. 7-12). pap. 6.95 (*0-88436-043-1*, 40280) EMC.
De Brunhoff, Laurent. La Fete de Celesteville. (gr. 4-6). 15.95 (*0-685-33969-6*) Fr & Eur.
Dumas, Alexandre. Georges. Rivers, W. Napoleon, et al, eds. (FRE.). 1990. 7.95 (*0-87498-082-8*); pap. 5.95 (*0-87498-083-6*) Assoc Pubs DC.
Filion, Pierre. Pikolo: L'Arbre Aux Mille Tresors. (ps-3). 1994. 15.95 (*1-55037-367-6*, Pub. by Annick CN); pap. 6.95 (*1-55037-366-8*, Pub. by Annick CN) Firefly Bks Ltd.
Flaubert, Gustave. Madame Bovary. (gr. 11 up). 1965. pap. 1.95 (*0-8049-0089-2*, CL-89) Airmont.
Fournier. Le Grand Meaulnes. (gr. 7-12). pap. 6.95 (*0-88436-110-1*, 40272) EMC.
Guillot, Rene. Wind of Chance. Dale, Norman, tr. Collot, Pierre, illus. (gr. 6-9). 1958. 21.95 (*0-87599-048-7*) S G Phillips.
Huneke, Barbara & Gay, Ilona. Bonjour, Tigre! 40p. (gr. 1). 1984. pap. 10.00 (*1-884488-00-5*) Bonjour Tigre.
—Bonjour, Tigre! 2nd ed. 40p. (gr. 1). 1985. pap. 12.00 (*1-884488-01-3*) Bonjour Tigre.
—Bonjour, Tigre! 3rd ed. 28p. (gr. 1). 1993. pap. 12.00 (*1-884488-03-X*) Bonjour Tigre.
Huneke, Barbara, et al. Oh la La! Let's Go to France with Tigre. 36p. (gr. 1). 1988. pap. 12.00 (*1-884488-02-1*) Bonjour Tigre.
Lear, Edward & De Paola, Tomie. Bonjour, Mister Satie. (Illus.). (ps-3). 1991. 15.95 (*0-399-21782-7*, Putnam) Putnam Pub Group.
McCann, Helen. What's French for Help, George? Eagle, Ellen, illus. LC 91-41563. 460p. (gr. 5-9). 1993. pap. 13.00 JR3 (*0-671-74689-8*, S&S BFYR) S&S Trade.
McGraw, Sheila. Je t'Aimera Toujours. (ps-3). 1988. pap. 4.95 (*0-920668-49-6*) Firefly Bks Ltd.
Maupassant. Mon Oncle Jules. (gr. 7-12). pap. 6.95 (*0-88436-044-X*, 40281) EMC.
Niedermayer, Walter. Into the Deep Misty Woods of the Ardennes. (Illus.). 170p. (Orig.). 1990. pap. text ed. 13.50 (*0-935648-30-5*) Halldin Pub.
Noonan, Diana. The Shepherd Who Planted a Forest. Campbell, Caroline, illus. LC 93-11828. 1994. write for info. (*0-383-03774-3*) SRA Schl Grp.
Renard, Jules. Poil de Carotte. (gr. 7-12). pap. 5.95 (*0-88436-046-6*, 40264) EMC.
Schnur, Steven. The Shadow Children. LC 94-5098. 1994. write for info. (*0-688-13281-2*); PLB write for info. (*0-688-13831-4*) Morrow Jr Bks.
Sempe, Jean-Jacques. Chronicles of Little Nicholas. 1993. 15.00 (*0-374-31275-3*) FS&G.
Simenon. Les Enigmes. (gr. 7-12). pap. 6.95 (*0-88436-058-X*, 40269) EMC.
Simenon, Georges. Maigret et le Clochard. pap. 6.95 (*0-88436-047-4*, 40270) EMC.
Smith, Duncan. Fred Goes to France. (Illus.). 25p. (gr. k-2). 1991. 11.95 (*0-237-51125-8*, Pub. by Evans Bros Ltd) Trafalgar.
Stevens, Biddy. Toto in France. (FRE.). 32p. (gr. 4-7). 1993. 12.95 (*0-8442-9180-3*, Natl Textbk) NTC Pub Grp.
Supervielle, Jules. Le Voleur D'enfants. pap. 5.95 (*0-88436-111-X*, 40265) EMC.
Wright, Nicola. Getting to Know: France & French. Wooley, Kim, illus. 32p. (gr. 3-7). 1993. 12.95 (*0-8120-6336-8*); pap. 5.95 (*0-8120-1532-0*) Barron.

FRANCE–HISTORY

Besson, Jean-Louis. Livre de l'Histoire de France. (FRE.). 124p. (gr. 4-9). 1986. 18.95 (*2-07-039525-1*) Schoenhof.
Charpentreau, J. & Borchers, E. Livre de Tous les Jours. (FRE.). (gr. 4-9). 1980. 17.95 (*2-07-039514-6*) Schoenhof.
Musee en Herbe Staff. Livre de la Tour Eiffel. (FRE.). 96p. (gr. 4-9). 1983. 14.95 (*2-07-039502-2*) Schoenhof.
Sookram, Brian. France. (Illus.). 128p. (gr. 5 up). 1990. 14.95 (*0-7910-1111-9*) Chelsea Hse.
Tissot, Olivier. Livre de Tous les Francais. Blachon, Roger, illus. (FRE.). 92p. (gr. 4-9). 1989. 15.95 (*2-07-039526-X*) Schoenhof.

FRANCE–HISTORY–BIOGRAPHY

Hoobler, Dorothy & Hoobler, Thomas. French Portraits. LC 93-38363. 1994. PLB 22.80 (*0-8114-6382-6*) Raintree Steck-V.

FRANCE–HISTORY–FICTION

Dumas, Alexandre. Three Musketeers. Price, Norman & Van Swearingen, Earl C., illus. (gr. 4-6). 1959. (G&D); deluxe ed. 13.95 (*0-448-06024-8*) Putnam Pub Group.
Haseley, Dennis. Horses with Wings. Curlee, Lynn, illus. LC 92-29869. 32p. (gr. k up). 1993. 16.00 (*0-06-022885-7*); PLB 15.89 (*0-06-022886-5*) HarpC Child Bks.
Storr, Catherine, as told by. The Three Musketeers. (Illus.). 32p. (gr. k-5). 1985. PLB 19.97 (*0-8172-2500-5*) Raintree Steck-V.

FRANCE–HISTORY–TO 1328

see also Celts

FRANCE–HISTORY–TO 1328–FICTION

Konigsburg, E. L. A Proud Taste for Scarlet & Miniver. Konigsburg, E. L., illus. LC 73-76320. 208p. (gr. 5-9). 1973. SBE 14.95 (*0-689-30111-1*, Atheneum Child Bk) Macmillan Child Grp.

FRANCE–HISTORY–HOUSE OF VALOIS, 1328-1589

see also Hundred Years' War, 1339-1453

Hugo, Victor. The Hunchback of Notre Dame. Shaw, Charles, illus. Stewart, Diana, adapted by. LC 81-5151. (Illus.). 48p. (gr. 4 up). 1983. PLB 20.70 (*0-8172-1671-5*) Raintree Steck-V.

FRANCE–HISTORY–HOUSE OF VALOIS, 1328-1589–FICTION

Dana, Barbara. Young Joan. LC 90-39494. 384p. (gr. 7 up). 1991. PLB 17.89 (*0-06-021423-6*) HarpC Child Bks.
Hugo, Victor. The Hunchback of Notre Dame. Shaw, Charles, illus. Stewart, Diana, adapted by. LC 81-5151. (Illus.). 48p. (gr. 4 up). 1983. PLB 20.70 (*0-8172-1671-5*) Raintree Steck-V.
Scott, Walter. Quentin Durward. Bennet, C. L., intro. by. (gr. 9 up). 1967. pap. 2.50 (*0-8049-0132-5*, CL-132) Airmont.
Sohl, Marcia & Dackerman, Gerald. Hunchback of Notre Dame: Student Activity Book. (Illus.). (gr. 4-10). 1976. wkbk 1.25 (*0-88301-189-1*) Pendulum Pr.

FRANCE–HISTORY–BOURBONS, 1589-1789–FICTION

Dumas, Alexandre. Man in the Iron Mask. Hillerich, R., intro. by. (gr. 9 up). 1967. pap. 2.75 (*0-8049-0150-3*, CL-150) Airmont.
—Three Musketeers. (gr. 8 up). 1966. pap. 3.95 (*0-8049-0127-9*, CL-127) Airmont.
—The Three Musketeers. Felder, Deborah, adapted by. LC 93-42782. 108p. (gr. 2-6). 1994. pap. 3.50 (*0-679-86017-7*, Bullseye Bks) Random Bks Yng Read.
Matas, Carol. The Burning Time. LC 94-443. 1994. 15.95 (*0-385-32097-3*) Delacorte.

FRANCE–HISTORY–REVOLUTION, 1789-1799

Balkwill, Richard. Trafalgar. LC 93-2650. (Illus.). 32p. (gr. 6 up). 1993. text ed. 13.95 RSBE (*0-02-726326-6*, New Discovery Bks) Macmillan Child Grp.
Banfield, Susan. The Rights of Man, the Reign of Terror: The Story of the French Revolution. LC 89-2742. 224p. (gr. 7 up). 1990. 15.00 (*0-397-32353-0*, Lipp Jr Bks); PLB 14.89 (*0-397-32354-9*, Lipp Jr Bks) HarpC Child Bks.
Cairns, Trevor. Power for the People. LC 76-30607. (Illus.). 96p. (gr. 7 up). 1978. pap. 13.95 (*0-521-20902-1*) Cambridge U Pr.
Hills, Ken. French Revolution. (Illus.). 32p. (gr. 3-9). 1988. PLB 10.95 (*0-86307-934-2*) Marshall Cavendish.
Marrin, Albert. Napoleon & the Napoleonic Wars. LC 93-13067. 288p. (gr. 7 up). 1993. pap. 5.99 (*0-14-036479-X*, Puffin) Puffin Bks.
Mitchell, Crohan. The Napoleonic Wars. (Illus.). 72p. (gr. 7-10). 1989. 19.95 (*0-7134-5729-5*, Pub. by Batsford UK) Trafalgar.
Mulvihill, Margaret. The French Revolution. Wood, Gerald, illus. LC 89-31564. 32p. (gr. 4-6). 1989. PLB 12.40 (*0-531-17167-1*, Gloucester Pr) Watts.
Otfinoski, Steven. Triumph & Terror: The French Revolution. LC 92-37131. (Illus.). 128p. (gr. 6-9). 1993. 16.95 (*0-8160-2762-5*) Facts on File.

FRANCE–HISTORY–REVOLUTION, 1789-1799–FICTION

Dickens, Charles. Tale of Two Cities. (gr. 9 up). 1964. pap. 2.95 (*0-8049-0021-3*, CL-21) Airmont.
—A Tale of Two Cities. Shaw, Charles, illus. Krapesh, Patti, adapted by. LC 79-24746. (Illus.). (gr. 4 up). 1983. PLB 20.70 (*0-8172-1658-8*) Raintree Steck-V.
Hess, Donna. In Search of Honor. 153p. (Orig.). (gr. 9 up). 1991. pap. 4.95 (*0-89084-595-6*) Bob Jones Univ Pr.
Hugo, Victor. Les Miserables. Kulling, Monica, adapted by. LC 94-15411. 1995. 3.50 (*0-679-86668-X*) Random.
Orczy, Emmuska. Scarlet Pimpernel. (gr. 7 up). 1964. pap. 2.95 (*0-8049-0028-0*, CL-28) Airmont.
Prowense, Mary J. Pamela & the Revolution. Schatz, Molly, ed. Kear, Suzanne, illus. 130p. (gr. 7 up). 1993. 12.95 (*0-9635107-2-X*) Marc Anthony.

FRANCE–HISTORY–1799-1914

Marrin, Albert. Napoleon & the Napoleonic Wars. LC 93-13067. 288p. (gr. 7 up). 1993. pap. 5.99 (*0-14-036479-X*, Puffin) Puffin Bks.
Milton, Nancy. The Giraffe That Walked to Paris. Roth, Roger, illus. LC 91-31767. 32p. (gr. k-4). 1992. 15.00 (*0-517-58132-9*); PLB 15.99 (*0-517-58133-7*) Crown Bks Yng Read.

FRANCE–HISTORY–CONSULATE AND EMPIRE, 1799-1815–FICTION

Wheeler, Thomas G. Fanfare for the Stalwart. LC 67-22813. (gr. 8 up). 1967. 21.95 (*0-87599-139-4*) S G Phillips.

FRANCE–SOCIAL LIFE AND CUSTOMS

Harris, Jonathan. The Land & People of France. LC 88-19211. (Illus.). 256p. (gr. 6 up). 1989. (Lipp Jr Bks); PLB 17.89 (*0-397-32321-2*, Lipp Jr Bks) HarpC Child Bks.
Kollay, Jocelyne. French Holiday Activity Workbook. (FRE & ENG., Illus.). 100p. (Orig.). (gr. 9-12). 1988. wkbk. 16.95 (*0-9617764-1-2*) PS Enterprises.
Loewen. Food in France. 1991. 11.95s.p. (*0-86625-344-0*) Rourke Pubns.
Powell, Jillian. France. LC 90-37568. (Illus.). 32p. (gr. k-3). 1991. PLB 12.40 (*0-531-18372-6*, Pub. by Bookwright Pr) Watts.

FRANCIS OF ASSISI, SAINT, 1182-1226

De Paola, Tomie. Francis: The Poor Man of Assisi. De Paola, Tomie, illus. LC 81-6984. 48p. (ps-3). 1982. reinforced bdg. 16.95 (*0-8234-0435-8*); pap. 6.95 (*0-8234-0812-4*) Holiday.
Hodges, Margaret. Brother Francis & the Friendly Beasts. Lewin, Ted, illus. LC 90-33206. 32p. (gr. 1-3). 1991. SBE 14.95 (*0-684-19173-3*, Scribners Young Read) Macmillan Child Grp.
Nichols, Terri V. Francis: The Knight of Assisi. CCC of America Staff, illus. 61p. (Orig.). (ps-6). 1990. incl. video 21.95 (*1-56814-002-9*); pap. text ed. 4.95 book (*0-685-62404-8*) CCC of America.
Schumann, Peter. St. Francis Preaches to the Birds. Schumann, Peter, illus. LC 92-7383. 36p. (gr. 3-10). 1992. Repr. of 1978 ed. 8.95 (*0-8118-0222-1*) Chronicle Bks.
Windeatt, Mary F. St. Francis of Assisi. Harmon, Gedge, illus. 32p. (gr. 1-5). 1989. Repr. of 1954 ed. wkbk. 3.00 (*0-89555-368-6*) TAN Bks Pubs.

FRANCIS OF ASSISI, SAINT, 1182-1126–FICTION

O'Dell, Scott. The Road to Damietta. 256p. (gr. 6 up). 1985. 14.45 (*0-395-38923-2*) HM.
—The Road to Damietta. 240p. 1987. pap. 3.99 (*0-449-70233-2*, Juniper) Fawcett.

FRANCISCANS–BIOGRAPHY

Stanton, Sue. Boston & the Feast of Saint Francis. (ps-3). 1994. pap. 4.95 (*0-8091-6616-X*) Paulist Pr.

FRANKLIN, BENJAMIN, 1706-1790

Adler, David A. Benjamin Franklin: Printer, Inventor, Statesman. Miller, Lyle, illus. LC 91-28816. 48p. (gr. 2-5). 1992. reinforced bdg. 14.95 (*0-8234-0929-5*) Holiday.

—A Picture Book of Benjamin Franklin. Wallner, John & Wallner, Alexandra, illus. LC 89-20059. 32p. (ps-3). 1990. reinforced bdg. 15.95 (*0-8234-0792-6*); pap. 5.95 (*0-8234-0882-5*) Holiday.

Alico, Stella H. Benjamin Franklin-Martin Luther King Jr. Cruz, E. R., illus. (gr. 4-12). 1979. pap. text ed. 2.95 (*0-88301-353-3*); wkbk 1.25 (*0-88301-377-0*) Pendulum Pr.

Aliki. The Many Lives of Benjamin Franklin. Aliki, illus. 32p. (ps-3). 1988. pap. 12.95 (*0-671-66119-1*, S&S BFYR); pap. 5.95 (*0-671-66491-3*, S&S BFYR) S&S Trade.

Cousins, Margaret. Ben Franklin of Old Philadelphia. LC 81-806. 160p. (gr. 5-9). 1981. Repr. of 1981 ed. 4.95 (*0-394-84928-0*) Random Bks Yng Read.

Feldman, Eve B. Benjamin Franklin: Scientist & Inventor. (Illus.). 64p. (gr. 5-8). 1990. PLB 12.90 (*0-531-10867-8*) Watts.

Franklin, Benjamin. Autobiography of Benjamin Franklin. Bigoness, J. W., intro. by. LC 80-26312. (gr. 8 up). 1965. pap. 2.75 (*0-8049-0071-X*, CL-71) Airmont.

Fritz, Jean. What's the Big Idea, Ben Franklin? (Illus.). 48p. (gr. 2-6). 1982. 13.95 (*0-698-20365-8*, Coward); pap. 6.95 (*0-698-20543-X*, Coward) Putnam Pub Group.

Graves, Charles P. Benjamin Franklin: Man of Ideas. (Illus.). 80p. (gr. 2-6). 1993. Repr. of 1960 ed. lib. bdg. 12.95 (*0-7910-1422-3*) Chelsea Hse.

Greene, Carol. Benjamin Franklin: A Man with Many Jobs. Dobson, Steven, illus. LC 88-15011. 48p. (gr. k-3). 1988. PLB 12.85 (*0-516-04202-5*); pap. 4.95 (*0-516-44202-3*) Childrens.

Kurland, Gerald. Benjamin Franklin: America's Universal Man. Rahmas, D. Steve, ed. LC 72-190250. 32p. (Orig.). (gr. 7-12). 1972. lib. bdg. 4.95 incl. catalog cards (*0-87157-533-7*) SamHar Pr.

Lawson, Robert. Ben & Me. (gr. 3-6). 1973. pap. 2.75 (*0-440-42038-5*, YB) Dell.

Looby, Christopher. Benjamin Franklin. Schlesinger, Arthur M., Jr. (Illus.). 112p. (gr. 5 up). 1990. 17.95x (*1-55546-808-X*) Chelsea Hse.

Meltzer, Milton. Benjamin Franklin: The New American. LC 88-17015. (Illus.). 288p. (gr. 6-9). 1988. PLB 15.40 (*0-531-10582-2*) Watts.

Osborne, Mary P. The Many Lives of Benjamin Franklin. (Illus.). (gr. 5 up). 1990. 13.95 (*0-685-31008-6*) Dial Bks Young.

—The Many Lives of Benjamin Franklin. LC 88-38369. (Illus.). 144p. (gr. 4-7). 1990. PLB 13.89 (*0-8037-0680-4*) Dial Bks Young.

Quackenbush, Robert. Benjamin Franklin & His Friends. Quackenbush, Robert, illus. 32p. (gr. 2-5). 1991. 14.95 (*0-945912-14-5*) Pippin Pr.

Santrey, Laurence. Young Ben Franklin. LC 81-23067. (Illus.). 48p. (gr. 4-6). 1982. PLB 10.79 (*0-89375-768-3*); pap. text ed. 3.50 (*0-89375-769-1*) Troll Assocs.

Scarf, Maggie. Meet Benjamin Franklin. Fogarty, Pat, illus. LC 88-17657. 64p. (gr. 2-4). 1989. pap. text ed. 3.50 (*0-394-81961-6*) Random Bks Yng Read.

Stevenson, Augusta. Benjamin Franklin: Young Printer. Quigley, Ray, illus. LC 86-10786. 192p. (gr. 2-6). 1986. pap. 3.95 (*0-02-041920-1*, Aladdin) Macmillan Child Grp.

Stewart, Gail B. Benjamin Franklin. LC 92-23315. (Illus.). 112p. (gr. 5-8). 1992. PLB 14.95 (*1-56006-026-3*) Lucent Bks.

Weinberg, Lawrence. Benjamin Franklin. Bloch, Alex, illus. 48p. (gr. 2-4). 1988. pap. 2.50 (*0-681-40347-0*) Longmeadow Pr.

FRANKLIN, BENJAMIN, 1706-1790–FICTION

Lawson, Robert. Ben & Me. Lawson, Robert, illus. 1939p. (gr. 7-10). 1988. 15.95 (*0-316-51732-1*); pap. 5.95 (*0-316-51730-5*) Little.

Stevens, Bryna. Ben Franklin's Glass Armonica. (ps-3). 1992. pap. 3.25 (*0-440-40584-X*) Dell.

FRAUD

see also Impostors and Imposture

FRAUD–FICTION

Colman, Hila. The Double Life of Angela Jones. LC 87-33246. 160p. (gr. 7 up). 1988. 12.95 (*0-688-06781-6*) Morrow Jr Bks.

Duncan, Lois. Stranger with My Face. (gr. 8 up). 1981. 15.95 (*0-316-19551-0*) Little.

Fleischman, Sid. McBroom Tells the Truth. Lorraine, Walter H., illus. LC 81-1035. 48p. (gr. 3-7). 1981. 12.45i (*0-316-28550-1*, Pub. by Atlantic Pr) Little.

Melville, Herman. Confidence Man. Grube, J., intro. by. (gr. 11 up). 1966. pap. 1.95 (*0-8049-0121-X*, CL-121) Airmont.

FREAKS

see Monsters

FREDERICK 2ND, DER GROSSE, KING OF PRUSSIA, 1712-1786

Kittredge, Mary. Frederick the Great. Schlesinger, Arthur M., Jr., intro. by. (Illus.). 112p. (gr. 5 up). 1988. lib. bdg. 17.95 (*0-87754-525-1*) Chelsea Hse.

FREE SPEECH

Evans, J. Edward. Freedom of Speech. (Illus.). 88p. (gr. 4 up). 1990. PLB 14.95 (*0-8225-1753-1*) Lerner Pubns.

Hentoff, Nat. The First Freedom: The Tumultuous History of Free Speech in America. LC 78-72860. (gr. 7 up). 1980. 11.95 (*0-440-03850-2*) Delacorte.

Lang, Susan S. & Lang, Paul. Censorship. (Illus.). 96p. (gr. 9-12). 1993. PLB 13.40 (*0-531-10999-2*) Watts.

Leone, Bruno, ed. Free Speech. LC 93-19855. 1994. lib. bdg. 16.95 (*1-56510-078-6*); pap. 9.95 (*1-56510-077-8*) Greenhaven.

Orr, Lisa, ed. Censorship: Opposing Viewpoints. LC 90-42854. (Illus.). 240p. (gr. 10 up). 1990. PLB 17.95 (*0-89908-479-6*); pap. text ed. 9.95 (*0-89908-454-0*) Greenhaven.

Pascoe, Elaine. Freedom of Expression: The Right to Speak Out in America. LC 92-7150. (Illus.). 128p. (gr. 7 up). 1992. PLB 15.90 (*1-56294-255-7*) Millbrook Pr.

Rappaport, Doreen. Tinker vs. Des Moines: Student Rights on Trial. Palencar, John J., illus. LC 92-25019. 160p. (gr. 5 up). 1993. 15.00 (*0-06-025117-4*); PLB 14.89 (*0-06-025118-2*) HarpC Child Bks.

Steele, Philip. Censorship. LC 91-40235. (Illus.). 48p. (gr. 6 up). 1992. text ed. 12.95 RSBE (*0-02-735404-0*, New Discovery) Macmillan Child Grp.

Steffens, Bradley. Free Speech: Identifying Propaganda Techniques. LC 92-23594. (Illus.). 32p. (gr. 4-7). 1992. PLB 10.95 (*0-89908-098-7*) Greenhaven.

Trager, Oliver, ed. The Arts & Media in America: Freedom or Censorship? 224p. 1991. 29.95x (*0-8160-2578-9*) Facts on File.

FREEBOOTERS

see Pirates

FREEDOM

see Liberty

FREEDOM MARCHES

see Blacks–Civil Rights

FREEDOM OF RELIGION

see Religious Liberty

FREEDOM OF SPEECH

see Free Speech

FREEDOM OF THE PRESS

Evans, J. Edward. Freedom of the Press. (Illus.). 72p. (gr. 5 up). 1990. PLB 14.95 (*0-8225-1752-3*) Lerner Pubns.

Pfeffer, Susan B. A Matter of Principle. LC 81-15288. 192p. (gr. 7 up). 1982. 11.95 (*0-385-28649-X*) Delacorte.

FREEDOM OF WORSHIP

see Religious Liberty

FREEZING

see Ice

FREIGHT AND FREIGHTAGE

see also Aeronautics, Commercial

FREMONT, JOHN CHARLES, 1813-1890

Harris, Edward D. John Charles Fremont & the Great Western Reconnaissance. Goetzmann, William H., ed. Collins, Michael, intro. by. (Illus.). 112p. (gr. 5 up). 1990. lib. bdg. 18.95 (*0-7910-1312-X*) Chelsea Hse.

FRENCH AND INDIAN WAR

see U. S.–History–French and Indian War, 1755-1763

FRENCH CANADIANS

Wartik, Nancy. French Canadians. (Illus.). 112p. (gr. 5 up). 1989. 17.95 (*0-87754-879-X*) Chelsea Hse.

FRENCH CANADIANS–FICTION

Pickthall, Marjorie. The Worker in Sandalwood: A Christmas Eve Miracle. Tyrrell, Frances, illus. LC 94-548. 32p. (gr. k-4). 1994. 14.99 (*0-525-45332-6*) Dutton Child Bks.

FRENCH CANADIANS IN THE U. S.–FICTION

London, Jonathan. The Sugaring-off Party. Pelletier, Gilles, illus. LC 93-21911. 1994. write for info. (*0-525-45187-0*, DCB) Dutton Child Bks.

FRENCH IN AMERICA

Kunz, Virginia B. The French in America. LC 66-10146. (Illus.). 96p. (gr. 5 up). PLB 15.95 (*0-8225-0204-6*); pap. 5.95 (*0-8225-1008-1*) Lerner Pubns.

Morrice, Polly. The French Americans. Moynihan, Daniel P. (Illus.). 112p. (gr. 5 up). 1988. lib. bdg. 17.95 (*0-87754-878-1*) Chelsea Hse.

FRENCH LANGUAGE

Amery, H. Usborne First Thousand Words in French. (gr. 4-7). 1994. Incl. cassette. pap. 19.95 (*0-88110-685-2*) EDC.

Amery, H. & Cartwright, S. First One Hundred Words French Sticker Book. (Illus.). 32p. (ps up). 1994. pap. 6.95 incl. 6 sticker pgs. (*0-7460-2117-8*, Usborne) EDC.

Atkin, K. Le Francais Sans Souci. 304p. (gr. 4-6). 1987. pap. text ed. 45.44 (*0-201-17624-6*) Addison-Wesley.

Bladon, Rachel. French for Beginners Workbook. (gr. 4-7). 1993. pap. 6.95 (*0-8442-1415-9*, Passport Bks) NTC Pub Grp.

Burchard, Elizabeth. French: In a Flash. 477p. (gr. 7-12). 1994. pap. 9.95 (*1-881374-09-2*) Flash Blasters.

Colvin, L. & Irving, N. Essential French. (Illus.). 64p. 1990. lib. bdg. 12.96 (*0-88110-420-5*); pap. 5.95 (*0-7460-0316-1*) EDC.

De Bruhoff, Jean, illus. A.B.C. de Babar. LC 94-5913. (gr. 3 up). 1994. write for info. (*0-679-86842-9*) Random Bks Yng Read.

De Brunhoff, Laurent. Babar's French & English Word Book. LC 93-27873. (Illus.). 128p. 1994. 16.00 (*0-679-83644-6*) Random Bks Yng Read.

Farris, Katherine, ed. Let's Speak French! A First Book of Words. rev. ed. Hendry, Linda, illus. LC 92-41737. (ENG & FRE.). 48p. (ps-5). 1993. 11.99 (*0-670-85042-X*) Viking Child Bks.

Gemmell, Kathy & Tyler, Jenny. First French at Home. (Illus.). 32p. (gr. 1-6). 1993. lib. bdg. 12.96 (*0-88110-643-7*, Usborne); pap. 5.95 (*0-7460-1049-4*, Usborne) EDC.

Grisewood, John. Fun to Learn French. Sleight, Katy, illus. LC 91-28240. 48p. (gr. 2-5). 1992. 12.95 (*0-531-15241-3*, Warwick); PLB 12.90 (*0-531-19120-6*, Warwick) Watts.

Hazzan, Anne-Francoise. Let's Learn French Coloring Book. (Illus.). 64p. (gr. 4 up). 1988. pap. 3.95 (*0-8442-1389-6*, Natl Textbk) NTC Pub Grp.

Irving, N. Learn French. (Illus.). 64p. (gr. 5 up). 1992. PLB 13.96 (*0-88110-596-1*); pap. 7.95 (*0-7460-0532-6*) EDC.

—Learn French Language Pack. (Illus.). 64p. (gr. 7 up). 1993. pap. 16.95 incl. tape (*0-7460-1439-2*, Usborne) EDC.

Lionni, Leo. Pouce par Pouce. (FRE., Illus.). (gr. k-1). 1961. 10.95 (*0-8392-3028-1*) Astor-Honor.

MacArthur, Barbara. Chantez Noel. Jensen, Robert, illus. (ENG & FRE.). 14p. (ps-12). 1993. pap. 12.95 incl. cass. (*1-881120-10-4*) Frog Pr WI.

Martinez, Eliseo R. & Martinez, Irma C. French Readiness Skills, Vol. 1. Mahak, Francine T., tr. (Illus.). 87p. 1987. wkbk. 9.50 (*1-878300-02-4*) Childrens Work.

Morgan-Williams, Louise. I Can Sing En Francais! Fun Songs for Learning French. (gr. 4-7). 1993. 8.95 (*0-8442-1457-4*, Natl Textbk) NTC Pub Grp.

—I Can Sing En Francais: Fun Songs for Learning French. (gr. 4-7). 1994. pap. 12.95 incl. cassette (*0-8442-1459-0*) NTC Pub Grp.

Needham, K. Essential French Dictionary. (Illus.). 64p. (gr. 6 up). 1994. PLB 12.96 (*0-88110-709-3*, Usborne); pap. 5.95 (*0-7460-1004-4*, Usborne) EDC.

Les Nombres. (FRE., Illus.). 3.50 (*0-7214-1427-3*) Ladybird Bks.

O'Halloran, Tim. Words Around Us in French. O'Halloran, Tim, illus. (FRE.). 48p. (ps-k). 1985. 10.95 (*0-88625-125-7*) Durkin Hayes Pub.

Rich, Beatrice. ABCDEFGHIJKLMNOPQRSTUVWXYZ in English & French. LC 81-20838. (Illus.). 64p. (gr. k-2). 1983. PLB 15.95 (*0-87460-353-6*) Lion Bks.

Root, Betty. Three Hundred First Words - Premiers Mots. Dann, Geoff, photos by. (ENG & FRE.). 156p. (ps). 1993. 9.95 (*0-8120-6357-0*) Barron.

Rosenstiehl, Agnes. Livre de la Langue Francaise. Gay, Pierre, illus. (FRE.). 93p. (gr. 4-9). 1985. 16.95 (*2-07-039524-3*) Schoenhof.

Slack, Anne, et al. French for Communication, One. LC 77-87429. (Illus.). (gr. 9). 1979. write for info. complete program HM.

Smith, Neraida. Let's Sing & Learn in French. (FRE.). 64p. 1991. pap. 4.95 (*0-8442-1455-8*, Natl Textbk); pap. 9.95 incl. audiocassette (*0-8442-1454-X*, Passport Bks) NTC Pub Grp.

Taylor, Maurie. Easy French Vocabulary Games. (FRE., Illus.). 64p. (gr. 4 up). 1988. pap. 4.95 (*0-8442-1323-3*, Natl Textbk) NTC Pub Grp.

Wilkes, Angela. French for Beginners. (Illus.). 48p. (gr. 4 up). 1988. 8.95 (*0-8442-1413-2*, Passport Bks) NTC Pub Grp.

Wordfinder in French. (Illus.). 48p. (gr. 2-6). 1984. 8.95 (*0-7460-0393-5*) EDC.

FRENCH LANGUAGE–CONVERSATION AND PHRASE BOOKS

Berlitz. Berlitz Jr. French. (FRE., Illus.). 64p. (Orig.). (ps-2). 1989. text ed. 19.95 incl. cassette (*0-689-71314-2*, Aladdin) Macmillan Child Grp.

Berlitz Jr., No. Two: French. LC 93-36123. (FRE & ENG.). 1995. pap. 19.95 (*0-689-71815-2*, Aladdin) Macmillan Child Grp.

Bovaird, Anne. Goodbye, U. S. A. - Bonjour la France, Vol. II: A Language Learning Adventure. Ballouhey, Pierre, illus. (gr. 3-8). 1994. 12.95 (*0-8120-6384-8*); pap. 5.95 (*0-8120-1390-5*) Barron.

Bowers, Irene & Weller, Linda. Bonjour, Mes Amis - Hello, My Friends. (Illus.). 32p. (ps-3). 1994. pap. 16.95 incl. 2 cassettes (*0-8120-8150-1*) Barron.

Bradley, Susannah, ed. Beginner's Guide to French. Archer, Rebecca, illus. 48p. (gr. 3-6). 1992. pap. 2.95 (*1-56680-004-8*) Mad Hatter Pub.

Farnes, C. Survive in Five Languages. (Illus.). 64p. (gr. 8 up). 1993. PLB 12.96 (*0-88110-623-2*); pap. 6.95 (*0-7460-1034-6*) EDC.

Garvy, Helen. Bingo Book, No. 5: French. LC 93-87239. 128p. 1994. pap. 6.00 (*0-918828-16-3*) Shire Pr.

Jacob, Suzanne, ed. Children's Living French. (Illus.). 1988. manual 4.95 (*0-517-56331-2*, Crown); pap. 4.95 dictionary (*0-517-56332-0*); cassettes 18.95 (*0-517-56329-0*) Crown Pub Group.

Kahn, Michele. My Everyday French Word Book. LC 79-89631. 44p. (gr. 1-6). 1981. 10.95 (*0-8120-5344-3*) Barron.

Lyric Language - French, Series 1 & 2. (Illus.). (ps-8). Series 1. 9.95 (*1-56015-225-7*) Series 2. 9.95 (*1-56015-238-9*) Penton Overseas.

60-minute audio cassette & illustrated book of French lyrics. Fun for any age, in the classroom or at home! A terrific way to teach colors, counting, animals & more. 26 original & traditional songs sung in a clear medium range. English spoken between songs to briefly explain each one & suggest coordinating activities & actions. Retail $14.95. SING, DANCE, LAUGH & LEARN SPANISH, (ISBN 1-881120-08-2) 1993. 30-minute audio cassette & illustrated lyric book. Perfect for the FLES or FLEX classroom, a summer school program or for learning at home. Counting in Spanish is easy when it's done rap-style with "Cuenta!". Or have fun parading around the room while chanting to the alphabet march. Retail $12.95. SING, DANCE, LAUGH & LEARN GERMAN, (ISBN 1-881120-11-2) 1993. 30-minute cassette & illustrated lyric book. From German foods to family members, these songs bring the German language to life! Sung in a clear, medium range which is easy to sing along with. Each song is introduced in English to assist the beginner. Retail $12.95. FOR MORE INFORMATION ON THESE & OTHER LANGUAGE LEARNING SONGS, CONTACT FROG PRESS, 2821 MILTON AVE., JANESVILLE, WI 53545, (608) 752-1112.
Publisher Provided Annotation.

Mealer, Tamara. My World in French Coloring Book. (FRE., Illus.). 64p. 1991. pap. 4.95 (*0-8442-1393-4*, Natl Textbk) NTC Pub Grp.

Munsch, Robert. Violet, Vert et Jaune: Purple, Green & Yellow in French. Desputeaux, Helene, illus. 32p. 1992. pap. 5.95 (*1-55037-272-6*, Pub. by Annick Pr) Firefly Bks Ltd.

Page, Brian. Franc-Parler. (FRE.). 208p. 1988. pap. 10.95 (*0-8219-0340-3*, 40306); tchr's. guide 5.95 (*0-8219-0341-1*, TG-40825) EMC.

Poulin, Stephane. As-Tu Vu Josephine? Poulin, Stephane, illus. LC 86-51044. (FRE.). 24p. (gr. k-4). 1988. 12.95 (*0-88776-188-7*); pap. 6.95 (*0-88776-224-7*) Tundra Bks.

—Have You Seen Josephine? Poulin, Stephane, illus. LC 86-51043. 24p. (gr. k-4). 1988. 12.95 (*0-88776-180-1*); pap. 6.95 (*0-88776-215-8*) Tundra Bks.

Price, Shirley S. Deviner et Appendre. 77p. (gr. 9-12). 1983. text ed. 20.95 (*0-88377-280-9*, Newbury) Heinle & Heinle.

Scibor, Teresa. It's Fun to Speak French with Zozo. (Illus.). 32p. (ps-3). 1993. pap. 12.95 (*0-8120-8012-2*) Barron.

Segal, Bertha E. Apprenons le Francais au Moyen de l'Action. Raileanu, Lia, tr. from ENG. (FRE.). 106p. (Orig.). (gr. 3-12). 1987. pap. text ed. 12.99 (*0-938395-13-0*) B Segal.

Waggoner, Carmen. Descriptions de Dessins: Picture Descriptions in French. Parr, Frederique & Winitz, Harris, eds. Baker, Syd, illus. (FRE.). 65p. (Orig.). (gr. 7 up). 1989. pap. text ed. 32.00 incl. 2 cassettes (*0-939990-77-6*) Intl Linguistics.

Watson, Carol & De Saulles, Janet. Five Hundred French Words & Phrases for Children. McNicholas, Shelagh, illus. 32p. (gr. 1-2). 1994. 8.95 (*0-7818-0267-9*) Hippocrene Bks.

White, Judith. Summer Talk: Phrase-a-Day French for Families. Macbain, Carol, illus. 27p. (ps-6). 1986. wkbk. 6.25 (*0-937531-01-4*) Fgn Lang Young Child.

FRENCH LANGUAGE–DICTIONARIES

A Child's Picture English-French Dictionary. LC 84-71800. 48p. (gr. k-6). 1984. 9.95 (*0-915361-12-4*) Modan-Adama Bks.

Cirker, Hayward & Steadman, Barbara. French Picture Word Book: Learn over Five Hundred Commonly Used French Words Through Pictures. (FRE & ENG., Illus.). 32p. (Orig.). 1993. pap. text ed. 2.95t (*0-486-27777-1*) Dover.

Davies, H. Beginner's French Dictionary. (Illus.). 128p. 1989. lib. bdg. 15.96 (*0-88110-346-2*); pap. 9.95 (*0-7460-0016-2*) EDC.

Let's Learn Picture Dictionaries: French. (Illus.). 72p. 1989. 9.95 (*0-8442-1392-6*, Natl Textbk) NTC Pub Grp.

Wilkes, Angela & Heminway, Annie. Mon Premier Livre des Mots en Francais. LC 92-56499. (FRE., Illus.). 64p. (ps-3). 1993. 12.95 (*1-56458-261-2*) Dorling Kindersley.

FRENCH LANGUAGE–DICTIONARIES–ENGLISH

Berlitz. Berlitz Jr. French Dictionary. LC 91-40123. (Illus.). 144p. (ps-2). 1992. pap. 11.95 POB (*0-689-71539-0*, Aladdin) Macmillan Child Grp.

Eastman, Philip D. The Cat in the Hat Beginner Book Dictionary in French & English. LC 65-22650. (Illus.). 144p. (gr. 2-3). 1965. 15.95 (*0-394-81063-5*) Beginner.

Faulkner, Keith. My First One Hundred Words in French & English. (Illus.). 14p. (ps-3). 1993. pap. 11.00 casebound (*0-671-86447-5*, S&S BFYR) S&S Trade.

Meyer, Jean-Christophe. Barron's Junior Illustrated Dictionary - French-English. Chmielewski, G., illus. (FRE & ENG.). 180p. (gr. 2 up). 1994. 14.95 (*0-8120-6458-5*) Barron.

Objets Familiers - Everyday Things. (ENG & FRE.). 63p. 1991. 19.95 (*2-07-057513-6*) Schoenhof.

Watermill Press Staff. Webster's English-French - Francais-Anglais Dictionary. 224p. (gr. 4-7). 1992. pap. 2.95 (*0-8167-2919-0*, Pub. by Watermill Pr) Troll Assocs.

FRENCH LANGUAGE–GRAMMAR

Gauduchon, Michaele. French Grammar Flipper, No. 2. 49p. (gr. 7 up). 1993. Repr. of 1990 ed. trade edition 6.25 (*1-878383-12-4*) C Lee Pubns.

Gutierrez, Marda L. Beginning Reading & Writing in French: A Children's French Grammar Workbook. Guiterrez, Marda L., illus. 64p. (Orig.). (gr. k-4). 1986. 8.95 (*0-938733-03-6*) Avantage Pub.

Roussy De Sales, R. Jeux de Grammaire. (FRE., Illus.). 64p. (gr. 5 up). 1983. pap. 4.95 (*0-8442-1380-2*, Natl Textbk) NTC Pub Grp.

Waggoner, Carmen. Basic Structures - French, Bk. 1: A Textbook for the Learnables. (FRE., Illus.). 127p. (gr. 7 up). 1991. incl. 4 cass. 45.00 (*0-939990-73-3*) Intl Linguistics.

FRENCH LANGUAGE–READERS

Amery, Heather. First Thousand Words in French. Cartwright, Stephen, illus. 50p. (ps-7). 1980. 11.95 (*0-86020-267-4*) EDC.

Conroy, Joseph F. Danger sur la Cote d'azur: Reader 4. Bakke, Eric, illus. LC 81-7820. (FRE.). 40p. (Orig.). (gr. 7-12). 1982. pap. 3.25 (*0-88436-857-2*, 40262) EMC.

—Destination: France! Reader 1. Bakke, Eric, illus. LC 81-7816. (FRE.). 40p. (Orig.). (gr. 7-12). 1982. pap. 3.25 (*0-88436-854-8*, 40259) EMC.

—Sur la Route de la Contrebande. Bakke, Eric, illus. LC 81-7817. (FRE.). 40p. (Orig.). (gr. 7-12). pap. 3.25 (*0-88436-856-4*, 40261) EMC.

De Roussy De Sales, Raoul. Easy French Crossword Puzzles. (FRE., Illus.). 64p. (gr. 5 up). 1983. pap. 4.95 (*0-8442-1330-6*, Natl Textbk) NTC Pub Grp.

Henry, Charles L., et al. French Study-Aid. 1974. pap. 2.75 (*0-87738-032-5*) Youth Ed.

Potter, Beatrix. Pierre Lapin: Peter Rabbit. (FRE., Illus.). (gr. 3-7). 1973. 5.00 (*0-7232-0650-3*) Warne.

Wilkes, Angela. Mon Premier Livre de Mots - My First French Word Book: A Bilingual Word Book. Heminway, Annie, tr. LC 92-54499. (ENG & FRE., Illus.). 48p. (gr. k-4). 1993. 12.95 (*1-56458-254-X*) Dorling Kindersley.

FRENCH LANGUAGE–STUDY AND TEACHING

Berlitz Jr., No. Two: French. LC 93-36123. (FRE & ENG.). 1995. pap. 19.95 (*0-689-71815-2*, Aladdin) Macmillan Child Grp.

Clem, Stephen D. Study Guide: Advanced Placement French Literature, Prose & Theater for the 1992 Exam. (FRE.). 304p. (Orig.). (gr. 11-12). 1991. pap. text ed. 17.27 (*1-877653-15-2*) Wayside Pub.

Criminale, Ulrike & The Language School of the American Cultural Exchange Staff. Springboard to French: Introduction to the French Language. rev. ed. Porter, Mary D., illus. 32p. (gr. k-4). 1991. Incl. cassettes. 19.95 (*1-880770-00-8*) ACE Pub.
SPRINGBOARD is a set of easy, encouraging foreign language lessons for young children ages 4-8. This popular series features two 90-minute cassettes on which a native speaker of the foreign language leads the child in short, playful sessions through a variety of actions by repeating simple commands in both the foreign language & in English. The child is not required to read or write the language. Instead, the language is absorbed almost effortlessly as the child enjoys a progression of music, games & activities. The program emphasizes well-planned lessons for the adult leader & can be enjoyed by anyone in the home setting as well as in class. Because the cassettes guide the activity, the adult is not required to know the language, but instead simply participates with the child. The accompanying Springboard books provide attractive illustrations & a word-for-word transcript of the cassettes along with a comprehensive Vocabulary Chart for review & an Activities Supplement with suggestions for further learning. The Series is available in French, German & Spanish, & will soon be available in Japanese. For information on placing orders, please call (206) 535-8104.
Publisher Provided Annotation.

Greuel, David P., ed. Anthology of Advanced Placement French Literature: For the 1992 Exam. (FRE.). 408p. (Orig.). (gr. 11-12). 1991. pap. text ed. 17.27 (*1-877653-14-4*) Wayside Pub.

Kendris, Christopher. How to Prepare for SAT II: French. 6th, rev. ed. LC 93-2558. 1994. pap. 11.95 incl. 60-min. cass. (*0-8120-1766-8*) Barron.

MacArthur, Barbara. Sing, Dance, Laugh & Eat Quiche 2. Jensen, Robert, illus. (FRE.). 35p. (Orig.). (ps-9). 1989. pap. text ed. 17.95 incl. cass. (*1-881120-01-5*) Frog Pr WI.

Mahoney, Judy. Teach Me More French. (FRE., Illus.). 20p. (ps-6). 1989. pap. 13.95 incl. audiocassette (*0-934633-11-8*); tchr's. ed. 6.95 (*0-934633-33-9*) Teach Me.

Mahoney, Judy, compiled by. Sing with Me in French: A Teach Me Tapes Songbook. Thiede, Carla R., contrib. by. (FRE & ENG., Illus.). 26p. (Orig.). (ps-6). 1994. pap. 7.95 (*0-934633-91-6*) Teach Me.

FRENCH LITERATURE

Becker, Sheila. VerbMaster: French. Collins, Stephen, ed. (FRE.). 28p. (Orig.). (gr. 9 up). 1990. pap. 4.95 (*0-9626328-2-1*) F One Servs.

FRENCH POETRY–COLLECTIONS

Bernos De Gasztold, Carmen. Prayers from the Ark: Selected Poems. Godden, Rumer, tr. Moser, Barry, illus. 32p. 1992. 16.00 (*0-670-84496-9*) Viking Child Bks.

FRENCH REVOLUTION

see France–History–Revolution, 1789-1799

FRESH-WATER ANIMALS

see also Aquariums; Marine Animals;
also names of individual fresh-water animal, e.g. Beavers, etc.

Aliki. My Visit to the Aquarium. Aliki, illus. LC 92-18678. 40p. (ps-3). 1993. 15.00 (*0-06-021458-9*); PLB 14.89 (*0-06-021459-7*) HarpC Child Bks.

Arvetis, Chris & Palmer, Carole. Lakes & Rivers. LC 93-499. (Illus.). 1993. write for info. (*0-528-83572-6*) Rand McNally.

Chinery, Michael. Questions & Answers about Freshwater Animals. Ford, Wayne & Robson, Eric, illus. LC 93-29415. 40p. (gr. 2-6). 1994. 10.95 (*1-85697-978-4*, Kingfisher LKC); pap. 5.95 (*1-85697-962-8*, Kingfisher LKC) LKC.

Curtis, Patricia. Aquatic Animals in the Wild & in Captivity. (Illus.). 64p. (gr. 3-8). 1992. 16.00 (*0-525-67384-9*, Lodestar Bks) Dutton Child Bks.

Deming, Susan. The River: A Nature Panorama. Deming, Susan, illus. 7p. (ps-3). 1991. bds. 5.95 (*0-87701-812-X*) Chronicle Bks.

Ganeri, Anita. Ponds & Pond Life. LC 92-6263. (Illus.). 32p. (gr. 5-7). 1993. PLB 11.90 (*0-531-14226-4*) Watts.

Gerstenfeld, Sheldon L. The Aquarium Take-Along Book. Harvey, Paul, illus. LC 93-23059. 128p. (gr. 2-5). 1994. 14.99 (*0-670-84386-5*) Viking Child Bks.

Grimmer, Glenna. Things That Swim in Texas Waters Alphabetically Speaking: And in Other Coastal States of the Gulf of Mexico. Eakin, Edwin M., ed. Hoese, H. Dickson, illus. 48p. (gr. 4-6). 1989. 11.95 (*0-89015-694-8*, Pub. by Panda Bks) Sunbelt Media.

Kaufman, Les & NEA Staff. Alligators to Zooplankton: A Dictionary of Water Babies. (Illus.). 64p. (gr. 5-7). 1991. PLB 15.90 (*0-531-10995-X*) Watts.

Peissel, Michel & Allen, Missy. Dangerous Water Creatures. (Illus.). 112p. (gr. 5 up). 1993. PLB 19.95 (*0-7910-1788-5*, Am Art Analog) Chelsea Hse.

Taylor, Kim. Hidden under Water. (gr. 4-7). 1990. 9.95 (*0-385-30184-7*) Delacorte.

Wood, John N. Nature Hide & Seek: Rivers & Lakes. Wood, John N. & Dean, Kevin, illus. LC 93-22501. (gr. 1-4). 1993. 13.00 (*0-679-83690-X*) Knopf Bks Yng Read.

FRESH-WATER BIOLOGY

see also Aquariums; Fresh-Water Animals; Fresh-Water Plants; Marine Biology

Aliki. My Visit to the Aquarium. Aliki, illus. LC 92-18678. 40p. (ps-3). 1993. 15.00 (*0-06-021458-9*); PLB 14.89 (*0-06-021459-7*) HarpC Child Bks.

Amos, William H. Life in Ponds & Streams. Crump, Donald J., ed. LC 81-47745. 32p. (ps-3). 1981. lib. bdg. 16.95 (*0-87044-404-2*); PLB 13.95 (*0-87044-409-3*) Natl Geog.

Bell, David O. Awesome Chesapeake. Ramsey, Marcy D., illus. 48p. (gr. 3-8).

1994. 11.95 (*0-87033-457-3*) Tidewater. The Chesapeake Bay is certainly an amazing body of water - the largest estuary in North America. This book, the first of its kind, stimulates elementary & middle school children's interest in the Bay by exposing them to the fascinating creatures & plants found in & around the Bay's 2,500 square miles. Concepts like watershed, airshed & food web are explained in concise, understandable terms to promote awareness of the human role in this vast system. Teachers will find this book a valuable resource for their students. How many children, for example, know about a prehistoric creature found in the Bay that help fight cancer? The readers may be surprised to learn that the critter in question is the horseshoe crab. This book is an effective means for children to discover the interesting traits of some of the plants, animals, birds & fish they are likely to find in & around the Bay. Outstanding drawings bring the estuary & its inhabitants to life. At Echo Hill Outdoor School in Worton, Maryland, David Owen Bell teaches Bay ecology to youngsters. Marcy Dunn Ramsey has illustrated more than twenty books. To order please contact Tidewater Publishers 800-638-7641.
Publisher Provided Annotation.

Curran, Eileen. Life in the Pond. Ellis, Elizabeth, illus. LC 84-16285. 32p. (gr. k-2). 1985. lib. bdg. 11.59 (*0-8167-0452-X*); pap. text ed. 2.95 (*0-8167-0453-8*) Troll Assocs.
Dewey, Jennifer O. At the Edge of the Pond. Dewey, Jennifer O., illus. 48p. (gr. 1-5). 1987. 14.95 (*0-316-18208-7*) Little.
Frame, Jeron A. Discovering Oceans, Lakes, Ponds & Puddles. (gr. 4-7). 1994. pap. 8.99 (*0-7459-2621-5*) Lion USA.
Headstrom, Richard. Adventures with Freshwater Animals. (Illus.). 217p. (gr. 5 up). 1983. pap. 5.95 (*0-486-24453-9*) Dover.
Jennings, Terry. Pond Life. LC 88-22880. (Illus.). 32p. (gr. 3-6). 1989. pap. 4.95 (*0-516-48406-0*) Childrens.
Kirkpatrick, Rena K. Look at Pond Life. rev. ed. Milne, Annabel & Stebbing, Peter, illus. LC 84-26249. 32p. (gr. 2-4). 1985. PLB 10.95 (*0-8172-2355-X*); pap. 4.95 (*0-8114-6901-8*) Raintree Steck-V.
Lavies, Bianca. Lily Pad Pond. Lavies, Bianca, photos by. LC 88-31697. (Illus.). 32p. (ps-2). 1989. 14.00 (*0-525-44483-1*, DCB) Dutton Child Bks.
Loewer, Peter. Pond Water Zoo: An Introduction to Microscopic Life. Jenkins, Jean, illus. LC 93-18468. (gr. 1-8). 1995. 13.95 (*0-689-31736-0*, Atheneum Child Bk) Macmillan Child Grp.
Mason, Helen. Life in a Pond. Rodgers, Gregg, illus. 32p. (Orig.). (gr. 3-6). 1992. pap. 3.50 (*0-88625-255-5*) Durkin Hayes Pub.
Michels, Tilde. At the Frog Pond. Ignatowicz, Nina, tr. from GER. Michl, Reinhard, illus. LC 88-37835. 32p. (ps-4). 1989. (Lipp Jr Bks) HarpC Child Bks.
Reid, George K. Pond Life. Zim, Herbert S., ed. Kaicher, Sally & Dolan, Tom, illus. (gr. 7 up). 1967. pap. write for info. (*0-307-24017-7*, Golden Pr) Western Pub.
Rockwell, Jane. All about Ponds. Veno, Joseph, illus. LC 83-4835. 32p. (gr. 3-6). 1984. lib. bdg. 10.59 (*0-89375-971-6*); pap. text ed. 2.95 (*0-89375-972-4*) Troll Assocs.
Sabin, Francene. Wonders of the Pond. Grant, Leigh, illus. LC 81-7407. 32p. (gr. 2-4). 1982. PLB 11.59 (*0-89375-576-1*); pap. text ed. 2.95 (*0-89375-577-X*); cassette 9.95 (*0-685-04956-6*) Troll Assocs.
Schwartz, David M. The Hidden Life of the Pond. Kuhn, Dwight, photos by. (Illus.). 40p. (gr. 1 up). 1988. PLB 15.00 (*0-517-57060-2*) Crown Bks Yng Read.
Snow, John. Secrets of Ponds & Lakes. Jack, Susan, ed. Dowling, Jak, intro. by. (Illus.). 96p. (Orig.). (gr. 4-10). 1982. pap. 3.95 (*0-930096-30-4*) G Gannett.
Snowball, Diane. Exploring Fresh Water Habitats. Belcher, Cynthia A., illus. 24p. (Orig.). (gr. 1-5). 1994. big bk. 21.95 (*1-879531-30-5*); PLB 9.95 (*1-879531-45-3*); pap. 4.95 (*1-879531-29-1*) Mondo Pubng.
Stone, Lynn M. Pond Life. LC 83-7311. (Illus.). 48p. (gr. k-4). 1983. PLB 12.85 (*0-516-01705-5*); pap. 4.95 (*0-516-41705-3*) Childrens.
Taylor, Barbara. River Life. Greenaway, Frank, photos by. LC 92-52822. (Illus.). 32p. (gr. 2-5). 1992. 9.95 (*1-56458-130-6*) Dorling Kindersley.
Tordjman, Nathalie. The Living Pond. Bogard, Vicki, tr. from FRE. Bour, Laura, illus. LC 90-50780. 38p. (gr. k-5). 1991. 5.95 (*0-944589-38-3*, 383) Young Discovery Lib.
Wells, Donna K. Pond Life: The Fishing Trip. Ching, illus. LC 90-1644. 32p. (ps-2). 1990. PLB 13.95 (*0-89565-581-0*) Childs World.
Wyler, Rose. Puddles & Ponds. Petruccio, Steven, illus. 32p. (gr. k-2). 1990. PLB 11.98 (*0-671-66348-8*, J Messner) S&S Trade.

FRESH-WATER PLANTS
see also Aquariums; Marine Plants

Arvetis, Chris & Palmer, Carole. Lakes & Rivers. LC 93-499. (Illus.). 1993. write for info. (*0-528-83572-6*) Rand McNally.

FREUD, SIGMUNND, 1856-1939

Mann, Barry. Sigmund Freud. LC 92-42548. 1993. 19.93 (*0-86625-491-9*); 14.95s.p. (*0-685-66534-8*) Rourke Pubns.

FRIENDS, SOCIETY OF

Brill, Marlene T. Allen Jay & the Underground Railroad. Porter, Janice L., illus. LC 92-25279. 1993. 14.95 (*0-87614-776-7*); pap. write for info. (*0-87614-605-1*) Carolrhoda Bks.
Hinshaw, Mary E. Quaker Adventures: Three Hundred Years in Carolina. (Illus.). 74p. (Orig.). (gr. 5-7). 1971. pap. 1.50x (*0-942727-01-0*) NC Yrly Pubns Bd.
Hinshaw, Seth B. Carolina Quakers. (Illus.). 74p. (Orig.). (gr. 5-7). 1971. pap. 1.50x (*0-942727-15-0*) NC Yrly Pubns Bd.

FRIENDS, SOCIETY OF–FICTION

Avi. Night Journeys. Cohn, Amy, ed. LC 93-50233. 160p. (gr. 5 up). 1994. write for info. (*0-688-05298-3*, Pub. by Beech Tree Bks); pap. 4.95 (*0-688-13628-1*, Pub. by Beech Tree Bks) Morrow.
Beatty, Patricia. Who Comes with Cannons? LC 92-6317. 192p. (gr. 5 up). 1992. 14.00 (*0-688-11028-2*) Morrow Jr Bks.
Clark, Marnie, et al, eds. Lighting Candles in the Dark. Thomas, Sylvia, illus. 215p. (Orig.). 1992. pap. 9.50 (*0-9620912-3-5*) Friends Genl Conf.
Cromer, Mary L. Stories for Jason. LC 93-37765. 110p. 1993. pap. 8.95 (*0-944350-28-3*) Friends United.
Luttrell, Ida. The Bear Next Door. Stapler, Sarah, illus. LC 90-4153. 64p. (gr. k-3). 1991. PLB 11.89 (*0-06-024024-5*) HarpC Child Bks.
Rinaldi, Ann. Finishing Becca: A Story of Peggy Shippen & Benedict Arnold. (gr. 7 up). 1994. pap. 3.95 (*0-15-200879-9*); 10.95 (*0-15-200880-2*) HarBrace.
Smith, Susan. Angela & the King-Size Crusade. (gr. 3-7). 1988. pap. 2.50 (*0-317-69592-4*) PB.
Turkle, Brinton. Obadiah the Bold. Turkle, Brinton, illus. LC 65-13350. (gr. k-3). 1977. pap. 3.95 (*0-14-050233-5*, Puffin) Puffin Bks.

FRIENDSHIP
see also Love

Amos, Janine. Feelings: Friendly. (gr. 4-7). 1994. 19.97 (*0-8114-9230-3*) Raintree Steck-V.
Barratt, Dorothy, et al. Becoming Friends, What Friends Believe. Eichorn, Chris & Nelson, Lois, illus. 78p. (gr. 5-6). 1990. tchr's. ed. 7.50 (*0-943701-16-3*) George Fox Pr.
Bennett, Marian & Stortz, Diane. My Family & Friends. Oliviera, Gerry, illus. 12p. (ps). 1992. deluxe ed. 4.99 (*0-87403-994-0*, 24-03114) Standard Pub.
Berry, Joy. Every Kid's Guide to Making Friends. Bartholemew, illus. 48p. (gr. 3-7). 1987. 5.95 (*0-516-21406-3*) Childrens.
Berry, Joy W. Teach Me about Friends. Dickey, Kate, ed. LC 85-45083. (Illus.). 36p. (ps). 1986. 4.98 (*0-685-10721-3*) Grolier Inc.
Borchers, Deena. Communicating with Friends. (Illus.). 48p. (gr. 9-12). 1992. pap. 8.99 (*1-55945-228-5*) Group Pub.
Brown, Pam. Lean on Me: How to Help a Friend with a Problem. Nelson, Becky, ed. (Orig.). (gr. 7-12). 1993. pap. text ed. 1.95 (*1-56309-068-6*) Womans Mission Union.
Bruzzone, Catherine & Morton, Lone. My Friends. Church, Caroline, illus. 24p. (Orig.). (gr. 1-3). 1994. pap. 3.95 (*0-8249-8650-4*, Ideals Child) Hambleton-Hill.
Crystal Clarity Staff. Little Secrets of Friendship. (gr. 4-7). 1993. 5.95 (*1-56589-602-5*) Crystal Clarity.
Daniel, Becky. Count on Your Friends. 32p. (ps-k). 1991. 8.95 (*0-86653-582-9*, GA1306) Good Apple.
Dann, Penny, illus. A Little Book of Friendship. LC 93-12918. (gr. 1-8). 1993. 12.95 (*1-56766-095-9*) Childs World.
DeFelice, Cynthia. The Light on Hogback Hill. LC 93-3507. 144p. (gr. 3-7). 1993. SBE 13.95 (*0-02-726453-X*, Macmillan Child Bk) Macmillan Child Grp.
Dellinger, Annetta E. Hugging. Williams, Jenny, illus. LC 84-21505. (ENG & SPA.). 32p. (ps-2). 1985. PLB 14.95 (*0-89565-301-X*) Childs World.
Families & Friends. (Illus.). 32p. (ps-2). 1985. 1.95 (*0-225-66390-2*) Harper SF.
Friendship. 1992. 3.98 (*0-8317-5009-X*) Smithmark.
Goley, Elaine. Friendship. (Illus.). 32p. (gr. 1-4). 1987. PLB 15.94 (*0-86592-376-0*); 11.95s.p. (*0-685-67575-0*) Rourke Corp.
Gouge, Betty, et al. KidSkills Interpersonal Skill Series, Let's Share: Friendship: Sharing. Morse, J. Thomas, et al, eds. Bleck, Linda & Bleck, Cathie, illus. LC 86-81270. 48p. (ps). 1986. PLB 8.95 (*0-934275-13-0*); bk. & cassette 11.95 (*0-934275-27-0*) Fam Skills.
Hallinan, P. K. That's What a Friend Is. 24p. (ps-2). 1990. pap. 4.95 (*0-8249-8492-7*, Ideals Child) Hambleton-Hill.
Jackson, Tim. Friends & Choices. Jackson, Tim, illus. & intro. by. 24p. (Orig.). (gr. 6-12). 1987. pap. 1.95 (*0-942675-05-3*) Creative License.
—Just Like a Happy Family. Jackson, Tim, illus. 17p. (gr. 4 up). 1985. pap. 1.95 (*0-942675-00-2*) Creative License.
—That's All They're Good For. Jackson, Tim, illus. & intro. by. 20p. (gr. 5-9). 1986. pap. 1.95 (*0-942675-02-9*) Creative License.
Johnson, Lois W. Thanks for Being My Friend. Peck, Virginia, illus. LC 88-60473. 180p. (Orig.). 1988. pap. 7.00 (*0-89109-234-X*) NavPress.
Joyce, Mary R. Friends: For Teens. (Illus.). 144p. (Orig.). (gr. 10-12). 1990. pap. text ed. 10.95 (*0-9615722-1-3*) LifeCom.
Kalman, Bobbie. Fun with My Friends. (Illus.). 32p. (gr. k-2). 1985. 15.95 (*0-86505-063-5*); pap. 7.95 (*0-86505-087-2*) Crabtree Pub Co.
Karlsberg, Elizabeth. How to Make & Keep Friends. Magnuson, Diana, illus. LC 90-48252. 128p. (gr. 5-9). 1991. lib. bdg. 10.89 (*0-8167-2295-1*); pap. text ed. 2.95 (*0-8167-2296-X*) Troll Assocs.
Kino Learning Center Staff, et al. My Relationships with Others. Mirocha, Kay, illus. 64p. (gr. 5-9). 1987. pap. 7.95 (*0-86653-419-9*, GA 1029) Good Apple.
Leshan, Eda. When Kids Drive Kids Crazy: How to Get Along with Your Friends & Enemies. (gr. 5 up). 1990. 12.95 (*0-8037-0866-1*) Dial Bks Young.
Macaulay, David. Mill. Macaulay, David, illus. 128p. (gr. 6 up). 1983. 15.45 (*0-395-34830-7*) HM.
MacGregor, Cynthia. Best Friends' Yearbook. 30p. (Orig.). (gr. 4-9). 1994. pap. 7.99 (*0-9640887-0-3*) Olive Tree Concepts.
Mahy, Margaret. Making Friends. LC 89-13246. (Illus.). 32p. (gr. k-3). 1990. SBE 13.95 (*0-689-50498-5*, M K McElderry) Macmillan Child Grp.
Marzollo, Jean & Marzollo, Claudio. Ruthie's Rude Friends. Meddaugh, Susan, illus. LC 84-1707. 48p. (ps-3). 1987. pap. 4.95 (*0-8037-0378-3*) Dial Bks Young.
Miller, E. Lorraine. Friendship. Browne, Rob, illus. LC 77-79105. (ps up). 1977. 5.00 (*0-89566-000-8*) Miller Ent.
Miller, Judi. How to be Friends with a Boy - How to be Friends with a Girl. 96p. (gr. 5-9). 1990. pap. 2.50 (*0-590-42806-3*) Scholastic Inc.
Morse, J. Thomas, et al. KidSkills Interpersonal Skill Series, A Lasting Friend: Friendship: Making Friends. Gouge, Betty, et al, eds. Bleck, Cathie, illus. LC 85-45422. 45p. (gr. 2-3). 1985. PLB 9.95 (*0-934275-06-8*); bk. & cassette 13.95 (*0-934275-20-3*) Fam Skills.
—KidSkills Interpersonal Skill Series, Lair of the Jade Tiger: Friendship: Keeping Friends. Gouge, Betty, et al, eds. Bleck, Cathie, illus. LC 85-81270. 48p. (gr. 2-3). 1986. PLB 9.95 (*0-934275-07-6*); bk. & cassette 13.95 (*0-934275-21-1*) Fam Skills.
My Best Friend, 4 bks. (Illus.). (gr. 3-5). 1989. Set, 48p. ea. lib. bdg. 39.92 (*0-671-94193-3*, J Messner) S&S Trade.
Noffs, David & Noffs, Laurie. The Daily Harold, Bk. 6. Lynch, Reg, illus. 24p. (Orig.). (gr. 6). 1987. wkbk. 2.50 (*0-929875-07-9*) Noffs Assocs.
—Harold Magazine, Bk. 4: Let's Be Friends. Noffs, Lauri A., illus. 24p. (Orig.). (gr. 4). 1987. wkbk. 2.50 (*0-929875-05-2*) Noffs Assocs.
Oxenbury, Helen. Friends. Oxenbury, Helen, illus. 14p. (ps-k). 1981. 3.95 (*0-671-42111-5*, Little Simon) S&S Trade.
Painter, Carol. Leading a Friends Helping Friends Program. Sorenson, Don L., ed. 160p. (Orig.). (gr. 9-12). 1989. pap. text ed. 8.95x (*0-932796-29-X*) Ed Media Corp.
Peck, Lee. Coping with Cliques. Rosen, Ruth, ed. LC 92-12380. (gr. 7-12). 1992. 14.95 (*0-8239-1412-7*) Rosen Group.
Powell, Richard. How to Deal with Friends. Snow, Alan, illus. LC 91-15164. 24p. (gr. k-3). 1992. PLB 9.59 (*0-8167-2422-9*); pap. text ed. 2.95 (*0-8167-2423-7*) Troll Assocs.
Preschool Color & Learn: Making Friends & Sharing. (ps). 1992. pap. 1.95 (*0-590-45059-X*) Scholastic Inc.
Rabinowich, Ellen. Underneath I'm Different. LC 82-14919. 192p. (gr. 7 up). 1983. 12.95 (*0-685-06447-6*) Delacorte.
Roberts, Sharon L. Friendship. Hohag, Linda, illus. LC 86-9641. (ENG & SPA.). 32p. (ps-2). 1986. PLB 14.95 (*0-89565-350-8*) Childs World.
Sachs, Marilyn. Just Like a Friend. LC 89-1168. 168p. (gr. 5-9). 1989. 14.95 (*0-525-44524-2*, DCB) Dutton Child Bks.
Schwartz, L. Feelings about Friends. (gr. 3-7). 1988. 4.95 (*0-88160-168-3*, LW 281) Learning Wks.
Sciacca, Fran & Sciacca, Jill. Burger, Fries & a Friend to Go. (gr. 7 up). 1987. pap. 3.95 (*0-89066-097-2*) World Wide Pubs.
Stone, J. David & Keefauver, Larry. Friend to Friend: Helping Your Friends Through Problems. rev. ed. LC 90-81968. 74p. (gr. 8-12). 1990. pap. 6.95x (*0-932796-31-1*) Ed Media Corp.
Varenhorst, Barbara B. Real Friends: Becoming the Friend You'd Like to Have. LC 82-48412. (Illus.). 160p. (Orig.). 1983. pap. 11.00 (*0-06-250890-3*, CN4048) Harper SF.

Wamberg, Steve & Wamberg, Annie. Building Better Friendships. (Illus.). 48p. (gr. 6-8). 1992. pap. 8.99 (*1-55945-138-6*) Group Pub.
Warburg, Sandol S. I Like You. Chwast, Jacqueline, illus. LC 65-11020. 48p. (gr. 1-3). 1965. 5.70 (*0-395-07176-3*) HM.
Wirths, Claudine G. & Bowman-Kruhm, Mary. Your Circle of Friends. (Illus.). 64p. (gr. 5-8). 1993. PLB 14.95 (*0-8050-2073-X*) TFC Bks NY.
Youngs, Bettie B. Friendship Is Forever, Isn't It? 141p. (Orig.). (gr. 4 up). 1990. pap. 8.95x (*0-940221-05-5*) Lrng Tools-Bilicki Pubns.
—Friendship Is Forever, Isn't It? 141p. (gr. 4-12). 1990. 8.95 (*0-915190-94-X*, JP 9094-X) Jalmar Pr.
Ziegler, Sandra. Friends: A Handbook about Getting Along Together. Fleishman, Seymour, illus. LC 81-17025. 112p. (gr. 2-6). 1980. PLB 14.95 (*0-89565-207-2*) Childs World.

FRIENDSHIP–FICTION

Aardema, Verna. Bimwili & the Zimwi. Meddaugh, Susan, illus. LC 85-4449. 32p. (Orig.). (ps-3). 1988. pap. 4.95 (*0-8037-0553-0*) Dial Bks Young.
—Oh, Kojo! How Could You! Brown, Marc T., illus. LC 84-1710. 32p. (ps-3). 1988. pap. 4.99 (*0-8037-0449-6*) Dial Bks Young.
—What's So Funny, Ketu? Brown, Marc T., illus. LC 82-70195. 32p. (ps-3). 1989. pap. 4.95 (*0-8037-0646-4*) Dial Bks Young.
Abbott, Jennie. Costume Party. Badenhop, Mary, illus. LC 87-14987. 96p. (gr. 5-8). 1988. PLB 9.89 (*0-8167-1189-5*); pap. text ed. 2.95 (*0-8167-1190-9*) Troll Assocs.
Ackerman, Karen. The Tin Heart. Hays, Michael, illus. LC 89-6528. 32p. (gr. 1-3). 1990. SBE 13.95 (*0-689-31461-2*, Atheneum Child Bk) Macmillan Child Grp.
Ada, Alma F. Sale el Oso (Small Book) Myers, Amy, illus. (SPA.). 16p. (Orig.). (gr. k-3). 1992. pap. text ed. 6.00 (*1-56334-079-8*) Hampton-Brown.
Adair, Peggy. Chance. LC 90-82750. 200p. (Orig.). (gr. 6-12). 1990. pap. 4.95 (*0-9626803-9-7*) Deep Riv Pr.
Adams, Pam. Playmates. (gr. 3 up). 1991. 6.95 (*0-85953-449-9*) Childs Play.
—Six in a Bath. (gr. 4 up). 1990. 4.95 (*0-85953-443-X*) Childs Play.
Adler, C. S. Always & Forever Friends. 176p. 1990. pap. 3.99 (*0-380-70687-3*, Camelot) Avon.
—Binding Ties. (gr. k-12). 1989. pap. 2.95 (*0-440-20413-5*, LFL) Dell.
—Mismatched Summer. 144p. 1991. 14.95 (*0-399-21776-2*, Putnam) Putnam Pub Group.
—Some Other Summer. (gr. 3-7). 1988. pap. 2.95 (*0-380-70515-X*, Camelot) Avon.
Adoff, Arnold. Flamboyan. Barbour, Karen, illus. 32p. (ps-3). 1988. 14.95 (*0-15-228404-4*, HB Juv Bks) HarBrace.
Adorjan, Carol. That's What Friends Are For. 1990. pap. 2.75 (*0-590-42454-8*) Scholastic Inc.
Aersten, Kristen. Count on Me. Aarsten, Kristen, illus. 24p. (Orig.). (ps-1). 1994. pap. 4.95 (*1-55037-362-5*, Pub. by Annick CN) Firefly Bks Ltd.
Ahlberg, Allan. Ten in a Bed. Amstutz, Andre, illus. 112p. 1989. pap. 12.95 (*0-670-82042-3*) Viking Child Bks.
Aiello, Barbara & Shulman, Jeffrey. Friends for Life: Featuring Amy Wilson. Barr, Loel, illus. LC 88-29251. 48p. (gr. 3-6). 1988. PLB 13.95 (*0-941477-03-7*) TFC Bks NY.
—Secrets Aren't (Always) for Keeps: Featuring Jennifer Hauser. Barr, Loel, illus. 48p. (gr. 3-6). 1988. PLB 13.95 (*0-8050-3069-7*) TFC Bks NY.
Akio, Terumasa. Me & Alves: A Japanese Journey. Matsui, Susan, tr. Oido, Yukio, illus. 24p. 1993. lib. bdg. 14.95 (*1-55037-223-8*, Pub. by Annick CN); pap. 4.95 (*1-55037-222-X*, Pub. by Annick CN) Firefly Bks Ltd.
Albright, Molly. Best Friends. DeRosa, Dee, illus. LC 87-13874. 96p. (gr. 3-6). 1988. PLB 9.89 (*0-8167-1151-8*); pap. text ed. 2.95 (*0-8167-1152-6*) Troll Assocs.
—The Big Showoffs. DeRosa, Dee, illus. LC 87-13872. 96p. (gr. 3-6). 1988. PLB 9.89 (*0-8167-1155-0*); pap. text ed. 2.95 (*0-8167-1156-9*) Troll Assocs.
—The Dream Team. DeRosa, Dee, illus. LC 87-13821. 96p. (gr. 3-6). 1988. PLB 9.89 (*0-8167-1153-4*); pap. text ed. 2.95 (*0-8167-1154-2*) Troll Assocs.
Alden, Joan. A Boy's Best Friend. Hopkins, Catherine, illus. LC 92-8061. 32p. (ps-2). 1992. 12.95 (*1-55583-203-2*, Alyson Wonderland) Alyson Pubns.
Alexander, Sue. Ellsworth & Millicent. Meier, David S., illus. LC 92-7705. 28p. (gr. k up). 1993. 14.95 (*0-88708-247-5*) Picture Bk Studio.
Aliki. Feelings. LC 84-4098. (Illus.). 32p. (ps up). 1986. 3.95 (*0-688-06518-X*, Mulberry) Morrow.
—Overnight at Mary Bloom's. Aliki, illus. LC 86-7719. 32p. (ps-3). 1987. 15.00 (*0-688-06764-6*); lib. bdg. 14.93 (*0-688-06765-4*) Greenwillow.
—We Are Best Friends. Aliki, illus. LC 81-6549. 32p. (gr. k-3). 1982. 16.00 (*0-688-00822-4*); PLB 15.93 (*0-688-00823-2*) Greenwillow.
—We Are Best Friends. LC 81-6549. (Illus.). 32p. (ps up). 1987. pap. 3.95 (*0-688-07037-X*, Mulberry) Morrow.
Allen, Richard E. Ozzy on the Outside. 1991. pap. 3.50 (*0-440-20767-3*) Dell.
Almon, Russell. Kid Can't Miss. 1992. pap. 3.50 (*0-380-76261-7*, Flare) Avon.
Alter, Judy. Katie & the Recluse. LC 90-23695. 192p. (gr. 4-9). 1991. pap. 5.95 (*0-936650-13-3*) E C Temple.
Althaus, Anne-Marie. A Touch of Sepia. LC 93-26299. (Illus.). 1994. 4.25 (*0-383-03781-6*) SRA Schl Grp.
Amdur, Nikki. One of Us. Sanderson, Ruth, illus. LC 81-65847. (gr. 3-6). 1981. Dial Bks Young.
Amstutz, Beverly. You Are Number One! (Illus.). 30p. (gr. k-9). 1982. pap. 2.50x (*0-937836-08-7*) Precious Res.
Anderson, Mary. Who Says Nobody's Perfect? LC 87-5336. 160p. (gr. 7 up). 1987. pap. 14.95 (*0-385-29582-0*) Delacorte.
Anglund, Joan W. A Friend Is Someone Who Likes You: Silver Anniversary Edition. Anglund, Joan W., illus. LC 58-8624. 32p. (ps up). 1983. 8.95 (*0-15-229678-6*, HB Juv Bks) HarBrace.
Anholt, Laurence. Camille & the Sunflowers. (Illus.). 32p. (ps-2). 1994. 13.95 (*0-8120-6409-7*) Barron.
Annikin Series, 3 bks, No. 12. (ps-1). 1992. Set. write for info. (*1-55037-251-3*, Pub. by Annick Pr) Firefly Bks Ltd.
Anzaldua, Gloria. Friends from the Other Side: Amigos del otro lado. Mendez, Consuelo, illus. LC 92-34384. 32p. (gr. 2-7). 1993. 13.95 (*0-89239-113-8*) Childrens Book Pr.
Ardizzone, Edward. Tim & Ginger. Ardizzone, Edward, illus. 48p. (ps-3). 1987. pap. 6.95 (*0-19-272113-5*) OUP.
—Tim's Friend Towser. Ardizzone, Edward, illus. 48p. (ps-3). 1987. pap. 6.95 (*0-19-272112-7*) OUP.
Ashford, Ann. If I Found a Wistful Unicorn: A Gift of Love. Drath, Bill, illus. 40p. 1992. 6.95 (*1-56145-047-2*) Peachtree Pubs.
Ashwill, Beverley. Marlina & McGee. Ashwill, Betty J., illus. LC 86-73031. 32p. (ps-3). 1987. pap. 5.95 (*0-941381-00-5*) BJO Enterprises.
—The Runaways. Ashwill, Betty, illus. LC 87-72441. 48p. (gr. 4-8). 1988. 12.95 (*0-941381-02-1*); pap. 5.95 (*0-941381-01-3*) BJO Enterprises.
Athkins, D. E. Mirror, Mirror. 144p. 1992. pap. 3.25 (*0-590-45246-0*, Point) Scholastic Inc.
Atkinson, John. Bamboo & Friends. Engel, Michael, illus. LC 88-50844. 104p. (gr. 1-12). 1988. 13.95 (*0-929155-05-X*) Windward Bks.
Auch, Mary J. Bird Dogs Can't Fly. Auch, Mary J., illus. LC 93-2746. (ps-3). 1993. reinforced bdg. 15.95 (*0-8234-1050-1*) Holiday.
—Seven Long Years Until College. LC 91-2094. 176p. (gr. 3-7). 1991. 13.95 (*0-8234-0901-5*) Holiday.
Avery, Lorraine. The Runaway Winner. Thomas, Linda, illus. LC 89-34369. 96p. (gr. 4-6). 1990. PLB 9.89 (*0-8167-1708-7*); pap. text ed. 2.95 (*0-8167-1709-5*) Troll Assocs.
Avi. S. O. R. Losers. 96p. (gr. 3-7). 1986. pap. 3.99 (*0-380-69993-1*, Camelot) Avon.
Babbitt, Natalie. Tuck Everlasting. LC 75-33306. 160p. (gr. 3 up). 1985. pap. 3.95 (*0-374-48009-5*, Sunburst) FS&G.
Baer, Judy. New Girl in Town. LC 88-71504. 176p. (Orig.). (gr. 10-12). 1988. pap. 3.99 (*1-55661-022-X*) Bethany Hse.
—Tomorrow's Promise. 144p. (Orig.). (gr. 6-9). 1990. pap. 3.99 (*1-55661-143-9*) Bethany Hse.
—Trouble with a Capital T. LC 88-71503. 176p. (Orig.). (gr. 10-12). 1988. pap. 3.99 mass market (*1-55661-021-1*) Bethany Hse.
—Yesterday's Dream. 144p. (Orig.). (gr. 8-10). 1990. pap. 3.99 (*1-55661-142-0*) Bethany Hse.
Baker, Barbara. Digby & Kate Again. Winborn, Marsha, illus. LC 88-25677. 48p. (ps-2). 1989. 9.95 (*0-525-44477-7*, DCB) Dutton Child Bks.
—N-O Spells No. LC 90-19714. (Illus.). 64p. (gr. 2-5). 1991. 10.95 (*0-525-44639-7*, DCB) Dutton Child Bks.
—The William Problem. Iosa, Ann, illus. LC 93-32598. 1994. write for info. (*0-525-45235-4*, DCB) Dutton Child Bks.
Baker, Barbara & Winborn, Martha. Digby & Kate Again. (Illus.). (gr. k-3). 1994. pap. 3.25 (*0-14-036665-2*) Puffin Bks.
Balian, Lorna. Wilbur's Space Machine. Balian, Lorna, illus. LC 90-55095. 32p. (ps-3). 1990. reinforced 14.95 (*0-8234-0836-1*) Holiday.
Bang, Molly. Sunshine's Book. 1994. write for info.; PLB write for info. Greenwillow.
Banks, Marcus. The Soup Kitchen. 32p. (gr. 9 up). 1993. pap. 5.95 (*0-8059-3322-0*) Dorrance.
Barrett, Joyce D. Willie's Not the Hugging Kind. Cummings, Pat, illus. LC 89-1868. 32p. (gr. k-3). 1989. 16.00 (*0-06-020416-8*); PLB 15.89 (*0-06-020417-6*) HarpC Child Bks.
Barrett, Mary B. Sing to the Stars. Speidel, Sandra, illus. LC 92-41773. 1994. 15.95 (*0-316-08224-4*) Little.
Bashful Bard. What Does It Mean to Be a Friend. (Illus.). 28p. (Orig.). (ps-1). 1989. Kenney Pubns.
Bastin, Marjolein. My Name Is Vera. (Illus.). 28p. (ps-2). 1985. 2.95 (*0-8120-5690-6*) Barron.
—Vera & Her Friends. (Illus.). 28p. (ps-2). 1985. 2.95 (*0-8120-5689-2*) Barron.
—Vera's Dresses Up. 28p. (ps-2). 1985. 2.95 (*0-8120-5691-4*) Barron.
Bates, A. Party Line. (gr. 6 up). 1989. pap. 3.25 (*0-590-44238-4*) Scholastic Inc.
—What's the Opposite of a Best Friend? (gr. 4-7). 1993. pap. 2.95 (*0-590-44145-0*) Scholastic Inc.
Bates, Betty. Thatcher Payne-in-the-Neck. (gr. k-6). 1987. pap. 3.25 (*0-440-48598-3*, YB) Dell.
Bauer, Marion D. On My Honor. (gr. k-6). 1987. pap. 3.99 (*0-440-46633-4*, YB) Dell.
Baum, Louis. One More Time. ALC Staff, ed. Bouma, Paddy, illus. LC 85-31050. 32p. (ps up). 1992. pap. 3.95 (*0-688-11698-1*, Mulberry) Morrow.
Bawden, Nina. The Robbers. LC 79-4152. (Illus.). 160p. (gr. 4-7). 1989. Repr. of 1979 ed. 12.95 (*0-688-41902-X*) Lothrop.
—The Witch's Daughter. 192p. (gr. 3-7). 1991. 13.45 (*0-395-58635-6*, Clarion Bks) HM.
Bayles, Miriam. Si Bantay, Si Puti, at Si Ngaw. Bayles, Arthur, illus. (TAG., Orig.). (gr. k-2). 1988. pap. 3.75x (*971-10-0359-7*, Pub. by New Day Pub PI) Cellar.
—Si Wayt at Ang Kanyang Mga Kaibigan. Tiano, Bethoven, illus. (TAG.). 35p. (Orig.). (gr. k-2). 1990. pap. 4.00x (*971-10-0416-X*, Pub. by New Day Pub PI) Cellar.
Baylis-White, Mary. Sheltering Rebecca. 112p. (gr. 5-9). 1993. pap. 3.99 (*0-14-036448-X*, Puffin) Puffin Bks.
Baylor, Byrd. And It Is Still That Way. Jelinek, Lucy, illus. 96p. (gr. k-8). 1987. pap. 6.95 (*0-939729-06-7*) Trails West Pub.
—Guess Who My Favorite Person Is. reissued ed. Parker, Robert A., illus. LC 77-7151. 32p. (gr. 1-4). 1992. RSBE 14.95 (*0-684-19514-3*, Scribners Young Read) Macmillan Child Grp.
Beatty, Patricia. Lupita Manana. LC 81-505. 192p. (gr. 6 up). 1992. pap. 4.95 (*0-688-11497-0*, Pub. by Beech Tree Bks) Morrow.
—O the Red Rose Tree. Cohn, Amy, ed. Dauber, Liz, illus. LC 93-50232. 208p. (gr. 5 up). 1994. write for info. (*0-688-21429-0*, Pub. by Beech Tree Bks); pap. 4.95 (*0-688-13627-3*) Morrow.
Bechard, Margaret. My Sister, My Science Report. 96p. (gr. 3-7). 1992. pap. 4.99 (*0-14-034408-X*, Puffin) Puffin Bks.
—Really No Big Deal. LC 93-31065. 144p. (gr. 3-7). 1994. 13.99 (*0-670-85444-1*) Viking Child Bks.
Beck, Amanda. The Pegasus Club & Me. Yoshi Miyake, illus. LC 91-38330. 32p. (gr. 2-6). 1992. PLB 19.97 (*0-8114-3577-6*) Raintree Steck-V.
Becker, Antoinette & Reuter, Eisabeth. Best Friends. (gr. 1-4). 1993. 12.95 (*0-943706-18-1*) Yllw Brick Rd.
Becker, Shirley. Buddy's Shadow. (Illus.). 32p. (ps-2). 1991. pap. 6.95 (*0-944727-08-5*) Jason & Nordic Pubs.
Behrens, Michael. At the Edge. 208p. (gr. 7 up). 1988. pap. 2.95 (*0-380-75610-2*, Flare) Avon.
Belpre, Pura. Perez & Martina. Sanchez, Carlos, illus. 64p. 1991. 15.95 (*0-670-84166-8*) Viking Child Bks.
Benard, Robert, ed. All Problems Are Simple. (Orig.). (gr. k-12). 1988. pap. 3.95 (*0-440-20164-0*, LFL) Dell.
Benchley, Nathaniel. Only Earth & Sky Last Forever. (gr. 7 up). 1992. 17.25 (*0-8446-6583-5*) Peter Smith.
Benjamin, Alan. Buck. Morley, Carol, illus. LC 93-31161. 1994. 15.00 (*0-671-88718-1*, S&S BFYR) S&S Trade.
Bennett, Cherie. Good-Bye, Best Friend. 1992. pap. 3.50 (*0-440-21247-2*) Dell.
—Good-Bye, Best Friend. 1993. pap. 3.50 (*0-06-106739-3*, Harp PBks) HarpC.
—Sunset, No. 05: Sunset Reunion. 1991. pap. 3.99 (*0-425-13318-4*, Splash) Berkley Pub.
Benning, Elizabeth. Please Don't Go. (gr. 9-12). 1993. pap. 3.50 (*0-06-106148-4*, Harp PBks) HarpC.
Berenstain, Michael. The Dwarks at the Mall. 48p. (Orig.). (gr. 2 up). 1985. pap. 2.25 (*0-553-15341-2*) Bantam.
Berenstain, Stan & Berenstain, Jan. The Berenstain Bears & the New Girl in Town. Berenstain, Jan & Berenstain, Stan, illus. LC 92-32570. 112p. (Orig.). (gr. 2-6). 1993. PLB 7.99 (*0-679-93613-0*); pap. 3.50 (*0-679-83613-6*) Random Bks Yng Read.
—Los Osos Berenstain y las Peleas Entre Amigos. Guibert, Rita, tr. Berenstain, Stan & Berenstain, Jan, illus. LC 92-14807. (SPA.). 32p. (ps-3). 1993. pap. 2.25 (*0-679-84006-0*) Random Bks Yng Read.
Bergen, J. P. Media Madness. LC 94-10859. (gr. 5 up). 1994. pap. 2.95 (*0-02-045472-4*, Collier) Macmillan.
Bergstrom, Corinne. Losing Your Best Friend. Rosamilia, Patricia, illus. LC 79-20622. 32p. (ps-3). 1980. 16.95 (*0-87705-471-1*) Human Sci Pr.
Bertrand, Cecile. Let's Pretend. LC 92-54431. (Illus.). (ps-3). 1993. 13.00 (*0-688-12377-5*) Lothrop.
Betancourt, Jeanne. More Than Meets the Eye. 1991. pap. 3.50 (*0-553-29351-6*) Bantam.
—My Name Is Brain Brian. LC 92-16513. 176p. (gr. 3-7). 1993. 13.95 (*0-590-44921-4*) Scholastic Inc.
Birch, Beverley & Gardner, Sally. Suzi, Sam, George & Alice. (Illus.). 32p. (ps-1). 1994. 17.95 (*0-370-31771-8*, Pub. by Bodley Head UK) Trafalgar.
Birdseye, Tom. I'm Going to Be Famous. LC 86-45401. 144p. (gr. 3-7). 1986. 14.95 (*0-8234-0630-X*) Holiday.
—Just Call Me Stupid. 128p. (gr. 4-7). 1993. 14.95 (*0-8234-1045-5*) Holiday.
Birdseye, Tom & Birdseye, Debbie. She'll Be Comin' Round the Mountain. Glass, Andrew, illus. LC 92-37641. 32p. (ps-3). 1994. reinforced bdg. 15.95 (*0-8234-1032-3*) Holiday.
Birnhack, Sara. Promise Me Tomorrow. LC 90-82061. (gr. 6 up). 1990. 12.95 (*1-56062-025-0*); pap. 9.95 (*1-56062-026-9*) CIS Comm.
Bissett, Isabel. Here Comes Annette! Vane, Mitch, illus. LC 92-27267. 1993. 3.75 (*0-383-03628-3*) SRA Schl Grp.
Blackburn. Waiting for Sunday. 1993. pap. 28.67 (*0-590-50158-5*) Scholastic Inc.
Blair, Cynthia. The Double-Dip Disguise. (gr. 4 up). 1988. pap. 3.50 (*0-449-70256-1*, Juniper) Fawcett.
Blair, Shannon. Kiss & Tell. 176p. (Orig.). (gr. 5 up). 1985. pap. 2.50 (*0-553-26843-0*) Bantam.

Blatchford, Claire. Por el Camino. Writer, C. C. & Nielsen, Lisa C., trs. Eagle, Mike, illus. (SPA.). 24p. (Orig.). (ps). 1992. pap. text ed. 3.00x (*1-56134-152-5*) Dushkin Pub.
—A Surprise for Reggie. Eagle, Mike, illus. 24p. (Orig.). (ps). 1992. pap. text ed. 3.00x (*1-56134-141-X*) Dushkin Pub.
Bloom, Hanya. Friendly Fangs. (gr. 4-7). 1991. pap. 2.95 (*0-06-106032-1*, Harp PBks) HarpC.
Blos, Joan W. A Gathering of Days: A New England Girl's Journal, 1830-1832. LC 90-32. 160p. (gr. 3-7). 1990. pap. 3.95 (*0-689-71419-X*, Aladdin) Macmillan Child Grp.
—Old Henry. Gammell, Stephen, illus. LC 86-21745. 32p. (ps up). 1990. pap. 4.95 (*0-688-09935-1*, Mulberry) Morrow.
Blume, Judy. Fudge, 3 vols. (gr. 4-7). 1992. Set. pap. 14. 00 boxed (*0-440-36051-X*) Dell.
—Fudge-a-Mania. 169p. 1991. text ed. 13.52 (*1-56956-235-0*) W A T Braille.
—Here's to You, Rachel Robinson. LC 93-9631. 208p. (gr. 5 up). 1993. 14.95 (*0-531-06801-3*); PLB 14.99 (*0-531-08651-8*) Orchard Bks Watts.
—It's Not the End of the World. 1979. pap. 1.95 (*0-553-13628-3*) Bantam.
—Judy Blume, 4 vols. (gr. 4-7). 1992. Set. pap. 14.00 boxed (*0-440-36053-6*) Dell.
—Just as Long as We're Together. LC 87-7980. 304p. (gr. 5-8). 1987. 12.95 (*0-531-05729-1*); PLB 12.99 (*0-531-08329-2*) Orchard Bks Watts.
—Just As Long As We're Together. 1988. pap. 3.50 (*0-440-70013-2*) Dell.
—Just As Long As We're Together. large type ed. (gr. 1-8). 1990. 16.95 (*0-7451-0826-1*, Galaxy Child Lrg Print) Chivers N Amer.
—The One in the Middle is the Green Kangaroo. Trivas, Irene, illus. (ps-3). 1992. pap. 4.99 (*0-440-40668-4*, YB) Dell.
Blyton, Enid. Five Get Into Trouble. large type ed. (gr. 1-8). 1993. 16.95 (*0-7451-1910-7*, Galaxy Child Lrg Print) Chivers N Amer.
Bobbie's Back, No. 2. 1993. pap. 3.50 (*0-553-56096-4*) Bantam.
Bock, Shelly V. Lonely Lyla. 1992. 7.95 (*0-533-09389-9*) Vantage.
Boegehold, Betty D. Fight. (ps-3). 1991. pap. 3.99 (*0-553-35206-7*) Bantam.
Boelts, Maribeth. Grace & Joe. Tucker, Kathy, ed. Gourbalt, Martine, illus. LC 93-45920. 32p. (ps-1). 1994. PLB 13.95 (*0-8075-3019-0*) A Whitman.
Bogart. Ten for Dinner. 1993. pap. 28.67 (*0-590-73173-4*) Scholastic Inc.
Bolinger, Camille J. The Forever Wreath. Bolinger, Paul F., illus. LC 92-81305. 40p. (ps-4). 1993. 17.95 (*0-9632777-6-6*) Dutch Run Pub.
Bond, Michael. Paddington on Screen. (gr. k-6). 1992. pap. 3.25 (*0-440-40029-5*, YB) Dell.
Bonnette, Jeanne. Three Friends. (ps-2). 1982. pap. 1.95 (*0-89992-066-7*) Coun India Ed.
Borg, Veronique. The Next Balcony Down. (Illus.). 32p. (gr. 3-5). 1991. 12.95 (*0-89565-757-0*) Childs World.
Borton, Lady. Junk Pile. Root, Kimberly B., illus. LC 94-6735. 1995. 15.95 (*0-399-22728-8*, Philomel Bks) Putnam Pub Group.
Botner, Barbara. The World's Greatest Expert on Everything...Is Crying. (gr. 3-7). 1986. pap. 2.95 (*0-440-49739-6*, YB) Dell.
Bottner, Barbara. Nothing in Common. (gr. 5 up). 1988. pap. 2.95 (*0-553-27060-5*, Starfire) Bantam.
Boughton, Richard. Rent-a-Puppy, Inc. LC 93-41688. 1995. pap. 3.95 (*0-689-71836-5*, Atheneum) Macmillan.
Boyd, Candy D. Forever Friends. (gr. 4-8). 1992. 17.25 (*0-8446-6571-1*) Peter Smith.
Bradbury, Ray. Switch on the Night. Dillon, Leo & Dillon, Diane, illus. LC 92-25321. 40p. (ps-2). 1993. 8.99 (*0-394-80486-4*); PLB 9.99 (*0-394-90486-9*) Knopf Bks Yng Read.
Bradford, Jan. Caroline Zucker Gets Even. Ramsey, Marcy D., illus. LC 89-20630. 96p. (gr. 2-5). 1991. lib. bdg. 9.89 (*0-8167-2015-0*); pap. text ed. 2.95 (*0-8167-2016-9*) Troll Assocs.
Bradley, Virginia. Wait & See. 1994. write for info. (*0-525-65158-6*, Cobblehill Bks) Dutton Child Bks.
Brandenberg, Franz. Leo & Emily. Aliki, illus. LC 80-19657. 56p. (gr. 1-3). 1981. 15.00 (*0-688-80292-3*) Greenwillow.
—Leo & Emily. (gr. k-6). 1990. pap. 2.95 (*0-440-40294-8*, YB) Dell.
—Nice New Neighbors. Aliki, illus. LC 77-1651. 56p. (gr. 1-4). 1977. PLB 13.88 (*0-688-84105-8*) Greenwillow.
Brandt, Betty. Special Delivery. Haubrich, Kathy, illus. 48p. (gr. k-4). 1988. lib. bdg. 14.95 (*0-87614-312-5*) Carolrhoda Bks.
Brennan, Melissa. Careless Kisses. 1991. pap. 3.50 (*0-06-106052-6*, Harp PBks) HarpC.
—Could This Be Love? 1991. pap. 3.50 (*0-06-106067-4*, Harp PBks) HarpC.
—Paradise Lost? 1991. pap. 3.50 (*0-06-106068-2*, Harp PBks) HarpC.
—The Real Thing. (gr. 7 up). 1992. pap. 3.50 (*0-06-106070-4*, Harp PBks) HarpC.
—Whispers & Rumors. 1991. pap. 3.50 (*0-06-106049-6*, Harp PBks) HarpC.
Brewster, Patience. Two Bushy Badgers. LC 92-40696. 1995. 14.95 (*0-316-10862-6*) Little.
Bridgers, Sue E. All Together Now. (gr. 7 up). 1990. pap. 3.99 (*0-553-24530-9*, Starfire) Bantam.
—Keeping Christina. LC 92-22061. 288p. (gr. 7 up). 1993. 15.00 (*0-06-021504-6*); PLB 14.89 (*0-06-021505-4*) HarpC Child Bks.
—Notes for Another Life. 208p. (gr. 7 up). 1989. pap. 2.95 (*0-553-27185-7*) Bantam.
Brimner, Larry D. Cory Coleman, Grade Two. Ritz, Karen, illus. 80p. (gr. 2-4). 1990. 12.95 (*0-8050-1312-1*, Bks Young Read) H Holt & Co.
—Max & Felix. 32p. (ps-3). 1993. 12.95 (*1-56397-010-4*) Boyds Mills Pr.
Brisson, Pat. Your Best Friend, Kate. Brown, Rick, illus. LC 88-6037. 40p. (gr. k-3). 1989. RSBE 13.95 (*0-02-714350-3*, Bradbury Pr) Macmillan Child Grp.
Broger, Achim. The Day Chubby Became Charles. Cafiero, Renee V., tr. from GER. McCully, Emily A., illus. LC 89-13112. 96p. (gr. 2-5). 1990. (Lipp Jr Bks); (Lipp Jr Bks) HarpC Child Bks.
Brook, Ruth. Jingle's Big Race. Kondo, Vala, illus. LC 86-30729. 32p. (gr. k-3). 1988. PLB 11.89 (*0-8167-0902-5*); pap. text ed. 2.95 (*0-8167-0903-3*) Troll Assocs.
—Jump for Joy, Betty. Kondo, Vala, illus. LC 86-30731. 32p. (gr. k-3). 1988. PLB 11.89 (*0-8167-0908-4*); pap. text ed. 2.95 (*0-8167-0909-2*) Troll Assocs.
—Sweet Hearts for Dolly. Kondo, Vala, illus. LC 86-30732. 32p. (gr. k-3). 1988. PLB 11.89 (*0-8167-0906-8*); pap. text ed. 2.95 (*0-8167-0907-6*) Troll Assocs.
Brooks, Bruce. Everywhere. LC 90-4073. 80p. (gr. 4 up). 1990. 13.00 (*0-06-020728-0*); PLB 12.89 (*0-06-020729-9*) HarpC Child Bks.
—Midnight Hour Encores. LC 86-45035. 288p. (gr. 7 up). 1986. 14.00 (*0-06-020709-4*); PLB 13.89 (*0-06-020710-8*) HarpC Child Bks.
—The Moves Make the Man. LC 83-49476. 288p. (gr. 7 up). 1987. pap. 3.95 (*0-06-447022-9*, Trophy) HarpC Child Bks.
—No Kidding. LC 88-22057. 224p. (gr. 7 up). 1991. pap. 4.95 (*0-06-447051-2*, Trophy) HarpC Child Bks.
Brooks, Chelsea. Don't Tell a Soul. 144p. (Orig.). (gr. 5 up). 1994. pap. 2.95 (*0-02-042783-2*, Collier Young Ad) Macmillan Child Grp.
Brooks, Martha. Two Moons in August. (gr. 7 up). 1992. 15.95 (*0-316-10979-7*) Little.
Broome, Errol. Dear Mr. Sprouts. LC 92-13490. 132p. (gr. 3-7). 1994. pap. 3.99 (*0-679-85394-4*) Random Bks Yng Read.
Brower, Jamil L. Do Unto Others. (gr. 4 up). 1992. 6.95 (*0-533-09665-0*) Vantage.
Brown, Marc T. The True Francine. Brown, Marc T., illus. 32p. (ps-3). 1981. 15.95 (*0-316-11212-7*, Joy St Bks) Little.
Browne, Anthony. Willy & Hugh. Browne, Anthony, illus. LC 90-4938. 32p. (ps-3). 1991. 13.00 (*0-679-81446-9*); lib. bdg. 13.99 (*0-679-91446-3*) Knopf Bks Yng Read.
Browne, Eileen. Where's That Bus? Browne, Eileen, illus. LC 90-20885. 32p. (ps-1). 1991. pap. 13.95 jacketed (*0-671-73810-0*, S&S BFYR) S&S Trade.
Brownrigg, Sheri. All Tutus Should Be Pink. Johnson, Meredith, illus. 32p. 1992. pap. 2.95 (*0-590-43904-9*, Cartwheel) Scholastic Inc.
—Best Friends Wear Pink Tutus. Johnson, Meredith, illus. LC 92-27569. 1993. write for info. (*0-590-46437-X*) Scholastic Inc.
Bryant, Bonnie. Horse Wise. (gr. 4 up). 1990. pap. 3.25 (*0-553-15805-8*) Bantam.
Buchan, Stuart. When We Lived with Pete. (Orig.). (gr. 4-7). 1986. pap. 2.95 (*0-440-49483-4*, YB) Dell.
Bunnett, Rochelle. Friends in the Park. Sahlhoff, Carl, illus. 32p. 1993. 7.95 (*1-56288-347-X*) Checkerboard.
Bunting, Eve. If I Asked You, Would You Stay? LC 82-49052. 160p. (gr. 7 up). 1987. (Trophy); pap. 3.95 (*0-06-447023-7*, Trophy) HarpC Child Bks.
—Maggie the Freak. (Illus.). 64p. (gr. 3-8). 1992. 8.95 (*0-89565-775-9*) Childs World.
—Our Sixth-Grade Sugar Babies. LC 90-5487. 160p. (gr. 4-6). 1992. pap. 3.95 (*0-06-440390-4*, Trophy) HarpC Child Bks.
—Sixth-Grade Sleepover. LC 86-4679. 96p. (gr. 4-7). 1986. 13.95 (*0-15-275350-8*, HB Juv Bks) HarBrace.
—Such Nice Kids. 160p. (gr. 4-9). 1990. 13.45 (*0-395-54998-1*, Clarion Bks) HM.
Burke, Timothy. Cocoa Puppy. Burke, Ann & Burke, Ann, illus. LC 89-50890. 32p. (Orig.). (ps-3). 1989. 5.00 (*0-9623227-0-9*) Thunder & Ink.
Burnett, Frances H. The Secret Garden. 1987. pap. 3.50 (*0-440-40055-4*) Dell.
—The Secret Garden. 1991. pap. 3.99 (*0-8125-1910-8*) Tor Bks.
—The Secret Garden. 288p. 1992. 9.49 (*0-8167-2558-6*); pap. 2.95 (*0-8167-2559-4*) Troll Assocs.
Burningham, John. Aldo. Burningham, John, illus. LC 91-19589. 32p. (ps-2). 1992. 15.00 (*0-517-58701-7*); PLB 15.99 (*0-517-58699-1*) Crown Bks Yng Read.
Bush, Max. Thirteen Bells of Boglewood. (Orig.). (gr. k-3). 1987. pap. 4.50 (*0-87602-272-7*) Anchorage.
Butler, Stephen. The Mouse & the Apple. Butler, Stephen, illus. LC 93-15951. 32p. (ps up). 1994. 15.00 (*0-688-12810-6*, Tambourine Bks); PLB 14.93 (*0-688-12811-4*, Tambourine Bks) Morrow.
Buttenwieser, Paul. Their Pride & Joy. (gr. 6 up). 1988. pap. 8.95 (*0-440-50073-7*, LE) Dell.
Butterworth, Nick. Making Faces. Butterworth, Nick, illus. LC 92-54578. 32p. (ps). 1993. 12.95 (*1-56402-212-9*) Candlewick Pr.
Byars, Betsy. Coast to Coast. (gr. 4-7). 1994. pap. 3.99 (*0-440-40926-8*) Dell.
Byars, Betsy C. Beans on the Roof. Rosales, Melodye, illus. 80p. (gr. k-3). 1988. pap. 13.95 (*0-440-50055-9*) Delacorte.
—Beans on the Roof. 1990. pap. 3.50 (*0-440-40314-6*, YB) Dell.
—A Blossom Promise. Rogers, Jacqueline, illus. 160p. (gr. k-6). 1989. pap. 3.50 (*0-440-40137-2*, YB) Dell.
—The Cybil War. Owens, Gail, illus. 144p. (gr. 3 up). 1990. pap. 3.99 (*0-14-034356-3*, Puffin) Puffin Bks.
—The Pinballs. LC 76-41518. 144p. (gr. 5 up). 1987. pap. 3.95 (*0-06-440198-7*, Trophy) HarpC Child Bks.
—Wanted...Mud Blossom. (gr. 4-7). 1993. pap. 3.50 (*0-440-40761-3*) Dell.
Cadnum, Michael. Breaking the Fall. LC 92-5829. 160p. (gr. 7 up). 1992. 15.00 (*0-670-84687-2*) Viking Child Bks.
Calder, Lyn. Blue-Ribbon Friends. LC 90-85433. (Illus.). 32p. (gr. k-3). 1991. 5.95 (*1-56282-034-6*) Disney Pr.
—Minnie 'n Me: That's What Friends Are For. Vaccaro Associates, Inc. Staff, illus. 24p. (ps-k). 1992. pap. write for info. (*0-307-11629-8*, 11629, Golden Pr) Western Pub.
Camp, Lindsay. Keeping Up with Cheetah. Newton, Jill, illus. LC 92-44162. (gr. k-4). 1993. 14.00 (*0-688-12655-3*) Lothrop.
Campbell, E. Year of the Leopard Song. 1992. write for info. (*0-15-299806-3*, HB Juv Bks) HarBrace.
Cantillon, Eli. Mysterious Pen Pal. (ps-5). 1994. 16.95 (*0-938971-83-2*) JTG Nashville.
Caple, Kathy. Fox & Bear. Caple, Kathy, illus. 40p. (gr. k-3). 1992. 13.45 (*0-395-55634-1*) HM.
Capote, Truman. Miriam: A Classic Story of Loneliness. (Illus.). (gr. 4 up). 1982. PLB 13.95 (*0-87191-829-3*) Creative Ed.
Carlson, Nancy. Harriet & Walt. LC 81-18137. (Illus.). 32p. (ps-3). 1982. lib. bdg. 13.50 (*0-87614-185-8*) Carolrhoda Bks.
—Harriet & Walt. Carlson, Nancy, illus. (gr. k-3). 1984. bk. & cassette 19.95 (*0-941078-59-0*); pap. 12.95 bk. & cassette (*0-317-14688-2*); cassette, 4 paperbacks & guide 27.95 (*0-317-14689-0*) Live Oak Media.
Carlsruh, Dan K. The Cannibals of Sunset Drive. LC 92-40568. 144p. (gr. 3-7). 1993. SBE 13.95 (*0-02-717110-8*, Macmillan Child Bk) Macmillan Child Grp.
Carlstrom, Nancy W. Fish & Flamingo. Desimini, Lisa, illus. (ps-3). 1993. 14.95 (*0-316-12859-7*) Little.
Carmelich, Christina M. Friends. 1993. 7.95 (*0-8062-4700-2*) Carlton.
Carpenter, Humphrey. Mr. Majeika. large type ed. Rodgers, Frank, illus. 96p. (gr. 1-8). 1992. 16.95 (*0-7451-1582-9*, Galaxy Child Lrg Print) Chivers N Amer.
Carrick, Carol. Some Friend. Carrick, Donald, illus. LC 79-11490. 112p. (gr. 3-6). 1987. pap. 5.70 (*0-89919-525-3*, Clarion Bks) HM.
Carter, Darleen. Uh-Oh Not Me. LC 90-71360. (Illus.). 44p. (gr. k-3). 1991. 5.95 (*1-55523-398-8*) Winston-Derek.
Carter, Peter. Borderlands. 1993. pap. 4.95 (*0-374-40883-1*) FS&G.
Caseley, Judith. Harry & Willy & Carrothead. LC 90-30291. (Illus.). 24p. (ps up). 1991. 13.95 (*0-688-09492-9*); PLB 13.88 (*0-688-09493-7*) Greenwillow.
—Sophie & Sammy's Library Sleepover. LC 91-48160. (Illus.). 32p. (ps up). 1993. 14.00 (*0-688-10615-3*); PLB 13.93 (*0-688-10616-1*) Greenwillow.
—Starring Dorothy Kane. LC 90-24172. (gr. 1 up). 1992. 13.00 (*0-688-10182-8*) Greenwillow.
—Starring Dorothy Kane. Caseley, Judith, illus. LC 93-6992. 160p. (gr. 3 up). 1994. pap. 4.95 (*0-688-12548-4*, Pub. by Beech Tree Bks) Morrow.
Cassedy, Sylvia. M. E. & Morton. LC 85-48251. 288p. (gr. 4-7). 1987. (Crowell Jr Bks); (Crowell Jr Bks) HarpC Child Bks.
Casterline, Charlotte L. My Friend Has Asthma. Zabroski, Patricia, illus. 24p. (Orig.). (ps-6). 1985. pap. 4.95 (*0-9617218-0-4*) Info All Bk.
—Sam the Allergen. (Illus.). 26p. (Orig.). (ps-6). 1985. pap. 4.95 (*0-9617218-1-2*) Info All Bk.
Cech, John. My Grandmother's Journey. McGinley-Nally, Sharon, illus. LC 90-35731. 40p. (ps-4). 1991. RSBE 14.95 (*0-02-718135-9*, Bradbury Pr) Macmillan Child Grp.
Chall, Marsha W. Mattie. 48p. 1994. pap. 3.50 (*0-380-72116-3*, Camelot Young) Avon.
Chambless, Jane. Tucker & the Bear. LC 89-30244. (ps-2). 1989. pap. 13.95 (*0-671-67357-2*, S&S BFYR) S&S Trade.
Champion, Joyce. Emily & Alice. Stevenson, Sucie, illus. LC 92-13575. 1993. 13.95 (*0-15-200588-9*) HarBrace.
—Emily & Alice Again. Stevenson, Sucie, illus. LC 93-5004. 1995. write for info. (*0-15-200439-4*, Gulliver Bks) HarBrace.
Chang, Heidi. Elaine & the Flying Frog. Chang, Heidi, illus. LC 90-33721. 64p. (Orig.). (gr. 2-4). 1991. PLB 6.99 (*0-679-90870-6*) Random Bks Yng Read.
Chapouton, Anne-Marie. Downy, Pistachio & Fanny. (Illus.). 48p. (gr. 3-8). 1990. 8.95 (*0-89565-808-9*) Childs World.
—Krustnkrum. (Illus.). 32p. (gr. k-2). 1991. 12.95 (*0-89565-744-9*) Childs World.
Chardiet, Bernice & Maccarone, Grace. Merry Christmas, What's Your Name School Friends. Karas, G. Brian, illus. 32p. (ps-2). 1991. 2.50 (*0-590-43306-7*) Scholastic Inc.

Child, A. My Best Friend & Me. 19p. (gr. 1). 1992. pap. text ed. 23.00 big bk. (*1-56843-022-1*); pap. text ed. 4.50 (*1-56843-072-8*) BGR Pub.

—Show Me a Face. 14p. (ps-k). 1992. pap. text ed. 23.00 big bk. (*1-56843-006-X*); pap. text ed. 4.50 (*1-56843-056-6*) BGR Pub.

Childress, Alice. A Hero Ain't Nothin' but a Sandwich. large type ed. 144p. 1989. lib. bdg. 15.95 (*1-55736-112-6*, Crnrstn Bks) BDD LT Grp.

Chottin, Ariane. Little Mouse's Rescue: Little Animal Adventures Ser. Dzierzawska, Malgorzata, illus. Jensen, Patricia, adapted by. LC 93-2949. (Illus.). 22p. (ps-3). 1993. 5.98 (*0-89577-505-0*) RD Assn.

Christian, Mary B. Penrod Again. Dyer, Jane, illus. LC 90-29. 56p. (gr. 1-4). 1990. pap. 3.95 (*0-689-71432-7*, Aladdin) Macmillan Child Grp.

Christiansen, C. B. Sycamore Street. Sweet, Melissa, illus. LC 92-33685. 48p. (gr. 1-3). 1993. SBE 13.95 (*0-689-31784-0*, Atheneum Child Bk) Macmillan Child Grp.

Clara Barton Elementary School First-Graders. I Need a Hug! (Illus.). 32p. (gr. k-3). 1992. pap. 3.50 (*0-87406-605-0*) Willowisp Pr.

Clardy, Andrea F. Dusty Was My Friend. Alexander, Eleanor, illus. 32p. (gr. 5 up). 1984. 16.95 (*0-89885-141-6*) Human Sci Pr.

Clarke, Gus. Eddie & Teddy. ALC Staff, ed. LC 90-5795. (Illus.). 32p. (ps up). 1992. pap. 3.95 (*0-688-11700-7*, Mulberry) Morrow.

Clarke, J. Al Capsella Takes a Vacation. 160p. (gr. 7 up). 1993. 14.95 (*0-8050-2685-1*, Bks Young Read) H Holt & Co.

—Riffraff. LC 92-9928. 96p. (gr. 9-12). 1992. 14.95 (*0-8050-1774-7*, Bks Young Read) H Holt & Co.

Clarke, Pauline. Return of the Twelve. (Orig.). (gr. 3-7). 1986. pap. 4.95 (*0-440-47536-8*) Dell.

Clayton, Elaine. Pup in School. Clayton, Elaine, illus. LC 92-18457. 24p. (ps-1). 1993. 12.00 (*0-517-59085-9*); PLB 12.99 (*0-517-59086-7*) Crown Bks Yng Read.

Cleary, Beverly. The Beezus & Ramona Diary. Tiegreen, Alan, illus. 224p. (gr. 5 up). 1986. pap. 9.95 (*0-688-06353-5*, Pub. by Beech Tree Bks) Morrow.

—Beverly Cleary, 4 vols. (gr. 4-7). 1991. Set. pap. 14.00 boxed (*0-380-71719-0*, Camelot) Avon.

—Henry & Beezus. 145p. 1992. Braille. 11.60 (*1-56956-356-X*) W A T Braille.

—Mitch & Amy. 224p. 1991. pap. 3.99 (*0-380-70925-2*, Camelot) Avon.

—Mitch & Amy. reissued ed. Marstall, Bob, illus. LC 67-10041. 224p. (gr. 2 up). 1991. 13.95 (*0-688-10806-7*); PLB 13.88 (*0-688-10807-5*) Morrow Jr Bks.

—Pen Pals, 6 vols. (gr. 4-7). 1990. pap. 17.70 boxed set (*0-440-36028-5*) Dell.

—Ramona & Her Friends. pap. 9.00 (*0-440-47222-9*) Dell.

Cleaver. Moonlake Angel. (gr. k-6). 1989. pap. 2.95 (*0-440-40165-8*, YB) Dell.

Clement, Claude. Little Squirrel's Special Nest. Jensen, Patricia, adapted by. LC 93-4243. (Illus.). 22p. (ps-3). 1993. 5.98 (*0-89577-542-5*, Reader's Digest Kids) RD Assn.

Clements, Bruce. Coming About. LC 83-47841. 180p. (gr. 5 up). 1984. 14.00 (*0-374-31457-8*) FS&G.

—Two Against the Tide. 224p. (gr. 4 up). 1987. pap. 3.50 (*0-374-48016-8*) FS&G.

Clifford, Eth. I Hate Your Guts, Ben Brooster. 112p. (gr. 3-7). 1989. 13.45 (*0-395-51079-1*) HM.

—Just Tell Me When We're Dead! (gr. 5-7). 1985. pap. 2.75 (*0-590-44010-1*, Apple Paperbacks) Scholastic Inc.

Clifton, Lucille. Everett Anderson's Friend. Grifalconi, Ann, illus. LC 92-8030. 32p. (ps-3). 1992. 14.95 (*0-8050-2246-5*, Bks Young Read) H Holt & Co.

—Everett Anderson's Goodbye. Grifalconi, Ann, illus. LC 82-23426. 32p. (Orig.). (ps-2). 1988. pap. 5.95 (*0-8050-0800-4*, Bks Young Read) H Holt & Co.

—Lucky Stone. Payson, Dale, illus. (gr. 2-5). 1986. pap. 3.50 (*0-440-45110-8*, YB) Dell.

—Three Wishes. (ps-3). 1994. pap. 4.99 (*0-440-40921-7*) Dell.

Cline, Don. Antrim & Billy. Metz, Leon, intro. by. LC 90-1598. (Illus.). 170p. 1990. 21.95 (*0-932702-48-1*) Creative Texas.

Clymer, E. The Spider, the Cave, & the Pottery Bowl. 80p. (gr. k-6). 1989. pap. 2.99 (*0-440-40166-6*, YB) Dell.

Clymer, Eleanor. Luke Was There. (gr. 4-6). 1992. 16.00 (*0-8446-6599-1*) Peter Smith.

Coburn, John B. Anne & the Sand Dobbies. LC 86-12650. 121p. (gr. 7-12). 1986. pap. 8.95 (*0-8192-1354-3*) Morehouse Pub.

Cockenpot, Marianne. Eugenio. (gr. 4-7). 1994. 15.95 (*0-316-14922-5*) Little.

Cohen, Barbara. Headless Roommate. (gr. 7-12). 1987. pap. 2.25 (*0-553-26679-9*) Bantam.

—The Long Way Home. Cohen, Barbara, illus. 1992. pap. 3.50 (*0-553-15984-4*) Bantam.

—Make a Wish, Molly. Jones, Jan N., illus. LC 93-17901. 1994. 14.95 (*0-385-31079-X*) Delacorte.

—Tell Us Your Secret. 1989. 13.95 (*0-553-05810-X*, Starfire) Bantam.

—Thank You, Jackie Robinson. Cuffari, Richard, illus. LC 87-29341. (gr. 3-6). 1988. PLB 15.00 (*0-688-07909-1*) Lothrop.

Cohen, Miriam. It's George. (gr. k-6). 1989. pap. 3.25 (*0-440-40198-4*) Dell.

—Liar, Liar, Pants on Fire! (gr. k-6). 1987. pap. 3.25 (*0-440-44755-0*, YB) Dell.

—Second Grade Friends. 1993. pap. 2.75 (*0-590-47463-4*) Scholastic Inc.

—Second Grade-Friends Again! (ps-3). 1994. pap. 2.95 (*0-590-45906-6*) Scholastic Inc.

—So What? (gr. k-6). 1988. pap. 3.25 (*0-440-40048-1*, YB) Dell.

Cole. Big Goof & Little Goof. 1992. pap. 3.95 (*0-590-41592-1*) Scholastic Inc.

Cole, Babette. Prince Cinders. Cole, Babette, illus. 32p. (ps-3). 1992. pap. 5.95 (*0-399-21882-3*, Sandcastle Bks) Putnam Pub Group.

Cole, Brock. Celine. 224p. (gr. 7 up). 1991. pap. 3.95 (*0-374-41082-8*, Sunburst) FS&G.

Cole, Joanna. Bully Trouble. Hafner, Marilyn, illus. LC 89-3757. 48p. (Orig.). (gr. 1-3). 1989. lib. bdg. 7.99 (*0-394-94949-8*); pap. 3.50 (*0-394-84949-3*) Random Bks Yng Read.

—The Missing Tooth. Hafner, Marilyn, illus. LC 88-1903. 48p. (Orig.). (gr. 1-3). 1988. lib. bdg. 7.99 (*0-394-99279-2*); pap. 3.50 (*0-394-89279-8*) Random Bks Yng Read.

Coleman, Nancy, et al. Hopes, Dreams & Wishes, 3 bks. Duris, Ellen, illus. 72p. (Orig.). (ps-k). 1991. pap. 8.95 Set (*0-8249-7419-0*, Ideals Child) Hambleton-Hill.

Conford, Ellen. Anything for a Friend. LC 78-27843. (gr. 3-7). 1979. 14.95 (*0-316-15308-7*) Little.

—Anything for a Friend. (gr. 4-7). 1992. pap. 3.50 (*0-553-48081-2*) Bantam.

—Why Me? 156p. (gr. 5 up). 1985. 14.95 (*0-316-15326-5*) Little.

Conrad, Pam. Holding Me Here. LC 85-45254. 192p. (gr. 7 up). 1986. PLB 11.89 (*0-06-021339-6*) HarpC Child Bks.

Cooney, Caroline B. Among Friends. 176p. (gr. 6 up). 1987. 13.95 (*0-553-05446-5*, Starfire) Bantam.

—Stranger. 1993. pap. 3.50 (*0-590-45680-6*) Scholastic Inc.

Cooney, Linda A. Breaking Away. 224p. 1991. pap. 2.95 (*0-590-44561-8*) Scholastic Inc.

—Playing Games. 1992. pap. 2.95 (*0-590-44565-0*, Point) Scholastic Inc.

Cooney, Linda A. & Cooney, Kevin. Making Changes. 176p. 1992. pap. 2.95 (*0-590-44563-4*) Scholastic Inc.

—Standing Alone. 176p. 1991. pap. 2.95 (*0-590-44562-6*) Scholastic Inc.

Cooper, Ilene. Choosing Sides. LC 89-13669. 224p. (gr. 4-7). 1990. 12.95 (*0-688-07934-2*) Morrow Jr Bks.

—Mean Streak. 192p. (gr. 3-7). 1992. pap. 3.99 (*0-14-034978-2*, Puffin) Puffin Bks.

—Trick or Trouble. (gr. 4 up). 1994. write for info. Viking Penguin.

Cooperman, Jeff & Salvadeo, Michele B. Waiting. (Illus.). 48p. (gr. 3-5). 1994. pap. 6.95 (*1-56721-062-7*) Twnty-Fifth Cent Pr.

Corcoran, Barbara. You Put up with Me, I'll Put up with You. 176p. (gr. 3-7). 1989. pap. 2.50 (*0-380-70558-3*, Camelot) Avon.

Corey, Deirdre. Friends 'til the Ocean Waves. 128p. (gr. 3-7). 1990. pap. 2.75 (*0-590-44028-4*) Scholastic Inc.

—Friends 'til the Thunder Claps. 144p. 1992. pap. 2.75 (*0-590-45112-X*, Apple Paperbacks) Scholastic Inc.

—Mysteriously Yours. (gr. 4-7). 1991. pap. 2.75 (*0-590-44030-6*, Apple Paperbacks) Scholastic Inc.

Cormier, Michael J. A Second Thought. Milone, Karen, illus. LC 91-41619. 32p. (gr. 2-6). 1992. PLB 19.97 (*0-8114-3578-4*) Raintree Steck-V.

Cormier, Robert. Other Bells For Us to Ring. 1990. 15.00 (*0-385-30245-2*) Delacorte.

—Take Me Where the Good Times Are. 1991. pap. 3.99 (*0-440-21096-8*, YB) Dell.

Cornish, Linda. Pong's Vists. LC 92-61596. (Illus.). 44p. (gr. k-3). 1993. 6.95 (*1-55523-565-4*) Winston-Derek.

Cosgrove, Stephen. Morgan Morning. James, Robin, illus. 32p. (Orig.). (gr. 1-4). 1982. pap. 2.95 (*0-8431-0591-7*) Price Stern.

—Raz-Ma-Taz. James, Robin, illus. 32p. (Orig.). (gr. 1-4). 1982. pap. 2.95 (*0-8431-0588-7*) Price Stern.

Cosgrove, Stephen & Cosgrove, Stephen. Morgan & Yew. James, Robin, illus. 32p. (Orig.). (gr. 1-4). 1982. pap. 3.95 (*0-8431-0589-5*) Price Stern.

Cosgrove, Stephen E. Hannah & Hickory. Edelson, Wendy, illus. 32p. (ps-3). 1990. PLB 14.95 (*0-89565-664-7*) Childs World.

—Persimmony. Edelson, Wendy, illus. 32p. (ps-3). 1990. PLB 14.95 (*0-89565-661-2*) Childs World.

Cossi, Olga. Adventure on the Graveyard of the Wrecks. LC 90-20686. 144p. (Orig.). (gr. 9-12). 1991. pap. 6.95 (*0-88289-808-6*) Pelican.

Cote, Nancy. Palm Trees. Cote, Nancy, illus. LC 92-18938. 40p. (ps-2). 1993. RSBE 14.95 (*0-02-724760-0*, Four Winds) Macmillan Child Grp.

Couch, Donna E. The Photograph. Kuchukian, J. Angele, illus. 40p. (gr. 1-6). 1992. 10.00g (*0-9634359-0-6*) Seabright Pr.

Craig, Janet A. Valentine's Day Mess. Morse, Debby, illus. LC 93-2211. 32p. (gr. k-2). 1993. PLB 11.59 (*0-8167-3254-X*); pap. text ed. 2.95 (*0-8167-3255-8*) Troll Assocs.

Craig, Lynn. New Friends in New Places. LC 94-1929. 1994. pap. 4.99 (*0-8407-9239-5*) Nelson.

—Summer of Choices. LC 94-4504. 1994. pap. 4.99 (*0-8407-9241-7*) Nelson.

Crawford, Diane M. Comedy of Errors. (gr. 4-7). 1992. pap. 2.99 (*0-553-29457-1*) Bantam.

Creech, Sharon. Walk Two Moons. LC 93-31277. 288p. (gr. 3-7). 1994. 16.00 (*0-06-023334-6*); PLB 15.89 (*0-06-023337-0*) HarpC Child Bks.

Cresswell, Helen. The Watchers: A Mystery at Alton Towers. LC 93-41683. (gr. 3-7). 1994. 14.95 (*0-02-725371-6*, Macmillan Child Bk) Macmillan Child Grp.

Cristaldi, Kathryn. Samantha the Snob: A Step 2 Book. Brunkus, Denise, illus. LC 93-19649. 48p. (Orig.). (gr. 1-3). 1994. 7.99 (*0-679-94640-3*); pap. 3.50 (*0-679-84640-9*) Random Bks Yng Read.

Croll, Carolyn. Too Many Babas. newly illus. ed. Croll, Carolyn, illus. LC 92-18779. 64p. (gr. k-4). 1994. pap. 3.50 (*0-06-444168-7*, Trophy) HarpC Child Bks.

Cross, Gillian. Chartbreaker. (gr. k-12). 1989. pap. 2.95 (*0-440-20312-0*, LFL) Dell.

—On the Edge. (gr. k-12). 1987. pap. 2.75 (*0-440-96666-3*, LFL) Dell.

Cross, Molly. Wait for Me! Mathieu, Joe, illus. LC 87-12926. 40p. (ps-3). 1993. pap. 2.99 (*0-679-83952-6*) Random Bks Yng Read.

Cruise, Beth. Kelly's Hero. LC 93-8706. (Illus.). 144p. (gr. 5 up). 1993. pap. 2.95 (*0-02-042769-7*, Collier Young Ad) Macmillan Child Grp.

Cullen, Lynn. The Backyard Ghost. LC 92-24580. 160p. (gr. 4-7). 1993. 13.95 (*0-395-64527-1*, Clarion Bks) HM.

Cummings, Carol. Sticks & Stones. Howatson, Melody, illus. 24p. (Orig.). (ps-3). 1992. pap. 4.99 (*0-9614574-8-1*) Teaching WA.

Cummings, Priscilla. Oswald & the Timberdoodles. Cohen, A. R., illus. LC 90-70723. 30p. (gr. k-5). 1990. 8.95 (*0-87033-411-5*) Tidewater.

Cusick, Richie T. Help Wanted. 224p. (Orig.). (gr. 7 up). 1993. pap. 3.99 (*0-671-79403-5*, Archway) PB.

Cuyler. Daisy Crazy Thanks. 1991. 14.95 (*0-8050-1557-4*) H Holt & Co.

Cuyler, Margery. From Here to There. 1994. write for info. (*0-8050-3191-X*) H Holt & Co.

Dahl, Roald. George's Marvelous Medicine. (gr. 2-4). 1987. pap. 2.75 (*0-553-15394-3*, Skylark) Bantam.

Dale. The Ivy. 1993. pap. 28.67 (*0-590-50128-3*) Scholastic Inc.

Dalton, Annie. The Real Tilly Beany. large type ed. Aldous, Kate, illus. 1993. 16.95 (*0-7451-1807-0*, Galaxy Child Lrg Print) Chivers N Amer.

Damon, Valerie H. Willo Mancifoot (and the Mugga Killa Whomps) Damon, Dave, ed. LC 83-50739. (Illus.). (gr. 2-6). 1985. 14.95 (*0-932356-07-9*); ltd. art ed. 100. 00 (*0-932356-08-7*) Star Pubns Mo.

Dana, Barbara. Zucchini. Christelow, Eileen, illus. 160p. (gr. 3-6). 1984. pap. 2.95 (*0-553-15437-0*, Skylark) Bantam.

Dana, Maggie. If Wishes Were Horses. Ruff, Donna, illus. LC 87-16201. 128p. (gr. 4-8). 1988. PLB 9.89 (*0-8167-1197-6*); pap. text ed. 2.95 (*0-8167-1198-4*) Troll Assocs.

—Jumping into Trouble. Ruff, Donna, illus. LC 87-16248. 128p. (gr. 4-8). 1988. PLB 9.89 (*0-8167-1193-3*); pap. text ed. 2.95 (*0-8167-1194-1*) Troll Assocs.

—No Time for Secrets. Ruff, Donna, illus. LC 87-19027. 128p. (gr. 4-8). 1988. PLB 9.89 (*0-8167-1191-7*); pap. text ed. 2.95 (*0-8167-1192-5*) Troll Assocs.

—Racing for the Stars. Ruff, Donna, illus. LC 87-16246. 128p. (gr. 4-8). 1988. PLB 9.89 (*0-8167-1195-X*); pap. text ed. 2.95 (*0-8167-1196-8*) Troll Assocs.

Danziger, Paula. Amber Brown Is Not a Crayon. Ross, Tony, illus. LC 92-34678. 80p. (gr. 1-4). 1994. 11.95 (*0-399-22509-9*, Putnam) Putnam Pub Group.

—Make Like a Tree & Leave. large type ed. (gr. 1-8). 1993. 16.95 (*0-7451-1912-3*, Galaxy Child Lrg Print) Chivers N Amer.

—Not for a Billion Gazillion Dollars. (gr. 4-7). 1994. pap. 3.99 (*0-440-40919-5*) Dell.

Danzinger, Paula. Make Like a Tree & Leave. (gr. 4-7). 1992. pap. 3.50 (*0-440-40577-7*) Dell.

Davidson, Doud P. Along the Endless Strip. 225p. (Orig.). 1992. pap. text ed. 5.95 (*0-9630884-2-4*) Team Effort.

Davidson, Linda. Fast Forward. (gr. 10 up). 1989. pap. 2.95 (*0-8041-0246-5*) Ivy Books.

Davis, Allison. Sesame Street: Imagine, a Wish for Grover. (ps-3). 1994. pap. 2.25 (*0-307-13130-0*, Golden Pr) Western Pub.

Davis, Gibbs. Swann Song. 176p. (gr. 7 up). 1989. pap. 2.50 (*0-380-75609-9*, Flare) Avon.

Davis, Russell B. & Ashabranner, Brent K. The Choctaw Code. (Illus.). 152p. (gr. 3-6). 1994. Repr. of 1961 ed. lib. bdg. 16.00 (*0-208-02377-1*, Pub. by Linnet) Shoe String.

Day, Alexandra. Frank & Ernest. Day, Alexandra, illus. 1991. pap. 3.95 (*0-590-41556-5*, Blue Ribbon Bks) Scholastic Inc.

Dean, Karen S. Cammy Takes a Bow. (gr. 3-7). 1988. pap. 2.50 (*0-380-75400-2*, Camelot) Avon.

Deaver, Julie R. First Wedding, Once Removed. LC 90-4184. 224p. (gr. 5-9). 1990. PLB 13.89 (*0-06-021427-9*) HarpC Child Bks.

DeClements, Barthe. Nothing's Fair in Fifth Grade. LC 80-54195. 144p. (gr. 3-7). 1981. pap. 12.95 (*0-670-51741-0*) Viking Child Bks.

Deem, James M. Three NBs of Julian Drew. LC 93-39306. 1994. 14.95 (*0-395-69453-1*) HM.

Deeter, Catherine. Seymour Bleu: A Space Odyssey. LC 92-24525. (Illus.). 32p. (ps-3). Date not set. 15.00 (*0-06-021524-0*); PLB 14.89 (*0-06-021525-9*) HarpC Child Bks.

Degen, Bruce. Jamberry. (ps-3). 1983. PLB 13.89 (*0-06-021417-1*) HarpC Child Bks.

De Goscinny, Rene & Uderzo, M. Obelix et Compagnie. (FRE., Illus.). 1990. 19.95 (*0-8288-5479-3*) Fr & Eur.

De la Mare, Walter. Visitors. LC 86-6244. 40p. (gr. 4 up). 1986. PLB 13.95s.p. (*0-88682-070-7*) Creative Ed.
Delton, Judy. Angel in Charge. (gr. k-6). 1990. pap. 2.95 (*0-440-40264-6*, YB) Dell.
—Angel's Mother's Boyfriend. Apple, Margot, illus. LC 82-27054. 176p. (gr. 2-5). 1986. 14.95 (*0-395-39968-8*) HM.
—Blue Skies, French Fries. 80p. (Orig.). (gr. k-6). 1988. pap. 3.25 (*0-440-40064-3*, YB) Dell.
—Merry Merry Huckleberry. Tiegreen, Alan, illus. (Orig.). 1990. pap. 2.95 (*0-440-40365-0*, Pub. by Yearling Classics) Dell.
—The Pee Wee Jubilee. (gr. k-6). 1989. pap. 3.25 (*0-440-40226-3*, YB) Dell.
—The Perfect Christmas Gift. McCue, Lisa, illus. LC 91-6549. 32p. (gr. k-3). 1992. RSBE 13.95 (*0-02-728471-9*, Macmillan Child Bk) Macmillan Child Grp.
—Rabbit's New Rug. Brown, Marc, illus. LC 93-15453. 1993. 13.27 (*0-8368-0972-6*) Gareth Stevens Inc.
—Rosy Noses, Freezing Toes. Tiegreen, Alan, illus. (Orig.). 1990. pap. 3.25 (*0-440-40384-7*, YB) Dell.
—Scary, Scary Huckleberry. Tiegreen, Alan, illus. (Orig.). (gr. k-6). 1990. pap. 2.95 (*0-440-40336-7*, YB) Dell.
De Maupassant, Guy. Two Friends. Redpath, Ann, ed. Delessert, Etienne, illus. 32p. (gr. 4 up). 1985. PLB 13.95 (*0-88682-003-0*) Creative Ed.
Demou, Doris B. More to Give. Meredith, Mary, ed. (Orig.). 1991. pap. 6.00 (*0-685-40721-7*) Doris Demou.
De Paola, Tomie. Bill & Pete. (ps-1). 1992. pap. 5.95 (*0-399-22402-5*, Sandcastle Bks) Putnam Pub Group.
—Bill & Pete Go Down the Nile. De Paola, Tomie, illus. 32p. (ps-1). 1987. 14.95 (*0-399-21395-3*, Putnam) Putnam Pub Group.
DePaolo, Paula. Rosie & the Yellow Ribbon. Wolf, Janet, illus. 32p. (ps-3). 1992. 14.95 (*0-316-18100-5*, Joy St Bks) Little.

Derby, Janice. Are You My Friend? Keenan, Joy D., illus. 40p. (ps-3). 1993. 12.95 (*0-8361-3609-8*) Herald Pr. The expressive watercolors of Joy Dunn Keenan dance across these pages as a boy & his grandfather spend a day at the park. Throughout the day they meet many people & the boy observes how they are different from him. He also notices that they are like him in the things they enjoy seeing & doing. He asks each one, "Are you my friend?" At the end, all the friends gather at the carousel. This book written by Janice Derby allows children to acknowledge characteristics such as language, skin color, being physically or mentally challenged, or having a different economic status that can separate us. By observing that others enjoy the same kinds of activities, children learn that the differences are minor compared to the many similarities we share. For children ages 4-to-8 & the adults who love them.
Publisher Provided Annotation.

De Regniers, Beatrice S. Going for a Walk. newly illus ed. Knox, Robert, illus. LC 91-43177. 32p. (ps-1). 1993. 15.00 (*0-06-022954-3*); PLB 14.89 (*0-06-022957-8*) HarpC Child Bks.
—How Joe the Bear & Sam the Mouse Got Together. Myers, Bernice, illus. LC 89-12110. 32p. (ps-2). 1990. 12.95 (*0-688-09079-6*); lib. bdg. 12.88 (*0-688-09080-X*) Lothrop.
—A Week in the Life of Best Friends: And Other Poems of Friendship. Doyle, Nancy, illus. LC 85-28680. 48p. (gr. 3-7). 1986. SBE 13.95 (*0-689-31179-6*, Atheneum Child Bk) Macmillan Child Grp.
De Trevino, Elizabeth B. Yo, Juan de Pareja. Borton, Enrique R. Trevino, tr. from ENG. (SPA.). 192p. (gr. 12 up). 1994. 16.00 (*0-374-38699-4*) FS&G.
Deuker, Carl. Heart of a Champion. LC 92-37231. 1993. 15.95 (*0-316-18166-8*, Joy St Bks) Little.
Devlin, Harry & Devlin, Wende. Cranberry Moving Day. LC 93-36279. (ps-1). 1994. pap. 2.95 (*0-689-71777-6*) MacMillan Child Grp.
Devlin, Wende & Devlin, Harry. Cranberry Valentine. Devlin, Wende & Devlin, Harry, illus. LC 85-24047. 32p. (gr. k-3). 1986. SBE 14.95 (*0-02-729200-2*, Four Winds) Macmillan Child Grp.
Dickinson, Peter. Heartease. (gr. 7 up). 1988. pap. 2.95 (*0-317-69490-1*, LFL) Dell.
Dines, Carol. Best Friends Tell the Best Lies. LC 88-29433. (gr. 7 up). 1989. 14.95 (*0-385-29704-1*) Delacorte.
Disney Famous Friends. (gr. 2 up). 1991. pap. 1.97 (*1-56297-122-0*) Lee Pubns KY.
Dobkin, Bonnie. Collecting. (Illus.). 32p. (ps-2). 1993. PLB 10.25 (*0-516-02015-3*); pap. 2.95 (*0-516-42015-1*) Childrens.
—Everybody Says. (Illus.). 32p. (ps-2). 1993. PLB 10.25 (*0-516-02019-6*); pap. 2.95 (*0-516-42019-4*) Childrens.
—Just a Little Different. Martin, Clovis, illus. LC 93-13024. 32p. (ps-2). 1994. PLB 13.80 (*0-516-02018-8*); pap. 2.95 (*0-516-42018-6*) Childrens.
Dodd, Lynley. Hairy Maclary's Bone. Dodd, Lynley, illus. LC 85-9772. 32p. (gr. 1-2). 1985. PLB 17.27 (*0-918831-06-7*) Gareth Stevens Inc.
—Slinky Malinki. Dodd, Lynley, illus. LC 90-44686. 32p. (gr. 1-2). 1991. PLB 17.27 (*0-8368-0197-0*) Gareth Stevens Inc.
Dodson, Susan. Shadows Across the Sand. (gr. 7 up). 1984. pap. 2.25 (*0-449-70114-X*, Juniper) Fawcett.
Doherty, Berlie. Willa & Old Miss Annie. Lewis, Kim, illus. LC 93-970. 96p. (gr. 3-6). 1994. 14.95 (*1-56402-331-1*) Candlewick Pr.
Doray, Andrea. Friends. Gress, Jonna, ed. LC 92-72842. (Illus.). 12p. (ps-2). 1992. pap. text ed. 14.25 (*0-944943-13-6*, CODE 19723-6) Current Inc.
Dubanevich, Arlene. Pig William. Dubanevich, Arlene, illus. LC 85-5776. 32p. (ps-2). 1985. RSBE 14.95 (*0-02-733200-4*, Bradbury Pr) Macmillan Child Grp.
Dudko, Mary A. & Larsen, Margie. BJ's Fun Week. Full, Dennis, photos by. LC 94-72001. (Illus.). 20p. (ps-k). 1994. bds. 3.95 (*1-57064-015-7*) Barney Pub.
Dugan, Barbara. Loop the Loop. Stevenson, James P., illus. LC 92-40168. 32p. (ps-3). 1993. pap. 4.99 (*0-14-054904-8*, Puffin) Puffin Bks.
Dunbar, Joyce. Seven Sillies. (ps-3). 1994. 13.95 (*0-307-17504-9*, Artsts Writrs) Western Pub.
Dunlop, Eileen. Finn's Search. LC 93-44880. 128p. (gr. 5-9). 1994. 14.95 (*0-8234-1099-4*) Holiday.
Dunrea, Olivier. Mogwogs on the March. Dunrea, Olivier, illus. LC 85-5493. 32p. (ps-1). 1985. pap. 5.95 (*0-8234-0845-0*) Holiday.
Dunster, Mark. Doricio. 11p. (Orig.). 1989. pap. 4.00 (*0-89642-170-8*) Linden Pubs.
Duplex, Mary. Trouble with a Capital T. 96p. 1992. pap. 7.95 (*0-8163-1057-2*) Pacific Pr Pub Assn.
Dygard, Thomas J. Backfield Package. LC 93-7721. 208p. (gr. 5 up). 1993. pap. 3.99 (*0-14-036348-3*, Puffin) Puffin Bks.
Echewa, T. Obinkaram. The Ancestor Tree. Hale, Christy, illus. 32p. (gr. k-3). 1994. 13.99 (*0-525-67467-5*, Lodestar Bks) Dutton Child Bks.
Edens, Cooper. With Secret Friends. LC 91-23642. (Illus.). 48p. (gr. 7-12). 1992. signed & numbered 20.00 (*0-671-75593-5*, Green Tiger); pap. 8.00 (*0-671-74970-6*, Green Tiger) S&S Trade.
Edwards, Michelle. Eve & Smithy. LC 92-44166. (gr. 4 up). 1995. 15.00 (*0-688-11825-9*); lib. bdg. 14.93 (*0-688-11826-7*) Lothrop.
Effinger, Marta. Bunker & Me: Summer Adventures of Best Friends, Vol. I. Lawrence & Penny, ed. Effinger, Michael, illus. Washington, Pat, intro. by. (Illus.). 30p. (gr. 3-5). 1990. 12.95x (*0-929917-02-2*) Magnolia PA.
Eggleston, Edward. Mister Blake's Walking Stick. 1988. Repr. of 1870 ed. lib. bdg. 59.00x (*0-7812-1170-0*) Rprt Serv.
Ehrlich, Amy. Leo, Zack & Emmie. Kellogg, Steven, illus. LC 81-2604. 64p. (ps-3). 1981. PLB 9.89 (*0-8037-4761-6*) Dial Bks Young.
—Leo, Zack & Emmie. Kellogg, Steven, illus. 64p. (ps-3). 1981. pap. 4.95 (*0-8037-4760-8*, Dial Easy to Read) Puffin Bks.
—Leo, Zack & Emmie Together Again. LC 86-16810. (Illus.). 56p. (ps-3). 1987. 9.95 (*0-8037-0381-3*); PLB 9.89 (*0-8037-0382-1*) Dial Bks Young.
—Leo, Zack, & Emmie Together Again. LC 86-16810. (Illus.). 56p. (ps-3). 1990. pap. 3.95 (*0-8037-0837-8*) Dial Bks Young.
Eisenberg, Lisa & Hall, Katy. Quickie Comebacks. 1992. pap. 1.95 (*0-590-44998-2*) Scholastic Inc.
Eitan, Ora. A Veces Grande, a Veces Pequeno. Writer, C. C. & Nielsen, Lisa C., trs. Elchanan, illus. (SPA.). 24p. (Orig.). (ps). 1992. pap. text ed. 3.00x (*1-56134-149-5*) Dushkin Pub.
Elliott, Paula. Fluffy & Sparky: A Story about True Buddies. Royall, Sandy, illus. 32p. (ps up). 1991. 12.95 (*1-879052-00-8*) Planetary Pubns.
Ellis, Jana. Never Stop Smiling. LC 88-12390. 160p. (gr. 7 up). 1988. pap. text ed. 2.50 (*0-8167-1360-X*) Troll Assocs.
Ellis, Sarah. Next-Door Neighbors. LC 89-37923. 160p. (gr. 4-7). 1990. SBE 13.95 (*0-689-50495-0*, M K McElderry) Macmillan Child Grp.
—Next-Door Neighbors. (gr. 4-7). 1992. pap. 3.25 (*0-440-40620-X*) Dell.
Endersby, Frank. Let's Talk Together. (Illus.). 32p. (ps-k). 1993. 15.95 (*0-460-88059-4*, Pub. by J M Dent & Sons) Trafalgar.
Engel, Diana. The Shelf-Paper Jungle. Engel, Diana, illus. LC 93-21772. 32p. (gr. k-3). 1994. pap. 14.95 RSBE (*0-02-733464-3*, Macmillan Child Bk) Macmillan Child Grp.
Enright, Elizabeth. The Saturdays. Enright, Elizabeth, illus. LC 41-30925. 196p. (gr. 4-6). 1988. 12.95 (*0-8050-0291-X*, Bks Young Read) H Holt & Co.
Erickson, Gina C. & Foster, Kelli C. Jeepers, Creepers. Gifford, Kerri, illus. 24p. (ps-3). 1994. pap. 3.50 (*0-8120-1841-9*) Barron.
Erickson, Russell E. A Toad for Tuesday. Di Fiori, Lawrence, photos by. LC 92-24595. (Illus.). 64p. (gr. 3 up). 1993. pap. 3.95 (*0-688-12276-0*, Pub. by Beech Tree Bks) Morrow.
Eriksson, Ake. Joel, Jesper, & Julia. Eriksson, Ake, illus. LC 89-25116. 32p. (ps-4). 1990. PLB 18.95 (*0-87614-419-9*) Carolrhoda Bks.
Escudie, Rene. Paul & Sebastian. Townley, Roderick, tr. from FRE. Wensell, Ulises, illus. LC 88-12768. 32p. (ps-3). 1988. 11.95 (*0-916291-19-7*) Kane-Miller Bk.
—Paul & Sebastian. (Illus.). 48p. (gr. 3-8). 1990. 8.95 (*0-89565-806-2*) Childs World.
Estes, Eleanor. Los Cien Vestidos. Mlawer, Teresa, tr. from ENG. Slobodkin, Louis, illus. (SPA.). 80p. (gr. 4). 1993. 13.95 (*1-880507-06-4*) Lectorum Pubns.
Ethridge, Kenneth E. Toothpick. LC 85-42883. 128p. (gr. 7 up). 1985. 13.95 (*0-8234-0585-0*) Holiday.
Evans, Sanford. Naomi's Geese. Chabrian, Deborah, illus. LC 92-44109. (gr. 5 up). 1993. pap. 15.00 (*0-671-75623-0*, S&S BFYR) S&S Trade.
Faber, Adele & Mazlish, Elaine. Bobby & the Brockles Go to School. Morehouse, Hank, illus. LC 93-42884. 64p. (Orig.). 1994. pap. 15.00 (*0-380-77068-7*) Avon.
Fabian, Margaret W. My Friend Luke, the Stenciller. Fabian, Margaret W., illus. LC 83-50689. 35p. (gr. 3-4). 1987. pap. 8.95 over boards (*0-931474-25-6*) TBW Bks.
Fabian, Stella. The Opal Mystery. LC 90-83465. (Illus.). 192p. (Orig.). (gr. 3-7). 1991. pap. 3.25 (*0-922434-39-5*) Brighton & Lloyd.
Farnette, Cherrie, et al. People Need Each Other. rev. ed. 80p. (gr. 4-7). 1989. pap. text ed. 7.95 (*0-86530-070-4*, IP 63-3) Incentive Pubns.
Farrar, Susan C. Samantha on Stage. Sanderson, Ruth, illus. 164p. (gr. 3 up). 1990. pap. 3.95 (*0-14-034328-8*, Puffin) Puffin Bks.
Farrington, Liz & Weil, Jennifer C. And Peter Said Goodbye. Scardova, Jaclyne, illus. Farrington, Liz, created by. LC 92-35977. (Illus.). 40p. (gr. k-4). 1993. 14.95 (*1-56844-000-6*) Enchante Pub.
Fassler, Joan. The Boy with a Problem: Johnny Learns to Share His Troubles. LC 78-147125. (Illus.). 32p. (ps-3). 1971. 16.95 (*0-87705-054-6*) Human Sci Pr.
The Fastest One of All. (Illus.). (ps-2). 1991. PLB 6.95 (*0-8136-5141-7*, TK3399); pap. 3.50 (*0-8136-5641-9*, TK3400) Modern Curr.
Feinberg, Anna. Wiggy & Boa. James, Ann, illus. 112p. (gr. 3-7). 1990. 13.95 (*0-395-53704-5*) HM.
Feldman, Eve. We Are Friends. (Illus.). 32p. (gr. 1-4). 1989. PLB 18.99 (*0-8172-3517-5*); pap. 3.95 (*0-8114-6716-3*) Raintree Steck-V.
Feldman, Eve B. That Cat! Ransome, James E., illus. LC 94-280. 1994. write for info. (*0-688-13310-X*, Tambourine Bks) Morrow.
Fender, Kay. Odette: A Springtime in Paris. Dumas, Philippe, illus. 32p. (ps-3). 1991. 10.95 (*0-916291-33-2*) Kane-Miller Bk.
Ferguson, Alane. Overkill. 176p. (gr. 5 up). 1994. pap. 3.99 (*0-380-72167-8*) Avon.
Ferris, Jean. Across the Grain. 212p. 1990. 15.00 (*0-374-30030-5*) FS&G.
—The Stainless Steel Rule. LC 85-45731. 192p. (gr. 7 up). 1986. 15.00 (*0-374-37212-8*) FS&G.
Ferry, Charles. Raspberry One. LC 82-25476. 224p. (gr. 7 up). 1983. 13.45 (*0-395-34069-1*) HM.
Fienberg, Anna. The Hottest Boy Who Ever Lived. Grant, Christy, ed. Gamble, Kim, illus. LC 94-6648. 32p. (gr. k-3). 1994. PLB 14.95 (*0-8075-3387-4*) A Whitman.
Find Simba. 10p. 1994. 6.98 (*1-57082-143-7*) Mouse Works.
Fitch, Janet. Kicks. LC 94-18592. Date not set. write for info. (*0-395-69624-0*, Clarion) HM.
Fleischman, Sid. The Scarebird. Sis, Peter, illus. LC 93-11726. 32p. (ps up). 1994. pap. 4.95 (*0-688-13105-0*, Mulberry) Morrow.
Fobes, Jacqueline. A Papago Boy & His Friends. (gr. 1-4). 1980. pap. 1.50 (*0-686-32641-5*) Impresora Sahuaro.
Fontenot, Mary A. Clovis Crawfish & the Curious Crapaud. Kidder, Christine, illus. LC 86-4997. 32p. (ps-3). 1986. 12.95 (*0-88289-610-5*) Pelican.
Foreman, Mary M., tr. from ENG. Encuentralo con Elena. King, Ed, illus. (SPA.). 24p. 1992. pap. 3.95 (*1-56288-238-4*) Checkerboard.
—Paseate con Paco. King, Ed, illus. (SPA.). 24p. 1929. pap. 3.95 (*1-56288-240-6*) Checkerboard.
Fosburgh, Liza. Bella Arabella. 112p. 1987. pap. 2.50 (*0-553-15484-2*, Skylark) Bantam.
The Fox & the Hound. 96p. 1988. 6.98 (*1-57082-038-4*) Mouse Works.
Fox, Paula. Lily & the Lost Boy. (gr. k-6). 1989. pap. 3.99 (*0-440-40235-2*, YB) Dell.
—Place Apart. 1993. pap. 3.95 (*0-374-45868-5*) FS&G.
Freeman, Don. Corduroy. Freeman, Don, illus. (gr. k-3). 1982. incl. cass. 19.95 (*0-941078-08-6*); pap. 12.95 incl. cass. (*0-941078-06-X*); user's guide incl. 4 pbs. & cass. 27.95 (*0-941078-07-8*) Live Oak Media.
—Corduroy: Edicion Espanola. (Illus.). 32p. (ps-3). 1990. pap. 4.50 (*0-14-054252-3*, Puffin) Puffin Bks.
—Corduroy: (Edicion Espanola) Freeman, Don, illus. (SPA.). (ps-3). 1990. incl. cass. 19.95 (*0-87499-192-7*); pap. 12.95 incl. cass. (*0-87499-213-3*); Set; incl. 4 bks., guide, & cass. pap. 27.95 (*0-87499-193-5*) Live Oak Media.
—Mop Top. Freeman, Don, illus. (gr. k-3). 1982. incl. cass. 19.95 (*0-941078-14-0*); pap. 12.95 incl. cass. (*0-941078-12-4*); user's guide incl. 6 pbs. & cass. 27.95 (*0-941078-13-2*) Live Oak Media.
—A Pocket for Corduroy. Freeman, Don, illus. (gr. k-3). 1982. incl. cass. 19.95 (*0-941078-17-5*); pap. 12.95 incl. cass. (*0-941078-15-9*); user's guide incl. 4 pbs. & cass. 27.95 (*0-941078-16-7*) Live Oak Media.

—A Rainbow of My Own. Freeman, Don, illus. (gr. k-3). 1982. incl. cass. 19.95 (0-941078-20-5); pap. 12.95 incl. cass. (0-941078-18-3); user's guide incl. 4 pbs. & cass. 27.95 (0-941078-19-1) Live Oak Media.

Freeman, Lydia. Corduroy's Day. McCue, Lisa, illus. LC 84-40477. 14p. (ps). 1985. pap. 3.99 (0-670-80521-1) Viking Child Bks.

French, Michael. Us Against Them. (gr. 7-12). 1989. pap. 2.95 (0-553-27647-6, Starfire) Bantam.

—Us Against Them. 1987. 13.95 (0-553-05440-6) Bantam.

Friends in Fern Hollow. (Illus.). (ps). 1985. bds. 1.49 (0-318-45846-2) Random Hse Value.

Fritz, Jean. Early Thunder. Ward, Lynd, illus. (gr. 5-9). 1987. pap. 4.99 (0-14-032259-0, Puffin) Puffin Bks.

Frost, Robert. You Come Too. Nason, Thomas W., illus. Hyde, Cox, frwd. by. LC 59-12940. (Illus.). 96p. (gr. 4-6). 1988. 14.95 (0-8050-0299-5, Bks Young Read); pap. 6.95 (0-8050-0316-9) H Holt & Co.

Fryar, Jane. The Locked-In Friend. Wilson, Deborah, illus. 32p. (ps-2). 1991. 7.99 (0-570-04195-3) Concordia.

Futcher, Jane. Promise Not to Tell. 192p. (Orig.). (gr. 4-5). 1991. pap. 2.95 (0-380-76037-1, Flare) Avon.

Gabhart, Ann. Only in Sunshine. (gr. 7 up). 1988. pap. 2.95 (0-380-75395-2, Flare) Avon.

—Two of a Kind. (gr. 4-7). 1992. pap. 3.50 (0-380-76153-X, Camelot) Avon.

Gackenbach, Dick. What's Claude Doing? LC 83-14983. (Illus.). 32p. (ps-3). 1986. pap. 4.95 (0-89919-464-8, Clarion Bks) HM.

Gaeddart, LouAnn. Your Former Friend, Matthew. 80p. 1985. pap. 2.25 (0-553-15345-5, Skylark) Bantam.

Galbraith, Kathryn O. Roommates Again. Graham, Mark, illus. LC 93-8709. 48p. (ps-2). 1994. SBE 14.95 (0-689-50592-2, M K McElderry) Macmillan Child Grp.

—Roommates Again. Graham, Mark, illus. LC 93-8709. 48p. (gr. 1-4). 1994. SBE 12.95 (0-689-50597-3, M K McElderry) Macmillan Child Grp.

Gantschev, Ivan. Good Morning, Good Night. Clements, Andrew, tr. Gantschev, Ivan, illus. LC 91-3603. 28p. (gr. k up). 1991. pap. 14.95 (0-88708-183-5) Picture Bk Studio.

Ganz, Yaffa. Sharing a Sunshine Umbrella: A Mimmy & Simmy Story. Klineman, Harvey, illus. 1989. 9.95 (0-87306-496-8) Feldheim.

Garcia, Maria. The Adventures of Connie & Diego Read-Along. 1988. incl. audiocassette 22.95 (0-89239-033-6) Childrens Book Pr.

Gardner, Theodore R., II. Something Nice to See. Hamlin, Peter, illus. LC 93-61121. 32p. (gr. 1 up). 1994. 15.95 (0-9627297-6-0) A A Knoll Pubs.

Garfield, Leon. Footsteps. (gr. k-6). 1988. pap. 3.25 (0-440-40102-X, YB) Dell.

—Smith. large type ed. (gr. 1-8). 1991. 16.95 (0-7451-0448-7, Galaxy Child Lrg Print) Chivers N Amer.

Garland, Sherry. I Never Knew Your Name. Greenberg, Sheldon, illus. LC 93-23703. 32p. (gr. k-3). 1994. 14. 95 (0-395-69686-0) Ticknor & Fields.

Garrigue, Sheila. The Eternal Spring of Mr. Ito. LC 85-5687. 176p. (gr. 5-7). 1985. SBE 14.95 (0-02-737300-2, Bradbury Pr) Macmillan Child Grp.

Garrigus, Charles B. Chas & the Summer of '26. 322p. (gr. 6-12). 1994. 12.50 (0-9638964-0-7) Cypress Hill.

Gauch, Patricia L. Tanya & Emily in a Dance for Two. Ichikawa, Satomi, illus. LC 93-5354. 40p. (ps-3). 1994. PLB 15.95 (0-399-22688-5, Philomel Bks) Putnam Pub Group.

Gauthier, Bertrand. Zachary in the Winner. Sylvestre, Daniel, illus. LC 93-7718. 1993. 15.93 (0-8368-1009-0) Gareth Stevens Inc.

Gelbart, Ofra. Sonidos Que Oigo. Writer, C. C. & Nielsen, Lisa C., trs. Eagle, Mike, illus. (SPA.). 24p. (Orig.). (ps). 1992. pap. text ed. 3.00x (1-56134-148-7) Dushkin Pub.

Gelbert, Ofra. Otra Cosa. Writer, C. C. & Nielsen, Lisa C., trs. Elchanan, illus. (SPA.). 24p. (Orig.). (ps). 1992. pap. text ed. 3.00x (1-56134-175-4) Dushkin Pub.

Geller, Mark. The Strange Case of the Reluctant Partners. LC 89-29409. 96p. (gr. 5-9). 1990. HarpC Child Bks.

George, Gail. The Popples' Pajama Party. Sustendal, Pat, illus. LC 85-19403. 32p. (ps-3). 1986. pap. 1.95 (0-394-88041-2) Random Bks Yng Read.

Geras, Adele. Pictures of the Night. LC 92-27425. 1993. write for info. (0-15-261588-1) HarBrace.

Gerson, Corinne. Passing Through. 208p. (gr. 8 up). 1980. pap. 1.50 (0-440-96958-1, LFL) Dell.

Gibbs, Bridget. What's in the Bag? 1990. 9.95 (1-55782-333-2, Pub. by Warner Juvenile Bks) Little.

—What's in the Box? 1990. 9.95 (1-55782-334-0, Pub. by Warner Juvenile Bks) Little.

Giff, Patricia R. All about Stacy. Sims, Blanche, illus. 80p. (Orig.). (gr. k-6). 1988. pap. 3.50 (0-440-40088-0, YB) Dell.

—B-E-S-T Friends. 80p. (Orig.). (gr. k-6). 1988. pap. 3.50 (0-440-40090-2, YB) Dell.

—The Candy Corn Contest. 80p. (Orig.). (ps-6). 1984. pap. 3.50 (0-440-41072-X, YB) Dell.

—December Secrets. Sims, Blanche, illus. 80p. (gr. k-6). 1984. pap. 3.50 (0-440-41795-3, YB) Dell.

—Fish Face. Sims, Blanche, illus. 80p. (Orig.). (gr. 1-4). 1984. pap. 3.25 (0-440-42557-3, YB) Dell.

—Love, from the Fifth-Grade Celebrity. (gr. k-6). 1987. pap. 3.50 (0-440-44948-0, YB) Dell.

—Tootsie Tanner, Why Don't You Talk. (gr. k-6). 1990. pap. 2.95 (0-440-40239-5, YB) Dell.

Gikow, Louise. Muppet Kids in I'm Mad at You! Chauhan, Manhar, illus. 24p. (ps-3). 1992. 1.95 (0-307-12648-X, 12648) Western Pub.

Gilden, Mel. Beverly Hills 90210: 'Tis the Season. 1992. pap. 3.99 (0-06-106786-5, Harp PBks) HarpC.

Gilligan, Shannon. Our Secret Gang, No. 6. 1992. pap. 2.99 (0-553-15994-1) Bantam.

Gilmer, Chris & Milam, June M. Let's All Be Friends. McIntosh, Chuck, illus. 20p. (ps-k). 1994. pap. text ed. 42.95 (1-884307-09-4); student's ed. 4.95 (1-884307-10-8) Dev Res Educ.

Gilson, Jamie. Sticks & Stones & Skeleton Bones. DeRosa, Dee, illus. (gr. 3-6). 1991. 14.00 (0-688-10098-8) Lothrop.

—You Don't Know Beans about Bats. De Groat, Diane, illus. LC 93-559. 1994. write for info. (0-395-67063-2, Clarion Bks) HM.

Gipson, Morrell & Mayer, Lene. Let's Be Friends. Stefoff, Rebecca, ed. LC 90-13795. (Illus.). 24p. (gr. k-3). 1990. PLB 14.60 (0-944483-92-5) Garrett Ed Corp.

Girion, Barbara. Portfolio to Fame. (Orig.). (gr. k-12). 1987. pap. 2.50 (0-440-97148-9, LFL) Dell.

—Prescription for Success. (gr. 7 up). 1987. pap. 2.50 (0-440-97165-9) Dell.

Glenn, Mel. My Friend's Got This Problem, Mr. Chandler. 1992. write for info. (Clarion Bks) HM.

Goffin, Josse. Yes. LC 92-54430. (Illus.). (ps-3). 1993. 13. 00 (0-688-12375-9) Lothrop.

Gold, Porter. Who's There? (Illus.). 32p. (gr. 1-4). 1989. PLB 18.99 (0-8172-3514-0); pap. 3.95 (0-8114-6717-1) Raintree Steck-V.

Goldberg, Whoopi. Alice. Rocco, John, illus. LC 92-15935. 48p. 1992. 15.00 (0-553-08990-0) Bantam.

Golding, Leila P. Rachel. LC 88-71304. 176p. (Orig.). (gr. 10-12). 1988. pap. 3.99 (0-87123-963-9) Bethany Hse.

—Shelly. LC 85-73424. 150p. (Orig.). (gr. 9-12). 1986. pap. 3.99 (0-87123-867-5) Bethany Hse.

Goldman, E. M. Money to Burn. LC 93-14584. 212p. (gr. 5-9). 1994. 14.99 (0-670-85339-9) Viking Child Bks.

Goofy & Friends Take a Trip. 16p. 1994. 9.98 (1-57082-151-8) Mouse Works.

Gordon, Christine W. Mee Glows with Health & Happiness. Gordon, Christine W., illus. LC 87-90587. 32p. (Orig.). (ps-2). 1987. pap. 5.00 (0-9618854-1-6) Mee Enterp.

—Mee, Who Is Hardly Any Size at All. Gordon, Christine W., illus. LC 87-90588. (Orig.). (ps-k). 1987. pap. 4.00 (0-9618854-0-8) Mee Enterp.

Gordon, Jeffie R. Muriel & Ruth: A Book about Friendship. Yerkes, Lane, illus. LC 91-728718. 24p. (ps-3). 1992. 8.95 (1-878093-18-5) Boyds Mills Pr.

Gordon, Sharon. Playground Fun. Karas, G. Brian, illus. LC 86-30854. 32p. (gr. k-2). 1988. lib. bdg. 7.89 (0-8167-0990-4); pap. text ed. 1.95 (0-8167-0991-2) Troll Assocs.

Gordon, Sheila. Waiting for the Rain. LC 87-7638. 224p. (gr. 7 up). 1987. 12.95 (0-531-05726-7); PLB 12.99 (0-531-08326-8) Orchard Bks Watts.

Gorman, Carol. Chelsey & the Green-Haired Kid. 1992. pap. 12.95 (0-395-44767-4) HM.

—Million Dollar Winner. Koehler, Ed, illus. LC 93-36935. 96p. (Orig.). (gr. 4-7). 1994. pap. 3.99 (0-570-04630-0) Concordia.

—Nobody's Friend. Nappi, Rudy, illus. LC 92-24936. 60p. (Orig.). (gr. 1-4). 1993. pap. 3.99 (0-570-04729-3) Concordia.

Gormley, Beatrice. Best Friend Insurance. McCully, Emily A., illus. LC 83-5713. 160p. (gr. 3-6). 1983. 10. 95 (0-525-44066-6, DCB) Dutton Child Bks.

—Best Friend Insurance. McCully, Emily A., illus. 160p. (gr. 3-7). 1985. pap. 2.50 (0-380-69854-4, Camelot) Avon.

Goudge, Eileen. Don't Say Goodbye. 153p. (Orig.). (gr. 6-12). 1985. pap. 2.25 (0-440-92108-2, LFL) Dell.

—Looking for Love. (Orig.). 1986. pap. 2.25 (0-440-94730-8, LFL) Dell.

—Night after Night. (gr. 6-12). 1986. pap. 2.25 (0-440-96369-9, LFL) Dell.

—Smart Enough to Know. (Orig.). (gr. 7-12). 1984. pap. 2.25 (0-440-98168-9, LFL) Dell.

Gould, Marilyn. Friends True & Periwinkle Blue. 160p. (Orig.). 1992. pap. 2.99 (0-380-76484-9, Camelot) Avon.

—The Twelfth of June. LC 85-45173. 183p. (gr. 4 up). 1994. PLB 12.95 (0-9632305-4-9) Allied Crafts.

Graber. Prouty & Me. Date not set. 15.00 (0-06-024251-5); PLB 14.89 (0-06-024252-3) HarpC Child Bks.

Graf, Rosanna & Graf, Virginia. Beary, Beary, Quite Contrary. Lawson, Laura, illus. (Orig.). Date not set. pap. 9.50 (1-882788-02-8) VanGar Pubs.

Graham, Bob. Pete & Roland. (ps-3). 1988. pap. 3.95 (0-318-32773-2, Puffin) Puffin Bks.

—Rose Meets Mr. Wintergarten. Graham, Bob, illus. LC 91-71824. 32p. (ps up). 1994. pap. 5.99 (1-56402-395-8) Candlewick Pr.

Grant, Cynthia D. Kumquat May, I'll Always Love You. (gr. 7-12). 1987. pap. 2.95 (0-553-26416-8, Starfire) Bantam.

Green, Kate. Between Friends. (Illus.). 32p. (gr. 1-4). 1992. 15.95 (0-89565-780-5) Childs World.

Greenberg, Jan. The Iceberg & Its Shadow. LC 80-20060. 132p. (gr. 7 up). 1980. 13.00 (0-374-33624-5) FS&G.

—Just the Two of Us. LC 88-45330. 128p. (gr. 5 up). 1991. pap. 3.95 (0-374-43982-6) FS&G.

Greenberg, Kenneth R. The Adventures of Tusky & His Friends, Bk. 1: A Jungle Adventure. Pearson, Allison K., illus. 51p. (gr. k-3). 1991. 13.95 (1-879100-00-2) Tusky Enterprises.

Greene, Constance C. A Girl Called Al. Barton, Byron, illus. (gr. 6-8). 1969. pap. 15.00 (0-670-34153-3) Viking Child Bks.

—I Know You, Al. 128p. (gr. 5-9). 1991. pap. 3.95 (0-14-034884-0, Puffin) Puffin Bks.

—Isabelle the Itch. 128p. (gr. 3-7). 1992. pap. 3.99 (0-14-036028-X) Puffin Bks.

—Your Old Pal, Al. 160p. (gr. k-6). 1981. pap. 2.95 (0-440-49862-7, YB) Dell.

Greenfield, Eloise. Big Friend, Little Friend. Gilchrist, Jan S., illus. 12p. (ps-1). 1991. bds. 4.95 (0-86316-204-5) Writers & Readers.

—First Pink Light. (ps-3). 1993. pap. 6.95 (0-86316-212-6) Writers & Readers.

Greenwald, Sheila. The Atrocious Two. (Orig.). (gr. k-6). 1989. pap. 2.95 (0-440-40141-0, YB) Dell.

—Here's Hermione: A Rosy Cole Production. (Illus.). (gr. 3-7). 1991. 13.95 (0-316-32715-8) Little.

—My Fabulous New Life. LC 92-44928. 160p. (gr. 3-7). 1993. 10.95 (0-15-277693-1, Browndeer Pr); pap. 3.95 (0-15-276716-9, Browndeer Pr) HarBrace.

Gregorich, Barbara. My Friend Goes Left. Hoffman, Joan, ed. John, Joyce, illus. 16p. (Orig.). (gr. k-2). 1984. pap. 2.25 (0-88743-008-2, 06008) Sch Zone Pub Co.

—My Friend Goes Left. Hoffman, Joan, ed. (Illus.). 32p. (gr. k-2). 1992. pap. 3.95 (0-88743-406-1, 06058) Sch Zone Pub Co.

Gregory, Valiska. Happy Burpday, Maggie McDougal! Porter, Pat, illus. 64p. (gr. 2-4). 1992. 11.95 (0-316-32777-8) Little.

Gretz, Susanna. Frog, Duck & Rabbit. Gretz, Susanna, illus. LC 91-16364. 32p. (ps-1). 1992. SBE 12.95 (0-02-737327-4, Four Winds) Macmillan Child Grp.

—Rabbit Rambles On. Gretz, Susanna, illus. LC 91-17069. 32p. (ps-1). 1992. SBE 12.95 (0-02-737325-8, Four Winds) Macmillan Child Grp.

Grodin, Charles. Freddie the Fly. Murdocca, Sal, illus. LC 92-5234. 32p. (ps-2). 1993. 12.00 (0-679-83847-3) Random Bks Yng Read.

Grove, Vicki. The Fastest Friend in the West. 176p. (gr. 4-8). 1990. 14.95 (0-399-22184-0, Putnam) Putnam Pub Group.

—Fastest Friend in the West. 176p. 1992. pap. 2.95 (0-590-44338-0, Apple Paperbacks) Scholastic Inc.

Gryspeerdt, Rebecca. Counting Friends. (Illus.). 24p. (ps-1). 1993. 13.95 (1-85681-092-5, Pub. by J MacRae UK) Trafalgar.

Gunn, Robin J. Sweet Dreams. LC 94-6239. 1994. write for info. (1-56179-255-1) Focus Family.

Guy, Rosa. Billy the Great. Binch, Caroline, illus. LC 92-34704. 32p. (gr. k-3). 1992. 15.00 (0-385-30666-0) Delacorte.

—The Friends. LC 72-11068. 208p. (gr. 4-6). 1973. 13.95 (0-8050-1742-9, Bks Young Read) H Holt & Co.

—The Friends. (gr. 7-12). 1983. pap. 2.95 (0-553-26519-9) Bantam.

—The Friends. 1981. pap. 3.99 (0-553-27326-4) Bantam.

Haas, Jessie. A Blue for Beware. Smith, Joseph A., photos by. LC 94-4572. (Illus.). 1995. write for info. RTE (0-688-13678-8) Greenwillow.

Hager, Betty. Marcie & the Monster of the Bayou. LC 93-44490. 112p. (gr. 3-7). 1994. pap. 4.99 (0-310-38431-1) Zondervan.

Hahn, Mary D. Tallahassee Higgins. 1988. pap. 3.50 (0-380-70500-1, Camelot) Avon.

Hale, Irina. How I Found a Friend. Hale, Irina, illus. 32p. (ps-1). 1992. PLB 12.50 (0-670-84286-9) Viking Child Bks.

Hallinan, P. K. A Rainbow of Friends. Hallinan, P. K., illus. LC 93-39257. 24p. (ps-2). 1994. PLB 11.00 (0-8249-8657-1, Ideals Child); pap. 4.95 (0-8249-8653-9, Ideals Child) Hambleton-Hill.

—That's What a Friend Is. Hallinan, P. K., illus. LC 76-27744. 32p. (gr. k-3). 1977. pap. 3.95 (0-516-43628-7) Childrens.

Halvorson, Marilyn. Let It Go. (gr. 5 up). 1988. pap. 2.95 (0-440-20053-9, LFL) Dell.

Hamilton, Dorothy. Bittersweet Days. Graber, Esther R., illus. LC 77-18867. 128p. (gr. 4-8). 1978. pap. 3.95 (0-8361-1846-4) Herald Pr.

—The Castle. Graber, Esther R., illus. LC 75-15599. 112p. (gr. 4-8). 1975. pap. 3.95 (0-8361-1776-X) Herald Pr.

—Holly's New Year. Graber, Esther R., illus. LC 81-4098. 112p. (gr. 3-9). 1981. pap. 3.95 (0-8361-1961-4) Herald Pr.

Hamilton, Gail. May the Best Man Win. (gr. 4-6). 1993. pap. 3.99 (0-553-48043-X) Bantam.

—Nothing Endures But Change. (gr. 4-7). 1993. pap. 3.99 (0-553-48037-5) Bantam.

Hamilton, Virginia. The Planet of Junior Brown. Pinkney, Jerry, photos by. LC 85-16651. (Illus.). 224p. (gr. 5-9). 1986. pap. 3.95 (0-02-043540-1, Collier Young Ad) Macmillan Child Grp.

—The Planet of Junior Brown. 2nd ed. LC 92-40350. 224p. (gr. 3-7). 1993. pap. 3.95 (0-689-71721-0, Aladdin) Macmillan Child Grp.

—White Romance. 233p. (gr. 7 up). 1989. pap. 3.95 (0-15-295888-6, Odyssey) HarBrace.

Hammond, Elizabeth. My Rainbow Friends. Taylor, Neil, illus. LC 87-51495. 44p. (ps). 1989. 5.95 (1-55523-023-7) Winston-Derek.

Hammond, Pearle L. The Prize in the Packard. La Mont, Violet, illus. 100p. (Orig.). (gr. 5-8). 1990. pap. 8.95 (0-9615161-6-X) Incline Pr.

Harbo, Gary. Bart Becomes a Friend: Advanced Reader. Harbo, Gary, illus. 33p. (gr. 1-4). 1992. text ed. 8.95 (1-884149-05-7) Kutie Kari Bks.

—My New Friend: Advanced Reader. Harbo, Gary, illus. 33p. (gr. 1-4). 1988. text ed. 8.95 (1-884149-01-4) Kutie Kari Bks.

Harmey, Barbara E. I Used to Be Older. (ps-k). pap. 4.95 (0-317-62508-X) St Martin.

Harrell, Janice. Betrayal. 1994. pap. 3.95 (0-590-47712-9) Scholastic Inc.

—Secret Diaries, Vol. 1: Temptation. 1994. pap. 3.95 (0-590-47692-0) Scholastic Inc.

—Tiffany, the Disaster. Ashby, Ruth, ed. 112p. (Orig.). (gr. 3-6). 1992. pap. 2.99 (0-671-72860-1, Minstrel Bks) PB.

Harris, Christine. The Silver Path. Ong, Helen, illus. 40p. (gr. 2-5). 1994. 14.95 (1-56397-338-3) Boyds Mills Pr.

Harris, Emily. Hilary & Lars. LC 88-50753. 82p. (gr. 5-8). 1988. 6.95 (1-55523-148-9) Winston-Derek.

Harvey, Dean. The Secret Elephant of Harlan Kooter. Richardson, Mark, illus. LC 91-45955. 160p. (gr. 2-5). 1992. 13.95 (0-395-62523-8) HM.

Haseley, Dennis. Ghost Catcher. Bloom, Lloyd, illus. LC 91-4426. 40p. (gr. 1-5). 1991. HarpC Child Bks.

Haskins. Black Gray & Blue. Date not set. 15.00 (0-06-023403-2); PLB 14.89 (0-06-023404-0) HarpC Child Bks.

Haskins, Francine. I Remember "121" LC 91-16647. (Illus.). 32p. (gr. k-5). 1991. 13.95 (0-89239-100-6) Childrens Book Pr.

Hassler, Jon. Jemmy. (gr. 5 up). 1988. pap. 3.95 (0-449-70302-9, Juniper) Fawcett.

Hathorn, Libby. The Surprise Box. Cutter, Priscilla, illus. LC 93-28957. 1994. 4.25 (0-383-03778-6) SRA Schl Grp.

—Way Home. Rogers, Gregory, illus. LC 93-48030. 32p. (gr. 1-5). 1994. 15.00 (0-517-59909-0) Crown Bks Yng Read.

Havill, Juanita. Jamaica & Brianna. O'Brien, Anne S., illus. LC 92-36508. 1993. 13.95 (0-395-64489-5) HM.

—Jamaica's Find. O'Brien, Anne S., illus. LC 85-14542. 32p. (gr. 4-8). 1987. pap. 4.80 (0-395-45357-7) HM.

Hawkins, Laura. The Cat That Could Spell Mississippi. LC 92-8025. 160p. (gr. 3-5). 1992. 13.95 (0-395-61627-1) HM.

Hay, John. Rover & Coo Coo. Solliday, Tim, illus. 32p. (gr. 3-6). 1991. 12.95 (0-88138-078-4, Green Tiger) S&S Trade.

Hayashi, Nancy. The Fantastic Stay-Home-from-School Day. Hayashi, Nancy, illus. LC 91-21095. 105p. (gr. 2-5). 1992. 12.00 (0-525-44864-0, DCB) Dutton Child Bks.

Hayes, Sheila. Zoe's Gift. LC 93-42621. 144p. 1994. 14. 99 (0-525-67484-5, Lodestar Bks) Dutton Child Bks.

Haynes, Betsy. The Boys Only Club. (gr. 4 up). 1990. pap. 2.95 (0-553-15809-0) Bantam.

—The Bragging War. 120p. (gr. 5-7). 1989. pap. 2.75 (0-553-15651-9) Bantam.

—Breaking Up. (gr. 4-7). 1991. pap. 2.99 (0-553-15873-2) Bantam.

—Celebrity Auction. (gr. 4 up). 1990. pap. 2.75 (0-553-15784-1) Bantam.

—Fabulous Five Minus One. (gr. 4-7). 1991. pap. 2.99 (0-553-15867-8) Bantam.

—The Fabulous Five, No. 30. 1992. pap. 2.99 (0-553-15875-9) Bantam.

—Grade Me. (gr. 7). 1989. pap. 2.75 (0-685-33584-4) Bantam.

—Melanie Edwards. 1992. pap. 2.99 (0-553-15874-0) Bantam.

—The Popularity Trap: The Fabulous Five, No. 3. (gr. 4-7). 1988. pap. 2.95 (0-553-15634-9, Skylark) Bantam.

—Scapegoat. (gr. 4-7). 1991. pap. 2.99 (0-553-15872-4) Bantam.

—Seventh-Grade Menace. (gr. 4 up). 1989. pap. 2.75 (0-553-15763-9) Bantam.

—Taffy Sinclair & the Melanie Makeover. (gr. 2-6). 1988. pap. 2.75 (0-553-15604-7, Skylark) Bantam.

—Taffy Sinclair & the Secret Admirer Epidemic. (gr. 2-6). 1988. pap. 2.50 (0-553-15582-2, Skylark) Bantam.

—Taffy Sinclair, Baby Ashley, & Me. 128p. (gr. 4-7). 1988. pap. 2.50 (0-553-15557-1, Skylark) Bantam.

Haywood, Carolyn. Eddie & His Big Deals. (Illus.). 192p. (gr. 3 up). 1990. Repr. of 1955 ed. 3.95 (0-688-10075-9, Pub. by Beech Tree Bks) Morrow.

Heine, Helme. Mollywoop. Manheim, Ralph, tr. (Illus.). 32p. (ps-3). 1991. bds. 14.95 bds. (0-374-35001-9) FS&G.

Henderson, Angela. JoJo Meets Scrappy. (Illus.). (ps-3). 1992. write for info. (1-882185-07-2) Crnrstone Pub.

Henkes, Kevin. Chester's Way. LC 87-14882. (Illus.). 32p. (ps-3). 1988. 15.00 (0-688-07607-6); lib. bdg. 14.93 (0-688-07608-4) Greenwillow.

—Jessica. LC 87-38087. (Illus.). 24p. (gr. k up). 1989. 14. 00 (0-688-07829-X); PLB 13.93 (0-688-07830-3) Greenwillow.

—A Weekend with Wendell. Henkes, Kevin, illus. LC 85-24822. 32p. (ps-3). 1986. 13.95 (0-688-06325-X); PLB 13.88 (0-688-06326-8) Greenwillow.

—Words of Stone. LC 91-28543. (gr. 5-12). 1992. 13.00 (0-688-11356-7) Greenwillow.

—Words of Stone. LC 93-7488. 160p. (gr. 4-7). 1993. pap. 3.99 (0-14-036601-6, Puffin) Puffin Bks.

Herlihy, Dirlie. Ludie's Song. 224p. (gr. 4 up). 1990. pap. 4.95 (0-14-034245-1, Puffin) Puffin Bks.

Hermes, Patricia. I Hate Being Gifted. 144p. 1990. 14.95 (0-399-21687-1, Putnam) Putnam Pub Group.

Herz, Roger J. Claude Humphrey Dwickens: The Old Man with the Mustache. Aldworth, Susan, illus. 32p. (Orig.). (ps-6). 1988. pap. text ed. 3.95 (0-9619560-0-3) TGNW Pr.

Herzig, Alison C. The Big Deal. 64p. (gr. 2-5). 1994. pap. 3.99 (0-14-034959-6) Puffin Bks.

Herzig, Alison C. & Mali, Jane L. Mystery on October Road. LC 93-7487. 64p. (gr. 3-7). 1993. pap. 3.99 (0-14-034614-7, Puffin) Puffin Bks.

Hesse, Karen. Phoenix Rising. 1994. 15.95 (0-8050-3108-1) H Holt & Co.

Hest, Amy. The Go-Between. DiSalvo-Ryan, DyAnne, illus. LC 90-24561. 32p. (gr. k-3). 1992. RSBE 14.95 (0-02-743632-2, Four Winds) Macmillan Child Grp.

—Nannies for Hire. Trivas, Irene, illus. LC 93-7040. 48p. (gr. 2 up). 1994. 15.00g (0-688-12527-1); PLB 14.93 (0-688-12528-X) Morrow Jr Bks.

—Pajama Party. Trivas, Irene, illus. LC 91-13676. 48p. (gr. 2 up). 1992. 14.00 (0-688-07866-4); PLB 13.93 (0-688-07870-2) Morrow Jr Bks.

—Pajama Party. Trivas, Irene, illus. 48p. (gr. 3 up). 1994. pap. 4.95 (0-688-12949-8, Pub. by Beech Tree Bks) Morrow.

—Pete & Lily. (gr. k-6). 1989. pap. 2.75 (0-440-40145-3, YB) Dell.

—Pete & Lily. LC 92-42319. 128p. (gr. 6 up). 1993. pap. 4.95 (0-688-12490-9, Pub. by Beech Tree Bks) Morrow.

Hicyilmaz, Gaye. Against the Storm. 1993. pap. 3.50 (0-440-40892-X) Dell.

Hill, David. See Ya, Simon. LC 93-39870. 120p. 1994. 14.99 (0-525-45247-8, DCB) Dutton Child Bks.

Hillert, Margaret. Four Good Friends. (Illus.). (ps-k). 1981. PLB 6.95 (0-8136-5061-5, TK2298); pap. 3.50 (0-8136-5561-7, TK2299) Modern Curr.

—Fun Days. (Illus.). (ps-k). 1982. PLB 6.95 (0-8136-5093-3, TK2162); pap. 3.50 (0-8136-5593-5, TK2163) Modern Curr.

Hilton, Nette. Andrew Jessup. Wilcox, Cathy, illus. LC 92-39799. 32p. (ps-2). 1993. PLB 13.95 (0-395-66900-6) Ticknor & Flds Bks Yng Read.

Hinton, Susie E. That Was Then, This Is Now. (gr. 7 up). 18.00 (0-8446-6371-9) Peter Smith.

Hirsch, Karen. Ellen Anders on Her Own. LC 93-13350. 96p. (gr. 3-7). 1994. SBE 13.95 (0-02-743975-5, Macmillan Child Bk) Macmillan Child Grp.

Hiser, Constance. The Missing Doll. Ramsey, Marcy, illus. 72p. (gr. 4-7). 1993. 13.95 (0-8234-1046-3) Holiday.

Hissey, Jane. Best Friends: More Old Bear Tales. Hissey, Jane, illus. 80p. (ps-3). 1989. 16.95 (0-399-21674-X, Philomel Bks) Putnam Pub Group.

Hite, Sid. It's Nothing to a Mountain. LC 93-42048. 1994. 15.95 (0-8050-2769-6) H Holt & Co.

Hoban, Lillian. Arthur's Pen Pal. Hoban, Lillian, illus. LC 75-6289. 64p. (gr. k-3). 1976. PLB 13.89 (0-06-022372-3) HarpC Child Bks.

—Arthur's Pen Pal. Hoban, Lillian, illus. 32p. (ps-2). 1990. pap. 6.95 (0-00-004236-6, Caedmon) HarperAudio.

Hoban, Russell. Best Friends for Frances. Hoban, Lillian, illus. LC 92-38401. 32p. (ps-3). 1976. pap. 4.95 (0-06-443008-1, Trophy) HarpC Child Bks.

Hockett, Betty M. Down a Winding Road. (Illus.). 80p. (gr. 3-8). 1985. pap. 3.50 (0-943701-11-2) George Fox Pr.

—From Here to There & Back Again. Cammack, Phyllis, illus. LC 84-81034. 80p. (Orig.). (gr. 3-8). 1984. pap. 3.50 (0-943701-09-0) George Fox Pr.

—Happiness under the Indian Trees. LC 86-81349. (Illus.). 80p. (gr. 3-8). 1986. pap. 3.50 (0-943701-12-0) George Fox Pr.

—What Will Tomorrow Bring? LC 85-70504. (Illus.). 80p. (gr. 3-8). 1985. pap. 3.50 (0-943701-10-4) George Fox Pr.

Hodgman, Ann. There's a Bat Wing in My Lunchbox. Pierard, John, illus. 96p. 1988. pap. 2.95 (0-380-75426-6, Camelot) Avon.

Hoff, Syd. Who Will Be My Friends? Hoff, Syd, illus. 32p. (gr. k-2). 1960. PLB 13.89 (0-06-022556-4) HarpC Child Bks.

Hoffius, Stephen. Winners & Losers. LC 92-42394. 123p. (gr. 6 up). 1993. pap. 15.00 (0-671-79194-X, S&S BFYR) S&S Trade.

Hofmann, Ginnie. The Bear Next Door: Story & Pictures. LC 93-616. (Illus.). (ps-3). 1994. 2.50 (0-679-83957-7) Random Bks Yng Read.

—One Teddy Bear Is Enough! Hofmann, Ginnie, illus. LC 88-18166. 32p. (Orig.). (ps-3). 1991. pap. 2.25 (0-394-89582-7) Random Bks Yng Read.

Hogan, Paula Z. I Hate Boys-I Hate Girls. Hockerman, Dennis, illus. McDonald, Paula & McDonald, Dickintro. by. LC 79-24056. (Illus.). 32p. (gr. k-6). 1980. PLB 19.97 (0-8172-1358-9) Raintree Steck-V.

Hogan, Ryan. Double Scoop in A Day at the Babysitter's. Hogan, Ryan, illus. LC 92-75373. 18p. (gr. 2-5). 1992. 12. 95 (0-9635529-0-2, 33001) Cult Exchange.

A DAY AT THE BABYSITTER'S tells about the excitement & adventures of meeting a new kid at the babysitter's. Double Scoop shows how two boys of different "flavors" meet, play & enjoy each other's company. Dreams of a sleepover, swimming together, riding bikes, & digging for treasures start wonderful plans for a very special friendship. The two main characters learn to get along with each other & a loving & lasting relationship starts. A DAY AT THE BABYSITTER'S is the first book in a series written & illustrated by Ryan Hogan, a third grader at Parkview Elementary School in White Bear Lake, MN. Double Scoop is Ryan's first book. It was made as a birthday present for his good friend, Michael Fowler. Double Scoop, in A DAY AT THE BABYSITTER'S is the real life story of how Michael & Ryan met. Hardcover. Call or write for information to order: Cultural Exchange Corporation, Suite 1760 - IDS Center, 80 South Eighth St., Minneapolis, MN 55402; 612-339-2113. ***Publisher Provided Annotation.***

Hoh, Diane. Funhouse. 1990. pap. 3.25 (0-590-43050-5) Scholastic Inc.

Holabird, Katharine. Angelina & Alice. Craig, Helen, illus. (ps-2). 1988. 15.00 (0-517-56074-7, Clarkson Potter) Crown Bks Yng Read.

Holcomb, Nan. Fair & Square. Yoder, Dot, illus. 32p. (ps-2). 1992. pap. 6.95 (0-944727-09-3) Jason & Nordic Pubs.

—Patrick & Emma Lou. Yoder, Dot, illus. 32p. (ps-2). 1989. pap. 6.95 (0-944727-03-4) Jason & Nordic Pubs.

Holl, Kristi D. First Things First. (gr. k-6). 1989. pap. 2.95 (0-440-40147-X, YB) Dell.

Holland, Alex N. Time for Us. Holland, Alex N., illus. 19p. (gr. k-3). 1994. pap. 11.95 (1-895583-70-5) MAYA Pubs.

Holland, Isabelle. Henry & Grudge. Guida, Liisa C., illus. 64p. (gr. 3-6). 1986. 10.95 (0-8027-6611-0); lib. bdg. 10.85 (0-8027-6612-9) Walker & Co.

—Now Is Not Too Late. 160p. (gr. 4 up). 1985. pap. 2.75 (0-553-15548-2) Bantam.

Hollander, Cass. A New Friend for Me. Ulrich, George, illus. 24p. (ps-2). 1992. pap. 0.99 (1-56293-108-3) McClanahan Bk.

Holman, Felice. Secret City, U. S. A. LC 92-44798. 208p. (gr. 4-7). 1993. pap. 3.95 (0-689-71755-5, Aladdin) Macmillan Child Grp.

Honeycutt, Natalie. The All New Jonah Twist. LC 85-28048. 128p. (gr. 3-5). 1986. SBE 13.95 (0-02-744840-1, Bradbury Pr) Macmillan Child Grp.

—Ask Me Something Easy. 160p. 1993. pap. 3.50 (0-380-71723-9, Flare) Avon.

—Invisible Lissa. 128p. (gr. 3-7). 1986. pap. 2.75 (0-380-70120-0, Camelot) Avon.

Hopkins, Lee B., ed. Best Friends. Watts, James, illus. LC 85-45257. 48p. (gr. k-4). 1986. PLB 14.89 (0-06-022562-9) HarpC Child Bks.

Hopper, Nancy J. The Queen of Put-Down. LC 92-19559. 112p. (gr. 4-6). 1993. pap. 3.95 (0-689-71670-2, Aladdin) Macmillan Child Grp.

Horstman, Lisa. Fast Friends: A Tail & Tongue Tale. Horstman, Lisa, illus. LC 93-28630. 40p. (ps-3). 1994. 13.00 (0-679-85404-5); PLB 13.99 (0-679-95404-X) Knopf Bks Yng Read.

Hossack, Sylvie A. Flying Chickens of Paradise Lane. LC 92-14527. 144p. (gr. 3-7). 1992. RSBE 13.95 (0-02-744565-8, Four Winds) Macmillan Child Grp.

Hot Dog & Friends. (Illus.). 1986. pap. 3.00 (0-440-85089-4) Dell.

Howard, Megan. I've Lost My Best Friend. LC 93-85681. 144p. (Orig.). (gr. 3-9). 1994. pap. 3.99 (0-679-85701-X) Random Bks Yng Read.

Howard, Milly. On Yonder Mountain. (Illus.). 127p. (Orig.). (gr. 1-6). 1989. pap. 5.50 (0-89084-462-3) Bob Jones Univ Pr.

Howe, James. I Wish I Were a Butterfly. Young, Ed, illus. LC 86-33635. 28p. (ps-3). 1987. 15.95 (0-15-200470-X, Gulliver Bks) HarBrace.

—A Night Without Stars. 192p. (gr. 7 up). 1985. pap. 2.95 (0-380-69877-3, Flare) Avon.

—Pinky & Rex. Sweet, Melissa, illus. 48p. (gr. 2). 1991. pap. 3.99 (0-380-71190-7, Pub. by Young Camelot) Avon.

—Pinky & Rex. LC 89-30786. (Illus.). 48p. (gr. k-3). 1990. SBE 12.95 (0-689-31454-X, Atheneum Child Bk) Macmillan Child Grp.

—Pinky & Rex & the Mean Old Witch. 48p. 1992. pap. 3.99 (0-380-71644-5, Camelot Young) Avon.

—Pinky & Rex & the Spelling Bee. Sweet, Melissa, illus. LC 89-78305. 48p. (gr. k-3). 1991. SBE 12.95 (*0-689-31618-6*, Atheneum Child Bk) Macmillan Child Grp.
—Pinky & Rex Get Married. Sweet, Melissa, illus. LC 89-406. 48p. (gr. k-3). 1990. SBE 11.95 (*0-685-58512-3*, Atheneum Child Bk); 12.95 (*0-689-31453-1*, Atheneum Childrens Bks) Macmillan Child Grp.
—Pinky & Rex Go to Camp. Sweet, Melissa, illus. LC 91-16123. 48p. (ps-3). 1992. SBE 12.95 (*0-689-31718-2*, Atheneum Child Bk) Macmillan Child Grp.
Howe, James & Sweet, Melissa. Pinky & Rex Get Married. (Illus.). 48p. (gr. 2). 1991. pap. 3.99 (*0-380-71191-5*, Pub. by Young Camelot) Avon.
Howe, Norma. In With the Out Crowd. 208p. (gr. 7 up). 1986. 12.95 (*0-395-40490-8*) HM.
Hughes, Dean. End of the Race. LC 92-37747. 160p. (gr. 5 up). 1993. SBE 13.95 (*0-689-31779-4*, Atheneum Child Bk) Macmillan Child Grp.
—Lucky Breaks Loose. LC 90-30850. 136p. (Orig.). (gr. 3-6). 1990. pap. 4.95 (*0-87579-194-8*) Deseret Bk.
—Lucky Fights Back. LC 91-31416. 150p. (Orig.). (gr. 3-6). 1991. pap. text ed. 4.95 (*0-87579-559-5*) Deseret Bk.
—Lucky's Crash Landing. LC 90-30991. 160p. (Orig.). (gr. 3-6). 1990. pap. 4.95 (*0-87579-193-X*) Deseret Bk.
—Nutty Can't Miss. 144p. (gr. 2-5). 1988. pap. 2.75 (*0-553-15584-9*, Skylark) Bantam.
Hughes, Shirley. The Alfie Collection: Alfie's Feet; An Evening at Alfie's; Alfie Gives a Hand; Alfie Gets in First, 4 bks. (Illus.). (ps up). 1993. Set. boxed, shrink-wrapped 16.95 (*0-688-12750-9*, Tupelo Bks) Morrow.
—Alfie Gives a Hand. LC 83-14883. (Illus.). (ps up). 1986. 4.95 (*0-688-06521-X*, Mulberry) Morrow.
—Angel Mae: A Tale of Trotter Street. ALC Staff, ed. LC 89-45288. (Illus.). 32p. (ps up). 1992. pap. 4.95 (*0-688-11847-X*, Mulberry) Morrow.
—Lucy & Tom's Day. Hughes, Shirley, illus. 32p. (ps-1). 1986. pap. 3.50 (*0-14-050068-5*, Puffin) Puffin Bks.
—Moving Molly. Hughes, Shirley, illus. LC 87-34250. 32p. (ps-2). 1988. 11.95 (*0-688-07982-2*); PLB 11.88 (*0-688-07984-9*) Lothrop.
Humphreys, Martha. Until Whatever. 176p. (gr. 9 up). 1991. 13.45 (*0-395-58022-6*, Clarion Bks) HM.
Hunt, Angela E. Cassie Perkins, No. 2: A Forever Friend. (gr. 4-7). 1991. pap. 4.99 (*0-8423-0462-2*) Tyndale.
—Cassie Perkins, No. 7: Star Light, Star Bright. LC 92-18796. 1993. 4.99 (*0-8423-1117-3*) Tyndale.
Hunt, Irene. No Promises in the Wind. 100p. 1987. pap. 3.99 (*0-425-09969-5*, Berkley-Pacer) Berkley Pub.
Hunt, Joyce. Four of Us & Victoria Chubb. (gr. 4-7). 1990. pap. 2.75 (*0-590-42976-0*) Scholastic Inc.
Hunter, Aileen. The Green Gang. 108p. (gr. 3-5). 1994. pap. 6.95 (*0-86241-364-8*, Pub. by Cnngt UK) Trafalgar.
Hurwitz, Johanna. Aldo Applesauce. Wallner, John, illus. LC 79-16200. 128p. (gr. 4-6). 1979. 12.95 (*0-688-22199-8*); PLB 12.88 (*0-688-32199-2*, Morrow Jr Bks) Morrow Jr Bks.
—Much Ado about Aldo. 63p. 1992. Braille. 5.04 (*1-56956-287-3*) W A T Braille.
—Russell Rides Again. Hoban, Lillian, illus. LC 85-7287. 96p. (ps-2). 1985. 12.95 (*0-688-04628-2*); lib. bdg. 12.88 (*0-688-04629-0*, Morrow Jr Bks) Morrow Jr Bks.
—Teacher's Pet. Hamamaka, Sheila, illus. LC 87-24003. 128p. (gr. 2-5). 1988. 12.95 (*0-688-07506-1*) Morrow Jr Bks.
—The Up & Down Spring. Owens, Gail, illus. LC 92-21337. 112p. (gr. 3 up). 1993. 14.00 (*0-688-11922-0*) Morrow Jr Bks.
—Yellow Blue Jay. Carrick, Donald, illus. LC 92-24597. 128p. (gr. 3 up). 1993. pap. 3.95 (*0-688-12278-7*, Pub. by Beech Tree Bks) Morrow.
Ikeda, Daisaku. Over the Deep Blue Sea. Wildsmith, Brian, illus. McCaughrean, Geraldine, tr. from JPN. LC 92-22557. (Illus.). 32p. (ps-3). 1993. 15.00 (*0-679-84184-9*); PLB 15.99 (*0-679-94184-3*) Knopf Bks Yng Read.
I'll Be Your Best Friend. (Illus.). 40p. (gr. k-5). 1994. pap. 4.95 (*0-685-71586-8*, 522) W Gladden Found.
In the Meadow, Unit 4. (gr. 1). 1991. 7.45 (*0-88106-728-8*) Charlesbridge Pub.
In the Meadow Activity Book, Unit 4. (gr. 1). 1991. 3.90 (*0-88106-730-X*) Charlesbridge Pub.
In the Meadow Activity Book (EV, Unit 4. (gr. 1). 1991. 3.90 (*0-88106-729-6*) Charlesbridge Pub.
Irwin, Hadley. Kim-Kimi. LC 86-21416. 208p. (gr. 7 up). 1987. SBE 14.95 (*0-689-50428-4*, M K McElderry) Macmillan Child Grp.
Isadora, Rachel. Friends. LC 88-11753. (Illus.). (ps up). 1990. 13.95 (*0-688-08264-5*); PLB 13.88 (*0-688-08265-3*) Greenwillow.
Jackson, Isaac. Somebody's New Pajamas. Soman, David, photos by. LC 93-32213. 1995. write for info. (*0-8037-1570-6*); lib. bdg. write for info. (*0-8037-1549-8*) Dial Bks Young.
Jacobs, Laurie A. So Much in Common. Gorbachev, Valeri, illus. 32p. (ps-3). 1994. 14.95 (*1-56397-115-1*) Boyds Mills Pr.
James, Betsy. Mary Ann. James, Betsy, illus. LC 93-13364. 32p. (ps-3). 1994. 13.99 (*0-525-45077-7*) Dutton Child Bks.
Jennings, Sharon. Jeremiah & Mrs. Ming. Levert, Mireille, illus. 24p. (ps). 1990. PLB 15.95 (*1-55037-079-0*, Pub. by Annick CN); pap. 5.95 (*1-55037-078-2*, Pub. by Annick CN) Firefly Bks Ltd.
—Jeremiah & Mrs. Ming Big Book. (Illus.). 24p. (ps). 1990. 21.95 (*1-55037-124-X*, Pub. by Annick CN) Firefly Bks Ltd.
Johnson, Frances R. Share with a Friend Love Above All. LC 92-61594. (Illus.). 44p. (gr. k-3). 1993. pap. 5.95 (*1-55523-564-6*) Winston-Derek.
Johnson, Pete. Catch You on the Flip Side. 135p. (gr. 7-9). 1989. pap. 9.95 (*0-233-98074-1*, Pub. by A Deutsch England) Trafalgar.
Johnson, Scott. One of the Boys. LC 91-19262. 256p. (gr. 7 up). 1992. SBE 16.00 (*0-689-31520-1*, Atheneum Child Bk) Macmillan Child Grp.
Johnson, Stacie. The Prince. 1992. pap. 3.50 (*0-553-29721-X*) Bantam.
—Sort of Sisters. 1992. pap. 3.50 (*0-553-29719-8*) Bantam.
Johnson, Stacy. Kwame's Girl. 1994. pap. 3.50 (*0-553-56313-0*) Bantam.
Johnston, Tony. Amber on the Mountain. Duncan, Robert, illus. LC 93-16292. (ps-6). 1994. write for info. (*0-8037-1219-7*); pap. write for info. (*0-8037-1220-0*) Dial Bks Young.
Jones, Linda K. Fear Strikes at Midnight. 128p. 1990. pap. 5.95 (*0-8361-3507-5*) Herald Pr.
Jones, Martha R. Willow Finds a Friend. (Illus.). 32p. (gr. 2-4). 1993. pap. 6.95 (*0-8059-3315-8*) Dorrance.
Jones, Rebecca C. Matthew & Tilly. Peck, Beth, illus. LC 90-3730. 32p. (ps-3). 1991. 13.95 (*0-525-44684-2*, DCB) Dutton Child Bks.
Jones, Rhodri. Different Friends. 122p. (gr. 6-9). 1990. pap. 9.95 (*0-233-98096-2*, Pub. by A Deutsch England) Trafalgar.
Joosse, Barbara M. The Losers Fight Back. Truesdell, Sue, illus. LC 92-40783. 1994. 13.95 (*0-395-62335-9*, Clarion Bks) HM.
Jordan, P. D. Cooper Street. 147p. (Orig.). (gr. 5-12). 1989. pap. 4.25 (*0-929885-21-X*) Haypenny Pr.
Jordan, Sherryl. Juniper Game. 1991. 13.95 (*0-590-44728-9*, Scholastic Hardcover) Scholastic Inc.
—Juniper Game. 1994. pap. 3.25 (*0-590-44729-7*) Scholastic Inc.
Jorgensen, Dan. Dawn's Diamond Defense. LC 87-11735. 1988. pap. 4.99 (*1-55513-062-3*, Chariot Bks) Chariot Family.
Jukes, Mavis. Getting Even. LC 87-25053. 160p. (gr. 4-7). 1988. PLB 12.99 (*0-394-99594-5*) Knopf Bks Yng Read.
—Getting Even. LC 87-25053. 176p. (gr. 4-7). 1989. pap. 2.95 (*0-394-82593-4*) Knopf Bks Yng Read.
—Like Jake & Me. Bloom, Lloyd, illus. LC 83-8380. 32p. (gr. 1-5). 1987. pap. 6.00 (*0-394-89263-1*) Knopf Bks Yng Read.
Kadish, Sharona. Discovering Friendship. Scribner, Joanne, illus. LC 93-34500. 1994. PLB 19.97 (*0-8114-4458-9*) Raintree Steck-V.
Kahaner, Ellen. Fourth Grade Loser. Henderson, David F., illus. LC 90-26791. 96p. (gr. 3-5). 1992. lib. bdg. 9.89 (*0-8167-2384-2*); pap. text ed. 2.95 (*0-8167-2385-0*) Troll Assocs.
Kaldhol, Marit. Goodbye Rune. Crosby-Jones, Michael, tr. from NOR. Yen, Wenche, illus. (NOR.). 32p. (ps-5). 1987. 13.95 (*0-916291-11-1*) Kane-Miller Bk.
Kamhi, Ralph. Hi Fives. (Illus.). 8p. (gr. 4-5). 1990. write for info. wkbk. (*0-9627292-1-3*) Extra NY.
—The Times of Your Life. 8p. (gr. 6-12). 1989. write for info. (*0-9627292-0-5*) Extra NY.
Kantenwein, Louise. Jean Marie. 1993. 7.95 (*0-533-10667-2*) Vantage.
Karr, Kathleen. It Ain't Always Easy. (Illus.). 236p. (gr. 5 up). 1990. 14.95 (*0-374-33645-8*) FS&G.
Kassem, Lou. Secret Wishes. 144p. (gr. 3-7). 1989. pap. 2.95 (*0-380-75544-0*, Camelot) Avon.
Kastner, Erich. Lisa & Lottie. Books, Cyrus, tr. De Larrea, Victoria, illus. 136p. (gr. 3-7). 1982. pap. 2.95 (*0-380-57117-X*, Camelot) Avon.
Kasza, Keiko. The Rat & the Tiger. (Illus.). 32p. (ps-3). 1993. PLB 14.95 (*0-399-22404-1*, Putnam) Putnam Pub Group.
Katchen, Carole. Your Friend Annie. 1989. pap. 2.75 (*0-590-42732-6*) Scholastic Inc.
Kaye, Marilyn. Cabin Six Plays Cupid. 128p. (Orig.). (ps-8). 1989. pap. 2.95 (*0-380-75701-X*, Camelot) Avon.
—Camp Sunnyside Friends, No. 16: Happily Ever After. 128p. (Orig.). 1992. pap. 3.50 (*0-380-76555-1*, Camelot) Avon.
—No Boys Allowed. 128p. (Orig.). (ps-8). 1989. pap. 2.95 (*0-380-75700-1*, Camelot) Avon.
—Three of a Kind, No. 1: With Friends Like These, Who Needs Enemies. (gr. 4-7). 1990. pap. 3.50 (*0-06-106001-1*, Harp PBks) HarpC.
—Three of a Kind, No. 4: Two's Company, Four's a Crowd. (gr. 4-7). 1991. pap. 3.50 (*0-06-106058-5*, Harp PBks) HarpC.
—Three of a Kind, No. 5: Cat Morgan, Working Girl. (gr. 4-7). 1991. pap. 3.50 (*0-06-106059-3*, Harp PBks) HarpC.
—Too Many Counselors. 128p. 1990. pap. 2.95 (*0-380-75913-6*, Camelot) Avon.
Keats, Ezra J. Louie. Keats, Ezra J., illus. LC 75-6766. 32p. (gr. k-3). 1983. PLB 14.88 (*0-688-02383-5*) Greenwillow.
—Maggie & the Pirate. Keats, Ezra J., illus. LC 85-29347. 32p. (gr. k-3). 1987. Repr. of 1979 ed. RSBE 13.95 (*0-02-749710-0*, Four Winds) Macmillan Child Grp.
Keene, Carolyn. A Mind of Her Own. Greenberg, Ann, ed. 160p. (Orig.). 1991. pap. 2.99 (*0-671-73117-3*, Archway) PB.
Kehret, Peg. Cages. MacDonald, Pat, ed. 160p. 1993. pap. 3.50 (*0-671-75879-9*, Minstrel Bks) PB.
—The Richest Kids in Town. LC 93-47271. 128p. (gr. 4 up). 1994. 13.99 (*0-525-65166-7*, Cobblehill Bks) Dutton Child Bks.
Kelley, Shirley. The Good, the Bad & the Two Cookie Kid. Herbst, Eric & Genee, Gloria, eds. Claridy, Jimmy, illus. Cash, Johnny, intro. by. (Illus.). 32p. (ps-4). 1993. Incl. audio cass. 9.95 (*1-882436-02-4*) Better Pl Pub.
—The Rainy Day Blues. Herbst, Eric & Genee, Gloria, eds. Claridy, Jimmy, illus. King, B. B., intro. by. (Illus.). 32p. (ps-4). 1993. Incl. audio cass. 9.95 (*1-882436-01-6*) Better Pl Pub.
Kellogg, Steven. Best Friends. Kellogg, Steven, illus. LC 85-15971. 32p. (ps-3). 1986. 13.95 (*0-8037-0099-7*); PLB 13.89 (*0-8037-0101-2*) Dial Bks Young.
—Pinkerton, Behave. giant ed. (ps-3). 1990. 17.99 (*0-8037-0841-6*) Dial Bks Young.
—Ralph's Secret Weapon. Kellogg, Steven, illus. LC 82-22115. 32p. (ps-3). 1986. pap. 4.95 (*0-8037-0024-5*) Dial Bks Young.
—Tallyho, Pinkerton! Kellogg, Steven, illus. LC 82-2341. 32p. (ps-3). 1985. 4.95 (*0-8037-0166-7*) Dial Bks Young.
Kent, Deborah. Why Me? (gr. 4-7). 1992. pap. 2.95 (*0-590-44179-5*) Scholastic Inc.
Kent, Jack. Socks for Supper. LC 93-7771. 1993. PLB 13.27 (*0-8368-0975-0*) Gareth Stevens Inc.

Kent, Richard. The Mosquito Test. Weinberger, Jane, ed. 250p. (Orig.). (gr. 8-12). 1994. pap. 8.95 (*1-883650-03-8*) Windswept Hse. Narrated by the main character, this young adult novel addresses two teenagers' vailiant efforts to overcome the emotional & physical setbacks of cancer & cystic fibrosis. Against the background of tennis courts, high school hallways & hospital wards, these boys discover the meaning of courage & the legacy of friendship. The author was Maine Teacher of the Year in 1993 & winner of the National Educator Award from the Milken Foundation in 1994. Over 20,000 sold to date. *Publisher Provided Annotation.*

Kerr, M. E. Fell Down. LC 90-49921. 208p. (gr. 7 up). 1993. pap. 3.95 (*0-06-447086-5*, Trophy) HarpC Child Bks.
—Little Little. LC 80-8454. 192p. (gr. 7 up). 1991. pap. 3.95 (*0-06-447061-X*, Trophy) HarpC Child Bks.
—Night Kites. LC 85-45386. 224p. (gr. 7 up). 1987. pap. 3.95 (*0-06-447035-0*, Trophy) HarpC Child Bks.
Kidd, Ronald. Dunker. 176p. (gr. 5 up). pap. 2.50 (*0-553-26431-1*) Bantam.
—Second Fiddle. 176p. (gr. 4-7). 1992. pap. 2.95 (*0-8167-1823-7*) Troll Assocs.
Kiesel, Stanley. Skinny Malinky Leads the War for Kidness. 176p. (gr. 7 up). 1985. pap. 2.50 (*0-380-69875-7*, Flare) Avon.
Kilborne, Sarah S. Peach & Blue. Fancher, Lou & Johnson, Steve, illus. LC 93-26562. 40p. (ps-2). 1994. 15.00 (*0-679-83929-1*); PLB 15.99 (*0-679-93929-6*) Knopf Bks Yng Read.
King, Deborah. Custer: The Story of a Horse. King, Deborah, illus. 32p. (ps-3). 1992. PLB 14.95 (*0-399-22147-6*, Philomel Bks) Putnam Pub Group.
King, Larry L. Because of Lozo Brown. (ps-3). 1990. pap. 3.95 (*0-14-050593-8*, Puffin) Puffin Bks.
Kiser, SuAnn. Hazel Saves the Day. Day, Betsy, illus. LC 92-34782. 1994. write for info. (*0-8037-1488-2*); PLB write for info. (*0-8037-1489-0*) Dial Bks Young.
Kitchen, Bert. And So They Build. Kitchen, Bert, illus. LC 92-54403. 32p. (ps up). 1993. 15.95 (*1-56402-217-X*) Candlewick Pr.
Klass, Sheila S. The Bennington Stitch. 144p. (gr. 7-12). 1986. pap. 2.50 (*0-553-26049-9*) Bantam.
—Page Four. 176p. 1988. pap. 2.95 (*0-553-26901-1*, Starfire) Bantam.
—Pork Bellies Are Down. LC 94-20235. 1995. 13.95 (*0-590-46686-0*) Scholastic Inc.
Klaveness, Jan O. The Griffin Legacy. (gr. 4-6). 1985. pap. 3.25 (*0-440-43165-4*, YB) Dell.
Klein, Norma. Just Friends. 160p. 1991. pap. 3.95 (*0-449-70352-5*, Juniper) Fawcett.
—Now That I Know. LC 87-32080. 160p. (gr. 7 up). 1988. 13.95 (*0-553-05472-4*) Bantam.
Klein, Robin. Enemies. (gr. 4-7). 1991. pap. 2.50 (*0-590-43689-9*) Scholastic Inc.
Kleven, Elisa. Ernst. (Illus.). 32p. (ps-3). 1993. pap. 4.50 (*0-14-054944-7*, Puff Unicorn) Puffin Bks.
Kline, Suzy. Herbie Jones & Hamburger Head. (gr. 4-7). 1991. pap. 3.95 (*0-14-034583-3*, Puffin) Puffin Bks.
—Horrible Harry in Room 2B. Remkiewicz, Frank, illus. 64p. (gr. 2-5). 1990. pap. 2.99 (*0-14-032825-4*, Puffin) Puffin Bks.
—Horrible Harry's Secret. Remkiewicz, Frank, illus. 64p. (gr. 2-5). 1992. pap. 2.99 (*0-14-032915-3*) Puffin Bks.

—Who's Orp's Girlfriend? 112p. (gr. 3-6). 1993. 13.95 (*0-399-22431-9*, Putnam) Putnam Pub Group.

Klugman, Miriam. Captain David. 100p. 1991. 9.95 (*1-56062-095-1*) CIS Comm.

Know When to Stop. (Illus.). (ps-2). 1991. PLB 6.95 (*0-8136-5083-6*, TK2320); pap. 3.50 (*0-8136-5583-8*, TK2321) Modern Curr.

Koertge, Ron. The Boy in the Moon. 176p. 1992. pap. 3.99 (*0-380-71474-4*, Flare) Avon.

Koller, Jackie F. Mole & Shrew Step Out. Ormai, Stella, illus. LC 91-20531. 32p. (ps-3). 1992. SBE 13.95 (*0-689-31713-1*, Atheneum Child Bk) Macmillan Child Grp.

Konigsburg, E. L. George. 160p. (gr. k-6). 1985. pap. 3.50 (*0-440-42847-5*, YB) Dell.

—Jennifer, Hecate, Macbeth, William McKinley & Me, Elizabeth. Konigsburg, E. L., illus. LC 67-10458. 128p. (gr. 3-5). 1971. SBE 13.95 (*0-689-30007-7*, Atheneum Child Bk) Macmillan Child Grp.

—Jennifer, Hecate, Macbeth, William McKinley & Me, Elizabeth. 128p. (gr. 3-6). 1985. pap. 3.50 (*0-440-44162-5*, YB) Dell.

—A Proud Taste for Scarlet & Miniver. 208p. (gr. 5-8). 1985. pap. 3.99 (*0-440-47201-6*, YB) Dell.

Kontoyiannaki, Elizabeth. Leo & His Friends. Kontoyiannaki, Elizabeth, illus. 12p. (gr. 1-4). 1992. pap. 12.95 (*1-56606-011-7*) Bradley Mann.

—Run, Don't Walk. Kontoyiannaki, Elizabeth, illus. (gr. k-3). Date not set. pap. 13.95 (*1-56606-016-8*) Bradley Mann.

Koontz, Robin M. Chicago & the Cat. Koontz, Robin M., illus. LC 91-34863. 32p. (gr. k-3). 1993. 12.00 (*0-525-65097-0*, Cobblehill Bks) Dutton Child Bks.

Korman, Gordon. Macdonald Hall Goes Hollywood. 176p. (gr. 3-7). 1991. 12.95 (*0-590-43940-5*, Scholastic Hardcover) Scholastic Inc.

—The War with Mr. Wizzle. 192p. (gr. 3-7). 1990. pap. 3.25 (*0-590-44206-6*) Scholastic Inc.

Korth-Sander, Irmtraut. Will You Be My Friend? Korth-Sander, Irmtraut, illus. Lanning, Rosemary, tr. from GER. LC 86-60485. (Illus.). 32p. (gr. k-2). 1986. 14.95 (*1-55858-071-9*) North-South Bks NYC.

Kraus, Robert. Three Friends. Arvego, Jose & Dewey, Ariane, illus. (gr. k-3). 1975. (Dutton); pap. 2.95 (*0-525-62346-9*) NAL-Dutton.

Kropp, Paul. Getting Even. 192p. 1986. pap. 3.50 (*0-7704-2112-1*) Bantam.

Krumgold, Joseph. Onion John. Shimin, Symeon, illus. LC 59-11395. 248p. (gr. 5 up). 1987. (Crowell Jr Bks); PLB 14.89 (*0-690-04698-7*, Crowell Jr Bks) HarpC Child Bks.

Kulling, Monica. Waiting for Amos. Lowe, Vicky, illus. LC 92-19550. 32p. (ps-2). 1993. SBE 13.95 (*0-02-751245-2*, Bradbury Pr) Macmillan Child Grp.

Kuskin, Karla. Just Like Everyone Else. LC 59-5320. (Illus.). 32p. (ps-3). 1982. pap. 5.95 (*0-06-443032-4*, Trophy) HarpC Child Bks.

Kwitz, Mary D. Little Chick's Friend Duckling. Degen, Bruce, illus. LC 90-5027. 32p. (ps-2). 1992. 13.00 (*0-06-023638-8*); PLB 13.89 (*0-06-023639-6*) HarpC Child Bks.

Lake, Simon. He Told Me To. 1993. pap. 3.50 (*0-553-56168-5*) Bantam.

Lamb, Nancy. The Great Mosquito, Bull, & Coffin Caper. Remkiewicz, Frank, illus. LC 91-31125. 160p. (gr. 3 up). 1992. reinforced bdg. 12.00 (*0-688-10933-0*) Lothrop.

Landis, James D. Joey & the Girls. 192p. (Orig.). (gr. 7-12). 1987. pap. 2.95 (*0-553-26415-X*, Starfire) Bantam.

Lansing, Karen E. Time to Be a Friend. LC 92-13010. 96p. (gr. 4-8). 1993. pap. 4.95 (*0-8361-3614-4*) Herald Pr.

Lantz, Frances. Dear Celeste, My Life Is a Mess. (gr. 4-7). 1992. pap. 3.25 (*0-553-15961-5*) Bantam.

—Making It on Our Own. (gr. 6-12). 1986. pap. 2.75 (*0-440-95202-6*, LFL) Dell.

Larocque, Jean-Paul. Life with Me. Larocque, Jean-Paul, illus. 14p. (gr. k-3). 1994. pap. 11.95 (*1-895583-67-5*) MAYA Pubs.

—Our Night Out. Larocque, Jean-Paul, illus. 12p. (gr. k-3). 1994. pap. 10.95 (*1-895583-66-7*) MAYA Pubs.

Larson, Kirby. Second Grade Pig Pals. Poydar, Nancy, illus. LC 93-16061. 96p. (gr. 1-5). 1994. 14.95 (*0-8234-1107-9*) Holiday.

Lasky, Kathryn. Home Free. (gr. 7 up). 1988. pap. 2.95 (*0-440-20038-5*, LFL) Dell.

—The Solo. McCarthy, Bobette, illus. LC 92-44456. 32p. (ps-2). 1994. RSBE 14.95 (*0-02-751664-4*, Macmillan Child Bk) Macmillan Child Grp.

Lattimore, Eleanor F. Little Pear & His Friends. (gr. 1-4). 1992. 17.00 (*0-8446-6575-4*) Peter Smith.

Lawlor, Laurie. Addie's Dakota Winter. Tucker, Kathy, ed. Gowing, Toby, illus. LC 89-5564. (Illus.). 160p. (gr. 2-6). 1989. PLB 11.95 (*0-8075-0171-9*) A Whitman.

—Addie's Long Summer. Tucker, Kathleen, ed. Gowing, Toby, illus. LC 91-34877. 176p. (gr. 3-6). 1992. PLB 11.95 (*0-8075-0167-0*) A Whitman.

—How To Survive Third Grade. Levine, Abby, ed. LC 87-25430. (Illus.). 72p. (gr. 2-5). 1988. PLB 9.95 (*0-8075-3433-1*) A Whitman.

Lebowitz, Fran. Mr. Chas & Lisa Sue Meet the Pandas. Graves, Michael, illus. LC 94-1132. 72p. (gr. 2-7). 1994. 15.00 (*0-679-86052-5*) Knopf Bks Yng Read.

Lee, Marie G. Saying Goodbye. LC 93-26092. 1994. write for info. (*0-395-67066-7*) HM.

LeMieux, A. C. Fruit Flies, Fish & Fortune Cookies. DeGroat, Diane, illus. LC 93-29606. 1994. write for info. (*0-688-13299-5*, Tambourine Bks) Morrow.

L'Engle, Madeleine. And Both Were Young. (Orig.). (gr. 7 up). 1983. pap. 3.99 (*0-440-90229-0*, LFL) Dell.

—And Both Were Young. LC 82-72751. 240p. (gr. 7 up). 1983. 14.95 (*0-385-29237-6*) Delacorte.

Leonard, Marcia. Take a Bow, Krissy! Long, Laurie S., illus. 64p. (gr. 1-4). 1994. PLB 7.99 (*0-448-40838-4*, G&D); pap. 3.95 (*0-448-40837-6*, G&D) Putnam Pub Group.

Leppard, Lois G. Mandie & the Charleston Phantom, Bk. 7. LC 86-7098. 128p. (Orig.). (gr. 4-7). 1986. pap. 3.99 (*0-87123-650-8*) Bethany Hse.

Lester, Helen. The Wizard, the Fairy, & the Magic Chicken. Munsinger, Lynn, illus. LC 82-21302. 32p. (gr. k-3). 1988. pap. 5.70 (*0-395-47945-2*) HM.

Levene, Nancy. Cherry Cola Champions. LC 88-12294. (Illus.). 120p. (gr. 3-7). 1988. pap. 4.99 (*1-55513-519-6*, Chariot Bks) Chariot Family.

—French Fry Forgiveness. LC 87-5268. (gr. 3-6). 1987. pap. 4.99 (*1-55513-302-9*, Chariot Bks) Chariot Family.

—Hot Chocolate Friendship. LC 87-5281. (gr. 3-6). 1987. pap. 4.99 (*1-55513-304-5*, Chariot Bks) Chariot Family.

—Peach Pit Popularity. LC 89-33900. (gr. 3-6). 1989. pap. 4.99 (*1-55513-529-3*, Chariot Bks) Chariot Family.

Levene, Nancy S. Mint Cookie Miracles. LC 88-11902. 120p. (gr. 3-7). 1988. pap. 4.99 (*1-55513-514-5*, Chariot Bks) Chariot Family.

Leverich, Kathleen. Best Enemies. Lamb, Susan C., illus. LC 88-19150. (gr. 1 up). 1989. 10.95 (*0-688-08316-1*) Greenwillow.

—Best Enemies Again. Lorraine, Walter, illus. LC 90-30303. 96p. (gr. 2 up). 1991. 12.95 (*0-688-09440-6*) Greenwillow.

Levine, Gloria. Cricket in Times Square: A Study Guide. (gr. 4-7). 1987. tchr's. ed. & wkbk. 14.95 (*0-88122-073-6*) LRN Links.

Levinson, Marilyn. The Fourth-Grade Four. Bowman, Leslie, illus. LC 89-31109. 64p. (gr. 2-4). 1989. 12.95 (*0-8050-1082-3*, Bks Young Read) H Holt & Co.

Levoy, Myron. Alan & Naomi. LC 76-41522. 176p. (gr. 6 up). 1987. pap. 3.95 (*0-06-440209-6*, Trophy) HarpC Child Bks.

Levy, Elizabeth. The Case of the Tattletale Heart. Eagle, Ellen, illus. 64p. (gr. 2-4). 1992. pap. 3.00 (*0-671-74064-4*, S&S BFYR) S&S Trade.

—Cheater, Cheater. LC 92-33455. 1993. 13.95 (*0-590-45865-5*) Scholastic Inc.

—Rude, Rowdy Rumors: A Brian & Pea Brain Mystery, No. 2. Ulrich, George, illus. LC 93-46792. 128p. (gr. 2-5). 1994. 13.00 (*0-06-023462-8*); PLB 12.89 (*0-06-023463-6*) HarpC Child Bks.

Levy, Marilyn. Remember to Remember Me. (gr. 5 up). 1988. pap. 2.95 (*0-449-70278-2*, Juniper) Fawcett.

Lewis, Beverly. Holly's First Love. LC 92-47055. 1993. pap. 2.99 (*0-310-38051-0*) Zondervan.

—Second-Best Friend. 160p. (gr. 6-9). 1994. pap. 4.99 (*0-310-43331-2*) Zondervan.

Lewis, Harriet. Pampoody & Max. 72p. 1977. pap. 4.50 (*0-933294-01-8*) Backroads.

Lexau, Joan M. Striped Ice Cream. LC 68-10774. (Illus.). 96p. (gr. k-3). 1968. PLB 13.89 (*0-397-31047-1*, Lipp Jr Bks) HarpC Child Bks.

Lieberman, Lillian. Comprehension. 64p. (gr. 2-5). 1987. 6.95 (*0-912107-66-9*) Monday Morning Bks.

Lillie, Patricia. Jake & Rosie. LC 87-14939. (Illus.). 24p. (ps up). 1989. 11.95 (*0-688-07624-6*); PLB 11.88 (*0-688-07625-4*) Greenwillow.

Lindberg, Anne. The Worry Week. (gr. 3-7). 1988. pap. 2.95 (*0-380-70394-7*, Camelot) Avon.

Lindberg, Becky T. Chelsea Martin Turns Green. Tucker, Kathy, ed. Poydar, Nancy, illus. LC 92-31613. 144p. (gr. 2-4). 1993. PLB 11.95 (*0-8075-1134-X*) A Whitman.

Lindbergh, Anne M. & Hoguet, Susan R. Next Time, Take Care. (Illus.). 32p. (ps-3). 1988. 13.95 (*0-15-257200-7*, HB Juv Bks) HarBrace.

Lindquist, Marie. Untamed Heart. 160p. (Orig.). (gr. 7-12). 1987. pap. 2.50 (*0-553-26474-5*, Starfire) Bantam.

Lionni, Leo. An Extraordinary Egg. LC 93-28565. (Illus.). 40p. (ps-2). 1994. 15.00 (*0-679-85840-7*); PLB 15.99 (*0-679-95840-1*) Knopf Bks Yng Read.

—It's Mine. Lionni, Leo, illus. LC 85-190. 32p. (ps-1). 1986. 15.00 (*0-394-87000-X*); lib. bdg. 15.99 (*0-394-97000-4*) Knopf Bks Yng Read.

—Little Blue & Little Yellow. Cohn, Amy, ed. LC 94-7324. (Illus.). 48p. (ps up). 1994. pap. 4.95 (*0-688-13285-5*, Mulberry) Morrow.

—Swimmy. LC 63-8504. (Illus.). 32p. (ps-6). 1987. 4.99 (*0-394-82620-5*) Knopf Bks Yng Read.

Lisle, Janet T. The Gold Dust Letters. LC 93-11806. 128p. (gr. 3-5). 1994. 14.95 (*0-531-06830-7*); lib. bdg. 14.99 RLB (*0-531-08680-1*) Orchard Bks Watts.

—Looking for Juliette. LC 94-6922. 128p. (gr. 3-5). 1994. 14.95 (*0-531-06870-6*); PLB 14.99 (*0-531-08720-4*) Orchard Bks Watts.

Little, Jean. Kate. LC 20-148419. 174p. (gr. 5-8). 1973. pap. 3.95 (*0-06-440037-9*, Trophy) HarpC Child Bks.

—Look Through My Window. Sandin, Joan, illus. LC 71-105470. 270p. (gr. 4-7). 1970. PLB 14.89 (*0-06-023924-7*) HarpC Child Bks.

Littleton, Mark. Winter Thunder. LC 92-5433. 1993. pap. 3.99 (*1-56507-008-9*) Harvest Hse.

Lobe, Mira. Ben & the Child of the Forest. Sklenitzka, Franz S., illus. 96p. (gr. 3-4). 1988. pap. 2.95 (*0-8120-3936-X*) Barron.

Lobel, Arnold. Days with Frog & Toad. LC 78-21786. (Illus.). 64p. (gr. k-3). 1979. 14.00i (*0-06-023963-8*); PLB 13.89 (*0-06-023964-6*) HarpC Child Bks.

—Days with Frog & Toad: (Dios con Sapo y Sepo) (SPA.). (gr. 1-6). 8.95 (*84-204-3743-3*) Santillana.

Lomasney, Eileen. What Do You Do with the Rest of the Day, Mary Ann? 1991. pap. 3.95 (*0-8091-6601-1*) Paulist Pr.

Long, Kathy. A Surprise for Mrs. Dodds: A Little Boy's Friendship Changes a Lonely Woman's Life. Rogers, Kathy, illus. LC 89-84939. 32p. (gr. 3-5). 1989. pap. 5.99 (*0-8066-2437-X*, 9-2437) Augsburg Fortress.

Loomis, Christine. In the Diner. Poydar, Nancy, illus. 32p. (ps-2). 1994. 14.95 (*0-590-46716-6*, Scholastic Hardcover) Scholastic Inc.

Lord, Wendy. Gorilla on the Midway. LC 93-1051. 1994. pap. 4.99 (*0-7814-0892-X*, Chariot Bks) Chariot Family.

—Pickle Stew. LC 93-19018. 1994. pap. 4.49 (*0-7814-0886-5*, Chariot Bks) Chariot Family.

Lovelace, Maud H. Betsy & Tacy Go Downtown. Lenski, Lois, illus. LC 43-51264. 192p. (gr. 2-5). 1979. pap. 3.95 (*0-06-440098-0*, Trophy) HarpC Child Bks.

—Betsy & Tacy Go over the Big Hill. Lenski, Lois, illus. LC 42-23557. 176p. (gr. 2-5). 1979. pap. 3.95 (*0-06-440099-9*, Trophy) HarpC Child Bks.

Lovelace, Maureen H. Betsy-Tacy. Lenski, Lois, illus. LC 40-30965. 128p. (gr. 2-5). 1979. pap. 3.95 (*0-06-440096-4*, Trophy) HarpC Child Bks.

—Betsy-Tacy & Tib. Lenski, Lois, illus. LC 41-18714. 144p. (gr. 2-5). 1979. pap. 3.95 (*0-06-440097-2*, Trophy) HarpC Child Bks.

Lowry, Lois. Find a Stranger, Say Good-Bye. LC 78-1024. 192p. (gr. 5 up). 1978. 16.95 (*0-395-26459-6*) HM.

—Switcharound. (gr. k-6). 1991. pap. 3.50 (*0-440-48415-4*, YB) Dell.

Lucien, Michele. Welcome to My World. 50p. (ps-k). 1993. pap. text ed. write for info. (*0-9639678-0-0*) Write For You.

Lukaszewski, David. Little Ms. Rosey & Friends. 1993. 7.75 (*0-8062-4622-7*) Carlton.

Lund, Doris. Eric. 268p. (gr. 7 up). 1979. pap. 2.95 (*0-440-94586-0*, LFL) Dell.

Lurie, Susan. Nutcracker. (ps-3). 1993. pap. 3.99 (*0-553-37293-9*) Bantam.

Lustig, Loretta, illus. Skip to My Lou. 1994. bk. & cassette 6.99 (*0-553-45908-2*) Bantam.

Luttrell, Ida. Ottie Slockett. Fogelman, Phyllis J., ed. Krause, Ute, illus. LC 88-30884. 40p. (ps-3). 1990. 9.95 (*0-8037-0709-6*); PLB 9.89 (*0-8037-0711-8*) Dial Bks Young.

Luttrell, Jean. Winning Isn't Everything. Luttrell, Chuck, illus. 76p. (Orig.). (gr. 3-5). 1990. pap. 6.95 (*0-9617609-2-3*) Shade Tree NV.

Lyon, George Ella. Together. Rosenberry, Vera, illus. LC 89-2892. 32p. (ps-1). 1994. pap. 5.95 (*0-531-07047-6*) Orchard Bks Watts.

McBrier, Page. First Course: Trouble. 128p. 1990. pap. 2.50 (*0-380-75783-4*, Camelot) Avon.

—The Great Rip-Off. 128p. 1990. pap. 2.95 (*0-380-75902-0*, Camelot) Avon.

—Rats. 128p. 1990. pap. 2.95 (*0-380-75901-2*, Camelot) Avon.

McCabe, Bernard. Bottle Rabbit & Friends. Scheffler, Axel, illus. 136p. (gr. 3-7). 1991. 14.95 (*0-571-15318-6*) Faber & Faber.

McCann, Helen. What's French for Help, George? Eagle, Ellen, illus. LC 91-41563. 460p. (gr. 5-9). 1993. pap. 13.00 JR3 (*0-671-74689-8*, S&S BFYR) S&S Trade.

McCaskill, Margaret. Please, Tell Me. 1993. 7.95 (*0-8062-4611-1*) Carlton.

McConnell, Christine. Don't Be Mad, Ivy. De Groat, Diane, photos by. (gr. 2-5). 1988. pap. 3.95 (*0-14-032329-5*, Puffin) Puffin Bks.

McDaniel, Lurlene. Goodbye Doesn't Mean Forever. (gr. 7 up). 1989. pap. 3.50 (*0-553-28007-4*, Starfire) Bantam.

—I Want to Live. 128p. (gr. 5-8). 1987. 2.99 (*0-87406-237-3*) Willowisp Pr.

—The Legacy: Making Wishes Come True. 1993. pap. 3.50 (*0-553-56134-0*) Bantam.

—Let Him Live. 1993. pap. 3.50 (*0-553-56067-0*) Bantam.

MacDonald, George. Alec Forbes & His Friend Annie. Phillips, Michael R., ed. 256p. (gr. 2-7). 1990. 10.99 (*1-55661-140-4*) Bethany Hse.

—The Peasant Girl's Dream. rev. ed. Phillips, Michael R., ed. LC 88-33336. 224p. (gr. 11 up). 1989. pap. 7.99 (*1-55661-023-8*) Bethany Hse.

Macdonald, Mary A. Hedgehog Bakes a Cake - Bank Street. (ps-3). 1990. pap. 3.99 (*0-553-34890-6*) Bantam.

Macdonald, Maryann. The Pink Party. LC 93-20989. (Illus.). 40p. (gr. k-3). 1994. 10.95 (*1-56282-620-4*); PLB 10.89 (*1-56282-621-2*) Hyprn Child.

McDonnell, Christine. Don't Be Mad, Ivy. DeGroat, Diane, illus. LC 81-65850. 80p. (gr. 1-5). 1981. Dial Bks Young.

—Friends First. LC 92-20290. 176p. (gr. 5 up). 1992. pap. 3.99 (*0-14-032477-1*) Puffin Bks.

—Just for the Summer. De Groat, Diane, illus. 128p. (gr. 2-6). 1989. pap. 3.95 (*0-14-032147-0*, Puffin) Puffin Bks.

McDonnell, Janet. Two Special Valentines. McCallum, Jodie, illus. LC 93-37097. 32p. (ps-2). 1994. PLB 12.30 (*0-516-00692-4*) Childrens.

—An XYZ Adventure in Alphabet Town. Hohag, Linda, illus. LC 92-2985. 32p. (ps-2). 1992. PLB 11.80 (*0-516-05424-4*) Childrens.
McGugan, Jim. Josepha. Kimber, Murray, illus. LC 94-6603. 1994. 13.95 (*0-8118-0802-5*) Chronicle Bks.
McHargue, Georgess. See You Later, Crocodile. 192p. (gr. 5-9). 1988. 14.95 (*0-440-50052-4*) Delacorte.
MacKeen, Leslie A. Who Can Fix It? Thatch, Nancy R., ed. MacKeen, Leslie A., illus. Melton, David, intro. by. LC 89-31819. (Illus.). 26p. (gr. k-3). 1989. PLB 14.95 (*0-933849-19-2*) Landmark Edns.
MacKinnon, Bernie. Meantime. 1992. pap. 4.95 (*0-395-61622-0*) HM.
MacLachlan, Patricia. Skylark. LC 93-33211. 64p. (gr. 3-5). 1994. 12.00 (*0-06-023328-1*); PLB 11.89 (*0-06-023333-8*) HarpC Child Bks.
McMullen, Shawn. That's What Friends Are For. Haley, Amanda, illus. LC 91-43656. (gr. 4-8). 1992. saddle-stitched 5.99 (*0-87403-975-4*, 24-03865) Standard Pub.
McNamara, John. Revenge of the Nerd. 128p. (gr. 5 up). 1985. pap. 2.50 (*0-440-97353-8*, LFL) Dell.
McOmber, Rachel B., ed. McOmber Phonics Storybooks: Hello Again. rev. ed. (Illus.). write for info. (*0-944991-84-X*) Swift Lrn Res.
—McOmber Phonics Storybooks: Jud & Nell. rev. ed. (Illus.). write for info. (*0-944991-33-5*) Swift Lrn Res.
—McOmber Phonics Storybooks: The Gal Pals. rev. ed. (Illus.). write for info. (*0-944991-42-4*) Swift Lrn Res.
McPhail, David. Annie & Company II. 1994. write for info. (*0-8050-2819-6*) H Holt & Co.
Madden, John. I've Got Your Nose! Bentley, Nancy, illus. 1991. 12.00 (*0-685-59973-6*) Dell.
Madgett, Naomi L. Pink Ladies in the Afternoon. 2nd ed. LC 90-60605. 75p. (gr. 7-10). 1990. pap. 7.00 (*0-916418-78-2*) Lotus.
Magorian, Michelle. Good Night, Mr. Tom. LC 80-8444. 336p. (gr. 5-9). 1986. pap. 3.95 (*0-06-440174-X*, Trophy) HarpC Child Bks.
Mahy, Margaret. Memory. (gr. k-12). 1989. pap. 3.50 (*0-440-20433-X*, LFL) Dell.
—The Tricksters. LC 86-33761. 272p. (gr. 9 up). 1987. 14.95 (*0-689-50400-4*, M K McElderry) Macmillan Child Grp.
Maifair, Linda. No Girls Allowed. Johnson, Meredith, illus. LC 93-40083. 1993. 3.99 (*0-8066-2688-7*, Augsburg) Augsburg Fortress.
Major, Kevin. Hold Fast. LC 79-17544. (gr. 9-12). 1980. 9.95 (*0-440-03506-6*) Delacorte.
Malkin, Michele. Blanche & Smitty, No. 1. 1988. pap. 3.95 (*0-553-05424-4*) Bantam.
—Blanche & Smitty, No. 2. 1988. 3.50 (*0-553-05478-3*) Bantam.
Maloney, Ray. The Impact Zone. (gr. k-12). 1987. pap. 2.95 (*0-440-94013-3*, LFL) Dell.
Mann, Peggy. Twelve Is Too Old. updated ed. 140p. (gr. 6-9). 1987. pap. 6.95 (*0-942493-00-1*) Woodmere Press.
Mariotti, Mario. Hands Off! (Illus.). 40p. (ps-4). 1990. 10. 95 (*0-916291-29-4*) Kane-Miller Bk.
Mark, Jan. Handles. large type ed. (gr. 1-8). 1991. 16.95 (*0-7451-0760-5*, Galaxy Child Lrg Print) Chivers N Amer.
Markus, Julia. Friends along the Way. (gr. k-12). 1987. pap. 4.95 (*0-440-32761-X*, LE) Dell.
Marron, Carol A. Someone Just Like Me. (ps-3). 1993. pap. 4.95 (*0-8114-8407-6*) Raintree Steck-V.
Marsden, John. Letters from the Inside. LC 93-41185. 1994. 13.95 (*0-395-68985-6*) HM.
Marshall, Edward. Fox All Week. Marshall, James, illus. LC 84-1708. (ps-3). 1984. 10.95 (*0-8037-0062-8*) Dial Bks Young.
Marshall, James. The Cut-ups Cut Loose. (Illus.). 32p. (ps-3). 1989. pap. 4.99 (*0-14-050672-1*, Puffin) Puffin Bks.
—George & Martha Round & Round. (ps-3). 1991. pap. 5.95 (*0-395-58410-8*) HM.
—George & Martha Tons of Fun. (Illus.). 48p. (gr. k-3). 1980. 13.95 (*0-395-29524-6*); pap. 4.80 (*0-395-42646-4*) HM.
Martin, Ann M. Claudia & the New Girl. large type ed. LC 93-15969. 176p. (gr. 4 up). 1993. PLB 15.93 (*0-8368-1016-3*) Gareth Stevens Inc.
—Claudia's Friend. (gr. 4-7). 1993. pap. 3.50 (*0-590-45665-2*) Scholastic Inc.
—Good-Bye, Stacy, Good-Bye. large type ed. LC 93-4345. 176p. (gr. 4 up). 1993. PLB 15.93 (*0-8368-1017-1*) Gareth Stevens Inc.
—Goodbye Stacey, Goodbye. 1993. pap. 3.25 (*0-590-43386-5*) Scholastic Inc.
—Hello Mallory. 1993. pap. 3.25 (*0-590-43385-7*) Scholastic Inc.
—Hello, Mallory. large type ed. 176p. (gr. 4 up). 1993. PLB 15.93 (*0-8368-1018-X*) Gareth Stevens Inc.
—Inside Out. (gr. 5-7). 1990. pap. 2.95 (*0-590-43621-X*) Scholastic Inc.
—Karen's New Friend. (gr. 4-7). 1993. pap. 2.95 (*0-590-45651-2*) Scholastic Inc.
—Karen's Pen Pal. 96p. 1992. pap. 2.95 (*0-590-44831-5*) Scholastic Inc.
—Secret Santa. LC 93-48981. 1994. 14.95 (*0-590-48295-5*) Scholastic Inc.
Martin, Bette. The Children's Material. (Illus.). 100p. (gr. k-4). 1980. pap. write for info. (*1-880436-02-7*) Miracle Exper.
—Help Is on the Way. (Illus.). 61p. (gr. 5-7). 1986. pap. write for info. (*1-880436-01-9*) Miracle Exper.
Martin, Bill, Jr. Words. (ps-6). 1993. 4.95 (*0-671-87174-9*, Little Simon) S&S Trade.
Martin, Bill, Jr. & Archambault, John. White Dynamite & Curly Kidd. Rand, Ted, illus. LC 85-27214. 48p. (ps-2). 1989. pap. 5.95 (*0-8050-1018-1*, Bks Young Read) H Holt & Co.
Martin, Linda. When Dinosaurs Go Visiting. LC 93-10207. 1993. 12.95 (*0-8118-0122-5*) Chronicle Bks.
Martinez, Carol. Paco y Ana Aprenden Acerca de la Amistad. Stillman, Peter, illus. (SPA., Orig.). (gr. 2-4). 1988. pap. 1.50 (*0-311-38589-3*, Edit Mundo) Casa Bautista.
Marzollo, Jean. Close Your Eyes. Jeffers, Susan, illus. (ps-k). 1981. 4.95 (*0-8037-1617-6*) Dial Bks Young.
Mason, Kate. My Friendship Bracelets. (ps-3). 1994. pap. 5.95 (*0-8167-3227-2*) Troll Assocs.
Mason, Laura L. Lots of Ways to Win. LC 91-68087. (Illus.). 44p. (gr. k-3). 1992. 7.95 (*1-55523-500-X*) Winston-Derek.
Mason, Margo C. Two Good Friends. (ps-3). 1990. 9.99 (*0-553-05869-X*) Bantam.
—Two Good Friends. (ps-3). 1990. pap. 3.50 (*0-553-34885-X*) Bantam.
Massi, Jeri. Abandoned. 136p. (Orig.). (gr. 5-8). 1989. pap. 4.95 (*0-89084-467-4*) Bob Jones Univ Pr.
Masterson, Audrey. The Day the Gypsies Came to Town. Oudekerk, Douglas, illus. LC 83-7319. 32p. (gr. 3-6). 1983. PLB 14.65 (*0-940742-22-5*) Raintree Steck-V.
Matas, Carol. Kris's War. 176p. 1992. pap. 3.25 (*0-590-45034-4*, Point) Scholastic Inc.
Mathers, Petra. Sophie & Lou. LC 90-37562. (Illus.). 32p. (ps-3). 1993. pap. 4.95 (*0-06-443331-5*, Trophy) HarpC Child Bks.
Mathis, Sharon B. Sidewalk Story. 64p. (gr. 2-6). 1986. pap. 3.99 (*0-14-032165-9*, Puffin) Puffin Bks.
Matranga, Frances C. One Step at a Time. (Illus.). (gr. 4-7). 1987. pap. 3.99 (*0-570-03642-9*, 39-1126) Concordia.
Matthews, Andrew. Mallory Cox & His Interstellar Socks. Ross, Tony, illus. 96p. (gr. 4-6). 1993. 18.95 (*0-460-88126-4*, Pub. by J M Dent & Sons) Trafalgar.
Matthews, Kay. I'm Glad You Asked. Sewards, Michele B., illus. 36p. (Orig.). (ps-3). 1994. pap. 7.50 (*0-940875-03-9*, Dist. by Gannon Distributing) Acequia Madre.
Matthews, Phoebe. Switchstance. 176p. (Orig.). (gr. 7 up). 1989. pap. 2.95 (*0-380-75729-X*, Flare) Avon.
Matula, Joyce. A Friend in Winter. LC 91-68091. (Illus.). 44p. (gr. k-4). 1992. pap. 6.95 (*1-55523-504-2*) Winston-Derek.
Mayer, Mercer. Appelard & Liverwurst. Kellogg, Steven, illus. LC 89-13803. 40p. (gr. k up). 1990. 13.95 (*0-688-09659-X*); PLB 13.88 (*0-688-09660-3*, Morrow Jr Bks) Morrow Jr Bks.
—This Is My Friend. (Illus.). 40p. (gr. k-2). 1989. write for info. (*0-307-11685-9*, Pub. by Golden Bks) Western Pub.
Mazer, Harry. When the Phone Rang. 192p. (gr. 7 up). 1986. pap. 2.95 (*0-590-44773-4*) Scholastic Inc.
Mazer, Norma F. E, My Name is Emily. 176p. 1991. 13. 95 (*0-590-43653-8*, Scholastic Hardcover) Scholastic Inc.
—Out of Control. LC 92-32516. 224p. (gr. 7 up). 1993. 14.00 (*0-688-10208-5*) Morrow Jr Bks.
—Out of Control. 224p. (gr. 5 up). 1994. pap. 3.99 (*0-380-71347-0*) Avon.
—Out of Control. large type ed. LC 93-47266. 1994. pap. write for info. (*0-7862-0159-2*) Thorndike Pr.
—Silver. LC 88-18652. 272p. (gr. 7 up). 1988. 12.95 (*0-688-06865-0*) Morrow Jr Bks.
Mazer, Norma F. & Mazer, Harry. Heartbeat. 1989. 16. 00 (*0-553-05808-8*, Starfire) Bantam.
Mebs, Gudren. Sunday's Child. (gr. k-6). 1989. pap. 2.95 (*0-440-40167-4*, YB) Dell.
Mega-Books Staff. My Friend Fang. 1992. pap. 3.99 (*0-553-37116-9*) Bantam.
Merriam, Eve. Blackberry Ink. Wilhelm, Hans, illus. LC 84-16633. 40p. (ps-2). 1985. 12.95 (*0-688-04150-7*); PLB 12.88 (*0-688-04151-5*, Morrow Jr Bks) Morrow Jr Bks.
—Jamboree. 96p. (Orig.). (ps-6). 1984. pap. 2.50 (*0-440-44199-4*, YB) Dell.
Michaels, Scott, ed. Freddy & Betty, Vol. 1. Morton, Tom, illus. (gr. 1-6). 1989. tchr's. ed. 2.50 (*0-317-93682-4*) S Michaels Pub.
Michals, Duane. Upside down, Inside Out, & Backwards. 80p. Date not set. pap. 19.95 (*0-685-68802-X*) Sonny Boy Bks.
Michels, Tilde. Who's That Knocking at My Door? Michl, Reinhard, illus. 28p. (ps-3). 1992. pap. 4.95 (*0-8120-1486-3*) Barron.
Miles, Betty. I Would If I Could. 120p. (gr. 3-6). 1983. pap. 2.95 (*0-380-63438-4*, Camelot) Avon.
—Maudie & Me & the Dirty Book. 140p. (gr. 4-7). 1981. pap. 2.95 (*0-380-55541-7*, Camelot) Avon.
—Maudie & Me & the Dirty Book. reissue ed. LC 79-19783. 144p. (gr. 4-7). 1989. pap. 3.99 (*0-394-82595-0*, Bullseye Bks) Random Bks Yng Read.
—The Trouble with Thirteen. LC 78-31678. (gr. 4-7). 1979. PLB 12.99 (*0-394-93930-1*) Knopf Bks Yng Read.
Millais, Raoul. Elijah & Pin-Pin. LC 91-20032. (Illus.). 48p. (ps-1). 1992. pap. 14.00 jacketed (*0-671-75543-9*, S&S BFYR) S&S Trade.
Miller, Frances A. The Truth Trap. 187p. 1986. pap. 3.95 (*0-449-70247-2*, Juniper) Fawcett.
Miller, Mary J. Upside Down. 121p. (gr. 3-7). 1994. pap. 3.99 (*0-14-034624-4*) Puffin Bks.
Miller, Shirley J. My House, Your House. Casey, Marjorie, illus. 60p. (Orig.). (gr. 2-6). 1993. pap. 6.95 (*1-878580-91-4*) Asylum Arts.
—School Days. Casey, Marjorie, illus. 80p. (Orig.). (gr. 2-6). 1993. pap. 6.95 (*1-878580-90-6*) Asylum Arts.
Millman, Malka. Too Tough to Care. 150p. (gr. 6). Date not set. 8.95 (*1-56062-237-7*) CIS Comm.
Mills, Claudia. Dynamite Dinah. LC 91-20651. 128p. (gr. 3-7). 1992. pap. 3.95 (*0-689-71591-9*, Aladdin) Macmillan Child Grp.
—Hannah on Her Way. LC 90-46532. 160p. (gr. 3-7). 1991. SBE 13.95 (*0-02-767011-2*, Macmillan Child Bk) Macmillan Child Grp.
Millward, David W. Jenny & Bob. (ps). 1991. 15.00 (*0-385-30431-5*) Delacorte.
Modarressi, Mitra. The Dream Pillow. LC 93-49400. (Illus.). 32p. (ps-2). 1994. 14.95 (*0-531-06855-2*); PLB 14.99 (*0-531-08705-0*) Orchard Bks Watts.
Modell, Frank. Look Out, It's April Fools' Day. Modell, Frank, illus. LC 84-4138. 24p. (ps up). 1985. 13.00 (*0-688-04016-0*); PLB 12.88 (*0-688-04017-9*) Greenwillow.
Moeri, Louise. The Forty-Third War. 208p. (gr. 5-9). 1989. 13.45 (*0-395-50215-2*) HM.
Mogensen, Jan. The Tiger's Breakfast. LC 91-3606. (Illus.). 32p. (ps-3). 1991. 14.95 (*0-940793-83-0*, Crocodile Bks) Interlink Pub.
Moncure, Jane B. Julie's New Home. Karch, Pat, illus. LC 82-19900. 32p. (gr. 3-4). 1983. lib. bdg. 8.45 (*0-89565-254-4*) Childs World.
—My Baby Brother Needs a Friend. Hook, Frances, illus. LC 78-21935. (ps-3). 1979. PLB 14.95 (*0-89565-019-3*) Childs World.
Monsell, Mary E. Toohy & Wood. Tryon, Leslie, illus. LC 91-38217. 64p. (gr. 2-5). 1992. SBE 12.95 (*0-689-31721-2*, Atheneum Child Bk) Macmillan Child Grp.
Monson, A. M. The Deer Stand. Pearson, Susan, ed. LC 91-32122. 160p. (gr. 4 up). 1992. reinforced bdg. 13. 00 (*0-688-11057-6*) Lothrop.
Montgomery, L. M. Anne of Green Gables. Felder, Deborah, adapted by. LC 93-36331. 108p. (Orig.). (gr. 2-6). 1994. pap. 2.99 (*0-679-85467-3*) Random Bks Yng Read.
—Rainbow Valley. 422p. 1992. text ed. 33.76 (*1-56956-121-4*) W A T Braille.
Montgomery, Lucy M. Anne of Green Gables. Mattern, Joanne, ed. Graef, Renee, illus. LC 92-12703. 48p. (gr. 3-6). 1992. PLB 12.89 (*0-8167-2866-6*); pap. text ed. 3.95 (*0-8167-2867-4*) Troll Assocs.
—Rainbow Valley. 240p. (gr. 6 up). 1985. pap. 2.95 (*0-553-25213-5*) Bantam.
Moore, Emily. Whose Side Are You On? 128p. (gr. 3-7). 1990. pap. 3.95 (*0-374-48373-6*, Sunburst) FS&G.
Moore, Lilian. Don't Be Afraid, Amanda. McCord, Kathleen, illus. LC 91-19661. 64p. (gr. 2-5). 1992. SBE 12.95 (*0-689-31725-5*, Atheneum Child Bk) Macmillan Child Grp.
—I'll Meet You at the Cucumbers. Wooding, Sharon, illus. (gr. 1-4). 1989. pap. 2.99 (*0-553-15705-1*, Skylark) Bantam.
Moreau, Patricia. Suzanne Masterson: Dangerous Games. 412p. 1994. pap. 8.99 (*0-88070-648-1*, Multnomah Bks) Questar Pubs.
Morpurgo, Michael. Waiting for Anya. 1991. 13.00 (*0-670-83735-0*) Viking Child Bks.
Morrison, Dorothy N. Whisper Goodbye. 192p. (gr. 2-9). 1988. pap. 2.95 (*0-8167-1045-7*) Troll Assocs.
Morrow, Catherine. The Jellybean Principal. Wummer, Amy, illus. LC 93-26537. 48p. (gr. 1-3). 1994. 7.99 (*0-679-94743-4*); pap. 3.50 (*0-679-84743-X*) Random Bks Yng Read.
Mueller, Charles. Almost Adult: Devotions for 9-12 Year Olds. LC 92-27014. 160p. (Orig.). (gr. 4-7). 1993. pap. 6.99 (*0-570-04598-3*) Concordia.
Mulford, Philippa G. Everything I Hoped For. 192p. (Orig.). (gr. 8-12). 1990. pap. 2.95 (*0-380-76074-6*, Flare) Avon.
—If It's Not Funny, Why Am I Laughing? LC 82-70321. 144p. (gr. 7 up). 1982. 9.95 (*0-440-03961-4*) Delacorte.
—The World Is My Eggshell. (gr. k-12). 1989. pap. 2.95 (*0-440-20243-4*, LFL) Dell.
Munro, Roxie. Blimps. Munro, Roxie, illus. LC 88-18138. 32p. (gr. 2-7). 1988. 12.95 (*0-525-44441-6*, DCB) Dutton Child Bks.
Munsch, Robert. Mortimer. Martchenko, Michael, illus. 24p. (gr. k-3). 1985. PLB 14.95 (*0-920303-12-9*, Pub. by Annick CN); pap. 4.95 (*0-920303-11-0*, Pub. by Annick CN) Firefly Bks Ltd.
—Murmel, Murmel, Murmel. Martchenko, Michael, illus. 32p. (gr. k-3). 1982. PLB 14.95 (*0-920236-29-4*, Pub. by Annick CN); pap. 4.95 (*0-920236-31-6*, Pub. by Annick CN) Firefly Bks Ltd.
—Something Good. Martchenko, Michael, illus. 24p. (ps-2). 1990. PLB 14.95 (*1-55037-099-5*, Pub. by Annick CN); pap. 4.95 (*1-55037-100-2*, Pub. by Annick CN) Firefly Bks Ltd.
Munsch, Robert & Kusugak, M. A Promise Is a Promise. Krykorka, Vladyana, illus. 32p. (gr. k-3). 1988. PLB 14.95 (*1-550370-09-X*, Pub. by Annick CN); pap. 4.95 (*1-550370-08-1*, Pub. by Annick CN) Firefly Bks Ltd.
Munsch, Robert & Martchenko, Michael. Wait & See. 24p. 1993. PLB 14.95 (*1-55037-335-8*, Pub. by Annick CN); pap. 4.95 (*1-55037-334-X*, Pub. by Annick CN) Firefly Bks Ltd.

Murphy, Elspeth C. Mary Jo Bennett. LC 85-17059. 107p. (Orig.). (gr. 3-7). 1985. pap. 4.99 (*0-89191-711-X*, 57117, Chariot Bks) Chariot Family.
Myers, Anna. Rosie's Tiger. LC 94-50814. 1994. write for info. (*0-8027-8305-8*) Walker & Co.
Myers, Bill & Johnson, Ken. McGee & Me! No. 2: Star in the Breaking. 1989. pap. 3.99 (*0-8423-4168-4*); video 19.95 (*0-8423-4153-6*) Tyndale.
—McGee & Me! No. 4: Skate Expectations. 1989. pap. 3.99 (*0-8423-4165-X*); video 19.95 (*0-8423-4155-2*) Tyndale.
—McGee & Me: The Big Lie. 1989. pap. 3.95 (*0-8423-4169-2*) Tyndale.
Myers, Bill & West, Robert E. Beauty in the Least. LC 93-14026. 1993. 3.99 (*0-8423-4124-2*) Tyndale.
Myers, Walter D. Dangerous Games. 1993. pap. 3.50 (*0-553-56269-X*) Bantam.
—Intensive Care. 1993. pap. 3.50 (*0-553-56268-1*) Bantam.
—Me, Mop, & the Moondance Kid. (gr. 4-7). 1988. 13.95 (*0-385-30147-2*) Doubleday.
—Me, Mop & the Moondance Kid. (gr. k-6). 1991. pap. 3.50 (*0-440-40396-0*, Pub. by Yearling Classics) Dell.
—Motown & Didi. (gr. k-12). 1987. pap. 3.99 (*0-440-95762-1*, LFL) Dell.
—The Righteous Revenge of Artemis Bonner. LC 91-42401. 144p. (gr. 5-9). 1994. pap. 3.95 (*0-06-440462-5*, Trophy) HarpC Child Bks.
Nabb, Magdalen. Josie Smith & Eileen. Vainio, Pirkko, illus. LC 91-31848. 96p. (gr. 1-5). 1992. SBE 12.95 (*0-689-50534-5*, M K McElderry) Macmillan Child Grp.
Naylor, Phyllis R. The Agony of Alice. LC 85-7957. 144p. (gr. 4-9). 1985. SBE 13.95 (*0-689-31143-5*, Atheneum Child Bk) Macmillan Child Grp.
—Josie's Troubles. Matheis, Shelley, illus. LC 90-47641. 128p. (gr. 3-7). 1992. SBE 13.95 (*0-689-31659-3*, Atheneum Child Bk) Macmillan Child Grp.
—One of the Third Thonkers. (gr. 4-7). 1991. pap. 3.99 (*0-440-40407-X*) Dell.
Nelson, Theresa. And One for All. (gr. 4-7). 1991. pap. 3.50 (*0-440-40456-8*) Dell.
Neville, Emily C. It's Like This, Cat. Weiss, Emil, illus. LC 62-21292. 192p. (gr. 5-9). 1964. 15.00 (*0-06-024390-2*); PLB 14.89 (*0-06-024391-0*) HarpC Child Bks.
Newman, Jerry. Green Earrings & a Felt Hat. Hewitt, Margaret, illus. LC 92-29056. 48p. (gr. 1-3). 1993. 14.95 (*0-8050-2392-5*, Bks Young Read) H Holt & Co.
Newton, Suzanne. Where Are You When I Need You? LC 92-31360. 208p. (gr. 7 up). 1993. pap. 3.99 (*0-14-034454-3*) Puffin Bks.
Nilsen, Alleen P. Presenting M. E. Kerr. (gr. k-8). 1990. pap. 3.95 (*0-440-20540-9*, LFL) Dell.
Nimeth, Albert J. I Like You, Just Because. LC 79-139971. (Illus.). (gr. 5 up). 1971. 5.00 (*0-8199-0422-8*, Frncscn Herld) Franciscan Pr.
Nister, Ernest. Special Days. Nister, Ernest, illus. (gr. k up). 1989. 5.95 (*0-399-21694-4*, Philomel Bks) Putnam Pub Group.
Nixon, Joan L. Maggie, Too. LC 84-19766. 101p. (gr. 3-7). 1985. 11.95 (*0-15-250350-1*, HB Juv Bks) HarBrace.
—A Place to Belong. 1990. pap. 3.50 (*0-553-28485-1*) Bantam.
Nobody Listens. (Illus.). (ps-2). 1991. pap. 3.50 (*0-8136-5959-0*, TK2349) Modern Curr.
Noelle of the Nutcracker. 1988. pap. 2.99 (*0-553-15673-X*, Skylark) Bantam.
Nones, Eric J. Caleb's Friend. (ps-3). 1993. 15.00 (*0-374-31017-3*) FS&G.
—Wendell. (ps up). 1989. 13.95 (*0-374-38266-2*) FS&G.
Nunes, Lygia B. My Friend the Painter. Pontiero, Giovanni, tr. from POR. 85p. (gr. 3-7). 1991. 13.95 (*0-15-256340-7*) HarBrace.
O'Brien, Teresa. Memories. LC 90-46155. 1985. 5.95 (*0-685-52310-1*) Childs Play.
O'Connor, Jane. Amy's (Not So) Great Camp-Out. Long, Laurie S., illus. LC 92-45881. 64p. (gr. 1-4). 1993. 7.99 (*0-448-40167-3*, G&D); pap. 3.95 (*0-448-40166-5*, G&D) Putnam Pub Group.
—Corrie's Secret Pal. Long, Laurie S., illus. LC 92-35602. 64p. (gr. 1-4). 1993. 7.99 (*0-448-40161-4*, G&D); pap. 3.95 (*0-448-40160-6*, G&D) Putnam Pub Group.
—Molly the Brave & Me. Hamanaka, Sheila, illus. LC 89-10864. 48p. (Orig.). (gr. 1-3). 1990. lib. bdg. 7.99 (*0-394-94175-6*); pap. 3.50 (*0-394-84175-1*) Random Bks Yng Read.
—Think, Corrie, Think! Long, Laurie S., illus. 64p. (gr. 1-4). 1994. 7.99 (*0-448-40466-4*, G&D); pap. 3.95 (*0-448-40465-6*, G&D) Putnam Pub Group.
O'Donnell, Peter. Pinkie Leaves Home. 1992. 13.95 (*0-590-45485-4*, Scholastic Hardcover) Scholastic Inc.
Okimoto, Jean D. Take a Chance, Gramps, Vol. 1. (gr. 4-7). 1990. 14.95 (*0-316-63812-9*, Joy St Bks) Little.
One Plus One Take Away Two! (ps-1). 1991. write for info. (*0-307-11575-5*, Golden Pr) Western Pub.
Oppenheim, Joanne. Rooter Remembers. (ps-3). 1991. 11.95 (*0-670-82865-3*) Viking Child Bks.
Orlev, Uri. The Island on Bird Street. Halkin, Hillel, tr. from HEB. 176p. (gr. 5 up). 1984. 13.45 (*0-395-33887-5*, 5-92515) HM.
Ormondroyd, Edward. Time at the Top. 1990. pap. 2.95 (*0-553-15420-6*) Bantam.
Osborne, Mary P. Mo & His Friends. (ps-3). 1991. pap. 3.95 (*0-8037-0924-2*, Dial Easy to Read) Puffin Bks.
O'Shaughnessy & McKenna. Eenie, Meenie, Murphy, No! 1992. pap. 2.95 (*0-590-42900-0*, Apple Paperbacks) Scholastic Inc.
Packard, M. Where Is Jake? (Illus.). 28p. (ps-2). 1990. PLB 10.50 (*0-516-05361-2*); pap. 3.95 (*0-516-45361-0*) Childrens.
Padoan, Gianni & Collini, Emanuela. Follow My Leader. (gr. 4 up). 1989. 11.95 (*0-85953-313-1*) Childs Play.
Page, David E. The Lemonade War. (Illus.). 64p. (gr. 1-3). 1993. pap. 2.50 (*0-87406-648-4*) Willowisp Pr.
Palmer, Mary R. Sharing Secrets. LC 91-65294. (Illus.). 60p. (ps-4). 1991. pap. 8.95 (*0-932433-82-0*) Windswept Hse.
Palmer, Todd S. Rhino & Mouse. Lanfredi, Judy, illus. LC 93-33299. 40p. (ps-3). 1994. 12.99 (*0-8037-1322-3*); PLB 12.89 (*0-8037-1323-1*) Dial Bks Young.
Pare, R. A Friend Like You. (Illus.). 24p. (ps-8). 1984. 12.95 (*0-920303-04-8*, Pub. by Annick CN); pap. 4.95 (*0-920303-05-6*, Pub. by Annick CN) Firefly Bks Ltd.
Pare, Roger. A Friend Like You. Pare, Roger, illus. 24p. (ps-2). 1989. pap. 0.99 (*0-920303-80-3*, Pub. by Annick CN) Firefly Bks Ltd.
Park, Barbara. Almost Starring Skinnybones. LC 87-28752. (gr. 3-7). 1988. lib. bdg. 11.99 (*0-394-99831-6*) Knopf Bks Yng Read.
—Beanpole. 160p. (gr. 5 up). 1984. pap. 2.95 (*0-380-69840-4*, Flare) Avon.
—Buddies. (gr. 7 up). 1986. pap. 2.95 (*0-380-69992-3*, Flare) Avon.
—The Kid in the Red Jacket. LC 86-20113. 128p. (gr. 3-7). 1988. Repr. of 1987 ed. 3.25 (*0-394-80571-2*) Knopf Bks Yng Read.
Parker, Cam. Camp Off-the-Wall. 128p. (gr. 3-7). 1987. pap. 2.50 (*0-380-75196-8*, Camelot) Avon.
Parry, Alan. Bruno Makes Friends. LC 91-70402. 16p. (ps-3). 1991. pap. 1.49 (*0-8066-2530-9*, 9-2530) Augsburg Fortress.
Parry, Alan & Parry, Linda. Bruno Makes Friends. Parry, Alan & Parry, Linda, illus. LC 91-70402. 16p. (ps-k). 1991. bds. 1.49 (*0-685-59565-X*, 9-2530, Augsburg) Augsburg Fortress.
Pascal, Francine. Alone in the Crowd. 1986. pap. 2.99 (*0-553-28087-2*) Bantam.
—Best Friends. 112p. (Orig.). (gr. 7-12). 1986. pap. 3.25 (*0-553-15655-1*, Skylark) Bantam.
—The Boyfriend War. 1994. pap. 3.50 (*0-553-29858-5*) Bantam.
—Danny Means Trouble. (gr. 3-6). 1990. pap. 3.25 (*0-553-15806-6*) Bantam.
—Elizabeth Betrayed. 1992. pap. 3.25 (*0-553-29235-8*) Bantam.
—Friend Against Friend. (gr. 9-12). 1990. pap. 3.50 (*0-553-28636-6*) Bantam.
—Hangin' out with Cici. 160p. (gr. 5 up). 1985. pap. 2.95 (*0-440-93364-1*, LFL) Dell.
—Jealous Lies. 1986. pap. 3.25 (*0-553-27558-5*) Bantam.
—Jessica Against Bruce. 1992. pap. 3.50 (*0-553-29232-3*) Bantam.
—Jessica's Unburied Treasure. (ps-3). 1992. pap. 2.99 (*0-553-15926-7*) Bantam.
—Lila's Music Video. (gr. 4-7). 1993. pap. 3.25 (*0-553-48059-6*) Bantam.
—The Morning After. 1993. pap. 3.50 (*0-553-29852-6*) Bantam.
—Nowhere to Run. 1986. pap. 2.99 (*0-553-27944-0*) Bantam.
—One of the Gang, No. 10. 1987. pap. 2.50 (*0-553-15531-8*, Skylark) Bantam.
—Promises, No. 15. 1985. pap. 3.25 (*0-553-27940-8*) Bantam.
—Robin in the Middle. (gr. 1-3). 1993. pap. 2.99 (*0-553-48014-6*) Bantam.
—Runaway. 176p. (Orig.). (gr. 5 up). 1985. pap. 2.75 (*0-553-26682-9*) Bantam.
—Sweet Valley: Choosing Sides. 1987. pap. 1.25 (*0-440-82085-5*) Dell.
—Sweet Valley Sneakin' 1987. pap. 1.25 (*0-440-82144-4*) Dell.
—Sweet Valley Trick or Treat. (gr. 4-7). 1990. pap. 2.99 (*0-553-15825-2*) Bantam.
—The Unicorns Go Hawaiian. (gr. 4-7). 1991. pap. 3.99 (*0-553-15948-8*) Bantam.
Paterson, Katherine. Bridge to Terabithia. Diamond, Donna, illus. LC 77-2221. (gr. 5 up). 1977. 14.00 (*0-690-01359-0*, Crowell Jr Bks) HarpC Child Bks.
—Bridge to Terabithia. Diamond, Donna, illus. LC 77-2221. 144p. (gr. 5-9). 1987. pap. 3.95 (*0-06-440184-7*, Trophy) HarpC Child Bks.
—Bridge to Terabithia. Diamond, Donna, illus. LC 77-2221. 144p. (gr. 5 up). 1987. Repr. of 1977 ed. PLB 13.89 (*0-690-04635-9*, Crowell Jr Bks) HarpC Child Bks.
—Bridge to Terabithia: (Puente Hasta Terabithia) (SPA.). (gr. 1-6). 8.95 (*84-204-3633-X*) Santillana.
—Come Sing, Jimmy Jo. 192p. (gr. 5 up). 1986. pap. 3.99 (*0-380-70052-2*, Flare) Avon.
—Flip-Flop Girl. 128p. (gr. 3-7). 1994. 13.99 (*0-525-67480-2*, Lodestar Bks) Dutton Child Bks.
Paulsen, Gary. The Crossing. (gr. k up). 1990. pap. 3.99 (*0-440-20582-4*, LFL) Dell.
—The Foxman. 128p. (gr. 4 up). 1990. pap. 3.99 (*0-14-034311-3*, Puffin) Puffin Bks.
Pearce, Philippa. Fresh. Zimdars, Berta, illus. 64p. 1987. PLB 13.95 (*0-88682-125-8*) Creative Ed.
Pearson, Gayle. The Fog Doggies & Me. LC 92-41069. 128p. (gr. 4-8). 1993. SBE 13.95 (*0-689-31845-6*, Atheneum Child Bk) Macmillan Child Grp.
Pearson, Kit. The Daring Game. (Illus.). 240p. (gr. 3-7). 1991. pap. 3.95 (*0-14-031932-8*, Puffin) Puffin Bks.
Peck, Richard. Remembering the Good Times. (gr. 5-12). 1986. pap. 3.99 (*0-440-97339-2*, LFL) Dell.
—Those Summer Girls I Never Met. (gr. k up). 1989. pap. 3.50 (*0-440-20457-7*, LFL) Dell.
Peck, Robert N. Soup. (gr. 3 up). 1979. pap. 3.50 (*0-440-48186-4*, YB) Dell.
—Soup. Gehm, Charles, illus. LC 73-15117. 104p. (gr. 3 up). 1974. PLB 10.99 (*0-394-92700-1*) Knopf Bks Yng Read.
—Soup & Me. Lilly, Charles, illus. LC 75-9514. 112p. (gr. 3-6). 1975. PLB 13.99 (*0-394-93157-2*) Knopf Bks Yng Read.
—Soup for President. Lewin, Ted, illus. LC 77-3548. (gr. 6 up). 1978. PLB 10.99 (*0-394-93675-2*) Knopf Bks Yng Read.
—Soup in the Saddle. Robinson, Charles, illus. LC 82-14010. 96p. (gr. 3-6). 1983. PLB 11.99 (*0-394-95294-4*) Knopf Bks Yng Read.
Peck, Sylvia. Kelsey's Raven. 240p. (gr. 5 up). 1992. 14.00 (*0-688-09583-6*) Morrow Jr Bks.
Peet, Bill. Zella, Zack, & Zodiac. (Illus.). 32p. (gr. k-3). 1989. pap. 4.80 (*0-395-52207-2*) HM.
Penelope's Pen Pal. (Illus.). 40p. (gr. k-5). 1994. pap. 4.95 (*0-685-71583-3*, 519) W Gladden Found.
Penner, Fred. Ebeneezer Sneezer. Hicks, Barbara, illus. 36p. (Orig.). (gr. 2-6). 1990. pap. 5.95 (*0-920534-37-6*, Pub. by Hyperion Pr Ltd CN) Sterling.
Pennywell, Sylvia C. The Gift of Hope. Dean, William R., illus. 21p. 1992. pap. 12.00 (*0-9637324-0-4*) Silver Grace Pubs.
Pepin, Muriel. Brave Little Fox. Jensen, Patricia, adapted by. Fichaux, Catherine, illus. LC 93-4238. 22p. (ps-3). 1993. 5.98 (*0-89577-541-7*, Readers Digest Kids) RD Assn.
Perkins, Mitali. The Sunita Experiment. LC 92-37267. 144p. (gr. 1-6). 1993. 14.95 (*0-316-69943-8*, Joy St Bks) Little.
—The Sunita Experiment. LC 93-28525. 192p. (gr. 5-9). 1994. pap. 4.50 (*1-56282-671-9*) Hyprn Ppbks.
Perkins, Myrna. Bored Betty's Wish. Perkins, William C. & Perkins, Lani, illus. 32p. (Orig.). (gr. 2-5). 1986. pap. 5.95 (*0-937729-02-7*) Markins Enter.
Perlman, Ruthy. Working It Out. LC 90-82185. (gr. 7 up). 1990. 13.95 (*1-56062-033-1*); pap. 9.95 (*1-56062-035-8*) CIS Comm.
Peters, Julie A. B.J.'s Billion Dollar Bet. LC 93-36132. 1994. 12.95 (*0-316-70254-4*) Little.
—Stinky Sneakers Contest. (ps-3). 1992. 13.95 (*0-316-70214-5*) Little.
Petersen, P. J. Corky & the Brothers Cool. (gr. 6 up). 1986. pap. 2.75 (*0-440-91624-0*, LFL) Dell.
—I Hate Camping. Remkiewicz, Frank, illus. 96p. (gr. 2-5). 1993. pap. 3.99 (*0-14-036446-3*, Puffin) Puffin Bks.
—Nobody Else Can Walk It for You. 224p. (gr. 6 up). 1984. pap. 2.95 (*0-440-96733-3*, LFL) Dell.
—The Sub. Johnson, Meredith, illus. LC 92-22269. (gr. 2-5). 1993. 12.99 (*0-525-45059-9*, DCB) Dutton Child Bks.
Peterson, George C. Stuck in the Mud, Vol. 1. Peterson, George, illus. 208p. (Orig.). (gr. 9-12). 1988. pap. write for info. (*0-9621320-0-4*) G Peterson.
Petroske, Mimi. Boy My Very Special Friend. Caroland, Mary, ed. (Illus.). 44p. (gr. k-3). 1991. 5.95 (*1-55523-381-3*) Winston-Derek.
Petty, Kate. Making Friends. Firmin, Charlotte, illus. 24p. (ps-2). 1991. pap. 4.95 (*0-8120-4660-9*) Barron.
Pevsner, Stella. The Night the Whole Class Slept Over. 176p. (gr. 4-9). 1991. 13.95 (*0-89919-983-6*, Clarion Bks) HM.
Pfeffer, Susan B. Just Between Us. 128p. (gr. k-6). 1981. pap. 2.25 (*0-440-44194-3*, YB) Dell.
—Most Precious Blood. 1993. pap. 3.99 (*0-553-56128-6*) Bantam.
—Rewind to Yesterday. (gr. 4-7). 1991. pap. 3.25 (*0-440-40474-6*) Dell.
—Starring Peter & Leigh. LC 78-72855. 1978. 7.95 (*0-440-08226-9*) Delacorte.
Pfister, Marcus. Chris & Croc. (Illus.). 32p. (gr. k-3). 1994. 14.95 (*1-55858-273-8*); lib. bdg. 14.88 (*1-55858-274-6*) North-South Bks NYC.
Philbrick, W. R. Freak the Mighty. LC 93-19913. 176p. (gr. 5-9). 1993. 13.95 (*0-590-47412-X*) Scholastic Inc.
Pierson, Jim. Just Like Everybody Else. Parks, Kathy, illus. Tada, Joni E., intro. by. (Illus.). 32p. (ps-3). 1993. 10.99 (*0-87403-842-1*, 24-03661) Standard Pub.
The Pigman & Me. 1993. pap. 3.99 (*0-553-56456-0*) Bantam.
Pike, Christopher. Fall into Darkness. 224p. 1991. pap. 3.99 (*0-671-73684-1*, Archway) PB.
—Weekend. 1986. pap. 2.75 (*0-590-42968-X*) Scholastic Inc.
Pilkey, Dav. A Friend for Dragon. LC 90-45219. (Illus.). 48p. (gr. 1-3). 1991. 12.95 (*0-531-05934-0*); PLB 12.99 (*0-531-08534-1*) Orchard Bks Watts.
Pinkwater, Daniel. Doodle Flute. Pinkwater, Daniel, illus. LC 90-6622. 32p. (gr. k-3). 1991. RSBE 13.95 (*0-02-774635-6*, Macmillan Child Bk) Macmillan Child Grp.
—Spaceburger: A Kevin Spoon & Mason Mintz Story. Pinkwater, Daniel, illus. LC 93-6658. 32p. (gr. k-3). 1993. RSBE 13.95 (*0-02-774643-7*, Macmillan Child Bk) Macmillan Child Grp.
Pinkwater, Daniel M. Big Orange Splot. (ps-3). 1993. pap. 3.95 (*0-590-44510-3*) Scholastic Inc.

Pinsker, Judith. A Lot Like You. (gr. 5 up). 1989. pap. 2.95 (*0-553-27852-5*, Starfire) Bantam.
—A Lot Like You. 1988. 13.95 (*0-553-05445-7*) Bantam.
Pittau, Francisco. Voyage under the Stars. Gervais, Bernadette, illus. LC 91-26075. 32p. (ps-3). 1992. 13.00 (*0-688-11328-1*); PLB 12.93 (*0-688-11329-X*) Lothrop.
Pitts, Paul. For a Good Time, Don't Call Claudia. 128p. (gr. 7 up). 1986. pap. 2.50 (*0-380-75117-8*, Flare) Avon.
Pizer, Abigail. It's a Perfect Day. Pizer, Abigail, illus. LC 89-37937. 32p. (ps-3). 1992. pap. 4.95 (*0-06-443302-1*, Trophy) HarpC Child Bks.
Plemons, Marti. Georgie & the New Kid. (Illus.). 128p. (gr. 3-6). 1992. pap. 4.99 (*0-87403-687-9*, 24-03727) Standard Pub.
Pochocki, Ethel. Mushroom Man. 1993. 15.00 (*0-671-75951-5*, Green Tiger) S&S Trade.
Polacco, Patricia. Chicken Sunday. Polacco, Patricia, illus. 32p. (ps-3). 1992. PLB 14.95 (*0-399-22133-6*, Philomel Bks) Putnam Pub Group.
—Just Plain Fancy. Polacco, Patricia, illus. (ps-3). 1990. 14.95 (*0-553-05884-3*, Little Rooster); (Little Rooster) Bantam.
—Mrs. Katz & Tush. 1992. 15.00 (*0-553-08122-5*, Little Rooster) Bantam.
—Pink & Say. LC 93-36340. (Illus.). 48p. (ps-3). 1994. PLB 15.95 (*0-399-22671-0*, Philomel Bks) Putnam Pub Group.
Poltarness, Weller. Martin & Tommy. Krestjanoff, illus. LC 93-13609. (gr. 4 up). 1994. 14.00 (*0-671-88067-5*, Green Tiger Pr) S&S Trade.
Polushkin, Maria. Mother, Mother, I Want Another. Dawson, Diane, illus. 32p. (ps-1). 1988. pap. 5.99 (*0-517-55947-1*) Crown Bks Yng Read.
Pomerantz, Charlotte. You're Not My Best Friend Anymore. LC 93-42595. 1995. write for info. (*0-8037-1559-5*); lib. bdg. write for info. (*0-8037-1560-9*) Dial Bks Young.
Porter, Gene S. Freckles. George, Jean C., afterword by. (gr. 5 up). 1988. pap. 4.95 (*0-317-68987-8*, Pub. by Yearling Classics) Dell.
Potter, Beatrix. Panache Petitgris. Potter, Beatrix, illus. (FRE.). 60p. 1990. 9.95 (*0-7859-3713-7*) Fr & Eur.
Precious Moments: A Friend Is... 12p. (ps). 1992. bds. write for info. (*0-307-06119-1*, 6119, Golden Pr) Western Pub.
Pryor, Bonnie. Amanda & April. DeGroat, Diane, illus. LC 85-15308. 32p. (ps-1). 1986. 15.95 (*0-688-05869-8*); lib. bdg. 15.88 (*0-688-05870-1*) Morrow Jr Bks.
Quattlebaum, Mary. Jackson Jones & the Puddle of Thorns. Rosales, Melodye, illus. LC 93-11433. (gr. 4-7). 1994. 13.95 (*0-385-31165-6*) Delacorte.
Quin-Harkin, Janet. The Graduates. 176p. (Orig.). (gr. 7-12). 1986. pap. 2.50 (*0-553-25723-4*) Bantam.
—Make Me a Star. (gr. 6 up). 1988. pap. 2.95 (*0-8041-0075-6*) Ivy Books.
—Old Friends, New Friends. 224p. (Orig.). (gr. 6 up). 1986. pap. 2.50 (*0-553-26186-X*) Bantam.
—On Our Own. 176p. (Orig.). (gr. 6 up). 1986. pap. 2.50 (*0-685-13234-X*) Bantam.
—One Step Too Far. 192p. (Orig.). (gr. 9-11). 1989. pap. text ed. 2.95 (*0-8041-0337-2*) Ivy Books.
—Roadtrip. (gr. 6 up). 1989. pap. 2.95 (*0-8041-0336-4*) Ivy Books.
—Roni's Dream Boy, No. 2. LC 93-50680. (Illus.). 176p. (gr. 3-6). 1994. pap. 2.95 (*0-8167-3415-1*) Troll Assocs.
—Tess & Ali & the Teeny Bikini. 1991. pap. 3.50 (*0-06-106064-X*, Harp PBks) HarpC.
Quinn, John. The Summer of Lily & Esme. 190p. (Orig.). (gr. 6 up). 1992. pap. 8.95 (*1-85371-208-6*, Pub. by Poolbeg Pr ER) Dufour.
Radley, Gail. The Golden Days. LC 92-19526. 160p. (gr. 5 up). 1992. pap. 3.99 (*0-14-036002-6*) Puffin Bks.
Ragan-Reid, Gale. Divine. LC 93-60229. (Illus.). 44p. (gr. 1-4). 1994. 7.95 (*1-55523-606-5*) Winston-Derek.
Rand, Suzanne. The Good Luck Girl. 192p. (Orig.). (gr. 7-12). 1986. pap. 2.50 (*0-553-25644-0*) Bantam.
Randle, Kristen D. The Only Alien on the Planet. LC 93-34594. 1994. 13.95 (*0-590-46309-8*) Scholastic Inc.
Ransom, Candice. Third Grade Detectives. LC 93-48920. (Illus.). 128p. (gr. 2-4). 1994. PLB 9.89 (*0-8167-2992-1*); pap. 2.95 (*0-8167-2993-X*) Troll Assocs.
Ransom, Candice F. Who Needs Third Grade? LC 92-30754. 128p. (gr. 2-4). 1992. PLB 9.89 (*0-8167-2988-3*); pap. text ed. 2.95 (*0-8167-2989-1*) Troll Assocs.
—Why Are Boys So Weird? LC 93-6222. (Illus.). 128p. (gr. 2-6). 1994. PLB 9.89 (*0-8167-2990-5*); pap. text ed. 2.95 (*0-8167-2991-3*) Troll Assocs.
Raschka, Chris. Yo! Yes? LC 92-25644. (Illus.). 32p. (ps-1). 1993. 14.95 (*0-531-05469-1*); PLB 14.99 (*0-531-08619-4*) Orchard Bks Watts.
Raskin, Ellen. Figgs & Phantoms. (Illus.). 160p. (gr. 5-9). 1989. pap. 5.99 (*0-14-032944-7*, Puffin) Puffin Bks.
Ravilious, Robin. Two in a Pocket. (ps-3). 1991. 14.95 (*0-316-73449-7*) Little.
Read, Lorna. The Lies They Tell. 160p. (gr. 6-9). 1990. pap. 7.95 (*0-233-98444-5*, Pub. by A Deutsch England) Trafalgar.
Reardon, Ruth & Rodegast, Roland. Listen to My Feelings. (Illus.). 1992. 8.95 (*0-8378-2499-0*) Gibson.
Reaver, Chap. Mote. 1992. pap. 3.50 (*0-440-21173-5*) Dell.
Reeves, Faye C. Howie Merton & the Magic Dust. Buller, Jon, illus. LC 90-38341. 64p. (Orig.). (gr. 2-4). 1991. lib. bdg. 6.99 (*0-679-91527-3*); pap. 2.50 (*0-679-81527-9*) Random Bks Yng Read.
Regan, Dian C. Game of Survival. 144p. (Orig.). 1989. pap. 2.75 (*0-380-75585-8*, Flare) Avon.
Reinsma, Carol. Friends Forever. Cori, Nathan, illus. 48p. (Orig.). (gr. 1-3). 1993. pap. 3.99 (*0-7847-0096-6*, 24-03946) Standard Pub.
Reiser, Lynn. Margaret & Margarita, Margarita y Margaret. LC 92-29012. 32p. (ps up). 1993. 14.00 (*0-688-12239-6*); lib. bdg. 13.93 (*0-688-12240-X*) Greenwillow.
Reiss, Kathryn. Glass House People. (gr. 7 up). 1992. pap. 6.95 (*0-15-231041-X*, HB Juv Bks) HarBrace.
Renauld, Christiane. A Pal for Martin. (Illus.). 32p. (gr. 3-5). 1991. 12.95 (*0-89565-756-2*) Childs World.
Repp, Gloria. Noodle Soup. Roberts, John, illus. LC 93-42417. 1994. write for info. (*0-89084-582-4*) Bob Jones Univ Pr.
Reynolds, Susan L. Strandia. (Illus.). 240p. (gr. 9-12). 1991. 14.95 (*0-374-37274-8*) FS&G.
Richardson, Arleta. New Faces, New Friends. LC 88-34639. (gr. 3-7). 1989. pap. 3.99 (*1-55513-985-X*, Chariot Bks) Chariot Family.
Richemont, Enid. The Glass Bird. Anstey, Caroline, illus. LC 92-54585. 112p. (gr. 3-6). 1993. 14.95 (*1-56402-195-5*) Candlewick Pr.
—The Time Tree. (gr. 3-7). 1990. 12.95 (*0-316-74452-2*) Little.
Richler, Mordecai. Jacob Two-Two Hooded Fang. (ps-7). 1987. pap. 2.50 (*0-317-64199-9*, Skylark) Bantam.
Richmond, Gary. The Forgotten Friend. (gr. 1-5). 1991. text ed. 6.99 (*0-8499-0913-9*) Word Inc.
Ripslinger, Jon. Triangle. (gr. 7 up). 1994. write for info. (*0-15-200048-8*); pap. write for info. (*0-15-200049-6*) HarBrace.
Rispin, Karen. Sabrina the Schemer. LC 93-39634. 1994. 4.99 (*0-8423-1296-X*) Tyndale.
Roberts, Brenda C. Sticks & Stones, Bobbie Bones. (gr. 4-7). 1993. pap. 2.95 (*0-590-46518-X*) Scholastic Inc.
Robins, Joan. Addie Meets Max. Truesdell, Sue, illus. LC 84-48329. 32p. (ps-3). 1985. PLB 13.89 (*0-06-025064-X*) HarpC Child Bks.
—Addie's Bad Day. Truesdell, Sue, illus. LC 92-13101. 32p. (ps-2). 1993. 14.00 (*0-06-021297-7*); PLB 13.89 (*0-06-021298-5*) HarpC Child Bks.
Robinson, Nancy K. Wendy on the Warpath. LC 93-32739. (gr. 3 up). 1994. 13.95 (*0-590-45571-0*) Scholastic Inc.
Rocard, Ann. Hobee Scrogneenee. Degano, Marino, illus. 28p. (ps-4). 1991. smythe sewn reinforced bdg. 9.95 (*1-56182-000-8*) Atomium Bks.
Rochman, Hazel. Who Do You Think You Are? Stories of Friends & Enemies. 1993. 15.95 (*0-316-75355-6*) Little.
Rocklin, Joanne. Three Smart Pals. Brunkus, Denise, illus. 48p. (ps-4). 1994. pap. 3.50 (*0-590-47431-6*, Cartwheel) Scholastic Inc.
Rodgers, Raboo. Magnum Fault. 192p. (gr. 5 up). 1984. 11.95 (*0-685-07882-5*, 5-95260) HM.
Rodowsky, Colby. P. S. Write Soon. 158p. (gr. 5 up). 1987. pap. 3.50 (*0-374-46032-9*) FS&G.
—What About Me? 144p. (gr. 3 up). 1989. pap. 3.50 (*0-374-48316-7*, Sunburst) FS&G.
Rogers, Fred. Making Friends. Judkis, Jim, photos by. (Illus.). (ps-1). 1987. 12.95 (*0-399-21382-1*, Putnam); pap. 5.95 (*0-399-21385-6*, Putnam) Putnam Pub Group.
Rogers, Jacqueline. Best Friends Sleep Over. LC 92-56895. 1993. write for info. (*0-590-44793-9*) Scholastic Inc.
Roos, Stephen. Fair-Weather Friends. 128p. (gr. 2-9). 1988. pap. 2.95 (*0-8167-1306-5*) Troll Assocs.
—Never Trust a Sister over Twelve. De Groat, Diane, illus. LC 92-34406. 1993. 13.95 (*0-385-31048-X*) Delacorte.
—You'll Miss Me When I'm Gone. (gr. k-12). 1989. pap. 2.95 (*0-440-20485-2*, LE) Dell.
Rosen, Michael. Mind Your Own Business. Blake, Quentin, illus. LC 74-9969. 96p. (gr. 3 up). 1974. 21.95 (*0-87599-209-9*) S G Phillips.
Rosenstock, D. Misfits & Miracles. 1994. pap. 3.99 (*0-553-48046-4*) Bantam.
Ross, Anna. Be My Friend. Gorbaty, Norman, illus. LC 89-24389. 24p. (ps). 1991. 3.95 (*0-394-85496-9*) Random Bks Yng Read.
Ross, Dave. A Book of Hugs. Ross, Dave, illus. LC 79-7896. 32p. (gr. k up). 1991. pap. 3.95 (*0-06-107418-7*) HarpC Child Bks.
Ross, Pat. M & M & the Super Child Afternoon. Hafner, Marylin, illus. 48p. (gr. 1-4). 1989. pap. 3.95 (*0-14-032145-4*, Puffin) Puffin Bks.
—M & M & the Superchild Afternoon. Hafner, Marylin, illus. LC 86-28128. (gr. 1-4). 1987. pap. 9.95 (*0-670-81208-0*) Viking Child Bks.
Ross, Ramon R. Harper & Moon. LC 92-17216. (Illus.). 192p. (gr. 4 up). 1993. SBE 14.95 (*0-689-31803-0*, Atheneum Child Bk) Macmillan Child Grp.
Ross, Tony. A Fairy Tale. Ross, Tony, illus. 32p. (ps-3). 1992. cancelled 13.95 (*0-316-75750-0*) Little.
Rostkowski, Margaret I. The Best of Friends. LC 88-33077. 192p. (gr. 7 up). 1989. HarpC Child Bks.
Rothstein, Chaya L. Mentchkins Make Friends. (gr. 4-8). 1988. pap. 4.95 (*0-87306-453-4*) Feldheim.
Rovetch, Lissa. Trigwater Did It. (Illus.). 32p. (ps-3). 1991. pap. 3.95 (*0-14-054238-8*, Puffin) Puffin Bks.
Rupert, Rona. Straw Sense. Dooling, Mike, illus. LC 92-8775. 1993. pap. 14.00 (*0-671-77047-0*, S&S BFYR) S&S Trade.
Russo, Marisabina. Alex Is My Friend. LC 90-24643. 32p. 1992. 14.00 (*0-688-10418-5*); PLB 13.93 (*0-688-10419-3*) Greenwillow.
—Waiting for Hannah. LC 87-37201. (Illus.). 32p. (ps up). 1989. 13.95 (*0-688-08015-4*); PLB 13.88 (*0-688-08016-2*) Greenwillow.
Ryan, Cheryl. Sally Arnold. Farnsworth, Bill, illus. LC 94-6455. 1995. write for info. (*0-525-65176-4*, Cobblehill Bks) Dutton Child Bks.
Ryden, Hope. Backyard Rescue. Rand, Ted, illus. LC 93-11683. 1994. write for info. (*0-688-12880-7*, Tambourine Bks) Morrow.
Rylant, Cynthia. Henry & Mudge: The First Book of Their Adventures. Stevenson, Suzie, illus. LC 86-13615. 40p. (gr. 1-3). 1987. RSBE 12.95 (*0-02-778001-5*, Bradbury Pr) Macmillan Child Grp.
—Missing May. 1993. pap. 3.99 (*0-440-40865-2*) Dell.
Sachar, Louis. The Boy Who Lost His Face. LC 88-22622. 192p. (gr. 5-9). 1989. 11.95 (*0-394-82863-1*) Knopf Bks Yng Read.
Sachs, Elizabeth-Ann. Kiss Me, Janie Tannenbaum. LC 91-28465. 144p. (gr. 5-9). 1992. SBE 13.95 (*0-689-31664-X*, Atheneum Child Bk) Macmillan Child Grp.
Sachs, Marilyn. Thunderbird. Spence, Jim, illus. LC 84-21252. 88p. (gr. 7 up). 1985. 10.95 (*0-525-44163-8*, 01063-320, DCB) Dutton Child Bks.
Sadler, Marilyn. P.J. The Spoiled Bunny. Bollen, Roger, illus. LC 85-19650. 32p. (ps-3). 1986. lib. bdg. 5.99 (*0-394-97245-7*); pap. 2.25 (*0-394-87245-2*) Random Bks Yng Read.
St. George, Judith. By George, Bloomers! Tomes, Margot, illus. LC 89-17898. 48p. (gr. 1-5). 1976. pap. 5.95 (*1-55870-135-4*, 70013) Shoe Tree Pr.
St. Germain, Sharon. The Terrible Fight. Zemke, Deborah, illus. 32p. (gr. k-3). 1990. 13.45 (*0-395-50069-9*) HM.
St. John, Charlotte. Red Hair Three. (gr. 7 up). 1992. pap. 3.99 (*0-449-70406-8*, Juniper) Fawcett.
St. John, Patricia. Friska, My Friend. 80p. (gr. 2-4). 1990. pap. 3.99 (*1-55661-151-X*) Bethany Hse.
Salassi, Otto R. Jimmy D. Sidewinder, & Me. (gr. 5 up). 1987. 11.75 (*0-688-05237-1*) Greenwillow.
Salat, Cristina. Alias Diamond Jones. Franke, Phil, illus. (gr. 4-7). 1993. pap. 3.50 (*0-553-37216-5*) Bantam.
—Living in Secret. LC 92-20889. 1993. 15.00 (*0-553-08670-7*, Skylark) Bantam.
—Living in Secret. (gr. 4-7). 1994. pap. 3.99 (*0-440-40950-0*) Dell.
Salem, Lynn & Stewart, Josie. Hope Not! (Illus.). 8p. (gr. 1). 1993. pap. 3.50 (*1-880612-04-6*) Seedling Pubns.
—Just Enough. Graham, Jennifer, illus. 12p. (gr. 1). 1992. pap. 3.50 (*1-880612-12-7*) Seedling Pubns.
—Never Be. (Illus.). 8p. (gr. 1). 1992. pap. 3.50 (*1-880612-00-3*) Seedling Pubns.
—No Luck. Collins, Tim, illus. 12p. (gr. 1). 1993. pap. 3.50 (*1-880612-07-0*) Seedling Pubns.
Samton, Sheila W. El Viaje de Jenny: Jenny's Journey. (Illus.). 32p. (ps-3). 1993. PLB 14.99 (*0-670-84843-3*) Viking Child Bks.
Samuels, Barbara. Duncan & Dolores. Samuels, Barbara, illus. LC 85-17119. 32p. (ps-2). 1986. RSBE 13.95 (*0-02-778210-7*, Bradbury Pr) Macmillan Child Grp.
Sandburg, Carl. Rootabaga Stories, Pt. 1. Hague, Michael, illus. 192p. (gr. 3-7). 1988. 19.95 (*0-15-269061-1*) HarBrace.
Santos, Antonio. Far Island. LC 93-87644. 94p. 1994. 8.00 (*0-9640825-0-0*) Naranga Bks.
Sargent, Dave. Best Friends. Sapaugh, Blaine, illus. 48p. (Orig.). (gr. k-8). 1993. text ed. 11.95 (*1-56763-056-1*); pap. text ed. 5.95 (*1-56763-057-X*) Ozark Pub.
—The Ties That Bind. 188p. 1992. write for info. Ozark Pub.
Saunders, Susan. Kate's Crush. 1989. pap. 2.50 (*0-590-42366-5*) Scholastic Inc.
—Kate's Sleepover Disaster. 1989. pap. 2.50 (*0-590-41846-7*) Scholastic Inc.
—Lauren I. 1990. pap. 2.50 (*0-590-42816-0*, SHLS) Scholastic Inc.
—Lauren Takes Charge. 1989. pap. 2.50 (*0-590-42300-2*) Scholastic Inc.
—Lauren's Big Mix-Up. 80p. (gr. 3-7). 1988. pap. 2.50 (*0-590-41336-8*, Apple Paperbacks) Scholastic Inc.
—Lauren's New Friend. (gr. 5-7). 1990. pap. 2.50 (*0-590-43194-3*) Scholastic Inc.
—The New Stephanie. (gr. 4-7). 1991. pap. 2.75 (*0-590-43924-3*) Scholastic Inc.
—Patti's Last Sleepover, No. 9. 96p. (gr. 3-7). 1988. pap. 2.50 (*0-590-41696-0*) Scholastic Inc.
—Patti's Luck. 96p. (gr. 4-6). 1987. pap. 2.50 (*0-590-40641-8*) Scholastic Inc.
—Starstruck Stephanie. 1990. pap. 2.50 (*0-590-42817-9*) Scholastic Inc.
—Stephanie. 1989. pap. 2.50 (*0-590-42814-4*) Scholastic Inc.
—Stephanie's Big Story. 1989. pap. 2.50 (*0-590-42299-5*) Scholastic Inc.
—Stephanie's Family Secret. 1989. pap. 2.50 (*0-590-41845-9*) Scholastic Inc.
Savin, Marcia. Will Lithuania Comstock Please Come to the Courtesy Phone? LC 93-28441. (Illus.). 160p. (gr. 5-9). 1993. PLB 13.95 (*0-8167-3324-4*); pap. 3.95 (*0-8167-3325-2*) BrdgeWater.

Sayles, Rasheeda A. Rasheeda's Visitors. 1990. 6.95 (*0-533-08920-4*) Vantage.
Schanback, Mindy. What's New in Sixth Grade? LC 90-26792. 96p. (gr. 4-6). 1992. lib. bdg. 9.89 (*0-8167-2388-5*); pap. text ed. 2.95 (*0-8167-2389-3*) Troll Assocs.
Schein, Jonah. Forget-Me-Not. Schein, Jonah, illus. 24p. 1988. 12.95 (*1-55037-001-4*, Pub. by Annick CN); pap. 4.95 (*1-55037-000-6*, Pub. by Annick CN) Firefly Bks Ltd.
Schenk De Regniers, Beatrice. The Way I Feel... Sometimes. Meddaugh, Susan, illus. (gr. 1-4). 1988. 13.95 (*0-318-35052-1*, Clarion Bks) HM.
Schneider, Meg F. The Practically Popular Crowd: Pretty Enough. 1992. 2.95 (*0-590-44804-8*, Apple Paperbacks) Scholastic Inc.
—The Practically Popular Crowd: Wanting More. 1992. pap. 2.95 (*0-590-44803-X*, Apple Paperbacks) Scholastic Inc.
Schories, Pat. Mouse Around. (ps-3). 1993. pap. 4.95 (*0-374-45414-0*, Sunburst) FS&G.
Schorsch, Laurence. Mr. Boffin. Spier, Nancy, illus. 32p. (gr. k-3). 1993. 6.95 (*1-56288-353-4*) Checkerboard.
Schotter, Roni. Captain Snap & the Children of Vinegar Lane. Sewall, Marcia, illus. LC 88-22489. 32p. (ps-3). 1989. 14.95 (*0-531-05797-6*); PLB 14.99 (*0-531-08397-7*) Orchard Bks Watts.
—Rhoda, Straight & True. LC 86-107. 192p. (gr. 6 up). 1986. 11.95 (*0-688-06157-5*) Lothrop.
Schubert, Ingrid & Schubert, Dieter. Little Big Feet. Schubert, Ingrid & Schubert, Dieter, illus. 32p. (ps-3). 1990. PLB 18.95 (*0-87614-426-1*) Carolrhoda Bks.
Schulman, Janet. The Big Hello. Hoban, Lillian, illus. LC 75-33672. (gr. 1-4). 1976. 13.95 (*0-688-80036-X*) Greenwillow.
Schulte, Elaine L. Melanie & the Modeling Mess. LC 93-45377. 1994. 4.99 (*1-55661-254-0*) Bethany Hse.
Schultz, Betty K. Chooch. Becicka, Lori, illus. LC 90-91639. 64p. (gr. 3-8). 1990. smythe-sewn 14.95 (*0-929568-00-1*) Raspberry IL.
Schurr, Cathleen. The Shy Little Kitten. reissued ed. Tenggren, Gustaf, illus. 24p. (ps-k). 1992. write for info. (*0-307-00145-8*, 312-10, Golden Pr) Western Pub.
Schutzer, Dena. Polka & Dot. Schutzer, Dena, illus. LC 93-29935. 1994. 14.00 (*0-679-84192-X*); PLB 14.99 (*0-679-94192-4*) Knopf Bks Yng Read.
Schwandt, Stephen. Holding Steady. 176p. 1990. pap. 2.95 (*0-380-70754-3*, Flare) Avon.
Schwartz, Amy. Camper of the Week. LC 90-23033. (Illus.). 32p. (gr. k-2). 1991. 14.95 (*0-531-05942-1*); RLB 14.99 (*0-531-08542-2*) Orchard Bks Watts.
—Oma & Bobo. LC 86-10665. (Illus.). 32p. (ps-2). 1987. RSBE 14.95 (*0-02-781500-5*, Bradbury Pr) Macmillan Child Grp.
Schwartz, Joel L. Best Friends Don't Come in Threes. (Illus.). 126p. (Orig.). (gr. 4-6). 1985. pap. 2.75 (*0-440-40603-X*, YB) Dell.
—Upchuck Summer. Degen, Bruce, illus. LC 81-69670. 144p. (gr. 4-8). 9.95 (*0-440-09264-7*); PLB 9.89 (*0-440-09269-8*) Delacorte.
—Upchuck Summer's Revenge. (gr. 4-7). 1991. pap. 3.50 (*0-440-40471-1*) Dell.
Schwartz, Linda. From Me to You. LC 93-86208. 32p. (gr. 1-6). 1994. 4.95 (*0-88160-237-X*, LW332) Learning Wks.
—How Can I Help? LC 93-86212. 184p. (gr. 4-8). 1994. 9.95 (*0-88160-213-2*, LW207) Learning Wks.
Schwartz, Sara. Head Trips. (ps-3). 1994. 11.95 (*1-55550-884-7*) Universe.
Scott, Carlton T. El Mensaje de Grin - Grin's Message. 2nd ed. Rosin, Laurie, ed. Fusco, Ginnie, tr. from ENG. Scott, Carlton T., illus. (SPA.). 32p. (ps-3). pap. 9.95 (*0-9636652-8-6*) C T Scott.
Scott, Sally. The Three Wonderful Beggars. LC 86-22825. (Illus.). 30p. (gr. k-3). 1988. Repr. of 1987 ed. 13.00 (*0-688-06656-9*); lib. bdg. 12.88 (*0-688-06657-7*) Greenwillow.
Seabrooke, Brenda. Jerry on the Line. LC 90-1745. 128p. (gr. 3-5). 1990. SBE 13.95 (*0-02-781432-7*, Bradbury Pr) Macmillan Child Grp.
—Jerry on the Line. 128p. (gr. 3-7). 1992. pap. 3.99 (*0-14-034868-9*) Puffin Bks.
Sebestyen, Ouida. IOU's. (gr. 7 up). 1986. pap. 2.75 (*0-440-93986-0*, LFL) Dell.
Selway, Martina. I Hate Roland Roberts. Selway, Martina, illus. LC 93-30916. 32p. (ps-2). 1994. 12.95 (*0-8249-8660-1*, Ideals Child) Hambleton-Hill.
—I Hate Roland Roberts. LC 93-30916. (Illus.). 32p. (ps-2). 1995. pap. 4.95 (*0-8249-8675-X*) Hambleton-Hill.
Semel, Nava. Flying Lessons. Halkin, Hillel, tr. LC 93-10811. 96p. (gr. 7 up). Date not set. 14.00 (*0-06-021470-8*); PLB 13.89 (*0-06-021471-6*) HarpC Child Bks.
Shalant, Phyllis. Transformation of Faith Futterman. LC 89-27563. 144p. (gr. 5 up). 1990. 13.95 (*0-525-44570-6*, DCB) Dutton Child Bks.
—The Transformation of Faith Futterman. 144p. (gr. 3-7). 1992. pap. 3.99 (*0-14-036026-3*) Puffin Bks.
Shannon, George. Seeds. Bjorkman, George, illus. LC 92-40738. 1994. 13.95 (*0-395-66990-1*) HM.
Shannon, Jacqueline. I Hate My Hero. LC 92-890. (gr. 4-7). 1992. pap. 13.00 (*0-671-75442-4*, S&S BFYR) S&S Trade.
—Too Much T. J. (gr. k-12). 1988. pap. 2.95 (*0-440-20222-1*, LFL) Dell.
Sharmat, Marjorie W. For Members Only. (Orig.). (gr. 5 up). 1986. pap. 2.50 (*0-440-92654-8*, LFL) Dell.
—Getting Something on Maggie Marmelstein. Shecter, Ben, illus. LC 78-157895. 110p. (gr. 4-6). 1971. PLB 13.89 (*0-06-025552-8*) HarpC Child Bks.
—I Saw Him First. 192p. (gr. 7 up). 1989. pap. 2.95 (*0-440-94009-5*, LFL) Dell.
—Mitchell Is Moving. Aruego, Jose & Dewey, Ariane, illus. LC 85-47782. 48p. (gr. 1-4). 1985. pap. 3.95 (*0-02-045260-8*, Aladdin) Macmillan Child Grp.
Sharp, Donna. The Name's Still Charlie. 1993. pap. 16.95 (*0-7022-2471-5*, Pub. by Univ Queensland Pr AT) Intl Spec Bk.
Sharpe, Susan. Spirit Quest. Sharpe, Kate & Sharpe, Alison, illus. LC 91-4417. 128p. (gr. 4-6). 1991. SBE 13.95 (*0-02-782355-5*, Bradbury Pr) Macmillan Child Grp.
—Spirit Quest. 128p. (gr. 3-7). 1993. pap. 3.99 (*0-14-036282-7*) Puffin Bks.
Sheehan, Patty. Kylie's Song. LC 88-16779. (Illus.). 32p. (gr. k-6). 1988. 16.95 (*0-911655-19-0*) Advocacy Pr.
Shelby, Anne. Potluck. Trivas, Irene, illus. LC 90-7757. 32p. (ps-2). 1994. pap. 5.95 (*0-531-07045-X*) Orchard Bks Watts.
Shelton, Rick. Hoggle's Christmas. Gates, Donald, illus. LC 92-37861. 80p. (gr. 2-6). 1993. 12.99 (*0-525-65129-2*, Cobblehill Bks) Dutton Child Bks.
Sherman, Eileen. Victor's Place. Trexler, Richard, illus. 598p. (Orig.). (gr. 10-12). 1989. pap. write for info. (*0-9604382-2-X*) Cornerstone Pr.
Shine, Deborah. The Race. 16p. (ps-2). 1992. pap. 14.95 (*1-56784-051-5*) Newbridge Comms.
Shinhav, Chaya. Adios, Berry. Writer, C. C. & Nielsen, Lisa C., trs. Eagle, Mike, illus. (SPA.). 24p. (Orig.). (ps). 1992. pap. text ed. 3.00x (*1-56134-154-1*) Dushkin Pub.
—Goodbye, Berry. Kriss, David, tr. from HEB. Eagle, Mike, illus. 24p. (Orig.). (ps). 1992. pap. text ed. 3.00x (*1-56134-144-4*) Dushkin Pub.
Shreve, Susan. The Gift of the Girl Who Couldn't Hear. LC 91-2247. 80p. (gr. 3 up). 1991. 12.95 (*0-688-10318-9*, Tambourine Bks) Morrow.
—The Gift of the Girl Who Couldn't Hear. LC 92-43763. 80p. (gr. 5 up). 1993. pap. 3.95 (*0-688-11694-9*, Pub. by Beech Tree Bks) Morrow.
Shreve, Susan R. Country of Strangers. 1990. pap. 9.95 (*0-385-26775-4*, Anchor NY) Doubleday.
Shub, Elizabeth. Seeing Is Believing. Isadora, Rachel, illus. LC 78-12378. 64p. 1994. 14.00 (*0-688-13647-8*) Greenwillow.
Shulman, Dee. The Visit. (Illus.). 32p. (ps-1). 1993. 15.95 (*0-370-31584-7*, Pub. by Bodley Head UK) Trafalgar.
Shura, Mary F. Don't Call Me Toad. 128p. 1988. pap. 2.95 (*0-380-70496-X*, Camelot) Avon.
Sibley, Brian. Little Give & Take. (gr. 4-7). 1994. 12.95 (*0-7459-2461-1*) Lion USA.
Siebert, Diane. Heartland. Minor, Wendell, illus. LC 87-29380. 32p. (gr. 2 up). 1992. pap. 6.95 (*0-06-443287-4*, Trophy) HarpC Child Bks.
Siegel, Beatrice. The Basket Maker & the Spinner. 64p. (gr. 3 up). 1987. 10.95 (*0-8027-6694-3*); PLB 11.85 (*0-8027-6695-1*) Walker & Co.
Silbert, Linda P. & Silbert, Alvin J. Agnes' Cardboard Piano. (Illus.). (gr. k-4). 1978. pap. 4.98 (*0-89544-054-7*) Silbert Bress.
—I'll Be Your Best Friend. (Illus.). (gr. k-4). 1978. pap. 4.98 (*0-89544-056-3*) Silbert Bress.
—Lost in the Cave. (Illus.). (gr. k-4). 1978. pap. 4.98 (*0-89544-057-1*) Silbert Bress.
—Penelope's Pen Pal. (Illus.). (gr. k-4). 1978. pap. 4.98 (*0-89544-053-9*) Silbert Bress.
—Tiger, Take off Your Hat. (Illus.). (gr. k-4). 1978. pap. 4.98 (*0-89544-051-2*) Silbert Bress.
—Tuffy's Bike Race. (Illus.). (gr. k-4). 1978. pap. 4.98 (*0-89544-058-X*) Silbert Bress.
—Tyrone Goes Camping. (Illus.). (gr. k-4). 1978. pap. 4.98 (*0-89544-055-5*) Silbert Bress.
—Whitney's New Glasses. (Illus.). (gr. k-4). 1978. pap. 4.98 (*0-89544-052-0*) Silbert Bress.
Silver, Jody. Rupert, Polly & Daisy. Silver, Jody, illus. LC 83-24979. 48p. (ps-3). 1984. 5.95 (*0-8193-1124-3*) Parents.
Simbal, Joanne. Long Shot. 134p. 1988. pap. 2.50 (*0-553-27594-1*) Bantam.
Simba's Adventure. 20p. 1994. 9.98 (*1-57082-152-6*) Mouse Works.
Simpson, Louis. Wei Wei & Other Friends. White, Robert, illus. 24p. 1990. pap. 25.00x (*0-930126-30-0*) Typographeum.
Singer, Marilyn. Several Kinds of Silence. LC 87-45304. 288p. (gr. 7 up). 1988. HarpC Child Bks.
—Twenty Ways to Lose Your Best Friend. Lindberg, Jeffrey, illus. LC 89-36576. 128p. (gr. 2-5). 1990. PLB 14.89 (*0-06-025643-5*) HarpC Child Bks.
—Twenty Ways to Lose Your Best Friend. Lindberg, Jeffrey, illus. LC 89-36576. 128p. (gr. 2-5). 1993. pap. 3.95 (*0-06-440353-X*, Trophy) HarpC Child Bks.
Sinykin, Sheri C. Next Thing to Strangers. LC 90-25991. 176p. (gr. 5 up). 1991. text ed. 12.95 (*0-688-10694-3*) Lothrop.
Skurzynski, Gloria. Good Bye, Billy Radish. LC 92-7577. (Illus.). 144p. (gr. 5 up). 1992. SBE 14.95 (*0-02-782921-9*, Bradbury Pr) Macmillan Child Grp.
Slaughter, Hope. A Cozy Place. Torrence, Susan, illus. LC 90-49715. 32p. (ps-2). 1990. 15.95 (*0-931093-13-9*) Red Hen Pr.
Sleator, William. The Duplicate. (gr. 5 up). 1990. pap. 3.99 (*0-553-28634-X*, Starfire) Bantam.
—Oddballs. LC 92-27666. (gr. 7 up). 1993. 14.99 (*0-525-45057-2*, DCB) Dutton Child Bks.
Slepian, Jan. The Alfred Summer. LC 79-24097. 132p. (gr. 6 up). 1980. SBE 13.95 (*0-02-782920-0*, Macmillan Child Bk) Macmillan Child Grp.
—Risk N' Roses. 160p. (gr. 3-7). 1992. pap. 2.95 (*0-590-45361-0*, Apple Paperbacks) Scholastic Inc.
Slote, Alfred. A Friend Like That. LC 87-35053. 160p. (gr. 3-7). 1988. (Lipp Jr Bks); (Lipp Jr Bks) HarpC Child Bks.
—A Friend Like That. LC 87-35053. 160p. (gr. 3-7). 1990. pap. 3.50 (*0-06-440266-5*, Trophy) HarpC Child Bks.
Small, David. Paper John. (ps up). 1989. pap. 3.95 (*0-374-45725-5*, Sunburst) FS&G.
Smith. Changing Places. 1993. pap. 2.95 (*0-590-44723-8*) Scholastic Inc.
Smith, Doris B. The Pennywhistle Tree. Bowman, Leslie, illus. LC 90-23119. 144p. (gr. 5-9). 1991. 14.95 (*0-399-21840-8*, Putnam) Putnam Pub Group.
Smith, K. Skeeter. (gr. 4-7). 1992. pap. 4.80 (*0-395-61621-2*) HM.
Smith, Kaitlin. Funny Things Happen. Smith, Kaitlin, illus. 15p. (gr. k-3). 1993. pap. 12.95 (*1-56606-020-6*) Bradley Mann.
—Take a Walk with Me. Smith, Kaitlin, illus. 12p. (gr. k-3). 1993. pap. 10.95 (*1-56606-019-2*) Bradley Mann.
Smith, Matthew V. Willie Goes to Town. Smith, Matthew V., illus. 15p. (gr. k-3). 1994. pap. 9.95 (*1-895583-65-9*) MAYA Pubs.
Smith, Mavis. I'm Going to Get You! (ps-3). 1991. pap. 5.99 (*0-14-054435-6*, Puffin) Puffin Bks.
Smith, Robert K. Squeaky Wheel. (gr. 3-7). 1990. 13.95 (*0-385-30155-3*) Delacorte.
Smith, Wendy. Say Hello, Tilly. (ps-3). 1991. 13.95 (*0-553-07160-2*) Bantam.
Smitt, Elizabeth. Lucca & Chester's Big Fight. (Illus.). 32p. (ps-2). 1995. 14.95 (*0-395-70930-X*) Ticknor & Flds Bks Yng Read.
Smucker, Barbara. Incredible Jumbo. 1991. 12.95 (*0-670-82970-6*) Viking Child Bks.
Smulders, Frank. Bigger Than Biggest. (Illus.). 24p. (Orig.). (ps-1). 1994. pap. 4.95 (*1-55037-360-9*, Pub. by Annick CN) Firefly Bks Ltd.
Sneaky Pete Big Book. (Illus.). 32p. (ps-3). 1990. pap. 22.95 (*0-516-49455-4*) Childrens.
Snell, Nigel. A Bird in the Hand. (Illus.). 32p. (ps-1). 1992. 13.95 (*0-237-60295-4*, Pub. by Evans Bros Ltd) Trafalgar.
Snyder, Zilpha K. Fool's Gold. (gr. 4-7). 1994. pap. 3.50 (*0-440-40952-7*) Dell.
—Libby on Wednesday. 1990. 14.95 (*0-385-29979-6*) Delacorte.
Soliven, Marivi. Pillow Tales. 1991. 6.95 (*0-533-09188-8*) Vantage.
Solomon, L. Ursa. The Friendship of Hesper & Rani. Mello, Marsha, illus. 60p. (gr. 1 up). 1985. spiral bdg. 7.95 (*0-9615756-1-1*) Henchanted Bks.
Sommer-Bodenburg, Angela. My Friend the Vampire. Glienke, Amelie, illus. LC 83-23930. 160p. (gr. 3-5). 1984. PLB 9.89 (*0-8037-0046-6*) Dial Bks Young.
Sommers, Tish. A Bird's Best Friend. Swanson, Maggie, illus. 32p. (ps-k). 1986. write for info. (*0-307-12018-X*, Pub. by Golden Bks) Western Pub.
Soto, Gary. Crazy Weekend. LC 93-13967. 144p. (gr. 3-7). 1994. 13.95 (*0-590-47814-1*) Scholastic Inc.
—Taking Sides. 1992. pap. 6.95 (*0-15-284077-X*) HarBrace.
Souci, Daniel S., illus. Song of Sedna. (gr. 5-9). 1994. 15.95 (*0-385-15866-1*) Doubleday.
Spier, Peter. Fast-Slow High-Low. Spier, Peter, illus. LC 72-76207. 24p. (ps-k). 1988. 5.95 (*0-385-24093-7*) Doubleday.
Spinelli, Eileen. Lizzie Logan Wears Purple Sunglasses. Durrell, Julie, illus. LC 93-29104. 1995. 13.00 (*0-671-74685-5*, S&S BFYR) S&S Trade.
—Somebody Loves You, Mr. Hatch. Yalowitz, Paul, illus. LC 90-33016. 32p. (ps-2). 1991. RSBE 13.95 (*0-02-786015-9*, Bradbury Pr) Macmillan Child Grp.
Spinelli, Jerry. Fourth Grade Rats. (ps-3). 1991. 13.95 (*0-590-44243-0*, Scholastic Hardcover) Scholastic Inc.
Spohn, Kate. Fanny & Margarita: Five Stories about Two Best Friends. LC 92-22208. (Illus.). 32p. (gr. 3-8). 1993. 13.99 (*0-670-84692-9*) Viking Child Bks.
Springer, Nancy. The Friendship Song. LC 91-9483. 144p. (gr. 4 up). 1992. SBE 13.95 (*0-689-31727-1*, Atheneum Child Bk) Macmillan Child Grp.
Stafford, Jean. The Scarlet Letter. LC 92-44056. 1994. 13.95 (*0-88682-588-1*) Creative Ed.
Stahl, Hilda. Big Trouble for Roxie. 160p. (gr. 4-7). 1992. pap. 3.99 (*0-89107-658-1*) Crossway Bks.
—Chelsea & the Outrageous Phone Bill. 160p. (gr. 4-7). 1992. pap. 3.99 (*0-89107-657-3*) Crossway Bks.
—Chelsea's Special Touch. LC 92-37203. 160p. (gr. 4-7). 1993. 3.99 (*0-89107-712-X*) Crossway Bks.
—Mystery at Bellwood Estate. LC 92-41738. 160p. (gr. 4-7). 1993. pap. 3.99 (*0-89107-713-8*) Crossway Bks.
—Sadie Rose & the Daring Escape. LC 88-70496. 144p. (gr. 4-7). 1988. pap. 4.99 (*0-89107-492-9*) Crossway Bks.
—Tough Choices for Roxie. LC 92-37055. 160p. (gr. 4 up). 1993. pap. 3.99 (*0-89107-711-1*) Crossway Bks.
Starbuck, Marnie. The Gladimals Learn about Friendship. 16p. (ps-3). 1991. pap. text ed. 0.75 (*1-56456-229-8*) W Gladden Found.
Starkman, Neal. The Riddle. Sasaki, Ellen J., illus. LC 89-25405. 50p. (Orig.). (gr. 2). 1989. pap. 11.00 (*0-935529-13-6*) Comprehen Health Educ.

Steel, Danielle. Martha's Best Friend. Rogers, Jacqueline, illus. (ps-2). 1989. 8.95 (*0-385-29801-3*) Delacorte.
Stefanik, Alfred. Copycat Sam: Developing Ties with a Special Child. Huff, Laura, illus. LC 81-20212. 32p. (gr. k-5). 1982. 16.95 (*0-89885-058-4*) Human Sci Pr.
Steig, William. Caleb & Katie. Steig, William, illus. 32p. (ps up). 1986. pap. 4.95 (*0-374-41038-0*) FS&G.
—Spinky Sulks. (gr. 4-8). 1991. pap. 4.95 (*0-374-46990-3*) FS&G.
Stevenson, James. No Friends. Stevenson, James, illus. LC 85-27247. 32p. (gr. k-3). 1986. 11.75 (*0-688-06506-6*); PLB 11.88 (*0-688-06507-4*) Greenwillow.
—The Worst Person in the World. LC 77-22141. (Illus.). 32p. (gr. k-3). 1978. PLB 13.88 (*0-688-84127-9*) Greenwillow.
Stine, R. L. The Best Friend. McDonald, Patricia, ed. 160p. (Orig.). (gr. 7 up). 1992. pap. 3.99 (*0-671-73866-6*, Archway) PB.
—Bozos on Patrol. 160p. 1992. pap. 2.75 (*0-590-44747-5*, Apple Paperbacks) Scholastic Inc.
—The Overnight. large type ed. (gr. 6 up). Date not set. PLB 14.60 (*0-8368-1158-5*) Gareth Stevens Inc.
Stolz, Mary. Bully of Barkham Street. Shortall, Leonard, illus. LC 68-2661. 224p. (gr. 3-6). 1963. PLB 14.89 (*0-06-025821-7*) HarpC Child Bks.
—Noonday Friends. Glanzman, Louis S., illus. LC 65-20257. 192p. (gr. 3-7). 1965. PLB 14.89 (*0-06-025946-9*) HarpC Child Bks.
—Noonday Friends. LC 65-20257. (Illus.). 192p. (gr. 4-7). 1971. pap. 3.95 (*0-06-440009-3*, Trophy) HarpC Child Bks.
Stone, Susheila. Where Is Batool? (Illus.). 25p. (gr. 2-4). 1991. 15.95 (*0-237-60157-5*, Pub. by Evans Bros Ltd) Trafalgar.
Strasser, Todd. A Very Touchy Subject. (gr. 6 up). 1986. pap. 2.95 (*0-440-98851-9*, LFL) Dell.
Strayer, Debbie. Jack & Stan, Winky, Blinky, & Pinky: Blend Book, 2 bks, Nos. 3 & 4. Majewski, Joy, illus. 16p. (gr. 1). 1992. Set. pap. 8.00 (*1-880892-12-X*) Fam Lrng Ctr.
—Sally & Sam, Mike & Spike: Blend Book, 2 bks, Nos. 5 & 6. Majewski, Joy, illus. 16p. (gr. 1). 1992. pap. 8.00 Set (*1-880892-13-8*) Fam Lrng Ctr.
Streatfeild, Noel. Good-Bye Gemma. (Orig.). (gr. k-6). 1987. pap. 3.25 (*0-440-42871-8*, YB) Dell.
Strete, Craig K. Big Thunder Magic. Brown, Craig, illus. LC 89-34613. 32p. (ps up). 1990. 12.95 (*0-688-08853-8*); PLB 12.88 (*0-688-08854-6*) Greenwillow.
Strommen, Judith B. Grady the Great. 160p. (gr. 4-6). 1990. 13.95 (*0-8050-1405-5*, Bks Young Read) H Holt & Co.
Sutton. Me & the Weirdos. (ps-7). 1987. pap. 2.25 (*0-553-15395-1*, Skylark) Bantam.
Sutton, Elizabeth H. Racing for Keeneland. LC 93-43385. (gr. 5-12). 1994. 14.95 (*1-56566-051-X*) Thomasson-Grant.
Suzanne, Jamie. Against the Rules. large type ed. Pascal, Francine, created by. 104p. (gr. 7-12). 1991. Repr. of 1987 ed. 9.95 (*1-55905-072-1*) Grey Castle.
—Best Friends. large type ed. Pascal, Francine, created by. 104p. (gr. 7-12). 1990. Repr. of 1986 ed. 9.95 (*1-55905-064-0*) Grey Castle.
Swallow, Pamela C. Wading Through Peanut Butter. (gr. 4-7). 1993. pap. 2.95 (*0-590-45793-4*) Scholastic Inc.
Sweeney, Joyce. Face the Dragon. 1990. 14.95 (*0-385-30164-2*) Delacorte.
T-Neck. 2nd, rev. & expanded ed. 180p. (gr. 5 up). 1993. pap. 7.95 (*0-9626608-5-X*) Magik NY.
Tada, Joni E. Meet My Friends. LC 87-22344. (gr. 3-7). 1987. pap. 4.99 (*1-55513-808-X*, Chariot Bks) Chariot Family.
Tafuri, Nancy. My Friends. Tafuri, Nancy, illus. LC 86-29388. 12p. (ps). 1987. Board book. 3.95 (*0-688-07187-2*) Greenwillow.
Talbert, Marc. The Purple Heart. 128p. (gr. 6). 1993. pap. 3.50 (*0-380-71985-1*, Camelot) Avon.
Talbott, Hudson. Going Hollywood! A Dinosaur's Dream. Talbott, Hudson, illus. LC 89-1190. 32p. (ps-3). 1989. 12.95 (*0-517-57354-7*) Crown Bks Yng Read.
Taylor, Lisa. Beryl's Box. Dann, Penny, illus. LC 92-44990. 32p. (ps-2). 1993. 12.95 (*0-8120-6355-4*); pap. 5.95 (*0-8120-1673-4*) Barron.
Taylor, Maureen. Without Warning. LC 91-12470. 144p. 1991. pap. 4.99 (*0-8066-2538-4*, 9-2538) Augsburg Fortress.
Taylor, Mildred D. The Friendship. Ginsburg, Max, illus. LC 86-29309. 56p. (gr. 2-6). 1987. 13.95 (*0-8037-0417-8*); PLB 13.89 (*0-8037-0418-6*) Dial Bks Young.
—The Friendship & the Gold Cadillac. (gr. 2-6). 1989. pap. 3.99 (*0-553-15765-5*, Skylark) Bantam.
Taylor, Theodore. The Odyssey of Ben O'Neal. 224p. 1991. pap. 3.50 (*0-380-71026-9*, Camelot) Avon.
Tempski, Armine von. Born in Paradise. LC 84-27345. 342p. 1985. 27.50 (*0-918024-65-X*); pap. 14.95 (*0-918024-34-X*) Ox Bow.
Terban, Marvin. It Figures. (gr. 4-7). 1993. pap. 5.95 (*0-395-66591-4*, Clarion Bks) HM.
Terrible Truth. 1984. pap. 2.25 (*0-440-78578-2*) Dell.
Testa, Fulvio. Wolf's Flavor. (ps-3). 1990. 3.95 (*0-8037-0744-4*, Dial) Doubleday.
Tharlet, Eve. Little Pig, Big Trouble. Clements, Andrew, tr. Tharlet, Eve, illus. LC 91-40637. 28p. (gr. k up). 1992. pap. 4.95 (*0-88708-227-0*) Picture Bk Studio.
Thomas, Janet. Newcomer. 33p. (Orig.). (gr. k-3). 1987. pap. 4.50 playscript (*0-87602-268-9*) Anchorage.
Thompson, Joan. The Mudpack & Me. MacDonald, Pat, ed. 160p. (Orig.). 1993. pap. 3.50 (*0-671-72862-8*, Minstrel Bks) PB.
Thompson, Julian F. The Fling. LC 93-33812. 1994. 15.95 (*0-8050-2881-1*) H Holt & Co.
—Gypsyworld. 172p. (gr. 7 up). 1992. 15.95 (*0-8050-1907-3*, Bks Young Read) H Holt & Co.
Thompson, Pat. My Friend Mr. Morris. (gr. k-6). 1988. pap. 2.50 (*0-440-40061-9*) Dell.
Thomson, Pat. Best Pest. (Illus.). 28p. (gr. 1-4). 1990. 13.95 (*0-575-04573-6*, Pub. by Gollancz UK) Trafalgar.
—No Trouble at All. Wild, Jocelyn, illus. 28p. (gr. 1-4). 1990. 13.95 (*0-575-04577-9*, Pub. by Gollancz UK) Trafalgar.
Thorpe, Jean J. Kirtpatrick's Kritters. Thorpe, Jean J., illus. 50p. (gr. k-6). 1988. pap. 7.95 (*0-317-93347-7*) Art & Earth.
Timm, Stephen A. The Floor That Said "No More" Neidigh, Sherry, illus. LC 86-60276. 48p. 1986. pap. 5.95 (*0-939728-12-5*) Steppingstone Ent.
Tolan, Stephanie S. A Good Courage. (gr. 7 up). 1989. pap. 1.50 (*0-449-70329-0*, Juniper) Fawcett.
—Pride of the Peacock. 176p. 1987. pap. 1.50 (*0-449-70207-3*, Juniper) Fawcett.
Tomkins, Jasper. Nimby. (Illus.). 60p. 1991. pap. 7.95 (*0-671-74973-0*, Green Tiger) S&S Trade.
Towne, Mary. Dive Through the Wave. LC 93-40999. (Illus.). 128p. (gr. 3-6). 1994. PLB 13.95 (*0-8167-3478-X*); pap. text ed. 2.95 (*0-8167-3479-8*) BrdgeWater.
Trevaskis, Ian. Periwinkle's Ride. Crossett, Warren, illus. LC 93-18049. 1994. write for info. (*0-383-03708-5*) SRA Schl Grp.
Trouble with Tuck. 1986. pap. 1.25 (*0-440-82064-2*) Dell.
Tryon, Thomas. The Adventures of Opal & Cupid. (Illus.). 224p. 1992. 14.00 (*0-670-82239-6*) Viking Child Bks.
Tsutsui, Yoriko. Anna's Special Present. Hayashi, Akiko, illus. 32p. (ps-3). 1988. pap. 11.95 (*0-670-81671-X*) Viking Child Bks.
Tuck Everlasting. 1987. pap. 1.25 (*0-440-84095-3*) Dell.
Turkle, Brinton. Thy Friend, Obadiah. (Illus.). 40p. (gr. k-3). 1982. pap. 4.99 (*0-14-050393-5*, Puffin) Puffin Bks.
Turner, Glennette T. Take a Walk in Their Shoes. Fax, Elton C., illus. LC 89-9700. 176p. (gr. 4-8). 1989. 15.00 (*0-525-65006-7*, Cobblehill Bks) Dutton Child Bks.
Tusa, Tricia. Stay Away from the Junkyard! Tusa, Tricia, illus. LC 91-38498. 32p. (gr. k-3). 1992. pap. 4.95 (*0-689-71626-5*, Aladdin) Macmillan Child Grp.
Twain, Mark. A Story Without an End. LC 85-30885. 32p. (gr. 4 up). 1986. PLB 13.95 (*0-88682-064-2*) Creative Ed.
Twohill, Maggie. Big Mouth. (gr. k-6). 1989. pap. 2.95 (*0-440-40223-9*, YB) Dell.
—Valentine Frankenstein. LC 90-24459. 144p. (gr. 3-6). 1991. SBE 13.95 (*0-02-789692-7*, Bradbury Pr) Macmillan Child Grp.
Uchida, Yoshiko. The Bracelet. Yardley, Joanna, illus. LC 92-26196. 32p. (ps-3). 1993. 14.95 (*0-399-22503-X*, Philomel Bks) Putnam Pub Group.
—The Happiest Ending. LC 85-6245. 120p. (gr. 3-7). 1985. SBE 13.95 (*0-689-50326-1*, M K McElderry) Macmillan Child Grp.
Underneath I'm Different. 1983. pap. 13.95 (*0-385-29234-1*) Doubleday.
Urbide, Fernando & Engler, Dan. Ben-Hur, A Race to Glory. CCC of America Staff, illus. 35p. (Orig.). (ps-8). 1992. incl. video 21.95 (*1-56814-006-1*); pap. text ed. 4.95 book (*0-685-62399-8*) CCC of America.
Ure, Jean. The Children Next Door. large type ed. (Illus.). (gr. 1-8). 1994. 15.95 (*0-7451-2271-X*, Galaxy etc.) Chivers N Amer.
—The Other Side of the Fence. LC 87-27184. 176p. (gr. 7 up). 1988. 14.95 (*0-385-29627-4*) Delacorte.
Vail, Rachel. Ever After. LC 93-29802. 176p. (gr. 6-9). 1993. 14.95 (*0-531-06838-2*); lib. bdg. 14.99 RLB (*0-531-08688-7*) Orchard Bks Watts.
—Wonder. LC 91-10576. 128p. (gr. 6 up). 1991. 13.95 (*0-531-05964-2*); RLB 13.99 (*0-531-08564-3*) Orchard Bks Watts.
—Wonder. 128p. (gr. 5 up). 1993. pap. 3.99 (*0-14-036167-7*, Puffin) Puffin Bks.
Valat, Pierre-Marie. Fun Faces. (Illus.). 32p. (ps up). 1989. 15.95 (*0-525-44544-7*, DCB) Dutton Child Bks.
Vallet, Muriel. Let's Take Turns. Vallet, Muriel, illus. 15p. (gr. k-3). 1993. pap. 10.95 (*1-895583-58-6*) MAYA Pubs.
Van Curen, Barbara. When the Zebras Came for Lunch. Manierre, Betsy, illus. 64p. (ps-2). 1989. pap. text ed. 5.95 (*0-922510-01-6*) Lucky Bks.
Van Kirk, Barbara D. The Person Who Had Feelings. Dunlap, Sam, illus. 44p. (Orig.). 1975. pap. 6.95 (*0-9631751-0-6*) New Begin OR.
Van Laan, Nancy. Round & Round Again. Westcott, Nadine B., illus. LC 93-45918. 32p. (ps-3). 1994. 13.95 (*0-7868-0009-7*); PLB 13.89 (*0-7868-2005-5*) Hyprn Child.
Van Loon, Paul. Party at Manny's. Spee, Gitte, illus. 24p. (Orig.). (ps-1). 1994. pap. 4.95 (*1-55037-361-7*, Pub. by Annick CN) Firefly Bks Ltd.
VerDorn, Bethea. Day Breaks. Graham, Thomas, illus. 32p. (ps-3). 1992. 14.95 (*1-55970-187-0*) Arcade Pub Inc.
Vesco, Anne-Marie. Charlotte & Leo. (Illus.). 32p. (gr. 3-5). 1991. 12.95 (*0-89565-818-6*) Childs World.
Vickery, Eugene L. New Friends in a New World: Thanksgiving Story of Children with New Friends. Tolpo, Lily, illus. 20p. (Orig.). (gr. k-8). 1986. pap. 1.95 (*0-937775-03-7*) Stonehaven Pubs.
Vincent, Gabrielle. Ernest & Celestine. LC 81-6392. (Illus.). 24p. (ps up). 1986. 3.95 (*0-688-06525-2*, Mulberry) Morrow.
Vinge, Joan D. Psion. 352p. (gr. k-12). 1985. pap. 2.95 (*0-440-97192-6*, LFL) Dell.
Viorst, Judith. If I Were in Charge of the World & Other Worries. LC 81-2342. (Illus.). 64p. (gr. 2 up). 1984. pap. 4.95 (*0-689-70770-3*, Aladdin) Macmillan Child Grp.
—Rosie & Michael. Tomei, Lorna, illus. LC 74-75571. 40p. (gr. 1-4). 1974. SBE 13.95 (*0-689-30439-0*, Atheneum Child Bk) Macmillan Child Grp.
—Rosie & Michael. 2nd ed. Tomei, Lorna, illus. LC 86-13969. 40p. (gr. 1-4). 1988. pap. 3.95 (*0-689-71272-3*, Aladdin) Macmillan Child Grp.
Voelker, Joyce. Dear Terry. (Illus.). 97p. (Orig.). (gr. 3-6). 1990. pap. 4.95 (*0-89084-526-3*) Bob Jones Univ Pr.
Voigt, Cynthia. David & Jonathan. 208p. 1992. 14.95 (*0-590-45165-0*, Scholastic Hardcover) Scholastic Inc.
—A Solitary Blue. LC 83-6007. 204p. (gr. 7 up). 1983. SBE 16.00 (*0-689-31008-0*, Atheneum Child Bk) Macmillan Child Grp.
—Tell Me if the Lovers Are Losers. LC 81-8079. 252p. (gr. 7 up). 1982. SBE 15.95 (*0-689-30911-2*, Atheneum Child Bk) Macmillan Child Grp.
Von Trutzschler, Wolf. Amanda. Von Trutzschler, Wolf, illus. LC 89-82473. 48p. (ps-2). 1990. Repr. of 1941 ed. 14.95 (*0-944439-19-5*) Clark City Pr.
Vulliamy, Clara. Ellen & Penguin. Vulliamy, Clara, illus. LC 92-54590. 32p. (ps up). 1993. 13.95 (*1-56402-193-9*) Candlewick Pr.
Wagner, Donald R. No Tears for My Mary. Horwitz, Janet, ed. LC 87-90522. 40p. (gr. 7 up). 1989. 8.95 (*0-910583-02-1*); pap. 4.95 (*0-318-32717-1*) Shamrock Pr.
Waite, Michael P. Buzzle Billy. LC 87-5282. (ps-2). 1987. 7.99 (*1-55513-218-9*, Chariot Bks) Chariot Family.
Wakeman, Cheryl A. Johnnie Ollie Carri III & His Friend. Womack, Fred, illus. 32p. (ps-3). 1985. 5.95 (*0-9614819-0-0*) R E Moen.
Walker, John C. In Other Words. Steiner, Connie, illus. 32p. 1993. lib. bdg. 14.95 (*1-55037-309-9*, Pub. by Annick CN); pap. 4.95 (*1-55037-310-2*, Pub. by Annick CN) Firefly Bks Ltd.
Wall, Dorothy. Tiny Story of Blinky Bill. (ps-3). 1993. 4.50 (*0-207-17468-7*, Pub. by Angus & Robertson AT) HarpC.
Wallace, Art. Toby & the Phantoms of the Fourth Grade. LC 93-760. (Illus.). (gr. 4-7). 1994. Repr. of 1971 ed. 11.95 (*0-89015-917-3*) Sunbelt Media.
Wallace, Bill. True Friends. LC 94-6449. 160p. (gr. 4-6). 1994. 14.95 (*0-8234-1141-9*) Holiday.
Walley, Susan. Best of Friends. Lyall, Elizabeth, ed. Halverson, Tom, illus. 156p. (Orig.). (gr. 4-8). 1989. pap. 4.95 (*0-89084-486-0*) Bob Jones Univ Pr.
Walter, Mildred P. Have a Happy... 96p. 1990. pap. 3.50 (*0-380-71314-4*, Camelot) Avon.
Ware, Martin E. Carly's & Amy's, Friends & Fables. (Illus.). 40p. (gr. 3-8). 1991. 7.50 (*0-8059-3194-5*) Dorrance.
Warner, Gertrude C., created by. The Haunted Cabin Mystery. (Illus.). (gr. 2-7). 1991. 10.95g (*0-8075-3179-0*); pap. 3.50g (*0-8075-3178-2*) A Whitman.
Warren, Jean. The Bear & the Mountain: A Totline Teaching Tale. Shimono, Judy & Tourtillotte, Barbara, illus. LC 93-38781. 32p. (gr. 2-8). 1994. 12.95 (*0-911019-99-5*); pap. 5.95 (*0-911019-98-7*) Warren Pub Hse.

Warren, Sandra & Pfleger, Deborah B. Arlie the Alligator. Thomas, Deborah, illus. LC 91-73758. 48p. (ps-3). 1992. PLB 13.95 casebound (*1-880175-13-4*); bk. & cass. 19.90 (*1-880175-11-8*); audiocassette 5.95 (*1-880175-12-6*) Arlie Enter.
Arlie is a very curious alligator who longs to make friends with the strange creatures at the beach. Find out who the strange creatures are & what happens when he attempts to talk to them. The 10-minute audio cassette is fully produced with actors & actresses in mini-musical style. Four catchy tunes have children singing along the first time they listen. In beautiful color, this casebound, open-ended story book also includes a page about real alligators & sheet music. A creative use of fonts signals the change from song lyrics to dialogue. Non-readers enjoy the audio tape & pictures, while young readers & middle readers love to follow along, singing & reading, word-for-

word, as the delightful story unfolds. Creative thinking is enhanced as children are encouraged to help Arlie find a way to communicate with the creatures. Unique in children's literature, ARLIE THE ALLIGATOR makes a great addition to the children's books-on-tape section of the library, elementary music libraries, elementary classrooms, in homes or for that long trip in the car. Activity guide also available, making that important classroom connection.
Publisher Provided Annotation.

Wartski, Maureen. Belonging. (Orig.). (gr. 7 up). 1993. pap. 3.99 (*0-449-70419-X*, Juniper) Fawcett.
Watch Out for Big Bad Brad. (gr. 2 up). 1991. pap. 1.97 (*1-56297-115-8*) Lee Pubns KY.
Watermill Pr. Staff. Como Dibujar Personajes Comicos. (ps-3). 1992. pap. 1.95 (*0-8167-2646-9*) Troll Assocs.
Watts, Carl. Steven Otto Nevets. LC 93-60236. (Illus.). 44p. (gr. k-3). 1993. 7.95 (*1-55523-602-2*) Winston-Derek.
Weaver-Gelzer, Charlotte. In the Time of Trouble. LC 92-11146. 224p. (gr. 7 up). 1993. 15.99 (*0-525-44973-6*, DCB) Dutton Child Bks.
Weber, Ane & Krueger, Ron. A Tailor-Made Friendship. French, Marty & Iwai, Noel, illus. 26p. (ps up). 1988. incl. cassette 7.95 (*1-55578-913-7*) Worlds Wonder.
Weber, Ane, et al. A Tailor-Made Friendship. French, Marty & Iwia, Noel, illus. 26p. (ps up). 1986. Book & Cassette. 7.95 (*1-55578-107-1*) Worlds Wonder.
Webster, Jean. Dear Enemy. (gr. 4-7). 1991. pap. 3.50 (*0-440-40440-1*) Dell.
Weinberg, Ben. Out to the Edge. Holmes, B., ed. 200p. (gr. 6-10). 1993. pap. 9.95 (*0-932433-47-2*) Windswept Hse.
Weiss, Anne E. Lies, Deception, & Truth. 160p. (gr. 5-9). 1988. 13.45 (*0-395-40486-X*) HM.
Weiss, Nicki. Hank & Dogie. (ps-3). 1991. pap. 2.75 (*0-553-15954-2*) Bantam.
—Maude & Sally. Weiss, Nicki, illus. LC 82-12003. 32p. (gr. k-3). 1983. 13.95 (*0-688-01859-9*); PLB 13.88 (*0-688-01861-0*) Greenwillow.
Wells, Rosemary. Stanley & Rhoda. Wells, Rosemary, illus. LC 78-51874. 40p. (ps-2). 1981. pap. 4.95 (*0-8037-7995-X*, 0383-120) Dial Bks Young.
—Stanley & Rhoda. LC 78-51874. (Illus.). (ps-2). 1985. 13.95 (*0-8037-8248-9*) Dial Bks Young.
Wersba, Barbara. Crazy Vanilla. LC 85-45956. 192p. (gr. 7 up). 1986. HarpC Child Bks.
West, Tracey. Mr. Peale's Bones. 80p. (gr. 4-6). 1994. PLB 12.95 (*1-881889-50-5*) Silver Moon.
Weyn, Suzanne. All Alone in the Eighth Grade. LC 91-10162. 128p. (gr. 6-9). 1992. lib. bdg. 9.89 (*0-8167-2394-X*); pap. text ed. 2.95 (*0-8167-2395-8*) Troll Assocs.
—Ashley's Big Mistake. LC 93-43505. (Illus.). 128p. (gr. 4-8). 1994. PLB 9.89 (*0-8167-3231-0*); pap. text ed. 2.95 (*0-8167-3232-9*) Troll Assocs.
—Nicole's Chance. LC 93-14022. (Illus.). 128p. (gr. 4-8). 1993. PLB 9.89 (*0-8167-3235-3*); pap. 2.95 (*0-8167-3236-1*) Troll Assocs.
—Star Magic. LC 90-11151. 128p. (gr. 4-8). 1991. lib. bdg. 9.89 (*0-8167-2013-4*); pap. text ed. 2.95 (*0-8167-2014-2*) Troll Assocs.
What's the Big Idea? 1923. pap. 1.50 (*0-440-86177-2*) Dell.
Whelan, Gloria. That Wild Berries Should Grow: The Story of a Summer. LC 93-41106. 122p. (gr. 4-6). 1994. 13.99 (*0-8028-3754-9*); pap. 4.99 (*0-8028-5091-X*) Eerdmans.
—Time to Keep Silent. (gr. 4-7). 1993. pap. 5.99 (*0-8028-0118-8*) Eerdmans.
Whisper's Rainbow Treasure. (gr. 4-7). 1990. pap. 2.50 (*0-89954-965-9*) Antioch Pub Co.
White, Ellen E. Life Without Friends. 256p. (gr. 7 up). 1988. pap. 3.25 (*0-590-44628-2*) Scholastic Inc.

Whitten, Wendy & McCullough, Herb. Someday...Someday, Bk. 1. Swerda, Mike, illus. 42p. (ps up). 1994. Incl. audio cass. 29.95 (*1-886184-00-3*) Ion Imagination.
Ion Imagination (tm) Entertainment, Inc. presents the first in a series of adventures with Flumpa (tm), a tree frog who introduces the children to the wonder of adventure as he meets new friends along the way. SOMEDAY... SOMEDAY has a twenty-one minute audiocassette incorporated into the outer hardcover. This cassette features a Sing Along Side: original "story" songs, sung by Wendy Whitten & recorded at Jack's Tracks-Nashville, TN, with lyrics in the back of the collectable book, & Read Along Side: narration with sound effects, from a powerful storm to the calming sounds of twilight, & page turn signals. This 9 3/4" x 12 3/4" full-color, perfect bound book has foil & metallic inks. SOMEDAY...SOMEDAY, mixed media only, $29.95, ISBN 1-886184-00-3. Published by Ion Imagination (tm) Entertainment, Inc. To order: call 1-800-3-FLUMPA or write P.O. Box 210943, Nashville, TN 37221-0943.
Publisher Provided Annotation.

Who's My Friend? 12p. (ps). 1994. 4.95 (*1-56458-736-3*) Dorling Kindersley.
Who's My Friend? Dial the Answer. 1992. pap. 3.99 (*0-517-06618-1*) Random Hse Value.
Wiethorn, Randall J. Rock Finds a Friend. Wiethorn, Randall J., illus. 32p. 1991. pap. 5.95 (*0-88138-110-1*, Green Tiger) S&S Trade.
Wild, Jocelyn. Florence & Eric Take the Cake. (ps-3). 1990. pap. 3.95 (*0-8037-0676-6*, Puff Pied Piper) Puffin Bks.
Wild, Margaret. Mr. Nick's Knitting. Huxley, Dee H., illus. 28p. (ps-3). 1989. 12.95 (*0-15-200518-8*, Gulliver Bks) HarBrace.
—Very Best of Friends. LC 89-36464. (ps-3). 1994. pap. 4.95 (*0-15-200077-1*, HB Juv Bks) HarBrace.
Wilde, Nicholas. Into the Dark. 1992. pap. 2.95 (*0-590-43423-3*, Apple Paperbacks) Scholastic Inc.
Wilde, Oscar. The Devoted Friend. LC 86-2609. 32p. (gr. 4 up). 1986. PLB 13.95 (*0-88682-067-7*) Creative Ed.
—The Devoted Friend. Batmanglij, N. Khalili, tr. from ENG. Fanta, illus. LC 87-31689. 28p. (gr. 4 up). 1988. 15.00 (*0-934211-16-7*); Bilingual Eng.-Persian. 15.00 (*0-934211-10-8*) Mage Pubs Inc.
Willard, Nancy. Highest Hit. LC 77-88970. (gr. 4-7). 1993. pap. 4.95 (*0-15-234279-6*) HarBrace.
Williams, Karen L. Applebaum's Garage. LC 92-31336. 1993. 13.95 (*0-395-65227-8*, Clarion Bks) HM.
Williams, Karen S. Best Friends Are for Keeps. LC 92-10988. 1992. write for info. (*0-8280-0660-1*) Review & Herald.
Williams, Vera B. Scooter. LC 90-38489. (Illus.). 160p. (gr. 4-7). 1993. 15.00 (*0-688-09376-0*); PLB 14.93 (*0-688-09377-9*) Greenwillow.
Willner-Pardo, Gina. Jason & the Losers. LC 93-44156. 1996. write for info. (*0-395-70160-0*, Clarion Bks) HM.
—When Jane-Marie Told My Secret. Poydar, Nancy, illus. LC 94-12820. (gr. 1-8). 1995. write for info. (*0-395-66382-2*, Clarion Bks) HM.
Winthrop, Elizabeth. The Best Friends Club. Weston, Martha, illus. LC 88-13406. 32p. (ps-3). 1989. PLB 12.88 (*0-688-07583-5*) Lothrop.
—Lizzie & Harold. Weston, Martha, illus. LC 83-14858. 32p. (gr. k-3). 1985. 12.95 (*0-688-02711-3*); PLB 12.88 (*0-688-02712-1*) Lothrop.
—Miranda in the Middle. (gr. 4 up). 1990. pap. 3.95 (*0-14-034392-X*, Puffin) Puffin Bks.
Wolf, Joyce. Between the Cracks. 176p. (gr. 5 up). 1992. 14.95 (*0-8037-1270-7*) Dial Bks Young.
Wolff, Virginia E. Make Lemonade. 160p. (gr. 5-9). 1993. 15.95 (*0-8050-2228-7*, Bks Young Read) H Holt & Co.
Wolkoff, Judie. In a Pig's Eye. (gr. k-6). 1989. pap. 2.95 (*0-440-40140-2*, YB) Dell.
Wolkstein, Diane. Step by Step. Smith, Joseph A., illus. LC 93-14667. 40p. (ps up). 1994. 15.00g (*0-688-10315-4*); PLB 14.93 (*0-688-10316-2*) Morrow Jr Bks.
Wollard, Kathy. How Come? Solomon, Pedra, illus. 256p. (Orig.). (gr. 3-7). 1993. pap. 10.95 (*1-56305-324-1*, 3324) Workman Pub.
Wood, Audrey. Orlando's Littlewhile Friends. Wood, Audrey, illus. LC 90-45723. (ps-2). 1989. 11.95 (*0-85953-111-2*); pap. 5.95 (*0-85953-106-6*) Childs Play.
Wood, Vivian B. You're a Very Special Person. Wood, David & Wood, Vivian B., illus. 38p. (Orig.). (gr. 1). 1988. pap. 5.95 (*0-9621567-0-1*) V B Wood.
Woodson, Jacqueline. Between Madison & Palmetto. LC 92-38783. (gr. 1-6). 1993. 13.95 (*0-385-30906-6*) Delacorte.
—I Hadn't Meant to Tell You This. LC 93-8733. 1994. 14.95 (*0-385-32031-0*) Delacorte.
—Last Summer with Maizon. 1990. 13.95 (*0-385-30045-X*) Doubleday.
—Maizon at Blue Hill. (gr. 4-7). 1994. pap. 3.50 (*0-440-40899-7*) Dell.
Worth, Bonnie. Way to Go, Chipmunk Cheeks. (gr. 4-7). 1991. pap. 3.25 (*0-440-40596-3*, YB) Dell.
Wright, Alexandra. Will We Miss Them? (Illus.). 32p. (ps-8). 1991. 14.95 (*0-88106-489-0*); PLB 15.88 (*0-88106-675-3*); pap. 6.95 (*0-88106-488-2*) Charlesbridge Pub.
Wrightson, Patricia. The Sugar-Gum Tree. Cox, David, illus. 64p. (gr. 2-6). 1992. 11.95 (*0-670-83910-8*) Viking Child Bks.
Wunderli, Stephen. The Blue Between the Clouds. LC 91-28010. 80p. (gr. 5 up). 1992. 13.95 (*0-8050-1772-0*, Bks Young Read) H Holt & Co.
Wurmfeld, Hope H. Baby Blues. LC 92-5828. 80p. (gr. 7 up). 1992. 14.00 (*0-670-84151-X*) Viking Child Bks.
Wyeth, Sharon D. Lisa, We Miss You. 1990. pap. 2.95 (*0-440-40393-6*) Dell.
—No Creeps Need Apply. (gr. k-6). 1989. pap. 2.95 (*0-440-40241-7*, YB) Dell.
—P. S. Forget It. (gr. k-6). 1989. pap. 2.95 (*0-440-40230-1*, YB) Dell.
—Palmer at Your Service. (gr. 4 up). 1990. pap. 2.95 (*0-440-40343-X*, YB) Dell.
—Pen Pals: Stolen Pen Pals, No. 9. (gr. 4-7). 1990. pap. 2.95 (*0-440-40342-1*) Dell.
—Super Pen Pals, No. 1. (Orig.). (gr. 4-7). 1990. pap. 3.50 (*0-440-40395-2*, Pub. by Yearling Classics) Dell.
—The Unknown Pen Pal. (Orig.). 1990. pap. 2.95 (*0-440-40345-6*) Dell.
Wynne, Carrie E. That Looks Like a Nice House. LC 94-898. (Illus.). 42p. (Orig.). (gr. 8). 1987. pap. 5.95 (*0-9613205-3-2*) Launch Pr.
Yates, Alma J. Ghosts in the Baker Mine. LC 91-45230. 197p. (Orig.). (gr. 3-7). 1992. pap. 4.95 (*0-87579-581-1*) Deseret Bk.
Yates, Elizabeth. Sound Friendships: The Story of Willa & Her Hearing Dog. Leaman, Christine, ed. Roberts, John, illus. O'Brien, Sheila, frwd. by. (Illus.). 113p. (Orig.). (gr. 7-12). 1992. pap. 4.95 (*0-89084-650-2*) Bob Jones Univ Pr.
Yeatman, Linda. Buttons. Casson, Hugh, illus. 64p. (gr. 2-5). 1988. pap. 2.95 (*0-8120-3956-4*) Barron.
Yolen, Jane. Owl Moon. Schoenherr, John, illus. (ps-1). 1987. 14.95 (*0-399-21457-7*, Philomel Bks) Putnam Pub Group.
Yorgason, Blaine M. & Yorgason, Brenton. Pardners: Three Stories on Friendship. Durfee, John C. & Durfee, Gaylie, illus. 64p. (Orig.). (gr. 9 up). 1988. pap. 3.95 (*0-929985-05-2*) Jackman Pubng.
Yorinks, Arthur. Sid & Sol. (gr. 4-8). 1991. pap. 3.95 (*0-374-46634-3*, Sunburst) FS&G.
York, Carol B. Miss Know It All... 96p. (Orig.). (gr. 4 up). 1985. pap. 2.50 (*0-553-15408-7*, Skylark) Bantam.
—Miss Know-It-All & the Three Ring Circus. (Illus.). 96p. (Orig.). 1988. pap. 2.75 (*0-553-15590-3*, Skylark) Bantam.
You Are Special! 36p. (ps-4). 1985. 8.95 (*0-88684-176-3*); cassette tape avail. Listen USA.
Young, Jean. Versions of the Truth. LC 91-67099. 45p. (gr. 7 up). 1992. pap. 5.95 (*1-55523-484-4*) Winston-Derek.
Young, Ruth. Golden Bear. Isadora, Rachel, illus. 32p. (ps-1). 1992. PLB 14.00 (*0-670-82577-8*) Viking Child Bks.
Zabar, Abbie. Fifty-Five Friends. LC 93-47366. (ps-2). 1994. 13.95 (*0-7868-0021-6*); pap. write for info. (*0-7868-2017-9*) Hyprn Child.
Zable, Rona S. Landing on Marvin Gardens. 1991. pap. 3.50 (*0-553-29288-9*) Bantam.
Zach, Cheryl. Benny & the No-Good Teacher. Wilson, Janet, illus. LC 91-30588. 80p. (gr. 2-6). 1992. SBE 12.95 (*0-02-793706-2*, Bradbury Pr) Macmillan Child Grp.
Zadra, Dan. Dare to Be Different. (Illus.). 32p. (gr. 6 up). 1986. PLB 12.95 (*0-88682-016-2*) Creative Ed.
—Mistakes Are Great! (Illus.). 32p. (gr. 6 up). 1986. PLB 12.95 (*0-88682-019-7*) Creative Ed.
—More Good Time for You. (Illus.). 32p. (gr. 6 up). 1986. PLB 12.95 (*0-88682-022-7*) Creative Ed.
Zalben, Jane B. Here's Looking at You, Kid. (gr. k-12). 1987. pap. 2.50 (*0-440-93573-3*, LFL) Dell.
Zeier, Joan T. Stick Boy. LC 92-23326. 144p. (gr. 2-6). 1993. SBE 13.95 (*0-689-31835-9*, Atheneum Child Bk) Macmillan Child Grp.
Zelonky, Joy. My Best Friend Moved Away. Adams, Angela, illus. Silverman, Manuel, intro. by. LC 79-24111. (Illus.). (gr. k-6). 1980. PLB 19.97 (*0-8172-1353-8*) Raintree Steck-V.
—My Best Friend Moved Away. (ps-3). 1993. pap. 3.95 (*0-8114-7157-8*) Raintree Steck-V.
Ziebel, Peter. Look Closer. (ps-3). 1993. pap. 5.95 (*0-395-66509-4*, Clarion Bks) HM.
Ziefert, Harriet. Mike & Tony: Best Friends. Siracusa, Catherine, illus. LC 93-25617. (ps-2). 1994. pap. 3.25 (*0-14-036853-1*, Puffin) Puffin Bks.
—Nicky Upstairs & Down. Brown, Richard, illus. (ps-3). 1987. (Puffin); pap. 3.50 (*0-14-050742-6*, Puffin) Puffin Bks.
—Stitches. Aitken, Amy, illus. 32p. (ps-3). 1990. pap. 3.50 (*0-14-054224-8*, Puffin) Puffin Bks.
Zindel, Bonnie. Hollywood Dream Machine. 192p. (gr. 7-12). 1985. pap. 2.50 (*0-553-25240-2*, Starfire) Bantam.
Zindel, Paul. A Begonia for Miss Applebaum. LC 88-11010. 192p. (gr. 7 up). 1989. 14.00i (*0-06-026877-8*); PLB 13.89 (*0-06-026878-6*) HarpC Child Bks.
—A Begonia for Miss Applebaum. (gr. 7 up). 1990. pap. 3.99 (*0-553-28765-6*, Starfire) Bantam.
—Fright Party. Mangiat, Jeff, illus. (gr. 4-7). 1993. pap. 3.50 (*0-553-48082-0*) Bantam.
—Harry & Hortense at Hormone High. 160p. (gr. 7-12). 1985. pap. 3.99 (*0-553-25175-9*, Starfire) Bantam.
Zolotow, Charlotte. The Hating Book. Shecter, Ben, illus. LC 69-14444. 32p. (ps-3). 1969. 14.00 (*0-06-026923-5*); PLB 13.89 (*0-06-026924-3*) HarpC Child Bks.
—The Hating Book. Schecter, Ben, illus. LC 69-14444. 32p. (gr. k-3). 1989. pap. 3.95 (*0-06-443197-5*, Trophy) HarpC Child Bks.

—Hold My Hand. Reissue. ed. Di Grazia, Thomas, illus. LC 72-76506. 32p. (gr. k-3). 1972. PLB 12.89 (*0-06-026952-9*) HarpC Child Bks.
—Janey. Himler, Ronald, illus. LC 72-9861. 24p. (ps-3). 1973. PLB 12.89 (*0-06-026928-6*) HarpC Child Bks.

FRIENDSHIP–POETRY

Grimes, Nikki. Meet Danitra Brown. Cooper, Floyd, illus. LC 92-43707. (gr. 4 up). 1995. 15.00 (*0-688-12073-3*); PLB 14.93 (*0-688-12074-1*) Lothrop.
Hallinan, P. K. That's What a Friend Is. Hallinan, P. K., illus. LC 76-27744. 32p. (gr. k-3). 1977. pap. 3.95 (*0-516-43628-7*) Childrens.
Kellogg, Steven. Best Friends. Fogelman, Phyllis J., ed. Kellogg, Steven, illus. LC 85-15971. 32p. (ps-3). 1990. pap. 4.99 (*0-8037-0829-7*) Dial Bks Young.
Livingston, Myra C. A Time to Talk: Poems of Friendship. Pinkney, Brian, illus. LC 91-42234. 128p. (gr. 7 up). 1992. SBE 13.95 (*0-689-50558-2*, M K McElderry) Macmillan Child Grp.
Maris, Ron. Is Anyone Home? Maris, Ron, illus. LC 85-5436. 32p. (ps-2). 1986. 16.00 (*0-688-05899-X*) Greenwillow.
Prelutsky, Jack. Rolling Harvey Down the Hill. Chess, Victoria, illus. LC 92-24606. 40p. (gr. 2 up). 1993. pap. 4.95 (*0-688-12270-1*, Mulberry) Morrow.
Roy, Cal. Friend Can Be. (Illus.). (gr. 2 up). 1969. 9.95 (*0-8392-3075-3*) Astor-Honor.

FROGMEN

see Skin Diving

FROGS

Back, Christine & Watts, Barrie. Tadpole & Frog. LC 86-10049. (Illus.). 25p. (gr. k-4). 1986. 5.95 (*0-382-09293-7*); PLB 7.95 (*0-382-09285-6*); pap. 3.95 (*0-382-24021-9*) Silver Burdett Pr.
Benedict, Kitty. The Toad: My First Nature Books. Felix, Monique, illus. 32p. (gr. k-2). 1993. pap. 2.95 (*1-56189-178-9*) Amer Educ Pub.
Berger, Melvin. Leaping Frogs. (Illus.). 16p. (ps-2). 1995. pap. text ed. 14.95 (*1-56784-023-X*) Newbridge Comms.
—Those Fabulous Frogs. 16p. (gr. 2-4). 1994. pap. 14.95 (*1-56784-208-9*) Newbridge Comms.
Butterfield, Moira. Frog. Johnson, Paul, illus. 24p. (ps-1). 1992. pap. 3.95 (*0-671-75893-4*, Little Simon) S&S Trade.
Clarke, Barry. Amazing Frogs & Toads. Young, Jerry, photos by. LC 90-31882. (Illus.). 32p. (Orig.). (gr. 1-5). 1990. lib. bdg. 9.99 (*0-679-90688-6*); pap. 7.99 (*0-679-80688-1*) Knopf Bks Yng Read.
Coldrey, Jennifer. Frog in the Pond. LC 85-30300. (Illus.). 32p. (gr. 4-6). 1987. 17.27 (*1-55532-059-7*) Gareth Stevens Inc.
—The World of Frogs. LC 85-30297. (Illus.). 32p. (gr. 2-3). 1987. 17.27 (*1-55532-024-4*) Gareth Stevens Inc.
Cole, Joanna. A Frog's Body. Wexler, Jerome, illus. LC 80-10705. 48p. (gr. k-3). 1980. PLB 12.88 (*0-688-32228-X*, Morrow Jr Bks) Morrow Jr Bks.
Dallinger, Jane & Johnson, Sylvia A. Frogs & Toads. LC 80-27667. (Illus.). 48p. (gr. 4 up). 1982. PLB 19.95 (*0-8225-1454-0*, First Ave Edns); pap. 5.95 (*0-8225-9502-8*, First Ave Edns) Lerner Pubns.
Fichter, George S. Turtles, Toads, & Frogs. Ambler, Barbara H., illus. 36p. (gr. k-3). 1993. 4.95 (*0-307-11433-3*, 11433, Golden Pr) Western Pub.
Fowler, Allan. Frogs & Toads, & Tadpoles, Too. LC 91-42178. (Illus.). 32p. (ps-2). 1992. PLB 10.75 (*0-516-04925-9*); PLB 22.95 big bk. (*0-516-49626-3*); pap. 3.95 (*0-516-44925-7*) Childrens.
—Ranas, Sapos y Renacuajos! Frogs & Toads, & Tadpoles, Too. LC 91-42178. (SPA., Illus.). 32p. (ps-2). 1992. PLB 10.75 (*0-516-34925-2*); pap. 3.95 (*0-516-54925-1*); big bk. 22.95 (*0-516-59626-8*) Childrens.
Gambill, Henrietta, ed. Who Made Frogs? (Illus.). 18p. 1994. 7.99 (*0-7847-0235-7*, 24-03125) Standard Pub.
Gibbons, Gail. Frogs. LC 93-269. (Illus.). 32p. (ps-3). 1993. reinforced bdg. 15.95 (*0-8234-1052-8*); pap. 5.95 (*0-8234-1134-6*) Holiday.
Hogan, Paula Z. The Frog. Strigenz, Geri K., illus. LC 78-21240. 32p. (gr. 1-4). 1979. PLB 19.97 (*0-8172-1253-1*); pap. 4.95 (*0-8114-8175-1*); pap. 9.95 incl. cassette (*0-8114-8183-2*) Raintree Steck-V.
—The Frog. LC 78-21240. (Illus.). 32p. (gr. 1-4). 1984. PLB 29.28 incl. cassette (*0-8172-2228-6*) Raintree Steck-V.
Johnson, Sylvia A. Tree Frogs. Masuda, Modoki, illus. LC 86-2721. 48p. (gr. 4 up). 1986. PLB 19.95 (*0-8225-1467-2*) Lerner Pubns.
Julivert, Maria A. El Fascinante Mundo, The Fascinating World: Las Ranas y Los Sapos, Of Frogs & Toads. Marcel Socias Studio Staff, ed. Arridondo, F., illus. 32p. (gr. 3-7). 1993. pap. 7.95 (*0-8120-1795-1*) Barron.
—The Fascinating World of Frogs & Toads. Marcel Socias Studio Staff & Arridondo, F., illus. 32p. (gr. 3-7). 1993. 11.95 (*0-8120-6345-7*); pap. 7.95 (*0-8120-1565-7*) Barron.
Kermit, Save the Swamp! 24p. (ps-2). 1992. 1.29 (*0-307-00131-8*, Golden Pr) Western Pub.
Lacey, Elizabeth A. The Complete Frog: A Guide for the Very Young Naturalist. Santoro, Christopher, illus. LC 88-9343. 72p. (gr. k-4). 1989. 12.95 (*0-688-08017-0*); PLB 12.88 (*0-688-08018-9*) Lothrop.
Lane, Margaret. The Frog. Corbett, Grahame, illus. LC 81-1228. 32p. (gr. k-4). 1994. 13.99 (*0-8037-2711-9*) Dial Bks Young.
Linley, Mike. The Frog & the Toad: Masters of Land & Water. Stefoff, Rebecca, ed. LC 92-10246. (Illus.). 31p. (gr. 3-6). 1992. PLB 17.26 (*1-56074-050-7*) Garrett Ed Corp.
Lovett, Sarah, text by. Extremely Weird Frogs. (Illus.). 48p. (gr. 3 up). 1991. 9.95 (*1-56261-006-6*) John Muir.
Michels, Tilde. At the Frog Pond. Ignatowicz, Nina, tr. from GER. Michl, Reinhard, illus. LC 88-37835. 32p. (ps-4). 1989. (Lipp Jr Bks) HarpC Child Bks.
Morris, Dean. Frogs & Toads. rev. ed. LC 87-16698. (Illus.). 48p. (gr. 2-6). 1987. PLB 10.95 (*0-8172-3208-7*) Raintree Steck-V.
Murray, Peter. Frogs. LC 92-32499. (gr. 2-6). 1993. 15.95 (*1-56766-010-X*) Childs World.
Oda, Hidetomo. The Tadpole. Pohl, Kathy, ed. LC 85-28202. (Illus.). 32p. (gr. 3-7). 1986. PLB 10.95 (*0-8172-2545-5*) Raintree Steck-V.
—The Tree Frog: Annual. annual Pohl, Kathy, ed. LC 85-28194. (Illus.). 32p. (gr. 3-7). 1986. PLB 10.95 (*0-8172-2546-3*) Raintree Steck-V.
Parker, Steve. Frogs & Toads. LC 93-38519. (Illus.). 60p. (gr. 3-6). 1994. 16.95 (*0-87156-466-1*) Sierra.
Petersen, Candyce A. Lucky Becomes a Frog. Stoffregen, Jill, illus. LC 92-6417. Date not set. 11.95 (*1-56065-096-6*) Capstone Pr.
Petty, Kate. Frogs & Toads. Baker, Alan, illus. 32p. (gr. k-3). 1990. pap. 3.95 (*0-531-15154-9*) Watts.
Pfeffer, Wendy. From Tadpole to Frog. Keller, Holly, illus. LC 93-3135. 32p. (ps-1). 1994. 15.00 (*0-06-023044-4*); PLB 14.89 (*0-06-023117-3*) HarpC Child Bks.
Riley, Helen. Frogs & Toads. LC 92-41476. 32p. (gr. 2-5). 1993. 14.95 (*1-56847-007-X*) Thomson Lrning.
Schultz, Ellen. I Can Read About Frogs & Toads. LC 78-73714. (Illus.). (gr. 2-5). 1979. pap. 2.50 (*0-89375-210-X*) Troll Assocs.
Selsam, Millicent E. & Hunt, Joyce. A First Look at Frogs, Toads & Salamanders. Spunger, Harriett, illus. 32p. (gr. 2-4). 1976. PLB 12.85 (*0-8027-6244-1*) Walker & Co.
Souza, D. M. Frogs, Frogs Everywhere. LC 94-6897. 1994. write for info. (*0-87614-825-9*) Carolrhoda Bks.
Stone, Lynn M. Toads. LC 93-15696. (gr. 4 up). 1993. write for info. (*0-86593-294-8*) Rourke Corp.
Taylor, Kim & Burton, Jane, photos by. See How They Grow: Frog. (Illus.). 24p. (gr. k-3). 1991. 6.95 (*0-525-67345-8*, Lodestar Bks) Dutton Child Bks.
White, William, Jr. All about the Frog. LC 91-40812. (Illus.). 72p. (gr. 7-12). 1992. 14.95 (*0-8069-8274-8*) Sterling.
Williams, John. The Life Cycle of a Frog. Caulkins, Janet, ed. LC 87-71472. (Illus.). 32p. (gr. k-6). 1988. PLB 11.90 (*0-531-18161-8*, Pub. by Bookwright Pr) Watts.

FROGS–FICTION

Aardema, Verna. The Vingananee & the Tree Toad. Weiss, Ellen, illus. (gr. 3-8). 1988. pap. 4.99 (*0-14-050890-2*, Puffin) Puffin Bks.
Adams, Pam. The Frog. 1985. 4.95 (*0-85953-259-3*) Childs Play.
—Froglet's Bathtime. (gr. 3 up). 1981. 9.95 (*0-85953-329-8*) Childs Play.
Alborough, Jez. Hide & Seek. LC 93-28542. (Illus.). 32p. (ps up). 1994. 5.99 (*1-56402-369-9*) Candlewick Pr.
Amir, Tami. The Brave Frog. Kriss, David, tr. from HEB. Elchanan, illus. 24p. (Orig.). (ps). 1992. pap. text ed. 3.00x (*1-56134-158-4*) Dushkin Pub.
Arnold, Tedd. Green Wilma. Arnold, Tedd, illus. LC 91-31501. 32p. (ps-3). 1993. 13.99 (*0-8037-1313-4*); PLB 13.89 (*0-8037-1314-2*) Dial Bks Young.
Bailey, Jill. Frogs in Three Dimensions. Bruandet, Jerome, illus. 12p. (ps). 1992. 16.00 (*0-670-84336-9*) Viking Child Bks.
Bancroft, Catherine & Gruenberg, Coale. That's Philomena. 1995. 15.00 (*0-02-708326-8*, Four Winds) Macmillan Child Grp.
Barkan, Joanne. Kermit's Mixed-up Message. Attinello, Lauren, illus. 32p. (Orig.). (gr. 1-4). 1987. pap. 2.75 (*0-590-44011-X*) Scholastic Inc.
Boericke, Arthur, et al. The Complete Adventures of Olga da Polga. Helweg, Hans, illus. LC 82-72753. 512p. (gr. 4-6). 1983. 16.95 (*0-440-00981-2*) Delacorte.
Brown, Marc T., illus. Can You Jump Like a Frog? 8p. (ps-k). 1989. 5.95 (*0-525-44463-7*, DCB) Dutton Child Bks.
Brown, Margaret W. Dream Book. (ps-3). 1991. pap. 4.99 (*0-440-40567-X*, YB) Dell.
Buller, Jon & Schade, Susan. Toad on the Road. Buller, Jon, illus. LC 91-4246. 32p. (Orig.). (ps-1). 1992. PLB 7.99 (*0-679-92689-5*); pap. 3.50 (*0-679-82689-0*) Random Bks Yng Read.
Burgess, Thornton W. The Adventures of Grandfather Frog. unabr. ed. Kliros, Thea, adapted by. Cady, Harrison, illus. LC 92-13146. 96p. 1992. pap. text ed. 1.00 (*0-486-27400-4*) Dover.
Carlson, Anna L. Toady Tales. 2nd. ed. LC 80-83018. 24p. (gr. k-4). 1983. pap. 1.95 (*0-939938-02-2*) Karwyn Ent.
Chalk, Gary. Mr. Frog Went A-Courting. (Illus.). 32p. (ps-3). 1994. 13.95 (*1-56458-622-7*) Dorling Kindersley.
Chenery, Janet. Toad Hunt. (ps-3). 1992. pap. 2.99 (*0-440-40561-0*) Dell.
Condit, A. Lloyd. Piffin. 1992. pap. 7.95 (*0-533-10143-3*) Vantage.
Conover, Chris. Froggie Went A-Courting. LC 86-45289. (Illus.). 32p. (ps up). 1986. 15.00 (*0-374-32466-2*) FS&G.
Costello, Gwen. Priscilla Tadpole. Kendzia, Mary C., ed. Read, Maryann, illus. 32p. (Orig.). 1992. pap. 4.95 (*0-89622-527-5*) Twenty-Third.
Coville, Bruce. Jennifer Murdley's Toad. Lippincott, Gary A., illus. 1992. 16.95 (*0-15-200745-8*, HB Juv Bks) HarBrace.
—Jennifer Murdley's Toad. MacDonald, Pat, ed. Lippincott, Gary A., illus. 176p. 1993. pap. 3.50 (*0-671-79401-9*, Minstrel Bks) PB.
Coxe, Molly. Maxie & Mirabel. LC 92-26528. (Illus.). 64p. (gr. k-3). 1994. 14.00 (*0-06-022868-7*); PLB 13.89 (*0-06-022869-5*) HarpC Child Bks.
Crowe, Robert. Tyler Toad & the Thunder. Chorao, Kay, illus. (ps-3). pap. 4.99 (*0-14-054791-6*, Puff Unicorn) Puffin Bks.
Dauer, Rosamond. Bullfrog & Gertrude Go Camping. 64p. (gr. k-6). 1988. pap. 2.95 (*0-440-40074-0*) Dell.
—Bullfrog Grows Up. (gr. k-6). 1988. pap. 2.95 (*0-440-40007-4*) Dell.
DeCremer, Shirley. Freddie the Frog. Overton, Amy, illus. LC 92-33094. 16p. Date not set. 14.95 (*0-935343-03-2*) Peartree.
DeLuca, June M. The Lily Pad Four & Friends. Faycheux, Wallace P., Jr., illus. 32p. (gr. k-2). 1992. pap. 2.95 (*0-8198-4431-4*) St Paul Bks.
Elliott, Donald. Frogs & Ballet. Arrowood, Clinton, illus. LC 78-19566. (gr. 1 up). 1979. (Pub. by Gambit); pap. 8.95 (*0-87645-119-9*) Harvard Common Pr.
Emery, C. F. Horny. Le Blanc, L., illus. LC 68-17304. 48p. (gr. 2 up). 1967. PLB 9.26 (*0-87783-017-7*) Oddo.
Erickson, Gina C. & Foster, Kelli C. Frog Knows Best. Gifford-Russell, Kerri, illus. 24p. (ps-2). 1992. pap. 3.50 (*0-8120-4855-5*) Barron.
Erickson, Russell E. A Toad for Tuesday. Di Fiori, Lawrence, photos by. LC 92-24595. (Illus.). 64p. (gr. 3 up). 1993. pap. 3.95 (*0-688-12276-0*, Pub. by Beech Tree Bks) Morrow.
—Warton & the Contest. Di Fiori, Lawrence, illus. LC 86-102. 96p. (ps-4). 1986. PLB 11.88 (*0-688-05819-1*) Lothrop.
Faulkner, Keith. Boastful Bullfrog. Lambert, Jonathan, illus. 22p. (gr. 1-3). 1991. 5.95 (*0-681-41051-5*) Longmeadow Pr.
Fox, Naomi. The Frog Prince. Fox, Neal, illus. 24p. (ps-1). 1992. Incl. cassette. pap. 9.95 (*1-882179-11-0*) Confetti Ent.
Freddy Frog. (Illus.). (ps). 1.79 (*0-517-46417-9*) Random Hse Value.
Freemont, Eleanor. Muppet Babies: Baby Kermit Is Afraid of the Dark. (ps-3). 1994. pap. 1.95 (*0-307-11618-2*, Golden Pr) Western Pub.
Gage, Wilson. Mike's Toads. Rounds, Glen, illus. LC 88-34907. 96p. (gr. 3 up). 1990. 12.95 (*0-688-08834-1*) Greenwillow.
—Mike's Toads. Rounds, Glen, illus. LC 88-34907. 96p. (gr. 3 up). 1991. pap. 3.95 (*0-688-10977-2*, Pub. by Beech Tree Bks) Morrow.
Garcia, Joseph G. Jump for the Apple! The Story of Lily Pond, a Soccer-Playing Frog with Long, Long Legs. Day, Rhonda, ed. Garcia, Joseph G., illus. 28p. (gr. 4up). 1983. pap. 5.95 (*0-9612350-0-4*) Goal Ent.
Gikow, Louise. I Am Kermit. (ps). 1993. 4.95 (*0-307-12170-4*, Golden Pr) Western Pub.
Gilbert, Jane. Grouchy Old Fuddley. 1991. 6.95 (*0-533-09110-1*) Vantage.
Gilmore. If Only Toad Could Fly. 1993. pap. 11.95 (*1-85756-029-9*, Pub. by Janus Pub UK) Intl Spec Bk.
Gregorich, Barbara. Jog, Frog, Jog. Hoffman, Joan, ed. Schneider, Rex, illus. 16p. (Orig.). (gr. k-2). 1984. pap. 2.25 (*0-88743-006-6*, 06006) Sch Zone Pub Co.
—Jog, Frog, Jog. Hoffman, Joan, ed. (Illus.). 32p. (gr. k-2). 1992. pap. 3.95 (*0-88743-404-5*, 06056) Sch Zone Pub Co.
Gretz, Susanna. Frog in the Middle. Gretz, Susanna, illus. LC 90-3842. 32p. (ps-1). 1991. RSBE 12.95 (*0-02-737471-8*, Four Winds) Macmillan Child Grp.
Greydanus, Rose. Federiquito el Sapo. Garcia, Tom, illus. (SPA.). 32p. (gr. k-2). 1981. PLB 7.89 (*0-89375-549-4*); pap. 1.95 (*0-685-04947-7*) Troll Assocs.
Griffith, Helen V. Emily & the Enchanted Frog. Lamb, Susan C., illus. LC 88-16511. 32p. (gr. 1 up). 1989. 12.95 (*0-688-08483-4*); PLB 12.88 (*0-688-08484-2*) Greenwillow.
Grimm, Jacob & Grimm, Wilhelm K. The Frog Prince & The Pear Tree. (Illus.). 48p. (gr. 1-4). 1985. 5.95 (*0-88110-251-2*) EDC.
Gwynne, Fred. Pondlarker. LC 90-9524. (Illus.). 40p. (gr. k-4). 1992. pap. 13.95 jacketed (*0-671-70846-5*, S&S BFYR); pap. 4.95 (*0-671-77818-8*, S&S BFYR) S&S Trade.
Henney, Carolee W. Calbert & His Adventures. Macneil, Melanie F., illus. LC 90-83140. 104p. (Orig.). (gr. 2-5). 1990. collector's first ed., numbered, signed by author, with dust jacket, sim. gold imprint title-author on spine 24.95 (*0-9626580-1-4*); pap. 9.95 (*0-9626580-0-6*) Aton Pr.
Horn, Karla. Frankie Frog. 1994. 7.95 (*0-533-10670-2*) Vantage.
Hunt, Joni P. A Chorus of Frogs. Leon, Vicki, ed. (Illus.). 40p. (Orig.). (gr. 5 up). 1992. pap. 7.95 (*0-918303-29-X*) Blake Pub.
Johnson, Annabel. I Am Leaper. 112p. 1992. pap. 2.75 (*0-590-43399-7*, Apple Paperbacks) Scholastic Inc.
Jordan, Tanis. Journey of the Red-Eyed Tree Frog. Jordan, Martin, illus. LC 91-29526. 40p. (ps-3). 1992. 16.00 (*0-671-76903-0*, Green Tiger) S&S Trade.

Joyce, William. Bently & Egg. Joyce, William, illus. LC 91-55499. 32p. (ps-3). 1992. 15.00 (*0-06-020385-4*); PLB 14.89 (*0-06-020386-2*) HarpC Child Bks.

Kasza, Keiko. Grandpa Toad's Last Secret. LC 93-44376. 1995. 14.95 (*0-399-22610-9*, Putnam) Putnam Pub Group.

Kellogg, Steven. The Mysterious Tadpole. Kellogg, Steven, illus. LC 77-71517. 32p. (ps-3). 1979. pap. 4.95 (*0-8037-6244-5*) Dial Bks Young.

Kepes, Juliet. Frogs Merry. Kepes, Juliet, illus. (ps-2). 1963. lib. bdg. 6.99 (*0-394-91176-8*) Pantheon.

Kherdian, David. Toad & the Green Princess. Hogrogian, Nonny, illus. LC 92-39314. 1994. 15.95 (*0-399-22539-0*, Philomel Bks) Putnam Pub Group.

Kilborne, Sarah S. Peach & Blue. Fancher, Lou & Johnson, Steve, illus. LC 93-26562. 40p. (ps-2). 1994. 15.00 (*0-679-83929-1*); PLB 15.99 (*0-679-93929-6*) Knopf Bks Yng Read.

Korman, Justine H. The Monster in Room 202. Chesworth, Michael D., illus. LC 93-2215. 32p. (gr. 2-4). 1993. pap. text ed. 9.59 (*0-8167-3182-9*); pap. 2.95 (*0-8167-3183-7*) Troll Assocs.

Krauss, Robert. Mert the Blurt. Aruego, Jose & Dewey, Ariane, illus. LC 80-14508. (ps). 1998. pap. 10.95 jacketed (*0-671-66537-5*, S&S BFYR); (S&S BFYR) S&S Trade.

Kuhn, Dwight R., photos by. Hungry Little Frog. Hirschi, Ron, text by. (Illus.). 32p. (ps-2). 1992. 9.95 (*0-525-65109-8*, Cobblehill Bks) Dutton Child Bks.

Kulling, Monica. Waiting for Amos. Lowe, Vicky, illus. LC 92-19550. 32p. (ps-2). 1993. SBE 13.95 (*0-02-751245-2*, Bradbury Pr) Macmillan Child Grp.

Lane, Margaret. The Frog. Corbett, Grahame, illus. 32p. (gr. k-4). 1994. pap. 4.99 (*0-14-050340-4*, Puff Pied Piper) Puffin Bks.

Langstaff, John & Rojankovsky, Feodor. Frog Went A-Courtin' Rojankovsky, Feodor, illus. LC 55-5237. 32p. (ps-3). 1972. pap. 4.95 (*0-15-633900-5*, Voyager Bks) HarBrace.

Larke, Joe. The Bullfrog & the Grasshopper & Other "Tails" Larke, Karol, illus. 72p. (gr. k-6). 1987. 10.00 (*0-9620112-0-7*) Grin A Bit.

Le Blanc, L. Little Frog Learns to Sing. Le Blanc, L., illus. LC 68-16394. 32p. (ps-2). 1967. PLB 9.95 (*0-87783-022-3*) cassette 7.94x (*0-87783-191-2*) Oddo.

Lee, Jeanne M., retold by. & illus. Toad Is the Uncle of Heaven. LC 85-5639. 32p. (ps-2). 1985. 13.95 (*0-8050-1146-3*, Bks Young Read) H Holt & Co.

Liebler, John. Frog Counts to Ten. LC 93-40116. (Illus.). 32p. (gr. k-3). 1994. 13.90 (*1-56294-436-3*) Millbrook Pr.

Lionni, Leo. An Extraordinary Egg. LC 93-28565. (Illus.). 40p. (ps-2). 1994. 15.00 (*0-679-85840-7*); PLB 15.99 (*0-679-95840-1*) Knopf Bks Yng Read.

Lobel, Arnold. Days with Frog & Toad. LC 78-21786. (Illus.). 64p. (gr. k-3). 1979. 14.00i (*0-06-023963-8*); PLB 13.89 (*0-06-023964-6*) HarpC Child Bks.

—Days with Frog & Toad. unabr. ed. (Illus.). (ps-3). 1990. pap. 6.95 incl. cassette (*1-55994-227-4*, Caedmon) HarperAudio.

—Frog & Toad All Year. LC 76-2343. (Illus.). 64p. (gr. k-3). 1976. 14.00 (*0-06-023950-6*); PLB 13.89 (*0-06-023951-4*) HarpC Child Bks.

—Frog & Toad All Year. unabr. ed. (Illus.). (ps-3). 1990. pap. 6.95 incl. cassette (*1-55994-228-2*, Caedmon) HarperAudio.

—Frog & Toad Are Friends. Lobel, Arnold, illus. LC 73-105492. 64p. (gr. k-3). 1970. 14.00 (*0-06-023957-3*); PLB 13.89 (*0-06-023958-1*) HarpC Child Bks.

—Frog & Toad are Friends. unabr. ed. (Illus.). (ps-3). 1990. pap. 6.95 incl. cassette (*1-55994-229-0*, Caedmon) HarperAudio.

—Frog & Toad Boxed Set, 4 bks. Lobel, Arnold, illus. 64p. (gr. k-3). Date not set. pap. 14.00 (*0-06-444167-9*, Trophy) HarpC Child Bks.

—The Frog & Toad Pop-Up Book. Lobel, Arnold, illus. LC 85-45373. 12p. (ps-3). 1986. 9.95i (*0-06-023986-7*) HarpC Child Bks.

—Frog & Toad Together. Lobel, Arnold, illus. LC 73-183163. 64p. (gr. k-3). 1972. 14.00 (*0-06-023959-X*); PLB 13.89 (*0-06-023960-3*) HarpC Child Bks.

—Frog & Toad Together. unabr. ed. (Illus.). (ps-3). 1990. pap. 6.95 incl. cassette (*1-55994-230-4*, Caedmon) HarperAudio.

—Frog & Toad Together: (Sapo y Sepo Inseparables) (SPA.). 8.95 (*84-204-3047-1*) Santillana.

London, Jonathan. Froggy Gets Dressed. Remkiewicz, Frank, illus. 32p. (ps-1). 1992. 13.00 (*0-670-84249-4*) Viking Child Bks.

—Let's Go, Froggy! Remkiewicz, Frank, illus. LC 93-24059. 32p. (ps-3). 1994. PLB 12.99 (*0-670-85055-1*) Viking Child Bks.

McCue, Lisa, illus. Froggie's Treasure. (ps-2). 1983. 2.95 (*0-671-45488-9*, Little Simon) S&S Trade.

McDonnell, Christine. Toad Food & Measle Soup. De Groat, Diane, illus. 112p. 1984. pap. 3.99 (*0-14-031724-4*, Puffin) Puffin Bks.

McOmber, Rachel B., ed. McOmber Phonics Storybooks: Boe E. Toad. rev. ed. (Illus.). write for info. (*0-944991-54-8*) Swift Lrn Res.

Maness, Malia. The Toad That Taught Flying. Hall, Patt, illus. LC 93-86144. 32p. (ps-3). 1993. 9.95 (*0-9633493-1-7*) Pacific Greetings.

Manushkin, Fran. Peeping & Sleeping. Plecas, Jennifer, illus. LC 93-26297. (ps-3). 1994. 14.95 (*0-395-64339-2*, Clarion Bks) HM.

Mayer, Mercer. A Boy, a Dog & a Frog. LC 67-22254. (Illus.). (ps-3). 1985. 9.95 (*0-8037-0763-0*); PLB 9.89 (*0-8037-0767-3*) Dial Bks Young.

—Boy, a Dog, & a Frog. (ps-3). 1992. pap. 3.50 (*0-14-054611-1*) Viking Child Bks.

—Frog Goes to Dinner. Mayer, Mercer, illus. LC 74-2881. 32p. (ps-2). 1974. 8.95 (*0-8037-3386-0*); PLB 8.89 (*0-8037-3381-X*) Dial Bks Young.

—Frog Goes to Dinner. Mayer, Mercer, illus. (gr. k-2). 1977. pap. 2.95 (*0-8037-2733-X*) Dial Bks Young.

—Frog on His Own. Mayer, Mercer, illus. LC 73-6018. 32p. (ps-2). 1973. 8.95 (*0-8037-2701-1*); PLB 8.89 (*0-8037-2695-3*) Dial Bks Young.

—Frog on His Own. Mayer, Mercer, illus. LC 73-6018. 32p. (ps-2). 1980. pap. 2.95 (*0-8037-2716-X*) Dial Bks Young.

—Frog, Where Are You? Mayer, Mercer, illus. LC 72-85544. (ps-3). 1969. 9.95 (*0-8037-2737-2*); PLB 9.89 (*0-8037-2732-1*) Dial Bks Young.

—Frog, Where Are You? Mayer, Mercer, illus. LC 72-85544. 32p. (ps-2). 1980. pap. 2.95 (*0-8037-2729-1*) Dial Bks Young.

Mayer, Mercer & Mayer, Marianna. One Frog Too Many. Mayer, Mercer, illus. LC 75-6325. 32p. (ps-2). 1985. 9.95 (*0-8037-4838-8*); PLB 9.89 (*0-8037-4858-2*) Dial Bks Young.

—One Frog Too Many. LC 75-6325. (Illus.). (ps-2). 1977. pap. 3.50 (*0-8037-6734-X*) Dial Bks Young.

Meisburger, W. F. History of Papa Frog. LC 93-74950. (Illus.). 24p. (ps-3). 1994. pap. 4.95x (*0-943864-72-0*) Davenport.

Mire, Betty. T-Pierre Frog & T-Felix Frog Go to School. Mire, Betty, illus. LC 93-74275. 32p. (Orig.). (gr. 1-3). 1994. PLB 6.95 (*0-9639378-0-4*) Cajun Bay Pr.

T-PIERRE FROG & T-FELIX FROG GO TO SCHOOL focuses on the importance of education & reading. This unique book is incorporated with the CAJUN FRENCH language (approximately one CAJUN FRENCH sentence on every page of text). And for every CAJUN FRENCH sentence there is a cute cartoon picture associated with it. It's a book that parents will enjoy reading to their children. The story begins with the first day of school on the Louisiana bayous. T-PIERRE FROG likes going to school & he loves to read. He tells his friend T-FELIX FROG that he wants to learn all he can, because he wants to one day become an astronaut. But T-FELIX FROG doesn't like school. And he tells T-PIERRE that he doesn't have to learn, because his only wish is to become a lazy hobo taking it easy in the shade. Sometimes wishes come true. T-FELIX finds that out, but not without woes. Although T-FELIX FROG is soon enlightened on the importance of an education through a dream or rather a nightmare. T-PIERRE FROG & T-FELIX FROG GO TO SCHOOL is simultaneously entertaining & educational. The book is complete with pronunciation guide. *Publisher Provided Annotation.*

Newman, Al. Fibber E. Frog. Doody, Jim, illus. LC 93-77685. 32p. (ps-3). 1993. text ed. 13.95 (*0-89334-213-0*); pap. 4.95 (*0-89334-217-3*) Humanics Ltd.

Nichols, Freeda B. Little Bug Eyes: The Little Frog Who Did. 2nd ed. LC 89-91965. (Illus.). 24p. (Orig.). (gr. k-6). 1991. pap. 4.95 (*0-9623980-0-4*) Baker Seaforth.

Owen, Annie. Wake up Frog! Owen, Annie, illus. LC 93-79578. 14p. (ps). 1994. bds. 4.95 (*1-85697-948-2*, Kingfisher LKC) LKC.

Parker, Nancy W. Working Frog. LC 90-24173. 40p. (gr. k up). 1992. 14.00 (*0-688-09918-1*); PLB 13.93 (*0-688-09919-X*) Greenwillow.

Paulsen, Gary. The Voyage of the Frog. 1990. pap. 3.99 (*0-440-40364-2*, Pub. by Yearling Classics) Dell.

—The Voyage of the Frog. large type ed. LC 93-30238. (gr. 9-12). 1993. 15.95 (*0-7862-0060-X*) Thorndike Pr.

Pavelko, Virginia & Scott, L. B. Five Little Speckled Frogs Big Book. Nichols, Barry, illus. (ps-2). 1988. pap. text ed. 14.00 (*0-922053-05-7*) N Edge Res.

Peabody, Paul. Blackberry Hollow. Peabody, Paul, illus. LC 92-8968. 160p. (gr. 3-7). 1993. 15.95 (*0-399-22500-5*, Philomel Bks) Putnam Pub Group.

Petty, Kate. Mr. Toad to the Rescue. Baker, Alan, illus. 24p. (ps-2). 1992. 8.95 (*0-8120-6273-6*) Barron.

—Mr. Toad's Narrow Escape. (ps-3). 1992. pap. 4.95 (*0-8120-1475-8*) Barron.

—Mr. Toad's Narrow Escapes. (ps-3). 1992. 8.95 (*0-8120-6289-2*) Barron.

—Stop, Look & Listen, Mr. Toad. Baker, Alan, illus. 24p. (ps-2). 1991. 8.95 (*0-8120-6230-2*) Barron.

Portlock, Rob. My Dad Ran over a Frog. Portlock, Rob, illus. LC 92-11584. 32p. (Orig.). (ps-1). 1992. pap. 4.99 (*0-8308-1901-0*, 1901) InterVarsity.

Potter, Beatrix. Jeremy Fisher. Twinn, Colin, illus. 10p. (ps-5). 1992. 5.99 (*0-7232-3999-1*) Warne.

—Meet Jeremy Fisher. (Illus.). 12p. (ps). 1987. bds. 2.95 (*0-7232-3453-1*) Warne.

—The Tale of Mr. Jeremy Fisher. Atkinson, Allen, illus. 1983. pap. 2.25 (*0-553-15221-1*) Bantam.

—The Tale of Mr. Jeremy Fisher. 1992. 3.99 (*0-517-07238-6*) Random Hse Value.

Priceman, Marjorie. Friend or Frog. Priceman, Marjorie, illus. (ps-3). 1989. 13.45 (*0-395-44523-X*) HM.

Rondon, Javier. The Absent-Minded Toad. Corbett, Kathryn, tr. from SPA. Cabrera, Marcela, illus. LC 94-14407. 32p. (ps-1). 1994. 9.95 (*0-916291-53-7*) Kane-Miller Bk.

Sadler, Marilyn. Alistair Underwater. 1990. pap. 13.95 jacketed (*0-671-69406-5*, S&S BFYR) S&S Trade.

Saunders, Susan. Kate the Winner! 128p. (gr. 3-7). 1991. pap. 2.75 (*0-590-43925-1*, Apple Paperbacks) Scholastic Inc.

Schertle, Alice. Little Frog's Song. Fisher, Leonard E., illus. LC 91-10405. 32p. (ps-2). 1992. 15.00 (*0-06-020059-6*); PLB 14.89 (*0-06-020060-X*) HarpC Child Bks.

Schindel, John. I'll Meet You Halfway. Watts, James, illus. LC 91-44019. 32p. (ps-2). 1993. SBE 14.95 (*0-689-50564-7*, M K McElderry) Macmillan Child Grp.

Schneider, Rex. The Wide-Mouthed Frog. LC 80-13449. (Illus.). 32p. (gr. k up). 1980. 13.95 (*0-916144-58-5*) Stemmer Hse.

Shannon, George. April Showers. Aruego, Jose & Dewey, Ariane, illus. LC 94-6266. 24p. 1995. write for info. (*0-688-13121-2*); PLB write for info. (*0-688-13122-0*) Greenwillow.

Show-&-Tell Frog. 1992. pap. 9.99 (*0-553-08134-9*) Bantam.

Show-&-Tell Frog. 1992. pap. 3.99 (*0-553-35147-8*) Bantam.

Snape, Juliet & Snape, Charles. Frog Friends. (Illus.). 32p. (ps-1). 1994. 17.95 (*1-85681-082-8*, Pub. by J MacRae UK) Trafalgar.

—Frog Odyssey. LC 91-4201. (Illus.). 32p. (ps-2). 1992. pap. 14.00 (*0-671-74741-X*, S&S BFYR) S&S Trade.

Solotareff, Gregoire. The Ogre & the Frog King. LC 87-8531. (FRE., Illus.). 32p. (ps-1). 1988. 11.95 (*0-688-07078-7*); lib. bdg. 11.88 (*0-688-07079-5*) Greenwillow.

Steig, William. Gorky Rises. (Illus.). 32p. (ps up). 1986. pap. 4.95 (*0-374-42784-4*) FS&G.

Stevenson, James. The Pattaconk Brook. LC 92-29404. 32p. (ps up). 1993. 14.00 (*0-688-11954-9*); lib. bdg. 13. 93 (*0-688-11955-7*) Greenwillow.

Teague, Mark. Frog Medicine. 1991. 13.95 (*0-590-44177-9*, Scholastic Hardcover) Scholastic Inc.

Temko, Florence. Paper Pandas & Jumping Frogs. Jackson, Paul, illus. Petersen, Richard, et al, photos by. LC 86-70960. (Illus.). 135p. (gr. 3-6). 1986. pap. 11.95 (*0-8351-1770-7*) China Bks.

Thompson, Richard. Frog's Riddle: And Other Draw-&-Tell Stories. Thompson, Richard, illus. 96p. 1990. 19. 95 (*1-55037-138-X*, Pub. by Annick CN) Firefly Bks Ltd.

Thomson, Pat. Thank You for the Tadpole. (gr. k-6). 1988. pap. 2.50 (*0-440-40027-9*, YB) Dell.

Twain, Mark. The Jumping Frog. (Illus.). 78p. (gr. 7 up). 1986. 25.00 (*0-932458-31-9*); pap. 6.95 (*0-932458-30-0*) Star Rover.

Velthuijs, Max. Frog & the Birdsong. (ps-3). 1991. bds. 13.95 jacketed (*0-374-32467-0*) FS&G.

—Frog & the Stranger. Velthuijs, Max, illus. LC 93-26401. 32p. 1994. 14.00 (*0-688-13267-7*, Tambourine Bks); PLB 13.93 (*0-688-13268-5*, Tambourine Bks) Morrow.

—Frog in Love. Bell, Anthea, tr. (ps up). 1991. pap. 4.95 (*0-374-42470-5*) FS&G.

—Frog in Winter. Velthuijs, Max, illus. LC 92-20545. 32p. (ps up). 1993. 14.00 (*0-688-12306-6*, Tambourine Bks); PLB 13.93 (*0-688-12307-4*, Tambourine Bks) Morrow.

Walsh, Ellen S. Hop Jump. LC 92-21037. 1993. 13.95 (*0-15-292871-5*) HarBrace.

Wang, Mary L. El Principe Rana (The Frog Prince) Connelly, Gwen, illus. LC 86-11796. (SPA.). 32p. (ps-2). 1989. pap. 3.95 (*0-516-53983-3*) Childrens.

Waricha, Jean. The Terror Toad. 64p. (gr. 1-6). 1994. pap. 3.95 (*0-448-40831-7*, G&D) Putnam Pub Group.

Warmsley, C. R. The Tale of Fleddy the Flog. (Illus.). 64p. 1995. pap. write for info. (*0-8059-3581-9*) Dorrance.

Weiss, Monica. The Biggest Pest, Comparisons. Berlin, Rosemary, illus. LC 91-16059. 24p. (gr. k-2). 1992. PLB 10.59 (*0-8167-2488-1*); pap. text ed. 2.95 (*0-8167-2489-X*) Troll Assocs.

—Birthday Cake Candles, Counting. Berlin, Rosemary, illus. LC 91-16033. 24p. (gr. k-2). 1992. PLB 10.59 (*0-8167-2496-2*); pap. text ed. 2.95 (*0-8167-2497-0*) Troll Assocs.

—Guess What! Drawing Conclusions. Berlin, Rosemary, illus. LC 91-17170. 24p. (gr. k-2). 1992. PLB 10.59 (*0-8167-2498-9*); pap. text ed. 2.95 (*0-8167-2499-7*) Troll Assocs.

—How Many? How Much? Measuring. Berlin, Rosemary, illus. LC 91-3992. 24p. (gr. k-2). 1992. PLB 10.59 (*0-8167-2500-4*); pap. text ed. 2.95 (*0-8167-2501-2*) Troll Assocs.

—Mmmm---Cookies! Simple Subtraction. Berlin, Rosemary, illus. LC 91-18648. 24p. (gr. k-2). 1992. PLB 10.59 (*0-8167-2486-5*); pap. text ed. 2.95 (*0-8167-2487-3*) Troll Assocs.

—Pop! ABC Letter & Sounds: Learning the Alphabet. Berlin, Rosemary, illus. LC 91-18704. 24p. (gr. k-2). 1992. PLB 10.59 (*0-8167-2492-X*); pap. text ed. 2.95 (*0-8167-2493-8*) Troll Assocs.

—Scoop! Fishbowl Fun, Simple Addition. Berlin, Rosemary, illus. LC 91-18657. 24p. (gr. k-2). 1992. PLB 10.59 (*0-8167-2484-9*); pap. text ed. 2.95 (*0-8167-2485-7*) Troll Assocs.

—Shopping Spree: Identifying Shapes. Berlin, Rosemary, illus. LC 91-3986. 24p. (gr. k-2). 1992. PLB 10.59 (*0-8167-2490-3*); pap. text ed. 2.95 (*0-8167-2491-1*) Troll Assocs.

—Snap! Charlie Gets the Whole Picture: Getting the Main Idea. Berlin, Rosemary, illus. LC 91-16499. (gr. k-2). 1992. PLB 10.59 (*0-8167-2494-6*); pap. 2.95 (*0-8167-2495-4*) Troll Assocs.

Whitten, Wendy & McCullough, Herb. Someday...Someday, Bk. 1. Swerda, Mike, illus. 42p. (ps up). 1994. Incl. audio cass. 29.95 (*1-886184-00-3*) Ion Imagination.
Ion Imagination (tm) Entertainment, Inc. presents the first in a series of adventures with Flumpa (tm), a tree frog who introduces the children to the wonder of adventure as he meets new friends along the way. SOMEDAY... SOMEDAY has a twenty-one minute audiocassette incorporated into the outer hardcover. This cassette features a Sing Along Side: original "story" songs, sung by Wendy Whitten & recorded at Jack's Tracks-Nashville, TN, with lyrics in the back of the collectable book, & Read Along Side: narration with sound effects, from a powerful storm to the calming sounds of twilight, & page turn signals. This 9 3/4" x 12 3/4" full-color, perfect bound book has foil & metallic inks. SOMEDAY...SOMEDAY, mixed media only, $29.95, ISBN 1-886184-00-3. Published by Ion Imagination (tm) Entertainment, Inc. To order: call 1-800-3-FLUMPA or write P.O. Box 210943, Nashville, TN 37221-0943. ***Publisher Provided Annotation.***

Wiesner, David. Tuesday. Briley, Dorothy, ed. Wiesner, David, illus. 32p. (gr. k up). 1991. 15.45 (*0-395-55113-7*, Clarion Bks) HM.

Williams, George J., III. Mark Twain: Jackass Hill & the Jumping Frog. Dalton, Bill, ed. (Illus.). 112p. (gr. 5 up). 1989. text ed. 14.95 (*0-935174-20-6*); pap. 6.95 (*0-935174-19-2*) Tree by River.

Wing, Natasha. Hippity Hop, Frog on Top. McGraw, DeLoss, illus. LC 93-11473. 1994. 15.00 (*0-671-87045-9*, S&S BFYR) S&S Trade.

Wood, Leslie. The Frog & the Fly. (Illus.). 16p. 1987. pap. 2.95 (*0-19-272154-2*) OUP.

Worth, Bonnie. If You Were Kermit. (ps-3). 1994. pap. 2.25 (*0-307-12814-8*, Golden Pr) Western Pub.

Yolen, Jane. Commander Toad & the Intergalactic Spy. Degen, Bruce, illus. 64p. (ps-4). 1986. (Coward); pap. 6.95 (*0-698-20623-1*, Coward) Putnam Pub Group.

—Commander Toad & the Planet of the Grapes. Degen, Bruce, illus. 64p. (gr. 1-4). 1982. (Coward); pap. 6.95 (*0-698-20540-5*) Putnam Pub Group.

—Commander Toad in Space. Degen, Bruce, illus. 64p. (gr. 3-5). 1980. (Coward); pap. 6.95 (*0-698-20522-7*) Putnam Pub Group.

Zakutinsky, Ruth. King David & the Frog. Kellman, A., ed. Backman, Aidel, illus. 32p. (gr. k-5). 1986. text ed. 9.95x (*0-911643-05-2*); pap. 5.95x (*0-911643-07-9*) Aura Bklyn.

FROGS–POETRY

Tryon, Leslie. One Gaping Wide-Mouthed Hopping Frog. Tryon, Leslie, illus. LC 92-11368. 32p. (ps-1). 1993. SBE 14.95 (*0-689-31785-9*, Atheneum Child Bk) Macmillan Child Grp.

FRONTIER AND PIONEER LIFE

see also Cowboys; Indians of North America–Captivities; Overland Journeys to the Pacific; Ranch Life

Anderson, Joan. Christmas on the Prairie. Ancona, George, illus. LC 85-4095. 48p. (gr. 2-6). 1985. 14.95 (*0-89919-307-2*, Clarion Bks) HM.

—Spanish Pioneers of the Southwest. Ancona, George, photos by. LC 88-16121. (Illus.). 64p. (gr. 3-6). 1989. 14.95 (*0-525-67264-8*, Lodestar Bks) Dutton Child Bks.

Anderson, Joan W. Pioneer Children of Appalachia. (gr. 4-7). 1990. pap. 5.70 (*0-395-54792-X*, Clarion Bks) HM.

Anderson, William & Kelly, Leslie A. Little House Country: A Photo Guide to the Homesites of Laura Ingalls Wilder. (Illus.). 48p. 1989. 9.95 (*0-9610088-8-1*) Anderson MI.

Bragg, Bea. The Very First Thanksgiving: Pioneers on the Rio Grande. LC 89-15562. (Illus.). 64p. (Orig.). (gr. 3-5). 1989. pap. 7.95 (*0-943173-22-1*) Harbinger AZ.

Chambers, Catherine E. Frontier Dream: Life on the Great Plains. Smolinski, Dick, illus. LC 83-18282. 32p. (gr. 5-9). 1984. PLB 11.59 (*0-8167-0039-7*); pap. text ed. 2.95 (*0-8167-0040-0*) Troll Assocs.

Cooper, James Fenimore. The Leatherstocking Saga. (gr. 5-6). 42.95 (*0-8488-0059-1*, Pub. by Amereon Hse) Amereon Ltd.

Fradin, Dennis. Pioneers. LC 84-9418. (Illus.). 48p. (gr. k-4). 1984. PLB 12.85 (*0-516-01927-9*) Childrens.

Gintzler, A. S. Rough & Ready Homesteaders. 48p. (gr. 4-7). 1994. text ed. 12.95 (*1-56261-154-2*) John Muir.

Gorsline, Marie & Gorsline, Douglas. The Pioneers. reissued ed. Gorsline, Marie & Gorsline, Douglas, illus. LC 78-54960. 32p. (gr. k-4). 1982. pap. 2.25 (*0-394-83905-6*) Random Bks Yng Read.

Gunby, Lise. Early Farm Life. (Illus.). 80p. (gr. 3-4). 1983. 15.95 (*0-86505-027-9*); pap. 7.95 (*0-86505-026-0*) Crabtree Pub Co.

Gurasich, Marj. Letters to Oma, a Young German Girl's Account of Her First Year in Texas, 1847. Whitehead, Barbara, illus. LC 88-38747. 162p. (gr. 4-8). 1989. pap. 9.95 (*0-87565-037-6*) Tex Christian.

Hamilton, Dorothy. Daniel Forbes: A Pioneer Boy. King, Barbara L., illus. (Orig.). (ps-4). 1980. pap. 3.95 (*0-686-32860-4*) Barnwood Pr.

Kalman, Bobbie. Early Artisans. (Illus.). 64p. (gr. 4-5). 1983. 15.95 (*0-86505-023-6*); pap. 7.95 (*0-86505-022-8*) Crabtree Pub Co.

—Early Christmas. (Illus.). 64p. (gr. 4-5). 1981. 15.95 (*0-86505-001-5*); pap. 7.95 (*0-86505-003-1*) Crabtree Pub Co.

—Early City Life. (Illus.). 64p. (gr. 4-5). 1983. 15.95 (*0-86505-029-5*); pap. 7.95 (*0-86505-028-7*) Crabtree Pub Co.

—The Early Family Home. (Illus.). 64p. (gr. 4-5). 1982. 15.95 (*0-86505-017-1*); pap. 7.95 (*0-86505-016-3*) Crabtree Pub Co.

—Early Pleasures & Pastimes. (Illus.). 96p. (gr. 4-5). 1983. 15.95 (*0-86505-025-2*); pap. 8.95 (*0-86505-024-4*) Crabtree Pub Co.

—Early Settler Children. (Illus.). 64p. (gr. 4-5). 1982. 15.95 (*0-86505-019-8*); pap. 7.95 (*0-86505-018-X*) Crabtree Pub Co.

—Early Settler Storybook. (Illus.). 64p. (gr. 4-5). 1982. 15.95 (*0-86505-021-X*); pap. 7.95 (*0-86505-020-1*) Crabtree Pub Co.

—Early Stores & Markets. (Illus.). 64p. (gr. 4-5). 1981. 15.95 (*0-86505-002-3*); pap. 7.95 (*0-86505-004-X*) Crabtree Pub Co.

—Early Travel. (Illus.). 64p. (gr. 4-5). 1981. 15.95 (*0-86505-007-4*); pap. 7.95 (*0-86505-008-2*) Crabtree Pub Co.

—Early Village Life. (Illus.). 64p. (gr. 4-5). 1981. 15.95 (*0-86505-009-0*); pap. 7.95 (*0-86505-010-4*) Crabtree Pub Co.

—Food for the Settler. (Illus.). 96p. (gr. 4-5). 1982. 15.95 (*0-86505-013-9*); pap. 8.95 (*0-86505-012-0*) Crabtree Pub Co.

—Settler Sayings. (Illus.). 32p. (Orig.). (gr. k-9). 1994. PLB 15.95 (*0-86505-498-3*); pap. 7.95 (*0-86505-518-1*) Crabtree Pub Co.

—Visiting a Village. (Illus.). 32p. (gr. 3-4). 1990. PLB 15.95 (*0-86505-487-8*); pap. 7.95 (*0-86505-507-6*) Crabtree Pub Co.

Kalman, Bobbie & Everts, Tammy. A Child's Day. (Illus.). 32p. (Orig.). (gr. k-9). 1994. PLB 15.95 (*0-86505-494-0*); pap. 7.95 (*0-86505-514-9*) Crabtree Pub Co.

—Customs & Traditions. LC 93-39882. (Illus.). 32p. (Orig.). (gr. k-9). 1994. PLB 15.95 (*0-86505-495-9*); pap. 7.95 (*0-86505-515-7*) Crabtree Pub Co.

Knight, Theodore. A Pioneer Woman. LC 94-741. 1994. write for info. (*1-55916-038-1*) Rourke Bk Co.

Lindbergh, Reeve. Johnny Appleseed. Jakoben, Kathy, illus. (ps-4). 1990. 15.95 (*0-316-52618-5*, Joy St Bks) Little.

Lindsley, Margaret. Andrew Henry: Mine & Mountain Major. (Illus.). 370p. 1990. 19.95 (*0-936204-79-6*); pap. 15.95 (*0-936204-78-8*) Jelm Mtn.

Mayers, Florence C. ABC: The Wild West Buffalo Bill Historical Center, Cody, Wyoming. LC 90-440. (Illus.). 32p. 1990. 12.95 (*0-8109-1903-6*) Abrams.

Miller, Robert H. The Story of "Stagecoach" Mary Fields. Hanna, Cheryl, illus. LC 93-46286. 1994. write for info. (*0-382-24394-3*) Silver.

Naden, C. J. I Can Read About Pioneers. LC 78-65835. (Illus.). (gr. 3-6). 1979. pap. 2.50 (*0-89375-214-2*) Troll Assocs.

Parish, Peggy. Let's Be Early Settlers with Daniel Boone. LC 67-14068. (Illus.). 96p. (gr. 3-5). 1967. PLB 14.89 (*0-06-024648-0*) HarpC Child Bks.

Perl, Lila. Hunter's Stew & Hangtown Fry. Cuffari, Richard, illus. LC 77-5366. 176p. (gr. 6 up). 1979. 13.95 (*0-395-28922-X*, Clarion Bks) HM.

Pioneers in Change, 15 bks. in 11 vols. (Illus.). (gr. 5-9). 1992. Set, 144p. ea. PLB 153.30 (*0-382-09930-3*); Set. pap. 76.45 (*0-382-24161-4*) Silver Burdett Pr.

Sabin, Francene. Pioneers. Frenck, Hal, illus. LC 84-2580. 32p. (gr. 3-6). 1985. PLB 9.49 (*0-8167-0120-2*); pap. text ed. 2.95 (*0-8167-0121-0*) Troll Assocs.

Smith, Carter, ed. Daily Life: A Sourcebook on Colonial America. LC 91-13941. (Illus.). 96p. (gr. 5-8). 1991. PLB 18.90 (*1-56294-038-4*); pap. 5.95 (*1-878841-68-8*) Millbrook Pr.

—Explorers & Settlers: A Sourcebook on Colonial America. (Illus.). 96p. (gr. 5-8). 1991. PLB 18.90 (*1-56294-035-X*); pap. 5.95 (*1-878841-64-5*) Millbrook Pr.

Stein, R. Conrad. The Oregon Trail. LC 93-36994. (Illus.). 32p. (gr. 3-6). 1994. PLB 12.30 (*0-516-06674-9*) Childrens.

Stenson, Elizabeth. Early Settler Activity Guide. (Illus.). 128p. (gr. 4-5). 1983. pap. 15.95 (*0-86505-036-8*) Crabtree Pub Co.

Stewart, Gail. Frontiersmen. (Illus.). 32p. (gr. 3-8). 1990. PLB 18.00 (*0-86625-406-4*); 13.50s.p. (*0-685-34709-5*) Rourke Corp.

—Lumberman. (Illus.). 32p. (gr. 3-8). 1990. lib. bdg. 18.00 (*0-86625-407-2*); 13.50s.p. (*0-685-58649-9*) Rourke Corp.

—Rivermen. (Illus.). 32p. (gr. 3-8). 1990. PLB 18.00 (*0-86625-409-9*); 13.50 (*0-685-58652-9*) Rourke Corp.

—Scouts. (Illus.). 32p. (gr. 3-8). 1990. PLB 18.00 (*0-86625-404-8*); 13.50 (*0-685-58651-0*) Rourke Corp.

—Trappers & Traders. (Illus.). 32p. (gr. 3-8). 1990. PLB 18.00 (*0-86625-401-3*); PLB 13.50s.p. (*0-685-58655-3*) Rourke Corp.

Tunis, Edwin. Frontier Living. Tunis, Edwin, illus. LC 75-29639. 168p. (gr. 7 up). 1976. 26.00 (*0-690-01064-8*, Crowell Jr Bks) HarpC Child Bks.

Vickery, Eugene L. Frontier Adventures: Stories in Verse of Young People in Kentucky & the South West. Vickery, Millie M., ed. Tolpo, Lily, illus. 40p. (Orig.). (gr. 1-8). 1987. pap. 4.95 perfect bdg. (*0-937775-06-1*) Stonehaven Pubs.

Wright, Courtni C. Wagon Train: A Black Family's Westward Journey in 1865. Griffith, Gershom, illus. LC 94-18975. Date not set. write for info. (*0-8234-1152-4*) Holiday.

FRONTIER AND PIONEER LIFE–ALASKA

DeGraf, Anna. Pioneering on the Yukon, 1892-1917. Brown, Roger S., ed. LC 92-14808. (Illus.). ix, 128p. 1992. lib. bdg. 19.50 (*0-208-02362-3*, Pub. by Archon Bks) Shoe String.

Miller, Luree & Miller, Scott. Alaska: Pioneer Stories of a Twentieth-Century Frontier. LC 91-10744. (Illus.). 144p. (gr. 6 up). 1991. 14.95 (*0-525-65050-4*, Cobblehill Bks) Dutton Child Bks.

FRONTIER AND PIONEER LIFE–BIOGRAPHY

Anderson, William. Laura Ingalls Wilder: A Biography. LC 91-33805. (Illus.). 240p. (gr. 3-7). 1992. 16.00 (*0-06-020113-4*); PLB 15.89 (*0-06-020114-2*) HarpC Child Bks.

Artman, John. Pioneers. Hyndman, Kathryn, illus. 64p. (gr. 4 up). 1987. pap. 8.95 (*0-86653-401-6*, GA 1027) Good Apple.

Clark, Thomas D. Simon Kenton, Kentucky Scout. 2nd ed. Hay, Melba P., intro. by. Shenton, Edward, illus. 256p. (gr. 6-12). 17.95 (*0-945084-38-2*); pap. 8.95 (*0-945084-39-0*) J Stuart Found.

Cooper, Ann K. Gallery of Pioneers. 68p. (gr. 9-12). 1986. pap. text ed. write for info. (*0-910463-05-0*) Edit Heliodor.

Crawford, Ann F. Jane Long - Frontier Woman. Baxter, Rosario, illus. 64p. (gr. 4-7). 1990. lib. bdg. 12.95 (*0-87443-090-9*) Benson.

—Lizzie - Queen of the Cattle Trails. Fain, Cheryl G., illus. 64p. (gr. 4-7). 1990. lib. bdg. 12.95 (*0-87443-091-7*) Benson.

Greene, Carol. John Chapman: The Man Who Was Johnny Appleseed. LC 91-12649. (Illus.). 48p. (gr. k-3). 1991. PLB 12.85 (*0-516-04223-8*); pap. 4.95 (*0-516-44223-6*) Childrens.

Hargrove, Jim. Daniel Boone: Pioneer Trailblazer. LC 85-13309. (Illus.). 124p. (gr. 5-7). 1985. PLB 14.40 (*0-516-03215-1*) Childrens.

Laura Ingalls Wilder. (gr. 2-6). 1988. pap. 3.99 (*0-14-032074-1*, Puffin) Puffin Bks.

Lindsley, Margaret. Andrew Henry: Mine & Mountain Major. (Illus.). 370p. 1990. 19.95 (*0-936204-79-6*); pap. 15.95 (*0-936204-78-8*) Jelm Mtn.

O'Rear, Sybil J. Charles Goodnight: Pioneer Cowman. LC 89-48652. (Illus.). 69p. (gr. 5-8). 1990. 10.95 (*0-89015-741-3*) Sunbelt Media.

Rowland, Mary C. & Loomis, F. A. As Long As Life: The Memoirs of a Frontier Woman Doctor, Mary Canaga Rowland, 1873-1966. LC 94-66409. (Illus.). 192p. (Orig.). (gr. 7 up). 1994. pap. 11.95 (*0-9641357-0-1*) Storm Peak.

Truman, Timothy. Wilderness: The True Story of Simon Girty. 1992. pap. 19.95 (*1-56060-167-1*) Eclipse Bks.

Whiteley, Opal. Only Opal: The Diary of a Young Girl. Boulton, Jane, adapted by. Cooney, Barbara, illus. 32p. (ps). 1994. 14.95 (*0-399-21990-0*, Philomel) Putnam Pub Group.

Zadra, Dan. Frontiersmen in America: Jim Bridgers. (gr. 2-4). 1988. 14.95 (*0-88682-179-7*) Creative Ed.

FRONTIER AND PIONEER LIFE–CALIFORNIA

Collins, William & Levene, Bruce. Black Bart: The True Story of California's Most Famous Stagecoach Robber. LC 91-67893. (Illus.). 224p. (Orig.). (gr. 4-7). 1992. pap. 15.95 (*0-933391-10-2*) Pac Transcript.

Rawls, Jim. Dame Shirley & the Gold Rush. Holder, John, illus. LC 92-18083. (gr. 2-5). 1992. PLB 19.97 (*0-8114-7222-1*) Raintree Steck-V.

FRONTIER AND PIONEER LIFE–FICTION

Ackerman, Karen. Araminta's Paint Box. Lewin, Betsy, illus. LC 88-35033. 32p. (gr. 1-3). 1990. pap. 13.95 SBE (*0-689-31462-0*, Atheneum Child Bk) Macmillan Child Grp.

Alter, Judith M. Luke & the Van Zandt County War. Conoly, Walli, illus. LC 84-101. 132p. (gr. 4 up). 1984. 10.95 (*0-912646-88-8*) Tex Christian.

Altsheler, Joseph A. Kentucky Frontiersmen: The Adventures of Henry Ware, Hunter & Border Fighter. rev. ed. Kenton, Nathaniel, ed. Doney, Todd, illus. LC 88-50581. 256p. (gr. 5-10). 1988. 16.95 (*0-929146-01-8*) Voyageur Pub.

—Riflemen of the Ohio. 1991. 13.95 (*0-929146-05-0*) Voyageur Pub.

Antle, Nancy. Beautiful Land: A Story of the Oklahoma Land Rush. Gampert, John, illus. 64p. (gr. 2-6). 1994. 12.99 (*0-670-85304-6*) Viking Child Bks.

Bagdon, Paul. Scrapper John: Valley of the Spotted Horse. (gr. 4-7). 1992. pap. 3.50 (*0-380-76416-4*, Camelot) Avon.

Baltazzi, Evan S. Dog Gone West: A Western for Dog Lovers. Kyziridis, Gregory, illus. 115p. (Orig.). (gr. 7 up). 1994. pap. 3.95 (*0-918948-05-3*) Evanel. DOG GONE WEST is a western for dog lovers, young & old. It is the story of a farmer & his family migrating from Pennsylvania to California in the middle of the last century, narrated by their dog Buck. The trip, with its few good times & many tribulations, follows a true itinerary, each part of which is seen through the eyes of the dog, who has some unusual comments about his masters, their fellow travellers, the Indians & even the landscapes the wagon train is going through. DOG GONE WEST is overflowing with the love of Buck for his masters & their love for him. He shares with the readers his feelings of puzzlement, wonder & affection as he saves more than once the lives of members of his "family." "'How about it?' Montana took Ann by the hand. That was it! I jumped from behind the bush growling & showing my teeth. My sudden appearance, size & fierce expression took them by surprise & gave Matt a chance to grab his rifle. Pointing it at them, he ordered: 'Better leave! Now!' Figuring the odds, they apologized sheepishly that they meant no harm & left."

Publisher Provided Annotation.

Bly, Stephen. Coyote True. LC 92-8224. 128p. 1992. pap. 4.99 (*0-89107-680-8*) Crossway Bks.

—The Dog Who Would Not Smile. 128p. (gr. 4-7). 1992. pap. 4.99 (*0-89107-656-5*) Crossway Bks.

—You Can Always Trust a Spotted Horse. LC 92-46667. 128p. (Orig.). (gr. 4-7). 1993. pap. 4.99 (*0-89107-716-2*) Crossway Bks.

Brink, Carol R. Caddie Woodlawn. Hyman, Trina S., illus. LC 73-588. 288p. (gr. 4-6). 1973. SBE 15.95 (*0-02-713670-1*, Macmillan Child Bk) Macmillan Child Grp.

—Caddie Woodlawn. 1970. pap. 3.95 (*0-02-041880-9*, Collier Young Ad) Macmillan Child Grp.

Brown, Irene B. Skitterbrain. Milam, Larry, illus. LC 78-18349. 128p. (gr. 4 up). 1992. pap. 6.95 (*0-936085-21-5*) Blue Heron OR.

Byars, Betsy C. The Golly Sisters Go West. Truesdell, Sue, illus. LC 84-48474. 64p. (gr. k-3). 1986. PLB 13.89 (*0-06-020884-8*) HarpC Child Bks.

—The Golly Sisters Ride Again. Truesdell, Sue, illus. & photos by LC 92-23394. 64p. (gr. k-3). 1994. 14.00 (*0-06-021563-1*); PLB 13.89 (*0-06-021564-X*) HarpC Child Bks.

—Hooray for the Golly Sisters! Truesdell, Sue, illus. LC 89-48147. 64p. (gr. k-3). 1990. 14.00 (*0-06-020898-8*); PLB 13.89 (*0-06-020899-6*) HarpC Child Bks.

—Trouble River. Negri, Rocco, illus. (gr. 3-7). 1969. pap. 13.95 (*0-670-73257-5*) Viking Child Bks.

—Trouble River. Negri, Rocco, illus. 160p. (gr. 3-7). 1989. pap. 3.99 (*0-14-034243-5*, Puffin) Puffin Bks.

Calvert, Patricia. Bigger. LC 93-14415. 144p. (gr. 4-6). 1994. SBE 14.95 (*0-684-19685-9*, Scribners Young Read) Macmillan Child Grp.

Canfield, Dorothy. The Bent Twig. 334p. 1981. Repr. PLB 17.95x (*0-89966-343-5*) Buccaneer Bks.

Chambers, Catherine E. California Gold Rush: Search for Treasure. Eitzen, Allan, illus. LC 83-18280. 32p. (gr. 5-9). 1984. PLB 11.59 (*0-8167-0051-6*); pap. text ed. 2.95 (*0-8167-0052-4*) Troll Assocs.

—Daniel Boone & the Wilderness Road. Guzzi, George, illus. LC 83-18291. 32p. (gr. 5-9). 1984. PLB 11.59 (*0-8167-0037-0*); pap. text ed. 2.95 (*0-8167-0038-9*) Troll Assocs.

—Flatboats on the Ohio: Westward Bound. Lawn, John, illus. LC 83-18278. 32p. (gr. 5-9). 1984. PLB 11.59 (*0-8167-0049-4*); pap. text ed. 2.95 (*0-8167-0050-8*) Troll Assocs.

—Frontier Farmer: Kansas Adventures. Epstein, Len, illus. LC 83-18279. 32p. (gr. 5-9). 1984. PLB 11.59 (*0-8167-0053-2*); pap. text ed. 2.95 (*0-8167-0054-0*) Troll Assocs.

—Frontier Village: A Town Is Born. Smolinski, Dick, illus. LC 83-18271. 32p. (gr. 5-9). 1984. PLB 11.59 (*0-8167-0045-1*); pap. text ed. 2.95 (*0-8167-0046-X*) Troll Assocs.

—Indiana Days: Life in a Frontier Town. Lawn, John, illus. LC 83-18283. 32p. (gr. 5-9). 1984. PLB 11.59 (*0-8167-0055-9*); pap. text ed. 2.95 (*0-8167-0056-7*) Troll Assocs.

—Log Cabin Home: Pioneers in the Wilderness. Eitzen, Allan, illus. LC 83-18277. 32p. (gr. 5-9). 1984. PLB 11.59 (*0-8167-0041-9*); pap. text ed. 2.95 (*0-8167-0042-7*) Troll Assocs.

—Texas Roundup: Life on the Range. Lawn, John, illus. LC 83-18281. 32p. (gr. 5-9). 1984. PLB 11.59 (*0-8167-0047-8*); pap. text ed. 2.95 (*0-8167-0048-6*) Troll Assocs.

—Wagons West: Off to Oregon. Smolinski, Dick, illus. LC 83-18276. 32p. (gr. 5-9). 1984. PLB 11.59 (*0-8167-0043-5*); pap. text ed. 2.95 (*0-8167-0044-3*) Troll Assocs.

Coerr, Eleanor. The Josefina Story Quilt. Degen, Bruce, illus. LC 85-45260. 64p. (gr. k-3). 1989. pap. 3.50 (*0-06-444129-6*, Trophy) HarpC Child Bks.

Cooper, James Fenimore. The Deerslayer. 528p. (gr. 9-12). 1991. pap. 3.50 (*0-553-21085-8*, Bantam Classics) Bantam.

—The Deerslayer: or The First War-Path. Wyeth, N. C., illus. LC 90-34326. 480p. 1990. (Scribners Young Read); SBE 24.95 (*0-684-19224-1*, Scribner) Macmillan Child Grp.

—Pathfinder. (gr. 6 up). 1964. pap. 2.95 (*0-8049-0035-3*, CL-35) Airmont.

—Pioneers. (gr. 8 up). 1964. pap. 1.95 (*0-8049-0049-3*, CL-49) Airmont.

—Prairie. (gr. 8 up). 1964. pap. 1.95 (*0-8049-0041-8*, CL-41) Airmont.

Dalgliesh, Alice. The Courage of Sarah Noble. Weisgard, Leonard, illus. LC 54-5922. 64p. (gr. 1-5). 1987. Repr. of 1954 ed. SBE 13.95 (*0-684-18830-9*, Scribners Young Read) Macmillan Child Grp.

—The Courage of Sarah Noble. 2nd ed. Weisgard, Leonard, illus. LC 91-15531. 64p. (gr. 1-5). 1991. pap. 4.95 (*0-689-71540-4*, Aladdin) Macmillan Child Grp.

Donahue, Marilyn C. The Valley in Between. (gr. 5 up). 1987. 14.95 (*0-8027-6731-1*); PLB 15.85 (*0-8027-6733-8*) Walker & Co.

Fleischman, Paul. The Borning Room. LC 91-4432. 80p. (gr. 6 up). 1991. 14.00 (*0-06-023762-7*); PLB 13.89 (*0-06-023785-6*) HarpC Child Bks.

Fontes, Ron & Korman, Justine. Calamity Jane at Fort Sanders. LC 92-52976. (Illus.). 80p. (gr. 1-4). 1992. PLB 12.89 (*1-56282-265-9*); pap. 3.50 (*1-56282-264-0*) Disney Pr.

—Davy Crockett & the Highwaymen. LC 92-52975. (Illus.). 80p. (gr. 1-4). 1992. PLB 12.89 (*1-56282-261-6*); pap. 3.50 (*1-56282-260-8*) Disney Pr.

Forbes, Esther. Johnny Tremain. 1987. pap. 4.50 (*0-440-44250-8*) Dell.

Fritz, Jean. The Cabin Faced West. Rojankovsky, Feodor, illus. (gr. 4-7). 1958. 13.95 (*0-698-20016-0*, Coward) Putnam Pub Group.

—The Cabin Faced West. Rojanovsky, Feodor, illus. (gr. 1-7). 1987. pap. 3.99 (*0-14-032256-6*, Puffin) Puffin Bks.

Gerrard, Roy. Rosie & the Rustlers. 32p. (ps up). 1991. pap. 4.95 (*0-374-46339-5*) FS&G.

Gipson, Fred. Old Yeller. 192p. 1992. Repr. PLB 15.95x (*0-89966-906-9*) Buccaneer Bks.

Glass, Andrew. Folks Call Me Appleseed John. LC 93-41046. 1995. write for info. (*0-385-32045-0*) Doubleday.

Gregory, Kristiana. Jimmy Spoon & the Pony Express. LC 93-47420. (gr. 4-7). 1994. 13.95 (*0-590-46577-5*) Scholastic Inc.

Grossman, Bill. Cowboy Ed. Wint, Florence, illus. LC 92-23393. 32p. (ps-2). 1993. 15.00 (*0-06-021570-4*); PLB 14.89 (*0-06-021571-2*) HarpC Child Bks.

Harrison, Nick. While Yet We Live. 224p. 1991. pap. 6.95 (*0-940652-08-0*) Sunrise Bks.

Harvey, Amanda. The Iron Needle. LC 93-32679. (Illus.). 1994. 15.00 (*0-688-13192-1*) Lothrop.

Howard, Ellen. The Chickenhouse House. LC 90-38007. (Illus.). 64p. (gr. 2-5). 1991. SBE 12.95 (*0-689-31695-X*, Atheneum Child Bk) Macmillan Child Grp.

Hunt, Irene. Trail of Apple Blossoms. Partridge, Sherri, illus. LC 92-46739. 64p. (gr. 4-6). 1993. PLB 12.95 (*0-382-24359-5*); 10.95 (*0-382-24368-4*) Silver Burdett Pr.

Hurmence, Belinda. Dixie in the Big Pasture. LC 93-9983. (gr. 4 up). 1994. write for info. (*0-395-52002-9*, Clarion) HM.

Ingoglia, Gina. Johnny Appleseed & the Planting of the West. LC 92-52978. (Illus.). 80p. (gr. 1-4). 1992. PLB 12.89 (*1-56282-259-4*); pap. 3.50 (*1-56282-258-6*) Disney Pr.

—Sacajawea & the Journey to the Pacific. LC 92-52977. (Illus.). 80p. (gr. 1-4). 1992. PLB 12.89 (*1-56282-263-2*); pap. 3.50 (*1-56282-262-4*) Disney Pr.

Irwin, Hadley. Jim-Dandy. LC 93-22611. 144p. (gr. 5-9). 1994. SBE 14.95 (*0-689-50594-9*, M K McElderry) Macmillan Child Grp.

Isaacs, Anne. Swamp Angel. Zelinsky, Paul O., illus. LC 93-43956. 40p. (ps-4). 1994. 14.99 (*0-525-45271-0*) Dutton Child Bks.

Karr, Kathleen. Oh, Those Harper Girls! 176p. (gr. 7 up). 1992. 16.00 (*0-374-35609-2*) FS&G.

Kerr, Rita. The Ghost of Panna Maria. Eakin, Ed, ed. Kerr, Rita, illus. 96p. (gr. 2-4). 1990. 10.95 (*0-89015-791-X*); pap. 3.95 (*0-89015-803-7*) Sunbelt Media.

—Texas Marvel. Roberts, Melissa, ed. 120p. (gr. 4-7). 1987. 10.95 (*0-89015-597-6*, Pub. by Panda Bks) Sunbelt Media.

Kingsley, Charles. Westward Ho! reissue ed. Wyeth, N. C., illus. LC 20-18930. 432p. (gr. 7 up). 1992. (Scribners Young Read); SBE 26.95 (*0-684-19444-9*, Scribners Young Read) Macmillan Child Grp.

Kinsey-Warnock, Natalie. Wilderness Cat. Graham, Mark, illus. LC 90-24250. 32p. (ps-3). 1992. 14.00 (*0-525-65068-7*, Cobblehill Bks) Dutton Child Bks.

Koller, Jackie F. The Primrose Way. 1992. write for info. (*0-15-256745-3*, Gulliver Bks) HarBrace.

Krensky, Stephen. The Iron Dragon Never Sleeps. Fulweiler, Frank, illus. LC 93-31167. 1994. 13.95 (*0-385-31171-0*) Delacorte.

Kudlinski, Kathleen V. Facing West: A Story of the Oregon Trail. Watling, James, illus. LC 93-41349. 64p. (gr. 2-6). 1994. 12.99 (*0-670-85451-4*) Viking Child Bks.

Larson, Dorothy W. Bright Shadows. Larson, Dorothy W., illus. LC 92-81679. 96p. (gr. 4-6). 1992. 14.95 (*0-9621779-0-3*) Sandstone Pub.

Lasky, Kathryn. The Bone Wars. 384p. (gr. 5-9). 1989. pap. 5.99 (*0-14-034168-4*, Puffin) Puffin Bks.

Laurgaard, Rachel K. Patty Reed's Doll: The Story of the Donner Party. Michaels, Elizabeth, illus. 144p. (gr. 3-6). 1989. pap. 7.95 (*0-9617357-2-4*) Tomato Enter.

Lawlor, Laurie. Addie Across the Prairie. MacDonald, Patricia, ed. Owens, Gail, illus. 128p. 1991. pap. 3.50 (*0-671-70147-9*, Minstrel Bks) PB.

—George on His Own. Tucker, Kathleen, ed. Gowing, Toby, illus. 144p. (gr. 3-7). 1993. 11.95g (*0-8075-2823-4*) A Whitman.

Levine, Ellen. If You Traveled West in a Covered Wagon. Freem, Elroy, illus. 80p. (gr. 3-5). 1992. pap. 4.95 (*0-590-45158-8*) Scholastic Inc.

Lightfoot, D. J. Trail Fever: The Life of a Texas Cowboy. Bobbish, John, illus. LC 92-5458. 1992. 11.00 (*0-688-11537-3*) Lothrop.

Liles, Maurine W. Rebecca of Blossom Prairie: Grandmother of a Vice President. Roberts, M., ed. (Illus.). 112p. 1990. 10.95 (*0-89015-754-5*) Sunbelt Media.

Little House Diary. 1986. pap. 4.95 (*0-440-82026-X*) Dell.

Luttrell, Wanda. Home on Stoney Creek. LC 93-47084. (gr. 4 up). 1994. write for info. (*0-7814-0901-2*) Chariot Family.

MacBride, Roger L. Little House on Rocky Ridge. Gilleece, David, illus. LC 92-39132. 368p. (gr. 3-7). 1993. 14.95 (*0-06-020842-2*); PLB 14.89 (*0-06-020843-0*) HarpC Child Bks.

—Little House on Rocky Ridge. Gilleece, David, illus. LC 92-39132. 368p. (gr. 3-7). 1993. pap. 3.95 (*0-06-440478-1*, Trophy) HarpC Child Bks.

McClung, Robert M. Hugh Glass: Mountain Man. LC 92-43790. 176p. (gr. 7 up). 1993. pap. 3.95 (*0-688-04595-2*, Pub. by Beech Tree Bks) Morrow.

Meyer, Carolyn. Where the Broken Heart Still Beats. LC 92-257. (gr. 4-7). 1992. write for info. (*0-15-200639-7*) HarBrace.

Moore, Robin. Maggie among the Seneca. rev. ed. LC 89-77110. 112p. (gr. 4-7). 1990. (Lipp Jr Bks); PLB 13.89 (*0-397-32456-1*, Lipp Jr Bks) HarpC Child Bks.

Morris, Neil. Home on the Prairie. LC 89-987. (Illus.). 32p. (gr. 4-8). 1989. PLB 9.95 (*1-85435-165-6*) Marshall Cavendish.

—On the Trapping Trail. LC 89-989. (Illus.). 32p. (gr. 3-8). 1989. PLB 9.95 (*1-85435-164-8*) Marshall Cavendish.

—Wagon Wheels Roll West. LC 89-988. (Illus.). 32p. (gr. 3-8). 1989. PLB 9.95 (*1-85435-167-2*) Marshall Cavendish.

Morrow, Honore. On to Oregon. Shenton, Edward, illus. LC 90-19554. 240p. (gr. 5 up). 1991. pap. 4.95 (*0-688-10494-0*, Pub. by Beech Tree Bks) Morrow.

Murrow, Liza K. West Against the Wind. LC 87-45337. 240p. (gr. 7 up). 1987. 15.95 (*0-8234-0668-7*) Holiday.

Nielsen, Shelly. More Victoria. LC 86-2280. 130p. (gr. 3-7). 1986. pap. 4.99 (*0-89191-453-6*, Chariot Bks) Chariot Family.

Nixon, Joan L. That's the Spirit, Claude. Pearson, Tracey C., illus. 32p. (ps-3). 1992. 13.00 (*0-670-83434-3*) Viking Child Bks.
Nolan, Cecile A. Journey West, on the Oregon Trail. (gr. 5 up). 1993. 16.95 (*0-9633168-2-6*) Rain Dance Pub.
O'Dell, Scott. Carlota. O'Dell, Scott, illus. LC 77-9468. 176p. (gr. 5-9). 1977. 13.45 (*0-395-25487-6*) HM.
Oke, Janette. A Bride for Donnigan. 224p. (Orig.). 1993. pap. 7.99 (*1-55661-327-X*) Bethany Hse.
—A Bride for Donnigan. large type ed. 224p. (Orig.). 1993. pap. 9.99 (*1-55661-328-8*) Bethany Hse.
—They Called Her Mrs. Doc. 224p. 1992. pap. 7.99 (*1-55661-246-X*) Bethany Hse.
—They Called Her Mrs. Doc. large type ed. 224p. 1992. pap. 9.99 (*1-55661-247-8*) Bethany Hse.
Pamplin, Laurel J. Masquerade on the Western Trail. Roberts, M., ed. (Illus.). 112p. (gr. 4-8). 1991. 9.95 (*0-89015-755-3*) Sunbelt Media.
Paulsen, Gary. Mr. Tucket. LC 93-31180. 1994. 14.95 (*0-385-31169-9*) Delacorte.
Penson, Mary. You're an Orphan, Mollie Brown: A Novel. Shaw, Charles, illus. LC 92-23407. 122p. (gr. 5-8). 1993. pap. 9.95 (*0-87565-111-9*) Tex Christian.
Pepper Bird Staff. Wild Frontier: Adventures of Jean Baptiste Du Sable. Rose, Ann C., illus. 48p. (Orig.). (gr. 4-7). 1993. pap. 4.95 (*1-56817-003-3*) Pepper Bird.
Phillips, Michael & Pella, Judith. Journals of Corrie Belle Hollister. (Orig., Set incls. My Father's World, Daughter of Grace, On the Trail of the Truth, A Place in the Sun & Sea to Shining Sea). 1992. Giftset. pap. 44.99 (*1-55661-766-6*) Bethany Hse.
Reuther, Ruth E. Meet at the Falls: The Story of the Pioneers. McCall, Jody, ed. (Illus.). 1989. pap. text ed. write for info. (*0-9622632-1-4*) Wee-Chee-Taw.
Rinaldi, Ann. A Stitch in Time. 304p. (gr. 7 up). 1994. 13.95 (*0-590-46055-2*, Scholastic Hardcover) Scholastic Inc.
—A Stitch in Time. LC 93-8964. 1994. 13.95 (*0-590-46056-0*) Scholastic Inc.
Sanders, Scott R. The Floating House. Cogancherry, Helen, illus. LC 94-15277. 1995. 15.00 (*0-02-778137-2*, BRadbury Pr) Macmillan Child Grp.
—Here Comes the Mystery Man. Cogancherry, Helen, illus. LC 92-24572. 32p. (gr. k-5). 1993. RSBE 15.95 (*0-02-778145-3*, Bradbury Pr) Macmillan Child Grp.
—Warm As Wool. LC 91-34987. (Illus.). 32p. (gr. k-5). 1992. RSBE 14.95 (*0-02-778139-9*, Bradbury Pr) Macmillan Child Grp.
Sauerwein, Leigh. The Way Home. LC 93-10097. 1993. 15.00 (*0-374-38247-6*) FS&G.
Schulte, Elaine L. Daniel Colton Kidnapped: Daniel Strikes a Bad Bargain - Now He Must Outsmart His Captors. (Illus.). 144p. (gr. 3-7). 1993. pap. 5.99 (*0-310-57261-4*, Pub. by Youth Spec) Zondervan.
Shay, Myrtle. Adventures of Ricky & Chub. Kennedy, Paul, illus. (gr. 4-8). PLB 7.19 (*0-685-02937-9*) Lantern.
Shefelman, Janice. A Paradise Called Texas. (Illus.). 128p. (gr. 4-7). 1983. 10.95 (*0-89015-409-0*, Pub. by Panda Bks); pap. 5.95 (*0-89015-506-2*) Sunbelt Media.
Speare, Elizabeth G. The Sign of the Beaver. 144p. (gr. 5-9). 1905. pap. 4.50 (*0-440-47900-2*, YB) Dell.
Stahl, Hilda. Kayla O'Brian & the Runaway Orphans. 128p. (gr. 4-7). 1991. pap. 4.95 (*0-89107-631-X*) Crossway Bks.
—Sadie Rose & the Champion Sharpshooter. 128p. (gr. 4-7). 1991. pap. 4.99 (*0-89107-630-1*) Crossway Bks.
—Sadie Rose & the Mad Fortune Hunters. LC 90-80619. 128p. (Orig.). (gr. 4-7). 1990. pap. 4.99 (*0-89107-578-X*) Crossway Bks.
—Sadie Rose & the Mysterious Stranger. 128p. (Orig.). (gr. 6-9). 1993. pap. 4.99 (*0-89107-747-2*) Crossway Bks.
Steele, William O. Buffalo Knife. 123p. (gr. 3-7). 1990. pap. 3.95 (*0-15-213212-0*, Odyssey) HarBrace.
—Flaming Arrows. 41p. (gr. 3-7). 1990. pap. 3.95 (*0-15-228427-3*, Odyssey) HarBrace.
Stewart, George R. The Pioneers Go West. LC 87-4568. 160p. (gr. 5-9). 1964. pap. 2.95 (*0-394-89180-5*, Random Juv) Random Bks Yng Read.
Stoutenburg, Adrien. American Tall Tales. Powers, Richard M., illus. (gr. 3-7). 1976. pap. 3.99 (*0-14-030928-4*, Puffin) Puffin Bks.
Tedrow, T. L. Days of Laura Ingalls Wilder, Vol. 2: Children of Promise. LC 92-1041. 1992. pap. 4.99 (*0-8407-3398-4*) Nelson.
—Days of Laura Ingalls Wilder, Vol. 3: Good Neighbors. 1992. pap. 4.99 (*0-8407-3399-2*) Nelson.
—Days of Laura Ingalls Wilder, Vol. 4: Home to the Prairie. 1992. pap. 4.99 (*0-8407-3401-8*) Nelson.
—Land of Promise. LC 92-28222. 1992. 4.99 (*0-8407-7735-3*) Nelson.
Turner, Ann. Dakota Dugout. Himler, Ronald, illus. 32p. (ps-3). 1989. pap. 3.95 (*0-689-71296-0*, Aladdin) Macmillan Child Grp.
Van Leeuwen, Jean. Going West. LC 90-20694. (Illus.). 48p. (ps-4). 1992. 15.00 (*0-8037-1027-5*); PLB 14.89 (*0-8037-1028-3*) Dial Bks Young.
Vogt, Esther L. A Race for Land. 112p. (Orig.). (gr. 4-7). 1992. pap. 4.95 (*0-8361-3575-X*) Herald Pr.
Waddell, Martin. Little Obie & the Kidnap. Lennox, Elsie, illus. LC 93-45959. 80p. (gr. 3-6). 1994. 14.95 (*1-56402-352-4*) Candlewick Pr.
Waters, Kate. Andrew McClure & the Headless Horseman: An Adventure in Prairietown, Indiana, 1836. LC 93-31876. (gr. 1-4). 1994. 14.95 (*0-590-45503-6*) Scholastic Inc.
Weidt, Maryann. Wild Bill Hickok. Casino, Steve, illus. LC 92-9732. 1992. 11.00 (*0-688-10089-9*) Lothrop.
Wells, Marian. Out of the Crucible. LC 88-21121. 256p. (Orig.). 1988. pap. 8.99 (*1-55661-037-8*) Bethany Hse.
Whelan, Gloria. Night of the Full Moon. Bowman, Leslie, illus. LC 93-6706. 64p. (gr. 2-4). 1993. 13.00 (*0-679-84464-3*); PLB 13.99 (*0-679-94464-8*) Knopf Bks Yng Read.
Wilder, Laura I. The Deer in the Wood. Graef, Renee, illus. LC 94-18684. 1995. 15.00 (*0-06-024881-5*, Festival); PLB 14.89 (*0-06-024882-3*) HarpC Child Bks.
—Going to Town. Graef, Renee, illus. LC 92-46722. (gr. k-3). Date not set. 15.00 (*0-06-023012-6*); PLB 14.89 (*0-06-023013-4*) HarpC Child Bks.
—The Little House on the Prairie. 250p. (gr. 4 up). 1991. Repr. lib. bdg. 19.95x (*0-89966-868-2*) Buccaneer Bks.
—On the Way Home. Lane, Rose W., ed. LC 62-17966. (Illus.). 112p. (gr. 7 up). 1962. 14.00 (*0-06-026489-6*); PLB 13.89 (*0-06-026490-X*) HarpC Child Bks.
—On the Way Home. Lane, Rose W., ed. LC 62-17966. (Illus.). 112p. (gr. 7 up). 1976. pap. 3.95 (*0-06-440080-8*, Trophy) HarpC Child Bks.
Wilder, Laura Ingalls. By the Shores of Silver Lake. rev. ed. Williams, Garth, illus. LC 52-7529. 304p. (gr. 3-7). 1961. 15.95 (*0-06-026416-0*); PLB 15.89 (*0-06-026417-9*) HarpC Child Bks.
—Dance at Grandpa's. Graef, Renee, illus. LC 93-24535. 40p. (ps-3). 1994. 12.00 (*0-06-023878-X*); PLB 11.89 (*0-06-023879-8*) HarpC Child Bks.
—Little House Books: Little House in the Big Woods; Little House on the Prairie; On the Banks of Plum Creek; By the Shores of Silver Lake; The Long Winter, 5 vols. Williams, Garth, illus. (gr. 3-7). 1993. pap. 19.75 Boxed Set (*0-06-440476-5*, Trophy) HarpC Child Bks.
—A Little House Christmas: Holiday Stories from the Little House Books. Williams, Garth, illus. LC 93-24537. 96p. (gr. 3-7). 1994. 18.95 (*0-06-024269-8*); PLB 18.89 (*0-06-024270-1*) HarpC Child Bks.
—Little House in the Big Woods. rev. ed. Williams, Garth, illus. LC 52-7525. 238p. (gr. 3-7). 1961. 15.95 (*0-06-026430-6*); PLB 15.89 (*0-06-026431-4*) HarpC Child Bks.
—Little House on the Prairie. rev. ed. Williams, Garth, illus. LC 52-7526. 336p. (gr. 3-7). 1961. 15.95 (*0-06-026445-4*); PLB 15.89 (*0-06-026446-2*) HarpC Child Bks.
—Little House on the Prairie. (gr. 4-6). 1975. pap. 5.00 (*0-06-080357-6*, P357, PL) HarpC.
—Little Town on the Prairie. rev. ed. Williams, Garth, illus. LC 52-7531. 308p. (gr. 3-7). 1961. 15.95 (*0-06-026450-0*); PLB 15.89 (*0-06-026451-9*) HarpC Child Bks.
—The Long Winter. rev. ed. Williams, Garth, illus. LC 52-7530. 334p. (gr. 3-7). 1961. 15.95 (*0-06-026460-8*); PLB 15.89 (*0-06-026461-6*) HarpC Child Bks.
—On the Banks of Plum Creek. rev. ed. Williams, Garth, illus. LC 52-7528. 340p. (gr. 3-7). 1961. 15.95 (*0-06-026470-5*); PLB 15.89 (*0-06-026471-3*) HarpC Child Bks.
—These Happy Golden Years. rev. ed. Williams, Garth, illus. LC 52-7532. 304p. (gr. 3-7). 1961. 15.95 (*0-06-026480-2*); PLB 15.89 (*0-06-026481-0*) HarpC Child Bks.
—Winter Days in the Big Woods. Graef, Renee, illus. LC 92-45883. 40p. (ps-3). 1994. 12.00 (*0-06-023014-2*); PLB 11.89 (*0-06-023022-3*) HarpC Child Bks.
Wilder, Laura Ingalls, adapted by. Christmas in the Big Woods. Graef, Renee, illus. LC 94-14478. 1995. 12.00 (*0-06-024752-5*, HarpT); PLB 11.89 (*0-06-024753-3*) HarpC Child Bks.
Williams, David. Grandma Essie's Covered Wagon. Sadowski, Wiktor, illus. 48p. (ps-3). 1993. 16.00 (*0-679-80253-3*); PLB 16.99 (*0-679-90253-8*) Knopf Bks Yng Read.
Wisler, G. Clifton. Jericho's Journey. LC 92-36701. 144p. (gr. 5-9). 1993. 13.99 (*0-525-67428-4*, Lodestar Bks) Dutton Child Bks.
Woodruff, Elvira. Dear Levi: Letters from the Overland Trail. Peck, Beth, illus. LC 93-5315. (gr. 3-7). 1994. 14.00 (*0-679-84641-7*); PLB 14.99 (*0-679-94641-1*) Knopf Bks Yng Read.
Wyman, Andrea. Red Sky at Morning. LC 91-55029. 240p. (gr. 3-7). 1991. 15.95 (*0-8234-0903-1*) Holiday.

FRONTIER AND PIONEER LIFE–SOUTHWEST

Heck, Bessie H. Danger on the Homestead. rev. ed. Anderson, Peggy P., illus. LC 93-71892. 160p. (gr. 3-6). 1993. Repr. of 1991 ed. 14.95 (*0-9637259-0-4*) Dinosaur Pr.
Hill, William E. & Hill, Jan C. Heading Southwest: Along the Santa Fe Trail. (Illus.). 32p. (Orig.). (gr. k-4). 1993. pap. 3.95 (*0-9636071-1-1*) HillHouse Pub.

FRONTIER AND PIONEER LIFE–THE WEST

Alter, Judith. Women of the Old West. LC 88-34549. (Illus.). 64p. (gr. 3-5). 1989. PLB 12.90 (*0-531-10756-6*) Watts.
Barker, Jane V. & Downing, Sybil. Martha Maxwell: Pioneer Naturalist. Jones, Ann, illus. 138p. 1982. pap. 6.95 (*1-878611-12-7*) Silver Rim Pr.
Bial, Raymond. Frontier Home. LC 92-36449. 40p. 1993. 15.95 (*0-395-64046-6*) HM.
Cox, Clinton. The Forgotten Heroes: The Story of the Buffalo Soldiers. LC 92-36622. 176p. 1993. 14.95 (*0-590-45121-9*) Scholastic Inc.
Cox, Mike. Texas Rangers. (Illus.). 144p. (gr. 6-9). 1992. 14.95 (*0-89015-818-5*) Sunbelt Media.
Davis, Nelle P. Stump Ranch Pioneer. Swetnam, Susan H., intro. by. LC 90-42417. 264p. (gr. 12). 1990. pap. 14.95 (*0-89301-141-X*) U of Idaho Pr.
Downing, Sybil & Barker, Jane V. Florence Sabin: Pioneer Scientist. Jones, Ann, illus. 100p. 1981. pap. 6.95 (*1-878611-11-9*) Silver Rim Pr.
Erickson, Paul. Daily Life in Covered Wagon. (gr. 4 up). 1994. write for info. (*0-89133-245-6*) Preservation Pr.
Fox, Mary V. The Story of Women Who Shaped the West. LC 90-21444. (Illus.). 32p. (gr. 3-6). 1991. PLB 12.85 (*0-516-04757-4*); pap. 3.95 (*0-516-44757-2*) Childrens.
Hill, William E. & Hill, Jan C. Heading West: An Activity Book for Children. Hill, William E. & Hill, Jan C., illus. 32p. (Orig.). (gr. k-4). 1992. pap. 3.95 (*0-9636071-0-3*) HillHouse Pub.
Jensen, Patricia A. Johnny Appleseed Goes a-Planting. Hogan, Patricia M., illus. LC 93-4811. 32p. (gr. k-2). 1993. PLB 11.59 (*0-8167-3159-4*); pap. text ed. 2.95 (*0-8167-3160-8*) Troll Assocs.
Kalman, Bobbie & Schimky, Dave. Fort Life. (Illus.). 32p. (Orig.). (gr. k-9). 1994. PLB 15.95 (*0-86505-496-7*); pap. 7.95 (*0-86505-516-5*) Crabtree Pub Co.
Landau, Elaine. Cowboys. LC 90-31025. (Illus.). 64p. (gr. 5-8). 1990. PLB 12.90 (*0-531-10866-X*) Watts.
Levinson, Nancy S. Snowshoe Thompson. Sandin, Joan, illus. LC 90-37401. 64p. (gr. k-3). 1992. 14.00 (*0-06-023801-1*); PLB 13.89 (*0-06-023802-X*) HarpC Child Bks.
Madsen, Susan A. I Walked to Zion: True Stories of Youth Who Walked the Mormon Trail. LC 94-404. (gr. 6-12). 1994. 12.95 (*0-87579-848-9*) Deseret Bk.
Matthews, L. Gunfighters. (Illus.). 32p. (gr. 3-8). 1989. PLB 18.00 (*0-86625-361-0*); 13.50s.p. (*0-685-58278-7*) Rourke Corp.
—Pioneers. (Illus.). 32p. (gr. 3-8). 1989. PLB 18.00 (*0-86625-362-9*); 13.50s.p. (*0-685-73975-9*) Rourke Corp.
Matthews, Leonard J. Pioneers & Trailblazers: Adventures of the Old West, 6 vols. 1990. 9.99 (*0-517-02537-X*) Random Hse Value.
Milligan, Bryce. The Lawmen: Stories of Men Who Tamed the West. Bill Smith Studio Staff, illus. 80p. (gr. 1-4). 1994. pap. 3.50 (*0-7868-4006-4*); PLB 12.89 (*0-7868-5005-1*) Disney Pr.
Petra Press Staff. A Multicultural Portrait of the Move West. LC 93-10317. 1993. 18.95 (*1-85435-658-5*) Marshall Cavendish.
Rice, James. Cowboy Rodeo. Rice, James, illus. LC 91-34924. 32p. 1992. 14.95 (*0-88289-903-1*) Pelican.
Rounds, Glen. The Prairie Schooners. (Illus.). 96p. (gr. 5 up). 1994. Repr. of 1968 ed. 15.95 (*0-8234-1086-2*) Holiday.
—The Prairie Schooners. Rounds, Glen, illus. (gr. 5 up). 1994. pap. 6.95 (*0-8234-1087-0*) Holiday.
Sandler, Martin W. Pioneers. Billington, James. LC 92-47495. (Illus.). 96p. (gr. 3 up). 1994. 19.95 (*0-06-023023-1*); PLB 20.89 (*0-06-023024-X*) HarpC Child Bks.
Shellenberger, Robert. Wagons West: Trail Tales - 1848. LC 91-72903. (Illus.). 96p. (Orig.). 1991. pap. 9.95 (*0-9623048-3-2*) Heritage West.
Steedman, Scott. A Frontier Fort on the Oregon Trail. Bergin, Mark, illus. 48p. 1994. 17.95 (*0-87226-371-1*); pap. 8.95 (*0-87226-264-2*) P Bedrick Bks.
Stickney, Joy. Young Pioneers on the Oregon Trail. Stickney, Joy, illus. 20p. (gr. 4-6). 1992. pap. 4.50 (*1-884563-01-5*) Canyon Creat.
Stiles, T. J. Jesse James. LC 92-45210. (Illus.). 1993. 18.95 (*0-7910-1737-0*, Am Art Analog); pap. write for info. (*0-7910-1738-9*, Am Art Analog) Chelsea Hse.
Tykal, Jack B. Etienne Provost: Man of the Mountains. Smith, Monte, ed. Smith, Ralph L., illus. Gowans, Fred, intro. by. LC 89-80549. (Illus.). 256p. (gr. 9 up). 1989. 15.95 (*0-943604-24-9*); pap. 9.95 perfect bdg. (*0-943604-23-0*) Eagles View.
Walker, Paul R. Great Figures of the Wild West. (Illus.). 128p. (gr. 7-12). 1992. lib. bdg. 16.95x (*0-8160-2576-2*) Facts on File.

FROST, ROBERT, 1874-1963

Bober, Natalie S. A Restless Spirit: The Story of Robert Frost. (Illus.). 192p. (gr. 5 up). 1991. 19.95 (*0-8050-1672-4*, Bks Young Read) H Holt & Co.
Loewen, Nancy & Berry, S. L. Robert Frost. (Illus.). 48p. (gr. 5-12). 1994. lib. bdg. 18.95 RLB smythe-sewn (*0-88682-613-6*, 97866-098) Creative Ed.

FRUIT

see also Citrus Fruit; Fruit Culture;
also names of fruits, e.g. Apple, etc.

De Bourgoing, Pascale. Fruit. (Illus.). 24p. 1991. pap. 10.95 (*0-590-45233-9*, Cartwheel) Scholastic Inc.
Dillion, Leo & Dillion, Diane. What Am I? LC 93-48835. (gr. 1 up). 1994. 13.95 (*0-590-47885-0*, Blue Sky Press) Scholastic Inc.
Dowden, Anne O., text by. & illus. From Flower to Fruit. LC 93-24972. 64p. (gr. 3 up). 1994. 15.95 (*0-395-68376-9*); pap. 8.95 (*0-395-68944-9*) Ticknor & Flds Bks Yng Read.
Ehlert, Lois. Eating the Alphabet: Fruits & Vegetables from A to Z. 32p. (ps-3). 1989. 14.95 (*0-15-224435-2*) HarBrace.
Fowler, Allan. Nos Gusta la Fruta! - We Love Fruit! LC 92-13312. (SPA., Illus.). 32p. (ps-2). 1993. big bk. 22.95 (*0-516-59633-0*); PLB 10.75 (*0-516-36006-X*); pap. 3.95 (*0-516-56006-9*) Childrens.
Lember, Barbara H., text by. & photos by Book of Fruit. LC 94-4067. (Illus.). 32p. (ps-2). 1994. PLB 14.95g (*0-395-66989-8*) Ticknor & Flds Bks Yng Read.

McMillan, Bruce. Growing Colors. McMillan, Bruce, photos by. LC 93-28804. (Illus.). 32p. (ps up). 1994. pap. 4.95 (*0-688-13112-3*, Mulberry) Morrow.
Mitgutsch, Ali. From Seed to Pear. Mitgutsch, Ali, illus. LC 81-83. 24p. (ps-3). 1981. PLB 10.95 (*0-87614-163-7*) Carolrhoda Bks.
Pef. Belles Lisses Poires de France. (FRE.). 56p. (gr. 1-5). 1990. pap. 8.95 (*2-07-031216-X*) Schoenhof.
Pohl, Kathleen. Gourds. (Illus.). 32p. (gr. 3-7). 1986. PLB 10.95 (*0-8172-2712-1*) Raintree Steck-V.
Robinson, Fay. We Love Fruit! LC 92-13312. (Illus.). 32p. (ps-2). 1992. PLB 10.75 (*0-516-06006-6*); big bk. 22.95 (*0-516-49633-6*) Childrens.
—We Love Fruit. LC 92-13312. (Illus.). 32p. (ps-2). 1993. pap. 3.95 (*0-516-46006-4*) Childrens.
Western Promotional Books Staff. Grapes. (ps). 1994. 0.95 (*0-307-13462-8*) Western Pub.

FRUIT–CANNING
see Canning and Preserving

FRUIT CULTURE
Handelsman, Judith F. Gardens from Garbage: How to Grow Plants from Recycled Kitchen Scraps. LC 92-9146. (Illus.). 48p. (gr. 4-6). 1993. PLB 13.90 (*1-56294-229-8*) Millbrook Pr.
Sanchez, Isidro & Peris, Carme. The Orchard. (Illus.). 32p. (ps). 1991. pap. 5.95 (*0-8120-4710-9*) Barron.
Walker, Lois. Get Growing! Exciting Plant Projects for Kids. 104p. 1991. pap. text ed. 9.95 (*0-471-54488-4*) Wiley.

FRUIT CULTURE–FICTION
Appelt. Watermelon Day. 1993. 14.95 (*0-8050-2304-6*) H Holt & Co.
Fukami, Haruo. An Orange for a Bellybutton. Fukami, Haruo, illus. 32p. (ps-3). 1990. PLB 18.95 (*0-87614-429-6*) Carolrhoda Bks.
Ghazi, Abidullah. Grandfather's Orchard. Ghazi, Tasneema, et al, eds. Van Patten, Michele, illus. 15p. (ps-k). Date not set. text ed. 14.95 (*1-56316-307-1*) Iqra Intl Ed Fdtn.
The Pineapple Story. LC 78-60645. (Illus.). 39p. (gr. 3 up). 1978. 5.00 (*0-916888-03-7*) Inst Basic Youth.
Riskind, Mary. Apple Is My Sign. 160p. (gr. 5-8). 1981. 14.95 (*0-395-30852-6*) HM.
Scheffler, Ursel. The Giant Apple. Brix-Henker, Silke, illus. 32p. (gr. k-3). 1990. PLB 18.95 (*0-87614-413-X*) Carolrhoda Bks.
Williams, Vera B. Cherries & Cherry Pits. Williams, Vera B., illus. LC 85-17156. 40p. (ps up). 1986. 16.00 (*0-688-05145-6*); PLB 15.93 (*0-688-05146-4*) Greenwillow.

FRUSTRATION
see Attitude (Psychology); Emotions

FRY, ELIZABETH (GURNEY) 1780-1845
Bull, Angela. Elizabeth Fry. (Illus.). 64p. (gr. 5-9). 1991. 11.95 (*0-237-60028-5*, Pub. by Evans Bros Ltd) Trafalgar.

FUEL
see also Wood
Baker, Susan. First Look at Using Energy. LC 91-2372. (Illus.). 32p. (gr. 1-2). 1991. PLB 17.27 (*0-8368-0680-8*) Gareth Stevens Inc.
Russell, William. Oil, Coal & Gas. LC 94-2401. (gr. 3 up). 1994. write for info. (*0-86593-357-X*) Rourke Corp.
Santrey, Laurence. Energy & Fuels. Burns, Raymond, illus. LC 84-2704. 32p. (gr. 3-6). 1985. PLB 9.49 (*0-8167-0290-X*); pap. text ed. 2.95 (*0-8167-0291-8*) Troll Assocs.

FULLER, RICHARD BUCKMINSTER, 1895-
Potter, Robert R. Buckminster Fuller. Gallin, Richard, ed. (Illus.). 144p. (gr. 5-9). 1990. PLB 10.95 (*0-382-09967-2*); pap. 6.95 (*0-382-09972-9*) Silver Burdett Pr.

FULTON, ROBERT, 1765-1815
Landau, Elaine. Robert Fulton. LC 90-47865. (Illus.). 64p. (gr. 3-5). 1991. PLB 12.90 (*0-531-20016-7*) Watts.
Landers-Henry, Joanne. Robert Fulton: Steamboat Builder. Mawicke, Tran, illus. 80p. (gr. 2-6). 1991. Repr. of 1975 ed. lib. bdg. 12.95 (*0-7910-1411-8*) Chelsea Hse.

FUND RAISING
Kleeberg, Irene C. Fund Raising. LC 88-5655. (Illus.). 72p. (gr. 4-9). 1988. 10.90 (*0-531-10583-0*) Watts.

FUNDS
see Finance

FUNERAL RITES AND CEREMONIES
Berrill, Margaret. Mummies, Masks, & Mourners. Molan, Chris, illus. LC 89-31822. 48p. (gr. 4-7). 1990. 14.95 (*0-525-67282-6*, Lodestar Bks) Dutton Child Bks.
Syme, Daniel B. Jewish Mourning. 1989. pap. 3.00 (*0-8074-0332-6*, 388494) UAHC.

FUNGI
see also Bacteriology; Mushrooms
Gattis, L. S., III. Fungi for Pathfinders: A Basic Youth Enrichment Skill Honor Packet. (Illus.). 20p. (Orig.). (gr. 5 up). 1987. pap. 5.00 tchr's. ed. (*0-936241-20-9*) Cheetah Pub.
Madgwick, Wendy. Fungi & Lichens. LC 90-9571. (Illus.). 48p. (gr. 5-9). 1990. PLB 21.34 (*0-8114-2728-5*) Raintree Steck-V.
Rotter, Charles M. Fungi. LC 92-44441. (gr. 4 up). 1993. 18.95 (*0-88682-593-8*) Creative Ed.
Tesar, Jenny. Fungi. (Illus.). 64p. (gr. 4-8). 1994. PLB 16.95 (*1-56711-044-4*) Blackbirch.

FUNNIES
see Comic Books, Strips, Etc.

FUR-BEARING ANIMALS
see also names of fur-bearing animals, e.g. Beavers, etc.

FUR SEALS
see Seals (Animals)

FUR TRADE
Siegel, Beatrice. Fur Trappers & Traders: The Indians, the Pilgrims, & the Beaver. Bock, William S., illus. LC 80-7671. 64p. (gr. 3-7). 1987. PLB 11.85 (*0-8027-6397-9*) Walker & Co.

FURNITURE
see also Wood Carving
also names of articles of furniture, e.g. Chairs; Mirrors; etc.
Mitgutsch, Ali. From Tree to Table. Mitgutsch, Ali, illus. LC 81-672. 24p. (ps-3). 1981. PLB 10.95 (*0-87614-165-3*) Carolrhoda Bks.

G

G.I.S.
see Soldiers–U. S.

GALAPAGOS ISLANDS
Blashfield, Jean F. Galapagos Islands. LC 94-3030. (Illus.). 64p. (gr. 5-8). 1994. PLB write for info. (*0-8114-6362-1*) Raintree Steck-V.
Litteral, Linda L. Bobos, Iguanas y Otros Animalejos - Boobies, Iguanas & Other Critters: Historia de la Naturaleza en los Galapagos - Nature's Story in the Galapagos. (SPA.). 72p. (gr. 4-9). 1993. 23.00 (*1-883966-02-7*) Am Kestrel Pr.
McGovern, Ann. Swimming with Sea Lions. 48p. 1992. 13.95 (*0-590-45282-7*, Scholastic Hardcover) Scholastic Inc.
Root, Phyllis & McCormick, Maxine. Galapagos. LC 89-7918. (Illus.). 48p. (gr. 4-5). 1989. text ed. 13.95 RSBE (*0-89686-434-0*, Crestwood Hse) Macmillan Child Grp.
Russell, William. The Galapagos Islands. LC 93-48335. 1994. write for info. (*1-55916-031-4*) Rourke Bk Co.
Schafer, Susan. The Galapagos Tortoise. LC 92-7396. (Illus.). 64p. (gr. 4 up). 1992. text ed. 13.95 RSBE (*0-87518-544-4*, Dillon) Macmillan Child Grp.

GALES
see Winds

GALILEI, GALILEO, 1564-1642
Fisher, Leonard E. Galileo. Fisher, Leonard E., illus. LC 91-31146. 32p. (gr. 2-6). 1992. SBE 15.95 (*0-02-735235-8*, Macmillan Child Bk) Macmillan Child Grp.
Hitzeroth, Deborah & Heerboth, Sharon. Galileo Galilei. LC 92-25957. (Illus.). 112p. (gr. 5-8). 1992. PLB 14.95 (*1-56006-027-1*) Lucent Bks.
Parker, Steve. Galileo & the Universe. Parker, Steve, illus. LC 91-28315. 32p. (gr. 3-7). 1992. 14.00 (*0-06-020735-3*) HarpC Child Bks.

GALLERIES (ART)
see Art–Galleries and Museums

GAMA, VASCO DA, 1469?-1524
Knight, David. Vasco Da Gama. LC 78-18057. (Illus.). 48p. (gr. 4-7). 1979. PLB 10.59 (*0-89375-175-8*); pap. 3.50 (*0-89375-167-7*) Troll Assocs.
Stefoff, Rebecca. Vasco da Gama & the Portuguese Explorers. Goetzmann, William H., ed. Collins, Michael, intro. by. (Illus.). 112p. (gr. 6-12). 1993. PLB 18.95 (*0-7910-1303-0*); pap. write for info. (*0-7910-1526-2*) Chelsea Hse.
Twist, Clint. Magellan & Da Gama. LC 93-19303. 1994. PLB 22.80 (*0-8114-7254-X*) Raintree Steck-V.
The Voyages of Vasco Da Gama. (Illus.). 32p. (gr. 5-6). 1992. PLB 12.40 (*0-531-14149-7*) Watts.

GAME AND GAME BIRDS
see also Hunting; Trapping
also names of animals and birds, e.g. Deer; Pheasants; etc.

GAME PRESERVES
Watts, Barrie. Twenty-Four Hours in a Game Reserve. Watts, Barrie, photos by. LC 91-23728. (Illus.). 48p. (gr. 4-6). 1992. PLB 12.90 (*0-531-14173-X*) Watts.

GAME PROTECTION–FICTION
London, Jonathan. Jackrabbit. Ray, Deborah K., illus. LC 94-1082. 1995. write for info. (*0-517-59657-1*, Crown); lib. bdg. write for info. (*0-517-59658-X*, Crown) Crown Pub Group.

GAMES
see also Amusements; Cards; Kindergarten; Olympic Games; Play; Singing Games; Sports;
also names of games, e.g. Chess; Tennis; etc.
Adams, Lynn, illus. Don Cooper's Musical Games. Cooper, Don, contrib. by. (Illus.). 32p. (Orig.). (ps-3). 1991. pap. 6.95 incl. 30-min. cassette (*0-679-81935-5*) Random Bks Yng Read.
Adams, Pam, illus. What Is It? (Orig.). (ps-2). 1975. pap. 3.95 (*0-85953-044-2*, Pub. by Child's Play England) Childs Play.
Adler, David A. Passover Fun Book: Puzzles, Riddles, Magic & More. (Illus.). (gr. k-5). 1978. saddlewire bdg. 3.95 (*0-88482-759-3*, Bonim Bks) Hebrew Pub.
Alderson, Frederick. Outdoor Games. (Illus.). 64p. (gr. 6 up). 1980. 14.95 (*0-7136-2031-5*) Dufour.
Anderson, Karen C. & Cumbaa, Stephen. The Bones & Skeleton Gamebook. (Illus.). 96p. (Orig.). (gr. 1-4). 1993. pap. 7.95 (*1-56305-497-3*, 3497) Workman Pub.
Anderson, Karen L. Games Magazine Presents Kids' Giant Book of Games. 1993. pap. 12.00 (*0-8129-2199-2*, Times Bks) Random.
Andrews, Ed. Caravans of Mars. Hasenauer, Richard, illus. 64p. (Orig.). 1989. pap. 8.00 (*1-55878-023-8*) Game Designers.
Aulson, Pam. Placemat Pets 'n Playmates. (Illus.). 24p. (gr. 6 up). 1980. pap. 3.00 (*0-9601896-2-9*) Patch As Patch.
Autobot Warriors Activity Book. (Illus.). 64p. (Orig.). (gr. 1-3). 1993. pap. 2.95 (*1-56144-378-6*, Honey Bear Bks) Modern Pub NYC.
Autobots' Advantage. (Illus.). 32p. (Orig.). (gr. 1-3). 1993. pap. 1.29 (*1-56144-342-5*, Honey Bear Bks) Modern Pub NYC.
Ball Games. 48p. (gr. 3-8). 1990. 15.95 (*1-85435-077-3*) Marshall Cavendish.
Barr, Marilynn G. Build-a-Board. (Illus.). 128p. (gr. 1-6). 1991. pap. 10.95 (*1-878279-32-7*) Monday Morning Bks.
—Gameboard Round-up. (Illus.). 128p. (gr. 1-6). 1991. pap. 10.95 (*1-878279-33-5*) Monday Morning Bks.
Barry, Sheila A. Super-Colossal Book of Puzzles, Tricks & Games. (Illus.). 640p. 1992. Repr. of 1978 ed. 9.99 (*0-517-07769-8*, Pub. by Wings Bks) Random Hse Value.
Baylor, Byrd. Guess Who My Favorite Person Is. Parker, Robert A., illus. LC 77-7151. 32p. (gr. 1-5). 1985. pap. 4.95 (*0-689-71052-6*, Aladdin) Macmillan Child Grp.
Beall, Pamela C. & Nipp, Susan H. Wee Sing & Play. (Illus.). 64p. (Orig.). (ps-2). 1983. pap. 2.95 (*0-8431-3812-2*); pap. 9.95 incl. cassette (*0-8431-3796-7*) Price Stern.
Beaver, Edmund. Travel Games. (gr. 4 up). 1974. pap. 1.00 (*0-910208-01-8*) Beavers.
Benarde, Anita. Games from Many Lands. Benarde, Anita, illus. Winskill, Mary, frwd. by. LC 71-86975. (Illus.). 64p. (gr. 3-7). 1971. PLB 13.95 (*0-87460-147-9*) Lion Bks.
Bentley, William G. Indoor & Outdoor Games. (gr. k-6). 1966. pap. 7.95 (*0-8224-3910-7*) Fearon Teach Aids.
Bergstrom, Joan M. & Bergstrom, Craig. All the Best Contests for Kids, 1992-1993. 3rd ed. 288p. (gr. k-9). 1992. pap. 9.95 (*0-89815-451-0*) Ten Speed Pr.
Bernstein, Bob. Friday Afternoon Fun. Schmidt, Ross, illus. 64p. (gr. 2-6). 1984. wkbk. 8.95 (*0-86653-206-4*, GA 558) Good Apple.
Blakey, Nancy. More Mudpies: One Hundred One Alternatives to Television. Watts, Melissah, illus. LC 94-11709. 144p. (ps-6). 1994. pap. 7.95 (*1-883672-11-2*) Tricycle Pr.
Blue Ranger. (Illus.). 8p. (gr. k-2). 1994. bds. write for info. (*1-56144-478-2*, Honey Bear Bks) Modern Pub NYC.
Boardman, Bob. Red Hot Peppers. Boardman, Diane, illus. 64p. (Orig.). (gr. 3 up). 1993. pap. 12.95 incl. speed rope (*0-912365-78-1*) Sasquatch Bks.
—Red Hot Peppers Book & Beaded Rope Kit: The Skoopum Book of Jump Rope Games, Rhymes, & Fancy Footwork. Boardman, Diane, illus. 64p. (Orig.). (gr. 2 up). 1993. pap. 11.95 (*0-912365-94-3*) Sasquatch Bks.
—Red Hot Peppers: Book, Audio, & Beaded Rope Kit. Boardman, Diane, illus. Shreave, Michael, contrib. by. (Illus.). 64p. (gr. 2 up). 1994. incl. rope & cass. 15.95 (*1-57061-003-7*) Sasquatch Bks.
—Red Hot Peppers: Book, Audio, & Speed Rope. Boardman, Diane, illus. Shreave, Michael, contrib. by. (Illus.). 64p. (gr. 2 up). 1994. incl. rope & cass. 15.95 (*1-57061-002-9*) Sasquatch Bks.
—Red Hot Peppers: The Skookum Book of Jump Rope Games, Rhymes, & Fancy Footwork. Boardman, Diane, illus. 64p. (Orig.). (gr. 3 up). 1993. pap. 8.95 (*0-912365-74-9*) Sasquatch Bks.
Boatness, Marie E. Travel Games for the Family. Westheimer, Mary, ed. Woodruff, Mark, illus. LC 93-90005. 144p. (Orig.). (gr. 1-8). 1993. pap. 9.95 (*0-9635619-0-1*) Canyon Creek.
Bond, Larry. Data Annex Upgrade. Venters, Steve, illus. 136p. (Orig.). 1990. pap. 10.00 (*1-55878-053-X*) Game Designers.
Brady, Maxine. The Monopoly Book. (Illus.). (gr. 7 up). 1976. pap. 4.95 (*0-679-14401-3*) McKay.
Brown, Marc T. Hand Rhymes. Brown, Marc T., illus. 32p. (ps-1). 1993. pap. 4.99 (*0-14-054939-0*, Puff Unicorn) Puffin Bks.
Brown, Marzella. Great Games for Cooperative Learning. Rivera, Doreen, et al, illus. 48p. (gr. 2-5). 1990. wkbk. 6.95 (*1-55734-108-7*) Tchr Create Mat.
Burroughs, Tracy S. Super Fun Kid's Games. LC 93-49449. 1994. 4.95 (*0-681-45556-X*) Longmeadow Pr.
Buskin, David. Outdoor Games. Kline, Dick, illus. Thompson, Morton, intro. by. (Illus.). (gr. k-4). 1966. PLB 13.95 (*0-87460-090-1*) Lion Bks.
Butterfield, M. Air Travel Games. (Illus.). 32p. (gr. 2 up). 1986. pap. 4.95 (*0-86020-997-0*) EDC.
Butterfield, S. Gold Medal Games. rev. ed. (gr. 1-3). 1992. Repr. of 1983 ed. 3.95 (*0-88160-106-3*, LW 125) Learning Wks.
Campbell, Andrea. Great Games for Great Parties: How to Throw a Perfect Party. LC 91-22983. (Illus.). 160p. (gr. 1-9). 1991. 14.95 (*0-8069-8318-3*) Sterling.
Campbell, Rod. My Presents. Campbell, Rod, illus. 24p. (ps-1). 1989. pap. 3.95 POB (*0-689-71286-3*, Aladdin) Macmillan Child Grp.
Caney, Steven. Steven Caney's Play Book. LC 75-9816. (Illus.). 240p. (ps-5). 1975. pap. 9.95 (*0-911104-38-0*, 050) Workman Pub.
Carlson, Chris. Troubled Waters. 80p. (Orig.). 1992. pap. 10.00 (*1-55878-098-X*) Game Designers.

Carnegie Museum of Natural History, Division of Education Staff. Dippy Diplodocus: Story & Gameboard. Kelley, Patte, illus. 16p. (Orig.). (ps-2). 1988. pap. 4.95 (*0-911239-23-5*) Carnegie Mus.

Cassidy, John & Stillinger, Scott. The New Official Koosh Book. Taber, Ed, illus. 88p. 1992. perfect bdg., incl. 3 mini-Koosh balls 9.95 (*1-878257-30-7*) Klutz Pr.

Chadwick, Frank. Cloud Captains of Mars. Aulisio, Janet, illus. 64p. (Orig.). 1989. pap. 8.00 (*1-55878-043-2*) Game Designers.

—Ironclads & Ether Flyers. Deitrick, David, illus. 112p. (Orig.). 1990. pap. 12.00 (*0-943580-96-X*) Game Designers.

Chadwick, Frank A. Conklin's Atlas. Ryan, Shea, illus. 80p. (Orig.). 1989. pap. 10.00 (*1-55878-024-6*) Game Designers.

—Twilight: Two Thousand. Harris, Dell, illus. 280p. (Orig.). 1990. pap. 20.00 (*1-55878-070-X*) Game Designers.

Chadwick, Frank S. Cadillacs & Dinosaurs. Schultz, Mark, illus. 144p. (Orig.). (gr. 9-12). 1990. pap. 18.00 (*1-55878-073-4*) Game Designers.

Charlton, S. Coleman. Creatures & Treasures. (Illus.). 96p. (gr. 10-12). 1985. 12.00 (*0-915795-30-2*, 1400) Iron Crown Ent Inc.

Charlton, S. Coleman & Ruemmler, John D. Middle-Earth Role Playing (MERP) (Illus.). 128p. (gr. 10-12). 1986. pap. 10.00 (*0-915795-31-0*, 8000) Iron Crown Ent Inc.

Chase, Richard. Singing Games & Playparty Games. Tolford, Joshua, illus. 63p. (gr. 1-4). 1949. pap. 2.50 (*0-486-21785-X*) Dover.

Chasing Games. 48p. (gr. 3-8). 1990. PLB 15.95 (*1-85435-078-1*) Marshall Cavendish.

Cherkerzian, Diane. Indoor Sunshine: Great Things to Make & Do on Rainy Days. LeHew, Ron, illus. LC 92-73628. 32p. (gr. 2-7). 1993. pap. 3.95 (*1-56397-163-1*) Boyds Mills Pr.

—Outdoor Fun: Great Things to Make & Do on Sunny Days. LeHew, Ron, illus. LC 92-74583. 32p. (gr. 2-7). 1993. pap. 3.95 (*1-56397-162-3*) Boyds Mills Pr.

Church, Ellen C. Learning Things: Games That Make Learning Fun for Children 3-8 Years Old. LC 81-82033. (ps-3). 1982. pap. 14.95 (*0-8224-4268-X*) Fearon Teach Aids.

Cobb, Vicki. How to Really Fool Yourself: Illusions for All Your Senses. LC 79-9620. (Illus.). 160p. (gr. 5 up). 1981. (Lipp Jr Bks); PLB 13.89 (*0-397-31907-X*, Lipp Jr Bks) HarpC Child Bks.

Colborn, Mark. Rolemaster Companion. Charlton, S. C., ed. McBride, Angus, illus. 96p. (gr. 10-12). 1986. pap. 12.00 (*0-915795-12-4*, 1500) Iron Crown Ent Inc.

Cole, Joanna & Calmenson, Stephanie. Crazy Eights: And Other Card Games. Tiegreen, Alan, illus. LC 93-5427. 80p. (gr. 2 up). 1994. 15.00 (*0-688-12199-3*); PLB 14.93 (*0-688-12200-0*); pap. 6.95 (*0-688-12201-9*, Pub. by Beech Tree Bks) Morrow Jr Bks.

—Pin the Tail on the Donkey & Other Party Games. Tiegreen, Alan, illus. LC 92-29786. 48p. (ps up). 1993. 15.00 (*0-688-11891-7*); PLB 14.93 (*0-688-11892-5*); pap. 6.95 (*0-688-12521-2*) Morrow Jr Bks.

Corbett, Pie. Playtime Treasury. 1990. 16.95 (*0-385-26448-8*) Doubleday.

Crazy Christmas Game. (Illus.). (gr. 1 up). 1993. 9 cards & box 2.95 (*0-8431-3507-7*) Price Stern.

Crisfield, Deborah. Gambling. LC 90-47961. (Illus.). 48p. (gr. 5-6). 1991. text ed. 12.95 RSBE (*0-89686-607-6*, Crestwood Hse) Macmillan Child Grp.

Decepticon Danger. (Illus.). 32p. (Orig.). (gr. 1-3). 1993. pap. 1.29 (*1-56144-343-3*, Honey Bear Bks) Modern Pub NYC.

Defenders of the Universe. (Illus.). 8p. (gr. k-2). 1994. bds. 4.95 (*1-56144-471-5*, Honey Bear Bks) Modern Pub NYC.

Deitrick, David R., illus. Tales from the Ether. 64p. (Orig.). (gr. 9-12). 1989. pap. 8.00 (*1-55878-011-4*) Game Designers.

Demi. Find Demi's Dinosaurs: An Animal Game Book. Demi, illus. 50p. (ps-3). 1989. 15.95 (*0-448-19020-6*, G&D) Putnam Pub Group.

Dinobots vs. Constructicons. (Illus.). 32p. (Orig.). (gr. 1-3). 1993. pap. 1.29 (*1-56144-344-1*, Honey Bear Bks) Modern Pub NYC.

Dobbs, Katy. My First Gamebook. Joyner, Jerry, illus. LC 85-40524. (ps-2). 1986. 6 bds. 5.95 (*0-89480-945-8*, 945) Workman Pub.

Donaldson, Judith E. Travel Games: Vol. 2, Five to Ten Years. Brown, George H., ed. Donaldson, Judith E., illus. 36p. (gr. k-5). pap. text ed. 1.50 (*0-939942-06-2*) Larkspur.

Dragonzord. (Illus.). 8p. (gr. k-2). 1994. bds. write for info. (*1-56144-475-8*, Honey Bear Bks) Modern Pub NYC.

Durlacher, Ed, ed. The Play Party Book: Singing Games for Children. Bare, Arnold E., illus. 38p. (ps-5). 1945. 9.50 (*0-8159-6505-2*) Devin.

Eickschen, Connie. Yestergames. 28p. (ps-7). 1991. pap. 4.95 (*0-9631442-0-0*) YesterCo.

Emerson, Sally & Corbett, Pie, eds. Action Rhymes. Maclean, Moira & Maclean, Colin, illus. LC 92-26445. 32p. (ps-k). 1993. pap. 4.95 (*1-85697-900-8*, Kingfisher LKC) LKC.

Fantasy Baseball. (Illus.). 64p. (gr. 3-7). 1992. pap. 2.95 (*0-307-22353-1*, 22353, Golden Pr) Western Pub.

Fantasy Basketball. (Illus.). 64p. (gr. 3-7). 1992. pap. 2.95 (*0-307-22363-9*, 22363, Golden Pr) Western Pub.

Fantasy Football. (Illus.). 64p. (gr. 3-7). 1992. pap. 2.95 (*0-307-22373-6*, 22373, Golden Pr) Western Pub.

Fenlon, Peter C. Moria. (Illus.). 72p. (gr. 10-12). 1984. 12.00 (*0-915795-27-2*, 2900) Iron Crown Ent Inc.

Fenlon, Peter C. & Colborn, Mark. Lords of Middle-Earth, Vol 1. McBride, Angus, illus. 96p. (Orig.). 1986. pap. 12.00 (*0-915795-26-4*, 8002) Iron Crown Ent Inc.

Findley, Nigel D. Native American Nations: A Shadowrun Sourcebook, Vol. 1. Ippolito, Donna & Mulvihill, Sharon T., eds. Laubenstein, Jeff & Bradstreet, Tim, illus. 136p. (gr. 7 up). 1991. pap. 12.00 (*1-55560-130-8*, 7202) FASA Corp.

Folsom, Marcia & Folsom, Michael. Easy As Pie: A Guessing Game of Sayings. Kent, Jack, illus. LC 84-14978. 64p. (ps-3). 1985. 13.95 (*0-89919-303-X*, Clarion Bks); pap. 5.95 (*0-89919-351-X*, Clarion Bks) HM.

Foster, Constance H. Polly's Magic Games: A Child's View of Obsessive-Compulsive Disorder. LC 93-74548. (Orig.). 1994. pap. 14.00 (*0-9639070-0-X*) Dilligaf Pubng.

Foster, Sally. Simon Says...Let's Play. Foster, Sally, photos by. LC 89-9776. (Illus.). 48p. (gr. 1-6). 1990. 13.95 (*0-525-65019-9*, Cobblehill Bks) Dutton Child Bks.

Freeman, W. B. My Anytime, Anyplace Activity Book, No. 02. (ps-3). 1994. pap. 6.99 (*0-8407-9196-8*) Nelson.

Frem, Margie, illus. Conversation Games: Vol. III, Solutions. Rev. ed. Freeman, Harold, Jr., intro. by. (Illus.). 134p. (ps-6). 1981. pap. 17.00 (*0-939632-23-3*) ILM.

Friedl, Michael. Ah...To Be A Kid: Three Dozen Aikido Games for Children of All Ages. Ransom, Stefan P., illus. 55p. (Orig.). 1994. pap. 9.95 (*0-9638530-1-5*, Castle Capers) Magical Michael.

Galeoti, Mike. Among the Dead. 80p. (Orig.). 1992. pap. 10.00 (*1-55878-107-2*) Game Designers.

Gambill, Hentietta D. Bible Learning Games. Wimmer, Sandy, illus. 16p. (gr. 1-7). 1993. 8.99 (*9-5032-0569-7*, 14-02259) Standard Pub.

Gamble, Donna T. Games to Go, 5 bklets. (ps-5). 1989. 29.95 (*1-55999-041-4*) LinguiSystems.

Gamec, Hazel S. The Disappearing ABC Game Book. Gamec, Hazel S., illus. 12p. write for info. (*0-938042-02-5*) Printek.

—Looking Out of the Window. Gamec, Hazel S., illus. 12p. 1980. write for info. (*0-938042-01-7*) Printek.

—The Magic Pencil Counting Book. Gamec, Hazel S., illus. 12p. 1980. write for info. (*0-938042-00-9*) Printek.

Games Children Play Series, 8 vols. LC 88-28773. (Illus.). 384p. (gr. 3-8). 1990. Set. 127.60 (*1-85435-076-5*) Marshall Cavendish.

Games of Skill & Strength. 48p. (gr. 3-8). 1990. PLB 15.95 (*1-85435-084-6*) Marshall Cavendish.

Games with Rope & String. 48p. (gr. 3-8). 1990. PLB 15.95 (*1-85435-081-1*) Marshall Cavendish.

Gannon, Charles E. Darktek Equipment Handbook. 104p. (Orig.). 1991. pap. 12.00 (*1-55878-084-X*) Game Designers.

Garden, Nancy. The Kid's Code & Cipher Book. Gomez, Victoria, illus. LC 80-10434. 176p. (gr. 5 up). 1981. 10.95 (*0-03-053856-4*, Bks Young Read); 4.95 (*0-03-059267-4*) H Holt & Co.

Garvy, Helen. Bingo Book, No. 1: Lower Grades. LC 93-85825. 80p. (Orig.). (gr. k-3). 1993. pap. 6.00 (*0-918828-12-0*) Shire Pr.

—Bingo Book, No. 2: Middle Grades. LC 93-85830. 80p. (Orig.). (gr. 3-6). 1993. pap. 6.00 (*0-918828-13-9*) Shire Pr.

—Bingo Book, No. 3: Upper Grades. LC 93-85829. 80p. (Orig.). (gr. 6-9). 1993. pap. 6.00 (*0-918828-14-7*) Shire Pr.

Gee, John. Hidden Pictures: Favorites by John Gee. (Illus.). 32p. (Orig.). (gr. 1-6). 1981. pap. 2.95 (*0-87534-230-2*) Highlights.

Gehman, Christian. Riders of Rohan. (Illus.). 48p. (gr. 10-12). 1985. pap. 12.00 (*0-915795-29-9*, 3100) Iron Crown Ent Inc.

Gifted & Talented: Puzzles & Games for Critical & Creative Thinking. 80p. (ps-1). 1994. pap. 3.95 (*1-56565-129-4*) Lowell Hse.

Gifted & Talented: Puzzles & Games for Critical & Creative Thinking. 80p. (gr. 1-3). 1994. pap. 3.95 (*1-56565-139-1*) Lowell Hse.

Goldar. (Illus.). 8p. (gr. k-2). 1994. bds. write for info. (*1-56144-476-6*, Honey Bear Bks) Modern Pub NYC.

Golden Staff. Sidewalk Chalk Games. (ps-3). 1994. pap. 5.95 (*0-307-16600-7*, Golden Pr) Western Pub.

Gould, Marilyn. Playground Sports: A Book of Ball Games. (Illus.). 62p. (gr. 2 up). 1991. 10.95 (*0-9632305-2-2*) Allied Crafts.

Great Games: More Than Two Hundred Games for All Ages. LC 93-85522. (Illus.). 256p. 1994. pap. 5.95 (*1-56138-383-X*) Running Pr.

Greenberg, Daniel & Siembieda, Kevin. Turtles Go Hollywood. Marciniszyn, Alex, ed. Long, Kevin, illus. 48p. (Orig.). (gr. 8 up). 1990. pap. 7.95 (*0-916211-46-0*, 510) Palladium Bks.

Greenwood, Donald J. Advanced Squad Leader: WWII Tactical Warfare. Keebler, Charlie, illus. 200p. (gr. 9 up). 1989. 45.00 (*0-911605-50-9*) Avalon Hill.

Griffiths, Rose. Games. Millard, Peter, photos by. LC 94-10038. (Illus.). 32p. (gr. 1 up). 1994. PLB 17.27 (*0-8368-1111-9*) Gareth Stevens Inc.

Grossman, Roz & Gewirtz, Gladys. Let's Play Dreidel. Springer, Sally, illus. LC 89-34892. 16p. (ps-3). 1989. incl. tape & dreidel 6.95 (*0-929371-00-3*) Kar Ben.

Grummer, Arnold E. The Great Balloon Game Book & More Balloon Activities. Wenger-Marsh, Beth, illus. 112p. (gr. 2 up). 1987. 12.95 (*0-938251-00-7*) G Markim.

Gryski, Camilla. Cat's Cradle, Owl's Eyes: A Book of String Games. Sankey, Tom, illus. LC 84-9075. 80p. (gr. 3 up). 1984. PLB 15.93 (*0-688-03940-5*) Morrow Jr Bks.

—Cat's Cradle, Owl's Eyes: A Book of String Games. Sankey, Tom, illus. 80p. (gr. 3 up). 1984. pap. 6.95 (*0-688-03941-3*, Pub. by Beech Tree Bks) Morrow.

—Many Stars & More String Games. Sankey, Tom, illus. LC 85-4875. 80p. (gr. 3 up). 1985. lib. bdg. 13.93 (*0-688-05793-4*) Morrow Jr Bks.

—Many Stars & More String Games. Sankey, Tom, illus. 80p. (gr. 3 up). 1985. pap. 7.95 (*0-688-05792-6*, Pub. by Beech Tree Bks) Morrow.

—Super String Games. Sankey, Tom, illus. LC 88-18365. 80p. (gr. 3 up). 1988. lib. bdg. 11.93 (*0-688-07685-8*) Morrow Jr Bks.

—Super String Games. Sankey, Tom, illus. LC 88-18365. 80p. (gr. 3 up). 1988. pap. 6.95 (*0-688-07684-X*, Pub. by Beech Tree Bks) Morrow.

Gygax, Gary. The Necropolis: And the Land of Egypt. Smith, Lester, ed. 208p. (Orig.). 1992. pap. 18.00 (*1-55878-143-9*) Game Designers.

Gygax, Gary & Smith, Lester. Mythus Magick. 384p. (Orig.). 1992. pap. 24.00 (*1-55878-133-1*) Game Designers.

Haddock, Eric W. New Orleans. 64p. (Orig.). 1991. pap. 10.00 (*1-55878-080-7*) Game Designers.

Hamilton, Leslie. Child's Play Six-Twelve: One Hundred Sixty Instant Activities, Crafts & Science Projects. 1992. 10.00 (*0-517-58354-2*, Crown) Crown Pub Group.

Handford, Martin. Find Waldo Now. Handford, Martin, illus. (ps up). 1988. 14.95 (*0-316-34292-0*) Little.

—The Great Waldo Search. Handford, Martin, illus. (ps up). 1989. 14.95 (*0-316-34282-3*) Little.

—Where's Waldo? (ps up). 1987. 14.95 (*0-316-34293-9*) Little.

Hargrave, et al. The Cthulhu Casebook: Adventures & Atmosphere for Call of Cthulhu. Petersen, Sandy, ed. Peterson, Sandy & Monroe, John B., eds. Gibbons, Lee, et al, illus. 130p. (Orig.). (gr. 12 up). 1990. pap. 18.95 (*0-933635-67-2*, 3305) Chaosium.

Harris, Frank. Great Games to Play with Groups. (gr. 1 up). 1989. 9.95 (*0-8224-3379-6*) Fearon Teach Aids.

Harris, Jack C. Adventure Gaming. LC 91-3885. (Illus.). 48p. (gr. 5-6). 1993. text ed. 12.95 RSBE (*0-89686-621-1*, Crestwood Hse) Macmillan Child Grp.

Harris, Steve, ed. Electronic Gaming - Fall Preview. 84p. 1990. pap. 3.95 (*1-878667-01-7*) Amer Dist Serv.

Hart, Bruce & Hart, Carole. Waiting Games. 320p. (gr. 7 up). 1981. pap. 3.50 (*0-380-79012-2*, Flare) Avon.

Heap of Trouble. (Illus.). 8p. (gr. k-2). 1994. bds. 4.95 (*1-56144-472-3*, Honey Bear Bks) Modern Pub NYC.

Heimann, Rolf. Bizarre Brain Benders. (Illus.). 32p. (gr. 4-7). 1993. pap. 3.95 (*0-8167-3035-0*, Pub. by Watermill Pr) Troll Assocs.

Herber, Keith & Morrison, Mark. Mansions of Madness: Mythos Mysteries in the Abodes of Man. Willis, Lynn, ed. Gibbons, Lee & Aulisio, Janet, illus. 130p. (Orig.). (gr. 12 up). 1990. pap. 17.95 (*0-933635-63-X*, 2327) Chaosium.

Highlights Editors. Hidden Pictures & Other Challengers. (Illus.). 32p. (Orig.). (gr. 1-6). 1981. pap. 2.95 (*0-87534-227-2*) Highlights.

—Hidden Pictures & Other Fun. (Illus.). 32p. (Orig.). (gr. 1-6). 1981. pap. 2.95 (*0-87534-178-0*) Highlights.

—Hidden Pictures & Other Puzzlers. (Illus.). 32p. (Orig.). (gr. 1-6). 1981. pap. 2.95 (*0-87534-180-2*) Highlights.

—Hidden Pictures Plus Brain Benders. (Illus.). 32p. (Orig.). (gr. 1-6). 1986. pap. 2.95 (*0-87534-104-7*) Highlights.

—Hidden Pictures Plus Brain Stretchers. (Illus.). 32p. (Orig.). (gr. 1-6). 1986. pap. 2.95 (*0-87534-103-9*) Highlights.

—Hidden Pictures Plus Brain Teasers. (Illus.). 32p. (Orig.). (gr. 1-6). 1986. pap. 2.95 (*0-87534-102-0*) Highlights.

—Hidden Pictures Plus Fun for Masterminds. (Illus.). 32p. (Orig.). (gr. 1-6). 1986. pap. 2.95 (*0-87534-101-2*) Highlights.

—Highlights Best Board Games from Around the World. Dugan, Robert, ed. (Illus.). 40p. (gr. 1-7). 1993. spiral bound 19.95 (*1-56397-244-1*) Boyds Mills Pr.

Highlights for Children Editors. Let's Make Games: Puzzles, Board Games, Games for Groups. (Illus.). 48p. (Orig.). (ps-3). 1993. pap. 5.95 (*1-56397-061-9*) Boyds Mills Pr.

Highlights Staff, ed. Hidden Pictures Plus Thinking Fun. (Illus.). 32p. (Orig.). (gr. 1-6). 1986. pap. 2.95 (*0-87534-105-5*) Highlights.

Hillery, Mable & Hall, Patricia. A Guide to the Use of Street-Folk-Musical Games in the Classroom: Chanting Games. rev. ed. Kendrick, John & May, Warren, illus. Freeman, Harold, Jr., intro. by. 77p. (ps-6). 1982. pap. 12.00 (*0-939632-05-5*) ILM.

Hodgson, Harriet. Gameworks. 64p. (gr. k-3). 1986. 6.95 (*0-912107-41-3*) Monday Morning Bks.

Home Alone Two - Lost in New York: Games & Puzzles. 64p. (gr. k-3). 1992. pap. 2.95 (*1-56144-229-1*, Honey Bear Bks) Modern Pub NYC.

Home Alone Two - Lost in New York: Puzzles & Mazes. 64p. (gr. k-3). 1992. pap. 2.95 (*1-56144-230-5*, Honey Bear Bks) Modern Pub NYC.

Hope, Cathy. Who's He & Who's Out. Kelly, Geoff, illus. LC 92-21396. 1993. 4.25 (*0-383-03607-0*) SRA Schl Grp.

Howell, Ann C. Tuskegee Airmen: Heroes in Flight for Dignity Inclusion & Citizenship Rights. Chandler, Alton, ed. Johannes, Greg, illus. 24p. (Orig.). (gr. 3-8). 1994. pap. text ed. 1.50 (*0-685-71995-2*) Chandler White.

Ingram, Anne & O'Donnell, Peggy. Family Car Book. Graham, Bob, illus. 48p. (gr. 4 up). 1992. pap. 6.95 (*0-920775-43-8*, Pub. by Greey dePencier CN) Firefly Bks Ltd.

—Rainy Day Book. Peters, Shirley, illus. 48p. (gr. 3 up). 1992. pap. 6.95 (*0-920775-44-6*, Pub. by Greey dePencier CN) Firefly Bks Ltd.

Isynwill, L. N. & Keith, Herbert. At Your Door: A Modern-Day Campaign. Willis, Lynn & Herber, Keith, eds. Gibbons, Lee, illus. 162p. (Orig.). (gr. 12 up). 1990. pap. 17.95 (*0-933635-64-8*, 2326) Chaosium.

Jackson, Steve & Livingstone, Ian. The Rings of Kether. (Orig.). (gr. 6-12). 1986. pap. 2.50 (*0-440-97407-0*, LFL) Dell.

Johanning, Jolynn. God Made All of Me: Activities for Young Children. (Illus.). 120p. 1992. pap. text ed. 11. 95 (*0-89390-210-1*) Resource Pubns.

Kauffman, Liz, ed. The Highlights Book of Travel Games. Palan, R. Michael, illus. 32p. (gr. 2-7). 1994. pap. 3.95 (*1-56397-273-5*) Boyds Mills Pr.

Keeler, Ronald F. Games for Children: For Indoors & Outdoors. 64p. (Orig.). (ps-2). 1982. pap. 3.99 (*0-8010-5478-8*) Baker Bk.

Kelemen, Julie. Advent Is for Children. 64p. (Orig.). (gr. 3 up). 1988. pap. 2.95 (*0-89243-292-6*) Liguori Pubns.

Kettler, Edward. South Atlantic War. 136p. (Orig.). 1991. pap. 12.00 (*1-55878-064-5*) Game Designers.

Klutz Press Staff. The Klutz Book of Jacks. (Illus.). 30p. (Orig.). 1989. pap. 7.95 incl. jacks, ball & pouch (*0-932592-21-X*) Klutz Pr.

—The Klutz Book of Marbles. (Illus.). 30p. (Orig.). 1989. pap. 7.95 incl. marbles, shooter & pouch (*0-932592-22-8*) Klutz Pr.

Korner, David. Come out & Play. Korner, David, illus. LC 86-2811. 56p. (gr. 1-5). 1987. pap. 9.95 (*0-939827-00-X*) Korn Kompany.

Kowitt, Holly. Road Trip: A Travel Activity Book. (ps-3). 1994. pap. 1.95 (*0-590-48105-3*) Scholastic Inc.

Kroll, Steven. The Tyrannosaurus Game. De Paola, Tomie, illus. 1988. bk. & cassette 19.95 (*0-87499-096-3*); bk. & cassette 12.95 (*0-87499-095-5*); 4 cassettes & guide 27.95 (*0-87499-097-1*) Live Oak Media.

Kubasch, Heike. Bree & the Barrow-Downs. (Illus.). 40p. (gr. 10-12). 1984. pap. 7.00 (*0-915795-16-7*, 8010) Iron Crown Ent Inc.

Lambord, Creede & Lambord, Sharleen. Heart of Darkness. 64p. (Orig.). 1991. pap. 10.00 (*0-685-61116-7*) Game Designers.

Landa, Norbert. Rabbit & Chicken Play Hide & Seek. Turk, Hanne, illus. LC 90-33484. (ps). 1992. bds. 4.95 (*0-688-09970-X*, Tambourine Bks) Morrow.

Langley, Andrew. Travel Games for Kids. rev. ed. LC 90-84702. (Illus.). 112p. (gr. k-8). 1992. pap. 10.95 (*0-936399-09-0*) Berkshire Hse.

Langstaff, Nancy & Langstaff, John. Sally Go Round the Moon & Other Revels Songs & Singing Games for Young Children. Pienkowski, Jan, illus. LC 86-90535. 127p. (ps-1). 1986. pap. 12.95 (*0-9618334-0-8*) Revels Pubns.

Lankford, Mary D. Hopscotch Around the World. Milone, Karen, illus. LC 91-17152. 48p. (gr. 4 up). 1992. 15.00 (*0-688-08419-2*); PLB 14.93 (*0-688-08420-6*) Morrow Jr Bks.

LaPlaca, Annette. Are We Almost There? The Kids' Book of Travel Fun. Bryer, Debbie, illus. 45p. (Orig.). (gr. 1-5). 1992. pap. 4.99 wkbk. (*0-87788-051-4*) Shaw Pubs.

Let's Play a Game Everyone Wins. 36p. (ps-4). 1985. 8.95 (*0-88684-178-X*); cassette tape avail. Listen USA.

Lieberman, Lillian. ABC: Board Games. Barr, Marilynn G., illus. 64p. (ps-2). 1991. pap. 7.95 (*1-878279-31-9*) Monday Morning Bks.

Lipscomb, Susan D. & Zuanich, Margaret A. BASIC Fun: Computer Games, Puzzles & Problems Children Can Write. 176p. (gr. k-7). 1982. pap. 2.95 (*0-380-80606-1*, Camelot) Avon.

Little People Big Book about Playtime. 64p. (ps-1). 1990. write for info. (*0-8094-7516-2*); lib. bdg. write for info. (*0-8094-7517-0*) Time-Life.

Liu, Sarah & Vittitow, Mary L. Learning Games Without Losers. (Illus.). 96p. (gr. 2-6). 1985. guide 8.95 (*0-86530-039-9*, IP 39-9) Incentive Pubns.

Loeffelbein, Robert L. The Recreation Handbook: Three-Hundred Forty-Two Games & Other Activities for Teams & Individuals. LC 92-50310. (Illus.). 255p. 1992. pap. 24.95x (*0-89950-744-1*) McFarland & Co.

Lopshire, Robert. ABC Games. Lopshire, Robert, illus. LC 85-47883. 64p. (ps-1). 1986. (Crowell Jr Bks) HarpC Child Bks.

Love, Marla. Twenty Decoding Games. (gr. 2-6). 1982. pap. 12.95 (*0-8224-5801-2*) Fearon Teach Aids.

—Twenty Word Structure Games. (gr. 2-6). 1983. pap. 12.95 (*0-8224-5802-0*) Fearon Teach Aids.

Love, Penelope & Morrison, Mark. Terror Australis: Cthulhu down Under. Willis, Lynn & Petersen, Sandy, eds. Sullivan, Tom & Leming, Ron, illus. 136p. (Orig.). (gr. 12 up). 1987. pap. 17.95 (*0-933635-40-0*, 2319) Chaosium.

McAlister, George A. & McLeod, Lloyd. Dominoes Texas Style. (Illus.). 164p. (Orig.). (gr. 9). 1977. pap. 5.95 (*0-924307-02-1*) Docutex Inc.

MacColl, Gail. The Book of Cards for Kids. LC 91-50962. (ps-3). 1992. pap. 10.95 (*1-56305-240-7*) Workman Pub.

McCoy, Elin. Cards for Kids: Games, Tricks & Amazing Facts. Huffman, Tom, illus. LC 91-11373. 160p. (gr. 1-7). 1991. SBE 13.95 (*0-02-765461-3*, Macmillan Child Bk) Macmillan Child Grp.

McKay, Sharon & MacLeod, David. Chalk Around the Block: A Somerville House Book. Mets, Marilyn, illus. LC 92-41495. 48p. 1993. incl. 5 pieces of sidewalk chalk 9.95 (*0-8362-4502-4*) Andrews & McMeel.

McKeage, Jeff. Hillmen of the Trollshaws. (Illus.). 36p. (gr. 10-12). 1984. pap. 7.00 (*0-915795-24-8*, 8040) Iron Crown Ent Inc.

Making Models & Games. LC 91-17039. (Illus.). 48p. (gr. 4-8). 1991. PLB 14.95 (*1-85435-409-4*) Marshall Cavendish.

Marchon-Arnaud, Catherine. A Gallery of Games. Schwartz, Marc, photos by. Collomb, Etienne. LC 93-25053. (Illus.). 60p. (gr. 3 up). 1994. 12.95 (*0-395-68379-3*) Ticknor & Flds Bks Yng Read.

Marsh, Carole. The Biltmore House Classroom Gamebook. (Illus., Orig.). (gr. 1-12). 1994. PLB 24.95 (*0-935326-83-9*) Gallopade Pub Group.

—The Lost Colony Classroom Gamebook. (Illus., Orig.). (gr. 3-12). 1994. pap. 19.95 (*0-935326-86-3*) Gallopade Pub Group.

—The Missing Head Mystery Classroom Gamebook. (Illus., Orig.). (gr. 3-6). 1994. pap. 19.95 (*0-935326-84-7*) Gallopade Pub Group.

Martin, Julia. Hellsgate. 64p. (Orig.). 1992. pap. 10.00 (*1-55878-097-1*) Game Designers.

—Rotten to the Core. Aulisio, Janet, illus. 64p. (Orig.). 1990. pap. 8.00 (*1-55878-059-9*) Game Designers.

Martin, Kathy. Party Shakers. Biancalana, Tim, illus. Martin, Kathy. LC 82-21729. (Illus.). 47p. (gr. k-8). 1982. pap. 3.95 (*0-942752-00-7*) C A M Co.

Marty, Sheree S. Chinese Jump Rope. LC 93-43812. (Illus.). 96p. 1994. pap. 3.95 (*0-8069-0352-X*) Sterling.

Mastodon. (Illus.). 8p. (gr. k-2). 1994. bds. write for info. (*1-56144-480-4*, Honey Bear Bks) Modern Pub NYC.

Maze Brain Twisters. (Illus.). 278p. 1991. pap. 2.99 (*0-517-02236-2*) Random Hse Value.

Megazord. (Illus.). 8p. (gr. k-2). 1994. bds. write for info. (*1-56144-477-4*, Honey Bear Bks) Modern Pub NYC.

Melton, Dana D. & Ledbetter, Frances M. Hooked on Games. Melton, Dana D., illus. 150p. (Orig.). (gr. k-6). 1989. pap. 9.95 (*0-685-29409-9*) Hooked Games.

Meyers, Carole T. Miles of Smiles: One Hundred One Great Car Games & Activities. (Illus.). 128p. (Orig.). 1992. pap. 8.95 (*0-917120-11-6*) Carousel Pr.

Miller, Marc W. ASW Forms. Venters, Steve, illus. 49p. (Orig.). 1990. pap. 8.00 (*1-55878-057-2*) Game Designers.

—Fighting Ships. Ellis, Kevin, illus. 96p. (Orig.). 1990. pap. 10.00 (*1-55878-050-5*) Game Designers.

—Sub Forms. Venters, Steve, illus. 49p. (Orig.). 1989. pap. 8.00 (*1-55878-019-X*) Game Designers.

Mills, Jane L. & Johnson, Larry D. Peek-a-Boo. Hebert, Kim T., illus. LC 86-60380. 13p. (Orig.). (ps). 1986. pap. 3.50 (*0-938155-04-0*); pap. 12.00 set of 3 bks. (*0-685-13530-6*) Read A Bol.

Mohr, Merilyn S. The Games Treasury: More Than Three Hundred Indoor & Outdoor Favorites with Strategies, Rules, & Traditions. Cooke, Roberta, illus. LC 93-3635. 352p. (Orig.). 1993. 29.95 (*1-881527-24-7*); pap. 19.95 (*1-881527-23-9*) Chapters Pub.

Monroe, John B., ed. Blood Brothers: B-Movie Monsters & Adventures. (Illus.). 128p. (Orig.). (gr. 12 up). 1990. pap. 18.95 (*0-933635-69-9*, 2329) Chaosium.

Nilsen, David. Ranger. Bostick, Angela, illus. 64p. (Orig.). 1989. pap. 8.00 (*1-55878-016-5*) Game Designers.

Novak, Greg. Over the Top. Doubet, Amy, illus. 120p. (Orig.). (gr. 9-12). 1990. pap. 12.00 (*1-55878-012-2*) Game Designers.

Nystul, Mike & Smith, Lester. Mechwarrior. 2nd ed. Ippolito, Donna & Mullvihill, Sharon T., eds. Venters, Steve & Knutson, Dana, illus. 167p. (Orig.). (gr. 7 up). 1991. pap. 15.00 (*1-55560-129-4*) FASA Corp.

Oakley, Ruth. Board & Card Games. LC 88-28710. (Illus.). 48p. (gr. 4-8). 1990. PLB 15.95 (*1-85435-082-X*) Marshall Cavendish.

—Chanting Games. LC 88-28774. (Illus.). 48p. (gr. 3-8). 1990. PLB 15.95 (*1-85435-080-3*) Marshall Cavendish.

—Games with Papers & Pencils. LC 88-28711. (Illus.). 48p. (gr. 3-8). 1989. PLB 15.95 (*1-85435-083-8*) Marshall Cavendish.

—Games with Sticks, Stones & Shells. LC 88-28773. (Illus.). 48p. (gr. 3-8). 1989. PLB 15.95 (*1-85435-079-X*) Marshall Cavendish.

Olney, Don. The Tops Discovery Kit. LC 93-87365. (Illus.). 64p. (gr. 3 up). 1994. incl. kit 17.95 (*1-56138-389-9*) Running Pr.

Owl Magazine Editors. My Summer Book. (Illus.). 64p. (gr. 3 up). 1992. pap. 8.95 (*0-920775-36-5*, Pub. by Greey dePencier CN) Firefly Bks Ltd.

—Nature What's It? Creatures, Plants, Nature's Oddities & More. (Illus.). 32p. (gr. 4 up). 1992. pap. 4.95 (*0-920775-38-1*, Pub. by Greey dePencier CN) Firefly Bks Ltd.

—Summer Fun. (Illus.). 128p. (gr. 4 up). 1992. pap. 8.95 (*0-919872-87-5*, Pub. by Greey dePencier CN) Firefly Bks Ltd.

—What's It? Gadgets, Objects, Machines & More. (Illus.). 32p. (gr. 3 up). 1992. pap. 4.95 (*0-920775-30-6*, Pub. by Greey dePencier CN) Firefly Bks Ltd.

Owl Magazine Editors & Chickadee Magazine Editors. Party Fun. (Illus.). 32p. (gr. 3 up). 1992. pap. 7.95 (*0-920775-41-1*, Pub. by Greey dePencier CN) Firefly Bks Ltd.

Pagnucci, Susan. Games to Cut. (Illus.). 20p. (Orig.). (gr. k-3). 1978. Incl. 5 reading & math games to make & use. 4.25 (*0-929326-03-2*) Bur Oak Pr Inc.

Pearson, Craig. Make Your Own Games Workshop. (gr. 3-8). 1982. pap. 10.95 (*0-8224-9782-4*) Fearon Teach Aids.

Peel, John. Where in America's Past Is Carmen Sandiego? Nez, John, illus. Vaccarello, Paul, contrib. by. (Illus.). 96p. (gr. 3-7). 1992. pap. 2.95 (*0-307-22205-5*, 22205, Golden Pr) Western Pub.

Perrin, Steve. Elfquest: The Official Roleplaying Game. 2nd ed. Chodak, Yurek, ed. Pini, Wendy & Schultz, Carolyn, illus. Pini, Richard, intro. by. 192p. (gr. 9 up). 1989. pap. 19.95 (*0-933635-54-0*, 2605) Chaosium.

Peterson, Steve & McDonald, George, eds. Enemies. Williams, Mark, illus. 24p. (gr. 10-12). 1986. pap. 6.00 (*0-915795-51-5*, 02) Iron Crown Ent Inc.

Phillips, Martin A. The Official National Table Hockey League Handbook, Vol. 1. Phillips, Zoe A., ed. Rullestad, Chris, illus. LC 89-91696. 66p. (Orig.). (gr. 12). 1989. write for info. (*0-9623588-0-0*); pap. write for info. (*0-9623588-1-9*) Gnu Wine Pr.

Pilurs, David B. Sun & Storm: The Codex. Caruso, Lenore & Caruso, Sara, eds. (Illus.). 96p. (gr. 7 up). 1993. pap. 12.95 perfect bound (*0-9636551-1-6*) Storm Pr.

—Sun & Storm: The Enchiridion. Caruso, Lenore R. & Caruso, Sara L., eds. (Illus.). 96p. (gr. 7 up). 1993. pap. 12.95 perfect bound (*0-9636551-0-8*) Storm Pr.

Pink Ranger. (Illus.). 8p. (gr. k-2). 1994. bds. write for info. (*1-56144-479-0*, Honey Bear Bks) Modern Pub NYC.

Pondsmith, Michael. Cyberpunk. Liu, Sam, et al, illus. Fisk, Colin, contrib. by. 98p. (gr. 10-12). 1988. game bk. 10.00 (*0-937279-05-6*, CP 3001) R Talsorian.

—Mekton II. 2nd ed. Bryant, Linda, et al, eds. Dunn, Benn, et al, illus. 93p. (gr. 7-12). 1987. game bk. 12.00 (*0-937279-04-8*, MK 1002) R Talsorian.

Potter, Beatrix. The Peter Rabbit Make-a-Mobile Book. 20p. 1991. pap. 5.95 (*0-7232-3764-6*) Warne.

Potter, T. Car Travel Games. (Illus.). 32p. (gr. 2 up). 1986. pap. 4.95 (*0-86020-926-1*) EDC.

Potter, T. & Butterfield, M. Travel Games. (Illus.). 64p. (gr. 2 up). 1986. pap. 7.95 (*0-86020-999-7*, Usborne) EDC.

Poynter, Margaret. Frisbee Fun. Poynter, Robert, illus. (gr. 3-6). 1978. (Archway); pap. 7.29 (*0-685-00479-1*) PB.

Price, Stern S. Spine-Tingling Puzzles & Games: Super Scary Activity Books. (Illus.). 48p. (Orig.). (gr. 3-5). 1993. pap. 2.95 (*0-8431-3622-7*) Price Stern.

Reid, Mary. Anytime Parties for Children. Arthur, Lorraine, illus. 80p. (gr. 1-5). 1987. wkbk. 5.99 (*0-87403-290-3*, 2802) Standard Pub.

Ripley, Catherine. Two Dozen Dinosaurs: A First Book of Dinosaur Facts & Mysteries, Games & Fun. Louie, Bo-Kim, illus. 32p. (gr. k up). 1992. pap. 7.95 (*0-920775-55-1*, Pub. by Greey dePencier CN) Firefly Bks Ltd.

Ripley Staff. Fun & Games. (Illus.). 48p. (gr. 3-6). 1991. 11.95 (*1-56065-062-1*) Capstone Pr.

Rita Repulsa's Revenge. (Illus.). 8p. (gr. k-2). 1994. bds. 4.95 (*1-56144-473-1*, Honey Bear Bks) Modern Pub NYC.

Robins, Deri & Buchanan, George. Santa's Sackful of Best Christmas Ideas. LC 92-41103. 32p. (gr. 2-6). 1993. pap. 5.95 (*1-85697-919-9*, Kingfisher LKC) LKC.

Robins, Deri, et al. The Kids Can Do It Book: Fun Things to Make and Do. Stowell, Charlotte, illus. LC 92-43345. 80p. (gr. k-4). 1993. pap. 9.95 (*1-85697-860-5*, Kingfisher LKC) LKC.

Robinson, Andrew M. The Gadgets! 48p. (gr. 10-12). 1986. pap. 8.00 (*0-915795-64-7*, 23) Iron Crown Ent Inc.

Rowen, Larry. Beyond Winning: Group Centered Games & Sports. (gr. 2-6). 1990. pap. 9.95 (*0-8224-3380-X*) Fearon Teach Aids.

Rowland, Marcus L. Canal Priests of Mars. Harris, Dell, illus. 64p. (Orig.). 1990. pap. 8.00 (*1-55878-039-4*) Game Designers.

Royer, Katherine. Nursery Happy Times Book. (Illus.). 48p. (ps). 1957. pap. 3.95x (*0-8361-1277-6*) Herald Pr.

Ruemmler, John D. Rangers of the North. (Illus.). 56p. (gr. 10-12). 1985. pap. 12.00 (*0-915795-22-1*, 3000) Iron Crown Ent Inc.

Runyan, Cathy C. Knuckles Down! A Fun Guide to Marble Play. 2nd ed. (Illus.). 36p. (gr. 1-6). 1990. pap. 4.95 (*0-935295-01-1*) Right Brain.

Saber Tooth Tiger. (Illus.). 8p. (gr. k-2). 1994. bds. write for info. (*1-56144-481-2*, Honey Bear Bks) Modern Pub NYC.

St. Andre, Ken & Perrin, Steve. Stormbringer: Fantasy Roleplaying in the World of Elric. 4th ed. Monroe, John B., ed. Whelan, Michael, et al, illus. 208p. (gr. 8 up). 1990. pap. 21.95 (*0-933635-66-4*, 2110) Chaosium.

Sargent, Carl. London Sourcebook. Ippolito, Donna & Mulvihill, Sharon T., eds. Biske, Joel & Nielson, Mike, illus. 152p. (gr. 7 up). 1991. pap. 15.00 (*1-55560-131-6*, 7203) FASA Corp.

Schick, Lawrence. Heroic Worlds: A History & Guide to Role-Playing Games. (Illus.). 448p. (Orig.). (gr. 6 up). 1991. 36.95 (*0-87975-652-7*); pap. 17.95 (*0-87975-653-5*) Prometheus Bks.
Schwartz, Linda. Fly & Find. (gr. 3 up). 1990. pap. 5.95 (*0-88160-194-2*, LW102) Learning Wks.
Search & Rescue Mission. (Illus.). 32p. (Orig.). (gr. 1-3). 1993. pap. 1.29 (*1-56144-345-X*, Honey Bear Bks) Modern Pub NYC.
Seddon, Sue & Gilgallon, Barbara. Family Matters: Travel Games. (Illus.). 96p. (gr. 2-10). 1993. pap. 4.95 (*0-7063-7093-7*, Pub. by Ward Lock UK) Sterling.
Shea, George. On the Road: Fun Travel Games & Activities. Sinclair, Jeff, illus. 48p. (gr. 3-10). 1992. pap. 4.95 (*0-8069-8228-4*) Sterling.
Sheeley, Craig. Special Operations. Wiseman, Loren K., ed. 104p. (Orig.). 1992. pap. 12.00 (*1-55878-108-0*) Game Designers.
Siegel, Mark, et al, eds. Gambling: Who Wins? 40p. 1992. pap. text ed. 11.95 (*1-878623-32-X*) Info Plus TX.
Siembieda, Kevin. Atlantis. Marciniszyn, Alex & Bartold, Thomas, eds. Long, Kevin & Parkinson, Keith, illus. 160p. (Orig.). (gr. 8 up). 1992. pap. 15.95 (*0-916211-54-1*, 804) Palladium Bks.
—Rifts Conversion Book. Marciniszyn, Alex & Bartold, Thomas, eds. Long, Kevin, et al, illus. 224p. (Orig.). (gr. 8 up). 1991. pap. 19.95 (*0-916211-53-3*, 803) Palladium Bks.
—Rifts Role-Playing Game. Marciniszyn, Alex & Bartold, Thomas, eds. Long, Kevin & Parkinson, Keith, illus. 256p. (Orig.). (gr. 8 up). 1990. pap. 24.95 (*0-916211-50-9*, 800) Palladium Bks.
—Rifts Sourcebook. Marciniszyn, Alex & Bartold, Thomas, eds. Long, Kevin, illus. 120p. (Orig.). (gr. 8 up). 1991. pap. 11.95 (*0-916211-51-7*, 801) Palladium Bks.
—The Vampire Kingdoms. Marciniszyn, Alex & Bartold, Thomas, eds. Long, Kevin, illus. 176p. (Orig.). (gr. 8 up). 1991. pap. 15.95 (*0-916211-52-5*, 802) Palladium Bks.
Siembieda, Kevin & Long, Kevin. Boxed Nightmares. Marciniszyn, Alex & Bartold, Thomas, eds. Long, Kevin & Beauvais, Denis, illus. 80p. (Orig.). (gr. 8 up). 1990. pap. 11.95 (*0-916211-41-X*, 701) Palladium Bks.
—Villains Unlimited. Marciniszyn, Alex & Bartold, Thomas, eds. Gustovich, Mike & Steranko, James, illus. 200p. (Orig.). (gr. 8 up). 1992. pap. 19.95 (*0-916211-49-5*, 501) Palladium Bks.
Smith, J. C. & McLean, J. Kidworks Series, No. 1. Horine, Billie & Seitz, Connie, illus. (ps-5). 1993. Set. PLB 32.65g (*1-882627-17-2*) KTS Pub.
Smith, Lester. Dark Conspiracy. 336p. (Orig.). 1991. pap. 22.00 (*1-55878-076-9*) Game Designers.
—Dark Races, Vol. 1. 104p. (Orig.). 1992. pap. 12.00 (*1-55878-105-6*) Game Designers.
—Proto-Dimensions, Vol. 1. 104p. (Orig.). 1992. pap. 12. 00 (*1-55878-114-5*) Game Designers.
Smith, Lester W. Beastman of Mars. Aulisio, Janet, illus. 64p. (Orig.). 1989. pap. 8.00 (*1-55878-022-X*) Game Designers.
—Deathwatch Program. Aulisio, Janet, illus. 64p. (Orig.). 1990. pap. 8.00 (*1-55878-051-3*) Game Designers.
Sochard, Ruth. Dagorlad & the Dead Marshes. (Illus.). 36p. (gr. 10-12). 1984. pap. 7.00 (*0-915795-20-5*, 8020) Iron Crown Ent Inc.
—Pirates of Pelargir. Fenlon, Peter, ed. McBride, Angus, illus. 32p. (Orig.). (gr. 10-12). 1987. pap. 6.00 (*0-915795-44-2*, 8104) Iron Crown Ent Inc.
Space Aliens Attack. (Illus.). 8p. (gr. k-2). 1994. bds. 4.95 (*1-56144-474-X*, Honey Bear Bks) Modern Pub NYC.
Sperling, Anita, et al. Funny Faces Tracing Fun. Wildman, George, illus. 24p. (gr. k-3). 1987. pap. 1.95 (*0-590-40889-5*) Scholastic Inc.
Spivak, Darlene. Sequence Fun. Wright, Theresa, illus. 32p. (gr. k-2). 1988. wkbk. 5.95 (*1-55734-121-4*) Tchr Create Mat.
Stackpole, Michael A. Evil Ascending. 320p. (Orig.). 1991. pap. 4.95 (*1-55878-099-8*) Game Designers.
—Evil Triumphant. 352p. (Orig.). 1992. pap. 4.95 (*1-55878-119-6*) Game Designers.
—A Gathering Evil. 328p. (Orig.). 1992. pap. 4.95 (*1-55878-092-0*) Game Designers.
Stafford, Greg. Prince Valiant: The Storytelling Game. Dunn, Bill & Willis, Lynn, eds. Foster, Hal, illus. 128p. (Orig.). (gr. 6 up). 1989. pap. 19.95 (*0-933635-50-8*, 2801) Chaosium.
Stafford, Greg & Dunn, Bill. Pendragon: Roleplaying in King Arthur's Britain. 3rd ed. Krinard, Sue, et al, illus. 208p. (gr. 9 up). 1990. pap. 21.95 (*0-933635-59-1*, 2) Chaosium.
Staplehurst, Graham. Robin Hood. Fenlon, Peter & Charlton, S. Coleman, eds. McBride, Angus, illus. 160p. (Orig.). (gr. 10-12). 1987. pap. 15.00 (*0-915795-28-0*, 1010) Iron Crown Ent Inc.
Steig, William. C D C? (Illus.). 64p. (gr. 3 up). 1986. pap. 3.95 (*0-374-41024-0*, Sunburst) FS&G.
Sterling, Mary E. Clothespin Games. Vasconcelles, Keith, illus. 28p. (ps-k). 1989. wkbk 7.95 (*1-55734-172-9*) Tchr Create Mat.
—File Folder Games. Vasconcelles, Keith, illus. 28p. (ps-k). 1989. wkbk 7.95 (*1-55734-171-0*) Tchr Create Mat.
—Synonym-Antonym-Homonym Word Games. Spence, Paula, illus. 48p. (gr. 2-5). 1988. wkbk. 6.95 (*1-55734-368-3*) Tchr Create Mat.
—Wheel Games. Vasconcelles, Keith, illus. 28p. (ps-k). 1989. wkbk 7.95 (*1-55734-170-2*) Tchr Create Mat.
Stevenson, James. Quick! Turn the Page! LC 89-34616. (Illus.). 32p. (ps up). 1990. 12.95 (*0-688-09308-6*); PLB 12.88 (*0-688-09309-4*) Greenwillow.
Stuart, Sally E. & Young, Woody. One-Hundred Plus Party Games. Dongarra, Kathryn, ed. White, Craig, illus. 96p. (Orig.). 1988. pap. text ed. 7.95 (*0-939513-61-7*) Joy Pub SJC.
Super Blockbusters Brain Builders. (Illus.). 278p. 1991. pap. 2.99 (*0-517-02242-7*) Random Hse Value.
Swerdlick, Harriet & Reiter, Edith. President Games: Puzzles, Quizzes, & Mind Teasers for Every George, Abe, & Lyndon! 48p. (Orig.). (gr. 3 up). 1988. pap. 2.95 incl. chipboard (*0-8431-2240-4*) Putnam Pub Group.
Taylor, Kevin. Fifty Nifty Travel Games. Yamamoto, Neal, illus. 64p. (gr. 3-7). 1994. pap. 4.95 (*1-56565-108-1*) Lowell Hse.
Theisen, John A. Steppelords of Mars. Harris, Dell, illus. 64p. (Orig.). 1989. pap. 8.00 (*1-55878-025-4*) Game Designers.
Thieme, Jeanne & Hansen, Robyn. The American Girls Games: Three Antique American Games That Kirsten, Samantha, & Molly Played. (Illus.). 32p. (Orig.). (gr. 2-5). 1989. pap. 17.95 (*0-937295-61-2*) Pleasant Co.
Tiner, John H. Acts Word Puzzles. (Illus.). 48p. 1986. pap. 2.95 (*1-56794-040-4*, C2300) Star Bible.
Toys & Games. (ARA., Illus.). (gr. 4-6). 1987. 3.95x (*0-86685-241-7*) Intl Bk Ctr.
Trapani, Iza. What Am I? An Animal Guessing Game. Trapani, Iza, illus. LC 92-15029. 32p. (ps-3). 1992. smythe sewn reinforced 13.95 (*1-879085-76-3*) Whsprng Coyote Pr.
Trent, Linda M. Games That Make Homework Fun! 80p. (Orig.). (gr. 2-8). 1991. pap. 9.95 (*0-9630470-2-7*) For-Kids.
Tyrannosaurus. (Illus.). 8p. (gr. k-2). 1994. bds. write for info. (*1-56144-482-0*, Honey Bear Bks) Modern Pub NYC.
Van der Meer, Ron. The World's First Ever Pop-Up Games Book. Van der Meer, Ron, illus. 8p. (gr. k-3). 1982. 9.95 (*0-440-06943-2*) Delacorte.
Vecchione, Glen. World's Best Outdoor Games. LC 92-19101. (Illus.). 128p. (gr. 6 up). 1992. 12.95 (*0-8069-8436-8*) Sterling.
—World's Best Outdoor Games. (Illus.). 128p. (gr. 3-10). 1993. pap. 4.95 (*0-8069-8437-6*) Sterling.
Verstraete, Elaine, illus. Games to Play. 32p. (ps-3). 1990. 4.95 (*1-56288-051-9*) Checkerboard.
Wallis, James & Siembieda, Kevin. Mutants in Avalon. Marciniszyn, Alex & Bartold, Thomas, eds. Fales, Kevin & MacDougall, Larry, illus. 80p. (Orig.). (gr. 8 up). 1991. pap. 9.95 (*0-916211-47-9*, 513) Palladium Bks.
Warren, Jean. Learning Games. 80p. (gr. k-2). 1983. 7.95 (*0-912107-06-5*) Monday Morning Bks.
Webb, Phila H. & Corby, Jane. Little Book of Hand Shadows. LC 90-52549. (Illus.). 80p. (gr. 1 up). 1990. 4.95 (*0-89471-852-5*) Running Pr.
Weiss, Ann E. Lotteries: Who Wins, Who Loses? LC 90-26525. 112p. (gr. 6 up). 1991. lib. bdg. 17.95 (*0-89490-242-3*) Enslow Pubs.
Wergin, Joseph P. Cribbage for Kids. Gansen, Ed, illus. Corvi, Becky S., intro. by. LC 90-82436. (Illus.). 116p. (Orig.). (gr. 4-6). 1990. pap. 12.50 (*0-9627003-0-4*); Deluxe gift set. 25.00 (*0-685-58857-2*) Intl Gamester.
Wergin, Joseph P. & Smith, Beatrice S. Poker for Kids & Everyone Else. Grube, Karl W., intro. by. 124p. 1992. pap. 10.00 (*0-685-60627-9*); tchr's. ed. 20.00 (*0-685-60628-7*) Intl Gamester.
Willner, Carl. Goblin-Gate & Eagle's Eyrie. (Illus.). 32p. (gr. 10-12). 1985. pap. 7.00 (*0-915795-40-X*, 8070) Iron Crown Ent Inc.
—Havens of Gondor, Land of Belfalas. Fenlon, Peter, ed. McBride, Angus, illus. 64p. (Orig.). (gr. 10-12). 1987. pap. 12.00 (*0-915795-25-6*, 3300) Iron Crown Ent Inc.
—Tower of Cirith Ungol & Shelob's Lair. (Illus.). 32p. (gr. 10-12). 1984. pap. 7.00 (*0-915795-21-3*, 8030) Iron Crown Ent Inc.
Wiseman, Loren K. American Combat Vehicle Handbook. Farley, A. C., illus. 104p. (Orig.). (gr. 9-12). 1990. pap. 12.00 (*1-55878-061-0*) Game Designers.
—Bangkok. 104p. (Orig.). 1991. pap. 12.00 (*1-55878-074-2*) Game Designers.
—Gazetteer. 64p. (Orig.). 1991. pap. 14.00 (*1-55878-078-5*) Game Designers.
—Heavy Weapons Handbook. Atlas, Nick, ed. 104p. (Orig.). 1992. pap. 12.00 (*1-55878-100-5*) Game Designers.
—Infantry Weapons of the World. Venters, Steve, illus. 104p. (Orig.). (gr. 9-12). 1991. pap. 12.00 (*1-55878-068-8*) Game Designers.
—Merc: Two Thousand. Larkin, Bob, illus. 120p. (Orig.). (gr. 9-12). 1990. pap. 16.00 (*1-55878-072-6*) Game Designers.
—More Tales from the Ether. Aulisio, Janet, illus. 64p. (Orig.). 1989. pap. 8.00 (*1-55878-028-9*) Game Designers.
—NATO Combat Vehicle Handbook. 104p. (Orig.). 1991. pap. 12.00 (*1-55878-077-7*) Game Designers.
—Nautical - Aviation Handbook. 104p. (Orig.). 1991. pap. 12.00 (*1-55878-088-2*) Game Designers.
—Soviet Combat Vehicle Handbook. Venters, Steve, illus. 104p. (Orig.). (gr. 9-12). 1990. pap. 12.00 (*1-55878-067-X*) Game Designers.
—Twilight Nightmares. 104p. (Orig.). 1991. pap. 12.00 (*1-55878-095-5*) Game Designers.
Wujcik, Erick. Mutants of the Yucatan. Marciniszyn, Alex, ed. Fales, Kevin & Dombrowski, James, illus. 48p. (Orig.). (gr. 8 up). 1990. pap. 7.95 (*0-916211-44-4*, 511) Palladium Bks.
Wujcik, Erick & Siembieda, Kevin. TMNT RPG Accessory Pack: Adventures in the Yucatan. Marciniszyn, Alex, ed. Dombrowski, James, illus. 24p. (Orig.). (gr. 8 up). 1990. pap. 11.95 (*0-916211-45-2*, 512) Palladium Bks.

GAMES–FICTION

Buller, Jon & Schade, Susan. The Video Kids. Buller, Jon & Schade, Susan, illus. LC 93-26923. 48p. (gr. 2-3). 1994. 7.99 (*0-448-40181-9*, G&D); pap. 3.50 (*0-448-40180-0*, G&D) Putnam Pub Group.
Cadnum, Michael. Breaking the Fall. LC 92-5829. 160p. (gr. 7 up). 1992. 15.00 (*0-670-84687-2*) Viking Child Bks.
Capote, Truman. Jug of Silver. Hoys, James, illus. LC 86-4230. 48p. (gr. 4 up). 1986. PLB 13.95 (*0-88682-076-6*) Creative Ed.
Chisholm, Sarah. My Christmas Star: A Hide & Seek Story. (ps). 1993. pap. 5.99 (*0-8066-2600-3*) Augsburg Fortress.
Cooke, Tom, illus. Hide-&-Seek with Big Bird: A Sesame Street Book. LC 89-64284. 14p. (ps). 1991. bds. 3.99 (*0-679-80785-3*) Random Bks Yng Read.
Cooney, Caroline B. Freeze Tag. 1992. 3.25 (*0-590-45681-4*, Point) Scholastic Inc.
Crutcher, Chris. The Crazy Horse Electric Game. (gr. k-12). 1988. pap. 3.99 (*0-440-20094-6*) Dell.
De Saint Mars, Dominique. Max Is Crazy about Video Games. Bloch, Serge, illus. LC 93-10987. (gr. 2-4). Date not set. 8.95 (*1-56766-102-5*) Childs World.
Dijs, Carla & Moerbeek, Kees. Hiding Places. (gr. 4 up). 1990. 9.95 (*0-85953-223-2*) Childs Play.
Dodds, Dayle Ann. Someone Is Hiding. 1994. PLB 8.95 (*0-671-75542-0*, Little Simon) S&S Trade.
Donaldson, Joan. The Real Pretend. Tudor, Tash, illus. 32p. (ps-3). 1992. 12.95 (*1-56288-158-2*) Checkerboard.
Frye, Tom. Scratchin' on the Eight Ball. 234p. 1994. 9.95 (*0-685-71640-6*, 787) W Gladden Found.
Hiller, B. B. Bingo Digest. 132p. 1991. pap. 2.75 (*0-590-45276-2*) Scholastic Inc.
Hoffman, Joan. The Last Game. (Illus.). 32p. (gr. k-2). 1992. pap. 3.95 (*0-88743-429-0*, 06081) Sch Zone Pub Co.
—The Last Game. (Illus.). 16p. (gr. k-2). 1992. pap. 2.25 (*0-88743-268-9*, 06035) Sch Zone Pub Co.
Hutchins, Pat. What Game Shall We Play? LC 89-34621. (Illus.). 24p. (ps up). 1990. 12.95 (*0-688-09196-2*); PLB 12.88 (*0-688-09197-0*) Greenwillow.
Jarrow, Gail. Beyond the Magic Sphere. LC 94-6884. (gr. 3-7). 1994. 15.95 (*0-15-200193-X*) HarBrace.
Justus. Jumping Jack. LC 73-87803. (Illus.). 32p. (gr. k-3). 1974. PLB 9.95 (*0-87783-123-8*); pap. 3.94 deluxe ed. (*0-87783-124-6*); cassette o.s.i. 7.94x (*0-87783-189-0*) Oddo.
Kay, Gene. Speedy O'Hare's Sun Valley Race. Kay, Gene, illus. 36p. (ps-7). 1987. pap. 8.95 (*0-945222-24-6*) Gazelle Prodns.
Kehne, Carroll. Tug of War. (gr. 4-7). 1994. 12.95 (*0-86316-216-9*) Writers & Readers.
Kendall, Carol. The Gammage Cup. (gr. 3 up). 1992. 17. 25 (*0-8446-6564-9*) Peter Smith.
Kessler, Leonard. Big Mile Race. (gr. 4-7). 1991. pap. 2.95 (*0-440-40413-4*) Dell.
Kusugak, Michael. Hide-&-Sneak. Krykorka, Vladyana, illus. 32p. (ps-3). 1992. PLB 14.95 (*1-55037-229-7*, Pub. by Annick CN); pap. 4.95 (*1-55037-228-9*, Pub. by Annick CN) Firefly Bks Ltd.
Leonard, Calista V. Guess Who. 36p. (ps-6). 1992. PLB write for info. (*0-9634165-0-2*) Vistoso Bks.
Locke, Joseph. Game Over. 1993. pap. 3.50 (*0-553-29652-3*) Bantam.
McCarthy, Bobette. Happy Hiding Hippos. McCarthy, Bobette, illus. LC 92-32599. 32p. (ps-1). 1994. RSBE 13.95 (*0-02-765446-X*, Bradbury Pr) Macmillan Child Grp.
Marney, Dean. Dirty Socks Don't Win Games. 128p. (gr. 3-7). 1992. pap. 2.95 (*0-590-44880-3*, Apple Paperbacks) Scholastic Inc.
Milios, Rita. Donde Esta Pedro? Sneaky Pete. Martin, Clovis, illus. LC 89-34666. (SPA.). 32p. (ps-2). 1991. PLB 10.25 (*0-516-32092-0*); pap. 2.95 (*0-516-52092-X*) Childrens.
Petty, Kate. Playing the Game. Firmin, Charlotte, illus. 24p. (ps-2). 1991. pap. 4.95 (*0-8120-4659-5*) Barron.
Reinsma, Carol. The Picnic Caper. Cori, Nathan, illus. LC 93-29567. 48p. (Orig.). (gr. k-3). 1994. pap. 3.99 (*0-7847-0006-0*, 24-03956) Standard Pub.
Rocklin, Joanne. Musical Chairs & Dancing Bears. De Matharel, Laure, illus. LC 92-41078. 32p. (ps-2). 1993. write for info. (*0-8050-2374-7*, Bks Young Read) H Holt & Co.
Rodda, Emily. Finders Keepers. LC 90-47850. (Illus.). (gr. 5 up). 1991. 13.95 (*0-688-10516-5*) Greenwillow.
Rose, Agatha. Hide-&-Seek in the Yellow House. Spohn, Kate, illus. 32p. (ps-1). 1992. PLB 14.00 (*0-670-84383-0*) Viking Child Bks.
Russo, Marisabina. Where Is Ben? LC 92-8627. (gr. 4 up). 1992. Repr. of 1990 ed. 4.50 (*0-14-054474-7*) Puffin Bks.
Salem, Lynn & Stewart, Josie. It's Game Day! (Illus.). 8p. (gr. 1). 1992. pap. 3.50 (*1-880612-02-X*) Seedling Pubns.

Stevenson, James. The Mud Flat Olympics. LC 93-28118. 56p. 1994. 15.00 (*0-688-12923-4*); PLB 14.93 (*0-688-12924-2*) Greenwillow.
Stiles, Norman & Berger, Lou. Elmo Goes Around the Corner - on Sesame Street. Mathieu, Joe, illus. LC 93-39056. 32p. (Orig.). (ps-3). 1994. pap. 2.50 (*0-679-85455-X*) Random Bks Yng Read.
Stine, Bob. Pork & Beans: Play Date. Aruego, Jose & Dewey, Ariane, illus. (ps-2). 1989. pap. 12.95 (*0-590-41579-4*) Scholastic Inc.
Ure, Jean. You Win Some, You Lose Some. (gr. k-12). 1988. pap. 2.95 (*0-440-99845-X*, LFL) Dell.
Wain, John. The Free Zone Starts Here. LC 83-14373. 196p. (gr. 7 up). 1984. 13.95 (*0-385-29315-1*) Delacorte.
Weyn, Suzanne. Full House: That's the Way It Crumbles, Cookie. (gr. 4-7). 1994. pap. 2.95 (*0-8167-3220-5*) Troll Assocs.
Wood, Don. Piggies. 28p. (ps-1). 1991. 13.95 (*0-15-256341-5*) HarBrace.

GAMES, OLYMPIC
see Olympic Games

GANDHI, INDIRA, 1917-
Fishlock, Trevor. Indira Gandhi. (Illus.). 64p. (gr. 5-9). 1991. 11.95 (*0-237-60025-0*, Pub. by Evans Bros Ltd) Trafalgar.

GANDHI, MOHANDAS KARAMCHAND, 1869-1948
Bains, Rae. Gandhi, Peaceful Warrior. Snow, Scott, illus. LC 89-5101. 48p. (gr. 4-6). 1990. lib. bdg. 10.79 (*0-8167-1767-2*); pap. text ed. 3.50 (*0-8167-1768-0*) Troll Assocs.
Clarke, Brenda. Gandhi. (Illus.). 32p. (gr. 3-8). 1988. PLB 10.95 (*0-86307-926-1*) Marshall Cavendish.
Faber, Doris & Faber, Harold. Mahatma Gandhi. LC 86-8734. (Illus.). 128p. (gr. 5 up). 1986. lib. bdg. 10.98 (*0-671-60176-8*, J Messner) S&S Trade.
Fischer, Louis. Gandhi: His Life & Message for the World. 192p. (gr. 9-12). 1982. pap. 4.50 (*0-451-62742-3*, Ment) NAL-Dutton.
Freitas, F. Bapu. Freitas, F., illus. (gr. 1-9). 1979. Pt. I. pap. 2.50 (*0-89744-173-7*); Pt. II. pap. 2.50 (*0-89744-174-5*) Auromere.
Gandhi, Mahatma. Mahatma Gandhi. Redpath, Ann, ed. Delessert, Etienne, illus. 32p. (gr. 4 up). 1985. PLB 12.95 (*0-88682-010-3*) Creative Ed.
Joshi, Uma. Stories from Bapu's Life. Patel, Mickey, illus. (gr. 1-9). 1979. pap. 2.50 (*0-89744-180-X*) Auromere.
Lazo, Caroline. Mahatma Gandhi. LC 92-14314. (Illus.). 64p. (gr. 4 up). 1993. text ed. 13.95 RSBE (*0-87518-526-6*, Dillon) Macmillan Child Grp.
Nicholoson, Michael. Mahatma Gandhi: Champion of Human Rights. Birch, Beverley, adapted by. LC 89-77589. (Illus.). 64p. (gr. 3-4). 1990. PLB 19.93 (*0-8368-0390-6*) Gareth Stevens Inc.
Rawding, F. W. Gandhi. LC 79-11008. (Illus.). 48p. (gr. 7 up). 1980. pap. 7.95 (*0-521-20715-0*) Cambridge U Pr.
Shankar, R. Story of Gandhi. (Illus.). 52p. (gr. 3-10). 1979. 5.00 (*0-89744-166-4*) Auromere.
Sherrow, Victoria. Mohandas Gandhi: The Power of the Spirit. (Illus.). 160p. (gr. 7 up). 1994. 15.90 (*1-56294-335-9*) Millbrook Pr.

GANGES RIVER
Cumming, David. The Ganges. LC 93-11987. (Illus.). 48p. (gr. 5-6). 1993. PLB 22.80 (*0-8114-3105-3*) Raintree Steck-V.

GANGS
see Crime and Criminals; Juvenile Delinquency

GANGS–FICTION
Allen, Stephen D. Reality: Drugs & Guns--No-Win Solutions. LC 92-64322. 126p. (gr. k-8). 1992. pap. 14.95 (*0-9634084-7-X*) S D A Pub.
Bannon, Troy. Mean Street. 1992. pap. 2.99 (*0-440-40588-2*, YB) Dell.
Bunting, Eve. Someone Is Hiding on Alcatraz Island. LC 84-5019. 144p. (gr. 5-8). 1984. 13.45 (*0-89919-219-X*, Clarion Bks) HM.
Collington, Peter. The Coming of the Surfman. Collington, Peter, illus. LC 92-41844. 32p. (gr. 3 up). 1994. 16.00 (*0-679-84721-9*) Knopf Bks Yng Read.
Cooper, Susan L. Dawn of Fear. Gill, Margery, illus. LC 71-115755. 157p. (gr. 5 up). 1988. 14.95 (*0-15-266201-4*, HB Juv Bks) HarBrace.
Crowley, Michael. Shack & Back. (ps-3). 1993. 14.95 (*0-316-16231-0*) Little.
Gould, Marilyn. Graffiti Wipeout. LC 91-90783. 112p. (gr. 5 up). 1992. pap. 6.95 (*0-9632305-0-6*) Allied Crafts.
Hinton, Susie E. Rumble Fish. LC 75-8004. 112p. (gr. 7 up). 1975. pap. 13.95 (*0-385-28675-9*) Delacorte.
Hutchens, Paul. On the Mexican Border. (gr. 2-7). 1968. pap. 4.99 (*0-8024-4818-6*) Moody.
—Sugar Creek Gang & the Cemetery Vandals. 128p. (gr. 3-7). 1972. pap. 4.99 (*0-8024-4829-1*) Moody.
Peck, Richard. Bel-Air Bambi & the Mall Rats. LC 92-29377. 1993. 15.95 (*0-385-30823-X*) Delacorte.
—Secrets of the Shopping Mall. 192p. (gr. k-6). 1989. pap. 3.99 (*0-440-40270-0*, LFL); pap. 3.99 (*0-440-98099-2*) Dell.
Spinelli, Jerry. Bathwater Gang. (gr. 4-7). 1990. 10.95 (*0-316-80720-6*) Little.
—The Bathwater Gang. Johnson, Meredith, illus. 64p. (gr. 2-4). 1992. pap. 3.95 (*0-316-80779-6*) Little.
—Bathwater Gang Gets down to Business. (ps-3). 1992. 12.95 (*0-316-80808-3*) Little.
Tanya Tinker & the Gizmo Gang: A Lift-the-Flap Book about How Things Work. LC 92-20859. 1992. write for info. (*0-8094-9315-2*); PLB write for info. (*0-8094-9316-0*) Time-Life.
Turner, Ann. Street Talk. (gr. 4-7). 1992. pap. 3.80 (*0-395-61625-5*) HM.
Wright, Richard. Rite of Passage. Rampersad, Arnold, afterword by. LC 93-2473. 128p. (gr. 7 up). 1994. 12.95 (*0-06-023419-9*); PLB 12.89 (*0-06-023420-2*) HarpC Child Bks.

GARAGES–FICTION
Myers, Laurie. Garage Sale Fever. Howell, Kathleen C., illus. LC 92-40342. 80p. (gr. 2-5). 1993. 13.00 (*0-06-022905-5*); PLB 12.89 (*0-06-022908-X*) HarpC.

GARBAGE
see Refuse and Refuse Disposal

GARDEN PESTS
see Insects, Injurious and Beneficial

GARDENING
Use for practical works on the cultivation of flowers, fruits, lawns, vegetables, etc.
see also Fruit Culture; Insects, Injurious and Beneficial; Organiculture; Plants; Plants, Cultivated; Vegetable Gardening; Weeds
Bigge, Tanya. Gardening Projects for Children. 1992. pap. 10.95 (*1-878767-31-3*) Murdoch Bks.
Birch, Beverley. Our Hidden Garden. (Illus.). 26p. (gr. 2-4). 1991. 12.95 (*0-237-60147-8*, Pub. by Evans Bros Ltd) Trafalgar.
Brown, Marc T. Your First Garden Book. Brown, Marc T., illus. (gr. 1 up). 1981. 12.45i (*0-316-11217-8*, Pub. by Atlantic Pr); pap. 6.95 (*0-316-11215-1*) Little.
Conteh-Morgan, Jane. My Garden. LC 94-10591. (Illus.). (gr. 1 up). 1995. write for info. (*0-553-09731-8*, Little Rooster) Bantam.
Creasy, Rosalind. Blue Potatoes, Orange Tomatoes: How to Grow a Rainbow Garden. Heller, Ruth, illus. LC 92-38800. 48p. (gr. 2-6). 1994. 15.95 (*0-87156-576-5*) Sierra.
Davenport, Zoe. Gardens. Davenport, Zoe, illus. 16p. (ps). 1995. 4.95 (*0-685-72231-7*) Ticknor & Flds Bks Yng Read.
—Gardens. LC 94-21456. (gr. 1-8). 1995. 4.95 (*0-395-71538-5*) Ticknor & Flds Bks Yng Read.
Fryer, Lee & Bradford, Leigh. A Child's Organic Garden. 88p. 1990. pap. 39.00x (*0-86439-097-1*, Pub. by Boolarong Pubns AT) St Mut.
Gaynor, Brigid. Backyard Attractions. Rollins, Nancy O., illus. (ps). 1993. Gift box set of 4 bks., 12p. ea. incl. seed packs. bds. 14.95 (*1-56828-043-2*) Red Jacket Pr.
Goldenberg, Janet. Weird Things You Can Grow. Gloeckner, Phoebe, illus. LC 93-43146. 48p. (Orig.). (gr. 3-7). 1994. pap. 10.00 (*0-679-85298-0*) Random Bks Yng Read.
Grow Lab: A Complete Guide to Gardening in the Classroom. LC 87-90726. 127p. (ps-8). 1988. pap. 19.95 (*0-915873-31-1*) Natl Gardening Assn.
Hershey, Rebecca. Ready, Set, Grow! A Kid's Guide to Gardening. 104p. (Orig.). (ps-6). 1995. pap. 13.95 (*0-673-36139-X*) GdYrBks.
Holstead, Christy & Linder, Pamela. Learn about Growing Friendships with Little Bud. rev. ed. Arlt, Bob, illus. (ps-3). 1993. activity bk. 3.98 (*1-881037-00-2*) McGreen Wisdom.
Huber, Judy. Gardening & Cooking with Children. 60p. (gr. 1-8). 1987. plastic comb. 4.95 (*0-944793-00-2*); pap. 2.95 (*0-944793-01-0*) Prairie Family Pubs.
Huff, Barbara A. Greening the City Streets: The Story of Community Gardens. Ziebel, Peter, photos by. (Illus.). 80p. (gr. 3-7). 1990. 15.45 (*0-89919-741-8*, Clarion Bks) HM.
Ideas from Nature. LC 91-17041. (Illus.). 48p. 1991. PLB 14.95 (*1-85435-410-8*) Marshall Cavendish.
Krementz, Jill. A Very Young Gardener. Krementz, Jill, photos by. LC 90-2766. (Illus.). 40p. (ps-3). 1991. 13.95 (*0-8037-0874-2*) Dial Bks Young.
Lopez, Ruth K. A Child's Garden Diary: Coloring & Activity Book. Lopez, Ruth K., illus. 56p. (Orig.). (gr. k-6). 1992. pap. 5.95 (*0-9627463-4-7*) Gardens Growing People.
McCann, Sean. Growing Things. LC 89-51018. 138p. (Orig.). 1989. pap. 5.95 (*1-85371-029-6*, Pub. by Poolbeg Press Ltd Eire) Dufour.
Maris, Ron. In My Garden. LC 87-8773. (Illus.). 32p. (ps-1). 1988. Repr. of 1987 ed. 13.00 (*0-688-07631-9*) Greenwillow.
Markmann, Erika. Grow It! An Indoor - Outdoor Gardening Guide for Kids. Konemund, Gisela, illus. LC 90-45043. 48p. (gr. 2-7). 1991. PLB 11.99 (*0-679-91528-1*); pap. 6.95 (*0-679-81528-7*) Random Bks Yng Read.
Morris, Ting & Morris, Neil. Growing Things. (Illus.). 32p. (gr. 2-4). 1994. PLB 12.40 (*0-531-14284-1*) Watts.
My Secret Garden Diary. (gr. 4-7). 1993. pap. 2.95 (*0-8167-3111-X*) Troll Assocs.
National Trust Staff. Investigating Gardens. (Illus.). 32p. (gr. 5-8). 1993. pap. 6.95 (*0-7078-0146-X*, Pub. by Natl Trust UK) Trafalgar.
NK Lawn & Garden Co. Staff. My First Garden Book. (Illus.). 80p. (Orig.). 1992. pap. 6.95 (*0-380-76667-1*) Avon.
Parkinson, Cornelia M. Alex Livingston, the Tomato Man. (Illus.). 20p. (gr. 4 up). 1985. pap. 1.50 (*0-938404-05-9*, AWL) Hist Tales.
Porter, Wes. The Garden Book & Greenhouse. LC 89-40372. (Illus.). 64p. (Orig.). (gr. k-5). 1992. Packaged in greenhouse with seed packets & peat pellets. pap. 10.95 (*0-89480-346-8*, 1346) Workman Pub.
Raferty, Kim G. & Raftery, Kevin. Kids Gardening: A Kid's Guide to Messing Around in the Dirt. M'Guinness, Jim, illus. 84p. (Orig.). 1989. pap. 12.95 incl. several varieties of seeds (*0-932592-25-2*) Klutz Pr.
Rangecroft, Derek. My First Garden Grows Nasturtiums. (ps-3). 1993. pap. 4.99 (*0-440-40834-2*) Dell.
—My First Garden Grows Pumpkins. (ps-3). 1993. pap. 4.99 (*0-440-40831-8*) Dell.
—My First Garden Grows Sunflowers. (ps-3). 1993. pap. 4.99 (*0-440-40837-7*) Dell.
—My First Garden Grows Tomatoes. (ps-3). 1993. pap. 4.99 (*0-440-40828-8*) Dell.
Rapp, Joel. Let's Get Growing: Twenty-Five Quick & Easy Gardening Projects for Kids. 1992. pap. 7.00 (*0-517-58880-3*, Crown) Crown Pub Group.
Robson, Denny A. Grow It for Fun: Hands-on Projects. LC 91-2737. (Illus.). 32p. (gr. k-4). 1991. PLB 11.90 (*0-531-17343-7*, Gloucester Pr) Watts.
Sanchez, Isidro & Peris, Carme. The Garden. (Illus.). 32p. (ps). 1991. pap. 5.95 (*0-8120-4708-7*) Barron.
Schnatz, Grace. A Child's Introduction to a Garden. Schnatz, Grace, illus. 33p. (gr. 4-8). 1984. PLB 4.75 (*0-9614145-0-2*) G Schnatz Pubns.
Stagg, Mildred A. & Lamb, Cecile. Song of the Seed. Faltico, Mary L., illus. 28p. (ps). 1992. 2.50 (*0-87403-956-8*, 24-03596) Standard Pub.
Stangl, Jean. Gardening Fun. (gr. k-3). 1991. pap. 10.95 (*0-8224-3381-8*) Fearon Teach Aids.
Walters, Jennie. Gardening with Peter Rabbit: A Gardening Kit. Potter, Beatrix, illus. 48p. (gr. k-4). 1992. pap. 14.50 (*0-7232-4024-8*) Warne.
Waters, Marjorie. The Victory Garden Kids' Book. Ulrich, George, illus. Mottau, Gary, photos by. LC 93-41043. (Illus.). 160p. 1994. pap. 15.95 (*1-56440-361-0*) Globe Pequot.
Wilkes, Angela. My First Garden Book. King, Dave, photos by. LC 90-40332. (Illus.). 48p. (gr. 2-5). 1992. 13.00 (*0-679-81412-4*) Knopf Bks Yng Read.
Wilner, Isabel. A Garden Alphabet. Wolff, Ashley, illus. LC 90-19619. 32p. (ps-2). 1991. 12.95 (*0-525-44731-8*, DCB) Dutton Child Bks.
Woggon, Guillermo. Cultivemos una Huerta. Granberry, Nola, tr. (SPA., Illus.). 16p. (gr. 1-3). 1987. pap. 1.40 (*0-311-38564-8*) Casa Bautista.

GARDENING–FICTION
Ada, Alma F. Una Semilla Nada Mas (Small Book) Remkiewicz, Frank, illus. (SPA.). 16p. (Orig.). (gr. k-3). 1992. pap. text ed. 6.00 (*1-56334-083-6*) Hampton-Brown.
Bar, Amos. Gary the Gardener. Kriss, David, tr. from HEB. Elchanan, illus. 24p. (Orig.). (ps). 1992. pap. text ed. 3.00x (*1-56134-162-2*) Dushkin Pub.
Barden, Helen. Busy Little Gardener. 1990. 5.99 (*0-517-03603-7*) Random Hse Value.
Bjork, Christina. Linnea in Monet's Garden. Sandin, Joan, tr. from SWE. Anderson, Lena, illus. 56p. (gr. 3-6). 1987. 13.00 (*91-29-58314-4*, Pub. by R & S Bks) FS&G.
Bond, Michael. Paddington's Garden. Lobban, John, illus. LC 92-24527. 32p. (ps-3). 1993. 8.95 (*0-694-00462-6*, Festival) HarpC Child Bks.
Brautigan, Richard. In Watermelon Sugar. 176p. (gr. 9 up). 1973. pap. 1.75 (*0-440-34026-8*) Dell.
Bunting, Eve. Flower Garden. Hewitt, Kathryn, illus. LC 92-25766. 1994. 13.95 (*0-15-228776-0*) HarBrace.
Burke-Weiner, Kimberly. The Maybe Garden. Roehm, Michelle, ed. Spillman, Fredrika, illus. 36p. (gr. 1-4). 1992. 14.95 (*0-941831-56-6*); pap. 7.95 (*0-941831-57-4*) Beyond Words Pub.
Burnett, Frances H. The Secret Garden. 288p. 1992. 9.49 (*0-8167-2558-6*); pap. 2.95 (*0-8167-2559-4*) Troll Assocs.
Caisley, Raewyn. The Leaf Raker. Power, Margaret, illus. LC 93-26218. 1994. 4.25 (*0-383-03756-5*) SRA Schl Grp.
Carlson, Nancy. Harriet & the Garden. LC 81-18136. (Illus.). 32p. (ps-3). 1982. lib. bdg. 13.50 (*0-87614-184-X*) Carolrhoda Bks.
—Harriet & the Garden. Carlson, Nancy, illus. (gr. k-3). 1985. bk. & cassette 19.95 (*0-941078-66-3*); pap. 12.95 bk. & cassette (*0-317-14686-6*); cassette, 4 paperbacks & guide 27.95 (*0-317-14687-4*) Live Oak Media.
Cartwright, Pauline. Jake Was a Pirate. Sofilas, Mark, illus. LC 93-26216. 1994. 4.25 (*0-383-03754-9*) SRA Schl Grp.
Cooke, Tom, illus. Bert's Little Garden: A Sesame Street Book. LC 90-61311. 22p. (ps). 1991. bds. 2.95 (*0-679-81061-7*) Random Bks Yng Read.
Coplans, Peta. Dottie. Coplans, Peta, illus. LC 92-41955. 1994. write for info. (*0-395-66788-7*) HM.
Cristini, Ermanno & Puricelli, Luigi. In My Garden. Cristini, Ermanno & Puricelli, Luigi, illus. LC 85-9402. 28p. (ps up). 1991. pap. 12.95 (*0-907234-05-4*) Picture Bk Studio.
Cushman, Doug. Mouse & Mole & the Year - Round Garden. LC 93-37202. (gr. 4 up). 1993. text ed. write for info. (*0-7167-6524-1*, Sci Am Yng Rdrs) W H Freeman.
De Brunhoff, Laurent. Babar Jardinier. (FRE.). (gr. 2-3). 15.95 (*0-685-11030-3*) Fr & Eur.
Edwards, Michelle. Eve & Smithy. LC 92-44166. (gr. 4 up). 1995. 15.00 (*0-688-11825-9*); lib. bdg. 14.93 (*0-688-11826-7*) Lothrop.
Ehlert, Lois. Growing Vegetable Soup. 40p. (ps-2). 1990. pap. 4.95 (*0-15-232580-8*, Voyager Bks) HarBrace.
—Growing Vegetable Soup. Ehlert, Lois, illus. 32p. (ps-3). 1991. pap. 19.95 (*0-15-232581-6*) HarBrace.

—Growing Vegetable Soup. (ps-3). 1987. 13.95 (*0-15-232575-1*, HB Juv Bks) HarBrace.
Florian, D. Vegetable Garden. 1991. 13.95 (*0-15-293383-2*, HB Juv Bks) HarBrace.
A Garden for Miss Mouse. 42p. (ps-3). 1993. PLB 13.27 (*0-8368-0891-6*) Gareth Stevens Inc.
Garland, Sarah. Doing the Garden. (Illus.). 32p. (ps-1). 1993. 15.95 (*0-370-31635-5*, Pub. by Bodley Head UK) Trafalgar.
Gerstein, Mordecai. Daisy's Garden. Date not set. 15.00 (*0-06-021141-5*, HarpT); PLB 14.89 (*0-06-021142-3*, HarpT) HarpC.
Gerstein, Mordicai & Harris, Susan Y. Daisy's Garden. LC 94-22123. (gr. 1-8). 1995. write for info. (*0-7868-0096-8*); write for info. (*0-7868-2080-2*) Hyprn Child.
Greene, George W. Gardening Storybox. Hatter, Laurie, illus. (ps). 1993. Activity kit incl. 2 bks., 12p. ea. 16. 95 (*1-56828-045-9*) Red Jacket Pr.
—Sal's Garden Trowell. Hatter, Laurie, illus. 12p. (ps). 1993. 4.95 (*1-56828-031-9*) Red Jacket Pr.
—Sam's Watering Can. Hatter, Laurie, illus. 12p. (ps). 1993. 4.95 (*1-56828-032-7*) Red Jacket Pr.
Greenstein, Elaine. Mrs. Rose's Garden. Greenstein, Elaine, illus. 28p. (gr. k up). 1993. 14.95 (*0-88708-264-5*) Picture Bk Studio.
Krauss. Carrot Seed. 1993. pap. 28.67 (*0-590-73301-X*) Scholastic Inc.
—La Semilla de Zanahoria. (SPA.). 1993. pap. 2.95 (*0-590-45092-1*) Scholastic Inc.
Krauss, Ruth. Carrot Seed Board Book. Johnson, Crockett, illus. LC 45-4530. 24p. (ps-2). 1993. 4.95 (*0-694-00492-8*, Festival) HarpC Child Bks.
Lewis, Richard, ed. In a Spring Garden. Keats, Ezra J., illus. 32p. (ps up). 1989. pap. 4.95 (*0-8037-4033-6*, Puff Pied Piper) Puffin Bks.
Light, John. Dig That Hole! LC 91-39036. (gr. 5 up). 1991. 3.95 (*0-85953-503-7*) Childs Play.
Lobel, Arnold. The Rose in My Garden. Lobel, Anita, illus. 40p. (ps-2). 1985. pap. 3.95 (*0-590-41530-1*) Scholastic Inc.
Lord, John V. Mr. Mead & His Garden. LC 74-20766. (Illus.). (gr. k-3). 1975. PLB 6.95 (*0-395-20278-7*) HM.
McKissack, Patricia & McKissack, Fredrick. Messy Bessey's Garden. Hackney, Richard, illus. LC 91-15333. 32p. (ps-2). 1991. PLB 10.25 (*0-516-02008-0*); pap. 2.95 (*0-516-42008-9*) Childrens.
Madenski, Melissa. In My Mother's Garden. Speidel, Sandra, illus. LC 93-40112. 1995. 15.95 (*0-316-54326-8*) Little.
Martin, Jacqueline M. The Second Street Gardens & the Green Truck Almanac. Gillman, Alec, illus. LC 94-10869. 1995. 15.95 (*0-02-762460-9*, Four Winds) Macmillan Child Grp.
Matthews, Cecily. Captain Orinoco's Onion. Smith, Craig, illus. LC 93-2802. 1994. write for info. (*0-383-03680-1*) SRA Schl Grp.
Moncure, Jane B. Word Bird's Rainy-Day Dance. Hohag, Linda, illus. LC 90-31693. 32p. (ps-2). 1990. PLB 14. 95 (*0-89565-579-9*) Childs World.
Moore, Elaine. Grandma's Garden. LC 90-6052. (ps-3). 1994. 15.00 (*0-688-08693-4*); 14.93 (*0-688-08694-2*) Lothrop.
Mosse, Richard. Bun-Bun's Garden. Sonstegard, Jeff, ed. (Illus.). 24p. (gr. 6-10). 1993. text ed. 12.95 (*0-9630328-4-4*) SDPI.
Muller, Gerda. The Garden in the City. Muller, Gerda, illus. 40p. (gr. k-5). 1992. 13.50 (*0-525-44697-4*, DCB) Dutton Child Bks.
Muntean, Michaela. A Garden for Miss Mouse. Santoro, Christopher, illus. LC 82-2135. 48p. (ps-3). 1982. 5.95 (*0-8193-1083-2*); lib. bdg. 5.95 (*0-8193-1084-0*) Parents.
Newman, Winifred B. The Secret in the Garden. (Illus.). 32p. (Orig.). (gr. k-5). 1980. Bahai.
Pearce, Philippa. Tom's Midnight Garden. (gr. k-6). 1991. pap. write for info. (Pub. by Yearling Classics) Dell.
Primavera, Elise. Plantpet. Primavera, Elise, illus. LC 93-36526. 32p. (ps-3). 1994. PLB 15.95 (*0-399-22627-3*, Putnam) Putnam Pub Group.
Quattlebaum, Mary. Jackson Jones & the Puddle of Thorns. Rosales, Melodye, illus. LC 93-11433. (gr. 4-7). 1994. 13.95 (*0-385-31165-6*) Delacorte.
Rockwell, Anne & Rockwell, Harlow. How My Garden Grew. LC 81-17145. (Illus.). 24p. (ps-k). 1982. RSBE 10.95 (*0-02-777660-3*, Macmillan Child Bk) Macmillan Child Grp.
Ryder, Joanne. First Grade Ladybugs. Lewin, Betsy, illus. LC 92-43528. 32p. (ps-2). 1993. PLB 9.79 (*0-8167-3006-7*); pap. text ed. 2.95 (*0-8167-3007-5*) Troll Assocs.
—My Father's Hands. Graham, Mark, illus. LC 93-27116. 1994. write for info. (*0-688-09189-X*); PLB write for info. (*0-688-09190-3*) Morrow Jr Bks.
Schaefer, Carole L. In the Children's Garden. Pauley, Lynn, illus. LC 93-15980. 1994. 14.95 (*0-8050-1958-8*) H Holt & Co.
Siracusa, Catherine. The Giant Zucchini. Siracusa, Catherine, illus. LC 92-72018. 48p. (gr. k-3). 1993. 10. 95 (*1-56282-286-1*); PLB 10.89 (*1-56282-287-X*) Hyprn Child.
Snyder, Zilpha K. Below the Root. 244p. (gr. 5 up). 1992. pap. 3.50 (*0-440-21266-9*, LFL) Dell.
Spurr, Elizabeth. The Gumdrop Tree. Gorton, Julia, illus. LC 93-38234. 32p. (ps-1). 1994. 13.95 (*0-7868-0008-9*); PLB 13.89 (*0-7868-2004-7*) Hyprn Child.
Stobbs, William. Gregory's Garden. (Illus.). 16p. 1987. pap. 2.95 (*0-19-272140-2*) OUP.
Walters, Jennie. Gardening with Peter Rabbit. Potter, Beatrix, illus. 48p. (gr. k-4). 1992. 9.00 (*0-7232-3998-3*) Warne.
Williams, Sarah, ed. Round & Round the Garden. Beck, Ian, illus. 48p. (ps). cassette 7.95 (*0-19-279852-9*) OUP.
Wolf, Janet. The Rosy Fat Magenta Radish. (ps-1). 1990. 14.95 (*0-316-95045-9*, Joy St Bks) Little.
Zavos, Judy. Murgatroyd's Garden. Zak, Drahos, illus. 32p. (gr. k-3). 1988. 9.95 (*0-312-01629-8*) St Martin.
Ziefert, Harriet. Little Bunny's Melon Patch. Ernst, Lisa C., illus. 20p. (ps-3). 1990. pap. 4.95 (*0-14-054262-0*, Puffin) Puffin Bks.
—Little Bunny's Noisy Friends. Ernst, Lisa C., illus. 20p. (ps-3). 1990. pap. 4.95 (*0-14-054263-9*, Puffin) Puffin Bks.

GARDENING–POETRY

Disch, Thomas M. The Tale of Dan De Lion. McClun, Rhonda, illus. 32p. (ps up). 1986. 9.95 (*0-918273-30-7*) Coffee Hse.
Steele, Mary Q. Anna's Garden Songs. Anderson, Lena, illus. LC 88-5660. 32p. (gr. k up). 1989. 11.95 (*0-688-08217-3*); PLB 11.88 (*0-688-08218-1*) Greenwillow.

GARDENS–FICTION

Ahlberg, Allan. It Was a Dark & Stormy Night. Ahlberg, Janet, illus. 32p. (ps-3). 1994. 13.99 (*0-670-85159-0*) Viking Child Bks.
Avery, Helen P. The Secret Garden. (Orig.). (gr. k-3). 1987. pap. 5.00 playscript (*0-87602-271-9*) Anchorage.
Balian, Lorna. A Garden for a Groundhog. Balian, Lorna, illus. 32p. (gr. k up). 1985. PLB 13.95 (*0-687-14009-9*) Humbug Bks.
Bassett, Lisa. Ten Little Bunnies. Bassett, Jeni, illus. LC 92-37986. (gr. 2 up). 1993. 3.99 (*0-517-08154-7*) Random Hse Value.
Burnett, Frances H. The Secret Garden. 302p. 1981. Repr. PLB 21.95x (*0-89966-326-5*) Buccaneer Bks.
—Secret Garden. (gr. k-6). 1990. pap. 3.50 (*0-440-47709-3*, Pub. by Yearling Classics); pap. 3.50 (*0-440-97709-6*, Dell Trade Pbks) Dell.
—The Secret Garden. (gr. 4-6). 1987. pap. 2.95 (*0-14-035004-7*, Puffin) Puffin Bks.
—The Secret Garden. Mitchell, Kathy, illus. 320p. (gr. 4 up). 1987. 13.95 (*0-448-06029-9*, G&D) Putnam Pub Group.
—The Secret Garden. Tudor, Tasha, illus. LC 62-17457. 256p. (gr. 4-8). 1987. pap. 3.50 (*0-06-440188-X*, Trophy) HarpC Child Bks.
—The Secret Garden. McNulty, Faith, afterword by. 1987. pap. 2.95 (*0-451-52417-9*, Sig Classics) NAL-Dutton.
—The Secret Garden. Allen, Thomas B., illus. Howe, James, adapted by. LC 86-17788. (Illus.). 72p. (gr. k-5). 1993. 13.95 (*0-394-86467-0*) Random Bks Yng Read.
—The Secret Garden. Howell, Troy, illus. 288p. (gr. k-6). 12.99 (*0-517-63225-X*) Random Hse Value.
—The Secret Garden. Hague, Michael, illus. LC 86-22780. 240p. (gr. 4-6). 1987. 19.95 (*0-8050-0277-4*, Bks Young Read) H Holt & Co.
—The Secret Garden. Lowry, Lois, intro. by. 256p. 1987. pap. 3.50 (*0-553-21201-X*, Bantam Classics) Bantam.
—The Secret Garden. Betts, Louise, adapted by. LC 87-15490. (Illus.). (gr. 3-6). 1988. PLB 12.89 (*0-8167-1203-4*); pap. 3.95 (*0-8167-1204-2*) Troll Assocs.
—The Secret Garden. 360p. 1987. pap. 4.95 (*0-19-281772-8*) OUP.
—The Secret Garden. Sanderson, Ruth, illus. LC 86-46002. 240p. 1988. 18.95 (*0-394-55431-0*) Knopf Bks Yng Read.
—The Secret Garden. Hughes, Shirley, illus. 240p. (gr. 5 up). 1989. pap. 18.95 (*0-670-82571-9*) Viking Child Bks.
—The Secret Garden. (gr. 5 up). 1989. pap. 2.50 (*0-451-52080-7*) NAL-Dutton.
—The Secret Garden. 304p. (gr. 4-7). 1987. pap. 2.95 (*0-590-43346-6*) Scholastic Inc.
—The Secret Garden. 1987. pap. 3.50 (*0-440-40055-4*) Dell.
—Secret Garden. 288p. 1990. pap. 2.50 (*0-8125-0501-8*) Tor Bks.
—The Secret Garden. 1991. pap. 3.99 (*0-8125-1910-8*) Tor Bks.
—The Secret Garden. 1979. pap. 3.25 (*0-440-77706-2*) Dell.
—The Secret Garden. 288p. (gr. 5-8). 1991. pap. 2.99 (*0-87406-575-5*) Willowisp Pr.
—The Secret Garden. 1993. 14.95 (*0-679-42309-5*, Everymans Lib) Knopf.
—The Secret Garden. Howe, James, adapted by. Allen, Thomas B., illus. LC 93-18509. 128p. (Orig.). (gr. 2-6). 1993. pap. 3.50 (*0-679-84751-0*, Bullseye Bks) Random Bks Yng Read.
—The Secret Garden. Bishop, Michael, illus. 200p. 1993. 25.00 (*0-88363-202-0*) H L Levin.
—Secret Garden. 20.95 (*0-8488-0692-1*) Amereon Ltd.
—The Secret Garden. Bauman, Jill, illus. LC 94-17836. 1994. 10.95 (*0-681-00646-3*) Longmeadow Pr.
Burnett, Frances Hodgson. The Secret Garden. (Illus.). 96p. (Orig.). (gr. 4-7). 1994. pap. 1.00 (*0-486-28024-1*) Dover.
Burnett, Francis H. The Secret Garden: A Young Reader's Edition of the Classic Story. Abr. ed. Crawford, Dale, illus. LC 90-80198. 56p. (gr. 1 up). 1990. 9.98 (*0-89471-860-6*) Courage Bks.
Cardinal, Catherine S. The Button Box. (Illus.). 40p. (Orig.). (gr. 3 up). 1992. write for info. (*0-9630655-1-3*); pap. write for info. Garden Gate.
—Mud Grape Pie. 29p. (gr. k-6). 1991. pap. 6.00 (*0-9630655-0-5*) Garden Gate.
Carlson, Nancy. Harriet & the Garden. Carlson, Nancy, illus. 32p. (ps-3). 1985. pap. 3.95 (*0-14-050466-4*, Puffin) Puffin Bks.
Carr, Jan. Secret Garden. (Illus.). (ps-3). 1993. pap. 3.25 (*0-590-47172-4*) Scholastic Inc.
Collette, Paul & Wright, Robert. Huddles. LC 91-51081. (Orig.). (gr. 3-12). 1985. pap. 6.00 play script (*0-88734-512-3*) Players Pr.
Cristaldi, Kathryn. The Secret Garden. (Illus.). (ps-3). 1993. pap. 2.95 (*0-590-47170-8*) Scholastic Inc.
Davis, Maggie S. A Garden of Whales. O'Connell, Jennifer B., illus. LC 92-34411. 32p. 1993. 16.95 (*0-944475-36-1*); pap. 6.95 (*0-944475-35-3*) Camden Hse Pub.
DiSalvo-Ryan, DyAnne. City Green. LC 93-27117. 1994. write for info. (*0-688-12786-X*); PLB write for info. (*0-688-12787-8*) Morrow Jr Bks.
Dyjak, Elisabeth. Bertha's Garden. Wilkins, Janet, illus. LC 93-28594. 1994. write for info. (*0-395-68715-2*) HM.
Hahn, Mary D. Doll in the Garden. 144p. 1990. pap. 3.50 (*0-380-70865-5*, Camelot) Avon.
Hamblen, Priscilla C. The Magic Garden. 1993. 7.95 (*0-8062-4596-4*) Carlton.
Ireland, Shep. Wesley & Wendell: In the Garden. Ireland, Shep, illus. 40p. (gr. 1). 1991. lib. bdg. 4.75 (*0-8378-0331-4*) Gibson.
El Jardin Secreto. (SPA.). 1990. casebound 3.50 (*0-7214-1404-4*) Ladybird Bks.
Johnston, Tony. Old Lady & the Birds. LC 91-45124. (ps-3). 1994. 14.95 (*0-15-257769-6*, HB Juv Bks) HarBrace.
Klipper, Ilse. My Magic Garden. Green, Maureen, et al, illus. 91p. (Orig.). (gr. 2-6). 1980. pap. 5.95 (*0-9605022-0-3*) Pathwys Pr CA.
Leonard, Marcia. Gregory & Mr. Grump. Brook, Bonnie, ed. Chambliss, Maxie & Iosa, Ann W., illus. 24p. (ps-1). 1990. 4.95 (*0-671-70406-0*); lib. bdg. 6.95 (*0-671-70402-8*) Silver Pr.
Molleson, Diane. Secret Garden, with Charm, Key-Shaped. (Illus.). (ps-3). 1993. pap. 12.95 (*0-590-47173-2*) Scholastic Inc.
Pearce, Philippa. Tom's Midnight Garden. Einzig, Susan, intro. by. LC 69-12008. (Illus.). 240p. (gr. 3-7). 1992. pap. 4.95 (*0-06-440445-5*, Trophy) HarpC Child Bks.
Quattlebaum, Mary. Jackson Jones & the Puddle of Thorns. Rosales, Melodye, illus. LC 93-11433. (gr. 4-7). 1994. 13.95 (*0-385-31165-6*) Delacorte.
Rice, Alice H. Mrs. Wiggs of the Cabbage Patch. 1992. Repr. lib. bdg. 19.95x (*0-89968-271-1*) Lightyear.
Ryder, Joanne. First Grade Ladybugs. Lewin, Betsy, illus. LC 92-43528. 32p. (ps-2). 1993. PLB 9.79 (*0-8167-3006-7*); pap. text ed. 2.95 (*0-8167-3007-5*) Troll Assocs.
Rylant, Cynthia. The Everyday Books: Everyday Garden. Rylant, Cynthia, illus. LC 92-40542. 14p. (ps-k). 1993. pap. 4.95 with rounded corners (*0-02-778023-6*, Bradbury Pr) Macmillan Child Grp.
—This Year's Garden. Szilagyi, Mary, illus. LC 86-22224. 32p. (ps-3). 1987. pap. 4.95 (*0-689-71122-0*, Aladdin) Macmillan Child Grp.
St. John, Patricia M. Rainbow Garden. (gr. 2-5). pap. 4.99 (*0-8024-0028-0*) Moody.
Saltzberg, Barney. Mrs. Morgan's Lawn. Saltzberg, Barney, illus. LC 92-54873. 32p. (ps-2). 1993. 13.95 (*1-56282-423-6*); PLB 13.89 (*1-56282-424-4*) Hyprn Child.
Schaefer, Carole L. In the Children's Garden. Pauley, Lynn, illus. LC 93-15980. 1994. 14.95 (*0-8050-1958-8*) H Holt & Co.
Shannon, George. Seeds. Bjorkman, George, illus. LC 92-40738. 1994. 13.95 (*0-395-66990-1*) HM.
Stevenson, James. Grandpas Too-Good Garden. LC 88-18786. (Illus.). 32p. (gr. k up). 1989. 12.95 (*0-688-08485-0*); PLB 12.88 (*0-688-08486-9*) Greenwillow.
Thesman, Jean. Nothing Grows Here. LC 93-45739. 208p. (gr. 4 up). 1994. 14.00 (*0-06-024457-7*); PLB 13.89 (*0-06-024458-5*) HarpC Child Bks.
Wainwright, Richard M. Garden of Dreams. Dvorsack, Carolyn S., illus. LC 93-17974. 1994. 14.00 (*0-9619566-6-6*) Family Life.
Widman, Christine. The Hummingbird Garden. Ransome, James, illus. LC 91-27338. 32p. (gr. k-3). 1993. RSBE 14.95 (*0-02-792761-X*, Macmillan Child Bk) Macmillan Child Grp.
Williams, Sophy. Nana's Garden. Williams, Sophy, illus. 32p. (ps-1). 1994. 14.99 (*0-670-85287-2*) Viking Child Bks.
Wolff, Ferida. The Emperor's Garden. Osborn, Kathy, illus. LC 93-14751. 1994. 15.00 (*0-688-11651-5*, Tambourine Bks); PLB 14.93 (*0-688-11652-3*) Morrow.

GARFIELD, JAMES ABRAM, PRESIDENT U. S., 1831-1881

Brown, Fern G. James A. Garfield: Twentieth President of the United States. Young, Richard G., ed. LC 89-39953. (Illus.). 128p. (gr. 5-9). 1990. PLB 17.26 (*0-944483-63-1*) Garrett Ed Corp.

Lillegard, Dee. James A. Garfield. LC 87-18200. (Illus.). 100p. (gr. 3 up). 1987. PLB 14.40 (*0-516-01394-7*) Childrens.

GARIBALDI, GIUSEPPE, 1807-1882

Viola, Herman & Viola, Susan. Giuseppe Garibaldi. (Illus.). 112p. (gr. 5 up). 1988. 17.95 (*0-87754-526-X*) Chelsea Hse.

GAS AND OIL ENGINES

see also Automobiles–Engines

Roth, Alfred C. Small Gas Engines. rev. ed. (Illus.). 352p. 1992. text ed. 26.60 (*0-87006-919-5*); instr's. guide 4.00 (*0-87006-921-7*); wkbk. 7.96 (*0-87006-920-9*) Goodheart.

GAS ENGINES

see Gas and Oil Engines

GASES

Bailey, Donna. Energy from Oil & Gas. LC 90-39300. (Illus.). 48p. (gr. 2-6). 1990. PLB 19.97 (*0-8114-2518-5*) Raintree Steck-V.

Barber, Jacqueline. Solids, Liquids, & Gases. Bergman, Lincoln & Fairwell, Kay, eds. Baker, Lisa H. & Peterson, Adria, illus. Barber, Jacqueline, et al, photos by. 56p. (Orig.). (gr. 3-6). 1986. pap. 15.00 (*0-912511-69-9*) Lawrence Science.

Mebane, Robert & Rybolt, Thomas. Air & Gasses. (Illus.). 64p. (gr. 5-8). 1995. bds. 15.95 (*0-8050-2839-0*) TFC Bks NY.

GASOLINE ENGINES

see Gas and Oil Engines

GASTRONOMY

see Cookery; Food

GAUCHOS

see Cowboys

GAUGUIN, PAUL, 1848-1903

Greenfeld, Howard. Paul Gauguin. LC 93-9454. 1993. 19. 95 (*0-8109-3376-4*) Abrams.

Venezia, Mike. Paul Gauguin. Venezia, Mike, illus. LC 91-35054. 32p. (ps-4). PLB 12.85, Apr. 1992 (*0-516-02295-4*); pap. 4.95, Jul. 1992 (*0-516-42295-2*) Childrens.

GAULLE, CHARLES DE, PRESIDENT FRANCE, 1890-1970

Whitelaw, Nancy. Charles de Gaulle: I Am France. LC 91-13095. (Illus.). 112p. (gr. 4-6). 1991. text ed. 13.95 RSBE (*0-87518-486-3*, Dillon) Macmillan Child Grp.

GAZETTEERS

see also Names, Geographical

GEESE

Ahlstrom, Mark. The Snow Goose. LC 85-29933. (Illus.). 48p. (gr. 5). 1986. text ed. 12.95 RSBE (*0-89686-293-3*, Crestwood Hse) Macmillan Child Grp.

Coste, Marion. Nene. Gray, Cissy, illus. LC 92-36543. 32p. 1993. 9.95 (*0-8248-1389-8*, Kolowalu Bk) UH Pr.

Fowler, Allan. Quack & Honk. LC 92-35056. (Illus.). 32p. (ps-2). 1993. big bk. 22.95 (*0-516-49643-3*); PLB 10.75 (*0-516-06012-0*); pap. 3.95 (*0-516-46012-9*) Childrens.

Kalas, Sybille. The Goose Family Book. Crampton, Patricia, tr. LC 85-30986. (Illus.). 53p. (gr. 1 up). 1991. pap. 15.95 (*0-88708-019-7*) Picture Bk Studio.

Rothaus, Jim. Ducks, Geese, & Swans. 24p. (gr. 3). 1988. PLB 14.95 (*0-88682-224-6*) Creative Ed.

Selsam, Millicent E. & Hunt, Joyce. A First Look at Ducks, Geese & Swans. Springer, Harriet, illus. 32p. (gr. 1-4). 1990. 11.95 (*0-8027-6975-6*); lib. bdg. 12.85 (*0-8027-6976-4*) Walker & Co.

GEESE–FICTION

Ahlstrom, Mark. The Canada Goose. LC 83-24015. (Illus.). 48p. (gr. 5). 1984. RSBE 12.95 (*0-89686-243-7*, Crestwood Hse) Macmillan Child Grp.

Auch, Mary J. Bird Dogs Can't Fly. Auch, Mary J., illus. LC 93-2746. (ps-3). 1993. reinforced bdg. 15.95 (*0-8234-1050-1*) Holiday.

Burningham, John. Borka: Adventures of a Goose with No Feathers. Burningham, John, illus. 32p. (ps-2). 1994. Repr. of 1964 ed. 4.99 (*0-517-58020-9*) Crown Bks Yng Read.

Coxe, Molly. Maxie & Mirabel. LC 92-26528. (Illus.). 64p. (gr. k-3). 1994. 14.00 (*0-06-022868-7*); PLB 13. 89 (*0-06-022869-5*) HarpC Child Bks.

Duvoisin, Roger. Petunia. Duvoisin, Roger, illus. (gr. k-3). 1962. lib. bdg. 10.99 (*0-394-90865-1*) Knopf Bks Yng Read.

—Petunia's Christmas. Duvoisin, Roger, illus. (gr. k-3). 1963. lib. bdg. 12.99 (*0-394-90868-6*) Knopf Bks Yng Read.

Evans, Sanford. Naomi's Geese. Chabrian, Deborah, illus. LC 92-44109. (gr. 5 up). 1993. pap. 15.00 (*0-671-75623-0*, S&S BFYR) S&S Trade.

Franklin, Kristine L. The Blue-Eyed Goose. LC 94-11978. 1995. write for info. (*0-688-13780-6*); PLB write for info. (*0-688-13781-4*) Lothrop.

Fredeking, Jean T. Gertrude: A Goose on the Loose. Weinberger, Jane, ed. LC 91-65295. (Illus.). 40p. 1991. 7.95 (*0-932433-81-2*) Windswept Hse.

Gallico, Paul. Snow Goose. (gr. 9 up). 1941. 12.00 (*0-394-44593-7*) Knopf Bks Yng Read.

—The Snow Goose. 50th anniversary ed. Peck, Beth, illus. LC 90-46880. 48p. 1992. 16.00 (*0-679-80683-0*); PLB 16.99 (*0-679-90683-5*) Knopf Bks Yng Read.

—Snow Goose. (Illus.). Date not set. pap. 5.99 (*0-517-11098-9*) Random Hse Value.

Grimm, Jacob & Grimm, Wilhelm K. The Golden Goose. Duntze, Dorothee, illus. Bell, Anthea, tr. LC 87-32108. (Illus.). 32p. (gr. k-3). 1988. 13.95 (*1-55858-047-6*) North-South Bks NYC.

Harris, Marian. Goose & the Mountain Lion. 1st ed. Harris, Jim, illus. LC 93-45424. 32p. (gr. k up). 1994. 14.95 (*0-87358-576-3*) Northland AZ.

Kent, Jack. Silly Goose. Kent, Jack, illus. LC 82-21441. 32p. (ps-3). 1986. 5.95 (*0-13-810177-9*) P-H.

—Silly Goose. LC 82-21441. (Illus.). 32p. (gr. k-4). 1982. PLB 10.95 (*0-671-66676-2*, S&S BFYR); pap. 5.95 (*0-671-66677-0*, S&S BFYR) S&S Trade.

Langton, Jane. The Fledgling. LC 79-2008. 192p. (gr. 3-7). 1981. pap. 3.95 (*0-06-440121-9*, Trophy) HarpC Child Bks.

Latimer, Jim. James Bear & the Goose Gathering. Franco-Feeney, Betsy, illus. LC 92-26190. 32p. (gr. k-2). 1994. SBE 14.95 (*0-684-19526-7*, Scribners Young Read) Macmillan Child Grp.

Lee, Paul A. Florence the Goose: A True Story for Children of All Ages. Smith, Page, illus. 47p. 1992. 14.95 (*0-937011-51-7*) Platonic Acad Pr.

Lindbergh, Reeve. Day the Goose Got Loose. Kellogg, Steven, illus. LC 87-28959. 32p. (ps-3). 1990. 12.95 (*0-8037-0408-9*); PLB 12.89 (*0-8037-0409-7*) Dial Bks Young.

Lishman, Bill. Father Goose & His Goslings. McMaster, Jack, illus. 72p. (Orig.). (gr. k-8). 1992. pap. 9.95 (*0-9623072-8-9*) S Ink WA.

McKelvey, David. Commander the Gander. Asklin, William O., illus. LC 84-72455. 48p. (gr. 4-6). 1984. lib. bdg. 10.95 (*0-931722-31-4*); pap. 3.95 (*0-931722-30-6*) Corona Pub.

Marshall-Noke, Dorothy. Feathers. Weinberger, Jane, ed. Christian, Marilynn V., illus. LC 88-51278. 64p. (gr. 1-4). 1990. pap. 7.95 (*0-932433-52-9*) Windswept Hse.

Newman, Al. Giggle E. Goose. Doody, Jim, illus. LC 93-77684. 32p. (ps-3). 1993. 13.95 (*0-89334-212-2*); pap. 4.95 (*0-89334-216-5*) Humanics Ltd.

Samton, Sheila W. Tilly & the Rhinoceros. (Illus.). 32p. (ps-3). 1993. PLB 14.95 (*0-399-21973-0*, Philomel Bks) Putnam Pub Group.

Saunders, Susan. The Golden Goose. Selzer, Isadore, illus. 32p. (gr. k-3). 1988. pap. 2.50 (*0-590-41715-0*) Scholastic Inc.

Schoenherr, John. Gone Goose. LC 94-15568. (gr. 1 up). 1995. write for info. (*0-399-22727-X*, Philomel Bks) Putnam Pub Group.

Silverman, Erica. The Freeze-in-Place Contest. Schindler, S. D., illus. LC 93-8707. (ps-2). 1994. 14.95 (*0-02-782685-6*) Macmillan.

Simon, Shirley. Foolish Goose. Gregorich, Barbara, ed. (Illus.). 16p. (Orig.). (gr. k-2). 1985. pap. 2.25 (*0-88743-015-5*, 06015) Sch Zone Pub Co.

—Foolish Goose. Gregorich, Barbara, ed. (Illus.). 32p. (gr. k-2). 1992. pap. 3.95 (*0-88743-413-4*, 06065) Sch Zone Pub Co.

Stevens, Kathleen. Aunt Skilly & the Stranger. Parker, Robert A., illus. LC 93-38235. 32p. (ps-2). 1994. 14.95 (*0-395-68712-8*, Ticknor & Flds Yng Read) Ticknor & Fields.

Taylor, E. J. Goose Eggs. LC 91-58809. (Illus.). (ps up). 1992. 12.95 (*1-56402-123-8*) Candlewick Pr.

Vainio, Pirkko. The Snow Goose. James, J. Alison, tr. from GER. Vainio, Pirkko, illus. LC 92-31330. 32p. (gr. k-3). 1993. 14.95 (*1-55858-194-4*); lib. bdg. 14.88 (*1-55858-195-2*) North-South Bks NYC.

Voake, Charlotte. Mrs. Goose's Baby. (ps). 1992. pap. 3.99 (*0-440-40615-3*) Dell.

Walsh, Ellen S. You Silly Goose. 1992. 13.95 (*0-15-299865-9*, HB Juv Bks) HarBrace.

Wangerin, Walter. Branta & the Golden Stone. Healey, Deborah, illus. LC 92-34891. 1993. pap. 16.00 (*0-671-79693-3*, S&S BFYR) S&S Trade.

White, Sylvia. Home Is Best. Weinberger, Jane & Black, Albert, eds. DeVito, Pamela, illus. LC 88-50315. 44p. (gr. 1-4). 1988. pap. 3.95 (*0-932433-48-0*) Windswept Hse.

Wickstrom, Thor. The Big Night Out. Wickstrom, Thor, illus. LC 91-46563. 32p. (ps-3). 1993. 13.99 (*0-8037-1170-0*); PLB 13.89 (*0-8037-1171-9*) Dial Bks Young.

Yolen, Jane. Honkers. Baker, Leslie, illus. LC 92-24302. 1993. 14.95 (*0-316-96893-5*) Little.

GEHRIG, HENRY LOUIS, 1903-1941

Brandt, Keith. Lou Gehrig, Pride of the Yankees. Lawn, John, illus. LC 85-1075. 48p. (gr. 4-6). 1986. lib. bdg. 10.79 (*0-8167-0549-6*); pap. text ed. 3.50 (*0-8167-0550-X*) Troll Assocs.

Curato, Guy, pseud. Batting One Thousand - Baseball's Leading Hitters: A Tribute to Lou Gehrig. LC 88-82916. 124p. (Orig.). (gr. 9). 1989. pap. write for info. (*0-9621591-0-7*) T Assicurato.

Rambeck, Richard. Lou Gehrig. LC 92-40673. (ENG & SPA.). (gr. 2-6). 1993. 14.95 (*1-56766-073-8*) Childs World.

Van Riper, Guernsey, Jr. Lou Gehrig: One of Baseball's Greatest. Robinson, Jerry, illus. LC 86-10951. 192p. (gr. 2-6). 1986. pap. 3.95 (*0-02-041930-9*, Aladdin) Macmillan Child Grp.

Weber, Bruce. Lou Gehrig: Classic Sports Shots. 1993. pap. 1.25 (*0-590-47023-X*) Scholastic Inc.

GEMS

For works on cut and polished precious stones treated from the point of view of art or antiquity. Works on uncut stones treated from the mineralogical point of view are entered under Precious Stones. Works on gems in which the interest is in the setting are entered under Jewelry.

see also Precious Stones

Gemstones. (gr. k-5). 1991. write for info. (*0-307-12853-9*, Golden Pr) Western Pub.

Jangl, James F. Birthstone Coloring Book: Birthstone Legends & Other Gem Folklore. Jangl, Alda M. & Jangl, James F., illus. 32p. (gr. k up). 1987. pap. 3.50 (*0-942647-03-3*) Prisma Pr.

Lutz, Tim. Gem Hunter's Kit. (Illus.). 64p. (Orig.). (gr. 3 up). 1990. package 17.95 (*0-89471-828-2*) Running Pr.

Swinburne, Laurence & Swinburne, Irene. The Deadly Diamonds. LC 77-10764. (Illus.). 48p. (gr. 4 up). 1983. PLB 20.70 (*0-8172-1064-4*) Raintree Steck-V.

GENEALOGY

see also Biography; Heraldry

Beller, Susan P. Roots for Kids: A Genealogy Guide for Young People. (Illus.). 128p. (Orig.). (gr. 6 up). 1989. pap. 7.95 (*1-55870-112-5*, 70093) Betterway Bks.

Bruzzone, Catherine. My First Family Tree Book. Church, Caroline, illus. 24p. (gr. k-2). 1992. pap. 3.95 (*0-8249-8546-X*, Ideals Child) Hambleton-Hill.

Burgeson, Nancy. My Family History. Janums, Aija, illus. LC 92-3086. 32p. (gr. 3-6). 1992. pap. text ed. 1.95 (*0-8167-2794-5*) Troll Assocs.

Chorzempa, Rosemary A. My Family Tree Workbook: Genealogy for Beginners. 64p. (gr. 5 up). 1982. pap. 2.50 (*0-486-24229-3*) Dover.

Cooper, Kay. Discover It Yourself: Where Did You Get Those Eyes? 80p. 1993. pap. 3.50 (*0-380-71304-7*, Camelot) Avon.

—Where Did You Get Those Eyes: A Guide to Discovering Your Family History. Accardo, Anthony, illus. (gr. 5 up). 1988. 13.95 (*0-8027-6802-4*); PLB 14. 85 (*0-8027-6803-2*) Walker & Co.

Crosby, Nina E. & Marten, Elizabeth H. Don't Teach Let Me Learn about Presidents, of the U. S. People, Genealogy, Immigrants. (Illus.). 80p. (Orig.). (gr. 3-9). 1979. pap. 8.95 tchr's. enrichment manual (*0-914634-67-4*, 7912) DOK Pubs.

Galloway-Blake, Jacqueline. My African Roots: A Child's Create Your Own Keepsake Book of Family History & African-Awareness. 32p. (ps-7). 1992. Wkbk. 5.95 (*0-9637243-6-3*) Brwn Sug & Spice.

Genealogy. (Illus.). 64p. (gr. 6-12). 1988. pap. 1.85 (*0-8395-3383-7*, 33383) BSA.

Lee, Kathleen. Tracing Our Italian Roots. Butler, Nate & Evans, Beth, illus. 48p. (gr. 4-7). 1993. text ed. 12.95 (*1-56261-149-6*) John Muir.
Nichols, Paul. Where in the World Did You Come From? Stallings, Scott, illus. 32p. (ps up). 1993. 17.95g (*1-884507-00-X*) Boyer-Caswell.
Perl, Lila. The Great Ancestor Hunt. LC 88-36211. (Illus.). 112p. (gr. 4 up). 1989. 15.45 (*0-89919-745-0*, Clarion Bks) HM.
—Great Ancestor Hunt: The Fun of Finding Out Who You Are. (gr. 4-7). 1990. pap. 5.70 (*0-395-54790-3*, Clarion Bks) HM.
Sagan, Miriam. Tracing Our Jewish Roots. Butler, Nate & Evans, Beth, illus. 48p. (gr. 4-7). 1993. text ed. 12.95 (*1-56261-151-8*) John Muir.
Silver, Leda. Tracing Our German Roots. Butler, Nate & Evans, Beth, illus. 48p. (gr. 4-7). 1993. text ed. 12.95 (*1-56261-150-X*) John Muir.
Styx, Sherrie A. Genealogy Just for Kids! (Illus.). 28p. (gr. k-4). 1989. wkbk. 2.50 (*1-882121-25-2*) Styx Enter.
—Our Colorful Family Tree. (Illus.). 10p. (ps-2). 1989. write for info. (*1-882121-00-7*) Styx Enter.
Thieme, Jeanne. The American Girls Album: A Picture Frame & Memory Book to Record Your Family History. (Illus.). 48p. (Orig.). (gr. 2-5). 1989. pap. 12.95 (*0-937295-57-4*) Pleasant Co.
Time Life Inc. Editors. The Family Tree: A Familiy History Book. Ward, Elizabeth & Kagan, Neil, eds. (Illus.). 56p. (ps-2). 1993. write for info.; PLB write for info. Time-Life.
Wolfman, Ira. Do People Grow on Family Trees? Genealogy for Kids & Other Beginners. LC 88-51586. (Illus.). 192p. (Orig.). (gr. 3-7). 1991. pap. 9.95 (*0-89480-348-4*, 1348) Workman Pub.

GENERALS

Applegate, Katherine. Story of Colin Powell & Benjamin Davis. (gr. 4-7). 1992. pap. 3.25 (*0-440-40595-5*) Dell.
Banta, Melissa. Colin Powell. LC 94-8349. 1994. write for info. (*0-7910-1770-2*); pap. write for info. (*0-7910-2142-4*) Chelsea Hse.
Blue, Rose. Colin Powell: Straight to the Top. (gr. 4-7). 1992. pap. 4.95 (*1-878841-80-7*) Millbrook Pr.
Brown, Warren. Colin Powell. (Illus.). 112p. (gr. 5 up). 1992. lib. bdg. 17.95 (*0-7910-1647-1*); pap. 9.95 (*0-7910-1648-X*) Chelsea Hse.
Caldwell, Willie W. Stonewall Jim: A Biography of General James A. Walker, C. S. A. Savage, Lon, ed. Butler, M. Caldwell, intro. by. (Illus.). 280p. (gr. 10-12). 1990. 24.95 (*0-9617256-4-8*); pap. 12.95 (*0-9617256-5-6*) Northcross Hse.
Everston, Jonathan. Colin Powell. (gr. 4-7). 1991. pap. 3.50 (*0-553-15966-6*) Bantam.
Fritz, Jean. Stonewall. (Illus.). (gr. 3-7). 1979. 15.95 (*0-399-20698-1*, Putnam) Putnam Pub Group.
Haskins, James S. Colin Powell: A Biography. 112p. 1992. pap. 2.95 (*0-590-45243-6*) Scholastic Inc.
Hughes, Libby. Norman Schwartzkopf: Hero with a Heart. LC 92-13598. (Illus.). 144p. (gr. 5 up). 1992. text ed. 13.95 RSBE (*0-87518-521-5*, Dillon) Macmillan Child Grp.
Landau, Elaine. Colin Powell: Four Star General. LC 91-12860. (Illus.). 64p. (gr. 5-8). 1991. PLB 12.90 (*0-531-20143-0*) Watts.
Pate, J'Nell L. Ranald Slidell Mackenzie: Brave Cavalry Colonel. LC 93-21952. (gr. 4-8). 1994. 14.95 (*0-89015-901-7*) Sunbelt Media.
Reef, Catherine. Benjamin Davis, Jr. (Illus.). 80p. (gr. 4-7). 1992. PLB 14.95 (*0-8050-2137-X*) TFC Bks NY.
—Colin Powell. (Illus.). 80p. (gr. 4-7). 1992. PLB 14.95 (*0-8050-2136-1*) TFC Bks NY.
Roth, David & Maifair, Linda L. Colin Powell. 112p. (gr. 3-7). 1993. 4.99 (*0-310-39851-7*, Pub. by Youth Spec) Zondervan.
Senna, Carl. Colin Powell: A Man of War & Peace. LC 92-16099. 150p. 1992. 15.95 (*0-8027-8180-2*); PLB 16.85 (*0-8027-8181-0*) Walker & Co.
Shelley, Mary V. Dr. Ed: The Story of General Edward Hand. Weatherlow, Regina, illus. LC 78-10331. 36p. (gr. 4-7). 1978. 5.75 (*0-915010-24-0*) Sutter House.
Stefoff, Rebecca. Norman Schwarzkopf. (Illus.). 112p. (gr. 5 up). 1992. lib. bdg. 17.95 (*0-7910-1725-7*) Chelsea Hse.
Super, Neil. Daniel "Chappie" James. (Illus.). 80p. (gr. 4-7). 1992. PLB 14.95 (*0-8050-2138-8*) TFC Bks NY.
Tracey, Patrick. Military Leaders of the Civil War. LC 92-34346. (Illus.). 128p. (gr. 6-9). 1993. 16.95x (*0-8160-2671-8*) Facts on File.
Valentine, E. J. H. Norman Schwarzkopf. (gr. 4-7). 1991. pap. 3.50 (*0-553-15967-4*) Bantam.
Wilkinson, Philip & Pollard, Michael. Generals Who Changed the World. Ingpen, Robert, illus. LC 93-31358. 1994. write for info. (*0-7910-2761-9*); pap. write for info. (*0-7910-2786-4*) Chelsea Hse.

GENERATION

see Reproduction

GENETICS

see also Adaptation (Biology); Evolution; Life (Biology); Reproduction

Asimov, Isaac. How Did We Find Out about Our Genes? Wool, David, illus. LC 83-1211. 64p. (gr. 5-8). 1983. PLB 10.85 (*0-8027-6500-9*) Walker & Co.
Balkwill, Fran. Amazing Schemes within Your Genes. Rolph, Mic, illus. LC 92-42942. (gr. 3 up). 1993. 17.50 (*0-87614-804-6*) Carolrhoda Bks.
—DNA Is Here to Stay. (gr. 4-7). 1994. pap. 8.95 (*0-87614-638-8*) Carolrhoda Bks.
Bornstein, Sandy. What Makes You What You Are? A First Look at Genetics. Steltenpohl, Jane, ed. (Illus.). 128p. (gr. 7 up). 1989. (J Messner); pap. 6.95 (*0-671-68650-X*) S&S Trade.
Byczynski, Lynn. Genetics: Nature's Blueprints. LC 91-15568. (Illus.). 96p. (gr. 5-8). 1991. PLB 15.95 (*1-56006-213-4*) Lucent Bks.
Dudley, William, ed. Genetic Engineering: Opposing Viewpoints. LC 89-25765. (Illus.). 264p. (gr. 10 up). 1990. lib. bdg. 17.95 (*0-89908-477-X*); pap. text ed. 9.95 (*0-89908-452-4*) Greenhaven.
Edelson, Edward. Genetics & Heredity. (Illus.). 112p. (gr. 6-12). 1991. 18.95 (*0-7910-0018-4*) Chelsea Hse.
Gerbi, Susan A. From Genes to Proteins. Head, J. J., ed. Steffen, Ann T., illus. LC 84-45830. 16p. (Orig.). (gr. 10 up). 1993. pap. text ed. 2.75 (*0-89278-358-3*, 45-9758) Carolina Biological.
Goldstein, Philip. Genetics Is Easy. rev. ed. (Illus.). (gr. 9 up). 8.05 (*0-8313-1539-3*) Lantern.
Gonick, Larry & Wheelis, Mark. The Cartoon Guide to Genetics. rev. ed. 1991. pap. 12.00 (*0-06-273099-1*, Harper Ref) HarpC.
Gutnik, Martin A. Genetics Projects for Young Scientists. 1989. pap. 6.95 (*0-531-15131-X*) Watts.
Higgins, Jane H. Discovering Genetics. West, James A., illus. 48p. (Orig.). (gr. 4-12). 1983. pap. text ed. 9.95 tchr's. enrichment bk. (*0-88047-033-X*, 8315) DOK Pubs.
Hooper, Tony. Genetics. LC 93-12060. (Illus.). 48p. (gr. 5-8). 1993. PLB 22.80 (*0-8114-2332-8*) Raintree Steck-V.
Jackson, John F. Genetics & You. (Illus.). 64p. (Orig.). (gr. 12). 1991. pap. 3.95 (*0-9628981-0-4*) Fenwick Pr.
Lampton, Christopher. Gene Technology: Confronting the Issues. LC 90-37572. (Illus.). 144p. (gr. 9-12). 1990. PLB 13.90 (*0-531-10951-8*) Watts.
Meredith, Sue. Why Are People Different? (Illus.). 24p. (gr. 1-5). 1993. lib. bdg. 11.96 (*0-88110-642-9*, Usborne); pap. 3.95 (*0-7460-1014-1*, Usborne) EDC.
Silverstein, Alvin & Silverstein, Virginia B. Genes, Medicine, & You. LC 88-37353. (Illus.). 160p. (gr. 6 up). 1989. lib. bdg. 18.95 (*0-89490-154-0*) Enslow Pubs.
Thro, Ellen. Genetic Engineering. (Illus.). 128p. (gr. 7 up). 1993. PLB 17.95x (*0-8160-2629-7*) Facts on File.
Van Loon, Borin. DNA - the Marvellous Molecule. 32p. 1991. pap. 7.95 (*0-906212-75-8*, Pub. by Tarquin UK) Parkwest Pubns.

GEODESY

see also Surveying

Lauber, Patricia. Seeing Earth from Space. LC 89-77523. (Illus.). 80p. (gr. 5 up). 1990. 19.95 (*0-531-05902-2*); PLB 19.99 (*0-531-08502-3*) Orchard Bks Watts.

GEOGRAPHICAL ATLASES

see Atlases

GEOGRAPHICAL DISTRIBUTION OF ANIMALS AND PLANTS

see also Animals–Migration; Birds–Migration; Desert Animals; Desert Plants; Fresh-Water Animals; Fresh-Water Plants; Marine Animals; Marine Plants

Animal Friends of the Northwest. (gr. 4-7). pap. 2.00 (*0-915266-08-3*) Awani Pr.
Animal Friends of the Rockies. (gr. 4-7). pap. 2.00 (*0-915266-09-1*) Awani Pr.
Animal Friends of the Sierra. (gr. 4-7). pap. 2.00 (*0-915266-06-7*) Awani Pr.
Animal Friends of the Southwest. (gr. 4-7). pap. 2.00 (*0-915266-07-5*) Awani Pr.
Animal Friends of the Yellowstone. (gr. 4-7). pap. 2.00 (*0-915266-10-5*) Awani Pr.
Discovery Atlas of Animals. LC 93-7252. 1993. write for info. (*0-528-83579-3*) Rand McNally.
Wolff, Robert. Animals of Europe. Dallet, Robert, illus. LC 77-78379. 160p. (gr. 3-9). 1969. PLB 29.95 (*0-87460-092-8*) Lion Bks.

GEOGRAPHICAL DISTRIBUTION OF MAN

see Anthropogeography; Ethnology

GEOGRAPHICAL NAMES

see Names, Geographical

GEOGRAPHY

For general works, frequently textbooks, which describe the surface of the earth with its various peoples, animals, natural products and industries. For travel books limited to one country or region, use the name of the place with the subdivision Description and Travel. Works that treat only of the physical features of the earth's surface and its atmosphere are entered under Physical Geography.
see also Anthropogeography; Atlases; Discoveries (In Geography); Ethnology; Maps; Physical Geography; Surveying; Voyages and Travels;
also names of countries, states, etc. with the subdivision Description and Travel, and Geography, e.g. U. S. –Description and Travel

Armstrong, B. Bodacious Borders. LC 92-81600. 68p. 1992. 9.95 (*0-88160-214-0*, LW208) Learning Wks.
Aten, Jerry. Understanding Our World Through Geography. 208p. (gr. 4-8). 1991. 14.95 (*0-86653-592-6*, GA1309) Good Apple.
Balsley, Irol W. Where on Earth? 144p. (gr. 4-8). 1986. wkbk. 12.95 (*0-86653-336-2*, GA 691) Good Apple.
Bender, Lionel. Geography. LC 91-29406. (Illus.). 96p. (gr. 1-5). 1992. pap. 13.00 (*0-671-75996-5*, S&S BFYR); pap. 8.00 (*0-671-75997-3*, S&S BFYR) S&S Trade.
Bresler, L. Earth Facts. (Illus.). 48p. (gr. 3-7). 1987. PLB 12.96 (*0-88110-239-3*); pap. 5.95 (*0-7460-0022-7*) EDC.
Brewton, Barney. California Studies. (gr. 4). 1987. text incl. activity program 229.00 (*0-318-41079-6*) Southwinds Pr.
Brown, Lawrence. Thinking about the World: Building Geography Foundations. 1993. pap. 16.00 (*0-201-45546-3*) Addison-Wesley.
Carratello, John & Carratello, Patty. World Geography. Chellton, Anna, illus. 48p. (gr. 3-6). 1989. wkbk. 6.95 (*1-55734-161-3*) Tchr Create Mat.
Cassidy, John. Earthsearch: A Kids' Geography Museum in a Book. 110p. Date not set. wire-o-bound, incl. rice, foreign coins, misc. inserts 19.95 (*1-878257-74-9*) Klutz Pr.
Churchill, E. Richard. Geography Flipper. 49p. (gr. 5 up). 1989. Repr. of 1987 ed. trade edition 5.95 (*1-878383-07-8*) C Lee Pubns.
Claridge, M. Geography Quizbook. (Illus.). 32p. (gr. 4 up). 1993. PLB 13.96 (*0-88110-535-X*, Usborne); pap. 6.95 (*0-7460-0710-8*, Usborne) EDC.
Cooper, Kay. Discover It Yourself: Where in the World Are You? Novak, Justin, illus. 96p. 1993. pap. 3.50 (*0-380-71299-7*, Camelot) Avon.
—Where in the World Are You? Novak, Justin, illus. 80p. (gr. 3-7). 1990. 13.95 (*0-8027-6912-8*); lib. bdg. 14.85 (*0-8027-6913-6*) Walker & Co.
Countries Facts. (Illus.). 48p. (gr. 3-7). 1986. PLB 12.96 (*0-88110-227-X*); pap. 5.95 (*0-86020-977-6*) EDC.
Crump, Donald J., ed. Books for Young Explorers: Along a Rocky Shore; Animal Families; Lions & Tigers & Leopards: The Big Cats; Our Amazing Animal Friends, 4 bks, Set 17. (gr. k-4). 1990. Set. 13.95 (*0-87044-821-8*); PLB 16.95 (*0-87044-826-9*) Natl Geog.
—Geo-Whiz! 104p. (gr. 3-8). 1988. 8.95 (*0-87044-657-6*); PLB 12.50 (*0-87044-662-2*) Natl Geog.
Cultures of the World, 6 vols. 128p. (gr. 5-10). 1992. Set. PLB 131.70 (*1-85435-543-0*) Marshall Cavendish.
Delf, Brian, illus. Picture Atlas of the World. LC 92-37056. 1992. write for info. (*0-528-83564-5*) Rand McNally.
Dempsey, Michael W. Children's First Geography Encyclopedia. 1985. 6.98 (*0-671-07746-5*) S&S Trade.
Dixon, Dougal. The Changing Earth. LC 93-6829. (Illus.). 32p. (gr. 4-6). 1993. 14.95 (*1-56847-052-5*) Thomson Lrning.
Dunn, Margery G., ed. Exploring Your World: The Adventure of Geography. rev. ed. LC 93-1849. (Illus.). 608p. (ps-6). 1993. PLB 40.00 (*0-87044-762-9*); deluxe ed. write for info. (*0-87044-959-1*) Natl Geog.
Fradin, Dennis. Continents. LC 86-9580. (Illus.). 48p. (gr. k-4). 1986. PLB 12.85 (*0-516-01291-6*); pap. 4.95 (*0-516-41291-4*) Childrens.
Frinks, Donna. All about Me. (gr. k). 1989. text incl. activity program 160.00 (*0-318-41077-X*) Southwinds Pr.
Gakken Co. Ltd. Editors. Famous Places. Time-Life Books Inc. Editors, tr. 90p. (gr. k-3). 1989. write for info. (*0-8094-4893-9*); PLB write for info. (*0-8094-4894-7*) Time-Life.
Gordon, Patricia & Snow, Reed C. Kids Learn America! Bringing Geography to Life with People, Places, & History. Williamson, Susan, ed. LC 91-27245. (Illus.). 176p. (Orig.). (gr. 1 up). 1991. pap. 12.95 (*0-913589-58-6*) Williamson Pub Co.
Green, David. Know the World. (Illus.). 32p. (Orig.). (gr. 5-6). 1992. pap. 6.95 (*0-906212-90-1*, Pub. by Tarquin UK) Parkwest Pubns.
Hargreaves, Margaret & Davis, Pat. At Home & School. (Illus.). (gr. 1). 1988. text incl. activity program 259.00 (*0-318-41078-8*) Southwinds Pr.
—Extending My World. (gr. 3). 1988. text incl. activity program 259.00 (*0-318-41080-X*) Southwinds Pr.
—My Neighborhood & Me. (gr. 2). 1988. text incl. activity program 259.00 (*0-318-41081-8*) Southwinds Pr.
Harte, J. P. & Dunbar, C. Skills in Geography. LC 93-27487. 1994. pap. write for info. (*0-521-44635-X*) Cambridge U Pr.
Hopper, Hilary L. Around the World Program Series. (gr. 4 up). 1993. Smyth sewn casebound. 17.95 (*0-939923-28-9*); Perfect bdg. 7.95 (*0-939923-27-0*); Family ed. 48.00 (*0-939923-26-2*) M & W Pub Co.
It's a Big Big World. (gr. 1-6). 1992. English ed., incl. audio cass. & crayons. 16.98 (*2-89429-007-1*); Spanish ed., incl. audio cass. & crayons. 16.98 (*2-89429-009-8*) Rincon Rodanthe.
James, Barbara. Use of Land. LC 93-8529. (Illus.). 32p. (gr. 4-6). 1993. 14.95 (*1-56847-119-X*) Thomson Lrning.
Jones, Earl, Sr. Map Rap: A Fun Way to Learn Geography Through Rap. Smallwood, James, illus. Coleman, Booker T., intro. by. LC 90-84037. (Illus.). 60p. (Orig.). (gr. 2-12). 1990. pap. 12.75 (*0-935132-18-X*) C H Fairfax.
The Julian Messner Color Illustrated Question & Answer Book: Where Is It? 128p. (gr. 5 up). 1985. (J Messner) S&S Trade.
Kalman, Bobbie. People & Places. (Illus.). 32p. (gr. 2-3). 1987. 15.95 (*0-86505-079-1*); pap. 7.95 (*0-86505-101-1*) Crabtree Pub Co.
Kinney, Karin, ed. Geography. LC 93-28237. (Illus.). 88p. (gr. k-3). 1994. write for info. (*0-8094-9462-0*); PLB write for info. (*0-8094-9463-9*) Time-Life.
Kruger, Herbert O., et al. World Geography Study Aid. 1986. pap. 1.95 (*0-87738-044-9*) Youth Ed.

LaMorte, Kathy & Lewis, Sharen. World Social Studies Yellow Pages for Students & Teachers. Newton, Rebecca, ed. LaMorte, Kathy, illus. 64p. (Orig.). 1993. pap. text ed. 7.95 (*0-86530-268-5*) Incentive Pubns.

Lands & Peoples, 6 vols, Vols. 1-6. LC 92-17742. 1993. Set. write for info. (*0-7172-8016-0*) Grolier Inc.

Lidstone, John, ed. Global Issues of Our Time. LC 93-34256. (Illus.). 192p. 1994. pap. write for info. (*0-521-42163-2*) Cambridge U Pr.

Little People Big Book about Faraway Places. 64p. (ps-1). 1990. write for info. (*0-8094-7504-9*); PLB write for info. (*0-8094-7505-7*) Time-Life.

Loredo, Betsy. Explorers Club Series. (Illus.). (gr. 4-6). 1993. PLB 21.95 (*1-881889-47-5*) Silver Moon.

Manley, Deborah. People & Places. (Illus.). 48p. (ps-6). 1990. 4.99 (*0-517-69614-2*) Random Hse Value.

Millea, Nicholas. Settlements. LC 93-24680. (Illus.). 32p. (gr. 4-6). 1993. 14.95 (*1-56847-057-6*) Thomson Lrning.

Moore, Jo E. Beginning Geography, Vol. 2: Landforms & Bodies of Water. (Illus.). 16p. (gr. k-2). 1993. pap. text ed. 5.95 incl. poster (*1-55799-253-3*) Evan-Moor Corp.

—Beginning Geography, Vol. 3: Continents & Oceans. (Illus.). 16p. (gr. k-2). 1993. pap. text ed. 5.95 incl. poster (*1-55799-254-1*) Evan-Moor Corp.

Nero, Ann B. Essential Skills in Geography. Radner, Barbara, ed. (Illus.). 94p. (Orig.). (gr. 4-9). 1987. pap. text ed. 3.96 (*0-528-17918-7*); tchrs. ed 7.92 (*0-528-17919-5*) Rand McNally.

O'Hare, Jeff. Globe Probe: Exciting Geographical Adventures All Around the World. 32p. (gr. 4-7). 1993. 10.95 (*1-56397-037-6*) Boyds Mills Pr.

People & Places Series, 24 bks. (Illus.). 1152p. (gr. 4-8). 1989. Set. PLB 358.80 (*0-382-09600-2*) Silver Burdett Pr.

Petty, Kate. Our Globe, Our World. (Illus.). 32p. (gr. 2-4). 1993. pap. 5.95 (*0-8120-1236-4*) Barron.

Rinard, Judith E. Along a Rocky Shore. (Illus.). (gr. k-4). 1990. Set. 13.95 (*0-87044-822-6*); lib. bdg. 16.95 (*0-87044-823-4*) Natl Geog.

Rosenthal, Paul. Where on Earth: A Geografunny Guide to the Globe. Rosenthal, Marc, illus. LC 92-1227. 112p. (Orig.). (gr. 3-7). 1992. PLB 15.99 (*0-679-90833-1*); pap. 11.00 (*0-679-80833-7*) Knopf Bks Yng Read.

Schroeder, Mary. Extending U. S. History & Geography. West, James A., illus. 32p. (Orig.). (gr. 3-6). 1984. 6.50 (*0-88047-041-0*, 8404) DOK Pubs.

Schwartz, L. U. S. Geography Journey. rev. ed. 48p. (gr. 4-8). 1992. Repr. of 1989 ed. 5.95 (*0-88160-181-0*, LW287) Learning Wks.

Silver Burdett Countries, 12 bks. 576p. (gr. 5 up). 1992. Set. PLB 129.50 (*0-382-09648-7*) Silver Burdett Pr.

Simon & Schuster Staff. Where Is It? Questions & Answers. 1989. pap. 7.95 (*0-671-68468-X*, S&S BFYR) S&S Trade.

Singer, Marilyn. Nine O'Clock Lullaby. Lessac, Frane, illus. LC 90-32116. 32p. (ps-3). 1991. PLB 14.89 (*0-06-025648-6*) HarpC Child Bks.

Steck-Vaughn Company Staff. Voices from Around the World. LC 90-10133. (Illus.). 128p. (gr. 5-9). 1990. PLB 22.80 (*0-8114-2772-2*) Raintree Steck-V.

Tallarico, Tony. I Didn't Know That about Famous People & Places. (Illus.). 32p. 1992. 9.95 (*1-56156 114-2*) Kidsbks.

Tyler, J., et al. Our World. (Illus.). 96p. (gr. 3-7). 1993. pap. text ed. 12.95 (*0-86020-571-1*, Usborne) EDC.

Tyler, Jenny. Usborne Book of World Geography. (Illus.). 160p. (gr. 4-7). 1986. 19.95 (*0-7460-1848-7*, Usborne) EDC.

Vallet, Roxanne. Geography Is Fun. Vallet, Roxanne, illus. 13p. (gr. k-3). 1992. pap. 10.95 (*1-895583-37-3*) MAYA Pubs.

VanCleave, Janice. Janice VanCleave's Geography for Every Kid. 240p. (gr. 3 up). 1993. text ed. 24.95 (*0-471-59841-0*); pap. text ed. 10.95 (*0-471-59842-9*) Wiley.

Varley, C. Geography Encyclopedia. (Illus.). 128p. (gr. 3-6). 1993. PLB 16.96 (*0-88110-600-3*); pap. 14.95 (*0-7460-0955-0*) EDC.

Waterlow, Julia. Journeys. LC 93-6819. (Illus.). 32p. (gr. 4-6). 1993. 14.95 (*1-56847-051-7*) Thomson Lrning.

Where It's At: Geography for the Quick. (gr. 4-8). 1987. 1.95 (*0-685-57931-X*) Trillium Pr.

Williams, Brian. Countries of the World: A Visual Factfinder. LC 92-40367. (Illus.). 96p. (gr. 5 up). 1993. 15.95 (*1-85697-844-3*, Kingfisher LKC); pap. 9.95 (*1-85697-816-8*) LKC.

—The Kingfisher Reference Atlas: An A-Z Guide to Countries of the World. Porter, Malcolm, illus. LC 92-54829. 216p. 1993. 19.95 (*1-85697-838-9*, Kingfisher LKC) LKC.

Wolfman, Ira. My World & Globe. LC 91-50382. (Illus.). 64p. (Orig.). 1991. pap. 12.95 (*0-89480-993-8*, 1993) Workman Pub.

Wood, Robert W. Thirty-Nine Easy Geography Activities. 1991. 16.95 (*0-8306-2493-7*); pap. 9.95 (*0-8306-2492-9*) TAB Bks.

Yoder, Walter D. Camino Real Activity Book: Spanish Settlers in the Southwest. (Illus.). 48p. (Orig.). (gr. 3-9). 1994. pap. 7.95 (*0-86534-218-0*) Sunstone Pr.

You Are Here: A First Book of Places. (gr. 2-4). 1991. write for info. (*0-307-11573-9*, Golden Pr) Western Pub.

Your School Report (TM) (Illus.). 51p. (gr. 5-11). 1994. 19.95 (*1-884618-00-6*) Unique Information.

GEOGRAPHY, BIBICAL

see Bible–Geography

GEOGRAPHY, COMMERCIAL

see also Economic Conditions; Trade Routes

Morris, Scott, ed. The Economy of the World. De Blij, Harm J., intro. by. LC 92-22291. (Illus.). 1993. 15.95 (*0-7910-1809-1*, Am Art Analog); pap. write for info. (*0-7910-1822-9*, Am Art Analog) Chelsea Hse.

—Industry of the World. De Blij, Harm J., intro. by. LC 92-22288. (Illus.). 1993. 15.95 (*0-7910-1807-5*, Am Art Analog); pap. write for info. (*0-7910-1820-2*, Am Art Analog) Chelsea Hse.

GEOGRAPHY–DICTIONARIES

Enciclopedia Geografica Juvenil, 13 vols. (SPA.). 1280p. 1974. Set. pap. 250.00 (*84-201-0410-8*) Fr & Eur.

Encyclopedia of World Geography. 1993. Set. 499.95 (*1-85435-632-1*) Marshall Cavendish.

Knowlton, Jack. Geography from A to Z: A Picture Glossary. Barton, Harriett, illus. LC 86-4594. 48p. (gr. 2-5). 1988. 14.00 (*0-690-04616-2*, Crowell Jr Bks); PLB 13.89 (*0-690-04618-9*) HarpC Child Bks.

GEOGRAPHY, ECONOMIC

see Geography, Commercial

GEOGRAPHY, HISTORICAL–MAPS

see Atlases, Historical

GEOGRAPHY, PHYSICAL

see Physical Geography

GEOGRAPHY–PICTORIAL WORKS

see Views

GEOGRAPHY, SOCIAL

see Anthropogeography

GEOGRAPHY–VOCATIONAL GUIDANCE

Sipiera, Paul. I Can Be a Geographer. LC 90-2198. (Illus.). 32p. (gr. k-3). 1990. PLB 11.80 (*0-516-01961-9*); pap. 3.95 (*0-516-41961-7*) Childrens.

GEOLOGICAL PHYSICS

see Geophysics

GEOLOGISTS

Higginson, Mel. Scientists Who Study the Earth. LC 94-7000. (gr. 4 up). 1994. write for info. (*0-86593-372-3*) Rourke Corp.

Wiggers, Raymond. The Amateur Geologist: Explorations & Investigations. (Illus.). (gr. 5-8). 1994. pap. 6.95 (*0-531-15695-8*) Watts.

GEOLOGY

see also Coral Reefs and Islands; Creation; Earth; Earthquakes; Glaciers; Mineralogy; Mountains; Oceanography; Physical Geography; Rocks; Submarine Geology; Volcanoes

Aylesworth, Thomas G. Moving Continents: Our Changing Earth. LC 89-33549. (Illus.). 64p. (gr. 6 up). 1990. lib. bdg. 15.95 (*0-89490-273-3*) Enslow Pubs.

Barrow, Lloyd H. Adventures with Rocks & Minerals: Geology Experiments for Young People. LC 90-30444. (Illus.). 96p. (gr. 4-9). 1991. lib. bdg. 16.95 (*0-89490-263-6*) Enslow Pubs.

Baylor, Byrd. If You Are a Hunter of Fossils. Parnall, Peter, illus. LC 79-17926. 32p. (ps-3). 1980. SBE 14.95 (*0-684-16419-1*, Scribners Young Read) Macmillan Child Grp.

Bell, Robert A. Crystals. Lopez, Paul, illus. 24p. (gr. k-5). 1992. pap. write for info. blister pk., incl. 3 crystal specimens & magnifying glass (*0-307-12856-3*, 12856, Golden Pr) Western Pub.

Boy Scouts of America. Geology. (Illus.). 96p. (gr. 6-12). 1985. pap. 1.85 (*0-8395-3284-9*, 33284) BSA.

Boyer, Robert E. & Snyder, P. B. Geology Fact Book. 2nd ed. LC 75-138627. (Illus.). 48p. (gr. 4-7). 1986. pap. text ed. 7.50 (*0-8331-0572-8*) Hubbard Sci.

Bryan, T. Scott. Geysers: What They Are & How They Work. (Illus.). 48p. (Orig.). 1990. pap. 5.95 (*0-911797-74-2*) R Rinehart.

Burchard, Elizabeth. Earth Science - Geology: In a Flash. 480p. (gr. 7-12). 1994. pap. 9.95 (*1-881374-07-6*) Flash Blasters.

Butler, Daphne. First Look under the Ground. LC 90-10250. (Illus.). 32p. (gr. 1-2). 1991. PLB 17.27 (*0-8368-0507-0*) Gareth Stevens Inc.

Catherall, Ed. Exploring Soil & Rocks. LC 90-10024. (Illus.). 48p. (gr. 4-8). 1990. PLB 22.80 (*0-8114-2595-9*) Raintree Steck-V.

Diagram Group & Lambert, David. The Field Guide to Geology. (Illus.). 256p. (gr. 8-12). 1988. 25.95x (*0-8160-1697-6*) Facts on File.

Diagram Group Staff & Lambert, David. The Field Guide to Geology. (Illus.). 256p. (gr. 8-12). 1989. pap. 14.95 (*0-8160-2032-9*) Facts on File.

Frahm, Randy. Canyons. LC 94-3156. 40p. 1994. 18.95 (*0-88682-707-8*) Creative Ed.

Goodman, Billy. Natural Wonders & Disasters. Goodman, Billy, illus. (gr. 3-7). 1991. 17.95 (*0-316-32016-1*) Little.

Grady, Sean M. Plate Tectonics: Earth's Shifting Crust. LC 91-16714. (Illus.). 96p. (gr. 5-8). 1991. PLB 15.95 (*1-56006-217-7*) Lucent Bks.

Horenstein, Sidney. Rocks Tell Stories. LC 92-16562. (Illus.). 72p. (gr. 4-6). 1993. PLB 15.40 (*1-56294-238-7*); pap. 6.95 (*1-56294-766-4*) Millbrook Pr.

Ingoglia, Gina. Look Inside the Earth. (Illus.). 16p. (ps-1). 1991. bds. 11.95 (*0-448-40087-1*, G&D) Putnam Pub Group.

Lauber, Pat. Dinosaurs Walked Here & Other Stories Fossils Tell. LC 91-40739. (Illus.). 64p. (gr. 2-5). 1992. pap. 5.95 (*0-689-71603-6*, Aladdin) Macmillan Child Grp.

Lye, Keith. The Earth. (Illus.). 64p. (gr. 4-6). 1991. PLB 15.40 (*1-56294-025-2*) Millbrook Pr.

McNulty, Faith. How to Dig a Hole to the Other Side of the World. Simont, Marc, illus. LC 78-22479. 32p. (ps-3). 1979. PLB 14.89 (*0-06-024148-9*) HarpC Child Bks.

Mariner, Tom. Continents. LC 89-17285. (Illus.). 32p. (gr. 3-8). 1990. PLB 9.95 (*1-85435-195-8*) Marshall Cavendish.

Mayes, S. What's under the Ground? (Illus.). 24p. (gr. 1-4). 1989. (Usborne); pap. 3.95 (*0-7460-0357-9*, Usborne) EDC.

National Wildlife Federation Staff. Geology: The Active Earth. (gr. k-8). 1991. pap. 7.95 (*0-945051-38-7*, 75032) Natl Wildlife.

Petty, Kate. The Ground Below Us. (Illus.). 32p. (gr. 2-4). 1993. pap. 5.95 (*0-8120-1232-1*) Barron.

Pomeroy, Johanna P. Content Area Reading Skills Geology: Detecting Sequence. (Illus.). (gr. 4). 1987. pap. text ed. 3.25 (*1-55737-085-0*) Ed Activities.

Sayre, April P. Tundra. (Illus.). 64p. (gr. 5-8). 1994. bds. 15.95 (*0-8050-2829-3*) TFC Bks NY.

Sipiera, Paul. I Can Be a Geologist. LC 86-9598. (Illus.). 32p. (gr. k-3). 1986. PLB 11.80 (*0-516-01897-3*); pap. 3.95 (*0-516-41897-1*) Childrens.

Skeem, Kenneth A. Genesis Fossil Booklet. Skeem, Jeanette, illus. (gr. 3-12). 1992. pap. text ed. 2.00 (*0-9606782-1-2*) Behemoth Pub.

Vogt, Gregory L. The Search for the Killer Asteroid. LC 93-47328. (Illus.). 72p. (gr. 4-6). 1994. PLB 15.90 (*1-56294-448-7*) Millbrook Pr.

Wiggers, Raymond. The Amateur Geologist: Explorations & Investigations. (Illus.). 144p. (gr. 6-9). 1993. PLB 12.90 (*0-531-11112-1*) Watts.

Zoehfeld, Kathleen W. How Mountains Are Made. Hale, James G., illus. LC 93-45436. 1995. 15.00 (*0-06-024509-3*); PLB 14.89 (*0-06-024510-7*) HarpC Child Bks.

GEOLOGY, DYNAMIC

see Geophysics

GEOLOGY, ECONOMIC

see also Mines and Mineral Resources; Soils

GEOLOGY, HISTORICAL

see Geology, Stratigraphic

GEOLOGY–MAPS

Raymo, Chet. Geologic & Topographic Profile of the United States along Interstate 80. Raymo, Chet, illus. 21p. (Orig.). (gr. 6-12). 1982. pap. text ed. 7.50 (*0-8331-1714-9*, 473) Hubbard Sci.

GEOLOGY–NORTH AMERICA

Frye, Keith. Roadside Geology of Virginia. Alt, David & Hyndman, Donald, eds. Venkatakrishnan, Rames, illus. Milici, Robert C., frwd. by. LC 86-8755. (Illus.). 256p. (Orig.). 1986. pap. 12.00 (*0-87842-199-8*) Mountain Pr.

Smith, W. Hovey. Guide to the Geology of Bartow County, Georgia. (Illus.). 46p. (Orig.). (gr. 8-12). 1985. pap. text ed. 5.00 (*0-916565-07-6*) Whitehall Pr.

GEOLOGY, STRATIGRAPHIC

see also Fossils

Reddy, Francis. Rand McNally Discovery Atlas of Dinosaurs & Prehistoric Creatures. Wills, Jan & Ortega, Pat, illus. LC 93-43086. 1994. write for info. (*0-528-83677-3*) Rand McNally.

Spizzirri Publishing Co. Staff. Paleozoic Life: An Educational Coloring Book. Spizzirri, Linda, ed. Spizzirri, Peter M., illus. 32p. (gr. 1-8). 1981. pap. 1.75 (*0-86545-024-2*) Spizzirri.

GEOLOGY, SUBMARINE

see Submarine Geology

GEOLOGY–VOCATIONAL GUIDANCE

Higginson, Mel. Scientists Who Study the Earth. LC 94-7000. (gr. 4 up). 1994. write for info. (*0-86593-372-3*) Rourke Corp.

GEOMETRICAL DRAWING

see also Graphic Methods; Mechanical Drawing

Macmahon, Horace. Stereogram Book of Contours. LC 74-188860. 32p. (gr. 1 up). 1972. pap. 5.10 plastic comb bdg. (*0-8331-1705-X*) Hubbard Sci.

GEOMETRY

see also Geometrical Drawing; Trigonometry

Barner, Bob. Space Race. LC 94-13267. (gr. 1 up). 1995. 6.95 (*0-553-37567-9*, Little Rooster) Bantam.

Brownlee, Juanita. Tangram Geometry in Metric. Merrick, Paul, illus. (Orig.). (gr. 5-10). 1976. pap. 7.95 (*0-918932-43-2*, 0140701407) Activity Resources.

Burchard, Elizabeth & Brick, Gary. Geometry: In a Flash. 478p. (gr. 7-12). 1994. pap. 9.95 (*1-881374-15-7*) Flash Blasters.

Callinan, Karen. Circles. Marden, Carol K., illus. 32p. (ps-2). Date not set. 11.95 (*1-56065-151-2*) Capstone Pr.

—Rectangles. Marden, Carol K., illus. 32p. (ps-2). Date not set. 11.95 (*1-56065-150-4*) Capstone Pr.

Churchill, Eric R. Geometry Flipper. 49p. (gr. 7 up). 1989. Repr. of 1988 ed. trade edition 5.95 (*1-878383-04-3*) C Lee Pubns.

Falwell, Cathryn. Shape Space. Falwell, Cathryn, illus. 32p. (ps-2). 1992. 13.45 (*0-395-61305-1*, Clarion Bks) HM.

Feldman, Judy. Shapes in Nature. LC 90-23091. (Illus.). 32p. (ps-2). 1991. PLB 13.35 (*0-516-05102-4*) Childrens.

Griffiths, Rose. Circles. Millard, Peter, photos by. LC 94-9592. (Illus.). 32p. (gr. 1 up). 1994. PLB 17.27 (*0-8368-1109-7*) Gareth Stevens Inc.

Healy, Christopher C. Build-a-Book Geometry. 239p. (gr. 9-12). 1993. pap. 9.95 (*1-55953-066-9*) Key Curr Pr.

Hewavisenti, Lakshmi. Shapes & Solids. LC 91-9170. (Illus.). 32p. (gr. k-4). 1991. PLB 11.90 (*0-531-17320-8*, Gloucester Pr) Watts.

Hoban, Tana. Circles, Triangles & Squares. Hoban, Tana, illus. LC 72-93305. 32p. (ps-2). 1974. RSBE 14.00 (*0-02-744830-4*, Macmillan Child Bk) Macmillan Child Grp.

—Shapes, Shapes, Shapes. Hoban, Tana, photos by. LC 85-17569. (Illus.). 32p. (ps-3). 1986. 16.00 (*0-688-05832-9*); PLB 15.93 (*0-688-05833-7*) Greenwillow.

Jenkins, Lee, et al. Geoblocks & Geojackets. (gr. 3-10). 1976. 9.50 (*0-918932-22-X*) Activity Resources.

Kirk, Jim. Environmental Geometry. (Illus.). (gr. 3-8). 1975. incl. activity cards 5.50 (*0-918932-61-0*) Activity Resources.

Komarc, Marilyn & Clay, Gwen. Exploring with Polydrons, Vol. 1. 48p. (gr. 3-9). 1991. pap. 7.95 (*0-938587-20-X*) Cuisenaire.

—Exploring with Polydrons, Vol. 2. 48p. (gr. 3-9). 1991. pap. 7.95 (*0-938587-21-8*) Cuisenaire.

Laycock, Mary & Dominques, Manuel. Discover It! 32p. (Orig.). (gr. 5-10). 1986. pap. 7.50 (*0-918932-87-4*) Activity Resources.

Lund, Charles. Dot Paper Geometry: With or Without a Geoboard. (Illus.). 84p. (gr. 4-8). 1980. pap. text ed. 9.50 (*0-914040-87-1*) Cuisenaire.

Mogensen, Sandra & Magarian-Gold, Judi. Exploring with Color Tiles. 48p. (gr. k-3). 1990. pap. text ed. 7.95 (*0-938587-17-X*) Cuisenaire.

Navarro, C. F. Early Geometry. (Illus.). 64p. (Orig.). (gr. 2-3). 1990. pap. text ed. 6.50 (*1-878396-04-8*) Start Smart Bks.

Nichols, Frank, illus. Circles. (Orig.). (ps-2). 1976. pap. 3.95 (*0-85953-047-7*) Childs Play.

Rogers, Paul. The Shapes Game. Tucker, Sian, illus. LC 89-19957. 32p. (ps-2). 1990. 12.95 (*0-8050-1280-X*, Bks Young Read) H Holt & Co.

Ross, Catherine S. Circles: Fun Ideas for Getting A-Round in Math. Slavin, Bill, illus. LC 92-40159. (gr. 4-7). 1993. pap. 9.57 (*0-201-62268-8*) Addison-Wesley.

Serra, Michael. Discovering Geometry: An Inductive Approach. 756p. (gr. 9-12). 1993. 32.29 (*0-913684-08-2*) Key Curr Pr.

—Patty Paper Geometry. (gr. 9-12). 1994. 18.95 (*1-55953-072-3*) Key Curr Pr.

—Patty Paper Geometry Student Workbook. (gr. 9-12). 1994. 3.25 (*1-55953-074-X*) Key Curr Pr.

Sharman, Lydia. The Amazing Book of Shapes. LC 93-34260. (Illus.). 40p. (gr. k-3). 1994. 14.95 (*1-56458-514-X*) Dorling Kindersley.

Smoothey, Marion. Angles. Evans, Ted, illus. LC 92-36222. 1993. 15.95 (*1-85435-466-3*) Marshall Cavendish.

—Circles. Evans, Ted, illus. 64p. (gr. 4-8). 1992. text ed. 16.95 (*1-85435-456-6*) Marshall Cavendish.

—Shape Patterns. Evans, Ted, illus. LC 92-36223. 1993. 15.95 (*1-85435-465-5*) Marshall Cavendish.

—Shapes. Evans, Ted, illus. LC 92-36224. 1993. 15.95 (*1-85435-464-7*) Marshall Cavendish.

—Solids. Evans, Ted, illus. LC 92-36220. 1993. 15.95 (*1-85435-469-8*) Marshall Cavendish.

—Triangles. Evans, Ted, illus. LC 92-12156. 1992. 15.95 (*1-85435-461-2*) Marshall Cavendish.

VanCleave, Janice. Janice VanCleave's Geometry for Every Kid: Easy Activities That Make Learning Geometry Fun. LC 93-43049. 1994. text ed. 24.95 (*0-471-31142-1*); pap. text ed. 10.95 (*0-471-31141-3*) Wiley.

Vellozi, Joseph A. Plane & Coordinate Geometry Study Aid. 1974. pap. 2.50 (*0-87738-040-6*) Youth Ed.

Wiley, Larry. Introductory Geometrics. 278p. (Orig.). (gr. 10-12). 1986. pap. text ed. 15.00 (*0-89824-065-4*); tchr's. ed. 7.50 (*0-89824-066-2*) Trillium Pr.

Zimmermann, H. Werner. Alphonse Knows...A Circle Is Not a Valentine. (Illus.). 24p. (ps-2). 1991. bds. 9.95 laminated (*0-19-540744-X*) OUP.

GEOMETRY, PLANE

see Geometry

GEOMETRY, SOLID

see Geometry

GEOPHYSICS

see also Meteorology; Oceanography

Farndon, John. How the Earth Works: One Hundred Ways Parents & Kids Can Share the Secrets of the Earth. LC 91-45004. (Illus.). 192p. (gr. 3 up). 1992. 24.00 (*0-89577-411-9*, Dist. by Random) RD Assn.

Ganeri, Anita. I Wonder Why the Wind Blows & Other Questions about Our Planet. LC 93-48559. 32p. (gr. k-3). 1994. 8.95 (*1-85697-996-2*, Kingfisher LKC) LKC.

Hehner, B. E. Blue Planet. 1992. write for info. (*0-15-200423-8*, Gulliver Bks) HarBrace.

Souza, D. M. Northern Lights. (gr. 4-7). 1994. pap. 7.95 (*0-87614-629-9*) Carolrhoda Bks.

GEORGE WASHINGTON BRIDGE–FICTION

Swift, Hildegarde H. & Ward, Lynd. Little Red Lighthouse & the Great Gray Bridge. Ward, Lynd, illus. LC 42-36286. (ps-3). 1942. 15.95 (*0-15-247040-9*, HB Juv Bks) HarBrace.

GEORGIA

Carole Marsh Georgia Books, 47 bks. 1994. lib. bdg. 1102.65 set (*0-7933-1285-X*); pap. 632.65 set (*0-7933-5142-1*) Gallopade Pub Group.

Carpenter, Allan. Georgia. LC 79-12095. (Illus.). 96p. (gr. 4 up). 1979. PLB 16.95 (*0-516-04110-X*) Childrens.

Fradin, Dennis. Georgia. LC 91-12101. 64p. (gr. 3-5). 1991. PLB 16.45 (*0-516-03810-9*) Childrens.

Fradin, Dennis B. The Georgia Colony. LC 89-34954. 160p. (gr. 4 up). 1989. PLB 17.95 (*0-516-00392-5*) Childrens.

Hepburn, Lawrence R. State Government in Georgia. 3rd ed. 200p. (gr. 8-12). 1991. text ed. 12.25 (*0-89854-176-X*) U of GA Inst Govt.

Hepburn, Mary A. Local Government in Georgia. 2nd ed. 240p. (gr. 8-12). 1991. text ed. 13.75 (*0-89854-148-4*) U of GA Inst Govt.

Jackson, Edwin L., et al. The Georgia Studies Book. (Illus.). 464p. (gr. 8). 1991. text ed. 19.85 (*0-89854-149-2*) U of GA Inst Govt.

Kent, Zachary A. Georgia. 204p. 1993. text ed. 15.40 (*1-56956-130-3*) W A T Braille.

Krull, Kathleen. Bridges to Change: How Kids Live on a South Carolina Sea Island. Hautzig, David, photos by. LC 93-42392. 1994. write for info. (*0-525-67441-1*, Lodestar Bks) Dutton Child Bks.

Loewen, N. Atlanta. (Illus.). 48p. (gr. 5 up). 1989. lib. bdg. 15.94 (*0-86592-543-7*); PLB 11.95s.p. (*0-685-58591-3*) Rourke Corp.

Marsh, Carole. Avast, Ye Slobs! Georgia Pirate Trivia. (Illus.). (gr. 3-12). 1994. PLB 24.95 (*0-7933-0328-1*); pap. 14.95 (*0-7933-0327-3*); computer disk 29.95 (*0-7933-0329-X*) Gallopade Pub Group.

—The Beast of the Georgia Bed & Breakfast. (Illus.). (gr. 3-12). 1994. PLB 24.95 (*0-7933-1512-3*); pap. 14.95 (*0-7933-1513-1*); computer disk 29.95 (*0-7933-1514-X*) Gallopade Pub Group.

—Bow Wow! Georgia Dogs in History, Mystery, Legend, Lore, Humor & More! (Illus.). (gr. 3-12). 1994. PLB 24.95 (*0-7933-3497-7*); pap. 14.95 (*0-7933-3498-5*); computer disk 29.95 (*0-7933-3499-3*) Gallopade Pub Group.

—Christopher Columbus Comes to Georgia! Includes Reproducible Activities for Kids! (Illus.). (gr. 3-12). 1994. PLB 24.95 (*0-7933-3650-3*); pap. 14.95 (*0-7933-3651-1*); computer disk 29.95 (*0-7933-3652-X*) Gallopade Pub Group.

—Georgia & Other State Greats (Biographies) (Illus.). (gr. 3-12). 1994. PLB 24.95 (*1-55609-392-6*); pap. 14.95 (*1-55609-391-8*); computer disk 29.95 (*0-7933-1520-4*) Gallopade Pub Group.

—Georgia Bandits, Bushwackers, Outlaws, Crooks, Devils, Ghosts, Desperadoes & Other Assorted & Sundry Characters! (Illus.). (gr. 3-12). 1994. PLB 24.95 (*0-7933-0310-9*); pap. 14.95 (*0-7933-0309-5*); computer disk 29.95 (*0-7933-0311-7*) Gallopade Pub Group.

—Georgia Classic Christmas Trivia: Stories, Recipes, Activities, Legends, Lore & More! (Illus.). (gr. 3-12). 1994. PLB 24.95 (*0-7933-0313-3*); pap. 14.95 (*0-7933-0312-5*); computer disk 29.95 (*0-7933-0314-1*) Gallopade Pub Group.

—Georgia Coastales. (Illus.). (gr. 3-12). 1994. PLB 24.95 (*1-55609-233-4*); pap. 14.95 (*1-55609-117-6*); computer disk 29.95 (*0-7933-1516-6*) Gallopade Pub Group.

—Georgia Coastales! 1994. lib. bdg. 24.95 (*0-7933-7275-5*) Gallopade Pub Group.

—Georgia Dingbats! Bk. 1: A Fun Book of Games, Stories, Activities & More about Our State That's All in Code! for You to Decipher. (Illus.). (gr. 3-12). 1994. PLB 24.95 (*0-7933-3803-4*); pap. 14.95 (*0-7933-3804-2*); computer disk 29.95 (*0-7933-3805-0*) Gallopade Pub Group.

—Georgia Festival Fun for Kids! (Illus.). (gr. 3-12). 1994. lib. bdg. 24.95 (*0-7933-3956-1*); pap. 14.95 (*0-7933-3957-X*); disk 29.95 (*0-7933-3958-8*) Gallopade Pub Group.

—The Georgia Hot Air Balloon Mystery. (Illus.). (gr. 2-9). 1994. 24.95 (*0-7933-2408-4*); pap. 14.95 (*0-7933-2409-2*); computer disk 29.95 (*0-7933-2410-6*) Gallopade Pub Group.

—Georgia Jeopardy! Answers & Questions about Our State! (Illus.). (gr. 3-12). 1994. PLB 24.95 (*0-7933-4109-4*); pap. 14.95 (*0-7933-4110-8*); computer disk 29.95 (*0-7933-4111-6*) Gallopade Pub Group.

—Georgia Jography: A Fun Run Through the Peach State. (Illus.). 50p. (Orig.). (gr. 4-8). 1994. pap. 14.95 (*0-935326-93-6*) Gallopade Pub Group.

—Georgia Kid's Cookbook: Recipes, How-To, History, Lore & More! (Illus.). (gr. 3-12). 1994. PLB 24.95 (*0-7933-0322-2*); pap. 14.95 (*0-7933-0321-4*); computer disk 29.95 (*0-7933-0323-0*) Gallopade Pub Group.

—Georgia Quiz Bowl Crash Course! (Illus.). (gr. 3-12). 1994. PLB 24.95 (*1-55609-384-5*); pap. 14.95 (*1-55609-383-7*); computer disk 29.95 (*0-7933-1515-8*) Gallopade Pub Group.

—Georgia Rollercoasters! (Illus.). (gr. 3-12). 1994. PLB 24.95 (*0-7933-5254-1*); pap. 14.95 (*0-7933-5255-X*); computer disk 29.95 (*0-7933-5256-8*) Gallopade Pub Group.

—Georgia School Trivia: An Amazing & Fascinating Look at Our State's Teachers, Schools & Students! (Illus.). (gr. 3-12). 1994. PLB 24.95 (*0-7933-0319-2*); pap. 14.95 (*0-7933-0318-4*); computer disk 29.95 (*0-7933-0320-6*) Gallopade Pub Group.

—Georgia Silly Basketball Sportsmysteries, Vol. I. (Illus.). (gr. 3-12). 1994. PLB 24.95 (*0-7933-0316-8*); pap. 14.95 (*0-7933-0315-X*); computer disk 29.95 (*0-7933-0317-6*) Gallopade Pub Group.

—Georgia Silly Basketball Sportsmysteries, Vol. II. (Illus.). (gr. 3-12). 1994. PLB 24.95 (*0-7933-1521-2*); pap. 14.95 (*0-7933-1522-0*); computer disk 29.95 (*0-7933-1523-9*) Gallopade Pub Group.

—Georgia Silly Football Sportsmysteries, Vol. I. (Illus.). (gr. 3-12). 1994. PLB 24.95 (*1-55609-394-2*); pap. 14.95 (*1-55609-393-4*); computer disk 29.95 (*0-7933-1508-5*) Gallopade Pub Group.

—Georgia Silly Football Sportsmysteries, Vol. II. (Illus.). (gr. 3-12). 1994. PLB 24.95 (*0-7933-1509-3*); pap. 14.95 (*0-7933-1510-7*); computer disk 29.95 (*0-7933-1511-5*) Gallopade Pub Group.

—Georgia Silly Trivia Book. (Illus.). 48p. (Orig.). (gr. 2-12). 1994. pap. 14.95 (*0-935326-61-8*) Gallopade Pub Group.

—Georgia's (Most Devastating!) Disasters & (Most Calamitous!) Catastrophies! (Illus.). (gr. 3-12). 1994. PLB 24.95 (*0-7933-0307-9*); pap. 14.95 (*0-7933-0306-0*); computer disk 29.95 (*0-7933-0308-7*) Gallopade Pub Group.

—The Hard-to-Believe-But-True! Book of Georgia History, Mystery, Trivia, Legend, Lore, Humor & More. (Illus.). (gr. 3-12). 1994. PLB 24.95 (*0-7933-0325-7*); pap. 14.95 (*0-7933-0324-9*); computer disk 29.95 (*0-7933-0326-5*) Gallopade Pub Group.

—If My Georgia Mama Ran the World! (Illus.). (gr. 3-12). 1994. PLB 24.95 (*0-7933-1517-4*); pap. 14.95 (*0-7933-1518-2*); computer disk 29.95 (*0-7933-1519-0*) Gallopade Pub Group.

—Jurassic Ark! Georgia Dinosaurs & Other Prehistoric Creatures. (gr. k-12). 1994. PLB 24.95 (*0-7933-7458-8*); pap. 14.95 (*0-7933-7459-6*); computer disk 29.95 (*0-7933-7460-X*) Gallopade Pub Group.

—Let's Quilt Georgia & Stuff It Topographically! (Illus.). (gr. 3-12). 1994. PLB 24.95 (*1-55609-382-9*); pap. 14.95 (*1-55609-054-4*); computer disk 29.95 (*0-7933-1507-7*) Gallopade Pub Group.

—Let's Quilt Our Georgia County. 1994. lib. bdg. 24.95 (*0-7933-7143-0*); pap. text ed. 14.95 (*0-7933-7144-9*); disk 29.95 (*0-7933-7145-7*) Gallopade Pub Group.

—Let's Quilt Our Georgia Town. 1994. lib. bdg. 24.95 (*0-7933-6993-2*); pap. text ed. 14.95 (*0-7933-6994-0*); disk 29.95 (*0-7933-6995-9*) Gallopade Pub Group.

—Meow! Georgia Cats in History, Mystery, Legend, Lore, Humor & More! (Illus.). (gr. 3-12). 1994. PLB 24.95 (*0-7933-3344-X*); pap. 14.95 (*0-7933-3345-8*); computer disk 29.95 (*0-7933-3346-6*) Gallopade Pub Group.

—Uncle Rebus: Georgia Picture Stories for Computer Kids. (Illus.). (gr. k-3). 1994. PLB 24.95 (*0-7933-4531-6*); pap. 14.95 (*0-7933-4532-4*); disk 29.95 (*0-7933-4533-2*) Gallopade Pub Group.

Pedersen, Anne. Kidding Around Atlanta: A Young Person's Guide to the City. (Illus.). 64p. (gr. 3 up). 1989. pap. 9.95 (*0-945465-35-1*) John Muir.

Snow, Pegeen. Atlanta. LC 88-20243. (Illus.). 60p. (gr. 3 up). 1989. text ed. 13.95 RSBE (*0-87518-389-1*, Dillon) Macmillan Child Grp.

Turner Programs Services, Inc. Staff & Clark, James I. Georgia. 48p. (gr. 3 up). 1985. pap. text ed. 19.97 (*0-8174-4281-2*) Raintree Steck-V.

GEORGIA–FICTION

Beatty, Patricia. Turn Homeward, Hannalee. LC 84-8960. 208p. (gr. 5-9). 1984. 12.95 (*0-688-03871-9*) Morrow Jr Bks.

Blackburn, Joyce. The Bloody Summer of Seventeen Forty-Two: A Colonial Boy's Journal. Graham, Critt, illus. 64p. (gr. 5-8). 1985. pap. 4.25 (*0-930803-00-0*) Fort Frederica.

Griffith, Helen V. Georgia Music. Stevenson, James, illus. LC 85-24918. 24p. (gr. k up). 1990. pap. 3.95 (*0-688-09931-9*, Mulberry) Morrow.

Krisher, Trudy. Spite Fences. LC 94-8665. 1994. 14.95 (*0-385-32088-4*) Delacorte.

Wilkinson, Brenda. Ludell. LC 75-9390. 176p. (gr. 7 up). 1975. PLB 14.89 (*0-06-026492-6*) HarpC Child Bks.

—Ludell & Willie. LC 76-18402. (gr. 7 up). 1977. PLB 13.89 (*0-06-026488-8*) HarpC Child Bks.

GEORGIA–HISTORY

Marsh, Carole. Chill Out: Scary Georgia Tales Based on Frightening Georgia Truths. (Illus.). 1994. lib. bdg. 24.95 (*0-7933-4684-3*); pap. 14.95 (*0-7933-4685-1*); disk 29.95 (*0-7933-4686-X*) Gallopade Pub Group.

—Georgia "Crinkum-Crankum" A Funny Word Book about Our State. (Illus.). 1994. lib. bdg. 24.95 (*0-7933-4837-4*); pap. 14.95 (*0-7933-4838-2*); disk 29.95 (*0-7933-4839-0*) Gallopade Pub Group.

—The Georgia Mystery Van Takes Off! Book 1: Handicapped Georgia Kids Sneak Off on a Big Adventure. (Illus.). (gr. 3-12). 1994. 24.95 (*0-7933-4991-5*); pap. 14.95 (*0-7933-4992-3*); computer disk 29.95 (*0-7933-4993-1*) Gallopade Pub Group.

—Georgia Timeline: A Chronology of Georgia History, Mystery, Trivia, Legend, Lore & More. (Illus.). (gr. 3-12). 1994. PLB 24.95 (*0-7933-5905-8*); pap. 14.95 (*0-7933-5906-6*); computer disk 29.95 (*0-7933-5907-4*) Gallopade Pub Group.

—Georgia's Unsolved Mysteries (& Their "Solutions") Includes Scientific Information & Other Activities for Students. (Illus.). (gr. 3-12). 1994. PLB 24.95 (*0-7933-5752-7*); pap. 14.95 (*0-7933-5753-5*); computer disk 29.95 (*0-7933-5754-3*) Gallopade Pub Group.

—My First Book about Georgia. (gr. k-4). 1994. PLB 24.95 (*0-7933-5599-0*); pap. 14.95 (*0-7933-5600-8*); computer disk 29.95 (*0-7933-5601-6*) Gallopade Pub Group.

GEOSCIENCE

see Geology

GERBILS

Barrett, Norman S. Gerbils. LC 89-21529. (Illus.). 32p. (gr. k-4). 1990. PLB 11.90 (*0-531-14030-X*) Watts.

Hearne, T. Gerbils. (Illus.). 32p. (gr. 2-5). 1989. lib. bdg. 15.94 (*0-86625-186-3*); 11.95s.p. (*0-685-58608-1*) Rourke Corp.

Piers, Helen. Taking Care of Your Gerbils: Young Pet Owner's Guides Ser. Vriends, Matthew M., ed. LC 92-26959. 32p. 1993. pap. 4.95 (*0-8120-1369-7*) Barron.

Wexler, Jerome. Pet Gerbils. Tucker, Kathy, ed. LC 89-5636. (Illus.). 48p. (gr. 3-6). 1990. PLB 14.95 (*0-8075-6523-7*) A Whitman.

GERBILS–FICTION

Adler, David A. Wacky Jacks: A Houdini Club Magic Mystery. Malone, Heather H., illus. LC 93-51259. 80p. (Orig.). (gr. 1-4). 1994. PLB 2.99 (*0-679-84696-4*); pap. 9.99 (*0-679-94696-9*) Random.

Manes, Stephen. The Great Gerbil Roundup. McKinley, John, illus. 105p. (gr. 3-7). 1988. 13.95 (*0-15-232490-9*, HB Juv Bks) HarBrace.

GERMAN LANGUAGE–CONVERSATIONS AND PHRASE BOOK

Amery, H. & Cartwright, S. First Hundred Words in German. (GER., Illus.). 32p. (ps-4). 1988. PLB 11.96 (*0-88110-324-1*, Usborne); pap. 7.95 (*0-7460-0365-X*, Usborne) EDC.

Beeck, Johannes, et al. Telefon. Baker, Syd, illus. Winitz, Harris, intro. by. (GER., Illus.). 50p. (gr. 7 up). 1990. Incls. cass. tape. pap. text ed. 22.00 (*0-939990-70-9*) Intl Linguistics.

Bladon, Rachel. German for Beginners Workbook. (gr. 4-7). 1993. pap. 6.95 (*0-8442-2181-3*, Passport Bks) NTC Pub Grp.

Brinckmann, Caren, et al. Beforderung. Baker, Syd, illus. Winitz, Harris, intro. by. (GER., Illus.). 40p. (gr. 7 up). 1990. Incls. cass. tape. pap. text ed. 22.00 (*0-939990-71-7*) Intl Linguistics.

Colvin, L. & Irving, N. Essential German. (Illus.). 64p. 1990. lib. bdg. 12.96 (*0-88110-419-1*); pap. 5.95 (*0-7460-0318-8*) EDC.

Criminale, Ulrike & Language School of the American Cultural Exchange Staff. Springboard to German: Introduction to the German Language. Porter, Mary D., illus. 32p. (gr. k-4). 1991. Incl. cassettes. 19.95 (*1-880770-01-6*) ACE Pub.

SPRINGBOARD is a set of easy, encouraging foreign language lessons for young children ages 4-8. This popular series features two 90-minute cassette tapes on which a native speaker of the foreign language leads the child in short, playful sessions through a variety of actions by repeating simple commands both in the foreign language & in English. The child is not required to read or write the language. Instead, the language is absorbed almost effortlessly as the child enjoys a progression of music, games & activities. The program emphasizes well-planned lessons for the adult leader & can be enjoyed by anyone in the home setting as well as in class. Because the cassettes guide the activity, the adult is not required to know the language, but instead simply participates with the child. The accompanying Springboard books provide attractive illustrations & a word-for-word transcript of the cassettes along with a comprehensive Vocabulary Chart for review & an Activities Supplement with suggestions for further learning. The Series is available in French, German & Spanish, & will soon be available in Japanese. For information on placing orders, please call (206) 535-8104.
Publisher Provided Annotation.

Farnes, C. Survive in Five Languages. (Illus.). 64p. (gr. 8 up). 1993. PLB 12.96 (*0-88110-623-2*); pap. 6.95 (*0-7460-1034-6*) EDC.

Gemmell, Kathy & Tyler, Jenny. First German at Home. (Illus.). 32p. (gr. 1-6). 1993. lib. bdg. 12.96 (*0-88110-644-5*, Usborne); pap. 5.95 (*0-7460-1051-6*, Usborne) EDC.

Hazzan, Anne-Francoise. Let's Learn German Coloring Book. (Illus.). 64p. (gr. 4 up). 1988. pap. 3.95 (*0-8442-2164-3*, Natl Textbk) NTC Pub Grp.

Hildebrand, Sigrid S. & Hildebrand, Eckart. Gehen. Rohrer, Josef, ed. Baker, Syd, illus. Winitz, Harris, intro. by. (GER., Illus.). 85p. (gr. 7 up). 1990. Incls. cass. tape. pap. 22.00 (*0-939990-64-4*) Intl Linguistics.

—Stellen, Legen und Setzen. Rohrer, Josef, ed. Baker, Syd, illus. Winitz, Harris, intro. by. (GER., Illus.). 80p. (Orig.). (gr. 7 up). 1990. Incls. cass. tape. pap. text ed. 22.00 (*0-939990-65-2*) Intl Linguistics.

Irving, N. Learn German. (Illus.). 64p. (gr. 5 up). 1992. PLB 13.96 (*0-88110-597-X*); pap. 7.95 (*0-7460-0534-2*) EDC.

—Learn German Language Pack. (Illus.). 64p. (gr. 7 up). 1993. pap. 16.95 incl. tape (*0-7460-1440-6*, Usborne) EDC.

Let's Learn Picture Dictionaries: German. (Illus.). 72p. 1991. 9.95 (*0-8442-2167-8*, Natl Textbk) NTC Pub Grp.

Liedloff, Helmut. Ohne Muhe! LC 79-84596. (Illus.). (gr. 9-10). 1980. pap. 7.84 (*0-395-27931-3*) HM.

Lyric Language - German, Series 1 & 2. (Illus.). (ps-8). Series 1. 9.95 (*1-56015-227-3*) Series 2. 9.95 (*1-56015-240-0*) Penton Overseas.

Mahoney, Judy. Teach Me More German. Kamstra, Angela, illus. (GER.). 20p. (ps-6). 1990. pap. 13.95 incl. audiocassette (*0-934633-23-1*); tchr's. ed. 6.95 (*0-934633-34-7*) Teach Me.

Mealer, Tamara. My World in German Coloring Book. (GER., Illus.). 96p. 1991. pap. 4.95 (*0-8442-2169-4*, Natl Textbk) NTC Pub Grp.

Nash, Rod. In Germany. (GER.). 80p. (gr. 7-12). 1984. pap. text ed. 8.95 (*0-8219-0056-0*, 45285); tchr's. wkbk. 5.95 (*0-8219-0274-1*, 45820); 4.95 (*0-8219-0273-3*, 45660) EMC.

Trim, John. Ganz Spontan! (GER.). 352p. 1988. pap. text ed. 11.50 (*0-8219-0346-2*, 45295); tchr's. guide 5.95 (*0-8219-0347-0*, TG-45823) EMC.

Wilkes, Angela. German for Beginners. (Illus.). 48p. (gr. 4 up). 1988. 8.95 (*0-8442-2165-1*, Passport Bks) NTC Pub Grp.

Winitz, Harris. Hauser und Gebaude: Houses & Buildings in German. Rohrer, Josef, ed. Baker, Syd, illus. (GER.). 50p. (Orig.). (gr. 7 up). 1989. pap. text ed. 22.00 incl. cass. (*0-939990-76-8*) Intl Linguistics.

Wright, Nicola. Getting to Know: Germany & German. Wooley, Kim, illus. 32p. (gr. 3-7). 1993. 12.95 (*0-8120-6337-6*); pap. 5.95 (*0-8120-1533-9*) Barron.

GERMAN LANGUAGE–DICTIONARIES–ENGLISH

Cirker, Hayward & Steadman, Barbara. German Picture Word Book: Learn over Five Hundred Commonly Used German Words Through Pictures. (GER & ENG., Illus.). 32p. (Orig.). 1993. pap. text ed. 2.95t (*0-486-27778-X*) Dover.

GERMAN LANGUAGE–GRAMMAR

Berlitz. Berlitz Jr. German: Ich Spreche Deutsch. (Illus.). 64p. (ps-2). 1992. pap. 19.95 POB (*0-689-71598-6*, Aladdin) Macmillan Child Grp.

Marsh, Carole. Jason Hewitt! German for Kids. 1994. lib. bdg. 24.95 (*0-7933-6879-0*); pap. text ed. 14.95 (*0-7933-6878-2*); disk 29.95 (*0-7933-6880-4*) Gallopade Pub Group.

GERMAN LANGUAGE–READERS

Amery, Heather. First Thousand Words in German. Cartwright, Stephen, illus. 50p. (ps-7). 1979. 11.95 (*0-86020-268-2*) EDC.

Civardi, Anne. Word Finder in German. Cartwright, Stephen, illus. 48p. (gr. k-3). 1984. 8.95 (*0-7460-0394-3*) EDC.

Cooper, Lee. Fun with German. Githens, Elizabeth, illus. (gr. 3 up). 1972. lib. bdg. 15.95 (*0-316-15588-8*) Little.

Curtis, David, et al. German Study-Aid. 1977. pap. 2.75 (*0-87738-034-1*) Youth Ed.

De Brunhoff, Laurent. Je Parle Allemand avec Babar. (FRE., Illus.). (gr. 4-6). 15.95 (*0-685-11271-3*) Fr & Eur.

Meyer, Ursula & Wolfson, Alice. Abenteur in Deutschland. (Illus.). (gr. 9-12). 1976. pap. text ed. 4.75 (*0-88345-276-6*, 18485) Prentice ESL.

GERMAN POETRY–COLLECTIONS

Busch, Wilhelm. Max & Moritz. Arndt, Walter, tr. LC 85-1241. (Illus.). (gr. 4 up). 1985. 9.95 (*0-915361-19-1*) Modan-Adama Bks.

GERMANS IN PENNSYLVANIA

see Pennsylvania Dutch

GERMANS IN THE U. S

Cook. German Americans. 1991. 13.95s.p. (*0-86593-140-2*); PLB 18.60 (*0-685-59184-0*) Rourke Corp.

Franck, Irene M. The German-American Heritage. (Illus.). 160p. 1988. 16.95x (*0-8160-1629-1*) Facts on File.

Galicich, Anne. The German Americans. Moynihan, Daniel P. (Illus.). 112p. (gr. 5 up). 1989. lib. bdg. 17.95 (*1-55546-141-7*); pap. 9.95 (*0-7910-0265-9*) Chelsea Hse.

Schouweiler, Thomas. Germans in America. LC 94-500. 1994. 15.95 (*0-8225-0245-3*); pap. 5.95 (*0-8225-1049-9*) Lerner Pubns.

GERMANS IN THE U. S.–FICTION

Hoff, Carol. Johnny Texas. Myers, Bob, illus. 150p. (gr. 4 up). 1992. lib. bdg. 15.95 (*0-937460-80-X*); pap. 9.95 (*0-937460-81-8*) Hendrick-Long.

Levitin, Sonia. Silver Days. LC 91-22581. 192p. (gr. 3-7). 1992. pap. 3.95 (*0-689-71570-6*, Aladdin) Macmillan Child Grp.

Lindsay, Mela M. The Story of Johann: The Boy Who Longed to Come to Amerika. Gentry, Diane, illus. LC 90-85324. 190p. 1991. 11.50 (*0-914222-18-X*) Am Hist Soc Ger.

GERMANY

Adler, Ann. A Family in West Germany. LC 85-6981. (Illus.). 32p. (gr. 2-5). 1985. PLB 13.50 (*0-8225-1658-6*) Lerner Pubns.

Ayer, Eleanor. Germany. (Illus.). 64p. (gr. 7 up). 1990. lib. bdg. 17.27 (*0-86593-093-7*); lib. bdg. 12.95s.p. (*0-685-36365-1*) Rourke Corp.

Bailey, Donna. Germany. LC 91-22763. (Illus.). 32p. (gr. 1-4). 1992. PLB 18.99 (*0-8114-2566-5*); pap. 3.95 (*0-8114-7176-4*) Raintree Steck-V.

First Book of Germany. (Illus.). 32p. (gr. 1-5). 1992. pap. 6.95 (*0-7460-1242-X*) EDC.

Flint, David. Germany. LC 93-631. (Illus.). 32p. (gr. 3-4). 1993. PLB 19.24 (*0-8114-3418-4*) Raintree Steck-V.

—Germany. LC 93-26534. 1993. PLB 22.80 (*0-8114-1845-6*) Raintree Steck-V.

Ganeri, Anita. Germany & the Germans. LC 92-37091. (Illus.). 32p. (gr. 5-8). 1993. PLB 12.40 (*0-531-17402-6*, Gloucester Pr) Watts.

Garrett, Dan & Drew-Bernstein, Charlotte. Germany. LC 91-20790. (Illus.). 96p. (gr. 6-12). 1992. PLB 22.80 (*0-8114-2446-4*) Raintree Steck-V.

Getting to Know Germany. 48p. 1990. 8.95 (*0-8442-2168-6*, Natl Textbk) NTC Pub Grp.

Hargrove, Jim. Germany. LC 91-22645. 128p. (gr. 5-9). 1991. PLB 20.55 (*0-516-02601-1*) Childrens.

Haskins, Jim. Count Your Way Through Germany. Byers, Helen, illus. 24p. (gr. 1-4). 1990. PLB 17.50 (*0-87614-407-5*) Carolrhoda Bks.

—Count Your Way Through Germany. LC 89-22232. (ps-3). 1991. pap. 5.95 (*0-87614-532-2*) Carolrhoda Bks.

Lerner Publications Company, Geography Department Staff. Germany - in Pictures. LC 93-40971. (Illus.). 64p. (gr. 5 up). 1994. PLB 18.95 (*0-8225-1873-2*) Lerner Pubns.

Loewen. Food in Germany. 1991. 11.95s.p. (*0-86625-347-5*) Rourke Pubns.

McHugh, Madeline & Balzert, Birgit. Guide to Germany. Brand, Maggie, illus. LC 93-39021. 32p. (gr. 1-4). 1994. 3.95 (*1-85697-959-8*, Kingfisher LKC) LKC.

Pfeiffer, Christine. Germany: Two Nations, One Heritage. LC 86-32954. (Illus.). 176p. (gr. 5 up). 1987. text ed. 14.95 RSBE (*0-87518-361-1*, Dillon) Macmillan Child Grp.

Phillpotts, Beatrice. Germany. (Illus.). 48p. (gr. 4-8). 1989. lib. bdg. 14.95 (*0-382-09794-7*) Silver Burdett Pr.

Schloredt, Valerie. Germany. (Illus.). 48p. (gr. 5 up). 1991. PLB 12.95 (*0-382-24245-9*) Silver Burdett Pr.

Stadtler, Christa. West Germany. LC 90-996. (Illus.). 32p. (gr. k-3). 1991. PLB 12.40 (*0-531-18371-8*, Pub. by Bookwright Pr) Watts.

Steele, Phillip. Germany. LC 92-39685. (Illus.). 32p. (gr. 5). 1993. text ed. 13.95 RSBE (*0-89686-777-3*, Crestwood Hse) Macmillan Child Grp.

GERMANY (FEDERAL REPUBLIC)

Dolan, Sean. West Germany: On the Road to Reunification. (Illus.). 128p. (gr. 5 up). 1991. 14.95 (*0-7910-1367-7*) Chelsea Hse.

Fuller, Barbara. Germany. LC 92-13447. 1992. 21.95 (*1-85435-530-9*) Marshall Cavendish.

Stadtler, Christa. West Germany. LC 90-996. (Illus.). 32p. (gr. k-3). 1991. PLB 12.40 (*0-531-18371-8*, Pub. by Bookwright Pr) Watts.

GERMANY–FICTION

Carter, Peter. Bury the Dead. LC 85-45995. 374p. (gr. 6 up). 1987. 17.00 (*0-374-31011-4*) FS&G.

Greene, Bette. Summer of My German. 1984. pap. 3.99 (*0-440-21892-6*) Dell.

Jerome, Jerome K. Three Men on the Bummel. (Illus.). 240p. (gr. 6-9). 1991. pap. 8.00 (*0-86299-029-7*) A Sutton Pub.

Kastner. Mein Onkel Franz. (gr. 7-12). pap. 5.95 (*0-88436-037-7*, 45259) EMC.

Kordon, Klaus. Brothers Like Friends. Crawford, Elizabeth D., tr. from GER. 192p. (gr. 5 up). 1992. 14.95 (*0-399-22137-9*, Philomel Bks) Putnam Pub Group.

Lenz. Lotte Soll Nicht Sterben. (gr. 7-12). pap. 5.95 (*0-88436-039-3*, 45260) EMC.

Roesler. Gansebraten. (gr. 7-12). pap. 5.95 (*0-88436-109-8*, 45262) EMC.

Roland, Donna. Grandfather's Stories from Germany. (gr. k-3). 1984. pap. 4.95x (*0-941996-03-4*); tchr's. ed. 5.50 (*0-941996-15-8*) Open My World.

—More of Grandfather's Stories from Germany. (gr. 1-3). 1984. pap. 4.95x (*0-941996-04-2*); tchr's. ed. 5.50 (*0-685-55723-5*) Open My World.

Schnurre. Die Tat - Ein Fall Fur Herrn Schmidt. pap. 6.95 (*0-88436-040-7*, 45272) EMC.

Townsend, Tom. Trader Wooly & the Ghost in the Colonel's Jeep. (Illus.). 110p. (gr. 6-8). 1991. 10.95 (*0-89015-807-X*) Sunbelt Media.

Winnig. Das Romerzimmer. (gr. 7-12). pap. 5.95 (*0-88436-041-5*, 45261) EMC.

Zweig. Novellen. (gr. 7-12). pap. 6.95 (*0-88436-042-3*, 45273) EMC.

GERMANY–HISTORY

Stewart, Gail B. Germany. LC 90-2244. (Illus.). 48p. (gr. 6-7). 1990. text ed. 12.95 RSBE (*0-89686-548-7*, Crestwood Hse) Macmillan Child Grp.

William, Spencer. Germany Then & Now. LC 93-29444. (Illus.). 176p. (gr. 9-12). 1994. PLB 13.90 (*0-531-11137-7*) Watts.

GERMANY–HISTORY–FICTION

Ray, Karen. To Cross a Line. LC 93-11813. 160p. (gr. 7 up). 1994. 14.95 (*0-531-06831-5*); lib. bdg. 14.99 RLB (*0-531-08681-X*) Orchard Bks Watts.

Richter, Hans P. I Was There. (gr. 5-9). 1987. pap. 4.99 (*0-14-032206-X*, Puffin) Puffin Bks.

GERMANY–HISTORY–20TH CENTURY

Finke, Blythe F. Konrad Adenauer: Architect of the New Germany. Rahmas, D. Steve, ed. LC 79-190241. 32p. (Orig.). (gr. 7-12). 1972. lib. bdg. 4.95 incl. catalog cards (*0-87157-523-X*) SamHar Pr.

GERMANY–HISTORY–1933-1945

Chrisp, Peter. Blitzkrieg. LC 90-42856. (Illus.). 64p. (gr. 7-10). 1991. PLB 13.40 (*0-531-18373-4*, Pub. by Bookwright Pr) Watts.

Heyes, Eileen. Adolf Hitler. LC 93-31269. (gr. 7 up). 1994. PLB 16.90 (*1-56294-343-X*) Millbrook Pr.

—Children of the Swastika: The Hitler Youth. LC 92-13204. (Illus.). 96p. (gr. 7 up). 1993. PLB 15.40 (*1-56294-237-9*) Millbrook Pr.

Marrin, Albert. Hitler. LC 93-13057. 256p. (gr. 7 up). 1993. pap. 5.99 (*0-14-036526-5*, Puffin) Puffin Bks.

Wolff, Marion F. The Shrinking Circle: Memories of Nazi Berlin, 1933-39. 128p. (gr. 7-9). 1989. pap. 7.95 (*0-8074-0419-5*, 147501); tchr's. guide 5.00 (*0-8074-0447-0*, 201500) UAHC.

GERMANY–HISTORY–1945-

Bradley, John F. & Bradley, Catherine. Germany: The Reunification of a Nation - Update. rev. ed. (Illus.). 40p. (gr. 6-8). 1993. PLB 12.90 (*0-531-17431-X*, Gloucester Pr) Watts.

Hargrove, Jim. The Story of the Unification of Germany. LC 91-12650. (Illus.). 32p. (gr. 3-6). 1991. PLB 12.30 (*0-516-04761-2*); pap. 3.95 (*0-516-44761-0*) Childrens.

GERMS

see Bacteriology; Microorganisms

GERONIMO, APACHE CHIEF, 1829-1909

Grosvenor, Richard. Geronimo. 8p. (gr. k-2). 1993. pap. write for info. (*1-882563-06-9*) Lamont Bks.

Jeffrey, David. Geronimo. Viola, Herman, intro. by. (Illus.). 32p. (gr. 3-6). 1990. PLB 19.97 (*0-8172-3404-7*); pap. 4.95 (*0-8114-4090-7*) Raintree Steck-V.

Kent, Zachary. The Story of Geronimo. LC 88-37005. (Illus.). 32p. (gr. 3-6). 1989. pap. 3.95 (*0-516-44743-2*) Childrens.

Sanford, William R. Geronimo: Apache Warrior. LC 93-42257. 48p. (gr. 4-10). 1994. lib. bdg. 14.95 (*0-89490-510-4*) Enslow Pubs.

Schwartz, Melissa. Geronimo. (Illus.). 128p. (gr. 5 up). 1992. lib. bdg. 17.95 (*0-7910-1701-X*) Chelsea Hse.

Wheeler, Jill. The Story of Geronimo. Deegan, Paul, ed. Dodson, Liz, illus. LC 89-84911. 32p. (gr. 4). 1989. PLB 11.96 (*0-939179-68-7*) Abdo & Dghtrs.

Zadra, Dan. Indians of America: Geronimo. rev. ed. (gr. 2-4). 1987. PLB 14.95 (*0-88682-159-2*) Creative Ed.

GERONTOLOGY

see Old Age

GERSHWIN, GEORGE, 1898-1937

Mitchell, Barbara. America, I Hear You: A Story about George Gershwin. Smith, Jan H., illus. 64p. (gr. 3-6). 1987. PLB 14.95 (*0-87614-309-5*) Carolrhoda Bks.

Venezia, Mike. George Gershwin. Venezia, Mike, illus. LC 94-9478. 48p. (gr. 4 up). 1994. PLB 17.20 (*0-516-04536-9*); pap. 4.95 (*0-516-44536-7*) Childrens.

GETTYSBURG, BATTLE OF, 1863

Coffey, Vincent J. The Battle of Gettysburg. LC 84-40834. (Illus.). 64p. (gr. 5 up). 1985. PLB 12.95 (*0-382-06830-0*); pap. 7.95 (*0-382-09911-7*) Silver Burdett Pr.

Johnson, Neil. The Battle of Gettysburg. Johnson, Neil, illus. LC 88-30414. 64p. (gr. 5 up). 1989. SBE 15.95 (*0-02-747831-9*, Four Winds) Macmillan Child Grp.

Kantor, MacKinlay. Gettysburg. LC 87-4576. (Illus.). (gr. 5-9). 1963. pap. 3.95 (*0-394-89181-3*) Random Bks Yng Read.

Murphy, Jim. The Long Road to Gettysburg. (Illus.). 128p. (gr. 4-7). 1992. 15.45 (*0-395-55965-0*, Clarion Bks) HM.

Reef, Catherine. Gettysburg. LC 91-43653. (Illus.). 72p. (gr. 4 up). 1992. text ed. 14.95 RSBE (*0-87518-503-7*, Dillon) Macmillan Child Grp.

Witherow, Diane L. Gettysburg Children's Activity Book. (Illus.). 40p. (gr. 1-6). 1990. pap. 3.00 (*0-939631-20-2*) Thomas Publications.

GETTYSBURG, BATTLE OF, 1863-FICTION

Gauch, Patricia L. Thunder at Gettysburg. (ps-3). 1990. pap. 3.25 (*0-553-15951-8*) Bantam.

GHANA

Barnett, Jeanie M. Ghana. (Illus.). 104p. (gr. 5 up). 1989. lib. bdg. 14.95 (*1-55546-789-X*) Chelsea Hse.

Hintz, Martin. Ghana. LC 86-29935. (Illus.). 128p. (gr. 5-9). 1987. PLB 20.55 (*0-516-02773-5*) Childrens.

Jacobsen, Karen. Ghana. LC 91-35273. (Illus.). 48p. (gr. k-4). 1992. PLB 12.85 (*0-516-01135-9*); pap. 4.95 (*0-516-41135-7*) Childrens.

Koslow, Philip. Ancient Ghana: The Land of Gold. LC 94-26192. (gr. 10 up). 1995. write for info. (*0-7910-3126-8*); pap. write for info. (*0-7910-2941-7*) Chelsea Hse.

Lerner Publications, Department of Geography Staff. Ghana in Pictures. (Illus.). 64p. (gr. 5 up). 1988. 17.95 (*0-8225-1829-5*) Lerner Pubns.

McKissack, Patricia. Royal Kingdoms of Ghana, Mali, & Soghay: Life in Medieval Africa. (Illus.). 128p. (gr. 5-9). 1994. 15.95 (*0-8050-1670-8*, Bks Young Read) H Holt & Co.

GHANA–FICTION

Wilkins, Verna & McLean, Gill, eds. Abena & the Rock: A Story from Ghana. Wilkinson, Barry, illus. Ramamurthy, Sita, contrib. by. LC 93-12122. (Illus.). 1993. 7.95 (*1-870516-08-7*) Childs Play.

GHOST STORIES

Abbott, Jennie. The Ghost of Hanover Hill. Badenhop, Mary, illus. LC 87-14983. 96p. (gr. 5-8). 1988. PLB 9.89 (*0-8167-1185-2*); pap. text ed. 2.95 (*0-8167-1186-0*) Troll Assocs.

Adler, C. S. Ghost Brother. 160p. (gr. 4-8). 1990. 14.95 (*0-395-52592-6*, Clarion Bks) HM.

—Ghost Brother. 144p. 1992. pap. 3.50 (*0-380-71386-1*, Camelot) Avon.

Ahlberg, Allan. Ghost Train. ALC Staff, ed. Amstutz, Andre, illus. LC 91-39838. 32p. (gr. k up). 1992. pap. 3.95 (*0-688-11659-0*, Mulberry) Morrow.

—Skeleton Crew. ALC Staff, ed. Amstutz, illus. LC 91-39161. 32p. (gr. k up). 1992. pap. 3.95 (*0-688-11660-4*, Mulberry) Morrow.

Aiken, Joan. A Foot in the Grave. Pienkowski, Jan, illus. 128p. (gr. 5 up). 1992. 15.95 (*0-670-84169-2*) Viking Child Bks.

—Return to Harken House. (gr. 5-9). 1990. 13.95 (*0-385-29975-3*) Delacorte.

—The Shadow Guests. (gr. 5 up). 1986. pap. 2.95 (*0-440-48226-7*, YB) Dell.

—The Shadow Guests. large type ed. (gr. 1-8). 1993. 16.95 (*0-7451-1913-1*, Galaxy Child Lrg Print) Chivers N Amer.

—The Shadow Guests: A Novel. LC 80-65830. 144p. (gr. 7 up). 1980. pap. 11.95 (*0-385-28889-1*) Delacorte.

Alcock, Vivien. The Haunting of Cassie Palmer. LC 81-15230. 160p. (gr. 4-6). 1982. pap. 11.95 (*0-385-28402-0*) Delacorte.

Alexander, Sue. Witch, Goblin & Ghost in the Haunted Woods. Winter, Jeanette, illus. LC 80-20863. 72p. (gr. 1-4). 1981. 6.95 (*0-394-84443-2*); lib. bdg. 7.99 (*0-394-94443-7*) Pantheon.

—Witch, Goblin, & Sometimes Ghost: Six Read-Alone Stories. Winter, Jeanette, illus. LC 76-8657. (ps-3). 1976. 6.95 (*0-394-83216-7*) Pantheon.

Allen, Laura J. Rollo & Tweedy & the Ghost at Dougal Castle. LC 89-26921. (Illus.). 64p. (gr. k-3). 1992. 13.00 (*0-06-020106-1*); PLB 13.89 (*0-06-020107-X*) HarpC Child Bks.

—Rollo & Tweedy & the Ghost at Dougal Castle. Allen, Laura J., illus. LC 89-26921. 64p. (gr. k-3). 1994. pap. 3.50 (*0-06-444182-2*, Trophy) HarpC Child Bks.

Alley, Robert. The Ghost in Dobbs Diner. Alley, Robert, illus. LC 81-4864. 48p. (ps-3). 1981. 5.95 (*0-8193-1055-7*); lib. bdg. 5.95 (*0-8193-1056-5*) Parents.

Alphin, Elaine M. Ghost Cadet. 192p. 1992. pap. 2.95 (*0-590-45244-4*, Apple Paperbacks) Scholastic Inc.

Anderson, Mary. Terror under the Tent. (gr. k-6). 1987. pap. 2.50 (*0-440-48633-5*, YB) Dell.

—The Three Spirits of Vandermeer Manor. (Orig.). (gr. k-6). 1987. pap. 2.75 (*0-440-48810-9*, YB) Dell.

Andrews, Jean F. The Ghost of Tomahawk Creek. Allard, Mike, illus. LC 93-86006. (Orig.). (gr. 2-6). 1993. pap. text ed. 5.95 (*1-883120-01-2*) Northern St U.

Astrop, John. John Astrop's Ghastly Games. Astrop, John, illus. 24p. (ps-3). 1983. pop-up bk. 9.95 (*0-385-29307-0*) Delacorte.

Avi. Something Upstairs: A Tale of Ghosts. LC 88-60094. 128p. (gr. 5-7). 1988. 13.95 (*0-531-05782-8*); PLB 13.99 (*0-531-08382-9*) Orchard Bks Watts.

Bang, Molly, ed. & illus. The Goblins Giggle & Other Stories. (gr. 3-5). 1988. 22.75 (*0-8446-6360-3*) Peter Smith.

Barkan, Joanne. A Very Scary Haunted House. Wheeler, Jodie, illus. 24p. 1991. pap. 3.95 (*0-590-44497-2*) Scholastic Inc.

Bauer, Marion D. Ghost Eye. 1992. 12.95 (*0-590-45298-3*, Scholastic Hardcover) Scholastic Inc.

—A Taste of Smoke. LC 92-32585. (gr. 5 up). 1993. 13.95 (*0-395-64341-4*, Clarion Bks) HM.

Bellairs, John. The Revenge of the Wizard's Ghost. Gorey, Edward, illus. LC 85-4550. 160p. (gr. 5 up). 1985. 13.95 (*0-8037-0170-5*) Dial Bks Young.

—The Revenge of the Wizard's Ghost. 160p. 1986. pap. 3.50 (*0-553-15451-6*) Bantam.

Benchley, Nathaniel. Ghost Named Fred. Shecter, Ben, illus. LC 68-24322. 64p. (gr. k-3). 1968. PLB 13.89 (*0-06-020474-5*) HarpC Child Bks.

—A Ghost Named Fred. Shecter, Ben, illus. LC 68-24322. 64p. (gr. k-3). 1979. pap. 3.50 (*0-06-444022-2*, Trophy) HarpC Child Bks.

Berenstain, Stan & Berenstain, Jan. The Berenstain Bears & the Galloping Ghost. Berenstain, Stan & Berenstain, Jan, illus. 112p. (Orig.). (gr. 2-6). 1994. 7.99 (*0-679-95815-0*); pap. 2.99 (*0-679-85815-6*) Random Bks Yng Read.

Black, J. R. The Ghost of Chicken Liver Hill. 120p. (Orig.). (gr. 3-7). 1993. pap. 3.50 (*0-679-85007-4*, Bullseye Bks) Random Bks Yng Read.

Blair, L. E. The Ghost of Eagle Mountain. 128p. (gr. 2 up). 1990. pap. write for info. (*0-307-22006-0*, Pub. by Golden Bks) Western Pub.

Block, Francesca L. Missing Angel Juan. Braun, Wendy, illus. LC 92-38299. 144p. (gr. 7 up). 1993. 14.00 (*0-06-023004-5*); PLB 13.89 (*0-06-023007-X*) HarpC Child Bks.

Bodie, Idella. Ghost in the Capitol. Kovach, Gay H., illus. 116p. (gr. 4-6). 1986. pap. 6.95 (*0-87844-072-0*) Sandlapper Pub Co.

—Ghost Tales for Retelling. Stone, Barbara, ed. (Illus.). 78p. (Orig.). (gr. 6). 1994. pap. 6.95 (*0-87844-125-5*) Sandlapper Pub Co.

To encourage young readers in the art - & pleasure - of storytelling, author Idella Bodie has pulled together twenty-seven tall tales she & her friends told around their backyard campfires when she was a girl. Older ghost story lovers will recognize old favorites like THE GOLDEN ARM. Ms. Bodie has organized these scary stories into five categories: flesh-tingling stories, spirits returning, supernatural stories, haunted places, & shapes & shadows. To assist the young storytellers, she has included a list of "Hints for Effective Storytelling." A retired English teacher, Ms. Bodie has previously written nine books for young readers: seven novels & two biographies. Call 1-800-849-7263 to order copies or request additional information.

Publisher Provided Annotation.

Bodkin, Odds. The Banshee Train. Rose, Ted, illus. LC 93-39635. Date not set. write for info. (*0-395-69426-4*, Clarion Bks) HM.

Bolton, Judy. Haunted Attic. (gr. 4-7). 1994. 12.95 (*1-55709-251-6*) Applewood.

Bright, Robert. Georgie. Bright, Robert, illus. 44p. (gr. k-1). 1944. pap. 7.95 (*0-385-07307-0*) Doubleday.

—Georgie. 48p. (gr. k-3). pap. 1.50 (*0-590-01617-2*) Scholastic Inc.

—Georgie & the Robbers. Bright, Robert, illus. LC 63-11384. 28p. (ps-1). 1963. pap. 5.95 (*0-385-04483-6*); pap. 2.50 (*0-385-13341-3*) Doubleday.

Brittain, Bill. The Ghost from Beneath the Sea. Chessare, Michele, illus. LC 92-1091. 148p. (gr. 4-7). 1992. 14.00 (*0-06-020827-9*); PLB 13.89 (*0-06-020828-7*) HarpC Child Bks.

—Who Knew There'd Be Ghosts? Chessare, Michele, illus. LC 84-48496. 128p. (gr. 4-7). 1985. PLB 13.89 (*0-06-020700-0*) HarpC Child Bks.

Brown. Springtime Ghost. (gr. 4-8). 1989. PLB 8.49 (*0-87386-059-4*); pap. 1.95 (*0-87386-063-2*) Jan Prods.

Buffie, Margaret. The Haunting of Frances Rain. 1989. pap. 12.95 (*0-590-42834-9*) Scholastic Inc.

—Someone Else's Ghost. LC 93-48015. (gr. 6 up). 1994. write for info. (*0-590-46922-3*) Scholastic Inc.
Bulla, Clyde R. Ghost of Windy Hill. Bolognese, Don, illus. LC 68-11059. (gr. 3-7). 1968. PLB 13.89 (*0-690-32764-1*, Crowell Jr Bks) HarpC Child Bks.
—The Ghost of Windy Hill. 96p. (Orig.). (gr. 2-5). 1990. pap. 2.75 (*0-590-43286-9*) Scholastic Inc.
Bunting, Eve. Ghost Behind Me. (gr. 7-9). 1986. pap. 2.50 (*0-671-62211-0*, Archway) PB.
—Ghost's Hour, Spook's Hour. Carrick, Donald, illus. LC 86-31674. 32p. (ps-1). 1987. 14.95 (*0-89919-484-2*, Clarion Bks) HM.
—Ghost's Hour, Spook's Hour. Carrick, Donald, illus. 1990. pap. 7.95 incl.cassette (*0-395-56244-9*, Clarion Bks) HM.
—In the Haunted House. Meddaugh, Susan, illus. LC 89-77663. 32p. (ps-3). 1990. 13.45 (*0-395-51589-0*, Clarion Bks) HM.
Burchill, James V., et al. Ghosts & Haunts from the Appalachian Foothills. LC 93-30419. 192p. (Orig.). 1993. pap. 9.95 (*1-55853-253-6*) Rutledge Hill Pr.
Butler, Linda P. Maxine & the Ghost Dog. Goldberg, Grace, illus. 24p. (ps-2). 1992. pap. 0.99 (*1-56293-114-8*) McClanahan Bk.
Cadwallader, Sharon. Cookie McCorkle & the Case of the Crooked Key. 112p. (Orig.). 1993. pap. 3.50 (*0-380-76896-8*, Camelot Young) Avon.
Calif, Ruth. The Over-the-Hill Ghost. Holub, Joan, illus. LC 87-30523. 160p. (gr. 3-8). 1988. 10.95 (*0-88289-667-9*) Pelican.
Carrie, Christopher. Mystery of the Forest Phantom. (Illus.). 40p. (gr. k up). 1990. pap. 1.59 (*0-86696-243-3*) Binney & Smith.
Carter, David A. In a Dark, Dark Wood: An Old Tale with a New Twist. (Illus.). 28p. (ps-3). 1991. pap. 10. 95 casebound, pop-up (*0-671-74134-9*, S&S BFYR) S&S Trade.
Cates, Emily. The Ghost in the Attic. Cates, Emily, illus. (gr. 3-7). 1990. pap. 2.95 (*0-553-15826-0*, Skylark) Bantam.
Catt, Louis. Little Ghost. Prater, John, illus. LC 93-29804. 32p. 1994. 4.99 (*1-56402-394-X*) Candlewick Pr.
Chambers, Aidan, ed. A Haunt of Ghosts. LC 86-45486. 192p. (gr. 7 up). 1987. HarpC Child Bks.
Chesworth, Michael. Party at the Ghost House. (ps-3). 1993. 9.95 (*0-89577-507-7*, Dist. by Random) RD Assn.
Clapp, Patricia. Jane-Emily. LC 92-46598. 160p. (gr. 7 up). 1993. pap. 3.95 (*0-688-04592-8*, Pub. by Beech Tree Bks) Morrow.
Cohen, Daniel. Great Ghosts. 48p. (gr. 4-7). 1992. pap. 1.95 (*0-590-45734-9*, Apple Paperbacks) Scholastic Inc.
—Railway Ghosts & Highway Horrors. Marchesi, Stephen, illus. LC 91-11161. 112p. (gr. 4 up). 1991. 13.95 (*0-525-65071-7*, Cobblehill Bks) Dutton Child Bks.
—Railway Ghosts & Railway Horrors. 112p. (gr. 3-7). 1993. pap. 2.95 (*0-590-45423-4*, Apple Paperbacks) Scholastic Inc.
—The World's Most Famous Ghosts. (Illus.). 112p. (gr. 3-6). 1989. pap. 2.99 (*0-671-69145-7*, Minstrel Bks) PB.
Cohen, Miriam. Starring First Grade. (gr. k-6). 1987. pap. 3.25 (*0-440-48250-X*, YB) Dell.
Colby, C. B. World's Best "True" Ghost Stories. LC 88-11703. (Illus.). 128p. (Orig.). (gr. 4 up). 1989. pap. 3.95 (*0-8069-6898-2*) Sterling.
Conrad, Pam. Stonewords: A Ghost Story. LC 89-36382. 144p. (gr. 5 up). 1990. 14.00 (*0-06-021315-9*); PLB 13.89 (*0-06-021316-7*) HarpC Child Bks.
—Stonewords: A Ghost Story. LC 89-36382. 144p. (gr. 5 up). 1991. pap. 3.95 (*0-06-440354-8*, Trophy) HarpC Child Bks.
Coombs, Patricia. Dorrie & the Haunted House. 48p. (gr. k-6). 1980. pap. 1.50 (*0-440-42212-4*, YB) Dell.
Courtney, Dayle. Secret of Pirates' Cave. rev. ed. 160p. (gr. 6-9). 1991. pap. 4.99 (*0-87403-834-0*, 24-03884) Standard Pub.
Coville, Bruce. The Ghost Wore Grey. 128p. (Orig.). 1988. pap. 3.50 (*0-553-15610-1*, Skylark) Bantam.
—Goblins in the Castle. MacDonald, Pat, ed. Coville, Katherine, illus. 176p. (Orig.). 1992. pap. 3.50 (*0-671-72711-7*, Minstrel Bks) PB.
Cresswell, Helen. Bagthorpes Haunted. (gr. 3-7). 1988. pap. 3.95 (*0-14-032172-1*, Puffin) Puffin Bks.
Crose, Mark. The Terminator. LC 90-28888. (Illus.). 48p. (gr. 5-6). 1991. text ed. 13.95 RSBE (*0-89686-580-0*, Crestwood Hse) Macmillan Child Grp.
Crume, Vic. The Ghost That Came Alive. reissued ed. 1992. pap. 2.95 (*0-590-46147-8*, Apple Paperbacks) Scholastic Inc.
Cullen, Lynn. The Backyard Ghost. LC 92-24580. 160p. (gr. 4-7). 1993. 13.95 (*0-395-64527-1*, Clarion Bks) HM.
Dadley, Debbie. Ghosts Don't Eat Potato Chips. (ps-3). 1992. pap. 2.75 (*0-590-45854-X*) Scholastic Inc.
Dahl, Roald, ed. Roald Dahl's Book of Ghost Stories. 235p. (gr. 5 up). 1984. pap. 9.00 (*0-374-51868-8*) FS&G.
Dearest Grand-Ma. 1991. pap. 13.95 (*0-385-41843-4*) Doubleday.
De Brunhoff, Laurent. Babar & the Ghost. De Brunhoff, Laurent, illus. LC 80-5753. 32p. (gr. k-3). 1981. Random Bks Yng Read.
Deem, James M. How to Find a Ghost. Kelley, True, illus. 144p. (gr. 5-9). 1988. 13.45 (*0-395-46846-9*) HM.
—How to Find a Ghost. 144p. 1990. pap. 3.25 (*0-380-70829-9*, Camelot) Avon.
Delton, Judy. Camp Ghost-Away. 80p. (Orig.). (gr. k-6). 1988. pap. 3.25 (*0-440-40062-7*, YB) Dell.
Denan, Corinne. Hair-Raising Tales. LC 79-66334. (Illus.). 48p. (gr. 5-7). 1980. PLB 9.89 (*0-89375-334-3*); pap. 2.95 (*0-89375-333-5*) Troll Assocs.
—Haunted House Tales. Toulmin-Rothe, Ann, illus. LC 79-66335. 48p. (gr. 5-7). 1980. PLB 9.89 (*0-89375-336-X*); pap. text ed. 2.95 (*0-89375-335-1*) Troll Assocs.
—Strange & Eerie Tales. new ed. LC 79-66336. (Illus.). 48p. (gr. 4-6). 1980. lib. bdg. 9.89 (*0-89375-338-6*); pap. 2.95 (*0-89375-337-8*) Troll Assocs.
Denholtz, Roni S. The Ghost in the New House. Fontalvo, Nelsy, illus. LC 86-81369. 32p. (gr. k-2). 1986. PLB 7.59 (*0-87386-017-9*); pap. 1.95 (*0-87386-013-6*) Jan Prods.
Detorie, Rick. Ghost in the Closet. 24p. (gr. k-3). 1989. pap. 1.95 (*0-8167-1457-6*) Troll Assocs.
—Haunted Elevator. 24p. (gr. k-3). 1989. pap. 1.95 (*0-8167-1459-2*) Troll Assocs.
—Haunted Tool Shed. 24p. (gr. k-3). 1989. pap. 1.95 (*0-8167-1456-8*) Troll Assocs.
—Red-Headed Gooseberry Ghost. 24p. (gr. k-3). 1989. pap. 1.95 (*0-8167-1458-4*) Troll Assocs.
Dickens, Charles. A Christmas Carol. Innocenti, Roberto, illus. 152p. (gr. 1-12). 1990. lib. bdg. 25.00 RLB smythe-sewn (*0-88682-327-7*, 97200-098) Creative Ed.
—The Signalman. Richardson, I. M., adapted by. Ashmead, Hal, illus. LC 81-19819. 32p. (gr. 5-10). 1982. PLB 10.79 (*0-89375-630-X*); pap. text ed. 2.95 (*0-89375-631-8*) Troll Assocs.
Disney, Walt, Productions Staff. Walt Disney Productions Presents "The Haunted House" LC 75-16430. (Illus.). 48p. (ps-3). 1976. 6.95 (*0-394-82570-5*); lib. bdg. 4.99 (*0-394-92570-X*) Random Bks Yng Read.
Dixon, Franklin W. Hardy Boys Ghost Stories. Greenberg, Ann, ed. 144p. (gr. 3-7). 1989. pap. 3.99 (*0-671-69133-3*, Minstrel Bks) PB.
Dodds, Dayle A. Ghost & Sam. (gr. 3 up). write for info. (*0-679-86199-8*) Random Bks Yng Read.
Drinkwater, Carol. The Haunted School. (gr. 5-9). 1988. pap. 3.95 (*0-317-69631-9*, Puffin) Puffin Bks.
Dubowski, Cathy E. Scrooge: Adapted from Charles Dickens' "A Christmas Carol" Dubowski, Mark, illus. LC 94-661. 48p. (gr. 1-3). 1994. PLB 7.99 (*0-448-40222-X*, G&D); pap. 3.50 (*0-448-40221-1*, G&D) Putnam Pub Group.
Dunlop, Eileen. Green Willow. LC 92-33402. 160p. (gr. 5-9). 1993. 14.95 (*0-8234-1021-8*) Holiday.
—House on the Hill. 160p. (gr. 2-9). 1989. pap. 2.95 (*0-8167-1323-5*) Troll Assocs.
Eldin, Peter. Spookster's Handbook. LC 89-32659. (Illus.). 96p. (Orig.). (gr. 4 up). 1990. 12.95 (*0-8069-5742-5*); pap. 3.95 (*0-8069-5743-3*) Sterling.
Estern, Anne G. The Picolinis & the Haunted House. Frenck, Hal, illus. 115p. (gr. 3-5). 1989. pap. 2.95 (*0-553-15771-X*, Skylark) Bantam.
Fager, Charles. Fire in the Valley: Six Quaker Ghost Stories. 90p. 1992. pap. 8.95 (*0-945177-10-0*) Kimo Pr.
Famous Ghost Stories. (gr. 4-7). 1993. pap. 2.95 (*0-89375-406-4*) Troll Assocs.
Farmer, Penelope. Thicker Than Water. LC 92-53133. 32p. (gr. 6-10). 1993. 14.95 (*1-56402-178-5*) Candlewick Pr.
Field, Eugene. Dibdin's Ghost. 1992. Repr. of 1893 ed. lib. bdg. 75.00 (*0-7812-2649-X*) Rprt Serv.
Fleischman, Sid. The Ghost in the Noonday Sun. Sis, Peter, illus. LC 88-11066. (gr. 5 up). 1989. 15.00 (*0-688-08410-9*) Greenwillow.
—The Ghost in the Noonday Sun. 144p. (gr. 3-7). 1991. pap. 2.75 (*0-590-43662-7*, Apple Paperbacks) Scholastic Inc.
—The Ghost on Saturday Night. Von Schmidt, Eric, illus. 64p. (gr. 4-6). 1974. 14.95 (*0-316-28583-8*, Joy St Bks) Little.
—Ghost on Saturday Night. 32p. 1992. pap. text ed. 2.56 (*1-56956-241-5*) W A T Braille.
Flora, James. Grandpa's Ghost Stories. LC 78-51999. (Illus.). 32p. (gr. k-4). 1980. SBE 13.95 (*0-689-50112-9*, M K McElderry) Macmillan Child Grp.
Foster, John. Never Say Boo to a Ghost. Paul, Korky, illus. 96p. 1991. pap. 2.75 (*0-590-45127-8*) Scholastic Inc.
Fox, J. N. Young Indiana Jones & the Pirates' Loot. LC 93-46831. 132p. (Orig.). (gr. 3-7). 1994. pap. 3.99 (*0-679-86433-4*, Bullseye Bks) Random Bks Yng Read.
Frost, Erica. I Can Read about Ghosts. LC 74-24964. (Illus.). (gr. 2-4). 1975. pap. 2.50 (*0-89375-065-4*) Troll Assocs.
Furman, Abraham L., ed. More Teen-Age Ghost Stories. (gr. 6-10). 1963. PLB 7.19 (*0-8313-0052-3*) Lantern.
—More Teen-Age Haunted Stories. (gr. 5-10). 1967. PLB 7.19 (*0-8313-0057-4*) Lantern.
Gabler, Mirko. Brackus, Krakus. Gabler, Mirko, illus. LC 92-25819. 32p. (ps-3). 1993. 14.95 (*0-8050-1963-4*, Bks Young Read) H Holt & Co.
Gage, Wilson. Mrs. Gaddy & the Ghost. Hafner, Marylin, illus. LC 78-16366. 56p. (gr. 1-3). 1979. 14.95 (*0-688-80179-X*) Greenwillow.
Gale, David, ed. Don't Give up the Ghost: The Delacorte Book of Original Ghost Stories. LC 92-47088. 1993. 14.95 (*0-385-31109-5*) Delacorte.
Gantz, David. The Spookiest Day. Gantz, David, illus. 32p. (Orig.). (gr. k-3). 1986. pap. 2.50 (*0-590-40325-7*) Scholastic Inc.
Garfield, Leon. Footsteps: A Novel. LC 80-65834. 192p. (gr. 7 up). 1980. 12.95 (*0-385-28294-X*) Delacorte.
—The Wedding Ghost. Keeping, Charles, illus. 66p. (gr. 6 up). 1987. bds. 16.00 laminated (*0-19-279779-4*) OUP.
The Ghost Train: Timeless Tales. 1992. 4.99 (*0-517-06972-5*) Random Hse Value.
Gilligan, Shannon. The Haunted Swamp. (gr. 4-7). 1991. pap. 2.95 (*0-553-15856-2*) Bantam.
Gleiter, Jan. Legend of Sleepy Hollow. (ps-3). 1993. pap. 3.95 (*0-8114-8351-7*) Raintree Steck-V.
Goode, Diane, illus. Diane Goode's Book of Scary Stories & Songs. LC 93-32610. 64p. (gr. 3 up). 1994. 15.99 (*0-525-45175-7*, DCB) Dutton Child Bks.
Great Ghost Stories. (gr. 4-7). 1993. pap. 2.95 (*0-8167-0468-6*) Troll Assocs.
Greene, Constance C. Nora: Maybe a Ghost Story. (gr. 4-7). 1993. pap. 3.95 (*0-15-276895-5*) HarBrace.
Greene, George W. What Haunts Hamlet's House? Hatter, Laurie, illus. 12p. (ps). 1992. 4.95 (*1-56828-003-3*) Red Jacket Pr.
Greenleaf, Ann G. Emily's New Ghost. LC 93-17779. (Illus.). 1993. 4.99 (*0-517-01959-0*, Pub. by Derrydale Bks) Random Hse Value.
Hahn, Mary D. The Doll in the Garden: A Ghost Story. 160p. (gr. 4-6). 1989. 13.45 (*0-89919-848-1*, Pub. by Clarion) HM.
—Look for Me by Moonlight. LC 94-21892. 1995. write for info. (*0-395-69843-X*); pap. write for info. (*0-395-69844-8*) HM.
—Wait Till Helen Comes: A Ghost Story. LC 86-2648. 192p. (gr. 4-7). 1986. 14.45 (*0-89919-453-2*, Clarion Bks) HM.
Hall, Lynn. The Mystery of Pony Hollow. Sanderson, Ruth, illus. LC 91-29861. 64p. (Orig.). (gr. 2-4). 1992. PLB 6.99 (*0-679-93052-3*); pap. 2.50 (*0-679-83052-9*) Random Bks Yng Read.
Hancock, Sibyl. Esteban & the Ghost. Zimmer, Dirk, illus. LC 82-22125. 32p. (ps-3). 1983. PLB 10.89 (*0-8037-2411-X*) Dial Bks Young.
Haunted House on Hoover Hill. 12p. (ps-3). 1990. pap. 2.95 (*0-8167-2192-0*) Troll Assocs.
Hawkins, Colin & Hawkins, Jacqui. Come for a Ride on the Ghost Train. Hawkins, Colin & Hawkins, Jacqui, illus. LC 92-54959. 40p. (ps up). 1993. 12.95 (*1-56402-236-6*) Candlewick Pr.
Hearne, Betsy G. Eli's Ghost. Himler, Ronald, illus. LC 86-21096. 112p. (gr. 3-7). 1987. SBE 13.95 (*0-689-50420-9*, M K McElderry) Macmillan Child Grp.
Hebert, Marie-Francine. A Ghost in My Mirror. (Illus.). 54p. (Orig.). 1992. pap. 5.95 (*0-929005-31-7*, Pub. by Second Story Pr CN) InBook.
Heuck, Sigrid. A Ghost in the Castle. Oberdieck, Bernard, tr. (Illus.). 26p. 1993. PLB 15.95 (*1-55037-328-5*, Pub. by Annick CN); pap. 6.95 (*1-55037-331-5*, Pub. by Annick CN) Firefly Bks Ltd.
Hezlep, William. Ghost Town. LC 91-51080. (Orig.). (gr. 3-12). 1985. pap. 5.00 play script (*0-88734-402-X*) Players Pr.
Highlights for Children Staff. The Ghostly Bell Ringer: And Other Mysteries. LC 90-85915. (Illus.). 96p. (gr. 3-7). 1992. pap. 2.95 (*1-878093-39-8*) Boyds Mills Pr.
Hildick, E. W. The Ghost Squad Breaks Through. LC 84-3985. 144p. (gr. 5-9). 1984. 12.95 (*0-525-44097-6*, 01063-320, DCB) Dutton Child Bks.
Hiser, Constance. Ghosts in the Fourth Grade. MacDonald, Pat, ed. Smith, Cat B., illus. 80p. 1992. pap. 2.99 (*0-671-75880-2*, Minstrel Bks) PB.
Hitchcock, Alfred, ed. Alfred Hitchcock's Ghostly Gallery. LC 62-14298. (Illus.). 272p. (gr. 5 up). 1984. pap. 4.99 (*0-394-86762-9*) Random Bks Yng Read.
—Alfred Hitchcock's Haunted Houseful. LC 84-15949. (Illus.). 272p. (gr. 4-9). 1985. pap. 4.99 (*0-394-87041-7*, Random Juv) Random Bks Yng Read.
Holzer, Hans. In Quest of Ghosts. (gr. 4-7). 1993. pap. 2.95 (*0-590-47346-8*) Scholastic Inc.
Homer, Larona. The Shore Ghosts & Other Stories of New Jersey. Bock, William S., illus. 154p. (gr. 4-8). 1986. 8.95 (*0-912608-14-5*) Mid Atlantic.
Hotze, Sollace. Acquainted with the Night. 256p. (gr. 7 up). 1992. 13.95 (*0-395-61576-3*, Clarion Bks) HM.
Howe, James. Nighty-Nightmare. 128p. (gr. 3-7). 1988. pap. 3.99 (*0-380-70490-0*, Camelot) Avon.
Hubner, Carol K. The Haunted Shul. Kramer, Devorah, illus. (gr. 3-8). 1979. 6.95 (*0-910818-14-2*) Judaica Pr.
Hughes, Dean. Nutty's Ghost. LC 92-8530. 144p. (gr. 3-7). 1993. SBE 13.95 (*0-689-31743-3*, Atheneum Child Bk) Macmillan Child Grp.
Hunter, Mollie. The Ghosts of Glencoe. 176p. (gr. 4 up). 1994. pap. 7.95 (*0-86241-467-9*, Pub. by Cnngt UK) Trafalgar.
Hutchinson, Duane. Storyteller's Ghost Stories. 4th ed. LC 89-23689. 112p. (gr. 4 up). 1989. pap. 6.95 (*0-934988-32-3*) Foun Bks.
—A Storyteller's Ghost Stories, Bk. 2. LC 90-3122. 96p. (gr. 4 up). 1990. pap. 6.95 (*0-934988-18-8*) Foun Bks.
Irving, Washington. The Headless Horseman: A Retelling of The Legend of Sleepy Hollow. Harding, Emma, illus. LC 94-10276. (gr. k-3). 1994. 15.95 (*0-8050-3584-2*) H Holt & Co.

—The Legend of Sleepy Hollow. Garland, Michael, illus. 64p. 1992. PLB 15.95 (*1-56397-027-9*) Boyds Mills Pr.
—The Legend of Sleepy Hollow. Flint, Ross, illus. 32p. (gr. k-4). 1992. pap. 4.95 (*0-8249-8574-5*, Ideals Child) Hambleton-Hill.
—The Legend of Sleepy Hollow. Kelley, Gary, illus. (gr. 4-12). 1990. lib. bdg. 19.95 RLB smythe-sewn (*0-88682-328-5*, 97206-098) Creative Ed.
—Legend of Sleepy Hollow & Other Stories. (gr. 6 up). 1964. pap. 2.95 (*0-8049-0050-7*, CL-50) Airmont.
—The Legend of Sleepy Hollow: Minibook Edition. Van Nutt, Robert, illus. LC 93-12153. 1993. incl. cass. 9.95 (*0-88708-321-8*, Rabbit Ears) Picture Bk Studio.
Jacques, Brian. Seven Strange & Ghostly Tales. (gr. 3 up). 1991. 14.95 (*0-399-22103-4*, Philomel Bks) Putnam Pub Group.
—Seven Strange & Ghostly Tales. 144p. 1993. pap. 3.50 (*0-380-71906-1*, Camelot) Avon.
James, Henry. Turn of the Screw. Andrews, C. A., intro. by. (gr. 9 up). 1967. pap. 1.75 (*0-8049-0155-4*, CL-155) Airmont.
—The Turn of the Screw. Shaw, Charles, illus. Stewart, Diana, adapted by. LC 81-5217. (Illus.). 48p. (gr. 4 up). 1983. PLB 20.70 (*0-8172-1672-3*) Raintree Steck-V.
—The Turn of the Screw. 160p. 1993. pap. 2.50 (*0-8125-3341-0*) Tor Bks.
James, Sara. Boots & the Spooky House. Barcita, Pamela, illus. 24p. 1993. PLB 3.98 (*1-56156-133-9*) Kidsbks.
Jensen, Patricia A. The Legend of Sleepy Hollow. Barnes-Murphy, Rowan S., illus. LC 93-24803. (gr. k-3). 1993. PLB 11.59 (*0-8167-3168-3*); pap. text ed. 2.95 (*0-8167-3169-1*) Troll Assocs.
Jerome, Jerome K. After Supper Ghost Stories: And Other Tales. 176p. (gr. 6-9). 1990. pap. 8.00 (*0-86299-762-3*) A Sutton Pub.
Jesep, Paul P. Lady-Ghost of the Isles of Shoals. LC 91-68204. 13p. (gr. 4). 1992. pap. 5.95 (*0-9634360-0-7*) Seacoast Pubns New Eng.
—Lady-Ghost of the Isles of Shoals. 2nd, rev. ed. Bowdrew, John, illus. LC 91-68204. 13p. (gr. 4). 1994. pap. 6.95 (*0-9634360-4-X*) Seacoast Pubns New Eng.
Jones, Louis C. Spooks of the Valley: Ghost Stories for Boys & Girls. Austin, Erwin H., illus. 111p. pap. 11.95 (*0-910746-10-9*, SOT01) Hope Farm.
Kahn, Joan. Ready or Not: Here Come Fourteen Frightening Stories! LC 86-31875. (Illus.). 176p. (gr. 7 up). 1987. 11.75 (*0-688-07167-8*) Greenwillow.
Kallen, Stuart A. Ghosts of the Seven Seas. LC 91-73060. 1991. 12.94 (*1-56239-041-4*) Abdo & Dghtrs.
—Haunted Hangouts of the Undead. LC 91-73065. 1991. 12.94 (*1-56239-036-8*) Abdo & Dghtrs.
—How to Catch a Ghost. Wallner, Rosemary, ed. LC 91-73063. 1991. 12.94 (*1-56239-038-4*) Abdo & Dghtrs.
—Phantoms of the Rich & Famous. LC 91-73064. 1991. 12.94 (*1-56239-037-6*) Abdo & Dghtrs.
—Witches, Magic & Spells. Wallner, Rosemary, ed. LC 91-73058. 1991. 12.94 (*1-56239-043-0*) Abdo & Dghtrs.
—World of the Bizarre. LC 91-73059. 202p. 1991. 12.94 (*1-56239-042-2*) Abdo & Dghtrs.
Kaplan, Carol B. The Haunted Picnic. Bolinske, Janet L., ed. Quenell, Midge, illus. LC 87-62999. 24p. (Orig.). (ps-k). 1988. 17.95 (*0-88335-754-2*); pap. write for info. (*0-88335-077-7*) Milliken Pub Co.
Kassem, Lou. A Haunting in Williamsburg: A Ghost Story. 112p. (gr. 5-6). 1990. pap. 3.50 (*0-380-75892-X*, Camelot) Avon.
Keene, Carolyn. Nancy Drew Ghost Stories. Greenberg, Ann, ed. 160p. (gr. 3-7). 1989. pap. 3.99 (*0-671-69132-5*, Minstrel Bks) PB.
Kehret, Peg. Horror at the Haunted House. 160p. (gr. 4 up). 1992. 14.00 (*0-525-65106-3*, Cobblehill Bks) Dutton Child Bks.
Klaveness, Jan O. Ghost Island. (gr. k-12). 1987. pap. 2.95 (*0-440-93097-9*, LFL) Dell.
Knudsen, Eric A. Spooky Stuffs: Hawaiian Ghost Stories. Kaye, Sally, ed. Buffet, Guy, illus. LC 74-80510. 64p. 1987. pap. 7.95 (*0-89610-047-2*) Island Heritage.
Landon, Lucinda. Meg MacKintosh & the Mystery At C. (gr. 4-7). 1990. 13.95 (*0-316-51367-9*, Joy St Bks) Little.
Lasky, Kathryn. Voice in the Wind: A Starbuck Family Adventure. (gr. 4-7). 1993. 16.95 (*0-15-294102-9*, HB Juv Bks); pap. 6.95 (*0-15-294103-7*) HarBrace.
Lehr, Norma. Shimmering Ghost of Riversend. (gr. 4-7). 1991. pap. 3.95 (*0-8225-9589-3*) Lerner Pubns.
Leppard, Lois G. Mandie & the Ghost Bandits, Bk. 3. LC 84-71151. 128p. (Orig.). (gr. 5-7). 1984. pap. 3.99 (*0-87123-442-4*) Bethany Hse.
Leroe, Ellen. Ghost Dog. Basso, Bill, illus. 64p. (gr. 2-5). 1994. pap. 2.95 (*0-7868-1003-3*) Hyprn Ppbks.
Levin, Betty. The Keeping Room. LC 80-23931. (Illus.). 248p. 1989. Repr. of 1981 ed. 11.95 (*0-688-80300-8*) Greenwillow.
Littledale, Freya, adapted by. The Legend of Sleepy Hollow. 1992. 3.95 (*0-590-45050-6*) Scholastic Inc.
Lively, Penelope. The Ghost of Thomas Kempe. Maitland, Anthony, illus. LC 73-77456. 192p. (gr. 3-6). 1973. 14.95 (*0-525-30495-9*, DCB) Dutton Child Bks.
Low, Alice, ed. Spooky Stories for a Dark & Stormy Night. Wilson, Gahan, illus. LC 93-33638. 128p. (gr. 3 up). 1994. 19.95 (*0-7868-0012-7*); PLB 19.89 (*0-7868-2008-X*) Hyprn Child.
Lynn, Ruth. Ester: The Story of a Small Ghost. Wagner, R. M., ed. Lynn, Ruth, illus. LC 81-69693. 28p. (gr. 5 up). 1981. 12.95 (*0-941674-00-2*) Woodcock Pr.
McBratney, Sam. The Ghosts of Hungryhouse Lane. Thiesing, Lisa, illus. 128p. (gr. 4-6). 1989. 13.95 (*0-8050-0985-X*, Bks Young Read) H Holt & Co.
McBrier, Page. Adventure in the Haunted House. Sims, Blanche, illus. LC 85-8436. 96p. (gr. 3-6). 1986. PLB 9.89 (*0-8167-0539-9*); pap. text ed. 2.95 (*0-8167-0540-2*) Troll Assocs.
Maccarone, Grace. Ghost on the Hill. 1990. pap. 2.75 (*0-590-42978-7*) Scholastic Inc.
—The Haunting of Grade Three. 96p. (Orig.). (gr. 2-5). 1987. pap. 2.75 (*0-590-43868-9*) Scholastic Inc.
—Return of the Third-Grade Ghosthunters. 1989. pap. 2.75 (*0-590-41944-7*) Scholastic Inc.
McKissack, Patricia. The Dark-Thirty: Southern Tales of the Supernatural. Pinkney, Brian, illus. LC 92-3021. 128p. (gr. 3-7). 1992. 15.00 (*0-679-81863-4*); PLB 15.99 (*0-679-91863-9*) Knopf Bks Yng Read.
Mahy, Margaret. Dangerous Spaces. 160p. (gr. 5 up). 1993. pap. 3.99 (*0-14-036362-9*, Puffin) Puffin Bks.
—The Haunting. LC 82-3983. 144p. (gr. 5-9). 1982. SBE 13.95 (*0-689-50243-5*, M K McElderry) Macmillan Child Grp.
Manes, Stephen. The Hooples' Haunted House. Weston, Martha, illus. LC 81-2216. 128p. (gr. 4-6). 1981. pap. 11.95 (*0-385-28416-0*) Delacorte.
Marar, Eve. More Haunted House Stories. (Illus.). 96p. (Orig.). 1988. pap. 1.95 (*0-942025-64-4*) Kidsbks.
Marquardt, Marsha. Little Ghost Goes to School. Marquardt, Marsha, illus. 12p. (Orig.). (gr. 1). 1993. pap. text ed. write for info. (*1-882225-12-0*) Tott Pubns.
Marshall, Edward. Four on the Shore. Marshall, James, illus. LC 84-1708. 48p. (ps-3). 1985. 9.95 (*0-8037-0155-1*); PLB 9.89 (*0-8037-0142-X*) Dial Bks Young.
Martin, Ann M. Dawn & the Surfer Ghost. (gr. 4-7). 1993. pap. 3.50 (*0-590-47050-7*) Scholastic Inc.
—Ghost at Dawn's House. 1993. pap. 3.50 (*0-590-43508-6*) Scholastic Inc.
—Kristy and the Haunted Mansion. (gr. 4-7). 1993. pap. 3.50 (*0-590-44958-3*) Scholastic Inc.
—Mallory & the Ghost Cat. 160p. 1992. pap. 3.25 (*0-590-44799-8*) Scholastic Inc.
Martin, Bill, Jr. & Archambault, John. The Ghost-Eye Tree. Rand, Ted, illus. LC 85-8422. 32p. (Orig.). (ps-2). 1985. 13.95 (*0-8050-0208-1*, Bks Young Read); pap. 5.95 (*0-8050-0947-7*) H Holt & Co.
May, Jim. The Boo Baby Girl Meets the Ghost of Mable's Gable. Finley, Shawn, illus. LC 92-72702. 32p. (ps-5). 1992. PLB 14.95 (*1-878925-03-2*) Brotherstone Pubs.
Mayer, Mercer. You're the Scaredy-Cat. Mayer, Mercer, illus. 40p. 1991. pap. 5.95 (*1-879920-01-8*) Rain Bird Prods.
Mega-Books Staff. Shadow & the Ghosts. 1992. pap. 3.99 (*0-553-37115-0*) Bantam.
Miller, Judi. Confessions of an Eleven-Year Old Ghost. (gr. 4-7). 1991. pap. 2.99 (*0-553-15932-1*) Bantam.
—Ghost a La Mode. (gr. 3-7). 1989. pap. 2.75 (*0-553-15755-8*, Skylark) Bantam.
—Ghost in My Soup. (gr. 3-7). 1985. pap. 2.99 (*0-553-15622-5*, Skylark) Bantam.
Miller, Leo. Ghost Stories. Costa, Gwen, ed. LC 91-33874. 1992. pap. 13.95 (*0-87949-358-5*) Ashley Bks.
Montgomery, Raymond A. The Haunted House. 64p. 1981. pap. 2.25 (*0-553-15428-1*) Bantam.
Moore, Ruth N. Ghost Town Mystery. Gerig, Sibyl G., illus. LC 87-2874. 144p. (gr. 4 up). 1987. pap. 5.95 (*0-8361-3445-1*) Herald Pr.
Mooser, Stephen. Shadows on the Graveyard Trail. (Orig.). (gr. 5-7). 1986. pap. 2.75 (*0-440-40805-9*, YB) Dell.
Mulligan, Mark. Ghost of Black's Island: The Screenplay. Thomas, Tim & Zorn, Vic, illus. 121p. (Orig.). (gr. 6-8). 1993. pap. 9.95x (*1-882444-01-9*) Blvd Bks FL.
Mullin, Penn. Ghosts of Black Point. Kratoville, Betty L., ed. (Illus.). 64p. (gr. 3-9). 1989. PLB 4.95 (*0-87879-653-3*) High Noon Bks.
Nash, Bruce, et al. Haunted Kids: True Ghost Stories. LC 93-14489. (Illus.). (gr. 4-9). 1993. pap. 2.95 (*0-8167-3266-3*) Troll Assocs.
Naylor, Phyllis R. Bernie & the Bessledorf Ghost. LC 88-29389. 144p. (gr. 3-7). 1990. SBE 13.95 (*0-689-31499-X*, Atheneum Child Bk) Macmillan Child Grp.
—Bernie & the Bessledorf Ghost. 144p. 1992. pap. 3.50 (*0-380-71351-9*, Camelot) Avon.
Nixon, Joan L. The Ghosts of Now. 192p. (gr. 7 up). 1986. pap. 3.50 (*0-440-93115-0*, LFL) Dell.
—Haunted House on Honeycutt Street. (gr. 4-7). 1991. pap. 2.99 (*0-440-40472-X*) Dell.
—Haunted Island. 128p. (Orig.). (gr. 3-7). 1987. pap. 2.95 (*0-590-43134-X*) Scholastic Inc.
—Specter. 1993. pap. 3.99 (*0-440-97740-1*) Dell.
O'Connor, Jane & O'Connor, Jim. The Ghost in Tent Nineteen. Williams, Richard, illus. LC 87-82372. 64p. (Orig.). (gr. 2-4). 1988. lib. bdg. 6.99 (*0-394-99800-6*); pap. 2.50 (*0-394-89800-1*) Random Bks Yng Read.
O'Connor, Jane, retold by. The Teeny Tiny Woman. Alley, R. W., illus. LC 86-485. 32p. (ps-1). 1986. lib. bdg. 7.99 (*0-394-98320-3*); pap. 3.50 (*0-394-88320-9*, Random Juv) Random Bks Yng Read.
Oetting. The Gray Ghosts of Gotham. LC 73-87804. (Illus.). 32p. (gr. 2-5). 1974. PLB 9.95 (*0-87783-135-1*); pap. 3.94 deluxe ed. (*0-87783-136-X*) Oddo.
O'Huigin, Sean. The Ghost Horse of the Mounties. Moser, Barry, illus. LC 87-46287. (gr. 4-6). 1991. 14.95 (*0-87923-721-X*) Godine.
O'Neal, Michael. Haunted Houses. LC 93-4330. 1994. 14.95 (*1-56510-095-6*) Greenhaven.
Ostheeren, Ingrid. Martin & the Pumpkin Ghost. adpt. ed. James, J. Alison, ed. & tr. Unzner-Fischer, Christa, illus. LC 93-42501. 32p. (gr. k-3). 1994. 14.95 (*1-55858-267-3*); PLB 14.88 (*1-55858-268-1*) North-South Bks NYC.
Packard, Edward. The Curse of the Haunted Mansion. 1982. pap. 3.50 (*0-553-27419-8*) Bantam.
Packard, Mary. Scaredy Ghost. Williams, Jennifer H., illus. LC 93-24845. 24p. (gr. k-2). 1993. pap. text ed. 1.50 (*0-8167-3246-9*) Troll Assocs.
Parish, Peggy. The Ghosts of Cougar Island. (Orig.). (gr. 2-4). 1986. pap. 3.50 (*0-440-42872-6*, YB) Dell.
—Haunted House. 160p. (gr. k-6). 1981. pap. 3.50 (*0-440-43459-9*, YB) Dell.
—Haunted House. (gr. 4-6). 1991. 16.50 (*0-8446-6391-3*) Peter Smith.
Pascal, Francine. The Carnival Ghost. (gr. 3-7). 1990. pap. 3.50 (*0-553-15859-7*) Bantam.
—Case of the Haunted Camp. (gr. 4-7). 1992. pap. 3.25 (*0-553-15894-5*) Bantam.
—Ghost in the Bell Tower. (gr. 4-7). 1992. pap. 3.99 (*0-553-15893-7*) Bantam.
—The Ghost of Tricia Martin. 1990. pap. 3.25 (*0-553-28487-8*) Bantam.
—Ghosts in the Graveyard. (gr. 4-7). 1990. pap. 3.99 (*0-553-15801-5*) Bantam.
—Jessica Gets Spooked. (ps-3). 1993. pap. 2.99 (*0-553-48094-4*) Bantam.
—Lila's Haunted House Party. (gr. 4-7). 1991. pap. 2.99 (*0-553-15919-4*) Bantam.
Paul, Korky. Pop-up Book of Ghost Tales. 24p. (gr. 3 up). 1991. 14.95 (*0-15-200589-7*, HB Juv Bks) HarBrace.
Paulsen, Gary. Dunc & the Flaming Ghost. 96p. (gr. 3-7). 1992. pap. 3.50 (*0-440-40686-2*, YB) Dell.
Pearce, Q. L. More Scary Stories for Sleep-Overs. LC 92-21705. (Illus.). 128p. (Orig.). 1992. pap. 4.95 (*0-8431-3451-8*) Price Stern.
—Still More Scary Stories for Sleepovers. LC 93-12822. (Illus.). 128p. (Orig.). (gr. 3-6). 1993. pap. 4.95 (*0-8431-3588-3*) Price Stern.
Pearson, Susan. The Spooky Sleepover. Fiammenghi, Gioia, illus. 64p. (gr. 1-3). 1991. pap. 12.00 jacketed (*0-671-74070-9*, S&S BFYR); pap. 3.00 (*0-671-74069-5*, S&S BFYR) S&S Trade.
Peck, Richard. The Ghost Belonged to Me. LC 74-34218. 184p. (gr. 7 up). 1975. pap. 14.95 (*0-670-33767-6*) Viking Child Bks.
—The Ghost Belonged to Me. (gr. k-6). 1987. pap. 3.99 (*0-440-42861-0*, YB) Dell.
—The Ghost Belonged to Me. large type ed. 230p. 1989. Repr. of 1975 ed. lib. bdg. 15.95 (*1-55736-116-9*, Crnrstn Bks) BDD LT Grp.
—Ghosts I Have Been. 256p. (gr. 5 up). 1979. pap. 3.50 (*0-440-92839-7*, LFL) Dell.
—Ghosts I Have Been. (gr. k-6). 1987. pap. 3.99 (*0-440-42864-5*, YB) Dell.
—Ghosts I Have Been. (gr. 5 up). 1992. 16.50 (*0-8446-6580-0*) Peter Smith.
Pellowski, Michael J. Ghost in the Library. Durham, Robert, illus. LC 88-1236. 48p. (Orig.). (gr. 1-4). 1989. PLB 10.59 (*0-8167-1337-5*); pap. text ed. 3.50 (*0-8167-1338-3*) Troll Assocs.
Perez, L. King. Ghoststalking. LC 93-41576. 1994. 18.95 (*0-87614-821-6*) Carolrhoda Bks.
Peters, Sharon. The Goofy Ghost. Garcia, Tom, illus. LC 81-2573. 32p. (gr. k-2). 1981. PLB 11.59 (*0-89375-533-8*); pap. 2.95 (*0-89375-534-6*) Troll Assocs.
Phillips, Ann. A Haunted Year. Flavin, Teresa, illus. LC 92-45638. 176p. (gr. 4-8). 1994. SBE 14.95 (*0-02-774605-4*, Macmillan Child Bk) Macmillan Child Grp.
Pienkowski, Jan. The Haunted House. (Illus.). 12p. (ps up). 1979. 14.95 (*0-525-31520-9*, DCB) Dutton Child Bks.
Pike, Christopher. The Midnight Club. MacDonald, Pat, ed. LC 93-20917. 256p. (Orig.). 1994. 14.00 (*0-671-87255-9*, Archway); pap. 3.99 (*0-671-87263-X*, Archway) PB.
—Remember Me. 1994. 14.00 (*0-671-50041-4*, Archway) PB.
Pinkwater, Daniel. The Phantom of the Lunch Wagon. LC 92-3051. (Illus.). 32p. (gr. k up). 1992. RSBE 13.95 (*0-02-774641-0*, Macmillan Child Bk) Macmillan Child Grp.
Platt, Kin. The Ghost of Hellsfire Street. LC 80-10446. 256p. (gr. 4-6). 1980. 12.95 (*0-385-28317-2*) Delacorte.
Pope, Elizabeth M. The Sherwood Ring. Ness, Evaline, illus. 272p. (gr. 7 up). 1992. pap. 3.99 (*0-14-034911-1*, Puffin) Puffin Bks.
Powling, Chris, compiled by. Faces in the Dark: A Book of Scary Stories. Bailey, Peter, illus. LC 93-46911. 80p. (gr. 2-6). 1994. 16.95 (*1-85697-986-5*, Kingfisher LKC) LKC.
Price, Susan. The Ghost Drum. 176p. (gr. 3 up). 1989. pap. 3.50 (*0-374-42547-7*, Sunburst) FS&G.

Rappaport, Doreen. A Scary Day. (ps-1). 1988. 8.49 (*0-87386-056-X*); incl. cassette 16.99 (*0-685-25200-0*); pap. 1.95 (*0-87386-052-7*); pap. 9.95 incl. cassette (*0-685-25201-9*) Jan Prods.

Razzi, Jim. The Ghost in the Mirror: And Other Ghost Stories. Kretschmann, Karin, illus. 64p. 1990. (G&D); pap. 2.95 (*0-448-40058-8*, G&D) Putnam Pub Group.

Reberg, Evelyne. The Old Woman & the Ghost. (Illus.). 48p. 1991. 8.95 (*0-89565-814-3*) Childs World.

Redmond, Marilyn. Henry Hamilton, Graduate Ghost. Redmond, Marilyn, illus. LC 81-22693. 159p. (gr. 6 up). 1982. 11.95 (*0-88289-303-3*) Pelican.

Redmond, Shirley-Raye. Grampa & the Ghost. 96p. (Orig.). (gr. 3 up). 1994. pap. 3.50 (*0-380-77382-1*, Camelot Young) Avon.

Robinson, Nancy K. The Ghost of Whispering Rock. Eagle, Ellen, illus. LC 92-52856. 64p. (gr. 2-6). 1992. 13.95 (*0-8234-0944-9*) Holiday.

Roddy, Lee. Ghost of the Moaning Mansion. 132p. (gr. 3-7). 1987. pap. 4.99 (*0-89693-349-0*, Victor Books) SP Pubns.

Ross, Pat. M & M & the Haunted House Game. Hafner, Marilyn, illus. 48p. (gr. 1-3). 1981. pap. 1.25 (*0-440-45544-8*, YB) Dell.

Rossetti, Christina. Goblin Market. (Illus.). 48p. (gr. 4-7). 1989. pap. 9.95 (*0-575-04389-X*, Pub. by Gollancz England) Trafalgar.

Sabin, Fran & Sabin, Lou. Secret of the Haunted House. Trivas, Irene, illus. LC 81-8751. 48p. (gr. 2-4). 1982. PLB 10.89 (*0-89375-598-2*); pap. text ed. 3.50 (*0-89375-599-0*) Troll Assocs.

St. George, Judith. Haunted. 160p. (gr. 6 up). 1986. pap. 2.50 (*0-553-26047-2*) Bantam.

San Souci, Robert D. Boy & the Ghost. LC 89-418. 40p. (ps-3). 1992. pap. 5.95 (*0-671-79248-2*, S&S BFYR) S&S Trade.

Sargent, Sarah. Jerry's Ghosts: The Mystery of the Blind Tower. LC 93-23700. (gr. 3-7). 1994. pap. 3.95 (*0-689-71839-X*, Atheneum) Macmillan.

Schrade, Arlene O. Gabriel, the Happy Ghost. Incl. Gabriel en Mexico (Gabriel Learns About the Day of the Dead) pap. 6.60 (*0-8442-7211-6*); Gabriel en Espana (Gabriel in Pampiona) pap. 6.60 (*0-8442-7222-1*); Gabriel en Puerto Rico (Gabriel in the Caribbean) pap. 6.60 (*0-8442-7224-8*). (ENG & SPA., Illus.). 32p. (gr. 4 up). 1988. pap. (Natl Textbk) NTC Pub Grp.

Schumacher, Claire W. Ghostly Tales of Lake Superior. Kopari, Catherine, illus. LC 87-91292. 94p. (Orig.). (gr. 9). 1987. PLB 6.95 (*0-917378-06-7*) Zenith City.

Schwartz, Alvin. Ghosts! Ghostly Tales from Folklore. Chess, Victoria, illus. LC 90-21746. 64p. (gr. k-3). 1991. 14.00 (*0-06-021796-0*); PLB 13.89 (*0-06-021797-9*) HarpC Child Bks.

—Scary Stories Three: More Tales to Chill Your Bones. Gammell, Stephen, illus. LC 90-47474. 128p. (gr. 4 up). 1991. 14.00 (*0-06-021794-4*); PLB 13.89 (*0-06-021795-2*) HarpC Child Bks.

Schwartz, Alvin, retold by. Ghosts! Ghostly Tales from Folklore. Chess, Victoria, illus. LC 90-21746. 64p. (gr. k-3). 1993. pap. 3.50 (*0-06-444170-9*, Trophy) HarpC Child Bks.

Seigel, Barbara & Seigel, Scott. Dark Fire. Greenberg, Ann, ed. 176p. (Orig.). 1992. pap. 2.99 (*0-671-70906-2*) PB.

Service, Pamela F. Phantom Victory. LC 93-37904. 128p. (gr. 5-7). 1994. SBE 14.95 (*0-684-19441-4*, Scribners Young Read) Macmillan Child Grp.

Seuling, Barbara. The Teeny Tiny Woman: An Old English Ghost Tale. Seuling, Barbara, illus. (gr. k-3). 1978. pap. 4.99 (*0-14-050266-1*, Puffin) Puffin Bks.

Sheldon, Ann. Linda Craig: The Haunted Valley. Barish, Wendy, ed. 192p. (gr. 3-7). 1982. 8.50 (*0-671-45551-6*) S&S Trade.

Showell, Ellen. The Trickster Ghost. 1992. 2.75 (*0-590-45795-0*, Little Apple) Scholastic Inc.

Siegal, Barbara & Siegal, Scott. Beyond Terror. MacDonald, Patricia, ed. 160p. (Orig.). 1991. pap. 3.50 (*0-671-70904-6*, Archway) PB.

—Midnight Chill. MacDonald, Patricia, ed. 176p. (Orig.). 1991. pap. 2.99 (*0-671-70905-4*, Archway) PB.

Sine, Megan & Sine, Willam H. Max Is Back. (Illus.). 80p. (gr. 4 up). 1989. pap. 3.95 (*0-449-90415-6*, Columbine) Fawcett.

Singer. Ghost Host. 1993. pap. 2.95 (*0-590-44505-7*) Scholastic Inc.

Smith, Janice L. There's a Ghost in the Coatroom: Adam Joshua's Christmas. Gackenbach, Dick, illus. LC 90-23068. 96p. (gr. 1-4). 1991. 12.95 (*0-06-022863-6*); PLB 12.89 (*0-06-022864-4*) HarpC Child Bks.

Snyder, Zilpha K. The Trespassers. LC 93-31168. 1994. write for info. (*0-385-31055-2*) Delacorte.

Spina, Russell, illus. Disney's Haunted Mansion Pop-up Book. 10p. (ps-8). 1994. 14.95 (*1-56282-499-6*) Disney Pr.

Stark, John. Haunted House Stories. (Illus.). 96p. (Orig.). 1988. pap. 1.95 (*0-942025-17-2*) Kidsbks.

Stine, Megan & Stine, H. William. Haunted Halloween. (Illus.). 80p. 1988. pap. 2.95 (*0-449-90327-3*, Columbine) Fawcett.

—Mysterious Max. (Illus.). 80p. 1988. pap. 2.95 (*0-449-90326-5*, Columbine) Fawcett.

Stine, Megan & Stine, William H. Baseball Card Fever. (Illus.). 80p. (gr. 4 up). 1989. pap. 3.95 (*0-449-90416-4*, Columbine) Fawcett.

—Max's Secret Formula. (Illus.). 80p. (gr. 4 up). 1989. pap. 3.95 (*0-449-90417-2*, Columbine) Fawcett.

Stine, R. L. Goosebumps: The Ghost Next Door. (gr. 4-7). 1993. pap. 2.95 (*0-590-49445-7*) Scholastic Inc.

—Goosebumps: The Haunted Mask. (gr. 4-7). 1993. pap. 2.95 (*0-590-49446-5*) Scholastic Inc.

—Haunted. large type ed. (gr. 6 up). Date not set. PLB 14.60 (*0-8368-1163-1*) Gareth Stevens Inc.

Storr, Catherine, as told by. The Flying Dutchman. LC 85-16711. (Illus.). 32p. (gr. k-5). 1985. PLB 19.97 (*0-8172-2501-3*) Raintree Steck-V.

Stridh, Kicki. The Horrible Spookhouse. Eriksson, Eva, illus. LC 93-22076. 1993. write for info. (*0-87614-811-9*) Carolrhoda Bks.

Sturrock, Walt, illus. Ghosts. 160p. 1990. 14.95 (*0-88101-269-6*) Unicorn Pub.

Supraner, Robyn. The Ghost in the Attic. LC 78-18039. (Illus.). 48p. (gr. 2-4). 1979. PLB 10.89 (*0-89375-095-6*); pap. 3.50 (*0-89375-083-2*) Troll Assocs.

Suzanne, Jamie. The Haunted House. large type ed. Pascal, Francine, created by. 106p. (gr. 7-12). 1990. Repr. of 1986 ed. 9.95 (*1-55905-066-7*) Grey Castle.

Tapp, Kathy K. The Ghostmobile. 160p. (gr. 3-7). 1988. pap. 2.75 (*0-590-43441-1*) Scholastic Inc.

Thacker, Nola. All on a Winter's Day. 144p. (gr. 7 up). 1990. pap. 2.95 (*0-590-43416-0*) Scholastic Inc.

Thayer, Jane. Gus Loved His Happy Home. Fleishman, Seymour, illus. LC 88-36962. 32p. (ps-2). 1989. PLB 15.00 (*0-208-02249-X*, Linnet) Shoe String.

Thesman, Jean. Cattail Moon. LC 93-6814. (gr. 4-7). 1994. write for info. (*0-395-67409-3*) HM.

Thompson, Jonathon J., Jr. Haunted House Hoax. 10p. (gr. 3-6). 1992. 2.50 (*0-933479-12-3*) Thompson.

Todd, H. E. The Silly Silly Ghost. Biro, Val, illus. 32p. (gr. k-3). 1989. 13.95 (*0-340-41155-4*, Pub. by Hodder & Stoughton UK) Trafalgar.

Tolan, Stephanie S. Who's There? LC 94-15384. 1994. write for info. (*0-688-04611-8*) Morrow Jr Bks.

Tomalin, Ruth. A Summer Ghost. 112p. (gr. 3-7). 1992. pap. 4.95 (*0-571-16221-5*) Faber & Faber.

Tropea, Maria. Look & Look Again, Lost in the Haunted Mansion. Tallarico, Anthony, illus. 24p. (Orig.). (gr. 4-7). 1990. pap. 1.95 (*1-878890-03-4*) Palisades Prodns.

Wainwright, Richard M. The Gift from Obadiah's Ghost. Crompton, Jack, illus. LC 89-25808. 40p. 1990. 13.00 (*0-9619566-2-3*) Family Life.

—A Tiny Miracle. Crompton, Jack, illus. 40p. 1986. Repr. 13.00g (*0-9619566-0-7*) Family Life.

Warner, Gertrude C., created by. The Mystery of the Singing Ghost. (Illus.). 192p. (gr. 2-7). 1992. 10.95g (*0-8075-5397-2*); pap. 3.50 (*0-8075-5398-0*) A Whitman.

Watermill. Midnight Fright: A Collection of Ghost Stories. (gr. 4-7). 1986. pap. 2.95 (*0-89375-405-6*) Troll Assocs.

Wedell, Robert F. Save the Haunted House. Swidor, M. J., illus. 124p. (Orig.). 1991. pap. 6.95 (*0-9625221-2-0*) Milrob Pr.

Weinberg, Larry. Ghost Hotel. LC 94-2970. (Illus.). 160p. (gr. 3-6). 1994. pap. 2.95 (*0-8167-3420-8*) Troll Assocs.

Weiner, Eric. Steer Clear of Haunted Hill. (gr. 1-3). 1993. pap. 3.50 (*0-553-48087-1*) Bantam.

Westall, Robert. Demons & Shadows: The Ghostly Best Stories. (gr. 4-7). 1993. 16.00 (*0-374-31768-2*) FS&G.

—Ghost Abbey. LC 88-23945. (gr. 7 up). 1989. pap. 12.95 (*0-590-41692-8*) Scholastic Inc.

—Ghost Abbey. 1990. pap. 2.95 (*0-590-41693-6*) Scholastic Inc.

—Shades of Darkness: More of the Ghostly Best Stories of Robert Westall. LC 93-42229. 1994. 17.00 (*0-374-36758-2*) FS&G.

Westall, Robert, selected by. Ghost Stories. Eckett, Sean, illus. LC 92-26451. 256p. (gr. 4-9). 1993. 6.95 (*1-85697-884-2*, Kingfisher LKC) LKC.

Weyn, Suzanne. My Brother the Ghost. Petersen, Eric, illus. 144p. (gr. 3-7). 1994. pap. 3.95 (*0-06-440557-5*, Trophy) HarpC Child Bks.

Wilde, Nicholas. Into the Dark. 1990. 13.95 (*0-590-43424-1*) Scholastic Inc.

—Into the Dark. 1992. pap. 2.95 (*0-590-43423-3*, Apple Paperbacks) Scholastic Inc.

Wilde, Oscar. The Canterville Ghost & Other Stories. (Illus.). 1991. pap. text ed. 6.50 (*0-582-03589-9*, 79118) Longman.

Windsor, Patricia. How a Weirdo & a Ghost Can Change Your Entire Life. (gr. k-6). 1988. pap. 2.75 (*0-440-40094-5*) Dell.

Wirkner, Linda. Mystery of the Blue-Gowned Ghost. (gr. 3-7). 1994. pap. 4.95 (*0-87935-128-4*) Williamsburg.

Woodyard, Chris. Haunted Ohio: Ghostly Tales from the Buckeye State. LC 91-75343. 224p. (Orig.). (gr. 6 up). 1991. pap. 9.95 (*0-9628472-0-8*) Kestrel Pubns.

Wright, Betty R. Christina's Ghost. LC 85-42880. 128p. (gr. 3-7). 1985. 14.95 (*0-8234-0581-8*) Holiday.

—Un Fantasma en la Casa. (gr. 4-7). 1993. pap. 2.95 (*0-590-46860-X*) Scholastic Inc.

—The Ghost Comes Calling. LC 93-13969. 128p. (gr. 2-6). 1994. 13.95 (*0-590-47353-0*) Scholastic Inc.

—The Ghost in the House. 160p. 1991. 13.95 (*0-590-43606-6*, Scholastic Hardcover) Scholastic Inc.

—A Ghost in the House. 176p. (gr. 3-7). 1993. pap. 2.95 (*0-590-43603-1*, Apple Paperbacks) Scholastic Inc.

—A Ghost in the Window. LC 87-45331. 160p. (gr. 3-7). 1987. 14.95 (*0-8234-0661-X*) Holiday.

—A Ghost in the Window. 1993. pap. 2.75 (*0-590-43442-X*) Scholastic Inc.

—The Ghost of Ernie P. LC 90-55108. 128p. (gr. 3-7). 1990. 14.95 (*0-8234-0835-3*) Holiday.

—The Ghost of Ernie P. 1992. pap. 2.95 (*0-590-45073-5*, Apple Paperbacks) Scholastic Inc.

—The Ghost of Popcorn Hill. Ritz, Karen, illus. LC 92-16391. 96p. (gr. 3-7). 1993. 14.95 (*0-8234-1009-9*) Holiday.

—Ghost Witch. LC 92-55055. 72p. (gr. 4-7). 1993. 13.95 (*0-8234-1036-6*) Holiday.

—Ghosts Beneath Our Feet. LC 84-47835. 144p. (gr. 3-7). 1984. 14.95 (*0-8234-0538-9*) Holiday.

—Ghosts Beneath Our Feet. 144p. (gr. 3-7). 1986. pap. 2.75 (*0-590-43444-6*) Scholastic Inc.

—The Ghosts of Mercy Manor. LC 92-21557. 1993. 13.95 (*0-590-43601-5*) Scholastic Inc.

Wyeth, Sharon D. The Ghost Show. 1990. pap. 2.75 (*0-553-15829-5*) Bantam.

Wyler, Rose & Ames, Gerald. Spooky Tricks. Schindler, S. D., illus. LC 92-47501. 64p. (ps-3). 1994. pap. 3.50 (*0-06-444172-5*, Trophy) HarpC Child Bks.

Wyss, Thelma H. A Stranger Here. LC 92-15307. 144p. (gr. 7 up). 1993. 14.00 (*0-06-021438-4*); PLB 13.89 (*0-06-021439-2*) HarpC Child Bks.

Zeplin, Zeno. The Cross-Eyed Ghost. Jones, Judy, illus. 154p. (gr. 3-6). 1991. PLB 14.95 casebound (*1-877740-05-5*); pap. text ed. 7.95 (*1-877740-06-3*) Nel-Mar Pub.

—The Haunted Classroom. Jones, Judy, illus. 136p. (gr. 4-7). 1989. text ed. 14.95 (*0-9615760-8-1*); pap. text ed. 7.95 (*0-9615760-9-X*) Nel-Mar Pub.

Zorn, Steven, retold by. Mostly Monsters. Bradley, John, illus. LC 93-70586. 56p. (gr. 3 up). 1994. 9.98 (*1-56138-333-3*) Courage Bks.

GHOST TOWNS

see Cities and Towns, Ruined, Extinct, Etc.

GHOSTS

see also Apparitions; Psychical Research; Superstition

Adams, Pam & Jones, Ceri, illus. A Book of Ghosts. LC 90-45584. 32p. (Orig.). (ps-2). 1974. (Pub. by Child's Play England); pap. 5.95 (*0-85953-028-0*) Childs Play.

Barry, Sheila A. The World's Most Spine-Tingling True Ghost Stories. Sharpe, Jim, illus. LC 92-19862. 96p. (gr. 3 up). 1992. 12.95 (*0-8069-8686-7*); pap. 3.95 (*0-8069-8687-5*) Sterling.

Beckett, John. World's Weirdest "True" Ghost Stories. Hayhurst, Steve, illus. LC 91-15408. 96p. (gr. 4 up). 1992. 12.95 (*0-8069-8410-4*); pap. 3.95 (*0-8069-8411-2*) Sterling.

Boston, Lucy M. The Chimneys of Green Knowe. large type ed. Boston, Peter, illus. 272p. (gr. 3 up). 1990. 18.95 (*0-7451-1175-0*) G K Hall.

Bradley, Susannah, ed. Ghosts, Monsters & Legends. Appleby, Barrie, illus. 48p. (gr. 3-6). 1992. pap. 2.95 (*1-56680-005-6*) Mad Hatter Pub.

Brittain, Bill. Who Knew There'd Be Ghosts? Chessare, Michele, illus. LC 84-48496. 128p. (gr. 4-7). 1988. pap. 3.95 (*0-06-440224-X*, Trophy) HarpC Child Bks.

Bursell, Susan. Haunted Houses. LC 93-4296. (gr. 3-5). 1994. 14.75 (*1-56006-153-7*) Lucent Bks.

Cohen, Daniel. Ghost in the House. Caponigro, John P., illus. LC 92-37858. (gr. 3-5). 1993. 13.99 (*0-525-65131-4*, Cobblehill Bks) Dutton Child Bks.

—The Ghost Of Elvis & Other Celebrity Spirits. LC 93-38030. 112p. (gr. 2-5). 1994. 14.95 (*0-399-22611-7*, Putnam) Putnam Pub Group.

—Ghostly Tales of Love & Revenge. 96p. (gr. 5-9). 1992. 14.95 (*0-399-22117-4*, Putnam) Putnam Pub Group.

—Ghosts of the Deep. LC 92-34669. 112p. (gr. 5-9). 1993. 14.95 (*0-399-22435-1*, Putnam) Putnam Pub Group.

—The Ghosts of War. 96p. (gr. 5-8). 1990. 13.95 (*0-399-22200-6*, Putnam) Putnam Pub Group.

—Great Ghosts. LC 90-34333. (Illus.). (gr. 4-7). 1990. 13.00 (*0-525-65039-3*, Cobblehill Bks) Dutton Child Bks.

—Phantom Animals. 96p. 1991. 14.95 (*0-399-22230-8*, Putnam) Putnam Pub Group.

—Phone Call from a Ghost: Strange Tales from Modern America. MacDonald, Patricia, ed. Lynn, David, illus. 112p. (gr. 5-7). 1990. pap. 3.50 (*0-671-68242-3*, Minstrel) PB.

—Real Ghosts. MacDonald, Pat, ed. 128p. (gr. 4-7). 1992. pap. 2.99 (*0-671-78622-9*, Minstrel Bks) PB.

—Young Ghosts. LC 93-45924. (Illus.). 122p. (gr. 4 up). 1994. PLB 13.99 (*0-525-65154-3*, Cobblehill Bks) Dutton Child Bks.

Coombs, Patricia. Dorrie & the Haunted House. 48p. (gr. k-6). 1980. pap. 1.50 (*0-440-42212-4*, YB) Dell.

Cox, Phil R. Ghost Train to Nowhere. (Illus.). 48p. (gr. 5 up). 1994. PLB 11.96 (*0-88110-519-8*, Usborne); pap. 4.95 (*0-7460-0677-2*, Usborne) EDC.

Deem, James M. Ghost Hunters. Biegel, Michael D., illus. 128p. (Orig.). 1992. pap. 3.50 (*0-380-76682-5*, Camelot) Avon.

Dolby, Karen. House of Shadows. (Illus.). 48p. (gr. 3 up). 1993. PLB 11.96 (*0-88110-520-1*, Usborne); pap. 4.95 (*0-7460-0679-9*, Usborne) EDC.

Emert, Phyllis R. Ghosts, Hauntings, & Mysterious Happenings. 128p. 1994. pap. 2.99 (*0-8125-2057-2*) Tor Bks.

Farrant, Don W. Real Ghosts Don't Wear Sheets. Kusmierz, James P., illus. 80p. (Orig.). 1985. pap. 7.00 (*0-935604-02-2*) Ivystone.

Fischel, E. Midnight Ghosts. (Illus.). 48p. (gr. 5 up). 1992. PLB 11.96 (*0-88110-521-X*, Usborne); pap. 4.95 (*0-7460-0651-9*, Usborne) EDC.

Friedhoffer, Robert & Brown, Harriet. How to Haunt a House for Halloween. Kaufman, Richard, illus. White, Timothy, photos by. (Illus.). 96p. (gr. 3 up). 1989. pap. 6.95 (*0-531-15122-0*) Watts.

Haskins, James. The Headless Haunt & Other African-American Ghost Stories. Otera, Ben, illus. LC 93-26223. 128p. (gr. 3-7). 1994. 14.00 (*0-06-022994-2*); PLB 13.89 (*0-06-022997-7*) HarpC Child Bks.

Hausman, Gerald, as told by. Duppy Talk: West Indian Tales of Mystery & Magic. LC 93-40586. (gr. 4 up). 1994. 14.00 (*0-671-89000-X*, S&S BFYR) S&S Trade.

Julien, Ophelia. Dead of Summer. LC 90-55256. 78p. (Orig.). (gr. 4 up). 1991. pap. 7.00 (*1-56002-065-2*) Aegina Pr.

Knight, David C. Best True Ghost Stories of the Twentieth Century. Waldman, Neil, illus. LC 83-23075. 64p. (gr. 3-7). 1984. pap. 11.95 jacketed (*0-671-66556-1*) S&S Trade.

Macklin, John. World's Most Bone-Chilling "True" Ghost Stories. LC 93-16616. (gr. 3 up). 1993. 12.95 (*0-8069-0390-2*) Sterling.

Mayard. Ghosts. 32p. (gr. k-6). 1977. pap. 5.95 (*0-86020-148-1*) EDC.

Nixon, Joan L. The Specter. LC 82-70322. 160p. (gr. 7 up). 1982. pap. 12.95 (*0-385-28948-0*) Delacorte.

Razzi, Jim. The Restless Dead: More Strange Real-Life Mysteries. Palencar, John J., illus. LC 93-34745. 96p. (gr. 3-7). 1994. pap. 3.95 (*0-06-440427-7*, Trophy) HarpC Child Bks.

Regan, Dana, illus. Baby Boo! 12p. (ps). 1992. 5.99 (*0-679-81544-9*) Random Bks Yng Read.

Reinstedt, Randall A. The Strange Case of the Ghosts of the Robert Louis Stevenson House. Bergez, John, ed. LC 88-81933. (Illus.). 70p. (gr. 3-6). 1988. casebound 12.95 (*0-933818-22-X*); pap. 8.95 (*0-933818-78-5*) Ghost Town.

Riehecky, Janet. Haunted Houses. Halverson, Lydia & Siculan, Dan, illus. LC 88-38780. 100p. (gr. 3-7). 1989. PLB 14.95 (*0-89565-454-7*) Childs World.

Roberts, Nancy. America's Most Haunted Places. (Illus.). 95p. (gr. 4 up). 1987. pap. 6.95 (*0-87844-074-7*) Sandlapper Pub Co.

—Ghosts & Specters of the Old South. Roberts, Bruce, photos by. LC 73-20909. (Illus.). 93p. (gr. 3 up). 1984. pap. 6.95 (*0-87844-058-5*) Sandlapper Pub Co.

—Southern Ghosts. (Illus.). 72p. (gr. 4 up). 1987. pap. 6.95 (*0-87844-075-5*) Sandlapper Pub Co.

Schnur, Steven. The Shadow Children. LC 94-5098. 1994. write for info. (*0-688-13281-2*); PLB write for info. (*0-688-13831-4*) Morrow Jr Bks.

Sharmat, Marjorie W. & Sharmat, Andrew. The Haunted Bus. (gr. 1-6). 1991. pap. 2.99 (*0-06-106030-5*, Harp PBks) HarpC.

Smith, Curtis W. Spirits of London: A Psychobiography for Travelers. LC 87-91611. 108p. (Orig.). (gr. 11 up). 1988. pap. 4.95 (*0-944208-00-2*) Seventh-Wing Pubns.

Sotnak, Lewann. Haunted Houses. LC 89-70792. (Illus.). 48p. (gr. 5-6). 1990. text ed. 11.95 RSBE (*0-89686-508-8*, Crestwood Hse) Macmillan Child Grp.

Stevenson, Drew. One Ghost Too Many: A Sarah Capshaw Mystery. Kelly, Kathleen M., illus. LC 90-47361. 128p. (gr. 4-6). 1991. 13.95 (*0-525-65052-0*, Cobblehill Bks) Dutton Child Bks.

Stine, R. L. Haunted. MacDonald, Patricia, ed. 176p. (Orig.). (gr. 6-9). 1991. pap. 3.99 (*0-671-74651-0*, Archway) PB.

Strete, Craig K. Big Thunder Magic. Brown, Craig, illus. LC 89-34613. 32p. (ps up). 1990. 12.95 (*0-688-08853-8*); PLB 12.88 (*0-688-08854-6*) Greenwillow.

Viviano, Christy L. Haunted Louisiana: True Tales of Ghosts & Other Unearthly Creatures. 164p. (gr. 5-12). 1992. pap. 10.95 (*1-881490-01-7*); audiocassette 16.95 (*1-881490-02-5*) Tree House Pr.

Weinberg, Alyce T. Spirits of Frederick. LC 79-54039. (Illus.). 73p. (Orig.). 1979. pap. 3.95x (*0-9604552-0-5*) A T Weinberg.

Windham, Kathryn T. Jeffrey Introduces Thirteen More Southern Ghosts. Foster, Sharon, illus. LC 70-170663. 120p. (gr. 6 up). 1987. pap. 9.50t (*0-8173-0381-2*) U of Ala Pr.

—Jeffrey's Latest Thirteen: More Alabama Ghosts. Gilbert, John, illus. LC 82-50029. 152p. 1987. pap. 9.50t (*0-8173-0380-4*) U of Ala Pr.

—Thirteen Georgia Ghosts & Jeffrey. Lanier, Frances, illus. LC 73-87004. 160p. (gr. 6 up). 1987. pap. 9.50t (*0-8173-0377-4*) U of Ala Pr.

—Thirteen Mississippi Ghosts & Jeffrey. Russell, H. R., illus. LC 74-15509. 152p. (gr. 6 up). 1987. pap. 9.50t (*0-8173-0379-0*) U of Ala Pr.

—Thirteen Tennessee Ghosts & Jeffrey. Brogdon, Lecia, illus. LC 73-87004. 160p. (gr. 6 up). 1987. pap. 9.50t (*0-8173-0378-2*) U of Ala Pr.

Windham, Kathryn T. & Figh, Margaret G. Thirteen Alabama Ghosts & Jeffrey. Atkins, Delores E., illus. LC 71-94443. 128p. (gr. 6 up). 1987. pap. 9.50t (*0-8173-0376-6*) U of Ala Pr.

Wright, Betty R. Christina's Ghost. 112p. (gr. 3-7). 1987. pap. 2.75 (*0-590-42709-1*) Scholastic Inc.

Zorn, Steven, as told by. Mostly Ghostly: Eight Spooky Tales to Chill Your Bones. Brodley, John, illus. LC 91-71087. 56p. (gr. 2 up). 1991. 9.98 (*1-56138-033-4*) Courage Bks.

GIANTS

Compton, Kenn & Compton, Joanne. Jack the Giant Chaser: An Appalachian Tale. LC 92-15911. (Illus.). 32p. (ps-3). 1993. reinforced bdg. 14.95 (*0-8234-0998-8*) Holiday.

Naden, C. J. I Can Read About All Kinds of Giants. LC 78-65833. (Illus.). (gr. 2-4). 1979. pap. 2.50 (*0-89375-201-0*) Troll Assocs.

GIANTS–FICTION

Amstutz, Beverly. Too Big for the Bag. (Illus.). (gr. k-7). 1981. pap. 2.50x (*0-937836-05-2*) Precious Res.

Beck, Ian. The Teddy Robber. (Illus.). 32p. (ps-3). 1993. 12.95 (*0-8120-6401-1*); pap. text ed. 5.95 (*0-8120-1711-0*) Barron.

Cincerelli, Carol J. The Selfish Giant by Oscar Wilde. 96p. (gr. 1-6). 1990. 10.95 (*0-86653-537-3*, GA1158) Good Apple.

Clayton, Sandra. The Giant. Hunnam, Lucinda, illus. LC 93-28992. 1994. 4.25 (*0-383-03745-X*) SRA Schl Grp.

Cole, Brock. The Giant's Toe. LC 85-20569. 32p. (ps up). 1986. 15.00 (*0-374-32559-6*) FS&G.

Coville, Bruce & Coville, Katherine. The Foolish Giant. LC 77-18522. (Illus.). (gr. k-2). 1978. PLB 12.89 (*0-397-31800-6*, Lipp Jr Bks) HarpC Child Bks.

Cuneo, Mary L. What Can a Giant Do? Huang, Benrei, illus. LC 92-8307. 32p. (ps-1). 1994. 15.00 (*0-06-021214-4*); PLB 14.89 (*0-06-021217-9*) HarpC Child Bks.

Dahl, Roald. The BFG. Blake, Quentin, illus. LC 85-566. 221p. (gr. 1 up). 1982. 16.00 (*0-374-30469-6*) FS&G.

—The BFG. Blake, Quentin, illus. 1989. pap. 4.50 (*0-14-034019-X*, Puffin) Puffin Bks.

—The BFG. LC 93-22605. 1993. 13.95 (*0-679-42813-5*, Everymans Lib) Knopf.

Denan, Corinne. Giant Tales. LC 79-66330. (Illus.). 48p. (gr. 3-6). 1980. lib. bdg. 9.89 (*0-89375-328-9*); pap. 2.95 (*0-89375-327-0*) Troll Assocs.

—Tales of the Ugly Ogres. Craft, Kinuko Y., illus. LC 79-66333. 48p. (gr. 3-6). 1980. PLB 9.89 (*0-89375-332-7*); pap. text ed. 2.95 (*0-89375-331-9*) Troll Assocs.

De Paola, Tomie. The Mysterious Giant of Barletta. De Paola, Tomie, illus. LC 83-18445. 32p. (ps-3). 1988. pap. 3.95 (*0-15-256349-0*, Voyager Bks) HarBrace.

De Regniers, Beatrice S. Jack the Giant Killer. Wilsdorf, Anne, illus. LC 86-3606. 32p. (gr. k-3). 1987. 13.95 (*0-689-31218-0*, Atheneum Child Bk) Macmillan Child Grp.

Du Bois, William P. The Giant. (Orig.). (gr. k-6). 1987. pap. 4.95 (*0-440-42994-3*, Pub. by Yearling Classics) Dell.

Feldman, Eve. A Giant Surprise. (Illus.). 32p. (gr. 1-4). 1989. PLB 18.99 (*0-8172-3527-2*); pap. 3.95 (*0-8114-6724-4*) Raintree Steck-V.

Galdone, Paul. Jack & the Beanstalk. Galdone, Paul, illus. LC 73-9726. 32p. (ps-3). 1982. pap. 5.95 (*0-89919-085-5*, Clarion Bks) HM.

The Giant's Child (EV, Unit 5. (gr. 2). 1991. 5-pack 21.25 (*0-88106-743-1*) Charlesbridge Pub.

Goffe, Toni. Giant That Sneezed. (ps-3). 1993. pap. 11.95 (*0-85953-927-X*) Childs Play.

Greenway, Jennifer, retold by. Jack & the Beanstalk. Bernal, Richard, illus. 1991. 6.95 (*0-8362-4903-8*) Andrews & McMeel.

Haley, Patrick. The Little Person. Kool, Jonna, illus. LC 81-65114. 64p. (gr. 2-3). 1981. PLB 9.00 (*0-9605738-0-1*) East Eagle.

Hao, Kuang-ts'ai. The Giant & the Spring. Wang, Eva, illus. (ENG & CHI.). 32p. (gr. 2-4). 1994. 14.95 (*1-57227-009-8*) Pan Asian Pubns.

—The Giant & the Spring. Wang, Eva, illus. (ENG & VIE.). 32p. (gr. 2-4). 1994. 16.95 (*1-57227-011-X*) Pan Asian Pubns.

—The Giant & the Spring. Wang, Eva, illus. (ENG & KOR.). 32p. (gr. 2-4). 1994. 16.95 (*1-57227-012-8*) Pan Asian Pubns.

—The Giant & the Spring. Wang, Eva, illus. (ENG & THA.). 32p. (gr. 2-4). 1994. 16.95 (*1-57227-013-6*) Pan Asian Pubns.

—The Giant & the Spring. Wang, Eva, illus. (ENG & TAG.). 32p. (gr. 2-4). 1994. 16.95 (*1-57227-014-4*) Pan Asian Pubns.

—The Giant & the Spring. Wang, Eva, illus. (ENG & CAM.). 32p. (gr. 2-4). 1994. 16.95 (*1-57227-015-2*) Pan Asian Pubns.

—The Giant & the Spring. Wang, Eva, illus. (ENG & LAO.). 32p. (gr. 2-4). 1994. 16.95 (*1-57227-016-0*) Pan Asian Pubns.

—The Giant & the Spring. Wang, Eva, illus. (ENG & KOR.). 32p. (gr. 2-4). 1994. 16.95 (*1-57227-017-9*) Pan Asian Pubns.

—The Giant & the Spring: El Gigante y el Nino Primavera. Zeller, Beatriz, tr. from CHI. Wang, Eva, illus. (ENG & SPA.). 32p. (gr. 2-4). 1994. 16.95 (*1-57227-010-1*) Pan Asian Pubns. What happens when a lonely Giant captures Spring & won't let it go? In this tale, the themes of selfishness & sharing are explored & the Giant's eventual realization of his error, coupled with his freeing of Spring, touchingly illustrate the value of making the right choice. The delicate illustrations in this book portray the gentle, although misguided nature of the Giant & the resilence of little Spring. Young readers will delight in the Giant's journey from greediness to generosity. Based on THE SELFISH GIANT by Oscar Wilde. Also available in English/Chinese, Vietnamese, Korean, Thai, Tagalog, Khmer, Lao & Hmong. For grades 2-4. Please specify language when ordering. Available exclusively from: Pan Asian Publications (USA) Inc., 29564 Union City Blvd., Union City, CA 94587. Order toll free: 1-800-853-ASIA, FAX: (510) 475-1489.
Publisher Provided Annotation.

Hawkes, Kevin. His Royal Buckliness. LC 91-40347. (Illus.). 32p. (ps up). 1992. 15.00 (*0-688-11062-2*); PLB 14.93 (*0-688-11063-0*); poster avail. Lothrop.

The Helpful Giant, Unit 5. (gr. 2). 1991. 5-pack 21.25 (*0-88106-745-8*) Charlesbridge Pub.

Hughes, Ted. The Iron Giant: A Story in Five Nights. Zimmer, Dirk, illus. LC 87-45089. 64p. (gr. 3-7). 1988. PLB 11.89 (*0-06-022639-0*) HarpC Child Bks.

—The Iron Giant: A Story in Five Nights. Zimmer, Dirk, illus. LC 87-45089. 64p. (gr. 3-7). 1988. pap. 4.95 (*0-06-440214-2*, Trophy) HarpC Child Bks.

Kellogg, Steven, retold by. & illus. Jack & the Beanstalk. LC 90-45990. 48p. 1991. 14.95 (*0-688-10250-6*); PLB 14.88 (*0-688-10251-4*) Morrow Jr Bks.

Kroll, Steven. Big Jeremy. Carrick, Donald, illus. LC 88-35812. 32p. (ps-3). 1989. reinforced bdg. 14.95 (*0-8234-0759-4*) Holiday.

Leonard, Marcia. The Giant Baby & Other Giant Tales. Alley, R. W., illus. LC 93-6225. (ps-4). 1994. pap. 2.95 (*0-590-46892-8*) Scholastic Inc.

Lomsky, Gerry. The Beanstalk Bandit: The Giant's Version of "Jack & the Beanstalk" Krug, Ken, illus. 30p. (gr. 2-7). 1993. pap. 4.95 (*1-883499-00-3*); Story cass. 6.95 (*1-883499-01-1*) Princess NJ.

McMullan, Kate & McMullan, Jim. The Noisy Giants' Tea Party. LC 92-52692. (Illus.). 32p. (ps-3). 1992. 15.00 (*0-06-205017-6*); PLB 14.89 (*0-06-205018-4*) HarpC Child Bks.

Martin, Melanie. Itsy-Bitsy Giant. Cushman, Doug, illus. LC 88-1234. 48p. (Orig.). (gr. 1-4). 1989. PLB 10.59 (*0-8167-1335-9*); pap. text ed. 3.50 (*0-8167-1336-7*) Troll Assocs.

Metaxas, Eric. Jack & the Beanstalk. Sorel, Ed, illus. LC 91-14176. 40p. (gr. k up). 1991. pap. 14.95 (*0-88708-188-6*, Rabbit Ears); incls. cassette 19.95 (*0-88708-189-4*, Rabbit Ears) Picture Bk Studio.

Moodie, Fiona. Boy & the Giants. (ps-3). 1993. 15.00 (*0-374-30927-2*) FS&G.

Morpurgo, Michael. The Sandman & the Turtles. LC 93-21531. 80p. (gr. 3-7). 1994. 14.95 (*0-399-22672-9*, Philomel Bks) Putnam Pub Group.

Muller, Gerda, illus. Jack & the Beanstalk. 48p. (gr. 2-6). 1991. 2.99 (*0-517-02421-7*) Random Hse Value.

Munsch, Robert. Giant. Tibo, Gilles, illus. 32p. (gr. k-3). 1989. PLB 15.95 (*1-550370-71-5*, Pub. by Annick CN); pap. 5.95 (*1-550370-70-7*, Pub. by Annick CN) Firefly Bks Ltd.

Porter, Sue. Little Wolf & the Giant. (ps-1). 1990. pap. 13.95 jacketed (*0-671-70363-3*, S&S BFYR) S&S Trade.

Roddie, Shen. Animal Stew. Gallagher, Patrick J., illus. 32p. (ps). 1992. 13.45 (*0-395-57582-6*) HM.

Wilde, Oscar. The Selfish Giant. Zwerger, Lisbeth, illus. LC 83-24930. 28p. (gr. 1 up). 1991. pap. 15.95 (*0-907234-30-5*) Picture Bk Studio.

—The Selfish Giant. LC 86-2593. 32p. (gr. 4 up). 1986. PLB 13.95 (*0-88682-068-5*) Creative Ed.

—The Selfish Giant. Mansell, Dom, illus. 1998. pap. 10.95 (*0-671-66847-1*) S&S Trade.

—The Selfish Giant. Zwerger, Lisbeth, illus. 1991. pap. 4.95 (*0-590-44460-3*) Scholastic Inc.

—The Selfish Giant. Gallagher, Saelig, illus. LC 93-10393. 1994. 15.95 (*0-399-22448-3*) Putnam Pub Group.

Willis, Jeanne. In Search of the Giant. Brown, Ruth, illus. LC 93-37589. 1994. write for info. (*0-525-45242-7*, DCB) Dutton Child Bks.

Wood, Audrey. Rude Giants. LC 91-13015. (Illus.). 32p. (ps-3). 1993. 13.95 (*0-15-269412-9*, HB Juv Bks) HarBrace.

GIBSON, ALTHEA, 1917-

Biracree, Tom. Althea Gibson. Horner, Matina, intro. by. (Illus.). 112p. (gr. 5 up). 1990. lib. bdg. 17.95 (*1-55546-654-0*) Chelsea Hse.

Fago, John N. & Farr, Naunerle C. Jim Thorpe - Althea Gibson. Redondo, Frank & Carrillo, Fred, illus. (gr. 4-12). 1979. pap. text ed. 2.95 (*0-88301-360-6*); wkbk. 1.25 (*0-88301-384-3*) Pendulum Pr.

GIFTED CHILDREN–FICTION

Brooks, Jerome. Knee Holes. LC 91-25398. 144p. (gr. 7 up). 1992. 14.95 (*0-531-05994-4*); lib. bdg. 14.99 (*0-531-08594-5*) Orchard Bks Watts.

Chesworth, Michael. Archibald Frisby. 1994. 15.00 (*0-374-30392-4*) FS&G.

Hutson, Joan. Legend of the Nine Talents. Hutson, Joan, illus. LC 92-26957. 1992. 4.95 (*0-8198-4468-3*) St Paul Bks.

Levy, Nathan & Levy, Janet. There Are Those. Edwards, Joan, illus. LC 82-81111. 32p. (ps up). 1990. 21.95 (*0-9608240-0-6*) NL Assoc Inc.

Nesbit, Jeffrey A. The Puzzled Prodigy. (Orig.). (gr. 3-6). 1992. pap. 4.99 (*0-89693-075-0*, Victor Books) SP Pubns.

Rimm, Sylvia B. & Priest, Christine. Gifted Kids Have Feelings Too: And Other Not-So-Fictitious Stories for & about Teenagers. Maas, Katherine, illus. LC 90-81442. 162p. (Orig.). (gr. 6-12). 1990. pap. text ed. 15.00 (*0-937891-06-1*); pap. text ed. 15.00 discussion book (*0-937891-07-X*) Apple Pub Wisc.

Warren, Sandra, ed. Being Gifted: Because You're Special from the Rest. 68p. (Orig.). (ps-6). 1987. pap. 9.99 (*0-89824-173-1*) Trillium Pr.

GIFTS

Amoss, Berthe. Car Seat Games. (Illus.). 10p. (ps-7). 1989. pap. 2.95 (*0-922589-14-3*) More Than Card.

Cheng, Andrea. Let's Make a Present! Easy to Make Gifts for Friends & Relatives of Any Age. Macdonald, Roland B. & Gray, Dan, illus. 128p. (gr. k-5). 1991. pap. 9.95 (*1-878767-16-X*) Murdoch Bks.

Corell, Brigitte. A Gift for You. LC 91-44377. (Illus.). 64p. PLB 15.40, apr. 1992 (*0-516-09260-X*); pap. 8.95, Jul. 1992 (*0-516-49260-8*) Childrens.

Darling, Harold. Happy Book. (Illus.). 48p. 1992. 6.95 (*0-9621131-5-8*) Blue Lantern Studio.

Dubuc, Suzanne. Make Your Own Gifts. (Illus.). 32p. (gr. 3-7). 1993. 7.95 (*2-7625-7159-6*, Pub. by Les Edits Herit CN) Adams Inc MA.

Lemke, Stefan & Pricken, Marie-Luise L. Making Toys & Gifts. LC 91-3880. (Illus.). 64p. 1991. PLB 15.40 (*0-516-09259-6*); pap. 8.95 (*0-516-49259-4*) Childrens.

Making Gifts. LC 91-17042. (Illus.). 48p. (gr. 4-8). 1991. PLB 14.95 (*1-85435-408-6*) Marshall Cavendish.

Silbert, Linda P. & Silbert, Alvin J. The Wonderful World of Gift Giving. (gr. 3-7). 1983. wkbk. 4.98 (*0-89544-024-5*) Silbert Bress.

The Wonderful World of Gift Giving. 32p. (gr. 3-7). 1994. 4.95 (*0-685-71921-9*, 515) W Gladden Found.

Wrap It up for Kids. (Illus.). 64p. 1992. pap. 10.00 (*0-688-11209-9*) Hearst Bks.

GIFTS–FICTION

Ada, Alma F. Serafina's Birthday. Bates, Louise, illus. LC 91-15389. 32p. (ps-2). 1992. SBE 13.95 (*0-689-31516-3*, Atheneum Child Bk) Macmillan Child Grp.

Boyd, Candy D. Circle of Gold. LC 93-19020. 128p. (gr. 3-7). 1994. 13.95 (*0-590-49426-0*) Scholastic Inc.

Branch, Hazel F. Just for Me. LC 92-62879. (Illus.). 57p. (Orig.). (gr. 4-9). 1992. pap. 3.95 (*0-931563-04-6*) Wishing Rm.

Brighton, Catherine. Hope's Gift. 1988. 12.95 (*0-385-24598-X*) Doubleday.

Bunting, Eve. The Mother's Day Mice. Brett, Jan, illus. LC 85-13991. (ps-3). 1986. 13.95 (*0-89919-387-0*, Clarion Bks) HM.

Caseley, Judith. Three Happy Birthdays. LC 92-24583. 40p. (gr. 1 up). 1993. pap. 4.95 (*0-688-11699-X*, Mulberry) Morrow.

Delton, Judy. No Time for Christmas. Mitchell, Anastasia, illus. 48p. (gr. k-4). 1988. PLB 14.95 (*0-87614-327-3*) Carolrhoda Bks.

—No Time for Christmas. Mitchell, Anastasia, illus. 48p. (gr. k-4). 1989. pap. 5.95 (*0-87614-503-9*, First Ave Edns) Lerner Pubns.

—The Perfect Christmas Gift. McCue, Lisa, illus. LC 91-6549. 32p. (gr. k-3). 1992. RSBE 13.95 (*0-02-728471-9*, Macmillan Child Bk) Macmillan Child Grp.

Edmiston, Jim. Little Eagle Lots of Owls. Ross, Jane, illus. LC 92-22683. 32p. (gr. k-3). 1993. 13.95 (*0-395-65564-1*) HM.

Emberley, Michael. Present, Vol. 1. (ps-3). 1991. 14.95 (*0-316-23411-7*) Little.

Gauthier, Bertrand. Zachary in the Present. Sylvestre, Daniel, illus. LC 93-7719. 1993. 15.93 (*0-8368-1010-4*) Gareth Stevens Inc.

Gettinger, Shifrah. A Very Special Gift. Leff, Tova, illus. 32p. (ps-3). 1993. 8.95 (*0-922613-52-4*); pap. text ed. 6.95 (*0-922613-53-2*) Hachai Pubns.

Gregory, Valiska. Happy Burpday, Maggie McDougal! Porter, Pat, illus. 64p. (gr. 2-4). 1992. 11.95 (*0-316-32777-8*) Little.

Hall, Donald. Lucy's Cristmas. McMurdy, Michael, illus. LC 92-46292. (gr. k-3). 1994. 14.95 (*0-15-276870-X*, Browndeer Pr) HarBrace.

Hansen, Joyce. The Gift-Giver. (gr. 3-6). 1989. pap. 6.70 (*0-89919-852-X*, Clarion Bks) HM.

Happy, Elizabeth. Bailey's Birthday. Chase, Andra, illus. LC 93-32519. 32p. (gr. 1-4). 1994. 16.95 (*1-55942-059-6*, 7658); video, tchr's. guide & storybook 79.95 (*1-55942-062-6*, 9377) Marshfilm.

Hughes, Shirley. Giving. Hughes, Shirley, illus. LC 92-53002. 24p. (ps). 1993. 12.95 (*1-56402-129-7*) Candlewick Pr.

Hunt, Angela E. Gift for Grandpa. LC 91-157544. (ps-3). 1991. 13.99 (*1-55513-425-4*, Chariot Bks) Chariot Family.

Kingman, Lee. The Best Christmas. Cooney, Barbara, illus. LC 92-21152. 96p. (gr. 5 up). 1993. pap. 4.95 (*0-688-11838-0*, Pub. by Beech Tree Bks) Morrow.

Kiser, SuAnn & Kiser, Kevin. The Birthday Thing. Abolafia, Yossi, illus. LC 87-38085. 24p. (gr. k up). 1989. 11.95 (*0-688-07772-2*); PLB 11.88 (*0-688-07773-0*) Greenwillow.

Klemin, Diana. How Do You Wrap a Horse? Demarest, Chris L., illus. 32p. (ps-3). 1993. 14.95 (*1-56397-187-9*) Boyds Mills Pr.

Little, Lessie J. & Greenfield, Eloise. I Can Do It by Myself. Byard, Carole, illus. LC 77-11554. (gr. k-2). 1978. (Crowell Jr Bks); PLB 15.89 (*0-690-03851-8*) HarpC Child Bks.

Lowry, Lois. Attaboy, Sam! De Groat, Diane, illus. 128p. (gr. 2-6). 1992. 13.45 (*0-395-61588-7*) HM.

McOmber, Rachel B., ed. McOmber Phonics Storybooks: A Box. rev. ed. (Illus.). write for info. (*0-944991-13-0*) Swift Lrn Res.

Mandrell, Louise & Collins, Ace. Jonathan's Gift. 32p. 1992. 12.95 (*1-56530-012-2*) Summit TX.

Martini, Teri. Christmas for Andy. (gr. 3 up). 1991. pap. 3.95 (*0-8091-6603-8*) Paulist Pr.

Marzollo, Jean. Best Present Ever. 1989. pap. 2.50 (*0-590-42724-5*) Scholastic Inc.

Mattozzi, Patricia R. The Greatest Gift. 1990. 4.50 (*0-8378-1887-7*) Gibson.

Mock, Dorothy. Worms for Winston: The Good News Kids Learn about Love. (Illus.). 32p. (Orig.). (ps-2). 1992. pap. 5.99 (*0-570-04716-1*) Concordia.

Mora, Pat. A Birthday Basket for Tia. Lang, Cecily, illus. LC 91-15753. 32p. (ps-1). 1992. RSBE 13.95 (*0-02-767400-2*, Macmillan Child Bk) Macmillan Child Grp.

Myers, Laurie. Garage Sale Fever. Howell, Kathleen C., illus. LC 92-40342. 80p. (gr. 2-5). 1993. 13.00 (*0-06-022905-5*); PLB 12.89 (*0-06-022908-X*) HarpC.

Naylor, Phyllis R. Keeping a Christmas Secret. Shiffman, Lena, illus. LC 93-12248. 32p. (gr. k-2). 1993. pap. 4.95 (*0-689-71760-1*, Aladdin) Macmillan Child Grp.

O. Henry. Gift of the Magi. Wheeler, Jody, illus. 24p. (ps-3). 1989. pap. 2.95 (*0-8249-8388-2*, Ideals Child) Hambleton-Hill.

—The Gift of the Magi. Sauber, Robert, illus. LC 91-7313. 48p. (gr. 1-6). 1991. 9.95 (*0-88101-116-9*) Unicorn Pub.

—The Gift of the Magi. Zwerger, Lisbeth, illus. LC 92-6632. 28p. 1992. pap. 5.95 (*0-88708-276-9*) Picture Bk Studio.

Oppenheim, Joanne. One Gift Deserves Another. (Illus.). 32p. (ps-1). 1992. 13.00 (*0-525-44975-2*, DCB) Dutton Child Bks.

Palumbo, Nancy. A Birthday Present for Ree-Ree: Un Cadeau d'Anniversaire Pour Ree-Ree. Weaver, Judith, illus. 32p. (Orig.). (ps-6). 1989. wkbk. 5.95 (*0-927024-15-2*) Crayons Pubns.

—A Birthday Present for Ree-Ree: Un Regalo Cumpleanos Para Ree-Ree. Weaver, Judith, illus. 32p. (Orig.). (gr. k-6). 1989. wkbk. 5.95 (*0-927024-14-4*) Crayons Pubns.

Patterson, Nancy R. The Christmas Cup. Bowman, Leslie W., illus. LC 88-29112. 80p. (gr. 3-5). 1989. 13.95 (*0-531-05821-2*); PLB 13.99 (*0-531-08421-3*) Orchard Bks Watts.

Plemons, Marti. Marty & the Mystery Gift. (Illus.). 128p. (gr. 3-6). 1992. pap. 4.99 (*0-87403-937-1*, 24-03767) Standard Pub.

Polacco, Patricia. Just Plain Fancy. (ps-3). 1994. pap. 4.99 (*0-440-40937-3*) Dell.

Porte, Barbara A. Harry's Birthday. Abolafia, Yossi, illus. LC 93-18189. 48p. (gr. k up). 1994. 14.00 (*0-688-12142-X*); PLB 13.93 (*0-688-12143-8*) Greenwillow.

Rinehart, Kimberly R. The Greatest Gift of All. Rettmer, Georgia M., illus. 70p. 1987. 12.95 (*0-942865-02-2*) It Takes Two.

Rodanas, Kristina. The Story of Wali Dad. Rodanas, Kristina, illus. LC 86-34423. 32p. (gr. k-3). 1988. 13.95 (*0-688-07262-3*); PLB 13.88 (*0-688-07263-1*) Lothrop.

Ross, Christine. Lily & the Present. Ross, Christine, illus. LC 91-41134. 28p. (ps-3). 1992. 13.95 (*0-395-61127-X*) HM.

Rylant, Cynthia. Mr. Putter & Tabby Bake the Cake. Howard, Arthur, illus. LC 94-9557. (gr. 1-5). 1994. 10.95 (*0-15-200205-7*); pap. 4.95 (*0-15-200214-6*) HarBrace.

Taha, Karen T. Gift for Tia Rosa. (gr. 4-7). 1991. pap. 2.99 (*0-553-15978-X*) Bantam.

Waite, Michael. Gilly Greenweed's Gift for Granny. LC 91-37443. (ps-3). 1992. pap. 7.99 (*0-7814-0035-X*, Chariot Bks) Chariot Family.

Warren, Jean. Huff & Puff's April Showers: A Totline Teaching Tale. Cubley, Kathleen, ed. Piper, Molly & Ekberg, Marion, illus. LC 93-5489. 32p. (Orig.). (ps-2). 1994. 12.95 (*0-911019-79-0*); pap. 5.95 (*0-911019-78-2*) Warren Pub Hse.

Waters, Mary. The Little Red Blanket. LC 93-61157. (Illus.). 40p. (ps-3). 1993. PLB 6.95 (*0-9638123-0-0*) WAI Pubng.

Wilkeshuis, Cornelis. The Best Gift of All. Van Bilsen, Rita, illus. LC 89-38122. 28p. (gr. k-2). 1989. 8.95 (*0-8198-1126-2*) St Paul Bks.

Wilkins, Joyce R. & Hawkins, Edeltraud. The Animal Market. LC 93-25202. 1993. 8.95 (*1-880373-06-8*) Pictorial Herit.

Williams, Vera B. Something Special for Me. LC 82-11884. (Illus.). 32p. (ps up). 1986. 4.95 (*0-688-06526-0*, Mulberry) Morrow.

Winthrop, Elizabeth. Bear's Christmas Surprise. Brewster, Patience, illus. LC 90-26414. 32p. (ps-3). 1991. reinforced 14.95 (*0-8234-0888-4*) Holiday.

GILBRETH FAMILY

Gilbreth, Frank B., Jr. & Carey, Ernestine G. Cheaper by the Dozen. rev. ed. Vasiliy, illus. LC 63-20411. 256p. (gr. 7 up). 1963. 20.00 (*0-690-18632-0*, Crowell Jr Bks) HarpC.

GILGAMESH

Zeman, Ludmila. Gilgamesh the King, Bk. 1. Zeman, Ludmila, illus. LC 91-67565. 24p. (gr. 3 up). 1992. 19.95 (*0-88776-283-2*) Tundra Bks.

—The Last Quest of Gilgamesh: Gilgamesh the King, Pt. III. Zeman, Ludmila, illus. LC 93-61787. 24p. (gr. 3 up). 1994. 19.95 (*0-88776-328-6*) Tundra Bks.

—Voyage au Pays Sous-Terrain: L'Epopee de Gilgamesh, Livre III. Boileau, Michele, tr. from ENG. Zeman, Ludmila, illus. LC 93-61788. (FRE.). 24p. (gr. 3 up). 1994. 19.95 (*0-88776-329-4*) Tundra Bks.

GIPSIES

see Gypsies

GIRAFFES

Arnold, Caroline. Giraffe. Hewett, Richard, illus. LC 87-1502. 48p. (gr. 2-5). 1987. 12.95 (*0-688-07069-8*); lib. bdg. 12.88 (*0-688-07070-1*, Morrow Jr Bks) Morrow Jr Bks.

—Giraffe. Hewett, Richard, photos by. LC 92-25549. (Illus.). 48p. (gr. 3 up). 1993. pap. 5.95 (*0-688-12272-8*, Mulberry) Morrow.

Bailey, Donna. Giraffes. LC 90-22108. (Illus.). (gr. 1-4). 1992. PLB 18.99 (*0-8114-2646-7*) Raintree Steck-V.

Denis-Huot, Christine & Denis-Huot, Michel. The Giraffe. 28p. (ps-3). 1993. pap. 6.95 (*0-88106-431-9*) Charlesbridge Pub.

Giraffes. 1991. PLB 14.95 (*0-88682-334-X*) Creative Ed.

Green, Carl R. & Sanford, William R. The Giraffe. LC 87-1363. (Illus.). 48p. (gr. 5). 1987. text ed. 12.95 RSBE (*0-89686-332-8*, Crestwood Hse) Macmillan Child Grp.

Hoffman, Mary. Giraffe. LC 86-6770. (Illus.). 24p. (gr. k-5). 1986. PLB 9.95 (*0-8172-2397-5*); pap. 3.95 (*0-8114-6875-5*) Raintree Steck-V.

Ling, Mary. Giraffe. LC 93-3041. (Illus.). 24p. (ps-1). 1993. 7.95 (*1-56458-311-2*) Dorling Kindersley.

Markert, Jenny. Giraffes. 32p. (gr. 2-6). 1991. 15.95 (*0-89565-723-6*) Childs World.

Milton, Nancy. The Giraffe That Walked to Paris. Roth, Roger, illus. LC 91-31767. 32p. (gr. k-4). 1992. 15.00 (*0-517-58132-9*); PLB 15.99 (*0-517-58133-7*) Crown Bks Yng Read.

Propper. Giraffe, Reading Level 3-4. (Illus.). 28p. (gr. 2-5). 1983. PLB 16.67 (*0-86592-860-6*); 12.50s.p. (*0-685-58817-3*) Rourke Corp.

Sattler, Helen R. Giraffes: The Sentinels of the Savannas. Santoro, Christopher, illus. LC 89-2287. 80p. (gr. 3 up). 1990. 14.95 (*0-688-08284-X*); PLB 14.88 (*0-688-08285-8*) Lothrop.

Stone, Lynn. Giraffes. (Illus.). 24p. (gr. k-5). 1990. lib. bdg. 11.94 (*0-86593-050-3*); lib. bdg. 8.95s.p. (*0-685-36346-5*) Rourke Corp.

Wildlife Education, Ltd. Staff. Giraffes. Francis, John, et al, illus. 20p. (Orig.). (gr. 5 up). 1982. pap. 2.75 (*0-937934-09-7*) Wildlife Educ.

Zingg, Eduard. Giraffes of Botswana. LC 93-10265. 1993. 14.96 (*1-56239-215-8*) Abdo & Dghtrs.

GIRAFFES–FICTION

Ada, Alma F. Los Seis Deseos de la Jirafa (Small Book) Roy, Doug, illus. (SPA.). 16p. (Orig.). (gr. k-3). 1992. pap. text ed. 6.00 (*1-56334-078-X*) Hampton-Brown.

Brenner, Barbara. Mr. Tall & Mr. Small. Shenon, Mike, illus. LC 93-8256. (gr. k-3). 1994. 14.95 (*0-8050-2757-2*) H Holt & Co.

Dahl, Roald. The Giraffe & the Pelly & Me. Blake, Quentin, illus. 80p. (gr. 2-5). 1994. pap. 3.99 (*0-14-037009-9*) Puffin Bks.

Dartez, Cecilia C. Jenny Giraffe & the Streetcar Party. Green, Andy, illus. LC 93-9924. 32p. (gr. k-3). 1993. 14.95 (*0-88289-962-7*) Pelican.

—Jenny Giraffe Discovers the French Quarter. Wilson, Shelby, illus. LC 90-48720. 32p. (ps-8). 1991. 12.95 (*0-88289-819-1*) Pelican.

Farmer, Nancy. The Warm Place. LC 94-21984. 1995. write for info. (*0-531-06888-9*) Orchard Bks Watts.

Grandma, Marian, pseud. Georgie the Jovial Giraffe. Sott, Donna, illus. LC 85-71331. 32p. (gr. 3 up). 1985. text ed. write for info. (*0-9614989-0-0*) Banmar Inc.

Lemaitre, Pascal. Emily the Giraffe. Lemaitre, Pascal, illus. LC 92-85508. 32p. (ps-2). 1993. 13.95 (*1-56282-403-1*); PLB 13.89 (*1-56282-404-X*) Hyprn Child.

Leslie-Melville, Betty. Daisy Rothschild: The Giraffe That Lives with Me. (gr. 2-6). 1992. 4.99 (*0-440-40671-4*, YB) Dell.

Morton, Lone. I'm Too Big (Je Suis Trop Gros) Weatherill, Steve, illus. Helie, Ide M., tr. from FRE. McCourt, Ella, concept by. LC 94-561. (ENG & FRE., Illus.). 28p. (ps up). 1994. 6.95 (*0-8120-6454-2*) Barron.

—I'm Too Big (Soy Demasiado Grande) Weatherill, Steve, illus. McCourt, Ella, concept by. LC 94-563. (ENG & SPA., Illus.). 28p. (ps up). 1994. 6.95 (*0-8120-6451-8*) Barron.

Rey, H. A. Cecily G. & the Nine Monkeys. Rey, H. A., illus. 32p. (gr. 1-3). 1974. 14.45 (*0-395-18430-4*) HM.

Riches, Judith. Giraffes Have More Fun. LC 91-21184. (Illus.). 32p. (ps-3). 1992. 14.00 (*0-688-11042-8*, Tambourine Bks); PLB 13.93 (*0-688-11043-6*, Tambourine Bks) Morrow.

Rogers. Josephine the Short Necked Giraffe. 1985. 3.95 (*0-8331-0036-X*) Hubbard Sci.

—Speedy Delivery. 1985. 3.95 (*0-8331-0037-8*) Hubbard Sci.

Rosenthal, Ellie. Why, Oh, Why Do You Laugh At Me? 1994. 7.95 (*0-533-10765-2*) Vantage.

GIRL SCOUTS

Brownie Girl Scout Handbook. 288p. (gr. 1-3). 1993. 7.95 (*0-88441-279-2*, 20-910) Girl Scouts USA.

Cadette & Senior Girl Scout Interest Projects. (Illus.). 160p. (gr. 6-12). 1987. pap. 6.00 (*0-88441-343-8*, 20-792) Girl Scouts USA.

Games for Girl Scouts. (Illus.). 128p. (ps up). 1990. pap. 6.00 (*0-88441-347-0*, 20-902) Girl Scouts USA.

Girl Scout Badges & Signs. (Illus.). 250p. (gr. 3-7). 1990. pap. 6.00 (*0-88441-346-2*, 20-914) Girl Scouts USA.

Girl Scouts of the U. S. A. Staff. Sing Together: A Girl Scout Songbook. (Illus.). 192p. (gr. 1-12). 1973. spiral bdg. 8.25 (*0-88441-309-8*, 20-206) Girl Scouts USA.

Junior Girl Scout Activity Book. (Illus.). 80p. 1992. 4.50 (*0-88441-348-9*, 20-904) Girl Scouts USA.

Kudlinski, Kathleen V. Juliette Gordon Low: America's First Girl Scout. Hamanaka, Sheila, illus. (gr. 2-6). 1988. pap. 10.95 (*0-670-82208-6*) Viking Child Bks.

My Daisy Girl Scout Activity Scrapbook. 64p. (gr. k-1). 1993. 5.95 (*0-88441-277-6*, 20-907) Girl Scouts USA.

Outdoor Education in Girl Scouting. (Illus.). 172p. (gr. 6-12). 1984. pap. 7.00 (*0-685-47514-X*, 26-217) Girl Scouts USA.

Steelsmith, Shari. Juliette Gordon Low: Founder of the Girl Scouts. Pope, Connie J., illus. LC 89-62673. 32p. (Orig.). (ps-4). 1990. lib. bdg. 16.95 (*0-943990-37-8*); pap. 5.95 (*0-943990-36-X*) Parenting Pr.

Who Is a Daisy Girl Scout? 32p. 1993. 14.95 (*0-88441-275-X*, 20-905) Girl Scouts USA.

Who Is a Daisy Girl Scout? 32p. (gr. k-1). 1993. 2.95 (*0-88441-276-8*, 20-906) Girl Scouts USA.

World Association of Girl Guides & Girl Scouts Staff. Trefoil 'Round the World. rev. ed. (Illus.). 304p. (gr. 4-12). 1992. 9.25 (*0-900827-50-5*, 23-967) Girl Scouts USA.

GIRL SCOUTS–FICTION

Leonard, Marcia. Take a Bow, Krissy! Long, Laurie S., illus. 64p. (gr. 1-4). 1994. PLB 7.99 (*0-448-40838-4*, G&D); pap. 3.95 (*0-448-40837-6*, G&D) Putnam Pub Group.

O'Connor, Jane. Amy's (Not So) Great Camp-Out. Long, Laurie S., illus. LC 92-45881. 64p. (gr. 1-4). 1993. 7.99 (*0-448-40167-3*, G&D); pap. 3.95 (*0-448-40166-5*, G&D) Putnam Pub Group.

—Corrie's Secret Pal. Long, Laurie S., illus. LC 92-35602. 64p. (gr. 1-4). 1993. 7.99 (*0-448-40161-4*, G&D); pap. 3.95 (*0-448-40160-6*, G&D) Putnam Pub Group.

—Make up Your Mind, Marsha! Long, Laurie S., illus. LC 92-45880. 64p. (gr. 1-4). 1993. 7.99 (*0-448-40165-7*, G&D); pap. 3.95 (*0-448-40164-9*, G&D) Putnam Pub Group.

—Sarah's Incredible Idea. Long, Laurie S., illus. LC 92-36803. 64p. (gr. 1-4). 1993. 7.99g (*0-448-40163-0*, G&D); pap. 3.95 (*0-448-40162-2*, G&D) Putnam Pub Group.

—Think, Corrie, Think! Long, Laurie S., illus. 64p. (gr. 1-4). 1994. 7.99 (*0-448-40466-4*, G&D); pap. 3.95 (*0-448-40465-6*, G&D) Putnam Pub Group.

GIRL SCOUTS–HANDBOOKS, MANUALS, ETC

Cadette & Senior Girl Scout Handbook. (Illus.). 176p. (gr. 6-12). 1987. pap. 7.25 (*0-88441-342-X*, 20-791) Girl Scouts USA.

Girl Scouts of the U. S. A. Staff. Wide World of Girl Guiding & Girl Scouting. (Illus.). 88p. (gr. 1-6). 1980. pap. text ed. 7.50 (*0-88441-143-5*, 19-713) Girl Scouts USA.

GIRLS

Blair, L. E. Peer Pressure Girl Talk, No. 9. 1991. pap. 2.95 (*0-307-22009-5*) Western Pub.

Cleary, Beverly. A Girl from Yamhill. (gr. k-6). 1989. pap. 4.50 (*0-440-40185-2*, YB) Dell.

—A Girl from Yamhill: A Memoir. LC 87-31554. (Illus.). 320p. (gr. 7 up). 1988. 15.95 (*0-688-07800-1*) Morrow Jr Bks.

Coerr, Eleanor. Sadako & the Thousand Paper Cranes. Himler, Ronald, illus. 64p. (gr. 2-5). 1979. pap. 3.50 (*0-440-47465-5*, YB) Dell.

Curro, Ellen. No Need to Be Afraid...First Pelvic Exam: A Handbook for Young Women & Their Mothers. Piccirilli, Charles, illus. 80p. (gr. 9-12). 1991. pap. text ed. 4.95 (*0-9629417-1-9*) Linking Ed Med.

Deaton, Wendy. My Own Thoughts: A Growth & Recovery Workbook for Young Girls. 32p. (gr. 2-6). 1993. wkbk. 5.95 (*0-89793-130-0*); practitioner packs 15.95 (*0-89793-133-5*) Hunter Hse.

Forrester, Victoria. Poor Gabriella: A Christmas Story. Boulet, Susan B., illus. LC 86-3607. 32p. 1986. SBE 14.95 (*0-689-31265-2*, Atheneum Child Bk) Macmillan Child Grp.

Galicich, Anne. Samantha Smith: A Journey for Peace. LC 87-13614. (Illus.). 64p. (gr. 3 up). 1988. text ed. 13.95 RSBE (*0-87518-367-0*, Dillon) Macmillan Child Grp.

Lukes, Bonnie L. How to Be a Reasonably Thin Teenage Girl (Without Starving, Losing Your Friends, or Running Away from Home) Niclaus, Carol, illus. LC 86-3347. 96p. (gr. 6 up). 1986. SBE 13.95 (*0-689-31269-5*, Atheneum) Macmillan Child Grp.

Madaras, Lynda & Madaras, Area. My Feelings, My Self: Lynda Madaras' Growing-Up Guide for Girls. Aher, Jackie, illus. LC 86-23719. 160p. (gr. 3-10). 1993. cancelled (*0-937858-87-0*); pap. 9.95 (*1-55704-157-1*) Newmarket.

Marzollo, Jean. Getting Your Period: A Book about Menstruation. Williams, Kent, illus. Storch, Marcia, intro. by. LC 88-3986. (Illus.). 112p. (gr. 4 up). 1989. 13.95 (*0-8037-0355-4*); 6.95 (*0-8037-0356-2*) Dial Bks Young.

Ransom, Candice F. So Young to Die: The Story of Hannah Senesh. (gr. 4-7). 1993. pap. 2.95 (*0-685-65620-9*) Scholastic Inc.

Rau, Margaret. Young Women in China. LC 88-31045. (Illus.). 160p. (gr. 6 up). 1989. lib. bdg. 18.95 (*0-89490-170-2*) Enslow Pubs.

Rodowsky, Colby. Julie's Daughter. LC 85-47589. 231p. (gr. 7 up). 1985. 15.00 (*0-374-33963-5*) FS&G.

Setterlund, Donna J. A Dream & a Promise: From a Child to a Woman with a Mother's Help along the Way. (Illus.). 240p. (gr. 8 up). 1990. write for info. (*0-9624342-2-1*); pap. write for info. Carriage Hse Studio Pubns.

Wadley, Verleen W. Four Winds of the Past. Webb, Glyn, ed. (Illus.). 215p. 1993. PLB 16.00x (*0-9604726-6-5*) Enterprise Pr.

Wanner, Donna T. Just for Me: The Self-Esteem & Wellness Guide for Girls. Noble, Claudia, ed. Moore, Candice, illus. LC 94-6134. 224p. (gr. 4-9). 1994. pap. 16.95 (*0-9630419-5-9*) Spiritseeker.

GIRLS–EMPLOYMENT

see Child Labor

GIRLS–FICTION

Abell. The Reward. Abell, et al, illus. 50p. (Orig.). (gr. 5 up). 1993. 25.00 (*1-56611-079-3*); pap. text ed. 15.00 (*1-56611-080-7*) Jonas.

Abell, Joan. Books for Young Ladies. rev. ed. Abell, Joan, illus. Date not set. 22.00 (*1-56611-028-9*); PLB 25.00 (*1-56611-072-6*); pap. 15.00 (*0-685-65772-8*) Jonas.

Ada, Alma F. My Name Is Maria Isabel. Cerro, Ana M., tr. from SPA. Thompson, K. Dyble, illus. LC 91-44910. 64p. (gr. 2-5). 1993. SBE 12.95 (*0-689-31517-1*, Atheneum Child Bk) Macmillan Child Grp.

Adams, Laurie. Alice Whipple Shapes Up. (gr. 4-7). 1990. pap. 2.75 (*0-553-15803-1*) Bantam.

Adler, C. S. If You Need Me. LC 87-36467. 160p. (gr. 4-8). 1988. SBE 13.95 (*0-02-700420-1*, Macmillan Child Bk) Macmillan Child Grp.

Adler, Susan S. Meet Samantha: An American Girl. Thieme, Jeanne, ed. Niles, Nancy & Lusk, Nancy M, illus. 72p. (gr. 2-5). 1986. PLB 12.95 (*0-937295-80-9*); pap. 5.95 (*0-937295-04-3*) Pleasant Co.

—Samantha Learns a Lesson: A School Story. Thieme, Jeanne, ed. Niles, Nancy & Lusk, Nancy N, illus. 72p. (gr. 2-5). 1986. PLB 12.95 (*0-937295-83-3*); pap. 5.95 (*0-937295-13-2*) Pleasant Co.

Adler, Susan S, et al. Samantha, 6 bks. Niles, Nancy, et al, illus. 432p. (gr. 2-5). 1991. Boxed Set. lib. bdg. 74.95 (*1-56247-050-7*); Boxed Set. pap. 34.95 (*0-937295-77-9*) Pleasant Co.

Agnes' Cardboard Piano. (Illus.). 40p. (gr. k-5). 1994. pap. 4.95 (*0-685-71584-1*, 520) W Gladden Found.

Agnew, Robin. Rebecca of Grand Hotel. Agnew, Robin, illus. 72p. 1990. text ed. 15.95 (*0-9627301-0-6*) Grand Hotel.

Ai-Ling, Louie, retold by. Yeh-Shen: A Cinderella Story from China. Young, Ed, illus. (ps-3). 1988. pap. 5.95 (*0-399-21594-8*, Sandcastle Bks) Putnam Pub Group.

Akiko Sueyoshi. Jessica's Friend. Young, Richard G., ed. Kaisei-sha, tr. Akiko Hayashi, illus. LC 89-12050. 32p. (gr. 1-3). 1989. PLB 14.60 (*0-944483-47-X*) Garrett Ed Corp.

Albright, Molly. Video Stars. Connor, Eulala, illus. LC 88-15880. 96p. (gr. 3-6). 1989. PLB 9.89 (*0-8167-1480-0*); pap. text ed. 2.95 (*0-8167-1481-9*) Troll Assocs.

Alcott, Louisa May. An Old-Fashioned Girl. (Orig.). (gr. k-6). 1987. pap. 4.95 (*0-440-46609-1*, Pub. by Yearling Classics) Dell.

—Old-Fashioned Girl. (gr. 4-7). 1991. pap. 2.95 (*0-14-035137-X*, Puffin) Puffin Bks.

—Rose in Bloom. (gr. k-6). 1986. pap. 4.95 (*0-440-47588-0*, YB) Dell.

—Rose in Bloom. 336p. (gr. 5 up). 1989. pap. 3.95 (*0-14-035125-6*, Puffin) Puffin Bks.

Alderson, Sueann. Bonnie McSmithers Is at It Again! Garrick, Fiona, illus. 24p. (Orig.). (ps-2). 1990. pap. 0.99 (*1-55037-110-X*, Pub. by Annick CN) Firefly Bks Ltd.

—Bonnie McSmithers You're Driving Me Dithers. Garrick, Fiona, illus. 24p. (Orig.). (ps-2). 1990. pap. 0.99 (*1-55037-108-8*, Pub. by Annick CN) Firefly Bks Ltd.

—Hurry Up, Bonnie! Garrick, Fiona, illus. 24p. (Orig.). (ps-2). 1990. pap. 0.99 (*1-55037-109-6*, Pub. by Annick CN) Firefly Bks Ltd.

Alexander, Martha. Sabrina. Alexander, Martha, illus. LC 72-134855. 32p. (ps-2). 1991. pap. 2.95 (*0-8037-0842-4*, Puff Pied Piper) Puffin Bks.

—Sabrina. Alexander, Martha, illus. 1991. 8.95 (*0-8037-7547-4*) Dial Bks Young.

Alexandra Keeper of Dreams. (Illus.). 36p. (ps-5). 1994. 14.95 (*0-685-71591-4*, 718) W Gladden Found.

Alice in Wonderland. (Illus.). 24p. (Orig.). (gr. k-3). 1993. pap. 2.50 (*1-56144-294-1*, Honey Bear Bks) Modern Pub NYC.

Allard, Harry & Marshall, James. Miss Nelson Is Back. (Illus.). (gr. k-3). 1986. 13.45 (*0-395-32956-6*); pap. 4.80 (*0-395-41668-X*) HM.

Allee, Marjorie H. Jane's Island. De Gogorza, Maitland, illus. 236p. (gr. 6 up). 1988. Repr. of 1931 ed. 13.95 (*0-9611374-2-8*) Woods Hole Hist.

Alpert, Lou. Emma Giggled. Alpert, Lou, illus. 32p. (ps-3). 1991. smythe sewn reinforced bdg. 12.95 (*1-879085-02-X*) Whsprng Coyote Pr.

Alter, Judy. Maggie & Devildust Ridin' High. Shaw, Charles, illus. LC 89-2683. 176p. (Orig.). (gr. 4-9). 1990. pap. 5.95 (*0-936650-10-9*) E C Temple.

Altman, Linda J. El Camino de Amelia. Santacruz, Daniel, tr. Sanchez, Enrique O., illus. LC 93-38627. (SPA.). 32p. (gr. k-3). 1994. 14.95 (*1-88000-007-5*); pap. 5.95 (*1-88000-010-5*) Lee & Low Bks.

Alvarez, Julia. How the Garcia Girls Lost Their Accents. 308p. (gr. 10 up). 1991. 16.95 (*0-945575-57-2*) Algonquin Bks.

Amir, Tami. La Rana Valiente. Writer, C. C. & Nielsen, Lisa C., trs. Elchanan, illus. (SPA.). 24p. (Orig.). (ps). 1992. pap. text ed. 3.00x (*1-56134-168-1*) Dushkin Pub.

Ammon, Richard. Growing up Amish. LC 88-27493. (Illus.). 80p. (gr. 3-7). 1989. SBE 13.95 (*0-689-31387-X*, Atheneum Child Bk) Macmillan Child Grp.

Anastasio, Dina. The Case of the Glacier Park Swallow. Saflund, Birgitta, illus. LC 94-65091. 96p. (Orig.). (gr. 4 up). 1994. pap. 8.95 (*1-879373-85-8*) R Rinehart.

—The Case of the Grand Canyon Eagle. Saflund, Birgitta, illus. LC 94-65090. 96p. (Orig.). (gr. 6 up). 1994. pap. 8.95 (*1-879373-84-X*) R Rinehart.

Anders, Jeanne. Leslie. LC 86-72892. 160p. (gr. 9 up). 1987. pap. 3.99 (*0-87123-927-2*) Bethany Hse.

Andersen, Hans Christian. The Little Match Girl. Isadora, Rachel, illus. 32p. (ps-3). 1990. 14.95 (*0-399-21336-8*, Sandcastle Bks); pap. 5.95 (*0-399-22007-0*, Sandcastle Bks) Putnam Pub Group.

Anderson, Jill. The Land of No. Blackwelder, Kathy, ed. Magnuson, Diana, illus. LC 87-51628. 40p. (gr. 1-4). 1990. PLB 14.95 (*0-9608284-5-1*) Timberline Pr.

Anderson, Mary. Suzy's Secret Snoop Society. (gr. 3-7). 1991. pap. 2.95 (*0-380-75917-9*, Camelot) Avon.

Angell, Judie. Dear Lola: How to Build Your Own Family. 144p. (gr. 5-9). 1986. pap. 1.95 (*0-440-91787-5*, LFL) Dell.

—Tina Gogo. 160p. (gr. 5 up). 1980. pap. 1.75 (*0-440-98738-5*, LFL) Dell.

Applegate, Katherine. The World's Best Jinx McGee. 80p. (Orig.). (gr. 2). 1992. pap. 2.99 (*0-380-76728-7*, Camelot Young) Avon.

Aragon, Jane C. Salt Hands. Rand, Ted, illus. 24p. (ps-2). 1994. pap. 4.99 (*0-14-050321-8*, Puff Unicorn) Puffin Bks.

Armstrong, Jennifer. Hilary to the Rescue. (gr. 3-6). 1990. pap. 2.75 (*0-553-15812-0*) Bantam.

Arnold, Katya, retold by. & illus. Baba Yaga & the Little Girl. LC 93-45752. 32p. (gr. k-3). 1994. 14.95 (*1-55858-287-8*); lib. bdg. 14.88 (*1-55858-288-6*) North-South Bks NYC.

Arrick, Fran. Nice Girl from Good Home. 208p. (gr. 7 up). 1986. pap. 2.75 (*0-440-96358-3*, LFL) Dell.

—Steffie Can't Come Out to Play. 160p. (gr. 7 up). 1979. pap. 2.50 (*0-440-97635-9*, LFL) Dell.

Ashwill, Beverley B. Heather & the New Baby. Ashwill, Betty J., illus. LC 88-63168. 23p. (Orig.). (gr. k-3). 1988. pap. 3.98 (*0-941381-03-X*) BJO Enterprises.

Auch, Mary J. Glass Slippers Give You Blisters. 1990. pap. 2.75 (*0-590-43501-9*) Scholastic Inc.

Avi. Bright Shadow. 2nd ed. LC 93-20918. 176p. (gr. 3-6). 1994. pap. 3.95 (*0-689-71783-0*, Aladdin) Macmillan Child Grp.

—The True Confessions of Charlotte Doyle. 240p. (gr. 6). 1992. pap. 3.99 (*0-380-71475-2*, Flare) Avon.

Axsom, Dora & Pelham, Erra. No Lace for Cricket: Sequel to Mountain Mama. 216p. (Orig.). (gr. 10 up). 1991. pap. 5.50 (*0-9621669-2-8*) Lil Red Hen OK.

Babbitt, Natalie. Phoebe's Revolt. LC 68-13679. (Illus.). 40p. (ps up). 1988. pap. 3.95 (*0-374-45792-1*) FS&G.

Baer, Judy. Adrienne. LC 87-71605. 176p. (Orig.). (gr. 7-12). 1987. pap. 3.99 (*0-87123-949-3*) Bethany Hse.

—Cedar River Daydreams 16-20 Giftset. 1993. 19.99 (*1-55661-772-0*) Bethany Hse.

—The Intruder. 160p. (Orig.). (gr. 7 up). 1989. pap. 3.99 (*1-55661-088-2*) Bethany Hse.

—Jennifer's Secret. LC 88-63463. 128p. (Orig.). (gr. 6 up). 1989. pap. 3.99 (*1-55661-058-0*) Bethany Hse.

—Lost & Found. 144p. (Orig.). (gr. 7-10). 1992. pap. 3.99 (*1-55661-243-5*) Bethany Hse.

—Unheard Voices. 144p. (Orig.). (gr. 7-10). 1992. pap. 3.99 (*1-55661-257-5*) Bethany Hse.

Baker, Barbara. Digby & Kate. Windborn, Marsha, illus. LC 93-6555. (gr. k-3). 1993. pap. 3.25 (*0-14-036547-8*, Puffin) Puffin Bks.

Ball, Nancy. Shy Ann. Christie, Robert D., illus. LC 88-51305. 55p. (Orig.). (gr. k-4). 1989. pap. 3.95 (*0-931563-03-8*) Wishing Rm.

Bang, Molly. Delphine. Bang, Molly, illus. LC 87-34958. 32p. (gr. 2 up). 1988. 12.95 (*0-688-05636-9*); PLB 12.88 (*0-688-05637-7*, Morrow Jr Bks) Morrow Jr Bks.

Banks, Lynne R. The Farthest-Away Mountain. 144p. 1992. pap. 3.99 (*0-380-71303-9*, Camelot) Avon.

Barkan, Joanne. Anna Marie's Blanket. Maze, Deborah, illus. 32p. 1990. 12.95 (*0-8120-6124-1*) Barron.

Barker, Cicely M. The Lord of the Rushie River & Simon the Swan. (Illus.). 98p. (ps-3). 1992. 14.00 (*0-7232-3980-0*) Warne.

Barrett, Pamela. Becky's Braces. 1993. 7.75 (*0-8062-4689-8*) Carlton.
Baum, L. Frank. Patchwork Girl of Oz. 1990. pap. 6.95 (*0-486-26514-5*) Dover.
Baumgardner, Mary A. Alexandra, Keeper of Dreams. Wheeler, Penny & Wilson, Miriam W., eds. Baumgardner, Mary A., illus. 37p. (gr. k-4). 1993. 12.95 (*0-944576-08-7*) Rocky River Pubs.
Bawden, Nina. Humbug. 144p. (gr. 5 up). 1994. pap. 3.99 (*0-14-036586-9*) Puffin Bks.
—The Outside Child. 240p. (gr. 5 up). 1994. pap. 3.99 (*0-14-036858-2*) Puffin Bks.
Bayer, Jane. A, My Name Is Alice. Kellogg, Steven, illus. LC 84-7059. 32p. (ps-2). 1987. pap. 4.95 (*0-8037-0130-6*) Dial Bks Young.
Beatty, Patricia. Be Ever Hopeful Hannalee. 216p. (gr. 5-9). 1990. pap. 2.95 (*0-8167-2259-5*) Troll Assocs.
—Sarah & Me & Lady from the Sea. LC 89-33624. 224p. (gr. 5 up). 1989. 11.95 (*0-688-08045-6*) Morrow Jr Bks.
—Turn Homeward, Hannalee. 193p. (gr. 5-9). 1990. pap. 2.95 (*0-8167-2260-9*) Troll Assocs.
Becker, Lois & Stratton, Mark. Mistress Mary. Alchemy II, Inc. Staff, illus. 26p. (ps). 1988. incl. cassette 9.95 (*1-55578-920-X*) Worlds Wonder.
Bee, Cindy. A Big House, a Little Girl & a Few Things That Made Them Laugh. Jesionowski, Mary & Schnickel, Jacob, illus. 20p. (Orig.). (ps-5). 1990. pap. 2.75 (*0-9616308-1-7*) Hearthstn Inn.
Begaye, Lisa S. Building a Bridge. Tracy, Libba, illus. LC 92-82138. 32p. (gr. k). 1993. 14.95 (*0-87358-557-7*) Northland AZ.
Beiler, Edna. Mattie Mae. Graber, E. R., illus. LC 67-24800. 128p. (gr. 3-7). 1967. pap. 5.95 (*0-8361-1789-1*) Herald Pr.
Belloc, Hilaire. Matilda Who Told Lies. Kellogg, Steven, illus. LC 78-121812. 32p. (ps up). 1992. pap. 3.99 (*0-14-054547-6*, Puff Pied Piper) Puffin Bks.
Bemelmans, Ludwig. Madeline. (Illus.). 32p. (ps-3). 1993. pap. 17.99 (*0-14-054845-9*, Puffin) Puffin Bks.
—Madeline. (Illus.). 1993. pap. 6.99 incl. cassette (*0-14-095120-2*, Puffin) Puffin Bks.
—Madeline. Grosman, Ernesto L., tr. (SPA., Illus.). 64p. (ps-3). 1993. 14.99 (*0-670-85154-X*) Viking Child Bks.
—Madeline's House: Includes: Madeline; Madeline's Rescue; Madeline & the Bad Hat. Bemelmans, Ludwig, illus. (ps-3). 1989. pap. 12.50 (*0-14-095028-1*, Puffin) Puffin Bks.
—Madeline's Rescue. (Illus.). 1993. pap. 6.99 incl. cassette (*0-14-095122-9*, Puffin) Puffin Bks.
Bender, Esther. Katie & the Lemon Tree. Keenan, Joy D., illus. 88p. (Orig.). (gr. 3-7). 1994. pap. 4.95 (*0-8361-3657-8*) Herald Pr.
Bennett, Cherie. Surviving Sixteen, No. 3: Did You Hear about Amber? 224p. (gr. 7 up). 1993. pap. 3.50 (*0-14-036318-1*, Puffin) Puffin Bks.
Bennett, Geraldine M. Katrina Tells about Bee Stings. (gr. k up). Date not set. pap. write for info. (*1-882786-07-6*) New Dawn NY.
—Katrina Tells of Healing a Kitten. (gr. k up). Date not set. pap. write for info. New Dawn NY.
—Monkey See, Monkey Do. (gr. k up). Date not set. pap. write for info. (*1-882786-09-2*) New Dawn NY.
Benning, Elizabeth. Life Without Alice. (gr. 4-7). 1993. pap. 3.50 (*0-06-106156-5*, Harp PBks) HarpC.
Benson, B. J. Tandy. LC 88-50930. 179p. 1989. pap. 9.95 (*1-55523-169-1*) Winston-Derek.
Benton, John. Debbie. 192p. (Orig.). (gr. 7-12). 1980. pap. 3.50 (*0-8007-8398-0*) J Benton Bks.
—Jackie. 192p. (Orig.). (gr. 7-12). 1981. pap. 3.50 (*0-8007-8406-5*) J Benton Bks.
—Terri. 192p. (gr. 7-12). 1981. pap. 3.50 (*0-8007-8408-1*) J Benton Bks.
Benziger, John. The Corpuscles: Adventurers in Inner Space. Benziger, John & Benziger, Mary, illus. LC 88-92390. 64p. (gr. k-6). 1989. 11.95 (*0-9620961-0-5*) Corpuscles Intergalactica.
Betancourt, Jeanne. Kate's Turn. (gr. 4-7). 1993. pap. 2.95 (*0-590-43104-8*) Scholastic Inc.
Birkenhead. Melanie Jane. Date not set. 15.00 (*0-06-023391-5*); PLB 14.89 (*0-685-68963-8*) HarpC Child Bks.
Bishop, Roma. Perfect Pom-Pom: Where Does It Belong? (ps-3). 1993. 9.95 (*0-307-17602-9*, Golden Pr) Western Pub.
Blackistone, Mick. Broken Wings Will Fly. Wharton, Jennifer H., illus. 32p. (gr. 2-6). 1992. 10.95 (*0-87033-439-5*) Tidewater.
Blackmore, Richard. Lorna Doone. 345p. 1981. Repr. PLB 24.95 (*0-89966-350-8*) Buccaneer Bks.
Blaine, Marge. The Terrible Thing That Happened at Our House. Wallner, John C., illus. 32p. (gr. 1-4). 1991. pap. 3.95 (*0-590-42371-1*) Scholastic Inc.
Blair, L. E. Baby Talk. 128p. (gr. 4-7). 1992. 2.95 (*0-307-22021-4*, 22021) Western Pub.
—Blue Ribbon. 128p. (gr. 3-7). 1992. pap. 2.95 (*0-307-22025-7*, 22025, Golden Pr) Western Pub.
—Center Stage. 128p. (gr. 3-7). 1992. pap. 2.95 (*0-307-22028-1*, 22028, Golden Pr) Western Pub.
—Party Central. 128p. (gr. 4-7). 1992. 2.95 (*0-307-22023-0*, 22023) Western Pub.
—Perfect Match. 128p. (gr. 3-7). 1992. pap. 2.95 (*0-307-22027-3*, 22027, Golden Pr) Western Pub.
—Rockin' Class Trip. 128p. (gr. 4-7). 1992. 2.95 (*0-307-22020-6*, 22020) Western Pub.
Blair, Susan M. Unexpected Company. Blair, Susan M., illus. 56p. (ps-7). 1992. 19.95 (*0-9631956-0-3*) Pendant Pr.
Blanca Nieves. (SPA.). 96p. 1994. 6.98 (*1-57082-140-2*) Mouse Works.
Blank, Grace W. Grace Delight & Tricksey. Witte, Suzanne, illus. LC 91-75093. 111p. (gr. k-3). 1992. 8.95 (*1-55523-459-3*) Winston-Derek.
—Jennie & Sue Visit a Kentucky Farm. Witte-Barrett, Suzanne, illus. 70p. (gr. 3-6). Date not set. write for info. (*0-9634122-5-6*) Feather Fables.
Blatchford, Claire. El Cielo Azul de Shawna. Writer, C. C. & Nielsen, Lisa C., trs. Eagle, Mike, illus. (SPA.). 24p. (Orig.). (ps). 1992. pap. text ed. 3.00x (*1-56134-174-6*) Dushkin Pub.
—Shawna's Bit of Blue Sky. Eagle, Mike, illus. 24p. (Orig.). (ps). 1992. pap. text ed. 3.00x (*1-56134-164-9*) Dushkin Pub.
Blegvad, Lenore. Anna Banana & Me. Blegvad, Erik, illus. LC 84-547. 32p. (gr. k-3). 1985. SBE 13.95 (*0-689-50274-5*, M K McElderry) Macmillan Child Grp.
Blos, Joan W. A Gathering of Days: A New England Girl's Journal, 1830-1832. LC 90-32. 160p. (gr. 3-7). 1990. pap. 3.95 (*0-689-71419-X*, Aladdin) Macmillan Child Grp.
Blume, Judy. Are You There, God? It's Me, Margaret. 156p. (gr. 5-8). 1972. pap. 3.99 (*0-440-40419-3*, YB) Dell.
—Blubber. LC 73-94116. 160p. (gr. 4-6). 1982. SBE 14.95 (*0-02-711010-9*, Bradbury Pr) Macmillan Child Grp.
—Deenie. LC 73-80197. 192p. (gr. 6-8). 1982. SBE 14.95 (*0-02-711020-6*, Bradbury Pr) Macmillan Child Grp.
—Judy Blume: Judy Blume & You, Friends for Life, 4 vols. (gr. 4-7). 1991. pap. 13.50 boxed set (*0-440-36013-7*) Dell.
—Otherwise Known As Sheila the Great. 128p. (gr. 3-6). 1976. pap. 3.99 (*0-440-46701-2*, YB) Dell.
—Starring Sally J. Freedman As Herself. LC 76-57805. 296p. (gr. 4-7). 1982. SBE 15.95 (*0-02-711070-2*, Bradbury Pr) Macmillan Child Grp.
—Superfudge. (gr. 4-7). 1993. pap. 1.99 (*0-440-21619-2*) Dell.
Bobo, Carmen P. Sarah's Growing-up Summer. LC 88-62111. 52p. 1989. 6.95 (*1-55523-187-X*) Winston-Derek.
Bodecker, N. M. Hurry, Hurry, Mary Dear! LC 76-14811. (Illus.). 128p. 1976. SBE 12.95 (*0-689-50066-1*, Pub. by M K McElderry) Macmillan Child Grp.
Bograd, Larry. Poor Gertie. Zimmer, Dirk, illus. LC 86-3091. 96p. (gr. 3-6). 1986. pap. 12.95 (*0-385-29487-5*) Delacorte.
Boolarong Publications Staff. Natasha's Dream. 1990. pap. 35.00x (*0-7316-3901-4*, Pub. by Boolarong Pubns AT) St Mut.
Borntrager, Mary C. Rebecca. 176p. (Orig.). (gr. 8-12). 1989. pap. 6.95 (*0-8361-3500-8*) Herald Pr.
Bourgeois, Paulette. Big Sarah's Little Boots. Clark, Brenda, illus. 1992. pap. 3.95 (*0-590-42623-0*, Blue Ribbon Bks) Scholastic Inc.
Boyd, Candy D. Charlie Pippin. LC 86-23780. 192p. (gr. 3-7). 1987. SBE 14.95 (*0-02-726350-9*, Macmillan Child Bk) Macmillan Child Grp.
Bradford, Jan. Caroline Zucker Makes a Big Mistake. Ramsey, Marcy, illus. LC 90-11160. 96p. (gr. 2-5). 1991. PLB 9.89 (*0-8167-2023-1*); pap. text ed. 2.95 (*0-8167-2024-X*) Troll Assocs.
Brand, Jill, ed. The Green Umbrella. (Illus.). 96p. (gr. 2-6). 1991. pap. 18.95 spiral bdg. (*0-7136-3390-5*, Pub. by A&C Black UK) Talman.
Brandt, Betty. The Adventures of Nicolet. Brandt, Laura, ed. Craig, Jennifer, illus. 160p. (Orig.). (gr. 8-12). 1991. 12.95 (*0-9622014-2-1*) Beaver Valley.
Brenner, Barbara A. Annie's Pet: Level 2. Ziegler, Jack, illus. (ps-3). 1989. 9.99 (*0-553-05833-9*); pap. 3.99 (*0-553-34693-8*) Bantam.
Bretecher, Claire. Agrippina. 50p. 1992. pap. 9.95 (*0-7493-0812-5*, Pub. by Mandarin UK) Heinemann.
Bridgers, Sue E. All Together Now. 192p. (gr. 7 up). 1980. pap. 2.75 (*0-553-26845-7*) Bantam.
Brillhart, Julie. Anna's Goodbye Apron. Mathews, Judith, ed. Brillhart, Julie, illus. LC 89-49362. 32p. (ps-1). 1990. PLB 13.95 (*0-8075-0375-4*) A Whitman.
Brinckloe, Julie. Playing Marbles. Brinckloe, Julie, illus. LC 88-1608. 32p. (gr. k-3). 1988. 12.95 (*0-688-07143-0*); PLB 12.88 (*0-688-07144-9*, Morrow Jr Bks) Morrow Jr Bks.
Brink, Carol R. Caddie Woodlawn. LC 89-18357. (Illus.). 288p. (gr. 4-6). 1990. pap. 3.95 (*0-689-71370-3*, Aladdin) Macmillan Child Grp.
Brodeur, Ruth W. Stories from the Big Chair. De Groat, Diane, illus. LC 88-35230. 48p. (gr. 1-4). 1989. SBE 12.95 (*0-689-50481-0*, M K McElderry) Macmillan Child Grp.
Bronte, Charlotte. Jane Eyre. (gr. 9 up). 1964. pap. 3.95 (*0-8049-0017-5*, CL-17) Airmont.
Brooks, Ilsley D. Jennifer Ilsley Deering Brooks. Stearns, Helen M., ed. Urbahn, Clara, illus. 48p. (ps up). 1987. 8.95 (*0-9614281-3-9*, Cricketfld Pr) Picton Pr.
Brooks, Jennifer. Princess Jessica Rescues a Prince. Flores, Lennie, illus. Ridley, Chas, ed. LC 93-92628. (Illus.). 40p. (ps-2). 1993. 15.95 (*0-9636335-0-3*) Nadja Pub.
Brophy, Hope F. A Letter to Sarah about God. LC 91-67504. (Illus.). 44p. (gr. 1-5). 1992. 7.95 (*1-55523-497-6*) Winston-Derek.
Brown. The House on Winchester Lane. (gr. 4-8). 1989. PLB 8.49 (*0-87386-061-6*); pap. 1.95 (*0-87386-062-4*) Jan Prods.
Brown, Marc T. The True Francine. Brown, Marc T., illus. (ps-3). 1987. pap. 5.95 (*0-316-11243-7*, Joy St Bks) Little.
Bulla, Clyde R. The Cardboard Crown. Chessare, Michele, illus. LC 83-45049. 96p. (gr. 2-5). 1984. (Crowell Jr Bks); (Crowell Jr Bks) HarpC Child Bks.
—Shoeshine Girl. Grant, Leigh, illus. LC 75-8516. 64p. (gr. 2-5). 1989. pap. 3.95 (*0-06-440228-2*, Trophy) HarpC Child Bks.
—Shoeshine Girl. LC 75-8516. (Illus.). 80p. (gr. 3-5). 1989. PLB 13.89 (*0-690-04830-0*, Crowell Jr Bks) HarpC Child Bks.
Bunting, Eve. Jane Martin, Dog Detective. Schwartz, Amy, illus. 44p. (ps-3). 1988. pap. 3.95 (*0-15-239587-3*, Voyager Bks) HarBrace.
—Karen Kepplewhite Is the World's Best Kisser. LC 83-2066. 96p. (gr. 3-6). 1983. 13.45 (*0-89919-182-7*, Clarion Bks) HM.
—Sharing Susan. LC 90-27097. 128p. (gr. 4-7). 1994. pap. 3.95 (*0-06-440430-7*, Trophy) HarpC Child Bks.
—Sixth Grade Sleepover. 112p. (gr. 3-7). 1987. pap. 2.95 (*0-590-42882-9*, Apple Paperbacks) Scholastic Inc.
—Two Different Girls. (Illus.). 64p. (gr. 3-8). 1992. 8.95 (*0-89565-772-4*) Childs World.
Burnett, Frances H. A Little Princess. Tudor, Tasha, illus. LC 63-15435. 240p. (gr. 4-8). 1987. pap. 3.95 (*0-06-440187-1*, Trophy) HarpC Child Bks.
—Sara Crewe. 96p. (gr. 3-7). 1986. pap. 2.75 (*0-590-42323-1*) Scholastic Inc.
Buss, Nancy. The Lobster & Ivy Higgins. Mulkey, Kim, illus. LC 91-72868. 64p. (gr. 3-7). 1992. 13.95 (*1-56397-011-2*) Boyds Mills Pr.
Busselle, Rebecca. Bathing Ugly. LC 88-17929. 192p. (gr. 7 up). 1989. 12.95 (*0-531-05801-8*); PLB 12.99 (*0-531-08401-9*) Orchard Bks Watts.
Butterworth, Oliver. Trouble with Jenny's Ear. (gr. 4-7). 1993. 4.95 (*0-316-11922-9*) Little.
Byars, Betsy C. The Glory Girl. LC 83-5927. 144p. (gr. 5-9). 1983. pap. 12.95 (*0-670-34261-0*) Viking Child Bks.
Cadwallader, Sharon. Cookie McCorkle & the Case of the Emerald Earrings. 128p. (Orig.). (gr. 3-4). 1991. pap. 2.95 (*0-380-76098-3*, Camelot Young) Avon.
—Cookie McCorkle & the Case of the Polka-Dot Safecracker. 128p. (Orig.). (gr. 3-4). 1991. pap. 2.95 (*0-380-76099-1*, Camelot Young) Avon.
Caines, Jeannette. Just Us Women. Cummings, Pat, illus. LC 81-48655. (gr. k-3). 1982. PLB 14.89 (*0-06-020942-9*) HarpC Child Bks.
Calhoun, Mary. Depend on Katie John. Frame, Paul, illus. LC 61-7328. 208p. (gr. 3-7). 1972. pap. 3.95 (*0-06-440029-8*, Trophy) HarpC Child Bks.
—Katie John. Frame, Paul, illus. LC 60-5775. (gr. 3-6). 1960. PLB 12.89 (*0-06-020951-8*) HarpC Child Bks.
Calvert, Patricia. Hadder MacColl. 144p. (gr. 5-9). 1986. pap. 3.95 (*0-14-032158-6*, Puffin) Puffin Bks.
—When Morning Comes. LC 89-5854. 160p. (gr. 7 up). 1989. SBE 13.95 (*0-684-19105-9*, Scribners Young Read) Macmillan Child Grp.
Cameron, Eleanor. Julia & the Hand of God. Owens, Gail, illus. 176p. (gr. 3-7). 1989. pap. 3.95 (*0-14-034042-4*, Puffin) Puffin Bks.
—Julia's Magic. Owens, Gail, illus. 160p. (gr. 3-7). 1989. pap. 3.95 (*0-14-034040-8*, Puffin) Puffin Bks.
—That Julia Redfern. Owens, Gail, illus. 144p. (gr. 3-7). 1989. pap. 3.95 (*0-14-034041-6*, Puffin) Puffin Bks.
Canfield, Dorothy. Understood Betsy. 219p. 1981. Repr. PLB 21.95 (*0-89966-342-7*) Buccaneer Bks.
—Understood Betsy. 213p. 1980. Repr. PLB 21.95 (*0-89967-016-4*) Harmony Raine.
Cannon, A. E. Amazing Gracie. LC 91-6781. 214p. (gr. 6-9). 1991. 15.00 (*0-385-30487-0*) Delacorte.
Caple, Kathy. The Purse. Caple, Kathy, illus. LC 86-2889. 32p. (gr. k-3). 1986. 13.95 (*0-395-41852-6*) HM.

Cardinal, Catherine S. Charlotte Pug: (The Walnut War) (Illus.). (gr. k-5). 1994. pap. 3.40 (*0-9630655-2-1*) Garden Gate.
Introducing CHARLOTTE PUG (The Walnut War) written by Catherine S. Cardinal who has brought to you MUD GRAPE PIE & THE BUTTON BOX. CHARLOTTE PUG deals with an age old conflict between the boys & the girls. This serious & sometimes comical situation has a positive conclusion & leaves the reader with a thought provoking lesson. The author's first collection, MUD GRAPE PIE, is a compilation of tales which deal with a fanciful herb garden & its fairy-like caretaker, Princess Jill. The Princess & her friends have many adventures, each one imparting a lesson about the herbs & imposing a moral applicable to life. THE BUTTON BOX (a gathering place for all sorts of odds & ends) holds a collection of stories. Liza,

Mary, Gladys, Sampson, Katie, & Grandpa Arthur are characters that are kept in this volume as is the assortment of buttons in the button box. Order from: Garden Gate Publishing, 1655 Washington Ave., Vincennes, IN 47591. Tel. 812-882-2626.
Publisher Provided Annotation.

Carlson, Rick. Spike's Big Blue Babble Balloon Machine Value: Sharing. 32p. 1992. pap. 1.95 saddle stitched (*0-310-58171-0*, Youth Bks) Zondervan.
Carney, Mary L. Wrestling with an Angel: A Devotional Novel for Junior Highers. rev. ed. 160p. (gr. 6-9). 1993. pap. 6.99 (*0-685-63320-9*, Pub. by Youth Spec) Zondervan.
Carratello, Patty. Dot's Pot. Spivak, Darlene, ed. Brostrom, Eileen, illus. 16p. (gr. k-2). 1988. wkbk. 1.95 (*1-55734-389-6*) Tchr Create Mat.
—Gail's Paint Pail. Spivak, Darlene, ed. Olsen, Shirley, illus. 16p. (gr. k-2). 1988. wkbk. 1.95 (*1-55734-385-3*) Tchr Create Mat.
—Skate, Kate, Skate. Spivak, Darlene, ed. Smythe, Linda, illus. 16p. (gr. k-2). 1988. wkbk. 1.95 (*1-55734-380-2*) Tchr Create Mat.
Carroll, Lewis & Baker, Kyle. Through the Looking-Glass. (Illus.). 52p. Date not set. pap. 4.95 (*1-57209-002-2*) Classics Int Ent.
Caseley, Judith. Chloe in the Know. LC 92-14757. (Illus.). 144p. (gr. 1 up). 1993. 14.00 (*0-688-11055-X*) Greenwillow.
—Cousins. LC 88-34903. (Illus.). 24p. (ps up). 1990. 12. 95 (*0-688-08433-8*); lib. bdg. 12.88 (*0-688-08434-6*) Greenwillow.
Cashman, Mary M. Amanda's Adventures. (gr. 2 up). 1994. 7.95 (*0-8062-4908-0*) Carlton.
Cathcart, Pamela B. History Hunt at Cold Harbor. Andrus, Michael J., frwd. by. (Illus.). 95p. (Orig.). 1994. 19.95 (*0-931563-15-1*); pap. 6.95 (*0-931563-14-3*) Wishing Rm.
Cavanna, Betty. Banner Year. 217p. (gr. 4-7). 1992. pap. 2.50 (*0-8167-1265-4*) Troll Assocs.
—Going on Sixteen. 188p. (gr. 6-9). 1992. pap. 2.50 (*0-8167-1266-2*) Troll Assocs.
—Paintbox Summer. 212p. 1981. Repr. PLB 19.95 (*0-89966-357-5*) Buccaneer Bks.
—Ruffles & Drums. (gr. 4-7). 1992. pap. 2.50 (*0-8167-1267-0*) Troll Assocs.
—Wanted: A Girl for the Horses. LC 83-19289. 224p. (gr. 7 up). 1984. 12.95 (*0-688-02757-1*) Morrow Jr Bks.
Chapouton, Anne-Marie. If Sophie... (Illus.). 32p. (gr. 3-5). 1991. 12.95 (*0-89565-760-0*) Childs World.
Child, Lydia Maria. Girls Own Book. LC 92-10815. (ps-3). 1991. 12.95 (*1-55709-134-X*) Applewood.
Chocolate, Debbi. Elizabeth's Wish. 1994. pap. 3.95 (*0-940975-45-9*) Just Us Bks.
Chriestenson, Shawna, et al. The Biggest Little Girl. French, Marty & Warter, Fred, illus. 26p. (ps up). 1988. incl. cassette 7.95 (*1-55578-916-1*) Worlds Wonder.
Christiansen, C. B. A Small Pleasure. 128p. (gr. 7 up). 1989. pap. 2.95 (*0-380-70699-7*, Flare) Avon.
Clancy, Lisa, ed. Stephanie: The Boy-Oh-Boy Next Door. (Orig.). 1993. pap. 3.50 (*0-671-88121-3*, Minstrel Bks) PB.
Clapp, Patricia. Constance. LC 85-43127. 256p. (gr. 7 up). 1991. pap. 3.95 (*0-688-10976-4*, Pub. by Beech Tree Bks) Morrow.
Clapp, Patricia C. Constance. 256p. (gr. 5 up). 1986. pap. 4.95 (*0-14-032030-X*, Puffin) Puffin Bks.
Clark, Cathy. Girl of the Year. (gr. 9-12). 1993. pap. 3.50 (*0-06-106744-X*, Harp PBks) HarpC.
Clark, Clara G. Annie's Choice. (Illus.). 196p. (gr. 5 up). 1993. 14.95 (*1-56397-053-8*) Boyds Mills Pr.
Cleary, Beverly. Beezus & Ramona. 160p. (gr. 5-6). 1990. pap. 3.99 (*0-380-70918-X*, Camelot) Avon.
—Ellen Tebbits. 160p. 1990. pap. 3.99 (*0-380-70913-9*, Camelot) Avon.
—The Luckiest Girl. 224p. (gr. 5-6). 1991. pap. 3.99 (*0-380-70922-8*, Flare) Avon.
—Ramona & Her Father. 192p. (gr. 5-6). 1990. pap. 3.99 (*0-380-70916-3*, Camelot) Avon.
—Ramona & Her Father. 1923. pap. 2.95 (*0-440-77241-9*) Dell.
—Ramona & Her Mother. 208p. 1990. pap. 3.99 (*0-380-70952-X*, Camelot) Avon.
—Ramona & Her Mother. 1923. pap. 2.95 (*0-440-77243-5*) Dell.
—Ramona, Forever. Tiegreen, Alan, illus. LC 84-704. 192p. (gr. 3-7). 1984. 13.95 (*0-688-03785-2*); PLB 13. 88 (*0-688-03786-0*, Morrow Jr Bks) Morrow Jr Bks.
—Ramona Forever. large type ed. 192p. 1989. Repr. of 1984 ed. lib. bdg. 15.95 (*1-55736-139-8*, Crnrstn Bks) BDD LT Grp.
—Ramona Forever. 1985. pap. 2.95 (*0-440-77210-9*) Dell.
—Ramona Forever. (gr. 4-7). 1993. pap. 1.99 (*0-440-21616-8*) Dell.
—Ramona Quimby, Age Eight. Tiegreen, Alan, illus. 192p. (gr. 3-7). 1982. pap. 3.25 (*0-440-47350-0*, YB) Dell.
—Ramona Quimby, Age Eight. 192p. 1992. pap. 3.99 (*0-380-70956-2*, Camelot) Avon.
—The Ramona Quimby Diary. Tiegreen, Alan, illus. 160p. (gr. 2 up). 1984. pap. 8.95 combbound (*0-688-03883-2*, Pub. by Beech Tree Bks) Morrow.
—Ramona the Brave. large type ed. (Illus.). 143p. (gr. k-6). 1989. Repr. lib. bdg. 15.95 (*1-55736-159-2*, Crnrstn Bks) BDD LT Grp.
—Ramona the Brave. 1984. pap. 2.95 (*0-440-77351-2*) Dell.
—Ramona the Pest. large type ed. (Illus.). 175p. (gr. k-6). 1990. Repr. PLB 15.95 (*1-55736-158-4*, Crnrstn Bks) BDD LT Grp.
—Ramona the Pest. 192p. 1992. pap. 3.99 (*0-380-70954-6*, Camelot) Avon.
—Ramona the Pest. 1923. pap. 2.95 (*0-440-77209-5*) Dell.
—Sister of the Bride. 128p. (gr. 6-9). 1981. pap. 2.75 (*0-440-97596-4*, LE) Dell.
Cleaver, Vera. Ellen Grae. Raskin, Ellen, illus. LC 67-10623. 96p. 1967. (Lipp Jr Bks) HarpC Child Bks.
—Moon Lake Angel. LC 86-15242. 160p. (gr. 7 up). 1987. 12.95 (*0-688-04952-4*) Lothrop.
Clements, Andrew. Big Al. Yoshi, illus. 1991. pap. 3.95 (*0-590-44455-7*, Blue Ribbon Bks) Scholastic Inc.
Coats, Laura J. Morning Window. LC 94-14515. 1995. 13.95 (*0-02-719055-2*) Macmillan.
Cohen, Barbara. The Christmas Revolution. De Groat, Diane, illus. LC 86-21340. 96p. (gr. 3-6). 1987. 12.95 (*0-688-06806-5*) Lothrop.
Cole, Babette. Hurray for Ethelyn. (Illus.). (ps-3). 1991. 14.95 (*0-316-15189-0*) Little.
—Princess Smartypants. Cole, Babette, illus. LC 86-12381. (ps-3). 1987. 13.95 (*0-399-21409-7*, Putnam) Putnam Pub Group.
—Princess Smartypants. (Illus.). 32p. (ps-3). 1991. pap. 5.95 (*0-399-21779-7*, Sandcastle Bks) Putnam Pub Group.
Cole, Brock. Celine. 1993. pap. 3.95 (*0-374-41083-6*) FS&G.
—Celine. Barbadillo, Pedro, tr. (SPA.). 172p. (gr. 9-12). 1992. pap. write for info. (*84-204-4711-0*) Santillana.
Collier, James L. & Collier, Christopher. Who Is Carrie? (gr. k-6). 1987. pap. 3.99 (*0-440-49536-9*, YB) Dell.
—The Winter Hero. 132p. (gr. 9 up). 1985. pap. 2.75 (*0-590-42604-4*) Scholastic Inc.
Collins, Sheila H. Jolie Blonde: A Cajun Twist to an Old Tale. Gorman, Carolyn P., ed. Diket, Chris, illus. 40p. (gr. 3). 1993. PLB 11.96x (*1-884725-00-7*) Blue Heron LA.
Conford, Ellen. And This Is Laura. (Illus.). 192p. (gr. 3-7). 1992. pap. 4.95 (*0-316-15354-0*) Little.
—Can Do, Jenny Archer. (gr. 4-7). 1993. pap. 3.95 (*0-316-15372-9*) Little.
—A Case for Jenny Archer. (ps-3). 1990. pap. 3.95 (*0-316-15352-4*) Little.
—Dreams of Victory. Rockwell, Gail, illus. 144p. (gr. 4-6). 1973. 14.95 (*0-316-15294-3*) Little.
—Felicia, the Critic. Stewart, Arvis, illus. (gr. 4-6). 1973. 14.95 (*0-316-15295-1*) Little.
—Felicia the Critic. (Illus.). 160p. (gr. 3-7). 1992. pap. 4.95 (*0-316-15358-3*) Little.
—Jenny Archer. (ps-3). 1991. pap. 2.95 (*0-316-15353-2*) Little.
—A Job for Jenny Archer. (gr. 2-4). 1990. pap. 2.95 (*0-316-15349-4*) Little.
—The Luck of Pokey Bloom. Lowenstein, Bernice, illus. 144p. (gr. 4-6). 1975. 14.95 (*0-316-15305-2*) Little.
—What's Cooking, Jenny Archer? (ps-3). 1991. pap. 3.95 (*0-316-15357-5*) Little.
Conkie, Heather. Sara's Homecoming. (gr. 4-7). 1993. pap. 3.99 (*0-553-48038-3*) Bantam.
Conlon-McKenna, Marita. Wildflower Girl. 176p. (gr. 5 up). 1994. pap. 3.99 (*0-14-036292-4*) Puffin Bks.
Conrad, Pam. Seven Silly Circles. Wimmer, Mike, illus. LC 85-45835. 64p. (gr. 2-5). 1987. HarpC Child Bks.
—Staying Nine. Wimmer, Mike, illus. LC 87-45862. 80p. (gr. 2-5). 1988. 13.00 (*0-06-021319-1*); PLB 12.89 (*0-06-021320-5*) HarpC Child Bks.
—What I Did for Roman. LC 86-45497. 224p. (gr. 7 up). 1987. PLB 14.89 (*0-06-021332-9*) HarpC Child Bks.
Coolidge, Susan. What Katy Did. 190p. 1988. Repr. lib. bdg. 19.95x (*0-89966-585-3*) Buccaneer Bks.
—What Katy Did Next. (gr. k-6). 1989. pap. 3.50 (*0-440-40244-1*, Pub. by Yearling Classics) Dell.
Cooney, Barbara. Miss Rumphius. LC 85-40447. (Illus.). 32p. (ps-3). 1985. pap. 4.99 (*0-14-050539-3*, Puffin) Puffin Bks.
Cooney, Caroline B. Twenty Pageants Later. (gr. 4-7). 1993. pap. 3.99 (*0-553-29672-8*) Bantam.
Cooper, Ilene. My Co-Star, My Enemy. 144p. (gr. 3-7). 1993. pap. 3.25 (*0-14-036156-1*) Puffin Bks.
—Trick or Trouble. 128p. (gr. 3-7). 1994. 13.99 (*0-670-85057-8*) Viking Child Bks.
Corcoran, Barbara. The Potato Kid. LC 89-14935. 192p. (gr. 3-7). 1989. SBE 14.95 (*0-689-31589-9*, Atheneum Child Bk) Macmillan Child Grp.
Cosgrove, Stephen. Heidi's Rose. Edelson, Wendy, illus. LC 90-71079. 32p. (gr. 3-6). 1991. 14.95 (*1-55868-033-0*) Gr Arts Ctr Pub.
Cossi, Olga. Firemate. rev. ed. LC 94-66085. 120p. (gr. 4-8). 1994. pap. 7.95 (*1-879373-87-4*) R Rinehart.
Cotton, Debie. Messy Marcy MacIntyre. LC 89-42629. 32p. (gr. 1-2). 1991. PLB 18.60 (*0-8368-0108-3*) Gareth Stevens Inc.
Cross, Gillian. Chartbreaker. LC 86-46199. 184p. (gr. 7 up). 1987. 14.95 (*0-8234-0647-4*) Holiday.
Cruise, Beth. Saved by the Bell: Girls' Night Out. LC 92-24648. 144p. (gr. 5 up). 1992. pap. 2.95 (*0-02-042766-2*, Collier Young Ad) Macmillan Child Grp.
Cunningham, Julia. Viollet. Cober, Alan E., illus. (gr. 4-7). 1966. PLB 6.99 (*0-394-91821-5*) Pantheon.
Cusick, Richie T. Buffy the Vampire Slayer. MacDonald, Pat, ed. 192p. 1992. pap. 3.99 (*0-671-79220-2*) PB.
—The Lifeguard. 192p. (Orig.). (gr. 9 up). 1988. pap. 3.25 (*0-590-43203-6*) Scholastic Inc.
Czernecki, Stefan & Rhodes, Timothy. Nina's Treasures. Czernecki, Stefan, illus. LC 93-26932. 40p. (gr. k-4). 1994. pap. 4.95 (*1-56282-487-2*) Hyprn Ppbks.
Dadey, Debbie & Jones, Marcia. Vampires Don't Wear Polka Dots. 96p. (Orig.). (gr. 2-5). 1990. pap. 2.50 (*0-590-43411-X*) Scholastic Inc.
Dahl, Roald. Matilda. large type ed. 1989. Repr. of 1988 ed. lib. bdg. 15.95 (*1-55736-123-1*, Crnrstn Bks) BDD LT Grp.
—Matilda. 240p. (gr. 3-7). 1990. pap. 4.99 (*0-14-034294-X*, Puffin) Puffin Bks.
Daly, Maureen. Seventeenth Summer. 293p. 1981. Repr. PLB 23.95 (*0-89966-355-9*) Buccaneer Bks.
Daneman, Meredith. Francie & the Boys. (Illus.). 192p. (gr. 6-9). 1989. 14.95 (*0-440-50137-7*) Delacorte.
Danenbert. Mary Dimple & Her Friends. 1994. 13.95 (*1-881116-58-1*) ICAN Pr.
Davis, Gibbs. Lucky Socks. (gr. 4-7). 1991. pap. 2.99 (*0-553-15865-1*) Bantam.
—Major-League Melissa. (gr. 4-7). 1991. pap. 3.25 (*0-553-15866-X*) Bantam.
—Maud Flies Solo. (gr. 4-7). 1990. pap. 3.50 (*0-553-15786-8*) Bantam.
—The Other Emily. Shute, Linda, illus. LC 83-18913. 32p. (gr. k-3). 1984. 14.45 (*0-395-35482-X*, 5-84351) HM.
—The Other Emily. Shute, Linda, illus. 32p. (gr. k-3). 1990. pap. 4.95 (*0-395-54947-7*) HM.
Day, S. Monica's Mother Said No. (Illus.). 24p. (ps-8). 1987. pap. 4.95 (*0-88753-158-X*, Pub. by Annick CN) Firefly Bks Ltd.
De Brunhoff, Laurent. Babar's Little Girl. De Brunhoff, Laurent, illus. LC 68-42962. 36p. (ps-3). 1987. 11.00 (*0-394-88689-5*) Random Bks Yng Read.
Deedy, Carmen A. Agatha's Feather Bed: Not Just Another Wild Goose Story. Seeley, Laura L., illus. 32p. (ps-3). 1991. 14.95 (*1-56145-008-1*) Peachtree Pubs.
De La Croix, Alice. Mattie's Whisper. LC 91-73885. 128p. (gr. 3-7). 1992. 14.95 (*1-56397-036-8*) Boyds Mills Pr.
Delton, Judy. I Never Win. (ps-3). 1991. pap. 2.95 (*0-440-40414-2*) Dell.
Demarest, Chris L. No Peas for Nellie. LC 87-14167. (Illus.). 32p. (ps-2). 1988. RSBE 14.95 (*0-02-728460-3*, Macmillan Child Bk) Macmillan Child Grp.
De Paola, Tomie. Marianna May & Nursey. De Paola, Tomie, illus. LC 82-9364. 32p. (ps-3). 1983. reinforced bdg. 15.95 (*0-8234-0473-0*); pap. 5.95 (*0-8234-0623-7*) Holiday.
Derby, Pat. Goodbye Emily, Hello. (gr. 7 up). 1989. 15. 00 (*0-374-32744-0*) FS&G.
De Regniers, Beatrice S. The Way I Feel... Sometimes. Meddaugh, Susan, illus. LC 87-18245. 48p. (gr. 1-4). 1988. 13.95 (*0-89919-647-0*, Clarion Bks) HM.
De Weese, Gene. The Calvin Nullifier. (gr. k-6). 1989. pap. 2.95 (*0-440-40214-X*, YB) Dell.
Dickens, Charles. Little Dorrit. (ps-8). 1990. Repr. lib. bdg. 39.95x (*0-89966-680-9*) Buccaneer Bks.
Dickens, Lucy. Dancing Class. Dickens, Lucy, illus. 32p. (ps-3). 1992. 14.00 (*0-670-84484-5*) Viking Child Bks.
Dickinson, Peter. Emma Tupper's Diary. 224p. (gr. 3 up). 1988. pap. 3.25 (*0-440-40080-5*, YB) Dell.
—Eva. (gr. 7 up). 1989. 14.95 (*0-440-50129-6*) Delacorte.
Dixon, Delores. The Tooth Fairy. 1991. 7.95 (*0-533-09433-X*) Vantage.
Dobrin, Arnold. Josephine's 'Magination. 48p. (gr. 2-5). 1991. pap. 4.95 (*0-590-43494-2*) Scholastic Inc.
Doherty, Berlie. Granny Was a Buffer Girl. LC 87-25080. 160p. (gr. 5 up). 1988. 12.95 (*0-531-05754-2*); PLB 12.99 (*0-531-08354-3*) Orchard Bks Watts.
Donahue, Marilyn. Reach with All Your Heart. LC 88-14807. 1988. pap. 4.49 (*1-55513-755-5*, Chariot Bks) Chariot Family.
Donovan, Stacey. Dive. 175p. (gr. 7 up). 1994. 14.99 (*0-525-45154-4*) Dutton Child Bks.
Dorris, Michael. Morning Girl. LC 92-52989. 80p. (gr. 3 up). 1992. 12.95 (*1-56282-284-5*); PLB 12.89 (*1-56282-285-3*) Hyprn Child.
Dotson, Williette D. Visions: The Story of a Black Girl Determined to Make It Despite the Odds. 190p. (gr. 9 up). 1993. text ed. 18.95 (*0-9635032-0-0*) SAC Pr.
Dott, A. Eric. Hide a Book: They Meet. Talbot, Jim, illus. 22p. (ps-1). 1987. PLB 5.95 (*0-939871-00-9*) Monarch Toy.
Douglas-Wiggins, Kate. Rebecca of Sunnybrook Farm. Hinkle, Don, ed. Elwell, Peter, illus. LC 87-15475. 48p. (gr. 3-6). 1988. PLB 12.89 (*0-8167-1217-4*); pap. text ed. 3.95 (*0-8167-1218-2*) Troll Assocs.
Doyle, Brian. Up to Low. 116p. (gr. 4-7). 1991. pap. 4.95 (*0-88899-088-X*, Pub. by Groundwood-Douglas & McIntyre CN) Firefly Bks Ltd.
—You Can Pick Me up at Peggy's Cove. 120p. (gr. 4-7). 1991. pap. 4.95 (*0-88899-116-9*, Pub. by Groundwood-Douglas & McIntyre CN) Firefly Bks Ltd.

Dragonwagon, Crescent. Always, Always. Zeldich, Arieh, illus. LC 83-22199. 32p. (gr. 1-4). 1984. RSBE 13.95 (*0-02-733080-X*, Macmillan Child Bk) Macmillan Child Grp.
—Annie Flies the Birthday Bike. McCully, Emily A., illus. LC 90-42861. 32p. (gr. k-3). 1993. RSBE 14.95 (*0-02-733155-5*, Macmillan Child Bk) Macmillan Child Grp.
—Margaret Ziegler Is Horse Crazy. Elwell, Peter, illus. LC 87-23975. 32p. (gr. 1-4). 1988. RSBE 13.95 (*0-02-733230-6*, Macmillan Child Bk) Macmillan Child Grp.
Driscoll, Debbie, adapted by. Jenny Came Along. Winter, Susan, illus. LC 94-17381. 1995. write for info. (*0-385-32054-X*) Doubleday.
Dubov, Christine. Aleksandra, Where Are Your Toes? Schnieder, Josef, photos by. (Illus.). 14p. (ps). 1986. 3.95 (*0-312-01717-0*) St Martin.
Duffy, James. Missing. LC 87-25295. 144p. (gr. 5-8). 1988. SBE 13.95 (*0-684-18912-7*, Scribners Young Read) Macmillan Child Grp.
Duke, Kate. Roseberry's Great Escape. LC 89-37847. (Illus.). 24p. (ps-1). 1990. 12.95 (*0-525-44597-8*, DCB) Dutton Child Bks.
Dunlop, Beverly. The Poetry Girl. 216p. (gr. 6-8). 1989. 13.45 (*0-395-49679-9*) HM.
Dunlop, Eileen. Clementina. LC 86-22913. 160p. (gr. 7 up). 1987. 12.95 (*0-8234-0642-3*) Holiday.
—The Valley of Deer. LC 89-1931. 152p. (gr. 4-7). 1989. 13.95 (*0-8234-0766-7*) Holiday.
Dunster, Mark. Emily, Pt. 3: Gib. 29p. (Orig.). 1994. pap. 5.00 (*0-89642-239-9*) Linden Pubs.
Easton, Patricia H. Stable Girl: Working for the Family. Ferguson, Herb, illus. 44p. (gr. 1-7). 1991. 18.95 (*0-15-278340-7*) HarBrace.
Edwards, Julie. Mandy. reissued ed. Brown, Judith G., illus. LC 76-157901. 192p. (gr. 4-7). 1990. PLB 13.89 (*0-06-021803-7*) HarpC Child Bks.
Edwards, Michelle. Dora's Book. Edwards, Michelle, illus. 32p. (gr. k-4). 1990. PLB 19.95 (*0-87614-411-3*) Carolrhoda Bks.
Ehrlich, Amy. The Dark Card. 180p. (gr. 7 up). 1993. pap. 3.99 (*0-14-036332-7*) Puffin Bks.
—Where It Stops, Nobody Knows. 224p. (gr. 6 up). 1990. pap. 3.95 (*0-14-034266-4*, Puffin) Puffin Bks.
Eisenberg, Lisa. Leave It to Lexie. 144p. (gr. 2-7). 1989. pap. 11.95 (*0-670-82844-0*) Viking Child Bks.
—Leave It to Lexie. 144p. (gr. 3-7). 1991. 3.95 (*0-14-034181-1*) Puffin Bks.
Emerson, Kathy L. The Mystery of the Missing Bagpipes. 128p. (Orig.). (gr. 5). 1991. pap. 2.95 (*0-380-76138-6*, Camelot) Avon.
Engel, Diana. Fishing. Engel, Diana, illus. LC 91-47705. 32p. (gr. k-3). 1993. RSBE 14.95 (*0-02-733463-5*, Macmillan Child Bk) Macmillan Child Grp.
Englebreit, Mary. Sweetie Pie. 1994. 7.95 (*0-89954-312-X*) Antioch Pub Co.
Ernst, Lisa C. Nattie Parsons' Good-Luck Lamb. LC 87-13700. (Illus.). 32p. (ps-3). 1988. pap. 11.95 (*0-670-81778-3*) Viking Child Bks.
Ewing. A Really Popular Girl. 1993. pap. 2.75 (*0-590-43202-8*) Scholastic Inc.
Ewing, Kathryn. Family Karate. Henderson, Dave, illus. 96p. (gr. 5 up). 1992. PLB 13.95 (*1-56397-117-8*) Boyds Mills Pr.
Farmer, Penelope. Charlotte Sometimes. (Orig.). (gr. k-6). 1987. pap. 4.95 (*0-440-41261-7*, Pub. by Yearling Classics) Dell.
—Emma in Winter. (gr. k-6). 1987. pap. 2.95 (*0-440-42308-2*, YB) Dell.
Fast, Freda. Anna. LC 90-67768. 63p. (Orig.). 1992. pap. 7.00 (*1-56002-169-1*, Univ Edtns) Aegina Pr.
Ferris, Jean. Invincible Summer. 176p. (gr. 7 up). 1989. pap. 3.50 (*0-380-70619-9*, Flare) Avon.
Field, Rachel. Calico Bush. Lewis, Allen, illus. LC 66-19095. 224p. (gr. 5-9). 1987. SBE 14.95 (*0-02-734610-2*, Macmillan Child Bk) Macmillan Child Grp.
—General Store. Laroche, Giles, illus. LC 87-37218. (ps-3). 1988. 15.95 (*0-316-28163-8*) Little.
—Hitty, Her First Hundred Years. (gr. k-6). 1990. pap. 3.95 (*0-440-40337-5*, YB) Dell.
Filichia, Peter. Girls Can't Do It. 224p. (Orig.). 1990. pap. 2.95 (*0-380-75784-2*, Flare) Avon.
Finley, Martha. Elsie Dinsmore. LC 74-15737. (Illus.). 342p. (gr. 7 up). 1975. Repr. of 1896 ed. 24.00x (*0-405-06372-5*) Ayer.
—Elsie Dinsmore. 332p. 1987. Repr. PLB 25.95x (*0-89966-332-X*) Buccaneer Bks.
—Elsie's Girlhood. 273p. 1981. Repr. PLB 25.95x (*0-89966-334-6*) Buccaneer Bks.
Fisher, Dorothy C. Understood Betsy. (gr. k-6). 1987. pap. 4.95 (*0-440-49179-7*, Pub. by Yearling Classics) Dell.
—Understood Betsy. (gr. 4-7). 1991. pap. 3.50 (*0-440-40796-6*) Dell.
—Understood Betsy. (gr. 4-7). 1994. pap. 3.25 (*0-590-48005-7*) Scholastic Inc.
Fisher, Juliet. Juliet Fisher & the Foolproof Plan. 96p. 1994. pap. 3.50 (*0-380-72066-3*, Camelot) Avon.
Fitzhugh, Louise. Harriet the Spy. 304p. (gr. 5 up). 1979. pap. 3.50 (*0-440-43447-5*, YB) Dell.
Fleishmann, Hedy & Fleishmann, Devorah E. Bittersweet Beginnings. LC 92-70696. 140p. 1992. write for info. (*1-56062-125-7*); pap. write for info. (*1-56062-126-5*) CIS Comm.
Foley, June. Susanna Siegelbaum Gives up Guys. 1992. pap. 3.25 (*0-590-43700-3*) Scholastic Inc.
Fox, Mem. Koala Lou. Lofts, Pamela, illus. LC 90-20620. (ps-3). 1994. pap. 4.95 (*0-15-200076-3*, HB Juv Bks) HarBrace.
French, Fiona. Snow White in New York. (Illus.). 32p. 1990. pap. 6.95 (*0-19-272210-7*) OUP.
Friedland, Joyce & Kessler, Rikki. Maggie Marmelstein for President: A Study Guide. (gr. 4-6). 1982. tchr's. ed. & wkbk. 14.95 (*0-88122-006-X*) LRN Links.
Friedman, Frieda. Dot for Short. 173p. 1981. Repr. PLB 14.95x (*0-686-73781-4*) Buccaneer Bks.
Fritz, Jean. Brady. Ward, Lynd, illus. (gr. 5-9). 1987. pap. 4.99 (*0-14-032258-2*, Puffin) Puffin Bks.
Frost, Marie. Hattie's Surprising Discovery. (gr. 4-7). 1991. pap. 5.99 (*1-56121-061-7*) Wolgemuth & Hyatt.
Funakoshi, Canna. One Evening. Izawa, Yohji, illus. LC 87-29243. (ps up). 1991. pap. 11.95 (*0-88708-063-4*) Picture Bk Studio.
Gabhart, Ann. For Sheila. 160p. (Orig.). 1991. pap. 2.95 (*0-380-75920-9*, Flare) Avon.
Gallaz, Chrsitophe. Rose Blanche: Based on the Original Idea of Roberto Innocenti. Delessert, Etienne & Redpath, Ann, eds. Coventry, Martha, tr. from FRE. LC 85-70219. (Illus.). 32p. (gr. 6 up). 1986. PLB 17.95 (*0-87191-994-X*) Creative Ed.
Garcia, Lola. A Girlfriend at Acoma, Siyu, & an Invitation to Supper. Aragon, Sherry, illus. 14p. (Orig.). (ps-7). 1981. pap. 3.75 (*0-915347-09-1*) Pueblo Acoma Pr.
Gardam, Jane. A Few Fair Days. LC 88-5477. 128p. (gr. 5 up). 1988. 11.95 (*0-688-07602-5*) Greenwillow.
Garfield, Vivien & Alcock, Vivien. The Sylvia Game. (gr. k-6). 1990. pap. 2.95 (*0-440-40266-2*, YB) Dell.
Gates, Doris. Blue Willow. Lantz, Paul, illus. LC 40-32435. (gr. 4-6). 1976. pap. 3.99 (*0-14-030924-1*, VS30, Puffin) Puffin Bks.
Gauch, Patricia L. C. K. & the Time She Quit the Family. Primavera, Elise, illus. 32p. (ps-3). 1992. pap. 5.95 (*0-399-22405-X*, Putnam) Putnam Pub Group.
Geller, Beverly M. Janice & Juanita. Whitaker, Kate, ed. DeVito, Pam, illus. LC 93-61633. 40p. (Orig.). (ps-3). 1994. pap. 7.95 (*1-883650-11-9*) Windswept Hse.
George, Jean C. One Day in the Woods. Allen, Gary, illus. LC 87-21712. 48p. (gr. 4-7). 1988. (Crowell Jr Bks); PLB 13.89 (*0-690-04724-X*, Crowell Jr Bks) HarpC Child Bks.
Gerber, Merrill J. Also Known As Sadzia! The Belly Dancer! LC 86-45484. 192p. (gr. 7 up). 1987. HarpC Child Bks.
Gerstein, Mordicai. The Story of May. Gerstein, Mordicai, illus. LC 90-22410. 48p. (ps-3). 1993. 16.00 (*0-06-022288-3*); PLB 15.89 (*0-06-022289-1*) HarpC Child Bks.
Getz, David. Almost Famous. 192p. (gr. 4-7). 1993. 13.95 (*0-8050-1940-5*, Bks Young Read) H Holt & Co.
Giff, Patricia R. Emily Arrow Promises to Do Better This Year. (Orig.). 1990. pap. 3.50 (*0-440-40369-3*, Pub. by Yearling Classics) Dell.
—The Girl Who Knew It All. Morrill, Leslie, illus. (gr. 4-6). 1984. 6.95 (*0-385-28362-8*); PLB 6.95 (*0-385-28363-6*) Delacorte.
—The Girl Who Knew It All. Morrill, Leslie, illus. LC 79-50677. (gr. 4-6). 1979. 6.95 (*0-440-03137-0*); PLB 6.89 (*0-440-03138-9*) Delacorte.
—Have You Seen Hyacinth Macaw? Kramer, Anthony, illus. (gr. 4-6). 1981. 11.95 (*0-385-28389-X*); pap. 12.95 (*0-385-28390-3*) Delacorte.
—I Love Saturday. Remkiewicz, Frank, illus. 32p. (ps-3). 1991. pap. 3.99 (*0-14-050653-5*) Puffin Bks.
Gikow, Louise. Shalom Sesame Presents a Chanukah Party for Kippi. Cooke, Tom, illus. 32p. 1994. 12.95 (*1-884857-06-X*) Comet Intl.
Gilman, Dorothy. Girl in Buckskin. 144p. (gr. 7 up). 1990. pap. 3.50 (*0-449-70380-0*, Juniper) Fawcett.
Gilman, Phoebe. Jillian Jiggs. Gilman, Phoebe, illus. 40p. (Orig.). (gr. k-3). 1988. pap. 2.50 (*0-590-41340-6*) Scholastic Inc.
—Jillian Jiggs. 1993. pap. 28.67 (*0-590-71823-1*) Scholastic Inc.
Gleeson, Kate. Kate Gleeson's Mary Had a Little Lamb. (ps). 1994. 2.25 (*0-307-06071-3*, Golden Pr) Western Pub.
Gleeson, Libby. I Am Susannah. ALC Staff, ed. 128p. (gr. 7 up). 1992. pap. 3.95 (*0-688-11636-1*, Pub. by Beech Tree Bks) Morrow.
Godden, Rumer. The Peacock Spring. 286p. (gr. 7 up). 1986. pap. 3.95 (*0-14-032005-9*, Penguin Bks) Viking Penguin.
Goldshlag-Cooks, Roberta. Gittel & the Bell. Martz, Susan, illus. LC 87-2828. (gr. k-4). 1987. 10.95 (*0-930494-68-7*) Kar Ben.

Good, Janis. Summer of the Lost Limb. Cates, Elizabeth, illus. 110p. (Orig.). 1994. pap. 7.95 (*0-9640365-5-X*) Christ Recollect.
Readers will step back 90 years in time to horse & buggy days. Young Mary & her people are of a religious sect similar to the Amish who live yet today as years ago. A tragic farm accident changes Mary's life, dashing her dreams of walking the half mile to her community school with other children. Readers follow Mary through a country operation on her own kitchen table, a trip to Washington, D.C., for an artificial limb, adjustments & struggles. They will feel with the limitations of the handicapped & even learn some valuable lessons & bits of history. Who believes teddy bears always existed? This book tells two stories behind the beginning of teddy bears. Then there are two strangers on horseback who meet Mary. Will she allow horses to cross the narrow swinging bridge that spans the river? Will she be able to perform a difficult duty on her wooden leg? Her faith makes all the difference. Christian Recollections, Rt. 1, Box 351, Mt. Solon, VA 22821.
Publisher Provided Annotation.

Goode, Diane, illus. The Nutcracker: The Story Based on the Ballet. LC 82-62170. 32p. 1988. pap. 1.50 (*0-394-81939-X*) Random Bks Yng Read.
Gormley, Beatrice. Ellie's Birthstone Ring. (Illus.). 128p. (gr. 2-4). 1992. 14.00 (*0-525-44969-8*, DCB) Dutton Child Bks.
Goss, Marilyn. Maggie Suzanne, Star of Christmas. Goss, Marilyn, illus. 36p. (gr. 3 up). 1988. 15.95 (*0-9620766-0-0*) Art Room Pubns.
Grabarits, Anne C. Kathy Needs Comfort & Timmy's New Outlook. (Illus.). 30p. 1993. saddlestitched 4.95 (*0-8059-3424-3*) Dorrance.
Granger, Michele. Eliza, the Hypnotizer: And Other Eliza & Francie Stories. (gr. 4-7). 1993. pap. 2.75 (*0-590-45506-0*) Scholastic Inc.
Gray, Luli. Falcon's Egg. Date not set. 13.95g (*0-685-72229-5*) Ticknor & Flds Bks Yng Read.
Green, Michelle Y. Willie Pearl. (gr. 4-7). 1991. pap. 9.95 (*0-9627697-0-3*) W Ruth Co.
Greenberg, Polly. I Know I'm Myself Because... Barrett, Jennifer, illus. 32p. (ps-3). 1986. 16.95 (*0-89885-045-2*); pap. 9.95 (*0-89885-200-5*) Human Sci Pr.
Greene, Bette. Philip Hall Likes Me, I Reckon Maybe. large type ed. (Illus.). 158p. 1989. PLB 15.95 (*1-55736-106-1*, Crnrstn Bks) BDD LT Grp.
Greene, Constance C. Al(exandra) the Great. 144p. (gr. 5-9). 1991. 3.95 (*0-14-034883-2*) Puffin Bks.
—Beat the Turtle Drum. 1128p. (gr. 5 up). 1994. pap. 3.99 (*0-14-036850-7*) Puffin Bks.
—Dotty's Suitcase. 144p. (gr. 3-7). 1982. pap. 1.95 (*0-440-42108-X*, YB) Dell.
—Dotty's Suitcase. 160p. (gr. 5-9). 1991. 3.95 (*0-14-034882-4*) Puffin Bks.
—A Girl Called Al. 128p. (gr. 5-9). 1977. pap. 2.95 (*0-440-42810-6*, YB) Dell.
—A Girl Called Al. large type ed. 1989. Repr. of 1969 ed. lib. bdg. 15.95 (*1-55736-145-2*, Crnrstn Bks) BDD LT Grp.
—I Know You, Al. (gr. k-6). 1977. pap. 2.95 (*0-440-44123-4*, YB) Dell.
—Isabelle Shows Her Stuff. (gr. 4-6). 1986. pap. 2.95 (*0-440-44152-8*, YB) Dell.
Greenwald, Sheila. Give Us a Great Big Smile, Rosy Cole. 80p. (gr. 5-7). 1982. pap. 2.50 (*0-440-42923-4*, YB) Dell.
—The Secret in Miranda's Closet. (gr. k-6). 1989. pap. 2.95 (*0-440-40128-3*, YB) Dell.
—Will the Real Gertrude Hollings Please Stand Up? 176p. (gr. k-6). 1985. pap. 2.95 (*0-440-49553-9*, YB) Dell.
Gregorich, Barbara. Sue Likes Blue. Hoffman, Joan, ed. (Illus.). 32p. (gr. k-2). 1992. pap. 3.95 (*0-88743-409-6*, 06061) Sch Zone Pub Co.
Grifalconi, Ann. Darkness & the Butterfly. Grifalconi, Ann, illus. 32p. (ps-3). 1987. 16.95 (*0-316-32863-4*) Little.
Griffin, Gail. An Afternoon at Emmi's. Eagle, Mike, illus. 24p. (Orig.). (ps). 1992. pap. text ed. 3.00x (*1-56134-163-0*) Dushkin Pub.
Griffin, Gail M. Una Tarde en la Casa de Emmi. Writer, C. C. & Nielsen, Lisa C., trs. Eagle, Mike, illus. (SPA.). 24p. (Orig.). (ps). 1992. pap. text ed. 3.00x (*1-56134-173-8*) Dushkin Pub.
Griffin, Peni R. The Switching Well. LC 92-38442. 224p. (gr. 5-9). 1993. SBE 15.95 (*0-689-50581-7*, M K McElderry) Macmillan Child Grp.
Griffith, Helen. Georgia Music. Stevenson, James, illus. LC 85-24918. 24p. (gr. k-3). 1986. 13.95 (*0-688-06071-4*); PLB 13.88 (*0-688-06072-2*) Greenwillow.
Grimm, Wilhelm K. Dear Mili. Sendak, Maurice, illus. Manheim, Ralph, tr. (Illus.). 40p. 1990. gift ed. 18.95 (*0-374-31766-6*); ltd. ed. 750.00 (*0-374-31763-1*); 1988 16.95, (*0-374-31762-3*) FS&G.
Gross, Sukey S. The Golden Gate. Shiman, Hedy, illus. 172p. (gr. 5-8). 1989. 11.95 (*1-56062-002-1*); pap. 8.95 (*1-56062-003-X*) CIS Comm.
—The Secret Diary. Backman, Aidel, illus. (gr. 5-8). 1989. 10.95 (*0-935063-67-6*); pap. 7.95 (*0-935063-68-4*) CIS Comm.

—The Silent Summer. Shiman, Hedy, illus. 139p. (gr. 7-9). 1989. 10.95 (*1-56062-004-8*); pap. 7.95 (*1-56062-005-6*) CIS Comm.
Grossman, Bill. Donna O'Neeshuck Was Chased by Some Cows. Truesdell, Sue, illus. LC 85-45823. 40p. (ps-3). 1991. pap. 5.95 (*0-06-443255-6*, Trophy) HarpC Child Bks.
Gryspeerdt, Rebecca. Colleen & the Hairy Beast. (Illus.). 32p. (gr. 1-4). 1992. 16.95 (*1-85681-101-8*, Pub. by J MacRae UK) Trafalgar.
Guthrie, Donna. Mrs. Gigglebelly Is Coming to Tea. Arnsteen, Katy K., illus. 32p. (ps-2). 1993. pap. 2.50 (*0-671-79605-4*, Little Simon) S&S Trade.
Guy, Rosa. Ruby. 1992. pap. 3.50 (*0-440-21130-1*) Dell.
Haas, Irene. The Maggie B. LC 74-18183. (Illus.). 32p. (ps-3). 1984. pap. 4.95 (*0-689-70764-9*, Aladdin) Macmillan Child Grp.
Hahn, Mary D. Daphne's Book. LC 83-20933. 192p. (gr. 4-8). 1983. 14.45 (*0-89919-183-5*, Clarion Bks) HM.
—Daphne's Book. 192p. 1985. pap. 2.50 (*0-553-15360-9*, Skylark) Bantam.
—The Jellyfish Season. 176p. (gr. 5). 1992. pap. 3.50 (*0-380-71635-6*, Camelot) Avon.
—The Sara Summer. 160p. (gr. 5 up). 1985. pap. 2.75 (*0-553-15481-8*) Bantam.
—The Sara Summer. 1985. pap. 2.99 (*0-553-15600-4*) Bantam.
—Stepping on the Cracks. 224p. 1992. pap. 3.99 (*0-380-71900-2*, Camelot) Avon.
Haines, Joan. A Banana for Rosie. Barker, Melissa & Logan, Ann, illus. 16p. (Orig.). (ps-1). 1985. pap. 2.65 (*0-936652-03-9*, Pub. by Ed Concern Pubns) Two Ems.
—Meet Rosie Posie. Barker, Melissa & Logan, Ann, illus. 16p. (Orig.). (ps-1). 1985. pap. 2.65 (*0-936652-00-4*, Pub. by Ed Concern Pubns) Two Ems.
—Rosie Posie Has a Bath. Barker, Melissa & Logan, Ann, illus. 16p. (ps-1). 1985. pap. 2.65 (*0-936652-02-0*, Pub. by Ed Concern Pubns) Two Ems.
—Rosie Posie Makes Friends. Berker, Melissa & Logan, Ann, illus. 16p. (Orig.). (ps-1). 1985. pap. 2.65 (*0-936652-01-2*, Pub. by Ed Concern Pubns) Two Ems.
Haith, Betty. Bonnie's Thirteenth Summer. 52p. 1992. pap. 4.95 (*1-882185-01-3*) Crnrstone Pub.
Hall, Jan. Maggie & Jumper. LC 92-61595. (Illus.). 44p. (ps-3). 1993. 6.95 (*1-55523-566-2*) Winston-Derek.
Hall, Lynn. In Trouble Again, Zelda Hammersmith. Cruz, Ray, illus. 138p. (gr. 3-5). 1987. 13.95 (*0-15-238780-3*) HarBrace.
—In Trouble Again, Zelda Hammersmith? 96p. (gr. 5 up). 1989. pap. 3.25 (*0-380-70612-1*, Camelot) Avon.
—The Leaving. 128p. (gr. 7 up). 1988. pap. 2.95 (*0-02-043310-7*, Collier Young Ad) Macmillan Child Grp.
—The Solitary. 128p. (gr. 7 up). 1989. pap. 2.95 (*0-02-043315-8*, Collier Young Ad) Macmillan Child Grp.
—Zelda Strikes Again! 151p. (gr. 3-7). 1988. 13.95 (*0-15-299966-3*) HarBrace.
Hallock, Rusty. Rita's Revenge! 64p. (gr. 1-6). 1994. pap. 3.95 (*0-448-40832-5*, G&D) Putnam Pub Group.
Hamilton, Dorothy. Anita's Choice. Moon, Ivan, illus. LC 70-131535. 96p. (gr. 4-9). 1971. pap. 3.95 (*0-8361-1741-7*) Herald Pr.
—Carlie's Pink Room. Graber, Esther Rose, illus. LC 83-26437. 88p. (gr. 7-9). 1984. pap. 3.95 (*0-8361-3354-4*) Herald Pr.
—Christmas for Holly. Graber, Esther R., illus. LC 72-141831. 112p. (gr. 4-9). 1971. pap. 3.95 (*0-8361-1658-5*) Herald Pr.
—Gina In-Between. Converse, James, illus. LC 81-13387. 128p. (Orig.). (gr. 5 up). 1982. pap. 3.95 (*0-8361-1986-X*) Herald Pr.
Hamilton, Gail. Felicity's Challenge. (gr. 4-7). 1992. pap. 3.99 (*0-553-48035-9*) Bantam.
Hamilton, Virginia. Willie Bea & the Time the Martians Landed. LC 89-6821. 224p. (gr. 4-7). 1989. pap. 3.95 (*0-689-71328-2*, Aladdin) Macmillan Child Grp.
Hamm, Anita M. Lisa & the Raindrops. (gr. 1-4). 1977. 3.50 (*0-935513-01-9*) Samara Pubns.
Hardy, Myronn E. Jenni & the Talking Tulip. (Illus.). 110p. (ps-3). 1989. pap. 4.95 (*0-9621696-3-3*) Ezra Pub Inc.
Harel, Nira. La Escuela de Maria. Writer, C. C. & Nielsen, Lisa C., trs. Eagle, Mike, illus. (SPA.). 24p. (Orig.). (ps). 1992. pap. text ed. 3.00x (*1-56134-153-3*) Dushkin Pub.
—Maria's School. Kriss, David, tr. from HEB. Eagle, Mike, illus. 24p. (Orig.). (ps). 1992. pap. text ed. 3.00x (*1-56134-143-6*) Dushkin Pub.
Harrah, Madge. Honey Girl. 128p. 1990. pap. 2.95 (*0-380-75828-8*, Camelot) Avon.
Harriet the Spy. 1975. pap. 2.95 (*0-440-73447-9*) Dell.
Harrison, Maggie. Lizzie's List. Matthews, Bethan, illus. LC 92-54580. 112p. (gr. 3-6). 1993. 14.95 (*1-56402-197-1*) Candlewick Pr.
Hart, Alison. Andie Out of Control. LC 93-86084. 132p. (Orig.). (gr. 3-7). 1994. pap. 3.50 (*0-679-85693-5*) Random Bks Yng Read.
—A Horse for Mary Beth. LC 93-86083. 132p. (Orig.). (gr. 3-7). 1994. pap. 3.50 (*0-679-85692-7*) Random Bks Yng Read.
—Jina Rides to Win. LC 93-86085. 132p. (Orig.). (gr. 3-7). 1994. pap. 3.50 (*0-679-85694-3*) Random Bks Yng Read.
Harvey, Brett. Immigrant Girl: Becky of Eldridge Street. Ray, Deborah K., illus. LC 86-15038. 40p. (gr. 1-4). 1987. reinforced bdg. 13.95 (*0-8234-0638-5*) Holiday.
Hatchigan, Jessica. Dinosaurs Aren't Forever. 112p. (Orig.). 1991. pap. 2.95 (*0-380-76137-8*, Camelot) Avon.
Hathorn, Libby. Freya's Fantastic Surprise. Thompson, Sharon, illus. 32p. (ps-3). 1989. 12.95 (*0-590-42442-4*, Scholastic Hardcover) Scholastic Inc.
Hausman, Gerald. Beth: The Little Girl of Pine Knoll. Totten, Bob, illus. LC 74-82228. 32p. (gr. 6 up). 1974. 15.00 (*0-912846-08-9*) Bookstore Pr.
Hautzig, Esther. The Endless Steppe. LC 68-13582. 256p. (gr. 7 up). 1987. pap. 3.95 (*0-06-447027-X*, Trophy) HarpC Child Bks.
Hawes, Louise. Nelson Malone Saves Flight 942. 160p. 1990. pap. 2.95 (*0-380-70758-6*, Camelot) Avon.
Hawks, Robert. The Twenty-Six Minutes. 190p. (Orig.). (gr. 8-12). 1988. pap. 4.95 (*0-938961-03-9*, Stamp Out Sheep Press) Sq One Pubs.
Haynes, Betsy. Nobody Likes Taffy Sinclair. (gr. 4-7). 1991. pap. 2.99 (*0-553-15877-5*) Bantam.
—Taffy Sinclair Goes to Hollywood. (gr. 4 up). 1990. pap. 2.95 (*0-553-15819-8*) Bantam.
Haywood, Carolyn. Betsy & Mr. Kilpatrick. (gr. k-6). 1989. pap. 3.25 (*0-440-40204-2*, YB) Dell.
—Betsy & the Boys. LC 45-35133. 140p. (gr. 1-5). 1945. 12.95 (*0-15-206944-5*, HB Juv Bks) HarBrace.
—Betsy's Busy Summer. (gr. k-6). 1989. pap. 3.25 (*0-440-40171-2*, YB) Dell.
—Betsy's Little Star. 160p. (gr. 3-6). 1989. pap. 3.25 (*0-440-40172-0*, YB) Dell.
—Betsy's Play School. (gr. k-6). 1989. pap. 3.25 (*0-440-40213-1*, YB) Dell.
—Betsy's Winterhouse. (gr. k-6). 1989. pap. 3.25 (*0-440-40227-1*, YB) Dell.
—Hello, Star. 64p. (gr. 2-4). 1992. pap. 2.50 (*0-8167-1310-3*) Troll Assocs.
—Snowbound with Betsy. (gr. k-6). 1992. 16.25 (*0-8446-6597-5*) Peter Smith.
Hearn, Diane D. Anna in the Garden. 1st ed. Hearn, Diane D., illus. LC 93-44204. 32p. (gr 1-3). 1994. PLB 15.95 (*1-881889-57-2*) Silver Moon.
Hedderwick, Mairi. Katie Morag & the New Pier. (Illus.). 32p. (ps-1). 1994. 19.95 (*0-370-31833-1*, Pub. by Bodley Head UK) Trafalgar.
Henkes, Kevin. Jessica. (Illus.). 32p. (ps-3). 1990. pap. 4.99 (*0-14-054194-2*, Puffin) Puffin Bks.
—Once Around the Block. Chess, Victoria, illus. LC 85-24901. 24p. (gr. k-3). 1987. 11.75 (*0-688-04954-0*); PLB 11.88 (*0-688-04955-9*) Greenwillow.
Her Honor, Katie Shannon. 128p. (gr. 5). 1989. pap. 2.95 (*0-553-15640-3*) Bantam.
Herman, Charlotte. Millie Cooper, Take a Chance. Cogancherry, Helen, illus. LC 88-11081. 112p. (gr. 3 up). 1989. 11.95 (*0-525-44442-4*, DCB) Dutton Child Bks.
Herman, Debbie. The Incredible Brocho Machine. (Illus.). 190p. (gr. 3-5). 1994. 8.95 (*1-56871-045-3*) Targum Pr.
Hermes, Patricia. You Shouldn't Have to Say Good-Bye. 128p. (gr. 3-7). 1989. pap. 2.75 (*0-590-43174-9*) Scholastic Inc.
Herzig, Alison & Mali, Jane L. The Wimp of the World. 130p. (gr. 2-6). 1994. 13.99 (*0-670-85208-2*) Viking Child Bks.
Hest, Amy. Getting Rid of Krista. Rogers, Jacqueline, illus. LC 87-23981. 80p. (gr. 2-5). 1988. 11.95 (*0-688-07149-X*) Morrow Jr Bks.
—Getting Rid of Krista. 80p. (gr. 4-7). 1992. pap. 2.95 (*0-8167-1841-5*) Troll Assocs.
Heyde, Christiane. The Happy Girl. Hawkins, Linda, illus. LC 89-85861. 40p. 1990. 11.95 (*0-87516-618-0*) DeVorss.
Hidaka, Masako. Girl from the Snow Country. Stinchecum, Amanda M., tr. from JPN. LC 86-10584. (Illus.). 32p. (ps-4). 1986. 13.95 (*0-916291-06-5*, Cranky Nell Bk) Kane-Miller Bk.
Hillam, Corbin. Jennifer of the Jungle. Hillam, Corbin, illus. 32p. (ps-2). 1990. text ed. 5.00 (*0-685-45916-0*) Concordia.
Hines, Anna. Boys Are Yucko! (gr. 4-7). 1990. pap. 2.95 (*0-590-43109-9*) Scholastic Inc.
Hines, Anna G. Tell Me Your Best Thing. Ritz, Karen, illus. 128p. (gr. 2-5). 1994. pap. 3.99 (*0-14-036447-1*) Puffin Bks.
Hoban, Julia. Amy Loves the Rain. Hoban, Lillian, illus. LC 87-45851. 24p. (ps). 1993. pap. 3.95 (*0-06-443293-9*, Trophy) HarpC Child Bks.
—Amy Loves the Snow. Hoban, Lillian, illus. LC 87-45852. 24p. (ps). 1993. pap. 3.95 (*0-06-443294-7*, Trophy) HarpC Child Bks.
Hoban, Russell. Bedtime for Frances. Williams, Garth, illus. LC 60-8347. (ps-2). 1976. pap. 4.95 (*0-06-443005-7*, Trophy) HarpC Child Bks.
Hodge, Lois L. A Season of Change. LC 87-18945. 108p. (Orig.). (gr. 7-12). 1987. pap. 2.95 (*0-930323-27-0*, Kendall Green Pubns) Gallaudet Univ Pr.
Hoehne, Marcia. A Pocket in My Heart. 160p. (Orig.). (gr. 4-7). 1994. pap. 4.99 (*0-89107-781-2*) Crossway Bks.
Hoffman, Mary. Nancy No-Size. Northway, Jennifer, illus. 32p. (gr. k-3). 1987. 9.95 (*0-19-520596-0*) OUP.
Holabird, Katharine. Angelina at the Fair. Craig, Helen, illus. LC 84-28931. 24p. (ps-2). 1988. 15.00 (*0-517-55744-4*, Clarkson Potter) Crown Bks Yng Read.
—Angelina Ballerina. Craig, Helen, illus. 24p. (ps-2). 1990. 4.99 (*0-517-57668-6*, Clarkson Potter) Crown Bks Yng Read.
Holcomb, Nan. Patrick & Emma Lou. Yoder, Dot, illus. 32p. (ps-3). 1992. Repr. of 1989 ed. 13.95 (*0-944727-14-X*) Jason & Nordic Pubs.
—Sarah's Surprise. Yoder, Dot, illus. 32p. (ps-2). 1990. pap. 6.95 (*0-944727-07-7*) Jason & Nordic Pubs.
—Sarah's Surprise. Yoder, Dot, illus. 32p. (ps-3). 1992. Repr. of 1990 ed. 13.95 (*0-944727-18-2*) Jason & Nordic Pubs.
Holl, Kristi. Rose Beyond the Wall. 160p. (gr. 2-9). 1988. pap. 2.95 (*0-8167-1309-X*) Troll Assocs.
Holl, Kristi D. Perfect or Not, Here I Come. 160p. (gr. 4-8). 1987. pap. 2.95 (*0-8167-1048-1*) Troll Assocs.
Holmes, Efner T. My Sadie. (Illus.). 128p. (gr. 3-6). 1993. pap. 3.50 (*1-56288-350-X*) Checkerboard.
Holtze, Sally H. Presenting Norma Fox Mazer. (gr. k-12). 1989. pap. 3.95 (*0-440-20486-0*, LE) Dell.
Honeycutt, Natalie. Josie's Beau. 128p. 1988. pap. 2.95 (*0-380-70524-9*, Camelot) Avon.
Hooks, William H. The Legend of the White Doe. Nolan, Denis, illus. LC 87-11176. 48p. (gr. 3 up). 1988. RSBE 14.95 (*0-02-744350-7*, Macmillan Child Bk) Macmillan Child Grp.
—Moss Gown. Carrick, Donald, illus. (gr. k-4). 1987. 13.95 (*0-89919-460-5*, Clarion Bks) HM.
Hopper, Nancy J. Carrie's Games. 128p. (gr. 7 up). 1989. pap. 2.50 (*0-380-70538-9*, Flare) Avon.
Horner, Althea J. Little Big Girl. Rosamilia, Patricia, illus. 32p. (ps-3). 1982. 14.95 (*0-89885-098-3*); pap. 9.95 (*0-89885-287-0*) Human Sci Pr.
Hotze, Sollace. A Circle Unbroken. LC 88-2569. 224p. (gr. 7 up). 1988. 13.95 (*0-89919-733-7*, Clarion Bks) HM.
Howard, Ellen. Edith Herself. Hinter, Ronald, illus. LC 86-10826. 144p. (gr. 3-7). 1987. SBE 13.95 (*0-689-31314-4*, Atheneum Child Bk) Macmillan Child Grp.
Howe, James. Pinky & Rex & the Spelling Bee. 48p. 1992. pap. 3.99 (*0-380-71643-7*, Camelot Young) Avon.
Hughes, Shirley. Bathwater's Hot. LC 84-14389. (Illus.). 24p. (gr. k-1). 1985. 4.95 (*0-688-04202-3*) Lothrop.
Hughes, Virginia E. Anna: The Little Peasant Girl. LC 92-91117. (Illus.). 64p. (gr. 4 up). 1994. pap. 8.00 (*1-56002-264-7*, Univ Edtns) Aegina Pr.
Hulme, Joy N. Climbing the Rainbow. LC 92-1109. 186p. (Orig.). (gr. 3-7). 1992. pap. 4.95 (*0-87579-584-6*) Deseret Bk.
Hunt, Angela E. Cassie Perkins: Love Burning Bright. 176p. (gr. 4-8). 1992. pap. text ed. 4.99 (*0-8423-1066-5*) Tyndale.
—Cassie Perkins, No. 1: No More Broken Promises. 1991. PLB 4.99 (*0-8423-0461-4*) Tyndale.
—Cassie Perkins, No. 3: A Basket of Roses. 1991. PLB 4.99 (*0-8423-0463-0*) Tyndale.
Hunt, Irene. Up a Road Slowly. 100p. 1987. pap. 3.99 (*0-425-10003-0*, Berkley-Pacer) Berkley Pub.
Hurd, Edith T. I Dance in My Red Pajamas. McCully, Emily A., illus. LC 81-47721. 32p. (gr. 1-3). 1982. PLB 14.89 (*0-06-022700-1*) HarpC Child Bks.
Hurmence, Belinda. A Girl Called Boy. (gr. 3-6). 1990. pap. 5.95 (*0-395-55698-8*, Clarion Bks) HM.
Hurwitz, Johanna. Busybody Nora. Hoban, Lillian, illus. LC 89-13649. 64p. (ps up). 1990. Repr. of 1976 ed. 12.95 (*0-688-09092-3*); PLB 12.88 (*0-688-09093-1*, Morrow Jr Bks) Morrow Jr Bks.
—DeDe Takes Charge! De Groat, Diane, illus. LC 84-9085. 128p. (gr. 3-7). 1984. 12.95 (*0-688-03853-0*) Morrow Jr Bks.
—DeDe Takes Charge! De Groat, Diane, illus. LC 84-9085. 128p. (gr. 4 up). 1992. pap. 3.95 (*0-688-11499-7*, Pub. by Beech Tree Bks) Morrow.
—Tough Luck Karen. LC 82-6443. (Illus.). 160p. (gr. 3 up). 1991. pap. 3.95 (*0-688-10974-8*, Pub. by Beech Tree Bks) Morrow.
Hutchins, H. Leanna Builds a Genie Trap. (Illus.). 24p. (ps-8). 1987. 12.95 (*0-920303-54-4*, Pub. by Annick CN); pap. 4.95 (*0-920303-55-2*, Pub. by Annick CN) Firefly Bks Ltd.
Impey, Rose. Who's a Bright Girl? Amstutz, Andre, illus. 42p. (gr. 2-4). 1989. 3.95 (*0-8120-6144-6*) Barron.
Isabelle the Itch. 1923. pap. 1.95 (*0-440-74345-1*) Dell.
Jackson, Dave & Jackson, Neta. Imprisoned in the Golden City. 128p. (Orig.). 1993. pap. 4.99 (*1-55661-269-9*) Bethany Hse.
James, Simon. Sally & the Limpet. James, Simon, illus. LC 90-40088. 32p. (ps-3). 1991. SBE 13.95 (*0-689-50528-0*, M K McElderry) Macmillan Child Grp.
Jenkin-Pearce, Susie. When I Was a Little Girl. (Illus.). 32p. (gr. k-2). 1993. 17.95 (*0-09-176359-2*, Pub. by Hutchinson UK) Trafalgar.
Johnson, Angela. Do Like Kyla. Ransome, James E., illus. LC 89-16229. 32p. (ps-2). 1993. pap. 5.95 (*0-531-07040-9*) Orchard Bks Watts.
Jones, Jay S. Rosalia, Be Proud. Jones, MariaElena G., illus. 41p. (gr. k-6). 1992. 14.95 (*0-9632040-0-9*); PLB 14.95 (*0-9632040-1-7*) Integrity Inst.
Jones, Jean R. Cassandra's Tale. McDougal, Paula, illus. (ps-9). Date not set. 35.00 (*0-936204-69-9*) Jelm Mtn.
Joosse, Barbara M. Anna, the One & Only. Mayo, Gretchen W., illus. LC 88-890. 144p. (gr. 2-6). 1990. pap. 3.95 (*0-06-440345-9*, Trophy) HarpC Child Bks.
Joseph, Lynn. Jasmine's Parlour Day. (Illus.). (ps-3). 1994. 15.00 (*0-688-11487-3*); 14.93 (*0-688-11488-1*) Lothrop.

Joyce, Rosemary. Anything to Win. 1994. pap. 4.05 (*1-56171-304-X*, S P I Bks) Shapolsky Pubs.
Judy Blume. Incl. Are You There, God? It's Me, Margaret; Blubber; Otherwise Known As Sheila the Great; Superfudge; Tales of a Fourth Grade Nothing. 1983. pap. 13.00 boxed set (*0-440-44348-2*) Dell.
Kaetler, Sarah. Stories from Grandpa's Rocking Chair. Klassen, Neil, illus. 64p. (Orig.). (gr. 1-5). 1984. pap. 3.95 (*0-919797-11-3*) Kindred Pr.
Kaner, Steve. I Am Not Jenny. Beinicke, Steve, illus. 32p. (ps-2). 1991. 13.95 (*0-88899-142-8*, Pub. by Groundwood-Douglas & McIntyre CN) Firefly Bks Ltd.
Kaplow, Robert. Alessandra in Love. LC 87-45883. 160p. (gr. 7 up). 1991. pap. 3.50 (*0-06-447053-9*, Trophy) HarpC Child Bks.
Katz, Illana. Sarah: Sexual Abuse. (ps-3). 1994. PLB 16.95 (*1-882388-07-0*); pap. 9.95 (*1-882388-08-9*) Real Life Strybks.
Kaye, Marilyn. Camp Sunnyside Friends: Balancing Act, No. 18. 128p. (Orig.). (gr. 5-12). 1992. pap. 3.50 (*0-380-76918-2*, Camelot) Avon.
—Camp Sunnyside Friends: The Tennis Trap, No. 12. 128p. (Orig.). (gr. 5). 1991. pap. 2.95 (*0-380-76184-X*, Camelot) Avon.
—Cassie. LC 87-11944. 134p. (gr. 3-7). 1987. 13.95 (*0-15-200421-1*, Gulliver Bks); pap. 4.95 (*0-15-200422-X*, Gulliver Bks) HarBrace.
—Daphne. LC 86-29420. (Illus.). 160p. (gr. 3-7). 1987. 13.95 (*0-15-200434-3*, Gulliver Bks); pap. 4.95 (*0-15-200433-5*) HarBrace.
—Katie Steals the Show. 128p. 1990. pap. 2.95 (*0-380-75910-1*, Camelot) Avon.
—Lydia. LC 87-12763. 129p. (gr. 3-7). 1987. 13.95 (*0-15-200510-2*, Gulliver Bks); pap. 4.95 (*0-15-200511-0*, Gulliver Bks) HarBrace.
—Mindy Wise. 144p. (gr. 5). 1993. pap. 3.50 (*0-380-71879-0*, Camelot) Avon.
—The New & Improved Sarah. 144p. (Orig.). 1990. pap. 2.95 (*0-380-76180-7*, Camelot) Avon.
—New Girl in Cabin Six. 128p. (Orig.). 1989. pap. 2.95 (*0-380-75703-6*, Camelot) Avon.
—Phoebe. 146p. (gr. 3-7). 1987. 13.95 (*0-15-200430-0*); pap. 4.95 (*0-15-200431-9*) HarBrace.
—Will the Real Becka Morgan Please Stand Up? (gr. 4-7). 1991. pap. 3.50 (*0-06-106041-0*, PL) HarpC.
—A Witch in Cabin Six. 128p. (gr. 3-4). 1990. pap. 2.95 (*0-380-75912-8*, Camelot) Avon.
Keene, Carolyn. The Legend of Miner's Creek. Greenberg, Anne, ed. 160p. (Orig.). 1992. pap. 3.99 (*0-671-73053-3*, Minstrel Bks) PB.
—Secret of the Tibetan Treasure. Winkler, Ellen, ed. 160p. (Orig.). 1992. pap. 3.99 (*0-671-73054-1*, Minstrel Bks) PB.
Keller, Beverly. Desdemona: Twelve Going on Desperate. LC 86-10655. 160p. (gr. 3-7). 1986. 13.00 (*0-688-06076-5*) Lothrop.
—Desdemona: Twelve Going on Desperate. LC 87-45287. 160p. (gr. 3-7). 1988. pap. 3.95 (*0-06-440226-6*, Trophy) HarpC Child Bks.
Keller, Holly. Geraldine's Big Snow. LC 87-14936. (Illus.). 24p. (ps-3). 1988. 11.95 (*0-688-07513-4*); lib. bdg. 11.88 (*0-688-07514-2*) Greenwillow.
—Lizzie's Invitation. LC 86-19380. (ps-3). 1987. 11.75 (*0-688-06124-9*); PLB 11.88 (*0-688-06125-7*) Greenwillow.
Kemp, Gene. The Room with No Windows. 114p. (gr. 3-6). 1989. pap. 4.95 (*0-571-16117-0*) Faber & Faber.
Kennedy, Richard. Amy's Eyes. Egielski, Richard, illus. LC 82-48841. 448p. (gr. 5 up). 1988. pap. 10.95 (*0-06-440220-7*, Trophy) HarpC Child Bks.
Kerr, M. E. Is That You, Miss Blue? LC 74-2627. 176p. (gr. 7 up). 1987. pap. 2.95 (*0-06-447033-4*, Trophy) HarpC Child Bks.
Kesselman, Wendy. Emma. 1993. pap. 4.99 (*0-440-40847-4*) Dell.
Kezzeiz, Ediba. Fatima's Surprise. Arostu, Salma, illus. 21p. (Orig.). (ps-1). 1991. pap. 3.50 (*0-89259-114-5*) Am Trust Pubns.
—When I Grow up. Shishani, Ami, illus. 17p. (Orig.). (ps-1). 1991. pap. 3.50 ea. (*0-89259-116-1*) Am Trust Pubns.
Kingman, Lee. Luck of the Miss L. (gr. 4-6). 1986. 12.95 (*0-685-11813-4*) HM.
King-Smith, Dick. Pretty Polly. large type ed. 1994. 16.95 (*0-7451-2036-9*, Galaxy Child Lrg Print) Chivers N Amer.
—Sophie Hits Six. 1st U.S. ed. Patkins, David, illus. LC 92-54692. 128p. (gr. k-4). 1993. 14.95 (*1-56402-216-1*) Candlewick Pr.
—Sophie's Tom. Parkins, David & Parkins, David, illus. LC 91-58756. 112p. (gr. k-4). 1992. 14.95 (*1-56402-107-6*) Candlewick Pr.
Kitamura, Satoshi. Lily Takes a Walk. LC 87-8894. (Illus.). 32p. (ps-1). 1991. pap. 3.95 (*0-525-44699-0*, Puffin) Puffin Bks.
Klass, Sheila S. Kool Ada. (gr. 4-7). 1993. pap. 2.95 (*0-590-43903-0*) Scholastic Inc.
Klein, Norma. Girls Can Be Anything. Doty, Roy, illus. LC 72-85258. 32p. (ps-1). 1975. 11.95 (*0-525-30662-5*, DCB); pap. 3.95 (*0-525-45029-7*, DCB) Dutton Child Bks.
Klein, Robin. All in the Blue Unclouded Weather. (gr. 3-7). 1992. 11.95 (*0-670-83909-4*) Viking Child Bks.
—Dresses of Red & Gold. 184p. (gr. 5-9). 1993. 12.50 (*0-670-84733-X*) Viking Child Bks.
Klusmeyer, Joann. Shelly from Rockytop Farm. Taylor, Neil, illus. 65p. (gr. 3-6). 1986. 5.95 (*1-55523-014-8*) Winston-Derek.
Kneeland, Linda. Cookie. Fargo, Todd, illus. 32p. (ps-3). 1992. Repr. of 1989 ed. 13.95 (*0-944727-16-6*) Jason & Nordic Pubs.
Komaiko, Leah. Annie Bananie. Cornell, Laura, illus. LC 86-45767. 32p. (ps-3). 1987. 15.00 (*0-06-023259-5*) HarpC Child Bks.
—Annie Bananie. Cornell, Laura, illus. LC 86-45767. 32p. (gr. k-3). 1989. pap. 4.95 (*0-06-443198-3*, Trophy) HarpC Child Bks.
Korman, Gordon. This Can't Be Happening at MacDonald Hall. 128p. 1990. pap. 2.95 (*0-590-44213-9*) Scholastic Inc.
Krakauer, Hoong Y. Rabbit Mooncakes. LC 92-23409. 1994. 15.95 (*0-316-50327-4*, Joy St Bks) Little.
Krause, Ute. Nora & the Great Bear. (Illus.). 32p. (ps-3). 1992. pap. 3.99 (*0-14-054565-4*, Puff Pied Piper) Puffin Bks.
Krementz, Jill. A Very Young Rider. (gr. k-6). 1987. pap. 6.95 (*0-440-49215-7*, YB) Dell.
Kriegman, Mitchell. Clarissa's All-in-One. (Illus.). 96p. 1993. pap. 2.95 (*0-448-40098-7*, G&D) Putnam Pub Group.
Kroll, Steven. Looking for Daniela: A Romantic Adventure. Lobel, Anita, illus. LC 87-29071. 32p. (ps-3). 1988. reinforced bdg. 14.95 (*0-8234-0695-4*) Holiday.
Kudeviz, Carol G. Sister Sarah: A New Baby Can Be Fun. Pease, Ken, illus. LC 94-66126. 24p. (ps-3). 1994. pap. 3.95 (*0-9639779-0-3*) Pigtail Pubng.
Kulling, Monica. I Hate You, Marmalade. Ayliffe, Alex, illus. 32p. (ps-3). 1992. 14.00 (*0-670-84480-2*) Viking Child Bks.
Kunsch de Sokoluk, M. Cristina. Cartas de Ester. (SPA.). 110p. (gr. 10 up). 1988. pap. 3.75 (*0-311-37027-6*) Casa Bautista.
Landon, Lucinda. Meg MacKintosh & the Case of the Curious Whale Watch. Landon, Lucinda, illus. 48p. (gr. 2-5). 1987. 14.95 (*0-316-51362-8*, Joy St Bks) Little.
Langley, Bob. Autumn Tiger. 256p. 1988. pap. 3.50 (*0-685-19806-5*) Bantam.
Lasky, Kathryn. Pageant. (gr. k-12). 1988. pap. 3.95 (*0-440-20161-6*, LFL) Dell.
—The Tantrum. McCarthy, Bobette, illus. LC 92-3701. 32p. (ps-1). 1993. RSBE 13.95 (*0-02-751661-X*, Macmillan Child Bk) Macmillan Child Grp.
Lawlor, Laurie. Addie's Dakota Winter. MacDonald, Patricia, ed. Gowing, Toby, illus. 160p. 1991. pap. 2.99 (*0-671-70148-7*, Minstrel Bks) PB.
Lehrman, Robert. The Store That Mama Built. LC 91-39983. 128p. (gr. 3-7). 1992. SBE 13.95 (*0-02-754632-2*, Macmillan Child Bk) Macmillan Child Grp.
L'Engle, Madeleine. Camila. Barbadillo, Pedro, tr. (SPA.). 197p. (gr. 9-12). 1992. pap. write for info. (*84-204-4555-X*) Santillana.
Leonard, Alison. Tina's Chance. 160p. (gr. 6 up). 1992. pap. 3.99 (*0-14-032882-3*) Puffin Bks.
Leppard, Lois G. Mandie & the Midnight Journey. 160p. (Orig.). (gr. 1-6). 1989. pap. 3.99 (*1-55661-084-X*) Bethany Hse.
—Mandie & the Shipboard Mystery, Bk. 14. 160p. (Orig.). (gr. 3-8). 1990. 3.99 (*1-55661-120-X*) Bethany Hse.
—Mandie & the Silent Catacombs. 160p. (gr. 3-8). 1990. 3.99 (*1-55661-148-X*) Bethany Hse.
—Mandie Books 16-20 Giftset. (Orig.). 1992. 19.99 (*1-55661-769-0*) Bethany Hse.
Lester, Helen. Lin's Backpack. 8p. (ps-1). 1994. text ed. 3.95 (*0-673-36194-2*) GdYrBks.
Leue, Mary M. Jessica Dragonette's Fiery Breath: A Fable for Little Girls Who Love Their Daddies. 2nd ed. Marceau, Melissa, illus. 46p. (gr. k-6). 1993. pap. 9.95 (*1-878115-00-6*) Dwn-To-Erth Bks.
Leverich, Kathleen. Hilary & the Troublemakers. Lorraine, Walter, illus. LC 91-13762. 144p. (Orig.). (gr. 3-7). 1993. pap. 3.99 (*0-679-84716-2*, Bullseye Bks) Random Bks Yng Read.
Levin, Betty. The Ice Bear. LC 86-254. 192p. (gr. 5 up). 1986. reinforced trade ed. 10.25 (*0-688-06431-0*) Greenwillow.
Levy, Elizabeth. Come Out Smiling: A Novel. LC 80-68734. 192p. (gr. 8-12). 1981. 8.95 (*0-440-01378-X*) Delacorte.
—World Class Gymnast. 112p. 1990. pap. 2.75 (*0-590-43832-8*) Scholastic Inc.
Lewis, Beverly. Sealed with a Kiss. 144p. (gr. 6-9). 1993. pap. 4.99 (*0-310-38071-5*, Pub. by Youth Spec) Zondervan.
—The Trouble with Weddings. 144p. (gr. 6-9). 1993. pap. 4.99 (*0-310-38081-2*, Pub. by Youth Spec) Zondervan.
Lewis, Linda. Pre-Teen Means Inbetween. MacDonald, Pat, ed. 160p. (Orig.). (gr. 3-6). 1993. pap. 2.99 (*0-671-74535-2*, Minstrel Bks) PB.
—Two Young Two Go Four Boys. (gr. 2-5). 1990. pap. 2.75 (*0-671-69560-6*, Archway) PB.
—We Hate Everything but Boys. (gr. 5-7). 1990. pap. 2.99 (*0-671-72225-5*, Archway) PB.
Lewis, Wendy. Sarah Scrap & Her Nature Trail. (Illus.). 32p. 1993. 13.95 (*0-237-51216-5*, Pub. by Evans Bros Ltd) Trafalgar.
—Sarah Scrap & Her Wonderful Heap! (Illus.). 32p. (gr. k-2). 1992. 13.95 (*0-237-51152-5*, Pub. by Evans Bros Ltd) Trafalgar.
Lightwood, Donald. The Baillie's Daughter. 160p. (gr. 3-5). 1994. pap. 6.95 (*0-86241-285-4*, Pub. by Cnngt UK) Trafalgar.
Lillington, Kenneth. Josephine. 148p. (gr. 3-6). 1991. pap. 4.95 (*0-571-16118-9*) Faber & Faber.
Lindbergh, Anne M. Hunky-Dory Dairy. 160p. (gr. 3-7). 1987. pap. 2.75 (*0-380-70320-3*, Camelot) Avon.
—The People in Pineapple Place. 160p. (gr. 4-5). 1990. pap. 2.95 (*0-380-70766-7*, Camelot) Avon.
Lindgren, Astrid. Lotta on Troublemaker Street. Brinckloe, Julie, illus. Bothmer, Gerry, tr. LC 90-25169. (Illus.). 64p. (gr. 1-4). 1991. pap. 2.95 (*0-689-71443-2*, Aladdin) Macmillan Child Grp.
—Pippi Goes on Board. 192p. 1981. Repr. PLB 16.95x (*0-89966-339-7*) Buccaneer Bks.
—Pippi Goes on Board. (Orig.). 1977. pap. 3.95 (*0-14-032774-6*, Puffin); pap. 3.99 (*0-14-030959-4*, Puffin) Puffin Bks.
—Pippi in the South Seas. (Orig.). 1988. pap. 3.95 (*0-14-032773-8*, Puffin) Puffin Bks.
—Pippi in the South Seas. Bothmer, Gerry, tr. Glanzman, Louis S., illus. 128p. (gr. 3-7). 1977. pap. 3.99 (*0-14-030958-6*, Puffin) Puffin Bks.
—Pippi Longstocking. 192p. 1981. Repr. PLB 21.95 (*0-89966-338-9*) Buccaneer Bks.
—Pippi Longstocking. (Orig.). 1988. pap. 3.95 (*0-14-032772-X*, Puffin) Puffin Bks.
—Pippi Longstocking. Lamborn, Florence, tr. Glanzman, Louis S., illus. 158p. (gr. 4-6). 1977. pap. 3.99 (*0-14-030957-8*, Puffin) Puffin Bks.
—Pippi Longstocking. large type ed. 127p. 1989. Repr. of 1945 ed. lib. bdg. 13.95 (*1-55736-152-5*, Crnrstn Bks) BDD LT Grp.
Linsenman-Schuh, Norma. Presenting Ali Marie in Cabin Fever. Rogers, Dennis, illus. 32p. (Orig.). (gr. k-5). 1993. pap. 5.95 (*1-884073-03-4*); pap. 24.95 incl. doll (*1-884073-00-X*) Esteem Intl.
—Presenting Jessica Lyn in King Purple. Quinlivan, Mary & Snyder, Deborah, illus. 32p. (Orig.). 1993. pap. 5.95 (*1-884073-04-2*); pap. 24.95 incl. doll (*1-884073-01-8*) Esteem Intl.
Little, Jean. Jess Was the Brave One. Wilson, Janet, illus. 32p. (ps-3). 1992. 13.95 (*0-670-83495-5*) Viking Child Bks.
Little Red Riding Hood. (FRE & SPA.). (gr. k-3). sp. ed. 4.95 (*0-685-28450-6*); fr. ed. 4.95 (*0-685-28451-4*) Fr & Eur.
Lloyd, David. The Sneeze. Wegner, Fritz, illus. LC 85-46022. 32p. (ps-2). 1986. PLB 11.89 (*0-685-12397-9*, Lipp Jr Bks) HarpC Child Bks.
Lobel, Arnold. Lucille. LC 64-11616. (Illus.). 64p. (gr. k-3). 1964. PLB 12.89 (*0-06-023966-2*) HarpC Child Bks.
Loehring, Wayne. The Athlete's Corner: Megan's Dilemma. 72p. (gr. 6-8). 1992. pap. 3.50 (*0-8059-3276-3*) Dorrance.
Loring, Patrick & Johnson, Joy. Ludy Lettuce: A Head of Her Time. Crider, Caroline, illus. (gr. 3 up). 1994. pap. write for info. (*1-56123-073-1*) Centering Corp.
Louie, Al-Ling. Yeh Shen: A Cinderella Story from China. Young, Ed, illus. 32p. (ps-2). 1990. 14.95 (*0-399-20900-X*, Philomel) Putnam Pub Group.
Lovelace, Maud H. Heaven to Betsy. Lenski, Lois, illus. LC 45-9806. 288p. (gr. 4-7). 1980. pap. 3.95 (*0-06-440110-3*, Trophy) HarpC Child Bks.
Lowe, George L. B. G., Vol. 1: The Little Drummer Girl Who Drums for the Sun. Montrell, Dan, illus. 21p. (Orig.). (ps). 1988. PLB 5.00x (*0-685-22681-6*) G L Lowe.
Lowry, Lois. Anastasia & Her Chosen Career. 192p. (gr. 3-7). 1987. 13.45 (*0-395-42506-9*) HM.
—Anastasia at This Address. 144p. (gr. 4-7). 1992. pap. 3.50 (*0-440-40652-8*, YB) Dell.
—Anastasia at Your Service. De Groat, Diane, illus. LC 82-9231. 160p. (gr. 3-6). 1982. 14.95 (*0-395-32865-9*) HM.
—Anastasia at Your Service. large type ed. 224p. 1988. lib. bdg. 15.95 (*1-55736-101-0*, Crnrstn Bks) BDD LT Grp.
—Anastasia Has the Answers. (gr. k-6). 1987. pap. 3.50 (*0-440-40087-2*, YB) Dell.
—Anastasia Krupnik. 128p. 1984. pap. 3.25 (*0-553-15534-2*) Bantam.
—Anastasia Krupnik. 160p. (gr. 3-6). 1979. 13.45 (*0-395-28629-8*) HM.
—Anastasia Krupnik. (gr. 4-7). 1984. pap. 3.50 (*0-440-40852-0*) Dell.
—Anastasia on Her Own. 144p. (gr. 2-6). 1986. pap. 3.50 (*0-440-40291-3*, YB) Dell.
—Anastasia on Her Own. large type ed. 184p. 1989. Repr. of 1985 ed. lib. bdg. 15.95 (*1-55736-135-5*, Crnrstn Bks) BDD LT Grp.
—Anastasia's Chosen Career. (gr. k-6). 1992. pap. 3.50 (*0-318-33286-8*, YB) Dell.
—The One Hundredth Thing about Caroline. 160p. (gr. 3-6). 1983. 14.45 (*0-395-34829-3*) HM.
—Taking Care of Terrific. large type ed. 208p. 1989. Repr. of 1983 ed. PLB 15.95 (*1-55736-119-3*, Crnrstn Bks) BDD LT Grp.
Lucas, Leanne. Addie McCormick & the Chicago Surprise. 1993. pap. 3.99 (*1-56507-082-8*) Harvest Hse.
—Addie McCormick & the Stolen Statue. (gr. 4 up). 1993. pap. 3.99 (*1-56507-080-1*) Harvest Hse.
Luger, Harriet. Lauren. 176p. (gr. 9 up). 1981. pap. 1.50 (*0-440-94700-6*, LE) Dell.

Luttrell, Ida. Ottie Slockett. LC 88-30884. (Illus.). 40p. (ps-3). 1992. pap. 3.99 (*0-8037-1215-4*, Dial Easy to Read) Puffin Bks.
McBrier, Page. Daphne Takes Charge. 1990. pap. 2.95 (*0-380-75899-7*, Camelot) Avon.
Maccarone, Grace & Chardiet, Bernice. Brenda's Private Swing. 32p. 1992. pap. 2.50 (*0-590-43304-0*) Scholastic Inc.
McCarthy, M. Dianne. The Maple Leaf. LC 92-91176. 168p. (gr. 3 up). 1994. pap. 9.00 (*1-56002-280-9*, Univ Edtns) Aegina Pr.
McCutchan, Betty. Rachel's Star. LC 91-75205. 97p. (gr. 6 up). 1992. 8.95 (*1-55523-464-X*) Winston-Derek.
McDaniel, Becky B. Fue Carmelita-Libro Grande: Katie Did It-Big Book. (Illus.). 32p. (ps-2). 1988. PLB 22.95 (*0-516-59512-1*) Childrens.
—Katie Did It Big Book. (Illus.). 32p. (gr. 5-9). 1988. PLB 22.95 (*0-516-49512-7*) Childrens.
McDaniel, Lurlene. Time to Let Go. (gr. 5 up). 1991. pap. 3.50 (*0-553-28350-2*, Starfire) Bantam.
MacDonald, Amy. Rachel Fister's Blister. Priceman, Marjorie, illus. 32p. (gr. k-3). 1993. pap. 4.80 (*0-395-65744-X*) HM.
MacDonald, George. A Daughter's Devotion. rev. ed. Phillips, Michael, ed. LC 88-19256. 320p. (gr. 11 up). 1988. pap. 7.99 (*0-87123-906-X*) Bethany Hse.
—The Princess & the Curdie. (Orig.). (gr. k-6). 1987. pap. 4.95 (*0-440-47182-6*, Pub. by Yearling Clasics) Dell.
Macdonald, Maryann. Fatso Jean, the Ice Cream Queen. (gr. 4 up). 1990. pap. 2.95 (*0-553-15797-3*) Bantam.
McFann, Jane. One More Chance. 192p. (gr. 6 up). 1988. pap. 2.50 (*0-380-75466-5*, Flare) Avon.
McKean, Thomas. The Search for Sara Sanderson. 160p. (gr. 3-7). 1987. pap. 2.50 (*0-380-75295-6*, Camelot) Avon.
McKissack, Patricia & McKissack, Fredrick. Messey Bessey Big Book. (Illus.). 32p. (ps-2). 1988. PLB 22.95 (*0-516-49508-9*) Childrens.
MacLachlan, Patricia. Cassie Binegar. LC 81-48641. 128p. (gr. 3-7). 1982. PLB 12.89 (*0-06-024034-2*) HarpC Child Bks.
—Cassie Binegar. LC 81-48641. 128p. (gr. 3-7). 1987. pap. 3.95 (*0-06-440195-2*, Trophy) HarpC Child Bks.
—Sarah, Plain & Tall. LC 83-49481. 64p. (gr. 3 up). 1987. pap. 3.95 (*0-06-440205-3*, Trophy) HarpC Child Bks.
McMahan, Dean. Ajuna's Star. LC 90-82569. (SPA., Illus.). 24p. (ps-2). 1990. pap. 4.95 (*0-9626254-3-4*) Ajuna Unlimited.
McNamara, John. Model Behavior. (gr. k-12). 1987. pap. 2.75 (*0-440-95569-6*, LFL) Dell.
Magorian, Michelle. Not a Swan. LC 91-19507. 416p. (gr. 7 up). 1992. 18.00 (*0-06-024214-0*); PLB 17.89 (*0-06-024215-9*) HarpC Child Bks.
Mahy, Margaret. The Catalogue of the Universe. 192p. (gr. 7 up). 1994. pap. 3.99 (*0-14-036600-8*) Puffin Bks.
Maiwald, Trudy. Missy & Her Nightlight. 16p. (Orig.). 1994. pap. write for info. (*1-56167-153-3*) Am Literary Pr.
Makris, Kathryn. Almost Sisters, No. 2: The Sisters War. 160p. (Orig.). 1991. pap. 3.50 (*0-380-76055-X*, Camelot) Avon.
—Almost Sisters: The Sisters Scheme. 144p. (Orig.). 1991. pap. 2.99 (*0-380-76035-5*, Camelot) Avon.
—Almost Sisters: The Sisters Team. 176p. (Orig.). (gr. 5 up). 1992. pap. 3.50 (*0-380-76056-8*, Camelot) Avon.
—Crosstown. 176p. (Orig.). 1993. pap. 3.50 (*0-380-76226-9*, Flare) Avon.
Mandrell, Louise. Mission for Jenny: A Story about the Meaning of Flag Day. (ps-3). 1993. 12.95 (*1-56530-038-6*) Summit TX.
Maple, Marilyn. On the Wings of a Butterfly: A Story about Life & Death. Haight, Sandy, illus. Grollman, Earl, afterword by. LC 91-50854. (Illus.). 32p. (Orig.). (gr. 1-6). 1992. 18.95 (*0-943990-69-6*); pap. 9.95 (*0-943990-68-8*) Parenting Pr.
Marino, Jan. The Day That Elvis Came to Town. 208p. (gr. 5). 1993. pap. 3.50 (*0-380-71672-0*, Camelot) Avon.
Marks, Alan. Thief's Daughter. (ps-3). 1994. 11.00 (*0-374-37481-3*) FS&G.
Martin, Ann. Rachel Parker Kingergarten Show-Off. Poydar, Nancy, illus. 1993. pap. 6.95 (*0-8234-1067-6*) Holiday.
Martin, Ann M. Baby-Sitters Little Sister Boxed Set, 4 bks, Bks. 25-28. 1992. Set. 11.00 (*0-590-66125-6*) Scholastic Inc.
—The Baby-Sitters Little Sister: School Scrapbook. (gr. 7-9). 1993. pap. 2.95 (*0-590-47677-7*) Scholastic Inc.
—Baby-Sitters Little Sisters: Secret Diary. (gr. 4-7). 1991. pap. 2.50 (*0-590-45010-7*) Scholastic Inc.
—California Girls! 240p. (gr. 3-7). 1990. pap. 3.75 (*0-590-43575-2*) Scholastic Inc.
—Claudia & Middle School. (gr. 4-7). 1991. pap. 3.25 (*0-590-44082-9*) Scholastic Inc.
—Dawn & the Big Sleepover. (gr. 4-7). 1991. pap. 3.50 (*0-590-43573-6*) Scholastic Inc.
—Jessi & the Dance School Phantom. 160p. (gr. 3-7). 1991. pap. 3.50 (*0-590-44083-7*, Apple Paperbacks) Scholastic Inc.
—Jessi & the Superbrat. (gr. 5 up). 1989. pap. 3.25 (*0-590-42502-1*, Apple Paperbacks) Scholastic Inc.
—Karen, Hannie, & Nancy: The Three Musketeers. 128p. (gr. 2-4). 1992. pap. 2.95 (*0-590-45644-X*, Little Apple) Scholastic Inc.
—Karen's Baby-Sitter. (gr. 4-7). 1994. pap. 2.95 (*0-590-47045-0*) Scholastic Inc.
—Karen's Big Joke. 1992. pap. 2.95 (*0-590-44829-3*) Scholastic Inc.
—Karen's Big Lie. (gr. 4-7). 1993. pap. 2.95 (*0-590-45655-5*) Scholastic Inc.
—Karen's Big Weekend. (gr. 4-7). 1993. pap. 2.95 (*0-590-47043-4*) Scholastic Inc.
—Karen's Birthday. (gr. 4-7). 1990. pap. 2.95 (*0-590-44257-0*) Scholastic Inc.
—Karen's Bully. 1992. 2.95 (*0-590-45646-6*, 053) Scholastic Inc.
—Karen's Cartwheel. 1992. pap. 2.75 (*0-590-44825-0*) Scholastic Inc.
—Karen's Ghost. 96p. (gr. 2-4). 1990. pap. 2.95 (*0-590-43649-X*) Scholastic Inc.
—Karen's Goldfish. 112p. (gr. 2-4). 1991. pap. 2.75 (*0-590-43644-9*) Scholastic Inc.
—Karen's Good-Bye. (gr. 4-7). 1991. pap. 2.95 (*0-590-43641-4*) Scholastic Inc.
—Karen's Home Run. (gr. 4-7). 1991. pap. 2.75 (*0-590-43642-2*) Scholastic Inc.
—Karen's in Love. (gr. 4-7). 1991. pap. 2.75 (*0-590-43645-7*) Scholastic Inc.
—Karen's Kite. (gr. 4-7). 1994. pap. 2.95 (*0-590-46913-4*) Scholastic Inc.
—Karen's Kittycat Club. 112p. (gr. 2-4). 1989. pap. 2.75 (*0-590-44264-3*) Scholastic Inc.
—Karen's Little Sister. 96p. (gr. 2-4). 1989. pap. 2.95 (*0-590-44298-8*) Scholastic Inc.
—Karen's Lucky Penny. (gr. 4-7). 1994. pap. 2.95 (*0-590-47048-5*) Scholastic Inc.
—Karen's New Friend. (gr. 4-7). 1993. pap. 2.95 (*0-590-45651-2*) Scholastic Inc.
—Karen's New Teacher. (gr. 4-7). 1991. pap. 2.95 (*0-590-44824-2*) Scholastic Inc.
—Karen's New Year. (gr. 4-7). 1991. pap. 2.75 (*0-590-43646-5*) Scholastic Inc.
—Karen's Newspaper. (gr. 4-7). 1993. pap. 2.95 (*0-590-47040-X*) Scholastic Inc.
—Karen's Pizza Party. 1993. pap. 2.95 (*0-590-47042-6*) Scholastic Inc.
—Karen's Roller Skates. 64p. (gr. 2-4). 1988. pap. 2.95 (*0-590-44259-7*) Scholastic Inc.
—Karen's School Picture. 112p. (gr. 2-4). 1989. pap. 2.95 (*0-590-44258-9*) Scholastic Inc.
—Karen's Secret. 1992. 2.95 (*0-590-45648-2*) Scholastic Inc.
—Karen's Sleepover. (gr. 4-7). 1990. pap. 2.95 (*0-590-43652-X*) Scholastic Inc.
—Karen's Stepmother. (gr. 4-7). 1994. pap. 2.95 (*0-590-47047-7*) Scholastic Inc.
—Karen's Surprise. 112p. (gr. 2-4). 1990. pap. 2.75 (*0-590-43648-1*) Scholastic Inc.
—Karen's Tea Party. 96p. 1992. pap. 2.75 (*0-590-44828-5*) Scholastic Inc.
—Karen's Toothache. (gr. 4-7). 1993. pap. 2.95 (*0-590-46912-6*) Scholastic Inc.
—Karen's Tuba. (gr. 4-7). 1993. pap. 2.95 (*0-590-45653-9*) Scholastic Inc.
—Karen's Wedding. (gr. 4-7). 1993. pap. 2.95 (*0-590-45654-7*) Scholastic Inc.
—Karen's Wish. 128p. (gr. 2-4). 1990. pap. 3.25 (*0-590-43647-3*) Scholastic Inc.
—Karen's Witch. 112p. (gr. 2-4). 1988. pap. 2.95 (*0-590-44300-3*) Scholastic Inc.
—Karen's Worst Day. 1993. pap. 2.95 (*0-590-44299-6*) Scholastic Inc.
—Keep Out, Claudia! 160p. (gr. 3-7). 1992. pap. 3.50 (*0-590-45657-1*, Apple Paperbacks) Scholastic Inc.
—Kristy & the Copycat. (gr. 4-7). 1994. pap. 3.50 (*0-590-47012-4*) Scholastic Inc.
—Kristy for President. 160p. 1992. pap. 3.25 (*0-590-44967-2*) Scholastic Inc.
—Kristy's Big Day. (gr. 4-7). 1987. pap. 3.25 (*0-590-43899-9*) Scholastic Inc.
—Mallory Hates Boys (& Gym) 1992. 3.25 (*0-590-45660-1*) Scholastic Inc.
—Mallory on Strike. (gr. 4-7). 1991. pap. 3.50 (*0-590-44971-0*) Scholastic Inc.
—Mary Anne & the Secret in the Attic. 160p. (gr. 3-7). 1992. pap. 3.25 (*0-590-44801-3*, Apple Paperbacks) Scholastic Inc.
—Mary Anne vs. Logan. (gr. 4-7). 1991. pap. 3.50 (*0-590-43570-1*) Scholastic Inc.
—Poor Mallory. 160p. 1990. pap. 3.25 (*0-590-43568-X*) Scholastic Inc.
—Slam Book. LC 87-45335. 160p. (gr. 7 up). 1987. 12.95 (*0-8234-0666-0*) Holiday.
—Stacey's Ex-Best Friend. 160p. 1992. pap. 3.25 (*0-590-44968-0*) Scholastic Inc.
—Yours Turly, Shirley. LC 88-6460. 144p. (gr. 3-7). 1988. 14.95 (*0-8234-0719-5*) Holiday.
Martin, Guenn. Remember the Eagle Day. Converse, James, illus. LC 83-26376. 128p. (gr. 7-9). 1983. pap. 4.95 (*0-8361-3351-X*) Herald Pr.
Marton, Jirina. Amelia's Celebration. Marton, Jirina, illus. 24p. (ps-3). 1992. PLB 15.95 (*1-55037-221-1*, Pub. by Annick CN); pap. 5.95 (*1-55037-220-3*, Pub. by Annick CN) Firefly Bks Ltd.
—Midnight Visit at Molly's House. (Illus.). 24p. (ps-8). 1988. 12.95 (*0-920303-99-4*, Pub. by Annick CN); pap. 4.95 (*0-920303-98-6*, Pub. by Annick CN) Firefly Bks Ltd.
Marzollo, Jean. Red Ribbon Rosie. Sims, Blanche, illus. LC 87-29641. 64p. (Orig.). (gr. 2-4). 1988. lib. bdg. 5.99 (*0-394-99608-9*); pap. 2.50 (*0-394-89608-4*) Random Bks Yng Read.
Marzollo, Jean & Marzollo, Claude. Ruthie's Rude Friends. 14p. 1991. Braille. 1.12 (*1-56956-311-X*) W A T Braille.
Masland, Skip. William Willya & the Washing Machine. Sheppard, Scott O., illus. 40p. (gr. k-5). 1993. 15.95 (*1-883016-01-0*) Moonglow Pubns.
Mason, Margo C. Ready, Alice? (gr. 4 up). 1990. pap. 3.50 (*0-553-34741-1*) Bantam.
Mayper, Monica. After Good-Night. Sis, Peter, illus. LC 86-45766. 32p. (ps-3). 1987. HarpC Child Bks.
Mazer, Norma F. Silver. 208p. 1989. pap. 3.99 (*0-380-75026-0*, Flare) Avon.
—Taking Terri Mueller. 192p. (gr. 8 up). 1981. pap. 3.99 (*0-380-79004-1*, Flare) Avon.
Meacham, Margaret. Boy on the Beach. Ramsey, Marcy D., illus. 144p. (Orig.). (gr. 4-8). 1992. pap. 8.95 (*0-87033-441-7*) Tidewater.
Meet Ramona Quimby. Incl. Ramona Quimby, Age Eight; Ramona the Pest; Ramona & Her Father; Ramona & Her Mother. 1983. pap. 11.20 boxed set (*0-440-45548-0*) Dell.
Meigs, Cornelia. Invisible Louisa. (gr. 4-7). 1988. pap. 2.95 (*0-590-44818-8*) Scholastic Inc.
Menzel, Barbara J. Would You Rather? Brahm, Sumishta, illus. LC 81-6810. 32p. (ps-3). 1982. 16.95 (*0-89885-076-2*) Human Sci Pr.
Merriam, Eve. Wise Woman & Her Secret. LC 90-42406. 1991. pap. 13.95 (*0-671-72603-X*, S&S BFYR) S&S Trade.
Messenger, Norman. Annabel's House. LC 88-60089. (Illus.). 28p. 1989. 18.95 (*0-531-05764-X*) Orchard Bks Watts.
Meyer, Carolyn. Because of Lissa. (gr. 7 up). 1990. pap. 2.95 (*0-553-28802-4*, Starfire) Bantam.
—Gillian's Choice. 1991. pap. 2.95 (*0-553-28835-0*) Bantam.
Migan, Helen. Nell's Story of Long Ago. LC 92-84106. 60p. (gr. 2-6). 1993. pap. 5.95 (*1-55523-593-X*) Winston-Derek.
Miklowitz, Gloria D. Desperate Pursuit. (gr. 7 up). 1992. pap. 3.99 (*0-553-29746-5*, Starfire) Bantam.
Miles, Miska. Annie & the Old One. Parnall, Peter, illus. (gr. 1-3). 1972. lib. bdg. 15.95i (*0-316-57117-2*, Joy St Bks) Little.
Miller, Judi. My Crazy Cousin Courtney. MacDonald, Pat, ed. 160p. (Orig.). (gr. 4-6). 1993. pap. 2.99 (*0-671-73821-6*, Minstrel Bks) PB.
Miller, Sandy. Smart Girl. 160p. (gr. 7 up). 1982. pap. 2.25 (*0-451-11887-1*, Sig Vista) NAL-Dutton.
Mills, Claudia. After Fifth Grade, the World! LC 88-26664. 128p. (gr. 3-7). 1989. SBE 13.95 (*0-02-767041-4*, Macmillan Child Bk) Macmillan Child Grp.
—Cally's Enterprise. 128p. (gr. 5 up). 1989. pap. 2.75 (*0-380-70693-8*, Camelot) Avon.
Mills, Diana. Crazy Hattie. (Illus.). 12p. (gr. 3-7). 1986. pap. 7.95 (*0-9616555-0-X*) Berry Good Child Bks.
Miner. Veronica. 1993. pap. 2.75 (*0-590-42134-4*) Scholastic Inc.
Miner, Jane C. Margaret. 224p. (Orig.). (gr. 7 up). 1988. pap. 2.75 (*0-590-41191-8*) Scholastic Inc.
Modiano, Patrick. Catherine Certitude. Rodarmor, William, tr. from FRE. Sempe, Jean-Jacques, illus. 64p. (gr. 4-9). Date not set. 18.95 (*0-87923-959-X*) Godine.
Moers, Hermann. Annie's Dancing Day. Unzner-Fischer, Christa, illus. Lanning, Rosemary, tr. from GER. LC 92-3612. (Illus.). 32p. (gr. k-3). 1992. 14.95 (*1-55858-160-X*); PLB 14.88 (*1-55858-161-8*) North-South Bks NYC.
Montfort, Elizabeth S. That Special Magic. LC 87-71719. (Illus.). 53p. (Orig.). (gr. 2-3). 1988. pap. 5.00 (*0-916383-37-7*) Aegina Pr.
Montgomery, L. M. Anne of Avonlea. (gr. 8 up). 1984. pap. 0.75 (*0-8049-0219-4*) Airmont.
—Anne of Green Gables. Lee, Jody, illus. (gr. 4 up). 1983. deluxe ed. 13.95 (*0-448-06030-2*, G&D) Putnam Pub Group.
—Anne of Green Gables. (gr. 7 up). 1984. pap. 1.95 (*0-8049-0218-6*) Airmont.
—Anne of Green Gables. Moore, Inga, illus. (gr. 4-8). 1994. 14.95 (*0-8050-3126-X*) H Holt & Co.
Montgomery, Lucy M. Anne of Green Gables. Atwood, Margaret, afterword by. 338p. 1993. pap. 4.95 (*0-7710-9883-9*) Firefly Bks Ltd.
—Anne of Green Gables. LC 93-70551. 240p. (gr. 4 up). 1993. 5.98 (*1-56138-324-4*) Courage Bks.
—Anne of Green Gables. 256p. (gr. 5 up). 1994. pap. 2.99 (*0-14-035148-5*) Puffin Bks.
—Anne of Green Gables, Vol. 1. (gr. 4-7). 1984. pap. 3.50 (*0-553-15327-7*) Bantam.
—Anne of Windy Poplars. (gr. 3-7). 1992. pap. 3.50 (*0-553-48065-0*) Bantam.
—Anne's House of Dreams, No. 5. 240p. (gr. 7-9). 1981. pap. 2.95 (*0-553-24195-8*) Bantam.
—Chronicles of Avonlea. Rubio, Mario, afterword by. 224p. 1988. pap. 2.95 (*0-451-52233-8*, Sig Classics) NAL-Dutton.
—Emily, 3 vols. (gr. 9-12). 1990. Boxed set. pap. 10.50 (*0-553-33308-9*) Bantam.
—Emily Climbs. 336p. (Orig.). 1983. pap. 3.99 (*0-553-26214-9*, Starfire) Bantam.
—Emily Climbs. 1976. 23.95 (*0-8488-0588-7*) Amereon Ltd.
—Emily of New Moon. 352p. (Orig.). 1988. pap. 3.50 (*0-318-33019-9*, Starfire) Bantam.
—Emily of New Moon. 1976. 23.95 (*0-8488-0589-5*) Amereon Ltd.

—Emily's Quest. 1976. 19.95 (*0-8488-0590-9*) Amereon Ltd.
—Further Chronicles of Avonlea. 208p. (Orig.). 1989. pap. 2.95 (*0-553-21381-4*, Starfire) Bantam.
—Jane of Lantern Hill. 1976. 19.95 (*0-8488-1434-7*) Amereon Ltd.
—Kilmeny of the Orchard. 1976. 20.95 (*0-8488-0721-9*) Amereon Ltd.
—Magic for Marigold. 1976. 21.95 (*0-8488-1102-X*) Amereon Ltd.
—Mistress Pat. 1976. 21.95 (*0-8488-1103-8*) Amereon Ltd.
—Rainbow Valley. 1985. pap. 3.50 (*0-553-26921-6*) Bantam.
—The Story Girl. 1989. pap. 2.95 (*0-553-21366-0*, Bantam Classics) Bantam.
Moody, Ralph. Mary Emma. 1976. 21.95 (*0-8488-1107-0*) Amereon Ltd.
—Mary Emma & Company. 1976. 24.95 (*0-8488-1513-0*) Amereon Ltd.
Moore, Elaine. Who Let Girls in the Boys' Locker Room? LC 94-820. (Illus.). 144p. (gr. 3-6). 1994. pap. text ed. 2.95 (*0-8167-3439-9*) Troll Assocs.
Moore, Yvette. Freedom Songs. LC 88-43073. 176p. (gr. 7 up). 1991. 14.95 (*0-531-05812-3*); PLB 14.99 (*0-531-08412-4*) Orchard Bks Watts.
Mora, Pat. A Birthday Basket for Tia. Lang, Cecily, illus. (gr. k-4). 1993. 13.95 (*0-685-64816-8*); audio cass. 11.00 (*1-882869-78-8*) Read Advent.
Morgan, Allan. Sadie & the Snowman. Clark, Brenda, illus. 32p. (ps-2). 1987. pap. 2.50 (*0-590-41826-2*) Scholastic Inc.
Morpurgo, Michael. Waiting for Anya. 1991. 13.00 (*0-670-83735-0*) Viking Child Bks.
Morris, Martha. Katherine & the Garbage Dump. Cathcart, Yvonne, illus. 24p. (gr. 1-4). 1992. 12.95 (*0-929005-39-2*, Pub. by Second Story Pr CN); pap. 5.95 (*0-929005-38-4*, Second Story Pr CN) InBook.
Munsch, Robert. Angela's Airplane. Martchenko, Michael, illus. 24p. (ps-1). 1986. pap. 0.99 (*0-920236-75-8*, Pub. by Annick CN) Firefly Bks Ltd.
—El Avion de Angela: (Angela's Airplane) Langer, Shirley, tr. Martchenko, Michael, illus. (SPA.). 32p. 1991. pap. 5.95 (*1-55037-189-4*, Pub. by Annick CN) Firefly Bks Ltd.
—Millicent & the Wind. Duranceau, Suzanne, illus. 32p. (gr. k-3). 1984. PLB 14.95 (*0-920236-98-7*, Pub. by Annick CN); pap. 4.95 (*0-920236-93-6*, Pub. by Annick CN) Firefly Bks Ltd.
—Millicent & the Wind. Duranceau, Suzanne, illus. 24p. (Orig.). (ps-2). 1989. pap. 0.99 (*1-55037-010-3*, Pub. by Annick CN) Firefly Bks Ltd.
Murphy, Catherine F. Alice Dodd & the Spirit of Truth. LC 92-32039. 176p. (gr. 3-7). 1993. SBE 14.95 (*0-02-767702-8*, Macmillan Child Bk) Macmillan Child Grp.
Nabb, Magdalen. Josie Smith. Vainio, Pirkko, illus. LC 88-8301. 80p. (gr. 1-4). 1989. SBE 12.95 (*0-689-50485-3*, M K McElderry) Macmillan Child Grp.
Nash, Ogden. Adventures of Isabel. (ps-3). 1994. 4.95 (*0-316-59883-6*) Little.
Nathan, Robert. Portrait of Jennie. 293p. 1981. Repr. PLB 18.95x (*0-89966-356-7*) Buccaneer Bks.
—Portrait of Jennie. 234p. 1981. Repr. PLB 16.95x (*0-89967-030-X*) Harmony Raine.
Naylor, Phyllis R. Alice in Rapture, Sort Of. LC 88-8174. 176p. (gr. 3-7). 1989. SBE 13.95 (*0-689-31466-3*, Atheneum Child Bk) Macmillan Child Grp.
—Alice in Rapture Sort Of. (gr. 4-7). 1991. pap. 3.50 (*0-440-40462-2*) Dell.
—All about Alice. (gr. 4-7). 1994. pap. 3.50 (*0-440-40918-7*) Dell.
—Josie's Troubles. (gr. 4-7). 1994. pap. 3.50 (*0-440-40862-8*) Dell.
—Reluctantly Alice. 196p. (gr. 5 up). 1992. pap. 3.50 (*0-440-40685-4*, YB) Dell.
Naylor-Reynolds, Phyllis. The Agony of Alice. (gr. k-6). 1988. pap. 3.50 (*0-440-40051-1*, YB) Dell.
Neville, Emily C. Berries Goodman. (gr. 5-9). 1992. 16.75 (*0-8446-6584-3*) Peter Smith.
Newcome, Zita. Rosie Goes Exploring. (Illus.). 32p. (ps-k). 1992. 11.95 (*1-85681-170-0*, Pub. by J MacRae UK) Trafalgar.
Newton, Suzanne. I Will Call It Georgie's Blues. (gr. 7 up). 1986. pap. 2.75 (*0-440-94090-7*, LFL) Dell.
Nielsen, Shelly. Just Victoria. LC 86-2294. 130p. (gr. 3-7). 1986. pap. 4.99 (*0-89191-609-1*, Chariot Bks) Chariot Family.
Nimmo, Jenny. Ultramarine. LC 91-43642. 192p. (gr. 6 up). 1992. 15.00 (*0-525-44869-1*, DCB) Dutton Child Bks.
Nixon, Joan L. And Maggie Makes Three. LC 85-16389. 112p. (gr. 3-7). 1986. 12.95 (*0-15-250355-2*, HB Juv Bks) HarBrace.
—And Maggie Makes Three. (gr. k-6). 1987. pap. 2.75 (*0-440-40127-5*, YB) Dell.
—Hollywood Daughters: Star Baby. 1991. pap. 3.50 (*0-553-28957-8*) Bantam.
—Maggie Too. (gr. k-6). 1987. pap. 2.50 (*0-440-45288-0*, YB) Dell.
Norris, Jerrie. Presenting Rosa Guy. 1992. pap. 3.99 (*0-440-21133-6*) Dell.
Norton, Ann. Brooke's Little Lies. 112p. (gr. 4-9). 1992. pap. 2.95 (*0-448-40491-5*, G&D) Putnam Pub Group.
O'Dell, Scott. Alexandra. LC 83-26390. 160p. (gr. 7 up). 1984. 13.45 (*0-395-35571-0*, 5-92366) HM.
—Carlotta. 144p. (gr. k-12). 1989. pap. 3.99 (*0-440-90928-7*, LFL) Dell.
—Janey. (gr. 7-12). 1986. write for info. HM.
—My Name Is Not Angelica. 144p. (gr. 5-9). 1989. 14.95 (*0-395-51061-9*) HM.
—My Name Is Not Angelica. (gr. k-6). 1990. pap. 3.99 (*0-440-40379-0*, YB) Dell.
—Sarah Bishop. 240p. (gr. 7up). 1991. pap. 3.25 (*0-590-44651-7*, Point) Scholastic Inc.
Ogburn, Jacqueline K. Scarlett Angelina Wolverton-Manning. Ajhar, Brian, illus. LC 92-41930. (gr. 4 up). 1994. 14.99 (*0-8037-1376-2*); PLB 14.89 (*0-8037-1377-0*) Dial Bks Young.
Oke, Janette. Julia's Last Hope. 224p. (Orig.). (gr. 8 up). 1990. pap. 7.99 (*1-55661-153-6*) Bethany Hse.
Oliver, Diana. Annie's Rainbow. 120p. (Orig.). (gr. 3-7). 1993. pap. 3.50 (*0-679-85006-6*, Bullseye Bks) Random Bks Yng Read.
—Desdemona Acts Up. 120p. (Orig.). (gr. 3-7). 1993. pap. 3.50 (*0-679-85293-X*, Bullseye Bks) Random Bks Yng Read.
—Get Lost, Sylvie! (Orig.). (gr. 3-7). 1993. pap. 3.50 (*0-679-84988-2*, Bullseye Bks) Random Bks Yng Read.
—Kathleen, Karate Queen. 120p. (Orig.). (gr. 3-7). 1993. pap. 3.50 (*0-679-85327-8*, Bullseye Bks) Random Bks Yng Read.
—Sharon Plays It Cool. LC 93-85235. 132p. (Orig.). (gr. 3-7). 1994. pap. 3.50 (*0-679-85476-2*) Random Bks Yng Read.
O'Neill, Laura. No More Little Miss Perfect. 112p. (gr. 4-9). 1992. pap. 2.95 (*0-448-40490-7*, G&D) Putnam Pub Group.
Orgel, Doris. Sarah's Room. Sendak, Maurice, illus. LC 63-13675. 48p. (ps-3). 1991. pap. 4.95 (*0-06-443238-6*, Trophy) HarpC Child Bks.
—Sarah's Room. reissued ed. Sendak, Maurice, illus. LC 63-13675. 48p. (gr. k-3). 1963. PLB 14.89 (*0-06-024606-5*) HarpC Child Bks.
—Starring Becky Suslow. (gr. 4-7). 1991. pap. 3.95 (*0-14-034063-7*, Puffin) Puffin Bks.
Otis, Sharon & Walker, Lois. Tammy's Smile. Porter, Debbie, illus. Goldman, Howard, pref. by. (Illus., Orig.). (ps-7). 1985. wkbk. 6.00 (*0-9617737-0-7*) Total Lrn.
Owens, Vivian W. Nadanda, the Wordmaker: Hide the Doll. Maxwell, Carolyn, ed. Watson, Richard J., illus. LC 93-74671. 248p. 1994. 16.95 (*0-9623839-3-7*) Eschar Pubns.
Page, Carole G. A Song for Kasey. 1992. pap. 4.99 (*0-8024-8176-0*) Moody.
—Summer of a Stranger. 1992. pap. 4.99 (*0-8024-8177-9*) Moody.
Palacios, Argentina. Christmas for Chabelita. Lohstoeter, Lori, illus. LC 94-9833. 32p. (gr. k-3). 1994. PLB 14.95 (*0-8167-3545-X*); pap. text ed. 3.95 (*0-8167-3541-7*) BrdgeWater.
Palumbo, Nancy. Meet Penelope P'Nutt: Conoza Penelope P'Nutt. Weaver, Judith, illus. 32p. (gr. k-6). 1989. wkbk. 5.95 (*0-927024-04-7*) Crayons Pubns.
—Meet Penelope P'Nutt: Viens Recontrer Penelope P'Nutt. Weaver, Judith, illus. 32p. (gr. k-6). 1989. wkbk. 5.95 (*0-927024-05-5*) Crayons Pubns.
—Penelope P'Nutt at Play: Los Juegos de Penelope P'Nutt. Weaver, Judith, illus. 32p. (gr. k-6). 1989. wkbk. 5.95 (*0-927024-16-0*) Crayons Pubns.
Parish, Peggy. Amelia Bedelia & the Surprise Shower. unabr. ed. Tripp, Wallace, illus. (ps-3). 1990. pap. 6.95 incl. cassette (*1-55994-216-9*, Caedmon) HarperAudio.
—Amelia Bedelia's Family Album. 48p. 1994. pap. 3.99 (*0-380-71698-4*, Camelot) Avon.
—Come Back, Amelia Bedelia. unabr. ed. Tripp, Wallace, illus. (ps-3). 1990. pap. 6.95 incl. cassette (*1-55994-225-8*, Caedmon) HarperAudio.
—Good Work, Amelia Bedelia. Sweat, Lynn, illus. LC 75-20360. 56p. (gr. 1-4). 1976. 14.00 (*0-688-80022-X*); PLB 13.93 (*0-688-84022-1*) Greenwillow.
—Play Ball, Amelia Bedelia. unabr. ed. Tripp, Wallace, illus. (ps-3). 1990. pap. 6.95 incl. cassette (*1-55994-241-X*, Caedmon) HarperAudio.
—Teach Us, Amelia Bedelia. Sweat, Lynn, illus. LC 76-22663. 56p. (gr. 1-4). 1977. 12.95 (*0-688-80069-6*); PLB 12.88 (*0-688-84069-8*) Greenwillow.
Park, Barbara. Beanpole. LC 83-111. 160p. (gr. 5 up). 1983. 13.00 (*0-394-85811-5*) Knopf Bks Yng Read.
Pascal, Francine. Amy's Pen Pal. 1990. pap. 3.25 (*0-553-15772-8*) Bantam.
—Booster Boycott. (gr. 4-7). 1991. pap. 3.25 (*0-553-15933-X*) Bantam.
—Boy Trouble. 1990. pap. 2.95 (*0-553-28317-0*) Bantam.
—Carolyn's Mystery Dolls. (gr. 4-7). 1991. pap. 2.99 (*0-553-15870-8*) Bantam.
—The Case of the Secret Santa. (gr. k-3). 1990. pap. 3.50 (*0-553-15860-0*) Bantam.
—Crybaby Lois. (gr. 4 up). 1990. pap. 2.99 (*0-553-15818-X*) Bantam.
—Dreams of Forever. 208p. (gr. 7 up). 1988. pap. 2.95 (*0-553-26700-0*, Starfire) Bantam.
—Elizabeth & Jessica Run Away. 1992. pap. 2.99 (*0-553-48004-9*) Bantam.
—Elizabeth & the Tattletale. 1994. pap. 2.99 (*0-553-48110-X*) Bantam.
—Elizabeth the Hero. (gr. 4-7). 1993. pap. 3.50 (*0-553-48060-X*) Bantam.
—Elizabeth's Broken Arm. (ps-3). 1993. pap. 2.99 (*0-553-48009-X*) Bantam.
—Elizabeth's New Hero. 1989. pap. 3.25 (*0-553-15753-1*) Bantam.
—Elizabeth's Super-Selling Lemonade. 1990. pap. 2.99 (*0-553-15807-4*) Bantam.
—Elizabeth's Valentine, No. 4. 1990. pap. 2.99 (*0-553-15761-2*) Bantam.
—Elizabeth's Video Fever. (ps-3). 1993. pap. 2.99 (*0-553-48010-3*) Bantam.
—Ellen Is Home Alone. (ps-3). 1993. pap. 2.99 (*0-553-48013-8*) Bantam.
—Enid's Story. (gr. 7 up). 1990. pap. 3.50 (*0-553-28576-9*) Bantam.
—Forever & Always. 176p. (gr. 6 up). 1988. pap. 2.95 (*0-553-26788-4*, Starfire) Bantam.
—Good-bye, Eva? (ps-3). 1993. pap. 2.99 (*0-553-48012-X*) Bantam.
—Hangin' Out with Cici. (gr. 4-7). 1991. pap. 3.95 (*0-14-034885-9*, Puffin) Puffin Bks.
—Jessica & Jumbo. (ps-3). 1991. pap. 2.99 (*0-553-15936-4*) Bantam.
—Jessica & the Money Mix-Up. (gr. 4-7). 1990. pap. 3.50 (*0-553-15798-1*) Bantam.
—Jessica & the Secret Star. (gr. 4-7). 1991. pap. 3.50 (*0-553-15911-9*) Bantam.
—Jessica the Nerd. 1992. pap. 3.50 (*0-553-15963-1*) Bantam.
—Jessica the Thief. (gr. 4-7). 1993. pap. 3.25 (*0-553-48054-5*) Bantam.
—Jessica the TV Star. (ps-3). 1991. pap. 2.99 (*0-553-15850-3*) Bantam.
—Jessica's Big Mistake. (ps-3). 1990. pap. 2.99 (*0-553-15799-X*) Bantam.
—Jessica's Mermaid. (gr. 1 up). 1994. pap. 2.99 (*0-553-48118-5*) Bantam.
—Jessica's New Look. (gr. 4-7). 1991. pap. 3.25 (*0-553-15869-4*) Bantam.
—Jessica's Snobby. 1992. pap. 2.99 (*0-553-15922-4*) Bantam.
—Jessica's Zoo Adventure. (ps-3). 1990. pap. 2.99 (*0-553-15802-3*) Bantam.
—Kidnapped by a Cult. 1992. pap. 3.25 (*0-553-29228-5*) Bantam.
—Left-Out Elizabeth. (ps-3). 1992. pap. 2.99 (*0-553-15921-6*) Bantam.
—Lila's April Fool. (gr. 4 up). 1994. pap. 2.99 (*0-553-48114-2*) Bantam.
—Lila's Secret, No. 6. 1990. pap. 2.99 (*0-553-15773-6*) Bantam.
—Lila's Story. (gr. 7 up). 1989. pap. 3.50 (*0-553-28296-4*) Bantam.
—Lois Strikes Back. 1990. pap. 3.25 (*0-553-15789-2*) Bantam.
—Mademoiselle Jessica. (gr. 4-7). 1991. pap. 3.25 (*0-553-15849-X*) Bantam.
—Mary Is Missing. 1990. pap. 3.25 (*0-553-15778-7*) Bantam.
—New Elizabeth. 1990. pap. 2.99 (*0-553-28385-5*) Bantam.
—The New Girl. 1987. pap. 3.50 (*0-553-15660-8*) Bantam.
—Patty's Last Dance. (gr. 4-7). 1993. pap. 3.25 (*0-553-48052-9*) Bantam.
—Power Play. 176p. (Orig.). (gr. 7 up). 1985. pap. 2.99 (*0-553-27493-7*) Bantam.
Rock Star's Girl. (gr. 9-12). 1991. pap. 3.25 (*0-553-28841-5*) Bantam.
—Rosa's Lie. 1992. pap. 3.50 (*0-553-29227-7*) Bantam.
—Second Best. 1988. pap. 3.25 (*0-553-15665-9*) Bantam.
—She's Not What She Seems. 1993. pap. 3.25 (*0-553-29849-6*) Bantam.
—Steven's Bride. 1992. pap. 3.25 (*0-553-29229-3*) Bantam.
—Sweet Valley. 1992. pap. 3.50 (*0-553-29230-7*) Bantam.
—Sweet Valley. 1992. pap. 3.25 (*0-553-29231-5*) Bantam.
—Sweet Valley Kids, No. 28: Elizabeth Meets Her Hero. (ps-3). 1992. pap. 2.99 (*0-553-15924-0*) Bantam.
—Sweet Valley Slumber Party. (gr. 4-7). 1991. pap. 2.99 (*0-553-15934-8*) Bantam.
—Together Forever. 176p. (gr. 7 up). 1988. pap. 2.95 (*0-553-26863-5*, Pub. by J C B Mohr GW) Bantam.
—The Twins' Little Sister. (gr. 4-7). 1991. pap. 3.25 (*0-553-15899-6*) Bantam.
—Won't Someone Help Anna? (gr. 4-7). 1993. pap. 3.25 (*0-553-48056-1*) Bantam.
Pascal, Francine & Stewart, Molly M. Jessica's Cat Trick. (ps-3). 1990. pap. 2.99 (*0-553-15768-X*, Skylark) Bantam.
Pascal, Francine, created by. Promises Broken. 176p. (gr. 7-12). 1986. pap. 2.95 (*0-553-26156-8*) Bantam.
—Tender Promises. 176p. (Orig.). (gr. 7-12). 1986. pap. 2.95 (*0-553-25812-5*, Starfire) Bantam.
Paterson, Katherine. The Great Gilly Hopkins. LC 77-27075. 192p. (gr. 5-9). 1987. pap. 3.95 (*0-06-440201-0*, Trophy) HarpC Child Bks.
Patterson, Francine. Koko's Kitten. 1993. pap. 4.95 (*0-590-44425-5*) Scholastic Inc.
Pavloff, George. A Rainbow for Suzanne. (Illus.). 72p. (gr. 1 up). 1991. 12.95 (*0-931474-40-X*) TBW Bks.
Pearson, Kit. A Handful of Time. (Illus.). 192p. (gr. 3-7). 1991. pap. 3.95 (*0-14-032268-X*, Puffin) Puffin Bks.
—Looking at the Moon. 224p. (gr. 5-9). 1992. 12.95 (*0-670-84097-1*) Viking Child Bks.
Peck, Harry T. The Adventures of Mabel. Rountree, Harry, illus. Cabaniss, Anne M., intro. by. (Illus.). 236p. (gr. k-5). 1986. Repr. of 1896 ed. 19.95 (*0-9616844-0-2*) Greenhouse Pub.
Peck, Richard. Representing Super Doll. 192p. (gr. 7 up). 1989. pap. 2.95 (*0-440-97362-7*, LFL) Dell.

Peek, Merle. Mary Wore Her Red Dress, & Henry Wore His Green Sneakers. 1988. pap. 5.95 (*0-89919-701-9*, Clarion Bks) HM.
Peel, John. Where in America Is Carmen Sandiego? (Illus.). 32p. (gr. 2-5). 1992. write for info. (*0-307-15859-4*, 15859) Western Pub.
Peet, Bill. Encore for Eleanor. Peet, Bill, illus. 48p. (gr. k-3). 1981. 13.45 (*0-395-29860-1*); pap. 3.95 (*0-317-18520-9*) HM.
—Pamela Camel. Peet, Bill, illus. LC 83-18594. 32p. (gr. k-3). 1984. 14.45 (*0-395-35975-9*, 5-93025) HM.
Pellowski, Michael J. Is That Arabella, No. 9. LC 91-58614. (Illus.). 128p. (Orig.). (gr. 4-8). 1992. pap. 2.99 (*1-56282-190-3*) Hyprn Child.
Pelton, Jeanette. Don't Call Me Emmy! 94p. (gr. 5-8). 1991. pap. 3.50 (*1-879564-02-5*) Long Acre Pub.
Penelope's Pen Pal. (Illus.). 40p. (gr. k-5). 1994. pap. 4.95 (*0-685-71583-3*, 519) W Gladden Found.
Peters, Lisa W. Tania's Trolls. 64p. (gr. 3). 1992. pap. 2.99 (*0-380-71444-2*, Camelot Young) Avon.
Pfeffer, Susan B. April Upstairs. 1992. pap. 3.50 (*0-553-15939-9*) Bantam.
—Darcy Downstairs. (ps-3). 1993. pap. 3.50 (*0-553-15942-9*) Bantam.
—Just Between Us. Tomei, Lorna, illus. LC 79-53606. 128p. (gr. 4-6). 1980. pap. 9.89 (*0-385-28594-9*) Delacorte.
—Kid Power. 121p. (gr. 3-7). 1988. pap. 2.95 (*0-590-42607-9*) Scholastic Inc.
—Make Believe. 160p. (gr. 4-7). 1993. 14.95 (*0-8050-1754-2*, Bks Young Read) H Holt & Co.
—Sara Kate Super Kid1. Hankins, Suzanne, illus. (gr. 2-4). 1994. 14.95 (*0-8050-3147-2*) H Holt & Co.
—Sara Kate Super Kid2. 1995. write for info. (*0-8050-3148-0*) H Holt & Co.
—The Sebastian Sisters: Evvie at Sixteen. (gr. 5 up). 1988. 13.95 (*0-553-05475-9*, Starfire) Bantam.
—Sebastian Sisters: Meg at Sixteen. 1991. pap. 3.50 (*0-553-28836-9*) Bantam.
—Sybil at Sixteen. (gr. 7 up). 1990. pap. 2.95 (*0-553-28614-5*, Starfire) Bantam.
—Turning Thirteen. (gr. 6-8). 1989. pap. 2.75 (*0-590-40765-1*, Apple Paperbacks) Scholastic Inc.
Phillips, Michael & Pella, Judith. Sea to Shining Sea. 304p. (Orig.). 1992. pap. 8.99 (*1-55661-227-3*) Bethany Hse.
Pike, Christopher. Slumber Party. 1985. pap. 3.50 (*0-590-43014-9*) Scholastic Inc.
Pinkwater, Jill. Buffalo Brenda. LC 88-31929. 192p. (gr. 5-9). 1989. SBE 14.95 (*0-02-774631-3*, Macmillan Child Bk) Macmillan Child Grp.
Pitcher, Valerie. Anya Astern, Come Down from the Sky. LC 90-71860. 44p. (gr. 6). 1991. 6.95 (*1-55523-412-7*) Winston-Derek.
Pittman, Helena C. Counting Jennie. (ps-3). 14.95 (*0-87614-745-7*) Carolrhoda Bks.
Plantos, T. Heather Hits Her First Home Run. (Illus.). 24p. (ps-8). 1989. pap. 4.95 (*0-88753-185-7*, Pub. by Black Moss Pr CN) Firefly Bks Ltd.
Pleasant Company Staff. My Trip to Felicity's Williamsburg: An American Girl's Journal. (Illus.). 14p. (gr. 2-5). 1991. 4.95 (*1-56247-028-0*); map, 2 sides & 6 panels 1.95 (*1-56247-029-9*) Pleasant Co.
Plummer, Louise. My Name Is Susan Smith, The 5 Is Silent. 1993. pap. 3.50 (*0-440-21451-3*) Dell.
Polacco, Patricia. The Keeping Quilt. Polacco, Patricia, illus. 32p. (ps-3). 1988. pap. 14.95 3-pc. bdg. (*0-671-64963-9*, S&S BFYR) S&S Trade.
Polakiewicz, David M. & Mellen, Stephanie. The Teeny Tiny Voice. Mellen, Stephanie, illus. 52p. (Orig.). (gr. k-12). 1992. pap. 5.95 (*1-878040-08-1*) Personal Growth.
Pollinger, Eileen. Stacey. LC 87-71604. 176p. (Orig.). (gr. 9-12). 1987. pap. 3.99 (*0-87123-943-4*) Bethany Hse.
Porter, Connie. Addy Learns a Lesson. Rosales, Melodye, illus. 70p. (Orig.). (gr. 2-5). 1993. PLB 12.95 (*1-56247-078-7*); pap. 5.95 (*1-56247-077-9*) Pleasant Co.
—Meet Addy. Rosales, Melodye, illus. 69p. (Orig.). (gr. 2-5). 1993. PLB 12.95 (*1-56247-076-0*); pap. 5.95 (*1-56247-075-2*) Pleasant Co.
Porter, Eleanor H. Pollyanna. (Orig.). (gr. k-6). 1987. pap. 4.95 (*0-440-45985-0*, Pub. by Yearling Classics) Dell.
—Pollyanna. 1988. pap. 2.25 (*0-14-035023-3*, Puffin) Puffin Bks.
—Pollyanna. (Illus.). (gr. k-9). 1987. pap. 2.95 (*0-590-44769-6*) Scholastic Inc.
—Pollyanna Grows Up. 308p. (gr. 4 up). 1980. Repr. of 1915 ed. lib. bdg. 20.95 (*0-89968-193-X*) Lightyear.
—Pollyanna Grows Up. 272p. (gr. 5 up). 1989. pap. 2.99 (*0-14-035024-1*, Puffin) Puffin Bks.
Porter, Gene S. A Girl of the Limberlost. (Orig.). (gr. 3-7). 1986. pap. 4.95 (*0-440-43090-9*, Pub. by Yearling Classics) Dell.
Porters, Eleanor H. Pollyanna. 176p. (gr. 6 up). 1993. pap. 5.95 (*1-55748-296-9*) Barbour & Co.
Portlock, Rob. Noon on the Moon. Portlock, Rob, illus. LC 93-19202. 32p. (Orig.). (ps-2). 1993. pap. 4.99 (*0-8308-1903-7*, 1903) InterVarsity.
Poulin, Stephane. Could You Stop Josephine? LC 88-50260. (Illus.). 24p. (ps-3). 1988. 12.95 (*0-88776-216-6*); pap. 6.95 (*0-88776-227-1*) Tundra Bks.
Powell, Mary C. Queen of the Air: The Story of Katherine Stinson. Petrick, Thomas W., ed. Driscoll, Martin, illus. 124p. (Orig.). (gr. 4-7). 1994. pap. 8.95 perfect bdg. (*1-880384-07-8*) Coldwater Pr.
Powell, Randy. Is Kissing a Girl Who Smokes Like Licking an Ashtray? 1994. pap. 3.95 (*0-374-43627-4*) FS&G.
Prenzlau, Sheryl. B. Y. Times Kid Sisters: Running Away, No. 5. Binyamini-Ariel, Liat, illus. Zakon, Miriam, contrib. by. (Illus.). 120p. (Orig.). (gr. 2-6). 1993. pap. 5.95 (*1-56871-018-6*) Targum Pr.
—B.Y. Times Kid Sisters, No. 6: Teacher's Pet. (Illus.). 115p. (Orig.). (gr. 3-7). 1993. pap. 6.95 (*1-56871-025-9*) Targum Pr.
Priebe, Vel. Wendy's Gift. Priebe, Vel, illus. 24p. (Orig.). (ps-2). 1988. pap. 1.50 (*0-919797-67-9*) Kindred Pr.
Prochazkova, Iva. The Season of Secret Wishes. Crawford, Elizabeth D., tr. from GER. LC 89-45291. 208p. (gr. 4-8). 1989. 12.95 (*0-688-08735-3*) Lothrop.
Qualey, Marsha. Everybody's Daughter. 208p. (gr. 6 up). 1993. pap. 4.95 (*0-395-65746-6*) HM.
Rabe, Berniece. The Balancing Girl. Hoban, Lillian, illus. LC 80-22100. 32p. (ps-2). 1988. pap. 4.99 (*0-525-44364-9*, 0382-120, DCB) Dutton Child Bks.
Radlauer, Ruth S. Breakfast by Molly. (gr. k-3). 1991. pap. 2.25 (*0-671-74021-0*, Little Simon) S&S Trade.
—Molly. (Illus.). (gr. k-3). 1991. pap. 2.50 (*0-671-74018-0*, Little Simon) S&S Trade.
—Molly at the Library. (Illus.). (gr. k-3). 1991. pap. 2.25 (*0-671-74019-9*, Little Simon) S&S Trade.
—Molly Goes Hiking. McCully, Emily A., illus. LC 86-18761. 32p. (ps-3). 1987. pap. 10.95 (*0-671-66860-9*) S&S Trade.
—Molly Goes Hiking. (Illus.). (gr. k-3). 1991. pap. 2.25 (*0-671-74022-9*, Little Simon) S&S Trade.
Rand, Suzanne. All American Girl. 208p. (Orig.). (gr. 7-12). 1986. pap. 2.50 (*0-553-25427-8*) Bantam.
Ransom. Sabrina. 1993. pap. 2.75 (*0-685-66034-6*) Scholastic Inc.
Ransom, Candice F. Emily, No. 11. 368p. (Orig.). (gr. 7 up). 1985. pap. 2.95 (*0-590-33410-7*) Scholastic Inc.
—Fourteen & Holding. 1990. pap. 2.95 (*0-590-43740-2*) Scholastic Inc.
—Nicole, No. 19. 224p. (Orig.). (gr. 7 up). 1986. pap. 2.25 (*0-590-40049-5*) Scholastic Inc.
—Thirteen. 192p. (Orig.). (gr. 6-8). 1990. pap. 2.95 (*0-590-43742-9*) Scholastic Inc.
Raskin, Ellen. Spectacles. 2nd ed. Raskin, Ellen, illus. LC 88-10363. 48p. (gr. k-4). 1988. pap. 4.95 (*0-689-71271-5*, Aladdin) Macmillan Child Grp.
Rawlings, Marjorie K. The Secret River. 3rd, facsimile ed. Weisgard, Leonard, illus. Bigham, Julia S., intro. by. (Illus.). 57p. (gr. 3-6). 1987. Repr. of 1955 ed. PLB 12.95 (*0-935259-02-3*) San Marco Bk.
Reed, Ronald F. Rebecca: A Novel for Children. Ham, Lisa K., illus. 37p. (Orig.). (ps-4). 1990. pap. 8.00 (*0-924303-00-X*) TX Wesleyan Coll.
Reiss, Johanna. The Upstairs Room. LC 77-187940. 192p. (gr. 7 up). 1987. pap. 3.95 (*0-06-447043-1*, Trophy) HarpC Child Bks.
Rema. 1991. 12.95 (*1-56062-090-0*) CIS Comm.
Robbins, Trina. Catswalk: The Growing of a Girl. (Illus.). 83p. (Orig.). (gr. 3-6). 1990. pap. 17.95 (*0-89087-608-8*) Celestial Arts.
Roberts, Willo D. Caroline, No. 7. 368p. (gr. 7 up). 1984. pap. 2.95 (*0-590-33239-2*) Scholastic Inc.
—The Girl with the Silver Eyes. 208p. (gr. 3-7). 1991. pap. 2.95 (*0-590-44248-1*) Scholastic Inc.
Robins, Joan. Addie's Bad Day. Truesdell, Sue, illus. 32p. (ps-2). 1994. pap. 3.50 (*0-685-71217-6*, Trophy) HarpC Child Bks.
Robinson, Nancy K. Angela & the Broken Heart. 1991. 12.95 (*0-590-43212-5*, Scholastic Hardcover) Scholastic Inc.
—Angela & the Broken Heart. 144p. 1992. pap. 2.95 (*0-590-43211-7*, Apple Paperbacks) Scholastic Inc.
—Oh Honestly, Angela! 128p. (gr. 4-6). 1985. pap. 10.95 (*0-590-41287-6*) Scholastic Inc.
—Oh Honestly, Angela! Williams, Richard, illus. 128p. 1991. pap. 2.95 (*0-590-44902-8*, Apple Paperbacks) Scholastic Inc.
—Veronica Knows Best. 128p. (gr. 4-6). 1987. pap. 10.95 (*0-590-40509-8*) Scholastic Inc.
—Veronica Knows Best. 160p. 1992. pap. 2.95 (*0-590-44900-1*, Apple Paperbacks) Scholastic Inc.
—Veronica Meets Her Match. (gr. 3-7). 1990. 12.95 (*0-590-41512-3*, Scholastic Hardcover) Scholastic Inc.
—Veronica Meets Her Match. 128p. 1992. pap. 2.95 (*0-590-45766-7*, Apple Paperbacks) Scholastic Inc.
—Veronica the Show-Off. LC 85-4483. 128p. (gr. 3-6). 1984. SBE 13.95 (*0-02-777360-4*, Four Winds) Macmillan Child Grp.
Rock, Gail. Addie & the King of Hearts. (gr. 4-6). 1986. pap. 2.50 (*0-440-40076-7*, YB) Dell.
—A Dream for Addie. (gr. 4-6). 1986. pap. 2.50 (*0-440-42151-9*, YB) Dell.
Rocklin, Joanne. Sonia Begonia. 112p. (gr. 3-7). 1987. pap. 2.50 (*0-380-70307-6*, Camelot) Avon.
Rockwell, Thomas. How to Fight a Girl. 144p. (gr. k-6). 1988. pap. 3.50 (*0-440-40111-9*, YB) Dell.
Roddy, Lee. The Gold Train Bandits. 176p. (Orig.). (gr. 3-8). 1992. pap. 5.99 (*1-55661-211-7*) Bethany Hse.
Rodgers, Mary. Summer Switch. LC 79-2690. 192p. (gr. 5 up). 1984. pap. 3.50 (*0-06-440140-5*, Trophy) HarpC Child Bks.
Rodowsky, Colby. Fitchett's Folly. LC 86-31859. 160p. (gr. 4 up). 1987. 15.00 (*0-374-32342-9*) FS&G.
—Julie's Daughter. (gr. 7 up). 1992. pap. 3.95 (*0-374-43973-7*) FS&G.
—Sydney, Herself. 176p. (gr. 7 up). 1989. 15.00 (*0-374-30649-4*) FS&G.
—Sydney, Herself. 1993. pap. 4.50 (*0-374-47390-0*) FS&G.
Rody, Lee. The Desperate Search. LC 88-63476. 160p. (gr. 2-6). 1989. pap. 5.99 (*1-55661-027-0*) Bethany Hse.
Roessel, Monty. Kinaalda: A Navajo Girl Grows Up. (gr. 4-7). 1993. pap. 3.95 (*0-8225-9641-5*) Lerner Pubns.
Rohmer, Harriet & Olivarez, Anna, eds. The Adventures of Connie & Diego Audiocassette. (SPA & ENG.). 1989. 8.95 (*0-89239-051-4*) Childrens Book Pr.
Romer, Ken. Dorothy & the Wooden Soldiers. (Illus.). 52p. (gr. 3-7). 1987. Colorina book with story. pap. 3.95 (*0-932458-35-1*) Star Rover.
Roos, Stephen. And the Winner Is... DeRosa, Dee, illus. LC 88-27519. 128p. (gr. 3-7). 1989. SBE 13.95 (*0-689-31300-4*, Atheneum Child Bk) Macmillan Child Grp.
Rosofsky, Iris. Miriam. LC 87-45859. 192p. (gr. 7 up). 1988. HarpC Child Bks.
Ross, Rhea B. Bet's on, Lizzie Bingman! 1992. pap. 3.95 (*0-395-64375-9*) HM.
Ross, Tony. I Want My Potty. LC 86-10568. (Illus.). 24p. (ps-k). 1986. 9.95 (*0-916291-08-1*, Cranky Nell Bk) Kane-Miller Bk.
Ross, William M. The Ticket to Harmony. 94p. (Orig.). (gr. 4-9). 1993. pap. 4.95 (*1-883787-00-9*, Dist. by Baker & Taylor Bks.); incl. tchr's. activities packet 7.95 (*1-883787-01-7*) Trolley Car.
Rostkowski, Margaret I. After the Dancing Days. LC 85-45810. 240p. (gr. 6-9). 1986. PLB 14.89 (*0-06-025078-X*) HarpC Child Bks.
Roth-Hano, Renee. Touch Wood: A Girlhood in Occupied France. LC 87-34326. 304p. (gr. 5-9). 1988. SBE 16.95 (*0-02-777340-X*, Four Winds) Macmillan Child Grp.
Rotner, Shelley & Kreisler, Ken. Ocean Day. Rotner, Shelley, illus. LC 92-6114. 32p. (ps-1). 1993. RSBE 14.95 (*0-02-777886-X*, Macmillan Child Bk) Macmillan Child Grp.
Rubin, Susan G. Emily Good as Gold. 192p. (gr. 5-9). 1993. 10.95 (*0-15-276632-4*, Browndeer Pr); pap. 3.95 (*0-15-276633-2*, Browndeer Pr) HarBrace.
Ruckman, Ivy. Melba the Brain. (gr. 4-7). 1991. pap. 3.25 (*0-440-40423-1*) Dell.
Russo, Marisabina. Why Do Grown-Ups Have All the Fun? Russo, Marisabina, illus. LC 86-4644. 24p. (ps-3). 1987. 11.75 (*0-688-06625-9*); PLB 11.88 (*0-688-06626-7*) Greenwillow.
Ryan, Mary C. The Voice from the Mendelsohns' Maple. 144p. (gr. 5). 1992. pap. 3.50 (*0-380-71140-0*, Camelot) Avon.
Rylant, Cynthia. A Blue-Eyed Daisy. (gr. k-6). 1987. pap. 3.50 (*0-440-40927-6*, YB) Dell.
—Missing May. LC 91-23303. 96p. (gr. 6 up). 1992. 13. 95 (*0-531-05996-0*); lib. bdg. 13.99 (*0-531-08596-1*) Orchard Bks Watts.
Sachar, Louis. Someday Angeline. 160p. (gr. 2-6). 1990. Repr. of 1983 ed. PLB 12.99 (*0-679-90412-3*) Knopf Bks Yng Read.
Sachs, Marilyn. Amy & Laura. 1993. pap. 2.95 (*0-590-44623-1*) Scholastic Inc.
—Dorrie's Book. 144p. 1991. pap. 2.95 (*0-380-76139-4*, Camelot) Avon.
—The Fat Girl. (gr. 7 up). 1986. pap. 2.75 (*0-440-92468-5*, LFL) Dell.
—Fran Ellen's House. 96p. 1989. pap. 2.75 (*0-380-70583-4*, Camelot) Avon.
—A Pocket Full of Seeds. (Illus.). 144p. (gr. 5 up). 1994. pap. 3.99 (*0-14-036593-1*) Puffin Bks.
St. John, Chris. Golden Girl. (gr. 5 up). 1989. pap. 3.50 (*0-449-13454-7*) Fawcett.
Salem, Lynn & Stewart, Josie. Taking Care of Rosie. Pendergast, Holly, illus. 8p. (gr. 1). 1992. pap. 3.50 (*1-880612-05-4*) Seedling Pubns.
Salter, Heidi. Taddy McFinley & the Great Grey Grimly. Thatch, Nancy R., ed. Salter, Heidi, illus. Melton, David, intro. by. LC 89-31820. (Illus.). 26p. (gr. 3-8). 1989. PLB 14.95 (*0-933849-21-4*) Landmark Edns.
Saltman, Judith. Goldie & the Sea. LaFave, Kim, illus. 32p. (ps-2). 1991. 4.95 (*0-88899-133-9*, Pub. by Groundwood-Douglas & McIntyre CN) Firefly Bks Ltd.
Sanchez, J. L. & Pacheco, M. A. La Nina Invisible (The Invisible Girl) Wensell, Uliises, illus. (SPA.). 42p. (gr. k-2). 1988. write for info. (*84-372-1829-2*) Santillana.
Sappenfield, John R. Liza & Mother Rug Bear. 1993. 7.95 (*0-8062-4842-4*) Carlton.
Sauer, Julia L. Fog Magic. Ward, Lynd, illus. 128p. (gr. 5-9). 1986. pap. 3.99 (*0-14-032163-2*, Puffin) Puffin Bks.
Saunders, Susan. Kate the Boss. (gr. 4-7). 1990. pap. 2.50 (*0-590-43189-7*) Scholastic Inc.
—Kate's Camp-Out. 96p. (Orig.). (gr. 3-7). 1988. pap. 2.50 (*0-590-41337-6*, Apple Paperbacks) Scholastic Inc.
—Kate's Surprise. 96p. (Orig.). (gr. 4-6). 1987. pap. 2.50 (*0-590-40643-4*, Apple Paperbacks) Scholastic Inc.
—Kate's Surprise Visitor. (gr. 5-7). 1990. pap. 2.50 (*0-590-42819-5*) Scholastic Inc.
—Lauren's Afterschool Job. 128p. (gr. 3-7). 1990. pap. 2.75 (*0-590-43928-6*) Scholastic Inc.
—Lauren's Double Disaster. (gr. 4-7). 1991. pap. 2.75 (*0-590-43926-X*) Scholastic Inc.
—Lauren's New Address. 1990. pap. 2.50 (*0-590-43191-9*) Scholastic Inc.
—Lauren's Sleepover Exchange. 112p. (gr. 3-7). 1989. pap. 2.50 (*0-590-41697-9*, Apple Paperbacks) Scholastic Inc.

—Stephanie Strikes Back. 96p. (gr. 3-7). 1988. pap. 2.50 (*0-590-41694-4*, Apple Paperbacks) Scholastic Inc.
Savitch, Jessica & Savitch, Stephanie. Ever after Ever. Staller, Laurie, et al, illus. 68p. (ps-7). 1993. write for info. (*1-883331-03-X*) Anderie Poetry.
Saylor, Melissa, illus. Mary Wore Her Red Dress Big Book. (ps-2). 1988. pap. text ed. 14.00 (*0-922053-17-0*) N Edge Res.
Scharer, Niko. Emily's House. Fitzgerald, Joanne, illus. 24p. 1992. pap. 4.95 (*0-88899-158-4*, Pub. by Groundwood-Douglas & McIntyre CN) Firefly Bks Ltd.
Schiller, Alexandra. The Raisin Eater. Martin, John J. & Schiller, Alexandra, eds. Schiller, Alexandra, illus. 44p. (gr. 3-4). 1984. 5.00 (*0-9618682-0-1*) A Schiller.
Schmidt, Annie M. Minnie. Salway, Lance, tr. from FRE. Sather, Kay, illus. LC 93-35924. 192p. (gr. 8-12). 1994. 14.95 (*1-57131-601-9*); pap. 6.95 (*1-57131-600-0*) Milkweed Ed.
Schnur, Steven. Hannah & Cyclops. (gr. 4-7). 1990. pap. 2.75 (*0-553-15796-5*) Bantam.
Schreiber, Perel. B.Y. High, No. 2: Making Her Mark. 160p. (gr. 7-10). 1994. 9.95 (*1-56871-040-2*) Targum Pr.
Schulte, Elaine. Cara's Beach Party. 144p. (Orig.). 1993. pap. 4.99 (*1-55661-252-4*) Bethany Hse.
—Here Comes Ginger. LC 88-38763. (gr. 3-7). 1989. pap. 4.99 (*1-55513-770-9*, Chariot Bks) Chariot Family.
—Here Comes Ginger. 1989. write for info. Prog Bapt Pub.
Schulte, Elaine L. Tricia's Got Trouble. (gr. 4-7). 1993. pap. 4.99 (*1-55661-253-2*) Bethany Hse.
Schurfranz, Vivian. Josie. 224p. (Orig.). (gr. 6-10). 1988. pap. 2.75 (*0-590-41207-8*) Scholastic Inc.
—Julie. 1993. pap. 2.50 (*0-590-42021-6*) Scholastic Inc.
—Rachel, No. 21. 224p. (Orig.). (gr. 7 up). 1986. pap. 2.50 (*0-590-40394-X*) Scholastic Inc.
Scott, Mike. Judith & the Traveller. 143p. (gr. 8-11). 1991. pap. 7.95 (*0-86327-299-1*, Pub. by Wolfhound Pr EIRE) Dufour.
Sebestyen, Ouida. The Girl in the Box: The Diary of Anne Frank. 160p. (gr. 7 up). 1988. 12.95 (*0-316-77935-0*, Joy St Bks) Little.
—Words by Heart. LC 78-27847. (gr. 5 up). 1979. 15.95 (*0-316-77931-8*, Joy St Bks) Little.
Segal, Lore. Tell Me a Mitzi. LC 69-14980. (Illus.). 40p. (ps-3). 1991. pap. 5.95 (*0-374-47502-4*) FS&G.
Selway, Martina. Don't Forget to Write. Selway, Martina, illus. LC 91-28430. 32p. (ps-2). 1994. pap. 4.95 (*0-8249-8636-9*, Ideals Child) Hambleton-Hill.
Seymour, Ruth G. & Grofe, Anne C. Sandy of Siam. 1992. 6.95 (*0-533-09667-7*) Vantage.
Sharmat, Marjorie W. Getting Closer. (Orig.). (gr. k-12). 1987. pap. 2.50 (*0-440-92828-1*, LFL) Dell.
—Getting Something on Maggie Marmelstein. Shecter, Ben, illus. LC 78-157895. 110p. (gr. 4-6). 1971. PLB 13.89 (*0-06-025552-8*) HarpC Child Bks.
—I Saw Him First. LC 82-14839. 128p. (gr. 7 up). 1983. pap. 12.95 (*0-385-29243-0*) Delacorte.
—Nobody Knows How Scared I Am. (Orig.). (gr. k-12). 1987. pap. 2.50 (*0-440-96267-6*, LFL) Dell.
Sharmat, Mitchell. A Girl of Many Parts. (Orig.). (gr. k-12). 1988. pap. 2.95 (*0-440-20209-4*, LFL) Dell.
Shaw, Janet. Changes for Kirsten: A Winter Story. Graef, Renee, illus. 65p. (Orig.). (gr. 2-5). 1988. pap. 5.95 (*0-937295-45-0*) Pleasant Co.
—Changes for Kirsten: A Winter Story. Thieme, Jeanne, ed. Graef, Renee, illus. 72p. (gr. 2-5). 1988. PLB 12.95 (*0-937295-94-9*) Pleasant Co.
—Happy Birthday Kirsten! A Springtime Story. Thieme, Jeanne, ed. Graef, Renne, illus. 72p. (gr. 2-5). 1987. PLB 12.95 (*0-937295-88-4*); pap. 5.95 (*0-937295-33-7*) Pleasant Co.
—Kirsten, 6 bks. Graef, Renee & Lackner, Paul, illus. 400p. (gr. 2-5). 1991. Boxed Set. lib. bdg. 74.95 (*1-56247-049-3*); Boxed Set. pap. 34.95 (*0-937295-76-0*) Pleasant Co.
—Kirsten Learns a Lesson: A School Story. Thieme, Jeanne, ed. Graef, Renee, illus. 72p. (gr. 2-5). 1986. PLB 12.95 (*0-937295-82-5*); pap. 5.95 (*0-937295-10-8*) Pleasant Co.
—Kirsten Saves the Day: A Summer Story. Thieme, Jeanne, ed. Graef, Renee, illus. 72p. (gr. 2-5). 1988. PLB 12.95 (*0-937295-91-4*); pap. 5.95 (*0-937295-39-6*) Pleasant Co.
—Kirsten's Surprise: A Christmas Story. Thieme, Jeanne, ed. Graef, Renee, illus. 72p. (gr. 2-5). 1986. PLB 12.95 (*0-937295-85-X*); pap. 5.95 (*0-937295-19-1*) Pleasant Co.
Shaw, Janet B. Meet Kirsten: An American Girl. Thieme, Jeanne, ed. Graef, Renee, illus. 72p. (gr. 2-5). 1986. PLB 12.95 (*0-937295-79-5*); pap. 5.95 (*0-937295-01-9*) Pleasant Co.
Sheldon, Dyan & De Lyman, Alicia G. Jack & Alice. (Illus.). 32p. (gr. k-2). 1992. 15.95 (*0-09-173638-2*, Pub. by Hutchinson UK) Trafalgar.
Shreve, Susan. Lily & the Runaway Baby. Truesdell, Sue, illus. LC 87-4684. 64p. (gr. 2-4). 1987. (Random Juv) Random Bks Yng Read.
Shulman. Karen Strange. 1991. 0.85 (*0-8050-2028-4*) H Holt & Co.
Shura, Mary F. Gentle Annie. (gr. 4-7). 1991. 12.95 (*0-590-44367-4*) Scholastic Inc.
—Jessica, No. 6. 368p. (gr. 7 up). 1984. pap. 2.95 (*0-590-33242-2*) Scholastic Inc.
—Polly Panic. 128p. (gr. 5 up). 1992. pap. 3.50 (*0-380-71334-9*, Camelot) Avon.
Sidney, Margaret. Phronsie Pepper. 250p. 1992. Repr. PLB 25.95x (*0-89966-967-0*) Buccaneer Bks.
Siegal, Aranka. Grace in the Wilderness: After the Liberation, 1945-1948. LC 85-20415. 220p. (gr. 5 up). 1985. 15.00 (*0-374-32760-2*) FS&G.
Silsbe, Brenda. Winning the Girl of the Sea. Priestley, Alice, illus. 32p. (gr. k-2). 1994. PLB 15.95 (*1-55037-313-7*, Pub. by Annick CN); pap. 5.95 (*1-55037-312-9*, Pub. by Annick CN) Firefly Bks Ltd.
Silverman, Erica. Fixing the Crack of Dawn. Spiedel, Sandra, illus. LC 93-33807. 32p. (gr. k-3). 1994. PLB 13.95 (*0-8167-3458-5*); pap. text ed. 3.95 (*0-8167-3459-3*) BrdgeWater.
Simon, Shirley. Get Lost, Becka! Gregorich, Barbara, ed. (Illus.). 32p. (gr. k-2). 1992. pap. 3.95 (*0-88743-411-8*, 06063) Sch Zone Pub Co.
Simpson, Holly. One Step Away. (gr. 6 up). 1989. pap. 2.95 (*0-449-14593-X*) Fawcett.
Skinner, David. You Must Kiss a Whale. LC 90-24079. 176p. (gr. 5-9). 1993. pap. 4.95 (*0-671-86697-4*, Half Moon Bks) S&S Trade.
Slightly Off-Center Writers Group, Ltd. Staff. A Girl Named Whoopie. (Illus.). 60p. (gr. 4-6). 1994. pap. 6.95 (*1-56721-080-5*) Twnty-Fifth Cent Pr.
—Girl Next Door. (Illus.). 60p. (gr. 4-6). 1994. pap. 6.95 (*1-56721-066-X*) Twnty-Fifth Cent Pr.
—Little Susan. (Illus.). 48p. (gr. 3-5). 1994. pap. 6.95 (*1-56721-079-1*) Twnty-Fifth Cent Pr.
Smith, Anne W. Blue Denim Blues. 128p. (gr. 6 up). 1988. pap. 2.75 (*0-380-70379-3*, Flare) Avon.
Smith, Kaitlin M. Sally Writes a Letter to Santa Claus. Smith, Kaitlin M., illus. 15p. (gr. 1-4). 1992. pap. 10.95 (*1-56606-005-2*) Bradley Mann.
—Skating with Katie. Smith, Kaitlin M., illus. 15p. (gr. k-3). 1992. pap. 17.95 (*1-895583-19-5*) MAYA Pubs.
Smith, Matthew V. Billy Jean. Smith, Matthew V., illus. 14p. (gr. k-3). 1993. pap. 9.95 (*1-895583-57-8*) MAYA Pubs.
—An Invitation to Sally's. Smith, Matthew V., illus. 18p. (gr. k-3). 1992. pap. 12.95 (*1-895583-07-1*) MAYA Pubs.
Snyder, Zilpha K. Janie's Private Eyes. (ps-3). 1989. 14.95 (*0-385-30146-4*) Doubleday.
Soike, Thomas E. Harriet's Chariot. LC 91-91311. 30p. (gr. 4-6). 1991. write for info. (*0-9631201-0-7*) T E Soike.
Solomon, Joan. Bobbi's New Year. (Illus.). 32p. (gr. 3-5). 1993. 12.95 (*0-237-60114-1*, Pub. by Evans Bros Ltd) Trafalgar.
Sommer, Susan. And I'm Stuck with Joseph. Moon, Ivan, illus. LC 84-611. 120p. (gr. 7-9). 1984. pap. 3.95 (*0-8361-3356-0*) Herald Pr.
Sonnenmark, Laura A. The Lie. 176p. 1992. 13.95 (*0-590-44740-8*, Scholastic Hardcover) Scholastic Inc.
Sorensen, Virginia. Plain Girl. Krush, Beth & Krush, Joe, illus. 151p. (gr. 3-7). 1988. pap. 5.95 (*0-15-262437-6*, Voyager Bks) HarBrace.
—Plain Girl. (gr. 3-7). 17.75 (*0-8446-6398-0*) Peter Smith.
Southall, Ivan. Rachel. LC 86-45509. 147p. (gr. 5 up). 1986. 14.00 (*0-374-36163-0*) FS&G.
Speregen, Devra. Blossom's Family Album. (gr. 4-7). 1993. pap. 4.95 (*0-590-47234-8*) Scholastic Inc.
Springer, Nancy. They're All Named Wildfire. LC 88 27497. 112p. (gr. 4 up). 1989. SBE 13.95 (*0-689-31450-7*, Atheneum Child Bk) Macmillan Child Grp.
Spyri, Johanna. Heidi. LC 85-13292. (gr. 5 up). 1964. pap. 1.95 (*0-8049-0018-3*, CL-18) Airmont.
—Heidi. LC 85-13292. (Illus.). (ps-3). 1985. 1.98 (*0-517-30779-0*) Random Hse Value.
—Heidi. Saunders, Susan, adapted by. Rowland, Jada, illus. LC 87-15466. 48p. (gr. 2-5). 1988. PLB 12.89 (*0-8167-1215-8*); pap. 3.95 (*0-8167-1216-6*) Troll Assocs.
—Heidi. 1988. 12.99 (*0-517-61814-1*) Random Hse Value.
—Heidi. (gr. 4 up). 1990. pap. 3.50 (*0-440-40357-X*) Dell.
—Heidi. 352p. 1992. 9.49 (*0-8167-2550-0*); pap. 2.95 (*0-8167-2551-9*) Troll Assocs.
Stahl, Hilda. Elizabeth Gail & Double Trouble, No. 11. 128p. 1989. pap. 4.99 (*0-8423-0801-6*) Tyndale.
—Elizabeth Gail & the Dangerous Double, No. 4. 128p. (gr. 5 up). 1988. 4.99 (*0-8423-0742-7*) Tyndale.
—Elizabeth Gail & the Great Canoe Conspiracy. 1991. PLB 4.99 (*0-8423-0815-6*) Tyndale.
—Elizabeth Gail & the Holiday Mystery. 128p. 1989. pap. 4.99 (*0-8423-0802-4*) Tyndale.
—Elizabeth Gail & the Music Camp Romance. 128p. 1989. pap. 4.99 (*0-8423-0808-3*) Tyndale.
—Elizabeth Gail & the Secret Love, No. 16. 128p. pap. 4.99 (*0-8423-0809-1*) Tyndale.
—Elizabeth Gail & the Strange Birthday Party. 128p. 1989. pap. 4.99 (*0-8423-0803-2*) Tyndale.
—Elizabeth Gail & the Terrifying News. 128p. 1989. pap. 4.99 (*0-8423-0812-1*) Tyndale.
—Elizabeth Gail & Time for Love. 128p. 1989. pap. 4.99 (*0-8423-0813-X*) Tyndale.
—Elizabeth Gail & Trouble at Sandhill Ranch. 128p. 1989. pap. 4.99 (*0-8423-0814-8*) Tyndale.
—Elizabeth Gail & Trouble from the Past. 128p. 1989. pap. 4.99 (*0-8423-0804-0*) Tyndale.
—Hannah & the Special 4th of July. 160p. (gr. 4-7). 1992. pap. 3.99 (*0-89107-660-3*) Crossway Bks.
—A Made-over Chelsea. 160p. (gr. 4-7). 1992. pap. 3.99 (*0-89107-683-2*) Crossway Bks.
Stanek, Lou W. Katy Did. 192p. (Orig.). (gr. 6 up). 1992. pap. 2.99 (*0-380-76170-X*, Flare) Avon.
Starring Sally J. Freedman: As Herself. (gr. 4 up). 1978. pap. 4.50 (*0-440-98239-1*) Dell.
Steig, William. Brave Irene. LC 86-80957. (Illus.). 32p. (ps-4). 1986. 17.00 (*0-374-30947-7*) FS&G.
—Ile d'Abel. (FRE.). 144p. (gr. 5-10). 1982. pap. 8.95 (*2-07-033156-3*) Schoenhof.
—Irene, la Valiente: Brave Irene. Mlawer, Teresa, tr. (SPA., Illus.). 32p. (ps-3). 1991. 16.00 (*0-374-30948-5*) FS&G.
—Irene, la Valiente: Brave Irene. (gr. 4-7). 1993. pap. 4.95 (*0-374-43620-7*) FS&G.
Stein, Gertrude. The World Is Round. Arenson, Roberta, illus. LC 93-562. 160p. 1993. Repr. of 1939 ed. 6.00 (*1-56957-905-9*) Shambhala Pubns.
Stephenson, Ruth M. Abigail. (Illus.). 32p. (Orig.). (ps-5). 1988. pap. 7.95 (*0-945705-00-X*) Young Life Pub.
Steptoe, John. Mufaro's Beautiful Daughters: An African Tale. Steptoe, John, illus. LC 84-7158. 32p. (gr. k-3). 1987. 16.00 (*0-688-04045-4*); PLB 15.93 (*0-688-04046-2*) Lothrop.
Steptoe, John L. Marcia. (Illus.). 80p. (gr. 7 up). 1991. pap. 3.99 (*0-14-034669-4*, Puffin) Puffin Bks.
Stevens, Carla. Lily & Miss Liberty. 80p. 1992. 12.95 (*0-590-44919-2*, Scholastic Hardcover) Scholastic Inc.
Stevenson, Laura C. Happily after All. 240p. 1993. pap. 3.50 (*0-380-71549-X*, Camelot) Avon.
Stiles, Martha B. Sarah the Dragon Lady. 96p. (gr. 3-7). 1988. pap. 2.75 (*0-380-70471-4*, Camelot) Avon.
Stine, R. L. The Girlfriend. 176p. 1991. pap. 3.50 (*0-590-44333-X*, Point) Scholastic Inc.
—The New Girl. (Orig.). (gr. 6-9). 1991. pap. 3.99 (*0-671-74649-9*, Archway) PB.
—The New Girl. large type ed. (gr. 6 up). Date not set. PLB 14.60 (*0-8368-1157-7*) Gareth Stevens Inc.
Stolz, Mary. Ivy Larkin. LC 86-4819. 226p. (gr. 7 up). 1986. 13.95 (*0-15-239366-8*, HB Juv Bks) HarBrace.
—Ivy Larkin. (gr. k-6). 1989. pap. 3.25 (*0-440-40175-5*, YB) Dell.
Storr, Catherine. Polly & the Wolf Again. large type ed. 1993. 16.95 (*0-7451-2035-0*, Galaxy Child Lrg Print) Chivers N Amer.
Strauss, Linda L. Alice Elizabeth Loved Surprises. (Illus.). 32p. (gr. k-3). 1993. pap. 2.99 (*0-87406-653-0*) Willowisp Pr.
Streatfeild, Noel. Gemma Alone. (Orig.). (gr. k-6). 1987. pap. 3.25 (*0-440-42865-3*, Yearling) Dell.
Streatfield, Noel. Ballet Shoes. Goode, Diane, illus. LC 89-24390. 288p. (gr. 4-9). 1993. pap. 3.99 (*0-679-84759-6*, Bullseye Bks) Random Bks Yng Read.
Stucky, Naomi R. Sara's Summer. 144p. (Orig.). (gr. 6-12). 1990. pap. 5.95 (*0-8361-3534-2*) Herald Pr.
Sullivan, Ann. Molly Maguire: Wide Receiver. 112p. (Orig.). 1992. pap. 2.99 (*0-380-76114-9*, Camelot) Avon.
Summer of Dreams: The Story of a World's Fair Girl. 64p. (gr. 4-6). 1993. incl. jacket 5.95 (*0-382-24335-8*); lib. bdg. 7.95 (*0-382-24332-3*); pap. 3.95 (*0-382-24354-4*) Silver Burdett Pr.
Suzanne, Jamie. The New Girl. large type ed. Pascal, Francine, created by. 105p. (gr. 7-12). 1990. Repr. of 1987 ed. 9.95 (*1-55905-069-1*) Grey Castle.
Swallow, Pamela C. Leave It to Christy. 160p. (gr. 5-8). 1987. 14.95 (*0-399-21482-8*, Putnam) Putnam Pub Group.
Sypher, Lucy J. The Edge of Nowhere. Abel, Ray, illus. 211p. (gr. 3-7). 1991. pap. 3.95 (*0-14-034550-7*, Puffin) Puffin Bks.
Szeker, Cyndy. Cyndy Szekere's Kisses. (ps). 1993. 2.25 (*0-307-06121-3*, Golden Pr) Western Pub.
Szekeres, Cyndy. Cyndy Szekeres' Hugs. 1990. bds. write for info. (*0-307-06108-6*, Golden Pr) Western Pub.
Taha, Karen T. Gift for Tia Rosa. (gr. 4-7). 1991. pap. 2.99 (*0-553-15978-X*) Bantam.
Taylor, Theodore. Maria. 80p. (gr. 4). 1993. pap. 3.50 (*0-380-72120-1*, Camelot) Avon.
Terris, Susan. Nell's Quilt. 176p. (gr. 7 up). 1988. pap. 2.50 (*0-590-41914-5*) Scholastic Inc.
Thesman, Jean. The Birthday Girls: I'm Not Telling. 128p. (Orig.). (gr. 4-8). 1992. pap. 2.99 (*0-380-76523-3*, Camelot) Avon.
—The Birthday Girls: Mirror, Mirror. 128p. (Orig.). (gr. 4-8). 1992. pap. 2.99 (*0-380-76271-4*, Camelot) Avon.
—The Birthday Girls: Who Am I, Anyway? 128p. (Orig.). (gr. 4-8). 1992. pap. 2.99 (*0-380-76524-1*, Camelot) Avon.
—The Last April Dancers. 224p. (gr. 7 up). 1987. 13.45 (*0-395-43024-0*) HM.
—Rachel Chance. 180p. (gr. 5-9). 1990. 13.45 (*0-395-50934-3*) HM.
—Rachel Chance. 192p. 1992. pap. 3.50 (*0-380-71378-0*, Flare) Avon.
—The Rain Catchers. 192p. 1992. pap. 3.50 (*0-380-71711-5*, Flare) Avon.
—The Whitney Cousins: Erin. 144p. (gr. 4-5). 1990. pap. 2.95 (*0-380-75875-X*, Flare) Avon.
—The Whitney Cousins: Heather. 160p. (gr. 4-5). 1990. pap. 2.95 (*0-380-75869-5*, Flare) Avon.
Thompson, Kay. Eloise. Knight, Hilary, illus. LC 55-11039. (gr. k-6). 1969. pap. 15.95 jacketed (*0-671-22350-X*, S&S BFYR) S&S Trade.
—Eloise. (Illus.). 66p. 1991. Repr. PLB 21.95x (*0-89966-833-X*) Buccaneer Bks.
—Eloise. (FRE.). 116p. (gr. 5-10). 1982. pap. 10.95 (*2-07-033223-3*) Schoenhof.

Thompson, R. Jenny's Neighbours. (Illus.). 24p. (ps-8). 1987. 12.95 (0-920303-73-0, Pub. by Annick CN); pap. 4.95 (0-920303-70-6, Pub. by Annick CN) Firefly Bks Ltd.
Thompson, Richard. Effie's Bath. Fernandes, Eugenie, illus. 1990. 14.95 (1-550370-55-3, Pub. by Annick CN); pap. 5.95 (1-550370-52-9, Pub. by Annick CN) Firefly Bks Ltd.
Tiffault, Benette W. A Quilt for Elizabeth. McConnell, Mary, illus. 32p. (Orig.). (gr. 2-5). 1992. pap. 8.95x (1-56123-034-0) Centering Corp.
Tilden, Ruth. Hazel Rides a Horse. (ps-3). 1994. 9.95 (0-307-17609-6, Artsts Writrs) Western Pub.
Tilly, Nancy. The Golden Girl. (gr. k-12). 1988. pap. 2.95 (0-440-20095-4, LFL) Dell.
Titherington, Jeanne. Where Are You Going, Emma? (Illus.). 24p. (ps-1). 1988. 11.95 (0-688-07081-7); lib. bdg. 11.88 (0-688-07082-5) Greenwillow.
Tomey, Ingrid. Savage Carrot. LC 93-7273. 192p. (gr. 5-7). 1993. SBE 14.95 (0-684-19633-6, Scribners Young Read) Macmillan Child Grp.
Travers, Pamela L. Mary Poppins & the House Next Door. Shepard, Mary, illus. (gr. 4 up). 1989. 12.95 (0-385-29749-1) Delacorte.
Tripp, Valerie. Changes for Felicity: A Winter Story. (Illus.). (gr. 2-5). 1992. PLB 12.95 (1-56247-038-8); pap. 5.95 (1-56247-037-X) Pleasant Co.
—Changes for Molly: A Winter Story. Backes, Nick, illus. 67p. (Orig.). (gr. 2-5). 1988. 12.95 (0-937295-96-5); pap. 5.95 (0-937295-49-3) Pleasant Co.
—Changes for Samantha: A Winter Story. Thieme, Jeanne, ed. Grace, Robert & Niles, Nancy, illus. 72p. (Orig.). (gr. 2-5). 1988. PLB 12.95 (0-937295-95-7); pap. 5.95 (0-937295-47-7) Pleasant Co.
—Felicity, 6 bks. (Illus.). (gr. 2-5). 1991. Boxed Set. PLB 74.95 (1-56247-045-0); Boxed Set. pap. 34.95 (1-56247-044-2) Pleasant Co.
—Felicity Saves the Day: A Summer Story. (Illus.). (gr. 2-5). 1992. PLB 12.95 (1-56247-035-3); pap. 5.95 (1-56247-034-5) Pleasant Co.
—Happy Birthday Felicity! A Springtime Story. (Illus.). 69p. (gr. 2-5). 1992. PLB 12.95 (1-56247-032-9); pap. 5.95 (1-56247-031-0) Pleasant Co.
—Happy Birthday Samantha! A Springtime Story. Thieme, Jeanne, ed. Grace, Robert & Niles, Nancy, illus. 72p. (gr. 2-5). 1987. PLB 12.95 (0-937295-89-2); pap. 5.95 (0-937295-35-3) Pleasant Co.
—Meet Molly: An American Girl. Thieme, Jeanne, ed. Payne, C. F., illus. 72p. (gr. 2-5). 1986. PLB 12.95 (0-937295-81-7); pap. 5.95 (0-937295-07-8) Pleasant Co.
—Molly, 6 bks. (Illus.). 432p. (gr. 2-5). 1991. Boxed Set. lib. bdg. 74.95 (1-56247-051-5); Boxed Set. pap. 34.95 (0-937295-78-7) Pleasant Co.
—Molly Learns a Lesson: A School Story. Thieme, Jeanne, ed. Payne, C. F., illus. 72p. (gr. 2-5). 1986. PLB 12.95 (0-937295-84-1); pap. 5.95 (0-937295-16-7) Pleasant Co.
—Molly Saves the Day: A Summer Story. Thieme, Jeanne, ed. Backes, Nick, illus. 72p. (gr. 2-5). 1988. PLB 12.95 (0-937295-93-0); pap. 5.95 (0-937295-43-4) Pleasant Co.
—Samantha Saves the Day: A Summer Story. Thieme, Jeanne, ed. Grace, Robert & Niles, Nancy, illus. 72p. (gr. 2-5). 1988. PLB 12.95 (0-937295-92-2); pap. 5.95 (0-937295-41-8) Pleasant Co.
Tritten, Charles. Heidi Grows Up. (gr. k-6). 1988. pap. 4.95 (0-440-40107-0, Pub. by Yearling Classics) Dell.
Turner, Ann. Nettie's Trip South. Himler, Ronald, illus. LC 86-18135. 32p. (gr. 1-5). 1987. SBE 13.95 (0-02-789240-9, Macmillan Child Bk) Macmillan Child Grp.
Tusa, Tricia. Stay Away from the Junkyard! Tusa, Tricia, illus. LC 87-15274. 32p. (gr. k-3). 1988. RSBE 14.95 (0-02-789541-6, Macmillan Child Bk) Macmillan Child Grp.
Udry, Janice M. What Mary Jo Shared. Sayles, Elizabeth, illus. 32p. (ps-3). 1991. pap. 3.95 (0-590-43757-7) Scholastic Inc.
Ulitsch, Laura. Lil Guard Angel. Crowder, Debbie, illus. LC 91-67738. 64p. 1993. pap. 8.00 (1-56002-137-3, Univ Edtns) Aegina Pr.
Vahnina, Galya. Den Meda: Annie's Day. Maidenberg, E., illus. (RUS.). 114p. (Orig.). 1987. pap. 14.95 (0-934393-16-8) Rector Pr.
Vail, Virginia. Happy Trails. Bode, Daniel, illus. LC 89-30584. 128p. (gr. 4-6). 1990. PLB 9.89 (0-8167-1627-7); pap. text ed. 2.95 (0-8167-1628-5) Troll Assocs.
—Riding Home. Bode, Daniel, illus. LC 89-34548. 128p. (gr. 4-6). 1990. PLB 9.89 (0-8167-1661-7); pap. text ed. 2.95 (0-8167-1662-5) Troll Assocs.
VanKempen, Corrigan. Emily Umily. (Illus.). 24p. (ps-8). 1984. 12.95 (0-920236-96-0, Pub. by Annick CN); pap. 4.95 (0-920236-99-5, Pub. by Annick CN) Firefly Bks Ltd.
Vaughan, Ruby, et al. Out of Ruby's Treasure Chest. Berger, Kathleen B. & Hutchison, Laura, illus. 32p. (Orig.). 1993. pap. 5.95 (1-881617-11-4) Teapot Tales.
Verzuh, Julie W. From the Heart of Lizzie. (gr. 7 up). 1983. pap. 7.50 (0-87839-039-1) North Star.
Vitalo, Valerie. Sweet Dreams, Sarah. DeVito, Pam, illus. LC 88-51277. 54p. (ps-4). 1989. 6.95 (0-932433-56-1) Windswept Hse.
Voigt, Cynthia. Seventeen Against the Dealer. LC 88-27488. 192p. (gr. 7 up). 1989. SBE 15.95 (0-689-31497-3, Atheneum Child Bk) Macmillan Child Grp.
Waas, Uli. Where's Molly? Waas, Uli, illus. Lanning, Rosemary, tr. from GER. LC 93-19736. (Illus.). 48p. (gr. 1-3). 1993. 12.95 (1-55858-229-0); lib. bdg. 12.88 (1-55858-230-4) North-South Bks NYC.
Walsh, Jill P. Grace. 1994. pap. 5.95 (0-374-42792-5, Sunburst) FS&G.
Walter, Mildred P. Girl on the Outside. (gr. 4-7). 1993. pap. 3.25 (0-590-46091-9) Scholastic Inc.
Ward, Cindy. Cookie's Week. De Paola, Tomie, illus. 32p. (ps-1). 1988. 11.95 (0-399-21498-4, Putnam) Putnam Pub Group.
—Cookie's Week. De Paola, Tomie, illus. 32p. (ps). 1992. pap. 4.95 (0-399-22406-8, Putnam) Putnam Pub Group.
Waterson, Betty. Starring Quincy Rumpel. 115p. (gr. 3-5). 1991. pap. 5.95 (0-88899-048-0, Pub. by Groundwood-Douglas & McIntyre CN) Firefly Bks Ltd.
Waterton, Betty. Morris Rumpel & the Wings of Icarus. 108p. (gr. 3-5). 1991. pap. 5.95 (0-88899-099-5, Pub. by Groundwood-Douglas & McIntyre CN) Firefly Bks Ltd.
—Quincy Rumpel. 96p. (gr. 3-5). 1991. pap. 5.95 (0-88899-036-7, Pub. by Groundwood-Douglas & McIntyre CN) Firefly Bks Ltd.
—Quincy Rumpel, P. I. 116p. (gr. 3-5). 1991. pap. 5.95 (0-88899-081-2, Pub. by Groundwood-Douglas & McIntyre CN) Firefly Bks Ltd.
Weber, Ane, et al. The Girl Who Wanted to Be Beautiful. French, Marty & Christman, Michael, illus. 26p. (ps up). 1986. Book & Cassette. 7.95 (1-55578-109-8) Worlds Wonder.
—The Girl Who Wanted to Be Beautiful. French, Marty & Christman, Michael, illus. 26p. (ps up). 1988. incl. cassette 7.95 (1-55578-915-3) Worlds Wonder.
—The Girl With the Pop-Up Garden. French, Marty, et al, illus. 26p. (ps up). 1986. Book & Cassette. 7.95 (1-55578-102-0) Worlds Wonder.
Wechter, Nell W. Taffy of Torpedo Junction. Sparks, Mary W., illus. LC 57-9312. 134p. (gr. 5-9). 1990. pap. 7.95 (0-89587-076-2) Blair.
Weedn, Flavia. Flavia & the Velveteen Rabbit. (Illus.). 52p. 1990. 16.00 (0-929632-10-9) Applause Inc.
Wells. Noisy Nora. 1993. pap. 28.67 (0-590-71436-8) Scholastic Inc.
Wells, Rosemary. Chut, Chut, Charlotte! (FRE.). 1990. pap. 8.95 (2-07-039001-2) Schoenhof.
—Noisy Nora. Wells, Rosemary, illus. 40p. (ps-2). 1980. pap. 3.99 (0-8037-6193-7) Dial Bks Young.
Wersba, Barbara. Just Be Gorgeous. LC 87-45858. 160p. (gr. 7 up). 1988. HarpC Child Bks.
—Just Be Gorgeous. 1991. pap. 3.25 (0-440-20810-6) Dell.
Westell, Kerry. Amanda's Book. Ohi, Ruth, illus. 24p. (ps-1). 1991. PLB 15.95 (1-55037-185-1, Pub. by Annick CN); pap. 5.95 (1-55037-182-7, Pub. by Annick CN) Firefly Bks Ltd.
Wetterer, Margaret. Kate Shelley & the Midnight Express. Ritz, Karen, illus. 48p. (gr. k-4). 1990. PLB 14.95 (0-87614-425-3) Carolrhoda Bks.
Weyn, Suzanne. The Makeover Club. 128p. (gr. 7 up). 1986. pap. 2.50 (0-380-75007-4, Flare) Avon.
—Patty's Big Problem. 96p. (gr. 2-5). 1992. pap. 2.75 (0-590-43564-7, Little Apple) Scholastic Inc.
—Stepping Out. Iskowitz, Joel, illus. LC 89-30586. 96p. (gr. 3-5). 1990. PLB 9.89 (0-8167-1619-6); pap. text ed. 2.95 (0-8167-1620-X) Troll Assocs.
—A Twist of Fate. Iskowitz, Joel, illus. LC 89-30585. 96p. (gr. 3-5). 1990. pap. text ed. 2.95 (0-8167-1622-6) Troll Assocs.
Whelan, Gloria. Next Spring an Oriole. Johnson, Pamela, illus. LC 87-4910. 64p. (gr. 2-4). 1987. lib. bdg. 6.99 (0-394-99125-7); pap. 2.99 (0-394-89125-2) Random Bks Yng Read.
White, Ruth. Sweet Creek Holler. 168p. (gr. 7 up). 1988. 16.00 (0-374-37360-4) FS&G.
Wickens, Elaine. Anna Day & the O-Ring. (Illus.). 24p. (ps-3). 1994. saddlestitched 6.95 (1-55583-252-0, Alyson Wonderland) Alyson Pubns.
Widman, Christine. The Willow Umbrella. Stock, Catherine, illus. LC 91-10989. 32p. (gr. k-3). 1993. RSBE 14.95 (0-02-792760-1, Macmillan Child Bk) Macmillan Child Grp.
Wiggan, Kate D. Rebecca of Sunnybrook Farm. 320p. 1992. 9.49 (0-8167-2556-X); pap. 2.95 (0-8167-2557-8) Troll Assocs.
Wiggin, Eric & Wiggin, Kate D. Rebecca of Sunnybrook Farm: The Girl. 256p. (gr. 4-7). 1990. 9.95 (1-56121-004-8) Wolgemuth & Hyatt.
—Rebecca of Sunnybrook Farm: The Woman. 256p. (gr. 6 up). 1991. pap. 9.95 (1-56121-013-7) Wolgemuth & Hyatt.
Wiggin, Kate D. Rebecca of Sunnybrook Farm. 239p. 1981. Repr. PLB 22.95x (0-89966-354-0) Buccaneer Bks.
—Rebecca of Sunnybrook Farm. (gr. k-6). 1986. pap. 4.95 (0-440-47533-3, Pub. by Yearling Classics) Dell.
—Rebecca of Sunnybrook Farm. 288p. (gr. 5-8). 1993. pap. 2.99 (0-87406-655-7) Willowisp Pr.
Wilder, Laura Ingalls. Little House Books: Little House in the Big Woods; Little House on the Prairie; On the Banks of Plum Creek; By the Shores of Silver Lake; The Long Winter, 5 vols. Williams, Garth, illus. (gr. 3-7). 1993. pap. 19.75 Boxed Set (0-06-440476-5, Trophy) HarpC Child Bks.
Wiley, Margaret. Melinda Zone. 1994. pap. 3.50 (0-440-21902-7) Dell.
Willard, Nancy. The Highest Hit. McCully, Emily A., illus. LC 77-88970. (gr. 4-7). 1978. 6.95 (0-15-234278-8, HB Juv Bks) HarBrace.
Williams-Garcia, Rita. Blue Tights. LC 87-17156. 160p. (gr. 7 up). 1988. 12.95 (0-525-67234-6, Lodestar Bks) Dutton Child Bks.
Wilson, Johniece M. Poor Girl, Rich Girl. (gr. 4-7). 1994. pap. 3.25 (0-590-44733-5) Scholastic Inc.
Wilson, Nancy H. Bringing Nettie Back. LC 92-7640. 160p. (gr. 3-7). 1992. SBE 13.95 (0-02-793075-0, Macmillan Child Bk) Macmillan Child Grp.
Wine, Jeanine. Silly Tillie. LC 87-38311. 32p. (gr. k-3). 1990. 12.95 (0-934672-62-8) Good Bks PA.
Winthrop, Elizabeth. Belinda's Hurricane. Watson, Wendy, illus. 64p. (gr. 2-6). 1989. pap. 3.95 (0-14-032985-4, Puffin) Puffin Bks.
Wittmann, Patricia. Scrabble Creek. Poydar, Nancy, illus. LC 92-10810. 32p. (gr. k-3). 1993. RSBE 14.95 (0-02-793225-7, Macmillan Child Bk) Macmillan Child Grp.
Wolde, Gunilla. Betsy's Fixing Day. Wolde, Gunilla, illus. LC 78-50056. 24p. (ps). 1990. 4.95 (0-394-83781-9) Random Bks Yng Read.
Wolff, Tobias. The Barracks Thief: And Selected Stories. 1989. pap. 7.95 (0-553-34675-X) Bantam.
Wolitzer, Meg. Operation: Save the Teacher: Saturday Night Toast. 128p. (Orig.). 1993. pap. 3.50 (0-380-76462-8, Camelot) Avon.
—Operation: Save the Teacher: Tuesday Night Pie. 128p. (Orig.). 1993. pap. 3.50 (0-380-76460-1, Camelot) Avon.
Wood, Audrey. Heckedy Peg. (ps-3). 1992. pap. write for info. (0-15-233679-6, HB Juv Bks) HarBrace.
—Silly Sally. LC 91-15839. (ps-3). 1994. pap. 19.95 (0-15-200072-0, HB Juv Bks) HarBrace.
Wooldridge, Rhoda. Hanah's Mill. LC 83-26515. (Illus.). (gr. 4-6). 1984. pap. 8.00 (0-8309-0386-0) Ind Pr MO.
Wooley, Catherine. Ginnie & Geneva. (gr. 5-7). 1988. pap. 3.95 (0-317-69651-3, Puffin) Puffin Bks.
Wright, Betty R. The Pike River Phantom. 160p. (gr. 3-7). 1990. pap. 3.25 (0-590-42808-X) Scholastic Inc.
—Rosie & the Dance of the Dinosaurs. LC 89-2083. 112p. (gr. 3-7). 1989. 14.95 (0-8234-0782-9) Holiday.
Wyeth, Sharon D. Annie K's Theater: The Dinosaur Tooth. (gr. 3-6). 1990. pap. 2.75 (0-553-15815-5) Bantam.
Yarbrough, Camille. The Shimmershine Queens. 128p. (gr. 5-8). 1989. 14.95 (0-399-21465-8, Putnam) Putnam Pub Group.
Yates, Elizabeth. Carolina's Courage. 131p. (Orig.). (gr. 2-4). 1989. pap. 4.95 (0-89084-482-8) Bob Jones Univ Pr.
Yeo. The Girl in the Window. 1993. pap. 2.75 (0-590-43153-6) Scholastic Inc.
York, Carol B. Miss Know It All Returns. 96p. 1985. pap. 2.50 (0-553-15351-X, Skylark) Bantam.
Young, Karen E. The Days of Josie. 19p. (gr. k). 1992. pap. text ed. 23.00 big bk. (1-56843-013-2); pap. text ed. 4.50 (1-56843-063-9) BGR Pub.
Zeplin, Zeno. Discovery on Dusty Creek. Jones, Judy, illus. 112p. (gr. 3-6). 1994. 14.95 (1-877740-23-3); pap. 7.95 (1-877740-24-1) Nel-Mar Pub.
Ziefert, Harriet. Penny Goes to the Movies. Rader, Laura, illus. 32p. (ps-3). 1990. pap. 3.50 (0-14-054225-6, Puffin) Puffin Bks.
Zolotow, Charlotte. I Like to Be Little. Blegvad, Erik, illus. LC 83-45056. 32p. (gr. k-4). 1987. (Crowell Jr Bks); PLB 13.89 (0-690-04674-X, Crowell Jr Bks) HarpC Child Bks.
—It's Not Fair. Reissue. ed. Du Bois, William P., illus. LC 76-3387. 32p. (gr. k-3). 1976. 13.00 (0-06-026934-0); PLB 12.89 (0-06-026935-9) HarpC Child Bks.
—Not a Little Monkey. Chessare, Michele, illus. LC 88-21457. 32p. (ps-1). 1989. HarpC Child Bks.
Zwicker, Linda. The Hope Chest of Arabella. (gr. 4-7). 1993. pap. 3.99 (0-553-48036-7) Bantam.

GIRLS' CLUBS–FICTION

Simpson, Juwairiah J. The Four Daughters of Yusuf the Dairy Farmer. Middendorf, Nancy, illus. 40p. (Orig.). (gr. 1-4). 1894. pap. 3.75 (0-89259-056-4) Am Trust Pubns.

GLACIAL EPOCH

Stille, Darlene R. Ice Age. LC 90-37681. (Illus.). 48p. (gr. k-4). 1990. PLB 12.85 (0-516-01107-3); pap. 4.95 (0-516-41107-1) Childrens.

GLACIAL EPOCH–FICTION

Kaye, Marilyn. Camp Sunnyside Friends, No. 15: Christmas Break. 128p. (Orig.). 1991. pap. 2.99 (0-380-76553-5, Camelot) Avon.
Thesman, Jean. When Does the Fun Start? 160p. (Orig.). 1991. pap. 3.50 (0-380-76129-7, Flare) Avon.

GLACIER NATIONAL PARK

Markert, Jenny. Glacier National Park. (SPA & ENG.). (gr. 2-6). 1992. PLB 15.95 (0-89565-858-5) Childs World.
Petersen, David. Waterton - Glacier International Peace Park. LC 92-9208. (Illus.). 48p. (gr. k-4). 1992. PLB 12.85 (0-516-01946-5) Childrens.
Radlauer, Ruth S. Glacier National Park. updated ed. LC 76-48993. (Illus.). 48p. (gr. 3 up). 1977. pap. 4.95 (0-516-47491-X) Childrens.
Root, Phyllis. Glacier. LC 88-18945. (Illus.). 48p. (gr. 4-5). 1988. text ed. 13.95 (0-89686-408-1, Crestwood Hse) Macmillan Child Grp.

GLACIERS

Bender, Lionel. Glacier. LC 88-50369. (Illus.). 32p. (gr. 3-5). 1989. PLB 11.90 (0-531-10647-0) Watts.

Bramwell, Martyn. Glaciers & Ice Caps. (Illus.). 32p. (gr. 5-8). 1994. PLB write for info. (*0-531-14302-3*) Watts.
George, Michael. Glaciers. LC 90-22068. (Illus.). 40p. (gr. 3-5). 1992. PLB 18.95 (*0-88682-401-X*) Creative Ed.
—Glaciers. 40p. (gr. 4-7). 1993. 15.95 (*1-56846-061-9*) Creat Editions.
Georges, D. V. Glaciers. LC 85-30884. (Illus.). 48p. (gr. k-4). 1986. PLB 12.85 (*0-516-01281-9*); pap. 4.95 (*0-516-41281-7*) Childrens.
Markert, Jenny. Glaciers & Icebergs. LC 92-32498. (ENG & SPA.). (gr. 2-6). 1993. 15.95 (*1-56766-004-5*) Childs World.
Patchett, Lynne. Glaciers. Burns, Robert, illus. LC 91-45080. 32p. (gr. 4-6). 1993. PLB 11.59 (*0-8167-2751-1*); pap. text ed. 3.95 (*0-8167-2752-X*) Troll Assocs.
Radlauer, Ruth & Gitkin, Lisa S. The Power of Ice. Gitkin, Lisa S., photos by. LC 85-5714. (Illus.). 48p. (gr. 3 up). 1985. pap. 4.95 (*0-516-47839-7*) Childrens.
Simon, Seymour. Icebergs & Glaciers. LC 86-18142. (Illus.). 32p. (ps-3). 1987. 14.95 (*0-688-06186-9*); lib. bdg. 14.88 (*0-688-06187-7*, Morrow Jr Bks) Morrow Jr Bks.
Tangborn, Wendell V. Glaciers. rev. ed. Simont, Marc, illus. LC 87-45306. 32p. (ps-3). 1988. pap. 4.50 (*0-06-445076-7*, Trophy) HarpC Child Bks.
—Glaciers. rev. ed. Simont, Marc, illus. LC 87-47696. 32p. (ps-3). 1988. (Crowell Jr Bks); (Crowell Jr Bks) HarpC Child Bks.
Walker, Sally M. Glaciers: Ice on the Move. (Illus.). 48p. (gr. 3-6). 1990. PLB 19.95 (*0-87614-373-7*) Carolrhoda Bks.
Wilson, Barbara. Icebergs & Glaciers. Leon, Vicki, ed. (Illus.). 40p. (Orig.). (gr. 5 up). 1990. pap. 7.95 (*0-918303-23-0*) Blake Pub.

GLANDS

Connelly, John P. You're Too Sweet. (gr. 4-9). 1968. 9.95 (*0-8392-1173-2*) Astor-Honor.

GLASS

Borowsky, Irvin J. Artists Confronting the Inconceivable. (Illus.). 136p. 1992. 100.00 (*1-881060-00-4*) Am Interfaith.
Chandler, Jane. Glass. Stefoff, Rebecca, ed. Barber, Ed, photos by. LC 91-18191. (Illus.). 32p. (gr. 3-5). 1991. PLB 15.93 (*1-56074-004-3*) Garrett Ed Corp.
Daniel, Jamie & Bonar, Veronica. Coping with - Glass Trash. Kenyon, Tony, illus. LC 93-32483. 32p. (gr. 2 up). 1994. PLB 17.27 (*0-8368-1057-0*) Gareth Stevens Inc.
Kolb, Kenneth E. & Kolb, Doris K. Glass: Its Many Facets. LC 86-32785. (Illus.). 64p. (gr. 6 up). 1988. lib. bdg. 15.95 (*0-89490-150-8*) Enslow Pubs.
Paterson, Alan J. How Glass Is Made. (Illus.). 32p. (gr. 7 up). 1986. 12.95x (*0-8160-0038-7*) Facts on File.
Songhurst, Hazel. Glass. LC 92-45670. (Illus.). 32p. (gr. 3-6). 1993. 13.95 (*1-56847-042-8*) Thomson Lrning.

GLASS, STAINED

see Glass Painting and Staining

GLASS MANUFACTURE

Healock, William, et al. Harry Northwood: The Wheeling Years, 1901-1925. (Illus.). 207p. (Orig.). 1991. 42.95 (*0-915410-75-3*, 3091); pap. 34.95 (*0-915410-74-5*, 3090) Antique Pubns.
Mitgutsch, Ali. From Sand to Glass. Mitgutsch, Ali, illus. LC 80-29572. 24p. (ps-3). 1981. PLB 10.95 (*0-87614-162-9*) Carolrhoda Bks.

GLASS PAINTING AND STAINING

Corning Museum of Glass Staff. Masterpieces of Glass from the Corning Museum: 24 Ready-to-Mail Full-Color. 12p. (Orig.). (gr. 7 up). 1984. pap. 3.95 (*0-486-24526-8*) Dover.
Healock, William, et al. Harry Northwood: The Wheeling Years, 1901-1925. (Illus.). 207p. (Orig.). 1991. 42.95 (*0-915410-75-3*, 3091); pap. 34.95 (*0-915410-74-5*, 3090) Antique Pubns.

GLASSWARE

Healock, William, et al. Harry Northwood: The Wheeling Years, 1901-1925. (Illus.). 207p. (Orig.). 1991. 42.95 (*0-915410-75-3*, 3091); pap. 34.95 (*0-915410-74-5*, 3090) Antique Pubns.

GLENN, JOHN HERSCHEL, 1921-

Cole, Michael D. John Glenn: Astronaut & Senator. LC 92-20285. (Illus.). 104p. (gr. 6 up). 1993. lib. bdg. 17.95 (*0-89490-413-2*) Enslow Pubs.

GLIDERS (AERONAUTICS)

Will-Harris, Toni. Hang Gliding. (Illus.). 48p. (gr. 3-6). 1992. PLB 12.95 (*1-56065-058-3*) Capstone Pr.

GLIDING AND SOARING

Barrett, Norman S. Hang Gliding. Franklin Watts Ltd., ed. LC 86-51223. (Illus.). 32p. (ps-9). 1988. 11.90 (*0-531-10350-1*) Watts.
Penzler, Otto. Hang Gliding: Riding the Wind. LC 75-21843. (Illus.). 32p. (gr. 5-10). 1976. PLB 10.79 (*0-89375-008-5*); pap. 2.95 (*0-89375-024-7*) Troll Assocs.

GLOBES

Broekel, Ray. Maps & Globes. LC 83-7509. (Illus.). 48p. (gr. k-4). 1983. PLB 12.85 (*0-516-01695-4*); pap. 4.95 (*0-516-41695-2*) Childrens.
Edson, Ann & Insel, Eunice. Reading Maps, Globes, Charts, Graphs. (gr. 4-6). 1982. wkbk. 2.69 (*0-89525-175-2*) Ed Activities.
Knowlton, Jack. Maps & Globes. Barton, Harriett, illus. LC 85-47537. 48p. (gr. 2-5). 1985. 15.00 (*0-690-04457-7*, Crowell Jr Bks); PLB 14.89 (*0-690-04459-3*) HarpC Child Bks.
—Maps & Globes. Barton, Harriett, illus. LC 85-47537. 48p. (gr. 2-5). 1986. pap. 4.95 (*0-06-446049-5*, Trophy) HarpC Child Bks.
Sipiera, Paul. Globes. LC 91-15869. 48p. (gr. k-4). 1991. PLB 12.85 (*0-516-01124-3*); pap. 4.95 (*0-516-41124-1*) Childrens.
Wolfman, Ira. My World & Globe. LC 91-50382. (Illus.). 64p. (Orig.). 1991. pap. 12.95 (*0-89480-993-8*, 1993) Workman Pub.

GLOSSARIES

see also names of language or subject with the subdivision dictionaries, e.g. English Language–Dictionaries; Chemistry–Dictionaries

GNOMES

see Fairies

GO KARTS

see Karts and Karting

GOATS

Burton, Jane. Caper the Kid. Burton, Jane, photos by. LC 89-11566. (Illus.). 32p. (gr. 2-3). 1989. PLB 17.27 (*0-8368-0203-9*) Gareth Stevens Inc.
Edwards, E. Dean. The American Pioneer. (Illus.). 36p. (Orig.). (gr. 1 up). 1988. pap. 2.95 (*0-685-44554-2*) E D Edwards.
Fowler, Allan. Ovejas Lanudas y Cabras Hambrientas: (Woolly Sheep & Hungry Goats) LC 92-36366. (SPA., Illus.). 32p. (ps-2). 1993. PLB 10.75 (*0-516-36014-0*); pap. 3.95 (*0-516-56014-X*) Childrens.
—Woolly Sheep & Hungry Goats. LC 92-36366. (Illus.). 32p. (ps-2). 1993. big bk. 22.95 (*0-516-49645-X*); PLB 10.75 (*0-516-06014-7*); pap. 3.95 (*0-516-46014-5*) Childrens.
Hall, Alice. Dairy Goats: Selecting, Fitting, Showing. Holleran, Betsy, illus. Jackson, Robert A., frwd. by. LC 77-153203. (Illus.). (gr. 7 up). 1975. pap. 4.00x (*0-932218-02-4*) Hall Pr.
Morris, Ann. Seven Hundred Kids on Grandpa's Farm. Heyman, Ken, photos by. (Illus.). 32p. (ps-3). 1994. 14.99 (*0-525-45162-5*, DCB) Dutton Child Bks.
Parkison, Ralph F. The Old Goat. Withrow, Marion O., ed. Bush, William, illus. 112p. (Orig.). (gr. 2-8). 1988. pap. write for info. Little Wood Bks.
Royston, Angela. Goat. (ps-3). 1990. PLB 10.90 (*0-531-19078-1*, Warwick) Watts.
Staub, Frank. Mountain Goats. LC 93-32491. 48p. (gr. 2-3). 1994. PLB 18.95 (*0-8225-3000-7*) Lerner Pubns.

GOATS–FICTION

Arnold, Caroline. Wild Goat. Hewett, Richard, photos by. LC 89-38958. (Illus.). 48p. (gr. 2 up). 1990. 13.95 (*0-688-08824-4*); PLB 13.88 (*0-688-08825-2*, Morrow Jr Bks) Morrow Jr Bks.
Asbjornsen, Peter C. & Moe, J. E. The Three Billy Goats Gruff. Brown, Marcia, illus. 28p. (ps-3). 1991. pap. 3.95 (*0-15-690150-1*) HarBrace.
Aushenker, Michael. Get That Goat! Thatch, Nancy R., ed. Aushenker, Michael, illus. Melton, David, intro. by. LC 90-5930. (Illus.). 26p. (gr. k-4). 1990. PLB 14.95 (*0-933849-28-1*) Landmark Edns.
Autry, Raz. Sam in Flight: Further Adventures of Bad Sam. Myers, Mary B., illus. LC 92-496. 64p. (Orig.). (gr. 1-6). 1992. pap. 5.95 (*1-56474-029-3*) Fithian Pr.
Chardiet, Jon. The Rough Gruff Goat Brothers. Suares, J. C., illus. (gr. k-3). 1993. pap. 5.95 incl. cass. (*0-590-69004-3*) Scholastic Inc.
Chottin, Ariane. Little Goat's New Horns. Jensen, Patricia, adapted by. Wirth, Pascale, illus. LC 93-4241. 22p. (ps-3). 1993. 5.98 (*0-89577-544-1*, Readers Digest Kids) RD Assn.
Cole, Brock. The Goats. large type ed. (Illus.). 208p. 1989. lib. bdg. 15.95 (*1-55736-113-4*, Crnrstn Bks) BDD LT Grp.
—The Goats. (gr. 5 up). 1990. pap. 3.95 (*0-374-42575-2*, Sunburst) FS&G.
—The Goats. (gr. 7 up). 1992. pap. 3.95 (*0-374-42576-0*) FS&G.
Dalokay, Vedat. Sister Shako & Kolo the Goat. 1994. 13.00 (*0-688-13271-5*) Lothrop.
Deloch-Hughes, Edye. I Like Gym Shoe Soup. Hughes, Darryl, illus. 16p. (gr. k-3). 1991. 10.25 (*0-941484-11-4*) Urban Res Pr.
Dominick, Bayard. Sam, a Goat. (Illus.). (gr. 3-5). 1968. 9.95 (*0-8392-3062-1*) Astor-Honor.
Dunn, Judy. The Little Goat. Dunn, Phoebe, illus. LC 77-91658. (ps-1). 1979. lib. bdg. 5.99 (*0-394-93872-0*) Random Bks Yng Read.
Galdone, Paul. The Three Billy Goats Gruff. Galdone, Paul, illus. 32p. (ps-3). 1981. pap. 4.95 (*0-89919-035-9*, Clarion Bks) HM.
Gregorich, Barbara. Up Went the Goat. Hoffman, Joan, ed. (Illus.). 32p. (gr. k-2). 1992. pap. 3.95 (*0-88743-400-2*, 06052) Sch Zone Pub Co.
Hillert, Margaret. The Boy & the Goats. (Illus.). (ps-k). 1982. PLB 6.95 (*0-8136-5092-5*, TK2160); pap. 3.50 (*0-8136-5592-7*, TK2161) Modern Curr.
Kaplan, Carol & Becker, Sandi. Three Nanny Goats Gruff. Mitter, Kathy, illus. 33p. (ps). 1989. 17.00 (*0-88734-409-7*) Players Pr.
Kratky, Lada J. El Chivo en la Huerta (Small Book) Remkiewicz, Frank, illus. (SPA.). 16p. (Orig.). (gr. k-3). 1992. pap. text ed. 6.00 (*1-56334-080-1*) Hampton-Brown.
Kroll, Steven. The Goat Parade. Kirk, Tim, illus. LC 82-10604. 48p. (ps-3). 1983. 5.50 (*0-8193-1099-9*); PLB 5.95 (*0-8193-1100-6*) Parents.
Leaf, Munro. Gordon the Goat. LC 87-26106. (Illus.). 48p. (ps-3). 1988. Repr. of 1944 ed. 14.50 (*0-208-02196-5*, Linnet) Shoe String.
McDonnell, Janet. Goat's Adventure in Alphabet Town. Dunnington, T., illus. LC 91-20548. 32p. (ps-2). 1992. PLB 11.80 (*0-516-05407-4*) Childrens.
Mahy, Margaret. The Queen's Goat. LC 90-46717. (Illus.). 32p. (ps-3). 1991. 12.95 (*0-8037-0938-2*) Dial Bks Young.
Milios, Rita. The Hungry Billy Goat. Walters, Mary C., illus. LC 88-673. 32p. (ps-2). 1989. PLB 10.25 (*0-516-02090-0*); pap. 2.95 (*0-516-42090-9*) Childrens.
Moncure, Jane B. Nanny Goat's Boat. Friedman, Joy, illus. LC 87-12839. (SPA & ENG.). 32p. (ps-2). 1987. PLB 14.95 (*0-89565-404-0*) Childs World.
Montgomery, Frances T. Billy Whiskers: Autobiography of a Goat. Fry, W. H., illus. 159p. (gr. 2 up). 1985. pap. 4.50 (*0-486-22345-0*) Dover.
Otfinoski, Steven. The Truth about Three Billy Goats Gruff. Barnes-Murphy, Rowan, illus. LC 93-42391. 32p. (gr. k-3). 1994. pap. text ed. 2.95 (*0-8167-3013-X*) Troll Assocs.
Pettigrew, Vera. Fionuala the Glendalough Goat. Myler, Terry, illus. 112p. (Orig.). (gr. 1-8). 1990. 10.95 (*0-947962-42-5*, Pub. by Anvil Bks Ltd Ireland); pap. 7.95 (*0-947962-43-3*, Pub. by Anvil Bks Ltd Ireland) Irish Bks Media.
Pevsner, Stella. Me, My Goat & My Sister's Wedding. (gr. 4-7). 1987. pap. 2.75 (*0-671-66206-6*, Minstrel Bks) PB.
Sharmat, Mitchell. Gregory, the Terrible Eater. Aruego, Jose & Dewey, Ariane, illus. LC 79-19172. 32p. (gr. k-3). 1984. RSBE 14.95 (*0-02-782250-8*, Four Winds) Macmillan Child Grp.
Starcher, Gwen. Christopher C. Kidd. Ross, Connie, illus. LC 93-61445. 96p. (Orig.). (gr. 2-6). 1994. pap. 4.95 (*1-878893-42-4*) Telcraft Bks.
Stevens, Janet. The Three Billy Goats Gruff. Stevens, Janet, illus. LC 86-33512. 40p. (ps-3). 1987. 12.95 (*0-15-286396-6*, HB Juv Bks) HarBrace.
—Three Billy Goats Gruff. 32p. (ps-3). 1990. pap. 4.95 (*0-15-286397-4*, Voyager Bks) HarBrace.
Tate, Susan. George Goat's Guardian Angel. Henium, Marian, illus. 40p. (Orig.). (gr. k-3). 1993. pap. 3.99 (*1-884395-02-3*) Clear Blue Sky.
Three Billy-Goats Gruff. (ARA., Illus.). (gr. 5-8). 1987. 3.95x (*0-86685-239-5*) Intl Bk Ctr.
The Three Billy Goats Gruff. (gr. 3-4). 1987. incl. cass. 6.95 (*0-317-64578-1*) HM.
Three Billy Goats Gruff. 24p. (ps-k). 1989. 2.25 (*1-56288-162-0*) Checkerboard.
Tinus, Arline W. Young Goat's Discovery. LC 93-38777. (Illus.). 32p. (ps-3). 1994. 13.95 (*1-878610-38-4*) Red Crane Bks.
Tucker, James C. & Wentworth, Anna. Goatie. (Illus.). 24p. (Orig.). (gr. 2-8). 1982. pap. 2.95 (*0-910341-00-1*) Blackwater Pub Co.

Willett, Fangette H. Jonah, the Mouse & the Goat. Jacobs, Jody, illus. 24p. (Orig.). (gr. 1 up). 1994. pap. 6.95 saddlestitched (*0-9642613-0-8*) Kinderword.
Join Jonah, the Mouse & the Goat on their wildly adventurous escapades. Set in the gorgeous aquamarine waters of the Caribbean, the three friends embark on a great sea adventure. The lush, full-color illustrations, sprinkled with hidden fairies, add sparkle & depth to the mystical creatures they encounter. They befriend a gigantic whale with smiling sapphire eyes, sea-foam witches & frolicking mermaids. Jonah & his friends are so bedazzled by their tropical fantasy that they fail to see an oncoming storm. They become trapped by the evil sea goblins who shred the sails of the boat & try to sink them. Jonah, terrified, calls to Amalie, who hears his cries & arises from the ocean floor to save them. This compelling tale, told in rhyme, embraces the West Indian culture & its love for magical stories. Ages 5 & up.
Publisher Provided Annotation.

GOBLINS

see Fairies

GOD

see also Christianity; Creation; Jesus Christ; Mythology; Religion; Theology

Anderson, Debby. God Loves Even Me. Beegle, Shirley, ed. Anderson, Debby, illus. 24p. (ps-3). 1994. pap. 1.89 (*0-7847-0254-3*, 24-04204) Standard Pub.
—Let's Talk about Children Around the World: God Made Them All. Norton, LoraBeth, ed. Anderson, Debby, illus. LC 94-9161. 32p. (ps-2). 1994. 7.99 (*0-7814-0178-X*, Chariot Bks) Chariot Family.
Bechtel, Faythelma. God's Marvelous Gifts. (gr. 5). 1982. 13.75x (*0-87813-920-6*) Christian Light.

Beers, V. Gilbert. Little Talks about God & You. 224p. (Orig.). (ps-2). 1986. pap. 9.99 (*0-89081-519-4*) Harvest Hse.
Boritzer, Etan. What Is God? Marantz, Robbie, illus. 32p. (Orig.). (gr. 1-7). 1990. 14.95 (*0-920668-89-5*); pap. 5.95 (*0-920668-88-7*) Firefly Bks Ltd.
Briscoe, Stuart & Briscoe, Jill. How Strong Is God? Marinin, Sally, illus. 12p. (Orig.). (gr. 4 up). 1993. pap. 2.99 (*0-8010-1037-3*) Baker Bk.
Brooks, Sandra. I Can Pray to God. Beegle, Shirley, ed. Axeman, Lois, illus. 24p. (ps-3). 1994. pap. 1.89 (*0-7847-0258-6*) Standard Pub.
Burgess, Beverly C. God Is My Best Friend. Linder, Elizabeth, illus. 32p. (Orig.). (gr. 1-3). 1986. pap. 1.98 (*0-89274-293-3*) Harrison Hse.
—How Can I Please You, God? Mckee, Vici, illus. 32p. (ps-5). 1991. Repr. of 1989 ed. 3.98 (*1-879470-00-4*) Burgess Pub.
Burrill, Richard, ed. Closest to God: The Life-Stories of Muhammad & the Five God-Men of History. (gr. 9-12). 1990. 17.95 (*1-878464-06-X*); pap. 10.95 (*1-878464-07-8*) Anthro Co.
Carlstrom, Nancy W. Does God Know How to Tie Shoes? McElrath-Eslick, Lori, illus. 40p. (ps-3). 1993. 14.99 (*0-8028-5074-X*) Eerdmans.
Caswell, Helen. God Must Like to Laugh. Caswell, Helen, illus. LC 87-1362. (ps-3). 1987. pap. 5.95 (*0-687-15188-0*) Abingdon.
—God's Love Is for Sharing. Caswell, Helen, illus. LC 87-11580. (gr. k-3). 1987. pap. 5.95 (*0-687-15335-2*) Abingdon.
Dean, Bessie. Aprendamos el Plan de Dios. Balderas, Eduardo, tr. Dean, Bessie, illus. LC 80-82256. (SPA.). 64p. (gr. k-3). 1980. pap. text ed. 5.98 (*0-88290-135-4*) Horizon Utah.
Deedat, Ahmed. What Is His Name. Obaba, Al I., ed. (Illus.). 49p. (Orig.). 1991. pap. text ed. 4.00 (*0-916157-74-1*) African Islam Miss Pubns.
Dick, Lois H. Discovering with God. Espe, Marvin, illus. 22p. (gr. k-6). 1984. pap. text ed. 4.25 (*1-55976-143-1*) CEF Press.
Erickson, Mary. God Can Do Anything. LC 92-33128. 1993. 9.99 (*0-7814-0001-5*, Chariot Bks) Chariot Family.
Fitzgerald, Annie. Dear God, Let's Play. LC 83-70495. 16p. (Orig.). (gr. 3-6). 1983. pap. 1.99 (*0-8066-2001-3*, 10-1852, Augsburg) Augsburg Fortress.
—Dear God, Thanks for Thinking up Love. LC 83-70499. 16p. (gr. 3-6). 1983. pap. 1.99 (*0-8066-2005-6*, 10-1853, Augsburg) Augsburg Fortress.
—Dear God, Thanks for Your Help. LC 83-70496. 16p. (gr. 3-6). 1983. pap. 1.99 (*0-8066-2002-1*, 10-1854, Augsburg) Augsburg Fortress.
—Dear God, We Just Love Christmas. LC 83-70494. 16p. (Orig.). (gr. 3-6). 1983. pap. 1.99 (*0-8066-2000-5*, 10-1855, Augsburg) Augsburg Fortress.
—Dear God, Where Do You Live? LC 83-70497. 16p. (gr. 3-6). 1983. pap. 1.99 (*0-8066-2003-X*, 10-1856, Augsburg) Augsburg Fortress.
—Dear God, Your World Is Wonderful. LC 83-70498. 16p. (gr. 3-6). 1983. pap. 1.99 (*0-8066-2004-8*, 10-1857, Augsburg) Augsburg Fortress.
Ford, Lauren. Little Book about God. Ford, Lauren, illus. LC 81-43749. 48p. (ps-3). 1985. pap. 9.95 (*0-385-17691-0*) Doubleday.
Gambill, Henrietta, ed. God Is Great! Acetate Window Book, No. 4. (Illus.). 16p. (ps-3). 1994. 6.99 (*0-7847-0154-7*, 24-03704) Standard Pub.
—Our Father in Heaven: Little Bible Window Book. (Illus.). 10p. (ps). 1994. 3.99 (*0-7847-0208-X*, 24-03148) Standard Pub.
—That's What God Is Like: Acetate Window Book, No. 3. (Illus.). 16p. 1994. 6.99 (*0-7847-0153-9*, 24-03703) Standard Pub.
Gellman, Marc. Does God Have a Big Toe? Stories about Stories in the Bible. De Mejo, Oscar, illus. LC 89-1893. 96p. (gr. 4-6). 1993. pap. 7.95 (*0-06-440453-6*, Trophy) HarpC Child Bks.
Gibson, Roxie C. Hey, God! Hurry! Gibson, James, illus. Harvey, Paul, intro. by. LC 82-60193. (Illus.). 52p. (gr. 3-5). 1982. 4.95 (*0-938232-08-8*, 32534) Winston-Derek.
—Hey, God! Listen! Gibson, James, illus. Harvey, Paul, intro. by. LC 82-60195. (Illus.). 68p. (gr. 3-5). 1982. 4.95 (*0-938232-06-1*, 32466) Winston-Derek.
—Hey, God! What Is America? Gibson, James, illus. Harvey, Paul, intro. by. LC 81-71025. (Illus.). 52p. (gr. 3-5). 1982. 4.95 (*0-938232-05-3*, 32795) Winston-Derek.
—Hey, God! What Is Christmas. Gibson, James, illus. LC 82-60192. 64p. (gr. 3-5). 1982. 4.95 (*0-938232-09-6*, 32752) Winston-Derek.
—Hey, God! Where Are You? Gibson, James, illus. Harvey, Paul, intro. by. LC 82-60194. (Illus.). 64p. (gr. 3-5). 1982. 4.95 (*0-938232-07-X*, 32485) Winston-Derek.
Goble, Paul. I Sing for the Animals. Goble, Paul, illus. LC 90-19812. 32p. 1991. SBE 9.95 (*0-02-737725-3*, Bradbury Pr) Macmillan Child Grp.
God Loves Me. 8p. (ps). 1983. bds. 3.99 (*0-85648-355-9*) Lion USA.
Godsey, Kyle. Object Lessons about God. 96p. (Orig.). (gr. 3-6). 1991. pap. 5.99 (*0-8010-3841-3*) Baker Bk.
Greene, Leia A. Where Is God? Greene, Leia A., illus. 40p. (gr. k-12). 1991. pap. text ed. 4.95 (*1-880737-05-1*) Crystal Jrns.
Groth, Lynn. God Cares for Me. 8p. (Orig.). (ps). 1985. pap. 1.25 (*0-938272-75-6*) Wels Board.
Hadley-Zelic, Patricia. God Is Love. Stevens, Rachel, illus. 24p. (Orig.). (ps). 1994. pap. 1.95 (*0-8198-3073-9*) St Paul Bks.
Heller, David. Dear God, What Religion Were the Dinosaurs: More Children's Letters to God. 1990. 14.95 (*0-385-26127-6*) Doubleday.
Hollingsworth, Mary. My Very First Book on God. Incrocci, Rick, illus. LC 94-10218. 1994. 4.99 (*0-7852-8020-0*) Nelson.
Hunt, Angela E. If God Is Real, Where in the World Is He? LC 90-21285. (Illus.). 188p. (Orig.). (gr. 7-12). 1991. pap. 7.99 (*0-8407-4411-0*) Nelson.
Hutson, Joan. Who? Hutson, Joan, illus. LC 92-31811. 32p. (ps-2). 1992. 3.50 (*0-8198-8266-6*) St Paul Bks.
Ingram, Robert D. Who Taught Frogs to Hop? A Child's Book about God. Goldsborough, June, illus. LC 89-82552. 32p. (ps). 1990. pap. 5.99 (*0-8066-2457-4*, 9-2457) Augsburg Fortress.
Is God Unfair? 48p. (gr. 6-8). 1990. pap. 8.99 (*1-55945-108-4*) Group Pub.
Kesler, Jay & Stafford, Tim. Making Life Make Sense: Answers to Hard Questions about God & You. 176p. 1991. pap. 7.99 (*0-310-71191-6*, Campus Life) Zondervan.
Kimball, Don. Who's Gonna Love Me? 160p. (Orig.). (gr. 9-12). 1988. pap. 5.95 (*0-89505-769-7*, 22027) Tabor Pub.
Kroll, Virginia L. I Wanted to Know All about God. Jenkins, Debra R., illus. LC 93-37382. 32p. 1994. 14.99 (*0-8028-5078-2*) Eerdmans.
Lippy, Elsie. God's Story. (Illus.). 10p. (gr. k-6). 1989. pap. text ed. 2.50 (*1-55976-128-8*) CEF Press.
The Lord Is My Shepherd. 1989. text ed. 3.95 cased (*0-7214-5199-3*) Ladybird Bks.
McAllister, Dawson & Miller, Rich. Who Are You, God? Varner, Charles, illus. (gr. 5-12). 1988. pap. 7.95 (*0-923417-11-7*) Shepherd Minst.
—Who Are You God? (gr. 5-12). 1990. pap. 5.95 tchr's. guide (*0-923417-13-3*) Shepherd Minst.
MacMaster, Eve. God's Family. Converse, James, illus. LC 81-6551. 168p. (gr. 3 up). 1981. pap. 5.95 (*0-8361-1964-9*) Herald Pr.
Martin, LaJoyce. Love's Golden Wings. Agnew, Tim & Kirchoff, Art, illus. LC 87-17346. 256p. (Orig.). (gr. 7 up). 1987. pap. 6.99 (*0-932581-19-6*) Word Aflame.
Marxhausen, Evelyn. When God Laid Down the Law. LC 59-1259. (gr. k-4). 1981. pap. 1.99 (*0-570-06142-3*) Concordia.
Mayfield, Larry. God's Power. (Illus.). (gr. k-6). 1980. visualized song 5.99 (*3-90117-017-0*) CEF Press.
Mees, Walter H., Jr. Who Is God? (Illus.). 48p. (gr. 9-12). 1991. pap. 8.99 (*1-55945-218-8*) Group Pub.
Mills, Charles. God's Special Promise to Me: A Devotional Book for Early Readers. LC 93-17945. 1993. 7.95 (*0-8163-1147-1*) Pacific Pr Pub Assn.
Murphy, Ann & Murphy, John. God's Gift of Life: A Child's First Book about Life. Cleary, Janice, illus. 32p. (Orig.). (gr. 1-3). 1994. pap. 4.95 (*0-8198-3070-4*) St Paul Bks.
Murphy, Campbell. David & I Talk to God Series. (ps-2). 1983. (Chariot Bks); pap. 2.95 (*0-686-45018-3*) Chariot Family.
Murphy, Elspeth C. Make Way for the King: Psalm 145 & 24. Nelson, Jane, illus. (ps-2). 1983. 3.99 (*0-89191-581-8*, Chariot Bks) Chariot Family.
—Sometimes Everything Feels Just Right. LC 86-2256. (Illus.). (ps-2). 1987. pap. 3.99 (*1-55513-038-0*, Chariot Bks) Chariot Family.
—Sometimes I Get Lonely. Nelson, Jane, illus. LC 80-70251. 24p. (ps-2). 1981. pap. 3.99 (*0-89191-367-X*, 53678, Chariot Bks) Chariot Family.
Nystrom, Carolyn. Who Is God? 32p. (ps-2). 1980. pap. 4.99 (*0-8024-6158-1*) Moody.
Odor, Ruth S. God Keeps His Promises. Chase, Andra, illus. LC 91-67212. 32p. (gr. 5-7). 1992. saddle-stitch 5.99 (*0-87403-931-2*, 24-03561) Standard Pub.
O'Rourke, Robert. What God Did for Zeke the Fuzzy Caterpillar. Loman, Roberta K., illus. 32p. (gr. k-2). 1991. pasted 2.50 (*0-87403-824-3*, 24-03924) Standard Pub.
Pearson, Mary R. All about God. LC 93-7692. 1993. 8.99 (*0-8423-1215-3*) Tyndale.
Peterson, Lorraine. If God Loves Me, Why Can't I Get My Locker Open? LC 80-27014. 141p. (Orig.). (gr. 6-12). 1980. pap. 7.99 (*0-87123-251-0*) Bethany Hse.
—Why Isn't God Giving Cash Prizes? Dugan, LeRoy, illus. LC 82-17866. 160p. (gr. 8-12). 1982. pap. 7.99 (*0-87123-626-5*) Bethany Hse.
Pitts, V. Peter, ed. Children's Pictures of God. LC 79-56298. (Illus.). (gr. 1-4). 1979. pap. 3.95 (*0-915744-20-1*) Character Res.
Poorten, Carolyn T. Can We See God. LC 91-68355. 42p. (gr. k-3). 1992. 6.95 (*1-55523-507-7*) Winston-Derek.
Rigmaiden, Paul. God Loves Us All. (Illus.). 32p. (Orig.). (gr. k-4). 1988. pap. 5.00 (*0-9621598-0-8*) Dada Pubns.
Rohwer, Lee O. What Is God Like? Muelken, Mary, illus. 64p. (Orig.). (gr. k-4). 1986. pap. 5.95 (*0-9617788-0-6*) Damon Pub.
—What Is God Like? 2nd, rev. ed. Muelken, Mary, illus. 68p. (Orig.). (gr. 8 up). 1989. pap. 7.95 (*0-9617788-1-4*) Damon Pub.
Round, Graham. God Creates. (ps). 1992. 5.99 (*0-8423-0994-2*) Tyndale.
Sasso, Sandy E. God's Paintbrush. Compton, Annette, illus. LC 92-15493. 32p. (gr. k-4). 1992. 15.95 (*1-879045-22-2*) Jewish Lights.
Shibley, David & Shibley, Naomi. Special Times with God. LC 81-14116. 160p. (ps). 1981. 6.99 (*0-8407-5780-8*) Nelson.
Stewart, Dana. God Feeds the Animals. Garris, Norma, illus. 12p. (ps). 1992. deluxe ed. 4.99 (*0-87403-998-3*, 24-03118) Standard Pub.
Stortz, Diane. God Cares for Me. Garris, Norma, illus. 12p. (ps). 1992. deluxe ed. 4.99 (*0-87403-992-4*, 24-03112) Standard Pub.
Swafford, Mrs. Z. W. Knowing God. rev. ed. 32p. (gr. k-2). 1980. tchr's. ed. 1.00 (*0-89114-090-5*); coloring bk. 0.50 (*0-89114-091-3*) Baptist Pub Hse.
Thomas, Mack. From God with Love. 63p. (ps-2). 1993. 13.99 (*0-945564-78-3*, Gold & Honey) Questar Pubs.
Walters, Julie & Kelly, Kathryn. God Loves Me: Three Psalms for Little Children. Kelly, Kathryn, illus. 96p. (gr. k-2). 1977. pap. 2.95 (*0-87793-138-0*) Ave Maria.
Webster, David. And God Created... (Illus.). 52p. (gr. k-6). 1992. 3.95 (*0-9633597-0-3*) Doodle-bug.
Willis, Doris. God's Wonderful World. (ps). 1990. 3.95 (*0-687-03121-4*) Abingdon.

GODS–FICTION

Aylott, Jane. The Soft Secret Word. Andersson, Benny, illus. 32p. 1992. 12.00 (*0-9631440-0-6*) Winged Peoples.
Gates, Doris. The Golden God: Apollo. CoConis, Constantine, illus. 110p. (gr. 3-7). 1983. pap. 4.99 (*0-14-031647-7*, Puffin) Puffin Bks.
—Two Queens of Heaven: Aphrodite & Demeter. CoConis, Constantine, illus. 94p. (gr. 3-7). 1983. pap. 4.99 (*0-14-031646-9*, Puffin) Puffin Bks.
Kezzeiz, Ediba. Inside & Under the World of Wonder. Mir, Anjum, illus. 38p. (Orig.). (ps). 1992. pap. text ed. 4.00 (*0-89259-112-9*) Am Trust Pubns.

GOETHALS, GEORGE WASHINGTON, 1858-1928

Latham, Jean L. George W. Goethals: Panama Canal Engineer. Green, Hamilton, illus. 80p. (gr. 2-6). 1991. Repr. of 1965 ed. lib. bdg. 12.95 (*0-7910-1440-1*) Chelsea Hse.

GOGH, VINCENT VAN, 1853-1890

Hughes, Andrew. Van Gogh. (Illus.). 32p. (gr. 5 up). 1994. 10.95 (*0-8120-6462-3*); pap. 5.95 (*0-8120-1999-7*) Barron.
Muhlberger, Richard, text by. What Makes a van Gogh a van Gogh? (Illus.). 48p. (gr. 5 up). 1993. 9.95 (*0-670-85198-1*) Viking Child Bks.
Raboff, Ernest. Vincent Van Gogh. LC 87-45300. (Illus.). 32p. (gr. 1 up). 1988. pap. 7.95 (*0-06-446077-0*, Trophy) HarpC Child Bks.

GOLD

see also Gold Mines and Mining; Jewelry; Money

Cohen, Daniel. Gold: The Fascinating Study of the Noble Metal Through the Ages. LC 76-18067. (Illus.). 192p. (gr. 7 up). 1976. 10.95 (*0-87131-218-2*) M Evans.
Fodor, R. V. Gold, Copper, Iron: How Metals Are Formed, Found, & Used. LC 87-24464. (Illus.). 96p. (gr. 6 up). 1989. lib. bdg. 16.95 (*0-89490-138-9*) Enslow Pubs.
Meltzer, Milton. Gold: The True Story of Why People Search for It, Mine It, Trade It, Fight for It, Mint It, Display It, Steal It, & Kill for It. LC 92-44497. (Illus.). 176p. (gr. 3-7). 1993. 15.00 (*0-06-022983-7*); PLB 14.89 (*0-06-022984-5*) HarpC Child Bks.
Mitgutsch, Ali. From Gold to Money. Mitgutsch, Ali, illus. LC 84-17488. 24p. (ps-3). 1985. PLB 10.95 (*0-87614-230-7*) Carolrhoda Bks.
Petralia, Joseph F. Gold! Gold! A Beginner's Handbook & Recreational Guide: How & Where to Prospect for Gold. 5th, rev. ed. Applegate, Jill, ed. Neri, Susan, illus. LC 81-126200. 144p. 1992. pap. 9.95 (*0-9605890-5-8*, AB92) Sierra Trading.
Russell, William. Gold & Silver. LC 94-504. (gr. 3 up). 1994. write for info. (*0-86593-359-6*) Rourke Corp.

GOLD FISH

see Goldfish

GOLD MINES AND MINING

see also Prospecting

Cooper, Michael. Klondike Fever: The Famous Gold Rush of 1898. (gr. 4-7). 1990. pap. 5.70 (*0-395-54784-9*, Clarion Bks) HM.
Van Steenwyk, Elizabeth. The California Gold Rush: West with the Forty-Niners. (Illus.). 64p. (gr. 5-8). 1991. PLB 12.90 (*0-531-20032-9*) Watts.

GOLD MINES AND MINING–FICTION

DeClements, Barthe. The Bite of the Gold Bug: A Story of the Alaskan Gold Rush. Andreasen, Dan, illus. 64p. (gr. 2-6). 1992. 13.00 (*0-670-84495-0*) Viking Child Bks.
Hollingsworth, Mary. Charlie & the Gold Mine. (Illus.). (ps-3). 1989. 5.99 (*0-915720-28-0*) Brownlow Pub Co.
Hoobler, Dorothy & Hoobler, Thomas. Treasure in the Stream: The Story of a Gold Rush Girl. Carpenter, Nancy, illus. 64p. (gr. 4-6). 1991. 5.95 (*0-382-24151-7*); PLB 7.95 (*0-382-24144-4*); pap. 3.95 (*0-382-24346-3*) Silver Burdett Pr.
Koranteng, Kwasi. Gold Diggers. (gr. 4-7). 1992. pap. 4.95 (*0-7910-2925-5*) Chelsea Hse.
Miller, Sherry. Snowskate Goes for Gold. Martinez, Jesse, illus. 32p. (Orig.). (gr. k-5). 1984. pap. 1.95 saddle-stitched (*0-913379-02-6*) Double M Pub.
Snyder, Zilpha K. Fool's Gold. (gr. 4-7). 1994. pap. 3.50 (*0-440-40952-7*) Dell.
Souter, John. Choice Adventures: Abandoned Gold Mine. 160p. (gr. 4-8). 1992. pap. 4.99 (*0-8423-5031-4*) Tyndale.
Thoene, Brock & Thoene, Bodie. Cannons of the Comstock. 224p. 1992. pap. 7.99 (*1-55661-166-8*) Bethany Hse.

Vandersteen, Willy. A Fool's Gold. Lahey, Nicholas J., tr. from FLE. LC 76-49377. (Illus., Orig.). (gr. 3-8). 1977. pap. 2.50 (*0-915560-08-9*, 08) Hiddigeigei.

Wells, Marian. Colorado Gold. LC 87-35333. 302p. (Orig.). (gr. 9-12). 1988. pap. 8.99 (*0-87123-966-3*) Bethany Hse.

Yates, Alma J. Ghosts in the Baker Mine. LC 91-45230. 197p. (Orig.). (gr. 3-7). 1992. pap. 4.95 (*0-87579-581-1*) Deseret Bk.

GOLD RUSH

see California–Gold Discoveries

GOLDFISH

Gilbert, Mariana. Your First Goldfish. (Illus.). 36p. (Orig.). 1991. pap. 1.95 (*0-86622-065-8*, YF-108) TFH Pubns.

O'Neal, Zibby. The Language of Goldfish. LC 79-19167. (gr. 6 up). 1980. pap. 14.95 (*0-670-41785-8*) Viking Child Bks.

Piers, Helen. Taking Care of Your Goldfish. Vriends, Matthew M., ed. LC 92-32170. 32p. 1993. pap. 4.95 (*0-8120-1368-9*) Barron.

GOLDMAN, EMMA, 1869-1940

Waldstreicher, David. Emma Goldman. Horner, Matina S., intro. by. (Illus.). 112p. (gr. 5 up). 1990. 17.95 (*1-55546-655-9*) Chelsea Hse.

GOLF

Blackstone, Margaret. This is Mini Golf. 1995. write for info. (*0-8050-2800-5*) H Holt & Co.

Merrins. Golf for the Young. 1983. pap. 9.95 (*0-689-70659-6*, Atheneum) Macmillan.

GOLF–BIOGRAPHY

Creighton, Susan. Greg Norman. LC 87-27565. (Illus.). 48p. (gr. 5-6). 1988. text ed. 11.95 RSBE (*0-89686-371-9*, Crestwood Hse) Macmillan Child Grp.

Gilbert, Thomas W. Lee Trevino. (Illus.). 112p. (gr. 5 up). 1992. lib. bdg. 17.95 (*0-7910-1256-5*) Chelsea Hse.

GOLF–FICTION

Mayer, Bill, illus. Golf-o-Rama: The Wacky Nine-Hole Pop-up Mini-Golf Book. 8p. 1994. 17.95 (*1-56282-635-2*) Hyprn Child.

Stiles, Norman & Berger, Lou. Elmo Goes Around the Corner - on Sesame Street. Mathieu, Joe, illus. LC 93-39056. 32p. (Orig.). (ps-3). 1994. pap. 2.50 (*0-679-85455-X*) Random Bks Yng Read.

Walker, David. Rick Tees Off. Wright, Malcolm, ed. Van Zandt, William, illus. Nicklaus, Jack, frwd. by. (Illus.). 112p. (Orig.). (gr. 4-9). 1985. pap. text ed. 3.95 (*0-9614856-0-4*) Pro Golfers.

Wojciechowska, Maia. Dreams of Golf. Karsky, A. K., illus. 52p. 1993. 14.50 (*1-883740-01-0*) Pebble Bch Pr Ltd.

GOMPERS, SAMUEL, 1850-1924

Kurland, Gerald. Samuel Gompers: Founder of the American Labor Movement. Rahmas, D. Steve, ed. LC 72-190242. 32p. (Orig.). (gr. 7-12). 1972. lib. bdg. 4.95 incl. catalog cards (*0-87157-524-8*) SamHar Pr.

GONZALES, RICHARD ALONZO (PANCHO), 1928-

Pancho Gonzalez. (ps-3). 1993. 18.95 (*0-7910-1782-6*) Chelsea Hse.

GOOD AND EVIL–FICTION

O'Connor, Frank. First Confession. 32p. (gr. 3 up). 1986. 13.95 (*0-88682-058-8*) Creative Ed.

GOOD GROOMING

see Beauty, Personal

GOOSE

see Geese

GORILLAS

Goodall, Jane. Jane Goodall's Animal World: Gorillas. LC 89-78064. (Illus.). 32p. (gr. 3-7). 1990. pap. 3.95 (*0-689-71396-7*, Aladdin) Macmillan Child Grp.

Gorillas. 1991. PLB 14.95 (*0-88682-423-0*) Creative Ed.

GORILLAS–FICTION

Aardema, Verna. Princess Gorilla & a New Kind of Water. Chess, Victoria, illus. LC 86-32888. 32p. (ps-3). 1991. pap. 3.95 (*0-8037-0914-5*, Puff Pied Piper) Puffin Bks.

Bailey, Jill. Gorilla Rescue. LC 90-9678. (Illus.). 48p. (gr. 3-7). 1990. PLB 21.34 (*0-8114-2705-6*); pap. 4.95 (*0-8114-6555-5*) Raintree Steck-V.

Bornstein, Ruth L. Little Gorilla. Bornstein, Ruth L., illus. LC 75-25508. 32p. (ps-3). 1986. 15.45 (*0-395-28773-1*, Clarion Bks); pap. 4.95 (*0-89919-421-4*, Clarion Bks) HM.

Brown, Anthony. Gorilla. Brown, Anthony, illus. LC 85-13. 32p. (ps-2). 1989. pap. 6.99 (*0-394-82225-0*) Knopf Bks Yng Read.

Hazen, Barbara S. The Gorilla Did It. Cruz, Ray, illus. LC 73-84828. 32p. (ps-1). 1974. RSBE 13.95 (*0-689-30138-3*, Atheneum Child Bk) Macmillan Child Grp.

Hoff, Syd. Julius. Hoff, Syd, illus. LC 59-8971. 64p. (gr. k-3). 1959. PLB 13.89 (*0-06-022491-6*) HarpC Child Bks.

Hoffman, Mary. Gorilla. LC 84-24906. (Illus.). 24p. (gr. k-5). 1985. PLB 9.95 (*0-8172-2413-0*); pap. 3.95 (*0-8114-6876-3*) Raintree Steck-V.

Kessler, Ethel. IS There a Gorilla in the Band? (ps). 1994. pap. 4.95 (*0-671-88303-8*, Little Simon) S&S Trade.

Leonard, Alain. Barnaby & the Big Gorilla. LC 91-25414. (Illus.). 32p. (ps-3). 1992. 15.00 (*0-688-11291-9*, Tambourine Bks); PLB 14.93 (*0-688-11292-7*, Tambourine Bks) Morrow.

Mauser, Pat R. Patti's Pet Gorilla. 64p. 1991. pap. 2.95 (*0-380-71039-0*, Camelot) Avon.

Mayer, Mercer. If I Had a Gorilla. (ps-3). 1994. pap. 5.95 (*1-879920-06-9*) Rain Bird Prods.

Morozumi, Atsuko. One Gorilla: A Counting Book. Morozumi, Atsuko, illus. 26p. (ps-1). 1990. 15.00 (*0-374-35644-0*) FS&G.

Oke, Janette. Who's New at the Zoo. Mann, Brenda, illus. 1994. pap. 4.99 (*0-934998-55-8*) Bethel Pub.

Thorne, Ian. King Kong. LC 76-51147. (Illus.). 48p. (gr. 3-5). 1977. text ed. 11.95 RSBE (*0-913940-69-0*, Crestwood Hse) Macmillan Child Grp.

Wallace, Jim. Search for the Mountain Gorillas. 128p. (gr. 6 up). 1985. pap. 2.25 (*0-553-26062-6*) Bantam.

GOVERNMENT, LOCAL

see Local Government

GOVERNMENT, RESISTANCE TO

Classrooms of Resistance. (Illus.). 168p. (gr. 3-6). 1980. 12.00 (*0-904613-10-0*); pap. 5.95 (*0-904613-01-1*) Writers & Readers.

GOVERNORS

Phillips, Margaret I. Governors of Tennessee. LC 77-26845. (Illus.). 193p. (gr. 6-12). 1978. 16.95 (*0-88289-169-3*) Pelican.

Sobol, Richard. Governor: In the Company of Ann W. Richards, Governor of Texas. LC 93-40426. (Illus.). 32p. (gr. 3-7). 1994. 14.99 (*0-525-65194-2*, Cobblehill Pr) Dutton Child Bks.

GOYA Y LUCIENTES, FRANCISCO JOSE DE, 1746-1828

Richardson, Martha. Francisco Jose De Goya: Spanish Painter. LC 93-2326. (Illus.). (ps-3). 1994. PLB 18.95 (*0-7910-1780-X*, Am Art Analog); write for info. (*0-7910-1799-0*) Chelsea Hse.

Venezia, Mike. Francisco Goya. Venezia, Mike, illus. LC 90-20887. 32p. (ps-4). 1991. PLB 12.85 (*0-516-02292-X*); pap. 4.95 (*0-516-42292-8*) Childrens.

Waldron, Ann. Francisco Goya. (Illus.). 92p. 1992. 19.95 (*0-8109-3368-3*) Abrams.

GRAAL

see Grail

GRACE, PRINCESS OF MONACO, 1929-

Surcouf, Elizabeth G. Grace Kelly, American Princess. LC 92-9626. 1992. 17.50 (*0-8225-0548-7*) Lerner Pubns.

GRAHAM, MARTHA

Pratt, Paula B. Martha Graham. LC 94-10883. (Illus.). 112p. (gr. 5-8). 1994. 14.95 (*1-56006-056-5*) Lucent Bks.

GRAHAM, WILLIAM FRANKLIN, 1918-

Aaseng, Nathan. Billy Graham. 112p. (gr. 3-7). 1993. 4.99 (*0-310-39841-X*, Pub. by Youth Spec) Zondervan.

Wilson, Jean. Crusader for Christ (Billy Graham) (gr. 6-9). 1979. pap. 3.95 (*0-87508-602-0*) Chr Lit.

GRAIL

see also Arthur, King

Pyle, Howard. The Story of the Grail & the Passing of Arthur. Pyle, Howard, illus. LC 85-40302. 340p. (gr. 7 up). 1985. SBE 19.95 (*0-684-18483-4*, Scribners Young Read) Macmillan Child Grp.

GRAIN

Grain. (Illus.). (gr. 5 up). 1984. lib. bdg. 17.27 (*0-86592-263-2*); 12.95s.p. (*0-685-58239-6*) Rourke Corp.

Greenaway, Theresa. Grasses & Grains. LC 90-9563. (Illus.). 48p. (gr. 5-9). 1990. PLB 21.34 (*0-8114-2729-3*) Raintree Steck-V.

Moncure, Jane B. What Was It Before It Was Bread? Hygaard, Elizabeth, illus. LC 85-11402. 32p. (ps-2). 1985. PLB 14.95 (*0-89565-323-0*) Childs World.

GRAMMAR

see also Language and Languages

also names of languages with the subdivision Grammar, e.g. English Language–Grammar

Gattegno, Caleb. Words in Color. rev. ed. (Orig.). (gr. k-12). 1977. mini-charts 8.75 (*0-87825-143-X*); Word Charts. 100.00 (*0-87825-131-6*); Phonic Code Charts. 40.00 (*0-87825-132-4*); Book R-0. 0.25 (*0-87825-127-8*); Book R-1. 0.65 (*0-87825-128-6*); Book R-2. 1.50 (*0-87825-129-4*); Book R-3. 1.50 (*0-87825-130-8*); Worksheets 1-7. 3.65 (*0-87825-178-2*); Worksheets 8-14. 1.65 (*0-87825-059-X*) Ed Solutions.

Smith, Carl B. Elementary Grammar: A Child's Resource Book. Reade, Eugene W., ed. 280p. (Orig.). (gr. 1-4). 1991. pap. 13.95 (*0-9628556-2-6*) Grayson Bernard Pubs.

Webb, Jane C. & Duckett, Barbara. RULES Phonological Evaluation. Seeland, Rene K., illus. 140p. (ps-3). 1990. text ed. 49.95 (*0-937857-12-2*, 1577) Speech Bin.

GRAMMAR SCHOOLS

see Education, Elementary; Public Schools

GRAMOPHONE

see Phonograph

GRAND CANYON

Cone, Patrick. Grand Canyon. Cone, Patrick, photos by. LC 93-31066. (Illus.). 1994. write for info. (*0-87614-820-8*) Carolrhoda Bks.

—Grand Canyon. (gr. 4-7). 1994. pap. 7.95 (*0-87614-628-0*) Carolrhoda Bks.

Diamond, Lynnell. Let's Discover the Grand Canyon. 32p. (gr. 1-6). 1990. pap. 3.95 (*0-89886-252-3*) Mountaineers.

Foster, Lynne. Exploring the Grand Canyon: Adventures of Yesterday & Today. (Illus.). 160p. (gr. 4 up). 1990. pap. 15.95 (*0-938216-33-3*) GCNHA.

Henry, Marguerite. Brighty: Of the Grand Canyon. Dennis, Wesley, illus. LC 53-7233. 224p. (gr. 3-7). 1991. SBE 13.95 (*0-02-743664-0*, Macmillan Child Bk) Macmillan Child Grp.

Markert, Jenny. Grand Canyon. (SPA & ENG.). (gr. 2-6). 1992. PLB 15.95 (*0-89565-856-9*) Childs World.

Mell, Jan. Grand Canyon. LC 88-18707. (Illus.). (gr. 4-5). 1988. text ed. 13.95 RSBE (*0-89686-406-5*, Crestwood Hse) Macmillan Child Grp.

Petersen, David. Grand Canyon National Park. LC 92-11343. (Illus.). 48p. (gr. k-4). 1993. pap. 4.95 (*0-516-42197-2*) Childrens.

Rawlins, Carol. The Grand Canyon. (Illus.). 64p. (gr. 5-8). 1994. PLB write for info. (*0-8114-6364-8*) Raintree Steck-V.

Salts, Bobbi. Grand Canyon Discovery: An Activity Book. (Illus.). 32p. (Orig.). (gr. 1-6). 1989. pap. 2.95 (*0-929526-03-1*) Double B Pubns.

Smith, Don. The Grand Canyon: Journey Through Time. new ed. LC 75-23413. (Illus.). 32p. (gr. 5-10). 1976. PLB 10.79 (*0-89375-007-7*); pap. 2.95 (*0-89375-023-9*) Troll Assocs.

GRAND CANYON–FICTION

Henry, Marguerite. Brighty: Of the Grand Canyon. Dennis, Wesley, illus. LC 90-28636. 224p. (gr. 3-7). 1991. pap. 3.95 (*0-689-71485-8*, Aladdin) Macmillan Child Grp.

Hogg, Gary. Happy Hawk Series, 6 bks. Anderson, Gary, illus. (gr. k-6). 1991. Set. 71.70 (*0-89868-243-6*); Set. pap. 29.70 (*0-89868-242-8*) ARO Pub.

Reese, Bob. Abert & Kaibab. Reese, Bob, illus. (gr. k-6). 1987. 7.95 (*0-89868-226-6*); pap. 2.95 (*0-89868-227-4*) ARO Pub.

—Abert & Kaibab. Reese, Bob, illus. (gr. k-6). 1987. pap. 20.00 (*0-685-50872-2*) ARO Pub.

—Cocos Berry Party. Reese, Bob, illus. (gr. k-6). 1987. 7.95 (*0-89868-193-6*); pap. 2.95 (*0-89868-194-4*) ARO Pub.

—Raven's Roost. Reese, Bob, illus. (gr. k-6). 1987. 7.95 (*0-89868-195-2*); pap. 2.95 (*0-89868-196-0*) ARO Pub.

—Sixty Word Grand Canyon Series, 6 bks. Reese, Bob, illus. (gr. k-6). 1987. Set. 47.70 (*0-89868-241-X*); Set. pap. 29.50 (*0-89868-240-1*) ARO Pub.

—Surefoot Mule. Reese, Bob, illus. (gr. k-6). 1987. 7.95 (*0-89868-197-9*); pap. 2.95 (*0-89868-198-7*) ARO Pub.

—Wild Turkey Run. Reese, Bob, illus. (gr. k-6). 1987. 7.95 (*0-89868-199-5*); pap. 2.95 (*0-89868-225-8*) ARO Pub.

Thompson-Hoffman, Susan. Tassel's Mission. Chapin, Tom, narrated by. Buzzanco, Eileen M., illus. LC 88-64151. 32p. (gr. 2-5). 1989. 11.95 (*0-924483-00-8*); incl. audiocassette 16.95 (*0-924483-03-2*); incl. audiocassette & toy combination 39.95 (*0-924483-06-7*); incl. audiocassette & small toy combination 25.95 (*0-924483-41-5*); write for info. audiocassette (*0-924483-09-1*) Soundprints.

GRAND OPERA

see Opera

GRANDPARENTS–FICTION

Ackerman, Karen. By the Dawn's Early Light: Al Amanecer. Ada, Alma F., tr. Stock, Catherine, illus. LC 93-34815. (ENG & SPA.). 40p. (ps-3). 1994. English ed. SBE 14.95 (*0-689-31788-3*, Atheneum Child Bk); Spanish ed. SBE 14.95 (*0-689-31917-7*) Macmillan Child Grp.

—Song & Dance Man. Gammell, Stephen, illus. LC 87-3200. 32p. (ps-2). 1988. 15.00 (*0-394-89330-1*); lib. bdg. 15.99 (*0-394-99330-6*) Knopf Bks Yng Read.

Ada, Alma F. I Love Saturdays y Domingos. Bryant, Michael, illus. LC 94-3362. 1995. 14.95 (*0-689-31819-7*, Atheneum) Macmillan.

Adams, Ken. When I Was Your Age. Biro, Val, illus. 32p. (ps-2). 1991. incl. dust jacket 12.95 (*0-8120-6249-3*) Barron.

Adams, Pam. Mrs Honey's Glasses. LC 93-12368. (Illus.). (ps-3). 1993. 7.95 (*0-85953-757-9*); pap. 3.95 (*0-85953-758-7*) Childs Play.

Alexander, M. Where Does the Sky End, Grandpa? 1992. 12.95 (*0-15-295603-4*, HB Juv Bks) HarBrace.

Aliki. The Two of Them. LC 79-10161. (Illus.). 32p. (gr. k-3). 1979. 14.95 (*0-688-80225-7*); PLB 14.88 (*0-688-84225-9*) Greenwillow.

Allen, Linda. When Grandfather's. 1992. pap. 2.99 (*0-553-15970-4*) Bantam.

Andersen, Honey & Reinholtd, Bill. Pop's Truck. Posey, Pam, illus. LC 93-18050. 1994. write for info. (*0-383-03709-3*) SRA Schl Grp.

Anderson, Janet. The Key into Winter. Soman, David, illus. LC 93-13017. 1993. write for info. (*0-8075-4170-2*) A Whitman.

Anderson, Lena. Stina's Visit. LC 89-77716. (Illus.). 32p. (ps up). 1991. 13.95 (*0-688-09665-4*); PLB 13.88 (*0-688-09666-2*) Greenwillow.

Arkin, Alan. Some Fine Grampa! Zimmer, Dirk, illus. LC 92-24436. 32p. (gr. k-3). 1995. 14.00 (*0-06-021533-X*); PLB 13.89 (*0-06-021534-8*) HarpC Child Bks.

Armstrong, Jennifer. Steal Away. LC 91-18504. 224p. (gr. 6 up). 1992. 15.95 (*0-531-05983-9*); lib. bdg. 15.99 (*0-531-08583-X*) Orchard Bks Watts.

Ash, Martha C. Grandmother's Visit with Sam. White, Regina, illus. LC 85-71540. 48p. (Orig.). (ps-2). 1985. pap. 4.25 (*0-933865-00-7*) Doris Pubns.

Aver, Kate. Joey's Way. Himler, Ronald, illus. LC 92-7830. 48p. (gr. 1-4). 1992. SBE 13.95 (*0-689-50552-3*, M K McElderry) Macmillan Child Grp.

Bahr, Mary. The Memory Box. Tucker, Kathleen, ed. Cunningham, David, illus. LC 91-21628. 32p. (gr. 1-4). 1992. PLB 13.95 (*0-8075-5052-3*) A Whitman.

Ball, Duncan. Grandfather's Wheeliething. Smith, Cat B., illus. LC 93-12524. 1994. pap. 15.00 (*0-671-79817-0*, S&S BFYR) S&S Trade.

Ballard, Robin. Granny & Me. LC 90-24170. (Illus.). 24p. (ps up). 1992. 14.00 (*0-688-10548-3*); PLB 13.93 (*0-688-10549-1*) Greenwillow.

Barrett, Elizabeth. Free Fall. LC 93-44160. 272p. (gr. 7 up). 1994. 15.00 (*0-06-024465-8*); PLB 14.89 (*0-06-024466-6*) HarpC Child Bks.

Bauer, Marion D. When I Go Camping with Grandma. Garns, Allen, illus. LC 93-33809. 32p. (gr. k-3). 1995. PLB 14.95 (*0-8167-3448-8*); pap. text ed. 4.95 (*0-8167-3449-6*) BrdgeWater.

Bawden, Nina. The Robbers. LC 79-4152. (Illus.). 160p. (gr. 4-7). 1989. Repr. of 1979 ed. 12.95 (*0-688-41902-X*) Lothrop.

Belton, Sandra. May'naise Sandwiches & Sunshine Tea. Carter, Gail G., illus. LC 93-46781. (ps-4). 1994. 14. 95 (*0-02-709035-3*, Four Winds) Macmillan Child Grp.

Berenstain, Stan & Berenstain, Janice. The Berenstain Bears & the Week at Grandma's. Berenstain, Stan & Berenstain, Janice, illus. LC 85-25743. (ps-1). 1986. lib. bdg. 5.99 (*0-394-97335-6*); pap. 2.25 (*0-394-87335-1*) Random Bks Yng Read.

Bianchi, John & Edwards, Frank B. Grandma Mooner Lost Her Voice. Bianchi, John, illus. 24p. (ps-2). 1992. PLB 14.95 (*0-921285-19-1*, Pub. by Bungalo Bks CN); pap. 4.95 (*0-921285-17-5*, Pub. by Bungalo Bks CN) Firefly Bks Ltd.

Blegvad, Lenore. Once upon a Time & Grandma. Blegvad, Lenore, illus. LC 92-7407. 32p. (ps-3). 1993. SBE 14.95 (*0-689-50548-5*, M K McElderry) Macmillan Child Grp.

Blos, Joan W. Grandpa Days. LC 88-19801. (ps-3). 1994. pap. 3.95 (*0-671-88244-9*, Halfmoon) S&S Trade.

Bobbi. Grandma's Teapot. Simbrom, Janine C., illus. 37p. 1992. pap. 3.95 (*0-9626608-3-3*) Magik NY.

Bobo, Carmen P. Sarah's Growing-up Summer. LC 88-62111. 52p. 1989. 6.95 (*1-55523-187-X*) Winston-Derek.

Bond, Ruskin. Grandfather's Private Zoo. (Illus.). 95p. (gr. 3-5). 1.00 (*0-88253-345-2*) Ind-US Inc.

Bonners, Susan. Wooden Doll. (Illus.). (ps-3). 1991. 13.95 (*0-688-08280-7*); PLB 13.88 (*0-688-08282-3*) Lothrop.

Boone, Debby. The Snow Angel. Ferrer, Gabri, illus. 32p. (ps-1). 1991. text ed. 12.99 (*0-89081-871-1*) Harvest Hse.

Booth, Barbara D. Mandy. LaMarche, Jim, illus. LC 90-19989. 32p. (gr. 1 up). 1991. 14.95 (*0-688-10338-3*); PLB 14.88 (*0-688-10339-1*) Lothrop.

Bornstein, Ruth L. A Beautiful Seashell. Bornstein, Ruth L., illus. LC 90-4032. 32p. (gr. k-3). 1990. HarpC Child Bks.

Brackett, Rona N. Harry's Grandpa Takes a Mysterious Journey. Johnson, Mackenzie, illus. LC 86-1233. 55p. (Orig.). (gr. 3-6). 1986. text ed. 12.50 (*0-916955-04-4*); pap. 6.75 (*0-916955-05-2*) Arcus Pub.

Brady, Kimberley S. Keeper for the Sea. LC 94-18506. 1995. 15.95 (*0-02-711851-7*) Macmillan Child Grp.

Brooks, Bruce. Everywhere. LC 90-4073. 80p. (gr. 4 up). 1992. pap. 3.95 (*0-06-440433-1*, Trophy) HarpC Child Bks.

Brown, Irene B. Before the Lark. Milam, Larry, illus. 180p. (gr. 4 up). 1992. pap. 7.95 (*0-936085-22-3*) Blue Heron OR.

Brown, Janet M. Thanksgiving at Obaachan's. Brown, Janet M., illus. LC 93-43933. 1994. 12.95 (*1-879965-07-0*) Polychrome Pub.

Buchanan, Joan. The Nana Rescue. Cooper-Brown, Jean, illus. LC 93-20803. 1994. 4.25 (*0-383-03740-9*) SRA Schl Grp.

Buckley, Helen E. Grandfather & I. Ormerod, Jan, illus. LC 93-22936. 1994. 13.00 (*0-688-12533-6*); PLB 12. 93 (*0-688-12534-4*) Lothrop.

—Grandmother & I. Ormerod, Jan, illus. LC 93-22937. (gr. 3 up). 1994. 13.00 (*0-688-12531-X*); PLB 12.93 (*0-688-12532-8*) Lothrop.

Bunting, Eve. A Day's Work. Himler, Ronald, illus. 1994. 14.95 (*0-395-67321-6*, Clarion Bks) HM.

—Sunshine Home. De Groat, Diane, illus. LC 93-570. (gr. k-3). 1994. 14.95 (*0-395-63309-5*, Clarion Bks) HM.

—The Wednesday Surprise. Garrick, Donald, illus. 32p. (gr. k-3). 1989. 14.45 (*0-89919-721-3*, Clarion Bks) HM.

Burnett, Frances H. Little Lord Fauntleroy. Butts, Dennis, intro. by. LC 92-13794. 208p. 1993. pap. 7.95 (*0-19-282961-0*) OUP.

—Little Lord Fauntleroy. 19.95 (*0-8488-0792-8*) Amereon Ltd.

Burningham, John. Granpa. Burningham, John, illus. LC 84-17464. 32p. (ps-1). 1985. 14.00 (*0-517-55643-X*) Crown Bks Yng Read.

—Granpa. (ps-2). 1992. pap. 4.99 (*0-517-58797-1*) Crown Bks Yng Read.

Butterworth, Nick. My Grandma Is Wonderful. Butterworth, Nick, illus. LC 91-58747. 32p. (ps up). 1992. pap. 4.99 (*1-56402-100-9*) Candlewick Pr.

—My Grandpa Is Amazing. Butterworth, Nick, illus. LC 91-58746. 32p. (ps up). 1992. pap. 4.99 (*1-56402-099-1*) Candlewick Pr.

Calmenson, Stephanie. Hotter Than a Hot Dog! Savadier, Elivia, illus. LC 93-313. (gr. 1-8). 1994. 14.95 (*0-316-12479-6*) Little.

Carlson, Nancy. Visit to Grandma's. (ps-3). 1991. 13.95 (*0-670-83288-X*) Viking Child Bks.

—A Visit to Grandma's. LC 93-18607. (Illus.). 32p. (ps-3). 1993. pap. 4.99 (*0-14-054243-4*, Puffin) Puffin Bks.

Carlson-Savage, Natalie. A Grandmother for the Orphelines. (gr. k-6). 1988. pap. 2.75 (*0-440-40016-3*, YB) Dell.

Carlstrom, Nancy W. Grandpappy. Molk, Laurel, illus. (ps-3). 1990. 14.95 (*0-316-12855-4*) Little.

—The Moon Came Too. Ormai, Stella, illus. LC 86-18046. 32p. (ps-1). 1987. SBE 13.95 (*0-02-717380-1*, Macmillan Child Bk) Macmillan Child Grp.

Carrick, Carol. Valentine. Bouma, Paddy, illus. LC 93-35911. 1995. write for info. (*0-395-66554-X*, Clarion Bks) HM.

Carris, Joan D. Stolen Bones: A Novel. LC 92-36479. 1993. 14.95 (*0-316-13018-4*) Little.

Caseley, Judith. Apple Pie & Onions. Caseley, Judith, illus. LC 86-9804. 32p. (gr. 1-4). 1987. 15.00 (*0-688-06762-X*); PLB 14.93 (*0-688-06763-8*) Greenwillow.

—Dear Annie. LC 90-39793. (Illus.). 32p. (ps up). 1991. 13.95 (*0-688-10010-4*); PLB 13.88 (*0-688-10011-2*) Greenwillow.

—Grandpa's Garden Lunch. LC 89-23325. (Illus.). 32p. (ps up). 1990. 12.95 (*0-688-08816-3*); PLB 12.88 (*0-688-08817-1*) Greenwillow.

—When Grandpa Came to Stay. Caseley, Judith, illus. LC 85-12616. 32p. (gr. k-2). 1986. 11.75 (*0-688-06128-1*); PLB 11.88 (*0-688-06129-X*) Greenwillow.

Casey, Barbara W. Grandma Jock & Christabelle. LC 93-60737. 61p. (gr. 7-12). 1993. pap. 6.95 (*1-55523-406-2*) Winston-Derek.

Castaneda, Omar S. El Tapiz de Abuela. Marcuse, Aida E., tr. Sanchez, Enrique O., illus. LC 93-38628. (SPA.). 32p. (gr. k-3). 1994. 14.95 (*1-88000-008-3*); pap. 5.95 (*1-88000-011-3*) Lee & Low Bks.

Castle, Caroline. Grandpa Baxter & the Photographs. Bowman, Peter, illus. LC 92-44192. 32p. (ps-1). 1993. 14.95 (*0-531-05487-X*); PLB 14.99 (*0-531-08637-2*) Orchard Bks Watts.

Cazet, Denys. Christmas Moon. Cazet, Denys, illus. LC 87-37434. 32p. (ps-2). 1988. pap. 4.95 (*0-689-71259-6*, Aladdin) Macmillan Child Grp.

Cech, John. My Grandmother's Journey. McGinley-Nally, Sharon, illus. LC 90-35731. 40p. (ps-4). 1991. RSBE 14.95 (*0-02-718135-9*, Bradbury Pr) Macmillan Child Grp.

Choi Sook Nyul. Halmoni & the Picnic. (ps-3). 1993. 14. 95 (*0-395-61626-3*) HM.

Christie, Sally & Kavanaugh, Peter. Mean & Mighty Me. LC 90-21200. (Illus.). 64p. (gr. 2-5). 1991. 10.95 (*0-525-44700-8*, DCB) Dutton Child Bks.

Cole, Norma. The Final Tide. LC 90-6072. 160p. (gr. 5 up). 1990. SBE 14.95 (*0-689-50510-8*, M K McElderry) Macmillan Child Grp.

Conley, Bruce H. Butterflies, Grandpa & Me. (Illus.). 25p. (gr. 4 up). 1976. pap. 2.00 (*0-685-65885-6*) Conley Outreach.

Conrad, Pam. The Tub Grandfather. Egielski, Richard, illus. LC 92-31770. 32p. (ps-3). 1993. 15.00 (*0-06-022895-4*); PLB 14.89 (*0-06-022896-2*) HarpC Child Bks.

Cosgrove, Stephen. Grampa-Lop. James, Robin, illus. LC 84-15078. 32p. (Orig.). (gr. 1-4). 1981. pap. 2.95 (*0-8431-0586-0*) Price Stern.

Cotter, Noreen. Definitely Different. Webb, Philip, illus. LC 93-133. 1994. write for info. (*0-383-03685-2*) SRA Schl Grp.

Creech, Sharon. Walk Two Moons. LC 93-31277. 288p. (gr. 3-7). 1994. 16.00 (*0-06-023334-6*); PLB 15.89 (*0-06-023337-0*) HarpC Child Bks.

Cross, Verda. Great-Grandma Tells of Threshing Day. Tucker, Kathleen, ed. Owens, Gail, illus. LC 90-28442. 40p. (gr. 1-6). 1992. 15.95 (*0-8075-3042-5*) A Whitman.

Cullen, Ruth V. My Letter from Grandma. Antonucci, Emil, illus. LC 92-34381. 32p. 1993. pap. 4.95 (*0-8091-6610-0*) Paulist Pr.

Curtis, Chara M. How Far to Heaven? Currier, Alfred, illus. 28p. 1993. 15.95 (*0-935699-06-6*) Illum Arts. HOW FAR TO HEAVEN? is the question Little One asks of her grandmother. To find the answer, they slip out the back gate into the woods & begin exploring the many signs of heaven found in nature. This moving story is greatly enhanced by Currier's museum-quality impressionistic paintings. Although designed as a children's book, this story is meant for readers of all ages. "The beauty & sensitivity of the illustrations & words will touch the very center of the heart of everyone who reads this book." - Gerald G. Jampolsky, M.D., Founder, The Center for Attitudinal Healing. "This wonderful little book is about enlightenment - waking up what is all around us. What could be more important?" - Larry Dossey, M.D., author. To order, call Atrium 1-800-275-2606.
Publisher Provided Annotation.

Czernecki, Stefan & Rhodes, Timothy. Nina's Treasures. LC 93-26932. 1994. PLB 14.89 (*1-56282-595-X*) Hyprn Child.

Dahl, Roald. The Witches. Blake, Quentin, illus. LC 85-519. 200p. (gr. 3-7). 1985. pap. 3.95 (*0-14-031730-9*) Viking Child Bks.

Daly, Niki. Papa Lucky's Shadow. Daly, Niki, illus. LC 91-24283. 32p. (gr. k-3). 1992. SBE 14.95 (*0-689-50541-8*, M K McElderry) Macmillan Child Grp.

Darling, Benjamin. Valerie & the Silver Pear. Lane, Dan, illus. LC 90-24945. 32p. (gr. k-3). 1992. RSBE 14.95 (*0-02-726100-X*, Four Winds) Macmillan Child Grp.

Davis, Jenny. Checking on the Moon. LC 91-8284. 224p. (gr. 6 up). 1991. 14.95 (*0-531-05960-X*); RLB 14.99 (*0-531-08560-0*) Orchard Bks Watts.

Davoll, Barbara. Grandpa's Secret. Hockerman, Dennis, illus. 24p. 1993. 6.99 (*1-56476-161-4*, Victor Books) SP Pubns.

DeFelice, Cynthia C. When Grampa Kissed His Elbow. Swanson, Karl, illus. LC 90-6696. 32p. (gr. k-3). 1992. RSBE 14.95 (*0-02-726455-6*, Macmillan Child Bk) Macmillan Child Grp.

Demarest, Dorothy E. Mrs. Cooderberry's Nine Grandchildren. 1992. text ed. 8.95 (*0-533-10117-4*) Vantage.

Denton, Kady M. Granny Is a Darling. LC 87-22635. (Illus.). 32p. (ps-3). 1988. SBE 13.95 (*0-689-50452-7*, M K McElderry) Macmillan Child Grp.

—Granny Is a Darling. Denton, Kady M., illus. LC 89-18397. 32p. (ps-2). 1990. pap. 4.95 (*0-689-71207-3*, Aladdin) Macmillan Child Grp.

De Paola, Tomie. Nana Upstairs & Nana Downstairs. new ed. De Paola, Tomie, illus. 32p. (ps-3). 1973. 13. 95 (*0-399-21417-8*, Putnam) Putnam Pub Group.

—Now One Foot, Now the Other. De Paola, Tomie, illus. 48p. (gr. 3-7). 1981. 13.95 (*0-399-20774-0*, Putnam) Putnam Pub Group.

—Watch Out for the Chicken Feet in Your Soup. LC 74-8201. (Illus.). (ps-3). 1985. (Pub. by Treehouse) P-H.

—Watch Out for the Chicken Feet in Your Soup. LC 74-8201. (Illus.). 32p. (gr. k-4). 1974. 12.95 (*0-685-35587-X*, S&S BFYR); pap. 5.95 (*0-685-35588-8*, S&S BFYR) S&S Trade.

Devlin, Wende & Devlin, Harry. Cranberry Autumn. LC 92-23237. (Illus.). 40p. (gr. k-3). 1993. RSBE 13.95 (*0-02-729936-8*, Four Winds) Macmillan Child Grp.

—The Trouble with Henriette. 1995. 15.00 (*0-02-729937-6*, Four Winds) Macmillan Child Grp.

Dexter, Alison. Grandma. Dexter, Alison, illus. LC 92-6473. 32p. (ps-2). 1993. 15.00 (*0-06-021143-1*); PLB 14.89 (*0-06-021144-X*) HarpC Child Bks.

Dickinson, Peter. Shadow of a Hero. LC 94-8667. 1994. 15.95 (*0-385-32110-4*) Delacorte.

Diller, Harriett. Grandaddy's Highway. (Illus.). 22p. (ps-3). 1993. 14.95 (*1-878093-63-0*) Boyds Mills Pr.

Dionetti, Michelle. Coal Mine Peaches. Riggio, Anita, illus. LC 90-28693. 32p. (ps-2). 1991. 14.95 (*0-531-05948-0*); RLB 14.99 (*0-531-08548-1*) Orchard Bks Watts.

Dodds, Siobhan. Grandpa Bud. Dodds, Siobhan, illus. LC 92-53135. 32p. (ps-3). 1993. 13.95 (*1-56402-175-0*) Candlewick Pr.

Doherty, Berlie. Granny Was a Buffer Girl. large type ed. (gr. 1-8). 1991. 16.95 (*0-7451-0725-7*, Galaxy Child Lrg Print) Chivers N Amer.

Dorros, Arthur. Abuela. Kleven, Elisa, illus. LC 90-21459. 40p. (ps-2). 1991. 14.00 (*0-525-44750-4*, DCB) Dutton Child Bks.

Dupre, Rick. The Wishing Chair. LC 92-38880. 32p. 1993. 18.95 (*0-87614-774-0*) Carolrhoda Bks.

Dyjak, Elisabeth. I Should Have Listened to Moon. LC 89-26739. 130p. (gr. 4-6). 1990. 13.45 (*0-395-52279-X*) HM.

Ernst, Lisa C. The Luckiest Kid on the Planet. (ps-2). 1994. 14.95 (*0-02-733566-6*, Bradbury Pr) Macmillan Child Grp.

Fakih, Kimberly O. Grandpa Putter & Granny Hoe. Pearson, Tracy C., illus. 128p. (gr. 2-5). 1992. 13.00 (*0-374-32762-9*) FS&G.

—High on the Hog. LC 93-34214. 1994. 16.00 (*0-374-33209-6*) FS&G.

Falwell, Cathryn. Nicky & Grandpa. Falwell, Cathryn, illus. 32p. (ps). 1991. 5.70 (*0-395-56917-6*, Clarion Bks) HM.

Fernandes, Kim. Visiting Granny. Fernandes, Kim, illus. Lacroix, Pat, photos by. (Illus.). 24p. (ps-k). 1990. 12. 95 (*1-55037-077-4*, Pub. by Annick CN); pap. 4.95 (*1-55037-084-7*, Pub. by Annik CN) Firefly Bks Ltd.

Fettig, Art. The Three Robots Find a Grandpa. Carpenter, Joe, illus. LC 84-80378. 96p. (Orig.). (gr. k-7). 1984. pap. 3.95 (*0-9601334-8-8*); cassette incl. Growth Unltd.

Flournoy, Valerie. Tanya's Reunion. Pinkey, Jerry, illus. LC 94-13067. 1995. write for info. (*0-8037-1604-4*); PLB write for info. (*0-8037-1605-2*) Dial Bks Young.

Foreman, Michael. Grandfather's Pencil & the Room of Stories. Foreman, Michael, illus. LC 93-6266. (ps-3). 1994. 13.95 (*0-15-200061-5*) HarBrace.

—Jack's Fantastic Voyage. 1992. write for info. (*0-15-239496-6*, HB Juv Bks) HarBrace.

Forward, Toby. Traveling Backward. Cornell, Laura, illus. LC 93-32514. 1994. write for info. RTE (*0-688-13076-3*, Tambourine Bks) Morrow.

Fox, Mem. Shoes from Grandpa. Mullins, Patricia, illus. LC 89-35401. 32p. (ps-1). 1992. pap. 4.95 (0-531-07031-X) Orchard Bks Watts.

—Sophie. Robinson, Aminah B. L., illus. LC 94-1976. (ps-3). 1994. 13.95 (0-15-277160-3) HarBrace.

Fox, Paula. Western Wind. LC 93-9629. 208p. (gr. 5 up). 1993. 14.95 (0-531-06802-1); PLB 14.99 (0-531-08652-6) Orchard Bks Watts.

Fraustino, Lisa R. Grass & Sky. LC 93-25210. 1994. write for info. (0-531-06823-4); lib. bdg. write for info. (0-531-08673-9) Orchard Bks Watts.

Friend, Catherine. Sawfin Stickleback. (Illus.). 32p. (ps-3). 1994. 13.95 (1-56282-473-2); PLB 13.89 (1-56282-474-0) Hyprn Child.

Gackenbach, Dick. With Love from Gran. (ps-3). 1990. pap. 5.70 (0-395-54775-X, Clarion Bks) HM.

Gantschev, Ivan. The Christmas Teddy Bear. Clements, Andrew, adapted by. LC 93-20121. (gr. 4 up). 1993. write for info. (0-88708-333-1) Picture Bk Studio.

—The Train to Grandma's. LC 87-13899. (Illus.). 36p. (ps up). 1991. pap. 16.95 (0-88708-053-7) Picture Bk Studio.

Garland, Sherry. The Silent Storm. LC 92-33690. 1992. write for info. (0-15-274170-4) HarBrace.

Geller, Norman. I Don't Want to Visit Grandma Anymore. Tomlinson, Albert J., illus. 28p. (gr. 1-4). 1984. pap. 4.95 (0-915753-05-7) N Geller Pub.

George, William T. & George, Lindsay B. Fishing at Long Pond. LC 89-77514. (Illus.). 24p. (ps up). 1991. 13.95 (0-688-09401-5); PLB 13.88 (0-688-09402-3) Greenwillow.

Geraghty, Paul. The Hunter. LC 93-22730. (Illus.). 32p. (ps-3). 1994. 15.00 (0-517-59692-X); PLB 15.99 (0-517-59693-8) Crown Bks Yng Read.

Gershator, Phillis. Sambalena Show-Off & the Iron Pot. Jenkins, Leonard, illus. LC 94-14413. 1995. 15.00 (0-02-735855-0) Macmillan.

Gibson, Andrew. Jemima, Grandma & the Great Lost Zone. Riddell, Chris, illus. 128p. (gr. 3-7). 1992. pap. 6.95 (0-571-16737-3) Faber & Faber.

Goldman, Susan. Grandma Is Somebody Special. Rubin, Caroline, ed. Golden, Susan, illus. LC 76-18980. 32p. (ps-1). 1976. PLB 10.95 (0-8075-3034-4) A Whitman.

Gould, Deborah. Grandpa's Slide Show. Harness, Cheryl, illus. LC 86-20981. 32p. (ps-3). 1987. 13.95 (0-688-06972-X); PLB 13.88 (0-688-06973-8) Lothrop.

Grandpa. Sir Reginald's Meeting. 1993. pap. 10.95 (0-533-10487-4) Vantage.

Greaves, Margaret. The Serpent Shell. Nesbitt, Jan, illus. 32p. (ps-3). 1993. 13.95 (0-8120-6350-3) Barron.

Greenfield, Eloise. Grandmama's Joy. Byard, Carole, illus. LC 79-11403. 32p. (gr. 2-5). 1980. 13.95 (0-399-21064-4, Philomel) Putnam Pub Group.

—Grandpa's Face. Cooper, Floyd, illus. LC 87-16729. 32p. (ps-2). 1988. 14.95 (0-399-21525-5, Philomel Bks) Putnam Pub Group.

—Grandpa's Face. Cooper, Floyd, illus. 32p. (ps-3). 1991. pap. 5.95 (0-399-22106-9, Sandcastle Bks) Putnam Pub Group.

—Grandpa's Face. Cooper, Floyd, illus. (SPA.). 32p. (ps up). 1993. pap. 5.95 (0-399-22511-0, Philomel Bks) Putnam Pub Group.

—William & the Good Old Days. Gilchrist, Jan S., illus. LC 91-47030. 32p. (gr. k-3). 1993. 15.00 (0-06-021093-1); PLB 14.89 (0-06-021094-X) HarpC Child Bks.

Griffin, Peni R. A Dig in Time. LC 90-47388. 192p. (gr. 4-7). 1991. SBE 14.95 (0-689-50525-6, M K McElderry) Macmillan Child Grp.

—A Dig in Time. LC 92-18958. 160p. (gr. 3-7). 1992. pap. 3.99 (0-14-036001-8) Puffin Bks.

Griffith, Helen V. Grandaddy's Place. Stevenson, James, illus. LC 86-19573. 40p. (gr. 1-4). 1987. 13.95 (0-688-06253-9); PLB 13.88 (0-688-06254-7) Greenwillow.

Guback, Georgia. Luka's Quilt. LC 93-12241. (Illus.). 32p. (ps up). 1994. 14.00 (0-688-12154-3); PLB 13.93 (0-688-12155-1) Greenwillow.

Haas, Jessie. Mowing. Smith, Joseph A., photos by. LC 93-12240. 32p. (ps up). 1994. 14.00 (0-688-11680-9); lib. bdg. 13.93 (0-688-11681-7) Greenwillow.

Halak, Glenn. A Grandmother's Story. LC 91-18058. (Illus.). 48p. (ps). 1992. 14.00 (0-671-74953-6, Green Tiger) S&S Trade.

Hall, Donald. Summer of 1944. Moser, Barry, illus. LC 92-38613. 32p. (gr. 1-5). 1994. 15.99 (0-8037-1501-3); PLB 15.89 (0-8037-1502-1) Dial Bks Young.

Harranth, Wolf. My Old Grandad. Oppermann-Dimow, Christina, illus. Carter, Peter, tr. (Illus.). 30p. (ps-6). 1987. 11.95 (0-19-279787-5) OUP.

Hartling, Peter. Old John. Crawford, Elizabeth D., tr. from GER. LC 89-12976. 128p. (gr. 4-9). 1990. 11.95 (0-688-08734-5) Lothrop.

Haseley, Dennis. Shadows. Bowman, Leslie, illus. 80p. (gr. 2-6). 1991. 12.95 (0-374-36761-2) FS&G.

Haskins, Francine. Things I Like about Grandma. Haskins, Francine, illus. 32p. (gr. 3-4). 1992. PLB 21.34 (0-89239-107-3) Childrens Book Pr.

Hathorn, Libby. Grandma's Shoes. Elivia, illus. LC 93-20776. (ps-3). 1994. 14.95 (0-316-35135-0) Little.

Hendershot, Judith. Up the Tracks to Grandma's. Allen, Thomas B., illus. LC 91-2749. 40p. (ps-2). 1993. 15.00 (0-679-81964-9); PLB 15.99 (0-679-91964-3) Knopf Bks Yng Read.

Hennessy, B. G. When You Were Just a Little Girl. Arnold, Jeanne, illus. 32p. (ps-3). 1994. pap. 4.99 (0-14-054172-1) Puffin Bks.

Hermes, Patricia. Someone to Count On. LC 93-13502. (ps-6). 1993. 14.95 (0-316-35925-4) Little.

—Take Care of My Girl: A Novel. LC 92-9819. 1992. 14.95 (0-316-35913-0) Little.

Hershey, Kathleen. Cotton Mill Town. Winter, Jeanette, illus. LC 92-7379. (ps-2). 1993. 12.99 (0-525-44966-3, DCB) Dutton Child Bks.

Hesse, Karen. Poppy's Chair. Life, Kay, illus. LC 91-47708. 32p. (gr. k-3). 1993. RSBE 14.95 (0-02-743705-1, Macmillan Child Bk) Macmillan Child Grp.

Hest, Amy. The Crack-of-Dawn Walkers. Schwartz, Amy, illus. 32p. (Orig.). (ps-3). 1988. pap. 3.99 (0-14-050829-5, Puffin) Puffin Bks.

—The Go-Between. DiSalvo-Ryan, DyAnne, illus. LC 90-24561. 32p. (gr. k-3). 1992. RSBE 14.95 (0-02-743632-2, Four Winds) Macmillan Child Grp.

—The Purple Coat. Schwartz, Amy, illus. LC 85-29186. 32p. (gr. k-3). 1986. RSBE 14.95 (0-02-743640-3, Four Winds) Macmillan Child Grp.

—The Purple Coat. Schwartz, Amy, illus. LC 91-38499. 32p. (gr. k-3). 1992. pap. 4.95 (0-689-71634-6, Aladdin) Macmillan Child Grp.

—Ruby's Storm. Cote, Nancy, illus. LC 92-31242. 32p. (ps-2). 1994. RSBE 14.95 (0-02-743160-6, Four Winds) Macmillan Child Grp.

Hickcox, RUth. Great-Grandmother's Apron. LC 93-42242. 1995. write for info. (0-8037-1513-7); lib. bdg. write for info. (0-8037-1514-5) Dial Bks Young.

Hickman, Janet. Jericho. LC 93-37309. 1994. write for info. (0-688-13398-3) Greenwillow.

Hill, Elizabeth S. The Street Dancers. 176p. (gr. 3-7). 1993. pap. 3.99 (0-14-034491-8, Puffin) Puffin Bks.

Hines, Anna G. Gramma's Walk. LC 92-30085. 32p. (ps up). 1993. 14.00 (0-688-11480-6); PLB 13.93 (0-688-11481-4) Greenwillow.

—Grandma Gets Grumpy. Hines, Anna G., illus. LC 87-17874. (ps-1). 1988. 13.95 (0-89919-529-6, Clarion Bks) HM.

—Grandma Gets Grumpy. Hines, Anna G., illus. LC 87-17874. 32p. (ps). 1990. pap. 4.80 (0-395-52595-0, Clarion Bks) HM.

Hippely, Hilary H. September Song. Baker, Leslie, illus. LC 93-32625. (gr. 5 up). 1995. 15.95 (0-399-22646-X, Putnam) Putnam Pub Group.

Hirschi, Ron. Harvest Song. Haeffele, Deborah, illus. LC 90-27009. 32p. (ps-3). 1991. 13.95 (0-525-65067-9, Cobblehill Bks) Dutton Child Bks.

Hite, Sid. It's Nothing to a Mountain. LC 93-42048. 1994. 15.95 (0-8050-2769-6) H Holt & Co.

Hoffman, Mary. My Grandma Has Black Hair. Burroughes, Joanna, illus. LC 87-24654. 32p. (ps-3). 1988. 9.95 (0-8037-0510-7) Dial Bks Young.

Hooks, William H. The Mighty Santa Fe. Thomas, Angela T., illus. LC 92-17026. 32p. (gr. k-3). 1993. RSBE 14.95 (0-02-744432-5, Macmillan Child Bk) Macmillan Child Grp.

Hoopes, Lyn L. Half a Button. Watts, Trish P., illus. LC 87-24949. 32p. (ps-2). 1989. HarpC Child Bks.

Houghton, Eric. The Backwards Watch. Abel, Simone, illus. LC 91-16951. 32p. (ps-2). 1992. 13.95 (0-531-05968-5); PLB 13.99 (0-531-08568-6) Orchard Bks Watts.

Houston, James R. Akavak. 80p. (gr. 5 up). 1990. pap. 8.95 (0-15-201731-3) HarBrace.

Howard, Kim. In Wintertime. LC 93-10979. 1994. 16.00 (0-688-11378-8); lib. bdg. 15.93 (0-688-11379-6) Lothrop.

Howe, Quincy. Streetsmart. LC 93-1397. 112p. (gr. 6-12). 1993. pap. 6.95 (0-932765-42-4, 1325-93); tchr's. guide 5.95 (0-685-70875-6, 1326-93) Close Up.

Hunt, Angela E. Gift for Grandpa. LC 91-157544. (ps-3). 1991. 13.99 (1-55513-425-4, Chariot Bks) Chariot Family.

Hurd, Edith T. I Dance in My Red Pajamas. McCully, Emily A., illus. LC 81-47721. 32p. (gr. 1-3). 1982. PLB 14.89 (0-06-022700-1) HarpC Child Bks.

Irwin, Hadley. What about Grandma? 176p. 1991. pap. 2.99 (0-380-71138-9, Flare) Avon.

Jam, Teddy. The Year of Fire. Wallace, Ian, illus. LC 92-2882. 48p. (gr. 1-5). 1993. SBE 14.95 (0-689-50566-3, M K McElderry) Macmillan Child Grp.

James, Sara. Boots Visits Grandma. Barcita, Pamela, illus. 24p. 1993. PLB 3.98 (1-56156-134-7) Kidsbks.

—Boots Visits Grandma. Barcita, Pamela, illus. 24p. (ps-k). 1993. 3.98 (0-8317-0603-1) Smithmark.

James, Simon. The Wild Woods. James, Simon, illus. LC 92-54582. 32p. (ps up). 1993. 13.95 (1-56402-219-6) Candlewick Pr.

Jenkins, Catherine. Monday Came. Thomas, Meredith, illus. LC 93-28982. 1994. 4.25 (0-383-03762-X) SRA Schl Grp.

Johnson, Angela. Toning the Sweep: A Novel. LC 92-34062. 112p. (gr. 6 up). 1993. 13.95 (0-531-05476-4); PLB 13.99 (0-531-08626-7) Orchard Bks Watts.

—When I Am Old with You. Soman, David, illus. LC 89-70928. 32p. (ps-2). 1993. pap. 4.95 (0-531-07035-2) Orchard Bks Watts.

Johnson, Dolores. Your Dad Was Just Like You. Johnson, Dolores, illus. LC 92-6347. 32p. (gr. k-3). 1993. RSBE 13.95 (0-02-747838-6, Macmillan Child Bk) Macmillan Child Grp.

Johnson, Herschel. A Visit to the Country. Bearden, Romare, illus. LC 87-25083. 32p. (ps-3). 1989. PLB 13.89 (0-06-022854-7) HarpC Child Bks.

Johnston, Tony. Grandpa's Song. Sneed, Brad, illus. LC 90-43836. 32p. (ps-3). 1991. 12.95 (0-8037-0801-7); lib. bdg. 12.89 (0-8037-0802-5) Dial Bks Young.

—Little Rabbit Goes to Sleep. Stevenson, Harvey, illus. LC 92-8543. 32p. (ps-k). 1994. 15.00 (0-06-021239-X); PLB 14.89 (0-06-021241-1) HarpC Child Bks.

Kastner, Jill. Snake Hunt. Kastner, Jill, illus. LC 92-32601. 32p. (ps-2). 1993. RSBE 14.95 (0-02-749395-4, Four Winds) Macmillan Child Grp.

Kasza, Keiko. Grandpa Toad's Last Secret. LC 93-44376. 1995. 14.95 (0-399-22610-9, Putnam) Putnam Pub Group.

Kehret, Peg. Night of Fear. LC 93-24051. 144p. (gr. 5 up). 1994. 13.99 (0-525-65136-5, Cobblehill Bks) Dutton Child Bks.

Keller, Holly. The Best Present. LC 87-38086. (Illus.). 32p. (gr. k up). 1989. 11.95 (0-688-07319-0); PLB 11.88 (0-688-07320-4) Greenwillow.

—Grandfather's Dream. LC 93-18186. (Illus.). 32p. (ps up). 1994. 14.00 (0-688-12339-2); PLB 13.93 (0-688-12340-6) Greenwillow.

Kerensky, Elaine. Far Away Gramma. Tremblay, Ruth, illus. 24p. (Orig.). (gr. k-3). 1990. pap. text ed. write for info. (0-9627228-0-4) Far Away Fam Playhse.

Ketteman, Helen. One Baby Boy. Flynn-Stanton, Maggie, illus. LC 93-23044. 1994. pap. 15.00 (0-671-87278-8, S&S BFYR) S&S Trade.

Kezzeiz, Ediba. Grandma's Garden. Hubbi, Mona, illus. 21p. (Orig.). (ps-4). 1991. pap. 3.50 (0-89259-113-7) Am Trust Pubns.

Khalsa, Dayal K. Tales of a Gambling Grandma. (Illus.). 32p. (gr. 1 up). 1991. 14.95 (0-88776-179-8) Tundra Bks.

Kibbey, Marsha. The Helping Place. Hagerman, Jennifer, illus. 40p. (gr. 1-4). 1991. PLB 13.50 (0-87614-680-9) Carolrhoda Bks.

—My Grammy. Ritz, Karen, illus. 32p. (gr. 1-4). 1988. PLB 13.50 (0-87614-328-1) Carolrhoda Bks.

Kinsey-Warnock, Natalie. The Canada Geese Quilt. Bowman, Leslie W., illus. 60p. (gr. 5 up). 1992. pap. 3.50 (0-440-40719-2, YB) Dell.

—The Fiddler of the Northern Lights. Bowman, Leslie W., illus. LC 92-36703. 1994. write for info. (0-525-65143-8, Cobblehill Bks) Dutton Child Bks.

Kirkpatrick, Patricia. Plowie. Kirkpatrick, Joey, illus. LC 93-13712. (ps-3). 1994. 14.95 (0-15-262802-9) HarBrace.

Klein, Norma. Going Backwards. 92p. (gr. 7 up). 1986. pap. 12.95 (0-590-40328-1) Scholastic Inc.

Kolanovic, Dubravka. A Special Day. Thatch, Nancy R., ed. Kolanovic, Dubravka, illus. Melton, David, intro. by. LC 93-13419. (Illus.). 29p. (gr. k-2). 1993. PLB 14.95 (0-933849-45-1) Landmark Edns.

Konigsburg, E. L. Amy Elizabeth Explores Bloomingdale's. Konigsburg, E. L., illus. LC 91-40132. 32p. (ps-3). 1992. SBE 14.95 (0-689-31766-2, Atheneum Child Bk) Macmillan Child Grp.

Kopen, Pamela A. Grandpa's Magic Drawer. Kopen, Pamela A., illus. Kopen, Dan F., intro. by. LC 91-91475. (Illus.). 32p. (ps-3). 1992. 14.95 (0-9628914-1-X) Padakami Pr.

Koralek, Jenny. The Boy & the Cloth of Dreams. Mayhew, James, illus. LC 93-23091. 32p. (ps up). 1994. 14.95 (1-56402-349-4) Candlewick Pr.

Kroll, Steven. Patrick's Tree House. Wilson, Roberta, illus. LC 93-4571. 64p. (gr. 2-5). 1994. RSBE 13.95 (0-02-751005-0, Macmillan Child Bk) Macmillan Child Grp.

Kurtz, Jane. Pulling the Lion's Tail. Cooper, Floyd, illus. LC 93-22836. 1995. pap. 15.00 (0-671-88183-3, S&S BFYR) S&S Trade.

Lasky, Kathryn. My Island Grandma. Schwartz, Amy, illus. LC 91-31000. 32p. (ps up). 1993. 15.00 (0-688-07946-6); PLB 14.93 (0-688-07948-2) Morrow Jr Bks.

Leonard, Marcia. The Giant Baby & Other Giant Tales. Alley, R. W., illus. LC 93-6225. (ps-4). 1994. pap. 2.95 (0-590-46892-8) Scholastic Inc.

LeShan, Eda. Grandparents: A Special Kind of Love. Taggart, Tricia, illus. LC 84-5673. 112p. (gr. 3-7). 1984. SBE 13.95 (0-02-756380-4, Macmillan Child Bk) Macmillan Child Grp.

Lester, Alison. Isabella's Bed. Lester, Alison, illus. LC 92-22935. 32p. (gr. k-3). 1993. Repr. of 1991 ed. 14.95 (0-395-65565-X) HM.

Levine, Arthur A. Bono & Nonno. Lanfredi, Judy, illus. LC 93-35931. 1995. write for info. (0-688-13233-2, Tambourine Bks); PLB write for info. (0-688-13234-0, Tambourine Bks) Morrow.

Levine, Evan. Not the Piano, Mrs. Medley! Schindler, Stephen D., illus. LC 90-29085. 32p. (ps-2). 1991. 14.95 (0-531-05956-1); RLB 14.99 (0-531-08556-2) Orchard Bks Watts.

Levinson, Riki. I Go with My Family to Grandma's. (ps-3). 1992. pap. 4.99 (0-14-054762-2) Puffin Bks.

—Watch the Stars Come Out. Goode, Diane, illus. LC 84-28672. 32p. (ps-3). 1985. 15.00 (0-525-44205-7, DCB) Dutton Child Bks.

Limb, Sue. Come Back, Grandma. Munoz, Claudio, illus. LC 92-43534. 32p. (ps-2). 1994. 13.00 (0-679-84720-0) Knopf Bks Yng Read.

London, Jonathan. Liplap & the Snowbunny. Long, Sylvia, illus. LC 93-31007. 1994. 13.95 (0-8118-0505-0) Chronicle Bks.

—The Sugaring-off Party. Pelletier, Gilles, illus. LC 93-21911. 1994. write for info. (0-525-45187-0, DCB) Dutton Child Bks.

Long, Evelyn. Grandma Tellmie about Ant, Wars Snake-Feeders, Blood-Drinking Bugs & Butterfly. Plott, Dave, et al, eds. 31p. 1984. pap. 4.00x (*0-931881-00-5*) Collaborare Pub.
Lyon, George-Ella. Come a Tide. Gammell, Stephen, illus. LC 89-35650. 32p. (ps-2). 1993. pap. 5.95 (*0-531-07036-0*) Orchard Bks Watts.
McAllister, Angela. The Wind Garden. Fletcher, Claire, illus. LC 93-37435. 1994. 15.00 (*0-688-13280-4*) Lothrop.
McBain, Ann F. My Very Own Quilt. 1993. 7.95 (*0-8062-4607-3*) Carlton.
McCartney, Jenny. Grandma's Hospital. Bruere, Julian, illus. LC 92-29958. 1993. 4.25 (*0-383-03570-8*) SRA Schl Grp.
McCormick, Maxine. Pretty As You Please. LC 92-39310. 1994. 15.95 (*0-399-22536-6*, Philomel Bks) Putnam Pub Group.
McCully, Emily A. The Grandma Mix-Up. McCully, Emily A., illus. LC 87-29378. 64p. (gr. k-3). 1988. PLB 13.89 (*0-06-024202-7*) HarpC Child Bks.
—The Grandma Mix-Up. McCully, Emily A., illus. LC 87-29378. 64p. (gr. k-3). 1991. pap. 3.50 (*0-06-444150-4*, Trophy) HarpC Child Bks.
—Grandmas at Bat. McCully, Emily A., illus. LC 92-8318. 64p. (gr. k-3). 1993. 14.00 (*0-06-021031-1*); PLB 13.89 (*0-06-021032-X*) HarpC Child Bks.
—Grandmas at the Lake. McCully, Emily A., illus. LC 89-26590. 64p. (gr. k-3). 1990. PLB 13.89 (*0-06-024127-6*) HarpC Child Bks.
McFarlane, Sheryl. Waiting for the Whales. Lightburn, Ron, illus. LC 92-25117. 32p. (ps-3). 1993. PLB 14.95 (*0-399-22515-3*, Philomel Bks) Putnam Pub Group.
McKay, Hilary. The Exiles. McKeating, Eileen, illus. LC 91-38220. 208p. (gr. 4-7). 1992. SBE 14.95 (*0-689-50555-8*, M K McElderry) Macmillan Child Grp.
—The Exiles at Home. LC 94-14225. (gr. 4-7). 1994. 15.95 (*0-689-50610-4*, M K McElderry) Macmillan Child Grp.
McKean, Thomas. Hooray for Grandma Jo! Demarest, Chris, illus. LC 93-16376. (ps-6). 1994. 14.00 (*0-517-57842-5*); PLB 14.99 (*0-517-57843-3*) Crown Bks Yng Read.
MacLachlan, Patricia. Three Names. Pertzoff, Alexander, illus. LC 90-4444. 32p. (gr. k-4). 1991. 14.95 (*0-06-024035-0*); PLB 14.89 (*0-06-024036-9*) HarpC Child Bks.
—Through Grandpa's Eyes. Ray, Deborah K., illus. LC 79-2019. 48p. (gr. k-3). 1983. pap. 4.95 (*0-06-443041-3*, Trophy) HarpC Child Bks.
Mac Laverty, Bernard. Andrew McAndrew. Smith, Duncan, illus. LC 92-52993. 80p. (gr. k-3). 1993. 13.95 (*1-56402-173-4*) Candlewick Pr.
McQuade, Susan. Great-Grandpa. Rogers, Gregory, illus. LC 92-27235. 1993. 3.75 (*0-383-03622-4*) SRA Schl Grp.
Mahy, Margaret. A Busy Day for a Good Grandmother. Chamberlain, Margaret, illus. LC 93-77331. 32p. (ps-3). 1993. SBE 14.95 (*0-689-50595-7*, M K McElderry) Macmillan Child Grp.
Manes, Stephen. An Almost Perfect Game. LC 94-18192. 1995. 13.95 (*0-590-44432-8*) Scholastic Inc.
Marie, Sharon. Granny's Crooked Teeth. 1993. 7.95 (*0-533-10602-8*) Vantage.
Marshall, Val & Tester, Bronwyn. And Grandpa Sat on Friday. Spavern, Marilyn, illus. LC 92-34159. 1993. 4.25 (*0-383-03610-0*) SRA Schl Grp.
Marshall, William. Adam's Island. (Illus.). (gr. 3-8). 1992. PLB 8.95 (*0-89565-889-5*) Childs World.
Martin, Ann M. Karen's Grandmother. (gr. 4-7). 1990. pap. 2.75 (*0-590-43651-1*) Scholastic Inc.
Martin, Bill, Jr. & Archambault, John. Knots on a Counting Rope. Rand, Ted, illus. LC 87-14832. 32p. (ps-2). 1987. 14.95 (*0-8050-0571-4*, Bks Young Read) H Holt & Co.
Martin, C. L. Down Dairy Farm Road. Hearn, Diane D., illus. LC 92-42848. 32p. (gr. k-3). 1994. RSBE 14.95 (*0-02-762450-1*, Macmillan Child Bk) Macmillan Child Grp.
Mason, Ann M. The Weird Things in Nanna's House. Wilcox, Cathy, illus. LC 91-16208. 32p. (ps-1). 1992. 13.95 (*0-531-05970-7*); lib. bdg. 13.99 (*0-531-08570-8*) Orchard Bks Watts.
Mason, Jane. River Day. Sorensen, Henri, illus. LC 93-26573. 32p. (gr. k-3). 1994. RSBE 14.95 (*0-02-762869-8*, Macmillan Child Bk) Macmillan Child Grp.
Mazer, Norma F. After the Rain. LC 86-33270. 304p. (gr. 7 up). 1987. 12.95 (*0-688-06867-7*) Morrow Jr Bks.
Menken, John. Grandpa's Gizmos. Skaggs, Keith A., ed. Davis, Tim, illus. 28p. (Orig.). (gr. 2-6). 1992. pap. 4.95 (*0-89084-663-4*) Bob Jones Univ Pr.
Miller, Rose. The Old Barn. Enik, Ted, illus. LC 92-35283. 32p. (gr. 2-6). 1992. PLB 19.97 (*0-8114-3581-4*) Raintree Steck-V.
Milstein, Linda. Grandma's Jewelry Box. Hirashima, Jean, illus. LC 91-66738. 24p. (ps-3). 1992. 8.00 (*0-679-81973-8*) Random Bks Yng Read.
Milstein, Linda B. Miami-Nanny Stories. Han, Oki, illus. LC 93-28680. 1994. 16.00 (*0-688-11151-3*, Tambourine Bks); PLB 15.93 (*0-688-11152-1*, Tambourine Bks) Morrow.
Mock, Dorothy. Springtime Special: The Good News Kids Learn about Patience. Mitter, Kathy, illus. LC 92-27010. 32p. (Orig.). (ps-2). 1993. pap. 5.99 (*0-570-04736-6*) Concordia.
Monjo, F. N. Grand Papa & Ellen Aroon. (gr. k-6). 1990. pap. 2.75 (*0-440-43004-6*, YB) Dell.
Moon, Nicola. Lucy's Pictures. Ayliffe, Alex, illus. LC 94-11178. (gr. 7-9). Date not set. write for info. (*0-8037-1833-0*) Dial Bks Young.
Moore, Elaine. Grandma's Garden. LC 90-6052. (ps-3). 1994. 15.00 (*0-688-08693-4*); 14.93 (*0-688-08694-2*) Lothrop.
—Grandma's House. Primavera, Elise, illus. LC 84-11233. 32p. (gr. k up). 1985. 15.00 (*0-688-04115-9*); PLB 14.93 (*0-688-04116-7*) Lothrop.
—Grandma's Promise. Primavera, Elise, illus. LC 86-33762. (gr. k-3). 1988. 15.00 (*0-688-06740-9*); lib. bdg. 14.93 (*0-688-06741-7*) Lothrop.
Mora, Pat. Pablo's Tree. Mora, Francisco X., illus. LC 92-27145. 32p. (ps-1). 1994. RSBE 14.95 (*0-02-767401-0*, Macmillan Child Bk) Macmillan Child Grp.
Moss, Marissa. In America. Moss, Marissa, illus. LC 93-26885. 1994. write for info. (*0-525-45152-8*, DCB) Dutton Child Bks.
Mower, Nancy A. I Visit My Tutu & Grandma. Wozniak, Patricia A., illus. LC 84-3280. (ps). 1984. 8.95 (*0-916630-41-2*) Pr Pacifica.
Murphy, Claire R. Gold Star Sister. LC 94-48135. 224p. (gr. 5-9). 1994. 14.99 (*0-525-67492-6*, Lodestar Bks) Dutton Child Bks.
Murrow, Liza K. Dancing on the Table. Himler, Ronald, illus. LC 89-46066. 128p. (gr. 3-7). 1990. 13.95 (*0-8234-0808-6*) Holiday.
Namioka, Lensey. April & the Dragon Lady. LC 93-27958. 1994. write for info. (*0-15-276644-8*, Browndeer Pr) HarBrace.
Neasi, Barbara. Listen to Me. Sharp, Gene, illus. LC 86-10664. 32p. (ps-2). 1986. PLB 10.25 (*0-516-02072-2*); pap. 2.95 (*0-516-42072-0*) Childrens.
Nelson, Vaunda M. Always Gramma. Uhler, Kimanne, illus. 32p. (ps-3). 1988. PLB 14.95 (*0-399-21542-5*, Putnam) Putnam Pub Group.
Nethery, Mary. Hannah & Jack. Morgan, Mary, illus. LC 93-4651. 1995. 15.95 (*0-02-768125-4*, Bradbury Pr) Macmillan Child Grp.
Nister, Ernest. Visiting Grandma. Nister, Ernest, illus. (gr. k up). 1989. 5.95 (*0-399-21695-2*, Philomel Bks) Putnam Pub Group.

Nobisso, Josephine. Grandma's Scrapbook. LC 91-23309. (Illus.). 1991. 12.95 (*0-671-74976-5*, Green Tiger) S&S Trade.
Readers have described the effect of GRANDMA'S SCRAPBOOK as "stunning in its beauty," "captivating & engrossing." In this companion volume to GRANDPA LOVED, a young girl tenderly shows us pages from the scrapbook her grandmother kept to chronicle their summers together. From the time grandmother pushes the girl in her stroller to the time the girl guides her grandmother's wheelchair, we follow their wonder-filled & zany exploits in densely atmospheric watercolors. So evocative & uplifting is the reverie that when we discover it is a posthumous one, we are filled with wonder & hope as the keeping of the scrapbook changes loving hands. Expect tears of longing & surprise, nostalgia & joy as readers finish the last page of this modern classic. Order from Simon & Schuster.
Publisher Provided Annotation.

—Grandpa Loved. 1991. 14.00 (*0-671-75265-0*, Green Tiger) S&S Trade.
Few picture books can elicit the kind of emotional charge & sense of wonder of GRANDPA LOVED. Named "One of the Best Kids Books of the Year" by Parents Magazine, & cited as one of the all-time picture books with "The Most Unforgettable Language," GRANDPA LOVED is quick becoming a modern classic. Tender & evocative watercolors render the relationship of a little boy & his grandfather as they savor life on the beach, in the forest, in a big city, & in the landscape of the family. When, in the end, we learn that the grandfather has died, we are uplifted, not only because the child cherishes the memories, but because he embraces the idea that his grandfather has become part of the mystery & spirit of the universe, imbuing all the people & places he loved with life. The nuances & language of GRANDPA LOVED & its companion, GRANDMA'S SCRAPBOOK, manage that delicate balance of tension & release that has left many readers forever affected. Order from Simon & Schuster.
Publisher Provided Annotation.

Nodar, Carmen M. Abuelita's Paradise. Mathews, Judith, ed. Paterson, Diane, illus. LC 91-42330. 32p. (gr. k-3). 1992. 13.95g (*0-8075-0129-8*) A Whitman.
—El Paraiso de Abuelita. Mathews, Judith, ed. Mlawer, Teresa, tr. Paterson, Diane, illus. LC 92-3767. (SPA.). 32p. (gr. k-3). 1992. 13.95g (*0-8075-6346-3*) A Whitman.
Nodar, Carmen S. Abuelita's Paradise. Paterson, Diane, illus. (gr. k-4). 1993. 13.95 (*0-685-66422-8*); audio cass. 11.00 (*1-882869-79-6*) Read Advent.
Noll, Sally. Lucky Morning. LC 93-18188. (Illus.). 32p. (ps up). 1994. 14.00 (*0-688-12474-7*); PLB 13.93 (*0-688-12475-5*) Greenwillow.
Nomura, Takaaki. Grandpa's Town. Stinchecum, Amanda M., tr. from JPN. (Illus.). 32p. (ps-3). 1991. 13.95 (*0-916291-36-7*) Kane-Miller Bk.
Nye, Naomi S. Dream Bottle. Yu Cha Pak, illus. LC 93-45675. 1995. 15.00 (*0-02-768467-9*, Four Winds) Macmillan Child Grp.
—Sitti's Secrets. Carpenter, Nancy, illus. LC 93-19742. 32p. (ps-3). 1994. RSBE 14.95 (*0-02-768460-1*, Four Winds) Macmillan Child Grp.
O'Callahan, Jay. Tulips. Santini, Debrah, illus. LC 91-41704. 28p. (gr. k up). 1992. pap. 14.95 (*0-88708-223-8*) Picture Bk Studio.
Okimoto, Jean D. Take a Chance, Gramps, Vol. 1. (gr. 4-7). 1990. 14.95 (*0-316-63812-9*, Joy St Bks) Little.
Olson, Arielle N. Hurry Home, Grandma! LC 84-1529. (Illus.). 32p. (ps-1). 1990. pap. 3.95 (*0-525-44650-8*, DCB) Dutton Child Bks.
Oppenheim, Shulamith L. Fireflies for Nathan. Ward, John, illus. LC 93-29568. 1994. 15.00 (*0-688-12147-0*, Tambourine Bks); lib. bdg. 14.93 (*0-688-12148-9*, Tambourine Bks) Morrow.
—Waiting for Noah. Hoban, Lillian, illus. LC 89-35561. 32p. (ps-2). 1990. 12.95 (*0-06-024633-2*) HarpC Child Bks.
Orr, Katherine. My Grandpa & the Sea. Orr, Katherine, illus. LC 89-23876. 32p. (gr. 1-4). 1990. PLB 18.95 (*0-87614-409-1*) Carolrhoda Bks.
—My Grandpa & the Sea. (ps-3). 1991. pap. 5.95 (*0-87614-525-X*) Carolrhoda Bks.
Ortiz, Mamie. My Grandfather & the Boys. Aragon, Sherry, illus. 14p. (Orig.). (ps-7). 1982. pap. 3.75 (*0-915347-03-2*) Pueblo Acoma Pr.
Ossorio, Nelson A., et al. Through Grandpa's Eyes. (Illus.). 60p. (gr. 4-6). 1994. pap. 6.95 (*1-56721-051-1*) Twenty-Fifth Cent Pr.
Oxenbury, Helen. Grandma & Grandpa. (Illus.). 24p. (ps-1). 1993. pap. 3.99 (*0-14-054978-1*, Puff Pied Piper) Puffin Bks.
Oxford, Mariesa. Going to Grandma's. (Illus.). (gr. 2-6). 1992. PLB 19.97 (*0-8114-3575-X*) Raintree Steck-V.
Padoan, Gianni. Remembering Grandad. 1989. 11.95 (*0-85953-311-5*) Childs Play.
Palacios, Argentina. A Christmas Surprise for Chabelita. Lohstoeter, Lori, photos by. LC 93-22336. (Illus.). 32p. (gr. k-4). 1993. PLB 14.95 (*0-8167-3131-4*); pap. 3.95 (*0-8167-3132-2*) Brdgewater.
Paraskevas, Betty. Monster Beach. Paraskevas, Michael, illus. LC 93-46927. 1995. write for info. (*0-15-292882-0*) HarBrace.
Patterson, Nancy R. The Christmas Cup. Bowman, Leslie W., illus. LC 88-29112. 80p. (gr. 3-5). 1989. 13.95 (*0-531-05821-2*); PLB 13.99 (*0-531-08421-3*) Orchard Bks Watts.
Paulsen, Gary. The Cookcamp. LC 90-7734. 128p. (gr. 5-7). 1991. 13.95 (*0-531-05927-8*); PLB 13.99 (*0-531-08527-9*) Orchard Bks Watts.
Pearson, Susan. Happy Birthday Grampie. Dillon, Leo D., ed. Dillon, Diane, illus. LC 86-31105. 32p. (ps-3). 1987. PLB 10.89 (*0-8037-3458-1*) Dial Bks Young.
Percy, Graham. Max and the Orange Door. LC 92-45563. (Illus.). (ps-3). 1993. 15.95 (*1-56766-076-2*) Childs World.
Perkins, Mitali. The Sunita Experiment. LC 92-37267. 144p. (gr. 1-6). 1993. 14.95 (*0-316-69943-8*, Joy St Bks) Little.
—The Sunita Experiment. LC 93-28525. 192p. (gr. 5-9). 1994. pap. 4.50 (*1-56282-671-9*) Hyprn Ppbks.
Perry, Katy. My Grandmother Wears Crazy Hats. Minor, Mary E., ed. (Illus.). 16p. (gr. k-5). 1993. pap. 4.95 (*0-9626823-4-9*) Perry ME.
Pittman, Helena C. One Quiet Morning: Story & Pictures. LC 93-49596. (Illus.). 1995. write for info. (*0-87614-838-0*) Carolrhoda Bks.
Polacco, Patricia & Polacco, Patricia. Babushka Baba Yaga. LC 92-30361. (Illus.). 32p. 1993. 14.95 (*0-399-22531-5*, Philomel Bks) Putnam Pub Group.

Polikoff, Barbara. Life's a Funny Proposition, Horatio. LC 91-28010. 144p. (gr. 4-7). 1992. 13.95 (*0-8050-1972-3*, Bks Young Read) H Holt & Co.

Polland, Barbara K. Grandma & Grandpa Are Special People. Reinertson, Barbara, illus. LC 80-66961. 80p. (gr. k-3). 1984. pap. 7.95 (*0-89087-343-7*) Celestial Arts.

Pomerantz, Charlotte. The Outside Dog. Plecas, Jennifer, illus. LC 91-6351. 64p. (gr. k-3). 1993. 14.00 (*0-06-024782-7*); PLB 13.89 (*0-06-024783-5*) HarpC Child Bks.

Porte, Barbara A. When Grandma Almost Fell off the Mountain & Other Stories. Chambliss, Maxie, illus. LC 91-41174. 32p. (ps-2). 1993. 14.95 (*0-531-05965-0*); PLB 14.99 (*0-531-08565-1*) Orchard Bks Watts.

Potaracke, Rochelle. Nanny's Special Gift. Mitchell, Mark, illus. LC 93-26093. 32p. (Orig.). (gr. 1-4). 1994. pap. 4.95 (*0-8091-6615-1*) Paulist Pr.

Prechtel, Martin. Grandmother Sweat Bath: A Story of the Tzutujil Mana. Prechtel, Martin, illus. Rodney, Janet, ed. (Illus.). 39p. (Orig.). (gr. 6 up). 1990. write for info. Weaselsleeves Pr.

Provost, Gary. Good If It Goes. LC 89-18339. 160p. (gr. 4-7). 1990. pap. 3.95 (*0-689-71381-9*, Aladdin) Macmillan Child Grp.

Pryor, Bonnie. Grandpa Bear. Degen, Bruce, illus. LC 84-25545. 32p. (ps-1). 1985. 12.95 (*0-688-04551-0*) Morrow Jr Bks.

Reddix, Valerie. Dragon Kite of the Autumn Moon. LC 91-1506. (ps-3). 1992. 14.00 (*0-688-11030-4*); PLB 14.93 (*0-688-11031-2*) Lothrop.

Redmond, Shirley-Raye. Grampa & the Ghost. 96p. (Orig.). (gr. 3 up). 1994. pap. 3.50 (*0-380-77382-1*, Camelot Young) Avon.

Reeder, Carolyn. Grandpa's Mountain. 176p. 1993. pap. 3.50 (*0-380-71914-2*, Camelot) Avon.

Rhodes, Judy C. The King Boy. LC 91-2159. 160p. (gr. 5-9). 1991. SBE 14.95 (*0-02-776115-0*, Bradbury Pr) Macmillan Child Grp.

Rice, Eve. At Grammy's House. LC 89-34617. (Illus.). 32p. (ps up). 1990. 12.95 (*0-688-08874-0*); lib. bdg. 12.88 (*0-688-08875-9*) Greenwillow.

Richardson, Arleta. The Grandma's Attic Storybook. LC 92-33823. 1993. pap. 9.99 (*0-7814-0070-8*, Chariot Bks) Chariot Family.

—Still More Stories from Grandma's Attic. (gr. 3-7). 1980. pap. 3.99 (*0-89191-252-5*, Chariot Bks) Chariot Family.

—Treasures from Grandma. LC 84-12736. (gr. 3-7). 1984. pap. 3.99 (*0-89191-934-1*, 59345, Chariot Bks) Chariot Family.

Riley, Janeway. Us...& Our Good Stuff. (Illus.). 176p. 1993. 19.95 (*0-9637378-1-3*) Janeway Riley.

Riley, Jocelyn. Crazy Quilt. 176p. (gr. 7-12). 1986. pap. 2.50 (*0-553-25640-8*) Bantam.

Roberts, Sarah. I Want to Go Home. Mathieu, Joe, illus. LC 84-11725. 40p. (ps-3). 1985. 4.95 (*0-394-87027-1*) Random Bks Yng Read.

Roberts, Willo D. To Grandmother's House We Go. LC 89-34972. 192p. (gr. 3-7). 1990. SBE 14.95 (*0-689-31594-5*, Atheneum Child Bk) Macmillan Child Grp.

Rochelle, Belinda. When Jo Louis Won the Title. Johnson, Larry, illus. LC 93-34317. (gr. 4 up). 1994. 14.95 (*0-395-66614-7*) HM.

Rodriguez, Gina M. Green Corn Tamales - Tamales de Elote. (SPA & ENG., Illus.). 40p. 1994. 14.95 (*0-938243-00-4*) Hispanic Bk Dist.

Rose, Kent & Rose, Alice. Cemetery Quilt. Kaloustian, Rosemary, illus. LC 94-17617. Date not set. write for info. (*0-395-70948-2*) HM.

Rosenberg, Liz. Grandmother & the Runaway Shadow. Peck, Beth, illus. LC 92-42349. 1994. write for info. (*0-399-22545-5*, Philomel Bks) Putnam Pub Group.

Rusk, Irene J. A Letter to Grandmother. Romanelli, Maryann, illus. LC 92-61973. 64p. (Orig.). 1994. pap. 8.00 (*1-56002-223-X*, Univ Edtns) Aegina Pr.

Russo, Marisabina. A Visit to Oma. LC 89-77716. (Illus.). 32p. (ps up). 1991. 13.95 (*0-688-09623-9*); PLB 13.88 (*0-688-09624-7*) Greenwillow.

Salem, Lynn & Stewart, Josie. Staying with Grandma Norma. Zala, Emma, illus. 16p. (gr. 1). 1993. pap. 3.50 (*1-880612-08-9*) Seedling Pubns.

Saull, D. L. The Sunchildren. 1992. 7.95 (*0-533-09619-7*) Vantage.

Say, Allen. Grandfather's Journey. LC 93-18836. 32p. 1993. 16.95 (*0-395-57035-2*) HM.

Scarffe, Bronwen. Walter Hottle Bottle. Crossett, Warren, illus. LC 92-34271. 1993. 14.00 (*0-383-03664-X*) SRA Schl Grp.

Scheller, Melanie. My Grandfather's Hat. Narahashi, Keiko, illus. LC 91-12486. 32p. (ps-3). 1992. SBE 13.95 (*0-689-50540-X*, M K McElderry) Macmillan Child Grp.

Schenker, Dona. Throw a Hungry Loop. LC 89-35496. 160p. (gr. 7 up). 1991. 12.95 (*0-679-80332-7*) Knopf Bks Yng Read.

Schertle, Alice. William & Grandpa. Stevenson, D., ed. Dabcovich, Lydia, illus. LC 88-666. 32p. (gr. k-3). 1988. 12.95 (*0-688-07580-0*); PLB 12.88 (*0-688-07581-9*) Lothrop.

Schnur, Steven. The Shadow Children. LC 94-5098. 1994. write for info. (*0-688-13281-2*); PLB write for info. (*0-688-13831-4*) Morrow Jr Bks.

Schwartz, David. Supergrandpa. (Illus.). (ps-3). 1991. 13.95 (*0-688-09898-3*); 13.88 (*0-688-09899-1*) Lothrop.

Scott, Ann H. Grandmother's Chair. Aubrey, Meg K., illus. 32p. (ps-1). 1990. 13.45 (*0-395-52001-0*, Clarion Bks) HM.

Scott, Blackie. It's Fun at Grandmother's House. LC 85-22021. (Illus.). 48p. (ps-3). 1992. 8.95 (*0-932419-01-1*) Peachtree Pubs.

Seabrooke, Brenda. The Bridges of Summer. LC 92-11642. 160p. (gr. 5 up). 1992. 14.00 (*0-525-65094-6*, Cobblehill Bks) Dutton Child Bks.

—Looking for Diamonds. Mantha, Nancy, illus. LC 93-36980. (gr. 4 up). 1995. write for info. (*0-525-65173-X*, Cobblehill Books) Dutton Child Bks.

Selway, Martina. Don't Forget to Write. Selway, Martina, illus. LC 91-28430. 32p. (ps-2). 1992. 12.95 (*0-8249-8543-5*, Ideals Child) Hambleton-Hill.

Sendak, Philip. In Grandpa's House. Barofsky, Semour, tr. from YID. Sendak, Maurice, illus. LC 85-42625. 48p. (ps up). 1985. 13.00 (*0-06-025462-9*); PLB 9.89 (*0-06-025463-7*) HarpC Child Bks.

Shanjar. Life with Grandfather. 9th ed. Shankar, illus. 54p. (Orig.). (gr. k-3). 1980. pap. 3.50 (*0-89744-212-1*, Pub. by Childrens Bk Trust IA) Auromere.

Shasha, Mark. Hall of Beasts. LC 92-39520. 1994. pap. 15.00 (*0-671-79893-6*) S&S Trade.

Sheldon, Dyan. The Whales' Song. Blythe, Gary, illus. LC 90-46722. 32p. (ps-3). 1991. 15.99 (*0-8037-0972-2*) Dial Bks Young.

Sherlock, Patti. Four of a Kind. LC 91-55038. 196p. (gr. 3-7). 1991. 13.95 (*0-8234-0913-9*) Holiday.

Shigekawa, Marlene. Bluejay in the Desert. Kikuchi, Isao, illus. LC 92-35424. 36p. (gr. k-4). 1993. 12.95 (*1-879965-04-6*) Polychrome Pub.

Silverman, Erica. On Grandma's Roof. Ray, Deborah K., illus. LC 89-31255. 32p. (ps-2). 1990. RSBE 13.95 (*0-02-782681-3*, Macmillan Child Bk) Macmillan Child Grp.

Sloss, Lesley. Anthony & the Aardvark. Clarke, Gus, illus. LC 90-6528. 32p. (ps up). 1991. 13.95 (*0-688-10302-2*); PLB 13.88 (*0-688-10303-0*) Lothrop.

Slote, Alfred. The Trading Game. LC 89-12851. 208p. (gr. 3-7). 1990. 15.00 (*0-397-32397-2*, Lipp Jr Bks); PLB 14.89 (*0-397-32398-0*, Lipp Jr Bks) HarpC Child Bks.

Smee, Nicola. The Tusk Fairy. Smee, Nicola, illus. LC 93-28444. 32p. (ps-2). 1993. PLB 14.95 (*0-8167-3311-2*); pap. 3.95 (*0-8167-3312-0*) BrdgeWater.

Smith, Barbara A. Somewhere Just Beyond. LC 93-14672. 96p. (gr. 3-7). 1993. SBE 12.95 (*0-689-31877-4*, Atheneum Child Bk) Macmillan Child Grp.

Smith, Doris B. Remember the Red-Shouldered Hawk. LC 93-14405. 160p. (gr. 5-9). 1994. 14.95 (*0-399-22443-2*, Putnam) Putnam Pub Group.

Smith, Maggie. My Grandma's Chair. LC 90-2278. (ps-3). 1992. 14.00 (*0-688-10663-3*); PLB 13.93 (*0-688-10664-1*) Lothrop.

Smith, Robert K. The War with Grandpa. Lauter, Richard, illus. LC 83-14366. 128p. (gr. 4-8). 1984. pap. 12.95 (*0-385-29314-3*) Delacorte.

—The War with Grandpa. Lauter, Richard, illus. 128p. (gr. 5-9). 1984. pap. 3.99 (*0-440-49276-9*, YB) Dell.

Smothers, Ethel F. Moriah's Pond. Ransome, James, illus. LC 94-6490. 128p. (gr. 3-8). 1995. 14.00 (*0-679-84504-6*); lib. bdg. write for info. (*0-679-94504-0*) Knopf Bks Yng Read.

Snyder, Carol. God Must Like Cookies, Too. Glick, Beth, illus. LC 92-26886. 32p. (ps-3). 1993. 16.95 (*0-8276-0423-8*) JPS Phila.

Sobel, Barbara. Great-Grandma, Heroine! LC 87-1235. (gr. 3-6). 1987. 7.59 (*0-87386-049-7*); bk. & cassette 16.99 (*0-317-55324-0*); pap. 1.95 (*0-87386-048-9*) Jan Prods.

Spyri, Johanna. Heidi. Dole, Helen B., tr. Sharp, William, illus. LC 93-50908. 1994. write for info. (*0-448-40563-6*, G&D) Putnam Pub Group.

Stahl, Hilda. Big Trouble for Roxie. 160p. (gr. 4-7). 1992. pap. 3.99 (*0-89107-658-1*) Crossway Bks.

Stallone, Linda. The Flood That Came to Grandma's House. Schooley, Joan, illus. LC 91-33955. 21p. (ps-3). 1992. 9.95 (*0-912975-02-4*) Upshur Pr.

Starnes, Gigi. Grandma's Tales: Storm of Darkness. Mitchell, Mark, illus. LC 94-16080. 1995. 11.95 (*0-89015-979-3*) Sunbelt Media.

Steel, Danielle. Max & Grandma & Grandpa Winky. (ps-3). 1991. 9.95 (*0-385-30165-0*) Delacorte.

Stephenson, Jean. Dogwood Stew & Catnip Tea. LC 92-40804. 160p. (Orig.). (gr. 4-7). 1993. pap. 4.99 (*0-89107-717-0*) Crossway Bks.

Stevens, Carla. Anna, Grandpa, & the Big Storm. Tomes, Margot, illus. 64p. (gr. 1-4). 1986. (Puffin); pap. 3.99 (*0-14-031705-8*, Puffin) Puffin Bks.

Stevenson, Harvey. Grandpa's House. LC 93-6318. (Illus.). 32p. (ps-3). 1994. 14.95 (*1-56282-588-7*); PLB 14.89 (*1-56282-589-5*) Hyprn Child.

Stevenson, James. Brrr! LC 89-34615. (Illus.). 32p. (ps up). 1991. 13.95 (*0-688-09210-1*); PLB 13.88 (*0-688-09211-X*) Greenwillow.

—Could Be Worse! Stevenson, James, illus. LC 76-28534. 32p. (gr. k-3). 1977. 13.95 (*0-688-80075-0*); PLB 13.88 (*0-688-84075-2*) Greenwillow.

—That's Exactly the Way It Wasn't. LC 90-30749. (Illus.). 30p. (ps up). 1991. 13.95 (*0-688-09868-1*); PLB 13.88 (*0-688-09869-X*) Greenwillow.

—There's Nothing to Do! Stevenson, James, illus. LC 85-8104. 32p. (gr. k-3). 1986. 11.75 (*0-688-04698-3*); PLB 11.88 (*0-688-04699-1*) Greenwillow.

—What's under My Bed? Stevenson, James, illus. LC 83-1454. 32p. (gr. k-3). 1983. 16.00 (*0-688-02325-8*); PLB 15.93 (*0-688-02327-4*) Greenwillow.

Stock, Catherine. Emma's Dragon Hunt. Stock, Catherine, illus. LC 83-25109. 32p. (gr. k up). 1984. 11.95 (*0-688-02696-6*); PLB 9.55 (*0-688-02698-2*) Lothrop.

Stolz, Mary. Coco Grimes. LC 93-34153. 128p. (gr. 3-6). 1994. 14.00 (*0-06-024232-9*); PLB 13.89 (*0-06-024233-7*) HarpC Child Bks.

—Go Fish. Cummings, Pat, illus. LC 90-4860. 80p. (gr. 2-6). 1991. 13.00 (*0-06-025820-9*); PLB 12.89 (*0-06-025822-5*) HarpC Child Bks.

—Go Fish. Cummings, Pat, illus. LC 90-4860. 80p. (gr. 2-6). 1993. pap. 3.95 (*0-06-440466-8*, Trophy) HarpC Child Bks.

—Stealing Home. LC 92-5226. 160p. (gr. 3-6). 1992. 14.00 (*0-06-021154-7*); PLB 13.89 (*0-06-021157-1*) HarpC Child Bks.

Strangis, Joel. Grandfather's Rock. Recht, Ruth, illus. LC 92-26525. 1993. 14.95 (*0-395-65367-3*) HM.

Stroud, Virginia. A Walk to the Great Mystery. LC 93-32340. 1993. write for info. (*0-8037-1636-2*); PLB write for info. (*0-8037-1637-0*) Dial Bks Young.

Stroud, Virginia A. Doesn't Fall off His Horse. (Illus.). (gr. 2 up). 1994. 14.99 (*0-8037-1634-6*); PLB 14.89 (*0-8037-1635-4*) Dial Bks Young.

Stuart, Jesse. The Beatinest Boy. Miller, Jim W., et al, eds. Henneberger, Robert, illus. Zornes, Rocky, contrib. by. (Illus.). 80p. (gr. 3-6). 1989. 10.00 (*0-945084-12-9*); pap. 5.00 (*0-945084-13-7*) J Stuart Found.

Sundvall, Viveca. Mimi Gets a Grandpa. Eriksson, Eva, illus. Fisher, Richard E., tr. (Illus.). 32p. (ps up). 1991. bds. 13.95 (*91-29-59864-8*, Pub. by R&S Bks) FS&G.

Swayne, Sam & Swayne, Zoa. Great-Grandfather in the Honey Tree. LC 81-90738. (Illus.). 53p. (gr. 3-5). 1982. pap. 4.95 perfect bdg. (*0-9608008-0-8*) Legacy Hse.

Tamboise, Pierre. A Trip by Torpedo. (Illus.). (gr. 3-8). 1992. PLB 8.95 (*0-89565-894-1*) Childs World.

Tan, Amy. The Moon Lady. Schields, Gretchen, illus. LC 91-22321. 32p. (gr. 1 up). 1992. RSBE 16.95 (*0-02-788830-4*, Macmillan Child Bk) Macmillan Child Grp.

Tarlton. Going to Grandma's. 1993. pap. 28.67 (*0-590-50159-3*) Scholastic Inc.

Temple, Charles. Cadillac. Lockhart, Lynne, illus. LC 93-42387. 1995. write for info. (*0-399-22654-0*) Putnam Pub Group.

Tews, Susan. Nettie's Gift. Sayles, Elizabeth, illus. 32p. (gr. k-3). 1993. 14.95 (*0-395-59027-2*, Clarion Bks) HM.

Thomas. Nana's Rocking Chair. 1993. 15.95 (*0-8050-2265-1*) H Holt & Co.

Thomas, Abigail. Wake up, Wilson Street. Low, William, illus. LC 92-10873. 32p. (gr. 5 up). 1993. 15.95 (*0-8050-2006-3*, Bks Young Read) H Holt & Co.

Thomas, Jane R. Saying Good-bye to Grandma. Sewall, Marcia, illus. LC 87-20826. 40p. (gr. 1-4). 1988. 15.45 (*0-89919-645-4*, Clarion Bks) HM.

—Saying Good-Bye to Grandma. LC 87-20826. 40p. (ps-3). 1990. pap. 5.70 (*0-395-54779-2*, Clarion Bks) HM.

Thompson, Colin. Looking for Atlantis. LC 93-24068. 1994. 16.00 (*0-679-85648-X*) Knopf Bks Yng Read.

Thomson, Pat. Can You Hear Me, Grandad? Alborough, Jez, illus. 32p. (gr. k-2). 1988. pap. 8.95 (*0-385-29599-5*) Delacorte.

—Can You Hear Me, Grandad? (gr. k-2). 1988. pap. 2.50 (*0-440-40025-2*, YB) Dell.

—Good Girl Granny. (gr. k-6). 1988. pap. 2.50 (*0-440-40026-0*, YB) Dell.

Tiller, Ruth. Cinnamon, Mint, & Mothballs: A Visit to Grandmother's House. Sogabe, Aki, illus. LC 92-32981. 1993. write for info. (*0-15-276617-0*) HarBrace.

Time Life Inc. Editors. CB: A Book about Time. Ward, Elizabeth & Kagan, Neil, eds. (Illus.). 30p. (ps-2). 1992. write for info. (*0-8094-9303-9*); lib. bdg. write for info. (*0-8094-9304-7*) Time-Life.

—The Search for the Seven Sisters: A Hidden-Picture Geography Book. (Illus.). 56p. (ps-2). 1991. write for info. (*0-8094-9287-3*); PLB write for info. (*0-8094-9288-1*) Time-Life.

Tomey, Ingrid. Grandfather's Day. McKay, Robert, illus. 64p. (gr. 3-7). 1992. PLB 12.95 (*1-56397-022-8*) Boyds Mills Pr.

Upham, Elizabeth. Grandmother's Locket. Hall, Maureen K., illus. 38p. (ps-1). 1985. 12.95 (*0-940696-10-X*) Monroe County Lib.

Vance, Joel M. Grandma & the Buck Deer. Colrus, Bill, illus. 173p. 1988. pap. text ed. 11.95 (*0-87691-322-2*) Cedar Glade Pr.

Van Hook, Beverly. Supergranny, No. 1: The Mystery of the Shrunken Heads. Wayson, Catherine, illus. 96p. (gr. 3-7). 1985. lib. bdg. 7.95 (*0-916761-11-8*); pap. 2.95 (*0-916761-10-X*) Holderby & Bierce.

—Supergranny, No. 2: The Case of the Riverboat Riverbelle. Wayson, Catherine, illus. 112p. (gr. 3-7). 1986. lib. bdg. 7.95 (*0-916761-09-6*); pap. 2.95 (*0-916761-08-8*) Holderby & Bierce.

—Supergranny, No. 3: The Ghost of Heidelberg Castle. Wayson, Catherine, illus. 112p. (gr. 3-7). 1987. lib. bdg. 7.95 (*0-916761-07-X*); pap. 2.95 (*0-916761-06-1*) Holderby & Bierce.

—Supergranny, No. 5: Character Who Came to Life. Nelken, Andrea, ed. Wayson, Catherine, illus. 112p. (Orig.). (gr. 3-6). 1989. lib. bdg. 7.95 (*0-916761-13-4*); pap. 2.95 (*0-916761-12-6*) Holderby & Bierce.
—Supergranny: Secret of Devil Mountain. Nelken, Andrea, ed. Wayson, Catherine, illus. 112p. (Orig.). (gr. 3-6). 1988. lib. bdg. 7.95 (*0-916761-05-3*); pap. 2.95 (*0-916761-04-5*) Holderby & Bierce.
—Supergranny 6: The Great College Caper, 6 bks. Nelken, Andrea, ed. Wayson, Catherine, illus. 112p. (gr. 3-7). 1991. Set. 53.00 (*0-916761-15-0*) Set. pap. 17.70 (*0-916761-14-2*) Holderby & Bierce.
Vigna, Judith. Grandma Without Me. Tucker, Kathleen, ed. Vigna, Judith, illus. LC 83-26031. 32p. (ps-3). 1984. PLB 13.95 (*0-8075-3030-1*) A Whitman.
Wahl, Jan. I Remember, Cried Grandma Pinky. Johnson, Arden, illus. LC 93-33806. 32p. (gr. k-2). 1994. PLB 14.95 (*0-8167-3456-9*); pap. text ed. 3.95 (*0-8167-3457-7*) BridgeWater.
Wahl, Mats. Grandfathers Laika. Nygren, Tord, illus. 32p. (gr. k-4). 1990. PLB 18.95 (*0-87614-434-2*) Carolrhoda Bks.
Waite, Michael. Gilly Greenweed's Gift for Granny. LC 91-37443. (ps-3). 1992. pap. 7.99 (*0-7814-0035-X*, Chariot Bks) Chariot Family.
Wallace, Ian. Chin Chiang & the Dragon's Dance. LC 83-13442. (Illus.). 32p. (gr. k-4). 1984. SBE 13.95 (*0-689-50299-0*, M K McElderry) Macmillan Child Grp.
Walsh, Jill P. When Grandma Came. Williams, Sophy, illus. 32p. (ps-3). 1992. 13.00 (*0-670-83581-1*) Viking Child Bks.
—When Grandma Came. Williams, Sophy, illus. 32p. (ps-3). 1994. pap. 4.99 (*0-14-054327-9*) Puffin Bks.
Walter, Mildred P. Trouble's Child. LC 84-16387. 128p. (gr. 4 up). 1985. 11.95 (*0-688-04214-7*) Lothrop.
Wardlaw, Lee. The Tales of Grandpa Cat. LC 92-39797. 32p. (gr. 2 up). 1994. 14.99 (*0-8037-1511-0*); PLB 14.89 (*0-8037-1512-9*) Dial Bks Young.
Watson. Grandpa's Slippers. 1993. pap. 28.67 (*0-590-75483-1*) Scholastic Inc.
Wayland, April H. It's Not My Turn to Look for Grandma. Booth, George, illus. LC 93-7018. 1994. 15.00 (*0-679-84491-0*); lib. bdg. 15.99 (*0-679-94491-5*) Knopf.
Welles, Laura & Welles, Ted. Will & Grandmother Change the Seashore. McCloskey, Maris, ed. Welles, Laura, illus. LC 92-62260. 40p. (Orig.). (gr. k-7). 1993. text ed. 24.00 (*0-915189-08-9*) Oceanus.
Weston, Martha. Apple Juice Tea. LC 93-17437. 1994. 14.95 (*0-395-65480-7*, Clarion Bks) HM.
What Time Is Grandma Coming? (Illus.). 24p. (ps-2). 1984. 6.95 (*0-8431-0645-X*) Price Stern.
Wiggin, Eric. Maggie: Life at the Elms. LC 93-27054. 1994. pap. 3.99 (*1-56507-133-6*) Harvest Hse.
Wild, Margaret. But Granny Did! Forss, Ian, illus. LC 92-31906. 1993. 3.75 (*0-383-03559-7*) SRA Schl Grp.
—Our Granny. Vivas, Julie, illus. LC 93-11950. 32p. (ps-2). 1994. reinforced bdg. 13.95 (*0-395-67023-3*) Ticknor & Flds Bks Yng Read.
Williams, Barbara. Kevin's Grandma. LC 74-23713. (Illus.). 32p. (ps-1). 1991. pap. 3.95 (*0-525-44785-7*, Puffin) Puffin Bks.
Williams, Carol L. Kelly & Me. LC 92-20492. 1993. 13.95 (*0-385-30897-3*) Delacorte.
Williams, Michael. The Genuine Half-Moon Kid. 192p. (gr. 7 up). 1994. 15.99 (*0-525-67470-5*, Lodestar Bks) Dutton Child Bks.
Williams, Sophy. Nana's Garden. Williams, Sophy, illus. 32p. (ps-1). 1994. 14.99 (*0-670-85287-2*) Viking Child Bks.
Willner-Pardo, Gina. Hunting Grandma's Treasures. Krudop, Walter L., illus. LC 94-13191. (gr. 4 up). 1994. pap. write for info. (*0-395-68190-1*, Clarion Bks) HM.
Wolff, Barbara M. Pappa & Me. Wolff, Barbara M., illus. 16p. (ps-1). 1991. PLB 13.95 (*1-879567-11-3*, Valeria Bks) Wonder Well.
Woodruff, Elvira. The Summer I Shrank My Grandmother. Coville, Katherine, illus. LC 90-55099. 160p. (gr. 3-7). 1990. 14.95 (*0-8234-0832-9*) Holiday.
—The Summer I Shrank My Grandmother. (gr. 4-7). 1992. 3.50 (*0-440-40640-4*, YB) Dell.
Wright, Betty R. Out of the Dark. LC 93-48025. (gr. 3-7). 1995. 13.95 (*0-590-43598-1*) Scholastic Inc.
Wyeth, Sharon D. Always My Dad. Colon, Raoul, illus. LC 93-43755. 40p. (ps-3). 1995. 15.00 (*0-679-83447-8*, Apple Soup Bks); PLB 15.99 (*0-679-93447-2*, Apple Soup Bks) Knopf Bks Yng Read.
Yep, Laurence. Child of the Owl. LC 76-24314. 224p. (gr. 7 up). 1977. PLB 12.89 (*0-06-026743-7*) HarpC Child Bks.
Zolotow, Charlotte. My Grandson Lew. LC 73-14335. (Illus.). 32p. (gr. k-3). 1974. PLB 13.89 (*0-06-026962-6*) HarpC Child Bks.

GRANGE, HAROLD EDWARD, 1903-

Spyri, Johanna. Heidi. (gr. k-1). 1986. 8.98 (*0-685-16841-7*, 618141) Random Hse Value.

GRANT, ULYSSES SIMPSON, PRESIDENT U. S. 1822-1885

Archer, Jules. A House Divided: The Lives of Ulysses S. Grant & Robert E. Lee. LC 93-38886. 1994. write for info. (*0-590-46102-8*) Scholastic Inc.
Bentley, Bill. Ulysses S. Grant. LC 93-416. (Illus.). 64p. (gr. 4-6). 1993. PLB 12.90 (*0-531-20162-7*) Watts.
Kent, Zachary. Ulysses S. Grant. LC 88-38056. (Illus.). 100p. (gr. 3 up). 1989. PLB 14.40 (*0-516-01364-5*); pap. 6.95 (*0-516-41364-3*) Childrens.
Marin, Albert. Unconditional Surrender: U. S. Grant & the Civil War. LC 93-20041. (Illus.). 208p. (gr. 5-9). 1994. SBE 19.95 (*0-689-31837-5*, Atheneum Child Bk) Macmillan Child Grp.
O'Brian, Steven. Ulysses S. Grant. Schlesinger, Arthur M., intro. by. (Illus.). 112p. (gr. 5 up). 1991. 17.95x (*1-55546-809-8*) Chelsea Hse.
Rickerby, Laura. Ulysses S. Grant & the Strategy of Victory. (Illus.). 160p. (gr. 5 up). 1990. lib. bdg. 12.95 (*0-382-09944-3*); pap. 7.95 (*0-382-24053-7*) Silver Burdett Pr.
Smith, Gene. Lee & Grant. 448p. (gr. 9-12). 1985. pap. 12.95 (*0-452-01000-4*, Mer) NAL-Dutton.
Zadra, Dan. Statesmen in America: Ulysses S. Grant. rev. ed. (gr. 2-4). 1988. PLB 14.95 (*0-88682-188-6*) Creative Ed.

GRAPHIC ARTS

see also Drawing; Painting; Printing
Belcher, J. A., ed. Sign Language Dot-to-Dot. new ed. 32p. (ps-3). 1979. 2.95 (*0-917002-40-7*) Joyce Media.
Graphing. (Illus.). 56p. (gr. 7-12). 1990. 8.80 (*0-941008-73-8*) Tops Learning.
Potter, T. & Peach, S. Graphic Design. (Illus.). 96p. (gr. 6 up). 1993. pap. 12.95 (*0-7460-0131-2*) EDC.

GRAPHIC ARTS–VOCATIONAL GUIDANCE

Roberson, Virginia L. Careers in Graphic Arts. rev. ed. (Illus.). (gr. 7-12). 1993. PLB 14.95 (*0-8239-1349-X*); pap. 9.95 (*0-8239-1715-0*) Rosen Group.

GRAPHIC METHODS

Blanchard, Robert. Graphiti, Bk. 1. rev. ed. 24p. (gr. 2-9). 1986. pap. 5.50 (*0-918932-89-0*) Activity Resources.
—Graphiti, Bk. 2. rev. ed. 24p. (gr. 2-9). 1986. wkbk. 5.50 (*0-918932-90-4*) Activity Resources.
Edson, Ann & Insel, Eunice. Reading Maps, Globes, Charts, Graphs. (gr. 4-6). 1982. wkbk. 2.69 (*0-89525-175-2*) Ed Activities.
Freeman, Marji. Creative Graphing. (gr. 4-7). 1992. pap. 7.95 (*0-201-48026-3*) Addison-Wesley.

GRAPHS

see Graphic Methods

GRASSES

Greenaway, Theresa. Grasses & Grains. LC 90-9563. (Illus.). 48p. (gr. 5-9). 1990. PLB 21.34 (*0-8114-2729-3*) Raintree Steck-V.
Pearce, Q. L. & Pearce, W. L. In the African Grasslands. Brook, Bonnie, ed. Bettoli, Delana, illus. 24p. (ps-1). 1990. 4.95 (*0-671-68831-6*); PLB 6.95 (*0-671-68827-8*) Silver Pr.

GRASSHOPPERS

see Locusts

GRASSLAND ECOLOGY

Amsel, Sheri. Grasslands. Amsel, Sheri, illus. LC 92-8788. 32p. 1992. lib. bdg. 19.24 (*0-8114-6302-8*) Raintree Steck-V.
Binato, Leonardo. What Lives in the Grass? 12p. (ps-3). 1993. 4.95 (*1-56566-028-5*) Thomasson-Grant.
Chinery, Michael. Grassland Animals. Butler, John & McIntyre, Brian, illus. LC 91-53145. 40p. (Orig.). (gr. 2-5). 1992. pap. 4.99 (*0-679-82045-0*) Random Bks Yng Read.
Collinson, Alan. Grasslands. LC 92-4021. (Illus.). 48p. (gr. 5 up). 1992. text ed. 13.95 RSBE (*0-87518-492-8*, Dillon) Macmillan Child Grp.
Cook, Kevin. Disappearing Grasslands. LC 93-1193. 1993. 17.27 (*0-8368-0483-X*) Gareth Stevens Inc.
Dvorak, David, Jr. A Sea of Grass: The Tallgrass Prairie. Dvorak, David, Jr., illus. LC 93-19507. 32p. (gr. 1-4). 1994. RSBE 14.95 (*0-02-733245-4*, Macmillan Child Bk) Macmillan Child Grp.
Goldstein, Natalie. Rebuilding Prairies & Forests. (Illus.). 96p. (gr. 3-6). 1994. PLB 23.20 (*0-516-05542-9*) Childrens.
Hirschi, Ron. Save Our Prairies & Grasslands. Bauer, Irwin A. & Bauer, Peggy, photos by. LC 93-4985. (Illus.). 1994. 17.95 (*0-385-31149-4*); pap. 9.95 (*0-385-31199-0*) Delacorte.
Knapp, Brian. What Do We Know about the Grasslands? LC 92-7888. (Illus.). 40p. (gr. 4-6). 1992. PLB 15.95 (*0-87226-359-2*) P Bedrick Bks.
Lambert, David. Grasslands. Furstinger, Nancy, ed. (Illus.). 48p. (gr. 5-8). 1989. PLB 12.95 (*0-382-09789-0*) Silver Burdett Pr.
Langley, Andrew. Grasslands. LC 93-77348. (Illus.). 32p. (gr. 4-7). 1993. 14.00 (*0-89577-515-8*, Dist. by Random) RD Assn.
Patent, Dorothy H. Prairie Dogs. Munoz, William, photos by. LC 92-34724. (Illus.). 1993. 15.45 (*0-395-56572-3*, Clarion Bks) HM.
Rotter, Charles M. The Prairie. LC 92-44822. (gr. 4 up). 1994. 18.95 (*0-88682-598-9*) Creative Ed.
Rowan, James P. Prairies & Grasslands. LC 83-7310. (Illus.). 48p. (gr. k-4). 1983. PLB 12.85 (*0-516-01706-3*); pap. 4.95 (*0-516-41706-1*) Childrens.
Sabin, Louis. Grasslands. Watling, James, illus. LC 84-2661. 32p. (gr. 3-6). 1985. PLB 9.49 (*0-8167-0214-4*); pap. text ed. 2.95 (*0-8167-0215-2*) Troll Assocs.
Sayre, April P. Grassland. (Illus.). 64p. (gr. 5-8). 1994. bds. 15.95 (*0-8050-2827-7*) TFC Bks NY.

GRAVES

see Cemeteries; Funeral Rites and Ceremonies; Mounds and Mound Builders

GRAVEYARDS

see Cemeteries

GRAVITATION

Ardley, Neil. The Science Book of Gravity. 1992. 9.95 (*0-15-200621-4*, Gulliver Bks) HarBrace.
Branley, Franklyn M. Gravity Is a Mystery. rev. ed. Madden, Don, illus. LC 85-48247. 32p. (ps-3). 1986. (Crowell Jr Bks); PLB 14.89 (*0-690-04527-1*) HarpC Child Bks.
Buegler, Marion E. Discovering Density. Bergman, Lincoln & Fairwell, Kay, eds. Klofkorn, Lisa, illus. Hoyt, Richard, photos by. (Illus.). 49p. (Orig.). (gr. 6-10). 1988. pap. 10.00 (*0-912511-17-6*) Lawrence Science.
Skurzynski, Gloria. Zero Gravity. LC 93-46735. (gr. 1-5). 1994. 14.95 (*0-02-782925-1*, Bradbury Pr) Macmillan Child Grp.
Taylor, Barbara. Weight & Balance. LC 89-21504. (Illus.). 32p. (gr. 5-8). 1990. PLB 12.40 (*0-531-14082-2*) Watts.

GRAVITY

see Gravitation

GREAT BRITAIN

Butterfield, Moira & Wright, Nicola. Getting to Know Britain: People, Places. Wooley, Kim, illus. LC 93-29716. (gr. 3-7). 1994. 12.95 (*0-8120-6392-9*); pap. 5.95 (*0-8120-1854-0*) Barron.
Flint, David. The United Kingdom. LC 93-13610. 1994. PLB 22.80 (*0-8114-1849-9*) Raintree Steck-V.
Goldstein, Frances. Children's Treasure Hunt Travel Guide to Britain. LC 78-71424. (Illus.). (gr. 1-12). 1979. pap. 6.95 (*0-933334-00-1*, Dist. by Hippocrene) Paper Tiger Pap.
Grant, Neil. United Kingdom. LC 88-18315. (Illus.). 48p. (gr. 4-8). 1988. PLB 14.95 (*0-382-09513-8*) Silver Burdett Pr.
Harris, Sarah. Finding Out about Life in Britain in the 1950's. (Illus.). 48p. (gr. 7-12). 1985. 19.95 (*0-7134-4424-X*, Pub. by Batsford UK) Trafalgar.
Jones, Lewis. Great Britain. (Illus.). 32p. (gr. 4-6). 1991. 17.95 (*0-237-60182-6*, Pub. by Evans Bros Ltd) Trafalgar.
Langley, Andrew. Passport to Great Britain. LC 93-21187. 1994. 13.90 (*0-531-14297-3*) Watts.
Sproule, Anna. Great Britain: The Land & Its People. LC 86-17674. (Illus.). 48p. (gr. 5 up). 1991. PLB 12.95 (*0-382-24243-2*) Silver Burdett Pr.
Stadtler, Christa. The United Kingdom. LC 91-6521. (Illus.). 32p. (gr. 2-4). 1992. PLB 12.40 (*0-531-18444-7*, Pub. by Bookwright Pr) Watts.
Steele, Philip. Great Britain. LC 93-4365. (Illus.). 32p. (gr. 4 up). 1994. text ed. 13.95 RSBE (*0-89686-774-9*, Crestwood Hse) Macmillan Child Grp.
Thavis, Richard. The Hilary & Lisa England Travel Journal. LC 93-43566. 1995. write for info. (*1-56766-119-X*) Childs World.

GREAT BRITAIN–ANTIQUITIES

Martell, Hazel M. The Vikings & Jorvik. LC 92-25215. (Illus.). 32p. (gr. 5 up). 1993. text ed. 13.95 RSBE (*0-87518-541-X*, Dillon) Macmillan Child Grp.

GREAT BRITAIN–BIOGRAPHY

Banks, David. Sarah Ferguson: The Royal Redhead. LC 87-15567. (Illus.). 64p. (gr. 3 up). 1988. text ed. 13.95 RSBE (*0-87518-369-7*, Dillon) Macmillan Child Grp.
Cooper, John & Morris, Susan. Cromwell Family. 52p. (gr. 6 up). 1987. pap. 7.95 (*0-85950-546-4*, Pub. by S Thornes UK) Dufour.
Courtney, Julia. Sir Peter Scott: Champion for the Environment & Founder of the World Wildlife Fund. LC 88-2076. (Illus.). 68p. (gr. 5-6). 1989. PLB 19.93 (*1-55532-819-9*) Gareth Stevens Inc.
Gilleo, Alma. Prince Charles. Endres, Helen, illus. LC 78-18938. (gr. k-4). 1978. PLB 13.95 (*0-89565-029-0*) Childs World.
Kantenwein, Louise. Danny Boy. 1992. 7.95 (*0-533-10175-1*) Vantage.
Licata, Renora. Princess Diana: Royal Ambassador. (Illus.). 64p. (gr. 3-7). 1993. PLB 14.95 (*1-56711-013-4*) Blackbirch.
—Princess Diana: Royal Ambassador. (Illus.). 64p. (gr. 3-7). 1993. pap. 7.95 (*1-56711-051-7*) Blackbirch.
Moriarty, Mary & Sweeney, Catherine. The Rebel Countess. Teskey, Donald, illus. 80p. (Orig.). (gr. 1-7). 1992. pap. 8.95 (*0-86278-211-2*, Pub. by OBrien Pr EIRE) Dufour.
Moskin, Marietta D. Margaret Thatcher. (Illus.). 128p. 1990. lib. bdg. 13.98 (*0-671-69632-7*, J Messner); pap. 7.95 (*0-671-69633-5*) S&S Trade.
St. John, Jetty. A Family in England. (Illus.). 32p. (gr. 2-5). 1988. lib. bdg. 13.50 (*0-8225-1679-9*) Lerner Pubns.
Wilson, Barbara K. Path Through the Woods. Stewart, Charles, illus. (gr. 7 up). 1958. 21.95 (*0-87599-129-7*) S G Phillips.

GREAT BRITAIN–FICTION

Alcott, Louisa May. Little Men. (Illus.). (gr. 5 up). 1969. pap. 1.95 (*0-8049-0194-5*, CL-194) Airmont.
Austen, Jane. Emma. Duffy, J. D., intro. by. (gr. 9 up). 1966. pap. 1.95 (*0-8049-0102-3*, CL-102) Airmont.
—Mansfield Park. Threapleton, M. M., intro. by. (gr. 10 up). 1967. pap. 1.95 (*0-8049-0131-7*, CL-131) Airmont.
—Persuasion. Duffy, J. D., intro. by. (gr. 10 up). 1966. pap. 1.50 (*0-8049-0107-4*, CL-107) Airmont.
—Pride & Prejudice. (gr. 10 up). 1962. pap. 3.50 (*0-8049-0001-9*, CL-1) Airmont.
—Pride & Prejudice. Cogancherry, Helen, illus. Stewart, Diana, adapted by. LC 81-5215. (Illus.). 48p. (gr. 4 up). 1983. PLB 20.70 (*0-8172-1673-1*) Raintree Steck-V.

—Sense & Sensibility. Spacks, Patricia M., afterword by. 352p. (gr. 9-12). 1983. pap. 3.50 (*0-553-21334-2*, Bantam Classics) Bantam.

Baylis-White, Mary. Sheltering Rebecca. 112p. (gr. 3-7). 1991. 14.95 (*0-525-67349-0*, Lodestar Bks) Dutton Child Bks.

Blackmore, Richard D. Lorna Doone. 272p. (gr. 4-6). 1984. pap. 2.95 (*0-14-035021-7*, Puffin) Puffin Bks.

Bond, Michael. More about Paddington. Fortnum, Peggy, illus. (gr. 4-6). 1962. 13.45 (*0-395-06640-9*) HM.

—Paddington at Work. Fortnum, Peggy, illus. LC 67-20372. (gr. 1-5). 1967. 13.95 (*0-395-06637-9*) HM.

—Paddington Goes to Town. 128p. (gr. 2-5). 1992. pap. 3.25 (*0-440-46793-4*, YB) Dell.

—Paddington Goes to Town. Fortnum, Peggy, illus. LC 68-28043. (gr. 1-5). 1977. 14.95 (*0-395-06635-2*) HM.

—Paddington Helps Out. Fortnum, Peggy, illus. (gr. 4-6). 1973. 13.45 (*0-395-06639-5*) HM.

—Paddington Marches On. (Illus.). (gr. 4-6). 1965. 13.45 (*0-395-06642-5*) HM.

Bronte, Charlotte. Jane Eyre. (gr. 9 up). 1964. pap. 3.95 (*0-8049-0017-5*, CL-17) Airmont.

—Jane Eyre. Shaw, Charlie, illus. Stewart, Diana, adapted by. LC 80-14426. (Illus.). 48p. (gr. 4 up). 1983. PLB 20.70 (*0-8172-1661-8*) Raintree Steck-V.

Bronte, Emily. Wuthering Heights. (gr. 9 up). 1964. pap. 2.95 (*0-8049-0011-6*, CL-11) Airmont.

—Wuthering Heights. Wright, Betty R., adapted by. Cogancherry, Helen, illus. LC 81-15786. 48p. (gr. 4 up). 1982. PLB 20.70 (*0-8172-1682-0*) Raintree Steck-V.

Brouwer, Sigmund. Barbarians from the Isle. 132p. (gr. 5-8). 1992. pap. 4.99 (*0-89693-116-1*) SP Pubns.

—Wings of an Angel. 132p. (gr. 5-8). 1992. pap. 4.99 (*0-89693-115-3*) SP Pubns.

Burnett, Frances H. Little Princess. Tudor, Tasha, illus. LC 63-15435. (gr. 4-6). 1963. 16.00 (*0-397-30693-8*, Lipp Jr Bks); PLB 15.89 (*0-397-31339-X*, Lipp Jr Bks) HarpC Child Bks.

—A Little Princess. 224p. (gr. 4-6). 1984. pap. 2.99 (*0-14-035028-4*, Puffin) Puffin Bks.

Butler, Samuel. Way of All Flesh. Rudzik, O. H., intro. by. (gr. 11 up). 1965. pap. 2.50 (*0-8049-0090-6*, CL-90) Airmont.

Cooper, Susan L. Over Sea, Under Stone. Gill, Margery, illus. LC 66-11199. (gr. 5 up). 1966. 14.95 (*0-15-259034-X*, HB Juv Bks) HarBrace.

Defoe, Daniel. Moll Flanders. (gr. 11 up). 1969. pap. 1.95 (*0-8049-0200-3*, CL-200) Airmont.

Dickens, Charles. Charles Dickens' A Christmas Carol. Richardson, I. M., ed. Kendall, Jane F., illus. LC 87-11270. 32p. (gr. 2-6). 1988. PLB 9.79 (*0-8167-1053-8*); pap. text ed. 1.95 (*0-8167-1054-6*) Troll Assocs.

—Christmas Carol. LC 85-15815. (gr. 7 up). 1963. pap. 2.25 (*0-8049-0026-4*, CL-26) Airmont.

—A Christmas Carol. Hildebrandt, Gregory, illus. LC 85-15815. 128p. 1983. pap. 14.95 (*0-671-45599-0*, S&S BFYR) S&S Trade.

—David Copperfield. (gr. 9 up). 1965. pap. 3.95 (*0-8049-0065-5*, CL-65) Airmont.

—David Copperfield. (Illus.). 32p. (gr. 6 up). 1994. 9.95 (*0-9638463-1-0*, Crtoon Mdia); pap. 3.99 (*0-9638463-0-2*) Cethial Commns.

—Great Expectations. Threapleton, M. M., intro. by. (gr. 9 up). 1965. pap. 3.95 (*0-8049-0068-X*, CL-68) Airmont.

—Great Expectations. rev. ed. Klischer, Beth, ed. Weikel, Cheryl, illus. 587p. (Orig.). (gr. 10 up). 1989. pap. 6.95 (*0-89084-504-2*) Bob Jones Univ Pr.

—Great Expectations. abr. ed. (Illus.). 172p. 1950. pap. text ed. 4.46 (*0-582-53003-2*) Longman.

—The Oxford Illustrated Dickens, 21 vols. Incl. The Old Curiosity Shop. Cattermole, George & Phiz, illus. 1951. 10.95 (*0-19-254506-X*); Our Mutual Friend. Stone, Marcus, illus. 1952. 13.95 (*0-19-254510-8*); The Personal History of David Copperfield. 10.95 (*0-19-254502-7*); The Posthumous Papers of the Pickwick Club. Dickens, Charles. (Illus.). 1947. 10.95 (*0-19-254501-9*); Sketches by Boz: Illustrative of Every-Day Life & Every-Day People. Cruickshank, George, illus. 1957. 10.95 (*0-19-254518-3*); A Tale of Two Cities. 1949. 10.95 (*0-19-254504-3*); The Uncommercial Traveller, & Reprinted Pieces. Dickens, Charles. 1958. 10.95 (*0-19-254521-3*); The Adventures of Oliver Twist. Cruickshank, George, illus. House, Humphy, intro. by. 1949. 10.95 (*0-19-254505-1*); American Notes & Pictures from Italy. Stone, Marcus, et al, illus. Sitwell, Sacheverell, intro. by. 1987. 10.95 (*0-19-254519-1*); Barnaby Rudge: A Tale of the Riots of 'Eighty. Dickens, Charles. 1954. 10.95 (*0-19-254513-2*); Bleak House. Phiz, illus. Sitwell, Osbert, intro. by. 1948. 14.95 (*0-19-254503-5*); Christmas Books. Farjeon, Eleanor, intro. by. (Illus.). 1954. 10.95 (*0-19-254514-0*); Christmas Stories. Dickens, Charles. (Illus.). 774p. 1956. 12.95 (*0-19-254517-5*); Dealings with the Firm of Dombey, & Son, Wholesale, Retail, & for Exploration. Phiz, illus. Garrod, H. W., intro. by. 1950. 14.95 (*0-19-254507-8*); Great Expectations. Dickens, Charles. (Illus.). 460p. 1987. 10.95 (*0-19-254511-6*); Hard Times for These Times. Walker, F. & Greiffenhagen, Maurice, illus. Foot, Dingle, intro. by. 1955. 10.95 (*0-19-254515-9*); The Life & Adventures of Martin Chuzzlewit. Phiz, illus. Russell, Geoffrey, intro. by. 1951. 13.95 (*0-19-254509-4*); The Life & Adventures of Nicholas Nickleby. Phiz, illus. Thorndike, Dame S., intro. by. 1950. 10.95 (*0-19-254508-6*); Little Dorrit. Dickens, Charles. (Illus.). 826p. 1953. 10.95 (*0-19-254512-4*); Master Humphrey's Clock & a Child's History of England. Dickens, Charles. (Illus.). 544p. 1958. 10.95 (*0-19-254520-5*); The Mystery of Edwin Drood. Fildes, Luke & Collins, Charles, illus. Roberts, S. C., intro. by. 294p. 1956. 10.95 (*0-19-254516-7*). 1987. Set. 200.00 (*0-19-254522-1*) OUP.

—Pickwick Papers. (gr. 10 up). 1968. pap. 2.95 (*0-8049-0191-0*, CL-191) Airmont.

Dickens, Charles & Geary, Rick. Great Expectations. (Illus.). 52p. Date not set. pap. 4.95 (*1-57209-001-4*) Classics Int Ent.

Eliot, George. Mill on the Floss. (gr. 10 up). 1964. pap. 2.95 (*0-8049-0043-4*, CL-43) Airmont.

—Mill on the Floss. Haight, G. S., ed. LC 62-16032. (gr. 9 up). 1972. pap. 9.96 (*0-395-05151-7*, RivEd) HM.

—Silas Marner. (gr. 9 up). 1964. pap. 2.50 (*0-8049-0014-0*, CL-14) Airmont.

Fielding, Henry. Tom Jones. Rowland, B., intro. by. (gr. 11 up). 1967. pap. 2.50 (*0-8049-0135-X*, CL-135) Airmont.

Goldsmith, Oliver. Vicar of Wakefield. (gr. 10 up). 1964. pap. 1.25 (*0-8049-0052-3*, CL-52) Airmont.

Hardy, Thomas. Far from the Madding Crowd. Gemme, F. R., intro. by. (gr. 11 up). 1967. pap. 2.50 (*0-8049-0136-8*, CL-136) Airmont.

—Jude the Obscure. Teitel, N. R., intro. by. (gr. 11 up). 1966. pap. 1.95 (*0-8049-0108-2*, CL-108) Airmont.

—Mayor of Casterbridge. Bigoness, J. W., intro. by. (gr. 11 up). 1965. pap. 1.95 (*0-8049-0063-9*, CL-63) Airmont.

—Return of the Native. (gr. 10 up). 1964. pap. 2.75 (*0-8049-0038-8*, CL-38) Airmont.

—Tess of the D'Urbervilles. Hogan, A. H., intro. by. (gr. 11 up). 1965. pap. 3.50 (*0-8049-0082-5*, CL-82) Airmont.

Hersom, Kathleen. The Half Child. LC 90-24079. 176p. (gr. 5-9). 1991. pap. 13.95 jacketed, 3-pc. bdg. (*0-671-74225-6*, S&S BFYR) S&S Trade.

—The Half Child. LC 91-30352. 104p. (gr. 5 up). 1993. pap. 4.95 (*0-671-86696-6*, Half Moon Bks) S&S Trade.

Hilton, James. Good-Bye, Mr. Chips. (Illus.). (gr. 7 up). 1962. 17.95 (*0-316-36420-7*, Pub. by Atlantic Monthly Pr) Little.

John, Mary. A Shilling for the Gate. 68p. 1991. pap. 23. 00x (*0-86383-763-8*, Pub. by Gomer Pr UK) St Mut.

King-Smith, Dick. Pigs Might Fly. (gr. 4 up). 1990. pap. 3.95 (*0-14-034537-X*, Puffin) Puffin Bks.

Kipling, Rudyard. Light That Failed. (gr. 8 up). 1969. pap. 1.50 (*0-8049-0199-6*, CL-199) Airmont.

Nesbit, Edith. Story of the Treasure Seekers. (gr. 4-6). 1987. pap. 2.25 (*0-685-03990-0*, Puffin) Puffin Bks.

Potter, Beatrix. The Tailor of Gloucester. Horden, Michael, read by. (Illus.). (ps-3). 1989. pap. 6.95 bk. & tape (*0-7232-3668-2*) Warne.

Scott, Walter, et al. Ivanhoe. (Illus.). 52p. Date not set. pap. 4.95 (*1-57209-023-5*) Classics Int Ent.

Sewell, Anna. Black Beauty. (gr. 5 up). 1963. pap. 1.50 (*0-8049-0023-X*, CL-23) Airmont.

—Black Beauty. new ed. Farr, Naunerle, ed. Nebres, Rudy, illus. LC 59-12495. 64p. (Orig.). (gr. 5-10). 1973. pap. 2.95 (*0-88301-094-1*) Pendulum Pr.

—Black Beauty. LC 59-12495. (gr. 3-7). 1983. pap. 2.25 (*0-14-035006-3*, Puffin) Puffin Bks.

—Black Beauty. Vance, Eleanor G., ed. Jeffers, Susan, illus. LC 84-27575. 72p. (ps-5). 1986. 16.00 (*0-394-86575-8*) Random Bks Yng Read.

—Black Beauty. LC 59-12495. (gr. 4-6). 1989. pap. 3.25 (*0-590-42354-1*) Scholastic Inc.

Sharp, Evelyn. Child's Christmas. 1991. 12.99 (*0-517-03369-0*) Random Hse Value.

Sohl, Marcia & Dackerman, Gerald. Black Beauty Student Activity Book. (Illus.). 16p. (gr. 4-10). 1976. pap. 1.25 (*0-88301-183-2*) Pendulum Pr.

Sterne, Laurence. Tristram Shandy. (gr. 11 up). 1967. pap. 1.95 (*0-8049-0152-X*, CL-152) Airmont.

Thackeray, William Makepeace. Vanity Fair. Threapleton, M. M., intro. by. (gr. 11 up). 1967. pap. 2.50 (*0-8049-0138-4*, CL-138) Airmont.

Westall, Robert. The Kingdom by the Sea. 176p. (gr. 5 up). 1991. 15.00 (*0-374-34205-9*) FS&G.

—Yaxley's Cat. 208p. 1992. 13.95 (*0-590-45175-8*, Scholastic Hardcover) Scholastic Inc.

GREAT BRITAIN–HISTORY

Baxter, Nicola. Invaders & Settlers. LC 93-46464. 1994. write for info. (*0-531-14338-4*) Watts.

Evans, Alan. On the Breadline. (Illus.). 48p. (gr. 6-9). 1994. 19.95 (*0-7134-6715-0*, Pub. by Batsford UK) Trafalgar.

The Georgians. (Illus.). (gr. 5 up). 1990. pap. 3.95 (*1-85543-011-8*) Ladybird Bks.

The Middle Ages. (Illus.). (gr. 5 up). 1990. pap. 3.95 (*1-85543-008-8*) Ladybird Bks.

Rawcliffe, Michael. Where You Live. (Illus.). 48p. (gr. 6-9). 1994. 19.95 (*0-7134-6714-2*, Pub. by Batsford UK) Trafalgar.

Sancha, Sheila. Walter Dragun's Town: Crafts & Trade in the Middle Ages. Sancha, Sheila, illus. LC 88-34066. 64p. (gr. 4 up). 1989. (Crowell Jr Bks); PLB 15.89 (*0-690-04806-8*, Crowell Jr Bks) HarpC Child Bks.

GREAT BRITAIN–HISTORY–FICTION

Bennett, John. Master Skylark. Hogan, Alice H., intro. by. (gr. 5 up). 1965. 1.95 (*0-8049-0092-2*, CL-92) Airmont.

Dick, Lois Hoadley. False Coin, True Coin. LC 92-39280. 1993. write for info. (*0-89084-664-2*) Bob Jones Univ Pr.

Dickens, Charles. Tale of Two Cities. 384p. 1989. pap. 2.50 (*0-8125-0506-9*) Tor Bks.

Gerrard, Jean. Matilda Jane. Gerrard, Roy, illus. LC 83-48082. 32p. (ps-3). 1983. 15.00 (*0-374-34865-0*) FS&G.

Kipling, Rudyard. Puck of Pook's Hill: And Rewards & Fairies. Mackenzie, Donald, ed. LC 92-14450. 496p. (gr. 4 up). 1993. pap. 7.95 (*0-19-282575-5*) OUP.

Konigsburg, E. L. A Proud Taste for Scarlet & Miniver. Konigsburg, E. L., illus. LC 73-76320. 208p. (gr. 5-9). 1973. SBE 14.95 (*0-689-30111-1*, Atheneum Child Bk) Macmillan Child Grp.

Magorian, Michelle. Back Home. LC 84-47629. 384p. (gr. 7 up). 1992. pap. 4.95 (*0-06-440411-0*, Trophy) HarpC Child Bks.

Reginald, R. & Menville, Douglas, eds. The Boyhood Days of Guy Fawkes: Or, the Conspirators of Old London. LC 75-46257. (Illus.). (gr. 7 up). 1976. Repr. of 1876 ed. lib. bdg. 18.00x (*0-405-08116-2*) Ayer.

Robin Hood. (FRE.). (gr. 3-8). 9.95 (*0-685-28453-0*) Fr & Eur.

Rodowsky, Colby. Keeping Time. LC 83-14122. 137p. (gr. 5 up). 1983. 14.00 (*0-374-34061-7*) FS&G.

Sutcliff, Rosemary. Eagle of the Ninth. 1993. pap. 4.95 (*0-374-41930-2*) FS&G.

GREAT BRITAIN–HISTORY–TO 1066

see also Celts

GREAT BRITAIN–HISTORY–TO 1066–FICTION

Alder, Elizabeth. The King's Shadow. 1994. 17.00 (*0-374-34182-6*) FS&G.

Sutcliff, Rosemary. The Lantern Bearers. LC 93-43116. 1994. pap. 4.95 (*0-374-44302-5*) FS&G.

—The Silver Branch. LC 93-7950. 1993. 4.95 (*0-374-46648-3*) FS&G.

GREAT BRITAIN–HISTORY–MEDIEVAL PERIOD, 1066-1485

De Angeli, Marguerite. The Door in the Wall: Story of Medieval London. De Angeli, Marguerite, illus. LC 64-7025. 111p. (gr. 3-6). 1989. pap. 14.95 (*0-385-07283-X*) Doubleday.

GREAT BRITAIN–HISTORY–NORMAN PERIOD, 1066-1154–FICTION

McGraw, Eloise. The Striped Ships. LC 91-7729. 240p. (gr. 7 up). 1991. SBE 15.95 (*0-689-50532-9*, M K McElderry) Macmillan Child Grp.

Scott, Walter. Ivanhoe. (gr. 9 up). 1964. pap. 2.95 (*0-8049-0034-5*, CL-34) Airmont.

GREAT BRITAIN–HISTORY–PLANTAGENETS, 1154-1399

Brooks, Polly S. Queen Eleanor: Independent Spirit of the Medieval World: a Biography of Eleanor of Aquitaine. LC 82-48776. 160p. (gr. 6 up). 1983. PLB 13.89 (*0-397-31995-9*, Lipp Jr Bks) HarpC Child Bks.

GREAT BRITAIN–HISTORY–PLANTAGENETS, 1154-1399–FICTION

Gray, Elizabeth J. Adam of the Road. Lawson, Robert, illus. 320p. (gr. 4-8). 1942. pap. 15.95 (*0-670-10435-3*) Viking Child Bks.

Ivanhoe. (Illus.). 48p. (gr. 4 up). 1988. PLB 20.70 (*0-8172-2765-2*) Raintree Steck-V.

Shakespeare, William. Henry IV, Pts. 1 & 2. Young, Archibald, intro. by. (gr. 10 up). pap. Pt. 1. pap. 1.25 (*0-8049-1018-9*, S18); Pt. 2. pap. 1.25 (*0-685-00150-4*, S19) Airmont.

—King John. Rowland, Beryl, intro. by. (gr. 9 up). 1968. pap. 1.95 (*0-8049-1024-3*, S24) Airmont.

—Richard Second. Young, Archibald M., intro. by. (gr. 9 up). 1966. pap. 0.60 (*0-8049-1014-6*, S14) Airmont.

Wheeler, Thomas G. All Men Tall. LC 70-77313. (gr. 8 up). 1969. 21.95 (*0-87599-157-2*) S G Phillips.

GREAT BRITAIN–HISTORY–LANCASTER AND YORK, 1399-1485–FICTION

Pyle, Howard. Men of Iron. Bennet, C. L., intro. by. (Illus.). (gr. 6 up). 1965. pap. 3.50 (*0-8049-0093-0*, CL-93) Airmont.

GREAT BRITAIN–HISTORY–WARS OF THE ROSES, 1455-1485–FICTION

Shakespeare, William. Richard Third. Willoughby, John, intro. by. (gr. 9 up). 1966. pap. 0.60 (*0-8049-1015-4*, S15) Airmont.

Stevenson, Robert Louis. Black Arrow. (gr. 6 up). 1964. pap. 2.95 (*0-8049-0020-5*, CL-20) Airmont.

GREAT BRITAIN–HISTORY–TUDORS, 1485-1603

Eames, Marion, ed. The Dark Land. 59p. 1991. pap. 30. 00x (*0-86383-741-7*, Pub. by Gomer Pr UK) St Mut.

Frost, Abigail. Elizabeth I. (Illus.). 32p. (gr. 3-8). 1989. PLB 10.95 (*1-85435-113-3*) Marshall Cavendish.

Ross, Stewart. Elizabethan Life. (Illus.). 72p. (gr. 7-11). 1991. 19.95 (*0-7134-6356-2*, Pub. by Batsford UK) Trafalgar.

Saraga, Jessica. Tudor Monarchs. (Illus.). 72p. (gr. 7-11). 1991. 19.95 (*0-7134-6350-3*, Pub. by Batsford UK) Trafalgar.

Snellgrove, L. E. Early Modern Age. (Illus.). 256p. (Orig.). (gr. 7-12). 1980. 19.92 (*0-582-31784-3*, 78447) Longman.

The Tudors. (Illus.). (gr. 5 up). 1990. pap. 3.95 (*1-85543-009-6*) Ladybird Bks.

GREAT BRITAIN–HISTORY–TUDORS, 1485-1603–FICTION

Kingsley, Charles. Westward Ho. (gr. 8 up). 1968. pap. 1.25 (*0-8049-0184-8*, CL-184) Airmont.

Scott, Walter. Kenilworth. new ed. (gr. 10 up). 1968. pap. 2.95 (*0-8049-0193-7*, CL-193) Airmont.

Twain, Mark. Prince & the Pauper. (gr. 5 up). 1964. pap. 2.50 (*0-8049-0032-9*, 32) Airmont.

GREAT BRITAIN–HISTORY–17TH CENTURY–FICTION

Blackmore, Richard D. Lorna Doone. Threapleton, M. M., intro. by. (gr. 8 up). 1967. pap. 2.50 (*0-8049-0149-X*, CL-149) Airmont.

GREAT BRITAIN–HISTORY–STUARTS, 1603-1714

Snellgrove, L. E. Early Modern Age. (Illus.). 256p. (Orig.). (gr. 7-12). 1980. 19.92 (*0-582-31784-3*, 78447) Longman.

GREAT BRITAIN–HISTORY–STUARTS, 1603-1714–FICTION

Wallace, M. Imelda, Sr. Outlaws of Ravenhurst. new ed. Schuster, L. A., illus. (gr. 6-10). 1950. 12.95 (*0-910334-25-0*); pap. 5.95 (*0-910334-26-9*) Cath Authors.

GREAT BRITAIN–HISTORY–CIVIL WAR AND COMMONWEALTH, 1642-1660

Kelly, Rosemary & Kelly, Tony. City at War: Oxford 1642-46. 52p. (gr. 11 up). 1987. pap. 7.95 (*0-85950-540-5*, Pub. by S Thornes UK) Dufour.

Kelly, Tony. Children in Tudor England. 52p. (gr. 6-9). 1987. pap. 7.95 (*0-85950-545-6*, Pub. by S Thornes UK) Dufour.

National Trust Staff. Investigating the Civil War. (Illus.). 32p. (gr. 5-8). 1993. pap. 6.95 (*0-7078-0111-7*, Pub. by Natl Trust UK) Trafalgar.

GREAT BRITAIN–HISTORY–1714-1837–FICTION

Forester, C. S. Lieutenant Hornblower. (gr. 7 up). 1984. 17.95 (*0-316-28907-8*); pap. 11.95 (*0-316-28921-3*) Little.

—Lord Hornblower, Vol. 1. (gr. 7 up). 1989. 17.95 (*0-316-28908-6*); pap. 11.95 (*0-316-28943-4*) Little.

Meyrick, Bette. Invasion! 70p. 1991. pap. 23.00x (*0-86383-773-5*, Pub. by Gomer Pr UK) St Mut.

GREAT BRITAIN–HISTORY–19TH CENTURY

Evans, David. How We Used to Live: Victorians Early & Late. (Illus.). 48p. (gr. 4-8). 14.95 (*0-7136-3310-7*, Pub. by A&C Black UK) Talman.

Inside a Victorian House. (Illus.). 32p. (gr. 3-6). 1994. pap. 8.95 (*0-7078-0169-9*, Pub. by Natl Trust UK) Trafalgar.

National Trust Staff. Investigating the Victorians. (Illus.). 32p. (gr. 3-6). 1994. pap. 6.95 (*0-7078-0167-2*, Pub. by Natl Trust UK) Trafalgar.

Rawcliffe, Michael. Finding out About: Life in Edwardian Britain. (Illus.). 48p. (gr. 7-10). 1989. 19.95 (*0-7134-5612-4*, Pub. by Batsford UK) Trafalgar.

—Victorian Town Life. (Illus.). 48p. (gr. 7-10). Date not set. 19.95 (*0-7134-6355-4*, Pub. by Batsford UK) Trafalgar.

Tames, Richard. Radicals, Reformers & Railways 1815-1851. (Illus.). 72p. (gr. 7-12). 1987. 19.95 (*0-7134-5264-1*, Pub. by Batsford UK) Trafalgar.

GREAT BRITAIN–HISTORY–20TH CENTURY

Britain in the 1950's. (Illus.). 72p. (gr. 7-10). 1989. 19.95 (*0-7134-5838-0*, Pub. by Batsford UK) Trafalgar.

Gilleo, Alma. Prince Charles. Endres, Helen, illus. LC 78-18938. (gr. k-4). 1978. PLB 13.95 (*0-89565-029-0*) Childs World.

Hodges, Michael. Britain in the 1970's. (Illus.). 72p. (gr. 7-10). 1989. 19.95 (*0-7134-5913-1*, Pub. by Batsford UK) Trafalgar.

Tames, Richard. Life in Wartime Britain. (Illus.). (gr. 7-10). 1993. 19.95 (*0-7134-6543-3*, Pub. by Batsford UK) Trafalgar.

GREAT BRITAIN–INDUSTRIES–HISTORY

Jones, Madeline. Finding Out about Industrial Britain. (Illus.). 64p. (gr. 7-12). 1984. 19.95 (*0-7134-4353-7*, Pub. by Batsford UK) Trafalgar.

GREAT BRITAIN–KINGS AND RULERS

Kings & Queens of England, 2 bks. (Illus.). (gr. 5 up). 3.50 (*0-317-03014-0*) Bk. 1 (*0-7214-0560-6*) Bk. 2 (*0-7214-0561-4*) Ladybird Bks.

Rand, Gloria. Prince William. LC 91-25180. (ps-3). 1994. pap. 5.95 (*0-8050-3384-X*) H Holt & Co.

Saraga, Jessica. Tudor Monarchs. (Illus.). 72p. (gr. 7-11). 1991. 19.95 (*0-7134-6350-3*, Pub. by Batsford UK) Trafalgar.

Wigner, Annabel. Elizabeth & Akbar: Portraits of Power. 52p. (gr. 11 up). 1987. pap. 7.95 (*0-85950-541-3*, Pub. by S Thornes UK) Dufour.

GREAT BRITAIN–NOBILITY

Bach, Julie. Princess Diana. Wallner, Rosemary, ed. LC 91-73026. 202p. 1991. 12.94 (*1-56239-081-3*) Abdo & Dghtrs.

Fox, Mary V. Princess Diana. LC 86-4451. (Illus.). 128p. (gr. 6 up). 1986. lib. bdg. 17.95 (*0-89490-129-X*) Enslow Pubs.

Giff, Patricia R. Diana: Twentieth-Century Princess. Laporte, Michele, illus. 64p. (gr. 3-5). 1992. pap. 3.99 (*0-14-034707-0*, Puffin) Puffin Bks.

Greene, Carol. Diana, Princess of Wales. LC 85-12751. (Illus.). 32p. (gr. 2-4). 1985. pap. 3.95 (*0-516-43538-8*) Childrens.

Ross, Josephine. Princess of Wales. (Illus.). 64p. (gr. 5-9). 1991. 11.95 (*0-237-60023-4*, Pub. by Evans Bros Ltd) Trafalgar.

GREAT BRITAIN–SOCIAL LIFE AND CUSTOMS

Inside a Victorian House. (Illus.). 32p. (gr. 3-6). 1994. pap. 8.95 (*0-7078-0169-9*, Pub. by Natl Trust UK) Trafalgar.

James. Lapps - Reindeer Herders of Lapland, Reading Level 5. (Illus.). 48p. (gr. 4-8). 1989. PLB 16.67 (*0-86625-263-0*); 12.50s.p. (*0-685-58811-4*) Rourke Corp.

National Trust Staff. Investigating the Victorians. (Illus.). 32p. (gr. 3-6). 1994. pap. 6.95 (*0-7078-0167-2*, Pub. by Natl Trust UK) Trafalgar.

Tames, Richard & Tames, Sheila. Great Britain. LC 93-49724. 1994. write for info. (*0-531-14313-9*) Watts.

GREAT LAKES

Aylesworth, Thomas G. & Aylesworth, Virginia L. Eastern Great Lakes: Ohio - Indiana - Michigan. (Illus.). 64p. (gr. 3 up). 1991. lib. bdg. 16.95 (*0-7910-1045-7*) Chelsea Hse.

—Western Great Lakes (Illinois, Iowa, Wisconsin, Minnesota) (Illus.). 64p. (Orig.). (gr. 3 up). 1987. lib. bdg. 16.95x (*1-55546-560-9*); pap. 6.95x (*0-7910-0549-6*) Chelsea Hse.

Henderson, Kathy. The Great Lakes. LC 88-34670. (Illus.). 48p. (gr. k-4). 1989. PLB 12.85 (*0-516-01163-4*); pap. 4.95 (*0-516-41163-2*) Childrens.

Murray, John. Lake Superior, Wow! A Kid's Guide to 99 Fun Things to Do in Duluth, Superior, & along Lake Superior's North Shore. (Illus.). 96p. 1993. pap. 7.95 (*0-943400-73-2*) Marlor Pr.

GREAT LAKES–FICTION

Holling, Holling C. Paddle-to-the-Sea. (Illus.). (gr. 4-6). 1980. 17.45 (*0-395-15082-5*); pap. 7.95 (*0-395-29203-4*) HM.

GREAT LAKES–HISTORY

Mitchell, John C. Great Lakes & Great Ships: An Illustrated History for Children. Woodruff, Thomas R., illus. 52p. (gr. 2-7). 1991. 15.95 (*0-9621466-1-7*) Suttons Bay Pubns.

GREAT PLAINS

Andryszewski, Tricia. The Dust Bowl: Disaster on the Plains. LC 92-15300. (Illus.). 64p. (gr. 4-6). 1993. PLB 15.40 (*1-56294-272-7*); pap. 5.95 (*1-56294-747-8*) Millbrook Pr.

Aylesworth, Thomas G. & Aylesworth, Virginia L. Great Plains (Montana, North Dakota, South Dakota, Wyoming, Nebraska) LC 87-18198. (Illus.). 64p. (gr. 3 up). 1988. lib. bdg. 16.95 (*1-55546-566-8*) Chelsea Hse.

Bullock, Robert. The Great Plains: A Young Reader's Journal. Bullock, Robert, illus. LC 86-81461. 64p. (Orig.). (gr. k-8). 1987. pap. 5.95 (*0-943972-10-8*) Homestead WY.

Harvey, Brett. My Prairie Year. Ray, Deborah K., illus. (ps-3). 1993. pap. 4.95 (*0-8234-1028-5*) Holiday.

Nielsen, Shelly. More Victoria. LC 86-2280. 130p. (gr. 3-7). 1986. pap. 4.99 (*0-89191-453-6*, Chariot Bks) Chariot Family.

Rounds, Glen. The Treeless Plains. (Illus.). 96p. (gr. 5 up). 1994. Repr. of 1967 ed. 15.95 (*0-8234-1084-6*) Holiday.

—The Treeless Plains. Rounds, Glen, illus. (gr. 5 up). 1994. pap. 6.95 (*0-8234-1085-4*) Holiday.

GREAT SMOKY MOUNTAINS

Bush, Florence C. Dorie: Woman of the Mountains. LC 91-12875. (Illus.). 254p. (gr. 6 up). 1992. text ed. 24. 95x (*0-87049-725-1*); pap. 11.95 (*0-87049-726-X*) U of Tenn Pr.

Radlauer, Ruth. Great Smoky Mountains National Park. updated ed. Zillmer, Rolf, photos by. LC 76-9839. (Illus.). 48p. (gr. 3 up). 1985. pap. 4.95 (*0-516-47489-8*) Childrens.

GREECE

Ardley, Brigette & Ardley, Neil. Greece. (Illus.). 48p. (gr. 4-8). 1989. lib. bdg. 14.95 (*0-382-09822-6*) Silver Burdett Pr.

Buchanan, David A. Greek Athletics. McLeish, Kenneth & McLeish, Valerie, eds. (Illus.). 48p. (gr. 7-12). 1976. pap. text ed. 9.00 (*0-582-20059-8*, 70659) Longman.

Chattington, Jenny & Firman, Mary. The Ancient Greeks. (Illus.). (gr. 2-6). pap. 3.95 (*0-7141-1283-6*, Pub. by Brit Mus UK) Parkwest Pubns.

Dicks, Brian. Greece. (Illus.). 32p. (gr. 4-6). 1991. 17.95 (*0-237-60192-3*, Pub. by Evans Bros Ltd) Trafalgar.

Fox, Mary V. Cyprus. LC 93-755. (Illus.). 128p. (gr. 5-9). 1993. PLB 20.55 (*0-516-02617-8*) Childrens.

Green, Roger L. Tales of Greek Heroes. (Orig.). (gr. 5-7). 1989. pap. 2.99 (*0-14-035099-3*, Puffin) Puffin Bks.

Jacobsen, Karen. Greece. LC 89-25343. (Illus.). 48p. (gr. k-4). 1990. PLB 12.85 (*0-516-01185-5*); pap. 4.95 (*0-516-41185-3*) Childrens.

Kontoyiannaki, Kosta. Agean Fun. Kontoyiannaki, Kosta, illus. 16p. (gr. k-3). 1992. pap. 12.95 (*1-895583-23-3*) MAYA Pubs.

—Can You Find Greece on the Map? Kontoyiannaki, Kosta, illus. 14p. (gr. k-3). 1992. pap. 14.95 (*1-895583-20-9*) MAYA Pubs.

Lerner Geography Department Staff, ed. Greece in Pictures. (Illus.). 64p. (gr. 5-12). 1991. PLB 17.50 (*0-8225-1882-1*) Lerner Pubns.

Naumoff, Olga. About the Splendid Macedonians: A Coloring Book & Much, Much More. Schindler, A. A., illus. 64p. 1982. pap. 4.95 (*0-941983-00-5*) Splendid Assocs.

Nichols, Roger & Nichols, Sarah. Greek Everyday Life. McLeish, Kenneth & McLeish, Valerie, eds. (Illus.). 48p. (gr. 7-12). 1978. pap. text ed. 9.00 (*0-582-20672-3*, 70819) Longman.

Spyropulos, Diana. Greece: A Spirited Independence. LC 85-25412. (Illus.). 128p. (gr. 5 up). 1990. text ed. 14. 95 RSBE (*0-87518-311-5*, Dillon) Macmillan Child Grp.

Stainer, Tom & Sutton, Harry. The Greeks. McEwan, Joseph, illus. 25p. (gr. 4-6). 1992. pap. 4.95 (*0-563-21174-1*, BBC-Parkwest) Parkwest Pubns.

Stein, R. Conrad. Greece. LC 87-13225. (Illus.). 128p. (gr. 5-9). 1987. PLB 20.55 (*0-516-02759-X*) Childrens.

GREECE–ANTIQUITIES

Terzi, Marinella. Ancient Greece. LC 92-7508. (Illus.). 36p. (gr. 3 up). 1992. PLB 14.95 (*0-516-08376-7*) Childrens.

GREECE–BIOGRAPHY

Hirokawa, Ryuichi. Children of the World: Greece. LC 87-42581. (Illus.). 64p. (gr. 5-6). 1987. PLB 21.26 (*1-55532-269-7*) Gareth Stevens Inc.

Plutarch. Plutarch's Lives. White, John S., ed. LC 66-28487. (Illus.). 468p. (gr. 7 up). 1900. 22.00 (*0-8196-0174-8*) Biblo.

GREECE–CIVILIZATION

see Civilization, Greek

GREECE–FICTION

Bawden, Nina. The Real Plato Jones. LC 92-43873. 1993. 13.95 (*0-395-66972-3*, Clarion Bks) HM.

Colum, Padraic. The Children's Homer: The Adventures of Odysseus & the Tale of Troy. Pogany, Willy, illus. LC 82-12643. 256p. (gr. 5 up). 1982. pap. 8.95 (*0-02-042520-1*, Collier Young Ad) Macmillan Child Grp.

Fenton, Edward. The Refugee Summer. LC 81-12593. 272p. (gr. 7 up). 1982. pap. 10.95 (*0-385-28854-9*) Delacorte.

Fox, Paula. Lily & the Lost Boy. LC 87-5778. 160p. (gr. 6-8). 1987. 12.95 (*0-531-05720-8*); PLB 12.99 (*0-531-08320-9*) Orchard Bks Watts.

Green, Roger L. The Luck of Troy. 176p. (gr. 5 up). 1993. pap. 2.25 (*0-14-035103-5*) Puffin Bks.

Hort, Lenny. Goatherd & the Shepherdess. Bloom, Lloyd, illus. LC 93-18178. 1994. 14.99 (*0-8037-1352-5*); PLB 14.89 (*0-8037-1353-3*) Dial Bks Young.

Keene, Carolyn. Greek Odyssey. Greenberg, Anne, ed. 160p. (Orig.). 1992. pap. 3.75 (*0-671-73078-9*, Archway) PB.

McLaren, Clemence. Women of Destiny: A Story of the Trojan War. LC 93-8127. 1996. 14.95 (*0-689-31820-0*, Atheneum Child Bk) Macmillan Child Grp.

Mara, Pam. The Greeks Pop-up. (Illus.). 32p. (Orig.). (gr. 3 up). 1985. pap. 7.95 (*0-906212-33-2*, Pub. by Tarquin UK) Parkwest Pubns.

Mayer, Albert I., Jr. Olympiad. LC 61-12875. (Illus.). (gr. 7 up). 1938. 18.00 (*0-8196-0115-2*) Biblo.

Orgel, Doris. Ariadne, Awake! Moser, Barry, illus. LC 93-24123. 80p. (ps-3). 1994. PLB 15.99 (*0-670-85158-2*) Viking Child Bks.

Pike, Christopher. The Immortal. MacDonald, Pat, ed. 256p. (Orig.). 1993. 14.00 (*0-671-87039-4*, Archway); pap. 3.99 (*0-671-74510-7*, Archway) PB.

—The Immortal. large type ed. LC 93-32608. (gr. 9-12). 1993. pap. 15.95 (*0-7862-0071-5*) Thorndike Pr.

Rosen, Billi. Andi's War. (Illus.). 144p. (gr. 5 up). 1991. pap. 3.95 (*0-14-034404-7*, Puffin) Puffin Bks.

GREECE–HISTORY

Ancient Greece & Rome. (Illus.). 20p. 1994. 6.95 (*1-56458-716-9*) Dorling Kindersley.

Artman, John. Ancient Greece. 64p. (gr. 4-8). 1991. 8.95 (*0-86653-583-7*, GA1310) Good Apple.

Ash, Maureen. Alexander the Great: Ancient Empire Builder. LC 91-1386. 128p. (gr. 3 up). 1991. PLB 20. 55 (*0-516-03063-9*) Childrens.

Bains, Rae. Ancient Greece. Frenck, Hal, illus. LC 84-2685. 32p. (gr. 3-6). 1985. PLB 9.49 (*0-8167-0244-6*); pap. text ed. 2.95 (*0-8167-0245-4*) Troll Assocs.

Descamps-Lequime, Sophie & Vernerey, Denise. The Ancient Greeks: In the Land of the Gods. LaRose, Mary K., tr. from FRE. Martin, Annie-Claude, illus. LC 91-35941. 64p. (gr. 4-6). 1992. PLB 15.40 (*1-56294-069-4*) Millbrook Pr.

Fisher, Leonard E. Olympians: Great Gods & Goddesses of Ancient Greece. Fisher, Leonard E., illus. LC 84-516. 32p. (gr. 1-4). 1984. reinforced bdg. 15.95 (*0-8234-0522-2*); pap. 5.95 (*0-8234-0740-3*) Holiday.

Household, Geoffrey. The Exploits of Xenophon. Fisher, Leonard E., illus. LC 89-12396. lx, 180p. (gr. 5-12). 1989. Repr. of 1955 ed. lib. bdg. 18.00 (*0-208-02224-4*, Linnet) Shoe String.

Little, Emily. The Trojan Horse: How the Greeks Won the War. Eagle, Michael, illus. LC 87-43118. 48p. (Orig.). (gr. 2-4). 1988. pap. 3.50 (*0-394-89674-2*) Random Bks Yng Read.

Loverance, Rowena. Ancient Greece. (Illus.). 48p. (gr. 3-7). 1993. 14.99 (*0-670-84754-2*) Viking Child Bks.

Millard, A. & Peach, S. The Greeks. (Illus.). 96p. 1990. PLB 16.96 (*0-88110-415-9*); pap. 10.95 (*0-7460-0342-0*) EDC.

Nardo, Don. Ancient Greece. LC 93-6904. (gr. 6-9). 1994. 14.95 (*1-56006-229-0*) Lucent Bks.

Odijk, Pamela. The Greeks. (Illus.). 48p. (gr. 5-8). 1989. PLB 12.95 (*0-382-09884-6*) Silver Burdett Pr.

Plutarch. Plutarch's Lives. White, John S., ed. LC 66-28487. (Illus.). 468p. (gr. 7 up). 1900. 22.00 (*0-8196-0174-8*) Biblo.

Polyzoides, G. Ancient Greek History. (GRE., Illus.). (gr. 4-6). 4.00 (*0-686-79636-5*) Divry.

Steele, Philip. Thermopylae. LC 93-2645. (Illus.). 32p. (gr. 6 up). 1993. text ed. 13.95 RSBE (*0-02-786887-7*, New Discovery Bks) Macmillan Child Grp.

Terzi, Marinella. Ancient Greece. LC 92-7508. (Illus.). 36p. (gr. 3 up). 1993. pap. 6.95 (*0-516-48376-5*) Childrens.

Tyler, Deborah. The Greeks & Troy. LC 93-18693. (Illus.). 32p. (gr. 6-8). 1993. text ed. 13.95 RSBE (*0-87518-537-1*, Dillon) Macmillan Child Grp.

Woodford, Susan. The Parthenon. (Illus.). 48p. (gr. 7 up). 1981. pap. 7.95 (*0-521-22629-5*) Cambridge U Pr.

GREECE–SOCIAL LIFE AND CUSTOMS

Chelepi, Chris. Growing up in Ancient Greece. Molan, Chris, illus. LC 91-14852. 32p. (gr. 3-5). 1993. PLB 11.89 (*0-8167-2719-8*); pap. text ed. 3.95 (*0-8167-2720-1*) Troll Assocs.

Loewen. Food in Greece. 1991. 11.95s.p. (*0-86625-348-3*) Rourke Pubns.

Pearson, Anne. Everyday Life in Ancient Greece. LC 93-37519. 1994. write for info. (*0-531-14310-4*) Watts.

Sauvain, Philip. Over Two Thousand Years Ago in Ancient Greece. LC 91-40072. (Illus.). 32p. (gr. 6 up). 1992. text ed. 13.95 RSBE (*0-02-781082-8*, New Discovery) Macmillan Child Grp.

Williams, A. Susan. The Greeks. LC 92-43639. 32p. (gr. 4-6). 1993. 14.95 (*1-56847-059-2*) Thomson Lrning.

GREECE, MODERN

Arnold, Frances. Greece. LC 91-24808. (Illus.). 96p. (gr. 6-12). 1992. PLB 22.80 (*0-8114-2448-0*) Raintree Steck-V.

Burrell, Roy. The Greeks. Connolly, Peter, illus. 112p. (gr. 7 up). 1990. 19.95 (*0-19-917161-0*) OUP.

GREECE, MODERN–HISTORY

Polyzoides, G. History of Byzantine & Modern Greece. (GRE., Illus.). (gr. 4-6). 4.00 (*0-686-79635-7*) Divry.

GREEK ART

see Art, Greek

GREEK CIVILIZATION

see Civilization, Greek

GREEK DRAMA–COLLECTIONS

Aristophanes. Four Major Plays. new ed. Teitel, N. R., intro. by. Incl. The Acharnians; The Birds; The Clouds; Lysistrata. (gr. 11 up). 1968. pap. 2.95 (*0-8049-0189-9*, CL-189) Airmont.

GREEK LANGUAGE, MODERN–CONVERSATION AND PHRASE BOOKS

Demertzis, Strati. The Power of Modern Greek: Basic Course I. 136p. (Orig.). (gr. 7-12). 1986. pap. text ed. 11.00 (*0-9618466-0-7*) Expressway Pubs.

—The Power of Modern Greek: Basic Course II. 164p. (Orig.). (gr. 7-12). 1986. pap. text ed. 12.00 (*0-9618466-1-5*) Expressway Pubs.

Groten, Frank J., Jr. & Finn, James K. A Basic Course for Reading Attic Greek. LC 85-234367. 284p. (gr. 9-12). 1990. Repr. of 1983 ed. 19.95x (*0-942573-50-1*) Hill School.

GREEK LANGUAGE, MODERN–GRAMMAR

Papantoniou, D. The Greek Children. (GRE., Illus.). (gr. 2-3). text ed. 4.00 (*0-686-79628-4*); wkbk. 2.50 (*0-686-79629-2*) Divry.

GREEK LITERATURE

Papantoniou, D. Greek Letters. (GRE.). 158p. (gr. 4-5). 4.00 (*0-686-79634-9*) Divry.

—Greek Stories. (GRE.). (gr. 3-4). 4.00 (*0-686-79633-0*) Divry.

GREEK MYTHOLOGY

see Mythology, Classical

GREEKS IN THE U. S.

Jones, Jayne C. The Greeks in America. rev. ed. LC 68-31504. (Illus.). 80p. (gr. 5 up). PLB 15.95 (*0-8225-0215-1*); pap. 5.95 (*0-8225-1010-3*) Lerner Pubns.

Monos, Dimitri. The Greek Americans. Moynihan, Daniel P., intro. by. 112p. (Orig.). (gr. 5 up). 1988. 17.95 (*0-87754-880-3*); pap. 9.95 (*0-7910-0266-7*) Chelsea Hse.

GREEN TURTLE

Cousteau Society Staff. Turtles. LC 91-32184. (Illus.). 24p. (ps-1). 1992. pap. 3.95 (*0-671-77059-4*, Little Simon) S&S Trade.

GREENBACKS

see Paper Money

GREENHOUSES

Porter, Wes. The Garden Book & Greenhouse. LC 89-40372. (Illus.). 64p. (Orig.). (gr. k-5). 1992. Packaged in greenhouse with seed packets & peat pellets. pap. 10.95 (*0-89480-346-8*, 1346) Workman Pub.

GREENLAND

Berg, Karin & Berg, Hans. Greenland Through the Year. LC 72-90689. (Illus.). 24p. (gr. k-4). 1973. 7.95 (*0-87592-023-3*) Scroll Pr.

Lepthien, Emilie U. Greenland. LC 88-37374. (Illus.). 128p. (gr. 5-9). 1989. PLB 20.55 (*0-516-02710-7*) Childrens.

GREENLAND–FICTION

Conrad, Pam. Call Me Ahnighito. 1995. 15.00 (*0-06-023322-2*); PLB 14.89 (*0-06-023323-0*) HarpC Child Bks.

Kortum, Jeanie & Stermer, Dugald. Ghost Vision. LC 82-19410. (Illus.). 144p. (gr. 5-9). o.s.i 10.95 (*0-685-42976-8*); PLB 10.99 (*0-685-42977-6*) Sierra.

GREETING CARDS

Crowther, Robert. Punchout Christmas Cards. 1989. pap. 5.95 (*0-671-68401-9*) S&S Trade.

Folmer, A. P. Fabulous Easter Fun Book. 16p. (gr. k-3). 1986. pap. 3.95 (*0-590-40207-2*) Scholastic Inc.

Kingshead Corporation Staff. Cut, Color & Create: Make Your Own: Christmas Cards. Kingshead Corporation Staff, illus. 24p. (gr. k-4). 1987. pap. 2.97 (*1-55941-021-3*) Kingshead Corp.

Suid, Murray. Greeting Cards. 64p. (gr. 2-6). 1988. 6.95 (*0-912107-74-X*, MM981) Monday Morning Bks.

GRIFFINS–FICTION

Marston, Elsa. A Griffin in the Garden. Daste, Larry, illus. LC 92-35399. 32p. (gr. k up). 1993. 15.00 (*0-688-10981-0*, Tambourine Bks); PLB 14.93 (*0-688-10982-9*, Tambourine Bks) Morrow.

Pickford, Susan T. It's up to You, Griffin! Ramsey, Marcy D., illus. 32p. (gr. k-4). 1993. bds. 10.95 (*0-87033-446-8*) Tidewater.

GROCERY TRADE

see also Supermarkets

Wilks, Shelley. What's It Like to Be a Grocer. Ramsey, Marcy D., illus. LC 89-34394. 32p. (gr. k-3). 1990. lib. bdg. 10.89 (*0-8167-1805-9*); pap. text ed. 2.95 (*0-8167-1806-7*) Troll Assocs.

GROOMING, PERSONAL

see Beauty, Personal

GROOMING FOR WOMEN

see Beauty, Personal

GROTTOES

see Caves

GROUND EFFECT MACHINES

see also Helicopters

GROUNDHOGS–FICTION

Balian, Lorna. A Garden for a Groundhog. Balian, Lorna, illus. 32p. (gr. k up). 1985. PLB 13.95 (*0-687-14009-9*) Humbug Bks.

Blair, Grandpa. Willie the Groundhog. 6p. (gr. 10 up). 1991. 4.75 (*0-930366-63-8*) Northcountry Pub.

Burgess, Thornton. The Adventures of Johnny Chuck. 1992. Repr. lib. bdg. 17.95x (*0-89966-991-3*) Buccaneer Bks.

Jensen, Patricia & Clement, Claude. Go to Sleep, Little Groundhog. Nouvelle, Catherine, illus. LC 91-46234. 24p. (ps-3). 1993. 6.99 (*0-89577-487-9*, Dist. by Random) RD Assn.

—Go to Sleep, Little Groundhog. Nouvelle, Catherine, illus. LC 91-46234. 24p. (ps-3). 1993. 6.99 (*0-89577-487-9*, Dist. by Random) RD Assn.

Kroll, Steven. It's Groundhog Day! Bassett, Jeni, illus. LC 86-22924. 32p. (ps-3). 1987. reinforced bdg. 14.95 (*0-8234-0643-1*) Holiday.

—It's Groundhog Day. (ps-3). 1991. pap. 2.50 (*0-590-44669-X*) Scholastic Inc.

McDonnell, Janet. Winter: Tracks in the Snow. Hohag, Linda, illus. LC 93-20172. 32p. (gr. 2 up). 1993. PLB 12.30 (*0-516-00679-7*) Childrens.

Moutran, Julia S. The Story of Punxsutawney Phil, "The Fearless Forecaster" Dubnansky, Marsha L., illus. LC 86-82950. 64p. (ps-5). 1987. 14.95 (*0-9617819-2-0*); pap. 8.95 (*0-9617819-0-4*); audiocassette 10.95 (*0-9617819-3-9*) Lit Pubns.

—Will Spring Ever Come to Gobbler's Knob? A Punxsutawney Phil Adventure Story. Sweetland, Marsha L., illus. 64p. (ps-5). 1992. Incl. Phil's Field Guide to Woodland Animals. 15.95 (*0-9617819-5-5*); Incl. Phil's Field Guide to Woodland Animals. pap. 9.95 (*0-9617819-4-7*); audiocass. 10.95 (*0-685-48131-X*) Lit Pubns.

Saltzman, Mark. Woodchuck Nation. Buller, Jon, illus. LC 93-4641. 1994. 15.00 (*0-679-85107-0*) Knopf Bks Yng Read.

Sargent, Dave & Sargent, Pat. Greta Groundhog. Sapaugh, Blaine, illus. 48p. (Orig.). (gr. k-8). 1993. text ed. 11.95 (*1-56763-040-5*); pap. text ed. 5.95 (*1-56763-041-3*) Ozark Pub.

GROUP LIVING

see Collective Settlements

GROUSE–FICTION

Nelson, Cathy. Being Grown up Is Not What I Thought! Nelson, Cathy, illus. 28p. (Orig.). (gr. 1-3). 1994. pap. 6.00 (*0-9637845-0-1*) Thumbprnt Pub.

GROWTH

For biological and psychological works on the growth and development of animal and human organisms.

see also Children–Growth; Growth (Plants)

Aliki. I'm Growing! Aliki, illus. LC 91-14087. 32p. (ps-1). 1992. 14.00 (*0-06-020244-0*); PLB 13.89 (*0-06-020245-9*) HarpC Child Bks.

—I'm Growing! Aliki, illus. LC 91-14087. 32p. (ps-1). 1993. pap. 4.95 (*0-06-445116-X*, Trophy) HarpC Child Bks.

Alpine Partners Staff. See How I Grow. Mitchell, Suzanne, ed. Matthews, Mozelle, illus. 32p. Date not set. 39.95 (*0-9637894-0-6*) Video Moments.

Althea. How Do Things Grow? Douglas, Julie, illus. LC 90-10923. 32p. (gr. k-3). 1991. PLB 11.59 (*0-8167-2118-1*); pap. text ed. 3.95 (*0-8167-2119-X*) Troll Assocs.

Bailey, Donna. All about Birth & Growth. LC 90-10134. (Illus.). 48p. (gr. 2-6). 1990. PLB 20.70 (*0-8114-2777-3*) Raintree Steck-V.

Bingham, Mindy, et al. Challenges: A Young Man's Journal for Self-Awareness & Personal Planning. updated ed. Greene, Barbara & Peters, Kathleen, eds. LC 84-70108. (Illus.). 240p. (gr. 8 up). 1993. 18.95 (*0-911655-26-3*, Dist. by Ingram Book Co Bookpeople); pap. 18.95 (*0-911655-24-7*, Dist. by Ingram Book Co Bookpeople); wkbk. 5.95 (*0-911655-25-5*, Dist. by Ingram Book Co Bookpeople) Advocacy Pr.

Birth & Growth. 48p. (gr. 5-8). 1988. PLB 10.95 (*0-382-09708-4*) Silver Burdett Pr.

Ganeri, Anita. Birth & Growth. (Illus.). 32p. (gr. 2-4). 1994. PLB 18.99 (*0-8114-5519-X*) Raintree Steck-V.

Gee, R. & Meredith, S. Growing Up: Adolescence, Body Changes & Sex. 48p. 1986. PLB 13.96 (*0-88110-337-3*); pap. 6.95 (*0-86020-837-0*) EDC.

Goennel, Heidi. While I Am Little. Goennel, Heidi, illus. LC 92-36795. 32p. (ps up). 1993. 14.00 (*0-688-12371-6*, Tambourine Bks); PLB 13.93 (*0-688-12372-4*, Tambourine Bks) Morrow.

Krauss, Ruth. Growing Story. Rowand, Phyllis, illus. LC 47-30688. (gr. k-3). 1947. 11.95i (*0-06-023380-X*) HarpC Child Bks.

Lemberg, Ray & Lemberg, Alexis. Daddy, Me & the Adventures of Growing Up. Evers, Melissa, illus. 32p. (Orig.). (gr. k-4). 1988. pap. 6.45 (*0-9619208-5-8*) Small Hands Pr.

Stine, Megan, et al. Hands-On Science: Things That Grow. Taback, Simms, illus. LC 92-56894. 1993. PLB 18.60 (*0-8368-0959-9*) Gareth Stevens Inc.

Taylor, Kim. Too Slow to See. (gr. 2-5). 1991. 9.95 (*0-385-30214-2*) Delacorte.

Wilkes, A. Growing Things. (Illus.). 14p. (gr. 2-6). 1986. pap. 4.50 (*0-7460-0122-3*) EDC.

Wilkes, Angela. See How I Grow. LC 93-27039. (Illus.). 32p. (ps). 1994. 13.95 (*1-56458-464-X*) Dorling Kindersley.

GROWTH (PLANTS)

Andersen, Honey. Which Comes First? Berry, Ruth, illus. LC 93-18113. 1994. write for info. (*0-383-03726-3*) SRA Schl Grp.

Maestro, Betsy. How Do Apples Grow? Maestro, Giulio, illus. LC 91-9468. 32p. (gr. k-3). 1993. pap. 4.95 (*0-06-445117-8*, Trophy) HarpC Child Bks.

Morris, Ting & Morris, Neil. Growing Things. (Illus.). 32p. (gr. 2-4). 1994. PLB 12.40 (*0-531-14284-1*) Watts.

Rowe, Julian & Perham, Molly. Watch It Grow! LC 94-12258. (Illus.). 32p. (gr. 1-4). 1994. PLB 18.60 (*0-516-08141-1*); pap. 4.95 (*0-516-48141-X*) Childrens.

Taylor, Barbara. Green Thumbs Up! The Science of Growing Plants. Bull, Peter, et al, illus. LC 91-4290. 40p. (Orig.). (gr. 2-5). 1992. pap. 4.95 (*0-679-82042-6*) Random Bks Yng Read.

—Growing Plants. LC 91-2568. (Illus.). 40p. (gr. k-4). 1991. PLB 12.90 (*0-531-19128-1*, Warwick) Watts.

GUADALCANAL, BATTLE OF, 1942-1943

Guadalcanal Diary. LC 78-50958. (gr. 4-12). 1978. pap. text ed. 2.25 (*0-88301-303-7*) Pendulum Pr.

GUAM

Eustaquio, Roque B. Islas: A Social Studies Workbook. 98p. (gr. 9-12). 1989. write for info wkbk. Marianas Red Pub.

Farrell, Don A. Liberation Nineteen Forty-Four: The Pictorial History of Guam. Koontz, Phyllis, ed. Dimalanta, Ariel, illus. (gr. 8-12). 1984. Repr. 15.95 (*0-930839-00-5*) Micronesian.

PSECC Staff. Hale'-Ta: Governing Guam: Before & After the Wars. 300p. (gr. 8). 1994. 40.00 (*1-883488-02-8*) Polit Status ECC.

—Hale'-Ta: Hestorian Taotao Tano' History of the Chamorro People. 100p. (gr. 5). 1993. 30.00 (*1-883488-00-1*) Polit Status ECC.

—Hale'-Ta: Issues in Guam's Political Development: The Chamorro Perspective. 100p. (gr. 9). 1994. 25.00 (*1-883488-03-6*) Polit Status ECC.

—Hale'Ta: Insights: The Chamorro Identity. 200p. (gr. 12). 1993. 25.00 (*1-883488-01-X*) Polit Status ECC.

GUATEMALA

Brill, Marlene T. & Targ, Harry R. Guatemala. LC 92-39099. (Illus.). 128p. (gr. 5-9). 1993. PLB 20.55 (*0-516-02614-3*) Childrens.

Cummins, Ronnie. Guatemala. Welch, Rose, illus. LC 89-40246. 64p. (gr. 5-6). 1990. PLB 21.26 (*0-8368-0120-2*) Gareth Stevens Inc.

Guatemala Is My Home. 48p. (gr. 2-8). 1992. PLB 18.60 (*0-8368-0901-7*) Gareth Stevens Inc.

Lazo, Caroline. Rigoberta Menchu. LC 93-8381. (Illus.). 64p. (gr. 4 up). 1994. text ed. 13.95 RSBE (*0-87518-619-X*, Dillon) Macmillan Child Grp.

Lerner Publications, Department of Geography Staff. Guatemala in Pictures. (Illus.). 64p. (gr. 5 up). 1987. PLB 17.50 (*0-8225-1803-1*) Lerner Pubns.

GUATEMALA–FICTION
Martin, Marilyn. Pedro. 152p. (gr. 3 up). 1980. 6.55 (*0-686-30765-8*) Rod & Staff.
GUERRILLA WARFARE
see also World War, 1939-1945–Underground Movements
GUIDANCE
see Counseling; Vocational Guidance
GUIDE BOOKS
see names of countries, states, etc. with the subdivision description and travel-guide books (e.g. U. S.–description and Travel etc.) and names of cities with the subdivision Description–Guide Books, e.g. New York–Description, etc.
GUIDE DOGS
Alexander, Sally H. Mom's Best Friend. Ancona, George, illus. LC 91-43809. 48p. (gr. 1-5). 1992. RSBE 14.95 (*0-02-700393-0*, Macmillan Child Bk) Macmillan Child Grp.
Arnold, Caroline. A Guide Dog Puppy Grows Up. Hewett, Richard, photos by. (Illus.). 43p. (gr. 1 up). 1991. 16.95 (*0-15-232657-X*) HarBrace.
Ring, Elizabeth. Assistance Dogs: In Special Service. LC 93-735. (Illus.). 32p. (gr. 2-4). 1993. PLB 13.40 (*1-56294-290-5*) Millbrook Pr.
Smith, Elizabeth S. A Guide Dog Goes to School: The Story of a Dog Trained to Lead the Blind. Dodson, Bert, illus. LC 87-11056. 64p. (gr. 1-4). 1987. 12.95 (*0-688-06844-8*); lib. bdg. 12.88 (*0-688-06846-4*, Morrow Jr Bks) Morrow Jr Bks.
GUIDE DOGS–FICTION
Garfield, James B. Follow My Leader. Greiner, Robert, illus. LC 57-1611. 192p. (gr. 4-6). 1957. pap. 13.95 (*0-670-32332-2*) Viking Child Bks.
GUIDE POSTS
see Signs and Signboards
GUIDED MISSILES
Nicholaus, J. Rockets & Missiles. (Illus.). 48p. (gr. 3-8). 1989. lib. bdg. 18.60 (*0-86592-418-X*); lib. bdg. 13. 95s.p. (*0-685-58577-8*) Rourke Corp.
GUILDS
see also Labor and Laboring Classes; Labor Unions
GUINEA PIGS
Bantam Staff. Guinea Pig: Baby Animal. (ps). 1994. 4.99 (*0-553-09549-8*) Bantam.
Barrett, Norman S. Guinea Pigs. LC 89-21528. (Illus.). 32p. (gr. k-4). 1990. PLB 11.90 (*0-531-14031-8*) Watts.
Bryant, Donna. My Guinea Pigs Pip & Gus. Wood, Jakki, illus. 20p. (ps-3). 1991. 8.95 (*0-8120-6213-2*) Barron.
Burton, Jane. Dazy the Guinea Pig. LC 89-11397. (Illus.). 32p. (gr. 2-3). 1989. PLB 17.27 (*0-8368-0206-3*) Gareth Stevens Inc.
Duke, Kate. Guinea Pigs Far & Near. Duke, Kate, illus. LC 84-1580. 24p. (ps-1). 1989. pap. 3.95 (*0-525-44480-7*, DCB) Dutton Child Bks.
Evans, Mark. Guinea Pigs. LC 92-52826. (Illus.). 48p. (gr. 2 up). 1992. 9.95 (*1-56458-125-X*) Dorling Kindersley.
Hansen, Elvig. Guinea Pigs. (gr. 4-7). 1993. pap. 6.95 (*0-87614-613-2*) Carolrhoda Bks.
Petty, Kate. Cobayos. Thompson, George, illus. LC 90-71412. (SPA.). 24p. (gr. k-4). 1991. PLB 10.90 (*0-531-07914-7*) Watts.
—Guinea Pigs. Thompson, George, illus. LC 94-26050. (gr. 1-4). 1995. write for info. (*0-8120-9080-2*) Barron.
Pope, Joyce. Taking Care of Your Guinea Pig. (Illus.). 32p. (gr. 4-9). 1990. pap. 3.95 o.s. (*0-531-15169-7*) Watts.
Steinkamp, Anja J. Your First Guinea Pig. (Illus.). 36p. (Orig.). 1991. pap. 1.95 (*0-86622-066-6*, YF-109) TFH Pubns.
GUINEA PIGS–FICTION
Bare, Colleen S. Guinea Pigs Don't Read Books. (Illus.). 32p. (ps-2). 1993. pap. 3.99 (*0-14-054995-1*, Puff Unicorn) Puffin Bks.
Duke, Kate. Guinea Pigs Far & Near. Duke, Kate, illus. LC 84-1580. 24p. (ps-1). 1984. 9.95 (*0-525-44112-3*, DCB) Dutton Child Bks.
Hughes, Barb. Spot, the Guinea Pig. Bogan, Rachel, ed. Baskerville, Leana, illus. (Illus.). 32p. (gr. k-3). 1992. pap. 7.95 (*1-878036-10-6*) Hughes Taylor.
Myers, Laurie. Guinea Pigs Don't Talk. Taylor, Cheryl, illus. LC 93-39642. 1994. 13.95 (*0-395-68967-8*, Clarion Bks) HM.
Smith, Emma. Emily the Traveling Guinea Pig. (gr. 1-5). 1960. 10.95 (*0-8392-3007-9*) Astor-Honor.
Wilson, A. N. Hazel the Guinea Pig. LC 91-71850. 96p. (gr. k-3). 1994. pap. 3.99 (*1-56402-372-9*) Candlewick Pr.
GUITAR
Bay, William. Children's Guitar Method, Vol. 1. (Illus.). 1993. 5.95 (*0-87166-386-4*, 93833); cass. 9.98 (*0-87166-387-2*, 93833); bk. & cass. 14.95 (*0-87166-388-0*, 93833) Mel Bay.
—Children's Guitar Method, Vol. 2. (Illus.). 1993. 5.95 (*0-87166-389-9*, 93834) Mel Bay.
—Children's Guitar Method, Vol. 3. 1993. 5.95 (*0-87166-392-9*, 93835) Mel Bay.
—Kids' Rock Guitar Method. 1993. 5.95 (*0-685-63861-8*, 94360); cass. 9.98 (*0-685-63862-6*, 94360); CD 14.95 (*0-685-63863-4*, 94360) Mel Bay.
Buckingham, Jack. The Accompaniment Guitar: A Beginner's Guide to Song Accompaniment for Individual or Classroom Use. (Illus.). 80p. 1979. pap. 7.00 (*0-8258-0003-X*, 05065) Fischer Inc NY.
Edwards, William H. Fretboard Logic, Vol. 1: The Reasoning Behind the Guitar's Unique Tuning System. rev. ed. (Illus.). 34p. (gr. 7-12). 1983. pap. 9.95 spiral bdg. (*0-685-29425-0*) Edwards Music Pub.
Ellis, Cathy. The Adventures of Gilly, the Guitar, Bk. 1. Moya, Patricia, illus. 40p. (ps-2). 1991. wkbk. incl. audiotape 15.95 (*1-879542-04-8*) Ellis Family Mus.
—Complete Guide for the Guitar. rev. ed. Lee, et al. (Illus.). 255p. (gr. 6-12). 1990. tchr's ed. 34.95 (*1-879542-01-3*); wkbk., student ed., spiral bd. 29.95 (*1-879542-00-5*) Ellis Family Mus.
—Holiday Guitar: Songs for Christmas & Hanukah. rev. ed. 48p. 1992. Repr. of 1985 ed. lab manual 18.95 (*1-879542-11-0*); audiotape 14.95 (*1-879542-12-9*) Ellis Family Mus.
—More Adventures with Gilly, the Guitar, Bk. 2. Moya, Patricia, illus. 48p. (ps-2). 1992. wkbk. 12.95 (*1-879542-08-0*); audiotape 14.95 (*1-879542-14-5*) Ellis Family Mus.
Erbsen, Wayne. The Complete & Painless Guide to the Guitar for Young Beginner. (Illus.). 64p. 1979. pap. 6.95 (*0-8258-0002-1*, PCB 111) Fischer Inc NY.
Isherwood, Millicent. The Guitar. 48p. (gr. 4-7). 1986. pap. 9.95 (*0-19-321334-6*) OUP.
Leanza, Frank. How to Get Started with the Guitar. (Illus.). 34p. 1993. pap. 3.95 (*0-934687-17-X*) Crystal Pubs.
Michelson, Sonia. New Dimensions in Classical Guitar for Children. 1993. 7.95 (*1-56222-115-9*, 94537); cass. 9.98 (*1-56222-259-7*, 94537) Mel Bay.
Smith, L. Learn to Play Guitar. (Illus.). 64p. (gr. 6-12). 1988. PLB 14.96 (*0-88110-384-5*); pap. 8.95 (*0-7460-0193-2*) EDC.
Vahila, Michael. Teaching Guitar to Children: A Complete Guide for Ages 5 to 12. LC 88-63797. (Illus.). 100p. (Orig.). (gr. k-7). 1988. pap. 9.95 (*0-942253-01-9*); book & cassette pkg. 18.95 (*0-942253-02-7*) PAZ Pub.
Zerbey, Richard J. Jam Plastic: Now You Can Play Lead Guitar with a Live Band. LC 85-754277. (Illus.). 24p. (Orig.). (gr. 7 up). 1986. lib. bdg. 21.95 incl. cassette (*0-935565-07-8*, JPHV-I); pap. 15.95 incl. cassette (*0-935565-04-3*); replacement (tape only) 7.99 (*0-935565-10-8*) Sound Ent.
—Jam Plastic: Now You Can Play Lead Guitar with a Live Band. LC 85-754101. (Illus.). 24p. (Orig.). (gr. 7 up). 1986. lib. bdg. 21.95 incl. cassette (*0-935565-08-6*); pap. 15.95 (*0-935565-05-1*); cassette incl.; replacement tape only 7.99 (*0-935565-11-6*) Sound Ent.
—Jam Plastic: Now You Can Play Lead Guitar with a Live Band. LC 85-754282. (Illus.). 24p. (Orig.). (gr. 7 up). 1986. lib. bdg. 21.95 incl. cassette (*0-935565-06-X*); pap. 15.95 (*0-935565-03-5*); cassette incl.; replacement tape only 7.99 (*0-935565-09-4*) Sound Ent.
GUITAR–FICTION
Ellis, Cathy. More Adventures of Gilly, the Guitar, Bk. 3. (Illus.). 48p. (ps-2). 1993. wkbk. 12.95 (*1-879542-26-9*); audiotape 14.95 (*1-879542-27-7*) Ellis Family Mus.
Robinson, Jan. The Story of Warple. Jewell, Jack, illus. 32p. (ps). 1990. 12.95 (*0-89334-137-1*) Humanics Ltd.
Rodriguez, Anita. Jamal & the Angel. Rodriguez, Anita, illus. LC 91-11636. 32p. (ps-2). 1992. 14.00 (*0-517-58601-0*); PLB 15.99 (*0-517-59115-4*) Crown Bks Yng Read.
Slightly Off-Center Writers Group, Ltd. Staff. Joy's Guitar. (Illus.). 48p. (gr. 3-6). 1994. pap. 6.95 (*1-56721-061-9*) Twnty-Fifth Cent Pr.
GULLS
O'Connor, Karen. The Herring Gull. LC 91-40856. (Illus.). 60p. (gr. 4 up). 1992. text ed. 13.95 RSBE (*0-87518-506-1*, Dillon) Macmillan Child Grp.
GULLS–FICTION
Bach, Richard. Jonathan Livingston Seagull. 128p. (gr. 7 up). 1976. pap. 4.99 (*0-380-01286-3*) Avon.
Benchley, Nathaniel. Kilroy & the Gull. Schoenherr, John, illus. LC 76-24309. (gr. 4-6). 1978. pap. 3.95 (*0-06-440090-5*, Trophy) HarpC Child Bks.
Hoff, Syd. The Lighthouse Children. LC 92-41172. (Illus.). 32p. (ps-2). 1994. 14.00 (*0-06-022958-6*); PLB 13.89 (*0-06-022959-4*) HarpC Child Bks.
Holling, Holling C. Seabird. (Illus.). (gr. 4-6). 1973. 17.95 (*0-395-18230-1*) HM.
Kelley, Rosemary S. Seavy Seagull & the Friendship Sloop Race. 2nd ed. Kelley, Rosemary S., illus. 39p. (ps-k). 1985. pap. 5.95 (*0-9616905-0-X*) R S Kelley.
O'Connor, Karen. The Green Team: The Adventures of Mitch & Molly. Chapin, Patrick O., illus. LC 92-24643. 80p. (Orig.). (gr. 1-4). 1993. pap. 4.99 (*0-570-04726-9*) Concordia.
GUNNING
see Hunting; Shooting
GUNS
see Firearms; Ordnance
GUTENBERG, JOHANN, 1397-1468
Burch, Joann J. Fine Print: A Story about Johann Gutenberg. (ps-3). 1992. pap. 5.95 (*0-87614-565-9*) Carolrhoda Bks.
GUTHRIE, WOODY, 1912-1967
Yates, Janelle. Woody Guthrie. (Illus.). 128p. (gr. 4 up). 1994. pap. 10.95 (*0-9623380-5-2*) Ward Hill Pr.
—Woody Guthrie. (Illus.). 128p. (gr. 4 up). 1994. PLB 14.95 (*0-9623380-0-1*) Ward Hill Pr.
GUYANA
Brill, Marlene T. Guyana. LC 94-7007. (Illus.). 128p. (gr. 5-9). 1994. PLB 27.40 (*0-516-02626-7*) Childrens.
Lerner Publications, Department of Geography Staff. Guyana in Pictures. (Illus.). 64p. (gr. 5 up). 1988. PLB 17.50 (*0-8225-1815-5*) Lerner Pubns.
GYMNASTICS
see also Physical Education and Training
Barrett, Norman. The World Cup. LC 93-21660. (Illus.). 48p. (gr. 4-8). 1993. 15.95 (*1-56847-124-6*) Thomson Lrning.
Barrett, Norman S. Gimnasia. LC 90-70888. (SPA., Illus.). 32p. (gr. k-4). 1990. PLB 11.90 (*0-531-07906-6*) Watts.
Bellew, Bob. Gymnastics. Kline, Marjory, ed. LC 91-9128. (Illus.). 32p. (gr. 2-5). 1992. PLB 11.90 (*0-531-18463-3*, Pub. by Bookwright Pr) Watts.
Boy Scouts of America. Cub Scout Sports: Gymnastics. (Illus.). 40p. (gr. 2-5). 1987. pap. 1.35 (*0-8395-4085-X*, 2110) BSA.
Carter, Eneida & Mikalac, Miriam. Break Dance: The Free & Easy Way! Forman, Jan A., illus. 32p. (gr. 7 up). 1984. pap. 9.95 (*0-916391-00-0*) Free & Easy Pubns.
Duden, Jane. Men's & Women's Gymnastics. LC 91-24682. (Illus.). 48p. (gr. 5). 1992. text ed. 11.95 RSBE (*0-89686-727-7*, Crestwood Hse) Macmillan Child Grp.
Durrant, Amanda. My Book of Gymnastics: Health & Movement. Fairclough, Chris, illus. LC 93-24978. 32p. (gr. k-4). 1993. 13.95 (*1-56847-125-4*) Thomson Lrning.
Haycock, Kate. Gymnastics. LC 91-16118. (Illus.). 48p. (gr. 6). 1991. text ed. 13.95 RSBE (*0-89686-666-1*, Crestwood Hse) Macmillan Child Grp.
Ivy, Elizabeth. Gymnast Commandos. (gr. 4-7). 1991. pap. 2.75 (*0-590-43835-2*) Scholastic Inc.
Kuklin, Susan. Going to My Gymnastics Class. Kuklin, Susan, illus. LC 90-20206. 40p. (ps-1). 1991. RSBE 13.95 (*0-02-751236-3*, Bradbury Pr) Macmillan Child Grp.
Levy, Elizabeth. Fear of Falling. 128p. (gr. 3-7). 1991. pap. 2.75 (*0-590-43834-4*, Apple Paperbacks) Scholastic Inc.
McLaughlin, Maria. Gymnastics. (Illus.). 64p. (gr. 7-12). 1984. 24.95 (*0-7134-4283-2*, Pub. by Batsford UK) Trafalgar.
McSweeney, Sean & Bunnett, Chris. Gymnastics. (Illus.). 64p. (gr. 7-10). 1993. 24.95 (*0-7134-7129-8*, Pub. by Batsford UK) Trafalgar.

Pakizer, Debi. Vaulting: The Art of Gymnastics on Horseback. Sears, Mary A., illus. Anderson, Julia & Barnette, Jackie, eds. (Illus.). 24p. (Orig.). (ps-5). 1993. pap. 8.00 (*0-9639785-6-X*) M A Sears. VAULTING: THE ART OF GYMNASTICS ON HORSEBACK - an offical demonstrator sport for the 1996 Summer Olympic games. The sport's origins have been traced to caveman drawings, Mongolian warriors & the Roman Cavalry. The book is an introduction & explanation of the sport's different facets of fun that can be had by all ages doing gymnastic-type moves on a moving horse. It is illustrated with line drawings, with copy to interest, & enlighten, anyone who reads it. Used as an activity book, it combines three facets of learning: kinesthetic (hand-eye coordination), visual, & audio skills to promote total learning & understanding of the sport. "A terrific new book...perfect for vaulters, friends or relatives...it tells all about vaulting!" - Young Equestrian Magazine. It is also very therapeutic for the handicapped, which is another benefit of this sport. The illustrator's daughter's successful progress toward living a more normal life, despite visual & minor cerebral palsy "challenges," is testimony to this fact. Vaulting is for all ages & physical abilities, & this book is a great introduction that ALL will enjoy. To order, write: Mountain Springs Vaulters, 555 W. Sierra Hwy., Acton, CA 93510.
Publisher Provided Annotation.

Roper, Gayle. The Puzzle of the Poison Pen. LC 94-6755. 1994. write for info. (*0-7814-1507-1*, Chariot Bks) Chariot Family.

U. S. A. Gymnastics Staff. I Can Do Gymnastics: Essential Skills for Intermediate Gymnasts. LC 92-43281. (Illus.). 144p. (Orig.). 1993. pap. 14.95 (*0-940279-54-1*) Masters Pr IN.

United States Gymnastics Federation Staff. I Can Do Gymnastics: Essential Skills for Beginning Gymnasts. Wilson, Lynn, et al, illus. Feeney, Rik, intro. by. LC 92-2441. 144p. (Orig.). (gr. 1-5). 1993. pap. 14.95 (*0-940279-51-7*) Masters Pr IN.

—I Can Do... Rhythmic Gymnastics: Student Workbook, Level 1-2. 88p. (gr. k-3). 1993. pap. 5.00 wkbk. (*1-885250-12-6*) USA Gymnastics.

—I Can Do...Rhythmic Gymnastics: Student Workbook, Levels 3 & 4. 91p. (gr. k-3). 1993. 5.00 (*1-885250-13-4*) USA Gymnastics.

—Make the Team: Gymnastics for Girls. (Illus.). (gr. 3-7). 1991. (Spts Illus Kids); pap. 5.95 (*0-316-88793-5*, Spts Illus Kids) Little.

GYPSIES

Sen, Abhijit & Raman, Papri Sri. Magic Bones. 264p. (gr. 9-10). 1992. 14.95 (*0-932377-49-1*) Facet Bks.

Strom, Yale. Uncertain Roads: Searching for the Gypsies. Strom, Yale, illus. LC 93-21962. 112p. (gr. 5-11). 1993. SBE 19.95 (*0-02-788531-3*, Four Winds) Macmillan Child Grp.

GYPSIES–FICTION

Bemelmans, Ludwig. Madeline & the Gypsies. Bemelmans, Ludwig, illus. 56p. (ps-3). 1977. pap. 4.50 (*0-14-050261-0*, Puffin) Puffin Bks.

Carlson, Natalie S. Family under the Bridge. Williams, Garth, illus. LC 58-5292. 112p. (gr. 3-7). 1958. PLB 14.89 (*0-06-020991-7*) HarpC Child Bks.

Pochocki, Ethel. The Gypsies' Tale. Kelly, Laura, illus. LC 93-3320. (gr. 4 up). 1994. pap. 15.00 (*0-671-79934-7*, S&S BFYR) S&S Trade.

Roth, Susan L. Gypsy Bird Song. (Illus.). 32p. (gr. 1 up). 1991. 14.95 (*0-374-32825-0*) FS&G.

Springer, Nancy. The Boy on a Black Horse. LC 92-27158. 176p. (gr. 5-9). 1994. SBE 14.95 (*0-689-31840-5*, Atheneum Child Bk) Macmillan Child Grp.

Worth, Valerie. Gypsy Gold. LC 83-20607. 176p. (gr. 12 up). 1986. pap. 3.45 (*0-374-42820-4*) FS&G.

H

HABITATIONS, HUMAN

see Architecture, Domestic; Houses; Housing

HABITATIONS OF ANIMALS

see Animals–Habitations

HABITS OF ANIMALS

see Animals–Habits and Behavior

HAIKU

Cassedy, Sylvia & Suetake, Kunihiro. Red Dragonfly on My Shoulder: Haiku. Bang, Molly, illus. LC 91-18443. 32p. (gr. k-5). 1992. 15.00 (*0-06-022624-2*); PLB 14.89 (*0-06-022625-0*) HarpC Child Bks.

Demi, selected by. & illus. In the Eyes of the Cat. Tze-Si Huang, tr. from JPN. LC 91-27729. 80p. (gr. 1-3). 1992. 15.95 (*0-8050-1955-3*, Bks Young Read) H Holt & Co.

Harter, Penny. Shadow Play, Night Haiku. Greene, Jeffrey, illus. LC 93-39887. (gr. 1-6). 1994. 15.00 (*0-671-88396-8*, S&S BFYR) S&S Trade.

Henderson, Harold G. Haiku in English. LC 67-16413. (Illus.). 75p. (gr. 9 up). 1967. pap. 7.95 (*0-8048-0228-9*) C E Tuttle.

Leivis, Edith M. Haiku Is... a Feeling. King, James B., illus. Leivis, Edith M., intro. by. LC 89-64144. (Illus.). 64p. (Orig.). (gr. 1-3). 1990. pap. 5.95 (*0-9624993-0-7*) Pippin Bks.

HAILE SELASSIE 1ST, EMPEROR OF ETHIOPIA, 1891-

Negash, Askale. Haile Selassie. Schlesinger, Arthur M., intro. by. (Illus.). 112p. (gr. 5 up). 1989. 17.95x (*1-55546-850-0*) Chelsea Hse.

Obaba, Al-Imam. Emperor Haile Selassie. (Illus.). 43p. (Orig.). 1989. pap. 3.95 (*0-916157-07-5*) African Islam Miss Pubns.

HAIR

Badt, Karin L. Hair There & Everywhere. LC 94-11652. (Illus.). 32p. (gr. 3-7). 1994. PLB 17.20 (*0-516-08187-X*); pap. 5.95 (*0-516-48187-8*) Childrens.

Bailey, Donna. All about Your Skin, Hair & Teeth. LC 90-10050. (Illus.). 48p. (gr. 2-6). 1990. PLB 20.70 (*0-8114-2783-8*) Raintree Steck-V.

Balasco, Dianne. Hair Flair. (gr. 4-7). 1994. pap. 6.95 (*0-8167-3366-X*) Troll Assocs.

Goldin, Augusta. Straight Hair, Curly Hair. Emberley, Ed E., illus. LC 66-12669. 40p. (gr. k-3). 1966. PLB 14.89 (*0-690-77921-6*, Crowell Jr Bks) HarpC Child Bks.

Hair. (Illus.). (gr. 5 up). 1987. lib. bdg. 15.94 (*0-86625-278-9*); 11.95s.p. (*0-685-67661-7*) Rourke Corp.

Howse, Cathy. Ultra Black Hair Growth II: Another Six Inches Longer One Year from Now. rev. ed. LC 90-90326. 125p. (Orig.). (gr. 8 up). 1994. pap. 12.95 (*0-9628330-1-0*) UBH Pubns.

—Ultra Black Hair Growth: Six Inches Longer One Year from Now. (Illus.). 92p. (Orig.). (gr. 8 up). 1990. pap. text ed. 10.95 (*0-9628330-0-2*) UBH Pubns.

Kroll, Virginia. Hats Off to Hair! Life, Kay, illus. 32p. (ps-4). 1995. 14.00 (*0-88106-869-1*); PLB 15.88 (*0-88106-870-5*); pap. 6.95 (*0-88106-868-3*) Charlesbridge Pub.

Kyle, Jamie. Great Hair for Girls. (Illus.). 32p. (gr. 3 up). 1993. 17.95 (*1-56288-414-X*) Checkerboard.

Punches, Laurie C. How to Simply Cut Hair. Martinez, Carla, et al, eds. Punches, Laurie C., illus. LC 88-92443. 109p. (Orig.). (gr. 11 up). 1989. pap. 8.95 (*0-929883-06-3*); VHS & Beta. video 29.95 (*0-929883-07-1*) Punches Prodns.

—How to Simply Cut Hair Even Better: Advanced Haircutting. Punches, Laurie C., illus. LC 88-92468. 129p. (Orig.). (gr. 11 up). 1989. pap. 9.95 (*0-929883-08-X*) Punches Prodns.

—How to Simply Highlight Hair. Punches, Laurie C., illus. LC 88-92469. 79p. (Orig.). (gr. 11 up). 1989. pap. 6.95 (*0-929883-02-0*); VHS & Beta. video 19.95 (*0-929883-03-9*) Punches Prodns.

—How to Simply Perm Hair. Punches, Laurie C., illus. LC 88-92467. 74p. (Orig.). (gr. 11 up). 1989. pap. 6.95 (*0-929883-04-7*); VHS & Beta. video 19.95 (*0-929883-05-5*) Punches Prodns.

HAIR–FICTION

Cisneros, Sandra. Hairs: Pelitos. Ybanez, Terry, illus. LC 93-32775. (ps-3). 1994. 15.00 (*0-679-86171-8*, Apple Soup Bks); PLB 15.99 (*0-679-96171-2*, Apple Soup Bks) Knopf Bks Yng Read.

Cote, Nancy. Palm Trees. Cote, Nancy, illus. LC 92-18938. 40p. (ps-2). 1993. RSBE 14.95 (*0-02-724760-0*, Four Winds) Macmillan Child Grp.

Damaris, Gypsy. Pink Hair. 20p. (Orig.). (gr. 1). 1984. pap. 2.35 (*0-914917-00-5*) Folk Life.

Dejoie, Paula. My Hair Is Beautiful...Because It's Mine. 1994. 5.95 (*0-86316-219-3*) Writers & Readers.

De Veaux, Alexis. An Enchanted Hair Tale. Hanna, Cheryl, illus. LC 85-45824. 40p. (gr. k-3). 1987. PLB 14.89 (*0-06-021624-7*) HarpC Child Bks.

Frandsen, Karen G. Michael's New Haircut. Frandsen, Karen G., illus. LC 86-11696. 32p. (ps-3). 1986. pap. 3.95 (*0-516-43545-0*) Childrens.

Gordon, Sharon. Mike's First Haircut. Fiammenghi, Gioia, illus. LC 87-10911. 32p. (gr. k-2). 1988. PLB 7.89 (*0-8167-1113-5*); pap. text ed. 1.95 (*0-8167-1114-3*) Troll Assocs.

Gray, Patricia. What a Haircut! Webb, Philip, illus. LC 93-26931. 1994. 4.25 (*0-383-03783-2*) SRA Schl Grp.

Holleyman, Sonia. Mona the Brilliant. LC 92-23332. 1993. pap. 13.95 (*0-385-30907-4*) Doubleday.

Martin, Ann M. Karen's Haircut. (gr. 4-7). 1990. pap. 2.75 (*0-590-42670-2*) Scholastic Inc.

Milstein, Linda B. Amanda's Perfect Hair. Meddaugh, Susan, illus. LC 92-34314. 32p. (ps up). 1993. 14.00 (*0-688-11153-X*, Tambourine Bks); PLB 13.93 (*0-688-11154-8*, Tambourine Bks) Morrow.

Portlock, Rob. Someone's Trying to Cut off My Head. Portlock, Rob, illus. LC 92-12483. 32p. (Orig.). (ps-1). 1992. pap. 4.99 (*0-8308-1902-9*, 1902) InterVarsity.

Robins, Joan. Addie's Bad Day. Truesdell, Sue, illus. LC 92-13101. 32p. (ps-2). 1993. 14.00 (*0-06-021297-7*); PLB 13.89 (*0-06-021298-5*) HarpC Child Bks.

Slightly Off-Center Writers Group, Ltd. Staff. Albert's Hair. (Illus.). 60p. (gr. 4-6). 1994. pap. 6.95 (*1-56721-081-3*) Twnty-Fifth Cent Pr.

Tusa, Tricia. Camilla's New Hairdo. (Illus.). 32p. (ps-3). 1991. 14.95 (*0-374-31021-1*) FS&G.

Vaughn-H, Shirley. Noby the Noble Nightwatchman with Three Strands of Hair. 1993. 7.95 (*0-533-10530-7*) Vantage.

Watts, Margaret. Trouble with Hairgrow. Smith, Craig, illus. LC 93-26298. 1994. 4.25 (*0-383-03782-4*) SRA Schl Grp.

HAITI

Anthony, Suzanne. Haiti. (Illus.). 112p. (gr. 5 up). 1989. lib. bdg. 14.95 (*1-55546-796-2*) Chelsea Hse.

Harner, Ruth. Ti-Fam: Witch Doctor's Daughter. (Illus.). 40p. (gr. k-6). 1986. pap. text ed. 8.99 (*1-55976-051-6*) CEF Press.

Lerner Publications, Department of Geography Staff. Haiti in Pictures. (Illus.). 64p. (gr. 5 up). 1987. PLB 17.50 (*0-8225-1816-3*) Lerner Pubns.

Santrey, Laurence. Toussaint l'Ouverture, Lover of Liberty. Griffith, Gershom, illus. LC 93-18971. 48p. (gr. 4-6). 1993. PLB 10.79 (*0-8167-2823-2*); pap. text ed. 3.50 (*0-8167-2824-0*) Troll Assocs.

Telemaque, Eleanor W. Haiti Through Its Holidays. Hill, Earl, illus. LC 79-52858. 64p. (gr. 4-6). 1980. 8.50x (*0-685-00779-0*) Blyden Pr.

HAITI–FICTION

Bontemps, Arna W. & Hughes, Langston. Popo & Fifina. Campbell, E. Simms, illus. Rampersad, Arnold & Rampersad, Arnoldintro. by. (Illus.). 120p. 1993. jacketed 14.95 (*0-19-508765-8*) OUP.

Temple, Frances. Taste of Salt: A Story of Modern Haiti. LC 92-6716. 192p. (gr. 7-12). 1992. 14.95 (*0-531-05459-4*); PLB 14.99 (*0-531-08609-7*) Orchard Bks Watts.

Van Laan, Nancy. Mama Rocks, Papa Sings. Smith, Roberta, illus. LC 93-39225. 40p. (ps-2). 1995. 15.00 (*0-679-84016-8*); PLB 15.99 (*0-679-94016-2*) Knopf Bks Yng Read.

Williams, Karen L. Tap-Tap. Stock, Catherine, illus. LC 93-13006. (gr. 1-4). 1994. 14.95 (*0-395-65617-6*, Clarion Bks) HM.

HALLOWEEN

Barkin, Carol & James, Elizabeth. The Scary Halloween Costume Book. Coville, Katherine, illus. LC 81-14249. (gr. 3-6). 1983. 13.00 (*0-688-00956-5*); PLB 12.93 (*0-688-00957-3*) Lothrop.

Barth, Edna. Witches, Pumpkins & Grinning Ghosts: The Story of the Halloween Symbols. Arndt, Ursula, illus. LC 72-75705. 96p. (gr. 3-6). 1981. 4.95 (*0-89919-040-5*, Clarion Bks); pap. 4.95 (*0-317-03145-7*, Clarion Bks) HM.

—Witches, Pumpkins & Grinning Ghosts: The Story of the Halloween Symbols. Arndt, Ursula, illus. LC 72-75705. 96p. (gr. 3-6). 1979. 14.95 (*0-395-28847-9*, Clarion Bks) HM.

Bauer, Caroline F., ed. Halloween: Stories & Poems. LC 88-2675. (Illus.). 96p. (gr. 2-5). 1989. 15.00 (*0-397-32300-X*, Lipp Jr Bks); PLB 14.89 (*0-397-32301-8*, Lipp Jr Bks) HarpC Child Bks.

Benjamin, Alan. Halloween Riddles Chubby Board Book. (ps-6). 1993. pap. 3.95 (*0-671-87067-X*, Little Simon) S&S Trade.

Borten. Halloween. Date not set. 15.00 (*0-06-023582-9*); PLB 14.89 (*0-06-023583-7*) HarpC Child Bks.

Brown, Marc T. Arthur's Halloween. Brown, Marc T., illus. LC 82-14286. 32p. (ps-3). 1983. (Joy St Bks); pap. 4.95 (*0-316-11059-0*, Joy St Bks) Little.

Buck, Nola. Creepy Crawly Critters & Other Halloween Tongue Twisters. Truesdell, Sue, illus. LC 94-15405. 1995. 14.00 (*0-06-024808-4*); PLB 13.89 (*0-06-024809-2*) HarpC.

Corwin, Judith H. Halloween Crafts. LC 93-6367. (Illus.). (gr. k-4). Date not set. PLB write for info. (*0-531-11148-2*) Watts.

—Halloween Fun. Corwin, Judith H., illus. LC 83-8289. 64p. (gr. 3 up). 1983. (J Messner); lib. bdg. 5.95 (*0-671-49756-1*); PLB 7.71s.p. (*0-685-47056-3*); pap. 4.46s.p. (*0-685-47057-1*) S&S Trade.

Cracchiolo, Rachelle & Smith, Mary D. Halloween Activities. Crachiolo, Rachelle & Smith, Mary D., illus. 32p. (gr. 1-3). 1980. wkbk. 4.95 (*1-55734-011-0*) Tchr Create Mat.

Davis, Nancy M, et al. October & Halloween. Davis, Nancy M., illus. 28p. (Orig.). (ps-4). 1986. pap. 4.95 (*0-937103-01-2*) DaNa Pubns.

Dewhirst, Carin & Dewhirst, Joan. My Tricks & Treats: Halloween Stories, Songs, Poems, Recipes, Crafts & Fun for Kids. Barnes-Murphy, Rowan, illus. 80p. (ps-3). 1993. 9.98 (*0-8317-5172-X*) Smithmark.

Edwards, Lindell H. Why Do We Have Halloween? (gr. 1 up). 1994. 8.95 (*0-8062-4853-X*) Carlton.

Folmer, A. P. Fabulous Halloween Fun Book. (gr. 4-7). 1993. pap. 4.95 (*0-590-47348-4*) Scholastic Inc.

Fradin, Dennis B. Halloween. LC 89-7681. (Illus.). 48p. (gr. 1-4). 1990. lib. bdg. 14.95 (*0-89490-234-2*) Enslow Pubs.

Gibbons, Gail. Halloween. Gibbons, Gail, illus. LC 84-519. 32p. (ps-3). 1984. reinforced bdg. 15.95 (*0-8234-0524-9*); pap. 5.95 (*0-8234-0577-X*) Holiday.

—Halloween. Gibbons, Gail, illus. (gr. k-3). 1985. incl. cassette 19.95 (*0-941078-87-6*); pap. 12.95 incl. cassette (*0-941078-85-X*); incl. cassette, 4 paperbacks guide 27.95 (*0-941078-86-8*) Live Oak Media.

Green, George W. Halloween Book & Masks. Hatter, Laurie, illus. (ps). 1993. Gift box set of 4 bks., 12p. ea. bds. 14.95 (*1-56828-040-8*) Red Jacket Pr.

Hallinan, P. K. Today Is Halloween. Hallinan, P. K., illus. 24p. (ps-3). 1992. PLB 11.45 (*1-878363-95-6*) Forest Hse.

Hart, Rhonda M. You Can Carve Fantastic Jack-o-Lanterns. Foster, Kim, ed. Noyes, Leslie, illus. LC 90-55042. 112p. 1990. pap. 6.95 (*0-88266-580-4*) Storey Comm Inc.

Haywood, Carolyn. Halloween Treats. De Larrea, Victoria, illus. LC 81-3959. 176p. (gr. 4-6). 1981. lib. bdg. 12.88 (*0-688-00709-0*) Morrow Jr Bks.

Hierstein-Morris, Jill. Halloween: Facts & Fun. Hierstein-Morris, Jill, illus. 72p. (gr. 1 up). 1988. pap. 9.95 (*1-877588-00-8*) Creatively Yours.

Hopkins, Lee B. Ragged Shadows: Poems of Halloween Night. (ps-3). 1993. 15.95 (*0-316-37276-5*) Little.

Hopkins, Lee B., ed. Hey-How for Halloween! McGaffrey, Janet, illus. LC 74-5601. 32p. (gr. 1-5). 1974. 12.95 (*0-15-233900-0*, HB Juv Bks) HarBrace.

Kalman, Bobbie. We Celebrate Halloween. (Illus.). 56p. (gr. 3-4). 1985. 15.95 (*0-86505-039-2*); pap. 7.95 (*0-86505-049-X*) Crabtree Pub Co.

Leiner, Katherine. Halloween. LC 92-39343. (Illus.). 48p. (gr. 2-6). 1993. SBE 15.95 (*0-689-31769-7*, Atheneum Child Bk) Macmillan Child Grp.

Limburg, Peter R. Weird! The Complete Book of Halloween Words. Lewin, Betsy, illus. LC 88-38678. 128p. (gr. 4-10). 1989. SBE 13.95 (*0-02-759050-X*, Bradbury Pr) Macmillan Child Grp.

—Weird! The Complete Book of Halloween Words. 176p. 1991. pap. 3.50 (*0-380-71172-9*, Camelot) Avon.

Maestro, Giulio. Halloween Howls: Riddles That Are a Scream. LC 83-1419. (Illus.). 64p. (gr. 2-7). 1992. pap. 4.99 (*0-14-036115-4*, Puff Unicorn) Puffin Bks.

—More Halloween Howls: Riddles That Come Back to Haunt You. LC 91-23505. (Illus.). 64p. (gr. 2-7). 1992. 12.00 (*0-525-44899-3*, DCB) Dutton Child Bks.

Marsh, Carole. Halloween: Silly Trivia. Marsh, Carole, illus. (Orig.). (gr. 2-9). 1994. PLB 24.95 (*1-55609-169-9*); pap. 14.95 (*1-55609-017-X*) Gallopade Pub Group.

Masters, Nanvy R. The Horrible, Homemade Halloween Costume. Warr, Debra H., illus. 32p. (gr. 2-4). 1993. 14.95 (*0-9623563-3-6*) J R Matthews.

May. Halloween, Reading Level 4. (Illus.). 48p. (gr. 3-8). 1989. PLB 15.94 (*0-86592-983-1*); 11.95s.p. (*0-685-58773-8*) Rourke Corp.
Moncure, Jane B. Our Halloween Book. rev. ed. Peltier, Pam, illus. LC 85-30868. 32p. (ps-3). 1986. PLB 13.95 (*0-89565-348-6*) Childs World.
Monroe, Lucy. Creepy Cuisine. Burke, Dianne O., illus. LC 92-41654. 80p. (gr. 4-7). 1993. pap. 4.99 (*0-679-84402-3*) Random Bks Yng Read.
Myra, Harold. Halloween, Is It For Real? Walles, Dwight, illus. LC 82-6323. 32p. (gr. 2-4). 1982. 8.99 (*0-8407-5268-7*) Nelson.
Nielsen, Shelly. Halloween. Wallner, Rosemary, ed. LC 91-73031. 1992. 13.99 (*1-56239-070-8*) Abdo & Dghtrs.
Osborne, Jill E. Make & Color Halloween Decoration. (ps-3). 1989. pap. 1.95 (*0-89375-644-X*) Troll Assocs.
Prelutsky, Jack. It's Halloween. Hafner, Marylin, illus. LC 77-2141. 56p. (gr. 1-4). 1977. 13.95 (*0-688-80102-1*); PLB 13.88 (*0-688-84102-3*) Greenwillow.
Reece, Colleen L. My First Halloween Book. Peltier, Pam, illus. LC 84-9431. 32p. (ps-2). 1984. pap. 3.95 (*0-516-42902-7*) Childrens.
Regan, Dian C. The Thirteen Hours of Halloween. Baeten, Lieve, illus. LC 92-41207. 1993. write for info. (*0-8075-7876-2*) A Whitman.
Ross, Kathy. Crafts for Halloween. Holm, Sharon L., illus. LC 93-37249. 48p. (gr. k-3). 1994. 15.40 (*1-56294-411-8*); pap. 6.95 (*1-56294-741-9*) Millbrook Pr.
Sandak, Cass. Halloween. LC 89-25396. (Illus.). 48p. (gr. 5-6). 1990. text ed. 12.95 (*0-89686-500-2*, Crestwood Hse) Macmillan Child Grp.
Stamper, Judith. Halloween Holiday Grab Bag. Girouard, Patrick, illus. LC 92-13224. 48p. (gr. 2-5). 1992. PLB 11.89 (*0-8167-2904-2*); pap. text ed. 3.95 (*0-8167-2905-0*) Troll Assocs.
Supraner, Robyn. Happy Halloween: Things to Make & Do. Barto, Renzo, illus. LC 80-23889. 48p. (gr. 1-5). 1981. lib. bdg. 11.89 (*0-89375-420-X*); pap. 3.50 (*0-89375-421-8*) Troll Assocs.
Van Blaricom, Colleen, ed. Halloween Craft Book: Spooky & Fun Things to Make. Palan, R. Michael, illus. 32p. (gr. 2-5). 1992. pap. 3.95 (*1-56397-119-4*) Boyds Mills Pr.
Venturi-Pickett, Stacy, illus. The Halloween Activity Book. 24p. (ps-3). 1992. pap. 4.95 (*0-8249-8573-7*, Ideals Child) Hambleton-Hill.
Willis, Abigail. Halloween Fun: Great Things to Make & Do. Spenceley, Annabel, illus. LC 93-21712. 32p. (gr. 2-6). 1993. pap. 4.95 (*1-85697-864-8*, Kingfisher LKC) LKC.
Ziefert, Harriet. What Is Halloween? Schumacher, Claire, illus. 16p. (ps). 1992. 5.95 (*0-694-00381-6*, Festival) HarpC Child Bks.

HALLOWEEN–FICTION

Abbott, Tony. Danger Guys: Hollywood Halloween. Scribner, Joanne & Chan, Suwin, illus. 80p. (gr. 2-5). 1994. pap. 3.95 (*0-06-440522-2*, Trophy) HarpC Child Bks.
Adams, Adrienne. A Halloween Happening. Adams, Adrienne, illus. LC 81-8969. 32p. (ps-3). 1981. SBE 13.95 (*0-684-17166-X*, Scribners Young Read) Macmillan Child Grp.
—A Halloween Happening. Adams, Adrienne, illus. LC 91-6907. 32p. (ps-3). 1991. pap. 3.95 (*0-689-71502-1*, Aladdin) Macmillan Child Grp.
—A Woggle of Witches. Adams, Adrienne, illus. LC 70-161536. 32p. (ps-3). 1971. RSBE 13.95 (*0-684-12506-4*, Scribners Young Read) Macmillan Child Grp.
Aiello, Barbara & Shulman, Jeffrey. Trick or Treat or Trouble: Featuring Brian McDaniel. Barr, Loel, illus. 56p. (gr. 3-6). 1989. PLB 13.95 (*0-941477-07-X*) TFC Bks NY.
Alden, Laura. Halloween Safety. McCallum, Jodie, illus. LC 93-7633. 32p. (ps-2). 1993. PLB 12.30 (*0-516-00684-3*); pap. 3.95 (*0-516-40684-1*) Childrens.
Alexander, Sue. Who Goes Out on Halloween-Bank Street? (ps-3). 1990. PLB 9.99 (*0-553-05891-6*, Little Rooster); pap. 3.99 (*0-553-34922-8*) Bantam.
Andrews, Sylvia. Rattlebone Rock. Plecas, Jennifer, illus. LC 93-4426. Date not set. 15.00 (*0-06-023451-2*); PLB 14.89 (*0-06-023452-0*) HarpC.
Appleby, Ellen. The Jolly Jack-O-Lantern. (Illus.). 5p. 1993. bds. 3.98 (*0-8317-9656-1*) Smithmark.
—Trick or Treat. (Illus.). 5p. 1993. bds. 3.98 (*0-8317-9657-X*) Smithmark.
Bacon, Joy. Oliver Bean. Weinberger, Jane, ed. DeVito, Pam, illus. LC 90-70907. 68p. (ps-3). 1991. 12.95 (*0-932433-71-5*); pap. 9.95 (*0-932433-73-1*) Windswept Hse.
Ball, Jacqueline A. Halloween Double Dare. (gr. 4-7). 1990. pap. 2.95 (*0-06-106006-2*, PL) HarpC.
Barkan, Joanne. The Very Scary Jack'O Lantern. Wheeler, Jodie, illus. 24p. 1991. pap. 3.95 (*0-590-44496-4*) Scholastic Inc.
Bauer, Caroline F. Halloween: Stories & Poems. Sis, Peter, illus. LC 88-2675. 96p. (gr. 2-5). 1992. pap. 4.95 (*0-06-446111-4*, Trophy) HarpC Child Bks.
Bender, Robert. A Little Witch Magic. LC 92-4054. (Illus.). 32p. (ps-3). 1992. 14.95 (*0-8050-2126-4*, Bks Young Read) H Holt & Co.
Benjamin, Alan. Hallowhat? A Chubby Board Book. (ps). 1992. pap. 3.95 (*0-671-77009-8*, Little Simon) S&S Trade.
—Howl-O-Ween Chubby Board Book. (ps-6). 1993. pap. 3.95 (*0-671-87066-1*, Little Simon) S&S Trade.
Berenstain, Stan & Berenstain, Janice. The Berenstain Bears Trick or Treat. Berenstain, Stan & Berenstain, Janice, illus. LC 89-30884. 32p. (Orig.). (ps-1). 1989. PLB 5.99 (*0-679-90091-8*); pap. 2.50 (*0-679-80091-3*) Random Bks Yng Read.
Bradbury, Ray. The Halloween Tree. Mugnaini, Joseph, illus. LC 72-2433. 160p. (gr. 6 up). 1988. Repr. of 1972 ed. 17.00 (*0-394-82409-1*); PLB 15.99 (*0-394-92409-6*) Knopf Bks Yng Read.
Brook, Ruth. Bitty's Halloween Surprise. Kondo, Vala, illus. LC 86-30730. 32p. (gr. k-3). 1988. PLB 11.89 (*0-8167-0916-5*); pap. text ed. 2.95 (*0-8167-0917-3*) Troll Assocs.
Brown, Ron. The Hag of Halloween. Shand, Jim & Brown, Ron, illus. LC 88-92081. 12p. (Orig.). (gr. 6). 1988. pap. 2.95 (*0-685-24339-7*) Deer Creek NY.
Buck, Nola. Not-Too-Sweet Trick or Treat, 8 bks. Karas, G. Brian, illus. 16p. (ps-3). 1993. 4.95 ea. (*0-694-00489-8*, Festival) HarpC Child Bks.
Bunting, Eve. Scary, Scary Halloween. Brett, Jan, illus. LC 86-2642. 32p. (ps-3). 1988. 12.95 (*0-89919-414-1*, Clarion Bks); pap. 5.95 (*0-89919-799-X*, Clarion Bks) HM.
Byars, Betsy C. McMummy. LC 93-16717. 160p. (gr. 5-9). 1993. 13.99 (*0-670-84995-2*) Viking Child Bks.
Calhoun, Mary. Wobble the Witch Cat. Duvoisin, Roger, illus. LC 58-5018. 32p. (gr. k-3). 1958. PLB 13.88 (*0-688-31621-2*) Morrow Jr Bks.
Carlson, Nancy. Harriet's Halloween Candy. LC 81-18140. (Illus.). 32p. (ps-3). 1982. lib. bdg. 13.50 (*0-87614-182-3*) Carolrhoda Bks.
—Harriet's Halloween Candy. 32p. (gr. k-3). 1984. pap. 3.99 (*0-14-050465-6*, Puffin) Puffin Bks.
—Harriet's Halloween Candy. Carlson, Nancy, illus. (gr. k-3). 1985. bk. & cassette 19.95 (*0-941078-53-1*); pap. 12.95 bk. & cassette (*0-941078-51-5*); cassette, 4 paperbacks & guide 27.95 (*0-941078-52-3*) Live Oak Media.
Carlson, Natalie S. Spooky & the Ghost Cat. Glass, Andrew, illus. LC 84-17146. 32p. (ps-1). 1985. 13.00 (*0-688-04316-X*) Lothrop.
—Spooky Night. Glass, Andrew, illus. LC 82-54. 32p. (ps-3). 1982. 16.00 (*0-688-00934-4*); PLB 15.93 (*0-688-00935-2*) Lothrop.
Carrick, Carol. Old Mother Witch. Carrick, Donald, illus. LC 75-4609. 32p. (ps-4). 1979. 14.45 (*0-395-28778-2*, Clarion Bks) HM.
Cassedy, Sylvia. Best Cat Suit of All. LC 87-24659. (ps-3). 1991. 10.95 (*0-8037-0516-6*); PLB 10.89 (*0-8037-0517-4*) Dial Bks Young.
Clifford, Eth. Scared Silly. 1989. pap. 2.75 (*0-590-42382-7*) Scholastic Inc.
Clymer, Susan. Halloween Echo. (gr. 4-7). 1993. pap. 2.75 (*0-590-46164-8*) Scholastic Inc.
Cole, Bruce. The Pumpkinville Mystery. Warhola, James, illus. LC 87-2533. 32p. (gr. 1-4). 1991. pap. 3.95 (*0-671-74199-3*, Little Simon) S&S Trade.
Coombs, Patricia. Dorrie & the Halloween Plot. LC 76-3643. (Illus.). 48p. (gr. 1-5). 1976. PLB 12.93 (*0-688-51764-1*) Lothrop.
Craig, Janet. Joey the Jack-O'-Lantern. Miller, Susan, illus. LC 87-10845. 32p. (gr. k-2). 1988. PLB 11.59 (*0-8167-1105-4*); pap. text ed. 2.95 (*0-8167-1106-2*) Troll Assocs.
Cusick, Richie T. Trick or Treat. 208p. (Orig.). (gr. 7 up). 1989. pap. 3.25 (*0-590-44235-X*) Scholastic Inc.
The Dancing Pumpkin. 1992. write for info. (*0-9634270-0-8*) Dancing Pumpkin.
Devlin, Wende & Devlin, Harry. Cranberry Halloween. LC 81-22134. (Illus.). 32p. (gr. k-3). 1984. RSBE 13.95 (*0-02-729910-4*, Four Winds) Macmillan Child Grp.
Dinardo, Jeffrey. Henry's Halloween. (ps-3). 1993. pap. 3.25 (*0-440-40854-7*) Dell.
Doyle, Tara. Trick-or-Treat Books, 4 vol. set. Kalish, Lionel & Weissman, Bari, illus. 16p. (ps-1). 1993. pap. 2.75 (*0-590-66583-9*, Cartwheel) Scholastic Inc.
Enderle, Judith R. & Tessler, Stephanie G. Six Creepy Sheep. O'Brien, John, illus. 24p. (ps-1). 1992. PLB 12.95 (*1-56397-092-9*) Boyds Mills Pr.
—Six Creepy Sheep. O'Brien, John, illus. LC 93-7140. 26p. (ps-1). 1993. pap. 4.99 (*0-14-054994-3*, Puffin) Puffin Bks.
Fass, Bernie & Wolfson, Mack. The Halloween Machine. (gr. k-9). 1984. pap. 15.95, 48 pgs. (*0-86704-009-2*); pap. 3.25 student's ed, 32 pgs. (*0-86704-010-6*) Clarus Music.
Feczko, Kathy. Halloween Party. Sims, Blanche, illus. LC 84-8635. 32p. (gr. k-2). 1985. PLB 11.59 (*0-8167-0354-X*); pap. text ed. 2.95 (*0-8167-0434-1*) Troll Assocs.
Foehl, Jamie L. Trick or Treat Taffy. Foehl, Barbara B., illus. LC 89-92436. 40p. (Orig.). (ps-6). 1989. write for info. (*0-9625337-0-X*); PLB write for info.; pap. write for info. B Bk Pub Co.
Freeman, Don. Tilly Witch. Freeman, Don, illus. (gr. k-3). 1969. pap. 13.95 (*0-670-71303-1*) Viking Child Bks.
Gezi, Kal & Bradford, Ann. The Mystery of the Live Ghosts. McLean, Mina G., illus. LC 78-8142. (gr. k-3). 1978. PLB 12.95 (*0-89565-026-6*) Childs World.
Giff, Patricia R. Beast & the Halloween Horror. Sims, Blanche, illus. (Orig.). (gr. k-6). 1990. pap. 3.50 (*0-440-40335-9*, YB) Dell.
Grambling, Lois. Elephant & Mouse Celebrate Halloween. Maze, Deborah, illus. (ps-1). 1991. 12.95 (*0-8120-6186-1*); pap. 5.95 (*0-8120-4761-3*) Barron.
Greenberg, Martin H. & Waugh, Charles G., eds. A Newbery Halloween: Thirteen Scary Stories by Newbery Award-Winning Authors. LC 92-43877. 1993. pap. 16.95 (*0-385-31028-5*) Doubleday.
Greene, Carol. The Thirteen Days of Halloween. LC 83-7347. (Illus.). 32p. (ps-2). 1983. PLB 11.80 (*0-516-08231-0*); pap. 3.95 (*0-516-48231-9*) Childrens.
Greene, George W. The Legend of Jack O'Lantern. Hatter, Laurie, illus. 12p. (ps). 1992. 4.95 (*1-56828-000-9*) Red Jacket Pr.
—Why Ghosts Like Halloween. Hatter, Laurie, illus. 12p. (ps). 1992. 4.95 (*1-56828-002-5*) Red Jacket Pr.
—Witch's Brew. Hatter, Laurie, illus. 12p. (ps). 1992. 4.95 (*1-56828-001-7*) Red Jacket Pr.
Greenleaf, Ann. Too Many Monsters. 1993. 4.99 (*0-517-09158-5*) Random Hse Value.
Greenleaf, Ann G. The Goblins Did It! LC 93-19746. (Illus.). 1993. 4.99 (*0-517-09157-7*) Random Hse Value.
Grubbs, T. Tori Had the Chicken-Pox: Halloween. Abell, J., ed. & illus. 36p. (Orig.). (gr. k-3). 1991. pap. 15.00 software looseleaf (*1-56611-002-5*); pap. 15.00 (*1-56611-226-5*) Jonas.
Hall, Zoe. It's Pumpkin Time! Halpern, Shari, illus. LC 93-35909. (ps-2). 1994. 14.95 (*0-590-47833-8*) Scholastic Inc.
Hallinan, P. K. Today Is Halloween! Hallinan, P. K., illus. 24p. (ps-2). 1992. pap. 4.95 perfect bdg. (*0-8249-8557-5*, Ideals Child) Hambleton-Hill.
Hanson, Don & Helfrich, R. L. Celebrate Halloween with Hog, Dog, & Frog. Helfrich, Nathan, illus. 64p. (Orig.). 1993. pap. 9.95 (*1-56883-018-1*) Colonial Pr AL.
Hartelius, Marge. Halloween Puzzle Bag. 32p. 1991. pap. 1.95 (*0-590-44581-2*) Scholastic Inc.
Haywood, Carolyn. Halloween Treats. (gr. 2-4). 1987. pap. 2.95 (*0-8167-1039-2*) Troll Assocs.
Helmrath, M. O. & Bartlett, J. L. Bobby Bear's Halloween. LC 68-56808. (Illus.). 32p. (ps-1). 1968. PLB 9.95 (*0-87783-004-5*); cassette 7.94x (*0-87783-183-1*) Oddo.
Hoban, Lillian. Arthur's Halloween Costume. LC 83-49465. (Illus.). 64p. (gr. k-3). 1984. PLB 13.89 (*0-06-022391-X*) HarpC Child Bks.
Howe, James. Scared Silly: A Halloween Treat. Morrill, Leslie, illus. LC 88-7837. 48p. (gr. k up). 1989. 13.95 (*0-688-07666-1*); PLB 13.88 (*0-688-07667-X*, Morrow Jr Bks) Morrow Jr Bks.
Huang, Benrei, illus. Pop-up Monster Party. 14p. (ps-1). 1992. 3.95 (*0-448-40255-6*, G&D) Putnam Pub Group.
Johnston, Tony. Soup Bone. (Illus.). 32p. (ps-3). 1990. 12.95 (*0-15-277255-3*) HarBrace.
Jones, Michael P. Halloween Bats. (Illus.). 24p. 1984. write for info. (*0-89904-065-9*) Crumb Elbow Pub.
—Halloween Ghosts. (Illus.). 24p. (ps-4). 1983. write for info. (*0-89904-064-0*); pap. text ed. write for info. (*0-89904-063-2*) Crumb Elbow Pub.
—Halloween Pumpkins. (Illus.). 24p. (ps-4). 1984. write for info. (*0-89904-067-5*); pap. text ed. write for info. (*0-89904-068-3*) Crumb Elbow Pub.
—Halloween Witches. (Illus.). 24p. (ps-4). 1983. write for info. (*0-89904-061-6*); pap. text ed. write for info. (*0-89904-062-4*) Crumb Elbow Pub.
Keats, Ezra. The Trip. Keats, Ezra, illus. LC 77-24907. 32p. (gr. k-3). 1978. PLB 15.93 (*0-688-84123-6*) Greenwillow.
Kessel, Joyce K. Halloween. Carlson, Nancy L., illus. LC 80-15890. 48p. (gr. k-4). 1980. PLB 14.95 (*0-87614-132-7*) Carolrhoda Bks.
Khdir, Kate & Nash, Sue. Little Ghost. Church, Caroline, illus. 32p. (ps-2). 1991. incl. dust jacket 12.95 (*0-8120-6203-5*); pap. 5.95 (*0-8120-4779-6*) Barron.
Kline, Suzy. Mary Marony, Mummy Girl. Sims, Blanche, illus. LC 93-14348. 80p. (gr. 1-4). 1994. 13.95 (*0-399-22609-5*, Putnam) Putnam Pub Group.
Koontz, Robin M. Chicago & the Cat: The Halloween Party. Koontz, Robin M., illus. LC 93-27043. 32p. (gr. k-3). 1994. 12.99 (*0-525-65138-1*, Cobblehill Bks) Dutton Child Bks.
Kraus, Robert. Daddy Long Ears' Halloween. (Illus.). 40p. (ps-1). 1990. 4.95 (*0-671-70352-8*, Little Simon) S&S Trade.
—How Spider Saved Halloween. (Illus.). 32p. (Orig.). (ps-2). 1988. pap. 2.50 (*0-590-42117-4*) Scholastic Inc.
—Jack O'Lantern's Scary Halloween. (ps-3). 1993. pap. 2.25 (*0-307-10016-2*, Golden Pr) Western Pub.
—Wise Old Owl's Halloween Adventure. LC 93-18686. (Illus.). 32p. (gr. k-3). 1993. PLB 10.89 (*0-8167-2949-2*); pap. text ed. 2.95 (*0-8167-2950-6*) Troll Assocs.
Kunhardt, Edith. Trick or Treat, Danny! LC 87-14963. (Illus.). 24p. (ps-1). 1988. 11.95 (*0-688-07310-7*); lib. bdg. 11.88 (*0-688-07311-5*) Greenwillow.
Laughlin, Florence. The Little Leftover Witch. 2nd ed. Greenwald, Sheila, illus. LC 88-10551. 96p. (gr. 2-6). 1988. pap. 3.50 (*0-689-71273-1*, Aladdin) Macmillan Child Grp.
Leedy, Loreen. The Dragon Halloween Party. Leedy, Loreen, illus. LC 86-286. 32p. (ps-3). 1986. reinforced bdg. 14.95 (*0-8234-0611-3*); pap. 5.95 (*0-8234-0765-9*) Holiday.
Maestro, Giulio. Halloween Howls: Riddles That Are a Scream. Maestro, Giulio, illus. LC 83-1419. 64p. (gr. 3-7). 1983. 10.95 (*0-525-44059-3*, DCB) Dutton Child Bks.

Mangas, Brian. You Don't Get a Carrot Unless You're a Bunny. Levitt, Sidney, illus. LC 88-19763. 32p. (ps-k). 1991. pap. 2.25 (*0-671-74200-0*, Little Simon) S&S Trade.
Mariana. Miss Flora McFlimsey's Halloween. rev. ed. Mariana, illus. LC 86-15270. 40p. (ps-2). 1987. 11.95 (*0-688-04549-9*) Lothrop.
Marzollo, Jean. Halloween Cats. (ps-3). 1992. pap. 2.50 (*0-590-46026-9*) Scholastic Inc.
Mayer, Gina. Trick or Treat, Little Critter. (ps-3). 1993. pap. 2.25 (*0-307-12791-5*, Golden Pr) Western Pub.
Meddaugh, Susan. The Witches' Supermarket. Meddaugh, Susan, illus. 32p. (gr. k-3). 1991. 13.95 (*0-395-57034-4*, Sandpiper) HM.
Meyers, Susan. P. J. Clover, Private Eye: The Case of the Halloween Hoot. Fiammenghi, Gioia, illus. 128p. (gr. 4-6). 1990. 13.95 (*0-525-67297-4*, Lodestar Bks) Dutton Child Bks.
Meyrick, Kathryn. Hazel's Healthy Halloween. LC 90-46517. 1989. 11.95 (*0-85953-296-8*); pap. 5.95 (*0-85953-308-5*) Childs Play.
Miller, Jayne. Too Much Trick or Treat. Thatch, Nancy R., ed. Miller, Jayna, illus. Melton, David, intro. by. LC 91-14930. (Illus.). 26p. (gr. k-4). 1991. PLB 14.95 (*0-933849-37-0*) Landmark Edns.
Mooser, Stephen. Disaster in Room 101. MacDougall, Rob, illus. LC 93-24055. 80p. (gr. 2-4). 1993. PLB 2.95 (*0-8167-3278-7*); pap. text ed. 2.95 (*0-8167-3279-5*) Troll Assocs.
—The Ghost with the Halloween Hiccups. De Paola, Tomie, illus. 32p. (gr. k-3). 1978. pap. 2.95 (*0-380-40287-4*, Camelot) Avon.
Mueller, Amelia. Jeremy's Jack-O-Lantern. Barb, Arlene, illus. 24p. (Orig.). (gr. k-3). 1992. pap. 5.95 (*0-945530-06-4*) Wordsworth KS.
Naylor, Phyllis R. The Girls Got Even. LC 92-43047. 1993. 13.95 (*0-385-31029-3*) Delacorte.
Packard, Mary. Scaredy Ghost. Williams, Jennifer H., illus. LC 93-24845. 24p. (gr. k-2). 1993. pap. text ed. 1.50 (*0-8167-3246-9*) Troll Assocs.
Packard, Mary E. The Witch Who Couldn't Fly. Cushman, Douglas E., illus. LC 93-2212. (gr. k-3). 1993. pap. 2.95 (*0-8167-3256-6*) Troll Assocs.
Pascal, Francine. Caroline's Halloween Spell. (ps-3). 1992. pap. 2.99 (*0-553-48006-5*) Bantam.
Paulsen, Gary. Dunc's Halloween. 96p. (gr. 3-7). 1992. pap. 3.50 (*0-440-40659-5*, YB) Dell.
Pearson, Susan. Porkchop's Halloween. Brown, Richard, illus. LC 88-4427. 32p. (gr. k-3). 1988. pap. 13.00 jacketed (*0-671-66732-7*, S&S BFYR) S&S Trade.
—Porkchop's Halloween. Brown, Richard, illus. 32p. (ps up). 1989. pap. 4.00 (*0-671-68872-3*, S&S BFYR) S&S Trade.
Peck, Richard. The Dreadful Future of Blossom Culp. (gr. 7 up). 1983. 15.00 (*0-385-29300-3*) Delacorte.
Peck, Robert N. Higbee's Halloween. 101p. (gr. 5-7). 1990. 13.95 (*0-8027-6968-3*); lib. bdg. 14.85 (*0-8027-6969-1*) Walker & Co.
Pilkey, Dav. Dragon's Halloween. LC 91-21107. (Illus.). 48p. (gr. 1-3). 1993. 12.95 (*0-531-05990-1*); PLB 12.99 (*0-531-08590-2*) Orchard Bks Watts.
Polette, Nancy. Eight Cinderellas. (Illus.). 48p. (gr. 3-6). 1994. pap. 5.95 (*1-879287-29-3*) Bk Lures.
Polisar, Barry L. The Haunted House Party: A Halloween Story. (Illus.). 40p. (gr. 3-6). 1987. 9.95 (*0-938663-02-X*); pap. 7.95 (*0-938663-11-9*) Rainbow Morn.
Prager, Annabelle. The Spooky Halloween Party. De Paola, Tomie, illus. LC 81-1945. 48p. (gr. 1-4). 1981. 6.95 (*0-394-84370-3*); lib. bdg. 7.99 (*0-394-94370-8*) Pantheon.
—The Spooky Halloween Party. reissue ed. De Paola, Tomie, illus. 48p. (gr. k-4). 1992. pap. 6.99 incl. cass. (*0-679-83056-1*) Random Bks Yng Read.
—The Spooky Halloween Party: A Step 2 Book. De Paola, Tomie, illus. LC 88-37571. 48p. (gr. 1-3). 1989. lib. bdg. 7.99 (*0-394-94961-7*); pap. 3.50 (*0-394-84961-2*) Random Bks Yng Read.
Prelutsky, Jack. It's Halloween. Hafner, Marylin, illus. 48p. (ps-3). 1987. pap. 2.50 (*0-590-41536-0*); Books & Cassette. 5.95 (*0-590-63252-3*) Scholastic Inc.
Quackenbush, Robert. Detective Mole & Halloween Mystery. 1989. pap. 3.95 (*0-671-67830-2*, Little Simon) S&S Trade.
Rao, Anthony, illus. Halloween Masks. 24p. (ps-3). 1984. pap. 3.99 saddle-stitched (*0-394-86126-4*) Random Bks Yng Read.
Ray, David. Pumpkin Light. Ray, David, illus. LC 92-25118. 32p. (ps-3). 1993. 14.95 (*0-399-22028-3*, Philomel Bks) Putnam Pub Group.
Rodger, Elizabeth. Boo to You, Too. LC 92-40023. 1993. write for info. (*0-671-86765-2*, S&S BFYR); pap. 2.95 (*0-671-86766-0*, S&S BFYR) S&S Trade.
Ross, Pat. M & M & the Halloween Monster. Hafner, Marylin, illus. LC 91-50294. 48p. (gr. 1-2). 1991. text ed. 10.95 (*0-670-83003-8*) Viking Child Bks.
—M & M & the Halloween Monster. Hafner, Marylin, illus. LC 93-15183. 64p. (gr. 2-5). 1993. pap. 3.99 (*0-14-034247-8*, Puffin) Puffin Bks.
Sears, Yvonne. Amber's Hallowe'en. Sears, Yvonne, illus. LC 87-90131. 36p. (gr. 2-5). 1988. 12.95 (*0-9618803-0-9*) Y-Knot.
Sharmat, Marjorie W. Nate the Great & the Halloween Hunt. (gr. k-6). 1990. pap. 3.50 (*0-440-40341-3*, YB) Dell.
Shute, Linda. Halloween Party. LC 93-25215. (gr. 1 up). 1994. 15.00 (*0-688-11714-7*); PLB 14.93 (*0-685-75783-8*) Lothrop.
Sierra, Judy. The House That Drac Built. Hillenbrand, Will, illus. LC 94-19002. Date not set. write for info. (*0-15-200015-1*) HarBrace.
Silverman, Erica. Big Pumpkin. Schindler, S. D., illus. LC 91-14053. 32p. (ps-3). 1992. RSBE 14.95 (*0-02-782683-X*, Macmillan Child Bk) Macmillan Child Grp.
Stain, Dan. Teddy Bears' Halloween Party. (gr. 1-7). 1989. pap. 2.50 (*0-89954-962-4*) Antioch Pub Co.
Stamper, Judith B. Totally Terrific Valentine Party Book. 1990. pap. 1.95 (*0-590-41713-4*) Scholastic Inc.
Stevenson, James. That Terrible Halloween Night. LC 79-27775. (Illus.). 32p. (ps). 1980. PLB 14.93 (*0-688-84281-X*) Greenwillow.
—That Terrible Halloween Night. LC 79-27775. (Illus.). 32p. (ps up). 1990. pap. 3.95 (*0-688-09932-7*, Mulberry) Morrow.
Stine, R. L. Halloween Night. (gr. 9-12). 1993. pap. 3.50 (*0-590-46098-6*) Scholastic Inc.
Stock, Catherine. Halloween Monster. Stock, Catherine, illus. LC 89-49530. 32p. (ps-1). 1990. SBE 11.95 (*0-02-788404-X*, Bradbury Pr) Macmillan Child Grp.
—Halloween Monster. Stock, Catherine, illus. LC 92-42987. 32p. (ps-1). 1993. pap. 3.95 (*0-689-71727-X*, Aladdin) Macmillan Child Grp.
Story Time Stories That Rhyme Staff. Halloween Stories That Rhyme. Story Time Stories That Rhyme Staff, illus. 38p. (Orig.). (gr. 4-7). 1992. GBC bdg. 15.95 (*1-56820-013-7*) Story Time.
Stout, Robert T. The Secret of Halloween. Stout, Robert T., illus. 24p. (Orig.). (ps-6). 1982. pap. 3.50 (*0-911049-02-9*) Yuletide Intl.
Stutson, Caroline. By the Light of the Halloween Moon. Hawkes, Kevin, illus. 32p. (ps-3). 1994. pap. 4.99 (*0-14-055305-3*) Puffin Bks.
Tester, Sylvia R. Magic Monsters Halloween. Bowman, Patricia, illus. LC 79-25183. (gr. k-3). 1980. PLB 13.95 (*0-89565-121-1*) Childs World.
Titherington, Jeanne. Pumpkin Pumpkin. LC 84-25334. (Illus.). 24p. (ps up). 1990. pap. 3.95 (*0-688-09930-0*, Mulberry) Morrow.
Troop, Beth, ed. A Simply Monstrous Time: And Other Halloween Stories from Highlights. (Illus.). 32p. (Orig.). (gr. 2-7). 1993. pap. 4.95 (*1-56397-085-6*) Boyds Mills Pr.
Trumbauer, Lisa. I Swear I Saw a Witch in Washington Square. LC 94-4371. 1994. write for info. (*0-681-00557-2*) Longmeadow Pr.
Van Leeuwen, Jean. Oliver & Amanda's Halloween. Schweninger, Ann, illus. LC 91-30941. 48p. (ps-3). 1992. 11.00 (*0-8037-1237-5*); PLB 10.89 (*0-8037-1238-3*) Dial Bks Young.
Varley, M. C. Wonderland Howl-oween. LC 93-71351. (gr. 4-7). 1993. pap. 3.95 (*1-56282-515-1*) Disney Pr.
Walley, Dean & Ingle, Annie. A Visit to the Haunted House. Noel, Arlene, illus. 14p. (ps-3). 1992. 7.99 (*0-679-82450-2*) Random Bks Yng Read.
Warren, Jean. Huff & Puff on Halloween: A Totline Teaching Tale. Cubley, Kathleen, ed. Isaacs, Jean & Tourtillotte, Barb, illus. LC 92-62824. 32p. (Orig.). (ps-2). 1993. 12.95 (*0-911019-68-5*); pap. text ed. 5.95 (*0-911019-69-3*) Warren Pub Hse.
Watson, Wendy. Boo! It's Halloween. Watson, Wendy, illus. 32p. (ps-3). 1992. 14.45 (*0-395-53628-6*, Clarion Bks) HM.
Wiseman, Bernard. Halloween with Morris & Boris. (gr. k-3). 1986. pap. 2.50 (*0-590-41498-4*) Scholastic Inc.
Wojciechowski, Susan. The Best Halloween of All. Meddaugh, Susan, illus. LC 91-9369. 32p. (ps-2). 1992. 10.00 (*0-517-57765-8*) Crown Bks Yng Read.
Wolff, Ferida & Kozielski, Dolores. The Halloween Grab Bag: A Book of Tricks & Treats. Neuhouse, David, illus. 96p. (gr. 2-5). 1993. pap. 5.95 (*0-06-446148-3*, Trophy) HarpC Child Bks.
—On Halloween Night. Avendano, Dolores, illus. LC 93-26859. 1994. 15.00 (*0-688-12972-2*, Tambourine Bks); PLB 14.93 (*0-688-12973-0*, Tambourine Bks) Morrow.
Wright, Betty R. Ghost Witch. LC 92-55055. 72p. (gr. 4-7). 1993. 13.95 (*0-8234-1036-6*) Holiday.
Ziefert, Harriet. Halloween Parade. James, Lillie, illus. 32p. (ps-3). 1992. 9.00 (*0-670-84568-X*) Viking Child Bks.
—Halloween Parade. James, Lillie, illus. 32p. (ps-3). 1992. pap. 3.50 (*0-14-054555-7*) Puffin Bks.
—Where's the Halloween Treat? Brown, Richard, illus. LC 85-3632. 20p. (ps). 1985. pap. 5.99 (*0-14-050556-3*, Puffin) Puffin Bks.

HAMER, FANNIE LOU

Colman, Penny. Fannie Lou Hamer & the Fight for the Vote. LC 92-21380. (Illus.). 32p. (gr. 2-4). 1993. PLB 12.90 (*1-56294-323-5*); pap. 4.95 (*1-56294-789-3*) Millbrook Pr.
Rubel, David. Fannie Lou Hamer: From Sharecropping to Politics. Gallin, Richard, ed. Young, Andrew, intro. by. (Illus.). 128p. (gr. 5 up). 1990. lib. bdg. 12.95 (*0-382-09923-0*); pap. 7.95 (*0-382-24061-8*) Silver Burdett Pr.

HAMILTON, ALEXANDER, 1757-1804

Kurland, Gerald. Alexander Hamilton: Architect of American Nationalism. Rahmas, D. Steve, ed. LC 73-190245. 32p. (gr. 7-12). 1972. lib. bdg. 4.95 incl. catalog cards (*0-87157-527-2*) SamHar Pr.
O'Brien, Steve. Alexander Hamilton. Schlesinger, Arthur M., Jr., intro. by. (Illus.). 112p. (gr. 5 up). 1989. 17.95 (*1-55546-810-1*) Chelsea Hse.

HAMILTON, ALICE, 1869-1905

McPherson, Stephanie S. Workers' Detective: A Story about Alice Hamilton. (ps-3). 1992. 14.95 (*0-87614-699-X*) Carolrhoda Bks.

HAMSTERS

Barrett, Norman S. Hamsters. LC 89-21518. (Illus.). 32p. (gr. k-4). 1990. PLB 11.90 (*0-531-14032-6*) Watts.
Evans, Mark. Hamster. Caras, Roger, intro. by. LC 92-53475. (Illus.). 48p. (gr. 3-7). 1993. 9.95 (*1-56458-223-X*) Dorling Kindersley.
Frisch. Hamsters. 1991. 11.95s.p. (*0-86625-191-X*) Rourke Pubns.
Petty, Kate. Hamsteres. Thompson, George, illus. LC 90-71413. (SPA.). 24p. (gr. k-4). 1991. PLB 10.90 (*0-531-07913-9*) Watts.
—Hamsters. Thompson, George, illus. LC 89-50455. 32p. (gr. k-2). 1989. PLB 10.90 (*0-531-17159-0*, Gloucester Pr) Watts.
—Hamsters. (Illus.). 24p. (ps-3). 1993. pap. 3.95 (*0-8120-1472-3*) Barron.
Piers, Helen. Taking Care of Your Hamster. 32p. 1992. pap. 4.95 (*0-8120-4695-1*) Barron.
Silverstein, Alvin & Silverstein, Virginia. Hamsters: All About Them. LC 74-8863. (Illus.). 128p. (gr. 3-6). 1974. PLB 14.93 (*0-688-50056-0*) Lothrop.
Smith, Peter. Your First Hamster. (Illus.). 36p. (Orig.). 1991. pap. 1.95 (*0-86622-067-4*, YF-110) TFH Pubns.
Watts, Barrie. Hamster. LC 86-10018. (Illus.). 25p. (gr. k-4). 1991. 5.95 (*0-382-09290-2*); pap. 3.95 (*0-382-09957-5*); PLB 7.95 (*0-382-09281-3*) Silver Burdett Pr.
Wexler, Jerome. Pet Hamsters. Tucker, Kathleen, ed. Wexler, Jerome, photos by. (Illus.). 48p. (gr. 2-6). 1992. PLB 14.95 (*0-8075-6525-3*) A Whitman.

HAMSTERS–FICTION

Baker, Alan. Benjamin's Balloon. (Illus.). 32p. 1990. 12.95 (*0-688-09744-8*) Lothrop.
—Benjamin's Portrait. Baker, Alan, illus. LC 86-10396. 32p. (ps-2). 1987. 11.93 (*0-688-06877-4*); PLB 11.93 (*0-688-06878-2*) Lothrop.
Banks, Lynne R. I, Houdini. 128p. (Orig.). 1989. pap. 3.99 (*0-380-70649-0*, Camelot) Avon.
Clarkson, Margaret. Susie's Babies: A Clear & Simple Explanation of the Everyday Miracle of Birth. 72p. 1992. pap. 7.99 (*0-8028-4053-1*) Eerdmans.
Erwin, Carolyn M. What Makes Danny Run? (Illus.). 32p. (Orig.). (gr. k-6). 1991. pap. 8.95 (*0-9630903-0-5*) Little Gems.
Kline, Suzy. Song Lee & the Hamster Hunt. Remkiewicz, Frank, illus. 64p. (gr. 2-6). 1994. 11.99 (*0-670-84773-9*) Viking Child Bks.
Pascal, Francine. Runaway Hamster. (ps-3). 1989. pap. 2.99 (*0-553-15759-0*, Skylark) Bantam.

HANCOCK, JOHN, 1737-1793

Fradin, Dennis B. John Hancock: First Signer of the Declaration of Independence. LC 88-31332. (Illus.). 48p. (gr. 3-6). 1989. lib. bdg. 14.95 (*0-89490-230-X*) Enslow Pubs.
Fritz, Jean. Will You Sign Here, John Hancock? Hyman, Trina S., illus. LC 75-33243. 48p. (gr. 2-6). 1982. 13.95 (*0-698-20308-9*, Coward); pap. 6.95 (*0-698-20539-1*, Coward) Putnam Pub Group.

HAND

Aliki. My Hands. rev. ed. Aliki, illus. LC 89-49158. 32p. (ps-1). 1990. 14.00 (*0-690-04878-5*, Crowell Jr Bks); PLB 13.89 (*0-690-04880-7*, Crowell Jr Bks) HarpC Child Bks.
—My Hands. rev. ed. Aliki, illus. LC 89-71728. 32p. (ps-1). 1992. pap. 4.50 (*0-06-445096-1*, Trophy) HarpC Child Bks.
Callahan, Rosemary. This Is Thumb Book. LC 92-56931. (Illus.). 35p. (gr. k-3). 1993. pap. 5.95 (*1-55523-571-9*) Winston-Derek.
Damon, Laura. Funny Fingers, Funny Toes. Kennedy, Anne, illus. LC 87-10915. 32p. (gr. k-2). 1988. PLB 11.59 (*0-8167-1089-9*); pap. text ed. 2.95 (*0-8167-1090-2*) Troll Assocs.
Gryski, Camilla. Hands On, Thumbs Up: Secret Handshakes, Fingerprints, Sign Languages, & More Handy Ways to Have Fun with Hands. 112p. 1991. pap. 8.61 (*0-201-56756-3*) Addison-Wesley.
Loman, Roberta K., illus. All about Hands. 28p. (ps). 1992. 2.50 (*0-87403-951-7*, 24-03591) Standard Pub.
Markham-David, Sally. Hands & Feet. Fleming, Leanne, illus. LC 93-28978. 1994. 4.25 (*0-383-03746-8*) SRA Schl Grp.
Perkins, Al. Hand, Hand, Fingers, Thumb. LC 76-77841. (Illus.). (ps-1). 1969. 6.95 (*0-394-81076-7*) Random Bks Yng Read.
Rourke, Arlene C. Los Manos y los Pies. LC 92-5661. (ENG & SPA.). 1992. 15.94 (*0-86625-290-8*); 11.95s.p. (*0-685-59319-3*) Rourke Pubns.

HANDEL, GEORGE FREDERICK, 1685-1759

Ludwig, Charles. George Frideric Handel: Composer of The Messiah. (Illus.). (gr. 3-6). 1987. pap. 6.95 (*0-88062-048-X*) Mott Media.
Rachlin, Ann. Handel. Hellard, Susan, illus. LC 92-11497. 1992. 5.95 (*0-8120-4992-6*) Barron.

HANDICAPPED

Adams, Pam. Disabled People. (gr. 4 up). 1990. 7.95 (*0-85953-361-1*); pap. 3.95 (*0-85953-351-4*) Childs Play.
American Institute for Research. Science Success for Students with Disabilities. 1993. pap. text ed. 18.50 (*0-201-81939-2*) Addison-Wesley.
Breakstone, Steve. Washington Walkabout. Marsh, Jerry & Hurt, Rory, eds. (Illus.). 256p. (Orig.). 1992. pap. 13.95 (*0-9632724-4-6*) Balance Pubns.

Brown, Fern G. Special Olympics. Rich, Mary P., ed. LC 91-31661. (Illus.). 64p. (gr. 3-5). 1992. PLB 12.90 (*0-531-20062-0*) Watts.

Buckel, Marian C. & Buckel, Tiffany. Mom, I Have a Staring Problem: A True Story of Petit Mal Seizures & the Hidden Problem It Can Cause: Learning Disability. LC 92-90113. (Illus.). 1992. pap. 3.95 saddle stitch (*0-317-04291-2*) M C Buckel.

Dwyer, Kathleen M. What Do You Mean I Have a Learning Disability? (Illus.). 32p. (gr. 5-9). 1991. 14.95 (*0-8027-8102-0*); PLB 15.85 (*0-8027-8103-9*) Walker & Co.

Gould, Marilyn. Golden Daffodils. LC 84-40758. 172p. (gr. 4 up). 1991. PLB 12.95 (*0-9632305-3-0*); pap. 6.95 (*0-9632305-1-4*) Allied Crafts.

Gravelle, Karen. Understanding Birth Defects. LC 90-32658. (Illus.). 126p. (gr. 7-12). 1990. PLB 13.40 (*0-531-10955-0*) Watts.

Harris, Jacqueline L. Learning Disorders. (Illus.). 64p. (gr. 5-8). 1993. PLB 14.95 (*0-8050-2604-5*) TFC Bks NY.

Holcomb, Nan. Fair & Square. Yoder, Dot, illus. 32p. (ps-2). 1992. pap. 6.95 (*0-944727-09-3*) Jason & Nordic Pubs.

—Fair & Square. Yoder, Dot, illus. 32p. (ps-2). 1992. 13. 95 (*0-944727-10-7*) Jason & Nordic Pubs.

Kettelkamp, Larry. High Tech for the Handicapped: New Ways to Hear, See, Talk, & Walk. LC 90-37527. (Illus.). 128p. (gr. 6 up). 1991. lib. bdg. 17.95 (*0-89490-202-4*) Enslow Pubs.

Kriegsman, Kay H., et al. Taking Charge: Teenagers Talk about Life & Physical Disabilities. (Illus.). 186p. (gr. 7-12). 1992. pap. 14.95 (*0-933149-46-8*) Woodbine House.

Marsh, Carole. The Alabama Mystery Van Takes Off! Book 1: Handicapped Alabama Kids Sneak Off on a Big Adventure. (Illus.). (gr. 3-12). 1994. 24.95 (*0-7933-4964-8*); pap. 14.95 (*0-7933-4965-6*); computer disk 29.95 (*0-7933-4966-4*) Gallopade Pub Group.

—The Alaska Mystery Van Takes Off! Book 1: Handicapped Alaska Kids Sneak Off on a Big Adventure. (Illus.). (gr. 3-12). 1994. 24.95 (*0-7933-4967-2*); pap. 14.95 (*0-7933-4968-0*); computer disk 29.95 (*0-7933-4969-9*) Gallopade Pub Group.

—The Arizona Mystery Van Takes Off! Book 1: Handicapped Arizona Kids Sneak Off on a Big Adventure. (Illus.). (gr. 3-12). 1994. 24.95 (*0-7933-4970-2*); pap. 14.95 (*0-7933-4971-0*); computer disk 29.95 (*0-7933-4972-9*) Gallopade Pub Group.

—The Arkansas Mystery Van Takes Off! Book 1: Handicapped Arkansas Kids Sneak Off on a Big Adventure. (Illus.). (gr. 3-12). 1994. 24.95 (*0-7933-4973-7*); pap. 14.95 (*0-7933-4974-5*); computer disk 29.95 (*0-7933-4975-3*) Gallopade Pub Group.

—The California Mystery Van Takes Off! Book 1: Handicapped California Kids Sneak Off on a Big Adventure. (Illus.). (gr. 3-12). 1994. 24.95 (*0-7933-4976-1*); pap. 14.95 (*0-7933-4977-X*); computer disk 29.95 (*0-7933-4978-8*) Gallopade Pub Group.

—The Colorado Mystery Van Takes Off! Book 1: Handicapped Colorado Kids Sneak Off on a Big Adventure. (Illus.). (gr. 3-12). 1994. 24.95 (*0-7933-4979-6*); pap. 14.95 (*0-7933-4980-X*); computer disk 29.95 (*0-7933-4981-8*) Gallopade Pub Group.

—The Connecticut Mystery Van Takes Off! Book 1: Handicapped Connecticut Kids Sneak Off on a Big Adventure. (Illus.). (gr. 3-12). 1994. 24.95 (*0-7933-4982-6*); pap. 14.95 (*0-7933-4983-4*); computer disk 29.95 (*0-7933-4984-2*) Gallopade Pub Group.

—The Delaware Mystery Van Takes Off! Book 1: Handicapped Delaware Kids Sneak Off on a Big Adventure. (Illus.). (gr. 3-12). 1994. 24.95 (*0-7933-4985-0*); pap. 14.95 (*0-7933-4986-9*); computer disk 29.95 (*0-7933-4987-7*) Gallopade Pub Group.

—The Florida Mystery Van Takes Off! Book 1: Handicapped Florida Kids Sneak Off on a Big Adventure. (Illus.). (gr. 3-12). 1994. 24.95 (*0-7933-4988-5*); pap. 14.95 (*0-7933-4989-3*); computer disk 29.95 (*0-7933-4990-7*) Gallopade Pub Group.

—The Georgia Mystery Van Takes Off! Book 1: Handicapped Georgia Kids Sneak Off on a Big Adventure. (Illus.). (gr. 3-12). 1994. 24.95 (*0-7933-4991-5*); pap. 14.95 (*0-7933-4992-3*); computer disk 29.95 (*0-7933-4993-1*) Gallopade Pub Group.

—The Hawaii Mystery Van Takes Off! Book 1: Handicapped Hawaii Kids Sneak Off on a Big Adventure. (Illus.). (gr. 3-12). 1994. 24.95 (*0-7933-4994-X*); pap. 14.95 (*0-7933-4995-8*); computer disk 29.95 (*0-7933-4996-6*) Gallopade Pub Group.

—The Idaho Mystery Van Takes Off! Book 1: Handicapped Idaho Kids Sneak Off on a Big Adventure. (Illus.). (gr. 3-12). 1994. 24.95 (*0-7933-4997-4*); pap. 14.95 (*0-7933-4998-2*); computer disk 29.95 (*0-7933-4999-0*) Gallopade Pub Group.

—The Illinois Mystery Van Takes Off! Book 1: Handicapped Illinois Kids Sneak Off on a Big Adventure. (Illus.). (gr. 3-12). 1994. 24.95 (*0-7933-5000-X*); pap. 14.95 (*0-7933-5001-8*); computer disk 29.95 (*0-7933-5002-6*) Gallopade Pub Group.

—The Indiana Mystery Van Takes Off! Book 1: Handicapped Indiana Kids Sneak Off on a Big Adventure. (Illus.). (gr. 3-12). 1994. 24.95 (*0-7933-5003-4*); pap. 14.95 (*0-7933-5004-2*); computer disk 29.95 (*0-7933-5005-0*) Gallopade Pub Group.

—The Iowa Mystery Van Takes Off! Book 1: Handicapped Iowa Kids Sneak Off on a Big Adventure. (Illus.). (gr. 3-12). 1994. 24.95 (*0-7933-5006-9*); pap. 14.95 (*0-7933-5007-7*); computer disk 29.95 (*0-7933-5008-5*) Gallopade Pub Group.

—The Kansas Mystery Van Takes Off! Book 1: Handicapped Kansas Kids Sneak Off on a Big Adventure. (Illus.). (gr. 3-12). 1994. 24.95 (*0-7933-5009-3*); pap. 14.95 (*0-7933-5010-7*); computer disk 29.95 (*0-7933-5011-5*) Gallopade Pub Group.

—The Kentucky Mystery Van Takes Off! Book 1: Handicapped Kentucky Kids Sneak Off on a Big Adventure. (Illus.). (gr. 3-12). 1994. 24.95 (*0-7933-5012-3*); pap. 14.95 (*0-7933-5013-1*); computer disk 29.95 (*0-7933-5014-X*) Gallopade Pub Group.

—The Louisiana Mystery Van Takes Off! Book 1: Handicapped Louisiana Kids Sneak Off on a Big Adventure. (Illus.). (gr. 3-12). 1994. 24.95 (*0-7933-5015-8*); pap. 14.95 (*0-7933-5016-6*); computer disk 29.95 (*0-7933-5017-4*) Gallopade Pub Group.

—The Maine Mystery Van Takes Off! Book 1: Handicapped Maine Kids Sneak Off on a Big Adventure. (Illus.). (gr. 3-12). 1994. 24.95 (*0-7933-5018-2*); pap. 14.95 (*0-7933-5019-0*); computer disk 29.95 (*0-7933-5020-4*) Gallopade Pub Group.

—The Maryland Mystery Van Takes Off! Book 1: Handicapped Maryland Kids Sneak Off on a Big Adventure. (Illus.). (gr. 3-12). 1994. 24.95 (*0-7933-5021-2*); pap. 14.95 (*0-7933-5022-0*); computer disk 29.95 (*0-7933-5023-9*) Gallopade Pub Group.

—The Massachusetts Mystery Van Takes Off! Book 1: Handicapped Massachusetts Kids Sneak Off on a Big Adventure. (Illus.). (gr. 3-12). 1994. 24.95 (*0-7933-5024-7*); pap. 14.95 (*0-7933-5025-5*); computer disk 29.95 (*0-7933-5026-3*) Gallopade Pub Group.

—The Michigan Mystery Van Takes Off! Book 1: Handicapped Michigan Kids Sneak Off on a Big Adventure. (Illus.). (gr. 3-12). 1994. 24.95 (*0-7933-5027-1*); pap. 14.95 (*0-7933-5028-X*); computer disk 29.95 (*0-7933-5029-8*) Gallopade Pub Group.

—The Minnesota Mystery Van Takes Off! Book 1: Handicapped Minnesota Kids Sneak Off on a Big Adventure. (Illus.). (gr. 3-12). 1994. 24.95 (*0-7933-5030-1*); pap. 14.95 (*0-7933-5031-X*); computer disk 29.95 (*0-7933-5032-8*) Gallopade Pub Group.

—The Mississippi Mystery Van Takes Off! Book 1: Handicapped Mississippi Kids Sneak Off on a Big Adventure. (Illus.). (gr. 3-12). 1994. 24.95 (*0-7933-5033-6*); pap. 14.95 (*0-7933-5034-4*); computer disk 29.95 (*0-7933-5035-2*) Gallopade Pub Group.

—The Missouri Mystery Van Takes Off! Book 1: Handicapped Missouri Kids Sneak Off on a Big Adventure. (Illus.). (gr. 3-12). 1994. 24.95 (*0-7933-5036-0*); pap. 14.95 (*0-7933-5037-9*); computer disk 29.95 (*0-7933-5038-7*) Gallopade Pub Group.

—The Montana Mystery Van Takes Off! Book 1: Handicapped Montana Kids Sneak Off on a Big Adventure. (Illus.). (gr. 3-12). 1994. 24.95 (*0-7933-5039-5*); pap. 14.95 (*0-7933-5040-9*); computer disk 29.95 (*0-7933-5041-7*) Gallopade Pub Group.

—The Nebraska Mystery Van Takes Off! Book 1: Handicapped Nebraska Kids Sneak off on a Big Adventure. (Illus.). (gr. 3-12). 1994. 24.95 (*0-7933-5042-5*); pap. 14.95 (*0-7933-5043-3*); computer disk 29.95 (*0-7933-5044-1*) Gallopade Pub Group.

—The Nevada Mystery Van Takes Off! Book 1: Handicapped Nevada Kids Sneak Off on a Big Adventure. (Illus.). (gr. 3-12). 1994. 24.95 (*0-7933-5045-X*); pap. 14.95 (*0-7933-5046-8*); computer disk 29.95 (*0-7933-5047-6*) Gallopade Pub Group.

—The New Hampshire Mystery Van Takes Off! Book 1: Handicapped New Hampshire Kids Sneak Off on a Big Adventure. (Illus.). (gr. 3-12). 1994. 24.95 (*0-7933-5048-4*); pap. 14.95 (*0-7933-5049-2*); computer disk 29.95 (*0-7933-5050-6*) Gallopade Pub Group.

—The New Jersey Mystery Van Takes Off! Book 1: Handicapped New Jersey Kids Sneak Off on a Big Adventure. (Illus.). (gr. 3-12). 1994. 24.95 (*0-7933-5051-4*); pap. 14.95 (*0-7933-5052-2*); computer disk 29.95 (*0-7933-5053-0*) Gallopade Pub Group.

—The New Mexico Mystery Van Takes Off! Book 1: Handicapped New Mexico Kids Sneak Off on a Big Adventure. (Illus.). (gr. 3-12). 1994. 24.95 (*0-7933-5054-9*); pap. 14.95 (*0-7933-5055-7*); computer disk 29.95 (*0-7933-5056-5*) Gallopade Pub Group.

—The New York Mystery Van Takes Off! Book 1: Handicapped New York Kids Sneak Off on a Big Adventure. (Illus.). (gr. 3-12). 1994. 24.95 (*0-7933-5057-3*); pap. 14.95 (*0-7933-5058-1*); computer disk 29.95 (*0-7933-5059-X*) Gallopade Pub Group.

—The North Carolina Mystery Van Takes Off! Book 1: Handicapped North Carolina Kids Sneak Off on a Big Adventure. (Illus.). (gr. 3-12). 1994. 24.95 (*0-7933-5060-3*); pap. 14.95 (*0-7933-5061-1*); computer disk 29.95 (*0-7933-5062-X*) Gallopade Pub Group.

—The North Dakota Mystery Van Takes Off! Book 1: Handicapped North Dakota Kids Sneak Off on a Big Adventure. (Illus.). (gr. 3-12). 1994. 24.95 (*0-7933-5063-8*); pap. 14.95 (*0-7933-5064-6*); computer disk 29.95 (*0-7933-5065-4*) Gallopade Pub Group.

—The Ohio Mystery Van Takes Off! Book 1: Handicapped Ohio Kids Sneak Off on a Big Adventure. (Illus.). (gr. 3-12). 1994. 24.95 (*0-7933-5066-2*); pap. 14.95 (*0-7933-5067-0*); computer disk 29.95 (*0-7933-5068-9*) Gallopade Pub Group.

—The Oklahoma Mystery Van Takes Off! Book 1: Handicapped Oklahoma Kids Sneak Off on a Big Adventure. (Illus.). (gr. 3-12). 1994. 24.95 (*0-7933-5069-7*); pap. 14.95 (*0-7933-5070-0*); computer disk 29.95 (*0-7933-5071-9*) Gallopade Pub Group.

—The Oregon Mystery Van Takes Off! Book 1: Handicapped Oregon Kids Sneak Off on a Big Adventure. (Illus.). (gr. 3-12). 1994. 24.95 (*0-7933-5072-7*); pap. 14.95 (*0-7933-5073-5*); computer disk 29.95 (*0-7933-5074-3*) Gallopade Pub Group.

—The Pennsylvania Mystery Van Takes Off! Book 1: Handicapped Pennsylvania Kids Sneak Off on a Big Adventure. (Illus.). (gr. 3-12). 1994. 24.95 (*0-7933-5075-1*); pap. 14.95 (*0-7933-5076-X*); computer disk 29.95 (*0-7933-5077-8*) Gallopade Pub Group.

—The Rhode Island Mystery Van Takes Off! Book 1: Handicapped Rhode Island Kids Sneak Off on a Big Adventure. (Illus.). (gr. 3-12). 1994. 24.95 (*0-7933-5078-6*); pap. 14.95 (*0-7933-5079-4*); computer disk 29.95 (*0-7933-5080-8*) Gallopade Pub Group.

—The South Carolina Mystery Van Takes Off! Book 1: Handicapped South Carolina Kids Sneak Off on a Big Adventure. (Illus.). (gr. 3-12). 1994. 24.95 (*0-7933-5081-6*); pap. 14.95 (*0-7933-5082-4*); computer disk 29.95 (*0-7933-5083-2*) Gallopade Pub Group.

—The South Dakota Mystery Van Takes Off! Book 1: Handicapped South Dakota Kids Sneak Off on a Big Adventure. (Illus.). (gr. 3-12). 1994. 24.95 (*0-7933-5084-0*); pap. 14.95 (*0-7933-5085-9*); computer disk 29.95 (*0-7933-5086-7*) Gallopade Pub Group.

—The Tennessee Mystery Van Takes Off! Book 1: Handicapped Tennessee Kids Sneak Off on a Big Adventure. (Illus.). (gr. 3-12). 1994. 24.95 (*0-7933-5087-5*); pap. 14.95 (*0-7933-5088-3*); computer disk 29.95 (*0-7933-5089-1*) Gallopade Pub Group.

—The Texas Mystery Van Takes Off! Book 1: Handicapped Texas Kids Sneak Off on a Big Adventure. (Illus.). (gr. 3-12). 1994. 24.95 (*0-7933-5090-5*); pap. 14.95 (*0-7933-5091-3*); computer disk 29.95 (*0-7933-5092-1*) Gallopade Pub Group.

—The Utah Mystery Van Takes Off! Book 1: Handicapped Utah Kids Sneak Off on a Big Adventure. (Illus.). (gr. 3-12). 1994. 24.95 (*0-7933-5093-X*); pap. 14.95 (*0-7933-5094-8*); computer disk 29.95 (*0-7933-5095-6*) Gallopade Pub Group.

—The Vermont Mystery Van Takes Off! Book 1: Handicapped Vermont Kids Sneak Off on a Big Adventure. (Illus.). (gr. 3-12). 1994. 24.95 (*0-7933-5096-4*); pap. 14.95 (*0-7933-5097-2*); computer disk 29.95 (*0-7933-5098-0*) Gallopade Pub Group.

—The Virginia Mystery Van Takes Off! Book 1: Handicapped Virginia Kids Sneak Off on a Big Adventure. (Illus.). (gr. 3-12). 1994. 24.95 (*0-7933-5099-9*); pap. 14.95 (*0-7933-5100-6*); computer disk 29.95 (*0-7933-5101-4*) Gallopade Pub Group.

—The Washington D. C. Mystery Van Takes Off! Book 1: Handicapped Washington D. C. Kids Sneak Off on a Big Adventure. (Illus.). (gr. 3-12). 1994. 24.95 (*0-7933-5105-7*); pap. 14.95 (*0-7933-5106-5*); computer disk 29.95 (*0-7933-5107-3*) Gallopade Pub Group.

—The Washington Mystery Van Takes Off! Book 1: Handicapped Washington Kids Sneak Off on a Big Adventure. (Illus.). (gr. 3-12). 1994. 24.95 (*0-7933-5102-2*); pap. 14.95 (*0-7933-5103-0*); computer disk 29.95 (*0-7933-5104-9*) Gallopade Pub Group.

—The West Virginia Mystery Van Takes Off! Book 1: Handicapped West Virginia Kids Sneak Off on a Big Adventure. (Illus.). (gr. 3-12). 1994. 24.95 (*0-7933-5108-1*); pap. 14.95 (*0-7933-5109-X*); computer disk 29.95 (*0-7933-5110-3*) Gallopade Pub Group.
—The Wisconsin Mystery Van Takes Off! Book 1: Handicapped Wisconsin Kids Sneak Off on a Big Adventure. (Illus.). (gr. 3-12). 1994. 24.95 (*0-7933-5111-1*); pap. 14.95 (*0-7933-5112-X*); computer disk 29.95 (*0-7933-5113-8*) Gallopade Pub Group.
—The Wyoming Mystery Van Takes Off! Book 1: Handicapped Wyoming Kids Sneak Off on a Big Adventure. (Illus.). (gr. 3-12). 1994. 24.95 (*0-7933-5114-6*); pap. 14.95 (*0-7933-5115-4*); computer disk 29.95 (*0-7933-5116-2*) Gallopade Pub Group.
Stewart, Jeffrey E. Work! A Reading Program. (Illus.). 116p. (Orig.). 1988. pap. 32.50 (*1-877866-02-4*) J E Stewart.
Walters, Gregory J. Equal Access: Safeguarding Disability Rights. LC 92-11523. 1992. PLB 22.60 (*0-86593-174-7*); 16.95s.p. (*0-685-59328-2*) Rourke Corp.
White, Peter. Disabled People. LC 88-83085. (Illus.). 64p. (gr. 5-7). 1990. 12.40 (*0-531-17146-9*, Gloucester Pr) Watts.

HANDICRAFT

see also Hobbies; Leather Work; Weaving

Adams, Adrienne. The Great Valentine's Day Balloon Race. Adams, Adrienne, illus. LC 80-19527. 32p. (ps-3). 1980. RSBE 14.95 (*0-684-16640-2*, Scribners Young Read) Macmillan Child Grp.
Alden, Laura. Something for Mother. Hohag, Linda, illus. LC 93-37096. 32p. (ps-2). 1994. PLB 12.30 (*0-516-00690-8*) Childrens.
Allison, Linda. The Reasons for Seasons: The Great Cosmic Megagalactic Trip Without Moving from Your Chair. Allison, Linda, illus. 128p. (gr. 4 up). 1975. pap. 9.95 (*0-316-03440-1*) Little.
—The Sierra Club Summer Book. Allison, Linda, illus. LC 93-41481. 1994. 7.99 (*0-517-10082-7*, Pub. by Wings Bks) Random Hse Value.
—Trash Artists Workshop. LC 80-84184. (gr. 3-8). 1981. pap. 10.95 (*0-8224-9780-8*) Fearon Teach Aids.
Amery, Heather. Fun with Paper. LC 92-51071. 1993. lib. bdg. 6.99 (*0-679-83493-1*); pap. 9.99 (*0-679-93493-6*) Random.
Applegate, Katherine. Disney's Christmas with All the Trimmings: Original Stories & Crafts from Mickey Mouse & Friends. Wilson, Phil, illus. 64p. (ps-3). 1994. 12.95 (*0-7868-3003-4*) Disney Pr.
Araki, Chiyo. Origami in the Classroom, 2 vols. LC 65-13412. (Illus.). (gr. 1 up). 1965-68. bds. Vol. 1. bds. 14.95 (*0-8048-0452-4*); Vol. 2. bds. 14.95 (*0-8048-0453-2*) C E Tuttle.
Armstrong, Beverly. Build a Doodle Circus. (Illus.). 32p. (gr. k-4). 1986. 2.95 (*0-88160-133-0*, LW138) Learning Wks.
—Build a Doodle Farm. (Illus.). 32p. (gr. k-4). 1986. 2.95 (*0-88160-130-6*, LW135) Learning Wks.
—Build a Doodle Ocean. (Illus.). 32p. (gr. k-4). 1986. 2.95 (*0-88160-131-4*, LW137) Learning Wks.
Arts & Crafts Discovery Units. Incl. Crayon. 9.95x; Mobiles. 9.95x; Paper. 9.95x; Papier Mache. 9.95x; Printing. 9.95x; Puppets. 9.95x; Tempera. 9.95x; Tissue. 9.95x; Watercolor. 9.95x; Weaving. 9.95x (*0-87628-532-9*). (gr. k-7). 1974. Ctr Appl Res.
Asden, Richard. The Professor's Stick Book & Toy. 16p. (gr. 3 up). 1993. pap. text ed. 19.95 (*1-883737-01-X*) Matey Pr.
Ashman, I. Make This Model: Haunted House. (Illus.). 32p. (gr. 4 up). 1991. pap. 9.95 (*0-7460-0647-0*, Usborne) EDC.
—Make This Model: Wizards Castle. (Illus.). 32p. (gr. 4 up). 1991. pap. 9.95 (*0-7460-0607-1*, Usborne) EDC.
Barr, Marilynn G. Dinosaur Days. (Illus.). 48p. (ps-1). 1993. pap. 5.95 (*1-878279-56-4*) Monday Morning Bks.
—Shortcuts for Fall. (Illus.). 80p. (ps-4). 1992. pap. 8.95 (*1-878279-43-2*) Monday Morning Bks.
—Shortcuts for Spring. (Illus.). 80p. (gr. k-4). 1992. pap. 8.95 (*1-878279-45-9*) Monday Morning Bks.
—Shortcuts for Winter. (Illus.). 80p. (gr. k-4). 1992. pap. 8.95 (*1-878279-44-0*) Monday Morning Bks.
Barraclough, Geoffrey. Challenging Artstraws. rev. ed. Doyle, Connie, ed. (Illus.). 28p. (gr. 3-6). Repr. 11.95 (*1-884461-07-7*) NES Arnold.
Bawden, Juliet. Fun with Fabric. Venus, Joanna, illus. Johnson, David, photos by. LC 92-51070. (Illus.). 48p. (gr. 1-5). 1993. PLB 9.99 (*0-679-93494-4*); pap. 6.99 (*0-679-83494-X*) Random Bks Yng Read.
—One Hundred One Things to Make: Fun Craft Projects with Everyday Materials. Pang, Alex, illus. LC 93-29633. 104p. 1994. 14.95 (*0-8069-0596-4*) Sterling.
Baxter, Nicola. Invaders & Settlers. LC 93-46464. 1994. write for info. (*0-531-14338-4*) Watts.
Beard, Daniel C. The American Boy's Handy Book: What to Do & How to Do It. Perrin, Noel, frwd. by. LC 82-3155. (Illus.). 320p. (gr. 4 up). 1983. pap. 10.95 (*0-87923-449-0*) Godine.
Bernstein, Bonnie & Blair, Leigh. Native American Crafts Workshop. LC 81-82041. (gr. 3-8). 1982. pap. 10.95 (*0-8224-9784-0*) Fearon Teach Aids.
Big Book of Boxes (cutouts) (gr. 2-6). 1992. 17.00 (*1-56021-140-7*) W J Fantasy.
Bingham, Caroline & Foster, Karen, eds. Crafts for Celebration. (Illus.). 48p. (gr. 2-6). 1993. PLB 14.40 (*1-56294-099-6*) Millbrook Pr.
—Crafts for Decoration. (Illus.). 48p. (gr. 2-6). 1993. PLB 14.40 (*1-56294-098-8*) Millbrook Pr.
—Crafts for Everyday Life. (Illus.). 48p. (gr. 2-6). 1993. PLB 14.40 (*1-56294-097-X*) Millbrook Pr.
—Crafts for Play. (Illus.). 48p. (gr. 2-6). 1993. PLB 14.40 (*1-56294-096-1*) Millbrook Pr.
Blakey, Nancy. The Mudpies Activity Book: Recipes for Invention. Watts, Melissah, illus. 144p. (ps-6). pap. 7.95 (*0-89815-576-2*) Ten Speed Pr.
Bolton, Jane. My Grandmother's Patchwork Quilt: A Book & Portfolio of Patchwork Pieces. LC 93-17279. 1994. 17.95 (*0-385-31155-9*) Doubleday.
Bonica, Diane. Hand-Shaped Art. Renard, Jan, illus. 112p. (ps-2). 1989. wkbk. 10.95 (*0-86653-474-1*, GA1079) Good Apple.
—Hand-Shaped Gifts. 144p. (ps-4). 1991. 11.95 (*0-86653-612-4*, GA1331) Good Apple.
Borchardt, Lois M. Learning about God's Love: Word-Picture Activities for Children in Grades 1 & 2. 48p. (gr. 1-2). 1986. pap. 2.99 (*0-570-04354-9*, 61-2017) Concordia.
Bottomley, Jim. Paper Projects for Creative Kids of All Ages. 160p. (gr. 5 up). 1983. pap. 12.95 (*0-316-10349-7*) Little.
Brackett, Karen & Manley, Rosie. Beautiful Junk. (gr. 1-6). 1990. pap. 10.95 (*0-8224-0626-8*) Fearon Teach Aids.
Bradley, Susannah. Busy Bee Pack. Banazi, Pauline, illus. (gr. 3-6). 1992. pap. 7.95 (*1-56680-503-1*) Mad Hatter Pub.
—Cuddly Teddies' Activity Book. Banazi, Pauline, illus. (gr. 3-6). 1992. pap. 5.95 (*1-56680-507-4*) Mad Hatter Pub.
—Freaky Frank's Cut Out Fun Book. Mostyn, David, illus. (gr. 3-6). 1992. pap. 3.95 (*1-56680-506-6*) Mad Hatter Pub.
Bridgewater, Alan. I Made It Myself: Kids Craft Projects. (Illus.). 192p. 1990. 19.95 (*0-8306-8339-9*, 3339); pap. 11.95 (*0-8306-3339-1*) TAB Bks.
Bridgewater, Alan & Bridgewater, Gill. Holiday Crafts: More Year-Round Crafts Kids Can Make. (Illus.). 256p. 1990. 25.95 (*0-8306-7409-8*, 3409); pap. 16.95 (*0-8306-3409-6*) TAB Bks.
Brigandi, Pat. String Magic: String Designs & How to Make Them. (gr. 4-7). 1993. pap. 2.95 (*0-590-46974-6*) Scholastic Inc.
Brinn, Ruth Esrig. Jewish Holiday Crafts for Little Hands. Kahn, Katherine Janus, illus. LC 92-39638. (gr. k up). 1993. pap. 10.95 (*0-929371-47-X*) Kar Ben.
Bronze, Lewis & Brown, Peter. Blue Peter Action Book. (Illus.). 65p. 1994. 8.95 (*0-563-36495-5*, BBC-Parkwest) Parkwest Pubns.
Brown, Ann. Handmade Christmas Gifts That Are Actually Usable. Small, Carol B., illus. LC 87-31993. 75p. (Orig.). (gr. k-6). 1987. pap. 6.95 (*0-938267-03-5*) Bold Prodns.
Brown, Jerome C. Folk Tale PaperCrafts. (gr. k-5). 1989. pap. 8.95 (*0-8224-3156-4*) Fearon Teach Aids.
—Holiday Art Projects. (gr. 3-12). 1984. pap. 5.95 (*0-8224-5190-5*) Fearon Teach Aids.
—Mother Goose PaperCrafts. (gr. k-5). 1989. pap. 8.95 (*0-8224-3154-8*) Fearon Teach Aids.
Bullach, Ivan & Chambers, Tony. Design. Maudlsley, Toby & Johnson, James, photos by. Bulloch, Ivan, designed by. LC 93-35626. (Illus.). 48p. (gr. 5-9). 1994. 16.95 (*1-56847-148-3*) Thomson Lrning.
Bulloch, Ivan. Play with Models. LC 94-14248. (gr. 1 up). 1994. write for info. (*0-87614-866-6*) Carolrhoda Bks.
Burgess, Anna. Do-It-Yourself Project Book. (gr. 4-7). 1994. pap. 5.95 (*0-8167-3343-0*) Troll Assocs.
Burt, Erica. Natural Materials. (Illus.). 32p. (gr. 2-6). 1990. lib. bdg. 15.94 (*0-86592-486-4*); lib. bdg. 11. 95s.p. (*0-685-46442-3*) Rourke Corp.
Butterfield, Moira. Fun with Paint. Venus, Joanna & Kerr, Elizabeth, illus. 48p. (gr. 1-5). 1993. PLB 9.99 (*0-679-93492-8*); pap. 6.99 (*0-679-83492-3*) Random Bks Yng Read.
—People & Places. Forsey, Chris, illus. LC 91-214. 40p. (Orig.). (gr. 2-5). 1991. pap. 3.99 (*0-679-80868-X*) Random Bks Yng Read.
Byrnes, Patricia & Krenz, Nancy. Southwestern Arts & Crafts Projects. Rev. ed. LC 77-18988. (Illus.). (gr. 1-8). 1979. pap. 9.95 (*0-913270-62-8*) Sunstone Pr.
Caldecott, Barrie. Jewelry Crafts. LC 91-9887. (Illus.). 48p. (gr. 5-8). 1992. PLB 12.40 (*0-531-14203-5*) Watts.
—Papier Mache. LC 92-6259. (Illus.). 48p. (gr. 4-6). 1993. PLB 12.40 (*0-531-14217-5*) Watts.
Caney, Steven. Steven Caney's Play Book. LC 75-9816. (Illus.). 240p. (ps-5). 1975. pap. 9.95 (*0-911104-38-0*, 050) Workman Pub.
Carlson, Laurie. EcoArt! Earth-Friendly Art & Craft Experiences for 3- to 9-Year-Olds. Braren, Loretta, illus. LC 92-21347. 160p. (Orig.). (ps-5). 1993. pap. 12.95 (*0-913589-68-3*) Williamson Pub Co.
—Kids Create! Art & Craft Experiences for 3- to 9-Year-Olds. Williamson, Susan, ed. Braren, Loretta T., illus. LC 90-33677. 160p. (Orig.). (gr. k-3). 1990. pap. 12.95 (*0-913589-51-9*) Williamson Pub Co.
Carroll, David. Make Your Own Chess Set. Carroll, David, photos by. (Illus.). (gr. 5 up). 1978. (Pub. by Treehouse) P-H.
Cheng, Andrea. Let's Make a Present! Easy to Make Gifts for Friends & Relatives of Any Age. Macdonald, Roland B. & Gray, Dan, illus. 128p. (gr. k-5). 1991. pap. 9.95 (*1-878767-16-X*) Murdoch Bks.
Cherkerzian, Diane. Christmas Fun: Holiday Crafts & Treats. Eitzen, Allen, illus. LC 92-75840. 32p. (ps-5). 1994. 4.95 (*1-56397-277-8*); prepack 14.95 (*1-56397-278-6*) Boyds Mills Pr.
—Indoor Sunshine: Great Things to Make & Do on Rainy Days. LeHew, Ron, illus. LC 92-73628. 32p. (gr. 2-7). 1993. pap. 3.95 (*1-56397-163-1*) Boyds Mills Pr.
—Outdoor Fun: Great Things to Make & Do on Sunny Days. LeHew, Ron, illus. LC 92-74583. 32p. (gr. 2-7). 1993. pap. 3.95 (*1-56397-162-3*) Boyds Mills Pr.
Churchill, E. Richard. Fantastic Paper Flying Machines. Michaels, James, illus. LC 93-44604. 128p. 1994. 14. 95 (*0-8069-0435-6*) Sterling.
—Holiday Paper Projects. Michaels, James, illus. LC 92-12100. 128p. (gr. 3-9). 1992. 14.95 (*0-8069-8512-7*) Sterling.
—Paper Science Toys. LC 90-9891. (Illus.). 128p. (gr. 3-10). 1990. 14.95 (*0-8069-5834-0*) Sterling.
Chwast, Seymour. Paper Pets: Make Your Own Three Dogs, 2 Cats, 1 Parrot, 1 Rabbit, 1 Monkey. LC 92-23609. (Illus.). 24p. 1993. pap. 19.95 (*0-8109-2531-1*) Abrams.
Conaway, Judith. Easy-to-Make Christmas Crafts. Barto, Renzo, illus. LC 85-16475. 48p. (gr. 1-5). 1986. PLB 11.89 (*0-8167-0674-3*); pap. text ed. 3.50 (*0-8167-0675-1*) Troll Assocs.
—Fun-to-Make Nature Crafts. Barto, Renzo, illus. LC 80-23999. 48p. (gr. 1-5). 1981. PLB 11.89 (*0-89375-440-4*); pap. 3.50 (*0-89375-441-2*) Troll Assocs.
—Great Gifts to Make. Barto, Renzo, illus. LC 85-16498. 48p. (gr. 1-5). 1986. PLB 11.89 (*0-8167-0676-X*); pap. text ed. 3.50 (*0-8167-0677-8*) Troll Assocs.
Consentino, Phyllis. Teddy Bear Junction: Stop Here for Fine Collector Bears. (Illus.). 104p. (Orig.). 1985. pap. 10.95 (*0-935855-00-9*) T B J Pubns.
Constable, David. Candlemaking. (Illus.). 80p. (Orig.). 1993. pap. 16.95 (*0-85532-683-2*, Pub. by Search Pr UK) A Schwartz & Co.
Corell, Brigitte. A Gift for You. LC 91-44377. (Illus.). 64p. PLB 15.40, apr. 1992 (*0-516-09260-X*); pap. 8.95, Jul. 1992 (*0-516-49260-8*) Childrens.
Corke, Philip. Handicrafts of the Arab World. (gr. 2-9). 1988. 7.95x (*0-86685-496-7*) Intl Bk Ctr.
Corwin, Judith H. African Crafts. LC 90-12493. (Illus.). 48p. (gr. k-4). 1990. PLB 12.90 (*0-531-10846-5*) Watts.
—Asian Crafts. Rosoff, Iris, ed. LC 91-13500. (Illus.). 48p. (gr. 1-4). 1992. PLB 12.90 (*0-531-11013-3*) Watts.
—Christmas Crafts. LC 93-6366. (Illus.). (gr. k-4). Date not set. PLB write for info. (*0-531-11149-0*) Watts.
—Easter Crafts. LC 93-21258. 1994. 12.90 (*0-531-11145-8*) Watts.
—Halloween Crafts. LC 93-6367. (Illus.). (gr. k-4). Date not set. PLB write for info. (*0-531-11148-2*) Watts.
—Latin American & Caribbean Crafts. Rosoff, Iris, ed. LC 91-13466. (Illus.). 48p. (gr. 1-4). 1992. PLB 12.90 (*0-531-11014-1*) Watts.
—Thanksgiving Crafts. LC 93-6369. (Illus.). (gr. k-4). Date not set. PLB write for info. (*0-531-11147-4*) Watts.
—Thanksgiving Fun. Corwin, Judith H., illus. 64p. (gr. 3 up). 1984. lib. bdg. 10.98 (*0-671-49422-8*, J Messner); lib. bdg. 5.95 (*0-671-50849-0*); PLB 7.71s.p. (*0-685-47062-8*); pap. 4.46s.p. (*0-685-47063-6*) S&S Trade.
—Valentine Crafts. LC 93-11970. 1994. 12.90 (*0-531-11146-6*) Watts.
Crafts in Action Series, 6 vols. (Illus.). (gr. 4-8). 1991. Set. PLB 89.70 (*1-85435-404-3*) Marshall Cavendish.
Craig, Diana. Making Models: Three-D Creations from Paper & Clay. LC 92-18413. (Illus.). 96p. (gr. 3-6). 1993. PLB 16.90 (*1-56294-204-2*); pap. 9.95 (*1-56294-710-9*) Millbrook Pr.
Cusick, Dawn. Fabric Lovers' Christmas Scrapcrafts. LC 93-10659. (Illus.). 128p. (gr. 10-12). 1993. 24.95 (*0-8069-0437-2*, Pub. by Lark Bks) Sterling.
Cuyler, Margery. All Around Pumpkin Book. McClintock, Barbara, illus. LC 79-4820. 96p. (ps-2). 1980. 8.95 (*0-03-047101-X*, Bks Young Read) H Holt & Co.
Dahlstrom, Lorraine M. Doing the Days: A Year's Worth of Creative Journaling, Drawing, Listening, Reading, Thinking, Arts & Crafts Activities for Children Ages 8-12. Wallner, Rosemary, ed. 240p. (Orig.). (gr. 3-7). 1994. pap. 21.95 (*0-915793-62-8*) Free Spirit Pub.
Daitz, Myrna. Crafty Ideas from Junk. Montgomery, Margaret, ed. Chapman, Gillian, illus. 48p. 1993. pap. 4.99 (*1-85015-393-0*) Exley Giftbooks.
D'Amato, Janet & D'Amato, Alex. Cardboard Carpentry. D'Amato, Jane & D'Amato, Alex, illus. Thompson, Morton, intro. by. (gr. 2-5). PLB 13.95 (*0-87460-085-5*) Lion Bks.
—Handicrafts for Holidays. D'Amato, Janet & D'Amato, Alex, illus. (gr. 1-4). 1967. PLB 13.95 (*0-87460-086-3*) Lion Bks.
—Indian Crafts. D'Amato, Janet & D'Amato, Alex, illus. (gr. 2-5). PLB 13.95 (*0-87460-088-X*) Lion Bks.
Daniel, Rebecca & Stegenga, Susan J. Christian Crafts from Cardboard Containers. (Illus.). 64p. (ps-5). 1992. 8.95 (*0-86653-703-1*, SS2833, Shining Star Pubns) Good Apple.

Darling, Kathy. Preschool Bible Crafts. (Illus.). 96p. (ps-1). 1992. 10.95 (*0-86653-699-X*, SS2829, Shining Star Pubns) Good Apple.
Dawson, Richard. Challenging Technology. rev. ed. Doyle, Connie, ed. (Illus.). 33p. (gr. 3-6). Repr. 11.95 (*1-884461-06-9*) NES Arnold.
Deshpande, Chris & Macleod-Brudenell, Iain. Festival Crafts. Mukhida, Zul, photos by. (Illus.). 32p. Date not set. lib. bdg. 18.60 (*0-8368-1153-4*) Gareth Stevens Inc.
Devonshire, Hilary. Moving Art. LC 90-31637. (Illus.). 48p. (gr. 5-8). 1990. PLB 12.40 (*0-531-14076-8*) Watts.
Dickenson, Gill. Face Painting: Art for Children. 1993. 12.98 (*1-55521-918-7*) Bk Sales Inc.
Diehn, Gwen & Krautwurst, Terry. Nature Crafts for Kids. LC 91-36387. (Illus.). 144p. 1992. 19.95 (*0-8069-8372-8*) Sterling.
—Science Crafts for Kids: 50 Fantastic Things to Invent & Create. LC 93-39112. 144p. 1993. 19.95 (*0-8069-0283-3*, Pub. by Lark Bks) Sterling.
Dondiego, Barbara L. After-School Crafts. Cawley, Jacqueline, illus. 144p. 1992. 22.95 (*0-8306-3868-7*, 4138); pap. 12.95 (*0-8306-3869-5*, 4138) TAB Bks.
Drake, Jane & Love, Ann. The Kids' Summer Handbook. Collins, Heather, illus. LC 93-2524. 208p. (gr. 3 up). 1994. 15.95 (*0-395-68711-X*); pap. 10.95 (*0-395-68709-8*) Ticknor & Flds Bks Yng Read.
Dubuc, Suzanne. Make Your Own Gifts. (Illus.). 32p. (gr. 3-7). 1993. 7.95 (*2-7625-7159-6*, Pub. by Les Edits Herit CN) Adams Inc MA.
Duch, Mabel. Easy-to-Make Puppets: Step-by-Step Instructions. Mohrmann, Gary, illus. LC 93-15320. 64p. (gr. 3-8). 1993. pap. 8.95 (*0-8238-0300-7*) Plays.
Eckstein, Joan & Gleit, Joyce. Fun with Making Things. 160p. 1991. pap. 2.99 (*0-380-76213-7*, Camelot) Avon.
Elliott, Deborah. Making a Book. LC 93-38569. (Illus.). 48p. (gr. 2-4). 1994. 15.95 (*1-56847-103-3*) Thomson Lrning.
Feller, Ron L. & Feller, Marsha Y. Fanciful Faces & Handbound Books: Fairy Tales. Ennes, Phyllis L., ed. Hastings, Kathryn K., illus. Smith, Andrew P., photos by. LC 88-34952. (Illus.). 72p. (Orig.). (gr. 2-9). 1989. pap. 9.95 (*0-9615873-1-8*) Arts Factory.
Fiarotta, Phyllis & Fiarotta, Noel. Cups, Cans & Paper Plate Fans. LC 91-41825. (Illus.). 192p. (gr. 9-12). 1992. 19.95 (*0-8069-8528-3*) Sterling.
Filkins, Vanessa. Gifts for Giving. 144p. (gr. k-5). 1991. 12.95 (*0-86653-611-6*, GA1330) Good Apple.
Fleischman, Paul. Copier Creations. LC 91-45413. (Illus.). 128p. (gr. 3-9). 1993. pap. 8.95 (*0-06-446152-1*, Trophy) HarpC Child Bks.
Ford, Marianne. Copycats & Artifacts. Pugh, Anna, illus. LC 86-45532. 96p. 1986. pap. 9.95 (*0-87923-645-0*) Godine.
Foreman, Gloria. Busy Hands. (Illus.). (gr. 3-8). 1959. pap. 1.00 (*0-915198-01-0*) G Foreman.
Forte, Imogene. December Patterns, Projects & Plans. 80p. (ps-1). 1989. pap. text ed. 7.95 (*0-86530-128-X*, IP 167-0) Incentive Pubns.
—November Patterns, Projects & Plans. 80p. (ps-1). 1989. pap. text ed. 7.95 (*0-86530-127-1*, IP 166-9) Incentive Pubns.
—October Patterns, Projects & Plans. 80p. (ps-1). 1989. pap. text ed. 7.95 (*0-86530-126-3*, IP 166-8) Incentive Pubns.
—September Patterns, Projects & Plans. 80p. (ps-1). 1989. pap. text ed. 7.95 (*0-86530-125-5*, IP 166-7) Incentive Pubns.
Forte, Imogene & Frank, Marge. Puddles & Wings & Grapevine Swings. LC 81-85014. (Illus.). 304p. (ps-6). 1982. pap. text ed. 16.95 (*0-86530-004-6*, IP-046) Incentive Pubns.
Foster, Karen. Rattles, Bells, & Chiming Bars. LC 92-5163. (Illus.). 48p. (gr. 2-6). 1992. PLB 14.40 (*1-56294-284-0*) Millbrook Pr.
Fun Wraps for Tots: Children's Gift Wraps. 1989. 9.99 (*0-517-68531-0*) Random Hse Value.
Gabriele. Christmas Arts & Crafts. 1985. pap. 1.95 (*0-911211-76-4*) Penny Lane Pubns.
Gakken Co. Ltd. Editors, ed. Things to Do. Time-Life Books Inc. Editors, tr. 90p. (gr. k-3). 1989. write for info. (*0-8094-4897-1*); PLB write for info. (*0-8094-4898-X*) Time-Life.
Ganeri, Anita & Wright, Rachel. India. LC 94-1395. 1994. write for info. (*0-531-14314-7*) Watts.
—Mexico. LC 94-7099. 1994. write for info. (*0-531-14316-3*) Watts.
Gardner, Beau. The Turn about, Think about, Look about Book. Gardner, Beau, illus. LC 80-12885. 32p. (gr. k-6). 1980. 15.00 (*0-688-41969-0*); PLB 14.93 (*0-688-51969-5*) Lothrop.
Gathings, Evelyn. Cut & Make Cat Masks in Full Color. 32p. (gr. 1 up). 1988. pap. 4.95 (*0-486-25804-1*) Dover.
Gendusa, Sam. Carving Jack-O-Lanterns. rev. ed. Ruse, Arnold, ed. Gendusa, Sam, illus. Ruse, Arnold, intro. by. LC 89-92605. (Illus.). 80p. 1989. pap. 9.95x (*0-9621071-1-5*) SG Prodns.
Gerson, Trina. Holiday Crafts. Gerson, Janice, illus. 80p. (ps-7). 1983. pap. text ed. write for info. (*0-9605878-1-0*) Anirt Pr.
Gibson, R. Decorating T-Shirts. (Illus.). 32p. (gr. 2-6). 1994. PLB 12.96 (*0-88110-710-7*, Usborne); pap. 5.95 (*0-7460-1696-4*, Usborne) EDC.
Giles, Nancy. Creative Food Box Crafts. Petty, Melissa, illus. 64p. (ps-2). 1989. wkbk. 8.95 (*0-86653-475-X*, GA1076) Good Apple.
—Creative Milk Carton Crafts. Petty, Melissa, illus. 64p. (ps-2). 1989. wkbk. 8.95 (*0-86653-462-8*, GA1075) Good Apple.
Gillis, Jennifer S. Hearts & Crafts: Over Twenty Projects for Fun-Loving Kids. Steege, Gwen, ed. Delmonte, Patti, illus. LC 93-4841. 64p. (gr. k-4). 1994. pap. 9.95 (*0-88266-844-7*) Storey Comm Inc.
Goodchild, Peter. The Spark in the Stone: Skills & Projects from the Native American Tradition. LC 90-27324. (Illus.). 144p. (Orig.). (gr. 5 up). 1991. pap. 11.95 (*1-55652-102-2*) Chicago Review.
Green, Jen. Making Crazy Animals. LC 91-33868. (Illus.). 32p. (gr. 2-4). 1992. PLB 12.40 (*0-531-17324-0*, Gloucester Pr) Watts.
—Making Mad Machines. (Illus.). 32p. (gr. 2-4). 1992. PLB 12.40 (*0-531-17326-7*, Gloucester Pr) Watts.
Grisewood, Sarah. Models. Robins, Jim, illus. LC 93-51045. 40p. 1994. PLB 10.95 (*1-85697-515-0*, Kingfisher LKC); pap. 5.95 (*1-85697-516-9*) LKC.
Gryski, Camilla. Friendship Bracelets. LC 92-31097. (Illus.). 48p. (gr. 5 up). 1993. 14.00 (*0-688-12435-6*); PLB 13.93 (*0-688-12436-4*) Morrow Jr Bks.
—Friendship Bracelets. LC 92-31097. (Illus.). (gr. 5 up). 1993. pap. 6.95 (*0-688-12437-2*, Pub. by Beech Tree Bks) Morrow.
—Lanyard: Having Fun with Plastic Lace. Hendry, Linda, illus. LC 93-35992. 32p. 1994. Repr. of 1993 ed. 15.00g (*0-688-13324-X*); PLB 14.93 (*0-688-13325-8*) Morrow Jr Bks.
Guerrier, Charlie. A Collage of Crafts. Schwartz, Marc, photos by. Colomb, Etienne, contrib. by. LC 93-24968. (Illus.). 60p. (gr. 3 up). 1994. 12.95 (*0-395-68377-7*) Ticknor & Flds Bks Yng Read.
Haas, Rudi & Blohm, Hans. The Egg-Carton Zoo, No. 1. Suzuki, David, intro. by. (Illus.). 64p. 1987. pap. 11.95 (*0-19-540513-7*) OUP.
Hamilton, Leslie. Child's Play Six-Twelve: One Hundred Sixty Instant Activities, Crafts & Science Projects. 1992. 10.00 (*0-517-58354-2*, Crown) Crown Pub Group.
Happy Wraps for Tots: Children's Gift Wraps. 1989. 9.99 (*0-517-68530-2*) Random Hse Value.
Harrison, Kathryn & Kohn, Valerie. Easy-to-Make Costumes. (Illus.). 80p. (gr. 4 up). 1993. pap. 12.16 (*1-895569-10-9*, Pub. by Tamos Bks CN) Sterling.
Hartelius, Margaret A. Knot Again! The Complete Lanyard Kit! Hartelius, Margaret A., illus. 24p. (gr. 1-7). 1993. pap. 7.95 (*0-448-40456-7*, G&D) Putnam Pub Group.
Hauser, Jill F. Kids' Crazy Conconctions: Fifty Mysterious Mixtures for Art & Craft Fun. Braren, Loretta T., illus. 160p. (Orig.). (ps-5). 1994. pap. 12.95 (*0-913589-81-0*) Williamson Pub Co.
Hauswald, Carol & Maskowski, Alice. Body Art: Holidays. (Illus.). 79p. (gr. k-1). 1992. pap. 8.95 (*1-878279-41-6*) Monday Morning Bks.
—Body Art: Nature. (Illus.). 80p. (ps-1). 1992. pap. 8.95 (*1-878279-40-8*) Monday Morning Bks.
—Body Art: People. (Illus.). 80p. (gr. k-1). 1992. pap. 8.95 (*1-878279-42-4*) Monday Morning Bks.
Hayes, Dympna & Lehman, Melanie. Fun with Things Around the House. Seeman, Tina, illus. 32p. (gr. 2). 1987. PLB 14.97 (*0-88625-166-4*); pap. 2.95 (*0-88625-155-9*) Durkin Hayes Pub.
Healton, Sarah H. & Whiteside, Kay H. Baskets, Beads, & Black Walnut Owls: Creative Crafts for Ages 9-12. Hartzog, Sherri, illus. LC 92-41247. (gr. 4-7). 1993. pap. 9.95 (*0-8306-4040-1*) TAB Bks.
Healton, Sarah H. & Whiteside, Kay H., eds. Look What I Made! Creative Crafts for Ages 6-8. (Illus.). 112p. (gr. 1-3). 1992. 16.95 (*0-8306-4037-1*, 4181); pap. 9.95 (*0-8306-4038-X*, 4181) TAB Bks.
Heiges, Shawn, illus. Jamestown Children's Activity Book. 40p. (gr. 1-6). 1992. pap. 2.00 (*0-939631-53-9*) Thomas Publications.
Heinz, Brian J. Beachcrafts Too. LC 87-35232. (Illus.). 112p. (Orig.). 1988. pap. 9.95 (*0-936335-01-7*) Ballyhoo Bks.
Hellman, Nina & Brouwer, Norman. A Mariner's Fancy: The Whaleman's Art of Scrimshaw. LC 92-20865. (Illus.). 96p. 1992. pap. 22.50 (*0-295-97212-2*) U of Wash Pr.
Helwig, Barbara & Stewart, Susan. Wishful Thinking. (Illus.). 44p. (gr. 2-5). 1991. spiral bound 4.95 (*1-881285-02-2*) Arbus Pub.
Hershoff, Evelyn G. It's Fun to Make Things from Scrap Materials. (Illus.). (gr. 4 up). 1944. pap. 6.95 (*0-486-21251-3*) Dover.
Highlights Editors. One Hundred Thirty-Two Gift Crafts Kids Can Make. (Illus.). 48p. (Orig.). (gr. 1-6). 1981. pap. 2.95 (*0-87534-308-2*) Highlights.
—One Hundred Twenty-Eight Holiday Crafts Kids Can Make. (Illus.). 48p. (Orig.). (gr. 1-6). 1981. pap. 2.95 (*0-87534-309-0*) Highlights.
—One Hundred Twenty-Seven Anytime Crafts Kids Can Make. (Illus.). 48p. (Orig.). (gr. 1-6). 1981. pap. 2.95 (*0-87534-307-4*) Highlights.
Highlights for Children Staff. One Hundred Eighteen Recyclable Crafts Kids Can Make. Highlights for Children Staff, illus. 40p. (gr. 1-5). 1993. pap. 2.95 (*0-87534-106-3*) Highlights.
—One Hundred Nineteen Any Time Crafts Kids Can Make. Highlights for Children Staff, illus. 40p. (gr. 1-5). 1993. pap. 2.95 (*0-87534-108-X*) Highlights.
—One Hundred Thirty-Six Party Ideas & Crafts Kids Can Make. Highlights for Children Staff, illus. 40p. (gr. 1-5). 1993. pap. 2.95 (*0-87534-110-1*) Highlights.
—One Hundred Twenty-One Holiday Crafts Kids Can Make. Highlights for Children Staff, illus. 40p. (gr. 1-5). 1993. pap. 2.95 (*0-87534-109-8*) Highlights.
—One Hundred Twenty-Three Gift Crafts Kids Can Make. Highlights for Children Staff, illus. 40p. (gr. 1-5). 1993. pap. 2.95 (*0-87534-107-1*) Highlights.
Hockenberry, Debra. The Craftmaker's Handbook. (Illus.). 60p. (Orig.). (gr. 12). 1990. pap. 8.00 (*1-878056-06-9*) D Hockenberry.
Hoffa, Darlene. Creation Crafts. (Illus.). 64p. (Orig.). 1993. pap. 5.99 (*0-570-04758-7*) Concordia.
Holdgate, Charles. Net Making. LC 72-84056. (Illus.). (gr. 7 up). 1972. 12.95 (*0-87523-180-2*) Emerson.
Holzenthaler, Jean. My Hands Can. Tafuri, Nancy, illus. (ps-k). 1978. 12.95 (*0-525-35490-5*, DCB) Dutton Child Bks.
Horn, Donna. Party & Holiday Decorations: A Handbook of Wafer Fun. Horn, Donna, illus. LC 87-50697. 88p. (Orig.). (gr. 4-12). 1988. pap. 14.95 (*0-935009-97-3*) Wafer Mache.
Ideas for Special Occasions. LC 91-17040. (Illus.). 48p. (gr. 4-8). 1991. PLB 14.95 (*1-85435-407-8*) Marshall Cavendish.
Ideas from Nature. LC 91-17041. (Illus.). 48p. 1991. PLB 14.95 (*1-85435-410-8*) Marshall Cavendish.
Irvine, Joan. Build It with Boxes. Hendry, Linda, illus. LC 91-45589. 96p. (gr. 3 up). 1993. 14.00 (*0-688-12081-4*); PLB 13.93 (*0-688-11524-1*) Morrow Jr Bks.
—Build It with Boxes. LC 91-45589. 96p. (gr. 3 up). 1993. pap. 6.95 (*0-688-11525-X*, Pub. by Beech Tree Bks) Morrow.
—How to Make Super Pop-Ups. (gr. 3 up). 1992. pap. 6.95 (*0-688-11521-7*, Pub. by Beech Tree Bks) Morrow.
Jayne, Caroline F. String Figures & How to Make Them. (Illus.). 407p. (gr. 7 up). 1906. pap. 5.95 (*0-486-20152-X*) Dover.
Jefferis, David. Making Kites. LC 92-42913. (Illus.). 40p. (gr. 3-7). 1993. 10.05 (*1-85697-923-7*, Kingfisher LKC); pap. 5.95 (*1-85697-922-9*) LKC.
Jenkins, Gerald & Bear, Magdalen. Tarquin Globe. (Illus.). 32p. (Orig.). (gr. 4-6). 1991. pap. 7.95 (*0-906212-55-3*, Pub. by Tarquin UK) Parkwest Pubns.
Jenkins, Gerald & Bear, Magdalene. Tarquin Starglobe. (Illus.). 32p. (Orig.). (gr. 4-6). 1991. pap. 6.95 (*0-906212-60-X*, Pub. by Tarquin UK) Parkwest Pubns.
Johanning, Jolynn. God Made All of Me: Activities for Young Children. (Illus.). 120p. 1992. pap. text ed. 11.95 (*0-89390-210-1*) Resource Pubns.
Jones. Creative Quickies. (Illus.). 100p. (gr. k-8). 1982. pap. 7.50 (*0-685-55702-2*) Arts Pubns.
Kallen, Stuart A. Eco-Arts & Crafts. LC 93-19059. (gr. 3 up). 1993. 14.96 (*1-56239-208-5*) Abdo & Dghtrs.
Kalman, Bobbie. Colonial Crafts. (Illus.). 32p. (gr. k-9). 1992. PLB 15.95 (*0-86505-490-8*); pap. 7.95 (*0-86505-510-6*) Crabtree Pub CO.
—Home Crafts. (Illus.). 32p. (gr. 3-4). 1990. PLB 15.95 (*0-86505-485-1*); pap. 7.95 (*0-86505-505-X*) Crabtree Pub Co.
Kelly, Emery. Kites on the Wind: Easy-to-Make Kites that Fly Without Sticks. Hagerman, Jennifer, illus. 64p. (gr. 4 up). 1991. PLB 22.95 (*0-8225-2400-7*) Lerner Pubns.
King, Virginia. Hello, Puppet. Mancini, Rob, illus. LC 92-21392. 1993. 2.50 (*0-383-03572-4*) SRA Schl Grp.
Kingshead Corporation Staff. Cut, Color & Create: Make Your Own: Alphabet Blocks. Kingshead Corporation Staff, illus. 24p. (ps-3). 1987. pap. 2.97 (*1-55941-005-1*) Kingshead Corp.
—Cut, Color & Create: Make Your Own: Alphabet Friends. Kingshead Corporation Staff, illus. 24p. (ps-3). 1987. pap. 2.97 (*1-55941-003-5*) Kingshead Corp.
—Cut, Color & Create: Make Your Own: Beach. Kingshead Corporation Staff, illus. 24p. (ps-4). 1987. pap. 2.97 (*1-55941-011-6*) Kingshead Corp.
—Cut, Color & Create: Make Your Own: Christmas Cards. Kingshead Corporation Staff, illus. 24p. (gr. k-4). 1987. pap. 2.97 (*1-55941-021-3*) Kingshead Corp.
—Cut, Color & Create: Make Your Own: Christmas Garland. Kingshead Corporation Staff, illus. 24p. (ps-2). 1987. pap. 2.97 (*1-55941-020-5*) Kingshead Corp.
—Cut, Color & Create: Make Your Own: Circus. Kingshead Corporation Staff, illus. 24p. (ps-4). 1987. pap. 2.97 (*1-55941-008-6*) Kingshead Corp.
—Cut, Color & Create: Make Your Own: Christmas Ornaments. Kingshead Corporation Staff, illus. 24p. (gr. 2 up). 1987. pap. 2.97 (*1-55941-018-3*) Kingshead Corp.
—Cut, Color & Create: Make Your Own: Christmas Snowflakes. Kingshead Corporation Staff, illus. 24p. (gr. k-3). 1987. pap. 2.97 (*1-55941-017-5*) Kingshead Corp.
—Cut, Color & Create: Make Your Own: Christmas Snowflakes. Kingshead Corporation Staff, illus. 24p. (gr. 3 up). 1987. pap. 2.97 (*1-55941-019-1*) Kingshead Corp.
—Cut, Color & Create: Make Your Own: Doll's Christmas. Kingshead Corporation Staff, illus. 24p. 1987. pap. 2.97 (*1-55941-013-2*) Kingshead Corp.
—Cut-Color-&-Create: Make Your Own: Easter Fun. Kingshead Corporation Staff, illus. 24p. (ps-1). 1989. pap. 2.97 (*1-55941-022-1*) Kingshead Corp.

—Cut-Color-&-Create: Make Your Own: Easter Fun. Kingshead Corporation Staff, illus. 24p. (ps-1). 1989. pap. 2.97 (*1-55941-023-X*) Kingshead Corp.
—Cut-Color-&-Create: Make Your Own: Easter Fun. Kingshead Corporation Staff, illus. 24p. (ps-1). 1989. pap. 2.97 (*1-55941-024-8*) Kingshead Corp.
—Cut, Color & Create: Make Your Own: Easy Christmas Ornaments. Kingshead Corporation Staff, illus. 24p. (ps-2). 1987. pap. 2.97 (*1-55941-016-7*) Kingshead Corp.
—Cut, Color & Create: Make Your Own: Farm. Kingshead Corporation Staff, illus. 24p. (ps-4). 1987. pap. 2.97 (*1-55941-007-8*) Kingshead Corp.
—Cut, Color & Create: Make Your Own: Masks. Kingshead Corporation Staff, illus. 24p. (ps-4). 1988. pap. 2.97 (*0-685-22520-8*) Kingshead Corp.
—Cut, Color & Create: Make Your Own: Number People. Kingshead Corporation Staff, illus. 24p. (ps-3). 1987. pap. 2.97 (*1-55941-004-3*) Kingshead Corp.
—Cut, Color & Create: Make Your Own: Number Blocks. Kingshead Corporation Staff, illus. 24p. (ps-3). 1987. pap. 2.97 (*1-55941-006-X*) Kingshead Corp.
—Cut, Color & Create: Make Your Own: Places to Go. Kingshead Corporation Staff, illus. 24p. (ps-4). 1987. pap. 2.97 (*1-55941-012-4*) Kingshead Corp.
—Cut, Color & Create: Make Your Own: Paperplate Puppets. Kingshead Corporation Staff, illus. 24p. (ps-3). 1987. pap. 2.97 (*1-55941-002-7*) Kingshead Corp.
—Cut, Color & Create: Make Your Own: Paperbag Puppets. Kingshead Corporation Staff, illus. 24p. (ps-3). 1987. pap. 2.97 (*1-55941-001-9*) Kingshead Corp.
—Cut-Color-&-Create: Make Your Own: Pumpkin Magic. Kingshead Corporation Staff, illus. 24p. (ps-1). 1988. pap. 2.97 (*1-55941-037-X*) Kingshead Corp.
—Cut, Color & Create: Make Your Own: Safari. Kingshead Corporation Staff, illus. 24p. (ps-4). 1987. pap. 2.97 (*1-55941-010-8*) Kingshead Corp.
—Cut, Color & Create: Make Your Own: Valentine Fun. Kingshead Corporation Staff, illus. 24p. (gr. k-3). 1987. pap. 2.97 (*1-55941-015-9*) Kingshead Corp.
—Cut, Color & Create: Make Your Own: Valentines. Kingshead Corporation Staff, illus. 24p. (gr. k-3). 1987. pap. 2.97 (*1-55941-014-0*) Kingshead Corp.
—Cut, Color & Create: Make Your Own: Zoo. Kingshead Corporation Staff, illus. 24p. (ps-4). 1987. pap. 2.97 (*1-55941-009-4*) Kingshead Corp.
Kirkman, Will. Nature Crafts Workshop. LC 80-84186. (gr. 3-8). 1981. pap. 10.95 (*0-8224-9781-6*) Fearon Teach Aids.
Klein, Bill. A Kid's Guide to Finding Good Stuff. (Illus.). 64p. (Orig.). (gr. 4-9). 1994. pap. 10.95 (*0-943173-96-5*) Harbinger AZ.
Klimo, Joan F. What Can I Do Today? A Treasury of Crafts for Children. Klimo, Joan F., illus. LC 73-15110. 64p. (gr. k-3). 1974. pap. 2.95 (*0-394-82809-7*) Pantheon.
Kohl, MaryAnn F. Mudworks: Creative Clay, Dough, & Modeling Experiences. LC 88-92897. (Illus.). 152p. (Orig.). (ps-6). 1989. pap. 14.95 (*0-935607-02-1*) Bright Ring.
Lamancusa, Jim. Dynamite Crafts for Special Occasions. (gr. 4-7). 1993. pap. 12.95 (*0-8306-4272-2*) TAB Bks.
Lambert, David & Wright, Rachel. Dinosaurs. LC 91-21118. (Illus.). 32p. (gr. 4-6). 1992. PLB 11.90 (*0-531-14159-4*) Watts.
Lancaster, John. Art with Found Materials. LC 91-2875. (Illus.). 48p. (gr. 5-8). 1991. PLB 12.40 (*0-531-14204-3*) Watts.
Langcaon, Jeff. Where's Kimo? Langcaon, Jeff, illus. 24p. (gr. k-2). 1993. pap. 5.95 (*1-880188-65-1*) Bess Pr.
LaRose-Weaver, Diane & Cusick, Dawn. Fireside Christmas: Celebrate the Holidays with More Than 120 Festive Projects to Make. LC 92-37316. (Illus.). 160p. (gr. 8 up). 1992. 26.95 (*0-8069-8378-7*, Pub. by Lark Bks) Sterling.
Leeuwen, M. & Moeskops, J. The Nature Corner: Celebrating the Year's Cycle with a Seasonal Tableau. Lawson, Polly, tr. (DUT., Illus.). 88p. (ps-3). 1990. pap. 12.95 (*0-86315-111-6*, Pub. by Floris Bks UK) Gryphon Hse.
Lehne, Judith L. The Never-Be-Bored Book: Quick Things to Make When There's Nothing to Do. Lipstein, Morissa G., illus. LC 92-16529. 128p. 1992. 17.95 (*0-8069-1254-5*) Sterling.
Lemke, Stefan & Pricken, Marie-Luise L. Making Toys & Gifts. LC 91-3880. (Illus.). 64p. 1991. PLB 15.40 (*0-516-09259-6*); pap. 8.95 (*0-516-49259-4*) Childrens.
Lipson, Michelle, et al. The Fantastic Costume Book: Forty Complete Patterns to Amaze & Amuse. LC 92-11365. (Illus.). 128p. (gr. 4 up). 1992. 19.95 (*0-8069-8376-0*) Sterling.
Lohf, Sabine. Christmas Crafts. LC 89-22255. 64p. 1989. lib. bdg. 15.40 (*0-516-09252-9*); pap. 8.95 (*0-516-49252-7*) Childrens.
—I Made It Myself. LC 89-22252. 64p. 1989. lib. bdg. 15.40 (*0-516-09254-5*); pap. 8.95 (*0-516-49254-3*) Childrens.
—Nature Crafts. LC 89-49552. (Illus.). 64p. 1990. pap. 8.95 (*0-516-49257-8*) Childrens.
—Things I Can Make. LC 93-40881. (ps-3). 1994. 12.95 (*0-8118-0667-7*) Chronicle Bks.
—Things I Can Make with Buttons. (Illus.). 32p. (ps-3). 1990. 6.95 (*0-87701-687-9*) Chronicle Bks.
—Things I Can Make with Cloth. (Illus.). 28p. (ps-3). 1989. 6.95 (*0-87701-666-6*) Chronicle Bks.
—Things I Can Make with Cork. (Illus.). 32p. (ps-3). 1990. 6.95 (*0-87701-726-3*) Chronicle Bks.
—Things I Can Make with Stones. (Illus.). 32p. (ps-2). 1990. 6.95 (*0-87701-769-7*) Chronicle Bks.
Lohf, Sabine & Schael, Hannelore. Making Things with Yarn. LC 89-22256. 64p. (gr. 2 up). 1989. pap. 8.95 (*0-516-49255-1*) Childrens.
Lye, Keith. Passport to Germany. LC 93-26680. (Illus.). 48p. (gr. 7 up). 1994. 13.90 (*0-531-14296-5*) Watts.
Lynn, Sara. I Can Make It! Dress Up. (ps-3). 1994. pap. 4.99 (*0-553-37260-2*) Bantam.
McClure, Nancee. Creative Egg Carton Crafts. McClure, Nancee, illus. 64p. (ps-2). 1989. wkbk. 8.95 (*0-86653-471-7*, GA1077) Good Apple.
McCoy, Sharon. Fifty Nifty Friendship Bracelets, Rings & Other Things. Olexiewicz, Charlene, illus. 64p. (gr. 3-7). 1994. pap. 4.95 (*1-56565-130-8*) Lowell Hse.
McDonnell, Janet. Two Special Valentines. McCallum, Jodie, illus. LC 93-37097. 32p. (ps-2). 1994. PLB 12.30 (*0-516-00692-4*) Childrens.
McGuire, Kevin. Woodworking for Kids: Forty Fabulous, Fun, & Useful Things for Kids to Make. LC 93-20489. (Illus.). 160p. (gr. 4 up). 1993. 19.95 (*0-8069-0429-1*, Pub. by Lark Bks) Sterling.
MacKenzie, Joy. The Big Book of Bible Crafts & Projects. Flint, Russ, illus. 212p. (Orig.). (ps-4). 1981. pap. 15.99 (*0-310-70151-1*, 14019P) Zondervan.
McKinnon, Elizabeth. Play & Learn with Rubber Stamps. Warren, Jean, ed. Mohrmann, Gary, illus. LC 93-61083. 64p. (Orig.). 1994. pap. text ed. 7.95 (*0-911019-93-6*) Warren Pub Hse.
McMillan, Mary. Christian Crafts from Hand-Shaped Art. 64p. (ps-5). 1991. 8.95 (*0-86653-629-9*, SS1886, Shining Star Pubns) Good Apple.
McOmber, Rachel B., ed. McOmber Phonics Storybooks: You Can Make It. rev. ed. (Illus.). write for info. (*0-944991-51-3*) Swift Lrn Res.
Making Gifts. LC 91-17042. (Illus.). 48p. (gr. 4-8). 1991. PLB 14.95 (*1-85435-408-6*) Marshall Cavendish.
Making Models & Games. LC 91-17039. (Illus.). 48p. (gr. 4-8). 1991. PLB 14.95 (*1-85435-409-4*) Marshall Cavendish.
Malone, Maggie. Christmas Scrapcrafts. (Illus.). 136p. (gr. 5-10). 1992. pap. 12.95 (*0-8069-6805-2*) Sterling.
Marchon-Arnaud, Catherine. A Gallery of Games. Schwartz, Marc, photos by. Collomb, Etienne. LC 93-25053. (Illus.). 60p. (gr. 3 up). 1994. 12.95 (*0-395-68379-3*) Ticknor & Flds Bks Yng Read.
Mason, Kate. Make Your Own Cool Crafts. (gr. 4-7). 1994. pap. 5.95 (*0-8167-3226-4*) Troll Assocs.
Meredith Corporation-Better Homes & Gardens Staff. At the Circus. (Illus.). 32p. (ps-12). 1991. PLB 10.95 (*1-878363-57-3*) Forest Hse.
—Let's Go Exploring. (Illus.). 32p. (ps-12). 1991. PLB 10.95 (*1-878363-58-1*) Forest Hse.
—Trains & Railroads. (Illus.). 32p. (ps-12). 1991. PLB 10.95 (*1-878363-59-X*) Forest Hse.
—Water Wonders. (Illus.). 32p. (ps-12). 1991. PLB 10.95 (*1-878363-60-3*) Forest Hse.
Michalski, Ute & Michalski, Tilman. Wind Crafts. LC 89-49553. (Illus.). 64p. 1990. 15.40 (*0-516-09258-8*); pap. 8.95 (*0-516-49258-6*) Childrens.
Mighty Morphin Power Rangers. (Illus.). 32p. (gr. k-4). 1994. pap. write for info. (*1-56144-456-1*, Honey Bear Bks) Modern Pub NYC.
Mighty Morphin Power Rangers. (Illus.). 32p. (gr. k-4). 1994. pap. write for info. (*1-56144-457-X*, Honey Bears Bks) Modern Pub NYC.
Mighty Morphin Power Rangers. (Illus.). 32p. (gr. k-4). 1994. pap. write for info. (*1-56144-458-8*, Honey Bear Bks) Modern Pub NYC.
Mighty Morphin Power Rangers. (Illus.). 32p. (gr. k-4). 1994. pap. write for info. (*1-56144-459-6*, Honey Bear Bks) Modern Pub NYC.
Mighty Morphin Power Rangers. (Illus.). 144p. (gr. k-4). 1994. pap. 4.95 (*1-56144-460-X*, Honey Bear Bks) Modern Pub NYC.
Mighty Morphin Power Rangers. (Illus.). 144p. (gr. k-4). 1994. pap. 4.95 (*1-56144-461-8*, Honey Bear Bks) Modern Pub NYC.
Mighty Morphin Power Rangers. (Illus.). 80p. (gr. k-2). 1994. pap. 2.95 (*1-56144-464-2*, Honey Bear Bks) Modern Pub NYC.
Mighty Morphin Power Rangers. (Illus.). 80p. (gr. k-2). 1994. pap. 2.95 (*1-56144-465-0*, Honey Bear Bks) Modern Pub NYC.
Mighty Morphin Power Rangers: Activity Book. (Illus.). 64p. (gr. k-4). 1994. pap. 2.95 (*1-56144-462-6*, Honey Bear Bks) Modern Pub NYC.
Milord, Susan. Tales Alive! Ten Multicultural Folk Tales, with Art, Craft & Creative Experiences. Donato, Michael, illus. 128p. (Orig.). (gr. k-6). 1994. pap. 15.95 (*0-913589-79-9*) Williamson Pub Co.
Mock, Dorothy. One Big Family: The Good News Kids Learn about Kindness. Mitter, Kathy, illus. LC 92-27012. 32p. (Orig.). (ps-2). 1993. pap. 3.99 (*0-570-04737-4*) Concordia.
Monroe, Lucy. Fifty Nifty Ways to Paint Your Face. Nolte, Larry, illus. LC 92-549. 1992. pap. 3.95 (*1-56565-029-8*) Lowell Hse.
Morris, Eileen. Crafts Kids Can Eat, Play with, or Wear. (gr. k-3). 1991. pap. 11.95 (*0-86653-979-4*) Fearon Teach Aids.
Morris, Ting & Morris, Neil. Animals. LC 93-20415. (Illus.). 32p. (gr. 2-4). 1993. PLB 12.40 (*0-531-14268-X*) Watts.
—Dinosaurs. LC 92-32915. 1993. 12.40 (*0-531-14258-2*) Watts.
—Masks. LC 92-32916. 1993. 12.40 (*0-531-14259-0*) Watts.
—Music. LC 93-20424. (Illus.). 32p. (gr. 2-4). 1993. PLB 12.40 (*0-531-14269-8*) Watts.
—Rain Forest. LC 93-26686. (Illus.). 32p. (gr. 2-4). 1994. PLB 12.40 (*0-531-14281-7*) Watts.
—Space. Levy, Ruth, illus. LC 93-24435. 32p. (gr. 2-4). 1994. PLB 12.90 (*0-531-14282-5*) Watts.
Moxley, Susan. Play with Papier-Mache. LC 94-14247. (gr. 1 up). 1994. write for info. (*0-87614-865-8*) Carolrhoda Bks.
Murphy, Corinne. Exploring the Hand Arts: For Juniors, Cadettes, Seniors, & Leaders. 112p. (gr. 4-12). 1955. pap. 5.00 (*0-88441-140-0*, 19-994) Girl Scouts USA.
Murray, Anna. My Christmas Craft Book. 1993. 9.99 (*0-307-16750-X*) Western Pub.
Murray, Beth. Gifts Children Can Make: Creative Presents for Family & Friends. Matsick, Anni, illus. LC 93-73301. 32p. (ps-5). 1994. 4.95 (*1-56397-324-3*); prepack 14.95 (*1-56397-397-9*) Boyds Mills Pr.
Murray, Beth, ed. Animal Craft Fun: Indoor & Outdoor Activities & Projects. LeHew, Ron, illus. 32p. (gr. k-5). 1994. pap. 3.95 (*1-56397-314-6*) Boyds Mills Pr.
National Wildlife Federation Staff. Wild & Crafty. (gr. k-8). 1991. pap. 7.95 (*0-945051-46-8*, 75043) Natl Wildlife.
Nature Crafts for Kids Book & Kit. (gr. 4-7). 1992. 40.00 (*0-8069-5699-2*) Sterling.
Newsome, Arden. Cork & Wood Crafts. Coner, Nancy, illus. LC 72-112370. 64p. (gr. k-3). 1971. PLB 12.95 (*0-87460-229-7*) Lion Bks.
Nowlin, Susan S. Fall Time Savers. Spence, Paula, et al, illus. 48p. (gr. k-6). 1989. wkbk. 6.95 (*1-55734-123-0*) Tchr Create Mat.
—Spring Time Savers. Spence, Paula, et al, illus. 48p. (gr. k-6). 1989. wkbk. 6.95 (*1-55734-125-7*) Tchr Create Mat.
—Winter Time Savers. Spence, Paula, et al, illus. 48p. (gr. k-6). 1989. wkbk. 6.95 (*1-55734-124-9*) Tchr Create Mat.
—Year-Round Open Worksheets. Spence, Paula, et al, illus. 48p. (gr. k-6). 1989. wkbk. 6.95 (*1-55734-126-5*) Tchr Create Mat.
O'Hare, Jeff. Hanukkah, Happy Hanukkah: Crafts, Recipes, Games, Puzzles, Songs, & More for the Joyous... Friedman, Arthur, illus. LC 93-73302. 32p. (ps-5). 1994. 4.95 (*1-56397-369-3*); 14.85 (*1-56397-396-0*) Boyds Mills Pr.
O'Neal, Debbie T. Easter Is Coming: Thirteen Fun Things to Make. (Illus.). 20p. (Orig.). (ps). 1993. pap. 6.99 (*0-8010-6759-6*) Baker Bk.
O'Reilly, Susie. Batik & Tie-Dye. LC 92-43264. 32p. (gr. 4-6). 1993. 14.95 (*1-56847-064-9*) Thomson Lrning.
Orr, Anne. Tatting with Anne Orr. 1989. pap. 2.50 (*0-486-25982-X*) Dover.
Overstreet, Charles. Indian & Mountain Man Crafts: Cuttin' & Stitchin' Smith, Monte, ed. Overstreet, Charles, illus. 106p. (Orig.). (gr. 8-12). 1994. pap. 10.95 perfect bdg. (*0-943604-41-9*) Eagles View.
Parkinson, Eric. Teaching Techniques. rev. ed. Doyle, Connie, ed. (Illus.). 45p. (gr. 3-6). Repr. 19.95 (*1-884461-05-0*) NES Arnold.
Party Wraps for Kids: Children's Gift Wraps. 1989. 9.99 (*0-517-68533-7*) Random Hse Value.
Peacock, Graham & Smith, Robin. Pulley Activities. rev. ed. Doyle, Connie, ed. (Illus.). 29p. (gr. 3-6). Repr. 11.95 (*1-884461-08-5*) NES Arnold.
Peak, Jan & Hennig, Anna. Trash to Treasure Crafts: From Recyclable Materials. Peak, Jan, illus. 80p. (gr. 3 up). 1992. wkbk. 8.99 (*0-87403-890-1*, 14-02146) Standard Pub.
Peaslee, Ann & Kille, Jullien. You Can Make It! You Can Do It! 101 E-Z Holiday Craft-Tivities for Children. Ball, Dave, illus. 120p. (Orig.). (gr. 3-6). 1991. pap. 9.95 (*0-89346-337-X*) Heian Intl.
Pelton, Jeanette & Pelton, Fawn. Crafts for a Long, Boring, What-Do-I-Do-Now Afternoon. Pelton, Dan, ed. (Illus.). 50p. (Orig.). (gr. 4-7). 1993. pap. 4.00 (*1-879564-04-1*) Long Acre Pub.

Pfiffner, George. Earth-Friendly Toys: How to Make Fabulous Toys & Games from Reusable Objects. (Illus.). 128p. (gr. 3-7). 1994. pap. text ed. 12.95 (*0-471-00822-2*) Wiley.
These days earth-savvy kids know the value of recycling. They're using old scraps of paper cardboard & foil to make their own erector sets. Or setting up a miniature space station for their action figures using old plastic bottles. Or maybe they're flying a sea plane made of discarded styrofoam. These are just a few of the imaginative toys you'll find in the first title of the exciting Earth-Friendly Series. Includes step-by-step instructions for creating 30 toys, including costumes, dolls, musical instruments, & much more. Lists interesting facts about recycling & other things kids can do to help clean

up the planet. Illustrated with over 200 line drawings. Other Earth-Friendly Books coming soon! Earth-Friendly Fashion (Fall 1994), Earth-Friendly Outdoor Fun (Spring 1995), & Earth-Friendly Holidays (Fall 1995). *Publisher Provided Annotation.*

—Earth-Friendly Wearables: How to Make Fabulous Clothes & Accessories from Reusable Objects. Date not set. pap. text ed. 12.95 (*0-471-00823-0*) Wiley.
Potter, Beatrix, illus. The Peter Rabbit Make-&-Play Book. 32p. (ps-5). 1992. pap. 6.99 (*0-7232-3991-6*) Warne.
Purves, Pamela. Decorating Eggs: In the Style of Faberge. Dace, Rosalind, ed. Search Press Studios Staff, illus. 96p. (Orig.). 1989. pap. 16.95 (*0-85532-644-1*, Pub. by Search Pr UK) A Schwartz & Co.
Randall, Ronne. Thanksgiving Fun: Great Things to Make & Do. Spenceley, Annabel, illus. LC 93-48615. 32p. (gr. 3-7). 1994. pap. 4.95 (*1-85697-500-2*, Kingfisher LKC) LKC.
Ransford, Lynn & Robinson, Phyllis. ABC Crafts & Cooking. (Illus.). 64p. (ps-2). 1987. wkbk. 7.95 (*1-55734-090-0*) Tchr Create Mat.
Robins, Deri. Papier Mache. LC 92-41102. (Illus.). 40p. (gr. 3-7). 1993. 10.95 (*1-85697-927-X*, Kingfisher LKC); pap. 5.95 (*1-85697-926-1*) LKC.
Robins, Deri & Buchanan, George. Santa's Sackful of Best Christmas Ideas. LC 92-41103. 32p. (gr. 2-6). 1993. pap. 5.95 (*1-85697-919-9*, Kingfisher LKC) LKC.
Robins, Deri & Stowell, Charlotte. Making Books. Robins, Jim, illus. LC 93-48560. 1994. PLB 10.95 (*1-85697-517-7*, Kingfisher LKC); pap. 5.95 (*1-85697-518-5*) LKC.
Robins, Deri, et al. The Kids Can Do It Book: Fun Things to Make and Do. Stowell, Charlotte, illus. LC 92-43345. 80p. (gr. k-4). 1993. pap. 9.95 (*1-85697-860-5*, Kingfisher LKC) LKC.
Robson, Denny A. Christmas: Activities & Projects. LC 92-3214. 1992. 11.90 (*0-531-17333-X*, Gloucester Pr) Watts.
—Jewelry: Arts & Crafts. LC 93-4835. (Illus.). 32p. (gr. 3-5). 1993. PLB 11.90 (*0-531-17427-1*, Gloucester Pr) Watts.
—Kites & Flying Objects. LC 91-75995. (Illus.). 32p. (gr. 2-4). 1992. PLB 11.90 (*0-531-17342-9*, Gloucester Pr) Watts.
—Paper Craft: Arts & Crafts. LC 93-8580. (Illus.). 32p. 1993. PLB 11.90 (*0-531-17428-X*, Gloucester Pr) Watts.
Rock, Lois. Simply Wonderful Craftbook. (Illus.). 48p. (gr. 3-6). 1993. 13.95 (*0-7459-2503-0*) Lion USA.
Rockwell, Harlow. I Did It. Rockwell, Harlow, illus. LC 86-22146. 64p. (gr. 1-3). 1987. pap. 3.95 (*0-689-71126-3*, Aladdin) Macmillan Child Grp.
—Look at This. Rockwell, Harlow, illus. LC 87-1033. 64p. (gr. 1-4). 1987. pap. 3.95 (*0-689-71165-4*, Aladdin) Macmillan Child Grp.
Rogler, Ingrid. Small Folk Quilters. Moss, Pamela, ed. Cordoba, Liglia, illus. 68p. (gr. 3-10). 1989. pap. text ed. 9.95 (*0-9622565-0-1*) Chitra Pubns.
Ross, Kathy. Crafts for Earth Day. Holm, Sharon L., illus. LC 94-9835. 1995. lib. bdg. write for info. (*1-56294-490-8*) Millbrook Pr.
—Crafts for Halloween. Holm, Sharon L., illus. LC 93-37249. 48p. (gr. k-3). 1994. 15.40 (*1-56294-411-8*); pap. 6.95 (*1-56294-741-9*) Millbrook Pr.
—Crafts for Kwanzaa. Holm, Sharon L., illus. LC 93-36690. 48p. (gr. k-3). 1994. 15.40 (*1-56294-412-6*); pap. 6.95 (*1-56294-740-0*) Millbrook Pr.
—Crafts for Valentine's Day. Holm, Sharon L., illus. LC 94-9834. 1995. lib. bdg. write for info. (*1-56294-489-4*) Millbrook Pr.
Roussel, Mike. Scrap Materials. (Illus.). 32p. (gr. 2-6). 1990. lib. bdg. 15.94 (*0-86592-487-2*); 11.95s.p. (*0-685-36305-8*) Rourke Corp.
Roussel, Mike, et al. Craft Projects, 6 bks. (Illus.). 192p. (gr. 2-6). 1990. Set. lib. bdg. 95.64 (*0-86592-482-1*); Set. lib. bdg. 71.70s.p. (*0-685-36300-7*) Rourke Corp.
Ruelle, Karen G. Seventy-Five Fun Things to Make & Do by Yourself. Haight, Sandy, illus. LC 93-5091. 80p. (gr. 2-10). 1993. 14.95 (*0-8069-0331-7*) Sterling.
Salts, Bobbi. Southwestern American Indian Discovery. Parker, Steve, illus. (gr. 2-8). 1991. pap. 3.95 (*0-929526-11-2*) Double B Pubns.
Sams, Kenneth. Flying Toys. (Illus.). (gr. 9-12). 1992. pap. 7.95 (*1-86351-038-9*, Pub. by S Milner AT) Sterling.
Sand Sculptures, Unit 11. (gr. 3). 1991. 7.45 (*0-88106-784-9*) Charlesbridge Pub.
Sand Sculptures Activity Book, Unit 11. (gr. 3). 1991. 3.90 (*0-88106-787-3*) Charlesbridge Pub.
Sand Sculptures Activity Book (EV, Unit 11. (gr. 3). 1991. 3.90 (*0-88106-786-5*) Charlesbridge Pub.
Sattler, Helen R. Recipes for Art & Craft Materials. rev. ed. Shohet, Marti, illus. LC 86-34271. 128p. (gr. 6 up). 1987. 14.00 (*0-688-07374-3*) Lothrop.
—Recipes for Art & Craft Materials. Shohet, Marti, illus. LC 93-26182. 144p. (gr. 5 up). 1994. pap. 4.95 (*0-688-13199-9*, Pub. by Beech Tree Bks) Morrow.
Schwartz, Linda. Build a Doodle Kit. (gr. k-4). 1990. pap. 10.95 (*0-88160-198-5*, LW152) Learning Wks.
Sea Castles Activity Book, Unit 9. (gr. 3). 1991. 3.90 (*0-88106-772-5*) Charlesbridge Pub.
Self, Margaret, ed. One Hundred Fifty-Eight Things to Make. LC 70-121625. (Orig.). (gr. 1-6). 1971. pap. 4.99 (*0-8307-0078-1*, 5002605) Regal.
Senterfitt, Marilyn. Christian Crafts with Egg Cartons. 64p. (ps-5). 1991. 8.95 (*0-86653-574-8*, SS1882, Shining Star Pubns) Good Apple.
Shaw, Sheila. Kaleidometrics: The Art of Making Beautiful Patterns from Circles. (Illus.). 32p. (gr. 5-9). 1986. pap. 7.50 (*0-906212-21-9*, Pub. by Tarquin UK) Parkwest Pubns.
Sinclair, Ellsworth Ed. Moods in Wire, Vol. 1: A Comprehensive Guide to the Fine Art of Wirewrapping. LC 94-7460. 112p. (gr. 9-12). 1994. pap. text ed. 24.95 (*0-9640483-0-2*) Orig Ellsworth.
Smith, A. G. Easy to Make Periscope. 1990. pap. 3.95 (*0-486-26426-2*) Dover.
—Easy to Make Pinwheels. 1990. pap. 2.95 (*0-486-26435-1*) Dover.
Sohi, Morteza E. Look What I Did with a Leaf. Sohi, Morteza E., illus. LC 92-35142. 32p. (gr. 4-8). 1993. 14.95 (*0-8027-8215-9*); PLB 15.85 (*0-8027-8216-7*) Walker & Co.
Solga, Kim. Make Clothes Fun! (Illus.). 48p. (gr. 1-6). 1992. 11.95 (*0-89134-421-7*, 30377) North Light Bks.
—Make Crafts! (Illus.). 48p. (ps). 1993. 11.95 (*0-89134-493-4*, 30525) North Light Bks.
—Make Sculptures! (Illus.). 48p. (gr. 1-6). 1992. 11.95 (*0-89134-420-9*, 30378) North Light Bks.
Somerville, L. & Gibson, R. How to Make Pop-Ups. (Illus.). 32p. (gr. 3-7). 1991. lib. bdg. 12.96 (*0-88110-627-5*, Usborne); pap. 5.95 (*0-7460-1273-X*, Usborne) EDC.
Steele, Philip. Collage. LC 92-42678. 40p. (gr. 3-7). 1993. 10.95 (*1-85697-921-0*, Kingfisher LKC); pap. 5.95 (*1-85697-920-2*) LKC.
Stevenson, Peter. Play Mask Book - Goldilocks & the Three Bears. 12p. (ps-3). 1991. pap. 5.95 (*0-8167-2372-9*) Troll Assocs.
Stohl, Anita. Christian Crafts Yarn Art. (Illus.). 64p. (ps-5). 1992. 8.95 (*0-86653-701-5*, SS2831, Shining Star Pubns) Good Apple.
Stuart, Sally E. & Young, Woody C. One Hundred Plus Craft & Gift Ideas: Fun & Easy Ideas for Any Occasion. White, Craig, illus. 96p. (Orig.). (gr. 1 up). 1990. pap. 9.95 (*0-939513-62-5*) Joy Pub SJC.
Suid, Anna. Holiday Crafts. 64p. (gr. k-2). 1985. 6.95 (*0-912107-31-6*) Monday Morning Bks.
Suid, Murray. Writing Hangups. 64p. (gr. 2-6). 1988. 6.95 (*0-912107-73-1*, MM980) Monday Morning Bks.
Sullivan, Dianna J. Paper Bag Art Projects. Adkins, Lynda, illus. 32p. (gr. 1-4). 1988. wkbk. 5.95 (*1-55734-100-1*) Tchr Create Mat.
—Paper Plate Art Projects. Adkins, Lynda, illus. 32p. (gr. 1-4). 1988. wkbk. 5.95 (*1-55734-101-X*) Tchr Create Mat.
Sullivan, S. Adams. Bats, Butterflies, & Bugs, Vol. 1. (ps-3). 1990. 14.95 (*0-316-82185-3*, Joy St Bks) Little.
Super Wraps for Kids: Children's Gift Wraps. 1989. 9.99 (*0-517-68532-9*) Random Hse Value.
Supraner, Robyn. Rainy Day Surprises You Can Make. LC 80-19858. (Illus.). 48p. (gr. 1-5). 1981. PLB 11.89 (*0-89375-428-5*); pap. 3.50 (*0-89375-429-3*) Troll Assocs.
Tabibian, Ina. Fearon's Refrigerator Display Rewards. (ps-1). 1989. pap. 6.95 (*0-8224-3152-1*) Fearon Teach Aids.
Tames, Richard & Tames, Sheila. Great Britain. LC 93-49724. 1994. write for info. (*0-531-14313-9*) Watts.
Terzian, Alexandra. The Kids' Multicultural Art Book: Art & Craft Experiences from Around the World. Trezzo-Braren Studio Staff, illus. 160p. (Orig.). (ps-6). 1993. pap. 12.95 (*0-913589-72-1*) Williamson Pub Co.
Things to Make: Arabic. (Illus.). (gr. 5-12). 1987. 3.95x (*0-86685-238-7*) Intl Bk Ctr.
Thomas, Meredith. Paper Shapes. Thomas, Meredith, illus. LC 93-27994. 1994. 4.25 (*0-383-03767-0*) SRA Schl Grp.
Thomson, Ruth. Collage. LC 94-12305. (Illus.). 24p. (ps-3). 1994. PLB 14.40 (*0-516-07988-3*); pap. 4.95 (*0-516-47988-1*) Childrens.
—Indians of the Plains. LC 90-46264. (Illus.). 32p. (gr. 4-6). 1991. PLB 11.90 (*0-531-14157-8*) Watts.
—Printing. LC 94-16913. (Illus.). 24p. (ps-3). 1994. PLB 14.40 (*0-516-07992-1*); pap. 4.95 (*0-516-47992-X*) Childrens.
—Spring. 1990. PLB 11.90 (*0-531-14018-0*) Watts.
—Summer. LC 89-36561. 1990. PLB 11.90 (*0-531-14019-9*) Watts.
Thumbelina. (Illus.). 32p. (gr. k-2). 1994. pap. 1.29 (*1-56144-283-6*, Honey Bear Bks) Modern Pub NYC.
Thumbelina. (Illus.). 32p. (gr. k-2). 1994. pap. 1.29 (*1-56144-284-4*, Honey Bear Bks) Modern Pub NYC.
Thumbelina. (Illus.). 32p. (gr. k-2). 1994. pap. 1.29 (*1-56144-285-2*, Honey Bear Bks) Modern Pub NYC.
Thumbelina. (Illus.). 32p. (gr. k-2). 1994. pap. 1.29 (*1-56144-286-0*, Honey Bear Bks) Modern Pub NYC.
Tofts, Hannah. Do-It-Yourself. LC 93-21218. (Illus.). 48p. (gr. 5-9). 1994. 16.95 (*1-56847-147-5*) Thomson Lrning.
Ullom, A. Thomas. Come Aboard Boats: Ship-Shape 3-D Activities. Art In-Forms Staff, ed. Ullom, A. Thomas, illus. 20p. (Orig.). 1983. pap. 8.95 wkbk. (*0-911835-00-8*) Art In-Forms.
Umnik, Sharon D., ed. One Hundred Seventy-Five Easy-to-Do Easter Crafts: Easy-to-Do Projects with Easy-to-Do Things. Cary, C., photos by. (Illus.). 64p. (gr. k-5). 1994. pap. 6.95 (*1-56397-316-2*) Boyds Mills Pr.
Using Paper & Paint. LC 91-17038. (Illus.). 48p. (gr. 4-8). 1991. PLB 14.95 (*1-85435-406-X*) Marshall Cavendish.
Using Yarn, Fabric & Thread. LC 91-17034. (Illus.). 48p. (gr. 4-8). 1991. PLB 14.95 (*1-85435-405-1*) Marshall Cavendish.
Van Blaricom, Colleen, ed. Christmas Crafts: Merry Things to Make. Louise, Anita, illus. 32p. (Orig.). (ps-5). 1993. pap. 3.95 (*1-56397-083-X*) Boyds Mills Pr.
—Crafts from Recyclables: Great Ideas from Throwaways. LeHew, Ron, illus. LC 91-72872. 48p. (gr. 1-5). 1992. pap. 4.95 (*1-56397-015-5*) Boyds Mills Pr.
—Easter Crafts. Riggio, Anita, illus. LC 91-72873. 32p. (ps-3). 1992. pap. 3.95 (*1-56397-014-7*) Boyds Mills Pr.
—Halloween Craft Book: Spooky & Fun Things to Make. Palan, R. Michael, illus. 32p. (gr. 2-5). 1992. pap. 3.95 (*1-56397-119-4*) Boyds Mills Pr.
Victor Vampire's Cut-Out Mask Book. (Illus.). 24p. (Orig.). (ps-k). 1991. pap. 3.95 (*0-8249-8348-3*, Ideals Child) Hambleton-Hill.
Volpe, Nancee. Good Apple & Seasonal Arts & Crafts. 144p. (gr. 3-7). 1982. 12.95 (*0-86653-087-8*, GA 438) Good Apple.
Vonk, Idalee W. Fifty-Two Elementary Patterns. Karch, Pat, illus. 48p. (Orig.). (gr. 1-6). 1979. pap. 6.99 (*0-87239-340-2*, 3366) Standard Pub.
Wallace, Mary. How to Make Great Stuff for Your Room. Wallace, Mary, illus. 88p. 1992. pap. 8.95 (*0-920775-85-3*, Pub. by Greey de Pencier CN) Firefly Bks Ltd.
Walter, F. Virginia. Great Newspaper Crafts. LC 90-20731. 80p. (gr. 4 up). 1993. pap. 9.95 (*0-920534-79-1*, Pub. by Tamos Bks CN) Sterling.
Waltner, Willard & Waltner, Elma. Hobbycraft for Juniors. (Illus.). (gr. 2-10). 7.95 (*0-8313-0096-5*) Lantern.
—New Look at Old Crafts. LC 70-143700. (Illus.). 142p. (gr. 9 up). 1971. 7.19 (*0-8313-0098-1*) Lantern.
Walton, Sally & Walton, Stewart. Stencil It! Over One Hundred Step-by-Step Projects. LC 92-36177. (Illus.). 80p. (gr. 4-10). 1993. 14.95 (*0-8069-0346-5*) Sterling.
Walton, Stewart & Walton, Sally. Wild Animal Paperchains. (Illus.). 32p. (gr. 3 up). 1993. pap. 6.95 (*0-688-12608-1*, Pub. by Beech Tree Bks) Morrow.
Warren, Jean. Crafts. 80p. (gr. k-2). 1983. 7.95 (*0-912107-04-9*) Monday Morning Bks.
—Huff & Puff Around the World: A Totline Teaching Tale. Cubley, Kathleen, ed. Piper, Molly & Ekberg, Marion, illus. LC 93-5490. 32p. (Orig.). (ps-2). 1994. 12.95 (*0-911019-81-2*); pap. 5.95 (*0-911019-80-4*) Warren Pub Hse.
—Huff & Puff on Thanksgiving: A Totline Teaching Tale. Cubley, Kathleen, ed. Piper, Molly & Ekberg, Marion, illus. LC 93-13545. 32p. (Orig.). (ps-2). 1993. 12.95 (*0-911019-70-7*); pap. 5.95 (*0-911019-71-5*) Warren Pub Hse.
—Huff & Puff's Foggy Christmas: A Totline Teaching Tale. Cubley, Kathleen, ed. Piper, Molly & Ekberg, Jean, illus. LC 93-38780. 32p. (Orig.). (ps-2). 1994. 12.95 (*0-911019-97-9*); pap. text ed. 5.95 (*0-911019-96-0*) Warren Pub Hse.
Watermill Press Staff. Make It with Balloons. (gr. 4-7). 1992. pap. 5.95 (*0-8167-2849-6*, Pub. by Watermill Pr) Troll Assocs.
Wegrzecki, Lester L. Christmas Decoration: Eggshell-Wydmuszki. Chrypinski, Anna, intro. by. (Illus., Orig.). (gr. 4 up). 1987. pap. write for info. (*0-9620774-0-2*) L L Wegrzecki.
Weiss, Andrea. Hanukkah Fun: Crafts & Games. Rhinelander, Mary F., illus. 32p. (gr. k-5). 1992. pap. 4.95 (*1-56397-059-7*) Boyds Mills Pr.
Wilkes, A. & Rosen, C. Simple Things to Make & Do. (Illus.). 72p. (gr. 2-6). 1986. pap. 8.95 (*0-7460-0549-0*, Usborne) EDC.
Willis, Abigail. Halloween Fun: Great Things to Make & Do. Spenceley, Annabel, illus. LC 93-21712. 32p. (gr. 2-6). 1993. pap. 4.95 (*1-85697-864-8*, Kingfisher LKC) LKC.
Wiseman, Ann. Making Things: The Hand Book of Creative Discovery. Wiseman, Ann, illus. 192p. (gr. 4 up). 1973. pap. 14.95 (*0-316-94849-7*) Little.
Wrap It up for Kids. (Illus.). 64p. 1992. pap. 10.00 (*0-688-11209-9*) Hearst Bks.
Wright, Rachel. Egyptians. LC 92-7840. (Illus.). 32p. (gr. 4-6). 1993. PLB 11.90 (*0-531-14209-4*) Watts.
—Knights. LC 91-20063. (Illus.). 32p. (gr. 4-6). 1992. PLB 11.90 (*0-531-14163-2*) Watts.
—Pirates. LC 90-46110. (Illus.). 32p. (gr. 4-6). 1991. PLB 11.90 (*0-531-14156-X*) Watts.
—Vikings. LC 92-4618. (Illus.). 32p. (gr. 5-8). 1993. PLB 11.90 (*0-531-14210-8*) Watts.
Yawger, Kathleen S. Bible Story Crafts. 96p. (ps-5). 1991. 10.95 (*0-86653-637-X*, SS1895, Shining Star Pubns) Good Apple.
Zweifel, Frances. The Make-Something Club: Fun with Crafts, Food & Gifts. Schweninger, Ann, illus. LC 93-2393. 32p. (ps-3). 1994. 13.99 (*0-670-82361-9*) Viking Child Bks.
—The Make-Something Club: Fun with Crafts, Food & Gifts. Schweninger, Ann, illus. 32p. (ps-3). 1994. pap. 4.99 (*0-14-050741-8*) Puffin Bks.

HANDWRITING
see Writing

HANGING
see Capital Punishment

HANUKKAH (FEAST OF LIGHTS)

Adler, David A. Hanukkah Fun Book: Puzzles, Riddles, Magic & More. LC 76-47459. (Illus.). (gr. 3-7). 1976. pap. 3.95 (*0-88482-754-2*, Bonim Bks) Hebrew Pub.

—Hanukkah Game Book: Games, Riddles, Puzzles & More. (Illus.). (gr. 1-5). 1978. pap. 3.95 (*0-88482-764-X*, Bonim Bks) Hebrew Pub.

—A Picture Book of Hanukkah. Heller, Linda, illus. LC 82-2942. 32p. (ps-3). 1982. pap. 5.95 (*0-8234-0574-5*) Holiday.

Backman, Aidel. One Night, One Hanukkah Night. (Illus.). 32p. (ps-2). 1990. 14.95 (*0-8276-0368-1*) JPS Phila.

Bearman, Jane. The Eight Nights: A Chanukah Counting Book. Bearman, Jane, illus. LC 78-60781. (gr. k-3). 1979. pap. 5.00 (*0-8074-0237-0*, 102562) UAHC.

Behrens, June. Hanukkah. Behrens, Terry, illus. LC 82-17890. 32p. (gr. k-4). 1983. PLB 11.60 (*0-516-02386-1*); pap. 3.95 (*0-516-42386-X*) Childrens.

Benjamin, Alan. Hanukkah Chubby Board Book. (ps-6). 1993. pap. 3.95 (*0-671-87069-6*, Little Simon) S&S Trade.

Block, Linda F. & Dubin, Debbie I. Chanukah on Noah's Ark. 72p. (Orig.). (gr. 1-7). 1987. pap. 6.95 (*0-9619082-0-3*) Noahs Ark.

Brokaw, Meredith & Gilbar, Annie. The Penny Whistle Christmas Party Book: Including Hanukkah, New Year's, & Twelfth Night Family Parties. Weber, Jill, illus. 128p. (Orig.). 1991. (Fireside); pap. 12.00 (*0-671-73794-5*, Fireside) S&S Trade.

Burns, Marilyn. The Hanukkah Book. Weston, Martha, illus. LC 80-27935. 128p. (gr. 3-7). 1984. SBE 13.95 (*0-02-716140-4*, Four Winds) Macmillan Child Grp.

—The Hanukkah Book. 128p. 1991. pap. 3.99 (*0-380-71520-1*, Camelot) Avon.

Chaikin, Miriam. Hanukkah. Weiss, Ellen, illus. LC 89-77512. 32p. (ps-3). 1990. reinforced bdg. 15.95 (*0-8234-0816-7*) Holiday.

—Hanukkah. Weiss, Ellen, illus. LC 89-77512. 32p. (ps-3). 1991. pap. 5.95 (*0-8234-0905-8*) Holiday.

—Light Another Candle: The Story & Meaning of Hanukkah. 1987 ed. Demi, illus. (gr. 7 up). 1981. pap. 6.95 (*0-89919-057-X*, Clarion Bks) HM.

Channen, Don. UH! OH! Hanukkah. (gr. 3-7). 1993. 12.95 (*0-943706-15-7*) Yllw Brick Rd.

Chiel, Kinneret. Complete Book of Hanukah. (Illus.). (gr. 6-8). pap. 6.95x (*0-87068-367-5*) Ktav.

Cooper, Don. Hanukkah Songs & Games. Cook, Donald, illus. 32p. (ps-3). 1989. pap. 6.95 incl. cassette (*0-679-80041-7*) Random Bks Yng Read.

Daniel, Frank, illus. Chanukah. 20p. (ps). 1993. pap. 3.95 (*0-689-71733-4*, Aladdin) Macmillan Child Grp.

De Paola, Tomie. My First Chanukah. De Paola, Tomie, illus. 12p. (ps-k). 1989. 5.95 (*0-399-21780-0*, Putnam) Putnam Pub Group.

Ehrlich, Amy. Story of Hanukkah. Sherman, Ori, illus. (ps up). 1989. 14.95 (*0-8037-0615-4*); PLB 14.89 (*0-8037-0616-2*) Dial Bks Young.

Fisher, Aileen L. My First Hanukkah Book. Kiedrowski, Priscilla, illus. LC 84-21510. 32p. (ps-2). 1985. pap. 3.95 (*0-516-42905-1*) Childrens.

Fradin, Dennis B. Hanukkah. LC 89-25643. (Illus.). 48p. (gr. 1-4). 1990. lib. bdg. 14.95 (*0-89490-259-8*) Enslow Pubs.

Gertz, Susan E. Hanukkah & Christmas at My House. Gertz, Susan E., illus. LC 91-73702. 32p. (ps-6). 1992. pap. 6.95 (*0-9630934-0-1*) Willow & Laurel.

Grishaver, Joel L. Building Jewish Life: Hanukkah Activity Book. (Illus.). 31p. 1988. pap. 1.85 (*0-933873-32-8*) Torah Aura.

Groner, Judye & Wikler, Madeline. All about Hanukkah. Schanzer, Rosalyn, illus. LC 88-13435. (gr. k-5). 1988. 10.95 (*0-930494-81-4*); pap. 4.95 (*0-930494-82-2*) Kar Ben.

—Hanukkah Fun: For Little Hands. Kahn, Katherine J., illus. 32p. (ps-2). 1992. pap. 3.95 (*0-929371-62-3*) Kar Ben.

Hirsh, Marilyn. I Love Hanukkah. Hirsh, Marilyn, illus. (gr. k-3). 1989. incl. cass. 19.95 (*0-87499-131-5*); pap. 12.95 incl. cass. (*0-87499-130-7*); Set; incl. 4 bks., cass., & guide. pap. 27.95 (*0-87499-132-3*) Live Oak Media.

Kalman, Bobbie. We Celebrate Hanukkah. (Illus.). 56p. (gr. 3-4). 1986. 15.95 (*0-86505-045-7*); pap. 7.95 (*0-86505-055-4*) Crabtree Pub Co.

Katz, Bobbi. A Family Hanukkah. Herzfeld, Caryl, illus. LC 91-51093. 40p. (ps-3). 1992. 7.99 (*0-679-83240-8*) Random Bks Yng Read.

Kimmelman, Leslie. Hanukkah Lights, Hanukkah Nights. Himmelman, John, illus. LC 91-15633. 32p. (ps-k). 1992. 12.00 (*0-06-020368-4*); PLB 11.89 (*0-06-020369-2*) HarpC Child Bks.

—Hanukkah Lights, Hanukkah Nights. Himmelman, John, illus. LC 91-15633. 32p. (ps-k). 1994. pap. 4.95 (*0-06-446164-5*, Trophy) HarpC Child Bks.

Koralek, Jenny. Hanukkah: The Festival of Lights. Wijngaard, Juan, illus. LC 89-8064. 32p. (gr. k-4). 1990. 14.00 (*0-688-09329-9*); lib. bdg. 13.93 (*0-688-09330-2*) Lothrop.

Kunin, Claudia. My Hanukkah Alphabet. (ps-3). 1993. 6.95 (*0-307-13719-8*, Golden Pr) Western Pub.

—My Hanukkah Book of Numbers. (ps-3). 1993. 6.95 (*0-307-13718-X*, Golden Pr) Western Pub.

Kuskin, Karla. A Great Miracle Happened There: A Chanukah Story. Parker, Robert A., illus. LC 92-17909. 32p. (gr. k-3). 1993. 15.00 (*0-06-023617-5*); PLB 14.89 (*0-06-023618-3*) HarpC Child Bks.

Lepon, Shoshana. Hanukkah Carousel. (ps-1). 1993. 12.95 (*0-943706-11-4*) Yllw Brick Rd.

Let's Celebrate Hanukkah! 5.98 (*0-943351-50-2*, XS2101) Astor Bks.

Nielsen, Shelly. Hanukkah. Wallner, Rosemary, ed. LC 91-73029. 1992. 13.99 (*1-56239-072-4*) Abdo & Dghtrs.

O'Hare, Jeff. Hanukkah, Happy Hanukkah: Crafts, Recipes, Games, Puzzles, Songs, & More for the Joyous... Friedman, Arthur, illus. LC 93-73302. 32p. (ps-5). 1994. 4.95 (*1-56397-369-3*); 14.85 (*1-56397-396-0*) Boyds Mills Pr.

Poskanzer, Susan. Riddles about Hannukah. Brook, Bonnie, ed. Gray, Rob, illus. 32p. (ps-3). 1990. 4.95 (*0-671-70555-5*); PLB 6.95 (*0-671-70553-9*) Silver Pr.

Rojany, Lisa. The Story of Hanukkah: A Lift-the-Flap Rebus Book. Jones, Holly, illus. 16p. (ps-3). 1993. 12.95 (*1-56282-420-1*) Hyprn Child.

Rosenfeld, Dina. A Chanukah Story for Night Number Three. Pape, David S., ed. Mandel, Harris, illus. 32p. (ps-1). 1989. 9.95 (*0-922613-16-8*); pap. 7.95 (*0-922613-17-6*) Hachai Pubns.

Schotter, Roni. Hanukkah! Hafner, Marylin, illus. (ps-3). 1990. 14.95 (*0-316-77466-9*, Joy St Bks) Little.

—Hanukkah! (gr. 4-8). 1993. pap. 5.95 (*0-316-77469-3*, Joy St Bks) Little.

Sidi, Smadar S. Chanukah A-Z. Nover, Teri, illus. (ps-2). 1988. 9.95 (*1-55774-041-0*) Modan-Adama Bks.

Silverman, Maida. Festival of Lights: The Story of Hanukkah. Ewing, Carolyn S., illus. LC 87-16076. (gr. 1-5). 1987. (Little Simon); pap. 2.95 (*0-671-64376-2*, Little Simon) S&S Trade.

Simon, Norma. Hanukah in My House. Gordon, Ayala, illus. (ps-k). 1960. plastic cover 4.50 (*0-8381-0705-2*) United Syn Bk.

The Story of Chanukah for Children. (ps-3). pap. 2.95 (*0-8249-8020-4*, Ideals Child) Hambleton-Hill.

Stuhlman, Daniel D. My Own Hanukah Story. Kuppersmith-Krause, Molly B., illus. (Orig.). (ps-5). 1980. pap. 3.95 personalized version (*0-934402-07-8*); decorations 1.00 (*0-934402-08-6*); trade version 2.50 (*0-934402-12-4*) BYLS Pr.

Sussman, Susan. Hanukkah: Eight Lights Around the World. Levine, Abby, ed. LC 87-25346. (Illus.). 40p. (gr. 2 up). 1988. PLB 11.95 (*0-8075-3145-6*) A Whitman.

—There's No Such Thing As a Chanukah Bush, Sandy Goldstein. Tucker, Kathleen, ed. LC 83-1291. (Illus.). 48p. (gr. 3-7). 1983. PLB 8.95 (*0-8075-7862-2*) A Whitman.

Vered, Ben. Why Is Hanukkah. (Illus.). (ps-5). 1961. pap. 2.50 (*0-914080-59-8*) Shulsinger Sales.

Weiss, Andrea. Hanukkah Fun: Crafts & Games. Rhinelander, Mary F., illus. 32p. (gr. k-5). 1992. pap. 4.95 (*1-56397-059-7*) Boyds Mills Pr.

Weiss, George D. Eight Days of Hanukah. 17p. 1991. incl. cassette 8.95 (*1-879756-00-5*) Holiday Time.

Wengrov, Charles. The Story of Hanukkah. (Illus.). (gr. k-7). 1965. pap. 2.50 (*0-914080-52-0*) Shulsinger Sales.

Zwebner, Janet. Animated Menorah. (Illus.). 48p. (gr. 1-4). 1989. 9.95 (*0-685-28790-4*) Shapolsky Pubs.

—Animated Menorah Chanukah Activity. (gr. 4-7). 1991. pap. 5.95 (*0-944007-61-9*) Shapolsky Pubs.

HANUKKAH (FEAST OF LIGHTS)–FICTION

Adler, David A. Happy Hanukkah Rebus. Palmer, Jan, illus. 32p. (ps-3). 1989. pap. 11.95 (*0-670-82419-4*) Viking Child Bks.

—Malke's Secret Recipe: A Chanukah Story from Chelm. LC 88-32019. (ps-3). 1989. 10.95 (*0-930494-88-1*); pap. 4.95 (*0-930494-89-X*) Kar Ben.

Armstrong, Beverly. The Hanukkah Happening. (Illus.). 24p. (gr. 2-6). 1987. 4.95 (*0-88160-150-0*, LW263) Learning Wks.

Birenbaum, Barbara. Candle Talk. Birenbaum, Barbara, illus. LC 90-33299. 54p. (gr. 2-5). 1991. 10.95 (*0-935343-10-5*); pap. 5.95g (*0-935343-15-6*) Peartree.

—The Lost Side of the Dreydl. Birenbaum, Barbara, illus. 50p. (gr. 3-5). 1987. 10.95 (*0-935343-17-2*); pap. 5.95 (*0-935343-16-4*) Peartree.

Fox, Terry. A Little Miracle: A Hanukah Story. Fox, David A., illus. LC 85-51615. 52p. (Orig.). (ps up). 1985. pap. 5.95 (*0-9615397-0-4*) Tenderfoot Pr.

Gantz, David. Davey's Hanukkah Golem. Gantz, David, illus. LC 91-2328. 32p. (gr. k-3). 1991. 13.95 (*0-8276-0380-0*) JPS Phila.

Gikow, Louise. Shalom Sesame Presents a Chanukah Party for Kippi. Cooke, Tom, illus. 32p. 1994. 12.95 (*1-884857-06-X*) Comet Intl.

Goldin, Barbara D. Just Enough Is Plenty: A Hannukkah Tale. Chwast, Seymour, illus. (ps-3). 1988. pap. 12.95 (*0-670-81852-6*) Viking Child Bks.

—Just Enough Is Plenty, a Hanukkah Tale. (ps-3). 1990. pap. 4.99 (*0-14-050787-6*, Puffin) Puffin Bks.

Greene, Jacqueline D. The Hanukah Tooth. Ouellet, Pauline A., illus. LC 81-90033. 28p. (ps-2). 1981. pap. 3.00 (*0-938836-02-1*) Pascal Pubs.

Herman, Gail. Count the Days of Hanukkah. Kalish, Lionel, illus. LC 92-82914. 16p. (ps-3). 1993. 3.95 (*0-590-47081-7*, Cartwheel) Scholastic Inc.

Hirsh, Marilyn. Potato Pancakes All Around: A Hanukkah Tale. (Illus.). 34p. (gr. k-3). 1982. pap. 6.95 (*0-8276-0217-0*) JPS Phila.

Kimmel, Eric A. The Chanukkah Guest. Carmi, Giora, illus. LC 89-20073. 32p. (ps-3). 1990. reinforced bdg. 15.95 (*0-8234-0788-8*); pap. 5.95 (*0-8234-0978-3*) Holiday.

McDonnell, Janet. Sharing Hanukkah. Endres, Helen, illus. LC 93-13250. 32p. (ps-2). 1993. PLB 12.30 (*0-516-00685-1*); pap. 3.95 (*0-516-40685-X*) Childrens.

Manushkin, Fran. Latkes & Applesauce. (Illus.). 1992. 4.95 (*0-590-42265-0*, Blue Ribbon Bks) Scholastic Inc.

—Latkes & Applesauce: A Hanukkah Story. Spowart, Robin, illus. (ps-3). 1990. 12.95 (*0-590-42261-8*, Scholastic Hardcover) Scholastic Inc.

Martin, Ann M. Secret Santa. LC 93-48981. 1994. 14.95 (*0-590-48295-5*) Scholastic Inc.

Rosen, Michael J. Elijah's Angel. Robinson, A., illus. 1992. 13.95 (*0-15-225394-7*, HB Juv Bks) HarBrace.

Rosenberg, Amye. Melly's Menorah. (Illus.). 24p. (ps-1). 1991. pap. 2.95 incl. stickers (*0-671-74495-X*, Little Simon) S&S Trade.

Rouss, Sylvia A. Sammy Spider's First Hanukkah. Kahn, Katherine J., illus. LC 92-39639. 1993. 13.95 (*0-929371-45-3*); pap. 5.95 (*0-929371-46-1*) Kar Ben.

Ryder, Joanne. First Grade Elves. Lewin, Betsy, illus. LC 93-25543. 32p. (ps-2). 1993. PLB 9.79 (*0-8167-3010-5*); pap. text ed. 2.95 (*0-8167-3011-3*) Troll Assocs.

Shostak, Myra. Rainbow Candles: A Chanukah Counting Book. Kahn, Katherine J., illus. LC 86-81718. 12p. (ps). 1986. bds. 4.95 (*0-930494-59-8*) Kar Ben.

Speregen, Devra. Arielle & the Hanukkah Surprise. 1992. pap. 2.50 (*0-590-46125-7*, Cartwheel) Scholastic Inc.

Sperling, Jerry. The Little Menorah Who Forgot Chanukah. Carmi, Giora, illus. (Orig.). 1993. pap. 12.95 incl. cassette (*0-8074-0508-6*, 101971) UAHC.

Stine, Megan. The Hanukkah Miracles. (Illus.). (ps-3). 1993. pap. 3.99 (*0-553-37294-7*) Bantam.

Sussman, Susan. There's No Such Thing As a Chanukah Bush, Sandy Goldstein. (gr. 4-7). 1993. pap. 3.50 (*0-8075-7863-0*) A Whitman.

Topek, Susan R. A Turn for Noah: A Hanukkah Story. Springer, Sally, illus. LC 92-22958. 1992. 12.95 (*0-929371-37-2*); pap. 4.95 (*0-929371-38-0*) Kar Ben.

Weilerstein, Sadie R. K'tonton in the Circus: A Hanukkah Adventure. Hirsh, Marilyn, illus. LC 81-11765. 96p. (gr. 2 up). pap. 8.95 (*0-8276-0303-7*) JPS Phila.

Wolfberg, Carrie. The Happy Dreidles: Hanukkah Adventure. Birenbaum, Barbara, illus. LC 86-12210. 28p. (ps-2). 1991. 8.50 (*0-935343-01-6*); pap. 3.50 (*0-935343-00-8*) Peartree.

HAPPINESS

Amos, Janine. Feelings: Happy. (gr. 4-7). 1994. 19.97 (*0-8114-9231-1*) Raintree Steck-V.

Brady, Janeen & Woolley, Diane. Standin' Tall Happiness. Wilson, Grant, illus. 22p. (Orig.). (ps-6). 1982. pap. text ed. 1.50 activity bk. (*0-944803-46-6*); cassette & bk. 9.95 (*0-944803-47-4*) Brite Music.

Crystal Clarity Staff. Little Secrets of Happiness. (gr. 4-7). 1993. 5.95 (*1-56589-604-1*) Crystal Clarity.

Dacquino, V. T. Kiss the Candy Days Good-Bye. (gr. 5-9). 1986. pap. 2.25 (*0-440-44369-5*) Dell.

Howard, Barbara. Journey of Joy. 157p. (gr. 5 up). 1990. pap. text ed. 11.00 (*0-8309-0562-6*) Herald Hse.

If You're Happy & You Know It. 24p. (ps-3). 1991. write for info. (*0-307-14162-4*, 14162) Western Pub.

Levinson, Nancy S. & Rocklin, Joanne. Feeling Great: Reaching Out to the World, Reaching in to Yourself--Without Drugs. 2nd, rev. ed. LC 92-16217. (Illus.). 112p. (gr. 8-12). 1992. pap. 7.95 (*0-89793-087-8*) Hunter Hse.

Mandino, Og. Og Mandino's Great Trilogy. 1993. 12.98 (*0-8119-0428-8*) Lifetime.

Vincent, Gabrielle. Smile, Ernest & Celestine. LC 82-1075. (Illus.). 24p. (ps-3). 1982. 10.75 (*0-688-01247-7*); PLB 11.88 (*0-688-01249-3*) Greenwillow.

HARBORS

see also Pilots and Pilotage

Carter, Katherine. Ships & Seaports. LC 82-4463. (Illus.). (gr. k-4). 1982. pap. 4.95 (*0-516-41656-1*) Childrens.

Crews, Donald. Harbor. Crews, Donald, illus. LC 81-6607. 32p. (ps-1). 1982. 11.75 (*0-688-00861-5*); PLB 14.93 (*0-688-00862-3*) Greenwillow.

Riegel, Martin P. Ghost Ports of the Pacific, Vol. I: California. LC 89-90772. (Illus.). 52p. (Orig.). 1989. 11.00 (*0-944871-18-6*); pap. 4.95 (*0-944871-19-4*) Riegel Pub.

—Ghost Ports of the Pacific, Vol. II: Oregon. LC 89-90772. (Illus.). 52p. (Orig.). 1989. 11.00 (*0-944871-20-8*); pap. 4.95 (*0-944871-21-6*) Riegel Pub.

HARBORS–FICTION

O'Hearn, Michael. Hercules the Harbor Tug. (Illus.). 32p. (ps-4). 1994. 15.95 (*0-88106-889-6*); PLB 16.00 (*0-88106-890-X*); pap. 7.95 (*0-88106-888-8*) Charlesbridge Pub.

HARDING, WARREN GAMALIEL, PRESIDENT U. S. 1865-1923

Canadeo, Anne. Warren G. Harding: Twenty-Ninth President of the United States. Young, Richard G., ed. LC 89-39952. (Illus.). 128p. (gr. 5-9). 1990. PLB 17.26 (*0-944483-64-X*) Garrett Ed Corp.

Wade, Linda R. Warren G. Harding. LC 88-38057. (Illus.). 100p. (gr. 3 up). 1989. PLB 14.40 (*0-516-01368-8*) Childrens.

HARES

see Rabbits

HARLEM, NEW YORK (CITY)–FICTION

Smalls-Hector, Irene. Irene & the Big, Fine Nickel, Vol. 1. (ps-3). 1991. 15.95 (*0-316-79871-1*) Little.

Wright, Richard. Rite of Passage. Rampersad, Arnold, afterword by. LC 93-2473. 128p. (gr. 7 up). 1994. 12. 95 (*0-06-023419-9*); PLB 12.89 (*0-06-023420-2*) HarpC Child Bks.

HARLEM, NEW YORK (CITY)–SOCIAL CONDITIONS

Cryan-Hicks, Kathryn, intro. by. Pride & Promise: The Harlem Renaissance. LC 93-72240. (Illus.). 52p. (Orig.). (gr. 5-12). 1994. pap. 4.95 (*1-878668-30-7*) Disc Enter Ltd.

HARRISON, BENJAMIN, PRESIDENT U. S. 1833-1901

Stevens, Rita. Benjamin Harrison: Twenty-Third President of the United States. Young, Richard G., ed. LC 88-24747. (Illus.). (gr. 5-9). 1989. PLB 17.26 (*0-944483-15-1*) Garrett Ed Corp.

HARRISON, WILLIAM HENRY, PRESIDENT U. S. 1773-1841

Fitz-Gerald, C. William Henry Harrison. LC 87-16842. (Illus.). 100p. (gr. 3 up). 1987. PLB 14.40 (*0-516-01392-0*) Childrens.

Stefoff, Rebecca. William Henry Harrison: Ninth President of the United States. Young, Richard G., ed. LC 89-25652. (Illus.). 128p. (gr. 5-9). 1990. PLB 17.26 (*0-944483-54-2*) Garrett Ed Corp.

HASTINGS, BATTLE OF, 1066

Sauvain, Philip. Hastings. LC 91-25369. (Illus.). 32p. (gr. 6 up). 1992. text ed. 13.95 RSBE (*0-02-781079-8*, New Discovery) Macmillan Child Grp.

HATS

Brenner, Martha. Abe Lincoln's Hat. Cook, Donald, illus. LC 93-31867. 48p. (Orig.). (gr. k-2). 1994. PLB 7.99 (*0-679-94977-1*); pap. 3.50 (*0-679-84977-7*) Random Bks Yng Read.

Morris, Ann. Hats, Hats, Hats. Heyman, Ken, photos by. LC 88-26676. (Illus.). 32p. (ps-2). 1989. 13.95 (*0-688-06338-1*); PLB 13.88 (*0-688-06339-X*) Lothrop.

—Hats, Hats, Hats. Heyman, Ken, photos by. LC 92-25548. (Illus.). 32p. (ps up). 1993. pap. 4.95 (*0-688-12274-4*, Mulberry) Morrow.

Newbold, Patt & Diebel, Anne. Paper Hat Tricks, Vol. 4: A Big Book of Hat Patterns, Folklore, Fairytales, Foreign Lands & Long Ago Hats. 39p. (ps-5). 1992. pap. text ed. 13.95 (*1-56422-996-3*, Pub. by Paper Hat) Start Reading.

HATS–FICTION

Adams, Pam. Mrs. Honey's Hat. LC 90-46604. (Illus.). 24p. (ps-2). 1980. 7.95 (*0-85953-099-X*, Pub. by Child's Play England); pap. 3.95 (*0-85953-325-5*) Childs Play.

Barkan, Joanne. That Fat Hat. Swanson, Maggie, illus. LC 92-7414. 1992. 2.95 (*0-590-45643-1*) Scholastic Inc.

Berenstain, Stan & Berenstain, Janice. Old Hat, New Hat. (Illus.). (ps-1). 1970. 6.95 (*0-394-80669-7*); lib. bdg. 7.99 (*0-394-90669-1*) Random Bks Yng Read.

Bland, Sue. Madame de Toucainville's Magnificent Hat. (Illus.). (gr. 4-7). 1993. 12.95 (*0-88995-115-2*, Pub. by Red Deer CN) Empire Pub Srvs.

Blos, Joan W. Martin's Hats. Simont, Marc, illus. LC 83-13389. 32p. (ps-3). 1984. 11.95 (*0-688-02027-5*); PLB 11.88 (*0-688-02033-X*, Morrow Jr Bks) Morrow Jr Bks.

—Martin's Hats. LC 83-13389. (Illus.). 32p. (ps up). 1984. pap. 4.95 (*0-688-07039-6*, Mulberry) Morrow.

Brown, Hayden & Dickins, Roberts. The Sombrero. Dickins, Robert, illus. LC 93-6633. 1994. write for info. (*0-383-03714-X*) SRA Schl Grp.

Christelow, Eileen. Olive & the Magic Hat. Christelow, Eileen, illus. LC 87-672. 32p. (gr. k-3). 1987. 12.95 (*0-89919-513-X*, Clarion Bks) HM.

Clark, Emma C. Catch That Hat! LC 89-34881. (Illus.). (ps-2). 1990. 12.95 (*0-316-14496-7*) Little.

Cushman, Doug. Uncle Foster's Hat Tree. Cushman, Doug, illus. LC 88-3573. 48p. (ps-3). 1988. 9.95 (*0-525-44410-6*, DCB) Dutton Child Bks.

Dr. Seuss. The Five Hundred Hats of Bartholomew Cubbins. LC 88-38412. (Illus.). 48p. (ps-3). 1989. Repr. of 1938 ed. 11.00 (*0-394-84484-X*); lib. bdg. 14. 99 (*0-394-94484-4*) Random Bks Yng Read.

Dudko, Mary A. & Larsen, Margie. Barney's Hats. Hartley, Linda, ed. Full, Dennis, photos by. LC 93-77016. (Illus.). 24p. (ps-1). 1993. pap. 2.25 (*1-57064-005-X*) Barney Pub.

Gill, Madelaine. The Spring Hat. LC 91-30556. (Illus.). 40p. (ps-1). 1993. pap. 13.00 (*0-671-75666-4*, S&S BYR) S&S Trade.

Hanel, Wolfram. The Extraordinary Adventures of an Ordinary Hat. James, J. Alison, tr. Unzner-Fischer, Christa, illus. LC 93-39756. 64p. (gr. 2-3). 1994. 13.95 (*1-55858-255-X*); PLB 13.88 (*1-55858-256-8*) North-South Bks NYC.

Hindley, Judy. Uncle Harold & the Green Hat. Utton, Peter, illus. 26p. (ps-3). 1991. bds. 13.95 (*0-374-38030-9*) FS&G.

Howard, Elizabeth F. Aunt Flossie's Hats (& Crab Cakes Later) Ransome, James E., illus. 32p. (ps-1). 1991. 14. 95 (*0-395-54682-6*, Clarion Bks) HM.

Johnson, Richard. Look at Me in a Funny Hat! Chatterton, Martin, illus. LC 93-32379. 14p. (ps up). 1994. 4.99 (*1-56402-414-8*) Candlewick Pr.

Keats, Ezra J. Jennie's Hat. Keats, Ezra J., illus. LC 66-15683. 32p. (gr. k-3). 1966. 15.00i (*0-06-023113-0*); PLB 14.89 (*0-06-023114-9*) HarpC Child Bks.

Krisher, Trudy. Kathy's Hats: A Story of Hope. Levine, Abby, ed. Westcott, Nadine B., illus. LC 92-2659. 32p. (gr. 1-5). 1992. 13.95g (*0-8075-4116-8*) A Whitman.

Lear, Edward. The Quangle Wangle's Hat. Stevens, Janet, illus. 32p. (ps-3). 1988. 12.95 (*0-15-264450-4*) HarBrace.

Leemis, Ralph. Mister Momboo's Hat. Bassett, Jeni, illus. LC 90-34397. 24p. (ps-k). 1991. 11.95 (*0-525-65045-8*, Cobblehill Bks) Dutton Child Bks.

Mariana. Miss Flora McFlimsey's Easter Bonnet. rev. ed. Mariana, illus. LC 86-15268. 40p. (gr. k-3). 1987. 9.95 (*0-688-04535-9*); PLB 8.88 (*0-688-04536-7*) Lothrop.

Miller, Margaret. Whose Hat? LC 86-18324. (Illus.). 40p. (ps-1). 1988. 14.00 (*0-688-06906-1*); lib. bdg. 13.93 (*0-688-06907-X*) Greenwillow.

Morris, Ann. Hats, Hats, Hats: Big Book Edition. 32p. (ps up). 1993. pap. 18.95 (*0-688-12938-2*, Mulberry) Morrow.

Porte, Barbara A. Harry's Birthday. Abolafia, Yossi, illus. LC 93-18189. 48p. (gr. k up). 1994. 14.00 (*0-688-12142-X*); PLB 13.93 (*0-688-12143-8*) Greenwillow.

Pratt, Pierre. Follow that Hat! Pratt, Pierre, illus. 32p. (ps-2). 1992. PLB 15.95 (*1-55037-261-0*, Pub. by Annick Pr); pap. 5.95 (*1-55037-259-9*, Pub. by Annick Pr) Firefly Bks Ltd.

—Leon sans Son Chapeau: Follow That Hat! Pratt, Pierre, illus. (FRE.). 32p. (ps-2). 1992. 15.95 (*1-55037-263-7*, Pub. by Annick Pr); pap. 6.95 (*1-55037-262-9*, Pub. by Annick Pr) Firefly Bks Ltd.

Reiss, Elayne & Friedman, Rita. Hat Helpers Hullabaloo. (gr. k-1). 12.50 (*0-89796-868-9*) New Dimens Educ.

Richardson, John. Jack's Hat. (Illus.). 32p. (gr. k-3). 1992. 16.95 (*0-09-174524-1*, Pub. by Hutchinson UK) Trafalgar.

Rohmer, Harriet, adapted by. Uncle Nacho's Hat: El sombrero del Tio Nacho. Ada, Alma F. & Zubizarreta, Rosalma, trs. (ENG & SPA., Illus.). 32p. (ps-5). 1993. pap. 5.95 (*0-89239-112-X*) Childrens Book Pr.

Rohmer, Harriet & Olivarez, Anna, eds. Uncle Nacho's Hat Read-Along. (ENG & SPA.). (ps-7). 1990. incl. audiocassette 22.95 (*0-89239-061-1*) Childrens Book Pr.

Roy, Ron. Whose Hat Is That? Hausherr, Rosemarie, photos by. (Illus.). 40p. (ps-3). 1990. pap. 5.70 (*0-395-54778-4*, Clarion Bks) HM.

Scarry, Richard. Be Careful, Mr. Frumble! Scarry, Richard, illus. LC 89-43154. 24p. (Orig.). (ps-2). 1990. pap. 2.25 (*0-679-80566-4*) Random Bks Yng Read.

—Mr. Frumble: Richard Scarry's Smallest Pop-up Book Ever! (Illus.). 10p. (ps-3). 1992. write for info. (*0-307-12463-0*, 12463, Golden Pr) Western Pub.

Scheller, Melanie. My Grandfather's Hat. Narahashi, Keiko, illus. LC 91-12486. 32p. (ps-3). 1992. SBE 13. 95 (*0-689-50540-X*, M K McElderry) Macmillan Child Grp.

Schneider, Howie. Uncle Lester's Hat. Schneider, Howie, illus. LC 92-20750. 32p. (ps-3). 1993. 14.95 (*0-399-22439-4*, Putnam) Putnam Pub Group.

Shelly, Walt & Stangl, Jean. Hats, Hats, & More Hats. (gr. 1-5). 1989. pap. 10.95 (*0-8224-3602-7*) Fearon Teach Aids.

Slobodkina, Esphyr. Caps for Sale. Slobodkina, Esphyr, illus. LC 84-43122. 1947. 13.00 (*0-201-09147-X*); PLB 12.89 (*0-06-025778-4*) HarpC Child Bks.

Smath, Jerry. A Hat So Simple. LC 93-22205. (Illus.). 32p. (ps-3). 1993. PLB 13.95 (*0-8167-3016-4*); pap. write for info. (*0-8167-3017-2*) BrdgeWater.

Smax, Willy. Big Pig's Hat. Ludlow, Keren, illus. LC 92-19442. (ps-3). 1993. 13.99 (*0-8037-1476-9*) Dial Bks Young.

Smith, William J. Ho for a Hat! Munsinger, Lynn, illus. LC 88-39864. (ps-1). 1989. 14.95 (*0-316-80120-8*, Joy St Bks) Little.

—Ho for a Hat! (gr. 3 up). 1993. pap. 4.95 (*0-316-80126-7*) Little.

Stoeke, Janet M. A Hat for Minerva Louise. LC 94-2139. (Illus.). 24p. (ps-1). 1994. 12.99 (*0-525-45328-8*) Dutton Child Bks.

Van der Meer, Ron & Van der Meer, Atie. Funny Hats: A Lift-the-Flap Book. Van der Meer, Ron & Van der Meer, Atie, illus. LC 91-62463. 16p. (ps). 1992. 7.99 (*0-679-82850-8*) Random Bks Yng Read.

Van Laan, Nancy. This Is the Hat: A Story in Rhyme. (ps). 1992. 14.95 (*0-316-89727-2*, Joy St Bks) Little.

Vicky's New Hat. 1989. 2.99 (*0-517-69124-8*) Random Hse Value.

Walbrecker, Dirk. Benny's Hat. Poppel, Hans, illus. 28p. (ps-1). 1991. smythe sewn reinforced bdg. 9.95 (*1-56182-028-8*) Atomium Bks.

Wildsmith, Brian & Wildsmith, Rebecca. Whose Hat Was That? LC 92-17237. 1993. 6.95 (*0-15-200691-5*); pap. write for info. (*0-15-200690-7*) HarBrace.

Wiltshire, Teri. The Tale of Pepper the Pony. Archer, Rebecca, illus. LC 92-46249. (ps). 1993. 8.95 (*1-85697-858-3*, Kingfisher LKC) LKC.

HAUNTED HOUSES

see Ghosts

HAWAII

Aka, Karen Y. Honolulu, Hawaii: The Travel Guide for Kids. Koch, Susan C., illus. 32p. (gr. k-4). 1992. pap. 4.95 (*0-945600-08-9*) Colormore Inc.

Aylesworth, Thomas G. & Aylesworth, Virginia L. Pacific: California, Hawaii. (gr. 3 up). 1992. lib. bdg. 16.95 (*0-7910-1050-3*) Chelsea Hse.

Bauer, Helen. Hawaii: The Aloha State. rev. ed. Rayson, Ann, rev. by. McCurdy, Bruce S., illus. LC 82-72319. 192p. (gr. 4-7). 1982. 25.95 (*0-935848-13-4*); pap. 16. 95 (*0-935848-15-0*); wkbk. 5.95 (*0-935848-34-7*); tchr's. manual 5.00 (*1-880188-46-5*) Bess Pr.

Bellerose, Albert J. Princess Kaiulani: Color Me Hawaii. (Illus.). 128p. (gr. k-6). 1990. pap. 3.95 (*0-935848-84-3*) Bess Pr.

Carole Marsh Hawaii Books, 44 bks. 1994. lib. bdg. 1027. 80 set (*0-7933-1286-8*); pap. 587.80 set (*0-7933-5144-8*) Gallopade Pub Group.

Carpenter, Allan. Hawaii. LC 79-9991. (Illus.). 96p. (gr. 4 up). 1979. PLB 16.95 (*0-516-04111-8*) Childrens.

Dunford, Elizabeth P. The Hawaiians of Old. rev. ed. Kudlak, Aimee A., illus. 220p. (gr. 4 up). 1990. text ed. 25.95 (*0-935848-43-6*); pap. text ed. 15.95 (*0-935848-01-0*); wkbk. 5.95 (*0-935848-08-8*); tchr's. manual 5.00 (*0-935848-09-6*) Bess Pr.

Durkin, Pat. The Kaua'i Guide to Beaches & Water Activities with Safety Tips. rev. ed. Ida, Gerald, et al, illus. 80p. pap. 2.50 (*0-942255-08-9*, G4-2) Magic Fishes Pr.

Feeney, Stephanie. A Is for Aloha. Reese, Jeff, photos by. LC 85-50569. (Illus.). 64p. (ps-3). 1985. 8.95 (*0-8248-0722-7*) UH Pr.

Fradin, Dennis. Hawaii: In Words & Pictures. LC 79-25605. (Illus.). 48p. (gr. 2-5). 1980. PLB 12.95 (*0-516-03913-X*); pap. 4.95 (*0-516-43913-8*) Childrens.

Fradin, Dennis B. Hawaii - From Sea to Shining Sea. LC 93-33861. (Illus.). 64p. (gr. 3-5). 1994. PLB 16.45 (*0-516-03811-7*) Childrens.

Hazlett, Richard W. Haleakala Discovery. rev. ed. Hazlett, Richard W., illus. 52p. (gr. 3-7). 1988. pap. 3.00 activity-color book (*0-940295-08-3*) HI Natural Hist.

Herda, D. J. Historical America: The Southwestern States. LC 92-28206. (Illus.). 64p. (gr. 5-8). 1993. PLB 15.40 (*1-56294-123-2*) Millbrook Pr.

Hoofnagle, Keith L. Hawaii Volcanoes Coloring Book. Hoofnagle, Keith L., illus. 32p. (ps-3). 1979. pap. 1.50 coloring book (*0-940295-07-5*) HI Natural Hist.

Ikemoto, Glenn Y. The Kaua'i Guide to Freshwater Sport Fishing. Boynton, David, photos by. (Illus.). 64p. (Orig.). 1989. pap. 2.50 (*0-942255-07-0*, G6) Magic Fishes Pr.

Jobson, Joy. The Kaua'i Guide to Kaua'i Products & Speciality Shopping. Stanger, Susan E., illus. 64p. (Orig.). 1988. pap. 2.50 (*0-942255-03-8*, G2) Magic Fishes Pr.

Johnston, Joyce. Hawaii. LC 93-46907. 1994. write for info. (*0-8225-2739-1*) Lerner Pubns.

Kaopuiki, Stacey. Peter Panini's Children's Guide to the Hawaiian Islands, 4 bks. (Illus.). (ps-5). 1991. Set. write for info. (*1-878498-01-0*) Hawaiian Isl Concepts.

The Kaua'i Guide. 96p. (Orig.). pap. 2.50 (*0-942255-01-1*, G1 & UP) Magic Fishes Pr.

Kikukawa, Cecily H. Ka Mea Ho'ala, the Awakener: The Story of Henry Obookiah. Burningham, Robin, illus. LC 82-70246. 100p. (Orig.). (gr. 7-10). 1982. pap. 6.95 (*0-935848-10-X*) Bess Pr.

Lano-Nellist, Cassandra. Child's First Book about Hawaii. Nellist, Cassandra L., illus. 24p. (ps). 1987. 8.95 (*0-916630-58-7*) Pr Pacifica.

Lovett, Sarah. Kidding Around the Hawaiian Islands: A Young Person's Guide to the Islands. Taylor, Michael, illus. 64p. (Orig.). (gr. 3 up). 1990. pap. 9.95 (*0-945465-37-8*) John Muir.

McNair, Sylvia. Hawaii. LC 89-35084. 144p. (gr. 4 up). 1989. PLB 20.55 (*0-516-00457-3*) Childrens.

—Hawaii. 187p. 1993. text ed. 15.40 (*1-56956-177-X*) W A T Braille.

Marsh, Carole. Avast, Ye Slobs! Hawaii Pirate Trivia. (Illus.). (gr. 3-12). 1994. PLB 24.95 (*0-7933-0352-4*); pap. 14.95 (*0-7933-0351-6*); computer disk 29.95 (*0-7933-0353-2*) Gallopade Pub Group.

—The Beast of the Hawaii Bed & Breakfast. (Illus.). (gr. 3-12). 1994. PLB 24.95 (*0-7933-1531-X*); pap. 14.95 (*0-7933-1532-8*); computer disk 29.95 (*0-7933-1533-6*) Gallopade Pub Group.

—Bow Wow! Hawaii Dogs in History, Mystery, Legend, Lore, Humor & More! (Illus.). (gr. 3-12). 1994. PLB 24.95 (*0-7933-3500-0*); pap. 14.95 (*0-7933-3501-9*); computer disk 29.95 (*0-7933-3502-7*) Gallopade Pub Group.

—Christopher Columbus Comes to Hawaii! Includes Reproducible Activities for Kids! (Illus.). (gr. 3-12). 1994. PLB 24.95 (*0-7933-3653-8*); pap. 14.95 (*0-7933-3654-6*); computer disk 29.95 (*0-7933-3655-4*) Gallopade Pub Group.

—The Hard-to-Believe-But-True! Book of Hawaii History, Mystery, Trivia, Legend, Lore, Humor & More. (Illus.). (gr. 3-12). 1994. PLB 24.95 (*0-7933-0349-4*); pap. 14.95 (*0-7933-0348-6*); computer disk 29.95 (*0-7933-0350-8*) Gallopade Pub Group.

—Hawaii & Other State Greats (Biographies) (Illus.). (gr. 3-12). 1994. PLB 24.95 (*1-55609-577-5*); pap. 14.95 (*1-55609-576-7*); computer disk 29.95 (*0-7933-1539-5*) Gallopade Pub Group.

—Hawaii Bandits, Bushwackers, Outlaws, Crooks, Devils, Ghosts, Desperadoes & Other Assorted & Sundry Characters! (Illus.). (gr. 3-12). 1994. PLB 24.95 (*0-7933-0334-6*); pap. 14.95 (*0-7933-0333-8*); computer disk 29.95 (*0-7933-0335-4*) Gallopade Pub Group.

—Hawaii Classic Christmas Trivia: Stories, Recipes, Activities, Legends, Lore & More! (Illus.). (gr. 3-12). 1994. PLB 24.95 (*0-7933-0337-0*); pap. 14.95 (*0-7933-0336-2*); computer disk 29.95 (*0-7933-0338-9*) Gallopade Pub Group.

—Hawaii Coastales. (Illus.). (gr. 3-12). 1994. PLB 24.95 (*1-55609-573-2*); pap. 14.95 (*1-55609-572-4*); computer disk 29.95 (*0-7933-1535-2*) Gallopade Pub Group.

—Hawaii Coastales! 1994. lib. bdg. 24.95 (*0-7933-7276-3*) Gallopade Pub Group.

—Hawaii Dingbats! Bk. 1: A Fun Book of Games, Stories, Activities & More about Our State That's All in Code! for You to Decipher. (Illus.). (gr. 3-12). 1994. PLB 24.95 (*0-7933-3806-9*); pap. 14.95 (*0-7933-3807-7*); computer disk 29.95 (*0-7933-3808-5*) Gallopade Pub Group.

—Hawaii Festival Fun for Kids! (Illus.). (gr. 3-12). 1994. lib. bdg. 24.95 (*0-7933-3959-6*); pap. 14.95 (*0-7933-3960-X*); disk 29.95 (*0-7933-3961-8*) Gallopade Pub Group.

—The Hawaii Hot Air Balloon Mystery. (Illus.). (gr. 2-9). 1994. 24.95 (*0-7933-2417-3*); pap. 14.95 (*0-7933-2418-1*); computer disk 29.95 (*0-7933-2419-X*) Gallopade Pub Group.

—Hawaii Jeopardy! Answers & Questions about Our State! (Illus.). (gr. 3-12). 1994. PLB 24.95 (*0-7933-4112-4*); pap. 14.95 (*0-7933-4113-2*); computer disk 29.95 (*0-7933-4114-0*) Gallopade Pub Group.

—Hawaii "Jography" A Fun Run Thru Our State! (Illus.). (gr. 3-12). 1994. PLB 24.95 (*1-55609-568-6*); pap. 14. 95 (*1-55609-567-8*); computer disk 29.95 (*0-7933-1525-5*) Gallopade Pub Group.

—Hawaii Kid's Cookbook: Recipes, How-to, History, Lore & More! (Illus.). (gr. 3-12). 1994. PLB 24.95 (*0-7933-0346-X*); pap. 14.95 (*0-7933-0345-1*); computer disk 29.95 (*0-7933-0347-8*) Gallopade Pub Group.

—Hawaii Quiz Bowl Crash Course! (Illus.). (gr. 3-12). 1994. PLB 24.95 (*1-55609-575-9*); pap. 14.95 (*1-55609-574-0*); computer disk 29.95 (*0-7933-1534-4*) Gallopade Pub Group.

—Hawaii Rollercoasters! (Illus.). (gr. 3-12). 1994. PLB 24.95 (*0-7933-5257-6*); pap. 14.95 (*0-7933-5258-4*); computer disk 29.95 (*0-7933-5259-2*) Gallopade Pub Group.

—Hawaii School Trivia: An Amazing & Fascinating Look at Our State's Teachers, Schools & Students! (Illus.). (gr. 3-12). 1994. PLB 24.95 (*0-7933-0343-5*); pap. 14. 95 (*0-7933-0342-7*); computer disk 29.95 (*0-7933-0344-3*) Gallopade Pub Group.

—Hawaii Silly Basketball Sports Mysteries. (Illus.). (gr. 3-12). 1994. PLB 24.95 (*0-7933-1540-9*); pap. 14.95 (*0-7933-1541-7*); computer disk 29.95 (*0-7933-1542-5*) Gallopade Pub Group.

—Hawaii: Silly Basketball Sportsmysteries, Vol. I. (Illus.). (gr. 3-12). 1994. PLB 24.95 (*0-7933-0340-0*); pap. 14. 95 (*0-7933-0339-7*); computer disk 29.95 (*0-7933-0341-9*) Gallopade Pub Group.

—Hawaii Silly Football Sportsmysteries, Vol. I. (Illus.). (gr. 3-12). 1994. PLB 24.95 (*1-55609-571-6*); pap. 14. 95 (*1-55609-570-8*); computer disk 29.95 (*0-7933-1527-1*) Gallopade Pub Group.

—Hawaii Silly Football Sportsmysteries, Vol. II. (Illus.). (gr. 3-12). 1994. PLB 24.95 (*0-7933-1528-X*); pap. 14. 95 (*0-7933-1529-8*); computer disk 29.95 (*0-7933-1530-1*) Gallopade Pub Group.

—Hawaii Silly Trivia! (Illus.). (gr. 3-12). 1994. PLB 24.95 (*1-55609-566-X*); pap. 14.95 (*1-55609-565-1*); computer disk 29.95 (*0-7933-1524-7*) Gallopade Pub Group.

—Hawaii's (Most Devastating!) Disasters & (Most Calamitous!) Catastrophies! (Illus.). (gr. 3-12). 1994. PLB 24.95 (*0-7933-0331-1*); pap. 14.95 (*0-7933-0330-3*); computer disk 29.95 (*0-7933-0332-X*) Gallopade Pub Group.

—If My Hawaii Mama Ran the World! (Illus.). (gr. 3-12). 1994. PLB 24.95 (*0-7933-1536-0*); pap. 14.95 (*0-7933-1537-9*); computer disk 29.95 (*0-7933-1538-7*) Gallopade Pub Group.

—Jurassic Ark! Hawaii Dinosaurs & Other Prehistoric Creatures. (gr. k-12). 1994. PLB 24.95 (*0-7933-7461-8*); pap. 14.95 (*0-7933-7462-6*); computer disk 29.95 (*0-7933-7463-4*) Gallopade Pub Group.

—Let's Quilt Hawaii & Stuff It Topographically! (Illus.). (gr. 3-12). 1994. PLB 24.95 (*1-55609-569-4*); pap. 14. 95 (*1-55609-093-5*); computer disk 29.95 (*0-7933-1526-3*) Gallopade Pub Group.

—Let's Quilt Our Hawaii County. 1994. lib. bdg. 24.95 (*0-7933-7146-5*); pap. text ed. 14.95 (*0-7933-7147-3*); disk 29.95 (*0-7933-7148-1*) Gallopade Pub Group.

—Let's Quilt Our Hawaii Town. 1994. lib. bdg. 24.95 (*0-7933-6996-7*); pap. text ed. 14.95 (*0-7933-6997-5*); disk 29.95 (*0-7933-6998-3*) Gallopade Pub Group.

—Meow! Hawaii Cats in History, Mystery, Legend, Lore, Humor & More! (Illus.). (gr. 3-12). 1994. PLB 24.95 (*0-7933-3347-4*); pap. 14.95 (*0-7933-3348-2*); computer disk 29.95 (*0-7933-3349-0*) Gallopade Pub Group.

—My First Book about Hawaii. (gr. k-4). 1994. PLB 24. 95 (*0-7933-5602-4*); pap. 14.95 (*0-7933-5603-2*); computer disk 29.95 (*0-7933-5604-0*) Gallopade Pub Group.

—Uncle Rebus: Hawaii Picture Stories for Computer Kids. (Illus.). (gr. k-3). 1994. PLB 24.95 (*0-7933-4534-0*); pap. 14.95 (*0-7933-4535-9*); disk 29. 95 (*0-7933-4536-7*) Gallopade Pub Group.

Oyama, Kaikilani E. The Kaua'i Guide on Ni'ihau: UniNi'ihau: M-m-m, What a Sweet Potato. Archives of the Kauai Museum Staff & Bernice P. Bishop Museum Staff, illus. (Orig.). 1988. pap. 2.50 (*0-942255-04-6*, G3) Magic Fishes Pr.

Penisten, John. Honolulu. LC 89-11973. (Illus.). 60p. (gr. 3 up). 1990. text ed. 13.95 RSBE (*0-87518-416-2*, Dillon) Macmillan Child Grp.

Potter, Norris & Kasdon, Lawrence. The Hawaiian Monarchy. LC 82-74176. (Illus.). 256p. (gr. 5-8). 1983. 25.95 (*0-935848-17-7*); pap. 16.95 (*0-935848-16-9*); wkbk. 5.95 (*0-935848-31-2*); Tchr's manual 5.00 (*1-880188-57-0*) Bess Pr.

Pratt, Helen G. The Hawaiians: An Island People. Morgan, Rosamond S. & Fraser, Juliette M., illus. 210p. (gr. 6 up). 1991. pap. 9.95 (*0-8048-1709-X*) C E Tuttle.

Radlauer, Ruth. Haleakala National Park. updated ed. Zillmer, Rolf, illus. LC 79-10500. 48p. (gr. 3 up). 1987. pap. 4.95 (*0-516-47499-5*) Childrens.

—Hawaii Volcanoes National Park. updated ed. Radlauer, Ed & Radlauer, Ruth, illus. LC 78-19718. 48p. (gr. 3 up). 1987. (Elk Grove Bks); pap. 4.95 (*0-516-47498-7*) Childrens.

Russell, William. Hawaii. LC 93-49340. 1994. write for info. (*1-55916-034-9*) Rourke Bk Co.

Stanley, Fay. The Last Princess: The Story of Princess Ka'iulani of Hawai'i. Stanley, Diane, illus. LC 89-71445. 40p. (gr. 1-4). 1991. RSBE 16.95 (*0-02-786785-4*, Four Winds) Macmillan Child Grp.

Thompson, Vivian L. Hawaiian Legends of Tricksters & Riddlers. Wozniak, Patricia A., illus. LC 90-44432. 112p. (Orig.). (gr. 4-8). 1990. pap. 8.50 (*0-8248-1302-2*, Kolowalu Bk) UH Pr.

Turner Educational Services, Inc. Staff & Clark, James I. Hawaii. 48p. (gr. 3 up). 1986. PLB 19.97 (*0-8174-4516-1*) Raintree Steck-V.

Twain, Mark. Roughing It. Girling, Z. N., intro. by. (Illus.). (gr. 8 up). 1967. pap. 2.95 (*0-8049-0134-1*, CL-134) Airmont.

Valier, Kathy. The Kaua'i Guide to Hiking Trails Less Traveled with Camping Information. (Illus.). 64p. (Orig.). 1989. pap. 2.50 (*0-942255-06-2*, G5) Magic Fishes Pr.

HAWAII–FICTION

Ehlers, Sabine. The Bossy Hawaiian Moon. Kiyabu, Walter H., illus. 32p. (ps-1). 1980. pap. 2.95 (*0-930492-15-3*) Hawaiian Serv.

Feeney, Stephanie. Hawaii Is a Rainbow. Hammid, Hella, illus. LC 80-5462. 64p. (ps-k). 1980. 12.95 (*0-8248-1007-4*) UH Pr.

Goodman, Robert & Spicer, Robert. Urashima Taro. 2nd ed. Suyeoka, George, illus. 72p. Date not set. 15.95 (*0-89610-276-9*, 24019-000) Island Heritage.

Goudge, Eileen. Hawaiian Christmas. (gr. 6 up). 1986. pap. 2.95 (*0-440-93649-7*, LFL) Dell.

Guback, Georgia. Luka's Quilt. LC 93-12241. (Illus.). 32p. (ps up). 1994. 14.00 (*0-688-12154-3*); PLB 13.93 (*0-688-12155-1*) Greenwillow.

Hober, David. Kobi the Elf, Magic & Adventure in Hawaii. Pickett, Timothy & Okaze, Kunio, eds. Nagaoki, Kobun, tr. Fontilis, Glen, illus. (ENG & JPN.). 32p. (Orig.). (gr. 1 up). 1990. pap. 4.95 (*0-9623215-0-8*) Moonbeam Magic Pub.

Hoobler, Dorothy & Hoobler, Thomas. Aloha Means Come Back: The Story of a World War II Girl. Bleck, Cathie, illus. 64p. (gr. 4-6). 1992. 5.95 (*0-382-24156-8*); PLB 7.95 (*0-382-24148-7*); pap. 3.95 (*0-382-24349-8*) Silver Burdett Pr.

Hughes, Dean. Lucky in Love. LC 93-33301. 161p. (Orig.). (gr. 3-7). 1993. pap. 4.95 (*0-87579-805-5*) Deseret Bk.

Koski, Mary. The Stowaway Fairy in Hawaii. (Illus.). 36p. (gr. k-5). 1991. 9.95 (*0-89610-225-4*) Island Heritage.

Lapka, Fay S. The Sea, the Song & the Trumpetfish. 160p. (Orig.). (gr. 7-12). 1991. pap. 6.99 (*0-87788-754-3*) Shaw Pubs.

McCay, William. Young Indiana Jones & the Mountain of Fire. LC 93-46118. 132p. (Orig.). (gr. 3-7). 1994. pap. 3.99 (*0-679-86384-2*, Bullseye Bks) Random Bks Yng Read.

Mower, Nancy. Tutu Kane & Granpa. Wozniak, Patricia, illus. 32p. (ps). 1989. 8.95 (*0-916630-66-8*) Pr Pacifica.

Oetting. Keiki of the Islands. LC 71-108728. (Illus.). 96p. (gr. 3 up). 1970. PLB 10.95 (*0-87783-018-5*); pap. 3.94 deluxe ed. (*0-87783-096-7*) Oddo.

Olsen, E. A. Killer in the Trap. Le Blanc, L., illus. LC 68-16399. 48p. (gr. 3 up). 1970. PLB 10.95 (*0-87783-019-3*); pap. 3.94 deluxe ed. (*0-87783-097-5*); cassette 10.60x (*0-87783-190-4*) Oddo.

Pitchford, Gene. Young Folks' Hawaiian Time. (Illus.). (ps). 1965. pap. 2.00 (*0-87505-275-4*) Borden.

Rappolt, Miriam. Queen Emma: A Woman of Vision. Rappolt, Miriam, prologue by. (Illus., Orig.). 1991. pap. 12.95 (*0-916630-68-4*) Pr Pacifica.

Rappolt, Miriam E. One Paddle, Two Paddle: Hawaiian Teen Age Mystery & Suspense Stories. Pultz, Jane W., ed. Frazer, Peg, illus. LC 82-24048. 190p. (gr. 7-9). 1994. pap. 10.95 (*0-916630-69-2*); wkbk. 4.00 (*0-916630-32-3*); tchr's. manual 2.00 (*0-916630-33-1*) Pr Pacifica.

From Hawaii comes the outstanding collection of mysteries & suspense stories with all the multi-cultural diversity that surrounds teen-age lives there. There are spooky encounters that defy logic & there is tragedy & fun. The tradition of folklore is rich in Hawaii & story telling is an important part of every social gathering. In keeping with the tradition, the author recreates the lives of young teenagers as they drive the car alone for the first time, engage in the popular outrigger canoe races, dedicate themselves to the ancient art of the hula,visit a Chinese cemetery at midnight, defy old superstitions, are forced to deal with a sinking catamaran at sea, visit a sacred heiau & much more. These stories are peopled with teenagers acting within their own groups & are an authentic reflection of their lives in this fascinating culture. For grades 7 through 9.

Publisher Provided Annotation.

Rattigan, Jama K. Dumpling Soup. Hsu-Flanders, Lillian, illus. 32p. (gr. 4-8). 1993. 15.95 (*0-316-73445-4*) Little.

Roddy, Lee. The Legend of Fire. 148p. (gr. 3-6). 1989. pap. 4.99 (*0-929608-17-8*) Focus Family.

Roop, Peter. The Cry of the Conch. Patric, illus. LC 84-4232. (gr. 3-5). 1984. 8.95 (*0-916630-39-0*) Pr Pacifica.

Salisbury, Graham. Blue Skin of the Sea: A Novel in Stories. (gr. 4-7). 1992. 15.95 (*0-385-30596-6*) Doubleday.

—Under the Blood Red Sun. LC 94-444. 1994. 15.95 (*0-385-32099-X*) Delacorte.

Salter-Mathieson, Nigel. Little Chief Mischief. Gruen, Chuck, illus. (gr. 2-7). 1962. 10.95 (*0-8392-3020-6*) Astor-Honor.

Slepian, Jan. The Broccoli Tapes. (gr. 3-7). 1989. 14.95 (*0-399-21712-6*, Philomel Bks) Putnam Pub Group.

—Broccoli Tapes. 225p. 1992. text ed. 18.00 (*1-56956-201-6*) W A T Braille.

Swanson, Helen M. Angel of Rainbow Gulch. 128p. (Orig.). (gr. 3-6). 1992. pap. 4.95 (*1-880188-08-2*) Bess PR.

Tabrah, Ruth M. Emily's Hawaii. Hall, Pat, illus. 191p. (gr. 4-7). 1994. pap. 8.95 (*0-916630-45-5*) Pr Pacifica. EMILY'S HAWAII by Ruth M. Tabrah is an exciting, multicultural adventure & suspense story popular with children grades 4-7. Both boys & girls will identify with the new friends 12-year-old Emily & her 10-year-old brother Beener find in their move to the Big Island of Hawaii. Japanese-American Dorothy Fujita introduces Emily & Beener to the colorful celebration of a midsummer Buddhist Bon Dance. Part-Hawaiian Alix & Hawaiian-Chinese Noelani take Emily into the special - & spooky - places of ancient Hawaii & its Polynesian traditions. Puerto Rican Tony Guzman helps Beener race his pet turtle. The children adventure through Hawaiian burial caves, immerse themselvs into the idyllic lifestyle of plantation Hawaii & learn by experience the importance of tolerance & mutual respect. Any child with a fear of "creepy, crawly" things will feel for Emily who confronts & overcomes her fears in order to save her brother's life. Now in its third printing, EMILY'S HAWAII has become a classic for a generation of young readers. The author's style is vivid; the narrative is strong. The broad range of realistic characters & the setting of Hawaii's aloha atmosphere make fascinating

reading. Ms. Tabrah, a well-known Hawaii author, has thirty books in print. Her other junior novel, THE RED SHARK, is popular with 12-16-year-olds.
Publisher Provided Annotation.

—The Red Shark. 2nd ed. Hall, Pat, illus. 224p. (gr. 5-10). 1991. pap. 7.95 (*0-916630-67-6*) Pr Pacifica.
Von Tempski, Armine. Bright Spurs. Brown, Paul, illus. LC 92-24540. x, 284p. 1992. pap. 14.95 (*0-918024-95-1*) Ox Bow.
—Pam's Paradise Ranch: A Story of Hawaii. Brown, Paul, illus. LC 92-24538. viii, 334p. 1992. pap. 14.95 (*0-918024-96-X*) Ox Bow.

HAWAII–HISTORY

Marsh, Carole. Chill Out: Scary Hawaii Tales Based on Frightening Hawaii Truths. (Illus.). 1994. lib. bdg. 24.95 (*0-7933-4687-8*); pap. 14.95 (*0-7933-4688-6*); disk 29.95 (*0-7933-4689-4*) Gallopade Pub Group.
—Hawaii "Crinkum-Crankum" A Funny Word Book about Our State. (Illus.). 1994. lib. bdg. 24.95 (*0-7933-4840-4*); pap. 14.95 (*0-7933-4841-2*); disk 29.95 (*0-7933-4842-0*) Gallopade Pub Group.
—The Hawaii Mystery Van Takes Off! Book 1: Handicapped Hawaii Kids Sneak Off on a Big Adventure. (Illus.). (gr. 3-12). 1994. 24.95 (*0-7933-4994-X*); pap. 14.95 (*0-7933-4995-8*); computer disk 29.95 (*0-7933-4996-6*) Gallopade Pub Group.
—Hawaii Timeline: A Chronology of Hawaii History, Mystery, Trivia, Legend, Lore & More. (Illus.). (gr. 3-12). 1994. PLB 24.95 (*0-7933-5908-2*); pap. 14.95 (*0-7933-5909-0*); computer disk 29.95 (*0-7933-5910-4*) Gallopade Pub Group.
—Hawaii's Unsolved Mysteries (& Their "Solutions") Includes Scientific Information & Other Activities for Students. (Illus.). (gr. 3-12). 1994. PLB 24.95 (*0-7933-5755-1*); pap. 14.95 (*0-7933-5756-X*); computer disk 29.95 (*0-7933-5757-8*) Gallopade Pub Group.
Stanley, Fay. The Last Princess: The Story of Princess Kaiulani of Hawaii. Stanley, Diane, illus. LC 93-45714. (gr. 1-4). 1994. pap. 5.95 (*0-689-71829-2*, Aladdin) Macmillan Child Grp.

HAWAII–HISTORY–FICTION

McLane, Gretel B. Kalia & the King's Horse. Wozniak, Patricia, illus. 88p. (gr. 4-7). 1994. pap. 8.95 (*0-916630-70-6*) Pr Pacifica.
KALIA & THE KING'S HORSE takes readers back to the island of Maui in Hawaii when that incredible creature, the horse, first arrived. Kalia, a 12-year-old Hawaiian girl, was fascinated with the horse & the men in charge of it, dreaming that one day she might ride an animal like it. But this horse was KAPU; only its handlers & the King could ride it. However, she watched from a nearby tree & learned all that she could about the horse. While in the tree she heard two men plotting against the King. Suddenly, she realized she must get the message to him on the other side of the island. Thus, the adventure begins. Written with a sensitive, deep understanding of the Hawaiian culture, it is probably the best book about Hawaii for 4th-6th graders. The first part of Kalia's story has been excerpted & printed in the children's magazine CRICKET & has been translated into the Polynesian language of Easter Island for use in their schools.
Publisher Provided Annotation.

Yamashita, Susan. The Menehune & the Nene. O'Connor, Barbara, illus. LC 84-3290. (gr. 3-6). 1984. 8.95 (*0-916630-42-0*) Pr Pacifica.

HAWAII–INDUSTRIES

Cadwallader, Sharon. Cookie McCorkle & the Case of the King's Ghost. 112p. (Orig.). 1991. pap. 2.99 (*0-380-76350-8*, Camelot) Avon.

HAWAIIAN LANGUAGE

Beamer, Nona. Helu Papa-Counting in Hawaiian: Pi'a Pa-Hawaiian Alphabet. Ching, Patrick, illus. 40p. 1991. text ed. write for info. (*0-9627294-0-X*) Hawaiian Resources.
Kawai'ae'a, Keiki C. Let's Learn to Count in Hawaiian. Tanaka, Cliff, illus. 24p. (ps-k). 1988. 7.95 (*0-89610-076-6*) Island Heritage.
—Let's Learn to Count in Hawaiian. Tanaka, Cliff, illus. 24p. (ps-k). 1988. incl. cassette 11.95 (*0-89610-080-4*) Island Heritage.
Murray, Patricia A. Let's Learn the Hawaiian Alphabet. Tanaka, Cliff, illus. 24p. (ps-k). 1987. 7.95 (*0-89610-075-8*) Island Heritage.
—Let's Learn the Hawaiian Alphabet. Tanaka, Cliff, illus. 24p. (ps-k). 1988. incls. cass. 11.95 (*0-89610-079-0*) Island Heritage.
Wren & Maile. Na 'Olelo Hawaii: Words. Wren, illus. (ENG & HAW.). 10p. (ps). 1992. bds. 3.95 (*1-880188-29-5*) Bess Pr.
—Pi'a'pa: Alphabet. Wren, illus. (ENG & HAW.). 10p. (ps). 1992. bds. 3.95 (*1-880188-30-9*) Bess Pr.
—Say It in Hawaiian: My Body. Wren, illus. (ENG & HAW.). 10p. (ps). 1992. bds. 3.95 (*1-880188-03-1*) Bess Pr.

HAWKS

Olsen, Penny. Falcons & Hawks. LC 92-11986. (Illus.). 72p. (gr. 5 up). 1992. PLB 17.95 (*0-8160-2843-5*) Facts on File.
Patent, Dorothy H. Osprey. Munoz, William, photos by. LC 92-30103. (Illus.). 64p. (gr. 4-9). 1993. 14.45 (*0-395-63391-5*, Clarion Bks) HM.

HAWKS–FICTION

Baylor, Byrd. Hawk, I'm Your Brother. reissued ed. Parnall, Peter, illus. LC 86-10742. 48p. (gr. 1-5). 1986. pap. 4.95 (*0-689-71102-6*, Aladdin) Macmillan Child Grp.
Dickinson, Peter. The Blue Hawk. (gr. 5-9). 1991. 21.50 (*0-8446-6478-2*) Peter Smith.
Le Sueur, Meridel. Sparrow Hawk. DesJarlait, Robert, illus. LC 87-80573. 176p. (gr. 7 up). 1987. Repr. of 1950 ed. 13.95 (*0-930100-22-0*) Holy Cow.
Mooy, John. The Tale of Boris: (A Fable of the Red-Tailed Hawk) Stroschin, Jane, illus. 32p. (gr. k-6). 1991. PLB 15.00 (*1-883960-06-1*); pap. 7.00 (*1-883960-07-X*) Henry Quill.
Walters-Lucy, Jean. Look Ma, I'm Flying. Tabesh, Delight, ed. & illus. LC 92-13953. 48p. (Orig.). (ps-5). 1992. pap. 6.95 perfect bdg. (*0-941992-28-4*) Los Arboles Pub.

HAYDN, FRANZ JOSEPH, 1732-1809

Greene, Carol. Franz Joseph Haydn: Great Man of Music. LC 93-37522. (Illus.). 48p. (gr. k-3). 1994. PLB 12.85 (*0-516-04260-2*) Childrens.
Rachlin, Ann. Haydn. Hellard, Susan, illus. LC 92-9521. 1992. 5.95 (*0-8120-4988-8*) Barron.

HAYES, RUTHERFORD BIRCHARD, PRESIDENT U. S. 1822-1893

Kent, Zachary. Rutherford B. Hayes. LC 88-8679. (Illus.). 100p. (gr. 3 up). 1989. PLB 14.40 (*0-516-01365-3*) Childrens.
Robbins, Neal E. Rutherford B. Hayes: Nineteenth President of the United States. Young, Richard G., ed. LC 88-24565. (Illus.). (gr. 5-9). 1989. PLB 17.26 (*0-944483-23-2*) Garrett Ed Corp.

HEALTH

see Hygiene

HEALTH, MENTAL

see Mental Health

HEALTH, PUBLIC

see Public Health

HEALTH EDUCATION

Arnold, Caroline. Pain: What Is It? How Do We Deal with It? LC 86-29815. (Illus.). 96p. (gr. 3-7). 1986. 12.95 (*0-688-05710-1*); lib. bdg. 12.88 (*0-688-05711-X*, Morrow Jr Bks) Morrow Jr Bks.
Carratello, Patricia. Let's Investigate Health & Safety. (Illus.). 48p. (gr. 1-4). 1984. wkbk. 6.95 (*1-55734-214-8*) Tchr Create Mat.
Health Facts, 8 bks. (gr. 2-3). 1992. Set 115.92 (*0-8114-2775-7*) Raintree Steck-V.
Ho, Betty Y. A Unique Health Guide for Children. Elkan, Betty, intro. by. Elkan, Amanda & Ho, Betty Y., illus. 60p. (Orig.). (gr. 3 up). 1994. pap. write for info. (*1-884996-00-0*) Juvenescent.
Muhammad, S. Ifetayo. Vitamin A Through Zinc: An Alphabet of Good Health. 16p. (Orig.). 1985. pap. 1.00 (*0-916157-13-X*) African Islam Miss Pubns.
Ransford, Lynn. Happy Healthy Bodies. (Illus.). 48p. (gr. 1-4). 1987. wkbk. 6.95 (*1-55734-223-7*) Tchr Create Mat.
Skolnick, Georgette B. To Be a Doctor: A Health Education Workbook. Barr, Charlotte & Cook, Tonya, illus. 215p. (Orig.). (gr. 6-9). 1982. student's wkbk. 8.00 (*0-913855-00-6*) GBS CA.
Sullivan, Dianna J. Big & Easy Health. Adkins, Lynda, illus. 48p. (ps-2). 1988. wkbk. 6.95 (*1-55734-104-4*) Tchr Create Mat.

HEALTH OF CHILDREN

see Children–Care and Hygiene

HEARING

see also Ear

Berry, Joy W. Teach Me about Listening. Dickey, Kate, ed. LC 85-45087. (Illus.). 36p. (ps). 1986. 4.98 (*0-685-10726-4*) Grolier Inc.
Bertrand, Cecile. Noni Hears. (ps). 1993. 4.95 (*0-307-15686-9*, Artsts Writrs) Western Pub.
Decker, Nan. The Caption Workbook. Drescher, Joan, illus. 27p. (gr. 5-8). 1984. pap. text ed. 1.95 (*0-913072-61-3*) Natl Assn Deaf.
Fowler, Allan. Hearing Things. LC 90-22524. (Illus.). 32p. (ps-2). 1991. PLB 10.75 (*0-516-04909-7*); pap. 3.95 (*0-516-44909-5*) Childrens.
—Lo Que Escuchas - Libro Grande: (Hearing Things Big Book) LC 90-22524. (SPA., Illus.). 32p. (ps-2). 1993. 22.95 (*0-516-59469-9*) Childrens.
Gardner, Karen A. My Life As an Ear. rev. ed. (Illus.). 37p. (ps-2). 1984. Set of 1-4. PLB 1.70 (*0-931421-01-2*) Psychol Educ Pubns.
Moncure, Jane B. Sounds All Around. Axeman, Lois, illus. LC 82-4516. 32p. (ps-3). 1982. pap. 3.95 (*0-516-43252-4*) Childrens.
Parramon, J. M. & Puig, J. J. Hearing. Rius, Maria, illus. 32p. (Orig.). (ps). 1985. pap. 6.95 (*0-8120-3563-1*); Span. ed. pap. 6.95 (*0-8120-3606-9*) Barron.
Pomeroy, Johanna P. Content Area Reading Skills Sound & Hearing: Detecting Sequence. (Illus.). (gr. 4). 1987. pap. text ed. 3.25 (*0-89525-860-9*) Ed Activities.
Showers, Paul. Ears Are for Hearing. Keller, Holly, illus. LC 89-17479. 32p. (gr. k-4). 1990. (Crowell Jr Bks); PLB 14.89 (*0-690-04720-7*, Crowell Jr Bks) HarpC Child Bks.
—Ears Are for Hearing. Keller, Holly, illus. LC 89-17479. 32p. (gr. k-4). 1993. pap. 4.50 (*0-06-445112-7*, Trophy) HarpC Child Bks.
—Listening Walk. Aliki, illus. LC 61-10495. 40p. (gr. k-3). 1961. PLB 13.89 (*0-690-49663-X*, Crowell Jr Bks) HarpC Child Bks.
Smith, Kathie B. & Crenson, Victoria. Hearing. Storms, Robert S., illus. LC 87-5854. 24p. (gr. k-3). 1988. PLB 10.59 (*0-8167-1006-6*); pap. text ed. 2.50 (*0-8167-1007-4*) Troll Assocs.
Snell, Nigel. Hearing. (Illus.). 32p. (gr. k-2). 1991. 10.95 (*0-237-60256-3*, Pub. by Evans Bros Ltd) Trafalgar.
Stoker, Richard G. & Gaydos, Janine. Hearing Aids for You & the Zoo. (Illus.). 32p. (gr. k-3). 1984. pap. 4.95 (*0-317-13888-X*) Alexander Graham.
Stuchbury, Dianne. Listen! Stuchbury, Dianne, illus. 24p. (ps-1). 1991. 4.99 (*0-7459-2001-2*) Lion USA.
Wright, Lillian. Hearing: First Starts Ser. LC 94-10719. (Illus.). 32p. (gr. 2-4). 1994. PLB 18.99 (*0-8114-5516-5*) Raintree Steck-V.

HEART

see also Blood–Circulation

Allison, Linda. Stethoscope Book & Kit. (gr. 2-7). 1991. pap. 12.45 (*0-201-57096-3*) Addison-Wesley.
Bailey, Donna. All about the Heart & Blood. LC 90-10052. (Illus.). 48p. (gr. 2-6). 1990. PLB 20.70 (*0-8114-2779-X*) Raintree Steck-V.
Gillis, Jennifer S. Hearts & Crafts: Over Twenty Projects for Fun-Loving Kids. Steege, Gwen, ed. Delmonte, Patti, illus. LC 93-4841. 64p. (gr. k-4). 1994. pap. 9.95 (*0-88266-844-7*) Storey Comm Inc.
Heart & Blood. 48p. (gr. 5-8). 1988. PLB 10.95 (*0-382-09700-9*) (*0-685-24608-6*) Silver Burdett Pr.
LeMaster, Leslie J. Your Heart & Blood. LC 84-7604. (Illus.). 48p. (gr. k-4). 1984. PLB 12.85 (*0-516-01933-3*); pap. 4.95 (*0-516-41933-1*) Childrens.
Parker, Steve. The Heart & Blood. rev. ed. (Illus.). 48p. (gr. 5 up). 1991. pap. 6.95 (*0-531-24604-3*) Watts.
Saunderson, Jane. Heart & Lungs. Farmer, Andrew & Green, Robina, illus. LC 90-42881. 32p. (gr. 4-6). 1992. PLB 11.89 (*0-8167-2096-7*); pap. text ed. 3.95 (*0-8167-2097-5*) Troll Assocs.

HEART–DISEASES

Arnold, Caroline. Heart Disease. LC 90-33609. (Illus.). 96p. (gr. 9-12). 1990. PLB 13.90 (*0-531-10884-8*) Watts.
Galperin, Anne. Stroke & Heart Disease. (Illus.). 112p. (gr. 6-12). 1991. 18.95 (*0-7910-0077-X*) Chelsea Hse.
Re'lem, Dyob & Melger, Boyd A. Hoge Bloeddruk, Myocardiale Infarct, Grafieken. (DUT., Illus.). 69p. (Orig.). (gr. 12 up). 1989. pap. write for info. (*0-9622463-1-X*) B Melger.
Silverstein, Alvin & Silverstein, Virginia B. Heart Disease: America's Number One Killer. rev. ed. LC 83-49495. (Illus.). 160p. (gr. 7 up). 1985. (Lipp Jr Bks); (Lipp Jr Bks) HarpC Child Bks.
Tiger, Steven. Heart Disease. LC 85-8949. (Illus.). 72p. (gr. 4-8). 1986. lib. bdg. 11.98 (*0-671-60021-4*, J Messner) S&S Trade.

HEAT

see also Fire; Temperature; Thermodynamics

Ardley, Neil. Heat. LC 91-29057. (Illus.). 48p. (gr. 6 up). 1992. text ed. 13.95 RSBE (*0-02-705666-X*, New Discovery) Macmillan Child Grp.
Dunn, Andrew. Heat. LC 93-7518. (Illus.). 32p. (gr. 3-6). 1993. 13.95 (*1-56847-018-5*) Thomson Lrning.
Fowler, Allan. Hot & Cold. LC 93-38588. (Illus.). 32p. (ps-2). 1994. PLB 10.14.40 (*0-516-06021-X*); pap. 3.95 (*0-516-46021-8*) Childrens.
Heat. (Illus.). 56p. (gr. 7-10). 1990. 8.80 (*0-941008-85-1*) Tops Learning.
Jennings, Terry. Heat. LC 88-22865. (Illus.). 32p. (gr. 3-6). 1989. pap. 4.95 (*0-516-48403-6*) Childrens.
Lafferty, Peter. Burning & Melting: Projects with Heat. (Illus.). 32p. (gr. 5-8). 1990. PLB 12.40 (*0-531-17235-X*, Gloucester Pr) Watts.
Maury, Jean-Pierre. Heat & Cold. 80p. (gr. 8 up). 1989. pap. 4.95 (*0-8120-4211-5*) Barron.
Mellett, Peter & Rossiter, Jane. Hot & Cold. LC 92-5141. (Illus.). 32p. (gr. 5-8). 1993. PLB 12.40 (*0-531-14236-1*) Watts.
Morgan, Sally & Morgan, Adrian. Using Energy. LC 93-20407. (gr. 4 up). 1993. write for info. (*0-8160-2984-9*) Facts on File.
Peacock, Graham. Heat. LC 93-34613. (Illus.). 32p. (gr. 2-4). 1994. 14.95 (*1-56847-075-4*) Thomson Lrning.
Richardson, Joy. Heat. LC 92-14419. (Illus.). (gr. k-4). 1993. 11.40 (*0-531-14239-6*) Watts.
Santrey, Laurence. Heat. Birmingham, Lloyd, illus. LC 84-2711. 32p. (gr. 3-6). 1985. PLB 9.49 (*0-8167-0306-X*); pap. text ed. 2.95 (*0-8167-0307-8*) Troll Assocs.

HEAT-EXPERIMENTS

Darling, David. Between Fire & Ice: The Science of Heat. LC 91-40966. (Illus.). 60p. (gr. 5 up). 1992. text ed. 13.95 RSBE (*0-87518-501-0*, Dillon) Macmillan Child Grp.

Gardner, Robert & Kemer, Eric. Temperature & Heat. LC 92-32367. (gr. 3-7). 1993. lib. bdg. 14.98 (*0-671-69040-X*, J Messner); pap. 9.95 (*0-671-69045-0*, J Messner) S&S Trade.

Gould, Alan. Convection: A Current Event. Bergman, Lincoln & Fairwell, Kay, eds. Klofkorn, Lisa, illus. Hoyt, Richard, photos by. (Illus.). 38p. (Orig.). (gr. 6-9). 1988. pap. 10.00 (*0-912511-15-X*) Lawrence Science.

Oleksy, Walter. Experiments with Heat. LC 85-30860. (Illus.). 48p. (gr. k-4). 1986. PLB 12.85 (*0-516-01277-0*); pap. 4.95 (*0-516-41277-9*) Childrens.

HEAT-FICTION

Fienberg, Anna. The Hottest Boy Who Ever Lived. Grant, Christy, ed. Gamble, Kim, illus. LC 94-6648. 32p. (gr. k-3). 1994. PLB 14.95 (*0-8075-3387-4*) A Whitman.

McAllister, Angela. The Ice Palace. Barrett, Angela, illus. LC 93-45255. 1994. 15.95 (*0-399-22784-9*, Putnam) Putnam Pub Group.

Rylant, Cynthia. Mr. Putter & Tabby Row the Boat. Howard, Arthur, illus. LC 93-41832. 1995. write for info. (*0-15-256257-5*) HarBrace.

HEAVEN

Delp, Debra. Packing for Heaven. Zoglio, Suzanne, ed. Larsen, Rob, illus. 32p. (Orig.). (gr. k-5). 1991. pap. text ed. 8.95 (*0-941668-03-7*) Tower Hill Pr.

Hillis, Don. Heaven Is Out of This World. (Illus.). 47p. 1982. pap. 1.00 (*0-89323-032-4*) Bible Memory.

Sinetar, Marsha. Why Can't Grownups Believe in Angels? LC 93-12906. (Illus.). 48p. 1993. text ed. 14.95 (*0-89243-551-8*, Triumph Books) Liguori Pubns.

Wilde, Gary. Heaven & Hell. (Illus.). 48p. (gr. 6-8). 1992. pap. 8.99 (*1-55945-131-9*) Group Pub.

HEBREW LANGUAGE

Amery & Haron. First Thousand Words in Hebrew. Cartwright, Stephen, illus. 62p. (ps-6). 1985. PLB 11. 95 (*0-86020-863-X*, Pub. by Usborne) EDC.

Bachrach, Kalman. Hasefer Alef-Beis Hametzuyar (In Color) Gordon, Ayalah, illus. (HEB.). 67p. (gr. 1). 1960. pap. text ed. 2.50x (*1-878530-01-1*) K Bachrach Co.

—Hasefer Chelek Rishon, Pt. 1: Alef-Beis. Soyer, Yitzhak, illus. (HEB.). 68p. (gr. 1). 1941. pap. text ed. 2.25x (*1-878530-00-3*) K Bachrach Co.

—Hasefer Chelek Sheini, Pt. 2. Krukman, Tsvi, illus. (HEB.). 91p. (gr. 2). 1942. pap. text ed. 2.25x (*1-878530-09-7*) K Bachrach Co.

—Hasefer Chelek Shlishi, Pt. 3. Krukman, Tsvi, illus. (HEB.). 74p. (gr. 3). 1947. pap. text ed. 2.25x (*1-878530-10-0*) K Bachrach Co.

—Me Ah P'Amim V'Echad - Asid (One Thousand Times & One - Future Tense) Dikduk L'Talmidim (Grammar for Students) (HEB.). 46p. (gr. 1-3). 1937. pap. text ed. 1.00x (*1-878530-21-6*) K Bachrach Co.

—Meyah P'Amim V'Echad - Haveh (One Thousand Times & One - Present Tense) Dikduk L'Talmidim (Grammar for Students) (HEB.). 32p. (gr. 1-3). 1937. pap. text ed. 1.00x (*1-878530-22-4*) K Bachrach Co.

—Meyah P'Amim V'Echad - Ovar (One Thousand Times & One - Past Tense) Dikduk L'Talmidim (Grammar for Students) (HEB.). 48p. (gr. 1-3). 1937. pap. text ed. 1.00x (*1-878530-20-8*) K Bachrach Co.

—Targilon Hasefer Chelek Rishon, Pt. 1. (HEB.). 42p. (gr. 1). 1950. wkbk. 2.25x (*1-878530-11-9*) K Bachrach Co.

—Targilon Hasefer Chelek Sheini, Pt. 2. (HEB.). 76p. (gr. 1). 1949. wkbk. 2.25x (*1-878530-12-7*) K Bachrach Co.

—Targilon Hasefer Chelek Shlishi, Pt. 3. (HEB.). 60p. (gr. 3). 1953. wkbk. 2.25x (*1-878530-13-5*) K Bachrach Co.

—Targilon Olami Sefer Rishon, Bk. 1. (HEB.). 54p. (gr. 2). 1936. wkbk. 2.00x (*1-878530-17-8*) K Bachrach Co.

—Targilon Olami Sefer Sheini, Bk. 2. (HEB.). 54p. (gr. 3-4). 1936. wkbk. 2.00x (*1-878530-18-6*) K Bachrach Co.

—Targilon Olami Sefer Shlishi, Bk. 3. (HEB.). 60p. (gr. 4-6). 1939. wkbk. 2.00x (*1-878530-19-4*) K Bachrach Co.

Bachrach, Kalman & Axelrod, Herman. Ketivoni Chelek Chamishi, Pt. 5. Vanner, Vera, illus. (HEB.). 64p. (gr. 6). 1972. pap. text ed. 3.50x (*1-878530-06-2*) K Bachrach Co.

—Ketivoni Chelek Rishon, Pt. 1. Krukman, Tsvi, illus. (HEB.). 72p. (gr. 2). 1957. pap. text ed. 3.50x (*1-878530-02-X*) K Bachrach Co.

—Ketivoni Chelek R'Viyi, Pt. 4. Vanner, Vera, illus. (HEB.). 55p. (gr. 5). 1972. pap. text ed. 3.50x (*1-878530-05-4*) K Bachrach Co.

—Ketivoni Chelek Sheni, Pt. 2. Krukman, Tsvi, illus. (HEB.). 62p. (gr. 3). 1958. pap. text ed. 3.50x (*1-878530-03-8*) K Bachrach Co.

—Ketivoni Chelek Shishi, Pt. 6. Herskowitz, Sarah, illus. (HEB.). 62p. (gr. 7). 1974. pap. text ed. 3.50x (*1-878530-07-0*) K Bachrach Co.

—Ketivoni Chelek Shlishi, Pt. 3. Hershkowitz, Sarah, illus. (HEB.). 64p. (gr. 4). 1959. pap. text ed. 3.50x (*1-878530-04-6*) K Bachrach Co.

—Ketivoni Chelek Sh'Viyi, Pt. 7. Hershkowitz, Sarah, illus. (HEB.). 64p. (gr. 8). 1974. pap. text ed. 3.50x (*1-878530-08-9*) K Bachrach Co.

Burstein, Chaya M. Jewish Kids Hebrew-English Wordbook. Burstein, Chaya M., illus. 40p. (gr. 1 up). 1993. 16.95 (*0-8276-0381-9*) JPS Phila.

Child's Picture Hebrew Dictionary. 1984. 9.95 (*0-915361-07-8*) Modan-Adama Bks.

Cohan, Leo M. The Hebrew Alphabet: From Generation to Generation. (Illus.). 21p. (Orig.). (gr. 4). 1989. pap. 5.95 (*0-9636415-0-6*) Kol Yisrael Pub.

Coopersmith, Harry, ed. More of the Songs We Sing. Oechsli, K., illus. (ENG & HEB.). 288p. (gr. 4-10). 1970. 9.50x (*0-8381-0217-4*) United Syn Bk.

Ducoff, Helen. Hebrew Alphabet: Twenty-Two Letters & Numbers to Color. (Illus.). (gr. k-3). pap. 4.95 (*0-8074-0457-8*, 101311) UAHC.

Edwards, Michelle. Alef-Bet: A Hebrew Alphabet Book. Edwards, Michelle, illus. LC 91-31011. 32p. (ps-3). 1992. 15.00 (*0-688-09724-3*); PLB 14.93 (*0-688-09725-1*) Lothrop.

Fernandez, Peter. My Hebrew Dinosaurus. (Illus.). 32p. (Orig.). (ps-2). pap. 3.95 (*0-929371-70-4*) Kar Ben.

Gaelen, Nina. The Hebrew Primer: Script Writing Workbook. 63p. (gr. 4-7). 1987. pap. text ed. 2.95x (*0-87441-416-4*) Behrman.

Ganz, Yaffa. Alef To Tav. Horen, Michael, illus. 48p. (gr. 1-6). 1989. 11.95 (*0-89906-962-2*); pap. 7.95 (*0-89906-963-0*) Mesorah Pubns.

Goldberg, Nathan. The New Illustrated Hebrew-English Dictionary for Young Readers. (HEB & ENG., Illus.). (gr. 4-7). 1958. pap. 6.95x (*0-87068-370-5*) Ktav.

Goldstein, Rose B. Songs to Share. Schloss, E., illus. (HEB & ENG.). 64p. (ps-5). 2.95x (*0-8381-0720-6*, 10-720) United Syn Bk.

Gordon, Yosi. In the Beginning God Created the Alef-Bet. Grishaver, Joel L., illus. 40p. (Orig.). (gr. 3-5). 1991. pap. 3.75 wkbk. (*0-933873-61-1*) Torah Aura.

Helfer, Judith. Aleph Bet for You. Helfer, Judith, illus. LC 70-88355. (ps-2). 1969. pap. 4.00 (*0-88400-024-9*) Shengold.

Kahn, Katherine J. Alef Is One: A Hebrew Alphabet & Counting Book. Kahn, Katherine J., illus. LC 89-24428. 48p. (ps-4). 1989. 12.95 (*0-929371-05-4*); pap. 7.95 (*0-929371-04-6*) Kar Ben.

Lapine, Jennifer & Lapine, Susan. My First Hebrew Alphabet Book. (Illus.). 48p. (ps-1). 1977. pap. 3.95 (*0-8197-0399-0*) Bloch.

Mahoney, Judy. Teach Me Hebrew. Horowitz, Shelly, tr. (Illus.). 20p. (ps-6). 1991. pap. 11.95 incl. audiocassette (*0-934633-54-1*); tchr's. ed. 5.95 (*0-934633-28-2*) Teach Me.

Markowitz, Endel. Kid-Ish Yiddish. Klein, Debby, illus. 44p. 1993. PLB 16.95 (*0-933910-05-3*) Haymark.

Mordechai, Tova. Good Night My Friend Aleph. Mordechai, Tova, illus. 32p. (ps-1). 1989. 9.95 (*0-922613-12-5*); pap. 7.95 (*0-922613-13-3*) Hachai Pubns.

Nover, Elizabeth Z. Reading Workbook for the Hebrew Primer. 60p. (gr. 4-7). 1987. pap. 2.95 (*0-317-60046-X*) Behrman.

Passport Books Editors. Let's Learn Hebrew Picture Dictionary. (gr. 4-7). 1993. 11.95 (*0-8442-8490-4*, Natl Textbk) NTC Pub Grp.

Rossel, Karen T. & Mason, Patrice G. Hebrew Through Prayer, Vol. 1. 65p. (gr. 4-7). 1980. pap. text ed. 3.45x (*0-87441-313-3*); wkbk. 3.25 (*0-87441-284-6*); tchr's ed. 14.95 (*0-685-18651-2*) Behrman.

—Hebrew Through Prayer, Vol. 2. 65p. (gr. 4-7). 1980. pap. text ed. 3.45x (*0-87441-314-1*); wkbk. 3.25 (*0-87441-285-4*); tchr's ed. 14.95 (*0-317-60048-6*) Behrman.

Sheheen, Dennis, ed. A Child's Picture English-Hebrew Dictionary. Meshi, Ita, illus. (gr. 1-3). 1987. 9.95 (*0-915361-75-2*) Modan-Adama Bks.

Sheheen, Dennis, illus. A Child's Picture English-Yiddish Dictionary. LC 85-15659. (gr. k-2). 1985. 9.95 (*0-915361-29-9*) Modan-Adama Bks.

Shumsky, Abraham & Shumsky, Adaia. Alef-Bet: A Hebrew Primer. Bass, Marilyn & Goldman, Marvin, illus. (gr. k-3). 1979. pap. text ed. 7.00 (*0-8074-0026-2*, 405309) UAHC.

Strauss, Ruby, et al. The Hebrew Primer. Brison-Stack, Guy, illus. 128p. (Orig.). (gr. 1-6). 1985. pap. 4.95 (*0-87441-392-3*); tchr's guide 12.50x (*0-87441-396-6*) Behrman.

Strauss, Ruby G. Let's Learn the Alef Bet: Reading Readiness Book for the Hebrew Primer. Stack-Brison, Guy, illus. 94p. (gr. 4-7). 1987. pap. text ed. 4.45x (*0-87441-439-3*) Behrman.

Weisfish, Chaya. Yedidut. (HEB.). 214p. (gr. 9-12). 1991. write for info. wkbk. (*0-9630241-0-8*) C Weisfish.

Winter, Magda & Peery, Meira. Heritage Language Program 1-3, 3 wkbks. pap. text ed. 4.25 (*0-685-73883-3*) Behrman.

Yonay, Shahar & Yonay, Rina. Systematic Hebrew, Pt. C. Einat, Tzvi, illus. (gr. 7). 1986. 13.45 (*0-9616783-0-5*) S Yonay.

—Systematic Hebrew, Pt. D. (gr. 8-9). 1987. 14.95 (*0-9616783-1-3*) S Yonay.

—Systematic Hebrew, Pt. B. (gr. 6). 1988. 11.95 (*0-9616783-3-X*) S Yonay.

—Systematic Hebrew, Pt. A. (gr. 5). 1988. 11.95 (*0-9616783-2-1*) S Yonay.

—The Test. (gr. 7-12). 1988. 14.95 (*0-9616783-4-8*) S Yonay.

HEBREW LITERATURE

May use same subdivisions and names of literary forms as for English Literature.

see also Bible; Jewish Literature

Cherney, Ila. My Haggadah. Paiss, Jana, illus. 66p. (gr. 4-7). 1985. pap. text ed. 4.25 (*0-317-60058-3*) Behrman.

Matov, G. Tales of Tzaddikim: Devarim. Weinbach, Shaindel, tr. Bardugo, Miriam, illus. 320p. (gr. 7-12). 1988. 14.95 (*0-89906-833-2*); pap. 10.95 (*0-89906-834-0*) Mesorah Pubns.

—Tales of Tzaddikim: Sh'emos. Weinbach, Shaindel, tr. from HEB. Bardvgo, Miriam, illus. 320p. (gr. 7-12). 1988. 14.95 (*0-89906-827-8*); pap. 10.95 (*0-89906-828-6*) Mesorah Pubns.

Nachman of Breslov. The Fixer. Succot, Miriam & Succot, Eliyah, trs. from HEB. Succot, Miriam & Succot, Eliyah, illus. (gr. 3-12). 1977. pap. 1.50 (*0-917246-04-7*) Maimes.

Saypol, Judyth R. & Wikler, Madeline, illus. My Very Own Simchat Torah. 24p. (gr. k-5). 1981. pap. 3.95 (*0-930494-11-3*) Kar Ben.

Scherman, Nosson. Reb Yitzchak's Jewel: Rashi's Father Gets a Reward. Dershowitz, Yosef & Horen, Michael, illus. 32p. (gr. k-6). 1988. 6.95 (*0-89906-525-2*) Mesorah Pubns.

Sears, David. Tales from Reb Nachman: Parables Told by Rabbi Nachman of Breslov. Sears, David, illus. 32p. (gr. k-6). 1987. 10.95 (*0-89906-808-1*); pap. 7.95 (*0-89906-809-X*) Mesorah Pubns.

Weinbach, Shaindel, tr. from HEB. Tales of Tzaddikim: Bamidbar. Bardugo, Miriam, illus. 320p. (gr. 7-12). 1988. 14.95 (*0-89906-831-6*); pap. 10.95 (*0-89906-832-4*) Mesorah Pubns.

—Tales of Tzaddikim: Vayikra. Bardugo, Miriam, illus. 320p. (gr. 7-12). 1988. 14.95 (*0-89906-829-4*); pap. 10. 95 (*0-89906-830-8*) Mesorah Pubns.

HEBREWS

see Jews

HEDGEHOGS-FICTION

Adshead, Paul. The Secret Hedgehog. LC 91-38897. (gr. 4 up). 1991. 7.95 (*0-85953-510-X*) Childs Play.

Cartwright, Ann. The Winter Hedgehog. Cartwright, Reg, illus. LC 90-5593. 32p. (ps-3). 1990. SBE 13.95 (*0-02-717775-0*, Macmillan Child Bk) Macmillan Child Grp.

Fredeking, Jean T. The Snuffling Hedgehog. 1987. pap. 20.00x (*0-317-59264-5*, Pub. by A H Stockwell England) St Mut.

Hoban, Russell. Bread & Jam for Frances: Big Book. Hoban, Lillian, illus. LC 92-13622. 32p. (ps-3). 1993. pap. 19.95 (*0-06-443336-6*, Trophy) HarpC Child Bks.

—Egg Thoughts & Other Frances Songs. newly illustrated ed. Hoban, Lillian, illus. LC 92-44004. 32p. (ps-3). 1994. pap. 4.95 (*0-06-443378-1*, Trophy) HarpC Child Bks.

—Jim Hedgehog & the Lonesome Tower. Lewin, Betsy, illus. 48p. (gr. 1-4). 1992. 12.95 (*0-395-59760-9*, Clarion Bks) HM.

Lawhead, Stephen R. Riverbank Stories: The Tale of Anabelle Hedgehog. 112p. 1994. pap. 3.50 (*0-380-72200-3*, Camelot) Avon.

—The Tale of Anabelle Hedgehog. (Illus.). 128p. (gr. 4-8). 1990. 9.99 (*0-7459-1924-3*) Lion USA.

Millais, Raoul. Elijah & Pin-Pin. LC 91-20032. (Illus.). 48p. (ps-1). 1992. pap. 14.00 jacketed (*0-671-75543-9*, S&S BFYR) S&S Trade.

Mistress Hedgehog Has an Adventure. (Illus.). (ps-1). 1.98 (*0-517-45737-7*) Random Hse Value.

Potter, Beatrix. Meet Mrs. Tiggy-Winkle. (Illus.). 12p. (ps). 1987. bds. 2.95 (*0-7232-3454-X*) Warne.

—The Tale of Mrs. Tiggy-Winkle. Potter, Beatrix, illus. 24p. (ps-2). 1991. incl. cassette 5.98 (*1-55886-058-4*) Smarty Pants.

—The Tale of Mrs. Tiggy-Winkle. 1992. 3.99 (*0-517-07237-8*) Random Hse Value.

Teitelbaum, Michael. Sonic the Hedgehog: Robotnik's Revenge. Hanson, Glen, illus. LC 93-48920. 64p. (gr. 2-4). 1994. pap. 2.50 (*0-8167-3438-0*) Troll Assocs.

Waddell, Martin. The Happy Hedgehog Band. Barton, Jill, illus. LC 91-71852. 32p. (ps up). 1994. pap. 4.99 (*1-56402-272-2*) Candlewick Pr.

HELICOPTERS

Baker, David. Helicopters. (Illus.). 48p. (gr. 3-8). 1987. PLB 18.60 (*0-86592-356-6*); 13.95s.p. (*0-685-67593-9*) Rourke Corp.

Croome, Angela. Hovercraft. Wilkinson, Gerald, illus. (gr. 5 up). 1962. 14.95 (*0-8392-3008-7*) Astor-Honor.

Graham, Ian. Helicopters. Hayward, Ron & Khan, Aziz, illus. 32p. (gr. 5-6). 1989. PLB 12.40 (*0-531-17171-X*, Gloucester Pr) Watts.

Helicopters. (Illus.). 64p. (gr. 3-9). 1990. PLB 16.95 (*1-85435-092-7*) Marshall Cavendish.

Ladd, James D. Military Helicopters. Gibbons, Tony, et al, illus. 48p. (gr. 5 up). 1987. PLB 14.95 (*0-8225-1382-X*) Lerner Pubns.

Maynard, Christopher. Helicopters. LC 92-32924. 32p. (gr. 1-4). 1993. 3.95 (*1-85697-893-1*, Kingfisher LKC) LKC.

Nielsen, Nancy J. Helicopter Pilots. LC 88-12007. (Illus.). 48p. (gr. 5-6). 1988. text ed. 11.95 RSBE (*0-89686-399-9*, Crestwood Hse) Macmillan Child Grp.

Petersen, David. Helicopters. LC 82-23502. (Illus.). 48p. (gr. k-4). 1983. PLB 12.85 (*0-516-01680-6*) Childrens.

Scarborough, Kate. How It Goes: Helicopters. Tegg, Simon & Thompson, Ian, illus. 32p. (gr. 3-7). 1994. 10.95 (*0-8120-6455-0*); pap. 4.95 (*0-8120-1993-8*) Barron.

Stephen, R. J. The Picture World of Helicopters. (Illus.). 32p. (gr. k-4). 1989. PLB 12.40 (*0-531-10726-4*) Watts.

—Picture World of Military Helicopters. (Illus.). 1990. PLB 12.40 (*0-531-14010-5*) Watts.
Sullivan, George. Modern Combat Helicopters. LC 92-31492. (Illus.). 128p. (gr. 6-9). 1993. 17.95x (*0-8160-2353-0*) Facts on File.
Supermachines. 112p. (gr. 4-9). 1989. 18.95 (*1-85435-075-7*) Marshall Cavendish.
White, D. Helicopters. (Illus.). 48p. (gr. 3-8). 1989. PLB 18.60 (*0-86592-451-1*); 13.95s.p. (*0-685-58295-7*) Rourke Corp.

HELICOPTERS–FICTION

Anderson, Joan. Harry's Helicopter. Ancona, George, photos by. LC 89-28601. (Illus.). 32p. (gr. k up). 1990. 13.95 (*0-688-09186-5*); PLB 13.88 (*0-688-09187-3*, Morrow Jr Bks) Morrow Jr Bks.
Budgie Goes to Sea. 40p. (ps-1). 1991. pap. 12.00 jacketed (*0-671-73474-1*, S&S BFYR) S&S Trade.

HEMINGWAY, ERNEST, 1899-1961

Lyttle, Richard B. Ernest Hemingway: The Life & the Legend. LC 91-11218. (Illus.). 224p. (gr. 7 up). 1992. SBE 15.95 (*0-689-31670-4*, Atheneum Child Bk) Macmillan Child Grp.
McDowell, N. Hemingway. (Illus.). (gr. 7 up). 1989. lib. bdg. 19.94 (*0-86592-298-5*); 14.95s.p. (*0-685-58634-0*) Rourke Corp.
Russell, Frazier. Ernest Hemingway: Romantic Adventurer. Pratt, George, illus. Wagner-Martin, Linda, frwd. by. (Illus.). 48p. (gr. 5-8). 1988. Kipling Pr.

HENRY 8TH, KING OF ENGLAND, 1509-1574

Dwyer, Frank. Henry VIII. Schlesinger, Arthur M., Jr., intro. by. (Illus.). 112p. (gr. 5 up). 1988. lib. bdg. 17.95 (*0-87754-530-8*) Chelsea Hse.

HENRY THE NAVIGATOR, PRINCE OF PORTUGAL, 1394-1460

Fisher, Leonard E. Prince Henry the Navigator. Fisher, Leonard E., illus. LC 89-28068. 32p. (gr. 2-6). 1990. 15.95 (*0-02-735231-5*, Macmillan Child Bk) Macmillan Child Grp.
Simon, Charnan. Henry the Navigator: Master Teacher of Explorers. LC 92-37048. (Illus.). 128p. (gr. 3 up). 1993. PLB 20.55 (*0-516-03071-X*) Childrens.

HENRY, PATRICK, 1736-1799

Fradin, Dennis B. Patrick Henry: "Give Me Liberty or Give Me Death!" LC 88-31330. (Illus.). 48p. (gr. 3-6). 1990. lib. bdg. 14.95 (*0-89490-232-6*) Enslow Pubs.
Fritz, Jean. Where Was Patrick Henry on the 29th of May? Tomes, Margot, illus. 48p. (gr. 3-5). 1982. 13.95 (*0-698-20307-0*, Coward); pap. 6.95 (*0-698-20544-8*, Coward) Putnam Pub Group.
Sabin, Louis. Patrick Henry: Voice of American Revolution. LC 81-23068. (Illus.). 48p. (gr. 4-6). 1982. PLB 10.79 (*0-89375-764-0*); pap. text ed. 3.50 (*0-89375-765-9*) Troll Assocs.

HENSON, MATTHEW ALEXANDER, 1866-1955

Campling, Elizabeth. Portrait of a Decade: The 1970s. (Illus.). 72p. (gr. 7-10). 1989. 19.95 (*0-7134-5988-3*, Pub. by Batsford UK) Trafalgar.
Dolan, Sean. Matthew Henson. (Illus.). 72p. (gr. 3-5). 1991. lib. bdg. 12.95 (*0-7910-1568-8*) Chelsea Hse.
Ferris, Jeri. Arctic Explorer: The Story of Matthew Henson. (Illus.). 80p. (gr. 3-6). 1989. PLB 17.50 (*0-87614-370-2*); pap. 5.95 (*0-87614-507-1*) Carolrhoda Bks.
Gleiter, Jan & Thompson, Kathleen. Matthew Henson. (Illus.). 32p. (Orig.). (gr. 2-5). 1988. PLB 19.97 (*0-8172-2676-1*) Raintree Steck-V.
Johnson, LaVerne C. Matthew Henson. Perry, Craig Rex, illus. LC 92-35253. 1992. 3.95 (*0-922162-94-8*) Empak Pub.
Rozakis, Laurie. Henson & Peary: The Race for the North Pole. (Illus.). 48p. (gr. 2-5). 1994. PLB 12.95 (*1-56711-066-5*) Blackbirch.
Williams, Jean. Matthew Henson: Polar Adventurer. LC 93-6101. (Illus.). 64p. (gr. 5-8). 1994. PLB 12.90 (*0-531-20006-X*) Watts.

HERALDRY

see also Chivalry; Decorations of Honor; Flags; Knights And Knighthood

Fradon, Dana. Harold the Herald: A Book about Heraldry. Fradon, Dana, illus. LC 89-49479. 40p. (gr. 4-7). 1990. PLB 14.95 (*0-525-44634-6*, DCB) Dutton Child Bks.
Manning, Rosemary. Heraldry. (Illus.). (gr. 7 up). 1975. 14.95 (*0-7136-0108-6*) Dufour.
Parker, James. Glossary of Terms Used in Heraldry. LC 77-94021. (Illus.). 692p. (gr. 9 up). 1970. 40.00 (*0-8048-0715-9*) C E Tuttle.

HERBAGE

see Grasses

HERBALS

see Botany; Herbs

HERBS

Bennett, Geraldine M. Sara Goes on an Herb Hunt. (Illus.). 72p. (Orig.). (gr. 3-8). 1994. pap. 7.98 (*1-882786-05-X*) New Dawn NY.
Cardinal, Catherine S. Mud Grape Pie. 29p. (gr. k-6). 1991. pap. 6.00 (*0-9630655-0-5*) Garden Gate.
Pallotta, Jerry. The Great Tasting Alphabet Book. LC 94-5178. (gr. k up). 1994. 14.95 (*0-685-72620-7*); PLB 15.00 (*0-685-72621-5*); pap. 6.95 (*0-685-72622-3*) Charlesbridge Pub.
—The Spice Alphabet Book: Herbs, Spices, & Other Natural Flavors. Evans, Leslie, illus. 32p. (Orig.). (ps-4). 1994. 14.95 (*0-88106-898-5*); PLB 15.00 (*0-88106-899-3*); pap. 6.95 (*0-88106-897-7*) Charlesbridge Pub.

HERBS, MEDICAL

see Botany, Medical

HERCULES

Bendall-Brunello, John. Seven-&-One-Half Labors of Hercules. Bendall-Brunello, John, illus. LC 91-36176. 64p. (gr. 2-5). 1991. 10.95 (*0-525-44780-6*, DCB) Dutton Child Bks.
Evslin, Bernard. Hercules. Smith, Joseph A., illus. LC 83-23834. 160p. (gr. 5up). 1984. 14.95 (*0-688-02748-2*) Morrow Jr Bks.
Gates, Doris. Mightiest of Mortals: Heracles. Cuffari, Richard, illus. 96p. (gr. 3-7). 1984. pap. 4.95 (*0-14-031531-4*, Puffin) Puffin Bks.
Richardson, I. M. The Adventures of Hercules. Baxter, Robert, illus. LC 82-16557. 32p. (gr. 4-8). 1983. PLB 11.79 (*0-89375-865-5*); pap. text ed. 2.95 (*0-89375-866-3*) Troll Assocs.

HEREDITY

Conway, Lorraine. Heredity & Embryology. (gr. 5 up). 1980. 7.95 (*0-916456-90-0*, GA 179) Good Apple.
Fradin, Dennis. Heredity. LC 87-831. (Illus.). 48p. (gr. k-4). 1987. PLB 12.85 (*0-516-01233-9*) Childrens.
Pomeroy, Johanna P. Content Area Reading skills Reproduction & Heredity: Main Idea. (Illus.). (gr. 4). 1988. pap. text ed. 3.25 (*1-55737-087-7*) Ed Activities.

HERMETIC ART AND PHILOSOPHY

see Astrology; Occult Sciences

HERMITS–FICTION

Roth, Arthur. Iceberg Hermit. 1989. pap. 2.95 (*0-590-44112-4*) Scholastic Inc.

HEROES

see also Courage; Explorers; Mythology; Saints

Canon, Jill & Archambault, Alan. Civil War Heroes. Archambault, Alan, illus. 48p. (Orig.). (gr. 7). 1988. pap. 3.95 (*0-88388-130-6*) Bellerophon Bks.
Donev, Mary K. & Donev, Stef. Acts of Courage. Anderian, Kaffi & Johannsen, Rob, illus. 48p. (gr. 5-9). 1985. pap. 5.95 (*0-88625-091-9*) Durkin Hayes Pub.
Gurasich, Marj. Did You Ever Meet a Texas Hero? LC 91-19544. (Illus.). (gr. 3-5). 1992. 12.95 (*0-89015-819-3*) Sunbelt Media.
Hentoff, Nat. American Heroes: In & Out of School. LC 86-29140. 192p. (gr. 7 up). 1987. pap. 14.95 (*0-385-29565-0*) Delacorte.
Hwa-I Publishing Co., Staff. Chinese Children's Stories, Vol. 76: The Stinky Emperor, The Hero Who Crawled. Ching, Emily, et al, eds. Wonder Kids Publications Staff, tr. from CHI. (Illus.). 28p. (gr. 3-6). 1991. Repr. of 1988 ed. 7.95 (*1-56162-076-9*) Wonder Kids.
Kaye, Marilyn. Real Heroes. 11th ed. (gr. 4-7). 1993. 13. 95 (*0-15-200563-3*) HarBrace.
Koslow, Philip. El Cid: Spanish Military Leader. LC 92-33377. (Illus.). 1993. PLB 18.95 (*0-7910-1239-5*, Am Art Analog); pap. write for info. (*0-7910-1266-2*, Am Art Analog) Chelsea Hse.
McSharry, Patra & Rosen, Roger, eds. On Heroes & the Heroic: In Search of Good Deeds. (gr. 7-12). 1993. 16.95 (*0-8239-1384-8*); pap. 8.95 (*0-8239-1385-6*) Rosen Group.
Masters, Anthony, compiled by. Heroic Stories. Molan, Chris, illus. LC 93-45413. 256p. (gr. 5-10). 1994. 6.95 (*1-85697-983-0*, Kingfisher LKC) LKC.
Nottridge, Rhoda. Adventure Films. LC 91-25839. (Illus.). 32p. (gr. 5). 1992. text ed. 13.95 RSBE (*0-89686-718-8*, Crestwood Hse) Macmillan Child Grp.
San Souci, Robert D. & Ginsburg, Max. Kate Shelley: Bound for Legend. LC 93-20438. (gr. 4-7). 1994. write for info. (*0-8037-1289-8*); write for info. (*0-8037-1290-1*) Dial Bks Young.
Saxby, Maurice. The Great Deeds of Heroic Women. Ingpen, Robert, illus. LC 91-11211. 152p. (gr. 4 up). 1992. 18.95 (*0-87226-348-7*) P Bedrick Bks.
—The Great Deeds of Superheroes. Ingpen, Robert, illus. 184p. (gr. 4 up). 1990. 24.95 (*0-87226-342-8*) P Bedrick Bks.
Shusterman, Neal. Kid Heroes: True Stories of Rescuers, Survivors & Achievers. 1991. 14.95 (*0-312-85081-6*) Tor Bks.
Wells, Candace & Carroll, Jeri. Legendary Heroes. Foster, Tom, illus. 64p. (gr. k-4). 1987. pap. 7.95 (*0-86653-380-X*, GA1007) Good Apple.

HEROES–FICTION

Ackermann, Jean. A Pride of Heroes: Candid Celebrations. v, 22p. (Orig.). (gr. 8-12). 1984. pap. 6.00 (*0-9614506-0-6*) Box Four Twenty-Four.
Cebulash, Mel. Snooperman. (gr. 3-8). 1992. PLB 8.95 (*0-89565-879-8*) Childs World.
Cole, Babette. Supermoo! LC 92-8967. (Illus.). 32p. (ps-3). 1993. 14.95 (*0-399-22422-X*, Putnam) Putnam Pub Group.
Estes, Eleanor. The Curious Adventures of Jimmy McGee. O'Brien, John, illus. LC 86-31793. 160p. (gr. 3-7). 1987. 14.95 (*0-15-221075-X*, HB Juv Bks) HarBrace.
Greene, Constance C. Odds on Oliver. Schindler, Stephen D., illus. LC 92-25932. 64p. (gr. 2-5). 1993. PLB 12. 99 (*0-670-84549-3*) Viking Child Bks.
Hautzig, Deborah. Night of Sentinels. 1994. 7.99 (*0-679-96029-5*); pap. 3.50 (*0-679-86029-0*) Random.
Hendrie, Alison. Rescue Nine One One Kid Heroes. (gr. 4-7). 1993. pap. 3.50 (*0-440-83074-5*) Dell.
Hudson, Eleanor. Teenage Mutant Ninja Turtles Pizza Party: A Step 1 Book - Preschool-Grade 1. Herbert, S. I., illus. LC 90-53243. 32p. (Orig.). (ps-1). 1991. PLB 7.99 (*0-679-91452-8*); pap. 3.50 (*0-679-81452-3*) Random Bks Yng Read.
Kaye, Marilyn. Real Heroes. 160p. (gr. 4). 1994. pap. 3.50 (*0-380-72283-6*, Camelot) Avon.
Kelleher, D. V. Defenders of the Universe. Brown, Jane C., illus. LC 92-1617. 128p. (gr. 3-5). 1993. 13.45 (*0-395-60515-6*) HM.
Kendall, Benjamin. Alien Invasions. Thatch, Nancy R., ed. Kendall, Benjamin, illus. Melton, David, intro. by. LC 93-13423. (Illus.). 29p. (gr. 2-4). 1993. PLB 14.95 (*0-933849-42-7*) Landmark Edns.
Kroll, Steven. Pride of the Rockets. 80p. (Orig.). (gr. 2). 1994. pap. 3.50 (*0-380-77369-4*, Camelot Young) Avon.
Kudlinski, Kathleen V. Hero over Here: A Story of World War I. Dodson, Bert, illus. 64p. (gr. 2-6). 1992. pap. 3.99 (*0-14-034286-9*, Puffin) Puffin Bks.
Ledney, Douglas. My Hero! 1994. 7.95 (*0-8062-4865-3*) Carlton.
Lipsyte, Robert. The Chemo Kid. LC 91-55500. 176p. (gr. 7 up). 1992. 14.00 (*0-06-020284-X*); PLB 13.89 (*0-06-020285-8*); pap. 3.95 (*0-685-59055-0*) HarpC Child Bks.
McKinley, Robin. The Hero & the Crown. LC 84-4074. 256p. (gr. 7 up). 1984. reinforced 15.00 (*0-688-02593-5*) Greenwillow.
Marino, Jan. Like Some Kind of Hero. 224p. 1993. pap. 3.50 (*0-380-72010-8*, Flare) Avon.
Paton Walsh, Jill. Grace. 256p. (gr. 7 up). 1992. 16.00 (*0-374-32758-0*) FS&G.
Prater, John. Tim & the Blanket Thief. Prater, John, illus. LC 93-6563. 32p. (ps-1). 1993. SBE 14.95 (*0-689-31881-2*, Atheneum Child Bk) Macmillan Child Grp.
Roop, Peter & Roop, Connie. Keep the Lights Burning, Abbie. Hanson, Peter E., illus. (gr. 2-4). 1989. incl. cass. 19.95 (*0-87499-135-8*); pap. 12.95 incl. cass. (*0-87499-134-X*); Set; incl. 4 bks., guide, & cass. pap. 27.95 (*0-87499-136-6*) Live Oak Media.
Shannon, Jacqueline. I Hate My Hero. LC 92-890. (gr. 4-7). 1992. pap. 13.00 (*0-671-75442-4*, S&S BFYR) S&S Trade.
Szymanski, Lois. A New Kind of Magic. 96p. (Orig.). (gr. 3). 1994. pap. 3.50 (*0-380-77349-X*, Camelot Young) Avon.
Wagner, Matt, et al. Grendel, No. 4. Wagner, Matt & Rankin, Rich, illus. 48p. (gr. 9-12). 1986. 29.95 (*0-936211-02-4*); pap. 5.95 (*0-938695-01-0*) Graphitti Designs.
Weiss, Ellen & Friedman, Mel. The Adventures of Ratman. Zimmer, Dirk, illus. LC 89-10869. 64p. (Orig.). (gr. 2-4). 1990. pap. 2.99 (*0-679-80531-1*) Random Bks Yng Read.
Windsor, Patricia. The Hero. LC 87-25658. 192p. (gr. 7 up). 1988. pap. 14.95 (*0-385-29624-X*) Delacorte.

HEROINES

see Heroes; Women in the Bible

HEROISM

see Courage; Heroes

HERONS–FICTION

Avi. Blue Heron. 192p. 1993. pap. 3.99 (*0-380-72043-4*, Camelot) Avon.
Burgess, Thornton. Longlegs the Heron. 1992. Repr. lib. bdg. 17.95x (*0-89966-979-4*) Buccaneer Bks.
Hall, N. & Packard, Mary. Spike & Mike. McCue, Lisa, illus. 40p. (ps-2). 1994. 12.00 (*0-679-85830-X*) Random Bks Yng Read.
Hall, Nancy & Packard, Mary. Spike & Mike. McCue, Lisa, illus. LC 93-13684. 40p. (ps-4). 1993. PLB 11.80 (*0-516-00830-7*) Childrens.

Krupinsky, Jacquelyn S. Henry, the Hesitant Heron. Cutri, Anne C., illus. (Illus.). 24p. (Orig.). (gr. k-3). 1987. pap. 6.95 (*0-912123-02-8*) Woodbury Pr.
HENRY, THE HESITANT HERON is afraid to fly. In fact, he is afraid to do almost everything until the forces of nature precipitate a crisis. A good friend, Freddy Swallow, comes to his aid. All ends happily with Henry snuggled down in the nest with his parents close by. Good for children who lack self-esteem & are also afraid to try their wings at new skills. Has a bibliography & a foreword from Audubon Canyon Ranch, Inc. (a heron sanctuary). Reviews - "Relates accurate information about Great Blue Heron habitat, but also gives young readers a look into the challenges of growing up." (Downeast Magazine). "A book that's going for classic status." (Courier-Gazette). Available from Woodbury Press, RR1, Box 700, Litchfield, ME 04350. When ordering, add $1.95 for shipping, $.25 for each additional book. Also available from the Maine Writers

& Publishers, Brunswick, ME 04011. *Publisher Provided Annotation.*

MacHaffie, Ingeborg. Henry the Heron. large type ed. Blumenstein, Amy, illus. Mouck, Mike, frwd. by. (Illus.). 55p. (Orig.). (ps). 1988. lib. bdg. 7.95 (*0-9609374-3-9*) Skribent.
This true short story for young children tells about a Great Blue Heron named Henry that comes to a suburban golf course every day &, oblivious of golfers, ducks, & seagulls, stays all day to fish in the small pond on the fifth fairway. A little lady named Fritzi sees that Henry cannot swallow the large fish & cuts the fish up into small pieces for him. Henry samples the various kinds of fish Fritzi feeds him & makes choices. Two children, Morten & Marianne, who come to visit, are excited to find a heron that knows his name & comes when they call. The story explains the normal habitat, food, & mating customs of great blue herons & why Henry is an unusual heron. The 9" x 12" book is printed in large type, the story told in easy-to-read form & amusingly illustrated. From this informative, fascinating story for children & adults alike, "Henry" has become a famous specimen of Portland, Oregon's official bird - the Great Blue Heron.
Publisher Provided Annotation.

Owen, Roy. The Ibis & the Egret. Sabuda, Robert, illus. LC 92-26220. 32p. (ps-3). 1993. 14.95 (*0-399-22504-8*, Philomel Bks) Putnam Pub Group.

Packard, Mary. Fairest of All. McCue, Lisa, illus. LC 93-11056. 40p. (ps-4). 1993. PLB 11.80 (*0-516-00826-9*) Childrens.

—Playing by the Rules. McCue, Lisa, illus. LC 93-4423. 40p. (ps-4). 1993. PLB 11.80 (*0-516-00827-7*) Childrens.

—Safe & Sound. McCue, Lisa, illus. LC 93-11058. 40p. (ps-4). 1993. PLB 11.80 (*0-516-00828-5*) Childrens.

—Save the Swamp. McCue, Lisa, illus. LC 93-11059. 40p. (ps-4). 1993. PLB 11.80 (*0-516-00829-3*) Childrens.

—Spike & Mike & the Treasure Hunt. McCue, Lisa, illus. LC 92-50295. 1993. write for info. (*0-679-93936-9*); lib. bdg. write for info. (*0-679-83936-4*) Random Bks Yng Read.

—Starting Over. McCue, Lisa & Scribner, Toni, illus. LC 93-11060. 40p. (ps-4). 1993. PLB 11.80 (*0-516-00831-5*) Childrens.

HESSE, HERMAN, 1877-1962

Fleissner, Else M. Herman N. Hesse: Modern German Poet & Writer. Rahmas, D. Steve, ed. LC 70-190244. 32p. (Orig.). (gr. 7-12). 1972. lib. bdg. 4.95 incl. catalog cards (*0-87157-526-4*) SamHar Pr.

HIAWATHA, IROQUOIS INDIAN

Bonvillain, Nancy. Hiawatha. (Illus.). 112p. (gr. 5 up). 1992. lib. bdg. 17.95 (*0-7910-1707-9*) Chelsea Hse.

Hagen. Hiawatha. 1995. 15.95 (*0-8050-1832-8*) H Holt & Co.

Wheeler, Jill. The Story of Hiawatha. Deegan, Paul, ed. Dodson, Liz, illus. LC 89-84908. 32p. (gr. 4). 1989. PLB 11.96 (*0-939179-71-7*) Abdo & Dghtrs.

HIBERNATION

see Animals–Hibernation

HICKOK, JAMES BUTLER, 1837-1876

Green, Carl R. & Sanford, William R. Wild Bill Hickok. LC 91-29856. (Illus.). 48p. (gr. 4-10). 1992. lib. bdg. 14.95 (*0-89490-366-7*) Enslow Pubs.

HIDALGO Y COSTILLA, MIGUEL, 1753-1811–FICTION

Father Hidalgo: Mini-Play. (gr. 5 up). 1978. 5.00 (*0-89550-326-3*) Stevens & Shea.

HIEROGLYPHICS

see also Picture Writing

Katan, Norma J. & Mintz, Barbara. Hieroglyphs: The Writing of Ancient Egypt. Katan, Norma J., illus. LC 80-13576. 96p. (gr. 4-7). 1981. SBE 14.95 (*0-689-50176-5*, M K McElderry) Macmillan Child Grp.

Scott, Joseph & Scott, Lenore. Egyptian Hieroglyphs for Everyone: An Introduction to the Writing of Ancient Egypt. reissued ed. Scott, Joseph & Scott, Lenore, illus. LC 68-13080. 96p. (gr. 7 up). 1990. PLB 14.89 (*0-690-04753-3*, Crowell Jr Bks) HarpC Child Bks.

HIGH SCHOOL EDUCATION

see Education, Secondary

HIGH SCHOOLS

Dentemaro, Christine & Kranz, Rachel. Straight Talk about Student Life. LC 92-31488. 1993. write for info. (*0-8160-2735-8*) Facts on File.

Dunnahoo, Terry. How to Survive High School. (Illus.). (gr. 9-12). 1994. pap. 6.95 (*0-531-15705-9*) Watts.

—How to Survive High School: A Student's Guide. LC 92-41700. (Illus.). 112p. (gr. 7-12). 1993. PLB 13.40 (*0-531-11135-0*) Watts.

Goldentyer, Debra. Dropping Out of School. LC 93-14251. (Illus.). 80p. (gr. 6-9). 1993. PLB 21.34 (*0-8114-3526-1*) Raintree Steck-V.

Haley, Beverly A. Focus on School: A Reference Handbook. 217p. 1990. lib. bdg. 39.50 (*0-87436-099-4*) ABC-CLIO.

Heun, Joseph H. Graduate High School - A Formula for Success. LC 91-71723. (Illus.). 150p. (gr. 10). 1991. pap. 19.95 (*0-9629317-0-5*) Ace Pub Prodns.

Krane, Stephen. New York City Specialized High School Entrance Examinations. LC 94-4838. 1994. write for info. (*0-671-89157-X*) P-H.

Robinson, Jacqueline, et al. High School Entrance Exams. LC 94-4836. 1994. write for info. (*0-671-89196-0*) P-H.

Souter, John C. Survive! (Orig.). (gr. 9-12). 1983. pap. 4.95 (*0-8423-6694-6*) Tyndale.

Steinberg, Eve P. Catholic High School Entrance Exams. 7th ed. LC 93-48701. 1994. 13.00 (*0-671-88149-3*, Arco Test) P-H Gen Ref & Trav.

Wirths, Claudine G. & Bowman-Kruhm, Mary. I Hate School! How to Hang In & When to Drop Out. Stren, Patti, illus. LC 85-48248. 128p. (gr. 7 up). 1986. (Crowell Jr Bks); (Crowell Jr Bks) HarpC Child Bks.

HIGH SPEED AERONAUTICS

see also Rockets (Aeronautics)

Taylor, Richard L. The First Supersonic Flight: Captain Charles E. Yeager Breaks the Sound Barrier. LC 94-57. (gr. 4 up). 1994. write for info. (*0-531-20177-5*) Watts.

HIGHER EDUCATION

see Education, Higher

HIGHWAY ACCIDENTS

see Traffic Accidents

HIGHWAY CONSTRUCTION

see Roads

HIGHWAY TRANSPORTATION

see Transportation, Highway

HIGHWAYMEN

see Robbers and Outlaws

HIGHWAYS

see Roads

HIKING

see also Backpacking; Walking

Bailey, Donna. Hiking. LC 90-23054. (Illus.). 32p. (gr. 1-4). 1991. PLB 18.99 (*0-8114-2905-9*); pap. 3.95 (*0-8114-4708-1*) Raintree Steck-V.

Evans, Jeremy. Hiking & Climbing. LC 91-4061. (Illus.). 48p. (gr. 5-6). 1992. text ed. 13.95 RSBE (*0-89686-684-X*, Crestwood Hse) Macmillan Child Grp.

Fisher, Ron. Mountain Adventure: Exploring the Appalachian Trail. Crump, Donald J., ed. (Illus.). 1988. 12.95 (*0-87044-668-1*); lib. bdg. 12.95 (*0-87044-673-8*) Natl Geog.

Foster, Lynne. Take a Hike! The Sierra Club Beginner's Guide to Hiking & Backpacking. (Illus.). 176p. (gr. 4-7). 1991. pap. 8.95 (*0-316-28948-5*, Joy St Bks) Little.

McMartin, Barbara. Adventures in Hiking. 110p. 1993. 12.50 (*0-925168-25-4*) North Country.

McVey, Vicki. The Sierra Club Wayfinding Book. Weston, Martha, illus. 96p. (gr. 4-7). 1991. 14.95 (*0-316-56340-4*); pap. 7.95 (*0-316-56342-0*) Little.

HILLARY, SIR EDMUND PERCIVAL, 1919-

Fraser, Mary A. On Top of the World: The Conquest of Mount Everest. Fraser, Mary A., illus. LC 90-48988. 40p. (gr. 2-5). 1991. 14.95 (*0-8050-1578-7*, Bks Young Read) H Holt & Co.

Gaffney, Timothy R. Edmund Hillary: First to Climb Mt. Everest. LC 89-28624. (Illus.). 128p. (gr. 3 up). 1990. PLB 20.55 (*0-516-03052-3*) Childrens.

HIMALAYA MOUNTAINS

Reynolds, Jan. Himalaya Vanishing Cultures. 32p. (gr. 2 up). 1991. 16.95 (*0-15-234465-9*); pap. 8.95 (*0-15-234466-7*) HarBrace.

HINDUISM

see also Yoga

Bennett, Olivia. Holi: Hindi Festival of Spring. (Illus.). 25p. (gr. 2-4). 1991. 11.95 (*0-237-60135-4*, Pub. by Evans Bros Ltd) Trafalgar.

Bhaktivedanta, Swami A. C. Prahlad, Picture & Story Book. LC 72-2032. (Illus.). (gr. 2-6). 1973. pap. 4.00 (*0-685-47513-1*) Bhaktivedanta.

Chatterjee, Debjani. The Elephant-Headed God & Other Hindu Tales. LC 92-20454. 1992. 13.00 (*0-19-508112-9*) OUP.

McLeod, W. H. Way of the Sikh. (gr. 4-8). 1986. pap. 7.95 (*0-7175-0731-9*) Dufour.

Madhu Bazaz Wangu. Hinduism. (Illus.). 128p. (gr. 7-12). 1991. 17.95x (*0-8160-2447-2*) Facts on File.

Mitchell, Pratima. Dance of Shiva. (Illus.). 25p. (gr. 2-4). 1991. 12.95 (*0-237-60148-6*, Pub. by Evans Bros Ltd) Trafalgar.

Nivedita, Sr. Cradle Tales of Hinduism. Noble, Margaret, ed. (Illus.). 329p. (gr. 3-12). 1972. pap. 5.95 (*0-87481-170-8*, Pub. by Advaita Ashram India); pap. 5.95 (*0-87481-131-7*) Vedanta Pr.

Ramakrishna, Swami. Tales from Ramakrishna. Chakravarty, Biswarajan, illus. Ray, Irene R. & Gupta, Mallika C.retold by. (Illus.). 54p. (Orig.). (gr. 1-5). 1975. pap. 1.95 (*0-87481-152-X*, Pub. by Advaita Ashram India) Vedanta Pr.

Smarananda, Swami. The Story of Ramakrishna. Chakravarty, Biswaranjan, illus. (Orig.). (gr. k-5). 1976. pap. 1.95 (*0-87481-168-6*, Pub. by Advaita Ashram India) Vedanta Pr.

Srinivasan, A. V. A Hindu Primer: Yaksha Prashna. Satchidananda, Swami, frwd. by. (Illus.). 78p. (gr. 6-12). 1984. pap. 7.70 (*0-86578-249-0*, 6203) Ind-US Inc.

Vishwashrayananda, Swami. Ramakrishna for Children. Chakravarty, Purhachandra, illus. Bagchi, Santosh, tr. from BEN. (Illus.). 40p. (gr. 3-6). 1975. pap. 1.95 (*0-87481-164-3*, Pub. by Advaita Ashram India) Vedanta Pr.

Yogeshananda, Swami. Way of the Hindu. (gr. 3-7). 1980. pap. 9.95 (*0-7175-0626-6*) Dufour.

HIPPOPOTAMUS

Arnold, Caroline. Hippo. Hewett, Richard, photos by. LC 88-39794. (Illus.). 48p. (gr. 2 up). 1989. 12.95 (*0-688-08145-2*); PLB 12.88 (*0-688-08146-0*, Morrow Jr Bks) Morrow Jr Bks.

Camel. 1989. 3.50 (*1-87865-733-X*) Blue Q.

Denis-Huot, Christine & Denis-Huot, Michel. The Hippopotamus: River Horse. (Illus.). 32p. (ps-4). 1994. pap. 6.95 (*0-88106-433-5*) Charlesbridge Pub.

Green, Carl R. & Sanford, William R. The Hippopotamus. LC 88-1830. (Illus.). 48p. (gr. 5). 1988. text ed. 12.95 RSBE (*0-89686-383-2*, Crestwood Hse) Macmillan Child Grp.

Hayes, Kenn. Let's Go Hippo. (ps). 1993. 14.95 (*1-56729-025-6*) Newport Pubs.

Hippos. 1991. PLB 14.95 (*0-88682-424-9*) Creative Ed.

Hoffman, Mary. Hippo. LC 84-24792. (Illus.). 24p. (gr. k-5). 1985. PLB 9.95 (*0-8172-2412-2*); pap. 3.95 (*0-8114-6877-1*) Raintree Steck-V.

Markert, Jenny M. Hippos. LC 92-29743. (gr. 2-6). 1993. PLB 15.95 (*1-56766-003-7*) Childs World.

Pouyanne. Hippo, Reading Level 3-4. (Illus.). 28p. (gr. 2-5). 1983. PLB 16.66 (*0-86592-855-X*); 12.50s.p. (*0-685-58819-X*) Rourke Corp.

Stone, Lynn. Hippopotamus. (Illus.). 24p. (gr. k-5). 1990. lib. bdg. 11.94 (*0-86593-051-1*); 8.95s.p. (*0-685-36347-3*) Rourke Corp.

HIPPOPOTAMUS–FICTION

Alexander, Sue. Ellsworth & Millicent. Meier, David S., illus. LC 92-7705. 28p. (gr. k up). 1993. 14.95 (*0-88708-247-5*) Picture Bk Studio.

Arnold, Caroline. Hippo. ALC Staff, ed. Hewett, Richard, illus. LC 88-39794. 48p. (gr. 3 up). 1992. pap. 5.95 (*0-688-11697-3*, Mulberry) Morrow.

Baker, Tanya & Holm, Carlton. Harvey the Hiccupping Hippopotamus. Wilkinson, Sue, illus. 32p. (ps-k). 1992. lib. bdg. 10.95 with dust jacket (*0-8120-6248-5*); pap. 5.95 (*0-8120-4927-6*) Barron.

Bowes, Clare. The Hippo Bus. Bowes, Clare, illus. LC 92-34264. 1993. 14.00 (*0-383-03629-1*) SRA Schl Grp.

Camp, Lindsay. Keeping Up with Cheetah. Newton, Jill, illus. LC 92-44162. (gr. k-4). 1993. 14.00 (*0-688-12655-3*) Lothrop.

Craig, Janet. Thump, Bump. Paterson, Diane, illus. LC 87-10933. 32p. (gr. k-2). 1988. PLB 11.59 (*0-8167-1077-5*); pap. text ed. 2.95 (*0-8167-1078-3*) Troll Assocs.

Dijs, Carla. Pretend You're a Hippo. (Illus.). 14p. (ps). 1992. pap. 6.95 pop-up bk. (*0-671-76057-2*, Little Simon) S&S Trade.

Gaban, Jesus. Harry Dresses Himself. Colorado, Nani, illus. 16p. (ps-1). 1992. PLB 13.27 (*0-8368-0715-4*) Gareth Stevens Inc.

—Harry the Hippo, 4 vols. Colorado, Nani, illus. 16p. (ps-1). 1992. Set. PLB 53.08 (*0-8368-0714-6*) Gareth Stevens Inc.

—Harry's Mealtime Mess. Colorado, Nani, illus. 16p. (ps-1). 1992. PLB 13.27 (*0-8368-0717-0*) Gareth Stevens Inc.

—Harry's Sandbox Surprise. Colorado, Nani, illus. 16p. (ps-1). 1992. PLB 13.27 (*0-8368-0716-2*) Gareth Stevens Inc.

—Tub Time for Harry. Colorado, Nani, illus. 16p. (ps-1). 1992. PLB 13.27 (*0-8368-0718-9*) Gareth Stevens Inc.

Gordon, Sharon. Playground Fun. Karas, G. Brian, illus. LC 86-30854. 32p. (gr. k-2). 1988. lib. bdg. 7.89 (*0-8167-0990-4*); pap. text ed. 1.95 (*0-8167-0991-2*) Troll Assocs.

Grant, Joan. The Blue Faience Hippopotamus. Day, Alexandra, illus. LC 91-17133. 32p. (Orig.). (gr. 7-9). 1991. Repr. of 1942 ed. 11.95 (*0-671-74977-3*, Green Tiger) S&S Trade.

Hadithi, Mwenye. Hot Hippo. Kennaway, Adrienne, illus. (ps-3). 1986. lib. bdg. 14.95 (*0-316-33722-6*) Little.

—Hot Hippo. (ps-3). 1994. 4.95 (*0-316-33718-8*) Little.

Heide, Florence P. The Bigness Contest. Chess, Victoria, illus. LC 92-12663. 1994. 14.95 (*0-316-35444-9*, Joy St Bks) Little.

Hurwitz, Johanna. Busybody Nora. Jeschke, Susan, illus. 64p. (gr. 1-5). 1982. pap. 1.50 (*0-440-41019-3*, YB) Dell.

Johnson, Doug. Never Babysit Hippos. 1993. write for info. (*0-8050-3026-3*) H Holt & Co.

—Never Babysit the Hippopotamuses! Carter, Abby, illus. LC 93-18341. 32p. (ps-2). 1993. 14.95 (*0-8050-1873-5*, Bks Young Read) H Holt & Co.

Kessler, Ethel & Kessler, Leonard. Are There Hippos on the Farm? (Illus.). 32p. (ps-k). 1986. casebound, padded cover 4.95 (*0-671-62066-5*, Little Simon) S&S Trade.

McCarthy, Bobette. Happy Hiding Hippos. McCarthy, Bobette, illus. LC 92-32599. 32p. (ps-1). 1994. RSBE 13.95 (*0-02-765446-X*, Bradbury Pr) Macmillan Child Grp.

—Ten Little Hippos: A Counting Book. McCarthy, Bobette, illus. LC 91-17175. 32p. (ps-2). 1992. SBE 13.95 (*0-02-765445-1*, Bradbury Pr) Macmillan Child Grp.

MacDonald, Maryann. Little Hippo Gets Glasses. LC 91-11971. (Illus.). 32p. (ps-3). 1992. 11.00 (*0-8037-0964-1*) Dial Bks Young.

McDonnell, Janet. Hippo's Adventure in Alphabet Town. McDonnell, J., illus. LC 91-20549. 32p. (ps-2). 1992. PLB 11.80 (*0-516-05408-2*) Childrens.

Marshall, James. George & Martha Encore. LC 73-5845. (Illus.). 48p. (gr. k-3). 1977. 14.95 (*0-395-17512-7*); pap. 5.95 (*0-395-25379-9*) HM.

—George & Martha Rise & Shine. Marshall, James, illus. (gr. k-3). 1979. 13.45 (*0-395-24738-1*); pap. 4.80 (*0-395-28006-0*) HM.

—George & Martha Tons of Fun. (Illus.). 48p. (gr. k-3). 1980. 13.95 (*0-395-29524-6*); pap. 4.80 (*0-395-42646-4*) HM.

Martin, Bill, Jr. The Happy Hippopotami. Johnston, Allyn, ed. Everitt, Betsy, illus. 32p. (ps-3). 1991. 12.95 (*0-15-233380-0*) HarBrace.

—Happy Hippopotami. (ps-3). 1992. pap. 4.95 (*0-15-233382-7*) HarBrace.

Marx, Trish. Hanna's Cold Winter. Knutson, Barbara, illus. LC 92-27143. 1993. 18.95 (*0-87614-772-4*) Carolrhoda Bks.

Matsuoka, Kyoko. There's a Hippo in My Bath! Hayashi, Akiko, illus. 1989. 12.95 (*0-385-26188-8*); PLB 12.95 (*0-385-26189-6*) Doubleday.

Mayer, Mercer. Hiccup. LC 76-2284. (Illus.). (ps-2). 1976. Dial Bks Young.

Minarik, Else H. Am I Beautiful? Abolafia, Yossi, illus. LC 91-32562. 24p. (ps-4). 1992. 14.00 (*0-688-09911-4*); PLB 13.93 (*0-688-09912-2*) Greenwillow.

Moncure, Jane B. Yes, No, Little Hippo. Gohman, Vera, illus. LC 87-21211. (SPA & ENG.). 32p. (ps-2). 1987. PLB 14.95 (*0-89565-411-3*) Childs World.

Morgan, Michaela. Helpful Betty to the Rescue. Kemp, Moira, illus. LC 93-39885. 1994. 18.95 (*0-87614-831-3*) Carolrhoda Bks.

Morgan, Michaela & Kemp, Moira. Helpful Betty Solves a Mystery. LC 93-39050. (gr. 3 up). 1994. 18.95 (*0-87614-832-1*) Carolrhoda Bks.

Most, Bernard. Hippopotamus Hunt. LC 93-39988. (ps-3). 1994. 14.95 (*0-15-234520-5*) HarBrace.

Schwartz, Linda. Hannah the Hippo. LC 90-62596. (Illus.). 32p. (ps-3). 1991. 4.95 (*0-88160-186-1*, LW 1200) Learning Wks.

Thaler, Mike. Come & Play, Hippo. Chambliss, Maxie, illus. LC 87-33489. 64p. (ps-3). 1993. pap. 3.50 (*0-06-444165-2*, Trophy) HarpC Child Bks.

—A Hippopotamus Ate the Teacher. Lee, Jared, illus. 32p. 1981. pap. 2.95 (*0-380-78048-8*, Camelot) Avon.

—There's a Hippopotamus under My Bed. (Illus.). 32p. (gr. k-3). 1978. pap. 2.95 (*0-380-40238-6*, Camelot) Avon.

—What Could a Hippopotamus Be? Grossman, Robert, illus. LC 89-77080. 40p. (ps-2). 1990. pap. 13.95 (*0-671-70847-3*, S&S BFYR) S&S Trade.

Waber, Bernard. You Look Ridiculous Said the Rhinoceros to the Hippopotamus. (Illus.). (gr. k-3). 1973. reinforced bdg. 16.95 (*0-395-07156-9*) HM.

Woychuk, Denis. The Other Side of the Wall. Howard, Kim, illus. LC 90-49415. 32p. (ps up). 1991. 13.95 (*0-688-09894-0*) Lothrop.

—Pirates! LC 91-3387. (Illus.). (ps-3). 1992. 14.00 (*0-688-10336-7*); PLB 13.93 (*0-688-10337-5*) Lothrop.

Ziefert, Harriet. Harry Takes a Bath. Smith, Mavis, illus. (ps-3). 1987. pap. 8.95 (*0-670-81721-X*, Puffin); pap. 3.50 (*0-14-050746-9*, Puffin) Puffin Bks.

HIROSHIMA

Black, Wallace B. & Blashfield, Jean F. Hiroshima & the Atomic Bomb. LC 92-33974. (Illus.). 48p. (gr. 5-6). 1993. text ed. 4.95 RSBE (*0-89686-571-1*, Crestwood Hse) Macmillan Child Grp.

Coerr, Eleanor. Sadako. Young, Ed, illus. LC 92-41483. 48p. (gr. 1-4). 1993. TLB 16.95 (*0-399-21771-1*, Putnam) Putnam Pub Group.

Farris, John. Hiroshima. McGovern, Brian, illus. LC 90-34064. 64p. (gr. 5-8). 1990. PLB 11.95 (*1-56006-015-8*) Lucent Bks.

McPhillips, Martin. Hiroshima. LC 85-40170. (Illus.). 64p. (gr. 5 up). 1985. PLB 12.95 (*0-382-06829-7*); pap. 7.95 (*0-382-06976-5*) Silver Burdett Pr.

Morimoto, Junko. My Hiroshima. (Illus.). 32p. (ps-3). 1992. pap. 5.99 (*0-14-054524-7*, Puffin) Puffin Bks.

O'Neal, Michael. President Truman & the Atomic Bomb: Opposing Viewpoints. LC 90-35611. (Illus.). 112p. (gr. 5-8). 1990. PLB 14.95 (*0-89908-079-0*) Greenhaven.

Sherrow, Victoria. Hiroshima. LC 93-30428. 1994. text ed. 14.95 (*0-02-782467-5*, New Discovery Bks) Macmillan Child Grp.

HIROSHIMA–FICTION

Morimoto, Junko. My Hiroshima. (Illus.). 32p. (ps up). 1990. pap. 13.95 (*0-670-83181-6*) Viking Child Bks.

HISPANO-AMERICAN WAR, 1898

see U. S.–History–War of 1898

HISTOLOGY

see Anatomy; Anatomy, Comparative; Botany–Anatomy; Cells

HISTORIANS

see also Archeologists

HISTORICAL ATLASES

see Atlases, Historical

HISTORICAL CHRONOLOGY

see Chronology, Historical

HISTORICAL DICTIONARIES

see History–Dictionaries

HISTORICAL GEOGRAPHY

see Atlases, Historical

HISTORICAL GEOGRAPHY

Crosby, Nina E. & Marten, Elizabeth H. Know Your State. West, James A., illus. 32p. (Orig.). (gr. 4-7). 1984. pap. 5.95 (*0-88047-036-4*, 8401) DOK Pubs.

HISTORIOGRAPHY

Cooper, Kay. Who Put the Cannon in the Courthouse Square: A Guide to Uncovering the Past. Accardo, Anthony, illus. LC 84-17251. (gr. 4 up). 1984. PLB 12.85 (*0-8027-6561-0*) Walker & Co.

Littlefield, Robert S. & Ball, Jane A. Tell Me the Way It Was... Stark, Steve, illus. 32p. (Orig.). (gr. 3-6). 1990. pap. text ed. 8.95 (*1-879340-07-0*, K0108) Kidspeak.

HISTORY, ANCIENT

see also Archeology; Bible; Civilization

Atkins, Sinclair. From Stone Age to Conquest. LC 85-73167. (Illus.). 96p. (gr. 5-8). 1984. pap. 12.95 (*0-7175-1305-X*) Dufour.

Baer, Ruth. Creation to Canaan, Bk. 1. (gr. 7). 1979. 9.80 (*0-686-30770-4*); tchr's. ed. avail. 6.40 (*0-686-30771-2*) Rod & Staff.

Burrell, Roy. Oxford First Ancient History. Connolly, Peter, illus. 320p. 1994. bds. 35.00 (*0-19-521058-1*) OUP.

Chisholm. Prehistoric Times. (gr. 2-5). 1983. pap. 4.50 (*0-88110-104-4*) EDC.

Cootes, R. J. & Snellgrove, L. E. Ancient World. 2nd ed. (Illus.). 208p. (gr. 6-12). 1991. pap. text ed. 23.00 (*0-582-31785-1*, 79165); wkbk. 11.72 (*0-582-36690-9*, 72482) Longman.

Corbishley, Mike. The Ancient World. (Illus.). 60p. (gr. 5 up). 1993. 17.95 (*0-87226-354-1*) P Bedrick Bks.

—Rome & the Ancient World. (Illus.). 80p. (gr. 2-6). 1993. 17.95x (*0-8160-2786-2*) Facts on File.

De Saint-Beauguat, Henri. The First People. LC 86-42657. (Illus.). 77p. (gr. 7 up). 1986. 12.95 (*0-382-09212-0*) Silver Burdett Pr.

De Saint-Beauquet, Henri. The First Settlements. LC 86-42659. (Illus.). 77p. (gr. 7 up). 1987. 12.95 (*0-382-09213-9*) Silver Burdett Pr.

Edom, H. & Brooks, F. Living Long Ago (B - U) (Illus.). 96p. (gr. 1-5). 1993. pap. 10.95 (*0-7460-1109-1*) EDC.

Martell, Hazel M. Over Six Thousand Years Ago: In the Stone Age. LC 91-39458. (Illus.). 32p. (gr. 6 up). 1992. text ed. 13.95 RSBE (*0-02-762429-3*, New Discovery) Macmillan Child Grp.

Milard, A. & Chisholm, J. Early Civilizations. (Illus.). 96p. 1992. PLB 16.96 (*0-88110-438-8*); pap. 10.95 (*0-7460-0328-5*) EDC.

Millard, A., et al. Ancient World. (Illus.). 288p. (gr. 7-12). 1992. pap. 24.95 (*0-7460-1233-0*) EDC.

Millard, Anne. Eyewitness Atlas of Ancient Worlds. Barnett, Russell, illus. 64p. (gr. 5 up). 1994. write for info. (*1-56458-679-0*) Dorling Kindersley.

Odijk, Pamela. The Ancient World, 12 bks. (Illus.). (gr. 5-8). 1991. Set, 48p. ea. lib. bdg. 155.40 (*0-382-09883-8*) Silver Burdett Pr.

Schroeder, Mary. Extending U. S. History & Geography. West, James A., illus. 32p. (Orig.). (gr. 3-6). 1984. 6.50 (*0-88047-041-0*, 8404) DOK Pubs.

Verges, Gloria & Verges, Oriol. The Greek & Roman Eras. Rius, Maria & Peris, Carme, illus. (ENG & SPA.). 32p. (gr. 2-4). 1988. pap. 6.95 (*0-8120-3388-4*); La Edad Antigua. pap. 6.95 (*0-8120-3389-2*) Barron.

—Prehistory to Egypt. Rius, Maria, illus. (SPA & ENG.). 32p. (gr. 2-4). 1988. pap. 4.95 (*0-8120-3390-6*); La Prehistoria y el Antiguo Egipto. pap. 6.95 (*0-8120-3391-4*) Barron.

HISTORY, ANCIENT–FICTION

Smith, Robert K. The Squeaky Wheel. (gr. 3-7). 1992. 3.50 (*0-440-40631-5*, YB) Dell.

Zeman, Ludmila. The Revenge of Ishtar, Bk. II: Gilgamesh the King. Zeman, Ludmila, illus. LC 93-60332. 24p. (gr. 3 up). Date not set. 19.95 (*0-88776-315-4*) Tundra Bks.

—Le Roi Gilgamesh. Boileau, Michele, tr. from ENG. Zeman, Ludmila, illus. LC 91-67565. (FRE.). 24p. (gr. 3 up). 1993. 19.95 (*0-88776-288-3*) Tundra Bks.

HISTORY–ATLASES

see Atlases, Historical

HISTORY, BIBLICAL

see Bible–History of Biblical Events

HISTORY–CHRONOLOGY

see Chronology, Historical

HISTORY, CHURCH

see Church History

HISTORY–CRITICISM

see Historiography

HISTORY–CURIOSA AND MISCELLANY

Arnsteen, Kathy K. & Guthrie, Donna. I Can't Believe It's History! Fun Facts from Around the World. (Illus.). 32p. (Orig.). (gr. 1-6). 1993. pap. 3.95 (*0-8431-3621-9*) Price Stern.

Carroll, Jeri & Wells, Candance. Pathfinders. Foster, Tom, illus. 64p. (gr. k-4). 1986. wkbk. 7.95 (*0-86653-357-5*, GA 696) Good Apple.

Claridge, M. History Quizbook. (Illus.). 32p. (gr. 4 up). 1992. PLB 13.96 (*0-88110-534-1*, Usborne); pap. 6.95 (*0-7460-0641-1*, Usborne) EDC.

Fast, Jonathan, adapted by. Newsies. LC 91-73973. (Illus.). 136p. (Orig.). (gr. 2-6). 1992. pap. 3.50 (*1-56282-115-6*) Disney Pr.

Manley, D. Look & Learn about People, Places & Things. (Illus.). (gr. 2-6). 5.98 (*0-517-45795-4*) Random Hse Value.

Manley, Deborah. Long Ago. (Illus.). 48p. (ps-6). 1990. 4.99 (*0-517-69615-0*) Random Hse Value.

Pringle, Laurence. The Earth Is Flat & Other Great Mistakes. LC 83-7966. (Illus.). 96p. (gr. 3-7). 1983. lib. bdg. 12.88 (*0-688-02467-X*, Morrow Jr Bks) Morrow Jr Bks.

HISTORY–DICTIONARIES

Mulvihill, Margaret, ed. People in the Past. LC 92-54483. (Illus.). 1993. write for info. (*1-56458-217-5*) Dorling Kindersley.

Silvani, Harold. Famous Places & Events. 56p. (gr. 3-6). 1975. wkbk. 6.95 (*1-878669-21-4*, 4014) Crea Tea Assocs.

HISTORY–HISTORIOGRAPHY

see Historiography

HISTORY, MILITARY

see Military History

HISTORY, MODERN

Here are entered works covering the period after 1453.

see also Civilization, Modern; Reformation; Renaissance

Blocksma, Mary. Ticket to the Twenties: A Time Traveler's Guide. Dennen, Susan, illus. LC 92-24303. 1993. 15.95 (*0-316-09974-0*) Little.

Brooman, Josh. The World Since Nineteen Hundred. 1989. pap. text ed. 16.00 (*0-582-00989-8*, 78443) Longman.

Campling, Elizabeth. Portrait of a Decade: Nineteen Eighties. (Illus.). 72p. (gr. 7-11). 1990. 19.95 (*0-7134-6209-4*, Pub. by Batsford UK) Trafalgar.

Cannon, Jim, et al. The Contemporary World: Conflict or Co-Operation? 2nd ed. (Illus.). 128p. (Orig.). (gr. 9-12). 1979. pap. text ed. 23.76 (*0-05-003734-X*, 70092) Longman.

Chaney, Lisa. Breakfast. (Illus.). 32p. (gr. 3-6). 1992. 12.95 (*0-7136-3186-4*, Pub. by A&C Black UK) Talman.

Colombo, Monica. The Islamic World. LC 93-31449. 1994. PLB 25.67 (*0-8114-3328-5*) Raintree Steck-V.

Duden, Jane. Nineteen Fifties. LC 89-34400. (Illus.). 48p. (gr. 6). 1989. text ed. 11.95 RSBE (*0-89686-476-6*, Crestwood Hse) Macmillan Child Grp.

—Nineteen Forties. LC 89-34401. (Illus.). 48p. (gr. 6). 1989. text ed. 11.95 RSBE (*0-89686-475-8*, Crestwood Hse) Macmillan Child Grp.

—Nineteen Ninety-Two. (Illus.). 48p. (gr. 5). 1993. RSBE 12.95 (*0-89686-852-4*, Crestwood Hse) Macmillan Child Grp.

—Nineteen Seventies. LC 89-34630. (Illus.). 48p. (gr. 6). 1989. text ed. 11.95 RSBE (*0-89686-478-2*, Crestwood Hse) Macmillan Child Grp.

—Nineteen Sixties. LC 89-34399. (Illus.). 48p. (gr. 6). 1989. text ed. 11.95 RSBE (*0-89686-477-4*, Crestwood Hse) Macmillan Child Grp.

Essential Facts. 48p. (gr. 3-6). 1992. pap. 2.95 (*1-56680-009-9*) Mad Hatter Pub.

Farrant, Don. Lure & Lore of the Golden Isles. LC 93-37413. (Illus.). 192p. (Orig.). (gr. 10 up). 1993. pap. 8.95 (*1-55853-262-5*) Rutledge Hill Pr.

Felder, Deborah G. The Kids' World Almanac of History. Lane, John, illus. 288p. (Orig.). 1991. 14.95 (*0-88687-496-3*); pap. 6.95 (*0-88687-495-5*) Wrld Almnc.

Fisher, Trevor. Portrait of a Decade: Nineteen Ten to Nineteen Nineteen. (Illus.). 72p. (gr. 7-11). 1990. 19.95 (*0-7134-6071-7*, Pub. by Batsford UK) Trafalgar.

Freeman, Charles. Portrait of a Decade: Nineteen Thirties. (Illus.). 72p. (gr. 7-11). 1990. 19.95 (*0-7134-6073-3*, Pub. by Batsford UK) Trafalgar.

Fyson, Nance L. Portrait of a Decade: The 1940s. (Illus.). 72p. (gr. 7-10). 1989. 19.95 (*0-7134-5628-0*, Pub. by Batsford UK) Trafalgar.

Greene, Janice, et al. Our Century: 1900-1910. LC 93-11445. (gr. 4 up). 1993. Repr. of 1989 ed. PLB 21.27 (*0-8368-1032-5*) Gareth Stevens Inc.

Hills, Ken. Nineteen Forties. LC 91-43852. (Illus.). 47p. (gr. 6-7). 1992. PLB 22.80 (*0-8114-3077-4*) Raintree Steck-V.

—Nineteen Sixties. LC 92-30367. (Illus.). 47p. (gr. 6-7). 1992. PLB 22.80 (*0-8114-3079-0*) Raintree Steck-V.

—Nineteen Thirties. LC 91-42164. (Illus.). 47p. (gr. 6-7). 1992. PLB 22.80 (*0-8114-3076-6*) Raintree Steck-V.

Hoare, Stephen & Dyson, Sue. The Modern World. LC 92-2405. (Illus.). 80p. (gr. 2-6). 1993. 17.95x (*0-8160-2792-7*) Facts on File.

The Human Story Series, 9 vols. 616p. (gr. 7 up). 1988. Set. 77.70 (*0-382-09625-8*) Silver Burdett Pr.

Jacobs, William J. Great Lives: World Government. LC 91-42368. (Illus.). 320p. (gr. 4-6). 1993. SBE 22.95 (*0-684-19285-3*, Scribners Young Read) Macmillan Child Grp.

Kuhn, Dwight. More Than Just a...Series, 2 vols. Kuhn, Dwight, photos by. (Illus.). 80p. (gr. 2 up). 1990. Set. 15.90 (*0-671-94439-8*); Set. PLB 21.90 (*0-671-94438-X*) Silver Pr.

Leonard, Marcia. How Did That Happen? Series, 4 vols. Chambliss, Maxie & Iosa, Ann W., illus. 96p. (ps-1). 1990. Set. 19.80 (*0-671-31235-9*); Set. PLB 27.80 (*0-671-31234-0*) Silver Pr.

Martell, Hazel M. The Age of Discovery, 1500-1650. LC 92-18621. (Illus.). 80p. (gr. 2-6). 1993. 17.95x (*0-8160-2789-7*) Facts on File.
Martinet, Jeanne. The Year You Were Born, 1986. Lanfredi, Judy, illus. 56p. (gr. 2 up). 1993. PLB 13.93 (*0-688-11969-7*, Tambourine Bks); pap. 7.95 (*0-688-11968-9*, Tambourine Bks) Morrow.
—The Year You Were Born, 1987. Lanfredi, Judy, illus. 56p. (gr. 2 up). 1993. PLB 13.93 (*0-688-11971-9*, Tambourine Bks); pap. 7.95 (*0-688-11970-0*, Tambourine Bks) Morrow.
Our Century, 9 titles. (gr. 4 up). 1993. Set. PLB 191.40 (*0-8368-1031-7*) Gareth Stevens Inc.
Our Century: 1910-1920. (gr. 4 up). 1993. PLB 21.27 (*0-8368-1033-3*) Gareth Stevens Inc.
Our Century: 1920-1930. (gr. 4 up). 1993. PLB 21.27 (*0-8368-1034-1*) Gareth Stevens Inc.
Our Century: 1930-1940. (gr. 4 up). 1993. PLB 21.27 (*0-8368-1035-X*) Gareth Stevens Inc.
Our Century: 1940-1950. (gr. 4 up). 1993. PLB 21.27 (*0-8368-1036-8*) Gareth Stevens Inc.
Our Century: 1950-1960. (gr. 4 up). 1993. PLB 21.27 (*0-8368-1037-6*) Gareth Stevens Inc.
Our Century: 1960-1970. (gr. 4 up). 1993. PLB 21.27 (*0-8368-1038-4*) Gareth Stevens Inc.
Our Century: 1970-1980. (gr. 4 up). 1993. PLB 21.27 (*0-8368-1039-2*) Gareth Stevens Inc.
Our Century: 1980-1990. (gr. 4 up). 1993. PLB 21.27 (*0-8368-1040-6*) Gareth Stevens Inc.
Pollard, Michael. The Nineteenth Century. LC 92-19080. (Illus.). 80p. (gr. 2-6). 1993. 17.95x (*0-8160-2791-9*) Facts on File.
Reynoldson, Fiona. Conflict & Change, 1650-1800. LC 92-20460. (Illus.). 80p. (gr. 2-6). 1993. 17.95 (*0-8160-2790-0*) Facts on File.
Ross, Stewart. The Nineteen Eighties. (Illus.). 72p. (gr. 7-11). 1991. 19.95 (*0-7134-6361-9*, Pub. by Batsford UK) Trafalgar.
Schroeder, Mary. Extending U. S. History & Geography. West, James A., illus. 32p. (Orig.). (gr. 3-6). 1984. 6.50 (*0-88047-041-0*, 8404) DOK Pubs.
Sharman, Margaret. Nineteen Fifties. LC 92-25916. (Illus.). 47p. (gr. 6-7). 1992. PLB 22.80 (*0-8114-3078-2*) Raintree Steck-V.
—Nineteen Hundred Tens. LC 92-17521. (Illus.). 47p. (gr. 6-7). 1992. PLB 22.80 (*0-8114-3074-X*) Raintree Steck-V.
—Nineteen Hundreds. LC 93-12034. (Illus.). 47p. (gr. 6-7). 1993. PLB 22.80 (*0-8114-3073-1*) Raintree Steck-V.
—Nineteen Twenties. LC 92-17526. (Illus.). 47p. (gr. 6-7). 1992. PLB 22.80 (*0-8114-3075-8*) Raintree Steck-V.
Stewart, Gail. Nineteen Hundreds. LC 89-9936. (Illus.). 48p. (gr. 6). 1989. text ed. 11.95 RSBE (*0-89686-471-5*, Crestwood Hse) Macmillan Child Grp.
—Nineteen Tens. LC 89-9946. (Illus.). 48p. (gr. 6). 1989. text ed. 11.95 RSBE (*0-89686-472-3*, Crestwood Hse) Macmillan Child Grp.
—Nineteen Thirties. LC 89-34405. (Illus.). 48p. (gr. 6). 1989. text ed. 11.95 RSBE (*0-89686-474-X*, Crestwood Hse) Macmillan Child Grp.
—Nineteen Twenties. (Illus.). 48p. (gr. 6). 1989. text ed. 11.95 RSBE (*0-89686-473-1*, Crestwood Hse) Macmillan Child Grp.
Tallarico, Tony. I Didn't Know That! about Famous People & Places. (Illus.). 1992. pap. 2.95 (*1-56156-106-1*) Kidsbks.
Thomson, Ruth. In the Post. (Illus.). 32p. (gr. 3-6). 1992. 12.95 (*0-7136-3184-8*, Pub. by A&C Black UK) Talman.
—Washday. (Illus.). 32p. (gr. 3-6). 1992. 12.95 (*0-7136-3183-X*, Pub. by A&C Black UK) Talman.
Twist, Clint. Nineteen Eighties. LC 92-40348. (Illus.). 47p. (gr. 6-7). 1993. PLB 22.80 (*0-8114-3081-2*) Raintree Steck-V.
—Nineteen Seventies. LC 92-39952. (Illus.). 47p. (gr. 6-7). 1993. PLB 22.80 (*0-8114-3080-4*) Raintree Steck-V.
Verges, Gloria & Verges, Oriol. The Contemporary Age (Nineteenth & Twentieth Century) Rius, Maria & Peris, Carme, illus. (ENG & SPA.). 32p. (gr. 2-4). 1988. pap. 4.50 (*0-8120-3394-9*); La Edad Contemporanea. pap. 6.95 (*0-8120-3395-7*) Barron.
—Modern Times (Seventeenth & Eighteenth Century) Rius, Maria & Peris, Carme, illus. 32p. (gr. 2-4). 1988. pap. 4.50 (*0-8120-3392-2*); La Edad Moderna. pap. 6.95 (*0-8120-3393-0*) Barron.
Williams, Betty. Portrait of a Decade: The 1920s. (Illus.). 72p. (gr. 7-10). 1989. 19.95 (*0-7134-5816-X*, Pub. by Batsford UK) Trafalgar.
Woodson, Jacqueline, et al. Let's Celebrate Series, 6 vols. Cooper, Floyd, et al, illus. 192p. (gr. k-2). 1990. Set. 29.70 (*0-671-31231-6*); Set. PLB 41.70 (*0-671-31230-8*) Silver Pr.

HISTORY, NATURAL
see Natural History

HISTORY, NAVAL
see Naval History;
see names of countries with the subdivision History, Naval e. g. U. S.–History, Naval

HISTORY–PHILOSOPHY
see also Civilization

HISTORY, UNIVERSAL
see World History

HISTORY–YEARBOOKS
Duden, Jane. Nineteen Ninety. LC 92-72890. (Illus.). 48p. (gr. 5). 1992. text ed. 12.95 RSBE (*0-89686-769-2*, Crestwood Hse) Macmillan Child Grp.

HISTRIONICS
see Acting; Theater

HITCHHIKING
see Walking

HITLER, ADOLF, 1889-1945
Heyes, Eileen. Adolf Hitler. LC 93-31269. (gr. 7 up). 1994. PLB 16.90 (*1-56294-343-X*) Millbrook Pr.
Italia, Bob. Adolf Hitler. Wallner, Rosemary, ed. LC 90-82613. (Illus.). 32p. (gr. 4). 1990. PLB 11.96 (*0-939179-79-2*) Abdo & Dghtrs.
Kerr, Judith. When Hitler Stole Pink Rabbit. (gr. 3 up). 1987. pap. 3.99 (*0-440-49017-0*, YB) Dell.
Marrin, Albert. Hitler. LC 93-13057. 256p. (gr. 7 up). 1993. pap. 5.99 (*0-14-036526-5*, Puffin) Puffin Bks.

HOAXES
see Impostors and Imposture

HOBBIES
see also Collectors and Collecting; Handicraft
Childress, Casey & McKenzie, Linda. A Kid's Guide to Collecting Baseball Cards. rev. ed. LC 93-39810. (Illus.). 80p. (gr. 3-9). 1994. pap. 9.95 (*0-943173-93-0*) Harbinger AZ.
Dartez, Cecilia C. The Louisiana Plantation Coloring Book. Arrigo, Joseph, illus. 32p. (Orig.). (ps-4). 1985. pap. 3.25 (*0-88289-473-0*) Pelican.
Kohn, Eugene. Photography: A Manual for Shutterbugs. Plasencia, Peter P., illus. Noa, Pedro A., photos by. (Illus.). (gr. 3-7). 1965. pap. 1.25 (*0-685-03891-2*) P-H.
Ziefert, Harriet. Dress Little Bunny. Ernst, Lisa C., illus. 12p. (ps-1). 1986. pap. text ed. 6.99 (*0-670-80358-8*) Viking Child Bks.

HOBBIES–FICTION
Bulla, Clyde R. Daniel's Duck. Sandin, Joan, illus. LC 77-25647. 64p. (gr. k-3). 1979. PLB 13.89 (*0-06-020909-7*) HarpC Child Bks.

HOCKEY
Babineau, Jeff. Tampa Bay Lightning. LC 94-4305. 32p. (gr. 3 up). 1994. 14.95 (*0-88682-688-8*) Creative Ed.
Bliss, Jonathan. The Centers. LC 93-42533. 1994. write for info. (*1-55916-014-4*) Rourke Bk Co.
—The Stanley Cup. LC 93-50579. 1994. write for info. (*1-55916-012-8*) Rourke Bk Co.
Brothers, Bruce. St. Louis Blues. LC 93-48456. 32p. 1994. PLB 14.95 (*0-88682-686-1*) Creative Ed.
Coffey, Wayne. The U. S. Hockey Team, 1980. (Illus.). 64p. (gr. 3-7). 1993. PLB 14.95 (*1-56711-007-X*) Blackbirch.
Everson, Mark. New York Islanders. LC 93-48435. 32p. 1994. 14.95 (*0-88682-680-2*) Creative Ed.
—New York Rangers. LC 93-48434. 32p. 1994. 14.95 (*0-88682-681-0*) Creative Ed.
Gilbert, John. Buffalo Sabres. LC 93-47952. 32p. 1994. 14.95 (*0-88682-670-5*) Creative Ed.
—Dallas Stars. LC 93-48448. 32p. 1994. PLB 14.95 (*0-88682-673-X*) Creative Ed.
—Philadelphia Flyers. LC 93-48455. 32p. 1994. PLB 14.95 (*0-88682-683-7*) Creative Ed.
—Pittsburgh Penguins. LC 93-48449. 32p. 1994. PLB 14.95 (*0-88682-684-5*) Creative Ed.
Goyens, Chris. Montreal Canadiens. LC 94-1362. 32p. 1994. 14.95 (*0-88682-678-0*) Creative Ed.
—Toronto Maple Leafs. LC 94-1361. 32p. 1994. 14.95 (*0-88682-689-6*) Creative Ed.
Gutman, Bill. Field Hockey. LC 89-7587. (Illus.). 64p. (gr. 3-8). 1990. PLB 14.95 (*0-942545-93-1*) Marshall Cavendish.
—Ice Hockey. LC 89-9714. (Illus.). 64p. (gr. 3-8). 1990. PLB 14.95 (*0-942545-86-9*) Marshall Cavendish.
Harris, Lisa. Hockey. LC 93-23282. 1993. PLB 21.34 (*0-8114-5781-8*) Raintree Steck-V.
Italia, Bob. The Montreal Canadiens: Nineteen Ninety Three Stanley Cup Champions. LC 93-30672. 1993. 14.96 (*1-56239-240-9*) Abdo & Dghtrs.
Jones, Terry. Calgary Flames. LC 93-48431. 32p. 1994. PLB 14.95 (*0-88682-671-3*) Creative Ed.
—Edmonton Oilers. LC 93-47950. 32p. 1994. 14.95 (*0-88682-675-6*) Creative Ed.
Kalb, Jonah. The Easy Hockey Book. Morrison, Bill, illus. 64p. (gr. 2-5). 1977. 13.95 (*0-395-25842-1*) HM.
Knapp, Ron. Top Ten Hockey Scorers. (Illus.). 48p. (gr. 4-10). 1994. lib. bdg. 14.95 (*0-89490-517-1*) Enslow Pubs.
Kupelian, Vartan. Boston Bruins. 32p. 1994. PLB 14.95 (*0-88682-669-1*) Creative Ed.
—Chicago Blackhawks. LC 93-48452. 32p. 1994. 14.95 (*0-88682-672-1*) Creative Ed.
—Detroit Red Wings. LC 93-47951. 32p. 1994. 14.95 (*0-88682-674-8*) Creative Ed.
McGuire, William. The Stanley Cup. 32p. (gr. 4). 1990. PLB 14.95 (*0-88682-316-1*) Creative Ed.
MacIntyre, Iain. Vancouver Canucks. LC 93-48447. 32p. 1994. PLB 14.95 (*0-88682-690-X*) Creative Ed.
Myers, Jess. Winnipeg Jets. LC 93-48451. 32p. 1994. PLB 14.95 (*0-88682-692-6*) Creative Ed.
Olson, Gary. Hartford Whalers. 32p. 1994. PLB 14.95 (*0-88682-676-4*) Creative Ed.
—Quebec Nordiques. LC 93-48453. 1994. PLB write for info. (*0-88682-685-3*) Creative Ed.
Rockwell, Bart. World's Strangest Hockey Stories. LC 92-25992. (Illus.). 96p. (gr. 3-7). 1992. PLB 9.89 (*0-8167-2936-0*); pap. text ed. 2.95 (*0-8167-2853-4*) Troll Assocs.
St. Peter, Joan. Los Angeles Kings. LC 93-48432. 32p. 1994. PLB 14.95 (*0-88682-677-2*) Creative Ed.
—San Jose Sharks. LC 98-48450. 1994. PLB 14.95 (*0-88682-687-X*) Creative Ed.
Smale, David. Washington Capitals. LC 94-4304. 32p. 1994. 14.95 (*0-88682-691-8*) Creative Ed.
Yannis, Alex. New Jersey Devils. 32p. 1994. PLB 14.95 (*0-88682-679-9*) Creative Ed.

HOCKEY–BIOGRAPHY
Bianchi, J. Champions of Hockey. (Illus.). 24p. (ps-8). 1989. 12.95 (*0-921285-18-3*, Pub. by Bungalo Bks CN); pap. 4.95 (*0-921285-16-7*, Pub. by Bungalo Bks CN) Firefly Bks Ltd.
Bliss, Jonathan. Great Goalies. LC 93-33591. 1994. write for info. (*1-55916-010-1*) Rourke Bk Co.
—The Legends. LC 93-42816. 1994. write for info. (*1-55916-015-2*) Rourke Bk Co.
—Wingmen Warriors. LC 93-39507. 1994. write for info. (*1-55916-013-6*) Rourke Bk Co.
Cox, Ted. Mario Lemieux (Super Mario) LC 93-19782. (Illus.). 48p. (gr. 2-8). 1993. PLB 11.95 (*0-516-04378-1*); pap. 3.95 (*0-516-44378-X*) Childrens.
Goldstein, Margaret J. Brett Hull: Hockey's Top Gun. (Illus.). 64p. (gr. 4-7). 1992. PLB 13.50 (*0-8225-0544-4*); pap. 3.95 (*0-8225-9599-0*) Lerner Pubns.
Gutman, Bill. Mario Lemieux: Wizard with a Puck. LC 92-5003. (Illus.). 48p. (gr. 3-6). 1992. PLB 13.40 (*1-56294-084-8*); pap. 4.95 (*1-56294-826-1*) Millbrook Pr.
—Mario Lemieux: Wizard with a Puck. (gr. 4-7). 1992. pap. 4.95 (*0-395-64544-1*) HM.
Italia, Bob. Hockey's Heroes. LC 93-21230. 1993. 14.96 (*1-56239-244-1*) Abdo & Dghtrs.
Leder, Jane M. Wayne Gretzky. LC 84-14980. (Illus.). 48p. (gr. 5-6). 1985. text ed. 11.95 RSBE (*0-89686-255-0*, Crestwood Hse) Macmillan Child Grp.
Raber, Tom. Wayne Gretzky: Hockey Great. (Illus.). 64p. (gr. 4-9). 1991. PLB 13.50 (*0-8225-0539-8*) Lerner Pubns.
—Wayne Gretzky: Hockey Great. 1992. pap. 4.95 (*0-8225-9601-6*) Lerner Pubns.
Rozens, Aleksandrs. Wayne Gretzky. LC 93-18132. 1993. 15.93 (*0-86592-119-9*); 11.95s.p. (*0-685-66586-0*) Rourke Enter.
Wayne Gretzky. (ps-3). 1992. pap. 1.25 (*0-590-45842-6*) Scholastic Inc.
Wolff, Craig T. Wayne Gretzky: Profil d'un Joueur de Hockey. Curtis, Bruce, photos by. (FRE., Illus.). 64p. (ps-5). 1984. pap. 2.25 (*0-380-85753-7*, Camelot) Avon.

HOCKEY–FICTION
Carrier, Roch. Le Chandail de Hockey. Cohen, Sheldon, illus. (FRE.). 24p. (Orig.). (gr. 1 up). 1985. pap. 6.95 (*0-88776-176-3*, Dist. by U of Toronto Pr); 14.95 (*0-88776-171-2*) Tundra Bks.
Christopher, Matt. The Hockey Machine. Schroeppel, Richard, illus. (gr. 4 up). 1986. 15.95 (*0-316-14055-4*) Little.
—Ice Magic. Goto, Byron, illus. (gr. 4-6). 1987. PLB 15.95 (*0-316-13958-0*); pap. 3.95 (*0-316-13991-2*) Little.
—Matt Christopher Hockey Boxed Set: Face-Off, Ice Magic, & the Hockey Machine. (gr. 4-7). 1993. 11.85 (*0-316-14271-9*) Little.
—Wingman on Ice. (gr. 4-7). 1993. pap. 3.95 (*0-316-14269-7*) Little.
Drumtra, Stacy. Face-off. 128p. (Orig.). 1992. pap. 3.50 (*0-380-76863-1*, Flare) Avon.
Godfrey, Martyn. Ice Hawk. 96p. (gr. 7-12). 1986. pap. text ed. 4.50 (*0-8219-0235-0*, 35361); 1.20 (*0-8219-0236-9*, 35720) EMC.
Godfrey, Martyn N. Please Remove Your Elbow from My Ear. 128p. (Orig.). 1993. pap. 3.50 (*0-380-76580-2*, Flare) Avon.
Gostick, Adrian R. Eddy & the Habs. LC 93-47424. (gr. 3-7). 1994. pap. 5.95 (*0-87579-832-2*) Deseret Bk.
Halecroft, David. Benched! 128p. (gr. 3-7). 1992. pap. 2.99 (*0-14-036038-7*) Puffin Bks.
—Blindside Blitz. (gr. 4-7). 1991. pap. 2.95 (*0-14-034906-5*, Puffin) Puffin Bks.
—Breaking Loose. LC 92-12084. 128p. (gr. 3-7). 1992. 13.00 (*0-670-84697-X*) Viking Child Bks.
—Hotshot on Ice. (gr. 4-7). 1991. pap. 2.95 (*0-14-034907-3*, Puffin) Puffin Bks.
—Power Play. (gr. 4 up). 1990. pap. 2.95 (*0-14-034549-3*, Puffin) Puffin Bks.
—Power Play. LC 92-12605. 128p. (gr. 3-7). 1992. 13.00 (*0-670-84698-8*) Viking Child Bks.
Jenkins, Jerry. The Bizarre Hockey Tournament. (Orig.). (gr. 7-12). 1986. pap. text ed. 4.99 (*0-8024-8236-8*) Moody.
Lynch, Chris. Iceman. LC 93-7776. 160p. (gr. 7 up). 1994. 15.00 (*0-06-023340-0*); PLB 14.89 (*0-06-023341-9*) HarpC Child Bks.
Morgan, Allen. Magic Hockey Skates. (ps-3). 1994. pap. 6.95 (*0-19-540851-9*) OUP.
Paulsen, Gary. Dancing Carl. LC 83-2663. 144p. (gr. 6-8). 1983. SBE 13.95 (*0-02-770210-3*, Bradbury Pr) Macmillan Child Grp.
Rocklin. Grandmaman Hockey. 1993. 15.95 (*0-8050-2322-4*) H Holt & Co.
Smith, Alias & Pelkowski, Robert. Hockey: Freddie Face-off & Fanny Falls in Ice Monster. 32p. (ps-3). 1989. pap. 3.95 (*0-8120-4243-3*) Barron.

HOGS
see also Pigs

Schmidt, Annemarie & Schmidt, Christian R. Pigs & Peccaries. LC 93-13051. (gr. 3 up). 1994. 18.60 (*0-8368-1003-1*) Gareth Stevens Inc.
Terry, John. Pigs in the Playground. Brewis, Henry, illus. 208p. 1986. pap. 7.95 (*0-85236-158-0*, Pub by Farming Pr UK); pap. text ed. 6.95 (*0-317-47058-2*, Pub. by Farming Pr UK) Diamond Farm Bk.

HOGS–FICTION

Aylesworth, Jim. Hanna's Hog. Rounds, Glen, illus. LC 87-11559. 32p. (gr. k-3). 1988. RSBE 13.95 (*0-689-31367-5*, Atheneum Child Bk) Macmillan Child Grp.
Blacke, Terry L. & Rider, Debra. Pabulum Pig: The Yule Swine. Blacke, Terry L., illus. LC 91-68193. 41p. (gr. 4). 1992. pap. 7.98 (*0-9630718-2-3*) New Dawn NY.
Hello, Piglet! LC 92-62558. 20p. (ps). 1993. 4.99 (*0-89577-483-6*, Dist. by Random) RD Assn.
Marks, Burton. Pig's Car. LC 92-62552. (Illus.). 10p. (ps-1). 1993. 4.99 (*0-89577-476-3*, Dist. by Random) RD Assn.

HOISTING MACHINERY

see also Elevators

HOLIDAY DECORATIONS

Churchill, E. Richard. Holiday Paper Projects. Michaels, James, illus. LC 92-12100. 128p. (gr. 3-9). 1992. 14.95 (*0-8069-8512-7*) Sterling.
Ross, Kathy. Crafts for Kwanzaa. Holm, Sharon L., illus. LC 93-36690. 48p. (gr. k-3). 1994. 15.40 (*1-56294-412-6*); pap. 6.95 (*1-56294-740-0*) Millbrook Pr.

HOLIDAYS

see also Fasts and Feasts;
also names of holidays, e.g. Fourth of July

Ainsworth, Catherine H. American Calendar Customs, Vol. I. LC 79-52827. 112p. (Orig.). (ps-12). 1979. pap. 12.00 (*0-933190-06-9*) Clyde Pr.
Alden, Laura. Father's Day. (Illus.). 32p. (ps-2). 1994. PLB 16.40 (*0-516-00693-2*); pap. 3.95 (*0-516-40693-0*) Childrens.
—President's Day. Friedman, Joy, illus. LC 93-37095. 32p. (ps-2). 1994. PLB 12.30 (*0-516-00691-6*) Childrens.
Alexander, Sue. America's Own Holidays: Mas de Fiesta de los Estados Unidos. Morrill, Leslie, illus. LC 86-32567. (SPA.). 48p. 1988. PLB 11.40 (*0-531-10293-9*) Watts.
Baker, James W. Presidents' Day Magic. Overlie, George, illus. 48p. (gr. 2-5). 1989. 11.95 (*0-8225-2232-2*) Lerner Pubns.
Banh Chung Banh Day: The New Year's Rice Cakes. (gr. 2-5). 1972. 2.50 (*0-686-10279-7*) Asia Resource.
Barkin, Carol & James, Elizabeth. The Holiday Handbook. LC 92-29846. 1993. 15.45 (*0-395-65011-9*, Clarion Bks) HM.
Bauman, Toni & Zinkgraf, June. Celebrations. Wunderlin, Linda W., illus. 240p. (gr. k-6). 1985. wkbk. 14.95 (*0-86653-330-3*, GA 666) Good Apple.
Behrens, June. Fiesta! Taylor, Scott, illus. LC 78-8468. 32p. (gr. k-4). 1978. PLB 11.60 (*0-516-08815-7*, Golden Gate); pap. 3.95 (*0-516-48815-5*) Childrens.
—Fiesta! Kratky, Lada, tr. LC 85-23271. (SPA., Illus.). 32p. (ps-3). 1986. PLB 11.60 (*0-516-38815-0*); pap. 3.95 (*0-516-58815-X*) Childrens.
Best Holiday Books Series, 20 bks. (Illus.). (gr. 1-4). Set. lib. bdg. 299.00 (*0-89490-337-3*) Enslow Pubs.
Blackwood, Alan. New Year. (Illus.). 48p. (gr. 3-8). 1987. PLB 15.94 (*0-86592-981-5*); 11.95s.p. (*0-685-67597-1*) Rourke Corp.
Bornstein, Harry. The Holiday Book. (Illus.). 48p. (ps-2). 1974. pap. 6.50 (*0-913580-30-9*, Kendall Green Pubs) Gallaudet Univ Pr.
Carrie, Christopher. Holiday Fun. (Illus.). 32p. (Orig.). (ps up). 1989. 1.99 (*0-685-27062-9*) Binney & Smith.
Carroll, Jeri A. & Wells, Candace B. Learning about Fall & Winter Holidays. 112p. (ps-2). 1988. wkbk. 10.95 (*0-86653-441-5*, GA1048) Good Apple.
Chiemroum, Sothea. Dara's Cambodian New Year. (ps-3). 1994. pap. 4.95 (*0-671-88607-X*, Half Moon Bks) S&S Trade.
Chocolate, Deborah M. Kwanzaa. Rosales, Melodye, illus. LC 89-25418. 32p. (ps-3). 1990. PLB 11.95 (*0-516-03991-1*); pap. 3.95 (*0-516-43991-X*) Childrens.
—My First Kwanzaa Book. 1992. bds. 10.95 (*0-590-45762-4*, Cartwheel) Scholastic Inc.
Corwin, Judith H. Messner Holiday Library, 9 bks. Corwin, Judith H., illus. (gr. 3 up). 1988. Set, 64p. ea. lib. bdg. 92.61 (*0-671-92641-1*, J Messner); Set, 64p. ea. pap. write for info. (*0-671-92642-X*) S&S Trade.
Cracchiolo, Rachelle. Holiday Cards. Darby's Designs, illus. 32p. (gr. 1-6). 1982. wkbk. 5.95 (*1-55734-031-5*) Tchr Create Mat.
Cracchiolo, Rachelle & Smith, Mary D. Holiday Hats. Cracchiolo, Rachelle & Smith, Mary D., illus. 16p. (gr. k-4). 1979. wkbk. 6.50 (*1-55734-002-1*) Tchr Create Mat.
D'Amato, Janet & D'Amato, Alex. Handicrafts for Holidays. D'Amato, Janet & D'Amato, Alex, illus. (gr. 1-4). 1967. PLB 13.95 (*0-87460-086-3*) Lion Bks.
Davis-Thompson, Helen. Let's Celebrate Kwanzaa: An Activity Book for Young Readers. Hall, Chris A., illus. 32p. (ps-5). 1993. pap. 5.95 (*0-936073-07-1*) Gumbs & Thomas.
Fox, Mary V. About Martin Luther King Day. LC 88-23230. (Illus.). 64p. (gr. 4-7). 1989. lib. bdg. 15.95 (*0-89490-200-8*) Enslow Pubs.
Freeman, Dorothy R. & MacMillan, Dianne M. Kwanzaa. LC 91-43100. (Illus.). 48p. (gr. 1-4). 1992. lib. bdg. 14.95 (*0-89490-381-0*) Enslow Pubs.
Frost, Ed & Frost, Roon. The Kids' Holiday Book: Activities Through the Seasons. Leach, Carol, illus. 176p. (Orig.). (ps-7). 1990. pap. 11.95 (*0-9618806-3-5*) Glove Compart Bks.
Garcia, Yolanda. Celebremos. (SPA., Illus.). (gr. 1-6). 10.95 (*0-935303-03-0*) Victory Pub.
Gerson, Trina. Holiday Crafts. Gerson, Janice, illus. 80p. (ps-7). 1983. pap. text ed. write for info. (*0-9605878-1-0*) Anirt Pr.
Glover, Susanne & Grewe, Georgeann. Holiday Happenings. (gr. 1-4). 1982. pap. 9.95 (*0-88160-046-6*, LW 231) Learning Wks.
Gore, Willma W. Earth Day. LC 91-43199. (Illus.). 48p. (gr. 1-4). 1992. lib. bdg. 14.95 (*0-89490-380-2*) Enslow Pubs.
Goss, Linda & Goss, Clay. It's Kwanzaa Time! LC 92-30380. 1994. 18.95 (*0-399-22505-6*, Philomel Bks) Putnam Pub Group.
Greene, Carol. Holidays Around the World. LC 82-9734. (Illus.). (gr. k-4). 1982. PLB 12.85 (*0-516-01624-5*); pap. 4.95 (*0-516-41624-3*) Childrens.
Hand, Phyllis. Celebrate Special Days. Hierstein, Judy, illus. 144p. (gr. k-6). 1985. wkbk. 11.95 (*0-86653-280-3*, SS 841, Shining Star Pubns) Good Apple.
Happy Holidays. (Illus.). (ps-5). 3.50 (*0-7214-0553-3*); o.p. (*0-317-03990-3*) Ladybird Bks.
Holidays Around the World. (Illus.). (ps-7). 1987. 5.95 (*0-553-05416-3*) Bantam.
Hoyt-Goldsmith, Diane. Celebrating Kwanzaa. Migale, Lawrence, photos by. LC 93-16799. (Illus.). 32p. (gr. 3-7). 1993. reinforced bdg. 15.95 (*0-8234-1048-X*); pap. 6.95 (*0-8234-1130-3*) Holiday.
Ideas for Special Occasions. LC 91-17040. (Illus.). 48p. (gr. 4-8). 1991. PLB 14.95 (*1-85435-407-8*) Marshall Cavendish.
Kalman, Bobbie. We Celebrate Christmas. (Illus.). 56p. (gr. 3-4). 1985. 15.95 (*0-86505-040-6*); pap. 7.95 (*0-86505-050-3*) Crabtree Pub Co.
—We Celebrate Family Days. (Illus.). 56p. (gr. 3-4). 1986. 15.95 (*0-86505-048-1*); pap. 7.95 (*0-86505-058-9*) Crabtree Pub Co.
—We Celebrate Harvest. (Illus.). 56p. (gr. 3-4). 1986. 15.95 (*0-86505-044-9*); pap. 7.95 (*0-86505-054-6*) Crabtree Pub Co.
Keefe, Betty. Fingerpuppets, Fingerplays & Holidays. (Illus.). 136p. (ps-3). 1984. spiral bdg. 17.95 (*0-938594-05-2*) Spec Lit Pr.
Kollay, Jocelyne. French Holiday Activity Workbook. (FRE & ENG., Illus.). 100p. (Orig.). (gr. 9-12). 1988. wkbk. 16.95 (*0-9617764-1-2*) PS Enterprises.
Kroll, Steven. Happy Mother's Day. Hafner, Marilyn, illus. LC 83-18498. 32p. (ps-3). 1985. reinforced bdg. 14.95 (*0-8234-0504-4*) Holiday.
Lasky, Kathryn. Days of the Dead. Knight, Christopher G., photos by. LC 93-47957. (Illus.). 48p. (gr. 3-7). 1994. 15.95 (*0-7868-0022-4*); PLB 15.89 (*0-7868-2018-7*) Hyprn Child.
LeGros, Lucy C. Instant Centers - Holidays. rev. ed. Legros, Ivor L., illus. 51p. (gr. k-2). 1988. tchr's ed. 5.95 (*0-317-65724-0*) Creat Res NC.
Lemelman, Martin. Chanukah Is... (Illus.). 10p. (ps-k). 1988. bds. 4.95 (*0-8074-0424-1*) UAHC.
Liestman, Vicki. Columbus Day. Hanson, Rick, illus. 56p. (gr. k-4). 1991. PLB 14.95 (*0-87614-444-X*) Carolrhoda Bks.
Lithuanian Photographers Staff. Lithuanian Celebrations: Lietuviu Sventes. Algimantas KEZYS Staff, ed. Bindokiene, Danute, intros. by. (ENG & LIT.). 250p. 1990. pap. text ed. 15.00 (*0-9617756-2-9*) Galerija.
Little People Big Book about Holidays & Celebrations. 64p. (ps-1). 1990. write for info. (*0-8094-7508-1*); PLB write for info. (*0-8094-7509-X*) Time-Life.
Livingston, Myra C. Celebrations. Fisher, Leonard E., illus. LC 84-19216. 32p. (ps-3). 1985. reinforced bdg. 15.95 (*0-8234-0550-8*); pap. 5.95 (*0-8234-0654-7*) Holiday.
Lizon, Karen H. Colonial American Holidays & Entertainment. LC 92-40262. 1993. 12.90 (*0-531-12546-7*) Watts.
Lowery, Linda. Earth Day. (Illus.). 48p. (gr. k-4). 1991. PLB 14.95 (*0-87614-662-0*) Carolrhoda Bks.
—Martin Luther King Day. Mitchell, Hetty, illus. (gr. 3-5). 1987. incl. cassette 19.95 (*0-87499-071-8*); pap. 12.95 incl. cassette (*0-87499-070-X*); 4 paperbacks, cassette & guide 27.95 (*0-87499-072-6*) Live Oak Media.
MacMillan, Dianne M. Martin Luther King, Jr. Day. LC 91-43097. (Illus.). 48p. (gr. 1-4). 1992. lib. bdg. 14.95 (*0-89490-382-9*) Enslow Pubs.
Madhubuti, Safisha. Story of Kwanzaa. (gr. 1). 1989. pap. 5.95 (*0-88378-001-1*) Third World.
Most, Bernard. Happy Holidaysaurus! 1992. 13.95 (*0-15-233386-X*, HB Juv Bks) HarBrace.
Packard, Ann & Stafford, Shirley. Holidays. 116p. 1983. write for info. (*0-9607580-4-6*) S Stafford.
Penner, Lucille R. Celebration: The Story of American Holidays. Ohlsson, Ib, illus. LC 92-25871. 80p. (gr. 1 up). 1993. SBE 15.95 (*0-02-770903-5*, Macmillan Child Bk) Macmillan Child Grp.
Perl, Lila & Ada, Alma F. Pinatas & Paper Flowers-Pinatas y Flores de Papel: Holidays of the Americas in English & Spanish. De Larrea, Victoria, illus. LC 82-12211. 91p. (gr. 3-6). 1983. 12.95 (*0-89919-112-6*, Clarion Bks); pap. 5.95 (*0-89919-155-X*, Clarion Bks) HM.
Pinkney, Andrea D. Seven Candles for Kwanzaa. Pinkney, Brian, illus. LC 92-3698. 32p. (gr. k up). 1993. 14.99 (*0-8037-1292-8*); lib. bdg. 14.89 (*0-8037-1293-6*) Dial Bks Young.
Plattner, Sandra S. Connecting with Holidays. (ps-k). 1991. pap. 10.95 (*0-8224-1634-4*) Fearon Teach Aids.
Poelker, Kathy. Look at the Holidays. Schiller, Juel K., illus. 64p. (ps-4). 1988. Repr. of 1980 ed. tchr's. ed. 7.95 (*0-317-91200-3*) LAM Co.
Porter, A. P. Kwanzaa. Van Buren, Bobby, illus. 48p. (gr. k-4). 1991. PLB 14.95 (*0-87614-668-X*); pap. 5.95 (*0-87614-545-4*) Carolrhoda Bks.
Reece, Colleen L. Mi Primer Libro de el Dia de las Brujas: My First Halloween Book. Kratky, Lada, tr. Peltier, Pam, illus. LC 85-31396. (SPA.). 32p. (ps-3). 1986. PLB 11.45 (*0-516-32902-2*); pap. 3.95 (*0-516-52902-1*) Childrens.
Renberg, Dalia H. The Complete Family Guide to Jewish Holidays. LC 84-11008. (Illus.). (gr. 4 up). 1985. pap. 22.95 (*0-915361-09-4*) Modan-Adama Bks.
Rozakis, Laurie. Celebrate! Holidays Around the World. LC 92-81915. (gr. k-4). 1993. pap. 4.95 (*0-88160-217-5*, LW107) Learning Wks.
Sandak, Cass. Patriotic Holidays. LC 89-25380. (Illus.). 48p. (gr. 5-6). 1990. text ed. 12.95 RSBE (*0-89686-501-0*, Crestwood Hse) Macmillan Child Grp.
Schaff, Joanne. Holidays & Celebrations: An Educational Activity Book. Schaff, Joanne, illus. 43p. (ps-2). 1993. pap. 4.95 (*0-9619365-1-7*) Tree City Pr.
Scott, Geoffrey. Memorial Day. Hanson, Peter E., illus. LC 83-1855. 48p. (gr. k-4). 1983. PLB 14.95 (*0-87614-219-6*) Carolrhoda Bks.
Shulz, Charles, illus. People & Customs of the World. LC 94-13723. 1994. write for info. (*0-517-11898-X*, Pub. by Derrydale Bks) Random Hse Value.
Sing, Rachel. Chinese New Year's Dragon. (ps-3). 1994. pap. 4.95 (*0-671-88602-9*, Half Moon Bks) S&S Trade.
Snelling, et al. Holidays & Festivals, 7 bks, Set I, Reading Level 4. (Illus.). 288p. (gr. 3-8). 1987. Set. PLB 111.58 (*0-86592-975-0*); Set. 83.65s.p. (*0-86592-982-3*) Rourke Corp.
Spies, Karen. Our National Holidays. LC 91-38894. (Illus.). 48p. (gr. 2-4). 1992. PLB 13.40 (*1-56294-109-7*); pap. 5.95 (*1-878841-88-2*) Millbrook Pr.
Sterling, Mary E. Holidays on Parade. Olsen, Shirley, illus. 64p. (gr. k-2). 1988. wkbk. 7.95 (*1-55734-377-2*) Tchr Create Mat.
Sullivan, Dianna J. Patriotic Holidays. Walhood, Darlene, illus. 48p. (gr. 1-5). 1986. wkbk. 6.95 (*1-55734-115-X*) Tchr Create Mat.
Tudor, Tasha. A Time to Keep: The Tasha Tudor Book of Holidays. 2nd ed. LC 77-9067. (Illus.). (gr. k-3). 1990. SBE 14.95 (*0-02-789502-5*, Macmillan Child Bk) Macmillan Child Grp.
Van Straalen, Alice. The Book of Holidays Around the World. LC 86-11674. (Illus.). 192p. (ps up). 1986. 16.95 (*0-525-44270-7*, DCB) Dutton Child Bks.
Wells, Candace B. & Carroll, Jeri A. Learning about Spring & Summer Holidays. 112p. (ps-2). 1988. wkbk. 10.95 (*0-86653-442-3*, GA1047) Good Apple.
Westberg, Barbara. Holiday Programs: Recitations, Exercises, Readings, Skits, Dramas, Musicals for All Ages, Vol. 2. Agnew, Tim, illus. LC 87-29786. 192p. (Orig.). 1993. pap. 7.99 (*1-56722-012-6*) Word Aflame.

HOLIDAYS–DRAMA

Gilfond, Henry & Blevins, George. Holiday Plays for Reading. (Illus.). 160p. (gr. 4 up). 1985. PLB 10.85 (*0-8027-6601-3*) Walker & Co.

HOLIDAYS–FICTION

Adler, David. The House on the Roof. Hirsh, Marilyn, illus. LC 84-12555. 32p. (ps-4). 1984. pap. 4.95 (*0-930494-35-0*) Kar-Ben.

Ballard, Bobbie. My Kwanzaa Story. Slay, Charles, illus. 48p. (gr. k-6). 1993. 6.95 (*0-9639349-0-2*) Ujamaa Ent.
MY KWANZAA STORY is new on the market! It is an 8 1/2 X 11, full-color, hardbound book that is available in both a PERSONALIZED & NON-PERSONALIZED format. MY KWANZAA STORY is produced by Ujamaa Enterprises, Inc., of Oak Ridge, TN. MY KWANZAA STORY centers around the celebration of Kwanzaa & explains the 7 guiding principles that are basic to the concept of Kwanzaa. In the story, a family is making preparation for the Karamu feast which is held on the last night of Kwanzaa. At this time, family & friends gather together to encourage & reaffirm family & cultural values. These values are presented as understood by the children in the story. The book is appropriate for k-5th or

6th grade. Wholesale price - (non-personalized) $6.95 per book plus shipping/handling. Wholesale price - (personalized) $8.95 (includes shipping/handling). Quality Books Inc. (a Dawson Company), 918 Sherwood Dr., Lake Bluff, IL 60044-2204; tel. 708-295-2010; fax 708-295-1556. *Publisher Provided Annotation.*

Burden-Patmon, Denise. Imani's Gift at Kwanzaa. Cooper, Floyd, illus. 32p. (gr. 2-5). 1993. pap. 4.95 (*0-671-79841-3*, S&S BYR) S&S Trade.

Chaikin, Miriam. Make Noise, Make Merry. (gr. 4-7). 1983. 11.95 (*0-89919-140-1*, Clarion Bks) HM.

Clements, Andrew. Santa's Secret Helper. Santini, Debrah, illus. LC 93-20119. (gr. 1-8). 1993. 4.95 (*0-88708-325-0*) Picture Bk Studio.

Denim, Sue. The Dumb Bunnies' Easter. Pilkey, Dav, illus. LC 94-15050. (gr. 1-8). 1995. write for info. (*0-590-20241-3*, Blue Sky Press) Scholastic Inc.

Foehl, Jamie L. Trick or Treat Taffy. Foehl, Barbara B., illus. LC 89-92436. 40p. (Orig.). (ps-6). 1989. write for info. (*0-9625337-0-X*); PLB write for info.; pap. write for info. B Bk Pub Co.

Hanson, Don & Helfrich, R. L. A Holiday on a Log with Hog, Dog & Frog: Greet the Easter Bunny. Helfrich, Nathan, illus. 64p. 1993. pap. 9.95 (*1-56883-020-3*) Colonial Pr AL.

Highlights Staff. Celebrate the Season: Holiday Stories from Highlights. LC 92-75838. (Illus.). 32p. (gr. 2-7). 1994. 4.95 (*1-56397-082-1*); prepack 14.85 (*1-56397-394-4*) Boyds Mills Pr.

Jaffe, Nina. In the Month of Kislev: A Story for Hanukkah. August, Louise, illus. 32p. (ps-3). 1992. 15.00 (*0-670-82863-7*) Viking Child Bks.

James, Elizabeth. Holiday Handbook. (gr. 4-7). 1994. pap. 8.95 (*0-395-67888-9*, Clarion Bks) HM.

Johnston, Annie F. The Little Colonel's Holidays. (gr. 5 up). 13.95 (*0-89201-038-X*) Zenger Pub.

Joosse, Barbara M. Fourth of July. McCully, Emily A., illus. LC 82-17301. 48p. (ps-2). 1985. PLB 11.99 (*0-394-95195-6*) Knopf Bks Yng Read.

Kaffa. The Best Ever Costume Party. 1993. pap. 6.95 (*0-590-46958-4*) Scholastic Inc.

Kallevig, Christine P. Holiday Folding Stories: Storytelling & Origami Together for Holiday Fun. LC 91-68161. (Illus.). 96p. (Orig.). 1992. pap. 11.50 (*0-9628769-1-7*) Storytime Ink.

Keller, Holly. Henry's Fourth of July. LC 84-13707. (Illus.). 32p. (ps-1). 1985. PLB 10.88 (*0-688-04013-6*) Greenwillow.

Kovitch, Lisa G. I Want to Decorate, Too! (Illus.). 34p. (Orig.). (ps). 1992. pap. 3.50 (*0-9635108-1-9*) Fragments Lghts.

Kroll, Steven. Mary McLean & the St. Patrick's Day Parade. Dooling, Michael, illus. 32p. (ps-3). 1991. 13.95 (*0-590-43701-1*, Scholastic Hardcover) Scholastic Inc.

—Mary McLean & the St. Patrick's Day Parade. (gr. 4-7). 1990. 3.95 (*0-590-43702-X*) Scholastic Inc.

McDonnell, Janet. Martin Luther King Day. Halverson, Lydia, illus. LC 93-13251. 32p. (ps-2). 1993. PLB 12.30 (*0-516-00687-8*); pap. 3.95 (*0-516-40687-6*) Childrens.

McOmber, Rachel B., ed. McOmber Phonics Storybooks: Bags... Bags (Holidays) rev. ed. (Illus.). write for info. (*0-944991-98-X*) Swift Lrn Res.

—McOmber Phonics Storybooks: Boyer's Toy Store. rev. ed. (Illus.). write for info. (*0-944991-69-6*) Swift Lrn Res.

Mandrell, Louise. All American Hero: A Story about the Meaning of Veterans Day. (gr. 4-7). 1993. 12.95 (*1-56530-010-6*) Summit TX.

—Candy's Frog Prince: A Story about the Meaning of Valentines Day. (gr. 4-7). 1993. 12.95 (*1-56530-046-7*) Summit TX.

—Eddie Finds a Hero: A Story about the Meaning of Memorial Day. (ps-3). 1993. 12.95 (*1-56530-037-8*) Summit TX.

—End of the Rainbow: A Story about the Meaning of St. Patrick's Day. (gr. 4-7). 1993. 12.95 (*1-56530-047-5*) Summit TX.

—Eye of an Eagle: A Story about the Meaning of Columbus Day. (gr. 4-7). 1993. 12.95 (*1-56530-009-2*) Summit TX.

—Kimi's American Dream: A Story about the Meaning of Martin Luther King Day. (gr. 4-7). 1993. 12.95 (*1-56530-045-9*) Summit TX.

—Mission for Jenny: A Story about the Meaning of Flag Day. (ps-3). 1993. 12.95 (*1-56530-038-6*) Summit TX.

—Twin Disasters: A Story about the Meaning of Labor Day. (gr. 4-7). 1993. 12.95 (*1-56530-041-6*) Summit TX.

Manes, Stephen. The Hooples' Horrible Holiday. 128p. (Orig.). (gr. 3-7). 1986. pap. 2.50 (*0-380-89740-7*, Camelot) Avon.

Mariana. Miss Flora McFlimsey's May Day. rev. ed. Mariana, illus. LC 86-15252. 40p. (ps-3). 1987. 9.95 (*0-688-04545-6*) Lothrop.

Marton, Jirina. Amelia's Celebration. Marton, Jirina, illus. 24p. (ps-3). 1992. PLB 15.95 (*1-55037-221-1*, Pub. by Annick CN); pap. 5.95 (*1-55037-220-3*, Pub. by Annick CN) Firefly Bks Ltd.

Moutran, Julia S. Will Spring Ever Come to Gobbler's Knob? A Punxsutawney Phil Adventure Story. Sweetland, Marsha L., illus. 64p. (ps-5). 1992. Incl. Phil's Field Guide to Woodland Animals. 15.95 (*0-9617819-5-5*); Incl. Phil's Field Guide to Woodland Animals. pap. 9.95 (*0-9617819-4-7*); audiocass. 10.95 (*0-685-48131-X*) Lit Pubns.

Pulver, Robin. The Holiday Handwriting School. Karas, G. Brian, illus. LC 89-77085. 32p. (gr. k-3). 1991. RSBE 13.95 (*0-02-775455-3*, Four Winds) Macmillan Child Grp.

Riehecky, Janet. Cinco de Mayo. Stasiak, Krystyna, illus. LC 93-13249. 32p. (ps-2). 1993. PLB 12.30 (*0-516-00681-9*); pap. 3.95 (*0-516-40681-7*) Childrens.

Salop, Byrd. The Kiddush Cup Who Hated Wine. Goldstein, Lil, illus. 32p. (gr. 1 up). 1981. pap. 5.95 (*0-8246-0265-X*) Jonathan David.

Schertle, Alice. Jeremy Bean's St. Patrick's Day. Shute, Linda, illus. LC 86-7403. 32p. (ps-2). 1987. 12.95 (*0-688-04813-7*); PLB 12.88 (*0-688-04814-5*) Lothrop.

Sidi, Smadar S. The Dreidle Champ & Other Holiday Stories. Evers, June V., illus. 120p. (gr. 3-9). 1987. 13.95 (*0-915361-89-2*) Modan-Adama Bks.

Tran, Kim-Lan. Tet: The New Year. Vo-Dinh, Mai, illus. 32p. (gr. 2-5). 1993. pap. 4.95 (*0-671-79843-X*, S&S BYR) S&S Trade.

Treasure Trunk. LC 90-10090. 1991. pap. 14.95 (*0-671-69203-8*, S&S BFYR) S&S Trade.

Tudor, Tasha. A Tasha Tudor's Sampler: A Tale for Easter, Pumpkin Moonshine, The Dolls' Christmas. Tudor, Tasha, illus. (gr. k-3). 1977. 9.95 (*0-679-20412-1*) McKay.

Wood, Audrey. The Horrible Holidays. Hoffman, Rosekrans, illus. LC 87-30617. 48p. (ps-3). 1988. 9.95 (*0-8037-0544-1*); PLB 9.89 (*0-8037-0546-8*) Dial Bks Young.

—Horrible Holidays. LC 87-30617. 48p. (ps-3). 1990. pap. 3.95 (*0-8037-0833-5*) Dial Bks Young.

Zalben, Jane B. Goldie's Purim. LC 90-43153. (Illus.). 32p. (ps-2). 1991. 13.95 (*0-8050-1227-3*, Bks Young Read) H Holt & Co.

HOLIDAYS–POETRY

Parkison, Ralph F. Days. Withrow, Marion O., ed. Bush, William, illus. 60p. (Orig.). (gr. 2-8). 1988. pap. write for info. Little Wood Bks.

HOLLYWOOD, CALIFORNIA

Killingray, David & Yapp, Malcolm. Hollywood. (Illus.). 32p. (gr. 6-11). 1980. pap. text ed. 3.45 (*0-89908-213-0*) Greenhaven.

HOLLYWOOD, CALIFORNIA–FICTION

Kalman, Maira. Max in Hollywood, Baby. Kalman, Maira, illus. 32p. 1992. 15.00 (*0-670-84479-9*) Viking Child Bks.

Weaver, Lydia. Child Star: When Talkies Came to Hollywood. Laporte, Michele, illus. 64p. (gr. 2-6). 1992. PLB 12.00 (*0-670-84039-4*) Viking Child Bks.

HOLOCAUST, JEWISH

Abells, Chana B. The Children We Remember. LC 85-24876. (Illus.). 48p. (ps up). 1986. 13.00 (*0-688-06371-3*); PLB 12.93 (*0-688-06372-1*) Greenwillow.

Adler, David A. Hilde & Eli, Children of the Holocaust. Ritz, Karen, illus. LC 93-38229. 32p. (gr. 3-7). 1994. reinforced bdg. 15.95 (*0-8234-1091-9*) Holiday.

—A Picture Book of Anne Frank. Ritz, Karen, illus. 32p. 1994. pap. 5.95 (*0-8234-1078-1*) Holiday.

Atkinson, Linda. In Kindling Flame: The Story of Hannah Senesh 1921-1944. LC 83-24392. 224p. (gr. 9 up). 1985. 15.00 (*0-688-02714-8*) Lothrop.

Auerbacher, Inge. I Am a Star: Child of the Holocaust. Bernbaum, Israel, illus. LC 92-31444. 80p. (gr. 3-7). 1993. pap. 4.99 (*0-14-036401-3*) Puffin Bks.

Ayer, Eleanor H. The Holocaust Museum: America Keeps the Memory Alive. LC 94-4585. 1994. text ed. 14.95 (*0-87518-649-1*, Dillon) Macmillan Child Grp.

Backrach, Susan D. Tell Them We Remember: The Story of the Holocaust with Images from the United States Holocaust Memorial Museum. LC 93-40090. (gr. 5 up). 1994. 19.95 (*0-316-69264-6*); pap. 10.95 (*0-316-07484-5*) Little.

Brown, Gene. Anne Frank: Child of the Holocaust. (Illus.). 64p. (gr. 3-7). 1993. pap. 7.95 (*1-56711-049-5*) Blackbirch.

Buchignani, Walter. Tell No One Who You Are: The Secret Childhood of Regine Miller. LC 92-80412. 160p. (gr. 5-8). 1994. 17.95 (*0-88776-286-7*); pap. 9.95 (*0-88776-303-0*) Tundra Bks.

Fersen-Osten, Renee. Don't They Know the World Stopped Breathing? Reminiscences of a Child During the Holocaust Years. 280p. (gr. 5-8). 1990. 16.95 (*1-56171-019-9*) Shapolsky Pubs.

Finkelstein, Norman H. Remember Not to Forget: A Memory of the Holocaust. Hokanson, Lois & Hokanson, Lars, illus. LC 92-24603. 32p. (gr. 2 up). 1993. pap. 4.95 (*0-688-11802-X*, Mulberry) Morrow.

Frank, Anne. Anne Frank: The Diary of a Young Girl. (gr. 4-7). 1988. lib. bdg. 15.95 (*1-55736-098-7*, Crnrstn Bks) BDD LT Grp.

—Diary of a Young Girl. large type ed. 1989. Repr. of 1947 ed. 15.95 (*0-685-47378-3*, Crnrstn Bks) BDD LT Grp.

Friedman, Ina R. The Other Victims: First-Person Stories of Non-Jews Persecuted by the Nazis. 224p. (gr. 5-9). 1990. 14.45 (*0-395-50212-8*) HM.

Galdone, Paul. Nightmare in History: The Holocaust 1933-1945. (ps). 1992. pap. 5.70 (*0-395-61579-8*, Clarion Bks) HM.

Greenfeld, Howard. The Hidden Children. LC 93-20326. 128p. (gr. 3 up). 1993. 15.95 (*0-395-66074-2*) Ticknor & Flds Bks Yng Read.

Handler, Andrew & Meschel, Susan V. Young People Speak: Surviving the Holocaust in Hungary. (Illus.). 160p. (gr. 9-12). 1993. PLB 13.90 (*0-531-11044-3*) Watts.

Hurwitz, Johanna. Anne Frank: Life in Hiding. Rosenberry, Vera, illus. LC 92-29826. 64p. (gr. 4 up). 1993. pap. 3.95 (*0-688-12405-4*, Pub. by Beech Tree Bks) Morrow.

Isaacman, Clara & Grossman, Joan A. Clara's Story. LC 84-14339. 180p. (gr. 3-7). 1984. 11.95 (*0-8276-0243-X*); pap. 9.95 (*0-8276-0506-4*) JPS Phila.

Landau, Elaine. We Survived the Holocaust. LC 91-16982. (Illus.). 144p. (gr. 9-12). 1991. 14.45 (*0-531-15229-4*); PLB 14.40 (*0-531-11115-6*) Watts.

Larsen, Anita. Raoul Wallenberg: Missing Diplomat. LC 91-19937. (Illus.). 48p. (gr. 5-6). 1992. text ed. 11.95 RSBE (*0-89686-616-5*, Crestwood Hse) Macmillan Child Grp.

Lazo, Caroline. Elie Wiesel. LC 93-44473. 1994. text ed. 13.95 (*0-87518-636-X*, Dillon) Macmillan Child Grp.

Leitner, Isabella & Leitner, Irving. The Big Lie: A True Story. 1992. 13.95 (*0-590-45569-9*, 025, Scholastic Hardcover) Scholastic Inc.

Meltzer, Milton. Never to Forget: The Jews of the Holocaust. LC 75-25409. (gr. 7 up). 1976. PLB 15.89 (*0-06-024175-6*) HarpC Child Bks.

—Never to Forget: The Jews of the Holocaust. LC 75-25409. (Illus.). 240p. (gr. 7 up). 1991. pap. 6.95 (*0-06-446118-1*, Trophy) HarpC Child Bks.

—Rescue: The Story of How Gentiles Saved Jews in the Holocaust. LC 87-47816. (Illus.). 224p. (gr. 7 up). 1988. 16.00 (*0-06-024209-4*); PLB 15.89 (*0-06-024210-8*) HarpC Child Bks.

—Rescue: The Story of How Gentiles Saved Jews in the Holocaust. LC 87-47816. (Illus.). 176p. (gr. 7 up). 1991. pap. 6.95 (*0-06-446117-3*, Trophy) HarpC Child Bks.

Neimark, Anne E. One Man's Valor: Leo Baeck & the Holocaust. LC 85-27366. (Illus.). 128p. (gr. 5-9). 1986. 14.95 (*0-525-67175-7*, Lodestar Bks) Dutton Child Bks.

Pariser, Michael. Elie Wiesel: Bearing Witness. LC 93-37126. (Illus.). 48p. (gr. 2-4). 1994. 12.90 (*1-56294-419-3*); pap. 6.95 (*1-56294-743-5*) Millbrook Pr.

Pettit, Jayne. Place to Hide: True Stories of Holocaust Rescues. (gr. 4-7). 1993. pap. 2.95 (*0-590-45353-X*) Scholastic Inc.

Raoul Wallenberg. LC 91-19712. (Illus.). 68p. (gr. 3-8). PLB 19.93 (*0-8368-0629-8*) Gareth Stevens Inc.

Resnick, Abraham. The Holocaust. LC 91-441. (Illus.). 112p. (gr. 5-8). 1991. PLB 14.95 (*1-56006-124-3*) Lucent Bks.

Rogasky, Barbara. Smoke & Ashes: The Story of the Holocaust. LC 87-28617. (Illus.). 192p. (gr. 5 up). 1988. 18.95 (*0-8234-0697-0*); pap. 9.95 (*0-8234-0878-7*) Holiday.

Rosenberg, Maxine B. Hiding to Survive: Fourteen Jewish Children & the Gentiles Who Rescued Them from the Holocaust. LC 93-28328. 1994. write for info. (*0-395-65014-3*, Clarion Bks) HM.

Rossel, Seymour. The Holocaust: The World & the Jews, 1933-1945. Altshuler, David, ed. 192p. (gr. 9-12). 1992. pap. text ed. write for info. (*0-87441-526-8*) Behrman.

Rossell, Seymour. The Holocaust: The Fire That Raged. LC 88-26718. (Illus.). 128p. (gr. 7-12). 1990. 13.40 (*0-531-10674-8*) Watts.

Roth-Hano, Renee. Touch Wood: A Girlhood Occupied In France. 304p. (gr. 5 up). 1989. pap. 4.99 (*0-14-034085-8*, Puffin) Puffin Bks.

Sender, Ruth M. The Cage. LC 86-8562. 252p. (gr. 7 up). 1986. SBE 16.95 (*0-02-781830-6*, Macmillan Child Bk) Macmillan Child Grp.

—The Holocaust Lady. LC 92-13268. 192p. (gr. 7 up). 1992. SBE 14.95 (*0-02-781832-2*, Macmillan Child Bk) Macmillan Child Grp.

—To Life. 240p. (gr. 6 up). 1990. pap. 4.95 (*0-14-034367-9*, Puffin) Puffin Bks.

Siegal, Aranka. Upon the Head of the Goat: A Childhood in Hungary, 1939-1944. 224p. (gr. 7 up). 1994. pap. 4.50 (*0-14-036966-X*) Puffin Bks.

Stadtler, Bea. The Holocaust: A History of Courage & Resistance. Bial, Morrison D., ed. Martin, David S., illus. Bauer, Yehuda, intro. by. LC 74-11469. (Illus.). 210p. (gr. 5-7). 1975. pap. text ed. 5.95x (*0-87441-231-5*); Discussion Guide: By Nancy Karkowsky. pap. text ed. 6.95 (*0-87441-257-9*) Behrman.

Tames, Richard. Anne Frank. LC 89-14609. (Illus.). 32p. (gr. 7-9). 1990. 12.40 (*0-531-10763-9*) Watts.

Tyler, Laura & Renna, Giani. Anne Frank. (Illus.). 104p. (gr. 5-8). 1990. lib. bdg. 9.95 (*0-382-09975-3*); pap. 5.95 (*0-382-24002-2*) Silver Burdett Pr.

Verhoeven, Rian & Van Der Rol, Ruud. Anne Frank: Beyond the Diary. (Illus.). 112p. (gr. 5 up). 1993. 17.00 (*0-670-84932-4*) Viking Child Bks.

Walshaw, Rachela & Walshaw, Sam. From Out of the Firestorm: A Memoir of the Holocaust. 260p. (gr. 5-8). 1990. pap. 10.95 (*1-56171-021-0*) Shapolsky Pubs.

HOLOCAUST, JEWISH–FICTION

Baylis-White, Mary. Sheltering Rebecca. 112p. (gr. 5-9). 1993. pap. 3.99 (*0-14-036448-X*, Puffin) Puffin Bks.

Cormier, Robert. Tunes for Bears to Dance To. LC 92-2734. 112p. (gr. 5 up). 1992. 15.00 (*0-385-30818-3*) Delacorte.

Drucker, Malka & Halperin, Michael. Jacob's Rescue: A Holocaust Story. LC 92-30523. 128p. (gr. 4-7). 1993. 15.95 (*0-553-08976-5*, Skylark) Bantam.

Malka, Drucker. Jacob's Rescue: A Holocaust Story. (gr. 4-7). 1994. pap. 3.99 (*0-440-40965-9*) Dell.

Matas, Carol. Daniel's Story. LC 92-27537. 144p. (gr. 4-9). 1993. 13.95 (*0-590-46920-7*) Scholastic Inc.

Nolan, Han. If I Should Die Before I Wake. LC 93-30720. 1994. 16.95 (*0-15-238040-X*, HB Juv Bks); pap. write for info. (*0-15-238041-8*, HB Juv Bks) HarBrace.

Schleimer, Sarah. Far from the Place We Called Home. LC 93-48519. 1994. 15.95 (*0-87306-667-7*) Feldheim.

Schnur, Steven. The Shadow Children. LC 94-5098. 1994. write for info. (*0-688-13281-2*); PLB write for info. (*0-688-13831-4*) Morrow Jr Bks.

Treseder, Terry W. Hear O Israel: A Story of the Warsaw Ghetto. Bloom, Lloyd, illus. LC 89-7029. 48p. (gr. 3 up). 1990. SBE 13.95 (*0-689-31456-6*, Atheneum Child Bk) Macmillan Child Grp.

Voigt, Cynthia. David & Jonathan. 208p. 1992. 14.95 (*0-590-45165-0*, Scholastic Hardcover) Scholastic Inc.

Vos, Ida. Anna Is Still Here. Edelstein, Terese & Smidt, Inez, trs. from DUT. LC 92-1618. 144p. (gr. 3-7). 1993. 13.45 (*0-395-65368-1*) HM.

HOLOGRAPHY

Graham, Ian. Lasers & Holograms. LC 91-10827. (Illus.). 32p. (gr. 5-8). 1991. PLB 12.40 (*0-531-17264-3*, Gloucester Pr) Watts.

Joval, Nomi. Room of Mirrors. Kubinyi, Laszlo, illus. 16p. (gr. k-4). 1991. PLB 13.95 (*1-879567-06-7*, Valeria Bks) Wonder Well.

HOLY GRAIL

see Grail

HOLY SCRIPTURES

see Bible

HOLY SEE

see Catholic Church; Popes

HOME

see also Home Economics; Marriage

Ask about the Home. 64p. (gr. 4-5). 1987. PLB 11.95 (*0-8172-2882-9*) Raintree Steck-V.

Klingel, Fitterer. Home Safety. (Illus.). 32p. (ps up). 1986. PLB 12.95 (*0-88682-081-2*) Creative Ed.

Rosen, Michael J., ed. Home: A Collaboration of Thirty Authors & Illustrators of Children's Books to Aid the Homeless. Williams, Vera, illus. LC 91-29125. 32p. (ps-3). 1992. 16.00 (*0-06-021788-X*); PLB 15.89 (*0-06-021789-8*) HarpC Child Bks.

Talkabout the Home. (ARA., Illus.). (gr. 1-3). 1987. 3.50x (*0-86685-233-6*) Intl Bk Ctr.

HOME–FICTION

Ackerman, Karen. I Know a Place. Ray, Deborah K., illus. 32p. (ps-3). 1992. 13.45 (*0-395-53932-3*) HM.

Asch, Frank. Goodbye House. Asch, Frank, illus. LC 85-19263. (ps-2). 1989. pap. 12.95 jacketed (*0-671-67054-9*, Little Simon); pap. 4.95 (*0-671-67927-9*, Little Simon) S&S Trade.

Atkinson, Kathie. Home & Safe. (ps-3). 1993. pap. 3.95 (*1-86373-373-6*, Pub. by Allen & Unwin Aust Pty AT) IPG Chicago.

Aubin, Michael. A Day at Home. (Illus.). 32p. (gr. 3-5). 1991. 12.95 (*0-89565-762-7*) Childs World.

Bellairs, John. The House with a Clock in Its Walls. 192p. (gr. 3 up). 1974. pap. 3.50 (*0-440-43742-3*, YB) Dell.

Betancourt, Jeanne. Home Sweet Home. (gr. 7 up). 1989. pap. 2.95 (*0-553-27857-6*, Starfire) Bantam.

—Home Sweet Home. 1988. 13.95 (*0-553-05469-4*) Bantam.

Boland, Janice. Annabel Again. Halsey, Megan, photos by. LC 94-189. (gr. 2 up). 1995. write for info. (*0-8037-1756-3*); pap. write for info. (*0-8037-1757-1*) Dial Bks Young.

Cole, Joanna. The Clown-Arounds Have a Party. Smath, Jerry, illus. LC 82-2128. 48p. (ps-3). 1982. 5.95 (*0-8193-1085-9*); PLB 5.95 (*0-8193-1086-7*) Parents.

—This Is the Place for Me. Van Horn, William, illus. 32p. (Orig.). (gr. k-3). 1986. pap. 2.50 (*0-590-33996-6*) Scholastic Inc.

Craig, Janet A. The Boo-Hoo Witch. Schories, Patricia L., illus. LC 93-2216. 32p. (gr. k-2). 1993. PLB 11.59 (*0-8167-3186-1*); pap. text ed. 2.95 (*0-8167-3187-X*) Troll Assocs.

Farmer, Nancy. The Warm Place. LC 94-21984. 1995. write for info. (*0-531-06888-9*) Orchard Bks Watts.

Ferris, Jean. Looking for Home. 1993. pap. 3.95 (*0-374-44566-4*) FS&G.

Fritz, Jean. Homesick: My Own Story. (gr. k-6). 1984. pap. 4.50 (*0-440-43683-4*, YB) Dell.

Hague, Kathleen. The Man Who Kept House. Hague, Michael, illus. LC 80-26258. 32p. (ps-3). 1988. pap. 4.95 (*0-15-251699-9*, Voyager Bks) HarBrace.

Hannah, Valerie. Little Jollys Find a Home. Herrick, George H., ed. Kokino, Olga, illus. 36p. (Orig.). (gr. k-3). 1991. pap. 5.95 (*0-941281-79-5*) V H Pub.

Lindbergh, Anne M. Tidy Lady. Hoguet, Susan R., illus. LC 88-10905. 30p. (gr. k-3). 1989. 13.95 (*0-15-287150-0*) HarBrace.

Ormerod, Jan. Sunshine. LC 80-84971. (Illus.). (ps up). 1990. pap. 3.95 (*0-688-09353-1*, Mulberry) Morrow.

Parker, Ann N. Home Is Where the Shade Tree Is. Vickery, Diane, illus. 18p. (gr. k-4). 1988. pap. 3.95 (*0-943487-13-7*) Sevgo Pr.

Reid, Margarette S. The Button Box. LC 89-38566. (Illus.). 24p. (ps-2). 1990. 13.99 (*0-525-44590-0*, DCB) Dutton Child Bks.

Rockwell, Anne. Our Garage Sale. Rockwell, Harlow, illus. LC 80-16704. 24p. (ps-1). 1984. 10.25 (*0-688-80278-8*); PLB 10.88 (*0-688-84278-X*) Greenwillow.

Rotenberg, Abie. The Place Where I Belong. Stern, Fruma, illus. (ps-1). 1988. 9.95 (*0-935063-43-9*) CIS Comm.

Smithson, Colin. Home Sweet Home. (Illus.). 32p. (ps-1). 1994. 15.95 (*1-85681-211-1*, Pub. by Bodley Head UK) Trafalgar.

HOME AND SCHOOL

Elovson, Allana. The Kindergarten Survival Handbook: The Before School Checklist & a Guide for Parents. rev. ed. Elovson, Andrea K., illus. 96p. (Orig.). (gr. k). 1993. Spanish ed. pap. text ed. 12.95 perfect bdg. (*1-879888-07-6*); English ed. pap. text ed. 12.95 (*1-879888-06-8*) Parent Ed.

Heacox, Diane. Up from Underachievement: How Teachers, Students, & Parents Can Work Together to Promote Student Success. Espeland, Pamela, ed. LC 91-19069. 144p. (Orig.). 1991. pap. 14.95 (*0-915793-35-0*) Free Spirit Pub.

HOME DECORATION

see Interior Decoration

HOME ECONOMICS

see also Consumer Education; Cookery; Dairying; Entertaining; Food; Fuel; Furniture; House Cleaning; Interior Decoration; Sewing; Shopping

Allen, Eleanor. Home Sweet Home: A History of Housework. (Illus.). 64p. (gr. 6 up). 1979. 14.95 (*0-7136-1927-9*) Dufour.

Alvarez Del Real, Maria E., ed. Como Reparar 500 Problemas De la Casa. (SPA., Illus.). 352p. (Orig.). 1988. pap. 4.50x (*0-944499-33-3*) Editorial Amer.

Chamberlain, Valerie M. & Buddinger, Peyton B. Teen Guide. 6th ed. O'Neill, Martha, ed. Evelyne Johnson Associates Staff, illus. 528p. 1985. text ed. 30.00 (*0-07-007842-4*); pap. text ed. 11.68 (*0-07-007831-9*) McGraw.

Endersby, Frank. Wash Day. (gr. 4 up). 1981. 3.95 (*0-85953-273-9*) Childs Play.

Van Tuyle, R. Helen. Timely Tips & Treats for the Tenderfoot Homemaker. Engle, Arch, illus. 108p. (Orig.). 1987. wkbk. 9.95 (*0-9617816-0-2*) R H Van Tuyle.

HOME ECONOMICS–EQUIPMENT AND SUPPLIES

see also Household Equipment and Supplies

HOME EDUCATION

see Self-Culture

HOME MISSIONS

see Missions

HOME REPAIRING

see Houses–Repairing

HOME STUDY COURSES

see Self-Culture

HOMER–ADAPTATIONS

Grant, Neil. The World of Odysseus. (Illus.). 48p. (gr. 7-9). 1992. 13.95 (*0-563-34414-8*, BBC-Parkwest); pap. 6.95 (*0-563-34415-6*, BBC-Parkwest) Parkwest Pubns.

Homer. Odyssey. (gr. 9 up). 1965. pap. 2.95 (*0-8049-0057-4*, CL-57) Airmont.

HOMER, WINSLOW, 1836-1910

Beneduce, Ann K. A Weekend with Winslow Homer. LC 93-12189. (Illus.). 64p. 1993. 19.95 (*0-8478-1622-2*) Rizzoli Intl.

HOMES

see Houses

HOMOSEXUALITY

Alyson, Sasha, ed. Young, Gay & Proud! rev. ed. (Illus.). 120p. (Orig.). (gr. 7-12). 1991. pap. 3.95 (*1-55583-001-3*) Alyson Pubns.

Cohen, Susan & Cohen, Daniel. When Someone You Know Is Gay. 196p. (gr. 7 up). 1992. pap. 3.99 (*0-440-21298-7*, LFL) Dell.

Dudley, William, ed. Homosexuality: Opposing Viewpoints. LC 92-40705. (Illus.). 264p. (gr. 10 up). 1993. PLB 17.95 (*0-89908-481-8*); pap. text ed. 9.95 (*0-89908-456-7*) Greenhaven.

Escoffier, Jeffrey. John Maynard Keynes. Duberman, Martin, intro. by. LC 94-1133. 1994. write for info. (*0-7910-2860-7*); pap. write for info. (*0-7910-2879-8*) Chelsea Hse.

Landau, Elaine. Different Drummer: Homosexuality in America. (gr. 7 up). 1986. lib. bdg. write for info. (*0-671-54997-9*, J Messner) S&S Trade.

McCauslin, Mark. Lesbian & Gay Rights. LC 91-40863. (Illus.). 48p. (gr. 5-6). 1992. text ed. 12.95 RSBE (*0-89686-751-X*, Crestwood Hse) Macmillan Child Grp.

Miller, Deborah. Coping When a Parent Is Gay. Rosen, Ruth, ed. (gr. 7-12). 1993. 14.95 (*0-8239-1404-6*) Rosen Group.

Snyder, Jane M. Sappho: Lives of Notable Gay Men & Lesbians. Duberman, Martin. LC 94-1134. 1994. write for info. (*0-7910-2308-7*) Chelsea Hse.

Sutton, Roger. Hearing Us Out: Voices from the Gay & Lesbian Community. Ebright, Lisa, photos by. LC 94-20206. (Illus.). (gr. 6-12). 1994. 16.95 (*0-316-82326-0*) Little.

HOMOSEXUALITY–FICTION

Bauer, Marion D. Am I Blue? Coming Out from the Silence. LC 93-29574. 224p. (gr. 9 up). 1994. 15.00 (*0-06-024253-1*); PLB 14.89 (*0-06-024254-X*) HarpC Child Bks.

Childress, Alice. Those Other People. 144p. (gr. 8 up). 1989. 14.95 (*0-399-21510-7*, Putnam) Putnam Pub Group.

Cohen, Richard A. Alfie's Home. Sherman, Elizabeth, illus. LC 93-78368. 30p. (gr. 3-12). 1993. 14.95 (*0-9637058-0-6*) Intl Healing.

Dhondy, Farrukh. Black Swan. LC 92-30425. 208p. (gr. 6 up). 1993. 14.95 (*0-395-66076-9*) HM.

Greene, Bette. Drowning of Stephan Jones. 1991. 16.00 (*0-553-07437-7*) Bantam.

Heron, Ann & Maran, Meredith. How Would You Feel If Your Dad Was Gay? Martins, George, illus. 32p. (gr. 1-5). 1991. text ed. 9.95 (*1-55583-188-5*) Alyson Pubns.

—How Would You Feel If Your Dad Was Gay? Kovick, Kris, illus. 48p. (gr. 1-5). 1994. pap. 6.95 (*1-55583-243-1*) Alyson Pubns.

Holland, Isabelle. The Man Without a Face. Reissue. ed. LC 71-37736. 144p. (gr. 7 up). 1988. Repr. of 1972 ed. (Lipp Jr Bks); PLB 12.89 (*0-397-32264-X*, Lipp Jr Bks) HarpC Child Bks.

Johnson-Calvo, Sarita. A Beach Party with Alexis. (Illus.). 32p. (Orig.). (gr. k-3). 1993. saddle-stitched wkbk. 2.95 (*1-55583-230-X*) Alyson Pubns.

McClain, Ellen J. No Big Deal. 160p. 1994. 14.99 (*0-525-67483-7*, Lodestar Bks) Dutton Child Bks.

Mosca, Frank. All American Boys. 116p. (Orig.). (gr. 7-12). 1983. pap. 5.95 (*0-932870-44-9*) Alyson Pubns.

Murrow, Liza K. Twelve Days in August: A Novel. LC 92-54489. 160p. (gr. 7 up). 1993. 14.95 (*0-8234-1012-9*) Holiday.

Newman, Leslea. Gloria Goes to Gay Pride. Crocker, Russell, illus. 48p. (Orig.). (ps-2). 1991. pap. 7.95 (*1-55583-185-0*) Alyson Pubns.

Salat, Cristina. Living in Secret. LC 92-20889. 1993. 15. 00 (*0-553-08670-7*, Skylark) Bantam.

Valentine, Johnny. Two Moms, the Zark, & Me. Lopez, Angelo, illus. 48p. (gr. k-3). 1993. 12.95 (*1-55583-236-9*) Alyson Pubns.

Walker, Kate. Peter. LC 92-18948. 176p. (gr. 7 up). 1993. 13.95 (*0-395-64722-3*) HM.

Willhoite, Michael. Daddy's Roommate. Willhoite, Michael, illus. 32p. (ps). 1990. 14.95 (*1-55583-178-8*) Alyson Pubns.

HONDURAS

Lerner Publications, Department of Geography Staff. Honduras in Pictures. (Illus.). 64p. (gr. 5 up). 1987. PLB 17.50 (*0-8225-1804-X*) Lerner Pubns.

HONEY

see also Bees

Hogan, Paula Z. The Honeybee. LC 78-21165. (Illus.). 32p. (gr. 1-4). 1984. PLB 29.28 incl. cassette (*0-8172-2229-4*) Raintree Steck-V.

Micucci, Charles, text by. & illus. Life & Times of the Honey Bee. LC 93-8135. 32p. (ps-3). 1995. 13.95g (*0-395-65968-X*) Ticknor & Flds Bks Yng Read.

Scarffe, Bronwen. Busy Bees. Costeloe, Brenda, illus. LC 92-31958. 1993. 3.75 (*0-383-03558-9*) SRA Schl Grp.

HONG KONG

Fyson, Nance L. Hong Kong. LC 89-26247. (Illus.). 96p. (gr. 6-12). 1990. PLB 22.80 (*0-8114-2433-2*) Raintree Steck-V.

McKenna, Nancy D. A Family in Hong Kong. (Illus.). 32p. (gr. 2-5). 1987. 13.50 (*0-8225-1676-4*) Lerner Pubns.

Murphy, Wendy & Murphy, Jack. Hong Kong. (Illus.). 64p. (gr. 3-7). PLB 14.95 (*1-56711-021-5*) Blackbirch.

Stein, R. Conrad. Hong Kong. LC 84-23199. (Illus.). 128p. (gr. 5-9). 1985. PLB 20.55 (*0-516-02765-4*) Childrens.

Wright, David K. Hong Kong. LC 90-9669. (Illus.). 64p. (gr. 5-6). 1991. PLB 21.26 (*0-8368-0382-5*) Gareth Stevens Inc.

HONG KONG–FICTION

McOmber, Rachel B., ed. McOmber Phonics Storybooks: A Package from Hong Kong. rev. ed. (Illus.). write for info. (*0-944991-61-0*) Swift Lrn Res.

HOOVER, JOHN EDGAR, 1895-1972

Deneberg, Barry. The True Story of J. Edgar Hoover & The F.B.I. LC 91-8021. 208p. (gr. 5 up). 1993. 13.95 (*0-590-43168-4*) Scholastic Inc.

HOOVER, HERBERT CLARK, PRESIDENT U. S. 1874-1964

Clinton, Susan. Herbert Hoover. LC 87-35711. (Illus.). 100p. (gr. 3 up). 1988. PLB 14.40 (*0-516-01355-6*); pap. 6.95 (*0-516-41355-4*) Childrens.

Hilton, Suzanne. The World of Young Herbert Hoover. Steins, Deborah, illus. (gr. 5-8). 1987. 12.95 (*0-8027-6708-7*); PLB 13.85 (*0-8027-6709-5*) Walker & Co.

Polikof, Barbara G. Herbert C. Hoover: Thirty-First President of the United States. Young, Richard G., ed. LC 89-39946. (Illus.). 128p. (gr. 5-9). 1990. PLB 17.26 (*0-944483-58-5*) Garrett Ed Corp.

HORMONES

Villee, Claude A., Jr. Human Hormones. Head, J. J., ed. Johnson, Patricia & Steffen, Ann T., illus. LC 86-72197. 16p. (Orig.). (gr. 10 up). 1987. pap. text ed. 2.75 (*0-89278-371-0*, 45-9771) Carolina Biological.

Young, John K. Hormones: Molecular Messengers. LC 92-40503. 1994. 13.40 (*0-531-12545-9*) Watts.

HORN (MUSICAL INSTRUMENT)

Johnson, Mark. The Complete Bugler: Practice & Performance Aid for the Young Bugler. Johnson, Mark, illus. 24p. (Orig.). (gr. 4-12). 1993. pap. 2.95 (*1-883988-10-1*); pap. 8.95 incl. cassette (*1-883988-04-7*) RSV Prods.

Leanza, Frank. How to Get Started with the Baritone Horn. (Illus.). 32p. 1993. pap. 3.95 (*0-934687-15-3*) Crystal Pubs.

—How to Get Started with the French Horn. (Illus.). 36p. 1993. pap. 3.95 (*0-934687-14-5*) Crystal Pubs.

HOROLOGY

see Clocks and Watches; Sundials

HOROSCOPE

see Astrology

HORROR STORIES

Aiken, Joan. A Fit of Shivers: Tales for Late at Night. LC 92-6130. 144p. (gr. 6 up). 1992. 15.00 (*0-385-30691-1*) Delacorte.

—Give Yourself a Fright. (gr. 7 up). 1989. 14.95 (*0-440-50120-2*) Delacorte.

—A Touch of Chill. LC 79-3331. 124p. (gr. 7 up). 1980. 9.95 (*0-385-29310-0*) Delacorte.

Albright, Molly. Fright Night. Connor, Eulala, illus. LC 88-12388. 96p. (gr. 3-6). 1989. PLB 9.89 (*0-8167-1486-X*); pap. text ed. 2.95 (*0-8167-1487-8*) Troll Assocs.

—Meet Miss Dracula. DeRosa, Dee, illus. LC 87-13871. 96p. (gr. 3-6). 1988. PLB 9.89 (*0-8167-1157-7*); pap. text ed. 2.95 (*0-8167-1158-5*) Troll Assocs.

Alexander, Sue. More Witch, Goblin & Ghost Stories. Winter, Jeanette, illus. LC 78-3280. (gr. 1-4). 1978. 6.95 (*0-394-83933-1*) Pantheon.

—Witch, Goblin, & Ghost Are Back. Winter, Jeanette, illus. LC 83-22157. 62p. (gr. 1-4). 1985. 6.95 (*0-394-86296-1*, Pant Bks Young); lib. bdg. 9.99 (*0-394-96296-6*) Pantheon.

Allen, Derek, retold by. Blood from the Mummy's Tomb. 160p. (gr. 6 up). 1988. pap. 2.95 (*0-8120-4074-0*) Barron.

Athkins, D. E. The Ripper. 1992. 3.25 (*0-590-45349-1*, Point) Scholastic Inc.

Barker, Clive & Niles, Steve. London, Vol. 1: Bloodline. Skulan, Tom, ed. Kastro, Carlos, illus. 48p. (Orig.). 1993. pap. 5.95 (*0-938782-25-8*) Fantaco.

—London, Vol. 2: End of the Line. Skulan, Tom, ed. Kastro, Carlos, illus. 48p. 1993. pap. 5.95 (*0-938782-26-6*) Fantaco.

Beach, Lynn. The Dark. MacDonald, Patricia, ed. 128p. (Orig.). 1991. pap. 2.99 (*0-671-74089-X*, Minstrel Bks) PB.

—Dead Man's Secret. MacDonald, Pat, ed. 128p. (Orig.). 1992. pap. 2.99 (*0-671-75924-8*, Minstrel Bks) PB.

—The Evil One. 128p. (Orig.). 1991. pap. 2.99 (*0-671-74088-1*, Minstrel Bks) PB.

—Phantom Valley: In the Mummy's Tomb. MacDonald, Pat, ed. 128p. (Orig.). 1992. pap. 2.99 (*0-671-75925-6*, Minstrel Bks) PB.

—Phantom Valley: The Headless Ghost. McDonald, Patricia, ed. 128p. (Orig.). (gr. 3-6). 1992. pap. 2.99 (*0-671-75926-4*, Minstrel Bks) PB.

—Scream of the Cat. MacDonald, Patricia, ed. 128p. (Orig.). 1992. pap. 2.99 (*0-671-74090-3*, Minstrel Bks) PB.

—The Spell. MacDonald, Pat, ed. 128p. (Orig.). 1992. pap. 2.99 (*0-671-75923-X*, Minstrel Bks) PB.

Bedard, Michael. A Darker Magic. 192p. 1989. pap. 2.95 (*0-380-70611-3*, Flare) Avon.

—Redwork. 224p. 1992. pap. 3.50 (*0-380-71612-7*, Flare) Avon.

Beere, Peter. School for Terror: Going to School Can Be Murder. 1994. pap. 3.50 (*0-590-48319-6*) Scholastic Inc.

Bellairs, John. Chessman of Doom. (gr. 4-7). 1991. pap. 3.50 (*0-553-15884-8*) Bantam.

—The Chessmen of Doom. (gr. 4-8). 1992. 16.50 (*0-8446-6579-7*) Peter Smith.

—The Figure in the Shadows. 192p. (gr. 4-7). 1977. pap. 3.50 (*0-440-42551-4*, YB) Dell.

Bennett, Jay. The Haunted One. (gr. 7 up). 1989. pap. 3.99 (*0-449-70314-2*, Juniper) Fawcett.

Black, J. R. Guess Who's Dating a Werewolf? 120p. (Orig.). (gr. 3-7). 1993. pap. 3.50 (*0-679-85008-2*, Bullseye Bks) Random Bks Yng Read.

—The Undead Express. 132p. (Orig.). (gr. 3-7). 1994. pap. 3.50 (*0-679-85408-8*, Bullseye Bks) Random Bks Yng Read.

Bone-Chilling Tales of Fright: Stories to Make You Scream. 128p. 1994. pap. 4.95 (*1-56565-167-7*) Lowell Hse Juvenile.

Brennan, J. H. Kingdom of Horror. (gr. 6-12). 1987. pap. 2.50 (*0-440-94540-2*) Dell.

Brightfield, Richard. The Gruesome Guests. LC 89-36334. 96p. (gr. 7 up). 1990. PLB 9.89 (*0-8167-1690-0*); pap. text ed. 2.95 (*0-8167-1691-9*) Troll Assocs.

Brouwer, Sigmund. Terror on Kamikaze Run. 144p. (Orig.). 1994. pap. 4.99 (*1-56476-159-2*, Victor Books) SP Pubns.

Brown, Roberta S. Queen of the Cold-Blooded Tales. 176p. (gr. 7 up). 1993. 19.00 (*0-685-67270-0*) August Hse.

Brown, Ruth. Dark Dark Tale. enl. ed. (ps-3). 1991. pap. 17.95 (*0-8037-1074-7*, Puff Pied Piper) Puffin Bks.

Bunting, Eve. Night of the Gargoyles. Wiesner, David, illus. LC 93-8160. 1994. 14.95 (*0-395-66553-1*, Clarion Bks) HM.

Burt, Katherine. The Scariest Stories You've Ever Heard, Pt. II. 96p. (gr. 4-8). 1988. 2.99 (*0-87406-419-8*, 39-19157-7) Willowisp Pr.

Campton, David, retold by. Frankenstein. 160p. (gr. 6 up). 1988. pap. 2.95 (*0-8120-4076-7*) Barron.

—The Vampyre. 160p. (gr. 6 up). 1988. pap. 2.95 (*0-8120-4070-8*) Barron.

Carusone, Al. Don't Open the Door after the Sun Goes Down: Tales of the Real & Unreal. Glass, Andrew, illus. LC 94-7406. (gr. 4 up). 1994. 13.95 (*0-395-65225-1*, Clarion Bks) HM.

Chance, Suzanne. Dig Me Up. 176p. (Orig.). 1992. pap. 3.50 (*0-380-76917-4*, Flare) Avon.

Cheetham, Ann. The Pit. 192p. (gr. 3-7). 1993. pap. 3.95 (*0-06-440448-X*, Trophy) HarpC Child Bks.

Cohen, Daniel. Southern Fried Rat & Other Gruesome Tales. 128p. (gr. 5). 1989. pap. 3.50 (*0-380-70655-5*, Flare) Avon.

Cooney, Caroline B. The Return of the Vampire. 176p. 1992. pap. 2.95 (*0-590-44884-6*, Point) Scholastic Inc.

—The Snow. 176p. (Orig.). (gr. 7 up). 1990. pap. 3.25 (*0-590-41640-5*) Scholastic Inc.

—Vampires Promise. 1993. pap. 3.50 (*0-590-45682-2*) Scholastic Inc.

Crider, Bill. A Vampire Named Fred. Shaw, Charles, illus. Alter, Judy, intro. by. LC 89-14524. (Illus.). 176p. (Orig.). (gr. 4-9). 1990. pap. 5.95 (*0-936650-11-7*) E C Temple.

Crisfield, Deborah. The Amityville Horror. LC 91-4528. (Illus.). 48p. (gr. 5-6). 1991. text ed. 13.95 RSBE (*0-89686-576-2*, Crestwood Hse) Macmillan Child Grp.

Crose, Mark. Halloween. LC 90-45854. (Illus.). 48p. (gr. 5-6). 1991. text ed. 13.95 (*0-89686-577-0*, Crestwood Hse) Macmillan Child Grp.

Davidson, Nicole. Demon's Beach. 160p. (Orig.). (gr. 7-12). 1992. pap. 3.50 (*0-380-76644-2*, Flare) Avon.

—Fan Mail. 176p. (Orig.). 1993. pap. 3.50 (*0-380-76995-6*, Flare) Avon.

De Balzac, Honore. La Grande Bretche. 48p. (gr. 6). 1990. PLB 13.95s.p. (*0-88682-306-4*) Creative Ed.

Doyle, Debra. Bad Blood: The Moon Is Full Beware the Beast. 1993. pap. 3.99 (*0-425-13953-0*) Berkley Pub.

Efron, Marshall & Olsen, Alfa-Betty. Really Scared Stiff: Three Creepy Tales. Medley, Linda, illus. 48p. (gr. 2-4). 1992. pap. write for info. (*0-307-11469-4*, 11469, Golden Pr) Western Pub.

Elfman, Eric. Three-Minute Thrillers: The Oozing Eyeball & Other Hasty Horrors. Suckow, Will, illus. 96p. (gr. 4-7). 1994. pap. 4.95 (*1-56565-138-3*) Lowell Hse Juvenile.

Ellis, Carol. Camp Fear. 1993. pap. 3.25 (*0-590-46411-6*) Scholastic Inc.

Elzbieta. Mimi's Scary Theater: A Play in Nine Scenes for Seven Characters & an Egg. Elzbieta, illus. LC 92-54868. 18p. (ps-3). 1993. 14.95 (*1-56282-415-5*) Hyprn Child.

Famous Tales of Mystery & Horror. (gr. 4-7). 1993. pap. 2.95 (*0-89375-369-6*) Troll Assocs.

Famous Tales of Terror. (gr. 4-7). 1993. pap. 2.95 (*0-89375-404-8*) Troll Assocs.

Faulkner, Keith. Dracula. Lambert, Jonathan, illus. 16p. (ps-2). 1993. 10.95 (*0-694-00559-2*, Festival) HarpC Child Bks.

Flood, E. L. The Fly. LC 91-7376. (Illus.). 48p. (gr. 5-6). 1991. text ed. 13.95 RSBE (*0-89686-574-6*, Crestwood Hse) Macmillan Child Grp.

—A Nightmare on Elm Street. LC 90-47425. (Illus.). 48p. (gr. 5-6). 1991. text ed. 13.95 RSBE (*0-89686-579-7*, Crestwood Hse) Macmillan Child Grp.

Fremont, Eleanor. Tales from the Crypt: Introduced by the Crypt-Keeper, Vol. 4. LC 90-23916. (Illus.). 96p. (Orig.). (gr. 4-7). 1992. pap. 2.99 (*0-679-83073-1*) Random Bks Yng Read.

—Tales from the Crypt: Introduced by the Old Witch, Vol. 5. LC 90-23916. (Illus.). 96p. (Orig.). (gr. 4-7). 1992. pap. 2.99 (*0-679-83074-X*) Random Bks Yng Read.

Fremont, Eleanor, adapted by. Tales from the Crypt, Vol. 1: Introduced by the Crypt-Keeper. Davis, Jack, illus. LC 90-23916. 96p. (Orig.). (gr. 4-7). 1991. pap. 2.99 (*0-679-81799-9*) Random Bks Yng Read.

—Tales from the Crypt, Vol. 2: Introduced by the Old Witch. Davis, Jack, illus. LC 90-23916. 96p. (Orig.). (gr. 4-7). 1991. pap. 2.99 (*0-679-81800-6*) Random Bks Yng Read.

Garden, Nancy. My Brother, the Werewolf. LC 93-46795. 1994. PLB write for info. (*0-679-95414-7*, Bullseye Bks); pap. write for info. (*0-679-85414-2*) Random Bks Yng Read.

—Prisoner of Vampires. (gr. 2-6). 1986. pap. 2.95 (*0-440-47194-X*, YB) Dell.

—Prisoner of Vampires. (gr. 4-7). 1993. pap. 3.95 (*0-374-46018-3*) FS&G.

Garth, G. G. Nightmare Matinee. 1994. pap. 3.50 (*0-553-56566-4*) Bantam.

Gorman, Carol. Die for Me. 144p. (Orig.). (gr. 7-12). 1992. pap. 3.50 (*0-380-76686-8*, Flare) Avon.

Gorog, Judith. In a Messy, Messy Room: And Other Strange Stories. Root, Kim, illus. 48p. (gr. 4-7). 1990. 14.95 (*0-399-22218-9*, Philomel Bks) Putnam Pub Group.

—On Meeting Witches at Wells. (gr. 3 up). 1991. 14.95 (*0-399-21803-3*, Philomel) Putnam Pub Group.

—When Nobody's Home: Thirteen Tales for Tonight. LC 93-34595. 1994. 13.95 (*0-590-46862-6*) Scholastic Inc.

Grant, Charles L. Fire Mask. (gr. 7 up). 1991. 14.95 (*0-553-07167-X*, Starfire) Bantam.

Great Tales of Terror. (gr. 4-7). 1993. pap. 2.95 (*0-89375-397-1*) Troll Assocs.

Griffiths, Barbara. Frankenstein's Hamster: Ten Spine-Tingling Tales. (gr. 4-7). 1992. 15.00 (*0-8037-0952-8*) Dial Bks Young.

Hahn, Mary D. Look for Me by Moonlight. LC 94-21892. 1995. write for info. (*0-395-69843-X*); pap. write for info. (*0-395-69844-8*) HM.

Halkin, John. Fangs of the Werewolf. 160p. (gr. 6 up). 1988. pap. 2.95 (*0-8120-4071-6*) Barron.

Harrah, Madge. No Escape. 112p. (Orig.). 1993. pap. 3.50 (*0-380-76569-1*, Camelot) Avon.

Hawks, Robert. Hall Pass. 160p. (Orig.). 1993. pap. 3.50 (*0-380-76951-4*, Flare) Avon.

Hawthorne, Nathaniel. House of the Seven Gables. (gr. 9 up). 1964. pap. 2.95 (*0-8049-0016-7*, CL-16) Airmont.

Hill, Mary, ed. Creepy Classics. Langeneckert, Mark, illus. LC 94-5079. 128p. (gr. 4-8). 1994. pap. 4.99 (*0-679-86692-2*) Random Bks Yng Read.

Hodgman, Ann. Dark Dreams. LC 93-15039. 224p. (gr. 7 up). 1993. pap. 3.50 (*0-14-036374-2*, Puffin) Puffin Bks.

—Dark Triumph. 224p. (gr. 7 up). 1994. pap. 3.50 (*0-14-036376-9*) Puffin Bks.

Hoh, Diane. Deadly Attraction. (gr. 9-12). 1993. pap. 3.50 (*0-590-46015-3*) Scholastic Inc.

—The Experiment. 1994. pap. 3.50 (*0-590-47703-X*) Scholastic Inc.

—Guilty. (gr. 12 up). 1993. pap. 3.50 (*0-590-49452-X*) Scholastic Inc.

—The Night Walker. 1994. pap. 3.50 (*0-590-47688-2*) Scholastic Inc.

—The Roommate. (gr. 9-12). 1993. pap. 3.50 (*0-590-47136-8*) Scholastic Inc.

—The Scream Team. 1993. pap. 3.50 (*0-590-47137-6*) Scholastic Inc.

—The Silent Scream. (gr. 9-12). 1993. pap. 3.50 (*0-590-46014-5*) Scholastic Inc.

—Sorority Sister. 1994. pap. 3.50 (*0-590-47689-0*) Scholastic Inc.

—The Train. 1992. 3.25 (*0-590-45640-7*, 068, Point) Scholastic Inc.

—The Whisperer. 1994. pap. 3.50 (*0-590-48154-1*) Scholastic Inc.

—The Wish. 1993. pap. 3.50 (*0-590-46013-7*) Scholastic Inc.

Howe, Imogen. Vicious Circle. (gr. 5-9). 1983. pap. 1.95 (*0-440-99318-0*, LFL) Dell.

Howe, James. Howliday Inn. Munsinger, Lynn, illus. 200p. 1983. pap. 3.99 (*0-380-64543-2*, Camelot) Avon.

—Scared Silly. 48p. 1990. pap. 5.99 (*0-380-70446-3*, Camelot) Avon.

Hurwood, Bernhardt J. Eerie Tales of Terror & Dread. 1992. 2.95 (*0-590-44650-9*, Point) Scholastic Inc.

Impey, Rose. Creepies Jumble Joan. (ps-3). 1991. pap. 3.25 (*0-440-40510-6*, YB) Dell.

—Creepies Scare Yourself to Sleep. (ps-3). 1991. pap. 3.25 (*0-440-40509-2*, YB) Dell.

The Invisible Man. 1993. pap. text ed. 6.50 (*0-582-08480-6*, 79820) Longman.

Irving, Washington. Rip Van Winkle. 1987. pap. 2.99 (*0-14-035051-9*, Puffin) Puffin Bks.

Johnson, Liliane & Dufton, Jo S. Children's Chillers & Thrillers. Bruhn, Joan, illus. 136p. (Orig.). Date not set. pap. 10.00 (*0-930069-04-8*) Jasmine Pr.

Jones, Lily. Whooo's There? 16p. (ps-3). 1992. 9.95 (*0-89577-439-9*) RD Assn.

Jordan, Cathleen, ed. Fun & Games at the Whacks Museum & Other Horror Stories: From Alfred Hitchcock Mystery Magazine & Ellery Queen's Mystery Magazine. LC 93-34862. (gr. 5-9). 1994. 15.00 (*0-671-89005-0*, S&S BFYR) S&S Trade.

Kallen, Stuart A. Vampires, Werewolves, & Zombies. LC 91-73062. 1991. 12.94 (*1-56239-039-2*) Abdo & Dghtrs.

Kash, Conrad, adapted by. The Addams Family in "Sir Pugsley" (Illus.). 24p. (ps-4). 1993. 20.00 (*0-307-74031-5*, 64031, Golden Pr) Western Pub.

Koltz, Tony. Vampire Express, No. 31. 1984. pap. 3.50 (*0-553-27053-2*) Bantam.

Kudalis, Eric. Dracula & Other Vampire Stories. 48p. (gr. 3-10). 1994. PLB 17.27 (*1-56065-212-8*) Capstone Pr.

—Frankenstein & Other Stories of Man-Made Monsters. 48p. (gr. 3-10). 1994. PLB 17.27 (*1-56065-213-6*) Capstone Pr.

—Stories of Mummies & the Living Dead. 48p. (gr. 3-10). 1994. PLB 17.27 (*1-56065-214-4*) Capstone Pr.

—Werewolves & Stories about Them. 48p. (gr. 3-10). 1994. PLB 17.27 (*1-56065-215-2*) Capstone Pr.

Lake, Simon. Something's Watching. 1993. pap. 3.50 (*0-553-29791-0*) Bantam.

Launchbury, Jane. Monster Stories. 1991. 3.99 (*0-517-06525-8*) Random Hse Value.

Lee, Samantha, retold by. Dr. Jekyll & Mr. Hyde. 160p. (gr. 6 up). 1988. pap. 2.95 (*0-8120-4072-4*) Barron.

Leroux, Gaston. The Phantom of the Opera. McMullan, Kate, adapted by. Jennis, Paul, illus. LC 88-34079. 96p. (Orig.). (gr. 3-7). 1993. lib. bdg. 5.99 (*0-394-93847-X*, Bullseye Bks); pap. 2.99 (*0-394-83847-5*, Bullseye Bks) Random Bks Yng Read.

Levy, Elizabeth. The Gorgonzola Zombies in the Park. Ulrich, George, illus. LC 92-11353. 96p. (gr. 2-5). 1994. pap. 3.95 (*0-06-440555-9*, Trophy) HarpC Child Bks.

Lewis, Shari. One-Minute Scary Stories. (ps-3). 1991. pap. 10.00 (*0-385-41778-0*) Doubleday.

Liebman, Arthur. The Ghosts, Witches & Vampires Quiz Book. Williams, Jack, illus. LC 91-23371. 128p. (gr. 3-10). 1992. pap. 4.95 (*0-8069-8409-0*) Sterling.
Lovelace, Delos W. King Kong. Conaway, Judith, ed. Van Munching, Paul, illus. LC 87-28354. 96p. (gr. 3-7). 1988. pap. 2.95 (*0-394-89789-7*) Random Bks Yng Read.
Low, Alice, ed. Spooky Stories for a Dark & Stormy Night. Wilson, Gahan, illus. LC 93-33638. 128p. (gr. 3 up). 1994. 19.95 (*0-7868-0012-7*); PLB 19.89 (*0-7868-2008-X*) Hyprn Child.
MacDonald, Caroline. Hostilities: Nine Bizarre Stories. LC 93-19019. 112p. (gr. 7 up). 1994. 13.95 (*0-590-46063-3*) Scholastic Inc.
McDonald, Collin. The Chilling Hour: Tales of the Real & Unreal. (Illus.). 128p. (gr. 4 up). 1992. 14.00 (*0-525-65101-2*, Cobblehill Bks) Dutton Child Bks.
—Nightwaves: Scary Tales for after Dark. LC 90-35234. (gr. 4-7). 1990. 12.95 (*0-525-65043-1*, Cobblehill Bks) Dutton Child Bks.
—Nightwaves: Scary Tales for after Dark. 112p. (gr. 3-7). 1992. pap. 3.95 (*0-06-440447-1*, Trophy) HarpC Child Bks.
—Shadows & Whispers: Tales from the Other Side. LC 94-2143. 160p. (gr. 4 up). 1994. 13.99 (*0-525-65184-5*, Cobblehill Bks) Dutton Child Bks.
McKinney, Nadine. Eyes in the Attic. LC 93-74952. 170p. (gr. 5-7). 1995. pap. 7.95x (*0-943864-73-9*) Davenport.
McKissack, Patricia. The Dark-Thirty: Southern Tales of the Supernatural. Pinkney, Brian, illus. LC 92-3021. 128p. (gr. 3-7). 1992. 15.00 (*0-679-81863-4*); PLB 15.99 (*0-679-91863-9*) Knopf Bks Yng Read.
Malcolm, Jahnna N. Freak Show. (gr. 4-7). 1993. pap. 2.95 (*0-590-45853-1*) Scholastic Inc.
—Scared Stiff. 128p. 1991. pap. 2.75 (*0-590-44996-6*, Apple Paperbacks) Scholastic Inc.
—Scared to Death. 144p. 1992. pap. 2.95 (*0-590-44995-8*, Apple Paperbacks) Scholastic Inc.
—The Slime That Ate Crestview. 1992. 2.95 (*0-590-45852-3*, Apple Paperbacks) Scholastic Inc.
Martin, Ann M. Kristy & the Vampires. (gr. 4-7). 1994. pap. 3.50 (*0-590-47053-1*) Scholastic Inc.
Mayne, William. Hob & the Goblins. (Illus.). 144p. (gr. 3-6). 1994. 12.95 (*1-56458-713-4*) Dorling Kindersley.
Milton, Hilary. Escape from High Doom. Schwartz, Betty, ed. Frame, Paul, illus. 128p. (Orig.). (gr. 3-7). 1984. PLB 5.97 (*0-685-08595-3*) S&S Trade.
—Fun House Terrors! Frame, Paul, illus. 128p. (gr. 3-7). 1984. (J Messner); pap. 2.95 (*0-685-09678-5*) S&S Trade.
Montgomery, Raymond A. The Haunted House. 1983. pap. 2.99 (*0-553-15679-9*) Bantam.
Mooser, Stephen. The Fright-Face Contest. (gr. k-6). 1989. pap. 2.75 (*0-685-26138-7*, YB) Dell.
—Hitchhiking Vampire. 1989. pap. 13.95 (*0-440-50134-2*) Dell.
—The Mummy's Secret. Morrill, Leslie, illus. LC 87-16152. 96p. (gr. 3-6). 1988. PLB 9.89 (*0-8167-1181-X*); pap. text ed. 2.95 (*0-8167-1182-8*) Troll Assocs.
—Night of the Vampire Kitty. (ps-3). 1991. pap. 2.95 (*0-440-40329-4*) Dell.
More Bone-Chilling Tales of Fright: Stories to Make You Scream. 128p. 1994. pap. 4.985 (*1-56565-181-2*) Lowell Hse Juvenile.
More Thrills, Chills, & Nightmares: Party Line; Prom Dress; The Baby-Sitter; & Trick or Treat. (gr. 7-12). 1991. pap. 11.80 boxed set (*0-590-63674-X*) Scholastic Inc.
Morey, Walt. Death Walk. 176p. 1993. pap. 7.95 (*0-936085-55-X*) Blue Heron OR.
Morissette, Oliver, et al. Prey. Morissette, Oliver, illus. (Orig.). Date not set. pap. 19.95 (*0-938782-29-0*) Fantaco.
Moser, Barry. Tales of Edgar Allan Poe. Glassman, Peter, afterword by. LC 91-3277. (Illus.). 312p. 1991. 19.95 (*0-688-07509-6*) Morrow Jr Bks.
Munsch, Robert. The Dark. Suomalainen, Sami, illus. 32p. (gr. k-3). 1984. pap. 4.95 (*0-920236-85-5*, Pub. by Annick CN) Firefly Bks Ltd.
Myers, Walter D. Un Lugar En las Sombras: Somewhere in the Darkness. 1994. pap. 3.25 (*0-590-47701-3*) Scholastic Inc.
Naha, Ed. Breakdown. (Orig.). 1988. pap. 3.50 (*0-440-20210-8*) Dell.
Namioka, Lensey. Village of the Vampire Cat: A Novel. LC 80-68737. 224p. (gr. 8-12). 1981. 9.95 (*0-440-09377-5*) Delacorte.
Nesbit, Edith. Five Children & It. 208p. (gr. 4-7). 1988. pap. 3.25 (*0-590-42146-8*, Apple Classics) Scholastic Inc.
Nixon. Edgar Winners Collection. Date not set. 14.00 (*0-06-023650-7*); PLB 13.89 (*0-06-023651-5*) HarpC Child Bks.
Nixon, Joan L. Secret, Silent Screams. LC 88-417. (gr. 7 up). 1988. 14.95 (*0-440-50059-1*) Delacorte.
Noonan, R. A. Critters. LC 90-45819. (Illus.). 48p. (gr. 5-6). 1991. text ed. 13.95 RSBE (*0-89686-575-4*, Crestwood Hse) Macmillan Child Grp.
Oakes, Terry, illus. A Pull-the-Tab Pop-Up Book of Classic Tales of Horror. Marshall, Ray, designed by. (Illus.). 10p. (ps up). 1988. 13.95 (*0-525-44418-1*, DCB) Dutton Child Bks.
O'Brien, Jane. Alien. (Illus.). 48p. (gr. 5-6). 1991. text ed. 13.95 RSBE (*0-89686-573-8*, Crestwood Hse) Macmillan Child Grp.
Outlet Staff. Lost in the Haunted Mansion. 1991. pap. 3.99 (*0-517-06138-4*) Random Hse Value.
Packard, Edward. Horror House. 1993. pap. 3.25 (*0-553-56008-5*) Bantam.
Park, Ruth. Things in Corners. 208p. (gr. 5 up). 1993. pap. 3.99 (*0-14-032713-4*, Puffin) Puffin Bks.
Paul, Korky. Pop-up Book of Ghost Tales. 24p. (gr. 3 up). 1991. 14.95 (*0-15-200589-7*, HB Juv Bks) HarBrace.
Payne, Bernal C., Jr. Experiment in Terror. (gr. 5-9). 1988. pap. 2.75 (*0-671-67261-4*, Archway) PB.
Pearce, J. C. Tug of War. LC 93-15037. 144p. (gr. 3-7). 1993. pap. 2.99 (*0-14-036663-6*, Puffin) Puffin Bks.
Peel, John. Alien Prey. Cherry, Eric, illus. 144p. (gr. 3-7). 1993. pap. 3.50 (*0-448-40529-6*, G&D) Putnam Pub Group.
—Blood Wolf. Cherry, Eric, illus. 144p. (gr. 3-7). 1993. pap. 2.95 (*0-448-40527-X*, G&D) Putnam Pub Group.
—Grave Doubts. Cherry, Eric, illus. 144p. (gr. 3-7). 1993. pap. 2.95 (*0-448-40528-8*, G&D) Putnam Pub Group.
—Night Wings. Cherry, Eric, illus. 144p. (gr. 3-7). 1993. pap. 2.95 (*0-448-40526-1*, G&D) Putnam Pub Group.
Pepper, Dennis, ed. The Oxford Book of Scary Tales. (Illus.). 160p. 1992. 20.00 (*0-19-278131-6*) OUP.
Pickford, Ted. Bobby's Watching. 1993. pap. 3.50 (*0-553-56089-1*) Bantam.
Pike, Christopher. The Eternal Enemy. MacDonald, Pat, ed. 224p. (Orig.). 1993. pap. 3.99 (*0-671-74509-3*) PB.
—Master of Murder. MacDonald, Pat, ed. (Orig.). 1992. pap. 3.99 (*0-671-69059-0*, Archway) PB.
—The Midnight Club. MacDonald, Pat, ed. LC 93-20917. 256p. (Orig.). 1994. 14.00 (*0-671-87255-9*, Archway); pap. 3.99 (*0-671-87263-X*, Archway) PB.
—Road to Nowhere. MacDonald, Pat, ed. 224p. (Orig.). (gr. 9 up). 1993. pap. 3.99 (*0-671-74508-5*, Archway) PB.
—Weekend. 230p. (Orig.). (gr. 9 up). 1986. pap. 3.50 (*0-590-44256-2*) Scholastic Inc.
—The Wicked Heart. MacDonald, Patricia, ed. 224p. (Orig.). 1993. 14.00 (*0-671-87314-8*, Archway); pap. 3.99 (*0-671-74511-5*, Archway) PB.
Pine, Nicholas. The New Kid. 1993. pap. 3.50 (*0-425-13970-0*) Berkley Pub.
—The Prom. 192p. (Orig.). 1994. pap. text ed. 3.50 (*0-425-14153-5*) Berkley Pub.
—Student Body. 1993. pap. 3.50 (*0-425-13983-2*) Berkley Pub.
Pinkwater, Daniel. Wempires. Pinkwater, Daniel, illus. LC 90-46925. 32p. (gr. k-3). 1991. RSBE 13.95 (*0-02-774411-6*, Macmillan Child Bk) Macmillan Child Grp.
Poe, Edgar Allan. The Cask of Amontillado. LC 80-21466. (Illus.). 32p. (gr. 9 up). 1980. PLB 13.95 (*0-87191-773-4*) Creative Ed.
—The Cask of Amontillado. Cutts, David E., adapted by. Toulmin-Rothe, Ann, illus. LC 81-15997. 32p. (gr. 5-10). 1982. PLB 10.79 (*0-89375-622-9*); pap. text ed. 2.95 (*0-89375-623-7*) Troll Assocs.
—Edgar Allan Poe's Tales of Terror. Martin, Les, adapted by. Chandler, Karen, illus. LC 90-52926. 96p. (gr. 2-6). 1991. pap. 2.99 (*0-679-81046-3*) Random Bks Yng Read.
—Ghostly Tales & Eerie Poems of Edgar Allan Poe. Schwinger, Larry, illus. LC 92-30884. 256p. 1993. 13.95 (*0-448-40533-4*, G&D) Putnam Pub Group.
—The Masque of the Red Death. Cutts, David E., adapted by. Lawn, John, illus. LC 81-15959. 32p. (gr. 5-10). 1982. PLB 10.79 (*0-89375-620-2*); pap. text ed. 2.95 (*0-89375-621-0*) Troll Assocs.
—The Masque of the Red Death. 1991. PLB 13.95 (*0-88682-477-X*) Creative Ed.
—The Pit & the Pendulum. (Illus.). 48p. (gr. 9 up). 1980. PLB 13.95 (*0-87191-771-8*) Creative Ed.
—The Pit & the Pendulum. Cutts, David E., adapted by. Eisenbery, Monroe, illus. LC 81-16432. 32p. (gr. 5-10). 1982. PLB 10.79 (*0-89375-626-1*); pap. text ed. 2.95 (*0-89375-627-X*) Troll Assocs.
—Tales of Edgar Allan Poe. Shaw, Charlie, illus. Stewart, Diana, adapted by. LC 80-14064. (Illus.). 48p. (gr. 4 up). 1980. PLB 20.70 (*0-8172-1662-6*) Raintree Steck-V.
—The Tell-Tale Heart. (Illus.). 32p. (gr. 9 up). 1980. PLB 13.95 (*0-87191-772-6*) Creative Ed.
Poe, Edgar Allan, et al. The Fall of the House of Usher. (Illus.). 52p. Date not set. pap. 4.95 (*1-57209-014-6*) Classics Int Ent.
Posner, Richard. Sweet Sixteen & Never Been Killed. MacDonald, Pat, ed. 256p. (Orig.). (gr. 5 up). 1993. pap. 3.50 (*0-671-86506-4*, Archway) PB.
Preiss, Byron. Vampire State Building. (gr. 4-7). 1992. pap. 3.50 (*0-553-15998-4*) Bantam.
Ransford, Lynn. Creepy Crawlies for Curious Kids. (Illus.). 48p. (gr. k-3). 1987. wkbk. 6.95 (*1-55734-217-2*) Tchr Create Mat.
Raphael, Morris. The Loup-Garou of Cote Gelee. Rodrigue, George, illus. 48p. (gr. 3-9). 1990. 12.95 (*0-9608866-7-2*) M Raphael.
Reaver, Chap. Little Bit Dead. 1994. pap. 3.99 (*0-440-21910-8*) Dell.
Rhyne, Nancy. The South Carolina Lizard Man. Magellan, Mauro, illus. LC 92-17289. 128p. (gr. 5-9). 1992. pap. 7.95 (*0-88289-907-4*) Pelican.
Rochman, H. Voices in the Dark. Date not set. 14.00 (*0-06-025024-0*); PLB 13.89 (*0-06-025025-9*) HarpC Child Bks.
Ross, Harriet, ed. Great Horror Stories. Bolle, Frank, illus. 160p. (gr. 3-9). 1992. pap. 11.95 (*0-87460-188-6*) Lion Bks.
Rubel, Nicole. It Came from the Swamp. Rubel, Nicole, illus. LC 87-24653. 32p. (ps-3). 1988. 10.95 (*0-8037-0513-1*); PLB 10.89 (*0-8037-0515-8*) Dial Bks Young.
Ruckman, Ivy. Melba the Mummy. (gr. 4-7). 1991. pap. 3.25 (*0-440-40437-1*) Dell.
Rue, T. S. The Attic. 1993. pap. 3.50 (*0-06-106157-3*, Harp PBks) HarpC.
—Nightmare Inn. (gr. 9-12). 1993. pap. 3.50 (*0-06-106740-7*, Harp PBks) HarpC.
—The Pool. 1993. pap. 3.50 (*0-06-106749-0*, Harp PBks) HarpC.
—Room Thirteen. (gr. 9-12). 1993. pap. 3.50 (*0-06-106746-6*, Harp PBks) HarpC.
Sanford, Willam R. & Green, Carl R. The Murders in the Rue Morgue. LC 86-24399. (Illus.). 48p. (gr. 3-5). 1987. text ed. 11.95 RSBE (*0-89686-308-5*, Crestwood Hse) Macmillan Child Grp.
Sanford, William & Green, Carl. Dracula's Daughter. LC 84-27462. (Illus.). 48p. (gr. 3-5). 1985. text ed. 10.95 RSBE (*0-89686-260-7*, Crestwood Hse) Macmillan Child Grp.
—Ghost of Frankenstein. LC 84-29231. (Illus.). 48p. (gr. 3-5). 1985. text ed. 10.95 RSBE (*0-89686-261-5*, Crestwood Hse) Macmillan Child Grp.
Sanford, William R. & Green, Carl R. The Black Cat. LC 86-24336. (Illus.). 48p. (gr. 3-5). 1987. text ed. 10.95 RSBE (*0-89686-310-7*, Crestwood Hse) Macmillan Child Grp.
Sanford, William R. & Green, Carl. R. House of Fear. LC 86-28768. (Illus.). 48p. (gr. 3-5). 1985. text ed. 10.95 RSBE (*0-89686-311-5*, Crestwood Hse) Macmillan Child Grp.
Sanford, William R. & Green, Carl R. The House of the Seven Gables. LC 86-16241. (Illus.). 48p. (gr. 3-5). 1987. text ed. 10.95 RSBE (*0-89686-312-3*, Crestwood Hse) Macmillan Child Grp.
—The Invisible Man. LC 86-24263. (Illus.). 48p. (gr. 3-5). 1987. text ed. 11.95 RSBE (*0-89686-307-7*, Crestwood Hse) Macmillan Child Grp.
—The Phantom of the Opera. LC 86-24272. (Illus.). 48p. (gr. 3-5). 1987. text ed. 11.95 RSBE (*0-89686-309-3*, Crestwood Hse) Macmillan Child Grp.
San Souci, Robert D. & Coville, Katherine. Short & Shivery: Thirty Chilling Tales. LC 86-29067. 192p. (gr. 4-6). 1987. 14.95 (*0-385-23886-X*) Doubleday.
Saunders, Susan. The Green Slime, No. 6. 1983. pap. 2.99 (*0-553-15680-2*) Bantam.
Scary Storytime. (Illus.). (ps-2). 1990. 3.50 (*0-7214-1340-4*) Ladybird Bks.
Schick, Joel & Schick, Alice. Bram Stoker's Dracula. Schick, Joel & Schick, Alice, illus. LC 80-13619. 48p. (gr. 4-6). 1980. PLB 12.95 (*0-685-42954-7*); pap. 6.95 (*0-385-28141-2*) Delacorte.
Schorsch, Laurence, ed. Evil Tales of Evil Things. Sperling, Thomas, illus. 128p. (gr. 3 up). 1993. pap. 3.50 (*1-56288-407-7*) Checkerboard.
—Tales of the Living Dead. Sperling, Thomas, illus. 128p. (gr. 3 up). 1993. pap. 3.50 (*1-56288-406-9*) Checkerboard.
Schwartz, Alvin. More Scary Stories to Tell in the Dark: Collected & Retold from Folklore. Gammell, Stephen, illus. LC 83-49494. 128p. (gr. 4-7). 1984. 14.00 (*0-397-32081-7*, Lipp Jr Bks); PLB 13.89 (*0-397-32082-5*, Lipp Jr Bks) HarpC Child Bks.
—Scary Stories, Boxed set. Gammell, Stephen, illus. (gr. 4-7). 1992. pap. 11.85 (*0-06-440465-X*, Trophy) HarpC Child Bks.
—Scary Stories Fright Box. (Illus.). 112p. (gr. 3-8). 1993. 14.95 (*0-694-00573-8*, Festival) HarpC Child Bks.
—Scary Stories Three: More Tales to Chill Your Bones. Gammell, Stephen, illus. LC 90-47474. 128p. (gr. 4 up). 1991. 14.00 (*0-06-021794-4*); PLB 13.89 (*0-06-021795-2*) HarpC Child Bks.
—Scary Stories Three: More Tales to Chill Your Bones. Gammell, Stephen, illus. LC 90-47474. 128p. (gr. 4 up). 1991. pap. 3.95 (*0-06-440418-8*, Trophy) HarpC Child Bks.
—Scary Stories to Tell in the Dark. (Illus.). 128p. (gr. 4 up). 1986. pap. 3.95 (*0-06-440170-7*, Trophy) HarpC Child Bks.
—Scary Stories to Tell in the Dark: Collected from American folklore. Gammell, Stephen, illus. LC 80-8728. 128p. (gr. 5 up). 1981. 14.00 (*0-397-31926-6*, Lipp Jr Bks); PLB 13.89 (*0-397-31927-4*, Lipp Jr Bks) HarpC Child Bks.
Seyki, Kofi. Haunted Taxi Driver. (gr. 4-7). 1992. pap. 3.95 (*0-7910-2914-X*) Chelsea Hse.
Shadows on the Grave. 1986. pap. 2.75 (*0-440-70805-2*) Dell.
Shelley, Mary Wollstonecraft. Frankenstein. (gr. 7 up). 1964. pap. 2.95 (*0-8049-0019-1*, CL-19) Airmont.
—Frankenstein. 256p. (gr. 9-12). 1989. pap. 2.50 (*0-8125-0457-7*) Tor Bks.
—Frankenstein. Weinberg, Larry, adapted by. Barr, Ken, illus. 96p. (gr. 3-7). 1992. pap. 6.99 incl. cass. (*0-679-82443-X*) Random Bks Yng Read.
Shusterman, Neal. Darkness Creeping: Tales to Trouble Your Sleep. Coy, Michael, illus. LC 93-13792. 128p. 1993. pap. 4.95 (*1-56565-069-7*) Lowell Hse.
Siegal, Barbara & Seigel, Scott. Cold Dread. MacDonald, Pat, ed. 176p. (Orig.). 1992. pap. 2.99 (*0-671-75946-9*) PB.
Sinte, R. L. One Day at Horror Land. (gr. 4-7). 1994. pap. 2.95 (*0-590-47738-2*) Scholastic Inc.
Slepian, Jan & Siedler, Ann. The Hungry Thing. Martin, Richard E., illus. 32p. (ps-3). 1988. pap. 3.95 (*0-590-42292-8*) Scholastic Inc.

Smith, L. J. Dark Reunion. 1992. pap. 3.99 (*0-06-106775-X*, Harp PBks) HarpC.
—The Kill. MacDonald, Pat, ed. 240p. (Orig.). 1994. pap. 3.50 (*0-671-87453-5*, Archway) PB.
Sommer-Bodenburg, Angela. If You Want to Scare Yourself. Cafiero, Renee V., tr. from GER. Spiess, Helga, illus. LC 87-45316. 112p. (gr. 2-5). 1989. (Lipp Jr Bks); PLB 12.89 (*0-397-32210-0*, Lipp Jr Bks) HarpC Child Bks.
—The Vampire in Love. Glienke, Amelie, illus. 128p. (gr. 2-6). 1991. 13.00 (*0-8037-0905-6*); lib. bdg. 12.89 (*0-8037-0906-4*) Dial Bks Young.
—The Vampire Takes a Trip. Glienke, Amelie, illus. LC 84-22995. 160p. (gr. 2-6). 1985. PLB 9.89 (*0-8037-0201-9*) Dial Bks Young.
Stamper, David A. More Night Frights. 1993. pap. 2.95 (*0-590-46045-5*) Scholastic Inc.
Stamper, Judith B. Even More Tales for the Midnight Hour. 112p. (gr. 4 up). 1992. pap. 2.75 (*0-590-44143-4*, Point) Scholastic Inc.
—Five Funny Frights. Raglin, Tim, illus. LC 92-44538. (gr. 4 up). 1993. pap. 2.95 (*0-590-46416-7*) Scholastic Inc.
—Night Frights: Thirteen Scary Stories. (gr. 4-7). 1993. pap. 2.95 (*0-590-46046-3*) Scholastic Inc.
—Still More Tales for the Midnight Hour. 1992. pap. 2.95 (*0-685-53518-5*, Point) Scholastic Inc.
—Tales for the Midnight Hour. 128p. 1992. pap. 2.95 (*0-590-45343-2*, Point) Scholastic Inc.
Steiber, Ellen. Fangs of Evil. LC 93-44043. 108p. (Orig.). (gr. 2-6). 1994. pap. 2.99 (*0-679-85466-5*, Bullseye Bks) Random Bks Yng Read.
—Shadow of the Fox. LC 94-1295. 108p. (gr. 2-6). 1994. pap. 3.50 (*0-679-86667-1*, Bullseye Bks) Random Bks Yng Read.
Steig, William. Shrek! (gr. 4-7). 1993. pap. 4.95 (*0-374-46623-8*) FS&G.
Steiner, Barbara. Night Cries. 144p. (Orig.). (gr. 4). 1993. pap. 3.50 (*0-380-76990-5*, Flare) Avon.
—The Photographer. 144p. 1989. pap. 3.50 (*0-380-75758-3*, Flare) Avon.
Stevenson, Robert Louis. Dr. Jekyll & Mr. Hyde. new ed. Platt, Kin, ed. Redondo, Nestor, illus. LC 73-75457. 64p. (Orig.). (gr. 5-10). 1973. pap. 2.95 (*0-88301-096-8*); student activity bk. 1.25 (*0-88301-176-X*) Pendulum Pr.
—Dr. Jekyll & Mr. Hyde. 1990. pap. 2.50 (*0-8125-0448-8*) Tor Bks.
—Dr. Jekyll & Mr. Hyde. 208p. 1991. pap. 3.25 (*0-590-45169-3*) Scholastic Inc.
Stine, Bob. Hit & Run. 1992. pap. 3.25 (*0-590-45385-8*, Point) Scholastic Inc.
Stine, Megan & Stine, H. William. Camp Zombie. LC 93-33748. 1994. write for info. (Bullseye Bks) Random Bks Yng Read.
—Camp Zombie. 108p. (Orig.). (gr. 2-6). 1994. pap. 2.99 (*0-679-85640-4*) Random Bks Yng Read.
Stine, R. L. Baby-Sitter III. 1993. pap. 3.50 (*0-590-46099-4*) Scholastic Inc.
—Beach House. 224p. (gr. 7 up). 1992. pap. 3.25 (*0-590-45386-6*, Point) Scholastic Inc.
—The Best Friend. McDonald, Patricia, ed. 160p. (Orig.). (gr. 7 up). 1992. pap. 3.99 (*0-671-73866-6*, Archway) PB.
—Call Waiting. 1994. pap. 3.50 (*0-590-47480-4*) Scholastic Inc.
—Dead Girlfriend. (gr. 9-12). 1993. pap. 3.50 (*0-590-45387-4*) Scholastic Inc.
—Deep Trouble. (gr. 4-7). 1994. pap. 3.25 (*0-590-47741-2*) Scholastic Inc.
—Double Date. 1994. pap. 3.99 (*0-671-78570-2*, Archway) PB.
—Fear Street Saga, No. 3: The Burning. 176p. (Orig.). (gr. 6-9). 1993. pap. 3.99 (*0-671-86833-0*, Archway) PB.
—The First Evil. MacDonald, Pat, ed. 176p. (Orig.). 1992. pap. 3.99 (*0-671-75117-4*, Archway) PB.
—Goodnight Kiss. MacDonald, Pat, ed. 224p. (Orig.). 1992. pap. 3.99 (*0-671-73823-2*, Archway) PB.
—Goosebumps: Say Cheese & Die! 1992. pap. 2.95 (*0-590-45368-8*, Apple Paperbacks) Scholastic Inc.
—Halloween Night. (gr. 9-12). 1993. pap. 3.50 (*0-590-46098-6*) Scholastic Inc.
—Hitchiker. 1993. pap. 3.50 (*0-590-46100-1*) Scholastic Inc.
—I Saw You That Night! (gr. 7 up). 1994. pap. 3.95 (*0-590-47481-2*) Scholastic Inc.
—Night of the Living Dummy. (gr. 3-7). 1993. pap. 2.95 (*0-590-46617-8*) Scholastic Inc.
—The Scarecrow Walks at Midnight. (gr. 4-7). 1994. pap. 3.25 (*0-590-47742-0*) Scholastic Inc.
—The Secret. MacDonald, Pat, ed. 176p. (Orig.). (gr. 5 up). 1993. pap. 3.99 (*0-671-86832-2*, Archway) PB.
—Stay Out of the Basement: Goose Bumps Ser. 128p. 1992. pap. 2.95 (*0-590-45366-1*, Apple Paperbacks) Scholastic Inc.
—The Third Evil: Fear Street. MacDonald, Pat, ed. 176p. (Orig.). 1992. pap. 3.99 (*0-671-75119-0*, Archway) PB.
—Welcome to Dead House. 128p. 1992. pap. 2.95 (*0-590-45365-3*, Apple Paperbacks) Scholastic Inc.
—Why I'm Afraid of Bess. (gr. 4-7). 1994. pap. 2.95 (*0-590-47739-0*) Scholastic Inc.
Stoker, Bram. Dracula. Lowndes, R. A., intro. by. LC 83-5471. (gr. 7 up). 1965. pap. 2.25 (*0-8049-0072-8*, CL-72) Airmont.
—Dracula. (gr. 4-6). 1986. pap. 3.50 (*0-14-035048-9*, Puffin) Puffin Bks.
—Dracula. Spinner, Stephanie, adapted by. Spence, Jim, illus. 96p. (gr. 3-7). 1992. pap. 6.99 incl. cass. (*0-679-82445-6*) Random Bks Yng Read.
—Dracula. Schwinger, Larry, illus. LC 93-50907. 1994. 15.95 (*0-448-40559-8*, G&D) Putnam Pub Group.
Stoker, Bram, et al. Dracula, Frankenstein, Dr. Jekyll & Mr. Hyde. King, Stephen, intro. by. 672p. (gr. 7). 1992. pap. 5.95 (*0-451-52363-6*, Sig Classics) NAL-Dutton.
Storm, Derek. Dead Zoo. 205p. (gr. 6-12). 1993. pap. 3.95 (*1-56969-353-6*) FamilyVision.
—Vampire Island. LC 93-71550. 175p. 1993. pap. 3.95 (*1-56969-350-1*) FamilyVision.
Strange Case of Dr. Jekyll & Mr. Hyde. 1993. pap. text ed. 6.50 (*0-582-08484-9*, 79829) Longman.
Strasser, Todd. Freaked. (gr. 4-7). 1993. pap. 4.50 (*0-440-40908-X*) Dell.
Sumner, M. C. Deadly Stranger. (gr. 9-12). 1993. pap. 3.50 (*0-06-106742-3*, Harp PBks) HarpC.
Tallis, Robyn. Horrorvid. (gr. 6 up). 1989. pap. 2.95 (*0-8041-0461-1*) Ivy Books.
Teitelbaum, Michael. Did You Hear Something? (Illus.). 1992. 2.98 (*0-685-60663-5*) Kidsbks.
—Don't Be Afraid of the Dark. (Illus.). 1992. 2.98 (*1-56156-090-1*) Kidsbks.
—There's No Such Thing As a Ghost. (Illus.). 1992. 2.98 (*1-56156-091-X*) Kidsbks.
—There's Something Weird in That Cave! (Illus.). 1992. 2.98 (*1-56156-092-8*) Kidsbks.
Teitelbaum, Mike. Universal Monsters: Dracula. Ruiz, Art, illus. 96p. (gr. 3-7). 1992. pap. 2.95 (*0-307-22331-0*, 22331, Golden Pr) Western Pub.
Tembo, John. Dead Men Don't Talk. (gr. 4-7). 1992. pap. 4.95 (*0-7910-2919-0*) Chelsea Hse.
Thompson, Richard. Don't Be Scared, Eleven. Fernandes, Eugenie, illus. 24p. 1993. lib. bdg. 14.95 (*1-55037-286-6*, Pub. by Annick CN); pap. 4.95 (*1-55037-287-4*, Pub. by Annick CN) Firefly Bks Ltd.
Thorne, Ian. The Deadly Mantis. LC 81-22074. (Illus.). 48p. (gr. 3-5). 1982. text ed. 11.95 RSBE (*0-89686-214-3*, Crestwood Hse) Macmillan Child Grp.
—Dracula. LC 76-51145. (Illus.). 48p. (gr. 3-5). 1977. text ed. 11.95 RSBE (*0-913940-67-4*, Crestwood Hse) Macmillan Child Grp.
—Frankenstein. LC 76-51144. (Illus.). 48p. (gr. 3-5). 1977. text ed. 11.95 RSBE (*0-913940-66-6*, Crestwood Hse); cass. 7.95 (*0-685-01269-7*) Macmillan Child Grp.
—Mad Scientists. LC 76-51149. (Illus.). 48p. (gr. 3-5). 1977. text ed. 11.95 RSBE (*0-913940-70-4*, Crestwood Hse); cassette o.s.i. 7.95 (*0-89686-487-1*) Macmillan Child Grp.
Villa, Mickie, ed. The Comics That Ate My Brain. Wooley, John, intro. by. (Illus.). 114p. 1991. pap. 9.95 (*0-944735-77-0*) Malibu Graphics.
Vivelo, Jacqueline. Chills Run Down My Spine. Eachus, Jennifer, illus. 128p. (gr. 3-6). 1994. 12.95 (*1-56458-712-6*) Dorling Kindersley.
Voigt, Cynthia. The Vandemark Mummy. 1992. pap. 3.99 (*0-449-70417-3*, Juniper) Fawcett.
Weinberg, Larry. Shivers & Shakes. Tavonatti, Mia, illus. LC 93-24445. 1993. pap. 2.95 (*0-8167-3281-7*) Troll Assocs.
Welch, R. C. Twisted Tales: The Dripping Head & Other Gruesome Stories. Fike, Scott, illus. 128p. (Orig.). (gr. 3-7). 1992. pap. 4.95 (*1-56288-314-3*) Checkerboard.
—Twisted Tales: The Slithering Corpse & Other Sinister Stories. Fike, Scott, illus. 128p. (Orig.). (gr. 3-7). 1992. pap. 4.95 (*1-56288-315-1*) Checkerboard.
Welch, Robert. Scary Stories for Sleep-Overs. (Illus.). 128p. (Orig.). (gr. 3-6). 1991. pap. 4.95 (*0-8431-2914-X*) Price Stern.
Wenk, Richard, adapted by. Tales from the Crypt, Vol. 3: Introduced by the Vault-Keeper. Davis, Jack, illus. LC 90-23916. 96p. (gr. 4-7). 1991. pap. 2.99 (*0-679-81801-4*) Random Bks Yng Read.
Westall, Robert. Demons & Shadows: The Ghostly Best Stories. (gr. 4-7). 1993. 16.00 (*0-374-31768-2*) FS&G.
—In Camera: And Other Stories. LC 92-13815. 176p. (gr. 7 up). 1993. 13.95 (*0-590-45920-1*) Scholastic Inc.
—Shades of Darkness: More of the Ghostly Best Stories of Robert Westall. LC 93-42229. 1994. 17.00 (*0-374-36758-2*) FS&G.
Westwood, Chris. Calling All Monsters. LC 91-19601. 224p. (gr. 7 up). 1993. 15.00 (*0-06-022461-4*); PLB 14.89 (*0-06-022462-2*) HarpC Child Bks.
—He Came from the Shadows. LC 90-38005. 224p. (gr. 7 up). 1991. 14.95 (*0-06-021658-1*); PLB 14.89 (*0-06-021659-X*) HarpC Child Bks.
—Shock Waves. 192p. (gr. 9 up). 1992. 13.45 (*0-395-63111-4*, Clarion Bks) HM.
Weyn, Suzanne. Rest in Pieces. Petersen, Eric, illus. 144p. (gr. 3-7). 1994. pap. 3.95 (*0-06-440558-3*, Trophy) HarpC Child Bks.
Whitcher, Susan. Real Mummies Don't Bleed: Friendly Tales for October Nights. (gr. 4-7). 1993. 15.00 (*0-374-36213-0*) FS&G.
Wierd & Spooky Tales. (Illus.). 192p. (gr. 3-8). 1993. pap. 13.95 (*0-87460-391-9*) Lion Bks.
Williamson, J. N. The Black School. (Orig.). 1989. pap. 3.50 (*0-440-20265-5*) Dell.
Windsor, Patricia. The Christmas Killer. 1992. pap. 3.25 (*0-590-43310-5*) Scholastic Inc.
Wright, Betty R. Scariest Night. (gr. 4-7). 1993. pap. 2.95 (*0-590-45918-X*) Scholastic Inc.
Wulffson, Don L. Time Fix: And Other Tales of Terror. 96p. 1994. 13.99 (*0-525-65140-3*, Cobblehill Bks) Dutton Child Bks.
Yolen, Jane & Greenberg, Martin H., eds. Vampires. LC 90-27888. 240p. (gr. 5 up). 1991. 15.00 (*0-06-026800-X*); PLB 14.89 (*0-06-026801-8*) HarpC Child Bks.
Young, Richard & Young, Judy D. Favorite Scary Stories of American Children. Hall, Wendell E., illus. 112p. (Orig.). (ps-5). 1990. pap. 8.95 (*0-87483-119-9*) August Hse.
—Favorite Scary Stories of American Children. Hall, Wendell E., illus. 110p. 1991. 19.95 (*0-87483-120-2*) August Hse.
Zindel, Paul. Attack of the Killer, No. 1. 1993. pap. 3.50 (*0-553-48084-7*) Bantam.
Zorn, Steven, as told by. Mostly Ghostly: Eight Spooky Tales to Chill Your Bones. Brodley, John, illus. LC 91-71087. 56p. (gr. 2 up). 1991. 9.98 (*1-56138-033-4*) Courage Bks.

HORSE

see Horses

HORSE RACING

Forbis, Judith E. Hoofbeats along the Tigris. Forbis, Judith E., illus. Forbis, Donald L., intro. by. (Illus.). 146p. (gr. 8 up). 1990. Repr. 34.95 (*0-9625644-1-9*) Ansata Pubns.
Harris, Jack. The Kentucky Derby. 32p. (gr. 4). 1990. PLB 14.95 (*0-88682-312-9*) Creative Ed.
Phillips, Louis. Willie Shoemaker. LC 88-14966. (Illus.). 48p. (gr. 5-6). 1988. text ed. 11.95 RSBE (*0-89686-381-6*, Crestwood Hse) Macmillan Child Grp.
Roth, Harold. A Day at the Races. LC 83-2345. (Illus.). 64p. (gr. 3-6). 1983. 10.95 (*0-394-85814-X*, Pant Bks Young) Pantheon.
Stone, Lynn M. Bluegrass Country. LC 93-23002. 1993. write for info. (*0-86593-306-5*) Rourke Corp.

HORSE RACING–FICTION

Bagnold, Enid. National Velvet. 272p. 1991. pap. 3.99 (*0-380-71235-0*, Flare) Avon.
Campbell, Joanna. Sierra's Steeplechase. (gr. 4-7). 1993. pap. 3.50 (*0-06-106164-6*, Harp PBks) HarpC.
Cocquyt, Kathryn. Little Freddie at the Kentucky Derby. Corbett, Sylvia, illus. LC 91-23540. 128p. (gr. 4-7). 1992. 13.95 (*0-88289-856-6*) Pelican.
—Little Freddie's Legacy. Corbett, Sylvia, illus. LC 93-5558. 1994. 13.95 (*1-56554-000-X*) Pelican.
Dugan, Michael. The Emu Who Wanted to Be a Horse. Smith, Craig, illus. LC 93-11736. 1994. 4.25 (*0-383-03743-3*) SRA Schl Grp.
Farley, Walter. Black Stallion. Ward, Keith, illus. LC 85-19927. (gr. 3-7). 1944. lib. bdg. 13.99 (*0-394-90601-2*) Random Bks Yng Read.
—Black Stallion Challenged. LC 64-15094. (Illus.). (gr. 5-9). 1980. Random Bks Yng Read.
—Black Stallion's Filly. LC 52-7216. (Illus.). (gr. 4-6). 1978. pap. 3.95 (*0-394-83916-1*) Random Bks Yng Read.
Henry, Marguerite. Black Gold. 2nd ed. LC 91-4907. (Illus.). 176p. (gr. 3-7). 1992. pap. 3.95 (*0-689-71562-5*, Aladdin) Macmillan Child Grp.
—Born to Trot. 2nd ed. LC 92-24139. (Illus.). 224p. (gr. 3-6). 1993. pap. 3.95 (*0-689-71692-3*, Aladdin) Macmillan Child Grp.
Hoppe, Joanne. Pretty Penny Farm. LC 86-1516. 224p. (gr. 7 up). 1987. 12.95 (*0-688-07201-1*) Morrow Jr Bks.
Loring, Philip A. The Miracle of the Blue Horse. (gr. 9-12). 1993. 7.95 (*0-8062-4606-5*) Carlton.
Pace, Mildred M. Kentucky Derby Champion. rev. ed. Gifford, James M., et al, eds. Dennis, Wesley, illus. 144p. (gr. 3 up). 1993. Repr. of 1955 ed. 12.00 (*0-945084-36-6*) J Stuart Found.
Reed, Kevin J. The Saratoga Yearling. Herold, Meri G., ed. Corrigan, Wendy O., illus. 110p. (Orig.). (gr. 5-9). 1985. pap. 3.95 (*0-9614546-0-1*) Chowder Pr.
Savage, Deborah. To Race a Dream. 1994. 15.95 (*0-395-69252-0*) HM.
Sutton, Elizabeth H. Racing for Keeneland. LC 93-43385. (gr. 5-12). 1994. 14.95 (*1-56566-051-X*) Thomasson-Grant.
Wojciechowska, Maia. Dreams of the Kentucky Derby. Karsky, A. K., illus. 52p. 1994. 14.50 (*1-883740-07-X*) Pebble Bch Pr Ltd.

HORSEBREAKING

see Horses–Training

HORSEMANSHIP

see also Rodeos

Bowlby, Linda A. & Thomas, Mary L. Side Saddle Riding: Four-H Manual. Frank, Gayle, illus. 23p. (Orig.). (gr. 9-12). 1984. pap. 5.00 (*1-884011-01-2*) Wrld Sidesaddle.
—Side Saddle Riding: Four-H Manual. 2nd, rev. ed. John-Petrie, Sandi, illus. 24p. (gr. 9-12). 1993. pap. 5.00 (*1-884011-06-3*) Wrld Sidesaddle.
Boy Scouts of America. Horsemanship. (Illus.). 64p. (gr. 6-12). 1986. pap. 1.85 (*0-8395-3298-9*, 33298) BSA.
Callahan, Dorothy M. Julie Krone: A Winning Jockey. LC 89-26061. (Illus.). 64p. (gr. 3 up). 1990. text ed. 13.95 (*0-87518-425-1*, Dillon) Macmillan Child Grp.
Clemens, Virginia P. Horse in Your Backyard: A First-Time Owner's Primer of Horse-Keeping. 1991. 19.95 (*0-13-395088-3*) P-H.
Corbett, Sue. Our Riding Centre. (Illus.). 25p. (gr. 2-4). 1991. 12.95 (*0-237-60145-1*, Pub. by Evans Bros Ltd) Trafalgar.

Damrell, Liz. With the Wind. Marchesi, Stephen, illus. LC 89-48942. 32p. (ps-2). 1991. 14.95 (*0-531-05882-4*); PLB 14.99 (*0-531-08482-5*) Orchard Bks Watts.
Edom, H. Starting Riding. (Illus.). 32p. (gr. k-3). 1992. PLB 12.96 (*0-88110-022-6*); pap. 4.95 (*0-7460-0980-1*) EDC.
Ettinger, Tom & Jaspersohn, William. My Riding Book: A Write-in-Me Bk. for Young Riders. (Illus.). 48p. (gr. 3-7). 1993. 10.95 (*0-694-00465-0*, Festival) HarpC Child Bks.
Evans, Jeremy. Horseback Riding. LC 91-23340. (Illus.). 48p. (gr. 5-6). 1992. text ed. 13.95 RSBE (*0-89686-683-1*, Crestwood Hse) Macmillan Child Grp.
Henriques, Pegotty. Dressage for the Young Rider. (Illus.). 160p. (gr. 6 up). 1990. 26.95 (*0-901366-99-4*, Pub. by Threshold Bks Uk) Half Halt Pr.
Kidd, Jane, ed. Learning to Ride. (Illus.). 208p. (gr. 4-9). 1993. 30.00 (*0-87605-961-2*) Howell Bk.
Kirksmith, Tommie. Ride Western Style: A Guide for Young Riders. (Illus.). 192p. (gr. 3-7). 1991. 16.95 (*0-87605-895-0*) Howell Bk.
—Western Performance: A Guide for Young Riders. Burt, Don, frwd. by. (Illus.). 224p. 1993. 24.00 (*0-87605-844-6*) Howell Bk.

Pakizer, Debi. Vaulting: The Art of Gymnastics on Horseback. Sears, Mary A., illus. Anderson, Julia & Barnette, Jackie, eds. (Illus.). 24p. (Orig.). (ps-5). 1993. pap. 8.00 (*0-9639785-6-X*) M A Sears. VAULTING: THE ART OF GYMNASTICS ON HORSEBACK - an offical demonstrator sport for the 1996 Summer Olympic games. The sport's origins have been traced to caveman drawings, Mongolian warriors & the Roman Cavalry. The book is an introduction & explanation of the sport's different facets of fun that can be had by all ages doing gymnastic-type moves on a moving horse. It is illustrated with line drawings, with copy to interest, & enlighten, anyone who reads it. Used as an activity book, it combines three facets of learning: kinesthetic (hand-eye coordination), visual, & audio skills to promote total learning & understanding of the sport. "A terrific new book...perfect for vaulters, friends or relatives...it tells all about vaulting!" - Young Equestrian Magazine. It is also very therapeutic for the handicapped, which is another benefit of this sport. The illustrator's daughter's successful progress toward living a more normal life, despite visual & minor cerebral palsy "challenges," is testimony to this fact. Vaulting is for all ages & physical abilities, & this book is a great introduction that ALL will enjoy. To order, write: Mountain Springs Vaulters, 555 W. Sierra Hwy., Acton, CA 93510.
Publisher Provided Annotation.

Robinson, Betty. A Guide to Arkansas Horse Trails. (Illus.). 82p. (Orig.). (gr. 8 up). 1991. pap. 8.95 (*0-929183-03-7*) Equestrian Unlimited.
Robinson, Betty & Gordon, Pat. The Horse Source: A Resource Guide for Mail Order Horse & Rider Supplies. 2nd ed. 60p. (gr. 8 up). 1991. pap. 6.95 (*0-929183-02-9*) Equestrian Unlimited.
Spataro, Lucian. Ride Across America: An Environmental Commitment. Baird, Tate, ed. Goodall, Jane, frwd. by. LC 90-72061. (Illus.). 183p. (gr. 9 up). 1991. 15.95 (*0-914127-44-6*, 1R-1) Univ Class.
Von Neumann-Cosel-Nebe, Isabelle. The Young Rider's Book of Horses & Horsemanship. Von Neumann-Cosel, Felicitas, ed. & tr. from GER. (Illus.). 208p. (gr. 4 up). 1992. 24.95 (*0-939481-24-3*) Half Halt Pr.
Watson, Mary G. Fields & Fencing. Vincer, Carole, illus. 24p. (Orig.). (gr. 3 up). 1988. pap. 10.00 (*0-901366-66-8*, Pub. by Threshold Bks) Half Halt Pr.
Winter, Ginny L. Riding Book. Winter, Ginny L., illus. (gr. k-3). 1963. 8.95 (*0-8392-3031-1*) Astor-Honor.

HORSEMANSHIP–FICTION

Beales, Valerie. Emma & Freckles. Rogers, Jacqueline, illus. LC 91-20751. 208p. (gr. 5-9). 1992. pap. 13.00 jacketed, 3-pc. bdg. (*0-671-74686-3*, S&S BFYR) S&S Trade.
Berenstain, Stan & Berenstain, Jan. The Berenstain Bears & the Galloping Ghost. Berenstain, Stan & Berenstain, Jan, illus. 112p. (Orig.). (gr. 2-6). 1994. 7.99 (*0-679-95815-0*); pap. 2.99 (*0-679-85815-6*) Random Bks Yng Read.
Bryant, Bonnie. Beach Ride. (gr. 4-7). 1993. pap. 3.50 (*0-553-48073-1*) Bantam.
—Bridle Path. (gr. 4-7). 1993. pap. 3.50 (*0-553-48074-X*) Bantam.
—Ranch Hands. (gr. 4-6). 1993. pap. 3.50 (*0-553-48076-6*) Bantam.
—Show Horse. (gr. 4-7). 1992. pap. 3.50 (*0-553-48072-3*) Bantam.
—Stable Manners. (gr. 4-6). 1993. pap. 3.50 (*0-553-48075-8*) Bantam.
—Star Rider. (gr. 4-7). 1991. pap. 3.50 (*0-553-15938-0*) Bantam.
Doty, Jean S. Dark Horse. Chhuy, Dorothy H., illus. LC 82-21651. 122p. (gr. 4-6). 1983. 12.95 (*0-688-01703-7*) Morrow Jr Bks.
Henry, Marguerite. White Stallion of Lipizza. Dennis, Wesley, illus. LC 93-34065. 112p. (gr. 3-7). 1994. pap. 9.95 (*0-689-71824-1*, Aladdin) Macmillan Child Grp.
Hewett, Joan. Laura Loves Horses. Hewett, Richard, photos by. (Illus.). 48p. (gr. 2-5). 1990. 14.45 (*0-89919-844-9*, Clarion Bks) HM.
Hudson, Jan. Dawn Rider. 176p. 1992. pap. 3.25 (*0-590-44987-7*, Point) Scholastic Inc.
Kirkland, Gelsey & Lawrence, Greg. Side Saddle Ballerina. Rogers, Jacqueline, illus. LC 93-20355. 1993. pap. 14.95 (*0-385-46978-0*) Doubleday.
Koda-Callan, Elizabeth. Good Luck Pony. LC 90-50366. 40p. (ps-3). 1990. 12.95 (*0-89480-859-1*, 1859) Workman Pub.
Pascal, Francine. Mansy Miller Fights Back. (gr. 4-7). 1991. pap. 3.50 (*0-553-15880-5*) Bantam.
Scott, Ann H. Someday Rider. Himler, Ronald, illus. 32p. (ps-3). 1991. pap. 4.95 (*0-395-58115-X*, Clarion Bks) HM.
Vail, Virginia. Happy Trails. Bode, Daniel, illus. LC 89-30584. 128p. (gr. 4-6). 1990. PLB 9.89 (*0-8167-1627-7*); pap. text ed. 2.95 (*0-8167-1628-5*) Troll Assocs.

HORSES

see also Ponies

Ancona, George. Man & Mustang. Ancona, George, illus. LC 91-29513. 48p. (gr. 3-7). 1992. RSBE 15.95 (*0-02-700802-9*, Macmillan Child Bk) Macmillan Child Grp.
Brady, Irene. America's Horses & Ponies. Brady, Irene, illus. 202p. (gr. 4 up). 1976. pap. 15.45 (*0-395-24050-6*, Sandpiper) HM.
Chapple, Judy. Your Horse: A Step-by-Step Guide to Horse Ownership. LC 84-22280. (Illus.). 144p. (gr. 8 up). 1984. (Garden Way Pub); pap. 12.95 (*0-88266-353-4*, Graden Way Pub) Storey Comm Inc.
Clayton, Michael & Howard, Tom. The Love of Horses. (Illus.). 96p. 1993. Repr. 12.98 (*0-8317-4597-5*) Smithmark.
Clemens, Virginia P. Horse in Your Backyard: A First-Time Owner's Primer of Horse-Keeping. 1991. 19.95 (*0-13-395088-3*) P-H.
Clutton-Brock, Juliet. Horse. Young, Jerry, photos by. LC 91-53132. (Illus.). 64p. (gr. 5 up). 1992. 16.00 (*0-679-81681-X*); PLB 16.99 (*0-679-91681-4*) Knopf Bks Yng Read.
Cole, Joanna. A Horse's Body. Wexler, Jerome, photos by. LC 80-28147. (Illus.). 48p. (gr. k-3). 1981. 13.95 (*0-688-00362-1*); PLB 13.88 (*0-688-00363-X*, Morrow Jr Bks) Morrow Jr Bks.
Davidson, Margaret. Five True Horse Stories. 1989. pap. 2.75 (*0-590-42400-9*) Scholastic Inc.
Eley, Janet. Understanding Your Horse's Health: A Practical Guide. (Illus.). 144p. (gr. 2 up). 1992. 24.95 (*0-7063-6963-7*, Pub. by Ward Lock UK) Sterling.
Evers, June V., ed. & illus. The Original Book of Horse Treats. 1994. 19.95 (*0-9638814-1-8*) Horse Hollow.
Fowler, Allan. Caballos, Caballos, Caballos: Horses, Horses, Horses. LC 91-35063. (SPA., Illus.). 32p. (ps-2). 1992. PLB 10.75 (*0-516-34921-X*); pap. 3.95 (*0-516-54921-9*); big bk. 22.95 (*0-516-59622-5*) Childrens.
—Horses, Horses, Horses. LC 91-35063. (Illus.). 32p. (ps-2). 1992. PLB 10.75 (*0-516-04921-6*); PLB 22.95 big bk. (*0-516-49622-0*); pap. 3.95 (*0-516-44921-4*) Childrens.
Frisch. Horses. 1991. 11.95s.p. (*0-86625-189-8*) Rourke Pubns.
Fry, Fiona S. Horses. (Illus.). (gr. 6up). 1981. 14.95 (*0-7136-2114-1*) Dufour.
Frydenborg, Kay. They Dreamed of Horses: Careers for Horse Lovers. Wood, Tanya, photos by. LC 93-33023. (Illus.). 128p. (gr. 4-6). 1994. 15.95 (*0-8027-8283-3*); PLB 16.85 (*0-8027-8284-1*) Walker & Co.
Gise, Joanne. A Picture Book of Horses. Pistolesi, Roseanna, illus. LC 90-40437. 24p. (gr. 1-4). 1991. lib. bdg. 9.59 (*0-8167-2152-1*); pap. text ed. 2.50 (*0-8167-2153-X*) Troll Assocs.
Green, Carl R. & Sanford, William R. The Wild Horses. LC 85-13276. (Illus.). 48p. (gr. 5). 1986. text ed. 12.95 RSBE (*0-89686-291-7*, Crestwood Hse) Macmillan Child Grp.
Greydanus, Rose. Horses. Snyder, Joel, illus. LC 82-20296. 32p. (gr. k-2). 1983. lib. bdg. 11.59 (*0-89375-900-7*); pap. 2.95 (*0-8167-1479-7*) Troll Assocs.
Harris, Richard. I Can Read About Horses. LC 72-96960. (Illus.). (gr. 2-4). 1973. pap. 2.50 (*0-89375-054-9*) Troll Assocs.
Henry, Marguerite. Album of Horses. Dennis, Wesley, illus. LC 92-33009. 112p. (gr. 2-5). 1993. pap. 9.95 (*0-689-71709-1*, Aladdin) Macmillan Child Grp.
Henry, Marguerite & Tucker, Ezra, illus. Marguerite Henry's Album of Horses: A Pop-up Book. 12p. (gr. k-3). 1993. pap. 14.95 (*0-689-71685-0*, Aladdin) Macmillan Child Grp.
Herriot, James. Bonny's Big Day. Brown, Ruth, illus. 32p. (gr. k up). 1987. 13.00 (*0-312-01000-1*) St Martin.
—Bonny's Big Day. Brown, Ruth, illus. 32p. 1991. pap. 6.95 (*0-312-06571-X*) St Martin.
Hirschi, Ron. Where Do Horses Live? 1989. 11.95 (*0-8027-6878-4*); lib. bdg. 12.85 (*0-8027-6879-2*) Walker & Co.
Honda, Tetsuya. Wild Horse Winter. (Illus.). 32p. (ps-3). 1992. 12.95 (*0-8118-0251-5*) Chronicle Bks.
Horse. LC 93-20819. (Illus.). 64p. (gr. 6 up). 1993. 15.95 (*1-56458-504-2*) Dorling Kindersley.
Horses: Superfacts. 1992. 4.99 (*0-517-07326-9*) Random Hse Value.
Isenbart, Hans-Heinrich. Birth of a Foal. David, Thomas, illus. LC 85-17406. 48p. (gr. 2-5). 1986. lib. bdg. 19.95 (*0-87614-239-0*) Carolrhoda Bks.
James, Shirley K. Going to a Horse Farm. (Illus.). 32p. (ps-8). 1992. 15.95 (*0-88106-477-7*) Charlesbridge Pub.
Jauck, Andrea & Points, Larry. Assateague: Island of the Wild Ponies. LC 92-5908. (Illus.). 32p. (gr. 1-5). 1993. RSBE 14.95 (*0-02-774695-X*, Macmillan Child Bk) Macmillan Child Grp.
Jones, Teri C. Little Book of Questions & Answers: My Home. Marsh, T. F., illus. 32p. (gr. k-3). 1992. PLB 10.95 (*1-56674-013-4*, HTS Bks) Forest Hse.
Jurmain, Suzanne. One upon a Horse: A History of Horses--& How They Shaped Our History. LC 88-17522. (Illus.). 176p. (gr. 4 up). 1989. 15.95 (*0-688-05550-8*) Lothrop.
Kalas, Sybille. The Wild Horse Family Book. Crampton, Patricia, tr. Kalas, Sybille, illus. LC 89-3929. (ps up). 1991. pap. 15.95 (*0-88708-110-X*) Picture Bk Studio.
Kidd, Jane. Horses & Ponies. (Illus.). 64p. 1989. 7.99 (*0-517-69206-6*) Random Hse Value.
Kidd, Jane, ed. A First Guide to Horse & Pony Care: What Every Young Rider Must Know about Feeding, Grooming & Handling. (Illus.). 208p. (gr. 3-7). 1991. 24.95 (*0-87605-833-0*) Howell Bk.
The Kids' Horse Book. pap. 8.95 (*1-895688-07-8*, Pub. by Greey dePencier CN) Firefly Bks Ltd.
LaBonte, Gail. The Miniature Horse. LC 89-26046. (Illus.). 60p. (gr. 3 up). 1990. text ed. 13.95 RSBE (*0-87518-424-3*, Dillon) Macmillan Child Grp.
Locker, Thomas. The Mare on the Hill. Locker, Thomas, illus. LC 85-1684. 32p. (gr. k-12). 1985. 15.95 (*0-8037-0207-8*); PLB 15.89 (*0-8037-0208-6*) Dial Bks Young.
Lucas, Zoe. Wild Horses of Sable Island. (Illus.). 36p. (gr. 2 up). 1992. pap. 4.95 (*0-919872-73-5*, Pub. by Greey de Pencier CN) Firefly Bks Ltd.
McFarland, Cynthia. Hoofbeats: The Story of a Thoroughbred. LC 92-14255. (Illus.). 32p. (gr. 1-3). 1993. SBE 14.95 (*0-689-31757-3*, Atheneum Child Bk) Macmillan Child Grp.
McGowan, E. M. Horses & Ponies, A Photo-Fact Book. (Illus., Orig.). 1988. pap. 1.95 (*0-942025-26-1*) Kidsbks.
Maynard, Christopher. Horses. LC 92-32264. 32p. (gr. 1-4). 1993. 3.95 (*1-85697-894-X*, Kingfisher LKC) LKC.
Morgan, Jenny. Herbs for Horses, No. 27: Threshold Picture Guide. Vincer, Carole, illus. 24p. (Orig.). 1993. pap. 12.00 (*1-872082-46-7*, Pub. by Kenilworth Pr UK) Half Halt Pr.
Morris, Dean. Horses. rev. ed. LC 87-16690. (Illus.). 48p. (Orig.). (gr. 2-6). 1987. PLB 10.95 (*0-8172-3209-5*) Raintree Steck-V.
Patent, Dorothy H. Appaloosa Horses. Munoz, William, photos by. LC 88-4470. (Illus.). 80p. (gr. 3-7). 1988. reinforced bdg. 14.95 (*0-8234-0706-3*) Holiday.
—Baby Horses. Munoz, William, photos by. 56p. (ps-1). 1991. PLB 17.50 (*0-87614-690-6*) Carolrhoda Bks.
—Horses. Munoz, William, photos by. LC 93-12329. 1993. 14.95 (*0-87614-766-X*) Carolrhoda Bks.
—Horses of America. LC 81-4165. (Illus.). 80p. (gr. 3-7). 1981. reinforced bdg. 15.95 (*0-8234-0399-8*) Holiday.
—Miniature Horses. Munoz, William, photos by. LC 90-38641. (Illus.). 48p. (gr. 3-7). 1991. 14.95 (*0-525-65049-0*, Cobblehill Bks) Dutton Child Bks.
Pope, Joyce. Horses. (Illus.). 32p. (gr. 4-6). 1991. 13.95 (*0-237-60173-7*, Pub. by Evans Bros Ltd) Trafalgar.
Posell, Elsa. Horses. LC 81-7741. (Illus.). 48p. (gr. k-4). 1981. PLB 12.85 (*0-516-01623-7*); pap. 4.95 (*0-516-41623-5*) Childrens.
Reynolds, Jan. Mongolia: Vanishing Cultures. LC 93-1351. (gr. 6 up). 1994. 16.95 (*0-15-255312-6*); pap. 8.95 (*0-15-255313-4*) HarBrace.
Rodenas, Paula. The Random House Book of Horses & Horsemanship. Cassels, Jean, illus. Farley, Walter, frwd. by. LC 86-42934. (Illus.). 192p. (gr. 3-7). 1991. 17.95 (*0-394-88705-0*); PLB 18.99 (*0-394-98705-5*) Random Bks Yng Read.
Rose, Marilyn S. My First Horse. 53p. (Orig.). (gr. 3-4). 1991. pap. 9.95 (*0-9632117-0-6*) AMI & Arabian Mktg.

Rounds, Glen. Wild Horses. Rounds, Glen, illus. LC 92-73608. 32p. (ps-3). 1993. reinforced bdg. 14.95 (*0-8234-1019-6*) Holiday.
Sale, Laurie. English Thoroughbred. (gr. 4-7). 1994. 10.95 (*0-8362-4217-3*) Andrews & McMeel.
Slade, Michael. Horses of Central Park. (gr. 4-7). 1994. pap. 2.95 (*0-590-44068-3*) Scholastic Inc.
Spector, Joanna. Horses & Ponies. (Illus.). 64p. (gr. 3 up). 1993. pap. 4.95 (*0-86020-255-0*, Usborne) EDC.
Spinelli, Eileen. Horses. (Illus.). 64p. (gr. k-4). 1992. PLB 13.75 (*1-878363-85-9*, HTS Bks) Forest Hse.
Stephens, Nancy. Horse Tails: A Look at Life with Horses. (Illus.). 220p. (Orig.). (gr. 7-12). 1990. pap. 9.95 (*0-685-29151-0*) Squared Away.
Stone, L. Caballos (Horses) 1991. 8.95s.p. (*0-86592-987-4*) Rourke Enter.
Stone, Lynn. Horses. (Illus.). 24p. (gr. k-5). 1990. lib. bdg. 11.94 (*0-86593-035-X*); lib. bdg. 8.95s.p. (*0-685-36311-2*) Rourke Corp.
Van der Linde, Laurel. From Mustangs to Movie Stars: Five True Horse Legends of Our Time. LC 94-25866. 1995. write for info. (*1-562-94456-8*) Millbrook Pr.
Von Neumann-Cosel-Nebe, Isabelle. The Young Rider's Book of Horses & Horsemanship. Von Neumann-Cosel, Felicitas, ed. & tr. from GER. (Illus.). 208p. (gr. 4 up). 1992. 24.95 (*0-939481-24-3*) Half Halt Pr.
Wallace, Jane. Poles & Gridwork, No. 26: Threshold Picture Guide. Vincer, Carole, illus. 24p. (Orig.). 1993. pap. 12.00 (*1-872082-44-0*, Pub. by Kenilworth Pr UK) Half Halt Pr.
—Solving Flatwork Problems, No. 25: Threshold Picture Guide. Vincer, Carole, illus. 24p. (Orig.). 1993. pap. 12.00 (*1-872082-43-2*, Pub. by Kenilworth Pr UK) Half Halt Pr.
Watson, Mary G. Feeds & Feeding. Vincer, Carole, illus. 24p. (Orig.). (gr. 3 up). 1988. pap. 10.00 (*0-901366-37-4*, Pub. by Threshold Bks) Half Halt Pr.
Wildlife Education, Ltd. Staff. Wild Horses. Hoopes, Barbara, illus. 20p. (Orig.). (gr. 5 up). 1982. pap. 2.75 (*0-937934-08-9*) Wildlife Educ.
Wilson, Kay. Arab Horses. (gr. 2-9). 1986. 7.95x (*0-86685-481-9*) Intl Bk Ctr.

HORSES–FICTION

Adler, Carole S. Riding Whiskey. LC 93-30196. 1994. 13.95 (*0-395-68185-5*, Clarion Bks) HM.
Allen, Adrianne T. Sheila's Show Biz Days. Shelia, illus. 64p. (Orig.). (gr. k-6). 1993. pap. 9.95 (*0-685-65119-3*) Colonial Pr AL.
Alter, Judy. Maggie & a Horse Named Devildust. Shaw, Charles, illus. LC 88-22815. 160p. (gr. 4-9). 1989. pap. 5.95 (*0-936650-08-7*) E C Temple.
—Maggie & the Search for Devildust. Shaw, Charles, illus. LC 88-8019. 160p. (gr. 4-9). 1989. pap. 5.95 (*0-936650-09-5*) E C Temple.
Anderson, C. W. Billy & Blaze: A Boy & His Pony. 2nd ed. LC 91-29882. (Illus.). 56p. (gr. k-3). 1992. pap. 3.95 (*0-689-71608-7*, Aladdin) Macmillan Child Grp.
—Blaze & Thunderbolt: Billy & Blaze Head West. Anderson, C. W., illus. LC 92-27153. 48p. (gr. k-3). 1993. pap. 3.95 PB (*0-689-71712-1*, Aladdin) Macmillan Child Grp.
Anderson, Ella. Jo-Jo. (gr. 2-7). 1979. pap. 2.95 (*0-87508-693-4*) Chr Lit.
Ayres, Becky H. Per & the Dala Horse. Gilbert, Yvonne, illus. LC 93-38596. 1995. write for info. (*0-385-32075-2*) Doubleday.
Baber, Carolyn S. Little Billy. Fleischman, Luke T., illus. 175p. (gr. 5-9). Date not set. PLB 14.95 (*0-944727-29-8*) Jason & Nordic Pubs.
Bagdon, Paul. Scrapper John: Valley of the Spotted Horse. (gr. 4-7). 1992. pap. 3.50 (*0-380-76416-4*, Camelot) Avon.
Bagnold, Enid. National Velvet. 293p. 1981. Repr. PLB 16.95x (*0-89966-359-1*) Buccaneer Bks.
—National Velvet. 339p. 1981. Repr. PLB 18.95 (*0-89967-033-4*) Harmony Raine.
—National Velvet. Lewin, Ted, illus. LC 85-2982. 207p. (gr. 3 up). 1985. 15.95 (*0-688-05788-8*) Morrow Jr Bks.
—National Velvet. 272p. 1991. pap. 3.99 (*0-380-71235-0*, Flare) Avon.
Balch, Glenn. Christmas Horse. Crowell, Pers, illus. Woodward, Tim, intro. by. (Illus.). 1990. pap. 9.95 (*0-931659-10-8*) Limberlost Pr.
Bashful Bard. Cricket & the Flying Horse. Bashful Bard, illus. LC 89-84946. 28p. (Orig.). (ps-1). 1989. Kenney Pubns.
Bauer, Marion D. Touch the Moon. Berenzy, Alix, illus. LC 87-663. 96p. (gr. 4-7). 1987. 14.95 (*0-89919-526-1*, Clarion Bks) HM.
Berg, Jean H. Mr. Koonan's Bargain. LC 70-158559. (gr. 1-4). 1971. 7.95 (*0-87874-002-3*, Nautilus) Galloway.
Berst, Barbara. We Are Farmers. Berst, Barbara, illus. 24p. (Orig.). (ps-2). 1990. acid-free cotton paper 25.00, (*0-9614126-3-1*); pap. 9.95 (*0-9614126-2-3*) Natl Lilac Pub.
Birch, Claire. High Stakes. (gr. 4-7). 1992. pap. 2.99 (*0-440-40583-1*) Dell.
Birkenhead. Biggest Horse You Ever Did See. Date not set. 15.00 (*0-06-023467-9*); PLB 14.89 (*0-06-023468-7*) HarpC Child Bks.
Black Beauty & Thirteen other Horse Stories. 544p. (gr. 2-10). 1991. 8.99 (*0-517-32104-1*) Random Hse Value.
Blanc, Esther S. Berchick, My Mother's Horse. Dixon, Tennessee, illus. LC 87-37172. 36p. (gr. k-5). 1989. 14.95 (*0-912078-81-2*) Volcano Pr.
Blumberg, Leda. Breezy. 96p. (gr. 3-7). 1988. pap. 2.50 (*0-380-89942-6*, Camelot) Avon.
Boegehold, Betty D. Horse Called Starfire. 1990. 9.99 (*0-553-05861-4*) Bantam.
Brett, Jan. Fritz & the Beautiful Horses. Brett, Jan, illus. 32p. (gr. k-3). 1981. 14.95 (*0-395-30850-X*); pap. 4.80 (*0-395-45356-9*) HM.
Bryant, Bonnie. Beach Ride. (gr. 4-7). 1993. pap. 3.50 (*0-553-48073-1*) Bantam.
—Bridle Path. (gr. 4-7). 1993. pap. 3.50 (*0-553-48074-X*) Bantam.
—Chocolate Horse. (gr. 4-7). 1994. pap. 3.50 (*0-553-48146-0*) Bantam.
—Fox Hunt. (gr. 4-7). 1992. pap. 3.50 (*0-553-15990-9*) Bantam.
—Ghost Rider. (gr. 4-7). 1992. pap. 3.50 (*0-553-48067-7*) Bantam.
—Hayride. (gr. 4-7). 1993. pap. 3.50 (*0-553-48145-2*) Bantam.
—High Horse. 1994. pap. 3.50 (*0-553-48147-9*) Bantam.
—Horse Games. (gr. 4-7). 1991. pap. 3.25 (*0-553-15882-1*) Bantam.
—Horse Shy, Bk. No. 2. (gr. 3-7). 1988. pap. 2.75 (*0-317-69287-9*) Bantam.
—Horse Trouble. 1992. pap. 3.50 (*0-553-48025-1*) Bantam.
—Pack Trip. (gr. 4-7). 1991. pap. 3.50 (*0-553-15928-3*) Bantam.
—Ranch Hands. (gr. 4-6). 1993. pap. 3.50 (*0-553-48076-6*) Bantam.
—Saddle Club. 1992. pap. 3.50 (*0-553-15983-6*) Bantam.
—Sea Horse. (gr. 4-7). 1991. pap. 3.50 (*0-553-15847-3*) Bantam.
—Show Horse. (gr. 4-7). 1992. pap. 3.50 (*0-553-48072-3*) Bantam.
—Snow Ride. 1992. pap. 3.50 (*0-553-15907-0*) Bantam.
—Stable Manners. (gr. 4-6). 1993. pap. 3.50 (*0-553-48075-8*) Bantam.
—Star Rider. (gr. 4-7). 1991. pap. 3.50 (*0-553-15938-0*) Bantam.
—Starlight Christmas. (gr. 4-7). 1990. pap. 3.50 (*0-553-15832-5*) Bantam.
—Team Play. (gr. 4-7). 1991. pap. 3.50 (*0-553-15862-7*) Bantam.
Bulla, Clyde R. Three-Dollar Mule. Lantz, Paul, illus. LC 94-18508. 96p. (gr. 1-3). 1995. pap. text ed. 2.95 (*0-8167-3598-0*) Troll Assocs.
Bunting, Eve. The Wild Horses. (Illus.). 64p. (gr. 3-8). 1992. 8.95 (*0-89565-778-3*) Childs World.
Bussolati, Emanuela. The Horse. Michelini, Carlo A., illus. LC 92-72118. 10p. (ps). 1993. 6.95 (*1-56397-201-8*) Boyds Mills Pr.
Byars, Betsy C. The Winged Colt of Casa Mia. Cuffari, Richard, illus. 132p. (gr. 3-7). 1981. pap. 2.95 (*0-380-00201-9*, Camelot) Avon.
Calvert, Patricia. The Snowbird. LC 80-19139. 160p. (gr. 7 up). 1989. SBE 13.95 (*0-684-19120-2*, Scribners Young Read) Macmillan Child Grp.
—The Stone Pony. 160p. (gr. 7-9). 1983. pap. 2.99 (*0-451-13729-9*, Sig) NAL-Dutton.
Campbell, Barbara. Taking Care of Yoki. LC 85-46040. 160p. (gr. 3-7). 1986. pap. 3.95 (*0-06-440173-1*, Trophy) HarpC Child Bks.
Campbell, Joanna. Ashleigh's Dream. (gr. 4-7). 1993. pap. 3.50 (*0-06-106737-7*, Harp PBks) HarpC.
—A Horse Called Wonder. (gr. 4-7). 1991. pap. 3.50 (*0-06-106120-4*, Harp PBks) HarpC.
—Star of Shadowbrook Farm. 1992. pap. 3.50 (*0-06-106783-0*, Harp PBks) HarpC.
—Thoroughbred: A Horse Called Wonder. 1992. pap. 3.50 (*0-06-106724-5*, Harp PBks) HarpC.
—The Wild Mustang. (gr. 3-5). 1989. pap. 3.50 (*0-553-15698-5*, Skylark) Bantam.
—Wonder's First Race. (gr. 6-9). 1991. pap. 3.50 (*0-06-106082-8*, Harp PBks) HarpC.
—Wonder's First Race. 1993. pap. 3.50 (*0-06-106704-0*, Harp PBks) HarpC.
—Wonder's Promise. 1991. pap. 3.50 (*0-06-106085-2*, Harp PBks) HarpC.
—Wonder's Promise. 1992. pap. 3.50 (*0-06-106705-9*, Harp PBks) HarpC.
—Wonder's Victory. (gr. 7-9). 1991. pap. 3.50 (*0-06-106083-6*, Harp PBks) HarpC.
—Wonder's Victory. (gr. 4-7). 1993. pap. 3.50 (*0-06-106703-2*, Harp PBks) HarpC.
—Wonder's Yearling. (gr. 4-7). 1993. pap. 3.50 (*0-06-106747-4*, Harp PBks) HarpC.
Cavanna, Betty. Banner Year. LC 87-23692. 224p. (gr. 7 up). 1987. 12.95 (*0-688-05779-9*) Morrow Jr Bks.
Christman, Ernest H. & Christman, Catherine. Darby's Stable: Cartoons & Stories, Level Two, Progressive Phonics. LC 84-50859. (Illus.). 88p. (Orig.). (gr. k-12). 1984. pap. text ed. 7.50 (*0-912329-04-1*) Tutorial Press.
Clymer, Eleanor. The Horse in the Attic. Lewin, Ted, illus. LC 83-6377. 96p. (gr. 3-6). 1983. SBE 14.00 (*0-02-719040-4*, Bradbury Pr) Macmillan Child Grp.
Cocquyt, Kathryn. Little Freddie at the Kentucky Derby. Corbett, Sylvia, illus. LC 91-23540. 128p. (gr. 4-7). 1992. 13.95 (*0-88289-856-6*) Pelican.
—Little Freddie's Legacy. Corbett, Sylvia, illus. LC 93-5558. 1994. 13.95 (*1-56554-000-X*) Pelican.
Coerr, Eleanor. Chang's Paper Pony. Ray, Deborah K., illus. LC 87-45679. 64p. (gr. k-3). 1988. 14.00 (*0-06-021328-0*); PLB 13.89 (*0-06-021329-9*) HarpC Child Bks.
Cole, Babette. Winni Allfours. Cole, Babette, illus. LC 93-28447. (gr. k-4). 1993. PLB 13.95 (*0-8167-3308-2*); pap. 3.95t (*0-8167-3307-4*) BrdgeWater.
Cosgrove, Stephen. Glitterby Baby. James, Robin, illus. LC 85-14354. 32p. (Orig.). (gr. 1-4). 1978. pap. 3.95 (*0-8431-1166-6*) Price Stern.
—Mumkin. James, Robin, illus. 32p. (Orig.). (gr. 1-4). 1986. pap. 2.95 (*0-8431-1431-2*) Price Stern.
—Nitter Pitter. James, Robin, illus. 32p. (Orig.). (gr. 1-4). 1978. pap. 3.95 (*0-8431-0570-4*) Price Stern.
Coville, Bruce. Herds of Thunder, Manes of Gold: A Collection of Horse Stories & Poems. Lewin, Ted, illus. LC 88-34651. 176p. (gr. 5-10). 1989. 15.95 (*0-385-24642-0*) Doubleday.
Currie, Quinn. Black Beauty. rev. ed. Ryan, Donna, illus. 126p. (gr. k-8). 1990. pap. 10.95 (*0-9623072-2-X*) S Ink WA.
Denton, Kady M. Janet's Horses. Denton, Kady M., illus. 32p. (ps-2). 1991. 12.70 (*0-395-51601-3*, Clarion Bks) HM.
Dickerson, Karle. Forgotten Filly. (gr. 4-7). 1993. pap. 3.50 (*0-06-106732-6*, Harp PBks) HarpC.
Doherty, Berlie. Snowy. Bowen, Keith, illus. LC 91-47519. 32p. (ps-3). 1993. 14.00 (*0-8037-1343-6*) Dial Bks Young.
Dryden, Pamela. Riding Home. 144p. (gr. 3-7). 1988. pap. 2.95 (*0-553-15591-1*) Bantam.
Duncan, Lois. Horses of Dreamland. Diamond, Donna, illus. 32p. (ps-3). 1986. 12.95 (*0-316-19554-5*) Little.
Easton, Patricia H. Rebel's Choice. 153p. (gr. 7 up). 1989. 14.95 (*0-15-200571-4*, Gulliver Bks) HarBrace.
Endersby, Frank. The Boy & the Horse. Endersby, Frank, illus. LC 90-46601. 16p. (ps-2). 1976. 11.95 (*0-85953-098-1*, Pub. by Child's Play England) Childs Play.
Escoula, Yvonne. Six Blue Horses. LC 70-103044. (gr. 5-9). 1970. 21.95 (*0-87599-162-9*) S G Phillips.
Eytcheson, Pat. Catch a Winner. Eakin, Edwin M., ed. Peacock, Joe, illus. 48p. (gr. 2-3). 1989. 10.95 (*0-89015-704-9*, Pub. by Panda Bks) Sunbelt Media.
—Catch a Winner Leaves the Ranch. Peacock, Joe, illus. 48p. (gr. 1-3). 1991. 10.95 (*0-89015-828-2*) Sunbelt Media.
Farley, Walter. Black Stallion. Ward, Keith, illus. LC 85-19927. (gr. 3-7). 1944. lib. bdg. 13.99 (*0-394-90601-2*) Random Bks Yng Read.
—Black Stallion Challenged. LC 64-15094. (Illus.). (gr. 5-9). 1980. Random Bks Yng Read.
—The Black Stallion Legend. LC 83-1870. (Illus.). 192p. (gr. 5-8). 1985. pap. 3.95 (*0-394-87500-1*) Random Bks Yng Read.
—The Black Stallion's Blood Bay Colt. reissued ed. LC 50-9584. 288p. (gr. 4-7). 1994. pap. 3.95 (*0-679-81347-0*) Random Bks Yng Read.
—Black Stallion's Filly. LC 52-7216. (Illus.). (gr. 4-6). 1978. pap. 3.95 (*0-394-83916-1*) Random Bks Yng Read.
—Black Stallion's Ghost. Draper, Angie, illus. (gr. 5-9). 1978. pap. 3.95 (*0-394-83919-6*) Random Bks Yng Read.
—The Horse-Tamer. LC 58-9030. 160p. (gr. 5-8). 1980. Random Bks Yng Read.
—Island Stallion. (Illus.). (gr. 5-6). 1980. pap. 4.95 (*0-394-84376-2*) Random Bks Yng Read.
—Little Black, a Pony. LC 61-7789. (Illus.). 62p. (gr. 1-2). 1961. lib. bdg. 7.99 (*0-394-90021-9*) Beginner.
—Man O' War. LC 62-9000. (Illus.). 352p. (gr. 5-9). 1983. 4.99 (*0-394-86015-2*) Knopf Bks Yng Read.
Farley, Walter & Farley, Steven. The Young Black Stallion. LC 89-42763. 192p. (gr. 5-9). 1989. 10.95 (*0-394-84562-5*) Random Bks Yng Read.
Feagles, Anita. Casey, the Utterly Impossible Horse. Wilson, Dagmar W., illus. LC 88-13871. 96p. (gr. 3-7). 1989. Repr. of 1960 ed. lib. bdg. 16.00 (*0-208-02239-2*, Linnet) Shoe String.
Fleischman, Paul. Path of the Pale Horse. LC 82-48611. 160p. (gr. 6 up). 1983. PLB 12.89 (*0-06-021905-X*) HarpC Child Bks.
Fleischman, Sid. Midnight Horse. (gr. 4-7). 1992. pap. 3.50 (*0-440-40614-5*) Dell.
Garland, Sherry. Best Horse on the Force. 112p. (gr. 4-6). 1991. 13.95 (*0-8050-1658-9*, Bks Young Read) H Holt & Co.
Gibson, Sylvia S. Latawnya, the Naughty Horse, Learns to Say "No" to Drugs. 1990. 6.95 (*0-533-09102-0*) Vantage.
Gilbert, Miriam. Rosie: The Oldest Horse in St. Augustine. Roch, J., illus. LC 67-30409. (FRE, SPA & ENG.). (gr. k-6). 1974. 6.95 (*0-87208-105-2*); pap. 5.95 (*0-87208-007-2*) Island Pr Pubs.
Goble, Paul. The Girl Who Loved Wild Horses. Goble, Paul, illus. LC 77-20500. 32p. (gr. k-3). 1982. SBE 14.95 (*0-02-736570-0*, Bradbury Pr) Macmillan Child Grp.
—The Girl Who Loved Wild Horses. Goble, Paul, illus. LC 92-29560. 32p. (ps-3). 1993. pap. 4.95 (*0-689-71696-6*, Aladdin) Macmillan Child Grp.
Goudge, Elizabeth. The Little White Horse. 1976. 25.95 (*0-89966-474-1*) Buccaneer Bks.
—The Little White Horse. 272p. (gr. 5 up). 1992. pap. 3.99 (*0-440-40734-6*, YB) Dell.
Greaves, Margaret. Star Horse. (ps-3). 1992. 13.95 (*0-8120-6294-9*) Barron.
Green, Timothy. Mystery of Navajo Moon. Green, Timothy, illus. LC 91-52600. 48p. (ps-4). 1991. pap. 7.95 (*0-87358-577-1*) Northland AZ.
Gruenberg, Linda. Hummer. 192p. (gr. 5-9). 1990. 13.45 (*0-395-51080-5*) HM.
Gwynne, Fred. The Sixteen-Hand Horse. Gwynne, Fred, illus. LC 79-13284. (gr. 1-5). 1987. P-H Gen Ref & Trav.

—The Sixteen Hand Horse. Gwynne, Fred, illus. LC 79-13284. (gr. 1-6). 1987. pap. 11.95 (*0-671-66291-0*, S&S BFYR); pap. 5.95 (*0-671-66968-0*, S&S BFYR) S&S Trade.
Haas, Jessie. A Blue for Beware. Smith, Joseph A., photos by. LC 94-4572. (Illus.). 1995. write for info. RTE (*0-688-13678-8*) Greenwillow.
—A Horse Like Barney. LC 92-34386. 176p. (gr. 5 up). 1993. 13.00 (*0-688-12415-1*) Greenwillow.
—No Foal Yet. Smith, Joseph A., illus. LC 94-6265. 32p. 1995. write for info. (*0-688-12925-0*); PLB write for info. (*0-688-12926-9*) Greenwillow.
—Uncle Daney's Way. LC 93-22192. (gr. 4 up). 1994. 14.00 (*0-688-12794-0*) Greenwillow.
Hall, Lynn. Flying Changes. D'Andrade, Diane, ed. 148p. (gr. 9 up). 1991. 13.95 (*0-15-228790-6*) HarBrace.
—Ride a Dark Horse. LC 87-12310. 176p. (gr. 7 up). 1987. 12.95 (*0-688-07471-5*) Morrow Jr Bks.
—The Something-Special Horse. Rabinowitz, Sandy, illus. LC 84-23636. 112p. (gr. 4-7). 1985. SBE 13.95 (*0-684-18343-9*, Scribners Young Read) Macmillan Child Grp.
Harding. Alvin's No Horse. 1994. pap. 4.95 (*0-8050-3274-6*) H Holt & Co.
Harris, Aurand. Ride a Blue Horse. 44p. (Orig.). (gr. k-3). 1986. pap. 4.50 playscript (*0-87602-264-6*) Anchorage.
Hart, Alison. A Horse for Mary Beth. LC 93-86083. 132p. (Orig.). (gr. 3-7). 1994. pap. 3.50 (*0-679-85692-7*) Random Bks Yng Read.
Haynes, Betsy. Taffy Sinclair, Queen of the Soaps. (ps-7). 1988. pap. 3.25 (*0-553-15647-0*, Skylark) Bantam.
Heilbroner, Joan. Robert the Rose Horse. LC 62-9218. (Illus.). 72p. (gr. 1-2). 1962. 6.95 (*0-394-80025-7*); lib. bdg. 7.99 (*0-394-90025-1*) Beginner.
Henning, Ann. The Connemara Stallion. 224p. (Orig.). (gr. 7-10). 1991. pap. 9.95 (*1-85371-158-6*, Pub. by Poolbeg Pr ER) Dufour.
Henry, Marguerite. Black Gold. 2nd ed. LC 91-4907. (Illus.). 176p. (gr. 3-7). 1992. pap. 3.95 (*0-689-71562-5*, Aladdin) Macmillan Child Grp.
—Born to Trot. 2nd ed. LC 92-24139. (Illus.). 224p. (gr. 3-6). 1993. pap. 3.95 (*0-689-71692-3*, Aladdin) Macmillan Child Grp.
—Justin Morgan Had a Horse. 2nd ed. Dennis, Wesley, illus. LC 91-13973. 176p. (gr. 3-7). 1991. pap. 3.95 (*0-689-71534-X*, Aladdin) Macmillan Child Grp.
—Marguerite Henry's Horseshoe Library: Stormy, Misty's Foal; Sea Star, Orphan of Chincoteague; Misty of Chincoteague, 3 bks. (Illus.). (gr. 3-7). 1992. Set. pap. 11.85 (*0-689-71624-9*, Aladdin) Macmillan Child Grp.
—Misty of Chincoteague. reissued ed. Dennis, Wesley, illus. LC 47-11404. 176p. (gr. 3-7). 1990. SBE 13.95 (*0-02-743622-5*, Macmillan Child Bk) Macmillan Child Grp.
—Misty of Chincoteague. Dennis, Wesley, illus. LC 90-27237. 176p. (gr. 3-7). 1991. pap. 3.95 (*0-689-71492-0*, Aladdin) Macmillan Child Grp.
—Misty's Twilight. Pre, Karen G., illus. LC 91-42582. 144p. (gr. 3-7). 1992. SBE 13.95 (*0-02-743623-3*, Macmillan Child Bk) Macmillan Child Grp.
—Mustang, Wild Spirit of the West. Lougheed, Robert, illus. LC 91-25187. 224p. (gr. 3-7). 1992. pap. 3.95 (*0-689-71601-X*, Aladdin) Macmillan Child Grp.
—Our First Pony. Rudish, Rich, illus. LC 84-13409. 64p. (gr. 1-5). 1995. 15.95 (*0-02-743625-X*) Macmillan Child Grp.
—A Pictorial Life Story of Misty. LC 76-41864. (Illus.). 112p. (gr. 3 up). 1995. 15.95 (*0-02-743626-8*) Macmillan Child Grp.
—San Domingo: The Medicine Hat Stallion. Lougheed, Robert, illus. LC 91-46020. 240p. (gr. 3-7). 1992. pap. 3.95 (*0-689-71631-1*, Aladdin) Macmillan Child Grp.
—Sea Star: Orphan of Chincoteague. LC 49-11474. (Illus.). 176p. (gr. 3-7). 1991. SBE 13.95 (*0-02-743627-6*); pap. 3.95 (*0-689-71530-7*, Aladdin) Macmillan Child Grp.
—Stormy: Misty's Foal. Dennis, Wesley, illus. LC 63-13334. 224p. (gr. 2-9). 1987. 8.95 (*0-528-82083-4*, Aladdin Bks); (Aladdin Bks) Macmillan Child Grp.
—Stormy, Misty's Foal. Dennis, Wesley, illus. LC 90-27306. 224p. (gr. 3-7). 1991. pap. 3.95 (*0-689-71487-4*, Aladdin) Macmillan Child Grp.
—The White Stallion of Lipizza. Dennis, Wesley, illus. LC 93-86024. 112p. (gr. 3-7). 1994. Repr. of 1964 ed. SBE 14.95 (*0-02-743628-4*, Macmillan Child Bk) Macmillan Child Grp.
—White Stallion of Lipizza. Dennis, Wesley, illus. LC 93-34065. 112p. (gr. 3-7). 1994. pap. 9.95 (*0-689-71824-1*, Aladdin) Macmillan Child Grp.
Highlights for Children Staff. Storm's Fury: And Other Horse Stories. LC 90-85910. (Illus.). 96p. (gr. 3-7). 1992. pap. 2.95 (*1-878093-31-2*) Boyds Mills Pr.
Hiller, B. B. Horse Crazy, No. 1. 144p. (Orig.). 1988. pap. 3.50 (*0-553-15594-6*, Skylark) Bantam.
—The Saddle Club, Bk. 2. 144p. (Orig.). 1988. pap. 3.50 (*0-553-15611-X*, Skylark) Bantam.
Hodges, Margaret. The Little Humpbacked Horse. Conover, Chris, illus. 32p. (ps up). 1987. pap. 3.95 (*0-374-44495-1*) FS&G.
Hoff, Syd. Barney's Horse. Hoff, Syd, illus. LC 87-66. 32p. (ps-3). 1987. PLB 13.89 (*0-06-022450-9*) HarpC Child Bks.
—Barney's Horse. Hoff, Syd, illus. LC 87-66. 32p. (ps-2). 1990. pap. 3.50 (*0-06-444142-3*, Trophy) HarpC Child Bks.
—Chester. Hoff, Syd, illus. LC 61-5768. 64p. (gr. k-3). 1961. PLB 13.89 (*0-06-022456-8*) HarpC Child Bks.
—Chester. Hoff, Syd, illus. LC 61-5768. 64p. (gr. k-3). 1986. pap. 3.50 (*0-06-444095-8*, Trophy) HarpC Child Bks.
—Horse in Harry's Room. Hoff, Syd, illus. LC 71-104753. 32p. (gr. k-3). 1970. PLB 13.89 (*0-06-022483-5*) HarpC Child Bks.
—The Horse in Harry's Room. Hoff, Syd, illus. LC 71-104753. 32p. (ps-2). 1985. pap. 3.50 (*0-06-444073-7*, Trophy) HarpC Child Bks.
—Thunderhoof. Hoff, Syd, illus. LC 75-129855. (gr. k-3). 1971. PLB 13.89 (*0-685-02069-X*) HarpC Child Bks.
Holland, Barbara. The Pony Problem. 128p. (gr. 3-7). 1993. pap. 3.99 (*0-14-036339-4*) Puffin Bks.
Holland, Isabelle. Toby the Splendid. LC 86-24681. 160p. (gr. 5 up). 1987. 13.95 (*0-8027-6674-9*); PLB 14.85 (*0-8027-6675-7*) Walker & Co.
Holmes, Frank, Jr. & Montgomery, K. C. Crystal's Vision. Wedel, Gail, ed. Montgomery, K. C., illus. 28p. (ps-3). 1992. 16.95x (*1-883005-00-0*) Holmes & Mont.
Hoppe, Joanne. Pretty Penny Farm. LC 86-1516. 224p. (gr. 7 up). 1987. 12.95 (*0-688-07201-1*) Morrow Jr Bks.
Hovde, Jeanne. A Horse for Cassie. LC 88-7355. 132p. (gr. 3-7). 1988. pap. 4.99 (*1-55513-587-0*, Chariot Bks) Chariot Family.
Irwin, Hadley. Jim-Dandy. LC 93-22611. 144p. (gr. 5-9). 1994. SBE 14.95 (*0-689-50594-9*, M K McElderry) Macmillan Child Grp.
James, Will. Smoky the Cow Horse. 2nd ed. James, Will, illus. LC 92-28753. 324p. (gr. 3-7). 1993. pap. 3.95 (*0-689-71682-6*, Aladdin) Macmillan Child Grp.
Jeffers, Susan. If Wishes Were Horses. LC 79-9986. (Illus.). 32p. (ps-3). 1987. pap. 3.95 (*0-525-44325-8*, 0383-120, DCB) Dutton Child Bks.
Johnson, Robin. Horse Stories. (Illus.). 96p. (Orig.). (gr. 5-9). 1988. pap. 1.95 (*0-942025-18-0*) Kidsbks.
Johnston, D. John & the Little Horse. 1993. 7.95 (*0-533-10264-2*) Vantage.
Kanno, Wendy. Sampson Horse. Reese, Bob, illus. (gr. k-2). 1984. 7.95 (*0-89868-163-4*); pap. 2.95 (*0-89868-164-2*) ARO Pub.
King, Deborah. Custer: The Story of a Horse. King, Deborah, illus. 32p. (ps-3). 1992. PLB 14.95 (*0-399-22147-6*, Philomel Bks) Putnam Pub Group.
King-Smith, Dick. Find the White Horse. large type ed. Wilkes, Larry, illus. 1993. 16.95 (*0-7451-1804-6*, Galaxy Child Lrg Print) Chivers N Amer.
—The Water Horse. large type ed. Parkins, David, illus. 124p. 1992. PLB 13.95 (*0-7451-1610-8*, Lythway Large Print) Hall.
Kirkland, Gelsey & Lawrence, Greg. Side Saddle Ballerina. Rogers, Jacqueline, illus. LC 93-20355. 1993. pap. 14.95 (*0-385-46978-0*) Doubleday.
Klemin, Diana. How Do You Wrap a Horse? Demarest, Chris L., illus. 32p. (ps-3). 1993. 14.95 (*1-56397-187-9*) Boyds Mills Pr.
Klusmeyer, Joann. Shelly from Rockytop Farm. Taylor, Neil, illus. 65p. (gr. 3-6). 1986. 5.95 (*1-55523-014-8*) Winston-Derek.
Koertge, Ron. The Arizona Kid. 224p. (gr. 7 up). 1989. pap. 3.99 (*0-380-70776-4*, Flare) Avon.
Kontoyiannaki, Kosta. Horse Rides for Homer. Kontoyiannaki, Kosta, illus. 15p. (gr. k-3). 1992. pap. 12.95 (*1-895583-21-7*) MAYA Pubs.
Krauss, Ruth. Charlotte & the White Horse. LC 55-8819. (Illus.). 24p. (gr. k-3). 1969. PLB 11.89 (*0-06-023361-3*) HarpC Child Bks.
Kudlinski, Kathleen V. Earthquake! A Story of Old San Francisco. Himler, Ronald, illus. 64p. (gr. 2-6). 1993. RB 12.99 (*0-670-84874-3*) Viking Child Bks.
Kuskin, Karla. Which Horse Is William? LC 90-24619. 24p. 1992. 14.00 (*0-688-10637-4*); lib. bdg. 13.93 (*0-688-10638-2*) Greenwillow.
Laundrie, Amy C. Whinny of the Wild Horses. Helmer, Jean C., illus. LC 88-21460. 128p. (gr. 3-6). 1990. SBE 13.95 (*0-02-754542-3*, Four Winds Press) Macmillan Child Grp.
Lawson, Robert. Mr. Revere & I. Lawson, Robert, illus. (gr. 7-10). 1953. 16.95 (*0-316-51739-9*) Little.
—Mr. Revere & I. Lawson, Robert, illus. 152p. (gr. 3-6). 1988. pap. 5.95 (*0-316-51729-1*) Little.
Lindman, Maj. Snipp, Snapp, Snurr & the Magic Horse. (Illus.). 32p. 1993. Repr. lib. bdg. 14.95x (*1-56849-001-1*) Buccaneer Bks.
Long, Olivia. A Horse of a Different Color. Long, Olivia, illus. 32p. (ps-4). Date not set. 9.95 (*1-880042-01-0*, SL12451) Shelf-Life Bks.
Luenn, Nancy, ed. A Horse's Tale: Ten Adventures in One Hundred Years. Megale, Marina & Schumacher, Sharon, illus. LC 88-61152. 96p. (Orig.). (gr. 2-6). 1988. lib. bdg. 16.95 (*0-943990-51-3*); pap. 7.95 (*0-943990-50-5*) Parenting Pr.
McClung, Cooky. Plugly, the Horse That Could Do Everything. Tyler, Barbara, illus. 48p. 1993. 16.95 (*0-939481-32-4*) Half Halt Pr.

MacDougall, Mary-Katherine. Black Jupiter. Gruver, Kate E., ed. Moyers, William, illus. 181p. (gr. 5 up). 1983. 8.95 (*0-940175-01-0*) Now Comns.
"It was late for the horses to be so high in the mountains. By this time in other years they had already found winter quarters in a lower area. But this fall they were waiting for a colt." That colt was Black Jupiter. Snow came. The horses had to leave through the rock gateway the black mare could not yet get through. The stallion stayed with her. The next dawn the colt came but did not move or make a sound. The horses left the newborn colt alone in the snow. Jim Peters, a prospector, living alone in his cabin, was sensitive to wildlife. He felt something was wrong when he heard two horses leaving a day after the herd. He found Black Jupiter alive but not strong. He took him to his cabin. There are Gregg & Jenine Jordan, children of a mining engineer, a threat to Jim & his mining plans. In turn, Jim is suspected of stealing from the surveying crew. Black Jupiter, set in the Rocky Mountains with a factual copper mining background, is a mystery story of distrust & misunderstanding, healed by love & a colt. There is a happy Christmas chapter. Black & white illustrations.
Publisher Provided Annotation.

McGraw, Robert. The Rogue & the Horse. McGraw, J. Darrin, illus. 32p. (Orig.). (ps-3). 1993. pap. 5.95 (*0-9633385-0-1*) Imagin Pr.
McHargue, Georgess. The Horseman's Word. LC 80-68736. 272p. (gr. 7 up). 1981. pap. 9.95 (*0-385-28472-1*) Delacorte.

McLane, Gretel B. Kalia & the King's Horse. Wozniak, Patricia, illus. 88p. (gr. 4-7). 1994. pap. 8.95 (*0-916630-70-6*) Pr Pacifica.
KALIA & THE KING'S HORSE takes readers back to the island of Maui in Hawaii when that incredible creature, the horse, first arrived. Kalia, a 12-year-old Hawaiian girl, was fascinated with the horse & the men in charge of it, dreaming that one day she might ride an animal like it. But this horse was KAPU; only its handlers & the King could ride it. However, she watched from a nearby tree & learned all that she could about the horse. While in the tree she heard two men plotting against the King. Suddenly, she realized she must get the message to him on the other side of the island. Thus, the adventure begins. Written with a sensitive, deep understanding of the Hawaiian culture, it is probably the best book about Hawaii for 4th-6th graders. The first part of Kalia's story has been excerpted & printed in the children's magazine CRICKET & has been translated into the Polynesian language of Easter Island for use in their schools.
Publisher Provided Annotation.

McPherson, Jan. In the Cold, Cold Dawn. LC 92-31918. 1993. 4.25 (*0-383-03578-3*) SRA Schl Grp.
Martin, Ann M. Mallory's Dream Horse. 160p. 1992. pap. 3.25 (*0-590-44965-6*) Scholastic Inc.
Martin, Jacqueline B. The Finest Horse in Town. Gaber, Susan, illus. LC 90-38596. 32p. (gr. k-5). 1992. 15.00 (*0-06-024151-9*); PLB 14.89 (*0-06-024152-7*) HarpC Child Bks.

Mawe, Sheelagh M. Dandelion: The Triumphant Life of a Misfit, a Story for All Ages. 165p. (Orig.). (gr. 4). 1994. pap. 6.95 (*0-9642168-0-9*) Totally Unique.
Dandelion is a lowly, mis-bred Irish farm horse. As is true of all creatures, she begins her life with a sense of her

own worth. But little by little, the "circumstances" of her life erode that belief. Dandelion becomes dispirited & eventually gives up her dreams. Nevertheless, given a chance at freedom, she has wits enough to pursue it, only to find that "freedom" was not quite what she was looking for! Dandelion's subsequent journey leads her to her true destination. It leads her to herself. In this enchanting book, readers of all ages will find in Dandelion an inspirational symbol of all those who have overcome poverty, prejudice, background & self-doubt to make a resounding success of their lives. To order contact: TOTALLY UNIQUE THOUGHTS, A Division of TUT Enterprises, 1713 Acme St., Orlando, FL 32805-3603. 407-246-7040.
Publisher Provided Annotation.

Mayer, Marianna. Black Horse. Thamer, Katie, illus. LC 83-25271. 42p. (ps-3). 1987. pap. 4.95 (*0-8037-0181-0*) Dial Bks Young.

Milne, A. A. Eeyore Loses a Tail. Shepard, Ernest H., illus. 32p. 1993. 4.99 (*0-525-45137-4*, DCB) Dutton Child Bks.

Moody, Ralph. Horse of a Different Color. 1976. 21.95 (*0-8488-1106-2*) Amereon Ltd.

Moore, Ruth N. Mystery of the Missing Stallions. Converse, James, illus. LC 84-19. 136p. (Orig.). (gr. 3-8). 1984. pap. 5.95 (*0-8361-3376-5*) Herald Pr.

Morrison, Dorothy N. Somebody's Horse. 224p. (gr. 4-8). 1987. pap. 2.95 (*0-8167-1046-5*) Troll Assocs.

Nabb, Magdalen. The Enchanted Horse. Heller, Julek, illus. LC 93-18423. 96p. (gr. 3-7). 1993. 14.95 (*0-531-06805-6*); PLB 14.99 (*0-531-08655-0*) Orchard Bks Watts.

O'Hara, Mary. My Friend Flicka. LC 87-45654. 272p. (gr. 7 up). 1988. pap. 5.00 (*0-06-080902-7*, P-902, PL) HarpC.

—Thunderhead. 320p. (gr. 5-9). 1967. pap. 1.75 (*0-440-98875-6*, LFL) Dell.

Osborne, Mary P. Moonhorse. Saelig, S. M., illus. LC 87-3818. 40p. (ps-3). 1991. 14.95 (*0-394-88960-6*); lib. bdg. 15.99 (*0-394-98960-0*) Knopf Bks Yng Read.

Ossorio, Nelson A. & Salvadeo, Michele B. Horse in the Bleachers. (Illus.). 60p. (gr. 4-6). 1994. pap. 6.95 (*1-56721-058-9*) Twenty-Fifth Cent Pr.

Outlet Staff. Black Beauty. 1993. 6.99 (*0-517-08777-4*) Random Hse Value.

Pace, Mildred M. Kentucky Derby Champion. rev. ed. Gifford, James M., et al, eds. Dennis, Wesley, illus. 144p. (gr. 3 up). 1993. Repr. of 1955 ed. 12.00 (*0-945084-36-6*) J Stuart Found.

Parker, Cam. A Horse in New York. 144p. (Orig.). (gr. 5 up). 1989. pap. 2.75 (*0-380-75704-4*, Camelot) Avon.

Patent, Dorothy H. Where the Wild Horses Roam. (gr. 4-7). 1993. pap. 6.95 (*0-395-66506-X*, Clarion Bks) HM.

Paterson, Katherine. Jacob Have I Loved. large type ed. 251p. (gr. k-6). 1990. Repr. lib. bdg. 15.95 (*1-55736-167-3*, Crnrstn Bks) BDD LT Grp.

Peterson, Jeanne W. Sometimes I Dream Horses. Schick, Eleanor, illus. LC 83-47710. 32p. (ps-3). 1987. HarpC Child Bks.

Peyton, K. M. Darkling. 1990. 14.95 (*0-385-30086-7*) Doubleday.

Pryor, Bonnie. Horses in the Garage. LC 92-7287. 160p. (gr. 4 up). 1992. 14.00 (*0-688-10567-X*) Morrow Jr Bks.

Rabinowitz, Sandy. How I Trained My Colt. (ps). 1991. pap. 2.75 (*0-553-15848-1*) Bantam.

Rappaport, Doreen. The Boston Coffee Party. McCully, Emily A., illus. LC 87-45301. 64p. (gr. k-3). 1990. pap. 3.50 (*0-06-444141-5*, Trophy) HarpC Child Bks.

Rawlings, Marjorie K. The Yearling. Wyeth, N. C., illus. LC 85-40301. 416p. 1985. (Scribners Young Read); SBE 25.00 (*0-684-18461-3*, Scribners) Macmillan Child Grp.

—The Yearling. 250p. 1991. Repr. lib. bdg. 19.95x (*0-89966-841-0*) Buccaneer Bks.

Ray, Lou. The Burros of Mavrick Gulch. (Illus.). 44p. (Orig.). (gr. k-5). 1983. pap. 7.95 (*0-9612346-0-1*, 83-090410) Ray-Foster.

Ray, Mary L. My Carousel Horse. Taxali, Gary, illus. LC 93-45876. 1900. write for info. (*0-15-200023-2*) HarBrace.

Richardson, Gale T. The Wings. (gr. 9-12). 1989. write for info. (*0-9614337-4-4*) Poetry Unltd.

Rockwood, Joyce. Groundhog's Horse. Kalin, Victor, illus. LC 77-22676. 128p. (gr. 2-4). 1978. reinforced ed. 12.95 (*0-8050-1173-0*, Bks Young Read) H Holt & Co.

Ross, Harriet, compiled by. Great Stories about Horses. Bolle, Frank, illus. LC 63-18759. 160p. (gr. 3-9). 1992. PLB 12.95 (*0-87460-202-5*) Lion Bks.

Rounds, Glen, adapted by. & illus. The Blind Colt. LC 89-1779. 84p. (gr. 3-6). 1989. 15.95 (*0-8234-0010-7*); pap. 5.95 (*0-8234-0758-6*) Holiday.

Sachar, Louis. There's a Boy in the Girls' Bathroom. large type ed. 1990. Repr. lib. bdg. 15.95 (*1-55736-174-6*, Crnrstn Bks) BDD LT Grp.

St. John, Chris. A Horse of Her Own. (gr. 5 up). 1989. pap. 2.95 (*0-449-13451-2*) Fawcett.

—Kate's Challenge. (gr. 5 up). 1989. pap. 2.95 (*0-449-13453-9*) Fawcett.

Scott, Bill. The Colt Who Had Never Been Ridden. LC 93-60919. (Illus.). 44p. 1994. 7.95 (*1-55523-648-0*) Winston-Derek.

Scott, Virginia C. Dream Horse: A Girl with No Roots, a Boy with a Bad Reputation, a Horse Nobody Wants. 1993. pap. 3.50 (*0-06-106149-2*, Harp PBks) HarpC.

Sewell, Anna. Black Beauty. (gr. 5 up). 1963. pap. 1.50 (*0-8049-0023-X*, CL-23) Airmont.

—Black Beauty. (Illus.). 320p. (gr. 4 up). 1945. 13.95 (*0-448-06007-8*, G&D); (G&D) Putnam Pub Group.

—Black Beauty. new ed. Farr, Naunerle, ed. Nebres, Rudy, illus. LC 59-12495. 64p. (Orig.). (gr. 5-10). 1973. pap. 2.95 (*0-88301-094-1*) Pendulum Pr.

—Black Beauty. LC 59-12495. (gr. 3-7). 1983. pap. 2.25 (*0-14-035006-3*, Puffin) Puffin Bks.

—Black Beauty. Vance, Eleanor G., ed. Jeffers, Susan, illus. LC 84-27575. 72p. (ps-5). 1986. 16.00 (*0-394-86575-8*) Random Bks Yng Read.

—Black Beauty. LC 59-12495. (gr. 4-6). 1989. pap. 3.25 (*0-590-42354-1*) Scholastic Inc.

—Black Beauty. (gr. 2-6). 1986. 7.98 (*0-685-16851-4*) Random Hse Value.

—Black Beauty. Dubowski, Cathy, adapted by. D'Andrea, Domenick, illus. LC 89-62772. 96p. (Orig.). (gr. 2-6). 1990. lib. bdg. 5.99 (*0-679-90370-4*, Bullseye Bks); pap. 3.50 (*0-679-80370-X*, Bullseye Bks) Random Bks Yng Read.

—Black Beauty. (gr. 4 up). 1990. pap. 3.50 (*0-440-40355-3*, Pub. by Yearling Classics) Dell.

—Black Beauty. 75p. (ps-8). 1986. pap. 3.50 (*0-451-52295-8*, Sig Classics) NAL-Dutton.

—Black Beauty. Keeping, Charles, illus. 216p. (gr. 5 up). 1990. 19.95 (*0-374-30776-8*) FS&G.

—Black Beauty. 256p. 1992. 9.49 (*0-8167-2548-9*); pap. 2.95 (*0-8167-2549-7*) Troll Assocs.

—Black Beauty. Needham, James, illus. 220p. 1992. 25. 00 (*0-88363-200-4*) H L Levin.

—Black Beauty. Lindskoog, Kathryn, ed. (gr. 3 up). 1992. pap. 4.99 (*0-88070-498-5*, Gold & Honey) Questar Pubs.

—Black Beauty. Simpson, Anne, ed. La Padula, Thomas, illus. LC 92-5805. 48p. (gr. 3-6). 1992. PLB 12.89 (*0-8167-2860-7*); pap. text ed. 3.95 (*0-8167-2861-5*) Troll Assocs.

—Black Beauty. Hollindale, Peter, intro. by. 240p. 1992. pap. 7.95 (*0-19-282812-6*) OUP.

—Black Beauty. abr. ed. Kliros, Thea, illus. LC 93-244. 96p. (gr. 1-9). 1993. pap. 1.00 (*0-486-27570-1*) Dover.

—Black Beauty. Ambrus, Victor, illus. LC 93-18939. 208p. (gr. 4-8). 1993. 14.95 (*0-8050-2772-6*, Bks Young Read) H Holt & Co.

—Black Beauty. 1993. 13.95 (*0-679-42811-9*, Everymans Lib) Knopf.

Shefelman, Janice. A Mare for Young Wolf. Shefelman, Tom, illus. LC 91-42749. 48p. (Orig.). (gr. 2-3). 1993. PLB 7.99 (*0-679-93445-6*); pap. 3.50 (*0-679-83445-1*) Random Bks Yng Read.

Sheldon, Ann. A Star in the Saddle. (Orig.). (gr. 3-6). 1989. pap. 2.75 (*0-318-41208-X*, Minstrel Bks) PB.

Sherlock, Patti. Four of a Kind. LC 91-55038. 196p. (gr. 3-7). 1991. 13.95 (*0-8234-0913-9*) Holiday.

Shub, Elizabeth. The White Stallion. Isadora, Rachel, illus. 64p. (gr. 1-4). 1984. pap. 2.50 (*0-553-15244-0*, Skylark) Bantam.

—The White Stallion. 1984. pap. 3.25 (*0-553-15615-2*) Bantam.

Signol, Anne. Norris on Broadway. (Illus.). 32p. (gr. 4-6). 1992. pap. 7.95 (*0-8059-3303-4*) Dorrance.

Simon, Carly. The Nightime Chauffeur. Datz, Margot, illus. LC 92-44934. 1993. pap. 16.00 (*0-385-47009-6*) Doubleday.

Simont, Marc. Polly's Oats. (ps-3). 1994. pap. 3.50 NOP (*0-440-40820-2*) Dell.

Slade, Michael. The Horses of Central Park. 96p. 1992. 12.95 (*0-590-44659-2*, Scholastic Hardcover) Scholastic Inc.

Slightly Off-Center Writers Group, Ltd. Staff. To Be Proud: or The Stallion's Tale. (Illus.). 48p. (gr. 3-5). 1994. pap. 6.95 (*1-56721-085-6*) Twnty-Fifth Cent Pr.

Snelling, Lauraine. Call for Courage. LC 92-16240. 160p. (Orig.). (gr. 7-10). 1992. pap. 5.99 (*1-55661-260-5*) Bethany Hse.

—Eagles' Wings. 160p. (Orig.). (gr. 7-10). 1991. pap. 5.99 (*1-55661-203-6*) Bethany Hse.

—Go for the Glory. 160p. (Orig.). (gr. 7-10). 1991. pap. 5.99 (*1-55661-218-4*) Bethany Hse.

—Kentucky Dreamer. 160p. (Orig.). 1992. pap. 5.99 (*1-55661-234-6*) Bethany Hse.

—The Race. 176p. (Orig.). (gr. 7-9). 1991. pap. 5.99 (*1-55661-161-7*) Bethany Hse.

—Second Wind. 1994. pap. 5.99 (*1-55661-401-2*) Bethany Hse.

—Shadow over San Mateo. 160p. (Orig.). (gr. 7-10). 1993. pap. 5.99 (*1-55661-292-3*) Bethany Hse.

Snyder, Zilpha K. A Season of Ponies. (gr. k-6). 1988. pap. 2.95 (*0-440-40006-6*) Dell.

Sohl, Marcia & Dackerman, Gerald. Black Beauty Student Activity Book. (Illus.). 16p. (gr. 4-10). 1976. pap. 1.25 (*0-88301-183-2*) Pendulum Pr.

Spinka, Penina K. White Hare's Horses. LC 90-42777. 160p. (gr. 5-9). 1991. SBE 13.95 (*0-689-31654-2*, Atheneum Child Bk) Macmillan Child Grp.

Spray, Carole. The Mare's Egg. La Fave, Kim, illus. Atwood, Margaret, afterword by. (Illus.). 56p. (Orig.). (gr. k-7). 1981. (Pub. by Camden Hse CN); pap. 9.95 (*0-920656-07-2*, Pub. by Camden Hse CN) Firefly Bks Ltd.

Springer, Nancy. The Boy on a Black Horse. LC 92-27158. 176p. (gr. 5-9). 1994. SBE 14.95 (*0-689-31840-5*, Atheneum Child Bk) Macmillan Child Grp.

—Colt. (gr. 4-7). 1991. 13.95 (*0-8037-1022-4*) Dial Bks Young.

—Colt. 128p. (gr. 5 up). 1994. pap. 3.99 (*0-14-036480-3*) Puffin Bks.

Stein, Jovial B. Son of Fury. (ps). 1991. pap. 2.75 (*0-553-15854-6*) Bantam.

Stevens, Mallory. Christmas Colt. (gr. 4-7). 1992. pap. 3.50 (*0-06-106721-0*, Harp PBks) HarpC.

Stover, Jill. Popsicle Pony. LC 93-79774. (ps-3). 1994. 14.00 (*0-688-12392-9*); 13.93 (*0-688-12393-7*) Morrow.

Swenson, May. The Centaur. Moser, Barry, illus. LC 92-14897. 32p. (gr. k-3). 1995. RSBE 14.95 (*0-02-788726-X*, Macmillan Child Bk) Macmillan Child Grp.

Swortzell, Lowell. The Little Humpback Horse. (Orig.). (gr. 1 up). 1984. pap. 5.00 (*0-87602-244-1*) Anchorage.

Szymanski, Lois. Patches. 96p. (Orig.). 1993. pap. 3.50 (*0-380-76841-0*, Camelot Young) Avon.

Tilden, Ruth. Hazel Rides a Horse. (ps-3). 1994. 9.95 (*0-307-17609-6*, Artsts Writrs) Western Pub.

Troll. Black Beauty Activity Book. 64p. (ps-3). 1991. pap. 1.95 (*0-8167-2290-0*) Troll Assocs.

Vail, Virginia. Horseback Summer. Bode, Daniel, illus. LC 89-30583. 128p. (gr. 4-6). 1990. lib. bdg. 9.89 (*0-8167-1625-0*); pap. text ed. 2.95 (*0-8167-1626-9*) Troll Assocs.

—Palomino. (gr. 4-7). 1992. pap. 3.50 (*0-06-106716-4*, Harp PBks) HarpC.

Vallet, Roxanne. Horses. Vallet, Roxanne, illus. 19p. (gr. k-3). 1992. pap. 10.95 (*1-895583-40-3*) MAYA Pubs.

Warner, Gertrude C. The Mystery Horse. (Illus.). 128p. (gr. 2-7). 1993. PLB 10.95 (*0-8075-5338-7*); pap. 3.50 (*0-8075-5339-5*) A Whitman.

Washburn, JoAnn. Maude the Mare. LC 87-51039. (Illus.). 44p. (gr. k-3). 1988. 6.95 (*1-55523-123-3*) Winston-Derek.

Watkins, Dawn L. Pulling Together. Cooper, Carolyn, ed. Pflug, Kathy, illus. 135p. (Orig.). (gr. 2-4). 1992. pap. 4.95 (*0-89084-609-X*) Bob Jones Univ Pr.

Wayland, April H. Night Horse. 1991. 12.95 (*0-590-42629-X*, Scholastic Hardcover) Scholastic Inc.

Welch, Sheila K. A Horse for All Seasons: Collected Stories. LC 93-94237. 160p. (gr. 4-8). 1994. 16.95 (*0-9638819-0-6*); pap. 9.95 (*0-9638819-1-4*) ShadowPlay Pr.

Wilbur, Frances. Horse Called Holiday. (gr. 4-7). 1992. pap. 2.95 (*0-590-44548-0*) Scholastic Inc.

Worcester, Donald E. Lone Hunter's Gray Pony & Lone Hunter & the Cheyennes & War Pony. 1992. Boxed set. 29.95 (*0-87565-109-7*) Tex Christian.

—War Pony. Pauley, Paige, illus. LC 83-40486. 96p. (gr. 4 up). 1984. Repr. of 1961 ed. 10.95 (*0-912646-85-3*) Tex Christian.

Yolen, Jane. Fever Dream. Pinkney, Jerry, illus. LC 93-10070. 32p. (gr. k-3). Date not set. 16.00 (*0-06-021482-1*); PLB 15.89 (*0-06-021483-X*) Harpc Child Bks.

Zeplin, Zeno & Jones, Judy. Apple Jack & the Big Storm: A Brave Horse to the Rescue. Ebersapacher, Margy, ed. Jones, Judy, illus. 48p. (gr. k-3). 1991. lib. bdg. 9.95 (*1-877740-10-1*); pap. text ed. 5.50 (*1-877740-11-X*) Nel-Mar Pub.

Zolotow, Charlotte. A Rose, a Bridge, & a Wild Black Horse. Spowart, Robin, illus. LC 86-25840. 32p. (ps-1). 1987. PLB 12.89 (*0-06-026939-1*, C Zolotow Bks) HarpC Child Bks.

HORSES–HISTORY

Anderson, John K. Horses & Riding. Conkle, Nancy, illus. 48p. (gr. 7-9). 1979. pap. 3.95 (*0-88388-066-0*) Bellerophon Bks.

Henry, Marguerite. King of the Wind: The Story of the Godolphin Arabian. 2nd ed. Dennis, Wesley, illus. LC 48-8773. 176p. (gr. 3-7). 1990. SBE 13.95 (*0-02-743629-2*, Macmillan Child Bk) Macmillan Child Grp.

—King of the Wind: The Story of the Godolphin Arabian. Dennis, Wesley, illus. 176p. (gr. 3-7). 1991. pap. 3.95 (*0-689-71486-6*, Aladdin) Macmillan Child Grp.

Viola, Herman J. After Columbus: The Horse's Return to America. Thomas, Peter, narrated by. Howland, Deborah, illus. LC 92-11038. 32p. (gr. 2-5). 1992. 11. 95 (*0-924483-61-X*); incl. audiocass. tape 16.95 (*0-924483-60-1*); incl. audiocass. tape & 13" stuffed mustang toy 39.95 (*0-924483-58-X*); incl. audiocass. tape & 9" stuffed mustang toy 25.95 (*0-924483-59-8*); audiocassette (*0-924483-74-1*) Soundprints.

HORSES–LEGENDS

Small, Howard I. Monty's Pal. Hengen, Nona, illus. LC 78-73621. viii, 120p. (gr. 3-8). 1979. 6.95 (*0-931474-08-6*) TBW Bks.

HORSES–PICTURES, ILLUSTRATIONS, ETC.
Henry, Marguerite. A Pictorial Life Story of Misty. LC 76-41864. (Illus.). 112p. (gr. 3 up). 1995. 15.95 (*0-02-743626-8*) Macmillan Child Grp.
Longstreet, Stephen, ed. Horse in Art. (Illus., Orig.). (ps). 1965. pap. 4.95 (*0-87505-198-7*) Borden.
Spizzirri Publishing Co. Staff. Horses: An Educational Coloring Book. Spizzirri, Linda, ed. (Illus.). 32p. (gr. k-5). 1985. pap. 1.75 (*0-86545-068-4*) Spizzirri.
HORSES–POETRY
Foster, John, ed. Horse Poems. (Illus.). 16p. (gr. 1 up). 1992. pap. 2.95 (*0-19-916421-5*) OUP.
Jeffers, Susan. If Wishes Were Horses: Mother Goose Rhymes. Jeffers, Susan, illus. LC 79-9986. 32p. (ps-3). 1979. 13.95 (*0-525-32531-X*, DCB) Dutton Child Bks.
HORSES–TRAINING
Freeman, Charlotte M. A Day in the Life of a Horse Trainer. Jann, Gayle, illus. LC 87-10681. 32p. (gr. 4-8). 1988. PLB 11.79 (*0-8167-1111-9*); pap. text ed. 2.95 (*0-8167-1112-7*) Troll Assocs.
Henderson, Kathy. I Can Be a Horse Trainer. LC 89-29203. (Illus.). 32p. (gr. k-3). 1990. pap. 3.95 (*0-516-41960-9*) Childrens.
Holderness-Roddam, Jane. Preparing for a Show. Vincer, Carole, illus. 24p. (gr. 3 up). 1989. pap. 10.00 (*0-901366-09-9*, Pub. by Threshold Bks) Half Halt Pr.
HORSESHOE CRABS
Day, Nancy. The Horseshoe Crab. LC 92-9772. (Illus.). 60p. (gr. 4 up). 1992. text ed. 13.95 RSBE (*0-87518-545-2*, Dillon) Macmillan Child Grp.
HORTICULTURE
see Gardening
HOSPITALITY
see Entertaining
HOSPITALS
see also Children–Hospitals; Nurses and Nursing
Butler, Daphne. First Look in the Hospital. LC 90-10245. (Illus.). 32p. (gr. 1-2). 1991. PLB 17.27 (*0-8368-0563-1*) Gareth Stevens Inc.
Carter, Sharon & Monnig, Judith. Coping with a Hospital Stay. Rosen, Ruth, ed. 128p. (gr. 7 up). 1987. PLB 14. 95 (*0-8239-0682-5*) Rosen Group.
Ciliotta, Claire & Livingston, Carole. Why Am I Going to the Hospital? Wilson, Dick, illus. (gr. k-7). 1992. pap. 8.95 (*0-8184-0568-6*, L Stuart) Carol Pub Group.
Coleman, William L. My Hospital Book. Walles, Dwight, illus. LC 81-10094. 96p. (Orig.). (gr. 2-7). 1981. pap. 5.99 (*0-87123-354-1*) Bethany Hse.
Elliott, Ingrid G. Hospital Roadmap: A Book to Help Explain the Hospital Experience to Young children. LC 82-80226. (Illus.). 36p. (Orig.). (gr. k-2). 1984. pap. 8.95 (*0-9608150-0-7*) Resources Children.
—Hospital Roadmap Manual: A Curriculum Guide to Explain the Hospital Experience to Young Children. 100p. (Orig.). (gr. k-2). 1986. pap. 11.95 (*0-9608150-1-5*) Resources Children.
Going into Hospital. (Illus.). (ps). 3.50 (*0-7214-0849-4*) Ladybird Bks.
Howe, James. The Hospital Book. Warshaw, Mal, photos by. LC 93-15701. (Illus.). 96p. (gr. 1 up). 1994. 16.00g (*0-688-12731-2*); pap. 7.95 (*0-688-12734-7*) Morrow Jr Bks.
Monroe, Betsy. My Visit to the Emergency Room: A Coloring Book for Kids. Monroe, Betsy, illus. (SPA.). 32p. (gr. k-4). 1990. pap. write for info. (*1-878083-03-1*) Color Me Well.
—My Visit to the Hospital: A Coloring Book for Kids. Monroe, Betsy, illus. 32p. (Orig.). (gr. k-4). 1986. pap. write for info. (*1-878083-02-3*) Color Me Well.
—My Visit to the Outpatient Department: A Coloring Book for Kids. Monroe, Betsy, illus. 24p. (gr. k-4). 1986. pap. write for info. (*1-878083-04-X*) Color Me Well.
Sauer, Sue, et al. Stevie Has His Heart Examined. Goldstein, Nancy, ed. Albury, Mary, illus. (ps-7). 1983. pap. text ed. 4.25 (*0-937423-00-9*) U M H & C.
—Stevie Has His Heart Repaired. Goldstein, Nancy, ed. Albury, Mary, illus. (ps-7). 1979. pap. text ed. 4.25 (*0-937423-01-7*) U M H & C.
Shepherd, Sue, et al. Color Me Special. Albury, Mary, illus. (ps-3). 1982. pap. text ed. 4.00 (*0-937423-02-5*) U M H & C.
Sigel, Lois S. New Careers in Hospitals. rev. ed. (Illus.). (gr. 7-12). 1990. PLB 14.95 (*0-8239-1172-1*) Rosen Group.
Stein, Sara B. A Hospital Story. LC 73-15269. (Illus.). 48p. (ps-8). 1984. pap. 8.95 (*0-8027-7222-6*) Walker & Co.
—A Hospital Story. LC 73-15269. (Illus.). 48p. (gr. 1 up). 1974. 12.95 (*0-8027-6173-9*) Walker & Co.
HOSPITALS–FICTION
Allan, Nicholas. Hilltop Hospital. (Illus.). 32p. (ps-1). 1994. 19.95 (*0-09-176438-6*, Pub. by Hutchinson UK) Trafalgar.
Balter, Lawrence. Alfred Goes to the Hospital. Schanzer, Roz, illus. 40p. (gr. 3-7). 1990. 5.95 (*0-8120-6150-0*) Barron.
Bucknall, Caroline. One Bear in the Hospital. Bucknall, Caroline, illus. LC 90-2994. 32p. (ps-2). 1991. 11.95 (*0-8037-0847-5*) Dial Bks Young.
Carlstrom, Nancy W. Barney Is Best. Hale, James G., illus. LC 92-30376. 32p. (ps-3). 1994. 15.00 (*0-06-022875-X*); PLB 14.89 (*0-06-022876-8*) HarpC Child Bks.
Carlyle, Carolyn. Mercy Hospital: Dr. Cute. 128p. (Orig.). 1993. pap. 3.50 (*0-380-76849-6*, Camelot) Avon.
—Mercy Hospital: Don't Tell Mrs. Harris. 128p. (Orig.). 1993. pap. 3.50 (*0-380-76848-8*, Camelot) Avon.
—Mercy Hospital: The Best Medicine. 128p. (Orig.). 1993. pap. 3.50 (*0-380-76847-X*, Camelot) Avon.
Civardi, Anne & Cartwright, Stephen. Going to the Hospital. 16p. (ps up). 1987. pap. 3.95 (*0-7460-1511-9*) EDC.
Davidson, Martine. Maggie & the Emergency Room. Hafner, Marylin, illus. LC 91-31413. 32p. (Orig.). (ps-2). 1992. PLB 5.99 (*0-679-91818-3*); pap. 2.25 (*0-679-81818-9*) Random Bks Yng Read.
—Rita Goes to the Hospital. Jones, John, illus. LC 91-43293. 32p. (Orig.). (ps-2). 1992. PLB 5.99 (*0-679-91820-5*); pap. 2.25 (*0-679-81820-0*) Random Bks Yng Read.
Hautzig, Deborah. A Visit to the Sesame Street Hospital. Mathieu, Joe, illus. LC 84-17852. 32p. (ps-4). 1985. lib. bdg. 5.99 (*0-394-97062-4*); pap. 2.25 (*0-394-87062-X*) Random Bks Yng Read.
—Una Visita Al Hospital De Sesame Street. Saunders, Paola B., tr. Mathieu, Joe, illus. LC 92-16610. (SPA.). 32p. (ps-3). 1993. pap. 2.25 (*0-679-83944-5*) Random Bks Yng Read.
Hogan, Paula Z. Hospital Scares Me. (ps-3). 1993. pap. 3.95 (*0-8114-7153-5*) Raintree Steck-V.
Hogan, Paula Z. & Hogan, Kirk. The Hospital Scares Me. Thelen, Mary, illus. Wilson, Jerrian M., intro. by. LC 79-23886. (Illus.). 32p. (gr. k-6). 1980. PLB 19.97 (*0-8172-1351-1*) Raintree Steck-V.
Howe, James. A Night Without Stars. LC 82-16278. 192p. (gr. 4-7). 1983. SBE 13.95 (*0-689-30957-0*, Atheneum Child Bk) Macmillan Child Grp.
Keller, Holly. The Best Present. LC 87-38086. (Illus.). 32p. (gr. k up). 1989. 11.95 (*0-688-07319-0*); PLB 11. 88 (*0-688-07320-4*) Greenwillow.
Kohlenberg, Sherry. Sammy's Mommy Has Cancer: A Story For Children Who Have a Loved One with Cancer. Crow, Lauri, illus. LC 93-38213. (gr. 2 up). 1994. 17.27 (*0-8368-1071-6*) Gareth Stevens Inc.
Martin, Charles E. Island Rescue. Martin, Charles E., illus. LC 84-13672. 32p. (gr. k-3). 1985. 11.75 (*0-688-04257-0*); PLB 11.88 (*0-688-04258-9*) Greenwillow.
Muratore, Carol. Scooter Goes to the Hospital. (Illus., Orig.). 1992. pap. text ed. 3.75 (*0-9628084-2-3*) Hlth Mngmnt Pubns.
Nelson, JoAnne. What Next? Katayama, Mits, illus. LC 91-35731. 24p. (Orig.). (gr. k-2). 1993. pap. 5.95 (*0-935529-19-5*) Comprehen Health Educ.
Roy, Ron. Move over, Wheelchairs Coming Through. Hausherr, Rosemarie, illus. LC 84-14314. 96p. (gr. 4-7). 1985. 15.45 (*0-89919-249-1*, Clarion Bks) HM.
Smith, Kaitlin M. Going to the Hospital. Smith, Kaitlin M., illus. 18p. (gr. k-3). 1992. pap. 13.95 (*1-895583-17-9*) MAYA Pubs.
Steel, Danielle. Max's Daddy Goes to the Hospital. Rogers, Jacqueline, illus. (ps-2). 1989. 8.95 (*0-385-29797-1*) Delacorte.
Wild, Margaret. Going Home. Harris, Wayne, illus. LC 93-22975. 32p. (ps-3). 1994. 14.95 (*0-590-47958-X*) Scholastic Inc.
HOSTESSES, AIR LINE
see Air Lines–Hostesses
HOT RODS
see Automobile Racing; Automobiles
HOTELS, MOTELS, ETC.–FICTION
Armstrong, Jennifer. Wild Rose Inn. 1994. pap. 3.99 (*0-553-29866-6*) Bantam.
—Wild Rose Inn, No. 3. (gr. 7 up). 1994. pap. 3.99 (*0-553-29909-3*) Bantam.
Brink, Carol R. The Pink Motel. Greenwald, Sheila, illus. LC 92-17953. 224p. (gr. 3-7). 1993. pap. 3.95 (*0-689-71677-X*, Aladdin) Macmillan Child Grp.
Dela Pena, Alba. Milas, the Innkeeper of Harvest Tree. Hough, Bonnie J. & Cook, Allen, illus. 28p. 1993. saddle stitched 8.95 (*1-56167-119-3*) Am Literary Pr.
DuQuette, Keith. Hotel Animal. DuQuette, Keith, illus. LC 93-14531. 32p. (ps-3). 1994. PLB 13.99 (*0-670-85056-X*) Viking Child Bks.
Fleischman, Paul. The Half-a-Moon Inn. Jacobi, Kathy, illus. LC 79-2010. 96p. (gr. 3-7). 1991. pap. 3.95 (*0-06-440364-5*, Trophy) HarpC Child Bks.
Gilson, Jamie. Soccer Circus. LC 92-9716. 1993. 12.00 (*0-688-12021-0*) Lothrop.
Graham, Alastair. Full Moon Soup: Or Fall of the Hotel Splendile. (ps-3). 1991. 14.95 (*0-8037-1045-3*) Dial Bks Young.
Hahn, Mary D. Look for Me by Moonlight. LC 94-21892. 1995. write for info. (*0-395-69843-X*); pap. write for info. (*0-395-69844-8*) HM.
Hinton, Nigel. Beaver Towers. large type ed. (Illus.). (gr. 1-8). 1994. 15.95 (*0-7451-2224-8*, Galaxy etc.) Chivers N Amer.
Hoban, Julia. Buzby. Himmelman, John, illus. LC 89-29408. 64p. (gr. k-3). 1990. PLB 11.89 (*0-06-022398-7*) HarpC Child Bks.
—Buzby to the Rescue. Himmelman, John, illus. LC 91-46085. 64p. (gr. k-3). 1993. 14.00 (*0-06-021025-7*); PLB 13.89 (*0-06-021024-9*) HarpC Child Bks.
Jamaica Inn. 1993. pap. text ed. 6.50 (*0-582-08482-2*, 79898) Longman.
Ruby, Lois. Pig-Out Inn. LC 86-21433. 180p. (gr. 5 up). 1987. 13.95 (*0-395-42714-2*) HM.
Schneider, Howie. No Dogs Allowed. LC 93-10395. 1994. write for info. (*0-399-22612-5*, Putnam) Putnam Pub Group.
Service, Pamela F. Phantom Victory. LC 93-37904. 128p. (gr. 5-7). 1994. SBE 14.95 (*0-684-19441-4*, Scribners Young Read) Macmillan Child Grp.
Stevenson, James. The Sea View Hotel. LC 78-2749. (Illus.). 48p. 1994. Repr. of 1974 ed. 15.00 (*0-688-13469-6*); PLB 14.93 (*0-688-13470-X*) Greenwillow.
Vaughan, Marcia & Mullins, Patricia. The Sea-Breeze Hotel. LC 91-22303. (Illus.). 32p. (ps-2). 1992. 14.00 (*0-06-020488-5*); PLB 13.89 (*0-06-020504-0*) HarpC Child Bks.
HOUDINI, HARRY, 1874-1926
Borland, Kathryn K. & Speicher, Helen R. Harry Houdini: Young Magician. LC 90-23321. (Illus.). 192p. (gr. 3-7). 1991. pap. 3.95 (*0-689-71476-9*, Aladdin) Macmillan Child Grp.
Fago, John N. & Toan, Debbie. Houdini - Walt Disney. Cruz, E. R. & Henson, Tenny, illus. (gr. 4-12). 1979. pap. text ed. 2.95 (*0-88301-350-9*); wkbk 1.25 (*0-88301-374-6*) Pendulum Pr.
Hass, Elizabeth. Houdini's Last Trick. LC 93-49866. (gr. 4 up). 1994. 2.99 (*0-685-71914-6*) Random Bks Yng Read.
Kraske, Robert. Harry Houdini: Master of Magic. (gr. 2-6). 1989. pap. 2.50 (*0-590-42402-5*) Scholastic Inc.
Sabin, Louis. The Great Houdini, Daring Escape Artist. Eitzen, Allan, illus. LC 89-5170. 48p. (gr. 4-6). 1990. PLB 10.79 (*0-8167-1769-9*); pap. text ed. 3.50 (*0-8167-1770-2*) Troll Assocs.
Woog, Adam. Harry Houdini. LC 93-47622. (Illus.). 112p. (gr. 5-8). 1994. 14.95 (*1-56006-053-0*) Lucent Bks.
HOUSE BOATS
see Houseboats
HOUSE CLEANING
Dasso, Margaret & Skelly, Maryan. Dirt Busters: The Best Little Cleaning Book Ever. rev. ed. 130p. (gr. 5 up). 1991. pap. 7.95 (*0-9621757-1-4*) Peter & Thorton Pubs.
HOUSE DECORATION
see Interior Decoration
HOUSE FLIES
see Flies
HOUSE FURNISHING
see Interior Decoration
HOUSE PAINTING
Painting. (Illus.). 32p. (gr. 6-12). 1983. pap. 1.85 (*0-8395-3372-1*, 33372) BSA.
HOUSE PLANTS
Gattis, L. S., III. Houseplants for Pathfinders: A Basic Youth Enrichment Skill Honor Packet. (Illus.). 24p. (Orig.). (gr. 5 up). 1989. pap. 5.00 tchr's. ed. (*0-936241-50-0*) Cheetah Pub.
HOUSE REPAIRING
see Houses–Repairing
HOUSEBOATS
Rickard, Graham. Mobile Homes. (Illus.). 32p. (gr. 2-5). 1989. 13.50 (*0-8225-2130-X*) Lerner Pubns.
HOUSEBOATS–FICTION
Warner, Gertrude C. Houseboat Mystery. Cunningham, David, illus. LC 67-26521. 128p. (gr. 2-7). 1966. PLB 10.95 (*0-8075-3412-9*); pap. 3.50 (*0-8075-3413-7*) A Whitman.
HOUSEHOLD APPLIANCES
see Household Equipment and Supplies
HOUSEHOLD EMPLOYEES–FICTION
Armstrong, Jennifer. Little Salt Lick & the Sun King. Goodell, Jon, illus. LC 93-18673. 32p. (ps-3). 1994. 15.00 (*0-517-59620-2*); 15.99 (*0-517-59621-0*) Crown Bks Yng Read.
Fine, Anne. Alias Madame Doubtfire. 1990. pap. 3.99 (*0-553-56615-6*) Bantam.
—Madame Doubtfire. Pena, Flora, tr (SPA.). 165p. (gr. 5-8). 1992. pap. write for info. (*84-204-4680-7*) Santillana.
Marino, Jan. For the Love of Pete: A Novel. LC 92-36465. 1993. 14.95 (*0-316-54627-5*) Little.
Maugham, W. Somerset. Appointment. Benjamin, Alan, adapted by. Essley, Roger, illus. LC 92-391. (ps-3). 1993. 16.00 (*0-671-75887-X*, Green Tiger) S&S Trade.
Parish, Peggy. Amelia Bedelia. Siebel, Fritz, illus. LC 91-10163. 64p. (gr. k-3). 1992. 14.00 (*0-06-020186-X*); PLB 13.89 (*0-06-020187-8*) HarpC Child Bks.
—Amelia Bedelia. Siebel, Fritz, illus. LC 91-10164. 64p. (gr. k-3). 1992. pap. 3.50 (*0-06-444155-5*, Trophy) HarpC Child Bks.
—Amelia Bedelia & the Baby. Sweat, Lynn, illus. 64p. (gr. k-3). 1982. pap. 3.99 (*0-380-57067-X*, Camelot) Avon.
—Amelia Bedelia & the Surprise Shower. Siebel, Fritz, illus. LC 66-18655. 64p. (gr. k-3). 1979. pap. 3.50 (*0-06-444019-2*, Trophy) HarpC Child Bks.
—Amelia Bedelia & the Surprise Shower. unabr. ed. Tripp, Wallace, illus. (ps-3). 1990. pap. 6.95 incl. cassette (*1-55994-216-9*, Caedmon) HarperAudio.
—Amelia Bedelia Helps Out. Sweat, Lynn, illus. 64p. (gr. k-3). 1981. pap. 3.99 (*0-380-53405-3*, Camelot) Avon.
—Amelia Bedelia's Family Album. 48p. 1994. pap. 3.99 (*0-380-71698-4*, Camelot) Avon.
—Come Back, Amelia Bedelia. unabr. ed. Tripp, Wallace, illus. (ps-3). 1990. pap. 6.95 incl. cassette (*1-55994-225-8*, Caedmon) HarperAudio.
—Good Work, Amelia Bedelia. Sweat, Lynn, illus. LC 75-20360. 56p. (gr. 1-4). 1976. 14.00 (*0-688-80022-X*); PLB 13.93 (*0-688-84022-1*) Greenwillow.
—Good Work, Amelia Bedelia. Sweat, Lynn, illus. 164p. (gr. k-5). 1980. pap. 3.99 (*0-380-49171-0*, Camelot) Avon.

—Play Ball, Amelia Bedelia. unabr. ed. Tripp, Wallace, illus. (ps-3). 1990. pap. 6.95 incl. cassette (*1-55994-241-X*, Caedmon) HarperAudio.
—Thank You, Amelia Bedelia. Siebel, Fritz, illus. LC 64-11835. (gr. k-3). 1964. PLB 12.89 (*0-06-024652-9*) HarpC Child Bks.
—Thank You, Amelia Bedelia. newly illus ed. Thomas, Barbara, illus. LC 92-5746. 64p. (gr. k-3). 1993. 14.00 (*0-06-022979-9*); PLB 13.89 (*0-06-022980-2*) HarpC Child Bks.
—Thank You, Amelia Bedelia: Newly Illustrated Edition. Siebel, Fritz, illus. LC 92-5746. 64p. (ps-3). 1993. pap. 3.50 (*0-06-444171-7*, Trophy) HarpC Child Bks.
Zelinsky, Paul O., adapted by. & illus. The Maid & the Mouse & the Odd-Shaped House. 32p. (ps-2). 1993. pap. 4.99 (*0-14-054946-3*, Puff Unicorn) Puffin Bks.
—The Maid & the Mouse & the Odd-Shaped House. 32p. (ps-2). 1993. 14.99 (*0-525-45095-5*, DCB) Dutton Child Bks.

HOUSEHOLD EQUIPMENT AND SUPPLIES

Berger, Melvin & Berger, Gilda. Telephones, Televisions, & Toilets: How They Work & What Can Go Wrong. Madden, Don, illus. LC 92-18198. (gr. k-3). 1993. 12.00 (*0-8249-8645-8*, Ideals Child); pap. 4.50 (*0-8249-8608-3*) Hambleton-Hill.
Parker, Steve. Everyday Things & How They Work. Bull, Peter & Moores, Ian, illus. LC 91-213. 40p. (Orig.). (gr. 2-5). 1991. pap. 4.99 (*0-679-80866-3*) Random Bks Yng Read.
Scarry, Richard. Richard Scarry Huckle's Book. Scarry, Richard, illus. (ps). 1979. 2.95 (*0-394-84130-1*) Random Bks Yng Read.
Weaver, Rebecca & Dale, Rodney. Machines in the Home. LC 92-21662. (Illus.). 64p. 1993. PLB 16.00 (*0-19-520965-6*) OUP.

HOUSEHOLD MANAGEMENT

see Home Economics

HOUSEKEEPING

see Home Economics

HOUSES

Here are entered general works on houses.
see also Building; Building-Repair and Reconstruction

Adkins, Jan. How a House Happens. (Illus.). 32p. (gr. 5 up). 1983. pap. 3.95 (*0-8027-7206-4*) Walker & Co.
Barton, Byron. Building a House. LC 80-22674. (Illus.). 32p. (ps-1). 1981. PLB 14.88 (*0-688-84291-7*) Greenwillow.
Bennett, Olivia. Our New Home. (Illus.). 26p. (gr. 2-4). 1991. 16.95 (*0-237-60149-4*, Pub. by Evans Bros Ltd) Trafalgar.
Bowyer. Houses & Homes. (gr. 4-9). 1978. (Usborne-Hayes); PLB 13.96 (*0-88110-117-6*); pap. 6.95 (*0-86020-191-0*) EDC.
Brown, Richard, illus. Muchas Palabras Sobre Mi Casa. (SPA.). 28p. (ps-1). 1989. pap. 3.95 (*0-15-200532-3*, Gulliver Bks) HarBrace.
—One Hundred Words about My House. (ps-1). 1989. pap. 3.95 (*0-15-200556-0*, Voy B) HarBrace.
Cartlidge, Michelle. Mouse's Christmas House: A Press-out Model House. (Illus.). 32p. (Orig.). 1992. pap. 9.95 (*0-8362-4500-8*) Andrews & McMeel.
Civardi, Anne. Moving House. (ps-3). 1993. pap. 3.95 (*0-7460-1281-0*, Usborne) EDC.
Cony, Sue, illus. Where Do We Live? 8p. (ps-k). 1991. bds. 4.95 (*1-56293-151-2*) McClanahan Bk.
Cumpiano, Ina. Homes Are for Living. (Illus.). 24p. (Orig.). (gr. 1-3). 1991. pap. text ed. 29.95 big bk. (*1-56334-047-X*); pap. text ed. 6.00 small bk. (*1-56334-053-4*) Hampton-Brown.
Dorros, Arthur. This is My House. (Illus.). (ps). 1992. 14.95 (*0-590-45302-5*, 019, Scholastic Hardcover) Scholastic Inc.
Drew, David. My House. Wood, Bill, illus. LC 92-30424. 1993. 2.50 (*0-383-03586-4*) SRA Schl Grp.
Emberley, Rebecca. My House, Mi Casa: A Book in Two Languages. Emberley, Rebecca, illus. LC 89-12893. (ps-2). 1990. 15.95 (*0-316-23637-3*) Little.
Felix, Monique. House. (ps up). 1993. 7.95 (*1-56846-074-0*) Creat Editions.
Gibbons, Gail. How a House Is Built. Gibbons, Gail, illus. LC 90-55107. 32p. (ps-3). 1990. reinforced bdg. 15.95 (*0-8234-0841-8*) Holiday.
Hamilton-MacLaren, Alistair. Houses & Homes. LC 91-23026. (Illus.). 48p. (gr. 5-7). 1992. PLB 12.90 (*0-531-18424-2*, Pub. by Bookwright Pr) Watts.
Hegene, Barbara M. Wood Homestead. (Illus.). 10p. (gr. 9-12). 1990. pap. write for info. (*0-9623847-5-5*) B Hegne.
Homes Theme Pack: Level 1 English, 12 bks. (Orig.). (gr. 1-3). 1992. pap. 129.95 set incl. 2 big bks., 12 small bks. & tchr's. guide (*1-56334-076-3*) Hampton-Brown.
Humberstone. Things at Home. (gr. 2-5). 1981. (Usborne-Hayes); pap. 4.50 (*0-86020-501-0*) EDC.
James, Alan. Homes in Cold Places. (Illus.). 32p. (gr. 2-5). 1989. 13.50 (*0-8225-2131-8*) Lerner Pubns.
—Homes in Hot Places. (Illus.). 32p. (gr. 2-5). 1989. 13.50 (*0-8225-2132-6*) Lerner Pubns.
—Homes on Water. (Illus.). 32p. (gr. 2-5). 1989. 13.50 (*0-8225-2127-X*) Lerner Pubns.
Jensen, P. My House. (Illus.). 28p. (ps-2). 1990. 10.50 (*0-516-05359-0*); pap. 3.95 (*0-516-45359-9*) Childrens.
Lambert, Mark. Homes in the Future. (Illus.). 32p. (gr. 2-5). 1989. 13.50 (*0-8225-2126-1*) Lerner Pubns.
Moving Day. (Illus.). 32p. (ps). 1990. 2.99 (*0-517-69195-7*) Random Hse Value.
Noonan, Diane. Houses That Move. Black, Don, illus. LC 92-27085. 1993. 14.00 (*0-383-03574-0*) SRA Schl Grp.
Rickard, Graham. Building Homes. (Illus.). 32p. (gr. 2-5). 1989. 13.50 (*0-8225-2129-6*) Lerner Pubns.
—Homes in Space. (Illus.). 32p. (gr. 2-5). 1989. 13.50 (*0-8225-2125-3*) Lerner Pubns.
—Mobile Homes. (Illus.). 32p. (gr. 2-5). 1989. 13.50 (*0-8225-2130-X*) Lerner Pubns.
Seltzer, Isadore. The House I Live In: At Home in America. Seltzer, Isadore, illus. LC 91-27469. 32p. (gr. 1-5). 1992. RSBE 14.95 (*0-02-781801-2*, Macmillan Child Bk) Macmillan Child Grp.
Steele, Philip. House Through the Ages. Howett, Andrew & Davidson, Gordon, illus. LC 91-36481. 32p. (gr. 3-6). 1993. PLB 11.89 (*0-8167-2733-3*); pap. text ed. 3.95 (*0-8167-2734-1*) Troll Assocs.
Tripp, Valerie. No Place Like Home. Callen, Liz, illus. 24p. (Orig.). (gr. 1-3). 1991. pap. text ed. 29.95 big bk. (*1-56334-046-1*); pap. text ed. 6.00 small bk. (*1-56334-052-6*) Hampton-Brown.
Tucker, Sian. Nursery Board: Homes. (ps). 1994. pap. 2.95 (*0-671-88261-9*, Little Simon) S&S Trade.
Weiss, Harvey. Shelters: From Tepee to Igloo. Weiss, Harvey, illus. LC 87-47698. 80p. (gr. 5-8). 1988. (Crowell Jr Bks); (Crowell Jr Bks) HarpC Child Bks.

HOUSES–FICTION

Ackerman, Karen. This Old House. Wickstrom, Sylvie, illus. LC 91-20449. 40p. (ps-1). 1992. SBE 14.95 (*0-689-31741-7*, Atheneum Child Bk) Macmillan Child Grp.
Around the House, What Can You Find? (ps). 1993. bds. 4.95 (*1-56458-268-X*) Dorling Kindersley.
Atkins, Rachel. At All Began with a Doormat. (Illus.). 32p. 1994. 11.95 (*1-56062-236-9*) CIS Comm.
Ballard, Robin. Good-bye, House. LC 93-252. (Illus.). 24p. (ps up). 1994. 14.00 (*0-688-12525-5*); PLB 13.93 (*0-688-12526-3*) Greenwillow.
Banks, Ann & Evans, Nancy. Goodbye, House. Russo, Marisabina, illus. 64p. (gr. 2-6). 1988. pap. 7.95 (*0-517-53907-1*, Harmony) Crown Pub Group.
Belcastro, Jani. The Old House on the Hill. Belcastro, Jani, illus. LC 92-59951. 44p. (gr. k-3). 1993. 6.95 (*1-55523-575-1*) Winston-Derek.
Blathwayt, Benedict. Little House by the Sea. (Illus.). 32p. (ps-1). 1994. 14.95 (*1-85681-002-X*, Pub. by J MacRae UK) Trafalgar.
Blume, Judy. Iggie's House. 128p. (gr. 3-6). 1986. pap. 3.99 (*0-440-44062-9*, YB) Dell.
Bour, Daniele. The House from Morning to Night. LC 84-21873. (Illus.). 16p. (ps-3). 1985. 9.95 (*0-916291-01-4*) Kane Miller Bk.
Brown, M. K. Sally's Room. (gr. 5-8). 1993. pap. 3.95 (*0-590-44710-6*) Scholastic Inc.
Brown, Marc. There's No Place Like Home. Brown, Marc, illus. LC 84-4229. 48p. (ps-3). 1984. 5.95 (*0-8193-1125-1*) Parents.
—There's No Place Like Home. LC 93-13040. 13.27 (*0-8368-0978-5*) Gareth Stevens Inc.
Bulla, Clyde R. Charlie's House. Flavin, Teresa, illus. LC 92-23998. 96p. (gr. 3-6). 1993. 14.00 (*0-679-83841-4*) Knopf Bks Yng Read.
Burton, Virginia L. The Little House. (Illus.). (gr. k-3). 1978. 13.95 (*0-395-18156-9*); pap. 4.95 (*0-395-25938-X*) HM.
Calhoun, Mary. Katie John. Frame, Paul, illus. LC 60-5775. (gr. 3-6). 1960. PLB 12.89 (*0-06-020951-8*) HarpC Child Bks.
Cameron, Ann. The Stories Julian Tells. Strugness, Ann, illus. LC 80-18023. 96p. (gr. k-5). 1981. 8.95 (*0-394-84301-0*); lib. bdg. 10.99 (*0-394-94301-5*) Pantheon.
Carle, Eric. My Apron. Carle, Eric, illus. LC 93-36342. 1994. 22.95 (*0-399-22685-0*, Philomel Bks) Putnam Pub Group.
Cassedy, Sylvia. Behind the Attic Wall. LC 82-45922. 320p. (gr. 3-7). 1983. (Crowell Jr Bks); PLB 14.89 (*0-690-04337-6*, Crowell Jr Bks) HarpC Child Bks.
—Lucie Babbidge's House. 256p. 1993. pap. 3.99 (*0-380-71812-X*, Camelot) Avon.
Christopher, John. Beyond the Burning Lands: The Sword of the Spirits Trilogy. LC 78-152288. 180p. (gr. 5-9). 1989. pap. 3.95 (*0-02-042572-4*, Collier Young Ad) Macmillan Child Grp.
Couture, Christin. The House on the Hill. (Illus.). 32p. (ps up). 1991. 13.95 (*0-374-33474-9*) FS&G.
De Brunhoff, Laurent. Chateau du Roi Babar. (FRE.). (gr. 3-8). 15.95 (*0-685-11078-8*) Fr & Eur.
Desimini, Lisa. My House. (gr. k-3). 1994. 15.95 (*0-8050-3144-8*) H Holt & Co.
Desputeaux, Helene. My House. (Illus.). 26p. (ps). 1993. bds. 2.95 (*2-921198-24-X*, Pub. by Les Edits Herit CN) Adams Inc MA.
Donaldson, Julia. A Squash & a Squeeze. Scheffler, Axel, illus. LC 92-16507. 32p. (ps-3). 1993. SBE 14.95 (*0-689-50571-X*, M K McElderry) Macmillan Child Grp.
Dragonwagon, Crescent. Home Place. Pinkney, Jerry, illus. LC 89-32911. 32p. (gr. k-3). 1990. SBE 14.95 (*0-02-733190-3*, Macmillan Child Bk) Macmillan Child Grp.
—Home Place. Pinkney, Jerry, illus. LC 92-46366. 40p. (gr. k-3). 1993. pap. 4.95 (*0-689-71758-X*, Aladdin) Macmillan Child Grp.
Emberley, Rebecca. My House Mi Casa. (ps-3). 1993. pap. 5.95 (*0-316-23448-6*) Little.
Erickson, Gina C. & Foster, Kelli C. What Rose Doesn't Know. Gifford, Kerri, illus. LC 93-36071. 24p. (ps-3). 1994. pap. 3.50 (*0-8120-1672-6*) Barron.
Felix, Monique. House: Mouse Books. (Illus.). 32p. (ps). 1993. pap. 2.95 (*1-56189-096-0*) Amer Educ Pub.
George, Jean C. One Day in the Desert. Brenner, Fred, illus. LC 82-45924. 48p. (gr. 5-7). 1983. PLB 13.89 (*0-690-04341-4*, Crowell Jr Bks) HarpC Child Bks.
Gliori, Debi. New Big House. Gliori, Debi, illus. LC 91-71829. 32p. (ps up). 1994. pap. 4.99 (*1-56402-371-0*) Candlewick Pr.
Goffstein, Brooke. A House, a Home. Goffstein, Brooke, illus. LC 88-37376. 32p. (ps up). 1989. HarpC Child Bks.
Herman, Charlotte. House on Walenska Street. (gr. 4-7). 1991. pap. 3.95 (*0-14-034405-5*, Puffin) Puffin Bks.
Hertz, Grete J. Yellow House. Clante, Iben, tr. (Illus.). (gr. 2-7). 1991. 12.95 (*0-920236-15-4*, Pub. by Annick CN) Firefly Bks Ltd.
Hillert, Margaret. House for Little Red. (Illus.). (ps-k). 1970. PLB 6.95 (*0-8136-5013-5*, TK2312); pap. 3.50 (*0-8136-5513-7*, TK2313) Modern Curr.
Hoberman, Mary A. A House Is a House for Me. Fraser, Betty, illus. 48p. (ps-3). 1982. pap. 3.99 (*0-14-050394-3*, Puffin) Puffin Bks.
—A House Is a House for Me. Fraser, Betty, illus. 1993. pap. 6.99 incl. cassette (*0-14-095116-4*, Puffin) Puffin Bks.
Hoberman, Mary Ann. A House Is a House for Me. Fraser, Betty, illus. (gr. k-3). 1984. incl. cassette 19.95 (*0-941078-33-7*); pap. 12.95 incl. cassette (*0-941078-31-0*); incl. 4 bks., cassette, & guide 27.95 (*0-317-07117-3*) Live Oak Media.
Holcroft, Anthony. The China Teacup. Webb, Philip, illus. LC 93-6620. 1994. write for info. (*0-383-03682-8*) SRA Schl Grp.
A House Is a House for Me. (ps-3). 1988. pap. 6.95 incl. cassette (*0-14-095065-6*, Puffin) Puffin Bks.
Hutchins, Pat. The House That Sailed Away. Hutchins, Lawrence, illus. LC 74-9823. 192p. (gr. 2-6). 1975. PLB 11.88 (*0-688-84013-2*) Greenwillow.
Katz, Avner. Tortoise Solves a Problem. Katz, Avner, illus. LC 91-32503. 40p. (gr. k-3). 1993. 13.00 (*0-06-020798-1*); PLB 12.89 (*0-06-020799-X*) HarpC Child Bks.
Keller, Beverly. Desdemona Moves On. LC 92-7127. 176p. (gr. 3-7). 1992. SBE 13.95 (*0-02-749751-8*, Bradbury Pr) Macmillan Child Grp.
Krauss, Ruth. Very Special House. Sendak, Maurice, illus. LC 53-7115. (ps-1). 1953. PLB 15.89 (*0-06-023456-3*) HarpC Child Bks.
L'Engle, Madeleine. A House Like a Lotus. (gr. 6-12). 1985. pap. 3.99 (*0-440-93685-3*, LFL) Dell.
Lepon, Shoshana. Hillel Builds a House. Barr, Marilyn, illus. LC 92-39383. 1993. cancelled (*0-929371-41-0*); pap. 5.95 (*0-929371-42-9*) Kar Ben.
Le Sieg, Theodore. In a People House. (Illus.). (ps-1). 1972. 6.95 (*0-394-82395-8*); lib. bdg. 7.99 (*0-394-92395-2*) Random Bks Yng Read.
Lindbergh, Reeve. If I'd Known Then What I Know Now. Root, Kimberly B., illus. LC 93-24058. 1994. 14.99 (*0-670-85351-8*) Viking Child Bks.
Lionni, Leo. Biggest House in the World. Lionni, Leo, illus. LC 68-12646. (gr. k-3). 1968. lib. bdg. 14.99 (*0-394-90944-5*) Pantheon.
Lobel, Arnold. Ming Lo Moves the Mountain. LC 92-47364. (Illus.). 32p. (ps up). 1993. pap. text ed. 4.95 (*0-688-10995-0*, Mulberry) Morrow.
Lodge, Bernard. Door to Door. Roffey, Maureen, illus. LC 93-22203. 32p. (ps-3). 1993. smythe sewn reinforced 14.95 (*1-879085-80-1*) Whsprng Coyote Pr.
Loelling, Carol. Whose House Is This? (Illus.). 24p. (gr. 3-6). 1978. 5.95 (*0-8431-0444-9*) Price Stern.
Lord, Bette B. In the Year of the Boar & Jackie Robinson. Simont, Marc, illus. LC 83-48440. 176p. (gr. 3-7). 1984. PLB 13.89 (*0-06-024004-0*) HarpC Child Bks.
Lunn, Janet. The Root Cellar. LC 83-3246. 256p. (gr. 5 up). 1983. SBE 14.95 (*0-684-17855-9*, Scribners Young Read) Macmillan Child Grp.
McGraw, S. This Old New House. (Illus.). 32p. (ps-8). 1989. 12.95 (*1-55037-035-9*, Pub. by Annick CN); pap. 4.95 (*1-55037-034-0*, Pub. by Annick CN) Firefly Bks Ltd.
McKean, Thomas. Secret of the Seven Willows. LC 91-4447. 160p. 1991. pap. 12.95 3-pc. bdg. (*0-671-72997-7*) S&S Trade.
McKillip, Patricia. The House on Parchment Street. Robinson, Charles, illus. LC 90-27119. 192p. (gr. 3-7). 1991. pap. 3.95 (*0-689-71471-8*, Aladdin) Macmillan Child Grp.
Manning, Mick. A Ruined House. LC 93-21295. 32p. (ps up). 1994. 14.95 (*1-56402-453-9*) Candlewick Pr.
Maxwell, William. Bun. Stevenson, James, illus. LC 93-42390. 1995. write for info. (*0-679-86053-3*); PLB write for info. (*0-679-96053-8*) Knopf Bks Yng Read.
Mitchell, Greg. Our Playhouse. Ridgeway, Jo A., illus. LC 92-21451. 1993. 3.75 (*0-383-03647-X*) SRA Schl Grp.
Monjo, F. N. House on Stink Alley. (gr. 4-7). 1991. pap. 3.25 (*0-440-43376-2*, YB) Dell.
Novak, Matt. Elmer Blunt's Open House. LC 91-38424. (Illus.). 24p. (ps-1). 1992. 14.95 (*0-531-05998-7*); PLB 14.99 (*0-531-08598-8*) Orchard Bks Watts.
Pinkwater, Daniel M. Big Orange Splot. (Illus.). 32p. 1992. Repr. of 1972 ed. 12.95 (*0-8038-9346-9*) Hastings.
Pryor, Bonnie. The House on Maple Street. Peck, Beth, illus. LC 86-12648. 32p. (gr. k-3). 1987. 15.95 (*0-688-06380-2*); lib. bdg. 14.88 (*0-688-06381-0*) Morrow Jr Bks.

Rogers, Paul & Rogers, Emma. Our House. Lamont, Priscilla, illus. LC 92-53015. 40p. (ps up). 1993. 14.95 (*1-56402-134-3*) Candlewick Pr.
Rusty's House. 1989. 2.99 (*0-517-69122-1*) Random Hse Value.
Saul, Carol P. Someplace Else. Root, Barrett, illus. (gr. 4 up). 1995. pap. 14.00 (*0-671-87283-4*, S&S BFYR) S&S Trade.
Schade, Susan & Buller, Jon. Snug House, Bug House. LC 93-34058. (Illus.). 48p. (ps-1). 1994. 6.95 (*0-679-85300-6*); PLB 7.99 (*0-679-95300-0*) Random Bks Yng Read.
Shinhav, Chaya. Cien Cuartos. Writer, C. C. & Nielsen, Lisa C., trs. Elchanan, illus. (SPA.). 24p. (Orig.). (ps). 1992. pap. text ed. 3.00x (*1-56134-169-X*) Dushkin Pub.
—A Hundred Rooms. Kriss, David, tr. from HEB. Elchanan, illus. 24p. (Orig.). (ps). 1992. pap. text ed. 3.00x (*1-56134-159-2*) Dushkin Pub.
Skiff, Andrea. Blueberry & the Victorian House. Peterson, Elizabeth J., ed. (Illus.). 27p. (Orig.). (gr. 2-5). 1992. pap. 5.95 (*0-938911-03-1*) Indiv Educ Syst.
Taylor, Dorothy L. Abigail's New Home. Schimmel, Beth, illus. LC 82-238196. 20p. (gr. k-3). 7.50 (*0-9610640-0-5*) D L Taylor.
Taylor, E. J. Ivy Cottage. LC 91-58810. (Illus.). (ps up). 1992. 12.95 (*1-56402-124-6*) Candlewick Pr.
Voelzke, Daryl E. Pierre Penguin: Finds a New Home. 24p. (ps-5). 1991. 11.95 (*0-9630803-0-X*) D E Voelzke.
York, Carol B. Pudmuddles. Thiesing, Lisa, illus. LC 91-23596. 48p. (gr. 2-5). 1993. 13.00 (*0-06-020436-2*); PLB 12.89 (*0-06-020437-0*) HarpC Child Bks.
—Pudmuddles. LC 91-23596. (gr. 4-7). 1994. pap. 3.95 (*0-06-440527-3*) HarpC Child Bks.
Yue, Charlotte & Yue, David. The Igloo. LC 88-6154. (Illus.). 128p. (gr. 3-7). 1988. 13.45 (*0-395-44613-9*) HM.
Zelinsky, Paul O., adapted by. & illus. The Maid & the Mouse & the Odd-Shaped House. 32p. (ps-2). 1993. pap. 4.99 (*0-14-054946-3*, Puff Unicorn) Puffin Bks.
—The Maid & the Mouse & the Odd-Shaped House. 32p. (ps-2). 1993. 14.99 (*0-525-45095-5*, DCB) Dutton Child Bks.

HOUSES–REPAIRING

Boy Scouts of America. Home Repairs. (Illus.). 42p. (gr. 6-12). 1961. pap. 1.85 (*0-8395-3329-2*, 33247) BSA.

HOUSES OF ANIMALS

see Animals–Habitations

HOUSING

see also City Planning

Berck, Judith. No Place to Be: Voices of Homeless Children. Coles, Robert, frwd. by. (Illus.). 144p. (gr. 5 up). 1992. 14.45 (*0-395-53350-3*) HM.
Davis, Bertha. America's Housing Crisis. LC 89-37028. (gr. 7-12). 1990. PLB 13.40 (*0-531-10917-8*) Watts.
Housing Choices. (gr. 7-12). 1989. Package of 10. 15.95 (*1-877844-02-0*, 2421) Meridian Educ.

HOUSING–FICTION

Beskow, Elsa. Peter's Old House. 28p. (ps-k). 1990. 14.95 (*0-86315-102-7*, 1479, Pub. by Floris Bks UK) Anthroposophic.
Holman, Felice. Secret City, U. S. A. LC 89-39841. 208p. (gr. 5-9). 1990. SBE 14.95 (*0-684-19168-7*, Scribners Young Read) Macmillan Child Grp.
Snyder, Carol. The Great Condominium Rebellion. Kramer, Anthony, illus. LC 81-65491. 128p. (gr. 4-6). 1981. PLB 11.95 (*0-385-28352-0*) Delacorte.
Zable, Rona S. Landing on Marvin Gardens. 1991. pap. 3.50 (*0-553-29288-9*) Bantam.

HOUSTON, SAMUEL, 1793-1863

Gleiter, Jan & Thompson, Kathleen. Sam Houston. LC 87-24161. (Illus.). 32p. (Orig.). (gr. 2-5). 1987. PLB 19.97 (*0-8172-2660-5*) Raintree Steck-V.
James, Marquis. The Raven: A Biography of Sam Houston. (Illus.). 527p. (gr. 10-12). 1988. pap. 12.95 (*0-292-77040-5*) U of Tex Pr.
Latham, Jean L. Sam Houston: Hero of Texas. (Illus.). 80p. (gr. 2-6). 1991. Repr. of 1965 ed. lib. bdg. 12.95 (*0-7910-1441-X*) Chelsea Hse.
Zadra, Dan. Statesmen in America: Sam Houston. rev. ed. (gr. 2-4). 1988. PLB 14.95 (*0-88682-187-8*) Creative Ed.

HUDSON, HENRY, d. 1611

Asimov, Isaac. Henry Hudson. LC 90-23948. (Illus.). 64p. (gr. 3-4). 1991. PLB 18.60 (*0-8368-0558-5*) Gareth Stevens Inc.
Harley, Ruth. Henry Hudson. new ed. LC 78-18053. (Illus.). 48p. (gr. 4-7). 1979. PLB 10.59 (*0-89375-171-5*); pap. 3.50 (*0-89375-163-4*) Troll Assocs.
Syme, Ronald. Henry Hudson. LC 90-49174. (Illus.). 152p. (gr. 6-10). 1991. PLB 13.95 (*1-55905-081-0*) Marshall Cavendish.
Weiner, Eric. Story of Henry Hudson. (gr. 4-7). 1991. pap. 2.99 (*0-440-40513-0*, YB) Dell.

HUDSON RIVER

Lourie, Peter. Hudson River: An Adventure from the Mountains to the Sea. LC 91-72870. (Illus.). 48p. (gr. 3-7). 1992. 15.95 (*1-878093-01-0*) Boyds Mills Pr.

HUGHES, JAMES LANGSTON, 1902-1967

AESOP Enterprises, Inc. Staff & Crenshaw, Gwendolyn J. Langston Hughes: The Poetic Rebirth of Self-Identity. 32p. (gr. 3-12). 1991. pap. write for info. incl. cassette (*1-880771-05-5*) AESOP Enter.
Berry, S. L. Langston Hughes. LC 93-741. 1994. PLB 18.95 (*0-88682-616-0*) Creative Ed.
Cooper, Floyd. Coming Home: From the Life of Langston Hughes. Cooper, Floyd, illus. LC 93-36332. 32p. (ps-5). 1994. PLB 15.95 (*0-399-22682-6*, Philomel Bks) Putnam Pub Group.
Dunham, Montrew. Langston Hughes: Young Poet. LC 93-21128. 1995. pap. 4.95 (*0-689-71787-3*, Aladdin) Macmillan Child Grp.
McKissack, Patricia & McKissack, Fredrick. Langston Hughes: Great American Poet. LC 92-2583. (Illus.). 32p. (gr. 1-4). 1992. lib. bdg. 12.95 (*0-89490-315-2*) Enslow Pubs.
Rummel, Jack. Langston Hughes. King, Coretta Scott, intro. by. (Illus.). 112p. (Orig.). (gr. 5 up). 1989. 17.95 (*1-55546-595-1*); pap. 9.95 (*0-7910-0201-2*) Chelsea Hse.
Walker, Alice. Langston Hughes, American Poet. LC 73-9565. (Illus.). 40p. (gr. 2-5). 1974. PLB 14.89 (*0-690-00219-X*, Crowell Jr Bks) HarpC Child Bks.

HULL HOUSE, CHICAGO

Kent, Deborah. Jane Addams & Hull House. LC 91-37882. (Illus.). 32p. (gr. 3-6). PLB 12.30, Apr. 1992 (*0-516-04852-X*); pap. 3.95, Jul. 1992 (*0-516-44852-8*) Childrens.

HUMAN BODY

see Anatomy

HUMAN FIGURE IN ART

see Anatomy

HUMAN RACE

see Anthropology; Man

HUMAN RELATIONS

Here are entered works that deal with the integration of people so that they can live and work together with psychological, social and economic satisfaction.

see also Behavior; Intercultural Education; Prejudices and Antipathies; Psychology, Applied; Social Adjustment; Toleration;

also interpersonal relations between individuals or group of individuals, e.g. Parent and Child

Carney, Mary L. Too Tough to Hurt. 128p. 1991. pap. 6.99 (*0-310-28621-2*, Youth Bks) Zondervan.
Carroll, Jeri A. Let's Learn about Getting Along with Others. 64p. (ps-2). 1988. wkbk 7.95 (*0-86653-439-3*, GA1042) Good Apple.
Crum, Thomas F. Magic of Conflict Workshop for Young People. Heffernan, Cheryl, illus. (gr. 6-12). 1989. multi-media kit 49.95 (*1-877803-04-9*) AIKI Works.

Curry, Jerri. The Swan: A Storybook for Adults & Other Children. Poppler, Sarah, illus. 21p. (gr. 7 up). 1989. incl. cassette 13.95g (*0-944586-00-7*) WIN Pub.
A Storybook for Adults & Other Children is a series of nine metaphoric family fairytales. The poetic stories have many meanings that allow the audience to explore life's issues. Published: THE SWAN (commitment) with seven-minute audio tape. Crystal learns about love on Puddle Pond as narrated by Thomas the toad. Work in progress: Shy Violet (self esteem) won't bloom because she doesn't think she is pretty. Old Ollie the Octopus (fear) is afraid to leave his rock & the Angel fish succeeds in helping Ollie let go of his rock. Snowflake (control) wants to know where she will land. Klinker the Clown (special needs) learns to accept his multi-striped face when the other clowns have solid color faces. Puffer (friendship) learns how her actions impact those around her. The Musical Miracle Merry-Go-Round (positive thinking) allows David to achieve the ability to believe. Buttercup & the butterflies (competition) want Mother Nature to make a decision about competition. Star (identity) wants to know who she is, so she searches throughout the universe to find out. There are questions & activities at the end of each story. Center for Family Mediation & Counseling, Jerri Curry, Ph.D. MFCC, 1530 Webster St., D, Fairfield, CA 94533; (707) 428-0228.
Publisher Provided Annotation.

Davis, Duane. My Friends & Me Story Book. rev. ed. (ps-k). 1988. pap. text ed. 73.25 (*0-88671-326-9*, 4605) Am Guidance.
Duplex, Mary. Trouble with a Capital T. 96p. 1992. pap. 7.95 (*0-8163-1057-2*) Pacific Pr Pub Assn.
Eager, George B. Peer Pressure: How to Handle It. Philbrook, Diana, illus. 29p. (Orig.). 1993. pap. 3.00x (*1-879224-10-0*) Mailbox.
—Relationships: How to be a Winner! Philbrook, Diana, illus. (Orig.). (gr. 6-12). 1993. pap. 3.00x (*1-879224-08-9*) Mailbox.
Educational Assessment Publishing Company Staff. Parent - Child Learning Library: Healthy Relationships. (Illus.). 32p. (gr. k-3). 1991. text ed. 9.95 (*0-942277-55-4*) Am Guidance.
—Parent - Child Learning Library: Healthy Relationships English Big Book. (Illus.). 32p. (gr. k-3). 1991. text ed. 16.95 (*0-942277-73-2*) Am Guidance.
—Parent - Child Learning Library: Health Relationships Spanish Big Book. (SPA., Illus.). 32p. (gr. k-3). 1991. text ed. 16.95 (*0-942277-74-0*) Am Guidance.
—Parent - Child Learning Library: Healthy Relationships Spanish Edition. (SPA.). 32p. (ps). 1991. text ed. 9.95 (*0-942277-91-0*) Am Guidance.
Elchoness, Monte. Why Can't Anyone Hear Me? A Guide for Surviving Adolescence. 2nd, rev. ed. Elchoness, Monte, illus. LC 86-737. 200p. (gr. 6-12). 1989. pap. 10.95 (*0-936781-06-8*, Dist. by Publishers Group West) Monroe Pr.
Fellows, Bob. Easily Fooled: New Insights & Techniques for Resisting Manipulation. rev. ed. Gray, Steve, illus. 64p. (Orig.). (gr. 7 up). 1989. pap. 5.95 (*0-9622879-0-3*) Mind Matters.
Friedl, Michael. Ah...To Be A Kid: Three Dozen Aikido Games for Children of All Ages. Ransom, Stefan P., illus. 55p. (Orig.). 1994. pap. 9.95 (*0-9638530-1-5*, Castle Capers) Magical Michael.

Garbarino, James. Let's Talk about Living in a World with Violence: An Activity Book for School-Age Children. Csaszar, Sonia, tr. Green, Phillip M., illus. (SPA.). 48p. (gr. k-8). 1993. Wkbk. 10.00 (*0-9639159-0-8*) Erikson Inst.
The new activity workbook for school-age children represents the latest step in a violence intervention program developed over the past seven years by Erikson Institute for Advanced Study in Child Development. Written by James Garbarino, Ph.D., the workbook combines reading, writing, drawing & discussion to help children clarify their thoughts, feelings & knowledge about violence. It seeks to help children discover the meaning of violence, that fear is normal & that there are things children can do to feel better & safer with help from caring adults. The workbook encourages a strengthening of the relationships with community resources that can create a positive change for children & families. Two guides--one for parents & one for teachers, counselors & other professionals--accompany the text to assist adults as they use the workbook with children.
Publisher Provided Annotation.

Hensel, Lila. Who Is My Neighbor? A Primer for Group Discussion. 32p. (Orig.). 1989. pap. 3.95 (*0-932727-29-8*) Hope Pub Hse.
Hislop, Julia. Coping with Rejection. LC 90-29123. 107p. (gr. 7-12). 1991. PLB 14.95 (*0-8239-1183-7*) Rosen Group.
Kramer, Patricia. The Dynamics of Relationships. rev. ed. (Illus.). 430p. (Orig.). (gr. 8-12). 1990. pap. text ed. 34.95 tchr's. manual (*0-317-90984-3*) Equal Partners.
—The Dynamics of Relationships: A Guide to Developing Self-Esteem & Social Skills for Teens & Young Adults, Bk. 1. rev. ed. (Illus.). 331p. (Orig.). (gr. 8-12). 1990. pap. text ed. 16.95 student manual (*0-317-90983-5*) Equal Partners.
—The Dynamics of Relationships: A Guide to Developing Self-Esteem & Social Skills for Teens & Young Adults, Bk. 2. rev. ed. (Illus.). 49p. (gr. 8-12). 1990. pap. text ed. 8.95 student manual (sexuality) (*0-317-90981-9*) Equal Partners.
Kramer, Patricia & Frazer, Linda. The Dynamics of Relationships. rev. ed. (Illus.). 125p. (gr. 4-7). 1990. pap. text ed. 13.95 student manual (*0-317-90982-7*) Equal Partners.
Moncure, Jane B. You & Me. Bolt, John, illus. LC 81-17009. 112p. (gr. 2-6). 1980. PLB 14.95 (*0-89565-212-9*) Childs World.
Morpugo, Michael. The War of Jenkins' Ear. LC 94-7602. 1995. 15.95 (*0-399-22735-0*, Philomel Bks) Putnam Pub Group.

Needle, Jan. The Bully. large type ed. (Illus.). (gr. 1-8). 1994. 15.95 (*0-7451-2223-X*, Galaxy etc.) Chivers N Amer.

Ottens, Allen J. Coping with Romantic Breakup. 147p. (gr. 7-12). 1987. PLB 14.95 (*0-8239-0649-3*) Rosen Group.

Packer, Alex J. Bringing up Parents: The Teenager's Handbook. Espeland, Pamela, ed. Pulver, Harry, Jr., illus. LC 92-36625. 272p. (gr. 7 up). 1993. pap. 12.95 (*0-915793-48-2*) Free Spirit Pub.

Peck, Lee. Coping with Cliques. Rosen, Ruth, ed. LC 92-12380. (gr. 7-12). 1992. 14.95 (*0-8239-1412-7*) Rosen Group.

Pincus, Debbie. Interactions. 96p. (gr. 4-9). 1988. wkbk. 10.95 (*0-86653-448-2*, GA1057) Good Apple.

Relationships. (gr. 7-12). 1989. Package of 10. 15.95 (*1-877844-05-5*, 2621) Meridian Educ.

Schmidt, Fran & Friedman, Alice. Creative Conflict Solving for Kids: Grades 3-4. 2nd ed. 90p. (gr. 3-4). 1993. Tchr's ed., incl. poster. 21.95 (*1-878227-17-3*); Wkbk. 11.95 (*0-685-64734-X*) Peace Educ.

—Peacemaking Skills for Little Kids. 2nd ed. (Illus.). 76p. (ps-2). 1993. Tchr's ed., incl. puppet, cass. & poster. 54.95 (*1-878227-16-5*); Wkbk. 11.95 (*1-878227-15-7*) Peace Educ.

Schwartz, L. Feelings about Friends. (gr. 3-7). 1988. 4.95 (*0-88160-168-3*, LW 281) Learning Wks.

Scott, Sharon. Too Smart for Trouble. Phillips, George, illus. 112p. (Orig.). (gr. k-5). 1990. pap. 7.95 (*0-87425-121-4*) Human Res Dev Pr.

Scott, Sharon & Nicholas. Not Better... Not Worse... Just Different. Phillips, George, illus. 118p. (Orig.). (gr. k-5). 1992. pap. 7.95 (*0-87425-195-8*) Human Res Dev Pr.

Spainhower, Steven D. School Smart: Behaviors & Skills for Student Success, 93-94. Wilson, Dana & Brown, Steven J., eds. (Illus.). 205p. (Orig.). (gr. 7-12). 1993. pap. text ed. 18.95 (*0-9637573-0-X*) Education Res.

Stanish, Bob. The Giving Book. 112p. (gr. 3-8). 1988. 10. 95 (*0-86653-459-8*, GA1065) Good Apple.

Webster-Doyle, Terrence. Why Is Everybody Always Picking on Me? A Guide to Handling Bullies. (Illus.). (gr. 5-12). 1991. 17.95 (*0-942941-23-3*); pap. 12.95 (*0-942941-22-5*) Atrium Soc Pubns.

Wirths, Claudine G. & Bowman-Kruhm, Mary. Your Power with Words. (Illus.). 64p. (gr. 5-8). 1993. PLB 14.95 (*0-8050-2075-6*) TFC Bks NY.

Ziegler, Sandra. Fairness. Endres, Helen, illus. LC 88-18976. (ENG & SPA.). 32p. (gr. k-3). 1989. PLB 14. 95 (*0-89565-390-7*) Childs World.

—Understanding. Williams, Jenny, illus. LC 88-23745. (SPA & ENG.). 32p. (ps-2). 1989. PLB 14.95 (*0-89565-452-0*) Childs World.

HUMAN RELATIONS–FICTION

Aiello. Secrets Aren't Always. 1991. 0.85 (*0-8050-2019-5*) H Holt & Co.

Asher, Sandy. Out of Here: A Senior Class Yearbook. LC 92-35188. 160p. (gr. 7 up). 1993. 14.99 (*0-525-67418-7*, Lodestar Bks) Dutton Child Bks.

Bell, Mary S. Sonata for Mind & Heart. LC 91-20588. 224p. (gr. 7 up). 1992. SBE 14.95 (*0-689-31734-4*, Atheneum Child Bk) Macmillan Child Grp.

Bunting, Eve. Smoky Night. Diaz, David, illus. LC 93-14885. (gr. 4 up). 1994. 14.95 (*0-15-269954-6*) Harbrace.

Cohen, Barbara. People Like Us. 1987. 13.95 (*0-553-05441-4*) Bantam.

Conly, Jane L. Crazy Lady! LC 92-18348. 192p. (gr. 5 up). 1993. 13.00 (*0-06-021357-4*); PLB 12.89 (*0-06-021360-4*) HarpC Child Bks.

Cornwell, Anita. The Girls of Summer. Caines, Kelly, illus. LC 88-64051. 100p. (Orig.). (gr. 6 up). 1989. pap. 12.95 (*0-938678-11-6*) New Seed.

Cruise, Beth. Exit, Stage Right. LC 94-16981. (gr. 5 up). 1994. pap. 3.95 (*0-02-042792-1*, Collier) Macmillan.

—Mistletoe Magic. 1994. pap. 3.95 (*0-02-042794-8*, Aladdin) Macmillan Child Grp.

—Saved by the Bell: Girls' Night Out. LC 92-24648. 144p. (gr. 5 up). 1992. pap. 2.95 (*0-02-042766-2*, Collier Young Ad) Macmillan Child Grp.

Duffy, James. The Graveyard Gang. LC 92-30990. 192p. (gr. 5-7). 1993. SBE 14.95 (*0-684-19449-X*, Scribners Young Read) Macmillan Child Grp.

Faber, Adele & Mazlish, Elaine. Bobby & the Brockles. Morehouse, Hank, illus. LC 93-42283. 64p. (Orig.). 1994. pap. 15.00 (*0-380-77067-9*) Avon.

Foley, June. Susanna Siegelbaum Gives up Guys. 160p. 1991. 13.95 (*0-590-43699-6*, Scholastic Hardcover) Scholastic Inc.

Galvin, Matthew R. Robby Really Transforms: A Story About Grown-ups Helping Children. Ferraro, Sandra, illus. LC 87-34883. 48p. (ps-6). 1988. lib. bdg. 16.95 (*0-945354-05-3*); pap. 6.95 (*0-945354-02-9*) Magination Pr.

Green, Kate. Between Friends. (Illus.). 32p. (gr. 1-4). 1992. 15.95 (*0-89565-780-5*) Childs World.

Greene, Constance C. I & Sproggy. McCully, Emily A., illus. 144p. (gr. 5 up). 1981. pap. 1.95 (*0-440-43986-8*, YB) Dell.

Greene, Graham. The Destructors. (gr. 4-9). 1989. 13.95 (*0-88682-348-X*, 97213-098) Creative Ed.

Guccione, Leslie D. Nobody Listens to Me. 176p. (gr. 3-7). 1991. pap. 2.75 (*0-590-43106-4*, Apple Paperbacks) Scholastic Inc.

Gunn, Robin J. Surprise Endings. 160p. (Orig.). 1991. pap. 4.99 (*1-56179-024-9*) Focus Family.

Hahn, Mary D. The Wind Blows Backwards. large type ed. LC 93-31870. (gr. 9-12). 1993. 15.95 (*0-7862-0064-2*) Thorndike Pr.

Hamanaka, Sheila. All the Colors of Earth. LC 93-27118. 1994. write for info. (*0-688-11131-9*); PLB write for info. (*0-688-11132-7*) Morrow Jr Bks.

Hess, Debra. Wilson Sat Alone. Greenseid, Diane, illus. LC 93-17616. (ps-2). 1994. pap. 14.00 (*0-671-87046-7*, S&S BFYR) S&S Trade.

Hopper, Nancy J. I Was a Fifth-Grade Zebra. LC 92-30731. (gr. 3-6). 1993. 13.99 (*0-8037-1420-3*); PLB 13.89 (*0-8037-1595-1*) Dial Bks Young.

Hosie, Bounar. Life Belts. LC 92-43048. 1993. 14.95 (*0-385-31074-9*) Delacorte.

Hughes, Dean. One-Man Team. LC 93-44676. (Orig.). (gr. 4-9). 1994. PLB write for info. (*0-679-95441-4*, Bullseye Bks); pap. 3.99 (*0-679-85441-X*) Random Bks Yng Read.

Hughes, Shirley. Chatting. LC 93-22747. 24p. (ps up). 1994. 13.95 (*1-56402-340-0*) Candlewick Pr.

Hurwitz, Johanna. New Neighbors for Nora. reissued ed. Hoban, Lillian, illus. LC 90-47882. 80p. (ps). 1991. Repr. of 1979 ed. 12.95 (*0-688-09947-5*); PLB 12.88 (*0-688-09948-3*, Morrow Jr Bks) Morrow Jr Bks.

Jones, Robin D. The Beginning of Unbelief. LC 92-22907. 160p. (gr. 7 up). 1993. SBE 13.95 (*0-689-31781-6*, Atheneum Child Bk) Macmillan Child Grp.

Levinson, Marilyn. No Boys Allowed. Leer, Rebecca, illus. LC 93-22335. 128p. (gr. 5-8). 1993. PLB 13.95 (*0-8167-3135-7*); pap. 2.95 (*0-8167-3136-5*) BrdgeWater.

Lowry, Lois. Your Move, J. P.! 128p. (gr. 3-7). 1990. 13. 45 (*0-395-53639-1*) HM.

McCullers, Carson. Sucker. Hayes, James, illus. LC 85-29114. 40p. (gr. 4 up). 1986. PLB 13.95 (*0-88682-053-7*) Creative Ed.

The Man Who Cooked for Himself. 1994. 13.27 (*0-8368-0984-X*) Gareth Stevens Inc.

Mango, Karin N. Portrait of Miranda. LC 92-8191. 240p. (gr. 7 up). 1993. 16.00 (*0-06-021777-4*); PLB 15.89 (*0-06-021778-2*) HarpC Child Bks.

Mazer, Norma F. & Mazer, Harry. Heartbeat. (gr. 7 up). 1990. pap. 3.50 (*0-553-28779-6*, Starfire) Bantam.

Miles, Betty. The Trouble with Thirteen. LC 78-31678. 112p. (gr. 3-7). 1989. pap. 2.95 (*0-394-82043-6*) Knopf Bks Yng Read.

Moll, Linda J. A Poison Tree: A Children's Fairy Tale. Moll, Linda J., illus. 40p. (gr. 1 up). 1994. PLB 12.95 (*0-9641641-1-6*) Punking Pr.
A POISON TREE is a children's fairy tale set in Ireland's countryside. Ian McGonagle feels rage for his wee brother, Malachy, after discovering his younger sibling ruined his birthday surprise. Ian vows revenge & calls on the evil fairies for help. Indeed, the evil fairies come with a black seed from which a poison tree will grow. But what happens next is not what Ian expected. Find out how sibling anger turns into forgiveness & how brotherly love prevails in this enchanting Irish fairy tale. A POISON TREE is a charming story for any child learning the sometimes difficult skill of getting along with others. Parents, caregivers, & teachers will find A POISON TREE a valuable social tool in the family, neighborhood or classroom. Children love the comical antics of the fairies & sit in anticipation of A POISON TREE's climactic ending. Teachers will find A POISON TREE a wonderful source for introducing literary devices & techniques to young scholars. A POISON TREE is rich in simile, metaphor, alliteration, rhyming verse,...Illustrations include quaint silhouettes & the text which is scripted in modified 4th-century celtic lettering. A Celtic knotwork border frames the page & completes the beauty of the book. To order A POISON TREE, contact Christopher Moll, P.O. Box 25, Williamson, NY 14589; 315-589-5119.
Publisher Provided Annotation.

Mueller, Karen. Beating Bully O'Brien. (gr. 3-7). 1991. pap. 2.95 (*0-380-75935-7*, Camelot) Avon.

Myers, Walter D. Somewhere in the Darkness. 224p. 1992. 14.95 (*0-590-42411-4*, Scholastic Hardcover) Scholastic Inc.

Obstfeld, Raymond. The Joker & the Thief. LC 92-9823. 1993. 15.00 (*0-385-30855-8*) Delacorte.

Park, Barbara. Operation: Dump the Chump. LC 81-8147. 128p. 1989. pap. 2.95 (*0-394-82592-6*) Knopf Bks Yng Read.

—Skinnybones. LC 81-20791. 112p. (gr. 3-6). 1989. pap. 3.95 (*0-394-82596-9*) Knopf Bks Yng Read.

Pascal, Francine. The Hand-Me-Down Kid. LC 79-5462. (gr. 5-9). 1980. pap. 12.95 (*0-670-35969-6*) Viking Child Bks.

Pevsner, Stella. And You Give Me a Pain, Elaine. (gr. 7-9). 1989. pap. 2.99 (*0-671-68838-3*, Archway) PB.

Posner, Richard. Goodnight, Cinderella. LC 89-17091. 242p. 1989. 13.95 (*0-87131-587-4*) M Evans.

Powell, Randy. Is Kissing a Girl Who Smokes Like Licking an Ashtray? 192p. 1992. 15.00 (*0-374-33632-6*) FS&G.

Reiss, Kathryn. The Glass House People. 1992. 16.95 (*0-15-231040-1*, HB Juv Bks) HarBrace.

Rogers, George L. Mac & Zach from Hackensack. Eskander, Stefanie C., illus. 32p. (gr. k-6). 1992. PLB 12.95 (*0-938399-07-1*); pap. 4.95 (*0-938399-06-3*) Acorn Pub MN.

Roos, Stephen. My Secret Admirer. Newsom, Carol, illus. LC 84-5010. 112p. (gr. 4-6). 1984. 14.95 (*0-385-29342-9*); PLB 13.95 (*0-385-29343-7*) Delacorte.

Silver, Norman. No Tigers in Africa. LC 91-29121. (Illus.). 100p. (gr. 7 up). 1992. 15.00 (*0-525-44733-4*, DCB) Dutton Child Bks.

Smith, Doris B. The Pennywhistle Tree. Bowman, Leslie, illus. LC 90-23119. 144p. (gr. 5-9). 1991. 14.95 (*0-399-21840-8*, Putnam) Putnam Pub Group.

Springstubb, Tricia. With a Name Like Lulu, Who Needs More Trouble? Kastner, Jill, illus. (gr. 5-9). 1989. 14. 95 (*0-385-29823-4*) Delacorte.

Voigt, Cynthia. The Runner. LC 84-21663. 192p. (gr. 8 up). 1985. SBE 15.95 (*0-689-31069-2*, Atheneum Child Bk) Macmillan Child Grp.

Wilkinson, Brenda. Ludell & Willie. 144p. (gr. 6 up). 1985. pap. 2.25 (*0-553-24995-9*) Bantam.

Wilson, Nancy H. The Reason for Janey. LC 93-22930. 176p. (gr. 3-7). 1994. SBE 14.95 (*0-02-793127-7*, Macmillan Child Bk) Macmillan Child Grp.

Wuthering Heights. 1993. pap. text ed. 6.50 (*0-582-09672-3*, 79835) Longman.

Wyss, Thelma H. A Stranger Here. LC 92-15307. 144p. (gr. 7 up). 1993. 14.00 (*0-06-021438-4*); PLB 13.89 (*0-06-021439-2*) HarpC Child Bks.

York, Carol B. Key to the Playhouse. Speirs, John, illus. LC 93-1800. 128p. (gr. 2-5). 1994. 13.95 (*0-590-46258-X*) Scholastic Inc.

Zelonky, Joy. I Can't Always Hear You. (ps-3). 1993. pap. 3.95 (*0-8114-5205-0*) Raintree Steck-V.

Zindel, Paul. David & Della. LC 93-12719. 176p. (gr. 7 up). 1993. 14.00 (*0-06-023353-2*); PLB 13.89 (*0-06-023354-0*) HarpC Child Bks.

HUMAN RIGHTS

see Civil Rights

HUMANISM

Here are entered works on culture founded on the study of the classics.

see also Learning and Scholarship; Renaissance

HUMBOLDT, ALEXANDER, FREIHERR VON, 1769-1859

Gaines, Ann. Alexander von Humboldt, Colossus of Exploration. Goetzmann, William H., ed. Collins, Michael, intro. by. (Illus.). 112p. (gr. 5 up). 1991. lib. bdg. 18.95 (*0-7910-1313-8*) Chelsea Hse.

HUMMING-BIRDS

Foster, Susan Q. The Hummingbird among the Flowers. Oxford Scientific Films Ser., photos by. LC 89-31912. (Illus.). 32p. (gr. 4-6). 1989. PLB 17.27 (*0-8368-0115-6*) Gareth Stevens Inc.

Greenewalt, Crawford H. Hummingbirds. (gr. 5 up). 1990. pap. 15.95 (*0-486-26431-9*) Dover.

Harrison, Virginia. The World of Hummingbirds. Oxford Scientific Films Staff, photos by. LC 89-31913. (Illus.). 32p. (gr. 2-3). 1989. PLB 17.27 (*0-8368-0140-7*) Gareth Stevens Inc.

Hummingbirds. 1991. PLB 14.95 (*0-88682-336-6*) Creative Ed.

Murray, Peter. Hummingbirds. LC 92-32320. (gr. 2-6). 1993. 15.95 (*1-56766-011-8*) Childs World.

Tyrrell, Esther Q. Hummingbirds: Jewels in the Sky. Tyrrell, Robert A., photos by. LC 91-40857. (Illus.). 36p. (gr. 1-5). 1992. 14.00 (*0-517-58390-9*); PLB 14. 99 (*0-517-58391-7*) Crown Bks Yng Read.

HUMORISTS

Colwell, Lynn H. Erma Bombeck: Writer & Humorist. LC 91-40924. (Illus.). 112p. (gr. 6 up). 1992. lib. bdg. 17.95 (*0-89490-384-5*) Enslow Pubs.

HUMOROUS PICTURES

see Cartoons and Caricatures; Comic Books, Strips, Etc.

HUMOROUS POETRY

see also Limericks; Nonsense Verses

Amery, H., compiled by. Funny Poems. (Illus.). 32p. (gr. 2-6). 1990. (Usborne); pap. 5.95 (*0-7460-0444-3*, Usborne) EDC.

Booth, David, selected by. Doctor Knickerbocker & Other Rhymes. Kovalski, Maryann, illus. LC 92-46266. 80p. (gr. 3 up). 1993. 16.95 (*0-395-67168-X*) Ticknor & Flds Bks Yng Read.

Cecil, Laura. Preposterous Pets. Clark, Emma C., photos by. LC 94-6527. (Illus.). 80p. 1995. write for info. RTE (*0-688-13581-1*) Greenwillow.
Cohen, Shari. Prime Time Rhyme. (gr. k-6). 1990. 10.95 (*0-9620467-4-4*) Forward March.
Cole, William E. Oh, How Silly! Ungerer, Tomi, illus. 80p. (gr. 2 up). 1990. pap. 3.95 (*0-14-034441-1*, Puffin) Puffin Bks.
—Oh, What Nonsense. Ungerer, Tomi, illus. 80p. (gr. 2 up). 1990. pap. 3.95 (*0-14-034442-X*, Puffin) Puffin Bks.
Florian, Douglas. Beast Feast. LC 93-10720. (gr. 5 up). 1994. write for info. (*0-15-295178-4*) HarBrace.
Jones, Tim. Wild Critters. Sturgis, Kent, ed. Newman, Leslie, illus. Walker, Tom, photos by. LC 91-7308. (Illus.). 48p. (Orig.). 1992. 15.95x (*0-945397-10-0*); pap. 7.95 (*0-945397-25-9*) Epicenter Pr.
Kennedy, X. J. Drat These Brats! Watts, James, illus. LC 92-33686. 48p. (gr. 3 up). 1993. SBE 12.95 (*0-689-50589-2*, M K McElderry) Macmillan Child Grp.
Kohen, Clarita. El Conejo y el Coyote. Menicucci, Gina, illus. (SPA.). 16p. (Orig.). (gr. k-5). 1993. PLB 7.50x (*1-56492-100-X*) Laredo.
Lansky, Bruce, compiled by. Kids Pick the Funniest Poems. LC 91-31072. (Illus.). 120p. 1991. 14.00 (*0-88166-149-X*) Meadowbrook.
Lear, Edward. Owl & the Pussycat. (ps-3). 1991. 3.95 (*0-8037-1044-5*) Dial Bks Young.
Marshall, James, compiled by. & illus. Pocketful of Nonsense. LC 93-18297. 1993. 12.95 (*0-307-17552-9*, Golden Pr) Western Pub.
Paraskevas, Betty. Junior Kroll & Company. Paraskevas, Michael, illus. LC 93-9138. (ps-6). 1994. 13.95 (*0-15-292855-3*) HarBrace.
Prelutsky, Jack. The New Kid on the Block. Stevenson, James, illus. LC 83-20621. 160p. (gr. 1 up). 1984. 15.95 (*0-688-02271-5*); PLB 15.88 (*0-688-02272-3*) Greenwillow.
—Rolling Harvey Down the Hill. Chess, Victoria, illus. LC 92-24606. 40p. (gr. 2 up). 1993. pap. 4.95 (*0-688-12270-1*, Mulberry) Morrow.
Prelutsky, Jack, compiled by. For Laughing Out Loud: Poems to Tickle Your Funnybone. Priceman, Marjorie, illus. LC 90-33010. 96p. (gr. 2-7). 1991. 14.95 (*0-394-82144-0*); PLB 15.99 (*0-394-92144-5*) Knopf Bks Yng Read.
Time-Life Inc. Editors. On Top of Spaghetti: A Lift-the-Flap Poetry Book. (Illus.). 20p. (ps-2). 1992. write for info. (*0-8094-9291-1*); PLB write for info. (*0-8094-9292-X*) Time-Life.
Wilbur, Richard. Opposites. Drescher, Henrik, illus. LC 92-39472. 1994. 15.95 (*0-15-230563-7*) HarBrace.
Wines, James, illus. Edward Lear's Nonsense. LC 93-20461. 32p. 1994. 12.95 (*0-8478-1682-6*) Rizzoli Intl.

HUMOROUS STORIES
see Wit and Humor

HUNDRED YEARS' WAR, 1339-1453
Lace, William W. The Hundred Years' War. LC 93-22871. (gr. 6-9). 1994. 14.95 (*1-56006-233-9*) Lucent Bks.

HUNDRED YEARS' WAR, 1339-1453–FICTION
Wheeler, Thomas G. All Men Tall. LC 70-77313. (gr. 8 up). 1969. 21.95 (*0-87599-157-2*) S G Phillips.

HUNGARIANS IN THE U. S.
Vardy, Steven B. The Hungarian Americans. Moynihan, Daniel P., intro. by. (Illus.). 112p. (gr. 5 up). 1990. lib. bdg. 17.95 (*0-87754-884-6*) Chelsea Hse.

HUNGARY
Geography Department. Hungary--in Picture. LC 93-3179. 1993. 17.50 (*0-8225-1883-X*) Lerner Pubns.
Hintz, Martin. Hungary. LC 88-10899. (Illus.). 128p. (gr. 5-9). 1988. PLB 20.55 (*0-516-02707-7*) Childrens.
Popescu, Julian. Hungary. (Illus.). 96p. (gr. 5 up). 1988. 14.95 (*0-222-00945-4*) Chelsea Hse.
St. John, Jetty. A Family in Hungary. (Illus.). 32p. (gr. 2-5). 1988. lib. bdg. 13.50 (*0-8225-1683-7*) Lerner Pubns.

HUNGARY–FICTION
Marx, Trish. Hanna's Cold Winter. Knutson, Barbara, illus. LC 92-27143. 1993. 18.95 (*0-87614-772-4*) Carolrhoda Bks.
Seredy, Kate. The Good Master. (Illus.). 196p. (gr. 5-9). 1986. pap. 4.95 (*0-14-030133-X*, Puffin) Puffin Bks.
—Singing Tree. (gr. 4 up). 1990. pap. 4.95 (*0-14-034543-4*, Puffin) Puffin Bks.
—White Stag. Seredy, Kate, illus. (gr. 7 up). 1937. pap. 13.00 (*0-670-76375-6*) Viking Child Bks.
Watkins, Dawn. Zoli's Legacy, Pt. 1: Inheritance. (Illus.). 190p. (Orig.). (gr. 7-12). 1991. pap. 4.95 (*0-89084-596-4*) Bob Jones Univ Pr.

HUNGARY–HISTORY
Blackwood, Alan. Hungarian Uprising, Reading Level 8. LC 86-20341. (Illus.). 80p. (gr. 7 up). 1988. 13.95s.p. (*0-86592-032-X*); PLB 18.60 (*0-685-58793-2*) Rourke Corp.
Handler, Andrew & Meschel, Susan V. Young People Speak: Surviving the Holocaust in Hungary. (Illus.). 160p. (gr. 9-12). 1993. PLB 13.90 (*0-531-11044-3*) Watts.
Siegal, Aranka. Upon the Head of the Goat: A Childhood in Hungary, 1939-1944. LC 81-12642. 214p. (gr. 7 up). 1981. 16.00 (*0-374-38059-7*) FS&G.

HUNGARY–HISTORY–REVOLUTION, 1956
Blackwood, Alan. Hungarian Uprising, Reading Level 8. LC 86-20341. (Illus.). 80p. (gr. 7 up). 1988. 13.95s.p. (*0-86592-032-X*); PLB 18.60 (*0-685-58793-2*) Rourke Corp.

HUNS
Bombarde, Odile. The Barbarians. Grant, Donald, illus. LC 87-34092. 38p. (gr. k-5). 1988. 5.95 (*0-944589-10-3*, 103) Young Discovery Lib.

HUNTING
see also Game Preserves; Tracking and Trailing; Trapping

Bonello, Kurt L. When Pappy Goes Hunting. Bonello, Christi S., illus. LC 94-72497. 24p. (ps-3). 1994. 12.95 (*0-9642248-0-1*) Bonello Studios. Hunting as an effective means of controlling certain animal populations has been part of wildlife conservation efforts around the world for centuries. Also, as a food source & as outdoor recreation, hunting has been a North American tradition for over 200 years. It is a tradition, however, that is seldom portrayed realistically in children's literature. Most wildlife scenarios portrayed in children's stories depict the wildlife Kingdom as illusion or fantasy. If hunting is discussed, it is almost always from a negative perspective & doesn't reflect the reality of hunting in America. While children's books depicting wildlife as fantasy are wonderful in their own way, the truth about hunting needed to be communicated, especially in rural communities where hunting is so much a part of community life. This book is an effective bridge between the wildlife fantasy & the reality of hunting deer. 24 pages & beautifully illustrated, WHEN PAPPY GOES HUNTING is a story that will help preserve the hunting heritage. BONELLO STUDIOS, H.C.R. 4 Box 111, Everett, PA 15537; 800-447-0110.
Publisher Provided Annotation.

Bulpin, Tom V. The Hunter Is Death. Astley-Maberly, C. T., illus. 348p. (gr. 10 up). 1987. Repr. of 1962 ed. 30.00 (*0-940143-08-9*) Safari Pr.
Fleckenstein, Henry A., Jr. Decoys of the Mid-Atlantic Region. LC 79-52438. (Illus.). 256p. (gr. 9-12). 1989. pap. 19.95 (*0-88740-174-0*) Schiffer.
Incredible Great Hunters. 32p. (ps-k). 1994. 4.95 (*1-56458-729-0*) Dorling Kindersley.
Patent, Dorothy H. A Family Goes Hunting. Munoz, William, photos by. (Illus.). 64p. (gr. 4-9). 1991. 14.45 (*0-395-52004-5*, Clarion Bks) HM.
Sobol, Donald J. Encyclopedia Brown's Book of the Wacky Outdoors. (Orig.). (gr. 5 up). 1988. pap. 2.50 (*0-553-15598-9*) Bantam.
Stelson, Caren B. Safari. Stelson, Kim A., illus. 40p. (gr. k-4). 1989. pap. 5.95 (*0-87614-512-8*, First Ave Edns) Lerner Pubns.

HUNTING–FICTION
Backovsky, Jan. Trouble in Paradise. LC 91-47930. (Illus.). 32p. (ps up). 1992. 14.00 (*0-688-11857-7*, Tambourine Bks); PLB 13.93 (*0-688-11858-5*, Tambourine Bks) Morrow.
Ball, Zachary. Bristle Face. LC 93-10394. 208p. (gr. 5 up). 1993. pap. 3.99 (*0-14-036444-7*, Puffin) Puffin Bks.
Bell, Sally. The Young Indiana Jones Chronicles: Safari in Africa. Vincente, Gonzalez, illus. 48p. (gr. 2-4). 1992. pap. write for info. (*0-307-11470-8*, 11470, Golden Pr) Western Pub.
Brady, Kathleen, illus. Oh, A-Hunting We Will Go Big Book. (ps-2). 1988. pap. text ed. 14.00 (*0-922053-14-6*) N Edge Res.
Burgess, Thornton W. The Adventures of Poor Mrs. Quack. (Illus.). 96p. 1993. pap. text ed. 1.00t (*0-486-27818-2*) Dover.
Cosgrove, Stephen. Trapper. James, Robin, illus. 32p. (Orig.). (gr. 1-4). 1982. pap. 2.95 (*0-8431-0587-9*) Price Stern.
Dahl, Roald. Doigt Magique. Galeron, Henri, illus. (FRE.). 63p. (gr. 1-5). 1989. pap. 9.95 (*2-07-031185-6*) Schoenhof.
—The Magic Finger. Ross, Tony, illus. LC 92-31443. 64p. (gr. 2-6). 1993. pap. 3.99 (*0-14-036303-3*) Puffin Bks.
De Paola, Tomie. The Hunter & the Animals: A Wordless Picture Book. LC 81-2875. (Illus.). 32p. (ps-3). 1981. reinforced bdg. 15.95 (*0-8234-0397-1*); pap. 5.95 (*0-8234-0428-5*) Holiday.
Easterling, Bill. Prize in the Snow. Owens, Mary B., illus. LC 92-23411. (ps-3). 1994. 15.95 (*0-316-22489-8*) Little.
Geraghty, Paul. The Hunter. LC 93-22730. (Illus.). 32p. (ps-3). 1994. 15.00 (*0-517-59692-X*); PLB 15.99 (*0-517-59693-8*) Crown Bks Yng Read.
Hughes, Monica. Hunter in the Dark. 144p. (gr. 7 up). 1984. pap. 2.95 (*0-380-67702-4*, Flare) Avon.
Hutchins, Pat. One Hunter. Hutchins, Pat, illus. LC 81-6352. 24p. (ps-1). 1982. 15.00 (*0-688-00614-0*); PLB 14.93 (*0-688-00615-9*) Greenwillow.
—One Hunter. LC 81-6352. (Illus.). 24p. (ps up). 1986. pap. 4.95 (*0-688-06522-8*, Mulberry) Morrow.
Leedy, Loreen. The Dragon ABC Hunt. Leedy, Loreen, illus. LC 85-21907. 36p. (ps-1). 1986. reinforced bdg. 14.95 (*0-8234-0596-6*) Holiday.
Mendoza, George. The Hunter I Might Have Been. (Illus.). 48p. (gr. 3-6). 1989. pap. 6.95 (*0-89815-333-6*) Ten Speed Pr.
Nordqvist, Sven. The Fox Hunt. Nordqvist, Sven, illus. LC 87-28197. 32p. (ps-2). 1988. 12.95 (*0-688-06881-2*); PLB 12.88 (*0-688-06882-0*, Morrow Jr Bks) Morrow Jr Bks.
Patent, Dorothy H. Family Goes Hunting. (gr. 4-7). 1993. pap. 6.95 (*0-395-66507-8*, Clarion Bks) HM.
Paulsen, Gary. Tracker. LC 83-22447. 96p. (gr. 6-8). 1984. SBE 13.95 (*0-02-770220-0*, Bradbury Pr) Macmillan Child Grp.
Peet, Bill. The Gnats of Knotty Pine. Peet, Bill, illus. LC 75-17024. 48p. (gr. k-3). 1984. 13.45 (*0-395-21405-X*); pap. 4.95 (*0-395-36612-7*) HM.
Rhodes, Judy C. The Hunter's Heart. LC 92-47025. 160p. (gr. 4-7). 1993. SBE 14.95 (*0-02-775935-0*, Bradbury Pr) Macmillan Child Grp.
Rohmer, Harriet, et al, eds. Invisible Hunters: Los Cazadores Invisibles. (SPA & ENG., Illus.). 32p. (gr. 2-7). 1993. pap. 5.95 (*0-89239-109-X*) Childrens Book Pr.
Standish, Burt L. Frank Merriwell's Hunting Tour. Rudman, Jack, ed. (gr. 9 up). Date not set. 9.95 (*0-8373-9307-8*); pap. 3.95 (*0-8373-9007-9*) F Merriwell.

Storm, Tom. Stormy Finds the New Forest. Powell, Lori, illus. 48p. (Orig.). (gr. 1-6). 1994. pap. 8.95 (*0-9643019-0-3*) T Storm. Tom Storm has written a mesmerizing children's book which contains endearing characters such as "Stormy," the whitetail fawn, & "Flapjack," the local beaver. Its many characters in bright vivid colors reach out & grasp children's attention from cover to cover. The story features Stormy & many other birds & animals. Because of deer overpopulation in their forest, Stormy & his mother must journey to find a new forest. They encounter many delightful animals & fun-filled experiences along the way. Finally, once settled into their new, abundant, & balanced forest, Stormy meets Joey, the son of a local hunter & soon to be a hunter himself. Joey & Stormy set out on their own adventures. Along the way, Joey gently educates Stormy on how hunting helps to sustain the quality environment for birds & animals by preventing overpopulation & starvation. Tom Storm's intent is to provide the public with a better understanding of the hunters' historic role in conservation & wildlife management of all birds & animals. Tom is able to strike a balanced approach between environmental & pro-hunting viewpoints, &, indeed, will please both sides with this charming story. There has never been anything like this book on the market. STORMY is unique, educational & fascinating - a charming story. Order from Storm Press, Box 2012, Great Falls, MT 59403.
Publisher Provided Annotation.

Troy, John. Ben at Large. 1990. pap. 12.50 (*1-55971-048-9*) NorthWord.

HURRICANES
Archer, Jules. Hurricane! LC 90-45369. (Illus.). 48p. (gr. 5-6). 1991. text ed. 12.95 RSBE (*0-89686-597-5*, Crestwood Hse) Macmillan Child Grp.
Barrett, Norman S. Huracanes y Tornados. LC 90-70889. (SPA., Illus.). 32p. (gr. k-4). 1990. PLB 11.90 (*0-531-07907-4*) Watts.

Bonilla, Jayne. If Hurricanes Were Candy Canes. Moss, Barbara, illus. 16p. (Orig.). (gr. k-6). 1992. pap. 4.95 (*0-9635105-0-9*) J R Bonilla.
Branley, Franklyn M. Hurricane Watch. Maestro, Giulio, illus. LC 85-47534. 32p. (ps-3). 1985. PLB 13.89 (*0-690-04471-2*, Crowell Jr Bks) HarpC Child Bks.
—Hurricane Watch. Maestro, Giulio, illus. LC 85-47534. 32p. (gr. k-3). 1987. pap. 4.50 (*0-06-445062-7*, Trophy) HarpC Child Bks.
Erlbach, Arlene. Hurricanes. LC 92-37811. (Illus.). 48p. (gr. k-4). 1993. PLB 12.85 (*0-516-01333-5*); pap. 4.95 (*0-516-41333-3*) Childrens.
Greenberg, Keith. Hurricanes & Tornadoes. (Illus.). 64p. (gr. 5-8). 1994. bds. 15.95 (*0-8050-3095-6*) TFC Bks NY.
Hamilton, Sue. Hurricane Hugo. Hamilton, John, ed. LC 90-82627. (Illus.). 32p. (gr. 4). 1990. PLB 11.96 (*0-939179-85-7*) Abdo & Dghtrs.
Hooker, Merrilee. Hurricanes. LC 92-42920. 1993. 12.67 (*0-86593-243-3*); 9.50s.p. (*0-685-67762-1*) Rourke Corp.
Hurricane! The Rage of Hurrican Andrew. LC 92-43613. 48p. (gr. 2 up). 1993. PLB 19.93 (*0-8368-0962-9*) Gareth Stevens Inc.
Kahl, Jonathan D. Storm Warning: The Power of Tornadoes & Hurricanes. LC 92-13627. 1993. 19.95 (*0-8225-2527-5*) Lerner Pubns.
Lampton, Christopher. Hurricane. (Illus.). 64p. (gr. 4-6). 1991. PLB 13.90 (*1-56294-030-9*); pap. 5.95 (*1-56294-780-X*) Millbrook Pr.
—Hurricane: A Disaster Book. (gr. 4-7). 1992. pap. 5.95 (*0-395-63643-4*) HM.
Lane, Rose W. Let the Hurricane Roar. LC 85-42742. 128p. (gr. 5-9). 1985. pap. 3.50 (*0-06-440158-8*, Trophy) HarpC Child Bks.
Lee, Sally. Hurricanes. LC 92-27367. (Illus.). 64p. (gr. 5-8). 1993. PLB 12.90 (*0-531-20152-X*); pap. 5.95 (*0-531-15665-6*) Watts.
Rotter, Charles M. Hurricanes. LC 92-44442. (gr. 6 up). 1994. 18.95 (*0-88682-597-0*) Creative Ed.
Stallone, Linda. The Flood That Came to Grandma's House. Schooley, Joan, illus. LC 91-33955. 21p. (ps-3). 1992. 9.95 (*0-912975-02-4*) Upshur Pr.
Twist, Clint. Hurricanes & Storms. LC 91-37269. (Illus.). 48p. (gr. 4-6). 1992. text ed. 13.95 RSBE (*0-02-789685-4*, New Discovery) Macmillan Child Grp.

HURRICANES–FICTION

Bottner, Barbara. Hurricane Music. Yalowitz, Paul, illus. LC 92-43697. 1994. 15.95 (*0-399-22544-7*, Putnam) Putnam Pub Group.
Garland, Sherry. The Silent Storm. LC 92-33690. 1992. write for info. (*0-15-274170-4*) HarBrace.
Hurwitz, Johanna. Hurricane Elaine. De Groat, Diane, illus. LC 86-12409. 112p. (gr. 5-8). 1986. 12.95 (*0-688-06461-2*) Morrow Jr Bks.
London, Jonathan. Island Hurricane. Sorensen, Henri, illus. LC 94-14518. 1994. write for info. (*0-688-08117-7*); PLB write for info. (*0-688-08118-5*) Lothrop.
Loredo, Betsy. Storm at the Shore. LC 93-16455. (Illus.). 64p. (Orig.). (gr. 3-5). 1993. PLB 12.95 (*1-881889-10-6*) Silver Moon.
Peck, Robert N. Arly's Run. 160p. (gr. 5-9). 1991. 16.95 (*0-8027-8120-9*) Walker & Co.
Watson, J. B. The Hurricane. Cocozza, Chris, illus. 160p. (gr. 3-7). 1994. pap. 3.50 (*0-448-40434-6*, G&D) Putnam Pub Group.
Weeks, Sarah. Hurricane City. Warhola, James, illus. LC 92-23389. 32p. (ps-1). 1993. 15.00 (*0-06-021572-0*); PLB 14.89 (*0-06-021573-9*) HarpC Child Bks.
Winthrop, Elizabeth. Belinda's Hurricane. Watson, Wendy, illus. LC 84-8028. 64p. (gr. 1-4). 1984. 10.95 (*0-525-44106-9*, DCB) Dutton Child Bks.

HUTCHINSON, ANNE (MARBURY), 1590-1643

Fradin, Dennis B. Anne Hutchinson: Fighter for Religious Freedom. LC 88-31329. (Illus.). 48p. (gr. 3-6). 1990. lib. bdg. 14.95 (*0-89490-229-6*) Enslow Pubs.
Nichols, Joan K. A Matter of Conscience: The Trial of Anne Hutchinson. Krovatin, Dan, illus. LC 92-18087. 101p. (gr. 2-5). 1992. PLB 21.34 (*0-8114-7233-7*) Raintree Steck-V.

HYDRAULIC ENGINEERING

see also Hydrostatics; Rivers; Water

HYDROELECTRIC POWER

see Water Power

HYDROFOIL BOATS

Stone, Jane. Challenge! The Big Thunderboats. new ed. LC 75-23408. (Illus.). 32p. (gr. 5-10). 1976. PLB 10.79 (*0-89375-003-4*); pap. 2.95 (*0-89375-019-0*) Troll Assocs.

HYDROLOGY

see Water

HYDROSTATICS

Rowe, Julina & Perham, Molly. Keep it Afloat! LC 93-8213. (Illus.). 32p. (gr. 1-4). 1993. PLB 13.95 (*0-516-08134-9*) Childrens.

HYENAS–FICTION

Daniells, Trenna. When Jokes Aren't Fun: The Hyena Who Teased Too Much. Braille International, Inc. Staff & Henry, James, illus. 20p. (Orig.). (gr. 1). 1992. pap. 10.95 (*1-56956-003-X*) W A T Braille.
—When Jokes Aren't Fun: The Hyena Who Teased Too Much. Braille International, Inc. Staff & Henry, James, illus. (Orig.). (gr. 2). 1992. pap. 10.95 (*1-56956-028-5*) W A T Braille.

McKissack, Patricia. Monkey-Monkey's Trick. Meisel, Paul, illus. LC 88-3072. 48p. (Orig.). (gr. 1-3). 1988. lib. bdg. 7.99 (*0-394-99173-7*); pap. 3.50 (*0-394-89173-2*) Random Bks Yng Read.

HYGIENE

see also Air; Children–Care and Hygiene; Clothing and Dress; Diet; Exercise; Food; Gymnastics; Mental Health; Narcotics; Physical Education and Training; Physiology; Sanitation; Sleep; Water–Pollution

Allen, Eleanor. Wash & Brush up. (Illus.). 64p. (gr. 7 up). 1984. 14.95 (*0-7136-1639-3*) Dufour.
Bains, Rae. Health & Hygiene. Zink-White, Nancy, illus. LC 84-2627. 32p. (gr. 3-6). 1985. PLB 9.49 (*0-8167-0180-6*); pap. text ed. 2.95 (*0-8167-0181-4*) Troll Assocs.
Baldwin, Dorothy. Health & Drugs. (Illus.). 32p. 1987. PLB 17.27 (*0-86592-292-6*); 12.95s.p. (*0-685-67609-9*) Rourke Corp.
—Health & Exercise. (Illus.). 32p. (gr. 3-8). 1987. PLB 17.27 (*0-86592-293-4*); 12.95s.p. (*0-685-67611-0*) Rourke Corp.
—Health & Feelings. (Illus.). 32p. (gr. 3-8). 1987. PLB 17.27 (*0-86592-290-X*); 12.95s.p. (*0-685-58167-5*) Rourke Corp.
—Health & Food. (Illus.). 32p. (gr. 3-8). 1987. PLB 17.27 (*0-86592-294-2*); 12.95s.p. (*0-685-67608-0*) Rourke Corp.
—Health & Friends. (Illus.). 32p. (gr. 3-8). 1987. PLB 17.27 (*0-86592-289-6*); 12.95s.p. (*0-685-67612-9*) Rourke Corp.
—Health & Hygiene. (Illus.). 32p. (gr. 3-8). 1987. PLB 17.27 (*0-86592-291-8*); 12.95s.p. (*0-685-67610-2*) Rourke Corp.
Berger, Gilda. Premenstrual Syndrome: A Guide for Young Women. 3rd, rev. ed. LC 91-34647. (Illus.). 96p. (gr. 7-12). 1991. pap. 7.95 (*0-89793-088-6*) Hunter Hse.
Bleich, Alan R. Coping with Health Risks & Risky Behavior. Rosen, Roger, ed. (gr. 7-12). 1990. PLB 14.95 (*0-8239-1072-5*) Rosen Group.
Bosworth, et al. Implementing BARN. (gr. 7-12). Date not set. write for info. incl. software (*0-912899-54-9*) Lrning Multi-Systs.
Brady, Janeen. Standin' Tall Cleanliness. Galloway, Neil, illus. 22p. (Orig.). (ps-6). 1984. pap. text ed. 1.50 activity bk. (*0-944803-54-7*); cassette & bk. 9.95 (*0-944803-55-5*) Brite Music.
Brown, Laurene K. & Brown, Marc T. Dinosaurs Alive & Well! A Guide to Good Health. (ps-3). 1990. 15.95 (*0-316-10998-3*, Joy St Bks) Little.
Catherall, Ed. Exploring the Human Body. (Illus.). 48p. (gr. 4-8). 1992. PLB 22.80 (*0-8114-2599-1*) Raintree Steck-V.
Chapman, Victoria, Associates Staff. Health on File. (Illus.). 288p. (gr. 7-12). 1994. loose-leaf binder 155.00x (*0-8160-2993-8*) Facts on File.
Cobb, Vicki. Brush, Comb, Scrub: Inventions to Keep You Clean. Hafner, Marylin, illus. LC 88-2930. 32p. (gr. 1-4). 1993. pap. 3.95 (*0-06-446107-6*, Trophy) HarpC Child Bks.
—Keeping Clean. Hafner, Marylin, illus. LC 88-2930. 32p. (gr. k-3). 1989. (Lipp Jr Bks); PLB 11.89 (*0-397-32313-1*) HarpC Child Bks.
Cole, Babette. Dr. Dog. LC 93-51077. (Illus.). 40p. (ps-1). 1994. 16.00 (*0-679-86720-1*) Knopf Bks Yng Read.
Collinson, Alan. Choosing Health. LC 90-25849. (Illus.). 48p. (gr. 5-8). 1991. PLB 22.80 (*0-8114-2801-X*) Raintree Steck-V.
Curro, Ellen. No Need to Be Afraid...First Pelvic Exam: A Handbook for Young Women & Their Mothers. Piccirilli, Charles, illus. 80p. (gr. 9-12). 1991. pap. text ed. 4.95 (*0-9629417-1-9*) Linking Ed Med.
Davies, Leah G. Kelly Bear Health. Davies, Joy D., illus. LC 89-85159. 28p. (Orig.). (ps-3). 1989. pap. 4.50 (*0-9621054-2-2*) Kelly Bear Pr.
Diehl, Harold S., et al. Health & Safety for You. 5th ed. 1980. text ed. 29.52 (*0-07-016863-6*) McGraw.
Elgin, Kathleen & Osterritter, John F. Twenty-Eight Days. LC 73-77779. (Illus.). 64p. (gr. 5 up). 1973. pap. 5.95 (*0-679-51382-5*) McKay.
Figtree, Dale. Eat Smart: A Guide to Good Health for Kids. LC 92-4550. 128p. 1992. 10.95 (*0-8329-0465-1*) New Win Pub.
Fraser, K. & Tatchell, J. Fitness & Health. (Illus.). 48p. (gr. 6-10). 1987. PLB 13.96 (*0-88110-234-2*); pap. 6.95 (*0-7460-0004-9*) EDC.
Friedland, Bruce. Childhood. (Illus.). 112p. (gr. 7-12). 1993. 18.95 (*0-7910-0036-2*) Chelsea Hse.
Gardner-Loulan, JoAnn, et al. Period. updated ed. Quackenbush, Marcia, illus. & LC 90-46065. 95p. (gr. 4-8). 1991. pap. 9.95 incl. removable parents' guide (*0-912078-88-X*) Volcano Pr.
Gay, Kathlyn. They Don't Wash Their Socks! (Illus.). (gr. 4-7). 1990. 13.95 (*0-8027-6916-0*); lib. bdg. 14.85 (*0-8027-6917-9*) Walker & Co.
Greenbaum, David & Wasser, Edward. My First Health & Nutrition Coloring Book: Mr. Carrots Coloring Book. Puglisi, Lou, illus. 40p. (Orig.). (gr. 2). 1988. pap. 0.99 (*0-9621833-0-X*) D Greenbaum.
Hawkes, Nigel. Medicine & Health. (Illus.). 32p. (gr. 5-8). PLB 13.95 (*0-8050-3417-X*) TFC Bks NY.
Hayes, Marilyn. Jumbo Health Yearbook: Grade 3. 96p. (gr. 3). 1978. 18.00 (*0-8209-0063-X*, JHY 3) ESP.
—Jumbo Health Yearbook: Grade 4. 96p. (gr. 4). 1979. 18.00 (*0-8209-0064-8*, JHY 4) ESP.
Houston, Jack. Jumbo Health Yearbook: Grade 5. 96p. (gr. 5). 1979. 18.00 (*0-8209-0065-6*, JHY 5) ESP.

—Jumbo Health Yearbook: Grade 6. 96p. (gr. 6). 1979. 18.00 (*0-8209-0066-4*, JHY 6) ESP.
—Jumbo Health Yearbook: Grade 7. 96p. (gr. 7). 1979. 18.00 (*0-8209-0067-2*, JHY 7) ESP.
—Jumbo Health Yearbook: Grade 8. 96p. (gr. 8). 1979. 18.00 (*0-8209-0068-0*, JHY 8) ESP.
Hunt, Angela E. & Calenberg, Laura K. Beauty from the Inside Out: Becoming the Best You Can Be. Herron, Sandra & White, Kim, illus. LC 93-7132. 1993. pap. 12.99 (*0-8407-6789-7*) Nelson.
Jones, Lorraine H. & Tsumura, Ted K. Health & Safety for You. 7th ed. 480p. 1987. text ed. 29.96 (*0-07-065386-0*) McGraw.
Katz, Illana & Rosenthal, Alan D. Show Me Where It Hurts, Chiropractic Care. Borowitz, Franz, illus. 40p. (gr. k-6). 1993. smythe sewn 16.95 (*1-882388-01-1*) Real Life Strybks.
McCoy, Kathy & Wibbelsman, Charles. The New Teenage Body Book. rev. ed. (Illus.). 288p. (Orig.). (gr. 9-12). 1992. pap. 15.00 (*0-399-51725-1*, Body Pr-Perigee) Berkley Pub.
McDonnell, Janet. Good Health: A Visit from Droopy. Dunnington, Tom, illus. LC 90-1871. 32p. (ps-2). 1990. PLB 13.95 (*0-89565-582-9*) Childs World.
McGreevey, Carla & Kelinson, Roberta. Blooming Health: Fun Health Activities for Language Enrichment Based on Bloom's Taxonomy. 80p. (ps-3). 1991. pap. 15.95 (*1-55999-204-2*) LinguiSystems.
Moncure, Jane B. Healthkins Help. Axeman, Lois, illus. LC 82-14713. 32p. (ps-2). 1982. PLB 13.95 (*0-89565-242-0*) Childs World.
—Magic Monsters Learn about Health. Endres, Helen, illus. LC 79-24240. (ps-3). 1980. PLB 14.95 (*0-89565-117-3*) Childs World.
Moss, Miriam. Be Positive. LC 92-26717. (Illus.). 32p. (gr. 6). 1993. text ed. 13.95 RSBE (*0-89686-786-2*, Crestwood Hse) Macmillan Child Grp.
Nardo, Don. Hygiene. (Illus.). (gr. 7-12). 1994. 19.95 (*0-7910-0020-6*, Am Art Analog) Chelsea Hse.
—Hygiene. Koop, C. Everett, intro. by. LC 92-32086. 1993. pap. write for info. (*0-7910-0460-0*) Chelsea Hse.
Nelson, JoAnne. It's up to Me! Magnuson, Diana, illus. LC 93-9349. 1994. 5.95 (*0-935529-63-2*) Comprehen Health Educ.

Noble, Elizabeth & Sorger, Leo. The Joy of Being a Boy. 115p. 1994. pap. 4.95 (*0-9641183-0-0*) New Life Images. The first book to reassure the young boy & his family that for his penis to remain intact as nature intended is the BEST way. Circumcision is the only surgical procedure where the decision to operate is made solely by parents who know little about the structure & function of the penis & foreskin. In simple words & photographs, THE JOY OF BEING A BOY explains these facts. It is an essential reading for: families with young boys, doctor's offices, libraries, day care centers & schools. This book will educate those who blindly follow tradition or believe in such medical fallacies that surgery is necessary for cleanliness & disease prevention. Even physicians often do not know that the foreskin should be left alone until it naturally retracts in childhood. The United States is the only country that circumcises most male infants for non-ritualistic reasons. According to the Universal Declaration of Human Rights & the United Nations Convention on the Rights of the Child "no-one shall be subjected to torture or to cruel, inhuman or degrading treatment or punishment." As well as psychological harm, for the adult male an average of twelve square inches of erogenous tissue is lost by this medically-unnecessary genital mutilation.
Publisher Provided Annotation.

Noffs, David & Noffs, Laurie. The Happy Healthy Harold, Bk. 1. Noffs, Laurie, illus. 24p. (Orig.). (gr. 1). 1987. wkbk. 2.50 (*0-929875-02-8*) Noffs Assocs.
—A Happy Healthy Harold, Bk. 2. Noffs, Laurie, illus. 24p. (Orig.). (gr. 2). 1987. wkbk. 2.50 (*0-929875-03-6*) Noffs Assocs.
Odor, Ruth S. What's a Body to Do? Letwenko, Ed, illus. LC 81-17031. 112p. (gr. 2-6). 1980. PLB 14.95 (*0-89565-209-9*) Childs World.

Orlandi, Mario, et al. Maintaining Good Health. 128p. (gr. 5 up). 1989. 18.95x (*0-8160-1667-4*) Facts On File.
Parker, Steve. Catching a Cold: How You Get Ill, Suffer & Recover. (Illus.). 32p. (gr. k-4). 1992. PLB 11.40 (*0-531-14146-2*) Watts.
Power, Vicki. Medicine & Health. LC 91-39578. (Illus.). 32p. (gr. 5-8). 1992. PLB 11.90 (*0-531-14198-5*) Watts.
Rayner, Claire. The Don't Spoil Your Body Book. King, Tony, tr. Lansdown, Richard, intro. by. (Illus.). 48p. (gr. 3 up). 1989. pap. 4.95 (*0-8120-6098-9*) Barron.
Rich, Ruth & D'Onofrio, Carol N. Decisions for Health. (Illus.). 488p. (gr. 9-12). 1993. text ed. 27.50 (*1-56269-053-1*); tchr's. manual, 520p. 39.25 (*1-56269-054-X*); Total tchr. support system. 208.75 (*1-56269-055-8*); write for info. audio pkg. (*1-56269-092-2*) Am Guidance.
Roettger, Doris. Growing up Healthy. (gr. k-3). 1991. pap. 8.95 (*0-86653-970-0*) Fearon Teach Aids.
Salter, Charles A. Looking Good, Eating Right: A Sensible Guide to Proper Nutrition & Weight Loss for Teens. (Illus.). 144p. (gr. 7 up). 1991. PLB 15.90 (*1-56294-047-3*) Millbrook Pr.
Sheehan, Angela, ed. Encyclopedia of Health, 14 vols. LC 89-17336. (Illus.). 900p. (gr. 4-8). 1991. PLB 299.95x (*1-85435-203-2*) Marshall Cavendish.
Simon, Nissa. Don't Worry, You're Normal. LC 81-43324. 192p. (gr. 7 up). 1982. (Crowell Jr Bks); (Crowell Jr Bks) HarpC Child Bks.
Sonder, Ben. Eating Disorders: When Food Turns Against You. LC 92-37547. (Illus.). 96p. (gr. 9-12). 1993. PLB 13.40 (*0-531-11175-X*) Watts.
Springate, Kay W. Let's Learn about Good Health. 64p. (ps-2). 1988. wkbk. 7.95 (*0-86653-438-5*, GA1041) Good Apple.
Stein, Sara. The Body Book. LC 91-50957. (Illus.). (gr. 4-7). 1992. 19.95 (*1-56305-298-9*, 3298); pap. 11.95 (*0-89480-805-2*, 1805) Workman Pub.
Tsumura, Ted K. & Jones, Lorraine H. Health & Safety for You. 6th ed O'Neill, Martha, ed. (Illus.). 288p. (gr. 7-12). 1984. 30.32 (*0-07-065378-X*) McGraw.
Visual Education Corporation Staff. Macmillan Encyclopedia of Health, 8 vols. (gr. 7-12). 1993. Set. text ed. 360.00 (*0-02-897439-5*) Macmillan.
—Macmillan Encyclopedia of Health, 8 vols. (gr. 7-12). 1993. Vol. 1. text ed. 40.00 ea. (*0-02-897431-X*) Vol. 2. text ed. 40.00 (*0-02-897432-8*); Vol. 3. text ed. 40.00 (*0-02-897433-6*); Vol. 4. text ed. 40.00 (*0-02-897434-4*); Vol. 5. text ed. 40.00 (*0-02-897435-2*); Vol. 6. text ed. 40.00 (*0-02-897436-0*); Vol. 7. text ed. 40.00 (*0-02-897437-9*); Vol. 8. text ed. 40.00 (*0-02-897438-7*) Macmillan.
Vitkus, Jessica. Beauty & Fitness with "Saved by the Bell" LC 91-42583. (Illus.). 64p. (Orig.). (gr. 5 up). 1992. pap. 6.95 (*0-02-045425-2*, Collier Young Ad) Macmillan Child Grp.
Wheeler, Jill C. Healthy Earth, Healthy Bodies. Kallen, Stuart A., ed. LC 91-73069. 202p. 1991. 12.94 (*1-56239-032-5*) Abdo & Dghtrs.

HYGIENE–FICTION

Bacon, Ron. Wash Day. Greenstein, Susan, illus. LC 92-34270. 1993. 2.50 (*0-383-03665-8*) SRA Schl Grp.
Battle-Lavert, Gwendolyn. The Barber's Cutting Edge. Holbert, Raymond, photos by. LC 94-4013. 1994. 14.95 (*0-89239-127-8*) Childrens Book Pr.
Berenstain, Stan & Berenstain, Janice. The Berenstain Bears & the Messy Room. Berenstain, Janice & Berenstain, Stan, illus. Lerner, Sharon, ed. 32p. (ps-2). 1983. lib. bdg. 5.99 (*0-394-95639-7*); pap. 2.50 (*0-394-85639-2*) Random Bks Yng Read.
Bottner, Barbara. Messy. Bottner, Barbara, illus. LC 78-50420. (gr. k-2). 1979. 6.95 (*0-440-05492-3*); pap. 6.46 (*0-440-05493-1*) Delacorte.
Bowling, David L. & Bowling, Patricia H. Dirty Dingy Daryl. Martz, John, ed. Bowling, Patricia H., illus. LC 81-83120. 24p. (ps-4). 1981. 6.00 (*0-939700-00-X*); pap. 3.95 (*0-939700-01-8*) I D I C P.
Bowling, HeBo D. & Bowling, Patricia H. Clean up Your Act, Dirty Dinjy Daryl. (Illus.). 32p. (Orig.). (gr. 1-4). 1994. pap. 4.95 perfect bdg. (*0-939700-04-2*) I D I C P.
Brown, M. K. Sally's Room. 32p. 1992. 13.95 (*0-590-44709-2*, Scholastic Hardcover) Scholastic Inc.
Buchanan, J. Taking Care of My Cold. (Illus.). 24p. (ps-8). 1990. pap. 4.95 (*0-88753-197-0*, Pub. by Black Moss Pr CN) Firefly Bks Ltd.
Burningham, John. Time to Get out of the Bath, Shirley. Burningham, John, illus. LC 76-58503. 32p. (gr. k-2). 1978. 13.95 (*0-690-01378-7*, Crowell Jr Bks); PLB 13.89 (*0-690-01379-5*) HarpC Child Bks.
Chapouton, Anne-Marie. Tim Tidies Up. (Illus.). 32p. (gr. 3-5). 1991. 12.95 (*0-89565-750-3*) Childs World.
Clean Team Staff & Campbell, Jeff. Spring Cleaning. (Orig.). (gr. 7 up). 1989. pap. 5.95 (*0-440-50162-8*, Dell Trade Pbks) Dell.
Curry, Jennifer. Measles & Sneezles. (Illus.). 96p. (gr. 4-6). 1992. 15.95 (*0-09-174082-7*, Pub. by Hutchinson UK) Trafalgar.
Dutton, Cheryl. Not in Here, Dad! Smith, Wendy, illus. 32p. (ps-2). 1989. 10.95 (*0-8120-6105-5*) Barron.
Edwards, Frank B. & Bianchi, John. Mortimer Mooner Stopped Taking a Bath. (Illus.). 24p. (ps-2). 1990. 14.95 (*0-921285-21-3*, Pub. by Bungalo Bks CN); pap. 4.95 (*0-921285-20-5*, Pub. by Bungalo Bks CN) Firefly Bks Ltd.
Ellison, Virginia. Pooh Get-Well Book. 1991. pap. 3.50 (*0-440-46971-6*) Dell.
ETR Associates Staff. The Golden Treasure. Paley, Nina, illus. LC 92-8360. 1992. write for info. (*1-56071-104-3*) ETR Assocs.
—In My Shoes. Paley, Nina, illus. LC 92-8359. 1992. write for info. (*1-56071-105-1*) ETR Assocs.
—Who Likes That Stuff? Paley, Nina, illus. LC 92-8356. 1992. write for info. (*1-56071-101-9*) ETR Assocs.
Faulkner, Keith. Monster in My Bathroom. Lambert, Tony, illus. 16p. (ps-3). 1993. 4.95 (*0-8431-3482-8*) Price Stern.
—Monster in My Toybox. Lambert, Tony, illus. 16p. (ps-3). 1993. 4.95 (*0-8431-3481-X*) Price Stern.
Frankel, Alona. Once upon a Potty: His. LC 79-53769. (Illus.). (ps-3). 1980. 5.50 (*0-8120-5371-0*); pkg., 1987 13.95 (*0-8120-7457-2*) Barron.
Gaspard, Helen. Doctor Dan the Bandage Man. Malvern, Corinne, illus. 24p. (ps-k). 1992. write for info. (*0-307-00142-3*, 312-07, Golden Pr) Western Pub.
Gorog, Judith. In a Messy, Messy Room: A Trophy Book. Root, Kimberly B., illus. 48p. (gr. 2-5). 1994. pap. 3.95 (*0-06-440480-3*, Trophy) HarpC Child Bks.
Greenblat, Rodney A. Slombo the Gross. LC 91-31235. (Illus.). 32p. (ps-3). 1993. 15.00 (*0-06-020775-2*); PLB 14.89 (*0-06-020776-0*) HarpC Child Bks.
Guymon, Maurine B. The Adventures of Micki Microbe. Zagone, Arlene T., illus. 88p. (gr. 2-5). 1987. 15.00 (*0-9618650-0-8*) MoDel Pubs.
Hamsa, Bobbie. Dirty Larry. LC 83-10079. (Illus.). 32p. (ps-2). 1983. PLB 10.25 (*0-516-02040-4*); pap. 2.95 (*0-516-42040-2*) Childrens.
Hellman-Hurpoil, Odile. Prince Oliver Doesn't Want to Take a Bath. (Illus.). (gr. 3-8). 1992. PLB 8.95 (*0-89565-887-9*) Childs World.
Henkes, Kevin. Clean Enough. Henkes, Kevin, illus. LC 81-6386. 24p. (gr. k-3). 1982. PLB 10.88 (*0-688-00829-1*) Greenwillow.
Houghton, Eric. The Backwards Watch. Abel, Simone, illus. LC 91-16951. 32p. (ps-2). 1992. 13.95 (*0-531-05968-5*); PLB 13.99 (*0-531-08568-6*) Orchard Bks Watts.
Howard, Neva. Tommy & James Cell. 32p. 1989. write for info. N Howard.
Huntley, Chris. The Beast in the Bathroom. Huntley, Chris, illus. 32p. (ps). 1991. write for info. Smythe bdg. (*0-9616679-2-3*) Aquarelle Pr.
Hutchins, Pat. Tidy Titch. LC 90-38483. (Illus.). 32p. (ps up). 1991. 15.00 (*0-688-09963-7*); PLB 14.93 (*0-688-09964-5*) Greenwillow.
Jacobs, Don. Happy Exercise: An Adventure into a Fit World. Speidel, Sandy, illus. LC 80-23547. 48p. (Orig.). (ps-5). 1980. pap. 4.95 (*0-89037-170-9*) Anderson World.
Kroll, Steven. The Pigrates Clean Up. Bassett, Jeni, illus. LC 92-21823. 32p. (ps-k). 1993. 14.95 (*0-8050-2368-2*, Bks Young Read) H Holt & Co.
Lawrence, Elizabeth H. Miss Muffin. 1993. 7.95 (*0-8062-4616-2*) Carlton.
Lewis, Rob. Tidy up, Trevor. LC 92-30327. (ps-3). 1993. 13.95 (*0-15-200626-5*) HarBrace.
McOmber, Rachel B., ed. McOmber Phonics Storybooks: The Haircut. rev. ed. (Illus.). write for info. (*0-944991-53-X*) Swift Lrn Res.
—McOmber Phonics Storybooks: The Tub. rev. ed. (Illus.). write for info. (*0-944991-24-6*) Swift Lrn Res.
McPhail, David. Andrew's Bath. McPhail, David, illus. (ps-3). 1984. 13.95 (*0-316-56319-6*, Joy St Bks) Little.
Mahy, Margaret. Keeping House. Smith, Wendy, illus. LC 90-37591. 32p. (gr. k-4). 1991. SBE 13.95 (*0-689-50515-9*, M K McElderry) Macmillan Child Grp.
Miller, Margaret. Where's Jenna? LC 93-13981. (ps-k). 1994. pap. 15.00 (*0-671-79167-2*, S&S BFYR) S&S Trade.
Moncure, Jane B. Caring for My Body. McCallum, Jodie, illus. 32p. (ps-2). 1990. PLB 12.95 (*0-89565-668-X*) Childs World.
Munsch, Robert. Jonathan Cleaned-up: Then He Heard a Sound. Martchenko, Michael, illus. 32p. (gr. 4-7). 1981. PLB 14.95 (*0-920236-22-7*, Pub. by Annick CN); pap. 4.95 (*0-920236-20-0*, Pub. by Annick CN) Firefly Bks Ltd.
Nelson, JoAnne. Good Grief! Good Grief! Thomsen, Ernie, illus. LC 92-6685. 24p. (Orig.). (gr. k-2). 1993. pap. 5.95 (*0-935529-18-7*) Comprehen Health Educ.
Nelson, Ray, Jr. The Internal Adventures of Donovan Willoughby. LC 91-18810. (Illus.). 48p. (ps-7). 1991. 12.95 (*0-89802-572-9*) Beautiful Am.
Parrett, Sherii & Brown, Sylvia. Slippy Cleans Up. (Illus.). 24p. (Orig.). (ps-6). 1992. pap. 5.99 (*1-56722-002-9*) Word Aflame.
Peters, Lisa W. The Room. Sneed, Brad, illus. LC 92-39807. (gr. 3 up). 1994. 14.99 (*0-8037-1431-9*); PLB 14.89 (*0-8037-1432-7*) Dial Bks Young.
Petty, Kate. New Shampoo. Barber, Ed, photos by. (Illus.). 32p. (gr. 2 up). 1992. bds. 12.95 (*0-7136-3481-2*, Pub. by A&C Black UK) Talman.
Sanschagrin, Joceline. Lollypop's Potty. (Illus.). 16p. (ps). 1993. bds. 5.95 (*2-921198-44-4*, Pub. by Les Edits Herit CN) Adams Inc MA.
Serfozo, Mary. Dirty Kurt. Poydar, Nancy, illus. LC 90-29065. 32p. (ps-3). 1992. SBE 13.95 (*0-689-50537-X*, M K McElderry) Macmillan Child Grp.
Smollin, Michael. Ernie's Bath Book. (ps-3). 1982. 3.95 (*0-394-85402-0*) Random Bks Yng Read.
Spinelli, Jerry. Who Put That Hair in My Toothbrush. (gr. 4-7). 1994. 4.95 (*0-316-80841-5*) Little.
Starbuck, Marnie. The Gladimals Learn Healthy Habits. 16p. (ps-3). 1991. pap. text ed. 0.75 (*1-56456-227-1*) W Gladden Found.
Teague, Mark. Pigsty. LC 93-21179. (gr. 1-4). 1994. 13.95 (*0-590-45915-5*) Scholastic Inc.
Wells, Rosemary. Fritz & the Mess Fairy. LC 90-26671. (Illus.). 32p. (ps-2). 1991. 14.00 (*0-8037-0981-1*); PLB 13.89 (*0-8037-0983-8*) Dial Bks Young.
Wilson, Sarah. Day That Henry Cleaned His Room. LC 89-11571. 1993. pap. 4.95 (*0-671-87168-4*, S&S BFYR) S&S Trade.
Wood, Audrey. King Bidgood's in the Bathtub. LC 85-5472. (ps-3). 1993. pap. 19.95 (*0-15-242732-5*) HarBrace.

HYGIENE, MENTAL

see Mental Health

HYGIENE, PUBLIC

see Public Health

HYGIENE, SOCIAL

see Hygiene; Public Health

HYMENOPTERA

see Ants; Bees; Wasps

HYMNOLOGY

see Hymns

HYMNS

see also Carols; Church Music

Barbold, M. Hymns in Prose for Children. 24p. (gr. 2-3). 1994. pap. 5.95 (*1-882427-24-6*) Aspasia Pubns.
Beautiful Ways Songs. (gr. k-6). pap. 0.50 (*0-686-29099-2*) Faith Pub Hse.
Bronstein, Nikki. Praise the Lord with Bells, Bk. I. 31p. (gr. k-7). 1992. spiral 13.00 (*1-880892-14-6*) Fam Lrng Ctr.
—Praise the Lord with Bells, Bk. II. 38p. (gr. k-7). 1992. spiral 13.00 (*1-880892-15-4*) Fam Lrng Ctr.
Griffin, Steve. Children's Guitar Hymnal. 32p. (gr. 4-10). 1978. wkbk. 2.95 (*0-89228-052-2*) Impact Bks MO.
Hartzler, Arlene & Gaeddert, John, eds. Children's Hymnary. LC 67-24327. (gr. k-7). 1967. 5.95 (*0-87303-095-8*) Faith & Life.
Henley, Karyn. My First Hymnal: Seventy-Five Favorite Bible Songs & What They Mean. Davis, Dennas, illus. 160p. 1994. incl. cass. 14.95 (*0-917143-35-3*) Sparrow TN.
Miner, Julia, illus. The Shepherd's Song: The Twenty-Third Psalm. LC 91-31067. 32p. 1993. 14.99 (*0-8037-1196-4*) Dial Bks Young.
Montgomery, Dorothy. Knowing Christ Song. Lautermilch, John, illus. 19p. (gr. k-6). 1981. visualized song 2.99 (*3-90117-025-1*) CEF Press.
Overholtzer, Ruth. Salvation Songs, Vol. I. 100p. (gr. k-6). 1975. pap. text ed. 2.99 (*3-90117-100-2*) CEF Press.
—Salvation Songs, Vol. II. 105p. (gr. k-4). 1979. pap. text ed. 2.99 (*1-55976-201-2*) CEF Press.
—Salvation Songs, Vol. III. 100p. (gr. k-6). 1975. pap. text ed. 2.99 (*1-55976-202-0*) CEF Press.
—Salvation Songs, Vol. IV. (Illus.). 96p. (gr. k-6). 1979. pap. text ed. 2.99 (*1-55976-203-9*) CEF Press.

HYPNOTISM

see also Mind and Body; Psychoanalysis

Ansari, Masud. Modern Hypnosis: Theory & Practice. Ansari, Said S., illus. 232p. (gr. 5). 1982. pap. 6.95 (*0-685-05553-1*) MAS Pr.

I

IBM PERSONAL COMPUTER

Schiller, David. My First Computer Book: IBM PC & Compatibles. LC 90-50367. 64p. (ps-2). 1991. pap. 17.95 (*0-89480-835-4*, 1835) Workman Pub.
Taitt, Jennifer. IBM, Vol. 1. 55p. (gr. 4-12). 1983. pap. text ed. 11.95 (*0-88193-031-8*) Create Learn.
—IBM, Vol. 2. 54p. (gr. 4-12). 1983. pap. text ed. 11.95 (*0-88193-032-6*) Create Learn.
—IBM, Vol. 3. 51p. (gr. 5-12). 1983. pap. text ed. 11.95 (*0-88193-033-4*) Create Learn.
—IBM, Vol. 4. 66p. (gr. 5-12). 1983. pap. text ed. 11.95 (*0-88193-034-2*) Create Learn.

ICE

see also Glaciers; Icebergs

Merk, Ann & Merk, Jim. Rain, Snow, & Ice. LC 94-13325. (gr. 3 up). 1994. write for info. (*0-86593-390-1*) Rourke Corp.
Palmer, Joy. Snow & Ice. LC 92-38438. (Illus.). 32p. (gr. 2-3). 1992. PLB 18.99 (*0-8114-3414-1*) Raintree Steck-V.
Stonehouse, Bernard. Snow, Ice, & Cold. LC 92-26298. (Illus.). 48p. (gr. 6 up). 1993. text ed. 13.95 RSBE (*0-02-788530-5*, New Discovery) Macmillan Child Grp.
Twist, Clint. Ice Caps to Glaciers: Projects with Geography. LC 92-33917. 1993. 12.40 (*0-531-17396-8*, Gloucester Pr) Watts.

ICE AGE

see Glacial Epoch

ICE CREAM, ICES, ETC.

Berger, Melvin. Make Mine Ice Cream. (Illus.). 16p. (ps-2). 1993. pap. text ed. 14.95 (*1-56784-007-8*) Newbridge Comms.
Greenberg, Keith E. Ben & Jerry: Ice Cream for Everyone! (Illus.). 48p. (gr. 2-5). 1994. pap. 6.95 (*1-56711-068-1*) Blackbirch.

Jaspersohn, William. Ice Cream. LC 87-38331. (Illus.). 48p. (gr. 3-7). 1988. RSBE 14.95 (*0-02-747821-1*, Macmillan Child Bk) Macmillan Child Grp.
Keller, Stella. Ice Cream. (Illus.). 32p. (gr. 1-4). 1989. PLB 18.99 (*0-8172-3523-X*); pap. 3.95 (*0-8114-6720-1*) Raintree Steck-V.
Mitgutsch, Ali. From Milk to Ice Cream. Mitgutsch, Ali, illus. LC 81-81. 24p. (ps-3). 1981. PLB 10.95 (*0-87614-158-0*) Carolrhoda Bks.
Neimark, Jill. Ice Cream. Milone, Karen, illus. LC 84-10915. (gr. 2-6). 1986. 11.95 (*0-8038-3440-3*); pap. 11.95 (*0-8038-9290-X*) Hastings.
Older, Jules. Ben & Jerry...The Real Scoop! Severance, Lyn, illus. LC 92-39649. 80p. (Orig.). (gr. 3-8). 1993. pap. 6.95 (*1-881527-04-2*) Chapters Pub.
Reece, Colleen L. What Was It Before It Was Ice Cream? Axeman, Lois, illus. LC 85-13262. 32p. (ps-2). 1985. PLB 14.95 (*0-89565-325-7*) Childs World.

ICE HOCKEY
see Hockey

ICE SKATING
see Skating

ICE SPORTS
see Winter Sports

ICEBERGS

Gans, Roma. Danger--Icebergs! Revised Edition of Icebergs. Rosenblum, Richard, illus. LC 87-45143. 32p. (ps-3). 1987. pap. 4.50 (*0-06-445066-X*, Trophy) HarpC Child Bks.
Markert, Jenny. Glaciers & Icebergs. LC 92-32498. (ENG & SPA.). (gr. 2-6). 1993. 15.95 (*1-56766-004-5*) Childs World.
Poole, Lynn & Poole, Gray. Danger, Iceberg Ahead. (Illus.). (gr. 1-4). 1961. lib. bdg. 4.39 (*0-394-90121-5*) Random Bks Yng Read.
Simon, Seymour. Icebergs & Glaciers. LC 86-18142. (Illus.). 32p. (ps-3). 1987. 14.95 (*0-688-06186-9*); lib. bdg. 14.88 (*0-688-06187-7*, Morrow Jr Bks) Morrow Jr Bks.
Wilson, Barbara. Icebergs & Glaciers. Leon, Vicki, ed. (Illus.). 40p. (Orig.). (gr. 5 up). 1990. pap. 7.95 (*0-918303-23-0*) Blake Pub.
Wood, Jenny. Icebergs: Titans of the Oceans. LC 90-55462. (Illus.). 32p. (gr. 3-4). 1991. PLB 17.27 (*0-8368-0470-8*) Gareth Stevens Inc.

ICELAND

Lepthien, Emilie U. Iceland. LC 86-29966. (Illus.). 128p. (gr. 5-9). 1987. PLB 20.55 (*0-516-02775-1*) Childrens.
McMillan, Bruce. Nights of the Pufflings. McMillan, Bruce, illus. LC 94-14808. (ps-3). Date not set. write for info. (*0-395-70810-9*) HM.
Russell, William. Iceland. LC 93-49326. 1994. write for info. (*1-55916-036-5*) Rourke Bk Co.

ICHTHYOLOGY
see Fishes

ICONOGRAPHY
see Art; Christian Art and Symbolism; Portraits

IDAHO

Bair, Elmer O. Elmer Bair's Story: 1899-1987, Vol. 1. Mangan, Velda B., ed. Chaffin, Maureen A., illus. LC 87-80294. 484p. (gr. 9 up). 1987. 20.00 (*0-9618269-0-8*) Elmer Bair.
Carole Marsh Idaho Books, 44 bks. 1994. lib. bdg. 1027.80 set (*0-7933-1287-6*); pap. 587.80 set (*0-7933-5146-4*) Gallopade Pub Group.
Carpenter, Allan. Idaho. new ed. LC 79-9804. (Illus.). 96p. (gr. 4 up). 1979. PLB 16.95 (*0-516-04112-6*) Childrens.
Davis, Nelle P. Stump Ranch Pioneer. Swetnam, Susan H., intro. by. LC 90-42417. 264p. (gr. 12). 1990. pap. 14.95 (*0-89301-141-X*) U of Idaho Pr.
Fisher, Ronald K. Beyond the Rockies: A Narrative History of Idaho. LC 89-83506. (Illus.). (gr. 4-9). 1989. text ed. 14.85 (*0-941734-00-5*) Alpha Om ID.
Fradin, Dennis. Idaho: In Words & Pictures. LC 80-14660. (Illus.). 48p. (gr. 2-5). 1980. PLB 12.95 (*0-516-03914-8*) Childrens.
Kent, Zachary. Idaho. LC 89-25280. (Illus.). 144p. (gr. 4 up). 1990. PLB 20.55 (*0-516-00458-1*) Childrens.
—Idaho. 192p. 1993. text ed. 15.40 (*1-56956-133-8*) W A T Braille.
Marsh, Carole. Avast, Ye Slobs! Idaho Pirate Trivia. (Illus.). (gr. 3-12). 1994. PLB 24.95 (*0-7933-0376-1*); pap. 14.95 (*0-7933-0375-3*); computer disk 29.95 (*0-7933-0377-X*) Gallopade Pub Group.
—The Beast of the Idaho Bed & Breakfast. (Illus.). (gr. 3-12). 1994. PLB 24.95 (*0-7933-1550-6*); pap. 14.95 (*0-7933-1551-4*); computer disk 29.95 (*0-7933-1552-2*) Gallopade Pub Group.
—Bow Wow! Idaho Dogs in History, Mystery, Legend, Lore, Humor & More! (Illus.). (gr. 3-12). 1994. PLB 24.95 (*0-7933-3503-5*); pap. 14.95 (*0-7933-3504-3*); computer disk 29.95 (*0-7933-3505-1*) Gallopade Pub Group.
—Chill Out: Scary Idaho Tales Based on Frightening Idaho Truths. (Illus.). 1994. lib. bdg. 24.95 (*0-7933-4690-8*); pap. 14.95 (*0-7933-4691-6*); disk 29.95 (*0-7933-4692-4*) Gallopade Pub Group.
—Christopher Columbus Comes to Idaho! Includes Reproducible Activities for Kids! (Illus.). (gr. 3-12). 1994. PLB 24.95 (*0-7933-3656-2*); pap. 14.95 (*0-7933-3657-0*); computer disk 29.95 (*0-7933-3658-9*) Gallopade Pub Group.
—The Hard-to-Believe-But-True! Book of Idaho History, Mystery, Trivia, Legend, Lore, Humor & More. (Illus.). (gr. 3-12). 1994. PLB 24.95 (*0-7933-0373-7*); pap. 14.95 (*0-7933-0372-9*); computer disk 29.95 (*0-7933-0374-5*) Gallopade Pub Group.
—Idaho & Other State Greats (Biographies) (Illus.). (gr. 3-12). 1994. PLB 24.95 (*1-55609-592-9*); pap. 14.95 (*1-55609-591-0*); computer disk 29.95 (*0-7933-1558-1*) Gallopade Pub Group.
—Idaho Bandits, Bushwackers, Outlaws, Crooks, Devils, Ghosts, Desperadoes & Other Assorted & Sundry Characters! (Illus.). (gr. 3-12). 1994. PLB 24.95 (*0-7933-0358-3*); pap. 14.95 (*0-7933-0357-5*); computer disk 29.95 (*0-7933-0359-1*) Gallopade Pub Group.
—Idaho Classic Christmas Trivia: Stories, Recipes, Activities, Legends, Lore & More! (Illus.). (gr. 3-12). 1994. PLB 24.95 (*0-7933-0361-3*); pap. 14.95 (*0-7933-0360-5*); computer disk 29.95 (*0-7933-0362-1*) Gallopade Pub Group.
—Idaho Coastales. (Illus.). (gr. 3-12). 1994. PLB 24.95 (*1-55609-588-0*); pap. 14.95 (*1-55609-587-2*); computer disk 29.95 (*0-7933-1554-9*) Gallopade Pub Group.
—Idaho Coastales! 1994. lib. bdg. 24.95 (*0-7933-7277-1*) Gallopade Pub Group.
—Idaho "Crinkum-Crankum" A Funny Word Book about Our State. (Illus.). 1994. lib. bdg. 24.95 (*0-7933-4843-9*); pap. 14.95 (*0-7933-4844-7*); disk 29.95 (*0-7933-4845-5*) Gallopade Pub Group.
—Idaho Dingbats! Bk. 1: A Fun Book of Games, Stories, Activities & More about Our State That's All in Code! for You to Decipher. (Illus.). (gr. 3-12). 1994. PLB 24.95 (*0-7933-3809-3*); pap. 14.95 (*0-7933-3810-7*); computer disk 29.95 (*0-7933-3811-5*) Gallopade Pub Group.
—Idaho Festival Fun for Kids! (Illus.). (gr. 3-12). 1994. lib. bdg. 24.95 (*0-7933-3962-6*); pap. 14.95 (*0-7933-3963-4*); disk 29.95 (*0-7933-3964-2*) Gallopade Pub Group.
—The Idaho Hot Air Balloon Mystery. (Illus.). (gr. 2-9). 1994. 24.95 (*0-7933-2426-2*); pap. 14.95 (*0-7933-2427-0*); computer disk 29.95 (*0-7933-2428-9*) Gallopade Pub Group.
—Idaho Jeopardy! Answers & Questions about Our State! (Illus.). (gr. 3-12). 1994. PLB 24.95 (*0-7933-4115-9*); pap. 14.95 (*0-7933-4116-7*); computer disk 29.95 (*0-7933-4117-5*) Gallopade Pub Group.
—Idaho "Jography" A Fun Run Thru Our State! (Illus.). (gr. 3-12). 1994. PLB 24.95 (*1-55609-583-X*); pap. 14.95 (*1-55609-582-1*); computer disk 29.95 (*0-7933-1544-1*) Gallopade Pub Group.
—Idaho Kid's Cookbook: Recipes, How-to, History, Lore & More! (Illus.). (gr. 3-12). 1994. PLB 24.95 (*0-7933-0370-2*); pap. 14.95 (*0-7933-0369-9*); computer disk 29.95 (*0-7933-0371-0*) Gallopade Pub Group.
—The Idaho Mystery Van Takes Off! Book 1: Handicapped Idaho Kids Sneak Off on a Big Adventure. (Illus.). (gr. 3-12). 1994. 24.95 (*0-7933-4997-4*); pap. 14.95 (*0-7933-4998-2*); computer disk 29.95 (*0-7933-4999-0*) Gallopade Pub Group.
—Idaho Quiz Bowl Crash Course! (Illus.). (gr. 3-12). 1994. PLB 24.95 (*1-55609-590-2*); pap. 14.95 (*1-55609-589-9*); computer disk 29.95 (*0-685-45925-X*) Gallopade Pub Group.
—Idaho Rollercoasters! (Illus.). (gr. 3-12). 1994. PLB 24.95 (*0-7933-5260-6*); pap. 14.95 (*0-7933-5261-4*); computer disk 29.95 (*0-7933-5262-2*) Gallopade Pub Group.
—Idaho School Trivia: An Amazing & Fascinating Look at Our State's Teachers, School & Students! (Illus.). (gr. 3-12). 1994. PLB 24.95 (*0-7933-0367-2*); pap. 14.95 (*0-7933-0366-4*); computer disk 29.95 (*0-7933-0368-0*) Gallopade Pub Group.
—Idaho Silly Basketball Sportsmysteries, Vol. I. (Illus.). (gr. 3-12). 1994. PLB 24.95 (*0-7933-0364-8*); pap. 14.95 (*0-7933-0363-X*); computer disk 29.95 (*0-7933-0365-6*) Gallopade Pub Group.
—Idaho Silly Basketball Sportsmysteries. (Illus.). (gr. 3-12). 1994. PLB 24.95 (*0-7933-1559-X*); pap. 14.95 (*0-7933-1560-3*); computer disk 29.95 (*0-7933-1561-1*) Gallopade Pub Group.
—Idaho Silly Football Sportsmysteries, Vol. I. (Illus.). (gr. 3-12). 1994. PLB 24.95 (*1-55609-586-4*); pap. 14.95 (*1-55609-585-6*); computer disk 29.95 (*0-7933-1546-8*) Gallopade Pub Group.
—Idaho Silly Football Sportsmysteries, Vol. II. (Illus.). (gr. 3-12). 1994. PLB 24.95 (*0-7933-1547-6*); pap. 14.95 (*0-7933-1548-4*); computer disk 29.95 (*0-7933-1549-2*) Gallopade Pub Group.
—Idaho Silly Trivia! (Illus.). (gr. 3-12). 1994. PLB 24.95 (*1-55609-581-3*); pap. 14.95 (*1-55609-580-5*); computer disk 29.95 (*0-7933-1543-3*) Gallopade Pub Group.
—Idaho Timeline: A Chronology of Idaho History, Mystery, Trivia, Legend, Lore & More. (Illus.). (gr. 3-12). 1994. PLB 24.95 (*0-7933-5911-2*); pap. 14.95 (*0-7933-5912-0*); computer disk 29.95 (*0-7933-5913-9*) Gallopade Pub Group.
—Idaho's (Most Devastating!) Disasters & (Most Calamitous!) Catastrophies! (Illus.). (gr. 3-12). 1994. PLB 24.95 (*0-7933-0355-9*); pap. 14.95 (*0-7933-0354-0*); computer disk 29.95 (*0-7933-0356-7*) Gallopade Pub Group.
—Idaho's Unsolved Mysteries (& Their "Solutions") Includes Scientific Information & Other Activities for Students. (Illus.). (gr. 3-12). 1994. PLB 24.95 (*0-7933-5758-6*); pap. 14.95 (*0-7933-5759-4*); computer disk 29.95 (*0-7933-5760-8*) Gallopade Pub Group.
—If My Idaho Mama Ran the World! (Illus.). (gr. 3-12). 1994. PLB 24.95 (*0-7933-1555-7*); pap. 14.95 (*0-7933-1556-5*); computer disk 29.95 (*0-7933-1557-3*) Gallopade Pub Group.
—Jurassic Ark! Idaho Dinosaurs & Other Prehistoric Creatures. (gr. k-12). 1994. PLB 24.95 (*0-7933-7464-2*); pap. 14.95 (*0-7933-7465-0*); computer disk 29.95 (*0-7933-7466-9*) Gallopade Pub Group.
—Let's Quilt Idaho & Stuff It Topographically! (Illus.). (gr. 3-12). 1994. PLB 24.95 (*1-55609-584-8*); pap. 14.95 (*1-55609-139-7*); computer disk 29.95 (*0-7933-1545-X*) Gallopade Pub Group.
—Let's Quilt Our Idaho County. 1994. lib. bdg. 24.95 (*0-7933-7149-X*); pap. text ed. 14.95 (*0-7933-7150-3*); disk 29.95 (*0-7933-7151-1*) Gallopade Pub Group.
—Let's Quilt Our Idaho Town. 1994. lib. bdg. 24.95 (*0-7933-6999-1*); pap. text ed. 14.95 (*0-7933-7000-0*); disk 29.95 (*0-7933-7001-9*) Gallopade Pub Group.
—Meow! Idaho Cats in History, Mystery, Legend, Lore, Humor & More! (Illus.). (gr. 3-12). 1994. PLB 24.95 (*0-7933-3350-4*); pap. 14.95 (*0-7933-3351-2*); computer disk 29.95 (*0-7933-3352-0*) Gallopade Pub Group.
—My First Book about Idaho. (gr. k-4). 1994. PLB 24.95 (*0-7933-5605-9*); pap. 14.95 (*0-7933-5606-7*); computer disk 29.95 (*0-7933-5607-5*) Gallopade Pub Group.
—Uncle Rebus: Idaho Picture Stories for Computer Kids. (Illus.). (gr. k-3). 1994. PLB 24.95 (*0-7933-4537-5*); pap. 14.95 (*0-7933-4538-3*); disk 29.95 (*0-7933-4539-1*) Gallopade Pub Group.
Pelta, Kathy. Idaho. LC 94-2235. 1994. lib. bdg. write for info. (*0-8225-2734-0*) Lerner Pubns.
Turner Program Services, Inc. Staff & Clark, James I. Idaho. LC 85-12151. 48p. (gr. 3 up). 1985. PLB 19.97 (*0-8174-4291-X*) Raintree Steck-V.
Walgamott, Charles S. Six Decades Back. Arrington, Leonard J., intro. by. LC 90-33649. (Illus.). 368p. 1990. pap. 15.95 (*0-89301-137-1*) U of Idaho Pr.
Young, Virgil M. Story of Idaho: Centennial Edition. LC 89-36899. (Illus.). 304p. (ps-4). 1990. 22.95 (*0-89301-131-2*); tchr's. guide 35.95x (*0-89301-159-2*) U of Idaho Pr.

IDAHO–FICTION

Beatty, Patricia. Bonanza Girl. LC 92-23317. 224p. (gr. 5 up). 1993. 14.00 (*0-688-12361-9*) Morrow Jr Bks.
—Bonanza Girl. LC 92-27682. 224p. 1993. 4.95 (*0-688-12280-9*) Morrow Jr Bks.
Wyss, Thelma H. A Stranger Here. LC 92-15307. 144p. (gr. 7 up). 1993. 14.00 (*0-06-021438-4*); PLB 13.89 (*0-06-021439-2*) HarpC Child Bks.

IDENTITY, PERSONAL
see Personality

IDIOCY
see Mentally Handicapped

IDIOMS
see names of languages with the subdivision Idioms, e.g. English Language–Idioms

ILLINOIS

Anderson, Kathy P. Illinois: Hello U. S. A. (gr. 4-7). 1993. 17.50 (*0-8225-2723-5*) Lerner Pubns.
Aylesworth, Thomas G. & Aylesworth, Virginia L. Western Great Lakes (Illinois, Iowa, Wisconsin, Minnesota) (Illus.). 64p. (gr. 3 up). 1992. lib. bdg. 16.95 (*0-7910-1046-5*) Chelsea Hse.
Carole Marsh Illinois Books, 44 bks. 1994. lib. bdg. 1027.80 set (*0-7933-1288-4*); pap. 587.80 set (*0-7933-5148-0*) Gallopade Pub Group.
Fradin, Dennis. Illinois. LC 91-13510. 64p. (gr. 3-5). 1991. PLB 16.45 (*0-516-03813-3*) Childrens.
—Illinois: In Words & Pictures. LC 76-7389. (Illus.). 48p. (gr. 2-5). 1976. PLB 12.95 (*0-516-03911-3*) Childrens.
Fradin, Dennis B. Illinois - De Mar A Mar: Illinois - from Sea to Shining Sea. LC 91-13510. (SPA., Illus.). 64p. (gr. 3-5). Date not set. PLB 21.27 (*0-516-33813-7*) Childrens.
Marsh, Carole. Avast, Ye Slobs! Illinois Pirate Trivia. (Illus.). (gr. 3-12). 1994. PLB 24.95 (*0-7933-0400-8*); pap. 14.95 (*0-7933-0399-0*); computer disk 29.95 (*0-7933-0401-6*) Gallopade Pub Group.
—The Beast of the Illinois Bed & Breakfast. (Illus.). (gr. 3-12). 1994. PLB 24.95 (*0-7933-1590-5*); pap. 14.95 (*0-7933-1591-3*); computer disk 29.95 (*0-7933-1592-1*) Gallopade Pub Group.
—Bow Wow! Illinois Dogs in History, Mystery, Legend, Lore, Humor & More! (Illus.). (gr. 3-12). 1994. PLB 24.95 (*0-7933-3506-X*); pap. 14.95 (*0-7933-3507-8*); computer disk 29.95 (*0-7933-3508-6*) Gallopade Pub Group.
—Chill Out: Scary Illinois Tales Based on Frightening Illinois Truths. (Illus.). 1994. lib. bdg. 24.95 (*0-7933-4693-2*); pap. 14.95 (*0-7933-4694-0*); disk 29.95 (*0-7933-4695-9*) Gallopade Pub Group.
—Christopher Columbus Comes to Illinois! Includes Reproducible Activities for Kids! (Illus.). (gr. 3-12). 1994. PLB 24.95 (*0-7933-3659-7*); pap. 14.95 (*0-7933-3660-0*); computer disk 29.95 (*0-7933-3661-9*) Gallopade Pub Group.
—The Hard-to-Believe-But-True! Book of Illinois History, Mystery, Trivia, Legend, Lore, Humor & More. (Illus.). (gr. 3-12). 1994. PLB 24.95 (*0-7933-0397-4*); pap. 14.95 (*0-7933-0396-6*); computer disk 29.95 (*0-7933-0398-2*) Gallopade Pub Group.
—If My Illinois Mama Ran the World! (Illus.). (gr. 3-12). 1994. PLB 24.95 (*0-7933-1595-6*); pap. 14.95 (*0-7933-1596-4*); computer disk 29.95 (*0-7933-1597-2*) Gallopade Pub Group.

—Illinois & Other State Greats (Biographies) (Illus.). (gr. 3-12). 1994. PLB 24.95 (*1-55609-416-7*); pap. 14.95 (*1-55609-415-9*); computer disk 29.95 (*0-7933-1598-0*) Gallopade Pub Group.
—Illinois Bandits, Bushwackers, Outlaws, Crooks, Devils, Ghosts, Desperadoes & Other Assorted & Sundry Characters! (Illus.). (gr. 3-12). 1994. PLB 24.95 (*0-7933-0382-6*); pap. 14.95 (*0-7933-0381-8*); computer disk 29.95 (*0-7933-0383-4*) Gallopade Pub Group.
—Illinois Classic Christmas Trivia: Stories, Recipes, Activities, Legends, Lore & More! (Illus.). (gr. 3-12). 1994. PLB 24.95 (*0-7933-0385-0*); pap. 14.95 (*0-7933-0384-2*); computer disk 29.95 (*0-7933-0386-9*) Gallopade Pub Group.
—Illinois Coastales. (Illus.). (gr. 3-12). 1994. PLB 24.95 (*1-55609-412-4*); pap. 14.95 (*1-55609-411-6*); computer disk 29.95 (*0-7933-1594-8*) Gallopade Pub Group.
—Illinois Coastales. 1994. lib. bdg. 24.95 (*0-7933-7278-X*) Gallopade Pub Group.
—Illinois "Crinkum-Crankum" A Funny Word Book about Our State. (Illus.). 1994. lib. bdg. 24.95 (*0-7933-4846-3*); pap. 14.95 (*0-7933-4847-1*); disk 29.95 (*0-7933-4848-X*) Gallopade Pub Group.
—Illinois Dingbats! Bk. 1: A Fun Book of Games, Stories, Activities & More about Our State That's All in Code! for You to Decipher. (Illus.). (gr. 3-12). 1994. PLB 24.95 (*0-7933-3812-3*); pap. 14.95 (*0-7933-3813-1*); computer disk 29.95 (*0-7933-3814-X*) Gallopade Pub Group.
—Illinois Festival Fun for Kids! (Illus.). (gr. 3-12). 1994. lib. bdg. 24.95 (*0-7933-3965-0*); pap. 14.95 (*0-7933-3966-9*); disk 29.95 (*0-7933-3967-7*) Gallopade Pub Group.
—The Illinois Hot Air Balloon Mystery. (Illus.). (gr. 2-9). 1994. 24.95 (*0-7933-2435-1*); pap. 14.95 (*0-7933-2436-X*); computer disk 29.95 (*0-7933-2437-8*) Gallopade Pub Group.
—Illinois Jeopardy! Answers & Questions about Our State! (Illus.). (gr. 3-12). 1994. PLB 24.95 (*0-7933-4118-3*); pap. 14.95 (*0-7933-4119-1*); computer disk 29.95 (*0-7933-4120-5*) Gallopade Pub Group.
—Illinois "Jography" A Fun Run Thru Our State! (Illus.). (gr. 3-12). 1994. PLB 24.95 (*1-55609-407-8*); pap. 14.95 (*1-55609-406-X*); computer disk 29.95 (*0-7933-1584-0*) Gallopade Pub Group.
—Illinois Kid's Cookbook: Recipes, How-to, History, Lore & More! (Illus.). (gr. 3-12). 1994. PLB 24.95 (*0-7933-0394-X*); pap. 14.95 (*0-7933-0393-1*); computer disk 29.95 (*0-7933-0395-8*) Gallopade Pub Group.
—The Illinois Mystery Van Takes Off! Book 1: Handicapped Illinois Kids Sneak Off on a Big Adventure. (Illus.). (gr. 3-12). 1994. 24.95 (*0-7933-5000-X*); pap. 14.95 (*0-7933-5001-8*); computer disk 29.95 (*0-7933-5002-6*) Gallopade Pub Group.
—Illinois Quiz Bowl Crash Course! (Illus.). (gr. 3-12). 1994. PLB 24.95 (*1-55609-414-0*); pap. 14.95 (*1-55609-413-2*); computer disk 29.95 (*0-7933-1593-X*) Gallopade Pub Group.
—Illinois Rollercoasters! (Illus.). (gr. 3-12). 1994. PLB 24.95 (*0-7933-5263-0*); pap. 14.95 (*0-7933-5264-9*); computer disk 29.95 (*0-7933-5265-7*) Gallopade Pub Group.
—Illinois School Trivia: An Amazing & Fascinating Look at Our State's Teachers, Schools & Students! (Illus.). (gr. 3-12). 1994. PLB 24.95 (*0-7933-0391-5*); pap. 14.95 (*0-7933-0390-7*); computer disk 29.95 (*0-7933-0392-3*) Gallopade Pub Group.
—Illinois Silly Basketball Sportsmysteries, Vol. I. (Illus.). (gr. 3-12). 1994. PLB 24.95 (*0-7933-0388-5*); pap. 14.95 (*0-7933-0387-7*); computer disk 29.95 (*0-7933-0389-3*) Gallopade Pub Group.
—Illinois Silly Basketball Sportsmysteries, Vol. II. (Illus.). (gr. 3-12). 1994. PLB 24.95 (*0-7933-1599-9*); pap. 14.95 (*0-7933-1600-6*); computer disk 29.95 (*0-7933-1601-4*) Gallopade Pub Group.
—Illinois Silly Football Sportsmysteries, Vol. I. (Illus.). (gr. 3-12). 1994. PLB 24.95 (*1-55609-410-8*); pap. 14.95 (*1-55609-409-4*); computer disk 29.95 (*0-7933-1586-7*) Gallopade Pub Group.
—Illinois Silly Football Sportsmysteries. (Illus.). (gr. 3-12). 1994. PLB 24.95 (*0-7933-1587-5*); pap. 14.95 (*0-7933-1588-3*); computer disk 29.95 (*0-7933-1589-1*) Gallopade Pub Group.
—Illinois Silly Trivia! (Illus.). (gr. 3-12). 1994. PLB 24.95 (*1-55609-405-1*); pap. 14.95 (*1-55609-113-3*); computer disk 29.95 (*0-7933-1583-2*) Gallopade Pub Group.
—Illinois Timeline: A Chronology of Illinois History, Mystery, Trivia, Legend, Lore & More. (Illus.). (gr. 3-12). 1994. PLB 24.95 (*0-7933-5914-7*); pap. 14.95 (*0-7933-5915-5*); computer disk 29.95 (*0-7933-5916-3*) Gallopade Pub Group.
—Illinois's (Most Devastating!) Disasters & (Most Calamitous!) Catastrophies! (Illus.). (gr. 3-12). 1994. PLB 24.95 (*0-7933-0379-6*); pap. 14.95 (*0-7933-0378-8*); computer disk 29.95 (*0-7933-0380-X*) Gallopade Pub Group.
—Illinois's Unsolved Mysteries (& Their "Solutions") Includes Scientific Information & Other Activities for Students. (Illus.). (gr. 3-12). 1994. PLB 24.95 (*0-7933-5761-6*); pap. 14.95 (*0-7933-5762-4*); computer disk 29.95 (*0-7933-5763-2*) Gallopade Pub Group.
—Jurassic Ark! Illinois Dinosaurs & Other Prehistoric Creatures. (gr. k-12). 1994. PLB 24.95 (*0-7933-7467-7*); pap. 14.95 (*0-7933-7468-5*); computer disk 29.95 (*0-7933-7469-3*) Gallopade Pub Group.
—Let's Quilt Illinois & Stuff It Topographically! (Illus.). (gr. 3-12). 1994. PLB 24.95 (*1-55609-408-6*); pap. 14.95 (*1-55609-097-8*); computer disk 29.95 (*0-7933-1585-9*) Gallopade Pub Group.
—Let's Quilt Our Illinois County. 1994. lib. bdg. 24.95 (*0-7933-7152-X*); pap. text ed. 14.95 (*0-7933-7153-8*); disk 29.95 (*0-7933-7154-6*) Gallopade Pub Group.
—Let's Quilt Our Illinois Town. 1994. lib. bdg. 24.95 (*0-7933-7002-7*); pap. text ed. 14.95 (*0-7933-7003-5*); disk 29.95 (*0-7933-7004-3*) Gallopade Pub Group.
—Meow! Illinois Cats in History, Mystery, Legend, Lore, Humor & More! (Illus.). (gr. 3-12). 1994. PLB 24.95 (*0-7933-3353-9*); pap. 14.95 (*0-7933-3354-7*); computer disk 29.95 (*0-7933-3355-5*) Gallopade Pub Group.
—My First Book about Illinois. (gr. k-4). 1994. PLB 24.95 (*0-7933-5608-3*); pap. 14.95 (*0-7933-5609-1*); computer disk 29.95 (*0-7933-5610-5*) Gallopade Pub Group.
Stein, R. Conrad. Illinois. (Illus.). 144p. (gr. 4 up). 1987. 20.55 (*0-516-00459-X*) Childrens.
—Illinois. 202p. 1993. text ed. 15.40 (*1-56956-169-9*) W A T Braille.
Stepien, William, et al. Discovering Illinois. rev. ed. (Illus.). 184p. (gr. 4). 1992. 16.95 (*0-87905-197-3*, Peregrine Smith) Gibbs Smith Pub.
Turner Educational Services, Inc. Staff & Clark, James I. Illinois. 48p. (gr. 3 up). 1986. PLB 19.97 (*0-8174-4524-2*) Raintree Steck-V.

ILLINOIS–FICTION

Hunt, Irene. Across Five Aprils. LC 92-46736. 212p. (gr. 4 up). 1993. PLB 10.95 (*0-382-24358-7*); 8.95 (*0-382-24367-6*) Silver Burdett Pr.
Marsh, Carole. Uncle Rebus: Illinois Picture Stories for Computer Kids. (Illus.). (gr. k-3). 1994. PLB 24.95 (*0-7933-4540-5*); pap. 14.95 (*0-7933-4541-3*); disk 29.95 (*0-7933-4542-1*) Gallopade Pub Group.

ILLUMINATION

see Lighting

ILLUSIONS

see Optical Illusions

ILLUSTRATION OF BOOKS

see also Drawing

Chimeric Inc. Staff. Illustory - Write & Illustrate Your Own Book! 12p. (gr. k-4). 19.95 (*0-9636796-0-0*) Chimeric.
Mitgutsch, Ali. From Picture to Picture Book. (Illus.). 24p. (ps-3). 1988. PLB 10.95 (*0-87614-353-2*) Carolrhoda Bks.
Wilson, Elizabeth. Bibles & Bestiaries: A Guide to Illuminated Manuscripts. LC 94-6687. 1994. write for info. (*0-374-30685-0*) FS&G.

ILLUSTRATIONS, HUMOROUS

see Cartoons and Caricatures

IMAGINARY ANIMALS

see Animals, Mythical

IMAGINATION

see also Creation (Literary, Artistic, etc.)

Berry, Joy W. Teach Me about Pretending. Dickey, Kate, ed. LC 85-45091. (Illus.). 36p. (ps). 1986. 4.98 (*0-685-10731-0*) Grolier Inc.
Jane, Pamela. Just Plain Penny. 160p. (gr. 3-7). 1990. 13.45 (*0-395-52807-0*) HM.
Little People Big Book about Imagination. 64p. (ps-1). 1990. write for info. (*0-8094-7479-4*); PLB write for info. (*0-8094-7480-8*) Time-Life.
Milios, Rita. Imagi-size: Activities to Exercise Your Students' Imaginations. (Illus.). 80p. (gr. k-4). 1993. pap. 8.95 (*1-880505-05-3*) Pieces of Lrning.
Neuberger, Phyllis J. Suppose You Were a Kitten. LC 82-91105. (Illus.). (gr. 1-3). 1982. pap. 2.95 (*0-9610050-0-9*) P J Neuberger.
Oram, Hiawyn. In the Attic. Kitamura, Satoshi, illus. LC 84-15570. 32p. (ps-2). 1985. 13.95 (*0-8050-0779-2*, Bks Young Read) H Holt & Co.
Short, David & Short, Pat. Entice Their Imaginations. Breviek, Phil, illus. 64p. (gr. k-6). 1985. wkbk. 7.95 (*0-86653-324-9*, GA 658) Good Apple.
Wassermann, Selma & Wassermann, Jack. The Book of Imagining. Smith, Dennis, illus. LC 89-77869. 32p. (gr. k-3). 1990. PLB 12.85 (*0-8027-6948-9*); pap. 4.95 (*0-8027-9454-8*) Walker & Co.

IMAGINATION–FICTION

Adams, Pam & Jones, Ceri. I Thought I Saw. LC 90-45582. (Illus., Orig.). (ps-2). 1974. 5.95 (*0-85953-074-4*, Pub. by Child's Play England); pap. 5.95 (*0-85953-029-9*) Childs Play.
Agell, Charlotte. Mud Makes Me Dance in the Spring. Agell, Charlotte, illus. LC 93-33610. 32p. (ps up). 1994. 7.95 (*0-88448-112-3*) Tilbury Hse.
Avi. Who Was That Masked Man, Anyway? LC 92-7942. 176p. (gr. 4 up). 1992. 14.95 (*0-531-05457-8*); PLB 14.99 (*0-531-08607-0*) Orchard Bks Watts.
Barron, Judy. I Want to Learn to Fly. Moore, Cyd, illus. LC 93-46696. 1994. write for info. (*0-590-49634-4*); write for info. (*0-590-72915-2*) Scholastic Inc.
Berger, Barbara H. When the Sun Rose. Berger, Barbara H., illus. LC 86-2484. 32p. (ps-2). 1986. 14.95 (*0-399-21360-0*, Philomel) Putnam Pub Group.
Bergman, Donna. Timmy Green's Blue Lake. Ohlsson, Ib, illus. LC 91-30232. 32p. (ps up). 1992. 14.00 (*0-688-10747-8*, Tambourine Bks); PLB 13.93 (*0-688-10748-6*, Tambourine Bks) Morrow.
Boyd, Lizi. Willy & the Cardboard Boxes. (Illus.). 32p. (ps-1). 1991. 11.95 (*0-670-83636-2*) Viking Child Bks.
Breitmeyer, Lois & Leithauser, Gladys. Who Should I Be? (gr. 4 up). 1991. pap. 2.95 (*0-8091-6599-6*) Paulist Pr.
Briggs, Raymond. The Bear. LC 94-8734. (Illus.). 48p. (ps up). 1994. 20.00 (*0-679-86944-1*); PLB 20.99 (*0-679-96944-6*) Random Bks Yng Read.
Brook, Leeanne. The Great Big, Enormous, Gigantic Cardboard Box. Vanzet, Gaston, illus. LC 92-29957. (gr. 3 up). 1993. 14.00 (*0-383-03571-6*) SRA Schl Grp.
Brown, Margaret W. David's Little Indian. Charlip, Remy, illus. 48p. (gr. 2-5). 1989. Repr. of 1954 ed. 10.95 (*0-929077-02-4*, Hopscotch Bks); PLB 10.95 (*0-317-92547-4*, Hopscotch Bks) Watermark Inc.
Browne, Anthony. Changes. Browne, Anthony, illus. LC 90-4283. 32p. (ps-3). 1991. 14.95 (*0-679-81029-3*); PLB 15.99 (*0-679-91029-8*) Knopf Bks Yng Read.
Burningham, John. Aldo. Burningham, John, illus. LC 91-19589. 32p. (ps-2). 1992. 15.00 (*0-517-58701-7*); PLB 15.99 (*0-517-58699-1*) Crown Bks Yng Read.
Bursik, Rose. Amelia's Fantastic Flight. Bursik, Rose, illus. LC 91-28809. 32p. (ps-2). 1992. 14.95 (*0-8050-1872-7*, Bks Young Read) H Holt & Co.
Bush, Timothy. James in the House of Aunt Prudence. Bush, Timothy, illus. LC 92-40127. 32p. (ps-2). 1993. 13.00 (*0-517-58881-1*); PLB 13.99 (*0-517-58882-X*) Crown Bks Yng Read.
Butler, Susan. A Trip to the Jungle. (Illus.). 40p. (Orig.). (ps-2). 1978. pap. 3.95 (*0-931416-00-0*) Open Books.
Cain, Barbara S. Double-Dip Feelings: A Book to Help Children Understand Emotions. O'Brien, Ann S., illus. LC 89-49382. 32p. 1990. 16.95 (*0-945354-23-1*); pap. 8.95 (*0-945354-20-7*) Magination Pr.
Cameron, John. Mummy I'm Bored. (Illus.). 32p. (ps-1). 1994. 15.95 (*0-86264-446-1*, Pub. by Andersen Pr UK) Trafalgar.
Camp, Lindsay. Dinosaurs at the Supermarket. Skilbeck, Clare, illus. LC 92-16936. 32p. (gr. 3-8). 1993. 13.99 (*0-670-84802-6*) Viking Child Bks.
Casey, Maude. Over the Water. 1994. 15.95 (*0-8050-3276-2*) H Holt & Co.
Chartier, Jack W. The Art of Whistling. (Illus.). 40p. (gr. 1 up). 1993. PLB 4.95 (*0-9636343-1-3*) Chartier.
Chesworth, Michael. Rainy Day Dream. (ps-3). 1992. 14.00 (*0-374-36177-0*) FS&G.
Cleary, Beverly. Beezus & Ramona. Darling, Louis, illus. LC 55-7623. 192p. (gr. 3-7). 1955. 12.95 (*0-688-21076-7*); PLB 12.88 (*0-688-31076-1*, Morrow Jr Bks) Morrow Jr Bks.
—Emily's Runaway Imagination. 224p. 1990. pap. 3.99 (*0-380-70923-6*, Camelot) Avon.
Cohen, Susan & Cohen, Dan. What You Can Believe. 1993. pap. 3.99 (*0-440-21890-X*) Dell.
Collier, John. In My Backyard. Collier, John, illus. 32p. (ps-3). 1993. reinforced bdg. 14.99 (*0-670-83609-5*) Viking Child Bks.
Collis, Annabel. You Can't Catch Me! LC 92-54486. 1993. 13.95 (*0-316-15237-4*) Little.
Cooper, Helen. The Bear under the Stairs. Cooper, Helen, illus. LC 92-23840. (ps-2). 1993. 12.99 (*0-8037-1279-0*) Dial Bks Young.
Cosgrove, Stephen. Tizzy. (ps-3). 1992. pap. 3.95 (*0-307-13453-9*) Western Pub.
Creighton, J. One Day There Was Nothing to Do. (Illus.). 24p. (ps-8). 1990. PLB 14.95 (*1-55037-091-X*, Pub. by Annick CN); pap. 4.95 (*1-55037-090-1*, Pub. by Annick CN) Firefly Bks Ltd.
Cummings, Pat. Jimmy Lee Did It. LC 84-21322. (Illus.). (ps-1). 1985. 13.95 (*0-688-04632-0*); PLB 12.88 (*0-688-04633-9*) Lothrop.
Cuneo, Mary L. How to Grow a Picket Fence. Westcott, Nadine B., illus. LC 91-36444. 32p. (ps-3). 1993. 15.00 (*0-06-020863-5*); PLB 14.89 (*0-06-020864-3*) HarpC Child Bks.
Desaix, Deborah D. In the Back Seat. (ps-3). 1993. 14.00 (*0-374-33639-3*) FS&G.
Desimini, Lisa. Moon Soup. Desimini, Lisa, illus. LC 92-55041. 32p. (ps-3). 1993. 14.95 (*1-56282-463-5*); PLB 14.89 (*1-56282-464-3*) Hyprn Child.
Dorros, Arthur. Abuela. Kleven, Elisa, illus. LC 90-21459. 40p. (ps-2). 1991. 14.00 (*0-525-44750-4*, DCB) Dutton Child Bks.
Dr. Seuss. Oh! The Thinks You Can Think! Dr. Seuss, illus. LC 75-1602. 48p. (ps-1). 1975. 6.95 (*0-394-83129-2*); lib. bdg. 7.99 (*0-394-93129-7*) Beginner.
Edwards, Roland. Tigers. Riches, Judith, illus. LC 91-40098. 32p. (ps-2). 1992. 15.00 (*0-688-11685-X*, Tambourine Bks); PLB 14.93 (*0-688-11686-8*, Tambourine Bks) Morrow.

Elwell, Sharon. Jeremy & the Wappo. Gentry, Debra, illus. 126p. (Orig.). (gr. 3-4). 1991. pap. 10.50 (*0-9626210-0-5*) Rattle OK Pubns.
Bored with Social Studies, a 4th grade boy falls asleep in class & awakes to find himself in a Native American village in the same location 150 years earlier. He is alarmed when the Wappo believe him to be a messenger from the gods & demand he give them instructions. He must find both a

message & a way home. During his stay in the Wappo village, he learns to hunt grasshoppers & fish without a hook. He learns authentic games & some of the language that was unique to this isolated triblet. He learns to leech toxins from acorns & catch woodpeckers in a basket. He is surprised that the Wappo are unimpressed with much that he tells them about "the land of the gods." Baseball, however, catches their interest & soon there is an unroarious Wappo version of the game. 4th graders love JEREMY & THE WAPPO: "This is my favorite book!" "I love the part where Jeremy doesn't know what he's eating!" "The baseball game is the funniest part!" "The fishing is the best!" "I cried at the end...but just a little bit." Teachers love it, too: "Beautiful book! It has made a difference." Order from Baker & Taylor or Rattle OK Publications, P.O. Box 5614, Napa, CA 94581, 707-253-9641.
Publisher Provided Annotation.

Emerson, Scott. The Magic Boots. Post, Howard, illus. LC 94-4036. 32p. (gr. k-4). 1994. 15.95 (*0-87905-603-7*) Gibbs Smith Pub.

Eversole, Robyn H. The Magic House. Palagonia, Peter, illus. LC 91-17824. 32p. (ps-2). 1992. 13.95 (*0-531-05924-3*); lib. bdg. 13.99 (*0-531-08524-4*) Orchard Bks Watts.

Farcot, Kimberly I. Imagine: A Journey Through the Child's Imagination. Farcot, Kimberly I., illus. LC 92-90202. 32p. (Orig.). (gr. k-4). 1992. pap. 8.95 (*0-9632372-2-5*) Custom Artwk.

Finney, La Rhue. Things Magical. Finney, La Rhue, illus. 22p. (Orig.). (gr. 2-4). 1992. pap. text ed. 6.95 (*0-9635276-0-6*) Taffey Apple.

Fitzgerald, John D. Great Brain. (gr. k-6). 1972. pap. 3.99 (*0-440-43071-2*, YB) Dell.

Foley, Diane. My Big Box. Quinn, Annie, illus. LC 92-31910. 1993. 3.75 (*0-383-03584-8*) SRA Schl Grp.

Franklin, Jonathan. Don't Wake the Baby. (Illus.). 32p. (ps-1). 1991. bds. 13.95 jacketed (*0-374-31826-3*) FS&G.

Givens, Terryl. Dragon Scales & Willow Leaves. Portwood, Andrew, illus. LC 93-665. Date not set. write for info. (*0-399-22619-2*, Putnam) Putnam Pub Group.

Glassman, Peter. The Wizard Next Door. Kellogg, Steven, illus. LC 92-21562. 40p. (gr. k up). 1993. 15.00 (*0-688-10645-5*); PLB 14.93 (*0-688-10646-3*) Morrow Jr Bks.

Gray, Nigel. A Country Far Away. LC 88-22360. (Illus.). 32p. (ps-1). 1991. pap. 5.95 (*0-531-07024-7*) Orchard Bks Watts.

Greenberg, David. Your Dog Might Be a Werewolf, Your Toes Could All Explode. (ps-3). 1992. pap. 2.99 (*0-553-15909-7*) Bantam.

Greenfield, Eloise. Daydreamers. Feelings, Tom, illus. LC 80-27262. (gr. k up). 1985. pap. 4.95 (*0-8037-0167-5*) Dial Bks Young.

—Me & Neesie. Barnett, Moneta, illus. LC 74-23078. 40p. (gr. 1-4). 1975. PLB 13.89 (*0-690-00715-9*, Crowell Jr Bks) HarpC Child Bks.

Gregorich, Barbara. A Different Tune. Hoffman, Joan, ed. (Illus.). 16p. (Orig.). (gr. k-2). 1991. pap. 2.25 (*0-88743-028-7*, 06028) Sch Zone Pub Co.

Grifalconi, Ann. Electric Yancy. LC 94-14596. 1995. write for info. (*0-688-13187-5*); PLB write for info. (*0-688-13188-3*) Lothrop.

Hall, Kirsten. Ballerina Girl. (Illus.). 28p. (ps-2). 1994. PLB 14.00 (*0-516-05363-9*); pap. text ed. 3.95 (*0-516-45363-7*) Childrens.

Harrison, Troon. The Long Weekend. Foreman, Michael, illus. LC 93-307. (gr. k). 1994. 14.95 (*0-15-248842-1*) HarBrace.

Henkes, Kevin. Jessica. LC 87-38087. (Illus.). 24p. (gr. k up). 1989. 14.00 (*0-688-07829-X*); PLB 13.93 (*0-688-07830-3*) Greenwillow.

Hessell, Jenny. Clouds. Ogden, Betina, illus. LC 92-27099. 1993. 3.75 (*0-383-03561-9*) SRA Schl Grp.

Hindley, Judy. Maybe It's a Pirate. Young, Selina, illus. LC 92-7261. 32p. (ps-3). 1992. 14.95 (*1-56566-016-1*) Thomasson-Grant.

Hoff, Syd. Horse in Harry's Room. Hoff, Syd, illus. LC 71-104753. 32p. (gr. k-3). 1970. PLB 13.89 (*0-06-022483-5*) HarpC Child Bks.

Hostetler, Jacob. My Backyard Giant. adpt. ed. Sawicki, Mary, adapted by. LC 93-29762. (Illus.). 32p. (ps-2). 1994. 10.95 (*0-8120-6399-6*); pap. 4.95 (*0-8120-1736-6*) Barron.

How to Get to Sesame Street. (Illus.). 24p. (ps-2). 1991. write for info. (*0-307-74006-4*, Golden Pr) Western Pub.

Howe, James. There's a Dragon in My Sleeping Bag. Rose, David S., illus. LC 93-26572. 1994. 14.95 (*0-689-31873-1*, Atheneum Child Bk) Macmillan Child Grp.

Jackson, Darcy. Another Fuzz Bugg Adventure. Sheppard, Scott O., illus. 40p. (gr. k-5). 1993. 15.95 (*1-883016-00-2*) Moonglow Pubns.

Johnston, Deborah. Mathew Michael's Beastly Day. LC 91-3084. (ps-3). 1992. write for info. (*0-15-200521-8*, HB Juv Bks) HarBrace.

Jones, Robin D. The Beginning of Unbelief. LC 92-22907. 160p. (gr. 7 up). 1993. SBE 13.95 (*0-689-31781-6*, Atheneum Child Bk) Macmillan Child Grp.

Keller, Debra. The Trouble with Mister. McNeill, Shannon, illus. LC 94-4048. 1995. 13.95 (*0-8118-0358-9*) Chronicle Bks.

Kherdian, David. By Myself. Hogrogian, Nonny, illus. LC 92-44366. 32p. (ps-2). 1993. 14.95 (*0-8050-2386-0*, Bks Young Read) H Holt & Co.

Klein, Robin. Seeing Things. 200p. (gr. 7 up). 1994. 12.50 (*0-670-85282-1*) Viking Child Bks.

Krauss, Ruth. I Can Fly. reissued ed. Blair, Mary, illus. 24p. (ps-k). 1992. write for info. (*0-307-00146-6*, 312-12, Golden Pr) Western Pub.

Kroll, Steven. I'd Like to Be. Appleby, Ellen, illus. LC 86-25215. 48p. (ps-3). 1987. 5.95 (*0-8193-1141-3*) Parents.

—The Magic Rocket. Hillenbrand, Will, illus. LC 91-10114. 32p. (ps-3). 1992. reinforced bdg. 14.95 (*0-8234-0916-3*) Holiday.

Laden, Nina. The Night I Followed the Dog. LC 93-31008. 1994. 13.95 (*0-8118-0647-2*) Chronicle Bks.

Leach, Maria. The Thing at the Foot of the Bed. 112p. (gr. 4-5). 1981. pap. 3.25 (*0-440-48773-0*, YB) Dell.

Lester, Alison. Imagine. Lester, Alison, illus. 32p. (gr. k-3). 1990. 13.45 (*0-395-53753-3*) HM.

—Imagine. (ps-3). 1993. pap. 6.95 (*0-395-66953-7*) HM.

Lewis, Hilda. Ship That Flew. Levrin, Nora, illus. LC 58-5903. (gr. 3-7). 1958. 25.95 (*0-87599-067-3*) S G Phillips.

Lewis, Kim. The Last Train. LC 93-32370. (Illus.). 32p. (ps up). 1994. 14.95 (*1-56402-343-5*) Candlewick Pr.

Lillegard, Dee. Sitting in My Box. Agee, Jon, illus. 32p. (ps-2). 1992. pap. 4.99 (*0-14-054819-X*, Puff Unicorn) Puffin Bks.

London, Jonathan. The Lion Who Had Asthma. Levine, Abby, ed. Westcott, Nadine B., illus. LC 91-16553. 32p. (ps-1). 1992. PLB 13.95 (*0-8075-4559-7*) A Whitman.

McAllister, Angela. Sleepy Ella. (ps-3). 1994. 13.95 (*0-385-32050-7*) Doubleday.

McConnachie, Brian. Elmer & the Chickens vs. the Big League. Stevenson, Harvey, illus. LC 91-2914. 32p. (ps-2). 1992. 14.00 (*0-517-57616-3*) Crown Bks Yng Read.

MacDonald, Marianne. The Pirate Queen. Smith, Jan, illus. 32p. (ps-3). 1992. incl. dust jacket 12.95 (*0-8120-6288-4*); pap. 5.95 (*0-8120-4952-7*) Barron.

McEwan, Ian. The Daydreamer. Browne, Anthony, illus. LC 93-44476. 128p. (gr. 5 up). 1994. 14.00 (*0-06-024426-7*); PLB 13.89 (*0-06-024427-5*) HarpC Child Bks.

McGilvray, Richard. Don't Climb out of the Window Tonight. Snow, Alan, illus. LC 92-28136. (ps-2). 1993. 13.99 (*0-8037-1373-8*) Dial Bks Young.

Mclerran, Alice. Roxaboxen. (ps-3). 1991. 14.95 (*0-688-07592-4*); PLB 14.88 (*0-688-07593-2*) Lothrop.

—Roxaboxen. Cooney, Barbara, illus. 32p. (ps-3). 1992. pap. 4.99 (*0-14-054475-5*, Puffin) Puffin Bks.

Mahy, Margaret. A Lion in the Meadow. Williams, Jenny, illus. 32p. (ps-3). 1992. 13.95 (*0-87951-446-9*) Overlook Pr.

Marks, Burton. Let's Go. Harvey, Paul, illus. LC 91-9986. 24p. (gr. k-2). 1992. lib. bdg. 9.89 (*0-8167-2413-X*); pap. text ed. 2.50 (*0-8167-2414-8*) Troll Assocs.

Marquez, Gabriel G. The Handsomest Drowned Man in the World: A Tale for Children. Rabazza, Gregory, tr. LC 92-44055. 1994. 13.95 (*0-88682-587-3*) Creative Ed.

Mayer, Mercer. Hiccup. (gr. 4-7). 1993. pap. 3.99 (*0-14-054641-3*) Puffin Bks.

Miller, Albert G. Captain Whopper. Komisarow, Donald, illus. (gr. 3-7). 1968. 10.95 (*0-8392-3058-3*) Astor-Honor.

Moerbeek, Kees. Fancy That! LC 91-39451. 1992. 9.95 (*0-85953-543-6*) Childs Play.

Monroy, Elizabeth. The Magical Mist. LC 93-91857. 52p. (ps-6). 1994. 15.95 (*0-9639760-0-1*) Going Home. THE MAGICAL MIST is a delightful story that teaches us all, large & small, the value of imagination. THE MAGICAL MIST is a beautifully illustrated fairy tale designed to empower the creative imagination of children. The story is about a young girl who loses a most precious & powerful part of herself in the process of growing & rediscovers it through her young daughter. Synopsis: Lauren's rag doll, Mirabelle, becomes magically alive & takes Lauren on a magical adventure to the World of Imagination, where she learns of the terrible peril facing her world. A cloud of disbelief has descended on the planet Earth & grows thicker every day. If nothing is done to stop it all the people of Earth will be consumed by despair. Lauren is presented with the Key to the World of Imagination. This magical key could free her world from the chains of disbelief. But forces are working against Lauren. Mrs. Grundy, Lauren's school teacher, sees Lauren's vivid imagination as nothing more than a disruption to the discipline & order of her classroom. To order contact: GOING HOME BOOKS, P.O. Box 688, Parker, AZ 85344. 1-800-410-1999, FAX: 619-665-5565.
Publisher Provided Annotation.

Morelli, Susan. Mrs. Funnywinkle. Weinberger, Jane, ed. (Illus.). 54p. (gr. 1-4). 1994. pap. 9.95 (*0-932433-62-6*) Windswept Hse.

Morgan, Lenore. Dragons & Stuff. LC 70-108725. (Illus.). 32p. (gr. 2-4). 1970. PLB 9.95 (*0-87783-012-6*); pap. 3.94 deluxe ed. (*0-87783-091-6*) Oddo.

Ness, E. Sam, Bangs, & Moonshine. (gr. 4 up). 1971. pap. 3.95 (*0-03-080111-7*) HR&W Schl Div.

Nightingale, Sandy. I'm a Little Monster. Nightingale, Sandy, illus. LC 94-18345. 1995. write for info. (*0-15-200309-6*) HarBrace.

Nixon, Joan L. When I am Eight. Gackenbach, Dick, photos by. LC 93-20023. (gr. 1-3). 1994. 13.99 (*0-8037-1499-8*) Dial Bks Young.

—When I Am Eight. LC 93-20023. (ps-3). 1994. 13.89 (*0-8037-1500-5*) Dial Bks Young.

Odgers, Sally F. Up the Stairs. Hunnam, Lucinda, illus. LC 92-21395. 1993. 4.25 (*0-383-03601-1*) SRA Schl Grp.

Ohanesian, Diane. Let's Pretend Teddy. (Illus.). 12p. (ps). 1992. bds. 9.95 gift boxed (*0-89577-450-X*, Dist. by Random) RD Assn.

Olsen, Ib S. The Grown-up Trap. LC 91-35251. (Illus.). 32p. (ps-4). 1990. 6.98 (*0-934738-96-3*) Thomasson-Grant.

Packard, Mary. I Am King! (Illus.). 28p. (ps-2). 1994. PLB 14.00 (*0-516-05365-5*); pap. 3.95 (*0-516-45365-3*) Childrens.

Paraskevas, Betty. Shamlanders. Paraskevas, Michael, illus. LC 92-32980. 1993. 13.95 (*0-15-292854-5*) HarBrace.

Parnall, Peter. Spaces. LC 92-1712. (Illus.). 32p. (gr. k-3). 1993. PLB 15.40 (*1-56294-336-7*) Millbrook Pr.

Paterson, Katherine. Bridge to Terabithia: (Puente Hasta Terabithia) (SPA.). (gr. 1-6). 8.95 (*84-204-3633-X*) Santillana.

—The Smallest Cow in the World. new ed. Brown, Jane C., illus. LC 90-30521. 64p. (gr. k-3). 1991. 14.00 (*0-06-024690-1*); PLB 13.89 (*0-06-024691-X*) HarpC Child Bks.

Peet, Bill. Wump World. Peet, Bill, illus. LC 72-124999. (gr. 3-5). 1974. 14.95 (*0-395-19841-0*); pap. 4.80 (*0-395-31129-2*) HM.

Peterson, Beth. Myrna Never Sleeps. LC 93-8301. 1995. 12.00 (*0-689-31893-6*, Atheneum Child Bk) Macmillan Child Grp.

Platt, Kin. Darwin & the Great Beasts. LC 90-39674. 64p. (gr. 2 up). 1992. 14.00 (*0-688-10030-9*) Greenwillow.

Ploetz, Craig T. Milo's Friends in the Dark. Koslowski, Richard K., illus. 32p. (ps-4). 1992. PLB 11.95 (*1-882172-00-0*) Milo Prods.

Polacco, Patricia. Appelemando's Dreams. Polacco, Patricia, illus. 32p. (ps-3). 1991. 14.95 (*0-399-21800-9*, Philomel) Putnam Pub Group.

Polette, Nancy. The Hole by the Apple Tree. Akgulian, Nishan, illus. LC 90-24646. 32p. 1992. 14.00 (*0-688-10557-2*); PLB 13.93 (*0-688-10558-0*) Greenwillow.

Portlock, Rob. Someone's Trying to Cut off My Head. Portlock, Rob, illus. LC 92-12483. 32p. (Orig.). (ps-1). 1992. pap. 4.99 (*0-8308-1902-9*, 1902) InterVarsity.

Raschka, Chris. Elizabeth Imagined an Iceberg. LC 93-4875. 1994. write for info. (*0-531-06817-X*); lib. bdg. write for info. (*0-531-08667-4*) Orchard Bks Watts.

Romack, Janice R. The Glass Jar. LC 93-85311. (Illus.). 40p. (gr. k-3). 1994. 6.95 (*1-55523-643-X*) Winston-Derek.

Rosen, Michael J. Goodnight Hands: A Bedtime Adventure. Hague, Scott, illus. LC 91-67933. 32p. (ps-3). 1992. pap. 14.95 (*1-880444-01-1*) Times to Treas.

Ross, Michael E. Become a Bird & Fly! Parnall, Peter, illus. LC 91-36562. 32p. (gr. k up). 1992. PLB 15.40 (*1-56294-074-0*) Millbrook Pr.

Samton, Sheila W. Jenny's Journey. LC 92-40724. (Illus.). 32p. (ps-3). 1993. pap. 4.99 (*0-14-054308-2*, Puffin) Puffin Bks.
Sandling, R. Harris. What Do You Do with a Cardboard Box on a Day When the Rain's Pourin' Down? Carter, Mary C., ed. Venema, Jon R., illus. 50p. (gr. 3 up). 1993. write for info. (*1-883194-00-8*) Emerald Hummngbrd.
Sharma, Rashmi. A Brahmin's Castles in the Air. LC 92-61764. (Illus.). 32p. (gr. k up). 1994. 14.95 (*1-878099-56-6*); pap. 6.95 (*1-878099-57-4*) Vidya Bks.
Slote, Elizabeth. Ana & Bold Berto. LC 93-37534. 1995. write for info. (*0-688-12980-3*, Tambourine Bks); PLB write for info. (*0-688-12981-1*, Tambourine Bks) Morrow.
Sun, Chyng F. On a White Pebble Hill. Chen, Chih-Sien, illus. LC 93-14495. 1994. 14.95 (*0-395-68395-5*) HM.
Sweeney, Jacqueline. Katie & the Night Noises. Johnson, Arden, illus. LC 93-22198. 32p. (ps-2). 1993. PLB 14.95 (*0-8167-3014-8*); pap. text ed. write for info. (*0-8167-3015-6*) BrdgeWater.
Swenson, May. The Centaur. Moser, Barry, illus. LC 92-14897. 32p. (gr. k-3). 1995. RSBE 14.95 (*0-02-788726-X*, Macmillan Child Bk) Macmillan Child Grp.
Tews, Susan. Nettie's Gift. Sayles, Elizabeth, illus. 32p. (gr. k-3). 1993. 14.95 (*0-395-59027-2*, Clarion Bks) HM.
Thompson, Colin. Looking for Atlantis. LC 93-24068. 1994. 16.00 (*0-679-85648-X*) Knopf Bks Yng Read.
Townsend, John R. Rob's Place. LC 86-27373. (gr. 4-9). 1988. PLB 12.95 (*0-688-07258-5*) Lothrop.
Utton, Peter. Jennifer's Room. LC 93-44482. 1995. 14.95 (*0-531-06842-0*) Orchard Bks Watts.
—What If. LC 93-38511. (Illus.). 32p. (gr. 3 up). 1994. 18.60 (*0-8368-1090-2*) Gareth Stevens Inc.
White, E. B. Trumpet of the Swan. Frascino, Edward, illus. LC 72-112484. (gr. 3-6). 1970. 13.00 (*0-06-026397-0*); PLB 12.89 (*0-06-026398-9*) HarpC Child Bks.
Wylie, Joanne & Wylie, David. So You Think You Saw a Monster? Learning about Make-Believe. LC 85-16594. (Illus.). 32p. (ps-2). 1985. pap. 3.95 (*0-516-44496-4*) Childrens.
—Y Tu Crees Que Viste un Monstruo? Un Cuento de Fantasia: So You Think You Saw a Monster? A Make Believe Story. LC 86-21604. (Illus.). 32p. (ps-2). 1986. pap. 3.95 (*0-516-54496-9*) Childrens.

IMBECILITY
see Mentally Handicapped

IMMERSION, BAPTISMAL
see Baptism

IMMIGRANTS
see Immigration and Emigration

IMMIGRATION AND EMIGRATION
Here are entered works on migration from one country to another. Works on the movement of population within a country for permanent settlements are entered under Migration, internal.
see also Anthropogeography; Refugees;
also names of countries with the subdivision Immigration And Emigration (e.g. U. S.–Immigration And Emigration, etc.); names of countries, cities, etc. with the subdivision Foreign Population (e.g. U. S.–Foreign Population, etc.); and names of nationalities, e.g. Italians In The U. S., etc.

Anderson, Kelly. Immigration. LC 92-44079. (Illus.). 112p. (gr. 5-8). 1993. PLB 14.95 (*1-56006-140-5*) Lucent Bks.
Auerbach, Susan. Vietnamese Americans. LC 91-15806. 104p. (gr. 5-9). 1991. 13.95s.p. (*0-86593-136-4*) Rourke Corp.
Bales, Carol A. Tales of the Elders: A Memory Book of Men & Women Who Came to America as Immigrants, 1900-1930. Bales, Carol A., photos by. LC 92-46729. (Illus.). 160p. (gr. 5 up). 1993. Repr. of 1977 ed. 5.45 (*0-8136-7215-5*); PLB 10.95 (*0-382-24364-1*) Silver Burdett Pr.
Bandon, Alexandra. Vietnamese Americans. LC 93-45497. 1994. text ed. 13.95 (*0-02-768146-7*, New Discovery Bks) Macmillan Child Grp.
—West Indian Americans. LC 93-27201. (Illus.). 112p. (gr. 6 up). 1994. text ed. 14.95 RSBE (*0-02-768148-3*, New Discovery Bks) Macmillan Child Grp.
Barbour, William, ed. Illegal Immigration. LC 93-1808. 1994. lib. bdg. 16.95 (*1-56510-072-7*); pap. 9.95 (*1-56510-071-9*) Greenhaven.
Berger, Melvin & Berger, Gilda. Where Did Your Family Come From? A Book about Immigrants. Quackenbush, Robert, illus. LC 92-28626. (gr. k-3). 1993. 12.00 (*0-8249-8647-4*, Ideals Child); pap. 4.50 (*0-8249-8610-5*) Hambleton-Hill.
Bode, Janet. New Kids in Town: Oral Histories of Immigrant Teens. 128p. 1991. pap. 2.95 (*0-590-44144-2*) Scholastic Inc.
Border Crossings: Emigration & Exile. (Illus.). (gr. 8 up). 1992. PLB 16.95 (*0-8239-1364-3*); pap. 8.95 (*0-8239-1365-1*) Rosen Group.
Caroli, Betty L. Immigrants Who Returned Home. (Illus.). (gr. 5 up). 1990. 17.95 (*0-87754-864-1*) Chelsea Hse.
Crosby, Nina E. & Marten, Elizabeth H. Don't Teach Let Me Learn about Presidents, of the U. S. People, Genealogy, Immigrants. (Illus.). 80p. (Orig.). (gr. 3-9). 1979. pap. 8.95 tchr's. enrichment manual (*0-914634-67-4*, 7912) DOK Pubs.
Dawson, Mildred L. Over Here It's Different: Carolina's Story. Ancona, George, photos by. LC 92-44515. (Illus.). 48p. (gr. 3-7). 1993. RSBE 14.95 (*0-02-726328-2*, Macmillan Child Bk) Macmillan Child Grp.
Dudley, William, ed. Immigration: Opposing Viewpoints. LC 90-13854. (Illus.). 240p. (gr. 10 up). 1990. PLB 17.95 (*0-89908-485-0*); pap. text ed. 9.95 (*0-89908-460-5*) Greenhaven.
Elias, Miriam L. Thanks to You! LC 94-44850. 1994. write for info. (*0-87306-663-4*); pap. write for info. (*0-87306-664-2*) Feldheim.
Fassler, David & Danforth, Kimberly. Coming to America: The Kids' Book about Immigration. (Illus.). 160p. (Orig.). (ps-6). 1992. pap. text ed. 12.95 (*0-914525-23-9*); tchr's. ed. plastic comb spiral bdg. 16.95 (*0-914525-24-7*) Waterfront Bks.
Freedman, Russell. Immigrant Kids. LC 79-20060. 64p. (gr. 3-7). 1980. 16.95 (*0-525-32538-7*, DCB) Dutton Child Bks.
Goldish, Meish. Immigration. (Illus.). 64p. (gr. 5-8). 1994. bds. 15.95 (*0-8050-3182-0*) TFC Bks NY.
Hillbrand, Percie V. The Norwegians in America. rev. ed. LC 67-15683. (Illus.). 80p. (gr. 5 up). PLB 15.95 (*0-8225-0243-7*); pap. 5.95 (*0-8225-1041-3*) Lerner Pubns.
Howlett, Bud. I'm New Here. LC 92-7478. 1993. 14.95 (*0-395-64049-0*) HM.
Hurwitz, Hilda A. & Wasburn, Hope. Dear Hope-- Love, Grandma. Wasburn, Mara H., ed. LC 93-2213. 1993. 12.95 (*1-88128-303-8*) Alef Design.
Jacobson, Gloria. Two for America: The True Story of a Swiss Immigrant. Cliff, Don, illus. 36p. (gr. 4). 1989. pap. 8.50 (*0-9618399-1-0*) G Jacobson.
Kurelek, William & Engelhart, Margaret S. They Sought a New World: The Story of European Immigration to North America. (Illus.). 48p. (gr. 4 up). 1985. 14.95 (*0-88776-172-0*, Dist. by U of Toronto Pr); pap. 7.95 (*0-88776-213-1*) Tundra Bks.
Kuropas, Myron B. Ukrainians in America. LC 94-14807. 1994. 17.50 (*0-8225-1955-0*); pap. 5.95 (*0-8225-3476-2*) Lerner Pubns.
Levine, Ellen. If Your Name Was Changed at Ellis Island. Parmenter, Wayne, illus. LC 92-27940. 80p. (gr. 2-5). 1993. 15.95 (*0-590-46134-6*) Scholastic Inc.
Mayberry, Jodine. Filipinos. Daniels, Roger, contrib. by. LC 90-12274. (Illus.). 64p. (gr. 5-8). 1990. PLB 13.40 (*0-531-10978-X*) Watts.
—Mexicans. Daniels, Roger, contrib. by. LC 90-32095. (Illus.). 64p. (gr. 5-8). 1990. PLB 12.40 (*0-531-10979-8*) Watts.
O'Connor, Karen. Dan Thuy's New Life in America. (Illus.). 40p. (gr. 4-8). 1992. PLB 17.50 (*0-8225-2555-0*) Lerner Pubns.
O'Neill, Teresa, ed. Immigration: Opposing Viewpoints. LC 92-21794. 288p. 1992. lib. bdg. 17.95 (*1-56510-007-7*); pap. 9.95 (*1-56510-006-9*) Greenhaven.
Patterson, Wayne. Koreans in America. 1992. pap. 5.95 (*0-8225-1045-6*) Lerner Pubns.
Perrin, Linda. Immigrants from the Far East. LC 80-65840. 192p. 1980. 12.95 (*0-385-28115-3*) Delacorte.
Reimers, David. The Immigrant Experience. Moynihan, Daniel P., intro. by. (Illus.). 112p. (gr. 5 up). 1989. 17.95x (*0-87754-881-1*) Chelsea Hse.
Robbins, Albert. Immigrants from Northern Europe. LC 80-68741. 224p. 1982. 9.95 (*0-385-28138-2*) Delacorte.
Rosenblum, Richard. Journey to the Golden Land. Rosenblum, Richard, illus. LC 91-44941. 32p. (gr. k-4). 1992. 14.95 (*0-8276-0405-X*) JPS Phila.
Sandler, Martin W. Immigrants. Billington, James, intro. by. LC 93-44126. 1995. 19.95 (*0-06-024507-7*); PLB 20.89 (*0-06-024508-5*) HarpC Child Bks.
Schreiner, Nikki B., et al. The Whole World Kit: American Dream Activity Cards. Weathers, Susan, et al, illus. 60p. (gr. 4-8). 1990. pap. text ed. 215.00 (*1-879218-29-1*) Touch & See Educ.
Sima, Patricia, et al. Immigration: A Thematic Unit. Welch, Sandy, illus. 80p. (gr. 3-5). 1993. wkbk. 8.95 (*1-55734-234-2*) Tchr Create Mat.
Steidl, Kim S. Portraits of Asian-Pacific Americans. 96p. (gr. 4-8). 1991. 12.95 (*0-86653-598-5*, GA1323) Good Apple.
Szumski, Bonnie. Immigration: Identifying Propaganda Techniques. LC 89-7508. (Illus.). 32p. (gr. 3-6). 1990. PLB 10.95 (*0-89908-639-X*) Greenhaven.

IMMIGRATION AND EMIGRATION–FICTION

Bartoletti, Susan C. Silver at Night. Ray, David, illus. 32p. (gr. k-4). 1994. 15.00 (*0-517-59426-9*); PLB 15.99 (*0-517-59427-7*) Crown Bks Yng Read.
Benson, Rita. Rosa's Diary. Campbell, Caroline, illus. LC 93-28972. 1994. 4.25 (*0-383-03772-7*) SRA Schl Grp.
Bosse, Malcolm. Ordinary Magic. LC 93-7956. 1993. 4.50 (*0-374-42517-5*) FS&G.
Brown, Irene B. Willow Whip. 208p. (Orig.). (gr. 5 up). pap. 8.95 (*0-936085-23-1*) Blue Heron OR.
Conlon-McKenna, Marita. Wildflower Girl. Teskey, Donald, illus. LC 92-52711. 176p. (gr. 5-9). 1992. 14.95 (*0-8234-0988-0*) Holiday.
Greenberg, Melanie H. Aunt Lilly's Laundromat. LC 93-42597. (Illus.). 24p. (ps-3). 1994. 12.99 (*0-525-45211-7*, DCB) Dutton Child Bks.
Gross, Virginia T. It's Only Goodbye. (gr. 4-8). 1990. 11.95 (*0-670-83289-8*) Viking Child Bks.
—It's Only Goodbye: An Immigrant Story. Raymond, Larry, illus. LC 92-18959. 64p. (gr. 2-6). 1992. pap. 3.99 (*0-14-034409-8*) Puffin Bks.
Hanson, Regina. The Tangerine Tree. Stevenson, Harvey, illus. LC 93-40530. 1995. write for info. (*0-395-68963-5*, Clarion Bks) HM.
Hart, Jan S. Hanna, the Immigrant. Roberts, Melissa, ed. Shaw, Charles, illus. 114p. (gr. 6-8). 1991. 12.95 (*0-89015-805-3*) Sunbelt Media.
—The Many Adventures of Minnie. Wilson, Kay, illus. LC 92-17740. 96p. (gr. 4-7). 1992. 12.95 (*0-89015-859-2*) Sunbelt Media.
Herold, Marrie R. A Very Important Day. Stock, Catherine, illus. LC 94-16647. 1995. write for info. (*0-688-13065-8*); PLB write for info. (*0-688-13066-6*) Morrow Jr Bks.
Hesse, Karen. Letters from Rifka. 192p. (gr. 4-7). 1992. 14.95 (*0-8050-1964-2*, Bks Young Read) H Holt & Co.
—Letters from Rifka. LC 93-7486. 160p. (gr. 3-7). 1993. pap. 3.99 (*0-14-036391-2*, Puffin) Puffin Bks.
Hoff, Carol. Johnny Texas. Myers, Bob, illus. 150p. (gr. 4 up). 1992. lib. bdg. 15.95 (*0-937460-80-X*); pap. 9.95 (*0-937460-81-8*) Hendrick-Long.
Joosse, Barbara M. The Morning Chair. Sewall, Marcia, illus. LC 93-4870. Date not set. write for info. (*0-395-62337-5*, Clarion Bks) HM.
Kavanagh, Katie. Home Is Where Your Family Is. Fitzhugh, Greg, illus. 1994. PLB 19.97 (*0-8114-4462-7*) Raintree Steck-V.
Klass, Sheila S. Pork Bellies Are Down. LC 94-20235. 1995. 13.95 (*0-590-46686-0*) Scholastic Inc.
Lawson, Robert. The Great Wheel. Lawson, Robert, illus. 180p. 1993. pap. 7.95 (*0-8027-7392-3*) Walker & Co.
Leighton, Maxinne R. An Ellis Island Christmas. Nolan, Dennis, illus. 32p. (gr. 1-4). 1992. 15.00 (*0-670-83182-4*) Viking Child Bks.
Levine, Ellen. I Hate English! Bjorkman, Steve, illus. (gr. k-2). 1989. pap. 13.95 (*0-590-42305-3*) Scholastic Inc.
Levinson, Riki. Soon, Annala. Downing, Julie, photos by. LC 92-44588. (Illus.). 32p. (ps-2). 1993. 14.95 (*0-531-05494-2*); PLB 14.99 (*0-531-08644-5*) Orchard Bks Watts.
Levitin, Sonia. Silver Days. LC 91-22581. 192p. (gr. 3-7). 1992. pap. 3.95 (*0-689-71570-6*, Aladdin) Macmillan Child Grp.
Lindsay, Mela M. The Story of Johann: The Boy Who Longed to Come to Amerika. Gentry, Diane, illus. LC 90-85324. 190p. 1991. 11.50 (*0-914222-18-X*) Am Hist Soc Ger.
Lingard, Joan. Between Two Worlds. 192p. (gr. 7 up). 1991. 14.95 (*0-525-67360-1*, Lodestar Bks) Dutton Child Bks.
—Between Two Worlds. 192p. (gr. 7 up). 1993. pap. 4.50 (*0-14-036505-2*, Puffin) Puffin Bks.
Mohr, Nicholas. Jaime & the Conch Shell. LC 93-30403. 1995. 13.95 (*0-590-47110-4*) Scholastic Inc.
Moss, Marissa. In America. Moss, Marissa, illus. LC 93-26885. 1994. write for info. (*0-525-45152-8*, DCB) Dutton Child Bks.
Munson, Sammye. Goodbye, Sweden, Hello Texas. LC 93-38928. 1994. 14.95 (*0-89015-948-3*) Sunbelt Media.
Nixon, Joan L. Land of Dreams. LC 93-8734. 1994. 14.95 (*0-385-31170-2*) Delacorte.
—Land of Promise. LC 92-28591. (gr. 4-7). 1993. 16.00 (*0-553-08111-X*) Bantam.
A Piece of Home. 1994. write for info. (*0-8037-1625-7*) Dial Bks Young.
Rosenberg, Liz. Grandmother & the Runaway Shadow. Peck, Beth, illus. LC 92-42349. 1994. write for info. (*0-399-22545-5*, Philomel Bks) Putnam Pub Group.
Ross, Lillian H. Buba Leah & Her Paper Children. Morgan, Mary, illus. 32p. (gr. k-3). 1991. 16.95 (*0-8276-0375-4*) JPS Phila.
—Sarah, Also Known As Hannah. Cogancherry, Helen, illus. LC 93-29601. 1994. write for info. (*0-8075-7237-3*) A Whitman.
Sachs, Marilyn. Call Me Ruth. LC 94-19695. 1995. write for info. (*0-688-13737-7*, Pub. by Beech Tree Bks) Morrow.
Sandin, Joan. The Long Way to a New Land. Sandin, Joan, illus. LC 80-8942. 64p. (gr. k-3). 1981. PLB 14.89 (*0-06-025194-8*) HarpC Child Bks.
Shapiro, Irwin. Joe Magarac & His U. S. A. Citizen Papers. Daugherty, James, illus. LC 78-66070. 58p. (gr. 1-8). 1979. pap. 7.95 (*0-8229-5305-6*) U of Pittsburgh Pr.
Shiefman, Vicky. Good-Bye to the Trees. LC 92-22260. 176p. (gr. 4-8). 1993. SBE 14.95 (*0-689-31806-5*, Atheneum Child Bk) Macmillan Child Grp.
Stevens, Carla. Lily & Miss Liberty. (gr. 4-7). 1993. pap. 2.75 (*0-590-44920-6*) Scholastic Inc.
Taylor, Sydney. All-of-a-Kind Family. John, Helen, illus. 189p. (gr. 3-6). 1988. Repr. of 1951 ed. 11.95 (*0-929093-00-3*) Taylor Prodns.
Van Laan, Nancy. People, People, Everywhere! Westcott, Nadine B., illus. LC 90-5303. 40p. (ps-2). 1992. 13.00 (*0-679-81063-3*); PLB 13.99 (*0-679-91063-8*) Knopf Bks Yng Read.
Whelan, Gloria. Goodbye, Vietnam. LC 91-3660. 112p. (gr. 3-7). 1992. 13.00 (*0-679-82263-1*); PLB 13.99 (*0-679-92263-6*) Knopf Bks Yng Read.
—Goodbye, Vietnam. LC 91-3660. 144p. (gr. 3-7). 1993. pap. 3.99 (*0-679-82376-X*, Bullseye Bks) Random Bks Yng Read.
Winter, Jeanette. Klara's New World. Winter, Jeanette, illus. LC 91-30212. 48p. (gr. 2-7). 1992. 15.00 (*0-679-80626-1*); PLB 15.99 (*0-679-90626-6*) Knopf Bks Yng Read.

Yates, Elizabeth. Hue & Cry. 182p. (gr. 7-12). 1991. pap. 4.95 (*0-89084-536-0*) Bob Jones Univ Pr.

IMMUNITY

see also Allergy; Communicable Diseases; Vaccination

Almonte, Paul & Desmond, Theresa. The Immune System. (Illus.). 48p. (gr. 5-6). 1991. text ed. 12.95 RSBE (*0-89686-661-0*, Crestwood Hse) Macmillan Child Grp.

Balkwill, Fran. Cell Wars. Rolph, Mic, illus. LC 92-6377. 1992. 17.50 (*0-87614-761-9*) Carolrhoda Bks.

Garvy, Helen. The Immune System: Your Magic Doctor. Bessie, Dan, illus. LC 91-91575. 76p. (gr. 4 up). 1992. lib. bdg. 15.00 (*0-918828-09-0*); pap. 10.00 (*0-918828-10-4*) Shire Pr.

Graham, Ian. Fighting Disease. LC 94-19981. Date not set. write for info. (*0-8114-3844-9*) Raintree Steck-V.

IMPLEMENTS, UTENSILS, ETC.

see Agricultural Machinery; Household Equipment and Supplies; Tools

IMPORTS

see Commerce

IMPOSTORS AND IMPOSTURE

Stewart, Gail B. Famous Hoaxes. LC 89-25422. (Illus.). 48p. (gr. 5-6). 1990. text ed. 11.95 RSBE (*0-89686-507-X*, Crestwood Hse) Macmillan Child Grp.

IMPRESSIONISM (ART)

Reyero, Carlos. The Key to Art from Romanticism to Impressionism. (Illus.). 80p. (gr. 8 up). 1990. PLB 21. 50 (*0-8225-2058-3*) Lerner Pubns.

IMPRISONMENT

see Prisons

INCAS

Alexander, Ellen. Chaska & the Golden Doll. LC 93-34691. (Illus.). 32p. (ps-3). 1994. 14.95 (*1-559702-41-9*) Arcade Pub Inc.

Appel, Benjamin. Shepherd of the Sun. Bryson, Bernarda, illus. (gr. 5 up). 1961. 10.95 (*0-8392-3033-8*) Astor-Honor.

Baquedano, Elizabeth. Aztec, Inca, & Maya. Zabe, Michel & Rudkin, David, illus. 64p. (gr. 5 up). 1993. 15.00 (*0-679-83883-X*); PLB 15.99 (*0-679-93883-4*) Knopf Bks Yng Read.

Gonzalez, Christina. Inca Civilization. LC 92-37021. (Illus.). 36p. (gr. 3 up). 1993. PLB 14.95 (*0-516-08380-5*); pap. 6.95 (*0-516-48380-3*) Childrens.

Harkonen, Reijo. The Grandchildren of the Incas. Pitkanen, Matti A., photos by. (Illus.). 40p. (gr. 3-6). 1991. PLB 19.95 (*0-87614-397-4*) Carolrhoda Bks.

Kendall, Sarita. The Incas. LC 91-513. (Illus.). 64p. (gr. 6 up). 1992. text ed. 14.95 RSBE (*0-02-750160-4*, New Discovery) Macmillan Child Grp.

Kuss, Daniele. Incas. LC 91-17741. (Illus.). 48p. (gr. 4-8). 1991. PLB 13.95 (*1-85435-267-9*) Marshall Cavendish.

McKissack, Patricia. The Inca. LC 85-6712. (Illus.). 45p. (gr. 2-3). 1985. PLB 12.85 (*0-516-01268-1*); pap. 4.95 (*0-516-41268-X*) Childrens.

—Los Incas (The Inca) LC 85-6712. (SPA.). 48p. (gr. k-4). 1987. PLB 12.85 (*0-516-31268-5*); pap. 4.95 (*0-516-51268-4*) Childrens.

Marrin, Albert. Inca & Spaniard: Pizarro & the Conquest of Peru. LC 88-29372. (Illus.). 192p. (gr. 5 up). 1989. SBE 15.95 (*0-689-31481-7*, Atheneum Child Bk) Macmillan Child Grp.

Newman, Shirlee P. The Incas. Rosoff, Iris, ed. LC 91-31378. (Illus.). 64p. (gr. 3-5). 1992. PLB 12.90 (*0-531-20004-3*) Watts.

—The Incas. (Illus.). 64p. (gr. 5-8). 1992. pap. 5.95 (*0-531-15637-0*) Watts.

Odijk, Pamela. The Incas. (Illus.). 48p. (gr. 5-8). 1990. PLB 12.95 (*0-382-09889-7*); 7.95 (*0-382-24264-5*); tchr's. guide 4.50 (*0-382-24279-3*) Silver Burdett Pr.

Skivington, Janice, illus. The Girl from the Sky: An Inca Folktale from South America. LC 91-42163. 24p. (ps-3). 1992. PLB 13.85 (*0-516-05138-5*); pap. 5.95 (*0-516-45138-3*) Childrens.

Steele, Philip. The Incas & Machu Picchu. LC 92-42283. (Illus.). 32p. (gr. 6-8). 1993. text ed. 13.95 RSBE (*0-87518-536-3*, Dillon) Macmillan Child Grp.

INCAS–FICTION

Clark, Ann N. Secret of the Andes. Charlot, Jean, illus. (gr. 3-7). 1976. pap. 4.99 (*0-14-030926-8*, Puffin) Puffin Bks.

—Secret of the Andes. Charlot, Jean, illus. (gr. 4-8). 1952. pap. 14.99 (*0-670-62975-8*) Viking Child Bks.

Lehtinen, Ritva. Grandchildren of the Incas. (gr. 4-7). 1992. pap. 6.95 (*0-87614-566-7*) Carolrhoda Bks.

Plenk, Dagmar. Sophie & the Incas. LC 90-71979. 72p. (Orig.). (gr. 3-7). 1991. pap. 9.00 (*1-56002-039-3*) Aegina Pr.

INCINERATION

see Refuse and Refuse Disposal

INDEPENDENCE DAY (U. S.)

see Fourth of July

INDEX LIBORUM PROHIBITORUM

see Catholic Literature

INDIA

Ardley, Brigette & Ardley, Neil. India. (Illus.). 48p. (gr. 4-8). 1989. lib. bdg. 14.95 (*0-382-09795-5*) Silver Burdett Pr.

Bawa, Ujagar S. Bichitra Naatik: A Part of Sikh Scriptures. 172p. (gr. 8-12). 1991. pap. 10.00x (*0-942245-06-7*) Wash Sikh Ctr.

—Sikhism: A Short Expose. 30p. (gr. 8-12). 1988. pap. 2. 00x (*0-942245-02-4*) Wash Sikh Ctr.

—Sri Sukhmani Sahib: A Part of Sikh Scriptures. 304p. (gr. 8-12). 1990. pap. 10.00x (*0-942245-05-9*) Wash Sikh Ctr.

Behal, J. K. India Today. 200p. (Orig.). (gr. 12). 1993. pap. text ed. 14.95 (*0-9628328-1-2*) Starlite Inc.

Braguet, Anne & Noblet, Martine. India. (Illus.). 76p. (gr. 5 up). 1994. 13.95 (*0-8120-6427-5*); pap. 7.95 (*0-8120-1866-4*) Barron.

Constitution of India for the Younger Reader. 1971. pap. 1.75 (*0-88253-410-6*) Ind-US Inc.

Cumming, David. India. (Illus.). 32p. (gr. k-4). 1991. 12. 40 (*0-531-18391-2*, Pub. by Bookwright Pr) Watts.

Das, Prodeepta. India. LC 89-38985. (Illus.). 32p. (gr. 5-8). 1990. PLB 11.90 (*0-531-14045-8*) Watts.

Dhanjal, Beryl. Amritsar. LC 93-31-45. (Illus.). 48p. (gr. 5 up). 1994. text ed. 13.95 RSBE (*0-87518-571-1*, Dillon) Macmillan Child Grp.

Galbraith, Catherine A. & Mehta, Rama. India Now & Through Time. 160p. (gr. 6 up). 1980. 16.45 (*0-395-29207-7*) HM.

Ganeri, Anita. I Remember India. LC 94-20925. 1994. write for info. (*0-8114-5609-9*) Raintree Steck-V.

—Journey Through India. Burns, Robert, illus. LC 91-46176. 32p. (gr. 3-5). 1993. PLB 11.89 (*0-8167-2761-9*); pap. text ed. 3.95 (*0-8167-2762-7*) Troll Assocs.

Ganeri, Anita & Wright, Rachel. India. LC 94-1395. 1994. write for info. (*0-531-14314-7*) Watts.

Ghose, Vijaya. Women in Society. LC 93-46880. (gr. 5 up). 1994. write for info. Set (*1-85435-559-7*) Marshall Cavendish.

Haskins, Jim. Count Your Way Through India. Dodson, Liz B., illus. 24p. (gr. 1-4). 1990. PLB 17.50 (*0-87614-414-8*) Carolrhoda Bks.

—Count Your Way Through India. (ps-3). 1992. pap. 5.95 (*0-87614-577-2*) Carolrhoda Bks.

Hussain, Shahrukh A. India. (Illus.). 32p. (gr. 4-8). 1992. 17.95 (*0-237-60185-0*, Pub. by Evans Bros Ltd) Trafalgar.

Jensen, Anne F. India: Its Culture & People. LC 90-23051. (Illus.). 272p. (Orig.). (gr. 1-8). 1991. pap. text ed. 18.32 (*0-8013-0343-5*) Longman.

Kalman, Bobbie. India: The Culture. (Illus.). 32p. (gr. 4-5). 1990. PLB 15.95 (*0-86505-212-3*); pap. 7.95 (*0-86505-292-1*) Crabtree Pub Co.

—India: The Land. (Illus.). 32p. (gr. 4-5). 1990. PLB 15. 95 (*0-86505-210-7*); pap. 7.95 (*0-86505-290-5*) Crabtree Pub Co.

—India: The People. (Illus.). 32p. (gr. 4-5). 1990. PLB 15. 95 (*0-86505-211-5*); pap. 7.95 (*0-86505-291-3*) Crabtree Pub Co.

Kaur, Sharon. Food in India. LC 88-31294. (Illus.). 32p. (gr. 3-6). 1989. lib. bdg. 15.94 (*0-86625-339-4*); 11. 95s.p. (*0-685-58500-X*) Rourke Corp.

Kublin, Hyman. India: Regional Study. rev. ed. (Illus.). 228p. (gr. 9-12). 1973. pap. 20.56 (*0-395-13928-7*) HM.

Lerner Publications, Department of Geography Staff, ed. India in Pictures. (Illus.). 64p. (gr. 5 up). 1989. 17.50 (*0-8225-1852-X*) Lerner Pubns.

McNair, Sylvia. India. LC 89-25435. (Illus.). 128p. (gr. 5-9). 1990. PLB 20.55 (*0-516-02719-0*) Childrens.

Nugent, Nicholas. India. LC 90-25300. (Illus.). 96p. (gr. 6-12). 1991. PLB 22.80 (*0-8114-2441-3*) Raintree Steck-V.

Parker, Lewis K. India. LC 94-614. 1994. write for info. (*1-55916-005-5*) Rourke Bk Co.

Schmidt, Jeremy. In the Village of the Elephants. Wood, Ted, photos by. LC 93-8545. (Illus.). 32p. (gr. 2-5). 1994. 15.95 (*0-8027-8226-4*); PLB 16.85 (*0-8027-8227-2*) Walker & Co.

Singh, Anne. Living in India. Matthews, Sarah, tr. from FRE. Riquier, Aline, illus. LC 87-31803. 38p. (gr. k-5). 1988. 5.95 (*0-944589-14-6*, 146) Young Discovery Lib.

Srinivasan, Rodbika. India. LC 89-25466. (Illus.). 128p. (gr. 5-9). 1991. PLB 21.95 (*1-85435-298-9*) Marshall Cavendish.

Stewart, Gail B. India. LC 91-34399. (Illus.). 48p. (gr. 6-7). 1992. text ed. 12.95 RSBE (*0-89686-745-5*, Crestwood Hse) Macmillan Child Grp.

INDIA–BIOGRAPHY

Allison, Carol. Ringu of India's Forest. Espe, Marvin, illus. 52p. (gr. k-6). 1987. pap. text ed. 8.99 (*1-55976-050-8*) CEF Press.

Ghosh, A. Chanakya. Vilas, Anil, illus. (gr. 1-8). 1979. pap. 3.00 (*0-89744-152-4*) Auromere.

Giff, Patricia R. Mother Teresa: A Sister to the Poor. Lewin, Ted, illus. LC 85-40885. 64p. (gr. 2-6). 1986. pap. 10.95 (*0-670-81096-7*) Viking Child Bks.

Haskins, James. India under Indira & Rajiv Gandhi. LC 88-21209. (Illus.). 104p. (gr. 6 up). 1989. lib. bdg. 17. 95 (*0-89490-146-X*) Enslow Pubs.

Singh, Mala. The Story of Guru Nanak. (Illus.). (gr. 2-9). 1979. 7.25 (*0-89744-138-9*) Auromere.

INDIA–DESCRIPTION AND TRAVEL

Ganeri, Anita. India. (Illus.). 32p. (gr. 5-8). 1994. PLB write for info. (*0-531-14272-8*) Watts.

Khanna, K. As They Saw India. Khanna, Krishna, illus. (gr. 1-9). 1979. pap. 2.50 (*0-89744-172-9*) Auromere.

Singh, Mala. Kashmir. Sharma, P. N., photos by. (Illus.). (gr. 1-10). 1979. pap. 2.50 (*0-89744-177-X*) Auromere.

Valiappa, Al. Story of Our Rivers: Book II. Chakravarty, Pranab, illus. (gr. 1-9). 1979. pap. 2.50 (*0-89744-184-2*) Auromere.

INDIA–FICTION

Anand, Mulk R. Maya of Mohenjo-Daro. 3rd ed. Biswas, Pulak, illus. 24p. (Orig.). (gr. k-3). 1980. pap. 2.50 (*0-89744-214-8*, Pub. by Childrens Bk Trust IA) Auromere.

Arnold, Marsha D. Heart of a Tiger. Henterly, Jamichael, illus. LC 94-17126. (gr. 1-8). 1995. write for info. (*0-8037-1695-8*); PLB write for info. (*0-8037-1696-6*) Dial Bks Young.

Axworthy, Anni. Anni's India Diary. Axworthy, Anni, illus. LC 92-17524. 32p. (gr. 1-5). 1992. smyth sewn reinforced 14.95 (*1-879085-59-3*) Whsprng Coyote Pr.

Basu, Romen. The Street Corner Boys. Hauge, Veronica, tr. 154p. (gr. 9-10). 1992. 14.95 (*0-932377-40-8*) Facet Bks.

Chaikin, Linda. Silk. 400p. (Orig.). 1993. pap. 9.99 (*1-55661-248-6*) Bethany Hse.

Cowcher, Helen. La Tigresa. Marcuse, Aida, tr. (SPA.). 32p. (gr. 4-8). 1993. pap. 5.95 (*0-374-47779-5*) FS&G.

—La Tigresa: Tigress. (ps-3). 1993. 16.00 (*0-374-37565-8*, Mirasol) FS&G.

—Tigress. Thomas, Peter, narrated by. Cowcher, Helen, illus. 32p. (gr. k-3). incls. cassette 19.95 (*0-924483-33-4*) Soundprints.

—Tigress. (ps-3). 1993. pap. 5.95 (*0-374-47781-7*) FS&G.

Dasa, Yogesvara & Dasi, Jyotirmayi-Devi. A Gift of Love: The Story of Sudama Brahmin. Dasa, Puskar, illus. LC 82-8874. 32p. (gr. 5-8). 1982. PLB 7.00 (*0-89647-015-6*) Bala Bks.

Dutta, S. & Hemalata. Harishchandra. Wheaton, Jaya, illus. (gr. 1-8). 1979. pap. 3.00 (*0-89744-155-9*) Auromere.

Gajadin, Chitra & Tagore, Rabindranath, eds. Amal & the Letter from the King: Adapted from a Play by Rabindranath Tagore. Ong, Helen, illus. LC 91-77712. 40p. 1992. PLB 14.95 (*1-56397-120-8*) Boyds Mills Pr.

Kipling, Rudyard. The Jungle Book. Detmold, Maurice, et al, illus. 320p. 1989. 12.99 (*0-517-67902-7*) Random Hse Value.

—The Jungle Book. Robson, W. W., intro. by. 432p. 1992. pap. 4.95 (*0-19-282901-7*) OUP.

—The Jungle Book. Ashachik, Diane M., ed. Hannon, Holly, illus. LC 92-5806. 48p. (gr. 3-6). 1992. PLB 12. 89 (*0-8167-2868-2*); pap. text ed. 3.95 (*0-8167-2869-0*) Troll Assocs.

—The Jungle Book. Weise, Kurt, illus. LC 94-5860. 1994. 13.95 (*0-679-43637-5*) Knopf.

—Jungle Books. (gr. 5 up). 1966. pap. 1.95 (*0-8049-0109-0*, CL-109) Airmont.

—The Jungle Books. 336p. 1961. pap. 3.95 (*0-451-52340-7*, Sig Classics) NAL-Dutton.

—Just So Stories. Brent, Isabelle, illus. Philip, Neil, frwd. by. (Illus.). 160p. 1993. 19.99 (*0-670-85196-5*) Viking Child Bks.

—Kim. 384p. (gr. 5 up). 1992. pap. 3.50 (*0-440-40695-1*, Pub. by Yearling Classics) Dell.

—The Maltese Cat. 1991. PLB 13.95 (*0-88682-475-3*) Creative Ed.

—The Miracle of Purun Bhagat. LC 85-26956. 40p. (gr. 6 up). 1986. PLB 13.95 (*0-88682-052-9*) Creative Ed.

—Mowgli Stories from "The Jungle Book" LC 94-467. (Illus.). 128p. (Orig.). 1994. pap. 1.00 (*0-486-28030-6*) Dover.

Rana, Indi. The Roller Birds of Rampur. 272p. (gr. 7 up). 1993. 15.95 (*0-8050-2670-3*, Bks Young Read) H Holt & Co.

Rankin, Louise. Daughter of the Mountains. Wiese, Kurt, illus. LC 92-26793. 192p. (gr. 5 up). 1993. pap. 4.99 (*0-14-036335-1*) Puffin Bks.

Shivkumar. Krishna & Sudama. Gupta, M. L. Dutta, illus. (gr. 1-8). 1979. pap. 2.00 (*0-89744-156-7*) Auromere.

Smarananda. Story of Sarada Devi. Chakravarty, Biswaranjan, illus. 36p. (Orig.). (gr. k-4). 1987. pap. 1.95 (*0-87481-229-1*, Pub. by Advaita Ashram India) Vedanta Pr.

Stewart, Mollie D. Noah's Land. 1991. 12.95 (*0-533-09336-8*) Vantage.

Stone, Susheila. Nadeem Makes Samosas. (Illus.). 25p. (gr. 2-4). 1991. 15.95 (*0-237-60155-9*, Pub. by Evans Bros Ltd) Trafalgar.

Wright, Meg, illus. Three Stories from India. (gr. 1-8). 1984. pap. text ed. 10.00 (*0-86508-166-2*) BCM Pubn.

INDIA–HISTORY

Ashton, Stephen. The British in India. (Illus.). 86p. (gr. 7-9). 1988. 19.95 (*0-7134-5475-X*, Pub. by Batsford UK) Trafalgar.

Ganeri, Anita. Exploration into India. LC 93-43716. 1994. text ed. 15.95 (*0-02-718082-4*, New Discovery Bks) Macmillan Child Grp.

Haskins, James. India under Indira & Rajiv Gandhi. LC 88-21209. (Illus.). 104p. (gr. 6 up). 1989. lib. bdg. 17. 95 (*0-89490-146-X*) Enslow Pubs.

Prabhakar, Vishnu. Story of Swarajya: Part I. (Illus.). (gr. 1-10). 1979. pap. 2.50 (*0-89744-185-0*) Auromere.

Prakash, Sumangal. Story of Swarajya: Part II. Khemraj, P., illus. (gr. 1-10). 1979. pap. 2.50 (*0-89744-186-9*) Auromere.

Rawding, F. W. The Rebellion in India, 1857. (Illus.). 48p. (gr. 7 up). 1977. pap. 7.95 (*0-521-20683-9*) Cambridge U Pr.

Sen, Abhijit & Raman, Papri Sri. Magic Bones. 264p. (gr. 9-10). 1992. 14.95 (*0-932377-49-1*) Facet Bks.

INDIA RUBBER

see Rubber

INDIANA

Baxter, Nancy N., ed. Hoosier Farmboy in Lincoln's Army: The Civil War Letters of Pvt. John R. McClure. 2nd ed. (Illus.). 67p. (gr. 6-10). 1971. 14.95 (*0-9617367-2-0*) Guild Pr IN.

Berry, S. L. Indianapolis. (Illus.). 60p. (gr. 3 up). 1990. text ed. 13.95 (*0-87518-426-X*, Dillon) Macmillan Child Grp.

Buchart & Associates, Inc. Staff. Indianapolis Guide Book for Kids. 36p. (ps-5). 1993. pap. 2.75 (*1-883900-01-8*) Buchart & Assocs.

Carole Marsh Indiana Books, 44 bks. 1994. lib. bdg. 1027.80 set (*0-7933-1289-2*); pap. 587.80 (*0-7933-5150-2*) Gallopade Pub Group.

Carpenter, Allan. Indiana. new ed. LC 78-12459. (Illus.). 96p. (gr. 4 up). 1979. PLB 16.95 (*0-516-04114-2*) Childrens.

Fradin, Dennis. Indiana: In Words & Pictures. LC 79-21383. (Illus.). 48p. (gr. 2-5). 1980. PLB 12.95 (*0-516-03912-1*) Childrens.

Fradin, Dennis B. & Fradin, Judith B. Indiana. LC 94-6234. (Illus.). 64p. (gr. 3-5). 1994. PLB 2.005 (*0-516-03814-1*) Childrens.

Hinshaw, Dorothy. When I Was Young in Indiana: A Country Life. (Illus.). 60p. 1994. 12.95 (*1-878208-38-1*) Guild Pr IN.

Marsh, Carole. Avast, Ye Slobs! Indiana Pirate Trivia. (Illus.). (gr. 3-12). 1994. PLB 24.95 (*0-7933-0424-5*); pap. 14.95 (*0-7933-0423-7*); computer disk 29.95 (*0-685-45926-8*) Gallopade Pub Group.

—The Beast of the Indiana Bed & Breakfast. (Illus.). (gr. 3-12). 1994. PLB 24.95 (*0-7933-1609-X*); pap. 14.95 (*0-7933-1610-3*); computer disk 29.95 (*0-7933-1611-1*) Gallopade Pub Group.

—Bow Wow! Indiana Dogs in History, Mystery, Legend, Lore, Humor & More! (Illus.). (gr. 3-12). 1994. PLB 24.95 (*0-7933-3509-4*); pap. 14.95 (*0-7933-3510-8*); computer disk 29.95 (*0-7933-3511-6*) Gallopade Pub Group.

—Chill Out: Scary Indiana Tales Based on Frightening Indiana Truths. (Illus.). 1994. lib. bdg. 24.95 (*0-7933-4696-7*); pap. 14.95 (*0-7933-4697-5*); disk 29.95 (*0-7933-4698-3*) Gallopade Pub Group.

—Christopher Columbus Comes to Indiana! Includes Reproducible Activities for Kids! (Illus.). (gr. 3-12). 1994. PLB 24.95 (*0-7933-3662-7*); pap. 14.95 (*0-7933-3663-5*); computer disk 29.95 (*0-7933-3664-3*) Gallopade Pub Group.

—The Hard-to-Believe-But-True! Book of Indiana History, Mystery, Trivia, Legend, Lore, Humor & More. (Illus.). (gr. 3-12). 1994. PLB 24.95 (*0-7933-0421-0*); pap. 14.95 (*0-7933-0420-2*); computer disk 29.95 (*0-7933-0422-9*) Gallopade Pub Group.

—If My Indiana Mama Ran the World! (Illus.). (gr. 3-12). 1994. PLB 24.95 (*0-7933-1613-8*); pap. 14.95 (*0-7933-1614-6*); computer disk 29.95 (*0-7933-1615-4*) Gallopade Pub Group.

—Indiana & Other State Greats (Biographies) (Illus.). (gr. 3-12). 1994. PLB 24.95 (*1-55609-437-X*); pap. 14.95 (*1-55609-436-1*); computer disk 29.95 (*0-7933-1616-2*) Gallopade Pub Group.

—Indiana Bandits, Bushwackers, Outlaws, Crooks, Devils, Ghosts, Desperadoes & Other Assorted & Sundry Characters! (Illus.). (gr. 3-12). 1994. PLB 24.95 (*0-7933-0406-7*); pap. 14.95 (*0-7933-0405-9*); computer disk 29.95 (*0-7933-0407-5*) Gallopade Pub Group.

—Indiana Classic Christmas Trivia: Stories, Recipes, Activities, Legends, Lore & More! (Illus.). (gr. 3-12). 1994. PLB 24.95 (*0-7933-0409-1*); pap. 14.95 (*0-7933-0408-3*); computer disk 29.95 (*0-7933-0410-5*) Gallopade Pub Group.

—Indiana Coastales. (Illus.). (gr. 3-12). 1994. PLB 24.95 (*1-55609-433-7*); pap. 14.95 (*1-55609-432-9*); computer disk 29.95 (*0-7933-1617-0*) Gallopade Pub Group.

—Indiana Coastales! 1994. lib. bdg. 24.95 (*0-7933-7279-8*) Gallopade Pub Group.

—Indiana "Crinkum-Crankum" A Funny Word Book about Our State. (Illus.). 1994. lib. bdg. 24.95 (*0-7933-4849-8*); pap. 14.95 (*0-7933-4851-X*); disk 29.95 (*0-7933-4852-8*) Gallopade Pub Group.

—Indiana Dingbats! Bk. 1: A Fun Book of Games, Stories, Activities & More about Our State That's All in Code! for You to Decipher. (Illus.). (gr. 3-12). 1994. PLB 24.95 (*0-7933-3815-8*); pap. 14.95 (*0-7933-3816-6*); computer disk 29.95 (*0-7933-3817-4*) Gallopade Pub Group.

—Indiana Festival Fun for Kids! (Illus.). (gr. 3-12). 1994. lib. bdg. 24.95 (*0-7933-3968-5*); pap. 14.95 (*0-7933-3969-3*); disk 29.95 (*0-7933-3970-7*) Gallopade Pub Group.

—The Indiana Hot Air Balloon Mystery. (Illus.). (gr. 2-9). 1994. 24.95 (*0-7933-2444-0*); pap. 14.95 (*0-7933-2445-9*); computer disk 29.95 (*0-7933-2446-7*) Gallopade Pub Group.

—Indiana Jeopardy! Answers & Questions about Our State! (Illus.). (gr. 3-12). 1994. PLB 24.95 (*0-7933-4121-3*); pap. 14.95 (*0-7933-4122-1*); computer disk 29.95 (*0-7933-4123-X*) Gallopade Pub Group.

—Indiana "Jography" A Fun Run Thru Our State! (Illus.). (gr. 3-12). 1994. PLB 24.95 (*1-55609-428-0*); pap. 14.95 (*1-55609-102-8*); computer disk 29.95 (*0-7933-1603-0*) Gallopade Pub Group.

—Indiana Kid's Cookbook: Recipes, How-to, History, Lore & More! (Illus.). (gr. 3-12). 1994. PLB 24.95 (*0-7933-0418-0*); pap. 14.95 (*0-7933-0417-2*); computer disk 29.95 (*0-7933-0419-9*) Gallopade Pub Group.

—The Indiana Mystery Van Takes Off! Book 1: Handicapped Indiana Kids Sneak Off on a Big Adventure. (Illus.). (gr. 3-12). 1994. 24.95 (*0-7933-5003-4*); pap. 14.95 (*0-7933-5004-2*); computer disk 29.95 (*0-7933-5005-0*) Gallopade Pub Group.

—Indiana Quiz Bowl Crash Course! (Illus.). (gr. 3-12). 1994. PLB 24.95 (*1-55609-435-3*); pap. 14.95 (*1-55609-434-5*); computer disk 29.95 (*0-7933-1612-X*) Gallopade Pub Group.

—Indiana Rollercoasters! (Illus.). (gr. 3-12). 1994. PLB 24.95 (*0-7933-5266-5*); pap. 14.95 (*0-7933-5267-3*); computer disk 29.95 (*0-7933-5268-1*) Gallopade Pub Group.

—Indiana School Trivia: An Amazing & Fascinating Look at Our State's Teachers, Schools & Students! (Illus.). (gr. 3-12). 1994. PLB 24.95 (*0-7933-0415-6*); pap. 14.95 (*0-7933-0414-8*); computer disk 29.95 (*0-7933-0416-4*) Gallopade Pub Group.

—Indiana Silly Basketball Sportsmysteries, Vol. I. (Illus.). (gr. 3-12). 1994. PLB 24.95 (*0-7933-0412-1*); pap. 14.95 (*0-7933-0411-3*); computer disk 29.95 (*0-7933-0413-X*) Gallopade Pub Group.

—Indiana Silly Basketball Sportsmysteries, Vol. II. (Illus.). (gr. 3-12). 1994. PLB 24.95 (*0-7933-1618-9*); pap. 14.95 (*0-7933-1619-7*); computer disk 29.95 (*0-7933-1620-0*) Gallopade Pub Group.

—Indiana Silly Football Sportsmysteries, Vol. I. (Illus.). (gr. 3-12). 1994. PLB 24.95 (*1-55609-431-0*); pap. 14.95 (*1-55609-430-2*); computer disk 29.95 (*0-7933-1605-7*) Gallopade Pub Group.

—Indiana Silly Football Sportsmysteries, Vol. II. (Illus.). (gr. 3-12). 1994. PLB 24.95 (*0-7933-1606-5*); pap. 14.95 (*0-7933-1607-3*); computer disk 29.95 (*0-7933-1608-1*) Gallopade Pub Group.

—Indiana Silly Trivia! (Illus.). (gr. 3-12). 1994. PLB 24.95 (*1-55609-427-2*); pap. 14.95 (*1-55609-101-X*); computer disk 29.95 (*0-7933-1602-2*) Gallopade Pub Group.

—Indiana Timeline: A Chronology of Indiana History, Mystery, Trivia, Legend, Lore & More. (Illus.). (gr. 3-12). 1994. PLB 24.95 (*0-7933-5917-1*); pap. 14.95 (*0-7933-5918-X*); computer disk 29.95 (*0-7933-5919-8*) Gallopade Pub Group.

—Indiana's (Most Devastating!) Disasters & (Most Calamitous!) Catastrophies! (Illus.). (gr. 3-12). 1994. PLB 24.95 (*0-7933-0403-2*); pap. 14.95 (*0-7933-0402-4*); computer disk 29.95 (*0-7933-0404-0*) Gallopade Pub Group.

—Indiana's Unsolved Mysteries (& Their "Solutions") Includes Scientific Information & Other Activities for Students. (Illus.). (gr. 3-12). 1994. PLB 24.95 (*0-7933-5764-0*); pap. 14.95 (*0-7933-5765-9*); computer disk 29.95 (*0-7933-5766-7*) Gallopade Pub Group.

—Jurassic Ark! Indiana Dinosaurs & Other Prehistoric Creatures. (gr. k-12). 1994. PLB 24.95 (*0-7933-7470-7*); pap. 14.95 (*0-7933-7471-5*); computer disk 29.95 (*0-7933-7472-3*) Gallopade Pub Group.

—Let's Quilt Indiana & Stuff It Topographically! (Illus.). (gr. 3-12). 1994. PLB 24.95 (*1-55609-429-9*); pap. 14.95 (*1-55609-096-X*); computer disk 29.95 (*0-7933-1604-9*) Gallopade Pub Group.

—Let's Quilt Our Indiana County. 1994. lib. bdg. 24.95 (*0-7933-7155-4*); pap. text ed. 14.95 (*0-7933-7156-2*); disk 29.95 (*0-7933-7157-0*) Gallopade Pub Group.

—Let's Quilt Our Indiana Town. 1994. lib. bdg. 24.95 (*0-7933-7005-1*); pap. text ed. 14.95 (*0-7933-7006-X*); disk 29.95 (*0-7933-7007-8*) Gallopade Pub Group.

—Meow! Indiana Cats in History, Mystery, Legend, Lore, Humor & More! (Illus.). (gr. 3-12). 1994. PLB 24.95 (*0-7933-3356-3*); pap. 14.95 (*0-7933-3357-1*); computer disk 29.95 (*0-7933-3358-X*) Gallopade Pub Group.

—My First Book about Indiana. (gr. k-4). 1994. PLB 24.95 (*0-7933-5611-3*); pap. 14.95 (*0-7933-5612-1*); computer disk 29.95 (*0-7933-5613-X*) Gallopade Pub Group.

—Uncle Rebus: Indiana Picture Stories for Computer Kids. (Illus.). (gr. k-3). 1994. PLB 24.95 (*0-7933-4543-X*); pap. 14.95 (*0-7933-4544-8*); disk 29.95 (*0-7933-4545-6*) Gallopade Pub Group.

Stein, R. Conrad. Indiana. LC 89-25281. (Illus.). 144p. (gr. 4 up). 1990. PLB 20.55 (*0-516-00460-3*) Childrens.

—Indiana. 194p. 1993. text ed. 15.40 (*1-56956-161-3*) W A T Braille.

Swain, Gwenyth. Indiana. Lerner Geography Department Staff, ed. (Illus.). 72p. (gr. 3-6). 1992. PLB 17.50 (*0-8225-2721-9*) Lerner Pubns.

Turner Program Services, Inc. Staff & Clark, James I. Indiana. LC 85-9977. 48p. (gr. 3 up). 1985. PLB 19.97 (*0-8174-4303-7*) Raintree Steck-V.

INDIANA–FICTION

Henry, Joanne L. A Clearing in the Forest: A Story about a Real Settler Boy. Robinson, Charles, illus. LC 91-18554. 64p. (gr. 3-6). 1992. RSBE 14.95 (*0-02-743671-3*, Four Winds) Macmillan Child Grp.

Porter, Gene S. Freckles. LC 93-42393. 1994. 7.99 (*0-517-10126-2*, Pub. by Gramercy) Random Hse Value.

Shay, Myrtle. Adventures of Ricky & Chub. Kennedy, Paul, illus. (gr. 4-8). PLB 7.19 (*0-685-02937-9*) Lantern.

Waters, Kate. Andrew McClure & the Headless Horseman: An Adventure in Prairietown, Indiana, 1836. LC 93-31876. (gr. 1-4). 1994. 14.95 (*0-590-45503-6*) Scholastic Inc.

INDIANAPOLIS SPEEDWAY RACE

Andretti, Michael, et al. Michael Andretti at Indianapolis. LC 91-38815. (Illus.). 64p. (gr. 3-7). 1992. pap. 15.00 jacketed (*0-671-75296-0*, S&S BFYR) S&S Trade.

—Michael Andretti at Indianapolis. Carver, Douglas, photos by. LC 91-38815. (Illus.). 64p. (gr. 3-7). 1993. pap. 5.95 (*0-671-79674-7*, S&S BFYR) S&S Trade.

Dregni, Michael. The Indianapolis 500. LC 93-44567. 1994. write for info. (*1-56065-205-5*) Capstone Pr.

Schleifer, Jay. Indy! The Great American Race. LC 94-761. 1994. text ed. 14.95 (*0-89686-819-2*, Crestwood Hse) Macmillan Child Grp.

Weber, Bruce. The Indianapolis Five Hundred. 32p. (gr. 4). 1990. PLB 14.95 (*0-88682-321-8*) Creative Ed.

INDIANS

see also Indians of Central America; Indians of Mexico; Indians of North America; Indians of South America

Artman, John. Indians: An Activity Book. 64p. (gr. 4 up). 1981. 8.95 (*0-86653-012-6*, GA 240) Good Apple.

Banks, Lynne R. The Indian in the Cupboard. Cole, Brock, illus. LC 80-2835. (gr. 4). 1985. 15.95 (*0-385-17051-3*) Doubleday.

Bendick, Jeanne. Tombs of the Ancient Americas. LC 92-24546. (Illus.). 64p. (gr. 5-8). 1993. PLB 12.40 (*0-531-20148-1*) Watts.

Bierhorst, John. The Way of the Earth: Native America & the Environment. LC 93-28971. (Illus.). 336p. (gr. 7 up). 1994. 15.00 (*0-688-11560-8*) Morrow Jr Bks.

Brandt, Keith. Indian Crafts. Guzzi, George, illus. LC 84-2588. 32p. (gr. 3-6). 1985. lib. bdg. 9.49 (*0-8167-0132-6*); pap. text ed. 2.95 (*0-8167-0133-4*) Troll Assocs.

McCall, Barbara. The European Invasion. LC 94-5530. (gr. 5 up). 1994. write for info. (*0-86625-535-4*) Rourke Pubns.

Rand McNally Discovery Atlas of Native Americans. LC 93-39472. 1994. pap. write for info. (*0-528-83678-1*) Rand McNally.

Ventura, Piero. Fourteen Ninety-Two: The Year of the New World. 96p. 1992. 19.95 (*0-399-22332-0*, Putnam) Putnam Pub Group.

Warren, Betsy. Let's Look Inside a Tepee. Warren, Betsy, illus. 28p. (Orig.). (gr. 3 up). 1989. pap. 3.50 (*0-9618660-2-0*) Ranch Gate Bks.

INDIANS, TREATMENT OF

Bealer, Alex. Only the Names Remain: The Cherokees & the Trail of Tears. Bock, William S., illus. (gr. 4-6). 1972. lib. bdg. 15.95 (*0-316-08520-0*) Little.

INDIANS OF CANADA

see Indians of North America–Canada

INDIANS OF CENTRAL AMERICA

De Larramendi Ruis, Alberto. Tropical Rain Forests of Central America. LC 92-35062. (Illus.). 36p. (gr. 3 up). 1993. PLB 14.95 (*0-516-08383-X*); pap. 6.75 (*0-516-48383-8*) Childrens.

Lazo, Caroline. Rigoberta Menchu. LC 93-8381. (Illus.). 64p. (gr. 4 up). 1994. text ed. 13.95 RSBE (*0-87518-619-X*, Dillon) Macmillan Child Grp.

INDIANS OF CENTRAL AMERICA–FICTION

Wisiniewski, David. Rain Player. Wisniewski, David, illus. 32p. (gr. k-4). 1991. 15.45 (*0-395-55112-9*, Clarion Bks) HM.

INDIANS OF CENTRAL AMERICA–MAYAS

see Indians of Mexico–Mayas

INDIANS OF MEXICO

Arnold, Caroline. Mexico's Ancient City of Teotihuacan: The First Metropolis in the Americas. Hewitt, Richard, photos by. LC 93-40811. (Illus.). 1994. 14.95 (*0-395-66584-1*, Clarion Bks) HM.

Birmingham, Duncan. The Maya, Aztecs & Incas Pop-up. (Illus.). 32p. (gr. 3 up). 1985. pap. 7.95 (*0-906212-37-5*, Pub. by Tarquin UK) Parkwest Pubns.

Lane, Sarah, et al. The Cora: People of the Sierra Madre. 51p. (gr. 6-12). 1989. pap. 9.95 (*0-941379-06-X*, 5114) World Eagle.

Wood, Marion. Growing up in Aztec Times. Hook, Richard, illus. LC 91-39444. 32p. (gr. 3-5). 1993. PLB 11.89 (*0-8167-2723-6*); pap. text ed. 3.95 (*0-8167-2724-4*) Troll Assocs.

INDIANS OF MEXICO–FICTION

Baker, Betty. Walk the World's Rim. LC 65-11458. 192p. (gr. 5 up). 1965. PLB 14.89 (*0-06-020381-1*) HarpC Child Bks.

McGee, Charmayne. So Sings the Blue Deer. LC 93-26580. 160p. (gr. 3-7). 1994. SBE 14.95 (*0-689-31888-X*, Atheneum Child Bk) Macmillan Child Grp.

O'Dell, Scott. The Feathered Serpent. 224p. (gr. 7 up). 1981. 16.95 (*0-395-30851-8*) HM.

Rhoads, Dorothy. The Corn Grows Ripe. Charlot, Jean, illus. LC 92-24888. (gr. 8-12). 1993. 4.99 (*0-14-036313-0*, Puffin) Puffin Bks.

Wisiniewski, David. Rain Player. Wisniewski, David, illus. 32p. (gr. k-4). 1991. 15.45 (*0-395-55112-9*, Clarion Bks) HM.

INDIANS OF MEXICO–LEGENDS

Bierhorst, John, ed. The Hungry Woman: Myths & Legends of the Aztecs. LC 92-22217. 1993. 9.00 (*0-688-12301-5*, Quill) Morrow.

Johnston, Tony. The Tale of Rabbit & Coyote. De Paola, Tomie, illus. LC 92-43652. 32p. (ps-3). 1994. 14.95 (*0-399-22258-8*, Putnam) Putnam Pub Group.

Lattimore, Deborah N. Why There Is No Arguing in Heaven: A Mayan Myth. Lattimore, Deborah N., illus. LC 87-35045. 40p. (gr. 1-5). 1989. PLB 13.89 (*0-06-023718-X*) HarpC Child Bks.

Lewis, Richard. All of You Was Singing. Young, Ed, illus. LC 93-44589. (gr. k-3). 1994. pap. 4.95 (*0-689-71853-5*, Alladin) Macmillan Child Grp.

McDermott, Gerald. Musicians of the Sun. LC 93-44050. 1994. 14.95 (*0-590-47337-9*, Blue Sky Press) Scholastic Inc.

Mike, Jan M. Opossum & the Great Firemaker: A Mexican Legend. Reasoner, Charles, illus. LC 92-36459. 32p. (gr. 2-5). 1993. lib. bdg. 11.89 (*0-8167-3055-5*); tchr's. ed. 3.95 (*0-8167-3056-3*) Troll Assocs.

Ober, Hal, retold by. How Music Came into the World. Ober, Carol, illus. LC 93-11330. 1994. 14.95 (*0-395-67523-5*) HM.

Vanden Broeck, Fabricio, illus. Ah Bak's Strange New Crop. Goldman, Judy, adapted by. LC 92-11322. (Illus.). 1995. 14.95 (*0-02-775657-2*) Macmillan.

Wolf, Bernard. Beneath the Stone: A Mexican Zapotec Tale. Wolf, Bernard, photos by. LC 92-27103. (Illus.). 48p. (gr. k-6). 1994. 15.95 (*0-531-06835-8*); lib. bdg. 15.99 RLB (*0-531-08685-2*) Orchard Bks Watts.

INDIANS OF MEXICO–AZTECS

Baquedano, Elizabeth. Aztec, Inca, & Maya. Zabe, Michel & Rudkin, David, illus. 64p. (gr. 5 up). 1993. 15.00 (*0-679-83883-X*); PLB 15.99 (*0-679-93883-4*) Knopf Bks Yng Read.

Bateman, Penny. The Aztecs Activity Book. (Illus.). 16p. 1994. pap. 5.95 (*0-500-27764-8*) Thames Hudson.

Berdan, Frances F. The Aztecs. Porter, Frank W., III, intro. by. (Illus.). 112p. (gr. 5 up). 1989. 17.95 (*1-55546-692-3*); pap. 9.95 (*0-7910-0354-X*) Chelsea Hse.

Bierhorst, John, ed. The Hungry Woman: Myths & Legends of the Aztecs. LC 92-22217. 1993. 9.00 (*0-688-12301-5*, Quill) Morrow.

Burell, Roy. Moctezuma & the Aztecs. McBride, Angus, illus. LC 92-5823. 63p. (gr. 6-7). 1992. PLB 24.26 (*0-8114-3351-X*) Raintree Steck-V.

Defrates, Joanna. What Do We Know about the Aztecs? Shone, Rob, illus. LC 92-16997. 40p. (gr. 3-6). 1993. 16.95 (*0-87226-357-6*) P Bedrick Bks.

Dineen, Jacqueline. The Aztecs. LC 91-36169. (Illus.). 64p. (gr. 6 up). 1992. text ed. 14.95 RSBE (*0-02-730652-6*, New Discovery) Macmillan Child Grp.

Gaudiano, Andrea. Azteca: The Story of a Jaguar Warrior. (SPA & ENG., Illus.). 160p. 1992. pap. 14.95 (*1-879373-05-X*) R Rinehart.

Greger, C. Shana. The Fifth & Final Sun. LC 93-11159. (Illus.). (ps-6). 1994. 14.95 (*0-395-67438-7*) HM.

Hicks, Peter. The Aztecs. LC 92-44377. 32p. (gr. 4-6). 1993. 14.95 (*1-56847-058-4*) Thomson Lrning.

Hughes, Jill. Aztecs. (Illus.). 32p. (gr. 4-6). 1991. 13.95 (*0-237-60172-9*, Pub. by Evans Bros Ltd) Trafalgar.

Larsen, Anita. Montezuma's Missing Treasure. LC 91-19259. (Illus.). 48p. (gr. 5-6). 1992. text ed. 11.95 RSBE (*0-89686-615-7*, Crestwood Hse) Macmillan Child Grp.

McDermott, Gerald. Musicians of the Sun. LC 93-44050. 1994. 14.95 (*0-590-47337-9*, Blue Sky Press) Scholastic Inc.

MacDonald, Fiona. Aztecs. (Illus.). 60p. (gr. 4 up). 1993. 15.95 (*0-8120-6377-5*) Barron.

McKissack, Patricia. The Aztec. LC 84-23142. (Illus.). 48p. (gr. k-4). 1985. PLB 12.85 (*0-516-01936-8*); pap. 4.95 (*0-516-41936-6*) Childrens.

Marrin, Albert. Aztecs & Spaniards: Cortes & the Conquest of Mexico. LC 85-28782. (Illus.). 224p. (gr. 5 up). 1986. SBE 15.95 (*0-689-31176-1*, Atheneum Child Bk) Macmillan Child Grp.

Millard. Crusaders, Aztecs & Samurai. (Illus.). (gr. 4-6). 1978. (Usborne-Hayes); PLB 13.96 (*0-88110-110-9*); pap. 6.95 (*0-86020-194-5*) EDC.

Nicholson, Robert. The Aztecs. LC 93-29445. 1994. write for info. (*0-7910-2701-5*); pap. write for info. (*0-7910-2725-2*) Chelsea Hse.

Nicholson, Robert & Watts, Claire. Los Aztecas. Araluce, Jose R., tr. from ENG. (SPA., Illus.). 24p. 1993. 14. 95x (*1-56492-091-7*) Laredo.

Ober, Hal, retold by. How Music Came into the World. Ober, Carol, illus. LC 93-11330. 1994. 14.95 (*0-395-67523-5*) HM.

Odijk, Pamela. The Aztecs. (Illus.). 48p. (gr. 5-8). 1990. PLB 12.95 (*0-382-09887-0*) Silver Burdett Pr.

Shepherd, Donna A. The Aztecs. Rosoff, Iris, ed. LC 91-28397. (Illus.). 64p. (gr. 5-8). 1992. PLB 12.90 (*0-531-20064-7*) Watts.

—The Aztecs. (Illus.). 64p. (gr. 5-8). 1992. pap. 5.95 (*0-531-15634-6*) Watts.

Wood, Marion. Growing up in Aztec Times. Hook, Richard, illus. LC 91-39444. 32p. (gr. 3-5). 1993. PLB 11.89 (*0-8167-2723-6*); pap. text ed. 3.95 (*0-8167-2724-4*) Troll Assocs.

Wood, Tim. The Aztecs. (Illus.). 48p. (gr. 3-7). 1992. 15. 00 (*0-670-84492-6*) Viking Child Bks.

INDIANS OF MEXICO–AZTECS–FICTION

Gaudiano, Andrea. Azteca: The Story of a Jaguar Warrior. (Illus.). 80p. 1992. pap. 7.95 (*1-879373-32-7*) R Rinehart.

Lattimore, Deborah N. The Flame of Peace: A Tale of the Aztecs. Lattimore, Deborah N., illus. LC 86-26934. 48p. (ps-3). 1991. pap. 5.95 (*0-06-443272-6*, Trophy) HarpC Child Bks.

O'Dell, Scott. The Feathered Serpent. 224p. (gr. 7 up). 1981. 16.95 (*0-395-30851-8*) HM.

INDIANS OF MEXICO–MAYAS

Baquedano, Elizabeth. Aztec, Inca, & Maya. Zabe, Michel & Rudkin, David, illus. 64p. (gr. 5 up). 1993. 15.00 (*0-679-83883-X*); PLB 15.99 (*0-679-93883-4*) Knopf Bks Yng Read.

Chrisp, Peter. The Maya. LC 93-46604. (Illus.). 32p. (gr. 4-6). 1994. 14.95 (*1-56847-170-X*) Thomson Lrning.

Greene, Jacqueline D. The Maya. Rosoff, Iris, ed. LC 91-29433. (Illus.). 64p. (gr. 3-5). 1992. PLB 12.90 (*0-531-20067-1*) Watts.

—The Maya. (Illus.). 64p. (gr. 5-8). 1992. pap. 5.95 (*0-531-15638-9*) Watts.

Hooper-Trout, Lawana. The Maya. (Illus.). 128p. (gr. 5 up). 1991. 17.95 (*1-55546-714-8*); pap. 9.95 (*0-7910-0387-6*) Chelsea Hse.

Lane, Sarah, et al. Batz'i K'op: True Speech. 93p. (gr. 6-12). 1988. pap. 11.95 (*0-941379-03-5*, 5115) World Eagle.

McKissack, Patricia. Los Mayas (The Maya) LC 85-9927. (Illus.). 48p. (gr. k-4). 1987. PLB 16.60 (*0-516-31270-7*); pap. 4.95 (*0-516-51270-6*) Childrens.

Odijk, Pamela. The Mayas. (Illus.). 48p. (gr. 5-8). 1990. PLB 12.95 (*0-382-09890-0*); 7.95 (*0-382-24265-3*); tchr's. guide 4.50 (*0-382-24280-7*) Silver Burdett Pr.

Sherrow, Victoria. The Maya Indians. LC 93-21751. (Illus.). (gr. 2-5). 1993. PLB 13.95 (*0-7910-1666-8*, Am Art Analog); pap. write for info (*0-7910-1994-2*, Am Art Analog) Chelsea Hse.

Tutor, Pilar. Mayan Civilization. LC 92-37022. (Illus.). 36p. (gr. 3 up). 1993. PLB 14.95 (*0-516-08381-3*); pap. 6.95 (*0-516-48381-1*) Childrens.

Vanden Broeck, Fabricio, illus. Ah Bak's Strange New Crop. Goldman, Judy, adapted by. LC 92-11322. (Illus.). 1995. 14.95 (*0-02-775657-2*) Macmillan.

Volkmer, Jane A. Song of Chirimia - La Musica de la Chirimia: A Guatemalan Folktale - Folklore Guatemalteco. Volkmer, Jame A., illus. (SPA & ENG.). 40p. (ps-4). 1990. PLB 18.95 (*0-87614-423-7*) Carolrhoda Bks.

INDIANS OF MEXICO–MAYAS–ANTIQUITIES

Putnam, James. Pyramid. Brightling, Geoff & Hayman, Peter, photos by. LC 94-8804. (Illus.). 64p. (gr. 5 up). 1994. 16.00 (*0-679-86170-X*); PLB 17.99 (*0-679-96170-4*) Knopf Bks Yng Read.

—Pyramid. (Illus.). (gr. 3-7). 1994. 16.95 (*1-56458-684-7*) Dorling Kindersley.

INDIANS OF MEXICO–MAYAS–FICTION

Brouwer, Sigmund. Sunrise at the Mayan Temple. (gr. 3-6). 1992. pap. 4.99 (*0-89693-057-2*, Victor Books) SP Pubns.

O'Dell, Scott. The Feathered Serpent. 224p. (gr. 7 up). 1981. 16.95 (*0-395-30851-8*) HM.

Rhoads, Dorothy. The Corn Grows Ripe. Charlot, Jean, illus. LC 92-24888. (gr. 8-12). 1993. 4.99 (*0-14-036313-0*, Puffin) Puffin Bks.

INDIANS OF NORTH AMERICA

see also Cliff Dwellers and Cliff Dwellings; Mounds and Mound Builders; Indians of North America–Canada

Alvarez, Juan. Chocolate, Chipmunks, & Canoes: An American Indian Words Coloring Book. Alvarez, Juan, illus. LC 90-60331. 32p. (gr. 1-3). 1991. pap. 3.95 (*1-878610-03-1*) Red Crane Bks.

American Indian Stories, 12 titles. (Illus.). (gr. 3-6). 1990. Set. 167.76 (*0-8114-6588-8*) Raintree Steck-V.

Ancona, George. Powwow. 48p. (gr. 4-7). 1993. pap. 8.95 (*0-15-263269-7*, HB Juv Bks) HarBrace.

Anderson, Joan. From Map to Museum: Uncovering Mysteries of the Past. Ancona, George, photos by. LC 87-31307. (Illus.). 64p. (gr. 3-7). 1988. 12.95 (*0-688-06914-2*); PLB 12.88 (*0-688-06915-0*, Morrow Jr Bks) Morrow Jr Bks.

Andrews, Elaine. Indians of the Plains. (Illus.). 96p. (gr. 5-8). 1991. lib. bdg. 18.95x (*0-8160-2387-5*) Facts on File.

The Arapaho Indians. (Illus.). 80p. (gr. 2-5). 1993. PLB 12.95 (*0-7910-1657-9*) Chelsea Hse.

Armitage, Peter. The Montagnais-Naskapi. (Illus.). (gr. 5 up). 1989. 17.95 (*1-55546-717-2*) Chelsea Hse.

Asch, Connie. Indians of the Americas Coloring Book. (Illus.). 32p. (Orig.). (gr. k-6). 1987. pap. 2.95 (*0-918080-33-9*) Treasure Chest.

Ashrose, Cara. The Very First Americans. Waldman, Bryna, illus. LC 92-38076. 32p. (ps-3). 1993. 7.99 (*0-448-40169-X*, G&D); pap. 2.25 (*0-448-40168-1*, G&D) Putnam Pub Group.

Ayer, Eleanor H. The Anasazi. LC 92-14701. 112p. 1993. 14.95 (*0-8027-8184-5*); PLB 15.85 (*0-8027-8185-3*) Walker & Co.

Bains, Rae. Indians of the Eastern Woodlands. Hannon, Mark, illus. LC 84-2664. 32p. (gr. 3-6). 1985. PLB 9.49 (*0-8167-0118-0*); pap. text ed. 2.95 (*0-8167-0119-9*) Troll Assocs.

—Indians of the Plains. Baxter, Robert, illus. LC 84-2645. 32p. (gr. 3-6). 1985. PLB 9.49 (*0-8167-0188-1*); pap. text ed. 2.95 (*0-8167-0189-X*) Troll Assocs.

—Indians of the West. Guzzi, George, illus. LC 84-2600. 32p. (gr. 3-6). 1985. PLB 9.49 (*0-8167-0134-2*); pap. text ed. 2.95 (*0-8167-0135-0*) Troll Assocs.

Baird, W. David. The Quapaws. Porter, Frank. (Illus.). 112p. (gr. 5 up). 1989. lib. bdg. 17.95 (*1-55546-728-8*) Chelsea Hse.

Bean, Lowell J. & Bourgeault, Lisa. The Cahuilla. Porter, Frank W., III, intro. by. (Illus.). 112p. (gr. 5 up). 1989. 17.95 (*1-55546-693-1*) Chelsea Hse.

Bellerophon Books Staff. California Indian Tribes, Vol. 1: Northern. (gr. 1-9). 1994. pap. 3.95 (*0-88388-153-5*) Bellerophon Bks.

—California Indian Tribes, Vol. 2: Southern. (gr. 4-7). 1992. pap. 3.95 (*0-88388-184-5*) Bellerophon Bks.

Bhi, Karen. The Lumbee: Southeast. (Illus.). (gr. 5 up). 1993. 18.95 (*1-55546-713-X*, Am Art Analog); pap. write for info. (*0-7910-0386-8*, Am Art Analog) Chelsea Hse.

Boule, Mary N. California's Native American Tribes, No. 1: Achumawi Tride. Liddell, Daniel, illus. 40p. (Orig.). (gr. 2-3). 1992. pap. 4.50 (*1-877599-25-5*) Merryant Pubs.

—California's Native American Tribes, No. 10: Maidu-KonKow Tribe. Liddell, Daniel, illus. 40p. (Orig.). (gr. 4-5). 1992. pap. 4.50 (*1-877599-34-4*) Merryant Pubs.

—California's Native American Tribes, No. 14: Ohlone Tribe. Liddell, Daniel, illus. 40p. (Orig.). (gr. 4-5). 1992. pap. 4.50 (*1-877599-38-7*) Merryant Pubs.

—California's Native American Tribes, No. 15: Patwin Tribe. Liddell, Daniel, illus. 60p. (Orig.). (gr. 3-5). 1992. pap. text ed. 4.50 (*1-877599-49-2*) Merryant Pubs.

—California's Native American Tribes, No. 18: Salinan Tribe. Liddell, Daniel, illus. 40p. (Orig.). (gr. 4-5). 1992. pap. 4.50 (*1-877599-41-7*) Merryant Pubs.

—California's Native American Tribes, No. 19: Shasta Tribe. Liddell, Daniel, illus. 40p. (Orig.). (gr. 2-4). 1992. pap. 4.50 (*1-877599-42-5*) Merryant Pubs.

—California's Native American Tribes, No. 2: Atsugewi Tribe. Liddell, Daniel, illus. 40p. (Orig.). (gr. 2-3). 1992. pap. 4.50 (*1-877599-26-3*) Merryant Pubs.

—California's Native American Tribes, No. 24: Foothill Yokuts Tribe. Liddell, Daniel, illus. 40p. (Orig.). (gr. 3-5). 1992. pap. 4.50 (*1-877599-46-8*) Merryant Pubs.

—California's Native American Tribes, No. 20: Tolowa Tribe. Liddell, Daniel, illus. 40p. (Orig.). (gr. 2-3). 1992. pap. 4.50 (*1-877599-43-3*) Merryant Pubs.

—California's Native American Tribes, No. 21: Tubatulabal Tribe. Liddell, Daniel, illus. 60p. (gr. 2-4). 1992. pap. 4.50 (*1-877599-24-7*) Merryant Pubs.

—California's Native American Tribes, No. 23: Valley Yokuts Tribe. Liddell, Daniel, illus. 40p. (Orig.). (gr. 4-5). 1992. pap. 4.50 (*1-877599-45-X*) Merryant Pubs.

—California's Native American Tribes, No. 22: Wintu Tribe. Liddell, Daniel, illus. 40p. (Orig.). (gr. 4-5). 1992. pap. 4.50 (*1-877599-44-1*) Merryant Pubs.

—California's Native American Tribes, No. 25: Yuki Tribe. Liddell, Daniel, illus. 40p. (Orig.). (gr. 2-3). 1992. pap. 4.50 (*1-877599-47-6*) Merryant Pubs.

—California's Native American Tribes, No. 26: Yurok Tribe. Liddell, Daniel, illus. 40p. (Orig.). (gr. 2-4). 1992. pap. 4.50 (*1-877599-48-4*) Merryant Pubs.

—California's Native American Tribes, No. 3: Cahuilla Tribe. Liddell, Daniel, illus. 40p. (Orig.). (gr. 2-4). 1992. pap. 4.50 (*1-877599-27-1*) Merryant Pubs.

—California's Native American Tribes, No. 5: Diegueno (Ipai-Tipai) Liddell, Daniel, illus. 40p. (Orig.). (gr. 2-4). 1992. pap. 4.50 (*1-877599-29-8*) Merryant Pubs.

—California's Native American Tribes, No. 6: Gabrielino Tribe. Liddell, Daniel, illus. 40p. (Orig.). (gr. 4-5). 1992. pap. 4.50 (*1-877599-30-1*) Merryant Pubs.

—California's Native American Tribes, No. 7: Hupa Tribe. Liddell, Daniel, illus. 40p. (Orig.). (gr. 2-4). 1992. pap. 4.50 (*1-877599-31-X*) Merryant Pubs.

—California's Native American Tribes, No. 8: Karok Tribe. Liddell, Daniel, illus. 40p. (Orig.). (gr. 2-3). 1992. pap. 4.50 (*1-877599-32-8*) Merryant Pubs.

—California's Native American Tribes, No. 9: Luiseno Tribe. Liddell, Daniel, illus. 40p. (Orig.). (gr. 4-5). 1992. pap. 4.50 (*1-877599-33-6*) Merryant Pubs.

Bovert, Howard E. & Baranzini, Marlene S. Book of the American Indians. Sanchez, Bill, illus. LC 93-3068. (gr. 1-8). 1994. 19.95 (*0-316-96921-4*); pap. 10.95 (*0-316-22208-9*) Little.

Brown, Fern G. Indians of North America. 1995. PLB write for info. (*0-8050-3251-7*); pap. write for info. (*0-8050-3250-9*) H Holt & Co.

Callaway, Colin G. Indians of the Northeast. (Illus.). 96p. (gr. 5-12). 1991. lib. bdg. 18.95x (*0-8160-2389-1*) Facts on File.

Calloway, Colin G. The Abenaki. Porter, Frank, intro. by. (Illus.). 112p. (gr. 5 up). 1989. lib. bdg. 17.95x (*1-55546-687-7*) Chelsea Hse.

Carlson, Laurie. More Than Moccasins: A Kid's Activity Guide to Traditional North American Indian Life. LC 93-39922. (Illus.). 176p. (Orig.). (ps-4). 1994. pap. 12. 95 (*1-55652-213-4*) Chicago Review.

Children's Atlas of Native Americans. 1992. 14.95 (*0-528-83494-0*) Rand McNally.

Clifton, James A. The Potawatomi. Porter, Frank, intro. by. (Illus.). 99p. (gr. 5 up). 1987. lib. bdg. 17.95x (*1-55546-725-3*) Chelsea Hse.

Cossi, Olga. Fire Mate. 85p. (gr. 3 up). 1988. pap. 7.95 (*0-89992-116-7*) Coun India Ed.

Crum, Robert. Eagle Drum: On the Powwow Trail with a Young Grass Dancer. LC 94-6034. (gr. 1-6). 1994. 16. 95 (*0-02-725515-8*) Macmillan Child Grp.

D'Apice, Rita, et al. Native American People, 6 bks, Set 11. (Illus.). 192p. (gr. 5-8). 1990. Set. lib. bdg. 95.64 (*0-86625-383-1*); Set. lib. bdg. 71.70s.p. (*0-685-36385-6*) Rourke Corp.

Davis, Maggie S. Roots of Peace, Seeds of Hope: A Journey for Peacemakers. Davis, Maggie S., illus. LC 93-80449. 60p. 1994. pap. 8.95 (*0-9638813-0-2*) Heartsong Bks.

Davis, Nancy M. & Moon, Teresa. Indians. Davis, Nancy M., illus. 33p. (Orig.). (ps-5). 1986. pap. 4.95 (*0-937103-03-9*) DaNa Pubns.
Demos, John. The Tried & True: Native American Women Confronting Colonization. (Illus.). 144p. 1995. 20.00 (*0-19-508142-0*) OUP.
Diamond, Arthur. Smallpox & the American Indian. LC 91-23066. (Illus.). 96p. (gr. 5-8). 1991. PLB 11.95 (*1-56006-018-2*) Lucent Bks.
Dobyns, Henry F. The Pima-Maricopa. (Illus.). 112p. (gr. 5 up). 1989. 17.95 (*1-55546-724-5*) Chelsea Hse.
Doherty, Katherine M. & Coherty, Craig A. The Zunis. (Illus.). 64p. (gr. 5-8). 1994. pap. 5.95 (*0-531-15704-0*) Watts.
Doherty, Katherine M. & Doherty, Craig A. The Chickasaw. LC 93-42163. 1994. write for info. (*0-86625-531-1*) Rourke Pubns.
—The Ute. LC 93-37999. 1994. write for info. (*0-86625-530-3*) Rourke Pubns.
—The Zunis. LC 93-18372. 1993. lib. bdg. 12.90 (*0-531-20157-0*) Watts.
Dolan, Terrance. The Kiowa Indians. LC 93-17696. (Illus.). (gr. 2-5). 1993. PLB 13.95 (*0-7910-1663-3*, Am Art Analog); pap. write for info. (*0-7910-2028-2*, Am Art Analog) Chelsea Hse.
Duvall, Jill D. The Cayuga. LC 91-3038. 48p. (gr. k-4). 1991. PLB 12.85 (*0-516-01123-5*); pap. 4.95 (*0-516-41123-3*) Childrens.
—The Oneida. LC 91-8893. 48p. (gr. k-4). 1991. PLB 12.85 (*0-516-01125-1*); pap. 4.95 (*0-516-41125-X*) Childrens.
—The Onondaga. LC 91-8894. 48p. (gr. k-4). 1991. PLB 12.85 (*0-516-01126-X*); pap. 4.95 (*0-516-41126-8*) Childrens.
—The Tuscarora. LC 91-3037. 48p. (gr. k-4). 1991. PLB 12.85 (*0-516-01128-6*); pap. 4.95 (*0-516-41128-4*) Childrens.
Emanuels, George. California Indians: An Illustrated Guide. (Illus.). 172p. (gr. 4-8). incl. study guide 19.95 (*0-9607520-5-6*); pap. 14.95 (*0-9607520-3-X*) Diablo Bks.
Faber, Gail & Lasagna, Michele. Pasquala: The Story of a California Indian Girl. Faber, Gail, illus. 95p. (Orig.). (gr. 4-8). 1990. 12.95 (*0-936480-07-6*); pap. 9.95 (*0-936480-06-8*); tchr's. guide 8.95 (*0-936480-08-4*) Magpie Pubns.
Feest, Christian F. The Powhatan Tribes. (Illus.). 112p. (gr. 5 up). 1990. 17.95 (*1-55546-726-1*) Chelsea Hse.
Fixico, Donald L. Urban Indians. (Illus.). 104p. (gr. 5 up). 1991. 17.95 (*1-55546-732-6*) Chelsea Hse.
The Flood. (gr. 4 up). 1976. 2.95 (*0-89992-020-9*) Coun India Ed.
Fowler, Loretta. The Arapaho. (Illus.). 128p. (gr. 5 up). 1989. 17.95 (*1-55546-690-7*) Chelsea Hse.
Fox, Frank. North American Indians Coloring Album. (Illus.). 32p. (Orig.). (gr. 1-6). 1978. pap. 4.50 (*0-8431-1727-3*, Troubador) Price Stern.
Fox, George & Puffer, Lela. Okemos: Story of a Fox Indian in His Youth. (gr. 3-9). 1976. 1.50 (*0-89992-036-5*) Coun India Ed.
Fradin, Dennis B. The Shoshoni. LC 88-11821. (Illus.). 48p. (gr. k-4). 1988. PLB 12.85 (*0-516-01156-1*); pap. 4.95 (*0-516-41156-X*) Childrens.
Freedman, Russell. Indian Chiefs. Freedman, Russell, photos by. LC 86-46198. (Illus.). 160p. (gr. 4 up). 1987. reinforced bdg. 18.95 (*0-8234-0625-3*); pap. 9.95 (*0-8234-0971-6*) Holiday.
—An Indian Winter. Bodmer, Karl, illus. LC 91-24205. 96p. (gr. 5 up). 1992. 21.95 (*0-8234-0930-9*) Holiday.
Frome, Shelly. Sun Dance for Andy Horn. 124p. (gr. 9-12). 1990. 14.95 (*0-89992-324-0*); pap. 9.95 (*0-89992-124-8*) Coun India Ed.
Gallant, Roy A. Ancient Indians: The First Americans. LC 87-36526. (Illus.). 128p. (gr. 6 up). 1989. lib. bdg. 17.95 (*0-89490-187-7*) Enslow Pubs.
Galloway, Anne. Tovangar. 1978. 3.00 (*0-939046-25-3*) Malki Mus Pr.
Gilliland, Hap. Broken Ice. (gr. 1-8). 1972. 5.95 (*0-89992-024-1*) Coun India Ed.
—No One Like a Brother. (gr. 4-12). 1970. 4.95 (*0-89992-003-9*) Coun India Ed.
Gilliland, Hap & Kovach, Tom. The Dark Side of the Moon. Hardgrove, Tanya, illus. 32p. (gr. 1-4). 1984. pap. 4.95 (*0-89992-086-1*) Coun India Ed.
Gilliland, Hap, et al. When We Went to the Mountains. (ENG, SPA, NAV, CRO & CHY.). 36p. (gr. 1-9). 1991. pap. 5.95 (*0-89992-103-5*) Coun India Ed.
Goldin, Barbara D., retold by. Coyote & the Firestick: A Northwest Coast Indian Legend. Hillenbrand, Will, illus. LC 94-5747. 1995. write for info. (*0-15-200438-6*) Harbrace.
Gorsline, Marie & Gorsline, Douglas. North American Indians. Gorsline, Douglas, illus. LC 77-79843. (ps-2). 1978. pap. 2.25 (*0-394-83702-9*) Random Bks Yng Read.
Grant, Bruce. Concise Encyclopedia of the American Indian. (Illus.). 352p. 1989. 8.99 (*0-517-69310-0*) Random Hse Value.
Green, Rayna. Women in American Indian Society. (Illus.). (gr. 5 up). 1992. 17.95 (*1-55546-734-2*) Chelsea Hse.
Grenier, Nicolas. Following Indian Trails. Grant, Donald, illus. LC 87-34597. 38p. (gr. k-5). 1988. 5.95 (*0-944589-09-X*, 09X) Young Discovery Lib.
Grisham, Noel & Warren, Betsy. Buffalo & Indians on the Great Plains. (Illus.). (gr. k-4). 1985. 12.95 (*0-89015-470-8*, Pub. by Panda Bks) Sunbelt Media.
Grumet, Robert S. The Lenapes. (Illus.). 112p. (gr. 5 up). 1990. 17.95 (*1-55546-712-1*); pap. 9.95 (*0-7910-0385-X*) Chelsea Hse.
Hakim, Joy. The First Americans. LC 92-50114. 1993. PLB 19.95 (*0-19-507745-8*); pap. 9.95 (*0-19-507746-6*) OUP.
Hale, Duane & Gibson, Arrell M. The Chickasaw. (Illus.). 112p. (gr. 5 up). 1991. 17.95 (*1-55546-697-4*); pap. 9.95 (*0-7910-0372-8*) Chelsea Hse.
Haluska, Vick. Arapaho Indians. (gr. 4-7). 1994. pap. 6.95 (*0-7910-1960-8*) Chelsea Hse.
Henry Tall Bull & Weist, Tom. Grandfather & the Popping Machine. (gr. 2-12). 1970. 4.95 (*0-89992-004-7*) Coun India Ed.
—The Spotted Horse. (gr. 2-10). 1970. 4.95 (*0-89992-002-0*) Coun India Ed.
—The Winter Hunt. 32p. (gr. 3-9). 1971. 4.95 (*0-89992-006-3*) Coun India Ed.
Hirschfelder, Arlene. Happily May I Walk: American Indians & Alaska Natives Today. LC 85-43349. 160p. (gr. 5 up). 1986. SBE 14.95 (*0-684-18624-1*, Scribners Young Read) Macmillan Child Grp.
Hirschi, Ron. Seya's Song. Bergum, Constance R., illus. LC 92-5029. 32p. (ps up). 1992. text ed. 14.95 (*0-912365-62-5*) Sasquatch Bks.
Holler, Anne. Pocahontas. (gr. 4-7). 1992. pap. 7.95 (*0-7910-1952-7*) Chelsea Hse.
Hooban, Louis. Indian Heritage Coloring Book. 50p. 1994. pap. 10.00 (*1-884710-05-0*) Indian Heritage.
Hornbeck-Tanner, Helen. The Ojibwa. (Illus.). 120p. (gr. 5 up). 1992. 17.95 (*1-55546-721-0*) Chelsea Hse.
Hubbard-Brown, Janet. A History Mystery: The Disappearance of the Anasazi. Saffioti, Lino, illus. 96p. (Orig.). 1992. pap. 3.50 (*0-380-76845-3*, Camelot) Avon.
Indian Canoeing. (Illus.). (gr. 6-12). 1976. 4.95 (*0-686-22273-3*) Coun India Ed.
Indian Lore. (Illus.). 90p. (gr. 6-12). 1959. pap. 1.85 (*0-8395-3358-6*, 33358) BSA.
Jacobs, Francine. The Tainos: The People Who Welcomed Columbus. Collins, Patrick, illus. 112p. (gr. 5-9). 1992. 15.95 (*0-399-22116-6*, Putnam) Putnam Pub Group.
Job, Kenneth. Indians in New York State. Whitman, Bernard, ed. Whitman, Shirley, illus. 48p. (Orig.). (gr. 4-7). 1989. pap. text ed. 5.00 (*0-918433-01-0*) In Educ.
Johnson, Gail E. Phantom Horse of Collister's Fields. (gr. 4-12). 1974. 1.50 (*0-89992-062-4*) Coun India Ed.
Jones, Jayne C. The American Indian in America, Vol. II. LC 73-13378. (Illus.). 96p. (gr. 5 up). 1973. PLB 11.95 (*0-8225-0227-5*); pap. 5.95 (*0-8225-1002-2*) Lerner Pubns.
—American Indian in America, Vol. 2. 1991. pap. 5.95 (*0-8225-1037-5*) Lerner Pubns.
The Junior Library of American Indians, 30 vols. (Illus.). (gr. 2-5). 1994. Set. PLB write for info. (*0-7910-1650-1*, Am Art Analog) Chelsea Hse.
Kennedy, John G. The Tarahumara. (Illus.). 112p. (gr. 5 up). 1990. 17.95 (*1-55546-730-X*) Chelsea Hse.
Keyworth, C. L. California Indians. (Illus.). 96p. (gr. 5-8). 1990. 18.95x (*0-8160-2386-7*) Facts on File.
Kindle, Patricia & Finney, Susan. American Indians. McKay, Ardis, illus. 64p. (gr. 4-8). 1985. wkbk. 8.95 (*0-86653-290-0*, GA 673) Good Apple.
Kniffen, Fred. Indians of Louisiana. LC 91-8499. (Illus.). 108p. (gr. 6-12). 1976. 13.95 (*0-911116-97-4*) Pelican.
Knobloch, Madge. Havasupai Years. (gr. 9 up). 1988. pap. 8.95 (*0-89992-117-5*, NO. 117-5) Coun India Ed.
Landau, Elaine. The Chilula. LC 93-31423. (Illus.). 64p. (gr. 5-8). 1994. PLB 12.90 (*0-531-20132-5*); pap. 5.95 (*0-531-15685-0*) Watts.
Lawlor, Laurie. Shadow Catcher: The Life & Work of Edward Sherriff Curtis. LC 93-40272. 1994. 16.95 (*0-8027-8288-4*); PLB 17.85 (*0-8027-8289-2*) Walker & Co.
Liptak, Karen. Indians of the Pacific Northwest. (Illus.). 96p. (gr. 5-8). 1990. 18.95x (*0-8160-2384-0*) Facts on File.
—Indians of the Southwest. (Illus.). 96p. (gr. 5-8). 1990. 18.95x (*0-8160-2385-9*) Facts on File.
—North American Indian Medicine People. LC 90-12337. (Illus.). 64p. (gr. 5-8). 1990. PLB 12.90 (*0-531-10868-6*) Watts.
—North American Indian Survival Skills. LC 90-12354. (Illus.). 64p. (gr. 5-8). 1990. PLB 12.90 (*0-531-10870-8*) Watts.
—North American Indian Survival Skills. (Illus.). 64p. (gr. 5-8). 1992. pap. 5.95 (*0-531-15642-7*) Watts.
—North American Indian Tribal Chiefs. (Illus.). 64p. (gr. 5-8). 1992. pap. 5.95 (*0-531-15643-5*) Watts.
Lyngheim, Linda. The Indians & the California Missions. rev. ed. Garber, Phyllis, illus. LC 84-80543. 160p. (gr. 4-6). 1990. 14.95 (*0-915369-04-4*); pap. 10.95 (*0-915369-00-1*) Langtry Pubns.
McCall, Barbara. Daily Life. LC 94-5528. 1994. write for info. (*0-86625-534-6*) Rourke Corp.
McCall, Barbara, et al. Native American People, 6 bks, Reading Level 4. (Illus.). 192p. (gr. 5-8). 1989. Set. PLB 95.64 (*0-86625-375-0*); lib. bdg. 71.70 (*0-685-58768-1*) Rourke Corp.
MacDonald, Fiona. Plains Indians. (Illus.). 60p. (gr. 4 up). 1993. 15.95 (*0-8120-6376-7*) Barron.
McIntosh, Jane. Native American. British Museum Staff, illus. 64p. (gr. 5 up). 1994. PLB 16.99 (*0-679-96169-0*); 16.00 (*0-679-86169-6*) Knopf Bks Yng Read.
Magorian, James. Keeper of Fire. Hardgrove, Tanya, illus. 78p. (Orig.). (gr. 4-12). 1984. pap. 6.95 (*0-89992-088-8*) Coun India Ed.
Mancini, Richard E. Indians of the Southeast. (Illus.). 96p. (gr. 5-8). 1991. lib. bdg. 18.95x (*0-8160-2390-5*) Facts on File.
Margolin, Malcolm, ed. Native Ways: California Indian Stories & Memories. (Illus.). 128p. (gr. 4-6). 1994. pap. 7.95 (*0-930588-73-8*) Heyday Bks.
Marsh, Jessie. Chinook. 32p. (ps-9). 1976. 4.95 (*0-89992-041-1*) Coun India Ed.
Martini, Teri. Indians. LC 81-15442. (Illus.). 48p. (gr. k-4). 1982. pap. 4.95 (*0-516-41628-6*) Childrens.
Mateo, Mary A. Portraits of Native American Indians. (Illus.). 96p. (gr. 4-7). 1992. 10.95 (*0-86653-669-8*, GA1322) Good Apple.
Matthews, L. Indians. (Illus.). 32p. (gr. 3-8). 1989. PLB 18.00 (*0-86625-364-5*); 13.50s.p. (*0-685-58279-5*) Rourke Corp.
May, Robin. Plains Indians of North America. (Illus.). 48p. (gr. 4-8). 1987. PLB 16.67 (*0-86625-258-4*); 12.50s.p. (*0-685-67607-2*) Rourke Corp.
Merrell, James H. The Catawbas. Porter, Frank W., III, intro. by. (Illus.). 112p. (gr. 5 up). 1989. 17.95 (*1-55546-694-X*) Chelsea Hse.
Mike, Jan. Chana, An Anasazi Girl: Historical Paperdoll Books to Read, Color & Cut. Lowmiller, Cathy, illus. 32p. (Orig.). (gr. k-4). 1991. pap. 3.95 (*0-918080-61-4*) Treasure Chest.
Miller, Jay. Native Americans. (Illus.). 48p. (gr. k-4). 1993. PLB 12.85 (*0-516-01192-8*); pap. 4.95 (*0-516-41192-6*) Childrens.
Mobley, Chuck & Mobley, Andrea. Navajo Rugs & Blankets Coloring Book. Mahan, Nancie, ed. Mike, Sam, illus. 32p. (Orig.). (ps up). 1994. pap. 2.95 (*0-918080-76-2*) Treasure Chest.
Morgan, Buford. Quest for Quivera: Coronado's Exploration into Southern U. S. 189p. (gr. 10 up). 1990. 15.95 (*0-89992-425-5*); pap. 9.95 (*0-89992-125-6*) Coun India Ed.
Muller, Carrel & Muller, Brenda. Louisiana Indians. Muller, Carrel & Muller, Brenda, illus. 64p. (gr. 3 up). 1985. 7.50 (*0-915785-01-3*) Bonjour Books.
Myers, Arthur. The Pawnee. LC 93-18369. (Illus.). 64p. (gr. 4-6). 1993. PLB 12.90 (*0-531-20165-1*) Watts.
—The Pawnee. (Illus.). 64p. (gr. 5-8). 1994. pap. 5.95 (*0-685-70385-1*) Watts.
North American Indian. (gr. 4-6). pap. 2.95 (*0-8431-4254-5*) Price Stern.
North American Indians: Illustrated History of the, 6 vols. (Illus.). 384p. 1990. Set. PLB 119.95 (*1-85435-137-0*) Marshall Cavendish.
Osinski, Alice. The Tlingit. LC 89-25345. (Illus.). 48p. (gr. k-4). 1990. PLB 12.30 (*0-516-01189-8*); pap. 4.95 (*0-516-41189-6*) Childrens.
Ourada, Patricia K. The Menominee. (Illus.). 112p. (gr. 5 up). 1990. 17.95 (*1-55546-715-6*) Chelsea Hse.
Penner, Lucille R. A Native American Feast. LC 94-10336. (Illus.). (gr. 1 up). 1994. 14.95 (*0-02-770902-7*) Macmillan.
Pennington, Dan. Itse Selu: Cherokee Harvest Festival. (Illus.). 32p. (ps-4). 1994. 14.95 (*0-88106-851-9*); PLB 15.00 (*0-88106-852-7*); pap. 6.95 (*0-88106-850-0*) Charlesbridge Pub.
The Plains Indian Book. (gr. 1-6). 1974. pap. 3.95 (*0-918858-02-X*) Fun Pub AZ.
Porter, Frank W. The Coast Salish Peoples. (Illus.). 104p. (gr. 5 up). 1989. 17.95 (*1-55546-701-6*) Chelsea Hse.
The Potawatomi: Great Lakes. 112p. (gr. 7-12). PLB 16.95 (*0-685-21873-2*, 201240) Know Unltd.
Prentzas, Scott. Tribal Law. LC 94-5531. 1994. write for info. (*0-86625-536-2*) Rourke Corp.
Rand McNally Staff & Reddy, Francis. Children's Atlas of Native Americans Rand McNally: Native Cultures of North & South America. Adelman, Elizabeth, ed. Cunningham, David, illus. 78p. (gr. 3-12). Date not set. 14.95 (*0-685-66563-1*); PLB 18.95 (*1-878363-99-9*) Forest Hse.
Roop, Peter. Little Blaze & the Buffalo Jump. Wells, Jesse, illus. 28p. (Orig.). (gr. 3-8). 1984. pap. 2.45 (*0-89992-089-6*) Coun India Ed.
Ruskin, Thelma. Indians of the Tidewater Country: Of Maryland, Virginia, Delaware & North Carolina. Buchanan, Carol & Ruskin, Robert, eds. Ruskin, Robert, illus. & intro. by. LC 85-73263. 132p. (gr. 4-5). 1986. casebound 15.00 (*0-917882-20-2*) MD Hist Pr.
Russell, George L. Map of American Indian Nations. 3rd ed. (gr. 6 up). 1993. pap. 15.00 (*1-881933-02-4*) Thundbird Ent.
Salts, Bobbi. Southwestern American Indian Discovery. Parker, Steve, illus. (gr. 2-8). 1991. pap. 3.95 (*0-929526-11-2*) Double B Pubns.
Schneider, Mary J. The Hidatsa. Porter, Frank W., III, intro. by. (Illus.). 112p. (gr. 5 up). 1989. 17.95 (*1-55546-707-5*) Chelsea Hse.
Schultz, John W. Famine Winter. (gr. 4-10). 1984. pap. 2.95 (*0-89992-094-2*) Coun India Ed.
Schuster, Helen H. The Yakima. (Illus.). 112p. (gr. 5 up). 1990. 17.95 (*1-55546-735-0*) Chelsea Hse.
Shemie, Bonnie. Houses of Bark: Tipi, Wigwam, & Longhouse. Shemie, Bonnie, illus. LC 90-70130. 24p. (gr. 3-7). 1990. 13.95 (*0-88776-246-8*) Tundra Bks.
—Maisons D'Ecorce: Tipi, Wigwam et Longue Maison. Shemie, Bonnie, illus. 24p. (gr. 3-7). 1990. 13.95 (*0-88776-256-5*) Tundra Bks.

Sherrow, Victoria. Indians of the Plateau & Great Basin. (Illus.). 96p. (gr. 5-8). 1991. lib. bdg. 18.95x (*0-8160-2388-3*) Facts on File.

Shields, Allan. Tragedy of Tenaya. (gr. 6). 1974. 5.95 (*0-89992-043-8*) Coun India Ed.

Siegel, Beatrice. Indians of the Northeast Woodlands Before & after the Pilgrims. 96p. 1992. 13.95 (*0-8027-8155-1*); lib. bdg. 14.85 (*0-8027-8157-8*) Walker & Co.

Silverberg, Robert. The Mound Builders. LC 85-25953. 276p. 1986. pap. 7.95 (*0-8214-0839-9*) Ohio U Pr.

Simmons, William S. The Narragansett. Porter, Frank W., III, intro. by. (Illus.). 112p. (gr. 5 up). 1989. 17.95 (*1-55546-718-0*) Chelsea Hse.

Smith, Carter, ed. Native Americans of the West: A Sourcebook on the American West. LC 91-31128. (Illus.). 96p. (gr. 5-8). 1992. PLB 18.90 (*1-56294-131-3*) Millbrook Pr.

Smith, Tom & Smith, Diane. Northwest Coast Indian Coloring Book. Smith, Tom, illus. 32p. (Orig.). (gr. 1-6). 1993. pap. 4.50 (*0-8431-3491-7*, Troubador) Price Stern.

Sneve, Virginia D. The Iroquois. Himler, Ronald, illus. (gr. 1-8). 1995. write for info. (*0-8234-1163-X*) Holiday.

Spizzirri Publishing Co. Staff. California Indians: An Educational Coloring Book. Spizzirri, Linda, ed. (Illus.). 32p. (gr. 1-8). 1986. pap. 1.75 (*0-86545-080-3*) Spizzirri.

—Plains Indians: An Educational Coloring Book. Spizzirri, Linda, ed. Spizzirri, Peter M., illus. 32p. (gr. 1-8). 1981. pap. 1.75 (*0-86545-025-0*) Spizzirri.

—Southeast Indians: An Educational Coloring Book. Spizzirri, Linda, ed. (Illus.). 32p. (gr. k-5). 1985. pap. 1.75 (*0-86545-065-X*) Spizzirri.

—Southwest Indians: An Educational Coloring Book. Spizzirri, Linda, ed. (Illus.). 32p. (gr. 1-8). 1986. pap. 1.75 (*0-86545-075-7*) Spizzirri.

Stan, S. The Ojibwe. (Illus.). 32p. (gr. 5-8). 1989. lib. bdg. 15.94 (*0-86625-381-5*); 11.95 (*0-685-58581-6*) Rourke Corp.

Stanley, Samuel & Oberg, Pearl. The Hunt. 32p. (gr. 5-9). 1976. pap. 1.50 (*0-89992-047-0*) Coun India Ed.

Tanner, Helen H. Ojibwa. (gr. 4-7). 1992. pap. 7.95 (*0-7910-0392-2*) Chelsea Hse.

Throssel, Richard. Blue Thunder. 32p. (gr. 6-12). 1976. 1.75 (*0-89992-046-2*) Coun India Ed.

Trafzer, Cliff. American Indians as Cowboys. (Illus.). 70p. (Orig.). (gr. 4-6). 1992. 10.95 (*0-940113-23-6*) Sierra Oaks Pub.

Trafzer, Clifford E. California's Indians & the Gold Rush. LC 89-64434. (Illus.). 61p. (Orig.). (gr. 4-7). 1990. pap. 10.95 (*0-940113-21-X*) Sierra Oaks Pub.

—The Chinook. Porter, Frank W., III, intro. by. (Illus.). 112p. (gr. 5 up). 1990. 17.95 (*1-55546-698-2*) Chelsea Hse.

Tunis, Edwin. Indians. rev. ed. Tunis, Edwin, illus. LC 78-60175. 160p. (gr. 5 up). 1979. Repr. of 1959 ed. PLB 24.89 (*0-690-01283-7*, Crowell Jr Bks) HarpC Child Bks.

Upton, Richard. The Indian As a Soldier at Fort Custer, Montana 1890-1895: Lieutenant Samuel C. Robertson's First Cavalry Crow Indian Contingent. Remington, Frederic & Goff, O. S., illus. LC 83-80826. 147p. (gr. 7-12). 1983. 27.50 (*0-912783-00-1*) Upton Sons.

Utter, Jack. American Indians: Answers to Today's Questions. LC 92-62877. (Illus.). xx, 331p. (gr. 7-12). 1993. 21.95 (*0-9628075-3-2*); pap. 14.95 (*0-9628075-2-4*) Natl Woodlands Pub.

Vallejo, Mariano, et al. Great Indians of California. Knill, Harry, ed. (Illus.). 48p. (gr. 6). 1981. pap. 3.95 (*0-88388-087-3*) Bellerophon Bks.

Vandervelde, Marjorie. Across the Tundra. (gr. 4-12). 1972. 1.50 (*0-89992-053-5*) Coun India Ed.

—Could It Be Old Hiari. (gr. 5-9). 1975. 4.95 (*0-89992-040-3*) Coun India Ed.

—Sam & the Golden People. (gr. 4-9). 1972. 1.50 (*0-89992-027-6*) Coun India Ed.

Waldman, Carl. Encyclopedia of Native American Tribes. Braun, Molly, illus. 308p. 1987. 45.00x (*0-8160-1421-3*) Facts on File.

Walens, Stanley. The Kwakiutl. (Illus.). (gr. 5 up). 1992. 17.95 (*1-55546-711-3*) Chelsea Hse.

Warren, Betsy. Indians Who Lived in Texas. Warren, Betsy, illus. LC 71-76607. 48p. (gr. 2 up). 1981. Repr. of 1970 ed. lib. bdg. 12.95 (*0-937460-02-8*) Hendrick-Long.

—Let's Remember...Indians of Texas. Warren, Betsy, illus. 32p. (gr. 3-7). 1981. pap. 5.95 (*0-937460-03-6*) Hendrick-Long.

Warren, Elizabeth. I Can Read About Indians. LC 74-24880. (Illus.). (gr. 2-4). 1975. pap. 2.50 (*0-89375-061-1*) Troll Assocs.

Weinstein-Farson, Laurie. The Wampanoag. Porter, Frank, intro. by. (Illus.). 96p. (gr. 5 up). 1988. lib. bdg. 17.95x (*1-55546-733-4*); pap. 9.95 (*0-7910-0368-X*) Chelsea Hse.

Weiss, Malcolm E. Sky Watchers of Ages Past. McFadden, Eliza, illus. (gr. 5-9). 1982. 14.45 (*0-395-29525-4*) HM.

Wheeler, M. J. First Came the Indians. Houston, James, illus. LC 82-13916. 32p. (gr. 1-5). 1983. SBE 12.95 (*0-689-50258-3*, M K McElderry) Macmillan Child Grp.

Whyte, Malcolm. Great Plains Indians Action Set. (Illus.). 24p. (gr. 1 up). 1994. pap. 6.99 (*0-8431-3396-1*, Troubador) Price Stern.

Wilson, James. Native Americans. LC 93-36059. (Illus.). 48p. (gr. 6-10). 1994. 16.95 (*1-56847-150-5*) Thomson Lrning.

Wilson, Terry P. The Osage. Porter, Frank, intro. by. (Illus.). 111p. (gr. 5 up). 1988. lib. bdg. 17.95x (*1-55546-722-9*) Chelsea Hse.

Wolfson, Evelyn. American Indian Tools & Ornaments. 1981. 8.95 (*0-679-20509-8*) McKay.

—From Abenaki to Zuni: A Dictionary of Native American Tribes. Bock, William S., photos by. (gr. 5 up). 1988. 17.95 (*0-8027-6789-3*); PLB 18.85 (*0-8027-6790-7*) Walker & Co.

World Book Staff, ed. Childcraft Supplement, 5 vols. LC 91-65174. (Illus.). (gr. 2-6). 1991. Set. write for info. (*0-7166-0666-6*) Prehistoric Animals, 304p. About Dogs, 304p. The Magic of Words, 304p. The Indian Book, 304p. The Puzzle Book, 304p. World Bk.

Wunder, John R. The Kiowa. (Illus.). 112p. (gr. 5 up). 1989. 17.95 (*1-55546-710-5*) Chelsea Hse.

INDIANS OF NORTH AMERICA–ABNAKI INDIANS–LEGENDS

Bruchac, Joseph, retold by. Gluskabe & the Four Wishes. Shrader, Christine, illus. LC 93-26924. 1995. write for info. (*0-525-65164-0*, Cobblehill Bks) Dutton Child Bks.

Witters, Judith. When the Earth Was Bare. Cammarata, Kathleen, illus. LC 93-26930. 1994. 4.25 (*0-383-03785-9*) SRA Schl Grp.

INDIANS OF NORTH AMERICA–ALGONQUIAN INDIANS

D'Apice, Rita & D'Apice, Mary. Algonquian. (Illus.). 32p. (gr. 5-8). 1990. lib. bdg. 15.94 (*0-86625-388-2*); lib. bdg. 11.95s.p. (*0-685-36386-4*) Rourke Corp.

Gregg, Andy. Great Rabbit & the Long-Tailed Wildcat. Grant, Christy, ed. Smith, Cat B., illus. LC 92-22950. 32p. (gr. 1-5). 1993. PLB 13.95 (*0-8075-3047-6*) A Whitman.

Holler, Anne. Chief Powhatan & Pocahontas. (Illus.). 112p. (gr. 5 up). 1993. PLB 17.95 (*0-7910-1705-2*) Chelsea Hse.

Quiri, Patricia R. The Algonquians. LC 91-29111. (Illus.). 64p. (gr. 3-5). 1992. PLB 12.90 (*0-531-20065-5*) Watts.

—The Algonquians. 64p. (gr. 5-8). 1992. pap. 5.95 (*0-531-15633-8*) Watts.

Siegel, Beatrice. Indians of the Northeast Woodlands Before & after the Pilgrims. 96p. 1992. 13.95 (*0-8027-8155-1*); lib. bdg. 14.85 (*0-8027-8157-8*) Walker & Co.

Thompson, Dorothea M. The Sokokis: Native Americans of New Hampshire. Thompson, Brownlow L., illus. 150p. (Orig.). (gr. 4). 1986. pap. 9.95x (*0-931947-50-2*) Thompson Pr.

INDIANS OF NORTH AMERICA–ALGONQUIAN INDIANS–FICTION

Lemieux, Margo. Full Worm Moon. Parker, Robert A., illus. LC 93-14728. 32p. 1994. 15.00 (*0-688-12105-5*, Tambourine Bks); PLB 14.93 (*0-688-12106-3*, Tambourine Bks) Morrow.

INDIANS OF NORTH AMERICA–AMUSEMENTS

see Indians of North America–Games; Indians of North America–Social Life and Customs

INDIANS OF NORTH AMERICA–ANTIQUITIES

see also Mounds and Mound Builders

Cordoba, Maria. PreColumbian Peoples of North America. LC 94-16112. (Illus.). 36p. (gr. 3 up). 1994. PLB 20.00 (*0-516-08393-7*); pap. 6.95 (*0-516-48393-5*) Childrens.

Johnson, Eileen & Dean, David K. Tales of the Ancient Watering Hole, Bk. 2: Protohistoric Life on the South Plains. Dean, David K., illus. 55p. (gr. 6-8). 1994. pap. 4.95 (*0-9640188-0-2*) Mus TX Tech.

Johnson, Elden. The Prehistoric Peoples of Minnesota. rev. ed. LC 87-32663. (Illus.). 35p. (gr. 9-12). 1988. pap. 3.95 (*0-87351-223-5*) Minn Hist.

Nichols, Peter & Nichols, Belia. Mastodon Hunters to Mound Builders: North American Archaeology. Battles-Herron, Linda & Newman, Beth, illus. 112p. (gr. 4-7). 1992. 12.95 (*0-89015-748-0*) Sunbelt Media.

Petersen, David. The Anasazi. LC 91-3036. 48p. (gr. k-4). 1991. PLB 12.85 (*0-516-01121-9*); pap. 4.95 (*0-516-41121-7*) Childrens.

Smith, Howard E., Jr. All about Arrowheads & Spear Points. Dewey, Jennifer O., illus. LC 88-39089. 80p. (gr. 4-6). 1989. 14.95 (*0-8050-0892-6*, Bks Young Read) H Holt & Co.

Snow, Dean R. The Archaeology of North America. Porter, Frank W., III, intro. by. (Illus.). 144p. (gr. 5 up). 1989. 17.95 (*1-55546-691-5*) Chelsea Hse.

Warren, Scott S. Cities in the Sand: The Ancient Civilizations of the Southwest. Warren, Scott S., illus. 64p. (gr. 4-8). 1991. 10.95 (*0-8118-0012-1*) Chronicle Bks.

Wheat, Pam & Whorton, Brenda, eds. Clues from the Past: A Resource Book on Archeology. Thompson, Eileen, illus. LC 90-4991. 200p. (gr. 3 up). 1990. pap. 17.95 (*0-937460-65-6*) Hendrick-Long.

Wood, Marian. Ancient America. 1990. 17.95 (*0-8160-2210-0*) Facts on File.

INDIANS OF NORTH AMERICA–APACHE INDIANS

Claro, Nicole. The Apache Indians. (Illus.). 80p. (gr. 2-5). 1993. PLB 12.95 (*0-7910-1656-0*) Chelsea Hse.

—Apache Indians: Southwest. (gr. 4-7). 1993. pap. 6.95 (*0-7910-1946-2*) Chelsea Hse.

Cuevas, Lou. Apache Legends: Songs of the Wind Dancer. Brown, Keven, ed. Cleveland, Fred, illus. 128p. (Orig.). 1991. pap. text ed. 8.95 (*0-87961-219-3*) Naturegraph.

Doherty, Craig A. & Doherty, Katherine M. The Apaches & Navajos. LC 89-9079. (Illus.). 64p. (gr. 3-5). 1989. PLB 12.90 (*0-531-10743-4*) Watts.

—The Apaches & Navajos. (Illus.). 64p. (gr. 5-8). 1991. pap. 5.95 (*0-531-15602-8*) Watts.

Levin, Beatrice & Vanderveld, Marjorie. Me Run Fast Good: Biographies of Tewanima (Hopi), Carlos Montezuma (Apache) & John Horse (Seminole) 32p. (gr. 5-9). 1983. pap. 1.95 (*0-89992-087-X*) Coun India Ed.

McCall, Barbara. Apache. (Illus.). 32p. (gr. 5-8). 1990. lib. bdg. 15.94 (*0-86625-384-X*); lib. bdg. 11.95s.p. (*0-685-36387-2*) Rourke Corp.

McKissack, Patricia. The Apache. LC 84-7803. (Illus.). 48p. (gr. k-4). 1984. PLB 12.85 (*0-516-01925-2*); pap. 4.95 (*0-516-41925-0*) Childrens.

Melody, Michael E. The Apache. Porter, Frank, intro. by. (Illus.). 112p. (gr. 5 up). 1989. 17.95 (*1-55546-689-3*); pap. 9.95 (*0-7910-0352-3*) Chelsea Hse.

Seymour, Tryntje V. N. The Gift of Changing Woman. LC 92-31833. (Illus.). 40p. (gr. 5-9). 1993. 16.95 (*0-8050-2577-4*, Bks Young Read) H Holt & Co.

Shaffer, Susan L., ed. Inde, the Western Apache. Harper-Marinick, Maria & Kinzie, Mable B., illus. (gr. 5 up). 1987. incl. 30 student bklts. & 1 tchr's. resource binder which contains poster, lesson plans, overhead transparencies, 1 realia, color slides & audio-cassette 294.43 (*0-934351-11-2*); tchr's. resource binder only 197.95 (*0-934351-22-8*); student bklt. only 4.95 (*0-934351-27-9*) Heard Mus.

Shorto, Russell. Geronimo. (Illus.). 144p. (gr. 5-7). 1989. PLB 10.95 (*0-382-09571-5*); pap. 7.95 (*0-382-09760-2*) Silver Burdett Pr.

INDIANS OF NORTH AMERICA–APACHE INDIANS–FICTION

Holmas, Stig. Son-of-Thunder. Born, Anne, tr. from NOR. Hurford, John, illus. LC 93-4211. 128p. (gr. 7 up). 1993. 16.95 (*0-943173-88-4*); pap. 10.95 (*0-943173-87-6*) Harbinger AZ.

Martinello, Marian, et al. Hopes, Prayers & Promises. Shelton, Caroline, illus. 48p. (gr. k-8). 1986. 12.95 (*0-935857-05-2*); pap. write for info. (*0-935857-06-0*) Texart.

INDIANS OF NORTH AMERICA–ART

Abbott, Lawrence. I Stand in the Center of the Good: Interviews with Contemporary Native American Artists. LC 93-36892. (Illus.). 347p. 1994. text ed. 40.00 (*0-8032-1037-X*) U of Nebr Pr.

Baylor, Byrd. When Clay Sings. Bahti, Tom, illus. LC 70-180758. 32p. (ps-3). 1987. Repr. of 1977 ed. SBE 13.95 (*0-684-18829-5*, Scribners Young Read) Macmillan Child Grp.

—When Clay Sings. Bahti, Tom, illus. LC 86-20587. 32p. (gr. 1-4). 1987. pap. 3.95 (*0-689-71106-9*, Aladdin) Macmillan Child Grp.

Gates, Frieda. North American Indian Masks. Gates, Frieda, illus. 64p. (gr. 5 up). 1982. 8.95 (*0-8027-6462-2*); lib. bdg. 9.85 (*0-8027-6463-0*) Walker & Co.

McNutt, Nan. The Bentwood Box. 3rd ed. Osawa, Yasu & Jackson, Nathan, illus. 36p. (Orig.). (gr. 3-8). 1989. pap. text ed. 9.95 (*0-9614534-0-0*) N McNutt Assocs.

—The Button Blanket. 2nd ed. Osawa, Yasu & Dawson, Nancy, illus. 44p. (gr. k-3). 1989. pap. 7.95 (*0-9614534-1-9*) N McNutt Assocs.

—The Button Blanket. 2nd ed. (Illus.). 44p. (gr. k-3). 1989. pap. 7.95 (*0-9614534-3-5*) Workshop Pubns.

—The Cedar Plank Mask. (Illus.). 34p. (gr. 3-6). 1991. pap. 9.95 (*0-9614534-2-7*) N McNutt Assocs.

—Northwest Coast Indian Art Series, 3 bks. rev. ed. Yasu Osawa, illus. 118p. (gr. k-8). 1992. Set. pap. text ed. 29.95 (*0-9614534-5-1*) N McNutt Assocs.

Moore, Reavis. Native Artists of North America. Burton, LeVar, frwd. by. (Illus.). 48p. (gr. 4-7). 1993. 14.95 (*1-56261-105-4*) John Muir.

Villasenor, David. Tapestries in Sand: The Spirit of Indian Sandpainting. rev. ed. (Illus.). 112p. (gr. 4 up). 1966. 16.95 (*0-911010-23-8*); pap. 8.95 (*0-911010-22-X*) Naturegraph.

Wesche, Alice. Wild Brothers of the Indians: As Pictured by the Ancient Americans. LC 77-79064. (Illus.). (gr. 3-8). 1977. pap. 4.95 (*0-918080-21-5*) Treasure Chest.

INDIANS OF NORTH AMERICA–BIOGRAPHY

Aaseng, Nathan. Athletes. LC 94-12469. 1995. write for info. (*0-8160-3019-7*) Facts on File.

Anderson, Peter. Charles Eastman: Physician, Reformer, & Native American Leader. LC 91-36654. (Illus.). 152p. (gr. 4 up). 1992. PLB 14.40 (*0-516-03278-X*); pap. 5.95 (*0-516-43278-8*) Childrens.

—Maria Martinez: Pueblo Potter. LC 92-4807. (Illus.). 32p. (gr. 2-5). 1992. PLB 11.80 (*0-516-04184-3*) Childrens.

Averill, Esther. King Philip, the Indian Chief. Belsky, Vera, illus. LC 92-32156. v, 147p. (gr. 6-12). 1993. lib. bdg. 17.50 (*0-208-02357-7*, Pub. by Linnet); (Pub. by Linnet) Shoe String.

Avery, Susan. Extraordinary American Indians. LC 92-11358. (Illus.). 260p. (gr. 4 up). 1992. PLB 24.65 (*0-516-00583-9*) Childrens.

The Aztec Indians. (Illus.). 80p. (gr. 2-5). 1993. PLB 12.95 (*0-7910-1658-7*); pap. write for info. (*0-7910-1963-2*) Chelsea Hse.

Bolton, Jonathan W. & Wilson, Claire M. Scholars, Writers, & Professionals. LC 93-31683. (Illus.). 128p. (gr. 4-11). 1994. 16.95x (*0-8160-2896-6*) Facts on File.
Brown, Marion M. Susette La Flesche: Advocate for Native American Rights. LC 91-35296. (Illus.). 152p. (gr. 4 up). 1992. PLB 14.40 (*0-516-03277-1*); pap. 5.95 (*0-516-43277-X*) Childrens.
Bulla, Clyde R. Squanto, Friend of the Pilgrims. 112p. 1990. pap. 2.95 (*0-590-44055-1*) Scholastic Inc.
Chief Joseph's Own Story As Told by Chief Joseph in 1879. (gr. 4 up). 1972. 4.95 (*0-89992-019-5*) Coun India Ed.
Cwiklik, Robert. Tecumseh: Shawnee Rebel. (Illus.). 112p. (gr. 5 up). 1994. PLB 18.95 (*0-7910-1721-4*, Am Art Analog) Chelsea Hse.
Eastman, Charles A. Indian Boyhood. Blumenschein, E. L., illus. LC 68-58282. (gr. 3-7). pap. 4.95 (*0-486-22037-0*) Dover.
Eckert, Allan W. Blue Jacket: War Chief of Shawnees. LC 69-10656. 177p. (gr. 7 up). 1983. pap. 6.95 (*0-913428-36-1*) Landfall Pr.
Erdrich, Heidi E. Maria Tallchief. Whipple, Rick, illus. LC 92-12256. 32p. (gr. 3-6). 1992. PLB 19.97 (*0-8114-6577-2*); pap. 4.95 (*0-8114-4099-0*) Raintree Steck-V.
Ferris, Jeri. Native American Doctor: The Story of Susan Laflesche Picotte. (gr. 4-7). 1991. pap. 6.95 (*0-87614-548-9*) Carolrhoda Bks.
Fox, Mary V. Chief Joseph of the Nez Perce Indians: Champion of Liberty. LC 92-35053. (Illus.). 152p. (gr. 4 up). 1992. PLB 14.40 (*0-516-03275-5*) Childrens.
Glassman, Bruce. Wilma Mankiller: Chief of the Cherokee Nation. (Illus.). 64p. (gr. 3-7). PLB 14.95 (*1-56711-032-0*) Blackbirch.
Hatheway, Flora. Chief Plenty Coups: Life of the Crow Indian Chief. (gr. 4). 1971. 4.95 (*0-89992-005-5*) Coun India Ed.
Holler, Anne. Pocahontas. (gr. 4-7). 1992. pap. 7.95 (*0-7910-1952-7*) Chelsea Hse.
Jackson, Jack & Jackson, Jack. Long Shadows: Indian Leaders Standing in the Path of Manifest Destiny, 1600-1900. Newcomb, W. W., Jr., frwd. by. (Illus.). 128p. (gr. 6 up). 1985. hardbound pictorial cover 17. 95 (*0-942376-07-2*) Paramount TX.
Jeffredo-Warden, Louise V. Ishi. Fujiwara, Kim, illus. LC 92-8602. 32p. (gr. 4-5). 1992. PLB 19.97 (*0-8114-6578-0*); pap. 4.95 (*0-8114-4096-6*) Raintree Steck-V.
Katz, William L. & Franklin, Paula A. Proudly Red & Black: Stories of Native & African Americans. LC 92-36119. (Illus.). 96p. (gr. 4-7). 1993. SBE 13.95 (*0-689-31801-4*, Atheneum Child Bk) Macmillan Child Grp.
Klausner, Janet. Sequoyah's Gift: A Portrait of the Cherokee Leader. King, Duane, afterword by. LC 92-24939. (Illus.). 128p. (gr. 4 up). 1993. 15.00 (*0-06-021235-7*); PLB 14.89 (*0-06-021236-5*) HarpC Child Bks.
Levin, Beatrice & Vanderveld, Marjorie. Me Run Fast Good: Biographies of Tewanima (Hopi), Carlos Montezuma (Apache) & John Horse (Seminole) 32p. (gr. 5-9). 1983. pap. 1.95 (*0-89992-087-X*) Coun India Ed.
Liptak, Karen. North American Indian Tribal Chiefs. Mathews, V., ed. LC 91-30261. (Illus.). 64p. (gr. 3-6). 1992. PLB 12.90 (*0-531-20101-5*) Watts.
Littlechild, George. This Land Is My Land. (Illus.). 32p. (gr. 3-8). 1993. 15.95 (*0-89239-119-7*) Childrens Book Pr.
Masson, Jean-Robert. The Great Indian Chiefs: Sitting Bull, Crazy Horse, Cochise, Geronimo. (Illus.). 80p. (gr. 4 up). 1994. 14.95 (*0-8120-6468-2*) Barron.

Matson, Emerson N. Legends of the Great Chiefs. (Illus.). 144p. (gr. 6-10). Date not set. pap. 5.95 (*0-9609940-0-9*) Storypole.
One of America's most-quoted legend books. In print since 1972. Authentic legends & little-known incidents recalled during first-hand interviews with actual descendants of some of the most famous Indian chiefs in American history. The author located surviving relatives of such famous Indian leaders as Sitting Bull, Red Cloud, Joseph, Leshi, Shelton, Swan, & Sampson. Each descendant recalls favorite legends & little-known facts about their famous ancestors. The legends were more than clever stories. To those who told them, they were a vital part of life itself. For today's reader, the legends are a window into ancient tribal lore. Sixteen-page photo section. Written for grades six through ten. Also used in college-level literature classes. Postage prepaid on orders of twelve or more books. Retail $5.95 paperback. Fax order-line 206-535-3889, Storypole Press, 11015 Bingham Ave. East, Tacoma, WA 98446-5225.
Publisher Provided Annotation.

Morrison, Dorothy N. Chief Sarah: Sarah Winnemucca's Fight for Indian Rights. (Illus.). 192p. (gr. 4 up). 1990. pap. 7.95 (*0-87595-204-6*) Oregon Hist.
North American Indians of Achievement, 24 vols. (Illus.). (gr. 5 up). 1994. Set. PLB write for info. (*0-7910-1700-1*, Am Art Analog) Chelsea Hse.
Petersen, David. Ishi: The Last of His People. LC 90-28887. (Illus.). 32p. (gr. 2-4). 1991. PLB 11.80 (*0-516-04179-7*); pap. 3.95 (*0-516-44179-5*) Childrens.
—Sequoyah: Father of the Cherokee Alphabet. LC 91-13313. 32p. (gr. 2-4). 1991. PLB 11.80 (*0-516-04180-0*); pap. 3.95 (*0-516-44180-9*) Childrens.
Prentzas, Scott. The Kwakiutl Indians. (Illus.). 80p. (gr. 2-5). 1993. PLB 12.95 (*0-7910-1664-1*) Chelsea Hse.
Rand, Jacki T. Wilma Mankiller. Still, Wayne A., illus. LC 92-12813. 32p. (gr. 4-5). 1992. PLB 19.97 (*0-8114-6576-4*); pap. 4.95 (*0-8114-4097-4*) Raintree Steck-V.
Richards, Dorothy F. Pocahontas, Child-Princess. Nelson, John, illus. LC 78-7719. (gr. k-4). 1978. PLB 13.95 (*0-89565-035-5*) Childs World.
Sanford, William R. Crazy Horse: Sioux Warrior. (Illus.). 48p. (gr. 4-10). 1994. lib. bdg. 14.95 (*0-89490-511-2*) Enslow Pubs.
Scordato, Ellen. Sarah Winnemucca. (Illus.). 112p. (gr. 5 up). 1992. lib. bdg. 17.95 (*0-7910-1710-9*) Chelsea Hse.
Seguin, Marilyn. Song of Courage, Song of Freedom: The Story of Mary Campbell. (Illus.). 120p. (Orig.). (gr. 4-9). 1993. pap. 12.95 (*0-8283-1952-9*) Branden Pub Co.
Sherrow, Victoria. Political Leaders & Peacemakers. LC 93-38383. (Illus.). 128p. (gr. 4-11). 1994. 16.95x (*0-8160-2943-1*) Facts on File.
Shumate, Jane. Chief Gall: Sioux War Chief. LC 94-13645. 1994. write for info. (*0-7910-1713-3*) Chelsea Hse.
Simon, Charnan. Wilma P. Mankiller: Chief of the Cherokee. LC 91-4334. 32p. (gr. 2-4). 1991. PLB 11. 80 (*0-516-04181-9*); pap. 3.95 (*0-516-44181-7*) Childrens.
Sonneborn, Liz. Performers. LC 94-25587. 1995. write for info. (*0-8160-3045-6*) Facts on File.
Thomson, Peggy. Katie Henio, Navajo Sheepherder. Conklin, Paul, photos by. LC 93-40430. 1994. write for info. (*0-525-65160-8*, Cobblehill Pr) Dutton Child Bks.
Trenholm, Virginia C. Omen of the Hawks. LC 89-63585. (Illus.). 312p. (gr. 9-12). 1989. 18.95 (*0-943255-26-0*); pap. 9.95 (*0-943255-35-X*) Portfolio Pub.
Upton, H. Indian Chiefs. (Illus.). 32p. (gr. 3-8). 1990. lib. bdg. 18.00 (*0-86625-400-5*); 13.50s.p. (*0-685-58654-5*) Rourke Corp.
Walker, Paul R. Spiritual Leaders. LC 93-31684. (Illus.). 128p. (gr. 4-11). 1994. 16.95x (*0-8160-2875-3*) Facts on File.
Wilker, Josh. The Lenape Indians. (Illus.). 80p. (gr. 2-5). 1993. PLB 13.95 (*0-7910-1665-X*, Am Art Analog); pap. 6.95 (*0-7910-2029-0*, Am Art Analog) Chelsea Hse.
Williams, Neva. Patrick des Jarlait: The Story of a Native American Artist. LC 94-6535. (gr. 5 up). 1994. write for info. (*0-8225-3151-8*) Lerner Pubns.
Wilson, Claire & Bolton, Jonathan. Joseph Brant. (Illus.). 112p. (gr. 5 up). 1992. lib. bdg. 17.95 (*0-7910-1709-5*) Chelsea Hse.
Wood, Ted & Wanbli Numpa Afraid of Hawk. A Boy Becomes a Man at Wounded Knee. 42p. 1992. 15.95 (*0-8027-8174-8*); lib. bdg. 16.85 (*0-8027-8175-6*) Walker & Co.
Yannuzzi, Della A. Wilma Mankiller: Leader of the Cherokee Nation. LC 93-44866. (Illus.). 128p. (gr. 6 up). 1994. lib. bdg. 17.95 (*0-89490-498-1*) Enslow Pubs.

INDIANS OF NORTH AMERICA–CANADA

Bemister, Margaret. Thirty Indian Legends of Canada. Tait, Douglas, illus. 158p. (gr. 3-7). 1991. pap. 9.95 (*0-88894-025-4*, Pub. by Groundwood-Douglas & McIntyre CN) Firefly Bks Ltd.
Littlechild, George. This Land Is My Land. (Illus.). 32p. (gr. 3-8). 1993. 15.95 (*0-89239-119-7*) Childrens Book Pr.
Younkin, Paula. Indians of the Arctic & Subarctic. (Illus.). 96p. (gr. 5-8). 1991. lib. bdg. 18.95x (*0-8160-2391-3*) Facts on File.

INDIANS OF NORTH AMERICA–CANADA–FICTION

Houston, James R. River Runners: A Tale of Hardship & Bravery. 160p. (gr. 5 up). 1992. pap. 4.50 (*0-14-036093-X*, Puffin) Puffin Bks.
Robinson, Margaret A. A Woman of Her Tribe. LC 90-31534. 144p. (gr. 7 up). 1990. SBE 13.95 (*0-684-19223-3*, Scribners Young Read) Macmillan Child Grp.

INDIANS OF NORTH AMERICA–CAPTIVITIES

Lenski, Lois. Indian Captive: The Story of Mary Jemison. Lenski, Lois, illus. LC 41-51956. 272p. (gr. 7-9). 1990. 16.00 (*0-397-30072-7*, Lipp Jr Bks); PLB 15.89 (*0-397-30076-X*, Lipp Jr Bks) HarpC Child Bks.
Seaver, James E. A Narrative of the Life of Mrs. Mary Jemison. Abrams, George, intro. by. 196p. 1990. pap. text ed. 12.95x (*0-8156-2491-3*) Syracuse U Pr.

INDIANS OF NORTH AMERICA–CAPTIVITIES–FICTION

Keehn, Sally. I Am Regina. 192p. 1991. 15.95 (*0-399-21797-5*, Philomel Bks) Putnam Pub Group.
Smith, Mary P. Boy Captive of Old Deerfield. (Illus.). (gr. 5-6). Repr. of 1904 ed. lib. bdg. 20.95x (*0-89190-961-3*, Pub. by River City Pr) Amereon Ltd.
Speare, Elizabeth G. Calico Captive. Mars, Witold T., illus. 288p. (gr. 7-9). 1957. 15.95 (*0-395-07112-7*) HM.

INDIANS OF NORTH AMERICA–CHEROKEE INDIANS

Bealer, Alex. Only the Names Remain: The Cherokees & the Trail of Tears. Bock, William S., illus. (gr. 4-6). 1972. lib. bdg. 15.95 (*0-316-08520-0*) Little.
Bruchac, Joseph & Ross, Gayle. The Story of the Milky Way: A Cherokee Tale. Stroud, Virginia A., illus. LC 94-20926. 1995. write for info. (*0-8037-1733-4*); PLB write for info. (*0-8037-1738-5*) Dial Bks Young.
Claro, Nicole. The Cherokee Indians. (Illus.). 80p. (gr. 2-5). 1991. lib. bdg. 12.95 (*0-7910-1652-8*) Chelsea Hse.
Fremon, David. The Trail of Tears. (Illus.). 96p. (gr. 6 up). 1994. text ed. 14.95 RSBE (*0-02-735745-7*, New Discovery Bks) Macmillan Child Grp.
Glassman, Bruce. Wilma Mankiller: Chief of the Cherokee Nation. (Illus.). 64p. (gr. 3-7). PLB 14.95 (*1-56711-032-0*) Blackbirch.
Hoyt-Goldsmith, Diane. Cherokee Summer. Migdale, Lawrence, photos by. LC 92-54416. (Illus.). 32p. (gr. 3-7). 1993. reinforced bdg. 15.95 (*0-8234-0995-3*) Holiday.
Johnson, Charles B. The Last Beloved Woman. 129p. (Orig.). (gr. 4 up). 1994. pap. 5.99 (*1-884505-00-7*) Amer Trail Bks.
Klausner, Janet. Sequoyah's Gift: A Portrait of the Cherokee Leader. King, Duane, afterword by. LC 92-24939. (Illus.). 128p. (gr. 4 up). 1993. 15.00 (*0-06-021235-7*); PLB 14.89 (*0-06-021236-5*) HarpC Child Bks.
Landau, Elaine. The Cherokees. Rosoff, Iris, ed. LC 91-30262. (Illus.). 64p. (gr. 3-5). 1992. PLB 12.90 (*0-531-20066-3*) Watts.
—The Cherokees. (Illus.). 64p. (gr. 5-8). 1992. pap. 5.95 (*0-531-15635-4*) Watts.
Lepthien, Emilie U. The Cherokee. LC 84-27476. (Illus.). 48p. (gr. k-4). 1985. PLB 12.85 (*0-516-01938-4*); pap. 4.95 (*0-516-41938-2*) Childrens.
—The Mandans. LC 89-22235. 48p. (gr. k-4). 1989. PLB 12.85 (*0-516-01180-4*); pap. 4.95 (*0-516-41180-2*) Childrens.
Lucas, Eileen. The Cherokees: People of the Southeast. LC 92-40874. (Illus.). 64p. (gr. 4-6). 1993. PLB 15.40 (*1-56294-312-X*) Millbrook Pr.
McCall, B. The Cherokee. (Illus.). 32p. (gr. 5-8). 1989. lib. bdg. 15.94 (*0-86625-376-9*); lib. bdg. 11.95s.p. (*0-685-58583-2*) Rourke Corp.
Meyers, Madeleine, intro. by. Cherokee Nation: Life Before the Tears. (Illus.). 64p. (Orig.). (gr. 5-12). 1993. pap. 4.95 (*1-878668-26-9*) Disc Enter Ltd.
Perdue, Thea. The Cherokee. Porter, Frank W., III, intro. by. (Illus.). 111p. (Orig.). (gr. 5 up). 1989. 17.95 (*1-55546-695-8*); pap. 9.95 (*0-7910-0357-4*) Chelsea Hse.
Petersen, David. Sequoyah: Father of the Cherokee Alphabet. LC 91-13313. 32p. (gr. 2-4). 1991. PLB 11. 80 (*0-516-04180-0*); pap. 3.95 (*0-516-44180-9*) Childrens.
Rand, Jacki T. Wilma Mankiller. Still, Wayne A., illus. LC 92-12813. 32p. (gr. 4-5). 1992. PLB 19.97 (*0-8114-6576-4*); pap. 4.95 (*0-8114-4097-4*) Raintree Steck-V.
Simon, Charnan. Wilma P. Mankiller: Chief of the Cherokee. LC 91-4334. 32p. (gr. 2-4). 1991. PLB 11. 80 (*0-516-04181-9*); pap. 3.95 (*0-516-44181-7*) Childrens.
Sober, Nancy H. The Intruders: The Illegal Residents of the Cherokee Nation, 1866-1907. 2nd ed. LC 90-84850. (Illus.). 222p. (gr. 12). 1991. PLB 24.95 (*0-9628188-0-1*) Cherokee Bks.
Steele, Phillip. The Last Cherokee Warriors. 2nd ed. LC 86-25348. (Illus.). 111p. (gr. 6-12). 1978. pap. 7.95 (*0-88289-203-7*) Pelican.
Stein, R. Conrad. The Trail of Tears. LC 92-33422. (Illus.). 32p. (gr. 3-6). 1993. PLB 12.30 (*0-516-06666-8*); pap. 3.95 (*0-516-46666-6*) Childrens.
Underwood, Tom. Cherokee Legends & the Trail of Tears. Crowe, Amanda, illus. 32p. (gr. 4-12). 1956. 3.50 (*0-935741-00-3*) Cherokee Pubns.
Underwood, Tom B. The Magic Lake: A Mystical Healing Lake of the Cherokee. Simmons, Shirley, illus. 20p. (gr. 1-3). 1982. 3.50 (*0-935741-08-9*) Cherokee Pubns.
Yannuzzi, Della A. Wilma Mankiller: Leader of the Cherokee Nation. LC 93-44866. (Illus.). 128p. (gr. 6 up). 1994. lib. bdg. 17.95 (*0-89490-498-1*) Enslow Pubs.

INDIANS OF NORTH AMERICA–CHEROKEE INDIANS–FICTION

Cohlene, Terri. Dancing Drum: A Cherokee Legend. 48p. (gr. 4-7). 1990. pap. 3.95 (*0-8167-2362-1*) Troll Assocs.
Pennington, Dan. Itse Selu: Cherokee Harvest Festival. (Illus.). 32p. (ps-4). 1994. 14.95 (*0-88106-851-9*); PLB 15.00 (*0-88106-852-7*); pap. 6.95 (*0-88106-850-0*) Charlesbridge Pub.

Rockwood, Joyce. Groundhog's Horse. Kalin, Victor, illus. LC 77-22676. 128p. (gr. 2-4). 1978. reinforced ed. 12.95 (*0-8050-1173-0*, Bks Young Read) H Holt & Co.

Roop, Peter & Roop, Connie. Ahyoka & the Talking Leaves. Miyake, Yoshi, illus. LC 91-3036. (gr. 1 up). 1992. text ed. 12.00 (*0-688-10697-8*) Lothrop.

Stewart, Elisabeth Jane. On the Long Trail Home. LC 93-34666. 1994. 13.95 (*0-395-68361-0*, Clarion Bks) HM.

Stroud, Virginia. A Walk to the Great Mystery. LC 93-32340. 1993. write for info. (*0-8037-1636-2*); PLB write for info. (*0-8037-1637-0*) Dial Bks Young.

The Trail on Which They Wept: The Story of a Cherokee Girl. 64p. (gr. 4-6). 1992. incl. jacket 5.95 (*0-382-24333-1*); lib. bdg. 7.95 (*0-382-24331-5*); pap. 3.95 (*0-382-24353-6*) Silver Burdett Pr.

INDIANS OF NORTH AMERICA–CHEYENNE INDIANS

Fradin, Dennis B. The Cheyenne. LC 87-33792. (Illus.). 48p. (gr. k-4). 1988. PLB 12.85 (*0-516-01211-8*); pap. 4.95 (*0-516-41211-6*) Childrens.

Gilliland, Hap. O'kohome: The Coyote Dog. Hardgrove, Tanya, illus. 47p. (Orig.). (gr. 4-9). 1989. pap. 5.95 (*0-89992-102-7*) Coun India Ed.

Henry Tall Bull & Weist, Tom. Cheyenne Legends of Creation. (gr. 4-9). 1972. 1.25 (*0-89992-025-X*) Coun India Ed.

—Cheyenne Warriors. (gr. 4-12). 1976. pap. 1.25 (*0-89992-015-2*) Coun India Ed.

Hoig, Stan. The Cheyenne. Porter, Frank W., III, intro. by. (Illus.). 112p. (gr. 5 up). 1989. 17.95 (*1-55546-696-6*); pap. 9.95 (*0-7910-0358-2*) Chelsea Hse.

—People of the Sacred Arrow. (Illus.). 144p. (gr. 6 up). 1992. 15.00 (*0-525-65088-1*, Cobblehill Bks) Dutton Child Bks.

Lodge, Sally. Cheyenne. (Illus.). 32p. (gr. 5-8). 1990. lib. bdg. 15.94 (*0-86625-387-4*); lib. bdg. 11.95s.p. (*0-685-36388-0*) Rourke Corp.

Meyers, Arthur. The Cheyenne. (Illus.). 64p. (gr. 5-8). 1992. pap. 5.95 (*0-531-15636-2*) Watts.

Myers, Arthur. The Cheyenne. LC 91-31010. (Illus.). 64p. (gr. 3-6). 1992. PLB 12.90 (*0-531-20069-8*) Watts.

Sonneborn, Liz. The Cheyenne Indians. (Illus.). 80p. (gr. 2-5). 1992. lib. bdg. 12.95 (*0-7910-1654-4*) Chelsea Hse.

INDIANS OF NORTH AMERICA–CHEYENNE INDIANS–FICTION

Finley, Mary Pearce. Soaring Eagle. LC 92-38263. (gr. 6 up). 1993. pap. 14.00 (*0-671-75598-6*, S&S BFYR) S&S Trade.

Goble, Paul. Death of the Iron Horse. Goble, Paul, illus. LC 85-28011. 32p. (gr. k-3). 1987. SBE 14.95 (*0-02-737830-6*, Bradbury Pr) Macmillan Child Grp.

—Death of the Iron Horse. Goble, Paul, illus. LC 92-1723. 32p. (ps-3). 1993. pap. 4.95 (*0-689-71686-9*, Aladdin) Macmillan Child Grp.

Irwin, Hadley. Jim-Dandy. LC 93-22611. 144p. (gr. 5-9). 1994. SBE 14.95 (*0-689-50594-9*, M K McElderry) Macmillan Child Grp.

INDIANS OF NORTH AMERICA–CHILDREN

Armstrong, Nancy. Navajo Children. (gr. 2-6). 1975. 1.95 (*0-89992-037-3*) Coun India Ed.

Chandonnet, Ann. Chief Stephen's Parky: One Year in the Life of an Athapascan Girl. Gilliland, Hap, ed. (Illus.). 72p. (Orig.). (gr. 4-12). 1989. pap. 7.95 (*0-89992-119-1*) Coun India Ed.

INDIANS OF NORTH AMERICA–CHIPPEWA INDIANS

Green, Jacqueline D. The Chippewa. LC 93-18371. (Illus.). 64p. (gr. 4-6). 1993. PLB 12.90 (*0-531-20122-8*); pap. 5.95 (*0-531-15700-8*) Watts.

—The Chippewa. LC 93-18371. (Illus.). 64p. (gr. 4-6). 1993. PLB 12.90 (*0-531-20122-8*); pap. 5.95 (*0-531-15700-8*) Watts.

Greene, Jacqueline D. The Chippewa. (Illus.). 64p. (gr. 5-8). 1994. pap. 5.95 (*0-531-15703-2*) Watts.

Osinski, Alice. The Chippewa. LC 86-32687. (Illus.). 48p. (gr. k-4). 1987. PLB 12.85 (*0-516-01230-4*); pap. 4.95 (*0-516-41230-2*) Childrens.

INDIANS OF NORTH AMERICA–CHIPPEWA INDIANS–FICTION

Dietrich, Wilson G. Muckwa: The Adventures of a Chippewa Indian Boy. Graves, Helen, ed. LC 89-52120. (Illus.). 71p. (gr. 3-10). 1990. pap. 6.95 (*1-55523-304-X*) Winston-Derek.

Wosmek, Frances. A Brown Bird Singing. Lewin, Ted, illus. LC 85-24002. 160p. (gr. 5-10). 1985. 11.95 (*0-688-06251-2*) Lothrop.

INDIANS OF NORTH AMERICA–CHOCTAW INDIANS

Lepthien, Emilie U. The Choctaw. LC 87-14583. (Illus.). 48p. (gr. k-4). 1987. PLB 12.85 (*0-516-01240-1*); pap. 4.95 (*0-516-41240-X*) Childrens.

McKee, Jesse O. The Choctaw. (Illus.). 104p. (gr. 5 up). 1989. 17.95 (*1-55546-699-0*) Chelsea Hse.

INDIANS OF NORTH AMERICA–CHUMASHAN INDIANS

Boule, Mary N. California's Native American Tribes, No. 4: Chumash Tribe. Liddell, Daniel, illus. 40p. (Orig.). (gr. 3-5). 1992. pap. 4.50 (*1-877599-28-X*) Merryant Pubs.

Duvall, Jill D. The Chumash. LC 93-36672. (Illus.). 48p. (gr. k-4). 1994. PLB 12.85 (*0-516-01052-2*) Childrens.

Gibson, Robert O. The Chumash. (Illus.). (gr. 5 up). 1991. 17.95 (*1-55546-700-8*) Chelsea Hse.

—The Chumash. (Illus.). 104p. (Orig.). (gr. 5 up). 1991. pap. 9.95 (*0-7910-0376-0*) Chelsea Hse.

Santa Barbara Museum of Natural History. California's Chumash Indians. rev. ed. Powell, Ann, et al, illus. 72p. (ps-4). 1988. pap. 5.95 (*0-945092-00-8*) EZ Nature.

Schwabacher, Martin. The Chumash Indians. LC 94-17181. (Illus.). 1995. write for info. (*0-7910-2488-1*); pap. write for info. (*0-7910-2490-3*) Chelsea Hse.

INDIANS OF NORTH AMERICA–CHUMASHAN INDIANS–FICTION

Spinka, Penina K. Mother's Blessing. LC 91-31342. 224p. (gr. 5-9). 1992. SBE 14.95 (*0-689-31758-1*, Atheneum Child Bk) Macmillan Child Grp.

INDIANS OF NORTH AMERICA–COMANCHE INDIANS

Alter, Judy. The Comanches. LC 93-23265. 1994. 12.90 (*0-531-20115-5*); pap. 5.95 (*0-531-15683-4*) Watts.

Hubbard-Brown, Janet. Comanche Indians: Great Plains. (gr. 4-7). 1993. pap. 6.95 (*0-7910-1957-8*) Chelsea Hse.

Mooney, Martin. The Comanche Indians. (Illus.). 80p. (gr. 2-5). 1993. PLB 12.95 (*0-7910-1653-6*) Chelsea Hse.

Rollings, Willard H. The Comanche. Porter, Frank W., III, intro. by. (Illus.). 112p. (gr. 5 up). 1989. 17.95 (*1-55546-702-4*); pap. 9.95 (*0-7910-0359-0*) Chelsea Hse.

Sanford, William R. Quanah Parker, Comanche Warrior. LC 93-42258. (Illus.). 48p. (gr. 4-10). 1994. lib. bdg. 14.95 (*0-89490-512-0*) Enslow Pubs.

INDIANS OF NORTH AMERICA–COMANCHE INDIANS–FICTION

Keith, Harold. The Sound of Strings: Sequel to Komantcia. LC 91-62777. 175p. (Orig.). (gr. 5 up). 1992. 17.00 (*0-927562-10-3*) Levite Apache.

Meyer, Carolyn. Where the Broken Heart Still Beats. LC 92-257. (gr. 4-7). 1992. write for info. (*0-15-200639-7*) HarBrace.

INDIANS OF NORTH AMERICA–COSTUME AND ADORNMENT

Authentic North American Arctic Circle Indian Clothing for Special Times. (ps-3). write for info. (*0-931363-10-1*) Celia Totus Enter.

Authentic North American California Indian Clothing for Special Times. (ps-3). write for info. (*0-931363-09-8*) Celia Totus Enter.

Authentic North American Columbia River Plateau & California Indian Cradleboards. (ps-5). write for info. (*0-931363-15-2*) Celia Totus Enter.

Authentic North American Columbia River Plateau Indian Clothing for Special Times. (ps-3). write for info. (*0-931363-01-2*) Celia Totus Enter.

Authentic North American Columbia River Plateau Yakima Indian Clothing for Special Times. (ps-3). write for info. (*0-931363-00-4*) Celia Totus Enter.

Authentic North American Great Basin Indian Clothing for Special Times. (ps-3). write for info. (*0-931363-06-3*) Celia Totus Enter.

Authentic North American Great Basin, Southwest, & Southeast Cradleboards. (ps-5). write for info. (*0-931363-13-6*) Celia Totus Enter.

Authentic North American Indian Baby Cradles. (ps-5). write for info. (*0-931363-16-0*) Celia Totus Enter.

Authentic North American Oregon Indian Clothing for Special Times. (ps-3). write for info. (*0-931363-11-X*) Celia Totus Enter.

Authentic North American Pacific Northwest Coast Indian Clothing for Special Times. (ps-3). write for info. (*0-931363-02-0*) Celia Totus Enter.

Authentic North American Pacific Northwest Coast, Woodlands & Arctic Circle Indian Cradles & Cradleboards. (ps-5). write for info. (*0-931363-14-4*) Celia Totus Enter.

Authentic North American Plains Indian Cradle Boards. (ps-3). write for info. (*0-931363-12-8*) Celia Totus Enter.

Authentic North American Plains Indian Clothing for Special Times. (ps-3). write for info. (*0-931363-03-9*) Celia Totus Enter.

Authentic North American Plains Indian Clothing for Special Times. (ps-3). write for info. (*0-931363-05-5*) Celia Totus Enter.

Authentic North American Southeast Indian Clothing for Special Times. (ps-3). write for info. (*0-931363-07-1*) Celia Totus Enter.

Authentic North American Southwest Indian Clothing for Special Times. (ps-3). write for info. (*0-931363-04-7*) Celia Totus Enter.

Authentic North American Woodland Indian Clothing for Special Times. (ps-3). write for info. (*0-931363-08-X*) Celia Totus Enter.

D'Amato, Janet & D'Amato, Alex. Indian Crafts. D'Amato, Janet & D'Amato, Alex, illus. (gr. 2-5). PLB 13.95 (*0-87460-088-X*) Lion Bks.

Hofsinde, Robert. Indian Costumes. Hofsinde, Robert, illus. LC 68-11895. (gr. 3-7). 1968. PLB 12.88 (*0-688-31614-X*) Morrow Jr Bks.

—Indian Warriors & Their Weapons. Hofsinde, Robert, illus. LC 65-11041. (gr. 4-7). 1965. PLB 11.88 (*0-688-31613-1*) Morrow Jr Bks.

White, George M. Craft Manual of North American Indian Footwear. 2nd, rev. ed. (Illus.). 72p. (gr. 4 up). 1992. 4.25 (*1-884693-00-8*) White Pubng.

INDIANS OF NORTH AMERICA–CREE INDIANS–FICTION

Mowat, Farley. Lost in the Barrens. (Illus.). (gr. 7 up). 1956. 15.95 (*0-316-58638-2*, Joy St Bks) Little.

Oliviero, Jamie. The Fish Skin. Morrisseau, Brent, illus. LC 92-85509. 40p. (ps-2). 1993. 14.95 (*1-56282-401-5*); PLB 14.89 (*1-56282-402-3*) Hyprn Child.

INDIANS OF NORTH AMERICA–CREEK INDIANS

Bruchac, Joseph. The Great Ball Game: A Muskogee Story. Roth, Susan L., illus. LC 93-6269. (gr. 4 up). 1994. 14.99 (*0-8037-1539-0*); PLB 14.89 (*0-8037-1540-4*) Dial Bks Young.

Green, Michael D. The Creeks. Porter, Frank, intro. by. (Illus.). 128p. (gr. 5 up). 1990. lib. bdg. 17.95x (*1-55546-703-2*) Chelsea Hse.

Scordato, Ellen. The Creek Indians. LC 92-35972. (Illus.). 80p. (gr. 2-5). 1993. PLB 12.95 (*0-7910-1660-9*); pap. write for info. (*0-7910-1974-8*) Chelsea Hse.

INDIANS OF NORTH AMERICA–CROW INDIANS

Ancona, George, photos by. Powwow. LC 92-15912. (Illus.). 48p. 1993. 16.95 (*0-15-263268-9*) HarBrace.

The Crow Indians. (Illus.). 80p. (gr. 2-5). 1993. PLB 12.95 (*0-7910-1661-7*); pap. write for info. (*0-7910-1964-0*) Chelsea Hse.

Hagman, Ruth. The Crow. LC 90-37679. (Illus.). 48p. (gr. k-4). 1990. PLB 12.85 (*0-516-01103-0*); pap. 4.95 (*0-516-41103-9*) Childrens.

Hatheway, Flora. Chief Plenty Coups: Life of the Crow Indian Chief. (gr. 4). 1971. 4.95 (*0-89992-005-5*) Coun India Ed.

Hoxie, Frederick E. The Crow. (Illus.). 128p. (gr. 5 up). 1989. 17.95 (*1-55546-704-0*); pap. 9.95 (*0-7910-0379-5*) Chelsea Hse.

INDIANS OF NORTH AMERICA–CROW INDIANS–FICTION

McGraw, Eloise J. Moccasin Trail. 256p. (gr. 5-9). 1986. pap. 4.99 (*0-14-032170-5*, Puffin) Puffin Bks.

Sobol, Rose. Woman Chief. 112p. (gr. 5-9). 1979. pap. 1.25 (*0-440-99657-0*, LFL) Dell.

INDIANS OF NORTH AMERICA–CUSTOMS

see Indians of North America–Social Life and Customs

INDIANS OF NORTH AMERICA–DAKOTA INDIANS

Bleeker, Sonia. The Sioux Indians: Hunters & Warriors of the Plains. Sasaki, Kisa N., illus. LC 62-7713. 160p. (gr. 3-6). 1962. PLB 11.88 (*0-688-31457-0*) Morrow Jr Bks.

Bruchac, Joseph. A Boy Called Slow. Baviera, Rocco, illus. LC 93-21233. 1994. write for info. (*0-399-22692-3*, Philomel Bks) Putnam Pub Group.

Sanford, William R. Sitting Bull: Sioux Warrior. LC 93-42255. (Illus.). 48p. (gr. 4-10). 1994. lib. bdg. 14.95 (*0-89490-514-7*) Enslow Pubs.

Stein, R. Conrad. The Story of Wounded Knee. LC 83-6584. (Illus.). 32p. (gr. 3-6). 1983. pap. 3.95 (*0-516-44665-7*) Childrens.

Wood, Ted & Wanbli Numpa Afraid of Hawk. A Boy Becomes a Man at Wounded Knee. 42p. 1992. 15.95 (*0-8027-8174-8*); lib. bdg. 16.85 (*0-8027-8175-6*) Walker & Co.

INDIANS OF NORTH AMERICA–DAKOTA INDIANS–FICTION

Bennett, James. Dakota Dream. LC 93-17854. 144p. (gr. 7 up). 1994. 14.95 (*0-590-46680-1*) Scholastic Inc.

Howe, James, adapted by. Dances with Wolves Storybook: A Story for Children. LC 91-20283. (Illus.). 64p. (ps-2). 1991. bds. 14.95 (*1-55704-104-0*) Newmarket.

Sandoz, Mari. The Story Catcher. LC 85-31810. (Illus.). 175p. (gr. 7-10). 1986. pap. 5.95 (*0-8032-9163-9*, Bison Books) U of Nebr Pr.

Sneve, Virginia D. The Chichi Hoohoo Bogeyman. Agard-Smith, Nadema, illus. LC 93-15909. 63p. (ps-6). 1993. pap. 6.95 (*0-8032-9219-8*, Bison Books) U of Nebr Pr.

—When Thunders Spoke. Lyons, Oren, illus. LC 93-10953. 95p. (gr. 5 up). 1993. pap. 7.95 (*0-8032-9220-1*, Bison Books) U of Nebr Pr.

Wangerin, Walter, Jr. The Crying for a Vision. LC 93-48589. (gr. 7 up). 1994. 16.00 (*0-671-79911-8*, S&S BFYR) S&S Trade.

INDIANS OF NORTH AMERICA–DAKOTA INDIANS–LEGENDS

Bernhard, Emery, retold by. Spotted Eagle & Black Crow: A Lakota Legend. Bernhard, Durga, illus. LC 92-23950. 32p. (ps-3). 1993. reinforced bdg. 15.95 (*0-8234-1007-2*) Holiday.

Goble, Paul. Crow Chief: A Plains Indian Story. Goble, Paul, illus. LC 90-28457. 32p. (ps-2). 1992. 14.95 (*0-531-05947-2*); lib. bdg. 14.99 (*0-531-08547-3*) Orchard Bks Watts.

Goble, Paul, retold by. Iktomi & the Buzzard: A Plains Indian Story. LC 93-24872. (Illus.). 1994. write for info. (*0-531-06812-9*); PLB write for info. (*0-531-08662-3*) Orchard Bks Watts.

Goble, Paul, illus. Adopted by the Eagles. LC 93-24247. (ps up). 1994. 15.95 (*0-02-736575-1*, Bradbury Pr) Macmillan Child Grp.

McGinnis, Mark W. Lakota & Dakota Animal Wisdom Stories. Kaizen, Pamela G., retold by. McGinnis, Mark W., illus. Bruguier, Leonard R., intro. by. (Illus.). 24p. 1994. pap. 11.98 (*1-877976-14-8*, 406-0016) Tipi Pr. LAKOTA & DAKOTA ANIMAL WISDOM STORIES is a compilation

of twelve traditional, northern plains Native American stories retold by Dakota storyteller, Pamela Greenhill Kaizen & are accompanied by twelve full-color illustrations by South Dakota artist & educator Mark W. McGinnis. Leonard R. Bruguier, a descendant of the Yankton chiefs War Eagle & Struck by the Ree, presents the introduction. The stories use animal characters to deal with the themes of compassion, greed, generosity, protection, survival, hard work, laziness, bravery, foolishness, trickery, & others. They range from simple humor as in THE FROG & THE TURTLE BROTHERS, where two close friends decide to jump in the lake rather than catch colds by getting wet in the rain, to the rich & complex story of THE CRANE, which weaves a tale of compassion & caring for one's neighbors. The animal characters give insightful guidance on human morals & ethics, & give a glimpse into the wonderful wit & wisdom of the Lakota & Dakota people. Mark McGinnis' paintings interpret a critical instant from each story, translating the oral moment to a visual expression of color, texture & shapes. This book is well suited to be read to younger children, to be read by older children, or for adults who enjoy new perspectives into Native American culture. Available for $11.98 plus $3.00 S/H from Tipi Press, St. Joseph's Indian School, Chamberlain, SD 57326; 605-734-3300.
Publisher Provided Annotation.

Rubalcaba, Jill, retold by. Uncegila's Seventh Spot: A Dakota Legend. Toddy, Irving, illus. LC 93-33350. 1995. write for info. (*0-395-68970-8*, Clarion Bks) HM.

INDIANS OF NORTH AMERICA–DANCES

DeCesare, Ruth. Myth, Music & Dance of the American Indian. Feldstein, Sandy, et al, eds. Seckler, Judy & Shelly, Walt, illus. 80p. (gr. 4-12). 1988. tchr's. ed. 12.95 (*0-88284-371-0*, 3518); student, 16p 3.95 (*0-88284-372-9*, 3520); Student Songbk., 24p 4.95 (*0-88284-373-7*, 3519); tchr's ed. with cassette 19.95 (*0-88284-383-4*, 3534) Alfred Pub.

Havnen-Finley, Jan. The Hoop of Peace. (Illus.). 1994. pap. 6.95 (*0-87961-239-8*) Naturegraph.
Geared to young readers, but suitable for all ages, THE HOOP OF PEACE shows by drawings & photographs how the Indian hoop dance is performed. It begins with a fascinating story of how a Lakota Indian, Kevin Locke, who from childhood had dreamed of becoming a hoop dancer, learned the art & many of its secret tricks from one of his friends. It was lucky that he did as there are very few of the traditional hoop dancers left & this friend passed on soon afterward. The book provides fascinating insight into the hoop dance & how the hoop, a circle, symbolizes peace to the Lakota & that each circular pattern in Locke's hoop dance represents something from nature, such as a butterfly, eagle, flower, sun & the moon. One Holy Man of the Lakota, Black Elk, had a vision years ago of a time in the future when the then broken hoop of the Lakota would be mended & interlocked with the hoops of many other nations, intertwined in one great circle representing the hoop of mankind. He depicts the world hoop, where the sacred tree blossoms anew in multi-color splendor.
Publisher Provided Annotation.

King, Sandra. Shannon: An Ojibway Dancer. Whipple, Catherine, photos by. Dorris, Michael, frwd. by. LC 92-27261. (Illus.). 48p. 1993. PLB 19.95 (*0-8225-2652-2*) Lerner Pubns.
Medearis, Angela S. Dancing with the Indians: A Reading Rainbow Review Book. Byrd, Samuel, illus. (ps-3). 1993. pap. 5.95 (*0-8234-1023-4*) Holiday.

INDIANS OF NORTH AMERICA–DELAWARE INDIANS

Miller, Jay. The Delaware. LC 93-36670. (Illus.). 48p. (gr. k-4). 1994. PLB 12.85 (*0-516-01053-0*) Childrens.
Myers, Albert C., ed. William Penn's Own Account of Lenni Lenape or Delaware Indians. (Illus.). 96p. (gr. 7 up). 1986. pap. 6.95 (*0-912608-13-7*) Mid Atlantic.

INDIANS OF NORTH AMERICA–DELAWARE INDIANS–FICTION

Harrington, M. R. The Indians of New Jersey: Dickon Among the Lenapes. LC 63-15519. (Illus.). (gr. 4-6). 1963. pap. 9.95x (*0-8135-0425-2*) Rutgers U Pr.

INDIANS OF NORTH AMERICA–DWELLINGS

Brandt, Keith. Indian Homes. Guzzi, George, illus. LC 84-2650. 32p. (gr. 3-6). 1985. PLB 9.49 (*0-8167-0126-1*); pap. text ed. 2.95 (*0-8167-0127-X*) Troll Assocs.
Nashone. Where Indians Live: American Indian Houses. Smith, Louise, illus. 37p. (Orig.). (gr. k-6). 1989. pap. 6.95 (*0-940113-16-3*) Sierra Oaks Pub.
Shemie, Bonnie. Houses of Bark. (Illus.). 24p. (gr. 3-7). 1993. pap. 6.95 (*0-88776-306-5*) Tundra Bks.
—Houses of Hide & Earth. (Illus.). 24p. (gr. 3-7). 1993. pap. 6.95 (*0-88776-307-3*) Tundra Bks.
—Houses of Snow, Skin & Bones. (Illus.). 24p. (gr. 3-7). 1993. pap. 6.95 (*0-88776-305-7*) Tundra Bks.
—Houses of Stone & Adobe: The Southwest. Shemie, Bonnie, illus. LC 93-61789. 24p. (gr. 3-7). 1994. 13.95 (*0-88776-330-8*) Tundra Bks.
—Houses of Wood: Northwest Coast. Shemie, Bonnie, illus. LC 92-80415. 24p. (gr. 3-7). 1994. pap. 6.95 (*0-88776-332-4*) Tundra Bks.
—Houses of Wood: The Northwest Coast. Shemie, Bonnie, illus. LC 92-80415. 24p. (gr. 3-6). 1992. 13.95 (*0-88776-284-0*) Tundra Bks.
—Maisons de Pierres et Adobe: Le Sud-Ouest. Melancon, Charlotte, tr. from ENG. Shemie, Bonnie, illus. LC 93-61790. (FRE.). 24p. (gr. 3-7). 1994. 13.95 (*0-88776-331-6*) Tundra Bks.
—Mounds of Earth & Shell: Native Sites: the Southeast. Shemie, Bonnie, illus. LC 93-60335. 24p. (gr. 3 up). 1993. 13.95 (*0-88776-318-9*) Tundra Bks.
Williamson, Ray A. & Monroe, Jean G. First Houses: Native American Homes & Sacred Structures. Carlson, Susan, illus. LC 92-34900. 160p. 1993. 14.95 (*0-395-51081-3*) HM.

INDIANS OF NORTH AMERICA–EDUCATION–FICTION

Chanin, Michael. Grandfather Four Winds & Rising Moon. Smith, Sally J., illus. LC 93-2689. 32p. 1994. 14.95 (*0-915811-47-2*) H J Kramer Inc.
Rodolph, Stormy. Quest for Courage. Lambert, Paulette L., illus. 112p. (gr. 4-6). 1993. pap. 8.95x (*1-879373-57-2*) R Rinehart.
Sheldon, Dyan. Under the Moon. Blythe, Gary, illus. LC 93-11711. 32p. (ps-3). 1994. 15.99 (*0-8037-1670-2*) Dial Bks Young.

INDIANS OF NORTH AMERICA–FICTION

Armstrong, Nancy. Navajo Long Walk. (gr. 4-9). 1983. pap. 7.95 (*0-89992-083-7*) Coun India Ed.
Asch, Connie. Tohono O'Odham Indian Coloring Book. rev. ed. (Illus.). 32p. (gr. 2-6). 1990. pap. 2.95 (*0-918080-60-6*) Treasure Chest.
Banks, Lynne R. The Indian in the Cupboard. Cole, Brock, illus. 192p. (gr. 4-7). 1982. pap. 3.99 (*0-380-60012-9*, Camelot) Avon.
—Return of the Indian. Geldart, William M., illus. LC 85-31119. 192p. (gr. 4-6). 1986. pap. 13.95 (*0-385-23497-X*) Doubleday.
—The Return of the Indian. (gr. 3-7). 1987. pap. 3.99 (*0-380-70284-3*, Camelot) Avon.
—The Return of the Indian. large type ed. (Illus.). 227p. 1989. PLB 15.95 (*1-55736-104-5*, Crnrstn Bks) BDD LT Grp.
—The Secret of the Indian. 160p. 1990. pap. 3.99 (*0-380-71040-4*, Camelot) Avon.
Banks, Sara H. Remember My Name. Saflund, Birgitta, illus. LC 92-61905. 120p. (Orig.). (gr. 4-8). 1993. pap. 8.95 (*1-879373-38-6*) R Rinehart.
Batdorf, Carol. Seawolf: Building a Canoe. Clark, Patricia, illus. 24p. (Orig.). (gr. 1-6). 1990. pap. 4.95 (*0-88839-247-8*) Hancock House.
—Tinka: A Day in a Little Girl's Life. Batdorf, Carol, illus. 32p. (Orig.). (gr. 1-6). 1990. pap. 5.95 (*0-88839-249-4*) Hancock House.
Baylor, Byrd. Hawk, I'm Your Brother. Parnall, Peter, illus. LC 75-39296. 48p. (ps-3). 1976. SBE 14.95 (*0-684-14571-5*, Scribners Young Read) Macmillan Child Grp.
Benchley, Nathaniel. Red Fox & His Canoe. Lobel, Arnold, illus. LC 64-16650. 64p. (gr. k-3). 1964. PLB 13.89 (*0-06-020476-1*) HarpC Child Bks.
—Small Wolf. Sandin, Joan, illus. LC 93-26717. 64p. (ps-3). 1986. 14.00 (*0-06-020491-5*); PLB 13.89 (*0-06-020492-3*) HarpC Child Bks.
Berry, Gail. Little Fox & the Golden Hawk. Arnold, Elaine, illus. Kremer, John, intro. by. (Illus.). 32p. (gr. 1-9). 1991. 9.50 (*0-912411-36-8*) Open Horizons.
Bird, E. J. The Rainmakers. LC 92-29789. 1993. 19.95 (*0-87614-748-1*) Carolrhoda Bks.
Blevins, Wade. And Then the Feather Fell. Blevins, Wade, illus. Sargent, Dave, intro. by. (Illus.). 48p. (Orig.). (gr. k-8). 1993. text ed. 11.95 (*1-56763-060-X*); pap. text ed. 5.95 (*0-685-67465-7*) Ozark Pub.
—Ganseti & the Legend of the Little People. Blevins, Wade, illus. Sargent, Dave, intro. by. (Illus.). 48p. (Orig.). (gr. k-8). 1993. text ed. 11.95 (*1-56763-065-0*); pap. text ed. 5.95 (*1-56763-066-9*) Ozark Pub.
Blood, Charles L. & Link, Martin. The Goat in the Rug. Parker, Nancy W., illus. LC 80-17315. 40p. (ps-3). 1984. Repr. of 1976 ed. RSBE 14.95 (*0-02-710920-8*, Four Winds) Macmillan Child Grp.
Bolognese, Don. Little Hawk's New Name. Bolognese, Don, illus. LC 93-40723. (gr. 3 up). 1995. pap. 2.95 (*0-590-48292-0*) Scholastic Inc.
Borland, Hal. When the Legends Die. 224p. (gr. 6-12). 1984. pap. 4.50 (*0-553-25738-2*) Bantam.
Brown, Margaret W. David's Little Indian. (ps-3). 1992. pap. 3.25 (*0-440-40587-4*) Dell.
Brown, Margaret Wise. David's Little Indian. LC 89-40295. (Illus.). 48p. (gr. k-4). 1992. Repr. 11.95 (*1-56282-209-8*) Hyprn Child.
Brown, Towana J. Raglagger. Brown, Becky, illus. LC 89-90647. 168p. (Orig.). (gr. 5-7). 1989. pap. 3.50 (*0-9622060-2-4*) T J Brown.
Brown, Vinson. Return of the Indian Spirit. Johnson, W. Cameron, illus. LC 81-65887. 64p. (gr. 5 up). 1982. pap. 7.95 (*0-89087-401-8*) Celestial Arts.
Bruchac, Joseph. Fox Song. Morin, Paul, illus. LC 92-24815. 32p. (ps). 1993. 14.95 (*0-399-22346-0*, Philomel Bks) Putnam Pub Group.
Bulla, Clyde R. Eagle Feather. Two Arrows, Tom, illus. 96p. (gr. 3-7). 1994. pap. 3.99 (*0-14-036730-6*) Puffin Bks.
—Pocahontas & the Strangers. (Illus.). 176p. (gr. 2-6). 1987. pap. 2.95 (*0-590-43481-0*) Scholastic Inc.
Burke, Wallace E. Night Hawk. E. P. Puffin & Co. Staff & Shupe, Bobbi, illus. 225p. (Orig.). 1994. pap. 10.95 (*0-9639014-1-9*) WEB Pubng.
Casler, Leigh. The Boy Who Dreamed of an Acorn. Begay, Shonto, illus. LC 92-44902. 32p. (ps up). 1994. PLB 15.95 (*0-399-22547-1*, Philomel) Putnam Pub Group.
Cavanagh, Helen. Panther Glade. LC 92-23406. 160p. (gr. 5-9). 1993. pap. 15.00 JR3 (*0-671-75617-6*, S&S BFYR) S&S Trade.
Chandonnet, Ann. Chief Stephen's Parky: One Year in the Life of An Athapascan Girl. 2nd ed. Kasl, Janette, illus. LC 92-61910. 80p. (gr. 4-6). 1993. pap. 7.95 (*1-879373-39-4*) R Rinehart.
Clark, Della R. Quiet One. Mignard, Phyllis D., illus. 64p. (ps-5). 1992. 15.00 (*0-9631252-0-6*) Desert Rose.
Clifford, Mary L. When the Great Canoes Came. Haynes, Joyce, illus. LC 92-27913. 1993. 12.95 (*0-88289-926-0*) Pelican.
Cochran, Sallie B. Brave Star & the Necklace. (Illus.). 23p. (Orig.). (gr. 4-7). 1991. pap. 10.95 (*0-9629612-0-5*) Isabels.
Connolly, Thomas E. A Coeur D'Alene Indian Story. 85p. pap. 4.50 (*0-87770-483-X*) Ye Galleon.
Cooper, James Fenimore. Deerslayer. (gr. 6 up). 1964. pap. 1.25 (*0-8049-0031-0*, CL31) Airmont.
—The Deerslayer. 528p. (gr. 9-12). 1991. pap. 3.50 (*0-553-21085-8*, Bantam Classics) Bantam.
—The Deerslayer: or The First War-Path. Wyeth, N. C., illus. LC 90-34326. 480p. 1990. (Scribners Young Read); SBE 24.95 (*0-684-19224-1*, Scribner) Macmillan Child Grp.
—Last of the Mohicans. (gr. 6 up). 1964. pap. 2.95 (*0-8049-0005-1*, CL-5) Airmont.
—The Last of the Mohicans. new & abr. ed. Farr, Naunerle, ed. Carrillo, Fred, illus. (gr. 4-12). 1977. pap. text ed. 2.95 (*0-88301-267-7*) Pendulum Pr.
—The Last of the Mohicans. reissue ed. Wyeth, N. C., illus. LC 86-17694. 376p. 1986. (Scribners Young Read); SBE 25.00 (*0-684-18711-6*, Scribner) Macmillan Child Grp.
—The Last of the Mohicans. 1989. 26.95 (*0-89968-254-5*) Buccaneer Bks.
—The Last of the Mohicans. Martin, Les, adapted by. Stirnweis, Shannon, illus. 96p. (Orig.). (gr. 2-7). 1993. cancelled (*0-679-94706-X*); pap. 3.50 (*0-679-84706-5*) Random Bks Yng Read.
—Pathfinder. (gr. 6 up). 1964. pap. 2.95 (*0-8049-0035-3*, CL-35) Airmont.
Cossi, Olga. Firemate. rev. ed. LC 94-66085. 120p. (gr. 4-8). 1994. pap. 7.95 (*1-879373-87-4*) R Rinehart.
Crew, Linda. Nekomah Creek. (gr. 4-7). 1993. pap. 3.50 (*0-440-40788-5*) Dell.
Curry, Jane L. Back in the Beforetime: Tales of the California Indians. Watts, James, illus. LC 86-21339. 144p. (gr. 3-7). 1987. SBE 13.95 (*0-689-50410-1*, M K McElderry) Macmillan Child Grp.
Cutler, Ebbitt. I Once Knew an Indian Woman. Johnson, Bruce, illus. 72p. (gr. 5 up). 1985. (Dist. by U of Toronto Pr); pap. 6.95 (*0-88776-068-6*) Tundra Bks.
Dalgliesh, Alice. The Courage of Sarah Noble. Weisgard, Leonard, illus. LC 54-5922. 64p. (gr. 1-5). 1987. Repr. of 1954 ed. SBE 13.95 (*0-684-18830-9*, Scribners Young Read) Macmillan Child Grp.

Darwin, Beatrice, illus. If You Lived with the Sioux Indians. 1992. pap. 4.95 (*0-590-45162-6*) Scholastic Inc.

Davis, R. Dell. Ashes & Sparks. LC 89-81718. (Illus.). 172p. (gr. 1-8). 1989. Set. text ed. 24.95 incl. audiotape & slipcase (*0-9616736-1-3*) J Franklin.

Davis, Russell B. & Ashabranner, Brent K. The Choctaw Code. (Illus.). 152p. (gr. 3-6). 1994. Repr. of 1961 ed. lib. bdg. 16.00 (*0-208-02377-1*, Pub. by Linnet) Shoe String.

Deans, Sis B. Blazing Bear. Comyns, Nantz, illus. LC 92-60478. 40p. (gr. 3-7). 1992. pap. 9.95 (*0-932433-94-4*) Windswept Hse.

De Paola, Tomie, ed. & illus. The Legend of the Indian Paintbrush. LC 87-20160. 40p. (ps-2). 1988. 14.95 (*0-399-21534-4*, Putnam) Putnam Pub Group.

Deschaine, Scott. Screaming Eagle. Roy, Mike, illus. 296p. 1993. pap. 11.95 (*1-878181-04-1*) Discovery Comics.

Dorris, Michael. Morning Girl. LC 92-52989. 80p. (gr. 3 up). 1994. 3.50 (*1-56282-661-1*) Hyprn Ppbks.

Downing, Sybil & Barker, Jane V. Mesas to Mountains. (Illus.). 47p. (ps-8). pap. 3.95 (*1-878611-04-6*) Silver Rim Pr.

Dygert, Janice. Red Horse & the Buffalo Robe Man. Gilliland, Hap, ed. (Illus.). (gr. 4-8). 1978. 1.95 (*0-89992-074-8*) Coun India Ed.

Edmiston, Jim. Little Eagle Lots of Owls. Ross, Jane, illus. LC 92-22683. 32p. (gr. k-3). 1993. 13.95 (*0-395-65564-1*) HM.

Elwell, Sharon. Jeremy & the Wappo. Gentry, Debra, illus. 126p. (Orig.). (gr. 3-4). 1991. pap. 10.50 (*0-9626210-0-5*) Rattle OK Pubns.
Bored with Social Studies, a 4th grade boy falls asleep in class & awakes to find himself in a Native American village in the same location 150 years earlier. He is alarmed when the Wappo believe him to be a messenger from the gods & demand he give them instructions. He must find both a message & a way home. During his stay in the Wappo village, he learns to hunt grasshoppers & fish without a hook. He learns authentic games & some of the language that was unique to this isolated triblet. He learns to leech toxins from acorns & catch woodpeckers in a basket. He is surprised that the Wappo are unimpressed with much that he tells them about "the land of the gods." Baseball, however, catches their interest & soon there is an unroarious Wappo version of the game. 4th graders love JEREMY & THE WAPPO: "This is my favorite book!" "I love the part where Jeremy doesn't know what he's eating!" "The baseball game is the funniest part!" "The fishing is the best!" "I cried at the end...but just a little bit." Teachers love it, too: "Beautiful book! It has made a difference." Order from Baker & Taylor or Rattle OK Publications, P.O. Box 5614, Napa, CA 94581, 707-253-9641.
Publisher Provided Annotation.

Fleischman, Paul. Saturnalia. LC 89-36380. 128p. (gr. 7 up). 1990. 14.00 (*0-06-021912-2*); PLB 13.89 (*0-06-021913-0*) HarpC Child Bks.

Fox, Robert B. The Land of the Long White Cloud. LC 92-60489. 169p. (gr. 7 up). 1993. 7.95 (*1-55523-532-8*) Winston-Derek.

Frame, Laurence A. The New Window, la Ventana Nueva, Vol. 1. Frame, Laurence A., illus. (ENG & SPA.). 30p. (gr. 2-8). 1994. pap. 12.00 (*1-884480-54-3*) Spts Curriculum.

Garaway, Margaret K. Dezbah & the Dancing Tumbleweeds. Lowmiller, Cathie, illus. 175p. (Orig.). (gr. 3-5). 1990. pap. 7.95 (*0-918080-50-9*) Treasure Chest.

George, Jean C. The Talking Earth. LC 82-48850. 160p. (gr. 5 up). 1987. pap. 3.95 (*0-06-440212-6*, Trophy) HarpC Child Bks.

Gilliland, Hap. Flint's Rock. Livers-Lambert, Pauline, illus. LC 94-65093. 144p. (Orig.). (gr. 4 up). 1994. pap. 8.95 (*1-879373-82-3*) R Rinehart.

Goble, Paul. Beyond the Ridge. Goble, Paul, illus. LC 92-39786. 32p. (gr. k-3). 1993. pap. 4.95 (*0-689-71731-8*, Aladdin) Macmillan Child Grp.

—The Girl Who Loved Wild Horses. Goble, Paul, illus. LC 92-29560. 32p. (ps-3). 1993. pap. 4.95 (*0-689-71696-6*, Aladdin) Macmillan Child Grp.

Goble, Paul, retold by. & illus. Iktomi & the Berries: A Plains Indian Story. LC 88-23353. 32p. (ps-2). 1992. pap. 5.95 (*0-531-07029-8*) Orchard Bks Watts.

—Iktomi & the Boulder: A Plains Indian Story. LC 87-35789. 32p. (ps-2). 1988. 14.95 (*0-531-05760-7*); PLB 14.99 (*0-531-08360-8*) Orchard Bks Watts.

Gregory, Kristiana. Jenny of the Tetons. 119p. (gr. 3-7). 1989. 13.95 (*0-15-200480-7*) HarBrace.

—Jenny of the Tetons. 140p. (gr. 3-7). 1991. pap. 4.95 (*0-15-200481-5*, HB Juv Bks) HarBrace.

—Legend of Jimmy Spoon. 165p. (gr. 3-7). 1990. 15.95 (*0-15-200506-4*) HarBrace.

Grutman, Jewel H. & Matthaei, Gay, eds. The Ledgerbook of Thomas Blue Eagle. LC 94-8966. (Illus.). 72p. 1994. 17.95 (*1-56566-063-3*) Thomasson-Grant.

Hale, Janet C. The Owl's Song. 144p. (gr. 7 up). 1976. pap. 2.50 (*0-380-00605-7*, 60212-1, Flare) Avon.

Hausman, Gerald. Ghost Walk: Native American Tales of the Spirit. Hausman, Sid, illus. 128p. (Orig.). 1991. pap. 9.95 (*0-933553-07-2*) Mariposa Print Pub.

Highwater, Jamake. ANPAO: An American Indian Odyssey. Scholder, Fritz, illus. LC 77-9264. 256p. (gr. 7 up). 1992. pap. 6.95 (*0-06-440437-4*, Trophy) HarpC Child Bks.

—The Ceremony of Innocence. LC 84-48334. 192p. (gr. 7 up). 1985. HarpC Child Bks.

—I Wear the Morning Star. LC 85-45258. 160p. (gr. 7 up). 1986. HarpC Child Bks.

Hill, Gerald N. The Year of the Indians. Hill, Gerald, Jr., illus. 54p. (Orig.). (gr. 4-7). 1985. pap. 4.95 (*0-912133-06-6*) Hilltop Pub Co.

Hobbs, Will. Bearstone. LC 89-6641. 144p. (gr. 6-9). 1989. SBE 14.95 (*0-689-31496-5*, Atheneum Child Bk) Macmillan Child Grp.

—Bearstone. 160p. (gr. 5). 1991. pap. 3.50 (*0-380-71249-0*, Camelot) Avon.

Hoff, Syd. Little Chief. Hoff, Syd, illus. LC 61-12098. 64p. (gr. k-3). 1961. PLB 13.89 (*0-06-022501-7*) HarpC Child Bks.

Houston, James. Drifting Snow: An Arctic Search. Houston, James, illus. LC 91-42674. 160p. (gr. 5 up). 1992. SBE 13.95 (*0-689-50563-9*, M K McElderry) Macmillan Child Grp.

Houston, James R. Long Claws: An Arctic Adventure. (Illus.). 32p. (ps-3). 1992. pap. 4.99 (*0-14-054522-0*, Puffin) Puffin Bks.

Hudson, Jan. Dawn Rider. 192p. (gr. 6 up). 1990. 14.95 (*0-399-22178-6*, Philomel Bks) Putnam Pub Group.

Huff, Gary. Indian Tales That Teach. 80p. (gr. k-4). 1988. saddle stitch 9.50x (*0-87322-129-X*, 4919, Pub. by YMCA USA) Human Kinetics.

Hull, Robert. Indian Stories. Bateman, Noel, illus. 48p. (gr. 5-9). 1994. 15.95 (*1-56847-189-0*) Thomson Lrning.

Irbinskas, Heather. How Jackrabbit Got His Very Long Ears. Spengler, Ken, illus. LC 93-38250. 32p. (gr. k up). 1994. 14.95 (*0-87358-566-6*) Northland AZ.

Irwin, Hadley. We Are Mesquakie, We Are One. LC 80-19000. 128p. (gr. 5 up). 1980. 10.95 (*0-912670-85-1*) Feminist Pr.

Jacobs, Shannon K. Boy Who Loved Morning. (ps-3). 1993. 15.95 (*0-316-45556-3*) Little.

James, Betsy. The Mud Family. Morin, Paul, illus. LC 92-43537. 32p. (ps-3). 1994. PLB 15.95 (*0-399-22549-8*, Putnam) Putnam Pub Group.

James, J. Alison. Sing for a Gentle Rain. LC 90-639. 224p. (gr. 7 up). 1990. SBE 14.95 (*0-689-31561-9*, Atheneum Child Bk) Macmillan Child Grp.

Kachel, Limana. Homer Littlebird's Rabbit: Cheyenne Indian Story for Children. 32p. (ps-2). 1983. pap. 2.45 (*0-89992-084-5*) Coun India Ed.

Katz, Welwyn W. False Face. LC 88-12847. 176p. (gr. 5-9). 1988. SBE 14.95 (*0-689-50456-X*, M K McElderry) Macmillan Child Grp.

Killingsworth, Monte. Circle Within a Circle. LC 93-17244. 176p. (gr. 7 up). 1994. SBE 14.95 (*0-689-50598-1*, M K McElderry) Macmillan Child Grp.

Kissinger, Rosemary. Quanah Parker: Comanche Chief. LC 90-23036. (Illus.). 96p. (ps-8). 1991. 12.95 (*0-88289-785-3*) Pelican.

Koller, Jackie F. The Primrose Way. 1992. write for info. (*0-15-256745-3*, Gulliver Bks) HarBrace.

Kroeber, Theodora. Ishi: Last of His Tribe. Robbins, Ruth, illus. 208p. 1964. PLB 14.45 (*0-395-27644-6*) HM.

Lampman, Evelyn S. Treasure Mountain. (Illus.). 207p. (gr. 4). 1990. pap. 6.95 (*0-87595-231-3*) Oregon Hist.

Larrabee, Lisa. Grandmother Five Baskets. Sawyer, Lori, illus. LC 93-10451. 64p. (gr. 3-7). 1993. 14.95 (*0-943173-86-8*); pap. 9.95 (*0-943173-90-6*) Harbinger AZ.

Lasky, Kathryn. Cloud Eyes. Moser, Barry, illus. LC 93-37805. (gr. k-5). 1994. 14.95 (*0-15-219168-2*) HarBrace.

Levin, Betty. Brother Moose. LC 89-34437. (gr. 5 up). 1990. 12.95 (*0-688-09266-7*) Greenwillow.

Lipsyte, Robert. The Brave. LC 90-25396. 208p. (gr. 7 up). 1993. pap. 3.95 (*0-06-447079-2*, Trophy) HarpC Child Bks.

—The Chief. LC 92-54502. 240p. (gr. 7 up). 1993. 15.00 (*0-06-021064-8*); PLB 14.89 (*0-06-021068-0*) HarpC Child Bks.

Locker, Thomas. The Land of Gray Wolf. Locker, Thomas, illus. LC 90-3915. 32p. (ps up). 1991. 15.95 (*0-8037-0936-6*); lib. bdg. 15.89 (*0-8037-0937-4*) Dial Bks Young.

Longfellow, Henry Wadsworth. Hiawatha. LC 83-26972. (Illus.). (gr. 2-5). 1984. PLB 19.97 (*0-8172-2106-9*); PLB 29.28 incl. cassette (*0-8172-2237-5*); pap. 23.95 incl. cassette (*0-8172-2265-0*) Raintree Steck-V.

MacGregor, Miles. The Sunflower. Thatch, Nancy R., ed. MacGregor, Miles, illus. Melton, David, intro. by. (Illus.). 29p. (gr. 3-6). 1994. PLB 14.95 (*0-933849-52-4*) Landmark Edns.

McNickle, D'Arcy. Runner in the Sun. Houser, Allan C., illus. LC 87-5986. 260p. 1987. pap. 11.95 (*0-8263-0974-7*) U of NM Pr.

Marsh, Carole. Those Whose Names Were Terrible. Rhodes, Priscilla, illus. (Orig.). (gr. 4-8). 1994. pap. 14.95 (*0-935326-48-0*) Gallopade Pub Group.

Martin, Bill, Jr. & Archambault, John. Knots on a Counting Rope. Rand, Ted, illus. LC 87-14832. 32p. (ps-2). 1987. 14.95 (*0-8050-0571-4*, Bks Young Read) H Holt & Co.

Matthews, Kay. An Anasazi Welcome. Belknap, Barbara, illus. LC 92-796. 40p. (gr. 1-6). 1992. pap. 6.95 (*1-878610-27-9*) Red Crane Bks.

Mayo, Gretchen W. North American Indian Stories, 4 vols. Mayo, Gretchen W., illus. 256p. (gr. 5 up). 1990. Set. pap. 23.80 (*0-8027-7341-9*) Walker & Co.

Meyer, Kathleen A. Tul-Tok-A-Na: The Small One. Hardgrove, Tanya, illus. 32p. (Orig.). (gr. 1-5). 1992. pap. 6.95 (*0-89992-105-1*) Coun India Ed.

Mikaelsen, Ben. Sparrow Hawk Red. LC 92-53458. 224p. (gr. 5-9). 1993. 14.95 (*1-56282-387-6*); PLB 14.89 (*1-56282-388-4*) Hyprn Child.

Mills, Jackie. Sirena of Salado. Mills, Jackie, illus. 32p. (gr. 2-7). 1991. 10.95 (*0-9629284-0-2*) Indian Trail.

Morris, Gilbert. The Rustlers of Panther Gap. LC 94-7128. (gr. 3-7). 1994. pap. 4.99 (*0-8423-4393-8*) Tyndale.

Murphy, Barbara B. Eagles in Their Flight. LC 93-11438. 1994. 14.95 (*0-385-32035-3*) Delacorte.

O'Dell, Scott. Island of the Blue Dolphins. Lewin, Ted, illus. 192p. (gr. 5 up). 1990. 18.45 (*0-395-53680-4*) HM.

—The Serpent Never Sleeps: A Novel of Jamestown & Pocahontas. Lewin, Ted, illus. 240p. (gr. 5 up). 1987. 16.95 (*0-395-44242-7*) HM.

—Streams to the River, River to the Sea: A Novel of Sacagawea. 1986. 14.45 (*0-395-40430-4*) HM.

—Streams to the River, River to the Sea: A Novel of Sacagawea. large type ed. 312p. (gr. 7 up). 1989. lib. bdg. 14.95 (*0-8161-4811-2*, Large Print Bks) Hall.

Osofsky, Audrey. Dreamcatcher. Young, Ed, illus. LC 91-20029. 32p. (ps-2). 1992. 14.95 (*0-531-05988-X*); lib. bdg. 14.99 (*0-531-08588-0*) Orchard Bks Watts.

Parish, Peggy. Good Hunting, Blue Sky. Watts, James, illus. LC 84-43143. 64p. (gr. k-3). 1988. PLB 14.89 (*0-06-024662-6*) HarpC Child Bks.

—Good Hunting, Blue Sky. Watts, James, illus. LC 84-43143. 64p. (gr. k-3). 1991. pap. 3.50 (*0-06-444148-2*, Trophy) HarpC Child Bks.

Peck, Robert. Jo Silver. LC 85-3720. 144p. (gr. 8-12). 1985. 9.95 (*0-910923-20-5*) Pineapple Pr.

Peyton, John L. Voices from the Ice. Peyton, John L., illus. 56p. (gr. k-4). 1990. pap. 7.95 (*0-939923-15-7*) M & W Pub Co.

Phillips, JoAnn. The Run According to Hawkeye. Holden, Tim P., illus. Ogle, John C., intro. by. (Illus.). 24p. (Orig.). 1993. pap. 9.95 (*0-9638403-0-4*) Cherokee Strip.

Pomerantz, Charlotte. Timothy Tall Feather. Stock, Catherine, illus. LC 85-24819. 32p. (gr. k-3). 1986. 11.75 (*0-688-04246-5*); PLB 11.88 (*0-688-04247-3*) Greenwillow.

Puffer, Darrick J. I'm Not Your Angel. LC 92-60490. 241p. (gr. 7 up). 1993. pap. 8.95 (*1-55523-533-6*) Winston-Derek.

Qualey, Marsha. Revolutions of the Heart. LC 92-24528. 192p. (gr. 6 up). 1993. 13.45 (*0-395-64168-3*) HM.

Reaver, Chap. A Little Bit Dead. LC 92-7185. 192p. (gr. 6 up). 1992. 15.00 (*0-385-30801-9*) Delacorte.

—A Little Bit Dead. large type ed. LC 93-42210. 1994. pap. 15.95 (*0-7862-0139-8*) Thorndike Pr.

Riddell, Chris. The Bear Dance. LC 90-9475. (Illus.). 32p. (ps-4). 1993. pap. 7.95 (*0-671-79852-9*, S&S BYR) S&S Trade.

Rodolph, Stormy. Quest for Courage. Lucero, Ruth, illus. 102p. (Orig.). (gr. 5-12). 1984. pap. 8.95 (*0-89992-092-6*) Coun India Ed.

Roop, Peter. Natosi: Strong Medicine. 32p. (gr. 3-8). 1984. pap. 2.45 (*0-89992-090-X*) Coun India Ed.

—Sik-Ki-Mi. 32p. (gr. 3-6). 1984. pap. 1.95 (*0-89992-091-8*) Coun India Ed.

Root, Phyllis. The Listening Silence. McDermott, Dennis, illus. LC 90-37425. 128p. (gr. 3-7). 1992. 14.00 (*0-06-025092-5*); PLB 13.89 (*0-06-025093-3*) HarpC Child Bks.

Ruemmler, John. Smoke on the Water: A Novel of Jamestown & the Powhatans. LC 91-42587. (Illus.). 176p. (gr. 7 up). 1992. pap. 6.95 (*1-55870-239-3*, 70099) Shoe Tree Pr.

Rumbaut, Hendle. Dove Dream. LC 93-26538. 1994. write for info. (*0-395-68393-9*) HM.

Run, Johnny, Run. (gr. 7 up). 1993. 19.95 (*0-9630328-6-0*) SDPI.

Russell, Sharman A. The Humpbacked Fluteplayer. LC 92-44492. 1994. 16.00 (*0-679-82408-1*) Knopf Bks Yng Read.

Sandoz, Mari. The Horsecatcher. LC 86-4360. 192p. (gr. 5-8). 1986. pap. 6.95 (*0-8032-9160-4*, Bison Books) U of Nebr Pr.
—The Story Catcher. LC 85-31810. (Illus.). 175p. (gr. 7-10). 1986. pap. 5.95 (*0-8032-9163-9*, Bison Books) U of Nebr Pr.
San Souci, Robert D. Legend of Scarface. San Souci, Daniel, illus. LC 77-15170. 40p. (gr. k-3). 1987. pap. 7.00 (*0-385-15874-2*, Pub. by Zephyr-BFYR) Doubleday.
Schultz, James W. The Loud Mouthed Gun. (gr. 4-8). 1984. pap. 4.95 (*0-89992-095-0*) Coun India Ed.
—Story of Running Eagle. (gr. 2-10). 1984. pap. 3.95 (*0-89992-093-4*) Coun India Ed.
Scieszka, Jon. The Good, the Bad, & the Goofy. Smith, Lane, illus. LC 93-15136. 80p. (gr. 2-5). 1993. pap. 2.99 (*0-14-036170-7*, Puffin) Puffin Bks.
Scott, Ann H. On Mother's Lap. Coalson, Glo, illus. 32p. (ps-k). 1992. 14.45 (*0-395-58920-7*, Clarion Bks); pap. 5.70 (*0-395-62976-4*, Clarion Bks) HM.
Searcy, Margaret Z. The Charm of the Bear Claw Necklace. Brough, Hazel, illus. LC 89-78044. 80p. (gr. 3-7). 1990. 13.95 (*0-88289-821-3*); pap. 6.95 (*0-88289-777-2*) Pelican.
—Wolf Dog of the Woodland Indians. Brough, Hazel, illus. LC 90-26215. 112p. (Orig.). (ps-8). 1991. pap. 6.95 (*0-88289-778-0*) Pelican.
Sharpe, Susan. Spirit Quest. Sharpe, Kate & Sharpe, Alison, illus. LC 91-4417. 128p. (gr. 4-6). 1991. SBE 13.95 (*0-02-782355-5*, Bradbury Pr) Macmillan Child Grp.
—Spirit Quest. 128p. (gr. 3-7). 1993. pap. 3.99 (*0-14-036282-7*) Puffin Bks.
Shefelman, Janice. A Mare for Young Wolf. Shefelman, Tom, illus. LC 91-42749. 48p. (Orig.). (gr. 2-3). 1993. PLB 7.99 (*0-679-93445-6*); pap. 3.50 (*0-679-83445-1*) Random Bks Yng Read.
Siberell, Anne. Whale in the Sky. Siberell, Anne, illus. LC 82-2483. 32p. (ps-3). 1985. 13.95 (*0-525-44021-6*, DCB); pap. 3.95 (*0-525-44197-2*, DCB) Dutton Child Bks.
Spinka, Penina K. Mother's Blessing. LC 91-31342. 224p. (gr. 5-9). 1992. SBE 14.95 (*0-689-31758-1*, Atheneum Child Bk) Macmillan Child Grp.
—White Hare's Horses. LC 90-42777. 160p. (gr. 5-9). 1991. SBE 13.95 (*0-689-31654-2*, Atheneum Child Bk) Macmillan Child Grp.
Strelkoff, Tatiana. The Changer. (Illus.). 96p. (gr. 4-6). 1994. pap. 8.95 (*0-945522-03-7*) Rebecca Hse.
Stroud, Virginia A. Doesn't Fall off His Horse. (Illus.). (gr. 2 up). 1994. 14.99 (*0-8037-1634-6*); PLB 14.89 (*0-8037-1635-4*) Dial Bks Young.
Tanaka, Beatrice. The Chase: A Kutenai Indian Tale. Gay, Michael, illus. LC 91-10790. 32p. (ps-2). 1991. lib. bdg. 14.99 (*0-517-58624-X*) Crown Bks Yng Read.
Taylor, C. J. Deux Plumes et la Solitude Disparue. Taylor, C. J., illus. 24p. (gr. 1-5). 1990. 13.95 (*0-88776-255-7*) Tundra Bks.
—How Two-Feather Was Saved from Loneliness. Taylor, C. J., illus. LC 90-70138. 24p. (gr. 1-5). 1990. 13.95 (*0-88776-254-9*) Tundra Bks.
Taylor, Morris. Top of the Hill. 64p. 1988. pap. 4.95 (*0-87961-183-9*) Naturegraph.
Thomasma, Kenneth. Kunu: Winnebago Boy Escapes. Fleuter, Craig, illus. LC 89-15074. 183p. (ps-8). 1992. 10.99 (*0-8010-8891-7*); pap. 6.99 (*0-8010-8892-5*) Baker Bk.
—Moho Wat: A Sheepeater Boy Attempts a Rescue. Brouwer, Jack, illus. LC 94-4074. 176p. (Orig.). (gr. 4-7). 1994. 10.99 (*0-8010-8918-2*); pap. 6.99 (*0-8010-8919-0*) Baker Bk.

—Moho Wat: Sheepeater Boy Attempts A Rescue. Brouwer, Jack, illus. 184p. 1994. 10.95 (*1-880114-14-3*); pap. 6.95 (*1-880114-13-5*) Grandview.
Moho Wat is a Sheepeater Indian boy living in what is now Yellowstone National Park. In a violent encounter with a mountain lion, the boy loses his left hand. Although devastated, Moho Wat struggles to overcome his loss & teaches himself to hunt using his feet to hold his bow & arrow. After a trip to the sacred Medicine Wheel, his courage & strength are tested when he makes a dangerous attempt to rescue the beautiful girl, Wind Flower, who was taken captive by a large enemy tribe. He does eveything he can to prove he is as good as any other boy. One day his father will say, "You have shown your bravery & skill. I am proud of my son, Moho Wat. To order call: 1-800-525-7344. Grandview Publishing, Box 2863, Jackson, WY 83001.
Publisher Provided Annotation.

—Pathki Nana: Kootenai Girl. (gr. 3-8). 1991. 9.95 (*1-880114-10-0*); pap. 6.95 (*1-880114-09-7*) Grandview.
Toussant, Eliza. Brave Little Blackfoot. Douglas, Cal, illus. 32p. (Orig.). (gr. 1 up). 1993. pap. text ed. write for info. (*0-9630583-3-9*) E Toussant.
Weechees. Sun Boy & His Hunter's Bow. 32p. (gr. 4-8). 1988. pap. 4.95 (*0-89992-115-9*) Coun India Ed.
—Sun Boy & the Angry Panther. 32p. (gr. 4-8). 1988. pap. 4.95 (*0-89992-114-0*) Coun India Ed.
—Sun Boy & the Monster of To-Oh-Pah. 32p. (gr. 4-8). 1988. pap. 4.95 (*0-89992-113-2*) Coun India Ed.
—Sun Boy: Cou-Yan-Nai: Comanche Indian Story for Children. 32p. (gr. 4-9). 1983. pap. 1.95 (*0-686-44422-1*) Coun India Ed.
Welsch, Roger. Uncle Smoke Stories: Four Fires in the Big Belly Lodge of the Nehawka. Bleck, Cathie, illus. LC 93-48309. 96p. (gr. 3-7). 1994. 15.00 (*0-679-85450-9*); PLB write for info. (*0-679-95450-3*) Knopf.
Wesche, Alice M. Runs Far, Son of the Chichimecs. (gr. 3-7). 1982. pap. 7.95 (*0-89013-133-3*) Museum NM Pr.
Whelan, Gloria. Night of the Full Moon. Bowman, Leslie, illus. LC 93-6706. 64p. (gr. 2-4). 1993. 13.00 (*0-679-84464-3*); PLB 13.99 (*0-679-94464-8*) Knopf Bks Yng Read.
White Deer of Autumn Staff. Native American Book of Knowledge. Roehm, Michelle, ed. (Illus.). 96p. (gr. 5-7). 1992. pap. 4.95 (*0-941831-42-6*) Beyond Words Pub.
—The Native American Book of Life. Roehm, Michelle, ed. (Illus.). 96p. (gr. 5-7). 1992. pap. 4.95 (*0-941831-43-4*) Beyond Words Pub.
White Deer of Autumn. Ceremony in the Circle of Life. San Souci, Daniel, illus. 32p. (gr. 2-6). 1991. pap. 6.95 (*0-941831-68-X*) Beyond Words Pub.
—The Great Change. (Illus.). 36p. (gr. k-5). 1992. 13.95 (*0-941831-79-5*) Beyond Words Pub.
Wisler, G. Clifton. The Raid. 128p. (gr. 5 up). 1994. pap. 3.99 (*0-14-036937-6*) Puffin Bks.
—Red Cap. 176p. (gr. 5 up). 1994. pap. 3.99 (*0-14-036936-8*) Puffin Bks.
Wisniewski, David. The Wave of the Sea-Wolf. LC 93-18265. 1994. 16.95 (*0-395-66478-0*, Clarion Bks) HM.
Worcester, Donald. Lone Hunter's Gray Pony. Pauley, Paige, illus. LC 84-16157. 70p. (gr. 4 up). 1985. 10.95 (*0-87565-001-5*) Tex Christian.
Worcester, Donald E. Lone Hunter's Gray Pony & Lone Hunter & the Cheyennes & War Pony. 1992. Boxed set. 29.95 (*0-87565-109-7*) Tex Christian.
—War Pony. Pauley, Paige, illus. LC 83-40486. 96p. (gr. 4 up). 1984. Repr. of 1961 ed. 10.95 (*0-912646-85-3*) Tex Christian.
Yerxa, Leo. Last Leaf First Snowflake to Fall. LC 93-5775. (Illus.). 32p. (gr. k-3). 1994. 14.95 (*0-531-06824-2*); lib. bdg. 14.99 (*0-531-08674-7*) Orchard Bks Watts.

INDIANS OF NORTH AMERICA–FOLKLORE

see Folklore, Indian

INDIANS OF NORTH AMERICA–GAMES

Whitney, Alex. Sports & Games the Indians Gave Us. Ostberg, Marie & Ostberg, Nils, illus. (gr. 7 up). 1977. 7.95 (*0-679-20391-5*) McKay.

INDIANS OF NORTH AMERICA–GOVERNMENT RELATIONS

Bealer, Alex. Only the Names Remain: The Cherokees & the Trail of Tears. Bock, William S., illus. (gr. 4-6). 1972. lib. bdg. 15.95 (*0-316-08520-0*) Little.
Kelly, Lawrence C. Federal Indian Policy. (Illus.). 112p. (gr. 5 up). 1990. 17.95 (*1-55546-706-7*) Chelsea Hse.
McClard, Megan & Ypsilantis, George. Hiawatha. Furstinger, Nancy, ed. (Illus.). 138p. (gr. 5-7). 1989. PLB 10.95 (*0-382-09568-5*); pap. 7.95 (*0-382-09757-2*) Silver Burdett Pr.
Sober, Nancy H. The Intruders: The Illegal Residents of the Cherokee Nation, 1866-1907. 2nd ed. LC 90-84850. (Illus.). 222p. (gr. 12). 1991. PLB 24.95 (*0-9628188-0-1*) Cherokee Bks.

INDIANS OF NORTH AMERICA–HAIDA INDIANS

Beck, Mary L. Heroes & Heroines in Tlingit-Haida Legend. DeWitt, Nancy, illus. LC 89-14931. 126p. (Orig.). (gr. 8 up). 1989. pap. 12.95 (*0-88240-334-6*) Alaska Northwest.
Bonvillain, Nancy. The Haidas: People of the Northwest Coast. LC 93-34902. 64p. (gr. 4-6). 1994. PLB 15.40 (*1-56294-491-6*) Millbrook Pr.

INDIANS OF NORTH AMERICA–HISTORY

see also Indians of North America–Wars

Aragon, Hilda, illus. A Pueblo Village. 8p. (Orig.). (ps-7). 1982. pap. 4.00 (*0-915347-17-2*) Pueblo Acoma Pr.
Armstrong, Nancy, et al. The Heritage. (gr. 3-6). 1977. 1.95 (*0-89992-065-9*) Coun India Ed.
Beyer, Don E. The Totem Pole Indians of the Northwest. (Illus.). 64p. (gr. 3 up). 1991. pap. 5.95 (*0-531-15607-9*) Watts.
Black, Sheila. Sitting Bull. Furstinger, Nancy, ed. (Illus.). 144p. (gr. 5-7). 1989. PLB 10.95 (*0-382-09572-3*); pap. 7.95 (*0-382-09761-0*) Silver Burdett Pr.
Bonvillain, Nancy. The Sac & Fox. LC 94-21846. 1995. write for info. (*0-7910-1684-6*) Chelsea Pub.
Boss-Ribs, Mary C. & Running-Crane, Jenny. Stories of Our Blackfeet Grandmothers. (Orig.). (gr. 1-6). 1984. pap. 4.95 (*0-89992-096-9*) Coun India Ed.
Brian, J. & Freeman, Jodi L. The Old Ones: A Children's Book about the Anasazi Indians. Flanagan, Terry, illus. LC 86-50383. 64p. (Orig.). (gr. k-4). 1986. pap. 2.95 (*0-937871-27-3*) Think Shop.
Brown, Dee. Wounded Knee: An Indian History of the American West. Ehrlick, Emy, adapted by. 192p. (gr. 7 up). 1975. pap. 1.50 (*0-440-95768-0*, LFL) Dell.
Cordoba, Maria. PreColumbian Peoples of North America. LC 94-16112. (Illus.). 36p. (gr. 3 up). 1994. PLB 20.00 (*0-516-08393-7*); pap. 6.95 (*0-516-48393-5*) Childrens.
Cwiklik, Robert. King Philip. Furstinger, Nancy, ed. (Illus.). 144p. (gr. 5-7). 1989. PLB 10.95 (*0-382-09573-1*); pap. 7.95 (*0-382-09762-9*) Silver Burdett Pr.
—Sequoyah. Furstinger, Nancy, ed. (Illus.). 142p. (gr. 5-7). 1989. PLB 10.95 (*0-382-09570-7*); pap. 7.95 (*0-382-09759-9*) Silver Burdett Pr.
Eargle, Dolan H., Jr. California Indian Country: The Land & the People. LC 91-67406. (Illus.). (gr. 4). 1992. pap. 12.70 (*0-937401-20-X*) Trees Co Pr.
—Earth Is Our Mother: A Guide to the Indians of California: Their Locales & Historic Sites. Record, Nancy, illus. LC 88-51438. (gr. 4). 1993. pap. 12.95 (*0-937401-09-9*) Trees Co Pr.
Egloff, Keith & Woodward, Deborah, eds. First People: The Early Indians of Virginia. (Illus.). 68p. (gr. 5-8). 1992. pap. 11.95 (*0-8139-1474-4*) U Pr of Va.
Fox, Mary V. Chief Joseph of the Nez Perce Indians: Champion of Liberty. LC 92-35053. (Illus.). 152p. (gr. 4 up). 1992. PLB 14.40 (*0-516-03275-5*) Childrens.
Guttmacher, Peter. Crazy Horse, Sioux War Chief. LC 93-38545. 1994. write for info. (*0-7910-1712-5*); pap. write for info. (*0-7910-2045-2*) Chelsea Hse.
Hardgrove, Tanya. Alaska in the Days That Were Before. (gr. 2-10). 1985. pap. 2.45 (*0-89992-098-5*) Coun India Ed.
Harvey, Karen D. & Harjo, Lisa D. Indian Country: A History of Native People in America. (Illus.). 400p. (gr. 4-12). 1994. 27.95x (*1-55591-911-1*, North Amer Pr) Fulcrum Pub.
Hirschfelder, Arlene. Artists & Craftspeople. (Illus.). 128p. (gr. 4-11). 1994. 16.95x (*0-8160-2960-1*) Facts on File.
Katz, William. Black Indians: A Hidden Heritage. LC 85-28770. (Illus.). 208p. (gr. 5 up). 1986. SBE 16.95 (*0-689-31196-6*, Atheneum Child Bk) Macmillan Child Grp.
Krull, Kathleen. One Nation, Many Tribes: How Kids Live in Milwaukee's Indian Community. Hautzig, David, photos by. LC 93-39538. 1994. write for info. (*0-525-67440-3*, Lodestar Bks) Dutton Child Bks.
Liptak, Karen. North American Indian Tribal Chiefs. Mathews, V., ed. LC 91-30261. (Illus.). 64p. (gr. 3-6). 1992. PLB 12.90 (*0-531-20101-5*) Watts.
Querry, Ron. Native American Struggle for Equality. LC 92-7474. 1992. 22.60 (*0-86593-179-8*); 16.95s.p. (*0-685-59320-7*) Rourke Corp.
Ruoff, A. LaVonne. Literatures of the American Indian. (Illus.). 112p. (gr. 5 up). 1991. PLB 17.95 (*1-55546-688-5*) Chelsea Hse.
Ruppel, Maxine. Vostaas: The Story of Montana's Indian Nations. (gr. 3-11). 1970. 5.95 (*0-89992-001-2*) Coun India Ed.
Sansom-Flood, Renee & Bernie, Shirley A. Remember Your Relatives, Vol. 1: Yankton Sioux Images, 1851 to 1904. Bruguier, Leonard R., ed. Flood, William J., et al, illus. Hoover, Herbert T., intro. by. 55p. (Orig.). (gr. 12). 1985. pap. 8.50 (*0-9621936-0-7*) Yankton Sioux Tribe.
Shuter, Jane, intro. by. Francis Parkman & the Plains Indians. LC 94-12853. (gr. 5 up). 1995. write for info. (*0-8114-8280-4*) Raintree Steck-V.
Stickney, Joy. Native Americans along the Oregon Trail. Stickney, Joy, illus. 24p. (Orig.). (gr. 4-6). 1993. pap. 4.50 (*1-884563-02-3*) Canyon Creat.
Swann, L. Marie. The Sacred Lake, 3 bks. Swann, L. Marie, illus. (gr. 3-4). 1992. Set. pap. text ed. 25.00 (*1-882156-05-6*) Eye Of The Eagle.
—The Sacred Lake: A History of the Washo Tribe (Native American) Prior to the Coming of the Europeans. 65p. (gr. 3-4). 1992. PLB 14.00 (*1-882156-01-3*); pap. text ed. 12.00 (*1-882156-00-5*) Eye Of The Eagle.
Swann, Marie L. The Sacred Lake Activity Book: Activities to Accompany Reading "The Sacred Lake" 51p. (gr. 3-4). 1992. Repr. of 1991 ed. wkbk. 8.00 (*1-882156-04-8*) Eye Of The Eagle.
Utter, Jack. Wounded Knee & the Ghost Dance Tragedy. LC 91-61211. (Illus.). iv, 29p. (Orig.). (gr. 10-12). 1991. pap. 3.95 (*0-9628075-1-6*) Natl Woodlands Pub.
Washburne, Carolyn K. A Multicultural Portrait of Colonial Life. LC 93-10320. (gr. 7 up). 1993. 18.95 (*1-85435-657-7*) Marshall Cavendish.
Yue, Charlotte. The Tipi: A Center of Native American Life. Yue, David, illus. LC 83-19529. 96p. (gr. 4-7). 1984. PLB 11.99 (*0-394-96177-3*) Knopf Bks Yng Read.

INDIANS OF NORTH AMERICA–HISTORY–FICTION

Goble, Paul. Death of the Iron Horse. Goble, Paul, illus. LC 92-1723. 32p. (ps-3). 1993. pap. 4.95 (*0-689-71686-9*, Aladdin) Macmillan Child Grp.

Thomasma, Kenneth. Amazing Indian Children. (gr. 3-8). 1991. 9.95 (*1-880114-12-7*); pap. 6.95

(*0-685-49336-9*) Grandview. AMAZING INDIAN CHILDREN is a series of five books, historic fiction written for a third grade read-ability. They are packed with Indian lore, history, geography & high adventure. Each book has a child as the central character who lives during a key time in that tribe's history. Through the Indian child's eyes the reader relives dramatic historic events. These books are accurately researched & are in use in over 1000 schools. They have been translated into Danish, Dutch, Eskimo & Spanish. Over 300,000 have been sold. NAYA NUKI: GIRL WHO RAN-ISBN 1-880114-01-1 cloth; 1-880114-00-3 pbk. With her friend, Sacagewea, a Shoshoni Indian Girl is taken prisoner, escapes & makes a 1000 mile wilderness journey back to her people. SOUN TETOKEN: NEZ PERCE BOY-ISBN 1-880114-08-9 cloth; 1-880114-07-0 pbk. Although mute since the death of his parents in a forest fire a young boy in Chief Joseph's band lives a happy adventurous life until the War of 1877 changes his life forever. OM-KAS-TOE OF THE BLACKFEET-ISBN 1-880114-06-2 cloth; 1-880114-05-4 pbk. Life changes dramatically for the Blackfeet people in the early 1700s when a twin brother & sister discover a strange animal & succeed in capturing it & returning it to their tribe. KUNU: ESCAPE ON THE MISSOURI-ISBN 1-880114-04-6 cloth; 1-880114-03-8 pbk. Following the forced removal of his people from Minnesota to South Dakota, a Winnebago Indian boy & his dying grandfather embark on a dangerous river journey back to their homeland. PATHKI NANA: KOOTENAI GIRL-ISBN 1-880114-10-0 cloth; 1-880114-09-7 pbk. A 9 year-old Kootenai girl with a very poor self-image leaves her village to seek her guardian spirit & finds herself in a life & death struggle with an evil man who seeks to end her life before she can return to her people. MOHO WAT: SHEEPEATER BOY ATTEMPTS A RESCUE; ISBN 1-880114-14-3 cloth; 1-880114-13-5 pbk. To order call 1-800-525-7344.
Publisher Provided Annotation.

INDIANS OF NORTH AMERICA–HOPI INDIANS

Hartley, Eugene L. Hopi Shields & the Best Defense. 32p. (gr. 3-8). 1991. pap. 4.95 (*0-89992-127-2*) Coun India Ed.

Levin, Beatrice & Vanderveld, Marjorie. Me Run Fast Good: Biographies of Tewanima (Hopi), Carlos Montezuma (Apache) & John Horse (Seminole) 32p. (gr. 5-9). 1983. pap. 1.95 (*0-89992-087-X*) Coun India Ed.

Mike, Jan M. Kachi; a Hopi Girl: Historical Paper Doll Book to Read, Color & Cut. Lowmiller, Cathie, illus. 32p. (gr. k-6). 1989. pap. 3.95 (*0-918080-47-9*) Treasure Chest.

Sherrow, Victoria. The Hopis: Pueblo People of the Southwest. LC 92-45055. (Illus.). 64p. (gr. 4-6). 1993. PLB 15.40 (*1-56294-314-6*) Millbrook Pr.

Tomchek, Ann. The Hopi. LC 87-8037. (Illus.). 48p. (gr. k-4). 1987. PLB 12.85 (*0-516-01234-7*); pap. 4.95 (*0-516-41234-5*) Childrens.

INDIANS OF NORTH AMERICA–HOPI INDIANS–FICTION

Landau, Elaine. The Hopi. LC 93-31964. 1994. 12.90 (*0-531-20098-1*); pap. 5.95 (*0-531-15684-2*) Watts.

Latterman, Terry. Little Joe, a Hopi Indian Boy, Learns a Hopi Indian Secret. Hawkins, Mary E., ed. Latterman, Terry, illus. LC 85-61836. 32p. (gr. 4-12). 1985. 12.95 (*0-934739-01-3*) Pussywillow Pub.

INDIANS OF NORTH AMERICA–HUPA INDIANS–FICTION

Oakley, Don. The Adventure of Christian Fast. Wiggins, D. Kevin, illus. LC 88-8001. 279p. (Orig.). (gr. 9 up). 1989. 12.95 (*0-9619465-1-2*); pap. 8.95 (*0-9619465-2-0*) Eyrie Pr.

INDIANS OF NORTH AMERICA–HURON INDIANS

Bonvillain, Nancy. The Huron. (Illus.). 112p. (gr. 5 up). 1989. 17.95 (*1-55546-708-3*) Chelsea Hse.

De Brebeuf, Jean. Huron Carol. Tyrrell, Frances, illus. LC 91-35965. 32p. (ps-6). 1992. 15.00 (*0-525-44909-4*, DCB) Dutton Child Bks.

INDIANS OF NORTH AMERICA–INDUSTRIES

Meiczinger, John. How to Draw Indian Arts & Crafts. Meiczinger, John, illus. LC 88-50807. 32p. (gr. 2-6). 1989. lib. bdg. 10.65 (*0-8167-1537-8*, Pub. by Watermill Pr); pap. text ed. 1.95 (*0-8167-1515-7*, Pub. by Watermill Pr) Troll Assocs.

Wilbur, C. Keith. Indian Handcrafts: How to Craft Dozens of Practical Objects Using Traditional Indian Techniques. LC 90-3522. (Illus.). 144p. (Orig.). 1990. pap. 13.95 (*0-87106-496-0*) Globe Pequot.

INDIANS OF NORTH AMERICA–IROQUOIS INDIANS

Doherty, Craig A. & Doherty, Katherine M. The Iroquois. LC 89-33055. (Illus.). 64p. (gr. 3-5). 1989. PLB 12.90 (*0-531-10747-7*) Watts.

—The Iroquois. (Illus.). 64p. (gr. 5-8). 1991. pap. 5.95 (*0-531-15603-6*) Watts.

Graymont, Barbara. The Iroquois. Porter, Frank, intro. by. (Illus.). 128p. (Orig.). (gr. 5 up). 1988. 17.95 (*1-55546-709-1*); pap. 9.95 (*0-7910-0361-2*) Chelsea Hse.

McCall, B. The Iroquois. (Illus.). 32p. (gr. 5-8). 1989. lib. bdg. 15.74 (*0-86625-378-5*); 11.95 (*0-685-58582-4*) Rourke Corp.

Ridington, Jillian & Ridington, Robin. People of the Longhouse: How the Iroquoian Tribes Lived. Bateson, Ian, illus. 48p. (gr. 3-7). 1992. pap. 7.95 (*1-55054-221-4*, Pub. by Groundwood-Douglas & McIntyre CN) Firefly Bks Ltd.

Sherrow, Victoria. Iroquois. (gr. 4-7). 1993. pap. 6.95 (*0-7910-2027-4*) Chelsea Hse.

—The Iroquois Indians. (Illus.). 80p. (gr. 2-5). 1993. PLB 12.95 (*0-7910-1655-2*) Chelsea Hse.

Sneve, Virginia D. The Iroquois. Himler, Ronald, illus. (gr. 1-8). 1995. write for info. (*0-8234-1163-X*) Holiday.

Wolfson, Evelyn. The Iroquois: People of the Northeast. LC 92-4642. (Illus.). 64p. (gr. 4-6). 1992. PLB 15.40 (*1-56294-076-7*) Millbrook Pr.

INDIANS OF NORTH AMERICA–IROQUOIS INDIANS–FICTION

Baker, Betty. Little Runner of the Longhouse. Lobel, Arnold, illus. LC 62-8040. 64p. (gr. k-3). 1962. PLB 13.89 (*0-06-020341-2*) HarpC Child Bks.

—Little Runner of the Longhouse. Lobel, Arnold, illus. LC 62-8040. 64p. (gr. k-3). 1989. pap. 3.50 (*0-06-444122-9*, Trophy) HarpC Child Bks.

Bruchac, Joseph. Iroquois Stories: Heroes & Heroines, Monsters & Magic. Burgevin, Daniel, illus. LC 85-5705. 198p. (gr. 3-7). 1985. pap. 8.95 (*0-89594-234-8*) Crossing Pr.

INDIANS OF NORTH AMERICA–KIOWA INDIANS–FICTION

Hurmence, Belinda. Dixie in the Big Pasture. LC 93-9983. (gr. 4 up). 1994. write for info. (*0-395-52002-9*, Clarion) HM.

Stroud, Virginia A. Doesn't Fall off His Horse. (Illus.). (gr. 2 up). 1994. 14.99 (*0-8037-1634-6*); PLB 14.89 (*0-8037-1635-4*) Dial Bks Young.

INDIANS OF NORTH AMERICA–KIOWA INDIANS–LEGENDS

Bullshows, Harry & Gilliland, Hap. Legends of Chief Bald Eagle. (gr. 2-10). 1977. 1.95 (*0-89992-034-9*) Coun India Ed.

Clark, Ella, ed. In the Beginning. (gr. 5 up). 1977. 1.95 (*0-89992-055-1*) Coun India Ed.

Gingras, Louie & Rainboldt, Jo. Coyote & Kootenai. (gr. 2-6). 1977. 1.95 (*0-89992-067-5*) Coun India Ed.

Morss, Willard N. & Herren, Janet M. Stolen Princess: A Northwest Indian Legend. Millard, Carolyn, illus. LC 83-82920. 79p. (Orig.). (gr. 4-8). 1983. pap. 8.95 (*0-9613025-0-X*) J M Herren.

INDIANS OF NORTH AMERICA–LEGENDS

see also Folklore, Indian

Bailey, John B. The Legend of the Cherokee Rose. Griffin, James D., Jr., ed. Smith, Rick, illus. 10p. (Orig.). (gr. k-8). 1991. pap. 3.00 (*0-9628023-1-X*) J Laina Pub.

Bass, Althea. Grandfather Grey Owl Told Me. (gr. 4 up). 1973. 1.75 (*0-89992-051-9*) Coun India Ed.

—Nightwalker & the Buffalo. (gr. 4-9). 1972. 4.95 (*0-89992-032-2*) Coun India Ed.

Bell, Rosemary. Yurok Tales. Webb, Kathy, illus. 90p. (Orig.). (gr. 4-8). 1992. pap. 9.95 (*1-880922-01-0*) Bell Bks CA.

Belting, Natalia M. Moon Was Tired of Walking on Air. Hillenbrand, Will, illus. LC 91-20946. 48p. (gr. 4-7). 1992. 15.95 (*0-395-53806-8*) HM.

Bemister, Margaret. Thirty Indian Legends of Canada. Tait, Douglas, illus. 158p. (gr. 3-7). 1991. pap. 9.95 (*0-88894-025-4*, Pub. by Groundwood-Douglas & McIntyre CN) Firefly Bks Ltd.

Berhard, Emery, retold by. The Tree That Rains: The Flood Myth of the Huichol Indians of Mexico. Bernhard, Durga, illus. LC 93-8294. 32p. (ps-3). 1994. reinforced bdg. 15.95 (*0-8234-1108-7*) Holiday.

Bierhorst, John. Is My Friend at Home? Pueblo Fireside Tales. Watson, Wendy, illus. LC 93-14249. 1996. 14. 95 (*0-02-709733-1*, Macmillan Child Bk) Macmillan Child Grp.

Bierhorst, John, ed. & tr. Lightning Inside You: And Other Native American Riddles. Brierley, Louise, illus. LC 91-21744. 112p. (gr. 2 up). 1992. 14.00 (*0-688-09582-8*) Morrow Jr Bks.

Bishop, James, Jr., et al. Experience Jerome & the Verde Valley Legends & Legacies, No. II. Henry, Ron, illus. LC 90-71606. 356p. (Orig.). (gr. 8-12). 1990. pap. 12. 95 (*0-9628329-1-X*) Thorne Enterprises.

Blevins, Wade. Legend of Little Deer. Blevins, Wade, illus. Sargent, Dave, intro. by. (Illus.). 48p. (Orig.). (gr. k-8). 1993. text ed. 11.95 (*1-56763-073-1*); pap. text ed. 5.95 (*1-56763-074-X*) Ozark Pub.

—Path of Destiny. Blevins, Wade, illus. Sargent, Dave, intro. by. (Illus.). 48p. (Orig.). (gr. k-8). 1993. text ed. 11.95 (*1-56763-071-5*); pap. text ed. 5.95 (*1-56763-072-3*) Ozark Pub.

—The Wisdom Circle. Blevins, Wade, illus. Sargent, Dave, intro. by. (Illus.). 48p. (Orig.). (gr. k-8). 1993. text ed. 11.95 (*1-56763-075-8*); pap. text ed. 5.95 (*1-56763-076-6*) Ozark Pub.

Brown, Virginia P. & Owens, Laurella, eds. Southern Indian Myths & Legends. Glick, Nathan, illus. 160p. (gr. 6-9). 1994. pap. 12.95 (*0-912221-05-4*) Beechwood.

Bruchac, Joseph. The Great Ball Game: A Muskogee Story. Roth, Susan L., illus. LC 93-6269. (gr. 4 up). 1994. 14.99 (*0-8037-1539-0*); PLB 14.89 (*0-8037-1540-4*) Dial Bks Young.

Bruchac, Joseph & Ross, Gayle. The Girl Who Married the Moon: Stories from Native North America. LC 93-43824. (Illus.). 128p. (gr. 5-8). 1994. PLB 13.95 (*0-8167-3480-1*); pap. text ed. 3.95 (*0-8167-3481-X*) BrdgeWater.

Bruchac, Joseph, as told by. Flying with Eagle, Racing the Great Bear: Stories from Native North America. LC 93-21966. (Illus.). 144p. (gr. 5-8). 1993. PLB 13.95 (*0-8167-3026-1*); pap. write for info. (*0-8167-3027-X*) BrdgeWater.

Bruchac, Joseph & London, Jonathan, eds. Thirteen Moons on Turtle's Back: A Native American Year of Moons. Locker, Thomas, illus. 32p. (ps-8). 1992. PLB 15.95 (*0-399-22141-7*, Philomel Bks) Putnam Pub Group.

Caduto, Michael J. & Bruchac, Joseph. Keepers of the Earth: Native American Stories, & Environmental Activities for Children. Fadden, John K. & Wood, Carol, illus. Momaday, N. Scott, intro. by. LC 88-3620. 209p. (gr. 1-6). 1988. indexed 19.95 (*1-55591-027-0*) Fulcrum Pub.

Cheyenne Short Stories: A Collection of Ten Traditional Stores of the Cheyenne. (CHY & ENG.). (gr. 2 up). 1977. 1.50 (*0-89992-057-8*) Coun India Ed.

Cohlene, Terri. Clamshell Boy. (Illus.). 48p. (gr. 4-8). 1990. lib. bdg. 19.93 (*0-86593-001-5*); lib. bdg. 14. 95s.p. (*0-685-46446-6*) Rourke Corp.

—Clamshell Boy: A Makah Legend. 48p. (gr. 4-7). 1990. pap. 3.95 (*0-8167-2361-3*) Troll Assocs.

—Dancing Drum. (Illus.). 48p. (gr. 4-8). 1990. lib. bdg. 19.93 (*0-86593-007-4*); lib. bdg. 14.95s.p. (*0-685-46447-4*) Rourke Corp.

—Ka-Ha-Si & the Loon. (Illus.). 48p. (gr. 4-8). 1990. lib. bdg. 19.93 (*0-86593-002-3*); lib. bdg. 14.95s.p. (*0-685-46448-2*) Rourke Corp.

—Little Firefly. (Illus.). 48p. (gr. 4-8). 1990. lib. bdg. 19. 93 (*0-86593-005-8*); lib. bdg. 14.95s.p. (*0-685-36333-3*) Rourke Corp.

—Little Firefly: An Algonquian Legend. 48p. (gr. 4-7). 1990. pap. 3.95 (*0-8167-2363-X*) Troll Assocs.

—Native American Legends, 6 bks. (Illus.). 288p. (gr. 4-8). 1990. Set. lib. bdg. 119.58 (*0-86593-000-7*); Set. lib. bdg. 89.70s.p. (*0-685-46445-8*) Rourke Corp.

—Quillworker. (Illus.). 48p. (gr. 4-8). 1990. lib. bdg. 19. 93 (*0-86593-004-X*); lib. bdg. 14.95s.p. (*0-685-36334-1*) Rourke Corp.

—Quillworker: A Cheyenne Legend. 48p. (gr. 4-7). 1990. pap. 3.95 (*0-8167-2358-3*) Troll Assocs.

—Turquoise Boy. (Illus.). 48p. (gr. 4-8). 1990. lib. bdg. 19.93 (*0-86593-003-1*); lib. bdg. 14.95s.p. (*0-685-36335-X*) Rourke Corp.

Connolly, James E., ed. Why the Possum's Tail Is Bare: And Other North American Indian Nature Tales. Adams, Andrea, illus. LC 84-26871. 64p. (gr. 4-8). 1992. 15.95 (*0-88045-069-X*); pap. 7.95 (*0-88045-107-6*) Stemmer Hse.

Crow, Moses N. Hoksila & the Red Buffalo. Provincial, Bernard W., illus. 40p. (Orig.). (gr. 3 up). 1991. pap. 4.95 (*1-877976-02-4*, 406-0017) Tipi Pr. Among the Lakota, this legend is called Enya-hoksei. It is told differently by every story-teller of every clan. The outline of the legend remains the same as it travels with time. The whole story changes with the changing of times. The significance of it, as it goes

through the ages, is that it has no horses in it. The story has to be very old. But like all legends, it keeps in tune with the passing of time. When Hoksila the young warrior begins his long journey, his hunt to rescue his wife & to rid his tribe of the red buffalo with the ugly black spots. Then he could free all the young maidens. This is a story of the battle of good & evil, & how it's been handed down by the Lakota. An engaging story for the young & those not so young.
Publisher Provided Annotation.

–A Legend from Crazy Horse Clan. Flood, Renee S., ed. Long Soldier, Daniel, illus. 36p. (Orig.). (gr. 3 up). 1987. pap. 4.95 (*1-877976-03-2*, 406-0010) Tipi Pr.
A LEGEND FROM CRAZY HORSE CLAN is a story for children of all ages. Beautiful illustrations by Daniel Long Soldier keep the legend alive in the reader's eye. The historian or student of Indian ways will enjoy the book as much as the child of seven, in whose imagination the baby raccoon Mesu embodies all that is faithful & loving in a small furry pet. Listen carefully to the words of Tashia. The symbolic role of man & woman is evident throughout the legend. Although the story essentially describes the life of a girl, the narrator is male. Clearly, the legend describes the male viewpoint of manhood, religion, courtship, aging & death. The characters are gentle, yet there is a strong underlying theme of tribal identity. Without a doubt, we are looking at life through the eyes of a warrior. Indian oral narration is spoken American literature in its finest form. When Lakota children of the 1990s become grandparents themselves, they will tell the legends again. Thanks to Moses Big Crow, one of those legends may well be A LEGEND FROM CRAZY HORSE CLAN.
Publisher Provided Annotation.

Crowder, Jack L. & Hill, Faith. Tonibah & the Rainbow. Tohtsonie, Clara & Wilson, Joe, trs. Crowder, Jack L., photos by. (ENG & NAV., Illus.). 32p. (Orig.). (gr. 7 up). 1986. pap. 6.95 (*0-9616589-1-6*) Upper Strata.

Crowl, Christine. The Hunter & the Woodpecker. (Illus.). 12p. (Orig.). (ps-6). 1990. pap. 2.50 (*1-877976-09-1*, 406-0015) Tipi Pr.
This children's book describes how the Sioux first discovered the flute, which makes magical music. The Red Headed Woodpecker tells a young brave of its powers to win over a beautiful maiden. A charming story, delightfully illustrated in four colors. A story for children of all ages.
Publisher Provided Annotation.

–White Buffalo Women. (Illus.). 18p. (Orig.). (gr. 6). 1991. pap. 2.50 (*1-877976-10-5*, 406-0014) Tipi Pr.
This story is a core legend of the Sioux & how the Sioux received the Sacred Prayer Pipe. The pipe was an important religious symbol among the Sioux. It was a "moveable" altar which was used in prayer & ceremony. It was the most cherished thing a man could own. The legend of WHITE BUFFALO WOMEN & the pipe originated with the Brule Sioux & is a story that has been handed down through the centuries. Beautifully told & illustrated in four color, a charming story for children young & old.
Publisher Provided Annotation.

Cuevas, Lou. Apache Legends: Songs of the Wind Dancer. Brown, Keven, ed. Cleveland, Fred, illus. 128p. (Orig.). 1991. pap. text ed. 8.95 (*0-87961-219-3*) Naturegraph.

De Angulo, Jaime. Indian Tales. De Angulo, Jaime, illus. 256p. (gr. 5 up). 1984. 10.95 (*0-374-52163-8*, Am Century) FS&G.

DeArmond, Dale. The Seal Oil Lamp. DeArmond, Dale, illus. 48p. (gr. k-4). 1988. 14.95 (*0-316-17786-5*) Little.

DeCesare, Ruth. Myth, Music & Dance of the American Indian. Feldstein, Sandy, et al, eds. Seckler, Judy & Shelly, Walt, illus. 80p. (gr. 4-12). 1988. tchr's. ed. 12. 95 (*0-88284-371-0*, 3518); student, 16p 3.95 (*0-88284-372-9*, 3520); Student Songbk., 24p 4.95 (*0-88284-373-7*, 3519); tchr's ed. with cassette 19.95 (*0-88284-383-4*, 3534) Alfred Pub.

DePaola, Tomie. La Leyenda Del Pincel Indio: The Legend of the Indian Paintbrush. DePaola, Tomie, illus. 32p. (ps-2). 1993. pap. 5.95 (*0-399-22604-4*, Putnam) Putnam Pub Group.

Dixon, Ann, retold by. How Raven Brought Light to People. Watts, James, illus. LC 90-28948. 32p. (gr. k-4). 1992. SBE 13.95 (*0-689-50536-1*, M K McElderry) Macmillan Child Grp.

Earring, Monica F., et al. Prairie Legends. Robinson, Pat, illus. (gr. 6-9). 1978. 1.95 (*0-89992-069-1*) Coun India Ed.

Egbert, Rebecca A. The Vision of the Spokane Prophet. Gilliland, Hap, ed. Hardgrove, Tanya, illus. 36p. (Orig.). (gr. 5-10). 1989. pap. 5.95 (*0-89992-118-3*) Coun India Ed.

Ehlert, Lois. Mole's Hill: A Woodland Tale. LC 93-31151. 1994. 14.95 (*0-15-255116-6*, HB Juv Bks) HarBrace.

Esbensen, Barbara J., retold by. The Great Buffalo Race: How the Buffalo Got His Hump: a Seneca Tale. David, Helen K., illus. LC 92-23410. (gr. k-4). 1994. 14.95 (*0-316-24982-3*) Little.

Galloway, Mary R. & Chiltosky, Mary U. Aunt Mary, Tell Me a Story: A Collection of Cherokee Legends & Tales. Galloway, John B., et al, illus. (Orig.). 1991. pap. 3.00 (*0-9628630-0-9*) Cherokee Comn.

Gerber, Will, et al. The Rings on Woot-Kew's Tail: Indian Legends of the Origin of the Sun, Moon & Stars. (gr. 3-9). 1973. 1.50 (*0-89992-059-4*) Coun India Ed.

Goble, Paul. Buffalo Woman. LC 83-15704. (Illus.). 32p. (gr. k up). 1984. RSBE 14.95 (*0-02-737720-2*, Bradbury Pr) Macmillan Child Grp.

—Buffalo Woman. Goble, Paul, illus. LC 86-20573. 32p. (gr. k up). 1987. pap. 4.95 (*0-689-71109-3*, Aladdin) Macmillan Child Grp.

—The Great Race. LC 90-39983. (Illus.). 32p. (gr. k-3). 1991. pap. 4.95 (*0-689-71452-1*, Aladdin) Macmillan Child Grp.

—Her Seven Brothers. Goble, Paul, illus. LC 92-40562. 32p. (gr. k-3). 1993. pap. 4.95 (*0-689-71730-X*, Aladdin) Macmillan Child Grp.

—The Love Flute. Goble, Paul, illus. LC 91-19716. 32p. (ps up). 1992. SBE 14.95 (*0-02-736261-2*, Bradbury Pr) Macmillan Child Grp.

Goble, Paul, retold by. & illus. Iktomi & the Berries: A Plains Indian Story. LC 88-23353. 32p. (ps-2). 1989. 14.95 (*0-531-05819-0*); PLB 14.99 (*0-531-08419-1*) Orchard Bks Watts.

Goble, Paul, as told by. & illus. Iktomi & the Buffalo Skull: A Plains Indian Story. LC 90-7716. 32p. (ps-2). 1991. 14.95 (*0-531-05911-1*); PLB 14.99 (*0-531-08511-2*) Orchard Bks Watts.

Goldin, Barbara D., retold by. Coyote & the Firestick: A Northwest Coast Indian Legend. Hillenbrand, Will, illus. LC 94-5747. 1995. write for info. (*0-15-200438-6*) Harbrace.

Greene, Jacqueline D. Manabozho's Gifts: Three Chippewa Tales. Hewitson, Jennifer, illus. LC 93-41738. 1994. 14.95 (*0-395-69251-2*) HM.

Gregg, Andy. Great Rabbit & the Long-Tailed Wildcat. Grant, Christy, ed. Smith, Cat B., illus. LC 92-22950. 32p. (gr. 1-5). 1993. PLB 13.95 (*0-8075-3047-6*) A Whitman.

Griffin, Arthur E., ed. Ah Mo: Indian Legends from Washington State. Malin, Edward, illus. 75p. (Orig.). (gr. 2-5). 1989. pap. write for info. Bainbridge Pr.

—The Legend of Tom Pepper & Other Stories. Malin, Edward, illus. 100p. (Orig.). (gr. 2-5). 1989. pap. write for info. Bainbridge Pr.

—Spelyi & Other Indian Legends. Malin, Edward, illus. (gr. 2-5). 1989. write for info. Bainbridge Pr.

Hausman, Gerald & Hausman, Gerald, eds. How Chipmunk Got Tiny Feet: Native American Animal Origin Stories. Hague, Michael, illus. LC 92-44186. (ps-6). 1995. 15.00 (*0-06-022906-3*, HarpT); PLB 14. 89 (*0-06-022907-1*) HarpC.

Heady, Eleanor B. Sage Smoke: Tales of the Shoshoni-Bannock Indians. Stewart, Arvis, illus. LC 92-46731. 94p. (gr. 4-6). 1993. PLB 10.95 (*0-382-24361-7*); 8.95 (*0-382-24370-6*) Silver Burdett Pr.

Henry Tall Bull & Weist, Tom. Cheyenne Legends of Creation. (gr. 4-9). 1972. 1.25 (*0-89992-025-X*) Coun India Ed.

—The Rolling Head: Cheyenne Tales. (gr. 3-9). 1971. 1.50 (*0-89992-013-6*) Coun India Ed.

Hilbert, Vi, as told by. Loon & Deer Were Traveling: A Story of the Upper Skagit. Nelson, Anita, illus. LC 92-5450. 24p. (ps-3). 1992. PLB 13.85 (*0-516-05140-7*); pap. 5.95 (*0-516-45140-5*) Childrens.

Hines, Donald M. The Forgotten Tribes: Oral Tales of the Teninos & Adjacent Mid-Columbia River Indian Nations. 142p. 1991. pap. 10.95 (*0-9629539-0-3*) Great Eagle Pub.

Holsinger, Rosemary. Karuk Tales. Piemme, P. I., illus. 70p. (gr. 4-8). 1992. pap. 7.95 (*1-880922-00-2*) Bell Bks CA.

Holthaus, Mary. The Hunter & the Ravens. 32p. (gr. 1-6). 1976. 2.00 (*0-89992-049-7*) Coun India Ed.

Houston, James R. The Falcon Bow: An Arctic Legend. (Illus.). 96p. (gr. 5 up). 1992. pap. 3.99 (*0-14-036078-6*, Puffin) Puffin Bks.

Hurmence, Belinda. The Nightwalker. LC 88-2827. 114p. (gr. 4-7). 1988. 12.95 (*0-89919-732-9*, Clarion Bks) HM.

Jaffe, Nina, adapted by. & tr. The Golden Flower: A Taino Myth from Puerto Rico. Moiles, Holly B., illus. LC 92-42364. 32p. (ps-3). 1995. RSBE 15.95 (*0-02-747585-9*, Macmillan Child Bk) Macmillan Child Grp.

Keeper, Berry. The Old Ones Told Me: American Indian Stories for Children. (Illus.). 36p. (Orig.). 1989. pap. 4.95 (*0-8323-0473-5*) Binford Mort.

Kerven, Rosalind. Earth Magic, Sky Magic: North American Indian Tales. (Illus.). 96p. 1991. 15.95 (*0-521-36235-0*); pap. 8.95 (*0-521-36806-5*) Cambridge U Pr.

Lacapa, Michael. Antelope Woman: An Apache Folktale. Lacapa, Michael, illus. LC 92-4198. 48p. (gr. 3 up). 1992. 14.95 (*0-87358-543-7*) Northland AZ.

—The Flute Player: An Apache Folktale. Lacapa, Michael, illus. LC 89-63749. 48p. (gr. 1-3). 1990. 14. 95 (*0-87358-500-3*) Northland AZ.

Larned, W. T. American Indian Fairy Tales. Rae, John, illus. LC 93-46940. 1994. 8.99 (*0-517-10177-7*, Pub. by Derrydale Bks) Random Hse Value.

Larry, Charles. Peboan & Seegwun. 32p. (ps-3). 1993. 16. 00 (*0-374-35773-0*) FS&G.

London, Jonathan & Pinola, Lanny. Fire Race: A Karuk Coyote Tale about How Fire Came to the People. Long, Sylvia, illus. Lang, Julian, afterword by. LC 92-32352. (Illus.). 1993. 13.95 (*0-8118-0241-8*) Chronicle Bks.

McDermott, Gerald. Raven: A Trickster Tale from the Pacific Northwest. LC 91-14563. (ps-3). 1993. 14.95 (*0-15-265661-8*, HB Juv Bks) HarBrace.

McDermott, Gerald, as told by. & illus. Coyote: A Trickster Tale from the Southwest. LC 92-32979. (ps-3). 1995. write for info. (*0-15-220724-4*) HarBrace.

McGinnis, Mark W. Lakota & Dakota Animal Wisdom Stories. Kaizen, Pamela G., retold by. McGinnis, Mark W., illus. Bruguier, Leonard R., intro. by. (Illus.). 24p. 1994. pap. 11.98 (*1-877976-14-8*, 406-0016) Tipi Pr.
LAKOTA & DAKOTA ANIMAL WISDOM STORIES is a compilation of twelve traditional, northern plains Native American stories retold by Dakota storyteller, Pamela Greenhill Kaizen & are accompanied by twelve full-color illustrations by South Dakota artist & educator Mark W. McGinnis. Leonard R. Bruguier, a descendant of the Yankton chiefs War Eagle & Struck by the Ree, presents the introduction. The stories use animal characters to deal with the themes of compassion, greed, generosity, protection, survival, hard work, laziness, bravery, foolishness, trickery, & others. They range from simple humor as in THE FROG & THE TURTLE BROTHERS, where two close friends decide to jump in the lake rather than catch colds by getting wet in the rain, to the rich & complex story of THE CRANE, which weaves a tale of compassion & caring for one's neighbors. The animal characters give insightful guidance on human morals & ethics, & give a glimpse into the wonderful wit & wisdom of the Lakota & Dakota people. Mark McGinnis' paintings interpret a critical instant

from each story, translating the oral moment to a visual expression of color, texture & shapes. This book is well suited to be read to younger children, to be read by older children, or for adults who enjoy new perspectives into Native American culture. Available for $11.98 plus $3.00 S/H from Tipi Press, St. Joseph's Indian School, Chamberlain, SD 57326; 605-734-3300. ***Publisher Provided Annotation.***

McGovern, Ann. The Defenders. 128p. (Orig.). (gr. 3-7). 1987. pap. 2.95 (*0-590-43866-2*) Scholastic Inc.

Marsh, Jessie. Indian Folk Tales from Coast to Coast. Cunningham, Tanya, illus. (gr. 3-6). 1978. 1.95 (*0-89992-068-3*) Coun India Ed.

Martin, Rafe. The Boy Who Lived with Seals. Shannon, David, illus. 32p. (ps-3). 1993. PLB 14.95 (*0-399-22413-0*, Putnam) Putnam Pub Group.

—The Rough-Face Girl. Shannon, David, illus. 32p. (ps-3). 1992. PLB 14.95 (*0-399-21859-9*, Putnam) Putnam Pub Group.

Martinez, Estefanita, as told by. The Naughty Little Rabbit & Old Man Coyote: A Tewa Story from San Juan Pueblo. Regan, Rick, illus. LC 92-8992. 24p. (ps-3). 1992. PLB 15.40 (*0-516-05141-5*); pap. 4.95 (*0-516-45141-3*) Childrens.

Masson, Marcelle. A Bag of Bones: Legends of the Wintu Indians of Northern California. LC 66-23398. 130p. (gr. 4 up). 1966. 16.95 (*0-911010-27-0*); pap. 8.95 (*0-911010-26-2*) Naturegraph.

Matson, Emerson N. Legends of the Great Chiefs. (Illus.). 144p. (gr. 6-10). Date not set. pap. 5.95 (*0-9609940-0-9*) Storypole.
One of America's most-quoted legend books. In print since 1972. Authentic legends & little-known incidents recalled during first-hand interviews with actual descendants of some of the most famous Indian chiefs in American history. The author located surviving relatives of such famous Indian leaders as Sitting Bull, Red Cloud, Joseph, Leshi, Shelton, Swan, & Sampson. Each descendant recalls favorite legends & little-known facts about their famous ancestors. The legends were more than clever stories. To those who told them, they were a vital part of life itself. For today's reader, the legends are a window into ancient tribal lore. Sixteen-page photo section. Written for grades six through ten. Also used in college-level literature classes. Postage prepaid on orders of twelve or more books. Retail $5.95 paperback. Fax order-line 206-535-3889, Storypole Press, 11015 Bingham Ave. East, Tacoma, WA 98446-5225.
Publisher Provided Annotation.

Mayo, Gretchen W. Star Tales: North American Indian Stories about the Stars. 96p. (gr. 5 up). 1987. 12.95 (*0-8027-6672-2*); PLB 13.85 (*0-8027-6673-0*) Walker & Co.

Mayo, Gretchen W., retold by. & illus. Here Comes Tricky Rabbit. LC 93-29763. 48p. (gr. 2-3). 1994. 12. 95 (*0-8027-8273-6*); PLB 13.85 (*0-8027-8274-4*) Walker & Co.

Moore, Elizabeth B. & Couvillon, Alice W. Louisiana Indian Tales. LC 89-71060. 112p. 1990. 11.95 (*0-88289-756-X*) Pelican.

Morgan, Pierr. Supper for Crow: A Northwest Coast Indian Tale. LC 93-41665. 1994. 15.00 (*0-517-59378-5*); PLB 15.99 (*0-517-59379-3*) Crown Pub Group.

Murphy, Claire R., retold by. The Prince & the Salmon People. Pasco, Duane, illus. LC 92-38394. 48p. 1993. 19.95 (*0-8478-1662-1*) Rizzoli Intl.

Nashone. Grandmother Stories of the Northwest: Northwestern Indian Tales. (Illus.). (gr. 5-12). 1987. pap. 6.95 (*0-940113-06-6*) Sierra Oaks Pub.

Nechodom, Kerry, adapted by. & illus. The Rainbow Bridge: A Chumash Legend. 32p. (Orig.). (gr. k-3). 1992. pap. 6.95 (*0-944627-36-6*) Sand River Pr.

Norman, Howard. How Glooskap Outwits the Ice Giants: And Other Tales of the Maritime Indians, Vol. 1. 1989. 14.95 (*0-316-61181-6*, Joy St Bks) Little.

Olin, Caroline & Dutton, Bertha P. Southwest Indians, Bk. 1: (Navajo, Pima, Apache, Bk. 1. (Illus.). (gr. 5). 1978. pap. 3.95 (*0-88388-049-0*) Bellerophon Bks.

Oughton, Jerrie. How the Stars Fell into the Sky. Desimini, Lisa, illus. 32p. (gr. k-3). 1992. 14.45 (*0-395-58798-0*) HM.

Piscataway Conoy Confederacy & Subtribes, Inc. Staff. A Piscataway Story: The Legend of Kittimuquinn. Seib-Toup, Rebecca, ed. Harley, Karen Y., illus. Savoy, Mervin A., intro. by. (Illus.). 96p. (gr. 4-6). 1994. 10.00 (*0-945253-09-5*) Thornsbury Bailey Brown.
The modern-day Piscataway Indians live in Southern Maryland near the present town of La Platta. They have a rich tradition & culture. This book is the first in a series of PISCATAWAY STORIES. It tells the story of Kittimuquinn, the progenitor of the Piscataways. The book is intended for school children between the ages of 10 & 12 years to acquaint them with the Piscataways & their culture & traditions. The text is written in poetry & is accompanied by a generous amount of original black & white pictures of Piscataway life & history. The pictures are keyed to the text to provide a visual interpretation of what the children read on each page. The book includes questions to help children test their reading & comprehension skills. It is also accompanied by a teacher's guide. Currently the book is used by the Maryland public schools to teach children about the Native American heritage of their area of the state. To order, contact: Thornsbury Bailey & Brown, Inc., P.O. Box 5169, Arlington, VA 22205.
Publisher Provided Annotation.

Pollock, Penny, retold by. The Turkey Girl: A Zuni Cinderella. Young, Ed, illus. LC 93-28947. 1995. 15. 95 (*0-316-71314-7*) Little.

Redhawk, Richard. Grandfather Origin Story: The Navajo Indian Begining. (Orig.). (gr. 3-6). 1988. pap. 6.95 (*0-940113-07-4*) Sierra Oaks Pub.

Red Hawk, Richard. Grandfather's Story of Navajo Monsters. Whitehorse, David, illus. (Orig.). (ps-7). 1988. pap. 6.95 (*0-940113-11-2*) Sierra Oaks Pub.

—A Trip to a Pow Wow. Brook, Anne C., illus. 45p. (Orig.). (gr. k-3). 1988. pap. 6.95 (*0-940113-14-7*) Sierra Oaks Pub.

Rodanas, Kristina. Dance of the Sacred Circle. LC 93-19626. (ps-3). 1994. 14.95 (*0-316-75358-0*) Little.

Rodanas, Kristina, retold by. & illus. Dragonfly's Tale. 32p. (gr. k-3). 1992. 14.45 (*0-395-57003-4*, Clarion Bks) HM.

Roper, William. Sequoia & His Miracle. (gr. 5-12). 1972. 4.95 (*0-89992-056-X*) Coun India Ed.

Ross, Gayle. How Rabbit Tricked Otter & Other Cherokee Trickster Stories. Jacob, Murv, illus. LC 93-3637. 80p. (gr. 1 up). 1994. 17.00 (*0-06-021285-3*, HarpT); PLB 16.89 (*0-06-021286-1*) HarpC.

Ross, Gayle, retold by. How Turtle's Back Was Cracked: A Traditional Cherokee Tale. Jacob, Murv, illus. LC 93-40657. 1995. write for info. (*0-8037-1728-8*); lib. bdg. write for info. (*0-8037-1729-6*) Dial Bks Young.

Roth, Susan. Ishi's Tale of Lizard. (gr. 4-7). 1992. 14.00 (*0-374-33643-1*) FS&G.

San Souci, Robert D., retold by. Sootface: An Ojibwa Indian Tale. San Souci, Daniel, illus. LC 93-10553. 1994. 14.95 (*0-385-31202-4*) Doubleday.

Scheer, George F., intro. by. Cherokee Animal Tales. rev. ed. Frankenberg, Robert, illus. LC 91-73537. 79p. (gr. 3-6). 1991. pap. 7.95 (*0-933031-60-2*) Coun Oak Bks.

Seymour, Tryntje V. N. The Gift of Changing Woman. LC 92-31833. (Illus.). 40p. (gr. 5-9). 1993. 16.95 (*0-8050-2577-4*, Bks Young Read) H Holt & Co.

Shetterly, Susan H. Raven's Light: A Myth from the People of the Northwest Coast. Shetterly, Robert, illus. LC 89-78183. 32p. (gr. 1-5). 1991. SBE 13.95 (*0-689-31629-1*, Atheneum Child Bk) Macmillan Child Grp.

Simms, Thomas E. Otokahekagapi (First Beginnings) Sioux Creation Story. (Illus.). 36p. (Orig.). 1987. pap. 3.50 (*1-877976-06-7*, 406-0005) Tipi Pr.
The first in a series of Lakota legends, is written & illustrated to foster greater respect for a proud people's tradition. This account in English & Lakota presents the profundity of the creation mystery. The pictures are Indian pictures, because this is the beginning of the Sioux Creation account. But it is for all children everywhere, because everyone asks about how things got started & how the World began. "So this picture book is like a little ball game. We shall learn that the book is a ball. Wakantanka will throw this ball to us, which is this book, & we shall catch it. Then we shall understand it. And we shall enjoy ourselves. Bring the ball -- this book -- to the Center, which is your Heart, then you will receive a present. The present is invisible, like a little secret. Good. That's all. Now I shall throw the ball to you. Catch it!"
Publisher Provided Annotation.

Stevens, Janet, retold by. & illus. Coyote Steals the Blanket: A Ute Tale. LC 92-54415. 32p. (ps-3). 1993. reinforced bdg. 15.95 (*0-8234-0996-1*); pap. 5.95 (*0-8234-1129-X*) Holiday.

Talashoema, Herschel. Coyote & Little Turtle: A Traditional Hopi Tale. Sekaquaptewa, Emory & Pepper, Barbara, eds. LC 93-21393. (Illus.). 95p. (gr. k-6). 1994. 14.95 (*0-940666-84-7*); pap. 9.95 (*0-940666-85-5*) Clear Light.

Taylor, C. J. Bones in the Basket. Taylor, C. J., illus. LC 93-61786. 32p. (gr. 1-5). 1994. 17.95 (*0-88776-327-8*) Tundra Bks.

—Le Secret Du Bison Blanc. Boileau, Michele, tr. from ENG. Taylor, C. J., illus. LC 93-60552. (FRE.). 24p. (gr. 3 up). 1993. 13.95 (*0-88776-322-7*) Tundra Bks.

—The Secret of the White Buffalo. Taylor, C. J., illus. LC 93-60551. 24p. (gr. 3 up). 1993. 13.95 (*0-88776-321-9*) Tundra Bks.

Taylor, Harriet P., retold by. & illus. Coyote Places the Stars. LC 92-46431. 32p. (ps-2). 1993. RSBE 14.95 (*0-02-788845-2*, Bradbury Pr) Macmillan Child Grp.

Tehanetorens. Sacred Song of the Hermit Thrush. Hutchens, Jerry L., illus. LC 93-945. 64p. (gr. 3 up). 1992. pap. 5.95 (*0-913990-36-1*) Book Pub Co.

Troughton, Joanna, retold by. & illus. How Rabbit Stole the Fire: A North American Indian Folk Tale. LC 85-15629. 32p. (gr. k-3). 1986. PLB 14.95 (*0-87226-040-2*, Bedrick Blackie) P Bedrick Bks.

—How the Seasons Came: A North American Indian Folk Tale. LC 91-40499. 32p. (gr. k-3). 1992. PLB 14. 95 (*0-87226-464-5*, Bedrick Blackie) P Bedrick Bks.

Ude, Wayne. Maybe I Will Do Something: Seven Coyote Tales. Rorer, Abigail, illus. LC 92-29392. 1993. 14.95 (*0-395-65233-2*) HM.

Walters, Anna L., retold by. The Two-Legged Creature: An Otoe Story. Bowles, Carol, illus. LC 92-56510. 32p. 1993. 14.95 (*0-87358-553-4*) Northland AZ.

Williamson, Ray A. & Monroe, Jean G. First Houses: Native American Homes & Sacred Structures. Carlson, Susan, illus. LC 92-34900. 160p. 1993. 14.95 (*0-395-51081-3*) HM.

Wood, Audrey. The Rainbow Bridge. Florczak, Robert, illus. LC 92-17661. 1993. write for info. (*0-15-265475-5*) HarBrace.

Wood, Marion. Spirits, Heroes & Hunters from North American Indian Mythology. Sibbick, John, illus. LC 91-38954. 132p. (gr. 6 up). 1992. 22.50 (*0-87226-903-5*) P Bedrick Bks.

Young, Ed, adapted by. Moon Mother: A Native American Creation Tale. LC 92-14981. (Illus.). 40p. (ps-3). 1993. 15.00 (*0-06-021301-9*); PLB 14.89 (*0-06-021302-7*) HarpC Child Bks.

Young, Richard & Young, Judy D. Race with the Buffalo & Other Native American Stories for Young Readers. 176p. 1993. 19.95 (*0-87483-343-4*) August Hse.

INDIANS OF NORTH AMERICA–MIWOK INDIANS

Boule, Mary N. California's Native American Tribes, No. 11: Coast Miwok. Liddell, Daniel, illus. 40p. (Orig.). (gr. 2-4). 1992. pap. 4.50 (*1-877599-35-2*) Merryant Pubs.

—California's Native American Tribes, No. 12: Eastern Miwok Tribe. Liddell, Daniel, illus. 40p. (Orig.). (gr. 3-5). 1992. pap. 4.50 (*1-877599-36-0*) Merryant Pubs.

—California's Native American Tribes, No. 13: Lake Miwok Tribe. Liddell, Daniel, illus. 40p. (Orig.). (gr. 3-5). 1992. pap. 4.50 (*1-877599-37-9*) Merryant Pubs.

INDIANS OF NORTH AMERICA–MOHAWK INDIANS

Bonvillain, Nancy. Mohawk. (Illus.). 112p. (gr. 5 up). 1992. lib. bdg. 17.95 (*0-7910-1636-6*) Chelsea Hse.

Duvall, Jill. The Mohawk. LC 90-21166. (Illus.). 48p. (gr. k-4). 1991. PLB 12.85 (*0-516-01115-4*); pap. 4.95 (*0-516-41115-2*) Childrens.

Hubbard-Brown, Janet. The Mohawk Indians. LC 93-18247. 1993. write for info. (*0-7910-1667-6*); pap. write for info. (*0-7910-1991-8*) Chelsea Hse.

Swamp, Jake. Giving Thanks: A Native American Good Morning Message. Printup, Erwin, Jr., illus. LC 94-5955. Date not set. 14.95 (*1-880000-15-6*) Lee & Low Bks.

INDIANS OF NORTH AMERICA–MUSIC

Bierhorst, John. A Cry from the Earth: Music of the North American Indians. LC 91-59002. (Illus.). 113p. 1992. pap. 14.95 (*0-941270-53-X*) Ancient City Pr.

DeCesare, Ruth. Myth, Music & Dance of the American Indian. Feldstein, Sandy, et al, eds. Seckler, Judy & Shelly, Walt, illus. 80p. (gr. 4-12). 1988. tchr's. ed. 12.95 (*0-88284-371-0*, 3518); student, 16p 3.95 (*0-88284-372-9*, 3520); Student Songbk., 24p 4.95 (*0-88284-373-7*, 3519); tchr's ed. with cassette 19.95 (*0-88284-383-4*, 3534) Alfred Pub.

Fichter, George S. American Indian Music & Musical Instruments. (gr. 5-10). 1978. 8.95 (*0-679-20443-1*) McKay.

INDIANS OF NORTH AMERICA–MYTHOLOGY

see Folklore, Indian; Indians of North America–Legends; Indians of North America–Religion and Mythology

INDIANS OF NORTH AMERICA–NAVAHO INDIANS

Aaseng, Nathan. Navajo Code Talkers. LC 92-11408. 114p. 1992. 14.95 (*0-8027-8182-9*); PLB 15.85 (*0-8027-8183-7*) Walker & Co.

Armstrong, Nancy. Navajo Children. (gr. 2-6). 1975. 1.95 (*0-89992-037-3*) Coun India Ed.

Bland, Celia. Peter McDonald: Former Chairman of The Navajo Nationa. LC 94-21856. 1995. pap. write for info. (*0-7910-1714-1*) (*0-7910-2071-1*) Chelsea Pub.

Clark, Ann N. Little Boy with Three Names: Stories of Taos Pueblo. reformatted ed. Lujan, Tonita, illus. LC 89-81747. 50p. (gr. 3 up). 1990. pap. 8.95 (*0-941270-59-9*) Ancient City Pr.

Doherty, Craig A. & Doherty, Katherine M. The Apaches & Navajos. LC 89-9079. (Illus.). 64p. (gr. 3-5). 1989. PLB 12.90 (*0-531-10743-4*) Watts.

—The Apaches & Navajos. (Illus.). 64p. (gr. 5-8). 1991. pap. 5.95 (*0-531-15602-8*) Watts.

Hoffman, Virginia. Lucy Learns to Weave: Gathering Plants. Denetsosie, Hoke, illus. LC 74-4894. 46p. (gr. 1-4). 1974. pap. 7.00 (*0-89019-009-7*) Rough Rock Pr.

Iverson, Peter. The Navajos. (Illus.). 112p. (gr. 5 up). 1990. 17.95 (*1-55546-719-9*); pap. 9.95 (*0-7910-0390-6*) Chelsea Hse.

Jayant, Amber. Silas & the Mad-Sad People. LC 80-83882. (Illus.). (gr. 1-5). 1981. 6.95 (*0-938678-08-6*) New Seed.

Kreischer, Elsie. Navaho Magic of Hunting. 32p. (gr. 4-10). 1988. pap. 4.95 (*0-89992-099-3*) Coun India Ed.

Lagerquist, Syble. Philip Johnston & the Navajo Code Talkers. (gr. 4-12). 1975. 4.95 (*0-89992-038-1*) Coun India Ed.

Mike, Jan M. Dolii; a Navajo Girl: Historical Paper Doll Book to Read, Color & Cut. Lowmiller, Cathie, illus. 32p. (gr. k-6). 1990. pap. 3.95 (*0-918080-54-1*) Treasure Chest.

New Mexico People & Energy Collective Staff, et al. Red Ribbons for Emma. LC 80-83883. (Illus.). 48p. (Orig.). (gr. 3 up). 1981. limited ed. 12.00 (*0-938678-07-8*) New Seed.

Osinski, Alice. The Navajo. (Illus.). (gr. k-4). 1987. PLB 15.40 (*0-516-01236-3*); pap. 4.95 (*0-516-41236-1*) Childrens.

Roessel, Monty, photos by & text by. Kinaalda: A Navajo Girl Grows Up. LC 92-35204. (Illus.). 48p. 1993. 19.95 (*0-8225-2655-7*) Lerner Pubns.

Sneve, Virginia Driving Hawk. The Navajos: A First Americans Book. Himler, Ronald, illus. LC 92-40330. 32p. (gr. 2-6). 1993. reinforced bdg. 15.95 (*0-8234-1039-0*) Holiday.

Stan, S. The Navajo. (Illus.). 32p. (gr. 5-8). 1989. lib. bdg. 15.94 (*0-86625-380-7*); lib. bdg. 11.95s.p. (*0-685-58580-8*) Rourke Corp.

Sundberg, Lawrence D. Dinetah: An Early History of the Navajo People. Smith, James C., Jr., ed. (Illus.). 128p. (Orig.). (gr. 5-12). 1994. pap. 14.95 (*0-86534-221-0*) Sunstone Pr.

Thomson, Peggy. Katie Henio, Navajo Sheepherder. Conklin, Paul, photos by. LC 93-40430. 1994. write for info. (*0-525-65160-8*, Cobblehill Pr) Dutton Child Bks.

Wood, Leigh H. The Navajo Indians. (Illus.). 80p. (gr. 2-5). 1991. lib. bdg. 12.95 (*0-7910-1651-X*) Chelsea Hse.

—Navajos. (gr. 4-7). 1993. pap. 6.95 (*0-7910-2026-6*) Chelsea Hse.

INDIANS OF NORTH AMERICA–NAVAHO INDIANS–FICTION

Armer, Laura A. Waterless Mountain. LC 92-32066. (Illus.). 240p. (gr. 3-5). 1993. 16.00 (*0-679-84502-X*) Knopf Bks Yng Read.

Armstrong, Nancy M. Navajo Long Walk. Livers-Lambert, Paulette, illus. 100p. (gr. 4-8). 1994. pap. 7.95 (*1-879373-56-4*) R Rinehart.

Blood, Charles L. & Link, Martin. The Goat in the Rug. Parker, Nancy W., illus. LC 89-77701. 40p. (ps-3). 1990. pap. 4.95 (*0-689-71418-1*, Aladdin) Macmillan Child Grp.

Clark, Ann N. Little Herder in Autumn. Harrington, John P., ed. Young, Robert W., tr. Denetsosie, Hoke, illus. LC 88-70848. (ENG & NAV.). 96p. (gr. 3 up). 1988. pap. 9.95 (*0-941270-46-7*) Ancient City Pr.

Crowder, Jack L. & Hill, Faith. Stephanie & the Coyote. 3rd, rev. ed. Morgan, William, tr. Holm, Wayne, intro. by. (NAV & ENG., Illus.). 32p. (gr. 3 up). pap. 4.95 (*0-9616589-0-8*) Upper Strata.

Garaway, Margaret K. Ashkii & His Grandfather. Warren, Harry, illus. LC 89-50604. 32p. (Orig.). (gr. k-6). 1989. pap. 5.95 (*0-918080-41-X*) Treasure Chest.

Gessner, Lynne. Malcolm Yucca Seed. rev. ed. Bock, William S. & Jensen, Debbie, illus. 64p. (gr. 3-8). pap. 5.95 (*0-918080-63-0*) Treasure Chest.

Grammer, Maurine. The Navajo Brothers & the Stolen Herd. Cleveland, Fred, illus. Rushing, Jack, frwd. by. LC 92-15018. (Illus.). 120p. (gr. 6-8). 1992. pap. 9.95 (*1-878610-23-6*) Red Crane Bks.

Green, Timothy. Mystery of Navajo Moon. Green, Timothy, illus. LC 91-52600. 48p. (ps-4). 1991. pap. 7.95 (*0-87358-577-1*) Northland AZ.

Momaday, Natachee S. Owl in the Cedar Tree. Perceval, Don, illus. LC 91-41866. viii, 117p. 1992. pap. 9.95 (*0-8032-8184-6*, Bison Books) U of Nebr Pr.

Moon, Sheila. Deepest Roots. Renfrew, Susan, illus. LC 86-19578. 240p. (gr. 8-12). 1986. pap. 8.95 (*0-917479-10-6*) Guild Psy.

—Knee-Deep in Thunder. Parnell, Peter, illus. LC 86-19534. 307p. (gr. 8-12). 1986. pap. 8.95 (*0-917479-08-4*) Guild Psy.

Pitts, Paul. Racing the Sun. 160p. 1988. pap. 3.50 (*0-380-75496-7*, Camelot) Avon.

Richardson, Jean. The Courage Seed. Finney, Pat, illus. LC 93-20182. 76p. (gr. 3-6). 1993. 14.95 (*0-89015-902-5*) Sunbelt Media.

Roessel, Monty. Kinaalda: A Navajo Girl Grows Up. (gr. 4-7). 1993. pap. 3.95 (*0-8225-9641-5*) Lerner Pubns.

Schulz, Beverly. The Adventures of Nelda Navajo & Her Forest Friends. 1993. 7.95 (*0-8062-4818-1*) Carlton.

Wilson, Bennett. The Magic Feather: An Adventure in Navajo Land. Wilson, Bennett, illus. 42p. (Orig.). (gr. 1-6). 1989. pap. 5.00 (*0-918080-48-7*) Treasure Chest.

Wunderli, Stephen. The Blue Between the Clouds. LC 91-28010. 80p. (gr. 5 up). 1992. 13.95 (*0-8050-1772-0*, Bks Young Read) H Holt & Co.

Yazzie, Earl. More Monster Stories from the Navajo Country, Vol. 3. (Illus.). 43p. (Orig.). (gr. k-5). 1989. pap. 6.95 (*0-940113-12-0*) Sierra Oaks Pub.

INDIANS OF NORTH AMERICA–NAVAHO INDIANS–LEGENDS

Begay, Shonto. Ma'ii & Cousin Horned Toad. (Illus.). 1992. 14.95 (*0-590-45391-2*, Scholastic Hardcover) Scholastic Inc.

Browne, Vee. Monster Slayer: A Navajo Folktale. Whitethorne, Baje, illus. LC 91-52603. 32p. (gr. k-6). 1991. 14.95 (*0-87358-525-9*) Northland AZ.

Cohlene, Terri. Turquoise Boy: A Navajo Legend. 48p. (gr. 4-7). 1990. pap. 3.95 (*0-8167-2360-5*) Troll Assocs.

Hausman, Gerald. Eagle Boy. Date not set. 15.00 (*0-06-021100-8*, HarpT); PLB 14.89 (*0-06-021101-6*, HarpT) HarpC.

Hausman, Gerald, compiled by. Coyote Walks on Two Legs. Cooper, Floyd, illus. LC 92-25115. 1994. 15.95 (*0-399-22018-6*, Philomel Bks) Putnam Pub Group.

Morgan, William. Navajo Coyote Tales. Thompson, Hildegard, ed. & tr. Lind, Jenny, illus. LC 88-72048. 50p. (gr. 2 up). 1988. pap. 8.95 (*0-941270-52-1*) Ancient City Pr.

Oughten, Jerrie. The Magic Weaver of Rugs. Desimini, Lisa, illus. LC 93-4850. 1994. write for info. (*0-395-66140-4*) HM.

Oughton, Jerrie. How the Stars Fell into the Sky. Desimini, Lisa, illus. 32p. (gr. k-3). 1992. 14.45 (*0-395-58798-0*) HM.

Rucki, Ani. Turkey's Gift to the People. Rucki, Ani, illus. LC 92-10764. 32p. (ps-4). 1992. 14.95 (*0-87358-541-0*) Northland AZ.

INDIANS OF NORTH AMERICA–NEZ PERCE INDIANS

Anderson, Madelyn K. The Nez Perce. LC 93-31422. (Illus.). 64p. (gr. 5-8). 1994. PLB 12.90 (*0-531-20063-9*); pap. 5.95 (*0-531-15686-9*) Watts.

Fox, Mary V. Chief Joseph of the Nez Perce Indians: Champion of Liberty. LC 92-35053. (Illus.). 152p. (gr. 4 up). 1992. PLB 14.40 (*0-516-03275-5*) Childrens.

Howes, Kathi. Nez Perce. (Illus.). 32p. (gr. 5-8). 1990. lib. bdg. 15.94 (*0-86625-379-3*); lib. bdg. 11.95s.p. (*0-685-36389-9*) Rourke Corp.

Osinski, Alice. The Nez Perce. LC 88-11822. (Illus.). 48p. (gr. k-4). 1988. PLB 12.85 (*0-516-01154-5*); pap. 4.95 (*0-516-41154-3*) Childrens.

Rifkin, Mark. The Nez Perce Indians. LC 93-12221. (Illus.). 80p. (gr. 2-5). 1993. PLB 13.95 (*0-7910-1668-4*, Am Art Analog); pap. write for info. (*0-7910-1992-6*, Am Art Analog) Chelsea Hse.

Schneider, Bill. The Flight of the Nez Perce. rev. ed. White, Dan, illus. LC 88-80227. 32p. 1993. pap. 5.95 (*0-937959-39-1*) Falcon Pr MT.

Scott, Robert A. Chief Joseph & the Nez Perces. (Illus.). 128p. (gr. 5 up). 1993. PLB 16.95x (*0-8160-2475-8*) Facts on File.

Sherrow, Victoria. The Nez Perces: People of the Far West. (Illus.). 64p. (gr. 4-6). 1994. 15.40 (*1-56294-315-4*) Millbrook Pr.

Sneve, Virginia. The Nez Perce. Himler, Ronald, illus. LC 93-38598. 32p. 1994. reinforced bdg. 15.95 (*0-8234-1090-0*) Holiday.

Trafzer, Clifford E. The Nez Perce: Northwest. (Illus.). (gr. 5 up). 1994. 18.95 (*1-55546-720-2*, Am Art Analog); pap. 7.95 (*0-7910-0391-4*, Am Art Analog) Chelsea Hse.

INDIANS OF NORTH AMERICA–NEZ PERCE INDIANS–FICTION

O'Dell, Scott & Hall, Elizabeth. Thunder Rolling in the Mountains. (Illus.). 144p. (gr. 5-9). 1992. 14.45 (*0-395-59966-0*) HM.

INDIANS OF NORTH AMERICA–OGLALA INDIANS

Greene, Carol. Black Elk: A Man with a Vision. LC 90-39480. (Illus.). 48p. (gr. k-3). 1990. PLB 12.85 (*0-516-04213-0*); pap. 4.95 (*0-516-44213-9*) Childrens.

Sanford, William R. Red Cloud: Sioux Warrior. LC 93-42256. (Illus.). 48p. (gr. 4-10). 1994. lib. bdg. 14.95 (*0-89490-513-9*) Enslow Pubs.

INDIANS OF NORTH AMERICA–OJIBWAY INDIANS–FICTION

Carter, Alden R. Dogwolf. LC 93-43518. (gr. 7 up). 1994. 14.95 (*0-590-46741-7*) Scholastic Inc.

Wosmek, Frances. A Brown Bird Singing. Lewin, Ted, illus. LC 92-43784. 128p. (gr. 5 up). 1993. pap. 4.95 (*0-688-04596-0*, Pub. by Beech Tree Bks) Morrow.

INDIANS OF NORTH AMERICA–ORIGIN

Sattler, Helen R. The Earliest Americans. Zallinger, Jean D., illus. 128p. (gr. 4-7). 1993. 16.95 (*0-395-54996-5*, Clarion Bks) HM.

INDIANS OF NORTH AMERICA–PAIUTE INDIANS

Bunte, Pamela A. & Franklin, Robert J. The Paiute. (Illus.). 112p. (gr. 5 up). 1990. 17.95 (*1-55546-723-7*) Chelsea Hse.

INDIANS OF NORTH AMERICA–PAPAGO INDIANS

Baylor, Byrd. The Desert Is Theirs. Parnall, Peter, illus. LC 74-24417. 32p. (ps-3). 1975. SBE 14.95 (*0-684-14266-X*, Scribners Young Read) Macmillan Child Grp.

INDIANS OF NORTH AMERICA–PAWNEE INDIANS–FICTION

Cohen, Caron L. Mud Pony. 1989. pap. 3.95 (*0-590-41526-3*) Scholastic Inc.

Cohen, Caron L., adapted by. The Mud Pony: A Traditional Skidi Pawnee Tale. Begay, Shonto, illus. LC 87-23451. 32p. (gr. k-4). 1988. pap. 14.95 (*0-590-41525-5*) Scholastic Inc.

Fradin, Dennis B. The Pawnee. LC 88-11820. (Illus.). 48p. (gr. k-4). 1988. PLB 12.85 (*0-516-01155-3*); pap. 4.95 (*0-516-41155-1*) Childrens.

Howell, War Cry. Gramma Curlychief's Pawnee Indian Stories. 3rd ed. Burns, Kathy, illus. LC 82-71948. 88p. (Orig.). (gr. 5-12). 1991. pap. 4.95x (*0-943864-22-4*) Davenport.

Paulsen, Gary. Mr. Tucket. LC 93-31180. 1994. 14.95 (*0-385-31169-9*) Delacorte.

INDIANS OF NORTH AMERICA–POETRY

Bierhorst, John, ed. In the Trail of the Wind: American Indian Poems & Ritual Orations. Bierhorst, Jane B., illus. (gr. 8 up). 1987. pap. 4.95 (*0-374-43576-6*) FS&G.

Bierhorst, John, selected by. On the Road of Stars: Native American Night Poems & Sleep Charms. Pedersen, Judy, illus. LC 92-20001. 40p. (gr. 1 up). 1994. RSBE 15.95 (*0-02-709735-8*, Macmillan Child Bk) Macmillan Child Grp.

Bruchac, Joseph & London, Jonathan, eds. Thirteen Moons on Turtle's Back: A Native American Year of Moons. Locker, Thomas, illus. 32p. (ps-8). 1992. PLB 15.95 (*0-399-22141-7*, Philomel Bks) Putnam Pub Group.

Clark, Ann N. In My Mother's House. Herrara, Velino, illus. 64p. 1992. pap. 4.99 (*0-14-054496-8*) Puffin Bks.

Jones, Hettie. The Trees Stand Shining: Poetry of the North American Indians. reissue ed. Parker, Robert A., illus. LC 79-142452. 32p. (gr. k up). 1993. 13.99 (*0-8037-9083-X*); PLB 13.89 (*0-8037-9084-8*) Dial Bks Young.

Longfellow, Henry Wadsworth. Hiawatha's Childhood. Le Cain, Errol, illus. 32p. (gr. k up). 1984. 15.00 (*0-374-33065-4*) FS&G.

—Hiawatha's Childhood. (ps-3). 1994. pap. 5.95 (*0-374-42997-9*, Sunburst) FS&G.

Sneve, Virginia H., selected by. Dancing Teepees: Poems of American Indian Youth. Gammell, Stephen, illus. LC 88-11075. 32p. (ps-4). 1991. pap. 5.95 (*0-8234-0879-5*) Holiday.

Wood, Nancy. Many Winters. Howell, Frank, illus. LC 74-3554. 80p. (gr. 6 up). 1974. pap. 15.95 (*0-385-02226-3*) Doubleday.

—Spirit Walker: Poems. Howell, Frank, illus. LC 92-29376. 80p. 1993. pap. 19.95 (*0-385-30927-9*) Doubleday.

INDIANS OF NORTH AMERICA–POMO INDIANS

Boule, Mary N. California's Native American Tribes, No. 17: East & S. E. Pomo Tribe. Liddell, Daniel, illus. 40p. (Orig.). (gr. 3-4). 1992. pap. 4.50 (*1-877599-40-9*) Merryant Pubs.

—California's Native American Tribes, No. 16: Western & N. E. Pomo Tribe. Liddell, Daniel, illus. 40p. (Orig.). (gr. 2-3). 1992. pap. 4.50 (*1-877599-39-5*) Merryant Pubs.

Brown, Vinson. Pomo Indians of California & Their Neighbors. Elsasser, Albert B., ed. Andrews, Douglas, illus. LC 78-13946. 64p. (Orig.). (gr. 4 up). 1969. 15.95 (*0-911010-31-9*); pap. 8.95 (*0-911010-30-0*) Naturegraph.

Worthylake, Mary M. The Pomo. LC 93-36666. (Illus.). 48p. (gr. k-4). 1994. PLB 12.85 (*0-516-01057-3*) Childrens.

INDIANS OF NORTH AMERICA–PUEBLO INDIANS

Anderson, Peter. Maria Martinez: Pueblo Potter. LC 92-4807. (Illus.). 32p. (gr. 2-5). 1992. PLB 11.80 (*0-516-04184-3*) Childrens.

Arnold, Caroline. The Ancient Cliff Dwellers of Mesa Verde. Hewett, Richard, illus. 64p. (gr. 3-6). 1992. 15.45 (*0-395-56241-4*, Clarion Bks) HM.

Clark, Ann N. Sun Journey: A Story of Zuni Pueblo. reissued ed. Sandy, Percy T., illus. LC 88-70955. 96p. (gr. 3 up). 1988. 19.95 (*0-941270-49-1*); pap. 9.95 (*0-941270-48-3*) Ancient City Pr.

D'Apice, Mary. Pueblo. (Illus.). 32p. (gr. 5-8). 1990. lib. bdg. 15.94 (*0-86625-385-8*); lib. bdg. 11.95s.p. (*0-685-36390-2*) Rourke Corp.

Folsom, Franklin. Red Power on the Rio Grande. Ortiz, Alfonso, intro. by. 144p. (gr. 4 up). 1989. 12.95 (*0-89992-421-2*); pap. 9.95 (*0-89992-121-3*) Coun India Ed.

Hoyt-Goldsmith, Diane. Pueblo Storyteller. Migdale, Lawrence, photos by. 1994. pap. 6.95 (*0-8234-1080-3*) Holiday.

Keegan, Marcia. Pueblo Boy: Growing up in Two Worlds. Keegan, Marcia, photos by. LC 90-45187. (Illus.). 48p. (gr. 2-6). 1991. 15.00 (*0-525-65060-1*, Cobblehill Bks) Dutton Child Bks.

Martell, Hazel M. Native Americans & Mesa Verde. LC 92-27758. (Illus.). 32p. (gr. 5 up). 1993. text ed. 13.95 RSBE (*0-87518-540-1*, Dillon) Macmillan Child Grp.

Ortiz, Alfonso. The Pueblo: Southwest. (Illus.). (gr. 5 up). 1994. 18.95 (*1-55546-727-X*, Am Art Analog); pap. 7.95 (*0-7910-0396-5*, Am Art Analog) Chelsea Hse.

Powell, Suzanne. The Pueblos. LC 93-18368. (Illus.). 64p. (gr. 4-6). 1993. PLB 12.90 (*0-531-20068-X*) Watts.

—The Pueblos. (Illus.). 64p. (gr. 5-8). 1994. pap. 5.95 (*0-685-70386-X*) Watts.

Stillman, Karen. The First Apartment Houses. LC 92-75994. (gr. 1-6). 1993. 9.95 (*0-383-03817-0*) CPI.

Trimble, Stephen. The Village of Blue Stone. Dewey, Jennifer O. & Reade, Deborah, illus. LC 88-34194. 64p. (gr. 3-7). 1990. RSBE 14.95 (*0-02-789501-7*, Macmillan Child Bk) Macmillan Child Grp.

Yoder, Walter D. American Pueblo Indian Activity Book. Smith, James C., Jr., ed. (Illus.). 48p. (Orig.). (gr. 3-9). 1994. pap. 7.95 (*0-86534-219-9*) Sunstone Pr.

Yue, Charlotte. The Pueblo. (gr. 4-7). 1990. pap. 6.95 (*0-395-54961-2*) HM.

INDIANS OF NORTH AMERICA–PUEBLO INDIANS–ANTIQUITIES

Buchanan, Ken. This House Is Made of Mud. LC 90-53589. (ENG & SPA., Illus.). 32p. (ps-2). 1994. 12.95 (*0-87358-593-3*); pap. 6.95 (*0-87358-580-1*) Northland AZ.

Petersen, David. The Anasazi. LC 91-3036. 48p. (gr. k-4). 1991. PLB 12.85 (*0-516-01121-9*); pap. 4.95 (*0-516-41121-7*) Childrens.

—Mesa Verde National Park. LC 91-35275. (Illus.). 48p. (gr. k-4). 1992. PLB 12.85 (*0-516-01136-7*); pap. 4.95 (*0-516-41136-5*) Childrens.

Radlauer, Ruth. Mesa Verde National Park. updated ed. Zillmer, Rolf, photos by. LC 76-27350. (Illus.). 48p. (gr. 3 up). 1984. pap. 4.95 (*0-516-47490-1*) Childrens.

Warren, Scott S. Cities in the Sand: The Ancient Civilizations of the Southwest. Warren, Scott S., illus. 64p. (gr. 4-8). 1991. 10.95 (*0-8118-0012-1*) Chronicle Bks.

INDIANS OF NORTH AMERICA–PUEBLO INDIANS–FICTION

Lyon, George-Ella. Dreamplace. Catalanotto, Peter, illus. LC 92-25102. 32p. (ps-2). 1993. 15.95 (*0-531-05466-7*); PLB 15.99 (*0-531-08616-X*) Orchard Bks Watts.

Mendel, Kathleen L. Whispering Clay. LC 92-71598. (Illus.). 40p. (Orig.). 1992. pap. 4.50x (*1-878142-29-1*) Telstar TX.

Stine, Megan & Stine, H. William. Young Indiana Jones & the Lost Gold of Durango. 132p. (Orig.). (gr. 3-7). 1993. pap. 3.50 (*0-679-84926-2*, Bullseye Bks) Random Bks Yng Read.

Strete, Craig K. Big Thunder Magic. Brown, Craig, illus. LC 89-34613. 32p. (ps up). 1990. 12.95 (*0-688-08853-8*); PLB 12.88 (*0-688-08854-6*) Greenwillow.

Vallo, Lawrence. Tales of a Pueblo Boy. LC 86-5876. (Illus.). 48p. (Orig.). 1987. pap. 5.95 (*0-86534-089-7*) Sunstone Pr.

Weisman, Joan. The Storyteller. Bradley, David, illus. LC 93-20460. 32p. 1993. 15.95 (*0-8478-1742-3*) Rizzoli Intl.

INDIANS OF NORTH AMERICA–PUEBLO INDIANS–LEGENDS

Mcdermott, Gerald. Flecha al Sol. (SPA.). (ps-3). 1991. 15.95 (*0-670-83748-2*) Viking Child Bks.

—Flecha al Sol: Un Cuento do Los Indios Pueblo. McDermott, Gerald, illus. (SPA.). 48p. (ps-3). 1991. pap. 4.99 (*0-14-054364-3*, Puffin) Puffin Bks.

INDIANS OF NORTH AMERICA–RECREATIONS

see Indians of North America–Games

INDIANS OF NORTH AMERICA–RELIGION AND MYTHOLOGY

see also Indians of North America–Dances; Totems and Totemism

Clark, Ella. Guardian Spirit Quest. (gr. 5-12). 1974. pap. 4.95 (*0-89992-045-4*) Coun India Ed.

Hildreth, Dolly, et al. The Money God. (gr. 6). 1972. 1.95 (*0-89992-031-4*) Coun India Ed.

Liptak, Karen. North American Indian Ceremonies. Mathews, V., ed. LC 90-12337. (Illus.). 64p. (gr. 3-6). 1992. PLB 12.90 (*0-531-20100-7*) Watts.

McDonald, W. H. Creation Tales from the Salish. (gr. 3-9). 1973. 1.25 (*0-89992-061-6*) Coun India Ed.

Medicine, Story. Children of the Morning Light: Wampanoag Tales As Told by Manitonquat. Arquette, Mary F., illus. LC 92-32328. 80p. (gr. 1 up). 1994. SBE 16.95 (*0-02-765905-4*, Macmillan Child Bk) Macmillan Child Grp.

Olin, Caroline & Dutton, Bertha P. Southwest Indians, Bk. 1: (Navajo, Pima, Apache, Bk. 1. (Illus.). (gr. 5). 1978. pap. 3.95 (*0-88388-049-0*) Bellerophon Bks.

Redhawk, Randy. The Pow Wow Book: A Must for Every Pow Wow. 2nd, rev. ed. LC 94-92187. (Illus.). 22p. (gr. 3 up). 1994. pap. 5.00x (*0-9641861-0-1*) Redhawk Pubng.

Villasenor, David. Tapestries in Sand: The Spirit of Indian Sandpainting. rev. ed. (Illus.). 112p. (gr. 4 up). 1966. 16.95 (*0-911010-23-8*); pap. 8.95 (*0-911010-22-X*) Naturegraph.

Walker, Paul R. Spiritual Leaders. LC 93-31684. (Illus.). 128p. (gr. 4-11). 1994. 16.95x (*0-8160-2875-3*) Facts on File.

Willoya, William & Brown, Vinson. Warriors of the Rainbow: Strange & Prophetic Dreams of the Indian Peoples. (Illus.). 94p. (gr. 4 up). 1962. 15.95 (*0-911010-25-4*); pap. 7.95 (*0-911010-24-6*) Naturegraph.

Wood, Marion. Spirits, Heroes & Hunters from North American Indian Mythology. Sibbick, John, illus. LC 91-38954. 132p. (gr. 6 up). 1992. 22.50 (*0-87226-903-5*) P Bedrick Bks.

INDIANS OF NORTH AMERICA–SALISH INDIANS–FICTION

Law, Katheryn. Salish Folk Tales. (gr. 2-8). 1972. 1.50 (*0-89992-028-4*) Coun India Ed.

McDonald, W. H. Creation Tales from the Salish. (gr. 3-9). 1973. 1.25 (*0-89992-061-6*) Coun India Ed.

INDIANS OF NORTH AMERICA–SAUK INDIANS

Bonvillain, Nancy. The Sac & Fox. LC 94-21846. 1995. write for info. (*0-7910-1684-6*) Chelsea Pub.

INDIANS OF NORTH AMERICA–SEMINOLE INDIANS

Brooks, B. The Seminole. (Illus.). 32p. (gr. 5-8). 1989. lib. bdg. 15.94 (*0-86625-377-7*); 11.95 (*0-685-58584-0*) Rourke Corp.

Garbarino, Merwyn S. The Seminole. Potter, Frank W., intro. by. (Illus.). 112p. (Orig.). (gr. 5 up). 1989. 17.95 (*1-55546-729-6*); pap. 9.95 (*0-7910-0367-1*) Chelsea Hse.

Koslow, Philip. The Seminole Indians. LC 93-35441. (Illus.). 80p. (gr. 2-5). 1994. PLB 13.95 (*0-7910-1672-2*, Am Art Analog); pap. write for info. (*0-7910-2486-5*, Am Art Analog) Chelsea Hse.

Lee, Martin. The Seminoles. (Illus.). 64p. (gr. 5-8). 1991. pap. 5.95 (*0-531-15604-4*) Watts.

Lepthien, Emilie U. The Seminole. LC 84-23141. (Illus.). 45p. (gr. 2-4). 1985. PLB 12.85 (*0-516-01941-4*); pap. 4.95 (*0-516-41941-2*) Childrens.

Levin, Beatrice & Vanderveld, Marjorie. Me Run Fast Good: Biographies of Tewanima (Hopi), Carlos Montezuma (Apache) & John Horse (Seminole) 32p. (gr. 5-9). 1983. pap. 1.95 (*0-89992-087-X*) Coun India Ed.

Sanford, William R. Crazy Horse: Sioux Warrior. (Illus.). 48p. (gr. 4-10). 1994. lib. bdg. 14.95 (*0-89490-511-2*) Enslow Pubs.

—Osceola: Seminole Warrior. LC 93-40964. (Illus.). 48p. (gr. 4-10). 1994. lib. bdg. 14.95 (*0-89490-535-X*) Enslow Pubs.

The Seminole: Southeast. 112p. (gr. 7-12). PLB 16.95 (*0-685-21874-0*, 201244) Know Unltd.

Sneve, Virginia D. The Seminoles. Himler, Ronald, illus. LC 93-14316. 32p. (gr. 2-6). 1994. reinforced bdg. 15.95 (*0-8234-1112-5*) Holiday.

INDIANS OF NORTH AMERICA–SEMINOLE INDIANS–FICTION

Kudlinski, Kathleen V. Night Bird: A Story of the Seminole Indians. Watling, James, illus. LC 92-25935. 64p. (gr. 2-6). 1990. PLB 12.99 (*0-670-83157-3*) Viking Child Bks.

Medearis, Angela S. Dancing with the Indians. Byrd, Samuel, illus. LC 90-28666. 32p. (ps-3). 1991. reinforced 14.95 (*0-8234-0893-0*) Holiday.

INDIANS OF NORTH AMERICA–SENECA INDIANS

Duvall, Jill. The Seneca. LC 90-21150. (Illus.). 48p. (gr. k-4). 1991. PLB 12.85 (*0-516-01119-7*); pap. 4.95 (*0-516-41119-5*) Childrens.

INDIANS OF NORTH AMERICA–SENECA INDIANS–FICTION

Harrington, M. R. The Iroquois Trail: Dickon among the Onondagas & Senecas. Perceval, Don, illus. 215p. 1991. pap. 9.95 (*0-8135-0480-5*) Rutgers U Pr.

INDIANS OF NORTH AMERICA–SHAWNEE INDIANS–FICTION

Watkins, Sherrin. White Bead Ceremony. Doner, Kim, illus. LC 93-50735. 40p. (gr. 3-6). 1994. 16.95 (*0-933031-92-0*); write for info. (*0-933031-26-2*) Coun Oak Bks.

WHITE BEAD CEREMONY is the first in a series about Mary Greyfeather, a contemporary Shawnee girl, whose world bridges two distinct cultures, that of the traditional Shawnee & that of a typical American child. Mary's mother wants her to learn about her Shawnee heritage, but she is more interested in Barbie dolls. Grandma suggests a Shawnee naming ceremony for Mary, complete with the traditional naming gift, a strand of white beads. Through whimsical pictures & words WHITE BEAD CEREMONY shows what happens when the Greyfeather clan gathers to try to decide upon a name for the little girl. Will she be named for the "mseewi womhsoomi," the grass-eaters, or for the "thepati womhsoomi," the claw-footed animals? In WHITE BEAD CEREMONY children everywhere can share in a traditional family celebration which becomes Mary's link to her rich Native heritage. "The book provides a welcome glimpse at how tribal traditions are woven into the fabric of modern-day life; its educational value is enhanced by the inclusion of Shawnee vocabulary cut-out "flashcards" & a thumbnail-sketch history of the Shawnee people." (PW) Call or write for information to order, Council Oak Publishing, 1350 E. 15th St., Tulsa, OK 74120 (918-587-6454) (800-247-8850).

Publisher Provided Annotation.

INDIANS OF NORTH AMERICA–SIGN LANGUAGE

Cody, Iron Eyes. Indian Talk: Hand Signals of the North American Indians. Cody, Iron Eyes, illus. LC 73-16246. 112p. (gr. 1 up). 1970. 15.95 (*0-911010-83-1*); pap. 7.95 (*0-911010-82-3*) Naturegraph.

Hofsinde, Robert. Indian Sign Language. Hofsinde, Robert, illus. LC 56-5178. (gr. 5 up). 1956. PLB 13.88 (*0-688-31610-7*) Morrow Jr Bks.

Liptak, Karen. North American Indian Sign Language. Berry, Don, illus. LC 90-12336. 64p. (gr. 5-8). 1990. PLB 12.90 (*0-531-10869-4*) Watts.

—North American Indian Sign Language. (Illus.). 64p. (gr. 5-8). 1992. pap. 5.95 (*0-531-15641-9*) Watts.

INDIANS OF NORTH AMERICA–SIKSIKA INDIANS–FICTION

Yolen, Jane. Sky Dogs. Moser, Barry, illus. LC 89-26960. 32p. (ps-3). 1990. 15.95 (*0-15-275480-6*); limited ed., numbered & s 100.00 (*0-15-275481-4*) HarBrace.

INDIANS OF NORTH AMERICA–SIOUX INDIANS

Bendix, Jane. Mi'Ca: Buffalo Hunter. Bendix, Jane, illus. 189p. (Orig.). (gr. 5-10). 1992. 14.95 (*0-89992-431-X*); pap. 9.95 (*0-89992-131-0*) Coun India Ed.

Brooks, B. The Sioux. (Illus.). 32p. (gr. 5-8). 1989. lib. bdg. 15.94 (*0-86625-382-3*); 11.95 (*0-685-58585-9*) Rourke Corp.

Crow, Moses N. Hoksila & the Red Buffalo. Provincial, Bernard W., illus. 40p. (Orig.). (gr. 3 up). 1991. pap. 4.95 (*1-877976-02-4*, 406-0017) Tipi Pr.

Among the Lakota, this legend is called Enya-hoksei. It is told differently by every story-teller of every clan. The outline of the legend remains the same as it travels with time. The whole story changes with the changing of times. The significance of it, as it goes through the ages, is that it has no horses in it. The story has to be very old. But like all legends, it keeps in tune with the passing of time. When Hoksila the young warrior begins his long journey, his hunt to rescue his wife & to rid his tribe of the red buffalo with the ugly black spots. Then he could free all the young maidens. This is a story of the battle of good & evil, & how it's been handed down by the Lakota. An engaging story for the

young & those not so young.
Publisher Provided Annotation.

–A Legend from Crazy Horse Clan. Flood, Renee S., ed. Long Soldier, Daniel, illus. 36p. (Orig.). (gr. 3 up). 1987. pap. 4.95 (*1-877976-03-2*, 406-0010) Tipi Pr.
A LEGEND FROM CRAZY HORSE CLAN is a story for children of all ages. Beautiful illustrations by Daniel Long Soldier keep the legend alive in the reader's eye. The historian or student of Indian ways will enjoy the book as much as the child of seven, in whose imagination the baby raccoon Mesu embodies all that is faithful & loving in a small furry pet. Listen carefully to the words of Tashia. The symbolic role of man & woman is evident throughout the legend. Although the story essentially describes the life of a girl, the narrator is male. Clearly, the legend describes the male viewpoint of manhood, religion, courtship, aging & death. The characters are gentle, yet there is a strong underlying theme of tribal identity. Without a doubt, we are looking at life through the eyes of a warrior. Indian oral narration is spoken American literature in its finest form. When Lakota children of the 1990s become grandparents themselves, they will tell the legends again. Thanks to Moses Big Crow, one of those legends may well be A LEGEND FROM CRAZY HORSE CLAN.
Publisher Provided Annotation.

Crowl, Christine. The Hunter & the Woodpecker. (Illus.). 12p. (Orig.). (ps-6). 1990. pap. 2.50 (*1-877976-09-1*, 406-0015) Tipi Pr.
This children's book describes how the Sioux first discovered the flute, which makes magical music. The Red Headed Woodpecker tells a young brave of its powers to win over a beautiful maiden. A charming story, delightfully illustrated in four colors. A story for children of all ages.
Publisher Provided Annotation.

–White Buffalo Women. (Illus.). 18p. (Orig.). (gr. 6). 1991. pap. 2.50 (*1-877976-10-5*, 406-0014) Tipi Pr.
This story is a core legend of the Sioux & how the Sioux received the Sacred Prayer Pipe. The pipe was an important religious symbol among the Sioux. It was a "moveable" altar which was used in prayer & ceremony. It was the most cherished thing a man could own. The legend of WHITE BUFFALO WOMEN & the pipe originated with the Brule Sioux & is a story that has been handed down through the centuries. Beautifully told & illustrated in four color, a charming story for children young & old.
Publisher Provided Annotation.

Hoover, Herbert T. The Yankton Sioux. Porter, Frank, intro. by. (Illus.). 112p. (gr. 5 up). 1988. lib. bdg. 17.95 (*1-55546-736-9*); pap. 9.95 (*0-7910-0369-8*) Chelsea Hse.

Landau, Elaine. The Sioux. (Illus.). 64p. (gr. 3 up). 1991. pap. 5.95 (*0-531-15606-0*) Watts.

Nicholson, Robert. Los Siux. Araluce, Jose R., tr. from ENG. (SPA., Illus.). 32p. 1993. 16.95x (*1-56492-092-5*) Laredo.

Osinski, Alice. The Sioux. LC 84-7629. (Illus.). 48p. (gr. k-4). 1984. PLB 12.85 (*0-516-01929-5*); pap. 4.95 (*0-516-41929-3*) Childrens.

Sandoz, Mari. These Were the Sioux. Kills Two & Amos Bad Heart Bull, illus. LC 85-8914. 118p. (gr. 6-12). 1985. pap. 5.95 (*0-8032-9151-5*, Bison Books) U of Nebr Pr.

Simms, Thomas E. Otokahekagapi (First Beginnings) Sioux Creation Story. (Illus.). 36p. (Orig.). 1987. pap. 3.50 (*1-877976-06-7*, 406-0005) Tipi Pr.
The first in a series of Lakota legends, is written & illustrated to foster greater respect for a proud people's tradition. This account in English & Lakota presents the profundity of the creation mystery. The pictures are Indian pictures, because this is the beginning of the Sioux Creation account. But it is for all children everywhere, because everyone asks about how things got started & how the World began. "So this picture book is like a little ball game. We shall learn that the book is a ball. Wakantanka will throw this ball to us, which is this book, & we shall catch it. Then we shall understand it. And we shall enjoy ourselves. Bring the ball -- this book -- to the Center, which is your Heart, then you will receive a present. The present is invisible, like a little secret. Good. That's all. Now I shall throw the ball to you. Catch it!"
Publisher Provided Annotation.

Wolfson, Evelyn. The Teton Sioux: People of the Plains. LC 92-4633. (Illus.). 64p. (gr. 4-6). 1992. PLB 15.40 (*1-56294-077-5*) Millbrook Pr.

INDIANS OF NORTH AMERICA–SIOUX INDIANS–FICTION

Shubert, J. Lansing. The Legacy of George Partridgeberry. Steele, Robert, ed. Shubert, Christiane, illus. 381p. (Orig.). (gr. 9-12). 1990. pap. 12.95 (*0-9627015-0-5*) J L Shubert.

INDIANS OF NORTH AMERICA–SOCIAL CONDITIONS

Campbell, Maria. People of the Buffalo: How the Plains Indians Lived. Tait, Douglas & Twofeathers, Shannon, illus. 48p. (gr. 3-7). 1992. pap. 7.95 (*0-88894-329-6*, Pub. by Groundwood-Douglas & McIntyre CN) Firefly Bks Ltd.

Ridington, Robin & Ridington, Jillian. People of the Trail: How the Northern Forest Indians Lived. Bateson, Ian, illus. 40p. (gr. 3-7). 1992. pap. 7.95 (*0-88894-412-8*, Pub. by Groundwood-Douglas & McIntyre CN) Firefly Bks Ltd.

INDIANS OF NORTH AMERICA–SOCIAL LIFE AND CUSTOMS

see also Indians of North America–Dances; Indians of North America–Games

Alter, Judy. The Comanches. LC 93-23265. 1994. 12.90 (*0-531-20115-5*); pap. 5.95 (*0-531-15683-4*) Watts.

Anderson, Madelyn K. The Nez Perce. LC 93-31422. (Illus.). 64p. (gr. 5-8). 1994. PLB 12.90 (*0-531-20063-9*); pap. 5.95 (*0-531-15686-9*) Watts.

Batdorf, Carol. Gifts of the Season: Life among the Northwest Indians. Graves, Katheryn, illus. 24p. (Orig.). (gr. 1-6). 1990. pap. 5.95 (*0-88839-246-X*) Hancock House.

Behrens, Terry. Powwow. LC 83-7274. (Illus.). 32p. (gr. k-4). 1983. pap. 3.95 (*0-516-42387-8*) Childrens.

Boss-Ribs, Mary C. & Running-Crane, Jenny. Stories of Our Blackfeet Grandmothers. (Orig.). (gr. 1-6). 1984. pap. 4.95 (*0-89992-096-9*) Coun India Ed.

Boule, Mary N. The California Native American Tribes, 26 vols. Harding, Virginia, ed. Liddell, Daniel, illus. (gr. 1-8). 1993. Boxed ed. pap. 94.00 (*1-877599-23-9*) Merryant Pubs.
CALIFORNIA NATIVE AMERICAN TRIBES is a series of 26 books, representing 26 groups of Native Americans living in what is today the state of California. Written at the third-through-fifth grade reading level, each book has a common chapter on California Native American people in general (to facilitate teachers' introduction of study unit), followed by a chapter containg succinct information on the everyday life of an individual band, or tribe, before the arrival of European explorers. Information is up-to-date & factual. Outstanding artwork is by Dan Liddell, one-quarter Chickasaw, whose exquisite line-drawings are rendered with an eye toward important details children often miss when looking at museum photos. An outline of each book's second chapter text is included, so students can write one of their first reports in a chronological, original style. Books available in boxed sets for classrooms or individually for custom sets. MERRYANT PUBLISHER, INC., 7615 SW 257th St., Vashon, WA 98070 (206-463-3879).
Publisher Provided Annotation.

Brandt, Keith. Indian Festivals. Guzzi, George, illus. LC 84-2644. 32p. (gr. 3-6). 1985. PLB 9.49 (*0-8167-0182-2*); pap. text ed. 2.95 (*0-8167-0183-0*) Troll Assocs.

Burrill, Richard. Protectors of the Land: An Environmental Journey to Understanding the Conservation Ethic. Macias, Regina, ed. Waters, Robyn & Ipina, David, illus. 300p. (gr. 3-12). 1993. pap. text ed. 22.95 (*1-878464-02-7*); write for info. (*1-878464-03-5*) Anthro Co.

Carter, Alden R. The Shoshoni. LC 89-31102. (Illus.). 64p. (gr. 3-5). 1989. PLB 12.90 (*0-531-10753-1*) Watts.

Eargle, Dolan H., Jr. California Indian Country: The Land & the People. LC 91-67406. (Illus.). (gr. 4). 1992. pap. 12.70 (*0-937401-20-X*) Trees Co Pr.

Echo-Hawk, Roger C. & Echo-Hawk, Walter R. Battlefields & Burial Grounds: The Indian Struggle to Protect Ancestral Graves & Human Remains in the United States. LC 92-39893. 1993. 19.95 (*0-8225-2663-8*) Lerner Pubns.

Gilliland, Hap. Coyote's Pow-Wow. (gr. 1-6). 1972. 4.95 (*0-89992-022-5*) Coun India Ed.

Goodchild, Peter. The Spark in the Stone: Skills & Projects from the Native American Tradition. LC 90-27324. (Illus.). 144p. (Orig.). (gr. 5 up). 1991. pap. 11.95 (*1-55652-102-2*) Chicago Review.

Hirschi, Ron. Seya's Song. Bergum, Constance R., illus. LC 92-5029. 32p. (ps up). 1992. text ed. 14.95 (*0-912365-62-5*) Sasquatch Bks.

Hofsinde, Robert. Indian Warriors & Their Weapons. Hofsinde, Robert, illus. LC 65-11041. (gr. 4-7). 1965. PLB 11.88 (*0-688-31613-1*) Morrow Jr Bks.

Hoyt-Goldsmith, Diane. Pueblo Storyteller. Migdale, Lawrence, illus. LC 90-46405. 32p. (gr. 3-7). 1991. reinforced bdg. 15.95 (*0-8234-0864-7*) Holiday.

Kalbacken, Joan. The Menominee. LC 93-36671. (Illus.). 48p. (gr. k-4). 1994. PLB 12.85 (*0-516-01054-9*) Childrens.

Keegan, Marcia. Pueblo Boy: Growing up in Two Worlds. Keegan, Marcia, photos by. LC 90-45187. (Illus.). 48p. (gr. 2-6). 1991. 15.00 (*0-525-65060-1*, Cobblehill Bks) Dutton Child Bks.

Krull, Kathleen. One Nation, Many Tribes: How Kids Live in Milwaukee's Indian Community. Hautzig, David, photos by. LC 93-39538. 1994. write for info. (*0-525-67440-3*, Lodestar Bks) Dutton Child Bks.

Landau, Elaine. The Chilula. LC 93-31423. (Illus.). 64p. (gr. 5-8). 1994. PLB 12.90 (*0-531-20132-5*); pap. 5.95 (*0-531-15685-0*) Watts.

—The Hopi. LC 93-31964. 1994. 12.90 (*0-531-20098-1*); pap. 5.95 (*0-531-15684-2*) Watts.

Liptak, Karen. North American Indian Ceremonies. Mathews, V., ed. LC 90-12337. (Illus.). 64p. (gr. 3-6). 1992. PLB 12.90 (*0-531-20100-7*) Watts.

McKeown, Martha F. Come to Our Salmon Feast. LC 59-9823. (Illus.). (gr. 4-9). 1959. 7.95 (*0-8323-0157-4*) Binford Mort.

McLain, Gary. The Indian Way: Learning to Communicate with Mother Earth. (Illus.). 114p. (Orig.). (gr. 3 up). 1990. pap. 9.95 (*0-945465-73-4*) John Muir.

Payne, Elizabeth. Meet the North American Indians. (Illus.). (gr. 2-6). 1965. 6.95 (*0-394-80060-5*); (Random Juv) Random Bks Yng Read.

Regguinti, Gordon. The Sacred Harvest: Ojibway Wild Rice Gathering. Kakkak, Dale, photos by. (Illus.). 48p. (gr. 3-6). 1992. PLB 19.95 (*0-8225-2650-6*) Lerner Pubns.

Rinebold, Analo T. & Rinebold, Albert. Aware Tribe for Kids: Growing up among Native Americans. 50p. (Orig.). 1994. pap. 10.00 (*0-9626135-4-1*) Aware Tribe.

Ruoff, A. LaVonne. Literatures of the American Indian. (Illus.). 112p. (gr. 5 up). 1991. PLB 17.95 (*1-55546-688-5*) Chelsea Hse.

Shuter, Jane, intro. by. Francis Parkman & the Plains Indians. LC 94-12853. (gr. 5 up). 1995. write for info. (*0-8114-8280-4*) Raintree Steck-V.

Sita, Lisa. The Rattle & the Drum: Native American Rituals & Celebrations. LC 93-27209. (Illus.). 80p. (gr. 3-6). 1994. PLB 16.90 (*1-56294-420-7*) Millbrook Pr.
Swentzell, Rina. Children of Clay: A Family of Pueblo Potters: We Are Still Here. (gr. 4-7). 1993. pap. 6.95 (*0-8225-9627-X*) Lerner Pubns.
Thomson, Peggy. Katie Henio, Navajo Sheepherder. Conklin, Paul, photos by. LC 93-40430. 1994. write for info. (*0-525-65160-8*, Cobblehill Pr) Dutton Child Bks.
Thomson, Ruth. Indians of the Plains. LC 90-46264. (Illus.). 32p. (gr. 4-6). 1991. PLB 11.90 (*0-531-14157-8*) Watts.
Trimble, Stephen. The Village of Blue Stone. Dewey, Jennifer O. & Reade, Deborah, illus. LC 88-34194. 64p. (gr. 3-7). 1990. RSBE 14.95 (*0-02-789501-7*, Macmillan Child Bk) Macmillan Child Grp.
Williams, Neva. Patrick des Jarlait: The Story of a Native American Artist. LC 94-6535. (gr. 5 up). 1994. write for info. (*0-8225-3151-8*) Lerner Pubns.
Wittstock, Laura W. Ininatig's Gift of Sugar: Traditional Native Sugarmaking. Kakkak, Dale, photos by. Dorris, Michael, frwd. by. LC 92-37980. (Illus.). 48p. 1993. 19.95 (*0-8225-2653-0*) Lerner Pubns.
Wolfson, Evelyn. Growing up Indian. Bock, William S., illus. LC 86-9053. 96p. (gr. 10 up). 1986. 10.95 (*0-8027-6643-9*); PLB 11.85 (*0-8027-6644-7*) Walker & Co.
Wood, Leigh. Childrearing. LC 94-5878. 1994. write for info. (*0-86625-537-0*) Rourke Bk Co.

INDIANS OF NORTH AMERICA–SPORTS
see Indians of North America–Games

INDIANS OF NORTH AMERICA–SUQUAMISH INDIANS
Jeffers, Susan, illus. Brother Eagle, Sister Sky: A Message from Chief Seattle. LC 90-27713. 32p. 1991. 16.00 (*0-8037-0969-2*); PLB 14.89 (*0-8037-0963-3*) Dial Bks Young.

INDIANS OF NORTH AMERICA–UTE INDIANS–FICTION
Hobbs, Will. Beardance. LC 92-44874. 208p. (gr. 5-9). 1993. SBE 14.95 (*0-689-31867-7*, Atheneum Child Bk) Macmillan Child Grp.

INDIANS OF NORTH AMERICA–WAMPANOAG INDIANS
Medicine, Story. Children of the Morning Light: Wampanoag Tales As Told by Manitonquat. Arquette, Mary F., illus. LC 92-32328. 80p. (gr. 1 up). 1994. SBE 16.95 (*0-02-765905-4*, Macmillan Child Bk) Macmillan Child Grp.
Peters, Russell M. Clambake: A Wampanoag Tradition. Madama, John, photos by. (Illus.). 48p. (gr. 3-6). 1992. PLB 19.95 (*0-8225-2651-4*) Lerner Pubns.

INDIANS OF NORTH AMERICA–WAMPANOAG INDIANS–FICTION
Fontes, Ron & Korman, Justine. Walt Disney Pictures Presents The Indian Warrior: A Novel. Fontes, Ron & Korman, Justine, illus. LC 93-48122. 32p. (gr. k-3). 1994. pap. 3.50 (*0-8167-2502-0*) Troll Assocs.

INDIANS OF NORTH AMERICA–WARS
see also U. S.–History–French and Indian War, 1755-1763
Brown, Dee. Wounded Knee: An Indian History of the American West. Ehrlich, Amy, adapted by. (Illus.). 224p. (gr. 7 up). 1993. pap. 9.95 (*0-8050-2700-9*, Bks Young Read) H Holt & Co.
Connell, Kate. These Lands Are Ours: Tecumseh's Fight for the Old Northwest. Jones, Jan N., illus. LC 92-14417. 96p. (gr. 2-5). 1992. PLB 21.34 (*0-8114-7227-2*) Raintree Steck-V.
Henry Tall Bull & Weist, Tom. Cheyenne Warriors. (gr. 4-12). 1976. pap. 1.25 (*0-89992-015-2*) Coun India Ed.
O'Neill, Laurie. Wounded Knee: Death of a Dream. LC 92-12998. (Illus.). 64p. (gr. 4-6). 1993. 15.40 (*1-56294-253-0*); pap. 5.95 (*1-56294-748-6*) Millbrook Pr.
Reedstrom, E. Lisle. Custer's Seventh Cavalry: From Fort Riley to the Little Big Horn. LC 92-26524. (Illus.). 176p. (gr. 10-12). 1992. pap. 14.95 (*0-8069-8762-6*) Sterling.
Stein, R. Conrad. The Story of Wounded Knee. LC 83-6584. (Illus.). 32p. (gr. 3-6). 1983. pap. 3.95 (*0-516-44665-7*) Childrens.
Utter, Jack. Wounded Knee & the Ghost Dance Tragedy. LC 91-61211. (Illus.). iv, 29p. (Orig.). (gr. 10-12). 1991. pap. 3.95 (*0-9628075-1-6*) Natl Woodlands Pub.

INDIANS OF NORTH AMERICA–WYAM INDIANS
McKeown, Martha F. Come to Our Salmon Feast. LC 59-9823. (Illus.). (gr. 4-9). 1959. 7.95 (*0-8323-0157-4*) Binford Mort.
—Linda's Indian Home. LC 56-8826. (Illus.). (gr. 3-7). 1969. 7.95 (*0-8323-0151-5*) Binford Mort.

INDIANS OF NORTH AMERICA–YUMA INDIANS
Bee, Robert L. The Yuma. (Illus.). 112p. (gr. 5 up). 1989. 17.95 (*1-55546-737-7*) Chelsea Hse.

INDIANS OF NORTH AMERICA–ZUNI INDIANS–FICTION
Hillerman, Tony. The Boy Who Made Dragonfly: A Zuni Myth. Grado, Janet, illus. LC 86-6996. 85p. (gr. 5 up). 1986. pap. 8.95 (*0-8263-0910-0*) U of NM Pr.

INDIANS OF SOUTH AMERICA
A Day with Tupi. (gr. 4). pap. 2.00 (*0-915266-01-6*) Awani Pr.
Flora. Feathers Like a Rainbow: An Amazon Indian Tale. Flora, illus. LC 88-26788. 32p. (gr. k-3). 1989. PLB 14.89 (*0-06-021838-X*) HarpC Child Bks.
Frost, Abigail. The Amazon. LC 89-17357. (Illus.). 48p. (gr. 4-8). 1990. PLB 13.95 (*1-85435-236-9*) Marshall Cavendish.
Kendall, Sarita. The Incas. LC 91-513. (Illus.). 64p. (gr. 6 up). 1992. text ed. 14.95 RSBE (*0-02-750160-4*, New Discovery) Macmillan Child Grp.
Lewington, Anna. Rain Forest Amerindians. LC 92-10560. (Illus.). 48p. (gr. 5-6). 1992. PLB 22.80 (*0-8114-2302-6*) Raintree Steck-V.
—What Do We Know about Amazonian Indians? LC 93-1736. (Illus.). 40p. (gr. 3 up). 1993. PLB 16.95 (*0-87226-367-3*); pap. 8.95 (*0-87226-262-6*) P Bedrick Bks.
Morrison, Marion. Indians of the Andes. (Illus.). 48p. (gr. 4-8). 1987. PLB 16.67 (*0-86625-260-6*); 12.50s.p. (*0-685-67605-6*) Rourke Corp.
Newman, Shirlee P. The Incas. Rosoff, Iris, ed. LC 91-31378. (Illus.). 64p. (gr. 3-5). 1992. PLB 12.90 (*0-531-20004-3*) Watts.
Rand McNally Staff & Reddy, Francis. Children's Atlas of Native Americans Rand McNally: Native Cultures of North & South America. Adelman, Elizabeth, ed. Cunningham, David, illus. 78p. (gr. 3-12). Date not set. 14.95 (*0-685-66563-1*); PLB 18.95 (*1-878363-99-9*) Forest Hse.
Redhawk, Richard. Grandmother's Christmas Story: A True Tale of the Quechan Indians. (Illus.). (ps-5). 1987. pap. 6.95 (*0-940113-08-2*) Sierra Oaks Pub.
Schwartz, David M. Yanomami: People of the Amazon. Englebert, Victor, photos by. LC 93-48616. (Illus.). 1994. 16.00 (*0-688-11157-2*); PLB 15.93 (*0-688-11158-0*) Lothrop.

INDIANS OF SOUTH AMERICA–FICTION
Blair, David N. Fear the Condor. 160p. (gr. 7 up). 1992. 15.00 (*0-525-67381-4*, Lodestar Bks) Dutton Child Bks.
Bosse, Malcolm. Deep Dream of the Rain Forest. large type ed. LC 93-42093. 1994. 15.95 (*0-7862-0145-2*) Thorndike Pr.
Kendall, Sarita. Ransom for a River Dolphin. LC 93-19929. 1993. 18.95 (*0-8225-0735-8*) Lerner Pubns.
O'Dell, Scott. The Amethyst Ring. LC 82-23388. 224p. (gr. 7 up). 1983. 14.45 (*0-395-33886-7*) HM.
Ritch, Ronald. Bones of Molech. Graves, Helen, ed. LC 86-51078. 240p. 1987. pap. 9.95 (*1-55523-061-X*) Winston-Derek.
Topooco, Eusebio. Waira's First Journey. LC 92-44158. (gr. 4 up). 1993. 15.00 (*0-688-12054-7*) Lothrop.

INDIANS OF SOUTH AMERICA–LEGENDS
Gifford, Douglas. Warriors, Gods & Spirits from Central & South American Mythology. Sibbeck, John & Dew, Heather, illus. LC 93-1013. 128p. (gr. 6 up). 1993. 22.50 (*0-87226-914-0*); pap. 14.95 sewn (*0-87226-915-9*) P Bedrick Bks.
Kuss, Daniele. Incas. LC 91-17741. (Illus.). 48p. (gr. 4-8). 1991. PLB 13.95 (*1-85435-267-9*) Marshall Cavendish.
McDermott, Gerald. Arrow to the Sun: A Pueblo Indian Tale. LC 73-16172. (Illus.). 48p. (gr. 1 up). 1974. pap. 14.95 (*0-670-13369-8*) Viking Child Bks.
Skivington, Janice, illus. The Girl from the Sky: An Inca Folktale from South America. LC 91-42163. 24p. (ps-3). 1992. PLB 13.85 (*0-516-05138-5*); pap. 5.95 (*0-516-45138-3*) Childrens.
Van Laan, Nancy. The Legend of El Dorado. Vidal, Beatriz, illus. LC 89-7998. 40p. (ps-4). 1991. 16.00 (*0-679-80136-7*) Knopf Bks Yng Read.

INDIANS OF SOUTH AMERICA–PERU
Alexander, Ellen. Chaska & the Golden Doll. LC 93-34691. (Illus.). 32p. (ps-3). 1994. 14.95 (*1-559702-41-9*) Arcade Pub Inc.

INDIC LITERATURE–COLLECTIONS
Das, Manoj. Books Forever. Chatterji, Sukumar, illus. (gr. 2-8). 1979. pap. 2.50 (*0-89744-175-3*) Auromere.

INDIVIDUALISM
see also Communism
Moore, Beverly. Echo's Song. Moore, Beverly, illus. 40p. (gr. k-3). 1993. PLB 13.95g (*0-9637288-7-3*) River Walker Bks.
Simon, Norma. Why Am I Different? Rubin, Caroline, ed. Leder, Dora, illus. LC 76-41172. 32p. (gr. k-2). 1976. PLB 11.95 (*0-8075-9074-6*) A Whitman.

INDIVIDUALITY
see also Personality
Barclay, Shinan N. Who Am I? What Am I? Where Do I Belong? The Storytale about the Search for Meaning, Identity & Purpose. (Illus.). 40p. (ps-4). 1990. 5.95 (*0-317-89505-2*); pap. write for info. (*0-945086-08-3*) Sunlight Prodns.
Clapman, Arnold. Angel the Pig. LC 94-20302. (Illus.). 1994. pap. 5.95 (*0-382-24662-4*) Silver Burdett Pr.
Danziger, Paula. Can You Sue Your Parents for Malpractice? LC 78-72856. 266p. (gr. 7 up). 1979. 14.95 (*0-385-28112-9*) Delacorte.
De Paola, Tomie. The Art Lesson. De Paola, Tomie, illus. 32p. (ps-3). 1989. 13.95 (*0-399-21688-X*, Putnam) Putnam Pub Group.
Discovering Personal Resources. 64p. (gr. 8 up). PLB 14.95 (*0-8239-1278-7*) Rosen Group.
Gaston, Blanche P. I Like Me, Vol. I. Kerns, Aaron, illus. 24p. (Orig.). (gr. k-3). 1982. 6.95x (*0-9608516-0-7*); pap. 4.95x (*0-9608516-1-5*) I Like Me Pub.
Grande Tabor, Nancy M. Are We Different? Somos Diferentes? Grande Tabor, Nancy M., illus. 32p. (ps-4). 1995. PLB 15.88 (*0-88106-814-4*); pap. 6.95 (*0-88106-813-6*) Charlesbridge Pub.
Konczal, Dee & Pesetski, Loretta. We All Come in Different Packages. 88p. (gr. 3-6). 1983. 8.95 (*0-88160-099-7*, LW 243) Learning Wks.
LeShan, Eda. What Makes You So Special? LC 91-16925. 160p. (gr. 3-7). 1992. 15.00 (*0-8037-1155-7*) Dial Bks Young.
Pevsner, Stella. I'm Emma, I'm a Quint. LC 92-36952. 1993. 13.95 (*0-395-64166-7*, Clarion Bks) HM.
Rotner, Shelley & Kreisler, Ken. Faces. Rotner, Shelley, photos by. LC 93-46758. (ps-1). 1994. 14.95 (*0-02-777887-8*) Macmillan.
Schwartz, Linda. I Am Special. 24p. (gr. 1-4). 1978. 3.95 (*0-88160-053-9*, LW 601) Learning Wks.
Spier, Peter. People. Spier, Peter, illus. LC 78-19832. 48p. (gr. 1-3). 1980. PLB 15.95 (*0-385-13181-X*) Doubleday.
Starkman, Neal. Personal Views. Gellos, Nancy, illus. LC 89-22302. 43p. (Orig.). (gr. 6-12). 1989. pap. 7.00 (*0-935529-12-8*) Comprehen Health Educ.
Thomasson, Merry. Hey Look at Me! Here We Go. Havens, Greg, illus. LC 85-62576. 20p. (ps-2). 1985. 9.95 (*0-9615407-0-2*) Thomasson-Grant.
—Hey Look at Me! I Can Be. Poole, Valerie, illus. LC 87-90455. 20p. (ps-2). 1987. 9.95 (*0-9615407-1-0*) Thomasson-Grant.
—Hey Look at Me! I Like to Dream. Poole, Valerie, illus. LC 87-90547. 20p. (ps-2). 1987. 9.95 (*0-9615407-2-9*) Thomasson-Grant.

INDOCHINA
see Asia, Southeastern

INDONESIA
Hassal, S. & Hassal, P. Brunei. (Illus.). 96p. (gr. 5 up). 1988. 14.95 (*0-7910-0158-X*) Chelsea Hse.
Jacobs, Judy. Indonesia: A Nation of Islands. (Illus.). 128p. (gr. 5 up). 1990. text ed. 14.95 RSBE (*0-87518-423-5*, Dillon) Macmillan Child Grp.
Lerner Publications, Department of Geography Staff, ed. Indonesia in Pictures. (Illus.). 64p. (gr. 5 up). 1990. PLB 17.50 (*0-8225-1860-0*) Lerner Pubns.
McNair, Sylvia. Indonesia. LC 93-3401. (Illus.). 128p. (gr. 5-9). 1993. PLB 20.55 (*0-516-02618-6*) Childrens.
Mirpuri, Gouri. Indonesia. LC 89-25457. (Illus.). 128p. (gr. 5-9). 1991. PLB 21.95 (*1-85435-294-6*) Marshall Cavendish.
Williams, Jeff T. Macao. (Illus.). 88p. (gr. 5 up). 1988. lib. bdg. 14.95 (*1-55546-786-5*) Chelsea Hse.

INDUCTION (LOGIC)
see Logic

INDUSTRIAL DRAWING
see Mechanical Drawing

INDUSTRIAL MANAGEMENT
see also Business; Machinery

INDUSTRIAL MATERIALS
see Materials

INDUSTRIAL PSYCHOLOGY
see Psychology, Applied

INDUSTRIAL REVOLUTION
see Great Britain–History–19th Century; Industry–History

INDUSTRIAL WASTES
see Waste Products

INDUSTRIES
see Industry

INDUSTRY
For general works on manufacturing and mechanical activities. Names of all individual industries are not included in this list but are to be added as needed, e.g. Steel Industry And Trade, etc.
see also Machinery in Industry; Manufactures
Morris, Scott, ed. Industry of the World. De Blij, Harm J., intro. by. LC 92-22288. (Illus.). 1993. 15.95 (*0-7910-1807-5*, Am Art Analog); pap. write for info. (*0-7910-1820-2*, Am Art Analog) Chelsea Hse.

INDUSTRY–HISTORY
Brownstone, David M. & Franck, Irene M. Manufacturers & Miners. (Illus.). 176p. 1988. 17.95x (*0-8160-1447-7*) Facts on File.
Clare, John D., ed. Industrial Revolution. LC 93-2554. 1994. 16.95 (*0-15-200514-5*) HarBrace.
Dale, Henry, et al. The Industrial Revolution. LC 92-21663. 1992. 16.00 (*0-19-520967-2*) OUP.

INDUSTRY AND ART
see Art Industries and Trade

INEBRIATES
see Alcoholism

INFANTILE PARALYSIS
see Poliomyelitis

INFANTS
For works about children in the earliest period of life, usually the first two years only.
Ahlberg, Janet & Ahlberg, Allan. The Baby's Catalogue. LC 82-9928. (Illus.). 32p. (gr. k up). 1983. 15.95i (*0-316-02037-0*, Joy St Bks) Little.
All about Baby! (Illus.). 20p. (ps). 1994. bds. 4.95 (*1-56458-530-1*) Dorling Kindersley.
Anholt, Catherine & Anholt, Laurence. Here Come the Babies. LC 92-54584. (Illus.). 32p. (ps up). 1993. 13.95 (*1-56402-209-9*) Candlewick Pr.
Asmann, Lynn & Sprague, Jane. Baby Basics. Asmann, Lynn, illus. (gr. 5 up). 1980. pap. 4.95 (*0-938416-00-6*) BCS Educ Aids.
Baby. LC 91-58213. (Illus.). 24p. (ps-3). 1992. 8.95 (*1-56458-004-0*) Dorling Kindersley.
Baby & Friends. (Illus.). 20p. (ps). 1994. bds. 4.95 (*1-56458-531-X*) Dorling Kindersley.
Berenstain, Stan & Berenstain, Janice. The Berenstain Bears' New Baby. Berenstain, Stan & Berenstain, Janice, illus. LC 74-2535. 32p. (Orig.). (ps-1). 1974. pap. 2.50 (*0-394-82908-5*) Random Bks Yng Read.

Bradley-Johnson, Sharon & Johnson, C. Merle. Baby Power: A New Addition. (Illus.). 32p. (Orig.). 1981. pap. 3.00 (*1-878526-05-7*) Pineapple MI.
Brandenberg, Aliki. Welcome Little Baby: Miniature Edition. Brandenberg, Aliki, illus. 24p. (ps up). 1993. Repr. text ed. 4.95 (*0-688-12665-0*, Tupelo Bks) Morrow.
Brinkley, Ginny & Sampson, Sherry. Usted y Su Nuevo Bebe: Un Libro Para Madres Jovenes. Salmon, Otilia & Rodriquez, Judy, trs. from ENG. Cooper, Gail S., illus. LC 92-80146. (SPA.). 80p. (gr. 7-12). 1992. pap. text ed. 4.95 (*0-9622585-2-0*) Pink Inc.
Cartwright, Stephen, illus. The New Baby. 16p. (ps up). 1994. 3.95 (*0-7460-1271-3*) EDC.
Cole, Joanna. How You Were Born. rev. ed. Miller, Margaret, photos by. LC 92-23970. (Illus.). 48p. (ps up). 1994. pap. 4.95 (*0-688-12061-X*, Mulberry) Morrow.
—How You Were Born: Illustrated with Photographs. rev. ed. Miller, Margaret, photos by. LC 92-23970. (Illus.). 48p. (ps up). 1993. 15.00 (*0-688-12059-8*); PLB 14.93 (*0-688-12060-1*) Morrow Jr Bks.
Dickman, Chareleen. Memories of Me, Baby. Hungerford, La Farne G., illus. (ps). 1993. pap. text ed. 34.95 (*1-882237-01-3*) Life Time Pubs.
Gee, R. Babies. 48p. (gr. 5-10). 1986. PLB 13.96 (*0-88110-336-5*); pap. 6.95 (*0-86020-839-7*) EDC.
Good Morning, Baby! (Illus.). 20p. (ps). 1994. bds. 4.95 (*1-56458-529-8*) Dorling Kindersley.
Good Night, Baby! (Illus.). 20p. (ps). 1994. bds. 4.95 (*1-56458-532-8*) Dorling Kindersley.
Hains, Harriet. My Baby Brother. LC 91-58199. (Illus.). 24p. (ps-3). 1992. 9.95 (*1-879431-76-9*) Dorling Kindersley.
Henderson, Kathy. The Baby's Book of Babies. Sieveking, Anthea, photos by. LC 88-20428. (Illus.). 24p. (ps-k). 1989. 9.95 (*0-8037-0634-0*) Dial Bks Young.
—The Baby's Book of Babies. Sieveking, Anthea, photos by. (Illus.). 24p. (ps-k). 1993. pap. 4.50 (*0-14-054882-3*, Puff Pied Piper) Puffin Bks.
Hendrickson, Karen. Baby & I Can Play & Fun with Toddlers. rev. ed. Steelsmith, Shari, ed. LC 89-64200. (Illus.). 56p. (ps-3). 1990. lib. bdg. 17.95 (*0-943990-57-2*); pap. 6.95 (*0-943990-56-4*) Parenting Pr.

Hyde, Sharon K. Babies Looking Book: Stimulation for the Newborn to Six Month Old Infant. (Illus.). 36p. (ps). 1992. 12.95 (*0-9624349-0-6*) S K Hyde. Babies tend to orient to faces more than other things around them. Using the technique of preferential looking, preferences have been ordered. For the newborn...color or pattern over grey... high contrast pattern over color... moderate complexity over high complexity...symmetrical over random. Interest in specific stimuli decreases over time & with the number of exposures. Visual stimulation is more effective when combined with auditory & tactile stimuli. Cognitive skills can be enhanced by appropriate stimulation. Also the nature of the interaction between the parent & the baby is developed. The baby is provided a safe, supportive & sensitive environment in which to see & learn. Reading to the baby allows focusing of attention, change of material as often as necessary, develops habit which remains valuable to relationship for years.
Publisher Provided Annotation.

Jacobsen, Mark & Kozlovski, Jane. Baby's Book. Jacobsen, Judith, ed. La Belle, Susan, illus. 1989. 24. 95 (*0-9623800-0-8*) Me Two Pubns.
—Baby's First Year. Jacobsen, Judith, ed. La Belle, Susan, illus. 1989. pap. 9.95 (*0-9623800-1-6*) Me Two Pubns.
Jonas, Ann. When You Were a Baby. Jonas, Ann, illus. LC 81-12800. 24p. (ps-1). 1982. 15.00 (*0-688-00863-1*); PLB 14.93 (*0-688-00864-X*) Greenwillow.
Knight, Margy Burns. Welcoming Babies. O'Brien, Anne S., illus. LC 94-6854. 19p. (gr. k up). 1994. 14.95 (*0-88448-123-9*) Tilbury Hse.
Kugler, Lisa. A New Baby for Us: Sibling Preparation & Activity Book for Big Brothers & Sisters. Kugler, Lisa, illus. 32p. (Orig.). (ps-1). 1990. pap. 5.95 (*0-944782-03-5*) Glover Pr.
Lawrence, John. Good Babies, Bad Babies: A Primer for Expectant Parents. (ps). 1990. 10.95 (*0-87923-823-2*) Godine.
MacKinnon, Debbie. Baby's First Year. Sieveking, Anthea, photos by. LC 92-21830. 26p. (ps). 1993. 11. 95 (*0-8120-6334-1*) Barron.
Ormerod, Jan. One Hundred One Things to Do with a Baby. LC 84-4401. (Illus.). 32p. (ps-2). 1984. lib. bdg. 15.93 (*0-688-03802-6*) Lothrop.
—One Hundred One Things to Do with a Baby. (Illus.). 32p. (ps up). 1994. pap. 4.95 (*0-688-12770-3*, Mulberry) Morrow.
Osofsky, Audrey. Dreamcatcher. Young, Ed, illus. LC 91-20029. 32p. (ps-2). 1992. 14.95 (*0-531-05988-X*); lib. bdg. 14.99 (*0-531-08588-0*) Orchard Bks Watts.
Oxenbury, Helen. Family. (Illus.). 14p. (ps-k). 1981. 3.95 (*0-671-42110-7*, Little Simon) S&S Trade.
Patent, Dorothy H. Babies! LC 87-26663. (Illus.). 40p. (ps-3). 1988. pap. 5.95 (*0-8234-0701-2*) Holiday.
Powell, Richard. How to Deal with Babies. Snow, Alan, illus. LC 91-3461. 24p. (gr. k-3). 1992. lib. bdg. 9.59 (*0-8167-2420-2*); pap. text ed. 2.95 (*0-8167-2421-0*) Troll Assocs.
Ragland, Teresa, illus. Baby Days & Lullabye Nights. 48p. 1993. 17.95 (*0-8249-8619-9*, Ideals Child); gift box incl. cass. 24.95 (*0-8249-7629-0*) Hambleton-Hill.
Rowland, Pleasant T. Our New Baby. Thieme, Jeanne, ed. Backes, Nick, illus. (ps). 1990. White Version. 19. 95 (*0-937295-64-7*); African-American Version. 19.95 (*0-937295-65-5*) Pleasant Co.
Schaffer, Patricia. How Babies & Family Are Made-There Is More Than One Way! Corbett, Susanne, illus. LC 86-23087. 64p. (gr. k-4). 1988. pap. 6.95 (*0-935079-17-3*) Tabor Sarah Bks.
Slier, Debby. Little Babies. 12p. (ps). 1989. 2.95 (*1-56288-148-5*) Checkerboard.
Stein, Sara B. That New Baby. LC 73-15271. (Illus.). 48p. 1984. pap. 8.95 (*0-8027-7227-7*) Walker & Co.
Stodden, Norma J. & McCormick, Linda. The All Gone Book. Levy, Gail, ed. Loui, Jill, illus. 18p. (ps). 1988. bds. 3.95 (*0-943693-05-5*) TRI Pubns.
—The Love Book. Levy, Gail, ed. Loui, Jill, illus. 18p. (ps). 1988. bds. 3.95 (*0-943693-04-7*) TRI Pubns.
—The More Book. Levy, Gail, ed. Loui, Jill, illus. 18p. (ps). 1988. bds. 3.95 (*0-943693-03-9*) TRI Pubns.
Stoppard, Miriam. First Food Made Fun. LC 93-34301. (Illus.). 64p. 1994. pap. 5.95 (*1-56458-546-8*) Dorling Kindersley.
Wabbes, Marie. How I Was Born. LC 91-8336. (Illus.). 32p. (gr. 1 up). 1991. 13.95 (*0-688-10734-6*, Tambourine Bks); PLB 13.88 (*0-688-10735-4*, Tambourine Bks) Morrow.
Who's My Baby? 12p. (ps). 1994. 4.95 (*1-56458-735-5*) Dorling Kindersley.
Wilburn, Kathy, illus. The Pudgy Book of Babies. 16p. (gr. k). 1984. pap. 2.95 (*0-448-10207-2*, G&D) Putnam Pub Group.
Wilkes, Angela. See How I Grow. LC 93-27039. (Illus.). 32p. (ps). 1994. 13.95 (*1-56458-464-X*) Dorling Kindersley.
Young, Mary M., illus. Bear with Me: Story & Coloring Book Adjusting to Life with a New Baby. 16p. (ps-3). 1989. pap. 7.95 (*0-943114-20-9*, CB100) Childbirth Graphics.

INFANTS–DISEASES
see Children–Diseases

INFANTS–FICTION
Adams, Pam. Baby Bubbles. (gr. 3 up). 1981. 5.95 (*0-85953-265-8*) Childs Play.
Ahlberg, Janet & Ahlberg, Allan. Adios Pequeno - Bye Bye, Baby. Puncel, Maria, tr. (SPA., Illus.). 28p. (gr. k-1). 1990. write for info. (*84-372-6613-0*) Santillana.
Aliki. Welcome, Little Baby. LC 86-7648. (Illus.). 24p. (ps up). 1987. 14.00 (*0-688-06810-3*); PLB 13.93 (*0-688-06811-1*) Greenwillow.
Andersen, Torsten. The Christmas Before: Adventures in Babyland & Beyond. 1992. text ed. 7.95 (*0-533-10136-0*) Vantage.
Anderson, Norma R. An Elfindale Story. Gonzales, Joe, illus. LC 81-5977. 36p. (Orig.). (gr. 1-6). 1981. pap. 5.95 (*0-913504-64-5*) Lowell Pr.
Andres, Katherine. Humphrey & Ralph. Day, Brant, illus. LC 93-11478. (ps-1). 1994. 14.00 (*0-671-88129-9*, S&S BFYR) S&S Trade.
Ariev, Lauren. Who Are Baby's Friends? Morgan, Mary, illus. 24p. (ps). 1992. bds. write for info. (*0-307-06142-6*, 6142, Golden Pr) Western Pub.
Armstrong, Jennifer. That Terrible Baby. Meddaugh, Susan, illus. LC 93-14727. 32p. 1994. 14.00 (*0-688-11832-1*, Tambourine Bks); PLB 13.93 (*0-688-11833-X*, Tambourine Bks) Morrow.
Arthur's Baby. (ps-3). 1993. pap. 7.95 incl. cass. (*0-316-11336-0*) Little.
Asch, Frank. Baby in the Box. Gibbons, Gail, illus. LC 88-16452. 32p. (ps-3). 1989. reinforced bdg. 12.95 (*0-8234-0725-X*) Holiday.
Auch, Mary J. Monster Brother. LC 93-41746. (Illus.). 32p. (ps-3). 1994. reinforced bdg. 15.95 (*0-8234-1095-1*) Holiday.
Benson, Rita. What Angela Needs. McClelland, Linda, illus. LC 92-34266. 1993. 14.00 (*0-383-03666-6*) SRA Schl Grp.
Berg, Eric. Baby Makes Four. LC 93-8909. 1993. write for info. (*1-56071-327-5*) ETR Assocs.
Birdseye, Tom. Waiting for Baby. Leedy, Loreen, illus. LC 90-29076. 32p. (ps-3). 1991. reinforced 14.95 (*0-8234-0892-2*) Holiday.
Boyd, Lizi. Sam Is My Half Brother. (Illus.). 32p. (ps-3). 1992. pap. 3.99 (*0-14-054190-X*, Puffin) Puffin Bks.
Bradman, Tony. Billy & the Baby. (ps-3). 1992. 11.95 (*0-8120-6328-7*); pap. 5.95 (*0-8120-1387-5*) Barron.
Brannon, Tom. Baby Natasha's Busy Day. (ps). 1993. pap. 2.25 (*0-307-06035-7*, Golden Pr) Western Pub.
Brannon, Tom, illus. What Does Baby Kermit Say? 12p. (ps). 1993. pap. 1.95 (*0-307-06036-5*, 6036, Golden Pr) Western Pub.
Breeze, Lynn, illus. This Little Baby Goes Out. Morris, Ann, text by. LC 92-30880. (Illus.). (ps). 1993. 5.95 (*0-316-10854-5*) Little.
—This Little Baby's Bedtime. Morris, Ann, text by. LC 92-30879. (Illus.). (ps). 1993. 5.95 (*0-316-58419-3*) Little.
—This Little Baby's Morning. Morris, Ann, text by. LC 92-30881. (Illus.). (ps). 1993. 5.95 (*0-316-58420-7*) Little.
—This Little Baby's Playtime. Morris, Ann, text by. LC 92-30878. (Illus.). (ps). 1993. 5.95 (*0-316-10855-3*) Little.
Bridge, Michael. Moses Goodleaf Learns to Walk: A Short Tale of Discovery. Brennan, Christine, illus. 32p. 1992. PLB 22.95 (*0-944963-18-8*); pap. 16.95 (*0-944963-19-6*); audio tape 7.95 (*0-944963-33-1*) Glastonbury Pr.
Brink, Carol R. Baby Island. Sewell, Helen, illus. LC 92-45577. 160p. (gr. 3-7). 1993. pap. 3.95 (*0-689-71751-2*, Aladdin) Macmillan Child Grp.
Brook, Ruth. Happy Birthday, Baby. Kondo, Vala, illus. LC 86-30750. 32p. (gr. k-3). 1988. PLB 11.89 (*0-8167-0912-2*); pap. text ed. 2.95 (*0-8167-0913-0*) Troll Assocs.
Brown, Craig. In the Spring. LC 92-17465. (Illus.). 24p. (ps up). 1994. 14.00 (*0-688-10983-7*); PLB 13.93 (*0-688-10984-5*) Greenwillow.
Brown, Marc T. Arthur's Baby, Vol. 1. 32p. 1987. 14.95 (*0-316-11123-6*, Joy St Bks) Little.
Browne, Anthony. The Big Baby. LC 93-20210. (Illus.). (gr. 1-3). 1994. 13.00 (*0-679-84737-5*) Knopf Bks Yng Read.
Bunting, Eve. Our Teacher's Having a Baby. De Groat, Diane, illus. 32p. (ps-3). 1992. 13.45 (*0-395-60470-2*, Clarion Bks) HM.
Butler, Dorothy. Another Happy Tale. Hurford, John, illus. LC 91-23133. 32p. (ps-3). 1991. 12.95 (*0-940793-88-1*, Crocodile Bks) Interlink Pub.
Byars, Betsy C. Bingo Brown, Gypsy Lover. 128p. (gr. 3-7). 1992. pap. 3.99 (*0-14-034518-3*) Puffin Bks.
Byrne, David. Stay up Late. Kalman, Maira, illus. LC 87-10399. (ps up). 1987. pap. 14.95 (*0-670-81895-X*) Viking Child Bks.
Carlstrom, Nancy W. Kiss Your Sister, Rose Marie! Wickstrom, Thor, illus. LC 90-48671. 32p. (ps-1). 1992. RSBE 13.95 (*0-02-717271-6*, Macmillan Child Bk) Macmillan Child Grp.
Caseley, Judith. Annie's Potty. LC 89-34717. (Illus.). 24p. (ps up). 1990. 12.95 (*0-688-09065-6*); lib. bdg. 12.88 (*0-688-09066-4*) Greenwillow.
—Harry & Arney. LC 93-20787. 1994. write for info. (*0-688-12140-3*) Greenwillow.
—Mama, Coming & Going. LC 92-29402. (Illus.). 32p. (ps up). 1994. 14.00 (*0-688-11441-5*); PLB 13.93 (*0-688-11442-3*) Greenwillow.
Chorao, Kay. The Cherry Pie Baby. Chorao, Kay, illus. LC 88-2630. 32p. (ps-3). 1989. 12.95 (*0-525-44435-1*, DCB) Dutton Child Bks.
—Rock, Rock, My Baby. Chorao, Kay, illus. LC 92-61268. 22p. (ps). 1993. 3.25 (*0-679-84333-7*) Random Bks Yng Read.
Cohn, Janice. Molly's Rosebush: A Concept Book. Tucker, Kathy, ed. Owens, Gail, illus. LC 93-50612. 32p. (ps-2). 1994. PLB 13.95 (*0-8075-5213-5*) A Whitman.
Conkie, Heather. Malcolm & the Baby. (gr. 4-7). 1992. pap. 3.99 (*0-553-48034-0*) Bantam.
Cook, Jean T. Hugs for Our New Baby. (Illus.). (ps-2). 1987. 5.99 (*0-570-04165-1*, 56-1622) Concordia.
Corey, Dorothy. Will There Be a Lap for Me? Levine, Abby, ed. Poydar, Nancy, illus. LC 91-20324. 24p. (ps-1). 1992. PLB 11.95 (*0-8075-9109-2*) A Whitman.
Cruickshank, Kathy. The Baby Book. Cruickshank, Kathy, illus. (ps-k). 1991. pap. 1.50 (*0-307-10029-4*, Golden Pr) Western Pub.
Curtis, Jamie L. When I Was Little: A Four-Year-Old's Memoir of Her Youth. Cornell, Laura, illus. LC 91-46188. 32p. (gr. k-3). 1993. 14.00 (*0-06-021078-8*); PLB 13.89 (*0-06-021079-6*) HarpC Child Bks.
Daly, Niki. Mary Malloy & the Baby Who Wouldn't Sleep. (ps-3). 1991. 14.95 (*0-307-17501-4*, Artsts Writrs) Western Pub.
Day, Alexandra. Carl's Afternoon in the Park. (Illus.). 32p. 1991. bds. 12.95 (*0-374-31109-9*) FS&G.
—Carl's Masquerade. 1992. 12.95 (*0-374-31094-7*) FS&G.
—Good Dog Carl. LC 91-25274. (Illus.). 36p. (Orig.). (ps up). 1991. 11.95 (*0-671-75204-9*, Green Tiger) S&S Trade.
Delton, Judy. Angel's Mother's Baby. (gr. 4-7). 1992. pap. 3.25 (*0-440-40586-6*) Dell.
Devlin, Wende & Devlin, Harry. A New Baby in Cranberryport. LC 93-45819. (ps-1). 1994. pap. 2.95 (*0-689-71780-6*, Aladdin) Macmillan Child Grp.
Dillow, John, illus. Baby's Day: Board Books. 10p. (ps). 1991. bds. 3.50 (*0-7214-9136-7*) Ladybird Bks.
Driscoll, Debbie. Baby Comes Home. Samuels, Barbara, illus. LC 91-2414. 40p. (ps-k). 1993. pap. 14.00 JRT (*0-671-75540-4*, S&S BFYR) S&S Trade.
Edwards, Michelle. Meera's Blanket. LC 94-14825. 1995. write for info. (*0-688-09710-3*); PLB write for info. (*0-688-09711-1*) Lothrop.
Eisberg, Tiffany B., et al. Mistery in the Nursery. (Illus.). 48p. (gr. 3-5). 1994. pap. 6.95 (*1-56721-056-2*) Twnty-Fifth Cent Pr.

Endersby, Frank. Our New Baby. (gr. 4 up). 1981. 3.95 (0-85953-231-3) Childs Play.
—Waiting for Baby. (gr. 4 up). 1981. 3.95 (0-85953-230-5) Childs Play.
Epstein, June. The Name. Power, Margaret, illus. LC 92-34161. 1993. 3.75 (0-383-03643-7) SRA Schl Grp.
Erickson, Gina K. Bat's Surprise. (ps-3). 1993. pap. 3.95 (0-8120-1735-8) Barron.
Falwell, Cathryn. Nicky & Grandpa. Falwell, Cathryn, illus. 32p. (ps). 1991. 5.70 (0-395-56917-6, Clarion Bks) HM.
—Nicky Loves Daddy. Falwell, Cathryn, illus. 32p. (ps). 1992. 5.70 (0-395-60820-1, Clarion Bks) HM.
—We Have a Baby. LC 92-40268. 1993. 13.45 (0-395-62038-4, Clarion Bks) HM.
—Where's Nicky? Briley, Cathryn, ed. Falwell, Cathryn, illus. 24p. (ps). 1991. 5.70 (0-395-56936-2, Clarion Bks) HM.
Fine, Anne. Flour Babies & the Boys of Room 8. LC 93-35698. 1994. Repr. of 1992 ed. 14.95 (0-316-28319-3) Little.
Fitzgerald, John. The Baby Brother. Power, Margaret, illus. LC 93-2803. 1994. write for info. (0-383-03677-1) SRA Schl Grp.
Fleischman, Paul. The Borning Room. LC 91-4432. 112p. (gr. 7 up). 1993. pap. 3.95 (0-06-447099-7, Trophy) HarpC Child Bks.
Fontes, Ron & Korman, Justine. Baby's Day Out. (ps-3). pap. 2.95 (0-8167-3528-X) Troll Assocs.
Franklin, Jonathan. Don't Wake the Baby. (Illus.). 32p. (ps-1). 1991. bds. 13.95 jacketed (0-374-31826-3) FS&G.
Galbraith, Kathryn O. Roommates & Rachel. 48p. (gr. 1). 1993. pap. 3.50 (0-380-71762-X, Camelot Young) Avon.
Garland, Sarah. Billy & Belle. Garland, Sarah, illus. 32p. (ps-3). 1992. 13.00 (0-670-84396-2) Viking Child Bks.
Gerstein, Mordicai. Arnold of the Ducks. Gerstein, Mordicai, illus. LC 82-47735. 64p. (gr. k-3). 1983. PLB 14.89 (0-06-022003-1) HarpC Child Bks.
—The Gigantic Baby. Levin, Arnie, illus. LC 90-35537. 32p. (gr. k-3). 1991. PLB 14.89 (0-06-022106-2) HarpC Child Bks.
Goodall, Jane & Van Lawick-Goodall, Hugo. Grub the Bush Baby. 80p. (ps up). 1988. 13.45 (0-395-48696-3, Sandpiper); (Sandpiper) HM.
Greenfield, Karen R. The Teardrop Baby. Collicott, Sharleen, illus. LC 93-29603. 40p. (ps-4). 1994. 16.00 (0-06-022943-8); PLB 15.89 (0-06-022944-6) HarpC Child Bks.
Guthrie, Donna. Not for Babies. Arnsteen, Katy K., illus. 24p. (ps-1). 1993. pap. 2.50 (0-685-63280-6, Little Simon) S&S Trade.
Haarhoff, Dorian. Desert December. Vermeulen, Leon, illus. 32p. (ps-3). 1992. 13.95 (0-395-61300-0, Clarion Bks) HM.
Harding, William J. Infant Child. LC 92-56939. (Illus.). 40p. (gr. k-3). 1993. 6.95 (1-55523-581-6) Winston-Derek.
Hassett, John & Hassett, Ann. We Got My Brother at the Zoo. LC 92-1681. 1993. 14.95 (0-395-62429-0) HM.
HeBo. Clean up Your Act! Dirty, Dingy, Daryl. LC 93-48306. 1994. pap. 4.95 (0-939700-29-8) I D I C P.
Henderson, Kathy. Bumpety Bump. Thompson, Carol, illus. LC 93-3541. 24p. (ps). 1994. 9.95 (1-56402-312-5) Candlewick Pr.
Henkes, Kevin. Julius, the Baby of the World. LC 88-34904. (Illus.). 32p. (ps up). 1990. 15.00 (0-688-08943-7); PLB 14.93 (0-688-08944-5) Greenwillow.
Hennessy, B. G. A, B, C, D, Tummy, Toes, Hands, Knees. Watson, Wendy, illus. 32p. (ps-1). 1989. pap. 13.95 (0-670-81703-1) Viking Child Bks.
Hest, Amy. Nannies for Hire. Trivas, Irene, illus. LC 93-7040. 48p. (gr. 2 up). 1994. 15.00g (0-688-12527-1); PLB 14.93 (0-688-12528-X) Morrow Jr Bks.
Hillert, Margaret. Funny Baby. (Illus.). (ps-k). 1963. PLB 6.95 (0-8136-5016-X, K2300); pap. 3.50 (0-685-50733-5, TK2301) Modern Curr.
Hoban, Russell. A Baby Sister for Frances. Hoban, Lillian, illus. LC 92-32603. 32p. (ps-3). 1976. pap. 4.95 (0-06-443006-5, Trophy) HarpC Child Bks.
Hoffman, Mary. Henry's Baby. Winter, Susan, illus. LC 92-53485. 32p. (gr. 1-4). 1993. 13.95 (1-56458-196-9) Dorling Kindersley.
Horowitz, Ruth. Mommy's Lap. LC 90-32626. (ps-3). 1993. 13.00 (0-688-07235-6); PLB 12.93 (0-688-07236-4) Lothrop.
Horton, Barbara S. What Comes in Spring? Young, Ed, illus. LC 89-39695. 40p. (ps-1). 1992. 14.00 (0-679-80268-1); PLB 14.99 (0-679-90268-6) Knopf Bks Yng Read.
Howe, James. Pinky & Rex & the New Baby. Sweet, Melissa, illus. LC 91-39801. 48p. (gr. k-3). 1993. SBE 12.95 (0-689-31717-4, Atheneum Child Bk) Macmillan Child Grp.
—Pinky & Rex & the New Baby. Sweet, Melissa, illus. 48p. 1994. pap. 3.99 (0-380-72083-3, Camelot Young) Avon.
Hutchins, Pat. Where's The Baby? Hutchins, Pat, illus. LC 86-33566. 32p. (ps-3). 1988. 11.95 (0-688-05933-3); lib. bdg. 11.88 (0-688-05934-1) Greenwillow.
Isaacs, Gwynne L. & Mott, Evelyn C. Baby Face: A Mirror Book. Isaacs, Gwynne L. & Mott, Evelyn C., illus. LC 93-84221. 14p. (ps). 1994. 4.99 (0-679-84981-5) Random Bks Yng Read.
Isadora, Rachel. Babies. LC 88-18782. (Illus.). (ps up). 1990. 13.95 (0-688-08031-6); PLB 13.88 (0-688-08032-4) Greenwillow.
—I Hear. Isadora, Rachel, illus. LC 84-6103. 32p. (ps). 1985. 15.00 (0-688-04061-6); PLB 14.93 (0-688-04062-4) Greenwillow.
—I See. Isadora, Rachel, illus. LC 84-6104. 32p. (ps). 1985. 15.00 (0-688-04059-4); PLB 14.93 (0-688-04060-8) Greenwillow.
—I See. LC 90-48254. (Illus.). 24p. (ps up). 1991. bds. 6.95 (0-688-10523-8) Greenwillow.
Jarrell, Mary. The Knee-Baby. Shimin, Symeon, illus. 32p. (ps up). 1988. pap. 4.95 (0-374-44244-4) FS&G.
Johnson, Stacy. Cindy's Baby. 1993. pap. 3.50 (0-553-56312-2) Bantam.
Jonas, Ann. When You Were a Baby. LC 90-47799. (Illus.). 24p. (ps up). 1991. bds. 6.95 (0-688-10525-4) Greenwillow.
Keller, Holly. Geraldine's Baby Brother. LC 93-34491. (ps up). 1994. 15.00 (0-688-12005-9); PLB 14.93 (0-688-12006-7) Greenwillow.
—What Alvin Wanted. LC 88-34917. (Illus.). 32p. (ps up). 1990. 12.95 (0-688-08933-X); lib. bdg. 12.88 (0-688-08934-8) Greenwillow.
Kherdian, David. Lullaby for Emily. 1995. write for info. (0-8050-2957-5) H Holt & Co.
Kingsley, Charles. Water Babies. Adam, G. Mercer, ed. Childers, Norman, illus. (gr. k-4). Repr. of 1905 ed. 12.95 (0-940561-09-3) White Rose Pr.
Knight, Joan. Opal in the Closet. Estrada, Pau, illus. LC 91-659. 28p. (gr. k up). 1992. pap. 14.95 (0-88708-174-6) Picture Bk Studio.
Koehler, Phoebe. The Day We Met You. LC 89-35344. 32p. (ps-k). 1990. SBE 14.00 (0-02-750901-X, Bradbury Pr) Macmillan Child Grp.
Kopper, Lisa. Daisy Thinks She's a Baby. LC 92-44539. (gr. 1-8). 1994. 10.00 (0-679-84723-5); PLB 10.99 (0-679-94723-X) Knopf Bks Yng Read.
Kopper, Lisa, illus. Ten Little Babies. LC 89-49478. 24p. (ps). 1990. 9.95 (0-525-44643-5, DCB) Dutton Child Bks.
Kubler, Annie. Rolling Along. 1991. 6.95 (0-85953-448-0) Childs Play.
Kudeviz, Carol G. Sister Sarah: A New Baby Can Be Fun. Pease, Ken, illus. LC 94-66126. 24p. (ps-3). 1994. pap. 3.95 (0-9639779-0-3) Pigtail Pubng.
Levinson, Riki. Me Baby! Hafner, Marylin, illus. LC 90-40372. 32p. (ps-1). 1991. 13.95 (0-525-44693-1, DCB) Dutton Child Bks.
Lewison, Wendy C. Bye-Bye, Baby. (ps). 1992. 4.95 (0-590-45172-3, Cartwheel) Scholastic Inc.
—Uh-oh, Baby. (ps). 1992. 4.95 (0-590-45171-5, Cartwheel) Scholastic Inc.
—Where's Baby. (ps). 1992. 4.95 (0-590-45170-7, Cartwheel) Scholastic Inc.
—Where's Baby? 1992. 4.95 (0-685-53516-9) Scholastic Inc.
Limmer, Milly J. Where Do Little Girls Grow? Levine, Abby, ed. Hoffman, Rosekrans, illus. LC 92-22936. 32p. (ps-2). 1993. PLB 14.95 (0-8075-8924-1) A Whitman.
Lindgren, Barbro. The Wild Baby. Prelutsky, Jack, tr. from SWE. Erikkson, Eva, illus. LC 81-2151. (gr. k-3). 1981. PLB 15.88 (0-688-00601-9) Greenwillow.
Lundell, Margo. Bedtime for Baby. (ps). 1994. 2.25 (0-307-06065-9, Golden Pr) Western Pub.
McAllister, Angela. The Babies of Cockle Bay. Jenkin-Pearce, Susie, illus. 32p. (ps-3). 1994. incl. dust jacket 13.95 (0-8120-6424-0); pap. 5.95 (0-8120-1952-0) Barron.
McClelland, Julia. This Baby. Brooks, Ron, illus. LC 92-43756. 1994. 13.95 (0-395-66613-9) HM.
MacCombie, Turi, illus. Hush, Little Baby. 1994. pap. 6.99 (0-553-45907-4) Bantam.
McDaniel, Lurlene. Baby Alicia Is Dying. 1993. pap. 3.50 (0-553-29605-1) Bantam.
McIlhenny, Robyn. Our Baby. Smith, Craig, illus. LC 92-27268. 1993. 3.75 (0-383-03646-1) SRA Schl Grp.
McKenna, Colleen O. Mother Murphy. 160p. (gr. 4-7). 1993. 13.95 (0-590-44820-X, Scholastic Hardcover); pap. 3.25 (0-590-44856-0, Scholastic Hardcover) Scholastic Inc.
MacLachlan, Patricia. Baby. LC 93-22117. (gr. 1-8). 1993. 13.95 (0-385-31133-8) Delacorte.
Megakinetics Staff. Baby Loves... (gr. k-5). 1991. pap. text ed. 15.00 (1-56495-007-7) Megakinetics.
Mennen, Ingrid. One Round Moon & a Star for Me. Daly, Niki, illus. LC 93-9628. 32p. (ps-2). 1994. 14.95 (0-531-06804-8); PLB 14.99 (0-531-08654-2) Orchard Bks Watts.
Moore, Elaine. Deep River. Sorensen, Henri, illus. LC 93-23043. 1994. pap. 14.00 (0-671-86534-X, S&S BFYR) S&S Trade.
Muldrow, Diane. Dearest Baby. Lundell, Margo & Lanza, Barbara, illus. 14p. (ps). 1993. bds. 3.95 (0-307-12394-4, 12394, Golden Pr) Western Pub.
Murdocca, Sal. Baby Wants the Moon. LC 94-14517. 1994. write for info. (0-688-13664-8); PLB write for info. (0-688-13665-6) Lothrop.
Nickelodeon Staff. Rugrats at the Movies. 1992. pap. 2.25 (0-448-40500-8, G&D) Putnam Pub Group.
—Rugrats Monster in the Garage. 1992. pap. 2.25 (0-448-40501-6, G&D) Putnam Pub Group.
North, Carol. Disney Babies: What Does Baby Mickey Find? Baker, Darrell, illus. (ps-k). 1991. bds. 1.80 (0-307-06113-2, Golden Pr) Western Pub.
O'Connor, Jane. Lauren & the New Baby. Long, Laurie S., illus. 64p. (gr. 1-4). 1994. 7.99 (0-448-40468-0, G&D); pap. 3.95 (0-448-40467-2, G&D) Putnam Pub Group.
Oppenheim, Joanne. Wake up, Baby! Sweat, Lynn, illus. (ps-3). 1990. PLB 9.99 (0-553-05907-6); pap. 3.50 (0-553-34914-7) Bantam.
Ormerod, Jan. Messy Baby. LC 84-12610. (Illus.). 24p. (ps). 1985. 4.95 (0-688-04128-0) Lothrop.
—Reading. LC 84-12628. (Illus.). 24p. (ps). 1985. 4.95 (0-688-04127-2) Lothrop.
—This Little Nose. Ormerod, Jan, illus. LC 87-2605. 24p. (ps). 1987. 5.95 (0-688-07276-3) Lothrop.
Parish, Peggy. Amelia Bedelia & the Baby. Sweat, Lynn, illus. LC 80-22263. 64p. (gr. 1-3). 1981. 14.00 (0-688-00316-8); PLB 13.93 (0-688-00321-4) Greenwillow.
Park, Barbara. Junie B. Jones & a Little Monkey Business. Brunkus, Denise, illus. LC 92-56706. 80p. (Orig.). (gr. 1-4). 1993. PLB 9.99 (0-679-93886-9); pap. 2.99 (0-679-83886-4) Random Bks Yng Read.
Paterson, Diane. Smile for Auntie. LC 76-2285. (Illus.). (gr. k-2). 1977. 7.95 (0-8037-8066-4); Pied Piper Bk. pap. 3.50 (0-8037-7981-X) Dial Bks Young.
Patrick, Denise L. Good Night, Baby. Lanza, Barbara, illus. 24p. (ps). 1993. bds. 3.50 (0-307-06144-2, 6144, Golden Pr) Western Pub.
Paxton, Tom. Where's the Baby? Graham, Mark, illus. LC 92-39875. 32p. (ps up). 1993. 15.00 (0-688-10692-7); PLB 14.93 (0-688-10693-5) Morrow Jr Bks.
Ross, Anna. Meet the Sesame Street Babies. LC 92-60973. 7p. (ps). 1993. bds. 3.95 (0-679-83486-9) Random Bks Yng Read.
Roth, Susan L. Thump, Creak, Bump! LC 94-14234. 1995. 14.95 (0-02-777916-5, Four Winds) Macmillan Child Grp.
Sage, Chris. Happy Baby. LC 89-78045. (Illus.). 12p. (ps). 1990. Dial Bks Young.
Sanschagrin, Joceline. Lollypop's Baby Sister. (Illus.). 16p. (ps). 1993. bds. 5.95 (2-921198-45-2, Pub. by Les Edits Herit CN) Adams Inc MA.
Schwartz, Amy. A Teeny, Tiny Baby. LC 93-4876. (Illus.). 32p. (ps-1). 1994. 15.95 (0-531-06818-8); PLB 15.99 (0-531-08668-2) Orchard Bks Watts.
Shott, Stephen, photos by. Bathtime. LC 91-11121. (Illus.). 12p. (ps). 1991. bds. 4.95 (0-525-44754-7, DCB) Dutton Child Bks.
—Look at Me. LC 91-11162. (Illus.). 12p. (ps). 1991. bds. 4.95 (0-525-44755-5, DCB) Dutton Child Bks.
Shreve, Susan. Lucy Forever, Miss Rosetree, & the Stolen Baby. Nones, Eric J., illus. LC 93-37187. 1994. PLB write for info. (0-688-12479-8, Tambourine Bks) Morrow.
Shute, Linda. How I Named the Baby. Grant, Christy, ed. Shute, Linda, illus. LC 92-33292. 32p. (ps-3). 1993. PLB 13.95 (0-8075-3417-X) A Whitman.
Simon, Norma. The Baby House. Samuels, Barbara, illus. LC 94-6637. 1995. 14.00 (0-671-87044-0, S&S BFYR) S&S Trade.
Sloss, Lesley. Anthony & the Aardvark. Clarke, Gus, illus. LC 90-6528. 32p. (ps up). 1991. 13.95 (0-688-10302-2); PLB 13.88 (0-688-10303-0) Lothrop.
Smith, Janice L. The Baby Blues: An Adam Joshua Story. Gackenbach, Dick, illus. LC 93-14492. 96p. (gr. 1-4). 1994. 12.00 (0-06-023642-6, HarpT); PLB 11.89 (0-06-023643-4, HarpT) HarpC.
Snyder, Carol. One Up, One Down. Chambliss, Maxie, illus. LC 93-36282. 1995. 16.00 (0-689-31828-6, Atheneum) Macmillan.
Soft as a Kitten. 24p. (ps). 1994. bds. 2.95 (0-448-40556-3, G&D) Putnam Pub Group.
Steptoe, John. Baby Says. ALC Staff, ed. LC 92-11524. (Illus.). 28p. (ps up). 1992. pap. 3.95 (0-688-11855-0, Mulberry) Morrow.
Stevenson, James. Rolling Rose. LC 90-24169. 24p. (ps up). 1992. 14.00 (0-688-10674-9); PLB 13.93 (0-688-10675-7) Greenwillow.
—Worse Than Willy! Stevenson, James, illus. LC 83-14201. 32p. (gr. k-3). 1984. 10.25 (0-688-02596-X); PLB 10.88 (0-688-02597-8) Greenwillow.
Stimson, Joan. Big Panda, Little Panda. Rutherford, Meg, illus. LC 93-36235. 32p. (ps-2). 1994. 12.95 (0-8120-6404-6); pap. 4.95 (0-8120-1691-2) Barron.
Stinnett, Leia. Color Me One. Stinnett, Leia, illus. 36p. (gr. 3 up). 1993. pap. text ed. 4.95 (1-880737-13-2) Crystal Jrns.
Szekeres, Cyndy. The New Baby. (Illus.). (ps-k). 1989. pap. write for info. (0-307-11998-X) Western Pub.
Takabayashi, Mari. Baby's Things. LC 93-31006. (ps-3). 1994. 17.95 (0-8118-0692-8) Chronicle Bks.
Taylor, Mark A. One Tiny Baby. Hutton, Kathryn, illus. 32p. (gr. k-2). 1989. 2.50 (0-87403-599-6, 3859) Standard Pub.
Taylor, Nicole. Baby. (Illus.). 40p. (gr. 6 up). 1994. 15.95 (1-56846-089-9) Creat Editions.
Thomasson, Merry F. Wee Babies. (ps). 1992. 9.95 (0-9615407-8-8) Merrybooks VA.
Thompson, R. Sky Full of Babies. (Illus.). 24p. (ps-8). 1987. 12.95 (0-920303-93-5, Pub. by Annick CN); pap. 4.95 (0-920303-92-7, Pub. by Annick CN) Firefly Bks Ltd.
Titherington, Jeanne. Baby's Boat. LC 91-10359. 24p. (ps up). 1992. 14.00 (0-688-08555-5); PLB 13.93 (0-688-08556-3) Greenwillow.
Van Laan, Nancy. Mama Rocks, Papa Sings. Smith, Roberta, illus. LC 93-39225. 40p. (ps-2). 1995. 15.00 (0-679-84016-8); PLB 15.99 (0-679-94016-2) Knopf Bks Yng Read.

Von Konigslow, A. Wayne. That's My Baby. (Illus.). 24p. (ps-8). 1986. 12.95 (*0-920303-56-0*, Pub. by Annick CN); pap. 4.95 (*0-920303-57-9*, Pub. by Annick CN) Firefly Bks Ltd.
Vulliamy, Clara. Bang & Shout. LC 93-28123. (Illus.). 14p. (ps). 1994. reinforced bdg. 4.95 (*1-56402-409-1*) Candlewick Pr.
—Boo, Baby, Boo! LC 93-22736. (Illus.). 14p. (ps). 1994. 4.95 (*1-56402-388-5*) Candlewick Pr.
—Yum Yum. LC 93-28124. (Illus.). 14p. (ps). 1994. 4.95 (*1-56402-408-3*) Candlewick Pr.
Wilds, Kazumi I. Hajime in the North Woods. Wilds, Kazumi I., ed. LC 93-34689. (Illus.). 32p. (ps-2). 1994. 15.95 (*1-559702-40-0*) Arcade Pub Inc.
Willis, Jeanne. Earthlets, As Explained by Professor Xargle. Ross, Tony, illus. LC 88-23692. 32p. (ps-2). 1989. 14.00 (*0-525-44465-3*, DCB) Dutton Child Bks.
Winer, Yvonne. Ssh, Don't Wake the Baby! Power, Margaret, illus. LC 92-34160. 1993. 3.75 (*0-383-03655-0*) SRA Schl Grp.
Yolen, Jane. Good Griselle. Christiana, David, illus. LC 93-11691. (gr. 2 up). 1994. write for info. (*0-15-231701-5*) HarBrace.
Ziefert, Harriet. Where Is My Baby? 16p. (ps-2). 1994. 10.95 (*0-694-00479-0*, Festival) HarpC Child Bks.

INFECTION AND INFECTIOUS DISEASES
see Communicable Diseases

INFIRMARIES
see Hospitals

INFORMATION SERVICES
Lambert, Mark. Information Technology. (Illus.). 48p. (gr. 5-8). 1991. PLB 12.90 (*0-531-18386-6*, Pub. by Bookwright Pr) Watts.

INFORMATION STORAGE AND RETRIEVAL SYSTEMS
Luehrmann, Arthur & Peckham, Herbert. Appleworks Date Bases: A Hands-On Guide. (Illus.). 166p. (Orig.). (gr. 7-12). 1987. pap. text ed. 11.95 (*0-941681-03-3*); tchr's. ed. 24.95 (*0-941681-11-4*); 5.25 inch disk 19.95 (*0-941681-00-9*); tchr's. guide 14.95 (*0-941681-08-4*) Computer Lit Pr.
—Hands-on Appleworks: A Guide to Word Processing, Data Bases & Spreadsheets, 3 bks. LC 87-836. (Illus.). 478p. (Orig.). (gr. 7-12). 1987. Set. pap. text ed. 21.95 (*0-941681-07-6*); Set. tchr's. ed. 34.95 (*0-941681-13-0*); tchr's. guide 14.95 (*0-685-58103-9*); 5.25 inch disk 19.95 (*0-685-67553-X*) Computer Lit Pr.

INITIAL TEACHING ALPHABET
The Alphabet Book. (Illus.). (ps-k). 3.50 (*0-7214-8100-0*) Ladybird Bks.
Lenski, Lois. Little Farm. Lenski, Lois, illus. LC 58-12902. (gr. k-3). 1980. 5.25 (*0-8098-1009-3*) McKay.
McConnell, Keith. The AnimAlphabet Encyclopedia. McConnell, Keith A., illus. 48p. (gr. 4 up). 1982. pap. 5.95 (*0-916144-97-6*) Stemmer Hse.

INJURIES
see First Aid

INJURIOUS INSECTS
see Insects, Injurious and Beneficial

INLAND NAVIGATION
see also Canals; Lakes

INOCULATION
see Vaccination

INQUISITION–FICTION
Rosen, Sidney & Rosen, Dorothy. The Magician's Apprentice. LC 93-10781. 1993. 19.95 (*0-87614-809-7*) Carolrhoda Bks.

INSANE
see Mental Illness

INSECTICIDES
see also Insects, Injurious and Beneficial
Baskin, Leonard. Leonard Baskin's Miniature Natural History. Baskin, Leonard, illus. 28p. (gr. k up). 1993. Repr. 14.95 (*0-88708-265-3*) Picture Bk Studio.

INSECTS
see also names of insects, e.g. Bees; Butterflies; Wasps
Amazing Insects. LC 92-50789. (Illus.). 32p. (gr. 3 up). 1993. 5.95 (*1-56138-226-4*) Running Pr.
Armstrong, Bev. Insects. (Illus.). 48p. (gr. 2-5). 1990. 5.95 (*0-88160-192-6*, LW 151) Learning Wks.
Arneson, D. J. Incredible Insects. (Illus.). 24p. (Orig.). 1990. pap. 2.50 (*0-942025-20-2*) Kidsbks.
Atkinson, Kathie. Creepy Crawlies. LC 92-31908. 1993. 3.75 (*0-383-03562-7*) SRA Schl Grp.
Bailes, Edith G. But Will It Bite Me? A Reference Book of Insects for Children & Their Grownups. 112p. (Orig.). (gr. 1-6). 1985. pap. 9.95 (*0-9611118-1-X*) Cardamom.
Baker, Nancy & Hoffman, Richard L. Exploring Virginia Insects: An Activity Book. 32p. (gr. 4-6). 1994. pap. 2.95 (*0-9625801-8-X*) VA Mus Natl Hist.
Be a Nature Detective, Be a Bug Detective. 1992. pap. 3.99 (*0-517-06724-2*) Random Hse Value.
Benedict, Kitty. The Gnat: My First Nature Books. Felix, Monique, illus. 32p. (gr. k-2). 1993. pap. 2.95 (*1-56189-171-1*) Amer Educ Pub.
Benton, Michael. Creepy Crawlies. LC 93-50177. 1994. 3.95 (*1-85697-502-9*, Kingfisher LKC) LKC.
Boy Scouts of America. Insect Study. (Illus.). 64p. (gr. 6-12). 1985. pap. 1.85 (*0-8395-3353-5*, 33353) BSA.
Brandt, Keith. Insects. Brickman, Robin, illus. LC 84-2659. 32p. (gr. 3-6). 1985. PLB 9.49 (*0-8167-0184-9*); pap. text ed. 2.95 (*0-8167-0185-7*) Troll Assocs.
Brenner, Barbara A. & Chardiet, Bernice. Where's That Insect? Hide & Seek Science. Schwartz, Carol, illus. LC 92-20906. 32p. 1993. 10.95 (*0-590-45210-X*) Scholastic Inc.
Bug. (Illus.). 20p. 1994. 6.95 (*1-56458-480-1*) Dorling Kindersley.
Bugs! Big Book. (Illus.). 32p. (ps-3). 1990. pap. 22.95 (*0-516-49451-1*) Childrens.
Compass Productions Staff. Incredible Insect Instincts. Mirocha, Paul, illus. 10p. (gr. k-4). 1992. 5.95 (*0-694-00412-X*, Festival) HarpC Child Bks.
Cooper, Don. Boogie-Woogie Bugs. Forrest, Sandra, illus. (ps-3). 1989. bk. & cassette 5.95 (*0-394-82950-6*) Random Bks Yng Read.
Cottam, Clarence & Zim, Herbert S. Insects. Irving, James G., illus. 160p. 1987. pap. write for info. (*0-307-24055-X*, Pub. by Golden Bks) Western Pub.
Day, O. M. ABCs of Bugs & Beasts. Day, O. M., illus. 31p. (Orig.). (gr. 3-12). 1991. pap. 11.95 (*0-9629795-1-1*) Klar-Iden Pub.
De Bourgoing, Pascale. Ladybug & Other Insects. Perols, Sylvie, illus. 24p. 1991. pap. 10.95 (*0-590-45235-5*, Cartwheel) Scholastic Inc.
Discovery PAC Insects. (gr. k-8). 1991. pap. 10.95 (*0-945051-35-2*, 75035) Natl Wildlife.
Dorling Kindersley Staff. Insects & Crawly Creatures. LC 92-12356. (Illus.). 24p. (ps-k). 1992. pap. 7.95 POB (*0-689-71645-1*, Aladdin) Macmillan Child Grp.
Embry, Lynn. Scientific Encounters of the Insect World. 64p. (gr. 4-7). 1988. wkbk. 8.95 (*0-86653-424-5*, GA 1039) Good Apple.
Eyewitness Explorers: Insects. (gr. 4-7). 1992. 9.95 (*1-56458-025-3*) Dorling Kindersley.
Facklam, Howard & Facklam, Margery. Insects. (Illus.). 64p. (gr. 5-8). 1994. bds. 15.95 (*0-8050-2859-5*) TFC Bks NY.
Facklam, Margery. The Biggest Bug Book. Facklam, Paul, illus. LC 92-24517. 1994. 15.95 (*0-316-27389-9*) Little.
Fascinating Insects. 20p. (gr. k up). 1992. laminated, wipe clean surface 9.95 (*0-88679-905-8*) Educ Insights.
Fine, Edith & Josephson, Judith. Big on Bugs. 24p. (ps). 1982. 2.95 (*0-88160-089-X*, LW 128) Learning Wks.
Fischer-Nagel, Andreas & Fischer-Nagel, Heiderose. Life of the Ladybug. Fischer-Nagel, Andreas & Fischer-Nagel, Heiderose, illus. LC 85-25467. 48p. (gr. 2-5). 1986. lib. bdg. 19.95 (*0-87614-240-4*) Carolrhoda Bks.
Forsyth, Adrian. Exploring the World of Insects: The Equinox Guide to Insect Behavior. Folkens, Pieter, illus. 64p. (gr. 5 up). 1992. PLB 17.95 (*0-921820-47-X*, Pub. by Camden Hse CN); pap. 9.95 (*0-921820-49-6*, Pub. by Camden Hse CN) Firefly Bks Ltd.
Fowler, Allan. It's a Good Thing There Are Insects. LC 90-2205. (Illus.). 32p. (ps-2). 1990. PLB 10.75 (*0-516-04905-4*); pap. 22.95 big bk. (*0-516-49465-1*); pap. 3.95 (*0-516-44905-2*) Childrens.
—Que Bueno Que Haya Insectos! It's a Good Thing There Are Insects. LC 90-2205. (SPA.). 32p. (ps-2). 1991. PLB 10.75 (*0-516-34905-8*); pap. 3.95 (*0-516-54905-7*) Childrens.
Ganeri, Anita. Insects. (Illus.). 32p. (gr. 5-7). 1993. PLB 11.90 (*0-531-14225-6*) Watts.
Gattis, L. S., III. Insects for Pathfinders: A Basic Youth Enrichment Skill Honor Packet. (Illus.). 24p. (Orig.). (gr. 5 up). 1987. pap. 5.00 tchr's. ed. (*0-936241-30-6*) Cheetah Pub.
George, Michael. Insects. 32p. 1991. 15.95 (*0-89565-703-1*) Childs World.
Glenn, George S., Jr. Start Exploring Insects: A Fact-Filled Coloring Book. Driggs, Helen, illus. 128p. (Orig.). (gr. 3 up). 1991. pap. 8.95 (*1-56138-043-1*) Running Pr.
Goor, Ron & Goor, Nancy. Insect Metamorphosis: From Egg to Adult. LC 89-15144. (Illus.). 32p. (gr. 2-6). 1990. SBE 14.95 (*0-689-31445-0*, Atheneum Child Bk) Macmillan Child Grp.
Gorey, Edward. The Bug Book. (Illus.). (gr. 4 up). 1987. 8.95 (*0-915361-69-8*) Modan-Adama Bks.
Greenbacker, Liz. Bugs: Stingers, Suckers, Sweeties, Swingers. LC 92-24963. (Illus.). 64p. (gr. 5-8). 1993. PLB 12.90 (*0-531-20072-8*) Watts.
—Bugs: Stingers, Suckers, Sweeties, Swingers. (Illus.). 64p. (gr. 5-8). 1993. pap. 6.95 (*0-531-15673-7*) Watts.
Hadden, Sue. Insects. LC 91-15625. (Illus.). 32p. (gr. 2-6). 1993. 14.95g (*1-56847-009-6*) Thomson Lrning.
Heller, Ruth. How to Hide a Butterfly: And Other Insects. Heller, Ruth, illus. 32p. (ps-3). 1992. pap. 2.25 (*0-448-40477-X*, Platt & Munk Pubs) Putnam Pub Group.
Hendryx, Brian, illus. One Hundred One Wacky Facts about Bugs & Spiders. 96p. 1992. pap. 1.95 (*0-590-44892-7*) Scholastic Inc.
Hickman, Pamela M. Bugwise. 1991. pap. 8.61 (*0-201-57074-2*) Addison-Wesley.
Hillyard, Paul. Insects & Spiders. LC 93-19074. (Illus.). 1993. write for info. (*1-56458-385-6*) Dorling Kindersley.
Holly, Brian. Bugs & Critters. Gruettner, Diane & Black, Diane, illus. 32p. (gr. 3-7). 1985. pap. 3.50 (*0-88625-118-4*) Durkin Hayes Pub.
Hunt, Joni P. Insects. Leon, Vicki, ed. Mitchell, Robert & Mitchell, Linda, photos by. LC 94-3046. (Illus.). 1994. pap. 9.95 (*0-918303-39-7*) Blake Pub.
Insect World. 88p. (ps-3). 1989. 15.93 (*0-8094-4841-6*); lib. bdg. 21.27 (*0-8094-4842-4*) Time-Life.
Insect World. LC 92-30847. 176p. 1993. 18.60 (*0-8094-9687-9*); lib. bdg. 24.60 (*0-8094-9688-7*) Time-Life.
Insects. (gr. 4-6). 1960. pap. 2.95 (*0-8431-4272-3*, Wonder-Treas) Price Stern.
Insects. (Illus.). 20p. (gr. k up). 1990. laminated, wipe clean surface 3.95 (*0-88679-590-7*) Educ Insights.
Insects. LC 91-58215. (Illus.). 24p. (ps-3). 1992. 8.95 (*1-56458-003-2*) Dorling Kindersley.
Insects. 1991. PLB 14.95 (*0-88682-335-8*) Creative Ed.
Insects. PLB 10.99 (*1-56458-026-1*) Dorling Kindersley.
Insects & Other Arthropods Activity Book. (Illus.). (ps-6). pap. 2.95 (*0-565-01099-9*, Pub. by Natural Hist Mus) Parkwest Pubns.
Insects of Arizona. (Illus.). 32p. (gr. 3 up). 1984. pap. 1.00 (*0-935810-14-5*) Primer Pubs.
Johnson, Sylvia A. Chirping Insects. Sato, Yuko, illus. LC 86-15380. 48p. (gr. 4 up). 1986. PLB 19.95 (*0-8225-1486-9*) Lerner Pubns.
—Chirping Insects. 1990. pap. 5.95 (*0-8225-9562-1*) Lerner Pubns.
—Ladybugs. Sato, Yuko, illus. LC 83-18777. 48p. (gr. 4 up). 1983. PLB 19.95 (*0-8225-1481-8*) Lerner Pubns.
—Water Insects. Masuda, Modoki, illus. 48p. (gr. 4 up). 1989. PLB 19.95 (*0-8225-1489-3*) Lerner Pubns.
Kirkpatrick, Rena K. Look at Insects. rev. ed. Farmer, Andrew, illus. LC 84-26228. 32p. (gr. 2-4). 1985. PLB 10.95 (*0-8172-2351-7*); pap. 4.95 (*0-8114-6897-6*) Raintree Steck-V.
Kneidel, Sally. Pet Bugs: A Kid's Guide to Catching & Keeping Touchable Insects. LC 93-39403. 1994. pap. text ed. 10.95 (*0-471-31188-X*) Wiley.
Lampton, Christopher. Insect Attack. LC 91-26155. (Illus.). 64p. (gr. 4-6). 1992. PLB 13.90 (*1-56294-127-5*) Millbrook Pr.
Lang, Susan S. Invisible Bugs & Other Creepy Creatures That Live with You. Lindstrom, Eric C., illus. 96p. (gr. 4-10). 1993. pap. 4.95 (*0-8069-8209-8*) Sterling.
Lantier-Sampon, Patricia. Flying Insects. LC 91-50347. (Illus.). 24p. (ps-2). 1991. PLB 15.93 (*0-8368-0542-9*) Gareth Stevens Inc.
Losito, Linda, et al. Insects & Spiders. (Illus.). 96p. 1989. 17.95x (*0-8160-1967-3*) Facts on File.
Lovett, Sarah. Extremely Weird Insects. Sundstrom, Mary & Evans, Beth, illus. LC 92-20098. 48p. (gr. 3 up). Date not set. pap. 9.95 (*1-56261-076-7*) John Muir.
McDonald, Megan. Insects Are My Life. Johnson, Paul B., illus. LC 94-21960. (gr. 1-8). 1995. write for info. (*0-531-06874-9*); pap. write for info. (*0-531-08724-7*) Orchard Bks Watts.
McKissack, Patricia & McKissack, Fredrick. Bugs! Martin, Clovis, illus. LC 88-22875. 32p. (ps-2). 1988. PLB 10.25 (*0-516-02088-9*); pap. 2.95 (*0-516-42088-7*) Childrens.
—Insectos! Bugs! LC 88-22875. (SPA., Illus.). 32p. (ps-2). 1991. PLB 10.25 (*0-516-32088-2*); pap. 2.95 (*0-516-52088-1*) Childrens.
Mattern, Joanne. A Picture Book of Insects. Kinnealy, Janice, illus. LC 90-11211. 24p. (gr. 1-4). 1991. PLB 9.59 (*0-8167-2154-8*); pap. 2.50 (*0-8167-2155-6*) Troll Assocs.
Merrians, Deborah. I Can Read About Insects. Nodel, Norman, illus. LC 76-54493. (gr. 2-5). 1977. pap. 2.50 (*0-89375-040-9*) Troll Assocs.
Meyers, Susan. Insect Zoo. Hewett, Richard, photos by. (Illus.). 48p. (gr. 3-7). 1991. 16.95 (*0-525-67325-3*, Lodestar Bks) Dutton Child Bks.
Mound, Laurence. Amazing Insects. LC 92-26735. 32p. (Orig.). (gr. 1-5). 1993. PLB 10.99 (*0-679-93925-3*); pap. 7.99 (*0-679-83925-9*) Knopf Bks Yng Read.
—Insect. Keates, Colin, et al, photos by. LC 89-15603. (Illus.). 64p. (gr. 5 up). 1990. 16.00 (*0-679-80441-2*); PLB 16.99 (*0-679-90441-7*) Knopf Bks Yng Read.
Naden, C. J. I Can Read About Creepy Crawly Creatures. LC 78-68469. (Illus.). (gr. 3-6). 1979. pap. 2.50 (*0-89375-207-X*) Troll Assocs.
National Wildlife Federation Staff. Incredible Insects. (gr. k-8). 1991. pap. 7.95 (*0-945051-39-5*, 75001) Natl Wildlife.
Natural History Museum Staff, compiled by. Creepy Crawlies: Ladybugs, Lobsters & Other Amazing Arthropods. LC 90-27531. (Illus.). 108p. (gr. 4-10). 1992. pap. 9.95 (*0-8069-8337-X*) Sterling.
Nayer, Judy. Insects. Goldberg, Grace, illus. 12p. (ps-2). 1993. bds. 6.95 (*1-56293-335-3*) McClanahan Bk.
Oda, Hidetomo. Insects & Their Homes. Pohl, Kathleen, ed. LC 85-28226. (Illus.). 32p. (gr. 3-7). 1986. PLB 10.95 (*0-8172-2528-5*) Raintree Steck-V.
Owen, Jennifer. Insect Life. Jackson, Ian & Harris, Alan, illus. 32p. (gr. 4-7). 1985. PLB 13.96 (*0-88110-173-7*, Pub. by Usborne); pap. 5.95 (*0-86020-843-5*) EDC.
Parker, Nancy W. & Wright, Joan R. Bugs. LC 86-29387. (Illus.). 40p. (gr. 1-4). 1987. 15.00 (*0-688-06623-2*); lib. bdg. 14.93 (*0-688-06624-0*) Greenwillow.
Parker, Steve. Beastly Bugs. Savage, Ann, illus. LC 92-43197. 38p. (gr. 3-6). 1993. PLB 19.97 (*0-8114-0689-X*) Raintree Steck-V.
—Creepy Creatures, 8 vols. (gr. 4-7). 1994. 111.84 (*0-8114-0711-X*) Raintree Steck-V.
Peissel, Michel & Allen, Missy. Dangerous Insects. (Illus.). 112p. (gr. 5 up). 1993. PLB 19.95 (*0-7910-1785-0*, Am Art Analog); pap. 9.95 (*0-7910-1933-0*, Am Art Analog) Chelsea Hse.
Podendorf, Illa. Insects. LC 81-7689. (Illus.). 48p. (gr. k-4). 1981. PLB 12.85 (*0-516-01627-X*); pap. 4.95 (*0-516-41627-8*) Childrens.
Pohl, Kathleen. Giant Water Bugs. (Illus.). 32p. (gr. 3-7). 1986. pap. text ed. 10.95 (*0-8172-2714-8*) Raintree Steck-V.

Pope, Joyce. Two Lives. Stilwell, Stella & Ward, Helen, illus. LC 91-17460. 48p. (gr. 4-8). 1992. PLB 22.80 (*0-8114-3153-3*); pap. 4.95 (*0-8114-6257-9*) Raintree Steck-V.

Quinn, Kaye. Bugs & Other Insects. (Illus.). 40p. (Orig.). (gr. k-4). 1989. pap. 2.95 (*0-8431-2375-3*) Price Stern.

Reidel, Marlene. From Egg to Butterfly. Reidel, Marlene, illus. LC 81-204. 24p. (ps-3). 1981. PLB 10.95 (*0-87614-153-X*) Carolrhoda Bks.

Richardson, Joy. Insects. LC 92-32189. 1993. 11.40 (*0-531-14248-5*) Watts.

Santa Fe Writers Group. Bizarre & Beautiful Feelers. Brigman, Chris, illus. LC 93-2034. 48p. 1993. text ed. 14.95 (*1-56261-125-9*) John Muir.

Selsam, Millicent E. Backyard Insects. Goor, Ronald, photos by. 40p. (ps-3). 1988. pap. 2.95 (*0-590-42256-1*) Scholastic Inc.

Selsam, Millicent E. & Hunt, Joyce. A First Look at Insects. Springer, Harriett, illus. LC 73-92451. 32p. (gr. 2-4). 1974. PLB 12.85 (*0-8027-6182-8*) Walker & Co.

Seymour, Peter. Insects: A Close-Up Look. Helmer, Jean C., illus. 10p. (gr. 2-5). 1985. pap. 8.95 SBE (*0-02-782120-X*, Macmillan Child Bk) Macmillan Child Grp.

Snedden, Robert. What Is an Insect? Oxford Scientific Films, photos by. LC 92-35060. (Illus.). 32p. (gr. 2-5). 1993. 13.95 (*0-87156-540-4*) Sierra.

Souza, Dorothy. Eight Legs. (Illus.). 40p. (gr. 1-4). 1991. PLB 17.50 (*0-87614-441-5*) Carolrhoda Bks.

—Insects Around the House. (Illus.). 40p. (gr. 1-4). 1991. PLB 17.50 (*0-87614-438-5*) Carolrhoda Bks.

—Insects in the Garden. (Illus.). 40p. (gr. 1-4). 1991. PLB 17.50 (*0-87614-439-3*) Carolrhoda Bks.

—What Bit Me? (Illus.). 40p. (gr. 1-4). 1991. PLB 17.50 (*0-87614-440-7*) Carolrhoda Bks.

Steele, Philip. Extinct Insects: And Those in Danger of Extinction. Kline, Marjory, ed. (Illus.). 32p. (gr. 4-7). 1992. PLB 11.90 (*0-531-11032-X*) Watts.

—Insects. LC 90-42016. (Illus.). 32p. (gr. 5-6). 1991. text ed. 3.95 RSBE (*0-89686-581-9*, Crestwood Hse) Macmillan Child Grp.

—Insects. 32p. (gr. 3-5). 1991. lib. bdg. 9.98 (*0-671-72235-2*, J Messner); pap. 4.95 (*0-671-72236-0*) S&S Trade.

Stidworthy, John. Insects. LC 89-31787. (Illus.). 32p. (gr. 4-6). 1989. PLB 12.40 (*0-531-17184-1*, Gloucester Pr) Watts.

Suzuki, David. Looking at Insects. (Illus.). 96p. 1992. text ed. 22.95 (*0-471-54747-6*); pap. text ed. 9.95 (*0-471-54050-1*) Wiley.

Tesar, Jenny. Insects. (Illus.). 64p. (gr. 4-8). 1993. PLB 16.95 (*1-56711-037-1*) Blackbirch.

—Insects. Felber, Michael, illus. 64p. (gr. 4-8). 1993. jacketed 14.95 (*1-56711-054-1*) Blackbirch.

Thomson, Ruth. Creepy Crawlies. Mansell, Dom, illus. LC 91-7482. 32p. (gr. k-3). 1991. pap. 5.95 (*0-689-71489-0*, Aladdin) Macmillan Child Grp.

Time Life Inc. Editors. How Far Can a Butterfly Fly? First Questions & Answers about Bugs. Lesk, Sara M., ed. (Illus.). 48p. (ps-k). 1994. write for info. (*0-7835-0882-4*); PLB write for info. (*0-7835-0883-2*) Time-Life.

Van der Meer, Ron, illus. Bugz: An Extraterrestrial Pop-up Book. LC 93-85507. 10p. 1994. 12.95 (*1-56138-339-2*) Running Pr.

Watts, Barrie. Stick Insects. Kline, Marjory, ed. Watts, Barrie, photos by. (Illus.). 32p. (gr. k-4). 1992. PLB 11.40 (*0-531-14220-5*) Watts.

—Wood Lice & Millipedes. Kline, Marjory, ed. Watts, Barrie, photos by. LC 91-16539. (Illus.). 32p. (gr. k-4). 1992. PLB 11.40 (*0-531-14162-4*) Watts.

Whayne, Susanne S. The World of Insects. Dudley, Ebet, illus. 48p. (gr. 3-7). 1990. pap. 9.95 (*0-671-69018-3*, S&S BFYR) S&S Trade.

Wildsmith, Brian & Wildsmith, Rebecca. Look Closer. LC 92-17241. 1993. 6.95 (*0-15-200477-5*, Gulliver Bks); pap. write for info. (*0-15-200478-5*, Gulliver Bks) HarBrace.

Woelflein, Luise. Ultimate Bug Book: A Unique Introduction to the Fascinating World of Insects. (ps-3). 1993. 19.95 (*0-307-17600-2*, Artsts Writrs) Western Pub.

The World in Your Backyard: And Other Stories of Insects & Spiders. (Illus.). 63p. (gr. 3-5). 1989. 10.95 (*0-88309-132-1*) Zaner-Bloser.

Wyse, Liz. Insects. LC 93-42983. (Illus.). 48p. 1994. 15.95 (*1-56847-257-9*) Thomson Lrning.

Yolla Bolly Press Staff. Big Bugs. Yolla Bolly Press Staff, illus. LC 93-27516. (gr. 3-7). 1994. pap. 14.95 (*0-15-200693-1*, Gulliver Bks) HarBrace.

INSECTS–COLLECTION AND PRESERVATION

Danks, Hugh. The Bug Book & the Bug Bottle. LC 86-40541. (Illus.). 64p. (Orig.). (gr. k-5). 1987. pap. 9.95 (*0-89480-314-X*, 1314) Workman Pub.

Yolla Bolly Press Staff. Big Bugs. Yolla Bolly Press Staff, illus. LC 93-27516. (gr. 3-7). 1994. pap. 14.95 (*0-15-200693-1*, Gulliver Bks) HarBrace.

INSECTS–FICTION

Ada, Alma F. Who's Hatching Here? - Quien Nacera Aqui? Escriva, Vivi, illus. (SPA & ENG.). 24p. (gr. k-2). 1989. English ed. 3.95 (*0-88272-811-3*); Spanish ed. 3.95 (*0-88272-800-8*) Santillana.

Asch, Frank & Vagin, Vladimir. Insects from Outer Space. Vagin, Vladimir, illus. LC 93-26876. 1994. 14.95 (*0-590-45489-7*) Scholastic Inc.

Aylesworth, Jim. Old Black Fly. Gammell, Stephen, illus. LC 91-26825. 32p. (ps-2). 1992. 15.95 (*0-8050-1401-2*, Bks Young Read) H Holt & Co.

Bersen, Dolores. The Adventures of Clyde Cockroach. 26p. (ps-4). 1994. 13.95 (*0-9640986-0-1*); PLB 14.95 (*0-9640986-1-X*); pap. 4.95 (*0-9640986-4-4*) DUB Pubng.

—Lynda Ladybug. 24p. (ps-2). 1995. 13.95 (*0-9640986-2-8*); PLB 14.95 (*0-9640986-3-6*); pap. 4.95 (*0-9640986-5-2*) DUB Pubng.

Bomans, Godfried. Eric in the Land of the Insects. Kornblith, Regina L., tr. from DUT. LC 93-24071. 1994. 14.95 (*0-395-65231-6*) HM.

Brown, Margaret W. The Walt Disney's the Grasshopper & the Ants. Moore, Larry, illus. LC 93-70938. 32p. 1993. 12.95 (*1-56282-534-8*); PLB 12.89 (*1-56282-535-6*) Disney Pr.

Brown, Ruth. Ladybug, Ladybug. Brown, Ruth, illus. LC 88-14852. 32p. (ps-1). 1988. 12.95 (*0-525-44423-8*, DCB) Dutton Child Bks.

Butler, Freddie L. Critter of the Cracks. (Illus.). 64p. 1994. pap. 8.00 (*0-8059-3572-X*) Dorrance.

Carle, Eric. The Eric Carle Slipcase Collection: The Very Hungry Caterpillar; the Very Bust Spider; the Very Quiet Cricket. Carle, Eric, illus. 32p. (ps-3). Date not set. 52.85 (*0-399-22623-0*, Philomel) Putnam Pub Group.

—The Grouchy Ladybug. Carle, Eric, illus. LC 77-3170. 48p. (ps-1). 1977. 15.00i (*0-690-01391-4*, Crowell Jr Bks); PLB 14.89 (*0-690-01392-2*) HarpC Child Bks.

Charles, Donald. Ugly Bug. LC 92-835. (ps-3). 1994. 13.99 (*0-8037-1204-9*); 13.89 (*0-8037-1205-7*) Dial Bks Young.

Clyne, Densey. Cicada Sing-Song. (gr. 4-7). 1994. pap. 6.95 (*1-86373-131-8*, Pub. by Allen & Unwin Aust Pty AT) IPG Chicago.

Cole, Joanna. Golly Gump Swallowed a Fly. Weissman, Bari, illus. LC 81-11072. 48p. (ps-3). 1982. 5.95 (*0-8193-1069-7*); lib. bdg. 5.95 (*0-8193-1070-0*) Parents.

Cosgrove, Stephen. Hucklebug. (Illus.). 32p. (Orig.). (gr. 1-4). 1978. pap. 2.95 (*0-8431-0556-9*) Price Stern.

Dobkin, Bonnie. The Great Bug Hunt. Dunnington, Tom, illus. LC 93-10333. 32p. (ps-2). 1993. PLB 10.25 (*0-516-02017-X*); pap. 2.95 (*0-516-42017-8*) Childrens.

Drew, David. The Big Brown Box. Ruth, Trevor, illus. LC 92-30673. 1993. 2.50 (*0-383-03619-4*) SRA Schl Grp.

Dubowski, Cathy E. & Dubowski, Mark. Snug Bug. LC 94-22489. (gr. 2 up). 1995. PLB write for info. (*0-448-40850-3*, G&D); pap. 3.50 (*0-448-40849-X*) Putnam Pub Group.

Duffy, William G., Jr. The Adventures of Grubber Bug. LC 82-71946. 45p. (ps-3). 1984. 3.50x (*0-943864-33-X*) Davenport.

Erickson, Gina C. & Foster, Kelli C. The Bug Club. Russell, Kerri G., illus. 24p. (ps-2). 1991. pap. 3.50 (*0-8120-4730-3*) Barron.

Fienberg, Anna. Ariel, Zed & the Secret of Life. (gr. 4-7). 1994. pap. 5.95 (*1-86373-276-4*, Pub. by Allen & Unwin Aust Pty AT) IPG Chicago.

Fowler, Richard. Ladybug on the Move. LC 92-19740. 1993. write for info. (*0-15-200475-0*) HarBrace.

Glugg, Professor. Glugg-A-Lug Bug. Glugg, Professor, illus. LC 92-74768. 32p. (Orig.). (ps up). 1993. pap. 3.95 (*1-881905-02-0*) Glue Bks.

Grodin, Charles. Freddie the Fly. Murdocca, Sal, illus. LC 92-5234. 32p. (ps-2). 1993. 12.00 (*0-679-83847-3*) Random Bks Yng Read.

Hafer, Todd. Carl Caterpillar's Wish for Wings. 12p. 1995. write for info. (*0-944943-56-X*, 254539) Current Inc.

Hooker, Irene H. & Brindle, Susan A. The Caterpillar That Came to Church - la Oruga Que Fue a Misa: A Story of the Eucharist - Un Cuento de la Eucaristia. Lademan, Miriam A., ed. Houtman, Jane F. & De Martinez, Luz M., trs. Hooker, Irene H. & Brindle, Susan A., illus. LC 92-63219. (ENG & SPA.). 64p. (Orig.). 1993. 9.95 (*0-87973-874-X*, 874); pap. 7.95 (*0-87973-875-8*, 875) Our Sunday Visitor.

Inkpen, Mick. Billy's Beetle. (ps-3). 1992. 13.95 (*0-15-200427-0*, HB Juv Bks) HarBrace.

James, Mary. Shoebag. (gr. 5-7). 1990. pap. 12.95 (*0-590-43029-7*) Scholastic Inc.

Jones, Michael P., ed. Andorff the Energy Ant's Coloring Book. abr. ed. (Illus.). 34p. 1984. text ed. 11.00 (*0-89904-071-3*); pap. text ed. 6.00 (*0-89904-072-1*) Crumb Elbow Pub.

Jones, Renata. The Little White Ladybug. De Tuerk, Lif, illus. LC 90-70475. 54p. (ps-3). 1990. 8.95 (*0-932433-67-7*) Windswept Hse.

Kelly, Karla, et al. Tales of Terratopia: The Secret of the Dragonfly & the Daring Dino Rescue. (Illus.). 36p. (gr. 1-6). 1993. 6.95 (*1-883871-00-X*) Nature Co.

Kent, Jack. The Caterpillar & the Polliwog. LC 82-7533. (Illus.). 32p. (gr. k-4). 1985. pap. 14.00 jacketed (*0-671-66280-5*, S&S BFYR); pap. 5.95 (*0-671-66281-3*, S&S BFYR) S&S Trade.

Kirk, David. Miss Spider's Tea Party. LC 93-15710. (Illus.). 32p. 1994. 15.95 (*0-590-47724-2*) Scholastic Inc.

Kline, Suzy. Horrible Harry & the Ant Invasion. Remkiewicz, Frank, illus. 64p. (gr. 2-5). 1991. 2.95 (*0-14-032914-5*) Puffin Bks.

Lokra. The Lady & the Fly. (Illus.). 48p. (gr. 3-8). 1990. 8.95 (*0-89565-812-7*) Childs World.

McLaughlin, Molly. Dragonflies. (gr. 1-5). 1989. 14.95 (*0-8027-6846-6*); PLB 15.85 (*0-8027-6847-4*) Walker & Co.

McOmber, Rachel B., ed. McOmber Phonics Storybooks: A Hum-Bug. rev. ed. (Illus.). write for info. (*0-944991-20-3*) Swift Lrn Res.

—McOmber Phonics Storybooks: Bug. rev. ed. (Illus.). write for info. (*0-944991-19-X*) Swift Lrn Res.

—McOmber Phonics Storybooks: The Hum-Bug Hop. rev. ed. (Illus.). write for info. (*0-944991-31-9*) Swift Lrn Res.

Marcroft, Karen. Fulbert Firefly. Marcroft, Renee, illus. LC 85-90463. 48p. (gr. 3-8). 1986. 14.95 (*0-935849-00-9*) Marcroft Prods.

Martin, Rafe. Will's Mammoth. Gammell, Stephen, illus. 32p. (ps-1). 1993. pap. 4.95 (*0-399-22603-6*, Putnam) Putnam Pub Group.

Maxner, Joyce. Lady Bugatti. Hawkes, Kevin, illus. LC 90-19127. 32p. (gr. k up). 1991. 13.95 (*0-688-10340-5*); PLB 13.88 (*0-688-10341-3*) Lothrop.

—Lady Bugatti. Hawkes, Kevin, illus. 32p. (ps-3). 1993. pap. 4.99 (*0-14-054832-7*) Puffin Bks.

Meade, Everard. Dragonfly. 1992. pap. 7.95 (*0-933905-20-3*) Claycomb Pr.

Mogensen, Jan. The Land of the Big. Mogensen, Jan, illus. LC 92-18302. 32p. (ps-3). 1993. 14.95 (*1-56656-111-6*, Crocodile Bks) Interlink Pub.

Most, Bernard. There's an Ant in Anthony. LC 79-23089. (Illus.). 32p. (ps up). 1992. pap. 3.95 (*0-688-11513-6*, Mulberry) Morrow.

Mound, Laurence. Paper Predators Spider & Fly. (gr. 4-7). 1993. pap. 8.00 (*0-440-40766-4*) Dell.

Nieto, Angel. Mosquito! Junco, Martha A., illus. Carter, Jackie, retold by. LC 94-55. (Illus.). 1994. write for info. (*0-590-29274-9*) Scholastic Inc.

Norman, Jane & Beazley, Frank. The Tale of the Tickle Bug. 24p. (ps-3). 1993. pap. write for info. (*1-883585-03-1*) Pixanne Ent.

Osborne, Mary P. Spider Kane & the Mystery at Jumbo Nightcrawler's. Chess, Victoria, illus. LC 91-10983. 128p. (gr. 1-5). 1993. 14.00 (*0-679-80856-6*) Knopf Bks Yng Read.

Peet, Bill. The Gnats of Knotty Pine. Peet, Bill, illus. LC 75-17024. 48p. (gr. k-3). 1984. 13.45 (*0-395-21405-X*); pap. 4.95 (*0-395-36612-7*) HM.

Pienkowski, Jan. Oh My, a Fly! (Illus.). 10p. (ps up). 1991. 4.95 (*0-8431-2965-4*) Price Stern.

Pinczes, Elinor J. A Remainder of One. MacKain, Bonnie, illus. LC 94-5446. Date not set. write for info. (*0-395-69455-8*) HM.

Poulet, Virginia. Blue Bug Goes to Paris. Anderson, Peggy P., illus. LC 85-31390. 32p. (ps-3). 1986. pap. 3.95 (*0-516-43480-2*) Childrens.

—Blue Bug's Beach Party. Fleming, Stan & Maloney, Mary, illus. LC 74-31224. 32p. (gr. k-3). 1975. PLB 11.80 (*0-516-03423-5*) Childrens.

Reese, Bob. Scary Larry the Very Very Hairy Tarantula. LC 81-3871. (Illus.). 24p. (ps-2). 1981. pap. 2.95 (*0-516-42306-1*) Childrens.

Reynolds-Naylor, Phyllis. Beetles Lightly Toasted. (gr. k-6). 1989. pap. 3.50 (*0-440-40143-7*, YB) Dell.

Roddie, Shen. The Terrible Itch. Roffey, Maureen, illus. 24p. (ps-1). 1993. pap. 13.00 casebound (*0-671-79169-9*, S&S BFYR) S&S Trade.

Rosman, Steven S. Deena the Damselfly. Carmi, Giora, illus. LC 91-43472. (gr. k-3). 1992. 10.95 (*0-8074-0477-2*, 101069) UAHC.

Ross, Katharine. Twinkle, Twinkle, Little Bug: A Sesame Street Book. Cooke, Tom, illus. LC 90-61760. 24p. (Orig.). (ps-2). 1991. pap. 2.25 (*0-679-81372-1*) Random Bks Yng Read.

Ryder, Joanne. My Father's Hands. Graham, Mark, illus. LC 93-27116. 1994. write for info. (*0-688-09189-X*); PLB write for info. (*0-688-09190-3*) Morrow Jr Bks.

—When the Woods Hum. LC 90-37879. (Illus.). 32p. (gr. 1 up). 1991. 13.95 (*0-688-07057-4*); PLB 13.88 (*0-688-07058-2*, Morrow Jr Bks) Morrow Jr Bks.

Santoro, Chris, illus. Lift a Rock, Find a Bug. LC 91-62580. 22p. (ps-k). 1993. 3.50 (*0-679-80904-X*) Random Bks Yng Read.

Sardegna, Jill. The Roly Poly Spider. Arnold, Tedd, illus. LC 93-40653. (ps-1). 1994. 13.95 (*0-590-47119-8*) Scholastic Inc.

Schade, Susan & Buller, Jon. Snug House, Bug House. LC 93-34058. (Illus.). 48p. (ps-1). 1994. 6.95 (*0-679-85300-6*); PLB 7.99 (*0-679-95300-0*) Random Bks Yng Read.

Singer, Marilyn. Wasp Is Not a Bee. 1994. write for info. (*0-8050-2820-X*) H Holt & Co.

Stone, Rosetta. Because a Little Bug Went Ka-Choo! Frith, Michael, illus. LC 75-1605. 48p. (gr. k-3). 1975. 6.95 (*0-394-83130-6*) Beginner.

Strejan, John. I Love to Eat Bugs. (Illus.). (ps up). 1992. pop-up 9.95 (*0-8431-3392-9*) Price Stern.

Stuart, et al. Thrilling Bug Stories. (Illus.). 21p. (Orig.). (gr. 4-8). 1994. pap. 2.95 (*0-9639985-0-1*) Fat Cat Pr.

Thomas, J. P. The Cricket Angel. 1992. 7.95 (*0-533-09713-4*) Vantage.

Turin, Adela & Selig, Syvie. Of Cannons & Caterpillars. (Illus.). 32p. (gr. 3-6). 1980. 4.95 (*0-904613-62-3*) Writers & Readers.

Wickstrom, Lois. Ladybugs for Loretta. Mion, Francie & Johnson, Priscilla M., illus. (gr. k-6). 1978. pap. 2.00 (*0-916176-04-5*) Sproing.

Wilkinson, Jack & Tubbs, Orrin. Spike Mosquito & the Flying Ants. Haigis, Debbie, ed. Tubbs, Orrin, illus. (Orig.). (gr. 1-6). 1991. pap. write for info. (*0-9629543-0-6*) Maine Heritage.

Wood, Leslie. The Frog & the Fly. (Illus.). 16p. 1987. pap. 2.95 (*0-19-272154-2*) OUP.

Yorinks, Arthur. Company's Coming. Small, David, illus. LC 87-13579. 32p. (ps-2). 1992. pap. 4.99 (*0-517-58858-7*) Crown Bks Yng Read.

INSECTS–HABITS AND BEHAVIOR

Bailey, Jill & Seddon, Tony. Mimicry & Camouflage. 64p. (gr. 5 up). 1988. 15.95x (*0-8160-1657-7*) Facts on File.

Harrison, Virginia. The World of Honeybees. Oxford Scientific Films Staff, photos by. LC 89-33936. (Illus.). 32p. (gr. 2-3). 1989. PLB 17.27 (*0-8368-0142-3*) Gareth Stevens Inc.

Hornblow, Leonora & Hornblow, Arthur. Insects Do the Strangest Things. Barlowe, Dorothy, illus. LC 88-30201. 64p. (gr. 2-4). 1990. lib. bdg. 6.99 (*0-394-94306-6*); pap. 4.99 (*0-394-84306-1*) Random Bks Yng Read.

Horton, et al. Amazing Fact Book of Insects. (Illus.). 32p. 1987. PLB 14.95 (*0-87191-845-5*) Creative Ed.

Morris, Dean. Insects That Live in Families. rev. ed. LC 87-16696. (Illus.). 48p. (gr. 2-6). 1987. PLB 10.95 (*0-8172-3210-9*) Raintree Steck-V.

Oda, Hidetomo. Insect Hibernation. Pohl, Kathy, ed. LC 85-2892. (Illus.). 32p. (Orig.). (gr. 3-7). 1986. text ed. 10.95 (*0-8172-2526-9*) Raintree Steck-V.

—Insects & Flowers. Pohl, Kathy, ed. LC 85-28206. (Illus.). 32p. (gr. 3-7). 1986. text ed. 10.95 (*0-8172-2527-7*) Raintree Steck-V.

—Insects in the Pond. Pohl, Kathy, ed. LC 85-28227. (Illus.). 32p. (gr. 3-7). 1986. text ed. 10.95 (*0-8172-2529-3*) Raintree Steck-V.

—The Ladybug. Pohl, Kathy, ed. LC 85-28199. (Illus.). 32p. (gr. 3-7). 1986. text ed. 10.95 (*0-8172-2538-2*) Raintree Steck-V.

Oram, Liz & Baker, R. Robin. Insect Migration. LC 91-12776. (Illus.). 48p. (gr. 4-8). 1992. PLB 22.80 (*0-8114-2926-1*) Raintree Steck-V.

O'Toole, Christopher. The Honeybee in the Meadow. Oxford Scientific Films Staff, photos by. LC 89-33935. (Illus.). 32p. (gr. 4-6). 1989. PLB 17.27 (*0-8368-0117-2*) Gareth Stevens Inc.

INSECTS–POETRY

Hopkins, Lee B., compiled by. Flit, Flutter, Fly! Poems about Bugs & Other Crawly Creatures. Palagonia, Peter, illus. LC 91-12441. 32p. (gr. k-4). 1992. pap. 14.00 (*0-385-41468-4*) Doubleday.

INSECTS, INJURIOUS AND BENEFICIAL

see also Insecticides

also names of insects, e.g. locusts; silkworms, etc.

Berger, Melvin. Stranger Than Fiction: Killer Bugs. 128p. (Orig.). 1990. pap. 3.50 (*0-380-76036-3*, Camelot) Avon.

Fichter, George S. Insect Pests. Strekalovsky, Nicholas, illus. (gr. 5 up). 1966. pap. write for info. (*0-307-24016-9*, Golden Pr.) Western Pub.

Godkin, Celia. What about Ladybugs? Godkin, Celia, illus. LC 93-4202. 40p. (ps-3). 1995. 14.95 (*0-87156-549-8*) Sierra.

Heymann, Georgianne, adapted by. Aphids. (Illus.). 32p. (gr. 3-7). 1986. PLB 10.95 (*0-8172-2717-2*) Raintree Steck-V.

Lampton, Christopher. Insect Attack: A Disaster Book. (gr. 4-7). 1992. pap. 5.95 (*0-395-62467-3*) HM.

Peissel, Michel & Allen, Missy. Dangerous Insects. (Illus.). 112p. (gr. 5 up). 1993. PLB 19.95 (*0-7910-1785-0*, Am Art Analog); pap. 9.95 (*0-7910-1933-0*, Am Art Analog) Chelsea Hse.

INSECTS AS CARRIERS OF DISEASE

see also Flies; Mosquitoes

INSPECTION OF SCHOOLS

see School Administration and Organization

INSPIRATION

see Creation (Literary, Artistic, etc.)

INSTRUCTION

see Education; Teaching

INSTRUMENTS, MUSICAL

see Musical Instruments

INSTRUMENTS, SCIENTIFIC

see Scientific Apparatus and Instruments

INSURANCE

Park, Jae S. Now What? Auto Accident Claims Guide. 100p. (Orig.). 1989. pap. text ed. 3.95 (*0-685-28055-1*) Park Pub Co.

INTEGRATION, RACIAL

see Race Problems

INTEGRATION IN EDUCATION

see Segregation in Education

INTELLECT

see also Creation (Literary, Artistic, etc.); Imagination; Knowledge, Theory of; Logic; Perception; Reasoning; Senses and Sensation; Thought and Thinking

Haggerty, Brian. Nurturing Intelligences. 1994. pap. 24.95 (*0-201-49056-0*) Addison-Wesley.

Sanford, Doris. Don't Look at Me: A Child's Book about Feeling Different. Evans, Graci, illus. LC 86-185484. 24p. (gr. k-6). 1986. 7.99 (*0-88070-150-1*, Gold & Honey) Questar Pubs.

Wenger, Win. A Method for Personal Growth & Development. (Illus.). 135p. (Orig.). (gr. 7-12). 1986. pap. 24.00 (*0-931865-09-3*) Psychegenics.

INTELLECTUAL LIFE

see Culture; Learning and Scholarship

INTELLIGENCE

see Intellect

INTELLIGENCE OF ANIMALS

see Animal Intelligence

INTELLIGENCE SERVICE–U. S.

Kronenwetter, Michael. Covert Action. LC 90-46209. (Illus.). (gr. 9-12). 1991. PLB 13.40 (*0-531-13018-5*) Watts.

Landau, Elaine. Big Brother Is Watching. 1992. 14.95 (*0-8027-8160-8*); lib. bdg. 15.85 (*0-8027-8161-6*) Walker & Co.

INTEMPERANCE

see Alcoholism

INTERCOLLEGIATE ATHLETICS

see Athletics

INTERCULTURAL EDUCATION

For works dealing with the eradication of racial and religious prejudices by showing the nature and effects of race, creed and immigrant cultures.

Branch, James H., III. Multicultural Stories. Ward, Dick, ed. Douglass, S., illus. LC 92-93449. 29p. 1992. 12.50 (*0-9635840-0-6*) Guttenburg Pub.

Clarke, Joy A. Multicultural Social Studies Unit: Who Am I? Blocker, Kearn, illus. 150p. (gr. 3-8). 1991. 3-ring binder 79.95 (*0-9626984-1-5*); pap. 69.95 (*0-685-62443-9*) Clarke Enterprise.

Cole, Ann, et al. Children Are Children Are Children: An Activity Approach to Exploring Brazil, France, Iran, Japan, Nigeria, & the U. S. S. R. (Illus.). (gr. 3-7). 1978. Little.

Hammer, Roger A. Hidden America: A Collection of Multi-Cultural Stories, 4 bks. rev. ed. Schlosser, Cy, et al, illus. (gr. 6 up). Set. pap. 29.95 (*0-932991-00-9*) Place in the Woods.

Jenness, Aylette. Come Home with Me: A Multicultural Treasure Hunt. LC 92-50699. (gr. 4-7). 1993. 16.95 (*1-56584-064-X*) New Press NY.

—Ven a Mi Casa. LC 93-83997. (gr. 4-7). 1993. 16.95 (*1-56584-118-2*) New Press NY.

Scott, Sharon & Nicholas. Not Better... Not Worse... Just Different. Phillips, George, illus. 118p. (Orig.). (gr. k-5). 1992. pap. 7.95 (*0-87425-195-8*) Human Res Dev Pr.

INTERIOR DECORATION

see also Coverlets; Furniture

Everett, F. & Woods, P., eds. Decorate Your Room. (Illus.). 48p. (gr. 6 up). 1989. lib. bdg. 13.96 (*0-88110-392-6*, Usborne); pap. 7.95 (*0-7460-0438-9*) EDC.

Greco, Gail. The Romance of Country Inns: A Decorating Book for Your Home. Bagley, Tom, photos by. LC 93-11708. (Illus.). 288p. (gr. 10 up). 1993. 29.95 (*1-55853-175-0*) Rutledge Hill Pr.

James, Elizabeth & Barkin, Carol. A Place of Your Own. Jacobs, Lou, Jr., illus. 96p. (gr. 9 up). 1981. (Dutton); pap. o.p. (*0-525-37099-4*) NAL-Dutton.

Rourke, A. Decorating Your Room. (Illus.). 32p. (gr. 5 up). 1989. lib. bdg. 15.94 (*0-86625-286-X*) Rourke Corp.

Sherrow, Victoria. Dream Rooms, Decorating with Flair. Magnuson, Diana, illus. LC 90-48241. 128p. (gr. 5-9). 1991. lib. bdg. 10.89 (*0-8167-2293-5*); pap. text ed. 2.95 (*0-8167-2294-3*) Troll Assocs.

Storm, Betsy. I Can Be an Interior Designer. LC 89-15758. 32p. (gr. k-3). 1989. pap. 3.95 (*0-516-41958-7*) Childrens.

Wood, Leslie. My House. (Illus.). 16p. (ps up). 1988. pap. 2.95 (*0-19-272186-0*) OUP.

INTERIOR DECORATION–FICTION

Berry, Liz. Mel. LC 93-7484. 224p. (gr. 7 up). 1993. pap. 3.99 (*0-14-036534-6*, Puffin) Puffin Bks.

Montenegro, Laura N. One Stuck Drawer. Montenegro, Laura N., illus. LC 90-46139. 32p. (gr. k-3). 1991. 14.45 (*0-395-57319-X*) HM.

INTERNAL-COMBUSTION ENGINES

see Gas and Oil Engines

INTERNATIONAL COOPERATION

For general works on international cooperative activities, with or without the participation of governments.

see also International Organization; United Nations

INTERNATIONAL ECONOMIC RELATIONS

Fisher, Barbara & Spiegel, Richard, eds. Streams Four. (Illus.). 150p. (Orig.). (gr. 9-12). 1990. pap. 5.00 (*0-934830-44-4*) Ten Penny.

INTERNATIONAL EDUCATION

For works on education for international understanding, world citizenship, etc.

see also Intercultural Education

INTERNATIONAL EXHIBITIONS

see Exhibitions

INTERNATIONAL FEDERATION

see International Organization

INTERNATIONAL LAW

see also International Organization; International Relations; Pirates; Salvage; Slave Trade; War

INTERNATIONAL ORGANIZATION

For works on plans leading towards political organizations of nations.

see also European Federation; World Politics

also names of specific organizations, e.g. United Nations, etc.

Kiang, John. The Early One World Movement. LC 91-68335. 360p. (Orig.). 1992. pap. 14.95 (*0-916301-03-6*) One World Pub.

INTERNATIONAL RELATIONS

see also Diplomats; Disarmament; International Economic Relations; International Organization; Peace also names of countries with the subdivision Foreign Relations, e.g. U. S.–Foreign Relations, etc.

Arnold, Terrell E. & Kennedy, Moorhead. Think about Terrorism: The New Warfare. LC 87-21158. (Illus.). 153p. (gr. 9-12). 1988. lib. bdg. 14.85 (*0-8027-6757-5*); pap. 5.95 (*0-8027-6758-3*) Walker & Co.

Bachrach, Deborah. Espionage. LC 92-37438. (Illus.). 112p. (gr. 5-8). 1992. PLB 14.95 (*1-56006-134-0*) Lucent Bks.

Edwards, R. International Terrorism. (Illus.). 48p. (gr. 5 up). 1988. PLB 18.60 (*0-86592-285-3*); 13.95s.p. (*0-685-58316-3*) Rourke Corp.

Galicich, Anne. Samantha Smith: A Journey for Peace. LC 87-13614. (Illus.). 64p. (gr. 3 up). 1988. text ed. 13.95 RSBE (*0-87518-367-0*, Dillon) Macmillan Child Grp.

Kronenwetter, Michael. The War Against Terrorism. Steltenpohl, Jane, ed. (Illus.). 138p. (gr. 7-10). 1989. lib. bdg. 13.98 (*0-671-69050-7*, J Messner) S&S Trade.

Martini, Teri. The Secret Is Out. 144p. (gr. 5). 1992. pap. 2.99 (*0-380-71465-5*, Camelot) Avon.

Milord, Susan. Hands Around the World: Three Hundred Sixty-Five Creative Ways to Build Cultural Awareness & Global Respect. LC 92-21753. (Illus.). 176p. (Orig.). (gr. 1-8). 1992. pap. 12.95 (*0-913589-65-9*) Williamson Pub Co.

Nabhan, Martin, et al. World Partners, 6 bks. (Illus.). 384p. (gr. 7 up). 1990. Set. lib. bdg. 95.58 (*0-86593-087-2*); Set. lib. bdg. 77.70s.p. (*0-685-36361-9*) Rourke Corp.

Plattner, Sandra S. Connecting Around the World. (ps-k). 1991. pap. 10.95 (*0-86653-978-6*) Fearon Teach Aids.

Polesetsky, Matthew & Dudley, William, eds. The New World Order: Opposing Viewpoints. LC 91-12374. (Illus.). 240p. (gr. 10 up). 1991. lib. bdg. 17.95 (*0-89908-183-5*); pap. 9.95 (*0-89908-158-4*) Greenhaven.

Pringle, Laurence. Living in a Risky World. LC 88-31686. (Illus.). 112p. (gr. 5 up). 1989. 12.95 (*0-688-04326-7*) Morrow Jr Bks.

Reynolds, Tony, et al. World Issues, 2 bks. (Illus.). 336p. (gr. 5 up). 1990. Set. lib. bdg. 126.00 (*0-86592-095-8*); Set. lib. bdg. 94.50s.p. (*0-685-36375-9*) Rourke Corp.

Stein, Conrad. The Iran Hostage Crisis. LC 94-9492. (Illus.). 32p. (gr. 3-6). 1994. PLB 16.40 (*0-516-06681-1*) Childrens.

INTERNATIONAL RELATIONS–FICTION

Blume, Judy. Iggie's House. large type, unabr. ed. 158p. (gr. 3-6). 1989. lib. bdg. 13.95 (*0-8161-4449-4*) G K Hall.

Jain, Ash. Don't Steal My Blocks! The Children's Storybook of Operation Desert Storm. Cavallotti, Carolina, illus. 12p. (Orig.). (ps-3). 1991. pap. 2.95 (*0-9629992-1-0*) Arlington Pr.

Wibberley, Leonard. Mouse That Roared. (gr. 6-12). 1971. pap. 3.50 (*0-553-24969-X*) Bantam.

INTERNATIONAL TRADE

see Commerce

INTERNMENT CAMPS

see Concentration Camps

INTERPERSONAL RELATIONS

see Human Relations

INTERPLANETARY COMMUNICATION

see Interstellar Communication

INTERPLANETARY VOYAGES

see also Outer Space–Exploration; Rockets (Aeronautics); Space Flight

Apfel, Necia H. Voyager to the Planets. (gr. 4-7). 1994. pap. 6.95 (*0-395-69622-4*, Clarion Bks) HM.

Blackman, Steven. Space Travel. LC 93-13310. (Illus.). 32p. (gr. 5-7). 1993. PLB 11.90 (*0-531-14275-2*) Watts.

Cameron, Eleanor. Mr. Bass's Planetoid. Darling, Louis, illus. (gr. 3-7). 1958. 14.95 (*0-316-12525-3*, Joy St Bks) Little.

—The Wonderful Flight to the Mushroom Planet. Henneberger, Robert, illus. (gr. 4-6). 1988. 15.95 (*0-316-12537-7*, Joy St Bks); pap. 5.95 (*0-316-12540-7*, Joy St Bks) Little.

Farrow, Peter & Lampert, Diane. Twyllyp. (Illus.). (gr. 3-7). 1963. 10.95 (*0-8392-3040-0*) Astor-Honor.

Helmrath, M. O. & Bartlett, J. L. Bobby Bear's Rocket Ride. LC 68-56809. (Illus.). 32p. (ps-1). 1968. PLB 12.35 prebound (*0-87783-008-8*); cassette 7.94x (*0-87783-186-6*) Oddo.

Petty, Kate. Into Space. Wood, Jakki, illus. 32p. (gr. 2-4). 1993. pap. 5.95 (*0-8120-1761-7*) Barron.

Yolen, Jane. Commander Toad & the Dis-Asteroid. Degen, Bruce, illus. LC 84-1897. 64p. (gr. 4). 1985. (Coward); pap. 6.95 (*0-698-20620-7*, Coward) Putnam Pub Group.

INTERSTELLAR COMMUNICATION

Marsh, Carole. The Backyard Searcher's Extra Terrestrial Log Book. (Illus.). (gr. 4-9). 1994. PLB 24.95 (*1-55609-282-2*); pap. 14.95 (*0-935326-27-8*) Gallopade Pub Group.

—How to Find an Extra Terrestrial in Your Own Backyard. (Illus.). 1994. 24.95 (*0-935326-09-X*) Gallopade Pub Group.

INSTELLAR VOYAGES

see Interplanetary Voyages

INTERVIEWING (JOURNALISM)

see Reporters and Reporting

INTOLERANCE

see Toleration

INTOXICATION

see Alcoholism; Narcotic Habit

INVALIDS

see Physically Handicapped

INVENTIONS

see also Creation (Literary, Artistic, etc.); Inventors

Andrews & McMeel Staff. Flintstones Wacky Inventions: How Things Work in the Modern Stone Age. (gr. 4-7). 1993. 15.95 (*1-878685-65-1*, Bedrock Pr) Turner Pub GA.

Bender, Lionel. Invention. King, Dave, photos by. LC 90-4888. (Illus.). 64p. (gr. 5 up). 1991. 16.00 (*0-679-80782-9*); PLB 16.99 (*0-679-90782-3*) Knopf Bks Yng Read.

Bendick, Jeanne. Eureka! It's a Telephone! Murdocca, Sal, illus. LC 92-5085. 48p. (gr. 2-6). 1993. PLB 15.40 (*1-56294-215-8*) Millbrook Pr.

Bendick, Jeanne & Bendick, Robert. Eureka! It's Television! Murdocca, Sal, illus. & designed by. LC 92-15652. 48p. (gr. 2-6). 1993. PLB 15.40 (*1-56294-214-X*); pap. 6.95 (*1-56294-718-4*) Millbrook Pr.

Boston's Museum of Science Inventor's Workshop. (Illus.). 64p. 1994. incl. kit 17.95 (*0-685-72752-1*) Running Pr.

Clements, Gillian. The Picture History of Great Inventors. LC 93-21705. 1994. 17.00 (*0-679-84788-X*); pap. 13.00 (*0-679-84787-1*) Knopf Bks Yng Read.

Crump, Donald J., ed. Small Inventions That Make a Big Difference. LC 83-23770. 104p. (gr. 3-8). 1984. 8.95 (*0-87044-498-0*); PLB 12.50 (*0-87044-503-0*) Natl Geog.

Dale, Rodney & Weaver, Rebecca. Home Entertainment. (Illus.). 64p. 1994. PLB 16.00 (*0-19-521001-8*) OUP.

—Machines in the Office. (Illus.). 64p. 1994. PLB 16.00 (*0-19-521000-X*) OUP.

Dale, Rodney, ed. Discoveries & Inventions, 8 vols. (Illus.). 512p. 1994. Set. PLB 128.00 (*0-19-520973-7*) OUP.

Dempsey, Michael, ed. Growing up with Science: The Illustrated Encyclopedia of Invention, 26 vols. rev. ed. LC 82-63047. (Illus.). (gr. 5-10). 1987. Set. 181.48 (*0-87475-841-6*) Stuttman.

Diagram Visual Information Staff. Historical Inventions on File. (Illus.). 288p. (gr. 5-10). 1994. loose-leaf binder 155.00x (*0-8160-2911-3*) Facts on File.

Filson, Brent. Superconductors & Other New Breakthroughs in Science. (Illus.). 128p. (gr. 5-9). 1989. lib. bdg. 13.98 (*0-671-65857-3*, J Messner); PLB 9.74s.p. (*0-685-24680-9*) S&S Trade.

Friddle, Sue. Jake Art. Friddle, Jacob, illus. (Orig.). (gr. k-7). 1989. pap. 5.00 (*0-9623308-1-7*) Anyones Pub.

Gardner, Robert. Experimenting with Inventions. LC 89-24788. (gr. 7-12). 1990. PLB 13.40 (*0-531-10910-0*) Watts.

Great Inventions. LC 92-54273. (Illus.). 24p. (gr. k-3). 1993. 8.95 (*1-56458-220-5*) Dorling Kindersley.

Great Inventions. LC 93-85988. 32p. 1994. 5.95 (*1-56138-199-3*) Running Pr.

Jacobs, Daniel. What Does It Do? Inventions Then & Now. (Illus.). 24p. (ps-2). 1990. PLB 17.10 (*0-8172-3586-8*); PLB 10.95 pkg. of 3 (*0-685-58554-9*) Raintree Steck-V.

Jones, Charlotte F. Mistakes That Worked. (gr. 4-7). 1994. pap. 9.95 (*0-385-32043-4*) Doubleday.

Konigsburg, E. L. Samuel Todd's Book of Great Inventions. Konigsburg, E. L., illus. LC 90-23688. 32p. (ps-2). 1991. SBE 13.95 (*0-689-31680-1*, Atheneum Child Bk) Macmillan Child Grp.

Lehman, James. Invendex, Inventors Index, Sparks the Flash of Genius. (Orig.). (gr. 8 up). 1993. pap. 7.95 (*0-9637633-0-X*) WLC Pub.

McCormack, Alan. Inventors Workshop. LC 80-84185. (gr. 3-8). 1981. pap. 10.95 (*0-8224-9783-2*) Fearon Teach Aids.

Markham, Lois. Inventions That Changed Modern Life. Gerstle, Gary, contrib. by. LC 93-17022. (Illus.). 48p. (gr. 5-7). 1993. PLB 22.80 (*0-8114-4930-0*) Raintree Steck-V.

Murphy, Jim. Guess Again: More Weird & Wacky Inventions. LC 85-24320. (Illus.). 64p. (gr. 3-6). 1986. SBE 13.95 (*0-02-767720-6*, Bradbury Pr) Macmillan Child Grp.

Peterson, Patricia R. The Know It All: Resource Book for Kids. (Illus.). 144p. (gr. 2 up). 1989. pap. 15.95 (*0-913705-45-4*) Zephyr Pr AZ.

Platt, Richard. The Smithsonian Visual Timeline of Inventions. (Illus.). 64p. (gr. 3-6). 1994. 15.95 (*1-56458-675-8*) Dorling Kindersley.

Prostano, Emanuel & Prostano, Joyce. Take Two Inventions & Two Patents. (Illus.). 130p. (Orig.). (gr. 8-12). 1991. pap. 19.95 (*0-944397-14-X*) In-Time Pubns.

Quinn, Kaye. Inventive Inventions. Quinn, Kaye, illus. 40p. (Orig.). (ps-4). 1986. pap. 2.95 (*0-8431-1893-8*) Price Stern.

Reid, S. Invention & Discovery. (Illus.). 128p. (gr. 6 up). 1987. PLB 15.96 (*0-88110-231-8*); pap. 9.95 (*0-86020-956-3*) EDC.

Reid, Struan. Inventions & Trade. (Illus.). 48p. (gr. 6 up). 1994. text ed. 15.95 RSBE (*0-02-726316-9*, New Discovery Bks) Macmillan Child Grp.

Ripley, Robert L. Inventions. Stott, Carol, illus. 48p. (gr. 3-6). Date not set. PLB 12.95 (*1-56065-125-3*) Capstone Pr.

Stanish, Bob. The Unconventional Invention Book. (gr. 3-12). 1981. 11.95 (*0-86653-035-5*, GA 263) Good Apple.

Stanish, Bob & Singletary, Carol. Inventioneering. Skiles, Janet, illus. 64p. (gr. 3-9). 1987. pap. 7.95 (*0-86653-402-4*, GA 1019) Good Apple.

Sylvester, D. Inventions. 40p. (gr. 4-8). 1992. 6.95 (*0-88160-252-3*, LW1401) Learning Wks.

Sylvester, Diane. Inventions, Robots, Future. 112p. (gr. 4-6). 1984. 9.95 (*0-88160-108-X*, LW 905) Learning Wks.

Tanner, Joey. Futuristics: A Time to Come. rev. ed. 73p. (gr. k-8). 1992. pap. text ed. 19.95 (*0-913705-16-0*) Zephyr Pr AZ.

Taylor, Barbara. Be an Inventor. Weekly Reader Staff, illus. 74p. (gr. 3-7). 1987. 11.95 (*0-15-205950-4*, Voyager Bks); pap. 7.95 (*0-15-205951-2*, Voyager Bks) HarBrace.

Turvey, Peter. Inventions: Inventors & Ingenious Ideas. (Illus.). 48p. (gr. 5-8). 1992. 13.95 (*0-531-15243-X*) Watts.

—Inventions: Inventors & Ingenious Ideas. (Illus.). 48p. (gr. 5-8). 1994. pap. 7.95 (*0-531-15713-X*) Watts.

Weiss, Harvey. How to Be an Inventor. LC 79-7823. (Illus.). 96p. (gr. 5 up). 1980. (Crowell Jr Bks) HarpC Child Bks.

World Book Editors, ed. Inventors & Inventions: A Supplement to Childcraft - the How & Why Library. LC 65-25105. (Illus.). 224p. (gr. 6 up). 1993. PLB write for info. (*0-7166-0693-3*) World Bk.

Wulffson, Don L. The Invention of Ordinary Things. Doty, Roy, illus. LC 80-17498. 96p. (gr. 3 up). 1981. PLB 14.93 (*0-688-51978-4*) Lothrop.

INVENTIONS–FICTION

Brouwer, Sigmund & Davidson, Wayne. Dr. Drabble's Amazing Invisibility Mirror. 24p. 1992. 5.99 (*0-89693-970-7*) SP Pubns.

—Dr. Drabble's Astounding Musical Mesmerizer. Bell, Bill, illus. 24p. (ps-2). 1991. 5.99 (*0-89693-904-9*) SP Pubns.

—Dr. Drabble's Incredible Identical Robot Innovation. Bell, Bill, illus. 24p. (ps-2). 1991. 5.99 (*0-89693-902-2*) SP Pubns.

—Dr. Drabble's Phenomenal Anti-Gravity Dust Machine. Bell, Bill, illus. 24p. (ps-2). 1991. 5.99 (*0-89693-901-4*) SP Pubns.

—Dr. Drabble's Spectacular Shrinker-Enlarger. 24p. 1992. 5.99 (*0-89693-969-3*) SP Pubns.

Buller, Jon & Schade, Susan. Twenty-Thousand Baseball Cards under the Sea. Buller, Jon, illus. LC 90-40704. 48p. (Orig.). (gr. 2-3). 1991. lib. bdg. 7.99 (*0-679-91569-9*); pap. 3.50 (*0-679-81569-4*) Random Bks Yng Read.

—The Video Kids. Buller, Jon & Schade, Susan, illus. LC 93-26923. 48p. (gr. 2-3). 1994. 7.99 (*0-448-40181-9*, G&D); pap. 3.50 (*0-448-40180-0*, G&D) Putnam Pub Group.

Collins, David R. Ara's Amazing Spinning Wheel. (Illus.). (ps-2). 1991. PLB 6.95 (*0-8136-5181-6*, TK7275); pap. 3.50 (*0-8136-5681-8*, TK7276) Modern Curr.

Crowley, Michael. New Kid on Spurwick Ave. Carter, Abby, illus. 32p. (gr. k-3). 1992. 14.95 (*0-316-16230-2*) Little.

Duffey, Betsy. The Gadget War. Wilson, Janet, illus. 80p. (gr. 2-5). 1994. pap. 3.99 (*0-14-034871-9*) Puffin Bks.

Fleming, Candace. Professor Fergus Fahrenheit & His Wonderful Weather Machine. Weller, Don, illus. LC 93-4432. (ps-3). 1994. pap. 14.00 (*0-671-87047-5*, S&S BFYR) S&S Trade.

Frank, John. Odds 'N Ends Alvy. Karas, G. Brian, illus. LC 92-27151. 32p. (gr. k-4). 1993. RSBE 14.95 (*0-02-735675-2*, Four Winds) Macmillan Child Grp.

Gackenbach, Dick. Tiny for a Day. Gackenbach, Dick, illus. LC 92-37580. 1993. 14.45 (*0-395-65616-8*, Clarion Bks) HM.

Haas, Dorothy. Burton's Zoom Zoom Va-Rooom Machine. Bobak, Cathy, illus. LC 89-77426. 144p. (gr. 5-8). 1990. SBE 13.95 (*0-02-738201-X*, Bradbury Pr) Macmillan Child Grp.

Hwa-I Publishing Co., Staff. Chinese Children's Stories, Vol. 36: Lu Ban & Old Sir Lee, Umbrellas. Ching, Emily, et al, eds. Wonder Kids Publications Staff, tr. from CHI. (Illus.). 28p. (gr. 3-6). 1991. Repr. of 1988 ed. 7.95 (*1-56162-036-X*) Wonder Kids.

MacGill-Callahan, Sheila. How the Boats Got Their Sails. LC 93-45966. 1995. write for info. (*0-8037-1541-2*); lib. bdg. write for info. (*0-8037-1542-0*) Dial Bks Young.

Morris, Gilbert. The Rustlers of Panther Gap. LC 94-7128. (gr. 3-7). 1994. pap. 4.99 (*0-8423-4393-8*) Tyndale.

Nelson, Jenny. Archibald & the Crunch Machine. Battersby, Sarah, illus. 40p. (gr. 2-4). 1990. pap. 5.95 (*1-55037-114-2*, Pub. by Annick CN) Firefly Bks Ltd.

Septimus Bean & His Amazing Machine. 42p. (ps-3). 1992. PLB 13.27 (*0-8368-0887-8*) Gareth Stevens Inc.

Skinner, David. The Wrecker. LC 93-46895. 1995. PLB 14.00 (*0-671-79771-9*, S&S BFYR) S&S Trade.

Small, David. Ruby Mae Has Something to Say. Small, David, illus. LC 91-33785. 40p. (ps-4). 1992. 12.00 (*0-517-58248-1*); PLB 12.99 (*0-517-58249-X*) Crown Bks Yng Read.

Snell, Gordon. Tom's Amazing Machine Zaps Back! (Illus.). 144p. (gr. 4-6). 1992. 15.95 (*0-09-173888-1*, Pub. by Hutchinson UK) Trafalgar.

Waite, Michael. Sammy's Gadget Galaxy. LC 91-38874. (ps-3). 1992. pap. 7.99 (*0-7814-0036-8*, Chariot Bks) Chariot Family.

Wonder Kids Publications Group Staff (USA) & Hwa-I Publishing Co., Staff. Inventions: Chinese Children's Stories, Vols. 36-40. Ching, Emily, et al, eds. Wonder Kids Publications Staff, tr. from CHI. Hwa-I Publishing Co., Staff, illus. LC 90-60799. (gr. 3-6). 1991. Repr. of 1988 ed. Five vol. set, 28p. ea. bk. 39. 75 (*0-685-58707-X*) Wonder Kids.

INVENTORS

see also Inventions

Aaseng, Nathan. The Inventors: Nobel Prizes in Chemistry, Physics, & Medicine. (Illus.). 80p. (gr. 5 up). 1988. PLB 17.50 (*0-8225-0651-3*) Lerner Pubns.

—Twentieth Century Inventors. (Illus.). 128p. (gr. 7-12). 1991. 16.95x (*0-8160-2485-5*) Facts on File.

Akinsheye, Dexter. African American Inventor Math Pack Workbook. Akinsheye, Dayo, ed. Akinsheye, Addae, illus. 20p. (Orig.). (gr. 2-5). 1992. pap. text ed. 2.50 (*1-877835-53-6*) TD Pub.

—Discovering American History. Akinsheye, Dayo, ed. Griffin, Charles, illus. 20p. (Orig.). (gr. 2-3). 1992. pap. 4.99 (*1-877835-70-6*) TD Pub.

Brophy, Ann. John Ericson & the Inventions of War. Gallin, Richard, ed. Steele, Henry, intro. by. (Illus.). 160p. (gr. 5 up). 1990. PLB 12.95 (*0-382-09943-5*); pap. 7.95 (*0-382-24052-9*) Silver Burdett Pr.

Carroll, Jeri & Wells, Candace. Inventors. Foster, Tom, illus. 64p. (gr. k-4). 1987. pap. 7.95 (*0-86653-381-8*, GA1006) Good Apple.

Chandler, Ann. Black Women: A Salute to Black Inventors. rev. ed. Ivery, Evelyn L., ed. Chandler, Alton, et al, illus. Chandler, Alton, intro. by. 24p. (gr. 3-7). 1992. pap. text ed. 1.50 (*1-877804-06-1*) Chandler White.

Clements, Gillian. The Picture History of Great Inventors. LC 93-21705. 1994. 17.00 (*0-679-84788-X*); pap. 13.00 (*0-679-84787-1*) Knopf Bks Yng Read.

Dommermuth-Costa, Carol. Nikola Tesla: A Spark of Genius. LC 93-43123. (Illus.). 144p. (gr. 5 up). 1994. 21.50 (*0-8225-4920-4*) Lerner Pubns.

Dunn, Andrew. Alexander Graham Bell. LC 90-2628. (Illus.). 48p. (gr. 5-7). 1991. PLB 12.40 (*0-531-18418-8*, Pub. by Bookwright Pr) Watts.

Gold, Rebecca. Steve Wozniak: A Wizard Called Woz. LC 94-859. (Illus.). 72p. (gr. 4-9). 1994. text ed. 17.50 (*0-8225-2881-9*) Lerner Pubns.

Hargrove, Jim. Dr. An Wang: Computer Pioneer. LC 92-35061. (Illus.). 152p. (gr. 4 up). 1993. PLB 14.40 (*0-516-03290-9*); pap. 5.95 (*0-516-43290-7*) Childrens.

Haskins, Jim. Outward Dreams: Black Inventors & Their Inventions. 128p. (gr. 7). 1991. 13.95 (*0-8027-6993-4*); PLB 14.85 (*0-8027-6994-2*) Walker & Co.

—Outward Dreams: Black Inventors & Their Inventions. (gr. 7 up). 1992. pap. 3.50 (*0-553-29480-6*, Starfire) Bantam.

Hayden, Robert. Nine African-American Inventors. rev. ed. (Illus.). 171p. (gr. 5-8). 1992. Repr. of 1972 ed. PLB 14.95 (*0-8050-2133-7*) TFC Bks NY.

Howell, Ann C. Communication: A Salute to Black Inventors. rev. ed. Ivery, Evelyn L., ed. Chandler, Alton, et al, illus. Chandler, Alton, intro. by. 24p. (gr. 3-7). 1992. pap. text ed. 1.50 (*1-877804-05-3*) Chandler White.

—Food: A Salute to Black Inventors. rev. ed. Ivery, Evelyn L., ed. Venable, James, et al, illus. Chndler, Alton, intro. by. 24p. (gr. 3-7). 1992. pap. text ed. 1.50 (*1-877804-01-0*) Chandler White.

—Old West: A Salute to Black Inventors. rev. ed. Ivery, Evelyn L., ed. Chandler, Alton, et al, illus. Chandler, Alton, pref. by. 24p. (gr. 3-7). 1992. pap. text ed. 1.50 (*1-877804-03-7*) Chandler White.

—Safety: A Salute to Black Inventors. rev. ed. Ivery, Evelyn L., ed. Chandler, Alton, et al, illus. Chandler, Alton H., intro. by. 24p. (gr. 3-7). 1992. pap. text ed. 1.50 (*1-877804-02-9*) Chandler White.

—Transportation - Food - Safety - Old West - Working Easier - Communication - Black Women: A Salute to Black Inventors. rev. ed. Ivery, Evelyn L., ed. Chandler, Alton, et al, illus. 24p. (gr. 3-7). 1992. pap. text ed. 10.50 (*1-877804-10-X*) Chandler White.

—Transportation: A Salute to Black Inventors. rev. ed. Ivery, Evelyn L., ed. Venable, James, et al, illus. Chandler, Alton, intro. by. 24p. (gr. 3-7). 1992. pap. text ed. 1.50 (*1-877804-00-2*) Chandler White.

—Working Easier: A Salute to Black Inventors. rev. ed. Ivery, Evelyn L., ed. Chandler, Alton, et al, illus. Chandler, Alton, intro. by. 24p. (gr. 3-7). 1992. pap. text ed. 1.50 (*1-877804-04-5*) Chandler White.

Jackson, Garnet N. Elijah McCoy, Inventor. Thomas, Gary, illus. LC 92-28797. 1992. 56.50 (*0-8136-5230-8*); pap. 28.50 (*0-8136-5703-2*) Modern Curr.

—Garrett Morgan, Inventor. Hudson, Thomas, illus. LC 92-28801. 1992. write for info. (*0-8136-5231-6*); pap. write for info. (*0-8136-5704-0*) Modern Curr.

Lafferty, Peter & Rowe, Julian. The Inventor Through History. Smith, Tony & Wheele, Steve, illus. LC 92-43262. 48p. 1993. 15.95 (*1-56847-013-4*) Thomson Lrning.

Lomask, Milton. Great Lives: Invention & Technology. LC 90-27619. (Illus.). 272p. (gr. 4-6). 1991. SBE 22.95 (*0-684-19106-7*, Scribners Young Read) Macmillan Child Grp.

McPartland, Scott. Edwin Land. LC 93-22077. (gr. 7-8). 1993. 15.93 (*0-86592-150-4*); 11.95s.p. (*0-685-66592-5*) Rourke Enter.

—Gordon Gould. LC 93-2819. 1993. 15.93 (*0-86592-079-6*); 11.95s.p. (*0-685-66585-2*) Rourke Enter.

Mitchell, Barbara. Shoes for Everyone: A Story about Jan Matzeliger. Mitchell, Hetty, illus. 64p. (gr. 3-6). 1986. PLB 14.95 (*0-87614-290-0*) Carolrhoda Bks.

Nirgiotis, Nicholas. Thomas Edison. LC 93-37028. (Illus.). 32p. (gr. 3-6). 1994. PLB 12.30 (*0-516-06676-5*) Childrens.

Noonan, Geoffrey J. Nineteenth-Century Inventors. 128p. (gr. 6-9). 1992. lib. bdg. 16.95x (*0-8160-2480-4*) Facts on File.
Oleksy, Walter. Inventors. (Illus.). 128p. (gr. 3-6). Date not set. 19.95 (*1-56065-118-0*) Capstone Pr.
Olsen, Frank H. Inventors Who Left Their Brand on America. 1991. pap. 3.50 (*0-553-29211-0*) Bantam.
Parker, Steve. Guglielmo Marconi & Radio. LC 94-8253. 1994. write for info. (*0-7910-3009-1*) Chelsea Hse.
—Thomas Edison & Electricity. LC 92-6805. (Illus.). 32p. (gr. 3-7). 1992. 14.00 (*0-06-020859-7*); PLB 13.89 (*0-06-021473-2*) HarpC Child Bks.
—Thomas Edison & Electricity. Parker, Steve, illus. LC 92-6805. 32p. (gr. 3-7). 1992. pap. 5.95 (*0-06-446144-0*, Trophy) HarpC Child Bks.
Patton, Sally J. & Maletis, Margaret. Inventors: A Source Guide for Self-Directed Units. rev. ed. 72p. (gr. 2-6). 1989. pap. text ed. 14.95 (*0-913705-35-7*) Zephyr Pr AZ.
Rozakis, Laurie. Steven Jobs. LC 92-43268. (gr. 5 up). 1993. 15.93 (*0-86592-001-X*); 11.95s.p. (*0-685-66327-2*) Rourke Corp.
St. Pierre, Stephanie. Gertrude Elion. LC 93-22315. (gr. 7-8). 1993. 15.93 (*0-86592-130-X*); 11.95s.p. (*0-685-66593-3*) Rourke Enter.
Swanson, June. David Bushnell & His Turtle: The Story of America's First Submarine. Eagle, Mike, illus. LC 90-628. 40p. (gr. 2-5). 1991. SBE 13.95 (*0-689-31628-3*, Atheneum Child Bk) Macmillan Child Grp.
Sweet, Dovie D. Red Light, Green Light: The Life of Garrett Morgan & His Invention of the Stop Light. 4th ed. (Orig.). (gr. 1-6). 1988. pap. 5.00 (*0-682-49088-1*) Kitwardo Pubs.
Taylor, Barbara. Charles Ginsburg. LC 93-494. (gr. 7-8). 1993. 15.93 (*0-86592-159-8*); 11.95s.p. (*0-685-66582-8*) Rourke Enter.
Towle, Wendy. The Real McCoy: The Life of an African-American Inventor. Clay, Wil, illus. LC 91-38895. 32p. (gr. k-4). 1993. 14.95 (*0-590-43596-5*) Scholastic Inc.
Van Steenwyk, Elizabeth. Levi Strauss: The Blue Jeans Man. (gr. 6-9). 1988. 13.95 (*0-8027-6795-8*); PLB 14.85 (*0-8027-6796-6*) Walker & Co.
Wade, Mary D. Milk, Meat Biscuits & The Terraqueous Machine: The Story of Gail Borden. Roberts, Melissa, ed. (Illus.). 64p. (gr. 4-7). 1987. 9.95 (*0-89015-605-0*) Sunbelt Media.
Weidt, Maryann N. & Anderson, Lydia M. Mr. Blue Jeans: A Story about Levi Strauss. (Illus.). 64p. (gr. 3-6). 1990. PLB 14.95 (*0-87614-421-0*) Carolrhoda Bks.
Williams, Brian. Karl Benz. LC 90-21744. (Illus.). 48p. (gr. 5-8). 1991. RLB 12.40 (*0-531-18404-8*, Pub. by Bookwright Pr) Watts.

INVENTORS–FICTION

Baker, Keith. The Magic Fan. 16p. (gr. k-3). 1989. 14.95 (*0-15-250750-7*) HarBrace.
Denslow, Sharon P. Radio Boy. Gillman, Alec, photos by. LC 93-36281. 1995. 14.00 (*0-02-728684-3*, Four Winds) Macmillan Child Grp.
Fenner, Carol. A Summer of Horses. LC 88-45878. 144p. (Orig.). (gr. 3-6). 1989. lib. bdg. 7.99 (*0-394-90480-X*); pap. 2.95 (*0-394-80480-5*) Knopf Bks Yng Read.
Haas, Dorothy. Burton's Zoom Zoom Va-Rooom Machine. Bobak, Cathy, illus. LC 89-77426. 144p. (gr. 5-8). 1990. SBE 13.95 (*0-02-738201-X*, Bradbury Pr) Macmillan Child Grp.
Lustig, Michael & Lustig, Esther. Willy Whyner, Cloud Designer. Lustig, Michael, illus. LC 93-21957. 40p. 1994. RSBE 14.95 (*0-02-761365-8*, Four Winds) Macmillan Child Grp.
Peabody, Paul. Blackberry Hollow. Peabody, Paul, illus. LC 92-8968. 160p. (gr. 3-7). 1993. 15.95 (*0-399-22500-5*, Philomel Bks) Putnam Pub Group.
Quin-Harkin, Janet. Septimus Bean & His Amazing Machine. Cumings, Art, illus. LC 79-163. 48p. (ps-3). 1980. 5.95 (*0-8193-0999-0*) Parents.
Skinner, David. You Must Kiss a Whale. LC 91-30352. 104p. (gr. 6 up). 1992. pap. 14.00 3-pc. bdg. (*0-671-74781-9*, S&S BFYR) S&S Trade.
Stevenson, Drew. Toying with Danger: A Sarah Capshaw Mystery. Ramsey, Marcy D., illus. LC 92-19325. (gr. 4-6). 1993. 14.00 (*0-525-65115-2*, Cobblehill Bks) Dutton Child Bks.
Weiss, E. & Friedman, M. The Poof Point. (gr. 3-7). 1992. 14.00 (*0-679-83257-2*) Knopf Bks Yng Read.

INVERTEBRATES

see also Corals; Insects; Mollusks; Worms

Aaseng, Nathan. Invertebrates. (Illus.). 112p. (gr. 7-12). 1993. PLB 13.40 (*0-531-12550-5*) Watts.
Bender, Lionel. Invertebrates. Khan, Aziz, illus. LC 87-82894. 40p. (gr. 1). 1988. 12.40 (*0-531-17092-6*) Watts.
Harlow, Rosie & Morgan, Gareth. Observing Minibeasts. Kuo Kang Chen, illus. 40p. (gr. 5-8). 1991. PLB 12.90 (*0-531-19125-7*, Warwick) Watts.
Hemsley, William. Jellyfish to Insects: Projects with Biology. LC 90-45657. (Illus.). 32p. (gr. 5-9). 1991. PLB 12.40 (*0-531-17293-7*, Gloucester Pr) Watts.
Illustrated Encyclopedia of Wildlife, Vol. 11: The Invertebrates, Pt. I. 240p. (gr. 7 up). 1990. lib. bdg. write for info. (*1-55905-047-0*) Grey Castle.
Illustrated Encyclopedia of Wildlife, Vol. 12: The Invertebrates, Pt. II. 184p. (gr. 7 up). 1990. lib. bdg. write for info. (*1-55905-048-9*) Grey Castle.
Illustrated Encyclopedia of Wildlife, Vol. 13: The Invertebrates, Pt. III. 184p. (gr. 7 up). 1990. lib. bdg. write for info. (*1-55905-049-7*) Grey Castle.
Illustrated Encyclopedia of Wildlife, Vol. 14: The Invertebrates, Pt. IV. 184p. (gr. 7 up). 1990. lib. bdg. write for info. (*1-55905-050-0*) Grey Castle.
Illustrated Encyclopedia of Wildlife, Vol. 15: The Invertebrates, Pt. V & Index. 192p. (gr. 7 up). 1990. lib. bdg. write for info. (*1-55905-051-9*) Grey Castle.
Landau, Elaine. Interesting Invertebrates: A Look at Some Animals Without Backbones. (Illus.). 64p. (gr. 5-8). 1991. PLB 12.90 (*0-531-20036-1*) Watts.
Losito, Linda, et al. Simple Animals. (Illus.). 96p. 1989. 17.95x (*0-8160-1968-1*) Facts on File.
Selsam, Millicent E. & Hunt, Joyce. A First Look at Animals Without Backbones. Springer, Harriett, illus. LC 76-12056. (gr. 2-4). 1976. PLB 9.85 (*0-8027-6269-7*) Walker & Co.
Shepherd, Elizabeth. No Bones: A Key to Bugs & Slugs, Worms, & Ticks, Spiders & Centipedes, & Other Creepy Crawlies. Patterson, Ippy, illus. LC 87-1549. 96p. (gr. 2-5). 1988. SBE 13.95 (*0-02-782880-8*, Macmillan Child Bk) Macmillan Child Grp.

INVESTIGATIONS

Spellman, Linda. Creative Investigations. 48p. (gr. 4-8). 1982. 5.95 (*0-88160-045-8*, LW 230) Learning Wks.

INVESTMENTS

see also Stock Exchange; Stocks

Young, Robin. The Stock Market. (Illus.). 80p. (gr. 5 up). 1991. PLB 21.50 (*0-8225-1780-9*) Lerner Pubns.

IOWA

Aylesworth, Thomas G. & Aylesworth, Virginia L. Western Great Lakes (Illinois, Iowa, Wisconsin, Minnesota) (Illus.). 64p. (gr. 3 up). 1992. lib. bdg. 16.95 (*0-7910-1046-5*) Chelsea Hse.
Canady, Robert & Annis, Scott. Color in Iowa Coloring Album. (Illus.). 32p. (Orig.). (gr. 1-5). 1984. pap. 3.95 (*0-9615584-0-7*) Little Gnome.
Carole Marsh Iowa Books, 45 bks. 1994. lib. bdg. 1052.75 set (*0-7933-1290-6*); pap. 602.75 set (*0-7933-5152-9*) Gallopade Pub Group.
Carpenter, Allan. Iowa. LC 79-11802. (Illus.). 96p. (gr. 4 up). 1979. PLB 16.95 (*0-516-04115-0*) Childrens.
Carter, Brian. State Government in Iowa. 5th ed. Institute of Public Affairs Staff, ed. (Illus.). (gr. 10). 1990. pap. text ed. 7.00 (*0-317-02886-3*) U Iowa IPA.
Comer, Fred R. Coming of Age: Teachers in Iowa 1954 to 1993. LC 93-78742. (Illus.). 240p. 1993. 20.00 (*0-9637413-0-6*) Iowa St Educ.
Fradin, Dennis. Iowa: In Words & Pictures. LC 79-19399. (Illus.). 48p. (gr. 2-5). 1980. PLB 12.95 (*0-516-03915-6*) Childrens.
Fradin, Dennis B. Iowa - From Sea to Shining Sea. LC 93-16331. (Illus.). 64p. (gr. 3-5). 1993. PLB 16.45 (*0-516-03815-X*) Childrens.
Jenison, Norma J. & Benjamin, Starr J. The Eyes of the Storm: Belmond, Iowa Recalls the 1966 Homecoming Day Tornado. LC 89-84423. (Illus.). 256p. (Orig.). 1989. pap. 8.95 (*0-9623288-0-4*) T Lydia Pr.
Kent, Deborah. Iowa. LC 90-21276. (Illus.). 144p. (gr. 5-8). 1991. PLB 20.55 (*0-516-00461-1*) Childrens.
—Iowa. 179p. 1993. text ed. 15.40 (*1-56956-149-4*) W A T Braille.
LaDoux, Rita C. Iowa. Lerner Geography Department Staff, ed. (Illus.). 72p. (gr. 3-6). 1992. PLB 17.50 (*0-8225-2724-3*) Lerner Pubns.
Marsh, Carole. Avast, Ye Slobs! Iowa Private Trivia. (Illus.). (gr. 3-12). 1994. PLB 24.95 (*0-7933-0448-2*); pap. 14.95 (*0-7933-0447-4*); computer disk 29.95 (*0-7933-0449-0*) Gallopade Pub Group.
—The Beast of the Iowa Bed & Breakfast. (Illus.). (gr. 3-12). 1994. PLB 24.95 (*0-7933-1628-6*); pap. 14.95 (*0-7933-1629-4*); computer disk 29.95 (*0-7933-1630-8*) Gallopade Pub Group.
—Bow Wow! Iowa Dogs in History, Mystery, Legend, Lore, Humor & More! (Illus.). (gr. 3-12). 1994. PLB 24.95 (*0-7933-3512-4*); pap. 14.95 (*0-7933-3513-2*); computer disk 29.95 (*0-7933-3514-0*) Gallopade Pub Group.
—Chill Out: Scary Iowa Tales Based on Frightening Iowa Truths. (Illus.). 1994. lib. bdg. 24.95 (*0-7933-4699-1*); pap. 14.95 (*0-7933-4700-9*); disk 29.95 (*0-7933-4701-7*) Gallopade Pub Group.
—Christopher Columbus Comes to Iowa! Includes Reproducible Activities for Kids! (Illus.). (gr. 3-12). 1994. PLB 24.95 (*0-7933-3665-1*); pap. 14.95 (*0-7933-3666-X*); computer disk 29.95 (*0-7933-3667-8*) Gallopade Pub Group.
—The Hard-to-Believe-But-True! Book of Iowa History, Mystery, Trivia, Legend, Lore, Humor & More. (Illus.). (gr. 3-12). 1994. PLB 24.95 (*0-7933-0445-8*); pap. 14.95 (*0-7933-0444-X*); computer disk 29.95 (*0-7933-0446-6*) Gallopade Pub Group.
—If My Iowa Mama Ran the World! (Illus.). (gr. 3-12). 1994. PLB 24.95 (*0-7933-1633-2*); pap. 14.95 (*0-7933-1634-0*); computer disk 29.95 (*0-7933-1635-9*) Gallopade Pub Group.
—Iowa & Other State Greats (Biographies) (Illus.). (gr. 3-12). 1994. PLB 24.95 (*1-55609-459-0*); pap. 14.95 (*1-55609-458-2*); computer disk 29.95 (*0-7933-1636-7*) Gallopade Pub Group.
—Iowa Bandits, Bushwackers, Outlaws, Crooks, Devils, Ghosts, Desperadoes & Other Assorted & Sundry Characters! (Illus.). (gr. 3-12). 1994. PLB 24.95 (*0-7933-0430-X*); pap. 14.95 (*0-7933-0429-6*); computer disk 29.95 (*0-7933-0431-8*) Gallopade Pub Group.
—Iowa Classic Christmas Trivia: Stories, Recipes, Activities, Legends, Lore & More! (Illus.). (gr. 3-12). 1994. PLB 24.95 (*0-7933-0433-4*); pap. 14.95 (*0-7933-0432-6*); computer disk 29.95 (*0-7933-0434-2*) Gallopade Pub Group.
—Iowa Coastales. (Illus.). (gr. 3-12). 1994. PLB 24.95 (*1-55609-455-8*); pap. 14.95 (*1-55609-454-X*); computer disk 29.95 (*0-7933-1632-4*) Gallopade Pub Group.
—Iowa Coastales! 1994. lib. bdg. 24.95 (*0-7933-7280-1*) Gallopade Pub Group.
—Iowa "Crinkum-Crankum" A Funny Word Book about Our State. (Illus.). 1994. lib. bdg. 24.95 (*0-7933-4853-6*); pap. 14.95 (*0-7933-4854-4*); disk 29.95 (*0-7933-4855-2*) Gallopade Pub Group.
—Iowa Dingbats! Bk. 1: A Fun Book of Games, Stories, Activities & More about Our State That's All in Code! for You to Decipher. (Illus.). (gr. 3-12). 1994. PLB 24.95 (*0-7933-3818-2*); pap. 14.95 (*0-7933-3819-0*); computer disk 29.95 (*0-7933-3820-4*) Gallopade Pub Group.
—Iowa Festival Fun for Kids! (Illus.). (gr. 3-12). 1994. lib. bdg. 24.95 (*0-7933-3971-5*); pap. 14.95 (*0-7933-3972-3*); disk 29.95 (*0-7933-3973-1*) Gallopade Pub Group.
—The Iowa Hot Air Balloon Mystery. (Illus.). (gr. 2-9). 1994. 24.95 (*0-7933-2453-X*); pap. 14.95 (*0-7933-2454-8*); computer disk 29.95 (*0-7933-2455-6*) Gallopade Pub Group.
—Iowa Jeopardy! Answers & Questions about Our State! (Illus.). (gr. 3-12). 1994. PLB 24.95 (*0-7933-4124-8*); pap. 14.95 (*0-7933-4125-6*); computer disk 29.95 (*0-7933-4126-4*) Gallopade Pub Group.
—Iowa "Jography" A Fun Run Thru Our State! (Illus.). (gr. 3-12). 1994. PLB 24.95 (*1-55609-450-7*); pap. 14.95 (*1-55609-085-4*); computer disk 29.95 (*0-7933-1622-7*) Gallopade Pub Group.
—Iowa Kid's Cookbook: Recipes, How-to, History, Lore & More! (Illus.). (gr. 3-12). 1994. PLB 24.95 (*0-7933-0442-3*); pap. 14.95 (*0-7933-0441-5*); computer disk 29.95 (*0-7933-0443-1*) Gallopade Pub Group.
—The Iowa Mystery Van Takes Off! Book 1: Handicapped Iowa Kids Sneak Off on a Big Adventure. (Illus.). (gr. 3-12). 1994. 24.95 (*0-7933-5006-9*); pap. 14.95 (*0-7933-5007-7*); computer disk 29.95 (*0-7933-5008-5*) Gallopade Pub Group.
—Iowa Quiz Bowl Crash Course! (Illus.). (gr. 3-12). 1994. PLB 24.95 (*1-55609-457-4*); pap. 14.95 (*1-55609-456-6*); computer disk 29.95 (*0-7933-1631-6*) Gallopade Pub Group.
—Iowa Rollercoasters! (Illus.). (gr. 3-12). 1994. PLB 24.95 (*0-7933-5269-X*); pap. 14.95 (*0-7933-5270-3*); computer disk 29.95 (*0-7933-5271-1*) Gallopade Pub Group.
—Iowa School Trivia: An Amazing & Fascinating Look at Our State's Teachers, Schools & Students! (Illus.). (gr. 3-12). 1994. PLB 24.95 (*0-7933-0439-3*); pap. 14.95 (*0-7933-0438-5*); computer disk 29.95 (*0-7933-0440-7*) Gallopade Pub Group.
—Iowa Silly Basketball Sportsmysteries, Vol. I. (Illus.). (gr. 3-12). 1994. PLB 24.95 (*0-7933-0436-9*); pap. 14.95 (*0-7933-0435-0*); computer disk 29.95 (*0-7933-0437-7*) Gallopade Pub Group.
—Iowa Silly Basketball Sportsmysteries, Vol. II. (Illus.). (gr. 3-12). 1994. PLB 24.95 (*0-7933-1637-5*); pap. 14.95 (*0-7933-1638-3*); computer disk 29.95 (*0-7933-1639-1*) Gallopade Pub Group.
—Iowa Silly Football Sportsmysteries, Vol. I. (Illus.). (gr. 3-12). 1994. PLB 24.95 (*1-55609-453-1*); pap. 14.95 (*1-55609-452-3*); computer disk 29.95 (*0-7933-1624-3*) Gallopade Pub Group.
—Iowa Silly Football Sportsmysteries, Vol. II. (Illus.). (gr. 3-12). 1994. PLB 24.95 (*0-7933-1625-1*); pap. 14.95 (*0-7933-1626-X*); computer disk 29.95 (*0-7933-1627-8*) Gallopade Pub Group.
—Iowa Silly Trivia! (Illus.). (gr. 3-12). 1994. PLB 24.95 (*1-55609-449-3*); pap. 14.95 (*1-55609-084-6*); computer disk 29.95 (*0-7933-1621-9*) Gallopade Pub Group.
—Iowa Timeline: A Chronology of Iowa History, Mystery, Trivia, Legend, Lore & More. (Illus.). (gr. 3-12). 1994. PLB 24.95 (*0-7933-5920-1*); pap. 14.95 (*0-7933-5921-X*); computer disk 29.95 (*0-7933-5922-8*) Gallopade Pub Group.
—Iowa's (Most Devastating!) Disasters & (Most Calamitous!) Catastrophies! (Illus.). (gr. 3-12). 1994. PLB 24.95 (*0-7933-0426-1*); pap. 14.95 (*0-7933-0427-X*); computer disk 29.95 (*0-7933-0428-8*) Gallopade Pub Group.
—Iowa's Unsolved Mysteries (& Their "Solutions") Includes Scientific Information & Other Activities for Students. (Illus.). (gr. 3-12). 1994. PLB 24.95 (*0-7933-5767-5*); pap. 14.95 (*0-7933-5768-3*); computer disk 29.95 (*0-7933-5769-1*) Gallopade Pub Group.
—Jurassic Ark! Iowa Dinosaurs & Other Prehistoric Creatures. (gr. k-12). 1994. PLB 24.95 (*0-7933-7473-1*); pap. 14.95 (*0-7933-7474-X*); computer disk 29.95 (*0-7933-7475-8*) Gallopade Pub Group.
—Let's Quilt Iowa & Stuff It Topographically! (Illus.). (gr. 3-12). 1994. PLB 24.95 (*1-55609-451-5*); pap. 14.95 (*1-55609-072-2*); computer disk 29.95 (*0-7933-1623-5*) Gallopade Pub Group.

—Let's Quilt Our Iowa County. 1994. lib. bdg. 24.95 (*0-7933-7158-9*); pap. text ed. 14.95 (*0-7933-7159-7*); disk 29.95 (*0-7933-7160-0*) Gallopade Pub Group.
—Let's Quilt Our Iowa Town. 1994. lib. bdg. 24.95 (*0-7933-7008-6*); pap. text ed. 14.95 (*0-7933-7009-4*); disk 29.95 (*0-7933-7010-8*) Gallopade Pub Group.
—Meow! Iowa Cats in History, Mystery, Legend, Lore, Humor & More! (Illus.). (gr. 3-12). 1994. PLB 24.95 (*0-7933-3359-8*); pap. 14.95 (*0-7933-3360-1*); computer disk 29.95 (*0-7933-3361-X*) Gallopade Pub Group.
—My First Book about Iowa. (gr. k-4). 1994. PLB 24.95 (*0-7933-5614-8*); pap. 14.95 (*0-7933-5615-6*); computer disk 29.95 (*0-7933-5616-4*) Gallopade Pub Group.
—Uncle Rebus: Iowa Picture Stories for Computer Kids. (Illus.). (gr. k-3). 1994. PLB 24.95 (*0-7933-4546-4*); pap. 14.95 (*0-7933-4547-2*); disk 29.95 (*0-7933-4548-0*) Gallopade Pub Group.
Turner Program Services, Inc. Staff & Clark, James I. Iowa. 48p. (gr. 3 up). 1985. PLB 19.97 (*0-8174-4311-8*) Raintree Steck-V.

IOWA–FICTION

Frost, Marie & Hanson, Bonnie C. Hattie's Cry for Help. (Illus.). 1992. pap. 5.99 (*1-56121-104-4*) Wolgemuth & Hyatt.

IRAN

Azerbaijan. (Illus.). (gr. 5 up). 1988. write for info. (*0-7910-0165-2*) Chelsea Hse.
Fox, Mary V. Iran. LC 90-21264. (Illus.). 128p. (gr. 5-9). 1991. PLB 20.55 (*0-516-02727-1*) Childrens.
Husain, A. Revolution in Iran. (Illus.). 80p. (gr. 7 up). 1988. PLB 18.60 (*0-86592-038-9*) Rourke Corp.
Lawson, Don. America Held Hostage: From the Teheran Embassy Takeover to the Iran-Contra Affair. LC 90-20515. (Illus.). 144p. (gr. 9-12). 1991. PLB 12.90 (*0-531-11009-5*) Watts.
Lerner Publications, Department of Geography Staff, ed. Iran in Pictures. (Illus.). 64p. (gr. 5 up). 1989. 17.50 (*0-8225-1848-1*) Lerner Pubns.
Rajendra, Vijeya & Kaplan, Gisela. Iran. LC 92-10207. 1992. 21.95 (*1-85435-534-1*) Marshall Cavendish.
Sanders, Renfield. Iran. (Illus.). 112p. (gr. 5 up). 1990. 14. 95 (*0-7910-1104-6*) Chelsea Hse.

IRAQ

Bratman, Fred. War in the Persian Gulf. (Illus.). 64p. (gr. 7 up). 1991. PLB 15.90 (*1-56294-051-1*); pap. 4.95 (*1-878841-61-0*) Millbrook Pr.
Claypool, Jane. Saddam Hussein. LC 92-46994. 1993. 19. 93 (*0-86625-477-3*); 14.95s.p. (*0-685-67775-3*) Rourke Pubns.
Deegan, Paul J. Saddam Hussein. Wallner, Rosemary, ed. LC 91-73076. (gr. 4 up). 1991. 13.99 (*1-56239-025-2*) Abdo & Dghtrs.
Dudley, William & Tipp, Stacey, eds. Iraq. LC 91-30036. 200p. (gr. 10 up). 1991. PLB 16.95 (*0-89908-575-X*); pap. text ed. 9.95 (*0-89908-581-4*) Greenhaven.
Foster, Leila M. Iraq. LC 90-2174. (Illus.). 128p. (gr. 5-9). 1991. PLB 20.55 (*0-516-02723-9*) Childrens.
Hassig, Susan M. Iraq. LC 92-12178. 1992. Set. write for info. (*1-85435-529-5*); 21.95 (*1-85435-533-3*) Marshall Cavendish.
Kent, Zachary. The Persian Gulf War: "The Mother of All Battles" LC 94-2533. (Illus.). 128p. (gr. 5 up). 1994. lib. bdg. 17.95 (*0-89490-528-7*) Enslow Pubs.
Lerner Publications, Department of Geography Staff. Iraq in Pictures. (Illus.). 64p. (gr. 5 up). 1990. PLB 17.50 (*0-8225-1847-3*) Lerner Pubns.
Renfrew, Nita. Saddam Hussein. (Illus.). 128p. (gr. 5 up). 1993. 18.95 (*0-7910-1776-1*, Am Art Analog) Chelsea Hse.
Stewart, Gail B. Iraq. LC 91-11893. (Illus.). 48p. (gr. 6-7). 1991. text ed. 12.95 RSBE (*0-89686-657-2*, Crestwood Hse) Macmillan Child Grp.

IRELAND

Bailey, Donna & Sproule, Anna. Ireland. LC 90-9645. (Illus.). 32p. (gr. 1-4). 1990. PLB 18.99 (*0-8114-2562-2*) Raintree Steck-V.
Byrne, Art & McMahon, Sean. Lives: One Hundred Thirteen Great Irishwomen & Irishmen. Short, John, illus. 230p. (Orig.). (gr. 9-12). 1990. pap. 16.95 (*1-85371-094-6*, Pub. by Poolbeg Pr ER) Dufour.
Chambers, John. One Hundred One Irish Lives. (Illus.). 348p. (Orig.). (gr. 4-8). 1992. pap. 21.95 (*0-7171-1725-1*, Pub. by Gill & Macmillan EIRE) Irish Bks Media.
Fradin, Dennis. The Republic of Ireland. LC 83-20960. (Illus.). 128p. (gr. 5-9). 1984. PLB 20.55 (*0-516-02767-0*) Childrens.
Grant, Neil. Ireland. (Illus.). 48p. (gr. 4-8). 1989. lib. bdg. 14.95 (*0-382-09819-6*) Silver Burdett Pr.
Ireland. LC 89-43187. (Illus.). 64p. (gr. 3-8). 1992. PLB 21.26 (*0-8368-0246-2*) Gareth Stevens Inc.
Ireland Is My Home. 48p. (gr. 2-8). 1992. PLB 18.60 (*0-8368-0902-5*) Gareth Stevens Inc.
Irish Question. (Illus.). (gr. 7 up). 1988. lib. bdg. 18.60 (*0-86592-027-3*); 13.95s.p. (*0-685-58241-8*) Rourke Corp.
Irvine, John. Treasury of Irish Saints. (gr. 1 up). 1984. 9.95 (*0-85105-902-3*, Pub. by Colin Smythe Ltd Britain) Dufour.
Levy, Patricia M. Ireland. LC 93-11026. (gr. 5 up). 1993. 21.95 (*1-85435-580-5*) Marshall Cavendish.
Lewis, John. Ireland: A Divided Country. LC 89-31550. (Illus.). 32p. (gr. 5-9). 1989. PLB 12.90 (*0-531-17169-8*) Watts.
Meyer, Carolyn. Voices of Northern Ireland: Growing up in a Troubled Land. LC 87-199. (Illus.). 212p. (gr. 7 up). 1987. 15.95 (*0-15-200635-4*, Gulliver Bks) HarBrace.
—Voices of Northern Ireland: Growing up in a Troubled Land. 1992. pap. 9.95 (*0-15-200636-2*) HarBrace.
—Voices of Northern Ireland: Growing Up in a Troubled Land. (gr. 7 up). 1992. pap. 9.95 (*0-15-200638-9*) HarBrace.
Moriarty, Mary & Sweeney, Catherine. Theobald Wolfe Tone. (Illus.). 64p. 1989. pap. 8.95 (*0-86278-160-4*, Pub. by O'Brien Press Ltd Eire) Dufour.
Peplow, Mary & Shipley, Debra. Ireland. LC 90-32821. (Illus.). 96p. (gr. 6-12). 1990. PLB 22.80 (*0-8114-2430-8*) Raintree Steck-V.
Pomeray, J. K. Ireland. (Illus.). 128p. (gr. 5 up). 1988. lib. bdg. 14.95x (*1-55546-794-6*) Chelsea Hse.

IRELAND–FICTION

Bell, Sam H. The Hollow Ball. 256p. (Orig.). (gr. 10-12). 1990. pap. 11.95 (*0-85640-452-7*, Pub. by Blackstaff Pr Belfast) Dufour.
Brightfield, Richard. Irish Rebellion. 1993. pap. 3.25 (*0-553-56349-1*) Bantam.
Conlon-McKenna, Marita. Under the Hawthorn Tree. Teskey, Donald, illus. LC 90-55097. 160p. (gr. 3-7). 1990. 13.95 (*0-8234-0838-8*) Holiday.
—Under the Hawthorn Tree: Children of the Famine. LC 92-18955. 160p. (gr. 5 up). 1992. pap. 3.99 (*0-14-036031-X*) Puffin Bks.
Considine, June. When the Luvenders Came to Merrick Town. LC 89-82487. 240p. (Orig.). (gr. 8-12). 1990. pap. 6.95 (*0-685-46916-6*, Pub. by Poolbeg Pr ER) Dufour.
Dhuibhne, Eilis N. Hugo & the Sunshine Girl. Betera, Carol, illus. 129p. (Orig.). (gr. 5-9). 1991. pap. 7.95 (*1-85371-160-8*, Pub. by Poolbeg Pr ER) Dufour.
Galt, Hugh. Horse Thief. 208p. (gr. 5-10). 1993. pap. 9.95 (*0-86278-278-3*, Pub. by OBrien Pr IE) Dufour.
Giff, Patricia R. The Great Shamrock Disaster. (ps-3). 1993. pap. 3.25 (*0-440-40778-8*) Dell.
Heneghan, James. Torn Away. (Illus.). 192p. (gr. 7 up). 1994. 14.99 (*0-670-85180-9*) Viking Child Bks.
Hoyal, Dawna T. Pat & the Leprechaun. 1992. 7.95 (*0-533-10158-1*) Vantage.
Hunt, Angela E. The Secret of Cravenhill Castle. LC 93-11181. Date not set. pap. 4.99 (*0-8407-6305-0*) Nelson.
Janoski, Elizabeth. What's Wrong with Eddie? 92p. (Orig.). (gr. 5-8). 1994. PLB 15.00 (*0-88092-041-6*); pap. 5.00 (*0-88092-040-8*) Royal Fireworks.
Joyce, James. The Encounter. 32p. (gr. 6 up). 1982. PLB 13.95 (*0-87191-896-X*) Creative Ed.
King-Smith, Dick. Paddy's Pot of Gold. Parkins, David, illus. LC 91-24586. 128p. (gr. 2-7). 1992. 14.00 (*0-517-58136-1*); PLB 14.99 (*0-517-58137-X*) Crown Bks Yng Read.
Lutzeier, Elizabeth. The Coldest Winter. LC 91-7159. 160p. (gr. 5-9). 1991. 13.95 (*0-8234-0899-X*) Holiday.
McCaughren, Tom. The Silent Sea. Myler, Terry, illus. 111p. (Orig.). 1988. pap. 7.95 (*0-947962-20-4*, Pub. by Children's Pr) Irish Bks Media.
McDermott, Gerald. Tim O'Toole & the Wee Folk. McDermott, Gerald, illus. 32p. (ps-3). 1992. pap. 3.99 (*0-14-050675-6*) Puffin Bks.
MacGrory, Yvonne. The Secret of the Ruby Ring. Miller, Terry, illus. LC 93-35950. 189p. 1994. pap. 6.95 (*0-915943-92-1*) Milkweed Ed.
Macken, Walter. Flight of the Doves. LC 91-3922. 1992. pap. 14.00 (*0-671-73801-1*, S&S BFYR) S&S Trade.
Malterre, Elona. The Last Wolf of Ireland. (gr. 4-9). 1990. 13.45 (*0-395-54381-9*, Clarion Bks) HM.
Mannion, Sean. Ireland's Friendly Dolphin. (Illus.). 128p. (Orig.) (gr. 7-11). 1991. pap. 9.95 (*0-86322-122-X*, Pub. by Brandon Bk Pubs ER) Irish Bks Media.

Moll, Linda J. A Poison Tree: A Children's Fairy Tale. Moll, Linda J., illus. 40p. (gr. 1 up). 1994. PLB 12.95 (*0-9641641-1-6*) Punking Pr.
A POISON TREE is a children's fairy tale set in Ireland's countryside. Ian McGonagle feels rage for his wee brother, Malachy, after discovering his younger sibling ruined his birthday surprise. Ian vows revenge & calls on the evil fairies for help. Indeed, the evil fairies come with a black seed from which a poison tree will grow. But what happens next is not what Ian expected. Find out how sibling anger turns into forgiveness & how brotherly love prevails in this enchanting Irish fairy tale. A POISON TREE is a charming story for any child learning the sometimes difficult skill of getting along with others. Parents, caregivers, & teachers will find A POISON TREE a valuable social tool in the family, neighborhood or classroom. Children love the comical antics of the fairies & sit in anticipation of A POISON TREE's climactic ending. Teachers will find A POISON TREE a wonderful source for introducing literary devices & techniques to young scholars. A POISON TREE is rich in simile, metaphor, alliteration, rhyming verse,...Illustrations include quaint silhouettes & the text which is scripted in modified 4th-century celtic lettering. A Celtic knotwork border frames the page & completes the beauty of the book. To order A POISON TREE, contact Christopher Moll, P.O. Box 25, Williamson, NY 14589; 315-589-5119.
Publisher Provided Annotation.

Morpurgo, Michael. Twist of Gold. LC 92-25928. 246p. (gr. 5-9). 1993. 14.99 (*0-670-84851-4*) Viking Child Bks.
Mullen, Michael. Sea Wolves from the North. Dunne, Jeannette, illus. 112p. (gr. 3-9). 1989. 10.95 (*0-905473-94-9*, Pub. by Wolfhound Pr EIRE); pap. 7.95 (*0-86327-023-9*, Pub. by Wolfhound Pr IE) Dufour.
Nimmo, Jenny, retold by. The Starlight Cloak. Todd, Justin, photos by. LC 92-26186. (Illus.). (ps-3). 1993. 14.99 (*0-8037-1508-0*) Dial Bks Young.
O'Shaughnessy, Peter. Con's Fabulous Journey to the Land of Gobel O'Glug. rev. ed. Myler, Terry, illus. 104p. (gr. 6-10). 1992. pap. 5.95 (*0-947962-68-9*, Pub. by Anvil Bks Ltd ER) Irish Bks Media.
Paine, Penelope C. Molly's Magic. Maeno, Itoko, illus. 32p. (gr. 1-4). 1994. 16.95 (*1-55942-068-5*, 7660) Marshfilm.
Rose, Deborah L. The People Who Hugged the Trees. Saflund, Birgitta, illus. LC 90-62832. 32p. (gr. 4-8). 1994. pap. 6.95 (*1-879373-50-5*) R Rinehart.
Scott, Michael. October Moon. LC 93-8693. 160p. (gr. 7 up). 1994. 14.95 (*0-8234-1110-9*) Holiday.
—The Seven Treasures: The Quest of the Sons of Tuireann. (Illus.). 158p. (gr. 3-7). 1993. pap. 9.95 (*0-86278-309-7*, Pub. by OBrien Pr IE) Dufour.
Stuart, Chad. The Ballymara Flood: A Tale from Old Ireland. Booth, George, illus. LC 94-15162. 1995. write for info. (*0-15-205698-X*) HarBrace.
Trevor, William. Juliet's Story. LC 93-21790. 1994. pap. 15.00 (*0-671-87442-X*) S&S Trade.
Wood, John. In a Secret Place. 112p. (gr. 5-9). 1994. pap. 7.95 (*0-86327-399-8*, Pub. by Wolfhound Pr ER) Dufour.

IRELAND–HISTORY

Furlong, Nicholas. A Foster Son for a King. (Illus.). 128p. (Orig.). (gr. 5-8). 1986. 9.95 (*0-947962-03-4*, Pub. by Childrens Pr); pap. 5.95 (*0-947962-04-2*, Pub. by Childrens Pr) Irish Bks Media.
Ingram, Cecil B. Ulsterheart: An Ancient Irish Habitation. LC 88-72366. (Illus.). 350p. (gr. 12). 1988. 60.00x (*0-9621544-0-7*) All Ireland Inc.
Joyce, P. W. A Child's History of Ireland. Harrison, Hank, ed. (Illus.). 225p. (gr. 8-12). 14.95 (*0-918501-24-5*); pap. write for info. (*0-918501-26-1*) Archives Pr.
McMahon, Sean. The Poolbeg Book of Irish Placenames. 113p. (Orig.). (gr. 10-12). 1990. pap. 8.95 (*1-85371-087-3*, Pub. by Poolbeg Pr ER) Dufour.
Newman, Roger C. Murtagh & the Vikings. (Illus.). 96p. (Orig.). (gr. 5-8). 1986. 9.95 (*0-947962-05-0*, Pub. by Childrens Pr); pap. 5.95 (*0-947962-06-9*, Pub. by Childrens Pr) Irish Bks Media.
Roche, Richard. The Call of the Wood Pigeon - Glaoch an Choluir Choille: A Day in the Life of a Monk in Pre-Viking Ireland. (Illus., Orig.). (gr. 1-8). 1990. pap. 9.95 (*1-85390-047-8*, Pub. by Veritas Pubns ER) Irish Bks Media.
Stein, Wendy. Ancient Ireland. Swanberg, Nancy & Anderson, L., illus. (gr. k). 1978. pap. text ed. 3.95 (*0-88388-060-1*) Bellerophon Bks.
Stewart, Gail B. Northern Ireland. LC 90-36291. (Illus.). 48p. (gr. 6-7). 1990. text ed. 12.95 RSBE (*0-89686-551-7*, Crestwood Hse) Macmillan Child Grp.

IRISH IN THE U. S.

Cavan, Seamus. The Irish-American Experience. Shenton, James, contrib. by. LC 92-7512. (Illus.). 64p. (gr. 4-6). 1993. PLB 15.40 (*1-56294-218-2*) Millbrook Pr.
Franck, Irene M. Irish-American Heritage. (Illus.). 160p. (gr. 5 up). 1989. 16.95x (*0-8160-1630-5*) Facts on File.
Johnson, James E. Irish in America. (gr. 4-7). 1994. pap. 5.95 (*0-8225-3475-4*) Lerner Pubns.
Johnson, James E. & Kavanagh, Jack. Irish in America. LC 93-25991. 1994. lib. bdg. 15.95 (*0-8225-1954-2*); pap. 5.95 (*0-8225-1975-5*) Lerner Pubns.
Moscinski, Sharon. Tracing Our Irish Roots. Butler, Nate & Evans, Beth, illus. LC 93-2070. 48p. 1993. text ed. 12.95 (*1-56261-148-8*) John Muir.
Watts, James. The Irish Americans. Moynihan, Daniel P., intro. by. 112p. (Orig.). (gr. 5 up). 1988. 17.95 (*0-87754-855-2*); pap. 9.95 (*0-7910-0267-5*) Chelsea Hse.

IRISH IN THE U. S.–FICTION
Conlon-McKenna, Marita. Wildflower Girl. Teskey, Donald, illus. LC 92-52711. 176p. (gr. 5-9). 1992. 14. 95 (*0-8234-0988-0*) Holiday.
Giff, Patricia R. The Gift of the Pirate Queen. Rutherford, Jenny, illus. LC 82-70310. 160p. (gr. 4-6). 1982. 11.95 (*0-385-28338-5*); PLB 11.95 (*0-385-28339-3*) Delacorte.
Griffith, Connie. The Shocking Discovery. 128p. (gr. 6-8). 1994. pap. 5.99 (*0-8010-3866-9*) Baker Bk.
Kroll, Steven. Mary McLean & the St. Patrick's Day Parade. Dooling, Michael, illus. 32p. (ps-3). 1991. 13. 95 (*0-590-43701-1*, Scholastic Hardcover) Scholastic Inc.
Lasky, Kathryn. Prank. (gr. 6 up). 1986. pap. 2.75 (*0-440-97144-6*, LFL) Dell.
Lawson, Robert. The Great Wheel. Lawson, Robert, illus. 180p. 1993. pap. 7.95 (*0-8027-7392-3*) Walker & Co.
Nixon, Joan L. Land of Promise. LC 92-28591. (gr. 4-7). 1993. 16.00 (*0-553-08111-X*) Bantam.

IRISH LITERATURE–COLLECTIONS
Brinn, Ross. To the Woods & Waters Wild: A Collection of Irish Writings. O'Mahony, Kieran, ed. LC 90-80516. 150p. (Orig.). 1990. pap. 9.95 (*0-944638-02-3*) Educare Pr.

IRISH POETRY–COLLECTIONS
Quinn, Bridie & Cashman, Seamus, eds. Wolfhound Book of Irish Poems for Young People. (Illus.). 192p. (ps-8). 1975. pap. 9.95 (*0-86327-002-6*, Pub. by Wolfhound Press Eire) Dufour.

IRON
Fodor, R. V. Gold, Copper, Iron: How Metals Are Formed, Found, & Used. LC 87-24464. (Illus.). 96p. (gr. 6 up). 1989. lib. bdg. 16.95 (*0-89490-138-9*) Enslow Pubs.
Lambert, M. Iron & Steel. (Illus.). 48p. (gr. 5 up). 1985. PLB 17.27 (*0-86592-268-3*); 12.95 (*0-685-58325-2*) Rourke Corp.

IRON CURTAIN COUNTRIES
see Communist Countries

IRON INDUSTRY AND TRADE
Martin, John H. A Day in the Life of a High-Iron Worker. Jann, Gayle, illus. LC 84-2449. 32p. (gr. 4-8). 1985. PLB 11.79 (*0-8167-0107-5*); pap. text ed. 2.95 (*0-8167-0108-3*) Troll Assocs.

IRRIGATION
see also Dams; Windmills

ISABEL 1ST, LA CATOLICA, QUEEN OF SPAIN, 1451-1504
Stevens, Paul. Ferdinand & Isabella. Schlesinger, Arthur M., Jr., intro. by. (Illus.). 112p. (gr. 5 up). 1988. lib. bdg. 17.95 (*0-87754-523-5*) Chelsea Hse.

ISAIAH, THE PROPHET
Head, Constance. Isaiah: The Prophet Prince. 384p. (Orig.). (ps-6). 1988. pap. 4.50 (*0-8423-1751-1*) Tyndale.

ISLAM
Abd al-Salam Nadvi. Umar bin Abd al-Aziz. 200p. (gr. 7-12). 1985. pap. 9.95 (*1-56744-406-7*) Kazi Pubns.
Abdul Waheed Khan. Beacon Lights, Bks. I-IV: True Tales for Children, 2 vol. set. 32p. (gr. 1-6). 1985. pap. 6.50 (*1-56744-222-6*) Kazi Pubns.
Abdur Rehman Shad. Uthman ibn Affan: The Third Caliph of Islam. 96p. (gr. 10-12). 1985. pap. 3.50 (*1-56744-409-1*) Kazi Pubns.
Ahmad, Fazl. Abu Bakr: First Caliph of Islam. 100p. (Orig.). (gr. 7-12). 1984. pap. 3.50 (*1-56744-240-4*) Kazi Pubns.
—Aisha: The Truthful. 140p. (Orig.). (gr. 7-12). 1984. pap. 3.50 (*1-56744-238-2*) Kazi Pubns.
—Ali, the Fourth Caliph of Islam. 103p. (Orig.). (gr. 7-12). 1984. pap. 3.50 (*1-56744-243-9*) Kazi Pubns.
—Husain: The Great Martyr. 150p. (Orig.). (gr. 7-12). 1984. pap. 3.50 (*1-56744-239-0*) Kazi Pubns.
—Khalid bin Walid: The Sword of Allah. 115p. (Orig.). (gr. 7-12). 1984. pap. 3.50 (*1-56744-244-7*) Kazi Pubns.
—Mahmood of Ghazni. 120p. (Orig.). (gr. 7-12). 1984. pap. 3.50 (*1-56744-246-3*) Kazi Pubns.
—Muhammad bin Qasim. 95p. (Orig.). (gr. 7-12). 1984. pap. 3.50 (*1-56744-245-5*) Kazi Pubns.
—Muhammad the Prophet of Islam. 125p. (Orig.). (gr. 7-12). 1984. pap. 3.50 (*1-56744-236-6*) Kazi Pubns.
—Muhy-ud Din Alamgir Aurangzeb. 103p. (Orig.). (gr. 7-12). 1984. pap. 3.50 (*1-56744-247-1*) Kazi Pubns.
—Omar: The Second Caliph of Islam. 100p. (Orig.). (gr. 7-12). 1984. pap. 3.50 (*1-56744-241-2*) Kazi Pubns.
—Othman, the Third Caliph of Islam. 95p. (Orig.). (gr. 7-12). 1984. pap. 3.50 (*1-56744-242-0*) Kazi Pubns.
—Some Companions of the Prophet, Pt. I. 115p. (gr. 4-10). 1985. pap. 3.50 (*1-56744-390-7*) Kazi Pubns.
—Some Companions of the Prophet, Pt. II. 115p. (gr. 4-10). 1985. pap. 3.50 (*1-56744-391-5*) Kazi Pubns.
—Some Companions of the Prophet, Pt. III. 115p. (gr. 4-10). 1985. pap. 3.50 (*1-56744-392-3*) Kazi Pubns.
—Sultan Tipi. 120p. (Orig.). (gr. 7-12). 1984. pap. 3.50 (*1-56744-237-4*) Kazi Pubns.
Ahmad, P. Color & Learn Salat. pap. 3.50 (*0-935782-58-3*) Kazi Pubns.
Ali, S. Ameer. Color & Learn the Names of the Family of Prophet Muhammad. 32p. (Orig.). (ps). Date not set. pap. 3.50 (*0-934905-13-4*) Kazi Pubns.
Al-Kausar, Tawfik, intro. by. Islamic Students Organizations: Role & Challenges, Proceedings of International Conference. 2nd ed. (ARA.). 425p. 1985. pap. write for info. (*1-882837-03-7*) Wamy Intl.
Al-Maudoodi, Abul A. Towards Understanding Islam. Ahmad, Khurshid, tr. & intro. by. 116p. 1985. pap. write for info. (*1-882837-25-8*) Wamy Intl.
Al-Sheikh, H. E., intro. by. Issues from the Contemporary Islamic Thoughts: Research Papers & Proceedings of the 2nd International Conference of Wamy. 3rd ed. (ARA.). 433p. 1984. pap. write for info. (*1-882837-01-0*) Wamy Intl.
Ashraf. Lessons in Islam, 5. 8.50 (*1-56744-121-1*) Kazi Pubns.
Athar, Alia N. Muhammad, the Last Prophet I. 32p. (gr. 2-4). 1992. pap. 3.00 wkbk. (*1-56744-209-9*) Kazi Pubns.
—Muhammad, the Last Prophet II. 32p. (gr. 3-5). 1992. pap. 3.00 (*1-56744-210-2*) Kazi Pubns.
—Prophets: Models for Humanity. 205p. 1993. pap. 14.50 (*1-56744-425-3*) Kazi Pubns.
Bakhtiar, Laleh. History of Islam, Pt. I. 205p. (gr. 10-12). 1993. pap. 19.95 (*1-56744-427-X*) Kazi Pubns.
—History of Islam, Pt. II. 205p. (gr. 10-12). 1993. pap. 19.95 (*1-56744-428-8*) Kazi Pubns.
—Muhammad's Companions: Essays on Those Who Bore Witness, Pt. I. 205p. (gr. 10-12). 1993. pap. 14.95 (*1-56744-426-1*) Kazi Pubns.
—Muhammad's Companions: Essays on Those Who Bore Witness, Pt. II. 205p. (gr. 10-12). 1993. pap. 12.95 (*1-56744-318-4*) Kazi Pubns.
Chaudhry, Saida. Call to Prophethood. (Illus.). (gr. 2-5). pap. 4.00 (*0-89259-046-7*) Am Trust Pubns.
—We Are Muslim Children. (gr. 4). 1984. pap. 4.00 (*0-89259-126-9*) Am Trust Pubns.
Color a Story: Adam. (ps). Date not set. pap. 3.50 (*0-934905-10-X*) Kazi Pubns.
Color & Learn Muslim Names. 32p. (ps). Date not set. pap. 3.50 (*0-933511-03-5*) Kazi Pubns.
Doray, S. J. Gateway to Islam, 4. pap. 10.00 (*1-56744-019-3*) Kazi Pubns.
Ghazi, Abidullah. The Salary of the Khalifah. Ghazi, Bushra Y. & Ghazi, Suhaib H., eds. Bisignani, Jill, illus. 20p. (Orig.). Date not set. pap. text ed. write for info. (*1-56316-370-5*) Iqra Intl Ed Fdtn.
Ghazi, Abidullah & Ghazi, Tasneema K. I Love Al-Madinah Al-Munawwarah. Azam, Hina & Abdulllah, Fadel, eds. Mazzoni, Jennifer, illus. 28p. (Orig.). (gr. 1-6). Date not set. pap. text ed. write for info. (*1-56316-362-4*) Iqra Intl Ed Fdtn.
—A True Promise. Ghazi, Bushra & Ghazi, Suhaib, eds. Rezac, Mike, illus. 25p. (Orig.). (gr. 1-7). Date not set. pap. text ed. write for info. (*1-56316-304-7*) Iqra Intl Ed Fdtn.
Ghazi, Suhaid H. The Prophets of Allah, Vol. I. Azam, Hina & Quraishi, Huda, eds. Rezac, Mike & Mazzoni, Jennifer, illus. 67p. (Orig.). (gr. k). Date not set. pap. text ed. write for info. (*1-56316-350-0*) Iqra Intl Ed Fdtn.
Gordon, Matthew S. Islam. (Illus.). 128p. (gr. 7-12). 1991. 17.95x (*0-8160-2443-X*) Facts on File.
Hablallah, Jeanette. Color a Story: Nuh. 32p. (ps). 1989. pap. 3.50 (*1-56744-251-X*) Kazi Pubns.
Hamid, J. Islamic Activity Book, Nos. I, II & III. 1988. pap. 3.50 ea. (*0-317-43011-4*) No. I (*0-933511-13-2*) No. II (*0-934905-08-8*) No. III (*0-933511-02-7*) Kazi Pubns.
Hamza, A. Color & Learn the Names of the Prophets. (Orig.). (ps). Date not set. pap. 3.50 (*0-934905-11-8*) Kazi Pubns.
Hashim, A. S. Eleven Surahs Explained. pap. 5.95 (*0-935782-90-7*) Kazi Pubns.
—Ibadat. pap. 5.95 (*1-56744-047-9*) Kazi Pubns.
—Iman, Basic Beliefs. pap. 5.95 (*1-56744-055-X*) Kazi Pubns.
—Islamic Arabic. pap. 5.95 (*1-56744-089-4*) Kazi Pubns.
Hassan, Syed K. Rhymes for Muslim Children. Ahmad, Saiyad F., ed. Mazzoni, Jennifer, illus. 48p. (Orig.). (gr. k). Date not set. pap. text ed. write for info. (*1-56316-315-2*) Iqra Intl Ed Fdtn.
Hayes, K. H. Stories of Great Muslims. 5.95 (*0-933511-63-9*) Kazi Pubns.
Hijazi, N. Color & Learn the Names of Animals. (Orig.). (ps). Date not set. pap. 3.50 (*0-934905-12-6*) Kazi Pubns.
Iqbal, Muhammad. Guiding Crescent. Aziz, Tariq, tr. 50p. (Orig.). (gr. 6-12). 1985. pap. 3.00 (*1-56744-285-4*) Kazi Pubns.
—Way of the Muslim. (gr. 3-7). 1983. pap. 7.95 (*0-7175-0632-0*) Dufour.
Ismaeel, Saeed. The Difference Between the Shiites & the Majority of Muslim Scholars. 35p. 1988. pap. write for info. Wamy Intl.
Kaahena, Yuhaayaa L. Children Style Quran: Stories for Children from Quran. Ismail, Latifa, ed. 22p. (Orig.). (gr. k-5). 1993. pap. 5.00 (*1-883781-04-3*) Yuhaaya.
Klaus, Sandra. Mustapha's Secret: A Muslim Boy's Search to Know God. Espe, Marvin, illus. 42p. (gr. 2-7). 1988. pressboard cover, plastic bdg. 9.95 (*0-9617490-1-6*) Gospel Missionary.
MacMillan, Dianne M. Ramadan & Id al-Fitr. LC 93-46185. (Illus.). 48p. (gr. 1-4). 1994. lib. bdg. 14.95 (*0-89490-502-3*) Enslow Pubs.
Massasati, Ahmad. Islamic Calligraphy Coloring Book. (Illus.). 57p. (Orig.). (gr. 3-6). 1991. pap. 4.95 (*0-89259-120-X*) Am Trust Pubns.
Mufassir, Sulayman. Biblical Studies from a Muslim Perspective. Obaba, Al I., ed. 49p. (Orig.). 1991. pap. text ed. 2.00 (*0-916157-61-X*) African Islam Miss Pubns.
Muhaiyaddeen, M. R. Treasures of the Heart: Sufi Stories for Young Children. Steele, Christine, ed. Balamore, Usha, tr. Deis, Ishaq, et al, illus. 110p. (ps). 1993. 10. 00 (*0-914390-33-3*) Fellowship Pr PA.
Numani, Shibli. Umar the Great, Vol. II. Saleem, M., tr. 200p. (gr. 7-12). 1985. 14.50 (*1-56744-407-5*) Kazi Pubns.
Obaba, Al I., ed. Sayings of the Honorable Elijah Muhammad, Vol. II. 49p. 1991. pap. text ed. 3.95 (*0-916157-86-5*) African Islam Miss Pubns.
Obaba, Al-Imam. The Aware Pages: Economic Unity a Must. (Illus.). 43p. (Orig.). 1988. pap. text ed. 2.50 (*0-916157-05-9*) African Islam Miss Pubns.
Obaba, Al-Imam & Abdullah. The Why & How of Burial & Death of a Muslim. (Illus.). 24p. (Orig.). 1985. pap. 1.50 (*0-916157-03-2*) African Islam Miss Pubns.
Perry, Rufus L. The Cushite: Or the Children of Ham (the Negro Race) Obaba, Al I., ed. 49p. (Orig.). 1991. pap. text ed. 4.00 (*0-916157-32-6*) African Islam Miss Pubns.
Qaderi, M. Taleem-Ul-Islam, 4. pap. 7.50 (*0-933511-72-8*) Kazi Pubns.
Saeed, Mahmud S. The Model of the Muslim Youth in the Story of Prophet Yusuf. Al-Johani, Maneh, intro. by. (ARA.). 32p. Date not set. pap. write for info. Wamy Intl.
Saqr, Abdul B. How to Call People to Islam. Ahmad, Shakil, tr. 154p. (Orig.). Date not set. pap. write for info. (*1-882837-16-9*) Wamy Intl.
Seyyed Hossein Nasr. A Young Muslim's Guide to the Modern World. 270p. 1993. text ed. 29.95 (*1-56744-495-4*); pap. text ed. 14.95 (*1-56744-478-4*) Kazi Pubns.
Siddiqui, A. A. Elementary Teachings of Islam. pap. 4.95 (*0-935782-89-3*) Kazi Pubns.
Studies & Research Unit of Wamy Staff. Principles of Dialogue. Al-Johani, Maneh, intro. by. (ARA.). 79p. Date not set. pap. write for info. (*1-882837-00-2*) Wamy Intl.
Zohny, Sophia. History of the Prophets: A Workbook. 40p. (Orig.). (gr. 1-12). 1991. 5.00 (*0-89259-111-0*) Am Trust Pubns.

ISLAM–HISTORY
Karim, F. Heroes of Islam, 16 bks. Incl. Bk. 1. Muhammad; Bk. 2. Abu Bakr; Bk. 3. Umar; Bk. 4. Othman; Bk. 5. Ali; Bk. 6. Khalid Bin Walid; Bk. 7. Mohammad Bin Qasim; Bk. 8. Mahmood of Ghazni; Bk. 9. Mohyuddin; Bk. 10. Sultan Tipu; Bk. 11. Aisha the Truthful; Bk. 12. Hussain the Martyr; Bk. 13. Some Companions of the Prophet-I; Bk. 14. Some Companions of the Prophet-II; Bk. 15. Some Companions of the Prophet-III. Set. pap. 45.00 (*1-56744-036-3*) Kazi Pubns.

ISLAND FLORA AND FAUNA
Balouet, Jean-Christopher & Behm, Barb. Endangered Animals of the Oceans & Seas. (Illus.). 32p. (gr. 3 up). Date not set. PLB 18.60 (*0-8368-1078-3*) Gareth Stevens Inc.

ISLANDS
see also Coral Reefs and Islands;
also names of islands and groups of islands, e.g. Cuba
Bates, Robin. Islands. LC 94-3155. 40p. 1994. 18.95 (*0-88682-711-6*) Creative Ed.
Bender, Lionel. Island. LC 89-5530. (Illus.). 32p. (gr. k-6). 1989. PLB 11.90 (*0-531-10820-1*) Watts.
Cape Verde. (Illus.). (gr. 5 up). 1989. 14.95 (*0-7910-0145-8*) Chelsea Hse.
Dean, Julia, text by. & photos by A Year on Monhegan Island. LC 93-24534. 48p. (gr. 2-4). 1994. 15.95 (*0-395-66476-4*) Ticknor & Flds Bks Yng Read.
Dicks, Brian. Lanzarote: Fire Island of the Canaries. (Illus.). 62p. (gr. 7-9). 1988. 22.95 (*0-85219-727-6*, Pub. by Batsford UK) Trafalgar.
Fyson, Nance L. Sri Lanka. (Illus.). 64p. (gr. 7-9). 1988. 19.95 (*0-85219-729-2*, Pub. by Batsford UK) Trafalgar.
Gibbons, Gail. Surrounded by Sea: Life on a New England Fishing Island. (ps-3). 1991. 14.95 (*0-316-30961-3*) Little.
Hassall, S. & Hassall, P. J. Seychelles. (Illus.). 96p. (gr. 5 up). 1988. 14.95 (*0-7910-0104-0*) Chelsea Hse.
Lasky, Kathryn. Surtsey: The Newest Place on Earth. Knight, Christopher G., photos by. (Illus.). 64p. (gr. 3-7). 1994. pap. 6.95 (*0-7868-1004-1*) Hyprn Ppbks.
Rydell, Wendy. All about Islands. Burns, Ray, illus. LC 83-4833. 32p. (gr. 3-6). 1984. lib. bdg. 10.59 (*0-89375-975-9*); pap. text ed. 2.95 (*0-89375-976-7*) Troll Assocs.
Solomon Islands. (Illus.). (gr. 5 up). 1989. 13.95 (*0-7910-0163-6*) Chelsea Hse.
Wildsmith, Brian. The Island. (Illus.). 16p. 1987. pap. 2.95 (*0-19-272137-2*) OUP.

ISLANDS–FICTION
Abolafia, Yossi. Yanosh's Island. LC 86-19462. 32p. (gr. k-3). 1987. 11.75 (*0-688-06816-2*); PLB 11.88 (*0-688-06817-0*) Greenwillow.
Avi. Smuggler's Island. LC 93-35964. 192p. (gr. 5 up). 1994. 14.00g (*0-688-12796-7*); pap. 3.95 (*0-688-12797-5*, Pub. by Beech Tree Bks) Morrow Jr Bks.
Binch, Caroline. Gregory Cool. LC 93-11845. (gr. 3 up). 1994. 14.99 (*0-8037-1577-3*) Dial Bks Young.
Brink, Carol R. Baby Island. Sewell, Helen, illus. LC 92-45577. 160p. (gr. 3-7). 1993. pap. 3.95 (*0-689-71751-2*, Aladdin) Macmillan Child Grp.
Bunting, Eve. The In-Between Days. Pertzoff, Alexander, illus. LC 93-45674. 96p. (gr. 3-7). 1994. 14.00 (*0-06-023609-4*); PLB 13.89 (*0-06-023612-4*) HarpC Child Bks.

Chetin, Helen. Angel Island Prisoner. Harvey, Catherine, tr. Lee, Jan, illus. LC 82-51170. (CHI & ENG.). (gr. 3 up). 1982. 7.95 (*0-938678-09-4*) New Seed.
Dunlop, Eileen. Finn's Island. LC 91-55027. 128p. (gr. 5-9). 1992. 13.95 (*0-8234-0910-4*) Holiday.
Field, Rachel. If Once You Have Slept on an Island. 32p. (ps-3). 1993. 14.95 (*1-56397-106-2*) Boyds Mills Pr.
Flood, E. L. Secret in the Moonlight: Welcome Inn. LC 93-50936. (Illus.). 144p. (gr. 3-6). 1994. pap. 2.95 (*0-8167-3427-5*) Troll Assocs.
Gibbons, Gail. Christmas on an Island. LC 93-50111. (gr. 3 up). 1994. write for info. (*0-688-09678-6*); PLB write for info. (*0-688-09679-4*) Morrow Jr Bks.
Harris, Aurand. Treasure Island. (gr. 4 up). 1983. pap. 4.50 (*0-87602-253-0*) Anchorage.
Hotze, Sollace. Acquainted with the Night. 256p. (gr. 7 up). 1992. 13.95 (*0-395-61576-3*, Clarion Bks) HM.
Ikeda, Daisaku. Over the Deep Blue Sea. Wildsmith, Brian, illus. McCaughrean, Geraldine, tr. from JPN. LC 92-22557. (Illus.). 32p. (ps-3). 1993. 15.00 (*0-679-84184-9*); PLB 15.99 (*0-679-94184-3*) Knopf Bks Yng Read.
Irwin, Hadley. The Original Freddie Ackerman. Hosten, James, illus. LC 91-43145. 192p. (gr. 5 up). 1992. SBE 14.95 (*0-689-50562-0*, M K McElderry) Macmillan Child Grp.
Jansson, Tove. Moominpappa at Sea. Hart, Kingsley, tr. from FIN. LC 93-1434. 1993. 17.00 (*0-374-35044-2*); pap. 4.95 (*0-374-45306-3*) FS&G.
Keller, Holly. Island Baby. LC 91-32491. (Illus.). 32p. (ps-8). 1992. 14.00 (*0-688-10579-3*); PLB 13.93 (*0-688-10580-7*) Greenwillow.
Kinsey-Warnock, Natalie. Wild Horses of Sweetbriar. LC 89-32280. (Illus.). (ps-3). 1990. 13.95 (*0-525-65015-6*, Cobblehill Bks) Dutton Child Bks.
Koci, Marta. Sarah's Bear. LC 86-30241. (Illus.). 28p. (ps). 1991. pap. 14.95 (*0-88708-038-3*) Picture Bk Studio.
Kontoyiannaki, Elizabeth. An Island Called Samos. Kontoyiannaki, Elizabeth, illus. 14p. (gr. k-3). 1992. pap. 9.95 (*1-895583-42-X*) MAYA Pubs.
Lasky, Kathryn. My Island Grandma. Schwartz, Amy, illus. LC 91-31000. 32p. (ps up). 1993. 15.00 (*0-688-07946-6*); PLB 14.93 (*0-688-07948-2*) Morrow Jr Bks.
Macdonald, G. The Little Island. 1993. pap. 4.99 (*0-440-40830-X*) Dell.
Macken, Walter. Island of the Great Yellow Ox. LC 90-22515. 192p. (gr. 5-9). 1991. pap. 14.00 jacketed, 3-pc. bdg. (*0-671-73800-3*, S&S BFYR) S&S Trade.
MacLachlan, Patricia. Baby. LC 93-22117. (gr. 1-8). 1993. 13.95 (*0-385-31133-8*) Delacorte.
Marshall, William. Adam's Island. (Illus.). (gr. 3-8). 1992. PLB 8.95 (*0-89565-889-5*) Childs World.
Martin, Charles E. For Rent. Martin, Charles E., illus. LC 85-864. 32p. (gr. k-3). 1986. 11.75 (*0-688-05716-0*); PLB 11.88 (*0-688-05717-9*) Greenwillow.
—Island Winter. Marten, Charles E., illus. LC 83-14098. 32p. (gr. k-3). 1984. 13.95 (*0-688-02590-0*); PLB 13.88 (*0-688-02592-7*) Greenwillow.
—Summer Business. Martin, Charles E., illus. LC 83-25422. 32p. (gr. k-3). 1984. PLB 14.88 (*0-688-03864-6*) Greenwillow.
Masters, Anthony. Klondyker. LC 92-351. 1992. pap. 15.00 (*0-671-79173-7*, S&S BFYR) S&S Trade.
Mazer, Harry. The Island Keeper. 176p. (gr. k-12). 1982. pap. 3.50 (*0-440-94774-X*, LFL) Dell.
Mitchell, Rita P. Hue Boy. Binch, Caroline, illus. LC 92-18560. 32p. (ps-3). 1993. 13.99 (*0-8037-1448-3*) Dial Bks Young.
Morley, Carol. A Spider & a Pig. LC 92-53215. 1993. 14.95 (*0-316-58405-3*) Little.
Murphy, Catherine F. Songs in the Silence. LC 93-26947. 192p. (gr. 3-7). 1994. SBE 14.95 (*0-02-767730-3*, Macmillan Child Bk) Macmillan Child Grp.
Ness, Evaline. Sam, Bangs & Moonshine. Ness, Evaline, illus. LC 66-10113. 48p. (ps-2). 1971. 14.95 (*0-8050-0314-2*, Bks Young Read); pap. 5.95 (*0-8050-0315-0*) H Holt & Co.
O'Dell, Scott. Island of the Blue Dolphins. 192p. (gr. k-6). 1987. pap. 4.50 (*0-440-43988-4*, YB) Dell.
—Island of the Blue Dolphins. large type ed. 161p. (gr. 2-6). 1987. Repr. of 1960 ed. lib. bdg. 14.95 (*1-55736-002-2*, Crnrstn Bks) BDD LT Grp.
Paulsen, Gary. The Island. LC 87-24761. 224p. (gr. 6-9). 1988. 13.95 (*0-531-05749-6*); PLB 13.99 (*0-531-08349-7*) Orchard Bks Watts.
—The Island. (gr. k up). 1990. pap. 3.99 (*0-440-20632-4*, LFL) Dell.
Peet, Bill. The Kweeks of Kookatumdee. Peet, Bill, illus. LC 84-22379. 32p. (gr. k-3). 1985. 13.95 (*0-395-37902-4*) HM.
Reid, Mary C. Come to the Island With Me. LC 92-73012. 32p. 1992. pap. 4.99 (*0-8066-2632-1*, 9-2632) Augsburg Fortress.
Roddy, Lee. Mystery of the Island Jungle. 160p. (Orig.). (gr. 3-7). 1989. pap. 4.99 (*0-929608-19-4*) Focus Family.
Seabrooke, Brenda. The Bridges of Summer. LC 92-11642. 160p. (gr. 5 up). 1992. 14.00 (*0-525-65094-6*, Cobblehill Bks) Dutton Child Bks.
Service, Pamela F. Phantom Victory. LC 93-37904. 128p. (gr. 5-7). 1994. SBE 14.95 (*0-684-19441-4*, Scribners Young Read) Macmillan Child Grp.
Steig, William. Abel's Island. LC 75-35916. (Illus.). 128p. (gr. 1 up). 1985. pap. 3.95 (*0-374-40016-4*, Sunburst Bks) FS&G.
Stieg, William. Rotten Island. (gr. 2 up). 1992. pap. 7.95 (*0-87923-960-3*) Godine.
Taylor, Theodore. Sweet Friday Island. LC 93-32435. (gr. 7 up). 1994. write for info. (*0-15-200009-7*); pap. write for info. (*0-15-200012-7*) HarBrace.
Verne, Jules. Mysterious Island. (gr. 8 up). 1965. pap. 1.95 (*0-8049-0077-9*, CL-77) Airmont.
Wallis, Lisa. Island Child. Haeffele, Deborah, illus. 32p. (gr. k-3). 1992. 14.00 (*0-525-67324-5*, Lodestar Bks) Dutton Child Bks.

ISLANDS OF THE PACIFIC

Lyle, Garry. Pacific Islands. (Illus.). 96p. (gr. 5 up). 1988. 14.95 (*0-222-01034-7*) Chelsea Hse.
Macdonald, Robert. Islands of the Pacific Rim & Their People. LC 94-7541. 48p. (gr. 5-8). 1994. 15.95 (*1-56847-167-X*) Thomson Lrning.
Phillips, Douglas A. & Levi, Steven C. The Pacific Rim Region: Emerging Giant. LC 88-3876. (Illus.). 160p. (gr. 6 up). 1988. lib. bdg. 18.95 (*0-89490-191-5*) Enslow Pubs.
Vilsoni, Patricia H. South Pacific Islanders. (Illus.). 48p. (gr. 4-8). 1987. PLB 16.67 (*0-86625-259-2*); 12.50 (*0-685-67606-4*) Rourke Corp.
Wright, David K. Brunei. LC 91-22511. 128p. (gr. 5-9). 1991. PLB 20.55 (*0-516-02602-X*) Childrens.

ISLANDS OF THE PACIFIC–FICTION

Bates, Gale. Tales of Tutu Nene & Nele. McCarthy, Carole H., illus. 36p. (ps-4). 1991. 7.95 (*0-89610-193-2*) Island Heritage.
Edens, Cooper. Santa Cow Island Vacation. Lane, Daniel, illus. LC 93-30899. (gr. 2 up). 1994. 14.00 (*0-671-88319-4*, Green Tiger) S&S Trade.
Gittins, Anne. Tales from the South Pacific Islands. LC 76-5411. (Illus.). 96p. (gr. 3 up). 1977. 7.95 (*0-916144-02-X*) Stemmer Hse.
Lang, W. Harold. Islands of the Pacific. Kubat, Frank J., Jr., ed. LC 87-83228. (Illus.). 168p. 1988. 44.95 (*0-945201-00-1*) Gannam-Kubat.
Von Tempski, Armine. Judy of the Islands: A Story of the South Seas. Burger, Carl, illus. LC 92-24539. viii, 280p. 1992. pap. 14.95 (*0-918024-97-8*) Ox Bow.

ISLANDS OF THE PACIFIC–HISTORY

Black, Wallace B. & Blashfield, Jean F. Island Hopping in the Pacific. LC 92-2505. (Illus.). 48p. (gr. 5-6). 1992. text ed. 12.95 RSBE (*0-89686-567-3*, Crestwood Hse) Macmillan Child Grp.

ISRAEL

Bamberger, David. A Young Person's History of Israel. Mandelkern, Nicholas, ed. (Illus.). 150p. (Orig.). (gr. 5-7). 1985. pap. 6.95 (*0-87441-393-1*); By Sara M. Schacheer & Priscilla Fishman. tchr's guide 12.50x (*0-87441-419-9*); student's activity bk. 4.25 (*0-87441-429-6*) Behrman.
Burstein, Chaya. Our Land of Israel. (Illus., Orig.). Date not set. pap. 8.00 (*0-8074-0527-2*, 127272); tchr's. guide 10.00 (*0-8074-0533-7*, 208037) UAHC.
Burstein, Chaya M. A Kid's Catalog of Israel. Burstein, Chaya, illus. 288p. (gr. 3 up). 1988. 14.95 (*0-8276-0263-4*) JPS Phila.
Cahill, Mary J. Israel. (Illus.). 112p. (gr. 5 up). 1988. lib. bdg. 14.95 (*1-55546-791-1*) Chelsea Hse.
Cozic, Charles P., ed. Israel: Opposing Viewpoints. LC 93-30964. (Illus.). 264p. (gr. 10 up). 1994. PLB 17.95 (*1-56510-133-2*); pap. text ed. 9.95 (*1-56510-132-4*) Greenhaven.
Department of Geography, Lerner Publications. Israel in Pictures. (Illus.). 64p. (gr. 5 up). 1988. PLB 17.50 (*0-8225-1833-3*) Lerner Pubns.
DuBois, Jill. Israel. LC 92-10208. 1992. 21.95 (*1-85435-531-7*) Marshall Cavendish.
Fisher, Leonard E. The Wailing Wall. Fisher, Leonard E., illus. LC 88-27192. 32p. (gr. 1-5). 1989. SBE 15.95 (*0-02-735310-9*, Macmillan Child Bk) Macmillan Child Grp.
Frankel, Max & Hoffman, Judy. I Live in Israel. Fishman, Priscilla, ed. LC 79-12833. (Illus.). (gr. 3-4). 1979. pap. text ed. 5.95x (*0-87441-317-6*) Behrman.
Gold-Vukson, Marji & Gold-Vukson, Michael. Imagine Exploring Israel: Creative Drawing Adventures. Gold-Vukson, Michael, illus. 48p. (Orig.). (gr. k-4). 1993. wkbk. 3.95 (*0-929371-64-X*) Kar Ben.
Hadary, Rivka. Israel. (Illus.). 32p. (gr. 4-6). 1991. 17.95 (*0-237-60190-7*, Pub. by Evans Bros Ltd) Trafalgar.
Haskins, Jim. Count Your Way Through Israel. Hanson, Rick, illus. 24p. (gr. 1-4). 1990. PLB 17.50 (*0-87614-415-6*) Carolrhoda Bks.
—Count Your Way Through Israel. (ps-3). 1992. pap. 5.95 (*0-87614-558-6*) Carolrhoda Bks.
Jones, Helen H. Israel. LC 85-5740. (Illus.). 128p. (gr. 5-9). 1986. PLB 20.55 (*0-516-02766-2*) Childrens.
Lange, Suzanne. The Year. LC 78-120787. (gr. 8 up). 1970. 21.95 (*0-87599-173-4*) S G Phillips.
Loewen. Food in Israel. 1991. 11.95s.p. (*0-86625-349-1*) Rourke Pubns.
Rogoff, Mike. Israel. LC 90-10027. (Illus.). 96p. (gr. 6-12). 1990. PLB 22.80 (*0-8114-2432-4*) Raintree Steck-V.
Sidon, et al. The Animated Israel. 54p. 1987. 14.95 (*0-8246-0326-5*) Jonathan David.
Taylor, Allegra. A Kibbutz in Israel. (Illus.). 32p. (gr. 2-5). 1987. 13.50 (*0-8225-1678-0*) Lerner Pubns.
Tolhurst, Marilyn. Israel. (Illus.). 48p. (gr. 4-8). 1989. lib. bdg. 14.95 (*0-382-09830-7*) Silver Burdett Pr.
Topek, Susan R. Israel Is... Kahn, Katherine J., illus. LC 88-83569. 12p. (ps). 1989. bds. 4.95 (*0-930494-92-X*) Kar Ben.

ISRAEL–FICTION

Banks, Lynne R. One More River. 256p. 1993. pap. 3.99 (*0-380-71563-5*, Camelot) Avon.
Edwards, Michelle. Chicken Man. (Illus.). (gr. k-3). 1991. 13.95 (*0-688-09708-1*); PLB 13.88 (*0-688-09709-X*) Lothrop.
—Chicken Man. Edwards, Michelle, illus. LC 93-11728. 32p. (ps up). 1994. pap. 4.95 (*0-688-13106-9*, Mulberry) Morrow.
McOmber, Rachel B., ed. McOmber Phonics Storybooks: Razz Visits Raz in Israel. rev. ed. (Illus.). write for info. (*0-944991-75-0*) Swift Lrn Res.
Meir, Mira. Alina: A Russian Girl Comes to Israel. Shapiro, Zeva, tr. from HEB. Rozen, Yael, illus. 48p. (gr. 2-4). 1982. 7.95 (*0-8276-0208-1*) JPS Phila.
Orlev, Uri. Lydia: Queen of Palestine. Halkin, Hillel, tr. from HEB. LC 93-12488. 1993. 13.95 (*0-395-65660-5*) HM.
Segal, Sheila F. Joshua's Dream: A Journey to the Land of Israel. Iskowitz, Joel, illus. LC 91-45513. (gr. k-3). 1992. 10.95 (*0-8074-0476-4*, 101062) UAHC.
Semel, Nava. Becoming Gershona. Simckes, Seymour, tr. 128p. (gr. 4 up). 1990. 12.95 (*0-670-83105-0*) Viking Child Bks.
—Becoming Gershona. Simckes, Seymour, tr. from HEB. LC 92-20306. 160p. (gr. 5 up). 1992. pap. 4.50 (*0-14-036071-9*) Puffin Bks.
—Flying Lessons. Halkin, Hillel, tr. LC 93-10811. 96p. (gr. 7 up). Date not set. 14.00 (*0-06-021470-8*); PLB 13.89 (*0-06-021471-6*) HarpC Child Bks.
Shalant, Phyllis. Shalom, Geneva Peace. 160p. (gr. 7 up). 1992. 15.00 (*0-525-44868-3*, DCB) Dutton Child Bks.
Steiner, Connie C. On Eagles Wings & Other Things. 32p. (gr. k-4). 1987. 12.95 (*0-8276-0274-X*) JPS Phila.

ISRAEL–HISTORY

Lehman, Emil. Israel: Idea & Reality. (Illus.). (gr. 8 up). 3.95x (*0-8381-0205-0*, 10-205) United Syn Bk.
Nover, Elizabeth Z. My Land of Israel. Rosenblum, Richard, illus. 35p. (Orig.). (gr. 1-2). 1987. pap. text ed. 4.25 (*0-87441-447-4*) Behrman.

ISRAEL–HISTORY–FICTION

Weilerstein, Sadie R. K'tonton in Israel, 3 bks. Safian, Elizabeth & Chernak, Judy, illus. (ps-6). 1988. Set of 3 bks. in zip loc bag. pap. 6.95 (*0-944633-32-3*); Set of 3 bks. & cassettes. pap. 29.95 (*0-685-43967-4*) Bk. 1: A Visit with K'tonton & K'tonton on Kibbutz, 40p. pap. 2.95 (*0-685-73935-X*); Bk. 2: K'tonton in Jerusalem-I: Adventure on Yom Ha'atzma'ut, Israel's Independence Day, 32p. pap. 2.95 (*0-685-73936-8*); Bk. 3: K'tonton in Jerusalem-II: Adventure in the Old City, 36p. pap. 2.95 (*0-685-73937-6*); pap. 10.95 (*0-685-73938-4*); 8.95 (*0-685-73939-2*) J Chernak.

ISRAEL-ARAB BORDER CONFLICTS

see Jewish-Arab Relations

ISRAEL-ARAB WAR, 1967-

Lawless, Richard & Bleaney, C. H. The First Day of the Six Day War. (Illus.). 64p. (gr. 7-11). 1990. 19.95 (*0-85219-820-5*, Pub. by Batsford UK) Trafalgar.

ISRAEL-ARAB WAR, 1967--FICTION

Banks, Lynne R. One More River. rev. ed. 256p. (gr. 5 up). 1992. 14.00 (*0-688-10893-8*) Morrow Jr Bks.
Reboul, Antoine. Thou Shalt Not Kill. Craig, Stephanie, tr. LC 77-77312. (gr. 5-8). 1969. 21.95 (*0-87599-161-0*) S G Phillips.

ISRAELITES

see Jews

ITALIAN LANGUAGE

Amery, H. & DiBello, P. The First Thousand Words in Italian. Cartwright, Stephen, illus. 64p. (gr. 1-6). 1983. 11.95 (*0-86020-768-4*) EDC.
Davies, H. Beginner's Italian Dictionary. (Illus.). 128p. (gr. 6 up). lib. bdg. 15.96 (*0-88110-423-X*, Usborne); pap. 9.95 (*0-7460-0764-7*) EDC.
De Brunhoff, Laurent. Je Parle Italien avec Babar. (FRE.). (gr. 4-6). 7.95 (*0-685-11274-8*) Fr & Eur.
Sheheen, Dennis, illus. A Child's Picture English-Italian Dictionary. LC 86-14052. (gr. k-2). 1986. 9.95 (*0-915361-57-4*) Modan-Adama Bks.
Wright, Nicola. Getting to Know: Italy & Italian. Wooley, Kim, illus. 32p. (gr. 3-7). 1993. 12.95 (*0-8120-6338-4*); pap. 5.95 (*0-8120-1534-7*) Barron.

ITALIAN LANGUAGE–CONVERSATION AND PHRASE BOOKS

Berlitz. Berlitz Jr. Italian: Parlo Italiano. LC 91-21143. (Illus.). 64p. (ps-2). 1992. pap. 19.95 POB (*0-689-71595-1*, Aladdin) Macmillan Child Grp.
Farnes, C. Survive in Five Languages. (Illus.). 64p. (gr. 8 up). 1993. PLB 12.96 (*0-88110-623-2*); pap. 6.95 (*0-7460-1034-6*) EDC.
Lyric Language - Italian, Series 1 & 2. (Illus.). (ps-8). Series 1. 9.95 (*1-56015-228-1*) Series 2. 9.95 (*1-56015-241-9*) Penton Overseas.

ITALIAN LANGUAGE–STUDY AND TEACHING

Hazzan, Anne-Francoise. Let's Learn Italian Coloring Book. (Illus.). 64p. (gr. 4 up). 1988. pap. 3.95 (*0-8442-8060-7*, Natl Textbk) NTC Pub Grp.
Mahoney, Judy. Teach Me Italian. Grifoni, Maria C., tr. (ITA., Illus.). 20p. (ps-6). 1992. pap. 11.95 incl. audiocassette (*0-934633-57-6*); tchr's. ed. 5.95 (*0-934633-29-0*) Teach Me.
Mealer, Tamara. My World in Italian Coloring Book. (ITA., Illus.). 96p. 1991. pap. 4.95 (*0-8442-8067-4*, Natl Textbk) NTC Pub Grp.
Wilkes, Angela. Italian for Beginners. 48p. (ps-1). 1988. 8.95 (*0-8442-8059-3*, Passport Bks) NTC Pub Grp.

ITALIANS IN THE U. S.
Di Franco, J. Philip. The Italian Americans. Moynihan, Daniel P., intro. by. 112p. (Orig.). (gr. 5 up). 1988. 17.95 (*0-87754-886-2*); pap. 9.95 (*0-7910-0268-3*) Chelsea Hse.
Grossman, Ronald P. Italians in America. LC 92-31325. 1993. lib. bdg. 15.95 (*0-8225-0244-5*); pap. 5.95 (*0-8225-1040-5*) Lerner Pubns.
Hoobler, Dorothy & Hoobler, Thomas. The Italian American Family Album. Cuomo, Mario M., intro. by. LC 93-46918. (Illus.). 128p. 1994. 19.95 (*0-19-509124-8*); PLB 22.95 (*0-19-508126-9*) OUP.
ITALY
Angilillo, Barbara W. Italy. LC 90-10191. (Illus.). 96p. (gr. 6-12). 1990. PLB 22.80 (*0-8114-2438-3*) Raintree Steck-V.
Bonomi, Kathryn. Italy. (Illus.). 128p. (gr. 5 up). 1991. 14.95 (*1-55546-752-0*) Chelsea Hse.
Borlenghi, Patricia & Wright, Rachel. Italy. LC 93-14702. (Illus.). 32p. (gr. 5-7). 1993. PLB 11.90 (*0-531-14264-7*) Watts.
Buckland, Simon. Guide to Italy. Downer, Maggie, illus. LC 93-39020. 32p. (gr. 1-4). 1994. 3.95 (*1-85697-960-1*, Kingfisher LKC) LKC.
Butler, Daphne. Italy. LC 92-16649. (Illus.). 32p. (gr. 3-4). 1992. PLB 19.24 (*0-8114-3677-2*) Raintree Steck-V.
Carricle, Noel. San Marino. (Illus.). 96p. (gr. 5 up). 1988. 14.95 (*0-7910-0101-6*) Chelsea Hse.
Clark, Colin. Journey Through Italy. Burns, Robert, illus. LC 91-46174. 32p. (gr. 3-5). 1993. PLB 11.89 (*0-8167-2763-5*); pap. text ed. 3.95 (*0-8167-2764-3*) Troll Assocs.
Getting to Know Italy. 48p. 1990. 8.95 (*0-8442-8066-6*, Natl Textbk) NTC Pub Grp.
Goldstein, Frances. Children's Treasure Hunt Travel Guide to Italy. Goldstein, Frances, illus. LC 79-67280. (Orig.). (gr. k-12). 1980. pap. 6.95 (*0-933334-01-X*, Dist. by Hippocrene) Paper Tiger Pap.
Haskins, Jim. Count Your Way Through Italy. Wright, Beth, illus. 24p. (gr. 1-4). 1990. PLB 17.50 (*0-87614-406-7*) Carolrhoda Bks.
—Count Your Way Through Italy. LC 89-37455. (ps-3). 1991. pap. 5.95 (*0-87614-533-0*) Carolrhoda Bks.
Hoobler, Dorothy & Hoobler, Thomas. Italian Portraits. Fujiwara, Kim, illus. LC 92-13641. 96p. (gr. 7-8). 1992. PLB 22.80 (*0-8114-6377-X*) Raintree Steck-V.
McLean, Virginia O. Pastatively Italy. (Illus.). 40p. (gr. k-6). 1994. incl. cassette 15.95 (*0-9606046-6-9*) Redbird.
Mariella, Cinzia. Passport to Italy. rev. ed. LC 93-21189. (Illus.). 48p. (gr. 5-8). 1994. PLB 13.90 (*0-531-14295-7*) Watts.
Powell, Jillian. Italy. LC 91-59. (Illus.). 32p. (gr. 2-4). 1992. PLB 12.40 (*0-531-18442-0*, Pub. by Bookwright Pr) Watts.
Sproule, Anna. Italy. (Illus.). 48p. (gr. 5 up). 1987. PLB 12.95 (*0-382-09473-5*) Silver Burdett Pr.
Stein, R. Conrad. Italy. LC 83-14259. (Illus.). 128p. (gr. 5-9). 1984. PLB 20.55 (*0-516-02768-9*) Childrens.
Travis, David. The Land & People of Italy. LC 91-9771. (Illus.). 256p. (gr. 6 up). 1992. 18.00 (*0-06-022778-8*); PLB 17.89 (*0-06-022784-2*) HarpC Child Bks.
Wright, David & Wright, Jill. Italy. (Illus.). 32p. (gr. 4-6). 1991. 17.95 (*0-237-60186-9*, Pub. by Evans Bros Ltd) Trafalgar.
Wright, Nicola. Getting to Know: Italy & Italian. Wooley, Kim, illus. 32p. (gr. 3-7). 1993. 12.95 (*0-8120-6338-4*); pap. 5.95 (*0-8120-1534-7*) Barron.
ITALY–ANTIQUITIES
Bisel, Sara. Secrets of Vesuvius: Exploring the Mysteries of an Ancient Buried City. (gr. 4-7). 1993. pap. 6.95 (*0-590-43851-4*) Scholastic Inc.
Jarvis, Mary B. The Leaning Tower of Pisa. 48p. (gr. 3-4). 1991. PLB 11.95 (*1-56065-031-1*) Capstone Pr.
ITALY–FICTION
Boccaccio, Giovanni. Chichibo & the Crane. Luzatti, Lele, illus. (gr. 1-6). 1961. 8.95 (*0-8392-3004-4*) Astor-Honor.
Brown, Regina. Little Brother. Bornschlegel, Ruth, illus. (gr. 3-7). 1962. 8.95 (*0-8392-3019-2*) Astor-Honor.
Caselli, Giovanni. A Roman Soldier. Sergio, illus. LC 86-4366. 32p. (gr. 3-6). 1991. PLB 12.95 (*0-87226-106-9*) P Bedrick Bks.
De Paola, Tomie. Jingle the Christmas Clown. (Illus.). 40p. (ps-3). 1992. 15.95 (*0-399-22338-X*, Putnam) Putnam Pub Group.
French, Simon. Change the Locks. LC 92-30194. 112p. (gr. 3-7). 1993. 13.95 (*0-590-45593-1*) Scholastic Inc.
Hooper, Maureen B. The Violin Man. LC 90-70417. 80p. (gr. 3-7). 1991. 12.95 (*1-878093-79-7*) Boyds Mills Pr.
Moravia. Sette Racconti. (gr. 7-12). pap. 6.95 (*0-88436-060-1*, 55258) EMC.
Stevens, Biddy. Toto in Italy. (ITA.). 32p. (gr. 4-7). 1992. 12.95 (*0-8442-9289-3*, Natl Textbk) NTC Pub Grp.
Strangis, Joel. Grandfather's Rock. Recht, Ruth, illus. LC 92-26525. 1993. 14.95 (*0-395-65367-3*) HM.
Ventura, Piero & Ventura, Marisa. The Painter's Trick. Ventura, Piero & Ventura, Marisa, illus. LC 76-54411. (gr. k-2). 1977. lib. bdg. 6.99 (*0-394-93320-6*) Random Bks Yng Read.
Vigna, Judith. Zio Pasquale's Zoo. LC 93-19360. 1993. write for info. (*0-8075-9488-1*) A Whitman.
ITALY–HISTORY–FICTION
Boccaccio. Andreuccio de Perugia. (gr. 7-12). pap. 5.95 (*0-88436-049-0*, 55250) EMC.
ITALY–HISTORY–1914-1946
Chrisp, Peter. The Rise of Fascism. LC 90-46774. (Illus.). 64p. (gr. 9-12). 1991. 13.40 (*0-531-18438-2*, Pub. by Bookwright Pr) Watts.
ITALY–SOCIAL LIFE AND CUSTOMS
Caselli, Giovanni. The Everyday Life of a Florentine Merchant. Caselli, Giovanni, illus. LC 86-4365. 32p. (gr. 3-6). 1991. PLB 12.95 (*0-87226-107-7*) P Bedrick Bks.
Hubley, John & Hubley, Penny. A Family in Italy. (Illus.). 32p. (gr. 2-5). 1987. PLB 13.50 (*0-8225-1673-X*) Lerner Pubns.
IWO JIMA, BATTLE OF, 1945
Black, Wallace B. & Blashfield, Jean F. Iwo Jima & Okinawa. LC 92-25868. (Illus.). 48p. (gr. 5-6). 1993. text ed. 4.95 RSBE (*0-89686-569-X*, Crestwood Hse) Macmillan Child Grp.

J

JACKSON, ANDREW, PRESIDENT U. S. 1767-1845
Coit, Margaret L. Andrew Jackson. LC 90-48986. (Illus.). 176p. (gr. 6-10). 1991. PLB 13.95 (*1-55905-082-9*) Marshall Cavendish.
Gutman, William. Andrew Jackson & the New Populism. (Illus.). 144p. (gr. 3-6). 1987. pap. 4.95 (*0-8120-3917-3*) Barron.
Hilton, Suzanne. The World of Young Andrew Jackson. Lynn, Patricia, illus. (gr. 5-8). 1988. 12.95 (*0-8027-6814-8*); PLB 13.85 (*0-8027-6815-6*) Walker & Co.
Meltzer, Milton. Andrew Jackson: And His America. (Illus.). 208p. (gr. 7-12). 1993. PLB 16.40 (*0-531-11157-1*) Watts.
Osinski, Alice. Andrew Jackson. LC 86-29983. (Illus.). 100p. (gr. 3 up). 1987. PLB 14.40 (*0-516-01387-4*); pap. 6.95 (*0-516-41387-2*) Childrens.
Parlin, John. Andrew Jackson: Pioneer & President. (Illus.). 80p. (gr. 2-6). 1991. Repr. of 1962 ed. lib. bdg. 12.95 (*0-7910-1442-8*) Chelsea Hse.
Sabin, Louis. Andrew Jackson, Frontier Patriot. Smolinski, Dick, illus. LC 85-1094. 48p. (gr. 4-6). 1986. lib. bdg. 10.79 (*0-8167-0547-X*); pap. text ed. 3.50 (*0-8167-0548-8*) Troll Assocs.
Sandak, Cass R. The Jacksons. LC 91-30363. (Illus.). 48p. (gr. 5). 1992. text ed. 12.95 RSBE (*0-89686-636-X*, Crestwood Hse) Macmillan Child Grp.
Stefoff, Rebecca. Andrew Jackson: 7th President of the United States. Young, Richard G., ed. LC 87-32878. (Illus.). (gr. 5-9). 1988. PLB 17.26 (*0-944483-08-9*) Garrett Ed Corp.
Wade. Andrew Jackson. (gr. 4-12). 1993. PLB 8.49 (*0-87386-091-8*); pap. 1.95 (*0-87386-090-X*) Jan Prods.
JACKSON, JESSE, 1941-
Celsi, Teresa. Jesse Jackson & Political Power. (Illus.). 32p. (gr. 2-4). 1991. PLB 12.90 (*1-56294-040-6*); pap. 4.95 (*1-878841-70-X*) Millbrook Pr.
Haskins, James. I Am Somebody! A Biography of Jesse Jackson. LC 91-34079. (Illus.). 112p. (gr. 6 up). 1992. lib. bdg. 17.95 (*0-89490-240-7*) Enslow Pubs.
Jakoubek, Robert. Jesse Jackson. King, Coretta Scott, intro. by. (Illus.). 112p. (gr. 5 up). 1991. PLB 17.95 (*0-7910-1130-5*) Chelsea Hse.
McKissack, Patricia C. Jesse Jackson: A Biography. 112p. (gr. 3-7). 1990. 2.95 (*0-590-42395-9*) Scholastic Inc.
Martin, Patricia S. Jesse Jackson: A Black Leader. (Illus.). 24p. (gr. 1-4). 1987. PLB 14.60 (*0-86592-170-9*); 10.95s.p. (*0-685-67565-3*) Rourke Corp.
Stone, Eddie. Jesse Jackson. rev. ed. (ps-10). 1988. pap. 3.95 (*0-87067-840-X*) Holloway.
Wilkinson, Brenda. Jesse Jackson: Still Fighting for the Dream. Gallin, Richard, ed. Young, Andrew, intro. by. (Illus.). 128p. (gr. 5 up). 1990. lib. bdg. 12.95 (*0-382-09926-5*); pap. 7.95 (*0-382-24064-2*) Silver Burdett Pr.
JACKSON, MAHALIA, 1911-1972
Dunham, Montrew. Mahalia Jackson: Young Gospel Singer. LC 93-34072. 1995. pap. 4.95 (*0-689-71786-5*, Aladdin) Macmillan Child Grp.
Witter, Evelyn. Mahalia Jackson: Born to Sing Gospel Music. (Illus.). (gr. 3-6). 1985. pap. 6.95 (*0-88062-045-5*) Mott Media.
Wolfe, Charles. Mahalia Jackson. Horner, Matina S., intro. by. 112p. (gr. 5 up). 1990. 17.95 (*1-55546-661-3*) Chelsea Hse.
—Mahalia Jackson: American Women of Achievement. (gr. 4-7). 1992. pap. 7.95 (*0-7910-0440-6*) Chelsea Hse.
JACKSON, RACHEL (DONELSON) 1767-1828
Sandak, Cass R. The Jacksons. LC 91-30363. (Illus.). 48p. (gr. 5). 1992. text ed. 12.95 RSBE (*0-89686-636-X*, Crestwood Hse) Macmillan Child Grp.
JACKSON, THOMAS JONATHAN, 1824-1863
Bennett, Barbara J. Stonewall Jackson: Lee's Greatest Lieutenant. (Illus.). 160p. (gr. 5 up). 1990. lib. bdg. 12.95 (*0-382-09939-7*); pap. 7.95 (*0-382-24048-0*) Silver Burdett Pr.
Fritz, Jean. Stonewall. (Illus.). (gr. 3-7). 1979. 15.95 (*0-399-20698-1*, Putnam) Putnam Pub Group.
Ludwig, Charles. Stonewall Jackson: Loved in the South Admired in the North. (Illus.). (gr. 3-6). 1989. pap. 6.95 (*0-88062-157-5*) Mott Media.
JACOB, THE PATRIARCH
Paamoni, Zev. The Adventures of Jacob. (Illus.). (gr. 5-10). 1970. 3.00 (*0-914080-26-1*) Shulsinger Sales.
Parry, Linda & Parry, Alan. Jacob & Esau. Parry, Linda & Parry, Alan, illus. LC 90-80555. 24p. (Orig.). (ps-2). 1990. pap. 1.99 (*0-8066-2490-6*, 9-2490, Augsburg) Augsburg Fortress.
JAGUARS–FICTION
Brusca, Maria C. When Jaguar's Moon. 1995. write for info. (*0-8050-2797-1*) H Holt & Co.
Herndon, Ernest. Night of the Jungle Cat. (gr. 5 up). 1994. pap. 4.99 (*0-310-38271-8*) Zondervan.
Ryde, Joanne. Jaguar in the Rain Forest. Rothman, Michael, illus. LC 94-16646. (gr. 3 up). 1995. write for info. (*0-688-12990-0*); pap. write for info. (*0-688-12991-9*) Morrow Jr Bks.
Vargo, Vanessa. Jaguar Talk. LC 92-4073. 1992. 5.95 (*0-85953-396-4*) Childs Play.
JAILS
see Prisons
JAM
Mitgutsch, Ali. From Fruit to Jam. Mitgutsch, Ali, illus. LC 81-58. 24p. (ps-3). 1981. PLB 10.95 (*0-87614-154-8*) Carolrhoda Bks.
JAMAICA
Hubley, John & Hubley, Penny. A Family in Jamaica. LC 85-6887. (Illus.). 32p. (gr. 2-5). 1985. PLB 13.50 (*0-8225-1657-8*) Lerner Pubns.
Lerner Publications, Department of Geography Staff. Jamaica in Pictures. (Illus.). 64p. (gr. 5 up). 1987. PLB 17.50 (*0-8225-1814-7*) Lerner Pubns.
Sheehan, Sean. Jamaica. LC 93-11019. (gr. 5-9). 1993. 21.95 (*1-85435-581-3*, Pub by Cavenidsh Bks UK); write for info. (*1-85435-578-3*) Marshall Cavendish.
JAMAICA–FICTION
Berry, James. Ajeemah & His Son. LC 92-6615. 96p. (gr. 7 up). 1992. 13.00 (*0-06-021043-5*); PLB 12.89 (*0-06-021044-3*) HarpC Child Bks.
—A Thief in the Village: And Other Stories of Jamaica. 156p. (gr. 4 up). 1990. pap. 4.99 (*0-14-034357-1*, Puffin) Puffin Bks.
Hanson, Regina. The Tangerine Tree. Stevenson, Harvey, illus. LC 93-40530. 1995. write for info. (*0-395-68963-5*, Clarion Bks) HM.
Havill, Juanita. Jamaica Tag-Along. O'Brien, Anne S., illus. 1990. pap. 4.80 (*0-395-54949-3*) HM.
McKenzie, Earl. A Boy Named Ossie: A Jamaican Childhood. (Illus.). 104p. (Orig.). 1991. pap. 8.95 (*0-435-98816-6*, 98816) Heinemann.
Pomerantz, Charlotte. Chalk Doll. Lessac, Frane, illus. LC 88-872. 32p. (ps-3). 1993. pap. 4.95 (*0-06-443333-1*, Trophy) HarpC Child Bks.
JAMES, JESSE WOODSON, 1847-1882
Green, Carl R. & Sanford, William R. Jesse James. LC 91-18123. (Illus.). 48p. (gr. 4-10). 1992. lib. bdg. 14.95 (*0-89490-365-9*) Enslow Pubs.
Love, Robertus. The Rise & Fall of Jesse James. Fellman, Michael, intro. by. LC 89-24965. xxiv, 446p. 1990. pap. 11.95 (*0-8032-7932-9*, Bison Books) U of Nebr Pr.
Stiles, T. J. Jesse James. LC 92-45210. (Illus.). 1993. 18.95 (*0-7910-1737-0*, Am Art Analog); pap. write for info. (*0-7910-1738-9*, Am Art Analog) Chelsea Hse.
JAMESTOWN, VIRGINIA–FICTION
O'Dell, Scott. The Serpent Never Sleeps: A Novel of Jamestown & Pocahontas. (gr. 8 up). 1988. pap. 3.99 (*0-449-70328-2*, Juniper) Fawcett.
Ruemmler, John. Smoke on the Water: A Novel of Jamestown & the Powhatans. LC 91-42587. (Illus.). 176p. (gr. 7 up). 1992. pap. 6.95 (*1-55870-239-3*, 70099) Shoe Tree Pr.
JAMESTOWN, VIRGINIA–HISTORY
Benjamin, Anne. Young Pocahontas: Indian Princess. Powers, Christine, illus. LC 91-32654. 32p. (gr. k-2). 1992. PLB 11.59 (*0-8167-2534-9*); pap. text ed. 2.95 (*0-8167-2535-7*) Troll Assocs.
Campbell, Elizabeth A. Jamestown: The Beginning. Bock, William S., illus. 96p. (gr. 4-6). 1974. lib. bdg. 15.95 (*0-316-12599-7*) Little.
Kay, Alan N. Jamestown Journey. Van Bergen, Jamie, illus. 56p. (gr. 4-7). 1992. pap. 4.95 (*0-939631-52-0*) Thomas Publications.
Mountain, Lee, et al. Jamestown Heritage Reader, Bk. A. (Illus.). 160p. (gr. 1). 1991. 12.10 (*0-89061-710-4*); pap. 9.10 (*0-89061-951-4*); tchr's. ed. 22.10 (*0-89061-961-1*) Jamestown Pubs.
—Jamestown Heritage Reader, Bk. C. 256p. (gr. 3). 1991. 14.95 (*0-89061-712-0*); pap. 11.95 (*0-89061-953-0*); tchr's. ed. 24.95 (*0-89061-963-8*) Jamestown Pubs.
—Jamestown Heritage Reader, Bk. E. 256p. (gr. 5). 1991. 16.50 (*0-89061-714-7*); pap. 13.50 (*0-89061-955-7*); tchr's. ed. 26.50 (*0-89061-965-4*) Jamestown Pubs.
—Jamestown Heritage Reader, Bk. F. 246p. (gr. 6). 1991. 17.20 (*0-89061-715-5*); pap. 14.20 (*0-89061-956-5*); tchr's. ed. 27.20 (*0-89061-966-2*) Jamestown Pubs.
Smith, Carter. The Jamestown Colony. (Illus.). 64p. (gr. 5 up). 1991. PLB 12.95 (*0-382-24121-5*); pap. 7.95 (*0-382-24116-9*) Silver Burdett Pr.
JAMESTOWN, VIRGINIA–HISTORY–FICTION
Knight, James E. Jamestown, New World Adventure. Wenzel, David, illus. LC 81-23086. 32p. (gr. 5-9). 1982. PLB 11.59 (*0-89375-724-1*); pap. text ed. 2.95 (*0-89375-725-X*) Troll Assocs.
JAPAN
Allen, Carol. Japan. (Illus.). 64p. (gr. 4-8). 1992. wkbk. 8.95 (*0-86653-684-1*, 1418) Good Apple.
Baines, John. Japan. LC 93-23948. (gr. 5 up). 1994. PLB 22.80 (*0-8114-1847-2*) Raintree Steck-V.

Coates, Bryan E. Japan. LC 91-40478. (Illus.). 32p. (gr. k-4). 1991. 12.40 (*0-531-18392-0*, Pub. by Bookwright Pr) Watts.
Dudley, William, ed. Japan: Opposing Viewpoints. LC 89-36620. (Illus.). 240p. (gr. 10 up). 1989. PLB 17.95 (*0-89908-444-3*); pap. 9.95 (*0-89908-419-2*) Greenhaven.
Flint, David. Japan. LC 92-43189. (Illus.). 32p. (gr. 3-4). 1992. PLB 19.24 (*0-8114-2940-7*) Raintree Steck-V.
Franco, Betsy. Around the World, Vol. 2: Japan. (Illus.). 48p. (gr. 1-3). 1993. pap. text ed. 7.95 (*1-55799-257-6*) Evan-Moor Corp.
Greene, Carol. Japan. LC 83-7603. (Illus.). 128p. (gr. 5-9). 1983. PLB 20.55 (*0-516-02769-7*) Childrens.
Haskins, Jim. Count Your Way Through Japan. (Illus.). 24p. (gr. 1-4). 1987. lib. bdg. 17.50 (*0-87614-301-X*); pap. 4.95 (*0-87614-485-7*) Carolrhoda Bks.
Howell, Melissa. Back Home in Japan: An Activity Book. Hackney, Rick, illus. 64p. (gr. 1-4). 1991. tchr's. ed. 1.95 (*981-3009-02-0*); wkbk. 3.95 (*981-3009-24-1*) OMF Bks.
Jacobsen, Karen. Japan. LC 82-4445. (Illus.). (gr. k-4). 1982. PLB 12.85 (*0-516-01630-X*); pap. 4.95 (*0-516-41630-8*) Childrens.
Kalman, Bobbie. Japan: The Land. (Illus.). 32p. (gr. 4-5). 1989. PLB 15.95 (*0-86505-204-2*); pap. 7.95 (*0-86505-284-0*) Crabtree Pub Co.
Lerner Publications, Department of Geography Staff. Japan in Pictures. (Illus.). 64p. (gr. 5 up). 1989. PLB 17.50 (*0-8225-1861-9*) Lerner Pubns.
Meeks, Christopher. Japan. (Illus.). 64p. (gr. 7 up). 1990. lib. bdg. 17.27 (*0-86593-089-9*); lib. bdg. 12.95s.p. (*0-685-36366-X*) Rourke Corp.
Meyer, Carolyn. A Voice from Japan: An Outsider Looks In. (Illus.). 212p. (gr. 7 up). 1988. 14.95 (*0-15-200633-8*, Gulliver Bks) HarBrace.
—Voice from Japan: An Outsider Looks In. 1992. pap. 9.95 (*0-15-200634-6*) HarBrace.
Omotani, Les M. Konnichi Wa, Japan: Middle School Through High School. (JPN.). 120p. (gr. 7-12). 1993. pap. 15.95 (*0-8442-8497-1*, Natl Textbk) NTC Pub Grp.
Ottenheimer, Laurence. Japan: Land of Samurai & Robots. Nikly, Michelle, illus. LC 87-34524. 38p. (gr. k-5). 1988. 5.95 (*0-944589-11-1*, 111) Young Discovery Lib.
Parker, Steve. Japan. Kossmann, Walter & Fink, Joanne, eds. (Illus.). 48p. (gr. 5 up). 1991. PLB 12.95 (*0-382-24246-7*) Silver Burdett Pr.
Pilbeam, Mavis. Japan. (Illus.). 32p. (gr. 4-8). 1992. 17.95 (*0-237-60187-7*, Pub. by Evans Bros Ltd) Trafalgar.
Shelley, Rex. Japan. LC 89-23877. (Illus.). 128p. (gr. 5-9). 1991. PLB 21.95 (*1-85435-297-0*) Marshall Cavendish.
Stefoff, Rebecca. Japan. (Illus.). 112p. (gr. 5 up). 1988. lib. bdg. 14.95 (*1-55546-199-9*) Chelsea Hse.
Takeshita, Jiro. Food in Japan. LC 88-31465. (Illus.). 32p. (gr. 3-6). 1989. lib. bdg. 15.94 (*0-86625-340-8*); 11. 95s.p. (*0-685-58501-8*) Rourke Corp.
Tames, Richard & Tames, Sheila. Japan. LC 93-42886. 1994. write for info. (*0-531-14315-5*) Watts.
Tyler, Deborah. Japan. LC 93-3268. (Illus.). 32p. (gr. 5). 1993. text ed. 13.95 RSBE (*0-89686-773-0*, Crestwood Hse) Macmillan Child Grp.
Uchida, Yoshiko. Samurai of Gold Hill. rev. ed. Forberg, Ati, illus. LC 84-20424. 128p. (gr. 4-12). 1985. pap. 5.95 (*0-916870-86-3*) Creative Arts Bk.
Walker, Richard. Japan. LC 92-10766. 96p. 1992. lib. bdg. 22.80 (*0-8114-2457-X*) Raintree Steck-V.

JAPAN–BIOGRAPHY

Honda, Maasaki. Shinichi Suzuki: Man of Love. Selden, Kyoko, tr. from JPN. 72p. (Orig.). (gr. 7-12). 1984. pap. text ed. 7.95 (*0-87487-199-9*, Suzuki Method) Summy-Birchard.
Hoobler, Dorothy & Hoobler, Thomas. Japanese Portraits. LC 93-39627. 1994. PLB 22.80 (*0-8114-6381-8*) Raintree Steck-V.
—Showa: The Age of Hirohito. 228p. (gr. 7 up). 1990. 15. 95 (*0-8027-6966-7*); lib. bdg. 16.85 (*0-8027-6967-5*) Walker & Co.
Hyman, Mark. Black Shogun of Japan - Sophonisa: Wife of Two Warring Kings & Other Stories from Antiquity. Massed, Cal, illus. 120p. (Orig.). (gr. 9-12). 1989. pap. 11.00 (*0-915515-01-6*) The Way Pub.
Italia, Bob. Emperor Hirohito. Walner, Rosemary, ed. LC 90-82620. (Illus.). 32p. (gr. 4). 1990. PLB 11.96 (*0-939179-80-6*) Abdo & Dghtrs.
Zimmerman, Julie & Torumasu, Kimiaki. Wishing on Daruma. LC 91-76745. (Illus.). 112p. (Orig.). (gr. 5 up). 1992. pap. 9.95 (*1-879418-05-3*) Biddle Pub.

JAPAN–CIVILIZATION

Gaskin, Carol. Camelot World: Secrets of the Samurai. 128p. (Orig.). 1990. pap. 2.95 (*0-380-76040-1*, Camelot) Avon.
Kalman, Bobbie. Japan: The Culture. (Illus.). 32p. (gr. 4-5). 1989. PLB 15.95 (*0-86505-206-9*); pap. 7.95 (*0-86505-286-7*) Crabtree Pub Co.
—Japan: The People. (Illus.). 32p. (gr. 4-5). 1989. PLB 15.95 (*0-86505-205-0*); pap. 7.95 (*0-86505-285-9*) Crabtree Pub Co.
Langone, John J. In the Shogun's Shadow: Understanding a Changing Japan. Parton, Steve, illus. LC 93-23999. 1994. 16.95 (*0-316-51409-8*) Little.
Metcalf, Florence E. A Peek at Japan: A Lighthearted Look at Japan's Language & Culture. 2nd, rev. ed. Tomoko, illus. 133p. (gr. 1-5). 1992. pap. text ed. 14. 95 (*0-9631684-3-6*) Metco Pub.
Waterlow, Julia. Japan. LC 93-20426. (Illus.). 32p. (gr. 5-8). 1994. PLB 12.40 (*0-531-14270-1*) Watts.
Westridge Young Writers Workshop Staff. Kids Explore America's Japanese Heritage. 112p. Date not set. pap. 8.95 (*1-56261-155-0*) John Muir.

JAPAN–FICTION

Baker, Keith. The Magic Fan. 16p. (gr. k-3). 1989. 14.95 (*0-15-250750-7*) HarBrace.
Compher, Catherine. Shoes on, Shoes Off. Gross, Karen, ed. 24p. (Orig.). (ps). 1993. pap. text ed. 6.95 (*1-56309-076-7*, New Hope) Womans Mission Union.
Crofford, Emily. Born in the Year of Courage. 184p. (gr. 4-6). 1991. PLB 19.95 (*0-87614-679-5*) Carolrhoda Bks.
Friedman, Ina R. How My Parents Learned to Eat. Say, Allen, illus. LC 84-18553. 32p. (gr. k-3). 1984. 14.95 (*0-395-35379-3*); pap. 4.80 (*0-395-44235-4*) HM.
Haugaard, Erik C. Samurai's Tale. 1990. pap. 4.95 (*0-395-54970-1*) HM.
Hosozawa-Nagano, Elaine. Chopsticks from America. Miyata, Masayuki, illus. LC 93-45795. 1994. 12.95 (*1-879965-11-9*) Polychrome Pub.
Hughes, Dean. Nutty & the Case of the Ski-Slope Spy. LC 90-176. 128p. (gr. 3-7). 1990. pap. 3.95 (*0-689-71438-6*, Aladdin) Macmillan Child Grp.
Ikeda, Daisaku. The Cherry Tree. McCaughrean, Geraldine, tr. Wildsmith, Brian, illus. LC 91-22148. 32p. (ps-3). 1992. 15.00 (*0-679-82669-6*); PLB 15.99 (*0-679-92669-0*) Knopf Bks Yng Read.
Jordan, June. Kimako's Story. Burford, Kay, illus. 42p. (gr. k-3). 1991. pap. 3.80 (*0-395-60338-2*, Sandpiper) HM.
Kalman, Maira. Sayonara, Mrs. Kackleman. Kalman, Maira, illus. 40p. (ps-5). 1989. pap. 14.95 (*0-670-82945-5*) Viking Child Bks.
Kroll, Virginia L. A Carp for Kimiko. Roundtree, Katherine, illus. LC 93-6940. 32p. 1993. 14.95 (*0-88106-412-2*); PLB 15.88 (*0-88106-413-0*) Charlesbridge Pub.
Levinson, Riki. Boys Here - Girls There. Ritz, Karen, illus. LC 92-5321. 1993. 13.00 (*0-525-67374-1*, Lodestar Bks) Dutton Child Bks.
Lifton, Betty J. Joji & the Dragon. Mitsui, Eiichi, illus. LC 88-8434. 64p. (gr. 1-3). 1989. Repr. of 1957 ed. lib. bdg. 16.00 (*0-208-02245-7*, Pub. by Linnet) Shoe String.
Lolling, Atsuko G. Aki & the Banner of Names: And Other Stories from Japan. (Orig.). (gr. 1-6). pap. 4.95 (*0-377-00218-6*) Friendship Pr.
Merrill, Jean. The Girl Who Loved Caterpillars. Cooper, Floyd, illus. 32p. (ps up). 1992. PLB 14.95 (*0-399-21871-8*, Philomel Bks) Putnam Pub Group.
Mitchetz, Marc. The Bloody Lotus. Hansom, Dick, tr. from FRE. Bosmans, Serge, illus. 49p. (Orig.). (gr. 12 up). 1990. pap. 7.95 (*0-87416-103-7*, Comcat Comics) Catalan Communs.
Mori, Hana. Jirohattan. Kurosaki, Tamiko & Crowe, Elizabeth, trs. from JPN. Crowe, Elizabeth, illus. LC 93-72833. 80p. (gr. 4-8). 1993. pap. 5.95 (*1-880188-69-4*) Bess Pr.
Mori, Kyoko. Shizuko's Daughter. LC 92-26956. 256p. (gr. 7 up). 1993. 15.95 (*0-8050-2557-X*, Bks Young Read) H Holt & Co.
Mosel, Arlene. The Funny Little Woman. Lent, Blair, illus. LC 75-179046. 40p. (ps-4). 1972. 16.00 (*0-525-30265-4*, 01258-370, DCB); pap. 4.95 (*0-525-45036-X*, DCB) Dutton Child Bks.
—Funny Little Woman. (ps-3). 1993. pap. 4.99 (*0-14-054753-3*, Puffin) Puffin Bks.
Nakawatari, Harutaka. The Sea & I. (Illus.). 32p. (ps-3). 1992. 15.00 (*0-374-36428-1*) FS&G.
Namioka, Lensey. The Coming of the Bear. LC 91-17331. 192p. (gr. 7 up). 1992. PLB 13.89 (*0-06-020289-0*) HarpC Child Bks.
—Island of Ogres. LC 88-22058. 208p. (gr. 7 up). 1989. HarpC Child Bks.
—Valley of the Broken Cherry Trees. LC 79-53605. (gr. 7 up). 1980. 8.95 (*0-440-09325-2*) Delacorte.
Nomura, Takaaki. Grandpa's Town. Stinchecum, Amanda M., tr. from JPN. (Illus.). 32p. (ps-3). 1991. 13.95 (*0-916291-36-7*) Kane-Miller Bk.
Paterson, Katherine. The Master Puppeteer. Wells, Haru, illus. LC 75-8614. 192p. (gr. 6 up). 1976. 15.00 (*0-690-00913-5*, Crowell Jr Bks) HarpC Child Bks.
—Of Nightingales That Weep. LC 74-8294. (Illus.). (gr. 5 up). 1974. 14.00 (*0-690-00485-0*, Crowell Jr Bks) HarpC Child Bks.
—Of Nightingales That Weep. Wells, Haru, illus. LC 74-8294. 192p. (gr. 4 up). 1989. pap. 3.95 (*0-06-440282-7*, Trophy) HarpC Child Bks.
Roe, JoAnn. Samurai Cat: Marco the Manx Ser. (Illus.). 64p. (gr. k-5). 1993. PLB 11.95 (*0-931551-08-0*); pap. 6.95 (*0-931551-07-2*) Montevista Pr.
Sakade, Florence. Kintaro's Adventures & Other Japanese Children's Stories. Hayashi, Yoshio, illus. 60p. (gr. 1-5). 1958. pap. 8.95 (*0-8048-0343-9*) C E Tuttle.
—Little One-Inch & Other Japanese Children's Favorite Stories. (Illus.). 60p. (gr. 1-5). 1958. pap. 8.95 (*0-8048-0384-6*) C E Tuttle.
—Peach Boy & Other Japanese Children's Favorite Stories. Kurosaki, Yoshisuke, illus. 58p. (gr. 1-5). 1958. pap. 8.95 (*0-8048-0469-9*) C E Tuttle.
Sakade, Florence, ed. Urashima Taro & Other Japanese Children's Stories. (Illus.). 58p. (gr. 1-6). 1958. pap. 8.95 (*0-8048-0609-8*) C E Tuttle.
Say, Allen. Grandfather's Journey. LC 93-18836. 32p. 1993. 16.95 (*0-395-57035-2*) HM.
—Tree of Cranes. Say, Allen, illus. 32p. (gr. k-3). 1991. 16.45 (*0-395-52024-X*, Sandpiper) HM.
Soto, Gary. Pacific Crossing. 1992. write for info. (*0-15-259187-7*, HB Juv Bks) HarBrace.
Steiber, Ellen. Shadow of the Fox. LC 94-1295. 108p. (gr. 2-6). 1994. pap. 3.50 (*0-679-86667-1*, Bullseye Bks) Random Bks Yng Read.
Talley, Carol. Hana's Year. Maeno, Itoko, illus. LC 92-19290. 32p. (gr. 1-4). 1992. 16.95 (*1-55942-034-0*, 7652); incl. video & tchr's. guide 79.95 (*1-55942-037-5*, 9371) Marshfilm.
Vaughan, Marcia K. Dorobo the Dangerous. Stone, Kazuko G., illus. LC 93-47891. 1994. 10.95 (*0-382-24076-6*); lib. bdg. 14.95 (*0-382-24070-7*); pap. 4.95 (*0-382-24453-2*) Silver Burdett Pr.
Watkins, Yoko K. So Far from the Bamboo Grove. (Illus.). 192p. (gr. 5 up). 1994. pap. 4.95 (*0-688-13115-8*, Pub. by Beech Tree Bks) Morrow.
Yashima, Taro. Crow Boy. (Illus.). (gr. k-3). 1976. pap. 3.99 (*0-14-050172-X*, Puffin) Puffin Bks.
—Crow Boy. Yashima, T., illus. (gr. k-3). 1955. pap. 14. 99 (*0-670-24931-9*) Viking Child Bks.

JAPAN–FOREIGN RELATIONS–U. S.

Blumberg, Rhoda. Commodore Perry in the Land of the Shogun. LC 84-21800. (Illus.). 128p. (gr. 4 up). 1985. 14.95 (*0-688-03723-2*) Lothrop.

JAPAN–HISTORY

Hyman, Mark. Black Shogun of Japan - Sophonisa: Wife of Two Warring Kings & Other Stories from Antiquity. Massed, Cal, illus. 120p. (Orig.). (gr. 9-12). 1989. pap. 11.00 (*0-915515-01-6*) The Way Pub.
Nardo, Don. Traditional Japan. LC 94-8376. (Illus.). 128p. (gr. 6-9). 1994. 14.95 (*1-56006-244-4*) Lucent Bks.
Odijk, Pamela. The Japanese. (Illus.). 48p. (gr. 5-8). 1991. PLB 12.95 (*0-382-09898-6*); 7.95 (*0-382-24272-6*); tchr's. guide 4.50 (*0-382-24286-6*) Silver Burdett Pr.
Roberts, Jenny. Samurai Warriors. LC 89-26020. 1990. PLB 12.40 (*0-531-17202-3*) Watts.
Tames, Richard. Japan since Nineteen Forty-Five. (Illus.). 72p. (gr. 7-10). 1989. 19.95 (*0-7134-5930-1*, Pub. by Batsford UK) Trafalgar.

JAPAN–HISTORY–1868-1945

Auakian, Monique. The Meiji Restoration & the Rise of Modern Japan. (Illus.). 64p. (gr. 7 up). 1991. PLB 12. 95 (*0-382-24132-0*); pap. 7.95 (*0-382-24139-8*) Silver Burdett Pr.
Morimoto, Junko. My Hiroshima. (Illus.). 32p. (ps-3). 1992. pap. 5.99 (*0-14-054524-7*, Puffin) Puffin Bks.

JAPAN–SOCIAL LIFE AND CUSTOMS

Cobb, Vicki. This Place Is Crowded: Japan. 32p. (gr. 2-4). 1992. 14.95 (*0-8027-8145-4*); lib. bdg. 15.85 (*0-8027-8146-2*) Walker & Co.
Elkin, Judith. A Family in Japan. (Illus.). 32p. (gr. 2-5). 1987. PLB 13.50 (*0-8225-1672-1*) Lerner Pubns.
Kuklin, Susan. Komodo: A Visit with Japanese Children. LC 94-15417. Date not set. write for info. (*0-399-22613-3*, Putnam) Putnam Pub Group.
Sugimoto, Etsu I. Daughter of the Samurai. LC 66-15849. (gr. 9 up). 1966. pap. 14.95 (*0-8048-1655-7*) C E Tuttle.

JAPANESE IN THE U. S.

Brimner, Larry D. Voices from the Camps: Japanese Americans during World War II. LC 93-31956. (Illus.). 160p. (gr. 9-12). 1994. PLB 13.90 (*0-531-11179-2*) Watts.
Brown, Tricia. Japanese American. 1994. write for info. (*0-8050-2353-4*) H Holt & Co.
Chin, Steven A. When Justice Failed: The Fred Korematsu Story. Tamura, David, illus. LC 92-18086. 105p. (gr. 2-5). 1992. PLB 21.34 (*0-8114-7236-1*) Raintree Steck-V.
Hamanaka, Sheila. The Journey: Japanese Americans, Racism, & Renewal. LC 89-22877. (Illus.). 40p. (gr. 5 up). 1990. 18.95 (*0-531-05849-2*); PLB 18.99 (*0-531-08449-3*) Orchard Bks Watts.
Japanese American Curriculum Project, Inc. Staff. Japanese American Journey: The Story of a People. Hongo, Florence M. & Burton, Miyo, eds. LC 85-80521. (Illus.). 181p. (Orig.). (gr. 5-8). 1985. 22.50x (*0-934609-00-4*); pap. 12.95x (*0-934609-01-2*) JACP Inc.
Kitano, Harry. Japanese Americans. (gr. 4-7). 1993. pap. 8.95 (*0-7910-0269-1*) Chelsea Hse.
Leathers, Noel L. The Japanese in America. LC 67-15684. (Illus.). 72p. (gr. 5 up). 1991. PLB 15.95 (*0-8225-0241-0*); pap. 5.95 (*0-8225-1014-6*) Lerner Pubns.
—Japanese in America. 1991. pap. 5.95 (*0-8225-1042-1*) Lerner Pubns.
Moynihan, Daniel P., ed. Japanese Americans. (Illus.). 112p. (gr. 7-12). PLB 16.95 (*0-685-44179-2*, 047831) Know Unltd.
Riehecky, Janet. Japanese Boys' Festival. Stasiak, Krystyna, illus. LC 93-47639. (Illus.). 32p. (ps-2). 1994. PLB 16.40 (*0-516-00695-9*); pap. 3.95 (*0-516-40695-7*) Childrens.
Rolater. Japanese Americans. 1991. 13.95s.p. (*0-86593-138-0*); 18.60 (*0-685-59186-7*) Rourke Corp.
Sagan, Miriam. Tracing Our Japanese Roots. (Illus.). 48p. (gr. 4-7). 1994. 12.95 (*1-56261-160-7*) John Muir.
Savage, Jeff. Kristi Yamaguchi: Pure Gold. LC 92-42190. (Illus.). 64p. (gr. 3 up). 1993. text ed. 13.95 RSBE (*0-87518-583-5*, Dillon) Macmillan Child Grp.
Stanley, Jerry. I Am an American: A True Story of the Japanese Internment. LC 93-41330. (Illus.). 112p. (gr. 4 up). 1994. 15.00 (*0-517-59786-1*); PLB 15.99 (*0-517-59787-X*) Crown Bks Yng Read.
Uchida, Yoshiko. Invisible Thread. 1991. 12.95 (*0-671-74164-0*, J Messner) S&S Trade.

—Journey to Topaz. rev. ed. Carrick, Donald, illus. LC 84-70422. 160p. (gr. 4-12). 1985. pap. 7.95 (*0-916870-85-5*) Creative Arts Bk.

JAPANESE IN THE U. S.–FICTION

Brown, Janet M. Thanksgiving at Obaachan's. Brown, Janet M., illus. LC 93-43933. 1994. 12.95 (*1-879965-07-0*) Polychrome Pub.

Hoobler, Dorothy & Hoobler, Thomas. Aloha Means Come Back: The Story of a World War II Girl. Bleck, Cathie, illus. 64p. (gr. 4-6). 1992. 5.95 (*0-382-24156-8*); PLB 7.95 (*0-382-24148-7*); pap. 3.95 (*0-382-24349-8*) Silver Burdett Pr.

Hosozawa-Nagano, Elaine. Chopsticks from America. Miyata, Masayuki, illus. LC 93-45795. 1994. 12.95 (*1-879965-11-9*) Polychrome Pub.

Kroll, Virginia. Pink Paper Swans. Clouse, Nancy L., illus. LC 93-41093. 32p. (gr. k-3). 1994. 14.99 (*0-8028-5081-2*) Eerdmans.

Kudlinski, Kathleen V. Pearl Harbor is Burning! A Story of World War II. Himler, Ronald, illus. LC 93-15135. 64p. (gr. 2-6). 1993. pap. 3.99 (*0-14-034509-4*, Puffin) Puffin Bks.

Means, Florence C. The Moved-Outers. LC 92-13706. 156p. 1993. pap. 6.95 (*0-8027-7386-9*) Walker & Co.

Salisbury, Graham. Under the Blood Red Sun. LC 94-444. 1994. 15.95 (*0-385-32099-X*) Delacorte.

Savin, Marcia. The Moon Bridge. 1992. 13.95 (*0-590-45873-6*, Scholastic Hardcover) Scholastic Inc.

Say, Allen. Grandfather's Journey. LC 93-18836. 32p. 1993. 16.95 (*0-395-57035-2*) HM.

Shigekawa, Marlene. Bluejay in the Desert. Kikuchi, Isao, illus. LC 92-35424. 36p. (gr. k-4). 1993. 12.95 (*1-879965-04-6*) Polychrome Pub.

Uchida, Yoshiko. A Jar of Dreams. LC 81-3480. 144p. (gr. 5-7). 1981. SBE 13.95 (*0-689-50210-9*, M K McElderry) Macmillan Child Grp.

—A Jar of Dreams. 2nd ed. LC 92-18803. 144p. (gr. 4-7). 1993. pap. 3.95 (*0-689-71672-9*, Aladdin) Macmillan Child Grp.

—Journey Home. Robinson, Charles, illus. LC 78-8792. 144p. (gr. 5-7). 1978. SBE 13.95 (*0-689-50126-9*, M K McElderry) Macmillan Child Grp.

—Journey Home. 2nd ed. Robinson, Charles, illus. LC 91-40149. 144p. (gr. 3-7). 1992. pap. 3.95 (*0-689-71641-9*, Aladdin) Macmillan Child Grp.

Yamate, Sandra S. Day of Remembrance. LC 93-45792. 1994. 12.95 (*1-879965-12-7*) Polychrome Pub.

Yashima, Taro. Umbrella. Yashima, Taro, illus. (ps-1). 1977. pap. 3.99 (*0-14-050240-8*, Puffin) Puffin Bks.

—Umbrella. Yashima, T., illus. (ps-1). 1958. pap. 15.99 (*0-670-73858-1*) Viking Child Bks.

JAPANESE LANGUAGE–CONVERSATION AND PHRASE BOOKS

Burchard, Elizabeth & Brick, Gary. Japanese: In a Flash. 445p. (gr. 7-12). 1994. pap. 9.95 (*1-881374-06-8*) Flash Blasters.

Goodman, Marlene, illus. Let's Learn Japanese Picture Dictionary: Elementary Through Junior High. (JPN.). 80p. (gr. 4-7). 1993. 11.95 (*0-8442-8494-7*, Natl Textbk) NTC Pub Grp.

Hirate, Susan H. & Kawaura, Noriko. Nihongo Daisuki! Japanese Language Activities for Children. LC 89-81822. (JPN & ENG., Illus.). 208p. (gr. k-6). 1990. tchr's ed. 19.95 (*0-935848-82-7*) Bess Pr.

Huntington, Seiko. Japanese "ABCs" Hiragana Learning Cards. Huntington, Seiko, illus. 128p. (Orig.). (gr. 1 up). 1988. pap. 16.95 (*0-936845-05-8*) Sakura Press.

Maeda, Jun. Let's Study Japanese. LC 64-24949. (Illus.). 130p. (gr. 9 up). 1965. pap. 6.95 (*0-8048-0362-5*) C E Tuttle.

Mahoney, Judy. Teach Me Japanese. Satoh, Naomi, tr. Bennett, Charlotte, illus. 20p. (ps-6). 1990. pap. 11.95 incl. audiocassette (*0-934633-17-7*); tchr's. ed. 5.95 (*0-934633-30-4*) Teach Me.

—Teach Me More Japanese. Satoh, Naomi, tr. Kamstra, Angela, illus. (JPN.). 20p. (ps-6). 1991. pap. 13.95 incl. audiocassette (*0-934633-20-7*); tchr's. ed. 6.95 (*0-934633-36-3*) Teach Me.

Metcalf, Florence E. A Peek at Japan: A Lighthearted Look at Japan's Language & Culture. 2nd, rev. ed. Tomoko, illus. 133p. (gr. 1-5). 1992. pap. text ed. 14.95 (*0-9631684-3-6*) Metco Pub.

Murray, D. M. & Wong, T. W. Noodle Words: An Introduction to Chinese & Japanese Characters. LC 79-147179. (Illus.). (gr. 9 up). 1971. pap. 6.95 (*0-8048-0948-8*) C E Tuttle.

Sheheen, Dennis, illus. A Child's Picture English-Japanese Dictionary. (gr. k-6). 1987. 9.95 (*1-55774-000-3*) Modan-Adama Bks.

Turkovich, Marilyn, et al. Omiyage. rev. ed. LC 90-42183. (Illus.). 220p. (gr. 6-12). 1990. looseleaf, incl. audio cass. 44.95 (*0-930141-37-7*) World Eagle.

JAPANESE LANGUAGE–GRAMMAR

Batt, Deleece. Hiragana Gambatte! Hulbert & Hirowatari, eds. (Illus.). 112p. 1994. pap. 10.00 (*4-7700-1797-9*) Kodansha.

Huntington, Seiko. Untangling Nihongo III: A Japanese Workbook, Vol. III. (Illus.). 135p. (Orig.). 1986. pap. 14.95 (*0-936845-02-3*) Sakura Press.

Huntington, Seiko & Huntington, Andrew S. Japanese "ABCs" II: Katakana Learning Cards. (Illus.). 128p. (Orig.). 1990. pap. 16.95 (*0-936845-06-6*) Sakura Press.

Kakutani, Akiko. Japanese for Today: Beginning Japanese Language Workbook. (Illus.). 229p. (Orig.). 1989. wkbk. 5.00 (*0-9619977-3-7*) Earlham College Pr.

Stacy, Selmarie. Ganbatte: (How to Read Japanese) (Illus.). 58p. (Orig.). (gr. 7 up). 1990. pap. 6.95 wkbk. (*0-935984-09-7*) Spheric Hse.

JAPANESE POETRY–COLLECTIONS

Demi, selected by. & illus. In the Eyes of the Cat. Tze-Si Huang, tr. from JPN. LC 91-27729. 80p. (gr. 1-3). 1992. 15.95 (*0-8050-1955-3*, Bks Young Read) H Holt & Co.

Lewis, Richard, ed. In a Spring Garden. Keats, Ezra J., illus. LC 65-23965. 32p. (ps up). 1989. Repr. of 1965 ed. 13.95 (*0-8037-4024-7*) Dial Bks Young.

Navasky, Bruno P., selected by. & tr. Festival in My Heart: Poems by Japanese Children. LC 93-18251. 1993. 29.95 (*0-8109-3314-4*) Abrams.

JAZZ MUSIC

Brown, Sandford. Louis Armstrong: Singing, Swinging Satchmo. LC 92-43192. (Illus.). 144p. (gr. 9-12). 1993. PLB 14.40 (*0-531-13028-2*) Watts.

—Louis Armstrong: Swinging, Singing Satchmo. (Illus.). (gr. 7-12). 1993. pap. 6.95 (*0-531-15680-X*) Watts.

Carlin, Richard. Jazz. (Illus.). 128p. (gr. 7-12). 1991. 17.95x (*0-8160-2229-1*) Facts on File.

Gourse, Leslie. Dizzy Gillespie & the Birth of Bebop. LC 93-30222. (Illus.). 160p. (gr. 7 up). 1994. SBE 14.95 (*0-689-31869-3*, Atheneum Child Bk) Macmillan Child Grp.

Monceaux, Morgan. Jazz. Monceaux, Morgan, illus. LC 93-38177. 1994. 18.00 (*0-679-86518-7*) Knopf Bks Yng Read.

Raschka, Chris. Charlie Parker Played Be Bop. LC 91-38420. (Illus.). 32p. (ps-1). 1992. 13.95 (*0-531-05999-5*); PLB 13.99 (*0-531-08599-6*) Orchard Bks Watts.

Terkel, Studs. Giants of Jazz. 2nd ed. LC 75-20024. (Illus.). 192p. (gr. 7 up). 1992. PLB 16.89 (*0-690-04917-X*, Crowell Jr Bks) HarpC Child Bks.

Wyman, Carolyn. Ella Fitzgerald: Jazz Singer Supreme. (Illus.). 144p. (gr. 9-12). 1993. PLB 14.40 (*0-531-13031-2*) Watts.

JAZZ MUSIC–FICTION

Collier, James L. The Jazz Kid. 1994. 15.95 (*0-8050-2821-8*) H Holt & Co.

Hurd, Thacher. Mama Don't Allow. LC 83-47703. (Illus.). 40p. (ps-3). 1984. 16.00 (*0-06-022689-7*); PLB 15.89 (*0-06-022690-0*) HarpC Child Bks.

Weik, Mary H. The Jazz Man. 2nd ed. Grifalconi, Ann, illus. LC 93-9965. 48p. (gr. 3-7). 1993. pap. 3.95 (*0-689-71767-9*, Aladdin) Macmillan Child Grp.

JAZZ MUSIC–HISTORY

Longstreet, Stephen. Magic Trumpets: The Story of Jazz for Young People. Longstreet, Stephen, illus. (Orig.). (gr. 7 up). 1989. pap. 16.95 (*0-913705-42-X*) Zephyr Pr AZ.

JEEPS

see Automobiles; Trucks

JEFFERSON, THOMAS, PRESIDENT U. S. 1743-1826

Adler, David A. A Picture Book of Thomas Jefferson. Wallner, John & Wallner, Alexandra, illus. LC 89-20076. 32p. (ps-3). 1990. reinforced bdg. 15.95 (*0-8234-0791-8*); pap. 5.95 (*0-8234-0881-7*) Holiday.

—Thomas Jefferson: Father of Our Democracy. Garrick, Jacqueline, illus. LC 87-45336. 48p. (gr. 2-5). 1987. reinforced bdg. 14.95 (*0-8234-0667-9*) Holiday.

Barrett, Marvin. Meet Thomas Jefferson. Fogarty, Pat, illus. LC 88-19069. 72p. (gr. 2-4). 1989. pap. 2.99 (*0-394-81964-0*) Random Bks Yng Read.

Bober, Natalie. Thomas Jefferson: Man on a Mountain. LC 87-37462. (Illus.). 288p. (gr. 7 up). 1988. SBE 15.95 (*0-689-31154-0*, Atheneum Child Bk) Macmillan Child Grp.

Bober, Natalie S. Thomas Jefferson: Man on a Mountain. LC 92-35604. (Illus.). 288p. (gr. 7 up). 1993. pap. 6.95 (*0-02-041797-7*, Collier Young Ad) Macmillan Child Grp.

Colver, Anne. Thomas Jefferson: Author of Independence. (Illus.). 80p. (gr. 2-6). 1993. Repr. of 1963 ed. lib. bdg. 12.95 (*0-7910-1443-6*) Chelsea Hse.

Crisman, Ruth. Thomas Jefferson, Man with a Vision. (gr. 4-7). 1992. pap. 2.95 (*0-590-44553-7*) Scholastic Inc.

Farr, Naunerle C. George Washington-Thomas Jefferson. Carrillo, Fred & Cruz, E. R., illus. (gr. 4-12). 1979. pap. text ed. 2.95 (*0-88301-355-X*); wkbk. 1.25 (*0-88301-379-7*) Pendulum Pr.

Giblin, James C. Thomas Jefferson: A Picture Book Biography. Dooling, Michael, illus. LC 93-23340. (gr. k-3). 1994. 14.95 (*0-590-44838-2*) Scholastic Inc.

Greene, Carol. Thomas Jefferson: Author, Inventor, President. LC 91-16363. (Illus.). 48p. (gr. k-3). 1991. PLB 12.85 (*0-516-04224-6*); pap. 4.95 (*0-516-44224-4*) Childrens.

Hargrove, Jim. Thomas Jefferson. LC 86-9658. (Illus.). 100p. (gr. 3 up). 1986. PLB 14.40 (*0-516-01385-8*); pap. 6.95 (*0-516-41385-6*) Childrens.

Hilton, Suzanne. The World of Young Tom Jefferson. Bock, William S., illus. 96p. (gr. 3-6). 1986. 12.95 (*0-8027-6621-8*); lib. bdg. 12.85 (*0-8027-6622-6*) Walker & Co.

Komroff, Manuel. Thomas Jefferson. LC 90-49177. (Illus.). 160p. (gr. 6-10). 1991. PLB 13.95 (*1-55905-083-7*) Marshall Cavendish.

Meltzer, Milton. Thomas Jefferson: The Revolutionary Aristocrat. LC 91-15943. (Illus.). 256p. (gr. 9-12). 1991. 16.45 (*0-531-15227-8*); PLB 16.40 (*0-531-11069-9*) Watts.

Monsell, Helen A. Tom Jefferson: The Third President of the United States. LC 89-37841. (Illus.). 192p. (gr. 2-6). 1989. pap. 3.95 (*0-689-71347-9*, Aladdin) Macmillan Child Grp.

Morris, Jeffrey. The Jefferson Way. LC 94-923. (Illus.). 112p. (gr. 5 up). 1994. 22.95 (*0-8225-2926-2*) Lerner Pubns.

Nardo, Don. Thomas Jefferson. LC 92-43913. (Illus.). 111p. (gr. 5-8). 1993. PLB 14.95 (*1-56006-037-9*) Lucent Bks.

Quackenbush, Robert. Pass the Quill; I'll Write a Draft: A Story of Thomas Jefferson. Quackenbush, Robert, illus. 32p. (gr. 2-6). 1989. PLB 14.95 (*0-945912-07-2*) Pippin Pr.

Reef, Catherine. Monticello. LC 91-15850. (Illus.). 72p. (gr. 4-6). 1991. text ed. 14.95 RSBE (*0-87518-472-3*, Dillon) Macmillan Child Grp.

Sabin, Francene. Young Thomas Jefferson. Baxter, Robert, illus. LC 85-1093. 48p. (gr. 4-6). 1985. lib. bdg. 10.79 (*0-8167-0561-5*); pap. text ed. 3.50 (*0-8167-0562-3*) Troll Assocs.

Sandak, Cass R. The Jeffersons. LC 91-33061. (Illus.). 48p. (gr. 5). 1992. text ed. 12.95 RSBE (*0-89686-637-8*, Crestwood Hse) Macmillan Child Grp.

Santrey, Laurence. Thomas Jefferson. Eitzen, Allan, illus. LC 84-2579. 32p. (gr. 3-6). 1985. PLB 9.49 (*0-8167-0176-8*); pap. text ed. 2.95 (*0-8167-0177-6*) Troll Assocs.

Shorto, Russell. Thomas Jefferson & the American Ideal. (Illus.). 144p. (gr. 3-6). 1987. pap. 5.95 (*0-8120-3918-1*) Barron.

Smith, Kathie B. Thomas Jefferson. Steltenpohl, Jane, ed. Seward, James, illus. 24p. (gr. 4-6). 1989. lib. bdg. 7.98 (*0-671-67512-5*, J Messner); PLB 5.99s.p. (*0-685-25428-3*) S&S Trade.

Smith, Kathie B. & Bradbury, Pamela Z. Thomas Jefferson. (Illus.). 32p. (ps up). 1989. pap. 2.25 (*0-671-64768-7*, Little Simon) S&S Trade.

Stefoff, Rebecca. Thomas Jefferson: 3rd President of the United States. Young, Richard G., ed. LC 87-32818. (Illus.). (gr. 5-9). 1988. PLB 17.26 (*0-944483-07-0*) Garrett Ed Corp.

Wade. Thomas Jefferson. (gr. 4-12). 1993. PLB 8.49 (*0-87386-035-7*); pap. 1.95 (*0-87386-084-5*) Jan Prods.

JEFFERSON, THOMAS, PRESIDENT U. S. 1743-1826–FICTION

Rinaldi, Ann. Wolf by the Ears. 1991. 13.95 (*0-590-43413-6*, Scholastic Hardcover) Scholastic Inc.

JELLYFISHES

Gowell, Elizabeth T. Sea Jellies: Rainbows in the Sea. LC 92-38515. (Illus.). 56p. (gr. 5-8). 1993. 15.95 (*0-531-15259-6*); PLB 15.90 (*0-531-11152-0*) Watts.

Kite, Patricia. Down in the Sea: The Jellyfish. Levine, Abby, ed. LC 92-12834. (Illus.). 24p. (ps-3). 1993. 13.95 (*0-8075-1712-7*) A Whitman.

Shale, David & Coldrey, Jennifer. The World of a Jellyfish. LC 86-5704. (Illus.). 32p. (gr. 2-3). 1986. 17.27 (*1-55532-073-2*) Gareth Stevens Inc.

Stone, Lynn M. Jellyfish. LC 93-19462. 1993. write for info. (*0-86593-284-0*) Rourke Corp.

JEMISON, MARY, 1743-1833

Lenski, Lois. Indian Captive: The Story of Mary Jemison. Lenski, Lois, illus. LC 41-51956. 272p. (gr. 7-9). 1990. 16.00 (*0-397-30072-7*, Lipp Jr Bks); PLB 15.89 (*0-397-30076-X*, Lipp Jr Bks) HarpC Child Bks.

JENGHIS KHAN, 1162-1227

Demi. Chingis Khan. Demi, illus. LC 90-28807. 64p. (gr. 3-5). 1991. 19.95 (*0-8050-1708-9*, Bks Young Read) H Holt & Co.

Lamb, Harold. Genghis Khan & the Mongol Horde. Fax, Elton, illus. LC 90-6328. viii, 182p. (gr. 5 up). 1990. Repr. of 1954 ed. lib. bdg. 16.50 (*0-208-02287-2*, Linnet) Shoe String.

JEROME, SAINT, 340?-420

Hodges, Margaret, retold by. St. Jerome & the Lion. Moser, Barry, illus. LC 90-22142. 32p. (ps-2). 1991. 14.95 (*0-531-05938-3*); RLB 14.99 (*0-531-08538-4*) Orchard Bks Watts.

JERUSALEM

Kuskin, Karla. Jerusalem, Shining Still. Frampton, David, illus. LC 86-25841. 32p. (ps up). 1987. 13.95 (*0-06-023548-9*); PLB 13.89 (*0-06-023549-7*) HarpC Child Bks.

Pirotta, Saviour. Jerusalem. LC 92-30130. (Illus.). 48p. (gr. 5 up). 1993. text ed. 13.95 RSBE (*0-87518-569-X*, Dillon) Macmillan Child Grp.

Shaw, Lee H., Jr. How to Live Forever in the New Jerusalem. 56p. (Orig.). (gr. 9-12). 1985. pap. 3.00x (*0-9614311-0-5*) Elijah-John.

Zanger, Walter. Jerusalem. (Illus.). 64p. (gr. 3-7). PLB 14.95 (*1-56711-022-3*) Blackbirch.

JERUSALEM–FICTION

Geras, Adele. Golden Windows: And Other Stories of Jerusalem. LC 92-39885. 160p. (gr. 3-7). 1993. 14.00 (*0-06-022941-1*); PLB 13.89 (*0-06-022942-X*) HarpC Child Bks.

Kimmel, Eric A. Asher & the Capmakers: A Hanukkah Story. Hillenbrand, Will, illus. LC 92-37978. 32p. (ps-3). 1993. reinforced bdg. 15.95 (*0-8234-1031-5*) Holiday.

Parker, Lois. Return to Jerusalem. Wheeler, Gerald, ed. 160p. (Orig.). 1988. pap. 6.95 (*0-8280-0426-9*) Review & Herald.

Weil, Judith. School for One. (gr. 4 up). 1992. 11.95 (*0-87306-620-0*); pap. 9.95 (*0-87306-621-9*) Feldheim.

JESUS CHRIST

see also Christianity

Aprendamos de Jesus: Learning about Jesus. (SPA.). 32p. 1987. pap. 1.50 (*0-311-26610-X*) Casa Bautista.

Balika, Susan S. Jesus Is My Special Friend. Beegle, Shirley, ed. Boldman, Craig, illus. 24p. (ps-3). 1994. pap. 1.89 (*0-7847-0261-6*) Standard Pub.

Ball, Ann. Holy Names of Jesus: Devotions, Litanies, Meditations. LC 90-60646. 192p. (Orig.). 1990. pap. 7.95 (*0-87973-428-0*, 428) Our Sunday Visitor.

Batchelor, Mary. The Story of Jesus. Haysom, John, illus. 192p. (gr. 1-6). 1992. 14.95 (*0-7459-1884-0*) Lion USA.

Berthier, Rene. Jesus, Friend of Children. (Illus.). 80p. (gr. 2-8). 1990. 9.99 (*0-85648-053-3*); pap. 6.99 (*0-85648-316-8*) Lion USA.

Bomer, John M., tr. from FRE. A Child's Life of Jesus. Napoli, Lizzi, illus. LC 89-81355. 40p. (Orig.). (ps-2). 1990. 8.95 (*0-87793-415-0*) Ave Maria.

Brennan-Nichols, Patricia. Getting to Know Jesus. Haberson, Lydia, illus. 68p. (Orig.). (gr. k-3). 1984. pap. 5.20 (*0-89505-130-3*, R0610) Tabor Pub.

—Learning to Love Jesus. (Illus.). 80p. (Orig.). (gr. 4-6). 1985. tchr's. guide 15.95 (*0-89505-329-2*, R0520); pap. 5.20 72p. (*0-89505-328-4*, R0510) Tabor Pub.

D. C. Cook Editors. The Big Picture Book about Jesus. Hook, Richard & Hook, Frances, illus. LC 77-72722. (ps-2). 1977. 13.99 (*0-89191-077-8*, 08292, Chariot Bks) Chariot Family.

Daniel, Rebecca. Book IV-the Teacher. McClure, Nancee, illus. 32p. (gr. 2-7). 1984. wkbk. 7.95 (*0-86653-225-0*, SS 827, Shining Star Pubns) Good Apple.

—Book VI-His Miracles. McClure, Nancee, illus. 32p. (gr. 2-7). 1984. wkbk. 7.95 (*0-86653-227-7*, SS 829, Shining Star Pubns) Good Apple.

—Book VII-His Parables. McClure, Nancee, illus. 32p. (gr. 2-7). 1984. wkbk. 7.95 (*0-86653-228-5*, SS 830, Shining Star Pubns) Good Apple.

—Book X-His Last Days. McClure, Nancee, illus. 32p. (gr. 2-7). 1984. wkbk. 6.95 (*0-86653-231-5*, SS 833, Shining Star Pubns) Good Apple.

—Book XI-His Last Hours. McClure, Nancee, illus. 32p. (gr. 2-7). 1984. wkbk. 7.95 (*0-86653-232-3*, SS 834, Shining Star Pubns) Good Apple.

—Book XII-His Resurrection. McClure, Nancee, illus. 32p. (gr. 2-7). 1984. wkbk. 7.95 (*0-86653-233-1*, SS 835, Shining Star Pubns) Good Apple.

—Jesus & His Miracles. 16p. (ps-3). 1991. 16.95 (*0-86653-634-5*, SS1879, Shining Star Pubns) Good Apple.

Daughters of St. Paul. I Learn about Jesus. LC 72-91979. Date not set. 9.95 (*0-8198-0246-8*); pap. 4.00 (*0-8198-0247-6*) St Paul Bks.
I LEARN ABOUT JESUS is a user-friendly child's first book about Jesus. In its simple dialogue & spare narratives, it would be appropriate to read to very young children. In addition, its large type, open formatting & full-page color illustrations could certainly appeal to young readers. Furthermore, the book would be a good preparation for a child's first formal religious instruction. Sr. Mary Elizabeth Tebo makes this story especially pertinent to young people by emphazing their personal relationship with God, that God loves them & is the source of their happiness. The book stands out in large part for its many beautiful illustrations by Sister C. Gondolfo, who expresses the Christian mysteries in a simplicity of form & composition. "By presenting Jesus in story-time, Sisters Tebo & Gondolfo engage children & parents alike in the life of Christ, & in the process help to keep going the story of our Redemption." - Paul Matthew St. Pierre, THE B.C. CATHOLIC. To order, please call 880-876-4463.
Publisher Provided Annotation.

Davis, Susan. Password to Heaven. 32p. (gr. k-3). 1980. pap. 2.50 (*0-8127-0298-0*) Review & Herald.

Dean, Bessie. Let's Learn about Jesus: A Child's Coloring Book of the Life of Christ. (Illus.). 72p. (ps-6). 1988. pap. 5.98 (*0-88290-131-1*) Horizon Utah.

Dede, Vivian. Jesus' First Miracle. LC 59-1445. (Illus.). 24p. (ps-4). 1990. pap. 1.99 (*0-570-09022-9*) Concordia.

Deedat, Ahmed. Was Jesus Crucified. Obaba, Al I., ed. 49p. (Orig.). 1991. pap. text ed. 2.00 (*0-916157-72-5*) African Islam Miss Pubns.

De Paola, Tomie. The Miracles of Jesus. De Paola, Tomie, illus. LC 86-18297. 32p. (gr. k-4). 1987. reinforced bdg. 15.95 (*0-8234-0635-0*) Holiday.

Downey, Melissa C. & Lingo, Susan L. Miracles of Jesus. Hayes, Theresa, ed. Green, Roy, illus. 32p. (Orig.). (gr. 1-5). 1994. wkbk. 3.99 (*0-7847-0141-5*) Standard Pub.

Enns, Peter & Forsberg, Glen. Jesus Is Alive! & Five Other Stories. Friesen, John H., illus. 24p. (ps-5). 1985. book & cassette 4.95 (*0-936215-06-2*) STL Intl.

Erickson, Mary E. Miracle in the Morning: The Wonderful Story of Easter. LC 92-20260. 1993. 10.99 (*0-7814-0779-6*, Chariot Bks) Chariot Family.

Evans, Helen K. Jesus, My Friend. 64p. (ps-3). 1988. 8.95 (*0-86653-428-8*, SS1856, Shining Star Pubns) Good Apple.

Fahs, Sophia L. Jesus - the Carpenter's Son. rev. ed. Baldridge, Cyrus L., illus. 160p. 1990. pap. 14.95 (*1-55896-191-7*) Unitarian Univ.

Fogle, Jeanne S. Symbols of God's Love: Codes & Passwords. Ducket, Mary Jean & Lane, W. Ben, eds. Weidner, Bea, illus. LC 86-12014. 32p. (Orig.). (gr. k-3). 1986. pap. 7.99 (*0-664-24050-X*, Westminster) Westminster John Knox.

Frank, Penny. The First Easter. Haysom, John & Morris, Tony, illus. Burow, Daniel, contrib. by. LC 92-31640. 1992. 6.95 (*0-7459-2607-X*) Lion USA.

—Jesus the King. (ps-3). 1984. 3.95 (*0-85648-771-6*) Lion USA.

—Secrets Jesus Told. (Illus.). 24p. (ps-4). 1982. 3.99 (*0-85648-762-7*) Lion USA.

Gambill, Henrietta, ed. Jesus Stills the Storm & Other Miracles: Little Moving Picture Book. (Illus.). 10p. 1994. 3.99 (*0-7847-0210-1*, 24-03150) Standard Pub.

Gangwer, Rosalie M. Jesus Calms the Storm: Matthew 8, 23-27 & Mark 4, 35-41 for the Beginning Reader. Mitter, Kathryn, illus. LC 93-17472. 32p. (ps-3). 1993. 6.50 (*0-8198-3955-8*) St Paul Bks.

Giampa, Linda. Jesus & Me, ABC Activity Book. (Illus.). 32p. (Orig.). (ps-2). 1991. pap. 2.99 (*0-570-04198-8*) Concordia.

Glavich, Mary K. A Child's Book of Miracles. LC 94-2378. (gr. 3 up). 1994. 2.50 (*0-8294-0802-9*) Loyola.

Griffin, Henry W. Jesus for Children. Swisher, Elizabeth, illus. 132p. 1986. 12.95 (*0-685-43036-7*) Harper SF.

Groth, Lynn. Jesus Loves Children. 16p. (Orig.). (ps). 1985. pap. 1.25 (*0-938272-78-0*) Wels Board.

—Reaching Tender Hearts, Vol. 1. Grunze, Richard, ed. May, Lawrence & Steele, Loren, illus. 157p. (ps-k). 1987. pap. 7.95 (*0-938272-42-X*) WELS Board.

—Reaching Tender Hearts, Vol. 2. Grunze, Richard, ed. May, Lawrence & Steele, Loren, illus. 176p. (ps-k). 1988. pap. 8.95 (*0-938272-43-8*) WELS Board.

—A Very Special Baby-Jesus. 8p. (Orig.). (ps). 1985. pap. 1.25 (*0-938272-76-4*) Wels Board.

Hall. Loaves & Fishes. 1992. 7.49 (*0-7814-0021-X*, Chariot Bks) Chariot Family.

Hardel, Dick. Jesus' Death & Resurrection. (Illus.). 48p. (gr. 9-12). 1991. pap. 8.99 (*1-55945-211-0*) Group Pub.

—Who Is Jesus? (Illus.). 48p. (gr. 9-12). 1991. pap. 8.99 (*1-55945-219-6*) Group Pub.

Harmon. My Jesus Pocket Book of Prayer. 1992. pap. 0.69 (*1-55513-733-4*, Chariot Bks) Chariot Family.

Hayes, Wanda. Jesus Makes Me Happy. Beegle, Shirley, ed. Hook, Frances, illus. 24p. (ps-3). 1994. pap. 1.89 (*0-7847-0263-2*) Standard Pub.

Holmes, Andy. Away in a Manger. (ps-3). 1992. 5.99 (*0-929216-49-0*) HSH Edu Media Co.

—Fairest Lord Jesus. (ps). 1992. 5.99 (*0-929216-58-X*) HSH Edu Media Co.

—Jesus Is All the World to Me. (ps-3). 1992. 5.99 (*0-929216-54-7*) HSH Edu Media Co.

—Jesus Loves Me. (ps-3). 1992. 5.99 (*0-929216-55-5*) HSH Edu Media Co.

—Jesus Loves the Little Children. (ps). 1992. 5.99 (*0-929216-56-3*) HSH Edu Media Co.

—O' How I Love Jesus. (ps). 1992. 5.99 (*0-929216-57-1*) HSH Edu Media Co.

—O' Little Town of Bethlehem. (ps-3). 1992. 5.99 (*0-929216-51-2*) HSH Edu Media Co.

—Silent Night. (ps-3). 1992. 5.99 (*0-929216-50-4*) HSH Edu Media Co.

—Tell Me the Stories of Jesus. (ps-3). 1992. 5.99 (*0-929216-59-8*) HSH Edu Media Co.

Hornsby, Sarah. Getting to Know Jesus from A to Z. LC 89-6109. 1989. 9.99 (*0-8007-1624-8*) Revell.

Hostetler, Marian. We Knew Jesus. 160p. (Orig.). (gr. 4-8). 1994. pap. 5.95 (*0-8361-3653-5*) Herald Pr.

Jesus Tambien Fue Joven - Jesus Was Also Young. (SPA.). 64p. (gr. 11 up). 1993. pap. 2.85 (*0-311-12255-8*) Casa Bautista.

Klug, Ron & Klug, Lyn. Jesus Lives. LC 82-72848. 32p. (Orig.). (ps). 1982. pap. 5.99 (*0-8066-1952-X*, 10-3527, Augsburg) Augsburg Fortress.

—Jesus Loves: Stories about Jesus for Children. Konsterile, Paul, illus. LC 86-81807. 32p. (Orig.). (gr. 3-8). 1986. saddlestitch 5.99 (*0-8066-2235-0*, 10-3526, Augsburg) Augsburg Fortress.

Lashbrook, Marilyn. The Best Day Ever: The Story of Jesus. Sharp, Chris, illus. LC 90-63764. (gr. k-3). 1991. 5.95 (*0-86606-444-3*, 875) Roper Pr.

Leone, Dee. The Miracles of Jesus. 48p. (ps-1). 1990. 7.95 (*0-86653-554-3*, SS1874, Shining Star Pubns) Good Apple.

Lindvall, Ella K. My Friend Jesus. Walles, Dwight, illus. 32p. (Orig.). (gr. 1-3). 1989. pap. 2.99 (*0-8024-5949-8*) Moody.

Lion Books Staff. Jesus on Trial. (ps-3). 1994. pap. 1.99 (*0-7459-1792-5*) Lion USA.

Lions Books Staff. Jesus the King. (ps-3). 1994. pap. 1.99 (*0-7459-1791-7*) Lion USA.

Logan, Anna & Koehler, Ed. The Jesus Tree Activity Book. (Illus.). 48p. (Orig.). (ps-2). 1991. pap. 4:99 (*0-570-04197-X*) Concordia.

The Lord Is My Shepherd. (Illus.). (gr. k-6). 1963. visualized song 4.99 (*3-90117-004-9*) CEF Press.

Lost & Found Kit. (gr. k-6). 1978. 19.99 (*1-55976-105-9*) CEF Press.

Lysne, Mary E. Come & See. Gambill, Henrietta, ed. Patterson, Kathleen, illus. 24p. (ps-3). 1993. wkbk. 2.39 (*0-7847-0104-0*, 23-02584) Standard Pub.

—Parables of Jesus. Gambill, Henrietta, ed. Patterson, Kathleen, illus. 24p. (ps-3). 1993. wkbk. 2.39 (*0-7847-0102-4*, 23-02582) Standard Pub.

—What Happened? Gambill, Henrietta, ed. Patterson, Kathleen, illus. 24p. (ps-3). 1993. wkbk. 2.39 (*0-7847-0103-2*, 23-02583) Standard Pub.

McAllister, Dawson. A Walk with Christ Through the Resurrection. Whitney, Roger, illus. (gr. 5-12). 1981. pap. 8.95 (*0-923417-14-1*) Shepherd Minst.

—A Walk with Christ to the Cross. Whitney, Roger, illus. (gr. 5-12). 1980. pap. 8.95 (*0-923417-09-5*) Shepherd Minst.

—Who Are You, Jesus? Lewis, Paul, illus. (gr. 5-12). 1986. pap. 7.95 (*0-923417-05-2*) Shepherd Minst.

McAllister, Dawson & Kimmel, Tim. Walk with Christ to the Cross. (gr. 5-12). 1981. pap. 5.95 tchr's. guide (*0-923417-20-6*) Shepherd Minst.

McAllister, Dawson & May, Tom. Who Are You Jesus? (gr. 5-12). 1986. pap. 7.95 tchr's. guide (*0-923417-03-6*) Shepherd Minst.

MacDonald, Kenneth B. & MacDonald, Agnes. The Second Coming: Tough Questions Answered. 300p. (Orig.). 1991. pap. text ed. 9.95 (*0-9626490-0-7*) Revivals & Missions.

McFadzean, Anita. One Special Star. Jaspers, Kate, illus. LC 90-21485. 32p. (ps-1). 1991. pap. 11.95 jacketed (*0-671-74023-7*, S&S BFYR); pap. 3.95 (*0-671-74024-5*, Little Simon) S&S Trade.

Marchand, Roger. Meeting Jesus in Holy Communion. 32p. (gr. 1-3). 1984. pap. 2.95 (*0-89243-202-0*) Liguori Pubns.

Marquart, M. Jesus' Second Family. (gr. k-2). 1977. pap. 1.99 (*0-570-06111-3*, 59-1229) Concordia.

My Book about Jesus. (Illus.). 32p. (ps-2). 1985. 1.95 (*0-225-66388-0*) Harper SF.

Nargi, Ben J. Are You He Who Is to Come. LC 88-51027. 138p. 1989. pap. 6.95 (*1-55523-177-2*) Winston-Derek.

Neff, Lavonne. Jesus Is Born! The Life of Christ for Children. (ps-3). 1994. 6.99 (*0-8423-1864-X*) Tyndale.

—Miracles of Jesus: The Life of Christ for Children. (ps-3). 1994. 6.99 (*0-8423-3970-1*) Tyndale.

Nystrom, Carolyn. Growing Jesus' Way. (ps-3). 1994. 5.99 (*0-8024-7860-3*) Moody.

—When Jesus Comes Back. (ps-3). 1994. 5.99 (*0-8024-7861-1*) Moody.

—Who Is Jesus? 32p. (ps-2). 1980. pap. 4.99 (*0-8024-6159-X*) Moody.

—Who Is Jesus? Children's Bible Basics. 30p. 1992. 5.99 (*0-8024-7856-5*) Moody.

Odor, Ruth S. Followers of Jesus. Williams, Karin, illus. LC 91-67210. 32p. (gr. 5-7). 1992. saddle-stitch 5.99 (*0-87403-933-9*, 24-03563) Standard Pub.

Oetting, R. When Jesus Was a Lad. LC 68-56816. (Illus.). 32p. (gr. 2-3). 1968. PLB 9.95x (*0-87783-047-9*) Oddo.

Pankow, Eleanor. Let's Talk about Jesus. (Illus.). (gr. k-6). 1963. 3.99 (*3-90117-015-4*) CEF Press.

Parry, Alan & Parry, Linda. Jesus is Alive! Parry, Alan, illus. 24p. (ps). 1990. pap. 0.99 (*0-8066-2479-5*, 9-2479) Augsburg Fortress.

—Paul Meets Jesus. Parry, Alan, illus. 24p. (ps). 1990. pap. 0.99 (*0-8066-2480-9*, 9-2480) Augsburg Fortress.

Parry, Linda & Parry, Alan. Jesus & You. Parry, Linda & Parry, Alan, illus. LC 91-71033. 10p. (ps-k). 1991. 3.99 (*0-8066-2557-0*, 9-2557, Augsburg) Augsburg Fortress.

—Jesus Loves You. Parry, Linda & Parry, Alan, illus. LC 91-71034. 10p. 1991. 5.99 (*0-8066-2558-9*, 9-2558, Augsburg) Augsburg Fortress.

Pennock, Michael. Jesus: Friend & Savior. LC 89-82459. (Orig.). (gr. 9-12). 1990. pap. text ed. 7.95 student text, 208p. (*0-87793-420-7*); tchr's. manual, 176p. 10. 95 (*0-87793-421-5*) Ave Maria.

Pipe, Rhona. The Easter Story. Spencely, Annabel, illus. LC 92-13325. 1993. 7.99 (*0-8407-3420-4*) Nelson.

Pipe, Rhona & Hunt. Where's Jesus? An Interactive Bible Storybook. (ps-3). 1993. 7.99 (*1-56507-146-8*) Harvest Hse.

Rosen, Ruth, ed. Jesus for Jews. Owens, Nate, illus. LC 87-20343. 336p. (Orig.). (gr. 12). 1987. 13.95 (*0-9616148-3-8*); pap. 7.95 (*0-9616148-4-6*); pap. 4.95 mass market (*0-9616148-2-X*) Purple Pomegranate.

Round, Graham. Jesus Saves. (ps). 1992. 5.99 (*0-8423-1873-9*) Tyndale.

Royer, Katherine. Nursery Stories of Jesus. (Illus.). 48p. (ps). 1957. pap. 3.95 (*0-8361-1276-8*) Herald Pr.

Sattgast, Elkins & Sattgast, Linda. Teach Me about Jesus. 160p. (ps-2). 1994. 9.99 (*0-88070-635-X*, Gold & Honey) Questar Pubs.

Seims, Tom. Miracles & Wonders. Arbuckle, Scott, illus. 32p. (Orig.). 1993. 7.99 (*1-56476-046-4*, Victor Books) SP Pubns.

—People & Places. Arbuckle, Scott, illus. 32p. (Orig.). 1993. 7.99 (*1-56476-047-2*, Victor Books) SP Pubns.
Senterfitt, Marilyn. Celebrate Jesus. 144p. (gr. 1-6). 1988. 11.95 (*0-86653-425-3*, SS845, Shining Star Pubns) Good Apple.
Simon, Mary M. Little Visits with Jesus. (Illus.). 256p. (ps-3). 1987. 12.99 (*0-570-03076-5*, 6-1191); pap. 9.99 (*0-570-03075-7*, 06-1190) Concordia.
—Sit Down! Mary & Martha. Jones, Dennis, illus. 24p. (Orig.). (ps-1). 1991. pap. 2.49 (*0-570-04701-3*) Concordia.
—Through the Roof. Jones, Dennis, illus. LC 93-36193. 32p. (Orig.). (gr. 1-3). 1994. pap. 3.99 (*0-570-04734-X*) Concordia.
—A Walk on the Waves: Matthew 14: 13-32: Jesus Walks on the Water. Jones, Dennis, illus. LC 92-21374. 32p. (Orig.). (gr. 1-3). 1993. pap. 3.99 (*0-570-04735-8*) Concordia.
—Where Is Jesus? Easter. Jones, Dennis, illus. 24p. (Orig.). (ps-1). 1991. pap. 2.49 (*0-570-04703-X*) Concordia.
Sparks, Judy, ed. Yes! Jesus Loves Me. Woggon, Bill, illus. 24p. (ps-2). 1985. 2.50 (*0-87239-882-X*, 3682) Standard Pub.
Stewart, Pat, illus. Jesus' Bethlehem Birthday. (ps-1). 1989. 9.99 (*1-55513-814-4*, Chariot Bks) Chariot Family.
Stirrup Associates, Inc. Staff. My Jesus Pocketbook of the Beginning. Harvey, Bonnie C. & Phillips, Cheryl M., eds. Burnett, Lindy, illus. LC 84-50918. 32p. (Orig.). (ps-3). 1984. pap. 0.69 (*0-937420-14-X*) Stirrup Assoc.
Stoner, Laura M. Jesus: A Story Color Book. (Illus.). 80p. (Orig.). (gr. 1-8). 1985. pap. 3.95 wkbk. (*0-934426-07-4*) Napsac Reprods.
Stortz, Diane. Five Small Loaves & Two Small Fish. Stites, Joe, illus. 28p. (ps). 1992. 2.50 (*0-87403-953-3*, 24-03593) Standard Pub.
—No Problem! Stuart, Don, illus. 28p. (ps). 1992. 2.50 (*0-87403-954-1*, 24-03594) Standard Pub.
Sumrall, Lester. Adventuring with Christ. 2nd ed. 161p. 1988. Repr. of 1938 ed. text ed. 11.95 (*0-937580-13-9*) LeSEA Pub Co.
Sutherland, E. A. Studies in Christian Education: Christ's Education Was Gained from Heaven-Appointed Sources, from Useful Work, from the Study of the Scriptures, from Nature, & from the Experiences of Life - God's Lesson Books. 160p. (gr. 9 up). 1989. pap. 6.95 (*0-945460-04-X*) Upward Way.
Tangvald, Christine. Jesus Is for Me. LC 88-70664. 24p. (ps-1). 1989. pap. 3.99 (*1-55513-740-7*, Chariot Bks) Chariot Family.
—What Is the Best Thing about Jesus? Stortz, Diane, ed. (Illus.). 32p. (ps-2). 1994. 12.99 (*0-7847-0164-4*) Standard Pub.
Taylor, Ken. Good News for Little People. (ps-2). 1991. 10.99 (*0-8423-6628-8*) Tyndale.
Taylor, Mark A. Breakfast with Jesus. Stiles, Andy, illus. 28p. (ps). 1993. PLB 4.99 (*0-7847-0037-0*, 24-03827) Standard Pub.
Thomas, Mack. What Would Jesus Do? Mortenson, Denis, illus. 253p. (ps-2). 1991. 12.99 (*0-945564-05-8*, Gold & Honey) Questar Pubs.
Waggoner, E. J. Christ & His Righteousness. 96p. (gr. 9 up). 1988. pap. 5.95 (*0-945460-01-5*) Upward Way.
Watson, E. Elaine. Jesus Loves Me All the Time. Beegle, Shirley, ed. Arthur, Lorraine, illus. 24p. (ps-3). 1994. pap. 1.89 (*0-7847-0262-4*) Standard Pub.
Watson, Elizabeth E. Tell Me about Jesus. (gr. 1 up). 1980. pap. 4.99 (*0-570-03484-1*, 56-1705) Concordia.
Wezeman, Phyllis & Weissner, Colleen. Seaside with the Savior. (Illus.). 144p. (gr. 1-6). 1989. 24.95 (*1-55513-186-7*, 68718) Cook.
Whalin, Terry. Never Too Busy. Faltico, Mary L., illus. 28p. (ps-k). 1993. 4.99 (*0-7847-0038-9*, 24-03828) Standard Pub.
White, E. G. Christ Our Savior. (Illus.). 160p. (gr. 5 up). 1989. pap. 8.95 (*0-945460-05-8*) Upward Way.
—Christ Our Savior. (SPA., Illus.). 176p. (gr. 5 up). 1990. pap. 8.95 (*0-945460-10-4*) Upward Way.
Willis, Doris. Jesus Grew. (ps). 1990. 3.95 (*0-687-03124-9*) Abingdon.
Winder, Linda. Jesus. (ps). 1993. 5.99 (*0-7814-0120-8*, Bible Discovery) Chariot Family.
Wyatt, Margaret. My Friend Jesus. Wyatt, Tracey, illus. LC 86-90051. 20p. (Orig.). (ps-12). 1986. pap. 2.25 (*0-9616117-0-7*) M Wyatt.
Young, Barbara. Jesus Is My Very Best Friend. (ps-k). 1984. 5.99 (*0-570-04097-3*, 56-1465) Concordia.
Yount, Christine. Telling Your Friends about Christ. (Illus.). 48p. (gr. 6-8). 1991. pap. 8.99 (*1-55945-114-9*) Group Pub.
Yzermans, Vincent A. Jesus & Caesar Augustus: A Legend. Yell, Vonett & Bergmann, Melvin, illus. LC 89-50566. 180p. (Orig.). (gr. 7-12). 1989. pap. 7.95 (*0-89622-396-5*) Twenty-Third.

JESUS CHRIST–ART

see also Bible–Pictorial Works; Christian Art and Symbolism

Jesus of Nazareth: Illustrated with Painting from the National Gallery in Washington. LC 93-35867. (ps up). 1994. 16.00 (*0-671-88651-7*, S&S BFYR) S&S Trade.
Johnson, Stephen & Johnson, Renae. Around the World with Jesus. (Illus.). 144p. (gr. 1-6). 1989. 24.95 (*1-55513-872-1*, 68726) Cook.

JESUS CHRIST–BIOGRAPHY

see also Jesus Christ–Nativity

Backhouse, Halcyon. The Incredible Journey. LC 92-33820. (Illus.). 1993. 9.99 (*0-8407-9403-7*) Nelson.
Bennett, Marian & Stortz, Diane. Jesus Grew. Munger, Nancy, illus. 12p. (ps). 1992. deluxe ed. 4.99 (*0-87403-995-9*, 24-03115) Standard Pub.
Brittain, Grady B. Platy: The Child in Us. McBoon, Linda, illus. LC 81-6503. 53p. (Orig.). (ps-8). 1981. pap. 2.00 (*0-86663-761-3*) Ide Hse.
Bull, Norman. Jesus the Nazarene. (gr. 2-7). 1984. pap. 10.95 (*0-7175-0981-8*) Dufour.
Carr, Dan. Our Savior Is Born. (gr. 1 up). 1984. 7.99 (*0-570-04092-2*, 56-1460) Concordia.
Daniel, Rebecca. Book VI-His Miracles. McClure, Nancee, illus. 32p. (gr. 2-7). 1984. wkbk. 7.95 (*0-86653-227-7*, SS 829, Shining Star Pubns) Good Apple.
—Book XI-His Last Hours. McClure, Nancee, illus. 32p. (gr. 2-7). 1984. wkbk. 7.95 (*0-86653-232-3*, SS 834, Shining Star Pubns) Good Apple.
—Book XII-His Resurrection. McClure, Nancee, illus. 32p. (gr. 2-7). 1984. wkbk. 7.95 (*0-86653-233-1*, SS 835, Shining Star Pubns) Good Apple.
—Jesus' Life. 48p. (ps-6). 1988. 7.95 (*0-86653-460-1*, SS855, Shining Star Pubns) Good Apple.
De Graaf, Anne. The Early Years of Jesus. (Illus.). 32p. 1989. 4.95 (*0-310-52720-1*) Zondervan.
Dickens, Charles. The Life of Our Lord. 128p. 1991. 15. 99 (*0-8407-9126-7*); audio cassette 12.99 (*0-8407-9965-9*) Nelson.
Doney, Meryl. Jesus: The Man Who Changed History. (Illus.). 48p. (gr. 4 up). 1988. text ed. 13.95 (*0-7459-1050-5*) Lion USA.
Downey, Melissa C. & Lingo, Susan L. Early Life of Jesus. Hayes, Theresa, ed. Green, Roy, illus. 32p. (Orig.). (gr. 1-5). 1994. wkbk. 3.99 (*0-7847-0140-7*) Standard Pub.
—New Life in Jesus. Hayes, Theresa, ed. Green, Roy, illus. 32p. (Orig.). (gr. 1-5). 1994. wkbk. 3.99 (*0-7847-0143-1*) Standard Pub.
Duntze, Dorothee, illus. The Life of Jesus. LC 93-28776. 105p. 1993. 14.95 (*0-8146-2303-4*) Liturgical Pr.
The Early Life of Jesus. (gr. 4-6). 1990. 1.55 (*0-89636-116-0*, JB 1C) Accent CO.
Egermeier, Elsie E. Egermeier's Picture-Story Life of Jesus. Inns, Kenneth, illus. (gr. k-6). 1969. 7.95 (*0-87162-008-1*, D2015) Warner Pr.
Ellis, Neil C. The Power of the Blood. 48p. (Orig.). 1991. pap. text ed. 7.95 (*0-925783-01-3*) Natl BIE Pub.
Fryar, Jane. The Easter Day Surprise. (Illus.). 24p. (Orig.). (ps-4). 1993. pap. 1.99 (*0-570-09033-4*) Concordia.
—Jesus Enters Jerusalem. (Illus.). 24p. (Orig.). (ps-4). 1993. pap. 1.99 (*0-570-09032-6*) Concordia.
Hershey, Katherine. Life of Christ, Vol. I. Banse, Charles & Chappell, David, illus. 54p. (gr. k-6). 1987. pap. text ed. 9.45 (*1-55976-000-1*) CEF Press.
—Life of Christ, Vol. III. Banse, Charles, illus. 51p. (gr. k-6). 1978. pap. text ed. 9.45 (*1-55976-002-8*) CEF Press.
—Life of Christ, Vol. IV. Banse, Charles, illus. 49p. (gr. k-6). 1978. pap. text ed. 9.45 (*1-55976-003-6*) CEF Press.
—Life of Christ, Vol. II. (Illus.). 55p. (gr. k-6). 1987. pap. 9.45 (*1-55976-001-X*) CEF Press.
Hill, Dave. Most Wonderful King. Wind, B., illus. (gr. 3-4). 1968. laminated bdg. 1.99 (*0-570-06032-X*, 59-1145) Concordia.
Hilliard, Dick & Valenti-Hilliard, Beverly. Happenings! Collopy, George F., illus. LC 81-52715. 60p. (gr. 1 up). 1981. pap. text ed. 4.95 (*0-89390-033-8*) Resource Pubns.
Hollingsworth, Mary. Journey to Jesus: A Four-in-One Story. Eubank, Mary G., illus. 32p. 1993. 13.99 (*0-8010-4371-9*) Baker Bk.
Huff, Brenda. A King Is Born. Fagan, Todd, et al, illus. 20p. 1993. 15.95 (*1-883909-01-5*) Wisdom Tree.
Jesus Is Born. 1991. 0.79 (*0-8307-0827-8*, 5608119) Regal.
Jesus Lives. 1991. 0.79 (*0-8307-0834-0*, 5608181) Regal.
Jesus of Nazareth: Illustrated with Painting from the National Gallery in Washington. LC 93-35867. (ps up). 1994. 16.00 (*0-671-88651-7*, S&S BFYR) S&S Trade.
Kageyama, Akiko. Journey to Bethlehem. 26p. (ps-3). 1983. 10.00 (*0-8170-1012-2*) Judson.
Kondeatis, Christos. Scenes from the Life of Jesus Christ: A Three-Dimensional Bible Storybook. LC 94-1732. (gr. 1 up). 1994. 19.95 (*0-8037-1786-5*) Dial Bks Young.
Larsen, Dan. Jesus. Bohl, Al, illus. 224p. (gr. 4-8). 1989. pap. text ed. 2.50 (*1-55748-100-8*) Barbour & Co.
L'Engle, Madeleine. The Glorious Impossible. Giotto, illus. 64p. (gr. 3 up). 1990. pap. 19.95 jacketed (*0-671-68690-9*, Little Simon) S&S Trade.
Life of Jesus. (Illus.). 32p. (Orig.). 1993. pap. 1.99 (*0-570-04756-0*) Concordia.
Lysne, Mary E. Mary & Elizabeth. Gambill, Henrietta, ed. Patterson, Kathleen, illus. 24p. (ps-3). 1993. wkbk. 2.39 (*0-7847-0101-6*, 23-02581) Standard Pub.
McMillan, Mary. The Story of Jesus. 48p. (ps-1). 1988. 7.95 (*0-86653-454-7*, SS1804, Shining Star Pubns) Good Apple.
Osborne, John T. Miracles. Osborne, John T., illus. 90p. 1988. pap. text ed. 5.75 (*0-929918-00-2*) Midstates Pub.
Otting, Rae. When Jesus Was a Lad. Marilue, illus. (gr. 1-2). 1978. pap. 1.25 (*0-89508-055-9*) Rainbow Bks.
Peterson, Esther A. A Child's Life of Christ. Lee, Nancy, illus. 44p. (gr. 3-8). 1987. 6.95 (*1-55523-045-8*) Winston-Derek.
Ralph, Margaret. Jesus: Historias de su Vida. King, Gordon, illus. LaValle, Teresa, tr. (Illus.). 28p. (gr. 4). 1979. 2.75 (*0-311-38536-2*, Edit Mundo) Casa Bautista.
Rich, George. Famous Interviews with Jesus Christ. (gr. 6 up). 1991. pap. text ed. 1.95 study guide, 32p. (*0-87227-157-9*); leader's guide, 24p. 1.95 (*0-87227-165-X*) Reg Baptist.
Savary, Louis. The Life of Jesus. Goodwill, Rita, illus. 43p. (ps-4). 1989. 5.59 (*0-88271-099-0*) Regina Pr.
Simon, Mary M. Thank you, Jesus: Luke 17: 11-19; Jesus Heals Ten Men with Leprosy. Jones, Dennis, illus. LC 93-36192. 32p. (gr. 1-3). 1994. pap. 3.99 (*0-570-04762-5*) Concordia.
Stirrup Associates, Inc. Staff. My Jesus Pocketbook of Scripture Pictures. Sherman, Erin, illus. LC 82-80351. 32p. (Orig.). (ps-3). 1982. pap. 0.69 (*0-937420-02-6*) Stirrup Assoc.
Story of Jesus Pop-Up Book. (Illus.). (ps-1). 1.98 (*0-517-43888-7*) Random Hse Value.
Tallach, Isobel. Life of Jesus. (Orig.). (ps-3). 1984. pap. 1.75 (*0-85151-345-X*) Banner of Truth.
Taylor, Kenneth N. Stories about Jesus. Munger, Nancy, illus. LC 94-4083. 112p. 1994. 7.99 (*0-8423-6093-X*) Tyndale.
Who Is Jesus? (gr. 4-6). 1990. 1.55 (*0-89636-117-9*, JB 2C) Accent CO.
Wolf, Bob. Just Like Jesus. (Illus.). 24p. (Orig.). (gr. 1-4). 1982. pap. 0.50 (*0-89323-034-0*) Bible Memory.

JESUS CHRIST–BIRTH

see Jesus Christ–Nativity

JESUS CHRIST–FICTION

Ahern, Denise. Bread & the Wine, No. Sixteen. (Illus.). (gr. k-4). 1979. 1.99 (*0-570-06127-X*, 59-1245) Concordia.
Alavedra, Joan. They Followed a Bright Star. Wensell, Ulises, illus. LC 93-6065. 40p. 1994. 15.95 (*0-399-22706-7*, Putnam) Putnam Pub Group.
Animals Gift. (ps-2). 1994. pap. 15.00 (*0-671-72962-4*) S&S Trade.
Aoki, Hisako. Santa's Favorite Story. 2nd ed. Gantschev, Ivan, illus. LC 82-60895. 28p. (gr. k up). 1991. pap. 4.95 (*0-88708-153-3*) Picture Bk Studio.
Barnes, Joyce B. Patches, the Blessed Beast of Burden. Ramirez-Walker, Linda J., illus. 36p. 1990. 15.00 (*0-9628493-0-8*) J B Barnes.
Black, Auguste R. Miracles at the Inn. Sherentz, Michael K., illus. 24p. (Orig.). (gr. 1-12). 1990. pap. 4.95 (*0-9628010-1-1*) A R Black.
Bosca, Francesca. Caspar & the Star. Ferri, Giuliano, illus. 40p. (gr. 1-8). 1991. 12.95 (*0-7459-2120-5*) Lion USA.
Fleetwood, Jenni. While Shepherds Watched. Melnyczuk, Peter, illus. LC 91-38779. 32p. (gr. k up). 1992. 14.00 (*0-688-11598-5*); PLB 13.93 (*0-688-11599-3*) Lothrop.
Fryar, Jane. Lost at the Mall: Morris the Mouse Adventure Ser. Wilson, Deborah, illus. 32p. (ps-1). 1991. 7.99 (*0-570-04196-1*, 56-1655) Concordia.
Gambill, Henrietta D. Little Christmas Animals. LC 94-10000. 1994. 1.89 (*0-7847-0274-8*) Standard Pub.
Head, Constance. The Man Who Carried the Cross for Jesus. (Illus.). (gr. k-4). 1979. 1.99 (*0-570-06124-5*, 59-1242) Concordia.
Heise, Robert F. Twas the Night Before Jesus. Wade, John, illus. 28p. (gr. 3-6). 1990. smyth-sewn 12.95 (*0-9627049-0-3*) Dogwood NC.
Helldorfer, M. C. Daniel's Gift. Downing, Julie, illus. LC 90-186. 32p. (gr. k-3). 1990. pap. 4.95 (*0-689-71440-8*, Aladdin) Macmillan Child Grp.
Hennessy, B. G. The First Night. Johnson, Steve & Fancher, Lou, illus. LC 93-9659. 32p. (ps-3). 1993. 13. 99 (*0-670-83026-7*) Viking Child Bks.
Herold, Ann B. The Mysterious Passover Visitors. (Illus.). 112p. (Orig.). (gr. 8-12). 1989. pap. 4.95 (*0-8361-3494-X*) Herald Pr.
Hunt, Angela E. Singing Shepherd. (Illus.). 32p. (ps-6). 1992. 13.95 (*0-7459-2224-4*) Lion USA.
Jeffs, Stephanie. The Little Christmas Tree. Barker, Chris, illus. 16p. (ps-8). 1991. 12.95 (*0-7459-2118-3*) Lion USA.
Kershaw, F. M. Heaven's Above. 1993. 13.95 (*0-533-10231-6*) Vantage.
Mathews, Nancy. Friends of Jesus: The Animals Tell Their Stories. (Illus.). 24p. (gr. 2-3). 1991. 9.99 (*0-8407-9609-9*) Nelson.
Nystrom, Carolyn. Growing Jesus' Way. (ps-2). 1982. 4.99 (*0-8024-6151-4*) Moody.
Sarlas-Fontana, Jane. The Adventures of Spero the Orthodox Church Mouse: The Nativity of Our Lord Christ's Birth. Simic, Tim, illus. 20p. (ps-4). 1992. pap. 6.95 (*0-937032-91-3*) Light&Life Pub Co MN.
Savitz, Harriet M. & Syring, K. Michael. The Pail of Nails. Shaw, Charles, illus. LC 88-7653. (gr. 3 up). 1990. 10.95 (*0-687-29974-8*) Abingdon.
Smith, Sally Ann. Candle, a Story of Love & Faith. Luther, Luana, ed. Jung, Mary, illus. LC 91-72745. 32p. (gr. 3-6). 1991. pap. 9.95 (*0-944875-22-X*) Doral Pub.
Speare, Elizabeth G. Bronze Bow. 256p. (gr. 6 up). 1961. 13.45 (*0-395-07113-5*) HM.
Tharlet, Eve. Simon & the Holy Night. Clements, Andrew, tr. (Illus.). 28p. (gr. k up). 1991. pap. 14.95 (*0-88708-185-1*) Picture Bk Studio.

—Simon & the Holy Night. Clements, Andrew, adapted by. Tharlet, Eve, illus. LC 93-306. 1993. 4.95 (*0-88708-324-2*) Picture Bk Studio.
Van DeWeyer, Robert & Spenceley, Annabel. The Shepherd's Son. LC 92-40284. 24p. (gr. k-3). 1993. 10.00 (*0-8170-1188-9*) Judson.
Van Horn, Brian & Van Horn, Chris. Lordy Lamb & the Twelve Lisciples. Mowdy, Sharon, ed. Scott, Rita & Van Horn, Brian, illus. 40p. (gr. k-5). 1989. 8.95 (*1-877765-00-7*) Lambgel Family.
Wallace, Lew. Ben Hur. Bennet, C. L., intro. by. (gr. 9 up). 1965. pap. 2.95 (*0-8049-0074-4*, CL-74) Airmont.
Wedeven, Carol S. The Christmas Crib That Zack Built. Fisher, Nell F., illus. LC 89-263. 1989. casebound 9.95 (*0-687-07816-4*) Abingdon.
Wells, Ruth & Van Dyke, Henry, eds. The Other Wise Man. Moser, Barry, illus. LC 93-16259. (ps-8). 1993. 16.95 (*0-88708-329-3*) Picture Bk Studio.
Westall, Robert. The Witness. Williams, Sophy, illus. 32p. 1994. 14.99 (*0-525-45331-8*) Dutton Child Bks.

JESUS CHRIST–ICONOGRAPHY
see Jesus Christ–Art

JESUS CHRIST–NATIVITY
see also Christmas
Allan, Nicholas. Jesus' Christmas Party. Allan, Nicholas, illus. LC 91-17092. 32p. 1992. 9.99 (*0-679-82688-2*) Random Bks Yng Read.
Anastasio, Dina. Joy to the World! Paterson, Bettina, illus. 32p. (ps-3). 1992. (G&D); pap. 2.25 (*0-448-40479-6*, G&D) Putnam Pub Group.
Bennett, Marian, ed. Baby Jesus. Karch, Paul, illus. 10p. (ps). 1985. 4.99 (*0-87239-907-9*, 2747) Standard Pub.
Bierhorst, John, tr. Spirit Child: A Story of the Nativity. Cooney, Barbara, illus. 32p. (ps up). 1990. pap. 4.95 (*0-688-09926-2*, Mulberry) Morrow.
Billington, Rachel. The First Christmas. Brown, Barbara, illus. LC 87-20383. 32p. (gr. k-5). 1987. pap. 6.95 (*0-8192-1410-8*) Morehouse Pub.
Briere, Euphemia. The Nativity of Our Lord: The Birth of the Messiah. Briere, Euphemia, illus. (Orig.). (gr. 1-3). 1993. pap. 6.00 (*0-913026-38-7*) St Nectarios.
Brown, Margaret W. Christmas in the Barn. Cooney, Barbara, illus. LC 52-7858. 32p. (gr. k-3). 1961. PLB 13.89 (*0-690-19272-X*, Crowell Jr Bks) HarpC Child Bks.
Daniel, Rebecca. Book I-His Birth. McClure, Nancee, illus. 32p. (gr. 2-7). 1984. wkbk. 6.95 (*0-86653-213-7*, SS 824, Shining Star Pubns) Good Apple.
De Vries, C. M. On the Way to Bethlehem. Vilain, Frederic, tr. from DUT. Muller, Anna-Hermine, illus. LC 90-43765. 16p. (Orig.). 1990. pap. 1.50 (*0-8198-5415-8*) St Paul Bks.
Evans, Helen K. Jesus Is Born. 64p. (ps-3). 1990. 8.95 (*0-86653-551-9*, SS894, Shining Star Pubns) Good Apple.
The First Christmas: Timeless Tales. 1992. 4.99 (*0-517-06971-7*) Random Hse Value.
Forell, Betty & Wind, Betty. Little Benjamin & the First Christmas. (Illus.). (ps-3). 1964. laminated bdg. 1.99 (*0-570-06005-2*, 59-1113) Concordia.
Frank, Penny. The First Christmas. (Illus.). 24p. (gr. 1 up). 1986. 3.99 (*0-85648-757-0*) Lion USA.
Gabriele. Nativity Story. 1985. pap. 1.95 (*0-911211-75-6*) Penny Lane Pubns.
Gambill, Henrietta, ed. I Can Draw the Nativity. (Illus.). 32p. 1994. pap. 4.99 (*0-7847-0221-7*, 24-03251) Standard Pub.
Gleeson, Brian. The Savior Is Born. Van Nutt, Robert, illus. LC 92-4577. 40p. 1992. pap. 14.95 (*0-88708-283-1*, Rabbit Ears); pap. 19.95 incl. cass. (*0-88708-284-X*, Rabbit Ears) Picture Bk Studio.
Hall, Susan T. Baby Jesus Is Born: Tickle Giggle Book. (ps). 1990. 7.49 (*1-55513-772-5*, Chariot Bks) Chariot Family.
Hartman, Bob. Birthday of a King: Jesus' Birthday. (ps-3). 1993. 7.99 (*1-56476-144-4*, Victor Books) SP Pubns.
Hayes, Theresa. Celebrate the Birth of Jesus. Chase, Andra, illus. 16p. (gr. 3-6). 1992. wkbk. 7.99 (*0-87403-930-4*, 14-03502) Standard Pub.
Heyer, Carol. The Christmas Story. Heyer, Carol, illus. LC 91-9101. 32p. (ps-1). 1991. 11.95 (*0-8249-8512-5*, Ideals Child) Hambleton-Hill.
Johnson, Pamela, illus. The Story of the First Christmas. LC 90-23154. 24p. (ps up). 1991. 2.95 (*0-694-00364-6*) HarpC Child Bks.
Klug, Ron & Klug, Lyn. Jesus Comes: the Story of Jesus' Birth for Children. Konsterile, Paul, illus. LC 86-81808. 32p. (Orig.). (gr. 3-8). 1986. pap. 5.99 saddlestitch (*0-8066-2234-2*, 10-3497, Augsburg) Augsburg Fortress.
LaFortune, Claude. Greeting Jesus: Let's Make the Nativity Scene. (Illus.). 24p. (Orig.). 1988. wkbk. 5.95 (*0-89622-384-1*) Twenty-Third.
Lashbrook, Marilyn. No Tree for Christmas: The Story of Jesus' Birth. Britt, Stephanie M., illus. LC 88-62025. 32p. (ps). 1989. 5.95 (*0-86606-434-6*, 866) Roper Pr.
Laughlin, Charlotte. Where's Baby Jesus? 1992. 9.99 (*0-8499-0902-3*) Word Inc.
Lesch, Christiane. In Bethlehem Long Ago. Lawson, Polly, tr. from GER. Lesch, Christiane, illus. 28p. (ps-2). Repr. of 1988 ed. 14.95 (*0-86315-076-4*, Pub. by Floris Bks UK) Gryphon Hse.
Lion Publishing Staff. Jesus Is Born. (ps). 1992. bds. 6.99 (*0-7459-2203-1*) Lion USA.
McCreary, Jane. Story of Christmas: A Trim a Tree Story Six Wonderful Ornaments Tell the Christmas Story. (ps-3). 1992. 10.99 (*0-87403-866-9*, 24-03556) Standard Pub.
McKissack, Patricia & McKissack, Frederick. All Paths Lead to Bethlehem. Shoemaker, Kathryn E., illus. LC 87-70472. 32p. (Orig.). (ps-3). 1987. pap. 5.99 (*0-8066-2265-2*, 10-0220, Augsburg) Augsburg Fortress.
McMillan, Mary. Baby Jesus. Grossmann, Dan, illus. 48p. (ps-1). 1986. wkbk. 7.95 (*0-86653-369-9*, SS 1800, Shining Star Pubns) Good Apple.
Moore, Yvette. The Birth of Christ. 16p. 1993. pap. 6.00 (*0-9637273-0-3*) Jubilee Yr Bks.
Moxley, Sheila, illus. The Christmas Story: A Lift-the-Flap Advent Calendar. LC 92-29520. 24p. 1993. 15.99 (*0-8037-1351-7*) Dial Bks Young.
Murphy, Mary. Mary Had a Baby. Amen! 16p. (Orig.). (ps-8). 1991. pap. text ed. 14.95 (*0-89243-339-6*); pap. text ed. 1.00 coloring bk. (*0-89243-340-X*) Liguori Pubns.
Odor, Ruth S. The Very Special Visitors. Clarke, Karen, illus. 28p. (ps). 1992. 2.50 (*0-87403-955-X*, 24-03595) Standard Pub.
Olson, Rachel. Twas the Night Before: A Picture-Story of the Nativity. Wray, Rhonda, ed. Zapel, Arthur L., illus. LC 93-26740. 24p. (Orig.). (gr. k-3). 1993. 14.95 (*0-916260-85-2*, B143) Meriwether Pub.
Parry, Alan & Parry, Linda. Baby Jesus. Parry, Alan, illus. 24p. (ps). 1990. pap. 0.99 (*0-8066-2478-7*, 9-2478) Augsburg Fortress.
Quaglini, Juliana. The Night of the Shepherds: A Christmas Experience. Flanagan, Anne J., tr. from ITA. De Vico, Elvira, illus. LC 93-25027. 32p. (Orig.). (gr. 4 up). 1993. pap. 3.95 (*0-8198-5128-0*) St Paul Bks.
Ray, Jane, illus. The Story of Christmas: Words from the Gospels of Matthew & Luke. LC 91-11357. 32p. (ps up). 1991. 15.95 (*0-525-44768-7*, DCB) Dutton Child Bks.
Shely, Patricia. El Nino Jesus. Granberry, Nola, tr. Karch, Pat, illus. (SPA.). 16p. (gr. 1-3). 1987. pap. 1.40 (*0-311-38563-X*) Casa Bautista.
Simon, Mary M. The First Christmas: Luke 2: 1-20: The Birth of Jesus. Jones, Dennis, illus. LC 92-21372. 32p. (Orig.). (gr. 1-3). 1993. pap. 3.99 (*0-570-04741-2*) Concordia.
Stewart, Pat. Away in a Manger. (Illus.). 32p. (gr. 3 up). 1989. 6.95 (*0-02-689338-X*) Checkerboard.
Stirrup Associates, Inc. Staff. My Jesus Pocketbook of a Very Special Birth Day. Harvey, Bonnie C. & Phillips, Cheryl M., eds. Burnett, Lindy, illus. LC 84-50919. 32p. (ps). 1984. pap. 0.69 (*0-937420-15-8*) Stirrup Assoc.
Storr, Catherine, retold by. The Birth of Jesus. Rowe, Gavin, illus. LC 82-9048. 32p. (gr. k-4). 1982. 14.65 (*0-8172-1977-3*) Raintree Steck-V.
Trent, Robbie. The First Christmas. rev. ed. Simont, Marc, illus. LC 89-29729. 32p. (ps-2). 1990. pap. 3.50 (*0-06-443249-1*, Trophy) HarpC Child Bks.
Vivas, Julie. The Nativity. Vivas, Julia, illus. 34p. (ps up). 1988. 13.95 (*0-15-200535-8*, Gulliver Bks) HarBrace.
Winthrop, Elizabeth. Story of the Nativity. 1986. pap. 2.25 (*0-671-63019-9*, Little Simon) S&S Trade.
Woggon, Guillermo. Alla en el Pesebre. Cranberry, Nola, tr. from ENG. (SPA., Illus.). 16p. (ps-2). 1987. pap. 1.40 (*0-311-38562-1*) Casa Bautista.

JESUS CHRIST–NATIVITY–DRAMA
Irsch, Ed. As It Was Told: A Play for Christmas. 16p. (Orig.). (gr. k-4). 1980. pap. text ed. 3.95 (*0-89536-439-5*, 0146) CSS OH.

JESUS CHRIST–NATIVITY–POETRY
Farber, Norma. When It Snowed That Night. Mathers, Petra, illus. LC 92-27414. 40p. (gr. k up). 1993. 16.00 (*0-06-021707-3*); PLB 15.89 (*0-06-021708-1*) HarpC Child Bks.
Kennedy, X. J. The Beasts of Bethlehem. McCurdy, Michael, illus. LC 91-38417. 48p. (gr. 1 up). 1992. SBE 13.95 (*0-689-50561-2*, M K McElderry) Macmillan Child Grp.

JESUS CHRIST–PARABLES
Benda, Andreas. The Good Samaritan. Jacobsen, Walter, illus. 10p. (gr. k-2). 1993. puzzle bk. 6.99 (*0-8028-5083-9*) Eerdmans.
—The Good Shepherd. Jacobsen, Walter, illus. 10p. (gr. k-2). 1993. puzzle bk. 6.99 (*0-8028-5084-7*) Eerdmans.
Butterworth, Nick. Stories Jesus Told. (ps-k). 1994. 10.99 (*0-88070-633-3*, Gold & Honey) Questar Pubs.
Butterworth, Nick & Inkpen, Mick. The Little Gate. Butterworth, Nick & Inkpen, Mick, illus. 32p. (ps-3). 1992. pap. 3.99 (*0-551-02506-9*) HarpC.
—The Rich Farmer. Butterworth, Nick & Inkpen, Mick, illus. 32p. (ps-3). 1992. pap. 3.99 (*0-551-02508-5*) HarpC.
Castagnola, Larry. More Parables for Little People. Muren, Nancy L., illus. LC 87-62532. 88p. (Orig.). (gr. 4-5). 1987. pap. 8.95 (*0-89390-095-8*) Resource Pubns.
Caswell, Helen. Parable of the Leaven. Caswell, Helen, illus. LC 92-15161. 24p. (ps-3). 1992. pap. 5.95 (*0-687-30024-X*) Abingdon.
—Parable of the Mustard Seed. Caswell, Helen, illus. LC 92-15160. 24p. (ps-3). 1992. pap. 5.95 (*0-687-30025-8*) Abingdon.
—Parable of the Sower. LC 90-23200. (ps-3). 1991. 11.95 (*0-687-30020-7*) Abingdon.
Cheasebro, Margaret. The Prodigal Son & Other Parables As Plays. LC 92-7232. (gr. 5 up). 1993. 6.99 (*0-8054-6065-9*) Broadman.
Daniel, Rebecca. Book VII-His Parables. McClure, Nancee, illus. 32p. (gr. 2-7). 1984. wkbk. 7.95 (*0-86653-228-5*, SS 830, Shining Star Pubns) Good Apple.
De Paola, Tomie. The Parables of Jesus. De Paola, Tomie, illus. LC 86-18323. 32p. (gr. k-4). 1987. reinforced bdg. 15.95 (*0-8234-0636-9*) Holiday.
Downey, Melissa C. & Lingo, Susan L. Parables of Jesus. Hayes, Theresa, ed. Green, Roy, illus. 32p. (Orig.). (gr. 1-5). 1994. wkbk. 3.99 (*0-7847-0142-3*) Standard Pub.
Glavich, Kathleen. Acting Out the Miracles & Parables: 52 Five-Minute Plays for Education & Worship. LC 88-50330. (Illus., Orig.). (gr. 4-6). 1988. pap. 12.95 (*0-89622-363-9*) Twenty-Third.
Glavich, Mary K. A Child's Book of Parables. LC 94-2383. 1994. 2.50 (*0-8294-0801-0*) Loyola.
The Good Samaritan. (Illus.). 32p. (gr. 2-12). 1975. incl. audiocassette 9.95 (*0-87510-101-1*) Christian Sci.
Grimes, Bobbie M. The Parable of Jesus & Santa. Cooley, Nance, illus. LC 84-90331. 40p. (ps-5). 1984. 14.95 (*0-9613328-0-8*) B & D Pub.
Hilliard, Dick & Valenti-Hilliard, Beverly. Wonders! Collopy, George F., illus. LC 81-52713. 64p. (Orig.). (gr. 1 up). 1981. pap. text ed. 4.95 (*0-89390-032-X*) Resource Pubns.
Jesus & the Donkey, 3 vols. (ps). 1991. Set. pap. 10.99 (*0-8007-7118-4*) Revell.
Kelly, Paul. Deciphering Jesus' Parables. (Illus.). 48p. (gr. 9-12). 1992. pap. 8.99 (*1-55945-237-4*) Group Pub.
Kramer, Janice & Mathews. Good Samaritan. LC 63-23369. (Illus.). (ps-k). 1964. laminated bdg. 1.99 (*0-570-06000-1*, 59-1102) Concordia.
Kratavil, Helen S. Parables of Christ. Butcher, Sam, illus. 64p. (gr. k-6). 1974. pap. text ed. 11.50 (*1-55976-015-X*) CEF Press.
Parry, Alan. The Lost Coin. (Illus.). 24p. (ps-k). 1994. 3.99 (*0-8499-1088-9*) Word Inc.
—The Lost Pearl. (Illus.). 24p. (ps-k). 1994. 3.99 (*0-8499-1087-0*) Word Inc.
—The Lost Son. (Illus.). 24p. (ps-k). 1994. 3.99 (*0-8499-1086-2*) Word Inc.
Powers, Isaias. Father Ike's Stories for Children: Teaching Christian Values Through Animal Stories. LC 88-50332. (Illus.). 64p. (Orig.). 1988. pap. 4.95 (*0-89622-370-1*) Twenty-Third.
Reid, John C. Parables from Nature: Earthly Stories with Heavenly Meanings. 2nd ed. Foley, Timothy, illus. 96p. (gr. k-4). 1991. pap. 7.99 (*0-8028-4052-3*) Eerdmans.
Taylor, Kenneth N. The Prodigal Son. (Illus.). 1989. bds. 3.99 (*0-8423-5040-3*, 755040-3) Tyndale.

JESUS CHRIST–POETRY
Farber, Norma. When It Snowed That Night. Mathers, Petra, illus. LC 92-27414. 40p. (gr. k up). 1993. 16.00 (*0-06-021707-3*); PLB 15.89 (*0-06-021708-1*) HarpC Child Bks.
Thomas, Joan G. If Jesus Came to My House. Thomas, Joan G., illus. 24p. (gr. k-3). 1951. 13.00 (*0-688-40981-4*) Lothrop.

JESUS CHRIST–SERMON ON THE MOUNT
see Sermon on the Mount

JESUS CHRIST–TEACHINGS
Dean, Bessie. Lessons Jesus Taught. Dean, Bessie, illus. 72p. (Orig.). (gr. k-5). 1980. pap. 5.98 (*0-88290-146-X*) Horizon Utah.
Kendrick, Rosalyn. In the Steps of Jesus: Insights into the Life & World of Jesus. 128p. (gr. 8-10). 1985. pap. 17.95x (*0-7175-1309-2*, Pub. by Stanley Thornes UK) Trans-Atl Phila.
Odor, Ruth S. Jesus Loves Us. Fagan, Wendy, illus. LC 91-67211. 32p. (gr. 5-7). 1992. saddle-stitched 5.99 (*0-87403-934-7*, 24-03564) Standard Pub.
Willis, Doris. Jesus, My Friend & Teacher. (ps). 1990. 3.95 (*0-687-03123-0*) Abingdon.

JESUS CHRIST IN ART
see Jesus Christ–Art

JEWELRY
see also Gems
Bergen, Lara R. Bead It! A Complete Jewelry Kit. Heins, Edward, illus. 24p. (gr. 3 up). 1994. pap. 13.95 (*0-448-40499-0*, G&D) Putnam Pub Group.
Caldecott, Barrie. Jewelry Crafts. LC 91-9887. (Illus.). 48p. (gr. 5-8). 1992. PLB 12.40 (*0-531-14203-5*) Watts.
Make Your Own Friendship Bracelets (with String in Five Colors) (gr. 4-7). 1993. pap. 5.95 (*0-8167-3112-8*, Pub. by Watermill Pr) Troll Assocs.
Zechlin, Katharina. Creative Enameling & Jewelry-Making. Kuttner, Paul, tr. LC 65-20877. (gr. 10 up). 1965. 6.95 (*0-8069-5062-5*); PLB 6.69 (*0-8069-5063-3*) Sterling.

JEWELS
see Gems; Jewelry; Precious Stones

JEWISH-ARAB RELATIONS
Abodaher, David J. Youth in the Middle East: Voices of Despair. (Illus.). 112p. (gr. 9-12). 1990. PLB 13.40 (*0-531-10961-5*) Watts.
Bernards, Neal. The Palestinian Conflict: Identifying Propaganda Techniques. LC 90-37741. (Illus.). 32p. (gr. 3-6). 1990. PLB 10.95 (*0-89908-602-0*) Greenhaven.
Deegan, Paul J. The Arab-Israeli Conflict. LC 91-73073. 202p. (gr. 4 up). 1991. 13.99 (*1-56239-028-7*) Abdo & Dghtrs.
Hills, Ken. Arab-Israeli Wars. (Illus.). 32p. (gr. 3-9). 1991. PLB 10.95 (*1-85435-261-X*) Marshall Cavendish.

Pimlott, John. Middle East: A Background to the Conflicts. LC 91-2673. (Illus.). 40p. (gr. 6-8). 1991. PLB 12.90 (*0-531-17329-1*, Gloucester Pr) Watts.
Reische, Diana. Arafat & the Palestine Liberation Organization. LC 90-46868. (Illus.). 160p. (gr. 9-12). 1991. PLB 14.40 (*0-531-11000-1*) Watts.

JEWISH HOLIDAYS

see Fasts and Feasts–Judaism

JEWISH LANGUAGE

see Hebrew Language

JEWISH LITERATURE

see also Bible; Hebrew Literature

Apelbaum, Shiffy. Moshe Mendel the Mitzva Maven & His Amazing Mitzva Quest. LC 94-4118. 1994. 12.95 (*0-87306-662-6*) Feldheim.
Atkin, Abraham. Chelkeinu. 200p. text ed. 6.50 (*0-914131-09-5*, A120) Torah Umesorah.
—Darkeinu Daled. text ed. 4.00 (*0-914131-13-3*, A102) Torah Umesorah.
Atkins, Abraham. Darkeinu Gimel. (gr. 4 up). text ed. 3.85 (*0-914131-14-1*, A101) Torah Umesorah.
Berman, Melanie. Building Jewish Life Prayers & Blessings. Bleicher, David, illus. 32p. (Orig.). (gr. k-2). 1991. pap. text ed. 1.85 (*0-933873-66-2*) Torah Aura.
Fields, Harvey J. Torah Commentary for Our Times, 3 vols. (Illus., Orig.). (gr. 7-9). 1994. pap. 35.00 Boxed Set (*0-8074-0530-2*, 164054) UAHC.
Fischer, Sophia M. & Eisenberg, Ruth P., eds. Reflections on the March of the Living: April 26 - May 10, 1992. Greenzweig, Gene, intros. by. 164p. (Orig.). (gr. 11-12). 1993. pap. 18.00 (*0-930029-07-0*) Central Agency.
Ginsburg, Marvell. Tattooed Torah. (Illus.). 32p. (gr. k-3). 1983. 6.95 (*0-8074-0252-4*, 104030) UAHC.
Grossman, Cheryl S. & Engman, Suzy. Jewish Literature for Children: A Teaching Guide. LC 85-70543. 230p. (Orig.). (gr. 4 up). 1985. text ed. 19.00 (*0-86705-018-7*); pap. text ed. 10.00 (*0-685-10172-X*) A R E Pub.
Haskelevich, B., ed. & tr. from ENG & HEB. My First Siddur: A Selection of Prayers for Jewish Boys & Girls. LC 90-82127. (RUS., Illus.). 32p. (Orig.). (gr. k-8). 1990. pap. 1.50 (*1-878860-01-1*) Noviysvet.
Hautzig, Esther, tr. from YID. The Seven Good Years & Other Stories of I. L. Peretz. Kogan, Deborah, illus. 96p. (gr. 3-6). 1984. 10.95 (*0-8276-0244-8*) JPS Phila.
Karkowsky, Nancy. The Ten Commandments: Text & Activity Book. (gr. 3-4). 5.95 (*0-317-70145-2*) Behrman.
Schur, Maxine. Hannah Szenes: A Song of Light. LC 85-5794. (Illus.). 104p. (gr. 3-7). 1985. 10.95 (*0-8276-0251-0*) JPS Phila.
Weilerstein, Sadie R. Ten & a Kid. Domanska, Janina, illus. LC 61-12600. 186p. (gr. 3 up). 1973. Repr. of 1961 ed. 8.95 (*0-8276-0009-7*) JPS Phila.
Zar, Rose. In the Mouth of the Wolf. 224p. (gr. 6 up). 1983. pap. 8.95 (*0-8276-0382-7*) JPS Phila.

JEWISH RELIGION

see Judaism

JEWS

see also Discrimination

Burstein, Chaya M. The Jewish Kids Catalog. Burstein, Chaya M., illus. 224p. (gr. 3-7). 1983. pap. 14.95 (*0-8276-0215-4*) JPS Phila.
Ganz, Yaffa. The Jewish Fact-Finder: A Bookful of Important Jewish Facts & Handy Information. (gr. 5-9). 1988. 12.95 (*0-87306-447-X*); pap. 9.95 (*0-87306-470-4*) Feldheim.
Gauz, Yaffa. Me & My Bubby, My Zeidy & Me. 1991. 9.95 (*0-87306-543-3*) Feldheim.
Gittelsohn, Roland B. How Do I Decide? (Orig.). (gr. 7-9). 1989. pap. text ed. 8.95x (*0-87441-488-1*) Behrman.
Guidelines for the Preschool Years. (ps). Date not set. pap. 20.00 (*0-685-72159-0*, 241120); Vol. 1, 3-hole punched lesson plan bk., 76p. 10.00 (*0-685-72160-4*, 241160) UAHC.
Guidelines for the Primary Years. Date not set. pap. 20. 00 (*0-685-72161-2*, 241130) UAHC.
Lemelman, Martin. My Jewish Home: Simchah Ba'ambatyah - Fun in the Bathtub. (Illus.). 10p. (ps). 1987. polyvinyl 3.95 (*0-8074-0327-X*, 102001) UAHC.
Moskowitz, Nachama S. Games, Games, & More Games for the Jewish Classroom. 306p. (Orig.). (gr. 4-6). 1994. pap. 8.00 (*0-8074-0504-3*, 201000) UAHC.
Raoul Wallenberg. LC 91-19712. (Illus.). 68p. (gr. 3-8). PLB 19.93 (*0-8368-0629-8*) Gareth Stevens Inc.
Roseman, Kenneth. All in My Jewish Family. Leipzig, Arthur, photos by. (Illus.). 32p. (gr. k-3). 1984. pap. 5.00 wkbk. (*0-8074-0266-4*, 103800) UAHC.
Rosenberg, Amye. Tzedakah. (Illus.). (gr. k-1). 1979. pap. text ed. 4.25 (*0-87441-279-X*) Behrman.
Saypol, Judyth R. & Wikler, Madeline. My Very Own Rosh Hashanah. (Illus.). 32p. (gr. k-6). 1978. pap. 3.95 (*0-930494-06-7*) Kar Ben.
Syme, Daniel & Bogot, Howard. I'm Growing. Compere, Janet, illus. 32p. (ps-1). 1982. pap. 4.00 (*0-8074-0167-6*, 101095) UAHC.
Synge, Ursula. The People & the Promise. LC 74-10661. 192p. (gr. 7-10). 1974. 22.95 (*0-87599-208-0*) S G Phillips.
Terry, Hilda. Does God Eat Us? A Contemporary Response to Old Questions. Terry, Hilda, illus. 271p. (Orig.). 1991. pap. 8.88 (*0-685-54234-3*) Art Ltd.
Thum, Robert & Dworski, Susan. My Jewish World. (Illus., Orig.). (gr. 3-4). 1989. pap. text ed. 7.95 (*0-87441-478-4*); tchr's. guide 14.95 (*0-87441-489-X*) Behrman.
Weilerstein, Sadie R. What the Moon Brought. (Illus.). 159p. (gr. 1-3). 1942. pap. 7.95 (*0-8276-0265-0*) JPS Phila.

JEWS–BIOGRAPHY

see also Rabbis

Adler, David A. Hilde & Eli, Children of the Holocaust. Ritz, Karen, illus. LC 93-38229. 32p. (gr. 3-7). 1994. reinforced bdg. 15.95 (*0-8234-1091-9*) Holiday.
Arem, Tzvi Z. The Story of Reb Baruch Ber: The Kamenitzer Rosh Yeshiba - Rabbi Baruch Ber Leibowitz & His Successor, Rabbi Reuven Grozovsky. (Illus.). 128p. (gr. 6-12). 1987. 11.95 (*0-89906-804-9*); pap. 8.95 (*0-89906-805-7*) Mesorah Pubns.
Auerbacher, Inge. I Am a Star: Child of the Holocaust. Bernbaum, Israel, illus. LC 92-31444. 80p. (gr. 3-7). 1993. pap. 4.99 (*0-14-036401-3*) Puffin Bks.
Brown, Gene. Anne Frank: Child of the Holocaust. (Illus.). 64p. (gr. 3-7). 1993. pap. 7.95 (*1-56711-049-5*) Blackbirch.
Bull, Angela. Anne Frank. (Illus.). 64p. (gr. 5-9). 1991. 11.95 (*0-237-60015-3*, Pub. by Evans Bros Ltd) Trafalgar.
Cytron, Phyllis. Myriam Mendilow: The Mother of Jerusalem. LC 93-15119. 1993. write for info. (*0-8225-4919-0*) Lerner Pubns.
Eisenberg, Azriel. Fill a Blank Page: A Biography of Solomon Schechter. (Illus.). (gr. 6-11). 3.75 (*0-8381-0730-3*, 10-730) United Syn Bk.
Feder, Harriet K. Judah Who Always Said, "No!" Kahn, Katherine J., illus. LC 90-4854. 32p. (ps-2). 1990. 12. 95 (*0-929371-13-5*); pap. 4.95 (*0-929371-14-3*) Kar Ben.
Finkelman, S. The Story of Reb Yosef Chaim: The Life & Times of Rabbi Yosef Chaim Sonnefield, the Guardian of Jerusalem. Dershowitz, Y., illus. 160p. (gr. 6-12). 1984. 11.95 (*0-89906-779-4*); pap. 8.95 (*0-89906-780-8*) Mesorah Pubns.
Finkelman, Shimon. The Story of Reb Elchonon: The Life of Rabbi Elchonon Wasserman. Dershowitz, Yosef, illus. 160p. (gr. 6-12). 1984. 11.95 (*0-89906-770-0*); pap. 8.95 (*0-89906-771-9*) Mesorah Pubns.
—The Story of Reb Nachum'ke: The Nineteen Century Tzaddik - A Legend in His Time. Dershowitz, Yosef, illus. 144p. (gr. 6-12). 1985. 11.95 (*0-89906-781-6*); pap. 8.95 (*0-89906-782-4*) Mesorah Pubns.
—The Story of Reb Yisrael Salanter: The Legendary Founder of the Mussar Movement. Dershowitz, Y., illus. 96p. (gr. 6-12). 1986. 11.95 (*0-89906-797-2*); pap. 8.95 (*0-89906-798-0*) Mesorah Pubns.
Fluek, Toby. Passover As I Remember It. Fluek, Toby, illus. LC 92-9020. 40p. (gr. k-5). 1994. 15.00 (*0-679-83876-7*) Knopf Bks Yng Read.
Frank, Anne. Diary of a Young Girl. large type ed. 1989. Repr. of 1947 ed. 15.95 (*0-685-47378-3*, Crnrstn Bks) BDD LT Grp.
Gurko, Miriam. Theodor Herzl: The Road to Israel. Weihs, Erika, illus. 96p. (gr. 3-7). 1988. 14.95 (*0-8276-0312-6*) JPS Phila.
Handler, Andrew & Meschel, Susan V. Young People Speak: Surviving the Holocaust in Hungary. (Illus.). 160p. (gr. 9-12). 1993. PLB 13.90 (*0-531-11044-3*) Watts.
Hurwitz, Hilda A. & Wasburn, Hope. Dear Hope-- Love, Grandma. Wasburn, Mara H., ed. LC 93-2213. 1993. 12.95 (*1-88128-303-8*) Alef Design.
Hurwitz, Johanna. Anne Frank: A Life in Hiding. Rosenberry, Vera, illus. 64p. (gr. 2-5). 1988. 12.95 (*0-8276-0311-8*) JPS Phila.
Karp, Deborah. Heroes of American Jew History. (Illus.). (gr. 6-7). 1966. pap. 7.95x (*0-87068-539-2*) Ktav.
Koehn, Ilse. Mischling, Second Degree: My Childhood in Nazi Germany. 240p. (gr. 6 up). 1990. pap. 4.95 (*0-14-034290-7*, Puffin) Puffin Bks.
Matov, G. Tales of Tzaddikim: Bereishis. Weinbach, Shaindel, tr. from HEB. Bardugo, Miriam, illus. 320p. (gr. 7-12). 1987. 14.95 (*0-89906-825-1*); pap. 10.95 (*0-89906-826-X*) Mesorah Pubns.
Perl, Lila. Isaac Bashevis Singer: The Life of a Storyteller. Ruff, Donna, illus. LC 93-45275. 1994. write for info. (*0-8276-0512-9*) JPS Phila.
Rosenberg, Maxine B. Hiding to Survive: Fourteen Jewish Children & the Gentiles Who Rescued Them from the Holocaust. LC 93-28328. 1994. write for info. (*0-395-65014-3*, Clarion Bks) HM.
Scherman, Nosson & Gevirtz, Eliezer. The Story of the Chofetz Chaim. Dershowitz, Yosef, illus. 160p. (gr. 6-12). 1987. 11.95 (*0-89906-766-2*); pap. 8.95 (*0-89906-767-0*) Mesorah Pubns.
Schwartz, Barry L. Honi the Circlemaker: Eco-Fables from Ancient Israel. LC 92-33715. 1992. pap. 8.95 (*0-377-00251-8*) Friendship Pr.
Shapolsky, Ian. The Jewish Trivia & Information Book. 400p. (gr. 6-12). 1985. pap. 5.95 (*0-933503-08-3*) Shapolsky Pubs.
Shurin, Yisroel. Morei Ha'Umah. (HEB.). 214p. 1992. text ed. 8.00 (*1-878895-02-8*, D451) Torah Umesorah.
Siegal, Aranka. Grace in the Wilderness: After the Liberation, 1945-1948. 224p. (gr. 7 up). 1994. pap. 4.50 (*0-14-036967-8*) Puffin Bks.
Teller, Hanoch. Sunset. 2nd ed. (Illus.). 288p. (gr. 12). 1988. Repr. of 1987 ed. 9.95 (*0-317-68545-7*) NYC Pub Co.
Theodor Herzl: Architect of a Nation. 120p. (gr. 5 up). 1991. PLB 21.50 (*0-8225-4913-1*) Lerner Pubns.

JEWS–FESTIVALS

see Fasts and Feasts–Judaism

JEWS–FICTION

Abrahamson, Ruth. The Kingston Castle. Shinan, Devora, illus. 102p. (gr. 3-8). 1991. 10.95 (*0-922613-42-7*); pap. 8.95 (*0-922613-43-5*) Hachai Pubns.
Adler, David A. The Number on My Grandfather's Arm. 28p. (gr. 1-3). 1987. 7.95 (*0-8074-0328-8*, 103641) UAHC.
—Rabbi & His Driver. Date not set. 14.95 (*0-06-020421-4*, HarpT); PLB 14.89 (*0-06-020422-2*, HarpT) HarpC.
Appleman, Harlene & Shapiro, Jane. A Seder for Tu B'Shevat. McLean, Chari R., illus. 32p. (ps up). 1984. pap. 2.95 (*0-930494-39-3*) Kar Ben.
Aroner, Miriam & Haas, Shelly O. The Kingdom of Singing Birds. LC 92-39382. 1993. 13.95 (*0-929371-43-7*); pap. 5.95 (*0-929371-44-5*) Kar Ben.
Bandes, Hanna. Reb Aharon's Treasure. Binyamini-Ariel, Liat, illus. 104p. (gr. 2-5). 1993. 9.95 (*1-56871-034-8*) Targum Pr.
Banks, Lynne R. One More River. rev. ed. 256p. (gr. 5 up). 1992. 14.00 (*0-688-10893-8*) Morrow Jr Bks.
Barrie, Barbara. Lone Star. 192p. (gr. 4-7). 1992. pap. 3.50 (*0-440-40718-4*, YB) Dell.
Baylis-White, Mary. Sheltering Rebecca. 112p. (gr. 3-7). 1991. 14.95 (*0-525-67349-0*, Lodestar Bks) Dutton Child Bks.
—Sheltering Rebecca. 112p. (gr. 5-9). 1993. pap. 3.99 (*0-14-036448-X*, Puffin) Puffin Bks.
Bush, Lawrence. Emma Ansky-Levine & Her Mitzvah Machine. Iskowitz, Joel, illus. (Orig.). (gr. 4-6). 1991. pap. 7.95 (*0-8074-0458-6*, 123933) UAHC.
—Rooftop Secrets & Other Stories of Anti-Semitism. Vorspan, Albert, commentary by. LC 86-1362. (Illus.). 144p. (Orig.). (gr. 7 up). 1986. pap. text ed. 7.95 (*0-8074-0314-8*, 121720); tchr's. guide 5.00 (*0-8074-0326-1*, 201441) UAHC.
Chapman, Carol. The Tale of Meshka the Kvetch. Lobel, Arnold, illus. LC 80-11225. 32p. (gr. k-3). 1980. 13.95 (*0-525-40745-6*, DCB) Dutton Child Bks.
Cohen, Sholom. The Lopsided Yarmulke. (ps-3). Date not set. pap. write for info. (*0-922613-51-6*) Hachai Pubns.
Cook-Waldron, Kathleen. Wilderness Passover. (Illus.). (gr. 4-7). 1993. 13.95 (*0-88995-112-8*, Pub. by Red Deer CN) Empire Pub Srvs.
Drucker, M. Grandma's Latkes. Chwast, E., ed. 1992. write for info. (*0-15-200468-8*, Gulliver Bks) HarBrace.
Drucker, Malka & Halperin, Michael. Jacob's Rescue: A Holocaust Story. LC 92-30523. 128p. (gr. 4-7). 1993. 15.95 (*0-553-08976-5*, Skylark) Bantam.
Edwards, Michelle. A Baker's Portrait. LC 90-41926. (Illus.). 32p. (gr. k up). 1991. 13.95 (*0-688-09712-X*); PLB 13.88 (*0-688-09713-8*) Lothrop.
—Chicken Man. Edwards, Michelle, illus. LC 93-11728. 32p. (ps up). 1994. pap. 4.95 (*0-688-13106-9*, Mulberry) Morrow.
Elias, Miriam L. Families, Etc. 1991. 12.95 (*0-87306-576-X*) Feldheim.
—Thanks to You! LC 94-44850. 1994. write for info. (*0-87306-663-4*); pap. write for info. (*0-87306-664-2*) Feldheim.
Elsant, Martin. Bar Mitzvah Lessons. LC 93-628. 1993. write for info. (*1-88128-301-1*) Alef Design.
Estrin, Leibel. The Man Who Rode with Eliyahu Hanavi. Stern, Ayala, illus. 32p. (ps-3). 1990. 9.95 (*0-922613-23-0*); pap. 7.95 (*0-922613-24-9*) Hachai Pubns.
—The Story of Danny Three Times. Zelcer, Amir, illus. 32p. (ps-1). 1989. 8.95 (*0-922613-10-9*); pap. 6.95 (*0-922613-11-7*) Hachai Pubns.
Feder, Harriet K. It Happened in Shushan: A Purim Story. Schanzer, Roz, illus. LC 88-2676. (Orig.). (ps-3). 1988. pap. 3.95 (*0-930494-75-X*) Kar Ben.
—Mystery in Miami Beach: A Vivi Hartman Adventure. 176p. (gr. 5-12). 1992. PLB 17.50 (*0-8225-0733-1*) Lerner Pubns.
Feund, Chanie. Read Me Berashis. Leff, Tora, illus. LC 90-83948. 32p. (ps-2). 1990. 9.95 (*0-685-46905-0*) CIS Comm.
Firer, Benzion. Saadiah Weissman. 140p. (gr. 5-12). 1982. 9.95 (*0-87306-294-9*); pap. 6.95 (*0-685-07830-2*) Feldheim.
—The Twins. Scae, Bracha, tr. from HEB. 230p. (gr. 4-8). 1983. 10.95 (*0-87306-279-5*); pap. 7.95 (*0-87306-340-6*) Feldheim.
Freund, Chavie. Read Me Beraiskis. LC 90-83948. 44p. Date not set. 10.95 (*1-56062-042-0*) CIS Comm.
Fuchs, Yitzchak Y. Halichos Bas Yisroel, Vol. 1. Dombey, Moshe, tr. from HEB. (gr. 7-12). 1987. 15. 95 (*0-87306-397-X*) Feldheim.
Gantz, David. Davey's Hanukkah Golem. Gantz, David, illus. LC 91-2328. 32p. (gr. k-3). 1991. 13.95 (*0-8276-0380-0*) JPS Phila.
Ganz, Yaffa. Hello Heddy Levi. (gr. 4-7). 1989. 8.95 (*0-87306-480-1*) Feldheim.
—Shukis Upsidedown Dream. Gewirtz, Bina, illus. (gr. k-3). 1986. 6.95 (*0-87306-384-8*) Feldheim.
Garfunkel, Debby. Baker's Dozen, No. 9: Through Thick & Thin. 144p. (Orig.). (gr. 4-9). 1993. pap. 7.95 (*1-56871-024-0*) Targum Pr.
Geller, Beverly. The Shalom Zachar. 47p. (ps-1). Date not set. 8.95 (*0-685-72701-7*) CIS Comm.

Geras, Adele. Golden Windows: And Other Stories of Jerusalem. LC 92-39885. 160p. (gr. 3-7). 1993. 14.00 (*0-06-022941-1*); PLB 13.89 (*0-06-022942-X*) HarpC Child Bks.
Gikow, Louise. A Sesame Street Passover: Kippi & the Missing Matzah. Brannon, Tom, illus. 36p. 1994. pap. 5.95 (*1-884857-02-7*) Comet Intl.
Goetz, Bracha. Nicanor Knew the Secret. Zakutinsky, Ruth, ed. Nodel, Norman, illus. 32p. (gr. 3). 1992. PLB 6.95 (*0-911643-14-1*) Aura Bklyn.
Gold, Auner. The Purple Ring. Hinlicky, Gregg, illus. 191p. (gr. 9-12). 1986. 10.95 (*0-935063-16-1*); pap. 8.95 (*0-935063-15-3*) CIS Comm.
Goldin, Barbara D. The Magician's Visit: A Passover Tale. Parker, Robert A., illus. LC 92-22903. 34p. 1993. 14.99 (*0-670-84840-9*) Viking Child Bks.
Goodman, David R. The Mitzvah Mouse. 24p. 1992. 8.95 (*0-317-06108-9*, Pub. by Gefen Pub Hse IS) Gefen Bks.
Goodman, Sarah. Shani Plus Three. 176p. (gr. 6-9). 1993. 9.95 (*1-56871-028-3*) Targum Pr.
Gottesman, Meir U. Chaimkel the Dreamer. Scheinberg, Shepsil, illus. 157p. (gr. 3-5). 1987. 9.95 (*0-935063-26-9*); pap. 7.95 (*0-935063-27-7*) CIS Comm.
Gottlieb, Yaffa L. My Upsheren Book. Bindel, Binah T., illus. 32p. (ps-1). 1991. 8.95 (*0-922613-37-0*); pap. 6.95 (*0-922613-38-9*) Hachai Pubns.
Greene, Jacqueline. One Foot Ashore. LC 93-22961. 144p. (gr. 4-6). 1994. 16.95 (*0-8027-8281-7*) Walker & Co.
Grishaver, Joel L. Tanta Teva & the Magic Booth. Bleicher, David, illus. LC 93-13193. 1993. 11.95 (*1-881283-00-3*) Alef Design.
Grode, Phyllis A. Sophie's Name. Haas, Shelly O., illus. LC 90-4833. 32p. (gr. k-3). 1990. 12.95 (*0-929371-18-6*); pap. 4.95 (*0-929371-19-4*) Kar Ben.
Gunsher, Cheryl. Lev the Lucky Lulav. (Illus.). 24p. (ps-k). 1993. 10.00 (*1-881602-01-X*) Prism NJ.
Halpern, Chaiky. The Dink That Stopped the Clock. 24p. (Orig.). (ps-3). 1985. pap. 2.95 (*0-87306-379-1*) Feldheim.
Hart, Jan S. Hanna, the Immigrant. Roberts, Melissa, ed. Shaw, Charles, illus. 114p. (gr. 6-8). 1991. 12.95 (*0-89015-805-3*) Sunbelt Media.
—The Many Adventures of Minnie. Wilson, Kay, illus. LC 92-17740. 96p. (gr. 4-7). 1992. 12.95 (*0-89015-859-2*) Sunbelt Media.
Hautzig, Esther. Riches. Diamond, Donna, illus. LC 89-26904. 32p. (gr. 3 up). 1992. PLB 13.89 (*0-06-022260-3*) HarpC Child Bks.
Heller, Linda. The Castle on Hester Street. Heller, Linda, illus. 32p. (gr. k-3). 1990. pap. 6.95t (*0-8276-0323-1*) JPS Phila.
Hesse, Karen. Letters from Rifka. 192p. (gr. 4-7). 1992. 14.95 (*0-8050-1964-2*, Bks Young Read) H Holt & Co.
—Letters from Rifka. LC 93-7486. 160p. (gr. 3-7). 1993. pap. 3.99 (*0-14-036391-2*, Puffin) Puffin Bks.
Hest, Amy. Love You, Soldier. LC 90-25161. 48p. (gr. 2-5). 1991. SBE 13.95 (*0-02-743635-7*, Four Winds) Macmillan Child Grp.
—Love You, Soldier. 48p. (gr. 2-6). 1993. pap. 3.99 (*0-14-036174-X*) Puffin Bks.
Hirsh, Marilyn. I Love Hanukkah. Hirsh, Marilyn, illus. LC 84-497. 32p. (ps-3). 1984. reinforced bdg. 13.95 (*0-8234-0525-7*); pap. 5.95 (*0-8234-0622-9*) Holiday.
Howe, Irving & Greenberg, Eliezer, eds. Favorite Yiddish Stories. 128p. 1992. Repr. 5.99 (*0-517-06656-4*, Pub. by Wings Bks) Random Hse Value.
Hubner, Carol K. Silent Shofar. Forst, Sigmund, illus. (gr. 3 up). 6.95 (*0-910818-53-3*); pap. 5.95 (*0-910818-54-1*) Judaica Pr.
—The Tattered Tallis. Kramer, Devorah, illus. 128p. (gr. 3-8). 1979. 5.95 (*0-910818-19-3*) Judaica Pr.
Hurwitz, Johanna. The Rabbi's Girls. Johnson, Pamela, illus. 160p. (gr. 3-7). 1989. pap. 3.95 (*0-14-032951-X*, Puffin) Puffin Bks.
Ish-Kishor, Sulamith. Our Eddie. reissued ed. LC 92-7719. 192p. (gr. 2-5). 1992. 15.00 (*0-394-81455-X*) Knopf Bks Yng Read.
Karkowsky, Nancy. Grandma's Soup. Haas, Shelly O., illus. LC 89-30875. 32p. (gr. k-5). 1989. 8.95 (*0-930494-98-9*) Kar Ben.
Kaye, Marilyn. The Atonement of Mindy Wise. Van Doren, Liz, ed. 160p. (gr. 7 up). 1991. 15.95 (*0-15-200402-5*, Gulliver Bks) HarBrace.
Kimmel, Eric A. Asher & the Capmakers: A Hanukkah Story. Hillenbrand, Will, illus. LC 92-37978. 32p. (ps-3). 1993. reinforced bdg. 15.95 (*0-8234-1031-5*) Holiday.
—The Chanukkah Tree. Carmi, Giora, illus. LC 88-4510. 32p. (ps-3). 1988. reinforced bdg. 14.95 (*0-8234-0705-5*) Holiday.
Klein, Leah. B. Y. Times, No. 1: Shani's Scoop. 1993. pap. 7.95 (*0-685-65290-4*) Feldheim.
—B. Y. Times, No. 10: The New Kids. 1993. pap. 7.95 (*0-685-65299-8*) Feldheim.
—B. Y. Times, No. 11: Dollars & Sense. 144p. 1993. pap. 7.95 (*1-56871-005-4*) Targum Pr.
—B. Y. Times, No. 12: Talking It Over. 149p. 1993. pap. 7.95 (*1-56871-010-0*) Targum Pr.
—B. Y. Times, No. 2: Batya's Search. 1993. pap. 7.95 (*0-685-65291-2*) Feldheim.
—B. Y. Times, No. 3: Twins in Trouble. 1993. pap. 7.95 (*0-685-65292-0*) Feldheim.
—B. Y. Times, No. 4: War! 1993. pap. 7.95 (*0-685-65293-9*) Feldheim.
—B. Y. Times, No. 5: Spring Fever. 1993. pap. 7.95 (*0-685-65294-7*) Feldheim.
—B. Y. Times, No. 6: Party Time. 1993. pap. 7.95 (*0-685-65295-5*) Feldheim.
—B. Y. Times, No. 7: Changing Times. 1993. pap. 9.95 (*0-685-65296-3*) Feldheim.
—B. Y. Times, No. 8: Summer Daze. 1993. pap. 7.95 (*0-685-65297-1*) Feldheim.
—B. Y. Times, No. 9: Here We Go Again. 1993. pap. 7.95 (*0-685-65298-X*) Feldheim.
—Kid Sisters, No. 1: The I-Can't-Cope Club. 1993. pap. 5.95 (*0-685-65300-5*) Feldheim.
—Kid Sisters, No. 2: The Treehouse Kids. 1993. pap. 5.95 (*0-685-65301-3*) Feldheim.
—Kid Sisters, No. 3: Ricky's Great Idea. 107p. 1993. pap. 5.95 (*1-56871-004-6*) Targum Pr.
—Kid Sisters, No. 4: Sarah's Room. 106p. 1993. pap. 5.95 (*1-56871-008-9*) Targum Pr.
—Nechama on Strike. 132p. (Orig.). (gr. 4-9). 1993. pap. 7.95 (*1-56871-029-1*) Targum Pr.
Klein-Ehlich, Tzvia. A Children's Treasure of Sephardic Tales. Galitzer, Channa, illus. 64p. (gr. 4-10). 1985. 11.95 (*0-89906-787-5*); pap. 8.95 (*0-89906-788-3*) Mesorah Pubns.
Kogan, Mark. Archivist, Vol. 1. Khotianovsky, Olga, ed. (RUS., Illus.). 300p. (Orig.). (gr. 9-12). 1990. pap. text ed. write for info. (*0-9624922-0-5*) Hazar NY.
Kranzler, Gershon. Yoshko the Dumbbell. (gr. 4-9). pap. 6.95 (*0-87306-246-9*) Feldheim.
Laird, Christa. Shadow of the Wall. LC 89-34469. (gr. 7 up). 1990. 12.95 (*0-688-09336-1*) Greenwillow.
Lanton, Sandy. Daddy's Chair. Haas, Shelly O., illus. LC 90-44908. 32p. (gr. k-4). 1991. 12.95 (*0-929371-51-8*) Kar Ben.
Lasky, Kathryn. The Night Journey. Hyman, Trina S., illus. 152p. (gr. 5-9). 1986. pap. 4.99 (*0-14-032048-2*, Puffin) Puffin Bks.
Lazewnik, Libby. Absolutely Shira. 190p. (gr. 6-9). 1993. 12.95 (*1-56871-032-1*) Targum Pr.
—Baker's Dozen, No. 1: On Our Own. 1993. pap. 7.95 (*0-685-65302-1*) Feldheim.
—Baker's Dozen, No. 5: The Inside Story. 1993. pap. 7.95 (*0-685-65306-4*) Feldheim.
Lazewnik, Libby, et al. Baker's Dozen, No. 6: Trapped. 1993. pap. 7.95 (*0-685-65307-2*) Feldheim.
Leader, R. L. Faithful Soldiers. (gr. 7 up). 1989. 12.95 (*0-944070-12-4*) Targum Pr.
Lehmann, Marcus. Family y Aguilar. Breuer, Jacob, adapted by. (gr. 7 up). 9.95 (*0-87306-122-5*) Feldheim.
Lepon, Shoshana. Hillel Builds a House. Barr, Marilyn, illus. LC 92-39383. 1993. cancelled (*0-929371-41-0*); pap. 5.95 (*0-929371-42-9*) Kar Ben.
Levitin, Sonia. The Golem & the Dragon Girl. LC 92-27665. 176p. (gr. 3-7). 1993. 14.99 (*0-8037-1280-4*); PLB 14.89 (*0-8037-1281-2*) Dial Bks Young.
—Journey to America. Robinson, Charles, illus. LC 86-22234. 160p. (gr. 3-6). 1987. pap. 3.95 (*0-689-71130-1*, Aladdin) Macmillan Child Grp.
—Journey to America. 2nd ed. LC 70-98616. (Illus.). 160p. (gr. 3-7). 1993. SBE 13.95 (*0-689-31829-4*, Atheneum Child Bk) Macmillan Child Grp.
—The Return. LC 86-25891. 224p. (gr. 5 up). 1987. SBE 14.95 (*0-689-31309-8*, Atheneum Child Bk) Macmillan Child Grp.
Lewis, Shari. One Minute Jewish Stories. 1993. pap. 4.99 (*0-440-40878-4*) Dell.
Lewis, Shari, adapted by. One-Minute Jewish Stories. Collier, Roberta, illus. (ps-3). 1989. 10.00 (*0-385-24447-9*) Doubleday.
Lieberman, Syd. The Wise Shoemaker of Studena. Lemelman, Martin, illus. LC 93-43481. 1994. write for info. (*0-8276-0509-9*) JPS Phila.
Marcus, Audrey F. & Zwerin, Raymond A. Like a Maccabee. Carmi, Giora, illus. (gr. k-3). 1991. 11.95 (*0-8074-0445-4*, 102564) UAHC.
Matas, Carol. Lisa's War. LC 88-29525. 128p. (gr. 7 up). 1989. SBE 13.95 (*0-684-19010-9*, Scribners Young Read) Macmillan Child Grp.
Mazer, Harry. The Last Mission. 192p. (gr. 7 up). 1981. pap. 3.99 (*0-440-94797-9*, LE) Dell.
Medoff, Francine. The Mouse in the Matzah Factory. Goldstein, David, illus. LC 82-23349. 40p. (ps-3). 1983. pap. 4.95 (*0-930494-19-9*) Kar Ben.
Miller, Deborah & Ostrove, Karen. Fins & Scales: A Kosher Tale. Ostrove, Karen, illus. LC 90-24388. 32p. (gr. 1-3). 1992. 8.95 (*0-929371-25-9*) Kar Ben.
Milstein, Linda B. Miami-Nanny Stories. Han, Oki, illus. LC 93-28680. 1994. 16.00 (*0-688-11151-3*, Tambourine Bks); PLB 15.93 (*0-688-11152-1*, Tambourine Bks) Morrow.
Nestlebaum, Chana. The Mookster's Mitzvah Mishaps. LC 91-75362. (Illus.). 32p. (gr. k-4). 1991. 11.95 (*0-910818-26-6*); pap. 8.95 (*0-910818-27-4*) Judaica Pr.
Neville, Emily C. Berries Goodman. LC 65-19485. (gr. 5-9). 1975. pap. 3.95 (*0-06-440072-7*, Trophy) HarpC Child Bks.
Nolan, Han. If I Should Die Before I Wake. LC 93-30720. 1994. 16.95 (*0-15-238040-X*, HB Juv Bks); pap. write for info. (*0-15-238041-8*, HB Juv Bks) HarBrace.
Oppenheim, Shulamith L. Appleblossom. Yolen, Jane, ed. Yardley, Joanna, illus. 28p. (gr. 1-7). 1991. 14.95 (*0-15-203750-0*, HB Juv Bks) HarBrace.
Orlev, Uri. Lydia: Queen of Palestine. Halkin, Hillel, tr. from HEB. LC 93-12488. 1993. 13.95 (*0-395-65660-5*) HM.
Panas, Peter, illus. The Shalom Sesame Players Present: The Story of Passover. 32p. 1994. 12.95 (*1-884857-00-0*); incl. audiocassette 14.95 (*1-884857-01-9*) Comet Intl.
Pape, David S., ed. The Story Hour, Vol. 1. Berg, David & Dershowitz, Yosef, illus. 166p. (ps-3). 1994. write for info. (*0-922613-64-8*) Hachai Pubns.
Polacco, Patricia. Mrs. Katz & Tush. 1992. 15.00 (*0-553-08122-5*, Little Rooster) Bantam.
Pushker, Gloria T. Toby Belfer Never Had a Christmas Tree. Hierstein, Judith, illus. LC 91-14514. 32p. 1991. 14.95 (*0-88289-855-8*) Pelican.
Ray, Karen. To Cross a Line. LC 93-11813. 160p. (gr. 7 up). 1994. 14.95 (*0-531-06831-5*); lib. bdg. 14.99 RLB (*0-531-08681-X*) Orchard Bks Watts.
Reiss, Johanna. The Upstairs Room. LC 77-187940. 208p. (gr. 7 up). 1990. pap. 3.95 (*0-06-440370-X*, Trophy) HarpC Child Bks.
Richter, Hans P. Friedrich. (gr. 5-9). 1987. pap. 4.99 (*0-14-032205-1*, Puffin) Puffin Bks.
Roseman, Kenneth. The Melting Pot. (Illus.). 144p. (Orig.). (gr. 4-6). 1984. pap. 7.95 (*0-8074-0269-9*, 146065) UAHC.
Rosenfeld, Dina. All about Us. Zelcer, Amir, illus. 32p. (ps-1). 1989. 8.95 (*0-922613-02-8*); pap. 6.95 (*0-922613-03-6*) Hachai Pubns.
—Labels for Laibel. Nodel, Norman, illus. 32p. (ps-1). 1990. 8.95 (*0-922613-35-4*); pap. 6.95 (*0-922613-36-2*) Hachai Pubns.
—A Little Boy Named Avram. Lederer, Ilene W., illus. 32p. (ps-1). 1989. 8.95 (*0-922613-08-7*); pap. 6.95 (*0-922613-09-5*) Hachai Pubns.
—Yossi & Laibel Hot on the Trail. Nodel, Norman, illus. 32p. (ps-1). 1991. 8.95 (*0-922613-47-8*); pap. 6.95 (*0-922613-48-6*) Hachai Pubns.
Ross, Lillian H. Buba Leah & Her Paper Children. Morgan, Mary, illus. 32p. (gr. k-3). 1991. 16.95 (*0-8276-0375-4*) JPS Phila.
Roth-Hano, Renee. Safe Harbors. LC 93-10782. 224p. (gr. 12 up). 1993. SBE 16.95 (*0-02-777795-2*, Four Winds) Macmillan Child Grp.
Rothstein, Chaya L. The Mentchkins Make Shabbos. Perlstein, Rivky, illus. (ps-2). 1986. pap. 2.95 (*0-317-42728-8*) Feldheim.
Rouss, Sylvia A. Sammy Spider's First Hanukkah. Kahn, Katherine J., illus. LC 92-39639. 1993. 13.95 (*0-929371-45-3*); pap. 5.95 (*0-929371-46-1*) Kar Ben.
Rubinstein, Reva. We Are One Family. Zakutinsky, Ruth, ed. (Illus.). 24p. (gr. 1-3). 1992. PLB 9.95x (*0-911643-15-X*) Aura Bklyn.
Sachs, Marilyn. Call Me Ruth. LC 94-19695. 1995. write for info. (*0-688-13737-7*, Pub. by Beech Tree Bks) Morrow.
Safran, Faigy. Uncle Moishy Visits Torah Island. Snowdone, Linda, illus. 32p. (gr. 2-8). 1987. incl. cassette 10.95 (*0-318-32597-7*); pap. 5.95 (*0-89906-807-3*) Mesorah Pubns.
Salop, Byrd. The Kiddush Cup Who Hated Wine. Goldstein, Lil, illus. 32p. (gr. 1 up). 1981. pap. 5.95 (*0-8246-0265-X*) Jonathan David.
Saypol, Judyth R. & Wikler, Madeline. My Very Own Shavuot Book. Wikler, Madeline & Fishman, Tamar, illus. 28p. (gr. k-6). 1982. pap. 2.95 (*0-930494-15-6*) Kar Ben.
Schanzer, Roz, illus. In the Synagogue. (ps). 1991. 4.95 (*0-929371-60-7*) Kar-Ben.
Schilder, Rosalind. Dayenu - Enough! How Uncle Murray Saved the Seder. Kahn, Katherine J., photos by. LC 88-1238. (Illus., Orig.). (ps-3). 1988. pap. 4.95 (*0-930494-76-8*) Kar Ben.
Schleimer, Sarah. Far from the Place We Called Home. LC 93-48519. 1994. 15.95 (*0-87306-667-7*) Feldheim.
Schnur, Steven. The Narrowest Bar Mitzvah. Lazzaro, Victor, illus. 48p. (Orig.). (gr. 4-6). 1986. pap. text ed. 6.95 (*0-8074-0316-4*, 123923) UAHC.
—The Return of Morris Schumsky. Lazzaro, Victor, illus. 48p. (gr. 4-6). 1987. pap. 6.95 (*0-8074-0358-X*, 123927) UAHC.
Schotter, Roni. Passover Magic. Hafner, Marylin, illus. LC 93-20053. (gr. 1-8). 1995. 14.95 (*0-316-77468-5*) Little.
Schur, Maxine R. Day of Delight: A Jewish Sabbath in Ethiopia. Pinkney, Brian, illus. LC 93-31451. (gr. 3 up). 1994. 15.99 (*0-8037-1413-0*); PLB 15.89 (*0-8037-1414-9*) Dial Bks Young.
Schwartz, Amy. Mrs. Moskowitz & the Sabbath Candlesticks. Schwartz, Amy, illus. 32p. (gr. k-5). 1983. pap. 6.95t (*0-8276-0231-6*) JPS Phila.
Segal, Jerry. The Place Where Nobody Stopped. Pilkey, Dav, illus. LC 90-43016. 160p. (gr. 6-8). 1991. 14.95 (*0-531-05897-2*); PLB 14.99 (*0-531-08497-3*) Orchard Bks Watts.
Sevela, Ephraim. We Were Not Like Other People. Bouis, Antonina W., tr. from RUS. LC 89-11015. 224p. (gr. 7 up). 1989. HarpC Child Bks.
Sherman, Eileen B. Independence Avenue. 164p. (gr. 5-8). 1990. 13.95 (*0-8276-0367-3*) JPS Phila.
—Monday in Odessa. (gr. 5-9). 1986. 11.95 (*0-8276-0262-6*) JPS Phila.
Shiefman, Vicky. Good-Bye to the Trees. LC 92-22260. 176p. (gr. 4-8). 1993. SBE 14.95 (*0-689-31806-5*, Atheneum Child Bk) Macmillan Child Grp.
Sholem-Aleykhem. Tevye the Dairyman: Complete, Illustrated. Simons, Joseph, ed. Katz, Miriam, tr. Bennett, Manuel, illus. (YID.). 160p. (gr. 10-12). 1994. pap. 12.95 (*0-934710-31-7*) J Simon.

Sidi, Smadar S. Little Daniel & the Jewish Delicacies. Schaer, Miriam, illus. (ps-5). 1988. 9.95 (*1-55774-028-3*) Modan-Adama Bks.

Siegel, Balky. Baker's Dozen, No. 2: Ghosthunters. 1993. pap. 7.95 (*0-685-65303-X*) Feldheim.

Silver, Norman. Python Dance. 192p. (gr. 8 up). 1993. 14.99 (*0-525-45161-7*, DCB) Dutton Child Bks.

Silverman, Maida. The Glass Menorah & Other Stories for Jewish Holidays. Levine, Marge, illus. LC 91-13890. 64p. (gr. 1-4). 1992. RSBE 14.95 (*0-02-782682-1*, Four Winds) Macmillan Child Grp.

Snyder, Carol. God Must Like Cookies, Too. Glick, Beth, illus. LC 92-26886. 32p. (ps-3). 1993. 16.95 (*0-8276-0423-8*) JPS Phila.

Sokoloff, David. Jewish Stories of Fun & Adventure. (Illus.). 96p. (gr. 1-3). 1990. pap. 5.95 (*0-685-35727-9*) Shapolsky Pubs.

Stein, Aidel. Baker's Dozen, No. 3: And the Winner Is... 1993. pap. 7.95 (*0-685-65304-8*) Feldheim.

—Baker's Dozen, No. 4: Stars in Their Eyes. 1993. pap. 7.95 (*0-685-65305-6*) Feldheim.

Steiner, Connie C. On Eagles Wings & Other Things. 32p. (gr. k-4). 1987. 12.95 (*0-8276-0274-X*) JPS Phila.

Tobias, Tobi. Pot Luck. Malone, Nola L., illus. LC 92-27678. 32p. (ps-3). 1993. pap. 15.00 (*0-688-09824-X*); PLB 14.93 (*0-688-09825-8*) Lothrop.

Topek, Susan R. A Holiday for Noah. Springer, Sally, illus. LC 89-48189. 24p. (ps). 1990. 10.95 (*0-929371-07-0*) Kar Ben.

Topek, Susan Remick. A Taste for Noah. Springer, Sally, illus. LC 92-39384. (gr. k up). 1993. 12.95 (*0-929371-39-9*); pap. 4.95 (*0-929371-40-2*) Kar Ben.

Travis, Lucille. Tirzah. Garber, S. David, ed. LC 90-23580. 160p. (Orig.). (gr. 3-7). 1991. pap. 5.95 (*0-8361-3546-6*) Herald Pr.

Treseder, Terry W. Hear O Israel: A Story of the Warsaw Ghetto. Bloom, Lloyd, illus. LC 89-7029. 48p. (gr. 3 up). 1990. SBE 13.95 (*0-689-31456-6*, Atheneum Child Bk) Macmillan Child Grp.

Tyberg, Sarah. Shaindy Strikes Again. (Illus.). 167p. (gr. 6-8). 1993. 10.95 (*1-56871-030-5*) Targum Pr.

Vineberg, Ethel. Grandmother Came from Dworitz: A Jewish Love Story. Briansky, Rita, illus. 44p. (gr. 4 up). 1987. Repr. of 1978 ed. text ed. 3.95 (*0-88776-195-X*) Tundra Bks.

Voigt, Cynthia. David & Jonathan. 208p. 1992. 14.95 (*0-590-45165-0*, Scholastic Hardcover) Scholastic Inc.

Weil, Judith. School for One. (gr. 4 up). 1992. 11.95 (*0-87306-620-0*); pap. 9.95 (*0-87306-621-9*) Feldheim.

Weilerstein, Sadie R. Best of K'tonton. Hirsh, Marilyn, illus. LC 80-20177. 96p. (gr. 1 up). 1980. pap. 9.95 (*0-8276-0187-5*) JPS Phila.

—K'tonton in the Circus: A Hanukkah Adventure. Hirsh, Marilyn, illus. LC 81-11765. 96p. (gr. 2 up). pap. 8.95 (*0-8276-0303-7*) JPS Phila.

—K'tonton's Sukkot Adventure. Boddy, Joe, illus. LC 93-2990. 34p. (ps-3). 1993. 12.95 (*0-8276-0502-1*) JPS Phila.

Weinbach, Shaindel. The Three Merchants: And Other Stories. Dershowitz, Y., illus. 160p. (gr. 6-12). 1983. 13.95 (*0-89906-768-9*); pap. 10.95 (*0-89906-769-7*) Mesorah Pubns.

Weissenberg, Fran. The Streets Are Paved with Gold. LC 89-24413. (Illus.). 160p. (Orig.). (gr. 5 up). 1990. pap. 6.95 (*0-943173-51-5*) Harbinger AZ.

Werlin, Nancy. Are You Alone on Purpose? 1994. 14.95 (*0-395-67350-X*) HM.

Wild, Margaret. Let the Celebrations Begin! Vivas, Julie, illus. LC 90-21606. 32p. (ps-1). 1991. 14.95 (*0-531-05937-5*); RLB 14.99 (*0-531-08537-6*) Orchard Bks Watts.

Winkler, Gershon. The Hostage Torah. Jones, Yochanan, illus. (gr. 7 up). 1981. pap. 5.95 (*0-910818-34-7*) Judaica Pr.

Wohl, Lauren L. Matzoh Mouse. Keavney, Pamela, illus. LC 90-31976. 32p. (gr. k-3). 1993. pap. 4.95 (*0-06-443323-4*, Trophy) HarpC Child Bks.

Yaffe, Rochel. Rambam: The Story of Rabbi Moshe Ben Maimon. Nodel, Norman, illus. 220p. (gr. 8 up). 1992. 10.95 (*0-922613-14-1*); pap. 8.95 (*0-922613-15-X*) Hachai Pubns.

Yolen, Jane. Devil's Arithmetic. 1990. pap. 3.99 (*0-14-034535-3*, Puffin) Puffin Bks.

Zakon, Miriam S. The Egyptian Star. Gaelen, Nina, illus. 114p. (gr. 3-9). 1983. o. p. 6.95 (*0-910818-47-9*); pap. 5.95 (*0-910818-48-7*) Judaica Pr.

Zakutinsky, Ruth. The Wonder Worm. Backman, Aidel, illus. 24p. (gr. k-3). 1992. PLB 6.95x (*0-911643-17-6*) Aura Bklyn.

Zalben. Happy Passover Rosie. (gr. 4 up). 1991. 13.95 (*0-8050-1442-X*) H Holt & Co.

Zalben, Jane B. The Fortuneteller in 5B. (Illus.). 144p. (gr. 4-7). 1991. 14.95 (*0-8050-1537-X*, Bks Young Read) H Holt & Co.

—Happy New Year, Beni. Zalben, Jane B., photos by. LC 92-25013. (Illus.). 32p. (gr. k-3). 1993. 13.95 (*0-8050-1961-8*, Bks Young Read) H Holt & Co.

Zemach, Margot. Siempre Puede Ser Peor: It Could Always Be Worse. Marcuse, Aida, tr. (SPA., Illus.). 32p. (ps-3). 1992. 17.00 (*0-374-36907-0*, Mirasol) FS&G.

Zusman, Evelyn. The Passover Parrot. Kahn, Katherine J., illus. LC 83-22182. 40p. (ps-3). 1984. pap. 4.95 (*0-930494-30-X*) Kar Ben.

JEWS–FOLKLORE

see Folklore, Jewish

JEWS–HISTORY

Abells, Chana B. The Children We Remember. LC 85-24876. (Illus.). 48p. (ps up). 1986. 13.00 (*0-688-06371-3*); PLB 12.93 (*0-688-06372-1*) Greenwillow.

Bull, Norman. Church of the Jews. (gr. 2-7). 1975. 10.95 (*0-7175-0450-6*) Dufour.

—Founders of the Jews. (gr. 2-7). 1985. pap. 10.95 (*0-7175-0977-X*) Dufour.

Charry, Elias & Segal, Abraham. The Eternal People. (Illus.). 448p. (gr. 9-11). 7.50x (*0-8381-0206-9*, 10-206) United Syn Bk.

Dimont, Max I. The Amazing Adventures of the Jewish People. LC 84-16806. 175p. (gr. 8 up). 1984. pap. 5.95 (*0-87441-391-5*) Behrman.

Drew, Margaret, ed. Holocaust & Human Behavior: Annotated Bibliography. 124p. 1989. lib. bdg. 15.85 (*0-8027-9411-4*) Walker & Co.

Eisenberg, Azriel. Fill a Blank Page: A Biography of Solomon Schechter. (Illus.). (gr. 6-11). 3.75 (*0-8381-0730-3*, 10-730) United Syn Bk.

Finkelstein, Norman H. The Other Fourteen Ninety-Two: Jewish Settlement in the New World. LC 89-6253. (Illus.). 100p. (gr. 6 up). 1992. pap. 4.95 (*0-688-11572-1*, Pub. by Beech Tree Bks) Morrow.

Goldin, Barbara D. The Passover Journey: A Seder Companion. Waldman, Neil, illus. LC 93-5133. 64p. 1994. 15.99 (*0-670-82421-6*) Viking Child Bks.

Goldwurm, Hersh & Holder, Meir. History of the Jewish People, Vol. I: The Second Temple Era. (Illus.). 226p. (gr. 7-8). 1993. 18.95 (*0-89906-454-X*); pap. 15.95 (*0-89906-455-8*) Mesorah Pubns.

Holder, Meir. History of the Jewish People, Vol. II: From Yavneh to Pumbedisa. Goldwurm, Hersh, ed. (Illus.). 332p. (gr. 7-8). 1993. 18.95 (*0-89906-499-X*); pap. 15.95 (*0-89906-475-2*) Mesorah Pubns.

Jones, Graham. How They Lived in Bible Times. Deverell, Richard & Deverell, Christine, illus. LC 91-30420. 48p. (gr. 1-8). 1992. 12.99 (*0-8307-1574-6*, 5112125) Regal.

Karp, Deborah. Heroes of American Jew History. (Illus.). (gr. 6-7). 1966. pap. 7.95x (*0-87068-539-2*) Ktav.

Lipson, Ruth. Modeh Ani Means Thank You. (Illus.). (ps-2). 1986. 7.95 (*0-87306-392-9*) Feldheim.

Meltzer, Milton. Never to Forget: The Jews of the Holocaust. LC 75-25409. (gr. 7 up). 1976. PLB 15.89 (*0-06-024175-6*) HarpC Child Bks.

Navon, Ziva B., ed. The Glorious Sephardic Heritage. 120p. (Orig.). (gr. 6-12). 1992. pap. text ed. 10.00 (*0-685-57455-5*) Central Agency.

Odijk, Pamela. The Israelites. (Illus.). 48p. (gr. 5-8). 1990. PLB 12.95 (*0-382-09888-9*); 7.95 (*0-382-24263-7*); tchr's. guide 4.50 (*0-382-24278-5*) Silver Burdett Pr.

Rosenfield, Geraldine. The Heroes of Masada. Sugarman, S. Allan, illus. 38p. (gr. 6-10). pap. 1.50 (*0-8381-0733-8*, 10-732) United Syn Bk.

Rossel, Seymour. Introduction to Jewish History. Kozodoy, Neil, ed. Kahn, Katherine, illus. 128p. (gr. 4-5). 1981. pap. text ed. 6.95 (*0-87441-335-4*); By Lenore C. Kipper. tchr's guide 12.50x (*0-87441-378-8*); Malkah L. Avrami. student's activity bk. 4.25 (*0-87441-363-X*) Behrman.

Sachar, A. L. History of the Jews. rev. ed. (gr. 6 up). 1967. pap. text ed. write for info. (*0-07-553559-9*); pap. text ed. 20.95 (*0-685-02836-4*) McGraw.

Stadtler, Bea. The Adventures of Gluckel of Hameln. LC 67-18814. (gr. 6-10). 3.75 (*0-8381-0731-1*, 10-731) United Syn Bk.

Synge, Ursula. The People & the Promise. LC 74-10661. 192p. (gr. 7-10). 1974. 22.95 (*0-87599-208-0*) S G Phillips.

Trepp, Leo. A History of the Jewish Experience: Eternal Faith, Eternal People. (gr. 9 up). 12.95 (*0-317-70167-3*) Behrman.

Weilerstein, Sadie R. Jewish Heroes, 2 bks. Cassel, Lili, illus. 208p. (gr. 2-3). Bk. 1. 4.25x (*0-8381-0180-1*); Bk. 2. 4.25x (*0-8381-0177-1*) United Syn Bk.

JEWS–HISTORY–FICTION

Atlas, Susan. Passover Passage. (gr. 4-7). 1991. 5.95 (*0-933873-46-8*) Torah Aura.

Cohen, Barbara. Yussel's Prayer. Deraney, Michael J., illus. LC 80-25377. 32p. (gr. k-4). 1981. PLB 14.93 (*0-688-00461-X*) Lothrop.

Cohen, Sholem. Yitzy & the G.O.L.E.M. 128p. (gr. 4-8). 1992. pap. text ed. 6.95 (*0-922613-50-8*) Hachai Pubns.

Gold, Avner. Envoy from Vienna. Hinlicky, Gregg, contrib. by. 185p. (gr. 9-12). 1986. 10.95 (*0-935063-22-6*); pap. 8.95 (*0-935063-21-8*) CIS Comm.

Levitin, Sonia. Escape from Egypt: A Novel. LC 93-29376. 1994. 16.95 (*0-316-52273-2*) Little.

Narell, Irena. Joshua: Fighter for Bar Kochba. LC 78-55959. (gr. 6-12). 1979. pap. 5.95 (*0-934764-01-8*) Akiba Pr.

Roseman, Kenneth. Escape from the Holocaust. 192p. (Orig.). (gr. 4-6). 1985. pap. 7.95 (*0-8074-0307-5*, 140070) UAHC.

Sender, Ruth M. To Life. LC 88-9312. 240p. (gr. 7 up). 1988. SBE 14.95 (*0-02-781831-4*, Macmillan Child Bk) Macmillan Child Grp.

Thoene, Bodie. Light in Zion. LC 88-4578. 352p. (Orig.). (gr. 11-12). 1988. pap. 9.99 (*0-87123-990-6*) Bethany Hse.

JEWS–LANGUAGE

see Hebrew Language

JEWS–LITERATURE

see Hebrew Literature; Jewish Literature

JEWS–PERSECUTIONS

Adler, David. We Remember the Holocaust. LC 87-21139. (Illus.). 144p. (gr. 6 up). 1989. 17.95 (*0-8050-0434-3*, Bks Young Read) H Holt & Co.

Meltzer, Milton. Never to Forget: The Jews of the Holocaust. LC 75-25409. (gr. 7 up). 1976. PLB 15.89 (*0-06-024175-6*) HarpC Child Bks.

Patterson, Charles. Anti-Semitism: The Road to the Holocaust & Beyond. 160p. (gr. 8). 1988. pap. 9.95 (*0-8027-7318-4*) Walker & Co.

JEWS–RELIGION

see Judaism

JEWS–RITES AND CEREMONIES

Chanover, Hyman & Zusman, Evelyn. A Book of Prayer for Junior Congregations: Sabbath & Festivals. (ENG & HEB.). 256p. (gr. 4-7). 4.50x (*0-8381-0174-7*, 10-174) United Syn Bk.

Chanover, Hyman, adapted by. Service for the High Holy Days Adapted for Youth. LC 72-2058. 192p. (gr. 8 up). 1972. pap. 4.95x (*0-87441-123-8*) Behrman.

Eisenberg, Azriel & Robinson, Jessie B. My Jewish Holidays. 208p. (gr. 5-6). 3.95x (*0-8381-0176-3*, 10-176) United Syn Bk.

Gersh, Harry. When a Jew Celebrates. Weihs, Erika, illus. LC 70-116678. 256p. (gr. 5-6). 1971. pap. text ed. 7.95x (*0-87441-091-6*); tchr's guide 14.95 (*0-685-41997-5*); student activity bk. 3.95 (*0-685-41998-3*); tchr's cassette 5.95 (*0-685-00740-5*) Behrman.

Grama, Shimon. Students' Yoman. (ENG & HEB.). 112p. (gr. 4-12). 1993. pap. text ed. 10.00 (*0-9635739-0-X*) Innovat NY.

Grossman, Miriam. The Wonder of Becoming You: How a Jewish Girl Grows Up. (gr. 6-8). 1988. 8.95 (*0-87306-438-0*) Feldheim.

Metter, Bert. Bar Mitzvah, Bat Mitzvah: How Jewish Boys & Girls Come of Age. Friedman, Marvin, illus. LC 83-23230. 64p. (Orig.). (gr. 4 up). 1984. (Clarion Bks) HM.

Neusner, Jacob. Mitzvah. (gr. 6-8). 5.95 (*0-317-70156-8*); tchr's guide 14.95 (*0-317-70157-6*) Behrman.

Oren, Rony. The Animated Haggadah (1990 Edition) (Illus.). 54p. 1990. 14.95 (*0-944007-43-0*) Shapolsky Pubs.

Patterson, Jose. Mazal-Tov: A Jewish Wedding. (Illus.). 25p. (gr. 2-4). 1991. 12.95 (*0-237-60140-0*, Pub. by Evans Bros Ltd) Trafalgar.

Rubenstein, Howard S. & Rubenstein, Judith S. Becoming Free: A Biblically Oriented Haggadah for Passover: The Permanent Relevance of the Ancient Lesson. LC 93-73663. 200p. 1993. pap. 9.95 (*0-9638886-0-9*) Granite Hills Pr.

Siegel, Danny. Tell Me a Mitzvah: Little & Big Ways to Repair the World. Friedman, Judith, illus. LC 93-7552. 64p. (Orig.). (gr. 2-6). 1993. pap. 7.95 (*0-929371-78-X*) Kar Ben.

Syme, Daniel B. Jewish Mourning. 1989. pap. 3.00 (*0-8074-0332-6*, 388494) UAHC.

Techner, David & Hirt-Manheimer, Judith. A Candle for Grandpa: A Guide to the Jewish Funeral for Children & Parents. Iskowitz, Joel, illus. (gr. k-3). 1993. 10.95 (*0-8074-0507-8*, 123070) UAHC.

Zlotowitz, M. My Blessings for Food: Birchas Hamozon. Horen, Michael, illus. 32p. (gr. 1-6). 7.95 (*0-89906-799-9*) Mesorah Pubns.

Zwebner, Janet. The Animated Haggadah Activity Book. 48p. (ps-8). 1990. pap. 5.95 (*0-944007-46-5*) Shapolsky Pubs.

JEWS IN GERMANY

Drucker, Olga L. Kindertransport. LC 92-14121. (gr. 5-8). 1992. 14.95 (*0-8050-1711-9*, Bks Young Read) H Holt & Co.

Koehn, Ilse. Mischling, Second Degree: My Childhood in Nazi Germany. LC 77-6189. 240p. (gr. 7 up). 1977. 15.00 (*0-688-80110-2*); PLB 14.93 (*0-688-84110-4*) Greenwillow.

—Mischling, Second Degree: My Childhood in Nazi Germany. 240p. (gr. 6 up). 1990. pap. 4.95 (*0-14-034290-7*, Puffin) Puffin Bks.

JEWS IN POLAND

Fluek, Toby. Passover As I Remember It. Fluek, Toby, illus. LC 92-9020. 40p. (gr. k-5). 1994. 15.00 (*0-679-83876-7*) Knopf Bks Yng Read.

Sender, Ruth M. The Cage. LC 86-8562. 252p. (gr. 7 up). 1986. SBE 16.95 (*0-02-781830-6*, Macmillan Child Bk) Macmillan Child Grp.

JEWS IN THE NETHERLANDS

Frank, Anne. Anne Frank: The Diary of a Young Girl. rev. ed. Mooyaart, B. M., tr. Roosevelt, Eleanor, intro. by. LC 52-6355. 312p. (gr. 7 up). 1967. 24.95 (*0-385-04019-9*) Doubleday.

—Diary of a Young Girl. large type ed. 1989. Repr. of 1947 ed. 15.95 (*0-685-47378-3*, Crnrstn Bks) BDD LT Grp.

Isaacman, Clara & Grossman, Joan A. Clara's Story. LC 84-14339. 180p. (gr. 3-7). 1984. 11.95 (*0-8276-0243-X*); pap. 9.95 (*0-8276-0506-4*) JPS Phila.

JEWS IN THE SOVIET UNION–FICTION

Matas, Carol. Sworn Enemies. LC 92-6188. 148p. 1993. 16.00 (*0-553-08326-0*) Bantam.

Schur, Maxine R. The Circlemaker. LC 93-17983. 1994. 13.99 (*0-8037-1354-1*) Dial Bks Young.

Segal, Jerry. The Place Where Nobody Stopped. Cohn, Amy, ed. Pilkey, Dar, illus. LC 94-86. 160p. (gr. 5 up). 1994. pap. 4.95 (*0-688-12567-0*, Pub. by Beech Tree Bks) Morrow.

JEWS IN THE U. S.

Bar-Lev, Geoffrey & Sakkal, Joyce. Jewish Amerian Struggle for Equality. LC 92-7473. 1992. 22.60 (*0-86593-182-8*); 16.95s.p. (*0-685-59291-X*) Rourke Corp.

Brownstone, David M. The Jewish-American Heritage. LC 87-19905. (Illus.). 128p. (gr. 7 up). 1988. 16.95x (*0-8160-1628-3*) Facts on File.

Butwin, Frances. The Jews in America. rev. ed. 87p. (gr. 5 up). 1991. PLB 15.95 (*0-8225-0217-8*) Lerner Pubns.

—Jews in America. 1991. pap. 5.95 (*0-8225-1044-8*) Lerner Pubns.

Finkelstein, Norman H. The Other Fourteen Ninety-Two: Jewish Settlement in the New World. LC 89-6253. (Illus.). 96p. (gr. 5-9). 1989. SBE 13.95 (*0-684-18913-5*, Scribners Young Read) Macmillan Child Grp.

Huttenbach, Henry. The Jewish Americans. Moynihan, Daniel P., intro. by. 112p. (Orig.). (gr. 5 up). 1989. 17. 95 (*0-87754-887-0*); pap. 9.95 (*0-7910-0270-5*) Chelsea Hse.

Kenvin, Helene. This Land of Liberty: A History of America's Jews. 216p. (gr. 7-9). 1986. pap. text ed. 8. 95x (*0-87441-421-0*) Behrman.

Leiman, Sondra. America: The Jewish Experience. Sarna, Jonathan, ed. (Illus., Orig.). (gr. 4-6). 1994. pap. text ed. 12.00x (*0-8074-0500-0*, 123938); tchr's. guide 10. 00 (*0-8074-0501-9*, 208034) UAHC.

Prophet, Mark L. & Prophet, Elizabeth C. Ascended Masters on Soul Mates & Twin Flames Bks I & II. 1985. 418p. 19.95, (*0-916766-85-3*); 404p. 19.95, (*0-916766-86-1*) Summit Univ.

JEWS IN THE U. S.–FICTION

Blos, Joan W. Brooklyn Doesn't Rhyme. Birling, Paul, illus. LC 93-31589. 96p. (gr. 3-6). 1994. SBE 12.95 (*0-684-19694-8*, Scribners Young Read) Macmillan Child Grp.

Blume, Judy. Starring Sally J. Freedman As Herself. LC 76-57805. 296p. (gr. 4-7). 1982. SBE 15.95 (*0-02-711070-2*, Bradbury Pr) Macmillan Child Grp.

Chapman, Carol. Tale of Meshka the Kvetch. (ps-3). 1993. pap. 4.99 (*0-14-054787-8*) Puffin Bks.

Cohen, Barbara. Make a Wish, Molly. Jones, Jan N., illus. LC 93-17901. 1994. 14.95 (*0-385-31079-X*) Delacorte.

Herman, Charlotte. What Happened to Heather Hopkowitz? LC 93-43628. 1994. pap. write for info. (*0-8276-0520-X*) JPS Phila.

Hurwitz, Johanna. Once I Was a Plum Tree. Fetz, Ingrid, illus. LC 79-23518. 160p. (gr. 4-6). 1980. PLB 12.88 (*0-688-32223-9*) Morrow Jr Bks.

Lakin, Patricia. Don't Forget. Rand, Ted, illus. LC 93-20341. 32p. 1994. 14.00 (*0-688-12075-X*, Tambourine Bks); PLB 13.93 (*0-688-12076-8*, Tambourine Bks) Morrow.

Lasky, Kathryn. Pageant. LC 86-12087. 240p. (gr. 7 up). 1986. SBE 14.95 (*0-02-751720-9*, Four Winds) Macmillan Child Grp.

Levinson, Riki. Soon, Annala. Downing, Julie, photos by. LC 92-44588. (Illus.). 32p. (ps-2). 1993. 14.95 (*0-531-05494-2*); PLB 14.99 (*0-531-08644-5*) Orchard Bks Watts.

Levitin, Sonia. Silver Days. LC 91-22581. 192p. (gr. 3-7). 1992. pap. 3.95 (*0-689-71570-6*, Aladdin) Macmillan Child Grp.

Little, Jean. Kate. LC 20-148419. 174p. (gr. 5-8). 1973. pap. 3.95 (*0-06-440037-9*, Trophy) HarpC Child Bks.

Lowry, Lois. Anastasia Krupnik. (gr. 4-7). 1984. pap. 3.50 (*0-440-40852-0*) Dell.

Moss, Marissa. In America. Moss, Marissa, illus. LC 93-26885. 1994. write for info. (*0-525-45152-8*, DCB) Dutton Child Bks.

Newman, Leslea. Fat Chance. LC 94-7692. 224p. (gr. 3-7). 1994. 14.95 (*0-399-22760-1*, Putnam) Putnam Pub Group.

Portnoy, Mindy A. Matzah Ball. Kahn, Katherine J., illus. LC 93-39402. 1994. 13.95 (*0-929371-68-2*); pap. 5.95 (*0-929371-69-0*) Kar Ben.

Roseman, Kenneth D. The Other Side of the Hudson. (Orig.). (gr. 4-6). 1993. pap. 7.95 (*0-8074-0506-X*, 140061) UAHC.

JIUJITSU

see Judo

JOAN OF ARC, SAINT, 1412-1431

Banfield, Susan. Joan of Arc. (Illus.). 112p. (gr. 5 up). 1985. lib. bdg. 17.95 (*0-87754-556-1*) Chelsea Hse.

Brooks, Polly S. Beyond the Myth: The Story of Joan of Arc. LC 89-37327. (Illus.). 192p. (gr. 7 up). 1990. 16. 00 (*0-397-32422-7*, Lipp Jr Bks); PLB 15.89 (*0-397-32423-5*, Lipp Jr Bks) HarpC Child Bks.

Christopher, Tracy. Joan of Arc: Soldier Saint. (Illus.). 80p. (gr. 3-5). 1993. PLB 13.95 (*0-7910-1767-2*, Am Art Analog) Chelsea Hse.

Smith, Dorothy. Saint Joan: The Girl in Armour. Broomfield, Robert, illus. 1990. 2.95 (*0-8091-6594-5*) Paulist Pr.

Storr, Catherine. Joan of Arc. Taylor, Robert, illus. LC 84-18346. 32p. (gr. 2-5). 1985. PLB 19.97 (*0-8172-2111-5*) Raintree Steck-V.

Williams, Brian. Joan of Arc. (Illus.). 32p. (gr. 3-8). 1989. PLB 10.95 (*1-85435-202-4*) Marshall Cavendish.

Windeatt, Mary F. St. Joan of Arc. Harmon, Gedge, illus. 32p. (gr. 1-5). 1989. Repr. of 1954 ed. wkbk. 3.00 (*0-89555-367-8*) TAN Bks Pubs.

JOAN OF ARC, SAINT, 1412-1431–FICTION

Dana, Barbara. Young Joan. LC 90-39494. 384p. (gr. 7 up). 1991. PLB 17.89 (*0-06-021423-6*) HarpC Child Bks.

JOB DISCRIMINATION

see Discrimination in Employment

JOBS

see Occupations; Professions

JOHN HENRY

Lester, Julius. John Henry. Pinkney, Jerry, illus. LC 93-34583. 40p. (ps-3). 1994. 16.99 (*0-8037-1606-0*); PLB 16.89 (*0-8037-1607-9*) Dial Bks Young.

JOHNSON, AMY, 1903-1941

Bailey, Eva. Amy Johnson. (Illus.). 64p. (gr. 5-9). 1991. 11.95 (*0-237-60032-3*, Pub. by Evans Bros Ltd) Trafalgar.

JOHNSON, ANDREW, PRESIDENT U. S. 1808-1875

Durwood, Thomas A. Andrew Johnson: Rebuilding the Union. Gallin, Richard, ed. Steele, Henry, intro. by. (Illus.). 160p. (gr. 5 up). 1990. PLB 12.95 (*0-382-09945-1*); PLB 12.74s.p. (*0-685-47042-3*); pap. 7.95 (*0-382-24054-5*) Silver Burdett Pr.

Kent, Zachary. Andrew Johnson. LC 88-39115. (Illus.). 100p. (gr. 3 up). 1989. PLB 14.40 (*0-516-01363-7*) Childrens.

Paley, Alan L. Andrew Johnson: The President Impeached. Rahmas, D. Steve, ed. LC 74-190248. 32p. (gr. 7-12). 1972. lib. bdg. 4.95 incl. catalog cards (*0-87157-531-0*) SamHar Pr.

Stevens, Rita. Andrew Johnson: Seventeenth President of the United States. Young, Richard G., ed. LC 88-28487. (Illus.). (gr. 5-9). 1989. PLB 17.26 (*0-944483-16-X*) Garrett Ed Corp.

JOHNSON, CLAUDIA ALTA (TAYLOR) 1912-

Flynn, Jean. Lady: The Story of Claudia Alta (Lady Bird) Johnson. 144p. (gr. 8-12). 1992. 14.95 (*0-89015-821-5*) Sunbelt Media.

JOHNSON, JAMES WELDON, 1871-1938

McKissack, Patricia & McKissack, Fredrick. James Weldon Johnson: Lift Every Voice & Sing. LC 89-77273. (Illus.). 32p. (gr. 2-5). 1990. PLB 11.80 (*0-516-04174-6*); pap. text ed. 3.95 (*0-516-44174-4*) Childrens.

Tolbert-Rouchaleau, Jane. James Weldon Johnson. King, Coretta Scott, intro. by. (Illus.). 112p. (Orig.). (gr. 5 up). 1988. 17.95 (*1-55546-596-X*); pap. 9.95 (*0-7910-0211-X*) Chelsea Hse.

JOHNSON, LYNDON BAINES, PRESIDENT U. S. 1908-1973

Devaney, John. Lyndon Baines Johnson, President. LC 85-31751. 128p. (gr. 5 up). 1986. 12.95 (*0-8027-6638-2*); PLB 13.85 (*0-8027-6639-0*) Walker & Co.

Eskow, Dennis. Lyndon Baines Johnson. LC 92-43687. (Illus.). 160p. (gr. 9-12). 1993. PLB 14.40 (*0-531-13019-3*) Watts.

Falkof, Lucille. Lyndon B. Johnson: Thirty-Sixth President of the United States. Young, Richard G., ed. LC 88-31003. (Illus.). (gr. 5-9). 1989. PLB 17.26 (*0-944483-20-8*) Garrett Ed Corp.

Flynn, Jean. Lady: The Story of Claudia Alta (Lady Bird) Johnson. 144p. (gr. 8-12). 1992. 14.95 (*0-89015-821-5*) Sunbelt Media.

Foster, Leila M. The Story of the Great Society. LC 90-22445. (Illus.). 32p. (gr. 3-6). 1991. PLB 12.30 (*0-516-04755-8*); pap. 3.95 (*0-516-44755-6*) Childrens.

Hargrove, Jim. Lyndon B. Johnson. LC 87-15890. (Illus.). 100p. (gr. 3 up). 1987. 14.40 (*0-516-01396-3*) Childrens.

Kaye, Tony. Lyndon B. Johnson. Schlesinger, Arthur M., Jr., intro. by. (Illus.). 112p. (gr. 5 up). 1988. lib. bdg. 17.95 (*0-87754-536-7*) Chelsea Hse.

Kurland, Gerald. Lyndon Baines Johnson: President Caught in an Ordeal of Power. Rahmas, D. Steve, ed. LC 76-190243. 32p. (Orig.). (gr. 7-12). 1972. lib. bdg. 4.95 incl. catalog cards (*0-87157-525-6*) SamHar Pr.

Lyndon B. Johnson: Mini-Play. (gr. 8 up). 1978. 6.50 (*0-685-42322-0*) Stevens & Shea.

Sandak, Cass R. The Lyndon Johnsons. LC 92-33522. (Illus.). 48p. (gr. 5). 1993. text ed. 4.95 RSBE (*0-89686-644-0*, Crestwood Hse) Macmillan Child Grp.

JOHNSTOWN, PENNSYLVANIA–FLOOD, 1889

Gross, Virginia T. The Day It Rained Forever: The Story of the Johnstown Flood. Himler, Ronald, illus. LC 92-44712. 64p. (gr. 2-6). 1993. pap. 3.99 (*0-14-034567-1*, Puffin) Puffin Bks.

Stein. Johnstown Flood. 1989. pap. 3.95 (*0-516-44680-0*) Childrens.

Walker, Paul R. Head for the Hills! The Amazing True Story of the Johnstown Flood. 96p. (Orig.). (gr. 2-5). 1993. pap. 2.99 (*0-679-84761-8*, Bullseye Bks) Random Bks Yng Read.

JOKES

see Wit and Humor

JOLIET, LOUIS, 1645-1700

Kent, Zachary. Jacques Marquette & Louis Jolliet: Mississippi River Voyagers. LC 92-36888. (Illus.). 128p. (gr. 3 up). 1994. PLB 20.55 (*0-516-03072-8*) Childrens.

JONAH, THE PROPHET

Amoss, Berthe. Jonah. (Illus.). 10p. (ps-7). 1989. pap. 2.95 (*0-922589-09-7*) More Than Card.

Briscoe, Jill. Jonah & the Worm. Armstrong, Tom & Davis, Florence, illus. 143p. (gr. 6). 1989. pap. write for info. Jilcoe.

Jonah. 1989. text ed. 3.95 cased (*0-7214-5260-4*) Ladybird Bks.

Jonah & the Whale, 3 vols. 1991. Set. pap. 10.99 (*0-8007-7119-2*) Revell.

Lashbrook, Marilyn. I Don't Want to: The Story of Jonah. Britt, Stephanie M., illus. LC 87-60264. 32p. (ps). 1987. 5.95 (*0-86606-428-1*, 844) Roper Pr.

Mills, Peter. Jonah's Adventure with the Big Fish: Bible Adventures. Mills, Peter, illus. 1991. bds. 8.99 with flaps (*0-8007-7121-4*) Revell.

Patterson, Geoffrey. Jonah & the Whale. (Illus.). (ps-3). 1992. 14.00 (*0-688-11238-2*); PLB 13.93 (*0-688-11239-0*) Lothrop.

Ryan, John. Jonah, a Whale of a Tale. Ryan, John, illus. 32p. (gr. 1-7). 1992. 11.95 (*0-7459-2150-7*) Lion USA.

Sanders, Nancy I. Jonah. (ps). 1994. pap. 6.99 (*0-8423-1885-2*) Tyndale.

Sant Bani School Children, illus. Book of Jonah. LC 84-50924. (gr. 1-6). 1984. pap. 6.95 (*0-89142-044-4*) Sant Bani Ash.

Spier, Peter. Book of Jonah. 1985. 14.00 (*0-385-19334-3*); PLB 12.99 (*0-385-19335-1*) Doubleday.

Stirrup Associates, Inc. Staff. My Jesus Pocketbook of Jonah & the Big Fish. Harvey, Bonnie C. & Phillips, Cheryl M., eds. Fulton, Ginger A., illus. LC 83-51679. 32p. (ps-3). 1984. pap. 0.69 (*0-937420-09-3*) Stirrup Assoc.

Tangvald, Christine H. Swish, Swish, Went the Giant Fish: And Other Bible Stories about Prayer. Griego, Tony, illus. LC 94-6709. Date not set. write for info. (*0-7814-0929-2*, Chariot Bks) Chariot Family.

Winder, Linda. Jonah. (ps). 1993. 5.99 (*0-7814-0119-4*, Chariot Bks) Chariot Family.

JONATHAN (BIBLICAL CHARACTER)

Bearman, Jane. Jonathan. Bearman, Jane, illus. LC 65-21754. (gr. 3 up). 1975. 3.95 (*0-8246-0089-4*) Jonathan David.

JONES, JOHN PAUL, 1747-1792

Brandt, Keith. John Paul Jones: Hero of the Seas. Swan, Susan, illus. LC 82-16045. 48p. (gr. 4-6). 1983. PLB 10.79 (*0-89375-849-3*); pap. text ed. 3.50 (*0-89375-850-7*) Troll Assocs.

Worcester, Donald E. John Paul Jones. (gr. 4-6). 1961. 4.36 (*0-395-01755-6*, Piper) HM.

Zadra, Dan. Statesmen in America: John Paul Jones. rev. ed. (gr. 2-4). 1988. PLB 14.95 (*0-88682-193-2*) Creative Ed.

JONES, MARY HARRIS, 1830-1930

Colman, Penny. Mother Jones & the March of the Mill Children. (Illus.). 48p. (gr. 3-6). 1994. 15.40 (*1-56294-402-9*) Millbrook Pr.

Hawxhurst, Joan C. Mother Jones. LC 92-22191. (Illus.). 128p. (gr. 7-10). 1992. PLB 22.80 (*0-8114-2327-1*) Raintree Steck-V.

JORDAN

Department of Geography, Lerner Publications. Jordan in Pictures. (Illus.). 64p. (gr. 5 up). 1988. PLB 17.50 (*0-8225-1834-1*) Lerner Pubns.

Foster, Leila M. Jordan. LC 91-8888. 128p. (gr. 5-9). 1991. PLB 20.55 (*0-516-02603-8*) Childrens.

JOSEPH, NEZ PERCE CHIEF, 1840-1904

Fox, Mary V. Chief Joseph of the Nez Perce Indians: Champion of Liberty. LC 92-35053. (Illus.). 152p. (gr. 4 up). 1993. pap. 5.95 (*0-516-43275-3*) Childrens.

Grant, Matthew G. & Zadra, Dan. Chief Joseph. LC 73-9816. 1987. PLB 14.95 (*0-88682-158-4*) Creative Ed.

Jassem, Kate. Chief Joseph, Leader of Destiny. new ed. LC 78-18048. (Illus.). 48p. (gr. 4-6). 1979. PLB 10.59 (*0-89375-155-3*); pap. 3.50 (*0-89375-145-6*) Troll Assocs.

Pollock, Dean. Joseph: Chief of the Nez Perce. 5th ed. (Illus.). 64p. (gr. 5 up). 1990. pap. 7.95 (*0-8323-0482-4*) Binford Mort.

Sanford, William R. Chief Joseph: Nez Perce Warrior. LC 93-41479. 48p. (gr. 4-10). 1994. lib. bdg. 14.95 (*0-89490-509-0*) Enslow Pubs.

Scott, Robert A. Chief Joseph & the Nez Perces. (Illus.). 128p. (gr. 5 up). 1993. PLB 16.95x (*0-8160-2475-8*) Facts on File.

Trafzer, Clifford E. Chief Joseph: Nez Perce Leader. (Illus.). 112p. (gr. 5 up). 1994. PLB 18.95 (*0-7910-1708-7*, Am Art Analog); pap. write for info. (*0-7910-1972-1*, Am Art Analog) Chelsea Hse.

Warburton, Lois. Chief Joseph. LC 92-28010. (Illus.). 112p. (gr. 5-8). 1992. PLB 14.95 (*1-56006-030-1*) Lucent Bks.

Yates, Diana. Chief Joseph: Thunder Rolling Down from the Mountains. (Illus.). 131p. (gr. 4 up). 1992. pap. 10. 95 (*0-9623380-8-7*) Ward Hill Pr.

—Chief Joseph: Thunder Rolling Down from the Mountains. (Illus.). 131p. (gr. 4 up). 1992. PLB 14.95 (*0-9623380-9-5*) Ward Hill Pr.

JOSEPH, SAINT

Hershey, Katherine. Joseph. (Illus.). 40p. (gr. k-6). 1979. pap. text ed. 9.45 (*1-55976-006-0*) CEF Press.

Patrignani. A Manual of Practical Devotion to St. Joseph. LC 82-50594. 328p. 1982. pap. 13.50 (*0-89555-175-6*) TAN Bks Pubs.

JOSEPH THE PATRIARCH

Frank, Penny. Joseph & the King of Egypt. Morris, Tony, et al, illus. 24p. (ps-3). 3.99 (*0-85648-733-3*) Lion USA.

—Joseph the Dreamer. Morris, Tony, et al, illus. 24p. (ps-3). 3.99 (*0-85648-732-5*) Lion USA.

Joseph. (ps-2). 3.95 (*0-7214-5067-9*) Ladybird Bks.

Lashbrook, Marilyn. Get Lost, Little Brother: The Story of Joseph. Britt, Stephanie M., illus. LC 87-62503. 32p. (ps). 1988. 5.95 (*0-86606-432-X*, 863) Roper Pr.

Lepon, Shoshona. Joseph the Dreamer. 32p. (gr. k-4). 1991. 11.95 (*0-910818-92-4*); pap. 8.95 (*0-910818-93-2*) Judaica Pr.

Olive, Teresa. Joseph & His Brothers. (Illus.). 24p. (Orig.). (ps-4). 1993. pap. 1.99 (*0-570-09030-X*) Concordia.
Tangvald, Christine H. Too Little - Too Big, & Other Bible Stories about Faith. Girouard, Patrick, illus. LC 93-42082. (gr. 2 up). 1994. write for info. (*0-7814-0928-4*, Chariot Bks) Chariot Family.
White, J. Edson. The Story of Joseph: From Shepherd Boy to a Ruler of Egypt. (Illus.). (gr. 3 up). 1990. pap. 4.95 (*0-945460-07-4*) Upward Way.
Williams, Rex. Joseph. (Illus.). 224p. (gr. 3 up). 1990. pap. 2.50 (*1-55748-116-4*) Barbour & Co.
Yenne, Bill, retold by. Joseph & the Coat of Many Colors. LC 93-37474. (Illus.). 1994. write for info. (*0-7852-8330-7*); pap. write for info. (*0-7852-8326-9*) Nelson.

JOURNALISM

Craig, Janet. What's It Like to Be a Newspaper Reporter. Kolding, Richard M., illus. LC 89-34384. 32p. (gr. k-3). 1989. lib. bdg. 10.89 (*0-8167-1807-5*); pap. text ed. 2.95 (*0-8167-1808-3*) Troll Assocs.
Dahlstrom, Lorraine M. Writing down the Days: Three Hundred Sixty-Five Creative Journaling Ideas for Young People. LC 89-29616. (Illus.). 176p. (gr. 6 up). 1990. pap. 12.95 (*0-915793-19-9*) Free Spirit Pub.
Goldstein, Bobbye S. & Goldstein, Gabriel F. Newspaper Fun Activities for Young Children. 128p. (ps-3). 1994. 10.95 (*0-685-71600-7*, 726) W Gladden Found.
Harwood, William N. Writing & Editing School News. 3rd, rev. ed. 364p. (gr. 11-12). 1990. pap. text ed. 17.33 (*0-931054-21-4*) Clark Pub.
Journalism. (Illus.). 40p. (gr. 6-12). 1983. pap. 1.85 (*0-8395-3350-0*, 33350) BSA.
Rothstein, Evelyn, et al. Editing Writes, Red Edition. Gompper, Gail, illus. 110p. (gr. 4-6). 1989. pap. 7.95 (*0-913935-45-X*) ERA-CCR.
Suid, Murray, et al. For the Love of Editing. (Illus.). 112p. (gr. 2-6). 1983. pap. 9.95 (*0-912107-00-6*) Monday Morning Bks.

JOURNALISM–FICTION

Bergen, J. P. Media Madness. LC 94-10859. (gr. 5 up). 1994. pap. 2.95 (*0-02-045472-4*, Collier) Macmillan.
Conford, Ellen. Dear Lovey Hart: I Am Desperate. 224p. (gr. 4-6). 1975. 14.95 (*0-316-15306-0*) Little.
Klein, Leah. B. Y. Times, No. 15: Secrets. 144p. (gr. 6-8). 1993. pap. 7.95 (*1-56871-036-4*) Targum Pr.
Lakin, Patricia. A True Partnership. Cushman, Doug, illus. LC 94-660. (gr. 5 up). 1994. write for info. (*0-8114-3869-4*) Raintree Steck-V.
McBrier, Page. The Great Rip-Off. 128p. 1990. pap. 2.95 (*0-380-75902-0*, Camelot) Avon.
—The Press Mess. 128p. (Orig.). (gr. 4-5). 1990. pap. 2.95 (*0-380-75900-4*, Camelot) Avon.
Pinkwater, Jill. Buffalo Brenda. LC 91-14806. 208p. (gr. 3-7). 1992. pap. 3.95 (*0-689-71586-2*, Aladdin) Macmillan Child Grp.
Quackenbush, Robert. Stop the Presses, Nellie's Got a Scoop! A Story of Nellie Bly. LC 91-4408. (gr. 4-7). 1992. pap. 13.00 (*0-671-76090-4*, S&S BFYR); pap. 3.95 (*0-671-76091-2*, S&S BFYR) S&S Trade.
Shannon, Jacqueline. I Hate My Hero. LC 92-890. (gr. 4-7). 1992. pap. 13.00 (*0-671-75442-4*, S&S BFYR) S&S Trade.

JOURNALISM–U. S.

Cormier, Robert. I Have Words to Spend: Reflections of a Small-Town Editor. (gr. 4-7). 1994. pap. 9.95 (*0-385-31204-0*) Delacorte.
Sherrow, Victoria. Image & Substance: The Media in U. S. Elections. LC 91-42067. (Illus.). 128p. (gr. 7 up). 1992. PLB 15.90 (*1-56294-075-9*) Millbrook Pr.

JOURNALISTS

Blue, Rose & Bernstein, Joanne E. Diane Sawyer: Super Newswoman. LC 89-16817. (Illus.). 104p. (gr. 6 up). 1990. lib. bdg. 17.95 (*0-89490-288-1*) Enslow Pubs.
Brown, Marzella. Newspaper Reporters. Coan, Sharon, ed. Apodaca, Blanqui, illus. 48p. (gr. 3-6). 1990. wkbk. 6.95 (*1-55734-137-0*) Tchr Create Mat.
Caras, Roger. A World Full of Animals: The Roger Caras Story. LC 93-31009. 1994. 12.95 (*0-8118-0654-5*); pap. 6.95 (*0-8118-0682-0*) Chronicle Bks.
Carlson, Judy. Nothing Is Impossible, Said Nelly Bly. (Illus.). 32p. (gr. 1-4). 1989. PLB 18.99 (*0-8172-3521-3*); pap. 3.95 (*0-8114-6721-X*) Raintree Steck-V.
Malone, Mary. Connie Chung: Broadcast Journalist. LC 91-25396. (Illus.). 128p. (gr. 6 up). 1992. lib. bdg. 17.95 (*0-89490-332-2*) Enslow Pubs.
Vonier, Sprague. Edward R. Murrow. LC 89-4344. (Illus.). 64p. (gr. 5-6). 1989. PLB 19.93 (*0-8368-0100-8*) Gareth Stevens Inc.

JOURNEYS

see Voyages around the World

JUAREZ, BENITO PABLO, 1806-1872

Benito Juarez: Mini-Play. (gr. 5 up). 1978. 5.00 (*0-89550-374-3*) Stevens & Shea.
Davis, Linda. A Purim Story. (Illus.). (ps-3). 1988. 7.95 (*0-317-68087-0*) Feldheim.
De Varona, Frank. Benito Juarez, President of Mexico. LC 92-19349. (Illus.). 32p. (gr. 2-4). 1993. PLB 12.90 (*1-56294-279-4*); pap. 4.95 (*1-56294-807-5*) Millbrook Pr.
Gleiter, Jan. Benito Juarez. De Varona, Frank, intro. by. (SPA & ENG., Illus.). 32p. (gr. 3-6). 1990. PLB 19.97 (*0-8172-3381-4*) Raintree Steck-V.
Palacios, Argentina. Viva Mexico! The Story of Benito Juarez & Cinco de Mayo. Berelson, Howard, illus. LC 92-18071. 32p. (gr. 2-5). 1992. PLB 18.51 (*0-8114-7214-0*) Raintree Steck-V.

JUDAISM

see also Jews; Sabbath; Synagogues

Abrams, Judith Z. Rosh Hashanah - A Family Service. Kahn, Katherine J., illus. LC 90-4855. 32p. (Orig.). (ps-4). 1990. pap. 3.95 (*0-929371-16-X*) Kar Ben.
—Selichot - A Family Service. Kahn, Katherine J., illus. LC 90-4863. 24p. (ps-4). 1990. pap. 3.95 (*0-929371-15-1*) Kar Ben.
—Shabbat: A Family Service. Kahn, Katherine J., illus. LC 91-31640. 24p. (Orig.). (gr. k-3). 1992. pap. text ed. 3.95 (*0-929371-29-1*) Kar Ben.
—Yom Kippur - A Family Service. Kahn, Katherine J., illus. LC 90-4862. 22p. (Orig.). (ps-4). 1990. pap. 3.95 (*0-929371-17-8*) Kar Ben.
Alper, Janis & Grishaver, Joel. Mah la'Asot: What Should I Do? A Book of Ethical Problems & Jewish Responses. Urbanovic, Jackie, illus. 64p. (Orig.). (gr. 4-8). 1992. pap. text ed. 4.95 (*0-933873-69-7*) Torah Aura.
Bamberger, David. Judaism & the World's Religions. (gr. 7-8). 7.95 (*0-317-70158-4*); tchr's guide 14.95 (*0-685-43978-X*) Behrman.
Beiner, Stan J. Sedra Scenes: Skits for Every Torah Portion. LC 82-71282. 225p. (Orig.). (gr. 6-12). 1982. pap. text ed. 9.75 (*0-86705-007-1*) A R E Pub.
Bennett, Alan D., ed. Journey Through Judaism: The Best of Keeping Posted. LC 90-19938. (gr. 10 up). 1991. pap. 12.00 (*0-8074-0311-3*, 160500) UAHC.
Bogot, Howard. Yoni. (ps). 1982. pap. 4.00 (*0-8074-0166-8*, 101980) UAHC.
Bogot, Howard I. My First One Hundred Hebrew Words: A Young Person's Dictionary of Judaism. Carmi, Giora, illus. (gr. k-3). 1993. 11.95 (*0-8074-0509-4*, 101716) UAHC.
Borovetz, Fran. Ha Motzi Bracha Kit. (Illus.). 32p. (Orig.). (gr. 3-4). 1985. pap. text ed. 4.95 (*0-933873-03-4*) Torah Aura.
Borowitz, Eugene & Patz, Naomi. Explaining Reform Judaism. 183p. (gr. 6-8). 1985. pap. text ed. 7.95 (*0-87441-394-X*); By Kerry Olitzky. tchr's. ed., 96pps. 14.95x (*0-87441-436-9*); wkbk., 90pps. 4.25 (*0-317-60043-5*) Behrman.
Burstein, Chaya M. The UAHC Kids Catalog of Jewish Living. Burstein, Chaya M., illus. LC 91-42815. (gr. 4-6). 1992. pap. 8.95 (*0-8074-0464-0*, 123934) UAHC.
Cedarbaum, Sophia. A First Book of Jewish Holidays. Ruthen, Marlene L., illus. LC 85-105348. 80p. (gr. 1-3). 1984. pap. text ed. 6.95 (*0-8074-0274-5*, 301500) UAHC.
Chaikin, Miriam. Menorahs, Mezuzas, & Other Jewish Symbols. Weihs, Erika, illus. 96p. (gr. 5 up). 1990. 14.95 (*0-89919-856-2*, Clarion Bks) HM.
Cook, Esky. Jewish Artwork by Esky: Children, Borders, Hebrew Alphabets. Whitman, Jonathan, intro. by. (Illus.). 128p. (Orig.). (gr. 1-8). Date not set. pap. 19.95 (*1-885143-02-8*) Preferred Ent.
—Jewish Artwork by Esky: Complete Set of Jewish Graphics. Whitman, Jonathan, intro. by. (Illus.). 384p. (Orig.). (gr. 1-8). Date not set. pap. 59.95 (*1-885143-00-1*) Preferred Ent.
—Jewish Artwork by Esky: Mitzvot, Animals, Food & Brachot. WHitman, Jonathan, ed. (Illus.). 128p. (Orig.). (gr. 1-8). Date not set. pap. 19.95 (*1-885143-03-6*) Preferred Ent.
—Jewish Artwork by Esky: Shabbat & Jewish Holidays. Whitman, Jonathan, ed. (Illus., Orig.). (gr. 1-8). Date not set. pap. 19.95 (*1-885143-01-X*) Preferred Ent.
Drucker, Malka. The Family Treasury of Jewish Holidays. Patz, Nancy, illus. LC 93-7549. (ps up). 1994. 21.95 (*0-316-19343-7*) Little.
Edwards, Michelle. Blessed Are You: Traditional Everyday Hebrew Prayers. LC 92-1666. (ps-3). 1993. 15.00 (*0-688-10759-1*); PLB 14.93 (*0-688-10760-5*) Lothrop.
Einstein, Stephen J. & Kukoff, Lydia. Every Person's Guide to Judaism. 196p. 1989. pap. 8.95 (*0-8074-0434-9*, 142610) UAHC.
Elias, Miriam L. Goodbye, My Friends. (gr. 6-9). 1989. 10.95 (*0-87306-491-7*); pap. 8.95 (*0-87306-492-5*) Feldheim.
Fields, Harvey J. A Torah Commentary for Our Times, Vol. 2: Exodus & Leviticus. Carmi, Giora, illus. LC 89-28478. (gr. 7-9). 1991. pap. text ed. 12.00x (*0-8074-0334-2*, 164010) UAHC.
Fine, Helen. At Camp Kee Tov: Ethics for Jewish Juniors. (Illus.). (gr. 4-6). Date not set. 6.95 (*0-8074-0128-5*, 121711) UAHC.
—Behold, the Land. (Illus.). 280p. (gr. 4-6). 1978. pap. 8.95 (*0-8074-0129-3*, 127270) UAHC.
—G'Dee. (Illus.). 164p. (gr. 4-6). 1958. 4.50 (*0-8074-0087-4*, 123702) UAHC.
Fishman, Joyce. Let's Learn about Jewish Symbols. (gr. k-3). wkbk. 6.00 (*0-8074-0171-4*, 101050) UAHC.
Fishman, Priscilla. Learn Mishnah Notebook. 128p. (gr. 7-8). 1983. pap. 3.50x (*0-87441-369-9*) Behrman.
Freund, Chavie. Read Me the Haggadah. Ieff, Tova, illus. (ps-2). 1990. 10.95 (*1-56062-021-8*) CIS Comm.
Ganz, Yaffa. Follow the Moon: A Journey Through the Jewish Year. Klineman, Harvey, illus. (gr. k-4). 1984. 10.95 (*0-87306-369-4*) Feldheim.
—The Jewish Fact-Finder: A Bookful of Important Jewish Facts & Handy Information. (gr. 5-9). 1988. 12.95 (*0-87306-447-X*); pap. 9.95 (*0-87306-470-4*) Feldheim.
—Who Knows One? A Book of Jewish Numbers. Klineman, Harvey, illus. (gr. k-4). 1981. 10.95 (*0-87306-285-X*) Feldheim.
Gates, Fay C. Judaism. (Illus.). 128p. (gr. 7-12). 1991. 17.95x (*0-8160-2444-8*) Facts on File.
Gates of Awe. (Illus.). 62p. (ps-8). 1991. 12.95 (*0-88123-014-6*) Central Conf.
Geller, Norman. It's Not the Jewish Christmas. Gruchow, Jane C., illus. 20p. (gr. 3-6). 1985. pap. 4.95 (*0-915753-09-X*) N Geller Pub.
Gellman, Ellie. Shai's Shabbat Walk. McLean, Chari, illus. LC 85-80780. 12p. (ps). 1985. bds. 4.95 (*0-930494-49-0*) Kar Ben.
Gittelsohn, Roland B. Love in Your Life: A Jewish View of Teenage Sexuality. (gr. 7-9). 1991. pap. 9.95 (*0-8074-0460-8*, 142685) UAHC.
Gold, Yeshara. Hurry, Friday's a Short Day: One Boy's Erev Shabbat in Jerusalem's Old City. (Illus.). 32p. (gr. 3-8). 1986. 10.95 (*0-89906-800-6*); pap. 7.95 (*0-89906-801-4*) Mesorah Pubns.
—Just a Week to Go: One Boy's Pesach Preparations in Jerusalem's Old City. (Illus.). 32p. (gr. 3-8). 1987. 10.95 (*0-89906-802-2*); pap. 7.95 (*0-89906-803-0*) Mesorah Pubns.
Goldin, Barbara. A Child's Book of Midrash: Fifty-Two Jewish Stories from the Sages. LC 90-39598. 124p. 1992. 25.00 (*0-87668-837-7*) Aronson.
Golomb, Morris. Know Jewish Living & Enjoy It. LC 78-54569. (Illus.). (gr. 5-9). 1981. 14.95 (*0-88400-054-0*) Shengold.
Gottesman, Meir U. Shpeter: Book One. (Illus.). (gr. 1-3). 1981. 5.95 (*0-910818-35-5*); pap. 4.95 (*0-910818-36-3*) Judaica Pr.
—Shpeter: Book Two. (Illus.). (gr. 1-3). 1981. 5.95 (*0-910818-39-8*); pap. 4.95 (*0-910818-40-1*) Judaica Pr.
Grand, Samuel & Grand, Tamar. The Children of Israel. (Illus.). 56p. (gr. k-3). 1972. text ed. 6.95 (*0-8074-0131-5*, 121320); tchr's. guide 2.25 (*0-8074-0132-3*, 201320); wkbk. 4.50 (*0-8074-0133-1*, 121322) UAHC.
Greenberg, Sidney & Silverman, Morris. Siddurenu. (gr. 3-7). 8.95x (*0-87677-099-5*) Prayer Bk.
Grishaver, Joel L. Being Torah Student Commentary, 2 Vols. (Illus.). 72p. (Orig.). (gr. 2-4). 1986. Vol. 1. pap. text ed. 4.95 (*0-933873-09-3*); Vol. 2. pap. text ed. 4.95 (*0-933873-10-7*) Torah Aura.
—Building Jewish Life: Siddur Commentary. Torah Aura Staff, photos by. (Illus.). 48p. (Orig.). (gr. 2-4). 1992. pap. text ed. 2.45 (*0-933873-74-3*) Torah Aura.
—Nineteen Out of Eighteen. Steinberger, Heidi, illus. (Orig.). (gr. 5-8). 1991. pap. 5.95 wkbk. (*0-685-50246-5*) Torah Aura.
—Shema & Company. rev. ed. Steinberger, Heidi, illus. (gr. 5-8). 1991. wkbk. 5.95 (*0-933873-62-X*) Torah Aura.
—Torah Toons I. (Illus.). 115p. (Orig.). (gr. 4 up). 1985. pap. text ed. 5.50 (*0-933873-01-8*) Torah Aura.
—Torah Toons II. (Illus.). 114p. (Orig.). (gr. 6 up). 1985. pap. text ed. 5.50 (*0-933873-02-6*) Torah Aura.
Grishaver, Joel L., et al. When I Stood on Mt. Sinai. Grishaver, Joel L., illus. 32p. (Orig.). (gr. 6 up). 1992. pap. text ed. 2.45 (*0-933873-70-0*) Torah Aura.
Gross, David C. Why Remain Jewish? 224p. (gr. 8 up). 1993. pap. 9.95 (*0-7818-0216-4*) Hippocrene Bks.
Grossman, Roz & Gewirtz, Gladys. Let's Play Dreidel. Springer, Sally, illus. LC 89-34892. 16p. (ps-3). 1989. incl. tape & dreidel 6.95 (*0-929371-00-3*) Kar Ben.
Guidelines: Lesson Plans for Lifelong Jewish Learning - The Intermediate Years, Grades 4-6. (gr. 4-6). Date not set. pap. 25.00 (*0-685-72162-0*, 241200); Vol. 3, 3-hole punched lesson plan bk., 80p. 10.00 (*0-685-72163-9*, 241170) UAHC.
Jacobs, Chana R. Take Care of Me. Rosenfeld, Dina, ed. Zelcer, Amir, illus. 32p. (ps-1). 1989. 8.95 (*0-922613-06-0*); pap. 6.95 (*0-922613-07-9*) Hachai Pubns.
Jacobs, Louis. The Book of Jewish Practice. (gr. 9 up). 8.95 (*0-317-70168-1*) Behrman.
—Hasidic Thought. (gr. 8-10). 8.95 (*0-317-70162-2*) Behrman.
—Jewish Personal & Social Ethics. 156p. (Orig.). (gr. 9). 1990. pap. text ed. 12.50 (*0-87441-510-1*) Behrman.
Karlinsky, Isaiah & Karlinsky, Ruth. My First Book of Mitzvos. (Illus.). (gr. k-3). 1986. 8.95 (*0-87306-388-0*) Feldheim.
Kasakove, David P. & Olitzky, Kerry M. Hebrew, Holidays, & Heroes: The Jewish Fun Book. Lerer, Mark, illus. (gr. 4-6). 1992. pap. 7.00 (*0-8074-0478-0*, 123937) UAHC.
Kipper, Lenore & Bogot, Howard. Alef-Bet of Jewish Values: Code Words of Jewish Life. Paiss, Jana, illus. 64p. (gr. 4-6). 1985. pap. text ed. 6.00 (*0-8074-0267-2*, 101087) UAHC.
Kitman, Carol & Hurwitz, Ann. One Mezuzah: A Jewish Counting Book. (gr. k). 6.95 (*0-317-70144-4*) Behrman.
Kobre, Faige. A Sense of Shabbat. LC 89-40361. (Illus.). 32p. 1990. 11.95 (*0-933873-44-1*) Torah Aura.
Kolatch, A. J. The Jewish Child's First Book of Why. LC 91-25352. 32p. 1992. 14.95 (*0-8246-0354-0*) Jonathan David.
Kripke, Dorothy K. & Levin, Meyer. God & the Story of Judaism. LC 62-17078. (gr. 4-6). 1962. By Toby K. Kurzband. 6.95x (*0-87441-000-2*) Behrman.
Kushner, Lawrence. The Book of Miracles: A Young Person's Guide to Jewish Spirituality. (Illus.). 96p. (Orig.). (gr. 4-6). 1987. pap. text ed. 7.95 (*0-8074-0323-7*, 123926) UAHC.

Learsi, Rufus. Prince of Judah & Other Stories of a Great Journey. 1962 ed. LC 62-21985. (Illus.). (gr. 6-10). 11. 95 (*0-88400-031-1*) Shengold.

Lemelman, Martin. My Jewish Home. Lemelman, Martin, illus. 10p. (ps-k). 1988. pap. 3.95 boardbk. (*0-8074-0415-2*, 102002) UAHC.

Levin, Meyer & Kurzband, Toby. Story of the Jewish Way of Life. LC 59-13487. (gr. 4-6). 1959. 6.95 (*0-87441-003-7*) Behrman.

Liebermann, M. Coloring Books on Events of the Jewish Months: Nisan. (ps-2). 1987. 2.50 (*0-914131-86-9*, D712) Torah Umesorah.

—Coloring Books on Events of the Jewish Months: Tishrei, Cheshvan. (ps-2). 1987. 2.50 (*0-914131-84-2*, D710) Torah Umesorah.

—Coloring Books on the Parshas Hashavua: Bereishis. (ps-2). 1987. 2.50 (*0-914131-79-6*, D700) Torah Umesorah.

—Coloring Books on the Parshas Hashavua: Devorim. (ps-2). 1987. 2.50 (*0-914131-83-4*, D704) Torah Umesorah.

—Coloring Books on the Parshas Hashavua: Shemos. (ps-2). 1987. 2.50 (*0-914131-80-X*, D701) Torah Umesorah.

—Coloring Books on the Parshas Hashavua: Vayikrah. (ps-2). 1987. 2.50 (*0-914131-81-8*, D702) Torah Umesorah.

—Learn as You Color Series III: Brachos. (ps-2). 1987. 2.50 (*0-914131-88-5*, D720) Torah Umesorah.

Lion The Printer. Seven Days a Week. (Illus.). (gr. k-5). 1977. spiral 2.00 (*0-914080-62-8*) Shulsinger Sales.

Meyer, Henye. The Exiles of Crocodile Island. Dershowitz, Yosef, illus. 224p. (gr. 6-12). 1984. 12.95 (*0-89906-772-7*); pap. 9.95 (*0-89906-773-5*) Mesorah Pubns.

Mitchel, Sue A. & Hughes, Barbara A. From the Bridegroom with Love. 144p. (gr. 8 up). 1992. pap. 6.95 (*0-9634469-0-8*) Chereb Pub.

Moskowitz, Nachama S. Bridge to Prayer: The Jewish Worship Workbook, Vol. II. (Illus.). 144p. (gr. 6-7). 1989. pap. text ed. 6.00 (*0-8074-0432-2*, 123596) UAHC.

Newman, Shirley. A Child's Introduction to Torah. Newman, Louis, ed. Zemsky, Jessica, illus. 128p. (Orig.). (gr. 4). 1972. pap. text ed. 12.50 (*0-87441-067-3*) Behrman.

Olomeinu: Our World Alphabetical Index of Themes & Personalities. 1987. 3.00 (*0-914131-72-9*, D050) Torah Umesorah.

Pasachoff, Naomi. Basic Judaism for Young People, Vol. 1: Israel. 150p. (gr. 4-5). 1987. pap. text ed. 7.95 (*0-87441-423-7*); By Lesley Silverstone. student activity bk., 90pgs. 4.25x (*0-87441-440-7*) Behrman.

—Basic Judaism for Young People, Vol 2: Torah. 150p. (gr. 5-6). 1986. pap. text ed. 7.95 (*0-87441-424-5*); By Lois M. Cohn. student activity bk., 92pps. 4.25x (*0-87441-442-3*) Behrman.

—Basic Judaism for Young People, Vol. 3: God. (gr. 6-7). 7.95 (*0-317-70146-0*); tchr's guide & dupl. masters 12. 50 (*0-317-70147-9*); student activity bk. 4.25 (*0-317-70148-7*) Behrman.

Polish, Daniel F., et al. Drugs, Sex, & Integrity: What Does Judaism Say? Diaz, Jose, illus. LC 90-28763. (gr. 7-9). 1991. pap. 10.00 (*0-8074-0459-4*, 168505) UAHC.

Portnoy, Mindy A. Mommy Never Went to Hebrew School. Haas, Shelly O., illus. LC 89-30874. 32p. (gr. k-5). 1989. pap. 4.95 (*0-930494-97-0*) Kar Ben.

Prager, Janice & LePoff, Arlene. Why Be Different: A Look into Judasim. 118p. (gr. 6-8). 1986. pap. text ed. 7.95 (*0-87441-427-X*) Behrman.

Rabinowitz, Jan. The Tzedakah Workbook. Golub, Jane & Grishaver, Joelrev. by. (Illus.). 32p. (Orig.). (gr. 4-5). 1986. pap. text ed. 3.95 (*0-933873-07-7*) Torah Aura.

Ray, Eric. Sofer: The Story of a Torah Scroll. LC 85-52420. (Illus.). 32p. (Orig.). (ps-4). 1986. pap. 4.95 (*0-933873-04-2*) Torah Aura.

Roseman, Kenneth D. The Tenth of Av. 96p. (Orig.). (gr. 4-6). 1988. pap. text ed. 7.95 (*0-8074-0359-8*, 123928) UAHC.

Rosen, Ruth, ed. Jesus for Jews. Owens, Nate, illus. LC 87-20343. 336p. (Orig.). (gr. 12). 1987. 13.95 (*0-9616148-3-8*); pap. 7.95 (*0-9616148-4-6*); pap. 4.95 mass market (*0-9616148-2-X*) Purple Pomegranate.

Rosenberg, Amye. Mitzvot. (Illus.). 30p. (gr. 1-5). pap. text ed. 4.25 (*0-87441-387-7*) Behrman.

Rosenthal, Yaffa. Mitzvos We Can Do. Kunda, Shmuel, illus. 32p. (gr. 1-8). 1982. 10.95 (*0-89906-775-1*); pap. 7.95 (*0-89906-776-X*) Mesorah Pubns.

—Thank You Hashem. Kunda, Shmuel, illus. 32p. (gr. 1-8). 1983. 10.95 (*0-89906-777-8*); pap. 7.95 (*0-89906-778-6*) Mesorah Pubns.

Rosner, Raphael, ed. Junior Judaica: Encyclopedia Judaica for Youth, 6 vols. 3rd ed. 1200p. 1994. Set 167.50 (*0-89563-816-9*, Pub. by Keter Pub IS) Coronet Bks.

Rossel, Seymour. When a Jew Seeks Wisdom: The Sayings of the Fathers. LC 75-14119. (gr. 7). pap. 7.95 (*0-87441-089-4*); student's encounter bk. 3.95 (*0-685-00741-3*); tchr's guide 14.95 (*0-685-41999-1*) Behrman.

Sagarin, James & Sagarin, Lori. Oseh Shalom. (Illus.). (gr. 4-6). 1990. wkbk. 6.00x (*0-8074-0351-2*, 123703) UAHC.

Saypol, Judyth R. & Wikler, Madeline. My Very Own Haggadah. Rev. ed. Burstein, Chaya, illus. LC 83-6. 32p. (ps-3). 1983. pap. text ed. 2.95 (*0-930494-23-7*) Kar Ben.

Schwartz, Linda. The Jewish Question Collection. LC 93-80430. 176p. (gr. 1 up). 1994. 7.95 (*0-88160-247-7*, LW342) Learning Wks.

Shamir, Ilana & Shavit, Shlomo, eds. The Young Reader's Encyclopedia of Jewish History. LC 87-10599. (gr. 7 up). 1987. pap. 17.95 (*0-670-81738-4*) Viking Child Bks.

Simms, Laura & Kozodoy, Ruth. Exploring Our Living Past. Harlow, Jules, ed. Rosenberg, Amye & Weihs, Erika, illus. (gr. k-2). 1978. pap. 7.95 (*0-87441-309-5*); tchr's guide 19.95x (*0-87441-276-5*) Behrman.

Simon, Solomon & Bial, Morrison D. The Rabbis' Bible, Vol. 1: Torah, 2 pts. (gr. 5-6). 6.95 (*0-317-70149-5*); tchr's guide 12.50 (*0-317-70150-9*); tchr's resource bk. 14.95 (*0-317-70151-7*); student activity bk. 3.50 (*0-317-70152-5*) Behrman.

—The Rabbis' Bible, Vol. 2: Early Prophets. (gr. 6-7). 6.95 (*0-317-70153-3*); tchr's guide 12.50 (*0-317-70154-1*); tchr's resource bk. 14.95 (*0-317-70155-X*) Behrman.

Simon, Solomon & Rothberg, Abraham. The Rabbis' Bible, Vol. 3: Later Prophets. (gr. 7-8). 6.95 (*0-317-70159-2*); tchr's guide 12.50 (*0-317-70160-6*); tchr's resource bk. 14.95 (*0-317-70161-4*) Behrman.

Singer, Ellen. Our Sacred Texts: Discovering the Jewish Classics. Zlotowitz, Bernard M., contrib. by. LC 92-16438. (gr. 4-6). 1992. pap. 8.00 (*0-8074-0479-9*, 123936); tchr's. guide 5.00 (*0-8074-0481-0*, 208031) UAHC.

Singer, Howard. With Mind & Heart. (gr. 8 up). 3.95x (*0-8381-0203-4*, 10-203) United Syn Bk.

Steinbock, Steven E. Torah: The Growing Gift. (Illus., Orig.). (gr. 4-6). 1994. pap. 8.00 (*0-8074-0502-7*, 123939); tchr's. guide 6.00 (*0-8074-0503-5*, 208035) UAHC.

Teich, Shmuel. The Rishonim: Biographical Sketches of the Prominent Early Rabbinic Sages & Leaders from the Tenth-Fifteenth Centuries. Goldwurm, Hersh, ed. & intro. by. (Illus.). 224p. (gr. 7-8). 1982. 16.95 (*0-89906-452-3*); pap. 13.95 (*0-89906-453-1*) Mesorah Pubns.

Teitelbaum, Chaya S. & Lederman, Raizel. Ich Lern Aleph-Beis. (YID., Illus.). 72p. (Orig.). 1991. pap. write for info wkbk.. (*0-9630821-0-8*) Ich Lern A-B.

Touger, Malka. Sefer Hamitzvot for Youth, Vols. 1 & 2. (gr. 7-10). 1988. 18.00 (*0-940118-26-2*) Vol. 1, 248 Positive Commandments, 95p. Vol. 2, 365 Negative Commandments, 144p. Moznaim.

Vorspan, Albert & Saperstein, David. Tough Choices: Jewish Perspectives on Social Justice. LC 92-31747. 1992. pap. 11.00 (*0-8074-0482-9*, 167275) UAHC.

Weinberg, Messody. Birds. Nodel, Norman, illus. Satat, Noah, photos by. (Illus.). 32p. (gr. 3-8). 1990. 10.95 (*0-922613-33-8*); pap. 8.95 (*0-922613-34-6*) Hachai Pubns.

Wise, Ira J. & Grishaver, Joel L. I Can Learn Torah, Vol. 2: Stories of the First Jewish Family. Blaicher, David, illus. 48p. (Orig.). (ps-2). 1992. pap. text ed. 2.45 (*0-933873-68-9*) Torah Aura.

Wolff, Ferida. Pink Slippers, Bat Mitzvah Blues. (gr. 3-7). 1989. 13.95 (*0-8276-0332-0*) JPS Phila.

Yedwab, Paul M. The Alef-Bet of Blessing. (Illus.). 80p. (Orig.). (gr. k-3). 1989. pap. text ed. 6.00x (*0-8074-0436-5*, 101094) 5.00 (*0-8074-0461-6*, 208029) UAHC.

Zalben, Jane & Breskin. Papa's Latkes. (ps-2). 1994. 5.95 (*0-8050-3099-9*) H Holt & Co.

Zelcer, Draizy. My Jewish A. B. C. Memeroff, Patti, illus. 32p. (ps-1). 1994. 8.95 (*0-922613-62-1*); pap. 6.95 (*0-922613-63-X*) Hachai Pubns.

JUDGES

see also Courts; Lawyers

Ayer, Eleanor H. Ruth Bader Ginsburg. LC 94-17854. 1994. text ed. 13.95 (*0-87518-651-3*, Dillon Pr) Macmillan Child Grp.

Deegan, Paul. Clarence Thomas. Italia, Bob, ed. LC 92-13717. 1992. PLB 13.99 (*1-56239-088-0*) Abdo & Dghtrs.

—Sandra Day O'Connor. Italia, Bob, ed. LC 92-13716. 1992. PLB 13.99 (*1-56239-089-9*) Abdo & Dghtrs.

Halliburton, Warren J. Clarence Thomas: Supreme Court Justice. LC 92-30951. (Illus.). 104p. (gr. 6 up). 1993. lib. bdg. 17.95 (*0-89490-414-0*) Enslow Pubs.

Italia, Bob. Anthony Kennedy. Deegan, Paul, ed. LC 92-13710. 40p. 1992. PLB 13.99 (*1-56239-094-5*) Abdo & Dghtrs.

—Antonin Scalia. Deegan, Paul, ed. LC 92-13712. 40p. 1992. PLB 13.99 (*1-56239-093-7*) Abdo & Dghtrs.

—Chief Justice William Rehnquist. Deegan, Paul, ed. LC 92-13709. 1992. PLB 13.95 (*1-56239-096-1*) Abdo & Dghtrs.

—Harry Blackmun. Deegan, Paul, ed. LC 92-13711. 1992. PLB 13.99 (*1-56239-090-2*) Abdo & Dghtrs.

Italia, Bob & Deegan, Paul. John Paul Stevens. LC 92-13713. 1992. PLB 13.99 (*1-56239-091-0*) Abdo & Dghtrs.

Stewart, Gail B. What Happened to Judge Crater? LC 91-16554. (Illus.). 48p. (gr. 5-6). 1992. text ed. 11.95 RSBE (*0-89686-617-3*, Crestwood Hse) Macmillan Child Grp.

Woods, Harold & Woods, Geraldine. Sandra Day O'Connor: Equal Justice: A Biography of Sandra Day O'Connor. LC 84-23042. (Illus.). 128p. (gr. 6 up). 1987. text ed. 13.95 RSBE (*0-87518-292-5*, Dillon) Macmillan Child Grp.

JUDO

see also Karate

Bailey, Donna. Judo. LC 90-23058. (Illus.). 32p. (gr. 1-4). 1991. PLB 18.99 (*0-8114-2900-8*); pap. 3.95 (*0-8114-4714-6*) Raintree Steck-V.

Barrett, Norman. Artes Marciales. LC 90-70884. (SPA., Illus.). 32p. (gr. k-4). 1990. PLB 11.90 (*0-531-07902-3*) Watts.

Casey, Kevin. Judo. LC 94-4090. (gr. 3 up). 1994. write for info. (*0-86593-369-3*) Rourke Corp.

Dando, Justin. Judo. rev. ed. (Illus.). 80p. (gr. 10-12). 1993. pap. 7.95 (*0-7137-2416-1*, Pub. by Blandford Pr UK) Sterling.

Kerr, George. Judo. LC 91-21215. (Illus.). 32p. (gr. 2-5). 1992. PLB 11.90 (*0-531-18465-X*, Pub. by Bookwright Pr) Watts.

Kobayashi, Kiyoshi & Sharp, Harold E. Sport of Judo: As Practiced in Japan. LC 57-75. (Illus.). 104p. (gr. 9 up). 1957. pap. 9.95 (*0-8048-0542-3*) C E Tuttle.

JUGGLERS AND JUGGLING

De Paola, Tomie. The Clown of God. De Paola, Tomie, illus. LC 78-3845. (gr. k up). 1978. 13.95 (*0-15-219175-5*, HB Juv Bks) HarBrace.

Finnigan, Dave. The Complete Juggler. 2nd, rev. ed. Edwards, Bruce, illus. Strong, Todd, contrib. by. LC 91-61138. (Illus.). 576p. (gr. 9-12). 1991. lib. bdg. 19. 95 (*0-9615521-1-5*); pap. 14.95 (*0-9615521-0-7*) Jugglebug.

—The Joy of Juggling. rev. ed. Edwards, Bruce, illus. 100p. (gr. 4-9). 1993. pap. 6.00 (*0-9615521-3-1*, 09001) Jugglebug.

—Scarf Juggling. Edwards, Bruce, illus. 24p. (Orig.). (gr. 2-7). 1991. pap. 7.95 (*0-9615521-8-2*, 04000) Jugglebug.

Meyer, Charles R. How to Be a Juggler. (Illus.). (gr. 4-7). 1977. 6.95 (*0-679-20407-5*) McKay.

Murray, Peter. You Can Juggle. LC 92-9504. (gr. 2-6). 1992. PLB 14.95 (*0-89565-966-2*) Childs World.

Pack, Robert. The Octopus Who Wanted to Juggle. Willard, Nancy, illus. (Orig.). (ps-7). 1990. text ed. 13. 95 (*0-913123-26-9*) Galileo.

JUMBO (ELEPHANT)

Blumberg, Rhoda. Jumbo. Hunt, Jonathan, illus. LC 91-34789. 48p. (gr. k-5). 1992. RSBE 15.95 (*0-02-711683-2*, Bradbury Pr) Macmillan Child Grp.

Smucker, Barbara. Incredible Jumbo. 1991. 12.95 (*0-670-82970-6*) Viking Child Bks.

JUNIPERUS OF ASSISI, BROTHER, 13TH CENTURY

Benedict, Rex. Oh, Brother Juniper. Berg, Joan, illus. (gr. 5-6). 1963. lib. bdg. 4.99 (*0-394-91457-0*) Pantheon.

JUNK

see Waste Products

JURISPRUDENCE

see Law

JURISTS

see Lawyers

JURY

Miller, Marvin. You Be the Jury: Courtroom Four. 1992. 2.50 (*0-590-45723-3*, 066) Scholastic Inc.

JUSTICE, ADMINISTRATION OF

see also Courts; Crime and Criminals

Adint, Victor. Drugs & Prison. LC 94-1025. 1994. 14.95 (*0-8239-1705-3*) Rosen Group.

Alberton, Kathleen. The ABCs of Family Court: A Children's Guide. Clarke, Dorothy J., illus. LC 88-120423. 54p. (gr. 1-12). 1987. pap. 1.50 (*0-9619599-0-8*) NYC Law Dept.

Almonte, Paul & Desmond, Theresa. Street Gangs. LC 93-25330. 1994. text ed. 13.95 (*0-89686-808-7*, Crestwood Hse) Macmillan Child Grp.

Green, Carl & Sanford, William. Judiciary. (Illus.). 96p. (gr. 7 up). 1990. lib. bdg. 18.60 (*0-86593-086-4*); lib. bdg. 13.95s.p. (*0-685-46457-1*) Rourke Corp.

Hjelmeland, Andy. Kids in Jail. Wolf, Dennis, photos by. (Illus.). 40p. (gr. 4-8). 1992. PLB 17.50 (*0-8225-2552-6*) Lerner Pubns.

Maybury, Richard J. Whatever Happened to Justice? Williams, Jane A., ed. (Illus.). 256p. (Orig.). (gr. 7 up). 1993. pap. 14.95 (*0-942617-10-X*) Blstckng Pr.

JUVENILE DELINQUENCY

see also Child Welfare

Alberton, Kathleen. The ABCs of Family Court: A Children's Guide. Clarke, Dorothy J., illus. LC 88-120423. 54p. (gr. 1-12). 1987. pap. 1.50 (*0-9619599-0-8*) NYC Law Dept.

Barden, Renardo. Gangs. LC 89-1413. (Illus.). 48p. (gr. 5-6). 1989. text ed. 12.95 RSBE (*0-89686-440-5*, Crestwood Hse) Macmillan Child Grp.

—Gangs. (Illus.). 64p. (gr. 7 up). 1990. lib. bdg. 17.27 (*0-86593-073-2*); 12.95s.p. (*0-685-36324-4*) Rourke Corp.

—Juvenile Violence. 1993. 14.95 (*1-85435-613-5*) Marshall Cavendish.

From Gangs to Grace: The Study Guide. (SPA., Illus.). (gr. 6-8). 1991. tchr's. guide 7.95 (*0-9630375-1-X*) Fam Comm Educ.

Garell, Dale C. & Snyder, Solomon H., eds. Delinquency & Criminal Behavior. (Illus.). 112p. (gr. 7-12). 1989. 18.95 (*0-7910-0045-1*) Chelsea Hse.

Gould, Marilyn. Graffiti Wipeout. LC 91-90783. 112p. (gr. 5 up). 1992. pap. 6.95 (*0-9632305-0-6*) Allied Crafts.

Greenberg, Keith E. Out of the Gang. (Illus.). 40p. (gr. 4-8). 1992. PLB 17.50 (*0-8225-2553-4*) Lerner Pubns.
Haskins, James. Street Gangs: Yesterday & Today. (Illus.). (gr. 6 up). 1977. pap. 4.95 (*0-8038-2662-1*) Hastings.
Hinojosa, Maria. Crews: Gang Members Talk to Maria Hinojosa. Perez, German, contrib. by. LC 94-12173. (Illus.). (gr. 7 up). 1994. 16.95 (*0-15-292873-1*); pap. 8.95 (*0-15-200283-9*) HarBrace.
Hjelmeland, Andy. Kids in Jail. Wolf, Dennis, photos by. (Illus.). 40p. (gr. 4-8). 1992. PLB 17.50 (*0-8225-2552-6*) Lerner Pubns.
Landau, Elaine. Teenage Violence. Steltenpohl, Jane, ed. (Illus.). 128p. (gr. 7 up). 1990. PLB 12.98 (*0-671-70153-3*, J Messner); pap. 5.95 (*0-671-70154-1*) S&S Trade.
Lang, Susan S. Teen Violence. (Illus.). 176p. (gr. 9-12). 1991. PLB 14.40 (*0-531-11057-5*) Watts.
McDonough, Jerome. Hoods. 22p. (Orig.). (gr. 7-12). 1992. pap. 3.00 (*0-88680-369-1*); royalty on application 35.00 (*0-685-62707-1*) I E Clark.
Oliver, Marilyn T. Gangs. (Illus.). 128p. (gr. 6 up). 1995. lib. bdg. 17.95 (*0-89490-492-2*) Enslow Pubs.
Redpath, Ann. What Happens If You Join a Street Gang? (Illus.). 48p. (gr. 3-6). Date not set. PLB 12.95 (*1-56065-139-3*) Capstone Pr.
Stark, Evan. Everything You Need to Know about Street Gangs. (gr. 7-12). 1992. PLB 14.95 (*0-8239-1319-8*) Rosen Group.
Street Gangs: Gaining Turf, Losing Ground. LC 91-22204. (gr. 7-12). 1991. PLB 16.95 (*0-8239-1332-5*); pap. 8.95 (*0-8239-1333-3*) Rosen Group.
Watson-Russell & Harvey. So, You've Been Busted! A Guide to Court Procedures for Adolescents Charged under the Young Offenders Act. 48p. 1989. pap. 10.00 (*0-409-80985-3*) Butterworth Legal Pubs.
Webb, Margot. Coping with Street Gangs. rev. ed. Rosen, Roger, ed. 64p. (gr. 7-12). 1992. PLB 14.95 (*0-8239-1600-6*) Rosen Group.
Wormser, Richard. Juveniles in Trouble. LC 93-35899. 1994. 16.00 (*0-671-86775-X*, J Messner); pap. write for info. (*0-671-86776-8*, J Messner) S&S Trade.

JUVENILE DELINQUENCY–FICTION

Fox, Paula. How Many Miles to Babylon? Giovanopoulos, Paul, illus. LC 79-25802. 128p. (gr. 5-7). 1982. SBE 13.95 (*0-02-735590-X*, Bradbury Pr) Macmillan Child Grp.
Grey, Harry. The Hoods. 1987. Repr. lib. bdg. 35.95x (*0-89966-549-7*) Buccaneer Bks.
Hinton, Susie E. Rumble Fish. LC 75-8004. 112p. (gr. 7 up). 1975. pap. 13.95 (*0-385-28675-9*) Delacorte.
Tunis, John R. City for Lincoln. 392p. (gr. 3-7). 1989. pap. 3.95 (*0-15-218580-1*, Odyssey) HarBrace.

JUVENILE LITERATURE

see Children'S Literature

K

K. K. K.

see Ku Klux Klan

KAIULANI, PRINCESS OF HAWAII, 1875-1899

Stanley, Fay. The Last Princess: The Story of Princess Kaiulani of Hawaii. Stanley, Diane, illus. LC 93-45714. (gr. 1-4). 1994. pap. 5.95 (*0-689-71829-2*, Aladdin) Macmillan Child Grp.

KANGAROOS

Arnold, Caroline. Kangaroo. Hewett, Richard, illus. LC 86-18103. 48p. (gr. 2-5). 1987. 12.95 (*0-688-06480-9*); lib. bdg. 12.88 (*0-688-06481-7*, Morrow Jr Bks) Morrow Jr Bks.
—Kangaroo. Hewett, Richard, photos by. LC 86-18103. (Illus.). 48p. (gr. 3 up). 1992. pap. 5.95 (*0-688-11502-0*, Mulberry) Morrow.
Barrett, Norman S. Kangaroos & Other Marsupials. (Illus.). 32p. (gr. k-4). 1991. pap. 4.95 (*0-531-15612-5*) Watts.
Dalmais. Kangaroo, Reading Level 3-4. (Illus.). 28p. (gr. 2-5). 1983. PLB 16.67 (*0-86592-864-9*); 12.50s.p. (*0-685-58820-3*) Rourke Corp.
Darling, Kathy. Kangaroos on Location. Darling, Tara, photos by. LC 92-38418. (Illus.). 1993. 14.00 (*0-688-09728-6*); lib. bdg. 13.93 (*0-688-09729-4*) Lothrop.
Eugene, Toni. Koalas & Kangaroos: Strange Animals of Australia. Crump, Donald J., ed. LC 81-607859. 32p. (ps-3). 1981. Set. 13.95 (*0-87044-403-4*); PLB 16.95 (*0-87044-408-5*) Natl Geog.
Fowler, Allan. Podria Ser un Mamifero - Libro Grande: (It Could Still Be a Mammal Big Book) LC 90-2161. (SPA., Illus.). 32p. (ps-2). 1993. 22.95 (*0-516-59463-X*) Childrens.
Hogan, Paula Z. The Kangaroo. Mayo, Gretchen, illus. LC 79-13660. (gr. 1-4). 1979. PLB 19.97 (*0-8172-1504-2*); pap. 4.95 (*0-8114-8181-6*); pap. 9.95 incl. cassette (*0-8114-8189-1*) Raintree Steck-V.
—The Kangaroo. LC 79-13660. (Illus.). 32p. (gr. 1-4). 1981. PLB 29.28 incl. cassette (*0-8172-1843-2*) Raintree Steck-V.
Kangaroos. 1991. PLB 14.95s.p. (*0-88682-425-7*) Creative Ed.
Markert, Jenny. Kangaroos. 32p. 1991. 15.95 (*0-89565-715-5*) Childs World.
Petty, Kate. Kangaroos. (ps-3). 1990. PLB 10.90 (*0-531-17195-7*, Gloucester Pr) Watts.
—Kangaroos. (Illus.). (gr. k-3). 1993. pap. 3.95 (*0-8120-1492-8*) Barron.
Rau, Margaret. The Gray Kangaroo at Home. Hulsmann, Eva, illus. LC 77-14942. (gr. 5-8). 1978. lib. bdg. 6.99 (*0-394-93451-2*) Knopf Bks Yng Read.
Ryden, Hope. Joey: The Story of a Baby Kangaroo. Ryden, Hope, photos by. LC 93-15419. (Illus.). 40p. 1994. 15.00 (*0-688-12744-4*, Tambourine Bks); PLB 14.93 (*0-688-12745-2*, Tambourine Bks) Morrow.
Sanford, William R. & Green, Carl R. Kangaroos. LC 86-32881. (Illus.). 48p. (gr. 5). 1987. text ed. 12.95 RSBE (*0-89686-322-0*, Crestwood Hse) Macmillan Child Grp.
Selsam, Millicent E. & Hunt, Joyce. A First Look at Kangaroos, Kaolas & Other Animals with Pouches. Springer, Harriet, illus. LC 85-3126. 32p. (gr. k-3). 1985. 9.95 (*0-8027-6600-5*); PLB 12.85 (*0-8027-6579-3*) Walker & Co.
Serventy, Vincent. Kangaroo. LC 84-17994. (Illus.). 24p. (gr. k-5). 1985. PLB 9.95 (*0-8172-2418-1*); pap. 3.95 (*0-8114-6878-X*) Raintree Steck-V.
Stone, Lynn. Kangaroos. (Illus.). 24p. (gr. k-5). 1990. lib. bdg. 11.94 (*0-86593-058-9*); lib. bdg. 8.95s.p. (*0-685-36371-6*) Rourke Corp.
Storms, John. Kelly the Kangaroo. Ooka, Dianne & Squellati, Liz, eds. Storms, Bob, illus. 24p. (Orig.). (gr. k-3). Date not set. pap. 4.95 (*0-89346-798-7*) Heian Intl.

KANGAROOS–FICTION

Blume, Judy. The One in the Middle Is the Green Kangaroo. Aitken, Amy, illus. 48p. (gr. k-2). 1982. pap. 3.99 (*0-440-46731-4*, YB) Dell.
—The One in the Middle Is the Green Kangaroo. 2nd ed. Trivas, Irene, illus. LC 80-29664. 32p. (gr. k-2). 1991. Repr. of 1981 ed. 14.95 (*0-02-711055-9*, Bradbury Pr) Macmillan Child Grp.
Brown, Margaret W. Young Kangaroo. Dewey, Jennifer, illus. LC 92-54866. 48p. (ps-3). 1993. 14.95 (*1-56282-409-0*); PLB 14.89 (*1-56282-410-4*) Hyprn Child.
Chottin, Ariane. Little Kangaroo Finds His Way. Jensen, Patricia, adapted by. Fichaux, Catherine, illus. LC 93-4242. 22p. (ps-3). 1993. 5.98 (*0-89577-543-3*, Readers Digest Kids) RD Assn.
Dahl, Roald. Matilda. Blake, Quentin, illus. 224p. (gr. 3-7). 1988. pap. 14.95 (*0-670-82439-9*) Viking Child Bks.
Flynn, Mary J. The Blue Kangaroo. Flynn, Mary J., illus. 24p. (Orig.). (ps-k). 1992. pap. text ed. 5.95 (*1-880812-03-7*) S Ink WA.
Kipling, Rudyard. The Sing-Song of Old Man Kangaroo. Rowe, John A., illus. LC 90-7382. 32p. (gr. k up). 1991. pap. 14.95 (*0-88708-152-5*) Picture Bk Studio.
Lehan, Daniel. Crocodile Snaps - Kangaroo Jumps. LC 92-50842. (Illus.). 32p. (ps-k). 1993. 13.95 (*0-531-05484-5*) Orchard Bks Watts.
Leonard, Marcia & Duell. Little Kangaroo's Bad Day. (ps-7). 1987. pap. 2.75 (*0-553-15461-3*) Bantam.
McDonnell, Janet. Kangaroo's Adventure in Alphabet Town. McCallum, J., illus. LC 91-20540. 32p. (ps-2). 1992. PLB 11.80 (*0-516-05411-2*) Childrens.
Meyer, Mercer. What Do You Do with a Kangaroo. (ps-3). 1993. pap. 199.51 (*0-590-21034-3*) Scholastic Inc.
—What Do You Do with a Kangaroo? (ps-3). 1993. pap. 19.95 (*0-590-72851-2*) Scholastic Inc.
Payne, Emmy. Katy No-Pocket. (gr. 1-3). 1973. reinforced bdg. 13.95 (*0-395-17104-0*) HM.
—Katy No-Pocket. Rey, H. A., illus. 32p. (gr. k-3). 1973. pap. 5.70 (*0-395-13717-9*, Sandpiper) HM.
Potash, Dorothy. The Tale of Ned & His Nose. Sperling, Thomas, illus. 24p. (gr. k-4). 1993. PLB 13.95 (*1-879567-23-7*, Valeria Bks) Wonder Well.
Roberts, Thom. Atlantic Free Balloon Race. (gr. 3-7). 1986. pap. 2.50 (*0-380-89868-3*, Camelot) Avon.
Rosenthal, Ellie. What Can I Do? Asked the Kangaroo. Rosenthal, David, illus. 1993. 7.95 (*0-533-10358-4*) Vantage.
Wiseman, Bernard. Little New Kangaroo. Burns, Theresa, illus. LC 92-21955. 1993. 14.95 (*0-395-65362-2*, Clarion Bks) HM.

KANSAS

Aylesworth, Thomas G. & Aylesworth, Virginia L. South Central (Louisiana, Arkansas, Missouri, Kansas, Oklahoma) (Illus.). 64p. (gr. 3 up). 1992. PLB 16.95 (*0-7910-1047-3*) Chelsea Hse.
Buntin, Phillip R., illus. Kansas Symbols Coloring Book. 12p. (Orig.). Date not set. pap. 2.25 (*1-882404-06-8*) KS Herit Ctr.
Carole Marsh Kansas Books, 44 bks. 1994. lib. bdg. 1027.80 set (*0-7933-1291-4*); pap. 587.80 set (*0-7933-5154-5*) Gallopade Pub Group.
Carpenter, Allan. Kansas. new ed. LC 79-12433. (Illus.). 96p. (gr. 4 up). 1979. PLB 16.95 (*0-516-04116-9*) Childrens.
Fradin, Dennis. Kansas: In Words & Pictures. Wahl, Richard, illus. LC 80-12576. 48p. (gr. 2-5). 1980. PLB 12.95 (*0-516-03916-4*) Childrens.
Fredeen, Charles. Kansas. Lerner Geography Department Staff, ed. (Illus.). 72p. (gr. 4-7). 1992. 17.50 (*0-8225-2716-2*) Lerner Pubns.
Isern, Thomas D. & Wilson, Raymond. Kansas Land. rev. ed. (Illus.). 237p. (gr. 7). 1992. 18.95 (*0-87905-275-9*, Peregrine Smith) Gibbs Smith Pub.
Kent, Zachary. Kansas. LC 90-35385. (Illus.). 144p. (gr. 4 up). 1990. PLB 20.55 (*0-516-00462-X*) Childrens.
—Kansas. 203p. 1993. text ed. 15.40 (*1-56956-145-1*) W A T Braille.
Marsh, Carole. Avast, Ye Slobs! Kansas Pirate Trivia. (Illus.). (gr. 3-12). 1994. PLB 24.95 (*0-7933-0472-5*); pap. 14.95 (*0-7933-0471-7*); computer disk 29.95 (*0-7933-0473-3*) Gallopade Pub Group.
—The Beast & the Kansas Bed & Breakfast. (gr. 3-12). 1994. 24.95 (*1-55609-371-3*); pap. 14.95 (*1-55609-372-1*); bk. on computer disk 29.95 (*1-55609-373-X*) Gallopade Pub Group.
—Bow Wow! Kansas Dogs in History, Mystery, Legend, Lore, Humor & More! (Illus.). (gr. 3-12). 1994. PLB 24.95 (*0-7933-3515-9*); pap. 14.95 (*0-7933-3516-7*); computer disk 29.95 (*0-7933-3517-5*) Gallopade Pub Group.
—Chill Out: Scary Kansas Tales Based on Frightening Kansas Truths. (Illus.). 1994. lib. bdg. 24.95 (*0-7933-4702-5*); pap. 14.95 (*0-7933-4703-3*); disk 29.95 (*0-7933-4704-1*) Gallopade Pub Group.
—Christopher Columbus Comes to Kansas! Includes Reproducible Activities for Kids! (Illus.). (gr. 3-12). 1994. PLB 24.95 (*0-7933-3668-6*); pap. 14.95 (*0-7933-3669-4*); computer disk 29.95 (*0-7933-3670-8*) Gallopade Pub Group.
—The Hard-to-Believe-But-True! Book of Kansas History, Mystery, Trivia, Legend, Lore, Humor & More. (Illus.). (gr. 3-12). 1994. PLB 24.95 (*0-7933-0469-5*); pap. 14.95 (*0-7933-0468-7*); computer disk 29.95 (*0-7933-0470-9*) Gallopade Pub Group.
—If My Kansas Mama Ran the World. (gr. 3-12). 1994. 24.95 (*1-55609-374-8*); pap. 14.95 (*1-55609-375-6*); bk. on computer disk 29.95 (*1-55609-376-4*) Gallopade Pub Group.
—Jurassic Ark! Kansas Dinosaurs & Other Prehistoric Creatures. (gr. k-12). 1994. PLB 24.95 (*0-7933-7476-6*); pap. 14.95 (*0-7933-7477-4*); computer disk 29.95 (*0-7933-7478-2*) Gallopade Pub Group.
—Kansas & Other State Greats (Biographies) (gr. 3-12). 1994. 24.95 (*1-55609-362-4*); pap. 14.95 (*1-55609-363-2*); bk. on computer disk 29.95 (*1-55609-364-0*) Gallopade Pub Group.
—Kansas Bandits, Bushwackers, Outlaws, Crooks, Devils, Ghosts, Desperadoes & Other Assorted & Sundry Characters! (Illus.). (gr. 3-12). 1994. PLB 24.95 (*0-7933-0454-7*); pap. 14.95 (*0-7933-0453-9*); computer disk 29.95 (*0-7933-0455-5*) Gallopade Pub Group.
—Kansas Classic Christmas Trivia: Stories, Recipes, Activities, Legends, Lore & More! (Illus.). (gr. 3-12). 1994. PLB 24.95 (*0-7933-0457-1*); pap. 14.95 (*0-7933-0456-3*); computer disk 29.95 (*0-7933-0458-X*) Gallopade Pub Group.
—Kansas Coastales. 1994. PLB 24.95 (*1-55609-365-9*); pap. 14.95 (*1-55609-366-7*); bk. on computer disk 29.95 (*1-55609-367-5*) Gallopade Pub Group.
—Kansas Coastales! 1994. lib. bdg. 24.95 (*0-7933-7281-X*) Gallopade Pub Group.
—Kansas "Crinkum-Crankum" A Funny Word Book about Our State. (Illus.). 1994. lib. bdg. 24.95 (*0-7933-4856-0*); pap. 14.95 (*0-7933-4857-9*); disk 29.95 (*0-7933-4858-7*) Gallopade Pub Group.
—Kansas Dingbats! Bk. 1: A Fun Book of Games, Stories, Activities & More about Our State That's All in Code! for You to Decipher. (Illus.). (gr. 3-12). 1994. PLB 24.95 (*0-7933-3821-2*); pap. 14.95 (*0-7933-3822-0*); computer disk 29.95 (*0-7933-3823-9*) Gallopade Pub Group.
—Kansas Festival Fun for Kids! (Illus.). (gr. 3-12). 1994. lib. bdg. 24.95 (*0-7933-3974-X*); pap. 14.95 (*0-7933-3975-8*); disk 29.95 (*0-7933-3976-6*) Gallopade Pub Group.
—The Kansas Hot Air Balloon Mystery. (Illus.). (gr. 2-9). 1994. 24.95 (*0-7933-2462-9*); pap. 14.95 (*0-7933-2463-7*); computer disk 29.95 (*0-7933-2464-5*) Gallopade Pub Group.
—Kansas Jeopardy! Answers & Questions about Our State! (Illus.). (gr. 3-12). 1994. PLB 24.95 (*0-7933-4127-2*); pap. 14.95 (*0-7933-4128-0*); computer disk 29.95 (*0-7933-4129-9*) Gallopade Pub Group.
—Kansas "Jography" A Fun Run Thru Your State. (gr. 3-12). 1994. PLB 24.95 (*1-55609-353-5*); pap. 14.95 (*1-55609-354-3*); bk. on computer disk 29.95 (*1-55609-355-1*) Gallopade Pub Group.
—Kansas Kid's Cookbook: Recipes, How-to, History, Lore & More! (Illus.). (gr. 3-12). 1994. PLB 24.95 (*0-7933-0466-0*); pap. 14.95 (*0-7933-0465-2*); computer disk 29.95 (*0-7933-0467-9*) Gallopade Pub Group.
—The Kansas Mystery Van Takes Off! Book 1: Handicapped Kansas Kids Sneak Off on a Big Adventure. (Illus.). (gr. 3-12). 1994. 24.95 (*0-7933-5009-3*); pap. 14.95 (*0-7933-5010-7*); computer disk 29.95 (*0-7933-5011-5*) Gallopade Pub Group.
—Kansas Quiz Bowl Crash Course. (gr. 3-12). 1994. PLB 24.95 (*1-55609-359-4*); pap. 14.95 (*1-55609-360-8*); bk. on computer disk 29.95 (*1-55609-361-6*) Gallopade Pub Group.
—Kansas Rollercoasters! (Illus.). (gr. 3-12). 1994. PLB 24.95 (*0-7933-5272-X*); pap. 14.95 (*0-7933-5273-8*); computer disk 29.95 (*0-7933-5274-6*) Gallopade Pub Group.
—Kansas School Trivia: An Amazing & Fascinating Look at Our State's Teachers, Schools & Students! (Illus.). (gr. 3-12). 1994. PLB 24.95 (*0-7933-0463-6*); pap. 14.95 (*0-7933-0462-8*); computer disk 29.95 (*0-7933-0464-4*) Gallopade Pub Group.

—Kansas Silly Basketball Sportsmysteries, Vol. I. (Illus.). (gr. 3-12). 1994. PLB 24.95 (*0-7933-0460-1*); pap. 14.95 (*0-7933-0459-8*); computer disk 29.95 (*0-7933-0461-X*) Gallopade Pub Group.

—Kansas Silly Basketball Sportsmysteries, Vol. II. (Illus.). (gr. 3-12). 1994. PLB 24.95 (*0-7933-1640-5*); pap. 14.95 (*0-7933-1641-3*); computer disk 29.95 (*0-7933-1642-1*) Gallopade Pub Group.

—Kansas Silly Football Mystery, Vol. I. (gr. 3-12). 1994. PLB 24.95 (*1-55609-368-3*); pap. 14.95 (*1-55609-369-1*); bk. on computer disk 29.95 (*1-55609-370-5*) Gallopade Pub Group.

—Kansas Silly Football Mystery, Vol. II. (gr. 3-12). 1994. PLB 24.95 (*1-55609-377-2*); pap. 14.95 (*0-318-41972-6*); bk. on computer disk 29.95 (*1-55609-379-9*) Gallopade Pub Group.

—Kansas Silly Trivia. (gr. 3-12). 1994. PLB 24.95 (*0-318-41973-4*); pap. 14.95 (*1-55609-351-9*); bk. on computer disk 29.95 (*1-55609-352-7*) Gallopade Pub Group.

—Kansas Timeline: A Chronology of Kansas History, Mystery, Trivia, Legend, Lore & More. (Illus.). (gr. 3-12). 1994. PLB 24.95 (*0-7933-5923-6*); pap. 14.95 (*0-7933-5924-4*); computer disk 29.95 (*0-7933-5925-2*) Gallopade Pub Group.

—Kansas's (Most Devastating!) Disasters & (Most Calamitous!) Catastrophies! (Illus.). (gr. 3-12). 1994. PLB 24.95 (*0-7933-0451-2*); pap. 14.95 (*0-7933-0450-4*); computer disk 29.95 (*0-7933-0452-0*) Gallopade Pub Group.

—Kansas's Unsolved Mysteries (& Their "Solutions") Includes Scientific Information & Other Activities for Students. (Illus.). (gr. 3-12). 1994. PLB 24.95 (*0-7933-5770-5*); pap. 14.95 (*0-7933-5771-3*); computer disk 29.95 (*0-7933-5772-1*) Gallopade Pub Group.

—Lets Quilt Kansas & Stuff It Topographically! (gr. 3-12). 1994. PLB 24.95 (*1-55609-356-X*); pap. 14.95 (*1-55609-357-8*); bk. on computer disk 29.95 (*1-55609-358-6*) Gallopade Pub Group.

—Let's Quilt Our Kansas County. 1994. lib. bdg. 24.95 (*0-7933-7161-9*); pap. text ed. 14.95 (*0-7933-7162-7*); disk 29.95 (*0-7933-7163-5*) Gallopade Pub Group.

—Let's Quilt Our Kansas Town. 1994. lib. bdg. 24.95 (*0-7933-7011-6*); pap. text ed. 14.95 (*0-7933-7012-4*); disk 29.95 (*0-7933-7013-2*) Gallopade Pub Group.

—Meow! Kansas Cats in History, Mystery, Legend, Lore, Humor & More! (Illus.). (gr. 3-12). 1994. PLB 24.95 (*0-7933-3362-8*); pap. 14.95 (*0-7933-3363-6*); computer disk 29.95 (*0-7933-3364-4*) Gallopade Pub Group.

—My First Book about Kansas. (gr. k-4). 1994. PLB 24.95 (*0-7933-5617-2*); pap. 14.95 (*0-7933-5618-0*); computer disk 29.95 (*0-7933-5619-9*) Gallopade Pub Group.

—Patch, the Pirate Dog: A Kansas Pet Story. (ps-4). 1994. PLB 24.95 (*0-7933-5464-1*); pap. 14.95 (*0-7933-5465-X*); computer disk 29.95 (*0-7933-5466-8*) Gallopade Pub Group.

—Uncle Rebus: Kansas Picture Stories for Computer Kids. (Illus.). (gr. k-3). 1994. PLB 24.95 (*0-7933-4549-9*); pap. 14.95 (*0-7933-4550-2*); disk 29.95 (*0-7933-4551-0*) Gallopade Pub Group.

Thompson, Kathleen. Kansas. LC 87-16406. 48p. (gr. 4 up). 1987. 19.97 (*0-8174-4648-6*) (*0-86514-091-X*) cancelled 3/4" video (*0-86514-241-6*) Raintree Steck-V.

KANSAS–FICTION

Brown, Irene B. Willow Whip. 208p. (Orig.). (gr. 5 up). pap. 8.95 (*0-936085-23-1*) Blue Heron OR.

Irwin, Hadley. Jim-Dandy. LC 93-22611. 144p. (gr. 5-9). 1994. SBE 14.95 (*0-689-50594-9*, M K McElderry) Macmillan Child Grp.

Rumbaut, Hendle. Dove Dream. LC 93-26538. 1994. write for info. (*0-395-68393-9*) HM.

Shannon, George. Climbing Kansas Mountains. Allen, Thomas B., illus. LC 89-38197. 32p. (ps-2). 1993. RSBE 15.95 (*0-02-782181-1*, Bradbury Pr) Macmillan Child Grp.

Wilder, Laura Ingalls. Little House on the Prairie. rev. ed. Williams, Garth, illus. LC 52-7526. 336p. (gr. 3-7). 1961. 15.95 (*0-06-026445-4*); PLB 15.89 (*0-06-026446-2*) HarpC Child Bks.

KARATE

Barrett, Norman. Artes Marciales. LC 90-70884. (SPA., Illus.). 32p. (gr. k-4). 1990. PLB 11.90 (*0-531-07902-3*) Watts.

Brightfield, Richard. Master of Karate. (gr. 9-12). 1990. pap. 3.50 (*0-553-28202-6*) Bantam.

Brimner, Larry D. Karate. LC 87-25341. (Illus.). 72p. (gr. 7-9). 1988. PLB 10.90 (*0-531-10480-X*) Watts.

Casey, Kevin. Karate. LC 94-4094. (gr. 3 up). 1994. write for info. (*0-86593-366-9*) Rourke Corp.

—Kung Fu. LC 94-4087. 1994. write for info. (*0-86593-368-5*) Rourke Corp.

Kozuki, Russell. Junior Karate. LC 71-167665. (Illus.). 128p. (gr. 11 up). 1971. 12.95 (*0-8069-4446-3*) Sterling.

Lewis, Tom G. Karate for Kids. 120p. (Orig.). (gr. 2-10). 1980. pap. 3.95 (*0-89826-005-1*) Natl Paperback.

Metil, Luana & Townsend, Jace. The Story of Karate: From Ancient Legends to Modern Heroes. LC 93-32006. 1994. 18.95 (*0-8225-3325-1*) Lerner Pubns.

Neff, Fred. Basic Karate Handbook. Reid, James, illus. LC 75-38471. 56p. (gr. 5 up). 1976. PLB 14.95 (*0-8225-1150-9*) Lerner Pubns.

—Karate Is for Me. Reid, James E., photos by. LC 79-16900. (Illus.). 48p. (gr. 2-5). 1980. PLB 13.50 (*0-8225-1090-1*) Lerner Pubns.

Nishiyama, Hidetaka & Brown, Richard C. Karate: Art of Empty-Hand Fighting. (Illus.). 246p. (gr. 9 up). 1991. pap. 17.95 (*0-8048-1668-9*) C E Tuttle.

Oldgate, Karl. Karate. rev. ed. (Illus.). 80p. (gr. 10-12). 1993. pap. 7.95 (*0-7137-2410-2*, Pub. by Blandford Pr UK) Sterling.

Park, Y. H. & Leibowitz, Jeff. Taekwondo for Children: The Ultimate Reference Guide for Children Interested in the World's Most Popular Martial Art. Choi, Butto, illus. 128p. (Orig.). (gr. 4-8). 1994. pap. 9.95 (*0-9637151-0-0*) YH Pk Taekwondo.

Pfluger, A. Karate: Basic Principles. Kuttner, Paul & Cunningham, Dale S., trs. LC 67-27760. (Illus.). (gr. 8 up). 1969. Repr. of 1967 ed. 6.95 (*0-8069-4432-3*); PLB 7.49 (*0-8069-4433-1*) Sterling.

Queen, J. Allen. Complete Karate. LC 93-24831. (Illus.). 192p. (gr. 10-12). 1993. 19.95 (*0-8069-8678-6*) Sterling.

—Karate Basics. (Illus.). 128p. (gr. 3 up). 1993. pap. 7.95 (*0-8069-8677-8*) Sterling.

—Karate for Kids. LC 93-45837. (Illus.). 96p. 1994. 12.95 (*0-8069-0614-6*) Sterling.

Savage, Jeff. Karate. LC 93-27206. 1995. text ed. 13.95 (*0-89686-854-0*, Crestwood Hse) Macmillan.

Sewalson, Don. Street Self-Defense. Sewalson, Don, illus. 81p. (gr. 6-12). 1986. pap. 6.75 (*0-938419-01-3*) DM Pub.

—Street Self-Defense. Sewalson, Don, illus. 63p. (gr. 6-12). 1986. pap. 6.75 (*0-938419-03-X*) DM Pub.

—Street Self-Defense. Sewalson, Don, illus. 58p. (gr. 6-12). 1986. pap. 6.75 (*0-938419-02-1*) DM Pub.

—Street Self-Defense: Complete Edition. Sewalson, Don, illus. 193p. (gr. 6-12). 1986. 27.00 (*0-938419-04-8*); pap. 16.95 (*0-938419-00-5*) DM Pub.

Teitelbaum, Michael. Jr. Karate, A Photo-Fact Book. (Illus.). 24p. (Orig.). 1988. pap. 1.95 (*0-942025-47-4*) Kidsbks.

—Tae Kwon Do. (Illus.). 24p. (Orig.). 1990. pap. 2.50 (*0-942025-88-1*) Kidsbks.

Webster-Doyle, Terrence. Facing the Double Edged Sword: The Art of Karate for Young People. Cameron, Rod, illus. LC 73-83919. 90p. (Orig.). (gr. 5-9). 1988. 17.95 (*0-942941-17-9*); pap. 12.95 (*0-942941-16-0*) Atrium Soc Pubns.

KARTS AND KARTING

Cazin, Lorraine. Karts. (Illus.). 48p. (gr. 3-6). 1992. PLB 12.95 (*1-56065-072-9*) Capstone Pr.

KELLER, HELEN ADAMS, 1880-1968

Adler, David A. A Picture Book of Helen Keller. Wallner, John & Wallner, Alexandra, illus. LC 89-77510. 32p. (ps-3). 1990. reinforced bdg. 15.95 (*0-8234-0818-3*) Holiday.

—A Picture Book of Helen Keller. Wallner, John & Wallner, Alexandra, illus. LC 89-77510. (ps-3). pap. 5.95 (*0-8234-0950-3*) Holiday.

Benjamin, Anne. Young Helen Keller: Woman of Courage. Durrell, Julie, illus. LC 91-26406. 32p. (gr. k-2). 1992. PLB 11.59 (*0-8167-2530-6*); pap. text ed. 2.95 (*0-8167-2531-4*) Troll Assocs.

Davidson, Margaret. Helen Keller. 1989. pap. 2.50 (*0-590-42404-1*) Scholastic Inc.

—Helen Keller's Teacher. 160p. 1992. pap. 2.95 (*0-590-44652-5*, Apple Paperbacks) Scholastic Inc.

Gibson, William. The Miracle Worker. (gr. 6-9). 1984. pap. 4.50 (*0-553-24778-6*) Bantam.

Graff, Stewart. Helen Keller. (ps-3). 1991. pap. 3.50 (*0-440-40439-8*) Dell.

Graff, Stewart & Graff, Polly A. Helen Keller. Frame, Paul, illus. 80p. (gr. 2-7). 1980. pap. 2.95 (*0-440-43566-8*, YB) Dell.

—Helen Keller: Toward the Light. (Illus.). 80p. (gr. 2-6). 1992. Repr. of 1965 ed. lib. bdg. 12.95 (*0-7910-1412-6*) Chelsea Hse.

Keller, Helen. Story of My Life. Barnett, M. R., intro. by. (gr. 8 up). 1965. pap. 2.95 (*0-8049-0070-1*, CL-70) Airmont.

Keller, Helen A. Story of My Life. (gr. 4-7). 1991. pap. 2.95 (*0-590-44353-4*) Scholastic Inc.

Kudlinski, Kathleen V. Helen Keller. Diamond, Donna, illus. 64p. (gr. 2-6). 1991. 3.95 (*0-14-032902-1*) Puffin Bks.

—Helen Keller: A Light for the Blind. Diamond, Donna, illus. 64p. (gr. 2-6). 1989. pap. 10.95 (*0-670-82460-7*) Viking Child Bks.

Markham, Lois. Helen Keller. LC 92-24942. (Illus.). 64p. (gr. 5-8). 1993. PLB 12.90 (*0-531-20104-X*) Watts.

Peare, Catherine O. The Helen Keller Story. LC 59-10979. 192p. (gr. 4-6). 1990. PLB 13.89 (*0-690-04793-2*, Crowell Jr Bks) HarpC Child Bks.

—The Helen Keller Story. LC 90-49173. (Illus.). 176p. (gr. 6-10). 1991. PLB 13.95 (*1-55905-084-5*) Marshall Cavendish.

Sabin, Francene. Courage of Helen Keller. LC 81-23109. (Illus.). 48p. (gr. 4-6). 1982. PLB 10.79 (*0-89375-754-3*); pap. text ed. 3.50 (*0-89375-755-1*) Troll Assocs.

St. George, Judith. Dear Dr. Bell - Your Friend, Helen Keller. 172p. (gr. 5-9). 1992. 15.95 (*0-399-22337-1*, Putnam) Putnam Pub Group.

—Dear Dr. Bell...Your Friend, Helen Keller. LC 93-9304. 96p. (gr. 6 up). 1993. pap. text ed. 4.95 (*0-688-12814-9*, Pub. by Beech Tree Bks) Morrow.

Santrey, Laurence. Helen Keller. Frenck, Hal, illus. LC 84-2682. 32p. (gr. 3-6). 1985. PLB 9.49 (*0-8167-0156-3*); pap. text ed. 2.95 (*0-8167-0157-1*) Troll Assocs.

Sloan, Carolyn. Helen Keller. (Illus.). 64p. (gr. 5-9). 1991. 11.95 (*0-237-60016-1*, Pub. by Evans Bros Ltd) Trafalgar.

Tames, Richard. Helen Keller. LC 89-29278. (Illus.). 32p. (gr. 5-6). 1989. PLB 12.40 (*0-531-10764-7*) Watts.

—Helen Keller. (Illus.). 32p. (gr. 5 up). 1991. pap. 5.95 (*0-531-24609-4*) Watts.

Wepman, Dennis. Helen Keller. Horner, Matina, intro. by. (Illus.). 112p. (Orig.). (gr. 5 up). 1987. 17.95 (*1-55546-662-1*); pap. 9.95 (*0-7910-0417-1*) Chelsea Hse.

Wilkie, Katharine E. Helen Keller: From Tragedy to Triumph. Doremus, Robert, illus. LC 86-10719. 192p. (gr. 2-6). 1986. pap. 3.95 (*0-02-041980-5*, Aladdin) Macmillan Child Grp.

KENNEDY, JOHN FITZGERALD, PRESIDENT U. S. 1917-1963

Adler, David A. A Picture Book of John F. Kennedy. Casilla, Robert, illus. LC 90-23589. 32p. (ps-3). 1991. reinforced 14.95 (*0-8234-0884-1*); pap. 5.95 (*0-8234-0976-7*) Holiday.

Anderson, Catherine C. John F. Kennedy. (Illus.). 112p. (gr. 5 up). 1991. PLB 21.50 (*0-8225-4904-2*) Lerner Pubns.

Denenberg, Barry. John Fitzgerald Kennedy: America's 35th President. 128p. (gr. 5-8). 1988. pap. 2.95 (*0-590-41344-9*) Scholastic Inc.

Falkof, Lucille. John F. Kennedy: 35th President of the United States. Young, Richard G., ed. LC 87-35954. (Illus.). (gr. 5-9). 1988. PLB 17.26 (*0-944483-03-8*) Garrett Ed Corp.

Frisbee, Lucy P. John Fitzgerald Kennedy: America's Youngest President. Fiorentinl, Al, illus. LC 86-10965. 192p. (gr. 2-6). 1986. pap. 3.95 (*0-02-041990-2*, Aladdin) Macmillan Child Grp.

Frolick, S. J. Once There Was a President. rev. ed. LC 80-69972. 64p. (gr. 3-7). 1980. pap. 6.95 (*0-9605426-0-4*) Black Star Pub.

Harrison, Barbara & Terris, Daniel. A Twilight Struggle: The Life of John Fitzgerald Kennedy. LC 91-1492. (Illus.). 224p. (gr. 5 up). 1992. 18.00 (*0-688-08830-9*) Lothrop.

John F. Kennedy: Mini Play. (gr. 8 up). 1977. 6.50 (*0-89550-372-7*) Stevens & Shea.

Kent, Zachary. John F. Kennedy. (Illus.). (gr. 3 up). 1987. PLB 14.40 (*0-516-01390-4*); pap. 6.95 (*0-516-41390-2*) Childrens.

Levine, I. E. John Kennedy: Young Man in the White House. LC 90-49180. (Illus.). 176p. (gr. 6-10). 1991. PLB 13.95 (*1-55905-085-3*) Marshall Cavendish.

Mills, Judie. John F. Kennedy. LC 87-29470. (Illus.). 384p. (gr. 7-12). 1988. PLB 17.40 (*0-531-10520-2*) Watts.

Richardson, Nigel. J. F. Kennedy. (Illus.). 64p. (gr. 5-9). 1991. 11.95 (*0-237-60029-3*, Pub. by Evans Bros Ltd) Trafalgar.

Sandak, Cass R. The Kennedys. LC 91-2911. (Illus.). 48p. (gr. 5). 1991. text ed. 4.95 RSBE (*0-89686-633-5*, Crestwood Hse) Macmillan Child Grp.

Smith, Kathie B. John F. Kennedy. Seward, James, illus. LC 86-33863. 24p. (gr. 4-6). 1987. lib. bdg. 7.98 (*0-671-64602-8*, J Messner); PLB 5.99s.p. (*0-685-18831-0*) S&S Trade.

White, Nancy B. Meet John F. Kennedy. (Illus.). (gr. 2-5). 1965. 7.99 (*0-394-80059-1*) Random Bks Yng Read.

—Meet John F. Kennedy. LC 93-20057. 80p. (gr. 2-6). 1993. pap. 2.99 (*0-679-83601-2*, Bullseye Bks) Random Bks Yng Read.

KENNEDY, JOHN FITZGERALD, PRESIDENT U. S. 1917-1963–ASSASSINATION

Donnelly, Judy. Who Shot the President? The Death of John F. Kennedy. LC 88-4418. (Illus.). 48p. (Orig.). (gr. 2-4). 1988. lib. bdg. 7.99 (*0-394-99944-4*); pap. 3.50 (*0-394-89944-X*) Random Bks Yng Read.

Hamilton, Sue. The Assassination of a President: John F. Kennedy. Hamilton, John, ed. LC 89-84903. (Illus.). 32p. (gr. 4). 1990. PLB 11.96 (*0-939179-55-5*) Abdo & Dghtrs.

Hayman, Leroy. Assassinations of John & Robert Kennedy. (gr. 4-7). 1993. pap. 2.95 (*0-590-46539-2*) Scholastic Inc.

Hoare, Stephen. The Assassination of John F. Kennedy. (gr. 7 up). 1989. 19.95 (*0-85219-766-7*, Pub. by Batsford UK) Trafalgar.

Landsman, Susan. A History Mystery: Who Shot JFK? 96p. (Orig.). 1992. pap. 3.50 (*0-380-77063-6*, Camelot) Avon.

Netzley, Patricia D. The Assassination of President John F. Kennedy. LC 93-20818. (Illus.). 96p. (gr. 6 up). 1994. text ed. 14.95 RSBE (*0-02-768127-0*, New Discovery Bks) Macmillan Child Grp.

Stein, R. Conrad. The Assassination of John F. Kennedy. LC 91-44546. (Illus.). 32p. (gr. 3-6). 1992. PLB 12.30 (*0-516-06652-8*) Childrens.

—The Assassination of John F. Kennedy. LC 91-44546. (Illus.). 32p. (gr. 3-6). 1993. pap. 3.95 (*0-516-46652-6*) Childrens.

Waggoner, Jeffrey. The Assassination of President Kennedy: Opposing Viewpoints. LC 89-37442. (Illus.). 112p. (gr. 5-8). 1989. PLB 14.95 (*0-89908-068-5*) Greenhaven.

KENNEDY, ROBERT FRANCIS, 1925-1968

Petrillo, Daniel J. Robert F. Kennedy. Schlesinger, Arthur M., Jr., intro. by. (Illus.). 112p. (Orig.). (gr. 5 up). 1989. 17.95 (*1-55546-840-3*); pap. 9.95 (*0-7910-0581-X*) Chelsea Hse.

KENNEDY, ROBERT FRANCIS, 1925-1968–ASSASSINATION

Hamilton, Sue. The Killing of a Candidate: Robert F. Kennedy. Hamilton, John, ed. LC 89-84905. (Illus.). 32p. (gr. 4). 1989. PLB 11.96 (*0-939179-57-1*) Abdo & Dghtrs.

Hayman, Leroy. Assassinations of John & Robert Kennedy. (gr. 4-7). 1993. pap. 2.95 (*0-590-46539-2*) Scholastic Inc.

KENNEDY FAMILY

Sandak, Cass R. The Kennedys. LC 91-2911. (Illus.). 48p. (gr. 5). 1991. text ed. 4.95 RSBE (*0-89686-633-5*, Crestwood Hse) Macmillan Child Grp.

Simonelli, Susan B. Rose Kennedy. (Illus.). 112p. (gr. 5 up). 1992. lib. bdg. 17.95 (*0-7910-1622-6*) Chelsea Hse.

KENNY, ELIZABETH, 1886-1952

Crofford, Emily. Healing Warrior: A Story about Sister Elizabeth Kenny. Ritz, Karen, illus. 64p. (gr. 3-6). 1989. PLB 14.95 (*0-87614-382-6*) Carolrhoda Bks.

KENTUCKY

Brown, Dottie. Kentucky. Lerner Geography Department Staff, ed. (Illus.). 72p. (gr. 4-7). 1992. 17.50 (*0-8225-2715-4*) Lerner Pubns.

Buchart & Associates, Inc. Staff. Louisville Guide Book for Kids. 36p. (ps-5). 1993. pap. 2.75 (*1-883900-02-6*) Buchart & Assocs.

Carpenter, Allan. Kentucky. new ed. LC 79-12696. (Illus.). 96p. (gr. 4 up). 1979. PLB 16.95 (*0-516-04117-7*) Childrens.

Clark, Thomas D. Simon Kenton, Kentucky Scout. 2nd ed. Hay, Melba P., intro. by. Shenton, Edward, illus. 256p. (gr. 6-12). 17.95 (*0-945084-38-2*); pap. 8.95 (*0-945084-39-0*) J Stuart Found.

Dunnigan, Alice A. The Fascinating Story of Black Kentuckians: Their Heritage & Tradition. 1990. 29.45 (*0-87498-088-7*); index 8.00 (*0-87498-089-5*) Assoc Pubs DC.

Fradin, Dennis. Kentucky: In Words & Pictures. Wahl, Richard, illus. LC 80-25810. 48p. (gr. 2-5). 1981. PLB 12.95 (*0-516-03917-2*) Childrens.

Fradin, Dennis B. Kentucky. LC 92-38810. (Illus.). 64p. (gr. 3-5). 1993. PLB 16.45 (*0-516-03817-6*) Childrens.

Klotter, James C. Our Kentucky; a Study of the Bluegrass State. LC 91-48220. 360p. 1992. 29.00 (*0-8131-1783-6*, F451) U Pr of Ky.

McNair, Sylvia. Kentucky. 199p. 1993. text ed. 15.40 (*1-56956-163-X*) W A T Braille.

Marsh, Carole. Avast, Ye Slobs! Kentucky Pirate Trivia. (Illus.). (gr. 3-8). 1994. PLB 24.95 (*0-7933-0496-2*); pap. 14.95 (*0-7933-0495-4*); disk 29.95 (*0-685-45938-1*) Gallopade Pub Group.

—The Beast of the Kentucky Bed & Breakfast. (Illus.). (gr. 3-8). 1994. PLB 24.95 (*0-7933-1650-2*); pap. 14.95 (*0-7933-1651-0*); disk 29.95 (*0-7933-1652-9*) Gallopade Pub Group.

—Bow Wow! Kentucky Dogs in History, Mystery, Legend, Lore, Humor & More! (Illus.). (gr. 3-12). 1994. PLB 24.95 (*0-7933-3518-3*); pap. 14.95 (*0-7933-3519-1*); computer disk 29.95 (*0-7933-3520-5*) Gallopade Pub Group.

—Carole Marsh Kentucky Books, 45 bks. (Illus.). (gr. 3-8). 1994. PLB 1052.75 set (*0-7933-1292-2*); pap. 602.75 (*0-7933-5156-1*) Gallopade Pub Group.

—Chill Out: Scary Kentucky Tales Based on Frightening Kentucky Truths. (Illus.). 1994. lib. bdg. 24.95 (*0-7933-4705-X*); pap. 14.95 (*0-7933-4706-8*); disk 29.95 (*0-7933-4707-6*) Gallopade Pub Group.

—Christopher Columbus Comes to Kentucky! Includes Reproducible Activities for Kids! (Illus.). (gr. 3-12). 1994. PLB 24.95 (*0-7933-3671-6*); pap. 14.95 (*0-7933-3672-4*); computer disk 29.95 (*0-7933-3673-2*) Gallopade Pub Group.

—The Hard-to-Believe-But-True! Book of Kentucky History, Mystery, Trivia, Legend, Lore, Humor & More. (Illus.). (gr. 3-8). 1994. PLB 24.95 (*0-7933-0493-8*); pap. 14.95 (*0-7933-0492-X*); disk 29.95 (*0-7933-0494-6*) Gallopade Pub Group.

—If My Kentucky Mama Ran the World! (Illus.). (gr. 3-8). 1994. lib. bdg. 24.95 (*0-7933-1655-3*); pap. 14.95 (*0-7933-1656-1*); disk 29.95 (*0-7933-1657-X*) Gallopade Pub Group.

—Jurassic Ark! Kentucky Dinosaurs & Other Prehistoric Creatures. (gr. k-12). 1994. PLB 24.95 (*0-7933-7479-0*); pap. 14.95 (*0-7933-7480-4*); computer disk 29.95 (*0-7933-7481-2*) Gallopade Pub Group.

—Kentucky & Other State Greats (Biographies) (Illus.). (gr. 3-8). 1994. PLB 24.95 (*1-55609-448-5*); pap. 14.95 (*1-55609-447-7*); disk 29.95 (*0-7933-1658-8*) Gallopade Pub Group.

—Kentucky Bandits, Bushwackers, Outlaws, Crooks, Devils, Ghosts, Desperadoes & Other Assorted & Sundry Characters! (Illus.). (gr. 3-8). 1994. PLB 24.95 (*0-7933-0478-4*); pap. 14.95 (*0-7933-0477-6*); disk 29.95 (*0-7933-0479-2*) Gallopade Pub Group.

—Kentucky Classic Christmas Trivia: Stories, Recipes, Activities, Legends, Lore & More! (Illus.). (gr. 3-8). 1994. PLB 24.95 (*0-7933-0481-4*); pap. 14.95 (*0-7933-0480-6*); disk 29.95 (*0-7933-0482-2*) Gallopade Pub Group.

—Kentucky Coastales. (Illus.). (gr. 3-8). 1994. PLB 24.95 (*1-55609-444-2*); pap. 14.95 (*1-55609-443-4*); disk 29.95 (*0-7933-1654-5*) Gallopade Pub Group.

—Kentucky Coastales! 1994. lib. bdg. 24.95 (*0-7933-7282-8*) Gallopade Pub Group.

—Kentucky "Crinkum-Crankum" A Funny Word Book about Our State. (Illus.). 1994. lib. bdg. 24.95 (*0-7933-4859-5*); pap. 14.95 (*0-7933-4860-9*); disk 29.95 (*0-7933-4861-7*) Gallopade Pub Group.

—Kentucky Festival Fun for Kids! (Illus.). (gr. 3-12). 1994. lib. bdg. 24.95 (*0-7933-3977-4*); pap. 14.95 (*0-7933-3978-2*); disk 29.95 (*0-7933-3979-0*) Gallopade Pub Group.

—The Kentucky Hot Air Balloon Mystery. (Illus.). (gr. 2-9). 1994. 24.95 (*0-7933-2471-8*); pap. 14.95 (*0-7933-2472-6*); computer disk 29.95 (*0-7933-2473-4*) Gallopade Pub Group.

—Kentucky Jeopardy! Answers & Questions about Our State! (Illus.). (gr. 3-12). 1994. PLB 24.95 (*0-7933-4130-2*); pap. 14.95 (*0-7933-4131-0*); computer disk 29.95 (*0-7933-4132-9*) Gallopade Pub Group.

—Kentucky "Jography" A Fun Run Thru Our State! (Illus.). (gr. 3-8). 1994. PLB 24.95 (*1-55609-439-6*); pap. 14.95 (*1-55609-109-5*); disk 29.95 (*0-7933-1644-8*) Gallopade Pub Group.

—Kentucky Kid's Cookbook: Recipes, How-To, History, Lore & More! (Illus.). (gr. 3-8). 1994. PLB 24.95 (*0-7933-0490-3*); pap. 14.95 (*0-7933-0489-X*); disk 29.95 (*0-7933-0491-1*) Gallopade Pub Group.

—The Kentucky Mystery Van Takes Off! Book 1: Handicapped Kentucky Kids Sneak Off on a Big Adventure. (Illus.). (gr. 3-12). 1994. 24.95 (*0-7933-5012-3*); pap. 14.95 (*0-7933-5013-1*); computer disk 29.95 (*0-7933-5014-X*) Gallopade Pub Group.

—Kentucky Quiz Bowl Crash Course! (Illus.). (gr. 3-8). 1994. PLB 24.95 (*1-55609-446-9*); pap. 14.95 (*1-55609-445-0*); disk 29.95 (*0-7933-1653-7*) Gallopade Pub Group.

—Kentucky Rollercoasters! (Illus.). (gr. 3-12). 1994. PLB 24.95 (*0-7933-5275-4*); pap. 14.95 (*0-7933-5276-2*); computer disk 29.95 (*0-7933-5277-0*) Gallopade Pub Group.

—Kentucky School Trivia: An Amazing & Fascinating Look at Our State's Teachers, Schools & Students! (Illus.). (gr. 3-8). 1994. PLB 24.95 (*0-7933-0487-3*); pap. 14.95 (*0-7933-0486-5*); disk 29.95 (*0-7933-0488-1*) Gallopade Pub Group.

—Kentucky Silly Basketball Sportsmysteries, Vol. I. (Illus.). (gr. 3-8). 1994. PLB 24.95 (*0-7933-0484-9*); pap. 14.95 (*0-7933-0483-0*); disk 29.95 (*0-7933-0485-7*) Gallopade Pub Group.

—Kentucky Silly Basketball Sportsmysteries, Vol. II. (Illus.). (gr. 3-8). 1994. PLB 24.95 (*0-7933-1659-6*); pap. 14.95 (*0-7933-1660-X*); disk 29.95 (*0-7933-1661-8*) Gallopade Pub Group.

—Kentucky Silly Football Sportsmysteries, Vol. I. (Illus.). (gr. 3-8). 1994. PLB 24.95 (*1-55609-442-6*); pap. 14.95 (*1-55609-441-8*); disk 29.95 (*0-7933-1646-4*) Gallopade Pub Group.

—Kentucky Silly Football Sportsmysteries, Vol. II. (Illus.). (gr. 3-8). 1994. PLB 24.95 (*0-7933-1647-2*); pap. 14.95 (*0-7933-1648-0*); disk 29.95 (*0-7933-1649-9*) Gallopade Pub Group.

—Kentucky Silly Trivia! (gr. 3-8). 1994. PLB 24.95 (*1-55609-438-8*); pap. 14.95 (*1-55609-040-4*); disk 29.95 (*0-7933-1643-X*) Gallopade Pub Group.

—Kentucky Timeline: A Chronology of Kentucky History, Mystery, Trivia, Legend, Lore & More. (Illus.). (gr. 3-12). 1994. PLB 24.95 (*0-7933-5926-0*); pap. 14.95 (*0-7933-5927-9*); computer disk 29.95 (*0-7933-5928-7*) Gallopade Pub Group.

—Kentucky's (Most Devastating!) Disasters & (Most Calamitous!) Catastrophies! LC 7933000476000008. (Illus.). (gr. 3-8). 1994. PLB 24.95 (*0-7933-0475-X*); pap. 14.95 (*0-7933-0474-1*); disk 29.95 (*0-685-45937-3*) Gallopade Pub Group.

—Kentucky's Unsolved Mysteries (& Their "Solutions") Includes Scientific Information & Other Activities for Students. (Illus.). (gr. 3-12). 1994. PLB 24.95 (*0-7933-5773-X*); pap. 14.95 (*0-7933-5774-8*); computer disk 29.95 (*0-7933-5775-6*) Gallopade Pub Group.

—Let's Quilt Our Kentucky County. 1994. lib. bdg. 24.95 (*0-7933-7164-3*); pap. text ed. 14.95 (*0-7933-7165-1*); disk 29.95 (*0-7933-7166-X*) Gallopade Pub Group.

—Let's Quilt Our Kentucky Town. 1994. lib. bdg. 24.95 (*0-7933-7014-0*); pap. text ed. 14.95 (*0-7933-7015-9*); disk 29.95 (*0-7933-7016-7*) Gallopade Pub Group.

—Meow! Kentucky Cats in History, Mystery, Legend, Lore, Humor & More! (Illus.). (gr. 3-12). 1994. PLB 24.95 (*0-7933-3365-2*); pap. 14.95 (*0-7933-3366-0*); computer disk 29.95 (*0-7933-3367-9*) Gallopade Pub Group.

—My First Book about Kentucky. (gr. k-4). 1994. PLB 24.95 (*0-7933-5620-2*); pap. 14.95 (*0-7933-5621-0*); computer disk 29.95 (*0-7933-5622-9*) Gallopade Pub Group.

—Patch, the Pirate Dog: A Kentucky Pet Story. (ps-4). 1994. PLB 24.95 (*0-7933-5467-6*); pap. 14.95 (*0-7933-5468-4*); computer disk 29.95 (*0-7933-5469-2*) Gallopade Pub Group.

—Uncle Rebus: Kentucky Picture Stories for Computer Kids. (Illus.). (gr. k-3). 1994. PLB 24.95 (*0-7933-4552-9*); pap. 14.95 (*0-7933-4553-7*); disk 29.95 (*0-7933-4554-5*) Gallopade Pub Group.

Ryen, Dag. Traces: The Story of Lexington's Past. Crow, James L. & Finkel, Becky, illus. 177p. (gr. 4 up). 1987. text ed. 13.95 (*0-912839-08-2*) Lexington-Fayette.

Stone, Lynn M. Bluegrass Country. LC 93-23002. 1993. write for info. (*0-86593-306-5*) Rourke Corp.

Stuart, Jesse. Kentucky Is My Land. Miller, Jim W., afterword by. LC 92-779. 107p. (gr. 10 up). 1987. Repr. of 1952 ed. 10.95 (*0-945084-01-3*) J Stuart Found.

—Strength from the Hills: The Story of Mick Stuart, My Father. rev. ed. Gifford, James M., intro. by. LC 92-3995. (Illus.). 175p. (gr. 3 up). 1992. Repr. of 1968 ed. 12.00 (*0-945084-29-3*) J Stuart Found.

Turner Educational Services, Inc. Staff, et al. Kentucky. 48p. (gr. 3 up). 1986. PLB 19.97 (*0-8174-4532-3*) Raintree Steck-V.

Wadley, Verleen W. Four Winds of the Past. Webb, Glyn, ed. (Illus.). 215p. 1993. PLB 16.00x (*0-9604726-6-5*) Enterprise Pr.

KENTUCKY–FICTION

Borden, Louise. Just in Time for Christmas. Lewin, Ted, illus. LC 93-40082. (ps-3). 1994. 14.95 (*0-590-45355-6*) Scholastic Inc.

Cannon, Bettie. A Bellsong for Sarah Raines. LC 87-4299. 192p. (gr. 7 up). 1987. 14.95 (*0-684-18839-2*, Scribners Young Read) Macmillan Child Grp.

Clark, Billy C. Goodbye Kate. Herndon, Jerry A., intro. by. Eldridge, Harold, illus. 288p. (gr. 6 up). 1994. Repr. of 1964 ed. 20.00 (*0-945084-41-2*) J Stuart Found.

—Song of the River. rev. ed. Gifford, James M., et al, eds. LC 92-31483. (Illus.). 176p. (gr. 7 up). 1993. Repr. of 1957 ed. 15.00 (*0-945084-35-8*) J Stuart Found.

Green, Michelle Y. Willie Pearl Series. 1992. write for info. (*0-9627697-6-2*) W Ruth Co.

Havill, Juanita. Kentucky Troll. LC 90-27850. (Illus.). (ps-3). 1993. 13.00 (*0-688-10457-6*); PLB 12.93 (*0-688-10458-4*) Lothrop.

Hines, Jane B. Kentucky Boy. Graves, Helen, ed. Taylor, Neil, illus. LC 86-40281. 155p. (Orig.). (gr. 4-8). 1986. pap. 7.95 (*1-55523-033-4*) Winston-Derek.

Luttrell, Wanda. Home on Stoney Creek. LC 93-47084. (gr. 4 up). 1994. write for info. (*0-7814-0901-2*) Chariot Family.

Snelling, Lauraine. Kentucky Dreamer. 160p. (Orig.). 1992. pap. 5.99 (*1-55661-234-6*) Bethany Hse.

Stuart, Jesse. Hie to the Hunters. 5th ed. Herndon, Jerry A. & Zornes, Rockyintro. by. LC 93-20063. 270p. (gr. 8 up). 1988. 20.00 (*0-945084-06-4*) J Stuart Found.

—A Penny's Worth of Character. 3rd ed. Miller, Jim W. & Herndon, Jerry A., eds. Zornes, Rocky, illus. LC 92-31438. 62p. (gr. 3-6). 1993. pap. 3.00 (*0-945084-32-3*) J Stuart Found.

—Plowshare in Heaven. 2nd ed. Herndon, Jerry A., et al, eds. LC 90-62718. (Illus.). 268p. (gr. 7 up). 1991. Repr. of 1958 ed. 20.00 (*0-945084-21-8*) J Stuart Found.

—Red Mule. 2nd ed. Herndon, Jerry A., ed. LC 92-31439. (Illus.). 96p. (gr. 3-6). 1993. 12.00 (*0-945084-34-X*); pap. text ed. 6.00 (*0-945084-33-1*) J Stuart Found.

KENYA

Bailey, Donna & Sproule, Anna. Kenya. LC 90-9644. (Illus.). 32p. (gr. 1-4). 1990. PLB 18.99 (*0-8114-2563-0*); pap. 3.95 (*0-8114-7178-0*) Raintree Steck-V.

Barysh, Ann, et al. The Suitcase Scholar Goes to Kenya. Lerner Geography Department Staff, ed. (gr. 4-6). Set incls. teaching guide, Kenya in Pictures, A Family in Kenya, Count Your Way Through Africa, Safari, Cooking the African Way & wall map. saddle-stitch bdg. 49.95 (*0-685-55161-X*); teaching guide 15.95 (*0-685-55162-8*) Lerner Pubns.

Blackburn, Roderic H. Okiek. (Illus.). 42p. (gr. 6-9). 1991. pap. 4.95 (*0-237-50631-9*, Pub. by Evans Bros Ltd) Trafalgar.

Isack, Hussein A. People of the North: Boran. (Illus.). 42p. (gr. 6-9). 1991. pap. 4.95 (*0-237-50724-2*, Pub. by Evans Bros Ltd) Trafalgar.

Jacobsen, Karen. Kenya. LC 90-20009. (Illus.). 48p. (gr. k-4). 1991. PLB 12.85 (*0-516-01112-X*); pap. 4.95 (*0-516-41112-8*) Childrens.

Kipkorir, Benjamin. People of the Rift Valley: Kalenjin. (Illus.). 43p. (gr. 6-9). 1991. pap. 4.95 (*0-237-50892-3*, Pub. by Evans Bros Ltd) Trafalgar.

Lerner Publications, Department of Geography Staff. Kenya in Pictures. (Illus.). 64p. (gr. 5 up). 1988. 17.50 (*0-8225-1830-9*) Lerner Pubns.

McLean, Virginia O. & Klyce, Katherine P. Kenya, Jambo! LC 88-63987. (Illus.). 36p. (gr. k-6). 1989. 15.95 (*0-9606046-4-2*); Incl. cassette. pap. 11.95 (*0-9606046-5-0*) Redbird.

Maren, Michael. The Land & People of Kenya. LC 88-22959. (Illus.). 208p. (gr. 6 up). 1989. 19.00 (*0-397-32334-4*, Lipp Jr Bks); PLB 18.89 (*0-397-32335-2*, Lipp Jr Bks) HarpC Child Bks.

Mwangudza, Johnson A. Mijikenda. (Illus.). 37p. (gr. 6-9). 1991. pap. 4.95 (*0-237-50490-1*, Pub. by Evans Bros Ltd) Trafalgar.

Ng'Weno, Fleur. Kenya. (Illus.). 32p. (gr. 7-10). 1992. 17.95 (*0-237-60194-X*, Pub. by Evans Bros Ltd) Trafalgar.

Ochieng, William R. People of the South-Western Highlands: Gusii. (Illus.). 34p. (gr. 6-9). 1991. pap. 4.95 (*0-237-49898-7*, Pub. by Evans Bros Ltd) Trafalgar.

—People Round the Lake: Luo. (Illus.). 32p. (gr. 6-9). 1991. pap. 4.95 (*0-237-50924-5*, Pub. by Evans Bros Ltd) Trafalgar.

Pateman, Robert. Kenya. LC 92-39263. 1993. 21.95 (*1-85435-572-4*) Marshall Cavendish.

Salim, Ahmed I. People of the Coast: Swahili. (Illus.). 40p. (gr. 6-9). 1991. pap. 4.95 (*0-237-50894-X*, Pub. by Evans Bros Ltd) Trafalgar.

Stein, R. Conrad. Kenya. LC 85-14949. (Illus.). 127p. (gr. 5-9). 1985. PLB 20.55 (*0-516-02770-0*) Childrens.

KENYA–FICTION

Brady, Jennifer. Jambi & the Lions. Thatch, Nancy R., ed. Brady, Jennifer, illus. Melton, David, intro. by. LC 92-17593. (Illus.). 26p. (gr. 3-5). 1992. PLB 14.95 (*0-933849-41-9*) Landmark Edns.

Dobkins, Lucy M. Daddy, There's a Hippo in the Grapes. Botero, Kirk, illus. LC 92-20321. 64p. (gr. 3-7). 1992. 12.95 (*0-88289-889-2*) Pelican.

Rispin, Karen. Ambush at Amboseli. LC 93-37801. 1994. 4.99 (*0-8423-1295-1*) Tyndale.

—Sabrina the Schemer. LC 93-39634. 1994. 4.99 (*0-8423-1296-X*) Tyndale.

Smith, Laura L. Sophisticated Josephine: The East African Bush Elephant. (Illus.). 32p. (gr. 3-5). 1993. pap. 6.95 (*0-8059-3311-5*) Dorrance.

Smith, Roland. Thunder Cave. LC 9-19714. 1995. 14.95 (*0-7868-0068-2*); 14.89 (*0-7868-2055-1*) Hyprn Child.

KEPLER, JOHANNES, 1571-1630

Tiner, John H. Johannes Kepler: Giant of Faith & Science. Burke, Rod, illus. LC 77-558. (gr. 3-6). 1977. pap. 6.95 (*0-915134-11-X*) Mott Media.

KEROSENE

see Petroleum

KEY, FRANCIS SCOTT, 1779-1843

Collins, David. Francis Scott Key. Van Seversen, Joe, illus. 113p. (gr. 3-6). 1982. pap. 6.95 (*0-915134-91-8*) Mott Media.

Kroll, Steven. By the Dawn's Early Light: The Story of the Star Spangled Banner. Andreasen, Dan, illus. LC 92-27101. 40p. (ps-5). 1994. 14.95 (*0-590-45054-9*) Scholastic Inc.

Patterson, Lillie. Francis Scott Key: Poet & Patriot. (Illus.). 80p. (gr. 2-6). 1991. Repr. of 1963 ed. lib. bdg. 12.95 (*0-7910-1461-4*) Chelsea Hse.

Whitcraft, Melissa. Francis Scott Key: A Gentleman of Maryland. LC 94-2571. 1994. write for info. (*0-531-20163-5*) Watts.

KEYNES, JOHN MAYNARD, 1883-1946

Escoffier, Jeffrey. John Maynard Keynes. Duberman, Martin, intro. by. LC 94-1133. 1994. write for info. (*0-7910-2860-7*); pap. write for info. (*0-7910-2879-8*) Chelsea Hse.

Victor, R. F. John Maynard Keynes: Father of Modern Economics. Rahmas, D. Steve, ed. 32p. (Orig.). (gr. 7-12). 1972. lib. bdg. 4.95 incl. catalog cards (*0-87157-517-5*) SamHar Pr.

KEYS

see Locks and Keys

KHRUSHCHEV, NIKITA SERGEEVICH, 1894-1971

Kallen, Stuart A. The Khrushchev Era. Wallner, Rosemary, ed. LC 92-13476. 1992. PLB 13.99 (*1-56239-103-8*) Abdo & Dghtrs.

KIBBUTZ

see Collective Settlements

KINDERGARTEN

Elovson, Allana. The Kindergarten Survival Handbook: The Before School Checklist & a Guide for Parents. rev. ed. Elovson, Andrea K., illus. 96p. (Orig.). (gr. k). 1993. Spanish ed. pap. text ed. 12.95 perfect bdg. (*1-879888-07-6*); English ed. pap. text ed. 12.95 (*1-879888-06-8*) Parent Ed.

Forte, Imogene. Think about It! Kindergarten. (Illus.). 80p. (ps-k). 1981. pap. text ed. 7.95 (*0-913916-96-X*, IP-96X) Incentive Pubn.

Gagnon, Constance. Help! for Preschoolers. 64p. (ps). 1982. 5.95 (*0-86653-061-4*, GA 412) Good Apple.

Grades K-1 Early Learner Workbook II. 192p. (gr. k-1). 1991. pap. 4.95 (*1-56144-047-7*) Modern Pub NYC.

Howe, James. When You Go to Kindergarten. rev. ed. Imershein, Betsy, photos by. LC 93-48152. (Illus.). 1994. 14.93 (*0-688-12912-9*); PLB 15.00 (*0-688-12913-7*) Morrow Jr Bks.

Issaroff, Penina. Kindergarten Carousel. (ps). 1993. 12.95 (*0-943706-12-2*) Yllw Brick Rd.

Kindergarten Vocabulary. (Illus.). 24p. (ps-k). 1986. 3.98 (*0-86734-069-X*, FS-3059) Schaffer Pubns.

Schaffer, Frank, Publications Staff. Kindergarten, Bk. 1. (Illus.). 48p. (gr. k). 1983. wkbk. 4.98 (*0-86734-024-X*, FS-2653) Schaffer Pubns.

—Kindergarten, Bk. 2. (Illus.). 48p. (ps-k). 1983. wkbk. 4.98 (*0-86734-025-8*, FS-2654) Schaffer Pubns.

—Kindergarten Skills. (Illus.). 24p. (ps-k). 1980. wkbk. 3.98 (*0-86734-012-6*, FS-3025) Schaffer Pubns.

Senisi, Ellen B. Kindergarten Kids. LC 94-6033. (ps-1). 1994. 2.50 (*0-590-47614-9*) Scholastic Inc.

Taulbee, Annette. Kindergarten Activities. (Illus.). 24p. (ps-k). 1986. 3.98 (*0-86734-065-7*, FS-3057) Schaffer Pubns.

—Kindergarten Math. (Illus.). 24p. (ps-k). 1986. 3.98 (*0-86734-070-3*, FS-3062) Schaffer Pubns.

—Kindergarten Thinking Skills. (Illus.). 24p. (ps-k). 1986. 3.98 (*0-86734-067-3*, FS-3060) Schaffer Pubns.

KINDERGARTEN–FICTION

Cazet, Denys. Born in the Gravy. Cazet, Denys, illus. LC 92-44523. 32p. (ps-1). 1993. 14.95 (*0-531-05488-8*); PLB 14.99 (*0-531-08638-0*) Orchard Bks Watts.

Cleary, Beverly. Ramona the Pest. Darling, Louis, illus. LC 68-12981. (gr. 3-7). 1968. 13.95 (*0-688-21721-4*); PLB 13.88 (*0-688-31721-9*) Morrow Jr Bks.

—Ramona the Pest. 1923. pap. 2.95 (*0-440-77209-5*) Dell.

Hinton, S. E. Big David, Little David. Daniel, Alan, illus. LC 93-32307. 1995. 14.95 (*0-385-31093-5*) Doubleday.

Martin, Ann. Rachel Parker Kingergarten Show-Off. Poydar, Nancy, illus. 1993. pap. 6.95 (*0-8234-1067-6*) Holiday.

Park, Barbara. Junie B. Jones & a Little Monkey Business. Brunkus, Denise, illus. LC 92-56706. 80p. (Orig.). (gr. 1-4). 1993. PLB 9.99 (*0-679-93886-9*); pap. 2.99 (*0-679-83886-4*) Random Bks Yng Read.

—Junie B. Jones & Her Big Fat Mouth. Brunkus, Denise, illus. LC 92-50957. 80p. (Orig.). (gr. 1-4). 1993. PLB 9.99 (*0-679-94407-9*); pap. 2.99 (*0-679-84407-4*) Random Bks Yng Read.

—Junie B. Jones & Some Sneaky Peeky Spying. Brunkus, Denise, illus. LC 93-5557. 80p. (Orig.). (gr. 1-4). 1994. PLB 9.99 (*0-679-95101-6*); pap. 2.99 (*0-679-85101-1*) Random Bks Yng Read.

Pryor, Bonnie. Jumping Jenny. Riggio, Anita, illus. 192p. (gr. 2 up). 1992. 14.00 (*0-688-09684-0*) Morrow Jr Bks.

Schaefer, Charles E. Cat's Got Your Tongue? A Story for Children Afraid to Speak. LC 91-42707. 32p. (ps-3). 1992. pap. 6.95 (*0-945354-46-0*); 16.95 (*0-945354-45-2*) Magination Pr.

—Cat's Got Your Tongue? A Story for Children Afraid to Speak. Friedman, Judith, illus. LC 92-56869. 1993. PLB 17.27 (*0-8368-0930-0*) Gareth Stevens Inc.

Schwartz, Amy. Annabelle Swift, Kindergartner. LC 87-15403. (Illus.). 32p. (ps-2). 1991. pap. 4.95 (*0-531-07027-1*) Orchard Bks Watts.

Serfozo, Mary. Benjamin Bigfoot. Smith, Joseph A., illus. LC 92-321. 32p. (ps-3). 1993. SBE 14.95 (*0-689-50570-1*, M K McElderry) Macmillan Child Grp.

KINDNESS TO ANIMALS

see Animals–Treatment

KINETICS

see Dynamics; Motion

KING, CORETTA SCOTT, 1927-

Henry, Sondra & Taitz, Emily. Coretta Scott King: Keeper of the Dream. LC 91-31082. (Illus.). 128p. (gr. 6 up). 1992. lib. bdg. 17.95 (*0-89490-334-9*) Enslow Pubs.

King, Coretta Scott. My Life with Martin Luther King, Jr. rev. ed. 256p. (gr. 6 up). 1993. 17.95 (*0-8050-2445-X*, Bks Young Read) H Holt & Co.

Medearis, Angela S. Dare to Dream: Coretta Scott King & the Civil Rights Movement. Rich, Anna, illus. LC 93-33573. 64p. (gr. 3-6). 1994. 13.99 (*0-525-67426-8*, Lodestar Bks) Dutton Child Bks.

Patrick, Diane. Coretta Scott King. LC 91-17032. (Illus.). 144p. (gr. 9-12). 1991. PLB 14.40 (*0-531-13005-3*) Watts.

Wheeler, Jill C. Coretta Scott King. LC 92-16677. 1992. 12.94 (*1-56239-116-X*) Abdo & Dghtrs.

KING, MARTIN LUTHER, 1929-1968

Adler, David A. Un Libro Ilustrado Sobre Martin Luther King, Hijo. Mlawer, Teresa, tr. from ENG. Casilla, Robert, illus. (SPA.). 32p. (ps-3). 1992. reinforced bdg. 14.95 (*0-8234-0982-1*); pap. 5.95 (*0-8234-0991-0*) Holiday.

—Martin Luther King, Jr. Free at Last. Casilla, Robert, illus. LC 86-4670. 48p. (gr. 2-5). 1986. reinforced bdg. 14.95 (*0-8234-0618-0*); pap. 4.95 (*0-8234-0619-9*) Holiday.

—A Picture Book of Martin Luther King, Jr. Casilla, Robert, illus. LC 89-1930. 32p. (ps-3). 1989. reinforced bdg. 15.95 (*0-8234-0770-5*); pap. 5.95 (*0-8234-0847-7*) Holiday.

AESOP Enterprises, Inc. Staff & Crenshaw, Gwendolyn J. Martin Luther King, Jr. Personalism & the Sacredness of the Human Personality. 16p. (gr. 3-12). 1991. pap. write for info. incl. cassette (*1-880771-01-2*) AESOP Enter.

Alico, Stella H. Benjamin Franklin-Martin Luther King Jr. Cruz, E. R., illus. (gr. 4-12). 1979. pap. text ed. 2.95 (*0-88301-353-3*); wkbk 1.25 (*0-88301-377-0*) Pendulum Pr.

Archer, Jules. They Had a Dream: The Civil Rights Struggle from Frederick Douglass to Marcus Garvey to Martin Luther King, Jr., & Malcolm X. (Illus.). 288p. (gr. 5 up). 1993. 15.99 (*0-670-84494-2*) Viking Child Bks.

Bains, Rae. Martin Luther King. Frenck, Hal, illus. LC 84-2666. 32p. (gr. 3-6). 1985. PLB 9.49 (*0-8167-0160-1*); pap. text ed. 2.95 (*0-8167-0161-X*) Troll Assocs.

Bray, Rosemary L. Martin Luther King. Zeldis, Malcah, illus. LC 93-41002. 48p. (gr. 2 up). 1995. write for info. (*0-688-13131-X*); PLB write for info. (*0-688-13132-8*) Greenwillow.

Cauper, Eunice. Martin Luther King, Jr. & Our January 15th Holiday for Children. Tonra, Ian, illus. 32p. (Orig.). (gr. k-3). 1991. pap. text ed. 6.00 (*0-9617551-3-X*) E Cauper.

Darby, Jean. Martin Luther King, Jr. (Illus.). 112p. (gr. 5 up). 1990. PLB 21.50 (*0-8225-4902-6*) Lerner Pubns.

—Martin Luther King, Jr. (gr. 4-7). 1992. pap. 6.95 (*0-8225-9611-3*) Lerner Pubns.

Davidson, Margaret. I Have a Dream: The Story of Martin Luther King. (gr. 4-7). 1991. pap. 2.75 (*0-590-44230-9*) Scholastic Inc.

De Kay, James T. Meet Martin Luther King, Jr. LC 88-26383. (Illus.). 72p. (gr. 2-4). 1989. PLB 6.99 (*0-394-91962-9*); pap. 2.99 (*0-394-81962-4*) Random Bks Yng Read.

DeKay, James T. Meet Martin Luther King, Jr. rev. ed. (Illus.). 112p. (gr. 3-5). 1993. 2.99 (*0-679-85411-8*, Bullseye Bks); PLB 9.99 (*0-679-95411-2*, Bullseye Bks) Random Bks Yng Read.

Faber, Doris & Faber, Donald. Martin Luther King, Jr. LC 90-49172. (Illus.). 128p. (gr. 6-10). 1991. PLB 13.95 (*1-55905-086-1*) Marshall Cavendish.

Fox, Mary V. About Martin Luther King Day. LC 88-23230. (Illus.). 64p. (gr. 4-7). 1989. lib. bdg. 15.95 (*0-89490-200-8*) Enslow Pubs.

Greene, Carol. Martin Luther King, Jr. A Man Who Changed Things. Dobson, Steven, illus. LC 88-37714. 48p. (gr. k-3). 1989. PLB 12.85 (*0-516-04205-X*); pap 4.95 (*0-516-44205-8*) Childrens.

Grubbs, J. E. Dr. Martin Luther King, Jr. Remembered. Abell, ed. Grubbs, T. G., illus. (gr. 1-4). 1994. 25.00 (*0-685-71479-9*); pap. 15.00 (*0-685-71480-2*) Jonas.

Hakim, Rita. Martin Luther King, Jr. And the March Toward Freedom. (Illus.). 32p. (gr. 2-4). 1991. PLB 12.90 (*1-878841-13-0*); pap. 4.95 (*1-878841-33-5*) Millbrook Pr.

Hamilton, Sue. The Killing of a Leader: Dr. Martin Luther King. Hamilton, John, ed. LC 89-84904. (Illus.). 32p. (gr. 4). 1989. PLB 11.96 (*0-939179-56-3*) Abdo & Dghtrs.

Haskins, James. The Life & Death of Martin Luther King, Jr. LC 77-3157. (Illus.). (gr. 5 up). 1977. PLB 14.93 (*0-688-51802-8*) Lothrop.

—The Life & Death of Martin Luther King, Jr. ALC Staff, ed. LC 77-3157. (Illus.). 176p. (gr. 6 up). 1992. pap. 3.95 (*0-688-11690-6*, Pub. by Beech Tree Bks) Morrow.

Haskins, Jim. I Have a Dream: The Life & Words of Martin Luther King, Jr. LC 91-42528. (Illus.). 112p. (gr. 5 up). 1992. PLB 19.90 (*1-56294-087-2*); pap. 8.95 (*1-56294-837-7*) Millbrook Pr.

—I Have a Dream: The Life & Words of Martin Luther King, Jr. 1992. pap. 8.70 (*0-395-64549-2*) HM.

Henry, Sondra & Taitz, Emily. Coretta Scott King: Keeper of the Dream. LC 91-31082. (Illus.). 128p. (gr. 6 up). 1992. lib. bdg. 17.95 (*0-89490-334-9*) Enslow Pubs.

Jakoubek, Robert. Martin Luther King, Jr. (gr. 5 up). 1990. pap. 9.95 (*0-7910-0243-8*) Chelsea Hse.

Jones, Kathryn. Happy Birthday Dr. King. (gr. 4-7). 1994. pap. 4.95 (*0-671-87523-X*, Half Moon Bks) S&S Trade.

Jones, Margaret. Martin Luther King, Jr. Scott, R., illus. LC 68-9483. 36p. (gr. 2-4). 1968. PLB 11.80 (*0-516-03524-X*); pap. 3.95 (*0-516-43524-8*) Childrens.

Kallen, Stuart A. Martin Luther King: A Man & His Dream. LC 93-2296. (gr. 7 up). 1993. 14.96 (*1-56239-256-5*) Abdo & Dghtrs.

Keyla Activity Book: Martin Luther King, Jr. 24p. (gr. 4-6). 1993. pap. text ed. 4.95 (*1-882962-05-2*) Keyla.

Lambert, Kathy. Martin Luther King, Jr. (Illus.). 80p. (gr. 3-5). 1993. PLB 12.95 (*0-7910-1759-1*) Chelsea Hse.

Lazo, Caroline. Martin Luther King, Jr. LC 93-9069. (Illus.). 64p. (gr. 4 up). 1994. text ed. 13.95 RSBE (*0-87518-618-1*, Dillon) Macmillan Child Grp.

Levine, Ellen. If You Lived At the Time of Martin Luther King. 1990. pap. 2.95 (*0-590-42582-X*) Scholastic Inc.

Lillegard, Dee. My First Martin Luther King Book. Endres, Helen, illus. LC 86-31670. 32p. (ps-2). 1987. PLB 11.45 (*0-516-02908-8*); pap. 3.95 (*0-516-42908-6*) Childrens.

Lowery, Linda. Martin Luther King Day. Mitchell, Hetty, illus. 56p. (gr. k-4). 1987. lib. bdg. 14.95 (*0-87614-299-4*) Carolrhoda Bks.

—Martin Luther King Day. Mitchell, Hetty, illus. (gr. 3-5). 1987. incl. cassette 19.95 (*0-87499-071-8*); pap. 12.95 incl. cassette (*0-87499-070-X*); 4 paperbacks, cassette & guide 27.95 (*0-87499-072-6*) Live Oak Media.

—Martin Luther King Day. Mitchell, Hetty, illus. 56p. (gr. k-4). 1987. pap. 5.95 (*0-87614-468-7*, First Ave Edns) Lerner Pubns.

McKissack, Patricia. Martin Luther King, Jr. A Man to Remember. LC 83-23933. (Illus.). 128p. (gr. 4 up). 1984. PLB 14.40 (*0-516-03206-2*); pap. 5.95 (*0-516-43206-0*) Childrens.

—Our Martin Luther King Book. Endres, Helen, illus. LC 86-6785. 32p. (ps-3). 1986. PLB 13.95 (*0-89565-342-7*) Childs World.

McKissack, Patricia & McKissack, Fredrick. Martin Luther King, Jr. Man of Peace. Ostendorf, Ned, illus. LC 90-19156. 32p. (gr. 1-4). 1991. lib. bdg. 12.95 (*0-89490-302-0*) Enslow Pubs.

MacMillan, Dianne M. Martin Luther King, Jr. Day. LC 91-43097. (Illus.). 48p. (gr. 1-4). 1992. lib. bdg. 14.95 (*0-89490-382-9*) Enslow Pubs.

Martin Luther King. 1992. 4.99 (*0-517-06993-8*) Random Hse Value.

Martin Luther King Jr: Mini Play. (gr. 5 up). 1977. 6.50 (*0-89550-363-8*) Stevens & Shea.

Martin Luther King Jr. Pop Up. 1991. 8.95 (*0-8167-2569-1*) Troll Assocs.

Marzollo, Jean. Feliz Cumpleanos, Martin Luther King: Happy Birthday, Martin Luther King. Romo, Alberto, tr. from ENG. Pinkney, J. Brian, illus. (SPA.). (gr. 3-7). 1994. pap. 4.95 (*0-590-47507-X*) Scholastic Inc.

—Happy Birthday, Martin Luther King. (ps-3). pap. 19.95 (*0-590-72828-8*) Scholastic Inc.

Mattern, Joanne. Young Martin Luther King, Jr. I Have a Dream. Eitzen, Allan, illus. LC 91-26478. 32p. (gr. k-2). 1992. text ed. 11.59 (*0-8167-2544-6*); pap. text ed. 2.95 (*0-8167-2545-4*) Troll Assocs.

Millender, Dharathula H. Martin Luther King, Jr. Young Man with a Dream. Fiorentino, Al, illus. LC 86-10739. 192p. (gr. 2-6). 1986. pap. 3.95 (*0-02-042010-2*, Aladdin) Macmillan Child Grp.

Milton, Joyce. Marching to Freedom: The Story of Martin Luther King Jr. (Orig.). (gr. k-6). 1987. pap. 3.50 (*0-440-45433-6*, YB) Dell.

Murphy, Carol. Martin Luther King, Jr. Reese, Bob, illus. (gr. k-6). 1991. 11.95 (*0-89868-230-4*) ARO Pub.

—Martin Luther King, Jr. Reese, Bob, illus. (gr. k-6). 1991. pap. 20.00 (*0-89868-231-2*) ARO Pub.

Myers, Walter D. Young Martin's Promise. Bond, Barbara H., illus. LC 92-18070. 32p. (gr. 2-5). 1992. PLB 18.51 (*0-8114-7210-8*) Raintree Steck-V.

Obaba, Al-Imam. Dr. Martin Luther King, Jr. (Illus.). 43p. (Orig.). 1989. pap. 3.95 (*0-916157-14-8*) African Islam Miss Pubns.

Ottenheimer. Martin Luther King, Jr. (gr. 2-5). 1987. pap. 2.50 (*0-671-63632-4*, Little Simon) S&S Trade.

Parker, Margot. What Is Martin Luther King, Jr. Day? Bates, Matt, illus. LC 89-29254. 48p. (ps-3). 1990. 11.80 (*0-516-03784-6*); pap. 4.95 (*0-516-43784-4*) Childrens.

Patrick, Diane. Martin Luther King, Jr. LC 89-24800. (Illus.). 1990. PLB 12.90 (*0-531-10892-9*) Watts.

Patterson, Lillie. Martin Luther King, Jr. & the Freedom Movement. 1989. 16.95x (*0-8160-1605-4*) Facts On File.

Peck, Ira. The Life & Words of Martin Luther King Jr. (Illus.). 96p. (Orig.). (gr. 3-7). 1991. pap. 2.95 (*0-590-43827-1*) Scholastic Inc.

Philosophy of Non-Violence: Martin Luther King Mini-Play. (gr. 8 up). 1978. 6.50 (*0-89550-313-1*) Stevens & Shea.

Plumpp, Sterling. Ballad of Harriet Tubman. Burrowes, Adjoa J., illus. 1993. 18.95 (*0-88378-062-3*) Third World.

Richardson, Nigel. Martin Luther King. (Illus.). 64p. (gr. 5-9). 1991. 11.95 (*0-237-60007-2*, Pub. by Evans Bros Ltd) Trafalgar.

Rowland, Della. Martin Luther King, Jr. The Dream of Peaceful Revolution. Gallin, Richard, ed. Young, Andrew, intro. by. (Illus.). 128p. (gr. 5 up). 1990. lib. bdg. 12.95 (*0-382-09924-9*); pap. 7.95 (*0-382-24062-6*) Silver Burdett Pr.

Schlank, Carol H. & Metzger, Barbara. Martin Luther King, Jr. A Biography for Young Children. Kastner, John, illus. 24p. (ps-3). 1989. pap. 3.95 (*0-9613271-2-X*) RAEYC.

—Martin Luther King, Jr. A Biography for Young Children. rev. ed. Kastner, John, illus. 32p. (ps-k). 1990. PLB 14.95 (*0-87659-123-3*); pap. 6.95 (*0-87659-122-5*) Gryphon Hse.

Schloredt, Valerie. Martin Luther King, Jr. LC 88-2211. (Illus.). 68p. (Orig.). (gr. 5-6). 1990. pap. 7.95 (*0-8192-1524-4*) Morehouse Pub.

—Martin Luther King, Jr. Leader in the Struggle for Civil Rights. Birch, Beverley, adapted by. LC 89-77587. (Illus.). 64p. (gr. 3-4). 1990. PLB 19.93 (*0-8368-0392-2*) Gareth Stevens Inc.

Schmidt, Fran & Friedman, Alice. Fighting Fair: Dr. Martin Luther King Jr. for Kids. Heyne, Chris, illus. 40p. (Orig.). (gr. 4-9). 1986. pap. text ed. 13.95 (*1-878227-01-7*) Peace Educ.

—Fighting Fair: Dr. Martin Luther King Jr. for Kids. rev. ed. Heyne, Chris, illus. (gr. 4-9). 1990. Set. pap. text ed. 74.95 69 p., incl. poster, video (*1-878227-02-5*); tchr's. ed., incl. poster 19.95 (*1-878227-07-6*); Set of 5. wkbk., 48p. 11.95 (*1-878227-08-4*) Peace Educ.

Schulke, Flip, ed. Martin Luther King, Jr. A Documentary...Montgomery to Memphis. King, Coretta S., intro. by. (Illus.). 224p. (gr. 8 up). 1976. limited ed. o.p. 100.00 (*0-685-62030-1*); pap. 15.95 (*0-393-07492-7*) Norton.

Smith, Kathie B. Martin Luther King, Jr. Seward, James, illus. LC 86-28059. 24p. (gr. 4-6). 1987. lib. bdg. 7.98 (*0-671-64149-2*, J Messner); PLB 5.99s.p. (*0-685-18830-2*) S&S Trade.

Tate, Eleanora E. Thank You, Dr. Martin Luther King, Jr. (gr. 4-7). 1992. pap. 3.99 (*0-553-15886-4*) Bantam.

Thompson, Margurite. Martin Luther King Jr. A Story For Children. 24p. (gr. k-3). 1983. 3.00 (*0-912444-25-8*) DARE Bks.

Thompson-Peters, Flossie E. Martin Luther King, Jr. Green, Ken, illus. Behrens, Debra J. & Jeffery, Lisa E., eds. (Illus.). 94p. (Orig.). (gr. 3-9). 1992. pap. 7.50 (*1-880784-06-8*) Atlas Pr.

Woodson, Jacqueline. Martin Luther King, Jr. Brook, Bonnie, ed. Cooper, Floyd, illus. 32p. (gr. k-2). 1990. 4.95 (*0-671-69112-0*); PLB 6.95 (*0-671-69106-6*) Silver Pr.

Yette, Samuel F. & Yette, Frederick W. Washington & Two Marches: 1963 & 1983. (Illus.). 1984. 25.00 (*0-911253-02-5*); pap. 16.95 (*0-911253-03-3*); deluxe ed. 50.00 deluxe ltd. ed (*0-317-11590-1*) Cottage Bks.

KING PHILIP'S WAR, 1675-1676

Averill, Esther. King Philip, the Indian Chief. Belsky, Vera, illus. LC 92-32156. v, 147p. (gr. 6-12). 1993. lib. bdg. 17.50 (*0-208-02357-7*, Pub. by Linnet); (Pub. by Linnet) Shoe String.

Cwiklik, Robert. King Philip. Furstinger, Nancy, ed. (Illus.). 144p. (gr. 5-7). 1989. PLB 10.95 (*0-382-09573-1*); pap. 7.95 (*0-382-09762-9*) Silver Burdett Pr.

Leach, Douglas E. Flintlock & Tomahawk: New England in King Philip's War. Morison, Samuel E., intro. by. LC 58-5467. 320p. 1992. pap. 12.50t (*0-940160-55-2*) Parnassus Imprints.

KINGS AND RULERS

see also Dictators; Queens;

also names of countries with the subdivision Kings and Rulers, e.g. Great Britain–Kings and Rulers; etc.; also names of individual kings and rulers, e.g. Elizabeth 2nd, Queen of Great Britain; etc.

Aliki. A Medieval Feast. LC 82-45923. (Illus.). 32p. (gr. 2-6). 1986. pap. 5.95 (*0-06-446050-9*, Trophy) HarpC Child Bks.

Barrett, Kevin. Imperial Crisis: House Devon in Turmoil. (Illus.). 56p. (gr. 10-12). 1985. pap. 12.00 (*0-915795-37-X*, 9300) Iron Crown Ent Inc.

Blackwood, Alan. Twenty Tyrants. LC 89-23853. (Illus.). 48p. (gr. 3-8). 1990. PLB 12.95 (*1-85435-255-5*) Marshall Cavendish.

Pollard, Michael. Absolute Rulers. Stefoff, Rebecca, ed. LC 91-33297. (Illus.). 48p. (gr. 5-8). 1992. PLB 19.93 (*1-56074-034-5*) Garrett Ed Corp.

KINGS AND RULERS–FICTION

Abell, Joan P. You Will Be King: Gallantry, Bk. 2: Age Three. rev. ed. Abell, Joan P., illus. 50p. (gr. 5-8). 1993. 22.00 (*1-56611-025-4*); PLB 25.00 (*0-685-65767-1*); pap. 15.00 (*1-56611-449-7*) Jonas.

Adams, Michael, illus. The Emperor's New Clothes. Ingram, John, ed. Adams, Michael, illus. 48p. (gr. 1-4). 1990. 5.95 (*0-88101-106-1*) Unicorn Pub.

Albright, Naomi. The Great White Forest-King. 170p. 1992. pap. 12.75 (*1-882218-01-9*) Blue Star Pubs.

Alexander, Lloyd. The Beggar Queen. (gr. 6-12). 1985. pap. 3.99 (*0-440-90548-6*, LFL) Dell.

—The High King. LC 68-11833. 288p. (gr. 4-6). 1968. 16.95 (*0-8050-1114-5*, Bks Young Read) H Holt & Co.

—The High King. 288p. (gr. k-6). 1969. pap. 3.99 (*0-440-43574-9*, YB) Dell.

Armstrong, Jennifer. King Crow. LC 93-39261. 1995. write for info. (*0-517-59634-2*); write for info. (*0-517-59635-0*) Crown Pub Group.

—Little Salt Lick & the Sun King. Goodell, Jon, illus. LC 93-18673. 32p. (ps-3). 1994. 15.00 (*0-517-59620-2*); 15.99 (*0-517-59621-0*) Crown Bks Yng Read.

Bauer, Marion D. Dream of Queens & Castles. (gr. 4-7). 1992. pap. 3.25 (*0-440-40554-8*) Dell.

Baum, L. Frank. Queen Zixi of Ix: Or, the Story of the Magic Cloak. Richardson, Frederick, illus. Gardner, M., intro. by. (Illus.). 231p. (gr. 1-3). 1971. pap. 4.95 (*0-486-22691-3*) Dover.

Bentheim, Rozelle. King Kid. LC 91-2058. (Illus.). 128p. (gr. 4-7). 1991. 13.95 (*0-8050-1633-3*, Bks Young Read) H Holt & Co.

Bond, Michael. Paddington Meets the Queen. Lobban, John, illus. LC 92-24938. 32p. (ps-3). 1993. 3.95 (*0-694-00460-X*, Festival) HarpC Child Bks.

Brenner, Peter. King for One Day. Wyss, Manspeter, illus. LC 74-151271. 36p. (ps-3). 7.95 (*0-87592-027-6*) Scroll Pr.

Brittain, Bill. My Buddy, the King. LC 88-35704. 144p. (gr. 5-8). 1989. 13.00 (*0-06-020724-8*); PLB 12.89 (*0-06-020725-6*) HarpC Child Bks.

—The Wish Giver: Three Tales of Coven Tree. Glass, Andrew, illus. LC 82-48264. 192p. (gr. 3-7). 1986. pap. 3.95 (*0-06-440168-5*, Trophy) HarpC Child Bks.

Burnett, Frances H. Little Lord Fauntleroy. 190p. (gr. 7 up). 1985. pap. 2.95 (*0-14-035025-X*, Puffin) Puffin Bks.

Charnas, Suzy M. The Bronze King. 208p. 1987. pap. 2.95 (*0-553-15493-1*, Skylark) Bantam.

Chew, Ruth. Royal Magic. 128p. 1991. pap. 2.75 (*0-590-44742-4*) Scholastic Inc.

Christian, Mary B. Penrod Again. Dyer, Jane, illus. LC 86-21846. 56p. (gr. 1-4). 1987. RSBE 11.95 (*0-02-718550-8*, Macmillan Child Bk) Macmillan Child Grp.

Cole, Brock. King at the Door. (ps-3). 1992. pap. 4.95 (*0-374-44041-7*) FS&G.

Derby, Sally. King Kendrick's Splinter. Gore, Leonid, illus. LC 94-4360. 1994. write for info. (*0-8027-8322-8*); Reinforced. write for info. (*0-8027-8323-6*) Walker & Co.

Ekwensi, Cyprian. King for Ever! (gr. 4-7). 1992. pap. 4.95 (*0-7910-2921-2*) Chelsea Hse.

Fletcher, Susan. Flight of the Dragon Kyn. LC 92-44787. 224p. (gr. 5-9). 1993. SBE 15.95 (*0-689-31880-4*, Atheneum Child Bk) Macmillan Child Grp.

Friedman, Aileen. The King's Commissioners. Guevara, Susan, illus. LC 94-11275. 1994. write for info. (*0-590-48989-5*) Scholastic Inc.

Gilbert, Lela. The Journey with the Golden Book. (Illus.). 1992. pap. 6.99 (*1-56121-070-6*) Wolgemuth & Hyatt.

Ginsburg, Mirra. The King Who Tried to Fry an Egg on His Head. Hillenbrand, Will, illus. LC 91-10099. 32p. (gr. k-3). 1994. RSBE 14.95 (*0-02-736242-6*, Macmillan Child Bk) Macmillan Child Grp.

Gleitzman, Morris. Two Weeks with the Queen. Bacha, Andy, illus. 144p. (gr. 3-7). 1993. pap. 3.95 (*0-06-440482-X*, Trophy) HarpC Child Bks.

Groves, Richard. Surprise, Surprise, Queen Loonia! Burgess, Mark, illus. 32p. (ps-1). 1992. pap. 5.95 (*0-8120-4582-3*) Barron.

Gwynne, Fred. The King Who Rained. (gr. 1-5). 11.95 (*0-317-62057-6*); pap. 5.95 (*0-317-62058-4*) P-H.

Hao, Kuang-ts'ai. The Emperor & the Nightingale. Chang, Shih-ming, illus. (ENG & CHI.). 32p. (gr. 2-4). 1994. 14.95 (*1-57227-018-7*) Pan Asian Pubns.

—The Emperor & the Nightingale. Chang, Shih-ming, illus. (ENG & VIE.). 32p. (gr. 2-4). 1994. 16.95 (*1-57227-020-9*) Pan Asian Pubns.

—The Emperor & the Nightingale. Chang, Shih-ming, illus. (ENG & KOR.). 32p. (gr. 2-4). 1994. 16.95 (*1-57227-021-7*) Pan Asian Pubns.

—The Emperor & the Nightingale. Chang, Shih-ming, illus. (ENG & THA.). 32p. (gr. 2-4). 1994. 16.95 (*1-57227-022-5*) Pan Asian Pubns.

—The Emperor & the Nightingale. Chang, Shih-ming, illus. (ENG & TAG.). 32p. (gr. 2-4). 1994. 16.95 (*1-57227-023-3*) Pan Asian Pubns.

—The Emperor & the Nightingale. Chang, Shih-ming, illus. (ENG & CAM.). 32p. (gr. 2-4). 1994. 16.95 (*1-57227-024-1*) Pan Asian Pubns.

—The Emperor & the Nightingale. Chang, Shih-ming, illus. (ENG & LAO.). 32p. (gr. 2-4). 1994. 16.95 (*1-57227-025-X*) Pan Asian Pubns.

—The Emperor & the Nightingale. Chang, Shih-ming, illus. (ENG & KOR.). 32p. (gr. 2-4). 1994. 16.95 (*1-57227-026-8*) Pan Asian Pubns.

—The Emperor & the Nightingale: El Emperador y el Ruisenor. Zeller, Beatriz, tr. from CHI. Chang, Shih-ming, illus. (ENG & SPA.). 32p. (gr. 2-4). 1994. 16.95 (*1-57227-019-5*) Pan Asian Pubns.

What price will an emperor, who wants to live forever, pay for immortality? Will he give up his favorite horse? His kingdom, perhaps? The answers to these questions are poignantly shown through this haunting & inspiring story about an emperor who ultimately decides to forsake immortality for the love of something greater than himself. This story is illustrated in dreamy details that enhance the story's lyrical power. Readers of all ages will be touched by the messages of love & life offered in THE EMPEROR & THE NIGHTINGALE. Based on Andersen's THE EMPEROR & THE NIGHTINGALE. Also available in English/Chinese, Vietnamese, Korean, Thai, Tagalog, Khmer, Lao & Hmong. For grades 2-4. Please specify the languages when ordering. Available exclusively from: Pan Asian Publications (USA) Inc., 29564 Union City Blvd., Union City, CA 94587. Order toll free: 1-800-853-ASIA, FAX: (510) 475-1489.

Publisher Provided Annotation.

Harris, Geraldine. Prince of the Godborn. (gr. k-12). 1987. pap. 2.50 (*0-440-95407-X*, LFL) Dell.

Hennessy, B. G. The Missing Tarts. Pearson, Tracey C., illus. 32p. (ps-3). 1991. pap. 3.95 (*0-14-050815-5*, Puffin) Puffin Bks.

Herge. King Ottokar's Sceptre. (Illus., Orig.). (gr. k up). 1974. pap. 7.95 (*0-316-35831-2*, Joy St Bks) Little.

Hillig, Chuck. The Magic King. Hesik, Blue, illus. LC 84-50928. 32p. (Orig.). (ps-2). 1984. 12.95 (*0-913299-07-3*, Dist. by PGW) Stillpoint.

Hoelscher, Gwen. Prince Skippy's Quest. (Illus.). 64p. (Orig.). (gr. 6 up). 1986. pap. 7.95 (*0-9617597-0-4*) Wright Monday Pr.

Hopkins, Lee B. Questions. Croll, Carolyn, illus. LC 90-21745. 64p. (gr. k-3). 1994. pap. 3.50 (*0-06-444181-4*, Trophy) HarpC Child Bks.

Kase, Judith B. The Emperor's New Clothes. (gr. k up). 1978. 4.50 (*0-87602-125-9*) Anchorage.

King-Smith, Dick. The Queen's Nose. Bennett, Jill, illus. LC 83-49480. 128p. (gr. 3-7). 1994. pap. 3.95 (*0-06-440450-1*, Trophy) HarpC Child Bks.

Kisling, Lee. The Fools' War. LC 91-47695. 176p. (gr. 5 up). 1992. 14.00 (*0-06-020836-8*); PLB 13.89 (*0-06-020837-6*) HarpC Child Bks.

Leonard, Marcia. King Lionheart's Castle. Wallner, Alexandra, illus. 24p. (ps-1). 1992. 5.95 (*0-382-72974-9*); PLB 9.98 (*0-382-72973-0*) Silver.

Lobel, Anita. Sven's Bridge. LC 91-29544. (Illus.). 32p. (ps-4). 1992. 14.00 (*0-688-11251-X*); PLB 13.93 (*0-688-11252-8*) Greenwillow.

Love, Ann. The Prince Who Wrote a Letter. Goffe, Toni, illus. LC 92-27587. 1992. 11.95 (*0-85953-398-0*, Pub. by Childs Play UK); pap. write for info. (*0-85953-399-9*, Pub. by Childs Play UK) Childs Play.

Lucado, Max. The Children of the King. Goffe, Toni, illus. 32p. (gr. 3-6). 1994. 12.99 (*0-89107-823-1*) Crossway Bks.

Luttrell, Ida. The Star Counters. Pretro, Korinna, illus. LC 93-20342. 32p. 1994. 15.00 (0-688-12149-7, Tambourine Bks); PLB 14.93 (0-688-12150-0, Tambourine Bks) Morrow.

McAllister, Angela. The King Who Sneezed. Henwood, Simon, illus. LC 88-6858. 32p. (gr. k-3). 1988. 12.95 (0-688-08327-7); PLB 12.88 (0-688-08328-5, Morrow Jr Bks) Morrow Jr Bks.

McKenzie, Ellen K. The King, the Princess, & the Tinker. Low, William, illus. LC 91-31316. 80p. (gr. 2-4). 1993. 14.95 (0-8050-1773-9, Redfeather BYR) H Holt & Co.

McMullen, Eunice & McMullen, Nigel. Dragon for Breakfast. (Illus.). 28p. (ps-3). 1990. PLB 18.95 (0-87614-650-7) Carolrhoda Bks.

Mahy, Margaret. Seventeen Kings & Forty-Two Elephants. Fogelman, Phyllis J., ed. MacCarthy, Patricia, illus. LC 87-5311. 32p. (ps-3). 1990. pap. 4.95 (0-8037-0781-9) Dial Bks Young.

Marriott, Michelle. Old King Cole & Friends. (gr. 4 up). 1990. 9.95 (0-85953-446-4) Childs Play.

Mayne, William. All the King's Men. LC 87-25659. 192p. (gr. 3-7). 1988. pap. 14.95 (0-385-29626-6) Delacorte.

Muntean, Michaela. Imagine: Ernie Is King. (ps-3). 1993. pap. 2.25 (0-307-13123-8, Golden Pr) Western Pub.

Neale, J. M. Good King Wenceslas. Henterly, Jamichael, illus. LC 88-3633. 24p. (ps up). 1988. 11.95 (0-525-44420-3, DCB) Dutton Child Bks.

—Good King Wenceslas. Henterly, Jamichael, illus. 24p. 1993. pap. 4.99 (0-14-054942-0, Puff Unicorn) Puffin Bks.

Newby, Robert. King Midas. Majewski, Dawn & Cozzolino, Sandra, illus. 64p. (gr. 1-6). 1990. PLB 15.95 (1-878363-25-5) Forest Hse.

Noonan, Janet & Calvert, Jacquelyn. Berries for the Queen. LC 92-32336. (ps-2). 1994. 8.99 (0-7814-0903-9, Chariot Bks) Chariot Family.

Oppenheim, Joanne. The Story Book Prince. Litzinger, Rosanne, illus. LC 85-31745. 32p. (ps-3). 1987. 12.95 (0-15-200590-0, Gulliver Bks) HarBrace.

Orczy, Emmuska. Lord Tony's Wife. 1986. Repr. lib. bdg. 19.95x (0-89966-553-5) Buccaneer Bks.

Packard, Mary. I Am King! (Illus.). 28p. (ps-2). 1994. PLB 14.00 (0-516-05365-5); pap. 3.95 (0-516-45365-3) Childrens.

Pienkowski, Jan, illus. Christmas: King James Version. LC 84-5719. 32p. (gr. 1 up). 1994. Repr. 18.95 (0-394-86923-0) Knopf Bks Yng Read.

Robbins, Ruth. Baboushka & the Three Kings. Sidjakov, Nicholas, illus. LC 60-15036. 32p. (ps-3). 1986. pap. 5.95 (0-395-42647-2) HM.

Rosenberg, Amye. Jewels for Josephine. Rosenberg, Amye, illus. 28p. (ps-2). 1993. 12.95 (0-448-40457-5, G&D) Putnam Pub Group.

Rothsteis, Shmuel. Heir to the Throne. Hinlicky, Gregg, illus. LC 90-83945. 224p. (gr. 5-8). 1990. 13.95 (1-56062-043-9); pap. 10.95 (1-56062-044-7) CIS Comm.

Ruskin, John. The King of the Golden River or the Black Brother. Doyle, Richard, illus. LC 74-82199. viii, 56p. (gr. 1 up). 1974. pap. 2.95 (0-486-20066-3) Dover.

Schneegans, Nicole. The King's Twins. (Illus.). 48p. (gr. 3-8). 1990. 8.95 (0-89565-813-5) Childs World.

Service, Pamela F. Being of Two Minds. LC 90-24097. 176p. (gr. 3-7). 1991. SBE 14.95 (0-689-31524-4, Atheneum Child Bk) Macmillan Child Grp.

Shankar, Alaka. The Seven Queens. Vyas, Anil, illus. 16p. (Orig.). (gr. k-3). 1980. pap. 2.50 (0-89744-217-2, Pub. by Childrens Bk Trust IA) Auromere.

Sharratt, Nick. The Green Queen. Sharratt, Nick, illus. LC 91-58735. 24p. (ps up). 1992. 5.95 (1-56402-093-2) Candlewick Pr.

Sheehan, Patty. Gwendolyn's Gifts. Bumgarner-Kirby, Claudia, illus. LC 91-12335. 32p. 1991. 14.95 (0-88289-845-0) Pelican.

Siekkinen, Raija. Mister King. Steffa, Tim, tr. Taina, Hannu, illus. 32p. (gr. k-4). 1987. lib. bdg. 18.95 (0-87614-315-X) Carolrhoda Bks.

Sikirycki, Igor. The Best Cook. Knobbe, Czeslaw, ed. & tr. from POL. Thoenes, Michael, illus. 26p. (gr. 1-6). 1993. text ed. 9.95 (0-9630328-2-8) SDPI.

Singer, Isaac Bashevis. Naftali, the Storyteller & His Horse, Sus. Zemach, Margot, illus. (gr. 3 up). 1987. pap. 3.50 (0-374-45487-6) FS&G.

Slightly Off-Center Writers Group, Ltd. Staff. King Saurus' Big Decision. (Illus.). 48p. (gr. 3-5). 1994. pap. 6.95 (1-56721-064-3) Twnty-Fifth Cent Pr.

Sprague, Gilbert M. The Nome King's Shadow in Oz. Abbott, Donald, illus. 120p. (gr. 3 up). 1992. 39.95 (0-929605-19-5); pap. 9.95 (0-929605-18-7) Books Wonder.

Stolz, Mary. King Emmett the Second. (gr. 4-7). 1993. pap. 3.25 (0-440-40777-X) Dell.

Storr, Catherine. King Midas. (ps-3). 1993. pap. 4.95 (0-8114-7148-9) Raintree Steck-V.

Tournier, Michel. Rois Mages. Charrier, Michel, illus. (FRE.). 160p. (gr. 5-10). 1978. pap. 7.95 (2-07-033280-2) Schoenhof.

Utz. The King, the Queen, & the Lima Bean. LC 73-93020. (Illus.). 32p. (gr. k-3). 1974. PLB 9.95 (0-87783-121-1); pap. 3.94 deluxe ed. (0-87783-122-X) Oddo.

Vandersteen, Willy. The King Drinks. Lahey, Nicholas J., tr. from FLE. LC 77-78696. (Illus., Orig.). (gr. 3-8). 1977. pap. 2.50 (0-915560-04-6) Hiddigeigei.

Van Jacobs, Gregory. The Polka Dot Queen. 1992. 7.95 (0-533-09669-3) Vantage.

Walsh, Jill P. The Emperor's Winding Sheet. 288p. (gr. 7 up). 1992. pap. 4.95 (0-374-42121-8, Sunburst) FS&G.

White, Ellen E. Long Live the Queen. 1990. pap. 2.95 (0-590-40851-8) Scholastic Inc.

Wild, Margaret. The Queen's Holiday. O'Loughlin, Sue, illus. LC 91-14024. 32p. (ps-1). 1992. 13.95 (0-531-05973-1); PLB 13.99 (0-531-08573-2) Orchard Bks Watts.

Wilkes, Larry. The King's Egg Dance. Wilkes, Larry, illus. 32p. (gr. k-4). 1990. PLB 18.95 (0-87614-446-6) Carolrhoda Bks.

Wolff, Ferida. The Emperor's Garden. Osborn, Kathy, illus. LC 93-14751. 1994. 15.00 (0-688-11651-5, Tambourine Bks); PLB 14.93 (0-688-11652-3) Morrow.

Wood, Audrey. King Bidgood's in the Bathtub. LC 85-5472. (ps-3). 1993. pap. 19.95 (0-15-242732-5) HarBrace.

Wrede, Patricia C. Calling on Dragons. LC 92-35469. 1993. write for info. (0-15-200950-7, J Yolen Bks) HarBrace.

—Talking to Dragons. LC 92-40719. 1993. 16.95 (0-15-284247-0, J Yolen Bks) HarBrace.

Ywing-Ming Yang. The Mask of the King. Dougall, Alan, ed. Xieu-Lin, Li, illus. 52p. (gr. 4 up). 1990. 4.95 (0-940871-11-4) Yangs Martial Arts.

KIPLING, RUDYARD, 1865-1936

Greene, Carol. Rudyard Kipling: Author of the Jungle Books. LC 94-11940. (Illus.). 32p. (gr. 2-4). 1994. PLB 17.20 (0-516-04266-1); pap. 4.95 (0-516-44266-X) Childrens.

Kamen, Gloria. Kipling: Storyteller of East & West. LC 85-7945. (Illus.). 80p. (gr. 3 up). 1985. SBE 13.95 (0-689-31195-8, Atheneum Child Bk) Macmillan Child Grp.

Rudyard Kipling. (Illus.). 700p. 8.98 (0-517-34798-9) Random Hse Value.

KITCHEN GARDENS

see Vegetable Gardening

KITCHEN UTENSILS

see Household Equipment and Supplies

KITCHENS

Kalman, Bobbie. The Kitchen. (Illus.). 32p. (gr. 3-4). 1990. PLB 15.95 (0-86505-484-3); pap. 7.95 (0-86505-504-1) Crabtree Pub Co.

Sendak, Maurice. In the Night Kitchen. Sendak, Maurice, illus. LC 70-105483. 48p. (ps-3). 1970. 16.00 (0-06-025489-0); PLB 15.89 (0-06-025490-4) HarpC Child Bks.

KITES

Evans, David. Fishing for Angels: The Magic of Kites. D'Arcy, Adele, illus. 88p. (Orig.). (gr. 5 up). 1991. pap. 12.95 (1-55037-162-2, Pub. by Annick CN) Firefly Bks Ltd.

Gattis, L. S., III. Kites for Pathfinders: A Basic Youth Enrichment Skill Honor Packet. Gattis, L. S., III, illus. 18p. (Orig.). (gr. 5 up). 1986. pap. 5.00 tchr's. ed. (0-936241-07-1) Cheetah Pub.

Gibbons, Gail. Catch the Wind! All about Kites. Gibbons, Gail, illus. LC 88-28820. (gr. k-3). 1989. 15.95 (0-316-30955-9) Little.

Jefferis, David. Making Kites. LC 92-42913. (Illus.). 40p. (gr. 3-7). 1993. 10.05 (1-85697-923-7, Kingfisher LKC); pap. 5.95 (1-85697-922-9) LKC.

Kelly, Emery. Kites on the Wind: Easy-to-Make Kites that Fly Without Sticks. Hageman, Jennifer, illus. 64p. (gr. 4 up). 1991. PLB 22.95 (0-8225-2400-7) Lerner Pubns.

Packard, M. The Kite. (Illus.). 28p. (ps-2). 1990. PLB 10.50 (0-516-05355-8); pap. 3.95 (0-516-45355-6) Childrens.

Pelham, David. Four Krazy Kites: To Make & Fly. Pelham, David, illus. 32p. 1994. 6.99 (0-525-45172-2) Dutton Child Bks.

Robson, Denny A. Kites & Flying Objects. LC 91-75995. (Illus.). 32p. (gr. 2-4). 1992. PLB 11.90 (0-531-17342-9, Gloucester Pr) Watts.

Somerville, L. How to Make Kites. (Illus.). 32p. (gr. 3-7). 1992. PLB 12.96 (0-88110-543-0, Usborne); pap. 5.95 (0-7460-0708-6, Usborne) EDC.

Troll. Kites That Really Fly. 14p. (gr. 5-9). 1991. pap. 5.95 (0-8167-2357-5) Troll Assocs.

Webber, Helen. My Kite Is the Magic Me. Webber, Helen, illus. (gr. k-6). 1968. 8.95 (0-8392-3055-9) Astor-Honor.

KITES–FICTION

Ada, Alma F. The Kite - El Papalote. Escriva, Vivi, illus. (SPA & ENG.). 23p. (gr. k-2). 1992. English ed. 6.95 (*1-56014-228-6*); Spanish ed. 6.95 (*1-56014-227-8*) Santillana. A resourceful mother helps her children make & fly a kite in this entertaining selection. A surprise ending adds to the reading experience. Predictable language patterns help young readers to decode the text easily. English & Spanish versions are available to delight children in both languages. To order: Santillana, 901 West Walnut, Compton, CA 90220. Telephone 1-800-245-8584. *Publisher Provided Annotation.*

Blanco, Alberto. Angel's Kite. Morales, Rodolfo, illus. Bellm, Dan, tr. from SPA. LC 93-42285. (ENG & SPA., Illus.). 1994. 13.95 (0-89239-121-9) Childrens Book Pr.

Brock, Ray. Go Fly a Kite. (Illus.). (gr. 4 up). 1976. pap. 8.00 (0-912846-17-8) Bookstore Pr.

Caraway, Jane. One Windy Day. Smath, Jerry, illus. 24p. (ps-2). 1990. PLB 17.10 (0-8172-3579-5); PLB 10.95 3 bk. set (0-685-67712-5) Raintree Steck-V.

Geisz, Janet W. Summer School Kites. LC 93-93776. (Illus.). 64p. 1994. pap. 6.00 (1-56002-311-2, Univ Edtns) Aegina Pr.

Haseley, Dennis. Kite Flier. Wiesner, David, illus. LC 92-22721. 32p. (ps-3). 1993. pap. 4.95 (0-689-71668-0, Aladdin) Macmillan Child Grp.

Lies, Brian. Hamlet & the Enormous Chinese Dragon Kite. LC 93-30726. 1994. 14.95 (0-395-68391-2) HM.

Loumaye, Jacqueline. The Tale of the Kite. (Illus.). 32p. (gr. 3-5). 1991. 12.95 (0-89565-759-7) Childs World.

Martin, Ann M. Karen's Kite. (gr. 4-7). 1994. pap. 2.95 (0-590-46913-4) Scholastic Inc.

Ostrovsky, Alexsandr. Paper Kite (Bumazhni Emei) Ostrovsky, Alexsandr, illus. (RUS.). 30p. (Orig.). 1987. pap. 14.95 (0-934393-18-4) Rector Pr.

Reddix, Valerie. Dragon Kite of the Autumn Moon. LC 91-1506. (ps-3). 1992. 14.00 (0-688-11030-4); PLB 14.93 (0-688-11031-2) Lothrop.

Rey, Margaret & Rey, H. A. Curious George Flies a Kite. (Illus.). 80p. (gr. k-3). 1973. 12.70 (0-395-16965-8) HM.

—Curious George Flies a Kite. Rey, H. A., illus. (gr. k-3). 1977. pap. 4.80 (0-395-25937-1) HM.

Ross, Katharine. Grover, Grover, Come on Over: A Step 1 Book - Preschool-Grade 1. Cooke, Tom, illus. LC 90-33947. 32p. (Orig.). (ps-1). 1991. PLB 7.99 (0-679-91117-0); pap. 3.50 (0-679-81117-6) Random Bks Yng Read.

Scott, Mavis. Little Ho & the Golden Kites. Reynolds, Pat, illus. 32p. (Orig.). (gr. k-2). 1993. pap. 6.95 (0-04-442242-3, Pub. by Allen & Unwin Aust Pty AT) IPG Chicago.

Spirn, Michele. The Kite Race. (ps-1). 1988. 8.49 (0-685-44566-6); incl. cassette 16.99 (0-685-25198-5); pap. 1.95 (0-87386-051-9); pap. 9.95 incl. cassette (0-685-25199-3) Jan Prods.

Vaughan, Marcia & Mullins, Patricia. The Sea-Breeze Hotel. LC 91-22303. (Illus.). 32p. (ps-2). 1992. 14.00 (0-06-020488-5); PLB 13.89 (0-06-020504-0) HarpC Child Bks.

Wise, Francis H. & Wise, Joyce M. Kites. (Illus.). (gr. 1). 1977. pap. 1.50 (0-915766-38-8) Wise Pub.

Yep, Laurence. Dragonwings. large type ed. 282p. 1990. Repr. of 1975 ed. lib. bdg. 15.95 (1-55736-168-1, Crnrstn Bks) BDD LT Grp.

Yolen, Jane. Emperor & the Kite. Young, Ed, illus. 32p. (ps up). 1992. pap. 5.95 (0-399-22512-9, Philomel Bks) Putnam Pub Group.

KLEE, PAUL, 1879-1940

Venezia, Mike. Paul Klee. Venezia, Mike, illus. LC 91-12554. 32p. (gr. 4). 1991. PLB 12.85 (0-516-02294-6); pap. 4.95 (0-516-42294-4) Childrens.

KLONDIKE GOLD FIELDS

Cooper, Michael. Klondike Fever: The Famous Gold Rush of 1898. LC 89-+013. (Illus.). 80p. (gr. 4 up). 1989. 14.45 (0-89919-803-1, Clarion Bks) HM.

Ray, Delia. Gold! the Klondike Adventure. (Illus.). (gr. 5-9). 1989. 14.95 (0-525-67288-5, Lodestar Bks) Dutton Child Bks.

KNIGHTHOOD

see Knights and Knighthood

KNIGHTS AND KNIGHTHOOD

see also Heraldry

Cairns, Trevor. Medieval Knights. (Illus.). 64p. (gr. 7 up). 1992. pap. 10.95 (0-521-38953-4) Cambridge U Pr.

Clare, John D., ed. Knights in Armor. (gr. 4-7). 1992. 16.95 (0-15-200508-0, Gulliver Bks) HarBrace.

Corbin, Carole L. Knights. 64p. (gr. 3-5). 1989. PLB 12.90 (0-531-10692-6) Watts.

Crawford, Tom. The Story of King Arthur. Green, John, illus. LC 94-3363. (gr. 4 up). 1994. pap. write for info. (0-486-28347-X) Dover.

Dann, Geoff & Gravett, Chris. Knight. LC 92-1590. 64p. (gr. 5 up). 1993. 15.00 (0-679-83882-1); PLB 15.99 (0-679-93882-6) Knopf Bks Yng Read.

Dines, Glen. Sir Cecil & the Bad Blue Beast. Dines, Glen, illus. LC 70-125868. (gr. k-2). 1970. 21.95 (0-87599-175-0) S G Phillips.

Frost, Abigail. The Age of Chivalry. LC 89-17396. (Illus.). 48p. (gr. 4-8). 1990. PLB 13.95 (1-85435-235-0) Marshall Cavendish.

Giblin, James C., retold by. The Dwarf, the Giant, & the Unicorn: A Tale of King Arthur. Ewart, Claire, illus. LC 92-34031. 1994. write for info. (0-395-60520-2, Clarion Bks) HM.

Heyer, Carol. Excalibur. Heyer, Carol, illus. LC 91-9100. 32p. (gr. k-4). 1991. 14.95 (0-8249-8487-0, Ideals Child) Hambleton-Hill.

Hindley. Knights & Castles. (gr. 4-6). 1976. (Usborne-Hayes); PLB 13.96 (0-88110-100-1); pap. 6.95 (0-86020-068-X) EDC.

Incredible Knights & Castles. 32p. (ps-k). 1994. 4.95 (1-56458-730-4) Dorling Kindersley.

Penner, Lucille R. Knights & Castles. Bell, Owain, illus. LC 93-45710. (gr. 4 up). 1994. PLB 2.50 (0-679-85095-3) Random.

Pyle, Howard. The Story of King Arthur & His Knights. Pyle, Howard, illus. xviii, 313p. (gr. 7 up). pap. 6.95 (0-486-21445-1) Dover.

—The Story of the Grail & the Passing of Arthur. unabr. ed. LC 92-29058. (Illus.). 272p. 1992. pap. text ed. 7.95 (*0-486-27361-X*) Dover.
Shannon, Mark. Gawain & the Green Knight. Shannon, David, illus. LC 93-13037. 32p. (ps-3). 1994. PLB 15.95 (*0-399-22446-7*, Putnam) Putnam Pub Group.
Weisberg, Barbara. The Big Golden Book of Knights & Castles. D'Achille, Gino, illus. 64p. (gr. 2-7). 1992. write for info. (*0-307-17874-9*, 17874, Golden Pr) Western Pub.
Wright, Rachel. Knights. LC 91-20063. (Illus.). 32p. (gr. 4-6). 1992. PLB 11.90 (*0-531-14163-2*) Watts.

KNIGHTS AND KNIGHTHOOD–FICTION

Bellairs, John. The Secret of the Underground Room. LC 92-17304. 128p. (gr. 5 up). 1992. pap. 3.99 (*0-14-034932-4*, Puffin) Puffin Bks.
Bellerophon Books Staff. Don Quixote. (gr. 4-7). 1992. pap. 3.95 (*0-88388-182-9*) Bellerophon Bks.
Blake, Quentin. Simpkin. Blake, Quentin, illus. 32p. (ps-1). 1994. 14.99 (*0-670-85371-2*) Viking Child Bks.
—Snuff. (ps-3). 1993. pap. 7.00 NOP (*0-00-663922-4*) Collins SF.
Bulla, Clyde R. The Sword in the Tree. Galdone, Paul, illus. LC 56-5699. 128p. (gr. 2-5). 1962. PLB 13.89 (*0-690-79909-8*, Crowell Jr Bks) HarpC Child Bks.
Cain, Michael. The Legend of Sir Miguel. Thatch, Nancy R., ed. Melton, David, intro. by. LC 90-5927. (Illus.). 26p. (gr. 3-6). 1990. PLB 14.95 (*0-933849-26-5*) Landmark Edns.
Craig, Helen. The Knight, the Princess & the Dragon. Craig, Helen, illus. LC 84-19419. 32p. (ps-2). 1985. lib. bdg. 8.99 (*0-394-97212-0*) Knopf Bks Yng Read.
De Paola, Tomie. The Knight & the Dragon. (Illus.). 32p. (gr. k-2). 1980. 14.95 (*0-399-20707-4*, Sandcastle Bks); (Sandcastle Bks) Putnam Pub Group.
Doyle, Debra & Macdonald, James D. The Knight's Wyrd. LC 92-53789. 1992. write for info. (*0-15-200764-4*, J Yolen Bks) HarBrace.
Eager, Edward. Knight's Castle. Bodecker, N. M., illus. (gr. 4-6). 17.00 (*0-8446-6232-1*) Peter Smith.
—Knight's Castle. Treherne, Katie T. & Bodecker, N. M., illus. 198p. (gr. 3-7). 1989. pap. 3.95 (*0-15-243105-5*, Odyssey) HarBrace.
Garrick, Liz. Quest for King Arthur, No. 23. Best, Charles, illus. 144p. (ps-6). 1988. pap. 2.50 (*0-553-27126-1*) Bantam.
Gerrard, Roy. Sir Cedric. LC 84-6111. (Illus.). 32p. (ps up). 1984. 14.95 (*0-374-36959-3*) FS&G.
—Sir Cedric. (Illus.). 32p. (gr. k up). 1986. pap. 4.95 (*0-374-46659-9*) FS&G.
Gross, Gwen. Knights of the Round Table. Green, Norman, illus. LC 85-2176. 96p. (gr. 2-6). 1993. (Bullseye Bks); pap. 2.99 (*0-394-87579-6*, Bullseye Bks) Random Bks Yng Read.
Hazen, Barbara S. The Knight Who Was Afraid of the Dark. Ross, Tony, illus. LC 88-18149. 32p. (ps-3). 1989. 12.95 (*0-8037-0667-7*); PLB 12.89 (*0-8037-0668-5*) Dial Bks Young.
—The Knight Who Was Afraid of the Dark. Ross, Tony, illus. LC 88-18149. 32p. (ps-3). 1992. pap. 3.99 (*0-14-054545-X*, Puff Pied Piper) Puffin Bks.
—The Knight Who Was Afraid to Fight. Goffe, Toni, photos by. LC 93-4608. 1994. write for info. (*0-8037-1591-9*); lib. bdg. write for info. (*0-8037-1592-7*) Dial Bks Young.
Hodges, Margaret, adapted by. Don Quixote & Sancho Panza. Marchesi, Stephen, illus. LC 90-24098. 80p. (gr. 6 up). 1992. SBE 16.95 (*0-684-19235-7*, Scribners Young Read) Macmillan Child Grp.
Hodges, Margaret, retold by. The Kitchen Knight. Hyman, Trina S., illus. LC 89-11215. 32p. (gr. 1-4). 1990. reinforced bdg. 15.95 (*0-8234-0787-X*) Holiday.
Hughes, Robert D. Gabriel's Trumpet. (Orig.). Date not set. pap. 6.99 (*0-8054-6059-4*) Broadman.
Hunter, Mollie. Day of the Unicorn. Diamond, Donna, illus. LC 91-44763. 96p. (gr. 2-5). 1994. 14.00 (*0-06-021062-1*, HarpT); PLB 13.89 (*0-06-021063-X*, HarpT) HarpC.
Lasker, Joe. Tournament of Knights. Lasker, Joe, illus. LC 85-48075. 32p. (gr. 3 up). 1986. (Crowell Jr Bks); PLB 13.89 (*0-690-04542-5*, Crowell Jr Bks) HarpC Child Bks.
McKinley, Robin. The Blue Sword. LC 82-2895. 288p. (gr. 7 up). 1982. reinforced 16.00 (*0-688-00938-7*) Greenwillow.
Madinaveitia, Horacio. Sir Robert's Little Outing. Madinaveitia, Horacio, illus. 32p. (gr. k-4). 1991. PLB 13.95 (*1-879567-01-6*, Valeria Bks); pap. text ed. 7.95 (*1-879567-00-8*) Wonder Well.

Marsano, Daniel T. Sun Day, the Not-Quite Knight. Stroschin, J. H., illus. 48p. (gr. k-6). 1994. PLB 15.00 (*1-883960-13-4*) Henry Quill. SUN DAY THE NOT-QUITE KNIGHT is the second book in this developing series. It has ever been said that the young ask, "Why?" & the old say, "Because!" In this story poem, Sir Day's son, Sun Day, questions the task that he must complete in order to attain knighthood. As he begins his quest, however, he learns that his greatest challenge is in meeting the test on his own terms while preserving who he is & who he wants to be. SIR DAY THE KNIGHT. Daniel T. Marsano. Illus. by Jane H. Stroschin. 48p. (Gr. k-6) 1993. $15.00 (1-883960-11-8). SIR DAY THE KNIGHT is a story of courage. The MICHIGAN READING JOURNAL, Volume 27, No. 3, Spring 1994, gave this review: "This story poem tells of a knight who embarks on a quest to defeat a dragon. He realizes how afraid he is, & finds that his fear is a greater problem than the reality of his quest. When he faces his dragon, he finds some pleasant surprises. Readers will be pleased with the delightful ending to this book by a Michigan author & illustrator." Call or write Henry Quill Press, Jane Stroschin, 7340 Lake Drive, Fremont, MI 49412-9146, (616) 924-3026.
Publisher Provided Annotation.

Mitgutsch, Ali. A Knight's Book. Crawford, Elizabeth D., tr. Mitgutsch, Ali, illus. 40p. (gr. 2-5). 1991. 16.45 (*0-395-58103-6*, Clarion Bks) HM.
Morpurgo, Michael. King Arthur. Foreman, Michael, illus. LC 93-33620. 1995. write for info. (*0-15-200080-1*) HarBrace.
Noonan, Janet & Calvert, Jacquelyn. A Crown for Sir Conrad. LC 92-32337. 1994. 8.99 (*0-7814-0317-0*, Chariot Bks) Chariot Family.
Oakeshott, R. Ewart. Knight & His Castle. Oakeshott, R. Ewart, illus. 108p. 1992. 16.95 (*0-8023-1294-2*) Dufour.
Osborne, Mary P. The Knight at Dawn. Murdocca, Sal, illus. LC 92-13075. 80p. (Orig.). (gr. 1-4). 1993. PLB 9.99 (*0-679-92412-4*); pap. 2.99 (*0-679-82412-X*) Random Bks Yng Read.
Peet, Bill. Cowardly Clyde. (Illus.). 48p. (gr. k-3). 1984. 13.45 (*0-395-27802-3*); pap. 5.95 (*0-395-36171-0*) HM.
Pierce, Tamora. In the Hand of the Goddess. LC 84-2946. 240p. (gr. 5 up). 1990. pap. 3.50 (*0-679-80111-1*) Random Bks Yng Read.
—In the Hand of the Goddess: Song of the Lioness, Bk. Two. LC 84-2946. 240p. (gr. 7 up). 1984. SBE 16.95 (*0-689-31054-4*, Atheneum Child Bk) Macmillan Child Grp.
—The Woman Who Rides Like a Man: Song of the Lioness, Book Three. LC 85-20054. 276p. (gr. 7 up). 1986. SBE 16.95 (*0-689-31117-6*, Atheneum Child Bk) Macmillan Child Grp.
Preiss, Byron & Gasperini, Jim. Secret of the Knights. Hescox, Richard, illus. 144p. (gr. 4 up). 1984. pap. 2.25 (*0-553-25368-9*) Bantam.
Pyle, Howard. Men of Iron. Hitchner, Earle, adapted by. Geehan, Wayne, illus. LC 89-33926. 48p. (gr. 3-6). 1990. PLB 12.89 (*0-8167-1871-7*); pap. text ed. 3.95 (*0-8167-1872-5*) Troll Assocs.
—The Story of the Champions of the Round Table. Pyle, Howard, illus. xviii, 329p. (ps-4). 1968. pap. 7.95 (*0-486-21883-X*) Dover.
Reeves, James, retold by. Exploits of Don Quixote. Ardizzone, Edward, illus. LC 85-11170. (gr. 5 up). 1985. 12.95 (*0-87226-025-9*, Bedrick Blackie); (Bedrick Blackie) P Bedrick Bks.
Rescue of Sir Clyde the Clumsy. 1991. pap. 1.97 (*1-56297-114-X*) Lee Pubns KY.
Ryan, John. Bad Year for Dragons. LC 89-37279. 28p. (gr. 1-4). 1989. 7.95 (*0-8192-1512-0*) Morehouse Pub.
Schurch, Maylan. The Sword of Denis Anwyck. LC 92-22127. 1992. pap. 7.95 (*0-8280-0658-X*) Review & Herald.
Scieszka, Jon. Knights of the Kitchen Table. Smith, Lane, illus. 64p. (gr. 3-7). 1991. 11.00 (*0-670-83622-2*) Viking Child Bks.
Scott, Dennis. Sir Gawain & the Green Knight. (gr. k up). 1978. 5.50 (*0-87602-202-6*) Anchorage.
Storr, Catherine. Sword & the Stone. (ps-3). 1993. pap. 4.95 (*0-8114-7147-0*) Raintree Steck-V.
Sutcliff, Rosemary. The Sword & the Circle. 256p. (gr. 4-7). 1981. 14.95 (*0-525-40585-2*, DCB) Dutton Child Bks.
Talbott, Hudson. King Arthur: The Sword in the Stone. LC 90-28104. (Illus.). 56p. (gr. 5 up). 1991. 14.95 (*0-688-09403-1*); PLB 14.88 (*0-688-09404-X*) Morrow Jr Bks.
Twain, Mark. Connecticut Yankee in King Arthur's Court. LC 83-9162. (gr. 5 up). 1964. pap. 3.25 (*0-8049-0029-9*, CL-29) Airmont.
—A Connecticut Yankee in King Arthur's Court. Hyman, Trina S., illus. LC 87-62879. 384p. (gr. 5 up). 1988. 19.95 (*0-688-06346-2*); signed ltd. ed. 100.00 (*0-688-08258-0*, Morrow Jr Bks) Morrow Jr Bks.
Williams, Marcia, adapted by. & illus. Don Quixote. LC 92-52995. 32p. (gr. 2 up). 1993. 13.95 (*1-56402-174-2*) Candlewick Pr.
Winthrop, Elizabeth. The Battle for the Castle. LC 92-54490. 160p. (gr. 3-7). 1993. 14.95 (*0-8234-1010-2*) Holiday.
—The Castle in the Attic. Hyman, Trina S., illus. LC 85-5607. 192p. (gr. 4-7). 1985. 14.95 (*0-8234-0579-6*) Holiday.

KNIGHTS AND KNIGHTHOOD–POETRY

Maloney, Marina. The Knight of the Sand Castle. LC 92-85410. (Illus.). 44p. (gr. k-4). 1993. pap. 5.95 (*1-55523-553-0*) Winston-Derek.

KNIGHTS OF THE ROUND TABLE

see Arthur, King

KNITTING

Baker, Wendy. Knitting. Baker, Wendy, illus. LC 93-21217. 48p. (gr. 5-9). 1994. 16.95 (*1-56847-146-7*) Thomson Lrning.
Coleman, Anne. Fabrics & Yarns. (Illus.). 32p. (gr. 2-6). 1990. lib. bdg. 15.94 (*0-86592-483-X*); lib. bdg. 11.95s.p. (*0-685-46441-5*) Rourke Corp.
Hansen, Robin. Sunny's Mittens: Learn to Knit - Lovikka Mittens. Stock, Lois L., illus. LC 90-61410. 48p. (gr. 3-6). 1990. pap. 12.95 wire-o bdg. (*0-89272-290-8*) Down East.
O'Reilly, Susie. Knitting & Crochet. Mukhida, Zul, photos by. (Illus.). 32p. (gr. 4-6). 1994. 14.95 (*1-56847-221-8*) Thomson Lrning.
Wilkes, A. & Garbera, C. Knitting. (Illus.). 48p. (gr. 6 up). 1986. PLB 14.96 (*0-88110-320-9*); pap. 7.95 (*0-86020-983-0*) EDC.

KNOTS AND SPLICES

Adkins, Jan. String: Tying It up, Tying It Down. Adkins, Jan, illus. LC 91-25786. 48p. (gr. 5 up). 1992. SBE 13.95 (*0-684-18875-9*, Scribners Young Read) Macmillan Child Grp.
Budworth, Geoffrey. The Knot Book. LC 84-26843. (Illus.). 160p. (gr. 7 up). 1985. pap. 8.95 (*0-8069-7944-5*) Sterling.
Gibson, Charles E. Handbook of Knots & Splices: & Other Work with Hempen & Wire Rope. (Illus.). (gr. 7 up). 12.95 (*0-87523-146-2*) Emerson.
Jackson, Ellen. Tie a String Around Your Finger: The History & Lore of Knots. Steele, Robert, illus. LC 93-41042. 1994. 14.95 (*0-395-68710-1*) Ticknor & Fields.
MacFarlan, Allan & MacFarlan, Paulette. Knotcraft: The Practical & Entertaining Art of Tying Knots. 186p. (gr. 6up). 1983. pap. 4.50 (*0-486-24515-2*) Dover.
Pioneering. (Illus.). 48p. (gr. 6-12). 1974. pap. 1.85 (*0-8395-3382-9*, 33377) BSA.
Severn, Bill. Bill Severn's Magic with Rope, Ribbon, & String. LC 93-17893. (Illus.). 224p. 1994. pap. 12.95 (*0-8117-2533-2*) Stackpole.

KNOWLEDGE, THEORY OF

Here are entered works that treat the origin, nature, methods and limits of human knowledge.
see also Belief and Doubt; Intellect; Perception; Senses and Sensation

Daniel, Becky & Daniel, Charlie. Thinker Sheets. 64p. (gr. 2-6). 1978. 7.95 (*0-916456-23-4*, GA78) Good Apple.
—What's Next? 64p. (gr. k-6). 1979. 7.95 (*0-916456-41-2*, GA116) Good Apple.
Lucas, Eileen. The Mind at Work: How to Make It Work Better for You. LC 92-34663. (Illus.). 96p. (gr. 7 up). 1993. PLB 15.40 (*1-56294-300-6*) Millbrook Pr.
Tyler, Sydney B. Young Think Program Two. 90p. (Orig.). (gr. k-1). 1988. pap. text ed. 25.00 report cover (*0-912781-13-0*) Thomas Geale.

KOALAS

Arnold, Caroline. Koala. Hewett, Richard, illus. LC 86-18092. 48p. (gr. 2-5). 1987. 13.95 (*0-688-06478-7*); lib. bdg. 13.88 (*0-688-06479-5*, Morrow Jr Bks) Morrow Jr Bks.
—Koala. Hewett, Richard, photos by. LC 86-18092. (Illus.). 48p. (gr. 3 up). 1992. pap. 5.95 (*0-688-11503-9*, Mulberry) Morrow.
Bright, Michael. Koalas. LC 90-3251. (Illus.). 32p. (gr. 5-8). 1990. PLB 12.40 (*0-531-17246-5*, Gloucester Pr) Watts.
Burt, Denise. Birth of a Koala. LC 88-14578. (Illus.). 40p. (gr. 3-7). 1988. Repr. of 1986 ed. 12.95 (*0-944176-02-X*) Terra Nova.
Eugene, Toni. Koalas & Kangaroos: Strange Animals of Australia. Crump, Donald J., ed. LC 81-607859. 32p. (ps-3). 1981. Set. 13.95 (*0-87044-403-4*); PLB 16.95 (*0-87044-408-5*) Natl Geog.
Green, Carl R. & Sanford, William R. The Koala. (Illus.). 48p. (gr. 5). 1987. text ed. 12.95 RSBE (*0-89686-334-4*, Crestwood Hse) Macmillan Child Grp.
Lee, Sandra. Koalas. LC 92-38807. (gr. 2-6). 1993. 15.95 (*1-56766-013-4*) Childs World.
Lepthien, Emilie U. Koalas. LC 90-2219. (Illus.). 48p. (gr. k-4). 1990. PLB 12.85 (*0-516-01108-1*); pap. 4.95 (*0-516-41108-X*) Childrens.
Reilly, Pauline. Koala. Rolland, Will, illus. 32p. (Orig.). 1993. pap. 6.95 (*0-86417-243-5*, Pub. by Kangaroo Pr AT) Seven Hills Bk Dists.
Rothaus, Jim. Koalas. 24p. (gr. 3). 1988. PLB 14.95 (*0-88682-227-0*) Creative Ed.
Selsam, Millicent E. & Hunt, Joyce. A First Look at Kangaroos, Kaolas & Other Animals with Pouches. Springer, Harriet, illus. LC 85-3126. 32p. (gr. k-3). 1985. 9.95 (*0-8027-6600-5*); PLB 12.85 (*0-8027-6579-3*) Walker & Co.
Serventy, Vincent. Koala. LC 84-17995. (Illus.). 24p. (gr. k-5). 1985. PLB 9.95 (*0-8172-2416-5*); pap. 3.95 (*0-8114-6879-8*) Raintree Steck-V.

Stone, Lynn. Koalas. (Illus.). 24p. (gr. k-5). 1990. lib. bdg. 11.94 (*0-86593-055-4*); lib. bdg. 8.95s.p. (*0-685-36372-4*) Rourke Corp.

Tibbitts, Alison & Roocroft, Alan. Koala. (Illus.). 24p. (ps-2). 1992. PLB 12.95 (*1-56065-103-2*) Capstone Pr.

Wildlife Education, Ltd. Staff. Koalas. Havlicek, Karel & Stuart, Walter, illus. 20p. (gr. 5 up). 1983. pap. 2.75 (*0-937934-13-5*) Wildlife Educ.

KOALAS–FICTION

Bassett, Lisa. Koala Christmas. Bassett, Jeni, illus. LC 90-47628. 32p. (ps-2). 1991. 12.95 (*0-525-65065-2*, Cobblehill Bks) Dutton Child Bks.

Broome, Errol. The Smallest Koala. Mason, Gwen, illus. (ps-1). 1988. 11.95 (*0-949447-65-X*) Terra Nova.

Case, Mary. Katie Koala Bear, Vol. 1: What Will Katie Wear to School? Shaffer, Dianna, illus. LC 89-83279. 28p. (gr. 2-4). 1989. pap. text ed. 4.95 (*0-685-28857-9*) Koala Pub Co.

—Katie Koala Bear, Vol. 2: Katie's Tree of Designs. Shaffer, Dianna, illus. 28p. (gr. 2-4). 1989. pap. text ed. 4.95 (*1-877995-00-2*) Koala Pub Co.

—Katie Koala Bear, Vol. 3: Katie & Karla Make Pizza. Shaffer, Dianna, illus. 28p. (gr. 2-4). 1989. pap. text ed. 4.95 (*1-877995-05-3*) Koala Pub Co.

—Katie Koala Bear, Vol. 4: Katie Loves Math. Shaffer, Dianna, illus. 28p. (gr. 2-4). 1989. pap. text ed. 4.95 (*1-877995-13-4*) Koala Pub Co.

—Katie Koala Bear, Vol. 5: Katie Learns to Read. Shaffer, Dianna, illus. 28p. (gr. 2-4). 1989. pap. text ed. 4.95 (*1-877995-04-5*) Koala Pub Co.

Case, Mary & Shaffer, Dianna. Katie Koala Bear in What Will Katie Wear to School? (Illus.). 20p. (Orig.). 1989. pap. 4.95 (*1-877995-06-1*) Koala Pub Co.

Fox, Mem. Koala Lou. 28p. (ps-1). 1989. 13.95 (*0-15-200502-1*) HarBrace.

Gelman, Rita G. A Koala Grows Up. Fiammenghi, Gioia, illus. 32p. (Orig.). (gr. k-3). 1986. pap. 3.95 (*0-590-41869-6*) Scholastic Inc.

Johnson, Debra A. I Dreamed I Was a Koala Bear. LC 94-6623. (gr. k up). 1994. write for info. (*1-56239-300-6*) Abdo & Dghtrs.

Mazzola, Toni & Guten, Mimi. Wally Koala & the Little Green Peach. Cohen, Keri, ed. McCoy, William M., illus. LC 93-94002. 22p. (ps-3). 1993. saddlestitch bdg. incl. cassette 9.95 (*1-883747-01-5*) WK Prods.
WALLY KOALA'S SLOGAN: "I'M WONDERFUL & SO ARE YOU." Books lovingly narrated by CHARLOTTE RAE (TV'S FACTS OF LIFE) who also sings original songs. IN WALLY KOALA & THE LITTLE GREEN PEACH, Farmer Jim picks all other peaches, leaving lonely little green peach at the top of the tree. Through the story of Mr. Big Peach Tree, Wally comforts Little Green Peach & previews all the changes he can expect during metamorphosis from green peach to glorious blossoming tree. (Vernon Woolf) "Magical journey into patience, trust in self, nature & process of life. A must for those who feel they're not blossoming as fast as their peers or their expectations." IN WALLY KOALA & FRIENDS, Wally travels from Australia to America with friends Sadie Kangaroo & Timmy Kookaburra. This book introduces the loveable characters. Self-esteem subtly emphasized. WALLY helps to make children aware that we all make mistakes, as he & Sadie did by sneaking Timmy on the plane. Mistakes are OK. We learn from them. (Vernon Woolf) "WALLY & FRIENDS teaches trust in the world of adult authority in an easy-going, delightful style." (BUSINESS STARTUPS mag) "Loveable koala from 'down under,' winning the hearts of North American children..." To order contact: W.K. Productions, P.O. Box 801504, Dallas, TX 75380-1504. Distributors: Baker & Taylor, Brodart Co., 717-326-2461, Hervey's Booklink, 214-480-9987, Ingram.
Publisher Provided Annotation.

Nobisso, Josephine & Krajnc, Anton C. For the Sake of a Cake. LC 92-38391. (Illus.). 28p. 1993. 9.95 (*0-8478-1685-0*) Rizzoli Intl.
Here's a multi-species cautionary tale for people who know how to share the work - or those who SHOULD know! Written in droll verse & illustrated with subtle drawings of sophisticated wit & whimsical zaniness, FOR THE SAKE OF A CAKE tells the tale of a Koala & an Alligator, already in bed, who argue whose turn it is to get up to check the cake baking in the oven. No holds are barred & no punches pulled as each lays claim to having already done too much work. Who's right? As in life, the reader is never sure. But one thing is certain: unless they find a way to cooperate, they're putting their very lives in danger! Written by the author of GRANDPA LOVED, GRANDMA'S SCRAPBOOK, & SSH! THE WHALE IS SMILING, FOR THE SAKE OF A CAKE crosses over from the children's fiction section to adult gift books to food & specialty shops, setting a delicious example & offering a rare Viennese cake recipe at the end. Order from Rizzoli International, 300 Park Ave., New York, NY 10010-5399, 1-800-462-2357.
Publisher Provided Annotation.

Oana, Katherine. Kippy Koala. Cooper, William, ed. Butrick, Lyn M., illus. LC 85-51823. 16p. (Orig.). (ps up). 1985. pap. text ed. 3.72 (*0-914127-21-7*) Univ Class.

Roc, Margaret. Little Koala. (ps-3). 1993. pap. 7.00 (*0-207-17039-8*, Pub. by Angus & Robertson AT) HarpC.

KORBUT, OLGA

Coffey, Wayne. Olga Korbut. (Illus.). 64p. (gr. 3-7). 1992. PLB 14.95 (*1-56711-002-9*) Blackbirch.

KOREA

Bandon, Alexandra. Korean Americans. LC 93-31059. 1994. text ed. 13.95 (*0-02-768147-5*, New Discovery Bks) Macmillan Child Grp.

Cho, Byung K. Korean Culture Tourism & Language: For Everything You Need to Know about Korea. 357p. (gr. 7 up). 1988. 29.00 (*0-685-30452-3*) B K Cho.

Dubois, Jill. South Korea. LC 93-4381. 1993. 21.95 (*1-85435-582-1*) Marshall Cavendish.

Farley, Carol. Korea: Land of the Morning Calm. (Illus.). 128p. (gr. 5 up). 1991. text ed. 14.95 RSBE (*0-87518-465-0*, Dillon) Macmillan Child Grp.

Han, Suzanne C. Let's Color Korea: Traditional Lifestyles. 24p. (gr. k-3). 1989. oversized 8.50x (*0-930878-94-9*) Hollym Intl.

Haskins, Jim. Count Your Way Through Korea. Hockerman, Dennis, illus. 24p. (gr. 1-4). 1989. 17.50 (*0-87614-348-6*); pap. 5.95 (*0-87614-516-0*) Carolrhoda Bks.

Jacobsen, Karen. Korea. LC 89-10043. 48p. (gr. k-4). 1989. PLB 12.85 (*0-516-01174-X*); pap. 4.95 (*0-516-41174-8*) Childrens.

Jones, B. J. Let's Color Korea: Everyday Life in Traditional. 24p. (gr. k-3). 1990. oversized 8.50x (*0-930878-98-1*) Hollym Intl.

Kim, Richard E. Lost Names: Scenes from a Boyhood in Japanese-Occupied Korea. 224p. 1988. 14.95 (*0-87663-678-4*) Universe.

Lerner Publications, Department of Geography Staff, ed. South Korea in Pictures. (Illus.). 64p. (gr. 5 up). 1989. PLB 17.50 (*0-8225-1868-6*) Lerner Pubns.

Loewen. Food in Korea. 1991. 11.95s.p. (*0-86625-345-9*) Rourke Pubns.

McNair, Sylvia. Korea. LC 85-23273. (Illus.). 127p. (gr. 5-6). 1986. PLB 20.55 (*0-516-02771-9*) Childrens.

Mayberry, Jodine. Koreans. LC 90-12987. (Illus.). 64p. (gr. 5-10). 1991. PLB 13.40 (*0-531-11106-7*) Watts.

Moffett, Eileen. Korean Ways. Moffett, Eileen, illus. 55p. (gr. k up). 1986. 10.95 (*0-8048-7013-6*, Pub. by Seoul Intl Tourist SK) C E Tuttle.

Mueller, M. Let's Color Korea: Traditional Games. 24p. (gr. k-3). 1989. oversized 8.50x (*0-930878-95-7*) Hollym Intl.

Nahm, Andrew C., et al, eds. I Love Korea! (Illus.). 86p. 1992. 22.50x (*0-930878-87-6*) Hollym Intl.

Pihl, Marshall R. Korean Word Book. Roschana, illus. LC 93-73161. (KOR & ENG.). 112p. (gr. k-6). 1993. 15.95 (*1-880188-53-8*); pap. 11.95 (*1-880188-52-X*) Bess Pr.

Shalant, Phyllis. Look What We've Brought You from Korea: Crafts, Games, Recipes, Stories & Other Cultural Activities from Korean-Americans. Park, Soyoo H., illus. LC 94-25829. 1994. write for info. (*0-671-88701-7*, J Messner) S&S Trade.

KOREA–FICTION

Adams, Edward B. Herdboy & Weaver. Choi, Dong-Ho, illus. 32p. (gr. 3). 1981. 8.95 (*0-8048-1470-8*, Pub by Seoul Intl Publishing House) C E Tuttle.

—Woodcutter & Nymph. Choi, Dong-Ho, illus. 32p. (gr. 3). 1982. 8.95 (*0-8048-1471-6*, Pub by Seoul Intl Publishing House) C E Tuttle.

Burkholder, Ruth C. Mi Jun's Difficult Decision. O'Dwyer, Chung S. & Fwhang, Duk S., illus. LC 83-20494. 14p. (Orig.). (gr. 4-6). 1984. pap. 4.95 (*0-377-00139-2*) Friendship Pr.

Choi, Sook N. Echoes of the White Giraffe. LC 92-17476. 144p. (gr. 5 up). 1993. 13.45 (*0-395-64721-5*) HM.

Dryer, Bonnie J. Steggie Saurus: Kindergartener in Korea. LC 92-60813. 44p. (gr. k-3). 1993. pap. 5.95 (*1-55523-547-6*) Winston-Derek.

Ilyon. The Birth of Tangun: The Legend of Korea's First King. Adams, Edward B., tr. from KOR. Yoon, Hak-Jung, illus. 28p. (gr. 5). 1986. 7.50 (*0-00-000006-X*, Pub. by Seoul Intl Tourist SK) C E Tuttle.

—The Death of Echadon: How Buddhism Came to Silla. Adams, Edward B., tr. Yoon, Hak-Jung, illus. 28p. (gr. 5). 1986. 7.50 (*0-00-000004-3*, Pub. by Seoul Intl Tourist SK) C E Tuttle.

—King Munmu of Silla: A Korean Ruler Who United His Country. Adams, Edward B., tr. Yoon, Hak-Jung, illus. 28p. (gr. 5). 1986. 7.50 (*0-00-000003-5*, Pub. by Seoul Intl Tourist SK) C E Tuttle.

—The Three Good Events. Adams, Edward B., tr. from KOR. Yoon, Hak-Jung, illus. 28p. (gr. 5). 1986. 7.50 (*0-00-000009-4*, Pub. by Seoul Intl Tourist SK) C E Tuttle.

Neuberger, Anne E. The Girl-Son. LC 94-6725. 1994. write for info. (*0-87614-846-1*) Carolrhoda Bks.

KOREA, PEOPLE'S DEMOCRATIC REPUBLIC OF

Ashby, Gwynneth. A Family in South Korea. (Illus.). 32p. (gr. 2-5). 1987. 13.50 (*0-8225-1675-6*) Lerner Pubns.

Nash, Amy. North Korea. (Illus.). 128p. (gr. 5 up). 1990. 14.95 (*0-7910-0157-1*) Chelsea Hse.

KOREA, REPUBLIC OF

Shepheard, Patricia. South Korea. (Illus.). 96p. (gr. 5 up). 1988. 14.95 (*0-7910-0118-0*) Chelsea Hse.

KOREA, REPUBLIC OF–FICTION

McMahon, Patricia. Chi-Hoon: A Korean Girl. O'Brien, Michael, photos by. LC 92-81331. (Illus.). 48p. (gr. 4-7). 1993. 16.95 (*1-56397-026-0*) Boyds Mills Pr.

Watkins, Yoko K. So Far from the Bamboo Grove. (Illus.). 192p. (gr. 5 up). 1994. pap. 4.95 (*0-688-13115-8*, Pub. by Beech Tree Bks) Morrow.

KOREAN WAR, 1950-1953

Bachrach, Deborah. The Korean War. LC 91-23065. (Illus.). 112p. (gr. 5-8). 1991. PLB 17.95 (*1-56006-409-9*) Lucent Bks.

Edwards, R. Korean War. (Illus.). 80p. (gr. 7 up). 1988. PLB 18.60 (*0-86592-036-2*); 13.95 (*0-685-58322-8*) Rourke Corp.

The Korean War Soldier at Heartbreak Ridge. 48p. (gr. 5-6). 1991. PLB 11.95 (*1-56065-006-0*) Capstone Pr.

McGowen, Tom. The Korean War. (Illus.). 64p. (gr. 5-8). 1993. pap. 5.95 (*0-531-15655-9*) Watts.

Smith, Carter. The Korean War. (Illus.). 64p. (gr. 5 up). 1990. PLB 12.95 (*0-382-09953-2*); pap. 7.95 (*0-382-09949-4*) Silver Burdett Pr.

Stein, R. Conrad. The Korean War: "The Forgotten War" LC 94-565. (Illus.). 128p. (gr. 5 up). 1994. lib. bdg. 17.95 (*0-89490-526-0*) Enslow Pubs.

KOREAN WAR, 1950-1953–FICTION

Sook Nyul Choi. Year of Impossible Goodbyes. 176p. (gr. 5 up). 1991. 13.45 (*0-395-57419-6*, Sandpiper) HM.

KOREANS IN THE U. S.–FICTION

Choi, Sook-Nyul. Gathering of Pearls. LC 94-10868. 1994. 13.95 (*0-395-67437-9*) HM.

Choi Sook Nyul. Halmoni & the Picnic. (ps-3). 1993. 14.95 (*0-395-61626-3*) HM.

Kline, Suzy. Song Lee & the Hamster Hunt. Remkiewicz, Frank, illus. 64p. (gr. 2-6). 1994. 11.99 (*0-670-84773-9*) Viking Child Bks.

—Song Lee in Room Two B. Remkiewicz, Frank, illus. 64p. (gr. 2-5). 1993. RB 10.99 (*0-670-84772-0*) Viking Child Bks.

Lee, Marie G. Saying Goodbye. LC 93-26092. 1994. write for info. (*0-395-67066-7*) HM.

Myers, Anna. Rosie's Tiger. LC 94-50814. 1994. write for info. (*0-8027-8305-8*) Walker & Co.

Rhie, Schi-Zhin. Soon-Hee in America. Rhie, Schi-Zhin, illus. LC 77-81780. 36p. (gr. k-3). 1977. PLB 6.50x (*0-930878-00-0*) Hollym Intl.

KOUFAX, SANFORD, 1935-

Grabowski, John. Sandy Koufax. Murray, Jim, intro. by. (Illus.). 64p. (gr. 3 up). 1992. lib. bdg. 14.95 (*0-7910-1180-1*) Chelsea Hse.

Sanford, William R. & Green, Carl R. Sandy Koufax. LC 92-31249. (Illus.). 48p. (gr. 5). 1993. text ed. 11.95 RSBE (*0-89686-780-3*, Crestwood Hse) Macmillan Child Grp.

KU KLUX KLAN

Cook, Fred J. The Ku Klux Klan: America's Recurring Nightmare. rev. ed. Steltenpohl, Jane, ed. (Illus.). 176p. (gr. 7 up). 1989. lib. bdg. 13.98 (*0-671-68421-3*, J Messner) S&S Trade.

Moore, Robert B. Violence, the KKK & the Struggle for Equality. 72p. (Orig.). (gr. 9 up). 1981. pap. 5.95 (*0-930040-38-4*) CIBC.

KUBLAI KHAN, EMPEROR OF CHINA, 1216-1294

Dramer, Kim. Kublai Khan. (Illus.). (gr. 5 up). 1990. 17.95 (*1-55546-812-8*) Chelsea Hse.

KUWAIT

Bratman, Fred. War in the Persian Gulf. (Illus.). 64p. (gr. 7 up). 1991. PLB 15.90 (*1-56294-051-1*); pap. 4.95 (*1-878841-61-0*) Millbrook Pr.

Caraccilo, Dominic J. The Ready Brigade of the Eighty-Second Airborne in Desert Storm: A Combat Memoir by a Headquarters Company Commander. LC 92-50945. 223p. (gr. 8-12). 1993. pap. 16.95x (*0-89950-829-4*) McFarland & Co.

Lerner Publications, Department of Geography Staff, ed. Kuwait in Pictures. (Illus.). 64p. (gr. 5 up). 1989. 17.50 (*0-8225-1846-5*) Lerner Pubns.

L

LABOR (OBSTETRICS)

see Childbirth

LABOR AND LABORING CLASSES

see also Child Labor; Communism; Labor Unions; Machinery in Industry; Migrant Labor; Occupations also names of classes of laborers e.g. Agricultural Laborers; Miners; etc.; and names of countries, cities, etc. with the subdivisions Economic Conditions and Social Conditions, e.g. U. S.–Economic Conditions; U. S.–Social Conditions

Boy Scouts of America. American Labor. (Illus.). 48p. (Orig.). (gr. 6-12). 1987. pap. 1.85 (*0-8395-3326-8*, 33326) BSA.

Bradley, Michael R. On the Job: Safeguarding Workers' Rights. LC 92-9015. 1992. 22.60 (*0-86593-175-5*); 16.95s.p. (*0-685-59322-3*) Rourke Corp.

Condon, Judith. Patterns of Work. LC 92-7838. (Illus.). 32p. (gr. 5-8). 1993. PLB 11.90 (*0-531-14228-0*) Watts.

Gelder, L. van, et al. Enciclopedia Juvenil Labor: Encyclopedia of Child Labor, 3 vols. (SPA.). 592p. 1977. 99.50 (*0-8288-5411-4*, S50474) Fr & Eur.

The Ludlow Massacre: Mini-Play. (gr. 5 up). 1978. 6.50 (*0-89550-321-2*) Stevens & Shea.

Lynd, Alice & Lynd, Staughton, eds. Rank & File: Personal Histories by Working-Class Organizers. Lynd, Alice, intro. by. 320p. (gr. 9-12). 1988. pap. 10.00 (*0-85345-752-2*) Monthly Rev.

McCombs, Barbara L. & Brannan, Linda. Consideration for Co-Worker Rights. (Illus.). 32p. (Orig.). (gr. 7-12). 1990. Set. 10 wkbks. & tchr's. guide 44.95 (*1-56119-063-2*); tchr's. guide 1.95 (*1-56119-010-1*); software 39.95 (*1-56119-105-1*) Educ Pr MD.

McNaught, Denise. When a Parent Loses a Job: A Workbook about My Parent's Job Loss. 1993. pap. 7.95 wkbk. (*0-385-30931-7*) Doubleday.

The Pullman Strike: Mini-Play. (gr. 5 up). 1978. 6.50 (*0-89550-322-0*) Stevens & Shea.

LABOR AND LABORING CLASSES–FICTION

Getzel. The Stone Cutter Who Wanted to Be Rich. LC 90-82859. (Illus.). 48p. (gr. 1-5). 1990. 9.95 (*0-685-45648-X*) CIS Comm.

Harry Bridges: Mini-Play. (gr. 5 up). 1978. 6.50 (*0-89550-327-1*) Stevens & Shea.

Hayford, James. Gridley Firing. Azarian, Mary, illus. LC 87-61473. 160p. (Orig.). (gr. 4 up). 1987. pap. 9.95 (*0-933050-49-6*) New Eng Pr VT.

Kessler, Leonard. Here Comes the Strikeout. Kessler, Leonard, illus. LC 65-10728. 64p. (gr. k-3). 1987. incl. cassette 5.98 (*0-694-00174-0*, Trophy) HarpC Child Bks.

Sebestyen, Ouida. On Fire. 192p. 1987. pap. 2.95 (*0-553-26862-7*, Starfire) Bantam.

Sinclair, Upton, et al. The Jungle. (Illus.). 52p. Date not set. pap. 4.95 (*1-57209-025-1*) Classics Int Ent.

Smyth, Gwenda. Les & the Laundry. Hunnam, Lucinda, illus. LC 93-26219. 1994. 4.25 (*0-383-03757-3*) SRA Schl Grp.

LABOR AND LABORING CLASSES–HOUSING

see Housing

LABOR AND LABORING CLASSES–U. S.

Altman, Linda J. The Pullman Strike of Eighteen Ninety-Four: Turning Point for American Labor. (Illus.). 64p. (gr. 4-6). 1994. 15.40 (*1-56294-346-4*) Millbrook Pr.

The Flint Sit-Down Strike: Mini-Play. (gr. 5 up). 1978. 6.50 (*0-89550-320-4*) Stevens & Shea.

Goldin, Barbara D. Fire! The Beginnings of the Labor Movement. Watling, James, illus. 64p. (gr. 2-6). 1992. RB 13.00 (*0-670-84475-6*) Viking Child Bks.

The Haymarket Affair: Mini-Play. (gr. 5 up). 1978. 6.50 (*0-89550-323-9*) Stevens & Shea.

LABOR DAY

Scott, Geoffrey. Labor Day. Wyman, Cherie R., illus. LC 81-15485. 48p. (gr. k-4). 1982. PLB 14.95 (*0-87614-178-5*) Carolrhoda Bks.

LABOR ORGANIZATIONS

see Labor Unions

LABOR SAVING DEVICES, HOUSEHOLD

see also Household Equipment and Supplies

LABOR UNIONS

Holmes, Burnham. Cesar Chavez. LC 92-18225. (Illus.). 128p. (gr. 7-10). 1992. PLB 22.80 (*0-8114-2326-3*) Raintree Steck-V.

Lazo, Caroline E. Lech Walesa. LC 92-39959. (Illus.). 64p. (gr. 4 up). 1993. text ed. 13.95 RSBE (*0-87518-525-8*, Dillon) Macmillan Child Grp.

Meltzer, Milton. Bread & Roses: The Struggle of American Labor, 1865-1915. (Illus.). 192p. 1990. 17.95x (*0-8160-2371-9*) Facts on File.

Vnenchak, Dennis. Lech Walesa & Poland. LC 92-40266. 1994. write for info. (*0-531-11128-8*) Watts.

LABORERS

see Labor and Laboring Classes

LADYBIRDS

Godkin, Celia. What about Ladybugs? Godkin, Celia, illus. LC 93-4202. 40p. (ps-3). 1995. 14.95 (*0-87156-549-8*) Sierra.

Pouyanne. Ladybug, Reading Level 3-4. (Illus.). 28p. (gr. 2-5). 1983. PLB 16.67 (*0-86592-863-0*); 12.50 (*0-685-58821-1*) Rourke Corp.

Watts, Barrie. Ladybug. (Illus.). 25p. (gr. k-4). 1991. PLB 7.95 (*0-382-09437-9*); pap. 3.95 (*0-382-09960-5*) Silver Burdett Pr.

—Ladybugs. Watts, Barrie, photos by. LC 88-50366. (Illus.). 32p. (gr. k-4). 1991. PLB 11.40 (*0-531-14043-1*); pap. 4.95 (*0-531-15616-8*) Watts.

LADYBIRDS–FICTION

Carle, Eric. La Mariquita Malhumorada. Carle, Eric, illus. LC 91-28582. 48p. (ps-3). 1992. 15.00 (*0-06-020549-0*); PLB 14.89 (*0-06-020569-5*) HarpC Child Bks.

Dotty the Ladybug Plays Hide-&-Seek. LC 93-85488. 20p. (ps-1). 1994. 3.99 (*0-89577-568-9*) RD Assn.

Down Ladybug Lane. LC 92-62555. (ps-k). 1992. 3.99 (*0-89577-481-X*, Dist. by Random) RD Assn.

Fowler, Richard. Ladybug on the Move. LC 92-19740. 1993. write for info. (*0-15-200475-0*) HarBrace.

LAFAYETTE, MARIE ADRIENNE FRANCOIS (DE NOAILLES) MARQUISE DE, 1759-1802

Zadra, Dan. Statesmen in America: Lafayette. (gr. 2-4). 1988. PLB 14.95 (*0-88682-190-8*) Creative Ed.

LAFAYETTE, MARIE JOSEPH PAUL YVES ROCH GILBERT DU MOTIER, MARQUIS DE, 1757-1834

Brandt, Keith. Lafayette, Hero of Two Nations. Snow, Scott, illus. LC 89-33981. 48p. (gr. 4-6). 1990. PLB 10.79 (*0-8167-1771-0*); pap. text ed. 3.50 (*0-8167-1772-9*) Troll Assocs.

LAFITTE, JEAN, 1782-1854

Tallant, Robert. The Pirate Lafitte & the Battle of New Orleans. Chase, John, illus. 192p. (gr. 5 up). 1994. pap. 7.95 (*0-88289-931-7*) Pelican.

LAFITTE, JEAN, 1782-1854–FICTION

Dewey, Ariane. Lafitte, the Pirate. LC 92-43787. (Illus.). 48p. (gr. 1 up). 1993. pap. 4.95 (*0-688-04578-2*, Mulberry) Morrow.

LAGUARDIA, FIORELLO HENRY, 1882-1947

Kurland, Gerald. Fiorello LaGuardia: The People's Mayor of New York. Rahmas, D. Steve, ed. LC 77-190238. 32p. (Orig.). (gr. 7-12). 1972. lib. bdg. 4.95 incl. catalog cards (*0-87157-520-5*) SamHar Pr.

LAKES

Arvetis, Chris & Palmer, Carole. Lakes & Rivers. LC 93-499. (Illus.). 1993. write for info. (*0-528-83572-6*) Rand McNally.

Behm, Barbara J. Exploring Lakeshores. LC 93-37060. 1994. 17.27 (*0-8368-1065-1*) Gareth Stevens Inc.

Bender, Lionel. Lake. LC 88-51613. (Illus.). 32p. (gr. 3-5). 1989. PLB 11.90 (*0-531-10708-6*) Watts.

Bramwell, Martyn. Rivers & Lakes. (Illus.). 32p. (gr. 5-8). 1994. PLB write for info. (*0-531-14305-8*) Watts.

Crump, Donald J., ed. The World's Wild Shores. (Illus.). 1990. 12.95 (*0-87044-716-5*); lib. bdg. 12.95 (*0-87044-721-1*) Natl Geog.

Frahm, Randy. Lakes. LC 93-46805. 40p. 1994. 18.95 (*0-88682-706-X*) Creative Ed.

Frame, Jeron A. Discovering Oceans, Lakes, Ponds & Puddles. (gr. 4-7). 1994. pap. 8.99 (*0-7459-2621-5*) Lion USA.

Santrey, Laurence. Lakes & Ponds. Moylan, Holly, illus. LC 84-2653. 32p. (gr. 3-6). 1985. PLB 9.49 (*0-8167-0206-3*); pap. text ed. 2.95 (*0-8167-0207-1*) Troll Assocs.

Snow, John. Secrets of Ponds & Lakes. Jack, Susan, ed. Dowling, Jak, intro. by. (Illus.). 96p. (Orig.). (gr. 4-10). 1982. pap. 3.95 (*0-930096-30-4*) G Gannett.

Wilkins, Marne. The Long Ago Lake. Weston, Martha, illus. 160p. (gr. 4 up). 1990. pap. 7.95 (*0-87701-632-1*) Chronicle Bks.

LAMPS–FICTION

Lang, Andrew. Aladdin. Le Cain, Errol, illus. 32p. (gr. k-3). 1983. pap. 4.95 (*0-14-050389-7*, Puffin) Puffin Bks.

LAND

Here are entered general works which cover such topics as types of land, the utilization, distribution and development of land and the economic factors which affect the value of land. Works which treat only of ownership of land are entered under Real Estate.

see also Agriculture; Farms; Feudalism

Cherrington, Mark. Degradation of the Land. (Illus.). (gr. 5 up). 1992. lib. bdg. 19.95 (*0-7910-1589-0*) Chelsea Hse.

Greene, Carol. Caring for Our Land. LC 91-10613. (Illus.). 32p. (gr. k-3). 1991. lib. bdg. 12.95 (*0-89490-354-3*) Enslow Pubs.

Newton, David E. Land Use A-Z. LC 89-78119. 128p. (gr. 6 up). 1991. lib. bdg. 17.95 (*0-89490-260-1*) Enslow Pubs.

Phinney, Margaret. Exploring Land Habitats. Talas, Terri, illus. 24p. (Orig.). (gr. 1-5). 1994. big bk. 21.95 (*1-879531-39-9*); PLB 9.95 (*1-879531-48-8*); pap. 4.95 (*0-685-74704-2*) Mondo Pubng.

Willis, Terri. Land Use & Abuse. LC 92-8842. (Illus.). 128p. (gr. 4-8). 1992. PLB 20.55 (*0-516-05507-0*) Childrens.

LAND SURVEYING

see Surveying

LAND USE

see Land

LANDFORMS

King, Celia. The Seven Natural Wonders of the World: A Pop-up Book. King, Celia, illus. 7p. (ps up). 1991. 8.95 (*0-8118-0001-6*) Chronicle Bks.

LANDMARKS, PRESERVATION OF

see Natural Monuments

LANDSCAPE ARCHITECTURE

see also Cemeteries

Landscape Architecture. (Illus.). 48p. (gr. 6-12). 1969. pap. 1.85 (*0-8395-3355-1*, 33355) BSA.

LANDSCAPE DESIGN

see Landscape Architecture

LANDSCAPE DRAWING

see also Landscape Painting

Arnosky, Jim. Sketching Outdoors in Summer. LC 87-29728. (gr. 5 up). 1988. PLB 12.95 (*0-688-06286-5*) Lothrop.

—Sketching Outdoors in Winter. LC 88-2202. (Illus.). 48p. (gr. 5 up). 1988. 12.95 (*0-688-06290-3*) Lothrop.

LANDSCAPE GARDENING

see also Landscape Architecture; Shrubs; Trees

LANDSCAPE PAINTING

see also Landscape Drawing

Blizzard, Gladys S. Come Look with Me: Exploring Landscape Art with Children. LC 91-34320. (Illus.). 32p. (gr. 1-8). 1992. 13.95 (*0-934738-95-5*) Thomasson-Grant.

LANGUAGE AND LANGUAGES

Here are entered general works on the history, philosophy, origin, etc. of language. Comparative studies of languages are entered under Philology, Comparative. see also Grammar; Phonetics; Rhetoric; Semantics; Speech; Voice; Writing also names of languages or groups of cognate languages, e.g. English Language; etc.; also classes of people with the subdivision Language, e.g. Children–Language; etc.

Bauman, Chris & Fishman, Sylvia E. Childhood Inventory of Language & Development Chart (CHILD) (ps-1). 1991. 7.50 (*0-937857-27-0*, 1592) Speech Bin.

Buddle, Jackie. Fun with Words. Davis, Annelies, illus. 32p. (gr. 2). 1988. PLB 14.97 (*0-88625-164-8*); pap. 2.97 (*0-88625-161-3*) Durkin Hayes Pub.

Charles, Arthur H., Jr. How to Learn a Foreign Language. LC 93-29573. (Illus.). 144p. (gr. 9-12). 1994. PLB 13.40 (*0-531-11098-2*) Watts.

Collins, Linda B. & Spangler, Carol S. The Communication Program Planning Book: A Plan Book for Speech-Language Pathologists. 200p. (gr. k-12). 1989. 21.95 (*0-937857-10-6*, 1567) Speech Bin.

Ege, Christine. Words for the World. Herbert, Janet, illus. LC 91-90679. 112p. (gr. k-6). 1992. Incl. 4 audio cass. 38.00 (*1-884161-00-6*) Comprehen Lang.

WORDS FOR THE WORLD introduces children to European languages & cultures. It is especially designed to meet the needs of parents & teachers who themselves have no foreign language background. Besides a detailed guide explaining how to adapt the material for different ages & grade levels, the book also features an introductory chapter for the children explaining the importance of learning about foreign countries & cultures. Based on the concept that languages come in families like people, the main body of the book spotlights eight different countries, including a narrative text on the lifestyle & culture as well as a foreign language vocabulary set (75 words & phrases for each language). All foreign words & phrases are pronounced on the audio cassettes. Countries featured are France, Spain, Italy, the former Soviet Union, Germany, Norway, Holland, & Sweden. WORDS FOR THE WORLD will enable children to recognize eight foreign languages by sight & sound. They will also get a taste of life in other countries! The book is

abundantly illustrated in full color with whimsical, imaginative drawings by Janet Herbert. To order, contact Comprehensive Language Communications, P.O. Box 242, Borger, TX 79008-0242; 806-273-2631. *Publisher Provided Annotation.*

Evans, Vicki. Be Like the Sun & Shine. (ENG, FRE & SPA., Illus.). 32p. (ps-5). 1993. pap. 9.00 (*0-9636367-0-7*) V Evans.

Forte, Imogene & MacKenzie, Joy. The Kids' Stuff: Book of Reading & Language Arts for the Primary Grades. (Illus.). 240p. (gr. 1-3). 1989. pap. text ed. 14.95 (*0-86530-121-2*, IP 01-3) Incentive Pubns.

Gelhay, Patrick & Marcantel, David E. Notre Langue Louisianaise: Our Louisiana Language, Bk. 1. Graeff, Benny, et al, illus. LC 85-81018. (ENG & FRE.). 180p. (gr. 4). 1985. text ed. 14.95 (*0-935085-00-9*); Tchr's ed. 14.95 (*0-935085-01-7*); write for info. Dialogue Booklet (*0-935085-03-3*); Cassette Tape Set 49.95 (*0-935085-02-5*) Ed Francaises.

Greene, Carol. Language. LC 83-7421. (Illus.). 48p. (gr. k-4). 1983. PLB 12.85 (*0-516-01694-6*) Childrens.

Marston, Bernice & Swiecki, Mark. In Plain English: A Game of Figurative Language. 1991. instr's manual 34. 95 (*1-55999-210-7*) LinguiSystems.

Moldenhauer, Janice. Developing Dictionary Skills. 64p. (gr. 3-8). 1979. 8.95 (*0-916456-48-X*, GA120) Good Apple.

Morris, Scott, ed. Languages of the World. De Blij, Harm J., intro. by. LC 92-22287. (Illus.). 1993. 15.95 (*0-7910-1811-3*, Am Art Analog); pap. write for info. (*0-7910-1824-5*, Am Art Analog) Chelsea Hse.

Robinson, Marc. Cock-a-Doodle Doo! What Does It Sound Like to You? Jenkins, Steve, illus. LC 92-30961. 32p. 1993. 12.95 (*1-55670-267-1*) Stewart Tabori & Chang.

Sandifer, Helga M. Alice in LanguageLand. large type ed. (SPA, FRE, GER & ENG., Illus.). 44p. 1994. Set, incl. bk., wkbk. & 2 audiocassettes. PLB 24.95 (*1-56650-997-1*) AIL Pub. ALICE IN LANGUAGELAND (R) is a series of ten (10) introduction into Basic Bilingual Education Subjects taught by Alice (Children teaching children). Each subject module consists of (1 textbook, 44p. w/audiocassette) (1 workbook, 60p. w/audiocassette), large bold 18pt. print in English-German, English-French & English Spanish. Retail $24.95. These books are full of graphics, hands on reading, writing, drawing, singing, it teaches major nouns & simple sentence structure. The author implemented great efforts into selecting subjects, vocabulary, structure & methodology. Two of the modules (A-B-C) & (Numbers 1-25) in all the above languages will be available in November of 1994. Review: Whether used at home or in school these books & tapes provide a wonderful & exciting introduction into the world of foreign language. ALICE IN LANGUAGELAND (R) (Diamond Word Booklets for Children of all ages in two languages) offer children an opportunity to experience a language other tahn their own in a way that is easy & fun & full of activity." Helga Carter, German Language Instructor, S.C. Public School System & USC. *Publisher Provided Annotation.*

Schwartz, Alvin. The Cat's Elbow: & Other Secret Languages. Zemach, Margot, illus. LC 81-5513. 96p. (gr. 3 up). 1982. 15.00 (*0-374-31224-9*) FS&G.

Shah, Bharat S. A Programmed Text to Learn Gujarati, Set. Kapadia, Madhusudan, frwd. by. 300p. (Orig.). (gr. 6 up). 1990. pap. text ed. 18.00 (*0-9623674-0-0*) Setubandh Pubns.

Swisher, Clarice. The Beginning of Language: Opposing Viewpoints. LC 89-7940. (Illus.). 112p. (gr. 5-8). 1989. PLB 14.95 (*0-89908-064-2*) Greenhaven.

Talley, Gene W. How to Learn a Foreign Language: Easy-to-Use, Diagrammed Study Techniques That Will Help You Learn a New Language. LC 89-91138. 52p. (Orig.). (gr. 11-12). 1989. pap. 6.75 (*0-9622222-0-8*) G Talley.

Tavzel, Carolyn. Blooming Holidays. (ps-5). 1989. pap. 15.95 (*1-55999-025-2*) LinguiSystems.

LANGUAGE ARTS

see Communication; English Language; Reading; Speech

Opie, Brenda & McAvinn, Douglas. Effective Language Arts Techniques for Middle Grades (4-8) An Integrated Approach. McAvinn, Douglas, illus. 84p. (Orig.). (gr. 4-8). 1989. pap. text ed. 7.95 (*0-685-26803-9*) Masterminds Pubns.

LANGUAGES AND VOCATIONAL OPPORTUNITIES

Kaplan, Andrew. Careers for Wordsmiths. (Illus.). 64p. (gr. 7 up). 1991. PLB 14.40 (*1-56294-024-4*); pap. 4.95 (*1-56294-774-5*) Millbrook Pr.

Shorto, Russell. Careers for Foreign Language Experts. LC 91-27661. (Illus.). 64p. (gr. 7 up). 1992. PLB 14.40 (*1-56294-159-3*); pap. 4.95 (*1-56294-769-9*) Millbrook Pr.

—Careers for Foreign Language Experts. 1992. pap. 4.95 (*0-395-63572-1*) HM.

LAOS

Diamond, Judith. Laos. LC 89-34279. 128p. (gr. 5-9). 1989. PLB 20.55 (*0-516-02713-1*) Childrens.

Jacobsen, Karen. Laos. LC 90-21034. (Illus.). 48p. (gr. k-4). 1991. PLB 12.85 (*0-516-01113-8*); pap. 4.95 (*0-516-41113-6*) Childrens.

Zickgraf, Ralph. Laos. (Illus.). 112p. (gr. 5 up). 1991. 14. 95 (*0-7910-0159-8*) Chelsea Hse.

LAPLAND

Reynolds, J. Far North: Vanishing Cultures. 1992. 16.95 (*0-15-227178-3*, HB Juv Bks); pap. 8.95 (*0-15-227179-1*, HB Juv Bks) HarBrace.

LAPPS

Vitebsky, Piers. Saami of Lapland. LC 93-32424. (Illus.). 48p. (gr. 6-10). 1994. 16.95 (*1-56847-159-9*) Thomson Lrning.

LARGE TYPE BOOKS

Banks, Lynne R. The Fairy Rebel. large type ed. (Illus.). 227p. 1989. lib. bdg. 15.95 (*1-55736-124-X*, Crnrstn Bks) BDD LT Grp.

Fitzgerald, John D. The Great Brain. large type ed. (Illus.). 219p. 1989. lib. bdg. 15.95 (*1-55736-102-9*, Crnrstn Bks) BDD LT Grp.

Jones, Ron. B-Ball: The Team that Never Lost a Game. (gr. 5 up). 1990. 14.95 (*0-553-05867-3*) Bantam.

Maybury, Anne. The Terracotta Palace. large type ed. LC 89-27151. 475p. 1989. lib. bdg. 19.95 (*0-89621-898-8*) Thorndike Pr.

Oke, Janette. Love Finds a Home. large type ed. 224p. (Orig.). 1989. Large type. pap. 8.99 (*1-55661-093-9*); pap. 6.99 (*1-55661-086-6*) Bethany Hse.

Oneal, Zibby. The Language of Goldfish. large type ed. PLB 15.95 (*0-685-29758-6*, Crnrstn Bks) BDD LT Grp.

Paulsen, Gary. The Voyage of the Frog. large type ed. LC 93-30238. (gr. 9-12). 1993. 15.95 (*0-7862-0060-X*) Thorndike Pr.

Peck, Robert N. Soup & Me. large type ed. 139p. 1990. Repr. lib. bdg. 15.95 (*1-55736-162-2*, Crnrstn Bks) BDD LT Grp.

Sholem-Aleykhem. Tevye the Dairyman: Complete, Illustrated. Simons, Joseph, ed. Katz, Miriam, tr. Bennett, Manuel, illus. (YID.). 160p. (gr. 10-12). 1994. pap. 12.95 (*0-934710-31-7*) J Simon.

Taylor, Theodore. The Cay. large type ed. 154p. (gr. k-6). 1990. Repr. lib. bdg. 15.95 (*1-55736-163-0*, Crnrstn Bks) BDD LT Grp.

Wilder, Laura I. By the Shores of Silver Lake. large type ed. 1990. Repr. lib. bdg. 15.95 (*1-55736-176-2*, Crnrstn Bks) BDD LT Grp.

Yep, Laurence. Dragonwings. large type ed. 282p. 1990. Repr. of 1975 ed. lib. bdg. 15.95 (*1-55736-168-1*, Crnrstn Bks) BDD LT Grp.

LA SALLE, ROBERT CAVELIER, SIEUR DE, 1643-1687

Coulter, Tony. La Salle & the Explorers of the Mississippi. Goetzmann, William H., ed. Collins, Michael, intro. by. (Illus.). 112p. (gr. 5 up). 1991. lib. bdg. 18.95 (*0-7910-1304-9*); pap. 9.95 (*0-7910-1527-0*) Chelsea Hse.

Jacobs, William J. La Salle: A Life of Boundless Adventure. LC 93-29699. (Illus.). 64p. (gr. 5-8). 1994. PLB 12.90 (*0-531-20141-4*) Watts.

Nolan, Jeannette C. La Salle & the Grand Enterprise. LC 90-48978. (Illus.). 176p. (gr. 6-10). 1991. PLB 13.95 (*1-55905-087-X*) Marshall Cavendish.

LASERS

Billings, Charlene W. Lasers: The New Technology of Light. LC 92-7324. (Illus.). 128p. 1992. PLB 17.95 (*0-8160-2630-0*) Facts on File.

French, P. M. & Taylor, J. W. How Lasers Are Made. (Illus.). 32p. (gr. 5-12). 1987. 12.95x (*0-8160-1690-9*) Facts on File.

Graham, Ian. Lasers & Holograms. LC 91-10827. (Illus.). 32p. (gr. 5-8). 1991. PLB 12.40 (*0-531-17264-3*, Gloucester Pr) Watts.

Lasers. 48p. (gr. 6 up). 1984. PLB 13.96 (*0-88110-165-6*); pap. 6.95 (*0-86020-722-6*) EDC.

McPartland, Scott. Gordon Gould. LC 93-2819. 1993. 15. 93 (*0-86592-079-6*); 11.95s.p. (*0-685-66585-2*) Rourke Enter.

Nardo, Don. Lasers: Humanity's Magic Light. LC 90-6269. (Illus.). 96p. (gr. 5-8). 1990. PLB 15.95 (*1-56006-200-2*) Lucent Bks.

Woods, et al. Lasers: Activities for the Classroom. (Illus.). 85p. (Orig.). 1990. pap. text ed. 13.81 (*0-87192-216-9*) Delmar.

LATIMER, LEWIS

Norman, Winifred L. & Patterson, Lily. Lewis Latimer: Scientist. LC 93-185. (Illus.). (gr. 5 up). 1994. PLB 18. 95 (*0-7910-1977-2*, Am Art Analog); pap. write for info. (*0-7910-1978-0*, Am Art Analog) Chelsea Hse.

Turner, Glennette. Lewis Howard Latimer. (Illus.). 144p. (gr. 5-9). 1990. PLB 10.95 (*0-382-09524-3*); pap. 6.95 (*0-382-24162-2*) Silver Burdett Pr.

LATIN AMERICA

see also South America

Lamb, Ruth S. Latin America: Sites & Insights. (gr. 9-12). 1963. pap. 4.00 (*0-912434-02-3*) Ocelot Pr.

LATIN AMERICA–BIOGRAPHY

Burch, Joann. Chico Mendes: Defender of the Rain Forest. (Illus.). 48p. (gr. 2-4). 1994. 12.90 (*1-56294-413-4*) Millbrook Pr.

Hispanics of Achievement, 34 vols. (Illus.). (gr. 5 up). 1991. lib. bdg. 610.30 (*0-7910-1231-X*) Chelsea Hse.

Jose Duarte. (Illus.). 112p. (gr. 6-12). 1991. PLB 17.95 (*0-7910-1241-7*) Chelsea Hse.

LATIN AMERICA–FICTION

Ada, Alma F. Barquitos de Papel. Torrecilla, Pablo, illus. (SPA.). 24p. (gr. 3-9). 1993. 16.95x (*1-56492-118-2*) Laredo.

—Barriletes. Torrecilla, Pablo, illus. (SPA.). 24p. (gr. 3-9). 1993. 16.95x (*1-56492-126-3*) Laredo.

—Dias de Circo. Torrecilla, Pablo, illus. (SPA.). 24p. (gr. 3-9). 1993. 16.95x (*1-56492-127-1*) Laredo.

—The Gold Coin. Waldman, Neil, illus. Randall, Bernice, tr. from SPA. LC 93-14403. (Illus.). 32p. (gr. k-3). 1994. pap. 4.95 (*0-689-71793-8*, Aladdin) Macmillan Child Grp.

—Pin, Pin, Sarabin. Torrecilla, Pablo, illus. (SPA.). 24p. (gr. 3-9). 1993. 16.95x (*1-56492-130-1*) Laredo.

—Pregones. Torrecilla, Pablo, illus. (SPA.). 24p. (gr. 3-8). 1993. 16.95x (*1-56492-110-7*) Laredo.

Baez, Josefina. Por Que Mi Nombre Es Marisol? Un Cuento De la Republica Dominicana. Guerrero, Alex, illus. (SPA.). 24p. (Orig.). (gr. k-3). 1993. pap. 12.95 (*1-882161-01-7*) Latinarte.

—Why Is My Name Marisol? A Dominican Children's Story. Guerrero, Alex, illus. 24p. (Orig.). (gr. k-3). 1993. pap. 12.95 (*1-882161-02-5*) Latinarte.

De Higuero, Cristina M. Los Payasos y Otros Cuentos. Higuero, Perez-Gambotti & De La Lastra, Achurra M., illus. LC 93-74473. (SPA.). 21p. (Orig.). (gr. 1-3). 1993. pap. 10.00 (*0-9605082-4-4*) Allied Ent.

Hurwitz, Johanna. New Shoes for Silvia. Pinkney, Jerry, illus. LC 92-40868. 32p. (ps up). 1993. 15.00 (*0-688-05286-X*); PLB 14.93 (*0-688-05287-8*) Morrow Jr Bks.

LATIN-AMERICANS IN THE U. S.

Cullison, Alan. The South Americans. Moynihan, Daniel P., intro. by. (Illus.). 112p. (gr. 5 up). 1991. lib. bdg. 17.95 (*0-87754-863-3*) Chelsea Hse.

LATIN LANGUAGE

Anderson, John A. & Groten, Frank J., Jr. Latin: A Course for Schools & Colleges. rev. ed. LC 71-102077. (Illus.). 357p. (gr. 7-12). 1988. Repr. of 1970 ed. 20. 00x (*0-942573-00-5*) Hill School.

DaParma, Charles W., et al. Latin Study Aid. 1987. pap. 2.75 (*0-87738-035-X*) Youth Ed.

Lebet, Philip E. & Perry, David J. Vocabula Et Sermones - Basic Vocabulary & Sample Conversations. (LAT.). 25p. (gr. 6-12). 1991. spiral 1.70 (*0-939507-19-6*, B4) Amer Classical.

Marsh, Carole. Latin for Kids: Of All the Gaul. (Illus.). (gr. 2-10). 1994. 24.95 (*0-935326-17-0*) Gallopade Pub Group.

Masciantonio, Rudolph. Latin, the Language of the Health Sciences. (Illus.). 42p. (Orig.). (gr. 7-12). 1992. spiral bound 3.10 (*0-939507-43-9*, B313) Amer Classical.

LATIN LITERATURE

Lind, Levi R., ed. Latin Poetry in Verse Translation. LC 57-59176. (gr. 9 up). 1957. pap. 9.96 (*0-395-05118-5*, RivEd) HM.

LATTER-DAY SAINTS

see Mormons and Mormonism

LAW

see also Courts; Judges; Jury; Lawyers; Police; also special branches of law, e.g. International Law; For laws on special subjects see names of subjects with the subdivision Laws and Regulations, e.g. Automobiles–Laws and Regulations

Adams, Pam. Law & Order. LC 90-25106. 1990. 7.95 (*0-685-52309-8*); pap. 3.95 (*0-85953-354-9*) Childs Play.

Fox, Ken. Everything You Need to Know about Your Legal Rights. (gr. 7-12). 1992. PLB 14.95 (*0-8239-1322-8*) Rosen Group.

Law. (Illus.). 64p. (gr. 6-12). 1975. pap. 1.85 (*0-8395-3389-6*, 33389) BSA.

Lipson, Greta & Lipson, Eric. Everyday Law for Young Citizens. 160p. (gr. 5 up). 1988. wkbk. 12.95 (*0-86653-447-4*, GA1056) Good Apple.

Miller, Marvin. You Be the Jury: Courtroom Two. (gr. 4-7). 1992. pap. 2.50 (*0-590-45725-X*) Scholastic Inc.

Sgarlata, Joseph. Law & Public Policy. 162p. (Orig.). (gr. 11-12). 1990. pap. text ed. 13.75x (*0-936826-34-7*) PS Assocs Croton.

Shuster, Albert H. & Miller, Russell R. The Young Citizen Observes the Law. Cooper, William H., ed. Butrick, Lyn M., illus. LC 83-80867. 93p. (gr. 4-8). 1983. pap. text ed. 5.27 (*0-914127-03-9*); tchr's. ed. 4.88 (*0-685-07834-5*) Univ Class.

Shuster, Albert H., et al. The Young Christian Observes the Law. Cooper, William H., ed. Butrick, Lyn M., illus. LC 83-80868. 106p. (gr. 4-8). 1983. pap. text ed. 5.27 (*0-914127-02-0*) Univ Class.

Summer, Lila & Woods, Samuel G. The Judiciary: Laws We Live By. LC 92-15199. (Illus.). 48p. (gr. 5-6). 1992. PLB 21.34 (*0-8114-7350-3*) Raintree Steck-V.

Wallace, L. Jean. What Every 18-Year-Old Needs to Know about California Law. Jones, Jewell, frwd. by. LC 93-28844. 192p. (gr. 12). 1994. text ed. 25.00x (*0-292-79084-8*); pap. 9.95 (*0-292-79085-6*) U of Tex Pr.

LAW–U. S.

Riekes, Linda & Ackerly, Sally M. Lawmaking. 2nd ed. (Illus.). 142p. (gr. 5-9). 1980. pap. text ed. 20.50 (*0-8299-1023-9*); tchr's. ed. 20.50 (*0-8299-1024-7*) West Pub.

Summer, Lila & Woods, Samuel G. The Judiciary: Laws We Live By. LC 92-15199. (Illus.). 48p. (gr. 5-6). 1992. PLB 21.34 (*0-8114-7350-3*) Raintree Steck-V.

Zerman, Melvyn B. Beyond a Reasonable Doubt: Inside the American Jury System. Caldwell, John, illus. LC 80-2451. 224p. (gr. 7 up). 1981. PLB 12.89 (*0-690-04095-4*, Crowell Jr Bks) HarpC Child Bks.

LAW ENFORCEMENT

see also Police

LAW ENFORCEMENT–BIOGRAPHY

Milligan, Bryce. The Lawmen: Stories of Men Who Tamed the West. Bill Smith Studio Staff, illus. 80p. (gr. 1-4). 1994. pap. 3.50 (*0-7868-4006-4*); PLB 12.89 (*0-7868-5005-1*) Disney Pr.

LAWN TENNIS

see Tennis

LAWS

see Law

LAWSON FAMILY

Lawson, Robert. They Were Strong & Good. Lawson, Robert, illus. (gr. 4-6). 1940. pap. 14.00 (*0-670-69949-7*) Viking Child Bks.

LAWYERS

see also Judges

Brownell, David. Great Lawyers. Conkle, Nancy, illus. 48p. (Orig.). (gr. 8). 1988. pap. 3.95 (*0-88388-133-0*) Bellerophon Bks.

Davie, John L. His Honor, the Buckaroo: The Autobiography of John L. Davie. rev. ed. LC 87-91072. (Illus.). 239p. (gr. 9-12). 1988. pap. 9.95 (*0-943077-12-5*) J Herzberg.

Fry, William R. & Hoopes, Roy. Legal Careers & the Legal System. LC 87-9298. (Illus.). 64p. (gr. 6 up). 1988. lib. bdg. 15.95 (*0-89490-142-7*) Enslow Pubs.

Hewett, Joan. Public Defender: Lawyer for the People. Hewett, Richard, photos by. (Illus.). 48p. (gr. 4-8). 1991. 14.95 (*0-525-67340-7*, Lodestar Bks) Dutton Child Bks.

LAWYERS–FICTION

Brown, Drollene. Belva Lockwood Wins Her Case. Levine, Abby, ed. LC 87-2114. (Illus.). 48p. (gr. 3-7). 1987. PLB 11.95 (*0-8075-0630-3*) A Whitman.

Killien, Christi. Artie's Brief: The Whole Truth & Nothing But. 112p. 1990. pap. 2.95 (*0-380-71108-7*, Camelot) Avon.

LAYOUT AND TYPOGRAPHY

see Printing

LEADERSHIP

Bartlett, Jaye. Freddy the Elephant: The Story of a Sensitive Leader. Dubina, Alan, illus. 45p. (Orig.). (ps up). 1991. pap. 11.95 incl. cassette (*1-878064-01-0*) New Age CT.

Bly, Léon. An Analysis of Leadership & How to Be a Better Leader. 117p. (Orig.). (gr. 9). 1988. text & wkbk. 24.95 (*0-9621505-0-9*) Schwarz Pauper.

Garrison, Thomas S., ed. Annual Directory of World Leaders, 1991, Vol. 3. 200p. (Orig.). (gr. 9-12). 1991. pap. 39.95 (*0-9610590-5-2*) IASB Enviro.

Lee, George L. Worldwide Interesting People: One Hundred Sixty-Two History Makers of African Descent. LC 91-50939. (Illus.). 144p. 1992. lib. bdg. 19.95 (*0-89950-670-4*) McFarland & Co.

Mayo, Cynthia R. Developing Tomorrow's Leaders Today: A Global Perspective: Leadership Development for Youths. 200p. (gr. 8 up). 1991. pap. 25.00 (*0-9630519-0-3*) M&M Pub.

Sanders, Bill. Stand Out: Becoming a Strong Leader. (Illus.). 176p. (Orig.). (gr. 9-12). 1994. pap. 7.99 (*0-8007-5533-2*) Revell.

LEAKEY, LOUIS SEYMOUR BAZETT, 1903-

Lambert, Lisa A. The Leakeys. LC 92-46046. 1993. 19.93 (*0-86625-492-7*); 14.95s.p. (*0-685-66536-4*) Rourke Pubns.

Willis, Delta. The Leakey Family: Leaders in the Search for Human Origins. LC 92-12522. (Illus.). 128p. 1992. PLB 16.95 (*0-8160-2605-X*) Facts on File.

LEAR, EDWARD, 1812-1888

Kamen, Gloria. Edward Lear: King of Nonsense. Lear, Edward, illus. LC 89-28023. 80p. (gr. 2-7). 1990. SBE 13.95 (*0-689-31419-1*, Atheneum Child Bk) Macmillan Child Grp.

LEARNING, ART OF

see Study, Method of

LEARNING AND SCHOLARSHIP

see also Culture; Education; Research

Almonte, Paul & Desmond, Theresa. Learning Disabilities. LC 91-22632. (Illus.). 48p. (gr. 5-6). 1992. text ed. 12.95 RSBE (*0-89686-721-8*, Crestwood Hse) Macmillan Child Grp.

Berry, Joy. Every Kid's Guide to Thinking & Learning. (Illus.). 48p. (gr. 3-7). 1987. 4.95 (*0-516-21424-1*) Childrens.

Berry, Marilyn. Help Is on the Way for Listening Skills. (Illus.). 48p. (gr. 4-6). 1987. pap. 4.95 (*0-516-43285-0*) Childrens.

Dickinson, Lavona & Watts, Ramona. Come Learn with Me. (ps). 1989. pap. 12.95 (*0-8224-1377-9*) Fearon Teach Aids.

Fullen, Dave. Lessons Learned: Students with Learning Disabilities, Ages 7-19, Share What They've Learned about Life & Learning. Farley, Brendon, illus. 40p. (Orig.). (gr. 1 up). 1993. pap. 6.95 (*1-881650-02-2*) Mntn Bks.

—A Nest in the Gale. Farley, Brendon, illus. LC 93-208563. 72p. (Orig.). (gr. 2-6). 1993. cancelled 24.95 (*1-881650-03-0*); pap. 18.95 incl. audio cassette (*1-881650-01-4*) Mntn Bks.

Hinsley, Sandra. Brain Gym Surfer. Corvey, Linda, illus. 6.00 (*0-685-64789-7*, 5) Edu-Kinesthetics.

Janover, Caroline. Josh: A Boy with Dyslexia. LC 88-10661. (Illus.). 100p. (gr. 3-6). 1988. pap. 7.95 (*0-914525-10-7*); 11.95 (*0-914525-18-2*) Waterfront Bks.

Maestro, Betsy & Maestro, Giulio. Traffic: A Book of Opposites. reissued ed. Maestro, Betsy & Maestro, Giulio, illus. LC 80-29641. 32p. (ps-1). 1991. 16.00 (*0-517-54427-X*) Crown Bks Yng Read.

Morris, Neil. I'm Big: A Fun Book of Opposites. Stevenson, Peter, illus. 32p. (ps-2). 1991. PLB 13.50 (*0-87614-674-4*) Carolrhoda Bks.

Murphy, Marsha A. Secrets of Making A's the Easy SpeedLearning Way: Powerful Learning Tools & Study Techniques Revealed. LC 92-75555. (Illus., Orig.). Date not set. Incl. audio tape. pap. 59.95 (*0-9635508-0-2*) DataQuest VA.

The author has coupled a learning resource guide & explanatory audio tape into a "LEARNING KIT" containing richly-informative tips for students of all ages on actually HOW to learn what they are INSTRUCTED to learn. These techniques are useful & adaptable for school, business & all life-long learners. In addition to the multitude of learning & memory techniques graphically explained & simplified here for easy understanding & instant application, there are also chapters included on organization of information, spelling, grammar, writing, reading comprehension, math shortcuts, library usage, study & relaxation tips, test-taking strategies, & speed-reading. Audio, visual, & tactile/kinesthetic techniques are clearly explained, showing students how to learn by circumventing rote memory alone. Mind pictures & mental movies are some of the powerful learning tools described here. These techniques are easy, fun, & will dramatically shorten learning time. Although this three-part guide is divided into sections generally applicable to different age groups, all students will find valuable information in each section. The text is lavishly illustrated & specially formatted for easy readability & understanding. TO ORDER: write DataQuest, P.O. Box 62692, Virginia Beach, VA 23466. *Publisher Provided Annotation.*

Roby, Cynthia. When Learning Is Tough: Kids Talk about Learning Disabilities. (ps-3). 1993. 12.95 (*0-8075-8892-X*) A Whitman.

Scholarship. (Illus.). 80p. (gr. 6-12). 1988. pap. 1.85 (*0-8395-3384-5*, 33384) BSA.

Spainhower, Steven D. School Smart: Behaviors & Skills for Student Success, 93-94. Wilson, Dana & Brown, Steven J., eds. (Illus.). 205p. (Orig.). (gr. 7-12). 1993. pap. text ed. 18.95 (*0-9637573-0-X*) Education Res.

Walt Disney Fun to Learn Library. 1985. write for info Bantam.

LEATHER WORK

Leatherwork. (Illus.). 48p. (gr. 6-12). 1983. pap. 1.85 (*0-8395-3310-1*, 33310) BSA.

LEAVES

Bellegarde, Ida R. Lisping Leaves. (gr. 9 up). 1976. 8.95 (*0-918340-03-9*) Bell Ent.

Corderoy, William. Leaves. Corderoy, William, illus. 32p. (gr. 1 up). 1994. 17.27 (*0-8368-1094-5*) Gareth Stevens Inc.

Fowler, Allan. It Could Still Be a Leaf. LC 93-882. (Illus.). 32p. (ps-2). 1993. PLB 10.75 (*0-516-06017-1*); pap. 3.95 (*0-516-46017-X*) Childrens.

Harlow, Rosie & Morgan, Gareth. Trees & Leaves. Peperell, Liz, illus. LC 91-7461. 40p. (gr. 5-8). 1991. PLB 12.90 (*0-531-19126-5*, Warwick) Watts.

Johnson, Sylvia A. How Leaves Change. Sato, Yuko, illus. 48p. (gr. 4 up). 1986. PLB 19.95 (*0-8225-1483-4*, First Ave Edns); pap. 5.95 (*0-8225-9513-3*, First Ave Edns) Lerner Pubns.

Kirkpatrick, Rena K. Look at Leaves. rev. ed. Milne, Annabel & Stebbing, Peter, illus. LC 84-26360. 32p. (gr. 2-4). 1985. PLB 10.95 (*0-8172-2353-3*); pap. 4.95 (*0-8114-6899-2*) Raintree Steck-V.

Maestro, Betsy. Why Do Leaves Change Color? Krupinski, Loretta, illus. LC 93-9611. 32p. (gr. k-4). 1994. 15.00 (*0-06-022873-3*); PLB 14.89 (*0-06-022874-1*) HarpC Child Bks.

Selsam, Millicent E. A First Look at Leaves. Selsam, Millicent E. & Hunt, Joyce, eds. Springer, Harriett, illus. LC 72-81376. 32p. (gr. 2-4). 1972. PLB 11.85 (*0-8027-6118-6*) Walker & Co.

Sohi, Morteza E. Look What I Did with a Leaf. Sohi, Morteza E., illus. LC 92-35142. 32p. (gr. 4-8). 1993. 14.95 (*0-8027-8215-9*); PLB 15.85 (*0-8027-8216-7*) Walker & Co.

Wiggers, Raymond. Picture Guide to Tree Leaves. LC 90-47859. (Illus.). 64p. (gr. 3-5). 1991. PLB 12.90 (*0-531-20025-6*) Watts.

—Picture Guide to Tree Leaves. (Illus.). 64p. (gr. 5-8). 1992. pap. 5.95 (*0-531-15646-X*) Watts.

LEBANON

Abood, Doris M. Lebanon: Bridge Between East & West. Art, Eve, illus. Thomas, Danny, intro. by. LC 73-84565. (Illus.). 40p. (gr. 5-10). 1973. 3.50 (*0-913228-07-9*) Dillon-Liederbach.

Foster, Leila M. Lebanon. LC 91-32230. 128p. (gr. 5-9). 1992. PLB 20.55 (*0-516-02612-7*) Childrens.

Lerner Publications, Department of Geography Staff, ed. Lebanon in Pictures. (Illus.). 64p. (gr. 5 up). 1988. 17.50 (*0-8225-1832-5*) Lerner Pubns.

Marston, Elsa. Lebanon: New Light in an Ancient Land. LC 93-5402. (Illus.). 128p. (gr. 5 up). 1994. text ed. 14.95 RSBE (*0-87518-584-3*, Dillon) Macmillan Child Grp.

Stewart, Gail B. Lebanon. LC 90-35499. (Illus.). 48p. (gr. 6-7). 1990. text ed. 12.95 RSBE (*0-89686-550-9*, Crestwood Hse) Macmillan Child Grp.

LEBANON–FICTION

Heide, Florence P. & Gilliland, Judith H. Sami & the Time of the Troubles. Lewin, Ted, illus. 32p. (gr. k-4). 1992. 13.45 (*0-395-55964-2*, Clarion Bks) HM.

LEE, ROBERT EDWARD, 1807-1870

Adler, David A. A Picture Book of Robert E. Lee. Wallner, John & Wallner, Alexandra, illus. LC 93-22998. 32p. (ps-3). 1994. reinforced bdg. 15.95 (*0-8234-1111-7*) Holiday.

Archer, Jules. A House Divided: The Lives of Ulysses S. Grant & Robert E. Lee. LC 93-38886. 1994. write for info. (*0-590-46102-8*) Scholastic Inc.

Bains, Rae. Robert E. Lee: Brave Leader. Smolinski, Dick, illus. LC 85-1092. 48p. (gr. 4-6). 1986. lib. bdg. 10.79 (*0-8167-0545-3*); pap. text ed. 3.50 (*0-8167-0546-1*) Troll Assocs.

Brandt, Keith. Robert E. Lee. Lawn, John, illus. LC 84-2687. 32p. (gr. 3-6). 1985. PLB 9.49 (*0-8167-0278-0*); pap. text ed. 2.95 (*0-8167-0279-9*) Troll Assocs.

Buchanan, Patricia. Robert E Lee: A Hero for Young Americans. LC 90-70314. 142p. (gr. 5-8). 1990. pap. 6.95 (*1-55523-334-1*) Winston-Derek.

Cannon, Marian G. Robert E. Lee: Defender of the South. LC 93-415. (Illus.). 64p. (gr. 4-6). 1993. PLB 12.90 (*0-531-20120-1*) Watts.

Commager, Henry S. America's Robert E. Lee. LC 90-48983. (Illus.). 128p. (gr. 6-10). 1991. PLB 13.95 (*1-55905-088-8*) Marshall Cavendish.

Dubowski, Cathy E. Robert E. Lee & the Rise of the South. (Illus.). 160p. (gr. 5 up). 1990. lib. bdg. 12.95 (*0-382-09942-7*); pap. 7.95 (*0-382-24051-0*) Silver Burdett Pr.

Graves, Charles P. Robert E. Lee: Hero of the South. (Illus.). 80p. (gr. 2-6). 1991. Repr. of 1964 ed. lib. bdg. 12.95 (*0-7910-1462-2*) Chelsea Hse.

Greene, Carol. Robert E. Lee: Leader in War & Peace. Dobson, Steven, illus. LC 89-33749. 48p. (gr. k-3). 1989. PLB 12.85 (*0-516-04209-2*); pap. 4.95 (*0-516-44209-0*) Childrens.

Kavanaugh, Jack & Murdoch, Eugene C. Robert E. Lee. LC 94-14732. 1994. write for info. (*0-7910-1768-0*) Chelsea Hse.

Marrin, Albert. Virginia's General: Robert E. Lee & the Civil War. LC 94-13353. (gr. 5-9). 1994. 19.95 (*0-689-31838-3*, Atheneum) Macmillan.

Monsell, Helen A. Robert E. Lee: Young Confederate. Arthur, James & Morrow, Gray, illus. LC 86-10736. 192p. (gr. 2-6). 1986. pap. 3.95 (*0-02-042020-X*, Aladdin) Macmillan Child Grp.

Morrison, Ellen E. Gentle Man of Destiny: A Portrait of Robert E. Lee. 2nd, rev. ed. LC 80-201289. (Illus.). 16p. (gr. 6). 1984. saddle-stitched 1.75 (*0-9622537-1-5*) Morielle Pr.

Robert E. Lee. (Illus.). (gr. 5 up). 1992. 17.95 (*1-55546-814-4*) Chelsea Hse.

Roddy, Lee. Robert E Lee: Gallant Christian Soldier. (Illus.). (gr. 3-6). 1977. pap. 6.95 (*0-915134-40-3*) Mott Media.

Smith, Gene. Lee & Grant. 448p. (gr. 9-12). 1985. pap. 12.95 (*0-452-01000-4*, Mer) NAL-Dutton.

Weidhorn, Manfred. Robert E. Lee. LC 87-14500. (Illus.). 160p. (gr. 5 up). 1988. SBE 14.95 (*0-689-31340-3*, Atheneum Child Bk) Macmillan Child Grp.

Zadra, Dan. Statesmen in America: Robert E. Lee. rev. ed. (gr. 2-4). 1988. PLB 14.95 (*0-88682-192-4*) Creative Ed.

LEFT- AND RIGHT-HANDEDNESS

Rehm, Karl & Koike, Kay. Left or Right? (Illus.). 32p. (gr. k-2). 1991. 13.45 (*0-395-58080-3*, Clarion Bks) HM.

LEGAL HOLIDAYS

see Holidays

LEGAL PROFESSION

see Lawyers

LEGAL TENDER

see Paper Money

LEGENDS

see also Fables; Fairy Tales; Folklore; Mythology

Asolon, Karel B., ed. The Phantom of Devil's Bridge & the Tale of Buffalo Castle. (Illus.). 41p. (Orig.). (gr. 4). 1985. pap. 12.00 (*0-930329-04-X*) Kabel Pubs.

Bailey, John, et al, eds. Gods & Men: Myths & Legends from the World's Religions. (Illus.). 144p. 1993. pap. 10.95 (*0-19-274145-4*) OUP.

Bellingham, David, et al. Goddesses, Heroes, & Shamans: The Young People's Guide to World Mythology. LC 94-1374. (Illus.). 160p. (gr. 5 up). 1994. 19.95 (*1-85697-999-7*, Kingfisher LKC) LKC.

Bradley, Susannah, ed. Ghosts, Monsters & Legends. Appleby, Barrie, illus. 48p. (gr. 3-6). 1992. pap. 2.95 (*1-56680-005-6*) Mad Hatter Pub.

De Coster, Charles T. Flemish Legends. Taylor, Harold, tr. Delstanche, Albert, illus. LC 78-74513. (gr. 7 up). 1979. Repr. of 1920 ed. 18.75x (*0-8486-0217-X*) Roth Pub Inc.

De Paola, Tomie, retold by. & illus. The Legend of the Bluebonnet: An Old Tale of Texas. LC 82-12391. 32p. (ps-3). 1983. 14.95 (*0-399-20937-9*, Putnam); (Putnam) Putnam Pub Group.

Ellis, Terry. The Legend of Willow Wood Springs. LC 85-63828. (Illus.). 180p. (Orig.). (gr. 4 up). 1989. pap. 4.75 (*0-915677-30-X*) Roundtable Pub.

French, Fiona. Anancy & Mr. Dry-Bone. (Illus.). (ps-3). 1991. 14.95 (*0-316-29298-2*) Little.

Lines, Kathleen, ed. The Faber Book of Greek Legends. Jacques, Faith, illus. 268p. (gr. 4 up). 1986. pap. 11.95 (*0-571-13920-5*) Faber & Faber.

Morgan, Robin. The Mer-Child: A Legend for Children & Other Adults. (Illus.). 64p. 1991. 17.95 (*1-55861-053-7*); 8.95 (*1-55861-054-5*) Feminist Pr.

Revich, S. J. Ibrahim the Magician. Hinlicky, Gregg, illus. 126p. (gr. 4-7). 1987. 9.95 (*0-935063-33-1*); pap. 7.95 (*0-935063-34-X*) CIS Comm.

Riordan, James & Lewis, Brenda R. An Illustrated Treasury of Myths & Legends. Ambrus, Victor, illus. 152p. (gr. 7 up). 1991. 12.95 (*0-87226-349-5*) P Bedrick Bks.

Ross, Harriet, compiled by. Heroes & Heroines of Many Lands. 160p. (gr. 3-9). 1992. Repr. of 1990 ed. PLB 14.95 (*0-87460-214-9*) Lion Bks.

Ruskin, John. The King of the Golden River or the Black Brother. Doyle, Richard, illus. LC 74-82199. viii, 56p. (gr. 1 up). 1974. pap. 2.95 (*0-486-20066-3*) Dover.

Urbide, Fernando & Engler, Dan. Ben-Hur, A Race to Glory. CCC of America Staff, illus. 35p. (Orig.). (ps-8). 1992. incl. video 21.95 (*1-56814-006-1*); pap. text ed. 4.95 book (*0-685-62399-8*) CCC of America.

Westphal, Patricia R. The Legend of Ice Breaker. LC 89-40245. 32p. (gr. 1-2). 1991. PLB 18.60 (*0-8368-0119-9*) Gareth Stevens Inc.

LEGENDS–AFRICA, WEST

Larungu, Rute. African-American Cultures: Myths & Legends from Ghana for Children. Turechek, Lou, illus. LC 92-81116. 96p. (gr. 3 up). 1992. lib. bdg. 14.95 (*1-878893-21-1*); pap. 8.95 (*1-878893-20-3*) Telcraft Bks. KIRKUS REVIEWS: "'A story, a story, let it go, let it come.' Three Hausa & five Ashanti tales...one can almost hear the teller's voice." BOOKLIST: "In an insightful, interactive manner, this collection provides a range of fast-paced tales... these stories should be read aloud, perhaps even dramatized, to be fully appreciated." SCHOOL LIBRARY JOURNAL: "...free verse...a fuller background to West African folklore than single-story books." To order: Quality Books, Inc. (libraries); Baker & Taylor (all). *Publisher Provided Annotation.*

LEGENDS–AUSTRALIA

Morgan, Sally. The Flying Emu & Other Australian Stories. Morgan, Sally, illus. LC 92-37880. 128p. (gr. k-7). 1993. 18.00 (*0-679-84705-7*) Knopf Bks Yng Read.

Troughton, Joanna, retold by. & illus. Whale's Canoe: A Folk Tale from Australia. LC 92-43616. 32p. (gr. k-3). 1993. 14.95 (*0-87226-509-9*) P Bedrick Bks.

LEGENDS–BRAZIL

Lippert, Margaret H. La Hija de la Serpiente Marina - the Sea Serpent's Daughter: Una Leyenda Brasilena. LC 92-21438. (gr. 4-7). 1993. PLB 11.89 (*0-8167-3124-1*); pap. 3.95 (*0-8167-3074-1*) Troll Assocs.

LEGENDS–CHINA

Chang, Florence C. Believe It or Not: An Anthology of Ancient Tales Retold. Chang, Shou-Jen, illus. LC 80-68258. 80p. (gr. 10-12). 1980. pap. 6.25x (wkbk. incl.) (*0-936620-02-1*) Ginkgo Hut.

LEGENDS–FRANCE

Picard, Barbara L. French Legends, Tales & Fairy Stories. Kiddell-Monroe, Joan, illus. 216p. (gr. 4 up). 1992. pap. 10.95 (*0-19-274149-7*) OUP.

LEGENDS–GERMANY

Browning, Robert. The Pied Piper of Hamelin: A Classic Tale. Jose, Eduard, adapted by. Suire, Diane D., tr. Rovira, Francesc, illus. LC 88-35313. 32p. (gr. k-2). 1988. PLB 19.95 (*0-89565-471-7*); PLB 13.95s.p. (*0-685-56031-7*) Childs World.

Pied Piper. (Illus.). (ps-1). 1985. 1.98 (*0-517-47105-1*) Random Hse Value.

The Pied Piper of Hamelin. (Illus.). (ps-3). 1985. 2.98 (*0-517-28805-2*) Random Hse Value.

Storr, Catherine, retold by. The Pied Piper of Hamelin. LC 84-26971. (Illus.). 32p. (gr. k-5). 1984. PLB 19.97 (*0-8172-2107-7*); PLB 29.28 incl. cassette (*0-8172-2238-3*) Raintree Steck-V.

LEGENDS–GREAT BRITAIN

Merrill, John N. Legends of Derbyshire. 2nd ed. Merrill, John N., illus. 71p. (Orig.). (gr. 6 up). 1975. pap. 3.00 (*0-913714-15-1*) Legacy Bks.

Pyle, Howard. The Story of King Arthur & His Knights. (Illus.). (gr. 7 up). 1978. Repr. of 1903 ed. lib. bdg. 12.00 luxury ed. (*0-932106-01-3*, Pub by Marathon Pr) S J Durst.

LEGENDS–HAWAII

Colum, Padraic. Legends of Hawaii. (Illus.). (gr. 8 up). 1937. text ed. 13.00x (*0-300-00376-5*) Yale U Pr.

LEGENDS–INDIA

Choudhary, Bani R. The Story of Krishna. (Illus.). (gr. 3-10). 1979. 7.25 (*0-89744-134-6*) Auromere.

—The Story of Ramayan. (Illus.). (gr. 3-10). 1979. 7.50 (*0-89744-133-8*) Auromere.

Ghosh, A. Legends from Indian History. Mukerji, Debrabrata, illus. (gr. 1-8). 1979. pap. 3.00 (*0-89744-157-5*); 4.50 (*0-685-00594-1*) Auromere.

Mehta, Hansa. Prince of Ayodhya. (Illus.). (gr. 1-9). 1979. pap. 2.50 (*0-89744-178-8*) Auromere.

Narayana, T. R. Bheesma. Sharma, Mukesh, illus. (gr. 1-8). 1979. pap. 3.00 (*0-89744-151-6*) Auromere.

Savitri. Savitri & Satyavan. Wheaton, Jaya, illus. (gr. 1-9). 1979. pap. 2.75 (*0-89744-160-5*) Auromere.

LEGENDS, INDIAN

see Indians of North America–Legends

LEGENDS–IRELAND

Donegan, Maureen. The Bedside Book of Irish Fables & Legends. 117p. (gr. 5 up). 1993. pap. 11.95 (*1-85635-063-0*, Pub. by Mercier Pr ER) Dufour.

LEGENDS–ITALY

De Paola, Tomie. The Clown of God. De Paola, Tomie, illus. LC 78-3845. (gr. k up). 1978. 13.95 (*0-15-219175-5*, HB Juv Bks) HarBrace.

—The Clown of God. De Paola, Tomie, illus. LC 78-3845. 45p. (ps-3). 1978. pap. 5.95 (*0-15-618192-4*, Voyager Bks) HarBrace.

LEGENDS–JAPAN

Harris, Rosemary. Child in the Bamboo Grove. Le Cain, Errol, illus. LC 72-4064. (gr. 1-3). 1972. 21.95 (*0-87599-194-7*) S G Phillips.

Pratt, Davis. Magic Animals of Japan. Kula, Elsa, illus. LC 67-17483. (gr. 1-4). 1967. (Pub. by Parnassus); PLB 5.88 (*0-87466-020-3*) HM.

Quayle, Eric, retold by. The Shining Princess & Other Japanese Legends. Foreman, Michael, illus. 112p. (gr. k-5). 1989. 15.95 (*1-55970-039-4*) Arcade Pub Inc.

LEGENDS, JEWISH

Chana Faiga Brander. A Blick of Tzurik. Bayer, Breindy, illus. 126p. (Orig.). (gr. 4). 1990. pap. text ed. 9.50 (*0-9629684-0-4*) K K Aharon.

Freehof, Lillian S. Bible Legends: An Introduction to Midrash, Vol. 1: Genesis. Schwartz, Howard, ed. (gr. 4-6). 1987. pap. text ed. 6.95 (*0-8074-0357-1*, 123050) UAHC.

Sherman, Josepha. Rachel the Clever: And Other Jewish Folktales. 171p. 1993. 18.95 (*0-87483-306-X*); pap. 9.95 (*0-87483-307-8*) August Hse.

LEGENDS–POLYNESIA

Sperry, Armstrong. Call It Courage. Sperry, Armstrong, illus. LC 40-4229. 96p. (gr. 5-7). 1968. SBE 13.95 (*0-02-786030-2*, Macmillan Child Bk) Macmillan Child Grp.

LEGENDS–SCANDINAVIA

Evans, C. & Millard, A. Greek & Norse Legends. (Illus.). 112p. (gr. 6-10). 1987. pap. 12.95 (*0-7460-0240-8*) EDC.

Lindgren, Astrid. The Tomten. Wiberg, Harold, illus. 32p. (ps-3). 1990. pap. 5.95 (*0-698-20680-0*, Sandcastle Bks) Putnam Pub Group.

LEGENDS–SOVIET UNION

Crouch, Marcus. Ivan: Stories of Old Russia. Dewar, Bob, illus. 80p. (gr. 3-7). 1989. jacketed 20.00 (*0-19-274135-7*) OUP.

LEGENDS–U. S.

Blair, Al. Moosewhopper: A Juicy, Moosey Min-Min-Minnesota Burger Tale. 3rd ed. McMurray, Chuck, illus. LC 83-61092. 32p. (gr. 3). 1983. pap. 3.95 (*0-930366-04-2*) Northcountry Pub.

Irving, Washington. Legend of Sleepy Hollow. Hitchner, Earle, adapted by. Van Buuren, John, illus. LC 89-33942. 48p. (gr. 3-6). 1990. PLB 12.89 (*0-8167-1869-5*); pap. text ed. 3.95 (*0-8167-1870-9*) Troll Assocs.

Kellogg, Steven. Johnny Appleseed. Kellogg, Steven, illus. LC 87-27317. 48p. (gr. 2 up). 1988. 14.95 (*0-688-06417-5*); PLB 14.88 (*0-688-06418-3*, Morrow Jr Bks) Morrow Jr Bks.

Rohmer, Harriet, adapted by. The Legend of Food Mountain (La montana del alimento) Carrillo, Graciela, illus. LC 81-71634. 24p. (gr. k-8). 1982. 13.95 (*0-89239-022-0*) Childrens Book Pr.

Rounds, David. Cannonball River Tales. Berenzy, Alix, illus. LC 92-11374. 104p. (gr. 4-7). 1992. 15.95 (*0-87156-577-3*) Sierra.

Small, Terry. Legend of John Henry. (gr. 4-7). 1994. 14.95 (*0-385-31168-0*) Doubleday.

LEGENDS–WALES

Alexander, Lloyd. Black Cauldron. LC 65-13868. (gr. 4-6). 1965. 16.95 (*0-8050-0992-2*, Bks Young Read) H Holt & Co.

—Book of Three. LC 64-18250. 224p. (gr. 4-6). 1964. 16.95 (*0-8050-0874-8*, Bks Young Read) H Holt & Co.

LEGENDS AND STORIES OF ANIMALS

see Animals–Fiction; Fables

LEGERDEMAIN

see Magic

LEIF ERICSSON, d. ca. 1020

Zadra, Dan. Explorers of America: Leif Erickson. (gr. 2-4). 1988. PLB 14.95 (*0-88682-180-0*) Creative Ed.

LEISURE

see also Hobbies; Recreation

LEMMINGS–FICTION

Arkin, Alan. The Lemming Condition. Sandin, Joan, illus. LC 75-6296. 64p. (gr. 4 up). 1976. 13.00 (*0-06-020133-9*) HarpC Child Bks.

LENIN, VLADIMIR ILYICH, 1870-1924

Kallen, Stuart A. The Lenin Era. Wallner, Rosemary, ed. LC 92-13473. 1992. PLB 13.99 (*1-56239-101-1*) Abdo & Dghtrs.

Rawcliffe, Michael. Lenin. (Illus.). 64p. (gr. 6-9). 1989. 19.95 (*0-7134-5611-6*, Pub. by Batsford UK) Trafalgar.

LENINGRAD–SIEGE, 1941-1944

Hanmer, Trudy J. Leningrad. LC 92-14. (Illus.). 96p. (gr. 6 up). 1992. text ed. 14.95 RSBE (*0-02-742615-7*, New Discovery) Macmillan Child Grp.

LENSES

Aust, Siegfried. Lenses! Take a Closer Look. Nyncke, Helge, illus. 32p. (gr. 2-5). 1991. PLB 18.95 (*0-8225-2151-2*) Lerner Pubns.

Berger, Melvin. All about Magnifying Glasses. (ps-3). 1993. pap. 4.95 (*0-590-45510-9*) Scholastic Inc.

Joval, Nomi. Color of Light. Kubinyi, Laszlo, illus. 16p. (ps-4). 1993. PLB 13.95 (*1-879567-19-9*, Valeria Bks) Wonder Well.

—Power of Glass. Kubinyi, Laszlo, illus. 16p. (ps-4). 1993. PLB 13.95 (*1-879567-21-0*, Valeria Bks) Wonder Well.

Murphy, Pat, et al. Bending Light: An Exploratorium Toolbook. Osborn, Stephen, illus. LC 92-20336. 1993. 15.95 (*0-316-25851-2*) Little.

Pusterla, Fred. My First Magnifier Book. Pusterla, Fred, illus. 12p. (ps-1). 1993. bds. 9.95 (*1-56293-140-7*) McClanahan Bk.

VanCleave, Janice. Janice VanCleave's Microscopes & Magnifying Lenses: Mind-Boggling Chemistry & Biology Experiments You Can Turn Into Science Fair Projects. 112p. (gr. 3 up). 1993. pap. text ed. 9.95 (*0-471-58956-X*) Wiley.

LEONARDO DA VINCI, 1452-1519

Hart, Tony. Leonardo Da Vinci. Hellard, Susan, illus. LC 93-2385. 24p. (ps-3). 1994. pap. 5.95 (*0-8120-1828-1*) Barron.

Lepscky, Ibi. Leonardo da Vinci. Cardoni, Paolo, illus. 24p. (gr. k-3). 1992. pap. 4.95 (*0-8120-1451-0*) Barron.

McLanathan, Richard B. Leonardo da Vinci. (Illus.). 72p. (gr. 7 up). 1990. 19.95 (*0-8109-1256-2*) Abrams.

Marshall, Norman F. & Ripamonti, Aldo. Leonardo da Vinci. (Illus.). 104p. (gr. 5-8). 1990. 9.95 (*0-382-09982-6*); pap. 5.95 (*0-382-24007-3*) Silver Burdett Pr.

Mason, Antony. Leonardo Da Vinci. (Illus.). 32p. (gr. 5 up). 1994. 10.95 (*0-8120-6460-7*); pap. 5.95 (*0-8120-1997-0*) Barron.

Provensen, Alice & Provensen, Martin. Leonardo da Vinci: The Artist, Inventor, Scientist in Three-Dimensional Movable Pictures. LC 83-26005. (Illus.). 12p. 1984. pap. 17.95 (*0-670-42384-X*) Viking Child Bks.

Skira-Venturi, Rosabianca. Weekend with Leonardo Da Vinci. (Illus.). 64p. (gr. 4-7). 1993. 19.95 (0-8478-1440-8) Rizzoli Intl.

Venezia, Mike. Da Vinci. Venezia, Mike, illus. LC 88-37715. 32p. (ps-4). 1989. PLB 12.85 (0-516-02275-X); pap. 4.95 (0-516-42275-8) Childrens.

LEONOWENS, ANNA HARRIETTE CRAWFORD

Landon, Margaret. Anna & the King of Siam. Ayer, M., illus. 1944. 16.95 (0-381-98135-5, A05201); 16.45 (0-685-02093-2) HarpC Child Bks.

LEOPARDS

Knutson, Barbara, retold by. & illus. Sungura & Leopard: A Swahili TricksterTale. LC 92-31905. 1993. 15.95 (0-316-50010-0) Little.

Scott, Jonathan. The Leopard Family Book. Scott, Jonathan, photos by. LC 91-14578. (Illus.). 56p. (gr. k up). 1991. pap. 15.95 (0-88708-186-X) Picture Bk Studio.

Stone, L. Leopards. (Illus.). 24p. (gr. k-5). 1989. lib. bdg. 11.94 (0-86592-502-X); 8.95s.p. (0-685-58630-8) Rourke Corp.

Tibbitts, Alison & Roocroft, Alan. Snow Leopard. (Illus.). 24p. (ps-2). 1992. PLB 12.95 (1-56065-106-7) Capstone Pr.

Urquhart, Jennifer C. Lions & Tigers & Leopards: The Big Cats. (Illus.). (gr. k-4). 1990. Set. 13.95 (0-87044-820-X); Set. PLB 16.95 (0-87044-825-0) Natl Geog.

LEOPARDS–FICTION

Achebe, Chinua & Iroaganachi, John. How the Leopard Got His Claws. Christiansen, Per, illus. LC 72-93382. 32p. (gr. 6 up). 1973. 11.95 (0-89388-056-6) Okpaku Communications.

Avent, Barbara P. The Leopard Speaks about Changes in Life. Alston, Nelson G., ed. Winchell, Karl, illus. LC 93-72214. 64p. (Orig.). 1993. pap. 9.95 (0-9632202-1-7) Alpha Bk Pr.

Bailey, Jill. Save the Snow Leopard. Green, John, illus. LC 90-45917. 48p. (gr. 3-7). 1991. PLB 21.34 (0-8114-2709-9); pap. 4.95 (0-8114-6557-8) Raintree Steck-V.

Cherry, Lynne, illus. Snow Leopard. LC 86-24033. 12p. (ps). 1987. (DCB); book & toy package 13.95 (0-685-14571-9, DCB) Dutton Child Bks.

Hadithi, Mwenye. Baby Baboon. Kennaway, Adrienne, illus. LC 92-56397. 1993. 15.95 (0-316-33729-3) Little.

Kipling, Rudyard. How the Leopard Got His Spots. Lohstoeter, Lori, illus. 64p. 1993. Repr. of 1989 ed. incl. cass. 9.95 (0-88708-301-3, Rabbit Ears) Picture Bk Studio.

Lester, Julius. How Many Spots Does a Leopard Have? (gr. 4-7). 1994. pap. 5.95 (0-590-41972-2) Scholastic Inc.

Levoy, Myron. A Shadow Like a Leopard. LC 79-2812. 192p. (gr. 4-7). 1994. pap. 3.95 (0-06-440458-7, Trophy) HarpC Child Bks.

Robertson, Janet. Oscar's Spots. LC 93-22199. (Illus.). 32p. (ps-2). 1993. PLB 13.95 (0-8167-3133-0); pap. write for info. (0-8167-3134-9) BrdgeWater.

LEPIDOPTERA

see Butterflies; Moths

LETTER WRITING

Cobb, Nancy. The Letter Writer Book: Have Fun, Be Heard, & Get Things Done -- By Letter. Cornell, Laura, illus. LC 94-2922. (gr. 2-6). 1994. 24.95 (0-89577-518-2, Readers Digest Kids) RD Assn.

James, Elizabeth & Barkin, Carol. Sincerely Yours: How to Write Great Letters. 192p. (gr. 4-8). 1993. 14.95 (0-395-58831-6, Clarion Bks); pap. 6.95 (0-395-58832-4, Clarion Bks) HM.

Leedy, Loreen. Messages in the Mailbox: How to Write a Letter. Leedy, Loreen, illus. LC 91-8718. 32p. (ps-3). 1991. reinforced bdg. 15.95 (0-8234-0889-2) Holiday.

—Messages in the Mailbox: How to Write a Letter. Leedy, Loreen, illus. 1994. pap. 5.95 (0-8234-1079-X) Holiday.

LETTER WRITING–FICTION

Brisson, Pat. Kate Heads West. Brown, Rick, illus. LC 89-27590. 40p. (gr. k-3). 1990. RSBE 13.95 (0-02-714345-7, Bradbury Pr) Macmillan Child Grp.

Caseley, Judith. Dear Annie. LC 90-39793. (Illus.). 32p. (ps up). 1991. 13.95 (0-688-10010-4); PLB 13.88 (0-688-10011-2) Greenwillow.

Cleary, Beverly. Dear Mr. Henshaw. large type ed. Zelinsky, Paul O., illus. 141p. (gr. 2-6). 1987. Repr. of 1983 ed. lib. bdg. 14.95 (1-55736-001-4, Crnrstn Bks) BDD LT Grp.

—Pen Pals, 6 vols. (gr. 4-7). 1990. pap. 17.70 boxed set (0-440-36028-5) Dell.

Dearest Grand-Ma. 1991. pap. 13.95 (0-385-41843-4) Doubleday.

Giff, Patricia R. Postcard Pest: Polk Street Special, No. 3. (ps-3). 1994. pap. 3.99 (0-440-40973-X) Dell.

—War Began at Supper: Letters to Miss Loria. (gr. 4-7). 1991. pap. 2.95 (0-440-40572-6) Dell.

Hesse, Karen. Letters from Rifka. 192p. (gr. 4-7). 1992. 14.95 (0-8050-1964-2, Bks Young Read) H Holt & Co.

—Letters from Rifka. LC 93-7486. 160p. (gr. 3-7). 1993. pap. 3.99 (0-14-036391-2, Puffin) Puffin Bks.

Hoban, Lillian. Arthur's Pen Pal. LC 75-6289. (Illus.). 64p. (gr. k-3). 1982. pap. 3.50 (0-06-444032-X, Trophy) HarpC Child Bks.

—Arthur's Pen Pal. unabr. ed. (Illus.). (ps-3). 1990. pap. 6.95 incl. cassette (1-55994-238-X, Caedmon) HarperAudio.

Keats, Ezra J. A Letter to Amy. LC 68-24329. (Illus.). 32p. (gr. k-3). 1984. pap. 5.95 (0-06-443063-4, Trophy) HarpC Child Bks.

Lowry, Lois. Anastasia at This Address. LC 90-48308. 112p. (gr. 3-7). 1991. 13.45 (0-395-56263-5) HM.

—Anastasia at This Address. large type ed. (gr. 1-8). 1994. sewn 16.95 (0-7451-2087-3, Galaxy Child Lrg Print) Chivers N Amer.

Marcus. Letters Ursula Nordstrom. Date not set. 17.00 (0-06-023625-6); PLB 17.00 (0-06-023624-8) HarpC Child Bks.

Nichol, Barbara. Beethoven Lives Upstairs. Cameron, Scott, illus. LC 93-5774. 1994. 15.95 (0-531-06828-5) Orchard Bks Watts.

Rusk, Irene J. A Letter to Grandmother. Romanelli, Maryann, illus. LC 92-61973. 64p. (Orig.). 1994. pap. 8.00 (1-56002-223-X, Univ Edtns) Aegina Pr.

Sloat, Teri. From Letter to Letter. Sloat, Teri, illus. LC 89-1135. 32p. (ps up). 1989. 13.95 (0-525-44518-8, DCB) Dutton Child Bks.

—From Letter to Letter. (Illus.). 32p. 1994. pap. 4.99 (0-14-055329-0, Puff Pied Piper) Puffin Bks.

Stone, Eddie. Donald Writes No More. (ps-12). 1988. pap. 2.95 (0-87067-733-0, BH733) Holloway.

Suarez, Maribel. La Letras: The Letters. (Illus.). 14p. (ps-1). 1990. 10.75 (970-05-0094-2) Hispanic Bk Dist.

Wild, Margaret. Thank You, Santa. (Illus.). 1992. 12.95 (0-590-45805-1, Scholastic Hardcover) Scholastic Inc.

Wyeth, Sharon D. Boy Project. (gr. 4-7). 1991. pap. 2.95 (0-440-40493-2) Dell.

—Palmer at Your Service. (gr. 4 up). 1990. pap. 2.95 (0-440-40343-X, YB) Dell.

—Sealed with a Kiss. (gr. k-6). 1990. pap. 2.95 (0-440-40272-7, YB) Dell.

York. Please Write... I Need Your Help! 1993. pap. 2.95 (0-590-46842-1) Scholastic Inc.

LETTERING

Aldous, Lynn. Lettering Pack. (Illus.). (gr. 3-6). 1992. pap. 7.95 (1-56680-505-8) Mad Hatter Pub.

Burgess, Anna. The Do-It-Yourself Lettering Book. (Illus.). 64p. (gr. 4-7). 1993. pap. 5.95 (0-8167-3036-9) Troll Assocs.

Tatchell, J. How to Draw Lettering. (Illus.). 32p. (gr. 4 up). 1991. PLB 12.96 (0-88110-537-6, Usborne); pap. 4.95 (0-7460-0635-7, Usborne) EDC.

LETTERS

Brisson, Pat. Your Best Friend, Kate. Brown, Rick, illus. LC 91-15245. 40p. (gr. 1-7). 1992. pap. 4.50 (0-689-71545-5, Aladdin) Macmillan Child Grp.

LETTERS OF CREDIT

see Credit

LETTERS OF THE ALPHABET

see Alphabet

LEVANT

see Near East

LEWIS, CLIVE STAPLES, 1898-1963

Sibley, Brian. Land of Narnia: Brian Sibley Explores the World of C. S. Lewis. Baynes, Pauline, illus. LC 90-4192. 96p. (gr. 5 up). 1990. 19.95 (0-06-025625-7); PLB 19.89 (0-06-025626-5) HarpC Child Bks.

LEWIS, JOHN LLEWELLYN, 1880-

John L. Lewis: Mini-Play. (gr. 5 up). 1978. 6.50 (0-89550-311-5) Stevens & Shea.

LEWIS, MERIWETHER, 1774-1809

Fitz-Gerald, Christine A. Meriwether Lewis & William Clark: The Northwest Expedition. LC 90-20696. (Illus.). 128p. (gr. 3 up). 1991. PLB 20.55 (0-516-03061-2); pap. 9.95 (0-516-43061-0) Childrens.

Kroll, Steven. Lewis & Clark: Explorers of the Far West. Williams, Richard, illus. LC 92-40427. 32p. (gr. 3-7). 1994. reinforced bdg. 16.95 (0-8234-1034-X) Holiday.

Noonan, Jon. Lewis & Clark. LC 92-9381. (Illus.). 48p. (gr. 5). 1993. text ed. 12.95 RSBE (0-89686-707-2, Crestwood Hse) Macmillan Child Grp.

Roop, Peter & Roop, Connie. Off the Map: The Journals of Lewis & Clark. Tanner, Tim, illus. LC 92-18340. 48p. (gr. 3-7). 1993. 14.95 (0-8027-8207-8); PLB 15.85 (0-8027-8208-6) Walker & Co.

Stefoff, Rebecca. Lewis & Clark. (Illus.). 80p. (gr. 3-5). 1992. lib. bdg. 12.95 (0-7910-1750-8) Chelsea Hse.

Twist, Clint. Lewis & Clark: Exploring North America. LC 93-33624. 1994. PLB 22.80 (0-8114-7255-8) Raintree Steck-V.

Zadra, Dan. Explorers of America: Lewis & Clark. rev. ed. (gr. 2-4). 1988. PLB 14.95 (0-88682-183-5) Creative Ed.

LEWIS AND CLARK EXPEDITION

Blumberg, Rhoda. The Incredible Journey of Lewis & Clark. LC 87-4235. (Illus.). 144p. (gr. 4 up). 1987. 17.95 (0-688-06512-0) Lothrop.

Brown, Marion M. Sacagawea: Indian Interpreter to Lewis & Clark. LC 87-33810. (Illus.). 119p. (gr. 4 up). 1988. PLB 14.40 (0-516-03262-3); pap. 5.95 (0-516-43262-1) Childrens.

Daugherty, James. Of Courage Undaunted: Across the Continent with Lewis & Clark. LC 90-49171. (Illus.). 168p. (gr. 6-10). 1991. PLB 13.95 (1-55905-089-6) Marshall Cavendish.

Edwards, Judith. Colter's Run. Potter, John, illus. 32p. (Orig.). 1993. pap. 5.95 (1-56044-178-X) Falcon Pr MT.

Fitz-Gerald, Christine A. Meriwether Lewis & William Clark: The Northwest Expedition. LC 90-20696. (Illus.). 128p. (gr. 3 up). 1991. PLB 20.55 (0-516-03061-2); pap. 9.95 (0-516-43061-0) Childrens.

Kroll, Steven. Lewis & Clark: Explorers of the Far West. Williams, Richard, illus. LC 92-40427. 32p. (gr. 3-7). 1994. reinforced bdg. 16.95 (0-8234-1034-X) Holiday.

McGrath, Patrick. The Lewis & Clark Expedition. LC 84-40381. (Illus.). 64p. (gr. 5 up). 1984. PLB 12.95 (0-382-06828-9); pap. 7.95 (0-382-09899-4) Silver Burdett Pr.

Moulton, Gary. Lewis & Clark & the Route to the Pacific. Goetzmann, William H., ed. Collins, Michael, intro. by. (Illus.). 112p. (gr. 5 up). 1991. lib. bdg. 18.95 (0-7910-1327-8) Chelsea Hse.

Noonan, Jon. Lewis & Clark. LC 92-9381. (Illus.). 48p. (gr. 5). 1993. text ed. 12.95 RSBE (0-89686-707-2, Crestwood Hse) Macmillan Child Grp.

Petersen, David & Coburn, Mark. Meriwether Lewis & William Clark: Soldiers, Explorers, & Partners in History. LC 88-14040. (Illus.). 152p. (gr. 4 up). 1988. PLB 14.40 (0-516-03264-X) Childrens.

Raphael, Elaine & Bolognese, Don. Sacajawea: The Journey West. LC 93-49002. (gr. 1-3). 1994. 12.95 (0-590-47898-2) Scholastic Inc.

Roop, Peter & Roop, Connie. Off the Map: The Journals of Lewis & Clark. Tanner, Tim, illus. LC 92-18340. 48p. (gr. 3-7). 1993. 14.95 (0-8027-8207-8); PLB 15.85 (0-8027-8208-6) Walker & Co.

Sabin, Francene. Lewis & Clark. Lawn, John, illus. LC 84-2642. 32p. (gr. 3-6). 1985. PLB 9.49 (0-8167-0224-1); pap. text ed. 2.95 (0-8167-0225-X) Troll Assocs.

Stein, R. Conrad. The Story of the Lewis & Clark Expedition. Aronson, Lou, illus. LC 78-4648. 32p. (gr. 3-6). 1978. pap. 3.95 (0-516-44620-7) Childrens.

Twist, Clint. Lewis & Clark: Exploring North America. LC 93-33624. 1994. PLB 22.80 (0-8114-7255-8) Raintree Steck-V.

LEWIS AND CLARK EXPEDITION–FICTION

Bohner, Charles. Bold Journey: West with Lewis & Clark. LC 84-19328. (Illus.). 171p. (gr. 5 up). 1985. 13.45 (0-395-36691-7); pap. 5.95 (0-395-54978-7) HM.

LEXINGTON, BATTLE OF, 1775

Nordstrom, Judy. Concord & Lexington. LC 92-23392. (Illus.). 72p. (gr. 4 up). 1993. text ed. 14.95 RSBE (0-87518-567-3, Dillon) Macmillan Child Grp.

LIBERIA

Department of Geography, Lerner Publications. Liberia in Pictures. (Illus.). 64p. (gr. 5 up). 1988. PLB 17.50 (0-8225-1837-6) Lerner Pubns.

Humphrey, Sally. A Family in Liberia. (Illus.). 32p. (gr. 2-5). 1987. PLB 13.50 (0-8225-1674-8) Lerner Pubns.

Stewart, Gail B. Liberia. LC 91-31532. (Illus.). 48p. (gr. 6-7). 1992. text ed. 4.95 RSBE (0-89686-746-3, Crestwood Hse) Macmillan Child Grp.

LIBERTY

see also Civil Rights; Religious Liberty

Deegan, Paul. Fights over Rights. Abbott, Phyllis, et al, eds. Wadsworth, Elaine, illus. LC 87-71091. 48p. (gr. 4). 1987. lib. bdg. 10.95 (0-939179-21-0) Abdo & Dghtrs.

—Right to Bear Arms. Abbott, Phyllis, et al, eds. Wadsworth, Elaine, illus. LC 87-71088. 32p. (gr. 4). 1987. lib. bdg. 10.95 (0-939179-24-5) Abdo & Dghtrs.

—Search & Seizure. Abbott, Phyllis, et al, eds. Wadsworth, Elaine, illus. LC 87-71090. 32p. (gr. 4). 1987. lib. bdg. 10.95 (0-939179-23-7) Abdo & Dghtrs.

Monroe, Judy. Censorship. LC 89-25407. (Illus.). 48p. (gr. 5-6). 1990. text ed. 4.95 RSBE (0-89686-490-1, Crestwood Hse) Macmillan Child Grp.

Moore, Ruth N. In Search of Liberty, Vol. 1. Converse, James, illus. LC 83-10827. 168p. (Orig.). (gr. 7-10). 1983. pap. 4.95 (0-8361-3340-4) Herald Pr.

Sabin, Francene. Freedom Documents. Dole, Bob, illus. LC 84-8596. 32p. (gr. 3-6). 1985. PLB 9.49 (0-8167-0238-1); pap. text ed. 2.95 (0-8167-0239-X) Troll Assocs.

Steffens, Bradley. Censorship. (Illus.). (gr. 5-8). 1994. 14.95 (1-56006-166-9) Lucent Bks.

Stewart, Bonnie. L Is for Liberty. Elder, John, illus. 32p. (gr. 1 up). 1993. 15.95g (1-879244-00-4) Windom Bks.

LIBERTY BELL

Boland, Charles M. Ring in the Jubilee: The Story of America's Liberty Bell. LC 72-80407. (Illus.). 96p. (gr. 6 up). 1973. pap. 5.95 (0-85699-055-8) Chatham Pr.

LIBERTY OF SPEECH

see Free Speech

LIBRARIANS

Johnson, Jean. Librarians A to Z. Johnson, Jean, photos by & illus. 48p. (gr. 1-3). 1989. 11.95 (0-8027-6841-5); lib. bdg. 12.85 (0-8027-6842-3) Walker & Co.

Paige, David. A Day in the Life of a Librarian. Ruhlin, Roger, illus. LC 84-8552. 32p. (gr. 4-8). 1985. PLB 11.79 (0-8167-0101-6); pap. text ed. 2.95 (0-8167-0102-4) Troll Assocs.

LIBRARIANS–FICTION

Pinkwater, Daniel. Aunt Lulu. Pinkwater, Daniel, illus. LC 88-1736. 32p. (gr. k-3). 1988. RSBE 13.95 (0-02-774661-5, Macmillan Child Bk) Macmillan Child Grp.

Thaler, Mike. Cannon the Librarian. Lee, Jared, illus. 32p. (Orig.). 1993. pap. 3.50 (0-380-76964-6, Camelot Young) Avon.

LIBRARIANSHIP

see Library Science

LIBRARIES

Cleary, Florence D. Discovering Books & Libraries: A Handbook for Students in the Middle & Upper Grades. 2nd ed. LC 76-55368. 196p. (gr. 7-12). 1977. pap. 10.00 (0-8242-0594-4) Wilson.

De Ponce, Blanca N. La Aventura de Estudiar: Programa para Desarrollar Destrezas de Estudio e Informacion en el nivel Elemental e Intermedio. Figueroa, Ivelisse, illus. (SPA.). 100p. (Orig.). (gr. 5-9). 1984. write for info. B Ponce.

Gibbons, Gail. Check It Out! The Book about Libraries. Gibbons, Gail, illus. 32p. (ps-3). 1988. pap. 3.95 (*0-15-216401-4*, Voyager Bks) HarBrace.

Gold, John C. Board of Education vs. Pico (1982) Book Banning. LC 93-23487. 1994. text ed. 14.95 (*0-02-736272-8*, New Discovery Bks) Macmillan Child Grp.

Hoffman, Jeanne & Prizzi, Elaine. Big Fearon Dictionary & Library Skills Kit. (gr. 4-8). 1989. pap. 20.95 (*0-8224-3055-X*) Fearon Teach Aids.

Jaspersohn, William. My Hometown Library. LC 92-17372. 1994. 14.95 (*0-395-55723-2*) HM.

Knowlton, Jack. Books & Libraries. Barton, Harriett, illus. LC 89-70804. 48p. (gr. 2-5). 1991. PLB 14.89 (*0-06-021610-7*) HarpC Child Bks.

—Books & Libraries. Barton, Harriett, illus. LC 89-70804. 48p. (gr. 2-5). 1993. pap. 5.95 (*0-06-446153-X*, Trophy) HarpC Child Bks.

Lakritz, Esther. Developing Library Skills. 112p. (gr. 4-8). 1989. 10.95 (*0-86653-481-4*, GA1081) Good Apple.

Lloyd, David & Geldard, William. Living in Love. 200p. (ps). 1993. pap. 16.00 (*0-89577-527-1*, Dist. by Random) RD Assn.

McCutcheon, Randall. Can You Find It? Twenty-Five Library Scavenger Hunts to Sharpen Your Research Skills. rev. ed. LC 91-30105. (Illus.). 208p. (gr. 9 up). pap. 10.95 (*0-915793-38-5*) Free Spirit Pub.

McInerney, Claire. Find It! The Inside Story at Your Library. Pulver, Harry, illus. 56p. (gr. 4-6). 1989. PLB 14.95 (*0-8225-2425-2*) Lerner Pubns.

Murtha, Philly. Library: Your Teammate. Redpath, Ann, ed. 32p. (gr. 4 up). 1984. PLB 11.95 (*0-87191-999-0*) Creative Ed.

Santrey, Laurence. Using the Library. Dole, Bob, illus. LC 84-2590. 32p. (gr. 3-6). 1985. PLB 9.49 (*0-8167-0122-9*); pap. text ed. 2.95 (*0-8167-0123-7*) Troll Assocs.

Shapiro, Lillian L. Teaching Yourself in Libraries: A Guide to the High School Media Center & Other Libraries. LC 78-16616. 180p. (gr. 7-12). 1978. 10.00 (*0-8242-0628-2*) Wilson.

Weil, Lisl. Let's Go to the Library. Weil, Lisl, illus. LC 90-55105. 32p. (ps-3). 1990. reinforced 13.95 (*0-8234-0829-9*) Holiday.

LIBRARIES, CHILDREN'S

see also Children–Books and Reading; Children's Literature

Tuma-Church, Deb. The Storytime Handbook. Tuma-Church, Deb, illus. 73p. (ps-5). 1988. wkbk. spiral bdg. 7.95 (*0-939644-37-1*) Media Pub.

LIBRARIES, CHILDREN'S–FICTION

Bonsall, Crosby N. Tell Me Some More. Siebel, Fritz, illus. LC 61-5773. 64p. (gr. k-3). 1961. PLB 13.89 (*0-06-020601-2*) HarpC Child Bks.

Freeman, Don. Quiet! There's a Canary in the Library. Freeman, Dan, illus. LC 69-15398. 48p. (gr. k-3). 1969. 11.45 (*0-516-08737-1*); pap. 3.95 (*0-516-48737-X*) Childrens.

LIBRARIES–FICTION

Alexander, Martha. How My Library Grew, By Dinah. Alexander, Martha, illus. 32p. (gr. k-5). 1983. 18.00 (*0-8242-0679-7*) Wilson.

Beatty, Patricia. The Nickel Plated Beauty. LC 92-27683. 272p. (gr. 5 up). 1993. pap. 4.95 (*0-688-12279-5*, Pub. by Beech Tree Bks) Morrow.

Clifford, Eth. Help! I'm a Prisoner in the Library. (Illus.). 112p. (gr. 2-5). 1979. 13.45 (*0-395-28478-3*) HM.

—Help! I'm a Prisoner in the Library. 96p. (gr. 4-6). 1991. pap. 2.95 (*0-590-44351-8*, Apple Paperbacks) Scholastic Inc.

Crow, Sherry R. Library Lightning. (Illus.). 128p. (gr. 3-6). 1990. pap. 12.95 (*0-913839-72-8*) Bk Lures.

Enerson, Laura. Our Library Lives in a Bus. Robin, illus. LC 77-71462. (gr. 3-5). 1977. 3.50 (*0-930480-01-5*) R H Barnes.

Furtado, Jo. Sorry, Miss Folio! Joos, Frederic, illus. (ps-3). 1992. pap. 6.95 (*0-916291-41-3*) Kane-Miller Bk.

Greenwald, Sheila. The Mariah Delany Lending Library Disaster. (gr. k-6). 1986. pap. 2.75 (*0-440-45327-5*, YB) Dell.

Hautzig, Deborah. Una Visita a la Biblioteca De Sesame Street. Saunders, Paola B., tr. Mathieu, Joe, illus. LC 92-16609. (SPA.). 32p. (ps-3). 1993. pap. 2.25 (*0-679-83943-7*) Random Bks Yng Read.

Houghton, Eric. Walter's Magic Wand. Teasdale, Denise, illus. LC 89-35400. 32p. (ps-1). 1990. 13.95 (*0-531-05851-4*); PLB 13.99 (*0-531-08451-5*) Orchard Bks Watts.

Hutchins, Hazel. Nicholas at the Library. Ohi, Ruth, illus. 32p. (ps-2). 1990. 14.95 (*1-55037-134-7*, Pub. by Annick CN); pap. 5.95 (*1-55037-132-0*, Pub. by Annick CN) Firefly Bks Ltd.

Landon, Lucinda. Meg MacKintosh & the Mystery in the Locked Library: A Solve-It-Yourself Mystery. LC 92-19948. 1993. 13.95 (*0-316-51374-1*, Joy St Bks) Little.

Loomis, Christine. At the Library. Poydar, Nancy, illus. LC 93-10882. 1994. 14.95 (*0-590-72831-8*); pap. 4.95 (*0-590-49489-9*) Scholastic Inc.

Loves, June. This Is the Book That I Borrowed. McClelland, Linda, illus. LC 92-31955. 1993. 4.25 (*0-383-03598-8*) SRA Schl Grp.

Pellowski, Michael J. Ghost in the Library. Durham, Robert, illus. LC 88-1236. 48p. (Orig.). (gr. 1-4). 1989. PLB 10.59 (*0-8167-1337-5*); pap. text ed. 3.50 (*0-8167-1338-3*) Troll Assocs.

Poulet, Virginia. Blue Bug Goes to the Library. Anderson, Peggy P., illus. LC 79-15219. 32p. (ps-3). 1979. PLB 11.80 (*0-516-03430-8*) Childrens.

Warner, Gertrude C., created by. The Deserted Library Mystery. (Illus.). (gr. 2-7). 1991. 10.95g (*0-8075-1561-2*); pap. 3.50g (*0-8075-1560-4*) A Whitman.

LIBRARIES–POETRY

Three Words a Day for Kids: A Fun & Helpful Calendar Journal. 366p. (gr. 1-6). 1993. spiral bdg. 8.50 (*1-882835-21-2*) STA-Kris.

LIBRARY SCIENCE

Here are entered general works on the organization and administration of libraries. Works about services offered by libraries to patrons are entered under Library Service.

Cook, Sybilla. Library Flipper: A Dewey Decimal System Guide. 49p. (gr. 4 up). 1988. trade edition 5.95 (*1-878383-08-6*) C Lee Pubns.

Daniels, Lolee & Pollard, Rita. The Library Experience: Sharing the Responsibility. Sullivan-Szarek, Mary, illus. (gr. 6-8). 1987. Teacher's manual, 130pp. 64.95 (*0-935637-08-7*); Student workbook, 120pp. 11.99 (*0-935637-09-5*); Transparency Set. 85.00 (*0-935637-10-9*) Cambridge Strat.

How to Use Your Library. 1972. pap. 1.95 (*0-87738-030-9*) Youth Ed.

Santa, Beauel M. & Hardy, Lois L. How to Use the Library. 2nd ed. LC 55-6606. (Illus.). 128p. (gr. 7-12). 1966. pap. text ed. 7.95x (*0-87015-145-2*) Pacific Bks.

LIBRARY SCIENCE–VOCATIONAL GUIDANCE

Puedo Ser Bibliotecaria: (I Can Be a Librarian) LC 87-35537. (SPA & ENG.). 32p. (gr. k-3). 1989. pap. 3.95 (*0-516-51913-1*) Childrens.

LIBRARY SERVICE

Mallett, Jerry & Bartch, Marian. Booker's Bunch, Bk. 1. 80p. (gr. 3-4). 1988. PLB 9.59 (*0-8000-4735-4*, 036417) Perma-Bound.

—Booker's Bunch, Bk. 2. 88p. (gr. 3-4). 1988. PLB 9.59 (*0-8000-4736-2*, 036418) Perma-Bound.

Windsor, Laura. Beating the Term Paper Deadline: A Student Guide to Getting Help at the Library - in Record Time. 24p. (Orig.). (ps-12). 1990. 4.95 (*0-918734-34-7*) Reymont.

LIBYA

Brill, Marlene T. Libya. LC 87-13192. (Illus.). 128p. (gr. 5-9). 1987. PLB 20.55 (*0-516-02776-X*) Childrens.

Gottfried, Ted. Libya: Desert Land in Conflict. LC 93-15096. (Illus.). 160p. (gr. 7 up). 1994. PLB 16.90 (*1-56294-351-0*) Millbrook Pr.

Malcolm, Peter. Libya. LC 92-38756. 1993. 21.95 (*1-85435-573-2*); Set. write for info. (*1-85435-571-6*) Marshall Cavendish.

LIFE

Alexander, Lloyd. The First Two Lives of Lukas-Kasha. 224p. (gr. 7 up). 1982. pap. 2.25 (*0-440-42784-3*, YB) Dell.

Aten, Jerry. Prime Time Life Skills. Filkins, Vanessa, illus. 64p. (gr. 2-5). 1983. wkbk. 8.95 (*0-86653-126-2*, GA 487) Good Apple.

George, Michael. Life. LC 93-12205. (gr. 4 up). 1994. PLB 18.95 (*0-88682-602-0*) Creative Ed.

Osei, G. K. The African Concept of Life & Death. Obaba, Al I., ed. (Illus.). 49p. (Orig.). 1991. pap. text ed. 3.00 (*0-916157-64-4*) African Islam Miss Pubns.

Pfeffer, Susan B. About David: A Novel. LC 80-65837. 176p. (gr. 7 up). 1980. 11.95 (*0-385-28013-0*) Delacorte.

Warburg, Sandol S. Growing Time. Weisgard, Leonard, illus. 48p. (gr. k-3). 1975. pap. 1.50 (*0-395-19971-9*, Sandpiper) HM.

LIFE (BIOLOGY)

see also Biology; Genetics; Old Age; Reproduction

Blueford, J. R., et al. Life Cycle - A Diversity in a Balance. (gr. k-6). 1992. 24.95 (*1-56638-157-6*) Math Sci Nucleus.

Burnie, David. Life. LC 93-33101. (gr. 3 up). 1994. 15.95 (*1-56458-477-1*) Dorling Kindersley.

Dahl, Tessa. Babies, Babies, Babies. Dodds, Siobhan, illus. 32p. (ps-2). 1991. 12.95 (*0-670-83921-3*) Viking Child Bks.

FS Staff & Gamlin, Linda. Life on Earth. Hayward, Ron, illus. LC 88-50508. 40p. (gr. 4-9). 1988. PLB 12.40 (*0-531-17120-5*, Gloucester Pr) Watts.

Raffi. Everything Grows. McMillan, Bruce, illus. LC 88-37162. 32p. (ps-2). 1989. 14.00 (*0-517-57387-3*) Crown Bks Yng Read.

Zoehfeld. What's Alive. 1995. 15.00 (*0-06-023443-1*); PLB 14.89 (*0-06-023444-X*) HarpC Child Bks.

LIFE, CHRISTIAN

see Christian Life

LIFE–ORIGIN

Asimov, Isaac. How Did We Find Out about the Beginning of Life? Wool, David, illus. LC 81-71196. 64p. (gr. 4-7). 1982. PLB 10.85 (*0-8027-6448-7*) Walker & Co.

Doney, Malcolm & Doney, Meryl. Who Made Me? Butterworth, Nick & Inkpen, Mick, illus. 38p. (ps-3). 1987. 9.99 (*0-310-55660-0*, 19064) Zondervan.

FS Staff & Gamlin, Linda. Origins of Life. Hayward, Ron, illus. LC 88-50509. 40p. (gr. 4-9). 1988. PLB 12.40 (*0-531-17119-1*, Gloucester Pr) Watts.

Garassino, Alessandro. Life: Origins & Evolution. Serini, Rocco, tr. from ITA. Gonano, Maria E. & Moriggia, Rosalba, illus. LC 94-8582. 48p. (gr. 6-8). 1994. PLB write for info. (*0-8114-3335-8*) Raintree Steck-V.

Lasky, Kathryn. Traces of Life: The Origins of Humankind. Powell, Whitney, illus. LC 89-12092. 144p. (gr. 5 up). 1990. 16.95 (*0-688-07237-2*) Morrow Jr Bks.

Wexo, John B. Life Begins. 24p. (gr. 3 up). 1991. PLB 14.95 (*0-88682-387-0*) Creative Ed.

LIFE, SPIRITUAL

see Spiritual Life

LIFE ON OTHER PLANETS

see also Interstellar Communication

Berger, Melvin. If You Lived on Mars. LC 88-9105. (Illus.). 80p. (gr. 4-6). 1989. 13.95 (*0-525-67260-5*, Lodestar Bks) Dutton Child Bks.

Branley, Franklyn M. Is There Life in Outer Space? Madden, Don, illus. LC 83-45057. 32p. (ps-3). 1984. (Crowell Jr Bks); PLB 14.89 (*0-690-04375-9*) HarpC Child Bks.

Crum, Wesley S. UFO Crash at Aztec: The Aztec Recovery, 25 March 1948. Stevens, Wendelle C., ed. (Illus.). 1p. (gr. 9-12). 1989. poster 3.95 (*0-934269-16-5*) UFO Photo.

Darling, David. Could You Ever Meet an Alien? (Illus.). 60p. (gr. 5 up). 1991. text ed. 14.95 RSBE (*0-87518-447-2*, Dillon) Macmillan Child Grp.

Dickinson, Terence. Extraterrestrials: A Field Guide for Earthlings. Schaller, Adolf, illus. 64p. (gr. 2 up). 1994. PLB 17.95 (*0-921820-86-0*, Pub. by Camden Hse CN); pap. 9.95 (*0-921820-87-9*, Pub. by Camden Hse CN) Firefly Bks Ltd.

What will THEY look like? That is the question addressed in this wonderfully illustrated book for young readers who want to explore beyond the cardboard aliens of television science fiction to find out what science says about our cosmic cousins from other planets - if they exist. Author Terence Dickinson, an astronomy instructor who has written extensively on subjects ranging from planetary exploration to cosmology, examines the picture we have absorbed from TV & movies about creatures from other planets, from the friendly visitor in E.T. THE EXTRA-TERRESTRIAL to the savage creature in ALIEN & the gaggle of other-worldly folk from Star Trek & its clones. Dickinson then explains how the variety of environments in the universe could give rise to creatures far more different from us than anything invented in Hollywood. Through the talents of illustrator Adolf Schaller, one of the chief artists for Carl Sagan's COSMOS television series, alien worlds come alive with plants, insects & animals never dreamed of before. A unique blend of science & imagination, EXTRA-TERRESTRIALS will compel anyone who has ever thought about what - & who - might be out there. *Publisher Provided Annotation.*

Fradin, Dennis. Search for Extraterrestrial Intelligence. LC 87-14618. (Illus.). 48p. (gr. k-4). 1987. pap. 4.95 (*0-516-41242-6*) Childrens.

Gutsch, William A., Jr. The Search for Extraterrestrial Life. (Illus.). 144p. (gr. 5-9). 1991. 14.00 (*0-517-57818-2*) Crown Bks Yng Read.

Kraus, John. Big Ear Two: Listening for Other-Worlds. (Illus.). 400p. (gr. 8 up). 1994. 24.95 (*1-882484-11-8*); pap. 14.95 (*1-882484-12-6*) CYGNUS-QUASAR Bks.

Marsh, Carole. The Backyard Searcher's Extra Terrestrial Log Book. (Illus.). (gr. 4-9). 1994. PLB 24.95 (*1-55609-282-2*); pap. 14.95 (*0-935326-27-8*) Gallopade Pub Group.

—How to Find an Extra Terrestrial in Your Own Backyard. (Illus.). 1994. 24.95 (*0-935326-09-X*) Gallopade Pub Group.

Rasmussen, Richard. Extraterrestrial Life. LC 91-15564. (Illus.). 112p. (gr. 5-8). 1991. PLB 14.95 (*1-56006-126-X*) Lucent Bks.

Stevens, Wendelle C. UFO Calendar 1990. (Illus.). 26p. (gr. 9-12). 1989. wkbk. 9.95 (*0-934269-19-X*) UFO Photo.

LIFE SUPPORT SYSTEMS (SPACE ENVIRONMENT)
see also Apollo Project
LIFESAVING
Dalton, J. W. The Life Savers of Cape Cod. Ackerman, Frank, intro. by. (Illus.). 176p. 1991. pap. 8.95 (*0-940160-49-8*) Parnassus Imprints.
Landau, Elaine. Why Are They Starving Themselves? Understanding Anorexia Nervosa & Bulimia. Schor, Ellen, intro. by. LC 82-24913. 160p. (gr. 7 up). 1983. lib. bdg. 13.98 (*0-671-45582-6*, J Messner); pap. 5.95 (*0-671-49492-9*) S&S Trade.
Lifesaving. (Illus.). 64p. (gr. 6-12). 1980. pap. 1.85 (*0-8395-3278-4*, 33297) BSA.
LIFTS
see Elevators
LIGHT
see also Color; Lasers; Optics; Radioactivity; X Rays
Anderson, L. W. Light & Color. rev. ed. LC 87-23225. (Illus.). 48p. (gr. 2-6). 1987. PLB 10.95 (*0-8172-3257-5*) Raintree Steck-V.
Ardley, Neil. Light. LC 91-25740. (Illus.). 48p. (gr. 8-9). 1992. text ed. 13.95 RSBE (*0-02-705667-8*, New Discovery) Macmillan Child Grp.
Asimov, Isaac. How Did We Find Out about the Speed of Light? Wool, David, illus. LC 86-4085. 64p. (gr. 5 up). 1986. 10.95 (*0-8027-6637-4*); PLB 11.85 (*0-8027-6613-7*) Walker & Co.
Bains, Rae. Light. Harriton, Chuck, illus. LC 84-2719. 32p. (gr. 3-6). 1985. PLB 9.49 (*0-8167-0202-0*); pap. text ed. 2.95 (*0-8167-0203-9*) Troll Assocs.
Cooper, Jason. Light. LC 92-8808. 1992. 12.67 (*0-86593-166-6*); 9.50s.p. (*0-685-59295-2*) Rourke Corp.
Crews, Donald. Light. LC 80-20273. (Illus.). 32p. (ps-1). 1981. PLB 13.88 (*0-688-00310-9*) Greenwillow.
Devonshire, Hilary. Light. LC 91-8401. (Illus.). 32p. (gr. 5-7). 1992. PLB 12.40 (*0-531-14126-8*) Watts.
Evans, David & Williams, Claudette. Color & Light. LC 92-53480. (Illus.). 24p. (gr. k-3). 1993. 9.95 (*1-56458-207-8*) Dorling Kindersley.
Houbre, Gilbert, illus. Light. Jeunesse, Gallimard, et al. LC 94-49003. (Illus.). (ps-2). 1994. 11.95 (*0-590-48327-7*) Scholastic Inc.
Hudson, Terry & Peacock, Graham. The Super Science Book of Light. LC 93-6837. (Illus.). 32p. (gr. 4-8). 1993. 14.95 (*1-56847-022-3*) Thomson Lrning.
Lauber, Patricia. What Do You See? Wexler, Jerome & Lessin, Leonard, photos by. LC 93-2388. (Illus.). 48p. (gr. 3-7). 1994. 17.00 (*0-517-59390-4*); PLB 17.99 (*0-517-59391-2*) Crown Bks Yng Read.
Light. (gr. 7-12). 1991. pap. 15.70 (*0-941008-87-8*) Tops Learning.
Mack, Karen. The Magical Adventures of Sun Beams. Johnson, Tani B., illus. 32p. (ps-4). 1992. pap. 5.95 (*0-9631644-0-6*) Shooting Star.
Morgan, Sally & Morgan, Adrian. Using Light. LC 93-21535. 1993. write for info. (*0-8160-2980-6*) Facts on File.
Murphy, Pat, et al. Bending Light: An Exploratorium Toolbook. Osborn, Stephen, illus. LC 92-20336. 1993. 15.95 (*0-316-25851-2*) Little.
Oxlade, Chris. Light. Thompson, Ian, illus. LC 94-5549. 30p. (gr. 2-5). 1994. 12.95 (*0-8120-6445-3*); pap. 4.95 (*0-8120-1984-9*) Barron.
Peacock, Graham. Light. LC 93-7522. (Illus.). 32p. (gr. 2-5). 1993. 14.95 (*1-56847-073-8*) Thomson Lrning.
Pomeroy, Johanna P. Content Area Reading Skills Light: Main Idea. (Illus.). (gr. 3). 1989. pap. text ed. 3.25 (*1-55737-687-5*) Ed Activities.
Richardson, Joy. Light. LC 92-14420. 1993. 11.40 (*0-531-14240-X*) Watts.
Robson, Pam. Light, Color & Optics Lenses. LC 92-37097. (Illus.). 32p. (gr. 4-7). 1993. PLB 12.40 (*0-531-17407-7*, Gloucester Pr) Watts.
Schoberle, Cecile. Day Lights, Night Lights. Stevenson, Harvey, illus. LC 93-18680. (gr. 4 up). 1994. pap. 14. 00 (*0-671-87439-X*, S&S BFYR) S&S Trade.
Searle-Barnes, Bonita. Light. (Illus.). 32p. (gr. k-3). 1993. 6.99 (*0-7459-2695-9*) Lion USA.
—The Wonder of God's World: Light. Smithson, Colin, illus. LC 92-44275. 1993. 6.99 (*0-7459-2022-5*) Lion USA.
Taylor, Barbara. Light. LC 92-7500. 1992. 12.40 (*0-531-17381-X*, Gloucester Pr) Watts.
Watson, Philip. Light Fantastic. Scruton, Clive & Fenton, Ronald, illus. LC 82-80989. 48p. (gr. 3-6). 1983. PLB 11.93 (*0-688-00969-7*) Lothrop.
Wilkins, Mary-Jane. Air, Light & Water. Bull, Peter, illus. LC 90-42620. 40p. (Orig.). (gr. 2-5). 1991. pap. 3.95 (*0-679-80859-0*) Random Bks Yng Read.
LIGHT–EXPERIMENTS
Ardley, Neil. Science Book of Light. 29p. (gr. 2-5). 1991. 9.95 (*0-15-200577-3*) HarBrace.
Broekel, Ray. Experiments with Light. LC 85-30888. (Illus.). 48p. (gr. k-4). 1986. PLB 12.85 (*0-516-01278-9*); pap. 4.95 (*0-516-41278-7*) Childrens.
Davis, Kay & Oldsfield, Wendy. Light. LC 91-30067. (Illus.). 32p. (gr. 2-5). 1991. PLB 19.97 (*0-8114-3006-5*); pap. 4.95 (*0-8114-1530-9*) Raintree Steck-V.
Devonshire, Hilary. Light. LC 91-8401. (Illus.). 32p. (gr. 5-7). 1992. PLB 12.40 (*0-531-14126-8*) Watts.
Edom, H. Science with Light & Mirrors. (Illus.). 24p. (gr. 1-4). 1992. PLB 12.96 (*0-88110-545-7*, Usborne); pap. 4.95 (*0-7460-0696-9*, Usborne) EDC.
Gardner, Robert. Light. (Illus.). 136p. (gr. 7 up). 1990. lib. bdg. 14.98 (*0-671-69037-X*, J Messner); pap. 9.95 (*0-671-69042-6*) S&S Trade.
—Science Projects about Light. LC 93-23719. (Illus.). 128p. (gr. 6 up). 1994. lib. bdg. 17.95 (*0-89490-529-5*) Enslow Pubs.
Glover, David. Sound & Light. LC 92-40213. 32p. (gr. 1-4). 1993. 10.95 (*1-85697-839-7*, Kingfisher LKC); pap. 5.95 (*1-85697-935-0*) LKC.
Murphy, Bryan. Experiment with Light. 32p. (gr. 2-5). 1991. PLB 17.50 (*0-8225-2454-6*) Lerner Pubns.
Murphy, Pat, et al. Bending Light: An Exploratorium Toolbook. Osborn, Stephen, illus. LC 92-20336. 1993. 15.95 (*0-316-25851-2*) Little.
Rowe, Julian & Perham, Molly. Colorful Light. LC 93-8217. (Illus.). 32p. (gr. 1-4). 1993. PLB 13.95 (*0-516-08131-4*) Childrens.
Searle-Barnes, Bonita. Light. (Illus.). 32p. (gr. k-3). 1993. 6.99 (*0-7459-2695-9*) Lion USA.
—The Wonder of God's World: Light. Smithson, Colin, illus. LC 92-44275. 1993. 6.99 (*0-7459-2022-5*) Lion USA.
Stine, Megan, et al. Hands-On Science: Color & Light. Taback, Simms, illus. LC 92-56889. 1993. PLB 18.60 (*0-8368-0954-8*) Gareth Stevens Inc.
Taylor, Barbara. Bouncing & Bending Light. LC 89-36213. (gr. 4-6). 1990. PLB 12.40 (*0-531-14014-8*) Watts.
—Color & Light. LC 91-9571. (Illus.). 40p. (gr. k-4). 1991. PLB 12.90 (*0-531-19127-3*, Warwick) Watts.
—Hear! Hear! The Science of Sound. Bull, Peter, et al, illus. LC 90-42617. 40p. (Orig.). (gr. 2-5). 1991. pap. 4.95 (*0-679-80813-2*) Random Bks Yng Read.
—Over the Rainbow! The Science of Color & Light. Bull, Peter, et al, illus. LC 91-4291. 40p. (Orig.). (gr. 2-5). 1992. pap. 4.95 (*0-679-82041-8*) Random Bks Yng Read.
Ward, Alan. Experimenting with Light & Illusions. Flax, Zena, illus. 48p. (gr. 2-7). 1991. lib. bdg. 12.95 (*0-7910-1514-9*) Chelsea Hse.
Williams, John. Simple Science Projects with Color & Light. LC 91-50544. (Illus.). 32p. (gr. 2-4). 1992. PLB 17.27 (*0-8368-0766-9*) Gareth Stevens Inc.
Zubrowski, Bernie. Mirrors. Doty, Roy, illus. LC 91-29142. 96p. (gr. 5 up). 1992. pap. 6.95 (*0-688-10591-2*, Pub. by Beech Tree Bks) Morrow.
—Mirrors: Finding Out about the Properties of Light. Doty, Roy, illus. LC 91-29142. 96p. (gr. 3 up). 1992. PLB 13.93 (*0-688-10592-0*) Morrow Jr Bks.
LIGHT AMPLIFICATION BY STIMULATED EMISSION OF RADIATION
see Lasers
LIGHT AND SHADE
see Shades and Shadows
LIGHTHOUSES
Cooper, J. Faros (Lighthouses) (SPA.). 1991. 8.95s.p. (*0-86592-936-X*) Rourke Enter.
—Lighthouses. 1991. 8.95s.p. (*0-86592-630-1*) Rourke Enter.
Gibbons, Gail. Beacons of Light: Lighthouses. Gibbons, Gail, illus. LC 89-33884. 32p. (gr. 1 up). 1990. 12.95 (*0-688-07379-4*); PLB 12.88 (*0-688-07380-8*, Morrow Jr Bks) Morrow Jr Bks.
Guiberson, Brenda Z. Lighthouses. 1995. write for info. (*0-8050-3170-7*) H Holt & Co.
LIGHTHOUSES–FICTION
Ardizzone, Edward. Tim to the Lighthouse. (Illus.). 48p. (gr. 1-4). 1987. pap. 6.95 (*0-19-272107-0*) OUP.
Biggar, Joan R. Shipwreck on the Lights. 160p. (Orig.). (gr. 5-8). 1992. pap. 3.99 (*0-570-04710-2*) Concordia.
Farrell, Vivian. Robert's Tall Friend: A Story of the Fire Island Lighthouse. Edwards, Christy, illus. LC 87-35246. 64p. (gr. 4-7). 1988. write for info. (*0-9619832-0-5*) Island-Metro Pubns.
Hoff, Syd. The Lighthouse Children. LC 92-41172. (Illus.). 32p. (ps-2). 1994. 14.00 (*0-06-022958-6*); PLB 13.89 (*0-06-022959-4*) HarpC Child Bks.
Jansson, Tove. Moominpappa at Sea. Hart, Kingsley, tr. from FIN. LC 93-1434. 1993. 17.00 (*0-374-35044-2*); pap. 4.95 (*0-374-45306-3*) FS&G.
McGough, Roger. The Lighthouse That Ran Away. (Illus.). 32p. (ps-2). 1992. 16.95 (*0-370-31471-9*, Pub. by Bodley Head UK) Trafalgar.
Roop, Peter & Roop, Connie. Keep the Lights Burning, Abbie. Hanson, Peter E., illus. (gr. 2-4). 1989. incl. cass. 19.95 (*0-87499-135-8*); pap. 12.95 incl. cass. (*0-87499-134-X*); Set; incl. 4 bks., guide, & cass. pap. 27.95 (*0-87499-136-6*) Live Oak Media.
Sargent, Ruth. The Littlest Lighthouse. Litchfield, Marion, illus. LC 81-66268. 32p. (Orig.). (ps-1). 1981. pap. 4.50 (*0-89272-119-7*) Down East.
LIGHTING
see also Candles
Aust, Siegfried. Light! A Bright Idea. Nyncke, Helge, illus. LC 92-9704. 1992. 18.95 (*0-8225-2155-5*) Lerner Pubns.
Cobb, Vicki & Cobb, Joshua. Light Action! Amazing Experiments with Optics. Cobb, Theo, illus. LC 92-25528. 208p. (gr. 6 up). 1993. 15.00 (*0-06-021436-8*); PLB 14.89 (*0-06-021437-6*) HarpC Child Bks.
LIGHTNING
Cutts, David. I Can Read About Thunder & Lightning. LC 78-66273. (Illus.). (gr. 2-6). 1979. pap. 2.50 (*0-89375-217-7*) Troll Assocs.
Kahl, Jonathan D. Thunderbolt: Learning about Lightning. LC 92-45177. 1993. 19.95 (*0-8225-2528-3*) Lerner Pubns.
Pearce, Q. L. Lightning & Other Wonders of the Sky. Steltenpohl, Jane, ed. Fraser, Mary A., illus. 64p. (gr. 4-6). 1989. PLB 12.98 (*0-671-68534-1*, J Messner); pap. 5.95 (*0-671-68648-8*) S&S Trade.
LIMERICKS
see also Nonsense Verses
Brown, Marc T., compiled by. & illus. Party Rhymes. LC 88-17680. 48p. (ps-3). 1988. 13.95 (*0-525-44402-5*, DCB) Dutton Child Bks.
Ciardi, John. The Hopeful Trout & Other Limericks. LC 87-23587. 1989. 13.45 (*0-395-43606-0*) HM.
—Hopeful Trout & Other Limericks. (gr. 4-7). 1992. pap. 3.80 (*0-395-61616-6*) HM.
Corbett, Scott. Jokes to Read in the Dark. Gusman, Annie, illus. LC 79-23129. 80p. (gr. 5-9). 1980. 12.95 (*0-525-32796-7*, 01063-320, DCB); (DCB) Dutton Child Bks.
Driver, Raymond. Animalimericks. 1994. pap. 5.95 (*0-671-87232-X*, Half Moon Bks) S&S Trade.
Gawron, Marlene. Busy Bodies: Finger Plays & Action Rhymes. rev. ed. (Illus.). 72p. (ps-1). 1985. pap. 5.50 (*0-913545-12-0*) Moonlight FL.
Lear, Edward. A Book of Nonsense. Lear, Edward, illus. LC 92-53176. 240p. 1992. 12.95 (*0-679-41798-2*, Evrymans Lib Childs Class) Knopf.
—Daffy Down Dillies: Silly Limericks. O'Brien, John, illus. LC 91-72986. 32p. 1992. 14.95 (*1-56397-007-4*) Boyds Mills Pr.
—A Little Book of Nonsense. Cott, Jonathan, ed. LC 93-24485. (Illus.). 224p. 1994. 6.00 (*1-56957-910-5*) Barefoot Bks.
—There Was an Old Man: A Gallery of Nonsense Rhythms, a Selection of Limericks. Lemieux, Michele, illus. LC 93-46492. 1994. write for info. (*0-688-10788-5*); PLB write for info. (*0-688-10789-3*) Morrow Jr Bks.
Lobel, Arnold. The Book of Pigericks. Lobel, Arnold, illus. LC 82-47730. 48p. (gr. k-3). 1983. PLB 14.89 (*0-06-023983-2*) HarpC Child Bks.
Palmer, Michele, ed. Rainy Day Rhymes: A Collection of Chants, Forecasts & Tales. Guerin, Penny, illus. LC 84-60412. 24p. (Orig.). (gr. k up). 1984. pap. 2.95 (*0-932306-02-0*) Rocking Horse.
Roehl, Harvey N. A Carousel of Limericks. Hyman, Pat, illus. LC 85-22538. 60p. (Orig.). (gr. 4-8). 1986. pap. 7.95 (*0-911572-47-3*) Vestal.
Thompson, Jonathon J., Jr. ABC Limericks. (Illus.). 40p. (gr. 3-6). 1992. 3.95 (*0-933479-04-2*) Thompson.
Wines, James, illus. Edward Lear's Nonsense. LC 93-20461. 32p. 1994. 12.95 (*0-8478-1682-6*) Rizzoli Intl.
Ziegler, Sandra K. Knock-Knocks, Limericks, & Other Silly Sayings. Magnuson, Diana, illus. LC 82-19764. 48p. (gr. 1-5). 1983. pap. 3.95 (*0-516-41872-6*) Childrens.
LIMITATION OF ARMAMENT
see Disarmament
LINCOLN, ABRAHAM, PRESIDENT U. S. 1809-1865
Abraham Lincoln. (Illus.). 24p. (gr. 2-5). 1987. pap. 2.50 (*0-671-62982-4*, Little Simon) S&S Trade.
Abraham Lincoln. (Illus.). (gr. 2-5). 1991. 8.95 (*0-8167-2568-3*) Troll Assocs.
Abraham Lincoln. 1992. 4.99 (*0-517-06996-2*) Random Hse Value.
Adler, David A. Un Libro Ilustrado sobre Abraham Lincoln. Mlawer, Teresa, tr. from ENG. Wallner, John & Wallner, Alexandra, illus. (SPA.). 32p. (ps-3). 1992. reinforced bdg. 14.95 (*0-8234-0980-5*); pap. 5.95 (*0-8234-0989-9*) Holiday.
—Picture Book of Abraham Lincoln. LC 88-16393. (Illus.). 32p. (ps-3). 1989. reinforced bdg. 15.95 (*0-8234-0731-4*); pap. 5.95 (*0-8234-0801-9*) Holiday.
Alden, Laura. President's Day. Friedman, Joy, illus. LC 93-37095. 32p. (ps-2). 1994. PLB 12.30 (*0-516-00691-6*) Childrens.
Bains, Rae. Abraham Lincoln. Smolinski, Dick, illus. LC 84-2581. 32p. (gr. 3-6). 1985. PLB 9.49 (*0-8167-0146-6*); pap. text ed. 2.95 (*0-8167-0147-4*) Troll Assocs.
Barkan, Joanne. Abraham Lincoln. Brook, Bonnie, ed. Miller, Lyle, illus. 32p. (gr. k-2). 1990. 4.95 (*0-671-69113-9*); PLB 6.95 (*0-671-69107-4*) Silver Pr.
Brandt, Keith. Abe Lincoln: The Young Years. LC 81-23172. (Illus.). 48p. (gr. 4-6). 1982. PLB 10.79 (*0-89375-750-0*); pap. text ed. 3.50 (*0-89375-751-9*) Troll Assocs.
Brenner, Martha. Abe Lincoln's Hat. Cook, Donald, illus. LC 93-31867. 48p. (Orig.). (gr. k-2). 1994. PLB 7.99 (*0-679-94977-1*); pap. 3.50 (*0-679-84977-7*) Random Bks Yng Read.
Cary, Barbara. Meet Abraham Lincoln. Marchesi, Stephen, illus. LC 88-19066. 72p. (gr. 2-4). 1989. pap. 3.50 (*0-394-81966-7*) Random Bks Yng Read.
Collins, David R. Abraham Lincoln. Quinton, Myron, illus. LC 76-2456. (gr. 3-6). 1976. pap. 6.95 (*0-915134-93-4*) Mott Media.
Colver, Anne. Abraham Lincoln: For the People. (Illus.). 80p. (gr. 2-6). 1992. Repr. of 1960 ed. lib. bdg. 12.95 (*0-7910-1414-2*) Chelsea Hse.
D'Aulaire, Ingri. Abraham Lincoln. (ps-3). 1987. pap. 10. 00 (*0-440-40690-0*) Dell.
D'Aulaire, Ingri & D'Aulaire, Edgar P. Abraham Lincoln. rev. ed. (gr. k-4). 1957. pap. 10.95 (*0-385-07669-X*) Doubleday.
Farr, Naunerle C. Abraham Lincoln - Franklin D. Roosevelt. Redondo, Nestor & LoFamia, Jun, illus. (gr. 4-12). 1979. pap. text ed. 2.95 (*0-88301-354-1*); wkbk. 1.25 (*0-88301-378-9*) Pendulum Pr.

Fradin, Dennis B. Lincoln's Birthday. LC 89-7665. (Illus.). 48p. (gr. 1-4). 1990. lib. bdg. 14.95 (0-89490-250-4) Enslow Pubs.

Freedman, Russell. Lincoln: A Photobiography. 160p. (gr. 4 up). 1987. 16.95 (0-89919-380-3, Clarion Bks) HM.

Gibbons, Ted. Lincoln & the Lady. 21p. 1989. pap. text ed. 2.50 (0-929985-11-7) Jackman Pubng.

Goodman, Ailene S. Abe Lincoln in Song & Story. LC 88-753827. (gr. 4-12). 1989. incl. audio cass. & guidebook 11.98 (0-9620704-0-8) A S Goodman.

Greene, Carol. Abraham Lincoln: President of a Divided Country. Dobson, Steven, illus. LC 89-33845. 48p. (gr. k-3). 1989. PLB 12.85 (0-516-04206-8); pap. 4.95 (0-516-44206-6) Childrens.

Hargrove, Jim. Abraham Lincoln (President's Biographies) (Illus.). 100p. (gr. 4-7). 1988. 14.40 (0-516-01359-9); pap. 6.95 (0-516-41359-7) Childrens.

Jacobs, William J. Lincoln. LC 90-8815. (Illus.). 48p. (gr. 4-6). 1991. SBE 13.95 (0-684-19274-8, Scribners Young Read) Macmillan Child Grp.

Kent, Zachary. The Story of the Election of Abraham Lincoln. Canaday, Ralph, illus. LC 85-23277. 32p. (gr. 3-6). 1986. pap. 3.95 (0-516-44669-X) Childrens.

Lee, Andrew. Lincoln. (Illus.). 64p. (gr. 6-9). 1989. 19.95 (0-7134-5662-0, Pub. by Batsford UK) Trafalgar.

McNeer, May. America's Abraham Lincoln. LC 90-48982. (Illus.). 128p. (gr. 6-10). 1991. PLB 13.95 (1-55905-090-X) Marshall Cavendish.

Melzer, Milton, ed. Lincoln, in His Own Words. Alcorn, Stephen, illus. LC 92-17431. 240p. 1993. 22.95 (0-15-245437-3); ltd. ed. 150.00 (0-15-245438-1) HarBrace.

Morgan, Lee & Cattaneo, Pietro. Abraham Lincoln. (Illus.). 104p. (gr. 5-8). 1990. 9.95 (0-382-09973-7); pap. 8.95 (0-382-24000-6) Silver Burdett Pr.

Murphy, Jim. The Long Road to Gettysburg. (Illus.). 128p. (gr. 4-7). 1992. 15.45 (0-395-55965-0, Clarion Bks) HM.

North, Sterling. Abe Lincoln: Log Cabin to White House. LC 87-4654. (Illus.). 160p. (gr. 5-9). 1987. pap. 4.99 (0-394-89179-1) Random Bks Yng Read.

Richards, Kenneth G. The Gettysburg Address. LC 91-43371. (Illus.). 32p. (gr. 3-6). 1992. PLB 12.30 (0-516-06654-4) Childrens.

—The Gettysburg Address. LC 91-43371. (Illus.). 32p. (gr. 3-6). 1993. pap. 3.95 (0-516-46654-2) Childrens.

Sandak, Cass R. The Lincolns. LC 92-6880. (Illus.). 48p. (gr. 5). 1992. text ed. 12.95 RSBE (0-89686-641-6, Crestwood Hse) Macmillan Child Grp.

Sandburg, Carl. Abe Lincoln Grows Up. Daugherty, James, illus. LC 74-17180. 222p. (gr. 7 up). 1985. 19.95 (0-15-201037-8, HB Juv Bks); pap. 5.95 (0-15-602615-5) HarBrace.

Shorto, Russell. Abraham Lincoln & the End of Slavery. (Illus.). 32p. (gr. 2-4). 1991. PLB 12.90 (1-878841-12-2); pap. 4.95 (1-878841-36-X) Millbrook Pr.

—Abraham Lincoln: To Preserve the Union. (Illus.). 160p. (gr. 5 up). 1990. lib. bdg. 12.95 (0-382-09937-0); pap. 7.95 (0-382-24046-4) Silver Burdett Pr.

Smith, Kathie B. Abraham Lincoln. Seward, James, illus. LC 86-28060. 24p. (gr. 4-6). 1987. (J Messner); PLB 5.99s.p. (0-685-18829-9) S&S Trade.

Sproule, Anna. Abraham Lincoln. LC 91-50540. (Illus.). 68p. (gr. 3-4). 1992. PLB 19.93 (0-8368-0620-4) Gareth Stevens Inc.

—Abraham Lincoln: Leader of a Nation in Crisis. LC 90-10374. (Illus.). 68p. (gr. 5-6). 1992. PLB 19.93 (0-8368-0216-0) Gareth Stevens Inc.

Stefoff, Rebecca. Abraham Lincoln: Sixteenth President of the United States. Young, Richard G., ed. LC 88-28488. (Illus.). (gr. 5-9). 1989. PLB 17.26 (0-944483-14-3) Garrett Ed Corp.

Stevenson, Augusta. Abraham Lincoln: The Great Emancipator. Robinson, Jerry, illus. 192p. (gr. 2-6). 1986. pap. 3.95 (0-02-042030-7, Aladdin) Macmillan Child Grp.

Trump, Fred. Lincoln's Little Girl. (Illus.). 184p. (gr. 5 up). 1994. 19.95 (1-56397-375-8) Boyds Mills Pr.

Wallower, Lucille. My Book about Abraham Lincoln. Gump, Patricia L., ed. (gr. 2-4). 1967. pap. 1.95 (0-931992-10-9) Penns Valley.

Woods, Andrew. Young Abraham Lincoln, Log-Cabin President. Schories, Pat, illus. LC 91-26570. 32p. (gr. k-2). 1992. text ed. 11.59 (0-8167-2532-2); pap. text ed. 2.95 (0-8167-2533-0) Troll Assocs.

Young, Robert. The Emancipation Proclamation: Why Lincoln Really Freed the Slaves. LC 94-9361. 1994. text ed. 14.95 (0-87518-613-0, Dillon) Macmillan Child Grp.

Zeldis, Malcah, illus. Honest Abe. Kunhardt, Edith, photos by. LC 91-47191. (Illus.). 32p. (gr. k up). 1993. 15.00 (0-688-11189-0); PLB 14.93 (0-688-11190-4) Greenwillow.

LINCOLN, ABRAHAM, PRESIDENT U. S. 1809-1865–ADDRESSES AND ESSAYS

Fritz, Jean. Just a Few Words, Mr. Lincoln: The Story of the Gettysburg Address. Robinson, Charles, illus. LC 92-35319. 48p. (gr. 2-3). 1993. 7.99 (0-448-40171-1, G&D); pap. 3.50 (0-448-40170-3, G&D) Putnam Pub Group.

LINCOLN, ABRAHAM, PRESIDENT U. S. 1809-1865–ASSASSINATION

Hamilton, Sue. The Assassination of Abraham Lincoln. Hamilton, John, ed. LC 89-84902. (Illus.). 32p. (gr. 4). 1990. PLB 11.96 (0-939179-54-7) Abdo & Dghtrs.

Hayman, Leroy. The Death of Lincoln: A Picture History of the Assassination. 128p. (gr. 4 up). 1989. pap. 2.95 (0-590-44570-7) Scholastic Inc.

Kent, Zachary. The Story of Ford's Theatre & the Death of Lincoln. LC 87-17662. (Illus.). 32p. (gr. 3-6). 1987. PLB 12.30 (0-516-04729-9); pap. 3.95 (0-516-44729-7) Childrens.

O'Neal, Michael. The Assassination of Abraham Lincoln: Opposing Viewpoints. LC 91-13682. (Illus.). 112p. (gr. 5-8). 1991. PLB 14.95 (0-89908-092-8) Greenhaven.

LINCOLN, ABRAHAM, PRESIDENT U. S. 1809-1865–DRAMA

Abraham Lincoln: Mini-Play, 2 pts. (gr. 5 up). 1978. Pt. 1. 6.50 (0-89550-317-4) Pt. 2. 6.50 (0-89550-325-5) Stevens & Shea.

LINCOLN, ABRAHAM, PRESIDENT U. S. 1809-1865–FICTION

McGovern, Ann. If You Grew up with Abraham Lincoln. Turkle, Brinton, illus. 64p. 1992. pap. 3.95 (0-590-45154-5) Scholastic Inc.

LINCOLN, MARY (TODD) 1818-1882

Anderson, LaVere. Mary Todd Lincoln: President's Wife. Cary, illus. 80p. (gr. 2-6). 1991. Repr. of 1975 ed. lib. bdg. 12.95 (0-7910-1415-0) Chelsea Hse.

Sandak, Cass R. The Lincolns. LC 92-6880. (Illus.). 48p. (gr. 5). 1992. text ed. 12.95 RSBE (0-89686-641-6, Crestwood Hse) Macmillan Child Grp.

Waldrop, Ruth. Mary Todd Lincoln: Mrs. Abraham Lincoln. Hendrix, Hurston H., illus. 110p. (gr. 3 up). 1994. write for info. (0-9616894-4-7) RuSK Inc.

Wilkie, Katharine E. Mary Todd Lincoln, Girl of the Bluegrass. Goldstein, Leslie, illus. LC 92-9782. 192p. (gr. 3-7). 1992. pap. 3.95 (0-689-71655-9, Aladdin) Macmillan Child Grp.

LINCOLN MEMORIAL, WASHINGTON, D. C.

Ashabranner, Brent. A Memorial for Mr. Lincoln. Ashabranner, Jennifer, illus. 128p. (gr. 5-9). 1992. 15.95 (0-399-22273-1, Putnam) Putnam Pub Group.

Reef, Catherine. The Lincoln Memorial. LC 93-13708. (Illus.). 72p. (gr. 4 up). 1994. text ed. 14.95 RSBE (0-87518-624-6, Dillon) Macmillan Child Grp.

LINDBERGH, CHARLES AUGUSTUS, 1902-

Collins, David R. Charles Lindbergh: Hero Pilot. Mays, Victor, illus. 80p. (gr. 2-6). 1991. Repr. of 1978 ed. lib. bdg. 12.95 (0-7910-1417-7) Chelsea Hse.

Demarest, Chris L. Lindbergh. Demarest, Chris L., illus. LC 92-41845. 40p. (ps-4). 1993. 15.00 (0-517-58718-1); PLB 15.99 (0-517-58719-X) Crown Bks Yng Read.

Farr, Naunerle C. & Fago, John N. Amelia Earhart - Charles Lindbergh. Vicatan, illus. (gr. 4-12). 1979. pap. text ed. 2.95 (0-88301-349-5); wkbk. 1.25 (0-88301-373-8) Pendulum Pr.

Lindbergh, Charles A. Boyhood on the Upper Mississippi: A Reminiscent Letter. LC 72-75804. (Illus.). 50p. (gr. 4-12). 1972. pap. 7.95 (0-87351-217-0) Minn Hist.

Stein, R. Conrad. The Spirit of St. Louis. LC 94-9491. (Illus.). 32p. 1994. PLB 16.40 (0-516-06682-X); pap. 3.95 (0-516-46682-8) Childrens.

—The Story of the Spirit of St. Louis. Meents, Len W., illus. LC 83-23174. 32p. (gr. 3-6). 1984. pap. 3.95 (0-516-44667-3) Childrens.

LINGUISTICS

see Language and Languages

LIONS

Cartwright, Ann & Cartwright, Reg. Proud & Fearless Lion. 32p. (ps-1). 1987. 8.95 (0-8120-5800-3) Barron.

Green, Carl R. & Sanford, William R. African Lion. LC 87-13648. (Illus.). 48p. (gr. 5). 1987. text ed. 12.95 RSBE (0-89686-328-X, Crestwood Hse) Macmillan Child Grp.

Hoffman, Mary. Lion. LC 84-24794. (Illus.). 24p. (gr. k-5). 1985. PLB 9.95 (0-8172-2411-4); pap. 3.95 (0-8114-6881-X) Raintree Steck-V.

Hughes, Jill. Lions & Tigers. (Illus.). 32p. (gr. 4-6). 1991. 13.95 (0-237-60164-8, Pub. by Evans Bros Ltd) Trafalgar.

Hurd, Edith T. Johnny Lion's Rubber Boots. Hurd, Clement, illus. LC 70-183165. 64p. (gr. k-3). 1972. PLB 13.89 (0-06-022710-9) HarpC Child Bks.

Lee, Sandra. Lions. 32p. 1991. 15.95 (0-89565-707-4) Childs World.

Lion. 1989. 3.50 (1-87865-730-5) Blue Q.

Lions. 1991. PLB 14.95 (0-88682-422-2) Creative Ed.

Mattern, Joanne. Lions & Tigers. Stone, Lynn M., illus. LC 92-19053. 24p. (gr. 4-7). 1992. (Pub. by Watermill Pr); pap. 1.95 (0-8167-2956-5, Pub. by Watermill Pr) Troll Assocs.

National Geographic Society Staff. Lion Cubs. (Illus.). Date not set. pap. 16.00 (0-87044-871-4) Natl Geog.

Petty, Kate. Lions. LC 89-26036. (ps-3). 1990. PLB 10.90 (0-531-17196-5, Gloucester Pr) Watts.

—Lions. 24p. (gr. k-3). 1993. pap. 3.95 (0-8120-1490-1) Barron.

Stone, L. Lions. (Illus.). 24p. (gr. k-5). 1989. lib. bdg. 11.94 (0-86592-501-1); 8.95s.p. (0-685-58629-4) Rourke Corp.

Storms, John. Lenny the Lion. Ooka, Dianne & Squellati, Liz, eds. Storms, Bob, illus. 24p. (Orig.). (gr. k-3). Date not set. pap. 4.95 (0-89346-799-5) Heian Intl.

Urquhart, Jennifer C. Lions & Tigers & Leopards: The Big Cats. (Illus.). (gr. k-4). 1990. Set. 13.95 (0-87044-820-X); Set. PLB 16.95 (0-87044-825-0) Natl Geog.

Wildlife Education, Ltd. Staff. Lions. Orr, Richard, illus. 24p. 1992. 13.95 (0-937934-81-X); pap. 2.75 (0-937934-42-9) Wildlife Educ.

Yee, Patrick. Baby Lion. (Illus.). 12p. (ps). 1994. bds. 3.99 (0-670-85289-9) Viking Child Bks.

Yoshida, Toshi. Young Lions. Yoshida, Toshi, illus. 40p. (gr. 1-5). 1989. 14.95 (0-399-21546-8, Philomel Bks) Putnam Pub Group.

LIONS–FICTION

Aardema, Verna. Rabbit Makes a Monkey of Lion. Pinkney, Jerry, illus. LC 86-11523. 32p. (ps-3). 1989. 11.95 (0-8037-0297-3); PLB 11.89 (0-8037-0298-1) Dial Bks Young.

Beittel, Kenneth R. & Beittel, Joan N. Ralph & Deno in Vermont. Beittel, Kenneth R., illus. LC 90-86028. 32p. (Orig.). (gr. 5 up). 1990. pap. 6.00 (0-9628511-0-8) HVHA.

Blagowidow, George. In Search of the Lady Lion Tamer. 249p. 1987. 15.95 (0-15-144500-1) HarBrace.

Brady, Jennifer. Jambi & the Lions. Thatch, Nancy R., ed. Brady, Jennifer, illus. Melton, David, intro. by. LC 92-17593. (Illus.). 26p. (gr. 3-5). 1992. PLB 14.95 (0-933849-41-9) Landmark Edns.

Brown, Margaret W. Don't Frighten the Lion! Rey, H. A., illus. 32p. (ps-2). 1993. pap. 4.95 (0-06-443262-9, Trophy) HarpC Child Bks.

Bulla, Clyde R. Lion to Guard Us. LC 80-2455. (Illus.). 128p. (gr. 3-5). 1989. pap. 3.95 (0-06-440333-5, Trophy) HarpC Child Bks.

Collins, David R. Leo's Amazing Paws & Jaws. (Illus.). (ps-2). 1987. PLB 6.95 (0-8136-5182-4, TK7269); pap. 3.50 (0-8136-5682-6, TK7270) Modern Curr.

Daniells, Trenna. Be True to Yourself: I Don't Want to Be a Lion Anymore. Braille International, Inc. Staff & Henry, James, illus. 11p. (Orig.). (gr. 1). 1992. pap. 10.95 (1-56956-001-3) W A T Braille.

—Be True to Yourself: I Don't Want to Be a Lion Anymore. Braille International, Inc. Staff & Henry, James, illus. (Orig.). (gr. 2). 1992. pap. 10.95 (1-56956-026-9) W A T Braille.

Daugherty, James. Andy & the Lion. Daugherty, James, illus. LC 38-27390. 80p. (gr. 1-4). 1938. pap. 13.95 (0-670-12433-8) Viking Child Bks.

—Andy & the Lion. (Illus.). 72p. (ps-3). 1989. pap. 4.99 (0-14-050277-7, Puffin) Puffin Bks.

De Angeli, Marguerite. The Lion in the Box. 1975. 12.95 (0-385-03317-6) Doubleday.

Desaix, Frank. Hilary & the Lions. (gr. 4-8). 1990. 15.00 (0-374-33237-1) FS&G.

Erickson, Gina C. & Foster, Kelli C. Bub & Chub. Gifford-Russell, Kerri, illus. 24p. (ps-2). 1992. pap. 3.50 (0-8120-4859-8) Barron.

Fields, Julia. The Green Lion of Zion Street. Pinkney, Jerry, illus. LC 92-24571. 32p. (gr. k-3). 1993. pap. 4.95 (0-689-71693-1, Aladdin) Macmillan Child Grp.

Freeman, Don. Dandelion. Freeman, Don, illus. LC 64-21472. 48p. (ps-2). 1964. pap. 14.00 (0-670-25532-7) Viking Child Bks.

Frost, Erica. Mr. Lion Goes to Lunch. Epstein, Len, illus. LC 85-14012. 48p. (Orig.). (gr. 1-3). 1986. PLB 10.59 (0-8167-0638-7); pap. text ed. 3.50 (0-8167-0639-5) Troll Assocs.

Greaves, Margaret. Sarah's Lion. (ps-3). 1992. 13.95 (0-8120-6279-5) Barron.

Guillot, Rene. Sirga. Kiddell-Monroe, Joan, illus. LC 59-12198. (gr. 6-9). 1959. 21.95 (0-87599-046-0) S G Phillips.

Hadithi, Mwenye. Lazy Lion. (ps-4). 1990. 15.95 (0-316-33725-0) Little.

Hogg, Gary. The Lion Who Couldn't Roar. Anderson, Gary, illus. (gr. k-6). 1991. 11.95 (0-89868-210-X); pap. 4.95 (0-89868-211-8) ARO Pub.

Hover, Margo. Disney's the Lion King. (ps-3). 1994. pap. 2.25 (0-307-12792-3, Golden Pr) Western Pub.

Hurd, Edith T. Johnny Lion's Bad Day. LC 78-85035. (Illus.). 64p. (gr. k-3). 1970. PLB 13.89 (0-06-022708-7) HarpC Child Bks.

—Johnny Lion's Book. Hurd, Clement, illus. LC 65-14490. 64p. (gr. k-3). 1965. PLB 13.89 (0-06-022706-0) HarpC Child Bks.

Ingoglia, Gina, adapted by. Disney's the Lion King. LC 93-71751. (Illus.). 96p. 1994. 14.95 (1-56282-628-X); PLB 14.89 (1-56282-629-8) Disney Pr.

—Disney's the Lion King. LC 93-71750. (Illus.). 64p. (gr. 2-6). 1994. 3.50 (1-56282-633-6) Disney Pr.

Kessel. Le Lion. (gr. 7-12). pap. 6.95 (0-88436-112-8, 40277) EMC.

Kimba the Lion. (ps). 1976. 2.50 (0-904494-30-6, Brimax Bks) Borden.

Kleven, Elisa. The Lion & the Little Red Bird. LC 91-36691. (Illus.). 32p. (ps-2). 1992. 13.50 (0-525-44898-5, DCB) Dutton Child Bks.

Koram, Gamal. When Lions Could Fly. (Illus.). 42p. (gr. 4-12). 1989. pap. 5.00 (1-877610-01-1) Sea Island.

Korman, Justine. Disney's the Lion King. (ps-3). 1994. 3.95 (0-307-12376-6, Golden Pr) Western Pub.

Kraus, Robert. Leo the Late Bloomer. Aruego, Jose, illus. LC 70-159154. 32p. (gr. k-3). 1994. pap. 4.95 (0-06-443348-X, Trophy) HarpC Child Bks.

La Fontaine. The Lion & the Rat. Wildsmith, Brian, illus. 32p. 1987. 16.00 (0-19-279607-0); pap. 7.50 (0-19-272167-4) OUP.

The Lion King, 4 bks. 40p. 1994. Set 6.98 (0-685-72088-8) Mouse Works.

The Lion King: Interlocking Board Book, 7 bks. 1994. bds. 5.98 Set (0-685-72089-6) Mouse Works.

Lyne, Sandy. The Lion & the Boy. Reilly, Kathy, illus. 48p. (gr. 4-7). 1988. 12.95 (0-933905-04-1); pap. 9.95 (0-933905-15-7) Claycomb Pr.

McIntire, Donald. The Pemaquid Loon from Temple. Bull, Kris F., illus. 1988. pap. 5.99 (*0-317-92307-2*) Herit Print Co.
McKean, Thomas. Hooray for Grandma Jo! Demarest, Chris, illus. LC 93-16376. (ps-6). 1994. 14.00 (*0-517-57842-5*); PLB 14.99 (*0-517-57843-3*) Crown Bks Yng Read.
McOmber, Rachel B., ed. McOmber Phonics Storybooks: Chatsworth. rev. ed. (Illus.). write for info. (*0-944991-74-2*) Swift Lrn Res.
McPhail, David. Snow Lion. McPhail, David, illus. LC 82-8119. 48p. (ps-3). 1987. 5.95 (*0-8193-1097-2*); PLB 5.95 (*0-8193-1098-0*) Parents.
—Snow Lion. McPhail, David, illus. 48p. (gr. 3-7). 1990. pap. 2.95 (*0-448-04335-1*, G&D) Putnam Pub Group.
Martin, Bill. Calendar Lion. 1993. write for info. (*0-8050-2417-4*) H Holt & Co.
Michael, Emory H. Androcles & the Lion. Hatchem, Mia, illus. LC 87-51492. 44p. (gr. k-4). 1988. 6.95 (*1-55523-132-2*) Winston-Derek.
Montenegro, Laura. Sweet Tooth. LC 93-49643. 1994. write for info. (*0-395-68078-6*) HM.
Mora, Emma. Cyril the Lion. 30p. (ps-1). 1987. 3.95 (*0-8120-5811-9*) Barron.
Newcome, Robert & Newcome, Zita. Little Lion. (Illus.). 32p. (ps-1). 1993. 17.95 (*1-85681-181-6*, Pub. by J MacRae UK) Trafalgar.
Peet, Bill. Eli. Peet, Bill, illus. LC 77-17500. 48p. (gr. k-3). 1978. 13.45 (*0-395-26454-5*) HM.
—Randy's Dandy Lions. (Illus.). (gr. k-3). 1979. 13.95 (*0-395-18507-6*); pap. 4.80 (*0-395-27498-2*) HM.
Pryor, Bonnie. Seth of the Lion People. LC 88-18747. 128p. (gr. 3-6). 1988. 11.95 (*0-688-07327-1*) Morrow Jr Bks.
Rogers, Paul T. Forget-Me-Not. Berridge, Celia, illus. 32p. (ps-k). 1986. pap. 3.50 (*0-685-43615-2*, Puffin) Puffin Bks.
Shaw, George Bernard. Androcles & the Lion. Storr, Catherine, ed. Hood, Philip, illus. LC 86-6665. 32p. (gr. 2-5). 1986. PLB 19.97 (*0-8172-2625-7*) Raintree Steck-V.
Silverstein, Shel. Lafcadio, the Lion Who Shot Back. Silverstein, Shel, illus. LC 62-13320. 112p. (gr. 3-6). 1963. 15.00 (*0-06-025675-3*); PLB 14.89 (*0-06-025676-1*) HarpC Child Bks.
Slater, Teddy. Disney's the Lion King: Morning at Pride Rock. (Illus.). 32p. (gr. 2-6). 1994. 12.95 (*1-56282-690-5*); PLB 12.89 (*1-56282-691-3*) Disney Pr.
The Snow Lion. 42p. (ps-3). 1992. PLB 13.27 (*0-8368-0888-6*) Gareth Stevens Inc.
Stinga, Frank, illus. The Carousel Lion. 12p. (ps). Date not set. 4.95 (*1-56828-064-5*) Red Jacket Pr.
Stone, Elaine M. Tekla & the Lion. LC 90-71366. (Illus.). 44p. (gr. 3-6). 1991. pap. 7.95 (*1-55523-388-0*) Winston-Derek.
Tate, Susan. Larry Lion Learns to Fear Not. Henium, Marian, illus. 40p. (gr. k-3). 1993. pap. 3.99 (*1-884395-03-1*) Clear Blue Sky.
Vaughn, Marcia. Riddle by the River. Ruffins, Reynold, illus. LC 93-46890. (gr. 1 up). 1994. write for info. (*0-382-24603-9*); pap. write for info. (*0-382-24451-6*); PLB write for info. (*0-382-24602-0*) Silver Burdett Pr.
Wells, Rosemary. A Lion for Lewis. Wells, Rosemary, illus. 32p. (ps-2). 1984. pap. 3.95 (*0-8037-0096-2*, Puff Pied Piper) Puffin Bks.
Zelinsky, Paul O. The Lion & the Stoat. Zelinsky, Paul O., illus. LC 83-16326. 40p. (gr. 1-3). 1984. PLB 10. 88 (*0-688-02563-3*) Greenwillow.
Zimelman, Nathan. Treed by a Pride of Irate Lions. Goffe, Toni, illus. LC 89-30344. (gr. k-3). 1990. Little.

LIONS–HABITS AND BEHAVIOR

Taylor, Dave. The Lion & the Savannah. (Illus.). 32p. (gr. 3-4). 1990. PLB 15.95 (*0-86505-364-2*); pap. 7.95 (*0-86505-394-4*) Crabtree Pub Co.

LIONS–POETRY

Peet, Bill. Hubert's Hair-Raising Adventure. (Illus.). 36p. (gr. k-3). 1959. 14.95 (*0-395-15083-3*) HM.

LIQUIDS

Agler, Leigh. Liquid Explorations. Bergman, Lincoln & Fairwell, Kay, eds. Klofkorn, Lisa, illus. Hoyt, Richard, photos by. (Illus.). 67p. (Orig.). (gr. 1-3). 1987. pap. 8.50 (*0-912511-51-6*) Lawrence Science.
Barber, Jacqueline. Solids, Liquids, & Gases. Bergman, Lincoln & Fairwell, Kay, eds. Baker, Lisa H. & Peterson, Adria, illus. Barber, Jacqueline, et al, photos by. 56p. (Orig.). (gr. 3-6). 1986. pap. 15.00 (*0-912511-69-9*) Lawrence Science.
Mebane, Robert. Water & Liquids. 1994. PLB write for info. H Holt & Co.
Mellett, Peter & Rossiter, Jane. Liquids in Action. LC 92-7649. (Illus.). 32p. (gr. 5-8). 1993. PLB 12.40 (*0-531-14235-3*) Watts.
Watson, Philip. Liquid Magic. Wood, Elizabeth & Fenton, Ronald, illus. LC 82-80988. 48p. (gr. 3-6). 1983. PLB 11.93 (*0-688-00967-0*) Lothrop.

LITERARY CHARACTERS

see Characters and Characteristics in Literature

LITERARY CRITICISM

see Criticism; Literature–History and Criticism

LITERATURE–BIO-BIBLIOGRAPHY

see also Authors

LITERATURE–BIOGRAPHY

see Authors

LITERATURE–CRITICISM

see Literature–History and Criticism

LITERATURE–EVALUATION

see Books and Reading; Books and Reading–Best Books; Criticism; Literature–History and Criticism

LITERATURE–HISTORY AND CRITICISM

see also Authors; Criticism

Danielson, Kathy. On My Honor: A Study Guide. Friedland, Joyce & Kessler, Rikki, eds. (gr. 3-6). 1991. pap. text ed. 14.95 (*0-88122-576-2*) LRN Links.
Diamond, Laurie. Little Soup's Hayride: A Study Guide. Friedland, J. & Kessler, R., eds. 20p. (gr. 1-3). 1992. pap. text ed. 14.95 (*0-88122-699-8*) Lrn Links.
—Next Spring an Oriole: A Study Guide. Friedland, Joyce & Kessler, Rikki, eds. (gr. 1-4). 1991. pap. text ed. 14.95 (*0-88122-565-7*) LRN Links.
—O'Diddy: A Study Guide. Friedland, Joyce & Kessler, Rikki, eds. (gr. 2-4). 1991. pap. text ed. 14.95 (*0-88122-570-3*) LRN Links.
Dobrow, Vicki. Johnny Tremain - Study Guide. Friedland, Joyce & Kessler, Rikki, eds. (gr. 7-10). 1993. pap. text ed. 14.95 (*0-88122-025-6*) Lrn Links.
Fischer, Elyse. The Silver Coach: A Study Guide. Friedland, Joyce & Kessler, Rikki, eds. (gr. 3-5). 1991. pap. text ed. 14.95 (*0-88122-577-0*) LRN Links.
Friedland, Joyce & Kessler, Rikki. The Pearl - Study Guide. Reeves, Barbara, ed. (gr. 6-10). 1993. pap. text ed. 14.95 (*0-88122-031-0*) Lrn Links.
—A Separate Peace - Study Guide. (gr. 7-10). 1993. pap. text ed. 14.95 (*0-88122-022-1*) Lrn Links.
—A Wrinkle in Time - Study Guide. (gr. 6-10). 1993. pap. text ed. 14.95 (*0-88122-014-0*) Lrn Links.
Gluzband, Cheryl. Rumble Fish - Study Guide. Friedland, Joyce & Kessler, Rikki, eds. (gr. 6-9). 1993. pap. text ed. 14.95 (*0-88122-128-7*) Lrn Links.
Golden, Michael. The Devil's Arithmetic: A Study Guide. Friedland, J. & Kessler, R., eds. 29p. (gr. 4-7). 1992. pap. text ed. 14.95 (*0-88122-697-1*) Lrn Links.
—Where the Red Fern Grows - Study Guide. Friedland, Joyce & Kessler, Rikki, eds. (gr. 6-8). 1993. pap. text ed. 14.95 (*0-88122-034-5*) Lrn Links.
Halverson, Patricia A. I Heard the Owl Call My Name - Study Guide. Friedland, Joyce & Kessler, Rikki, eds. (gr. 6-10). 1993. pap. text ed. 14.95 (*0-88122-100-7*) Lrn Links.
Harwayne. Writers Shelf: Literature Through. 1992. Pt. I. 174.05 (*0-06-027097-7*, Festival); Pt. II. 154.55 (*0-06-027098-5*, Festival) HarpC Child Bks.
Levine, Gloria. Roll of Thunder, Hear My Cry - Study Guide. Friedland, Joyce & Kessler, Rikki, eds. (gr. 6-10). 1993. pap. text ed. 14.95 (*0-88122-126-0*) Lrn Links.
Levine, Gloria & Fischer, Kathleen M. The Wave - Study Guide. Friedland, Joyce & Kessler, Rikki, eds. (gr. 6-10). 1993. pap. text ed. 14.95 (*0-88122-132-5*) Lrn Links.
McGee, Brenda. Felita: A Study Guide. Friedland, Joyce & Kessler, Rikki, eds. (gr. 1-4). 1991. pap. text ed. 14. 95 (*0-88122-567-3*) LRN Links.
Murphy, Michael. My Brother Sam Is Dead - Study Guide. Friedland, Joyce & Kessler, Rikki, eds. (gr. 5-8). 1993. pap. text ed. 14.95 (*0-88122-119-8*) Lrn Links.
Norris, Crystal. I Am the Cheese - Study Guide. Friedland, Joyce & Kessler, Rikki, eds. (gr. 7-10). 1993. pap. text ed. 14.95 (*0-88122-101-5*) Lrn Links.
—Julie of the Wolves - Study Guide. Friedland, Joyce & Kessler, Rikki, eds. (gr. 6-9). 1993. pap. text ed. 14.95 10 (*0-88122-099-X*) Lrn Links.
—The Light in the Forest - Study Guide. Friedland, Joyce & Kessler, Rikki, eds. (gr. 6-9). 1993. pap. text ed. 14.95 (*0-88122-117-1*) Lrn Links.
—One Flew over the Cuckoo's Nest - Study Guide. Friedland, Joyce & Kessler, Rikki, eds. (gr. 10-12). 1993. pap. text ed. 14.95 (*0-88122-121-X*) Lrn Links.
—Ordinary People - Study Guide. Friedland, Joyce & Kessler, Rikki, eds. (gr. 9-12). 1993. pap. text ed. 14. 95 (*0-88122-122-8*) Lrn Links.
—The Picture of Dorian Gray - Study Guide. Friedland, Joyce & Kessler, Rikki, eds. (gr. 10-12). 1993. pap. text ed. 14.95 (*0-88122-123-6*) Lrn Links.
—Shane - Study Guide. Friedland, Joyce & Kessler, Rikki, eds. (gr. 7-10). 1993. pap. text ed. 14.95 (*0-88122-129-5*) Lrn Links.
Reeves, Barbara. Number the Stars: A Study Guide. Friedland, Joyce & Kessler, Rikki, eds. (gr. 5-8). 1991. pap. text ed. 14.95 (*0-88122-579-7*) LRN Links.
Ripley, Robert L. Literature. Stott, Carol, illus. 48p. (gr. 3-6). 1992. PLB 12.95 (*1-56065-130-X*) Capstone Pr.
Rowbotham, Judith. Good Girls Make Good Wives: Guidance for Girls in Victorian Fiction. (Illus.). 256p. (gr. 9-12). 1989. text ed. 45.00 (*0-631-16395-6*); pap. text ed. 24.95 (*0-631-16396-4*) Blackwell Pubs.
Schmidt, Gary D. Hugh Lofting. LC 92-11256. 200p. 1992. text ed. 22.95 (*0-8057-7023-2*, Twayne) Macmillan.
Spencer, Anne. Molly's Pilgrim: A Study Guide. Friedland, J. & Kessler, R., eds. 19p. (gr. 2-4). 1992. pap. text ed. 14.95 (*0-88122-700-5*) Lrn Links.
—The Trumpet of the Swan: A Study Guide. Friedland, J. & Kessler, R., eds. 24p. (gr. 4-6). 1992. pap. text ed. 14.95 (*0-88122-710-2*) Lrn Links.
Sussman, Linda. A Raisin in the Sun - Study Guide. Friedland, Joyce & Kessler, Rikki, eds. (gr. 8-12). 1993. pap. text ed. 14.95 (*0-88122-124-4*) Lrn Links.
Tretler, Marcia. The Outsiders - Study Guide. Friedland, Joyce & Kessler, Rikki, eds. (gr. 6-9). 1993. pap. text ed. 14.95 (*0-88122-030-2*) Lrn Links.
—Sounder - Study Guide. Friedland, Joyce & Kessler, Rikki, eds. (gr. 6-9). 1993. pap. text ed. 14.95 (*0-88122-130-9*) Lrn Links.
—The Summer of My German Soldier - Study Guide. Friedland, Joyce & Kessler, Rikki, eds. (gr. 6-9). 1993. pap. text ed. 14.95 (*0-88122-131-7*) Lrn Links.
Villanella, Rosemary. The Yearling - Study Guide. Friedland, Joyce & Kessler, Rikki, eds. (gr. 7-11). 1993. pap. text ed. 14.95 (*0-88122-061-2*) Lrn Links.
Williams, Brian. Literature. LC 90-36113. (Illus.). 48p. (gr. 6-11). 1990. PLB 11.95 (*0-8114-2365-4*) Raintree Steck-V.

LITERATURE–STORIES, PLOTS, ETC.

Albert, Toni. Ben & Me: A Study Guide. Friedland, Joyce & Kessler, Rikki, eds. (gr. 2-5). 1991. pap. text ed. 14.95 (*0-88122-566-5*) LRN Links.
—The War with Grandpa: A Study Guide. Friedland, Joyce & Kessler, Rikki, eds. (gr. 3-6). 1991. pap. text ed. 14.95 (*0-88122-578-9*) LRN Links.
Allison, Christine. Teach Your Children Well: A Parent's Guide to the Stories, Poems, Fables, & Tales that Instill Traditional Values. LC 92-42762. 1993. 22.95 (*0-385-30290-8*) Delacorte.
Bell, Irene W. Literature Cross-A-Word Book I: Crossword Learning Experiences with Animal Stories, Modern Fantasy, & Space & Time. Kirby, Keith, illus. 96p. 1982. pap. 14.75 (*0-89774-062-9*) Oryx Pr.

---

reading are provided, & numerous illustrations are interspersed throughout.
Publisher Provided Annotation.

Christopher, Garrett. Ira Sleeps Over: A Study Guide. Friedland, Joyce & Kessler, Rikki, eds. (gr. k-3). 1991. pap. text ed. 14.95 (*0-88122-590-8*) LRN Links.
—The Story of Ferdinand: A Study Guide. Friedland, Joyce & Kessler, Rikki, eds. (gr. k-3). 1991. pap. text ed. 14.95 (*0-88122-594-0*) LRN Links.
—Tales of a Fourth-Grade Nothing: A Study Guide. Friedland, Joyce & Kessler, Rikki, eds. (gr. 2-5). 1991. pap. text ed. 14.95 (*0-88122-575-4*) LRN Links.
Holz, Laurie, ed. Words of Love. Blake, Michael, intro. by. 144p. (gr. 8 up). 1992. lib. bdg. 15.00 (*1-56508-001-7*) Seven Wolves.
Island of the Blue Dolphins: L-I-T Guide. (gr. 4-7). 1993. 8.95 (*1-56644-950-2*) Educ Impress.
Magill, Frank N., ed. Masterplots II, 4 vols. LC 92-44708. 1695p. (gr. 8 up). 1991. Set. PLB 365.00 (*0-89356-579-2*, Magill Bks); CD-ROM avail.; Vol. 1. write for info. (*0-89356-580-6*); Vol. 2. write for info. (*0-89356-581-4*); Vol. 3. write for info. (*0-89356-582-2*); Vol. 4. write for info. 335 (*0-89356-583-0*) Salem Pr.
Preston-Foster, Mary. Fun With Fiction. (gr. 2-5). 1988. pap. 8.95 (*0-8224-3173-4*) Fearon Teach Aids.
Swann, Marie L. The Sacred Lake Activity Book: Activities to Accompany Reading "The Sacred Lake" 51p. (gr. 3-4). 1992. Repr. of 1991 ed. wkbk. 8.00 (*1-882156-04-8*) Eye Of The Eagle.

LITERATURE AS A PROFESSION
see Authors; Authorship; Journalism; Journalists

LITTERING
see Refuse and Refuse Disposal

LITTLE, MALCOLM, 1925-1965
Adoff, Arnold. Malcolm X. Wilson, John, illus. LC 85-42974. 40p. (gr. 2-5). 1985. pap. 5.95 (*0-06-446015-0*, Trophy) HarpC Child Bks.
—Malcolm X. Wilson, John, illus. LC 70-94787. 48p. (gr. 2-5). 1970. PLB 14.89 (*0-690-51414-X*, Crowell Jr Bks) HarpC Child Bks.
—Malcolm X. (gr. 1-4). 1992. 18.25 (*0-8446-6587-8*) Peter Smith.
AESOP Enterprises, Inc. Staff & Crenshaw, Gwendolyn J. Malcolm X: Developing Self-Esteem, Self-Love, & Self-Dignity. 27p. (gr. 3-12). 1991. pap. write for info. incl. cassette (*1-880771-00-4*) AESOP Enter.
Archer, Jules. They Had a Dream: The Civil Rights Struggle from Frederick Douglass to Marcus Garvey to Martin Luther King, Jr., & Malcolm X. (Illus.). 288p. (gr. 5 up). 1993. 15.99 (*0-670-84494-2*) Viking Child Bks.
Barr, Roger. Malcolm X. LC 93-17853. (gr. 5-8). 1994. 14.95 (*1-56006-044-1*) Lucent Bks.
Collins, David R. Malcolm X: Center of the Storm. LC 91-39951. (Illus.). 104p. (gr. 5 up). 1992. text ed. 13.95 RSBE (*0-87518-498-7*, Dillon) Macmillan Child Grp.
Cwiklik, Robert. Malcolm X & Black Pride. LC 92-23687. (Illus.). 32p. (gr. 2-4). 1991. PLB 12.90 (*1-56294-042-2*); pap. 4.95 (*1-878841-73-4*) Millbrook Pr.
Davies, Mark. Malcolm X: Another Side of the Movement. Gallin, Richard, ed. Young, Andrew, intro. by. (Illus.). 128p. (gr. 5 up). 1990. lib. bdg. 12.95 (*0-382-09925-7*); pap. 7.95 (*0-382-24063-4*) Silver Burdett Pr.
Diamond, Arthur. Malcolm X: A Voice for Black America. LC 93-8431. (Illus.). 128p. (gr. 6 up). 1994. lib. bdg. 17.95 (*0-89490-435-3*) Enslow Pubs.
Dinero, G. Who's Hot! Malcolm X. 1993. pap. 1.49 (*0-440-21480-7*) Dell.
Grimes, Nikki. Malcolm X: A Force for Change. (gr. 7 up). 1992. pap. 4.00 (*0-449-90803-8*) Fawcett.
Keyla Activity Book: Malcolm X. 24p. (gr. 4-6). 1992. pap. text ed. 4.95 (*1-882962-01-X*) Keyla.
Mack-Williams, Kibibi. Malcolm X. LC 92-46767. 1993. 19.93 (*0-86625-493-5*); 14.95s.p. (*0-685-66548-8*) Rourke Pubns.
Myers, Walter D. Malcolm X: By Any Means Necessary. 1994. pap. 3.95 (*0-590-48109-6*) Scholastic Inc.
Myers, Walter Dean. Malcolm X: By Any Means Necessary. LC 92-13480. 224p. (gr. 5 up). 1993. 13.95 (*0-590-46484-1*) Scholastic Inc.
Obaba, Al-Imam. Malcolm X Great Nubian Quiz. (Illus.). 43p. (Orig.). 1988. pap. 3.95 (*0-916157-16-4*) African Islam Miss Pubns.
Rummel, Jack. Malcolm X. King, Coretta Scott, intro. by. (Illus.). 112p. (gr. 5 up). 1989. lib. bdg. 17.95x (*1-55546-600-1*); pap. 9.95 (*0-7910-0227-6*) Chelsea Hse.
Shirley, David. Malcolm X: Racial Spokesman. LC 93-17700. (Illus.). 1993. 13.95 (*0-7910-2106-8*, Am Art Analog); pap. 4.95 (*0-7910-2112-2*, Am Art Analog) Chelsea Hse.
Slater, Jack. Malcolm X. LC 93-12687. (Illus.). 32p. (gr. 3-6). 1993. PLB 12.30 (*0-516-06669-2*); pap. 3.95 (*0-516-46669-0*) Childrens.
Sprott, Maxine. Malik: The History the Legend the Myth (the Story of Malcolm X) Allen, James R., intro. by. (Illus.). 66p. (Orig.). (gr. 5). 1991. pap. 8.00 (*0-9629982-9-X*) Vital Edits.
Stine, Megan. Story of Malcolm X, Civil Rights Leader. (gr. 4-7). 1994. pap. 3.50 (*0-440-40900-4*) Dell.
Thompson-Peters, Flossie E. El-Hajj Malik El-Shabazz: The Biography of Malcolm X. Behrens, Debra J. & Jeffery, Lisa E., eds. Green, Kenneth L., illus. 65p. (Orig.). (gr. 4-12). 1994. pap. 8.00 (*1-880784-08-4*) Atlas Pr.

LITTLE BIG HORN, BATTLE OF THE, 1876
Goble, Paul. Red Hawk's Account of Custer's Last Battle. Goble, Paul, illus. LC 91-231701. 64p. 1992. pap. 9.95 (*0-8032-7033-X*, Bison Books) U of Nebr Pr.
Henckel, Mark. Battle of the Little Bighorn. Potter, John, illus. 32p. (Orig.). (gr. 3-7). 1992. pap. 5.95 (*1-56044-042-2*) Falcon Pr MT.
Steele, Philip. Little Bighorn. LC 91-24065. (Illus.). 32p. (gr. 6 up). 1992. text ed. 13.95 RSBE (*0-02-786885-0*, New Discovery) Macmillan Child Grp.
Stein, R. Conrad. The Story of Little Bighorn. LC 83-6594. (Illus.). 32p. (gr. 3-6). 1983. pap. 3.95 (*0-516-44663-0*) Childrens.
Willis, Charles. Battle of Little Big Horn. (Illus.). 64p. 1990. PLB 12.95 (*0-382-09952-4*); pap. 7.95 (*0-382-09948-6*) Silver Burdett Pr.

LITTLE LEAGUE BASEBALL
Kruetzer, Peter. Little League's Official How-to-Play Baseball Book. 1990. pap. 12.95 (*0-385-41278-9*) Doubleday.
—Little League's Official How-to-Play Baseball Handbook. 1990. pap. 9.95 (*0-385-24700-1*) Doubleday.
Newman, Gerald. Happy Birthday, Little League. LC 88-38158. 64p. (gr. 3-6). 1989. PLB 12.90 (*0-531-10687-X*) Watts.
Stotz, Carl E. A Promise Kept: The Story of the Founding of Little League Baseball. Loss, Kenneth D. & Zebrowski, Stephanie R., eds. (Illus.). 208p. (gr. 7-12). 1992. 16.95 (*1-880484-05-6*) Zebrowski Hist.

LITTLE LEAGUE BASEBALL–FICTION
Benchley, Nathaniel. Only Earth & Sky Last Forever. LC 72-82891. 204p. (gr. 7 up). 1974. pap. 4.95 (*0-06-440049-2*, Trophy) HarpC Child Bks.
Konigsburg, E. L. About the B'nai Bagels. Konigsburg, E. L., illus. LC 69-13529. 176p. (gr. 4-6). 1971. SBE 14.95 (*0-689-20631-3*, Atheneum Child Bk) Macmillan Child Grp.

LIVESTOCK
see also Cattle; Cows; Dairying; Domestic Animals; Hogs; Horses; Sheep; Veterinary Medicine
Whyte, Malcolm. Farm Animals. (Illus.). 32p. (Orig.). (gr. 1-4). 1989. pap. 2.95 (*0-8431-1960-8*, Troubador) Price Stern.

LIVING FOSSILS
Martin, James. Living Fossils. LC 94-7926. 1995. write for info. (*0-517-59866-3*); PLB write for info. (*0-517-59867-1*) Crown Bks Yng Read.
Pope, Joyce. Living Fossils. Stillwell, Stella & Ward, Helen, illus. LC 91-13998. 48p. (gr. 4-8). 1992. PLB 22.80 (*0-8114-3151-7*); pap. 4.95 (*0-8114-6256-0*) Raintree Steck-V.
Sandak, Cass R. Living Fossils. LC 91-34423. (Illus.). 64p. (gr. 3-6). 1992. PLB 12.90 (*0-531-20048-5*) Watts.

LIVINGSTONE, DAVID, 1813-1873
Clinton, Susan. Henry Stanley & David Livingstone: Explorers of Africa. LC 90-2172. (Illus.). 128p. (gr. 3 up). 1990. PLB 20.55 (*0-516-03055-8*) Childrens.
Humble, Richard. The Travels of Livingstone. LC 90-32379. (Illus.). 32p. (gr. 5-8). 1991. PLB 12.40 (*0-531-14101-2*) Watts.
Twist, Clint. Stanley & Livingstone: Expeditions Through Africa. LC 94-21642. 1995. write for info. (*0-8114-3976-3*) Raintree Steck-V.

LIZARDS
Bailey, Donna. Lizards. LC 90-22988. (Illus.). (gr. 1-4). 1992. PLB 18.99 (*0-8114-2645-9*) Raintree Steck-V.
Barrett, Norman S. Dragons & Lizards. LC 90-43335. (Illus.). 32p. (gr. k-4). 1991. PLB 11.90 (*0-531-14111-X*) Watts.
Beers, Dorothy S. The Gecko. (Illus.). 60p. (gr. 3 up). 1990. text ed. 13.95 RSBE (*0-87518-441-3*, Dillon) Macmillan Child Grp.
Creighton, Susan. The Giant Lizard. LC 88-16128. (Illus.). 48p. (gr. 5). 1988. text ed. 12.95 RSBE (*0-89686-394-8*, Crestwood Hse) Macmillan Child Grp.
Fichter, George S. Snakes & Lizards: A Golden Junior Guide. (ps-3). 1993. 4.95 (*0-307-11432-5*, Golden Pr) Western Pub.
Gerholdt, James E. Lizards. LC 94-6355. 1994. write for info. (*1-56239-306-5*) Abdo & Dghtrs.
Gravelle, Karen. Lizards. LC 91-4665. (Illus.). 64p. (gr. 5-8). 1991. PLB 12.90 (*0-531-20026-4*) Watts.
Harrison, Virginia. The World of Lizards. Oxford Scientific Films Staff, photos by. LC 87-42608. (Illus.). 32p. (gr. 2-3). 1988. PLB 17.27 (*1-55532-307-3*) Gareth Stevens Inc.
Hawcock, David. Lizard. (ps). 1994. 3.95 (*0-307-17300-3*, Artsts Writrs) Western Pub.
Linley, Mike. The Lizard in the Jungle. Oxford Scientific Films, photos by. LC 87-42612. (Illus.). 32p. (gr. 4-6). 1988. PLB 17.27 (*1-55532-303-0*) Gareth Stevens Inc.
Martin, L. Chameleons. (Illus.). 24p. (gr. k-5). 1989. lib. bdg. 11.94 (*0-86592-576-3*) Rourke Corp.
—Iguanas. (Illus.). 24p. (gr. k-5). 1989. lib. bdg. 11.94 (*0-86592-575-5*); 8.95s.p. (*0-685-58606-5*) Rourke Corp.
—Komodo Dragons. (Illus.). 24p. (gr. k-5). 1989. lib. bdg. 11.94 (*0-86592-574-7*); 8.95s.p. (*0-685-58604-9*) Rourke Corp.
—Lizards. (Illus.). 24p. (gr. k-5). 1989. lib. bdg. 11.94 (*0-86592-577-1*); 8.95s.p. (*0-685-58605-7*) Rourke Corp.
Morris, Dean. Snakes & Lizards. rev. ed. LC 87-16697. (Illus.). 48p. (gr. 2-6). 1987. PLB 10.95 (*0-8172-3212-5*) Raintree Steck-V.
Reilly, Pauline. Frillneck: An Australian Dragon. Rolland, Will, illus. 32p. (Orig.). 1993. pap. 6.95 (*0-86417-414-4*, Pub. by Kangaroo Pr AT) Seven Hills Bk Dists.
Schnieper, Claudia. Lizards. Meirer, Max, illus. 48p. (gr. 2-6). 1990. PLB 19.95 (*0-87614-405-9*) Carolrhoda Bks.
Serventy, Vincent. Lizard. (Illus.). 24p. (gr. k-5). 1986. PLB 9.95 (*0-8172-2706-7*); pap. 3.95 (*0-8114-6882-8*) Raintree Steck-V.
Smith, Trevor. Amazing Lizards. Young, Jerry, photos by. LC 90-31884. (Illus.). 32p. (Orig.). (gr. 1-5). 1990. lib. bdg. 9.99 (*0-679-90819-6*); pap. 7.99 (*0-679-80819-1*) Knopf Bks Yng Read.
Storms, John. Tony the Tokay Gecko. Storms, Robert, illus. 24p. (Orig.). (gr. k-4). 1993. pap. 4.95 (*0-89346-531-3*) Heian Intl.
Walls, Jerry G. Your First Lizard. 34p. (Orig.). (gr. 1-6). 1991. pap. 1.95 (*0-86622-068-2*, YF-111) TFH Pubns.

LIZARDS–FICTION
Carle, Eric. The Mixed-up Chameleon. 2nd ed. Carle, Eric, illus. LC 83-45950. 32p. (ps-3). 1984. 15.00 (*0-690-04396-1*, Crowell Jr Bks); PLB 14.89 (*0-690-04397-X*) HarpC Child Bks.
Covington, Dennis. Lizard. 1993. pap. 3.50 (*0-440-21490-4*) Dell.
DuQuette, Keith. Hotel Animal. DuQuette, Keith, illus. LC 93-14531. 32p. (ps-3). 1994. PLB 13.99 (*0-670-85056-X*) Viking Child Bks.
Gardner, Richard A. Dorothy & the Lizard of Oz. Richmond, Frank, illus. LC 80-12787. 108p. (gr. 1-6). 1980. 14.95 (*0-933812-03-5*) Creative Therapeutics.
Hale, Bruce. The Legend of the Laughing Gecko: A Hawaiian Fantasy. Hale, Bruce, illus. Brown, Susana, concept by. (Illus.). 32p. (Orig.). (ps-3). 1989. pap. write for info. Geckostufs.
—Surf Gecko to the Rescue! Hale, Bruce, illus. 32p. (ps-4). 1991. write for info. (*0-9621280-1-5*) Geckostufs.
Herndon, Ernest. The Secret of Lizard Island. LC 93-5011. 144p. 1994. pap. 4.99 (*0-310-38251-3*) Zondervan.
Hooks, William H. Mr. Dinosaur. Meisel, Paul, illus. LC 92-33476. 1994. (Little Rooster); pap. 3.99 (*0-553-37234-3*, Little Rooster) Bantam.
Horstman, Lisa. Fast Friends: A Tail & Tongue Tale. Horstman, Lisa, illus. LC 93-28630. 40p. (ps-3). 1994. 13.00 (*0-679-85404-5*); PLB 13.99 (*0-679-95404-X*) Knopf Bks Yng Read.
Kemvichanuvat, Cherdchai. The Poor Lizard. Rodriguez, Gloria F., ed. Chang, Phillip, illus. Pinta, Thanom, tr. (Illus.). (gr. k-3). 1979. pap. 3.50 (*0-686-26621-8*, Pub. by New Day Pub PI) Cellar.
McBarnet, Gill. Gecko Hide & Seek. McBarnet, Gill, illus. 24p. (ps-2). Date not set. 7.95 (*0-9615102-7-7*) Ruwanga Trad.
—The Goodnight Gecko. (Illus.). 32p. 1991. 7.95 (*0-9615102-6-9*) Ruwanga Trad.
Magellan, Mauro. Cambio Chameleon. Magellan, Mauro, illus. LC 89-19995. 32p. 1990. 12.95 (*0-89334-118-5*) Humanics Ltd.
Massie, Diane R. Chameleon Was a Spy. Massie, Diane R., illus. LC 78-19510. (gr. 2-6). 1979. (Crowell Jr Bks) HarpC Child Bks.
Monsell, Mary E. Toohy & Wood. Tryon, Leslie, illus. LC 91-38217. 64p. (gr. 2-5). 1992. SBE 12.95 (*0-689-31721-2*, Atheneum Child Bk) Macmillan Child Grp.
Reynolds, Pat. Tom's Friend. LC 93-170. 1994. write for info. (*0-383-03797-2*) SRA Schl Grp.
Ryder, Joanne. Lizard in the Sun. Rothman, Michael, illus. LC 89-33886. 32p. (gr. k up). 1990. 13.95 (*0-688-07172-4*); PLB 13.88 (*0-688-07173-2*, Morrow Jr Bks) Morrow Jr Bks.
—Lizard in the Sun. (ps-3). 1994. pap. 4.95 (*0-688-13081-X*, Mulberry) Morrow.
Scholes, Katherine. Blue Chameleon. 176p. (gr. 7-12). 1994. 11.95 (*0-85572-192-8*, Pub. by Hill Content Pubng AT) Seven Hills Bk Dists.
Shannon, George. Lizard's Song. Aruego, Jose & Dewey, Ariane, illus. LC 80-21432. 32p. (gr. k-3). 1981. 14.95 (*0-688-80310-5*); PLB 14.88 (*0-688-84310-7*) Greenwillow.
—Lizard's Song. Arvego, Jose & Dewey, Ariane, illus. LC 80-21432. 32p. (ps up). 1992. pap. 3.95 (*0-688-11516-0*, Mulberry) Morrow.
Sis, Peter. Komodo! LC 92-25811. (Illus.). 32p. (ps up). 1993. 15.00 (*0-688-11583-7*); PLB 14.93 (*0-688-11584-5*) Greenwillow.
Wallace, Bill. Ferret in the Bedroom, Lizards in the Fridge. LC 85-21996. 144p. (gr. 3-7). 1986. 14.95 (*0-8234-0600-8*) Holiday.

LLAMAS
Arnold, Caroline. Llama. Hewett, Richard, photos by. LC 87-27130. (Illus.). 48p. (gr. 2-5). 1988. 12.95 (*0-688-07540-1*); PLB 12.88 (*0-688-07541-X*) Morrow Jr Bks.
Bare, Colleen S. Love a Llama. LC 92-39928. (Illus.). 32p. (gr. 1-4). 1994. 13.99 (*0-525-65146-2*, Cobblehill Bks) Dutton Child Bks.

Barkman, Betty & Barkman, Paul. A Well Trained Llama: A Trainers Guide. rev. ed. LC 88-93027. (Illus.). 95p. (Orig.). (gr. 9 up). 1989. pap. text ed. 25.00 (*0-945860-01-3*) Birch Bark Pr.
Hart, Rosana. Living with Llamas: Tales from Juniper Ridge. rev. ed. (Illus.). 192p. 1991. pap. 11.95 (*0-916289-13-3*) Juniper Ridge.
Jones, Susan L. Llamas: Woolly, Winsome & Wonderful. LC 87-29279. (Illus.). 68p. (Orig.). 1987. pap. text ed. 12.95 (*0-942280-47-4*) Pub Horizons.
Kienlen, Helen & Sandercock, Lois. Llamas. Bower, J. R., illus. 16p. (Orig.). (gr. k-4). 1989. pap. text ed. 4.00 (*0-9626864-0-9*) Holistic Learning.
LaBonte, Gail. The Llama. LC 88-16407. (Illus.). 60p. (gr. 3 up). 1988. text ed. 13.95 RSBE (*0-87518-393-X*, Dillon) Macmillan Child Grp.

LLAMAS–FICTION

Guarino, Deborah. Is Your Mama a Llama? Kellogg, Steven, illus. 1991. pap. 3.95 (*0-590-44725-4*, Blue Ribbon Bks) Scholastic Inc.
Massi, Jeri. The Myth of the Llama. Thompson, Del & Thompson, Dana, illus. 118p. (Orig.). (gr. 6). 1989. pap. 5.95 (*1-877778-00-1*) Llama Bks.
Palacios, Argentina. El Secreto de la Llama - the Llama's Secret: Una Leyenda Peruana. LC 93-21436. (gr. 4-7). 1993. PLB 11.89 (*0-8167-3123-3*); pap. 3.95 (*0-8167-3072-5*) Troll Assocs.
Shine, Michael. Mama Llama's Pajamas. Villegas, Carene, illus. 45p. (Orig.). (ps-3). 1990. pap. 8.95 (*0-945265-32-8*) Accord Comm.

LOBSTER FISHERIES–FICTION

Guiberson, Brenda Z. Lobster Boat. Lloyd, Megan, illus. LC 92-4055. 32p. (ps-3). 1993. 14.95 (*0-8050-1756-9*, Bks Young Read) H Holt & Co.

LOBSTERS–FICTION

Harriman, Edward. Leroy the Lobster & Crabby Crab. (Illus.). (ps-1). 1967. pap. 7.95 (*0-89272-000-X*) Down East.
Hartman, Bob. Lobster for Lunch. Stammen, JoEllen M., illus. LC 91-77671. 32p. (gr. k-3). 1992. 14.95 (*0-89272-302-5*) Down East.
MacDonald, High. Chung Lee Loves Lobsters. Wales, Johnny, illus. 24p. (gr. k-3). 1992. PLB 14.95 (*1-55037-217-3*, Pub. by Annick CN); pap. 4.95 (*1-55037-214-9*, Pub. by Annick CN) Firefly Bks Ltd.
Olsen, E. A. Lobster King. LC 68-16400. (Illus.). 48p. (gr. 3 up). 1970. PLB 10.95 (*0-87783-024-X*); pap. 3.94 deluxe ed. (*0-87783-099-1*); cassette 10.60x (*0-87783-192-0*) Oddo.

LOCAL GOVERNMENT

see also Cities and Towns
Feinberg, Barbara S. Local Governments. LC 92-27366. 1993. lib. bdg. 12.90 (*0-531-20153-8*) Watts.
Hepburn, Mary A. Local Government in Georgia. 2nd ed. 240p. (gr. 8-12). 1991. text ed. 13.75 (*0-89854-148-4*) U of GA Inst Govt.
Santrey, Laurence. State & Local Government. Dole, Bob, illus. LC 84-8440. 32p. (gr. 3-6). 1985. PLB 9.49 (*0-8167-0270-5*); pap. text ed. 2.95 (*0-8167-0271-3*) Troll Assocs.

LOCH NESS, SCOTLAND

Abels, Harriette S. Loch Ness Monster. LC 87-9027. (Illus.). 48p. (gr. 5-6). 1987. text ed. 12.95 RSBE (*0-89686-343-3*, Crestwood Hse) Macmillan Child Grp.
Berke, Sally. Monster at Loch Ness. LC 77-24715. (Illus.). 48p. (gr. 4 up). 1983. PLB 20.70 (*0-8172-1054-7*) Raintree Steck-V.
Hezlep, William. Nessie. (gr. 3-12). 1980. pap. 5.00 play script (*0-88734-401-1*) Players Pr.
Landau, Elaine. The Loch Ness Monster. LC 92-35145. (Illus.). 48p. (gr. 3-6). 1993. PLB 14.40 (*1-56294-347-2*) Millbrook Pr.
San Souci, Robert D. The Loch Ness Monster: Opposing Viewpoints. LC 89-12026. (Illus.). 112p. (gr. 5-8). 1989. PLB 14.95 (*0-89908-072-3*) Greenhaven.
Steffens, Bradley. The Loch Ness Monster. LC 94-2120. 1995. 14.95 (*1-56006-159-6*) Lucent Bks.

LOCKS AND KEYS

Hughes, Shirley. Alfie Gets in First. Hughes, Shirley, illus. LC 81-8427. 32p. (ps-1). 1982. 13.95 (*0-688-00848-8*); PLB 13.88 (*0-688-00849-6*) Lothrop.
Sharmat, Marjorie W. Nate the Great & the Missing Key. Simont, Marc, illus. 48p. (gr. 1-4). 1982. pap. 3.50 (*0-440-46191-X*, YB) Dell.
Tchudi, Stephen. Lock & Key: The Secrets of Locking Things up, in, & Out. LC 92-43252. (Illus.). 128p. (gr. 5 up). 1993. SBE 14.95 (*0-684-19363-9*, Scribners Young Read) Macmillan Child Grp.

LOCOMOTION

see Aeronautics; Automobiles; Boats and Boating; Flight; Navigation; Transportation; Walking

LOCOMOTIVES

Brown, James E. Old Freight Train Coloring Book. (SPA & ENG.). 24p. (Orig.). 1992. pap. 0.50 (*0-9632358-0-X*) J E Brown.
Chant, Chris. Steam Locomotives. Batchelor, John, illus. LC 88-28763. 63p. (gr. 3-9). 1989. PLB 16.95 (*1-85435-087-0*) Marshall Cavendish.

LOCOMOTIVES–FICTION

Burton, Virginia L. Choo Choo. (Illus.). 48p. (gr. k-3). 1973. 14.45 (*0-395-17684-0*) HM.
Fleming, Ian. Chitty Chitty Bang Bang. 159p. (gr. 5-6). Repr. of 1964 ed. lib. bdg. 17.95 (*0-88411-983-1*, Pub. by Aeonian Pr) Amereon Ltd.
Peet, Bill. Smokey. (Illus.). (gr. k-3). 1962. 14.45 (*0-395-15992-X*) HM.

LOCUSTS

Bailey, Jill. Life Cycle of a Grasshopper. (ps-3). 1990. PLB 11.90 (*0-531-18314-9*, Pub. by Bookwright Pr) Watts.
Dallinger, Jane. Grasshoppers. LC 80-27806. (Illus.). (gr. 4 up). 1981. PLB 19.95 (*0-8225-1455-9*) Lerner Pubns.
—Grasshoppers. Sato, Yuko, photos by. (Illus.). 48p. (gr. 4 up). pap. 5.95 (*0-8225-9568-0*) Lerner Pubns.
Hasegawa, Yo. The Grasshopper. Pohl, Kathy, ed. LC 85-28228. (Illus.). 32p. (gr. 3-7). 1986. text ed. 10.95 (*0-8172-2536-6*) Raintree Steck-V.
Stowe, Lynn M. Grasshoppers. LC 93-7586. 1993. write for info. (*0-86593-286-7*) Rourke Corp.
Watts, Barrie. Grasshoppers & Crickets. LC 90-45996. (Illus.). 32p. (gr. k-4). 1991. PLB 11.40 (*0-531-14161-6*); pap. 4.95 (*0-531-15618-4*) Watts.

LOCUSTS–FICTION

Fontenot, Mary A. Clovis Crawfish & the Singing Cigales. Vincent, Eric, illus. LC 81-5608. 32p. (ps-3). 1981. 12.95 (*0-88289-270-3*) Pelican.
Loves, June. The Grasshopper. Forss, Ian, illus. LC 92-34263. 1993. 4.25 (*0-383-03626-7*) SRA Schl Grp.
Sushiela. The Ant & the Grasshopper: A Love Story. Sushiela, illus. LC 89-92067. 129p. (Orig.). (gr. 5 up). 1990. pap. 15.95 (*0-9623363-1-9*) Running Water.
Turner, Ann. Grasshopper Summer. LC 88-13847. 144p. (gr. 3-7). 1989. SBE 14.95 (*0-02-789511-4*, Macmillan Child Bk) Macmillan Child Grp.
—Grasshopper Summer. 166p. (gr. 5-9). 1990. pap. 2.95 (*0-8167-2262-5*) Troll Assocs.

LOG CABINS

Danforth, Helen H. A Tale of Two Cabins. (Illus.). 36p. (Orig.). (gr. 7 up). 1985. pap. 4.95 (*0-9614899-0-1*) Pioneer Farm.

LOGGING

see Lumber and Lumbering

LOGIC

see also Knowledge, Theory of; Probabilities; Reasoning; Thought and Thinking
Birmingham, Duncan. Look Twice: Mirror Reflections, Logical Thinking. (gr. 3 up). 1991. pap. 6.95 (*0-906212-86-3*, Pub. by Tarquin UK) Parkwest Pubns.
Butrick, Lyn M. Logic for Space Age Kids. Cooper, William H., ed. Butrick, Lyn M., illus. LC 84-50892. 32p. (gr. 3-6). 1984. pap. 5.27 (*0-914127-16-0*) Univ Class.
Daniel, Becky. Logic Thinker Sheets. 64p. (gr. 4-8). 1989. 8.95 (*0-86653-505-5*, GA1099) Good Apple.
Eads, Sandra & Post, Beverly. Logic in the Round. (gr. 5 up). 1989. pap. 8.95 (*0-8224-4206-X*) Fearon Teach Aids.
Lieberman, Lillian. Making Inferences. 64p. (gr. 2-5). 1989. 6.95 (*0-912107-88-X*, MM1905) Monday Morning Bks.
Post, Beverly & Eads, Sandra. Logic, Anyone? One Hundred Sixty-Five Brain-Stretching Problems. (gr. 5-12). 1982. pap. 12.95 (*0-8224-4326-0*); wkbk. 5.95 (*0-8224-4327-9*) Fearon Teach Aids.
Rothstein, Erica L. & Renineke, eds. Dell Book of Logic Problems, No. 3. (Orig.). 1988. pap. 10.99 (*0-440-50068-0*, Dell Trade Pbks) Dell.
Schoenfield, Mark & Rosenblatt, Jeanette. Adventures with Logic. (gr. 5-7). 1985. pap. 8.95 (*0-8224-0285-8*) Fearon Teach Aids.
—Discovering Logic. (gr. 4-6). 1985. pap. 8.95 (*0-8224-1915-7*) Fearon Teach Aids.
—Playing with Logic. (gr. 3-5). 1985. pap. 8.95 (*0-8224-5310-X*) Fearon Teach Aids.
Sloane, Paul & MacHale, Des. Logical Thinking Puzzles. Miller, Myron, illus. LC 92-19095. 96p. (gr. 5 up). 1992. 12.95 (*0-8069-8670-0*) Sterling.
Tilkin, Sheldon L. & Conoway, Judith. Predicting Outcomes. (Illus.). 24p. (gr. 3-4). 1980. wkbk. 2.95 (*0-89403-575-4*) EDC.
—Predicting Outcomes. (Illus.). 24p. (gr. 4-5). 1980. wkbk. 2.95 (*0-89403-585-1*) EDC.

LONDON, JACK, 1876-1916

Bains, Rae. Jack London: A Life of Adventure. Geehan, Wayne, illus. LC 91-3927. 48p. (gr. 4-6). 1992. PLB 10.79 (*0-8167-2513-6*); pap. text ed. 3.50 (*0-8167-2514-4*) Troll Assocs.
Gleiter, Jan & Thompson, Kathleen. Jack London. LC 87-23578. (Illus.). 32p. (Orig.). (gr. 2-5). 1987. PLB 19.97 (*0-8172-2661-3*) Raintree Steck-V.
Jack London. (Illus.). (gr. 2-5). 1989. PLB 29.28 incl. cassette (*0-8172-2952-3*) Raintree Steck-V.
Powell, John. The Arts - Jack London. LC 92-46766. 1993. 19.93 (*0-86625-486-2*); 14.95s.p. (*0-685-66540-2*) Rourke Pubns.
Schroeder, Alan. Jack London. (Illus.). 128p. (gr. 5 up). 1992. lib. bdg. 17.95 (*0-7910-1623-4*) Chelsea Hse.

LONDON

Book of London. (Illus.). 64p. (gr. 5 up). 1987. PLB 13.96 (*0-88110-260-1*); pap. 8.95 (*0-7460-0050-2*) EDC.
Davis, James E. & Hawke, Sharryl D. London. (Illus.). 64p. (gr. 4-9). 1990. PLB 11.95 (*0-8172-3027-0*) Raintree Steck-V.
Hughes, Richard. Lost in London. Wheeler, Jill, ed. Lowery, Carol, illus. LC 88-71732. 48p. (gr. 4). 1988. lib. bdg. 10.95 (*0-939179-47-4*) Abdo & Dghtrs.
Lovett, Sarah. Kidding Around London: A Young Person's Guide to the City. Taylor, Michael, illus. 64p. (Orig.). (gr. 3 up). 1989. pap. 9.95 (*0-945465-24-6*) John Muir.
Marker, Sherry. London. (Illus.). 64p. (gr. 3-7). PLB 14.95 (*1-56711-023-1*) Blackbirch.
Munro, Roxie. The Inside-Outside Book of London. LC 89-12023. (Illus.). 48p. (ps up). 1989. 13.95 (*0-525-44522-6*, DCB) Dutton Child Bks.
Wild, Anne. Pop-up London. (Illus.). 32p. (gr. 3 up). 1985. pap. 7.95 (*0-906212-30-8*, Pub. by Tarquin UK) Parkwest Pubns.
Wittich, John. Discovering London Street Names. 96p. (Orig.). (gr. 6 up). 1977. pap. 3.00 (*0-913714-09-7*) Legacy Bks.

LONDON–FICTION

Alcock, Vivien. The Cuckoo Sister. LC 85-20648. 158p. (gr. 4-6). 1986. pap. 14.95 (*0-385-29467-0*) Delacorte.
Ashley, Bernard. Terry on the Fence. Keeping, Charles, illus. LC 76-39898. (gr. 5-9). 1977. 21.95 (*0-87599-222-6*) S G Phillips.
Bawden, Nina. The Robbers. LC 79-4152. (Illus.). 160p. (gr. 4-7). 1989. Repr. of 1979 ed. 12.95 (*0-688-41902-X*) Lothrop.
Bemelmans, Ludwig. Madeline in London. Bemelmans, Ludwig, illus. 56p. (ps-3). 1977. pap. 4.50 (*0-14-050199-1*, Puffin) Puffin Bks.
Blacker, Terence. Homebird. LC 92-23536. 144p. (gr. 7 up). 1993. SBE 13.95 (*0-02-710685-3*, Bradbury Pr) Macmillan Child Grp.
Bond, Michael. Paddington Meets the Queen. Lobban, John, illus. LC 92-24938. 32p. (ps-3). 1993. 3.95 (*0-694-00460-X*, Festival) HarpC Child Bks.
Buckley, Joe. Donny in London. 160p. (gr. 7-11). 1993. pap. 9.95 (*0-86327-360-2*, Pub. by Wolfhound Pr EIRE) Dufour.
Burnett, Frances H. Little Princess. (gr. 3 up). 1993. pap. 4.99 (*0-88070-527-2*, Gold & Honey) Questar Pubs.
—A Little Princess. Dubowski, Cathy E., adapted by. 108p. (Orig.). (gr. 2-6). 1994. pap. 2.99 (*0-685-71036-X*) Random Bks Yng Read.
—Little Princess. 14.95 (*0-8488-1253-0*) Amereon Ltd.
Cutler, Lynn W. Baggage to London. Ohi, Ruth, illus. 24p. (Orig.). (ps-1). 1994. pap. 0.99 (*1-55037-345-5*, Pub. by Annick CN) Firefly Bks Ltd.
Danziger, Paula. You Can't Eat Your Chicken Pox, Amber Brown. Ross, Tony, illus. LC 93-37761. (gr. 3 up). 1995. write for info. (*0-399-22702-4*, Putnam) Putnam Pub Group.
Dickens, Charles. Dombey & Son. (ps-8). 1990. Repr. lib. bdg. 29.95x (*0-89966-678-7*) Buccaneer Bks.
—Little Dorrit. (ps-8). 1990. Repr. lib. bdg. 39.95x (*0-89966-680-9*) Buccaneer Bks.
—Oliver Twist. (gr. 9 up). 1964. pap. 3.50 (*0-8049-0009-4*, CL-9) Airmont.
—Oliver Twist. Martin, Les, adapted by. Zallinger, Jean, illus. LC 89-24279. 96p. (gr. 2-6). 1990. PLB 5.99 (*0-679-90391-7*); pap. 2.99 (*0-679-80391-2*) Random Bks Yng Read.
Disney, Walt. Oliver & Company. (ps-3). 1990. 6.98 (*0-8317-6574-7*) Viking Child Bks.
Doherty, Berlie. Street Child. large type ed. (Illus.). (gr. 1-8). 1994. 15.95 (*0-7451-2225-6*, Galaxy etc.) Chivers N Amer.
—Street Child. LC 94-5020. 160p. (gr. 3-7). 1994. 14.95 (*0-531-06864-1*); PLB 14.99 (*0-531-08714-X*) Orchard Bks Watts.
Eure, Wesley. Red Wings of Christmas. Paolillo, Ronald G., illus. LC 92-5457. 160p. (gr. 3-7). 1992. 19.95 (*0-88289-902-3*); audiocassette 14.95 (*0-88289-998-8*) Pelican.
Godden, Rumer. An Episode of Sparrows. 208p. (gr. 7 up). 1989. pap. 4.95 (*0-14-034024-6*, Puffin) Puffin Bks.
Pascal, Francine. Love & Death in London. 1994. pap. 3.50 (*0-553-56227-4*) Bantam.
Richemont, Enid. The Magic Skateboard. Ormerod, Jan, illus. LC 92-53010. 80p. (gr. 3-6). 1993. 13.95 (*1-56402-132-7*) Candlewick Pr.
Slobodkin, Louis. The Space Ship Returns to the Apple Tree. Slobodkin, Louis, illus. LC 93-10747. 128p. (gr. 3-7). 1994. pap. 3.95 (*0-689-71768-7*, Aladdin) Macmillan Child Grp.
Ure, Jean. Plaque. 218p. (gr. 5 up). 1991. 16.95 (*0-15-262429-5*, HB Juv Bks) HarBrace.

LONDON–HISTORY

Kronenwetter, Michael. London. LC 91-30306. (Illus.). 96p. (gr. 6 up). 1992. text ed. 14.95 RSBE (*0-02-751050-6*, New Discovery) Macmillan Child Grp.

LONDON–HISTORY–FICTION

De Angeli, Marguerite. The Door in the Wall: Story of Medieval London. De Angeli, Marguerite, illus. LC 64-7025. 111p. (gr. 3-6). 1989. pap. 14.95 (*0-385-07283-X*) Doubleday.
Paton-Walsh, Jill. Fireweed. LC 73-109554. 144p. (gr. 6 up). 1970. 14.95 (*0-374-32310-0*) FS&G.

LONDON–POETRY

Bemmelmans, Ludwig. Madeline in London. Bemelmans, Ludwig, illus. (gr. k-3). 1961. pap. 15.00 (*0-670-44648-3*) Viking Child Bks.

LONDON–POLICE

Wilkes, J. The London Police in the Nineteenth Century. LC 76-57247. (Illus.). 48p. (gr. 7 up). 1977. pap. 7.95 (*0-521-21406-8*) Cambridge U Pr.

LONDON. TOWER

Fisher, Leonard E. The Tower of London. Fisher, Leonard E., illus. LC 87-1629. 32p. (gr. 1-5). 1987. SBE 15.95 (*0-02-735370-2*, Macmillan Child Bk) Macmillan Child Grp.
Saunders, Susan. The Tower of London. (gr. 2-4). 1984. pap. 2.25 (*0-553-15490-7*, Skylark) Bantam.

LONELINESS–FICTION
Ardizzone, Edward. Tim All Alone. (Illus.). 48p. (ps-7). 1990. pap. 6.95 (*0-19-272125-9*) OUP.
Ballard, Robin. My Father Is Far Away. LC 91-29580. (Illus.). 32p. (ps-6). 1992. 14.00 (*0-688-10953-5*); PLB 13.93 (*0-688-10954-3*) Greenwillow.
Crompton, Anne E. The Snow Pony. 128p. (gr. 4-6). 1991. 14.95 (*0-8050-1573-6*, Bks Young Read) H Holt & Co.
Fienberg, Anna. The Hottest Boy Who Ever Lived. Grant, Christy, ed. Gamble, Kim, illus. LC 94-6648. 32p. (gr. k-3). 1994. PLB 14.95 (*0-8075-3387-4*) A Whitman.
Fritz, Jean. Homesick: My Own Story. Tomes, Margot, illus. 160p. (gr. 3-7). 1982. 14.95 (*0-399-20933-6*, Putnam) Putnam Pub Group.
Hall, Donald. The Man Who Lived Alone. Azarian, Mary, illus. LC 84-47655. 36p. (gr. 2 up). 1984. 12.50 (*0-87923-538-1*) Godine.
Peck, Richard. Close Enough to Touch. LC 81-65498. 192p. (gr. 7 up). 1981. 15.00 (*0-385-28145-5*) Delacorte.
Petty, Kate. Feeling Left Out. Firmin, Charlotte, illus. 24p. (ps-2). 1991. pap. 4.95 (*0-8120-4658-7*) Barron.
Ryan, Cheryl. Sally Arnold. Farnsworth, Bill, illus. LC 94-6455. 1995. write for info. (*0-525-65176-4*, Cobblehill Bks) Dutton Child Bks.
Rylant, Cynthia. An Angel for Solomon Singer. Catalanotto, Peter, illus. LC 91-15957. 32p. 1992. 14. 95 (*0-531-05978-2*); lib. bdg. 14.99 (*0-531-08578-3*) Orchard Bks Watts.
Stevenson, James. Mr. Hacker. Modell, Frank, illus. LC 89-30479. 32p. (gr. k up). 1990. 12.95 (*0-688-09216-0*); PLB 12.88 (*0-688-09217-9*) Greenwillow.
LONG ISLAND–FICTION
Fitzhugh, Louise. Long Secret. Fitzhugh, Louise, illus. LC 65-23370. (gr. 5 up). 1965. PLB 14.89 (*0-06-021411-2*) HarpC Child Bks.
The Great Gatsby. 1993. pap. text ed. 6.50 (*0-582-08485-7*, 79818) Longman.
Hosie, Bounar. Life Belts. LC 92-43048. 1993. 14.95 (*0-385-31074-9*) Delacorte.
LONG ISLAND–HISTORY
Shodell, Elly, ed. Particles of the Past: Sandmining on Long Island 1870s-1980s. 2nd ed. Pope, Genoroso, pref. by. (Illus.). 43p. (gr. 9-12). pap. 8.95 (*0-9615059-0-7*) Pt WA Pub Lib.
Stoff, Joshua. From Canoes to Cruisers: The Maritime Heritage of Long Island. Stoff, Joshua, illus. LC 93-40844. 112p. (Orig.). 1994. 18.00 (*1-55787-110-8*, Empire State Bks); pap. 10.00 (*1-55787-111-6*, Empire State Bks) Heart of the Lakes.
LONGEVITY
see Old Age
LOOKING GLASSES
see Mirrors
LOONS
Green, Ivah J. Loon. LC 65-22310. (Illus.). 32p. (gr. 4 up). 1968. PLB 9.95 (*0-87783-025-8*) Oddo.
Josephson, Judith P. The Loon. LC 88-9599. (Illus.). 48p. (gr. 5). 1988. text ed. 12.95 RSBE (*0-89686-390-5*, Crestwood Hse) Macmillan Child Grp.
Klein, Tom. Loon Magic for Kids. 48p. 1990. 14.95 (*1-55971-047-0*); pap. 6.95 (*1-55971-121-3*) NorthWord.
—Loon Magic for Kids. LC 90-9860. (Illus.). 48p. (gr. 3-4). 1990. PLB 18.60 (*0-8368-0402-3*) Gareth Stevens Inc.
LOONS–FICTION
Hassett, John & Hassett, Ann. Junior - A Little Loon Tale. Hassett, John, illus. 32p. (gr. 2-5). 1993. 14.95 (*0-89272-322-X*) Down East.
Krupinsky, Jacquelyn S. Look Out for Loons. Krupinsky, Lisa A., ed. Arbuckle, Jane & Krupinsky, Lisa, illus. 28p. (Orig.). (gr. k-3). 1983. pap. 5.95 (*0-912123-01-X*) Woodbury Pr.

Loon, Joan & Loon, John. The Lunettes. (Illus.). 16p. (gr. 1-4). 1984. 25.00 (*1-56611-503-5*); pap. 18.00 (*1-56611-504-3*) Jonas.
Our modern society looks to protection of the environment. Two Loons decide to find the best nesting area & begin a trip that takes them over historic London, New York City &, of course, over the sea & through the air. Thinking at last to have found a suitable place to land, an unfortunate accident of the environment happens to them; not spelled out, some creative thinking evolves from today's "select schools" programs. In graded schools best for grades 1-4. Teacher read, explained 1-2. It is done in black & white to cut down on toners throw-off often required by Cannon copiers. Call or write for information. To order: Jonas Publishing, 2603 W. 60th, Indianapolis, IN 46208 (317-255-5220). Prepaid only; checks must accompany. No refunds or returns. Include $2.00 min. for shipping & handling.
Publisher Provided Annotation.

Martin, Jacqueline B. Birdwashing Song: The Willow Tree Loon. Carpenter, Nancy, illus. LC 94-11787. 1995. 15.95 (*0-02-762442-0*) Macmillan.
LORD'S DAY
see Sabbath
LORD'S PRAYER
Dumelle, Grace. The Lord's Prayer: Explained for Little Ones. Williams, Abbie, illus. 24p. (Orig.). 1990. pap. text ed. 4.95 (*0-937739-08-1*) Roman IL.
Le Tord, Bijou. The River & the Rain: The Lord's Prayer. LC 93-20730. 1994. 15.95 (*0-385-32034-5*) Doubleday.
The Lord's Prayer. (ps-2). 3.95 (*0-7214-5015-6*) Ladybird Bks.
Lucy, Reda, pseud. The Lord's Prayer for Children. Nannie, illus., pseud. 24p. (Orig.). (ps-3). 1981. pap. 2.25 (*0-87516-437-4*) DeVorss.
Meyer, David & Meyer, Alice, eds. The Lord's Prayer: An Illustrated Bible Passage for Young Children. Katsma, Candi, illus. LC 91-90826. 32p. (Orig.). (ps-4). 1991. pap. 10.95 incl. cassette (*1-879099-05-5*) Thy Word.
Rock, Lois. The Lord's Prayer for Children. (Illus.). 32p. (gr. k-2). 1993. 8.99 (*0-7459-2542-1*) Lion USA.
Tudor, Tasha. Give Us This Day, the Lord's Prayer. (Illus.). (ps up). 1989. 9.95 (*0-399-21442-9*, Philomel Bks) Putnam Pub Group.
Webb, Barbara O. The Lord's Prayer: The Prayer Jesus Taught. (Illus.). 24p. (Orig.). (gr. k-4). 1986. saddle stitch 3.99 (*0-570-08529-2*, 56-1556) Concordia.
LOS ANGELES
Bishop, Kathleen. A White Face Painted Brown: A Young Girl's Journey into the Bosom of a Black & Mexican Los Angeles Ghetto Called Aliso Village. Shwed, Joanne, ed. 180p. (Orig.). (gr. 8-12). 1993. pap. text ed. 12.95 (*0-9636217-1-8*) Pallas Athena.
Cash, Judy. Kidding Around Los Angeles: A Young Person's Guide to the City. (Illus.). 64p. (gr. 3 up). 1989. pap. 9.95 (*0-945465-34-3*) John Muir.
Davis, James E. & Hawke, Sharryl D. Los Angeles. (Illus.). 64p. (gr. 4-9). 1990. PLB 11.95 (*0-8172-3028-9*) Raintree Steck-V.
Los Angeles Children's Museum Staff. Color Your Way Through L. A. Polsky, Carol, ed. U. S.-Japan Cross Culture Center & Opinion Editors, trs. Rubin, Marvin, illus. (ENG, SPA & JPN.). 56p. (Orig.). (gr. k up). 1983. 3.95 (*0-914953-00-1*) Los Angeles.
Rodriguez, Luis J. Always Running: Gang Days in L. A. LC 92-39002. (Orig.). (gr. 9 up). 1993. 19.95 (*1-880684-06-3*) Curbstone.
St. George, Mark. Los Angeles: City of Dreams II. rev. ed. (Illus.). 160p. 1989. 16.95 (*0-9620541-4-3*); pap. 9.95 (*0-9620541-5-1*) Proteus LA.
Stewart, G. Los Angeles. (Illus.). 48p. (gr. 5 up). 1989. lib. bdg. 15.94 (*0-86592-540-2*); 11.95 (*0-685-58589-1*) Rourke Corp.
Zach, Cheryl. Los Angeles. (Illus.). 60p. (gr. 3 up). 1990. text ed. 13.95 RSBE (*0-87518-415-4*, Dillon) Macmillan Child Grp.
Zelver, Patricia. The Wonderful Towers of Watts. Lessac, Frane, illus. LC 93-20344. 32p. 1994. 15.00 (*0-688-12649-9*, Tambourine Bks); PLB 14.93 (*0-688-12650-2*, Tambourine Bks) Morrow.
LOS ANGELES–FICTION
Block, Francesca L. The Hanged Man. LC 94-720. 128p. (gr. 7 up). 1994. 14.00 (*0-06-024536-0*); PLB 13.89 (*0-06-024537-9*) HarpC Child Bks.
—Weetzie Bat. LC 88-6214. 96p. (gr. 7 up). 1989. 12.95 (*0-06-020534-2*); PLB 14.89 (*0-06-020536-9*) HarpC Child Bks.
—Witch Baby. LC 90-28916. 112p. (gr. 7 up). 1991. 14. 00 (*0-06-020547-4*); PLB 13.89 (*0-06-020548-2*) HarpC Child Bks.
Bray, Marian F. Stars over East L. A. (Orig.). (gr. 8-12). 1993. pap. 6.99 (*0-87788-798-5*) Shaw Pubs.
Bunting, Eve. Smoky Night. Diaz, David, illus. LC 93-14885. (gr. 4 up). 1994. 14.95 (*0-15-269954-6*) Harbrace.
Fitch, Janet. Kicks. LC 94-18592. Date not set. write for info. (*0-395-69624-0*, Clarion) HM.
Koertge, Ron. Harmony Arms. 1992. 15.95 (*0-316-50104-2*, Joy St Bks) Little.
Mills, Bart. Melrose Place - Off the Record. 1992. pap. 3.99 (*0-06-106787-3*, Harp PBks) HarpC.
Nelson, Peter. Melrose Place. 1992. pap. 3.99 (*0-06-106788-1*, Harp PBks) HarpC.
Rocklin, Joanne. Jace the Ace. De Groat, Diane, illus. LC 90-34095. 112p. (gr. 2-6). 1990. SBE 13.95 (*0-02-777445-7*, Macmillan Child Bk) Macmillan Child Grp.
Somtow, S. P. The Wizard's Apprentice. Jainschigg, Nicholas, illus. LC 93-12384. 144p. (gr. 7 up). 1993. SBE 14.95 (*0-689-31576-7*, Atheneum Child Bk) Macmillan Child Grp.
Weisberg, Valerie H. Three Jolly Stories Include: Three Jollys, Jollys Visit L. A., Jolly Gets Mugged: An ESL Adult-Child Reader. Kolino, Olga, illus. 76p. (Orig.). (gr. 4 up). 1985. pap. text ed. 6.95x (*0-9610912-4-X*) V H Pub.
LOS ANGELES–RACE RELATIONS
Salak, John. The Los Angeles Riots: America's Cities in Crisis. LC 92-30572. (Illus.). 64p. (gr. 5-8). 1993. 15. 90 (*1-56294-373-1*) Millbrook Pr.
LOS ANGELES DODGERS (BASEBALL TEAM)
Goodman, Michael. Los Angeles Dodgers. 48p. (gr. 4-10). 1992. PLB 14.95 (*0-88682-458-3*) Creative Ed.
The Los Angeles Dodgers. 1991. pap. 2.99 (*0-517-05787-5*) Random Hse Value.
Los Angeles Dodgers. (gr. 4-7). 1993. pap. 1.49 (*0-553-56432-3*) Bantam.
Sanford, William R. & Green, Carl R. Sandy Koufax. LC 92-31249. (Illus.). 48p. (gr. 5). 1993. text ed. 11.95 RSBE (*0-89686-780-3*, Crestwood Hse) Macmillan Child Grp.
LOTUS 1-2-3 (COMPUTER PROGRAM)
Blanc, Iris. Lotus 1-2-3 (Ver. 2.2) Quick Reference Guide. (gr. 9-12). 1990. spiral bdg. 8.95 (*1-56243-000-9*, L2-17); transparencies 225.00 (*1-56243-026-2*, TT19) DDC Pub.
LOUIS 14TH, KING OF FRANCE, 1638-1715
Aliki. King's Day: Louis XIV of France. LC 88-38179. (Illus.). 32p. (gr. 2-6). 1989. 13.95 (*0-690-04588-3*, Crowell Jr Bks); PLB 13.89 (*0-690-04590-5*, Crowell Jr Bks) HarpC Child Bks.
—The King's Day: Louis XIV of France. Aliki, illus. LC 88-38179. 32p. (gr. 2-6). 1991. pap. 4.95 (*0-06-443268-8*, Trophy) HarpC Child Bks.
LOUISIANA
Aylesworth, Thomas G. & Aylesworth, Virginia L. South Central (Louisiana, Arkansas, Missouri, Kansas, Oklahoma) (Illus.). 64p. (gr. 3 up). 1992. PLB 16.95 (*0-7910-1047-3*) Chelsea Hse.
Carpenter, Allan. Louisiana. LC 78-3390. (Illus.). 96p. (gr. 4 up). 1978. PLB 16.95 (*0-516-04118-5*) Childrens.
Dartez, Cecilia C. The Louisiana Plantation Coloring Book. Arrigo, Joseph, illus. 32p. (Orig.). (ps-4). 1985. pap. 3.25 (*0-88289-473-0*) Pelican.
Gelhay, Patrick & Marcantel, David E. Notre Langue Louisianaise: Our Louisiana Language, Bk. 1. Graeff, Benny, et al, illus. LC 85-81018. (ENG & FRE.). 180p. (gr. 4). 1985. text ed. 14.95 (*0-935085-00-9*); Tchr's ed. 14.95 (*0-935085-01-7*); write for info. Dialogue Booklet (*0-935085-03-3*); Cassette Tape Set 49.95 (*0-935085-02-5*) Ed Francaises.
Kent, Deborah. Louisiana. 196p. 1993. text ed. 15.40 (*1-56956-166-4*) W A T Braille.
LaDoux, Rita C. Louisiana. LC 92-13365. 1993. PLB 17. 50 (*0-8225-2740-5*) Lerner Pubns.
Marsh, Carole. Avast, Ye Slobs! Louisiana Pirate Trivia. (Illus.). (gr. 3-8). 1994. PLB 24.95 (*0-7933-0520-9*); pap. 14.95 (*0-7933-0519-5*); disk 29.95 (*0-7933-0521-7*) Gallopade Pub Group.
—The Beast of the Louisiana Bed & Breakfast. (Illus.). (gr. 3-8). 1994. PLB 24.95 (*0-7933-1669-3*); pap. 14.95 (*0-7933-1670-7*); disk 29.95 (*0-7933-1671-5*) Gallopade Pub Group.
—Bow Wow! Louisiana Dogs in History, Mystery, Legend, Lore, Humor & More! (Illus.). (gr. 3-12). 1994. PLB 24.95 (*0-7933-3521-3*); pap. 14.95 (*0-7933-3522-1*); computer disk 29.95 (*0-7933-3523-X*) Gallopade Pub Group.
—Carole Marsh Louisiana Books, 44 bks. (Illus.). (gr. 3-8). 1994. PLB 1027.80 set (*0-7933-1293-0*); pap. 587.80 set (*0-7933-5158-8*) Gallopade Pub Group.
—Christopher Columbus Comes to Louisiana! Includes Reproducible Activities for Kids! (Illus.). (gr. 3-12). 1994. PLB 24.95 (*0-7933-3674-0*); pap. 14.95 (*0-7933-3675-9*); computer disk 29.95 (*0-7933-3676-7*) Gallopade Pub Group.
—The Hard-to-Believe-But-True! Book of Louisiana History, Mystery, Trivia, Legend, Lore, Humor & More. (Illus.). (gr. 3-8). 1994. PLB 24.95 (*0-7933-0517-9*); pap. 14.95 (*0-7933-0516-0*); disk 29. 95 (*0-7933-0518-7*) Gallopade Pub Group.
—If My Louisiana Mama Ran the World! (Illus.). (gr. 3-8). 1994. lib. bdg. 24.95 (*0-7933-1674-X*); pap. 14.95 (*0-7933-1675-8*); disk 29.95 (*0-7933-1676-6*) Gallopade Pub Group.
—Jurassic Ark! Louisiana Dinosaurs & Other Prehistoric Creatures. (gr. k-12). 1994. PLB 24.95 (*0-7933-7482-0*); pap. 14.95 (*0-7933-7483-9*); computer disk 29.95 (*0-7933-7484-7*) Gallopade Pub Group.
—Let's Quilt Louisiana & Stuff It Topographically! (Illus.). (gr. 3-8). 1994. PLB 24.95 (*1-55609-397-7*); pap. 14.95 (*1-55609-075-7*); disk 29.95 (*0-7933-1664-2*) Gallopade Pub Group.
—Let's Quilt Our Louisiana Parish. 1994. lib. bdg. 24.95 (*0-7933-7167-8*); pap. text ed. 14.95 (*0-7933-7168-6*); disk 29.95 (*0-7933-7169-4*) Gallopade Pub Group.
—Let's Quilt Our Louisiana Town. 1994. lib. bdg. 24.95 (*0-7933-7017-5*); pap. text ed. 14.95 (*0-7933-7018-3*); disk 29.95 (*0-7933-7019-1*) Gallopade Pub Group.
—Louisiana! A(lligator) to Z(ydeco) 1994. PLB 24.95 (*0-7933-7321-2*); pap. text ed. 14.95 (*0-7933-7320-4*); disk 29.95 (*0-7933-7322-0*) Gallopade Pub Group.
—Louisiana & Other State Greats (Biographies) (Illus.). (gr. 3-8). 1994. lib. bdg. 24.95 (*1-55609-404-3*); pap. 14.95 (*1-55609-403-5*); disk 29.95 (*0-685-45939-X*) Gallopade Pub Group.
—Louisiana Bandits, Bushwackers, Outlaws, Crooks, Devils, Ghosts, Desperadoes & Other Assorted & Sundry Characters! (Illus.). (gr. 3-8). 1994. PLB 24.95 (*0-7933-0502-0*); pap. 14.95 (*0-7933-0501-2*); disk 29. 95 (*0-7933-0503-9*) Gallopade Pub Group.

—Louisiana Classic Christmas Trivia: Stories, Recipes, Activities, Legends, Lore & More! (Illus.). (gr. 3-8). 1994. PLB 24.95 (*0-7933-0505-5*); pap. 14.95 (*0-7933-0504-7*); disk 29.95 (*0-7933-0506-3*) Gallopade Pub Group.

—Louisiana Coastales. (Illus.). (gr. 3-8). 1994. PLB 24.95 (*1-55609-400-0*); pap. 14.95 (*1-55609-119-2*); disk 29.95 (*0-7933-1673-1*) Gallopade Pub Group.

—Louisiana Coastales. 1994. lib. bdg. 24.95 (*0-7933-7283-6*) Gallopade Pub Group.

—Louisiana Dingbats! Bk. 1: A Fun Book of Games, Stories, Activities & More about Our State That's All in Code! for You to Decipher. (Illus.). (gr. 3-12). 1994. PLB 24.95 (*0-7933-3827-1*); pap. 14.95 (*0-7933-3828-X*); computer disk 29.95 (*0-7933-3829-8*) Gallopade Pub Group.

—Louisiana Festival Fun for Kids! (Illus.). (gr. 3-12). 1994. lib. bdg. 24.95 (*0-7933-3980-4*); pap. 14.95 (*0-7933-3981-2*); disk 29.95 (*0-7933-3982-0*) Gallopade Pub Group.

—The Louisiana Hot Air Balloon Mystery. (Illus.). (gr. 2-9). 1994. 24.95 (*0-685-37850-0*); pap. 14.95 (*0-7933-2481-5*); computer disk 29.95 (*0-7933-2482-3*) Gallopade Pub Group.

—Louisiana Jeopardy! Answers & Questions about Our State! (Illus.). (gr. 3-12). 1994. PLB 24.95 (*0-7933-4133-7*); pap. 14.95 (*0-7933-4134-5*); computer disk 29.95 (*0-7933-4135-3*) Gallopade Pub Group.

—Louisiana "Jography" A Fun Run Thru Our State! (Illus.). (gr. 3-8). 1994. lib. bdg. 24.95 (*1-55609-396-9*); pap. 14.95 (*1-55609-108-7*); disk 29.95 (*0-7933-1663-4*) Gallopade Pub Group.

—Louisiana Kid's Cookbook: Recipes, How-to, History, Lore & More! (Illus.). (gr. 3-8). 1994. PLB 24.95 (*0-7933-0514-4*); pap. 14.95 (*0-7933-0513-6*); disk 29.95 (*0-7933-0515-2*) Gallopade Pub Group.

—Louisiana Quiz Bowl Crash Course! (Illus.). (gr. 3-8). 1994. PLB 24.95 (*1-55609-402-7*); pap. 14.95 (*1-55609-401-9*); disk 29.95 (*0-7933-1672-3*) Gallopade Pub Group.

—Louisiana Rollercoasters! (Illus.). (gr. 3-12). 1994. PLB 24.95 (*0-7933-5278-9*); pap. 14.95 (*0-7933-5279-7*); computer disk 29.95 (*0-7933-5280-0*) Gallopade Pub Group.

—Louisiana School Trivia: An Amazing & Fascinating Look at Our State's Teachers, Schools & Students! (Illus.). (gr. 3-8). 1994. PLB 24.95 (*0-7933-0511-X*); pap. 14.95 (*0-7933-0510-1*); disk 29.95 (*0-7933-0512-8*) Gallopade Pub Group.

—Louisiana Silly Basketball Sportsmysteries, Vol. I. (Illus.). (gr. 3-8). 1994. PLB 24.95 (*0-7933-0508-X*); pap. 14.95 (*0-7933-0507-1*); disk 29.95 (*0-7933-0509-8*) Gallopade Pub Group.

—Louisiana Silly Basketball Sportsmysteries, Vol. II. (Illus.). (gr. 3-8). 1994. PLB 24.95 (*0-7933-1678-2*); pap. 14.95 (*0-7933-1679-0*); disk 29.95 (*0-7933-1680-4*) Gallopade Pub Group.

—Louisiana Silly Football Sportsmysteries, Vol. I. (Illus.). (gr. 3-8). 1994. PLB 24.95 (*1-55609-399-3*); pap. 14.95 (*1-55609-398-5*); disk 29.95 (*0-7933-1665-0*) Gallopade Pub Group.

—Louisiana Silly Football Sportsmysteries, Vol. II. (Illus.). (gr. 3-8). 1994. PLB 24.95 (*0-7933-1666-9*); pap. 14.95 (*0-7933-1667-7*); disk 29.95 (*0-7933-1668-5*) Gallopade Pub Group.

—Louisiana Silly Trivia! (Illus.). (gr. 3-8). 1994. PLB 24.95 (*1-55609-395-0*); pap. 14.95 (*1-55609-041-2*); disk 29.95 (*0-7933-0522-5*) Gallopade Pub Group.

—Louisiana Timeline: A Chronology of Louisiana History, Mystery, Trivia, Legend, Lore & More. (Illus.). (gr. 3-12). 1994. PLB 24.95 (*0-7933-5929-5*); pap. 14.95 (*0-7933-5930-9*); computer disk 29.95 (*0-7933-5931-7*) Gallopade Pub Group.

—Louisiana's (Most Devastating!) Disasters & (Most Calamitous!) Catastrophies! (Illus.). (gr. 3-8). 1994. PLB 24.95 (*0-7933-0499-7*); pap. 14.95 (*0-7933-0498-9*); disk 29.95 (*0-685-45940-3*) Gallopade Pub Group.

—Meow! Louisiana Cats in History, Mystery, Legend, Lore, Humor & More! (Illus.). (gr. 3-12). 1994. PLB 24.95 (*0-7933-3368-7*); pap. 14.95 (*0-7933-3369-5*); computer disk 29.95 (*0-7933-3370-9*) Gallopade Pub Group.

—Uncle Rebus: Louisiana Picture Stories for Computer Kids. (Illus.). (gr. k-3). 1994. PLB 24.95 (*0-7933-4555-3*); pap. 14.95 (*0-7933-4556-1*); disk 29.95 (*0-7933-4557-X*) Gallopade Pub Group.

Muller, Carrel & Muller, Brenda. Explore Louisiana. (Illus.). 32p. (gr. 4 up). 1984. 5.50 (*0-915785-00-5*) Bonjour Books.

Norwood, David, et al, illus. Children's Tour of Red Stick City. 32p. (gr. 1-6). 1980. pap. text ed. 2.00 (*0-9608282-2-2*) YWCO.

Turner Program Services, Inc. Staff & Clark, James I. Louisiana. LC 85-9976. 48p. (gr. 3 up). 1985. PLB 19.97 (*0-86514-432-X*) Raintree Steck-V.

LOUISIANA–FICTION

Cusick, Richie T. Evil on the Bayou. 160p. (gr. 7 up). 1992. pap. 3.50 (*0-440-92431-6*, LFL) Dell.

Edler, Timothy. Crawfish-Man Rescues Ron Guidry. (Illus.). (gr. k-8). 1980. lea. 6.00 (*0-931108-05-5*) Little Cajun Bks.

Fontenot, Mary A. Clovis Crawfish & Batiste Bete Puante. Blazek, Scott R., illus. LC 93-1249. 32p. (gr. k-3). 1993. 14.95 (*0-88289-952-X*) Pelican.

—Clovis Crawfish & Bertile's Bon Voyage. Blazek, Scott R., illus. LC 90-22160. 32p. (ps-3). 1991. 12.95 (*0-88289-825-6*) Pelican.

—Clovis Crawfish & Bidon Box Turtle. Blazek, Scott R., illus. LC 93-44340. 1996. write for info. (*1-56554-057-3*) Pelican.

—Clovis Crawfish & Etienne Escargot. Blazek, Scott R., illus. LC 91-26896. 32p. (ps-3). 1992. 12.95 (*0-88289-826-4*) Pelican.

—Clovis Crawfish & Simeon Suce-Fleur. Blazek, Scott R., illus. LC 89-35370. 32p. (ps-3). 1990. 12.95 (*0-88289-751-9*) Pelican.

—Mardi Gras in the Country. Soper, Patrick, illus. LC 93-44341. 1994. 12.95 (*1-56554-033-6*) Pelican.

Hughes, Alice D. Cajun Columbus. rev. ed. Rice, James, illus. LC 91-16783. 40p. 1991. 12.95 (*0-88289-875-2*) Pelican.

Johnson, Zenobia M. & Broussard, Lucretia-del J. Louisiana Reading Adventures. (Illus.). 32p. (Orig.). (gr. 4-7). 1984. 3.50 (*0-9617411-0-4*) Z M Johnson.

Kovacs, Deborah. Brewster's Courage. Mathieu, Joe, illus. LC 91-21481. 112p. (gr. 2-6). 1992. pap. 14.00 jacketed, 3-pc. bdg. (*0-671-74016-4*, S&S BFYR) S&S Trade.

Kroll, Virginia. Sweet Magnolia. Jacques, Laura, illus. LC 93-11966. 32p. (ps-4). 1994. 14.95 (*0-88106-415-7*); PLB 15.88 (*0-88106-416-5*); pap. 6.95 (*0-88106-414-9*) Charlesbridge Pub.

Landry, Tom. The Ballad of Tont Lala. (Illus.). 32p. (gr. k-8). leather 6.00 (*0-931108-11-X*) Little Cajun Bks.

Mire, Betty. T-Pierre Frog & T-Felix Frog Go to School. Mire, Betty, illus. LC 93-74275. 32p. (Orig.). (gr. 1-3). 1994. PLB 6.95 (*0-9639378-0-4*) Cajun Bay Pr.
T-PIERRE FROG & T-FELIX FROG GO TO SCHOOL focuses on the importance of education & reading. This unique book is incorporated with the CAJUN FRENCH language (approximately one CAJUN FRENCH sentence on every page of text). And for every CAJUN FRENCH sentence there is a cute cartoon picture associated with it. It's a book that parents will enjoy reading to their children. The story begins with the first day of school on the Louisiana bayous. T-PIERRE FROG likes going to school & he loves to read. He tells his friend T-FELIX FROG that he wants to learn all he can, because he wants to one day become an astronaut. But T-FELIX FROG doesn't like school. And he tells T-PIERRE that he doesn't have to learn, because his only wish is to become a lazy hobo taking it easy in the shade. Sometimes wishes come true. T-FELIX finds that out, but not without woes. Although T-FELIX FROG is soon enlightened on the importance of an education through a dream or rather a nightmare. T-PIERRE FROG & T-FELIX FROG GO TO SCHOOL is simultaneously entertaining & educational. The book is complete with pronunciation guide.
Publisher Provided Annotation.

Raphael, Morris. The Loup-Garou of Cote Gelee. Rodrigue, George, illus. 48p. (gr. 3-9). 1990. 12.95 (*0-9608866-7-2*) M Raphael.

—Maria: Goddess of the Teche. Ferry, Kate, illus. 48p. (gr. 4-9). 1991. 13.95 (*0-9608866-8-0*) M Raphael.

Snellings, M. L. Jessie Strikes Louisiana Gold. (gr. 3-7). 1969. 3.95 (*0-87511-116-5*) Claitors.

Thomassie, Tynia. Feliciana Feydra LeRoux. Smith, Cat B., illus. LC 93-30347. 1995. 14.95 (*0-316-84125-0*) Little.

Wallace, Bill. Blackwater Swamp. LC 93-28439. 208p. 1994. 15.95 (*0-8234-1120-6*) Holiday.

LOUISIANA–HISTORY

Amoss, Berthe. The Loup Garou. Amoss, Berthe, illus. LC 79-20536. 48p. (ps-4). 1979. 9.95 (*0-88289-189-8*) Pelican.

Bridges, L. T. Flags of Louisiana. (ps-8). 1971. 3.95 (*0-87511-010-X*) Claitors.

Frois, Jeanne. Louisianians All. Carley, Nathan B., illus. LC 92-19208. 96p. 1991. 11.95 (*0-88289-824-8*) Pelican.

Marsh, Carole. Chill Out: Scary Louisiana Tales Based on Frightening Louisiana Truths. (Illus.). 1994. lib. bdg. 24.95 (*0-7933-4708-4*); pap. 14.95 (*0-7933-4709-2*); disk 29.95 (*0-7933-4710-6*) Gallopade Pub Group.

—Louisiana "Crinkum-Crankum" A Funny Word Book about Our State. (Illus.). 1994. lib. bdg. 24.95 (*0-7933-4862-5*); pap. 14.95 (*0-7933-4863-3*); disk 29.95 (*0-7933-4864-1*) Gallopade Pub Group.

—The Louisiana Mystery Van Takes Off! Book 1: Handicapped Louisiana Kids Sneak Off on a Big Adventure. (Illus.). (gr. 3-12). 1994. 24.95 (*0-7933-5015-8*); pap. 14.95 (*0-7933-5016-6*); computer disk 29.95 (*0-7933-5017-4*) Gallopade Pub Group.

—My First Book about Louisiana. (gr. k-4). 1994. PLB 24.95 (*0-7933-5623-7*); pap. 14.95 (*0-7933-5624-5*); computer disk 29.95 (*0-7933-5625-3*) Gallopade Pub Group.

—Patch, the Pirate Dog: A Louisiana Pet Story. (ps-4). 1994. PLB 24.95 (*0-7933-5470-6*); pap. 14.95 (*0-7933-5471-4*); computer disk 29.95 (*0-7933-5472-2*) Gallopade Pub Group.

Phares, Ross. Cavalier in the Wilderness. Hastings, Jack, illus. LC 76-1409. 290p. (gr. 6-12). 1976. 16.95 (*0-88289-128-6*); pap. 11.95 (*0-88289-127-8*) Pelican.

Pitre, Verne. Grandma Was a Sailmaker: Tales of the Cajun Wetlands. Ledet, Billy, illus. 160p. (Orig.). (gr. 9). 1991. pap. 12.95 (*0-9621724-5-6*) Blue Heron LA.

Raphael, Morris. The Battle in the Bayou Country. Minvielle, Chestee H., illus. 199p. (gr. 5-12). 1976. 12.95 (*0-9608866-0-5*) M Raphael.

LOURDES (SHRINE)

Urbide, Fernando & Engler, Dan. Bernadette: The Princess of Lourdes. CCC of America Staff, illus. 35p. (Orig.). (ps-6). 1990. incl. video 21.95 (*1-56814-004-5*); pap. text ed. 4.95 book (*0-685-62403-X*) CCC of America.

LOVE, NAT, 1854?-1921?

Miller, Robert H. The Story of Nat Love. Bryant, Michael, illus. LC 93-46287. 1994. 10.95 (*0-382-24398-6*); pap. 4.95 (*0-382-24393-5*); PLB 14.95 (*0-382-24389-7*) Silver Burdett Pr.

LOVE

see also Dating (Social Customs); Friendship; Marriage

Alvarez Del Real, Maria E., ed. Como Escribir Cartas De Amor. (SPA., Illus.). 288p. (Orig.). 1988. pap. 4.00x (*0-944499-38-4*) Editorial Amer.

Bacher, June M. Love Is a Gentle Stranger. LC 82-83839. 160p. (gr. 10 up). 1992. pap. 3.99 (*1-56507-975-2*); pap. 4.99 (*0-89081-975-0*) Harvest Hse.

Batchelor, Phil. Love Is a Verb. 1991. pap. 3.99 (*0-312-92427-5*) St Martin.

Berry, Linda. The Sincere Milk...That You May Grow. 102p. 1993. pap. 5.00 (*0-9636797-0-8*) Christ Covenant.
Wish you had the power to change things? And that you knew how to use that power? Here is a book written especially for pre-teens, teenagers, & young adults to help them understand about love & relationships. It is written in everyday language so it is easy to understand. It's about the greatest love relationship in the whole world. The love that true marriage (the happily ever after kind), is patterned after. THE SINCERE MILK...THAT YOU MAY GROW is written in two parts. Part one is all about the basics of getting to know the one you love & "how to" act on it. Part two is all about "why" & a history of weddings, traditions, covenants, & where they come from. Everyone knows someone who needs to read this book & benefit from it by putting its principles to use every day. It is full of wisdom, power, & revelations, & how to obtain & use them all towards a better life. To order: CCB, Rt. #5, Box #28, Council Bluffs, IA 51503. Add $1.00 P&H. Discounts.
Publisher Provided Annotation.

Coleman, William L. Cupid is Stupid! How to Fall in Love Without Falling on Your Face. LC 91-21852. 164p. (Orig.). (gr. 9 up). 1991. pap. 7.99 (*0-8308-1335-7*, 1335) InterVarsity.

Dickenson, Celia. Too Many Boys. 160p. (Orig.). (gr. 5-6). 1984. pap. 2.50 (*0-553-26615-2*) Bantam.

Eager, George B. What Is Real Love? Philbrook, Diana, illus. (Orig.). (gr. 6-12). 1993. pap. 3.00x (*1-879224-06-2*) Mailbox.

Edmark, Tomima. Kissing: Everything You Ever Wanted to Know. (Illus.). 144p. (Orig.). 1991. pap. 6.95 (*0-671-70883-X*, Fireside) S&S Trade.

Everly, Kathleen & Gordon, Sol. How Can You Tell If You're Really in Love? Cohen, Vivien, illus. 20p. (gr. 7-12). 1983. pap. 1.95 (*0-934978-06-9*) Ed-U Pr.

Everything You Need to Know about Romantic Breakup. (Illus.). 1991. lib. bdg. 14.95 (*0-8239-1219-1*) Rosen Group.
Field, Mary & Field, Elliot. A Loving Guide to the World As a Two Year-Old Says It. Taklender, Sharon, illus. 14p. (Orig.). (ps up). 1983. pap. 5.95 (*0-914445-00-6*) Palm Springs Pub.
Goley, Elaine. Love. (Illus.). 32p. (gr. 1-4). 1987. PLB 132.66 10 bk. set (*0-317-60399-X*); PLB 15.94 (*0-86592-380-9*); 11.95s.p. (*0-685-67578-5*) Rourke Corp.
Johnson, Helen M. How Do I Love Me? 2nd ed. 105p. (gr. 10 up). 1986. pap. text ed. 9.95 (*0-88133-224-0*) Sheffield WI.
Lewis, Linda. Loving Two Is Hard to Do. 160p. (gr. 6-9). 1990. pap. 2.95 (*0-671-70587-3*, Archway) PB.
Loving. 64p. (gr. 3-8). 1984. 8.95 (*0-86653-180-7*, GA 540, Dist. by Ingram) Good Apple.
Makris, Kathryn. Mission: Love. 192p. (Orig.). (gr. 7-12). 1986. pap. 2.25 (*0-553-25470-7*) Bantam.
Moncure, Jane B. Caring. rev. ed. Endes, Helen, illus. LC 80-27506. (ENG & SPA.). (ps-2). 1981. PLB 14.95 (*0-89565-201-3*) Childs World.
Morris, Ann. Loving. (Illus.). 32p. 1990. 15.00 (*0-688-06340-3*); PLB 14.93 (*0-688-06341-1*) Lothrop.
Nappa, Amy. Love or Infatuation? (Illus.). 48p. (gr. 6-8). 1992. pap. 8.99 (*1-55945-128-9*) Group Pub.
Paulson, Nancy. Preschool Program, Pt. 1: Loving God - Loving Others. (Illus.). 140p. (ps). 1992. pap. 24.99 incl. cassette (*1-55945-400-8*); pap. 18.99 bk. only (*1-55945-819-4*); cassette only 7.99 (*1-55945-816-X*) Group Pub.
RanDelle, B. J. & Marshbum, Sandra. Lessons in Love. Dodd, John & Taylor, Leigh, illus. LC 24-476. 64p. (gr. k-4). 1982. text ed. 5.95 (*0-910445-00-1*) Randelle Pubns.
Rennert, Maggie. I Love You. Frankel, Alona, illus. (ps up). 1987. 9.95 (*0-915361-71-X*) Modan-Adama Bks.
Reynolds, Elizabeth. The Perfect Boy. 176p. (Orig.). (gr. 7-12). 1986. pap. 2.25 (*0-553-25469-3*) Bantam.
St. Clair, Barry & Jones, Bill. Love: Making It Last. 140p. (Orig.). 1993. pap. 5.99 (*1-56476-188-6*, Victor Books) SP Pubns.
Sciacca, Fran & Sciacca, Jill. Is This the Real Thing? What Love Is & Isn't. 64p. 1992. pap. 3.99 saddle stitch bdg. (*0-310-48081-7*) Zondervan.
Stefoff, Rebecca. Friendship & Love. (Illus.). 104p. (gr. 6-12). 1989. 18.95 (*0-7910-0039-7*) Chelsea Hse.
Tudor, Tasha, ed. & illus. All for Love. LC 83-21959. 96p. (gr. 6-8). 1984. 16.95 (*0-399-21012-1*, Philomel) Putnam Pub Group.
Wyatt, Molly. Kim's Winter. (gr. 7 up). 1982. pap. 1.75 (*0-317-00342-9*, Sig Vista) NAL-Dutton.

LOVE–FICTION

Adams, K. J. Crazy in Love. 1993. pap. 3.50 (*0-06-106161-1*, Harp PBks) HarpC.
Aiken, Joan. Black Hearts in Battersea. 224p. (gr. 5 up). 1981. pap. 1.75 (*0-440-90648-2*, LFL) Dell.
Aks, Patricia. Impossible Love. 144p. (Orig.). (gr. 9-12). 1991. pap. 3.50 (*0-449-70297-9*, Juniper) Fawcett.
All Night Long. 128p. (Orig.). (gr. 7-12). 1984. pap. 3.50 (*0-553-27568-2*) Bantam.
Ames, Diane. Never Say Good-Bye. 1992. pap. 3.50 (*0-06-106077-1*, Harp PBks) HarpC.
Anderson, Mary. Catch Me, I'm Falling in Love. (gr. k-12). 1987. pap. 2.50 (*0-440-91122-2*, LFL) Dell.
—Do You Call That a Dream Date? LC 86-908. 176p. (gr. 7 up). 1987. pap. 14.95 (*0-385-29488-3*) Delacorte.
Andrews, Kristi. Upstaged, No. 7. 176p. (Orig.). (gr. 6 up). 1988. pap. 2.50 (*0-553-26704-3*) Bantam.
Anson, Mandy. Focus on Love. 1991. pap. 2.99 (*0-553-29290-0*) Bantam.
Applegate, Katherine. Love Shack. 1993. pap. 3.50 (*0-06-106793-8*, Harp PBks) HarpC.
—My Sister's Boyfriend. 1992. pap. 3.50 (*0-06-106717-2*, Harp PBks) HarpC.
—Ocean City. 1993. pap. 3.50 (*0-06-106748-2*, Harp PBks) HarpC.
—The Unbelievable Truth. (gr. 7 up). 1992. pap. 3.50 (*0-06-106774-1*, Harp PBks) HarpC.
Asher, Sandy. Everything Is Not Enough. (gr. k-12). 1988. pap. 2.75 (*0-440-20002-4*, LFL) Dell.
Avi. Romeo & Juliet - Together (& Alive!) at Last. LC 87-7680. 128p. (gr. 6-8). 1987. 13.95 (*0-531-05721-6*); PLB 13.99 (*0-531-08321-7*) Orchard Bks Watts.
Baer, Judy. Dear Judy, Did You Ever Like a Boy Who Didn't Like You? 1993. pap. 7.99 (*1-55661-341-5*) Bethany Hse.
—The Discovery. 144p. (Orig.). 1993. pap. 3.99 (*1-55661-330-X*) Bethany Hse.
—Riddles of Love-Sweet Dreams No. 63: Kiss Me Creep. 1991. pap. 2.50 (*0-553-30233-7*) Bantam.
Baker, Jennifer. Good-Bye to Love, Bk. 2. (gr. 7). 1994. pap. 3.95 (*0-590-48324-2*) Scholastic Inc.
—A Time to Love, Bk. 1. (gr. 7). 1994. pap. 3.95 (*0-590-48323-4*) Scholastic Inc.
Balian, Lorna. I Love You, Mary Jane. Balian, Lorna, illus. 48p. (ps-3). 1988. Repr. of 1966 ed. 7.50 (*0-687-37100-7*) Humbug Bks.
Banks, Lynne R. Lynne Reid Banks, 3 vols. (gr. 4-7). 1991. pap. 11.97 Boxed Set (*0-380-71680-1*) Avon.
Beauty & the Beast: Be Our Guest. 4p. 1994. 5.98 (*1-57082-000-7*) Mouse Works.
Becker, Eve. The Love Potion. (gr. 4-7). 1989. pap. 2.75 (*0-553-15731-0*, Skylark) Bantam.
Beecham, Jahnna. Dance With Me. 192p. 1987. pap. 2.50 (*0-317-65473-X*, Sweet Dreams) Bantam.
—The Right Combination, No. 139. 192p. (Orig.). (gr. 5 up). 1988. pap. 2.50 (*0-553-27005-2*, Sweet Dreams) Bantam.
Bellairs, John. Trolley to Yesterday. (gr. 4-7). 1990. pap. 3.99 (*0-553-15795-7*) Bantam.
Benchley, Nathaniel. Only Earth & Sky Last Forever. (gr. 7 up). 1992. 17.25 (*0-8446-6583-5*) Peter Smith.
Bennett, Cherie. Only Love Can Break Your Heart, No. 3. 224p. (gr. 7 up). 1993. pap. 3.50 (*0-14-036320-3*) Puffin Bks.
—Sunset Heart. 224p. (Orig.). (ps-3). 1994. pap. 3.99 (*0-425-14183-7*, Splash) Berkley Pub.
—Sunset Revenge. 224p. (Orig.). 1994. pap. 3.99 (*0-425-14228-0*) Berkley Pub.
—Sunset Touch. 1993. pap. 3.99 (*0-425-13708-2*) Berkley Pub.
—Wild Hearts on Fire. 1994. pap. 3.50 (*0-671-86514-5*, Archway) PB.
Bennett, James. I Can Hear the Mourning Dove. 1993. pap. 3.25 (*0-590-45691-1*) Scholastic Inc.
Benning, Elizabeth. Dying of the Light. 1993. pap. 3.50 (*0-06-106796-2*, Harp PBks) HarpC.
—Losing David. 1994. pap. 3.50 (*0-06-106147-6*, Harp PBks) HarpC.
Bernard, Elizabeth. Changing Partners. (gr. 6 up). 1988. pap. 2.95 (*0-449-13303-6*, Girls Only) Fawcett.
Bischoff, David. Some Kind of Wonderful: Movie Tie-In. (gr. 9 up). 1987. pap. 2.50 (*0-440-98042-9*) Dell.
Blair, Alison. Love by the Book. (gr. 10 up). 1989. pap. 2.95 (*0-8041-0331-3*) Ivy Books.
Blake, Susan. A Change of Heart. 224p. (Orig.). (gr. 7-12). 1986. pap. 2.95 (*0-553-26168-1*) Bantam.
Blume, Judy. Fudge-a-Mania. (gr. 4-7). 1991. pap. 3.99 (*0-440-40490-8*, YB) Dell.
—It's Not the End of the World. (gr. k-6). 1982. pap. 3.99 (*0-440-94140-7*) Dell.
—Just As Long As We're Together. 304p. (gr. k-6). 1988. pap. 4.50 (*0-440-40075-9*, YB) Dell.
—Just As Long As We're Together. (gr. 4-7). 1991. pap. 3.99 (*0-440-21094-1*, YB) Dell.
Boies, Janice. Heart & Soul. 192p. (gr. 7 up). 1988. pap. 2.50 (*0-553-26949-6*) Bantam.
—Just the Way You Are. 176p. (Orig.). (gr. 7-12). 1986. pap. 2.50 (*0-553-25815-X*) Bantam.
—Love on Strike. (gr. 9-12). 1990. pap. 2.75 (*0-553-28633-1*) Bantam.
—Wright Boy, Wrong Girl. LC 88-91249. 186p. (gr. 6 up). 1989. pap. 2.95 (*0-8041-0239-2*) Ivy Books.
Boje, Shirley. Cry Softly Thule Nene. (gr. 4-7). 1992. pap. 4.95 (*0-7910-2926-3*) Chelsea Hse.
Boritzer, Etan. What Is Love? Marantz, Robbie, illus. LC 93-94066. 32p. (gr. k-5). 1994. 14.95 (*0-9637597-2-8*); pap. 5.95 (*0-9637597-3-6*) V Lane Bks.
Boulding, J. Russell. Thora's Saga: A Tale of Old Iceland. LC 85-73124. (Illus.). 184p. (Orig.). (gr. 6-12). 1986. pap. 4.95 (*0-936001-00-3*) Peaceable Pr.
Bracale, Carla. Fair-Weather Love. 1992. pap. 2.99 (*0-553-29449-0*) Bantam.
—Puppy Love. (gr. 9-12). 1991. pap. 2.95 (*0-553-28830-X*) Bantam.
Brennan, Melissa. Careless Kisses. 1991. pap. 3.50 (*0-06-106052-6*, Harp PBks) HarpC.
—Could This Be Love? 1991. pap. 3.50 (*0-06-106067-4*, Harp PBks) HarpC.
—Paradise Lost? 1991. pap. 3.50 (*0-06-106068-2*, Harp PBks) HarpC.
—Whispers & Rumors. 1991. pap. 3.50 (*0-06-106049-6*, Harp PBks) HarpC.
Bridgers, Sue E. Permanent Connections. LC 86-45491. 288p. (gr. 7 up). 1988. pap. 3.95 (*0-06-447020-2*, Trophy) HarpC Child Bks.
Bronte, Charlotte. Jane Eyre. Mitchell, Kathy, illus. (gr. 4 up). 1983. deluxe ed. 15.95 (*0-448-06031-0*, G&D) Putnam Pub Group.
Bronte, Emily. Wuthering Heights. Wright, Betty R., adapted by. Cogancherry, Helen, illus. LC 81-15786. 48p. (gr. 4 up). 1982. PLB 20.70 (*0-8172-1682-0*) Raintree Steck-V.
—Wuthering Heights. 224p. 1989. pap. 2.50 (*0-8125-0516-6*) Tor Bks.
Bronte, Emily & Geary, Rick. Wuthering Heights. (Illus.). 52p. Date not set. pap. 4.95 (*1-57209-011-1*) Classics Int Ent.
Brooks, Chelsea. Beauty & the Blues. 144p. (Orig.). (gr. 5 up). 1994. pap. 2.95 (*0-02-041974-0*, Collier Young Ad) Macmillan Child Grp.
—The Dream Team. 144p. (Orig.). (gr. 5 up). 1994. pap. 2.95 (*0-02-041976-7*, Collier Young Ad) Macmillan Child Grp.
—Power of Love. 144p. (Orig.). (gr. 5 up). 1994. pap. 2.95 (*0-02-041975-9*, Collier Young Ad) Macmillan Child Grp.
Brown, Charlotte, adapted by. The Taming of the Shrew. (Illus.). 32p. (gr. 5 up). 1987. pap. 2.50 (*0-88680-276-8*); royalty on application 20.00 (*0-685-67659-5*) I E Clark.
Bryan, Ashley. Sh-Ko & His Eight Wicked Brothers. Yoshimura, Fumio, illus. LC 88-892. 32p. (ps-3). 1988. SBE 13.95 (*0-689-31446-9*, Atheneum Child Bk) Macmillan Child Grp.
Bunting, Eve. Oh, Rick. (Illus.). 64p. (gr. 3-8). 1992. 8.95 (*0-89565-774-0*) Childs World.
—Will You Be My POSSLQ. LC 87-322. 181p. (gr. 7 up). 1987. 12.95 (*0-15-297399-0*, HB Juv Bks) HarBrace.
Byars, Betsy. Bingo Brown's Guide to Romance. large type ed. 1994. 16.95 (*0-7451-2037-7*, Galaxy Child Lrg Print) Chivers N Amer.
Byars, Betsy C. Bingo Brown & the Language of Love. large type ed. 152p. 1989. lib. bdg. 15.95 (*1-55736-146-0*, Crnrstn Bks) BDD LT Grp.
—Bingo Brown's Guide to Romance. 160p. (gr. 3-7). 1992. 14.00 (*0-670-84491-8*) Viking Child Bks.
Cadwallader, Sharon. Star-Crossed Love. 176p. (Orig.). (gr. 7-12). 1987. pap. 2.50 (*0-553-26339-0*) Bantam.
Cahn, Julie. Spotlight on Love. (gr. 2-7). 1984. pap. 2.95 (*0-671-52625-1*) S&S Trade.
Cameron, Ann. The Most Beautiful Place in the World. Allen, Thomas B., illus. LC 88-4228. 64p. (ps-3). 1988. 13.00 (*0-394-89463-4*); lib. bdg. 12.99 (*0-394-99463-9*) Knopf Bks Yng Read.
Castillo, Steve. Maximum Happiness: Jack & Jill Discover True Love. Castillo, Steve, illus. 58p. (Orig.). (gr. 9). 1989. 5.95 (*0-317-93187-3*) Paisley Bks.
Caudell, Marian. Listen to Your Heart. 176p. (Orig.). (gr. 7-12). 1986. pap. 2.50 (*0-553-25727-7*) Bantam.
Caudill, Rebecca. Did You Carry the Flag Today, Charley? (gr. k-6). 1988. pap. 3.25 (*0-440-40092-9*) Dell.
Chief Little Summer & Warm Night Rain. The Misfit. 300p. (gr. 8-12). 1991. 10.95 (*1-880440-03-2*) Piqua Pr.
—Reflections on a Rainy April Day. 23p. (gr. 1-5). 1991. 7.95 (*1-880440-02-4*) Piqua Pr.
Chisholm, Gloria. Andrea. LC 83-71614. 160p. (Orig.). (gr. 9 up). 1983. pap. 3.99 (*0-87123-297-9*) Bethany Hse.
Choi, Sook N. Year of Impossible Goodbyes. (gr. 4-7). 1993. pap. 3.99 (*0-440-40759-1*) Dell.
Clark, Marnie, et al, eds. Lighting Candles in the Dark. Thomas, Sylvia, illus. 215p. (Orig.). 1992. pap. 9.50 (*0-9620912-3-5*) Friends Genl Conf.
Cleary, Beverly. Jean & Johnny. 240p. 1991. pap. 3.99 (*0-380-70927-9*, Flare) Avon.
—The Luckiest Girl. 224p. (gr. 5-6). 1991. pap. 3.99 (*0-380-70922-8*, Flare) Avon.
Clements, Bruce. Tom Loves Anna Loves Tom. (gr. 7 up). 1992. pap. 3.95 (*0-374-47939-9*) FS&G.
Clifford, Eth. The Remembering Box. ALC Staff, ed. LC 85-10851. 64p. (gr. 5 up). 1992. pap. 3.95 (*0-688-11777-5*, Pub. by Beech Tree Bks) Morrow.
Cloverdale Press Staff. Cheating Heart. 1992. pap. 2.99 (*0-553-29451-2*) Bantam.
—Love on the Upbeat. 1992. pap. 2.99 (*0-553-29453-9*) Bantam.
—Lucky in Love. 1992. pap. 2.99 (*0-553-29456-3*) Bantam.
—Play Me a Love Song. 1992. pap. 2.99 (*0-553-29450-4*) Bantam.
—Sweet Dreams. 1992. pap. 2.99 (*0-553-29452-0*) Bantam.
—Trust in Love. 176p. (Orig.). 1988. pap. 2.50 (*0-553-27229-2*, Sweet Dreams) Bantam.
Conford, Ellen. If This Is Love, I'll Take Spaghetti. 1990. pap. 2.95 (*0-590-43819-0*) Scholastic Inc.
—Loving Someone Else. 1992. pap. 3.50 (*0-553-29787-2*) Bantam.
—The Things I Did for Love. 144p. 1988. pap. 2.95 (*0-553-27374-4*, Starfire) Bantam.
—Things I Did Love. 1987. 13.95 (*0-553-05431-7*) Bantam.
Conkie, Heather. Old Quarrels, Old Love. (gr. 4-6). 1993. pap. 3.99 (*0-553-48041-3*) Bantam.
Conrad, Barnaby. Time Is All We Have. 1989. pap. 4.95 (*0-440-20245-0*) Dell.
Conrad, Pam. Holding Me Here. 160p. (gr. 7 up). 1987. pap. 2.95 (*0-553-26525-3*, Starfire) Bantam.
Cooney. Last Dance. 1992. pap. 3.25 (*0-590-45785-3*, Point) Scholastic Inc.
—Saturday Night. 1992. pap. 3.25 (*0-590-45784-5*, Point) Scholastic Inc.
—Summer Nights. 1992. pap. 3.25 (*0-590-45786-1*, Point) Scholastic Inc.
Cooney, Caroline B. Forbidden. (gr. 9-12). 1993. pap. 3.50 (*0-590-46574-0*) Scholastic Inc.
—Party's Over. 1991. 13.95 (*0-590-42552-8*, Scholastic Hardcover) Scholastic Inc.
—The Party's Over. 192p. (gr. 7 up). 1992. pap. 3.25 (*0-590-42553-6*, Point) Scholastic Inc.
—The Perfume. 1992. pap. 3.25 (*0-590-45402-1*, Point) Scholastic Inc.
Cooney, Linda A. Freshman Feud. 1992. pap. 3.50 (*0-06-106141-7*, Harp PBks) HarpC.
—Freshman Follies. 1992. pap. 3.50 (*0-06-106142-5*, Harp PBks) HarpC.
—Freshman Promises. 1992. pap. 3.99 (*0-06-106134-4*, Harp PBks) HarpC.
—Freshman Summer. 1992. pap. 3.99 (*0-06-106780-6*, Harp PBks) HarpC.
—Freshman Wedding. 1992. pap. 3.50 (*0-06-106135-2*, Harp PBks) HarpC.
Cooper, J. B. Picture Perfect Romance. 1993. pap. 2.99 (*0-553-29983-2*) Bantam.
Crawford, Diane M. Comedy of Errors. (gr. 4-7). 1992. pap. 2.99 (*0-553-29457-1*) Bantam.
Cutburth, Ronald W. Love from the Sea. Naumann, Cynthia E., ed. Persels, Beth, illus. Tostado, Rocio G., tr. (SPA., Illus.). 27p. (gr. 5-8). 1990. pap. write for info. (*1-878291-09-2*) Love From Sea.
—Love from the Sea. Naumann, Cynthia E., ed. West, Bobbie, tr. Persels, Beth, illus. (CHI.). 27p. (gr. 5-8). 1990. pap. write for info. (*1-878291-11-4*) Love From Sea.
—Love from the Sea. Naumann, Cynthia E., ed. Percels, Beth, illus. 27p. (Orig.). (gr. 4-7). 1990. pap. 3.50 (*1-878291-01-7*) Love From Sea.

D'Abreo, Brendan. Heads & Hearts. (gr. 3-6). 1994. pap. 10.95 (*0-8059-3522-3*) Dorrance.
Daley, Dan. A Song for Linda, No. 122. 144p. (Orig.). (gr. 7-12). 1987. pap. 2.50 (*0-553-26419-2*) Bantam.
Daly, Maureen. Acts of Love. LC 86-1863. 176p. (gr. 7 up). 1986. pap. 12.95 (*0-590-33873-0*) Scholastic Inc.
—Acts of Love. 192p. (gr. 7 up). 1987. pap. 2.75 (*0-590-43631-7*) Scholastic Inc.
—Seventeenth Summer. (gr. 7-9). 1985. pap. 3.50 (*0-671-61931-4*, Archway) PB.
D'Anard, Elizabeth. Cinderella Summer. (gr. 7 up). 1992. pap. 3.50 (*0-06-106776-8*, Harp PBks) HarpC.
Daniel, Kate. Sweet Dreams. 1992. pap. 3.50 (*0-06-106720-2*, Harp PBks) HarpC.
—Sweetheart. 1993. pap. 3.50 (*0-06-106735-0*, Harp PBks) HarpC.
—Teen Idol. 1992. pap. 3.50 (*0-06-106779-2*, Harp PBks) HarpC.
DeClements, Barthe. How Do You Lose Ninth Grade Blues? 144p. (gr. 5 up). 1993. pap. 3.99 (*0-14-036333-5*, Puffin) Puffin Bks.
De Gale, Ann. Island Encounter. (Orig.). (gr. 6 up). 1986. pap. 2.50 (*0-440-94026-5*, LFL) Dell.
Delessert, Etienne. Ashes, Ashes. Delessert, Etienne, illus. 32p. (gr. 1-12). 1990. lib. bdg. 16.95 RLB smythe-sewn (*0-88682-628-4*, 97855-098) Creative Ed.
De Saint Mars, Dominique. Lily Is in Love. Bloch, Serge, illus. LC 93-10988. (gr. 2-4). Date not set. 8.95 (*1-56766-101-7*) Childs World.
Devore, Cynthia D. Do Rainbows Last Forever? LC 93-7720. (gr. 5 up). 1993. 14.96 (*1-56239-248-4*) Abdo & Dghtrs.
Dickert, Barbara K. I Love You More. (gr. 5 up). 1993. 7.95 (*0-8062-4716-9*) Carlton.
Dickinson, Peter. The Changes: A Trilogy, 3 vols. Incl. The Devil's Children. 192p. 1986. pap. 14.95 (*0-385-29449-2*); Heartsease. 192p. 1986. pap. 14.95 (*0-385-29451-4*); The Weathermonger. 244p. 1986. pap. 14.95 (*0-385-29450-6*). (gr. 7 up). 1986. pap. Delacorte.
Disney Staff. Disney's Beauty & the Beast. 1991. 6.98 (*0-8317-2434-X*) Viking Child Bks.
Donahue, Marilyn. Somebody Special to Love. LC 88-14809. 1988. pap. 4.49 (*0-89191-360-2*, Chariot Bks) Chariot Family.
Double Love. (gr. 7-12). 1984. pap. 3.50 (*0-553-27567-4*) Bantam.
Duane, Diane E. So You Want to Be a Wizard. (gr. 5-8). 1986. pap. 2.75 (*0-440-98252-9*, LFL) Dell.
Dube, Hope. Love Is a Challenge. (gr. 4-7). 1992. pap. 4.95 (*0-7910-2923-9*) Chelsea Hse.
DuKore, Jesse. Long Distance Love. (gr. 7-12). 1983. pap. 2.25 (*0-553-17853-9*) Bantam.
Eires, Anita. Summer Awakening. (gr. 6 up). 1986. pap. 2.50 (*0-440-98369-X*, LFL) Dell.
Elkins, Stephen. Stories That End with a Hug. Menck, Kevin, illus. 32p. (gr. k-8). 1993. 12.98 (*1-56919-002-X*) Wonder Wkshop.
Ellis, Albert. My Secret Admirer. 1993. pap. 3.25 (*0-590-44768-8*) Scholastic Inc.
Ellis, Lucy. Pink Parrots, No. 3: Mixed Signals. (gr. 4-7). 1991. pap. 3.50 (*0-316-18566-3*, Spts Illus Kids) Little.
Everett, Percival. One That Got Away. (ps-3). 1992. 14. 95 (*0-395-56427-1*, Clarion Bks) HM.
Falk, Bonnie H. Forget-Me-Not. Huber, Nancy D., illus. LC 84-90501. 192p. (gr. 4-8). 1984. pap. 7.95 (*0-9614108-0-9*) BHF Memories.
Favors, Jean. Tough Choices. 112p. (Orig.). (gr. 4-9). 1992. pap. 2.95 (*0-448-40492-3*, G&D) Putnam Pub Group.
Fields, Terri. The Other Me. 160p. (Orig.). (gr. 7-12). 1987. pap. 2.50 (*0-553-26196-7*) Bantam.
Finney, Shan. Geared for Romance. 192p. (Orig.). (gr. 7-12). 1987. pap. 2.50 (*0-553-26902-X*) Bantam.
Foley, June. Falling in Love Is No Snap. LC 86-1990. 144p. (gr. 7 up). 1986. pap. 14.95 (*0-385-29490-5*) Delacorte.
—Falling in Love Is No Snap. 144p. (gr. 6 up). 1989. pap. 2.95 (*0-440-20349-X*, LFL) Dell.
—It's No Crush, I'm in Love. LC 81-15214. 224p. (gr. 7 up). 1982. 12.95 (*0-385-28465-9*) Delacorte.
—Love by Any Other Name. LC 82-72752. 224p. (gr. 7 up). 1983. pap. 13.95 (*0-385-29245-7*) Delacorte.
Foster, Sharon. Stormy Leigh. 368p. (Orig.). (gr. 9 up). 1988. pap. 6.95 (*1-56292-535-0*) Honor Bks Ok.
Foster, Stephanie. A Chance at Love, No. 6. 192p. (gr. 5 up). 1988. pap. 2.95 (*0-553-27017-6*, Sweet Dreams) Bantam.
Fowler, Ruth. Lights! Camera! Love in Action! Smothers, Mark, illus. 64p. (Orig.). (gr. 4-6). 1989. pap. text ed. 3.95 (*0-936625-68-6*) Womans Mission Union.
Freeman, Lory. Loving Touches. Deach, Carol, illus. LC 85-62434. 32p. (Orig.). (ps). 1985. PLB 15.95 (*0-943990-21-1*); pap. 4.95 (*0-943990-20-3*) Parenting Pr.
From the Heart. 1988. 7.95 (*0-89954-776-1*) Antioch Pub Co.
Galbraith, Kathryn O. Laura Charlotte. Cooper, Floyd, illus. 32p. (ps up). 1993. pap. 5.95 (*0-399-22514-5*, Philomel Bks) Putnam Pub Group.
Gantschev, Ivan. Moon Lake. (ps-3). 1991. pap. 14.95 (*0-907234-08-9*) Picture Bk Studio.
Garfield, Leon. The Night of the Comet. LC 79-50670. (gr. 7 up). 1979. 8.95 (*0-685-01396-0*); pap. 7.45 (*0-385-28753-4*) Delacorte.
Geras, Adele. The Tower Room. 1992. 15.95 (*0-15-289627-9*, HB Juv Bks) HarBrace.
Geringer, Laura. A Three Hat Day. Lobel, Arnold, illus. LC 85-42640. 32p. (ps-3). 1985. PLB 14.89 (*0-06-021989-0*) HarpC Child Bks.
Giff, Patricia R. Love, from the Fifth-Grade Celebrity. Morrill, Leslie, illus. LC 85-46075. 144p. (gr. 4-6). 1986. 13.95 (*0-385-29486-7*) Delacorte.
—Tootsie Tanner, Why Don't You Talk? An Abby Jones, Junior Detective, Mystery. Kramer, Anthony, illus. LC 86-32910. 144p. (gr. 4-6). 1987. pap. 13.95 (*0-385-29579-0*) Delacorte.
Gorman, Susan. The Game of Love. (gr. 6 up). 1988. pap. 2.50 (*0-553-27476-7*) Bantam.
—This Time for Real. 192p. (Orig.). (gr. 7 up). 1988. pap. 2.50 (*0-553-27175-X*) Bantam.
Goudge, Eileen. Against the Rules. (Orig.). (gr. 6 up). 1986. pap. 2.25 (*0-440-90096-4*, LFL) Dell.
—Deep-Sea Summer. (Orig.). (gr. k-12). 1988. pap. 2.95 (*0-440-20123-3*) Dell.
—Heart for Sale. (Orig.). (gr. 7-12). 1986. pap. 2.25 (*0-440-93382-X*, LFL) Dell.
—Kiss & Make Up. 154p. (Orig.). (gr. 6-12). 1986. pap. 2.25 (*0-440-94514-3*, LFL) Dell.
—Presenting Superhunk. (Orig.). (gr. 6-12). 1985. pap. 2.25 (*0-440-97172-1*, LFL) Dell.
—Something Borrowed, Something Blue. (Orig.). (gr. k-12). 1988. pap. 2.95 (*0-440-20055-5*, LFL) Dell.
—Sweet Talk. (Orig.). (gr. k-12). 1986. pap. 2.25 (*0-440-98411-4*, LFL) Dell.
—Sweet Talk. 160p. 1986. pap. 2.95 (*0-553-17220-4*) Bantam.
—A Touch of Ginger. (Orig.). (gr. 7-12). 1985. pap. 2.25 (*0-440-98816-0*, LFL) Dell.
—Treat Me Right. (Orig.). (gr. 6 up). 1986. pap. 2.25 (*0-440-98845-4*, LFL) Dell.
Graham, Heather X. Sweet Savage Eden. (Orig.). 1989. pap. 5.99 (*0-440-20235-3*) Dell.
Greenberg, Jan. Exercises of the Heart. LC 86-11977. 160p. (gr. 6 up). 1986. 14.00 (*0-374-32237-6*) FS&G.
Greene, Bette. Philip Hall Likes Me, I Reckon, Maybe. Lilly, Charles, illus. 144p. 1975. pap. 3.99 (*0-440-45755-6*, YB) Dell.
Greene, C. The Golden Locket. Sewall, Marcia, illus. 1992. 13.95 (*0-15-231220-X*, HB Juv Bks) HarBrace.
Greene, Constance C. The Love Letters of J. Timothy Owen. LC 85-45846. 192p. (gr. 7 up). 1988. pap. 2.75 (*0-06-447026-1*, Trophy) HarpC Child Bks.
Greene, Yvonne. Little Sister. (gr. 11 up). 1981. pap. 2.50 (*0-553-26613-6*) Bantam.
—The Love Hunt. 192p. (Orig.). (gr. 5 up). 1985. pap. 2.25 (*0-553-25070-1*) Bantam.
Greenwald, Sheila. Valentine Rosy. (gr. 3-7). 1986. pap. 2.50 (*0-440-49203-3*, YB) Dell.
Gregory, Diana. Two's a Crowd. 144p. (Orig.). (gr. 6 up). 1985. pap. 2.25 (*0-553-24992-4*) Bantam.
Grimes, Frances H. Sweet Dreams: Love Lines, No. 154. (gr. 6 up). 1988. pap. 2.50 (*0-318-37112-X*) Bantam.
Grove, Vicki. Goodbye My Wishing Star. 1989. pap. 2.95 (*0-590-42152-2*) Scholastic Inc.
Guest, Elissa H. The Handsome Man. 160p. (gr. 7 up). 1981. pap. 1.95 (*0-440-93437-0*, LFL) Dell.
Haith, Betty. Bonnie's Thirteenth Summer. 52p. 1992. pap. 4.95 (*1-882185-01-3*) Crnrstone Pub.
Hallinan, P. K. How Do I Love You? (Illus.). 24p. (ps-2). 1990. pap. 4.95 perfect bdg. (*0-8249-8505-2*, Ideals Child) Hambleton-Hill.
Hamilton, Kersten. Natalie Jean & Tag-along Tessa. 1991. 2.99 (*0-8423-4621-X*) Tyndale.
—Natalie Jean & the Flying Machine. 1991. 2.99 (*0-8423-4620-1*) Tyndale.
Hamilton, Virginia. A White Romance. 200p. (gr. 8 up). 1987. 14.95 (*0-399-21213-2*, Philomel Bks) Putnam Pub Group.
Hanes, Betsy. Taffy Sinclair & the Romance Machine Disaster. 128p. (Orig.). 1987. pap. 2.75 (*0-553-15644-6*, Skylark) Bantam.
Hart, Bruce & Hart, Carole. Cross Your Heart. 256p. (Orig.). (gr. 6 up). 1988. pap. 3.50 (*0-380-89971-X*, Flare) Avon.
Hastings, Catt. Romance on the Run. 1993. pap. 3.50 (*0-553-29987-5*) Bantam.
Hatonn & L-L Research Staff. What Is Love? A Coloring Book for Kids. (Illus.). 34p. (ps-2). 1984. pap. 6.95 (*0-945007-05-1*) L-L Resrch.
Hawley, Richard. Shining Still. (Illus.). 192p. 1989. 12.95 (*0-374-36811-2*) FS&G.
Haynes, Betsy. Taffy Sinclair's Romance. 1992. pap. 3.25 (*0-553-15494-X*) Bantam.
Hazen, Barbara S. Even If I Did Something Awful? Kincade, Nancy, illus. LC 91-23143. 32p. (ps-2). 1992. pap. 3.95 (*0-689-71600-1*, Aladdin) Macmillan Child Grp.
Heart to Heart. 176p. (Orig.). (gr. 7-12). 1987. pap. 2.50 (*0-553-26293-9*) Bantam.
Hermes, Patricia. Be Still My Heart. MacDonald, Patricia, ed. 160p. 1991. pap. 2.99 (*0-671-70645-4*, Archway) PB.
—You Shouldn't Have to Say Good-Bye. LC 82-47933. 117p. (gr. 3-7). 1982. 11.95 (*0-15-299944-2*, HB Juv Bks) HarBrace.
Herrick, Ann. The Perfect Guy. (gr. 5 up). 1989. pap. 2.95 (*0-553-27927-0*) Bantam.
Hill, Grace L. Marcia Schuyler. 1992. 9.95 (*1-55748-261-6*) Barbour & Co.
—Phoebe Deane. 1992. 9.95 (*1-55748-262-4*) Barbour & Co.
Hodgman, Ann. Dark Music, No. 2. 224p. (gr. 7 up). 1994. pap. 3.50 (*0-14-036375-0*) Puffin Bks.
Hoh, Diane. The Fever. 176p. 1992. pap. 3.25 (*0-590-45401-3*, Point) Scholastic Inc.
Holcomb, Nan. How about a Hug. Taggart, Tricia, illus. 32p. (ps-2). 1992. Repr. of 1988 ed. 13.95 (*0-944727-12-3*) Jason & Nordic Pubs.
Hooper, Mary. Follow That Dream. (Orig.). (gr. 6 up). 1986. pap. 2.50 (*0-440-92644-0*, LFL) Dell.
—Friends & Rivals. (Orig.). (gr. 6 up). 1986. pap. 2.50 (*0-440-92660-2*, LFL) Dell.
Hope in Darkness. 1988. 7.95 (*0-89954-775-3*) Antioch Pub Co.
Hudson, Anne & Daniels, Neil. Ozzie: An Odyssey of Love. Daniels, Neil, illus. LC 83-81305. 72p. (Orig.). (gr. 1-6). 1983. pap. 3.95 (*0-940258-10-2*) Kripalu Pubns.
Humphreys, Martha. Until Whatever. 1993. pap. 3.25 (*0-590-46616-X*) Scholastic Inc.
Island, John. World of the Heart. Redford, Jim L., illus. 48p. (ps-6). Date not set. text ed. 14.95 (*0-9637712-0-5*) Island Flowers.
Jacobs, Barbara. Stolen Kisses. (Orig.). (gr. 6 up). 1986. pap. 2.50 (*0-440-97734-7*, LFL) Dell.
Jam, Teddy. Dr. Kiss Says Yes. Fitzgerald, Joanne, illus. 32p. (ps-1). 1992. 12.95 (*0-88899-141-X*, Pub. by Groundwood-Douglas & McIntyre CN) Firefly Bks Ltd.
James, Emily. Hillside Live! 128p. (Orig.). (gr. 3-9). 1993. pap. 2.95 (*0-448-40495-8*, G&D) Putnam Pub Group.
James, Robin. Sadie. James, Robin, illus. 32p. (Orig.). (gr. 1-4). 1994. pap. 3.95 (*0-8431-3611-1*) Price Stern.
Jarnow, Jill. Lifeguard Summer, No. 142. 192p. (Orig.). (gr. 7-9). 1988. pap. 2.50 (*0-553-27124-5*, Sweet Dreams) Bantam.
Jenner, Caryn. Clashing Hearts. 1992. pap. 2.99 (*0-553-29458-X*) Bantam.
Johnston, Norma. The Watcher in the Mist. 208p. 1986. pap. 2.95 (*0-553-26032-4*, Starfire) Bantam.
Jones, Adrienne. Long Time Passing. LC 90-4046. 256p. (gr. 7 up). 1993. pap. 3.95 (*0-06-447070-9*, Trophy) HarpC Child Bks.
Joosse, Barbara M. Mama, Do You Love Me? Lavallee, Barbara, illus. 32p. (ps-1). 1991. 13.95 (*0-87701-759-X*) Chronicle Bks.
Kamenetz. The Pool of Nectar. (gr. 4 up). 1993. 22.50 (*0-8050-2226-0*) H Holt & Co.
Kaplow, Robert. Alessandra in Love. LC 88-23141. 160p. (gr. 7 up). 1989. (Lipp Jr Bks); (Lipp Jr Bks) HarpC Child Bks.
Kasza, Keiko. A Mother for Choco. Kasza, Keiko, illus. 32p. (ps-1). 1992. PLB 14.95 (*0-399-21841-6*, Putnam) Putnam Pub Group.
Kaye, Marilyn. Choose Me. 1992. pap. 3.50 (*0-06-106714-8*, Harp PBks) HarpC.
—Runaway. (gr. 7 up). 1992. pap. 3.50 (*0-06-106782-2*, Harp PBks) HarpC.
Kayne, Sheryl W. Queen of the Kisses. Blonski, Meribeth, illus. LC 94-75985. 32p. (ps-2). 1994. 14.95 (*1-880851-13-X*) Greene Bark Pr.
Keene, Carolyn. Greek Odyssey. Greenberg, Anne, ed. 160p. (Orig.). 1992. pap. 3.75 (*0-671-73078-9*, Archway) PB.
—Heart of Danger. (gr. 7 up). 1991. pap. 3.50 (*0-671-73665-5*, Archway) PB.
—Love Times Three. (Orig.). (gr. 9-12). 1991. pap. 3.50 (*0-671-96703-7*, Archway) PB.
—A Mind of Her Own. Greenberg, Ann, ed. 160p. (Orig.). 1991. pap. 2.99 (*0-671-73117-3*, Archway) PB.
—Rendezvous in Rome. Greenberg, Anne, ed. 160p. (Orig.). 1992. pap. 3.75 (*0-671-73077-0*, Archway) PB.
—Stolen Kisses. 160p. 1990. pap. 2.95 (*0-671-67762-4*, Archway) PB.
—Swiss Secrets. Greenberg, Anne, ed. 160p. 1992. pap. 3.99 (*0-671-73076-2*, Archway) PB.
Kellogg, Marjorie. Tell Me That You Love Me, Junie Moon. 224p. 1993. pap. 3.95 (*0-374-47510-5*) FS&G.
Kent, Deborah. Talk to Me, My Love. (Orig.). (gr. k-12). 1987. pap. 2.75 (*0-440-97810-6*, LFL) Dell.
Kerr, M. E. Gentlehands. LC 77-11860. 192p. (gr. 7 up). 1990. pap. 3.95 (*0-06-447067-9*, Trophy) HarpC Child Bks.
—If I Love You, Am I Trapped Forever? 192p. (gr. 7 up). 1974. pap. 2.25 (*0-440-94320-5*, LFL) Dell.
—If I Love You, Am I Trapped Forever? LC 72-9860. 192p. (gr. 7 up). 1988. pap. 3.95 (*0-06-447032-6*, Trophy) HarpC Child Bks.
Keyes, Daniel. Flowers for Algernon: A Classic Story of Struggle. (Illus.). (gr. 4 up). 1987. PLB 13.95 (*0-88682-007-3*) Creative Ed.
Kidd, Ronald. Sammy Carducci's Guide to Women. 112p. (gr. 3-7). 1991. 14.95 (*0-525-67363-6*, Lodestar Bks) Dutton Child Bks.
—Sammy Carducci's Guide to Women. 112p. (gr. 3-7). 1994. pap. 3.99 (*0-14-036481-1*) Puffin Bks.
Killien, Christi. All of the Above. LC 86-27872. (gr. 5-9). 1987. 13.95 (*0-395-43023-2*) HM.
Kirby, Susan. Partners in Love. 1993. pap. 2.99 (*0-553-29460-1*) Bantam.
Kiss Me Creep. 1985. pap. 1.75 (*0-440-82009-X*) Dell.
Klein, Norma. Older Men. 192p. 1988. pap. 2.95 (*0-449-70261-8*, Juniper) Fawcett.
Knudson, R. R. Just Another Love Story. (gr. 7 up). 1984. pap. 2.50 (*0-380-65532-2*, 60172-9, Flare) Avon.
Koechlin, Lionel. The Love Affair of Mr. Ding & Mrs. Dong. (Illus.). 32p. (gr. k-2). 1991. 12.95 (*0-89565-817-8*) Childs World.
Koertge, Ron. Where the Kissing Never Stops. (gr. k-12). 1988. pap. 2.95 (*0-440-20167-5*) Dell.

Koosak, Tara. Boy Girl Daze Craze. Koosak, Tara, illus. LC 91-91469. 60p. (Orig.). (gr. 4-8). 1992. pap. 3.50 (*0-934426-44-9*) NAPSAC Reprods.
Lamb, Jane M. Sharing with Thumpy: My Story of Love & Grief. Dodge, Nancy C., illus. 48p. (gr. k-12). 1985. pap. 8.95 workbook (*0-918533-10-4*) Prairie Lark.
Landis, James D. Looks Aren't Everything. 1991. pap. 3.50 (*0-553-28860-1*) Bantam.
Lantz, Frances. Truth about Making Out. (gr. 4 up). 1990. pap. 3.50 (*0-553-15813-9*) Bantam.
Larrison, Roxann. A Garden of Bitter Herbs. (Orig.). 1993. pap. 3.95 (*0-87067-389-0*) Holloway.
Lawrence, D. H. You Touched Me. 48p. (gr. 6 up). 1982. PLB 13.95 (*0-87191-894-3*) Creative Ed.
Leroe, Ellen. Have a Heart, Cupid Delaney. 160p. (gr. 5 up). 1988. pap. 2.95 (*0-553-27002-8*, Starfire) Bantam.
—Personal Business. 144p. (gr. 6 up). 1987. pap. 2.95 (*0-553-26652-7*, Starfire) Bantam.
Levitin, Sonia. Man Who Kept His Heart in a Bucket. Pinkney, Jerry, illus. (ps-3). 1991. 14.95 (*0-8037-1029-1*); PLB 14.89 (*0-8037-1030-5*) Dial Bks Young.
Levy, Elizabeth. First Date. 1990. pap. 2.75 (*0-590-42825-X*) Scholastic Inc.
Lewis, Linda. All for the Love of That Boy. 224p. (gr. 7-9). 1989. pap. 2.95 (*0-671-68243-1*, Archway) PB.
—Dedicated to That Boy I Love. 168p. (gr. 6-9). 1990. pap. 2.75 (*0-671-68244-X*, Archway) PB.
—We Love only Older Boys. 176p. (Orig.). (gr. 7 up). 1990. pap. 2.95 (*0-671-69558-4*, Archway) PB.
Lexau, Joan M. Don't Be My Valentine. Hoff, Syd, illus. LC 85-42621. 64p. (gr. k-3). 1985. PLB 14.89 (*0-06-023873-9*) HarpC Child Bks.
Likken, Laurie. Winner Takes All. 192p. 1987. pap. 2.50 (*0-317-65474-8*, Sweet Dreams) Bantam.
Lowry, Lois. Autumn Street. 192p. (gr. 4-7). 1986. pap. 3.50 (*0-440-40344-8*, YB) Dell.
—Summer to Die. 1984. pap. 3.50 (*0-553-27395-7*) Bantam.
Lykken, Laurie. Priceless Love. 192p. (Orig.). (gr. 7 up). 1988. pap. 2.50 (*0-553-27174-1*) Bantam.
—The Truth about Love. 1991. pap. 2.95 (*0-553-28862-8*) Bantam.
Lyons, Pam. Danny's Girl. (Orig.). (gr. 6 up). 1986. pap. 2.50 (*0-440-91830-8*, LFL) Dell.
—Love Around the Corner. (Orig.). (gr. k-12). 1987. pap. 2.50 (*0-440-94726-X*, LFL) Dell.
—Tug of Love. (Orig.). (gr. 6 up). 1986. pap. 2.50 (*0-440-98818-7*, LFL) Dell.
MacBain, Carol. Heartbreak Hill. 192p. (Orig.). (gr. 7-12). 1987. pap. 2.50 (*0-553-26195-9*) Bantam.
—Stand By for Love. 192p. (Orig.). (gr. 7-12). 1987. pap. 2.50 (*0-553-26903-8*) Bantam.
McCullers, Carson. A Tree, a Rock, a Cloud. (gr. 4-12). 1989. 13.95 (*0-88682-349-8*, 97225-098) Creative Ed.
McDaniel, Lurlene. Happily Ever after. 1992. pap. 3.50 (*0-553-29056-8*) Bantam.
MacDonald, George. The Landlady's Master. Phillips, Michael R., ed. 208p. (Orig.). (gr. 11 up). 1989. pap. 7.99 (*0-87123-904-3*) Bethany Hse.
McDonnell, Christine. Just for the Summer. De Groat, Diane, illus. LC 87-8201. (gr. 2-5). 1987. pap. 11.95 (*0-670-80059-7*) Viking Child Bks.
McFann, Jane. Be Mine. (gr. 12 up). 1994. pap. 3.50 (*0-590-46690-9*) Scholastic Inc.
McHugh, Elisabet. The Real Thing. 1991. pap. 2.99 (*0-553-29186-6*) Bantam.
McHugh, Fiona. Of Corsets & Secrets & True, True Love. (gr. 4-7). 1993. pap. 3.99 (*0-553-48040-5*) Bantam.
MacKay, Judy F. Tales of a Nuf in the Land of Doon. Langley, William A., illus. 84p. (Orig.). (gr. 4-7). 1992. pap. 9.95 perfect bdg. (*1-882748-00-X*) MacKay-Langley.
MacLachlan, Patricia. Seven Kisses in a Row. Marrella, Maria P., illus. LC 82-47718. 64p. (gr. 2-5). 1988. pap. 3.95 (*0-06-440231-2*, Trophy) HarpC Child Bks.
McLerran, Alice. Kisses. Morgan, Mary, illus. 32p. (ps-3). 1993. 4.95 (*0-590-44711-4*) Scholastic Inc.
Mahon, K. L. Just One Tear. LC 93-80198. (gr. 4-7). 1994. 14.00 (*0-688-13519-6*) Lothrop.
Malcolm, Jahnna N. Too Hot to Handle. 1991. pap. 2.99 (*0-553-28262-X*) Bantam.
Mandelstein, Paul. Nightingale & the Wind. Silin-Palmer, Pamela, illus. LC 93-31056. 32p. (gr. 4 up). 1994. 17. 95 (*0-8478-1787-3*) Rizzoli Intl.
Mark, Jan. Handles. LC 86-43076. 160p. (gr. 5-9). 1987. pap. 3.95 (*0-14-031587-X*, Puffin) Puffin Bks.
Marshall, Mollie. Ready for Romance. 192p. (Orig.). (gr. 6-12). 1982. pap. 1.95 (*0-8439-1129-8*) Dorchester Pub Co.
Martin, Ann M. Dawn & the Older Boy. (gr. 4-7). 1990. pap. 3.25 (*0-590-43566-3*) Scholastic Inc.
—Just a Summer Romance. LC 86-46201. 170p. (gr. 7 up). 1987. 13.95 (*0-8234-0649-0*) Holiday.
—Just a Summer Romance. 1988. pap. 2.75 (*0-590-43999-5*, NAL) Scholastic Inc.
—Stacey's Big Crush. (gr. 4-7). 1993. pap. 3.50 (*0-590-45667-9*) Scholastic Inc.
Martin, LaJoyce. Heart-Shaped Pieces. Agnew, Tim, illus. LC 90-22517. 160p. (Orig.). (gr. 9 up). 1991. pap. 6.99 (*0-932581-78-1*) Word Aflame.
Mazer, Harry. The Girl of His Dreams. LC 86-47749. 192p. (gr. 7 up). 1987. (Crowell Jr Bks); (Crowell Jr Bks) HarpC Child Bks.
Mazer, Norma F. Someone to Love. LC 82-72755. 256p. (gr. 7 up). 1983. 13.95 (*0-685-06446-8*) Delacorte.
—Summer Girls, Love Boys & Other Short Stories. LC 82-70320. 192p. (gr. 7 up). 1982. pap. 11.95 (*0-385-28930-8*) Delacorte.
—When We First Met. 1991. pap. 2.95 (*0-590-43823-9*) Scholastic Inc.
Mazer, Norma F. & Mazer, Harry. Heartbeat. (gr. 7 up). 1990. pap. 3.50 (*0-553-28779-6*, Starfire) Bantam.
Mercuri, Carmela. Beauty & the Beast: Story with Music. Polomski, R., illus. 24p. (Orig.). (gr. 8-12). 1976. pap. 4.95 (*0-935474-24-2*) Carousel Pubns Ltd.
Michaels, Fran. Mr. Wonderful. 192p. (Orig.). (gr. 7-12). 1987. pap. 2.50 (*0-553-26340-4*) Bantam.
Miklowitz, Gloria D. Goodbye Tomorrow. LC 86-23948. 192p. (gr. 7 up). 1987. 13.95 (*0-385-29562-6*) Delacorte.
—Goodbye Tomorrow. (gr. k-12). 1988. pap. 3.25 (*0-440-20081-4*, LFL) Dell.
—Love Story, Take Three. (gr. k-12). 1987. pap. 2.75 (*0-440-95084-8*, LFL) Dell.
—The War Between the Classes. (gr. 6 up). 1986. pap. 3.99 (*0-440-99406-3*, LFL) Dell.
Mills, Claudia. Dinah in Love. LC 93-19256. 144p. (gr. 3-7). 1993. SBE 13.95 (*0-02-766998-X*, Macmillan Child Bk) Macmillan Child Grp.
Miner, Jane C. Roxanne, Vol. 15. 368p. (Orig.). (gr. 11 up). 1985. pap. 2.95 (*0-590-33686-X*) Scholastic Inc.
—Winter Love Story. 1993. pap. 3.50 (*0-590-47610-6*) Scholastic Inc.
Montgomery, Lucy M. Anne of Avonlea: An Anne of Green Gables Story. Sieffert, Clare, illus. 320p. 1990. 13.95 (*0-448-40063-4*, G&D) Putnam Pub Group.
Moreau, Patricia. Suzanne Masterson: Dangerous Games. 412p. 1994. pap. 8.99 (*0-88070-648-1*, Multnomah Bks) Questar Pubs.
Morgan, Mary, illus. Guess Who I Love? 18p. (ps). 1992. bds. 2.95 (*0-448-40313-7*) Putnam Pub Group.
Morris, Kimberly. Wild Hearts. 1992. pap. 3.50 (*0-06-106781-4*, Harp PBks) HarpC.
Morrison, Dorothy N. Whisper Again. 208p. (gr. 2-9). 1989. pap. 2.95 (*0-8167-1307-3*) Troll Assocs.
Mount, Guy. Lady Ocean: A Love Story for Children. (Illus.). (gr. k-6). 1986. pap. 3.00 (*0-9604462-2-2*) Sweetlight.
Munsch, Robert. Siempre Te Querre (Love You Forever) McGraw, Sheila, illus. 32p. 1992. pap. 4.95 (*1-895565-01-4*) Firefly Bks Ltd.
Munsil, Janet. Il N'y a Pas De Fumee - Where There's Smoke. Martchenko, Michael, illus. (ENG & FRE.). 24p. 1993. PLB 14.95 (*1-55037-291-2*, Pub. by Annick CN); French ed. pap. 4.95 (*1-55037-311-0*, Pub. by Annick CN); English ed. pap. 4.95 (*1-55037-290-4*, Pub. by Annick CN) Firefly Bks Ltd.
Murphy, Lorraine. The Prize. 192p. (gr. 8). 1993. pap. text ed. 7.95 (*1-883511-02-X*) Veritas Pr CA.
Murrow, Liza K. Fire in the Heart. 255p. (gr. 5-9). 1990. pap. 2.95 (*0-8167-2261-7*) Troll Assocs.
Myers, Walter D. Motown & Didi: A Love Story. LC 84-3632. 192p. (gr. 7 up). 1984. pap. 14.95 (*0-670-49062-8*) Viking Child Bks.
Namm, Diane. First Love. LC 94-14502. (Illus.). 224p. (gr. 6 up). 1994. pap. text ed. 3.50 (*0-8167-3440-2*) Troll Assocs.
—Good-Bye Kiss. LC 94-16883. (Illus.). 224p. (gr. 6 up). 1994. pap. text ed. 3.50 (*0-8167-3441-0*) Troll Assocs.
—Senior Kisses. LC 94-25436. 224p. 1994. pap. text ed. 3.50 (*0-8167-3442-9*, WestWind) Troll Assocs.
Nielsen, Virginia. La Sauvage. (Orig.). 1988. pap. 3.95 (*0-440-20190-X*) Dell.
Nimmo, Jenny. Orchard of the Crescent Moon. 170p. (gr. 5-9). 1990. pap. 2.95 (*0-8167-2265-X*) Troll Assocs.
Nister, Ernest. Keepsake Carousel. 1993. 7.95 (*1-56397-081-3*) Boyds Mills Pr.
Nixon, Joan L. A Family Apart. 176p. (gr. 5 up). 1988. pap. 3.99 (*0-553-27478-3*, Starfire) Bantam.
No More Boys. 176p. (gr. 5-6). 1986. pap. 2.25 (*0-553-25643-2*) Bantam.
Nobile, Jeanett. Portrait of Love. 166p. (gr. 6-8). 1983. pap. 2.25 (*0-553-17846-6*) Bantam.
O'Banyon, Constance. Song of the Nightingale. 1992. pap. 8.99 (*0-06-104122-X*, Harp PBks) HarpC.
O'Connell, June. Love on the Upbeat. 1992. pap. 2.99 (*0-553-29455-5*) Bantam.
O'Connor, Jane. Yours till Niagara Falls, Abby. 128p. (Orig.). (gr. 3-7). 1991. pap. 2.75 (*0-590-42854-3*) Scholastic Inc.
Oke, Janette. Love Comes Softly. large type ed. 188p. (gr. 4 up). 1985. pap. 8.99 (*0-87123-828-4*) Bethany Hse.
—Love Takes Wing. LC 88-19276. 224p. (Orig.). (gr. 8 up). 1988. pap. 6.99 (*1-55661-035-1*) Bethany Hse.
—Spring's Gentle Promise. large type ed. 224p. (Orig.). 1989. pap. 8.99 (*1-55661-074-2*) Bethany Hse.
Okimoto, Jean D. Jason's Women. LC 85-28655. 210p. (gr. 7up). 1986. 14.95 (*0-316-63809-9*, 638099, Joy St Bks) Little.
Oldham, June. Grow Up Cupid. (gr. k-12). 1989. pap. 2.95 (*0-440-20256-6*, LFL) Dell.
O'Neal, Zibby. In Summer Light. LC 85-50806. 180p. (gr. 7 up). 1985. pap. 12.95 (*0-670-80784-2*) Viking Child Bks.
Oniell, Laura. The Ski Trip. 128p. (Orig.). (gr. 3-9). 1993. pap. 2.95 (*0-448-40494-X*, G&D) Putnam Pub Group.
Orgel, Doris. Crack in the Heart. (gr. 7 up). 1989. pap. 2.95 (*0-449-70204-9*, Juniper) Fawcett.
Ormondroyd, Edward. Theodore's Rival. Larrecq, John M., illus. (gr. 4-8). 1986. pap. 3.80 (*0-395-41669-8*, Sandpiper) HM.
Overton, Jenny. The Ship from Simnel Street. LC 85-21965. 224p. (gr. 5 up). 1986. reinforced trade ed. 10. 25 (*0-688-06182-6*) Greenwillow.
Park, Ruth. Playing Beatie Bow. LC 81-8097. 204p. (gr. 5-9). 1982. SBE 14.95 (*0-689-30889-2*, Atheneum Child Bk) Macmillan Child Grp.
Parkison, Ralph F. Eovl. Withrow, Marion O., ed. Bush, William, illus. 36p. (Orig.). (gr. 2-8). 1988. pap. write for info. Little Wood Bks.
Pascal, Francine. All Night Long. large type ed. 134p. (gr. 5-8). 1989. Repr. of 1984 ed. PLB 10.50 (*1-55905-014-4*, Dist. by Gareth Stevens); 9.50 (*1-55905-004-7*) Grey Castle.
—Amy's True Love. 1991. pap. 2.99 (*0-553-28963-2*) Bantam.
—Anything for Love. 1994. pap. 3.50 (*0-553-56311-4*) Bantam.
—Are We in Love. 1993. pap. 3.25 (*0-553-29851-8*) Bantam.
—Dangerous Love. (gr. 7 up). 1984. pap. 3.50 (*0-553-27741-3*) Bantam.
—The Dating Game. 1991. pap. 2.99 (*0-553-29187-4*) Bantam.
—Dear Sister. (gr. 7 up). 1984. pap. 3.50 (*0-553-27672-7*) Bantam.
—Don't Go Home with John. 1993. pap. 3.50 (*0-553-29236-6*) Bantam.
—Forbidden Love. 1987. pap. 2.99 (*0-553-27521-6*) Bantam.
—Girl They Both Loved. 1991. pap. 3.25 (*0-553-29226-9*) Bantam.
—The Great Boyfriend Switch. (gr. 4-7). 1993. pap. 3.50 (*0-553-48053-7*) Bantam.
—Head over Heels. (Orig.). (gr. 5). 1985. pap. 3.25 (*0-553-27444-9*) Bantam.
—Heartbreaker. 176p. (gr. 7 up). 1984. pap. 3.50 (*0-553-27569-0*) Bantam.
—In Love Again. (gr. 7 up). 1989. pap. 3.50 (*0-553-28193-3*) Bantam.
—In Love with a Prince. 1993. pap. 3.25 (*0-553-29237-4*) Bantam.
—Jessica the Rock Star. (gr. 5 up). 1989. pap. 3.25 (*0-553-15766-3*) Bantam.
—Love & Betrayal & Hold the Mayo! (gr. 5-9). 1986. pap. 2.95 (*0-440-94735-9*, LFL) Dell.
—Love Letters. 160p. (gr. 6 up). 1985. pap. 2.75 (*0-553-26883-X*) Bantam.
—Love Letters for Sale. (gr. 4-7). 1992. pap. 3.25 (*0-553-29234-X*) Bantam.
—Love, Lies & Jessica Wakefield. 1993. pap. 3.50 (*0-553-56306-8*) Bantam.
—The Love Potion. (gr. 4-6). 1993. pap. 3.25 (*0-553-48058-8*) Bantam.
—Memories. 1985. pap. 2.99 (*0-553-27492-9*) Bantam.
—My Best Friend's Boyfriend. 1992. pap. 3.50 (*0-553-29233-1*) Bantam.
—My First Love & Other Disasters. 176p. (gr. 7 up). 1986. pap. 2.95 (*0-440-95447-9*, LFL) Dell.
—My First Love & Other Disasters. (gr. 4-7). 1991. pap. 3.95 (*0-14-034886-7*, Puffin) Puffin Bks.
—Operation Love. (gr. 7 up). 1994. pap. 3.50 (*0-553-29860-7*) Bantam.
—The Perfect Girl. 1991. pap. 3.25 (*0-553-28901-2*) Bantam.
—Perfect Summer. 256p. (Orig.). (gr. 6 up). 1985. pap. 3.50 (*0-553-25072-8*) Bantam.
—Regina's Legacy. 1991. pap. 3.25 (*0-553-28863-6*) Bantam.
—Showdown. 160p. (gr. 6). 1985. pap. 3.25 (*0-553-27589-5*) Bantam.
—Sweet Valley: Three's a Crowd. 1987. pap. 1.25 (*0-440-82193-2*) Dell.
—Taking Sides. 1986. pap. 3.25 (*0-553-27490-2*) Bantam.
—Too Good to Be True. 592p. (Orig.). (gr. 7 up). 1984. pap. 2.75 (*0-553-26824-4*) Bantam.
—The Wakefield Legacy: The Untold Story. (gr. 7 up). 1992. pap. 3.99 (*0-553-29794-5*, Starfire) Bantam.
—Wrong Kind of Girl. (gr. 7 up). 1984. pap. 3.50 (*0-553-27668-9*) Bantam.
Pascal, Francine, created by. Loving. 208p. (Orig.). (gr. 7-12). 1991. pap. 3.50 (*0-553-24716-6*) Bantam.
—The Older Boy. (gr. 3-7). 1988. pap. 3.25 (*0-553-15664-0*, Skylark) Bantam.
Past Perfect. 192p. (Orig.). (gr. 7-12). 1987. pap. 2.50 (*0-553-26789-2*) Bantam.
Paton Walsh, Jill. Torch. LC 87-45995. 176p. 1988. 15.00 (*0-374-37684-0*) FS&G.
Peart, Jane. Dreams of a Longing Heart. LC 90-38382. 192p. (Orig.). (gr. 10 up). 1990. pap. 7.99 (*0-8007-5373-9*) Revell.
—Quest for Lasting Love. LC 90-40569. (Orig.). (gr. 10 up). 1990. pap. 7.99 (*0-8007-5372-0*) Revell.
Peck, Robert N. Soup in Love. (gr. 4-7). 1993. pap. 3.50 (*0-440-40755-9*) Dell.
Petersen, P. J. The Boll Weevil Express. 92p. (gr. 6 up). 1984. pap. 2.95 (*0-440-91040-4*, LFL) Dell.
Peyton, K. M. The Edge of the Cloud. 192p. (gr. 7 up). 1989. pap. 3.99 (*0-14-030905-5*, Puffin) Puffin Bks.
—Flambards. 224p. (gr. 7 up). 1989. pap. 3.95 (*0-14-034153-6*, Puffin) Puffin Bks.
Phelps, Lauren M. The News Is Love. 1992. pap. 2.99 (*0-553-29459-8*) Bantam.
Pierce, David. Forever Yours. 1994. pap. 3.50 (*0-06-106174-3*, Harp PBks) HarpC.
Pitt, Jane. Secret Hearts. (Orig.). (gr. 6 up). 1986. pap. 2.50 (*0-440-97722-3*, LFL) Dell.
Playing Games. 176p. (gr. 5-6). 1986. pap. 2.25 (*0-553-25642-4*) Bantam.

Playing with Fire. 149p. (gr. 7-12). 1984. pap. 3.50 (0-553-27669-7) Bantam.

Polcovar, Jane. Hey, Good Looking! 144p. (gr. 6 up). 1985. pap. 2.25 (0-553-24383-7) Bantam.

Pryor, Bonnie. Rats, Spiders & Love. Higgenbottom, J. Winslow, illus. LC 85-25831. 128p. (gr. 4-6). 1986. 13.95 (0-688-05867-1) Morrow Jr Bks.

Quin-Harkin, Janet. Best Friends Forever, No. 6. 176p. (Orig.). (gr. 7-12). 1986. pap. 2.50 (0-553-26111-8) Bantam.

—Dream Come True. (gr. 6 up). 1988. pap. 2.95 (0-8041-0334-8) Ivy Books.

—Graduation Day. 1992. pap. 3.50 (0-06-106096-8, Harp PBks) HarpC.

—Growing Pains. 176p. (Orig.). (gr. 6 up). 1986. pap. 2.50 (0-553-26034-0) Bantam.

—Home Sweet Home. (gr. 6 up). 1988. pap. 2.95 (0-8041-0333-X) Ivy Books.

—Karen's Perfect Match. LC 94-14327. 176p. (gr. 4-7). 1994. pap. 2.95 (0-8167-3416-X, Rainbow NJ) Troll Assocs.

—My Phantom Love. (gr. 7 up). 1992. pap. 3.50 (0-06-106770-9, Harp PBks) HarpC.

—My Secret Love. 224p. (Orig.). (gr. 7-12). 1986. pap. 2.95 (0-553-25884-2) Bantam.

—On My Own. 1992. pap. 3.50 (0-06-106722-9, Harp PBks) HarpC.

—One Hundred One Ways to Meet Mr. Right. 176p. (Orig.). (gr. 6 up). 1985. pap. 2.25 (0-553-24946-0) Bantam.

—Out of Love. 208p. (Orig.). (gr. 6 up). 1986. pap. 2.50 (0-553-25937-7) Bantam.

—The Trouble with Toni. 192p. (Orig.). (gr. 6 up). 1986. pap. 2.50 (0-553-25724-2) Bantam.

Rand, Suzanne. The Boy She Left Behind. 192p. (Orig.). (gr. 6). 1985. pap. 2.25 (0-553-24890-1) Bantam.

Rathbun, Carolyn R. Sara Bear's Surprise. Harvey, Chuck, illus. (Orig.). (ps). 1993. 12.95 (0-9634808-0-4); pap. 4.50 (0-9634808-1-2) Endless Love.

Raymond, Patrick. Daniel & Esther. LC 89-49588. 176p. (gr. 7 up). 1990. SBE 13.95 (0-689-50504-3, M K McElderry) Macmillan Child Grp.

Redish, Jane. Promise Me Love. 176p. (Orig.). (gr. 7-12). 1986. pap. 2.50 (0-553-26158-4) Bantam.

Reit, Ann. The First Time. (Orig.). (gr. 5 up). 1986. pap. 2.50 (0-440-92560-6, LFL) Dell.

Reynolds, Elizabeth. Stolen Kisses. 144p. (Orig.). (gr. 7-12). 1986. pap. 2.50 (0-553-25726-9) Bantam.

Romance on the Run. 1993. pap. 3.50 (0-553-29988-3) Bantam.

Roos, Stephen. Confessions of a Wayward Preppie. LC 85-16241. 144p. (gr. 7 up). 1986. 13.95 (0-385-29454-9) Delacorte.

—My Secret Admirer. (gr. k-12). 1991. pap. 3.25 (0-440-45950-8, YB) Dell.

Ross, Dave. A Book of Hugs. Ross, Dave, illus. LC 79-7896. 32p. (gr. k up). 1991. pap. 3.95 (0-06-107418-7) HarpC Child Bks.

Rowe, Jeanine C. Eyes of Desire. Hannan, R., ed. 370p. 1991. pap. 5.99 (0-9626415-0-2) Intl Info NY.

Rue, Nancy. Stop in the Name of Love. Rosen, Roger, ed. (gr. 7 up). 1988. PLB 12.95 (0-8239-0794-5) Rosen Group.

Ryan, Mary E. Dance a Step Closer. 1988. pap. 2.95 (0-440-20127-6, LFL) Dell.

Ryland, Cynthia. Couple of Kooks: And Other Stories about Love. 1992. pap. 3.50 (0-440-21210-3) Dell.

Rylant, Cynthia. A Couple of Kooks: And Other Stories about Love. LC 90-30646. 112p. (gr. 7 up). 1990. 14.95 (0-531-05900-6); PLB 14.99 (0-531-08500-7) Orchard Bks Watts.

—A Kindness. LC 88-1454. 128p. (gr. 7 up). 1988. 13.95 (0-531-05767-4); PLB 13.99 (0-531-08367-5) Orchard Bks Watts.

Saal, Jocelyn & Burman, Margaret. On Thin Ice. 181p. (gr. 6 up). 1983. pap. 1.95 (0-553-17070-8) Bantam.

Sachs, Marilyn. Almost Fifteen. LC 86-29209. (gr. 4-9). 1987. 12.95 (0-525-44285-5, DCB) Dutton Child Bks.

—Baby Sister. LC 85-16171. (gr. 7-11). 1986. 13.95 (0-525-44213-8, DCB) Dutton Child Bks.

—Fourteen. 128p. (gr. 7 up). 1985. pap. 2.95 (0-380-69842-0, Flare) Avon.

Sadler, Mike. Lonely Stranger. (gr. 4-7). 1992. pap. 4.95 (0-7910-2922-0) Chelsea Hse.

St. Pierre, Stephanie. Project Boyfriend. 1991. pap. 2.95 (0-553-28900-4) Bantam.

—Sun Kissed. 1990. pap. 2.75 (0-553-28517-3) Bantam.

Sainz, Frances. Carino. 23p. (ps-1). 1992. pap. text ed. 23.00 big bk. (1-56843-047-7); pap. text ed. 4.50 (1-56843-094-9) BGR Pub.

Sampson, Emma S. Miss Minerva & William Green Hill. 275p. 1992. Repr. lib. bdg. 21.95x (0-89966-922-0) Buccaneer Bks.

Schurfranz, Vivian. Danielle, No. 4. 368p. (gr. 7 up). 1984. pap. 2.95 (0-590-33156-6) Scholastic Inc.

—Megan, No. 16. 224p. (Orig.). (gr. 7 up). 1986. pap. 2.75 (0-590-41468-2) Scholastic Inc.

Secret Heart. 1993. 3.50 (0-553-29986-7) Bantam.

Secrets. 118p. (gr. 6 up). 1984. pap. 3.50 (0-553-27578-X) Bantam.

Service, Pamela F. Tomorrow's Magic. (gr. 5 up). 1988. pap. 3.95 (0-449-70305-3, Juniper) Fawcett.

Shakespeare, William. Romeo & Juliet. Shaw, Charles, illus. Stewart, Diana, adapted by. LC 79-24465. (Illus.). 48p. (gr. 4 up). 1983. PLB 20.70 (0-8172-1653-7) Raintree Steck-V.

Shannon, Jacqueline. Big Guy, Little Women. (gr. 6-8). 1989. pap. 2.75 (0-590-41685-5, Apple Paperbacks) Scholastic Inc.

Sharmat, Marjorie W. Fighting over Me. (Orig.). (gr. 6 up). 1986. pap. 2.50 (0-440-92530-4, LFL) Dell.

—He Noticed I'm Alive & Other Hopeful Signs. (Orig.). (gr. k-12). 1989. pap. 2.95 (0-440-93809-0, LFL) Dell.

—Here Comes Mr. Right. (gr. 5 up). 1987. pap. 2.50 (0-440-93841-4) Dell.

—I Think I'm Falling in Love. (Orig.). (gr. 6 up). 1986. pap. 2.50 (0-440-94011-7, LFL) Dell.

—I'm Going to Get Your Boyfriend. (Orig.). (gr. k-12). 1987. pap. 2.50 (0-440-94004-4, LFL) Dell.

—Snobs Beware. (Orig.). (gr. 6 up). 1986. pap. 2.50 (0-440-98092-5, LFL) Dell.

—Two Guys Noticed Me...& Other Miracles. (gr. k up). 1989. pap. 2.95 (0-440-98846-2, LFL) Dell.

Sheldon, Dyan. Tall, Thin, & Blonde. LC 92-53021. 176p. (gr. 6-10). 1993. 14.95 (1-56402-139-4) Candlewick Pr.

Shura, Mary F. Diana. 224p. (gr. 6-10). 1988. pap. 2.75 (0-590-41416-X) Scholastic Inc.

—Marilee, No. 9. 368p. (Orig.). (gr. 7 up). 1985. pap. 2.95 (0-590-33433-6) Scholastic Inc.

Simbal, Joanne. Gifts from the Heart, No. 146. 176p. (Orig.). 1988. pap. 2.50 (0-553-27228-4, Sweet Dreams) Bantam.

Simons, Scott & Simons, Evelyn. Opening a Can of Words. 1994. pap. 3.50 (0-8125-2948-0) Tor Bks.

Singer, Marilyn. Storm Rising. 1989. pap. 12.95 (0-590-42173-5) Scholastic Inc.

Singleton, Linda J. Love to Spare. 1993. pap. 2.99 (0-553-29979-4) Bantam.

Sloate, Susan. Racing Hearts. (gr. 7 up). 1991. pap. 2.99 (0-553-28962-4) Bantam.

Smith, K. T. Beverly Hills, 90210: Fantasies. 1992. pap. 3.99 (0-06-106727-X, Harp PBks) HarpC.

Smith, Sherri C. Wrong-Way Romance. (gr. 9-12). 1991. pap. 2.95 (0-553-28840-7) Bantam.

Snelling, Lauraine. Out of the Mist. 1993. pap. 5.99 (1-55661-338-5) Bethany Hse.

Snyder, Zilpha K. The Headless Cupid. Raible, Alton, illus. (gr. 3-7). 1985. pap. 3.50 (0-440-43507-2, YB) Dell.

Soliven, Marivi. Pillow Tales. 1991. 6.95 (0-533-09188-8) Vantage.

Sommer-Bodenburg, Angela. The Vampire in Love. 144p. (gr. 3-6). 1993. pap. 2.99 (0-671-75877-2, Minstrel Bks) PB.

South, Sheri C. The Cinderella Game. 1992. pap. 2.99 (0-553-29454-7) Bantam.

—That Certain Feeling. 1991. pap. 2.99 (0-553-29354-0) Bantam.

Spector, Debra. Secret Admirer. 160p. (gr. 6 up). 1985. pap. 2.25 (0-553-24688-7) Bantam.

Speed, Toby. One Leaf Fell. 1993. 14.95 (1-55670-271-X) Stewart Tabori & Chang.

Spinelli, Jerry. Jason & Marceline. (gr. k-12). 1988. pap. 3.50 (0-440-20166-7, LFL) Dell.

Spyropulos, Diana. Cornelius & the Dog Star. Williams, Ray, illus. LC 94-32335. 48p. (gr. k-5). 1995. 15.95 (*0-935699-08-2*) Illum Arts. CORNELIUS & THE DOG STAR is the tale of a dignified but grouchy old basset hound named Cornelius. Arriving one evening at the Gates of Heaven, he is dismayed when Saint Bernard says he cannot enter until he has learned to open his heart. Feeling lost & alone, he encounters Sirius, the Dog Star, who guides him on a wondrous adventure of the heart. In the end, Cornelius learns to love even Tucker, a hobo he had treated badly on Earth. Featuring Williams' fantastical illustrations, this story will capture the hearts of young & old. To order call Atrium at 1-800-275-2606. "Adults & children alike will enjoy reading this quirky & fun story...Beautiful, full-color illustrations enhance the fantasy experience." - NAPRA Trade Journal. *Publisher Provided Annotation.*

Stahl, Hilda. Elizabeth Gail & the Missing Love Letters, No. 13. 128p. 1989. pap. 4.99 (0-8423-0807-5) Tyndale.

—Sadie Rose & the Secret Romance. 128p. (gr. 4-7). 1992. pap. 4.99 (0-89107-661-1) Crossway Bks.

Steinke, Ann. My Cheating Heart. 1993. pap. 3.50 (0-06-106733-4, Harp PBks) HarpC.

Stevens, Mallory. Can't Buy Me Love. 1992. pap. 3.50 (0-06-106710-5, Harp PBks) HarpC.

Stewart, A. C. Elizabeth's Tower. LC 72-4063. 220p. (gr. 6-9). 1972. 21.95 (0-87599-193-9) S G Phillips.

Stine, Megan. Dylan's Secret. 112p. (Orig.). (gr. 4-9). 1992. pap. 2.95 (0-448-40493-1, G&D) Putnam Pub Group.

Stine, R. L. Blind Date. 1986. pap. 3.50 (0-590-43125-0, Point) Scholastic Inc.

—The Boyfriend. 176p. (gr. 7 up). 1990. pap. 3.50 (0-590-43279-6, Point) Scholastic Inc.

—First Date. MacDonald, Pat, ed. 176p. (Orig.). 1992. pap. 3.99 (0-671-73865-8, Archway) PB.

Stowe, Aurelia, ed. Love Will Come: Stories of Romance. 1963. lib. bdg. 4.99 (0-394-91363-9) Random Bks Yng Read.

Strasser, Todd. Workin' for Peanuts. LC 82-14070. 192p. (gr. 7 up). 1983. pap. 12.95 (0-385-29236-8) Delacorte.

Stuart, Jesse. Daughter of the Legend. Spurlock, John H., ed. Marsh, Jim, illus. Dykeman, Wilma & Kennedy, Brentintro. by. (Illus.). 256p. (gr. 8 up). 1994. Repr. of 1965 ed. 20.00 (0-945084-42-0) J Stuart Found.

Sunshine, Tina. An X-Rated Romance. 142p. (gr. 7 up). 1982. pap. 2.50 (0-380-79905-7, Flare) Avon.

Sweeney, Joyce. Dream Collector. 1991. pap. 3.50 (0-440-21131-X, YB) Dell.

Sweet Dreams. 1994. pap. 3.50 (0-553-29989-1) Bantam.

Tab, Joan & Jon. Etruscans: Valentine's Day. rev. ed. Abel, J., illus. 20p. (gr. 5-8). 1992. pap. 25.00 (1-56611-007-6); pap. 10.00 (1-56611-299-0) Jonas.

Tamar, Erika. Fair Game. 1993. pap. 3.95 (0-15-227065-5) HarBrace.

—The Things I Did Last Summer. LC 93-32556. (gr. 7 up). 1994. write for info. (0-15-282490-1); pap. write for info. (0-15-200020-8) HarBrace.

Taylor, Mildred D. Let the Circle Be Unbroken. (gr. 7-12). 1983. pap. 3.50 (0-553-23436-6) Bantam.

Taylor, Theodore. Waking up a Rainbow. LC 85-16239. 224p. (gr. 7 up). 1986. pap. 14.95 (0-385-29435-2) Delacorte.

Taylor, William. Paradise Lane. 176p. (gr. 7 up). 1989. pap. 2.75 (0-590-41014-8) Scholastic Inc.

Tedesco, Donna. Do You Know How Much I Love You? Tedesco, Donna, illus. LC 92-7856. 32p. (ps-1). 1994. SBE 13.95 (0-02-789120-8, Bradbury Pr) Macmillan Child Grp.

Thesman, Jean. Couldn't I Start Over? 176p. (Orig.). (gr. 7 up). 1989. pap. 2.95 (0-380-75717-6, Flare) Avon.

Thompson, Julian F. Shepherd. 176p. (gr. 8 up). 1993. 15.95 (0-8050-2106-X, Bks Young Read) H Holt & Co.

Thrash, Jacquelyn R. Heart o' Desire. 1992. write for info. (0-9635247-2-0) Three Pines.

Turner. In the Heart. Date not set. 15.00 (0-06-023730-9); PLB 14.89 (0-06-023731-7) HarpC Child Bks.

Ullman, James R. Banner in the Sky. LC 54-7296. 256p. (gr. 7 up). 1988. pap. 3.95 (0-06-447048-2, Trophy) HarpC Child Bks.

Ure, Jean. See You Thursday. LC 83-5217. 224p. (gr. 7 up). 1983. pap. 12.95 (0-385-29303-8) Delacorte.

Vail, Linda. My Wicked Valentine. (Orig.). 1989. pap. 3.95 (0-440-20233-7) Dell.

Voigt, Cynthia. Dicey's Song. LC 82-3882. 204p. (gr. 6 up). 1982. SBE 15.95 (0-689-30944-9, Atheneum Child Bk) Macmillan Child Grp.

Voyer, Kelly. For Love of Rock. Voyer, Kelly, illus. 24p. (Orig.). (ps-1). 1994. pap. 0.99 (1-55037-349-8, Pub. by Annick CN) Firefly Bks Ltd.

Walton, Rick. Will You Still Love Me? Teare, Brad, illus. LC 92-341. 32p. (ps). 1992. 11.95 (0-87579-582-X) Deseret Bk.

Ward, James M. & Hong, Jane C. Pool of Radiance. LC 88-51726. 352p. (Orig.). 1989. pap. 3.95 (0-88038-735-1) TSR Inc.

Warren, Andrea. Searching for Love. 240p. (Orig.). (gr. 7-12). 1987. pap. 2.95 (0-553-26292-0) Bantam.

Warren, Peggy. Where Love Goes. (Illus.). 36p. (gr. k-3). 1992. 5.95 (0-9628710-3-6) Art After Five.

—Where Love Is. (Illus.). (gr. k-3). 1992. 5.95 (0-9628710-2-8) Art After Five.

Watts, Alycyn. Moonlight Melody. 1993. pap. 2.99 (0-553-29985-9) Bantam.

Weekend Romance. 1993. pap. 3.50 (0-685-65928-3) Bantam.

Weisinger, Steve. The Little Book of Hugs. Davies, Sumiko, illus. LC 90-60083. 28p. (ps). 1991. bds. 3.25 (0-679-80755-1) Random Bks Yng Read.

—The Little Book of Kisses. Davies, Sumiko, illus. LC 90-60082. 28p. (ps). 1991. bds. 3.25 (0-679-80754-3) Random Bks Yng Read.

Weitzman, Geri. Bead Dazzled. (gr. 4-7). 1994. pap. 6.95 (0-8167-3469-0) Troll Assocs.

Wersba, Barbara. Beautiful Losers. LC 87-7590. 192p. (gr. 7 up). 1988. HarpC Child Bks.

—Just Be Gorgeous. 1991. pap. 3.25 (0-440-20810-6) Dell.

—Love Is the Crooked Thing. 1990. 3.50 (0-440-20542-5, LFL) Dell.

Westall, Robert. The Promise. 208p. (gr. 5 up). 1991. 13.95 (0-590-43760-7, Scholastic Hardcover) Scholastic Inc.

White, Joe. Looking for Love in All the Wrong Places. rev. & updated ed. 1991. pap. 3.95 (0-8423-3829-2) Tyndale.

Wilde, Oscar. The Nightingale & the Rose. Wright, Freire & Foreman, Michael, illus. (gr. 4 up). 1981. 14.95 (0-19-520231-7) OUP.

Willard, Barbara. The Iron Lily. (gr. k-12). 1989. pap. 3.25 (0-440-20434-8, LFL) Dell.

Wine, Jeanine. Mrs. Tibbles & the Special Someone. LC 87-14966. 32p. (ps-3). 1987. 12.95 (*0-934672-54-7*) Good Bks PA.
Winfield, Julia. Only Make-Believe. 176p. (Orig.). (gr. 7-12). 1987. pap. 2.50 (*0-553-26418-4*) Bantam.
—Private Eyes. 160p. (Orig.). (gr. 7-12). 1989. pap. 2.75 (*0-553-25814-1*) Bantam.
Winthrop, Elizabeth. Sloppy Kisses. Burgess, Anne, illus. LC 90-105. 32p. (gr. k-3). 1990. pap. 4.95 (*0-689-71410-6*, Aladdin) Macmillan Child Grp.
Wolfe, Anne H. Wings of Love. (gr. 4-7). 1993. pap. 2.99 (*0-553-29978-6*) Bantam.
Wolitzer, Hilmer. Wish You Were Here. 180p. (gr. 5 up). 1986. pap. 3.45 (*0-374-48412-0*, Sunburst) FS&G.
Woodson, Jacqueline. Dear One. 1993. pap. 3.50 (*0-440-21420-3*) Dell.
Wyeth, Sharon D. Boy Crazy. (gr. 4-7). 1991. pap. 3.25 (*0-440-40426-6*, YB) Dell.
—Boy Project. (gr. 4-7). 1991. pap. 2.95 (*0-440-40493-2*) Dell.
—Heartbreak Guy. (gr. 4-7). 1991. pap. 2.95 (*0-440-40412-6*) Dell.
—Rocky Romance, No. 137. 192p. (Orig.). (gr. 7-12). 1988. pap. 2.50 (*0-553-26948-8*, Sweet Dreams) Bantam.
—Sealed with a Kiss. (gr. k-6). 1990. pap. 2.95 (*0-440-40272-7*, YB) Dell.
Zable, Rona S. Love at the Laundromat. 160p. (gr. 7 up). 1992. pap. 3.50 (*0-553-27225-X*, Starfire) Bantam.
Zach, Cheryl. Looking Out for Lacy. 1992. pap. 3.50 (*0-06-106772-5*, Harp PBks) HarpC.
Zadra, Dan. Talk Like an Eagle. (Illus.). 32p. (gr. 6 up). 1986. PLB 12.95 (*0-88682-021-9*) Creative Ed.
—There Will Never Be Another You. (Illus.). 32p. (gr. 6 up). 1986. PLB 12.95 (*0-88682-015-4*) Creative Ed.
Zolotow, Charlotte. If You Listen. Reissue. ed. Simont, Marc, illus. LC 79-2688. 32p. (gr. k-3). 1980. PLB 13.89 (*0-06-027050-0*) HarpC Child Bks.
—Some Things Go Together. Gundersheimer, Karen, illus. LC 82-48694. 24p. (ps-3). 1989. (Crowell Jr Bks); (Crowell Jr Bks) HarpC Child Bks.

LOVE (THEOLOGY)

Baden. The Greatest Gift Is Love. LC 59-1314. 24p. (gr. k-4). 1985. pap. 1.89 (*0-570-06196-2*) Concordia.
Crook, Carol. Overflowing with Love. 19p. (Orig.). (gr. 7 up). 1989. pap. 0.95x (*0-939399-06-7*) Bks of Truth.
Hutchcroft, Vera. Give What You Can. Butcher, Sam, illus. 20p. (gr. k-6). 1984. pap. text ed. 4.25 (*1-55976-142-3*) CEF Press.
McCaw, Mabel. What Is Loving? Todd, Barbara, illus. 12p. (ps). 1987. 3.25 (*0-8378-5208-0*) Gibson.
Moncure, Jane B. Love. rev. ed. Hohag, Linda, illus. LC 80-27479. (ENG & SPA.). 32p. (ps-2). 1981. PLB 14.95 (*0-89565-205-6*) Childs World.
Nighswander, Ada. The Little Martins Learn to Love. (ps-4). 1982. 6.95 (*0-686-30775-5*) Rod & Staff.

LOVE POETRY

Fletcher, Ralph. I Am Wings: Poems about Love. Baker, Joe, illus. 48p. (gr. 5-9). 1994. SBE 12.95 (*0-02-735395-8*, Bradbury Pr) Macmillan Child Grp.
Greenfield, Eloise. Honey, I Love: And Other Love Poems. Dillon, Diane & Dillon, D., illus. LC 77-2845. 48p. (gr. 1-3). 1978. 13.00 (*0-690-01334-5*, Crowell Jr Bks); PLB 12.89 (*0-690-03845-3*) HarpC Child Bks.
Marsh, James. From the Heart: Light-Hearted Verse. LC 92-17912. (Illus.). 32p. 1993. 6.99 (*0-8037-1449-1*) Dial Bks Young.
Watson, Wendy. A Valentine for You. Briley, Dorothy, ed. Watson, Wendy, illus. 32p. (ps-1). 1991. 14.45 (*0-395-53625-1*, Clarion Bks) HM.

LOVE POETRY–COLLECTIONS

Manushkin, Fran, compiled by. Disney Babies Somebody Loves You: Poems of Friendship & Love. Shelly, Jeff, illus. LC 92-53436. 32p. (ps-k). 1993. 9.95 (*1-56282-370-1*) Disney Pr.

LOW, JULIETTE (GORDON) 1860-1927

Behrens, June. Juliette Low: Founder of the Girl Scouts of America. LC 88-11976. (Illus.). 32p. (gr. 2-4). 1988. PLB 11.80 (*0-516-04171-1*); pap. 3.95 (*0-516-44171-X*) Childrens.
Steelsmith, Shari. Juliette Gordon Low: Founder of the Girl Scouts. Pope, Connie J., illus. LC 89-62673. 32p. (Orig.). (ps-4). 1990. lib. bdg. 16.95 (*0-943990-37-8*); pap. 5.95 (*0-943990-36-X*) Parenting Pr.

LOW TEMPERATURES

Stonehouse, Bernard. Snow, Ice, & Cold. LC 92-26298. (Illus.). 48p. (gr. 6 up). 1993. text ed. 13.95 RSBE (*0-02-788530-5*, New Discovery) Macmillan Child Grp.

LULLABIES

Aliki. Hush Little Baby. Aliki, illus. (ps-1). 1972. (Pub. by Treehouse) P-H.
—Hush Little Baby: A Folk Lullaby. LC 68-12194. (Illus.). 32p. (gr. k-4). 1972. (S&S BFYR); pap. 5.95 (*0-671-66742-4*, S&S BFYR) S&S Trade.
Amoss, Berthe. Lullaby & Good Night. (Illus.). 10p. (ps-7). 1989. pap. 2.95 (*0-922589-13-5*) More Than Card.
Bang, Molly. Ten, Nine, Eight. Bang, Molly, illus. LC 81-20106. 24p. (ps-1). 1983. 15.00 (*0-688-00906-9*); PLB 14.93 (*0-688-00907-7*) Greenwillow.
Bozylinsky, Hannah H. Lala Salama. LC 92-23928. (Illus.). 40p. (ps-2). 1993. PLB 14.95 (*0-399-22022-4*, Philomel Bks) Putnam Pub Group.
Brady, Janeen & Woolley, Diane. Brite Dreams. Twede, Evan, illus. 32p. (Orig.). (ps). 1988. pap. 2.50 (*0-944803-79-2*); pap. 10.95 incl. cassette (*0-944803-80-6*) Brite Music.
Brown, J. Aaron, ed. A Child's Gift of Lullabyes. Vienneau, Jim, illus. 14p. (ps). 1987. Book packaged with cassette. 12.95 (*0-927945-01-0*) Someday Baby.
—Un Regalo de Arrullos Para Ninos. Vienneau, Jim, illus. Pineda, Sysy, tr. (SPA., Illus.). 14p. (ps). 1988. Book with cassette. 12.95 (*0-927945-02-9*) Someday Baby.
Carlson. A Christmas Lullaby. 24p. (gr. k-4). 1985. pap. 1.99 (*0-570-06195-4*, 59-1296) Concordia.
Carlstrom, Nancy. Northern Lullaby. Dillon, Leo & Dillon, Diane, illus. 32p. (ps-3). 1992. PLB 15.95 (*0-399-21806-8*, Philomel Bks) Putnam Pub Group.
Cassatt, Mary, illus. Lullabies & Good Night. 32p. 1989. 13.95 (*0-8249-8441-2*, Ideals Child); incl. 60-min. cassette 17.95 (*0-8249-7351-8*) Hambleton-Hill.
Chusid, Nancy. Favorite Lullabies. Chusid, Nancy, illus. 32p. (Orig.). (gr. 2-6). 1990. pap. 6.95 incl. cassette (*1-878624-06-7*) McClanahan Bk.
Dyer, Jane, selected by. & illus. Babyland: A Book for Babies. LC 93-4244. 1995. 17.95 (*0-316-19766-1*) Little.
Goodman, Joan E. Hush Little Darling. 1992. 4.95 (*0-590-45247-9*, Cartwheel) Scholastic Inc.
Gutmann, Bessie P. Nursery Songs & Lullabies. (Illus.). 32p. 1990. 9.95x (*0-448-23457-2*, G&D) Putnam Pub Group.
Hague, Michael, compiled by. & illus. Sleep, Baby, Sleep: Lullabies & Night Poems. LC 93-27119. 1994. PLB write for info. (*0-688-10877-6*) Morrow Jr Bks.
Headington, Christopher. Sweet Sleep: A Collection of Lullabies & Cradle Songs. LC 88-26898. (Illus.). 96p. 1990. (Clarkson Potter) Crown Pub Group.
Hughes, Margaret A. Mother Goose Favorite Lullabies. HIcks, Russell, et al, illus. 26p. (ps). 1987. 9.95 (*0-934323-51-8*); pre-programmed audio cass. tapes avail. Alchemy Comms.
Marzollo, Jean. Close Your Eyes. Jeffers, Susan, illus. LC 76-42935. (ps-2). 1978. PLB 12.89 (*0-8037-1610-9*) Dial Bks Young.
Merriam, Eve. Goodnight to Annie: An Alphabet Lullaby. Schwartz, Carol, illus. 32p. (ps-2). 1994. pap. 4.95 (*0-7868-1005-X*) Hyprn Ppbks.
Muir, Jim. Little Girls Have to Sleep. Barwick, Mary, illus. Moore, Robert, contrib. by. LC 92-37456. (Illus.). 1994. 16.00 (*1-881320-03-0*) Black Belt Pr.
Paxton, Tom. The Animals' Lullaby. Ingraham, Erick, illus. LC 92-18841. 40p. (ps up). 1993. 15.00 (*0-688-10468-1*); PLB 14.93 (*0-688-10469-X*) Morrow Jr Bks.
Plotz, Helen. A Week of Lullabies. Russo, Marisabina, illus. LC 86-18458. 32p. (ps-3). 1988. 11.95 (*0-688-06652-6*); lib. bdg. 11.88 (*0-688-06653-4*) Greenwillow.
Plume, Ilse, ed. & illus. Lullaby & Goodnight: Songs & Poems for Babies. LC 93-4425. 32p. (ps-1). 1994. 12.00 (*0-06-023501-2*); PLB 11.89 (*0-06-023502-0*) HarpC Child Bks.
Roth, Kevin. Lullabies for Little Dreamers. De Groat, Diane, illus. 24p. (ps-1). 1992. incl. cassette 9.95 (*0-679-82382-4*) Random Bks Yng Read.
Sing a Lullaby, Unit 3. (gr. 1). 1991. 29.50 (*0-88106-717-2*) Charlesbridge Pub.
Stanley, Diane. Birdsong Lullaby. Stanley, Diane, illus. LC 85-5654. 32p. (ps-2). 1985. 12.95 (*0-688-05804-3*) Morrow Jr Bks.
Van Laan, Nancy. Country Lullaby: All Around the World. Meade, Holly, illus. LC 93-44484. (gr. 1-4). 1995. 14.95 (*0-316-89732-9*) Little.

LUMBER AND LUMBERING

see also Forests and Forestry; Trees; Wood

Adams, Peter D. Early Loggers & the Sawmill. (Illus.). 64p. (gr. 4-5). 1981. 15.95 (*0-86505-005-8*); pap. 7.95 (*0-86505-006-6*) Crabtree Pub Co.
Appelbaum, Diana. Giants in the Land. McCurdy, Michael, illus. LC 92-26526. 32p. 1993. 14.95 (*0-395-64720-7*) HM.
Bentley, Judith. Railroad Workers & Loggers. (Illus.). 96p. (gr. 5-8). 1995. bds. 16.95 (*0-8050-2997-4*) TFC Bks NY.
Gintzler, A. S. Rough & Ready Loggers. (Illus.). 48p. (gr. 4-7). 1994. 12.95 (*1-56261-164-X*) John Muir.
Silverstein, Alvin, et al. The Spotted Owl. LC 93-42624. (Illus.). 48p. (gr. 4-6). 1994. PLB 13.40 (*1-56294-415-0*) Millbrook Pr.

LUMBER AND LUMBERING–FICTION

Hines, Gary. The Day of the High Climber. Hines, Anna G., illus. LC 93-12254. 32p. (ps up). 1994. 14.00 (*0-688-11494-6*); PLB 13.93 (*0-688-11495-4*) Greenwillow.
Paulsen, Gary. The Winter Room. LC 89-42541. 128p. (gr. 6-9). 1989. 13.95 (*0-531-05839-5*); PLB 13.99 (*0-531-08439-6*) Orchard Bks Watts.

LUMBER AND LUMBERING–LEGENDS

Kurelek, William. Lumberjack. (Illus.). 48p. (gr. 5 up). text ed. 17.95 (*0-88776-052-X*, Dist. by U of Toronto Pr) Tundra Bks.
McCormick, Dell J. Paul Bunyan Swings His Axe. McCormick, Dell J., illus. LC 36-33409. (gr. 4-6). 1936. 11.95 (*0-87004-093-6*) Caxton.
—Tall Timber Tales: More Paul Bunyan Stories. Livesley, Lorna, illus. LC 39-20778. (gr. 4-6). 1939. 11.95 (*0-87004-094-4*) Caxton.
Shephard, Esther. Paul Bunyan. Kent, Rockwell, illus. LC 85-5448. 233p. (gr. 7 up). 1985. 12.95 (*0-15-259749-2*, HB Juv Bks) HarBrace.
Turney, Ida V. Paul Bunyan, the Work Giant. (Illus.). (gr. 3 up). 1969. 7.95 (*0-8323-0163-9*) Binford Mort.

LUMINESCENCE, ANIMAL

see Bioluminescence

LUNAR EXPEDITIONS

see Space Flight to the Moon

LUNAR EXPLORATION

see Moon–Exploration

LUNAR PROBES

see also names of space projects, e.g. Mariner Project; etc.

LUNCH ROOMS

see Restaurants, Bars, etc.

LUNCHEONS

Bodily, Jolene & Kreiswirth, Kinny. The Lunch Book & Bag: A Fit Kid's Guide to Making Delicious (& Nutritious) Lunches. Kreiswirth, Kinny, illus. LC 92-2815. 56p. (gr. 2-6). 1992. pap. 12.95 (*0-688-11624-8*, Tambourine Bks) Morrow.

LUTHER, MARTIN, 1483-1546

Fearon, Mike. Martin Luther. 144p. 1993. 4.99 (*1-55661-306-7*) Bethany Hse.
Fehlauer, Adolph. Life & Faith of Martin Luther. (gr. 6-9). 1981. pap. 6.95 (*0-8100-0125-X*, 15N0376) Northwest Pub.
Nohl, Frederick. Martin Luther: Hero of Faith. LC 62-14146. (Illus.). (gr. 4-6). 1962. pap. 5.99 (*0-570-03727-1*, 12-2629) Concordia.
Schwiebert, Ernest G. Luther & His Times: The Reformation from a New Perspective. (Illus.). (gr. 9 up). 1950. 26.95 (*0-570-03246-6*, 15-1164) Concordia.

LUXEMBOURG

Carrick, Noel. Luxembourg. (Illus.). 96p. (gr. 5 up). 1988. 14.95 (*0-222-01144-0*) Chelsea Hse.
Lepthien, Emilie U. Luxembourg. LC 89-34664. 128p. (gr. 5-9). 1989. PLB 20.55 (*0-516-02714-X*) Childrens.

LYING

see Truthfulness and Falsehood

LYME DISEASE

Landau, Elaine. Lyme Disease. LC 89-70514. (Illus.). 1990. PLB 12.90 (*0-531-10931-3*) Watts.
Mactire, Sean P. Lyme Disease & Other Pest-Borne Illnesses. LC 91-40895. (Illus.). 112p. (gr. 7-12). 1991. PLB 13.40 (*0-531-12523-8*) Watts.
Silverstein, Alvin, et al. Lyme Disease, the Great Imitator: How to Prevent & Cure It. Sigal, Leonard H., pref. by. LC 90-81250. (Illus.). 126p. (gr. 5 up). 1990. pap. 5.95 (*0-9623653-9-4*) Avstar Pub.

LYNX

Bonners, Susan. Hunter in the Snow: The Lynx. LC 93-24975. (gr. 1-5). 1994. 14.95 (*0-316-10201-6*) Little.
Savarin, Julian J. Lynx. 240p. 1986. 15.95 (*0-8027-0890-0*) Walker & Co.
Schneider, Jost. Lynx. LC 94-2119. 1994. write for info. (*0-87614-844-5*) Carolrhoda Bks.

LYON, MARY, 1797-1849

Rosen, Dorothy S. A Fire in Her Bones: The Story of Mary Lyon. LC 94-1978. 1994. write for info. (*0-87614-840-2*) Carolrhoda Bks.

LYSERGIC ACID DIETHYLAMIDE

Gunn, Jeffrey. Pen Pals, Vol. 8: Facts about Acid. Wolfe, Debra, illus. (Orig.). (gr. 3). 1990. pap. write for info. (*1-879146-08-8*) Knowldg Pub.

M

MACARTHUR, DOUGLAS, 1880-1964

Darby, Jean. Douglas MacArthur. (Illus.). 112p. (gr. 5 up). 1989. 21.50 (*0-8225-4901-8*) Lerner Pubns.
Finkelstein, Norman. Douglas MacArthur: The Emperor General: A Biography of Douglas MacArthur. LC 88-22863. (Illus.). 128p. (gr. 5 up). 1989. text ed. 13.95 RSBE (*0-87518-396-4*, Dillon) Macmillan Child Grp.

MACHINE TOOLS

Cohen, Lynn. Energy & Machines. 64p. (ps-2). 1988. 6.95 (*0-912107-78-2*, MM982) Monday Morning Bks.
Erickson, Sheldon, et al. Machine Shop. Cordel, Betty, et al, eds. (Illus.). 169p. (Orig.). (gr. 5-9). 1993. pap. text ed. 14.95 (*1-881431-39-8*, 1311) AIMS Educ Fnd.

MACHINERY

see also Agricultural Machinery; Engines; Inventions; Locomotives; Machine Tools; Mechanical Drawing; Mechanics; Steam Engines

Ardley, Neil. Science Book of Machines. (gr. 4-7). 1992. 9.95 (*0-15-200613-3*, HB Juv Bks) HarBrace.
Bains, Rae. Simples Machines. Veno, Joseph, illus. LC 84-2607. 32p. (gr. 3-6). 1985. PLB 9.49 (*0-8167-0166-0*); pap. text ed. 2.95 (*0-8167-0167-9*) Troll Assocs.
Barton, Byron. Machines at Work. Barton, Byron, illus. LC 86-24221. 32p. (ps-1). 1987. 15.00 (*0-694-00190-2*, Crowell Jr Bks); PLB 14.89 (*0-690-04573-5*) HarpC Child Bks.
Boy Scouts of America. Machinery. (Illus.). 58p. (gr. 6-12). 1983. pap. 1.85 (*0-8395-3337-3*, 33337) BSA.
Breverton, David. Here Comes Bulldozer. Bartle, Brian, illus. 12p. (ps-1). 1992. 4.95 (*0-448-40590-3*, G&D) Putnam Pub Group.
Burnie, David. Machines: How They Work. LC 93-44070. (Illus.). 48p. 1994. 14.95 (*0-8069-0744-4*) Sterling.
Carratello, John & Carratello, Patty. Hands on Science: Simple Machines. Wright, Terry & Spence, Paula, illus. 32p. (gr. 2-5). 1988. wkbk. 5.95 (*1-55734-227-X*) Tchr Create Mat.

Diggers & Dump Trucks. LC 91-16119. (Illus.). 24p. (ps-k). 1991. pap. 7.95 POB (*0-689-71516-1*, Aladdin) Macmillan Child Grp.
Diggers & Dumpers. 32p. (ps-3). 1994. 4.95 (*1-56458-731-2*) Dorling Kindersley.
Gardner, Robert. Forces & Machines. (Illus.). 136p. (gr. 7 up). 1991. lib. bdg. 14.98 (*0-671-69041-8*, J Messner); pap. 9.95 (*0-671-69046-9*) S&S Trade.
Gifford, C. Machines. (Illus.). 32p. (gr. 5-8). 1994. PLB 13.95 (*0-88110-699-2*, Usborne); pap. 6.95 (*0-7460-1962-9*, Usborne) EDC.
Glover, David. Machines. Baker, Wendy & Haslam, Andrew, illus. LC 93-42984. 48p. 1994. 15.95 (*1-56847-256-0*) Thomson Lrning.
Hennessy, B. G. Road Builders. Taback, Simms, illus. 32p. (ps-2). 1994. 14.99 (*0-670-83390-8*) Viking Child Bks.
Horton, et al. Amazing Fact Book of Machines. (Illus.). 32p. 1987. PLB 14.95 (*0-87191-846-3*) Creative Ed.
Horvatic, Anne. Simple Machines. Bruner, Stephen, photos by. LC 88-29997. (Illus.). 32p. (gr. 1-4). 1989. 13.95 (*0-525-44492-0*, DCB) Dutton Child Bks.
Illustrated Guides Series, 8 vols. LC 88-28764. (Illus.). 512p. (gr. 3-9). 1990. Set. 135.60 (*1-85435-085-4*) Marshall Cavendish.
Jennings, Terry. Cranes, Dump Trucks, Bulldozers & Other Building Machines. LC 92-23370. 1993. RLB 10.95 (*1-85697-866-4*, Kingfisher LKC); pap. 5.95 (*1-85697-865-6*) LKC.
Lambert, Mark & Hamilton-MacLaren, Alistair. Machines. (Illus.). 48p. (gr. 5-8). 1991. 12.90 (*0-531-18413-7*, Pub. by Bookwright Pr) Watts.
Machines. (Illus.). 48p. (gr. 7-12). 1989. pap. 6.95 (*0-941008-99-1*) Tops Learning.
Machines, Cars, Boats, & Airplanes. 224p. (ps-1). 1989. 5.99 (*0-517-68232-X*) Random Hse Value.
MacKenzie, Carol. Whirr Pop Click Clang. Given, Rebecca, illus. LC 94-8525. 1994. write for info. (*0-688-13292-8*, Tambourine Bks); Limited Ed. write for info. (*0-688-13293-6*) Morrow.
Pape, Donna L. The Book of Foolish Machinery. Winkowski, Frederic, illus. 32p. (gr. 2-5). 1988. pap. 2.50 (*0-590-40907-7*) Scholastic Inc.
Pomeroy, Johanna P. Content Area Reading Skills Machines: Detecting Sequence. (Illus.). (gr. 3). 1989. pap. text ed. 3.25 (*1-55737-690-5*) Ed Activities.
Radford, Derek. Building Machines & What They Do. Radford, Derek, illus. LC 91-71860. 32p. (ps-3). 1994. pap. 4.99 (*1-56402-364-8*) Candlewick Pr.
Rawson. How Machines Work. (gr. 2-5). 1976. PLB 13.96 (*0-88110-115-X*); pap. 6.95 (*0-86020-197-X*) EDC.
Robbins, Ken, photos by & text by. Power Machines. LC 92-30649. (Illus.). 32p. (gr. k-3). 1993. 15.95 (*0-8050-1410-1*, Bks Young Read) H Holt & Co.
Rockwell, Anne & Rockwell, Harlow. Machines. LC 72-185149. (Illus.). 24p. (ps-2). 1972. RSBE 13.95 (*0-02-777520-8*, Macmillan Child Bk) Macmillan Child Grp.
Rojany, Lisa. Hands-On Book of Big Machines. (ps-3). 1992. 11.95 (*0-316-41904-4*) Little.
Royston, Angela. Big Machines. Pastor, Terry, illus. LC 93-16019. (gr. 3 up). 1994. 12.95 (*0-316-76070-6*) Little.
Seller, Mick. Wheels, Pulleys & Levers. (Illus.). 32p. (gr. 5-7). 1993. PLB 12.40 (*0-531-17420-4*, Gloucester Pr) Watts.
Stickland, Paul. Machines As Tall As Giants. Stickland, Paul, illus. LC 88-34695. (gr. k-3). 1989. PLB 10.99 (*0-394-95375-4*) Random Bks Yng Read.
Stine, Megan, et al. Hands-On Science: Fun Machines. Taback, Simms, illus. LC 92-56891. 1993. PLB 18.60 (*0-8368-0956-4*) Gareth Stevens Inc.
Taylor, Barbara. Get It in Gear! The Science of Movement. Bull, Peter, et al, illus. LC 90-42617. 40p. (Orig.). (gr. 2-5). 1991. pap. 4.95 (*0-679-80812-4*) Random Bks Yng Read.
Wilkin, Fred. Machines. LC 85-30936. (Illus.). 48p. (gr. k-4). 1986. PLB 12.85 (*0-516-01283-5*) Childrens.
Williams, John. Simple Science Projects with Machines. LC 91-50547. (Illus.). 32p. (gr. 2-4). 1992. PLB 17.27 (*0-8368-0769-3*) Gareth Stevens Inc.
Working Hard with the Mighty Loader. Date not set. pap. write for info. (*0-590-47302-6*) Scholastic Inc.
The World of Machines. (Illus.). 80p. (gr. k-6). 1986. per set 199.00 (*0-8172-2591-9*) Raintree Steck-V.
Young, C. Diggers. (Illus.). 12p. (ps). 1993. bds. 4.50 (*0-7460-1096-6*) EDC.
—Diggers & Cranes. (Illus.). 32p. (ps-2). 1991. PLB 13.96 (*0-88110-552-X*, Usborne); pap. 5.95 (*0-7460-0625-X*, Usborne) EDC.
Young, Caroline & Castor, Harriet. Machines That Work. (Illus.). 96p. (gr. k-5). 1993. pap. 14.95 (*0-7460-0990-9*, Usborne) EDC.

MACHINERY, AUTOMATIC
see Automation

MACHINERY–MODELS
see also Airplanes–Models; Automobiles–Models; Railroads–Models
Green, Jen. Making Mad Machines. (Illus.). 32p. (gr. 2-4). 1992. PLB 12.40 (*0-531-17326-7*, Gloucester Pr) Watts.

MACHINERY IN INDUSTRY
Hoban, Tana. Dig, Drill, Dump, Fill. LC 75-11987. (Illus.). 32p. (ps-3). 1975. 13.88 (*0-688-84016-7*) Greenwillow.

MACHINES
see Machinery

MACINTOSH (COMPUTER)
Schepp, Debra & Schepp, Brad. Mac Club! Ellinger, Debra, illus. LC 93-8520. 1993. 19.60 (*0-8306-4253-6*) TAB Bks.
—Mac Party! Ellinger, Debra, illus. LC 93-8519. 1993. 19.60 (*0-8306-4250-1*) TAB Bks.

MACKENZIE, SIR ALEXANDER, 1764-1820
Manson, Ainslie. A Dog Came, Too: A True Story. Blades, Ann, illus. LC 91-44891. 32p. (gr. 1-5). 1993. SBE 13.95 (*0-689-50567-1*, M K McElderry) Macmillan Child Grp.

MACKINAC ISLAND
Penrod, John S. Straits of Mackinac & Mackinac Island. rev. ed. (gr. 7 up). 1989. pap. 4.49 (*0-942618-20-3*) Penrod-Hiawatha.

MCKINLEY, WILLIAM, PRESIDENT U. S. 1843-1901
Collins, David R. William McKinley: Twenty-Fifth President of the United States. Young, Richard G., ed. LC 89-39954. (Illus.). 128p. (gr. 5-9). 1990. PLB 17.26 (*0-944483-55-0*) Garrett Ed Corp.
Kent, Zachary. William McKinley. LC 88-10881. (Illus.). 100p. (gr. 3 up). 1988. PLB 14.40 (*0-516-01361-0*) Childrens.

MCKINLEY, MOUNT
Gonzales, Rod & Faurot, Chip. To the Summit. McDonald, Mike, ed. Gonzales, Rod, illus. 32p. (Orig.). (gr. 5-10). 1993. pap. 3.95 (*1-882724-00-3*) Alaska Comics.

MACRAME
Gryski, Camilla. Friendship Bracelets. LC 92-31097. (Illus.). 48p. (gr. 5 up). 1993. 14.00 (*0-688-12435-6*); PLB 13.93 (*0-688-12436-4*) Morrow Jr Bks.
—Friendship Bracelets. LC 92-31097. (Illus.). (gr. 5 up). 1993. pap. 6.95 (*0-688-12437-2*, Pub. by Beech Tree Bks) Morrow.

MADAGASCAR
Department of Geography, Lerner Publications. Madagascar in Pictures. (Illus.). 64p. (gr. 5 up). 1988. PLB 17.50 (*0-8225-1841-4*) Lerner Pubns.
Powzyk, Joyce. Madagascar Journey. LC 94-21053. (gr. 9-12). 1995. write for info. (*0-688-09487-2*); pap. write for info. (*0-688-13964-7*) Lothrop.
Stevens, Rita. Madagascar. (Illus.). 112p. (gr. 5 up). 1988. lib. bdg. 14.95 (*1-55546-195-6*) Chelsea Hse.

MADISON, DOROTHY (PAYNE) TODD, 1768-1849
Klingel, Cindy. Women of America: Dolly Madison. (gr. 2-4). 1987. PLB 14.95 (*0-88682-167-3*) Creative Ed.
Quiri, Patricia R. Dolley Madison. LC 92-28300. 1993. 12.90 (*0-531-20097-3*) Watts.
Sandak, Cass R. The Madisons. LC 92-14040. (Illus.). 48p. (gr. 5). 1992. text ed. 12.95 RSBE (*0-89686-642-4*, Crestwood Hse) Macmillan Child Grp.
Waldrop, Ruth. Dolly Madison. LC 89-61360. (Illus.). 112p. (gr. 3 up). 1989. PLB 10.95 (*0-318-50084-1*); pap. 6.95 (*0-9616894-3-9*) Rusk Inc.

MADISON, JAMES PRESIDENT U. S. 1751-1836
Clinton, Susan. James Madison. LC 86-13630. (Illus.). 100p. (gr. 3 up). 1986. PLB 14.40 (*0-516-01382-3*); pap. 6.95 (*0-516-41382-1*) Childrens.
Fritz, Jean. The Great Little Madison. (Illus.). 160p. (gr. 5 up). 1989. 15.95 (*0-399-21768-1*, Putnam) Putnam Pub Group.
Kelly, Regina Z. James Madison: Statesman & President. LC 90-49166. (Illus.). 144p. (gr. 6-10). 1991. PLB 13.95 (*1-55905-091-8*) Marshall Cavendish.
Leavell, Perry. James Madison. Schlesinger, Arthur M., intro. by. (Illus.). 112p. (gr. 5 up). 1988. 17.95 (*1-55546-815-2*) Chelsea Hse.
Polikof, Barbara G. James Madison: Fourth President of the United States. Young, Richard G., ed. LC 88-24537. (Illus.). (gr. 5-9). 1989. PLB 17.26 (*0-944483-22-4*) Garrett Ed Corp.
Quiri, Patricia R. Dolley Madison. LC 92-28300. 1993. 12.90 (*0-531-20097-3*) Watts.
Sandak, Cass R. The Madisons. LC 92-14040. (Illus.). 48p. (gr. 5). 1992. text ed. 12.95 RSBE (*0-89686-642-4*, Crestwood Hse) Macmillan Child Grp.
Wade. James Madison. (gr. 4-12). 1993. PLB 8.49 (*0-87386-087-X*); pap. 1.95 (*0-87386-086-1*) Jan Prods.

MADONNA
see Mary, Virgin

MAGAZINES
see Periodicals

MAGELLAN, FERDINAND, d. 1521
Asimov, Isaac. Ferdinand Magellan. LC 91-9207. (Illus.). 64p. (gr. 3-4). 1991. PLB 18.60 (*0-8368-0560-7*) Gareth Stevens Inc.
Brewster, Scott & Baraldi, Giani. Ferdinand Magellan. (Illus.). 104p. (gr. 5-8). 1990. lib. bdg. 9.95 (*0-382-09979-6*); pap. 5.95 (*0-382-24005-7*) Silver Burdett Pr.
Brownlee, Walter. The First Ships Round the World. LC 73-91815. (Illus.). 48p. (gr. 7 up). 1974. pap. 7.95 (*0-521-20438-0*) Cambridge U Pr.
Harley, Ruth. Ferdinand Magellan. new ed. LC 78-18058. (Illus.). 48p. (gr. 4-7). 1979. PLB 10.59 (*0-89375-176-6*); pap. 3.50 (*0-89375-168-5*) Troll Assocs.
Jacobs, William J. Magellan: Voyager with a Dream. LC 93-29698. (Illus.). 64p. (gr. 5-8). 1994. PLB 12.90 (*0-531-20139-2*) Watts.
Noonan, Jon. Ferdinand Magellan. (Illus.). 48p. (gr. 5). 1993. text ed. 12.95 RSBE (*0-89686-706-4*, Crestwood Hse) Macmillan Child Grp.
Schecter, Darrow. I Can Read About Magellan. LC 78-73713. (Illus.). (gr. 3-6). 1979. pap. 2.50 (*0-89375-209-6*) Troll Assocs.
Stefoff, Rebecca. Ferdinand Magellan & the Discovery of the World Ocean. Goetzmann, William H., ed. Collins, Michael, intro. by. (Illus.). 128p. (gr. 5 up). 1990. lib. bdg. 18.95 (*0-7910-1291-3*) Chelsea Hse.
Twist, Clint. Magellan & Da Gama. LC 93-19303. 1994. PLB 22.80 (*0-8114-7254-X*) Raintree Steck-V.
Wilkie, Katherine. Ferdinand Magellan: Noble Captain. Coyle, P., illus. (gr. 4-6). 1963. pap. 2.44 (*0-395-01751-3*, Piper) HM.

MAGIC
see also Card Tricks; Occult Sciences
Adams, Pam, illus. Magic. LC 90-46518. 32p. (Orig.). (ps-2). 1978. 11.95 (*0-85953-104-X*, Pub. by Child's Play England); pap. 5.95 (*0-85953-081-7*) Childs Play.
Alexander, Martha. Three Magic Flip Books. Incl. The Magic Hat; The Magic Picture; The Magic Box. (Illus.). (ps-k). 1984. Three bks. in a shrink-wrapped slipcase. 5.95 (*0-8037-0051-2*, 0578-170) Dial Bks Young.
Ames, Gerald & Wyler, Rose. Magic Secrets. Stubis, Talivaldis, illus. LC 67-4229. 64p. (gr. k-3). 1967. PLB 10.89 (*0-06-020069-3*) HarpC Child Bks.
Bailey, Vanessa. Magic Tricks: Games & Projects for Children. LC 90-32664. (Illus.). 32p. (gr. k-4). 1990. PLB 11.90 (*0-531-17256-2*, Gloucester Pr) Watts.
Baker, James W. Illusions Illustrated: A Professional Magic Show for Young Performers. Ayres, Carter M., photos by. Swofford, Jeanette, illus. LC 83-19549. 120p. (gr. 6 up). 1984. PLB 22.95 (*0-8225-0768-4*, First Ave Edns); pap. 6.95 (*0-8225-9512-5*, First Ave Edns) Lerner Pubns.
—Presidents' Day Magic. Overlie, George, illus. 48p. (gr. 2-5). 1989. 11.95 (*0-8225-2232-2*) Lerner Pubns.
—Thanksgiving Magic. Overlie, George, illus. 48p. (gr. 2-5). 1989. 11.95 (*0-8225-2233-0*) Lerner Pubns.
Beisner, Monika. Secret Spells & Curious Charms. Beisner, Monika, illus. LC 85-45323. 32p. (ps up). 1986. 15.00 (*0-374-36692-6*) FS&G.
Bernstein, Bob. Monday Morning Magic. 64p. (gr. k-6). 1982. 8.95 (*0-86653-080-0*, GA 425) Good Apple.
Bird, Malcolm & Dart, Alan. The Magic Handbook. (Illus.). 96p. (gr. 1-5). 1992. pap. 12.95 (*0-8118-0284-1*) Chronicle Bks.
Blackstone, Harry, Jr., et al. The Blackstone Book of Magic & Illusion. Bradbury, Ray, frwd. by. Mason, Eric, illus. LC 84-29486. 248p. (gr. 7 up). 1985. 22.95 (*0-937858-45-5*) Newmarket.
Border, Rosy. Beginners Guide to Magic. Everett, Mimi, illus. 48p. (gr. 3-6). 1992. pap. 2.95 (*1-56680-008-0*) Mad Hatter Pub.
Boy Scouts of America. Cub Scout Magic. (Illus.). 146p. (gr. 3-5). 1960. pap. 7.00x (*0-8395-3219-9*, 33219) BSA.
Brandreth, Gyles. Quick & Easy Magic Tricks. (Illus.). 96p. (Orig.). 1988. pap. 1.95 (*0-942025-33-4*) Kidsbks.
Cailloux, Michel. Learning Magic with Michel the Magician. (Illus.). 32p. (gr. 3-7). 1993. 7.95 (*2-7625-6854-4*, Pub. by Les Edits Herit CN) Adams Inc MA.
Charles, Kirk. Amazing Card Tricks. LC 92-5482. (Illus.). (gr. 2-6). 1992. PLB 14.95 (*0-89565-965-4*) Childs World.
—Amazing Coin Tricks. Woodworth, Viki, illus. LC 93-29259. (gr. 2-6). 1994. 14.95 (*1-56766-084-3*) Childs World.
—Magic Tricks. LC 92-9012. (Illus.). (gr. 2-6). 1992. PLB 14.95 (*0-89565-964-6*) Childs World.
Churchill, E. Richard. Paper Tricks & Toys. LC 91-38789. 128p. 1992. 14.95 (*0-8069-8416-3*) Sterling.
Cobb, Vicki. Magic...Naturally: Science Entertainments & Amusements. new ed. Kalish, Lionel, illus. LC 90-21829. 160p. (gr. 4 up). 1993. pap. 4.95 (*0-06-446031-2*, Trophy) HarpC Child Bks.
—Magic...Naturally! Science Entertainments & Amusements. Kalish, Lionel, illus. LC 90-21829. 160p. (gr. 4 up). 1993. 15.00 (*0-06-022474-6*); PLB 14.89 (*0-06-022475-4*) HarpC Child Bks.
Cobb, Vicki & Darling, Kathy. Wanna Bet! Science Challenges Bound to Fool You. LC 92-8962. 1992. 13.00 (*0-688-11213-7*) Lothrop.
Collis, Len. Magic Tricks for Children. Carter, Terry & George, Bob, illus. 96p. (gr. 3 up). 1989. pap. 4.95 (*0-8120-4289-1*) Barron.
Conaway, Judith. More Magic Tricks You Can Do. LC 86-11351. (Illus.). 48p. (gr. 1-5). 1987. PLB 11.89 (*0-8167-0864-9*); pap. text ed. 3.50 (*0-8167-0865-7*) Troll Assocs.
Crosby, Nina E. & Marten, Elizabeth H. Don't Teach! Let Me Learn about Fantasy, Magic, Monkeys & Monsters. Rossi, Richard, illus. 72p. (Orig.). (gr. 3-10). 1984. 8.95 (*0-88047-045-3*, 8410) DOK Pubs.
Day, Jon. Let's Make Magic: Over Forty Tricks You Can Do. Fisher, Chris, illus. LC 92-53093. 96p. (Orig.). (gr. 2-6). 1992. 14.95 (*1-85697-834-6*, Kingfisher LKC); pap. 9.95 (*1-85697-806-0*) LKC.
Disney, Walt, Productions Staff. The Mickey Mouse Magic Book. LC 74-16420. (Illus.). 48p. (gr. 1-2). 1975. 6.95 (*0-394-82567-5*) Random Bks Yng Read.
Duncan, Lois. A Gift of Magic. Stewart, Arvis, illus. (gr. 4-6). 1971. 15.95 (*0-316-19545-6*) Little.
Eldin, Peter. The Magic Handbook. Colville, Jeane, et al, illus. LC 85-171061. 192p. (gr. 4 up). 1985. lib. bdg. 9.79 (*0-671-55040-3*, J Messner); pap. 6.95 (*0-685-42988-1*) S&S Trade.

Evans, C. & Keable-Elliott, I. Complete Book of Magic. (Illus.). 64p. 1989. PLB 13.96 (*0-88110-383-7*); pap. 7.95 (*0-7460-0300-5*) EDC.

Evans, C., et al. Complete Book of Magic & Magic Tricks. (Illus.). 128p. 1992. 15.95 (*0-7460-0742-6*) EDC.

Fabian, Stella. A Handful of Magic. Mejia, Roger, illus. 125p. (gr. 2-6). 1988. pap. 3.25 (*0-922434-36-0*) Brighton & Lloyd.

Firestone, Allan L. Mr. Luckypennys Magic Book. Katz, Deborah, illus. LC 77-71450. (gr. 2-7). 1977. pap. 4.95 (*0-934682-01-1*) Emmett.

Forte, Imogene. Rainy Day: Magic for Wonderful Wet Weather. LC 83-82332. (Illus.). 80p. (gr. k-6). 1983. pap. text ed. 3.95 (*0-86530-094-1*, IP94-1) Incentive Pubns.

Friedhoffer, Robert. The Magic Show: A Guide for Young Magicians. Eisenberg, Linda, illus. LC 93-42272. 80p. (gr. 4-6). 1994. PLB 14.40 (*1-56294-355-3*) Millbrook Pr.

—Magic Tricks, Science Facts. LC 89-28487. 1990. PLB 12.90 (*0-531-10902-X*) Watts.

—Magic Tricks, Science Facts. 1990. pap. 6.95 (*0-531-15186-7*) Watts.

Fulves, Karl. The Children's Magic Kit: Sixteen Easy-to-Do Tricks Complete with Cardboard Cutouts. Schmidt, Joseph K., illus. 32p. (Orig.). (gr. 3-6). 1981. pap. 3.95 (*0-486-24019-3*) Dover.

—Easy-to-Do Magic Tricks for Children. Schmidt, Joseph K., illus. LC 93-9675. 48p. (Orig.). 1993. pap. 2.95 (*0-486-27613-9*) Dover.

—Self-Working Table Magic: Ninety-Seven Foolproof Tricks with Everyday Objects. Schmidt, Joseph K., illus. 128p. (Orig.). 1981. pap. 3.95 (*0-486-24116-5*) Dover.

Gill, Shelley R. Mammoth Magic. Cartwright, Shannon, illus. 36p. (Orig.). (gr. k-6). 1986. pap. 7.95 (*0-934007-01-2*) Paws Four Pub.

Gormley, Beatrice. The Magic Mean Machine. McCully, Emily A., illus. 128p. (Orig.). (gr. 5 up). 1989. pap. 2.95 (*0-380-75519-X*, Camelot) Avon.

Heddle, R. & Keable-Elliott, I. Book of Magic Tricks. (Illus.). 64p. (gr. 4-12). 1992. PLB 13.96 (*0-88110-509-0*, Usborne); pap. 7.95 (*0-7460-0653-5*, Usborne) EDC.

Hoyt, Marie A. Work-Game Sheets for Magnet Magic Etc. Bye, C. J., et al, illus. 28p. (Orig.). (gr. 2-8). 1984. pap. text ed. 2.50 (*0-914911-03-1*) Educ Serv Pr.

Johnson, Stephanie. Hoppin' Magic: My First Card & Coin Magic Tricks. Manwaring, Kerry, illus. 32p. 1993. pap. 5.95 (*1-56565-089-1*) Lowell Hse.

—My First Kitchen Kaper Magic Tricks. 1992. 3.98 (*0-8317-6240-3*) Smithmark.

—My First Strings & Knots Magic Tricks. 1992. 3.98 (*0-8317-6241-1*) Smithmark.

Kallen, Stuart A. Tricky Tricks. LC 92-14775. 1992. 12.94 (*1-56239-127-5*) Abdo & Dghtrs.

Kettelkamp, Larry. Magic Made Easy. rev. ed. Eutemey, Loring, illus. Klotzbeacher, Donovan, photos by. LC 80-22947. (Illus.). 96p. (gr. 3-7). 1981. 13.95 (*0-688-00458-X*); PLB 13.88 (*0-688-00377-X*, Morrow Jr Bks) Morrow Jr Bks.

Kiraithe, Jackie. Magic Links: Manual. Gonzales, Linda, ed. 200p. Date not set. 48.00 (*0-942787-95-1*) Binet Intl.

Klein, Tom & Wolpert, Tom. Animal Magic for Kids Series, 6 vols. (Illus.). (gr. 1-6). 1991. Set. PLB 111.60 (*0-8368-0659-X*) Gareth Stevens Inc.

Knoles, David. Spooky Magic Tricks. Knoles, David, illus. LC 93-1642. 128p. (gr. 3-10). 1993. 12.95 (*0-8069-0418-6*) Sterling.

—Spooky Magic Tricks. (Illus.). 128p. 1994. pap. 4.95 (*0-8069-0419-4*) Sterling.

Kronzek, Allan Z. A Book of Magic for Young Magicians: The Secrets of Alkazar. (Illus.). 128p. 1992. pap. 6.95t (*0-486-27134-X*) Dover.

Lagercrantz, Rose & Lagercrantz, Samuel. Is It Magic? Norlen, Paul, tr. from SWE. Eriksson, Eva, illus. LC 89-63054. (gr. k-3). 1990. 13.95 (*91-29-59182-1*, Pub. by R & S Bks) FS&G.

Levy, Robert & Joseph, Joan. Robert Levy's Magic Book. LC 76-16016. (Illus.). 216p. (gr. 5 up). 1976. 10.95 (*0-87131-219-0*) M Evans.

Lewis, Shari & Zimmerman, Dick. Shari Lewis Presents One Hundred-One Magic Tricks for Kids to Do. Buller, Jon, illus. LC 89-10360. 96p. (Orig.). 1990. PLB 9.99 (*0-394-92059-7*); pap. 6.95 (*0-394-82059-2*) Random Bks Yng Read.

Leyton, Lawrence. My First Magic Book. LC 93-22104. (Illus.). 48p. (gr. k-4). 1993. 13.95 (*1-56458-319-8*) Dorling Kindersley.

Lipson, Greta & Bolkosky, Sidney. Mighty Myth. 152p. (gr. 5-12). 1982. 12.95 (*0-86653-064-9*, GA 419) Good Apple.

Longe, Bob. Easy Magic Tricks. LC 94-11207. (Illus.). 128p. 1994. 12.95 (*0-8069-1264-2*) Sterling.

—Nutty Challenges & Zany Dares. Longe, Bob, illus. LC 93-32391. 128p. 1994. pap. 4.95 (*0-8069-0454-2*) Sterling.

Magic Pack. (gr. 3-6). 1992. pap. 7.95 (*1-56680-500-7*) Mad Hatter Pub.

Magnet Magic. (Illus.). (ps-2). 1991. PLB 6.95 (*0-8136-5193-X*, TK7263); pap. 3.50 (*0-8136-5693-1*, TK7264) Modern Curr.

Maria & Mr. Feathers. (Illus.). (ps-2). 1991. PLB 6.95 (*0-8136-5124-7*, TK2610); pap. 3.50 (*0-8136-5624-9*, TK2609) Modern Curr.

Miller, Marvin. Your Own Christmas Magic Show. 1993. pap. 6.95 (*0-590-47558-4*) Scholastic Inc.

—Your Own Super Magic Show. 1993. pap. 4.95 (*0-590-33044-6*) Scholastic Inc.

Nozaki, Akihiro & Anno, Mitsumasa. Anno's Hat Tricks. LC 84-18900. (Illus.). 44p. (gr. 3 up). 1985. 15.95 (*0-399-21212-4*, Philomel Bks) Putnam Pub Group.

OWL Magazine Editors & Chickadee Magazine Editors. Magic Fun: Mystery Potions, Card Magic, Vanishing Tricks Plus Puzzles, Treats, & Much More. (Illus.). 32p. (gr. 1-5). 1992. 14.95 (*0-316-67741-8*, Joy St Bks) Little.

OWL Magazine Staff & Chickadee Magazine Staff. Magic Fun: Mystery Potions, Card Magic, Vanishing Tricks Plus Puzzles, Treats, & Much More. 32p. (gr. 1-5). 1992. pap. 5.95 (*0-316-67739-6*, Joy St Bks) Little.

Oxlade, Chris. Air. Thompson, Ian, illus. LC 94-5547. 30p. (gr. 2-5). 1994. 12.95 (*0-8120-6444-5*); pap. 4.95 (*0-8120-1983-0*) Barron.

—Light. Thompson, Ian, illus. LC 94-5549. 30p. (gr. 2-5). 1994. 12.95 (*0-8120-6445-3*); pap. 4.95 (*0-8120-1984-9*) Barron.

—Science Magic with Sound. Thompson, Ian, illus. LC 94-5550. 30p. (gr. 2-5). 1994. 12.95 (*0-8120-6446-1*); pap. 4.95 (*0-8120-1985-7*) Barron.

—Water. Thompson, Ian, illus. LC 94-5548. 30p. (gr. 2-5). 1994. 12.95 (*0-8120-6448-8*); pap. 4.95 (*0-8120-1986-5*) Barron.

Popcorn Magic. (Illus.). (ps-2). 1991. PLB 6.95 (*0-8136-5195-6*, TK7261); pap. 3.50 (*0-8136-5695-8*, TK7262) Modern Curr.

Rigney, Francis J. A Beginner's Book of Magic. (Illus.). (gr. 6 up). 1963. 9.95 (*0-8159-5103-5*) Devin.

Seuling, Barbara. Abracadabra! Creating Your Own Magic Show from Beginning to End. (gr. 3-6). 1977. (Archway) PB.

Severn, Bill. Magic with Rope, Ribbon, & String. 224p. (gr. 6 up). 1981. 9.95 (*0-679-20813-5*) McKay.

Shadow Magic. (Illus.). (ps-2). 1991. PLB 6.95 (*0-8136-5192-1*, TK7257); pap. 3.50 (*0-8136-5692-3*, TK7258) Modern Curr.

Shalit, Nathan. Science Magic Tricks: Over 50 Fun Tricks That Mystify & Dazzle. Ulan, Helen C., illus. LC 79-18645. 128p. (gr. 6 up). 1981. 9.95 (*0-03-047116-8*, Bks Young Read); pap. 6.95 (*0-8050-0234-0*) H Holt & Co.

Stoddard, Edward. The First Book of Magic. (Illus.). 80p. (gr. 4-7). 1980. pap. 2.95 (*0-380-49221-0*, Camelot) Avon.

Supraner, Robyn. Magic Tricks You Can Do! Barto, Renzo, illus. LC 80-19780. 48p. (gr. 1-5). 1981. PLB 11.89 (*0-89375-418-8*); pap. text ed. 3.50 (*0-89375-419-6*) Troll Assocs.

Tarr, Bill. One Hundred One Easy-to-Do Magic Tricks. unabr., unaltered ed. Daniel, Frank, illus. LC 92-22895. 224p. 1992. pap. text ed. 7.95t (*0-486-27367-9*) Dover.

Townsend, Charles B. World's Best Magic Tricks. LC 91-41310. (Illus.). 128p. (gr. 6-12). 1992. 12.95 (*0-8069-8582-8*) Sterling.

—World's Best Magic Tricks. LC 91-41310. (Illus.). 128p. (gr. 3-9). 1993. pap. 4.95 (*0-8069-8583-6*) Sterling.

Van Rensselaer, Alexander. Your Book of Magic. (gr. 9 up). 1968. 7.95 (*0-571-06939-8*) Transatl Arts.

Waldron, Linda & Montana, LeRoy. The Children's Handbook of Real Magic. 32p. (gr. 3-4). 1993. pap. 10.00 (*1-883783-00-3*) Crystal Oracle.

Water Magic. (Illus.). (ps-2). 1991. PLB 6.95 (*0-8136-5196-4*, TK7343); pap. 3.50 (*0-8136-5696-6*, TK7344) Modern Curr.

Watermill Press Staff. Kid's Book of Magic Tricks. 80p. (gr. 4-7). 1992. pap. 4.95 (*0-8167-2739-2*, Pub. by Watermill Pr) Troll Assocs.

Watts, Barry. More Amazing Magic: Fantastic Tricks to Amuse, Confuse, & Mystify. (gr. 4-7). 1993. pap. 3.95 (*0-207-18172-1*, Pub. by Angus & Robertson AT) HarpC.

White, Larry & Broekel, Ray. Razzle Dazzle! Magic Tricks for You. Fay, Ann, ed. Seltzer, Meyer, illus. LC 87-6114. 48p. (gr. 3-8). 1987. PLB 11.95 (*0-8075-6857-0*) A Whitman.

White, Laurence B. Math-a-Magic: Number Tricks for Magicians. (gr. 4-7). 1994. pap. 4.95 (*0-8075-4995-9*) A Whitman.

Williams, Randall. The Rosen Photo Guide to a Career in Magic. (Illus.). (gr. 7-12). 1988. lib. bdg. 12.95 (*0-8239-0817-8*) Rosen Group.

Wilson, Mark. Mark Wilson's Complete Course in Magic. LC 87-73058. (Illus.). 472p. 1988. Repr. of 1975 ed. 18.98 (*0-89471-623-9*) Courage Bks.

Wolpert, Tom. Whale Magic for Kids. Nicklin, Flip, illus. LC 90-50718. 48p. (gr. 3-4). 1991. PLB 18.60 (*0-8368-0660-3*) Gareth Stevens Inc.

Wood, Elizabeth. Fifty Nifty Magic Tricks. Yamamoto, Neal, illus. 64p. (ps-3). 1992. pap. 4.95 (*0-929923-93-6*) Lowell Hse.

Wyler, Rose & Ames, Gerald. Magic Secrets. rev. ed. Dorros, Arthur, illus. LC 89-35841. 64p. (gr. k-3). 1990. 14.00 (*0-06-026646-5*); PLB 13.89 (*0-06-026647-3*) HarpC Child Bks.

—Magic Secrets. rev. ed. Dorros, Arthur, illus. LC 89-35841. 64p. (gr. k-3). 1991. pap. 3.50 (*0-06-444153-9*, Trophy) HarpC Child Bks.

—Spooky Tricks. Schindler, Stephen D., illus. LC 92-47501. 64p. (gr. k-3). 1994. 14.00 (*0-06-023025-8*); PLB 13.89 (*0-06-023026-6*) HarpC Child Bks.

MAGIC–FICTION

Adler, David A. Onion Sundaes: A Houdini Club Magic Mystery. Malone, Heather H., illus. LC 93-5878. 80p. (Orig.). (gr. 1-4). 1994. PLB 9.99 (*0-679-94697-7*); pap. 2.99 (*0-679-84697-2*) Random Bks Yng Read.

Alexander, Lloyd. The Wizard in the Tree. 144p. (gr. 5 up). 1981. pap. 3.25 (*0-440-49556-3*, Pub. by Yearling Classics) Dell.

Alvarez, Cynthia. The Candy Land Mystery. (Illus.). 24p. (ps up). 1994. 9.99 (*0-679-86200-5*) Random Bks Yng Read.

Anderson, Joy. Juma & the Magic Jinn. Mikolaycak, Charles, illus. LC 85-23815. 40p. (gr. 1-3). 1986. 12.95 (*0-688-05443-9*); PLB 12.88 (*0-688-05444-7*) Lothrop.

Andrews, Kristi. All That Glitters, No. 2: Take Two. 176p. (Orig.). 1987. pap. 2.50 (*0-553-26417-6*) Bantam.

Armstrong, Jennifer. The Whittler's Tale. Vasiliev, Valery, illus. LC 93-14749. 1994. 16.00 (*0-688-10751-6*, Tambourine Bks); PLB 15.93 (*0-688-10752-4*) Morrow.

Arnold, Tim. The Winter Mittens. LC 88-2736. (Illus.). 32p. (gr. 3-6). 1988. RSBE 13.95 (*0-689-50449-7*, M K McElderry) Macmillan Child Grp.

Ayers, Becky H. Victoria Flies High. Koontz, Robin M., illus. LC 89-694. 32p. (ps-3). 1990. 12.95 (*0-525-65014-8*, Cobblehill Bks) Dutton Child Bks.

Baker, Dianne. Ted Bear's Magic Swing. Krum, Ronda, illus. LC 91-65819. 32p. (gr. 1-3). 1992. 12.95 (*0-87159-162-6*) Unity Bks.

Banks, Lynne R. The Mystery of the Cupboard. Newsom, Tom, illus. LC 92-39295. 256p. (gr. 5 up). 1993. 13.95 (*0-688-12138-1*); PLB 13.88 (*0-688-12635-9*) Morrow Jr Bks.

Bauer, Marion D. Touch the Moon. Berenzy, Alix, illus. LC 87-663. 96p. (gr. 4-7). 1987. 14.95 (*0-89919-526-1*, Clarion Bks) HM.

Becker, Eve. The Magic Mix-Up. (gr. 4-7). 1989. pap. 2.75 (*0-553-15770-1*, Skylark) Bantam.

—The Sneezing Spell. (gr. 4-7). 1990. pap. 2.75 (*0-553-15774-4*, Skylark) Bantam.

—Thirteen Means Magic. (gr. 4-7). 1989. pap. 2.75 (*0-553-15730-2*, Skylark) Bantam.

—Too Much Magic. (gr. 4-7). 1990. pap. 2.75 (*0-553-15785-X*) Bantam.

Bedard, Michael. A Darker Magic. LC 86-28829. 208p. (gr. 5-9). 1987. SBE 14.95 (*0-689-31342-X*, Atheneum Child Bk) Macmillan Child Grp.

Beisert, Heide H. My Magic Cloth: A Story for a Whole Week. Beisert, Heide H., illus. Lewis, Naomi, tr. LC 86-60490. (Illus.). 32p. (gr. k-3). 1986. 14.95 (*1-55858-069-7*) North-South Bks NYC.

Bellairs, John. The Dark Secret of Weatherend. Gorey, Edward, illus. 208p. (gr. 5 up). 1984. 13.95 (*0-8037-0072-5*) Dial Bks Young.

—The Figure in the Shadows. Mayer, Mercer, illus. LC 74-2885. 168p. (gr. 4-7). 1975. Dial Bks Young.

—The Figure in the Shadows. Mayer, Mercer, illus. LC 92-31362. 160p. (gr. 3 up). 1993. pap. 3.99 (*0-14-036337-8*, Puffin) Puffin Bks.

—The House with a Clock in Its Walls. Gorey, Edward, illus. LC 92-26794. 192p. (gr. 3 up). 1993. pap. 3.99 (*0-14-036336-X*, Puffin) Puffin Bks.

—The Mansion in the Mist. LC 91-29639. 176p. (gr. 5 up). 1992. 15.00 (*0-8037-0845-9*); PLB 14.89 (*0-8037-0846-7*) Dial Bks Young.

—The Spell of the Sorcerer's Skull. 176p. 1985. pap. 2.75 (*0-553-15357-9*, Skylark) Bantam.

Benjamin, Saragail K. My Dog Ate It. LC 93-25218. 128p. (gr. 3-7). 1994. 14.95 (*0-8234-1047-1*) Holiday.

Berry, James R. Magicians of Erianne. LC 85-45833. 256p. (gr. 7 up). 1988. HarpC Child Bks.

Blacker, Terence. In Control, Ms. Wiz? Goffe, Toni, illus. 64p. (gr. 2-5). 1990. pap. 2.95 (*0-8120-4500-9*) Barron.

Bolton, Elizabeth. Secret of the Magic Potion. Sims, Blanche, illus. LC 84-8881. 48p. (gr. 2-4). 1985. PLB 10.89 (*0-8167-0420-1*); pap. text ed. 3.50 (*0-8167-0421-X*) Troll Assocs.

Brenner, Barbara A. The Magic Box, Level 3. Boix, Manuel, illus. 1990. PLB 9.99 (*0-553-05896-7*, Little Rooster); pap. 3.50 (*0-553-34926-0*, Little Rooster) Bantam.

Bridwell, Norman. The Witch Goes to School. LC 92-12091. (ps-3). 1992. pap. 2.95 (*0-590-45831-0*) Scholastic Inc.

Brittain, Bill. Devil's Donkey. Glass, Andrew, illus. LC 80-7907. 128p. (gr. 3-7). 1981. PLB 13.89 (*0-06-020683-7*) HarpC Child Bks.

—The Mystery of the Several Sevens. Warhola, James, illus. LC 93-47076. 96p. (gr. 2-5). 1994. 11.95 (*0-06-024459-3*); PLB 11.89 (*0-06-024462-3*) HarpC Child Bks.

—The Wish Giver: Three Tales of Coven Tree. Glass, Andrew, illus. LC 82-48264. 192p. (gr. 3-7). 1983. PLB 13.89 (*0-06-020687-X*) HarpC Child Bks.

—The Wizards & the Monster. Warhola, James, illus. LC 93-47077. 96p. (gr. 2-5). 1994. 11.95 (*0-06-024454-2*); PLB 11.89 (*0-06-024456-9*) HarpC Child Bks.

Broekel, Ray & White, Laurence B., Jr. Hocus Pocus: Magic You Can Do. Fay, Anne, ed. Thelen, Mary, illus. LC 83-26096. 48p. (gr. 3 up). 1984. PLB 11.95 (*0-8075-3350-5*) A Whitman.

Brooke, William J. A Brush with Magic. LC 92-41744. (Illus.). 160p. (gr. 3 up). 1993. 15.00 (*0-06-022973-X*); PLB 14.89 (*0-06-022974-8*) HarpC Child Bks.

Brown, Marc T. Arthur's April Fool. LC 82-20368. (Illus.). 32p. (ps-3). 1985. 15.95 (*0-316-11196-1*, Joy St Bks); pap. 4.95 (*0-316-11234-8*, Joy St Bks) Little.

Buchwald, Emilie. Gildaen: The Heroic Adventures of a Most Unusual Rabbit. Flynn, Barbara, illus. LC 93-16255. 192p. 1993. 14.95 (*0-915943-38-7*); pap. 6.95 (*0-915943-75-1*) Milkweed Ed.

Buffett, Jimmy & Buffett, Savannah J. Trouble Dolls. Ingber, Bonnie V., intro. by. Davis, Lambert, illus. 32p. (gr. 1 up). 1991. 14.95 (*0-15-290790-4*) HarBrace.

Buller, Jon & Schade, Susan. Yo! It's Captain Yo-Yo. Buller, Jon & Schade, Susan, illus. LC 92-44306. 48p. (gr. 2-3). 1993. 7.99 (*0-448-40192-4*, G&D); pap. 3.50 (*0-448-40191-6*, G&D) Putnam Pub Group.

Burbank, Linda. Sylvan: The Magic Tree. Van Treese, James B., ed. Upman, Michael, illus. 30p. 1993. pap. 7.95 (*1-56901-201-6*) NW Pub.

Butenhoff, Lisa K. Nina's Magic. Thatch, Nancy R., ed. Butenhoff, Lisa K., illus. Melton, David, intro. by. LC 92-18293. (Illus.). 26p. (gr. 3-4). 1992. PLB 14.95 (*0-933849-40-0*) Landmark Edns.

Calmenson, Stephanie. The Little Witch Sisters. Alley, R. W., illus. LC 93-15454. 1993. 13.27 (*0-8368-0970-X*) Gareth Stevens Inc.

Cartwright, Pauline. The Bird Chain. Cooper-Brown, Jean, illus. LC 93-20805. 1994. 4.25 (*0-383-03736-0*) SRA Schl Grp.

Chardiet, Jon. The Magic Fish Rap. 1993. incl. cassette 5.95 (*0-590-66152-3*) Scholastic Inc.

—The Magic Fish Rap. 1993. pap. 3.95 (*0-590-45859-0*) Scholastic Inc.

Charnas, Suzy M. The Golden Thread. 1989. 13.95 (*0-553-05821-5*, Starfire) Bantam.

Chetwin, Grace. Friends in Time. LC 91-33178. 144p. (gr. 3-7). 1992. SBE 13.95 (*0-02-718318-1*, Bradbury Pr) Macmillan Child Grp.

Chew, Ruth. Royal Magic. 128p. 1991. pap. 2.75 (*0-590-44742-4*) Scholastic Inc.

—Wrong Way Around Magic. (gr. 4-7). 1993. pap. 2.75 (*0-590-46023-4*) Scholastic Inc.

Chitwood, Deb. The Magic Ring. Fraydas, Stan, illus. LC 82-62432. 32p. (ps-3). 1983. 9.95 (*0-942044-01-0*) Polestar.

Christelow, Eileen. Olive & the Magic Hat. Christelow, Eileen, illus. LC 87-672. 32p. (gr. k-3). 1987. 12.95 (*0-89919-513-X*, Clarion Bks) HM.

Clifton, Lucille. The Lucky Stone. Payson, Dale, illus. LC 78-72862. 64p. (gr. 4-6). 1979. pap. 6.46 (*0-385-28600-7*) Delacorte.

Coates, Anna. Dog Magic. (gr. 4-7). 1991. pap. 2.99 (*0-553-15910-0*, Skylark) Bantam.

Cole, Joanna. Mixed-Up Magic. Donnelly, Judy, ed. Kelley, True, illus. LC 87-14965. 32p. (gr. k-3). 1987. 8.95 (*0-8038-9298-5*) Hastings.

Colum, Padraic. The Boy Apprenticed to an Enchanter. Leight, Edward, illus. (gr. 3-7). 1991. 20.00 (*0-8446-6482-0*) Peter Smith.

Conrad, Pam. Prairie Songs. reissue ed. Zudeck, Darryl S., illus. LC 85-42633. 176p. (gr. 5 up). 1987. pap. 3.95 (*0-06-440206-1*, Trophy) HarpC Child Bks.

Cooper, Margaret C. The Riddle of Changewater Pond. LC 93-15699. 128p. (gr. 4-7). 1993. SBE 13.95 (*0-02-724495-4*, Bradbury Pr) Macmillan Child Grp.

Coville, Bruce. Jennifer Murdley's Toad. Lippincott, Gary A., illus. 1992. 16.95 (*0-15-200745-8*, HB Juv Bks) HarBrace.

Cresswell, Helen. The Watchers: A Mystery at Alton Towers. LC 93-41683. (gr. 3-7). 1994. 14.95 (*0-02-725371-6*, Macmillan Child Bk) Macmillan Child Grp.

Cresswell, Helen & Brown, Judy. Almost Goodbye. LC 91-33464. (Illus.). 64p. (gr. 2-5). 1992. 11.00 (*0-525-44858-6*, DCB) Dutton Child Bks.

Cretan, Gladys. Joey's Head. Sims, Blanche, illus. LC 90-41592. 48p. (gr. 2-4). 1991. pap. 13.95 jacketed (*0-671-73201-3*, S&S BFYR) S&S Trade.

Dahl, Roald. Doigt Magique. Galeron, Henri, illus. (FRE.). 63p. (gr. 1-5). 1989. pap. 9.95 (*2-07-031185-6*) Schoenhof.

—The Magic Finger. Ross, Tony, illus. LC 92-31443. 64p. (gr. 2-6). 1993. pap. 3.99 (*0-14-036303-3*) Puffin Bks.

Davis, Gibbs. Christy's Magic Glove. (ps-3). 1992. pap. 3.25 (*0-553-15988-7*) Bantam.

Davis, Maggie S. Something Magic. LC 90-10062. (gr. k-3). 1991. pap. 13.95 (*0-671-69627-0*, S&S BFYR) S&S Trade.

Degroat, Florence. A Fairy's Workday. Wilson, Patricia, illus. 65p. (gr. 1-6). 1983. pap. 2.25 (*0-87516-508-7*) DeVorss.

De Paola, Tomie. Strega Nona's Magic Lessons. De Paola, Tomie, illus. LC 80-28260. 32p. (gr. k up). 1982. 13.95 (*0-15-281785-9*, HB Juv Bks) HarBrace.

—Strega Nona's Magic Lessons. De Paola, Tomie, illus. 32p. (gr. k up). 1984. pap. 4.95 (*0-15-281786-7*, Voyager Bks) HarBrace.

Derby, Sally. Jacob & the Stranger. Gore, Leonid, illus. LC 93-11022. 32p. (ps-3). 1994. 11.95 (*0-395-66897-2*) Ticknor & Flds Bks Yng Read.

Dexter, Catherine. The Gilded Cat. 208p. (gr. 4 up). 1992. 14.00 (*0-688-09425-2*) Morrow Jr Bks.

Dicks, Terrance. The MacMagics: A Spell for My Sister. Canning, Celia, illus. 96p. (gr. 3-6). 1992. pap. 3.50 (*0-8120-4881-4*) Barron.

—The MacMagics: My Brother the Vampire. Canning, Celia, illus. 96p. (ps-3). 1992. pap. 3.50 (*0-8120-4883-0*) Barron.

—Meet the MacMagics. Canning, Celia, illus. 96p. (gr. 3-6). 1992. pap. 3.50 (*0-8120-4882-2*) Barron.

Dillon, Barbara. A Mom by Magic. Lindberg, Jeffrey, illus. LC 89-29410. 144p. (gr. 3-7). 1990. (Lipp Jr Bks); PLB 13.89 (*0-397-32449-9*, Lipp Jr Bks) HarpC Child Bks.

Duane, Diane E. Deep Wizardry. LC 84-15566. 288p. (gr. 7 up). 1985. 15.95 (*0-385-29373-9*) Delacorte.

Dubowski, Cathy W. Pretty Good Magic. Dubowski, Mark, illus. LC 87-4784. 48p. (gr. 1-3). 1987. lib. bdg. 7.99 (*0-394-99068-4*); 3.50 (*0-394-89068-X*) Random Bks Yng Read.

Duncan, Lois. A Gift of Magic. (gr. 5-7). 1990. pap. 3.50 (*0-671-72649-8*, Archway) PB.

Dutton, Sandra. The Magic of Myrna C. Waxweather. (gr. 2-6). 1990. pap. 2.75 (*0-553-15788-4*, Skylark) Bantam.

Eager, Edward. Half Magic. Bodecker, N. M., illus. LC 54-5153. 217p. (gr. 3-7). 1954. 14.95 (*0-15-233078-X*, HB Juv Bks) HarBrace.

—Half Magic. Treherne, Katie T. & Bodecker, N. M., illus. 192p. (gr. 3-7). 1989. pap. 4.95 (*0-15-233081-X*, Odyssey) HarBrace.

—Magic by the Lake. Treherne, Katie T. & Bodecker, N. M., illus. 190p. (gr. 3-7). 1989. pap. 3.95 (*0-15-250444-3*, Odyssey) HarBrace.

—Magic or Not? Bodecker, N. M., illus. (gr. 4-6). 1984. 17.00 (*0-8446-6154-6*) Peter Smith.

—Magic or Not? Treherne, Katie T. & Bodecker, N. M., illus. 197p. (gr. 3-7). 1989. pap. 3.95 (*0-15-251160-1*, Odyssey) HarBrace.

—Seven-Day Magic. (gr. 4-6). 17.25 (*0-8446-6381-6*) Peter Smith.

—Seven-Day Magic. Treherne, Katie T. & Bodecker, N. M., illus. 190p. (gr. 3-7). 1989. pap. 4.95 (*0-15-272916-X*, Odyssey) HarBrace.

Eastman, David. The Sorcerer's Apprentice. Jones, John, illus. LC 87-13767. 32p. (gr. k-4). 1988. PLB 9.79 (*0-8167-1067-8*); pap. text ed. 1.95 (*0-8167-1068-6*) Troll Assocs.

Eastman, David, adapted by. Aladdin & the Wonderful Lamp. Waldman, Bryna, illus. LC 87-13756. 32p. (gr. 1-4). 1988. PLB 9.79 (*0-8167-1073-2*); pap. text ed. 1.95 (*0-8167-1074-0*) Troll Assocs.

Ernst, Lisa C. & Ernst, Lee. The Tangram Magician. (Illus.). 24p. 1990. 19.95 (*0-8109-3851-0*) Abrams.

Everitt, Betsy. Frida the Wondercat. 32p. (ps-3). 1990. 13.95 (*0-15-229540-2*) HarBrace.

Faber, Roger A. What Happened to Milly? Monroe, John, illus. (gr. 3 up). Date not set. pap. write for info. (*1-880122-07-3*) White Stone.

Fields, Frever. Frumpy McDoogle: The Boy Who Made a Poem. 32p. (gr. 1-3). 1992. 12.95 (*0-9632675-0-7*) Kimberlite.

Fienberg, Anna. The Magnificent Nose: And Other Marvels. Gamble, Kim, illus. (ps-3). 1992. 13.95 (*0-316-28195-6*, Joy Street) Little.

Forward, Toby. Traveling Backward. Cornell, Laura, illus. LC 93-32514. 1994. write for info. RTE (*0-688-13076-3*, Tambourine Bks) Morrow.

Gabler, Mirko. Brackus, Krakus. Gabler, Mirko, illus. LC 92-25819. 32p. (ps-3). 1993. 14.95 (*0-8050-1963-4*, Bks Young Read) H Holt & Co.

Galchutt, David. There Was Magic Inside. LC 91-44107. (Illus.). 40p. (ps-2). 1993. pap. 14.00 JRT (*0-671-75978-7*, S&S BFYR) S&S Trade.

Galdone, Paul. The Magic Porridge Pot. Galdone, Paul, illus. LC 76-3531. 32p. (ps-3). 1979. 13.45 (*0-395-28805-3*, Clarion Bks) HM.

Gaskin, Carol. The War of the Wizards. Price, T. Alexander, illus. LC 84-2663. 128p. (gr. 3-7). 1985. PLB 9.49 (*0-8167-0318-3*); pap. text ed. 2.95 (*0-8167-0319-1*) Troll Assocs.

Gathorne-Hardy, Jonathan. Jane's Adventures In & Out of the Book. Hill, Nicholas, illus. LC 80-29185. 192p. (gr. 5 up). 1981. 13.95 (*0-87951-122-2*) Overlook Pr.

Glassman, Peter. The Wizard Next Door. Kellogg, Steven, illus. LC 92-21562. 40p. (gr. k up). 1993. 15. 00 (*0-688-10645-5*); PLB 14.93 (*0-688-10646-3*) Morrow Jr Bks.

Gono & the Magic Hat. 36p. (ps-4). 1985. 8.95 (*0-88684-179-8*); cassette tape avail. Listen USA.

Gormley, Beatrice. Fifth Grade Magic. McCully, Emily A., illus. 128p. (gr. 3-7). 1984. pap. 3.50 (*0-380-67439-4*, Camelot) Avon.

—The Ghastly Glasses. McCully, Emily A., illus. LC 85-10112. 128p. (gr. 2-6). 1985. 12.95 (*0-525-44215-4*, DCB) Dutton Child Bks.

Gouge, Elizabeth. Linnets & Valerians. (gr. 4-7). 1992. pap. 3.50 (*0-440-40590-4*, YB) Dell.

Green, Phyllis. Eating Ice Cream with a Werewolf. Stern, Patti, illus. LC 82-47727. 128p. (gr. 3-7). 1983. HarpC Child Bks.

Greenfield, Karen R. The Teardrop Baby. Collicott, Sharleen, illus. LC 93-29603. 40p. (ps-4). 1994. 16.00 (*0-06-022943-8*); PLB 15.89 (*0-06-022944-6*) HarpC Child Bks.

Gregorich, Barbara. It's Magic. Hoffman, Joan, ed. (Illus.). 16p. (Orig.). (gr. k-2). 1991. pap. 2.25 (*0-88743-029-5*, 06029) Sch Zone Pub Co.

Greydanus, Rose. Hocus Pocus, Magic Show! Goodman, Joan, illus. LC 81-2637. 32p. (gr. k-2). 1981. PLB 11. 59 (*0-89375-539-7*); pap. text ed. 2.95 (*0-89375-540-0*) Troll Assocs.

Hamilton, Virginia. The Magical Adventures of Pretty Pearl. LC 82-48629. 320p. (gr. 7 up). 1983. PLB 17.89 (*0-06-022187-9*) HarpC Child Bks.

Hastings. Rufus & Christopher & the Magic Bubble. LC 73-87799. (Illus.). 32p. (gr. k-2). 1974. PLB 9.95 (*0-87783-127-0*); pap. 3.94 deluxe ed. (*0-87783-128-9*); cassette 7.94x (*0-87783-197-1*) Oddo.

Hazen, Barbara S. The Magic Stick. 16p. (ps-2). 1992. pap. 14.95 (*1-56784-053-1*) Newbridge Comms.

Herman, Charlotte. Max Malone the Magnificent. Smith, Cat B., illus. LC 92-14123. 64p. (gr. 2-4). 1993. 14.95 (*0-8050-2282-1*, Bks Young Read) H Holt & Co.

Hill, Douglas. Penelope's Pendant. (gr. 5-7). 1991. 12.95 (*0-385-41641-5*) Doubleday.

Hillert, Margaret. Magic Beans. (Illus.). (ps-k). 1966. PLB 6.95 (*0-8136-5053-4*, TK2338); pap. 3.50 (*0-8136-5553-6*, TK2339) Modern Curr.

Hindley, Judy. Uncle Harold & the Green Hat. Utton, Peter, illus. 26p. (ps-3). 1991. bds. 13.95 (*0-374-38030-9*) FS&G.

Hiser, Constance. The Missing Doll. Ramsey, Marcy, illus. 72p. (gr. 4-7). 1993. 13.95 (*0-8234-1046-3*) Holiday.

—No Bean Sprouts, Please! Ewing, Carolyn, illus. LC 89-1817. 64p. (gr. 2-5). 1989. 13.95 (*0-8234-0760-8*) Holiday.

Hooks, William H. Freedom's Fruit. Ransome, James E., illus. LC 93-235. 1995. write for info. (*0-679-82438-3*); lib. bdg. write for info. (*0-679-92438-8*) Knopf.

Horn, Myrna. Krista's Magic Hat. LC 90-71359. (Illus.). 44p. (gr. k-3). 1991. 5.95 (*1-55523-397-X*) Winston-Derek.

Houck, Eric L., Jr. Rabbit Surprise. Catalano, Dominic, illus. LC 92-1318. 32p. (ps-2). 1993. 14.00 (*0-517-58777-7*); PLB 14.99 (*0-517-58778-5*) Crown Bks Yng Read.

Howe, James. Rabbit-Cadabra! 48p. 1994. pap. 5.99 (*0-380-71336-5*, Camelot Young) Avon.

Hunter, Mollie. Day of the Unicorn. Diamond, Donna, illus. LC 91-44763. 96p. (gr. 2-5). 1994. 14.00 (*0-06-021062-1*, HarpT); PLB 13.89 (*0-06-021063-X*, HarpT) HarpC.

Hurd, Inis I. The Magic Lamp. Gesner, Ethel & Irvine, Bonnie, illus. LC 87-30728. 140p. (gr. 4-7). 1989. PLB 14.50 (*0-944517-00-5*) Christian Center.

Hutchins, Hazel. Anastasia Morningstar. 96p. (gr. 2-5). 1992. pap. 3.99 (*0-14-034343-1*) Puffin Bks.

Jacobs, W. W. The Monkey's Paw. LC 86-2329. 48p. (gr. 6 up). 1986. PLB 13.95 (*0-88682-060-X*) Creative Ed.

Johnson, Paul B. Frank Fister's Hidden Talent: Story & Pictures. LC 93-4883. 1994. write for info. (*0-531-06813-7*); lib. bdg. write for info. (*0-531-08663-1*) Orchard Bks Watts.

Jones, Diana W. The Ogre Downstairs. LC 89-11741. 192p. (gr. 5 up). 1990. 12.95 (*0-688-09195-4*) Greenwillow.

—Yes, Dear. Philpot, Graham, illus. LC 91-17733. 32p. (ps-6). 1992. 14.00 (*0-688-11195-5*) Greenwillow.

Kaufman, John. Milk Rock. (gr. k-2). 1994. 14.95 (*0-8050-2814-5*) H Holt & Co.

Koda-Callan, Elizabeth. The Magic Locket. Koda-Callan, Elizabeth, illus. LC 88-5508. 40p. (ps-3). 1988. 12.95 (*0-89480-602-5*, 1602) Workman Pub.

Krakoff, S. B. The Magick Cave. 175p. (Orig.). (gr. 6-7). 1989. pap. write for info. Charcoal St Pr.

Krensky, Stephen. Ghostly Business. LC 89-29584. 160p. (gr. 4-7). 1990. pap. 3.95 (*0-689-71364-9*, Aladdin) Macmillan Child Grp.

Kroll, Steven. The Big Bunny & the Magic Show. Stevens, Janet, illus. 32p. (ps-2). 1987. pap. 3.95 (*0-590-44633-9*) Scholastic Inc.

Lavranos, Destini & Ritchie, Sheri. The Magical Tree. Elston, Dino, illus. 2p. (ps-k). 1993. 14.95 (*0-9638393-0-6*) Bedtime Bks.

Lecher, Doris. Angelita's Magic Yarn. (Illus.). 32p. (ps-3). 1992. 14.00 (*0-374-30332-0*) FS&G.

Lee, Tanith. Black Unicorn. Cooper, Heather, illus. LC 91-15646. 144p. (gr. 7 up). 1991. SBE 14.95 (*0-689-31575-9*, Atheneum Child Bk) Macmillan Child Grp.

Le Landgren. A Touch of Magic: A Fantasy Adventure. LC 90-8183. (Orig.). (gr. 2-7). 1990. pap. 7.95 (*0-943367-03-4*) Princess Pub.

Leroe, Ellen. Leap Frog Friday. DeRosa, Dee, illus. LC 92-8284. 48p. (gr. 2-5). 1992. 12.00 (*0-525-67370-9*, Lodestar Bks) Dutton Child Bks.

Lester, Helen. The Revenge of the Magic Chicken. Munsinger, Lynn, illus. 32p. (gr. k-3). 1990. 13.45 (*0-395-50929-7*) HM.

—The Wizard, the Fairy, & the Magic Chicken. Munsinger, Lynn, illus. LC 82-21302. 32p. (gr. k-3). 1988. pap. 5.70 (*0-395-47945-2*) HM.

Lewis, J. Patrick. The Christmas of the Reddle Moon. Kelley, Gary, illus. LC 93-28049. (gr. 3 up). 1994. 15. 99 (*0-8037-1566-8*); PLB 15.89 (*0-8037-1567-6*) Dial Bks Young.

Lindbergh, Anne M. Travel Far, Pay No Fare. LC 91-35886. 192p. (gr. 5-8). 1992. 14.00 (*0-06-021775-8*); PLB 13.89 (*0-06-021776-6*) HarpC Child Bks.

McClintock, Barbara. The Battle of Luke & Longnose. LC 93-12815. 1994. 14.95 (*0-395-65751-2*) HM.

McDermott, Gerald. Tim O'Toole & the Little People. (ps-3). 1990. pap. 13.95 (*0-670-80393-6*) Viking Child Bks.

MacDonald, Betty. Hello, Mrs. Piggle-Wiggle. LC 57-5613. (Illus.). (gr. 1-3). 1985. pap. 3.95 (*0-06-440149-9*, Trophy) HarpC Child Bks.

—Mrs. Piggle-Wiggle. rev. ed. LC 47-1876. (Illus.). 120p. (gr. 1-3). 1985. pap. 3.95 (*0-06-440148-0*, Trophy) HarpC Child Bks.

—Mrs. Piggle-Wiggle's Farm. LC 54-7299. (Illus.). 132p. (gr. 1-3). 1985. pap. 3.95 (*0-06-440150-2*, Trophy) HarpC Child Bks.
—Mrs. Piggle-Wiggle's Magic. LC 49-11124. (Illus.). 144p. (gr. 1-3). 1985. pap. 3.95 (*0-06-440151-0*, Trophy) HarpC Child Bks.
McGowen, Tom. A Trial of Magic. 144p. (gr. 5-9). 1992. 15.00 (*0-525-67376-8*, Lodestar Bks) Dutton Child Bks.
McKean, Thomas. The Haunted Circus. LC 92-32713. 176p. (gr. 4-7). 1993. pap. 13.00 JRT (*0-671-72998-5*, S&S BFYR) S&S Trade.
—Secret of the Seven Willows. LC 91-4447. 160p. 1991. pap. 12.95 3-pc. bdg. (*0-671-72997-7*) S&S Trade.
McOmber, Rachel B., ed. McOmber Phonics Storybooks: The Magic e. rev. ed. (Illus.). write for info. (*0-944991-37-8*) Swift Lrn Res.
—McOmber Phonics Storybooks: The Neat Trick. rev. ed. (Illus.). write for info. (*0-944991-55-6*) Swift Lrn Res.
—McOmber Phonics Storybooks: The Prime Time Trick. rev. ed. (Illus.). write for info. (*0-944991-56-4*) Swift Lrn Res.
McPhail, David. Moony B. Finch, Fastest Draw in the West. LC 93-37408. 1994. lib. bdg. 12.95 (*0-307-17554-5*, Artsts Writrs) Western Pub.
Madden, Don. The Wartville Wizard. LC 92-22246. (Illus.). 32p. (gr. k-3). 1993. pap. 4.95 (*0-689-71667-2*, Aladdin) Macmillan Child Grp.
Madsen, Ross M. Perrywinkle & the Book of Magic Spells. Zimmer, Dirk, illus. LC 85-15932. 48p. (ps-3). 1988. pap. 4.95 (*0-8037-0501-8*) Dial Bks Young.
Magorian, James. The Magic Pretzel. LC 88-71603. (Illus.). 32p. (gr. 2-5). 1988. pap. 3.00 (*0-930674-28-6*) Black Oak.
Mahy, Margaret. The Girl with the Green Ear: Stories about Magic in Nature. Hughes, Shirley, illus. LC 91-14992. 112p. (gr. 3-7). 1992. 15.00 (*0-679-82231-3*); PLB 15.99 (*0-679-92231-8*) Knopf Bks Yng Read.
Marilue. Bobby Bear's Magic Show. Marilue, illus. LC 89-62707. 32p. (ps-2). 1990. PLB 12.95 (*0-87783-253-6*) Oddo.
Martin, Bill, Jr. & Archambault, John. The Magic Pumpkin. Lee, Robert J., illus. LC 89-11162. 32p. (ps-2). 1989. 14.95 (*0-8050-1134-X*, Bks Young Read) H Holt & Co.
Mathers, Petra. Victor & Christabel. Mathers, Petra, illus. LC 92-33468. 40p. (ps-3). 1993. 15.00 (*0-679-83060-X*); PLB 15.99 (*0-679-93060-4*) Knopf Bks Yng Read.
Matthews, Morgan. Houdini, the Vanishing Hare. Gustafson, Dana, illus. LC 88-1286. 48p. (Orig.). (gr. 1-4). 1989. PLB 10.59 (*0-8167-1343-X*); pap. text ed. 3.50 (*0-8167-1344-8*) Troll Assocs.
May, Ingrid. Magic Ears Sandy. 1991. 7.95 (*0-533-09382-1*) Vantage.
Mayer, Mercer. A Special Trick. LC 69-18220. (Illus.). (gr. k-3). 1976. pap. 4.95 (*0-8037-8103-2*) Dial Bks Young.
Melling, Orla. The Druid's Tune. rev. ed. (Illus.). 195p. (gr. 7 up). 1993. pap. 9.95 (*0-86278-285-6*, Pub. by OBrien Pr IE) Dufour.
Milton, John. Comus. Hyman, Trina S., illus. Hodges, Margaret, adapted by. LC 94-13618. (Illus.). (gr. 1-8). 1995. write for info. (*0-8234-1146-X*) Holiday.
Moffit, Linda L. The Magic Mirror. LC 89-50125. (Illus.). 80p. (Orig.). (gr. k-7). 1989. pap. 8.95 (*0-87516-615-6*) DeVorss.
Moncure, Jane B. Word Bird's Magic Wand. Hohag, Linda, illus. LC 90-1645. 32p. (ps-2). 1990. PLB 14.95 (*0-89565-580-2*) Childs World.
Montgomery, Lucy M. Jane of Lantern, Magic for Marigold. (gr. 7 up). 1989. pap. 2.95 (*0-318-41644-1*, Starfire) Bantam.
Mora, Francisco X. Juan Tuza & the Magic Pouch. Mora, Francisco X., illus. 32p. (ps-1). 1993. PLB 15.00 (*0-917846-24-9*, 95563) Highsmith Pr.
Moss, Marissa. But Not Kate. Donovan, Melanie, ed. Moss, Marissa, illus. LC 90-25751. 32p. (ps-3). 1992. 14.00 (*0-688-10600-5*); PLB 13.93 (*0-688-10601-3*) Lothrop.
Muller, Robin. The Magic Paintbrush. 1992. pap. 8.50 (*0-385-25373-7*) Doubleday.
Muntean, Michaela. Imagine: Grover's Magic Carpet Ride. (ps-3). 1993. pap. 2.25 (*0-307-13120-3*, Golden Pr) Western Pub.
Naylor, Phyllis R. Beetles, Lightly Toasted. LC 87-911. 144p. (gr. 3-7). 1987. SBE 13.95 (*0-689-31355-1*, Atheneum Child Bk) Macmillan Child Grp.
Nesbit, Edith. Enchanted Castle. 231p. 1981. Repr. PLB 10.95x (*0-89966-361-3*) Buccaneer Bks.
—Five Children & It. 188p. 1981. Repr. PLB 21.95 (*0-89966-362-1*) Buccaneer Bks.
Nister, Ernest. Merry Magic-Go-Round. (Illus.). (gr. k up). 1983. PLB 12.95 (*0-399-20946-8*, Philomel) Putnam Pub Group.
Nixon, Jean L. A Deadly Game of Magic. LC 83-8379. 148p. (gr. 7 up). 1983. 13.95 (*0-15-222954-X*, HB Juv Bks) HarBrace.
—A Deadly Game of Magic. (gr. 6-12). 1985. pap. 3.99 (*0-440-92102-3*, LFL) Dell.
Odgers, Sally F. Wiz. Sofilas, Mark, illus. LC 92-31952. 1993. 3.75 (*0-383-03608-9*) SRA Schl Grp.
Osborne, Mary P. The Knight at Dawn. Murdocca, Sal, illus. LC 92-13075. 80p. (Orig.). (gr. 1-4). 1993. PLB 9.99 (*0-679-92412-4*); pap. 2.99 (*0-679-82412-X*) Random Bks Yng Read.
—Pirates Past Noon. Murdocca, Sal, illus. LC 93-2039. 80p. (gr. 1-4). 1994. PLB 9.99 (*0-679-92425-6*); pap. 2.99 (*0-679-82425-1*) Random.
Ostheeren, Ingrid. Jonathan Mouse & the Magic Box. Mathieu, Agnes, illus. Lanning, Rosemary, tr. from GER. LC 89-43248. (Illus.). 32p. (gr. k-3). 1990. 13.95 (*1-55858-087-5*) North-South Bks NYC.
Parkin, Rex. The Red Carpet. Parkin, Rex, illus. LC 92-19912. 48p. (gr. k-3). 1993. pap. 4.95 (*0-689-71678-8*, Aladdin) Macmillan Child Grp.
Pascal, Francine. The Case of the Magic Christmas Bell. (ps-3). 1991. pap. 3.25 (*0-553-15964-X*) Bantam.
Pastore, Michael. Lark's Magic. Warde, Ann, illus. LC 89-51204. 113p. (gr. 4-12). 1990. pap. 10.00 (*0-927379-36-8*, ZP36) Zorba Pr.
Pearson, Carol L. I Believe in Make Believe. (Orig.). (gr. k up). 1984. pap. 4.50 (*0-87602-255-7*) Anchorage.
Pellowski, Michael J. Magic Broom. Garry-McCord, Kathi, illus. LC 85-14054. 48p. (Orig.). (gr. 1-3). 1986. PLB 10.59 (*0-8167-0636-0*); pap. text ed. 3.50 (*0-8167-0637-9*) Troll Assocs.
—Mixed-up Magic. Cushman, Doug, illus. LC 88-1312. 48p. (Orig.). (gr. 1-4). 1989. PLB 10.59 (*0-8167-1327-8*); pap. text ed. 3.50 (*0-8167-1328-6*) Troll Assocs.
Persall, Holli C. The Magic Corn. Haley, Laura M., illus. 24p. (gr. k-4). 1990. 10.95 (*0-9628486-0-3*) Rhyme Time.
Petersen, P. J. The Amazing Magic Show. Williams-Andriani, Renee, illus. LC 93-34861. (gr. 2-5). 1994. 14.00 (*0-671-86581-1*, S&S BFYR) S&S Trade.
Pugh, Charles. The Griot. (ps-12). 1993. pap. 3.95 (*0-87067-697-0*) Holloway.
Quin-Harkin, Janet. Magic Growing Powder. Cumings, Art, illus. LC 80-18019. 48p. (ps-3). 1981. 5.95 (*0-8193-1037-9*); PLB 5.95 (*0-8193-1038-7*) Parents.
Raney, Ken. Stick Horse. (Illus.). 32p. (ps-1). 1991. 9.95 (*0-9625261-4-2*, Green Tiger) S&S Trade.
Ransford, Sandy. Master Magician: An Action Book. (Illus.). 64p. 1994. incl. kit 19.95 (*1-56138-460-7*) Running Pr.
Reuter, Bjarne. Buster's World. (Illus.). 154p. (gr. 5-9). 1991. pap. 3.95 (*0-14-034471-3*, Puffin) Puffin Bks.
Richemont, Enid. The Magic Skateboard. Ormerod, Jan, illus. LC 92-53010. 80p. (gr. 3-6). 1993. 13.95 (*1-56402-132-7*) Candlewick Pr.
Roberts, Jane. Emir's Education in the Proper Use of Magical Powers. Cherry, Lynne, illus. 138p. (gr. 3 up). 1984. pap. 8.95 (*0-913299-08-1*, Dist. by PGW) Stillpoint.
Roberts, Willo D. The Magic Book. LC 85-20056. 156p. (gr. 3-7). 1986. SBE 13.95 (*0-689-31120-6*, Atheneum Child Bk) Macmillan Child Grp.
—The Magic Book. LC 88-19360. 160p. (gr. 2-6). 1988. pap. 3.95 (*0-689-71284-7*, Aladdin) Macmillan Child Grp.
Robertson, Janet. Oscar's Spots. LC 93-22199. (Illus.). 32p. (ps-2). 1993. PLB 13.95 (*0-8167-3133-0*); pap. write for info. (*0-8167-3134-9*) BrdgeWater.
Rodriguez, Anita. Aunt Martha & the Golden Coin. Rodrigues, Anita, illus. LC 92-7316. 32p. (ps-2). 1993. 14.00 (*0-517-59337-8*, Clarkson Potter); PLB 14.99 (*0-517-59338-6*, Clarkson Potter) Crown Bks Yng Read.
Ross, Tony. A Fairy Tale. Ross, Tony, illus. 32p. (ps-3). 1992. cancelled 13.95 (*0-316-75750-0*) Little.
Sabin, Francene. The Magic String. Snyder, Joel, illus. LC 81-4076. 32p. (gr. k-2). 1981. PLB 11.59 (*0-89375-547-8*); pap. 2.95 (*0-89375-548-6*) Troll Assocs.
Schwartz, Alvin, ed. Tales of Trickery from the Land of Spoof. Christiana, David, illus. LC 85-16004. 87p. (gr. 4 up). 1985. 14.00 (*0-374-37378-7*) FS&G.
Selznick, Brian. The Houdini Box. Selznick, Brian, illus. LC 90-5387. 64p. (gr. 1-6). 1994. pap. 2.99 (*0-679-85448-7*) Random Bks Yng Read.
Shettle, Andrea. Flute Song Magic. (gr. 7 up). 1990. pap. 2.95 (*0-380-76225-0*, Flare) Avon.
Shura, Mary F. Shoefull of Shamrock. 96p. 1991. pap. 2.95 (*0-380-76169-6*, Camelot Young) Avon.
Shusterman, Neal. The Eyes of Kid Midas. LC 92-17897. 1992. 15.95 (*0-316-77542-8*) Little.
Silbey, Uma. Paul & Mary & their Magic Crystals. Chien-Erikson, Nancy, illus. 48p. (Orig.). (ps-3). 1988. pap. 9.95 (*0-938925-07-5*) U-Music.
Smith, Janice L. Wizard & Wart. Meisel, Paul, illus. LC 92-41170. 64p. (gr. k-3). 1994. 14.00 (*0-06-022960-8*); PLB 13.89 (*0-06-022961-6*) HarpC Child Bks.
—Wizard & Wart at Sea. LC 94-3200. 1995. 14.00 (*0-06-024754-1*); PLB 13.89 (*0-06-024755-X*) HarpC.
Snyder, Dianne. George & the Dragon Word. Lies, Brian, illus. 56p. (gr. 2-4). 1991. 13.45 (*0-395-55129-3*, Sandpiper) HM.
Snyder, Zilpha K. Black & Blue Magic. Holtan, Gene, illus. LC 66-12850. 192p. (gr. 3-7). 1972. Spartan ed. 5.95 (*0-689-30075-1*, Atheneum) Macmillan Child Grp.
—Black & Blue Magic. (gr. k-6). 1994. pap. 3.99 (*0-440-40053-8*, YB) Dell.
—Black & Blue Magic. Holtan, Gene, illus. LC 94-791. (gr. 3-7). 1994. pap. 3.95 (*0-689-71848-9*, Aladdin) Macmillan.
—The Headless Cupid. Raible, Alton, illus. LC 78-154763. 208p. (gr. 4-6). 1971. SBE 15.95 (*0-689-20687-9*, Atheneum Child Bk) Macmillan Child Grp.
Sobol, Donald J. The Amazing Power of Ashur Fine. (gr. 4-8). 1987. pap. 2.95 (*0-8167-1049-X*) Troll Assocs.
Somtow, S. P. The Wizard's Apprentice. Jainschigg, Nicholas, illus. LC 93-12384. 144p. (gr. 7 up). 1993. SBE 14.95 (*0-689-31576-7*, Atheneum Child Bk) Macmillan Child Grp.
Sorensen, LaDawn. Magical Mr. E. (Illus.). 44p. (gr. k-2). 1991. pap. 5.95 (*1-55523-360-0*) Winston-Derek.
Steele, Mary Q. Because of the Sand Witches There. Galdone, Paul, illus. LC 75-5932. 192p. (gr. 3-7). 1975. 11.75 (*0-688-80001-7*); PLB 11.88 (*0-688-84001-9*) Greenwillow.
Steig, William. Amazing Bone. (ps-3). 1993. pap. 4.95 (*0-374-40358-9*, Sunburst) FS&G.
—El Hueso Prodigioso: The Amazing Bone. (ps-3). 1993. 17.00 (*0-374-33504-4*, Mirasol) FS&G.
—Silvestre y la Piedrecita Magica. Mlawer, Teresa, tr. from ENG. Steig, William, illus. 40p. (gr. 3). 1990. PLB 12.95 (*0-9625162-0-1*); pap. 5.95 (*0-9625162-7-9*) Lectorum Pubns.
Sterman, Betsy & Sterman, Samuel. Backyard Dragon. Wenzel, David, illus. LC 92-26292. 192p. (gr. 3-7). 1993. 14.00 (*0-06-020783-3*); PLB 13.89 (*0-06-020784-1*) HarpC Child Bks.
—Too Much Magic. Glasser, Judy, illus. LC 85-45861. 160p. (gr. 3-7). 1994. pap. 3.95 (*0-06-440404-8*, Trophy) HarpC Child Bks.
Strasser, Todd & Duke, Richard. Disney's It's Magic: Stories from the Films. DiCicco, Gil, illus. 80p. 1994. 14.95 (*0-7868-3001-8*); PLB 14.89 (*0-7868-5000-0*) Disney Pr.
Sutton, Scott E. The Secret of GorBee Grotto. (Illus.). 60p. (gr. 2-4). 1987. 13.95x (*0-9617199-3-1*) Sutton Pubns.
Talbert, Marc. Double Or Nothing. (gr. 3-7). 1990. 15.00 (*0-8037-0832-7*) Dial Bks Young.
Theriot, David. Leola et la pirogue. Easterling, Mae L., illus. (FRE.). 39p. (gr. 3). 1979. pap. text ed. 1.25 (*0-911409-03-3*) Natl Mat Dev.
Travers, Pamela L. Mary Poppins. rev. ed. (gr. 4-7). 1991. pap. 4.50 (*0-440-40406-1*) Dell.
—Mary Poppins Comes Back. (gr. 4-7). 1991. pap. 3.50 (*0-440-40418-5*) Dell.
Trotman, Felicity, as told by. The Sorcerer's Apprentice. (Illus.). 32p. (gr. k-5). 1985. PLB 19.97 (*0-8172-2505-6*) Raintree Steck-V.
Turkle, Brinton. Do Not Open. Turkle, Brinton, illus. LC 80-10289. 32p. (ps-2). 1981. pap. 13.95 (*0-525-28785-X*, 01258-370, DCB) Dutton Child Bks.
Twohill, Maggie. Jeeter, Mason & the Magic Headset. (gr. 3-6). 1986. pap. 2.75 (*0-440-44220-6*, YB) Dell.
Valens, Amy. Danilo the Fruit Man. Valens, Amy, illus. LC 91-46893. 32p. (ps-3). 1993. 12.99 (*0-8037-1151-4*); PLB 12.89 (*0-8037-1152-2*) Dial Bks Young.
Van Allsburg, Chris. The Sweetest Fig. Van Allsburg, Chris, illus. LC 93-12692. (gr. 4 up). 1993. 17.95 (*0-395-67346-1*) HM.
—The Widow's Broom. LC 92-7110. (Illus.). 32p. (gr. k-4). 1992. 17.95 (*0-395-64051-2*) HM.
Walt Disney Staff. Sorcerer's Apprentice. (ps-3). 1992. 5.98 (*0-453-03025-4*) Viking-Penguin.
Walters, Catherine. Max & Minnie. Walters, Catherine, illus. 32p. 1994. 12.95 (*0-87226-377-0*) P Bedrick Bks.
Wangerin, Walter. Branta & the Golden Stone. Healey, Deborah, illus. LC 92-34891. 1993. pap. 16.00 (*0-671-79693-3*, S&S BFYR) S&S Trade.
Ward, Nick. A Bag of Tricks. (Illus.). 16p. 1987. pap. 2.95 (*0-19-272143-7*) OUP.
Warren, Jean. The Wishing Fish: A Totline Teaching Tale. Cubley, Kathleen, ed. Tourtillotte, Barbara, illus. LC 93-12523. 32p. (Orig.). (ps-2). 1994. 12.95 (*0-911019-73-1*); pap. 5.95 (*0-911019-74-X*) Warren Pub Hse.
Welch, Fay. The Magic Swap Shop. rev. ed. (gr. 3-12). 1985. pap. 6.00 play script (*0-88734-509-3*) Players Pr.
Wellin Magic. 36p. (ps-4). 1985. 8.95 (*0-88684-180-1*); cassette tape avail. Listen USA.
Wells, Rosemary. Morris's Disappearing Bag. LC 75-9202. (ps-3). 1990. 17.99 (*0-8037-0839-4*) Dial Bks Young.
Willard, Nancy. The Marzipan Moon. Sewall, Marcia, illus. LC 80-24221. 48p. (gr. 2-5). 1981. 9.95 (*0-15-252962-4*, HB Juv Bks) HarBrace.
—The Sorcerer's Apprentice. Dillon, Leo D., et al, eds. Dillon, Diane & Dillon, Lee, illus. LC 93-19912. 32p. (ps-6). 1993. 15.95 (*0-590-47329-8*) Scholastic Inc.
Williamson, Tracey. Magic Shadow Show: Four Stories - Four Plays, 2 bks. (Illus.). 24p. (gr. k-4). 1991. 17.95 (*0-525-44765-2*, DCB) Dutton Child Bks.
Wolkstein, Diane. The Banza. Brown, Marc T., illus. LC 81-65845. 32p. (ps-3). 1981. Dial Bks Young.
—The Magic Wings: A Tale from China. Parker, Robert A., illus. LC 83-1611. 32p. (gr. 2-4). 1983. (DCB); pap. 4.95 (*0-525-44275-8*, DCB) Dutton Child Bks.
Wood, Audrey. Magic Shoelaces. Wood, Audrey, illus. LC 90-49097. 32p. (ps-2). 1989. 7.95 (*0-85953-109-0*); pap. 3.95 (*0-85953-321-2*) Childs Play.
Woodruff, Elvira. Back in Action. Hillenbrand, Will, illus. LC 91-2093. 160p. (gr. 3-7). 1991. 13.95 (*0-8234-0897-3*) Holiday.
Wrede, Patricia C. Calling on Dragons. LC 92-35469. 1993. write for info. (*0-15-200950-7*, J Yolen Bks) HarBrace.
—Talking to Dragons. LC 92-40719. 1993. 16.95 (*0-15-284247-0*, J Yolen Bks) HarBrace.
Wyler, Rose & Ames, Gerald. Spooky Tricks. LC 68-16822. (Illus.). 64p. (ps-3). 1968. PLB 11.89 (*0-06-026634-1*) HarpC Child Bks.

Wyllie, Stephen. The Wizards' Revenge. Heller, Julek, illus. LC 93-14494. (gr. 4 up). 1994. 18.95 (*0-8037-1690-7*) Dial Bks Young.

Wynne-Jones, Tim. Zoom at Sea. Beddows, Eric, illus. LC 92-14738. 32p. (ps-2). 1993. 15.00 (*0-06-021448-1*); PLB 14.89 (*0-06-021449-X*) HarpC Child Bks.

Yolen, Jane. The Girl in the Golden Bower. Dyer, Jane, illus. LC 92-37284. (gr. 5 up). 1994. 15.95 (*0-316-96894-3*) Little.

—Wizard's Hall. Ingber, Bonnie V., ed. 133p. (gr. 3-7). 1991. 13.95 (*0-15-298132-2*) HarBrace.

York, Carol B. Miss Know-It-All & the Magic House. Stock, Catherine, illus. (gr. 3-7). 1989. pap. 2.75 (*0-318-41641-7*, Skylark) Bantam.

Young, Tommy S. Tommy Scott Young Spins Magical Tales, 2 vols. Irvin, Nathanial, Jr., ed. Incl. Vol. I. Barney McCabe. LC 85-61698. 44p. 7.95 (*0-685-10585-7*); Vol. II. Tiny Hooty & the Percher. LC 85-61699. 36p. PLB 10.00 (*0-685-10586-5*). LC 85-6198. (gr. 1-8). 1985. PLB 13.95 Barney McCabe, vol. I, 44pgs. (*0-934721-01-7*); PLB 13.95 Tiny Hooty & the Percher, Vol. II, 36 pgs. (*0-934721-02-5*); PLB 29.95 Cassette & Book Package (*0-934721-07-6*); Cassette Tape Vol. I, 17 min. 30 sec. 11.95, Vol. II 18 min. 22 sec. (*0-934721-00-9*) Raspberry Rec.

Zambreno, M. A Plague of Sorcerers. 257p. (gr. 4-9). 1991. 16.95 (*0-15-262430-9*, HB Juv Bks) HarBrace.

Zambreno, Mary F. Journeyman Wizard: A Magical Mystery. LC 93-37449. 1994. 16.95 (*0-15-200022-4*, Yolen Bks) HarBrace.

Zeplin, Zeno. Secret Magic. Jones, Judy, illus. 56p. (gr. 3-6). 1990. lib. bdg. 9.95 casebound (*1-877740-03-9*); pap. text ed. 5.50g (*1-877740-04-7*) Nel-Mar Pub.

Ziefert, Harriet. The Small Potatoes Club & the Small Potatoes & the Magic Show. Brown, Richard, illus. 64p. (Orig.). (gr. k-6). 1984. pap. 2.99 (*0-440-48034-5*, YB) Dell.

MAGICIANS

Borland, Kathryn K. & Speicher, Helen R. Harry Houdini: Young Magician. LC 90-23321. (Illus.). 192p. (gr. 3-7). 1991. pap. 3.95 (*0-689-71476-9*, Aladdin) Macmillan Child Grp.

Hass, Elizabeth. Houdini's Last Trick. LC 93-49866. (gr. 4 up). 1994. 2.99 (*0-685-71914-6*) Random Bks Yng Read.

Lawrence, Ann. Merlin the Wizard. Hunter, Susan, illus. 32p. (gr. 2-5). 1986. PLB 19.97 (*0-8172-2628-1*) Raintree Steck-V.

Nickell, Joe. Wonderworkers! How They Perform the Impossible. Nickell, Joe, illus. 80p. (Orig.). 1991. pap. 12.95 (*0-87975-688-8*) Prometheus Bks.

MAGICIANS–FICTION

Alexander, Lloyd. The Wizard in the Tree. Kubinyi, Laszlo, illus. 144p. (gr. 4-7). 1974. 14.95 (*0-525-43128-4*, DCB) Dutton Child Bks.

Bazaldua, Barbara. Disney's Aladdin: Monkey Business. (ps-3). 1993. pap. 2.25 (*0-307-12788-5*, Golden Pr) Western Pub.

Binato, Leonardo. What's in the Magician's Hat? 12p. (ps-3). 1992. 4.95 (*1-56566-008-0*) Thomasson-Grant.

Braybrooks, Ann. Disney's Aladdin: The Cave of Wonders. (ps-3). 1993. 4.95 (*0-307-11565-8*, Golden Pr) Western Pub.

—Disney's Aladdin: The Cave of Wonders. (ps-3). 1993. pap. 3.50 (*0-307-15974-4*, Golden Pr) Western Pub.

Coombs, Patricia. The Magician & McTree. Coombs, Patricia, illus. LC 83-11984. (gr. 1-4). 1984. 11.95 (*0-688-02109-3*) Lothrop.

Disney, Walt. Aladdin en Espanol. 1993. 6.98 (*0-453-03164-1*) Mouse Works.

—Aladdin: Travels with Genie. (ps-3). 1993. 6.98 (*0-453-03138-2*) Mouse Works.

Grejniec, Michael. Who Is My Neighbor? LC 93-39248. (Illus.). 40p. (ps-2). 1994. 8.99 (*0-679-85801-6*); PLB 9.99 (*0-679-95801-0*) Knopf Bks Yng Read.

Howe, James. Rabbit Cadabra! Daniel, Alan, illus. LC 91-34656. 48p. (gr. k up). 1993. 15.00 (*0-688-10402-9*); PLB 14.93 (*0-688-10403-7*) Morrow Jr Bks.

Jones, Diana W. Archer's Goon. LC 83-17199. 256p. (gr. 7 up). 1984. reinforced 10.25 (*0-688-02582-X*) Greenwillow.

Langenus, Ron. Merlin's Return. Delmonte, Niesje C., tr. from DUT. (Illus.). 175p. (gr. 5-8). 1994. pap. 7.95 (*0-86327-383-1*, Pub. by Wolfhound Pr ER) Dufour.

Laurin, Anne. Perfect Crane. Mikolaycak, Charles, illus. LC 80-7912. 32p. (gr. 1-4). 1981. PLB 13.89 (*0-06-023744-9*) HarpC Child Bks.

McGowen, Tom. The Magicians' Challenge. LC 89-32333. 144p. (gr. 5-9). 1989. 13.95 (*0-525-67289-3*, Lodestar Bks) Dutton Child Bks.

Milton, John. Comus. Hyman, Trina S., illus. Hodges, Margaret, adapted by. LC 94-13618. (Illus.). (gr. 1-8). 1995. write for info. (*0-8234-1146-X*) Holiday.

Pearson, Susan. The Green Magician Puzzle. Fiammenghi, Gioia, illus. LC 90-22436. 1991. pap. 11. 95 (*0-671-74054-7*, S&S BFYR); pap. 2.95 (*0-671-74053-9*, S&S BFYR) S&S Trade.

Peretz, I. L. & Shulevitz, Uri. The Magician. LC 85-42955. (Illus.). 32p. (gr. k-6). 1985. RSBE 12.95 (*0-02-782770-4*, Macmillan Child Bk) Macmillan Child Grp.

Roessler, Mark. The Last Magician in Blue Haven. Hundgen, Donald, illus. 52p. (Orig.). (gr. 4-8). 1994. pap. 12.95 (*0-9638293-0-0*) Hundelrut Studio.

THE LAST MAGICIAN is an imaginative tale for children & adults, filled with numerous delicate pen drawings by Donald Hundgen. A sophisticated city doctor comes to Blue Haven to serve the rural community but ends up becoming a thorn in their side. The simple villagers love magic. The doctor, Fortunamus Gengeloof, drives off all the magicians by revealing their secrets, until one comes along who is a match for the doctor. For prepublication order & general information: Write: Hundelrut Studio, 10 Hawthorne Street, Plymouth, NH 03264. USA. Phone: 603-536-4396. *Publisher Provided Annotation.*

Selznick, Brian. The Houdini Box. Selznick, Brian, illus. LC 90-5387. 64p. (gr. 1-6). 1991. 13.00 (*0-679-81429-9*); PLB 13.99 (*0-679-91429-3*) Knopf Bks Yng Read.

Willard, Nancy. The Sorcerer's Apprentice. Dillon, Leo D., et al, eds. Dillon, Diane & Dillon, Lee, illus. LC 93-19912. 32p. (ps-6). 1993. 15.95 (*0-590-47329-8*) Scholastic Inc.

MAGNETISM

see also Electricity; Electromagnetism; Magnets

Challand, Helen. Experiments with Magnets. LC 85-30851. (Illus.). 48p. (gr. k-4). 1986. PLB 12.85 (*0-516-01279-7*); pap. 4.95 (*0-516-41279-5*) Childrens.

Challoner, Jack. My First Batteries & Magnets. LC 92-52825. (Illus.). 48p. (gr. k-4). 1992. 12.95 (*1-56458-133-0*) Dorling Kindersley.

Cooper, Jason. Magnetism. LC 92-8807. 1992. 11.94 (*0-86593-165-8*); 8.95s.p. (*0-685-59294-4*) Rourke Corp.

Davis, Kay & Oldsfield, Wendy. Electricity & Magnetism. LC 91-30069. (Illus.). 32p. (gr. 2-5). 1991. PLB 19.97 (*0-8114-3004-9*); pap. 4.95 (*0-8114-1532-5*) Raintree Steck-V.

Gardner, Robert. Electricity & Magnetism. (Illus.). 96p. (gr. 5-8). 1994. bds. 16.95 (*0-8050-2850-1*) TFC Bks NY.

Kerrod, Robin. Electricity & Magnetism. Evans, Ted, illus. LC 93-46013. 1994. 16.95 (*1-85435-626-7*) Marshall Cavendish.

Magnetism. (gr. 7-12). 1991. pap. 12.30 (*0-941008-90-8*) Tops Learning.

Parramon Staff. Magnets & Electric Current. (Illus.). 48p. (gr. 5 up). 1994. 12.95 (*0-8120-6436-4*) Barron.

Pomeroy, Johanna P. Content Area Reading Skills Electricity & Magnetism. (Illus.). (gr. 4). 1987. pap. text ed. 3.25 (*0-89525-859-5*) Ed Activities.

Robson, Pam. Magnetism. LC 92-37098. (Illus.). 32p. (gr. 5-8). 1993. PLB 12.40 (*0-531-17399-2*, Gloucester Pr) Watts.

Rowe, Julian & Perham, Molly. Amazing Magnets. LC 94-16942. (Illus.). 32p. (gr. 1-4). 1994. PLB 18.60 (*0-516-08137-3*); pap. 4.95 (*0-516-48137-1*) Childrens.

Taylor, Barbara. Batteries & Magnets. LC 91-2558. (Illus.). 40p. (gr. k-4). 1991. PLB 12.90 (*0-531-19130-3*, Warwick) Watts.

—Electricity & Magnets. LC 90-31021. (Illus.). 32p. (gr. 5-8). 1990. PLB 12.40 (*0-531-14083-0*) Watts.

—More Power to You! The Science of Batteries & Magnets. Bull, Peter, et al, illus. LC 91-4293. 40p. (Orig.). (gr. 2-5). 1992. pap. 4.95 (*0-679-82040-X*) Random Bks Yng Read.

Ward, ALan. Experimenting with Magnetism. Flax, Zena, illus. 48p. (gr. 2-7). 1991. lib. bdg. 12.95 (*0-7910-1509-2*) Chelsea Hse.

Weilbacher, Mike. The Magnetism Exploration Kit: Discover One of Nature's Most Astonishing Forces. (Illus.). 64p. (gr. 3 up). 1993. incl. kit 17.95 (*1-56138-240-X*) Running Pr.

Wong, Ovid K. Experimenting with Electricity & Magnetism. LC 92-37672. (gr. 7-12). 1993. 13.40 (*0-531-12547-5*) Watts.

—Experimenting with Electricity & Magnetism. (Illus.). 128p. (gr. 7-12). 1993. pap. 6.95 (*0-531-15681-8*) Watts.

Zubrowski, Bernie. Blinkers & Buzzers: Building & Experimenting with Electricity & Magnetism. Doty, Roy, illus. LC 90-44519. 112p. (gr. 3 up). 1991. PLB 12.88 (*0-688-09966-1*) Morrow Jr Bks.

MAGNETS

Adler, David. Amazing Magnets. Lawler, Dan, illus. LC 82-17377. 32p. (gr. 3-6). 1983. PLB 10.59 (*0-89375-894-9*); pap. text ed. 2.95 (*0-89375-895-7*) Troll Assocs.

Amery, H. & Littler, A. Batteries & Magnets. (Illus.). 32p. (gr. 3-6). 1977. pap. 6.95 (*0-86020-008-6*) EDC.

Ardley, Neil. Science Book of Magnets. 29p. (gr. 2-5). 1991. 9.95 (*0-15-200581-1*, HB Juv Bks) HarBrace.

Berger, Melvin. The Mystery of Magnets. (Illus.). 16p. (ps-2). 1995. pap. text ed. 14.95 (*1-56784-022-1*) Newbridge Comms.

Bittinger, Gayle. Play & Learn with Magnets. Warren, Jean, ed. Mohrmann, Gary, illus. LC 93-61084. 64p. (Orig.). 1994. pap. text ed. 7.95 (*0-911019-92-8*) Warren Pub Hse.

Edom, H. Science with Magnets. (Illus.). 24p. (gr. 1-4). 1991. PLB 12.96 (*0-88110-629-1*, Usborne); pap. 4.95 (*0-7460-1259-4*, Usborne) EDC.

Fitzpatrick, Julie. Magnets. (Illus.). 30p. (gr. 3-5). 1991. 13.95 (*0-237-60208-3*, Pub. by Evans Bros Ltd) Trafalgar.

Gardner, Robert. Science Projects about Electricity & Magnets. LC 93-45252. (Illus.). 128p. (gr. 6 up). 1994. lib. bdg. 17.95 (*0-89490-530-9*) Enslow Pubs.

Glover, David. Batteries, Bulbs & Wires. LC 92-40215. 32p. (gr. 1-4). 1993. 10.95 (*1-85697-837-0*, Kingfisher LKC); pap. 5.95 (*1-85697-933-4*) LKC.

Kirkpatrick, Rena K. Look at Magnets. rev. ed. Knight, Ann, illus. LC 84-26252. 32p. (gr. 2-4). 1985. PLB 10. 95 (*0-8172-2354-1*); pap. 4.95 (*0-8114-6900-X*) Raintree Steck-V.

Krensky, Stephen. All about Magnets. (ps-3). 1993. pap. 4.95 (*0-590-45567-2*) Scholastic Inc.

Pressling, Robert. My Magnet. Pragoff, Fiona, photos by. LC 94-7110. (Illus.). 32p. (gr. 1 up). 1994. PLB 17.27 (*0-8368-1117-8*) Gareth Stevens Inc.

Rowe, Julian & Perham, Molly. Amazing Magnets. LC 94-16942. (Illus.). 32p. (gr. 1-4). 1994. PLB 18.60 (*0-516-08137-3*); pap. 4.95 (*0-516-48137-1*) Childrens.

Santrey, Laurence. Magnets. Veno, Joseph, illus. LC 84-2597. 32p. (gr. 3-6). 1985. PLB 9.49 (*0-8167-0140-7*); pap. text ed. 2.95 (*0-8167-0141-5*) Troll Assocs.

VanCleave, Janice. Janice VanCleave's Magnets. 87p. (Orig.). 1993. pap. text ed. 9.95 (*0-471-57106-7*) Wiley.

Whalley, Margaret. Experiment with Magnets & Electricity. LC 92-41109. 1993. 17.50 (*0-8225-2457-0*) Lerner Pubns.

MAINE

Cayford, John E. Maine Firsts. 3rd, rev. & enl. ed. LC 79-56551. 68p. (Orig.). pap. text ed. 18.50 (pack of 10) (*0-941216-11-X*); tchr's. ed. incl. pack of 10 20.00 (*0-941216-12-8*) Cay-Bel.

Dean, Julia, text by. & photos by A Year on Monhegan Island. LC 93-24534. 48p. (gr. 2-4). 1994. 15.95 (*0-395-66476-4*) Ticknor & Flds Bks Yng Read.

Engfer, LeeAnne. Maine. (Illus.). 72p. (gr. 3-6). 1991. PLB 17.50 (*0-8225-2701-4*) Lerner Pubns.

Fendler, Donn. Lost on a Mountain in Maine. Egan, Joseph, as told to. LC 77-99178. (Illus.). 128p. (gr. 4 up). 1992. pap. 3.95 (*0-688-11573-X*, Pub. by Beech Tree Bks) Morrow.

Fradin, Dennis. Maine: In Words & Pictures. LC 79-25122. (Illus.). 48p. (gr. 2-5). 1980. PLB 12.95 (*0-516-03919-9*) Childrens.

Fradin, Dennis B. Maine - From Sea to Shining Sea. LC 93-32680. (Illus.). 64p. (gr. 3-5). 1994. PLB 16.45 (*0-516-03819-2*) Childrens.

Gibbons, Gail. Surrounded by Sea: Life on a New England Fishing Island. (ps-3). 1991. 14.95 (*0-316-30961-3*) Little.

Harrington, Ty. Maine. LC 88-38399. (Illus.). 144p. (gr. 4 up). 1989. PLB 20.55 (*0-516-00465-4*) Childrens.

—Maine. 179p. 1993. text ed. 15.40 (*1-56956-157-5*) W A T Braille.

Howard, Jean G. Bound by the Sea: A Summer Diary. LC 86-50255. (Illus.). 96p. (gr. 6-12). 1986. text ed. 15.00 (*0-930954-25-4*); pap. 10.00 (*0-930954-26-2*) Tidal Pr.

McMillan, Bruce. Finestkind O'Day, Lobstering in Maine. (Illus.). 48p. (gr. 3-8). 1990. 15.00 (*0-685-35117-3*) Apple Isl Bks.

Marsh, Carole. Avast, Ye Slobs! Maine Pirate Trivia. (Illus.). (gr. 3-8). 1994. PLB 24.95 (*0-7933-0545-4*); pap. 14.95 (*0-7933-0544-6*); disk 29.95 (*0-7933-0546-2*) Gallopade Pub Group.

—The Beast of the Maine Bed & Breakfast. (Illus.). (gr. 3-8). 1994. PLB 24.95 (*0-7933-1681-2*); pap. 14.95 (*0-7933-1682-0*) (*0-7933-1683-9*) Gallopade Pub Group.

—Bow Wow! Maine Dogs in History, Mystery, Legend, Lore, Humor & More! (Illus.). (gr. 3-12). 1994. PLB 24.95 (*0-7933-3524-8*); pap. 14.95 (*0-7933-3525-6*); computer disk 29.95 (*0-7933-3526-4*) Gallopade Pub Group.

—Carole Marsh Maine Books, 44 bks. (Illus.). (gr. 3-8). 1994. PLB 1027.80 set (*0-7933-1294-9*); pap. 587.80 set (*0-7933-5160-X*) Gallopade Pub Group.

—Christopher Columbus Comes to Maine! Includes Reproducible Activities for Kids! (Illus.). (gr. 3-12). 1994. PLB 24.95 (*0-7933-3677-5*); pap. 14.95 (*0-7933-3678-3*); computer disk 29.95 (*0-7933-3679-1*) Gallopade Pub Group.

—The Hard-to-Believe-But-True! Book of Maine History, Mystery, Trivia, Legend, Lore, Humor & More. (Illus.). (gr. 3-8). 1994. PLB 24.95 (*0-7933-0542-X*); pap. 14.95 (*0-7933-0541-1*); disk 29.95 (*0-7933-0543-8*) Gallopade Pub Group.

—If My Maine Mama Ran the World! (Illus.). (gr. 3-8). 1994. lib. bdg. 24.95 (*0-7933-1687-1*); pap. 14.95 (*0-7933-1688-X*); disk 29.95 (*0-7933-1689-8*) Gallopade Pub Group.

—Jurassic Ark! Maine Dinosaurs & Other Prehistoric Creatures. (gr. k-12). 1994. PLB 24.95 (*0-7933-7485-5*); pap. 14.95 (*0-7933-7486-3*); computer disk 29.95 (*0-7933-7487-1*) Gallopade Pub Group.

—Let's Quilt Maine & Stuff It Topographically! (Illus.). (gr. 3-8). 1994. PLB 24.95 (*1-55609-599-6*); pap. 14.95 (*1-55609-068-4*); disk 29.95 (*1-55609-601-1*) Gallopade Pub Group.

—Let's Quilt Our Maine County. 1994. lib. bdg. 24.95 (*0-7933-7170-8*); pap. text ed. 14.95 (*0-7933-7171-6*); disk 29.95 (*0-7933-7172-4*) Gallopade Pub Group.
—Let's Quilt Our Maine Town. 1994. lib. bdg. 24.95 (*0-7933-7020-5*); pap. text ed. 14.95 (*0-7933-7021-3*); disk 29.95 (*0-7933-7022-1*) Gallopade Pub Group.
—Maine & Other State Greats (Biographies) (Illus.). (gr. 3-8). 1994. PLB 24.95 (*1-55609-614-3*); pap. 14.95 (*1-55609-615-1*); disk 29.95 (*1-55609-616-X*) Gallopade Pub Group.
—Maine Bandits, Bushwackers, Outlaws, Crooks, Devils, Ghosts, Desperadoes & Other Assorted & Sundry Characters! (Illus.). (gr. 3-8). 1994. PLB 24.95 (*0-7933-0527-6*); pap. 14.95 (*0-7933-0526-8*); disk 29. 95 (*0-7933-0528-4*) Gallopade Pub Group.
—Maine Classic Christmas Trivia: Stories, Recipes, Activities, Legends, Lore & More! (Illus.). (gr. 3-8). 1994. PLB 24.95 (*0-7933-0530-6*); pap. 14.95 (*0-7933-0529-2*); disk 29.95 (*0-7933-0531-4*) Gallopade Pub Group.
—Maine Coastales! (Illus.). (gr. 3-8). 1994. PLB 24.95 (*1-55609-608-9*); pap. 14.95 (*1-55609-609-7*); disk 29. 95 (*1-55609-610-0*) Gallopade Pub Group.
—Maine Coastales! 1994. lib. bdg. 24.95 (*0-7933-7284-4*) Gallopade Pub Group.
—Maine Dingbats! Bk. 1: A Fun Book of Games, Stories, Activities & More about Our State That's All in Code! for You to Decipher. (Illus.). (gr. 3-12). 1994. PLB 24. 95 (*0-7933-3830-1*); pap. 14.95 (*0-7933-3831-X*); computer disk 29.95 (*0-7933-3832-8*) Gallopade Pub Group.
—Maine Festival Fun for Kids! (Illus.). (gr. 3-12). 1994. lib. bdg. 24.95 (*0-7933-3983-9*); pap. 14.95 (*0-7933-3984-7*); disk 29.95 (*0-7933-3985-5*) Gallopade Pub Group.
—The Maine Hot Air Balloon Mystery. (Illus.). (gr. 2-9). 1994. 24.95 (*0-7933-2489-0*); pap. 14.95 (*0-7933-2490-4*); computer disk 29.95 (*0-7933-2491-2*) Gallopade Pub Group.
—Maine Jeopardy! Answers & Questions about Our State! (Illus.). (gr. 3-12). 1994. PLB 24.95 (*0-7933-4136-1*); pap. 14.95 (*0-7933-4137-X*); computer disk 29.95 (*0-7933-4138-8*) Gallopade Pub Group.
—Maine "Jography" A Fun Run Thru Our State! (Illus.). (gr. 3-8). 1994. PLB 24.95 (*1-55609-596-1*); pap. 14.95 (*1-55609-597-X*); disk 29.95 (*1-55609-598-8*) Gallopade Pub Group.
—Maine Kid's Cookbook: Recipes, How-to, History, Lore & More! (Illus.). (gr. 3-8). 1994. PLB 24.95 (*0-7933-0539-X*); pap. 14.95 (*0-7933-0538-1*); disk 29. 95 (*0-7933-0540-3*) Gallopade Pub Group.
—Maine Quiz Bowl Crash Course! (Illus.). (gr. 3-8). 1994. PLB 24.95 (*1-55609-611-9*); pap. 14.95 (*1-55609-612-7*); disk 29.95 (*1-55609-613-5*) Gallopade Pub Group.
—Maine Rollercoasters! (Illus.). (gr. 3-12). 1994. PLB 24. 95 (*0-7933-5281-9*); pap. 14.95 (*0-7933-5282-7*); computer disk 29.95 (*0-7933-5283-5*) Gallopade Pub Group.
—Maine School Trivia: An Amazing & Fascinating Look at Our State's Teachers, Schools & Students! (Illus.). (gr. 3-8). 1994. PLB 24.95 (*0-7933-0536-5*); pap. 14.95 (*0-7933-0535-7*); disk 29.95 (*0-7933-0537-3*) Gallopade Pub Group.
—Maine Silly Basketball Sportsmysteries, Vol. I. (Illus.). (gr. 3-8). 1994. PLB 24.95 (*0-7933-0533-0*); pap. 14.95 (*0-7933-0532-2*); disk 29.95 (*0-7933-0534-9*) Gallopade Pub Group.
—Maine Silly Basketball Sportsmysteries, Vol. II. (Illus.). (gr. 3-8). 1994. PLB 24.95 (*0-7933-1684-7*); pap. 14.95 (*0-7933-1685-5*); disk 29.95 (*0-7933-1686-3*) Gallopade Pub Group.
—Maine Silly Football Sportsmysteries, Vol. I. (Illus.). (gr. 3-8). 1994. PLB 24.95 (*1-55609-602-X*); pap. 14. 95 (*1-55609-604-6*); disk 29.95 (*1-55609-606-2*) Gallopade Pub Group.
—Maine Silly Football Sportsmysteries, Vol. II. (Illus.). (gr. 3-8). 1994. PLB 24.95 (*1-55609-603-8*); pap. 14.95 (*1-55609-605-4*); disk 29.95 (*1-55609-607-0*) Gallopade Pub Group.
—Maine Silly Trivia! (Illus.). (gr. 3-8). 1994. PLB 24.95 (*1-55609-593-7*); pap. 14.95 (*1-55609-594-5*); disk 29. 95 (*1-55609-595-3*) Gallopade Pub Group.
—Maine's (Most Devastating!) Disasters & (Most Calamitous!) Catastrophies! (Illus.). (gr. 3-8). 1994. PLB 24.95 (*0-7933-0524-1*, 0-7933-0525-X); pap. 14. 95 (*0-7933-0523-3*); disk 29.95 (*0-685-45941-1*) Gallopade Pub Group.
—Meow! Maine Cats in History, Mystery, Legend, Lore, Humor & More! (Illus.). (gr. 3-12). 1994. PLB 24.95 (*0-7933-3371-7*); pap. 14.95 (*0-7933-3372-5*); computer disk 29.95 (*0-7933-3373-3*) Gallopade Pub Group.
—Uncle Rebus: Maine Picture Stories for Computer Kids. (Illus.). (gr. k-3). 1994. PLB 24.95 (*0-7933-4558-8*); pap. 14.95 (*0-7933-4559-6*); disk 29.95 (*0-7933-4560-X*) Gallopade Pub Group.
Thaxter, Celia. Celia's Island Journal. (ps-3). 1992. 15.95 (*0-316-83921-3*) Little.
Turner Program Services, Inc. Staff & Clark, James I. Maine. LC 85-9975. 48p. (gr. 3 up). 1985. PLB 19.97 (*0-86514-433-8*) Raintree Steck-V.

MAINE–FICTION

Baker, Marybeth. Maynard's Allagash Friends. 1989. pap. 7.95 (*0-929906-25-X*) G Gannett.
Campbell, Louise A. & Bowers, Grace A. Muffin, The Maine Puffin. Mason, MacAdam L., illus. 40p. (Orig.). (gr. k-3). 1988. pap. 9.95 (*0-9621949-0-5*) Muffin Enter.
Flanagan, James M. Builders of Maine. LC 91-58091. 400p. 1994. 15.95 (*0-932433-87-1*) Windswept Hse.
Fox, J. N. Young Indiana Jones & the Pirates' Loot. LC 93-46831. 132p. (Orig.). (gr. 3-7). 1994. pap. 3.99 (*0-679-86433-4*, Bullseye Bks) Random Bks Yng Read.
Futcher, Jane. Promise Not to Tell. 192p. (Orig.). (gr. 4-5). 1991. pap. 2.95 (*0-380-76037-1*, Flare) Avon.
Hahn, Mary D. Look for Me by Moonlight. LC 94-21892. 1995. write for info. (*0-395-69843-X*); pap. write for info. (*0-395-69844-8*) HM.
Hotze, Sollace. Acquainted with the Night. 256p. (gr. 7 up). 1992. 13.95 (*0-395-61576-3*, Clarion Bks) HM.
Irwin, Hadley. The Original Freddie Ackerman. Hosten, James, illus. LC 91-43145. 192p. (gr. 5 up). 1992. SBE 14.95 (*0-689-50562-0*, M K McElderry) Macmillan Child Grp.
Koller, Jackie F. The Last Voyage of the Misty Day. LC 91-17482. 160p. (gr. 4-8). 1992. SBE 13.95 (*0-689-31731-X*, Atheneum Child Bk) Macmillan Child Grp.
Kroll, Steven. Patrick's Tree House. Wilson, Roberta, illus. LC 93-4571. 64p. (gr. 2-5). 1994. RSBE 13.95 (*0-02-751005-0*, Macmillan Child Bk) Macmillan Child Grp.
McCloskey, Robert. Burt Dow: Deep-Water Man. McCloskey, Robert, illus. LC 68-364. 64p. (gr. 4-6). 1963. pap. 15.95 (*0-670-19748-3*) Viking Child Bks.
—One Morning in Maine. (ps-3). 1976. pap. 3.99 (*0-14-050174-6*, Puffin) Puffin Bks.
—One Morning in Maine. McCloskey, Robert, illus. (gr. k-3). 1952. pap. 14.00 (*0-670-52627-4*) Viking Child Bks.
—Time of Wonder. McCloskey, Robert, illus. (gr. k-3). 1957. pap. 16.00 (*0-670-71512-3*) Viking Child Bks.
Murphy, Catherine F. Songs in the Silence. LC 93-26947. 192p. (gr. 3-7). 1994. SBE 14.95 (*0-02-767730-3*, Macmillan Child Bk) Macmillan Child Grp.
Simpson, Dorothy. Island in the Bay. 184p. (Orig.). (gr. 7-12). 1993. 9.95 (*0-942396-62-6*) Blackberry ME.
Wiggin, Eric. Katy. (Illus.). 1992. pap. 8.99 (*1-56121-078-1*) Wolgemuth & Hyatt.
—Maggie: Life at the Elms. LC 93-27054. 1994. pap. 3.99 (*1-56507-133-6*) Harvest Hse.
—Maggie's Homecoming. LC 93-27053. 1994. pap. 3.99 (*1-56507-134-4*) Harvest Hse.

MAINE–HISTORY

Kuller, Alison M. An Outward Bound School. Stewart, Thomas R. & Kuller, Alison M., illus. LC 89-5169. 32p. (gr. 3-6). 1990. PLB 10.79 (*0-8167-1731-1*); pap. text ed. 2.95 (*0-8167-1732-X*) Troll Assocs.
Marsh, Carole. Chill Out: Scary Maine Tales Based on Frightening Maine Truths. (Illus.). 1994. lib. bdg. 24. 95 (*0-7933-4711-4*); pap. 14.95 (*0-7933-4712-2*); disk 29.95 (*0-7933-4713-0*) Gallopade Pub Group.
—Maine "Crinkum-Crankum" A Funny Word Book about Our State. (Illus.). 1994. lib. bdg. 24.95 (*0-7933-4865-X*); pap. 14.95 (*0-7933-4866-8*); disk 29. 95 (*0-7933-4867-6*) Gallopade Pub Group.
—The Maine Mystery Van Takes Off! Book 1: Handicapped Maine Kids Sneak Off on a Big Adventure. (Illus.). (gr. 3-12). 1994. 24.95 (*0-7933-5018-2*); pap. 14.95 (*0-7933-5019-0*); computer disk 29.95 (*0-7933-5020-4*) Gallopade Pub Group.
—Maine Timeline: A Chronology of Maine History, Mystery, Trivia, Legend, Lore & More. (Illus.). (gr. 3-12). 1994. PLB 24.95 (*0-7933-5932-5*); pap. 14.95 (*0-7933-5933-3*); computer disk 29.95 (*0-7933-5934-1*) Gallopade Pub Group.
—My First Book about Maine. (gr. k-4). 1994. PLB 24.95 (*0-7933-5626-1*); pap. 14.95 (*0-7933-5627-X*); computer disk 29.95 (*0-7933-5628-8*) Gallopade Pub Group.
—Patch, the Pirate Dog: A Maine Pet Story. (ps-4). 1994. PLB 24.95 (*0-7933-5473-0*); pap. 14.95 (*0-7933-5474-9*); computer disk 29.95 (*0-7933-5475-7*) Gallopade Pub Group.
Rolde, Neil. Maine: A Narrative History. (Illus.). 368p. (Orig.). 1990. pap. 19.95 (*0-88448-069-0*) Tilbury Hse.
Tingay, Graham I. & Badcock, John. These Were the Romans. LC 86-11654. (Illus.). 196p. (gr. 10-12). 1987. pap. 14.95 (*0-8023-1280-2*) Dufour.

MAIZE

see Corn

MAKE-UP (COSMETICS)

see Cosmetics

MAKE-UP, THEATRICAL

Boucher, Helene & Major, Henriette. Make up Magic. (Illus.). 32p. (gr. 3-7). 1993. 7.95 (*2-7625-5270-2*, Pub. by Les Edits Herit CN) Adams Inc MA.
Freeman, Ron. Makeup Art. LC 90-38305. (Illus.). 48p. (gr. 5-8). 1991. PLB 12.90 (*0-531-14133-0*) Watts.
Snazaroo. Five Minute Faces: Fantastic Face-Painting Ideas. LC 91-26669. (Illus.). 48p. (Orig.). 1992. 7.99 (*0-679-82810-9*); PLB 10.99 (*0-679-92810-3*) Random Bks Yng Read.

MALADJUSTED CHILDREN

see Problem Children

MALAWI

Department of Geography, Lerner Publications. Malawi in Pictures. (Illus.). 64p. (gr. 5 up). 1988. PLB 17.50 (*0-8225-1842-2*) Lerner Pubns.
Lane, Martha S. Malawi. LC 89-25433. (Illus.). 128p. (gr. 5-9). 1990. PLB 20.55 (*0-516-02720-4*) Childrens.
Sanders, Renfield. Malawi. (Illus.). 104p. (gr. 5 up). 1988. lib. bdg. 14.95 (*1-55546-193-X*) Chelsea Hse.

MALAYA–FICTION

Conrad, Joseph. Lord Jim. Gemme, F. R., intro. by. (gr. 10 up). 1965. pap. 1.95 (*0-8049-0054-X*, CL-54) Airmont.
—Outcast of the Islands. Teitel, N. R., intro. by. (gr. 9 up). 1966. pap. 1.50 (*0-8049-0113-9*, CL-113) Airmont.

MALAYSIA, FEDERATION OF

Lerner Publications, Department of Geography Staff, ed. Malaysia in Pictures. (Illus.). 64p. (gr. 5 up). 1989. 17. 50 (*0-8225-1854-6*) Lerner Pubns.
Major, John S. The Land & People of Malaysia & Brunei. LC 90-20124. (Illus.). 272p. (gr. 6 up). 1991. 17.95 (*0-06-022488-6*); PLB 17.89 (*0-06-022489-4*) HarpC Child Bks.
Munan, Heidi. Malaysia. LC 89-25464. (Illus.). 128p. (gr. 5-9). 1991. PLB 21.95 (*1-85435-296-2*) Marshall Cavendish.
Wright, David K. Malaysia. LC 87-33784. (Illus.). 128p. (gr. 5-9). 1988. PLB 20.55 (*0-516-02702-6*) Childrens.

MALCOLM X

see Little, Malcolm, 1925-1965

MAMMALS

see also Primates;
also names of mammals, e.g. Bats

Arnosky, Jim. Crinkleroot's Twenty-Five Mammals Every Child Should Know. Arnosky, Jim, illus. LC 93-7585. 32p. (ps-3). 1994. RSBE 12.95 (*0-02-705845-X*, Bradbury Pr) Macmillan Child Grp.
Bender, Lionel. Birds & Mammals. Khan, Aziz, illus. LC 87-82896. 40p. (gr. 6-8). 1988. PLB 12.40 (*0-531-17091-8*, Gloucester Pr) Watts.
Bramwell, Martyn, ed. Mammals. LC 93-4336. 48p. (gr. k-3). 1993. 12.95 (*1-56458-386-4*) Dorling Kindersley.
Brownell, M. Barbara. Mammals. LC 93-19467. (gr. 1-3). 1993. write for info. (*0-87044-890-0*); incl. Reptiles & Amphibians 24.95 (*0-685-70103-4*) Natl Geog.
Burnie, David. Mammals. LC 92-54312. (Illus.). 64p. (gr. 3 up). 1993. 9.95 (*1-56458-228-0*) Dorling Kindersley.
Burton, John. Mammals. (gr. 5 up). 1992. 9.98 (*0-8317-6973-4*) Smithmark.
Chermayeff, Ivan. Furry Facts. LC 93-30147. 1994. 10.95 (*0-15-230425-8*, Gulliver Bks) HarBrace.
Crump, Donald J., ed. Giants from the Past. LC 81-47893. 104p. (gr. 3-8). 1983. PLB 12.50 (*0-87044-429-8*) Natl Geog.
Dewey, Jennifer. Mammals on the Rise: A Prehistoric Southwest Coloring Book. (ps-3). 1992. pap. 4.95 (*0-89013-238-0*) Museum NM Pr.
Endangered Mammals - Africa: An Educational Coloring Book. (gr. 3 up). pap. 1.75 (*0-86545-213-X*) Spizzirri.
Endangered Mammals - Asia & China: An Educational Coloring Book. (gr. 3 up). pap. 1.75 (*0-86545-214-8*) Spizzirri.
Endangered Mammals - South America: An Educational Coloring Book. pap. 1.75 (*0-86545-215-6*) Spizzirri.
Esbensen, Barbara J. Baby Whales Drink Milk. Davis, Lambert, illus. LC 92-30375. 32p. (ps-1). 1994. 15.00 (*0-06-021551-8*); PLB 14.89 (*0-06-021552-6*) HarpC Child Bks.
Fowler, Allan. It Could Still Be a Mammal. LC 90-2161. (Illus.). 32p. (ps-2). 1990. PLB 10.75 (*0-516-04903-8*); pap. 22.95 big bk. (*0-516-49463-5*); pap. 3.95 (*0-516-44903-6*) Childrens.
—Podria Ser un Mamifero: It Could Still Be a Mammal. LC 90-2161. (SPA.). 32p. (ps-2). 1991. PLB 10.75 (*0-516-34903-1*); pap. 3.95 (*0-516-54903-0*) Childrens.
Ganeri, Anita. Small Mammals. LC 92-32706. 1993. 11. 90 (*0-531-14249-3*) Watts.
George, Michael. Mammals. (gr. 2-6). 1992. PLB 15.95 (*0-89565-846-1*) Childs World.
Grace, Theresa. A Picture Book of Underwater Life. Pistolesi, Roseanna, illus. LC 89-37330. 24p. (gr. 1-4). 1990. lib. bdg. 9.59 (*0-8167-1906-3*); pap. text ed. 2.50 (*0-8167-1907-1*) Troll Assocs.
Hiller, Ilo. Introducing Mammals to Young Naturalists. LC 89-35523. (Illus.). 112p. (gr. 6). 1990. 9.00 (*0-89096-427-0*); pap. 4.50 (*0-89096-428-9*) Tex A&M Univ Pr.
Illustrated Encyclopedia of Wildlife, Vol. 1: The Mammals, Pt. I. 184p. (gr. 7 up). 1990. lib. bdg. write for info. (*1-55905-037-3*) Grey Castle.
Illustrated Encyclopedia of Wildlife, Vol. 2: The Mammals, Pt. II. 184p. (gr. 7 up). 1990. lib. bdg. write for info. (*1-55905-038-1*) Grey Castle.
Illustrated Encyclopedia of Wildlife, Vol. 3: The Mammals, Pt. III. 184p. (gr. 7 up). 1990. lib. bdg. write for info. (*1-55905-039-X*) Grey Castle.
Illustrated Encyclopedia of Wildlife, Vol. 4: The Mammals, Pt. IV. 192p. (gr. 7 up). 1990. lib. bdg. write for info. (*1-55905-040-3*) Grey Castle.
Kalman, Bobbie. Forest Mammals. Loates, Glen, illus. 56p. (gr. 3-4). 1987. 15.95 (*0-86505-165-8*); pap. 7.95 (*0-86505-185-2*) Crabtree Pub Co.
Large Mammals Activity Book. (Illus.). (ps-6). pap. 2.95 (*0-565-01014-X*, Pub. by Natural Hist Mus) Parkwest Pubns.
Lovett, Sarah. Extremely Weird Mammals. (Illus.). 48p. (Orig.). (gr. 3 up). 1993. pap. 9.95 (*1-56261-107-0*) John Muir.
McCord. Prehistoric Mammals. (Illus.). (gr. 4-6). 1977. (Usborne-Hayes); pap. 13.96 (*0-88110-120-6*); pap. 6.95 (*0-86020-128-7*) EDC.

Mammals. 32p. (ps-8). pap. 29.50 (*0-87474-335-4*) Smithsonian.

Mammals of Arizona. (Illus.). 32p. (gr. 3 up). 1984. pap. 1.00 (*0-935810-16-1*) Primer Pubs.

Mammals: Superdoodles. LC 92-74100. (gr. 1-6). 1993. pap. 4.95 (*0-88160-219-1*, LW303) Learning Wks.

Minelli, Giuseppe. Mammals. (Illus.). 64p. 1988. 15.95x (*0-8160-1560-0*) Facts on File.

Nayer, Judy. Mammals. Goldberg, Grace, illus. 12p. (ps-2). 1993. bds. 6.95 (*1-56293-337-X*) McClanahan Bk.

Neuman, Pearl. When Winter Comes. (Illus.). 32p. (gr. 1-4). 1989. PLB 18.99 (*0-8172-3519-1*); pap. 4.95 (*0-8114-6723-6*) Raintree Steck-V.

O'Neill, Mary. Life after the Dinosaurs. Bindon, John, illus. LC 89-31164. 32p. (gr. 3-7). 1989. lib. bdg. 12.89 (*0-8167-1639-0*); pap. text ed. 3.95 (*0-8167-1640-4*) Troll Assocs.

Oram, Liz & Baker, R. Robin. Mammal Migration. LC 91-12181. (Illus.). 48p. (gr. 4-8). 1992. PLB 22.80 (*0-8114-2927-X*) Raintree Steck-V.

Palmer, S. Manatees. (Illus.). 24p. (gr. k-5). 1989. lib. bdg. 11.94 (*0-86592-359-0*); 8.95s.p. (*0-685-58620-0*) Rourke Corp.

Parker, Steve. Mammal. Burton, Jane & King, Dave, photos by. LC 88-22656. (Illus.). 64p. (gr. 5 up). 1989. 16.00 (*0-394-82258-7*); lib. bdg. 16.99 (*0-394-92258-1*) Knopf Bks Yng Read.

Parsons, Alexandra. Amazing Mammals. Young, Jerry, photos by. LC 89-38831. (Illus.). 32p. (gr. 1-5). 1990. 7.99 (*0-679-80224-X*); PLB 9.99 (*0-679-90224-4*) Knopf Bks Yng Read.

Peissel, Michel & Allen, Missy. Dangerous Mammals. (Illus.). 112p. (gr. 5 up). 1993. PLB 19.95 (*0-7910-1790-7*, Am Art Analog) Chelsea Hse.

Richardson, Joy. Mammals. LC 92-32913. 1993. 11.40 (*0-531-14253-1*) Watts.

Sabin, Francene. Mammals. Veno, Joseph, illus. LC 84-2658. 32p. (gr. 3-6). 1985. PLB 9.49 (*0-8167-0208-X*); pap. text ed. 2.95 (*0-8167-0209-8*) Troll Assocs.

Schneider, Jeff. My Friend the Manatee: An Ocean Magic Book. Spoon, Wilfred, illus. LC 90-61576. 12p. (ps). 1991. 4.95g (*1-877779-08-3*) Schneider Educational.

Sea Mammals-Coloring Book. 1985. pap. 3.95 (*0-88388-067-9*) Bellerophon Bks.

The Sierra Club Book of Great Mammals. LC 92-11373. 72p. (gr. 5 up). 1992. 16.95 (*0-87156-507-2*) Sierra.

The Sierra Club Book of Small Mammals. LC 92-28859. (Illus.). 72p. (gr. 5 up). 1993. 16.95 (*0-87156-525-0*) Sierra.

Snedden, Robert. What Is a Mammal? Lascom, Adrian, illus. Oxford Scientific Films Staff, photos by. LC 93-26145. (Illus.). 32p. (gr. 2-5). 1994. 14.95 (*0-87156-468-8*) Sierra.

Spizzirri Publishing Co. Staff. Mammals: An Educational Coloring Book. Spizzirri, Linda, ed. Spizzirri, Peter M., et al, illus. 32p. (gr. 1-8). 1981. pap. 1.75 (*0-86545-027-7*) Spizzirri.

Steele, Philip. Mammals. 32p. (gr. 3-5). 1991. (J Messner); pap. 4.95 (*0-671-72234-4*) S&S Trade.

—Wild Animals. LC 90-42014. (Illus.). 32p. (gr. 5-6). 1991. text ed. 3.95 RSBE (*0-89686-584-3*, Crestwood Hse) Macmillan Child Grp.

Stone, Lynn. Hyenas. (Illus.). 24p. (gr. k-5). 1990. lib. bdg. 11.94 (*0-86593-049-X*); lib. bdg. 8.95s.p. (*0-685-36348-1*) Rourke Corp.

—Wombats. (Illus.). 24p. (gr. k-5). 1990. lib. bdg. 11.94 (*0-86593-059-7*); lib. bdg. 8.95s.p. (*0-685-36374-0*) Rourke Corp.

Tee-Van, Helen D. Small Mammals Are Where You Find Them. (Illus.). (gr. 3-7). 1967. lib. bdg. 5.99 (*0-394-91643-3*) Knopf Bks Yng Read.

Tesar, Jenny. Mammals. (Illus.). 64p. (gr. 4-8). 1993. PLB 16.95 (*1-56711-042-8*) Blackbirch.

—Mammals. Kray, Robert, illus. 64p. (gr. 4-8). 1993. jacketed 14.95 (*1-56711-055-X*) Blackbirch.

Torbit, Stephen C. Large Mammals of the Central Rockies: A Guide to Their Locations & Ecology. Torbit, Stephen C., illus. 72p. (gr. 12). 1987. pap. 7.95 (*0-9618450-0-7*) Bennet Creek.

Wexo, John B. Mammals, Pt. II. 24p. (gr. 3 up). 1991. PLB 14.95 (*0-88682-396-X*) Creative Ed.

Zoehfeld, Kathleen W. Manatee Winter. Petruccio, Steven J., illus. LC 94-158. 32p. (ps-2). 1994. 14.95 (*1-56899-075-8*); incl. audiocassette 19.95 (*1-56899-079-0*); incl. 15" plush toy 26.95 (*1-56899-077-4*); mini-sized bk. 4.50 (*1-56899-076-6*); mini-sized bk., incl. 6" plush toy 12.95 (*1-56899-078-2*); audiocassette avail. (*1-56899-080-4*) Soundprints.

MAMMALS, FOSSIL

see also names of extinct animals, e.g. Mastodon; etc.

Hawcock, David. Wooly Mammoth. 1994. 5.95 (*0-8050-3195-2*) H Holt & Co.

Kerrod, Robin. Primates, Insect Eaters & Baleen Whales. (Illus.). 96p. 1988. 17.95x (*0-8160-1961-4*) Facts on File.

Losito, Linda, et al. Mammals: Small Plant-Eaters. (Illus.). 96p. 1988. 17.95x (*0-8160-1958-4*) Facts on File.

Matthews, Rupert. Age of Mammals. LC 89-9800. (ps-3). 1990. PLB 12.40 (*0-531-18311-4*) Watts.

O'Toole, Christopher & Stidworthy, John. Mammals: The Hunters. (Illus.). 96p. 1988. 17.95x (*0-8160-1959-2*) Facts on File.

Stidworthy, John, et al. Mammals: Large Plant-Eaters. (Illus.). 96p. 1988. 17.95x (*0-8160-1960-6*) Facts on File.

Wexo, John B. Mammals, Pt. I. 24p. (gr. 3 up). 1991. PLB 14.95 (*0-88682-395-1*) Creative Ed.

MAN

Disney, Walt, Productions Staff. All about People. LC 85-43075. 80p. (Orig.). 1985. pap. 5.95 (*0-553-05536-4*) Bantam.

Hall, Donald. Oxcart Man. Cooney, Barbara, tr. (gr. 1-5). 1984. incl. cassette 19.95 (*0-941078-41-8*); pap. 12.95 incl. cassette (*0-941078-40-X*); pap. 27.95 4 bks, cassette & guide (*0-941078-42-6*) Live Oak Media.

MAN–ANTIQUITY

see Man–Origin and Antiquity

MAN–COLOR

see Color of Man

MAN–INFLUENCE OF ENVIRONMENT

see also Color of Man

Anderson, Madelyn K. Environmental Diseases. LC 87-8117. (Illus.). 72p. (gr. 4-9). 1987. PLB 10.90 (*0-531-10382-X*) Watts.

Group for Environmental Education, Inc. Staff. Our Man-Made Environment, Book 7. (gr. 7). 1973. pap. 7.95x (*0-262-07050-2*) MIT Pr.

MacQuitty, Miranda. Desert. LC 93-21068. 1994. 16.00 (*0-679-86003-7*); PLB 16.99 (*0-679-96003-1*) Knopf Bks Yng Read.

MAN–INFLUENCE ON NATURE

Blashfield, Jean F. & Black, Wallace B. Endangered Species. LC 92-9083. (Illus.). 128p. (gr. 4-8). 1992. PLB 20.55 (*0-516-05514-3*) Childrens.

Cherry, Lynne. A River Ran Wild. 1992. 14.95 (*0-15-200542-0*, HB Juv Bks) HarBrace.

Duggleby, John. Pesticides. LC 90-35496. (Illus.). 48p. (gr. 6). 1990. text ed. 12.95 RSBE (*0-89686-540-1*, Crestwood Hse) Macmillan Child Grp.

George, Jean C. The Everglades. Minor, Wendell, illus. LC 92-9517. Date not set. 15.00 (*0-06-021228-4*); PLB 14.89 (*0-06-021229-2*) HarpC Child Bks.

Hare, Tony. Habitat Destruction. LC 91-8402. (Illus.). 32p. (gr. 5-8). 1991. PLB 12.40 (*0-531-17307-0*, Gloucester Pr) Watts.

Hoff, Mary & Rodgers, Mary M. Life on Land. (Illus.). 72p. (gr. 4-6). 1992. PLB 21.50 (*0-8225-2507-0*) Lerner Pubns.

Pollock, Steve. The Atlas of Endangered Places. LC 92-20388. (Illus.). 64p. 1993. 17.95 (*0-8160-2857-5*) Facts on File.

Raintree Steck-Vaughn Staff. Atlas of the Environment. Coote, Roger, ed. LC 92-8196. (Illus.). 96p. (gr. 6-7). 1992. PLB 26.99 (*0-8114-7250-7*) Raintree Steck-V.

Rand McNally Staff. Children's Atlas of the Environment. (gr. 4-7). 1991. 14.95 (*0-528-83438-X*) Rand McNally.

Silver, Donald. Extinction Is Forever. Wynne, Patricia J., illus. LC 93-32567. 1995. 12.00 (*0-671-86769-5*, J Messner); pap. 6.95 (*0-671-86770-9*, J Messner) S&S Trade.

Stidworthy, John. Environmentalist. LC 91-34608. (Illus.). 32p. (gr. 4-7). 1992. PLB 12.40 (*0-531-17268-6*, Gloucester Pr) Watts.

Tesar, Jenny. Endangered Habitats. (Illus.). 128p. (gr. 7-12). 1991. lib. bdg. 18.95x (*0-8160-2493-6*) Facts on File.

Wheeler, Jill C. The People We Live With. Kallen, Stuart A., ed. LC 91-73067. 1991. 12.94 (*1-56239-034-1*) Abdo & Dghtrs.

Willis, Terri. Land Use & Abuse. LC 92-8842. (Illus.). 128p. (gr. 4-8). 1992. PLB 20.55 (*0-516-05507-0*) Childrens.

MAN–INFLUENCE ON NATURE–FICTION

Boyle, Doe & Thomas, Peter, eds. Big Town Trees: From an Original Article which Appeared in Ranger Rick Magazine, Copyright National Wildlife Federation. Beylon, Cathy, illus. LC 92-34778. 20p. (gr. k-3). 1993. 6.95 (*0-924483-83-0*); incl. audio tape 9.95 (*0-924483-84-9*); incl. audio tape & 13 inch plush toy 35.95 (*0-924483-87-3*); incl. 9 inch plush toy 21.95 (*0-924483-89-X*) Soundprints.

—Earth Day Every Day: From an Original Article which Appeared in Ranger Rick Magazine, Copyright National Wildlife Federation. Beylon, Cathy, illus. LC 92-27292. 20p. (gr. k-3). 1993. 6.95 (*0-924483-82-2*); incl. audio tape 9.95 (*0-924483-85-7*); incl. audio tape & 13 inch plush toy 35.95 (*0-924483-86-5*); incl. 9 inch plush toy 21.95 (*0-924483-88-1*) Soundprints.

Cole, Babette. Supermoo! LC 92-8967. (Illus.). 32p. (ps-3). 1993. 14.95 (*0-399-22422-X*, Putnam) Putnam Pub Group.

Locker, Thomas. The Land of Gray Wolf. Locker, Thomas, illus. LC 90-3915. 32p. (ps up). 1991. 15.95 (*0-8037-0936-6*); lib. bdg. 15.89 (*0-8037-0937-4*) Dial Bks Young.

London, Jonathan. Voices of the Wild. McLoughlin, Wayne, illus. LC 92-27651. 32p. (ps up). 1993. 15.00 (*0-517-59217-7*); PLB 15.99 (*0-517-59218-5*) Crown Bks Yng Read.

MacGill-Callahan, Sheila. And Still the Turtle Watched. (ps-3). 1991. 14.95 (*0-8037-0931-5*); PLB 14.89 (*0-8037-0932-3*) Dial Bks Young.

Schaffer, Ulrich. Zilya's Secret Plan. Shoji, Takashi, illus. 32p. (ps-6). 1991. pap. 4.99 (*0-7459-1957-X*) Lion USA.

Thompson, Colin. The Paper Bag Prince. Thompson, Colin, illus. LC 91-27453. 32p. (gr. 2-7). 1992. 15.00 (*0-679-83048-0*); PLB 15.99 (*0-679-93048-5*) Knopf Bks Yng Read.

MAN–ORIGIN AND ANTIQUITY

see also Anatomy, Comparative; Evolution; Man, Prehistoric

Asimov, Isaac. How Did We Find Out about Our Human Roots? Wool, David, illus. (gr. 4-8). 1979. PLB 10.85 (*0-8027-6361-8*) Walker & Co.

Lambert, Lisa A. The Leakeys. LC 92-46046. 1993. 19.93 (*0-86625-492-7*); 14.95s.p. (*0-685-66536-4*) Rourke Pubns.

Lewin, Roger. The Origin of Modern Humans: A Scientific American Library Volume. LC 93-17647. 1993. text ed. write for info. (*0-7167-5039-2*, Sci Am Yng Rdrs) W H Freeman.

McCaughrean, Geraldine. A Little Lower than the Angels. 144p. (gr. 6-9). 1987. 15.00 (*0-19-271561-5*) OUP.

Ronen, Avraham. Stones & Bones! How Archaeologists Trace Human Origins. LC 93-2480. (gr. 6 up). 1993. lib. bdg. write for info. (*0-8225-3207-7*, Runestone Pr) Lerner Pubns.

Warburton, Lois. Human Origins: Tracing Humanity's Evolution. LC 92-24990. (Illus.). 96p. (gr. 5-8). 1992. PLB 15.95 (*1-56006-221-5*) Lucent Bks.

Willis, Delta. The Leakey Family: Leaders in the Search for Human Origins. LC 92-12522. (Illus.). 128p. 1992. PLB 16.95 (*0-8160-2605-X*) Facts on File.

MAN, PREHISTORIC

see also Cave Dwellers; Man–Origin and Antiquity; also names of countries, cities, etc. with the subdivision Antiquities, e.g. U. S–Antiquities; etc.

Both, Zilpha. Stories on Rocks. Weinberger, Jane, ed. (Illus.). 80p. (gr. 2-5). 1994. 10.95 (*1-883650-08-9*) Windswept Hse.

Caselli, Giovanni. An Ice Age Hunter. Caselli, Giovanni, illus. LC 91-33261. 32p. (gr. 3-6). 1992. lib. bdg. 12.95 (*0-87226-103-4*) P Bedrick Bks.

Corbishley, Mike. Where People Came From? LC 94-16651. 1995. write for info. (*0-8114-3880-5*) Raintree Steck-V.

Getz, David. The Frozen Man. 1994. write for info. (*0-8050-3261-4*) H Holt & Co.

Lessem, Don. The Iceman. LC 93-31534. (Illus.). 32p. (gr. 2-6). 1994. 14.00 (*0-517-59596-6*); lib. bdg. 14.99 (*0-517-59597-4*) Crown Bks Yng Read.

McCord. Early Man. (Illus.). (gr. 4-6). 1977. (Usborne-Hayes); PLB 13.96 (*0-88110-121-4*); pap. 6.95 (*0-86020-130-9*) EDC.

Parker, Steve. Prehistoric Life. Sergio, illus. LC 92-54452. 64p. (gr. 3-7). 1993. 12.95 (*1-56458-238-8*) Dorling Kindersley.

People of Long Ago. (Illus.). 80p. (gr. k-6). 1986. per set 199.00 (*0-8172-2587-0*) Raintree Steck-V.

Ronen, Avraham. Stones & Bones! How Archaeologists Trace Human Origins. LC 93-2480. (gr. 6 up). 1993. lib. bdg. write for info. (*0-8225-3207-7*, Runestone Pr) Lerner Pubns.

Santrey, Laurence. Prehistoric People. Smolinski, Dick, illus. LC 84-8464. 32p. (gr. 3-6). 1985. PLB 9.49 (*0-8167-0242-X*); pap. text ed. 2.95 (*0-8167-0243-8*) Troll Assocs.

MAN, PREHISTORIC–FICTION

Andrews & McMeel Inc. Staff. Pebbles & Bamm-Bamm's Wedding Album. (ps-3). 1993. 9.95 (*1-878685-62-7*) Turner Pub GA.

Baylor, Byrd. One Small Blue Bead. 2nd ed. Himler, Ronald, illus. LC 90-28160. 32p. (gr. 2-5). 1992. SBE 13.95 (*0-684-19334-5*, Scribners Young Read) Macmillan Child Grp.

Brennan, J. H. Shiva Accused: An Adventure of the Ice Age. LC 90-25888. 288p. (gr. 5 up). 1991. 16.95 (*0-06-020741-8*) HarpC Child Bks.

—Shiva: An Adventure of the Ice Age. LC 89-77654. 192p. (gr. 5 up). 1990. (Lipp Jr Bks); (Lipp Jr Bks) HarpC Child Bks.

—Shiva: An Adventure of the Ice Age. LC 89-77654. 208p. (gr. 5 up). 1992. pap. 3.95 (*0-06-440392-0*, Trophy) HarpC Child Bks.

—Shiva's Challenge: An Adventure of the Ice Age. LC 91-40676. 224p. (gr. 5 up). 1992. 17.00 (*0-06-020825-2*); PLB 16.89 (*0-06-020826-0*) HarpC Child Bks.

Cowley, Marjorie. Dar & the Spear Thrower. (gr. 4-7). 1994. 13.95 (*0-395-68132-4*, Clarion Bks) HM.

Dickinson, Peter. A Bone from a Dry Sea. LC 92-20491. 1993. 16.00 (*0-385-30821-3*) Delacorte.

—A Bone from a Dry Sea. large type ed. LC 93-43769. 1994. pap. 15.95 (*0-7862-0154-1*) Thorndike Pr.

Evarts, Hal. Jay-Jay & the Peking Monster. (gr. 5-9). 1984. 15.25 (*0-8446-6166-X*) Peter Smith.

Hoff, Syd. Stanley. newly illus. ed. Hoff, Syd, illus. LC 91-15034. 64p. (gr. k-3). 1962. 13.00 (*0-06-022535-1*); PLB 12.89 (*0-06-022536-X*) HarpC Child Bks.

—Stanley. newly illus. ed. Hoff, Syd, illus. LC 91-12266. 64p. (gr. k-3). 1978. pap. 3.50 (*0-06-444010-9*, Trophy) HarpC Child Bks.

Matus, Joel. Leroy & the Caveman. LC 92-24647. 144p. (gr. 3-7). 1993. SBE 13.95 (*0-689-31812-X*, Atheneum Child Bk) Macmillan Child Grp.

Sathre, Vivian. J. B. Wigglebottom & the Parade of Pets. O'Neill, Catherine, illus. LC 92-17375. 96p. (gr. 2-6). 1993. SBE 12.95 (*0-689-31811-1*, Atheneum Child Bk) Macmillan Child Grp.

Scieszka, Jon. Your Mother Was a Neanderthal. Smith, Lane, illus. 64p. (gr. 2-6). 1993. PLB 10.99 (*0-670-84481-0*) Viking Child Bks.

Seidler, Tor. The Tar Pit. 160p. 1991. pap. 3.95 (*0-374-47452-4*) FS&G.

Turnbull, Ann. Maroo of the Winter Caves. LC 84-4327. 144p. (gr. 4-7). 1984. 14.95 (*0-89919-304-8*, Clarion Bks) HM.
—Maroo of the Winter Caves. (gr. 4-7). 1990. pap. 4.80 (*0-395-54795-4*, Clarion Bks) HM.
Wood, Audrey. The Tickleoctopus. Wood, Don, illus. LC 93-26868. 1994. 14.95 (*0-15-287000-8*) HarBrace.

MAN IN SPACE
see Manned Space Flight

MANAGEMENT OF CHILDREN
see Children–Management

MANGROVE
Lavies, Bianca. Mangrove Wilderness: Nature's Nursery. Lavies, Bianca, photos by. (Illus.). 32p. (gr. 4 up). 1994. 15.99 (*0-525-45186-2*, DCB) Dutton Child Bks.

MANN, HORACE, 1796-1859
Sawyer, Kem K. Horace Mann. (Illus.). 112p. (gr. 5 up). 1993. PLB 17.95 (*0-7910-1741-9*) Chelsea Hse.

MANNED SPACE FLIGHT
see also Astronauts; Outer Space–Exploration; Space Medicine;
also names of projects, e.g. Gemini Project; etc.
Biel, Timothy L. The Challenger. McGovern, Brian, illus. LC 90-6255. 64p. (gr. 5-8). 1990. PLB 11.95 (*1-56006-013-1*) Lucent Bks.
Bondar, Barbara & Bondar, Roberta. On the Shuttle: Eight Days in Space. 64p. Date not set. PLB 16.95 (*1-895688-12-4*, Pub. by Greey dePencier CN); pap. 8.95 (*1-895688-10-8*, Pub. by Greey dePencier CN) Firefly Bks Ltd.
Murray, Peter. La Lanzadera Espacial. LC 93-17916. (gr. 2-6). 1993. 15.95 (*1-56766-038-X*) Childs World.
Shorto, Russell. How to Fly the Space Shuttle. Keating, Edward, photos by. (Illus.). 48p. (Orig.). (gr. 4-7). 1992. pap. 9.95 (*1-56261-063-5*) John Muir.

MANNERS
see Courtesy; Etiquette

MANNERS AND CUSTOMS
see also Chivalry; Clothing and Dress; Costume; Etiquette; Funeral Rites and Ceremonies; Holidays; Marriage Customs and Rites; Travel
Anderson, Debby. Let's Talk about Children Around the World: God Made Them All. Norton, LoraBeth, ed. Anderson, Debby, illus. LC 94-9161. 32p. (ps-2). 1994. 7.99 (*0-7814-0178-X*, Chariot Bks) Chariot Family.
Branson, Mary K. A Carousel of Countries: Games, Songs, Recipes & Customs from Around the World. (Illus.). 96p. (Orig.). (gr. 1-6). 1986. pap. 5.95 (*0-936625-53-8*, New Hope AL) Womans Mission Union.
Brown, Marc T. & Krensky, Stephen. Perfect Pigs: An Introduction to Manners. LC 83-746. (Illus.). 32p. (ps-3). 1983. 15.95 (*0-316-11079-5*, Joy St Bks); pap. 6.95 (*0-316-11080-9*, Joy St Bks) Little.
Family Ties Series. (Illus.). (gr. 1-3). 1993. PLB 21.95 (*1-881889-46-7*) Silver Moon.
Hallinan, P. K. I'm Thankful Each Day! Hallinan, P. K., illus. 24p. (ps-2). 1989. pap. 4.95 perfect bdg. (*0-8249-8535-4*, Ideals Child) Hambleton-Hill.
Hoving, Walter. Tiffany's Table Manners for Teenagers. Eula, Joe, illus. LC 88-23964. 96p. (gr. 5 up). 1989. Repr. of 1962 ed. 14.00 (*0-394-82877-1*) Random Bks Yng Read.
Knight, Margy Burns. Welcoming Babies. O'Brien, Anne S., illus. LC 94-6854. 19p. (gr. k up). 1994. 14.95 (*0-88448-123-9*) Tilbury Hse.
Le Sieg, Theodore. Come Over to My House. Erdoes, R., illus. LC 66-10686. 72p. (gr. k-3). 1966. Beginner.
Steele, Philip. Between the Two World Wars. LC 94-10692. (gr. 3 up). 1994. text ed. 14.95 (*0-02-726322-3*, New Discovery Bks) Macmillan Child Grp.
Super, Gretchen. Family Traditions. De Kiefte, Kees, illus. 48p. (gr. k-3). 1992. PLB 15.95 (*0-8050-2218-X*) TFC Bks NY.

MANNERS AND CUSTOMS–FICTION
Gray, Nigel. A Country Far Away. LC 88-22360. (Illus.). 32p. (ps-1). 1989. 14.95 (*0-531-05792-5*); PLB 14.99 (*0-531-08392-6*) Orchard Bks Watts.
Huffman, Marlys B. A Cave to Share. Faucheux, Wallace, illus. 22p. (Orig.). 1991. pap. 3.95 (*0-8198-0733-8*) St Paul Bks.
Wildsmith, Brian & Wildsmith, Rebecca. Whose Hat Was That? LC 92-17237. 1993. 6.95 (*0-15-200691-5*); pap. write for info. (*0-15-200690-7*) HarBrace.

MANTLE, MICKEY CHARLES, 1931-
Weber, Bruce. Mickey Mantle: Classic Sports Shots. 1993. pap. 1.25 (*0-590-47024-8*) Scholastic Inc.
Wolff, Rick. Mickey Mantle. Murray, Jim, illus. 64p. (gr. 3 up). 1991. lib. bdg. 14.95 (*0-7910-1181-X*) Chelsea Hse.

MANUFACTURES
see also Machinery; Waste Products
Crump, Donald J., ed. How Things Are Made. LC 79-3242. (Illus.). 104p. (gr. 3-8). 1981. 8.95 (*0-87044-334-8*); PLB 12.50 (*0-87044-339-9*) Natl Geog.
Parker, Steve. How Things Are Made. LC 92-21676. (Illus.). 128p. (ps-3). 1993. 7.00 (*0-679-83695-0*); PLB 11.99 (*0-679-93695-5*) Random Bks Yng Read.
Steele, Philip. Factory Through the Ages. Lapper, Ivan, et al, illus. LC 91-33262. 32p. (gr. 3-6). 1993. PLB 11.89 (*0-8167-2729-5*); pap. text ed. 3.95 (*0-8167-2730-9*) Troll Assocs.

MAO, TSE-TUNG, 1893-
Garza, Hedda. Mao Zedong. (Illus.). 112p. (gr. 5 up). 1988. lib. bdg. 17.95 (*0-87754-564-2*) Chelsea Hse.
Kurland, Gerald. Mao Tse-Tung: Founder of Communist China. Rahmas, D. Steve, ed. LC 75-190232. 32p. (Orig.). (gr. 7-12). 1972. lib. bdg. 4.95 incl. catalog cards (*0-87157-514-0*) SamHar Pr.
Marrin, Albert. Mao Tse-Tung & His China. (Illus.). 284p. (gr. 7 up). 1989. pap. 14.95 (*0-670-82940-4*) Viking Child Bks.
—Mao Tse-Tung & His China. LC 93-3799. 288p. (gr. 7 up). 1993. pap. 5.99 (*0-14-036478-1*, Puffin) Puffin Bks.

MAORIS–FICTION
Lattimore, Deborah N. Punga: The Goddess of Ugly. LC 92-23191. 32p. 1993. 14.95 (*0-15-292862-6*) HarBrace.
Savage, Deborah. A Stranger Calls Me Home. 240p. (gr. 5-9). 1992. 14.45 (*0-395-59424-3*) HM.

MAP DRAWING
see also Atlases
Beasant, Pam & Smith, Alastair. How to Draw Maps & Charts. (Illus.). 32p. (gr. 3 up). 1993. lib. bdg. 12.96 (*0-88110-650-X*, Usborne); pap. 4.95 (*0-7460-1002-8*, Usborne) EDC.
Chapman, Gillian & Robson, Pam. Maps & Mazes: A First Guide to Mapmaking. LC 93-1234. (Illus.). 32p. (gr. 2-4). 1993. PLB 13.40 (*1-56294-405-3*); pap. 6.95 (*1-56294-715-X*) Millbrook Pr.
Mango, Karin N. Mapmaking. Corwin, Judith H., illus. LC 83-25084. 112p. (gr. 4 up). 1984. lib. bdg. 9.29 (*0-671-45518-4*, J Messner) S&S Trade.
Petty, Kate. Maps & Journals. (Illus.). 32p. (gr. 2-4). 1993. pap. 5.95 (*0-8120-1235-6*) Barron.
Ryan, Peter. Explorers & Mapmakers. Molan, Chris, illus. LC 89-31824. 48p. (gr. 4-7). 1990. 14.95 (*0-525-67285-0*, Lodestar Bks) Dutton Child Bks.

MAPLE
Metcalf, Rosamond S. The Sugar Maple. Hearn, James, photos by. LC 82-595. (Illus.). 40p. (gr. 3-5). 1982. pap. 3.50x (*0-914016-87-3*) Phoenix Pub.
Thornhill, Jan. A Tree in a Forest. LC 91-25857. (Illus.). 40p. (ps-3). 1992. pap. 15.00 (*0-671-75901-9*, S&S BFYR) S&S Trade.

MAPS
Aten, Jerry. Maptime... U. S. A. 64p. (gr. 4 up). 1982. 7.95 (*0-86653-093-2*, GA 422) Good Apple.
—Prime Time Maps. Filkins, Vanessa, illus. 64p. (gr. 2-5). 1983. wkbk. 7.95 (*0-86653-108-4*, GA 470) Good Apple.
Baynes, John. How Maps Are Made. (Illus.). 32p. (gr. 5-12). 1987. 12.95x (*0-8160-1691-7*) Facts on File.
Berger, Melvin & Berger, Gilda. The Whole World in Your Hands: Looking at Maps. Quackenbush, Robert, illus. LC 92-18199. (gr. k-3). 1993. 12.00 (*0-8249-8646-6*, Ideals Child); pap. 4.50 (*0-8249-8609-1*) Hambleton-Hill.
Broekel, Ray. Maps & Globes. LC 83-7509. (Illus.). 48p. (gr. k-4). 1983. PLB 12.85 (*0-516-01695-4*); pap. 4.95 (*0-516-41695-2*) Childrens.
Cobb, Annie. Going Places Series, 4 vols. Wilburn, Kathy, illus. (gr. k-3). 1991. Set, 32p. ea. 19.80 (*0-671-31248-0*); Set, 32p. ea. lib. bdg. 27.80 (*0-671-31247-2*) Silver Pr.
—Squirrel's Treasure Hunt. Wilburn, Kathy, illus. 32p. (gr. k-3). 1991. PLB 6.95 (*0-671-70391-9*); 4.95 (*0-671-70395-1*) Silver Pr.
Edson, Ann & Insel, Eunice. Reading Maps, Globes, Charts, Graphs. (gr. 4-6). 1982. wkbk. 2.69 (*0-89525-175-2*) Ed Activities.
Frisch, Carlienne. Destinations: How to Use All Kinds of Maps. LC 93-10577. 1993. 13.95 (*0-8239-1607-3*) Rosen Group.
Hartman, Gail. As the Crow Flies: A First Book of Maps. Stevenson, Harvey, illus. LC 90-33982. 32p. (ps-1). 1991. RSBE 13.95 (*0-02-743005-7*, Bradbury Pr) Macmillan Child Grp.
—As the Crow Flies: A First Book of Maps. Stevenson, Harvey, illus. LC 93-22101. 32p. (ps-1). 1993. pap. 4.95 (*0-689-71762-8*, Aladdin) Macmillan Child Grp.
—As the Roadrunner Runs: A First Book of Maps. Bobak, Cathy, illus. LC 94-13. (ps-1). 1994. 14.95 (*0-02-743092-8*, Bradbury Pr) Macmillan Child Grp.
Kennedy, Christine & Smith, Mark. The Pathfinder's Adventure Kit. Kimber, William, illus. LC 92-34711. 56p. (Orig.). (gr. 4-7). 1993. pap. 15.00 (*0-679-83491-5*) Random Bks Yng Read.
Klawitter, P. Mapworks. LC 92-81914. 48p. (gr. 4-8). 1992. 5.95 (*0-88160-206-X*, LW254) Learning Wks.
Knowlton, Jack. Maps & Globes. Barton, Harriett, illus. LC 85-47537. 48p. (gr. 2-5). 1985. 15.00 (*0-690-04457-7*, Crowell Jr Bks); PLB 14.89 (*0-690-04459-3*) HarpC Child Bks.
—Maps & Globes. Barton, Harriett, illus. LC 85-47537. 48p. (gr. 2-5). 1986. pap. 4.95 (*0-06-446049-5*, Trophy) HarpC Child Bks.
Larson, Russell J. Africa by Four: Coloring Book. (Illus.). 14p. (Orig.). (gr. k-6). 1992. pap. text ed. 1.85 (*1-881087-01-8*) Storm Moutain.
Lye, Keith. Measuring & Maps: Projects with Geography. LC 91-2296. (Illus.). 32p. (gr. 5-8). 1991. PLB 12.40 (*0-531-17325-9*, Gloucester Pr) Watts.
Morris, Scott. How to Read a Map. De Blij, Harm J., intro. by. LC 92-22824. (Illus.). 1993. 15.95 (*0-7910-1812-1*, Am Art Analog); pap. write for info. (*0-7910-1825-3*, Am Art Analog) Chelsea Hse.
Petty, Kate. Maps & Journals. (Illus.). 32p. (gr. 2-4). 1993. pap. 5.95 (*0-8120-1235-6*) Barron.
—Our Globe, Our World. (Illus.). 32p. (gr. 2-4). 1993. pap. 5.95 (*0-8120-1236-4*) Barron.
Porter, Malcolm, contrib. by. The Dillon Press Children's Atlas. LC 93-15593. (Illus.). 96p. (gr. 5 up). 1993. text ed. 16.95 RSBE (*0-87518-606-8*, Dillon) Macmillan Child Grp.
Rand McNally Discovery Atlas of Native Americans. LC 93-39472. 1994. pap. write for info. (*0-528-83678-1*) Rand McNally.
Riffel, Paul. Reading Maps. LC 79-13628. (Illus.). (gr. 7 up). 1973. pap. 8.95 plastic comb bdg. (*0-8331-1300-3*) Hubbard Sci.
Rushdoony, Haig A. Language of Maps: A Map Skills Program for Grades 4-6. (gr. 4-6). 1983. pap. 12.95 (*0-8224-4242-6*) Fearon Teach Aids.
Starkey, Dinah. Scholastic Atlas of Exploration. LC 93-41402. 1994. 14.95 (*0-590-27548-8*, Scholastic Reference) Scholastic Inc.
Stefoff, Rebecca. The Young Oxford Companion to Maps & Mapmaking. (Illus.). 320p. 1994. lib. bdg. 35.00 (*0-19-508042-4*) OUP.
Taylor, Barbara. Be Your Own Map Expert. LC 93-31692. 48p. 1994. 14.95 (*0-8069-0664-2*) Sterling.
—Maps & Mapping: Geography Facts & Experiments. LC 92-23373. (Illus.). 32p. (ps-3). 1993. 10.95 (*1-85697-863-X*, Kingfisher LKC); pap. 5.95 (*1-85697-936-9*) LKC.
Weiss, Harvey. Maps: Getting from Here to There. Weiss, Harvey, illus. 64p. (gr. 2-5). 1991. 14.45 (*0-395-56264-3*, Sandpiper) HM.
Wentrcek, Ginger. Marvelous Maps & Graphs. (gr. 1-3). pap. 5.95 (*0-8224-6332-6*) Fearon Teach Aids.

MAPS, HISTORICAL
see Atlases, Historical

MARCHES FOR NEGRO CIVIL RIGHTS
see Blacks–Civil Rights

MARCONI, GUGLIELMO, MARCHESE, 1874-1937
Morgan, Nina. Guglielmo Marconi. LC 90-1268. (Illus.). 48p. (gr. 5-7). 1991. PLB 12.40 (*0-531-18417-X*, Pub. by Bookwright Pr) Watts.
Tames, Richard. Guglielmo Marconi. LC 89-29277. (Illus.). 32p. (gr. 5-8). 1990. PLB 12.40 (*0-531-14024-5*) Watts.

MARFAN'S SYNDROME
Bernhardt, Barbara A., et al. The Marfan Syndrome: A Booklet for Teenagers. LeHew, Ronald, illus. 20p. 1988. pap. 1.00 (*0-918335-03-5*) Natl Marfan Foun.

MARIHUANA
Cohen, Miriam. Marijuana: Its Effects on Mind & Body. (Illus.). 32p. (gr. 5 up). 1991. pap. 4.49 (*0-7910-0000-1*) Chelsea Hse.
Gunn, Jeffrey. Pen Pals, Vol. 4: Facts about Pot. Wolfe, Debra, illus. (Orig.). (gr. 3). 1990. pap. write for info. (*1-879146-04-5*) Knowldg Pub.
Leahy, Barbara H. Marijuana: A Dangerous "High" Way. rev. ed. Farrell, Lee & Jensen, Rosemary D., eds. Moles, Danna, illus. LC 82-62440. 173p. (Orig.). (gr. 4-9). 1983. pap. 6.95 (*0-9610312-1-2*) B Leahy.
Mann, Peggy & Houlton, Betsy. Ms. Cramm on Pot: The Real Story about Marijuana. Hanson, Eric, illus. 21p. (gr. 6-12). 1991. pap. 1.75 (*0-89486-738-5*, 5512B) Hazelden.
Marijuana. rev. ed. (Illus.). 64p. (gr. 7-12). 1993. PLB 14.95 (*0-8239-1683-9*) Rosen Group.
Stronck, David. Marijuana - The Real Story. Nelson, Mary & Clark, Kay, eds. Ransom, Robert D., illus. 30p. (gr. 5-8). 1987. pap. text ed. 2.95 (*0-941816-36-2*) ETR Assocs.
Tobias, Ann. Pot: What It Is, What It Does. Huffman, Tom, illus. LC 78-10817. 48p. (gr. 3-4). 1979. PLB 12.88 (*0-688-84200-3*) Greenwillow.
—Pot: What It Is, What It Does. Huffman, Tom, illus. LC 78-10817. 48p. (ps up). 1991. pap. 4.95 (*0-688-00463-6*, Mulberry) Morrow.
Zeller, Paula K. Alerta a la Marihuana: Focus on Marijuana. Neuhaus, David, illus. (SPA.). 56p. (gr. 3-7). 1991. PLB 16.40 (*0-516-37354-4*) Childrens.

MARINE ANIMALS
see also Corals; Fishes; Fresh-Water Animals
Aliki. My Visit to the Aquarium. Aliki, illus. LC 92-18678. 40p. (ps-3). 1993. 15.00 (*0-06-021458-9*); PLB 14.89 (*0-06-021459-7*) HarpC Child Bks.
Aquatic Life. LC 92-25074. 176p. 1993. 18.60 (*0-8094-9679-8*); lib. bdg. 24.60 (*0-8094-9680-1*) Time-Life.

a multitude of marine activities. Colorful sea anemones & shy octopuses undulate their tentacles on the sea floor, while orca whales breach & yachts & ferry boats wend their watery ways at the surface. ADVENTURES IN GREATER PUGET SOUND includes concise & definitive information on a host of creatures & boats from wrinkled whelks to eagles to oil freighters. The activities are designed to reinforce text information. The book is illustrated with more than 150 pen & ink drawings. To order: Northwest Island Associates, 444 Guemes Island Road, Anacortes, WA 98221; (206) 293-3721.
Publisher Provided Annotation.

Atkinson, Kathie. The Blue Layer. LC 93-28993. 1994. 4.25 (*0-383-03747-6*) SRA Schl Grp.
—Worms, Wonderful Worms. LC 93-28968. 1994. 4.25 (*0-383-03788-3*) SRA Schl Grp.
Barrett, Norman S. Monsters of the Deep. (Illus.). 32p. (gr. k-4). 1991. PLB 11.90 (*0-531-14150-0*) Watts.
Baskin, Leonard. Leonard Baskin's Miniature Natural History. Baskin, Leonard, illus. 28p. (gr. k up). 1993. Repr. 14.95 (*0-88708-265-3*) Picture Bk Studio.
Berger, Melvin. Stranger Than Fiction: Sea Monsters. 96p. 1991. pap. 2.95 (*0-380-76054-1*, Camelot) Avon.
Carlisle, Madelyn W. Let's Investigate Slippery, Splendid Sea Creatures. Banek, Yvette S., illus. LC 92-45206. 32p. (gr. 3-7). 1993. pap. 4.95 (*0-8120-4974-8*) Barron.
Carwardine, Mark. Water Animals. Young, Richard G., ed. Camm, Martin, illus. LC 89-7879. 45p. (gr. 3-5). 1989. PLB 14.60 (*0-944483-31-3*) Garrett Ed Corp.
Chinery, Michael. Ocean Animals. Robson, Eric, illus. LC 91-53144. 40p. (Orig.). (gr. 2-5). 1992. pap. 4.99 (*0-679-82046-9*) Random Bks Yng Read.
—Questions & Answers about Seashore Animals. LC 93-29428. (Illus.). 40p. (gr. 2-6). 1994. 10.95 (*1-85697-981-4*, Kingfisher LKC); pap. 5.95 (*1-85697-965-2*, Kingfisher LKC) LKC.
Coldrey, Jennifer. Life in the Sea. LC 90-38113. (Illus.). 32p. (gr. 4-7). 1991. PLB 12.40 (*0-531-18360-2*) Watts.
Cole, Joanna. The Magic School Bus on the Ocean Floor. (Illus.). (ps up). 1992. 14.95 (*0-590-41430-5*, 003, Scholastic Hardcover) Scholastic Inc.
Colin, Patrick L. Marine Invertebrates & Plants of the Living Reef. (Illus.). 512p. (gr. 7 up). 1988. lib. bdg. 29.95 (*0-86622-875-6*, H-971) TFH Pubns.
Corey, Donna. Manatee: A First Book. rev. ed. Corey, Donna, illus. Strykowski, Joe, photos by. LC 92-60557. (Illus.). 48p. (ps-6). 1993. pap. 5.00 (*1-882533-15-1*) Star Thrower.
—Manati: Un Libro Inicial. Strykowski, Joe, illus. LC 92-64397. 48p. (ps-6). 1992. pap. 4.95 (*1-879488-01-9*) Sundiver.
Cousteau Society Staff. Manatees. LC 92-34180. (Illus.). (ps-1). 1993. pap. 3.95 POB (*0-671-86566-8*, Little Simon) S&S Trade.
Creatures of the Deep. (Illus.). 48p. (Orig.). (ps-2). 1989. pap. 2.95 (*0-8431-2726-0*) Price Stern.
Curtis, Patricia. Aquatic Animals in the Wild & in Captivity. (Illus.). 64p. (gr. 3-8). 1992. 16.00 (*0-525-67384-9*, Lodestar Bks) Dutton Child Bks.
Cuthbert, Susan. Deep Sea Creatures. (Illus.). 16p. (gr. 1-6). 1992. pap. 1.99 activity bk. (*0-7459-2143-4*) Lion USA.
Darling, Kathy. Manatee: On Location. (Illus.). (gr. 4-7). 1991. 14.95 (*0-688-09031-1*); PLB 14.88 (*0-685-75778-1*) Lothrop.
Deming, Susan. The Ocean: A Nature Panorama. Deming, Susan, illus. 7p. (ps-3). 1992. bds. 5.95 (*0-8118-0158-6*) Chronicle Bks.
Doubilet, Anne. Under the Sea from A to Z. Doubilet, David, photos by. LC 90-1355. (Illus.). 32p. (gr. k-6). 1991. 16.00 (*0-517-57836-0*); PLB 16.99 (*0-517-57837-9*) Crown Bks Yng Read.
Downer, Ann. Don't Blink Now! Capturing the Hidden World of Sea Creatures. (Illus.). 40p. (gr. 5-8). 1991. PLB 14.90 (*0-531-11072-9*) Watts.
Esbensen, Barbara J. Sponges Are Skeletons. Keller, Holly, illus. LC 92-9740. 32p. (gr. k-4). 1993. 15.00 (*0-06-021034-6*); PLB 14.89 (*0-06-021037-0*) HarpC Child Bks.
Fine, John C. Creatures of the Sea. LC 89-34. (Illus.). 32p. (ps-3). 1989. RSBE 14.95 (*0-689-31420-5*, Atheneum Child Bk) Macmillan Child Grp.
Ganeri, Anita. Sea Mammals. Ovendon, Dennis & McGregor, Malcolm, illus. LC 93-19706. 32p. (gr. 4-6). 1993. PLB 19.97 (*0-8114-6159-9*) Raintree Steck-V.
Geistdoefer, Patrick. Undersea Giants. Boucher, Joelle, illus. LC 87-34531. 38p. (gr. k-5). 1988. 5.95 (*0-944589-02-2*, 022) Young Discovery Lib.
Gelman, Rita G. Monsters of the Sea, Vol. 1. (ps-3). 1990. 12.95 (*0-316-30738-6*, Joy St Bks) Little.
Gibson, Barbara & Pinkney, Jerry. Creatures of the Desert World & Strange Animals of the Sea, 2 bks. Crump, Donald J., ed. (Illus.). 20p. (gr. 3-8). 1987. Set. 21.95 (*0-87044-688-6*) Natl Geog.
Greene, Carol. Reading about the Manatee. LC 92-26811. (Illus.). 32p. (gr. k-3). 1993. lib. bdg. 13.95 (*0-89490-424-8*) Enslow Pubs.
Hirschi, Ron. Ocean. (ps-3). 1991. 12.00 (*0-553-07470-9*); pap. 4.99 (*0-553-35214-8*) Bantam.
Holling, Holling C. Pagoo. Holling, Lucille W., illus. (gr. 3-9). 1957. 16.45 (*0-395-06826-6*) HM.
Jacobs, Francine. Sam the Sea Cow. 32p. (gr. 1-3). 1992. lib. bdg. 14.85 (*0-8027-8147-0*); pap. 7.95 (*0-8027-7373-7*) Walker & Co.
Johnson, Jinny. Ocean Wildlife. (Illus.). 24p. (gr. 4-7). 1993. 9.95 (*0-89577-536-0*, Dist. by Random) RD Assn.
Kindersley, Dorling. Sea Animals. LC 91-27724. (Illus.). 24p. (ps-k). 1992. pap. 7.95 POB (*0-689-71565-X*, Aladdin) Macmillan Child Grp.
Kite, Patricia. Down in the Sea: The Sea Slug. LC 93-3765. 1994. write for info. (*0-8075-1717-8*) A Whitman.
Lepthien, Emilie U. Manatees. LC 90-21138. (Illus.). 48p. (gr. k-4). 1991. PLB 12.85 (*0-516-01114-6*); pap. 4.95 (*0-516-41114-4*) Childrens.
Lovett, Sarah. Extremely Weird Sea Creatures. Sundstrom, Mary & Blakemore, Sally, illus. LC 92-18383. 48p. (Orig.). (gr. 3 up). Date not set. pap. 9.95 (*1-56261-077-5*) John Muir.
McNulty, Faith. Dancing with Manatees. Shiffman, Lena, illus. LC 93-7593. 48p. (ps-4). 1994. pap. 2.95 (*0-590-46401-9*) Scholastic Inc.
Mallory, Kenneth. The Red Sea. (Illus.). 48p. (gr. 5-7). 1991. 14.95 (*0-531-15213-8*); PLB 14.90 (*0-531-10993-3*) Watts.
Mark, Sara, ed. The Mystery of the Sunken Treasure: Sea Math. (Illus.). 64p. 1993. write for info. (*0-8094-9994-0*) Time-Life.
Martin, James. Tentacles: Octopus, Squid, & Their Relatives. LC 92-22234. 32p. (gr. 2-6). 1993. 14.00 (*0-517-59149-9*); PLB 14.99 (*0-517-59150-2*) Crown Bks Yng Read.
Milton, Joyce. Whales & Other Creatures of the Sea. Deal, Jim, illus. LC 92-2409. 32p. (ps-4). 1993. PLB 7.99 (*0-679-93899-0*); pap. 2.50 (*0-679-83899-6*) Random Bks Yng Read.
Nayer, Judy. Sea Creatures. Goldberg, Grace, illus. 10p. (ps-2). 1992. bds. 6.95 (*1-56293-222-5*) McClanahan Bk.
Oram, Liz & Baker, R. Robin. Migration in the Sea. LC 91-12765. (Illus.). 48p. (gr. 4-8). 1992. PLB 22.80 (*0-8114-2928-8*) Raintree Steck-V.
Palmer, S. Manaties (Manatees) 1991. 8.95s.p. (*0-86592-672-7*) Rourke Enter.
—Spanish Language Books, Set 4: Mamifero Marino (Sea Mammals, 6 bks. 1991. 53.70s.p. (*0-86592-835-5*) Rourke Enter.
Palmer, Sarah. Sea Mammal Discovery Library, 6 bks, Reading Level 2. (Illus.). 144p. (gr. k-5). 1989. Set. PLB 71.60 (*0-86592-357-4*); PLB 53.70s.p. (*0-685-58759-2*) Rourke Corp.
Pearce, Q. L. Giants of the Deep. Petruccio, Steven J., illus. 48p. (gr. 3-7). 1993. pap. 5.95 (*1-56565-042-5*) Lowell Hse.
Peissel, Michel & Allen, Missy. Dangerous Water Creatures. (Illus.). 112p. (gr. 5 up). 1993. PLB 19.95 (*0-7910-1788-5*, Am Art Analog) Chelsea Hse.
Penny, Malcolm. Exploiting the Sea. LC 90-38112. (Illus.). 32p. (gr. 4-7). 1991. PLB 12.40 (*0-531-18359-9*, Pub. by Bookwright Pr) Watts.
Phillips, Gina. First Facts about Giant Sea Creatures. Persico, F. S., illus. 24p. 1991. 2.98 (*1-56156-084-7*) Kidsbks.
—First Facts about Giant Sea Creatures. Persico, F. S., illus. 24p. 1992. pap. 2.50 (*1-56156-156-8*) Kidsbks.
Pick, C. Undersea. (Illus.). 32p. 1976. PLB 13.96 (*0-88110-437-X*); pap. 6.95 (*0-86020-092-2*) EDC.
Podendorf, Illa. Animals of Sea & Shore. LC 81-38453. (Illus.). 48p. (gr. k-4). 1982. PLB 12.85 (*0-516-01615-6*); pap. 4.95 (*0-516-41615-4*) Childrens.
Posell, Elsa. Whales & Other Sea Mammals. LC 82-4451. (gr. k-4). 1982. 12.85 (*0-516-01663-6*); pap. 4.95 (*0-516-41663-4*) Childrens.
Rabin, Staton. Monster Myths: The Truth about Water Monsters. LC 91-34420. (Illus.). 40p. (gr. 5-8). 1992. PLB 15.90 (*0-531-11074-5*) Watts.
Reinstedt, Randall A. Otters, Octopuses, & Odd Creatures of the Deep. Bergez, John, ed. LC 87-82106. (Illus.). 64p. (gr. 3-6). 1987. casebound 12.95 (*0-933818-21-1*); pap. 8.95 (*0-933818-76-9*) Ghost Town.
Rinard, Judy. Amazing Animals of the Sea. Crump, Donald J., ed. LC 80-8796. (Illus.). 104p. (gr. 3-8). 1981. 8.95 (*0-87044-382-8*); PLB 12.50 (*0-87044-387-9*) Natl Geog.
Roberts, M. L. World's Weirdest Underwater Creatures. LC 93-21053. 1993. PLB 11.89 (*0-8167-3230-2*, Pub. by Watermill Pr); pap. 2.95 (*0-8167-3222-1*, Pub. by Watermill Pr) Troll Assocs.
Sammon, Rick. Hide & Seek under the Sea: A Photo Book of Marine Predator & Prey & the Amazing Tricks They Use in Their Fight for Survival. LC 94-14817. (Illus.). 64p. 1994. 14.95 (*0-89658-254-X*) Voyageur Pr.
Sea Animals. 32p. (Orig.). (ps-1). 1984. pap. 1.25 (*0-8431-1517-3*) Price Stern.
Sea Otters. 1991. PLB 14.95 (*0-88682-415-X*) Creative Ed.
Shale, David & Coldrey, Jennifer. Man-of-War at Sea. LC 86-5703. (Illus.). 32p. (gr. 4-6). 1987. PLB 17.27 (*1-55532-069-4*) Gareth Stevens Inc.
Spizzirri Publishing Co. Staff. Prehistoric Sea Life: An Educational Coloring Book. Spizzirri, Linda, ed. Kohn, Arnie, illus. 32p. (gr. 1-8). 1981. pap. 1.75 (*0-86545-020-X*) Spizzirri.
Steele, Philip. Sharks & Other Creatures of the Deep. LC 91-72484. (Illus.). 64p. (gr. 3 up). 1991. 11.95 (*1-879431-16-5*); PLB 12.99 (*1-879431-31-9*) Dorling Kindersley.
Swanson, Diane. Safari Beneath the Sea: The Wonder World of the North Pacific Coast. Royal British Columbia Museum Staff, photos by. LC 94-1465. 64p. (gr. 4-7). 1994. 16.95 (*0-87156-415-7*) Sierra.
Taylor, Dave. Endangered Ocean Animals. Kalman, Bobbie, ed. (Illus.). 32p. (Orig.). (gr. 3-6). 1992. PLB 15.95 (*0-86505-533-5*); pap. 7.95 (*0-86505-543-2*) Crabtree Pub Co.
Turbak, Gary. Ocean Animals in Danger. Ormsby, Lawrence, illus. 32p. (gr. 1 up). 1994. 14.95 (*0-87358-574-7*) Northland AZ.
Wallace, Karen. Think of an Eel. Bostock, Mike, illus. LC 92-53131. 32p. (ps up). 1993. 14.95 (*1-56402-180-7*) Candlewick Pr.
Wexo, John B. Swimmers. 24p. (gr. 3 up). 1991. PLB 14.95 (*0-88682-390-0*) Creative Ed.
Whyte, Malcolm. Sea Creatures. (Illus.). 32p. (Orig.). (gr. 1-4). pap. 3.95 (*0-8431-1959-4*, Troubador) Price Stern.
Wu, Norbert. Beneath the Waves: Exploring the World of the Kelp Forest. Wu, Norbert, illus. (gr. 3-7). 1992. 12.95 (*0-87701-835-9*) Chronicle Bks.
Wyler, Rose. Seashore Surprises. (Illus.). 32p. (gr. k-3). 1991. lib. bdg. 11.98 (*0-671-69165-1*, J Messner); pap. 4.95 (*0-671-69167-8*) S&S Trade.

MARINE ANIMALS–FICTION

Anderson, Joan. Sally's Submarine. Ancona, George, contrib. by. LC 94-16644. (gr. 4-7). Date not set. write for info. (*0-688-12690-1*); PLB write for info. (*0-688-12691-X*) Morrow Jr Bks.
Coatsworth, Elizabeth. Under the Green Willow. Domanska, Janina, illus. LC 84-1471. 24p. (gr. k-3). 1984. 9.25 (*0-688-03845-X*); PLB 8.59 (*0-688-03846-8*) Greenwillow.
Craft, Mary. Sea Otters Cruz & Slick. Craft, Mary, illus. 24p. (Orig.). (ps-4). 1991. pap. write for info. (*0-9624842-2-9*) M Craft.
Fontenot, Mary A. Clovis Crawfish & the Spinning Spider. LC 86-23778. (Illus.). 32p. (ps-3). 1987. 12.95 (*0-88289-644-X*) Pelican.
Kimmel, Eric A. One Good Tern Deserves Another. LC 94-4505. 160p. (gr. 5-7). 1994. 14.95 (*0-8234-1138-9*) Holiday.
Leditschke, Anna. Tiny Timothy Turtle. McLean-Carr, Carol, illus. 32p. (ps-2). 1991. PLB 18.60 (*0-8368-0667-0*) Gareth Stevens Inc.
Limmer, Milly J. Where Will You Swim Tonight? Fay, Ann, ed. Pittman, Helena C., illus. LC 90-38938. 32p. (ps-1). 1991. 14.95 (*0-8075-8949-7*) A Whitman.
Mannino, Marc P. & Mannino, Angelica L. Marjorie's Magical Tail. LC 93-86041. (Illus.). 32p. (Orig.). (ps-5). 1993. pap. 7.95 (*0-9638340-0-2*) Sugar Sand.
Mulligan, Mark. Manatee: The Screenplay. Thomas, Tim & Zorn, Vic, illus. 121p. (Orig.). (gr. 9-12). 1993. pap. 9.95x (*1-882444-00-0*) Blvd Bks FL.
Ryder, Joanne. A House by the Sea. Sweet, Melissa, illus. LC 93-22149. 32p. (ps up). 1994. 15.00g (*0-688-12675-8*); PLB 14.93 (*0-688-12676-6*) Morrow Jr Bks.
—One Small Fish. Schwartz, Carol, illus. LC 92-21563. 32p. (gr. k up). 1993. 15.00 (*0-688-07059-0*); PLB 14.93 (*0-688-07060-4*) Morrow Jr Bks.
Stevenson, James. Which One Is Whitney? LC 89-34614. (Illus.). 40p. (gr. k up). 1990. 12.95 (*0-688-09061-3*); lib. bdg. 12.88 (*0-688-09062-1*) Greenwillow.
Tate, Suzanne. Crabby's Water Wish: A Tale of Saving Sea Life. Melvin, James, illus. LC 91-60262. 28p. (Orig.). (gr. k-3). 1991. pap. 3.95 (*1-878405-04-7*) Nags Head Art.
—Mary Manatee: A Tale of Sea Cows. Melvin, James, illus. LC 90-60102. 28p. (Orig.). (gr. k-3). 1990. pap. 3.95 (*0-9616344-9-9*) Nags Head Art.
Weir, Bob & Weir, Wendy. Baru Bay. LC 93-23325. (Illus.). 1995. incl. cassette 19.95 (*1-56282-622-0*); PLB 14.95 (*1-56282-623-9*) Hyprn Child.

MARINE BIOLOGY

see also Fresh-Water Biology; Marine Animals; Marine Ecology; Marine Plants; Marine Resources

Ancona, George. The Aquarium Book. (Illus.). 48p. (gr. 3-6). 1991. 14.95 (*0-89919-655-1*, Clarion Bks) HM.
Anson, August. Marine Biology & Ocean Science. (Illus.). 340p. (gr. 9-12). 1990. text ed. 24.95 (*0-9624094-0-5*); pap. text ed. 18.95 (*0-9624094-1-3*) Balaena Bks.
Arnold, Caroline. A Walk on the Great Barrier Reef. Arnold, Arthur, illus. 48p. (gr. 2-5). 1988. pap. 6.95 (*0-87614-501-2*, First Ave Edns) Lerner Pubns.
Baker, Lucy. Life in the Oceans. (gr. 4-7). 1993. pap. 4.95 (*0-590-46132-X*) Scholastic Inc.
Be an Underwater Detective. 40p. (gr. 2 up). 1989. 3.99 (*0-517-68913-8*) Random Hse Value.

Bell, David O. Awesome Chesapeake. Ramsey, Marcy D., illus. 48p. (gr. 3-8). 1994. 11.95 (*0-87033-457-3*) Tidewater.

Berger, Melvin. Life in the Sea. (Illus.). 16p. (ps-2). 1993. pap. text ed. 14.95 (*1-56784-013-2*) Newbridge Comms.

Binato, Leonardo. What Swims in the Sea? 12p. (ps-3). 1993. 4.95 (*1-56566-027-7*) Thomasson-Grant.

Bloch, C. Ocean Life Sticker Book. M. J. Studios Staff, illus. 32p. (Orig.). (gr. k-6). 1993. pap. 3.95 (*1-879424-61-4*) Nickel Pr.

Center for Marine Conservation Staff. The Ocean Book: Aquarium & Seaside Activities & Ideas for All Ages. (gr. k-6). 1989. pap. text ed. 12.95 (*0-471-62078-5*) Wiley.

Cole, Joanna. Magic School Bus on the Ocean Floor. (ps-3). pap. 19.95 (*0-590-72836-9*) Scholastic Inc.

Conway, Lorraine. Marine Biology. 64p. (gr. 5 up). 1982. 7.95 (*0-86653-056-8*, GA 400) Good Apple.

Craig, Janet. What's under the Ocean. Harvey, Paul, illus. LC 81-11425. 32p. (gr. k-2). 1982. PLB 11.59 (*0-89375-652-0*); pap. 2.95 (*0-89375-653-9*) Troll Assocs.

Curran, Eileen. Life in the Sea. Snyder, Joel, illus. LC 84-16190. 32p. (gr. k-2). 1985. lib. bdg. 11.59 (*0-8167-0448-1*); pap. text ed. 2.95 (*0-8167-0449-X*) Troll Assocs.

De Larramendi Ruis, Alberto. Coral Reefs. LC 93-3438. (Illus.). 36p. (gr. 3 up). 1993. PLB 14.95 (*0-516-08384-8*); pap. 6.95 (*0-516-48384-6*) Childrens.

Feeney, Stephanie & Fielding, Ann. Sand to Sea: Marine Life of Hawaii. LC 88-38669. 1989. 12.95 (*0-8248-1180-1*, Kolowalu Bk) UH Pr.

Gunzi, Christiane. Tide Pool. Greenaway, Frank, photos by. LC 92-52823. (Illus.). 32p. (gr. 2-5). 1992. 9.95 (*1-56458-131-4*) Dorling Kindersley.

Gutnik, Martin J. & Browne-Gutnik, Natalie. Great Barrier Reef. LC 94-3029. (gr. 4 up). 1994. write for info. (*0-8114-6369-9*) Raintree Steck-V.

Higginson, Mel. Scientists Who Study Ocean Life. LC 94-6999. 1994. write for info. (*0-86593-371-5*) Rourke Corp.

Jaspersohn, William. A Day in the Life of a Marine Biologist. (Illus.). 96p. (gr. 5 up). 1982. 15.95 (*0-316-45814-7*) Little.

Lavies, Bianca. The Atlantic Salmon. Lavies, Bianca, photos by. LC 91-27990. (Illus.). 32p. (gr. 2-5). 1992. 14.50 (*0-525-44860-8*, DCB) Dutton Child Bks.

McAlarv, Florence & Cohen, Judith L. You Can Be a Woman Marine Biologist. Kate, David A., illus. 40p. (Orig.). (gr. 4-7). 1992. pap. 6.00 (*1-880599-06-6*) Cascade Pass.

McAlary, Florence & Cohen, Judith L. Tu Puedes Ser Biologa Marina. Katz, David A. & Yanez, Juan, illus. (SPA.). 40p. (gr. 4-7). 1992. pap. 6.00 (*1-880599-07-4*) Cascade Pass.

Maidoff, Ilka. Let's Explore the Shore. (Illus.). (gr. 5 up). 1962. 9.95 (*0-8392-3017-6*) Astor-Honor.

Mallory, Kenneth. The Red Sea. (Illus.). 48p. (gr. 5-7). 1991. 14.95 (*0-531-15213-8*); PLB 14.90 (*0-531-10993-3*) Watts.

Mills, Dick. Encyclopedia of the Marine Aquarium. 1988. 12.99 (*0-517-63378-7*) Random Hse Value.

Morris, Dean. Underwater Life. rev. ed. LC 87-16693. (Illus.). 48p. (gr. 2-6). 1987. PLB 10.95 (*0-8172-3214-1*) Raintree Steck-V.

Ocean Life. (Illus.). 64p. 1991. 4.99 (*0-517-05151-6*) Random Hse Value.

Paige, David. A Day in the Life of a Marine Biologist. Ruhlin, Roger, photos by. LC 80-54097. (Illus.). 32p. (gr. 4-8). 1981. PLB 11.79 (*0-89375-446-3*); pap. 2.95 (*0-89375-447-1*) Troll Assocs.

Parker, Steve. Seashore. King, Dave, illus. LC 88-27173. 64p. (gr. 5 up). 1989. 16.00 (*0-394-82254-4*); PLB 16.99 (*0-394-92254-9*) Knopf Bks Yng Read.

Ricciuti, Edward. Crustacea. (Illus.). 64p. (gr. 4-8). 1994. PLB 16.95 (*1-56711-046-0*) Blackbirch.

Sea Creatures. LC 92-54274. (Illus.). 24p. (gr. k-3). 1993. 8.95 (*1-56458-221-3*) Dorling Kindersley.

Sea Life. (Illus.). 20p. (gr. k up). 1990. laminated, wipe clean surface 3.95 (*0-88679-818-3*) Educ Insights.

Sea Life. (Illus.). 16p. (gr. k up). 1990. laminated, wipe clean surface 9.95 (*0-88679-662-8*) Educ Insights.

Seashore Walk. LC 92-50791. (Illus.). 32p. (gr. 3 up). 1993. 5.95 (*1-56138-228-0*) Running Pr.

Selberg, Ingrid. Secrets of the Deep. Fogelman, Phyllis J., ed. McGuiness, Doreen, illus. 12p. (gr. 1-5). 1990. 14.95 (*0-8037-0766-5*) Dial Bks Young.

Seymour, Peter. What Lives in the Sea. (Illus.). 10p. (gr. 2-5). 1985. pap. 8.95 SBE (*0-02-782170-6*, Macmillan Child Bk) Macmillan Child Grp.

Shannon, George. Sea Gifts. Azarian, illus. LC 88-45429. (gr. 2-4). 1989. 11.95 (*0-87923-770-8*) Godine.

Smith, Sue. Exploring Salt Water Habitats. Belcher, Cynthia A., illus. 24p. (Orig.). (gr. 1-5). 1994. big bk. 21.95 (*1-879531-33-X*); PLB 9.95 (*1-879531-46-1*); pap. 4.95 (*1-879531-32-1*) Mondo Pubng.

Swanson, Diane. Safari Beneath the Sea: The Wonder World of the North Pacific Coast. Royal British Columbia Museum Staff, photos by. LC 94-1465. 64p. (gr. 4-7). 1994. 16.95 (*0-87156-415-7*) Sierra.

Thompson, Brenda & Overbeck, Cynthia. Under the Sea. Beisner, Monica, illus. LC 76-22470. 24p. (gr. k-3). 1977. PLB 7.95 (*0-8225-1363-3*) Lerner Pubns.

Twist, Clint. Seas & Oceans. LC 91-18086. (Illus.). 48p. (gr. 4-6). 1991. text ed. 13.95 RSBE (*0-87518-491-X*, Dillon) Macmillan Child Grp.

Waters, John F. Deep-Sea Vents: Living Worlds Without Sun. LC 92-41111. (Illus.). 48p. (gr. 5 up). 1994. 14.99 (*0-525-65145-4*, Cobblehill Bks) Dutton Child Bks.

Wood, Jenny. Under the Sea. Livingstone, Malcolm, illus. LC 91-7484. 32p. (gr. k-3). 1991. pap. 5.95 (*0-689-71488-2*, Aladdin) Macmillan Child Grp.

Wood, John N. Nature Hide & Seek: Oceans. Harrison, Mark, illus. LC 85-73. 24p. (gr. 1-4). 1985. 13.00 (*0-394-87583-4*) Knopf Bks Yng Read.

Wu, Norbert. Fish Faces. LC 92-27343. (Illus.). 32p. (ps-2). 1993. 15.95 (*0-8050-1668-6*, Bks Young Read) H Holt & Co.

—Life in the Oceans. (gr. 4-7). 1991. 17.95 (*0-316-95638-4*) Little.

Zim, Herbert S. & Ingle, Lester. Seashores. Barlowe, Dorothea & Barlowe, Sy, illus. (gr. 5 up). 1955. pap. write for info. (*0-307-24496-2*, Golden Pr) Western Pub.

MARINE BIOLOGY–FICTION

Lewis, Gary A. The Clean-up of Codfish Cove. William Langley Studios Staff, illus. 32p. (gr. k-3). 1994. 5.95 (*1-884506-05-4*) Third Story.

—Shamu's Best Friend. William Langley Studios Staff, illus. 32p. (gr. k-4). 1994. 5.95 (*1-884506-04-6*) Third Story.

Lonergan, Elaine. Sir Winston Walrus & the Great Rescue. William Langley Studios Staff, illus. 32p. (gr. k-3). 1994. 5.95 (*1-884506-06-2*) Third Story.

Montgomery, Raymond A. Journey under the Sea. large type ed. Granger, Paul, illus. 117p. (gr. 3-7). 1987. Repr. of 1977 ed. 8.95 (*0-942545-04-4*); PLB 9.95 (*0-942545-10-9*, Dist. by Grolier) Grey Castle.

Olsen, E. A. Mystery at Salvage Rock. LC 68-16401. (Illus.). 48p. (gr. 3 up). 1970. PLB 10.95 (*0-87783-027-4*); pap. 3.94 deluxe ed. (*0-87783-101-7*); cassette 10.60x (*0-87783-195-5*) Oddo.

Resnick, Jane. All about Training Shamu. (Illus.). 32p. (Orig.). (gr. 1-8). 1994. pap. 3.95 (*1-884506-11-9*) Third Story.

—Shamu's Secrets of the Sea. Lopez, Paul, illus. 12p. (ps-k). 1994. 6.95 (*1-884506-03-8*) Third Story.

Tate, Suzanne. Pearlie Oyster: A Tale of an Amazing Oyster. Melvin, James, illus. LC 89-92226. 28p. (Orig.). (gr. k-3). 1989. pap. 3.95 (*0-9616344-7-2*) Nags Head Art.

Weiss, Ellen. Shamu & His Friends. (Illus.). (ps-k). 1994. 5.95 (*1-884506-00-3*) Third Story.

MARINE ECOLOGY

Armstrong, Beverly. Marine Life - Superdoodles. LC 93-80432. 32p. (gr. 1-6). 1994. 4.95 (*0-88160-227-2*, LW322) Learning Wks.

Collins, Elizabeth. The Living Ocean. Train, Russell E., intro. by. LC 93-26205. 1994. write for info. (*0-7910-1586-6*); pap. write for info. (*0-7910-1611-0*) Chelsea Hse.

Hare, Tony. Polluting the Sea. LC 90-43993. (Illus.). 32p. (gr. 4-8). 1991. PLB 12.40 (*0-531-17290-2*, Gloucester Pr) Watts.

Hogan, Paula. Dying Oceans. LC 91-10216. (Illus.). 32p. (gr. 3-4). 1991. PLB 17.27 (*0-8368-0476-7*) Gareth Stevens Inc.

Morgan, Nina. The Sea. LC 94-9084. (Illus.). 128p. (gr. k-4). 1994. pap. 5.95 (*1-85697-526-6*, Kingfisher LKC) LKC.

Wright, Alexandra. At Home in the Tide Pool. (Illus.). 32p. (ps-4). 1993. 14.95 (*0-88106-483-1*); PLB 15.88 (*0-88106-481-5*) Charlesbridge Pub.

MARINE FAUNA
see Marine Animals

MARINE FLORA
see Marine Plants

MARINE GEOLOGY
see Submarine Geology

MARINE PLANTS
see also Algae; Fresh-Water Plants

Deming, Susan. The Ocean: A Nature Panorama. Deming, Susan, illus. 7p. (ps-3). 1992. bds. 5.95 (*0-8118-0158-6*) Chronicle Bks.

Dewhurst, William. Your First Aquarium Plants. (Illus.). 34p. (Orig.). (gr. 9-12). 1991. pap. 1.95 (*0-86622-112-3*, YF-101) TFH Pubns.

Doubilet, Anne. Under the Sea from A to Z. Doubilet, David, photos by. LC 90-1355. (Illus.). 32p. (gr. k-6). 1991. 16.00 (*0-517-57836-0*); PLB 16.99 (*0-517-57837-9*) Crown Bks Yng Read.

Hall, Howard. The Kelp Forest. Leon, Vicki, ed. (Illus.). 40p. (Orig.). (gr. 5 up). 1990. pap. 7.95 (*0-918303-21-4*) Blake Pub.

Swanson, Diane. Safari Beneath the Sea: The Wonder World of the North Pacific Coast. Royal British Columbia Museum Staff, photos by. LC 94-1465. 64p. (gr. 4-7). 1994. 16.95 (*0-87156-415-7*) Sierra.

Wu, Norbert. Beneath the Waves: Exploring the World of the Kelp Forest. Wu, Norbert, illus. (gr. 3-7). 1992. 12.95 (*0-87701-835-9*) Chronicle Bks.

MARINE RESOURCES
see also Fisheries

Baker, Susan. First Look under the Sea. (Illus.). 32p. (gr. 1-2). 1991. PLB 17.27 (*0-8368-0702-2*) Gareth Stevens Inc.

Conservation of the Sea. LC 93-19872. 1994. write for info. (*0-7910-2102-5*) Chelsea Hse.

Koch, Frances K. Mariculture: Farming the Fruits of the Sea. (Illus.). 56p. (gr. 5-8). 1992. PLB 15.90 (*0-531-11116-4*) Watts.

Markert, Jenny. Ocean Resources. LC 93-12204. (gr. 5 up). 1994. PLB 18.95 (*0-88682-599-7*) Creative Ed.

MARINE ZOOLOGY
see Marine Animals

MARINER PROJECT

Simon, Seymour. Mercury. LC 91-17404. (Illus.). 24p. (gr. k up). 1992. 14.00 (*0-688-10544-0*); PLB 13.93 (*0-688-10545-9*) Morrow Jr Bks.

MARINERS
see Seamen

MARION, FRANCIS, 1732-1795

Zadra, Dan. Frontiersmen in America: Francis Marion. rev. ed. (gr. 2-4). 1988. 14.95 (*0-88682-196-7*) Creative Ed.

MARIONETTES
see Puppets and Puppet Plays

MARITIME DISCOVERIES
see Discoveries (In Geography)

MARKET GARDENING
see Vegetable Gardening

MARKETING (HOME ECONOMICS)
see Shopping

MARKETS
see also Fairs

MARKETS–FICTION

Carlstrom, Nancy W. Baby-O. Stevenson, Sucie, illus. 32p. (ps-3). 1992. 14.95 (*0-316-12851-1*) Little.

Haseley, Dennis. The Thieves' Market. Desimini, Lisa, illus. LC 90-38440. 32p. (gr. 1-5). 1991. HarpC Child Bks.

Rondon, Javier. The Absent-Minded Toad. Corbett, Kathryn, tr. from SPA. Cabrera, Marcela, illus. LC 94-14407. 32p. (ps-1). 1994. 9.95 (*0-916291-53-7*) Kane-Miller Bk.

Williams, Karen L. Tap-Tap. Stock, Catherine, illus. LC 93-13006. (gr. 1-4). 1994. 14.95 (*0-395-65617-6*, Clarion Bks) HM.

MARKSMANSHIP
see Shooting

MARMOTS

Lepthien, Emilie U. Woodchucks. LC 91-35276. (Illus.). 48p. (gr. k-4). 1992. PLB 12.85 (*0-516-01140-5*); pap. 4.95 (*0-516-41140-3*) Childrens.

MARMOTS–FICTION

Johnson, Crockett. Will Spring Be Early or Will Spring Be Late? Johnson, Crockett, illus. LC 59-9424. 48p. (gr. k-3). 1961. PLB 13.89 (*0-690-89423-6*, Crowell Jr Bks) HarpC Child Bks.

MARQUETTE, JACQUES, 1637-1675

Kent, Zachary. Jacques Marquette & Louis Jolliet: Mississippi River Voyagers. LC 92-36888. (Illus.). 128p. (gr. 3 up). 1994. PLB 20.55 (*0-516-03072-8*) Childrens.

MARRIAGE
see also Dating (Social Customs); Domestic Relations; Family; Family Life; Family Life Education; Sex; Sexual Ethics

Almonte, Paul & Desmond, Theresa. Interracial Marriage. LC 91-45251. (Illus.). 48p. (gr. 5-6). 1992. text ed. 12.95 RSBE (*0-89686-749-8*, Crestwood Hse) Macmillan Child Grp.

(*0-9636797-0-8*) Christ Covenant. Wish you had the power to change things? And that you knew how to use that power? Here is a book written especially for pre-teens, teenagers, & young adults to help them understand about love & relationships. It is written in everyday language so it is easy to understand. It's about the greatest love relationship in the whole world. The love that true marriage (the happily ever after kind), is patterned after. THE SINCERE MILK...THAT YOU MAY GROW is written in two parts. Part one is all about the basics of getting to know the one you love & "how to" act on it. Part two is all about "why" & a history of weddings, traditions, covenants, & where they come from. Everyone knows someone who needs to read this book & benefit from it by putting its principles to use every day. It is full of wisdom, power, & revelations, & how to obtain & use them all towards a better life. To order: CCB, Rt. #5, Box #28, Council Bluffs, IA 51503. Add $1.00 P&H. Discounts.
Publisher Provided Annotation.

Buhay, Debra. Black & White of Marriage. 30p. (gr. 12). 1990. pap. 2.00 (*1-878056-04-2*) D Hockenberry.
Center for Learning Network Staff. Marriage: A Shared Sacrament. 65p. (gr. 9-12). 1993. tchr's. ed. 12.95 (*1-56077-286-7*) Ctr Learning.
Everything You Need to Know about Teen Marriage. (Illus.). 1991. lib. bdg. 14.95 (*0-8239-1221-3*) Rosen Group.
Friedrich, Liz. Teen Guide to Married Life. (Illus.). 64p. (gr. 7-12). 1989. PLB 13.40 (*0-531-10836-8*) Watts.
—Teen Guide to Married Life. 1990. pap. 4.95 (*0-531-15209-X*) Watts.
Landau, Elaine. Interracial Dating. LC 92-44814. (gr. 7 up). 1993. lib. bdg. 13.98 (*0-671-75258-8*, J Messner); lib. bdg. 7.95 (*0-671-75261-8*) S&S Trade.
Lindsay, Jeanne W. Caring, Commitment & Change: How to Build a Relationship That Lasts. Crawford, David, photos by. (Illus.). 192p. (Orig.). (gr. 7 up). 1995. 15.95 (*0-930934-92-X*); pap. 9.95 (*0-930934-93-8*); tchr's quide 15.95 (*0-685-75787-0*); wkbk. 2.50 (*0-685-75788-9*) Morning Glory.
—Teenage Couples - Coping with Reality: Handling Money, In-Laws, Babies & Other Details of Daily Life. Crawford, David, photos by. (Illus.). 192p. (Orig.). (gr. 7 up). 1995. 15.95 (*0-930934-87-3*); pap. 9.95 (*0-930934-86-5*); wkbk. 2.50 (*0-930934-88-1*); tchr's guide 15.95 (*0-930934-89-X*) Morning Glory.
Miller, Cynthia P. Challenges of the Heart. Agnew, Tim, illus. LC 90-21432. 144p. (Orig.). 1991. pap. 6.99 (*0-932581-79-X*) Word Aflame.
Mitchel, Sue A. & Hughes, Barbara A. From the Bridegroom with Love. 144p. (gr. 8 up). 1992. pap. 6.95 (*0-9634469-0-8*) Chereb Pub.
Packard, Gwen K. Coping in an Interfaith Family. LC 92-39454. 1993. 14.95 (*0-8239-1452-6*) Rosen Group.
Russell, Bob. Marriage by the Book: Biblical Models for Marriage Today. 112p. (Orig.). 1992. pap. 6.99 (*0-87403-906-1*, 29-03156) Standard Pub.
Sister, Fatimatu. The Do's & Dont's of a Happy Marriage. 16p. (Orig.). 1987. pap. 0.50 (*0-916157-10-5*) African Islam Miss Pubns.

MARRIAGE–FICTION

Balter, Lawrence. The Wedding: Adjusting to a Parent's Remarriage. Schanzer, Roz, illus. 40p. (ps-2). 1989. 5.95 (*0-8120-6118-7*) Barron.
Barnes, Frances. Figaro. Fairbridge, John, illus. LC 93-132. 1994. write for info. (*0-383-03686-0*) SRA Schl Grp.
Bedrock Press Staff. Pebbles & Bamm-Bamm's Wedding Album. 1993. 39.95 (*1-878685-64-3*, Bedrock Press) Turner Pub GA.
Bridesmaids, No. 3. 1993. pap. 3.50 (*0-553-56097-2*) Bantam.
Brooks, Bruce. What Hearts? LC 92-5305. 208p. (gr. 5 up). 1992. 14.00 (*0-06-021131-8*); PLB 13.89 (*0-06-021132-6*) HarpC Child Bks.
Cooper, Ilene. Mean Streak. 192p. (gr. 3-7). 1992. pap. 3.99 (*0-14-034978-2*, Puffin) Puffin Bks.
Crane, Stephen. Bride Comes to Yellow Sky. Johnson, V. C., illus. 40p. (gr. 6 up). 1982. PLB 13.95 (*0-87191-827-7*) Creative Ed.
Delton, Judy. Angel's Mother's Wedding. 128p. (gr. 3-7). 1987. 14.95 (*0-395-44470-5*) HM.
Drescher, Joan. My Mother's Getting Married. (ps-3). 1989. pap. 4.99 (*0-14-054667-7*, Puff Pied Piper) Puffin Bks.
Emecheta, Buchi. The Moonlight Bride. LC 82-17816. 77p. (gr. 6-10). 1983. pap. 6.95 (*0-8076-1063-1*) Braziller.
Freeman, Mary E. The Revolt of Mother. (gr. 5 up). 1992. PLB 13.95 (*0-88682-495-8*) Creative Ed.
Hennessy, B. G. Jake Baked the Cake. Morgan, Mary, illus. 32p. (ps-3). 1992. pap. 3.99 (*0-14-050882-1*) Puffin Bks.
Lindbergh, Anne M. Travel Far, Pay No Fare. LC 91-35886. 192p. (gr. 5-8). 1992. 14.00 (*0-06-021775-8*); PLB 13.89 (*0-06-021776-6*) HarpC Child Bks.
Miklowitz, Gloria D. The Day the Senior Class Got Married. 160p. (gr. 6 up). 1985. pap. 2.75 (*0-440-92096-5*, LFL) Dell.
Muchmore, Jo Ann. Johnny Rides Again. LC 94-19466. 1995. write for info. (*0-8234-1156-7*) Holiday.
Peterson, John. The Littles Have a Wedding. (gr. 4-7). 1993. pap. 2.75 (*0-590-46224-5*) Scholastic Inc.
Porte, Barbara A. Harry Gets an Uncle. Abolafia, Yossi, illus. LC 90-39562. 48p. (gr. k up). 1991. 13.95 (*0-688-09389-2*); PLB 13.88 (*0-688-09390-6*) Greenwillow.
Sharmat, Marjorie W. How to Have a Gorgeous Wedding. 144p. (gr. k-12). 1989. pap. 2.95 (*0-440-93794-9*, LFL) Dell.
Smith, Barry. Minnie & Ginger: A Twentieth-Century Romance. Smith, Barry, illus. LC 90-40330. 32p. (ps-3). 1991. 13.95 (*0-517-58253-8*, Clarkson Potter) Crown Bks Yng Read.
Wolkoff, Judie. Happily Ever after...Almost. 224p. (gr. 5-9). 1984. pap. 2.95 (*0-440-43366-5*, YB) Dell.

MARRIAGE, MIXED–FICTION

Davol, Marguerite. Black, White, Just Right. Trivas, Irene, illus. LC 93-19932. 1993. write for info. (*0-8075-0785-7*) A Whitman.

MARRIAGE COUNSELING

Lindsay, Jeanne W. Teenage Marriage: Coping with Reality. rev. ed. LC 83-19638. (Illus.). 208p. 1988. pap. 9.95 (*0-930934-30-X*) Morning Glory.

MARRIAGE CUSTOMS AND RITES

Bennett, Olivia. Sikh Wedding. (Illus.). 27p. (gr. 2-4). 1991. 12.95 (*0-237-60128-1*, Pub. by Evans Bros Ltd) Trafalgar.
Compton, Anita. Marriage Customs. LC 93-16317. (Illus.). 32p. (gr. 4-8). 1993. 13.95 (*1-56847-033-9*) Thomson Lrning.
Larson, Heidi. Wedding Time. (Illus.). 25p. (gr. 2-4). 1991. 12.95 (*0-237-60146-X*, Pub. by Evans Bros Ltd) Trafalgar.

MARRIAGE CUSTOMS AND RITES–FICTION

Lewin, Hugh. Jafta & the Wedding. Kopper, Lisa, illus. LC 82-12836. 24p. (ps-3). 1983. pap. 4.95 (*0-87614-497-0*) Carolrhoda Bks.
—Jafta's Father. Kopper, Lisa, illus. 24p. (ps-3). 1989. pap. 4.95 (*0-87614-496-2*, First Ave Edns) Lerner Pubns.
McCullers, Carson. Member of the Wedding. (gr. 9-12). 1985. pap. 4.50 (*0-553-25051-5*) Bantam.
Martin, Ann M. Karen's Wedding. (gr. 4-7). 1993. pap. 2.95 (*0-590-45654-7*) Scholastic Inc.
Pascal, Francine. The Wedding. 1993. pap. 3.50 (*0-553-29855-0*) Bantam.
Slightly Off-Center Writers Group, Ltd. Staff. Maid of Honor. 120p. 1994. pap. 6.95 (*1-56721-067-8*) Twnty-Fifth Cent Pr.

Thomas, Charlotte E. Our Little Flower Girl: A Child Has Her First Experience Participating in a Wedding. Jonsson, Deborah, illus. LC 92-72538. 32p. (ps-3). 1992. PLB 16.95 singer-sewn (*0-9633607-0-1*) Golden Rings. Finally, a delightful story written specifically to help little girls selected to take part in a wedding ceremony. While informing them of what their role will entail, it also entertains them with a charming story. The tale begins with her invitation to join the bridal party & proceeds through the many preparations & customs leading up to THE BIG DAY. Her finery is chosen & she discovers it must be ordered, which is a new experience for her. She solicits her friends & their toys to help her practice for her exciting role. The meanings of rehearsal & reception are also made known. An apprehensive child in the beginning ends up eagerly anticipating becoming a bride herself someday. This must have book is beautifully illustrated in full color & contains a page for her photo & one for signatures of the wedding party & special friends. This KEEPSAKE book is available for $19.95 incl. S&H. Please send check or money order payable to: Golden Rings Publishing Co., 6173 Doe Haven Dr., Farmington, NY 14425 or call 1-800-433-6173 for MC/VISA orders.
Publisher Provided Annotation.

—The Ring Bearer's Big Day: A Child Has His First Experience Participating in a Wedding. Jonsson, Deborah, illus. LC 94-79366. 1994. 19.95 (*0-9633607-1-X*) Golden Rings. Finally, a delightful storybook written specifically to help little boys selected to take part in a wedding ceremony. While informing them of what their role will entail, it also entertains them with a charming story about a little boy who is in love with his old sneakers & climbing trees. The tale begins with his invitation to join the bridal party & proceeds through the many preparations & customs leading up to THE BIG DAY. He tries on his tuxedo & tries to convince the salesman he could wear his sneaks, as they are black. His worries are greatly reduced when he finds a kindly neighbor who gives him some insight into the joys of joining the wedding party. In finality, he has a great time & is really proud to have been chosen. This must have book is beautifully illustrated in full color & contains a page for his photo & one for signatures of the wedding party & special friends. This KEEPSAKE BOOK IS AVAILABLE FOR $19.95 incl. S&H. Please send check or money order payable to: Golden Rings Publishing Co., 6173 Doe Haven Dr., Farmington, NY 14425 or call 1-800-433-6173 for MC/VISA orders.
Publisher Provided Annotation.

MARS (PLANET)

Asimov, Isaac, et al. The Red Planet: Mars. rev. & updated ed. (Illus.). (gr. 3 up). 1994. PLB 17.27 (*0-8368-1132-1*) Gareth Stevens Inc.
Baker, David. Exploring Mars. (Illus.). 48p. (gr. 3-8). 1987. PLB 18.60 (*0-86592-404-X*); lib. bdg. 13.95s.p. (*0-685-67598-X*) Rourke Corp.
Berger, Melvin. Discovering Mars: The Amazing Story of the Red Planet. (gr. 4-7). 1992. pap. 3.95 (*0-590-45221-5*) Scholastic Inc.
British Museum, Geological Department Staff. Moon, Mars & Meteorites. (Illus.). 36p. (gr. 7 up). 1986. pap. 5.95 (*0-521-32414-9*) Cambridge U Pr.
Corrick, James A. Mars. (Illus.). 128p. (gr. 7-12). 1991. PLB 13.40 (*0-531-12528-9*) Watts.
Fradin, Dennis B. Mars. LC 88-39122. (Illus.). 48p. (gr. k-4). 1989. PLB 12.85 (*0-516-01164-2*); pap. 4.95 (*0-516-41164-0*) Childrens.
George, Michael. Mars. (ENG & SPA.). (gr. 2-6). 1992. PLB 15.95 (*0-89565-852-6*) Childs World.
Kelch, Joseph W. Millions of Miles to Mars. Byrne, Connell, illus. LC 93-33798. (gr. 3 up). 1995. 17.00 (*0-671-88249-X*, J Messner); pap. 10.95 (*0-671-88250-3*, J Messner) S&S Trade.
Landau, Elaine. Mars. LC 90-13097. (Illus.). 64p. (gr. 3-5). 1991. PLB 12.90 (*0-531-20012-4*) Watts.
Simon, Seymour. Mars. LC 86-31106. (Illus.). 32p. (ps-3). 1987. 13.00 (*0-688-06584-8*); lib. bdg. 12.88 (*0-688-06585-6*, Morrow Jr Bks) Morrow Jr Bks.
—Mars. LC 86-31106. (Illus.). 32p. (gr. k up). 1990. pap. 5.95 (*0-688-09928-9*, Mulberry) Morrow.
Vogt, Gregory L. Mars. LC 93-11219. (Illus.). 32p. (gr. 2-4). 1994. PLB 12.90 (*1-56294-392-8*) Millbrook Pr.
Young, Ruth. A Trip to Mars. Cocca-Leffler, Maryann, illus. LC 89-70936. 32p. (ps-1). 1990. 14.95 (*0-531-05892-1*); PLB 14.99 (*0-531-08492-2*) Orchard Bks Watts.

MARS (PLANET)–FICTION

Ghrist, Julie, illus. Taelly's Counting Adventures: On Mars. 12p. (ps). 1993. 4.95 (*1-56828-028-9*) Red Jacket Pr.
Hamilton, Virginia. Willie Bea & the Time the Martians Landed. LC 83-1659. 224p. (gr. 5-9). 1983. reinforced bdg. 15.00 (*0-688-02390-8*) Greenwillow.
Timlin, William M. The Ship That Sailed to Mars. (Illus.). 104p. (gr. 4-5). 1992. Repr. of 1923 ed. 25.00 (*0-9633212-6-9*) V Wagner Pubns.

MARSHALL, GEORGE CATLETT, 1880-1959

Lubetkin, Wendy. George Marshall. (Illus.). (gr. 5 up). 1990. 17.95 (*1-55546-843-8*) Chelsea Hse.

MARSHALL, THURGOOD, 1908-

Bains, Rae. Thurgood Marshall: Fight for Justice. Griffith, Gershom, illus. LC 92-37302. 48p. (gr. 4-6). 1993. 10. 79 (*0-8167-2827-5*); tchr's. ed. 3.50 (*0-8167-2828-3*) Troll Assocs.

Cavan, Seamus. Thurgood Marshall & Equal Rights. LC 92-12995. (Illus.). 32p. (gr. 2-4). 1993. PLB 12.40 (*1-56294-277-8*); pap. 4.95 (*1-56294-793-1*) Millbrook Pr.

Greene, Carol. Thurgood Marshall: First Black Supreme Court Justice. LC 91-4798. (Illus.). 48p. (gr. k-3). 1991. PLB 12.85 (*0-516-04225-4*); pap. 4.95 (*0-516-44225-2*) Childrens.

Haskins, James. Thurgood Marshall: A Life for Justice. 172p. (gr. 7 up). 1992. 14.95 (*0-8050-2095-0*, Bks Young Read) H Holt & Co.

Hess, Debra. Thurgood Marshall: The Fight for Equal Justice. Gallin, Richard, ed. Young, Andrew, intro. by. (Illus.). 128p. (gr. 5 up). 1990. lib. bdg. 12.95 (*0-382-09921-4*); pap. 7.95 (*0-382-24058-8*) Silver Burdett Pr.

Prentzes, G. S. Thurgood Marshall: Champion of Justice. LC 92-34222. (Illus.). 1993. 13.95 (*0-7910-1769-9*, Am Art Analog); pap. 4.95 (*0-7910-1969-1*, Am Art Analog) Chelsea Hse.

MARSHES

Amsel, Sheri. A Wetland Walk. Amsel, Sheri, illus. LC 92-5105. 32p. (gr. k-3). 1993. PLB 15.40 (*1-56294-213-1*); pap. 6.95 (*1-56294-719-2*) Millbrook Pr.

Caitlin, Stephen. Wonders of Swamps & Marshes. Watling, James, illus. LC 89-4967. 32p. (gr. 2-4). 1990. PLB 11.59 (*0-8167-1765-6*); pap. text ed. 2.95 (*0-8167-1766-4*) Troll Assocs.

Cobb, Vicki. This Place Is Wet. Lavallee, Barbara, illus. 32p. (Orig.). (gr. 2-5). 1993. pap. 6.95 (*0-8027-7399-0*) Walker & Co.

Gore, Sheila. Swamps. Burns, Robert, illus. LC 91-45081. 32p. (gr. 4-6). 1993. PLB 11.59 (*0-8167-2755-4*); pap. text ed. 3.95 (*0-8167-2756-2*) Troll Assocs.

Grace, Theresa. A Picture Book of Swamp & Marsh Animals. Pistolesi, Roseanna, illus. LC 91-16034. 24p. (gr. 1-4). 1992. lib. bdg. 9.59 (*0-8167-2434-2*); pap. text ed. 2.50 (*0-8167-2435-0*) Troll Assocs.

Greenaway, Theresa. Swamp Life. Taylor, Kim & Burton, Jane, photos by. LC 92-53489. (Illus.). 32p. (gr. 2-5). 1993. 9.95 (*1-56458-211-6*) Dorling Kindersley.

Guiberson, Brenda Z. Spoonbill Swamp. Lloyd, Megan, illus. LC 91-8555. 32p. (ps-3). 1992. 14.95 (*0-8050-1583-3*, Bks Young Read) H Holt & Co.

Hirschi, Ron. Save Our Wetlands. Bauer, Irwin A. & Bauer, Peggy, photos by. LC 93-4984. (Illus.). 1994. 17.95 (*0-385-31152-4*); pap. 9.95 (*0-385-31197-4*) Delacorte.

Lavies, Bianca. Mangrove Wilderness: Nature's Nursery. Lavies, Bianca, photos by. (Illus.). 32p. (gr. 4 up). 1994. 15.99 (*0-525-45186-2*, DCB) Dutton Child Bks.

Liptak, Karen. Saving Our Wetlands & Their Wildlife. LC 91-4682. (Illus.). 64p. (gr. 5-8). 1991. PLB 12.90 (*0-531-20092-2*) Watts.

Luenn, Nancy. Squish! A Wetland Walk. Himler, Ronald, illus. LC 93-22628. 1994. 14.95 (*0-689-31842-1*, Atheneum Child Bk) Macmillan Child Grp.

McCormick, Anita L. Vanishing Wetlands. (Illus.). (gr. 5-8). 1995. 14.95 (*1-56006-162-6*) Lucent Bks.

Matthews, Downs. Wetlands. Guravich, Dan, photos by. LC 93-3439. 1994. pap. 15.00 (*0-671-86562-5*, S&S BFYR) S&S Trade.

National Wildlife Federation Staff. Wading into Wetlands. (gr. k-8). 1991. pap. 7.95 (*0-945051-44-1*, 75025) Natl Wildlife.

Rood, Ronald. Wetlands. Donnelly, Marlene H., illus. LC 92-47140. 48p. (gr. 2-5). 1994. 15.00 (*0-06-023010-X*); PLB 14.89 (*0-06-023011-8*) HarpC Child Bks.

Rotter, Charles M. & Taylor, Nicole. Wetlands. LC 92-41339. 1994. 18.95 (*0-88682-594-6*) Creative Ed.

Sabin, Francene. Swamps & Marshes. Flynn, Barbara, illus. LC 84-2717. 32p. (gr. 3-6). 1985. PLB 9.49 (*0-8167-0280-2*); pap. text ed. 2.95 (*0-8167-0281-0*) Troll Assocs.

Staub, Frank. America's Wetlands. LC 94-3872. 1994. write for info. (*0-87614-827-5*) Carolrhoda Bks.

MARSHES–FICTION

Dominick, Bayard. Joe, a Porpoise. (Illus.). (gr. 3-5). 1968. 10.95 (*0-8392-3067-2*) Astor-Honor.

Edler, Timothy J. Coocan: Boy of the Swamp. (Illus.). 40p. (gr. k-8). 1983. pap. 6.00 (*0-931108-09-8*) Little Cajun Bks.

—Dark Gator. (Illus.). 48p. (gr. k-8). 1980. pap. 6.00 (*0-931108-06-3*) Little Cajun Bks.

Erickson, Gina C. & Foster, Kelli C. Frog Knows Best. Gifford-Russell, Kerri, illus. 24p. (ps-2). 1992. pap. 3.50 (*0-8120-4855-5*) Barron.

Guiberson, Brenda Z. Spoonbill Swamp. LC 91-8555. (ps-3). 1994. pap. 4.95 (*0-8050-3385-8*) H Holt & Co.

Porter, Gene S. Freckles. LC 93-42393. 1994. 7.99 (*0-517-10126-2*, Pub. by Gramercy) Random Hse Value.

Vaughan, Marsha K. Whistling Dixie. Date not set. 15.00 (*0-06-021030-3*, HarpT); 14.89 (*0-06-021029-X*, HarpT) HarpC.

Wallace, Bill. Blackwater Swamp. LC 93-28439. 208p. 1994. 15.95 (*0-8234-1120-6*) Holiday.

MARSUPIALIA

Barrett, Norman S. Kangaroos & Other Marsupials. LC 90-42383. (Illus.). 32p. (gr. k-4). 1991. PLB 11.90 (*0-531-14113-6*) Watts.

MARTINIQUE–FICTION

Zobel, Joseph. Black Shack Alley. Warner, Keith Q., tr. from FRE. LC 78-13852. (Illus., Orig.). (gr. 9 up). 1991. 20.00 (*0-914478-67-2*); pap. 12.00 (*0-914478-68-0*) Three Continents.

MARX, HEINRICH KARL, 1818-1883

Kort, Michael. Marxism in Power: The Rise & Fall of a Doctrine. LC 92-15697. (Illus.). 176p. (gr. 7 up). 1993. PLB 16.90 (*1-56294-241-7*) Millbrook Pr.

MARXISM

see Communism

MARY, VIRGIN

Bodker, Cecil. Mary of Nazareth. 1989. 14.95 (*91-29-59178-3*, Pub. by R & S Bks) FS&G.

Father Robert J. Fox. The Day the Sun Danced: The True Story of Fatima. CCC of America Staff, illus. 60p. (Orig.). (gr. k-6). 1989. incl. video 21.95 (*1-56814-001-0*); book 4.95 (*0-685-62401-3*) CCC of America.

Hintze, Barbara. Mary: Mother of Jesus. Padgett, James R., illus. (gr. 1-6). 1977. bds. 5.99 (*0-8054-4232-4*, 4242-32) Broadman.

Hronas, G. H. The Illustrated Life of the Theotokos for Children. 1990. pap. 5.95 (*0-937032-73-5*) Light&Life Pub Co MN.

Lysne, Mary E. Mary & Elizabeth. Gambill, Henrietta, ed. Patterson, Kathleen, illus. 24p. (ps-3). 1993. wkbk. 2.39 (*0-7847-0101-6*, 23-02581) Standard Pub.

Mulqueen, Jack & Chatton, Ray. God's Mother Is My Mother. Chatton, Ray, illus. 28p. (Orig.). (gr. 1-3). 1978. pap. 2.50 (*0-913382-49-3*, 103-13) Prow Bks-Franciscan.

Tangvald, Christine H. Swish, Swish, Went the Giant Fish: And Other Bible Stories about Prayer. Griego, Tony, illus. LC 94-6709. Date not set. write for info. (*0-7814-0929-2*, Chariot Bks) Chariot Family.

Windeatt, Mary F. The Children of Fatima & Our Lady's Message to the World. Harmon, Gedge, illus. LC 90-71828. 161p. (gr. 5-9). 1991. pap. 6.00 (*0-89555-419-4*) TAN Bks Pubs.

—The Miraculous Medal: The Story of Our Lady's Appearances to Saint Catherine of Laboure. Harmon, Gedge, illus. LC 90-71823. 107p. (gr. 5-9). 1991. pap. 5.00 (*0-89555-417-8*) TAN Bks Pubs.

—Our Lady of Banneux. Harmon, Gedge, illus. 32p. (gr. 1-5). 1989. Repr. of 1954 ed. wkbk. 3.00 (*0-89555-364-3*) TAN Bks Pubs.

—Our Lady of Beauraing. Harmon, Gedge, illus. 32p. (gr. 1-5). 1989. Repr. of 1954 ed. wkbk. 3.00 (*0-89555-363-5*) TAN Bks Pubs.

—Our Lady of Fatima. Harmon, Gedge, illus. 32p. (gr. 1-5). 1989. Repr. of 1954 ed. wkbk. 3.00 (*0-89555-357-0*) TAN Bks Pubs.

—Our Lady of Guadalupe. Harmon, Gedge, illus. 32p. (gr. 1-5). 1989. Repr. of 1954 ed. wkbk. 3.00 (*0-89555-359-7*) TAN Bks Pubs.

—Our Lady of Knock. Harmon, Gedge, illus. 32p. (gr. 1-5). 1989. Repr. of 1954 ed. wkbk. 3.00 (*0-89555-362-7*) TAN Bks Pubs.

—Our Lady of la Salette. Harmon, Gedge, illus. 32p. (gr. 1-5). 1989. Repr. of 1954 ed. wkbk. 3.00 (*0-89555-361-9*) TAN Bks Pubs.

—Our Lady of Lourdes. Harmon, Gedge, illus. 32p. (gr. 1-5). 1989. Repr. of 1954 ed. wkbk. 3.00 (*0-89555-358-9*) TAN Bks Pubs.

—Our Lady of Pellevoisin. Harmon, Gedge, illus. 32p. (gr. 1-5). 1989. Repr. of 1954 ed. wkbk. 3.00 (*0-89555-366-X*) TAN Bks Pubs.

—Our Lady of Pontmain. Harmon, Gedge, illus. 32p. (gr. 1-5). 1989. Repr. of 1954 ed. wkbk. 3.00 (*0-89555-365-1*) TAN Bks Pubs.

—Our Lady of the Miraculous Medal. Harmon, Gedge, illus. 32p. (gr. 1-5). 1989. Repr. of 1954 ed. wkbk. 3.00 (*0-89555-360-0*) TAN Bks Pubs.

MARYLAND

Carpenter, Allan. Maryland. new ed. LC 78-14892. (Illus.). 96p. (gr. 4 up). 1979. PLB 16.95 (*0-516-04120-7*) Childrens.

Eagen, Jane & McGinnis, Jeanne. Our Maryland. rev. ed. (Illus.). 288p. (gr. 4). 1992. 22.00 (*0-87905-233-3*, Peregrine Smith) Gibbs Smith Pub.

Fradin, Dennis. Maryland: In Words & Pictures. LC 80-15185. (Illus.). 48p. (gr. 2-5). 1980. PLB 12.95 (*0-516-03920-2*) Childrens.

Fradin, Dennis B. & Fradin, Judith B. Maryland. LC 94-6551. (Illus.). 64p. (gr. 3-5). 1994. PLB 22.00 (*0-516-03820-6*) Childrens.

Johnston, Joyce. Maryland. 72p. (gr. 3-6). 1991. PLB 17. 50 (*0-8225-2713-8*) Lerner Pubns.

Kent, Deborah. Maryland. LC 89-25282. (Illus.). 144p. (gr. 4 up). 1990. PLB 20.55 (*0-516-00466-2*) Childrens.

—Maryland. 184p. 1993. text ed. 15.40 (*1-56956-136-2*) W A T Braille.

Marsh, Carole. Avast, Ye Slobs! Maryland Pirate Trivia. (Illus.). (gr. 3-8). 1994. PLB 24.95 (*0-7933-0569-1*); pap. 14.95 (*0-7933-0568-3*); disk 29.95 (*0-7933-0570-5*) Gallopade Pub Group.

—The Beast of the Maryland Bed & Breakfast. (Illus.). (gr. 3-8). 1994. PLB 24.95 (*0-7933-1690-1*); pap. 14.95 (*0-7933-1691-X*); disk 29.95 (*0-7933-1692-8*) Gallopade Pub Group.

—Bow Wow! Maryland Dogs in History, Mystery, Legend, Lore, Humor & More! (Illus.). (gr. 3-12). 1994. PLB 24.95 (*0-7933-3527-2*); pap. 14.95 (*0-7933-3528-0*); computer disk 29.95 (*0-7933-3529-9*) Gallopade Pub Group.

—Christopher Columbus Comes to Maryland! Includes Reproducible Activities for Kids! (Illus.). (gr. 3-12). 1994. PLB 24.95 (*0-7933-3680-5*); pap. 14.95 (*0-7933-3681-3*); computer disk 29.95 (*0-7933-3682-1*) Gallopade Pub Group.

—The Hard-to-Believe-But-True! Book of Maryland History, Mystery, Trivia, Legend, Lore, Humor & More. (Illus.). (gr. 3-8). 1994. PLB 24.95 (*0-7933-0566-7*); pap. 14.95 (*0-7933-0565-9*); disk 29. 95 (*0-7933-0567-5*) Gallopade Pub Group.

—If My Maryland Mama Ran the World! (Illus.). (gr. 3-8). 1994. lib. bdg. 24.95 (*0-7933-1693-6*); pap. 14.95 (*0-7933-1694-4*); disk 29.95 (*0-7933-1695-2*) Gallopade Pub Group.

—Jurassic Ark! Maryland Dinosaurs & Other Prehistoric Creatures. (gr. k-12). 1994. PLB 24.95 (*0-7933-7488-X*); pap. 14.95 (*0-7933-7489-8*); computer disk 29.95 (*0-7933-7490-1*) Gallopade Pub Group.

—Let's Quilt Maryland & Stuff It Topographically! (Illus.). (gr. 3-8). 1994. PLB 24.95 (*1-55609-622-4*); pap. 14.95 (*1-55609-058-7*); disk 29.95 (*1-55609-623-2*) Gallopade Pub Group.

—Let's Quilt Our Maryland County. 1994. lib. bdg. 24.95 (*0-7933-7173-2*); pap. text ed. 14.95 (*0-7933-7174-0*); disk 29.95 (*0-7933-7175-9*) Gallopade Pub Group.

—Let's Quilt Our Maryland Town. 1994. lib. bdg. 24.95 (*0-7933-7023-X*); pap. text ed. 14.95 (*0-7933-7024-8*); disk 29.95 (*0-7933-7025-6*) Gallopade Pub Group.

—Maryland & Other State Greats (Biographies) (Illus.). (gr. 3-8). 1994. PLB 24.95 (*1-55609-636-4*); pap. 14.95 (*1-55609-637-2*); disk 29.95 (*1-55609-638-0*) Gallopade Pub Group.

—Maryland Bandits, Bushwackers, Outlaws, Crooks, Devils, Ghosts, Desperadoes & Other Assorted & Sundry Characters! (Illus.). (gr. 3-8). 1994. PLB 24.95 (*0-7933-0551-9*); pap. 14.95 (*0-7933-0550-0*); disk 29. 95 (*0-7933-0552-7*) Gallopade Pub Group.

—Maryland Classic Christmas Trivia: Stories, Recipes, Activities, Legends, Lore & More! (Illus.). (gr. 3-8). 1994. PLB 24.95 (*0-7933-0554-3*); pap. 14.95 (*0-7933-0553-5*); disk 29.95 (*0-7933-0555-1*) Gallopade Pub Group.

—Maryland Coastales! (Illus.). (gr. 3-8). 1994. PLB 24.95 (*1-55609-630-5*); pap. 14.95 (*1-55609-631-3*); disk 29. 95 (*1-55609-632-1*) Gallopade Pub Group.

—Maryland Coastales! 1994. lib. bdg. 24.95 (*0-7933-7285-2*) Gallopade Pub Group.

—Maryland Dingbats! Bk. 1: A Fun Book of Games, Stories, Activities & More about Our State That's All in Code! for You to Decipher. (Illus.). (gr. 3-12). 1994. PLB 24.95 (*0-7933-3833-6*); pap. 14.95 (*0-7933-3834-4*); computer disk 29.95 (*0-7933-3835-2*) Gallopade Pub Group.

—Maryland Festival Fun for Kids! (Illus.). (gr. 3-12). 1994. lib. bdg. 24.95 (*0-7933-3986-3*); pap. 14.95 (*0-7933-3987-1*); disk 29.95 (*0-7933-3988-X*) Gallopade Pub Group.

—The Maryland Hot Air Balloon Mystery. (Illus.). (gr. 2-9). 1994. 24.95 (*0-7933-2498-X*); pap. 14.95 (*0-7933-2499-8*); computer disk 29.95 (*0-7933-2500-5*) Gallopade Pub Group.

—Maryland Jeopardy! Answers & Questions about Our State! (Illus.). (gr. 3-12). 1994. PLB 24.95 (*0-7933-4139-6*); pap. 14.95 (*0-7933-4140-X*); computer disk 29.95 (*0-7933-4141-8*) Gallopade Pub Group.

—Maryland "Jography" A Fun Run Thru Our State! (Illus.). (gr. 3-8). 1994. PLB 24.95 (*1-55609-619-4*); pap. 14.95 (*1-55609-620-8*); disk 29.95 (*1-55609-621-6*) Gallopade Pub Group.

—Maryland Kid's Cookbook: Recipes, How-to, History, Lore & More! (Illus.). (gr. 3-8). 1994. PLB 24.95 (*0-7933-0563-2*); pap. 14.95 (*0-7933-0562-4*); disk 29. 95 (*0-7933-0564-0*) Gallopade Pub Group.

—Maryland Quiz Bowl Crash Course! (Illus.). (gr. 3-8). 1994. PLB 24.95 (*1-55609-633-X*); pap. 14.95 (*1-55609-634-8*); disk 29.95 (*1-55609-635-6*) Gallopade Pub Group.

—Maryland Rollercoasters! (Illus.). (gr. 3-12). 1994. PLB 24.95 (*0-7933-5284-3*); pap. 14.95 (*0-7933-5285-1*); computer disk 29.95 (*0-7933-5286-X*) Gallopade Pub Group.

—Maryland School Trivia: An Amazing & Fascinating Look at Our State's Teachers, Schools & Students! (Illus.). (gr. 3-8). 1994. PLB 24.95 (*0-7933-0560-8*); pap. 14.95 (*0-7933-0559-4*); disk 29.95 (*0-7933-0561-6*) Gallopade Pub Group.

—Maryland Silly Basketball Sportsmysteries, Vol. I. (Illus.). (gr. 3-8). 1994. PLB 24.95 (*0-7933-0557-8*); pap. 14.95 (*0-7933-0556-X*); disk 29.95 (*0-7933-0558-6*) Gallopade Pub Group.

—Maryland Silly Basketball Sportsmysteries, Vol. II. (Illus.). (gr. 3-8). 1994. PLB 24.95 (*0-7933-1696-0*); pap. 14.95 (*0-7933-1697-9*); disk 29.95 (*0-7933-1698-7*) Gallopade Pub Group.

—Maryland Silly Football Sportsmysteries, Vol. I. (Illus.). (gr. 3-8). 1994. PLB 24.95 (*1-55609-624-0*); pap. 14.95 (*1-55609-625-9*); disk 29.95 (*1-55609-626-7*) Gallopade Pub Group.

—Maryland Silly Football Sportsmysteries, Vol. II. (Illus.). (gr. 3-8). 1994. PLB 24.95 (*1-55609-627-5*); pap. 14.95 (*1-55609-628-3*); disk 29.95 (*1-55609-629-1*) Gallopade Pub Group.
—Maryland Silly Trivia! (Illus.). (gr. 3-8). 1994. PLB 24.95 (*1-55609-617-8*); pap. 14.95 (*1-55609-042-0*); disk 29.95 (*1-55609-618-6*) Gallopade Pub Group.
—Maryland Timeline: A Chronology of Maryland History, Mystery, Trivia, Legend, Lore & More. (Illus.). (gr. 3-12). 1994. PLB 24.95 (*0-7933-5935-X*); pap. 14.95 (*0-7933-5936-8*); computer disk 29.95 (*0-7933-5937-6*) Gallopade Pub Group.
—Maryland's (Most Devastating!) Disasters & (Most Calamitous!) Catastrophies! (Illus.). (gr. 3-8). 1994. PLB 24.95 (*0-7933-0548-9*); pap. 14.95 (*0-7933-0547-0*); disk 29.95 (*0-7933-0549-7*) Gallopade Pub Group.
—Maryland's Unsolved Mysteries (& Their "Solutions") Includes Scientific Information & Other Activities for Students. (Illus.). (gr. 3-12). 1994. PLB 24.95 (*0-7933-5782-9*); pap. 14.95 (*0-7933-5783-7*); computer disk 29.95 (*0-7933-5784-5*) Gallopade Pub Group.
—Meow! Maryland Cats in History, Mystery, Legend, Lore, Humor & More! (Illus.). (gr. 3-12). 1994. PLB 24.95 (*0-7933-3374-1*); pap. 14.95 (*0-7933-3375-X*); computer disk 29.95 (*0-7933-3376-8*) Gallopade Pub Group.
—My First Book about Maryland. (gr. k-4). 1994. PLB 24.95 (*0-7933-5629-6*); pap. 14.95 (*0-7933-5630-X*); computer disk 29.95 (*0-7933-5631-8*) Gallopade Pub Group.
—Patch, the Pirate Dog: A Maryland Pet Story. (ps-4). 1994. PLB 24.95 (*0-7933-5476-5*); pap. 14.95 (*0-7933-5477-3*); computer disk 29.95 (*0-7933-5478-1*) Gallopade Pub Group.
—Uncle Rebus: Maryland Picture Stories for Computer Kids. (Illus.). (gr. k-3). 1994. PLB 24.95 (*0-7933-4561-8*); pap. 14.95 (*0-7933-4562-6*); disk 29.95 (*0-7933-4563-4*) Gallopade Pub Group.
Reef, Catherine. Baltimore. LC 89-25695. (Illus.). 60p. (gr. 3 up). 1990. text ed. 13.95 (*0-87518-427-8*, Dillon) Macmillan Child Grp.
Rollo, Vera F. Maryland Today: A Geography. (Illus.). 188p. (gr. 4). 1994. 19.50 (*0-917882-37-7*); tchr's. guide, 60p. 10.00 (*0-685-71072-6*) MD Hist Pr.
Seiden, Art. Michael Shows off Baltimore. Seiden, Art, illus. 32p. (gr. 1-5). 1982. 5.95 (*0-942806-01-8*) Outdoor Bks.
Turner Program Services, Inc. Staff & Clark, James I. Maryland. 48p. (gr. 3 up). 1985. PLB 19.97 (*0-86514-434-6*) Raintree Steck-V.
Wilson, Richard & Bridner, E. L., Jr. Maryland: Its Past & Present. 4th ed. 234p. (gr. 4). 1992. casebound 17.75 (*0-917882-34-2*) MD Hist Pr.

MARYLAND–HISTORY

Boyce-Ballweber, Hettie. The First People of Maryland. LC 87-61066. 110p. (gr. 1-6). 1987. casebound 15.00 (*0-917882-24-5*) MD Hist Pr.
Fradin, Dennis B. The Maryland Colony. LC 90-2210. (Illus.). 160p. (gr. 4 up). 1990. PLB 17.95 (*0-516-00394-1*) Childrens.
Marck, John T. Maryland, the Seventh State: A History. 2nd ed. (Illus.). 230p. (Orig.). (gr. 9-12). 1993. pap. 24.95 (*1-884604-02-1*) Creative Impress.
Marsh, Carole. Chill Out: Scary Maryland Tales Based on Frightening Maryland Truths. (Illus.). 1994. lib. bdg. 24.95 (*0-7933-4714-9*); pap. 14.95 (*0-7933-4715-7*); disk 29.95 (*0-7933-4716-5*) Gallopade Pub Group.
—Maryland "Crinkum-Crankum" A Funny Word Book about Our State. (Illus.). 1994. lib. bdg. 24.95 (*0-7933-4868-4*); pap. 14.95 (*0-7933-4869-2*); disk 29.95 (*0-7933-4870-6*) Gallopade Pub Group.
—The Maryland Mystery Van Takes Off! Book 1: Handicapped Maryland Kids Sneak Off on a Big Adventure. (Illus.). (gr. 3-12). 1994. 24.95 (*0-7933-5021-2*); pap. 14.95 (*0-7933-5022-0*); computer disk 29.95 (*0-7933-5023-9*) Gallopade Pub Group.
Schaun, George & Schaun, Virginia. Everyday Life in Colonial Maryland. 130p. (gr. k-12). 1982. casebound 14.75 (*0-917882-11-3*) MD Hist Pr.
Weinberg, Alyce T. Spirits of Frederick. LC 79-54039. (Illus.). 73p. (Orig.). 1979. pap. 3.95x (*0-9604552-0-5*) A T Weinberg.

MASAI

Margolies, Barbara A. Olbalbal: A Day in Maasailand. Margolies, Barbara A., illus. LC 93-19744. 32p. (gr. 1-4). 1994. RSBE 15.95 (*0-02-762284-3*, Four Winds) Macmillan Child Grp.

MASAI–FICTION

Kroll, Virginia. Masai & I. Carpenter, Nancy, illus. LC 91-24561. 32p. (gr. k-2). 1992. RSBE 14.95 (*0-02-751165-0*, Four Winds) Macmillan Child Grp.
Smith, Roland. Thunder Cave. LC 9-19714. 1995. 14.95 (*0-7868-0068-2*); 14.89 (*0-7868-2055-1*) Hyprn Child.

MASERS, OPTICAL

see Lasers

MASKS (FOR THE FACE)

Davies, Kate. Play Mask Book - Wizard of Oz. 12p. (ps-3). 1991. pap. 5.95 (*0-8167-2373-7*) Troll Assocs.
Dubuc, Suzanne. Make up Funny Masks. (Illus.). 32p. (gr. 3-7). 1993. 7.95 (*2-7625-6740-8*, Pub. by Les Edits Herit CN) Adams Inc MA.
Gelber, Carol. Masks Tell Stories. LC 92-15595. (Illus.). 72p. (gr. 4-6). 1993. PLB 15.40 (*1-56294-224-7*); pap. 6.95 (*1-56294-765-6*) Millbrook Pr.
Green, George W. Halloween Book & Masks. Hatter, Laurie, illus. (ps). 1993. Gift box set of 4 bks., 12p. ea. bds. 14.95 (*1-56828-040-8*) Red Jacket Pr.
Green, Jen. Making Masks & Crazy Faces. LC 92-9813. 1992. 12.40 (*0-531-17365-8*, Gloucester Pr) Watts.
Holroyd, Angela. The Big Book of Animal Masks. Anstey, David, illus. 32p. (gr. k-4). 1990. pap. 8.95 heavy card (*0-671-72580-7*, Little Simon) S&S Trade.
—The Big Book of Monster Masks. Anstey, David, illus. 32p. (gr. k-4). 1990. pap. 8.95 heavy card (*0-671-72579-3*, Little Simon) S&S Trade.
Mah, Ronald. North America Animal Masks & Hats. Werges, Rosanne, ed. (Illus.). 48p. (Orig.). (gr. k-4). 1988. pap. 4.95 (*0-9615903-2-7*) Symbiosis Bks.
Morris, Ting & Morris, Neil. Masks. LC 92-32916. 1993. 12.40 (*0-531-14259-0*) Watts.
Robson, Denny A. Masks & Funny Faces. LC 91-75994. (Illus.). 32p. (gr. 2-4). 1992. PLB 11.90 (*0-531-17345-3*, Gloucester Pr) Watts.
Stevenson, Peter. Play Mask Book - Goldilocks & the Three Bears. 12p. (ps-3). 1991. pap. 5.95 (*0-8167-2372-9*) Troll Assocs.
—Play Mask Book: Little Red Riding Hood. 12p. (ps-3). 1991. pap. 5.95 (*0-8167-2370-2*) Troll Assocs.
Supraner, Robyn. Great Masks to Make. Barto, Renzo, illus. LC 80-24077. 48p. (gr. 1-5). 1981. PLB 11.89 (*0-89375-436-6*); pap. 3.50 (*0-89375-437-4*) Troll Assocs.
Valat, Pierre-Marie. Animal Faces: Fifteen Punch-Out Masks. (Illus.). 32p. (ps up). 1988. pap. 17.99 (*0-525-44440-8*, DCB) Dutton Child Bks.

MASONRY

Boy Scouts of America. Masonry. (Illus.). 64p. (gr. 6-12). 1980. pap. 1.85 (*0-8395-3339-X*, 33339) BSA.

MASS COMMUNICATION

see Communication

MASSACHUSETTS

Carpenter, Allan. Massachusetts. new ed. LC 78-3785. (Illus.). 96p. (gr. 4 up). 1978. PLB 16.95 (*0-516-04121-5*) Childrens.
Fradin, Dennis. Massachusetts. LC 91-541. 64p. (gr. 3-5). 1991. PLB 16.45 (*0-516-03821-4*) Childrens.
Higgins, Deck, photos by. A Walk Through Walden Woods. Henley, Don, afterword by. LC 94-1802. 1994. 14.95 (*0-590-48505-9*) Scholastic Inc.
Kent, Deborah. Massachusetts. LC 87-9402. (Illus.). 144p. (gr. 4 up). 1987. PLB 20.55 (*0-516-00467-0*) Childrens.
—Massachusetts. 212p. 1993. text ed. 15.40 (*1-56956-134-6*) W A T Braille.
Marsh, Carole. Avast, Ye Slobs! Massachusetts Pirate Trivia. (Illus.). (gr. 3-8). 1994. PLB 24.95 (*0-7933-0593-4*); pap. 14.95 (*0-7933-0592-6*); disk 29.95 (*0-7933-0594-2*) Gallopade Pub Group.
—The Beast of the Massachusetts Bed & Breakfast. (Illus.). (gr. 3-8). 1994. PLB 24.95 (*0-7933-1699-5*); pap. 14.95 (*0-7933-1700-2*); disk 29.95 (*0-7933-1701-0*) Gallopade Pub Group.
—Bow Wow! Massachusetts Dogs in History, Mystery, Legend, Lore, Humor & More! (Illus.). (gr. 3-12). 1994. PLB 24.95 (*0-7933-3530-2*); pap. 14.95 (*0-7933-3531-0*); computer disk 29.95 (*0-7933-3532-9*) Gallopade Pub Group.
—Carole Marsh Massachusetts Books, 44 bks. (Illus.). (gr. 3-8). 1994. PLB 1027.80 set (*0-7933-1296-5*); pap. 587.80 set (*0-7933-5164-2*) Gallopade Pub Group.
—Christopher Columbus Comes to Massachusetts! Includes Reproducible Activities for Kids! (Illus.). (gr. 3-12). 1994. PLB 24.95 (*0-7933-3683-X*); pap. 14.95 (*0-7933-3684-8*); computer disk 29.95 (*0-7933-3685-6*) Gallopade Pub Group.
—The Hard-to-Believe-But-True! Book of Massachusetts History, Mystery, Trivia, Legend, Lore, Humor & More. (Illus.). (gr. 3-8). 1994. PLB 24.95 (*0-7933-0590-X*); pap. 14.95 (*0-7933-0589-6*); disk 29.95 (*0-7933-0591-8*) Gallopade Pub Group.
—If My Massachusetts Mama Ran the World! (Illus.). (gr. 3-8). 1994. lib. bdg. 24.95 (*0-7933-1702-9*); pap. 14.95 (*0-7933-1703-7*); disk 29.95 (*0-7933-1704-5*) Gallopade Pub Group.
—Jurassic Ark! Massachusetts Dinosaurs & Other Prehistoric Creatures. (gr. k-12). 1994. PLB 24.95 (*0-7933-7491-X*); pap. 14.95 (*0-7933-7492-8*); computer disk 29.95 (*0-7933-7493-6*) Gallopade Pub Group.
—Let's Quilt Massachusetts & Stuff It Topographically! (Illus.). (gr. 3-8). 1994. PLB 24.95 (*1-55609-684-4*); pap. 14.95 (*1-55609-685-2*); disk 29.95 (*1-55609-686-0*) Gallopade Pub Group.
—Let's Quilt Our Massachusetts Town. 1994. lib. bdg. 24.95 (*0-7933-7026-4*); pap. text ed. 14.95 (*0-7933-7027-2*); disk 29.95 (*0-7933-7028-0*) Gallopade Pub Group.
—Massachusetts & Other State Greats (Biographies) (Illus.). (gr. 3-8). 1994. PLB 24.95 (*1-55609-699-2*); pap. 14.95 (*1-55609-700-X*); disk 29.95 (*1-55609-701-8*) Gallopade Pub Group.
—Massachusetts Bandits, Bushwackers, Outlaws, Crooks, Devils, Ghosts, Desperadoes & Other Assorted & Sundry Characters! (Illus.). (gr. 3-8). 1994. PLB 24.95 (*0-7933-0575-6*); pap. 14.95 (*0-7933-0574-8*); disk 29.95 (*0-7933-0576-4*) Gallopade Pub Group.
—Massachusetts Classic Christmas Trivia: Stories, Recipes, Activities, Legends, Lore & More! (Illus.). (gr. 3-8). 1994. PLB 24.95 (*0-7933-0578-0*); pap. 14.95 (*0-7933-0577-2*); disk 29.95 (*0-7933-0579-9*) Gallopade Pub Group.
—Massachusetts Coastales. (Illus.). (gr. 3-8). 1994. PLB 24.95 (*1-55609-693-3*); pap. 14.95 (*1-55609-694-1*); disk 29.95 (*1-55609-695-X*) Gallopade Pub Group.
—Massachusetts Coastales! 1994. lib. bdg. 24.95 (*0-7933-7286-0*) Gallopade Pub Group.
—Massachusetts Dingbats! Bk. 1: A Fun Book of Games, Stories, Activities & More about Our State That's All in Code! for You to Decipher. (Illus.). (gr. 3-12). 1994. PLB 24.95 (*0-7933-3836-0*); pap. 14.95 (*0-7933-3837-9*); computer disk 29.95 (*0-7933-3838-7*) Gallopade Pub Group.
—Massachusetts Festival Fun for Kids! (Illus.). (gr. 3-12). 1994. lib. bdg. 24.95 (*0-7933-3989-8*); pap. 14.95 (*0-7933-3990-1*); disk 29.95 (*0-7933-3991-X*) Gallopade Pub Group.
—The Massachusetts Hot Air Balloon Mystery. (Illus.). (gr. 2-9). 1994. 24.95 (*0-7933-2507-2*); pap. 14.95 (*0-7933-2508-0*); computer disk 29.95 (*0-7933-2509-9*) Gallopade Pub Group.
—Massachusetts Jeopardy! Answers & Questions about Our State! (Illus.). (gr. 3-12). 1994. PLB 24.95 (*0-7933-4142-6*); pap. 14.95 (*0-7933-4143-4*); computer disk 29.95 (*0-7933-4144-2*) Gallopade Pub Group.
—Massachusetts "Jography" A Fun Run Thru Our State! (Illus.). (gr. 3-8). 1994. PLB 24.95 (*1-55609-682-8*); pap. 14.95 (*1-55609-111-7*); disk 29.95 (*1-55609-683-6*) Gallopade Pub Group.
—Massachusetts Kid's Cookbook: Recipes, How-to, History, Lore & More! (Illus.). (gr. 3-8). 1994. PLB 24.95 (*0-7933-0587-X*); pap. 14.95 (*0-7933-0586-1*); disk 29.95 (*0-7933-0588-8*) Gallopade Pub Group.
—Massachusetts' (Most Devastating!) Disasters & (Most Calamitous!) Catastrophies! (Illus.). (gr. 3-8). 1994. PLB 24.95 (*0-7933-0572-1*); pap. 14.95 (*0-7933-0571-3*); disk 29.95 (*0-7933-0573-X*) Gallopade Pub Group.
—Massachusetts Quiz Bowl Crash Course! (Illus.). (gr. 3-8). 1994. PLB 24.95 (*1-55609-696-8*); pap. 14.95 (*1-55609-697-6*); disk 29.95 (*1-55609-698-4*) Gallopade Pub Group.
—Massachusetts Rollercoasters! (Illus.). (gr. 3-12). 1994. PLB 24.95 (*0-7933-5287-8*); pap. 14.95 (*0-7933-5288-6*); computer disk 29.95 (*0-7933-5289-4*) Gallopade Pub Group.
—Massachusetts School Trivia: An Amazing & Fascinating Look at Our State's Teachers, Schools & Students! (Illus.). (gr. 3-8). 1994. PLB 24.95 (*0-7933-0584-5*); pap. 14.95 (*0-7933-0583-7*); disk 29.95 (*0-7933-0585-3*) Gallopade Pub Group.
—Massachusetts Silly Basketball Sportsmysteries, Vol. I. (Illus.). (gr. 3-8). 1994. PLB 24.95 (*0-7933-0581-0*); pap. 14.95 (*0-7933-0580-2*); disk 29.95 (*0-7933-0582-9*) Gallopade Pub Group.
—Massachusetts Silly Basketball Sportsmysteries, Vol. II. (Illus.). (gr. 3-8). 1994. PLB 24.95 (*0-7933-1705-3*); pap. 14.95 (*0-7933-1706-1*); disk 29.95 (*0-7933-1707-X*) Gallopade Pub Group.
—Massachusetts Silly Football Sportsmysteries, Vol. I. (Illus.). (gr. 3-8). 1994. PLB 24.95 (*1-55609-687-9*); pap. 14.95 (*1-55609-688-7*); disk 29.95 (*1-55609-689-5*) Gallopade Pub Group.
—Massachusetts Silly Football Sportsmysteries, Vol. II. (Illus.). (gr. 3-8). 1994. PLB 24.95 (*1-55609-690-9*); pap. 14.95 (*1-55609-691-7*); disk 29.95 (*1-55609-692-5*) Gallopade Pub Group.
—Massachusetts Silly Trivia! (Illus.). (gr. 3-8). 1994. PLB 24.95 (*1-55609-680-1*); pap. 14.95 (*1-55609-110-9*); disk 29.95 (*1-55609-681-X*) Gallopade Pub Group.
—Meow! Massachusetts Cats in History, Mystery, Legend, Lore, Humor & More! (Illus.). (gr. 3-12). 1994. PLB 24.95 (*0-7933-3377-6*); pap. 14.95 (*0-7933-3378-4*); computer disk 29.95 (*0-7933-3379-2*) Gallopade Pub Group.
—My First Book about Massachusetts. (gr. k-4). 1994. PLB 24.95 (*0-7933-5632-6*); pap. 14.95 (*0-7933-5633-4*); computer disk 29.95 (*0-7933-5634-2*) Gallopade Pub Group.
—Patch, the Pirate Dog: A Massachusetts Pet Story. (ps-4). 1994. PLB 24.95 (*0-7933-5479-X*); pap. 14.95 (*0-7933-5480-3*); computer disk 29.95 (*0-7933-5481-1*) Gallopade Pub Group.
—Uncle Rebus: Massachusetts Picture Stories for Computer Kids. (Illus.). (gr. k-3). 1994. PLB 24.95 (*0-7933-4564-2*); pap. 14.95 (*0-7933-4565-0*); disk 29.95 (*0-7933-4566-9*) Gallopade Pub Group.
Norton, Bettina A. Neighborhood Trivia Hunt for Concord, Massachusetts. (Illus.). 20p. (gr. 7-12). 1985. pap. 4.95 (*0-938357-02-6*) BAN Pub Boston.
Turner Program Services, Inc. Staff & Clark, James I. Massachusetts. LC 85-11915. 48p. (gr. 3 up). 1985. PLB 19.97 (*0-86514-435-4*) Raintree Steck-V.
Warner, J. F. Massachusetts. LC 93-37203. (Illus.). 72p. (gr. 3-6). 1994. 17.50 (*0-8225-2737-5*); pap. 5.95 (*0-8225-9666-0*) Lerner Pubns.

MASSACHUSETTS–FICTION

Avi. Emily Upham's Revenge. ALC Staff, ed. Zelinsky, Paul, illus. LC 92-9572. 192p. (gr. 5 up). 1992. pap. 3.95 (*0-688-11899-2*, Pub. by Beech Tree Bks) Morrow.
Corcoran, Barbara. The Hideaway. LC 86-28849. 128p. (gr. 5-9). 1987. SBE 13.95 (*0-689-31353-5*, Atheneum Child Bk) Macmillan Child Grp.
Paterson, Katherine. Lyddie. 240p. (gr. 5-9). 1991. 15.00 (*0-525-67338-5*, Lodestar Bks) Dutton Child Bks.
—Lyddie. LC 92-20304. 192p. (gr. 7 up). 1992. pap. 3.99 (*0-14-034981-2*) Puffin Bks.

Pedicini, John G. Slow Moe. Serino, John, ed. Marderosian, Mark, illus. 32p. (gr. k-2). 1991. 9.95 (*0-9627436-7-4*) Je Suis Derby.

MASSACHUSETTS–HISTORY

Anderson, Joan. The First Thanksgiving Feast. Ancona, George, photos by. LC 84-5803. (Illus.). 48p. (gr. 2-6). 1984. 14.95 (*0-89919-287-4*, Clarion Bks) HM.

Beatty, Jerome. Arctic Rovings: Or the Adventures of a New Bedford Boy on Sea & Land by Daniel Weston Hall. Hogarth, William, illus. LC 91-40359. xiv, 144p. (gr. 7-10). 1992. Repr. of 1968 ed. lib. bdg. 17.50 (*0-208-02324-0*, Pub. by Linnet) Shoe String.

George, Jean C. First Thanksgiving. Locker, Thomas, illus. LC 91-46643. 32p. (ps up). 1993. PLB 15.95 (*0-399-21991-9*, Philomel Bks) Putnam Pub Group.

Glover, Janice. Those Billington Boys: A Pilgrim Story. Howard, Susie, illus. 48p. (Orig.). (gr. 3-6). 1994. pap. text ed. 10.00 (*1-883613-02-7*) Byte Size.

Marsh, Carole. Chill Out: Scary Massachusetts Tales Based on Frightening Massachusetts Truths. (Illus.). 1994. lib. bdg. 24.95 (*0-7933-4717-3*); pap. 14.95 (*0-7933-4718-1*); disk 29.95 (*0-7933-4719-X*) Gallopade Pub Group.

—Massachusetts "Crinkum-Crankum" A Funny Word Book about Our State. (Illus.). 1994. lib. bdg. 24.95 (*0-7933-4871-4*); pap. 14.95 (*0-7933-4872-2*); disk 29. 95 (*0-7933-4873-0*) Gallopade Pub Group.

—The Massachusetts Mystery Van Takes Off! Book 1: Handicapped Massachusetts Kids Sneak Off on a Big Adventure. (Illus.). (gr. 3-12). 1994. 24.95 (*0-7933-5024-7*); pap. 14.95 (*0-7933-5025-5*); computer disk 29.95 (*0-7933-5026-3*) Gallopade Pub Group.

—Massachusetts Timeline: A Chronology of Massachusetts History, Mystery, Trivia, Legend, Lore & More. (Illus.). (gr. 3-12). 1994. PLB 24.95 (*0-7933-5938-4*); pap. 14.95 (*0-7933-5939-2*); computer disk 29.95 (*0-7933-5940-6*) Gallopade Pub Group.

—Massachusetts's Unsolved Mysteries (& Their "Solutions") Includes Scientific Information & Other Activities for Students. (Illus.). (gr. 3-12). 1994. PLB 24.95 (*0-7933-5785-3*); pap. 14.95 (*0-7933-5786-1*); computer disk 29.95 (*0-7933-5787-X*) Gallopade Pub Group.

Smith, M. L., ed. Diary of Ruth Anna Hatch, Woods Hole, 1881. Tappan, Eva M., illus. 1992. text ed. write for info. (*0-9611374-3-6*) Woods Hole Hist.

Stamper, Judith B. New Friends in a New Land: A Thanksgiving Story. Jezierski, Chet, illus. LC 92-18072. 32p. (gr. 2-5). 1992. PLB 18.51 (*0-8114-7213-2*) Raintree Steck-V.

MASSACHUSETTS–HISTORY–COLONIAL PERIOD

Bowen, Gary. One Year at Plimoth Plantation 1626. Bowen, Gary, illus. LC 93-31016. 88p. (gr. 3-7). 1994. 19.95 (*0-06-022541-6*); PLB 19.89 (*0-06-022542-4*) HarpC Child Bks.

Dunnahoo, Terry J. The Plymouth Plantation. LC 93-39625. 1995. text ed. 14.95 (*0-87518-627-0*, Dillon) Macmillan Child Grp.

Fradin, Dennis B. The Massachusetts Colony. LC 86-9753. (Illus.). 160p. (gr. 4 up). 1986. PLB 17.95 (*0-516-00386-0*) Childrens.

Wade, L. Plymouth: Pilgrims' Story of Survival. 1991. 11. 95s.p. (*0-86592-469-4*) Rourke Enter.

Waters, Kate. Samuel Eaton's Day: A Day in the Life of a Pilgrim Boy. Kendall, Russell, photos by. LC 92-32325. (gr. 4 up). 1993. 14.95 (*0-590-46311-X*) Scholastic Inc.

—Sarah Morton's Day: A Day in the Life of a Pilgrim Girl. Kendall, Russell, photos by. (Illus.). 32p. 1991. pap. 4.95 (*0-590-44871-4*, Blue Ribbon Bks) Scholastic Inc.

MASSACHUSETTS–HISTORY–FICTION

Daugherty, James. The Landing of the Pilgrims. LC 80-21430. (Illus.). 160p. (gr. 5-9). 1963. PLB 8.99 (*0-394-90302-1*); pap. 3.95 (*0-394-84697-4*) Random Bks Yng Read.

Harness, Cheryl. Three Young Pilgrims. Harness, Cheryl, illus. LC 91-7289. 40p. (gr. k-5). 1992. RSBE 15.95 (*0-02-742643-2*, Bradbury Pr) Macmillan Child Grp.

Rinaldi, Ann. A Break with Charity: A Story about the Salem Witch Trials. LC 92-8858. 1992. 16.95 (*0-15-200353-3*, Gulliver Bks) HarBrace.

Smith, Mary P. Boy Captive of Old Deerfield. (Illus.). (gr. 5-6). Repr. of 1904 ed. lib. bdg. 20.95x (*0-89190-961-3*, Pub. by River City Pr) Amereon Ltd.

—Boys & Girls of Seventy-Seven. 2nd ed. Silvester, Susan B., ed. Grunwald, C., illus. LC 86-30607. 333p. (gr. 5 up). 1987. Repr. of 1909 ed. 17.00 (*0-913993-08-5*) Paideia MA.

MASSACHUSETTS–POLITICS AND GOVERNMENT–REVOLUTION

Cox, Clinton. The Undying Glory. 176p. 1991. 14.95 (*0-590-44170-1*, Scholastic Hardcover) Scholastic Inc.

MASTERSON, WILLIAM BARCLAY, 1853-1921

Green, Carl R. & Sanford, William R. Bat Masterson. LC 91-29857. (Illus.). 48p. (gr. 4-10). 1992. lib. bdg. 14.95 (*0-89490-362-4*) Enslow Pubs.

MATERIA MEDICA

see also Poisons

MATERIALS

Charman, Andrew. Materials. LC 92-6078. (Illus.). 32p. (gr. 5-8). 1993. PLB 12.40 (*0-531-14232-9*) Watts.

Jennings, Terry. Materials. LC 88-22884. (Illus.). 32p. (gr. 3-6). 1989. pap. 4.95 (*0-516-48405-2*) Childrens.

Morgan, Sally & Morgan, Adrian. Materials. LC 93-31722. (Illus.). 48p. (gr. 5-9). 1994. 14.95x (*0-8160-2985-7*) Facts on File.

Peacock, Graham & Chambers, Cally. The Super Science Book of Materials. LC 93-30779. (Illus.). 32p. (gr. 4-8). 1993. 14.95 (*1-56847-096-7*) Thomson Lrning.

Quinn, John & Kualter, Anne. Materials. LC 93-51024. (Illus.). 32p. (gr. 2-4). 1994. 14.95 (*1-56847-076-2*) Thomson Lrning.

Riley, Peter D. Materials. (Illus.). 48p. (gr. 7-12). 1986. 17.95 (*0-85219-628-8*, Pub. by Batsford UK) Trafalgar.

Taylor, Barbara. Structures & Materials. LC 91-8740. (Illus.). 32p. (gr. 4-6). 1991. PLB 12.40 (*0-531-14186-1*) Watts.

MATERNITY

see Mothers

MATHEMATICAL DRAWING

see Geometrical Drawing; Mechanical Drawing

MATHEMATICAL RECREATIONS

Anno, Mitsumasa. Anno's Magic Seed. LC 92-39309. 1994. write for info. (*0-399-22538-2*, Philomel Bks) Putnam Pub Group.

—Anno's Math Games, No. III. (Illus.). 112p. (ps-3). 1991. 19.95 (*0-399-22274-X*, Philomel Bks) Putnam Pub Group.

Aten, Jerry. Good Apple & Math Fun. 144p. (gr. 3-7). 1981. 12.95 (*0-86653-023-1*, GA 279) Good Apple.

Azzolino, Agnes. Math Games for Adult & Child: Math Games for 2 Through 7-Year-Olds. rev. ed. LC 93-7994. (Illus.). 84p. (Orig.). (ps-2). 1993. Incl. 3 game boards, a set of cards & plastic game pieces. pap. text ed. 20.00 (*0-9623593-4-3*) Mathematical.

Barner, Bob. Space Race. LC 94-13267. (gr. 1 up). 1995. 6.95 (*0-553-37567-9*, Little Rooster) Bantam.

Baxter, Roberta. Number Fun. Sagasti, Miriam, illus. 32p. (ps-2). Date not set. 11.95 (*1-56065-147-4*) Capstone Pr.

Bernstein, Bob. Math Thinking Motivators. 96p. (gr. 2-7). 1988. wkbk. 10.95 (*0-86653-431-8*, GA1049) Good Apple.

Blum, Ray. Math Tricks, Puzzles, & Games. Sinclair, Jeff, illus. LC 93-46750. 96p. 1994. 12.95 (*0-8069-0582-4*) Sterling.

Blum, Raymond. Mathemagic. Sinclair, Jeff, illus. LC 91-22523. 128p. (gr. 4-11). 1991. 12.95 (*0-8069-8354-X*) Sterling.

—Mathemagic. Sinclair, Jeff, illus. LC 91-22523. 128p. (gr. 8 up). 1992. pap. 4.95 (*0-8069-8355-8*) Sterling.

Book, David L. Problems for Puzzlebusters. LC 92-90284. (Illus.). 358p. (gr. 7-12). 1992. 24.95 (*0-9633217-0-6*) Enigmatics.

Bryant-Mole, Karen & Gee, Robyn. Multiplying & Dividing Puzzles. (Illus.). 32p. (gr. 2-6). 1993. pap. 4.95 (*0-7460-1073-7*, Usborne) EDC.

Bureloff, Morris & Johnson, Connie. Calculators, Number Patterns, & Magic. Roes, Ruth, illus. (gr. 4-12). 1977. pap. text ed. 7.95 (*0-918932-49-1*) Activity Resources.

Burns, Marilyn. The I Hate Mathematics! Book. Hairston, Martha, illus. 128p. (gr. 5 up). 1975. 17.95 (*0-316-11740-4*); pap. 10.95 (*0-316-11741-2*) Little.

Callaghan, Steven. Brainercise Mental Exercise Program: Arithmetic, Vol. 1, Bk. 8. large type ed. 25p. (gr. k up). 1991. comb binding 5.00 (*0-925395-23-4*) SGC Biomedical.

—Brainercise Mental Exercise Program: Arithmetic, Vol. 1, Bk. 7. large type ed. 25p. (gr. k up). 1991. comb binding 5.00 (*0-925395-22-6*) SGC Biomedical.

—Brainercise Mental Exercise Program: Arithmetic, Vol. 1, Bk. 9. large type ed. 25p. (gr. k up). 1991. comb binding 5.00 (*0-925395-29-3*) SGC Biomedical.

—Brainercise Mental Exercise Program: Arithmetic, Vol. 1, Bk. 10. large type ed. 25p. (gr. k up). 1991. comb binding 5.00 (*0-925395-30-7*) SGC Biomedical.

—Brainercise Mental Exercise Program: Arithmetic, Vol. 2, Bk. 1. large type ed. 25p. (gr. k up). 1991. comb binding 5.00 (*0-925395-27-7*) SGC Biomedical.

—Brainercise Mental Exercise Program: Arithmetic, Vol. 2, Bk. 3. large type ed. 25p. (gr. k up). 1991. comb binding 5.00 (*0-925395-32-3*) SGC Biomedical.

—Brainercise Mental Exercise Program: Arithmetic, Vol. 2, Bk. 2. large type ed. 25p. (gr. k up). 1991. comb binding 5.00 (*0-925395-31-5*) SGC Biomedical.

—Brainercise Mental Exercise Program: Arithmetic, Vol. 3, Bk. 1. large type ed. 25p. (gr. k up). 1991. comb binding 5.00 (*0-925395-28-5*) SGC Biomedical.

Carroll, Lewis. A Tangled Tale. Frost, Arthur B., illus. LC 87-50437. 208p. (gr. 5-12). 1987. pap. 7.95 (*0-940561-06-9*) White Rose Pr.

Challoner, J. The Science Book of Numbers. 1992. 9.95 (*0-15-200623-0*, Gulliver Bks) HarBrace.

Daniel, Becky. Logic Brain Boosters. (Illus.). 64p. (gr. 1-4). 1992. 7.95 (*0-86653-652-3*, GA1347) Good Apple.

—Math Thinker Sheets. 64p. (gr. 4-8). 1988. wkbk. 8.95 (*0-86653-429-6*, GA1036) Good Apple.

Dobson, Eileen. The First Maths Games File. 40p. (ps-4). 1986. pap. 7.50 (*0-906212-42-1*, Pub. by Tarquin UK) Parkwest Pubns.

Egsgard, John, et al. Making Connections: With Mathematics. (Illus.). 102p. (gr. 9-12). 1989. pap. 19. 95 (*0-939765-27-6*, G116) Janson Pubns.

Fun with Numbers. 1992. pap. 1.95 (*0-590-45058-1*) Scholastic Inc.

Giblin, Peter, ed. Mathematical Challenges: Puzzles & Problems in Secondary School Mathematics. (Illus.). 59p. (gr. 9-12). 1989. pap. 19.95 (*0-939765-28-4*, G118) Janson Pubns.

Ginns, Russell. Puzzlooney: Really Ridiculous Math Puzzles. LC 93-42178. 1994. pap. text ed. write for info. (*0-7167-6532-2*, Sci Am Yng Rdrs) W H Freeman.

Griffiths, Rose. Games. Millard, Peter, photos by. LC 94-10038. (Illus.). 32p. (gr. 1 up). 1994. PLB 17.27 (*0-8368-1111-9*) Gareth Stevens Inc.

Heafford, Philip. Great Book of Math Puzzles. LC 93-25890. (Illus.). 96p. (gr. 10-12). 1993. pap. 4.95 (*0-8069-8814-2*) Sterling.

Helwig, Barbara & Stewart, Susan. Math Mysteries. (Illus.). 40p. (gr. 2-5). 1991. spiral bound 4.95 (*1-881285-00-6*) Arbus Pub.

—Math Mysteries. rev. ed. (Illus.). 90p. (gr. 2-6). 1992. spiral bdg. 4.95 (*1-881285-03-0*) Arbus Pub.

Hewavisenti, Lakshmi. Counting. LC 91-9189. (Illus.). 32p. (gr. k-4). 1991. PLB 11.90 (*0-531-17266-X*, Gloucester Pr) Watts.

Hovanec, Helene. Numbzzles. 48p. (Orig.). (gr. 2 up). 1993. pap. 2.95 incl. chipboard (*0-8431-3493-3*) Price Stern.

Kallen, Stuart A. Mathmagical Fun. LC 92-14777. 1992. 12.94 (*1-56239-129-1*) Abdo & Dghtrs.

McCarthy, Donald. Fun with Math-E-Magic. Cooper, William H., ed. McCarthy, Donald W., illus. 65p. (gr. 4-9). 1984. pap. 2.60 (*0-914127-01-2*) Univ Class.

Mark, Sara, ed. Mystery Mansion: House Math. LC 93-25398. (Illus.). 64p. (gr. k-2). 1993. write for info. (*0-8094-9986-X*) Time-Life.

Norman, L. C. Mathland: The Expert Version. (Illus.). 80p. Date not set. pap. write for info. (*0-521-46802-7*) Cambridge U Pr.

—Mathland: The Novice Version. (Illus.). 88p. 1995. pap. write for info. (*0-521-46801-9*) Cambridge U Pr.

Plonsky, Lydia, et al. Math for the Very Young: A Handbook of Activities for Parents & Children. LC 94-20861. 1995. write for info. (*0-471-01671-3*); pap. write for info. (*0-471-01647-0*) Wiley.

Ross, Catherine S. Circles: Fun Ideas for Getting A-Round in Math. Slavin, Bill, illus. LC 92-40159. (gr. 4-7). 1993. pap. 9.57 (*0-201-62268-8*) Addison-Wesley.

Smoothey, Marion. Circles. Evans, Ted, illus. 64p. (gr. 4-8). 1992. text ed. 16.95 (*1-85435-456-6*) Marshall Cavendish.

—Number Patterns. Evans, Ted, illus. 64p. (gr. 4-8). 1992. text ed. 16.95 (*1-85435-458-2*) Marshall Cavendish.

—Numbers. Evans, Ted, illus. 64p. (gr. 4-8). 1992. text ed. 16.95 (*1-85435-457-4*) Marshall Cavendish.

Spizman, Robyn. Bulletin Boards: To Reinforce Basic Math Skills. Pesiri, Evelyn, illus. 64p. (gr. k-6). 1984. wkbk. 7.95 (*0-86653-208-0*, GA 573) Good Apple.

Time-Life Bks. Editors. Alice in Numberland: Fantasy Math. Mark, Sara, et al, eds. LC 93-9136. (Illus.). 64p. (ps-4). 1993. write for info. (*0-8094-9978-9*); lib. bdg. write for info. (*0-8094-9979-7*) Time-Life.

Time Life Inc. Editors. From Head to Toe: Body Math. Crawford, Jean B. & Daniels, Patricia, eds. LC 92-34974. (Illus.). 64p. (gr. k-2). 1993. write for info. (*0-8094-9966-5*); PLB write for info. (*0-8094-9967-3*) Time-Life.

—Look Both Ways: City Math. Crawford, Jean B., et al, eds. (Illus.). 64p. (gr. k-2). 1992. write for info. (*0-8094-9958-4*); lib. bdg. write for info. (*0-8094-9959-2*) Time-Life.

Time-Life Inc. Editors. Play Ball: Sports Math. Mark, Sara, et al, eds. (Illus.). 64p. (gr. k-4). 1993. write for info. (*0-8094-9970-3*); lib. bdg. write for info. (*0-8094-9971-1*) Time-Life.

Time Life Inc. Editors. The Search for the Mystery Planet: Space Math. Crawford, Jean B., ed. (Illus.). 64p. (gr. k-2). 1993. write for info. (*0-8094-9982-7*); lib. bdg. write for info. (*0-8094-9983-5*) Time-Life.

Time-Life Inc. Editors. See You Later Escalator: Mall Math. Crawford, Jean B., et al, eds. LC 93-6494. (Illus.). 64p. (gr. k-2). 1993. write for info. (*0-8094-9974-6*); PLB write for info. (*0-8094-9975-4*) Time-Life.

Time Life Inc Staff. Right in Your Own Backyard: Nature Math. Ward, Elizabeth, et al, eds. LC 92-27222. (Illus.). 64p. (gr. k-4). 1992. write for info. (*0-8094-9962-2*); PLB write for info. (*0-8094-9963-0*) Time-Life.

Valentine. Educational Play: Math. (gr. 4-6). 1992. 8.00 (*0-89824-140-5*) Trillium Pr.

VanCleave, Janice. Janice VanCleave's Geometry for Every Kid: Easy Activities That Make Learning Geometry Fun. LC 93-43049. 1994. text ed. 24.95 (*0-471-31142-1*); pap. text ed. 10.95 (*0-471-31141-3*) Wiley.

Warren, Jean. One-Two-Three Math: Pre-Math Activities for Working with Young Children. Ekberg, Marion, illus. LC 92-80528. 160p. (Orig.). (ps-1). 1992. 14.95 (*0-911019-52-9*) Warren Pub Hse.

Wyler, Rose & Elting, Mary. Math Fun: Test Your Luck. LC 91-3919. (Illus.). 64p. (gr. 4-7). 1992. lib. bdg. 10. 98 (*0-671-74311-2*, J Messner); pap. 5.95 (*0-671-74312-0*, J Messner) S&S Trade.

—Math Fun: With Pocket Calculator. LC 91-16265. (Illus.). 64p. (gr. 4-7). 1992. PLB 10.98 (*0-671-74308-2*, J Messner); pap. 5.95 (*0-671-74309-0*, J Messner) S&S Trade.

MATHEMATICAL SETS

see Set Theory

MATHEMATICIANS

Reimer, Luetta & Reimer, Wilbert. Mathematicians Are People, Too: Stories from the Lives of Great Mathematicians. (Illus.). 143p. (Orig.). (gr. 3-10). 1990. pap. 11.95 (*0-86651-509-7*, DS01032) Seymour Pubns.

—Mathematicians Are People, Too, Vol. 2: Stories from the Lives of Great Mathematicians. (Illus.). 150p. (Orig.). (gr. 3 up). 1994. pap. 11.95 (*0-86651-823-1*, DS21326) Seymour Pubns.

MATHEMATICS

see also Algebra; Arithmetic; Calculus; Geometry; Mechanics; Mensuration; Numbers Theory; Set Theory; Trigonometry

Adair, R., et al. Brinca de Alegria Hacia la Primavera con las Matematicas y Ciencias. (SPA & ENG.). 94p. (gr. k-1). 1988. pap. text ed. 16.95 (*1-881431-21-5*) AIMS Educ Fnd.

—Caete de Gusto Hacid el Otono con las Matematicas y Ciencias. (SPA & ENG.). 116p. (gr. k-1). 1988. pap. text ed. 16.95 (*1-881431-19-3*) AIMS Educ Fnd.

—Patine al Invierno con Matematicas y Ciencias. (SPA & ENG.). 105p. (gr. k-1). 1988. pap. text ed. 16.95 (*1-881431-20-7*) AIMS Educ Fnd.

Alberti, Delbert & Mason, George. Laboratory Laughter. Firmhand, Zelda, illus. (Orig.). (gr. 2-9). 1974. pap. 7.95 (*0-918932-25-4*) Activity Resources.

Allasio, John, et al. Sequential Math 2: A Workbook. 141p. (gr. 9-12). 1990. pap. 7.95 (*0-937820-65-2*); answer key 3.25 (*0-937820-66-0*) Westsea Pub.

—Sequential Math 3: A Workbook. 156p. (gr. 10-12). 1993. pap. 7.95 (*0-937820-67-9*); answer key 3.25 (*0-937820-68-7*) Westsea Pub.

Analysis. (gr. 7-12). 1991. pap. 6.95 (*0-941008-80-0*) Tops Learning.

Anno, Mitsumasa. Anno's Math Games. 104p. (ps-3). 1987. 19.95 (*0-399-21151-9*, Philomel Bks) Putnam Pub Group.

—Anno's Math Games II. Anno, Mitsumasa, illus. 104p. (gr. 1-4). 1989. 19.95 (*0-399-21615-4*, Philomel Bks) Putnam Pub Group.

Aten, Jerry. Prime Time Math Skills. Filkins, Vanessa, illus. 64p. (gr. 2-5). 1984. wkbk. 8.95 (*0-86653-155-6*, GA 524) Good Apple.

Aydelott, Jimmie. Art & Math Throughout the Year. (gr. 1-6). 1989. pap. 8.95 (*0-8224-0104-5*) Fearon Teach Aids.

Azzolino, Agnes. Math Games for the Young Child. Vinik, Michael, illus. (Orig.). (ps-2). 1987. pap. text ed. 8.40 (*0-9623593-1-9*) Mathematical.

Bank Street College of Education Editors. Let's Do Math. (gr. 1-2). 1986. pap. 3.95 (*0-8120-3627-1*) Barron.

Baxter, Roberta. The Shape of Your World. Sagasti, Miriam, illus. 32p. (ps-2). Date not set. 11.95 (*1-56065-144-X*) Capstone Pr.

Becker, Jan, et al. Enhance Chance. (Illus., Orig.). (gr. k-9). 1973. pap. 7.95 (*0-918932-10-6*) Activity Resources.

Bell, Jo G. The Day Small Circle Changed His Shape. Conahan, Carolyn, illus. 32p. (ps-2). Date not set. 11. 95 (*1-56065-160-1*) Capstone Pr.

Bernstein, Bob. Mathemativities. 112p. (gr. 2-7). 1991. 10.95 (*0-86653-617-5*, GA1336) Good Apple.

Blakely, April. Middle School Math Challenge. 144p. (gr. 6-9). Date not set. 7.95 (*0-88160-267-1*, LW1010) Learning Wks.

Bloom, Edgar B. It All Starts with Counting: A Short Guide to Old-Fashioned Arithmetic & Other Mathematical Concepts. Holliman, Mary C., ed. viii, 122p. (Orig.). (gr. 6-12). 1993. pap. 10.00 (*0-936015-26-8*) Pocahontas Pr.

Bogad, Carolyn. Fraction Fantasy. (gr. 5-7). 1979. pap. 3.95 (*0-88160-067-9*, LW 707) Learning Wks.

Bold, Ethan. The Flip Chart of Math Tips. Bold, Mary, ed. 20p. (Orig.). (gr. 6-7). 1992. pap. 10.00 (*0-938267-09-4*) Bold Prodns.

Brooks, Lloyd D., et al. Business Mathematics. 10th ed. 576p. (gr. 9-12). 1987. text ed. 24.96 (*0-07-008166-2*) McGraw.

Bryant-Mole, K. Chart & Graph Puzzles. (Illus.). 32p. (gr. 1-5). 1994. pap. 4.95 (*0-7460-1724-3*, Usborne) EDC.

Bulloch, Ivan. Games. LC 94-6461. (Illus.). 32p. (gr. k-3). 1994. 14.95 (*1-56847-231-5*) Thomson Lrning.

—Patterns. LC 94-7414. (Illus.). 32p. (gr. k-3). 1994. 14. 95 (*1-56847-230-7*) Thomson Lrning.

Burk, Donna, et al. Math Excursions K: Project-Based Mathematics for Kindergartners. 2nd & rev. ed. (Illus.). (gr. k). pap. text ed. 29.50 (*0-685-70397-5*, 08345) Heinemann.

Burma-Washington, Marcay & Schroeder, Mary A. Math in Bloom (Addition & Subtraction) (gr. 1-4). 1989. spiral wkbk. 39.95 (*1-55999-058-9*) LinguiSystems.

—Math in Bloom (Multiplication & Division) (gr. 2-6). 1989. spiral wkbk. 39.95 (*1-55999-059-7*) LinguiSystems.

Burns, Marilyn. Collection of Math Lessons: Grades Six to Eight. (gr. 6-8). 1990. pap. 15.95 (*0-201-48042-5*) Addison-Wesley.

—Collection of Math Lessons: Grades Three to Six. (gr. 3-6). 1987. pap. 15.95 (*0-201-48040-9*) Addison-Wesley.

—Math for Smarty Pants: Or Who Says Mathematicians Have Little Pig Eyes. Weston, Martha, illus. 140p. (gr. 7 up). 1982. 15.95 (*0-316-11738-2*); pap. 10.95 (*0-316-11739-0*) Little.

Butterfield, Sherri. Following Directions Connections. 32p. (gr. 4-6). 1994. 3.95 (*0-88160-265-5*, LW814) Learning Wks.

—I'm Following Directions. 32p. (gr. 1-3). 1994. 3.95 (*0-88160-266-3*, LW815) Learning Wks.

Clark, Clara E. A Tangram Diary. (Illus.). 64p. (Orig.). (gr. 3-6). 1980. pap. 6.95 (*0-934734-05-4*) Construct Educ.

Clark, Clara E. & Sternberg, Betty J. Math in Stride, Bk. 1. (Illus.). 166p. (Orig.). (gr. k-2). 1980. pap. 5.95 (*0-934734-06-2*); tchr's. manual 19.95 (*0-934734-12-7*) Construct Educ.

—Math in Stride, Bk. 2. (Illus.). 203p. (Orig.). (gr. 1-3). 1980. pap. 6.50 (*0-934734-07-0*); tchr's. manual 19.95 (*0-934734-13-5*) Construct Educ.

—Math in Stride, Bk. 3. (Illus.). 219p. (Orig.). (gr. 2-4). 1980. pap. 6.95 (*0-934734-08-9*) Construct Educ.

Clement, Rod. Counting on Frank. LC 90-27558. (Illus.). 32p. (gr. 1-3). 1991. PLB 18.60 (*0-8368-0358-2*) Gareth Stevens Inc.

CMSP Projects. Applied Math Concepts: Lines & Perimeters Area & Volume. rev. ed. (Illus.). 91p. pap. text ed. write for info. (*0-942851-01-3*) CMSP Projects.

Cook, Sue C. The Numbers Book: Student Syllabus, 2 vols. (gr. k-2). 1974. Vol. 1. pap. text ed. 11.85 (*0-89420-081-X*, 193050); Vol. 2. pap. text ed. 11.85 (*0-89420-082-8*, 193051); cass. recordings 17.38 (*0-89420-208-1*, 193000) Natl Book.

Cotter, Joan A. Worksheets for the Abacus, Complete Volume. (Illus.). 320p. (gr. k-4). 1990. 24.95 (*0-9609636-6-9*) Activities Learning.

Craig, Linda & Praytor, Phyllis. Criterion Referenced Test Kit: Math. Reed, Tom, illus. 54p. (gr. 4). 1978. write for info. (*0-936394-01-3*) Education Serv.

Crary, Elizabeth. My Name Is Not Dummy. Horosko, Marina M., illus. LC 83-24983. 32p. (Orig.). (ps-2). 1983. PLB 15.95 (*0-9602862-9-2*); pap. 4.95 (*0-9602862-8-4*) Parenting Pr.

Crawford, Jean B., ed. Pterodactyl Tunnel: Amusement Park Math. (Illus.). 64p. (gr. k-2). 1993. write for info. (*0-8094-9990-8*) Time-Life.

Daniel, Becky. Hooray for the Big Book of Math Facts! 288p. (gr. 1-4). 1990. 24.95 (*0-86653-533-0*, GA1148) Good Apple.

—Math Brainstorms. 80p. (gr. 1-4). 1990. 9.95 (*0-86653-565-9*, GA1170) Good Apple.

Daniel, Becky & Daniel, Charlie. Big Addition Book. 64p. (gr. k-3). 1979. 8.95 (*0-916456-44-7*, GA118) Good Apple.

—Big Subtraction Book. 64p. (gr. k-3). 1979. 8.95 (*0-916456-43-9*, GA117) Good Apple.

—The Division Book. 64p. (gr. 3-6). 1980. 8.95 (*0-916456-77-3*, GA 190) Good Apple.

—The Multiplication Book. 64p. (gr. 2-6). 1980. 8.95 (*0-916456-76-5*, GA 191) Good Apple.

Davis, James A. Times Table Secrets. Davis, James A., illus. 12p. (gr. 3-5). 1994. incls. flash cards 10.00 (*0-9634088-1-X*) Simp Solns.

Davis, Richard C., et al. Rational Numbers Study Aid. 1976. pap. 3.00 (*0-87738-039-2*) Youth Ed.

The Division Wipe-Off Book. 24p. (gr. 1 up). 1988. pap. 1.95 (*0-590-42041-0*) Scholastic Inc.

Douglas, Vincent. Math. Robison, Don, illus. 48p. (Orig.). (gr. 4). 1993. wkbk. 1.99 (*1-56189-074-X*) Amer Educ Pub.

—Math. Robison, Don, illus. 48p. (Orig.). (gr. 5). 1993. wkbk. 1.99 (*1-56189-075-8*) Amer Educ Pub.

—Math. Robison, Don, illus. 48p. (Orig.). (gr. 6). 1993. wkbk. 1.99 (*1-56189-076-6*) Amer Educ Pub.

Duncan, Jim. Practical Math Skills - Intermediate Level. Tom, Darcy, illus. 64p. (gr. 4-6). 1989. wkbk. 8.95 (*0-86653-465-2*, GA1070) Good Apple.

—Practical Math Skills - Junior High Level. Tom, Darcy, illus. 64p. (gr. 7-9). 1989. wkbk. 8.95 (*0-86653-466-0*, GA1071) Good Apple.

—Practical Math Skills - Primary Level. Tom, Darcy, illus. 64p. (gr. 1-3). 1989. wkbk. 8.95 (*0-86653-464-4*, GA1069) Good Apple.

Dunn, Patricia. Math Trivial Pursuit - Intermediate Level. Dunn, Patricia, illus. 64p. (gr. 4-6). 1989. wkbk. 12.95 (*0-86653-468-7*, GA1073) Good Apple.

—Math Trivial Pursuit - Junior High Level. Dunn, Patricia, illus. 64p. (gr. 7-9). 1989. wkbk. 12.95 (*0-86653-469-5*, GA1074) Good Apple.

—Math Trivial Pursuit - Primary Level. Dunn, Patricia, illus. 64p. (gr. 1-3). 1989. wkbk. 12.95 (*0-86653-492-X*, GA1072) Good Apple.

Eicholz, Robert, et al. Extending the Ideas Enrichment Workbook. 2nd ed. (gr. 4). 1980. pap. text ed. write for info. (*0-201-16035-8*); pap. text ed. write for info. (*0-201-16045-5*); Grade 4. write for info. tchr's ed. (*0-201-16046-3*) Addison-Wesley.

—Extending the Ideas Enrichment Workbook. 2nd ed. (gr. 5-6). 1980. pap. text ed. write for info. (*0-201-16055-2*); Grade 5. write for info. tchr's ed. (*0-201-16056-0*); pap. text ed. write for info. (*0-201-16065-X*) Addison-Wesley.

Erdtmann, Greta. The Path to Math. Erdtmann, Greta, illus. Doman, Glenn, intro. by. (Illus.). 60p. (ps). 1981. 8.95 (*0-936676-11-6*) Better Baby.

Finnegan, Thomas J., et al. Mathematics Study Aid. 1975. pap. 2.50 (*0-87738-036-8*) Youth Ed.

Forsthoefel, John. Utilizing Problem Solving in Math. Zilliox, Elaine, illus. 40p. (Orig.). (gr. 3-8). 1984. 5.95 (*0-88047-039-9*, 8405) DOK Pubs.

Frank, Marjorie. The Kids' Stuff: Book of Math for the Middle Grades. (Illus.). 240p. (gr. 4-6). 1988. pap. text ed. 14.95 (*0-86530-012-7*, IP 13-1) Incentive Pubns.

—The Kids' Stuff: Book of Math for the Primary Grades. (Illus.). 240p. (gr. 1-3). 1988. pap. text ed. 14.95 (*0-86530-040-2*, IP 13-0) Incentive Pubns.

Fun with Addition. (Illus.). (gr. 1-3). 3.50 (*0-7214-0704-8*) Ladybird Bks.

Fun with Division. (Illus.). (gr. 1-3). 3.50 (*0-7214-0707-2*) Ladybird Bks.

Gee, R. & Bryant-Mole, K. Adding & Subtraction Puzzles. (Illus.). 32p. (gr. 2-6). 1993. pap. 4.95 (*0-7460-1074-5*) EDC.

Goodman, Jan M. Group Solutions. Bergman, Lincoln & Fairwell, Kay, eds. (Illus.). 144p. (gr. k-4). 1992. pap. 15.00 (*0-912511-81-8*) Lawrence Science.

Goodwin, Irene & Silvers, Ruth. Polka Dotted Pencil Pushers: Math. Goodwin, Irene, illus. LC 79-63129. 156p. (Orig.). 1979. pap. 8.95 tchr's. guide (*0-932970-08-7*) Prinit Pr.

Greenes, Carole, et al. Mathletics: Gold Medal Problems. (Illus.). 149p. (gr. 8-10). 1989. pap. 19.95 (*0-939765-31-4*, G119) Janson Pubns.

Gregorich, Barbara. Basic Math: First Grade. Hoffman, Joan, ed. Koontz, Robin M., illus. 32p. (gr. 1). 1990. wkbk. 2.29 (*0-88743-181-X*) Sch Zone Pub Co.

—Basic Math: Second Grade. Hoffman, Joan, ed. Koontz, Robin M., illus. 32p. (gr. 2). 1990. wkbk. 2.29 (*0-88743-187-9*) Sch Zone Pub Co.

—Story Problems: Grades 1-2 Math. Hoffman, Joan, ed. Cook, Chris, illus. 32p. (gr. 1-2). 1982. wkbk. 1.99 (*0-938256-45-9*) Sch Zone Pub Co.

—Story Problems: Grades 3-4 Math. Hoffman, Joan, ed. Cook, Chris, illus. 32p. (gr. 3-4). 1982. wkbk. 1.99 (*0-938256-46-7*) Sch Zone Pub Co.

Griesbach, Ellen & Taylor, Jerry. The Prentice-Hall Encyclopedia of Mathematics. Taylor, Louis, ed. (Illus., Orig.). (gr. 6 up). 1982. 39.50 (*0-13-696013-8*) P-H.

Griffiths, Rose. Boxes. Millard, Peter, photos by. (Illus.). 32p. (gr. 1 up). 1995. PLB 17.27 (*0-8368-1179-8*) Gareth Stevens Inc.

—First Step Math, 4 vols. Millard, Peter, photos by. (Illus.). (gr. 1 up). 1994. PLB 69.08 (*0-8368-1108-9*) Gareth Stevens Inc.

—First Step Math, 4 vols. Millard, Peter, photos by. (Illus.). (gr. 1 up). 1995. PLB 69.08 (*0-8368-1178-X*) Gareth Stevens Inc.

—First Step Math, 8 vols. Millard, Peter, photos by. (Illus.). (gr. 1 up). Date not set. PLB 138.18 (*0-8368-1183-6*) Gareth Stevens Inc.

—Printing. Millard, Peter, photos by. (Illus.). 32p. (gr. 1 up). 1995. PLB 17.27 (*0-8368-1181-X*) Gareth Stevens Inc.

Grimm, Gary & Mitchell, Don. Good Apple Math Book. 220p. (gr. 3-8). 1975. 14.95 (*0-916456-00-5*, GA59) Good Apple.

Guy, Richard K. Fair Game: How to Play Impartial Combinatorial Games. Malkevitch, Joseph, ed. Joliffe, Dale, illus. 113p. (Orig.). (gr. 9-12). 1989. pap. text ed. 12.95 (*0-912843-16-0*) COMAP Inc.

Haugo, John E. Math Regrouping Games: Apple Set. 32p. (gr. 4-6). 1982. Set. 71.92 (*0-07-079118-X*) McGraw.

—Math Regrouping Games: TRS-80 Model III Set. (Illus.). 32p. (gr. 4-6). 1982. Set. 71.92 (*0-07-079224-0*) McGraw.

—Math Skill Games: Apple Set. (Illus.). 40p. (gr. 4-6). 1982. Set. 71.92 (*0-07-079116-3*) McGraw.

—Math Skill Games: TRS-80 Model III Set. Kovaleik, Terry, illus. 40p. (gr. 4-6). 1982. Set. 71.92 (*0-07-079222-4*) McGraw.

Heath, Royal V. Mathemagic: Magic, Puzzles & Games with Numbers. (Illus.). 128p. (gr. 2 up). pap. 3.95 (*0-486-20110-4*) Dover.

Hewavisenti, Latshmi. Problem Solving. (Illus.). 32p. (gr. k-4). 1991. PLB 11.90 (*0-531-17318-6*, Gloucester Pr) Watts.

Hillen, Judith A. Piezas y Disenos, un Mosaico de Matematicas y Ciencias. (SPA & ENG.). 160p. (gr. 5-9). 1992. pap. text ed. 16.95 (*1-881431-31-2*) AIMS Educ Fnd.

Hughes, Benjamin B. Multiplication Table by the "Method of Tricks" A Pictorially Rapid & Permanent Mastery. (Illus.). 24p. (gr. k up). 1994. pap. text ed. 10.00 (*1-885028-00-8*) Wings of Freedom.
Color. First copyrighted 1991. Powerful Conceptual Development. Hailed as the FASTEST METHOD EVER DEVISED...ANY child who can count forward to 30 & backward from 10 can, in only 4 flips of the page, excitedly & permanently master the Multiplication Table in only a couple of hours by this 1ST-TIME-EVER "revolutionary" ground-breaking strategy using cartoon picture mnemonics - a method first created by the author in 1990 for severe learning disabled children which has NEVER missed with ANY of the well over 1000

"academically challenged" children "emancipated" across 3 states. A 1991 Talk Show Sensation...Powerful enough for a National Award winning Elementary School Principal of the Year in Science to offer to promote the book nationally...Powerful enough for the largest school district in UTAH to not only offer to help publish the method but also fly the author down from ALASKA to showcase the method in classrooms for a solid 2-week period before a steady stream of key educators from throughout UTAH'S Salt Lake Valley...Powerful enough to induce others to subsequently try cartoon picture strategies of their own with perfectly predictable acclaim... Book follows author's EVERY CHILD A CHAMPION NATIONAL CAMPAIGN providing FREE inner-city "festival of success" clinics all across America. Teacher-Manuals, Posters, Flash-Cards, Games. Orders only: 1-800-MATH*JOY. Info: Brent Hughes, Times Table Tricks, Inc., P.O. Box 20355, Boulder, CO 80308-3355. *Publisher Provided Annotation.*

Jenkins, Gerald & Wild, Anne. Make Shapes One. (Illus.). 24p. (Orig.). (gr. 4 up). 1985. pap. 4.95 (*0-906212-00-6*, Pub. by Tarquin UK) Parkwest Pubns.

—Make Shapes Three. 24p. (Orig.). (gr. 4 up). 1985. pap. 4.95 (*0-906212-02-2*, Pub. by Tarquin UK) Parkwest Pubns.

—Make Shapes Two. (Illus.). 24p. (Orig.). (gr. 4 up). 1985. pap. 4.95 (*0-906212-01-4*, Pub. by Tarquin UK) Parkwest Pubns.

—Mathematical Curiosities Three. (Illus.). 60p. (gr. 5-9). 1986. pap. 5.95 (*0-906212-25-1*, Pub. by Tarquin UK) Parkwest Pubns.

Jenkins, Lee. The Balance Book. (Illus., Orig.). (gr. 2-8). 1974. pap. 7.95 (*0-918932-02-5*) Activity Resources.

Jenkins, Lee & McLean, Peggy. It's a Tangram World. rev. ed. Laycock, Mary, ed. 48p. (gr. 3-6). 1981. pap. 7.95 (*0-918932-70-X*) Activity Resources.

Johnson, Donovan A. Mathmagic with Flexagons. Kaz, Diane, ed. (Orig.). (gr. 4-12). 1974. pap. 7.95 (*0-918932-30-0*) Activity Resources.

Jonson, Liz & Silliman, Emery. Beginning Math. Nayer, Judith E., ed. Cocca, Maryann, illus. 32p. (gr. k-1). 1991. wkbk. 1.95 (*1-878624-59-8*) McClanahan Bk.

Joseph, Andre. The Psycho-Mathematical Basic Skills Learning Workbooklet. 67p. (gr. 6-7). 1980. 8.00 (*0-936264-00-4*); write for info. (*0-936264-01-2*) Andres & Co.

Justus, Fred. Jumbo Math Yearbook: Grade 1. 96p. (gr. 1). 1980. 18.00 (*0-8209-0030-3*, JMY 1) ESP.

Keston, Louise, ed. Math Skills by Objectives. 240p. (gr. 7-9). 1985. pap. text ed. 5.25 (*0-317-46527-9*) Cambridge Bk.

Kiaie, Catherine C. Workbook - Math 1: Basic Skills, Grade 1-2. (ps-3). 1984. pap. 2.50 (*0-307-23541-6*, Golden Pr) Western Pub.

Kopp, Jaine. Frog Math. Bergman, Lincoln & Fairwell, Kay, eds. (Illus.). 106p. (gr. k-3). 1992. pap. 12.50 (*0-912511-79-6*) Lawrence Science.

Kuczma, Marcin E., compiled by. Problems: One Hundred Forty-Four Problems of the Austrian-Polish Mathematics Competition, 1978-1993. Mientka, Walter E., frwd. by. 164p. (gr. 7-12). 1994. pap. 20.00 (*0-9640959-0-4*) Acad Distrib.

Kumbaraci, Turkan & Gardenier, George H. Fun with Numbers: Statistical Methods: Games & Song. Gardenier, Turhan K., illus. LC 89-90944. 15p. (gr. 1-8). 1989. 20.00x (*0-685-29038-7*, 0002) Teka Trends.

—Time: Statistical Methods: Games & Songs. Gardenier, Turhan K., illus. LC 89-90944. 19p. (gr. 1-8). 1989. 20.00 (*0-685-29041-7*, 0005) Teka Trends.

—Two-by-Two: Statistical Methods: Games & Songs. Gardenier, Turhan K., illus. LC 89-90944. 19p. (gr. 1-8). 1989. 20.00 (*0-685-29042-5*, 0006) Teka Trends.

Lacret-Subirat, Fabian. Lacret Mathematics Basic Skills. (Illus.). 467p. (gr. 7-12). 1986. text ed. 15.00 softcover (*0-943144-17-5*) Lacret Pub.

—Mastering HSPT-Math Skills. (Illus.). 250p. (gr. 7-12). 1986. pap. 15.00 (*0-943144-19-1*); answer key school use only avail. Lacret Pub.

—Mastering Math Basic Skills Workbook. (Illus.). 251p. (gr. 7). 1987. pap. 8.48 (*0-943144-21-3*) Lacret Pub.

Lafferty, Peter. Archimedes. LC 90-21749. (Illus.). 48p. (gr. 5-8). 1991. RLB 12.40 (*0-531-18403-X*, Pub. by Bookwright Pr) Watts.

Laycock, Mary. Base Ten Mathematics. Jung, Tom, photos by. Moray, Joe, intro. by. (gr. 1-9). 1976. pap. 7.95 (*0-918932-03-3*) Activity Resources.

—Bucky for Beginners. Kyzer, Martha, illus. 64p. (Orig.). (gr. 4-12). 1984. pap. text ed. 7.95 (*0-918932-82-3*) Activity Resources.

Laycock, Mary & Smart, Margaret. Solid Sense of Mathematics, 3 vols. (Illus.). 64p. (Orig.). (gr. 4-9). 1981. pap. text ed. 7.95 (*0-918932-74-2*) Activity Resources.

Laycock, Mary, et al. Geoblocks & Geojackets: Metric Version. rev., 2nd ed. Laycock, Mary, et al, illus. 96p. (Orig.). (gr. 3-10). 1988. pap. 8.95 (*0-918932-91-2*) Activity Resources.

Learning Forum Staff. Success Through Math Mastery. (gr. 8-12). 1989. 24.95 (*0-945525-11-7*) Supercamp.

Lenchner, George. Mathematical Olympiad Contest Problems for Children (Also for Teachers, Parents, & Other Adults) Lenchner, George, illus. LC 90-83825. 176p. (Orig.). (gr. 3-8). 1990. pap. 18.95 (*0-9626662-0-3*) Glenwood Pubns.

Lund, Charles & Smart, Margaret. Focus on Calculator Math. Kyzer, Martha, illus. Laycock, Mary, intro. by. (Illus.). (gr. 4-12). 1979. pap. text ed. 8.50 (*0-918932-66-1*) Activity Resources.

McCabe, J. L. Everyday Mathematics: A Study Guide. (Illus.). 168p. (Orig.). 1988. pap. text ed. 13.95 (*0-942465-11-3*, 2 323 279) Summertree Bks.

McCoy, Leah P. Elementary Math Flipper, No. I. 39p. (gr. 4 up). 1989. trade edition 6.25 (*1-878383-13-2*) C Lee Pubns.

McGreevey, Carla & Kelinson, Roberta M. Blooming Math: Fun Activities for Beginning Math Based on Benjamin Bloom's Taxonomy. (ps-3). 1988. pap. 15.95 (*1-55999-027-9*) LinguiSystems.

McLaughlin, Jack. People Piece Puzzles. (Illus.). (gr. 2-8). 1973. pap. 7.95 (*0-918932-38-6*) Activity Resources.

McLean, P., et al. Building Understanding (Primary) (gr. 1-3). 1990. 7.95 (*0-918932-96-3*) Activity Resources.

McLean, Peggy & Sternberg, Betty. People Piece Primer. (Orig.). (gr. k-3). 1975. pap. 7.50 (*0-918932-37-8*) Activity Resources.

McLean, Peggy, et al. Let's Pattern Block It. (Illus., Orig.). (gr. k-8). 1973. pap. 12.50 (*0-918932-26-2*) Activity Resources.

Mark, Sara, ed. Mystery Mansion: House Math. LC 93-25398. (Illus.). 64p. (gr. k-2). 1993. write for info. (*0-8094-9986-X*) Time-Life.

—The Mystery of the Sunken Treasure: Sea Math. (Illus.). 64p. 1993. write for info. (*0-8094-9994-0*) Time-Life.

Marsh, Carole. Math for Boys: A Book with the Number or Getting Boys to Love & Excel in Math! (Illus.). (gr. 4-12). 1994. PLB 24.95 (*1-55609-806-5*); pap. 14.95 (*1-55609-830-8*); computer disk 29.95 (*1-55609-878-2*) Gallopade Pub Group.

—Math for Girls: The Book with the Number to Get Girls to Love & Excel in Math! (Illus.). 60p. (gr. 3-9). 1994. PLB 24.95 (*1-55609-343-8*); pap. 14.95 (*1-55609-344-6*); computer disk 29.95 (*1-55609-345-4*) Gallopade Pub Group.

Martinez, Eliseo R. & Martinez, Irma C. Supplemental Studies in Math, Vol. 1. (Illus.). 73p. (ps-1). 1985. wkbk. 8.75 (*1-878300-00-8*) Childrens Work.

Math for Fall: Level A. (Illus.). 88p. (gr. 1-2). 1993. pap. text ed. 14.95 (*1-55799-259-2*) Evan-Moor Corp.

Math for Spring: Level A. (Illus.). 88p. (gr. 1-2). 1993. pap. text ed. 14.95 (*1-55799-261-4*) Evan-Moor Corp.

Math for Summer: Level A. (Illus.). 88p. (gr. 1-2). 1993. pap. text ed. 14.95 (*1-55799-262-2*) Evan-Moor Corp.

Math for Winter: Level A. (Illus.). 88p. (gr. 1-2). 1993. pap. text ed. 14.95 (*1-55799-260-6*) Evan-Moor Corp.

Math Yellow Pages for Students & Teachers. LC 87-82071. 64p. (gr. k-6). 1988. pap. text ed. 6.95 (*0-86530-008-9*) Incentive Pubns.

Mathews, Louise. Bunches & Bunches of Bunnies. Bassett, Jeni, illus. 32p. (gr. k-3). 1991. pap. 3.95 (*0-590-44766-1*) Scholastic Inc.

Miller, Don. Mental Math & Estimation. 80p. (gr. 3-8). 1993. pap. text ed. 9.50 (*0-938587-30-7*) Cuisenaire.

Mogard, Sue & McDonnell, Ginny. Gobble up Math. LC 94-75876. 136p. (gr. k-3). 1994. 9.95 (*0-88160-262-0*, LW105) Learning Wks.

Moore, Jo E. Shoebox Center: Math Activities. (Illus.). 64p. (gr. 1-3). 1993. pap. text ed. 7.95 (*1-55799-252-5*) Evan-Moor Corp.

Murray, Tom. Estimation Exploration. (gr. 3-8). 1994. pap. text ed. 7.95 (*1-882293-02-9*) Activity Resources.

Palmer, Martha. Transition Math. Hoffman, Joan, ed. Cook, Chris, illus. 32p. (gr. k-1). 1979. wkbk. 1.99 (*0-938256-27-0*) Sch Zone Pub Co.

Perry, Cheryl & Faulkner, Hal. Holiday Mathemagic. (Illus.). (gr. 4-10). 1977. pap. text ed. 7.95 (*0-918932-50-5*) Activity Resources.

Peterson, Elizabeth J. Beginning Math at Home. Dewagian, Jeanette, illus. 75p. (ps-1). 4 sets 10.95, (*0-938911-01-5*) Indiv Educ Syst.

Quinn, Dan & Davis, Larry. Multiplication Memorization Made Fun & Easy. 128p. (gr. 1-3). 1993. tchr's. ed. 9.95 (*0-9629746-1-7*) Texas Trends.

Ripley, Robert L. Math & Science Facts. Stott, Carol, illus. 48p. (gr. 3-6). 1992. PLB 12.95 (*1-56065-128-8*) Capstone Pr.

Rohrer, Doug. Thought Provokers. 57p. (gr. 9-12). 1993. pap. 9.95 (*1-55953-065-0*) Key Curr Pr.

Sachar, Louis. Sideways Arithmetic from Wayside School. 96p. (gr. 4-8). 1992. pap. 2.95 (*0-590-45726-8*, Apple Paperbacks) Scholastic Inc.

Sachs, Leroy, ed. Projects to Enrich School Mathematics: Level 2. LC 88-5259. (Illus.). 96p. (Orig.). (gr. 7-9). 1988. pap. 8.00 (*0-87353-260-0*) NCTM.

—Projects to Enrich School Mathematics: Level 3. LC 88-5129. (Illus.). 128p. (Orig.). (gr. 10-12). 1988. pap. 11.00 (*0-87353-261-9*) NCTM.

Schneider, Anthony J. Wonders in Numbers. (Illus.). 134p. (Orig.). (gr. 7-12). 1994. pap. 9.75 (*0-9640218-0-3*) Schneider Assocs.

Presents math & science in a manner that helps junior & senior high school students understand the basic relationships between numbers & real-life situations. A delightful adventure in numeracy - the gatekeeper to higher education & our modern workforce. Contains 21 thought-provoking, easy-to-read, generously illustrated chapters that are loaded with historical perspectives: A Space Odyssey; How We Count; Taking A Chance; From Here To Infinity; The Right Size; Planets In Motion; Let's Talk Percentages; A Number Is A Number, Or Is It?; Scientific Notation; Mean, Median, Mode; Pi All Over; Destination Moon; Radiation All Around; e-Gads; Go Gaussian; Let's Take A Poll; Mathematics In Art; Zany World Of Weights & Measures; Demon dB; Frequency Analysis; Calculus 001. Makes otherwise rote learning come to life, fills a void in the supplementary reading market for Grades 7-12, & is a lifelong reference. Also of interest to teachers. SCHNEIDER ASSOCIATES, 458 Camino Alondra, San Clemente, CA 92672. Phone or FAX (714) 661-2671. *Publisher Provided Annotation.*

Schwartz, Linda. Hot Fudge Fractions. (gr. 3-4). 1979. pap. 3.95 (*0-88160-065-2*, LW 705) Learning Wks.

—Math Marathon. (gr. 5-7). 1979. pap. 3.95 (*0-88160-066-0*, LW 706) Learning Wks.

Sharp, Richard M. & Metzner, Seymour. The Sneaky Square & 113 Other Math Activities For Kids. (Illus.). 126p. (ps up). 1990. 15.95 (*0-8306-8474-3*, 3474); pap. 8.95 (*0-8306-3474-6*) TAB Bks.

Shepherd, Glenn. Whole Numbers. Bell-Jarrett, Kaytee, illus. 76p. (gr. 6-12). 1994. pap. text ed. 5.75 (*1-885120-01-X*) F E Braswell.

Smart, M., et al. Building Understanding (Middle) (gr. 4-8). 1990. 8.95 (*0-918932-97-1*) Activity Resources.

Smart, Margaret. Focus on Percent. Laycock, Mary, ed. (Illus.). (gr. 5-9). 1978. pap. text ed. 7.95 (*0-918932-54-8*) Activity Resources.

Smart, Margaret A. Focus on Pre-Algebra. Laycock, Mark, intro. by. (Illus.). 48p. (Orig.). (gr. 6-9). 1983. pap. text ed. 7.95 (*0-918932-81-5*) Activity Resources.

Smoothey, Marion. Let's Investigate Series, 6 vols. Evans, Ted, illus. 64p. (gr. 4-8). 1993. Set, Group 1. PLB 101.70 (*1-85435-455-8*); Set, Group 2. PLB write for info. (*1-85435-463-9*) Marshall Cavendish.

—Number Patterns. Evans, Ted, illus. 64p. (gr. 4-8). 1992. text ed. 16.95 (*1-85435-458-2*) Marshall Cavendish.

—Numbers. Evans, Ted, illus. 64p. (gr. 4-8). 1992. text ed. 16.95 (*1-85435-457-4*) Marshall Cavendish.

Solutions. (Illus.). 72p. (gr. 7-12). 1990. 12.30 (*0-941008-82-7*) Tops Learning.

Spancer, Cookie. Gifted & Talented Math Workbook. Whitten, Leesa, illus. 96p. (ps-3). 1992. pap. 3.95 (*0-929923-82-0*) Lowell Hse.

Speiser, E. & Weiser, Marjorie P., eds. Math Skills by Objectives. 352p. (gr. 7-9). 1988. pap. text ed. 6.00 (*0-8428-0202-9*) Cambridge Bk.

Sternberg, Betty. Attribute Acrobatics. (Illus., Orig.). (gr. 1-9). 1974. pap. 9.95 (*0-918932-01-7*) Activity Resources.

—Colored Cubes Activity Cards. (Illus., Orig.). (gr. 2-8). 1973. pap. 6.50 (*0-918932-06-8*) Activity Resources.

Story Time Stories That Rhyme Staff. Math in Stories That Rhyme. Story Time Stories That Rhyme Staff, illus. 50p. (Orig.). (gr. 4-7). 1992. GBC bdg. 19.95 (*1-56820-017-X*) Story Time.

Taulbee, Annette. Kindergarten Math. (Illus.). 24p. (ps-k). 1986. 3.98 (*0-86734-070-3*, FS-3062) Schaffer Pubns.

Taylor, Anne. Math in Art. Taylor, Anne, illus. (Orig.). (gr. 1-9). 1974. pap. 7.95 (*0-918932-28-9*) Activity Resources.

Thompson, Denisse & Van Loy, Merrie. Fundamental Skills of Mathematics. Howland, Joe & Savige, Katherine, eds. Howland, Thomas, illus. LC 87-50098. 536p. (gr. 9-12). 1987. text ed. 19.95 (*0-943202-16-7*) H & H Pub.

Time-Life Bks. Editors. Alice in Numberland: Fantasy Math. Mark, Sara, et al, eds. LC 93-9136. (Illus.). 64p. (ps-4). 1993. write for info. (*0-8094-9978-9*); lib. bdg. write for info. (*0-8094-9979-7*) Time-Life.

Time Life Inc. Editors. From Head to Toe: Body Math. Crawford, Jean B. & Daniels, Patricia, eds. LC 92-34974. (Illus.). 64p. (gr. k-2). 1993. write for info. (*0-8094-9966-5*); PLB write for info. (*0-8094-9967-3*) Time-Life.

—Look Both Ways: City Math. Crawford, Jean B., et al, eds. (Illus.). 64p. (gr. k-2). 1992. write for info. (*0-8094-9958-4*); lib. bdg. write for info. (*0-8094-9959-2*) Time-Life.

Time-Life Inc. Editors. Play Ball: Sports Math. Mark, Sara, et al, eds. (Illus.). 64p. (gr. k-4). 1993. write for info. (*0-8094-9970-3*); lib. bdg. write for info. (*0-8094-9971-1*) Time-Life.

Time Life Inc. Editors. The Search for the Mystery Planet: Space Math. Crawford, Jean B., ed. (Illus.). 64p. (gr. k-2). 1993. write for info. (*0-8094-9982-7*); lib. bdg. write for info. (*0-8094-9983-5*) Time-Life.

Time-Life Inc. Editors. See You Later Escalator: Mall Math. Crawford, Jean B., et al, eds. LC 93-6494. (Illus.). 64p. (gr. k-2). 1993. write for info. (*0-8094-9974-6*); PLB write for info. (*0-8094-9975-4*) Time-Life.

Time Life Inc Staff. Right in Your Own Backyard: Nature Math. Ward, Elizabeth, et al, eds. LC 92-27222. (Illus.). 64p. (gr. k-4). 1992. write for info. (*0-8094-9962-2*); PLB write for info. (*0-8094-9963-0*) Time-Life.

Trinkle, Timothy, et al. Practice, Practice, Practice, Plus, Bk. II: Proportions, Percents, Integers, Rationals, Equations, Area, Volume, Problem Solving, Combinations. 2nd ed. 224p. 1990. pap. 10.75 (*0-685-35051-7*); answer book 2.50 (*0-685-35052-5*) ST Two.

Usher, Michael A. & Bormuth, Robert. Experiencing Life Through Mathematics, Vol. 1. rev. ed. (Illus.). 128p. (Orig.). (gr. 8-12). 1978. pap. text ed. 4.92 (*0-913688-18-5*); tchrs. ed. 8.00x (*0-913688-19-3*) Pawnee Pub.

Vancleave, Janice P. Janice Vancleave's Math for Every Kid: Easy Activities That Make Learning Math Fun. 224p. 1991. text ed. 24.95 (*0-471-54693-3*); pap. text ed. 10.95 (*0-471-54265-2*) Wiley.

Vaughn, JIm. Jumbo Math Yearbook: Grade 3. 96p. (gr. 3). 1978. 18.00 (*0-8209-0032-X*, JMY 3) ESP.

Vervoort & Mason. Calculator Math, 3 vols. (gr. 7-12). 1980. Beginning Grades 5-7. pap. 10.95 (*0-8224-1200-4*) Intermediate Grades 6-8. pap. 10.95 (*0-8224-1201-2*); Advanced Grades 8-10. pap. 10.95 (*0-8224-1202-0*) Fearon Teach Aids.

Walker, Dava J. Mathematics. Nolte, Larry, illus. 48p. (gr. 3-6). Date not set. PLB 12.95 (*1-56065-113-X*) Capstone Pr.

Wardlaw, Lee. Me Plus Math Equals Headache. Hoy, Joanne H., illus. LC 86-20305. (Orig.). (gr. 1-3). 1986. pap. 3.50 (*0-931093-07-4*) Red Hen Pr.

Welchman-Tischler, Rosamond. The Mathematical Toolbox. (Illus.). 90p. (gr. 1-8). 1992. pap. 9.95 (*0-938587-27-7*) Cuisenaire.

Wells, David. Can You Solve These?, No. 2: Mathematical Problems to Test Your Thinking Powers. (Illus.). 80p. (Orig.). (gr. 5 up). 1985. pap. 6.95 (*0-906212-34-0*, Pub. by Tarquin UK) Parkwest Pubns.

White, Laurence B. Math-a-Magic: Number Tricks for Magicians. (gr. 4-7). 1994. pap. 4.95 (*0-8075-4995-9*) A Whitman.

White, Laurence B., Jr. & Broekel, Ray. Math-a-Magic: Number Tricks for Magicians. Mathews, Judith, ed. Seltzer, Meyer, illus. LC 89-35395. 48p. (gr. 3-6). 1990. 11.95 (*0-8075-4994-0*) A Whitman.

Wiebe, Arthur. Domino Math, 2 bks. Creative Teaching Assocs. Staff, illus. 60p. Bks. A & B. write for info. set (*1-878669-18-4*, 4145) Bk. A, Grades 1-4, 1973. pap. text ed. 6.95 (*1-878669-19-2*, 4145); Bk. B, Grades 2-6, 1974. pap. text ed. 6.95 (*0-685-74216-4*, 4146) Crea Tea Assocs.

World Book Editors. The World Book of Math Power Activities 2. LC 93-61456. (Illus.). 64p. (gr. 3-5). 1994. PLB write for info. (*0-7166-4895-4*) World Bk.

World Book Editors, ed. The World Book of Math Power Activities 1. LC 93-61407. (Illus.). 64p. (gr. k-2). 1994. PLB write for info. (*0-7166-3894-0*) World Bk.

World Book Staff, ed. The World Book of Math Power, 2 vols. rev. ed. LC 90-70044. (Illus.). 800p. (gr. 6 up). 1992. write for info. (*0-7166-1392-1*) World Bk.

Zaslavsky, Claudia. Count on Your Fingers African Style. Pinkney, Jerry, illus. LC 77-26586. 32p. (gr. k-3). 1980. (Crowell Jr Bks); (Crowell Jr Bks) HarpC Child Bks.

MATHEMATICS–DATA PROCESSING

Cummings, Robert. Basketmath: For IBM Computers. Cummings, Robert, illus. (Orig.). (gr. 6-12). 1993. pap. 69.00 (*0-9623926-5-0*) Sci Academy Soft.

Glatzer, David & Glatzer, Joyce. The Casio SL-450: A Tool for Teaching Mathematics. Sobel, Max, ed. (Illus.). 72p. (gr. k-6). 1993. wkbk. 9.95 (*1-878532-05-7*) Casio Inc.

MATHEMATICS–DICTIONARIES

Abdelnoor, R. E. The Silver Burdett Mathematical Dictionary. LC 86-45568. (Illus.). 126p. (gr. 5-12). 8.95 (*0-382-09485-9*); pap. 5.95 (*0-382-09309-7*) Silver Burdett Pr.

Chenier, Norman J. Chenier Math Method: A Practical Math Dictionary & Workbook-Textbook. (Illus.). 268p. (gr. 9 up). 1989. text ed. 24.95 (*0-9626061-0-3*) Chenier Educ Enter.

Dyches, Richard W. & Shaw, Jean M. First Math Dictionary. Sornat, Czeslaw, illus. LC 91-7527. 104p. (gr. k-4). 1991. PLB 15.90 (*0-531-11111-3*) Watts.

MATHEMATICS–STUDY AND TEACHING

Beckmann, Beverly. Numbers in God's World. (ps). 1983. 6.99 (*0-570-04083-3*, 56-1438) Concordia.

Casolaro, Nancy. The Gifted & Talented Math Workbook. Whitten, Leesa, illus. 96p. (gr. 1-3). 1993. pap. 3.95 (*1-56565-039-5*) Lowell Hse.

Chenier, Norman J. Chenier Math Method: A Practical Math Dictionary & Workbook-Textbook. (Illus.). 268p. (gr. 9 up). 1989. text ed. 24.95 (*0-9626061-0-3*) Chenier Educ Enter.

Conrad, Steven R. & Flegler, Daniel. Math Contests - Grades Seven & Eight, Vol. 2: School Years: 1982-83 Through 1990-91. 166p. (Orig.). (gr. 5-8). 1992. pap. 12.95 (*0-940805-05-7*) Math Leagues.

—Math Contests - Grades 4, 5, & 6, Vol. 2: School Years: 1986-87 Through 1990-91. 102p. (Orig.). (gr. 3-8). 1991. pap. 12.95 (*0-940805-03-0*) Math Leagues.

—Math Contests - High School, Vol. 2: School Years: 1982-83 Through 1990-91. 118p. (Orig.). (gr. 9-12). 1992. pap. 12.95 (*0-940805-04-9*) Math Leagues.

Embry, Lynn & Bobo, Betty. Math America. Skiles, Janet, illus. 128p. (gr. 4-6). 1987. pap. 12.95 (*0-86653-378-8*, GA1015) Good Apple.

—Math Around the World. 144p. (gr. 4-6). 1991. 12.95 (*0-86653-600-0*, GA1319) Good Apple.

Gardenier, George E. Statistical Methods: Games & Songs. Gardenier, T. K., ed. Gardenier, Jason C., illus. 99p. (gr. 3 up). 1989. 89.00 (*0-685-29043-3*) Teka Trends.

Geoffrion, Sondra. Power Study to up Your Grades in Math. LC 88-61284. 60p. (gr. 11 up). 1989. pap. text ed. 3.95 (*0-88247-783-8*) R & E Pubs.

Gerber, Carole. Master Math Workbook Grade Five. (gr. 4-7). 1990. pap. 4.95 (*1-56189-015-4*) Amer Educ Pub.

—Master Math Workbook Grade Four. (gr. 4-7). 1990. pap. 4.95 (*1-56189-014-6*) Amer Educ Pub.

—Master Math Workbook Grade K. (ps-3). 1990. pap. 4.95 (*1-56189-010-3*) Amer Educ Pub.

—Master Math Workbook Grade One. (ps-3). 1990. pap. 4.95 (*1-56189-011-1*) Amer Educ Pub.

—Master Math Workbook Grade Six. (gr. 4-7). 1990. pap. 4.95 (*1-56189-016-2*) Amer Educ Pub.

—Master Math Workbook Grade Three. (ps-3). 1990. pap. 4.95 (*1-56189-013-8*) Amer Educ Pub.

—Master Math Workbook Grade Two. (ps-3). 1990. pap. 4.95 (*1-56189-012-X*) Amer Educ Pub.

Glatzer, David & Glatzer, Joyce. The Casio SL-450: A Tool for Teaching Mathematics. Sobel, Max, ed. (Illus.). 72p. (gr. k-6). 1993. wkbk. 9.95 (*1-878532-05-7*) Casio Inc.

Hoban, Tana. Count & See. Hoban, Tana, illus. LC 72-175597. 40p. (ps-2). 1972. RSBE 14.95 (*0-02-744800-2*, Macmillan Child Bk) Macmillan Child Grp.

Kumbaraci, Turkan & Gardenier, George H. Branching Trees: Statistical Methods: Games & Songs. Gardenier, Turhan K., illus. LC 89-90944. 27p. (gr. 1-8). 1989. 30.00x (*0-685-29039-5*, 0003) Teka Trends.

Lucas, Jerry. Becoming a Mental Math Wizard. LC 91-19472. (Illus.). 192p. (Orig.). (gr. 7 up). 1991. pap. 8.95 (*1-55870-216-4*, 70009) Shoe Tree Pr.

North Carolina School of Science & Mathematics, Department of Mathematics & Computer Science Staff. Data Analysis. LC 88-5305. (Illus.). 132p. (Orig.). (gr. 11-12). 1988. pap. 12.00 (*0-87353-263-5*) NCTM.

—Geometric Probability. LC 88-5305. (Illus.). 40p. (Orig.). (gr. 11-12). 1988. pap. 11.00 (*0-87353-259-7*) NCTM.

Rodriguez, David & Rodriguez, Judy. Times Tables the Fun Way: A Picture Method of Learning the Multiplication Facts. Bagley, Val & Barwald, Diana, illus. 86p. (gr. 2-8). 1992. 19.95 (*1-883841-25-9*) Key Pubs UT.

Schaffer, Frank, Publications Staff. Multiplication. (Illus.). 24p. (gr. 3-5). 1978. wkbk. 3.98 (*0-86734-010-X*, FS-3011) Schaffer Pubns.

Spizman, Robyn. Bulletin Boards: To Reinforce Basic Math Skills. Pesiri, Evelyn, illus. 64p. (gr. k-6). 1984. wkbk. 7.95 (*0-86653-208-0*, GA 573) Good Apple.

Trowell, Judith M., ed. Projects to Enrich School Mathematics: Level I. LC 89-14017. (Illus.). 168p. (gr. 4-6). 1990. pap. 14.50 (*0-87353-280-5*) NCTM.

Zeman, Anne & Kelly, Kate. Everything You Need to Know about Math Homework. LC 93-49351. 1994. write for info. (*0-590-49358-2*); pap. 8.95 (*0-590-49359-0*) Scholastic Inc.

MATHEWSON, CHRISTOPHER, 1880-1925

Macht, Norm. Christy Mathewson. Murray, Jim, intro. by. (Illus.). 64p. (gr. 3 up). 1991. lib. bdg. 14.95 (*0-7910-1182-8*) Chelsea Hse.

MATISSE, HENRI, 1869-1954

Rodari, Florian. A Weekend with Matisse. Knight, Joan, tr. from FRE. LC 93-41671. 64p. 1994. 19.95 (*0-8478-1792-X*) Rizzoli Intl.

MATRIMONY

see Marriage

MATTER

Darling, David. From Glasses to Gases: The Science of Matter. LC 91-38233. (Illus.). 60p. (gr. 5 up). 1992. text ed. 13.95 RSBE (*0-87518-500-2*, Dillon) Macmillan Child Grp.

Glover, David. Solids & Liquids. LC 92-40214. 32p. (gr. 1-4). 1993. 10.95 (*1-85697-845-1*, Kingfisher LKC); pap. 5.95 (*1-85697-934-2*) LKC.

Morgan, Sally & Morgan, Adrian. Materials. LC 93-31722. (Illus.). 48p. (gr. 5-9). 1994. 14.95x (*0-8160-2985-7*) Facts on File.

Parramon Editorial Team Staff. The Elements. (Illus.). 96p. (ps-1). 1994. 16.95 (*0-8120-6440-2*) Barron.

Pomeroy, Johanna P. Content Area Reading Skills Matter: Locating Details. (Illus.). (gr. 4). 1988. pap. text ed. 3.25 (*1-55737-086-9*) Ed Activities.

Time Life Books Staff. Structure of Matter. 1992. 18.95 (*0-8094-9662-3*) Time-Life.

Wilkin, Fred. Matter. LC 85-30882. (Illus.). 48p. (gr. k-4). 1986. PLB 12.85 (*0-516-01284-3*) Childrens.

MATTER–PROPERTIES

Cobb, Vicki. Why Can't You Unscramble an Egg? Enik, Ted, illus. LC 89-33465. 40p. (gr. 2-5). 1990. 12.95 (*0-525-67293-1*, Lodestar Bks) Dutton Child Bks.

MAXIMS

see Proverbs

MAYAS

see Indians of Mexico–Mayas

MAYFLOWER (SHIP)

Felloney, Nanette. Meet Me on the Mayflower. (Illus.). 21p. (gr. 3 up). 1992. pap. 3.95 (*1-882684-00-1*) True Tales.

MAYFLOWER (SHIP)–FICTION

Gay, David. Voyage to Freedom: Story of the Pilgrim Fathers. 149p. 1984. pap. 8.95 (*0-85151-384-0*) Banner of Truth.

McGovern, Ann. If You Sailed on the May Flower. Devito, Anna, illus. 80p. 1991. pap. 3.95 (*0-590-45161-8*) Scholastic Inc.

Shaffer, Elizabeth. Daughter of the Dawn. 1992. write for info. (*0-936369-72-8*) Son-Rise Pubns.

MAYO, CHARLES HORACE, 1865-1939

Crofford, Emily. Frontier Surgeons: A Story about the Mayo Brothers. Ritz, Karen, illus. 64p. (gr. 3-6). 1989. PLB 14.95 (*0-87614-381-8*) Carolrhoda Bks.

MAYO, WILLIAM JAMES, 1861-1939

Crofford, Emily. Frontier Surgeons: A Story about the Mayo Brothers. Ritz, Karen, illus. 64p. (gr. 3-6). 1989. PLB 14.95 (*0-87614-381-8*) Carolrhoda Bks.

MAYORS

Krueger, Martin T. Two Speeches of the Mayor: Martin T. Krueger. Rinehart, Betty M., intro. by. 44p. (Orig.). (gr. 8 up). 1989. pap. text ed. 2.00 (*0-935549-13-7*) MI City Hist.

Kurland, Gerald. Fiorello LaGuardia: The People's Mayor of New York. Rahmas, D. Steve, ed. LC 77-190238. 32p. (Orig.). (gr. 7-12). 1972. lib. bdg. 4.95 incl. catalog cards (*0-87157-520-5*) SamHar Pr.

—Richard Daley: The Strong Willed Mayor of Chicago. Rahmas, D. Steve, ed. LC 70-190236. 32p. (Orig.). (gr. 7-12). lib. bdg. 4.95 incl. catalog cards (*0-87157-518-3*) SamHar Pr.

Roberts, Naurice. Henry Cisneros: A Leader for the Future. rev. ed. LC 91-2330. 32p. (gr. 2-4). 1991. PLB 11.80 (*0-516-04175-4*); pap. 3.95 (*0-516-44175-2*) Childrens.

—Henry Cisneros: Alcalde Mexico-Americano. LC 85-29057. 32p. (gr. 2-5). 1987. pap. 3.95 (*0-516-53485-8*) Childrens.

MAYS, WILLIE HOWARD, 1931-

Sabin, Louis. Willie Mays, Young Superstar. Jones, John R., illus. LC 89-33979. 48p. (gr. 4-6). 1990. PLB 10.79 (*0-8167-1775-3*); pap. text ed. 3.50 (*0-8167-1776-1*) Troll Assocs.

Weber, Bruce. Willie Mays: Classical Sports Shots. 1993. pap. 1.25 (*0-590-47020-5*) Scholastic Inc.

MAZE PUZZLES

Bullock, Waneta B. & Loveless, Ganelle. ABC Mazes. (Illus.). 56p. (gr. k-1). 1979. pap. 8.00 (*0-87879-713-0*, Ann Arbor Div) Acad Therapy.

Drew, David. Jock Jerome. Culio, Ned, illus. LC 92-31133. 1993. 2.50 (*0-383-03636-4*) SRA Schl Grp.

Gamiello, Elvira. Haunted Mazes. (Illus.). 96p. (Orig.). 1988. pap. 1.95 (*0-942025-29-6*) Kidsbks.

—Maze Madness. (Illus.). 64p. (Orig.). (gr. 4-6). 1988. pap. 1.95 (*0-942025-93-8*) Kidsbks.

—Space Age Mazes. (Illus., Orig.). (gr. 4-6). 1989. pap. 1.95 (*0-942025-94-6*) Kidsbks.

Haunted Bronco Ranch. 48p. (Orig.). (gr. 1-4). 1993. pap. 2.95 (*0-8431-3537-9*) Price Stern.

Kingston, Peter. My First Book of Mazes. (ps-1). 1992. pap. 2.95 (*0-8431-3457-7*) Price Stern.

Latta, Richard. More Dinosaur Mazes. (Illus.). 48p. (Orig.). (gr. 2 up). 1992. pap. 2.95 incl. chipboard (*0-8431-3420-8*) Price Stern.

McCreary, Paul. The Maze Book. (Illus.). (gr. 2-4). 1979. pap. 8.00 (*0-87879-712-2*, Ann Arbor Div) Acad Therapy.

Madgwick, Wendy. Animaze! A Collection of Amazing Nature Mazes. Hussey, Lorna, illus. LC 91-46892. 40p. (ps-3). 1992. 13.00 (*0-679-82665-3*); PLB 13.99 (*0-679-92665-8*) Knopf Bks Yng Read.

Nevins, Dan. Three-Dee Mouse Mazes. (Illus.). 48p. (Orig.). (gr. 8-11). 1987. pap. 2.95 (*0-8431-1883-0*) Price Stern.

Phillips, Dave. Mother Goose Mazes. LC 92-17679. 1992. pap. write for info. (*0-486-27319-9*) Dover.

RGA Publishing Staff. Mystery of Pirate Island. 48p. (Orig.). (gr. 1-4). 1993. pap. 2.95 (*0-8431-3536-0*) Price Stern.
San Jose, Christine & Taylor, Jody. The Adventures of the Amazing Mazers: Hidden Pictures & Maze Games. Jordan, Charles, illus. 32p. (gr. 2-7). 1994. pap. 4.95 (*1-56397-335-9*) Boyds Mills Pr.
Schanzer, Rosalyn. Ezra in Pursuit: A Book of Mazes. LC 92-25815. 1993. pap. 10.95 (*0-385-30884-1*) Doubleday.
—Ezra on a Quest: A Maze Chase Medieval. LC 93-19537. 1994. 12.95 (*0-385-32262-3*) Doubleday.
Snape, Charles & Scott, Heather. How Amazing. (Illus.). 48p. 1993. pap. 9.95 (*0-521-35672-5*) Cambridge U Pr.
Speirs, John. The Quest for the Golden Mane. Speirs, John, illus. LC 91-33894. 32p. (gr. k-6). 1991. 9.95 (*0-89577-394-5*, Dist. by Random) RD Assn.
Strong & Guastella. Wandering Through the Wild Nature Mazes. 1992. pap. 2.50 (*0-590-45016-6*) Scholastic Inc.
Sullivan, Scott. Tough Mazes. (Illus.). 40p. (Orig.). (gr. 1 up). 1989. pap. 3.50 (*0-8431-2332-X*, Troubador) Price Stern.
Tallarico, A. Stop & Find: Space Race Mazes. (Illus.). 12p. (Orig.). 1991. pap. 1.95 (*1-56156-030-8*) Kidsbks.
Tallarico, Anthony. Stop & Find Maze Madness. Tallarico, Anthony, illus. 12p. (Orig.). (gr. 4-7). 1990. pap. 1.95 (*1-878890-00-X*) Palisades Prodns.
Taylor, Jody, ed. Mazes, Mazes, Mazes. 64p. (gr. 2-7). 1994. pap. 6.95 (*1-56397-334-0*) Boyds Mills Pr.
Walne, Sarah W. Memphis Mazes. 32p. (gr. 1-6). 1992. text ed. 12.95 (*1-881207-00-5*); pap. text ed. 8.95 (*1-881207-01-3*); tchr's. manual 9.95 (*1-881207-02-1*); tape 7.95 (*1-881207-03-X*) City Mazes.

MEAD, MARGARET, 1901-

Castiglia, Julie. Margaret Mead. (Illus.). 144p. (gr. 5-9). 1989. PLB 10.95 (*0-382-09525-1*) Silver Burdett Pr.
Saunders, Susan. Margaret Mead: The World Was Her Family. Lewin, Ted, illus. (Orig.). (gr. 2-6). 1988. pap. 3.99 (*0-14-032063-6*) Viking Child Bks.
Ziesk, Edra. Margaret Mead. Horner, Matina S., intro. by. (Illus.). 112p. (gr. 5 up). 1990. lib. bdg. 17.95 (*1-55546-667-2*) Chelsea Hse.

MEAL PLANNING

see Nutrition

MEASURES

see Weights and Measures

MEASURING

see Mensuration

MECHANICAL BRAINS

see Computers

MECHANICAL DRAWING

see also Geometrical Drawing; Graphic Methods; Lettering

Boy Scouts of America. Drafting. (Illus.). 32p. (gr. 6-12). 1965. pap. 1.85 (*0-8395-3273-3*, 33262) BSA.
Peach, S. Technical Drawing. (Illus.). 48p. (gr. 6 up). 1987. PLB 14.96 (*0-88110-247-4*); pap. 7.95 (*0-7460-0094-4*) EDC.

MECHANICAL ENGINEERING

see also Engines; Machinery; Power (Mechanics)

MECHANICAL MODELS

see Machinery–Models

MECHANICS

see also Dynamics; Force and Energy; Hydrostatics; Liquids; Machinery; Motion; Power (Mechanics); Steam Engines

Everyday Things. LC 92-52830. 24p. (ps-3). 1993. 8.95 (*1-56458-134-9*) Dorling Kindersley.
Herman, Gail. Cro Knows: All about Levers, Pulleys, Gears, Wheels, Bridges & Scales. LC 94-3118. (Illus.). 1994. write for info. (*0-679-86747-3*) Random Bks Yng Read.
Humberstone. Things That Go. (gr. 2-5). 1981. (Usborne-Hayes); pap. 4.50 (*0-86020-493-6*) EDC.
Macaulay, David. The Way Things Work. Macaulay, David, illus. 400p. (ps up). 1988. 29.45 (*0-395-42857-2*) HM.
Parker, Steve. Dime Como Funciona (How Things Work) (SPA., Illus.). 164p. (gr. 4 up). 1992. PLB 19.90 (*1-56294-179-8*) Millbrook Pr.
Pomeroy, Johanna P. Content Area Reading Skills Mechanics: Cause & Effect. (Illus.). (gr. 4). 1988. pap. text ed. 3.25 (*1-55737-088-5*) Ed Activities.
Richardson, Peter & Richardson, Bob. Great Careers for People Interested in How Things Work, 6 vols. LC 93-78076. (Illus.). 48p. (gr. 6-9). 1993. 16.95 (*0-8103-9389-1*, 102107, UXL) Gale.
Tallarico, Tony. I Didn't Know That about How Things Work. (Illus.). 32p. 1992. 9.95 (*1-56156-116-9*); pap. 2.95 (*1-56156-176-2*) Kidsbks.

MECHANICS (PERSONS)

Florian, Douglas. An Auto Mechanic. LC 90-48809. (Illus.). 24p. (ps up). 1991. 13.95 (*0-688-10635-8*); PLB 13.88 (*0-688-10636-6*) Greenwillow.
Gaskin, Carol. A Day in the Life of a Racing Car Mechanic. Klein, John F., illus. LC 84-2430. 32p. (gr. 4-8). 1985. PLB 11.79 (*0-8167-0091-5*); pap. 2.95 (*0-8167-0092-3*) Troll Assocs.

MEDAL OF HONOR

Beyer, W. F. & Keydel, D. F., eds. Deeds of Valor: How America's Civil War Heroes Won the Congressional Medal of Honor. (Illus.). 544p. (gr. 3-7). 1992. 9.98 (*0-681-41567-3*) Longmeadow Pr.

MEDICAL BOTANY

see Botany, Medical

MEDICAL CENTERS

see also Hospitals

MEDICAL PROFESSION

see Medicine; Physicians

MEDICAL TECHNOLOGY–VOCATIONAL GUIDANCE

Bryan, Jenny. Medical Technology. LC 90-25027. (Illus.). 48p. (gr. 5-7). 1991. 12.90 (*0-531-18398-X*, Pub. by Bookwright Pr) Watts.
Garell, Dale C. & Snyder, Solomon H., eds. Medical Technology. (Illus.). (gr. 6-12). 1993. 18.95 (*0-7910-0087-7*) Chelsea Hse.

MEDICINAL PLANTS

see Botany, Medical

MEDICINE

see also Anatomy; Bacteriology; Botany, Medical; Hospitals; Hygiene; Hypnotism; Mind and Body; Pathology; Pharmacy; Physiology
also headings beginning with the word Medical

Aaseng, Nathan. The Disease Fighters: The Nobel Prize in Medicine. (Illus.). 80p. (gr. 5 up). 1987. PLB 17.50 (*0-8225-0652-1*) Lerner Pubns.
Baron, Connie. The Physically Disabled. LC 88-21554. (Illus.). 48p. (gr. 5-6). 1988. text ed. 12.95 RSBE (*0-89686-417-0*, Crestwood Hse) Macmillan Child Grp.
Barrett, Norman S. Picture World of Ambulances. LC 90-31223. (Illus.). 32p. (gr. k-4). 1991. PLB 12.40 (*0-531-14090-3*) Watts.
Benziger, John. The Corpuscles Meet the Virus Invaders. Benziger, John & Benziger, Mary, illus. LC 90-80327. 30p. (gr. 3-6). 1990. 14.95 (*0-9620961-1-3*) Corpuscles Intergalactica.
Berger, Melvin. Sports Medicine. LC 81-43891. (Illus.). 128p. (gr. 5 up). 1982. (Crowell Jr Bks); (Crowell Jr Bks) HarpC Child Bks.
Bernards, Neal, ed. Euthanasia: Opposing Viewpoints. LC 89-2181. (Illus.). 235p. (gr. 10 up). 1989. PLB 17.95 (*0-89908-442-7*); pap. 9.95 (*0-89908-417-6*) Greenhaven.
Boy Scouts of America Staff. Medicine. (Illus.). 70p. (gr. 6-12). 1991. pap. 1.85 (*0-8395-3244-X*, 33244) BSA.
Buchman, Dian D. Medical Mysteries: Six Deadly Cases. (gr. 4-7). 1993. pap. 2.75 (*0-590-43468-3*) Scholastic Inc.
Center for Attitudinal Healing Staff. Advice to Doctors & Other Big People...from Kids. Jampolsky, Gerald, intro. by. (Illus.). 164p. (Orig.). (gr. 8-12). 1990. pap. 7.95 (*0-89087-618-5*) Celestial Arts.
Drotar, David L. The Fire Curse & Other Medical Mysteries. LC 94-5659. 1994. write for info. (*0-8027-8326-0*); write for info. (*0-8027-8327-9*) Walker & Co.
Finn, Jeffrey. Health Care Delivery. (Illus.). (gr. 6-12). 1993. 18.95 (*0-7910-0084-2*) Chelsea Hse.
Fradin, Dennis B. Medicine: Yesterday, Today, & Tomorrow. LC 88-15336. 194p. (gr. 4 up). 1989. PLB 19.95 (*0-516-00538-3*) Childrens.
Galperin, Ann. Gynecological Disorders. (Illus.). 112p. (gr. 6-12). 1991. 18.95 (*0-7910-0075-3*) Chelsea Hse.
Garell, Dale C. & Snyder, Solomon H., eds. Arthritis. (Illus.). (gr. 6-12). 1992. 18.95 (*0-7910-0057-5*) Chelsea Hse.
—Medical Disorders & Their Treatment Series, 27 vols. (Illus.). 2542p. (gr. 6-12). 1994. Set. 511.65x (*0-7910-0011-7*, Am Art Analog) Chelsea Hse.
—Medical Issues Series, 8 vols. (Illus.). 756p. (gr. 6-12). 1994. Set. PLB 208.45x (*0-7910-0012-5*, Am Art Analog) Chelsea Hse.
Gordon, James S. Holistic Medicine. (Illus.). 120p. (gr. 6-12). 1988. lib. bdg. 18.95x (*0-7910-0085-0*) Chelsea Hse.
Graham, Ian. Fighting Disease. LC 94-19981. Date not set. write for info. (*0-8114-3844-9*) Raintree Steck-V.
Grauer, Neil. Medicine & the Law. (Illus.). 120p. (gr. 6-12). 1990. 18.95 (*0-7910-0088-5*) Chelsea Hse.
Hawkes, Nigel. Medicine & Health. (Illus.). 32p. (gr. 5-8). PLB 13.95 (*0-8050-3417-X*) TFC Bks NY.
Jussim, Daniel. Medical Ethics. (Illus.). 144p. (gr. 7 up). 1990. lib. bdg. 13.98 (*0-671-70015-4*, J Messner) S&S Trade.
Kittredge, Mary. The Common Cold. (Illus.). 104p. (gr. 6-12). 1990. 18.95 (*0-7910-0060-5*) Chelsea Hse.
—Headaches. (Illus.). 104p. (gr. 6-12). 1989. 18.95 (*0-7910-0064-8*) Chelsea Hse.
Kusinitz, Mark. Folk Medicine. (Illus.). 112p. (gr. 6-12). 1992. 18.95 (*0-7910-0083-4*) Chelsea Hse.
Levine, Saul V. & Wilcox, Kathleen. Dear Doctor. LC 86-21335. 256p. (gr. 7 up). 1987. PLB 12.88 (*0-688-07094-9*); pap. 6.95 (*0-688-07095-7*) Lothrop.
Maloney, Michael. Straight Talk about Eating Disorders. 1993. pap. 3.99 (*0-440-21350-9*) Dell.
Marshall, Eliot & Finn, Jeffrey. Medical Ethics. (Illus.). 128p. (gr. 6-12). 1990. 18.95 (*0-7910-0086-9*) Chelsea Hse.
O'Neil, Karen E. Health & Medicine Projects for Young Scientists. LC 92-42745. (Illus.). 128p. (gr. 8-9). 1993. PLB 13.90 (*0-531-11050-8*); pap. 6.95 (*0-531-15668-0*) Watts.
Oxenbury, Helen. The Checkup. (Illus.). 24p. (ps-1). 1994. pap. 3.99 (*0-14-055275-8*, Puff Pied Piper) Puffin Bks.
Power, Vicki. Medicine & Health. LC 91-39578. (Illus.). 32p. (gr. 5-8). 1992. PLB 11.90 (*0-531-14198-5*) Watts.
Rockwell, Harlow. My Doctor. Rockwell, Harlow, illus. LC 91-27163. 24p. (ps-2). 1992. pap. 3.95 (*0-689-71606-0*, Aladdin) Macmillan Child Grp.
Rosenthal, Alan & Katz, Illana. Show Me Where It Hurts! Chiropractic Care. (ps-3). 1993. pap. 9.95 (*1-882388-10-0*) Real Life Strybks.
Savage, Eileen D. Winning over Asthma. Savage, Eileen D., illus. Plaut, Thomas F., intro. by. LC 89-50551. (Illus.). 32p. (gr. k-3). 1993. pap. 6.95 (*0-914625-09-8*) Pedipress.
Senior, Kathryn. Medicine: Doctors, Demons & Drugs. LC 93-10608. (Illus.). 48p. (gr. 5-8). 1993. 13.95 (*0-531-15263-4*) Watts.
Shoecraft, William D. Dr. Charles Drew. Gullatte, David, illus. 32p. 1994. text ed. 11.99 (*0-9633151-1-0*) Did You Know Pub.
Sirimarco, Elizabeth. Eating Disorders. 1993. pap. 14.95 (*1-85435-614-3*) Marshall Cavendish.
Stewart, Gail B. Alternative Healing: Opposing Viewpoints. LC 90-3807. (Illus.). 112p. (gr. 5-8). 1990. PLB 14.95 (*0-89908-083-9*) Greenhaven.
Sully, Nina. Looking at Medicine. (Illus.). 72p. (gr. 7-12). 1984. 19.95 (*0-7134-3847-9*, Pub. by Batsford UK) Trafalgar.
Tartakoff, Katy. Burned & Beautiful. Shields, Laurie, illus. 54p. (Orig.). Date not set. wkbk. 14.95 (*0-9629365-1-0*) Childrens Lgcy.
—Let Me Show You My World. Shields, Laurie, illus. 54p. (Orig.). Date not set. wkbk. 14.95 (*0-9629365-2-9*) Childrens Lgcy.
World Book Staff, ed. The World Book Health & Medical Annual - 1993. LC 87-648075. (Illus.). 400p. (gr. 6 up). 1992. PLB write for info. (*0-7166-1193-7*) World Bk.
Yancey, Diane. The Hunt for Hidden Killers: Ten Cases of Medical Mystery. LC 93-16638. (Illus.). 128p. (gr. 7 up). 1994. PLB 15.90 (*1-56294-389-8*) Millbrook Pr.

MEDICINE–BIOGRAPHY

see also Nurses and Nursing; Physicians; Surgeons

AESOP Enterprises, Inc. Staff & Crenshaw, Gwendolyn J. Charles Richard Drew: A Navigator on the River of Life. 16p. (gr. 3-12). 1991. pap. write for info. incl. cassette (*1-880771-06-3*) AESOP Enter.
Curtis, Robert H. Great Lives: Medicine. LC 92-5387. (Illus.). 336p. (gr. 4-6). 1993. SBE 22.95 (*0-684-19321-3*, Scribners Young Read) Macmillan Child Grp.

MEDICINE, DENTAL

see Dentistry; Teeth

MEDICINE–DICTIONARIES

Alstetter, Billy. Speech & Hearing. (Illus.). 112p. (gr. 6-12). 1991. 18.95 (*0-7910-0029-X*) Chelsea Hse.
Edelson, Edward. Sports Medicine. (Illus.). 112p. (gr. 6-12). 1988. 18.95 (*0-7910-0030-3*); pap. 9.95 (*0-7910-0470-8*) Chelsea Hse.
Garell, Dale C. & Snyder, Solomon H., eds. The Encyclopedia of Health, 79 vols. (Illus.). 8848p. (gr. 5 up). 1988. Set. lib. bdg. 1497.05 (*0-7910-0007-9*) Chelsea Hse.
Kittredge, Mary. Pain. (Illus.). 112p. (gr. 6-12). 1992. 18.95 (*0-7910-0072-9*) Chelsea Hse.
Kusinitz, Marc. Tropical Medicine. (Illus.). 112p. (gr. 6-12). 1990. 18.95 (*0-7910-0079-6*) Chelsea Hse.
Miller, Martha. Kidney Disorders. (Illus.). (gr. 6-12). 1992. 18.95 (*0-7910-0066-4*) Chelsea Hse.
Murphy, Wendy & Murphy, Jack. Nuclear Medicine. Garell, Dale C. & Snyder, Solomon H., eds. (Illus.). (gr. 6-12). 1994. 19.95 (*0-7910-0070-2*, Am Art Analog); pap. write for info. (*0-7910-0497-X*, Am Art Analog) Chelsea Hse.
Nardo, Don. Medical Diagnosis. (Illus.). (gr. 6-12). 1993. 18.95 (*0-7910-0067-2*) Chelsea Hse.
Wax, Nina. Occupational Health. Garell, Dale C. & Snyder, Solomon H., eds. LC 93-3903. (Illus.). (gr. 6-12). 1994. PLB 19.95 (*0-7910-0089-3*, Am Art Analog); pap. write for info. (*0-7910-0527-5*) Chelsea Hse.
Zonderman, John & Shader, Laurel. Mononucleosis & Other Infectious Diseases. (Illus.). 112p. (gr. 6-12). 1989. 18.95 (*0-7910-0069-9*) Chelsea Hse.

MEDICINE–FICTION

Benjamin, Cynthia. I Am a Doctor. Sagasti, Miriam, illus. 24p. (ps). 1994. 7.95 (*0-8120-6380-5*) Barron.
—Yo Soy un Medico. Sagasti, Miriam, illus. 24p. (ps). 1994. 7.95 (*0-8120-6414-3*) Barron.
Brandenberg, Franz. I Wish I Was Sick, Too! Aliki, illus. LC 75-46610. 32p. (gr. k-3). 1976. PLB 15.88 (*0-688-84047-7*) Greenwillow.
Cherry, Lynne. Who's Sick Today? Cherry, Lynne, illus. LC 87-22185. 24p. (ps-1). 1988. 11.95 (*0-525-44380-0*, 01160-350, DCB) Dutton Child Bks.
Cole, Joanna. Get Well, Clown-Arounds! Smath, Jerry, illus. LC 82-8148. 48p. (ps-3). 1983. 5.95 (*0-8193-1095-6*); PLB 5.95 (*0-8193-1096-4*) Parents.
Cooney, Caroline B. Emergency Room. 1994. pap. 3.25 (*0-590-45740-3*) Scholastic Inc.
Dahl, Roald. George's Marvelous Medicine. (gr. 4-7). 1991. pap. 3.99 (*0-14-034641-4*, Puffin) Puffin Bks.
Davidson, Martine. Kevin & the School Nurse. Hafner, Marylin, illus. LC 91-30194. 32p. (Orig.). (ps-2). 1992. PLB 5.99 (*0-679-91821-3*); pap. 2.25 (*0-679-81821-9*) Random Bks Yng Read.
—Maggie & the Emergency Room. Hafner, Marylin, illus. LC 91-31413. 32p. (Orig.). (ps-2). 1992. PLB 5.99 (*0-679-91818-3*); pap. 2.25 (*0-679-81818-9*) Random Bks Yng Read.
—Rita Goes to the Hospital. Jones, John, illus. LC 91-43293. 32p. (Orig.). (ps-2). 1992. PLB 5.99 (*0-679-91820-5*); pap. 2.25 (*0-679-81820-0*) Random Bks Yng Read.

—Robby Visits the Doctor. Stevenson, Nancy, illus. LC 91-30193. 32p. (Orig.). (ps-2). 1992. PLB 5.99 (*0-679-91819-1*); pap. 2.25 (*0-679-81819-7*) Random Bks Yng Read.
Fleischman, Paul. Path of the Pale Horse. LC 82-48611. 160p. (gr. 5 up). 1992. pap. 3.95 (*0-06-440442-0*, Trophy) HarpC Child Bks.
Hurd, Thacher. Tomato Soup. Hurd, Thacher, illus. LC 90-21421. 40p. (ps-3). 1992. 15.00 (*0-517-58237-6*); PLB 15.99 (*0-517-58238-4*) Crown Bks Yng Read.
Koeleman, Paul. Dr. Paul's Amazing Eyewear. (ps-3). 1993. 12.95 (*0-8478-5707-7*) Rizzoli Intl.
Loomis, Christine. One Cow Coughs: A Counting Book for the Sick & Miserable. Dypold, Pat, illus. LC 93-1836. 32p. (ps-2). 1994. 14.95g (*0-395-67899-4*) Ticknor & Flds Bks Yng Read.
Maccarone, Grace. Itchy, Itchy Chickenpox. Lewin, Betsy, illus. 32p. 1992. pap. 2.95 (*0-590-44948-6*) Scholastic Inc.
Pollack, Eileen. Whisper Whisper Jesse, Whisper Whisper Josh: A Story about AIDS. Templeman, Kristine, ed. Gilfoy, Bruce, illus. LC 92-72471. (Illus.). 32p. (ps up). 1992. PLB 16.95 (*0-9624828-4-6*); pap. 5.95 (*0-9624828-3-8*) Advantage-Aurora.
Robison, Deborah & Perez, Carla. Your Turn, Doctor. Robison, Deborah, illus. LC 81-68778. 32p. (ps-2). 1982. Dial Bks Young.
Rockwell, Anne & Rockwell, Harlow. Sick in Bed. Rockwell, Anne & Rockwell, Harlow, illus. LC 81-15637. 24p. (ps-k). 1982. RSBE 10.95 (*0-02-777730-8*, Macmillan Child Bk) Macmillan Child Grp.
Ruby, Lois. Miriam's Well. LC 91-46301. 288p. (gr. 7 up). 1993. 13.95 (*0-590-44937-0*) Scholastic Inc.
Shafner, R. L. & Weisberg, Eric J. The Hearty Treatment. LC 92-43369. 1993. 13.50 (*0-8225-2103-2*) Lerner Pubns.
Squeaky Sneaker Books Staff. Chicken Pox Panic. (ps-3). 1993. pap. 3.95 (*1-56233-176-0*, Squeaky Sneaker) Star Song TN.
Taylor, C. J. Little Water & the Gift of the Animals. Taylor, C. J., illus. LC 92-8413. 24p. (gr. 1-5). 1992. PLB 13.95 (*0-88776-285-9*) Tundra Bks.
Weaver, Lydia. Close to Home: A Story of the Polio Epidemic. Arrington, Aileen, illus. LC 92-25937. 64p. (gr. 2-6). 1993. PLB 12.99 (*0-670-84511-6*) Viking Child Bks.

MEDICINE–HISTORY

Bender, Lionel. Frontiers of Medicine. (Illus.). 32p. (gr. 4-6). 1991. PLB 12.40 (*0-531-17298-8*, Gloucester Pr) Watts.
Brownstone, David M. & Franck, Irene M. Healers. (Illus.). 240p. (gr. 6-10). 1989. 17.95x (*0-8160-1446-9*) Facts on File.
Cohen, Daniel. The Last Hundred Years: Medicine. LC 81-14357. (Illus.). 192p. (gr. 5 up). 1981. 8.95 (*0-87131-356-1*) M Evans.
Facklam, Margery & Facklam, Howard. Pharmacology: The Good Drugs. LC 92-9198. (Illus.). 128p. 1992. PLB 17.95x (*0-8160-2627-0*) Facts on File.
Garza, Hedda. Women in Medicine. (Illus.). 176p. (gr. 9-12). 1994. lib. bdg. 13.93 (*0-531-11204-7*) Watts.
Kalman, Bobbie. Early Health & Medicine. (Illus.). 64p. (gr. 4-5). 1983. 15.95 (*0-86505-031-7*); pap. 7.95 (*0-86505-030-9*) Crabtree Pub Co.
Ritchie, David. Health & Medicine. LC 94-17793. 1994. write for info. (*0-7910-2839-9*) Chelsea Hse.
Terkel, Susan N. Colonial American Medicine. LC 92-43988. 1993. 12.90 (*0-531-12539-4*) Watts.

MEDICINE, POPULAR

Here are entered medical books for the layman.

Hodgson, Karen. Boop! Boop! I'm Better. Davis, Wesley, illus. 12p. 1993. pap. 1.25 (*1-56794-046-3*, C2316) Star Bible.
Reid, Ace. Cowpokes Home Remedies. 7th ed. Reid, Ace, illus. 56p. (gr. k-5). pap. 5.95 (*0-917207-07-6*) Reid Ent.

MEDICINE, PEDIATRIC

see Children–Diseases

MEDICINE, PREVENTIVE

see Bacteriology; Hygiene; Immunity; Public Health

MEDICINE–U. S.

Wekesser, Carol, ed. Health Care in America: Opposing Viewpoints. LC 93-30963. (Illus.). 264p. (gr. 10 up). 1994. PLB 17.95 (*1-56510-135-9*); pap. text ed. 9.95 (*1-56510-134-0*) Greenhaven.

MEDICINE, VETERINARY

see Veterinary Medicine

MEDICINE–VOCATIONAL GUIDANCE

Carter, Adam. A Day in the Life of a Medical Detective. Duncan, Bob, illus. LC 84-8851. 32p. (gr. 4-8). 1985. PLB 11.79 (*0-8167-0097-4*); pap. text ed. 2.95 (*0-8167-0098-2*) Troll Assocs.
Edwards, Lois. Great Careers for People Interested in the Human Body, 6 vols. LC 93-78078. (Illus.). 48p. (gr. 6-9). 1993. 16.95 (*0-8103-9386-7*, 102104, UXL) Gale.
Epstein, Rachel. Careers in Health Care. Koop, C. Everett, intro. by. (Illus.). 112p. (gr. 6-12). 1989. 18.95 (*0-7910-0081-8*) Chelsea Hse.
Simpson, Carolyn & Hall, Penelope. Exploring Careers in Medicine. 1993. PLB 14.95 (*0-8239-1711-8*); pap. 9.95 (*0-8239-1712-6*) Rosen Group.

MEDICINE MAN

Liptak, Karen. North American Indian Medicine People. (Illus.). 64p. (gr. 5-8). 1992. pap. 5.95 (*0-531-15640-0*) Watts.

MEDIEVAL CIVILIZATION

see Civilization, Medieval

MEDITATIONS

Bean, Vaughan. The ABCs of Meditation & More: How to Maximize Your Child's Innate Intelligence. Miuru, illus. 96p. (Orig.). (gr. 2-6). 1994. pap. 11.95 (*0-9631740-1-0*) Millinnium-Holographic.
Each child born into our world arrives with their own individual & innate brand of intelligence. Before a child grows old enough to stop using his or her active imagination, you can instill positive & beneficial concepts inside them. In the opinion of the author, children who learn the art of meditation will usually & grow into adulthood with an expanded spiritual awareness & will possess the positive psychological tools necessary to help them be successful in adult life. THE ABC'S OF MEDITATION & MORE is designed to help develop a child's innate intelligence by introducing them to elementary concepts of meditation, creative visualization, guardian angels, lucid dreaming, the power of intuition, positive self image, & other beneficial concepts. Meditation can also help to temporarily calm children & reduce their stress level. THE ABC'S OF MEDITATION & MORE is recommended for children between the ages of 7 & 11 & is published by Books That Teach (an imprint of Holographic Books). Illustrations by Sri Lankan Artist Miuru. For additional information, contact: Holographic Books, P.O. Box 101862, Ft. Worth, TX 76185 or call 817-377-3303.
Publisher Provided Annotation.

Christian, S. Rickly. Alive: Daily Devotions for Young People. (Illus.). 1990. pap. 8.99 (*0-310-71031-6*, Campus Life) Zondervan.
—Alive Two. (Illus.). 1990. pap. 8.99 (*0-310-71041-3*, Campus Life) Zondervan.
Cristo Vive en Me. (SPA & ENG.). (gr. 2). 1983. pap. text ed. 2.00 (*0-8198-1426-1*); 1.00 (*0-8198-1427-X*) St Paul Bks.
Garth, Maureen. Starbright: Meditations for Children. LC 90-56458. 96p. (Orig.). 1991. pap. 10.00 (*0-06-250398-7*) Harper SF.
Hazen, Barbara S. World, World, What Can I Do? LC 90-43764. 32p. (ps-3). 1991. 8.95 (*0-8192-1537-6*) Morehouse Pub.
Hodgson, Joan. Our Father. Ripper, Peter, illus. (ps-3). 1977. pap. 2.95 (*0-85487-040-7*) DeVorss.
Hornsby, Sarah. At the Name of Jesus. Hornsby, Sarah, illus. LC 83-26245. 256p. 1986. 12.99 (*0-8007-9078-2*) Chosen Bks.
Jacobs, Mildred Spires. Come unto Me. (Illus.). 56p. (Orig.). (gr. 5-6). 1982. pap. 2.95 (*0-9609612-0-8*) Enrich Enter.
Johnson, Barry L. The Visit of the Tomten. 46p. 1990. pap. 7.95 (*0-8358-0439-9*) Upper Room.
Kelly, Robert. How Do I Make up My Mind, Lord? LC 82-70948. 112p. (Orig.). (gr. 3-7). 1982. pap. 5.99 (*0-8066-1923-6*, 10-3168, Augsburg) Augsburg Fortress.
Kerl, Mary A. Where Are You, Lord? LC 82-70949. 112p. (Orig.). (gr. 3-6). 1982. pap. 5.99 (*0-8066-1924-4*, 10-7069, Augsburg) Augsburg Fortress.
Langford, Anne. Meditation for Little People. Bethards, David, illus. LC 75-46191. 40p. (gr. k-4). 1976. pap. 6.95 (*0-87516-211-8*) DeVorss.
Manley, Stephen. More Than Words. 32p. 1988. pap. 1.95 (*0-8341-1236-1*) Beacon Hill.
O'Connor, Francine M. My Lenten Walk with Jesus. (Illus.). 32p. (gr. 1-3). 1992. pap. 1.95 incl. cut-out Lenten calendar (*0-89243-421-X*); pap. 9.95 incl. tchr's. packet (*0-89243-420-1*) Liguori Pubns.
Richter, Betts. Something Special Within. 2nd ed. Jacobsen, Alice, illus. 48p. (ps-5). 1982. pap. 6.95 (*0-87516-488-9*) DeVorss.
Sanders, Bill. Outtakes: Devotions for Girls. LC 88-18283. 160p. (gr. 7-12). 1988. pap. 7.99 (*0-8007-5284-8*) Revell.
Skold, Betty W. Lord, I Need An Answer: Story Devotions for Girls. LC 81-52279. 112p. (gr. 3-8). 1985. pap. 5.99 (*0-8066-1911-2*, 10-4099, Augsburg) Augsburg Fortress.
Swanson, Steve. Faith Journeys: Youth Devotions by Nine Youth Writers. LC 91-19369. 152p. (gr. 4 up). 1991. pap. 8.99 (*0-8066-2562-7*, 9-2562) Augsburg Fortress.

MEDITERRANEAN REGION

Lyle, Garry. Cyprus. (Illus.). 96p. (gr. 5 up). 1988. 14.95 (*0-222-00942-X*) Chelsea Hse.

MEIR, GOLDA (MABOVITZ), 1898-

Adler, David A. Our Golda: The Story of Golda Meir. Ruff, Donna, illus. LC 83-16798. 64p. (gr. 3-7). 1984. pap. 11.95 (*0-670-53107-3*) Viking Child Bks.
—Our Golda: The Story of Golda Meir. Ruff, Donna, illus. 64p. (gr. 2-6). 1986. pap. 4.50 (*0-14-032104-7*, Puffin) Puffin Bks.

MELVILLE, HERMAN, 1819-1891

Stefoff, Rebecca. Herman Melville. LC 93-11751. 1994. PLB 15.00 (*0-671-86771-7*, J Messner); pap. write for info. (*0-671-86772-5*, J Messner) S&S Trade.

MEMOIRS

see Autobiographies; Biography

MEMORY

Reid, S. Memory Skills. (Illus.). 48p. (gr. 6-10). 1988. PLB 12.96 (*0-88110-305-5*); pap. 5.95 (*0-7460-0162-2*) EDC.
Wartik, Nancy. Memory & Learning. (Illus.). (gr. 6-12). 1992. 18.95 (*0-7910-0022-2*) Chelsea Hse.

MEN

see Man

MENDESIA, GRACIA, 1510-1569

Stadtler, Bea. Story of Dona Gracia Mendes. Shevo, Aharon, illus. LC 70-83166. (gr. 6-9). 1969. 4.50 (*0-8381-0734-6*) United Syn Bk.

MENNONITES

Bial, Raymond. Amish Home. Bial, Raymond, illus. 40p. (gr. 4-7). 1993. 14.95 (*0-395-59504-5*) HM.
Kenna, Kathleen. Four Seasons. Stawicki, Andrew, photos by. (Illus.). 1995. 14.95g (*0-395-67344-5*) Ticknor & Flds Bks Yng Read.
Vernon, Louise A. Night Preacher. LC 73-94378. (Illus.). 134p. (gr. 3-8). 1969. pap. 5.95 (*0-8361-1774-3*) Herald Pr.

MENNONITES–FICTION

Mitchell, Barbara. Down Buttermilk Lane. LC 90-46876. 32p. (ps-3). 1993. 15.00 (*0-688-10114-3*); PLB 14.93 (*0-688-10115-1*) Lothrop.
Tallarico, Beatrice & Stone, S. C. Tindel's Blue Door. 2nd ed. (Illus.). 19p. (gr. 2-8). 1986. pap. 2.95 (*0-936191-14-7*) Tallstone Pub.
Vernon, Louise A. Beggars Bible: An Illustrated Historical Fiction of John Wycliffe for the 9-14 Age-Group. LC 77-131534. (Illus.). 128p. (gr. 4-9). 1971. 5.95 (*0-8361-1732-8*) Herald Pr.
—Secret Church. LC 67-15988. (Illus.). 128p. (gr. 3-8). 1967. pap. 5.95 (*0-8361-1783-2*) Herald Pr.
Vogt, Esther L. A Race for Land. 112p. (Orig.). (gr. 4-7). 1992. pap. 4.95 (*0-8361-3575-X*) Herald Pr.

MENSURATION

see also Geodesy; Surveying; Weights and Measures

Griffiths, Rose. Facts & Figures. Millard, Peter, photos by. LC 94-7984. (Illus.). 32p. (gr. 1 up). 1994. PLB 17.27 (*0-8368-1110-0*) Gareth Stevens Inc.
Hewavisenti, Lakshmi. Measuring. LC 91-10767. (Illus.). 32p. (gr. k-4). 1991. PLB 11.90 (*0-531-17319-4*, Gloucester Pr) Watts.
Hoban, Tana. Over, under & Through. Hoban, Tana, photos by. LC 72-81055. (Illus.). 32p. (ps-2). 1973. RSBE 13.95 (*0-02-744820-7*, Macmillan Child Bk) Macmillan Child Grp.
Markle, Sandra. Measuring Up: Experiments, Puzzles & Games Exploring Measurement. LC 94-19240. 1995. 16.00 (*0-689-31904-5*, Atheneum) Macmillan.
Measuring Length. (gr. 7-12). 1991. pap. 6.95 (*0-941008-72-X*) Tops Learning.
Sneider, Cary & Gould, Alan. Height-O-Meters. Bergman, Lincoln & Fairwell, Kay, eds. Klofkorn, Lisa, illus. Hoyt, Richard. (Illus.). 60p. (gr. 6-10). 1989. pap. 10.00 (*0-912511-22-2*) Lawrence Science.
Tyler, J. & Round, G. Starting to Measure. (Illus.). 24p. (ps up). 1991. pap. 3.50 (*0-7460-0624-1*, Usborne) EDC.
Westcott, Alvin & Schluep, J. Fun with Timothy Triangle. LC 66-11445. (Illus.). 64p. (gr. 4 up). 1970. pap. 3.94 deluxe ed. (*0-87783-014-2*); answer key 0.39x (*0-87783-164-5*) Oddo.

MENTAL DEFICIENCY

see Mentally Handicapped

MENTAL DISEASES

see Mental Illness; Psychology, Pathological

MENTAL HEALTH

see also Mental Illness; Mind and Body; Psychology, Pathological

Barbour, William, ed. Mental Illness: Opposing Viewpoints. LC 94-4977. (Illus.). 264p. (gr. 10 up). 1995. PLB 17.95 (*1-56510-209-6*); pap. text ed. 9.95 (*1-56510-208-8*) Greenhaven.
Chiles, John. Teenage Depression & Drugs. updated ed. (Illus.). (gr. 5 up). 1992. lib. bdg. 19.95 (*0-685-52254-7*); pap. 9.95 (*0-685-52255-5*) Chelsea Hse.
Clayton, Lawrence & Carter, Sharon. Coping with Depression. rev. ed. Rosen, Ruth, ed. (gr. 7-12). 1992. 14.95 (*0-8239-1488-7*) Rosen Group.
Cush, Cathie. Depression. LC 93-14252. (Illus.). (gr. 6-9). 1993. PLB 21.34 (*0-8114-3529-6*) Raintree Steck-V.
Hales, Dianne. Depression. LC 88-34176. (Illus.). 104p. (gr. 6-12). 1989. 18.95 (*0-7910-0046-X*) Chelsea Hse.

Mallick, Joan. Anorexia. Head, J. J., ed. Steffen, Ann T. & Slifko, Fran, illus. LC 86-72198. 16p. (Orig.). (gr. 10 up). 1987. pap. text ed. 2.75 (*0-89278-373-7*, 45-9773) Carolina Biological.

Maloney, Michael & Kranz, Rachel. Straight Talk about Anxiety & Depression. 128p. (gr. 5-12). 1991. lib. bdg. 16.95x (*0-8160-2434-0*) Facts on File.

Moss, Miriam. Be Positive. LC 92-26717. (Illus.). 32p. (gr. 6). 1993. text ed. 13.95 RSBE (*0-89686-786-2*, Crestwood Hse) Macmillan Child Grp.

Perry, Susan. How Are You Feeling Today? (Illus.). (gr. 2-6). 1992. PLB 14.95 (*0-89565-876-3*) Childs World.

Silverstein, Herma. Teenage Depression. (Illus.). 128p. (gr. 9-12). 1990. 13.45 (*0-531-15183-2*); PLB 13.40 (*0-531-10960-7*) Watts.

MENTAL HYGIENE

see Mental Health

MENTAL ILLNESS

see also Mental Health

Bergman, Thomas. We Laugh, We Love, We Cry: Children Living with Mental Retardation. LC 88-42971. (Illus.). 48p. (gr. 4-5). 1989. PLB 18.60 (*1-55532-914-4*) Gareth Stevens Inc.

Byck, Robert. Treating Mental Illness. updated ed. (Illus.). (gr. 5 up). 1992. lib. bdg. 19.95 (*0-685-52256-3*) Chelsea Hse.

Dinner, Sherry H. Nothing to Be Ashamed Of: Growing up with Mental Illness in Your Family. LC 88-13244. 160p. (gr. 5 up). 1989. pap. 7.95 (*0-688-08493-1*, Pub. by Beech Tree Bks) Morrow.

—Nothing to Be Ashamed Of: Growing up with Mental Illness in Your Family. 160p. (ps-3). 1989. PLB 12.93 (*0-688-08482-6*) Lothrop.

Fullen, Dave. The Mountain Song. Farley, Brendon, illus. Oremus, Earl, contrib. by. (Illus.). 20p. (Orig.). (gr. 1-6). 1992. pap. 14.95 incl. cass. (*1-881650-00-6*) Mntn Bks.

Goldman, M. Nikki. Emotional Disorders. LC 93-42609. 1994. write for info. Set; 14.95 (*1-85435-619-4*) Marshall Cavendish.

Greenberg, Harvey R. Emotional Illness in Your Family: Helping Your Relatives, Helping Yourself. LC 89-31042. 304p. (gr. 6 up). 1989. SBE 16.95 (*0-02-736921-8*, Macmillan Child Bk) Macmillan Child Grp.

Johnson, Julie T. Understanding Mental Illness: For Teens Who Care about Someone with Mental Illness. 70p. (gr. 6 up). Repr. of 1989 ed. 4.95g (*0-8225-9574-5*) Lerner Pubns.

Lundy, Alan. Diagnosing & Treating Mental Illness. (Illus.). 136p. (gr. 6-12). 1990. 18.95 (*0-7910-0047-8*) Chelsea Hse.

Markosian, Becky T. & Thayne, Emma L. Hope & Recovery: A Mother-Daughter Story about Anorexia Nervosa, Bulimia, & Manic Depression. Rosoff, Iris, ed. LC 91-36619. (Illus.). 176p. (gr. 9-12). 1992. PLB 14.40 (*0-531-11140-7*) Watts.

Sessions, Deborah. My Mom Is Different. Chalkley, Ausan, illus. 32p. (Orig.). 1994. pap. 8.95 (*0-9629164-3-9*) Sidran Pr.

Smith, Douglas W. Schizophrenia. LC 92-21140. (Illus.). (gr. 7-12). 1993. PLB 13.40 (*0-531-12514-9*) Watts.

MENTAL ILLNESS–FICTION

Bennett, James. I Can Hear the Mourning Dove. 224p. (gr. 7 up). 1990. 14.45 (*0-395-53623-5*) HM.

Berry, Liz. Mel. LC 93-7484. 224p. (gr. 7 up). 1993. pap. 3.99 (*0-14-036534-6*, Puffin) Puffin Bks.

Fran, Renee & Freshman, Floris, illus. What Happened to Mommy? 32p. (Orig.). (ps-6). 1994. pap. 5.95 (*0-9640250-0-0*) Eastman NY.

Hamilton-Paterson, James. House in the Waves. LC 76-103043. (gr. 8 up). 1970. 21.95 (*0-87599-171-8*) S G Phillips.

Joosse, Barbara M. Anna & the Cat Lady. Mayo, Gretchen W., illus. LC 91-12510. 176p. (gr. 3-7). 1992. 14.00 (*0-06-020242-4*) HarpC Child Bks.

Neufeld, John. Lisa, Bright & Dark. (gr. 7 up). 1969. 21.95 (*0-87599-153-X*) S G Phillips.

Riley, Jocelyn. Crazy Quilt. 176p. (gr. 7-12). 1986. pap. 2.50 (*0-553-25640-8*) Bantam.

Streatfeild, Noel. Thursday's Child. (Orig.). (gr. 5 up). 1986. pap. 3.50 (*0-440-48687-4*, YB) Dell.

Zindel, Paul. Harry & Hortense at Hormone High. 160p. (gr. 7-12). 1985. pap. 3.99 (*0-553-25175-9*, Starfire) Bantam.

MENTAL PHILOSOPHY

see Philosophy; Psychology

MENTAL TELEPATHY

see Thought Transference

MENTALLY HANDICAPPED

see also Mental Illness

Amenta, Charles A. Russell Is Extra Special: A Book about Autism for Children. LC 91-41863. 32p. (ps-3). 1992. pap. 8.95 (*0-945354-44-4*); 16.95 (*0-945354-43-6*) Magination Pr.

Clinkscale, Lonnie J. Hey Dummy! A Testimony of an Overcomer. LC 94-94507. 112p. (gr. 3 up). 1994. pap. 6.95 (*0-9640311-0-8*) Clinkscale Pubns. There are few things more devastating to a child's fragile self-esteem than being humiliated before classmates & called a "dummy" by friends, teachers & even family members. But millions of bright, sensitive, yet learning disabled children live this nightmare every day...clinging to the hope that one day, perhaps, they can achieve their life's goals. Everyone has a turning point in their life. For Lonnie Clinkscale, author of HEY DUMMY!, it was a newly discovered faith in God & the help of one special teacher. He'll tell you how he was given the strength to overcome incredible odds: * A paralyzing learning disability that prevented him from spelling his name or adding 2 plus 2 on the blackboard. * Severe stuttering, rendering even simple sentences almost unintelligible. * Insensitive taunting from fellow students, & even a guidance counselor who encouraged him to join the army because he "wasn't college material." * A deprived childhood, marred by family tensions, divorce & poverty. Once encouraged & made to feel like a "somebody," Clinkscale's natural abilities blossomed & he progressed from being unable to read aloud to winning speech tournaments & becoming an honors student. Today, he is an administrative executive at Ohio's 12th largest hospital. The books can be purchased through Clinkscale Publications & Productions, Inc. by calling 1-800-505-6464 or by writing to Clinkscale Publications & Productions, Inc., P.O. Box 5696, Youngstown, OH 44504 (volume discounts are available). ***Publisher Provided Annotation.***

Dick, Jean. Mental & Emotional Disabilities. LC 88-21555. (Illus.). 48p. (gr. 5-6). 1988. text ed. 12.95 RSBE (*0-89686-418-9*, Crestwood Hse) Macmillan Child Grp.

Dolce, Laura. Mental Retardation. (Illus.). (gr. 6-12). 1994. 19.95 (*0-7910-0050-8*, Am Art Analog); pap. write for info. (*0-7910-0530-5*, Am Art Analog) Chelsea Hse.

Dunbar, Robert E. Mental Retardation. LC 91-18513. (Illus.). 96p. (gr. 9-12). 1991. PLB 13.40 (*0-531-12502-5*) Watts.

Exley, Helen. What It's Like to Be Me. 2nd ed. (Illus.). 127p. (gr. 4-11). 1984. pap. 10.95 (*0-377-00144-9*) Friendship Pr.

Fullen, Dave. A Nest in the Gale. Farley, Brendon, illus. LC 93-208563. 72p. (Orig.). (gr. 2-6). 1993. cancelled 24.95 (*1-881650-03-0*); pap. 18.95 incl. audio cassette (*1-881650-01-4*) Mntn Bks.

Geraghty, Helen M. Chris Burke: Actor. (Illus.). 1994. 18.95 (*0-7910-2081-9*, Am Art Analog); pap. write for info. (*0-7910-2094-0*, Am Art Analog) Chelsea Hse.

Lee, Gregory. Chris Burke: He Overcame Down Syndrome. LC 93-18213. 1993. 14.60 (*0-86593-263-8*); 10.95s.p. (*0-685-66611-5*) Rourke Corp.

Sobol, Harriet L. My Brother Steven Is Retarded. Agre, Patricia, illus. LC 76-46996. 32p. (gr. 3-6). 1977. RSBE 13.95 (*0-02-785990-8*, Macmillan Child Bk) Macmillan Child Grp.

MENTALLY HANDICAPPED–EDUCATION

Crowther, Jean D. What Do I Do Now, Mom? Growing-up Guidance for Young Teen-age Girls. Bagley, Val C., illus. LC 80-82257. 86p. (gr. 9-12). 1980. 8.98 (*0-88290-134-6*) Horizon Utah.

Fullen, Dave. Lessons Learned: Students with Learning Disabilities, Ages 7-19, Share What They've Learned about Life & Learning. Farley, Brendon, illus. 40p. (Orig.). (gr. 1 up). 1993. pap. 6.95 (*1-881650-02-2*) Mntn Bks.

Gehret, Jeanne. Eagle Eyes: A Child's Guide to Paying Attention. 2nd ed. Covert, Susan, illus. 40p. (gr. 1-5). 1991. 13.95 (*0-9625136-5-2*); pap. 8.95 perfect bdg. (*0-9625136-4-4*) Verbal Images Pr.

Harris. Learning Disorders. 1993. write for info. (*0-8050-3043-3*) H Holt & Co.

Howard, Diane W. Swimming Upstream: A Complete Guide to the College Application Process for the Learning Disabled Student. Lord, J. R., intro. by. (Illus.). 140p. (Orig.). (gr. 8-12). 1989. pap. write for info. wkbk. Hunt Hse Pub.

MENTALLY HANDICAPPED–FICTION

Berkus, Clara W. Charlsie's Chuckle. Dodd, Margaret, illus. LC 91-46655. 32p. (gr. k-6). 1992. 14.95 (*0-933149-50-6*) Woodbine House.

Booth, Zilpha M. Finding a Friend. Breeden, Teisha, illus. LC 86-50987. 54p. (gr. 1-5). 1987. pap. 3.95 (*0-932433-22-7*) Windswept Hse.

Brown, Towana J. Leave, Retard, Leave! Brown, Becky, illus. 127p. (Orig.). (gr. 8-12). 1988. pap. 3.50 (*0-9622060-0-8*) T J Brown.

Buchanan, Dawna L. The Falcon's Wing. LC 91-22545. 144p. (gr. 5 up). 1992. 13.95 (*0-531-05986-3*); lib. bdg. 13.99 (*0-531-08586-4*) Orchard Bks Watts.

Conly, Jane L. Crazy Lady! LC 92-18348. 192p. (gr. 5 up). 1993. 13.00 (*0-06-021357-4*); PLB 12.89 (*0-06-021360-4*) HarpC Child Bks.

Fassler, Joan. One Little Girl. Smyth, M. Jane, illus. LC 76-80120. 32p. (ps-3). 1969. 16.95 (*0-87705-008-2*) Human Sci Pr.

Fitzgerald, John & Fitzgerald, Lyn. Barnaby's Birthday. Posey, Pam, illus. LC 92-34275. 1993. 14.00 (*0-383-03618-6*) SRA Schl Grp.

Fleming, Virginia. Be Good to Eddie Lee. Cooper, Floyd, illus. 32p. (ps-3). 1993. PLB 14.95 (*0-399-21993-5*, Philomel Bks) Putnam Pub Group.

Griffith, Connie. Secret Behind Locked Doors. LC 93-8420. 128p. (gr. 5-8). 1994. pap. 5.99 (*0-8010-3864-2*) Baker Bk.

—The Shocking Discovery. 128p. (gr. 6-8). 1994. pap. 5.99 (*0-8010-3866-9*) Baker Bk.

Hesse, Karen. Wish on a Unicorn. LC 92-26792. 112p. (gr. 3-7). 1993. pap. 3.99 (*0-14-034935-9*) Puffin Bks.

Jasmine, Cairo. Our Brother Has Down's Syndrome. (Illus.). 24p. (ps-8). 1985. PLB 14.95 (*0-920303-30-7*, Pub. by Annick CN); pap. 4.95 (*0-920303-31-5*, Pub. by Annick CN) Firefly Bks Ltd.

Keyes, Daniel. Flowers for Algernon. (gr. 8 up). 1970. pap. 3.50 (*0-553-25665-3*) Bantam.

Klein, Robin. Boss of the Pool. 96p. (gr. 3-7). 1992. pap. 3.99 (*0-14-036037-9*) Puffin Bks.

Lund, Lauren. Bunny: A Storybook for Children Who Have a Parent with Multiple Personalities. Lund, Lauren, illus. 36p. (Orig.). 1993. pap. text ed. 5.95 (*0-9637149-1-0*) Soft Words.

Nelson, JoAnne. Friends All Around. DuCharme, Tracy, illus. LC 92-4657. 24p. (Orig.). (gr. k-2). 1993. pap. 5.95 (*0-935529-17-9*) Comprehen Health Educ.

Nystrom, Carolyn. The Trouble with Josh. Rees, Gary, illus. 48p. (gr. 6-12). 1989. text ed. 7.99 (*0-7459-1621-X*) Lion USA.

O'Shaughnessy, Ellen. Somebody Called Me a Retard Today - & My Heart Felt Sad. Garner, David, illus. LC 92-10812. 24p. 1992. 13.95 (*0-8027-8196-9*); PLB 14.85 (*0-8027-8197-7*) Walker & Co.

Radley, Gail. Oakley Duster Day. LC 94-10858. 1995. 14.00 (*0-02-775792-7*) Macmillan Child Grp.

Tamar, Erika. No Defense. LC 93-3248. (gr. 9-12). 1993. write for info. (*0-15-278537-X*) HarBrace.

Testa, Maria. Thumbs Up, Rico! Paterson, Diane, illus. 1994. write for info. (*0-8075-7906-8*) A Whitman.

Wilson, Nancy H. The Reason for Janey. LC 93-22930. 176p. (gr. 3-7). 1994. SBE 14.95 (*0-02-793127-7*, Macmillan Child Bk) Macmillan Child Grp.

Wood, June R. The Man Who Loved Clowns. 192p. (gr. 5-9). 1992. 14.95 (*0-399-21888-2*, Putnam) Putnam Pub Group.

Wright, Betty R. My Sister Is Different. Cogancherry, Helen, illus. Nietupski, John, intro. by. LC 80-25508. (Illus.). 32p. (gr. k-6). 1981. PLB 16.67 (*0-8172-1369-4*) Raintree Steck-V.

MENTALLY RETARDED

see Mentally Handicapped

MERCHANDISING

see Retail Trade

MERCHANTS

Caselli, Giovanni. The Everyday Life of a Florentine Merchant. Caselli, Giovanni, illus. LC 86-4365. 32p. (gr. 3-6). 1991. PLB 12.95 (*0-87226-107-7*) P Bedrick Bks.

MERCURY (PLANET)

Baker, David. Exploring Venus & Mercury. LC 88-33707. (Illus.). 48p. (gr. 4-6). 1989. PLB 18.60 (*0-86592-371-X*); lib. bdg. 13.95s.p. (*0-685-58638-3*) Rourke Corp.

Brewer, Duncan. Mercury. LC 90-40807. (Illus.). 64p. (gr. 5-9). 1992. PLB 13.95 (*0-685-57609-4*) Marshall Cavendish.

Daily, Robert. Mercury. LC 93-6097. (Illus.). 64p. (gr. 5-8). 1994. PLB 12.90 (*0-531-20164-3*) Watts.

Fradin, Dennis B. Mercury. LC 89-25359. (Illus.). 48p. (gr. k-4). 1990. PLB 12.85 (*0-516-01186-3*); pap. 4.95 (*0-516-41186-1*) Childrens.

Simon, Seymour. Mercury. LC 91-17404. (Illus.). 24p. (gr. k up). 1992. 14.00 (*0-688-10544-0*); PLB 13.93 (*0-688-10545-9*) Morrow Jr Bks.

Vogt, Gregory L. Mercury. LC 93-11218. (Illus.). 32p. (gr. 2-4). 1994. PLB 12.90 (*1-56294-390-1*) Millbrook Pr.

MERMAIDS–FICTION

Andersen, Hans Christian. The Little Mermaid. Treherne, Katie T., adapted by. & illus. LC 89-31602. 42p. (gr. k-3). 1989. 15.95 (*0-15-246320-8*) HarBrace.

—The Little Mermaid. Iwasaki, Chihiro, illus. 1991. pap. 3.95 (*0-590-44456-5*) Scholastic Inc.

—Little Mermaid. pap. 2.95 (*0-88388-039-3*) Bellerophon Bks.

—The Little Mermaid. Hague, Michael, illus. LC 92-29807. 1994. 16.95 (*0-8050-1010-6*, Bks Young Read) H Holt & Co.

—The Little Mermaid: The Original Story. Santore, Charles, illus. LC 93-20375. 1993. 14.00 (*0-517-06495-2*) Random Hse Value.

—La Sirenita - The Little Mermaid. (ps-3). 1994. pap. 2.95 (*0-486-28001-2*) Dover.

Another Fine Mess. write for info. (*1-56326-170-7*, 05-21) Disney Bks By Mail.
Applegate, Katherine. Boyfriend Mix-up. LC 93-72888. (Illus.). 80p. (gr. 1-4). 1994. pap. 3.50 (*1-56282-642-5*) Disney Pr.
—The Haunted Palace. Barnhart, Philo, illus. LC 93-70936. 80p. (gr. 1-4). 1993. pap. 3.50 (*1-56282-503-8*) Disney Pr.
—King Triton, Beware! Barnhart, Philo, illus. LC 93-71030. 80p. (gr. 1-4). 1993. pap. 3.50 (*1-56282-502-X*) Disney Pr.
Ariel & Sebastian: Serpent Teen. (Illus.). 48p. (gr. 3-7). 1992. pap. 2.95 (*1-56115-266-8*, 21807, Golden Pr) Western Pub.
Ariel's Painting Party. write for info. (*1-56326-173-1*, 05-24) Disney Bks By Mail.
As Fun As You Feel. write for info. (*1-56326-153-7*, 05-04) Disney Bks By Mail.
Balducci, Rita. Disney's the Little Mermaid. (ps). 1993. 3.95 (*0-307-12537-8*, Golden Pr) Western Pub.
Bee Nice. write for info. (*1-56326-167-7*, 05-18) Disney Bks By Mail.
The Big Switch. write for info. (*1-56326-159-6*, 05-10) Disney Bks By Mail.
Blanco, Alberto. Desert Mermaid (La sirena del desierto) LC 92-1105. (Illus.). 32p. (gr. k-5). 1992. 13.95 (*0-89239-106-5*) Childrens Book Pr.
Calmenson, Stephanie, adapted by. Walt Disney Pictures Presents the Little Mermaid. Maten, Frenc, illus. (ps-k). 1991. pap. write for info. (*0-307-10027-8*, Golden Pr) Western Pub.
Carpenter, Mimi G. Mermaid in a Tidal Pool. Carpenter, Mimi G., illus. 32p. (Orig.). (ps-6). 1985. pap. 8.95 (*0-9614628-0-9*) Beachcomber Pr.

—Of Lucky Pebbles & Mermaid's Tears. Carpenter, Mimi G., illus. 32p. (ps-5). 1994. pap. 9.95 (*0-9614628-2-5*) Beachcomber Pr.
Author/Illustrator Mimi Gregoire Carpenter (What The Sea Left Behind, 1981), presents a rhyming fantasy with an environmental theme for children through fifth grade (Includes a shell identification page). "Mimi Gregoire Carpenter conveys a child-like sense of wonder in her artwork & writing. As revealed in her work, her inspiration comes from the sea & its creatures. Mimi's philosophy, spirituality & love... of the environment are embodied in her beautiful illustrations & storylines."--New England Science Center, Worcester, Mass. Don't miss this unusual bunch of creatures - Sea Uglies & Sandcreatures, Tidal Pool Trolls & Lagoonies. Learn about the environment, mischief, being different, being creative - about things you can change & about things you cannot & while you're at it - learn about why we call beachglass "Mermaid's Tears" & why pebbles with rings around them are called "Lucky." Shorah, a "non-traditional" mermaid & the story's main character, learns to face the consequences of her actions after she conjures a storm that disrupts the sea world. 8 1/2" X 10 1/2" - detailed opaque watercolors & graphite - durable coated paper - stapled binding - paperback 32pp. $9.95. Write or call Beachcomber "Studio" Press, RR3, Box 2220, Oakland, ME 04963; 207-465-7197.
Publisher Provided Annotation.

Carr, M. J. Ariel the Spy. LC 92-54512. (Illus.). 80p. (gr. 1-4). 1993. pap. 3.50 (*1-56282-372-8*) Disney Pr.
—Arista's New Boyfriend. LC 92-54511. (Illus.). 80p. (gr. 1-4). 1993. pap. 3.50 (*1-56282-371-X*) Disney Pr.
Castles in the Sand. write for info. (*1-56326-161-8*, 05-12) Disney Bks By Mail.
A Charmed Life. write for info. (*1-56326-150-2*, 05-01) Disney Bks By Mail.
Cheer-up Sebastian. write for info. (*1-56326-151-0*, 05-02) Disney Bks By Mail.
Christopher, Jess. Alana's Secret Friend. Marvin, Fred & Barnhart, Philo, illus. 80p. (gr. 1-4). 1994. pap. 3.50 (*0-7868-4002-1*) Disney Pr.
Climo. If You Meet a Mermaid. Date not set. 15.00 (*0-06-023876-3*); PLB 14.89 (*0-06-023877-1*) HarpC Child Bks.
Colmenson, Stephanie. Walt Disney Pictures Presents the Little Mermaid: Ariel above the Sea. Mateu, Franc, illus. (gr. k-2). 1991. 4.25 (*0-307-11697-2*, Golden Pr) Western Pub.
The Crabby Conductor. write for info. (*1-56326-163-4*, 05-14) Disney Bks By Mail.
Dale, Nora. Nan & the Sea Monster. (Illus.). 32p. (gr. 1-4). 1989. PLB 18.99 (*0-8172-3526-4*); pap. 3.95 (*0-8114-6728-7*) Raintree Steck-V.
Daniells, Trenna. All Things Change: Maylene the Mermaid. Braille International, Inc. Staff & Henry, James, illus. (Orig.). (gr. 1). 1992. pap. 10.95 (*1-56956-004-8*) W A T Braille.
—All Things Change: Maylene the Mermaid. Braille International, Inc. Staff & Henry, James, illus. (Orig.). (gr. 2). 1992. pap. 10.95 (*1-56956-029-3*) W A T Braille.
Dear Diary. write for info. (*1-56326-157-X*, 05-08) Disney Bks By Mail.
Detective Sebastian. write for info. (*1-56326-165-0*, 05-16) Disney Bks By Mail.
Disney, Walt. The Little Mermaid: A Visit with Friends Storyboard; Ariel's Story, Sebastian's Story. (ps-3). 1993. 6.98 (*0-453-03127-7*) Mouse Works.
—Little Mermaid under the Sea. (gr. 4-7). 1991. pap. 2.25 (*0-307-21805-8*, Golden Pr) Western Pub.
Disney's Little Mermaid. (Illus.). 128p. 1992. 5.95 (*1-56138-154-3*) Running Pr.
Disney's The Little Mermaid. 20p. (ps-4). 1993. 24.00 (*0-307-74304-7*, 64304, Golden Pr) Western Pub.
Disney's The Little Mermaid: Tales from under the Sea. LC 90-85427. 80p. (gr. 2-7). 1991. 10.95 (*1-56282-014-1*) Disney Pr.
A Dragon's Tail. write for info. (*1-56326-166-9*, 05-17) Disney Bks By Mail.
Flounder, My Hero. write for info. (*1-56326-155-3*, 05-07) Disney Bks By Mail.
Flounder's Folly. write for info. (*1-56326-152-9*, 05-03) Disney Bks By Mail.
The Good Sport. write for info. (*1-56326-171-5*, 05-22) Disney Bks By Mail.
Goodman, Beth. Meet Crystal Starr: A Coloring Activity Book. (ps-3). 1993. pap. 1.95 (*0-590-46605-4*) Scholastic Inc.
Her Majesty, Ariel. write for info. (*1-56326-154-5*, 05-05) Disney Bks By Mail.
How Does Your Garden Grow? write for info. (*1-56326-168-5*, 05-19) Disney Bks By Mail.
Hughes, Linda. Disney's the Little Mermaid. (ps-3). 1993. pap. 2.25 (*0-307-12787-7*, Golden Pr) Western Pub.
Kaye, Marilyn. Reflections of Arsulu. LC 92-53935. (Illus.). 80p. (gr. 1-4). 1992. pap. 3.50 (*1-56282-248-9*) Disney Pr.
—The Same Old Song. LC 92-53936. (Illus.). 80p. (gr. 1-4). 1992. pap. 3.50 (*1-56282-249-7*) Disney Pr.
Korman, Justine. The Little Mermaid. Ong, Cristina, illus. 32p. (ps-1). 1993. pap. 2.50 (*0-590-46448-5*, Cartwheel) Scholastic Inc.
—Little Mermaid: Best Baby-Sitter under the Sea. (ps-3). 1994. pap. 2.25 (*0-307-12818-0*, Golden Pr) Western Pub.
Little Mermaid. (Illus.). 24p. (ps-2). 1991. write for info. (*0-307-74014-5*, Golden Pr) Western Pub.
The Little Mermaid. 16p. (gr. 3 up). 1992. Incl. xylotone. 14.95 (*0-7935-1390-1*, 00824001) H Leonard.
Littledale, Freya, as told by. The Little Mermaid. San Souci, Daniel, illus. 40p. (Orig.). (gr. k-3). 1986. pap. 3.95 (*0-590-44358-5*) Scholastic Inc.
Ludier, Carol. Little Mermaid: What's under the Sea? (ps-3). 1993. 9.95 (*0-307-06077-2*, Golden Pr) Western Pub.
The Magic Melody. write for info. (*1-56326-169-3*, 05-20) Disney Bks By Mail.
Martin, Kerry, illus. Disney's The Little Mermaid. LC 90-85428. 12p. (gr. 2-6). 1991. 9.95 (*1-56282-017-6*) Disney Pr.
Marvin, Fred, illus. Disney's the Little Mermaid Novels, 4 bks. (gr. 1-4). 1993. Boxed set incl. Green-Eyed Pearl, Nefazia Visits the Palace, Reflections of Arsulu & The Same Old Song. pap. 11.80 (*1-56282-562-3*) Disney Pr.
Melendez, Francisco. The Mermaid & the Major: or, the True Story of the Invention of the Submarine. Melendez, Francisco, illus. 64p. 1991. 24.95 (*0-8109-3619-4*) Abrams.
Noble, Trinka H. Hansy's Mermaid. Noble, Trinka H., illus. LC 82-45509. 32p. (ps-2). 1983. PLB 10.89 (*0-8037-3606-1*) Dial Bks Young.
Paradise Island. write for info. (*1-56326-160-X*, 05-11) Disney Bks By Mail.
Patrick, Denise L. Disney's The Little Mermaid: Ariel's Secret. DiCicco, Sue, illus. 14p. (ps-k). 1992. bds. write for info. (*0-307-12393-6*, 12393, Golden Pr) Western Pub.
Rodriguez, K. S. The Dolphins of Coral Dove, No. 11. Marvin, Fred & Barnhart, Philo, illus. 80p. (gr. 1-4). 1994. pap. 3.50 (*0-685-70832-2*) Disney Pr.
St. Pierre, Stephanie. Practical-Joke War. LC 93-73812. (Illus.). 80p. (gr. 1-4). 1994. pap. 3.50 (*1-56282-641-7*) Disney Pr.
San Souci, Robert D. Sukey & the Mermaid. Pinkney, Brian, illus. LC 90-24559. 32p. (gr. k-3). 1992. RSBE 15.00 (*0-02-778141-0*, Four Winds) Macmillan Child Grp.
Scared Silly. write for info. (*1-56326-162-6*, 05-13) Disney Bks By Mail.
Scuttle's Last Flight. write for info. (*1-56326-158-8*, 05-09) Disney Bks By Mail.
Singer, A. L., adapted by. Disney's the Little Mermaid. Dias, Ron, illus. LC 92-74259. 96p. 1993. 14.95 (*1-56282-429-5*); PLB 14.89 (*1-56282-430-9*) Disney Pr.
—Disney's the Little Mermaid. Dias, Ron, illus. LC 92-74260. 64p. (gr. 2-6). 1993. pap. 3.50 (*1-56282-436-8*) Disney Pr.
A Slippery Deck. write for info. (*1-56326-172-3*, 05-23) Disney Bks By Mail.
Smith, Donald. Tiny Mermaid's Hide & Seek Adventure. (Illus.). 16p. (ps-2). 1993. 12.95 (*0-590-46673-9*) Scholastic Inc.
Stapleton, John T. The Littlest Mermaid. Flanigan, Ruth J., illus. 24p. (ps-2). 1992. pap. 0.99 (*1-56293-109-1*) McClanahan Bk.
Teitelbaum, Michael. Little Mermaid: Ariel's New Friend. (ps-3). 1994. pap. 2.25 (*0-307-12817-2*, Golden Pr) Western Pub.
Teitlbaum, Michael. Little Mermaid. (ps-3). 1991. 3.50 (*0-307-12335-9*, Golden Pr) Western Pub.
Thomas, Iolette. Mermaid Janine. (ps-3). 1993. pap. 4.95 (*0-590-46594-5*) Scholastic Inc.
An Undersea Wish. write for info. (*1-56326-164-2*, 05-15) Disney Bks By Mail.
Walt Disney Staff. La Sirenita (The Little Mermaid) (SPA.). (ps-3). 1992. 6.98 (*0-453-03017-3*) Viking-Penguin.
Walt Disney's the Little Mermaid. (ps-3). 1991. write for info. (*0-307-12345-6*, Golden Pr) Western Pub.
Weyn, Suzanne. Green-Eyed Pearl. LC 92-53938. (Illus.). (gr. 1-4). 1992. pap. 3.50 (*1-56282-250-0*) Disney Pr.
—Nefazia Visits the Palace. LC 92-53937. (Illus.). (gr. 1-4). 1992. pap. 3.50 (*1-56282-247-0*) Disney Pr.
Whistles & Doubloons. write for info. (*1-56326-156-1*, 05-06) Disney Bks By Mail.
Willis, Val. The Mystery in the Bottle. Shelley, John, illus. 32p. (gr. k-3). 1991. bds. 14.95 (*0-374-35194-5*) FS&G.

MERRIMAC (FRIGATE)

Carter, Alden R. Battle of the Ironclads: The Monitor & the Merrimack. LC 93-417. (Illus.). 64p. (gr. 4-6). 1993. PLB 12.90 (*0-531-20091-4*) Watts.
Stein. Monitor & Merrimac. 1989. pap. 3.95 (*0-516-44662-2*) Childrens.

MERRY-GO-ROUNDS–FICTION

Bolton, Mimi D. Merry-Go-Round Family. 2nd ed. (Illus.). 225p. (gr. 3-7). 1990. Repr. of 1954 ed. 14.95x (*0-9614274-2-6*) Wisla Pubs.
Chorao, Kay. Carousel Round & Round. LC 93-35520. 1995. write for info. (*0-395-63632-9*, Clarion Bks) HM.
Cummings, Pat. Carousel. Cummings, Pat, illus. LC 93-8708. 32p. (ps-3). 1994. RSBE 14.95 (*0-02-725512-3*, Bradbury Pr) Macmillan Child Grp.
Edens, Cooper. Shawnee Bill's Enchanted Five-Ride Carousel. 1994. 15.00 (*0-671-75952-3*, Green Tiger) S&S Trade.
Foster, Elizabeth. Gigi in America: The Further Adventures of a Merry-Go-Round Horse. Cote, Phyllis N., illus. 130p. (gr. 4-8). pap. 9.95 (*0-913028-69-X*) North Atlantic.
—Gigi: The Story of a Merry-Go-Round Horse. Birchoff, Ilse, illus. 124p. (gr. 4-8). pap. 9.95 (*0-913028-55-X*) North Atlantic.

—Gigi: The Story of a Merry-Go-Round Horse. Israel, Nancy M. & Israel, Nancy M.frwd. by. (Illus.). 118p. (gr. 2-6). 1990. Repr. of 1943 ed. 14.95 (*0-9626165-0-8*) Paper Memories.
1990 edition of an enduring 1943 children's classic. Foreword by Nancy M. Israel, author's daughter. $14.95 plus $2.00 shipping. Paper Memories, Box 234, Glen Echo, MD 20812. 40% discount on orders of 5 or more copies. When he first comes to the Prater in Vienna as a new horse for the carousel, Gigi is shy, lonely & frightened of the gold ring. But through his friendship with Lili, the first child to climb into his saddle, he gains skill & confidence & becomes the children's favorite horse. Suddenly, with the outbreak of World War I, the merry-go-round is dismantled, & Lili & Gigi say a sad goodbye to each other. Gigi then finds himself on a small merry-go-round in Paris where a new young friend teaches him to speak French. But this pleasant time ends also when the little carousel is sold & Gigi is carted off to a London fleamarket. How Gigi eventually comes to America where he finds a happy surprise brings a heart-warming conclusion to this charming story. A "must read" for carousel lovers of all

ages.
Publisher Provided Annotation.

Greaves, Margaret. Star Horse. (ps-3). 1992. 13.95 (*0-8120-6294-9*) Barron.
Hegarty, Sue & Geoghegan, Judy. Carousel Coloring Book. Hennigh, Susan, illus. 32p. (Orig.). (gr. k-8). 1989. pap. 4.50 (*0-9622526-1-1*) Freels Fndtn.
Jarvis McGraw, Eloise & McGraw, Lauren. Merry Go Round in Oz. Martin, Dick, illus. 303p. (gr. 3-6). 1989. 24.95 (*0-929605-06-3*) Books Wonder.
Martin, Bill, Jr. & Archambault, John. Up & Down on the Merry-Go-Round. Rand, Ted, illus. LC 87-28836. 32p. (ps-2). 1991. pap. 4.95 (*0-8050-1638-4*, Bks Young Read) H Holt & Co.
Nelson, JoAnne. Friends All Around. DuCharme, Tracy, illus. LC 92-4657. 24p. (Orig.). (gr. k-2). 1993. pap. 5.95 (*0-935529-17-9*) Comprehen Health Educ.
Ray, Mary L. My Carousel Horse. Taxali, Gary, illus. LC 93-45876. 1900. write for info. (*0-15-200023-2*) HarBrace.
Samstag, Nicholas. Kay Kay Comes Home. Shahn, Ben, illus. (gr. 5-7). 1962. 10.95 (*0-8392-3015-X*) Astor-Honor.
Walter, Mildred P. Tiger Ride. LC 92-40281. (Illus.). 32p. (ps-2). 1995. RSBE 17.00 (*0-02-792303-7*, Bradbury Pr) Macmillan Child Grp.

MESMERISM
see Hypnotism

METABOLISM
see also Nutrition

METAL WORK
see Metalwork

METALLURGY
see also Mineralogy
also names of metals, e.g. Gold; etc.

Mitgutsch, Ali. From Ore to Spoon. Mitgutsch, Ali, illus. LC 80-28862. 24p. (ps-3). 1981. PLB 10.95 (*0-87614-161-0*) Carolrhoda Bks.

METALS

Billings, Charlene W. Superconductivity: From Discovery to Breakthrough. LC 90-20782. (Illus.). 64p. (gr. 3-7). 1991. 15.95 (*0-525-65048-2*, Cobblehill Bks) Dutton Child Bks.
Daniel, Jamie & Bonar, Veronica. Coping with - Metal Trash. Kenyon, Tony, illus. LC 93-32482. 32p. (gr. 2 up). 1994. PLB 17.27 (*0-8368-1058-9*) Gareth Stevens Inc.
Mebane, Robert & Rybolt, Thomas. Metals. (Illus.). 64p. (gr. 5-8). 1995. bds. 15.95 (*0-8050-2842-0*) TFC Bks NY.
Reymond, Jean-Pierre. Metals: Born of Earth & Fire. Prunier, James, illus. LC 87-34596. 38p. (gr. k-5). 1988. 5.95 (*0-944589-19-7*, 197) Young Discovery Lib.
Story of Metals. (ARA., Illus.). (gr. 5-12). 1987. 3.95x (*0-86685-227-1*) Intl Bk Ctr.

METALWORK
see also Jewelry; Steel

Boy Scouts of America. Metalwork. (Illus.). 36p. (gr. 6-12). 1969. pap. 1.85 (*0-8395-3312-8*, 33312) BSA.
Groneman, Chris H. & Feirer, John L. Getting Started in Metalworking. (Illus.). 1979. text ed. 9.52 (*0-07-024998-9*) McGraw.
Hawkins, Leslie V. Art Metal & Enameling. 234p. (gr. 9-12). 1974. text ed. 17.60 (*0-02-662240-8*) Bennett IL.
Mitgutsch, Ali. From Ore to Spoon. Mitgutsch, Ali, illus. LC 80-28862. 24p. (ps-3). 1981. PLB 10.95 (*0-87614-161-0*) Carolrhoda Bks.
Walker, John R. Metal Projects, Bk. 3. LC 77-21602. (Illus.). 96p. 1977. pap. 9.60 (*0-87006-238-7*); pap. 7.20 (*0-685-01929-2*) Goodheart.

METAMORPHIC ROCKS
see Rocks

METEORITES

Branley, Franklyn M. Shooting Stars. Keller, Holly, illus. LC 88-14190. 32p. (ps-1). 1989. 13.95 (*0-690-04701-0*, Crowell Jr Bks); PLB 13.89 (*0-690-04703-7*, Crowell Jr Bks) HarpC Child Bks.
British Museum, Geological Department Staff. Moon, Mars & Meteorites. (Illus.). 36p. (gr. 7 up). 1986. pap. 5.95 (*0-521-32414-9*) Cambridge U Pr.
Carlisle, Madelyn. Let's Investigate Magical, Mysterious Meteorites. Banek, Yvette, illus. LC 92-12776. (gr. 4-7). 1992. pap. 4.95 (*0-8120-4733-8*) Barron.
Lauber, Patricia. Voyagers from Space: Meteors & Meteorites. Eagle, Mike, illus. LC 86-47745. 80p. (gr. 5 up). 1989. (Crowell Jr Bks); PLB 15.89 (*0-690-04634-0*, Crowell Jr Bks) HarpC Child Bks.
Sipiera, Paul P. Meteorites. LC 94-10947. (Illus.). 48p. (gr. k-4). 1994. PLB 17.20 (*0-516-01068-9*); pap. 4.95 (*0-516-41068-7*) Childrens.

METEOROLOGISTS

Mogil, H. Michael & Levine, Barbara G. The Amateur Meteorologist: Explorations & Investigations. (Illus.). (gr. 5-8). 1994. pap. 6.95 (*0-531-15696-6*) Watts.
Witty, Margot & Witty, Ken. A Day in the Life of a Meteorologist. Sanacore, Stephen, photos by. LC 80-54098. (Illus.). 32p. (gr. 4-8). 1981. PLB 11.79 (*0-89375-450-1*); pap. 2.95 (*0-89375-451-X*) Troll Assocs.

METEOROLOGY
see also Air; Atmosphere; Climate; Clouds; Floods; Hurricanes; Lightning; Rain and Rainfall; Seasons; Snow; Solar Radiation; Storms; Thunderstorms; Tornadoes; Weather; Weather Forecasting; Winds

Berger, Melvin & Berger, Gilda. How's the Weather? A Look at Weather & How It Changes. Cymerman, John, illus. LC 93-16686. 48p. (gr. k-3). 1993. PLB 12.00 (*0-8249-8641-5*, Ideals Child); pap. 4.50 (*0-8249-8599-0*) Hambleton-Hill.
Bower, Miranda. Experiment with Weather. LC 92-41126. 1993. 17.50 (*0-8225-2458-9*) Lerner Pubns.
Bramwell, Martyn. Weather. (Illus.). 32p. (gr. 5-8). 1994. PLB write for info. (*0-531-14306-6*) Watts.
Casey, Denise. Weather Everywhere. Gilmore, Jackie, photos by. LC 92-23239. (Illus.). 40p. (gr. k-4). 1995. RSBE 15.00 (*0-02-717777-7*, Bradbury Pr) Macmillan Child Grp.
Gakken Co. Ltd. Staff, ed. Wind & Weather. Time-Life Books Inc. Editors, tr. (Illus.). 90p. (gr. k-3). 1989. 15.93 (*0-8094-4829-7*); PLB 21.27 (*0-8094-4830-0*) Time-Life.
Ganeri, Anita. Outdoor Science. LC 93-13125. (Illus.). 48p. (gr. 5 up). 1993. text ed. 13.95 RSBE (*0-87518-579-7*, Dillon) Macmillan Child Grp.
—The Weather. LC 92-26987. 1993. 11.90 (*0-531-14250-7*) Watts.
Graf, Mike. The Weather Report. (gr. 3-6). 1989. pap. 13.95 (*0-8224-7511-1*) Fearon Teach Aids.
Green, Ivah. Splash & Trickle. Connor, Bil, illus. (gr. 2-3). 1978. pap. 1.25 (*0-89508-062-1*) Rainbow Bks.
McVey, Vicki. Sierra Club Book of Weatherwisdom. (gr. 4-7). 1991. 16.95 (*0-316-56341-2*) Little.
Mogil, H. Michael & Levine, Barbara G. The Amateur Meteorologist: Explorations & Investigations. LC 93-17506. (Illus.). 144p. (gr. 6-9). 1993. PLB 12.90 (*0-531-11045-1*) Watts.
Petty, Kate. The Sky Above Us. (Illus.). 32p. (gr. 2-4). 1993. pap. 5.95 (*0-8120-1234-8*) Barron.
Pluckrose, Henry A. Weather. LC 93-45660. 1994. PLB 11.95 (*0-516-08123-3*) Childrens.
Simon, Seymour. Weather. LC 92-31069. (Illus.). 40p. (gr. k up). 1993. 15.00 (*0-688-10546-7*); PLB 14.93 (*0-688-10547-5*) Morrow Jr Bks.
Souza, D. M. Northern Lights. (gr. 4-7). 1994. pap. 7.95 (*0-87614-629-9*) Carolrhoda Bks.
Steele, Philip. Heatwave: Causes & Effects. LC 90-46263. (Illus.). 32p. (gr. 5-8). 1991. PLB 12.40 (*0-531-11023-0*) Watts.
Taylor, Michael. Aircraft Carriers. 1989. pap. 3.95 (*0-590-41997-8*) Scholastic Inc.
Welch, Catherine A. Clouds of Terror. (ps-3). 1994. pap. 5.95 (*0-87614-639-6*) Carolrhoda Bks.

METEORS
see also Meteorites

Asimov, Isaac. Comets & Meteors. (gr. 4-7). 1991. pap. 4.99 (*0-440-40450-9*, YB) Dell.
—What is a Shooting Star? LC 90-25922. (Illus.). 24p. (gr. 2-3). 1991. PLB 15.93 (*0-8368-0436-8*) Gareth Stevens Inc.
Bendick, Jeanne. Comets & Meteors: Visitors from Space. (Illus.). 32p. (gr. k-2). 1991. PLB 12.90 (*1-56294-001-5*); pap. 4.95 (*1-878841-55-6*) Millbrook Pr.
Branley, Franklyn M. Shooting Stars. Keller, Holly, illus. LC 88-14190. 32p. (ps-1). 1991. pap. 4.50 (*0-06-445103-8*, Trophy) HarpC Child Bks.
Simon, Seymour. Comets, Meteors, & Asteroids. LC 93-51251. 1994. write for info. (*0-688-12709-6*); PLB write for info. (*0-688-12710-X*) Morrow Jr Bks.
Sorensen, Lynda. Comets & Meteors. LC 93-15690. (gr. 5 up). 1993. write for info. (*0-86593-277-8*) Rourke Corp.

METHOD OF STUDY
see Study, Method of

METHODOLOGY
see special subjects with the subdivision Methodology, e.g. Science–Methodology; etc.

METRIC SYSTEM

Brady, Janeen. The Metrics Are Coming! (gr. k-4). 1980. cassette 8.95 (*0-944803-14-8*) Brite Music.
Brownlee, Juanita. Tangram Geometry in Metric. Merrick, Paul, illus. (Orig.). (gr. 5-10). 1976. pap. 7.95 (*0-918932-43-2*, 0140701407) Activity Resources.
Camilli, Thomas. Make It Metric. (Illus.). 32p. (gr. 4-6). 1993. pap. text ed. 4.95 (*1-55799-251-7*) Evan-Moor Corp.
Donovan, Frank. Let's Go Metric. (Illus.). 192p. 1974. 6.95 (*0-679-40057-5*, Weybright) McKay.
Finnegan, Thomas J., et al. Metric System Study Aid. 1976. pap. 2.50 (*0-87738-042-2*) Youth Ed.
Metric Measure. (gr. 7-12). 1992. pap. 8.80 (*0-941008-76-2*) Tops Learning.
Ross, Frank, Jr. The Metric System: Measures for All Mankind. Galster, Robert, illus. LC 74-14503. 128p. (gr. 7-10). 1974. 29.95 (*0-87599-198-X*) S G Phillips.

METROLOGY
see Mensuration; Weights and Measures

METROPOLITAN AREAS
see also Cities and Towns

METTERNICH-WINNEBURG, CLEMENS LOTHAR WENZEL, FURST VON, 1773-1859

Von der Heide, John. Klemens von Metternich. Schlesinger, Arthur M., Jr., intro. by. (Illus.). 112p. (gr. 5 up). 1988. lib. bdg. 17.95 (*0-87754-541-3*) Chelsea Hse.

MEXICAN WAR, 1845-1848
see U. S.–History–War with Mexico, 1845-1848

MEXICAN AMERICANS
see also Mexicans in the U. S.

Alvarez, Everett, Jr. & Clinton, Susan. Everett Alvarez, Jr. A Hero for Our Times. LC 90-38375. (Illus.). 32p. (gr. 2-4). 1990. PLB 11.80 (*0-516-04277-7*); pap. 3.95 (*0-516-44277-5*) Childrens.
Atkin, S. Beth. Voices from the Fields: America's Migrant Children. LC 92-32248. 96p. 1993. 16.95 (*0-316-05633-2*) Little.
Bandon, Alexandra. Mexican Americans. LC 92-41001. (Illus.). 112p. (gr. 6 up). 1993. text ed. 14.95 RSBE (*0-02-768142-4*, New Discovery Bks) Macmillan Child Grp.
Bishop, Kathleen. A White Face Painted Brown: A Young Girl's Journey into the Bosom of a Black & Mexican Los Angeles Ghetto Called Aliso Village. Shwed, Joanne, ed. 180p. (Orig.). (gr. 8-12). 1993. pap. text ed. 12.95 (*0-9636217-1-8*) Pallas Athena.
Brimner, Larry D. A Migrant Family. (Illus.). 40p. (gr. 4-8). 1992. PLB 17.50 (*0-8225-2554-2*) Lerner Pubns.
Catalano, Julie. Mexican Americans. Moynihan, Daniel P., intro. by. 112p. (Orig.). (gr. 5 up). 1988. 17.95 (*0-87754-857-9*); pap. 9.95 (*0-7910-0272-1*) Chelsea Hse.
Emiliano Zapata: Mini Play. (gr. 5 up). 1977. 5.00 (*0-89550-357-3*) Stevens & Shea.
Green, Carl R. Oscar de la Hoya. LC 93-33583. 1994. text ed. 13.95 (*0-89686-835-4*, Crestwood Hse) Macmillan Child Grp.
Hewett, Joan. Hector Lives in the United States Now: The Story of a Mexican-American Child. Hewett, Richard R., illus. LC 89-36572. 48p. (gr. 2-5). 1990. (Lipp Jr Bks); PLB 13.89 (*0-397-32278-X*, Lipp Jr Bks) HarpC Child Bks.
Krull, Kathleen. The Other Side: How Kids Live in a California Latino Neighborhood. Hautzig, David, photos by. LC 93-15845. (Illus.). (ps-6). 1994. write for info. (*0-525-67438-1*, Lodestar Bks) Dutton Child Bks.
Lannert. Mexican Americans. 1991. 13.95s.p. (*0-86593-139-9*); PLB 18.60 (*0-685-59187-5*) Rourke Corp.
Marquez, Nancy & Perez, Theresa. Portraits of Mexican Americans. 96p. (gr. 4-8). 1991. 10.95 (*0-86653-605-1*, GA1324) Good Apple.
Martinez, Elizabeth C. Henry Cisneros: Mexican-American Leader. LC 92-21384. (Illus.). 32p. (gr. 2-4). 1993. PLB 12.90 (*1-56294-368-5*); pap. 4.95 (*1-56294-810-5*) Millbrook Pr.
Morey, Janet N. & Dunn, Wendy. Famous Mexican Americans. LC 89-7218. (Illus.). (gr. 5 up). 1989. 14.99 (*0-525-65012-1*, Cobblehill Bks) Dutton Child Bks.
Nicholson, Loren. Romualdo Pacheco's California! The Mexican-American Who Won. (Illus.). 112p. (Orig.). (gr. 10-12). 1991. pap. text ed. 12.95 (*0-9623233-2-2*) CA HPA.
Rodriguez, Consuelo. Cesar Chavez. (Illus.). 112p. (gr. 5 up). 1991. lib. bdg. 17.95 (*0-7910-1232-8*) Chelsea Hse.
Sylvester, Diane. The Hispanic Question Collection. 120p. (gr. 4-8). 1994. 6.95 (*0-88160-263-9*, LW202) Learning Wks.

MEXICAN AMERICANS–FICTION

Ada, Alma F. I Love Saturdays y Domingos. Bryant, Michael, illus. LC 94-3362. 1995. 14.95 (*0-689-31819-7*, Atheneum) Macmillan.
Bunting, Eve. A Day's Work. Himler, Ronald, illus. 1994. 14.95 (*0-395-67321-6*, Clarion Bks) HM.
Cazet, Denys. Born in the Gravy. Cazet, Denys, illus. LC 92-44523. 32p. (ps-1). 1993. 14.95 (*0-531-05488-8*); PLB 14.99 (*0-531-08638-0*) Orchard Bks Watts.
Dorros, Arthur. Radio Man - Don Radio: A Story in English & Spanish. Dorros, Sandra M., tr. LC 92-28369. (Illus.). 40p. (gr. 1-5). 1993. 16.00 (*0-06-021547-X*); PLB 15.89 (*0-06-021548-8*) HarpC Child Bks.
Havill, Juanita. Treasure Nap. Savadier, Elivia, illus. 32p. (gr. k-3). 1992. 14.95 (*0-395-57817-5*) HM.
Jones, Jay S. Rosalia, Be Proud. Jones, MariaElena G., illus. 41p. (gr. k-6). 1992. 14.95 (*0-9632040-0-9*); PLB 14.95 (*0-9632040-1-7*) Integrity Inst.
Levene, Nancy S. Hero for a Season. Reck, Sue, ed. LC 93-21126. 96p. (gr. 3-6). 1994. pap. 4.99 (*0-7814-0702-8*, Chariot Bks) Cook.
Martini, Teri. Feliz Navidad, Pablo. McNichols, William H., illus. (gr. 4 up). 1990. 2.95 (*0-8091-6597-X*) Paulist Pr.
Marvin, Isabel R. Josefina & the Hanging Tree. LC 91-34501. 128p. (gr. 6-9). 1992. pap. 9.95 (*0-87565-103-8*) Tex Christian.
Mora, Pat. A Birthday Basket for Tia. Lang, Cecily, illus. LC 91-15753. 32p. (ps-1). 1992. RSBE 13.95 (*0-02-767400-2*, Macmillan Child Bk) Macmillan Child Grp.
Paley, Nina, illus. Inside-Out Feelings. LC 93-8953. 1993. write for info. (*1-56071-315-1*) ETR Assocs.
Perez, L. King. Ghoststalking. LC 93-41576. 1994. 18.95 (*0-87614-821-6*) Carolrhoda Bks.
Politi, Leo. Three Stalks of Corn. Politi, Leo, illus. LC 93-19737. 32p. (gr. k-3). 1994. pap. 4.95 (*0-689-71782-2*, Aladdin) Macmillan Child Grp.
Quin-Harkin, Janet. Roni's Dream Boy, No. 2. LC 93-50680. (Illus.). 176p. (gr. 3-6). 1994. pap. 2.95 (*0-8167-3415-1*) Troll Assocs.
Soto, Gary. Baseball in April: And Other Stories. 111p. (gr. 7 up). 1990. 14.95 (*0-15-205720-X*) HarBrace.
—Baseball in April & Other Stories. 137p. (gr. 3-7). 1991. pap. 4.95 (*0-15-205721-8*, Odyssey) HarBrace.
—Local News. LC 92-37905. 1993. 13.95 (*0-15-248117-6*) HarBrace.

—The Mustache. Hinojosa, Celina, illus. LC 93-42395. 1995. 14.95 (*0-399-22617-6*, Putnam) Putnam Pub Group.
—Pacific Crossing. 1992. write for info. (*0-15-259187-7*, HB Juv Bks) HarBrace.
—The Pool Party. Casilla, Robert, illus. LC 92-34407. 1993. 13.95 (*0-385-30890-6*) Delacorte.
—The Shirt. Velasquez, Eric, illus. LC 91-26145. 64p. (gr. 2-5). 1992. 14.95 (*0-385-30665-2*) Delacorte.
—Too Many Tamales. Martinez, Ed, illus. 32p. (ps-3). 1993. 14.95 (*0-399-22146-8*, Putnam) Putnam Pub Group.
Stafford, Jean. The Scarlet Letter. LC 92-44056. 1994. 13.95 (*0-88682-588-1*) Creative Ed.
Taylor, T. Maria: A Christmas Story. 1992. 13.95 (*0-15-217763-9*, HB Juv Bks) HarBrace.
Thomas, Jane R. Lights on the River. Dooling, Michael, illus. LC 93-33636. 32p. (ps-3). 1994. 15.95 (*0-7868-0004-6*); PLB 15.89 (*0-7868-2003-9*) Hyprn Child.

MEXICANS IN THE U. S.

Pinchot, Jane. The Mexicans in America. rev. ed. LC 72-3587. (Illus.). 104p. (gr. 5 up). 1989. PLB 15.95 (*0-8225-0222-4*); pap. 5.95 (*0-8225-1016-2*) Lerner Pubns.

MEXICO

Barysh, Ann, et al. The Suitcase Scholar Goes to Mexico. Lerner Geography Department Staff, ed. (Illus.). (gr. 4-6). 1992. Set incls. teaching guide, Mexico in Pictures, A Family in Mexico, Count Your Way Through Mexico, Cooking the Mexican Way, Focus on Mexico: Modern Life in an Ancient Land & wall map. saddle-stitch bdg. 49.95 (*0-8225-4003-7*); teaching guide 15.95 (*0-685-55160-1*) Lerner Pubns.
Benitez, Mirna. How Spider Tricked Snake. (Illus.). 32p. (gr. 1-4). 1989. PLB 18.99 (*0-8172-3524-8*); pap. 3.95 (*0-8114-6725-2*) Raintree Steck-V.
Brandt, Keith. Mexico & Central America. Eitzen, Allan, illus. LC 84-2668. 32p. (gr. 3-6). 1985. PLB 9.49 (*0-8167-0264-0*); pap. text ed. 2.95 (*0-8167-0265-9*) Troll Assocs.
Department of Geography, Lerner Publications Company Staff. Mexico in Pictures. (Illus.). 64p. (gr. 5 up). 1988. PLB 17.50 (*0-8225-1801-5*) Lerner Pubns.
Fincher, Ernest B. Mexico & the United States: Their Linked Destinies. LC 82-45581. (Illus.). 224p. (gr. 7 up). 1983. (Crowell Jr Bks); (Crowell Jr Bks) HarpC Child Bks.
Flint, David. Mexico. LC 93-7529. (Illus.). 32p. (gr. 3-4). 1993. PLB 19.24 (*0-8114-3419-2*) Raintree Steck-V.
Franco, Betsy. Around the World, Vol. 1: Mexico. (Illus.). 48p. (gr. 1-3). 1993. pap. text ed. 7.95 (*1-55799-256-8*) Evan-Moor Corp.
Ganeri, Anita & Wright, Rachel. Mexico. LC 94-7099. 1994. write for info. (*0-531-14316-3*) Watts.
Garver, Susan & McGuire, Paula. From Mexico, Cuba, & Puerto Rico. (gr. 7-11). pap. 2.50 (*0-317-13311-X*, LFL) Dell.
Getting to Know Mexico. 48p. 1991. 8.95 (*0-8442-7623-5*, Natl Textbk) NTC Pub Grp.
Haskins, Jim. Count Your Way Through Mexico. Byers, Helen, illus. 24p. (gr. 1-4). 1989. 17.50 (*0-87614-349-4*); pap. 5.95 (*0-87614-517-9*) Carolrhoda Bks.
Howard, John. Mexico. (Illus.). 48p. (gr. 5 up). 1992. PLB 12.95 (*0-382-24247-5*) Silver Burdett Pr.
Irizarry, Carmen. Passport to Mexico. rev. ed. LC 93-46692. 1994. write for info. (*0-531-14322-8*) Watts.
Jacobsen, Karen. Mexico. Kratky, Lada, tr. from ENG. LC 82-4437. (SPA., Illus.). 48p. (gr. k-4). 1984. PLB 12.85 (*0-516-31632-X*); pap. 4.95 (*0-516-51632-9*) Childrens.
Jacobson, Karen. Mexico. LC 82-4437. (Illus.). (gr. k-4). 1982. PLB 12.85 (*0-516-01632-6*); pap. 4.95 (*0-516-41632-4*) Childrens.
James, Ian. Mexico. LC 89-50383. (Illus.). 32p. (gr. 4-6). 1989. PLB 11.90 (*0-531-10761-2*) Watts.
Kalman, Bobbie. Mexico - the Land. LC 93-37747. (Illus.). 32p. (Orig.). (gr. 4-9). 1993. PLB 15.95 (*0-86505-214-X*); pap. 7.95 (*0-86505-294-8*); Span. ed. pap. 7.95 (*0-86505-398-7*) Crabtree Pub Co.
—Mexico - The People. LC 93-34764. (Illus.). 32p. (Orig.). (gr. 4-9). 1993. PLB 15.95 (*0-86505-215-8*); pap. 7.95 (*0-86505-295-6*); Span. ed. pap. 7.95 (*0-86505-399-5*) Crabtree Pub Co.
Paltrowitz, Stuart & Paltrowitz, Donna. Content Area Reading Skills-Competency Mexico: Locating Details. (Illus.). (gr. 4). 1987. pap. text ed. 3.25 (*0-89525-854-4*) Ed Activities.
Parker, Lewis. Dropping in on Mexico. LC 93-42777. 1994. write for info. (*1-55916-001-2*) Rourke Bk Co.
Poulet, Virginia. Azulin Visita a Mexico (Blue Bug Visits Mexico) Anderson, Peggy P., illus. LC 89-25420. (SPA.). 32p. (ps-3). 1990. PLB 11.80 (*0-516-33429-8*); pap. 3.95 (*0-516-53429-7*) Childrens.
Reilly, Mary J. Mexico. LC 90-22469. (Illus.). 128p. (gr. 5-9). 1991. PLB 21.95 (*1-85435-385-3*) Marshall Cavendish.
Rummel, Jack. Mexico. (Illus.). 128p. (gr. 5 up). 1990. 14.95 (*0-7910-1110-0*) Chelsea Hse.
Stein, R. Conrad. Mexico. LC 83-21049. (Illus.). 128p. (gr. 5-9). 1984. PLB 20.55 (*0-516-02772-7*) Childrens.
Widdows, Richard. Mexico. (Illus.). 48p. (gr. 4-8). 1987. PLB 14.95 (*0-382-09506-5*) Silver Burdett Pr.

MEXICO–ANTIQUITIES

Arnold, Caroline. Mexico's Ancient City of Teotihuacan: The First Metropolis in the Americas. Hewitt, Richard, photos by. LC 93-40811. (Illus.). 1994. 14.95 (*0-395-66584-1*, Clarion Bks) HM.

MEXICO–BIOGRAPHY

Bains, Rae. Benito Juarez, Hero of Modern Mexico. Davis, Allen, illus. LC 92-2291. 48p. (gr. 4-6). 1992. lib. bdg. 10.79 (*0-8167-2825-9*); pap. 3.50 (*0-8167-2826-7*) Troll Assocs.
De Varona, Frank. Miguel Hidalgo y Costilla - Father of Mexican Independence. LC 92-36562. (Illus.). 32p. (gr. 2-4). 1993. PLB 12.90 (*1-56294-370-7*) Millbrook Pr.
Hoobler, Dorothy & Hoobler, Thomas. Mexican Portraits. Kuester, Robert, illus. LC 92-13642. 96p. (gr. 7-8). 1992. PLB 22.80 (*0-8114-6376-1*) Raintree Steck-V.
Roman, Joseph. Octavio Paz: Mexican Poet & Critic. LC 92-47051. (Illus.). 1994. PLB 18.95 (*0-7910-1249-2*, Am Art Analog); pap. write for info. (*0-7910-1276-X*, Am Art Analog) Chelsea Hse.
Stein, R. Conrad. The Mexican Revolution, 1910-1920. LC 93-17259. (Illus.). 144p. (gr. 4-7). 1994. RSBE 14.95 (*0-02-786950-4*, New Discovery Bks) Macmillan Child Grp.

MEXICO (CITY)

Davis, James E. & Hawke, Sharryl D. Mexico City. (Illus.). 64p. (gr. 4-9). 1990. PLB 11.95 (*0-8172-3029-7*) Raintree Steck-V.

MEXICO–FICTION

Ancona, George. Pinata Maker el Pinatero. LC 93-2389. (gr. 4-7). 1994. pap. 8.95 (*0-15-200060-7*, HB Juv Bks) HarBrace.
Bovaird, Anne. Goodbye U. S. A. - Ola Mexico! Ballouhey, Pierre, illus. (gr. 3-7). 1994. 12.95 (*0-8120-6374-0*); pap. 5.95 (*0-8120-1388-3*) Barron.
Bunting, Eve. A Part of the Dream. (Illus.). 64p. (gr. 3-8). 1992. 8.95 (*0-89565-771-6*) Childs World.
Ets, Marie H. Gilberto & the Wind. Ets, Marie H., illus. LC 63-8527. (gr. k-3). 1978. pap. 3.99 (*0-14-050276-9*, Puffin) Puffin Bks.
Ets, Marie H. & Labastida, Aurora. Nine Days to Christmas. Ets, Marie H., illus. (ps-2). 1959. pap. 13.95 (*0-670-51350-4*) Viking Child Bks.
Flora, James. The Fabulous Firework Family. Flora, James, illus. LC 93-11472. 32p. (gr. k-4). 1994. SBE 14.95 (*0-689-50596-5*, M K McElderry) Macmillan Child Grp.
George, Jean C. Shark Beneath the Reef. LC 88-25194. 192p. (gr. 7 up). 1989. 13.00 (*0-06-021992-0*); PLB 12.89 (*0-06-021993-9*) HarpC Child Bks.
Gollub, Matthew. The Moon Was at a Fiesta. Martinez, Leovigildo, illus. LC 93-14750. 32p. 1994. 15.00 (*0-688-11637-X*, Tambourine Bks); PLB 14.93 (*0-688-11638-8*) Morrow.
Gordon, Alvin J. Tortillas. DeGrazia, Ted, illus. 20p. (Orig.). (gr. 1-3). 1971. pap. 6.95 (*0-916955-06-0*) ARCUS Pub.
Johnston, Terry C. Lorenzo the Naughty Parrot. Politi, L., illus. 1992. write for info. (*0-15-249350-6*, HB Juv Bks) HarBrace.
Johnston, Tony. Old Lady & the Birds. LC 91-45124. (ps-3). 1994. 14.95 (*0-15-257769-6*, HB Juv Bks) HarBrace.
Krull, Kathleen. Maria Molina & the Days of the Dead. LC 94-14535. (gr. k-3). 1994. 15.95 (*0-02-750999-0*, Macmillan Child Bk) Macmillan Child Grp.
Lewis, Thomas P. Hill of Fire. Sandin, Joan, illus. LC 70-121802. 64p. (gr. k-3). 1971. PLB 13.89 (*0-06-023804-6*) HarpC Child Bks.
McGee, Charmayne. So Sings the Blue Deer. LC 93-26580. 160p. (gr. 3-7). 1994. SBE 14.95 (*0-689-31888-X*, Atheneum Child Bk) Macmillan Child Grp.
Maitland, Katherine. Ashes for Gold: A Tale from Mexico. Mills, Elise, illus. LC 94-14349. 24p. (Orig.). (gr. k-4). 1994. big bk. 21.95 (*1-879531-14-3*); PLB 9.95 (*1-879531-43-7*); pap. 4.95 (*1-879531-22-4*) Mondo Pubng.
Matthews, Billie P. & Chichester, A. Lee. Secret of the Cibolo. Roberts, Melissa, ed. (Illus.). 104p. (gr. 4-7). 1988. 9.95 (*0-89015-638-7*, Pub. by Panda Bks) Sunbelt Media.
Merino, Jose M. The Gold of Dreams. Lane, Helen, tr. 224p. (gr. 7 up). 1992. 15.00 (*0-374-32692-4*) FS&G.
Merino, Jose Maria. Beyond the Ancient Cities. Lane, Helen, tr. from SPA. LC 93-35482. 1994. 16.00 (*0-374-34307-1*) FS&G.
Mora, Francisco X. Juan Tuza & the Magic Pouch. Mora, Francisco X., illus. 32p. (ps-1). 1993. PLB 15.00 (*0-917846-24-9*, 95563) Highsmith Pr.
Poulet, Virginia. Blue Bug Visits Mexico. Anderson, Peggy P., illus. LC 89-25420. 32p. (ps-2). 1990. PLB 11.80 (*0-516-03429-4*); pap. 3.95 (*0-516-43429-2*) Childrens.
Rhoads, Dorothy. The Corn Grows Ripe. Charlot, Jean, illus. LC 92-24888. (gr. 8-12). 1993. 4.99 (*0-14-036313-0*, Puffin) Puffin Bks.
Strasser, Todd. The Diving Bell. 192p. 1992. 13.95 (*0-590-44620-7*, Scholastic Hardcover) Scholastic Inc.
Toepperwein, Emilie & Toepperwein, Fritz A. Jose & the Mexican Jumping Bean. (Illus.). (gr. 4-7). 1965. PLB 2.95 (*0-910722-05-6*) Highland Pr.
Williams, Jeanne. Tame the Wild Stallion. Conoly, Walle, illus. LC 84-16257. 182p. (gr. 4 up). 1985. 14.95 (*0-87565-002-3*); pap. 8.95 (*0-87565-009-0*) Tex Christian.

MEXICO–HISTORY

Antonio Lopez de Santa Anna. (Illus.). 112p. (gr. 6-12). 1993. PLB 17.95 (*0-7910-1245-X*) Chelsea Hse.
Department of Geography, Lerner Publications Company Staff. Mexico in Pictures. (Illus.). 64p. (gr. 5 up). 1988. PLB 17.50 (*0-8225-1801-5*) Lerner Pubns.
Fisher, Leonard E. Pyramid of the Sun - Pyramid of the Moon. Fisher, Leonard E., illus. LC 88-1410. 32p. (gr. 1-5). 1988. SBE 15.95 (*0-02-735300-1*) Macmillan Child Grp.
Grier, Paula. The Early Mexicans. (Illus.). 47p. (Orig.). (gr. 6-8). 1982. pap. text ed. 14.95 (*1-878550-03-9*) Inter Dev Res Assn.
Killingray, David. The Mexican Revolution. Yapp, Malcolm, et al, eds. (Illus.). 32p. (gr. 6-11). 1980. pap. text ed. 3.45 (*0-89908-112-6*) Greenhaven.
Miguel Hidalgo y Costilla. (Illus.). 32p. (gr. 3-6). 1988. PLB 19.97 (*0-8172-2905-1*) Raintree Steck-V.
Ochoa, George. The Fall of Mexico City. (Illus.). 64p. (gr. 5 up). 1989. PLB 12.95 (*0-382-09836-6*); pap. 7.95 (*0-382-09853-6*) Silver Burdett Pr.
Simpson, Lesley B. Many Mexicos: Silver Anniversary Edition. 4th, rev. ed. (gr. 9 up). 1966. pap. 15.00x (*0-520-01180-5*) U CA Pr.
Stefoff, Rebecca. Independence & Revolution in Mexico, 1810-1940. (Illus.). 160p. (gr. 6-9). 1993. 16.95 (*0-8160-2841-9*) Facts on File.
Stein, R. Conrad. The Mexican Revolution, 1910-1920. LC 93-17259. (Illus.). 144p. (gr. 4-7). 1994. RSBE 14.95 (*0-02-786950-4*, New Discovery Bks) Macmillan Child Grp.

MEXICO–HISTORY–CONQUEST, 1519-1540

Larsen, Anita. Montezuma's Missing Treasure. LC 91-19259. (Illus.). 48p. (gr. 5-6). 1992. text ed. 11.95 RSBE (*0-89686-615-7*, Crestwood Hse) Macmillan Child Grp.
Stein, R. Conrad. Hernando Cortes: Conqueror of Mexico. LC 90-20655. (Illus.). 128p. (gr. 3 up). 1991. PLB 20.55 (*0-516-03059-0*) Childrens.

MEXICO–HISTORY–CONQUEST, 1519-1540–FICTION

Jacobs, William J. Cortes: Conquerer of Mexico. LC 93-31177. (Illus.). 64p. (gr. 5-8). 1994. PLB 12.90 (*0-531-20138-4*) Watts.
Mathews, Sally S. The Sad Night: The Story of an Aztec Victory & a Spanish Loss. Mathews, Sally S., illus. LC 92-25119. (gr. 1-4). 1994. 16.95 (*0-395-63035-5*, Clarion Bks) HM.

MEXICO–HISTORY–SPANISH COLONY, 1540-1810–FICTION

Gray, Genevieve. How Far, Felipe? Grifalconi, Ann, illus. LC 77-11846. 64p. (gr. k-3). 1978. PLB 11:89 (*0-06-022108-9*) HarpC Child Bks.

MEXICO–HISTORY–WARS OF INDEPENDENCE, 1810-1821–FICTION

Borton De Trevino, Elizabeth. Leona, a Love Story. LC 93-38751. 1994. 15.00 (*0-374-34382-9*) FS&G.

MEXICO–PRESIDENTS

Antonio Lopez de Santa Anna. (Illus.). 112p. (gr. 6-12). 1993. PLB 17.95 (*0-7910-1245-X*) Chelsea Hse.
Bains, Rae. Benito Juarez, Hero of Modern Mexico. Davis, Allen, illus. LC 92-2291. 48p. (gr. 4-6). 1992. lib. bdg. 10.79 (*0-8167-2825-9*); pap. 3.50 (*0-8167-2826-7*) Troll Assocs.
Lazaro Cardenas: Mini Play. (gr. 5 up). 1977. 5.00 (*0-89550-358-1*) Stevens & Shea.

MEXICO–SOCIAL LIFE AND CUSTOMS

Ancona, George. Pablo Remembers. LC 92-22819. (gr. 4 up). 1993. 15.00 (*0-688-11249-8*); lib. bdg. 14.93 (*0-688-11250-1*) Lothrop.
Casagrande, Louis B. & Johnson, Sylvia A. Focus on Mexico: Modern Life in an Ancient Land. (Illus.). 96p. (gr. 5up). 1986. lib. bdg. 21.50 (*0-8225-0645-9*) Lerner Pubns.
Hoyt-Goldsmith, Diane. Day of the Dead: A Mexican-American Celebration. Migdale, Lawrence, photos by. LC 93-42106. (Illus.). 32p. (gr. 3-7). 1994. reinforced bdg. 15.95 (*0-8234-1094-3*) Holiday.
Kalman, Bobbie. Mexico - the Culture. LC 93-34765. (Illus.). 32p. (Orig.). (gr. 4-9). 1993. PLB 15.95 (*0-86505-216-6*); pap. 7.95 (*0-86505-296-4*); Span. ed. pap. 7.95 (*0-86505-400-2*) Crabtree Pub Co.
Lasky, Kathryn. Days of the Dead. Knight, Christopher G., photos by. LC 93-47957. (Illus.). 48p. (gr. 3-7). 1994. 15.95 (*0-7868-0022-4*); PLB 15.89 (*0-7868-2018-7*) Hyprn Child.
Moran, Tom. A Family in Mexico. (Illus.). 32p. (gr. 2-5). 1987. 13.50 (*0-8225-1677-2*) Lerner Pubns.
Silverthorne, Elizabeth. Fiesta: Mexico's Great Celebrations. LC 91-37178. (Illus.). 64p. (gr. 3-6). 1992. PLB 14.40 (*1-56294-055-4*); pap. 6.95 (*1-56294-836-9*) Millbrook Pr.
Wolf, Bernard. Beneath the Stone: A Mexican Zapotec Tale. Wolf, Bernard, photos by. LC 92-27103. (Illus.). 48p. (gr. k-6). 1994. 15.95 (*0-531-06835-8*); lib. bdg. 15.99 RLB (*0-531-08685-2*) Orchard Bks Watts.

MICE

Burton, Robert. The Mouse in the Barn. Oxford Scientific Films, photos by. LC 87-42614. (Illus.). 32p. (gr. 4-6). 1988. PLB 17.27 (*1-55532-305-7*) Gareth Stevens Inc.
Cartlidge, Michelle. Mouse in the House. Cartlidge, Michelle, illus. 12p. (ps). 1991. bds. 3.50 (*0-525-44678-8*, DCB) Dutton Child Bks.
Fischer-Nagel, Heiderose & Fischer-Nagel, Andreas. A Look Through the Mouse Hole. Fischer-Nagel, Heiderose & Fischer-Nagel, Andreas, illus. 48p. (gr. 2-5). 1989. lib. bdg. 19.95 (*0-87614-326-5*) Carolrhoda Bks.

Harrison, Virginia. The World of Mice. Oxford Scientific Films Staff, photos by. LC 87-42609. (Illus.). 32p. (gr. 2-3). 1988. PLB 17.27 (*1-55532-309-X*) Gareth Stevens Inc.

Kirby, Mansfield. The Secret of Thut-Mouse III: or Basil Beaudesert's Revenge. Post, Mance, illus. LC 85-47588. 64p. (ps up). 1985. 14.00 (*0-374-36677-2*) FS&G.

Watts, Barrie, photos by. Mouse. (Illus.). 24p. (gr. k-3). 1992. 6.95 (*0-525-67357-1*, Lodestar Bks) Dutton Child Bks.

Wexler, Jerome. Pet Mice. Tucker, Kathleen, ed. LC 88-2. (Illus.). 48p. (gr. 2-8). 1989. PLB 14.95 (*0-8075-6524-5*) A Whitman.

MICE–FICTION

Aesop. The City Mouse & the Country Mouse. Wheeler, Jody, illus. LC 85-70290. 18p. (ps). 1985. 3.95 (*0-448-10226-9*, G&D) Putnam Pub Group.

Aliki. At Mary Bloom's. Aliki, illus. LC 75-45482. 32p. (gr. k-3). 1983. 11.25 (*0-688-02480-7*); PLB 14.93 (*0-688-02481-5*) Greenwillow.

Anderson, Myra. Kathryn's Mouse. Chapman, Shirley, illus. 48p. (gr. k-6). 1991. 16.95 (*0-9625620-4-1*) DOT Garnet.

Andrews & McMeel Inc. Staff. Tom & Jerry Friends to the End. (ps-3). 1993. 14.95 (*1-878685-26-0*) Turner Pub GA.

Archambault, John & Martin, Bill, Jr. A Beautiful Feast for a Big King Cat. Degen, Bruce, illus. LC 92-32331. 32p. (ps-3). 1994. 13.00 (*0-06-022903-9*); PLB 12.89 (*0-06-022904-7*) HarpC Child Bks.

Asch, Frank. Pearl's Promise. Asch, Frank, illus. LC 83-17153. 160p. (gr. 4-6). 1984. PLB 12.95 (*0-385-29321-6*); pap. 12.95 (*0-385-29325-9*) Delacorte.

Baehr, Patricia. Mouse in the House. Lydecker, Laura, illus. LC 93-4068. 32p. (ps-3). 1994. reinforced bdg. 15.95 (*0-8234-1102-8*) Holiday.

Baker, Alan. Two Tiny Mice. Baker, Alan, illus. LC 90-13939. 32p. (ps-1). 1991. 12.95 (*0-8037-0973-0*) Dial Bks Young.

—Where's Mouse? Baker, Alan, illus. LC 92-53117. 16p. (ps-k). 1992. 12.95 (*1-85697-821-4*, Kingfisher LKC) LKC.

Barklem, Jill. Autumn Story. Barklem, Jill, illus. LC 80-15433. 32p. (gr. 1 up). 1986. 8.95 (*0-399-20745-7*, Philomel Bks) Putnam Pub Group.

—Spring Story. Barklem, Jill, illus. LC 80-15300. 32p. (gr. 1 up). 1986. 10.95 (*0-399-20746-5*, Philomel) Putnam Pub Group.

—Summer Story. Barklem, Jill, illus. LC 80-15423. 32p. (gr. 1 up). 1986. 10.95 (*0-399-20747-3*, Philomel) Putnam Pub Group.

—Winter Story. Barklem, Jill, illus. LC 80-15422. 32p. (gr. 1 up). 1986. 10.95 (*0-399-20748-1*, Philomel) Putnam Pub Group.

—World of Brambly Hedge. LC 92-25306. (Illus.). 24p. (ps up). 1993. 17.95 (*0-399-22012-7*, Philomel Bks) Putnam Pub Group.

Bebe Mickey - Juega a Las Escondillas. (SPA.). (ps-3). 1993. pap. 2.95 (*0-307-96097-8*, Golden Pr) Western Pub.

Bech, Bente, illus. Hot on the Scent. Lind, Peter, contrib. by. LC 92-8782. (Illus.). 32p. (ps-3). 1993. PLB 17.27 (*0-8368-0510-0*) Gareth Stevens Inc.

Beeson, Bob. What Time Is It, Mr. Wolf? Beeson, Bob, illus. 32p. (ps). 1994. 12.95 (*0-8249-8649-0*, Ideals Child) Hambleton-Hill.

Beguinot, Brigitte. The Mouse Party: An Open-the-Door Book. Beguinot, Brigitte, illus. 12p. (ps-3). 1992. bds. 10.95 (*1-878093-50-9*) Boyds Mills Pr.

Belle's Surprise Party. 10p. 1994. 6.98 (*1-57082-142-9*) Mouse Works.

Berger, Thomas. The Mouse & the Potato. Lawson, Polly, tr. Grillis, Carla, illus. (DUT.). 32p. (ps-2). 1990. Repr. 14.95 (*0-86315-103-5*, Pub. by Floris Bks UK) Gryphon Hse.

Bishop & Leechman. The Adventures of Jozedek. Nudd, Stacy, illus. LC 86-72946. 62p. (Orig.). (gr. 4-5). 1987. pap. 6.00 (*0-916383-23-7*) Aegina Pr.

Boegehold, Betty D. Pippa Pops Out! Szekeres, Cyndy, illus. 64p. (ps-3). 1980. pap. 0.95 (*0-440-46865-5*, YB) Dell.

Boyd, Lizi. Mouse in a House: A Toy, Book, & Crafts Kit. (ps-3). 1993. 12.95 (*0-316-10444-2*) Little.

Brandenberg, Franz. Nice New Neighbors. Aliki, illus. LC 77-1651. 56p. (gr. 1-4). 1977. PLB 13.88 (*0-688-84105-8*) Greenwillow.

—Nice New Neighbors. Aliki, illus. 32p. (ps-2). 1990. pap. 2.75 (*0-590-44117-5*) Scholastic Inc.

Braybrooks, Ann. Disney's Mickey Mouse Reading Kit. (Illus.). 24p. 1993. kit 19.95 (*1-56138-145-4*) Running Pr.

Brenner, Barbara. Mr. Tall & Mr. Small. Shenon, Mike, illus. LC 93-8256. (gr. k-3). 1994. 14.95 (*0-8050-2757-2*) H Holt & Co.

Browne, Eileen. No Problem. Parkins, David, illus. LC 92-53134. 40p. (ps up). 1993. bk. ed. 14.95 (*1-56402-176-9*); bk. & kit ed. 14.99 (*1-56402-200-5*) Candlewick Pr.

Buchanan, Heather S. George & Matilda Mouse & the Floating School. LC 89-22036. (Illus.). 40p. (ps-3). 1990. pap. 13.95 (*0-671-70613-6*) S&S Trade.

—George & Matilda Mouse & the Moon Rocket. LC 91-24318. (Illus.). 40p. (ps-3). 1992. pap. 14.00 jacketed (*0-671-75864-0*, S&S BFYR) S&S Trade.

Bullock, Kathleen. A Friend for Mitzi Mouse. LC 90-31559. (Illus.). 40p. (ps-1). 1990. pap. 13.95 jacketed (*0-671-68867-7*, Little Simon) S&S Trade.

Burgess, Thornton. Whitefoot the Wood Mouse. 1992. Repr. lib. bdg. 17.95x (*0-89966-980-8*) Buccaneer Bks.

Burgess, Thornton W. The Adventures of Danny Meadow Mouse. Cady, Harrison & Kliros, Thea, illus. LC 92-36950. 96p. 1993. pap. 1.00 (*0-486-27565-5*) Dover.

—Adventures of Danny Meadow Mouse. 18.95 (*0-8488-0377-9*) Amereon Ltd.

—Whitefoot the Wood Mouse. 18.95 (*0-8488-0395-7*) Amereon Ltd.

Burningham, John. Trubloff: The Mouse Who Wanted to Play the Balalaika. Burningham, John, illus. LC 93-13279. (ps-2). 1994. pap. 4.99 (*0-517-59435-8*) Crown Bks Yng Read.

Butler, Stephen. The Mouse & the Apple. Butler, Stephen, illus. LC 93-15951. 32p. (ps up). 1994. 15.00 (*0-688-12810-6*, Tambourine Bks); PLB 14.93 (*0-688-12811-4*, Tambourine Bks) Morrow.

Calmenson, Stephanie. Tom & Jerry: The Movie--Digest Novelization. (gr. 4-7). 1993. pap. 3.25 (*0-590-47115-5*) Scholastic Inc.

Carle, Eric. Do You Want to Be My Friend? Carle, Eric, illus. LC 70-140643. 32p. (ps-2). 1971. 15.00 (*0-690-24276-X*, Crowell Jr Bks); PLB 14.89 (*0-690-01137-7*, Crowell Jr Bks) HarpC Child Bks.

Carratello, Patty. Mice on Ice. Spivak, Darlene, ed. Smythe, Linda, illus. 16p. (gr. k-2). 1988. wkbk. 1.95 (*1-55734-382-9*) Tchr Create Mat.

Carter, Noelle. Peek-a-Boo, Little Mouse. Carter, David, illus. LC 91-78193. 12p. (ps). 1992. 10.95 (*0-8050-2253-8*, Bks Young Read) H Holt & Co.

Cartlidge, Michelle. Mouse Birthday. Cartlidge, Michelle, illus. 24p. (ps). 1994. 4.99 (*0-525-45237-0*) Dutton Child Bks.

—Mouse House. (Illus.). 24p. (ps). 1990. 4.95 (*0-525-44638-9*, DCB) Dutton Child Bks.

—Mouse Letters. Cartlidge, Michelle, illus. 24p. (ps). 1993. 4.99 (*0-525-45089-0*, DCB) Dutton Child Bks.

—Mouse Theater. (Illus.). 22p. (ps). 1992. 4.95 (*0-525-44980-9*, DCB) Dutton Child Bks.

—Mouse Time. Cartlidge, Michelle, illus. 24p. (ps). 1991. 3.95 (*0-525-44766-0*, DCB) Dutton Child Bks.

Cartlidge, Michelle & Cartlidge, Michelle. A Mouse's Diary. (Illus.). 32p. (ps-2). 1994. 4.50 (*0-525-45195-1*, DCB) Dutton Child Bks.

Cauley, Lorinda B. Three Blind Mice. (Illus.). 32p. (ps-3). 1991. 14.95 (*0-399-21775-4*, Putnam) Putnam Pub Group.

Cauley, Lorinda B., retold by. The Town Mouse & the Country Mouse. (Illus.). 32p. (ps-3). 1990. pap. 5.95 (*0-399-22009-7*, Sandcastle Bks) Putnam Pub Group.

Chardiet, Bernice. Come Out, Mouse. Dinardo, Jeffrey, illus. 20p. (ps-1). 1994. pap. 4.99 (*0-14-054997-8*) Puffin Bks.

Chorao, Kay. Cathedral Mouse. Chorao, Kay, illus. LC 87-33398. 32p. (ps-2). 1988. 12.95 (*0-525-44400-9*, DCB) Dutton Child Bks.

—Cathedral Mouse. LC 87-33398. (Illus.). 32p. (ps-2). 1991. pap. 4.95 (*0-525-44823-3*, Puffin) Puffin Bks.

Chottin, Ariane. Little Mouse's Rescue: Little Animal Adventures Ser. Dzierzawska, Malgorzata, illus. Jensen, Patricia, adapted by. LC 93-2949. (Illus.). 22p. (ps-3). 1993. 5.98 (*0-89577-505-0*) RD Assn.

The City Mouse & the Country Mouse, Unit 7. (gr. 2). 1991. 5-pack 21.25 (*0-88106-758-X*) Charlesbridge Pub.

Cleary, Beverly. Lucky Chuck. Higginbottom, J. Winslow, illus. LC 83-13386. 40p. (gr. k-3). 1984. 13.95 (*0-688-02736-9*); PLB 13.88 (*0-688-02738-5*, Morrow Jr Bks) Morrow Jr Bks.

—The Mouse & the Motorcycle. Darling, Louis, illus. LC 65-20956. (gr. 2-6). 1965. 13.95 (*0-688-21698-6*); PLB 13.88 (*0-688-31698-0*) Morrow Jr Bks.

—The Mouse & the Motorcycle. large type ed. 1989. Repr. of 1965 ed. lib. bdg. 15.95 (*1-55736-137-1*, Crnrstn Bks) BDD LT Grp.

—The Mouse & the Motorcycle. 160p. 1990. pap. 3.99 (*0-380-70924-4*, Camelot) Avon.

—Mouse House Trio, 3 vols. (gr. 4-7). 1990. pap. 9.75 (*0-440-36016-1*) Dell.

—Ralph S. Mouse. Zelinsky, Paul O., illus. LC 82-3516. 160p. (gr. 4-6). 1982. 14.95 (*0-688-01452-6*); lib. bdg. 14.88 (*0-688-01455-0*) Morrow Jr Bks.

—Ralph S. Mouse. large type ed. 160p. 1989. Repr. of 1982 ed. lib. bdg. 15.95 (*1-55736-136-3*, Crnrstn Bks) BDD LT Grp.

—Ralph S. Mouse. 160p. (gr. 5). 1993. pap. 3.99 (*0-380-70957-0*, Camelot) Avon.

—Ramona, Mouse, 4 vols. (gr. 4-7). 1990. Boxed Set. pap. 14.00 (*0-380-71483-3*, Camelot) Avon.

—Runaway Ralph. 176p. 1991. pap. 3.99 (*0-380-70953-8*, Camelot) Avon.

Clohe, Rene. Fairyland Favorites: Town Mouse & Country Mouse. 1989. 2.98 (*0-671-06188-7*) S&S Trade.

Conly, Jane L. Racso & the Rats of NIMH. Lubin, Leonard, illus. LC 85-42634. 288p. (gr. 4-7). 1988. pap. 3.95 (*0-06-440245-2*, Trophy) HarpC Child Bks.

Coon, Alma S. The Mouse & the Mill & the Bottle Babies. Shoemaker, Kathryn, illus. 44p. (ps-1). 1982. 5.95 (*0-87935-061-X*) Williamsburg.

Cormier, Robert. I Am the Cheese. LC 76-55948. 224p. (gr. 7-12). 1977. 18.95 (*0-394-83462-3*) Pantheon.

Cosgrove, Stephen. Little Mouse on the Prairie. James, Robin, illus. 32p. (Orig.). (gr. 1-4). 1978. pap. 2.95 (*0-8431-0569-0*) Price Stern.

Cousins, Lucy. Maisy Goes to School. Cousine, Lucy, illus. LC 91-58743. 16p. (ps). 1992. 12.95 (*1-56402-085-1*) Candlewick Pr.

—Maisy Goes to the Playground. Cousine, Lucy, illus. LC 91-58742. 16p. (ps). 1992. 12.95 (*1-56402-084-3*) Candlewick Pr.

Craig, Janet. Max & Maggie in Summer: Nice Mice. (ps-3). 1994. pap. 2.25 (*0-8167-3353-8*) Troll Assocs.

—Windy Day. Durrell, Julie, illus. LC 87-10909. 32p. (gr. k-2). 1988. PLB 7.89 (*0-8167-0982-3*); pap. text ed. 1.95 (*0-8167-0983-1*) Troll Assocs.

Craig, Janet A. Valentine's Day Mess. Morse, Debby, illus. LC 93-2211. 32p. (gr. k-2). 1993. PLB 11.59 (*0-8167-3254-X*); pap. text ed. 2.95 (*0-8167-3255-8*) Troll Assocs.

Crust, Linda. Melvin's Cold Feet. Brindle, John, illus. LC 90-47201. 32p. (gr. 2-3). 1991. PLB 18.60 (*0-8368-0356-6*) Gareth Stevens Inc.

Cushman. Mouse & Mole & the Christmas Walk. 1994. text ed. write for info. (*0-7167-6560-8*) W H Freeman.

Dashney, John. The Adventures of Walter the Weremouse. Somerville, Sheila, illus. 164p. (Orig.). (gr. 4-8). 1992. pap. 6.50x (*0-9633236-0-1*) J Dashney.

Davoll, Barbara. The Christopher Churchmouse Treasury. Hockerman, Dennis, illus. (Orig.). 1992. pap. 12.99 (*0-89693-078-5*, Victor Books) SP Pubns.

Derby, Sally. The Mouse Who Owned the Sun. Henstra, Friso, illus. LC 91-40965. 32p. (ps-3). 1993. RSBE 14.95 (*0-02-766965-3*, Four Winds) Macmillan Child Grp.

Dickinson, Peter. Time & the Clock Mice, Etcetera. Chichester-Clark, Emma, illus. LC 93-11434. 1994. 16.95 (*0-385-32038-8*) Delacorte.

DiFiori, Larry. Muffin Mouse's New House. DiFiori, Larry, illus. (ps-k). 1991. pap. write for info. (*0-307-10028-6*, Golden Pr) Western Pub.

Disney, Walt. Great Mouse Detective. (ps-3). 1988. 6.98 (*0-453-03188-9*) NAL-Dutton.

—Mickey's Costume Party: A Mix & Match Book. (ps-3). 1993. 6.98 (*0-453-03124-2*) Mouse Works.

—Perils of Mickey: The Mail Must Go Through. (ps-3). 1993. 6.98 (*0-453-03096-3*) Mouse Works.

Drew, David. Nibbly Mouse. Newman, Penny, illus. LC 92-21397. 1993. 4.25 (*0-383-03587-2*) SRA Schl Grp.

Drew, James. Rackstraw: The Magical Thoughts & Adventures of A Brilliant Young Art Mouse. George, Mary G., ed. Drew, James, illus. LC 93-71718. 168p. (gr. 2-9). 1994. 18.95 (*0-9625023-9-1*) Art Pr Intl.

Dubanevich, Arlene. Tom's Tail. (ps-3). 1990. 13.95 (*0-670-83021-6*) Viking Child Bks.

—Tom's Tail. LC 92-8615. (gr. 4 up). 1992. 4.50 (*0-14-054177-2*) Puffin Bks.

Dunbar, Joyce. Ten Little Mice. 24p. (ps-1). 1990. 13.95 (*0-15-200601-X*) HarBrace.

—Ten Little Mice. (ps). 1992. 19.95 (*0-15-284614-X*) HarBrace.

entertaining murine fantasy." (Library Journal).
Publisher Provided Annotation.

Edwards, Richard. A Mouse in My Roof. Venice, illus. (ps up). 1990. write for info. Delacorte.
—A Mouse in My Roof. 1990. PLB 14.99 (*0-385-30127-8*) Dell.
Emberley, Michael. Ruby, Vol. 1. (ps-3). 1990. 14.95 (*0-316-23643-8*) Little.
Erkel, Cynthia R. The Farmhouse Mouse. Erkel, Michael, illus. LC 92-27040. 32p. (ps-3). 1994. PLB 14.95 (*0-399-22444-0*, Putnam) Putnam Pub Group.
Ezra, Mark. The Sleepy Dormouse. (Illus.). 32p. (ps-3). 1994. pap. 14.95 (*1-56656-153-1*, Crocodile Bks) Interlink Pub.
Felix, Monique. The Alphabet. Felix, Monique, illus. 32p. (ps-12). 1993. 7.95 (*1-56846-003-1*) Creative Ed.
—The Boat. (Illus.). 32p. (ps-12). 1993. 7.95 (*1-56846-080-5*) Creat Editions.
—The Colors. 1992. PLB 10.95s.p. (*0-88682-404-4*) Creative Ed.
—Colors: Mouse Books. (Illus.). 32p. (ps). 1993. pap. 2.95 (*1-56189-093-6*) Amer Educ Pub.
—The House. 1992. PLB 10.95 (*0-88682-405-2*) Creative Ed.
—Mouse Book Series, 6 bks. Felix, Monique, illus. 32p. (Orig.). (ps-k). 1993. Set. pap. 17.70 (*1-56189-077-4*) Amer Educ Pub.
—The Numbers. Felix, Monique, illus. 32p. (ps-12). 1993. 7.95 (*1-56846-001-5*) Creat Editions.
—The Opposites. Felix, Monique, illus. 32p. (ps-12). 1993. 7.95 (*1-56846-002-3*) Creat Editions.
—The Plane. (Illus.). 32p. (ps-12). 1993. 7.95 (*1-56846-079-1*) Creat Editions.
—The Wind. 1992. PLB 10.95 (*0-88682-406-0*) Creative Ed.
Field, Rachel. Road Might Lead to Anywhere, Vol. 1. LC 89-32815. (ps-3). 1990. 14.95 (*0-316-28178-6*) Little.
Fisher, Maxine P. The Country Mouse & the City Mouse: "Christmas Is Where the Heart Is" Smath, Jerry, illus. LC 93-26488. 48p. (ps-2). 1994. 13.00 (*0-679-84684-0*) Random Bks Yng Read.
Fleming, Denise. Lunch. LC 92-178. (Illus.). 32p. (ps-2). 1992. 14.95 (*0-8050-1636-8*, Bks Young Read) H Holt & Co.
The Fourteen Forest Mice, 4 bks. (Illus.). (ps-3). Complete set. PLB 69.08 (*0-8368-0495-3*) Gareth Stevens Inc.
Fowler, Richard. There's a Mouse about the House. (Illus.). 24p. (ps-1). 1984. 9.95 (*0-88110-154-0*) EDC.
Frankel, Julie E. Mice! Venezia, Mike, illus. LC 86-1008. 32p. (ps-2). 1986. PLB 10.25 (*0-516-02070-6*); pap. 2.95 (*0-516-42070-4*) Childrens.
Freeman, Don. Norman the Doorman. Freeman, Don, illus. (ps-2). 1959. pap. 15.95 (*0-670-51515-9*) Viking Child Bks.
Fryar, Jane. Lost at the Mall: Morris the Mouse Adventure Ser. Wilson, Deborah, illus. 32p. (ps-1). 1991. 7.99 (*0-570-04196-1*, 56-1655) Concordia.
Fuchshuber, Annegert. Giant Story - Mouse Tale: A Half Picture Book. (Illus.). 32p. (ps-3). 1988. lib. bdg. 18.95 (*0-87614-319-2*) Carolrhoda Bks.
A Garden for Miss Mouse. 42p. (ps-3). 1993. PLB 13.27 (*0-8368-0891-6*) Gareth Stevens Inc.
Gaudreau, Carmen. Bernard et Bridget: A la Cabane a Sacre. LeBlanc, Lorraine, illus. (FRE.). 40p. (gr. k-1). 1979. pap. text ed. 1.50 (*0-911409-47-5*); of 53 2x2 slides 13.25 set (*0-686-42727-0*) Natl Mat Dev.
Gee, R. & Borton, P. Cat & Mouse in Space. (Illus.). 24p. (ps up). 1994. PLB 11.95 (*0-88110-708-5*, Usborne); pap. 3.95 (*0-7460-1417-1*, Usborne) EDC.
Gentile, Gennaro L. The Mouse in the Manger. McKissack, Vernon, illus. LC 78-72944. 80p. (gr. k-4). 1978. pap. 5.95 (*0-87793-165-8*) Ave Maria.
Geraghty, Paul. Look Out, Patrick! Geraghty, Paul, illus. LC 89-77850. 32p. (ps-1). 1990. 13.95 (*0-02-735822-4*, Macmillan Child Bk) Macmillan Child Grp.
Gibson, R. Cat & Mouse Get a Pet. (Illus.). 24p. (ps up). 1994. PLB 11.96 (*0-88110-697-6*, Usborne); pap. 3.95 (*0-7460-1419-8*, Usborne) EDC.
Ginsburg, Mirra. Four Brave Sailors. Tafuri, Lynn, illus. LC 86-7555. 24p. (ps-1). 1987. 11.75 (*0-688-06514-7*); PLB 11.88 (*0-688-06515-5*) Greenwillow.
Gomi, Taro. Hide & Seek. Young, Richard G., ed. Kaisei-sha, tr. LC 89-12049. (Illus.). 32p. (gr. 1-3). 1989. PLB 14.60 (*0-944483-45-3*) Garrett Ed Corp.
Gordon, Sharon. Maxwell Mouse. Rosenberg, Amye, illus. LC 81-4653. 32p. (gr. k-2). 1981. PLB 11.59 (*0-89375-501-X*); pap. 2.95 (*0-89375-502-8*) Troll Assocs.
Graham, John. I Love You, Mouse. De Paola, Tomie, illus. LC 78-6214. 32p. (ps-2). 1990. pap. 3.95 (*0-15-644106-3*, Voyager Bks) HarBrace.
Grambling, Lois. Elephant & Mouse Celebrate Halloween. Maze, Deborah, illus. (ps-1). 1991. 12.95 (*0-8120-6186-1*); pap. 5.95 (*0-8120-4761-3*) Barron.
Grambling, Lois G. Elephant & Mouse Get Ready for Christmas. Maze, Deborah, illus. 32p. 1990. with dust jacket 12.95 (*0-8120-6185-3*) Barron.
Gregorich, Barbara. Mouse & Owl. Hoffman, Joan, ed. (Illus.). 16p. (Orig.). (gr. k-2). 1991. pap. 2.25 (*0-88743-025-2*, 06025) Sch Zone Pub Co.
Hao, Kuang-ts'ai. Dance, Mice, Dance! Tartarotti, Stefano, illus. (ENG & CHI.). 32p. (gr. 2-4). 1994. 14.95 (*1-57227-000-4*) Pan Asian Pubns.
—Dance, Mice, Dance! Tartarotti, Stefano, illus. (ENG & VIE.). 32p. (gr. 2-4). 1994. 16.95 (*1-57227-002-0*) Pan Asian Pubns.
—Dance, Mice, Dance! Tartarotti, Stefano, illus. (ENG & KOR.). 32p. (gr. 2-4). 1994. 16.95 (*1-57227-003-9*) Pan Asian Pubns.
—Dance, Mice, Dance! Tartarotti, Stefano, illus. (ENG & THA.). 32p. (gr. 2-4). 1994. 16.95 (*1-57227-004-7*) Pan Asian Pubns.
—Dance, Mice, Dance! Tartarotti, Stefano, illus. (ENG & TAG.). 32p. (gr. 2-4). 1994. 16.95 (*1-57227-005-5*) Pan Asian Pubns.
—Dance, Mice, Dance! Tartarotti, Stefano, illus. (ENG & CAM.). 32p. (gr. 2-4). 1994. 16.95 (*1-57227-006-3*) Pan Asian Pubns.
—Dance, Mice, Dance! Tartarotti, Stefano, illus. (ENG & LAO.). 32p. (gr. 2-4). 1994. 16.95 (*1-57227-007-1*) Pan Asian Pubns.
—Dance, Mice, Dance! Tartarotti, Stefano, illus. (ENG & KOR.). 32p. (gr. 2-4). 1994. 16.95 (*1-57227-008-X*) Pan Asian Pubns.

—Dance, Mice, Dance! Bailen, Ratones, Bailen! Zeller, Beatriz, tr. from CHI. Tartarotti, Stefano, illus. (ENG & SPA.). 32p. (gr. 2-4). 1994. 16.95 (*1-57227-001-2*) Pan Asian Pubns. DANCE, MICE, DANCE! is an entertaining story about a magical flute player who becomes proud & lazy after being highly praised by the townspeople. Although the town folk soon desert him because of his bad ways, the town mice befriend him & teach him the value of his talent & the importance of friendship. Readers will also enjoy the whimsical illustrations that accompany this worthwhile story. Based on THE PIED PIPER OF HAMELIN. Also available in English/ Chinese, Vietnamese, Korean, Thai, Tagalog, Khmer, Lao & Hmong. For grades 2-4. Please specify language when ordering. Available exclusively from: Pan Asian Publications (USA) Inc., 29564 Union City Blvd., Union City, CA 94587. Order toll free: 1-800-853-ASIA, FAX: (510) 475-1489.
Publisher Provided Annotation.

Harvey, Jane. Marvin the Mouse Look & Find Book. (Illus.). 64p. (ps-1). 1991. 6.99 (*0-517-05389-6*) Random Hse Value.
Hellings, Colette. Too Little, Too Big: Trop Petite, Trop Grande. Maes, Dominique, illus. 40p. (ps-3). 1993. 10.95 (*0-8118-0530-1*) Chronicle Bks.
Henrietta. A Mouse in the House. LC 91-60514. (Illus.). 32p. (ps-3). 1991. 13.95 (*1-879431-11-4*); PLB 14.99 (*1-879431-26-2*) Dorling Kindersley.
—Un Raton en Casa - A Mouse in the House. Puncel, Maria & Vasquez, Juan J., eds. Puncel, Maria, tr. (SPA., Illus.). 29p. (gr. k-1). 1992. write for info. (*84-372-6619-X*) Santillana.
Herman, Gail. Fievel's Big Showdown. Lazor-Bahr, Beverly, illus. Kirschner, David, created by. (Illus.). 32p. (ps-3). 1992. pap. 3.50 (*0-448-40392-7*, G&D) Putnam Pub Group.
—Fievel's Big Showdown: An American Tail. (ps-3). 1992. 9.95 (*0-448-40379-X*, G&D) Putnam Pub Group.
Hernandez, Betsy & Monk, Donny. Silent Night: A Mouse Tale. Boddy, Joe, illus. 48p. (ps-5). 1992. write for info. (*0-917143-17-5*) Sparrow TN.
—The Story of Silent Night: A Mouse Tale. (Illus.). 48p. (ps-5). 1992. 12.95 (*0-917143-10-8*) Sparrow TN.
Hibbard, Ann. Dangerous Journey to Emerald Island: Adventures of Gus the Gutter Mouse. (gr. 4-7). 1991. pap. 5.99 (*1-56121-047-1*) Wolgemuth & Hyatt.
Himmelman, John. Montigue on the High Seas. (Illus.). 32p. (ps-3). 1990. pap. 3.95 (*0-14-050789-2*, Puffin) Puffin Bks.
Hirashima, Jean, illus. Wee Mouse's Peekaboo House. LC 89-64279. 14p. (ps). 1991. bds. 3.99 (*0-679-80786-1*) Random Bks Yng Read.
Hoban, Russell. The Mouse & His Child. (gr. k-6). 1990. pap. 3.50 (*0-440-40293-X*, YB) Dell.
Hoff, Syd. Mrs. Brice's Mice. Hoff, Syd, illus. LC 87-45680. 32p. (ps-2). 1988. PLB 13.89 (*0-06-022452-5*) HarpC Child Bks.
—Mrs. Brice's Mice. Hoff, Syd, illus. LC 87-45680. 32p. (ps-2). 1991. pap. 3.50 (*0-06-444145-8*, Trophy) HarpC Child Bks.
Holabird, Katharine. Angelina Ballerina. Craig, Helen, illus. LC 83-8233. (ps-2). 1988. 15.00 (*0-517-55083-0*, Clarkson Potter) Crown Bks Yng Read.
—Angelina Book & Doll Package. Craig, Helen, illus. LC 83-8233. 32p. (ps-2). 1989. book & doll 25.00 (*0-517-57089-0*, Clarkson Potter) Crown Bks Yng Read.
—Angelina Dances. Craig, Helen, illus. LC 92-80524. 6p. (ps-k). 1992. bds. 5.99 (*0-679-83484-2*) Random Bks Yng Read.
—Angelina on Stage. Craig, Helen, illus. 24p. (ps-2). 1988. 15.00 (*0-517-56073-9*, Clarkson Potter) Crown Bks Yng Read.
—Angelina's Birthday Surprise. Craig, Helen, illus. LC 89-3513. 32p. (ps-2). 1989. 15.00 (*0-517-57325-3*, Clarkson Potter) Crown Bks Yng Read.
Hollier, Jo. Charlie Churchmouse Finds a Home. Kichejian, Janet, ed. Pullig, Louis, illus. 16p. 1989. 14.95 (*0-685-29440-4*) Silver Pubns.
Hollingsworth, Mary. Charlie & the Jinglemouse. (Illus.). (ps-3). 1989. 5.99 (*0-915720-25-6*) Brownlow Pub Co.
Hopkins, Margaret. Sleepytime for Baby Mouse. Schmidt, Karen L., illus. 12p. (ps-3). 1985. 3.95 (*0-448-40875-9*, G&D) Putnam Pub Group.
Horowitz, Jordan. Tom & Jerry: The Movie. (ps-3). 1993. pap. 2.95 (*0-590-47116-3*) Scholastic Inc.
Hurd, Thacher. Little Mouse's Big Valentine. Hurd, Thacher, illus. LC 89-34515. 32p. (ps-1). 1990. 13.00 (*0-06-026192-7*); PLB 12.89 (*0-06-026193-5*) HarpC Child Bks.
—Little Mouse's Big Valentine. Hurd, Thacher, illus. LC 89-34515. 32p. (ps-1). 1992. pap. 3.95 (*0-06-443281-5*, Trophy) HarpC Child Bks.
—Little Mouse's Birthday Cake. Hurd, Thacher, illus. LC 91-11919. 32p. (ps-1). 1992. 15.00 (*0-06-020215-7*); PLB 14.89 (*0-06-020216-5*) HarpC Child Bks.
—Tomato Soup. Hurd, Thacher, illus. LC 90-21421. 40p. (ps-3). 1992. 15.00 (*0-517-58237-6*); PLB 15.99 (*0-517-58238-4*) Crown Bks Yng Read.
Ireland, Vicky. The Town Mouse, & the Country Mouse. 38p. (Orig.). (gr. k-3). 1987. pap. 4.50 playscript (*0-87602-266-2*) Anchorage.
Iwamura, Kazuo. The Fourteen Forest Mice & the Harvest Moon Watch. Knowlton, Mary L., tr. from JPN. Iwamura, Kazuo, illus. LC 90-50706. 32p. (gr. k-3). 1991. PLB 17.27 (*0-8368-0497-X*) Gareth Stevens Inc.
—The Fourteen Forest Mice & the Spring Meadow Picnic. Knowlton, Mary L., tr. from JPN. Iwamura, Kazuo, illus. LC 90-50704. 32p. (gr. k-3). 1991. PLB 17.27 (*0-8368-0498-8*) Gareth Stevens Inc.
—The Fourteen Forest Mice & the Summer Laundry Day. Knowlton, Mary L., tr. from JPN. Iwamura, Kazuo, illus. LC 90-50705. 32p. (gr. k-3). 1991. PLB 17.27 (*0-8368-0576-3*) Gareth Stevens Inc.
—The Fourteen Forest Mice & the Winter Sledding Day. Knowlton, Mary L., tr. from JPN. Iwamura, Kazuo, illus. LC 90-50707. 32p. (gr. k-3). 1991. PLB 17.27 (*0-8368-0499-6*) Gareth Stevens Inc.
Jacques, Brian. Mariel of Redwall. 400p. (gr. 5-9). 1992. 17.95 (*0-399-22144-1*, Philomel Bks) Putnam Pub Group.
—Martin the Warrior. Chalk, Gary, illus. 400p. (gr. 5-9). 1994. 16.95 (*0-399-22670-2*, Philomel) Putnam Pub Group.
Janice. Little Bear Marches in the Saint Patrick's Day Parade. Mariana, illus. LC 67-15712. 40p. (gr. k-3). PLB 13.93 (*0-688-51075-2*) Lothrop.
Jensen, Patricia. Little Mouse's Rescue. (ps-3). 1994. 6.99 (*0-89577-581-6*, Readers Digest Kids) RD Assn.
Johnson, Pamela. A Mouse's Tale. D'Andrade, Diane, ed. (Illus.). 32p. (ps-3). 1991. 11.95 (*0-15-256032-7*) HarBrace.
Johnson, Patricia. Mistletoe. 1992. 7.95 (*0-533-09706-1*) Vantage.
Jose, Eduard, adapted by. The Vain Little Mouse: A Classic Tale. Riehecky, Janet, tr. Asensio, Augusti, illus. LC 88-35214. 32p. (gr. 1-4). 1988. PLB 13.95 (*0-89565-464-4*) Childs World.
Joubert, Jean. White Owl & Blue Mouse. Levertov, Denise, tr. from FRE. Gay, Michel, illus. LC 90-70710. 64p. (gr. 1-3). 1990. 13.95 (*0-944072-13-5*) Zoland Bks.
Los Juguetes De Bebe Mickey. (SPA.). (ps-3). 1993. pap. 2.95 (*0-307-96098-6*, Golden Pr) Western Pub.
Kahalewai, Marilyn. Maui Mouse's Supper. LC 87-92276. (Illus.). 16p. (Orig.). (ps-3). 1989. 7.95 (*0-935848-57-6*); pap. 5.95 (*1-880188-68-6*) Bess Pr.
Keller, Holly. The New Boy. LC 90-41757. (Illus.). 24p. (ps up). 1991. 13.95 (*0-688-09827-4*); PLB 13.88 (*0-688-09828-2*) Greenwillow.
Kellogg, Steven. The Island of the Skog. LC 73-6019. (Illus.). (gr. k-3). 1976. pap. 4.95 (*0-8037-4122-7*) Dial Bks Young.
—The Island of the Skog. Kellogg, Steven, illus. LC 73-6019. 32p. (ps-3). 1973. 15.00 (*0-8037-3842-0*); PLB 13.89 (*0-8037-3840-4*) Dial Bks Young.
Kerr, Rita. A Wee Bit of Texas. Kerr, Rita, illus. 80p. (gr. 1-4). 1991. 10.95 (*0-89015-809-6*) Sunbelt Media.
Kezzeiz, Ediba. Ramadan Adventures of Fasfoose Mouse. Shishani, Ami, illus. 36p. (Orig.). (gr. 1-6). 1991. pap. 3.00 ea. (*0-89259-117-X*) Am Trust Pubns.
King-Smith, Dick. Martin's Mice. Alborough, Jez, illus. LC 88-20359. 128p. (gr. 3 up). 1988. 13.00 (*0-517-57113-7*) Crown Bks Yng Read.
—Martin's Mice. large print ed. (gr. 4-7). 1989. lib. bdg. 16.50 (*0-7451-0956-X*, Lythway Large Print) Hall.
—Martin's Mice. 1990. pap. 3.25 (*0-440-40380-4*, Pub. by Yearling Classics) Dell.
—The Mouse Butcher. Smith, Wendy, illus. 144p. (gr. 3-7). 1992. pap. 3.99 (*0-14-031457-1*) Puffin Bks.
Kraus, Robert. Another Mouse to Feed. Aruego, Jose & Dewey, Ariane, illus. 32p. (ps-1). 1988. pap. 6.95 bk. & cassette (*0-671-67146-4*, S&S BFYR) S&S Trade.

—Another Mouse to Feed. Aruego, Jose & Dewey, Ariane, illus. LC 78-21259. (ps). 1987. pap. 13.95 jacketed (*0-671-66522-7*, S&S BFYR); pap. 5.95 (*0-671-66688-6*, S&S BFYR) S&S Trade.
—Dr. Mouse, Bungle Jungle Doctor. (Illus.). 32p. (ps-2). 1992. pap. write for info. (*0-307-15964-7*, 15964) Western Pub.
—Noel the Coward. Aruego, Jose & Dewey, Ariane, illus. 32p. (ps-3). 1988. pap. 12.95 jacketed (*0-671-66845-5*, S&S BFYR); pap. 5.95 (*0-671-66846-3*, S&S BFYR) S&S Trade.
—Where Are You Going, Little Mouse? Aruego, Jose & Dewey, Ariane, illus. LC 84-25868. 32p. (ps-1). 1986. 15.00 (*0-688-04294-5*); PLB 14.93 (*0-688-04295-3*) Greenwillow.
—Where Are You Going, Little Mouse? Dewey, Jose & Dewey, Ariane, illus. LC 84-25868. (ps up). 1989. 4.95 (*0-688-08747-7*, Mulberry) Morrow.
—Whose Mouse Are You? Aruego, Jose, illus. LC 70-89931. 32p. (ps-k). 1986. pap. 4.95 (*0-689-71142-5*, Aladdin) Macmillan Child Grp.
—Whose Mouse Are You? Aruego, Jose, illus. LC 70-89931. 32p. (ps-k). 1970. RSBE 13.95 (*0-02-751190-1*, Macmillan Child Bk) Macmillan Child Grp.
Kroll, Steven. The Biggest Pumpkin Ever. Bassett, Jeni, illus. LC 83-18492. 32p. (ps-3). 1984. reinforced bdg. 15.95 (*0-8234-0505-2*) Holiday.
Kwitz, Mary D. Bell Tolls at Mousehaven Manor. (gr. 4-7). 1993. pap. 3.25 (*0-590-43841-7*) Scholastic Inc.
Langley, Andy. The Hungry Mice. (Illus.). 8p. 1992. bds. 3.95 (*0-681-41517-7*) Longmeadow Pr.
—The Naughty Mice. (Illus.). 8p. 1992. bds. 3.95 (*0-681-41516-9*) Longmeadow Pr.
Lawton, Helen. Moggy the Mouser. McAllan, Marina, illus. LC 93-6571. 1994. write for info. (*0-383-03702-6*) SRA Schl Grp.
Leigh, Oretta. Aloysius Sebastian Mozart Mouse. DeLacre, Lulu, illus. 32p. (gr. k-2). 1984. 6.95 (*0-685-09671-8*, J Messner) S&S Trade.
Leonard, Marcia. Catch a Mouse. 1988. 4.95 (*0-553-05425-2*, Little Rooster) Bantam.
Leonard, Marcia & Schmidt, Karen L. Little Mouse Makes a Mess. 32p. (Orig.). (gr. 1). 1985. pap. 2.50 (*0-553-15301-3*) Bantam.
Lewison, Wendy. Happy Thanksgiving! Morgan, Mary, illus. 24p. (ps). 1993. bds. 2.95 (*0-448-40552-0*, G&D) Putnam Pub Group.
Lewison, Wendy C. Shy Vi. Smith, Stephen J., illus. LC 91-39658. 40p. (ps-2). 1993. pap. 14.00 JRT (*0-671-76968-5*, S&S BFYR) S&S Trade.
Lionni, Leo. Alexander & the Wind-up Mouse. Lionni, Leo, illus. LC 76-77423. 32p. (ps-2). 1969. 15.00 (*0-394-80914-9*); lib. bdg. 15.99 (*0-394-90914-3*) Knopf Bks Yng Read.
—A Busy Year. LC 91-29149. (Illus.). 36p. (ps-2). 1992. 7.99 (*0-679-82464-2*); PLB 10.99 (*0-679-92464-7*) Knopf Bks Yng Read.
—Frederick. Lionni, Leo, illus. LC 66-10355. 32p. (gr. k-3). 1973. pap. 4.99 (*0-394-82614-0*) Knopf Bks Yng Read.
—Mr. McMouse. Lionni, Leo, illus. LC 92-8963. 40p. (ps-1). 1992. 15.00 (*0-679-83890-2*); PLB 15.99 (*0-679-93890-7*) Knopf Bks Yng Read.
—Tillie & the Wall. Lionni, Leo, illus. LC 88-9316. 32p. (ps-2). 1989. 12.95 (*0-394-82155-6*); lib. bdg. 13.99 (*0-394-92155-0*) Knopf Bks Yng Read.
Lobel, Arnold. Martha the Movie Mouse. Lobel, Arnold, illus. LC 66-18654. 32p. (ps-3). 1993. pap. 4.95 (*0-06-443318-8*, Trophy) HarpC Child Bks.
—Mouse Soup. Lobel, Arnold, illus. LC 76-41517. 64p. (gr. k-3). 1977. 14.00 (*0-06-023967-0*); PLB 13.89 (*0-06-023968-9*) HarpC Child Bks.
—Mouse Tales. Lobel, Arnold, illus. LC 72-76511. 64p. (ps-3). 1978. pap. 3.50 (*0-06-444013-3*, Trophy) HarpC Child Bks.
Lundell, Margo. The Wee Mouse Who Was Afraid of the Dark. McQueen, Lucinda, illus. 32p. 1991. pap. 1.95 (*0-448-40060-X*, Platt & Munk Pubs) Putnam Pub Group.
McCully, Emily A. The Christmas Gift. McCully, Emily A., illus. LC 87-45758. 32p. (ps-1). 1988. PLB 12.89 (*0-06-024212-4*) HarpC Child Bks.
McDonnell, Janet. Mouse's Adventure in Alphabet Town. Williams, Jenny, illus. LC 91-47717. 32p. (ps-2). 1992. PLB 11.80 (*0-516-05413-9*) Childrens.
—Spring: New Life Everywhere. Hohag, Linda, illus. LC 93-10309. 32p. (gr. 2 up). 1993. PLB 12.30 (*0-516-00677-0*) Childrens.
—Summer, a Growing Time. Hohag, Linda, illus. LC 93-1182. 32p. (gr. 2 up). 1993. PLB 12.30 (*0-516-00678-9*) Childrens.
—Winter: Tracks in the Snow. Hohag, Linda, illus. LC 93-20172. 32p. (gr. 2 up). 1993. PLB 12.30 (*0-516-00679-7*) Childrens.
McGrath, Meggan. My Grapes. McGrath, Meggan, illus. LC 93-24057. 48p. (Orig.). 1993. pap. 16.95 (*0-938586-99-8*) Pfeifer-Hamilton.
McKissack, Patricia & McKissack, Fredrick. Country Mouse & City Mouse. Sikorski, Anne, illus. LC 85-12759. (ps-2). 1985. PLB 10.25 (*0-516-02362-4*); pap. 3.95 (*0-516-42362-2*) Childrens.
—El Ratoncito del Campo y el Ratoncito de la Ciudad: Country Mouse & City Mouse. LC 86-21565. 32p. (ps-2). 1986. pap. 3.95 (*0-516-52362-7*) Childrens.
McMillan, Bruce. Mouse Views: What the Class Pet Saw. LC 92-25921. (Illus.). 32p. (ps-3). 1993. reinforced bdg. 15.95 (*0-8234-1008-0*); pap. 5.95 (*0-8234-1132-X*) Holiday.
Maisner, Heather. Find Mouse in the House. Hard, Charlotte, illus. LC 93-3638. 20p. (ps up). 1994. 9.95 (*1-56402-351-6*) Candlewick Pr.
—Find Mouse in the Yard. Hard, Charlotte, illus. LC 93-12825. 20p. (ps up). 1994. 9.95 (*1-56402-350-8*) Candlewick Pr.
Majewski, Joe. A Friend for Oscar Mouse. Majewski, Maria, illus. LC 87-5365. 32p. (ps-2). 1991. pap. 3.99 (*0-8037-0913-7*, Puff Pied Piper) Puffin Bks.
Malotki, Ekkehart, retold by. The Mouse Couple. Lacapa, Michael, illus. LC 88-60916. 64p. (gr. 2-7). 1988. 14.95 (*0-87358-473-2*) Northland AZ.
Martin, Melanie. Madison Moves to the Country. Karas, G. Brian, illus. LC 88-1313. 48p. (Orig.). (gr. 1-4). 1989. PLB 10.59 (*0-8167-1345-6*); pap. text ed. 3.50 (*0-8167-1346-4*) Troll Assocs.
—Morris, the Millionaire Mouse. LC 88-1235. (Illus.). 48p. (Orig.). (gr. 1-4). 1989. PLB 10.59 (*0-8167-1339-1*); pap. text ed. 3.50 (*0-8167-1340-5*) Troll Assocs.
Matthews, Joan. Mindy Mouse & the A-Frame House. 1994. 7.95 (*0-533-10683-4*) Vantage.
Michaels, Ski. The Big Surprise. Paterson, Diane, illus. LC 85-14017. 48p. (gr. 1-3). 1986. PLB 10.59 (*0-8167-0576-3*); pap. text ed. 3.50 (*0-8167-0577-1*) Troll Assocs.
Mickey Mouse. (Illus.). 204p. 1991. 17.99 (*0-517-69715-7*) Random Hse Value.
Mickey Mouse & Friends. 1990. write for info. (*0-307-15535-8*, Golden Pr) Western Pub.
Miller, Edna. Mousekin Finds a Friend. Miller, Edna, illus. (ps-3). 1971. (Pub. by Treehouse) P-H.
—Mousekin's ABCs. LC 72-176159. (Illus.). 32p. (gr. k-4). 1974. pap. 5.95 (*0-671-66473-5*, S&S BFYR) S&S Trade.
—Mousekin's Close Call. Miller, Edna, illus. LC 77-27571. (gr. k-3). 1980. 9.95x (*0-13-604207-4*, Pub. by Treehouse) P-H.
—Mousekin's Family. Miller, Edna, illus. (gr. k-3). 1972. (Pub. by Treehouse); PLB 9.95x (*0-13-604462-X*) P-H.
—Mousekin's Frosty Friend. LC 89-29892. (Illus.). 32p. (gr. k-4). 1990. pap. 12.95 jacketed (*0-671-70445-1*, S&S BFYR) S&S Trade.
—Mousekin's Golden House. Miller, Edna, illus. (gr. k-3). 1971. (Pub. by Treehouse) P-H.
—Mousekin's Golden House. LC 64-16429. (Illus.). 32p. (gr. k-4). 1971. pap. 5.95 (*0-671-66972-9*, S&S BFYR) S&S Trade.
—Mousekin's Golden House. LC 87-32111. (ps-3). 1990. pap. 12.95 (*0-671-66282-1*, S&S BFYR) S&S Trade.
—Mousekin's Lost Woodland. LC 91-4201. (Illus.). 40p. (ps-3). 1992. pap. 13.00 jacketed (*0-671-74938-2*, S&S BFYR) S&S Trade.
—Mousekin's Woodland Sleepers. (Illus.). (gr. k-3). 1977. (Pub. by Treehouse) P-H.
—Mousekin's Woodland Sleepers. 1987. 11.95 (*0-13-604505-7*) P-H.
Miller, Moira. Oscar Mouse Finds a Home. (ps-3). 1992. pap. 4.99 (*0-14-054682-0*) Viking Child Bks.
—The Proverbial Mouse. LC 86-16737. (Illus.). 32p. (ps-3). 1992. pap. 4.99 (*0-8037-1072-0*, Puff Pied Piper) Puffin Bks.
Minnie 'n Me: What Will I Wear? (ps-1). 1991. write for info. (*0-307-11584-4*, Golden Pr) Western Pub.
Minnie's Tea Party. 24p. 1994. 9.98 (*1-57082-156-9*) Mouse Works.
Montague, William A. Little Mouse: The Mouse Who Lived with Henry David Thoreau at Walden Pond. Roof, Christopher, ed. Payne, Maxine & Montague, William A., illus. LC 93-73231. 56p. (Orig.). (gr. 2-4). 1993. pap. text ed. 7.95 (*0-9638644-0-8*) Concord MouseTrap.
Moore, Lilian. Don't Be Afraid, Amanda. McCord, Kathleen, illus. LC 91-19661. 64p. (gr. 2-5). 1992. SBE 12.95 (*0-689-31725-5*, Atheneum Child Bk) Macmillan Child Grp.
—I'll Meet You at the Cucumbers. Wooding, Sharon, illus. LC 87-15195. 72p. (gr. 2-6). 1988. SBE 13.95 (*0-689-31243-1*, Atheneum Child Bk) Macmillan Child Grp.
Morgan, Mary, illus. Guess Who I Love? 18p. (ps). 1992. bds. 2.95 (*0-448-40313-7*) Putnam Pub Group.
Morimoto, Junko. Mouse's Marriage. (Illus.). 32p. (Orig.). (ps-1). 1988. pap. 4.99 (*0-14-050678-0*, Puffin) Puffin Bks.
Mousekin's Fables. (Illus.). 32p. 1985. pap. 5.95 (*0-671-66475-1*, S&S BFYR) S&S Trade.
Myers, Walter D. The Mouse Rap. Bacha, Andy. LC 89-35419. 192p. (gr. 5-9). 1992. pap. 3.95 (*0-06-440356-4*, Trophy) HarpC Child Bks.
Nash, Corey. Little Treasury of Walt Disney: Mickey & Friends. 1988. 5.99 (*0-517-61639-4*) Random Hse Value.
Naylor, Phyllis R. Maudie in the Middle. 1990. pap. 3.25 (*0-440-40324-3*, Pub. by Yearling Classics) Dell.
Noll, Sally. Watch Where You Go. LC 88-35591. (Illus.). 32p. (ps up). 1990. 12.95 (*0-688-08498-2*); lib. bdg. 12.88 (*0-688-08499-0*) Greenwillow.
—Watch Where You Go. LC 92-25333. 1993. pap. 3.99 (*0-14-054884-X*) Puffin Bks.
Novak, Matt. Mouse TV. LC 93-49399. (Illus.). 32p. (ps-1). 1994. 14.95 (*0-531-06856-0*); PLB 14.99 (*0-531-08706-9*) Orchard Bks Watts.
Numeroff, Laura J. If You Give a Mouse a Cookie. Bond, Felicia, illus. LC 84-48343. 32p. (ps-2). 1985. 13.00 (*0-06-024586-7*); PLB 12.89 (*0-06-024587-5*) HarpC Child Bks.
—If You Give a Mouse a Cookie. 1993. pap. 28.67 (*0-590-71885-1*) Scholastic Inc.
Oakley, Graham. The Church Mice Spread Their Wings. Oakley, Graham, illus. LC 75-15102. 40p. (gr. k-3). 1976. SBE 13.95 (*0-689-30496-X*, Atheneum Child Bk) Macmillan Child Grp.
O'Brien, Robert C. Mrs. Frisby & the Rats of NIMH. Bernstein, Zena, illus. LC 74-134818. 240p. (gr. 3-7). 1971. SBE 15.95 (*0-689-20651-8*, Atheneum Child Bk) Macmillan Child Grp.
Oechsli, Kelly. Mice at Bat. Oechsli, Kelly, illus. LC 85-45266. 64p. (gr. 1-3). 1986. HarpC Child Bks.
—Mice at Bat. Oechsli, Kelly, illus. LC 85-45266. 64p. (gr. k-3). 1990. pap. 3.50 (*0-06-444139-3*, Trophy) HarpC Child Bks.
Ormondroyd, Edward. Broderick. Larrecq, John M., illus. LC 77-83752. (gr. k-3). 1969. (Pub. by Parnassus); PLB 4.77 (*0-686-86580-4*) HM.
Ostheeren, Ingrid. Jonathan Mouse. Lanning, Rosemary, tr. from GER. LC 85-10501. (Illus.). 32p. (gr. k-3). 1986. 13.95 (*1-55858-064-6*) North-South Bks NYC.
—Jonathan Mouse & the Baby Bird. Mathieu, Agnes, illus. Lanning, Rosemary, tr. from GER. LC 91-6614. (Illus.). 32p. (gr. k-3). 1991. 14.95 (*1-55858-108-1*) North-South Bks NYC.
—Jonathan Mouse & the Magic Box. Mathieu, Agnes, illus. Lanning, Rosemary, tr. from GER. LC 89-43248. (Illus.). 32p. (gr. k-3). 1990. 13.95 (*1-55858-087-5*) North-South Bks NYC.
—Jonathan Mouse, Detective. Mathieu, Agnes, illus. Lanning, Rosemary, tr. from GER. LC 92-29023. (Illus.). 32p. (gr. k-3). 1993. 14.95 (*1-55858-164-2*); pap. 14.95 (*1-55858-141-3*) North-South Bks NYC.
Packard, Mary. Sleep-over Mouse. (Illus.). 28p. (ps-2). 1994. PLB 14.00 (*0-516-05367-1*); pap. 3.95 (*0-516-45367-X*) Childrens.
Palmer, Todd S. Rhino & Mouse. Lanfredi, Judy, illus. LC 93-33299. 40p. (ps-3). 1994. 12.99 (*0-8037-1322-3*); PLB 12.89 (*0-8037-1323-1*) Dial Bks Young.
Parish, Peggy. Play Ball, Amelia Bedelia. Tripp, Wallace, illus. LC 71-85028. 64p. (ps-3). 1985. (Trophy); pap. 3.50 (*0-06-444005-2*, Trophy) HarpC Child Bks.
Parkison, Ralph F. The Twig & the Mouse, Bk. 2. Withrow, Marion O., ed. Bush, William, illus. 17p. (Orig.). (gr. 2-6). 1988. pap. 4.25 (*0-929949-01-3*) Little Wood Bks.
Peppe, Rodney. Mice on the Moon. (gr. 4 up). 1993. pap. 13.95 (*0-385-30839-6*) Doubleday.
Pilkey, Dav. Dogzilla. LC 92-37906. (gr. 4 up). 1993. 10.95 (*0-15-223944-8*); pap. 5.95 (*0-15-223945-6*) HarBrace.
—Kat Kong. LC 92-14483. (ps-3). 1993. 10.95 (*0-15-242036-3*); pap. 5.95 (*0-15-242037-1*) HarBrace.
Pochicki, Ethel. Attic Mice. (ps-3). 1993. pap. 3.50 (*0-440-40745-1*) Dell.
Pochocki, Ethel. The Attic Mice. Catrow, David, illus. LC 90-32064. 128p. (gr. 2-4). 1990. 13.95 (*0-8050-1298-2*, Bks Young Read) H Holt & Co.
Potter, Beatrix. El Cuento de Juanito Raton de Ciudad. (SPA., Illus.). 64p. 1988. 5.95 (*0-7232-3560-0*) Warne.
—El Cuento de los Dos Malvados Ratones. (SPA., Illus.). 64p. 1988. 5.95 (*0-7232-3559-7*) Warne.
—Deux Vilaines Souris. (FRE.). 59p. 1990. 10.95 (*2-07-056070-8*) Schoenhof.
—Deux Vilaines Souris. (FRE.). 59p. 1990. 9.95 (*0-7859-3625-4*, 2070560708) Fr & Eur.
—Mouse Tales. (Illus.). 128p. 1989. 8.95 (*0-7232-3543-0*) Warne.
—The Tailor of Gloucester. (Illus.). 57p. (gr. k-3). 1973. pap. 1.75 (*0-486-20176-7*) Dover.
—The Tailor of Gloucester. Atkinson, Allen, illus. 1984. pap. 2.25 (*0-553-15220-3*) Bantam.
—The Tale of Johnny Town-Mouse. (ps-3). 1987. 5.95 (*0-7232-3472-8*); pap. 2.25 (*0-7232-3497-3*) Warne.
—The Tale of Mrs. Tittlemouse. 1987. 5.95 (*0-7232-3470-1*); pap. 2.25 (*0-7232-3495-7*) Warne.
—The Tale of Mrs. Tittlemouse & Other Mouse Stories. LC 85-40386. (Illus.). 80p. (ps-3). 1985. 10.95 (*0-7232-3324-1*) Warne.
—The Tale of Pigling Bland. 1987. 5.95 (*0-7232-3474-4*); pap. 2.25 (*0-7232-3499-X*) Warne.
—The Tale of Two Bad Mice. LC 74-75268. (Illus.). 59p. (gr. 2-4). 1974. pap. 1.75 (*0-486-23065-1*) Dover.
—The Tale of Two Bad Mice. 64p. (Orig.). (ps). 1984. pap. 2.25 (*0-553-15219-X*) Bantam.
—The Tale of Two Bad Mice. (Illus.). (ps-3). 1987. 5.95 (*0-7232-3464-7*); pap. 2.25 (*0-7232-3489-2*) Warne.
—The Tale of Two Bad Mice. 1992. 3.99 (*0-517-07241-6*) Random Hse Value.
—The Tale of Two Bad Mice. (Illus.). 32p. (gr. k-3). 1992. pap. 2.99 (*0-87406-620-4*) Willowisp Pr.
—Tom Kitten: Bath Book. 1989. 3.50 (*0-7232-3585-6*) Warne.
Potter, Beatrix, created by. Two Bad Mice. Marsh, T. F., et al, illus. 24p. (gr. 2-4). 1992. PLB 10.95 (*1-56674-011-8*, HTS Bks) Forest Hse.
Powhida, Elizabeth C. Anthony Mouse Goes Swimming. Peterson, Nancy M., illus. 40p. (ps-5). 1993. pap. write for info. (*0-9625842-1-5*, TXU538146) Kinderhook Pubs.
Pryor, Bonnie. The Porcupine Mouse. Begin, Maryjane, illus. LC 87-12305. 32p. (ps-2). 1988. 13.95 (*0-688-07153-8*); PLB 13.88 (*0-688-07154-6*, Morrow Jr Bks) Morrow Jr Bks.
Que Hace Bebe Mickey? (SPA.). (ps-3). 1993. pap. 2.95 (*0-307-96113-3*, Golden Pr) Western Pub.

Roberts, Bethany. Cat Parade! Greenseid, Diane, illus. LC 93-26726. 1995. write for info. (*0-395-67893-5*, Clarion Bks) HM.
—Halloween Mice! Cushman, Doug, illus. LC 93-17192. 1994. write for info. (*0-395-67064-0*, Clarion Bks) HM.
Roche, P. K. Webster & Arnold Go Camping. (Illus.). 32p. (ps-3). 1991. pap. 3.95 (*0-14-050806-6*, Puffin) Puffin Bks.
Rosenbluth, Rosalyn. The Brave Little Mouse. Borgo, Deborah, illus. 24p. (ps-2). 1993. pap. text ed. 0.99 (*1-56293-346-9*) McClanahan Bk.
Ross, Dave. Little Mouse's Valentine. LC 85-15357. (Illus.). 32p. (ps-k). 1986. 11.95 (*0-688-06224-5*); (Morrow Jr Bks) Morrow Jr Bks.
Roth, Carol. Quiet As a Mouse. Schories, Pat, illus. 32p. (ps-3). 1991. 6.95 (*1-56288-121-3*) Checkerboard.
Rowe, Amy & Rowe, Philip. Ernest the Fierce Mouse. rev. ed. Norton, Andrea, illus. 32p. (gr. k-2). 1990. Repr. of 1985 ed. PLB 10.95 (*1-878363-08-5*) Forest Hse.
Samton, Sheila W. Oh No! A Naptime Adventure. Samton, Sheila W., illus. 32p. (ps-1). 1993. RB 13.99 (*0-670-84250-8*) Viking Child Bks.
Sarlas-Fontana, Jane. The Adventures of Spero the Orthodox Church Mouse: The Nativity of Our Lord Christ's Birth. Simic, Tim, illus. 20p. (ps-4). 1992. pap. 6.95 (*0-937032-91-3*) Light&Life Pub Co MN.
—Spero Learns of Palm Sunday & Jesus' Love. 28p. (ps-4). 1993. pap. 5.95 (*0-9638336-0-X*) Spero & Me.
Sathre, Vivian. Mouse Chase. Schumaker, Ward, illus. LC 94-17010. Date not set. write for info. (*0-15-200105-0*) HarBrace.
Schories, Pat. Mouse Around. (ps-3). 1991. bds. 13.00 (*0-374-35080-9*) FS&G.
Schrecker, Judie. The Pet Shop Mouse. LC 93-60231. (Illus.). 44p. (ps-3). 1994. 8.95 (*1-55523-605-7*) Winston-Derek.
Scoltock, Jack. Jeremy's Adventure. (Illus.). 91p. (Orig.). (gr. 2-5). 1991. pap. 7.95 (*0-86327-305-X*, Pub. by Wolfhound Pr EIRE) Dufour.
Seidler, Tor. A Rat's Tale. Marcellino, Fred, illus. 187p. (gr. 1-8). 1986. 16.00 (*0-374-36185-1*) FS&G.
Severn, Jeffrey. George & His Giant Shadow. Severn, Jeffrey, illus. 32p. (ps-1). 1990. 12.95 (*0-87701-634-8*) Chronicle Bks.
Sharp, Margery. Miss Bianca. Williams, Garth, illus. (gr. 2-4). 1923. 0.95 (*0-440-45761-0*, YB) Dell.
—Miss Bianca in the Salt Mines. 1978. pap. 1.25 (*0-440-45717-3*, YB) Dell.
Slaughter, Hope. Windmill Hill. Frascino, Edward, illus. 64p. (gr. 2-5). 1993. 14.95 (*0-945912-21-8*) Pippin Pr.
Smith, Wendy. The Lonely, Only Mouse. (Illus.). 32p. 1988. pap. 3.50 (*0-14-050651-9*, Puffin) Puffin Bks.
Snyder, Zilpha K. Squeak Saves the Day. (ps-3). 1992. pap. 3.25 (*0-440-40585-8*, YB) Dell.
Soto, Gary. Chato's Kitchen. Guevara, Susan, illus. LC 93-43503. 1995. write for info. (*0-399-22658-3*, Putnam) Putnam Pub Group.
Spring, Grace J. The Fabulous House of Marcella Mouse. Spring, Grace J., illus. LC 85-7518. 24p. (gr. 1-6). 1985. pap. 3.95 (*0-317-39846-6*) Andrew Mtn Pr.
Steig, William. Abel's Island. Steig, William, illus. LC 75-35916. 128p. (gr. 1 up). 1976. 15.00 (*0-374-30010-0*) FS&G.
Steptoe, John. The Story of Jumping Mouse. Steptoe, John, illus. LC 82-14848. 40p. (gr. k-3). 1984. 15.00 (*0-688-01902-1*); PLB 14.93 (*0-688-01903-X*) Lothrop.
—The Story of Jumping Mouse. LC 82-14848. (Illus.). 40p. (gr. 1 up). 1989. pap. 4.95 (*0-688-08740-X*, Mulberry) Morrow.
Sternburg, Sharon. Suzie Q. Mouse Adventures. Coyne, John P., illus. 39p. (Orig.). (ps-1). 1993. pap. 5.99 (*0-9633513-1-1*) S M Resar Pub.
—Suzie Q. Mouse Adventures: Coloring Book. Coyne, John P., illus. 39p. (Orig.). (ps-1). Date not set. pap. 1.99x (*0-9633513-0-3*) S M Resar Pub.
Stevens, Janet, adapted by. & illus. The Town Mouse & the Country Mouse. LC 86-14276. 32p. (ps-3). 1987. reinforced bdg. 15.95 (*0-8234-0633-4*); pap. 5.95 (*0-8234-0733-0*) Holiday.
Stevenson, James. The Stowaway. LC 89-25861. (Illus.). 32p. (ps up). 1990. 12.95 (*0-688-08619-5*); PLB 12.88 (*0-688-08620-9*) Greenwillow.
Stoddard, Sandol. Bedtime Mouse. (ps-3). 1993. pap. 4.95 (*0-395-67436-0*) HM.
Stolz, Mary. Belling the Tiger. Montresor, Beni, illus. LC 61-5776. 64p. (gr. 2-5). 1990. PLB 12.89 (*0-06-025863-2*) HarpC Child Bks.
—Tales at the Mousehole. Johnson, Pamela, illus. LC 88-46130. 96p. (gr. 2-4). 1992. 15.95 (*0-87923-789-9*) Godine.
Stone, Bernard. Quasimodo Mouse. Steadman, Ralph, illus. 32p. (gr. 1-4). 1987. 15.95 (*0-86264-072-5*, Pub. by Anderson Pr UK) Trafalgar.
Stortz, Diane. Barnaby Mouse, Detective, & the Mystery of the Big Book. Girouard, Patrick, illus. LC 93-14425. 28p. (ps). 1994. 4.99 (*0-7847-0004-4*, 24-03870) Standard Pub.
Szekeres, Cyndy. Cyndy Szekeres' Teeny Mouse Counts Herself. Szekeres, Cyndy, illus. 12p. (ps). 1992. bds. write for info. (*0-307-06118-3*, 6118, Golden Pr) Western Pub.
Taylor, Judy. The Adventures of Dudley Dormouse. Cross, Peter, illus. & created by. LC 91-58717. 80p. (ps up). 1992. 9.95 (*1-56402-043-6*) Candlewick Pr.
Timm, Stephen A. The Dragon & the Mouse: Together Again. Lalo, illus. LC 81-90230. 46p. (ps-8). 1981. 12.95 (*0-939728-03-6*); pap. 4.95 (*0-939728-04-4*) Steppingstone Ent.
Titus, Eve. Anatole & the Thirty Thieves. (ps-3). 1990. pap. 4.95 (*0-553-34889-2*) Bantam.
Tompert, Ann. A Carol for Christmas. Kelly, Laura, illus. LC 94-9039. (gr. k-3). 1994. 14.95 (*0-02-789402-9*) Macmillan.
—Just a Little Bit. Munsinger, Lynn, illus. LC 92-31857. 1993. 14.95 (*0-395-51527-0*) HM.
Town Mouse & Country Mouse. 24p. (ps-3). 1989. write for info. (*1-56288-161-2*) Checkerboard.
Tudor, Tasha. Mouse Mills Catalogue for Spring. Tudor, Tasha, illus. Mouse, Timothy D., tr. LC 89-50061. (Illus.). 40p. (gr. k up). 1989. pap. text ed. 6.95 (*0-9621753-2-3*) Jenny Wren Pr.
Tulku, Chagdud. The Kind King & the Magnanimous Mice: A Tibetan Folktale. 1993. pap. 9.95 (*1-881847-03-9*) Chagdud Gonpa-Padma.
Van Laan, Nancy. A Mouse in My House. Priceman, Marjorie, illus. LC 89-15591. 32p. (ps-3). 1990. 9.95 (*0-679-80043-3*); PLB 10.99 (*0-679-90043-8*) Knopf Bks Yng Read.
Van Leeuwen, Jean. The Great Christmas Kidnapping Caper. Kellogg, Steven, illus. LC 75-9201. 144p. (gr. 2-6). 1975. 12.95 (*0-685-01454-1*) Dial Bks Young.
—The Great Rescue Operation. Apple, Margot, illus. LC 81-65851. 176p. (gr. 2-6). 1982. 10.95 (*0-685-01455-X*); PLB 10.89 (*0-685-01456-8*) Dial Bks Young.
—The Great Rescue Operation. Apple, Margot, illus. 144p. (gr. 3 up). 1990. pap. 3.95 (*0-14-034288-5*, Puffin) Puffin Bks.
—The Great Summer Camp Catastrophe. DeGroat, Diane, illus. LC 91-18487. 192p. (gr. 2-6). 1992. 13.00 (*0-8037-1106-9*); PLB 12.89 (*0-8037-1107-7*) Dial Bks Young.
Vargus, Jane A. Ashmouse & the Wrong Side of the Bed. Vargus, Jane A., illus. LC 92-61365. 44p. 1993. pap. 5.95 (*1-55523-557-3*) Winston-Derek.
Waddell, Martin & Miller, Virginia. Squeak-a-Lot. LC 90-3568. (Illus.). 32p. (ps up). 1991. 13.95 (*0-688-10244-1*); PLB 13.88 (*0-688-10245-X*) Greenwillow.
Wahl, Jan. Pleasant Fieldmouse. Sendak, Maurice, illus. LC 64-14684. 80p. (gr. k-3). 1964. PLB 14.89 (*0-06-026331-8*) HarpC Child Bks.
—Pleasant Fieldmouse. Sendak, Maurice, illus. LC 64-14684. 72p. (gr. k-3). 1992. pap. 7.95 (*0-06-443226-2*, Trophy) HarpC Child Bks.
—The Six Voyages of Pleasant Field Mouse. (Orig.). 1994. pap. 3.50 (*0-8125-2403-9*) Tor Bks.
Wallis, Diz. A Jar Full of Mice. Wallis, Diz, illus. LC 90-85919. 24p. 1991. 5.95 (*1-878093-42-8*) Boyds Mills Pr.
Wallner, John. City Mouse - Country Mouse & Two More Tales from Aesop. Wallner, John, illus. 32p. (Orig.). (gr. k-3). 1987. pap. 2.50 (*0-590-41155-1*) Scholastic Inc.
Walsh, Ellen S. Mouse Paint. Walsh, Ellen S., illus. 32p. (ps-1). 1989. 11.95 (*0-15-256025-4*) HarBrace.
Walt Disney Productions. Rescuers Down Under. 1990. 6.98 (*0-8317-7389-8*) Viking Child Bks.
Walt Disney Staff. Perils of Mickey: The Mail Pilot. (ps-3). 1993. pap. 2.25 (*0-307-12794-X*, Pub. by Golden Bks) Western Pub.
—Perils of Mickey: The Seven Ghosts. (ps-3). 1993. pap. 2.25 (*0-307-12793-1*, Pub. by Golden Bks) Western Pub.
—The Rescuers. (gr. 5-8). 1989. 6.98 (*0-8317-7388-X*) Viking Child Bks.
Walt Disney's Mickey Mouse Tales. (Illus.). 128p. 1992. 5.95 (*1-56138-155-1*) Running Pr.
Walt Disney's Mickey's Christmas Carol. (ps-3). 1990. write for info. (*0-307-12179-8*) Western Pub.
Waters, Tony. Sailor's Bride. (ps-3). 1991. pap. 13.95 (*0-385-41440-4*) Doubleday.
Weinberger, Jane. Vim, a Very Important Mouse. 8th ed. Allen, Rosemary, illus. LC 84-50872. 40p. (ps-4). 1989. 4.95 (*0-932433-01-4*) Windswept Hse.
Wells, Claudia E. Whiskers, the Bank Mouse. Shardin, Arthur, illus. LC 77-10823. (gr. 1-4). 1981. 4.50 (*0-930506-00-6*); pap. write for info. (*0-930506-01-4*) Popcorn Pubs.
Wells, Rosemary. Shy Charles. LC 87-27247. (Illus.). 32p. (ps-3). 1992. pap. 3.99 (*0-14-054537-9*, Puff Pied Piper) Puffin Bks.
—Shy Charles. (Illus.). 32p. (ps-3). 1992. pap. 17.99 giant bk. (*0-14-054570-0*, Puff Pied Piper) Puffin Bks.
White, E. B. E. B. White Boxed Set. Incl. Charlotte's Web; The Trumpet of the Swan; Stuart Little. (Illus.). (gr. 3 up). 1972. 39.00 (*0-06-026399-7*) HarpC Child Bks.
—E. B. White Boxed Set. Incl. Charlotte's Web; The Trumpet of the Swan; Stuart Little. (Illus.). (gr. 3 up). 1974. pap. 11.85 (*0-06-440061-1*, Trophy) HarpC Child Bks.
—Stuart Little. Williams, Garth, illus. LC 45-9585. 132p. (gr. 3-6). 1945. 13.00 (*0-06-026395-4*); PLB 12.89 (*0-06-026396-2*) HarpC Child Bks.
—Stuart Little. LC 45-9585. (Illus.). 132p. (gr. 3-7). 1974. pap. 3.95 (*0-06-440056-5*, Trophy) HarpC Child Bks.
White, Joseph A. The Three Little Mousies. LC 93-70959. 20p. (gr. k-3). 1993. pap. 3.95 (*0-9636278-0-5*) White DEI.

Willett, Fangette H. Jonah, the Mouse & the Goat. Jacobs, Jody, illus. 24p. (Orig.). (gr. 1 up). 1994. pap. 6.95 saddlestitched (*0-9642613-0-8*) Kinderword.
Join Jonah, the Mouse & the Goat on their wildly adventurous escapades. Set in the gorgeous aquamarine waters of the Caribbean, the three friends embark on a great sea adventure. The lush, full-color illustrations, sprinkled with hidden fairies, add sparkle & depth to the mystical creatures they encounter. They befriend a gigantic whale with smiling sapphire eyes, sea-foam witches & frolicking mermaids. Jonah & his friends are so bedazzled by their tropical fantasy that they fail to see an oncoming storm. They become trapped by the evil sea goblins who shred the sails of the boat & try to sink them. Jonah, terrified, calls to Amalie, who hears his cries & arises from the ocean floor to save them. This compelling tale, told in rhyme, embraces the West Indian culture & its love for magical stories. Ages 5 & up.
Publisher Provided Annotation.

Williams, Jill. An Adventure in Mouseland. Christie, Robert D., illus. LC 92-61769. 61p. (gr. k-6). 1992. pap. 3.95 (*0-931563-10-0*) Wishing Rm.
Wohl, Lauren L. Matzoh Mouse. Keavney, Pamela, illus. LC 90-31976. 32p. (gr. k-3). 1993. pap. 4.95 (*0-06-443323-4*, Trophy) HarpC Child Bks.
Wolkstein, Diane. Little Mouse's Painting. Begin, Maryjane, illus. LC 91-16017. 32p. (ps up). 1992. 15.00 (*0-688-07609-2*); PLB 14.93 (*0-688-07610-6*) Morrow Jr Bks.
Wood, A. J. The Treasure Hunt. Downer, Maggie, illus. LC 92-5515. 32p. (ps-4). 1992. 13.95 (*1-56566-018-8*) Thomasson-Grant.
Wood, Audrey & Wood, Audrey. Tugford Wanted to Be Bad. LC 83-318. (Illus.). 32p. (ps-3). 1983. 9.95 (*0-15-291083-2*, HB Juv Bks) HarBrace.
Worthington, Denise. En Nuestra Casa Habia un Raton. (Illus.). 8p. (gr. 1). 1993. 3.50 (*1-880612-16-X*) Seedling Pubns.
—Our House Had a Mouse. (Illus.). 8p. (gr. 1). 1993. pap. 3.50 (*1-880612-29-1*) Seedling Pubns.
Woychuk, Denis. The Other Side of the Wall. Howard, Kim, illus. LC 90-49415. 32p. (ps up). 1991. 13.95 (*0-688-09894-0*) Lothrop.
—Pirates! LC 91-3387. (Illus.). (ps-3). 1992. 14.00 (*0-688-10336-7*); PLB 13.93 (*0-688-10337-5*) Lothrop.
York, Carol B. The Good Day Mice. De Larrea, Victoria, illus. 112p. (gr. 3-7). 1989. pap. 2.75 (*0-553-15373-0*, Skylark) Bantam.
Zeldin, Florence. A Mouse in Our Jewish House. Rauchwerger, Lisa, illus. LC 89-40362. 32p. (ps). 1990. 11.95 (*0-933873-43-3*) Torah Aura.
Zelinsky, Paul O., adapted by. & illus. The Maid & the Mouse & the Odd-Shaped House. 32p. (ps-2). 1993. pap. 4.99 (*0-14-054946-3*, Puff Unicorn) Puffin Bks.
—The Maid & the Mouse & the Odd-Shaped House. 32p. (ps-2). 1993. 14.99 (*0-525-45095-5*, DCB) Dutton Child Bks.
Ziefert, Harriet. A Clean House for Mole & Mouse. Prebenna, David, illus. (Orig.). (ps-3). 1988. pap. 3.50 (*0-14-050810-4*, Puffin) Puffin Bks.
—New House for Mouse & Mole. Prebenna, David, illus. (ps-3). 1987. pap. 8.95 (*0-670-81720-1*) Viking Child Bks.
Zimelman, Nathan. Shaughnessy. Davenport, May, ed. Bd. with Humanization of Freddie Mouse. Blake, Richard. LC 81-71551. 64p. (Orig.). (gr. 3-5). 1984. pap. 3.50x (*0-943864-38-0*) Davenport.

MICE–POETRY

Fisher, Aileen. The House of a Mouse. Sandin, Joan, illus. LC 87-24947. 32p. (ps-3). 1988. HarpC Child Bks.
Foster, John, ed. Mouse Poems. (Illus.). 16p. (gr. 1 up). 1992. pap. 2.95 (*0-19-916430-4*) OUP.
Howard, Jean G. Of Mice & Mice. limited ed. Howard, Jean G., illus. LC 78-50486. (gr. k-4). 1978. 5.50 (*0-930954-03-3*); deluxe ed. 35.00 deluxe ed. (*0-930954-04-1*) Tidal Pr.

MICHELANGELO BUONARROTI, 1475-1564

Green, Jen. Michelangelo. (Illus.). 32p. (gr. 5 up). 1994. 10.95 (*0-8120-6461-5*); pap. 5.95 (*0-8120-1998-9*) Barron.
Hart, Tony. Michelangelo. Hellard, Susan, illus. LC 93-2384. 24p. (ps-3). 1994. pap. 5.95 (*0-8120-1827-3*) Barron.
Lace, William W. Michelangelo. LC 92-46996. (Illus.). 111p. (gr. 5-8). 1993. PLB 14.95 (*1-56006-038-7*) Lucent Bks.
McLanathan, Richard B. Michelangelo. LC 92-27688. (Illus.). 92p. 1993. 19.95 (*0-8109-3634-8*) Abrams.

Richmond, Robin. Introducing Michelangelo. (Illus.). 32p. (gr. 2-5). 1992. 14.95 (*0-316-74440-9*) Little.
Venezia, Mike. Michelangelo. Venezia, Mike, illus. LC 91-555. 32p. (ps-4). 1991. PLB 12.85 (*0-516-02293-8*); pap. 4.95 (*0-516-42293-6*) Childrens.

MICHIGAN

Blinks, William, et al. Memories of Early Michigan City. Lewis, Patricia, ed. (Orig.). (gr. 6 up). 1990. pap. 2.00 (*0-935549-14-5*) MI City Hist.
Carole Marsh Michigan Books, 44 bks. PLB 1027.80 set (*0-7933-1297-3*); pap. 587.80 set (*0-7933-5166-9*) Gallopade Pub Group.
Carpenter, Allan. Michigan. LC 78-8001. (Illus.). 96p. (gr. 4 up). 1978. PLB 16.95 (*0-516-04122-3*) Childrens.
Fradin, Dennis. Michigan: In Words & Pictures. LC 79-225356. (Illus.). 48p. (gr. 2-5). 1980. PLB 12.95 (*0-516-03922-9*) Childrens.
Fradin, Dennis B. Michigan. LC 91-32920. 64p. (gr. 3-5). 1992. PLB 16.45 (*0-516-03822-2*) Childrens.
Hall, Betty L. Michigan Survival. rev. ed. 160p. (gr. 10-12). 1986. pap. text ed. 5.84 (*0-936159-02-2*) Westwood Pr.
Hildebrand, Janice. Sheboygan County: One Hundred Fifty Years of Progress: An Illustrated History. (Illus.). 208p. (gr. 7 up). 1988. 29.95 (*0-89781-252-2*) Preferred Mktg.
Kachaturoff, Grace. Michigan! 2nd ed. (Illus.). 298p. (gr. 4). 1992. 23.00 (*0-87905-228-7*, Peregrine Smith) Gibbs Smith Pub.
McConnell, David B. Discover Michigan. Rasmussen, George L., illus. LC 81-6722. 144p. (gr. 4). 1989. text ed. 18.70x (*0-910726-07-8*); tchr's. guide 7.45x (*0-910726-33-7*) Hillsdale Educ.
—Explore Michigan A to Z. McConnell, Stella M., ed. Rasmussen, George L., illus. LC 93-17430. 48p. (Orig.). (gr. 3-4). 1993. pap. 7.95 (*0-910726-55-8*) Hillsdale Educ.
Marsh, Carole. Avast, Ye Slobs!: Michigan Pirate Trivia. (Illus.). (gr. 3 up). 1994. PLB 24.95 (*0-7933-0617-5*); pap. 14.95 (*0-7933-0616-7*); computer disk 29.95 (*0-7933-0618-3*) Gallopade Pub Group.
—The Beast of the Michigan Bed & Breakfast. (Illus.). (gr. 3 up). 1994. PLB 24.95 (*0-7933-1708-8*); pap. 14.95 (*0-7933-1709-6*); computer disk 29.95 (*0-7933-1710-X*) Gallopade Pub Group.
—Bow Wow! Michigan Dogs in History, Mystery, Legend, Lore, Humor & More! (Illus.). (gr. 3-12). 1994. PLB 24.95 (*0-7933-3533-7*); pap. 14.95 (*0-7933-3534-5*); computer disk 29.95 (*0-7933-3535-3*) Gallopade Pub Group.
—Chill Out: Scary Michigan Tales Based on Frightening Michigan Truths. (Illus.). 1994. lib. bdg. 24.95 (*0-7933-4720-3*); pap. 14.95 (*0-7933-4721-1*); disk 29.95 (*0-7933-4722-X*) Gallopade Pub Group.
—Christopher Columbus Comes to Michigan! Includes Reproducible Activities for Kids! (Illus.). (gr. 3-12). 1994. PLB 24.95 (*0-7933-3686-4*); pap. 14.95 (*0-7933-3687-2*); computer disk 29.95 (*0-7933-3688-0*) Gallopade Pub Group.
—The Hard-to-Believe-But-True! Book of Michigan History, Mystery, Trivia, Legend, Lore, Humor & More. (Illus.). (gr. 3 up). 1994. PLB 24.95 (*0-7933-0614-0*); pap. 14.95 (*0-7933-0613-2*); computer disk 29.95 (*0-7933-0615-9*) Gallopade Pub Group.
—If My Michigan Mama Ran the World! (Illus.). (gr. 3 up). 1994. lib. bdg. 24.95 (*0-7933-1723-1*); pap. 14.95 (*0-7933-1724-X*); computer disk 29.95 (*0-7933-1725-8*) Gallopade Pub Group.
—Jurassic Ark! Michigan Dinosaurs & Other Prehistoric Creatures. (gr. k-12). 1994. PLB 24.95 (*0-7933-7494-4*); pap. 14.95 (*0-7933-7495-2*); computer disk 29.95 (*0-7933-7496-0*) Gallopade Pub Group.
—Let's Quilt Michigan & Stuff It Topographically! (Illus.). (gr. 3 up). 1994. PLB 24.95 (*1-55609-669-0*); pap. 14.95 (*1-55609-138-9*); computer disk 29.95 (*1-55609-670-4*) Gallopade Pub Group.
—Let's Quilt Our Michigan County. 1994. lib. bdg. 24.95 (*0-7933-7179-1*); pap. text ed. 14.95 (*0-7933-7180-5*); disk 29.95 (*0-7933-7181-3*) Gallopade Pub Group.
—Let's Quilt Our Michigan Town. 1994. lib. bdg. 24.95 (*0-7933-7029-9*); pap. text ed. 14.95 (*0-7933-7030-2*); disk 29.95 (*0-7933-7031-0*) Gallopade Pub Group.
—Meow! Michigan Cats in History, Mystery, Legend, Lore, Humor & More! (Illus.). (gr. 3-12). 1994. PLB 24.95 (*0-7933-3380-6*); pap. 14.95 (*0-7933-3381-4*); computer disk 29.95 (*0-7933-3382-2*) Gallopade Pub Group.
—Michigan & Other State Greats (Biographies) (Illus.). (gr. 3 up). 1994. PLB 24.95 (*1-55609-677-1*); pap. 14.95 (*1-55609-678-X*); computer disk 29.95 (*1-55609-679-8*) Gallopade Pub Group.
—Michigan Bandits, Bushwackers, Outlaws, Crooks, Devils, Ghosts, Desperadoes & Other Assorted & Sundry Characters! (Illus.). (gr. 3 up). 1994. PLB 24.95 (*0-7933-0599-3*); pap. 14.95 (*0-7933-0598-5*); computer disk 29.95 (*0-7933-0600-0*) Gallopade Pub Group.
—Michigan Classic Christmas Trivia: Stories, Recipes, Activities, Legends, Lore & More! (Illus.). (gr. 3 up). 1994. PLB 24.95 (*0-685-45942-X*); pap. 14.95 (*0-7933-0601-9*); computer disk 29.95 (*0-7933-0603-5*) Gallopade Pub Group.
—Michigan Coastales. (Illus.). (gr. 3 up). 1994. PLB 24.95 (*1-55609-671-2*); pap. 14.95 (*1-55609-672-0*); computer disk 29.95 (*1-55609-673-9*) Gallopade Pub Group.
—Michigan Coastales! 1994. lib. bdg. 24.95 (*0-7933-7287-9*) Gallopade Pub Group.
—Michigan "Crinkum-Crankum" A Funny Word Book about Our State. (Illus.). 1994. lib. bdg. 24.95 (*0-7933-4874-9*); pap. 14.95 (*0-7933-4875-7*); disk 29.95 (*0-7933-4876-5*) Gallopade Pub Group.
—Michigan Dingbats! Bk. 1: A Fun Book of Games, Stories, Activities & More about Our State That's All in Code! for You to Decipher. (Illus.). (gr. 3-12). 1994. PLB 24.95 (*0-7933-3839-5*); pap. 14.95 (*0-7933-3840-9*); computer disk 29.95 (*0-7933-3841-7*) Gallopade Pub Group.
—Michigan Festival Fun for Kids! (Illus.). (gr. 3-12). 1994. lib. bdg. 24.95 (*0-7933-3992-8*); pap. 14.95 (*0-7933-3993-6*); disk 29.95 (*0-7933-3994-4*) Gallopade Pub Group.
—The Michigan Hot Air Balloon Mystery. (Illus.). (gr. 2-9). 1994. 24.95 (*0-7933-2516-1*); pap. 14.95 (*0-7933-2517-X*); computer disk 29.95 (*0-7933-2518-8*) Gallopade Pub Group.
—Michigan Jeopardy! Answers & Questions about Our State! (Illus.). (gr. 3-12). 1994. PLB 24.95 (*0-7933-4145-0*); pap. 14.95 (*0-7933-4146-9*); computer disk 29.95 (*0-7933-4147-7*) Gallopade Pub Group.
—Michigan "Jography" A Fun Run Thru Our State. (Illus.). (gr. 3 up). 1994. PLB 24.95 (*1-55609-666-6*); pap. 14.95 (*1-55609-667-4*); computer disk 29.95 (*1-55609-668-2*) Gallopade Pub Group.
—Michigan Kid's Cookbook: Recipes, How-To, History, Lore & More! (Illus.). (gr. 3 up). 1994. PLB 24.95 (*0-7933-0611-6*); pap. 14.95 (*0-7933-0610-8*); computer disk 29.95 (*0-7933-0612-4*) Gallopade Pub Group.
—The Michigan Mystery Van Takes Off! Book 1: Handicapped Michigan Kids Sneak Off on a Big Adventure. (Illus.). (gr. 3-12). 1994. 24.95 (*0-7933-5027-1*); pap. 14.95 (*0-7933-5028-X*); computer disk 29.95 (*0-7933-5029-8*) Gallopade Pub Group.
—Michigan Quiz Bowl Crash Course! (Illus.). (gr. 3 up). 1994. PLB 24.95 (*1-55609-674-7*); pap. 14.95 (*1-55609-675-5*); computer disk 29.95 (*1-55609-676-3*) Gallopade Pub Group.
—Michigan Rollercoasters! (Illus.). (gr. 3-12). 1994. PLB 24.95 (*0-7933-5290-8*); pap. 14.95 (*0-7933-5291-6*); computer disk 29.95 (*0-7933-5292-4*) Gallopade Pub Group.
—Michigan School Trivia: An Amazing & Fascinating Look at Our State's Teachers, Schools & Students! (Illus.). (gr. 3 up). 1994. PLB 24.95 (*0-7933-0608-6*); pap. 14.95 (*0-7933-0607-8*); computer disk 29.95 (*0-7933-0609-4*) Gallopade Pub Group.
—Michigan Silly Basketball Sportsmysteries, Vol. I. (Illus.). (gr. 3 up). 1994. PLB 24.95 (*0-7933-0605-1*); pap. 14.95 (*0-7933-0604-3*); computer disk 29.95 (*0-7933-0606-X*) Gallopade Pub Group.
—Michigan Silly Basketball Sportsmysteries, Vol. II. (Illus.). (gr. 3 up). 1994. PLB 24.95 (*0-7933-1711-8*); pap. 14.95 (*0-7933-1712-6*); computer disk 29.95 (*0-7933-1713-4*) Gallopade Pub Group.
—Michigan Silly Football Sportsmysteries, Vol. I. (Illus.). (gr. 3 up). 1994. PLB 24.95 (*1-55609-702-6*); pap. 14.95 (*1-55609-703-4*); computer disk 29.95 (*1-55609-704-2*) Gallopade Pub Group.
—Michigan Silly Football Sportsmysteries, Vol. II. (Illus.). (gr. 3 up). 1994. PLB 24.95 (*1-55609-705-0*); pap. 14.95 (*1-55609-706-9*); computer disk 29.95 (*1-55609-707-7*) Gallopade Pub Group.
—Michigan Silly Trivia! (Illus.). (gr. 3 up). 1994. PLB 24.95 (*1-55609-663-1*); pap. 14.95 (*1-55609-664-X*); computer disk 29.95 (*1-55609-665-8*) Gallopade Pub Group.
—Michigan Timeline: A Chronology of Michigan History, Mystery, Trivia, Legend, Lore & More. (Illus.). (gr. 3-12). 1994. PLB 24.95 (*0-7933-5941-4*); pap. 14.95 (*0-7933-5942-2*); computer disk 29.95 (*0-7933-5943-0*) Gallopade Pub Group.
—Michigan's (Most Devastating!) Disasters & (Most Calamitous!) Catastrophies! (Illus.). (gr. 3 up). 1994. PLB 24.95 (*0-7933-0596-9*); pap. 14.95 (*0-7933-0595-0*); computer disk 29.95 (*0-7933-0597-7*) Gallopade Pub Group.
—Michigan's Unsolved Mysteries (& Their "Solutions") Includes Scientific Information & Other Activities for Students. (Illus.). (gr. 3-12). 1994. PLB 24.95 (*0-7933-5788-8*); pap. 14.95 (*0-7933-5789-6*); computer disk 29.95 (*0-7933-5790-X*) Gallopade Pub Group.
—My First Book about Michigan. (gr. k-4). 1994. PLB 24.95 (*0-7933-5635-0*); pap. 14.95 (*0-7933-5636-9*); computer disk 29.95 (*0-7933-5637-7*) Gallopade Pub Group.
—Patch, the Pirate Dog: A Michigan Pet Story. (ps-4). 1994. PLB 24.95 (*0-7933-5482-X*); pap. 14.95 (*0-7933-5483-8*); computer disk 29.95 (*0-7933-5484-6*) Gallopade Pub Group.
—Uncle Rebus: Michigan Picture Stories for Computer Kids. (Illus.). (gr. k-3). 1994. PLB 24.95 (*0-7933-4567-7*); pap. 14.95 (*0-7933-4568-5*); disk 29.95 (*0-7933-4569-3*) Gallopade Pub Group.
Mitchell, John C. Michigan: An Illustrated History for Children. 2nd ed. Woodrutt, Thomas R., illus. 52p. (gr. 1-6). 1987. Repr. 14.95 (*0-9621466-0-9*) Suttons Bay Pubns.
Parker, Lois & McConnell, David. A Little Peoples' Beginning on Michigan. Deeter, Theresa, illus. 32p. (Orig.). (gr. 1-2). 1981. pap. 5.50 (*0-910726-06-X*) Hillsdale Educ.
Sirvaitis, Karen. Michigan. LC 92-44847. 1993. PLB 17.50 (*0-8225-2722-7*) Lerner Pubns.
Stein, R. Conrad. Michigan. LC 87-9383. (Illus.). 144p. (gr. 4 up). 1987. PLB 20.55 (*0-516-00468-9*) Childrens.
—Michigan. 188p. 1993. text ed. 15.40 (*1-56956-175-3*) W A T Braille.
Thompson, Kathleen. Michigan. LC 87-16373. 48p. (gr. 3 up). 1987. 19.97 (*0-86514-465-6*) Raintree Steck-V.
Weddon, Willah. Michigan Governors Growing Up. Terry, Kathi, illus. 100p. (Orig.). (gr. 1-8). 1994. pap. text ed. write for info. (*0-9638376-1-3*) Weddon Pr.
Zimmerman, Chanda K. Detroit. LC 88-35914. (Illus.). 60p. (gr. 3 up). 1989. text ed. 13.95 RSBE (*0-87518-409-X*, Dillon) Macmillan Child Grp.

MICHIGAN–ANTIQUITIES

Penrod, John S. Tahquamenon in Michigan's Upper Peninsula. (gr. 7 up). 1988. pap. 4.49 (*0-942618-12-2*) Penrod-Hiawatha.
—The Upper Peninsula of Michigan. rev. ed. (gr. 7 up). 1988. pap. 4.49 (*0-942618-11-4*) Penrod-Hiawatha.

MICHIGAN–FICTION

Bolton, Mimi D. Merry-Go-Round Family. 2nd ed. (Illus.). 225p. (gr. 3-7). 1990. Repr. of 1954 ed. 14.95x (*0-9614274-2-6*) Wisla Pubs.
Richardson, Arleta. The Grandma's Attic Storybook. LC 92-33823. 1993. pap. 9.99 (*0-7814-0070-8*, Chariot Bks) Chariot Family.
Whelan, Gloria. Night of the Full Moon. Bowman, Leslie, illus. LC 93-6706. 64p. (gr. 2-4). 1993. 13.00 (*0-679-84464-3*); PLB 13.99 (*0-679-94464-8*) Knopf Bks Yng Read.

MICROBES

see Bacteriology; Microorganisms; Viruses

MICROBIOLOGY

see also Bacteriology; Microorganisms; Microscope and Microscopy

Dashefsky, H. Steven. Microbiology: Forty-Nine Science Fair Projects. (gr. 3 up). 1994. text ed. 19.95 (*0-07-015659-X*) McGraw.
Dashevsky, H. Steven. Microbiology: Forty-Nine Science Fair Projects. (gr. 4-7). 1994. pap. text ed. 10.95 (*0-07-015660-3*) McGraw.

MICROCOMPUTERS

Ault, Rosalie S. BASIC Programming for Kids. LC 83-12773. (Illus.). 192p. (gr. 5 up). 1983. 10.95 (*0-685-06975-3*) HM.
Bitter, Gary G. & Camuse, Ruth A. Using a Microcomputer in the Classroom. (gr. k-12). 1983. pap. text ed. 25.00 (*0-8359-8144-4*, Reston) P-H.

Borman, Jami L. A Computer Dictionary for Kids...And Their Parents. (Illus.). (gr. 4-6). Date not set. write for info. (*0-8120-9079-9*) Barron.
Are your kids' questions about "graphical user interfaces" driving you berserk? Frustrated with arcane computer manuals? Don't have the time to be bothered? Jami Lynne Borman's fun & exciting new book, A COMPUTER DICTIONARY FOR KIDS...AND THEIR PARENTS, is the perfect solution! Using illustrations & simple, non-technical language, she makes over 600 computer-related terms clear to kids...AND THEIR PARENTS! From Abbreviation to Zip, each entry uses either a game or an example to make learning EASY & FUN! A COMPUTER DICTIONARY FOR KIDS...AND THEIR PARENTS will make kids comfortable with computers & will answer the questions of parents who've wondered "Am I still smarter than my children?" Jami Lynne Borman is a professional computer consultant, the author of four other books on computers & a mother.. .the perfect author for your perfect solution!
Publisher Provided Annotation.

Johnson, Jay. What's Inside the Magic Box? Using Personal Computers in the 21st Century. (gr. 4 up). 1991. 14.00 (*0-910609-24-1*) Gifted Educ Pr.
Kemnitz, T. M. & Mass, Lynne. Kids Working with Computers: Acorn BASIC. (gr. 2-6). 1984. 4.99 (*0-89824-086-7*) Trillium Pr.
Kemnitz, Thomas M. & Mass, Lynne. Kids Working with Computers: The Apple BASIC Manual. Schlendorf, Lori, illus. 42p. (gr. 4-7). 1983. pap. 4.99 (*0-89824-092-1*) Trillium Pr.

—Kids Working with Computers: The Atari BASIC Manual. Schlendorf, Lori, illus. 48p. (gr. 4-7). 1983. pap. 4.99 (*0-89824-062-X*) Trillium Pr.
Liebowitz, Jay & Zelde, Janet S. Kids & Computers. 2nd ed. Rogers, Nip, illus. 70p. (gr. 3-6). 1989. write for info. (*0-9623252-0-1*); pap. write for info. (*0-9623252-2-8*) J Liebowitz.
Pantiel, Mindy & Petersen, Becky. Kids, Teachers, & Computers: A Guide to Computers in the Elementary School. (Illus.). 176p. 1984. pap. text ed. 25.00 (*0-13-515420-0*); pap. text ed. 16.95 (*0-13-515396-4*) P-H.
Rathbone, R. Andrew. PC Secrets: Tips & Tricks to Make Your Computer More Effective. Lingham, Gretchen & Steward-Shahan, Leah, eds. 200p. (Orig.). 1991. pap. text ed. 8.95 (*0-945776-23-3*) Comptr Pub Enterprises.
Rathbone, Tina. Hundreds of Fascinating Uses for Your Computer. Lingham, Gretchen & Steward-Shahan, Leah, eds. 200p. (Orig.). 1991. pap. text ed. 8.95 (*0-945776-22-5*) Comptr Pub Enterprises.
Sterchele, Norman. Beginning at the Beginning with Your MS-DOS Microcomputer: An Introduction to: The Machine, DOS & Procedures. (Illus.). 96p. (Orig.). (gr. 10). 1989. pap. 11.95 (*0-9624107-0-5*) Compu-Aid.
Taitt, Jennifer. IBM, Vol. 1. 55p. (gr. 4-12). 1983. pap. text ed. 11.95 (*0-88193-031-8*) Create Learn.
—IBM, Vol. 2. 54p. (gr. 4-12). 1983. pap. text ed. 11.95 (*0-88193-032-6*) Create Learn.
—IBM, Vol. 3. 51p. (gr. 5-12). 1983. pap. text ed. 11.95 (*0-88193-033-4*) Create Learn.
—IBM, Vol. 4. 66p. (gr. 5-12). 1983. pap. text ed. 11.95 (*0-88193-034-2*) Create Learn.
Taitt, Kathy. Apple, Vol. 1. 59p. (gr. 4-12). 1983. pap. text ed. 11.95 (*0-88193-001-6*) Create Learn.
—Apple, Vol. 2. 61p. (gr. 4-12). 1983. pap. text ed. 11.95 (*0-88193-002-4*) Create Learn.
—Apple, Vol. 3. 55p. (gr. 5-12). 1983. pap. text ed. 11.95 (*0-88193-003-2*) Create Learn.
—Apple, Vol. 4. 57p. (gr. 5-12). 1983. pap. text ed. 11.95 (*0-88193-004-0*) Create Learn.
—Apple, Vol. 5. 57p. (gr. 6-12). 1983. pap. text ed. 11.95 (*0-88193-005-9*) Create Learn.
—Apple, Vol. 6. 68p. (gr. 6-12). 1984. pap. text ed. 11.95 (*0-88193-006-7*) Create Learn.
Wert, Debra. Mac's Choice Workbook. Anfenson-Vance, Deborah, et al, eds. Wilson, Miriam J., intro. by. (Illus.). 36p. (gr. 2-6). 1989. pap. 5.00 (*0-944576-03-6*) Rocky River Pubs.

MICROCOMPUTERS–PROGRAMMING

Nance, Douglas W. Pascal: Introduction to Programming & Problem Solving. (Illus.). 639p. (gr. 9-12). 1989. Repr. of 1986 ed. text ed. 34.25 (*0-314-93206-2*) West Pub.

MICROELECTRONICS

Levine, Janice R. Microcomputers in Elementary & Secondary Education: A Guide to Resources. 64p. (gr. k-12). 1983. 3.75 (*0-937597-06-6*, IR-65) ERIC Clear.

MICROGRAPHIC ANALYSIS

see Microscope and Microscopy

MICROMINIATURE ELECTRONIC EQUIPMENT

see Microelectronics

MICROMINIATURIZATION (ELECTRONICS)

see Microelectronics

MICROORGANISMS

see also Bacteriology; Microbiology; Microscope and Microscopy; Viruses

Bender, Lionel. Around the Home. LC 91-9764. (Illus.). 32p. (gr. 4-6). 1991. PLB 12.40 (*0-531-17348-8*, Gloucester Pr) Watts.
Loewer, Peter. Pond Water Zoo: An Introduction to Microscopic Life. Jenkins, Jean, illus. LC 93-18468. (gr. 1-8). 1995. 13.95 (*0-689-31736-0*, Atheneum Child Bk) Macmillan Child Grp.
Nardo, Don. Germs: Mysterious Microorganisms. LC 91-15569. (Illus.). 96p. (gr. 5-8). 1991. PLB 15.95 (*1-56006-214-2*) Lucent Bks.
Parker, Steve. Mysterious Microbes. Orr, Chris, Illustration Staff & Savage, Ann, illus. LC 93-36476. 1994. 19.97 (*0-8114-2344-1*) Raintree Steck-V.
Sabin, Francene. Microbes & Bacteria. Acosta, Andres, illus. LC 84-2749. 32p. (gr. 3-6). 1985. PLB 9.49 (*0-8167-0232-2*); pap. text ed. 2.95 (*0-8167-0233-0*) Troll Assocs.

MICROPROCESSORS

CES Industries, Inc. Staff. Ed-Lab Experiment Manual: CES 380-85 Microprocessors. (Illus., Orig.). (gr. 9-12). 1984. pap. write for info. (*0-86711-076-7*) CES Industries.

MICROSCOPE AND MICROSCOPY

see also Microbiology

Bender, Lionel. Around the Home. LC 91-9764. (Illus.). 32p. (gr. 4-6). 1991. PLB 12.40 (*0-531-17348-8*, Gloucester Pr) Watts.
—Frontiers of Medicine. (Illus.). 32p. (gr. 4-6). 1991. PLB 12.40 (*0-531-17298-8*, Gloucester Pr) Watts.
Bleifeld, Maurice. Experimenting with a Microscope. Rasof, Henry, ed. LC 88-14043. (Illus.). 112p. (gr. 7-12). 1988. PLB 13.40 (*0-531-10580-6*) Watts.
Canault, Nina. Incredibly Small. LC 93-9337. (Illus.). 48p. (gr. 6 up). 1993. text ed. 14.95 RSBE (*0-02-716455-1*, New Discovery Bks) Macmillan Child Grp.
Edwards, Frank B. Close Up: Microscopic Photographs of Everyday Stuff. (Illus.). 48p. 1992. lib. bdg. 17.95 (*0-921285-25-6*, Pub. by Bungalo Bks CN); pap. 6.95 (*0-921285-24-8*, Pub. by Hedgehog Prods CN) Firefly Bks Ltd.
Kumin, Maxine. The Microscope. Lobel, Arnold, illus. LC 82-47728. 32p. (ps-3). 1984. PLB 13.89 (*0-06-023524-1*) HarpC Child Bks.
Oxlade, C. & Stockley, C. The World of the Microscope. (Illus.). 48p. 1989. PLB 13.96 (*0-88110-364-0*); pap. 7.95 (*0-7460-0289-0*) EDC.
Riley, Peter. Looking at Microscopes. (Illus.). 48p. (gr. 5-8). 1985. 19.95 (*0-7134-4632-3*, Pub. by Batsford UK) Trafalgar.
Selsam, Millicent E. Greg's Microscope. Lobel, Arnold, illus. LC 63-8002. 64p. (gr. k-3). 1963. PLB 13.89 (*0-06-025296-0*) HarpC Child Bks.
Sneider, Cary I. More Than Magnifiers. Bergman, Lincoln & Fairwell, Kay, eds. Bevilacqua, Carol, illus. Hoyt, Richard, photos by. (Illus.). 47p. (Orig.). (gr. 6-9). 1988. pap. 8.50 (*0-912511-62-1*) Lawrence Science.
Stewart, Gail B. Microscopes: Bringing the Unseen World into Focus. LC 92-17316. (Illus.). 96p. (gr. 5-8). 1992. PLB 15.95 (*1-56006-211-8*) Lucent Bks.
Stwertka, Eve & Stwertka, Albert. Microscope: How to Use It & Enjoy It. LC 88-23127. (Illus.). (gr. 4-7). 1988. lib. bdg. 9.98 (*0-671-63705-3*, J Messner); pap. 4.95 (*0-671-67060-3*) S&S Trade.
Taylor, Ron. Through the Microscope. (Illus.). 64p. (gr. 4-7). 1985. 15.95x (*0-8160-1075-7*) Facts on File.
Tomb, Howard. Microaliens: Dazzling Journeys with an Electron Microscope. (gr. 4-7). 1993. 16.00 (*0-374-34960-6*) FS&G.
VanCleave, Janice. Janice VanCleave's Microscopes & Magnifying Lenses: Mind-Boggling Chemistry & Biology Experiments You Can Turn Into Science Fair Projects. 112p. (gr. 3 up). 1993. pap. text ed. 9.95 (*0-471-58956-X*) Wiley.

MICROSCOPIC ANALYSIS

see Microscope and Microscopy

MICROSCOPIC ORGANISMS

see Microorganisms

MICROSOFT (COMPUTER PROGRAM)

Finkel, LeRoy, et al. Microsoft Works Through Applications: IBM PC Version 2.0. LC 90-38911. (Illus.). 352p. (gr. 7 up). 1991. text ed. 27.95 (*0-941681-23-8*); pap. text ed. 21.95 spiral bdg. (*0-941681-18-1*); tchr's. ed. 34.95 (*0-941681-19-X*); 5.25 in. disk 19.95 (*0-941681-22-X*); tchr's. guide 14.95 (*0-941681-24-6*) Computer Lit Pr.
Schwartz, Karl. Microsoft Windows 3.0 Quick Reference Guide. (gr. 9-12). 1991. pap. 8.95 spiral bdg. (*1-56243-032-7*, N-17); transparencies 265.00 (*1-56243-014-9*, NT-19) DDC Pub.

MICROWAVE COOKERY

Betty Crocker Editors. Betty Crocker's Boys & Girls Microwave Cookbook. 160p. 1992. pap. 15.00 (*0-13-085549-9*, B Crocker Ckbks) P-H Gen Ref & Trav.
Cappelloni, Nancy. Ethnic Cooking the Microwave Way. Wolfe, Robert L. & Wolfe, Diane, photos by. LC 93-29543. (Illus.). 48p. (gr. 4-7). 1994. PLB 14.95 (*0-8225-0929-6*); pap. 5.95 (*0-8225-9660-1*) Lerner Pubns.
Lansky, Vicky. Microwave Cooking for Kids. 1992. 6.95 (*0-590-44203-1*) Scholastic Inc.
Stancil, Rosemary D. & Wilkins, Lorela N. Kids' Simply Scrumptious Microwaving. 1987. pap. 7.95 (*0-449-90226-9*, Columbine) Fawcett.

MIDDLE AGES

see also Chivalry; Civilization, Medieval; Knights and Knighthood; Renaissance

Adams, Brian. Medieval Castles. LC 88-83092. (Illus.). 32p. (gr. 4-6). 1989. PLB 12.40 (*0-531-17155-8*, Gloucester Pr) Watts.
Caselli, Giovanni. The Middle Ages. LC 87-27105. 48p. (gr. 5 up). 1988. 16.95 (*0-87226-176-X*) P Bedrick Bks.
—Middle Ages. (gr. 4-7). 1993. pap. 8.95 (*0-87226-263-4*) P Bedrick Bks.
Chamberlain, E. R. Florence in the Time of the Medici. Reeves, Marjorie, ed. (Illus.). 96p. (Orig.). (gr. 7-12). 1982. pap. 8.76 (*0-582-20489-5*, 70771) Longman.
Conway, Lorraine. The Middle Ages. Akins, Linda, illus. 64p. (gr. 4-8). 1987. pap. 8.95 (*0-86653-400-8*, GA 1022) Good Apple.
Cootes, R. J. Middle Ages. 2nd ed. 208p. (gr. 6-12). 1989. pap. text ed. 21.52 (*0-582-31783-5*, 78446) Longman.
Corbishley, Mike. The Medieval World. LC 92-31445. (Illus.). 60p. (gr. 5 up). 1993. PLB 17.95 (*0-87226-362-2*) P Bedrick Bks.
Corrick, James A. The Early Middle Ages. LC 94-8778. (Illus.). 128p. (gr. 6-9). 1994. 14.95 (*1-56006-246-0*) Lucent Bks.
Early Middle Ages. (gr. 4-7). 1990. 25.67 (*0-8172-3307-5*) Raintree Steck-V.
Farre, Marie. Long Ago in a Castle. Matthews, Sarah, tr. from FRE. Thibault, Dominique, illus. LC 87-33996. 38p. (gr. k-5). 1988. 5.95 (*0-944589-06-5*, 065) Young Discovery Lib.
Golden, Michael. Journeying Through the Middle Ages: A Study Guide. (gr. 5-8). 1991. pap. text ed. 19.95 (*0-88122-687-4*) LRN Links.
Gregory, Tony. The Dark Ages. LC 91-43093. (Illus.). 80p. (gr. 2-6). 1993. 17.95x (*0-8160-2787-0*) Facts on File.
Howarth, Sarah. Medieval People. (Illus.). 48p. (gr. 4-6). 1992. PLB 14.40 (*1-56294-153-4*) Millbrook Pr.
—Medieval Places. (Illus.). 48p. (gr. 4-6). 1992. PLB 14.40 (*1-56294-152-6*) Millbrook Pr.
—The Middle Ages. (Illus.). 48p. (gr. 3-7). 1993. 14.99 (*0-670-85098-5*) Viking Child Bks.
Late Middle Ages. (gr. 4-7). 1990. 25.67 (*0-8172-3308-3*) Raintree Steck-V.
Lyttle, Richard B. Land Beyond the River: Europe in the Age of Migration. LC 85-28758. (Illus.). 192p. (gr. 5 up). 1986. SBE 15.95 (*0-689-31199-0*, Atheneum Child Bk) Macmillan Child Grp.
MacDonald, Fiona. The Middle Ages. (Illus.). 80p. (gr. 2-6). 1993. 17.95x (*0-8160-2788-9*) Facts on File.
The Middle Ages. (Illus.). (gr. 5 up). 1990. pap. 3.95 (*1-85543-008-8*) Ladybird Bks.
Oakes, Catherine. The Middle Ages. Biesty, Stephen, illus. 28p. (gr. 3-7). 1989. 14.95 (*0-15-200451-3*, Gulliver Bks) HarBrace.
Polette, Nancy. Middle Ages: Learning Through Literature. (Illus.). 48p. (gr. 3-6). 1994. pap. 5.95 (*1-879287-27-7*) Bk Lures.
Sabin, Louis. Middle Ages. Frenck, Hal, illus. LC 84-2670. 32p. (gr. 3-6). 1985. PLB 9.49 (*0-8167-0174-1*); pap. text ed. 2.95 (*0-8167-0175-X*) Troll Assocs.
Verges, Gloria & Verges, Oriol. The Middle Ages. Rius, Maria & Peris, Carme, illus. 32p. (gr. 2-4). 1988. pap. 6.95 (*0-8120-3386-8*); La Edad Media. pap. 6.95 (*0-8120-3387-6*) Barron.
Weber, Sally & Glasscock, Paula. Castles, Pirates, Knights & Other Learning Delights. 104p. (gr. 5-8). 1980. 10.95 (*0-916456-92-7*, GA 158) Good Apple.

MIDDLE AGES–FICTION

Anno, Mitsumasa. Anno's Medieval World. Anno, Mitsumasa, illus. LC 79-28367. 56p. (gr. 3 up). 1990. 16.95 (*0-399-20742-2*, Philomel Bks) Putnam Pub Group.
Brittain, Bill. The Wizards & the Monster. Warhola, James, illus. LC 93-47077. 96p. (gr. 2-5). 1994. 11.95 (*0-06-024454-2*); PLB 11.89 (*0-06-024456-9*) HarpC Child Bks.
Cosman, Madeleine P. The Medieval Baker's Daughter: A Bilingual Adventure in Medieval Life with Costumes, Banners, Music, Food, & a Mystery Play. LC 84-71590. (ENG & SPA., Illus.). 112p. (gr. 3-12). 1984. pap. 7.95 (*0-916491-18-8*) Bard Hall Pr.
Cushman, Karen. Catherine, Called Birdy. 224p. (gr. 7 up). 1994. 14.95 (*0-395-68186-3*, Clarion Bks) HM.
—The Midwife's Apprentice. LC 94-13792. 1994. pap. write for info. (*0-395-69229-6*, Clarion Bks) HM.
Doyle, Debra & Macdonald, James D. The Knight's Wyrd. LC 92-53789. 1992. write for info. (*0-15-200764-4*, J Yolen Bks) HarBrace.
Gerrard, Roy. Sir Cedric. LC 84-6111. (Illus.). 32p. (ps up). 1984. 14.95 (*0-374-36959-3*) FS&G.
Gray, Elizabeth J. Adam of the Road. Lawson, Robert, illus. 320p. (gr. 4-8). 1942. pap. 15.95 (*0-670-10435-3*) Viking Child Bks.
Kelly, Eric P. The Trumpeter of Krakow. Domanska, Janina, illus. LC 91-26879. 224p. (gr. 3-7). 1992. pap. 3.95 (*0-689-71571-4*, Aladdin) Macmillan Child Grp.
Osborne, Mary P. The Knight at Dawn. Murdocca, Sal, illus. LC 92-13075. 80p. (Orig.). (gr. 1-4). 1993. PLB 9.99 (*0-679-92412-4*); pap. 2.99 (*0-679-82412-X*) Random Bks Yng Read.
Rosen, Sidney & Rosen, Dorothy. The Magician's Apprentice. LC 93-10781. 1993. 19.95 (*0-87614-809-7*) Carolrhoda Bks.
Sherman, Josepha. Windleaf. LC 93-615. 128p. (gr. 7 up). 1993. 14.95 (*0-8027-8259-0*); cancelled (*0-8027-8260-4*) Walker & Co.
Temple, Frances. The Ramsay Scallop. LC 93-29697. 352p. (gr. 6-9). 1994. 15.95 (*0-531-06836-6*); lib. bdg. 15.99 RLB (*0-531-08686-0*) Orchard Bks Watts.
Waite, Michael. Sylvester the Jester. LC 91-38875. (ps-3). 1992. pap. 8.99 (*0-7814-0033-3*, Chariot Bks) Chariot Family.

MIDDLE ATLANTIC STATES

see Atlantic States

MIDDLE EAST

see Asia; Near East

MIDDLE STATES

see Atlantic States

MIDDLE WEST

Bial, Raymond. Corn Belt Harvest. (Illus.). 48p. (gr. 3-6). 1991. 14.45 (*0-395-56234-1*, Sandpiper) HM.
Herda, D. J. Environmental America: The North Central States. (Illus.). 64p. (gr. 5-8). 1991. PLB 15.40 (*1-878841-08-4*) Millbrook Pr.
Siebert, Diane. Heartland. Minor, Wendell, illus. LC 87-29380. 32p. (ps-3). 1989. 16.00 (*0-690-04730-4*, Crowell Jr Bks); PLB 15.89 (*0-690-04732-0*) HarpC Child Bks.

MIDDLE WEST–FICTION

Lawlor, Laurie. Addie's Long Summer. Tucker, Kathleen, ed. Gowing, Toby, illus. LC 91-34877. 176p. (gr. 3-6). 1992. PLB 11.95 (*0-8075-0167-0*) A Whitman.

MIDDLE WEST–HISTORY

Herda, D. J. Historical America: The North Central States. LC 92-16311. (Illus.). 64p. (gr. 5-8). 1993. PLB 15.40 (*1-56294-120-8*) Millbrook Pr.
Stanley, Jerry. Children of the Dust Bowl: The True Story of the School at Weedpatch Camp. LC 92-323. (Illus.). 96p. (gr. 4 up). 1993. pap. 6.99 (*0-517-88094-6*) Crown Bks Yng Read.

MIDGETS

see Dwarfs

MIDWAY, BATTLE OF, 1942

Sauvain, Philip. Midway. LC 92-29566. (Illus.). 32p. (gr. 6 up). 1993. text ed. 13.95 RSBE (*0-02-781090-9*, New Discovery) Macmillan Child Grp.

MIDWEST
see Middle West
MIDWIFERY
see Childbirth
MIGRANT LABOR
Here are entered works dealing with casual or seasonal workers who move from place to place in search of employment. Works on the movement of population within a country for permanent settlement are entered under Migration, Internal.
Altman, Linda J. Migrant Farm Workers: The Temporary People. LC 93-11921. 1994. 13.40 (*0-531-13033-9*) Watts.
Atkin, S. Beth. Voices from the Fields: America's Migrant Children. LC 92-32248. 96p. 1993. 16.95 (*0-316-05633-2*) Little.
De Ruiz, Dana C. & Larios, Richard. La Causa: The Migrant Farmworkers' Story. Gutierrez, Rudy, illus. LC 92-12806. 92p. (gr. 2-5). 1992. PLB 21.34 (*0-8114-7231-0*) Raintree Steck-V.
Holmes, Burnham. Cesar Chavez. LC 92-18225. (Illus.). 128p. (gr. 7-10). 1992. PLB 22.80 (*0-8114-2326-3*) Raintree Steck-V.
MIGRANT LABOR–FICTION
Dorros, Arthur. Radio Man - Don Radio: A Story in English & Spanish. Dorros, Sandra M., tr. LC 92-28369. (Illus.). 40p. (gr. 1-5). 1993. 16.00 (*0-06-021547-X*); PLB 15.89 (*0-06-021548-8*) HarpC Child Bks.
Gates, Doris. Blue Willow. Lantz, Paul, illus. LC 40-32435. 176p. (gr. 4-7). 1940. pap. 14.00 (*0-670-17557-9*) Viking Child Bks.
Peck, Robert N. Arly's Run. 160p. (gr. 5-9). 1991. 16.95 (*0-8027-8120-9*) Walker & Co.
Thomas, Jane R. Lights on the River. Dooling, Michael, illus. LC 93-33636. 32p. (ps-3). 1994. 15.95 (*0-7868-0004-6*); PLB 15.89 (*0-7868-2003-9*) Hyprn Child.
Williams, S. Working Cotton. Byard, C., ed. 1992. 14.95 (*0-15-299624-9*, HB Juv Bks) HarBrace.
MIGRANT LABOR–U. S.
Brimner, Larry D. A Migrant Family. (Illus.). 40p. (gr. 4-8). 1992. PLB 17.50 (*0-8225-2554-2*) Lerner Pubns.
Stanley, Jerry. Children of the Dustbowl: The True Story of the School at Weedpatch Camp. LC 92-393. (Illus.). 96p. (gr. 4 up). 1992. 15.00 (*0-517-58781-5*); PLB 15.99 (*0-517-58782-3*) Crown Bks Yng Read.
MIGRATION
see Immigration and Emigration
MIGRATION OF ANIMALS
see Animals–Migration
MIGRATION OF BIRDS
see Birds–Migration
MIGRATORY WORKERS
see Migrant Labor
MILITARY AERONAUTICS
see Aeronautics, Military
MILITARY AIRPLANES
see Airplanes, Military
MILITARY ART AND SCIENCE
see also Aeronautics, Military; Arms and Armor; Battles; Disarmament; Fortification; Ordnance; Signals and Signaling; Soldiers; Spies; War
also headings beginning with the word Military
Baker. Soviet Air Force. LC 88-12121. (Illus.). 48p. (gr. 3-8). 1987. PLB 18.60 (*0-86625-331-9*); PLB 13.95s.p. (*0-685-58301-5*) Rourke Corp.
—Soviet Forces in Space. LC 88-14050. (Illus.). 48p. (gr. 3-8). 1987. PLB 18.60 (*0-86625-335-1*); PLB 13.95s.p. (*0-685-58299-X*) Rourke Corp.
Cross, Robin. Modern Military Weapons. LC 91-12317. (Illus.). 32p. (gr. 5-8). 1991. PLB 12.40 (*0-531-11174-1*) Watts.
Dolan, Edward F. Military. 1995. PLB write for info. (*0-8050-2865-X*) H Holt & Co.
Gander, Terry. Artillery. Gibbons, Tony, et al, illus. 48p. (gr. 5 up). 1987. PLB 14.95 (*0-8225-1380-3*) Lerner Pubns.
Ladd, James D. Amphibious Techniques. Sarson, Peter & Bryan, Tony, illus. LC 84-10003. 48p. (gr. 5 up). 1985. PLB 13.50 (*0-8225-1379-X*, First Ave Edns); pap. 4.95 (*0-8225-9505-2*, First Ave Edns) Lerner Pubns.
Lowe, Malcolm V. Bombers. Gibbons, Tony, et al, illus. 48p. (gr. 5 up). 1987. PLB 13.50 (*0-8225-1381-1*, First Ave Edns); pap. 4.95 (*0-8225-9541-9*, First Ave Edns) Lerner Pubns.
Miller. Soviet Navy. LC 88-11327. (Illus.). 48p. (gr. 3-8). 1988. PLB 18.60 (*0-86625-336-X*); PLB 13.95s.p. (*0-685-58300-7*) Rourke Corp.
—Soviet Rocket Forces. LC 88-11367. (Illus.). 48p. (gr. 3-8). 1988. PLB 18.60 (*0-86625-333-5*); PLB 13.95s.p. (*0-685-58297-3*) Rourke Corp.
—Soviet Submarines. (Illus.). 48p. (gr. 3-8). 1987. PLB 18.60 (*0-86625-332-7*); PLB 13.95s.p. (*0-685-58296-5*) Rourke Corp.
Smith, Chris & Harbor, Bernard. Military Technology. (Illus.). 48p. (gr. 5-8). 1991. 12.90 (*0-531-18456-0*, Pub. by Bookwright Pr) Watts.
Wood. Soviet Army. (Illus.). 48p. (gr. 3-8). 1987. PLB 18.60 (*0-86625-334-3*); PLB 13.95s.p. (*0-685-58298-1*) Rourke Corp.
MILITARY ART AND SCIENCE–STUDY AND TEACHING
see Military Education
MILITARY BIOGRAPHY
see Generals
MILITARY COSTUME
see Uniforms, Military
MILITARY EDUCATION
see also names of military schools, e.g. U. S. Military Academy, West Point; etc.
Collins, Robert F. Qualifying for Admission to the Service Academies: A Student's Guide. rev. ed. Rosen, Ruth, ed. (Illus.). 154p. (gr. 7 up). 1990. lib. bdg. 14.95 (*0-8239-1187-X*) Rosen Group.
MILITARY ENGINEERING
see also Fortification
Cross, Robin. Technology of War. LC 93-48234. (Illus.). 48p. (gr. 5-9). 1994. 14.95 (*1-56847-177-7*) Thomson Lrning.
MILITARY HISTORY
see also Battles; Naval History;
also names of countries with the subdivision Army or History, Military
Anderson, Dale. Battles That Changed the Modern World. Gerstle, Gary, contrib. by. LC 93-17028. (Illus.). 48p. (gr. 5-7). 1993. PLB 22.80 (*0-8114-4928-9*) Raintree Steck-V.
Wars That Changed the World, 6 vols. LC 87-36748. (Illus.). 192p. (gr. 3-9). 1988. Set. 65.70 (*0-86307-929-6*) Marshall Cavendish.
Wilkinson, Philip & Pollard, Michael. Generals Who Changed the World. Ingpen, Robert, illus. LC 93-31358. 1994. write for info. (*0-7910-2761-9*); pap. write for info. (*0-7910-2786-4*) Chelsea Hse.
Yue, Charlotte & Yue, David. Armor. LC 93-50601. 1994. 14.95 (*0-395-68101-4*) HM.
MILITARY LIFE
see Soldiers
MILITARY POWER
see Disarmament; Military Art and Science; Sea Power
MILITARY SCHOOLS
see Military Education
MILITARY SCIENCE
see Military Art and Science
MILITARY SERVICE, COMPULSORY
Simons, Donald L. I Refuse: Memories of a Vietnam War Objector. List, David, intro. by. LC 91-70992. 184p. (Orig.). (gr. 12 up). 1992. 27.50 (*0-9620024-2-9*); pap. 13.95 (*0-9620024-3-7*) Broken Rifle Pr.
MILITARY SERVICE–VOCATIONAL GUIDANCE
Macdonald, Robert W. Exploring Careers in the Military Services. rev. ed. Rosen, Ruth, ed. (Illus.). 190p. (gr. 7 up). 1991. 14.95 (*0-8239-1358-9*) Rosen Group.
Slappey, Mary M. Exploring Military Service for Women. rev. ed. (Illus.). 168p. (gr. 9-12). 1989. PLB 14.95 (*0-8239-0996-4*) Rosen Group.
MILITARY SIGNALING
see Signals and Signaling
MILITARY TRAINING
see Military Education
MILITARY UNIFORMS
see Uniforms, Military
MILITARY VEHICLES
see Vehicles, Military
MILK
Aliki. Milk from Cow to Carton. rev. ed. LC 91-23807. (Illus.). 32p. (gr. k-4). 1992. 14.00 (*0-06-020434-6*); PLB 13.89 (*0-06-020435-4*) HarpC Child Bks.
—Milk from Cow to Carton. rev. ed. LC 91-23807. (Illus.). 32p. (gr. k-4). 1992. pap. 4.50 (*0-06-445111-9*, Trophy) HarpC Child Bks.
Carrick, Donald. Milk. Carrick, Donald, illus. LC 84-25879. 24p. (ps-1). 1985. lib. bdg. 13.88 (*0-688-04823-4*) Greenwillow.
Fowler, Allan. Gracias a las Vacas: Thanks to Cows. LC 91-35062. (SPA., Illus.). 32p. (ps-2). 1992. PLB 10.75 (*0-516-34924-4*); pap. 3.95 (*0-516-54924-3*); big bk. 22.95 (*0-516-59625-X*) Childrens.
—Thanks to Cows. LC 91-35062. (Illus.). 32p. (ps-2). 1992. PLB 10.75 (*0-516-04924-0*); PLB 22.95 big bk. (*0-516-49625-5*); pap. 3.95 (*0-516-44924-9*) Childrens.
Giblin, James C. Milk: The Fight for Purity. LC 85-48252. (Illus.). 128p. (gr. 3-7). 1986. (Crowell Jr Bks); PLB 12.89 (*0-690-04574-3*, Crowell Jr Bks) HarpC Child Bks.
Robbins, Ken. Make Me a Peanut Butter Sandwich & a Glass of Milk. (Illus.). (ps up). 1992. 14.95 (*0-590-43550-7*, 023, Scholastic Hardcover) Scholastic Inc.
Ross, Catherine S. Amazing Milk Book. 1991. pap. 6.68 (*0-201-57087-4*) Addison-Wesley.
Turner, Dorothy. Milk. Yates, John, illus. 32p. (gr. 1-4). 1989. PLB 14.95 (*0-87614-361-3*) Carolrhoda Bks.
MILL AND FACTORY BUILDINGS
see Factories
MILLAY, EDNA ST. VINCENT, 1892-1950
Daffron, Carolyn. Edna St. Vincent Millay. Horner, Matina S., intro. by. (Illus.). 112p. (gr. 5 up). 1990. 17.95 (*1-55546-668-0*) Chelsea Hse.
MILWAUKEE BREWERS (BASEBALL TEAM)
Milwaukee Brewers. (gr. 4-7). 1993. pap. 1.49 (*0-553-56411-0*) Bantam.
Rambeck, Richard. Milwaukee Brewers. 48p. (gr. 4-10). 1992. PLB 14.95 (*0-88682-441-9*) Creative Ed.
MIND
see Intellect; Psychology
MIND AND BODY
see also Dreams; Hypnotism; Nervous System; Psychoanalysis; Psychology, Pathological; Sleep
Bosworth, et al. Stress Management. (gr. 7-12). Date not set. incl. software 120.00 (*0-912899-57-3*) Lrning Multi-Systs.
Brandreth, Gyles. Amazing Facts about Your Body. Craig, Bobby, illus. LC 80-1088. 32p. (gr. 5-8). 1981. pap. 2.95 (*0-385-17018-1*, Zephyr-BFYR) Doubleday.
Check, William A. The Mind-Body Connection. (Illus.). 112p. (gr. 6-12). 1990. 18.95 (*0-7910-0068-0*) Chelsea Hse.
Feldman, Robert S. Understanding Stress. (Illus.). 96p. (gr. 7-12). 1992. PLB 12.90 (*0-531-12531-9*) Watts.
Kettelkamp, Larry. A Partnership of Mind & Body: Biofeedback. LC 76-24818. (Illus.). (gr. 5-9). 1976. PLB 12.88 (*0-688-32088-0*) Morrow Jr Bks.
Youngs, Bettie B. A Stress Management Guide for Young People. 6th ed. Nelson, Trish, illus. 88p. (gr. 6-12). 1986. pap. text ed. 9.95x (*0-940221-00-4*) Lrng Tools-Bilicki Pubns.
MIND CURE
see Christian Science; Mind and Body
MINERAL INDUSTRIES
see Mines and Mineral Resources
MINERAL LANDS
see Mines and Mineral Resources
MINERAL OIL
see Petroleum
MINERAL RESOURCES
see Mines and Mineral Resources
MINERALOGY
see also Gems; Precious Stones
Arem, Joel. Rocks & Minerals. Boltin, Lee & Arem, Joel, photos by. LC 91-74106. (Illus.). 160p. (gr. 7-12). 1991. pap. 8.95 (*0-945005-06-7*) Geoscience Pr.
Arem, Joel E. Descubre Rocas y Minerales. University of Mexico City Staff, tr. from SPA. O'Neill, Pablo M. & Robare, Lorie, illus. 48p. (gr. 3-8). 1993. PLB 16.95 (*1-56674-051-7*, HTS Bks) Forest Hse.
Arneson, D. J. Rocks & Minerals. Friedman, Howard, illus. 32p. (Orig.). 1990. pap. 2.50 (*0-942025-90-3*) Kidsbks.
Bains, Rae. Rocks & Minerals. Maccabe, Richard, illus. LC 84-8644. 32p. (gr. 3-6). 1985. PLB 9.49 (*0-8167-0186-5*); pap. text ed. 2.95 (*0-8167-0187-3*) Troll Assocs.
Beattie, Laura C. Discover Rocks & Minerals: Activity Book. Creative Company Staff, illus. 24p. (gr. 3-8). 1991. wkbk. 2.95 (*0-911239-36-7*) Carnegie Mus.
Benanti, Carol. Rocks & Minerals. (Illus.). 32p. (gr. 3 up). 1994. pap. 10.00 (*0-679-85072-4*) Random Bks Yng Read.
Brown, Vinson, et al. Rocks & Minerals of California. 3rd. rev. ed. LC 72-13423. (Illus.). 200p. (gr. 4 up). 1972. 17.95 (*0-911010-59-9*); pap. 9.95 (*0-911010-58-0*) Naturegraph.
Clark, John O. Mining to Minerals: Projects with Geography. LC 91-34411. (Illus.). 32p. (gr. 5-9). 1992. PLB 12.40 (*0-531-17272-4*, Gloucester Pr) Watts.
Gattis, L. S., III. Rocks & Minerals for Pathfinders: A Basic Youth Enrichment Skill Honor Packet. (Illus.). 22p. (Orig.). (gr. 5 up). 1987. pap. 5.00 tchr's. ed. (*0-936241-29-2*) Cheetah Pub.
Hyler, Nelson W. Rocks & Minerals. Shannon, Kenyon, illus. (gr. 4-6). pap. 2.95 (*0-8431-4274-X*, Wonder-Treas) Price Stern.
Lye, Keith. Rocks & Minerals. LC 92-31817. (Illus.). 32p. (gr. 2-3). 1992. PLB 18.99 (*0-8114-3411-7*) Raintree Steck-V.
—Rocks, Minerals & Fossils. (Illus.). 48p. (gr. 5-8). 1991. PLB 12.95 (*0-382-24226-2*) Silver Burdett Pr.
Marcus, Elizabeth. Rocks & Minerals. Lawler, Dan, illus. LC 82-17424. 32p. (gr. 3-6). 1983. PLB 10.59 (*0-89375-876-0*); pap. text ed. 2.95 (*0-89375-877-9*) Troll Assocs.
Minerals. (gr. k-5). 1991. write for info. (*0-307-12851-2*, Golden Pr) Western Pub.
Morris, Scott, ed. Rocks & Minerals of the World. De Blij, Harm J., intro. by. LC 92-22910. (Illus.). 1993. 15.95 (*0-7910-1803-2*, Am Art Analog); pap. write for info. (*0-7910-1816-4*, Am Art Analog) Chelsea Hse.
Parker, Steve. Rock & Minerals. LC 93-12643. (Illus.). 64p. (gr. 3-6). 1993. 9.95 (*1-56458-394-5*) Dorling Kindersley.
Podendorf, Illa. Rocks & Minerals. LC 81-38494. (Illus.). 48p. (gr. k-4). 1982. PLB 12.85 (*0-516-01648-2*); pap. 4.95 (*0-516-41648-0*) Childrens.
Russell, William. Rocks & Minerals. LC 94-507. (gr. 3 up). 1994. write for info. (*0-86593-362-6*) Rourke Corp.
Shedenhelm, W. R. Discover Rocks & Minerals. (Illus.). 48p. (gr. 3-6). 1992. PLB 14.95 (*1-878363-70-0*, HTS Bks) Forest Hse.
Woolley, Alan. Rocks & Minerals. (Illus.). 64p. (gr. 7 up). 1992. pap. 4.95 (*0-86020-112-0*) EDC.
Zim, Herbert S. & Shaffer, Paul R. Rocks & Minerals. Perlman, Raymond, illus. (gr. 6 up). 1957. pap. write for info. (*0-307-24499-7*, Golden Pr) Western Pub.
MINERALS
see Mineralogy
MINERS–FICTION
Leppard, Lois G. Mandie & the Abandoned Mine, Bk. 8. LC 87-70883. 144p. (Orig.). (gr. 5-8). 1987. pap. 3.99 (*0-87123-932-9*) Bethany Hse.
Lyon, George E. Mama is a Miner. Catalanotto, Peter, illus. LC 93-49398. 32p. (gr. k-3). 1994. 15.95 (*0-531-06853-6*); PLB 15.99 (*0-531-08703-4*) Orchard Bks Watts.
Rappaport, Doreen. Trouble at the Mines. Sandin, Joan, illus. LC 84-45339. 96p. (gr. 3-7). 1987. (Crowell Jr Bks); PLB 13.89 (*0-690-04446-1*, Crowell Jr Bks) HarpC Child Bks.
Weber, Kathryn. Molly Moonshine & Timothy. Downey, Jane, illus. 44p. (gr. 2-4). 1990. pap. 2.95 (*1-878438-01-8*) Ranch House Pr.

MINES AND MINERAL RESOURCES
see also Mineralogy; Mining Engineering; Prospecting also specific types of mines and mining, e.g. Coal Mines and Mining; etc.
Bates, Robert L. The Challenge of Mineral Resources. LC 90-35948. (Illus.). 64p. (gr. 6 up). 1991. lib. bdg. 15.95 (*0-89490-245-8*) Enslow Pubs.
—Industrial Minerals: How They Are Found & Used. LC 87-36537. (Illus.). 64p. (gr. 6 up). 1988. lib. bdg. 15.95 (*0-89490-174-5*) Enslow Pubs.
—Mineral Resources A-Z. LC 90-34301. 128p. (gr. 6 up). 1991. lib. bdg. 17.95 (*0-89490-244-X*) Enslow Pubs.
Bentley, Judith. Miners, Merchants, & Maids. (Illus.). 96p. (gr. 5-8). 1995. bds. 16.95 (*0-8050-2998-2*) TFC Bks NY.
Brownstone, David M. & Franck, Irene M. Manufacturers & Miners. (Illus.). 176p. 1988. 17.95x (*0-8160-1447-7*) Facts on File.
Lye, Keith. Rocks, Minerals & Fossils. (Illus.). 48p. (gr. 5-8). 1991. PLB 12.95 (*0-382-24226-2*) Silver Burdett Pr.
Makela, Constance E. Iron Mining Fun Book for Children: Featuring Orville Ore. Makela, Constance E., illus. 44p. (Orig.). (gr. k-6). 1982. pap. 2.00x (*0-9608686-0-7*) Happy Thoughts & Rainbow.
Metcalf, Doris & Marson, Ron. Rocks & Minerals. Marson, Peg, illus. 88p. (gr. 7-12). 1989. tchr's. ed. 15.70 (*0-941008-23-1*) Tops Learning.
Mitgutsch, Ali. From Ore to Spoon. Mitgutsch, Ali, illus. LC 80-28862. 24p. (ps-3). 1981. PLB 10.95 (*0-87614-161-0*) Carolrhoda Bks.
Natural History Museum Staff. Rocks & Minerals. Keates, Colin & Einsiedel, Andreas, photos by. LC 87-26514. (Illus.). 64p. (gr. 5 up). 1988. 16.00 (*0-394-89621-1*); lib. bdg. 16.99 (*0-394-99621-6*) Knopf Bks Yng Read.
Williams, Brian. Mining. Morris, Tony, illus. LC 92-29906. 48p. (gr. 5-8). 1993. PLB 21.34 (*0-8114-4789-8*) Raintree Steck-V.

MINES AND MINERAL RESOURCES–FICTION
Beatty, Patricia. Bonanza Girl. LC 92-23317. 224p. (gr. 5 up). 1993. 14.00 (*0-688-12361-9*) Morrow Jr Bks.
—Bonanza Girl. LC 92-27682. 224p. 1993. 4.95 (*0-688-12280-9*) Morrow Jr Bks.
Clymer, Eleanor. Santiago's Silver Mine. 80p. (Orig.). (gr. k-6). 1989. pap. 2.75 (*0-440-40157-7*, YB) Dell.
Fink, Dale B. Mr. Silver & Mrs. Gold. Chan, Shirley, illus. LC 79-15924. 32p. (ps-3). 1980. 16.95 (*0-87705-447-9*) Human Sci Pr.
Ghost Mines of Yosemite. (gr. 6 up). pap. 2.00 (*0-915266-02-4*) Awani Pr.
Gleitzman, Morris. Worry Warts. LC 92-22631. 1993. 12.95 (*0-15-299666-4*) HarBrace.
Harris, Jeanette M. & Harben, Peter W. Mined It! A Fairy Tale with Mineral Content. 60p. (gr. 1-12). 1992. pap. text ed. 12.98 (*0-9632303-0-1*) Butternut Bks.

MINIATURE CAMERAS
see Cameras

MINIATURE OBJECTS
see Dollhouses; Models and Model Making; Toys; see names of objects with the subdivision Models, e.g. Airplanes–Models

MINING
see Mines and Mineral Resources; Mining Engineering

MINING ENGINEERING
Brownstone, David M. & Franck, Irene M. Manufacturers & Miners. (Illus.). 176p. 1988. 17.95x (*0-8160-1447-7*) Facts on File.
Clark, John O. Mining to Minerals: Projects with Geography. LC 91-34411. (Illus.). 32p. (gr. 5-9). 1992. PLB 12.40 (*0-531-17272-4*, Gloucester Pr) Watts.

MINISTERS (DIPLOMATIC AGENTS)
see Diplomats

MINISTERS OF THE GOSPEL
see Clergy

MINKS–FICTION
Burgess, Thornton. Billy Mink. 91p. 1981. Repr. PLB 17.95x (*0-89966-352-4*) Buccaneer Bks.
—Billy Mink. 178p. 1981. Repr. PLB 17.95 (*0-89967-026-1*) Harmony Raine.
Burgess, Thornton W. Billy Mink. 18.95 (*0-8488-0397-3*) Amereon Ltd.
Lyon, David. The Crumbly Coast. LC 93-41083. 1995. write for info. (*0-385-32079-5*) Doubleday.

MINNESOTA
Aylesworth, Thomas G. & Aylesworth, Virginia L. Western Great Lakes (Illinois, Iowa, Wisconsin, Minnesota) (Illus.). 64p. (gr. 3 up). 1992. lib. bdg. 16.95 (*0-7910-1046-5*) Chelsea Hse.
Carlson, Jeffrey D. A Historical Album of Minnesota. LC 92-41136. (Illus.). 64p. (gr. 4-8). 1994. PLB 15.90 (*1-56294-006-6*); pap. 6.95 (*1-56294-757-5*) Millbrook Pr.
Carole Marsh Minnesota Books, 44 bks. 1994. PLB 1027.80 set (*0-7933-1298-1*); pap. 587.80 set (*0-7933-5168-5*) Gallopade Pub Group.
Carpenter, Allan. Minnesota. new ed. LC 78-8000. (Illus.). 96p. (gr. 4 up). 1978. PLB 16.95 (*0-516-04123-1*) Childrens.
Fradin, Dennis. Minnesota: In Words & Pictures. LC 79-21543. (Illus.). 48p. (gr. 2-5). 1980. PLB 12.95 (*0-516-03923-7*) Childrens.
Gilman, Rhoda R. The Story of Minnesota's Past. LC 91-11189. (Illus.). 231p. 1991. pap. 22.50 (*0-87351-267-7*) Minn Hist.
Johnson, Elden. The Prehistoric Peoples of Minnesota. rev. ed. LC 87-32663. (Illus.). 35p. (gr. 9-12). 1988. pap. 3.95 (*0-87351-223-5*) Minn Hist.
King, Sandra. Shannon: An Ojibway Dancer. Whipple, Catherine, photos by. Dorris, Michael, frwd. by. LC 92-27261. (Illus.). 48p. 1993. PLB 19.95 (*0-8225-2652-2*) Lerner Pubns.
Marsh, Carole. Avast, Ye Slobs!: Minnesota Pirate Trivia. (Illus.). (gr. 3 up). 1994. PLB 24.95 (*0-7933-0641-8*); pap. 14.95 (*0-7933-0640-X*); computer disk 29.95 (*0-7933-0642-6*) Gallopade Pub Group.
—The Beast of the Minnesota Bed & Breakfast. (Illus.). (gr. 3 up). 1994. PLB 24.95 (*0-7933-1714-2*); pap. 14.95 (*0-7933-1715-0*); computer disk 29.95 (*0-7933-1716-9*) Gallopade Pub Group.
—Bow Wow! Minnesota Dogs in History, Mystery, Legend, Lore, Humor & More! (Illus.). (gr. 3-12). 1994. PLB 24.95 (*0-7933-3536-1*); pap. 14.95 (*0-7933-3537-X*); computer disk 29.95 (*0-7933-3538-8*) Gallopade Pub Group.
—Chill Out: Scary Minnesota Tales Based on Frightening Minnesota Truths. (Illus.). 1994. lib. bdg. 24.95 (*0-7933-4723-8*); pap. 14.95 (*0-7933-4724-6*); disk 29.95 (*0-7933-4725-4*) Gallopade Pub Group.
—Christopher Columbus Comes to Minnesota! Includes Reproducible Activities for Kids! (Illus.). (gr. 3-12). 1994. PLB 24.95 (*0-7933-3689-9*); pap. 14.95 (*0-7933-3690-2*); computer disk 29.95 (*0-7933-3691-0*) Gallopade Pub Group.
—The Hard-to-Believe-But-True! Book of Minnesota History, Mystery, Trivia, Legend, Lore, Humor & More. (Illus.). (gr. 3 up). 1994. PLB 24.95 (*0-7933-0638-8*); pap. 14.95 (*0-7933-0637-X*); computer disk 29.95 (*0-7933-0639-6*) Gallopade Pub Group.
—If My Minnesota Mama Ran the World! (Illus.). (gr. 3 up). 1994. lib. bdg. 24.95 (*0-7933-1717-7*); pap. 14.95 (*0-7933-1718-5*); computer disk 29.95 (*0-7933-1719-3*) Gallopade Pub Group.
—Jurassic Ark! Minnesota Dinosaurs & Other Prehistoric Creatures. (gr. k-12). 1994. PLB 24.95 (*0-7933-7497-9*); pap. 14.95 (*0-7933-7498-7*); computer disk 29.95 (*0-7933-7499-5*) Gallopade Pub Group.
—Let's Quilt Minnesota & Stuff It Topographically! (Illus.). (gr. 3 up). 1994. PLB 24.95 (*1-55609-645-3*); pap. 14.95 (*1-55609-099-4*); computer disk 29.95 (*1-55609-647-X*) Gallopade Pub Group.
—Let's Quilt Our Minnesota County. 1994. lib. bdg. 24.95 (*0-7933-7182-1*); pap. text ed. 14.95 (*0-7933-7183-X*); disk 29.95 (*0-7933-7184-8*) Gallopade Pub Group.
—Let's Quilt Our Minnesota Town. 1994. lib. bdg. 24.95 (*0-7933-7032-9*); pap. text ed. 14.95 (*0-7933-7033-7*); disk 29.95 (*0-7933-7034-5*) Gallopade Pub Group.
—Meow! Minnesota Cats in History, Mystery, Legend, Lore, Humor & More! (Illus.). (gr. 3-12). 1994. PLB 24.95 (*0-7933-3383-0*); pap. 14.95 (*0-7933-3384-9*); computer disk 29.95 (*0-7933-3385-7*) Gallopade Pub Group.
—Minnesota & Other State Greats (Biographies) (Illus.). (gr. 3 up). 1994. PLB 24.95 (*1-55609-660-7*); pap. 14.95 (*1-55609-661-5*); computer disk 29.95 (*1-55609-662-3*) Gallopade Pub Group.
—Minnesota Bandits, Bushwackers, Outlaws, Crooks, Devils, Ghosts, Desperadoes & Other Assorted & Sundry Characters! (Illus.). (gr. 3 up). 1994. PLB 24.95 (*0-7933-0623-X*); pap. 14.95 (*0-7933-0622-1*); computer disk 29.95 (*0-7933-0624-8*) Gallopade Pub Group.
—Minnesota Classic Christmas Trivia: Stories, Recipes, Activities, Legends, Lore & More! (Illus.). (gr. 3 up). 1994. PLB 24.95 (*0-7933-0626-4*); pap. 14.95 (*0-7933-0625-6*); computer disk 29.95 (*0-7933-0627-2*) Gallopade Pub Group.
—Minnesota Coastales! 1994. lib. bdg. 24.95 (*0-7933-7288-7*) Gallopade Pub Group.
—Minnesota "Crinkum-Crankum" A Funny Word Book about Our State. (Illus.). 1994. lib. bdg. 24.95 (*0-7933-4877-3*); pap. 14.95 (*0-7933-4878-1*); disk 29.95 (*0-7933-4879-X*) Gallopade Pub Group.
—Minnesota Dingbats! Bk. 1: A Fun Book of Games, Stories, Activities & More about Our State That's All in Code! for You to Decipher. (Illus.). (gr. 3-12). 1994. PLB 24.95 (*0-7933-3842-5*); pap. 14.95 (*0-7933-3843-3*); computer disk 29.95 (*0-7933-3844-1*) Gallopade Pub Group.
—Minnesota Festival Fun for Kids! (Illus.). (gr. 3-12). 1994. lib. bdg. 24.95 (*0-7933-3995-2*); pap. 14.95 (*0-7933-3996-0*); disk 29.95 (*0-7933-3997-9*) Gallopade Pub Group.
—The Minnesota Hot Air Balloon Mystery. (Illus.). (gr. 2-9). 1994. 24.95 (*0-7933-2525-0*); pap. 14.95 (*0-7933-2526-9*); computer disk 29.95 (*0-7933-2527-7*) Gallopade Pub Group.
—Minnesota Jeopardy! Answers & Questions about Our State! (Illus.). (gr. 3-12). 1994. PLB 24.95 (*0-7933-4148-5*); pap. 14.95 (*0-7933-4149-3*); computer disk 29.95 (*0-7933-4150-7*) Gallopade Pub Group.
—Minnesota "Jography" A Fun Run Thru Our State. (Illus.). (gr. 3 up). 1994. PLB 24.95 (*1-55609-642-9*); pap. 14.95 (*1-55609-643-7*); computer disk 29.95 (*1-55609-644-5*) Gallopade Pub Group.
—Minnesota Kid's Cookbook: Recipes, How-To, History, Lore & More. (Illus.). (gr. 3 up). 1994. PLB 24.95 (*0-7933-0635-3*); pap. 14.95 (*0-7933-0634-5*); computer disk 29.95 (*0-7933-0636-1*) Gallopade Pub Group.
—The Minnesota Mystery Van Takes Off! Book 1: Handicapped Minnesota Kids Sneak Off on a Big Adventure. (Illus.). (gr. 3-12). 1994. 24.95 (*0-7933-5030-1*); pap. 14.95 (*0-7933-5031-X*); computer disk 29.95 (*0-7933-5032-8*) Gallopade Pub Group.
—Minnesota Quiz Bowl Crash Course! (Illus.). (gr. 3 up). 1994. PLB 24.95 (*1-55609-657-7*); pap. 14.95 (*1-55609-658-5*); computer disk 29.95 (*1-55609-659-3*) Gallopade Pub Group.
—Minnesota Rollercoasters! (Illus.). (gr. 3-12). 1994. PLB 24.95 (*0-7933-5293-2*); pap. 14.95 (*0-7933-5294-0*); computer disk 29.95 (*0-7933-5295-9*) Gallopade Pub Group.
—Minnesota School Trivia: An Amazing & Fascinating Look at Our State's Teachers, Schools & Students! (Illus.). (gr. 3 up). 1994. PLB 24.95 (*0-7933-0632-9*); pap. 14.95 (*0-7933-0631-0*); computer disk 29.95 (*0-7933-0633-7*) Gallopade Pub Group.
—Minnesota Silly Basketball Sportsmysteries, Vol. I. (Illus.). (gr. 3 up). 1994. PLB 24.95 (*0-7933-0629-9*); pap. 14.95 (*0-7933-0628-0*); computer disk 29.95 (*0-7933-0630-2*) Gallopade Pub Group.
—Minnesota Silly Basketball Sportsmysteries, Vol. II. (Illus.). (gr. 3 up). 1994. PLB 24.95 (*0-7933-1720-7*); pap. 14.95 (*0-7933-1721-5*); computer disk 29.95 (*0-7933-1722-3*) Gallopade Pub Group.
—Minnesota Silly Football Sportsmysteries, Vol. I. (Illus.). (gr. 3 up). 1994. PLB 24.95 (*1-55609-648-8*); pap. 14.95 (*1-55609-649-6*); computer disk 29.95 (*1-55609-650-X*) Gallopade Pub Group.
—Minnesota Silly Trivia! (Illus.). (gr. 3 up). 1994. PLB 24.95 (*1-55609-639-9*); pap. 14.95 (*1-55609-640-2*); computer disk 29.95 (*1-55609-641-0*) Gallopade Pub Group.
—Minnesota Timeline: A Chronology of Minnesota History, Mystery, Trivia, Legend, Lore & More. (Illus.). (gr. 3-12). 1994. PLB 24.95 (*0-7933-5944-9*); pap. 14.95 (*0-7933-5945-7*); computer disk 29.95 (*0-7933-5946-5*) Gallopade Pub Group.
—Minnesota's (Most Devastating!) Disasters & (Most Calamitous!) Catastrophies! (Illus.). (gr. 3 up). 1994. PLB 24.95 (*0-7933-0620-5*); pap. 14.95 (*0-7933-0619-1*); computer disk 29.95 (*0-7933-0621-3*) Gallopade Pub Group.
—Minnesota's Unsolved Mysteries (& Their "Solutions") Includes Scientific Information & Other Activities for Students. (Illus.). (gr. 3-12). 1994. PLB 24.95 (*0-7933-5791-8*); pap. 14.95 (*0-7933-5792-6*); computer disk 29.95 (*0-7933-5793-4*) Gallopade Pub Group.
—My First Book about Minnesota. (gr. k-4). 1994. PLB 24.95 (*0-7933-5638-5*); pap. 14.95 (*0-7933-5639-3*); computer disk 29.95 (*0-7933-5640-7*) Gallopade Pub Group.
—Patch, the Pirate Dog: A Minnesota Pet Story. (ps-4). 1994. PLB 24.95 (*0-7933-5485-4*); pap. 14.95 (*0-7933-5486-2*); computer disk 29.95 (*0-7933-5487-0*) Gallopade Pub Group.
—Uncle Rebus: Minnesota Picture Stories for Computer Kids. (Illus.). (gr. k-3). 1994. PLB 24.95 (*0-7933-4570-7*); pap. 14.95 (*0-7933-4571-5*); disk 29.95 (*0-7933-4572-3*) Gallopade Pub Group.
Paulsen, Gary. Woodsong. Paulsen, Ruth W., illus. LC 89-70835. 160p. (gr. 7 up). 1990. SBE 15.00 (*0-02-770221-9*, Bradbury Pr) Macmillan Child Grp.
Porter, A. P. Minnesota. Lerner Geography Department Staff, ed. (Illus.). 72p. (gr. 4-7). 1992. PLB 17.50 (*0-8225-2718-9*) Lerner Pubns.
Sansome, Constance J. Minnesota in Maps: A Trailblazer Atlas. Sansome, Constance J. & Jefferson, Lisa E., illus. 32p. (gr. 3 up). 1990. 17.95 (*0-9626025-0-7*); pap. 12.95 (*0-9626025-1-5*) Trailblazer Bks.
Stein, R. Conrad. Minnesota. LC 90-35384. (Illus.). 144p. (gr. 4 up). 1990. PLB 20.55 (*0-516-00469-7*) Childrens.
—Minnesota. 199p. 1993. text ed. 15.40 (*1-56956-147-8*) W A T Braille.
Thompson, Kathleen. Minnesota. LC 87-16405. 48p. (gr. 3 up). 1988. 19.97 (*0-86514-466-4*) Raintree Steck-V.

MINNESOTA–FICTION
Blair, Yogi. Minnesota Fortune Cookies. 5th ed. 26p. (gr. 11 up). 1993. 8.95 (*0-930366-73-5*) Northcountry Pub.
Lovelace, Maud H. Betsy & Joe. Neville, Vera, illus. LC 48-8096. 256p. (gr. 5 up). 1948. 14.95 (*0-690-13378-2*, Crowell Jr Bks) HarpC Child Bks.
—Betsy & Tacy Go Downtown. Lenski, Lois, illus. LC 43-51264. 192p. (gr. 2-5). 1966. PLB 14.89 (*0-690-13450-9*, Crowell Jr Bks) HarpC Child Bks.
—Betsy & Tacy Go over the Big Hill. Lenski, Lois, illus. LC 42-23557. 176p. (gr. 2-5). 1966. PLB 14.89 (*0-690-13521-1*, Crowell Jr Bks) HarpC Child Bks.
—Betsy's Wedding. Neville, Vera, illus. LC 55-11108. 241p. (gr. 5 up). 1955. 14.95 (*0-690-13733-8*, Crowell Jr Bks) HarpC Child Bks.
Lovelace, Maureen H. Betsy-Tacy. Lenski, Lois, illus. LC 40-30965. 128p. (gr. 2-5). 1966. PLB 14.89 (*0-690-13805-9*, Crowell Jr Bks) HarpC Child Bks.
—Betsy-Tacy & Tib. Lenski, Lois, illus. LC 41-18714. 144p. (gr. 2-5). 1966. PLB 14.89 (*0-690-13876-8*, Crowell Jr Bks) HarpC Child Bks.

McColley, Kevin. Pecking Order. LC 93-17768. 224p. (gr. 7 up). 1994. 16.00 (*0-06-023554-3*); PLB 15.89 (*0-06-023555-1*) HarpC Child Bks.

Marsh, Carole. Minnesota Coastales. (Illus.). (gr. 3 up). 1994. PLB 24.95 (*1-55609-654-2*); pap. 14.95 (*1-55609-655-0*); computer disk 29.95 (*1-55609-656-9*) Gallopade Pub Group.

—Minnesota Silly Football Sportsmysteries, Vol. II. (Illus.). (gr. 3 up). 1994. PLB 24.95 (*1-55609-651-8*); pap. 14.95 (*1-55609-652-6*); computer disk 29.95 (*1-55609-653-4*) Gallopade Pub Group.

Marvin, Isabel R. A Bride for Anna's Papa. LC 93-41175. (Illus.). 144p. 1994. pap. 6.95 (*0-915943-93-X*) Milkweed Ed.

Nixon, Joan L. Land of Dreams. LC 93-8734. 1994. 14. 95 (*0-385-31170-2*) Delacorte.

Paulsen, Gary. The Winter Room. LC 89-42541. 128p. (gr. 6-9). 1989. 13.95 (*0-531-05839-5*); PLB 13.99 (*0-531-08439-6*) Orchard Bks Watts.

Qualey, Marsha. Come in from the Cold. LC 93-42064. 1994. 14.95 (*0-395-68986-4*) HM.

Riddell, Ruth. Ice Warrior. LC 91-29506. 144p. (gr. 4-7). 1992. SBE 13.95 (*0-689-31710-7*, Atheneum Child Bk) Macmillan Child Grp.

Thomas, Jane R. Courage at Indian Deep. LC 83-14404. (Illus.). 128p. (gr. 3-7). 1984. 13.95 (*0-89919-181-9*, Clarion Bks) HM.

Wareing, Eleanor J. The Cat Who Was Named Twice. Lynn, Susan K., illus. 141p. (Orig.). (gr. 3-6). 1990. pap. 6.95 (*0-9629175-0-8*) E J Wareing.

Wilder, Laura Ingalls. On the Banks of Plum Creek. rev. ed. Williams, Garth, illus. LC 52-7528. 340p. (gr. 3-7). 1961. 15.95 (*0-06-026470-5*); PLB 15.89 (*0-06-026471-3*) HarpC Child Bks.

Wosmek, Frances. A Brown Bird Singing. Lewin, Ted, illus. LC 92-43784. 128p. (gr. 5 up). 1993. pap. 4.95 (*0-688-04596-0*, Pub. by Beech Tree Bks) Morrow.

MINORITIES

see also Discrimination; Race Problems

Brown, Gene. Discovery & Settlement: Europe Meets the New World (1490-1700) LC 93-8537. (Illus.). 64p. (gr. 5-8). 1993. PLB 15.95 (*0-8050-2574-X*) TFC Bks NY.

Dudley, William & Cozic, Charles. Racism in America: Opposing Viewpoints. LC 91-14293. (Illus.). 240p. (gr. 10 up). 1991. lib. bdg. 17.95 (*0-89908-182-7*); pap. 9.95 (*0-89908-157-6*) Greenhaven.

Hammer, Roger A. Hidden America: A Collection of Multi-Cultural Stories, 4 bks. rev. ed. Schlosser, Cy, et al, illus. (gr. 6 up). Set. pap. 29.95 (*0-932991-00-9*) Place in the Woods.

Katz, William L. From World War Two to the New Frontier, 1940-1963. LC 92-42801. (Illus.). 96p. (gr. 7-8). 1993. PLB 22.80 (*0-8114-6280-3*) Raintree Steck-V.

—The Great Society to the Reagan Era, 1964-1993. LC 92-43709. (Illus.). 96p. (gr. 7-8). 1993. PLB 22.80 (*0-8114-6282-X*) Raintree Steck-V.

—Minorities Today. LC 92-47438. (Illus.). 96p. (gr. 7-8). 1992. PLB 22.80 (*0-8114-6281-1*) Raintree Steck-V.

—The New Freedom to the New Deal, 1913-1939. LC 92-39948. (Illus.). 96p. (gr. 7-8). 1993. PLB 22.80 (*0-8114-6279-X*) Raintree Steck-V.

Koreans in America. rev. ed. (Illus.). 64p. (gr. 5 up). 1992. 15.95 (*0-8225-0248-8*) Lerner Pubns.

Langone, John J. Spreading Poison: A Book about Racism & Prejudice. LC 92-17847. 1993. 15.95 (*0-316-51410-1*) Little.

Marvis, Barbara J. Contemporary American Success Stories: Famous People of Asian Ancestry, Vol. III. LC 93-78991. (Illus.). 96p. (gr. 5-12). 1993. 15.95 (*1-883845-02-5*); pap. 8.95 (*1-883845-08-4*); tchr's. ed. 5.95 (*1-883845-05-X*) M Lane Pubs.

—Contemporary American Success Stories: Famous People of Asian Ancestry, Vol. I. LC 93-78991. (Illus.). 96p. (gr. 5-12). 1993. 15.95 (*1-883845-00-9*) M Lane Pubs.

—Contemporary American Success Stories: Famous People of Asian Ancestry, Vol. II. LC 93-78991. (Illus.). 96p. (gr. 5-12). 1993. 15.95 (*1-883845-01-7*) M Lane Pubs.

Meier, Gisela. Minorities. LC 91-11651. 64p. (gr. 5-7). 1991. 12.95s.p. (*0-86593-124-0*); lib. bdg. 17.27 (*0-685-59203-0*) Rourke Corp.

Petra Press Staff. A Multicultural Portrait of the Move West. LC 93-10317. 1993. 18.95 (*1-85435-658-5*) Marshall Cavendish.

Piggins, Carol A. A Multicultural Portrait of the Civil War. LC 93-10319. 1993. 18.95 (*1-85435-660-7*, Pub. by M Cavendish Bks UK) Marshall Cavendish.

Press, David P. A Multicultural Portrait of Professional Sports. LC 93-10316. 1993. 18.95 (*1-85435-661-5*) Marshall Cavendish.

Siegel, Mark, et al, eds. Minorities: America's Rich Culture. 72p. 1992. pap. text ed. 12.95 (*1-878623-33-8*) Info Plus TX.

Stanek, Muriel. We Came from Vietnam. Fay, Ann, ed. McMahon, W. Franklin, illus. LC 84-29927. 48p. (gr. 1-6). 1985. PLB 10.50 (*0-8075-8699-4*) A Whitman.

Steins, Richard. A Nation Is Born: Rebellion & Independence in America (1700-1820) LC 93-24994. (Illus.). 64p. (gr. 5-8). 1993. PLB 15.95 (*0-8050-2582-0*) TFC Bks NY.

Washburne, Carolyn K. A Multicultural Portrait of Colonial Life. LC 93-10320. (gr. 7 up). 1993. 18.95 (*1-85435-657-7*) Marshall Cavendish.

Witkoski, Michael. Italian Americans. LC 91-15428. (Illus.). 104p. (gr. 5-9). 1991. 13.95s.p. (*0-86593-137-2*); PLB 18.60 (*0-685-59185-9*) Rourke Corp.

Wright, David K. A Multicultural Portrait of Life in the Cities. LC 93-10318. 1993. 18.95 (*1-85435-659-3*) Marshall Cavendish.

MIRACLE PLAYS

see Mysteries and Miracle Plays

MIRRORS

Edom, H. Science with Light & Mirrors. (Illus.). 24p. (gr. 1-4). 1992. PLB 12.96 (*0-88110-545-7*, Usborne); pap. 4.95 (*0-7460-0696-9*, Usborne) EDC.

Fitzpatrick, Julie. Mirrors. (Illus.). 30p. (gr. 3-5). 1991. 13.95 (*0-237-60209-1*, Pub. by Evans Bros Ltd) Trafalgar.

Fowler, Allan. Mirror, Mirror. LC 93-38591. (Illus.). 32p. (ps-2). 1994. PLB 10.75 (*0-516-06023-6*) Childrens.

McDonough, Jerome. Mirrors. (Illus.). 32p. (gr. 7 up). 1987. pap. 3.00 (*0-88680-278-4*); royalty on application 35.00 (*0-685-67656-0*) I E Clark.

McLean, Peggy. Mirror Explorations. (gr. k-4). 1994. pap. text ed. 7.95 (*1-882293-01-0*) Activity Resources.

Simon, Seymour. Mirror Magic. Matsick, Anni, illus. LC 90-85921. 32p. (gr. 2-5). 1991. Repr. 9.95 (*1-878093-07-X*) Boyds Mills Pr.

Taylor, Barbara. Bouncing & Bending Light. LC 89-36213. (gr. 4-6). 1990. PLB 12.40 (*0-531-14014-8*) Watts.

Zubrowski, Bernie. Mirrors. Doty, Roy, illus. LC 91-29142. 96p. (gr. 5 up). 1992. pap. 6.95 (*0-688-10591-2*, Pub. by Beech Tree Bks) Morrow.

—Mirrors: Finding Out about the Properties of Light. Doty, Roy, illus. LC 91-29142. 96p. (gr. 3 up). 1992. PLB 13.93 (*0-688-10592-0*) Morrow Jr Bks.

MISDEMEANORS (LAW)

see Criminal Law

MISSILES, GUIDED

see Guided Missiles

MISSING PERSONS

Anderson, Carolyn. How to Protect Your Child from Becoming a Missing Person. 46p. (ps-7). 1992. wkbk., incl. audiotape 12.00 (*1-883778-00-X*); audiotape 5.00 (*0-685-68073-8*) Starlite Prods.

Bren Guernsey, JoAnn. Missing Children. LC 89-25210. (Illus.). 48p. (gr. 4 up). 1990. text ed. 12.95 RSBE (*0-89686-494-4*, Crestwood Hse) Macmillan Child Grp.

Christensen, Loren. Missing Children. (Illus.). 64p. (gr. 7 up). 1990. lib. bdg. 17.27 (*0-86593-076-7*); lib. bdg. 12. 95s.p. (*0-685-46440-7*) Rourke Corp.

Cooney, Caroline B. Face on the Milk Carton. 1991. pap. 3.99 (*0-553-28958-6*) Bantam.

Hoobler, Dorothy & Hoobler, Tom. Vanished. 144p. (gr. 7 up). 1992. 16.95 (*0-8027-8148-9*); PLB 17.85 (*0-8027-8149-7*) Walker & Co.

Larsen, Anita. Amelia Earhart: Missing, Declared Dead. LC 91-19246. (Illus.). 48p. (gr. 5-6). 1992. text ed. 11. 95 RSBE (*0-89686-613-0*, Crestwood Hse) Macmillan Child Grp.

Stewart, Gail B. What Happened to Judge Crater? LC 91-16554. (Illus.). 48p. (gr. 5-6). 1992. text ed. 11.95 RSBE (*0-89686-617-3*, Crestwood Hse) Macmillan Child Grp.

MISSIONARIES

Beck, Margaret. Madugu. Whitney, Dick, illus. 26p. (gr. k-6). 1987. pap. text ed. 5.50 (*1-55976-052-4*) CEF Press.

Bostrom, Alice. David Livingstone, Missionary to Africa. Lautermilch, John, illus. 32p. (Orig.). 1982. pap. 1.30 (*0-89323-027-8*) Bible Memory.

Briscoe, Jill. Paint the Prisons Bright: Corrie Ten Boom. (gr. 5 up). 1991. pap. 4.99 (*0-8499-3308-0*) Word Inc.

Chamberlain, Eugene. Loyd Corder: Traveler for God. LC 82-73663. (gr. 4-6). 1983. 5.99 (*0-8054-4284-7*, 4242-84) Broadman.

Chudnovsky, Elynne, illus. Bare, Beautiful Feet & Other Missionary Stories. (gr. 1-5). 1992. 3.99 (*0-87509-485-6*) Chr Pubns.

—The Potato Story & Other Missionary Stories. LC 91-78295. (gr. 1-5). 1992. 3.99 (*0-87509-484-8*) Chr Pubns.

Craig, Mary. Mother Theresa. (Illus.). 64p. (gr. 5-9). 1991. 11.95 (*0-237-60008-0*, Pub. by Evans Bros Ltd) Trafalgar.

Cutts, Grace. To China & Back. 27p. (ps-2). 1991. 3.99 (*0-87509-453-8*) Chr Pubns.

Cutts, William A. Weak Thing in Moni Land: The Story of Bill & Gracie Cutts. Richardson, Don, frwd. by. LC 90-80454. (Illus.). 168p. (Orig.). 1990. pap. 7.99 (*0-87509-429-5*) Chr Pubns.

Davis, Rebecca H. With Daring Faith. 187p. (Orig.). 1987. pap. 4.95 (*0-89084-414-3*) Bob Jones Univ Pr.

Dick, Lois H. I Dare. Lombard, Lynette, illus. 42p. (gr. k-6). 1971. pap. text ed. 9.45 (*1-55976-034-6*) CEF Press.

—Run Ma Run. Butcher, Sam, illus. 57p. (gr. k-6). 1978. pap. text ed. 8.99 (*1-55976-055-9*) CEF Press.

Harner, Ruth. Rejoicing with Joy. Butcher, Sam, illus. 21p. (gr. k-6). 1988. pap. text ed. 4.25 (*1-55976-145-8*) CEF Press.

Heath, Lou. Ed Taylor: Father of Migrant Missions. LC 81-70911. (gr. k-3). 1982. 5.99 (*0-8054-4278-2*, 4242-78) Broadman.

Hibschman, Barbara. I Want to Be a Missionary. Wulf, Barbara L., illus. 24p. (Orig.). (gr. 1-6). 1990. pap. 4.99 (*0-87509-436-8*) Chr Pubns.

—One Shall Chase a Thousand. 30p. (gr. k-3). 1993. pap. 3.99 (*0-87509-516-X*) Chr Pubns.

Hillam, Corbin. Jennifer of the City. Hillam, Corbin, illus. 32p. (ps-2). 1990. text ed. 5.00 (*0-570-04183-X*) Concordia.

Hockett, Betty M. Outside Doctor on Call: The Life-Story of Dr. Ezra & Frances DeVol. Loewen, Janelle, illus. 80p. (Orig.). (gr. 3-6). 1992. pap. 4.95 (*0-943701-20-1*) George Fox Pr.

—Whistling Bombs & Bumpy Trains: The Life-Story of Anna Nixon. Loewen, Janelle, illus. LC 89-84572. 80p. (Orig.). (gr. 3-6). 1989. pap. 3.50 (*0-943701-15-5*) George Fox Pr.

Hollaway, Lee. Los Orr: Duo Misionero. 64p. 1987. pap. 2.75 (*0-311-01073-3*) Casa Bautista.

Howard, Mildred T. These Are My People. (Illus.). 152p. (Orig.). (gr. 3). 1984. pap. 6.94 (*0-89084-242-6*) Bob Jones Univ Pr.

Jacobs, William J. Mother Teresa: Helping the Poor. (Illus.). 48p. (gr. 2-4). 1991. PLB 12.90 (*1-56294-020-1*) Millbrook Pr.

Kent, Renee. You Can Be a Musician & a Missionary, Too. McClain, Cindy, ed. Sealy, Kathy, illus. 64p. (Orig.). (gr. 4-6). 1988. pap. 3.95 (*0-936625-37-6*, PZ7.K419Y) Womans Mission Union.

Kiefer, James. Hudson Taylor. Beerhorst, Adrian, illus. 53p. (gr. k-6). 1973. pap. text ed. 8.99 (*1-55976-054-0*) CEF Press.

Lazo, Caroline. Mother Teresa. LC 92-23765. (Illus.). 64p. (gr. 4 up). 1993. text ed. 13.95 RSBE (*0-87518-559-2*, Dillon) Macmillan Child Grp.

Ludwig, Charles. Jason Lee. (gr. 3-6). 1992. pap. 6.95 (*0-88062-161-3*) Mott Media.

Marxhausen, Joanne. Some of My Best Friends Are Trees. LC 56-1640. (Illus., Orig.). (ps-4). 1990. pap. 7.99 (*0-570-04182-1*, 56-1640) Concordia.

Massey, Barbara. Virginia Wingo: Teacher & Friend. LC 82-73665. (gr. k-3). 1983. 5.99 (*0-8054-4282-0*, 4242-82) Broadman.

Miller, S. My Book about Hudson. 1989. 5.95 (*9971-972-69-7*) OMF Bks.

Mouillesseaux, Claire & Seger, Doris. Devil-Kings & Cannibals. (Illus.). 52p. (gr. k-4). 1962. pap. text ed. 8.99 (*1-55976-053-2*) CEF Press.

Philips, Martha & Hadden, Mary. Behind Stone Walls & Barbed Wire. Lynn, Claire, ed. (Illus.). 176p. (Orig.). (gr. 5 up). 1991. pap. 2.25 (*0-89323-057-X*) Bible Memory.

Strawn, Kathy. Matthew's Dad Is a Missionary. Sealy, Kathy, illus. 32p. (Orig.). (gr. 1-3). 1988. pap. 2.95 (*0-936625-38-4*) Womans Mission Union.

Swift, Catherine. Gladys Aylward. LC 89-61792. 128p. 1989. pap. 4.99 (*1-55661-090-4*) Bethany Hse.

Timyan, Janis, illus. A Happy Day for Ramona & Other Missionary Stories for Children. LC 87-71018. (Orig.). (gr. 1-5). 1987. pap. 3.99 (*0-87509-392-2*) Chr Pubns.

—The Pink & Green Church & Other Missionary Stories for Children. LC 87-71019. (gr. 1-5). 1988. pap. 3.99 (*0-87509-393-0*) Chr Pubns.

Walsh, Vincent M. Prepare My People. 100p. (Orig.). 1986. pap. text ed. 5.00 (*0-943374-13-8*) Key of David.

Weinrich, Mark. Meet the Missionary. (Illus.). 24p. (Orig.). (gr. k-3). 1993. pap. 4.99 (*0-87509-517-8*) Chr Pubns.

—The Missing Missionary. (Illus.). 24p. (Orig.). (gr. k-3). 1993. pap. 4.99 (*0-87509-518-6*) Chr Pubns.

Whittlesey, Marjorie T. The Dragon Will Survive. LC 89-17585. 1991. 13.95 (*0-87949-315-1*) Ashley Bks.

Zook, Mary R. Little Missionaries. 184p. (ps-5). 1979. 6.95 (*0-686-30764-X*) Rod & Staff.

MISSIONARIES–FICTION

Buckwalter, Leoda. Road to Chumba. Johns, Helen, ed. LC 94-71563. 188p. (Orig.). 1994. pap. 8.95 (*0-916035-60-3*) Evangel Indiana.

Martin, Mildred A. Missionary Stories & the Millers. Burkholder, Edith, illus. 208p. (gr. 3 up). 1993. 9.50 (*0-9627643-7-X*) Green Psturs Pr.

Myers, Bill. My Life As Crocodile Junk Food. (gr. 3-7). 1993. pap. 4.99 (*0-8499-3405-2*) Word Inc.

Repp, Gloria. A Question of Yams: A Missionary Story Based on True Events. Daniels, Karen, ed. Bruckner, Roger, illus. 67p. (Orig.). (gr. 2-4). 1992. pap. 4.95 (*0-89084-614-6*) Bob Jones Univ Pr.

Rispin, Karen. Sabrina the Schemer. LC 93-39634. 1994. 4.99 (*0-8423-1296-X*) Tyndale.

Wilkinson, Barbara. Apples for the Missionaries. Dillard, Karen, illus. 32p. (Orig.). (gr. 1-3). 1989. pap. text ed. 2.95 (*0-936625-67-8*) Womans Mission Union.

MISSIONS

see also Missionaries;

also names of churches, denominations, religious orders, etc. with the subdivision Missions, e.g. Catholic Church–Missions; etc.

Beasley, Mrs. Jim. Missions Studies: Brazil. (Illus.). 32p. (Orig.). (ps). 1985. pap. 2.25 (*0-89114-155-3*) Baptist Pub Hse.

Becker, Melissa. My Family Helps: A Missions Activity Book for Preschoolers. Gross, Karen, ed. 24p. (Orig.). (ps). 1993. pap. text ed. 3.95 (*1-56309-080-5*, New Hope) Womans Mission Union.

California Missions Fact Cards. (Illus.). 24p. (gr. 3-6). 1992. looseleaf binder 22.00 (*0-9634017-3-4*); card set 18.00 (*0-9634017-7-7*) Toucan Valley.

Douglass, Herbert E. Why Jesus Waits: How the Sanctuary Message Explains the Mission of the Seventh-Day Adventist Church. rev. ed. LC 76-10925. 96p. (gr. 10 up). 1987. pap. 3.95 (*0-945460-00-7*) Upward Way.

Driskill, J. Lawrence. Mission Adventures in Many Lands. Jackson, Russ, illus. LC 92-15689. (gr. 3-6). 1992. PLB 17.95 (*0-932727-57-3*); pap. 11.95 (*0-932727-56-5*) Hope Pub Hse.

—Mission Stories from Around the World. LC 93-39413. 192p. (gr. 4-8). 1994. PLB 19.95 (*0-932727-72-7*); pap. 11.95 (*0-932727-71-9*) Hope Pub Hse.

Lyngheim, Linda. The Indians & the California Missions. rev. ed. Garber, Phyllis, illus. LC 84-80543. 160p. (gr. 4-6). 1990. 14.95 (*0-915369-04-4*); pap. 10.95 (*0-915369-00-1*) Langtry Pubns.

McIndoo, Ethel. Missions Adventures 1. Massey, Barbara, ed. 32p. (Orig.). (gr. 1-6). 1991. pap. text ed. 1.50 (*1-56309-026-0*) Womans Mission Union.

—Missions Adventures 2. Massey, Barbara, ed. 32p. (Orig.). (gr. 1-6). 1991. pap. text ed. 1.50 (*1-56309-027-9*) Womans Mission Union.

—Missions Adventures 3. Massey, Barbara, ed. 32p. (gr. 1-6). 1991. pap. text ed. 1.50 (*1-56309-028-7*) Womans Mission Union.

—Missions Adventures 4. Massey, Barbara, ed. 32p. (Orig.). (gr. 1-6). 1991. pap. text ed. 1.50 (*1-56309-029-5*) Womans Mission Union.

—Missions Adventures 5. Massey, Barbara, ed. 32p. (Orig.). (gr. 1-6). 1991. pap. text ed. 1.50 (*1-56309-030-9*) Womans Mission Union.

—Missions Adventures 6. Massey, Barbara, ed. 32p. (Orig.). (gr. 1-6). 1991. pap. text ed. 1.50 (*1-56309-031-7*) Womans Mission Union.

Newberry, Tina T. Kelli Tyler Extraordinaire. 120p. (Orig.). (gr. 4-6). 1990. pap. text ed. 3.50 (*0-936625-91-0*, New Hope AL) Womans Mission Union.

Pratt, Anne H. Junior Missionary Handbook. 64p. (Orig.). (gr. 3-6). 1987. pap. 5.98 (*0-88290-318-7*) Horizon Utah.

Richardson, Freida. Madagascar's Miracle Story. Richardson, Jerry, intros. by. LC 89-32335. (Illus.). 156p. (Orig.). 1989. pap. 6.99 (*0-932581-47-1*) Word Aflame.

Smith, Anne. Get into the Action: An Activity Book for Children on Mission Action. 31p. (Orig.). (gr. 1-6). 1990. pap. text ed. 2.95 (*0-936625-84-8*) Womans Mission Union.

Spizzirri Publishing Co. Staff & Spizzirri, Linda. California Missions: An Educational Coloring Book. (Illus.). 32p. (gr. k-5). 1985. pap. 1.75 (*0-86545-062-5*) Spizzirri.

Steere, D'Ann. Choice Adventures, No. 4: The Rain Forest Mission. (gr. 3-7). 1991. PLB 4.99 (*0-8423-5028-4*) Tyndale.

Stienecker, David. A Mission Padre. LC 94-743. (gr. 4 up). 1994. write for info. (*1-55916-040-3*) Rourke Bk Co.

Stone, Lynn M. Missions. LC 93-18638. (Illus.). (gr. 3-7). 1993. 15.93 (*0-86625-445-5*); 11.95s.p. (*0-685-66595-X*) Rourke Pubns.

Sutton, Jan. One Giant Step: Putting Feet to Missions. 80p. (Orig.). (gr. 7-12). 1990. pap. text ed. 3.95 (*0-936625-85-6*) Womans Mission Union.

Tapp, Sandra. Missions Day Camp: Language Missions. McClain, Cindy, ed. 23p. (Orig.). (gr. 4-6). 1990. pap. text ed. 1.95 (*0-936625-99-6*) Womans Mission Union.

Thomason, Kendra. My Family Plays & Prays: Mission Activity Book for Preschoolers. Gross, Karen, ed. 32p. (Orig.). (ps). 1992. pap. text ed. 3.95 (*1-56309-050-3*, New Hope) Womans Mission Union.

MISSISSIPPI

Braynard, Frank O. U. S. Steamships: A Picture Postcard History. Cronkite, Walter, intro. by. (Illus.). 144p. (Orig.). 1991. pap. 14.95 (*0-930256-20-4*) Almar.

Carole Marsh Mississippi Books, 45 bks. 1994. PLB 1052.75 set (*0-7933-1299-X*); pap. 602.75 set (*0-7933-5170-7*) Gallopade Pub Group.

Carson, Robert. Mississippi. LC 88-11747. (Illus.). 144p. (gr. 4 up). 1988. PLB 20.55 (*0-516-00470-0*) Childrens.

—Mississippi. 193p. 1993. text ed. 15.40 (*1-56956-167-2*) W A T Braille.

Marsh, Carole. Avast, Ye Slobs!: Mississippi Pirate Trivia. (Illus.). (gr. 3 up). 1994. PLB 24.95 (*0-7933-0666-3*); pap. 14.95 (*0-7933-0665-5*); computer disk 29.95 (*0-7933-0667-1*) Gallopade Pub Group.

—The Beast of the Mississippi Bed & Breakfast. (Illus.). (gr. 3 up). 1994. PLB 24.95 (*0-7933-0644-2*); pap. 14.95 (*0-7933-1726-6*); computer disk 29.95 (*0-7933-1727-4*) Gallopade Pub Group.

—Bow Wow! Mississippi Dogs in History, Mystery, Legend, Lore, Humor & More! (Illus.). (gr. 3-12). 1994. PLB 24.95 (*0-7933-3539-6*); pap. 14.95 (*0-7933-3540-X*); computer disk 29.95 (*0-7933-3541-8*) Gallopade Pub Group.

—Chill Out: Scary Mississippi Tales Based on Frightening Mississippi Truths. (Illus.). 1994. lib. bdg. 24.95 (*0-7933-4726-2*); pap. 14.95 (*0-7933-4727-0*); disk 29.95 (*0-7933-4728-9*) Gallopade Pub Group.

—Christopher Columbus Comes to Mississippi! Includes Reproducible Activities for Kids! (Illus.). (gr. 3-12). 1994. PLB 24.95 (*0-7933-3692-9*); pap. 14.95 (*0-7933-3693-7*); computer disk 29.95 (*0-7933-3694-5*) Gallopade Pub Group.

—The Hard-to-Believe-But-True! Book of Mississippi History, Mystery, Trivia, Legend, Lore, Humor & More. (Illus.). (gr. 3 up). 1994. PLB 24.95 (*0-7933-0663-9*); pap. 14.95 (*0-7933-0662-0*); computer disk 29.95 (*0-7933-0664-7*) Gallopade Pub Group.

—If My Mississippi Mama Ran the World! (Illus.). (gr. 3 up). 1994. lib. bdg. 24.95 (*0-7933-1728-2*); pap. 14.95 (*0-7933-1729-0*); computer disk 29.95 (*0-7933-1730-4*) Gallopade Pub Group.

—Jurassic Ark! Mississippi Dinosaurs & Other Prehistoric Creatures. (gr. k-12). 1994. PLB 24.95 (*0-7933-7500-2*); pap. 14.95 (*0-7933-7501-0*); computer disk 29.95 (*0-7933-7502-9*) Gallopade Pub Group.

—Let's Quilt Mississippi & Stuff It Topographically! (Illus.). (gr. 3 up). 1994. PLB 24.95 (*1-55609-710-7*); pap. 14.95 (*1-55609-074-9*); computer disk 29.95 (*1-55609-716-6*) Gallopade Pub Group.

—Let's Quilt Our Mississippi County. 1994. lib. bdg. 24.95 (*0-7933-7185-6*); pap. text ed. 14.95 (*0-7933-7186-4*); disk 29.95 (*0-7933-7187-2*) Gallopade Pub Group.

—Let's Quilt Our Mississippi Town. 1994. lib. bdg. 24.95 (*0-7933-7035-3*); pap. text ed. 14.95 (*0-7933-7036-1*); disk 29.95 (*0-7933-7037-X*) Gallopade Pub Group.

—Meow! Mississippi Cats in History, Mystery, Legend, Lore, Humor & More! (Illus.). (gr. 3-12). 1994. PLB 24.95 (*0-7933-3386-5*); pap. 14.95 (*0-7933-3387-3*); computer disk 29.95 (*0-7933-3388-1*) Gallopade Pub Group.

—Mississippi & Other State Greats (Biographies) (Illus.). (gr. 3 up). 1994. PLB 24.95 (*1-55609-725-5*); pap. 14.95 (*1-55609-726-3*); computer disk 29.95 (*1-55609-727-1*) Gallopade Pub Group.

—Mississippi Bandits, Bushwackers, Outlaws, Crooks, Devils, Ghosts, Desperadoes & Other Assorted & Sundry Characters! (Illus.). (gr. 3 up). 1994. PLB 24.95 (*0-7933-0648-5*); pap. 14.95 (*0-7933-0647-7*); computer disk 29.95 (*0-7933-0649-3*) Gallopade Pub Group.

—Mississippi Classic Christmas Trivia: Stories, Recipes, Activities, Legends, Lore & More. (Illus.). (gr. 3 up). 1994. PLB 24.95 (*0-7933-0651-5*); pap. 14.95 (*0-7933-0650-7*); computer disk 29.95 (*0-7933-0652-3*) Gallopade Pub Group.

—Mississippi Coastales. (Illus.). (gr. 3 up). 1994. PLB 24.95 (*1-55609-720-4*); pap. 14.95 (*1-55609-122-2*); computer disk 29.95 (*1-55609-721-2*) Gallopade Pub Group.

—Mississippi Coastales! 1994. lib. bdg. 24.95 (*0-7933-7289-5*) Gallopade Pub Group.

—Mississippi "Crinkum-Crankum" A Funny Word Book about Our State. (Illus.). 1994. lib. bdg. 24.95 (*0-7933-4880-3*); pap. 14.95 (*0-7933-4881-1*); disk 29.95 (*0-7933-4882-X*) Gallopade Pub Group.

—Mississippi Dingbats! Bk. 1: A Fun Book of Games, Stories, Activities & More about Our State That's All in Code! for You to Decipher. (Illus.). (gr. 3-12). 1994. PLB 24.95 (*0-7933-3845-X*); pap. 14.95 (*0-7933-3846-8*); computer disk 29.95 (*0-7933-3847-6*) Gallopade Pub Group.

—Mississippi Festival Fun for Kids! (Illus.). (gr. 3-12). 1994. lib. bdg. 24.95 (*0-7933-3998-7*); pap. 14.95 (*0-7933-3999-5*); disk 29.95 (*0-7933-4000-4*) Gallopade Pub Group.

—The Mississippi Hot Air Balloon Mystery. (Illus.). (gr. 2-9). 1994. 24.95 (*0-7933-2534-X*); pap. 14.95 (*0-7933-2535-8*); computer disk 29.95 (*0-7933-2536-6*) Gallopade Pub Group.

—Mississippi Jeopardy! Answers & Questions about Our State! (Illus.). (gr. 3-12). 1994. PLB 24.95 (*0-7933-4151-5*); pap. 14.95 (*0-7933-4152-3*); computer disk 29.95 (*0-7933-4153-1*) Gallopade Pub Group.

—Mississippi "Jography" A Fun Run Thru Our State. (Illus.). (gr. 3 up). 1994. PLB 24.95 (*1-55609-709-3*); pap. 14.95 (*1-55609-091-9*); computer disk 29.95 (*1-55609-715-8*) Gallopade Pub Group.

—Mississippi Kid's Cookbook: Recipes, How-To, History, Lore & More. (Illus.). (gr. 3 up). 1994. PLB 24.95 (*0-7933-0660-4*); pap. 14.95 (*0-7933-0659-0*); computer disk 29.95 (*0-7933-0661-2*) Gallopade Pub Group.

—The Mississippi Mystery Van Takes Off! Book 1: Handicapped Mississippi Kids Sneak Off on a Big Adventure. (Illus.). (gr. 3-12). 1994. 24.95 (*0-7933-5033-6*); pap. 14.95 (*0-7933-5034-4*); computer disk 29.95 (*0-7933-5035-2*) Gallopade Pub Group.

—Mississippi Quiz Bowl Crash Course! (Illus.). (gr. 3 up). 1994. PLB 24.95 (*1-55609-722-0*); pap. 14.95 (*1-55609-723-9*); computer disk 29.95 (*1-55609-724-7*) Gallopade Pub Group.

—Mississippi Rollercoasters! (Illus.). (gr. 3-12). 1994. PLB 24.95 (*0-7933-5296-7*); pap. 14.95 (*0-7933-5297-5*); computer disk 29.95 (*0-7933-5298-3*) Gallopade Pub Group.

—Mississippi School Trivia: An Amazing & Fascinating Look at Our State's Teachers, Schools & Students! (Illus.). (gr. 3 up). 1994. PLB 24.95 (*0-7933-0657-4*); pap. 14.95 (*0-7933-0656-6*); computer disk 29.95 (*0-7933-0658-2*) Gallopade Pub Group.

—Mississippi Silly Basketball Sports Mysteries, Vol. II. (Illus.). (gr. 3 up). 1994. PLB 24.95 (*0-7933-1731-2*); pap. 14.95 (*0-7933-1732-0*); computer disk 29.95 (*0-685-45944-6*) Gallopade Pub Group.

—Mississippi Silly Basketball Sportsmysteries, Vol. I. (Illus.). (gr. 3 up). 1994. PLB 24.95 (*0-7933-0654-X*); pap. 14.95 (*0-7933-0653-1*); computer disk 29.95 (*0-7933-0655-8*) Gallopade Pub Group.

—Mississippi Silly Football Sportsmysteries, Vol. I. (Illus.). (gr. 3 up). 1994. PLB 24.95 (*1-55609-711-5*); pap. 14.95 (*1-55609-712-3*); computer disk 29.95 (*1-55609-713-1*) Gallopade Pub Group.

—Mississippi Silly Football Sportsmysteries, Vol. II. (Illus.). (gr. 3 up). 1994. PLB 24.95 (*1-55609-717-4*); pap. 14.95 (*1-55609-718-2*); computer disk 29.95 (*1-55609-719-0*) Gallopade Pub Group.

—Mississippi Silly Trivia! (Illus.). (gr. 3 up). 1994. PLB 24.95 (*1-55609-708-5*); pap. 14.95 (*1-55609-039-0*); computer disk 29.95 (*1-55609-714-X*) Gallopade Pub Group.

—Mississippi Timeline: A Chronology of Mississippi History, Mystery, Trivia, Legend, Lore & More. (Illus.). (gr. 3-12). 1994. PLB 24.95 (*0-7933-5947-3*); pap. 14.95 (*0-7933-5948-1*); computer disk 29.95 (*0-7933-5949-X*) Gallopade Pub Group.

—Mississippi's (Most Devastating!) Disasters & (Most Calamitous!) Catastrophies! (Illus.). (gr. 3 up). 1994. PLB 24.95 (*0-7933-0645-0*); pap. 14.95 (*0-7933-0643-4*); computer disk 29.95 (*0-7933-0646-9*) Gallopade Pub Group.

—Mississippi's Unsolved Mysteries (& Their "Solutions") Includes Scientific Information & Other Activities for Students. (Illus.). (gr. 3-12). 1994. PLB 24.95 (*0-7933-5794-2*); pap. 14.95 (*0-7933-5795-0*); computer disk 29.95 (*0-7933-5796-9*) Gallopade Pub Group.

—My First Book about Mississippi. (gr. k-4). 1994. PLB 24.95 (*0-7933-5641-5*); pap. 14.95 (*0-7933-5642-3*); computer disk 29.95 (*0-7933-5643-1*) Gallopade Pub Group.

—Patch, the Pirate Dog: A Mississippi Pet Story. (ps-4). 1994. PLB 24.95 (*0-7933-5488-9*); pap. 14.95 (*0-7933-5489-7*); computer disk 29.95 (*0-7933-5490-0*) Gallopade Pub Group.

—River Rogues! Natchez Pirates, Playboys, & the Rest of the Cock-o-the-Walk Crowd under-the-Hill & along the Trace. 1994. lib. bdg. 24.95 (*0-7933-7584-3*); pap. 14.95 (*0-7933-7323-9*) Gallopade Pub Group.

—Uncle Rebus: Mississippi Picture Stories for Computer Kids. (Illus.). (gr. k-3). 1994. PLB 24.95 (*0-7933-4573-1*); pap. 14.95 (*0-7933-4574-X*); disk 29.95 (*0-7933-4575-8*) Gallopade Pub Group.

Ready, Anna. Mississippi. LC 92-31056. 1993. PLB 17.50 (*0-8225-2743-X*) Lerner Pubns.

Thompson, Kathleen. Mississippi. LC 87-16440. 48p. (gr. 3 up). 1987. 19.97 (*0-86514-467-2*) Raintree Steck-V.

MISSISSIPPI–FICTION

Ball, Zachary. Bristle Face. LC 93-10394. 208p. (gr. 5 up). 1993. pap. 3.99 (*0-14-036444-7*, Puffin) Puffin Bks.

Naylor, Phyllis R. Night Cry. LC 83-15569. 168p. (gr. 5-9). 1984. SBE 14.95 (*0-689-31017-X*, Atheneum Child Bk) Macmillan Child Grp.

Taylor, Mildred D. Mississippi Bridge. Ginsberg, Max, illus. (gr. 4-7). 1992. pap. 3.50 (*0-553-15992-5*, Skylark) Bantam.

—The Road to Memphis. 304p. (gr. 5-9). 1992. pap. 3.99 (*0-14-036077-8*, Puffin) Puffin Bks.

Twain, Mark. Adventures of Huckleberry Finn. (Illus.). (gr. 4-7). 1991. pap. 6.50 (*0-582-03585-6*) Longman.

—The Adventures of Tom Sawyer. Moser, Barry, illus. Glassman, Peter, afterword by. LC 89-60838. (Illus.). 272p. (ps up). 1989. 21.95 (*0-688-07510-X*) Morrow Jr Bks.

—Adventures of Tom Sawyer. 1991. pap. text ed. 6.50 (*0-582-03588-0*) Longman.

MISSISSIPPI RIVER

Holling, Holling C. Minn of the Mississippi. (Illus.). (gr. 4-6). 1992. 16.95 (*0-395-17578-X*) HM.

McCall, Edith. Biography of a River: The Mississippi. (Illus.). (gr. 7 up). 1990. 16.95 (*0-8027-6914-4*); lib. bdg. 17.85 (*0-8027-6915-2*) Walker & Co.

—Mississippi Steamboatman: The Story of Henry Miller Shreve. LC 85-13795. (Illus.). 115p. (gr. 5-8). 1986. 11.95 (*0-8027-6597-1*) Walker & Co.

Middleton, Pat. Mississippi River Activity Guide. (Illus.). 32p. (gr. 4-7). 1993. pap. 5.50 (*0-9620823-5-X*) Heritage WI.

Morgan, Nina. The Mississippi. Fordyce, Lawrence, illus. LC 92-39950. 48p. (gr. 5-6). 1993. PLB 22.80 (*0-8114-3103-7*) Raintree Steck-V.

MISSISSIPPI RIVER–FICTION

Adventures of Tom Sawyer. 1993. pap. text ed. 6.50 (*0-582-09677-4*, 79814) Longman.

Clemens, Samuel. Huckleberry Finn. Farr, Naunerle, ed. Redondo, Francisco, illus. LC 73-75468. 64p. (Orig.). (gr. 5-10). 1973. pap. 2.95 (*0-88301-098-4*) Pendulum Pr.

—Tom Sawyer. new ed. Shapiro, Irwin, ed. Cruz, E. R., illus. LC 73-75465. 64p. (Orig.). (gr. 5-10). 1973. pap. 2.95 (*0-88301-103-4*); student activity bk. 1.25 (*0-88301-179-4*) Pendulum Pr.

Clements, Bruce. I Tell a Lie Every So Often. LC 73-22356. 160p. (gr. 5 up). 1984. pap. 3.50 (*0-374-43539-1*) FS&G.

Fichter, George S. First Steamboat down the Mississippi. Boddy, Joe, illus. LC 88-30308. 112p. (gr. 4-6). 1989. 9.95 (*0-88289-715-2*) Pelican.

Holling, Holling C. Minn of the Mississippi. Holling, Holling C., illus. (gr. 4-6). 1978. pap. 7.70 (*0-395-27399-4*) HM.

Koste, Virginia G. The Trial of Tom Sawyer. (gr. 4 up). 1978. 4.50 (*0-87602-213-1*) Anchorage.
Stevermer, C. River Rats. 1992. 16.95 (*0-15-200895-0*, HB Juv Bks) HarBrace.
Twain, Mark. The Adventures of Huckleberry Finn. LC 85-9576. (gr. 5 up). 1962. pap. 2.75 (*0-8049-0004-3*, CL-4) Airmont.
—Adventures of Huckleberry Finn. McKay, Donald & Polseno, Jo, illus. LC 85-9576. 448p. (gr. 4-6). 1981. 14.95 (*0-448-06000-0*, G&D); (G&D) Putnam Pub Group.
—Adventures of Huckleberry Finn. LC 85-9576. (gr. 3-7). 1983. pap. 2.99 (*0-14-035007-1*, Puffin Bks) Puffin Bks.
—Adventures of Huckleberry Finn. Kellogg, Steven, illus. Glassman, Peter, afterword by. LC 92-27398. (Illus.). 1993. write for info. (*0-688-10656-0*) Morrow Jr Bks.
—Adventures of Huckleberry Finn. Date not set. pap. 2.95 (*0-590-43389-X*) Scholastic Inc.
—The Adventures of Tom Sawyer. LC 63-19420. (gr. 5 up). 1964. pap. 2.95 (*0-8049-0006-X*, CL-6) Airmont.
—Adventures of Tom Sawyer. McKay, Donald & Polseno, Jo, illus. LC 62-19420. (gr. 4-6). 1981. 13.95 (*0-448-06002-7*, G&D); (G&D) Putnam Pub Group.
—The Adventures of Tom Sawyer. LC 62-19420. 224p. (gr. 3-7). 1983. pap. 2.99 (*0-14-035003-9*, Puffin) Puffin Bks.
Twain, Mark, pseud. Adventures of Tom Sawyer. Gise, Joanne, adapted by. James, Raymond, illus. LC 89-20559. 48p. (gr. 3-6). 1990. lib. bdg. 12.89 (*0-8167-1859-8*); pap. text ed. 3.95 (*0-8167-1860-1*) Troll Assocs.
Twain, Mark. Adventures of Tom Sawyer. 1989. 12.99 (*0-517-68813-1*) Random Hse Value.
—The Adventures of Tom Sawyer. Aagaard, Gary, illus. 304p. (gr. 5 up). 1992. 24.95 (*1-879329-08-5*) Time Warner Libraries.
—Adventures of Tom Sawyer. 1993. pap. 2.95 (*0-590-43352-0*) Scholastic Inc.
Twain, Mark, pseud. The Adventures of Tom Sawyer. McKay, Donald & Wimmer, Michael, illus. LC 93-50909. 1994. 14.95 (*0-448-40560-1*, G&D) Putnam Pub Group.
Twain, Mark. Adventures of Tom Sawyer & Adventures of Huckleberry Finn. Dickey, James, intro. by. 1979. pap. 4.95 (*0-451-52272-9*) NAL-Dutton.
Twain, Mark, pseud. Aventures de Tom Sawyer. Lapointe, Claude, illus. (FRE.). 296p. (gr. 5-10). 1987. pap. 9.95 (*2-07-033449-X*) Schoenhof.
Twain, Mark. Huckleberry Finn. Stewart, Diana, adapted by. Neidigh, Sherry, illus. LC 79-24312. 48p. (gr. 4 up). 1983. PLB 20.70 (*0-8172-1651-0*) Raintree Steck-V.
Twain, Mark, pseud. Huckleberry Finn. Vogel, Nathaele, illus. (FRE.). 380p. (gr. 5-10). 1990. pap. 10.95 (*2-07-033230-6*) Schoenhof.
—Huckleberry Finn. (gr. 4-7). 1993. pap. 4.95 (*0-8114-6826-7*) Raintree Steck-V.
Twain, Mark. Life on the Mississippi. Willoughby, J., intro. by. (gr. 9 up). 1965. pap. 1.95 (*0-8049-0055-8*, CL-55) Airmont.
—Reader's Digest Best Loved Books for Young Readers: The Adventures of Huckleberry Finn. Ogburn, Jackie, ed. Falter, John, illus. 192p. (gr. 4-12). 1989. 3.99 (*0-945260-30-X*) Choice Pub NY.
—Reader's Digest Best Loved Books for Young Readers: The Adventures of Tom Sawyer. Ogburn, Jackie, ed. Falter, John, illus. 136p. (gr. 4-12). 1989. 3.99 (*0-945260-19-9*) Choice Pub NY.
Twain, Mark, pseud. Tom Sawyer. (gr. 4-7). 1993. pap. 4.95 (*0-8114-6843-7*) Raintree Steck-V.
Twain, Mark. Tom Sawyer Abroad. Rowland, B., intro. by. Bd. with Tom Sawyer Detective. (gr. 5up). 1966. pap. 1.50 (*0-8049-0126-0*, CL-126) Airmont.
Twain, Mark & Ploog, Michael. Tom Sawyer. (Illus.). 52p. Date not set. pap. 4.95 (*1-57209-007-3*) Classics Int Ent.
Warner, Gertrude C., created by. The Haunted Cabin Mystery. (Illus.). (gr. 2-7). 1991. 10.95g (*0-8075-3179-0*); pap. 3.50g (*0-8075-3178-2*) A Whitman.

MISSISSIPPI VALLEY

see also Middle West

Morgan, Nina. The Mississippi. Fordyce, Lawrence, illus. LC 92-39950. 48p. (gr. 5-6). 1993. PLB 22.80 (*0-8114-3103-7*) Raintree Steck-V.

MISSISSIPPI VALLEY–HISTORY

Badt, Karin L. The Mississippi Flood of 1993. LC 94-9493. (Illus.). 32p. (gr. 3-6). 1994. PLB 16.40 (*0-516-06680-3*) Childrens.

MISSOURI

Aylesworth, Thomas G. & Aylesworth, Virginia L. South Central (Louisiana, Arkansas, Missouri, Kansas, Oklahoma) (Illus.). 64p. (gr. 3 up). 1992. PLB 16.95 (*0-7910-1047-3*) Chelsea Hse.
Bradley, Melvin. Mules: Missouri's Long Eared Miners. Gwin, Paul, ed. (Illus.). 116p. (Orig.). 1987. pap. 7.50 (*0-933842-06-6*) Extension Div.
Carole Marsh Missouri Books, 44 bks. 1994. PLB 1027.80 set (*0-7933-1300-7*); pap. 587.80 (*0-7933-5172-3*) Gallopade Pub Group.
Carpenter, Allan. Missouri. LC 78-3551. (Illus.). 96p. (gr. 4 up). 1978. PLB 16.95 (*0-516-04125-8*) Childrens.
Fradin, Dennis. Missouri: In Words & Pictures. Wahl, Richard, illus. LC 80-12249. 48p. (gr. 2-5). 1980. PLB 12.95 (*0-516-03925-3*) Childrens.
Fradin, Dennis B. Missouri - From Sea to Shining Sea. LC 93-32675. (Illus.). 64p. (gr. 3-5). 1994. PLB 16.45 (*0-516-03825-7*) Childrens.
McCandless, Perry & Foley, William E. Missouri: Then & Now. rev. ed. LC 90-32545. (Illus.). 328p. (gr. 4). 1992. text ed. 19.95 (*0-8262-0825-8*) U of Mo Pr.
Marsh, Carole. Avast, Ye Slobs!: Missouri Pirate Trivia. (Illus.). (gr. 3 up). 1994. PLB 24.95 (*0-7933-0690-6*); pap. 14.95 (*0-7933-0689-2*); computer disk 29.95 (*0-7933-0691-4*) Gallopade Pub Group.
—The Beast of the Missouri Bed & Breakfast. (Illus.). (gr. 3 up). 1994. PLB 24.95 (*0-7933-1734-7*); pap. 14.95 (*0-7933-1735-5*); computer disk 29.95 (*0-685-45946-2*) Gallopade Pub Group.
—Bow Wow! Missouri Dogs in History, Mystery, Legend, Lore, Humor & More! (Illus.). (gr. 3-12). 1994. PLB 24.95 (*0-7933-3542-6*); pap. 14.95 (*0-7933-3543-4*); computer disk 29.95 (*0-7933-3544-2*) Gallopade Pub Group.
—Chill Out: Scary Missouri Tales Based on Frightening Missouri Truths. (Illus.). 1994. lib. bdg. 24.95 (*0-7933-4729-7*); pap. 14.95 (*0-7933-4730-0*); disk 29.95 (*0-7933-4731-9*) Gallopade Pub Group.
—Christopher Columbus Comes to Missouri! Includes Reproducible Activities for Kids! (Illus.). (gr. 3-12). 1994. PLB 24.95 (*0-7933-3695-3*); pap. 14.95 (*0-7933-3696-1*); computer disk 29.95 (*0-7933-3697-X*) Gallopade Pub Group.
—The Hard-to-Believe-But-True! Book of Missouri History, Mystery, Trivia, Legend, Lore, Humor & More. (Illus.). (gr. 3 up). 1994. PLB 24.95 (*0-7933-0687-6*); pap. 14.95 (*0-7933-0686-8*); computer disk 29.95 (*0-7933-0688-4*) Gallopade Pub Group.
—If My Missouri Mama Ran the World! (Illus.). (gr. 3 up). 1994. lib. bdg. 24.95 (*0-7933-1737-1*); pap. 14.95 (*0-7933-1738-X*); computer disk 29.95 (*0-7933-1739-8*) Gallopade Pub Group.
—Jurassic Ark! Missouri Dinosaurs & Other Prehistoric Creatures. (gr. k-12). 1994. PLB 24.95 (*0-7933-7503-7*); pap. 14.95 (*0-7933-7504-5*); computer disk 29.95 (*0-7933-7505-3*) Gallopade Pub Group.
—Let's Quilt Missouri & Stuff It Topographically! (Illus.). (gr. 3 up). 1994. PLB 24.95 (*1-55609-733-6*); pap. 14.95 (*1-55609-734-4*); computer disk 29.95 (*1-55609-735-2*) Gallopade Pub Group.
—Let's Quilt Our Missouri County. 1994. lib. bdg. 24.95 (*0-7933-7188-0*); pap. text ed. 14.95 (*0-7933-7189-9*); disk 29.95 (*0-7933-7190-2*) Gallopade Pub Group.
—Let's Quilt Our Missouri Town. 1994. lib. bdg. 24.95 (*0-7933-7038-8*); pap. text ed. 14.95 (*0-7933-7039-6*); disk 29.95 (*0-7933-7040-X*) Gallopade Pub Group.
—Meow! Missouri Cats in History, Mystery, Legend, Lore, Humor & More! (Illus.). (gr. 3-12). 1994. PLB 24.95 (*0-7933-3389-X*); pap. 14.95 (*0-7933-3390-3*); computer disk 29.95 (*0-7933-3391-1*) Gallopade Pub Group.
—Missouri & Other State Greats (Biographies) (Illus.). (gr. 3 up). 1994. PLB 24.95 (*1-55609-748-4*); pap. 14.95 (*1-55609-749-2*); computer disk 29.95 (*1-55609-750-6*) Gallopade Pub Group.
—Missouri Bandits, Bushwackers, Outlaws, Crooks, Devils, Ghosts, Desperadoes & Other Assorted & Sundry Characters! (Illus.). (gr. 3 up). 1994. PLB 24.95 (*0-7933-0672-8*); pap. 14.95 (*0-7933-0671-X*); computer disk 29.95 (*0-7933-0673-6*) Gallopade Pub Group.
—Missouri Classic Christmas Trivia: Stories, Recipes, Activities, Legends, Lore & More. (Illus.). (gr. 3 up). 1994. PLB 24.95 (*0-7933-0675-2*); pap. 14.95 (*0-7933-0674-4*); computer disk 29.95 (*0-7933-0676-0*) Gallopade Pub Group.
—Missouri Coastales. (Illus.). (gr. 3 up). 1994. PLB 24.95 (*1-55609-742-5*); pap. 14.95 (*1-55609-743-3*); computer disk 29.95 (*1-55609-744-1*) Gallopade Pub Group.
—Missouri Coastales! 1994. lib. bdg. 24.95 (*0-7933-7290-9*) Gallopade Pub Group.
—Missouri "Crinkum-Crankum" A Funny Word Book about Our State. (Illus.). 1994. lib. bdg. 24.95 (*0-7933-4883-8*); pap. 14.95 (*0-7933-4884-6*); disk 29.95 (*0-7933-4885-4*) Gallopade Pub Group.
—Missouri Dingbats! Bk. 1: A Fun Book of Games, Stories, Activities & More about Our State That's All in Code! for You to Decipher. (Illus.). (gr. 3-12). 1994. PLB 24.95 (*0-7933-3848-4*); pap. 14.95 (*0-7933-3849-2*); computer disk 29.95 (*0-7933-3850-6*) Gallopade Pub Group.
—Missouri Festival Fun for Kids! (Illus.). (gr. 3-12). 1994. lib. bdg. 24.95 (*0-7933-4001-2*); pap. 14.95 (*0-7933-4002-0*); disk 29.95 (*0-7933-4003-9*) Gallopade Pub Group.
—The Missouri Hot Air Balloon Mystery. (Illus.). (gr. 2-9). 1994. 24.95 (*0-7933-2543-9*); pap. 14.95 (*0-7933-2544-7*); computer disk 29.95 (*0-7933-2545-5*) Gallopade Pub Group.
—Missouri Jeopardy! Answers & Questions about Our State! (Illus.). (gr. 3-12). 1994. PLB 24.95 (*0-7933-4154-X*); pap. 14.95 (*0-7933-4155-8*); computer disk 29.95 (*0-7933-4156-6*) Gallopade Pub Group.
—Missouri "Jography" A Fun Run Thru Our State. (Illus.). (gr. 3 up). 1994. PLB 24.95 (*1-55609-730-1*); pap. 14.95 (*1-55609-731-X*); computer disk 29.95 (*1-55609-732-8*) Gallopade Pub Group.
—Missouri Kid's Cookbook: Recipes, How-To, History, Lore & More. (Illus.). (gr. 3 up). 1994. PLB 24.95 (*0-7933-0684-1*); pap. 14.95 (*0-7933-0683-3*); computer disk 29.95 (*0-7933-0685-X*) Gallopade Pub Group.
—The Missouri Mystery Van Takes Off! Book 1: Handicapped Missouri Kids Sneak Off on a Big Adventure. (Illus.). (gr. 3-12). 1994. 24.95 (*0-7933-5036-0*); pap. 14.95 (*0-7933-5037-9*); computer disk 29.95 (*0-7933-5038-7*) Gallopade Pub Group.
—Missouri Quiz Bowl Crash Course! (Illus.). (gr. 3 up). 1994. PLB 24.95 (*1-55609-745-X*); pap. 14.95 (*1-55609-746-8*); computer disk 29.95 (*1-55609-747-6*) Gallopade Pub Group.
—Missouri Rollercoasters! (Illus.). (gr. 3-12). 1994. PLB 24.95 (*0-7933-5299-1*); pap. 14.95 (*0-7933-5300-9*); computer disk 29.95 (*0-7933-5301-7*) Gallopade Pub Group.
—Missouri School Trivia: An Amazing & Fascinating Look at Our State's Teachers, Schools & Students! (Illus.). (gr. 3 up). 1994. PLB 24.95 (*0-7933-0681-7*); pap. 14.95 (*0-7933-0680-9*); computer disk 29.95 (*0-7933-0682-5*) Gallopade Pub Group.
—Missouri Silly Basketball Sportsmysteries, Vol. II. (Illus.). (gr. 3 up). 1994. PLB 24.95 (*0-7933-1740-1*); pap. 14.95 (*0-7933-1741-X*); computer disk 29.95 (*0-7933-1742-8*) Gallopade Pub Group.
—Missouri Silly Football Sportsmysteries, Vol. II. (Illus.). (gr. 3 up). 1994. PLB 24.95 (*1-55609-739-5*); pap. 14.95 (*1-55609-740-9*); computer disk 29.95 (*1-55609-741-7*) Gallopade Pub Group.
—Missouri Silly Trivia! (Illus.). (gr. 3 up). 1994. PLB 24.95 (*1-55609-728-X*); pap. 14.95 (*1-55609-100-1*); computer disk 29.95 (*1-55609-729-8*) Gallopade Pub Group.
—Missouri Timeline: A Chronology of Missouri History, Mystery, Trivia, Legend, Lore & More. (Illus.). (gr. 3-12). 1994. PLB 24.95 (*0-7933-5950-3*); pap. 14.95 (*0-7933-5951-1*); computer disk 29.95 (*0-7933-5952-X*) Gallopade Pub Group.
—Missouri's (Most Devastating!) Disasters & (Most Calamitous!) Catastrophies! (Illus.). (gr. 3 up). 1994. PLB 24.95 (*0-7933-0669-8*); pap. 14.95 (*0-7933-0668-X*); computer disk 29.95 (*0-7933-0670-1*) Gallopade Pub Group.
—Missouri's Unsolved Mysteries (& Their "Solutions") Includes Scientific Information & Other Activities for Students. (Illus.). (gr. 3-12). 1994. PLB 24.95 (*0-7933-5797-7*); pap. 14.95 (*0-7933-5798-5*); computer disk 29.95 (*0-7933-5799-3*) Gallopade Pub Group.
—My First Book about Missouri. (gr. k-4). 1994. PLB 24.95 (*0-7933-5644-X*); pap. 14.95 (*0-7933-5645-8*); computer disk 29.95 (*0-7933-5646-6*) Gallopade Pub Group.
—Patch, the Pirate Dog: A Missouri Pet Story. (ps-4). 1994. PLB 24.95 (*0-7933-5491-9*); pap. 14.95 (*0-7933-5492-7*); computer disk 29.95 (*0-7933-5493-5*) Gallopade Pub Group.
—Uncle Rebus: Missouri Picture Stories for Computer Kids. (Illus.). (gr. k-3). 1994. PLB 24.95 (*0-7933-4576-6*); pap. 14.95 (*0-7933-4577-4*); disk 29.95 (*0-7933-4578-2*) Gallopade Pub Group.
Sanford, William R. & Green, Carl R. Missouri. LC 89-35082. 144p. (gr. 4 up). 1989. PLB 20.55 (*0-516-00471-9*) Childrens.
—Missouri. 205p. 1993. text ed. 15.40 (*1-56956-171-0*) W A T Braille.
Stacy, Darryl. Missouri: Studies. Stacy, Darryl, illus. 56p. (gr. 7-9). 1988. wkbk. 5.25 (*0-911981-51-9*) Cloud Pub.
Stacy, Darryl & Bimes, James D. Missouri: Studies: Government & Constitution. Stacy, Darryl, illus. 120p. (gr. 7-9). 1989. Repr. of 1988 ed. text ed. 15.95 (*0-911981-50-0*) Cloud Pub.
Sturman, Susan. Kansas City. LC 90-25614. (Illus.). 60p. (gr. 3 up). 1990. text ed. 13.95 RSBE (*0-87518-432-4*, Dillon) Macmillan Child Grp.
Thompson, Kathleen. Missouri. 48p. (gr. 3 up). 1985. PLB 19.97 (*0-86514-436-2*) Raintree Steck-V.

MISSOURI–FICTION

Clemens, Samuel. Huckleberry Finn. Farr, Naunerle, ed. Redondo, Francisco, illus. LC 73-75468. 64p. (Orig.). (gr. 5-10). 1973. pap. 2.95 (*0-88301-098-4*) Pendulum Pr.
—Tom Sawyer. new ed. Shapiro, Irwin, ed. Cruz, E. R., illus. LC 73-75465. 64p. (Orig.). (gr. 5-10). 1973. pap. 2.95 (*0-88301-103-4*); student activity bk. 1.25 (*0-88301-179-4*) Pendulum Pr.
Clements, Bruce. I Tell a Lie Every So Often. LC 73-22356. 160p. (gr. 5 up). 1984. pap. 3.50 (*0-374-43539-1*) FS&G.
MacBride, Roger L. Little House on Rocky Ridge. Gilleece, David, illus. LC 92-39132. 368p. (gr. 3-7). 1993. 14.95 (*0-06-020842-2*); PLB 14.89 (*0-06-020843-0*) HarpC Child Bks.
—Little House on Rocky Ridge. Gilleece, David, illus. LC 92-39132. 368p. (gr. 3-7). 1993. pap. 3.95 (*0-06-440478-1*, Trophy) HarpC Child Bks.
Marsh, Carole. Missouri Silly Basketball Sportsmysteries, Vol. I. (Illus.). (gr. 3 up). 1994. PLB 24.95 (*0-7933-0678-7*); pap. 14.95 (*0-7933-0677-9*); computer disk 29.95 (*0-685-45947-0*) Gallopade Pub Group.
Nixon, Joan L. A Dangerous Promise. LC 94-464. 1994. 15.95 (*0-385-32073-6*) Delacorte.

Tedrow, T. L. Days of Laura Ingalls Wilder, Vol. 2: Children of Promise. LC 92-1041. 1992. pap. 4.99 (*0-8407-3398-4*) Nelson.
—Days of Laura Ingalls Wilder, Vol. 3: Good Neighbors. 1992. pap. 4.99 (*0-8407-3399-2*) Nelson.
—Days of Laura Ingalls Wilder, Vol. 4: Home to the Prairie. 1992. pap. 4.99 (*0-8407-3401-8*) Nelson.
—Land of Promise. LC 92-28222. 1992. 4.99 (*0-8407-7735-3*) Nelson.
Twain, Mark. The Adventures of Huckleberry Finn. LC 85-9576. (gr. 5 up). 1962. pap. 2.75 (*0-8049-0004-3*, CL-4) Airmont.
—Adventures of Huckleberry Finn. McKay, Donald & Polseno, Jo, illus. LC 85-9576. 448p. (gr. 4-6). 1981. 14.95 (*0-448-06000-0*, G&D); (G&D) Putnam Pub Group.
—Adventures of Huckleberry Finn. LC 85-9576. (gr. 3-7). 1983. pap. 2.99 (*0-14-035007-1*, Puffin Bks) Puffin Bks.
—The Adventures of Huckleberry Finn. LC 85-9576. 384p. (gr. 4-6). 1986. pap. 4.95 (*0-14-039046-4*, Penguin Classics) Viking Penguin.
—Adventures of Huckleberry Finn. Kellogg, Steven, illus. Glassman, Peter, afterword by. LC 92-27398. (Illus.). 1993. write for info. (*0-688-10656-0*) Morrow Jr Bks.
—Adventures of Huckleberry Finn. Date not set. pap. 2.95 (*0-590-43389-X*) Scholastic Inc.
—The Adventures of Tom Sawyer. LC 63-19420. (gr. 5 up). 1964. pap. 2.95 (*0-8049-0006-X*, CL-6) Airmont.
—Adventures of Tom Sawyer. McKay, Donald & Polseno, Jo, illus. LC 62-19420. (gr. 4-6). 1981. 13.95 (*0-448-06002-7*, G&D); (G&D) Putnam Pub Group.
—The Adventures of Tom Sawyer. LC 62-19420. 224p. (gr. 3-7). 1983. pap. 2.99 (*0-14-035003-9*, Puffin) Puffin Bks.
Twain, Mark, pseud. Adventures of Tom Sawyer. Gise, Joanne, adapted by. James, Raymond, illus. LC 89-20559. 48p. (gr. 3-6). 1990. lib. bdg. 12.89 (*0-8167-1859-8*); pap. text ed. 3.95 (*0-8167-1860-1*) Troll Assocs.
Twain, Mark. Adventures of Tom Sawyer. 1989. 12.99 (*0-517-68813-1*) Random Hse Value.
—The Adventures of Tom Sawyer. Aagaard, Gary, illus. 304p. (gr. 5 up). 1992. 24.95 (*1-879329-08-5*) Time Warner Libraries.
Twain, Mark, pseud. The Adventures of Tom Sawyer. McKay, Donald & Wimmer, Michael, illus. LC 93-50909. 1994. 14.95 (*0-448-40560-1*, G&D) Putnam Pub Group.
Twain, Mark. Adventures of Tom Sawyer & Adventures of Huckleberry Finn. Dickey, James, intro. by. 1979. pap. 4.95 (*0-451-52272-9*) NAL-Dutton.
—Huckleberry Finn. Stewart, Diana, adapted by. Neidigh, Sherry, illus. LC 79-24312. 48p. (gr. 4 up). 1983. PLB 20.70 (*0-8172-1651-0*) Raintree Steck-V.
—Life on the Mississippi. Willoughby, J., intro. by. (gr. 9 up). 1965. pap. 1.95 (*0-8049-0055-8*, CL-55) Airmont.
—Tom Sawyer Abroad. Rowland, B., intro. by. Bd. with Tom Sawyer Detective. (gr. 5up). 1966. pap. 1.50 (*0-8049-0126-0*, CL-126) Airmont.

MISSOURI VALLEY
Freedman, Russell. An Indian Winter. Bodmer, Karl, illus. LC 91-24205. 96p. (gr. 5 up). 1992. 21.95 (*0-8234-0930-9*) Holiday.
Wilder, Laura I. On the Way Home. Lane, Rose W., ed. LC 62-17966. (Illus.). 112p. (gr. 7 up). 1962. 14.00 (*0-06-026489-6*); PLB 13.89 (*0-06-026490-X*) HarpC Child Bks.

MITCHELL, MARIA, 1818-1889
McPherson, Stephanie. Rooftop Astronomer: A Story about Maria Mitchell. Mitchell, Hetty, illus. 32p. (gr. 3-6). 1990. PLB 14.95 (*0-87614-410-5*) Carolrhoda Bks.

MOBILES (SCULPTURE)
Williams, Guy R. Making Mobiles. (Illus.). (gr. 7 up). 1969. 11.95 (*0-87523-167-5*) Emerson.
Zubrowski, Bernie. Mobiles. LC 92-28408. (gr. 5 up). 1993. pap. 6.95 (*0-688-10589-0*, Pub. by Beech Tree Bks) Morrow.
—Mobiles: Building & Experimenting with Balancing Toys. Doty, Roy, illus. LC 92-28408. 104p. (gr. 3 up). 1993. Repr. PLB 13.93 (*0-688-10590-4*) Morrow Jr Bks.

MOBS
see Riots

MOCKINGBIRDS
Doughty, Robin W. The Mockingbird. LC 88-736. (Illus.). 80p. (gr. 10-12). 1988. 14.95 (*0-292-75099-4*) U of Tex Pr.

MODEL CAR RACING
Murphy, Fred. Radio-Controlled Action Cars. (Illus.). 24p. (Orig.). 1990. pap. 2.50 (*0-942025-87-3*) Kidsbks.

MODELING
see also Sculpture–Technique
Gibson, R. & Tyler, J. Playdough. (Illus.). 32p. (ps-3). 1989. lib. bdg. 13.96 (*0-88110-413-2*, Usborne); pap. 5.95 (*0-7460-0465-6*) EDC.
Hull, Jeannie. Clay. Fairclough, Chris, photos by. LC 89-9959. (Illus.). 48p. (gr. 3-6). 1989. PLB 12.40 (*0-531-10757-4*) Watts.
Making Models & Games. LC 91-17039. (Illus.). 48p. (gr. 4-8). 1991. PLB 14.95 (*1-85435-409-4*) Marshall Cavendish.
O'Reilly, Susie. Modeling. Mukhida, Zul, photos by. LC 93-7517. (Illus.). 32p. (gr. 4-6). 1993. 14.95 (*1-56847-066-5*) Thomson Lrning.
Slade, Richard. Your Book of Modelling. (gr. 4 up). 1968. 7.95 (*0-571-08387-0*) Transatl Arts.

MODELS, FASHION
Basford, Teri M. Ten Steps to Becoming a Model. (Illus.). 50p. (Orig.). (gr. 9). 1989. pap. write for info.; pap. text ed. write for info. T Mack Glamour.
Keith, Evan. Who's Hot -- Cindy Crawford. (gr. 4-7). 1993. pap. 1.49 (*0-440-21592-7*) Dell.
Moss, Miriam. Fashion Model. LC 90-15082. (Illus.). 32p. (gr. 5-6). 1991. text ed. 13.95 RSBE (*0-89686-609-2*, Crestwood Hse) Macmillan Child Grp.

MODELS, FASHION–FICTION
Green, Yvonne. Rising Star: Kelly Blake, Teen Model, No. 2. 176p. (gr. 7-12). 1986. pap. 2.50 (*0-553-25639-4*) Bantam.
Greene, Yvonne. Double Trouble. 160p. (Orig.). (gr. 7-12). 1986. pap. 2.50 (*0-553-26154-1*) Bantam.
—Hard to Get-Kelly Blake. 176p. (Orig.). (gr. 7-12). 1986. pap. 2.50 (*0-553-26037-5*) Bantam.
—Headliners-Kelly Blake. 160p. (Orig.). (gr. 7-12). 1986. pap. 2.50 (*0-553-26112-6*) Bantam.
—Paris Nights, No. 6. 160p. (Orig.). (gr. 7-12). 1987. pap. 2.50 (*0-553-26199-1*) Bantam.
Hunt, Angela E. Cassie Perkins, No. 7: Star Light, Star Bright. LC 92-18796. 1993. 4.99 (*0-8423-1117-3*) Tyndale.
Weyn, Suzanne. Chloe Mania! LC 93-42853. (Illus.). 128p. (gr. 4-8). 1994. PLB 9.89 (*0-8167-3233-7*); pap. text ed. 2.95 (*0-8167-3234-5*) Troll Assocs.
—Nicole's Chance. LC 93-14022. (Illus.). 128p. (gr. 4-8). 1993. PLB 9.89 (*0-8167-3235-3*); pap. 2.95 (*0-8167-3236-1*) Troll Assocs.
—Tracey's Tough Choice. LC 93-25185. (Illus.). 128p. (gr. 4-8). 1993. PLB 9.89 (*0-8167-3237-X*); pap. 2.95 (*0-8167-3238-8*) Troll Assocs.

MODELS, FASHION–VOCATIONAL GUIDANCE
Lee, Anna. Modeling & You! Lee, Tommy, illus. 117p. (Orig.). (gr. 6-12). 1991. pap. 12.95 (*0-9629647-0-0*) CUE Pubns.

MODELS, MECHANICAL
see Machinery–Models

MODELS AND MODEL MAKING
see also names of objects with the subdivision Models, e.g. Airplanes–Models
Bawden, Juliet. One Hundred One Things to Make: Fun Craft Projects with Everyday Materials. Pang, Alex, illus. LC 93-29633. 104p. 1994. 14.95 (*0-8069-0596-4*) Sterling.
Boy Scouts of America. Model Design & Building. (Illus.). 44p. (gr. 6-12). 1964. pap. 1.85 (*0-8395-3280-6*, 33280) BSA.
Bulloch, Ivan. Play with Models. LC 94-14248. (gr. 1 up). 1994. write for info. (*0-87614-866-6*) Carolrhoda Bks.
Cummings, Richard. Make Your Own Model Forts & Castles. Cummings, Richard, illus. (gr. 6 up). 1977. 8.95 (*0-679-20400-8*) McKay.
Goodman, Michael E. Radio Control Models. LC 91-47750. (Illus.). 48p. (gr. 5-6). 1993. text ed. 12.95 RSBE (*0-89686-622-X*, Crestwood Hse) Macmillan Child Grp.
Green, Jen. Making Mad Machines. (Illus.). 32p. (gr. 2-4). 1992. PLB 12.40 (*0-531-17326-7*, Gloucester Pr) Watts.
Hamilton-MacLaren, Alistair. Houses & Homes. LC 91-23026. (Illus.). 48p. (gr. 5-7). 1992. PLB 12.90 (*0-531-18424-2*, Pub. by Bookwright Pr) Watts.
—Water Transportation. LC 91-16195. (Illus.). 48p. (gr. 4-8). 1992. PLB 12.90 (*0-531-18414-5*, Pub. by Bookwright Pr) Watts.
Harris, Jack C. Plastic Model Kits. LC 91-25201. (Illus.). 48p. (gr. 5-6). 1993. text ed. 12.95 RSBE (*0-89686-623-8*, Crestwood Hse) Macmillan Child Grp.
Lambert, David & Wright, Rachel. Dinosaurs. LC 91-21118. (Illus.). 32p. (gr. 4-6). 1992. PLB 11.90 (*0-531-14159-4*) Watts.
Marks, Leonard. Make a Model Starship Enterprise. 1990. pap. 5.99 (*0-517-06030-2*) Random Hse Value.
Maxwell, Colin. Model Making. (Illus.). 48p. (gr. 5-8). 1992. PLB 12.40 (*0-531-14195-0*) Watts.
Oxlade, Chris. Canals & Waterways. Pyke, Jeremy, illus. Chillmaid, Marty, photos by. LC 93-49749. (Illus.). 1994. write for info. (*0-531-14331-7*) Watts.
Smolinsky, Jill. Super Models. 32p. (Orig.). (gr. 3-7). 1993. pap. 2.95 (*1-56565-055-7*) Lowell Hse.
Ward, Brian. Flying Models. LC 92-9908. 1993. 12.40 (*0-531-14241-8*) Watts.
Watermill Press Staff. Columbus Model Book. (gr. 4-7). 1992. pap. 9.95 (*0-8167-2748-1*) Troll Assocs.

MODERN CIVILIZATION
see Civilization, Modern

MODERN HISTORY
see History, Modern

MODERN PHILOSOPHY
see Philosophy, Modern

MOHAMMED, 570?-632
Alladin, Bilzik. Story of Mohammad the Prophet. Anand, B. M., illus. (gr. 3-10). 1979. 7.25 (*0-89744-139-7*) Auromere.
Burrill, Richard, ed. Closest to God: The Life-Stories of Muhammad & the Five God-Men of History. (gr. 9-12). 1990. 17.95 (*1-878464-06-X*); pap. 10.95 (*1-878464-07-8*) Anthro Co.
Hashim, A. S. Life of Prophet Muhammad-I. pap. 7.50 (*1-56744-125-4*) Kazi Pubns.
—Life of Prophet Muhammad-II. pap. 6.50 (*1-56744-126-2*) Kazi Pubns.

MOLECULAR BIOCHEMISTRY
see Molecular Biology

MOLECULAR BIOLOGY
Newton, David. James Watson & Francis Crick. (Illus.). 128p. (gr. 7-12). 1992. lib. bdg. 16.95x (*0-8160-2558-4*) Facts on File.

MOLECULAR BIOPHYSICS
see Molecular Biology

MOLECULES
Bains, Rae. Molecules & Atoms. Harriton, Chuck, illus. LC 84-2712. 32p. (gr. 3-6). 1985. PLB 9.49 (*0-8167-0284-5*); pap. text ed. 2.95 (*0-8167-0285-3*) Troll Assocs.
Mebane, Robert C. & Rybolt, Thomas R. Adventures with Atoms & Molecules, Bk. I: Chemistry Experiments for Young People. Perkins, Ronald I., intro. by. LC 85-10177. (Illus.). 82p. (gr. 4-9). 1985. lib. bdg. 16.95 (*0-89490-120-6*) Enslow Pubs.
—Adventures with Atoms & Molecules, Bk. II: Chemistry Experiments for Young People. Perkins, Ronald I., intro. by. LC 85-10177. (Illus.). 96p. (gr. 4-9). 1987. lib. bdg. 16.95 (*0-89490-164-8*) Enslow Pubs.
—Adventures with Atoms & Molecules, Bk. III: Chemistry Experiments for Young People. LC 85-10177. (Illus.). 96p. (gr. 4-9). 1991. lib. bdg. 16.95 (*0-89490-254-7*) Enslow Pubs.
—Adventures with Atoms & Molecules, Bk. IV: Chemistry Experiments for Young People. LC 85-10177. (Illus.). 96p. (gr. 4-9). 1992. lib. bdg. 16.95 (*0-89490-336-5*) Enslow Pubs.
Roxbee-Cox, P. Atoms & Molecules. (Illus.). 32p. (gr. 6-9). 1993. PLB 13.96 (*0-88110-589-9*); pap. 6.95 (*0-7460-0988-7*) EDC.

MOLES (ANIMALS)
George, Jean C. The Moon of the Moles. Rothman, Michael, illus. LC 91-14535. 48p. (gr. 3-7). 1992. 15.00 (*0-06-020258-0*); PLB 14.89 (*0-06-020259-9*) HarpC Child Bks.

MOLES (ANIMALS)–FICTION
Bos, Burny. Meet the Molesons. De Beer, Hans, illus. James, J. Alison, tr. (Illus.). 48p. (gr. 2-4). 1994. 12.95 (*1-55858-257-6*); lib. bdg. 12.88 (*1-55858-258-4*) North-South Bks NYC.
Buchanan, Elizabeth. Mole Moves House. 1989. 9.95 (*0-385-26538-7*); PLB 10.99 (*0-385-26539-5*) Doubleday.
Cushman. Mouse & Mole & the Christmas Walk. 1994. text ed. write for info. (*0-7167-6560-8*) W H Freeman.
Edwards, Richard. Moles Can Dance. Anstey, Caroline, illus. LC 93-2462. 32p. (ps up). 1994. 13.95 (*1-56402-361-3*) Candlewick Pr.
Finger, Charles J. Tales from Silver Lands. 1989. pap. 3.25 (*0-590-42447-5*) Scholastic Inc.
Greenleaf, Ann. Max & Molly's Fall. 1993. 4.99 (*0-517-09155-0*) Random Hse Value.
—Max & Molly's Winter. 1993. 4.99 (*0-517-09152-6*) Random Hse Value.
Himmelman, John. Montigue on the High Seas. (Illus.). 32p. (ps-3). 1990. pap. 3.95 (*0-14-050789-2*, Puffin) Puffin Bks.
Hoban, Lillian. Silly Tilly's Thanksgiving Dinner. Hoban, Lillian, illus. LC 89-29287. 64p. (gr. k-3). 1991. pap. 3.50 (*0-06-444154-7*, Trophy) HarpC Child Bks.
Holzwarth, Werner & Erlbruch, Wolf. The Story of the Little Mole who Went in Search of Whodunit. LC 93-17676. (ENG.). 24p. (gr. 3 up). 1993. 12.95 (*1-55670-348-1*) Stewart Tabori & Chang.
Hunt, Rod. Mole Wins a Prize. Gordon, Mike, illus. 32p. (ps-k). 1987. 6.95 (*0-09-167520-0*, Pub. by Hutchinson UK) Trafalgar.
Johnston, Tony. Happy Birthday Mole & Troll. (gr. k-6). 1989. pap. 2.95 (*0-440-40217-4*, YB) Dell.
Koller, Jackie F. Mole & Shrew Step Out. Ormai, Stella, illus. LC 91-20531. 32p. (ps-3). 1992. SBE 13.95 (*0-689-31713-1*, Atheneum Child Bk) Macmillan Child Grp.
McDonnell, Janet. Mouse's Adventure in Alphabet Town. Williams, Jenny, illus. LC 91-47717. 32p. (ps-2). 1992. PLB 11.80 (*0-516-05413-9*) Childrens.
Millais, Raoul. Elijah & Pin-Pin. LC 91-20032. (Illus.). 48p. (ps-1). 1992. pap. 14.00 jacketed (*0-671-75543-9*, S&S BFYR) S&S Trade.
Mole & His New Red Hat. (gr. 3-7). 1974. 9.50 (*0-686-23317-4*) Rochester Folk Art.
Pochocki, Ethel. Mushroom Man. 1993. 15.00 (*0-671-75951-5*, Green Tiger) S&S Trade.
Townsend, Sue. The Secret Diary of Adrian Mole, Aged 13 3-4. 208p. (gr. 8 up). 1984. pap. 4.99 (*0-380-86876-8*, Flare) Avon.
Tripp, C. J. Just Mole. Hudd, Stacy, illus. LC 87-71721. 137p. (Orig.). (gr. 4-6). 1989. pap. 7.00 (*0-916383-39-3*) Aegina Pr.
Wouters, Anne. This Book Is for Us. Wouters, Anne, illus. LC 91-23742. 32p. (ps-1). 1992. 8.95 (*0-525-44882-9*, DCB) Dutton Child Bks.
Yolen, Jane. Eeny, Meeny, Miney Mole. Brown, K., illus. 1992. 13.95 (*0-15-225350-5*, HB Juv Bks) HarBrace.
Ziefert, Harriet. New House for Mouse & Mole. Prebenna, David, illus. (ps-3). 1987. pap. 8.95 (*0-670-81720-1*) Viking Child Bks.

MOLLUSKS
see also Shells
Oda, Hidetomo. Snails. LC 85-28211. (Illus.). 32p. (gr. 3-7). 1986. PLB 10.95 (*0-8172-2544-7*) Raintree Steck-V.
Richardson, Joy. Mollusks. LC 93-18542. (Illus.). 32p. (gr. 2-4). 1993. PLB 11.40 (*0-531-14263-9*) Watts.

MONARCHS
see Kings and Rulers; Queens

MONASTICISM AND RELIGIOUS ORDERS–FICTION

Carlsruh, Dan K. The Cannibals of Sunset Drive. LC 92-40568. 144p. (gr. 3-7). 1993. SBE 13.95 (*0-02-717110-8*, Macmillan Child Bk) Macmillan Child Grp.

Stolz, Mary. Pangur Ban. Johnson, Pamela, illus. LC 87-35049. 196p. (gr. 7 up). 1988. PLB 13.89 (*0-06-025862-4*) HarpC Child Bks.

MONASTICISM AND RELIGIOUS ORDERS FOR WOMEN

Gray, Charlotte. Mother Teresa. LC 88-2226. (Illus.). 68p. (gr. 5-6). 1990. pap. 7.95 (*0-8192-1523-6*) Morehouse Pub.

—Mother Teresa: Servant to the World's Suffering People. Ullstein, Susan, adapted by. LC 89-49750. (Illus.). 64p. (gr. 3-4). 1990. PLB 19.93 (*0-8368-0393-0*) Gareth Stevens Inc.

Jacobs, William J. Mother Teresa: Helping the Poor. (gr. 4-7). 1992. pap. 4.95 (*1-878841-57-2*) Millbrook Pr.

Mohan, Claire J. Mother Teresa's Someday: The Young Life of Mother Teresa of Calcutta. Gallagher, Patricia C., ed. Thomes, Susannah H., illus. 60p. (Orig.). (gr. k-6). 1990. PLB 14.95 (*0-9621500-6-1*); pap. 6.95 (*0-9621500-7-X*) Young Sparrow Pr.

MONETARY QUESTION

see Money

MONEY

see also Banks and Banking; Coins; Credit; Gold; Paper Money

Bank Street College of Education Editors. Let's Learn about Money. (gr. 1-2). 1986. pap. 3.95 (*0-8120-3626-3*) Barron.

Banks, Ann. It's My Money: A Kid's Guide to the Green Stuff. Natti, Susanna, illus. LC 93-12618. (gr. 3-7). 1993. 3.99 (*0-670-36086-4*) Puffin Bks.

Berg, Adriane G. & Bochner, Arthur B. Totally Awesome Money Book for Kids (& Their Parents) (Illus.). 176p. (gr. 4-12). 1993. 18.95 (*1-55704-183-0*); pap. 9.95 (*1-55704-176-8*) Newmarket.

Berger, Melvin & Berger, Gilda. Round & Round the Money Goes: What Money Is & How We Use It. Cymerman, John, illus. LC 93-14770. 48p. (gr. 1-3). 1993. PLB 12.00 (*0-8249-8640-7*, Ideals Child); pap. 4.50 (*0-8249-8598-2*) Hambleton-Hill.

Bungum, Jane. Money & Financial Institutions. (Illus.). 88p. (gr. 5 up). 1991. PLB 21.50 (*0-8225-1781-7*) Lerner Pubns.

Byers, Patricia & Preston, Julia. The Kids' Money Book. LC 82-184275. (Illus.). 144p. (gr. 2-6). 1983. pap. 4.95 (*0-89709-041-1*) Liberty Pub.

Chromey, Rick. Money: A Christian Perspective. (Illus.). 48p. (gr. 9-12). 1991. pap. 8.99 (*1-55945-212-9*) Group Pub.

Cribb, Joe. Money. British Museum, illus. LC 89-15589. 64p. (gr. 5 up). 1990. 16.00 (*0-679-80438-2*); PLB 16.99 (*0-679-90438-7*) Knopf Bks Yng Read.

Elkin, Benjamin. Money. LC 83-7436. (Illus.). 48p. (gr. k-4). 1983. PLB 12.85 (*0-516-01697-0*) Childrens.

Godfrey, Neale S. The Kid's Money Book. Novak, Justin, illus. 128p. (gr. 3 up). 1991. 12.95 (*1-56288-002-0*) Checkerboard.

Jones, David. Your Book of Money. (gr. 7 up). 1971. 7.95 (*0-571-09341-8*) Transatl Arts.

Kain, Carolyn. The Story of Money. Wood, Gerry, illus. LC 91-38898. 32p. (gr. 3-6). 1993. PLB 11.89 (*0-8167-2711-2*); pap. text ed. 3.95 (*0-8167-2712-0*) Troll Assocs.

Knowledge Unlimited Staff, ed. What Is Money: From Barter to Banking. (Illus.). 21p. (gr. 4-12). incl. 2 filmstrips, 2 cass., 2 guides 66.00 (*0-915291-34-7*) Know Unltd.

—What Is Money: The Ups & Downs of the Money Supply. (Illus.). 27p. (gr. 4-12). 1984. incl. 2 filmstrips, 2 cass., 2 guides 66.00 (*0-915291-27-4*) Know Unltd.

Kyte, Kathy S. The Kids' Complete Guide to Money. Brown, Richard, illus. LC 84-3962. 96p. (gr. 5 up). 1984. lib. bdg. 10.99 (*0-394-96672-4*) Knopf Bks Yng Read.

Lee, Mary P. Coping with Money. Rosen, Ruth, ed. (gr. 7 up). 1988. PLB 14.95 (*0-8239-0783-X*) Rosen Group.

Lewis, Brenda R. Coins & Currency. LC 92-46359. (Illus.). 80p. (gr. 5 up). 1993. 13.00 (*0-679-82662-9*); PLB 13.99 (*0-679-92662-3*) Random Bks Yng Read.

Mitgutsch, Ali. From Gold to Money. Mitgutsch, Ali, illus. LC 84-17488. 24p. (ps-3). 1985. PLB 10.95 (*0-87614-230-7*) Carolrhoda Bks.

Ockenga, Earl & Rucker, Walt. Money. Dawson, Dave, illus. 16p. (gr. 1). 1990. pap. text ed. 1.25 (*1-56281-125-8*, M125) Extra Eds.

Pellowski, Michael J. Moosey Saves Money. Harvey, Paul, illus. LC 85-14053. 48p. (Orig.). (gr. 1-3). 1986. PLB 10.59 (*0-8167-0628-X*); pap. text ed. 3.50 (*0-8167-0629-8*) Troll Assocs.

Piltch, Benjamin & Smergut, Peter. Money Matters. 64p. (gr. 7-12). 1983. 3.95 (*0-934618-03-8*) Learning Well.

Price, Ray B. & Cox, Gale R. How to Acquire Wealth: One Man's Odyssey. LC 90-61189. 87p. (Orig.). 1990. pap. text ed. 8.95 (*0-9626318-0-9*) Price Pub SC.

Rendon, Marion B. & Kranz, Rachel. Straight Talk about Money. Ryan, Elizabeth A., ed. 128p. (gr. 7-12). 1992. lib. bdg. 16.95x (*0-8160-2612-2*) Facts on File.

Resnick, Abraham. Money. (Illus.). (gr. 5-8). 1994. 14.95 (*1-56006-165-0*) Lucent Bks.

Silver, A. David. A Young Person's First Book of Wealth. (Illus.). 300p. (gr. 7-12). 1987. wkbk. 15.95x (*0-945214-00-6*) Silver Prescrip Pr.

Smith, Allan H., ed. Teenage Money Making Guide. Trachsler, Don, illus. LC 84-90126. 281p. (Orig.). (ps-12). 1984. pap. 10.00 (*0-931113-00-8*) Success Publ.

Spies, Karen B. Our Money. LC 91-43231. (Illus.). 48p. (gr. 2-4). 1992. PLB 13.40 (*1-56294-212-3*); pap. 5.95 (*1-56294-815-6*) Millbrook Pr.

Urton, Andrea. Fifty Nifty Ways to Earn Money. Manwaring, Kerry, illus. 80p. (gr. 4-7). 1993. pap. 4.95 (*1-56565-043-3*) Lowell Hse.

Wilkinson, Elizabeth. Making Cents: Every Kid's Guide to Money, Vol. 1. 1989. pap. 8.95 (*0-316-94102-6*) Little.

Wool, John D. Using Money Series, 3 bks. rev. ed. Incl. Bk. 1: Counting My Money. 96p. (gr. 1 up). 1994. pap. text ed. 4.50 (*0-88323-259-6*, 171); Bk. 2: Making My Money Count. 96p. 1994. pap. text ed. 4.50 (*0-88323-260-X*, 172); Bk. 3: Buying Power. 96p. (gr. 3 up). 1993. pap. text ed. 4.50 (*0-88323-258-8*, 173). pap. text ed. tchr's. answer key 1.50 (*0-88323-173-5*, 224) Pendergrass Pub.

Young, Woody. Moneywise. White, Craig, illus. 48p. (Orig.). (gr. 1-5). 1986. pap. text ed. 4.95 (*0-939513-30-7*) Joy Pub SJC.

MONEY–FICTION

Adams, Barbara J. The Go-Around Dollar. Zarins, Joyce A., illus. LC 90-26269. 32p. (gr. 1-4). 1992. RSBE 13.95 (*0-02-700031-1*, Four Winds) Macmillan Child Grp.

Assimaku-Idun, Aba. Kofi & Ama Make a Fortune. 1994. 8.75 (*0-8062-4880-7*) Carlton.

Axelrod, Amy. Pigs Will Be Pigs. McGinley-Nally, Sharon, illus. LC 93-7640. 40p. (gr. k-3). 1994. RSBE 14.95 (*0-02-765415-X*, Four Winds) Macmillan Child Grp.

Boyd, Candy D. Circle of Gold. LC 93-19020. 128p. (gr. 3-7). 1994. 13.95 (*0-590-49426-0*) Scholastic Inc.

Brancato, Robin F. Uneasy Money. Hendrix, Bryan, designed by. LC 86-45296. (Illus.). 256p. (gr. 7-10). 1989. Repr. of 1986 ed. PLB 11.99 (*0-394-96954-5*) Knopf Bks Yng Read.

Brisson, Pat. Benny's Pennies. (gr. 4 up). 1993. pap. 14.95 (*0-385-41602-4*) Doubleday.

Brittain, Bill. All the Money in the World. LC 77-25635. (Illus.). 160p. (gr. 3-7). 1979. PLB 14.89 (*0-06-020676-4*) HarpC Child Bks.

—All the Money in the World. Robinson, Charles, illus. LC 77-25635. 160p. (gr. 4-7). 1982. pap. 3.95 (*0-06-440128-6*, Trophy) HarpC Child Bks.

Caple, Kathy. The Purse. 32p. (gr. k-3). 1992. pap. 4.80 (*0-395-62981-0*, Sandpiper) HM.

Danziger, Paula. Not for a Billion Gazillion Dollars. LC 92-2735. 127p. (gr. 4-6). 1992. 14.95 (*0-385-30819-1*) Delacorte.

Ellis, Jana. Sweet Success. LC 89-36348. 160p. (gr. 7 up). 1989. pap. text ed. 2.50 (*0-8167-1673-0*) Troll Assocs.

Giff, Patricia R. Count Your Money with the Polk Street School. (ps-3). 1994. pap. 3.99 (*0-440-40929-2*) Dell.

Goldman, E. M. Money to Burn. LC 93-14584. 212p. (gr. 5-9). 1994. 14.99 (*0-670-85339-9*) Viking Child Bks.

Gorman, Carol. The Richest Kid in the World. Nappi, Rudy, illus. LC 92-24935. 60p. (Orig.). (gr. 1-4). 1993. pap. 3.99 (*0-570-04728-5*) Concordia.

Hautzig, Esther. Riches. Diamond, Donna, illus. LC 89-26904. 32p. (gr. 3 up). 1992. PLB 13.89 (*0-06-022260-3*) HarpC Child Bks.

—Riches. LC 89-26904. (gr. 4-7). 1994. pap. 3.95 (*0-06-440550-8*) HarpC Child Bks.

Haywood, Carolyn. Here's a Penny. Rev. ed. Haywood, Carolyn & Yakovetic, Joe, illus. LC 44-7329. 150p. (gr. 1-5). 1986. pap. 4.95 (*0-15-640062-6*, Voyager Bks) HarBrace.

Heide, Florence P. Treehorn's Treasure. Gorey, Edward, illus. LC 81-4043. 64p. (gr. 3-6). 1981. reinforced bdg. 13.95 (*0-8234-0425-0*) Holiday.

Herman, Charlotte. Max Malone Makes a Million. Smith, Cat B., illus. LC 90-46373. 80p. (gr. 2-4). 1991. 13.95 (*0-8050-1374-1*, Redfeather BYR) H Holt & Co.

Hoban, Lillian. Arthur's Funny Money. Hoban, Lillian, illus. LC 80-7903. 64p. (gr. k-3). 1981. PLB 13.89 (*0-06-022344-8*) HarpC Child Bks.

Kimenye, Barbara. Money Game. (gr. 4-7). 1992. pap. 4.95 (*0-7910-2927-1*) Chelsea Hse.

Kimmel, Eric A. Four Dollars & Fifty Cents. Rounds, Glen, illus. (ps-3). 1993. pap. 5.95 (*0-8234-1024-2*) Holiday.

Lantz, Francess. Marissa's Dance. LC 93-43225. (Illus.). 128p. (gr. 3-7). 1994. pap. text ed. 2.95 (*0-8167-3475-5*) Troll Assocs.

Leedy, Loreen. The Monster Money Book. Leedy, Loreen, illus. LC 91-18168. 32p. (ps-3). 1992. reinforced bdg. 14.95 (*0-8234-0922-8*) Holiday.

Medearis, Angela S. Picking Peas for a Penny. Shaw, Charles G., illus. 40p. (gr. 1-4). 1993. pap. 4.95 (*0-590-45942-2*) Scholastic Inc.

Merrill, Jean. Toothpaste Millionaire. (gr. 4-7). 1993. pap. 4.95 (*0-395-66954-5*) HM.

Moody, Ralph. Shaking the Nickel Bush. 1976. 20.95 (*0-8488-1108-9*) Amereon Ltd.

Pellowski, Michael J. Good-bye Millions, No. 10. LC 91-58617. (Illus.). 128p. (Orig.). (gr. 4-8). 1992. pap. 2.99 (*1-56282-191-1*) Hyprn Child.

Perkins, Anne T. Nan's Nickel. Perkins, Anne T. & Lomax, James, illus. 8p. 1993. 12.00 (*1-884204-04-X*) Teach Nxt Door.

Pfeffer, Susan B. The Ring of Truth. LC 92-25272. 1993. 15.95 (*0-553-09224-3*) Bantam.

Reynolds, Malvina. Magic Penny Big Book. Draper, Tani, illus. (ps-2). 1988. pap. text ed. 14.00 (*0-922053-19-7*) N Edge Res.

Rockwell, Thomas. How to Get Fabulously Rich. Frammenghi, Gioia, illus. 128p. (gr. 5-8). 1990. 13.95 (*0-531-15180-8*); PLB 13.90 (*0-531-10877-5*) Watts.

—How to Get Fabulously Rich. (gr. 4-7). 1991. pap. 3.50 (*0-440-40546-7*, YB) Dell.

Schwartz, David A. If You Made a Million. Kellogg, Steven, illus. 40p. (gr. 1-5). 1989. 16.00 (*0-688-07017-5*); PLB 15.93 (*0-685-75780-3*) Lothrop.

Silverstein, Herma. Mad, Mad Monday. (gr. 7-9). 1989. pap. 2.99 (*0-671-67403-X*, Archway) PB.

Smith, Matthew V. A Penny for the Gum Machine. Smith, Matthew V., illus. 12p. (gr. k-3). 1992. pap. 9.95 (*1-895583-09-8*) MAYA Pubs.

Stewart, Sarah. The Money Tree. Small, David, illus. 32p. (gr. k up). 1991. 14.95 (*0-374-35014-0*) FS&G.

—Money Tree. (ps-3). 1994. pap. 4.95 (*0-374-45295-4*, Sunburst) FS&G.

The Stonecutter Who Wanted to Be Rich. 1990. 10.95 (*0-685-61053-5*) CIS Comm.

Viorst, Judith. Alexander, Who Used to Be Rich Last Sunday, Vol. 1. LC 77-1579. (Illus.). 32p. (ps-4). 1978. RSBE 13.95 (*0-689-30602-4*, Atheneum Child Bk) Macmillan Child Grp.

Vosper, Alice. Rags to Riches. 222p. (gr. 7 up). 1983. pap. 2.25 (*0-380-83873-7*, Flare) Avon.

Weyn, Suzanne. Three for the Show. Iskowitz, Joel, illus. LC 89-34547. 96p. (gr. 3-5). 1990. pap. text ed. 2.95 (*0-8167-1656-0*) Troll Assocs.

White, Cristine A. Matthew's Allowance. LC 89-51091. 44p. (gr. k-3). 1989. 5.95 (*1-55523-249-3*) Winston-Derek.

Williams, Vera B. A Chair for My Mother. Williams, Vera B., illus. LC 81-7010. 32p. (gr. k-3). 1982. 15.00 (*0-688-00914-X*); PLB 14.93 (*0-688-00915-8*) Greenwillow.

Wilson, Johnniece M. Poor Girl, Rich Girl. 176p. 1992. 13.95 (*0-590-44732-7*, Scholastic Hardcover) Scholastic Inc.

MONEY–HISTORY

Kain, Carolyn. The Story of Money. Wood, Gerry, illus. LC 91-38898. 32p. (gr. 3-6). 1993. PLB 11.89 (*0-8167-2711-2*); pap. text ed. 3.95 (*0-8167-2712-0*) Troll Assocs.

Maestro, Betsy. The Story of Money. Maestro, Giulio, illus. 48p. (gr. 4-7). 1993. 15.95 (*0-395-56242-2*, Clarion Bks) HM.

—The Story of Money. Cohn, Amy, ed. Maestro, Guilio, illus. 1995. pap. 4.95 (*0-688-13304-5*, Mulberry) Morrow.

Oppenheim, Joanne. Money. LC 94-12740. 1995. 15.00 (*0-689-31910-X*, Atheneum) Macmillan.

Sold! The Origins of Money & Trade. LC 93-37782. 1994. PLB write for info. (*0-8225-3206-9*, Runestone Pr) Lerner Pubns.

MONEY, PAPER

see Paper Money

MONEY RAISING

see Fund Raising

MONGOLS

Reynolds, Jan. Mongolia: Vanishing Cultures. LC 93-1351. (gr. 6 up). 1994. 16.95 (*0-15-255312-6*); pap. 8.95 (*0-15-255313-4*) HarBrace.

MONGOOSES–FICTION

Kipling, Rudyard. Rikki-Tikki-Tavi. 1992. 16.95 (*0-15-267015-7*, HB Juv Bks) HarBrace.

Montgomery, H. Mongoose Magoo. LC 68-56822. (Illus.). 64p. (gr. 2-5). 1968. PLB 10.95 (*0-87783-026-6*); pap. 3.94 deluxe ed. (*0-87783-100-9*) Oddo.

MONITOR (IRONCLAD)

Carter, Alden R. Battle of the Ironclads: The Monitor & the Merrimack. LC 93-417. (Illus.). 64p. (gr. 4-6). 1993. PLB 12.90 (*0-531-20091-4*) Watts.

Stein. Monitor & Merrimac. 1989. pap. 3.95 (*0-516-44662-2*) Childrens.

MONKEYS

Ancona, George. The Golden Lion Tamarin Comes Home. LC 93-23705. (gr. 2-6). 1994. 15.95 (*0-02-700905-X*, Macmillan Child Bk) Macmillan Child Grp.

Arnold, Caroline. Monkey. Hewett, Richard, photos by. LC 92-31094. (Illus.). 48p. (gr. 2 up). 1993. 15.00 (*0-688-11344-3*); PLB 14.93 (*0-688-11345-1*) Morrow Jr Bks.

—Orangutan. Hewett, Richard, photos by. LC 89-38957. (Illus.). 48p. (gr. 2 up). 1990. 13.95 (*0-688-08826-0*); PLB 13.88 (*0-688-08827-9*, Morrow Jr Bks) Morrow Jr Bks.

Barrett, Norman S. Monos y Simios. LC 90-71420. (SPA., Illus.). 32p. (gr. k-4). 1991. PLB 11.90 (*0-531-07918-X*) Watts.

Carwardine, Mark. Monkeys & Apes. Young, Richard G., ed. Camm, Martin, illus. LC 89-32808. 45p. (gr. 3-5). 1989. PLB 14.60 (*0-944483-28-3*) Garrett Ed Corp.

Crosby, Nina E. & Marten, Elizabeth H. Don't Teach! Let Me Learn about Fantasy, Magic, Monkeys & Monsters. Rossi, Richard, illus. 72p. (Orig.). (gr. 3-10). 1984. 8.95 (*0-88047-045-3*, 8410) DOK Pubs.

Haldane, Suzanne. Helping Hands: How Monkeys Assist People Who Are Disabled. Haldane, Suzanne, photos by. LC 90-27382. (Illus.). 48p. (gr. 3-7). 1991. 14.95 (*0-525-44723-7*, DCB) Dutton Child Bks.

Hansard, Peter. I Like Monkeys Because. Casey, Patricia, illus. LC 92-54409. 32p. (ps up). 1993. 14.95 (*1-56402-196-3*) Candlewick Pr.

Hoffman, Mary. Monkey. LC 84-15117. (Illus.). 24p. (gr. k-5). 1985. PLB 9.95 (*0-8172-2406-8*); pap. 3.95 (*0-8114-6883-6*) Raintree Steck-V.
Lemmon, Tess. Monkeys. LC 91-7590. (Illus.). 32p. (gr. 2-5). 1992. PLB 12.40 (*0-531-18454-4*, Pub. by Bookwright Pr) Watts.
Lumley, Kathryn W. Monkeys & Apes. LC 82-12779. (Illus.). (gr. k-4). 1982. PLB 12.85 (*0-516-01633-4*); pap. 4.95 (*0-516-41633-2*) Childrens.
Mattern, Joanne. Monkeys & Apes. LC 92-28080. (Illus.). 24p. (gr. 4-7). 1992. pap. text ed. 1.95 (*0-8167-2962-X*) Troll Assocs.
Maynard, Thane. Primates: Apes, Monkeys, Prosimians. (Illus.). 56p. (gr. 2 up). 1994. PLB 14.91 (*0-531-11169-5*) Watts.
Morris, Dean. Monkeys & Apes. rev. ed. LC 87-16688. (Illus.). 48p. (gr. 3). 1987. PLB 10.95 (*0-8172-3211-7*) Raintree Steck-V.
Old World Monkeys. 1991. PLB 14.95 (*0-88682-419-2*) Creative Ed.
Overbeck, Cynthia. Monkeys. LC 81-1961. (Illus.). 48p. (gr. 4 up). 1981. PLB 19.95 (*0-8225-1464-8*) Lerner Pubns.
Rau, Margaret. The Snow Monkey at Home. Hulsmann, Eva, illus. LC 78-31550. (gr. 4-7). 1979. lib. bdg. 6.99 (*0-394-93976-X*) Knopf Bks Yng Read.
Richmond, Gary. Zookeeper Looks at Monkeys. 1991. pap. 3.99 (*0-8499-0861-2*) Word Inc.
Steedman, Scott. Amazing Monkeys. Young, Jerry, photos by. LC 90-19238. (Illus.). 32p. (Orig.). (gr. 1-5). 1991. PLB 9.99 (*0-679-91517-6*); pap. 6.95 (*0-679-81517-1*) Knopf Bks Yng Read.
Stone, Lynn. Gibbons. (Illus.). 24p. (gr. k-5). 1990. lib. bdg. 11.94 (*0-86593-062-7*); lib. bdg. 8.95s.p. (*0-685-36317-1*) Rourke Corp.
—Monkey Discovery Library, 6 bks. (Illus.). 144p. (gr. k-5). 1990. Set. lib. bdg. 71.60 (*0-86593-061-9*); Set. lib. bdg. 53.70s.p. (*0-685-36314-7*) Rourke Corp.
—Orangutans. (Illus.). 24p. (gr. k-5). 1990. lib. bdg. 11.94 (*0-86593-065-1*); lib. bdg. 8.95s.p. (*0-685-36319-8*) Rourke Corp.
—Snow Monkeys. (Illus.). 24p. (gr. k-5). 1990. lib. bdg. 11.94 (*0-86593-066-X*); lib. bdg. 8.95s.p. (*0-685-36320-1*) Rourke Corp.
Whitehead, Patricia. Monkeys. Dodson, Bert, illus. LC 81-11439. 32p. (gr. k-2). 1982. PLB 11.59 (*0-89375-670-9*); pap. text ed. 2.95 (*0-89375-671-7*) Troll Assocs.
Wilmot, Zoe. Monkey. LC 93-77345. (Illus.). (ps). 1993. 3.99 (*0-89577-510-7*, Dist. by Random) RD Assn.
Yee, Patrick. Baby Monkey. (Illus.). 12p. (ps). 1994. bds. 3.99 (*0-670-85290-2*) Viking Child Bks.

MONKEYS–FICTION

Allen, Helen S. A Letter to Lynn: Mandy's Day at the Beach. 16p. (ps). 1992. pap. text ed. 5.00 (*1-881907-03-1*) Two Bytes Pub.
—A Valentine Letter to Lynn: Mandy's Adventure in the Snow. 16p. (ps). 1992. pap. text ed. 5.00 (*1-881907-02-3*) Two Bytes Pub.
Bierhorst, John, ed. The Monkey's Haircut: And Other Stories Told by the Maya. Parker, Robert A., illus. LC 85-28471. 160p. (gr. 5 up). 1986. 13.00 (*0-688-04269-4*) Morrow Jr Bks.
Bornstein. Gorilita. (SPA.). 1993. pap. 3.95 (*0-590-12086-7*) Scholastic Inc.
Brown, Marc T., illus. Two Little Monkeys. 8p. (ps-k). 1989. 5.95 (*0-525-44533-1*, DCB) Dutton Child Bks.
Calmenson, Stephanie. One Little Monkey. Appleby, Ellen, illus. LC 82-7958. 48p. (ps-3). 1982. pap. 5.95 (*0-8193-1091-3*); PLB 5.95 (*0-8193-1092-1*) Parents.
Christelow, Eileen. Don't Wake up Mama! Another Five Little Monkeys Story. Christelow, Eileen, illus. 32p. (ps-3). 1992. 13.95 (*0-395-60176-2*, Clarion Bks) HM.
—Five Little Monkeys Jumping on the Bed. Christelow, Eileen, illus. (ps-3). 1993. pap. 5.70 (*0-395-55701-1*, Clarion Bks); pap. 7.95 incl. cassette (*0-395-60115-0*, Clarion Bks) HM.
—Five Little Monkeys Sitting in a Tree. Christelow, Eileen, illus. 32p. (gr. k-3). 1993. pap. 5.70 (*0-395-66413-6*, Clarion Bks) HM.
Clifford, Eth. Harvey's Marvelous Monkey Mystery. LC 86-20837. (gr. 3-6). 1987. 13.45 (*0-395-42622-7*) HM.
Crozat, Francois. I Am a Little Monkey. (Illus.). (ps-3). 1991. large 8.95 (*0-8120-6149-7*); miniature 2.95 (*0-8120-6221-3*) Barron.
Dodds, Dayle A. The Color Box. Laroche, Giles, illus. 32p. (ps-1). 1992. 12.95 (*0-316-18820-4*) Little.
Erickson, Gina C. & Foster, Kelli C. Pip & Kip. Russell, Kerri G., illus. LC 92-29864. 24p. (ps-2). 1993. pap. 3.50 (*0-8120-1454-5*) Barron.
Franklin, Kristine L. Cuando Regresaron los Monos. Roth, Robert, illus. Zubizarreta, Rosa, tr. from ENG. LC 93-46783. (SPA., Illus.). (gr. k-3). 1994. 14.95 (*0-689-31950-9*, Atheneum) Macmillan.
—When the Monkeys Came Back. Roth, Robert, illus. LC 92-33684. 1994. 14.95 (*0-689-31807-3*, Atheneum) Macmillan.
Galdone, Paul. The Turtle & the Monkey. Galdone, Paul, illus. 32p. (ps-3). 1990. pap. 6.95 (*0-395-54425-4*, Clarion Bks) HM.
Gantos, Jack. Rotten Ralph's Show & Tell. Rubel, Nicole, illus. 32p. (ps-3). 1989. 13.45 (*0-395-44312-1*) HM.
Gao, R. L., tr. from CHI. The Adventures of Monkey King. Allen, Rita, illus. 132p. (Orig.). (gr. 2-5). 1989. pap. 6.95 (*0-9620765-1-1*) Victory Press.
Gave, Marc. Monkey See, Monkey Do. Rogers, Jacqueline, illus. 32p. (ps-2). 1993. pap. 2.95 (*0-590-45801-9*) Scholastic Inc.
Gelman, Rita G. More Spaghetti, I Say! Gerberg, Mort, illus. 32p. (ps-3). 1993. pap. 2.95 (*0-590-45783-7*) Scholastic Inc.
Hale, Hanna. Zelda Orangutan. Hale, Hanna, illus. 64p. (gr. 4-6). 1994. Perfect bdg. pap. 12.95 (*0-9638724-0-0*) Cando Pubng.
Jacobs, W. W. The Monkey's Paw. Richardson, I. M., adapted by. Lawn, John, illus. LC 81-19824. 32p. (gr. 5-10). 1982. PLB 10.79 (*0-89375-628-8*); pap. text ed. 2.95 (*0-89375-629-6*) Troll Assocs.
—The Monkey's Paw. rev. ed. (gr. 9-12). 1989. Repr. of 1905 ed. multi-media kit 35.00 (*0-685-31128-7*) Balance Pub.
Jones, Charles. Monkey, Monkey. 25p. (Orig.). (gr. k-3). 1986. pap. 4.50 playscript (*0-87602-265-4*) Anchorage.
Kraus, Robert. Klunky Monkey, New Kid in Class. Brook, Bonnie, ed. Kraus, Robert, illus. 48p. (ps-3). 1990. lib. bdg. 5.95 (*0-671-70853-8*); pap. 3.95 (*0-671-70854-6*) Silver Pr.
LaFleur, Tom & Brennan, Gale. Spunky the Monkey. Murtagh, Betty, illus. 16p. (Orig.). (gr. k-6). 1981. pap. 1.25 (*0-685-02457-1*) Brennan Bks.
Leibold, Jay. Surf Monkeys. (gr. 4-7). 1993. pap. 3.25 (*0-553-29301-X*) Bantam.
Little, Karen E. Monkey Match. (ps-1). 1981. 4.50 (*0-913545-03-1*) Moonlight FL.
McAllister, Angela. Matepo. Newton, Jill, illus. LC 90-33113. 32p. (ps-3). 1991. 12.95 (*0-8037-0838-6*) Dial Bks Young.
Marshall, James. George & Martha One Fine Day. Marshall, James, illus. 48p. (gr. k-3). 1978. 14.45 (*0-395-27154-1*); pap. 4.80 (*0-395-32921-3*) HM.
Martin. Monkey Mothers. Date not set. 15.00 (*0-06-023515-2*); PLB 14.89 (*0-06-023516-0*) HarpC Child Bks.
Mathiesen, Egon. Oswald the Monkey. (Illus.). (gr. k-3). 1959. 9.95 (*0-8392-3025-7*) Astor-Honor.
Mayhar, Ardath & Fortier, Ron. Monkey Station. LC 88-51729. 320p. (Orig.). 1989. pap. 3.95 (*0-88038-743-2*) TSR Inc.
One Hundred Monkeys. LC 90-22446. 40p. 1991. pap. 13.95 incl. jacket (*0-671-73564-0*, Little Simon) S&S Trade.
One Little Monkey. 1994. 13.27 (*0-8368-0988-2*) Gareth Stevens Inc.
Rawls, Wilson. Summer of the Monkeys. (gr. 4-7). 1992. pap. 4.50 (*0-553-29818-6*) Bantam.
Rey, H. A. Cecily G. & the Nine Monkeys. Rey, H. A., illus. (ps-3). 1989. pap. 3.95 (*0-395-50651-4*, Sandpiper) HM.
—Curious George. (Illus.). 56p. (gr. k-3). 1973. 12.70 (*0-395-15993-8*) HM.
—Curious George. Rey, H. A., illus. 48p. (gr. k-3). 1973. pap. 4.80 (*0-395-15023-X*, Sandpiper) HM.
—Curious George. LC 93-40088. 1994. pap. 19.95 (*0-395-69803-0*) HM.
—Curious George Gets a Medal. (Illus.). 48p. (gr. k-3). 1957. 12.70 (*0-395-16973-9*) HM.
—Curious George Learns the Alphabet. (Illus.). 72p. (gr. k-3). 1963. 12.70 (*0-395-16031-6*) HM.
—Curious George Learns the Alphabet. Rey, H. A., illus. LC 62-12261. 72p. (gr. k-3). 1973. pap. 4.80 (*0-395-13718-7*, Sandpiper) HM.
—Curious George Rides a Bike. (Illus.). 48p. (gr. k-3). 1952. 12.95 (*0-395-16964-X*) HM.
—Curious George Rides a Bike. new ed. (Illus.). 48p. (gr. k-3). 1973. pap. 4.80 (*0-395-17444-9*, Sandpiper) HM.
—Curious George Takes a Job. (Illus.). 48p. (gr. k-3). 1973. 13.45 (*0-395-15086-8*) HM.
—Curious George Takes a Job. Rey, H. A., illus. 48p. (gr. k-3). 1974. pap. 4.80 (*0-395-18649-8*, Sandpiper) HM.
—Jorge el Curioso. (SPA., Illus.). (gr. k-3). 1961. 13.95 (*0-395-17075-3*) HM.
Rey, H. A. & Rey, Margaret. Curious George Goes to the Hospital. (Illus.). 48p. (gr. 1-5). 1973. 14.95 (*0-395-18158-5*); pap. 4.80 (*0-395-07062-7*) HM.
Rey, Margaret. Curious George & the Pizza. LC 85-2434. 32p. (ps-2). 1985. 9.95 (*0-395-39039-7*); pap. 3.95 (*0-395-39033-8*) HM.
Rey, Margaret & Rey, H. A. Curious George Flies a Kite. Rey, H. A., illus. (gr. k-3). 1977. pap. 4.80 (*0-395-25937-1*) HM.
Rey, Margaret & Shalleck, Allan J. Curious George & the Dinosaur. (Illus.). (ps-3). 1990. pap. 7.70 incl. cassette (*0-395-56484-0*, Clarion Bks) HM.
—Curious George & the Pizza. 1988. pap. 7.70 incl. cass. (*0-395-48874-5*) HM.
—Curious George at the Beach. (Illus.). 32p. (ps-2). 1988. HM.
—Curious George at the Fire Station. 1988. pap. 7.70 incl. cass. (*0-395-48875-3*) HM.
—Curious George Bakes a Cake. (Illus.). 32p. (ps-2). 1990. HM.
—Curious George Goes Camping. (Illus.). 32p. (ps-2). 1990. HM.
—Curious George Goes to a Restaurant. (Illus.). 32p. (ps-2). 1988. HM.
—Curious George Goes to a Toy Store. (Illus.). 32p. (ps-2). 1990. HM.
—Curious George Goes to an Air Show. (Illus.). 32p. (ps-2). 1990. HM.
—Curious George Goes to School. (Illus.). (ps-3). 1990. Bk. & cass. pap. 7.95 (*0-395-56483-2*) HM.
Rey, Margaret, ed. Curious George & the Dump Truck. (Illus.). 32p. (ps-2). 1984. pap. 3.80 (*0-395-36629-1*) HM.
—Curious George at the Fire Station. LC 85-2471. 32p. (ps-2). 1985. 9.95 (*0-395-39037-0*); pap. 3.95 (*0-395-39031-1*) HM.
—Curious George Goes to the Aquarium. (Illus.). 32p. (ps-2). 1984. 9.95 (*0-395-36634-8*); pap. 3.95 (*0-395-36628-3*) HM.
—Curious George Visits the Zoo. LC 85-2415. 32p. (ps-2). 1985. 8.70 (*0-395-39036-2*); pap. 3.80 (*0-395-39030-3*) HM.
Rey, Margaret & Shalleck, Allan J., eds. Curious George at the Airport. (Illus.). 32p. (ps-2). 1987. pap. 2.80 (*0-395-45368-2*) HM.
—Curious George Plays Baseball. LC 86-10609. (Illus.). 32p. (ps-2). 1986. 8.95 (*0-395-39041-9*); pap. 3.95 (*0-395-39035-4*) HM.
—Curious George Visits the Police Station. (Illus.). 32p. (ps-2). 1987. HM.
—Curious George Walks the Pets. LC 86-7470. (Illus.). 32p. (ps-2). 1986. HM.
Rey, Margret. Curious George & the Dinosaur. (ps-3). 1989. 9.95 (*0-395-51942-X*) HM.
Schubert, Dieter. Where's My Monkey? LC 86-16578. (Illus.). 32p. (ps-2). 1992. pap. 3.99 (*0-8037-1071-2*, Puff Pied Piper) Puffin Bks.
Slobodkina, Esphyr. Caps for Sale. 32p. (gr. k-3). 1989. Big Book. 28.67 (*0-590-64643-5*); pap. 2.95 (*0-590-71775-8*) Scholastic Inc.
Spacone, Carl. No Monkey Too Big. Hoffman, John, ed. Brophy, Paul, illus. 224p. (Orig.). (gr. 9 up). 1987. 8.95 (*0-944712-00-2*); pap. text ed. 8.95 (*0-318-23727-X*) Spacone Pub.
Spunky the Monkey. (Illus.). (ps-2). 1991. PLB 6.95 (*0-8136-5175-1*, TK3883); pap. 3.50 (*0-8136-5675-3*, TK3884) Modern Curr.
Travers, Pamela L. Friend Monkey. Keeping, Charles, illus. LC 70-161389. (ps up). 1971. 6.95 (*0-15-229555-0*, HB Juv Bks) HarBrace.
—Friend Monkey. (Orig.). (gr. k-6). 1987. pap. 4.95 (*0-440-42817-3*, Pub. by Yearling Classics) Dell.
Van Gulik, Robert H. Monkey & the Tiger. 1980. pap. 2.95 (*0-684-16737-9*, Scribner) Macmillan.
Weiss, Monica. Stop That Monkey! (ps-3). 1994. 9.95 (*0-89577-551-4*, Readers Digest Kids) RD Assn.
Wolo & Wolo. Sir Archibald. LC 91-73411. (Illus.). 56p. (ps-1). 1991. Repr. of 1944 ed. 14.95 (*0-944439-22-5*) Clark City Pr.
Wriggins, Sally. White Monkey King: A Chinese Fable. Solbert, Ronni, illus. LC 76-44281. (gr. 1-5). 1977. 5.95 (*0-394-83450-X*) Pantheon.

MONOLOGS

Gaffigan, Catherine, ed. By Kids, for Kids. LC 93-31562. 64p. (Orig.). (gr. 4-6). 1994. pap. 7.95 (*0-9627226-8-5*) Excalibur Publishing.
Karshner, Roger. Teenage Mouth. 64p. (Orig.). (gr. 8-12). 1991. pap. 7.95 (*0-940669-17-X*) Dramaline Pubns.
Majeski, Bill. Fifty Great Monologs for Student Actors. Zapel, Arthur L., ed. LC 87-14103. 144p. (Orig.). (gr. 10 up). 1987. pap. 9.95 (*0-916260-43-7*, B-197) Meriwether Pub.
Murray, John. Modern Monologues for Young People. rev. ed. 150p. (gr. 7-12). 1982. pap. 12.00 (*0-8238-0255-8*) Plays.
Roddy, Ruth M. Kids' Stuff. 64p. (Orig.). (gr. 1-7). 1993. pap. 7.95 (*0-940669-23-4*, D30) Dramaline Pubns.
—More Monologues for Kids. 64p. (Orig.). (gr. 6-9). 1992. pap. 7.95 (*0-940669-18-8*) Dramaline Pubns.

MONOPLANES

see Airplanes

MONROE, JAMES, PRESIDENT U. S. 1758-1831

Bains, Rae. James Monroe, Young Patriot. Frenck, Hal, illus. LC 85-1071. 48p. (gr. 4-6). 1986. lib. bdg. 10.79 (*0-8167-0557-7*); pap. text ed. 3.50 (*0-8167-0558-5*) Troll Assocs.
Fitz-Gerald, Christine M. James Monroe. LC 86-33436. (Illus.). 100p. (gr. 3 up). 1987. PLB 14.40 (*0-516-01383-1*); pap. 6.95 (*0-516-41383-X*) Childrens.
Sandak, Cass R. The Monroes. LC 92-34408. (Illus.). 48p. (gr. 5). 1993. text ed. 12.95 RSBE (*0-89686-645-9*, Crestwood Hse) Macmillan Child Grp.
Stefoff, Rebecca. James Monroe: 5th President of the United States. Young, Richard G., ed. LC 87-32845. (Illus.). (gr. 5-9). 1988. PLB 17.26 (*0-944483-11-9*) Garrett Ed Corp.
Wade. James Monroe. (gr. 4-12). 1993. PLB 8.49 (*0-87386-089-6*); pap. 1.95 (*0-87386-083-7*) Jan Prods.
Wetzel, Charles. James Monroe. (Illus.). (gr. 5 up). 1989. 17.95 (*1-55546-817-9*) Chelsea Hse.

MONSTERS

see also Dwarfs; Giants

Abels, Harriette S. Loch Ness Monster. LC 87-9027. (Illus.). 48p. (gr. 5-6). 1987. text ed. 12.95 RSBE (*0-89686-343-3*, Crestwood Hse) Macmillan Child Grp.
Antoupoulos, Barbara. The Abominable Snowman. LC 77-21387. (Illus.). 48p. (gr. 4 up). 1983. PLB 20.70 (*0-8172-1053-9*) Raintree Steck-V.
Ballinger, Erich. Monster Manual: A Complete Guide to Your Favorite Creatures. LC 93-34219. (Illus.). 144p. (gr. 5 up). 1994. PLB 18.95 (*0-8225-0722-6*) Lerner Pubns.
Berger, Melvin. Monsters. 128p. 1991. pap. 2.95 (*0-380-76053-3*, Camelot) Avon.
Bradley, Susannah, ed. Ghosts, Monsters & Legends. Appleby, Barrie, illus. 48p. (gr. 3-6). 1992. pap. 2.95 (*1-56680-005-6*) Mad Hatter Pub.

Cabat, Erni, illus. Erni Cabat's Magical World of Monsters. Cohen, Daniel, text by. (Illus.). 32p. (gr. 4 up). 1992. 14.00 (*0-525-65087-3*, Cobblehill Bks) Dutton Child Bks.

Emert, Phyllis R. Monsters, Strange Dreams, & UFO's. 128p. 1994. pap. 2.50 (*0-8125-9425-8*) Tor Bks.

Evslin, Bernard. Fentis: Monsters of Mythology. 1992. 19.95 (*1-55546-248-0*) Chelsea Hse.

Garinger, Alan. Water Monsters: Opposing Viewpoints. LC 91-15174. (Illus.). 112p. (gr. 5-8). 1991. PLB 14.95 (*0-89908-087-1*) Greenhaven.

Grahame, Kenneth. Little Treasury of the Wind in the Willows, 6 vols. in 1. 1988. boxed 5.99 (*0-517-65353-2*) Random Hse Value.

Horton, et al. Amazing Fact Book of Monsters. (Illus.). 32p. 1987. PLB 14.95 (*0-87191-847-1*) Creative Ed.

Kallen, Stuart A. Monsters, Dinosaurs & Beasts. LC 91-73061. 202p. 1991. 12.94 (*1-56239-040-6*) Abdo & Dghtrs.

M. J. Studios Staff, illus. Monster Madness Sticker Pad. 32p. (gr. k-6). 1993. pap. 2.95 (*1-879424-56-8*) Nickel Pr.

Miller. Monsters. Francis, John, illus. 32p. (gr. k-6). 1977. PLB write for info. (*0-86020-146-5*); pap. 5.95 (*0-685-73598-2*) EDC.

Namm, D. Monsters! (Illus.). 28p. (ps-2). 1990. PLB 10. 50 (*0-516-05358-2*); pap. 3.95 (*0-516-45358-0*) Childrens.

Rabin, Staton. Monster Myths: The Truth about Water Monsters. LC 91-34420. (Illus.). 40p. (gr. 5-8). 1992. PLB 15.90 (*0-531-11074-5*) Watts.

Seltzer, Meyer. Hide-&-Go Shriek Monster Riddles. Levine, Abby, ed. Seltzer, Meyer, illus. LC 89-49379. 32p. (gr. 1-4). 1990. PLB 8.95 (*0-8075-3273-8*) A Whitman.

Spellman, Linda. Monsters, Mysteries, UFOs. 112p. (gr. 4-6). 1984. 9.95 (*0-88160-095-4*, LW 903) Learning Wks.

Stallman, Birdie. Learning about Dragons. Halverson, Lydia, illus. LC 81-4746. 48p. (gr. 2-6). 1981. pap. 4.95 (*0-516-46531-7*) Childrens.

Tallarico, Tony. Drawing & Cartooning Monsters: A Step-by-Step Guide for the Aspiring Monster-Maker. (Illus.). 128p. (Orig.). 1992. pap. 7.95 (*0-399-51785-5*, Perigee Bks) Berkley Pub.

—Things You Always Wanted to Know about Monsters: But Were Afraid to Ask. (Illus.). 64p. (Orig.). 1988. pap. 1.95 (*0-942025-59-8*) Kidsbks.

Walker, P. Bigfoot & other Legendary Creatures. Noonan, W., illus. 1992. 15.95 (*0-15-207147-4*, HB Juv Bks) HarBrace.

MONSTERS–FICTION

Adams, Pam. The Green-Eyed Monster. (gr. 4 up). 1985. 8.95 (*0-85953-195-3*) Childs Play.

—The Red-Eyed Monster. (gr. 4 up). 1985. 8.95 (*0-85953-196-1*) Childs Play.

Ahlberg, Allan. The Ghost Train. Amstutz, Andre, illus. LC 91-39838. 32p. (ps-6). 1992. 14.00 (*0-688-11435-0*) Greenwillow.

Alcock, Vivien. The Monster Garden. LC 88-6900. 160p. (gr. 5-9). 1988. 13.95 (*0-440-50053-2*) Delacorte.

—The Monster Garden. (gr. k-6). 1990. pap. 2.95 (*0-440-40257-3*, YB) Dell.

Alexander, Liza. Sesame Street: My Name Is Oscar the Grouch. (ps-3). 1994. pap. 1.95 (*0-307-11617-4*, Golden Pr) Western Pub.

Allen, Constance. My Name Is Elmo. Swanson, Maggie, illus. 24p. (ps-k). 1993. pap. 1.45 (*0-307-11541-0*, 11541, Golden Pr) Western Pub.

Andersen, Torsten. Debbie Dare. 1992. 7.95 (*0-533-10279-0*) Vantage.

Anderson, Ken. Nessie & the Little Blind Boy of Loch Ness. Fiott, Steve, intro. by. (Illus.). 72p. 1992. collector's ed. 49.95 (*0-941613-27-5*) Stabur Pr.

Anderson, Mary. The Curse of the Demon. (gr. k-6). 1989. pap. 2.95 (*0-440-40203-4*, YB) Dell.

—The Hairy Beast in the Woods. (gr. 8-12). 1989. pap. 2.75 (*0-318-42743-5*, Pub. by Yearling Classics) Dell.

—Mostly Monsters, No. 1. (gr. k-6). 1989. pap. 2.95 (*0-440-40178-X*, YB) Dell.

—Mostly Monsters, No. 2. (Orig.). (gr. k-6). 1989. pap. 2.95 (*0-440-40181-X*, YB) Dell.

Ashby, Ruth, ed. Monster Mix-Up. 128p. (Orig.). 1991. pap. 3.50 (*0-671-74201-9*, Archway) PB.

Auch, Mary J. Monster Brother. LC 93-41746. (Illus.). 32p. (ps-3). 1994. reinforced bdg. 15.95 (*0-8234-1095-1*) Holiday.

Avery, Lorraine. Secret in the Lake. Thomas, Linda, illus. LC 89-5119. 96p. (gr. 4-6). 1990. PLB 9.89 (*0-8167-1710-9*); pap. text ed. 2.95 (*0-8167-1711-7*) Troll Assocs.

Bad Ben & the Monster. (gr. k-2). 1990. text ed. 3.95 cased (*0-7214-5266-3*) Ladybird Bks.

Bartels, Alice. The Beast. Tibo, Gilles, illus. 32p. (ps-2). 1990. 14.95 (*1-55037-101-0*, Pub. by Annick CN); pap. 5.95 (*1-55037-102-9*, Pub. by Annick CN) Firefly Bks Ltd.

Bellairs, John. Mummy, Will & Crypt. 1985. pap. 3.99 (*0-553-15701-9*) Bantam.

Berlan, Kathryn H. Andrew's Amazing Monsters. Chambliss, Maxie, illus. LC 91-39131. 32p. (ps-2). 1993. SBE 13.95 (*0-689-31739-5*, Atheneum Child Bk) Macmillan Child Grp.

Bird, Malcolm. The School in Murky Wood. (Illus.). 40p. (ps-3). 1993. 10.95 (*0-8118-0544-1*) Chronicle Bks.

Bloom, Hanya. Friendly Fangs. (gr. 4-7). 1991. pap. 2.95 (*0-06-106032-1*, Harp PBks) HarpC.

—Science Spook. (gr. 4-7). 1990. pap. 2.95 (*0-06-106020-8*, PL) HarpC.

Borovsky, Paul. The Strange Blue Creature. Borovsky, Paul, illus. LC 92-54864. 32p. (ps-2). 1993. 13.95 (*1-56282-434-1*); PLB 13.89 (*1-56282-435-X*) Hyprn Child.

Boynton, Sandra. Boynton on Board: Birthday Monsters! Boynton, Sandra, illus. 24p. (ps). 1993. bds. 6.95 (*1-56305-443-4*, 3443) Workman Pub.

Brennan, Herbie. Emily & the Werewolf. Pace, David, illus. 96p. (gr. 3-7). 1993. SBE 16.95 (*0-689-50593-0*, M K McElderry) Macmillan Child Grp.

Broun, Heywood. The Fifty-First Dragon. Redpath, Ann, ed. Delessert, Etienne, illus. 32p. (gr. 4 up). 1985. PLB 13.95s.p. (*0-88682-005-7*) Creative Ed.

Byars, Betsy C. The Blossoms & the Green Phantom. Rogers, Jacqueline, illus. 160p. (gr. k-6). 1988. pap. 3.50 (*0-440-40069-4*) Dell.

Carey, Valerie S. Harriet & William & the Terrible Creature. LC 90-13721. (Illus.). 32p. (ps-1). 1990. pap. 3.95 (*0-525-44652-4*, DCB) Dutton Child Bks.

Chevalier, Christa. Spence & the Sleepytime Monster. Tucker, Kathleen, ed. Chevalier, Christa, illus. LC 83-25988. 32p. (ps-1). 1984. PLB 11.95 (*0-8075-7574-7*) A Whitman.

Christian, Mary B. Go West, Swamp Monsters. Brown, Marc T., illus. LC 84-12686. 48p. (ps-3). 1985. 8.95 (*0-8037-0091-1*) Dial Bks Young.

—Go West, Swamp Monsters. LC 84-12686. (Illus.). 48p. (ps-3). 1987. pap. 4.95 (*0-8037-0438-0*) Dial Bks Young.

—Swamp Monsters. Brown, Marc T., illus. LC 82-1574. 56p. (ps-3). 1983. pap. 4.95 (*0-8037-7614-4*) Dial Bks Young.

—Swamp Monsters. Brown, Marc T., illus. LC 93-25616. (gr. 1-4). 1994. pap. 3.25 (*0-14-036841-8*, Puffin) Puffin Bks.

Clarke, Gus. Ten Green Monsters. (ps-3). 1994. 10.95 (*0-307-17605-3*, Artsts Writrs) Western Pub.

Cohen, Milton. Ilana & the Monsters. Elfring, Harriet, illus. 40p. (Orig.). Date not set. pap. 3.00 (*0-9616076-0-2*) Jomilt Pubns.

Cohen, Miriam. Jim Meets the Thing. 49p. (gr. k-6). 1989. pap. 3.25 (*0-440-40149-6*, YB) Dell.

Cole, Joanna. Monster Valentines. 1990. pap. 2.50 (*0-590-42216-2*) Scholastic Inc.

Cooney, Nancy E. Go Away Monsters, Lickety Split! Chambliss, Maxie, illus. 32p. (ps-1). 1990. 13.95 (*0-399-21935-8*, Putnam) Putnam Pub Group.

Cosgrove, Stephen. Creole. (Illus.). 32p. (Orig.). (gr. 1-4). 1975. pap. 2.95 (*0-8431-0552-6*) Price Stern.

—Serendipity. James, Robin, illus. LC 94-25575. 1995. write for info. (*0-8431-3819-X*) Price Stern.

Coville, Bruce. Bruce Coville's Book of Monsters: Tales to Give You the Creeps. (gr. 4-7). 1993. pap. 2.95 (*0-590-46159-1*) Scholastic Inc.

—The Monster's Ring. Coville, Katherine, illus. LC 82-3436. 96p. (gr. 8-11). 1982. lib. bdg. 9.99 (*0-394-95320-7*) Pantheon.

Craig, Helen. Night of the Paper Bag Monsters. Craig, Helen, illus. LC 92-44610. 32p. (Orig.). (ps up). 1994. pap. 4.99 (*1-56402-120-3*) Candlewick Pr.

Creighton, J. Maybe a Monster. (Illus.). 24p. (ps-8). 1989. 12.95 (*1-55037-037-5*, Pub. by Annick CN); pap. 4.95 (*1-55037-036-7*, Pub. by Annick CN) Firefly Bks Ltd.

Crowe, Robert L. Clyde Monster. Chorao, Kay, illus. LC 76-10733. 32p. (ps-3). 1987. (DCB); pap. 3.95 (*0-525-44289-8*, DCB) Dutton Child Bks.

—Clyde Monster. (ps-3). 1993. pap. 4.99 (*0-14-054743-6*) Puffin Bks.

Cuyler, Margery. Weird Wolf. Zimmer, Dirk, illus. LC 89-1541. 80p. (gr. 2-4). 1991. pap. 4.95 (*0-8050-1643-0*, Bks Young Read) H Holt & Co.

Dadey, Debbie. Frankenstein Doesn't Plant Petunias. (gr. 9-12). 1993. pap. 2.75 (*0-590-47071-X*) Scholastic Inc.

Dadey, Debbie & Jones, Marcia. Aliens Don't Wear Braces. 1993. pap. 2.95 (*0-590-47070-1*) Scholastic Inc.

Daniells, Trenna. Travis & the Dragon: Accepting Others As They Are. Braille International, Inc. Staff & Henry, James, illus. (Orig.). (gr. 1). 1992. pap. 10.95 (*1-56956-005-6*) W A T Braille.

—Travis & the Dragon: Accepting Others As They Are. Braille International, Inc. Staff & Henry, James, illus. (Orig.). (gr. 2). 1992. pap. 10.95 (*1-56956-030-7*) W A T Braille.

DeBeer, Liz. Ming's Monster. Fahey, Cathy, illus. LC 92-70985. 44p. (gr. k-3). 1993. 7.95 (*1-55523-521-2*) Winston-Derek.

DeGroat, Diane. Annie Pitts, Swamp Monster. LC 93-2474. 1994. pap. 13.00 (*0-671-87004-1*, S&S BFYR) S&S Trade.

Delessert, Etienne. Dance! Delessert, Etienne, illus. 32p. (gr. 1-8). 1994. RLB smythe-sewn 16.95 (*0-88682-627-6*, 97938-098) Creative Ed.

Demarest, Chris L. Morton & Sidney. Demarest, Chris L., illus. LC 92-44153. 32p. (gr. k-2). 1993. pap. 4.95 (*0-689-71740-7*, Aladdin) Macmillan Child Grp.

Denan, Corinne. Dragon & Monster Tales. new ed. LC 79-66329. (Illus.). 48p. (gr. 3-6). 1980. PLB 9.89 (*0-89375-326-2*); pap. 2.95 (*0-89375-325-4*) Troll Assocs.

Deschaine, Scott. Monster Love. Donovan, Bob, illus. 36p. 1993. pap. 2.50 (*1-878181-05-X*) Discovery Comics.

Drescher, Henrik. The Little Boy Who Ate Around. LC 93-40848. (Illus.). 40p. (ps-3). 1994. 14.95 (*0-7868-0014-3*); 14.89 (*0-7868-2011-X*) Hyprn Child.

—Pat the Beastie: A Pull-&-Poke Book. Drescher, Henrik, illus. 18p. (ps). 1993. 9.95 (*1-56282-407-4*) Hyprn Child.

—Simon's Book. LC 82-24931. (Illus.). 32p. (ps up). 1991. pap. 3.95 (*0-688-10484-3*, Mulberry) Morrow.

Druce, Arden. Witch, Witch. LC 91-29763. 1991. 11.95 (*0-85953-780-3*); pap. 5.95 (*0-685-52311-X*) Childs Play.

Duncan, Jane. Janet Reachfar & the Kelpie. Hedderwick, Mairi, illus. LC 75-44166. 32p. (ps-3). 1976. 7.50 (*0-685-02316-8*, Clarion Bks) HM.

Eccles, Jane. Maxwell's Birthday. LC 91-16290. (Illus.). 32p. (ps-3). 1992. 14.00 (*0-688-11036-3*, Tambourine Bks); PLB 13.93 (*0-688-11037-1*, Tambourine Bks) Morrow.

Emberley, Ed. Go Away, Big Green Monster! (ps-3). 1993. 12.95 (*0-316-23653-5*) Little.

Euvremer, Teryl. Triple Whammy. Euvremer, Teryl, illus. LC 91-44240. 32p. (gr. k-4). 1993. 15.00 (*0-06-021060-5*); PLB 14.89 (*0-06-021061-3*) HarpC Child Bks.

Evelyn-Marie. Daniel Scott & the Monster. Lang, Irene, illus. LC 85-13369. 32p. (gr. k-3). 1985. 7.95 (*0-9614746-1-0*); PLB 9.95 (*0-9614746-2-9*); bk. & cassette 11.95 (*0-9614746-0-2*); pap. 3.00 (*0-9614746-4-5*) Berry Bks.

Faulkner, Keith. Monster in My Bathroom. Lambert, Tony, illus. 16p. (ps-3). 1993. 4.95 (*0-8431-3482-8*) Price Stern.

—Monster in My Toybox. Lambert, Tony, illus. 16p. (ps-3). 1993. 4.95 (*0-8431-3481-X*) Price Stern.

Fisher, Leonard E. Cyclops. Fisher, Leonard E., illus. 1993. pap. 5.95 (*0-8234-1062-5*) Holiday.

Fisher, Lucretia. Two Monsters: A Fable. Jardine, Thomas, illus. LC 76-21684. 48p. (ps up). 1976. pap. 3.95 (*0-916144-08-9*) Stemmer Hse.

Garden, Nancy. The Mystery of the Night Raiders. LC 87-45829. 144p. (gr. 4-6). 1987. 14.00 (*0-374-35221-6*) FS&G.

—Mystery of the Night Raiders. MacDonald, Patricia, ed. 176p. 1991. pap. 2.99 (*0-671-76064-5*, Minstrel Bks) PB.

Geringer, Laura. Look Out, Look Out, It's Coming! Truesdell, Sue, illus. LC 91-4707. 40p. (ps-2). 1992. PLB 14.89 (*0-06-021712-X*) HarpC Child Bks.

Giff, Patricia R. The Beast in Ms. Rooney's Room. 80p. (Orig.). (gr. 1-4). 1984. pap. 3.50 (*0-440-40485-1*, YB) Dell.

Gilden, Mel. Fifth Grade Monsters, No. 12: Werewolf Come Home. 1990. pap. 2.75 (*0-380-75908-X*, Camelot) Avon.

—Fifth Grade Monsters, No. 13: Monster Boy. 96p. 1991. pap. 2.95 (*0-380-76305-2*, Camelot) Avon.

—Fifth Grade Monsters, No. 14: Troll Patrol. 96p. (Orig.). 1991. pap. 2.95 (*0-380-76306-0*, Camelot) Avon.

—How to Be a Vampire in One Easy Lesson. 1990. pap. 2.75 (*0-380-75906-3*, Camelot) Avon.

—Island of the Weird. 96p. 1990. pap. 2.95 (*0-380-75907-1*, Camelot) Avon.

—M Is for Monster. 96p. 1987. pap. 2.75 (*0-380-75423-1*, Camelot) Avon.

—The Monster in Creeps Head Bay. 96p. 1990. pap. 2.75 (*0-380-75905-5*, Camelot) Avon.

—The Pet of Frankenstein. 96p. (gr. 3-7). 1988. pap. 2.50 (*0-380-75185-2*, Camelot) Avon.

—Z Is for Zombie. 96p. (gr. 3-7). 1988. pap. 2.75 (*0-380-75686-2*, Camelot) Avon.

Godfrey, Martyn. Is It Ok If This Monster Stays for Lunch? (ps-3). 1994. pap. 6.95 (*0-19-540882-9*) OUP.

Gordon, Sharon. The Jolly Monsters. Cushman, Doug, illus. LC 87-10867. 32p. (gr. k-2). 1988. PLB 11.59 (*0-8167-1079-1*); pap. text ed. 2.95 (*0-8167-1080-5*) Troll Assocs.

Graham, Richard. Jack & the Monster. Varley, Susan, illus. (ps-3). 1989. 13.45 (*0-395-49680-2*) HM.

Greaves, Margaret. The Serpent Shell. Nesbitt, Jan, illus. 32p. (ps-3). 1993. 13.95 (*0-8120-6350-3*) Barron.

Green, Carl & Sanford, William. Tarantula. LC 84-20067. (Illus.). 48p. (gr. 3-5). 1985. RSBE 10.95 (*0-89686-264-X*, Crestwood Hse) Macmillan Child Grp.

Greenberg, Jan. No Dragons to Slay. LC 83-17200. 152p. (gr. 7 up). 1984. pap. 3.50 (*0-374-45509-0*) FS&G.

Greenblat, Rodney A. Slombo the Gross. LC 91-31235. (Illus.). 32p. (ps-3). 1993. 15.00 (*0-06-020775-2*); PLB 14.89 (*0-06-020776-0*) HarpC Child Bks.

Greenleaf, Ann. Too Many Monsters. 1993. 4.99 (*0-517-09158-5*) Random Hse Value.

The Grumpus under Rug. (Illus.). (ps-2). 1991. PLB 6.95 (*0-8136-5114-X*, TK2262); pap. 3.50 (*0-8136-5614-1*, TK2263) Modern Curr.

Haley, Gail E., retold by. & illus. Jack & the Fire Dragon. 40p. (gr. k-4). 1988. PLB 14.95 (*0-517-56814-4*) Crown Bks Yng Read.

Harry & the Hendersons. 1987. pap. 1.50 (*0-440-82048-0*) Dell.

Harvey, Jayne. Great-Uncle Dracula. Carter, Abby, illus. LC 91-31460. 80p. (Orig.). (gr. 2-4). 1992. PLB 6.99 (*0-679-92448-5*); pap. 2.50 (*0-679-82448-0*) Random Bks Yng Read.

Hawkins, Colin. Monsters. (gr. 4-7). 1993. pap. 7.00 NOP (*0-00-664020-6*) HarpC Child Bks.

Hayward, Linda. The Biggest Cookie in the World. Ewers, Joe, illus. LC 88-36247. 24p. (Orig.). (ps-1). 1989. pap. 2.25 (*0-394-84049-6*) Random Bks Yng Read.

—The Biggest Cookie in the World. Ewers, Joe, illus. LC 94-21151. 1995. write for info. (*0-679-87146-2*); PLB write for info. (*0-679-97146-7*) Random Bks Yng Read.

Heller, Nicholas. The Monster in the Cave. Heller, Nicholas, illus. LC 86-29598. 32p. (ps-3). 1987. 11.75 (*0-688-07313-1*); lib. bdg. 11.88 (*0-688-07314-X*) Greenwillow.

Herbert the Timid Dragon. (gr. 1-3). 1991. write for info. (*0-307-11463-5*, Golden Pr) Western Pub.

Herman, Gail. Double-Header. Smath, Jerry, illus. LC 92-34175. 32p. (ps-1). 1993. PLB 7.99 (*0-448-40156-8*, G&D); pap. 3.50 (*0-448-40157-6*, G&D) Putnam Pub Group.

Hird, Nancy E. Marty's Monster. Damon, Valerie, illus. 48p. (Orig.). (gr. 1-3). 1993. pap. 3.99 (*0-7847-0098-2*, 24-03948) Standard Pub.

Hitchcock, Alfred, ed. Alfred Hitchcock's Monster Museum. LC 81-13883. (Illus.). 224p. (gr. 5 up). 1982. pap. 4.99 (*0-394-84899-3*) Random Bks Yng Read.

Hoban, Russell. Monsters. Blake, Quentin, illus. 1990. 13.95 (*0-590-43422-5*) Scholastic Inc.

—Monsters. Blake, Quentin, illus. 32p. (ps-2). 1993. pap. 4.95 (*0-590-43421-7*) Scholastic Inc.

Hodges, Margaret. St. George & the Dragon. (ps-4). 1990. pap. 6.95 (*0-316-36795-8*) Little.

Hoh, Diane. Monster. 1994. pap. 3.95 (*0-590-48321-8*) Scholastic Inc.

Holland, Jeffrey. Chessie, the Sea Monster That Ate Annapolis. Ramsey, Marcy D., illus. 32p. (gr. k-4). 1990. 8.95 (*0-9618461-0-0*) BaySailor Bks.

Hooks, William H. Mr. Monster, Level 3. Meisel, Paul, illus. 1990. PLB 9.99 (*0-553-05897-5*, Little Rooster); pap. 3.50 (*0-553-34927-9*, Little Rooster) Bantam.

Howe, James. There's a Monster under My Bed. Rose, David S., illus. LC 85-20026. 32p. (ps-2). 1986. SBE 13.95 (*0-689-31178-8*, Atheneum Child Bk) Macmillan Child Grp.

—There's a Monster under My Bed. Rose, David, illus. LC 89-18664. 32p. (gr. k-3). 1990. pap. 4.95 (*0-689-71409-2*, Aladdin) Macmillan Child Grp.

Huntley, Chris. The Beast in the Bathroom. Huntley, Chris, illus. 32p. (ps). 1991. write for info. Smythe bdg. (*0-9616679-2-3*) Aquarelle Pr.

Hutchins, Pat. Silly Billy! LC 91-32561. (Illus.). 32p. (ps-6). 1992. 14.00 (*0-688-10817-2*); PLB 13.93 (*0-688-10818-0*) Greenwillow.

—Three-Star Billy. LC 93-26517. 32p. 1994. 15.00 (*0-688-13078-X*); lib. bdg. 14.93 (*0-688-13079-8*) Greenwillow.

—The Very Worst Monster. Hutchins, Pat, illus. LC 84-5928. 32p. (gr. k-3). 1985. 16.95 (*0-688-04010-1*); PLB 16.88 (*0-688-04011-X*) Greenwillow.

—The Very Worst Monster. LC 84-5928. (Illus.). (gr. 1 up). 1989. pap. 7.95 bk. & cassette (*0-688-09038-9*, Mulberry) Morrow.

Ingle, Annie. The Monster That Glowed in the Dark. Petach, Heidi, illus. LC 92-30144. 16p. (ps-1). 1993. pap. 5.99 (*0-679-84194-6*) Random Bks Yng Read.

Jackson, Daniel & Summers-Dawes, Kate. Monsters You've Never Heard of & Never Will Unless You Read This Book. (gr. 1-5). 1991. pap. 5.95 (*1-880722-00-3*) S L Jackson.

Johnston, Tony. Night Noises & Other Mole & Troll Stories. (gr. k-6). 1989. pap. 2.95 (*0-440-40232-8*, YB) Dell.

Jonsen, George. Favorite Tales of Monsters & Trolls. O'Brien, John, illus. Lerner, Sharon, ed. LC 76-24182. (Illus.). (ps-2). 1977. lib. bdg. 5.99 (*0-394-93477-6*) Random Bks Yng Read.

Jungman, Ann. Vlad the Drac. large type ed. (Illus.). (gr. 1-8). 1994. 15.95 (*0-7451-2221-3*, Galaxy etc.) Chivers N Amer.

Kline, Suzy. Horrible Harry in Room Two B. 31p. 1992. text ed. 2.48 (*1-56956-113-3*) W A T Braille.

—Horrible Harry in Room 2B. Remkiewicz, Frank, illus. (gr. 2-5). 1988. pap. 10.95 (*0-670-82176-4*) Viking Child Bks.

Knief, William. The Golden Monster. Weber, Susan M., illus. 32p. (Orig.). 1971. pap. 1.00 staple bound (*0-685-30030-7*) Cottonwood KS.

Koltz, Tony. Vampire Express. 128p. (Orig.). (gr. 4-7). 1984. pap. text ed. 2.25 (*0-553-26185-1*) Bantam.

Kracht, Susan. The Sloppy Monster. Corns, Marvin A., illus. LC 92-60289. 44p. (ps-3). 1992. 5.95 (*1-55523-527-1*) Winston-Derek.

Kudalis, Eric. Frankenstein & Other Stories of Man-Made Monsters. 48p. (gr. 3-10). 1994. PLB 17.27 (*1-56065-213-6*) Capstone Pr.

Leedy, Loreen. The Monster Money Book. Leedy, Loreen, illus. LC 91-18168. 32p. (ps-3). 1992. reinforced bdg. 14.95 (*0-8234-0922-8*) Holiday.

Leetham, Helen. Sir Percy & the Dragon. (Illus.). 32p. (ps-1). 1994. 17.95 (*0-86264-273-6*, Pub. by Andersen Pr UK) Trafalgar.

L'Engle, Madeleine. Dragons in the Waters. 288p. (gr. 7 up). 1982. pap. 4.50 (*0-440-91719-0*, LFL) Dell.

Lerner, Sharon. Follow the Monsters. Cooke, Tom, illus. LC 84-18031. 32p. (ps-1). 1985. pap. 3.50 (*0-394-87126-X*) Random Bks Yng Read.

Lester, Alison. Monsters Are Knocking. 16p. (ps-1). 1999. pap. 4.99 (*0-14-054967-6*, Puffin) Puffin Bks.

Levy, Elizabeth. Frankenstein Moved in on the Fourth Floor. Gerstein, Mordicai, illus. LC 78-19830. (gr. 1-5). 1979. PLB 12.89 (*0-06-023811-9*) HarpC Child Bks.

—Frankenstein Moved in on the Fourth Floor. Gerstein, Mordicai, illus. LC 78-19830. 64p. (gr. 2-5). 1981. pap. 3.95 (*0-06-440122-7*, Trophy) HarpC Child Bks.

—Gorgonzola Zombies in the Park. Ulrich, George, illus. LC 92-11353. 96p. (gr. 2-5). 1993. 14.00 (*0-06-021461-9*); PLB 13.89 (*0-06-021460-0*) HarpC Child Bks.

Lowe. Beasts by Bunches. 1987. 10.95 (*0-385-23794-4*) Doubleday.

McCormick, Bob. The Story of Tahoe Tessie: The Original Lake Tahoe Monster. 5th, rev. ed. Lambert, Eileen, illus. (gr. 1-4). 1990. pap. 5.95 (*0-9626792-6-7*) Tahoe Tourist.

McHargue, Georgess. The Beasts of Never. Bozzo, Frank, illus. LC 86-29374. 128p. (gr. 7 up). 1987. pap. 14.95 (*0-385-29573-1*) Delacorte.

Mana, Tawa & Youyouseyah. When Hopi Children Were Bad: A Monster Story. Coates, Ross, illus. 41p. (Orig.). (gr. k-5). 1989. pap. 6.95 (*0-940113-20-1*) Sierra Oaks Pub.

Marsh, Carole. Ghost of the Bed & Breakfast. (Illus.). 48p. (ps-7). 1994. 24.95 (*1-55609-155-9*); pap. 14.95 (*1-55609-239-3*) Gallopade Pub Group.

Mathews, Judith. An Egg & Seven Socks. Hafner, Marylin, illus. LC 91-11476. 32p. (ps-2). 1993. 14.00 (*0-06-020207-6*); PLB 13.89 (*0-06-020208-4*) HarpC Child Bks.

Mathias, Robert. Beauty & the Beast. 1991. 4.99 (*0-517-06693-9*) Random Hse Value.

Mayer, Mercer. Liza Lou & the Yeller Belly Swamp. Mayer, Mercer, illus. LC 80-16605. 48p. (gr. k-3). 1984. Repr. of 1976 ed. RSBE 14.95 (*0-02-765220-3*, Four Winds) Macmillan Child Grp.

—There's a Nightmare in My Closet. 1992. pap. 4.99 (*0-14-054712-6*, Puffin) Puffin Bks.

Meddaugh, Susan. Beast. Meddaugh, Susan, illus. 32p. (gr. k-3). 1985. 13.95 (*0-395-30349-4*); pap. 3.95 (*0-317-18511-X*) HM.

Mega-Books Staff. My Friend Fang. 1992. pap. 3.99 (*0-553-37116-9*) Bantam.

Michelson, Richard. Did You Say Ghosts? Baskin, Leonard, illus. LC 92-30134. 32p. (ps up). 1993. RSBE 14.95 (*0-02-766915-7*, Macmillan Child Bk) Macmillan Child Grp.

Miller, Judi. Vampire Named Murray. (gr. 4-7). 1991. pap. 2.99 (*0-553-15885-6*) Bantam.

Moncure, Jane B. Magic Monsters Count to Ten. Fudala, Rosemary, illus. LC 78-23634. (ps-3). 1979. PLB 14.95 (*0-89565-058-4*) Childs World.

—Magic Monsters Look for Colors. Magnuson, Diana, illus. LC 78-23792. (ps-3). 1979. PLB 14.95 (*0-89565-056-8*) Childs World.

—Magic Monsters Look for Shapes. Magnuson, Diana, illus. LC 78-21529. (ps-3). 1979. PLB 14.95 (*0-89565-057-6*) Childs World.

A Monster Followed Me to School. (gr. 1-3). 1991. write for info. (*0-307-11466-X*, Golden Pr) Western Pub.

The Monster Mystery. (Illus.). 64p. (gr. k-2). 1989. 6.95 (*0-87449-511-3*) Modern Pub NYC.

Monsters. 16p. 1990. pap. 3.99 (*0-517-03348-8*) Random Hse Value.

Mooser, Stephen. Creepy Creature Club, No. 3: Monster Holiday. 1989. pap. 2.75 (*0-440-40251-4*) Dell.

—My Halloween Boyfriend. (gr. k-6). 1989. pap. 2.75 (*0-440-40231-X*, YB) Dell.

—Secrets of Scary Fun. (Orig.). (gr. k-6). 1990. pap. 2.99 (*0-440-40338-3*, YB) Dell.

Mosel, Arlene. Funny Little Woman. (ps-3). 1993. pap. 4.99 (*0-14-054753-3*, Puffin) Puffin Bks.

Moss, Marissa. After-School Monster. LC 90-49416. (Illus.). 32p. (gr. k up). 1991. 13.95 (*0-688-10116-X*); PLB 13.88 (*0-688-10117-8*) Lothrop.

—After-School Monster. 32p. (ps-3). 1993. pap. 4.99 (*0-14-054829-7*, Puffin) Puffin Bks.

Mueller, Virginia. Monster & the Baby. Fay, Ann, ed. Munsinger, Lynn, illus. LC 85-3127. 24p. (ps-1). 1985. PLB 11.95 (*0-8075-5253-4*) A Whitman.

—Monster Can't Sleep. Munsinger, Lynn, illus. (ps-1). 1988. pap. 3.95 (*0-14-050878-3*, Puffin) Puffin Bks.

—A Playhouse for Monster. Fay, Ann, ed. Munsinger, Lynn, illus. LC 85-3144. 24p. (ps-1). 1985. PLB 11.95 (*0-8075-6541-5*) A Whitman.

—A Playhouse for Monster. Munsinger, Lynn, illus. (ps-1). 1988. pap. 3.95 (*0-14-050877-5*, Puffin) Puffin Bks.

Nightingale, Sandy. I'm a Little Monster. Nightingale, Sandy, illus. LC 94-18345. 1995. write for info. (*0-15-200309-6*) HarBrace.

Osborne, Dwight. The Squiggly Wiggly Head Family. Ablin, Barry, illus. 16p. 1992. pap. 5.95 (*0-9632817-0-4*) Osborne Bks.

Packard, Edward. You Are a Monster. 128p. (gr. 4). 1988. pap. 2.75 (*0-553-27474-0*) Bantam.

Paraskevas, Betty. Monster Beach. Paraskevas, Michael, illus. LC 93-46927. 1995. write for info. (*0-15-292882-0*) HarBrace.

Parish, Peggy. No More Monsters for Me! Simont, Marc, illus. LC 81-47111. 64p. (gr. k-3). 1987. pap. 3.50 (*0-06-444109-1*, Trophy) HarpC Child Bks.

Pascal, Francine. Jessica's Monster Nightmare. (gr. 1-3). 1993. pap. 2.99 (*0-553-48008-1*) Bantam.

Pellowski, Michael J. The Messy Monster. Paterson, Diane, illus. LC 85-14064. 48p. (Orig.). (gr. 1-3). 1986. PLB 10.59 (*0-8167-0570-4*); pap. text ed. 3.50 (*0-8167-0571-2*) Troll Assocs.

Pienkowski, Jan. Little Monsters. (Illus.). 10p. (ps up). 1986. 9.95 (*0-8431-1241-7*) Price Stern.

—Little Monsters. (Illus.). 10p. (ps up). 1991. 4.95 (*0-8431-2964-6*) Price Stern.

Pilkey, Dav. Dogzilla. LC 92-37906. (gr. 4 up). 1993. 10.95 (*0-15-223944-8*); pap. 5.95 (*0-15-223945-6*) HarBrace.

—Dragon's Fat Cat. LC 91-16369. (Illus.). 48p. (gr. 1-3). 1992. 12.95 (*0-531-05982-0*); lib. bdg. 12.99 (*0-531-08582-1*) Orchard Bks Watts.

Pinkwater, Daniel M. I Was a Second Grade Werewolf. LC 82-17715. (Illus.). 32p. (ps-2). 1983. 12.95 (*0-525-44038-0*, DCB) Dutton Child Bks.

Polidori, John. The Vampire. reissue ed. Martin, Les, adapted by. Munching, Paul V., illus. LC 88-34078. 96p. (gr. 2-6). 1989. lib. bdg. 5.99 (*0-394-93844-5*, Bullseye Bks); pap. 3.50 (*0-394-83844-0*, Bullseye Bks) Random Bks Yng Read.

Powell, Richard. How to Deal with Monsters. Snow, Alan, illus. LC 91-14975. 24p. (gr. k-3). 1992. PLB 9.59 (*0-8167-2424-5*); pap. text ed. 2.95 (*0-8167-2425-3*) Troll Assocs.

Prelutsky, Jack. The Dragons Are Singing Tonight. Sis, Peter, illus. LC 92-29013. 40p. (ps up). 1993. 15.00 (*0-688-09645-X*); PLB 14.93 (*0-688-12511-5*) Greenwillow.

Rainey, Richard. The Monster Factory. LC 92-26191. (Illus.). 128p. (gr. 6 up). 1993. text ed. 13.95 RSBE (*0-02-775663-7*, New Discovery) Macmillan Child Grp.

Razzi, Jim. Dragons. 64p. (Orig.). (gr. 1-3). 1984. pap. text ed. 2.25 (*0-553-15465-6*, Skylark) Bantam.

Richler, Mordecai. Jacob Two-Two Meets the Hooded Fang. (gr. 4-7). 1994. pap. 3.50 (*0-679-85403-7*) Knopf Bks Yng Read.

Rodgers, Frank. Looking after Your First Monster. (ps-3). 1992. pap. 3.95 (*0-590-45695-4*) Scholastic Inc.

Roos, Stephen. Love Me, Love My Werewolf. (gr. 4-7). 1993. pap. 3.50 (*0-440-40812-1*) Dell.

Ross, Dave. How to Prevent Monster Attacks. LC 83-26536. (Illus.). 64p. (gr. 4 up). 1984. 7.00 (*0-688-03790-9*) Morrow Jr Bks.

Ryan, John. Pugwash & the Sea Monster. (Illus.). 32p. (gr. k-2). 1994. 19.95 (*0-370-10793-4*, Pub. by Bodley Head UK) Trafalgar.

Sanford, William & Green, Carl. Dracula's Daughter. LC 84-27462. (Illus.). 48p. (gr. 3-5). 1985. text ed. 10.95 RSBE (*0-89686-260-7*, Crestwood Hse) Macmillan Child Grp.

—Ghost of Frankenstein. LC 84-29231. (Illus.). 48p. (gr. 3-5). 1985. text ed. 10.95 RSBE (*0-89686-261-5*, Crestwood Hse) Macmillan Child Grp.

—The Mole People. LC 84-23913. (Illus.). 48p. (gr. 3-5). 1985. text ed. 10.95 RSBE (*0-89686-262-3*, Crestwood Hse) Macmillan Child Grp.

—Werewolf of London. LC 84-19910. (Illus.). 48p. (gr. 3-5). 1985. text ed. 10.95 RSBE (*0-89686-265-8*, Crestwood Hse) Macmillan Child Grp.

Saunders, Susan. Attack of the Monster Plants. 64p. (gr. 4). 1986. pap. 2.25 (*0-553-15399-4*) Bantam.

Schick, Joel & Schick, Alice. Mary Shelley's Frankenstein. Schick, Joel & Schick, Alice, illus. LC 80-385. 48p. (gr. 4-6). 1981. PLB 11.95 (*0-385-28302-4*) Delacorte.

Schreier, Joshua. Hank's Work. LC 92-15205. (ps-2). 1993. 13.50 (*0-525-44970-1*, DCB) Dutton Child Bks.

Sendak, Maurice. Seven Little Monsters. Sendak, Maurice, illus. LC 76-18400. (gr. 1 up). 1977. PLB 14.89 (*0-06-025478-5*) HarpC Child Bks.

—Where the Wild Things Are. LC 91-45366. (Illus.). 48p. (gr. k up). 1992. incl. mini Bernard doll 16.95 (*0-694-00432-4*, Festival); incl. mini Max doll 16.95 (*0-694-00431-6*, Festival) HarpC Child Bks.

—Where the Wild Things Are: (Donde Viven los Monstruos) Sendak, Maurice, illus. (SPA.). (gr. 1-6). 22.95 (*84-204-3022-6*) Santillana.

Shannon, Margaret, text by. & illus. Elvira. LC 92-39784. 32p. (ps-2). 1993. PLB 13.95 (*0-395-66597-3*) Ticknor & Flds Bks Yng Read.

Sharmat, Marjorie W. Pizza Monster. 1989. pap. 12.95 (*0-440-50086-9*) Dell.

—Scarlet Monster Lives Here. Kendrick, Dennis, illus. LC 78-19484. 64p. (gr. k-3). 1979. PLB 11.89 (*0-06-025527-7*) HarpC Child Bks.

—Scarlet Monster Lives Here. Kendrick, Dennis, illus. LC 78-19484. 64p. (gr. k-3). 1986. pap. 3.50 (*0-06-444098-2*, Trophy) HarpC Child Bks.

Sharmat, Marjorie W. & Sharmat, Mitchell. The Pizza Monster. Bruncus, Denise, illus. (ps up). 1989. 12.95 (*0-385-29722-X*) Delacorte.

Shebar, Sharon. Night Monsters. Reese, Bob, illus. (gr. k-3). 1979. pap. 20.00 (*0-685-50869-2*) ARO Pub.

Shelley, Mary Wollstonecraft. Frankenstein. Schick, Alice & Schick, Joel, eds. LC 80-385. (Illus.). 48p. (gr. 3 up). 1980. PLB 10.89 (*0-440-02693-8*); pap. 4.95 (*0-440-02692-X*) Delacorte.

—Frankenstein. Binder, Otto, ed. Cruz, Nardo, illus. LC 73-75462. 64p. (Orig.). (gr. 5-10). 1973. pap. 2.95 (*0-88301-097-6*); student activity bk. 1.25 (*0-88301-177-8*) Pendulum Pr.

—Frankenstein. Kelley, Gary, illus. Stewart, Diana, adapted by. LC 81-5216. (Illus.). 48p. (gr. 4 up). 1983. PLB 20.70 (*0-8172-1674-X*) Raintree Steck-V.

—Frankenstein. Weinberg, Larry, adapted by. Barr, Ken, illus. LC 87-23543. 96p. (gr. 2-6). 1982. (Bullseye Bks); pap. 3.50 (*0-394-84827-6*, Bullseye Bks) Random Bks Yng Read.

—Frankenstein. Arneson, D. J., retold by. Clift, Eva, illus. 128p. 1992. pap. 2.95 (*1-56156-142-8*) Kidsbks.

Silverman, Erica. Big Pumpkin. Schindler, S. D., illus. LC 91-14053. 32p. (ps-3). 1992. RSBE 14.95 (*0-02-782683-X*, Macmillan Child Bk) Macmillan Child Grp.

Skwarek, Skip. The Weirdies of Wailing Wood. Compass Productions Staff, illus. LC 91-46916. 10p. (gr. k-4). 1992. 4.95 (*0-8037-1188-3*) Dial Bks Young.

Slater, Jim. Big Snowy. Slater, Christopher, illus. LC 80-53066. (ps-3). 1981. pap. 1.25 (*0-394-84736-9*) Random Bks Yng Read.

Slepian, Jan. Hungry Thing Returns. (ps-3). 1993. pap. 3.95 (*0-590-42891-8*) Scholastic Inc.

Smith, Dona. Shock Shots: Ghosts. (gr. 4-7). 1993. pap. 1.25 (*0-590-47568-1*) Scholastic Inc.

—Shock Shots: Monsters. (gr. 4-7). 1993. pap. 1.25 (*0-590-47566-5*) Scholastic Inc.

—Shock Shots: Mummies. (gr. 4-7). 1993. pap. 1.25 (*0-590-47571-1*) Scholastic Inc.

—Shock Shots: Vampires. (gr. 4-7). 1993. pap. 1.25 (*0-590-47569-X*) Scholastic Inc.

—Shock Shots: Werewolves. (gr. 4-7). 1993. pap. 1.25 (*0-590-47570-3*) Scholastic Inc.

—Shock Shots: Zombies. (gr. 4-7). 1993. pap. 1.25 (*0-590-47567-3*) Scholastic Inc.

Smith, Janice L. The Monster in the Third Dresser Drawer. Gackenbach, Dick, illus. LC 81-47109. 96p. (gr. 1-4). 1981. 13.00 (*0-06-025734-2*); PLB 12.89 (*0-06-025739-3*) HarpC Child Bks.

—The Monster in the Third Dresser Drawer: And Other Stories about Adam Joshua. Gackenbach, Dick, illus. LC 81-47109. 96p. (gr. 1-4). 1988. pap. 3.95 (*0-06-440223-1*, Trophy) HarpC Child Bks.

Smith, Kaitlin M. Big Monster Learns about Manners. Smith, Kaitlin M., illus. 18p. (gr. 1-5). 1992. pap. 10.95 (*1-56606-006-0*) Bradley Mann.

Stanish, Bob. A Monster's Shoe & the Cat. Stanish, Bob, illus. 44p. (gr. 1-4). 1983. pap. 9.95 tchr's. enrichment bk. (*0-88047-018-6*, 8303) DOK Pubs.

Stern, Steve. Hershel & the Beast. Gills, K. King, illus. LC 86-27789. 64p. (Orig.). (gr. 1-5). 1987. text ed. 13.95 (*0-938507-05-2*) Ion Books.

Stevens, Kathleen. The Beast in the Bathtub. Bowler, Ray, illus. LC 85-12691. 32p. (gr. 2-3). 1985. PLB 18.60 (*0-918831-15-6*) Gareth Stevens Inc.

—Bully for the Beast! Bowler, Ray, illus. LC 88-33090. 32p. (gr. 2-3). 1990. PLB 18.60 (*0-8368-0020-6*) Gareth Stevens Inc.

Stimson, Joan. Monster: Stories for under Fives. Hawksley, Gerald, illus. 44p. (ps-k). 1992. 3.50 (*0-7214-1505-9*) Ladybird Bks.

Stine, Megan & Stine, H. William. Camp Zombie. LC 93-33748. 1994. write for info. (Bullseye Bks) Random Bks Yng Read.

—Camp Zombie. 108p. (Orig.). (gr. 2-6). 1994. pap. 2.99 (*0-679-85640-4*) Random Bks Yng Read.

Stine, R. L. The Girl Who Cried Monster. (gr. 4-7). 1993. pap. 2.95 (*0-590-46618-6*) Scholastic Inc.

—Monster Blood Two. (gr. 4-7). 1994. pap. 3.25 (*0-590-47740-4*) Scholastic Inc.

—The Werewolf of Fever Swamp. (gr. 8-12). 1993. pap. 23.95 (*0-590-49449-X*) Scholastic Inc.

Stoker, Bram. Dracula. Schick, Alice & Schick, Joel, eds. LC 83-5471. (Illus.). 48p. (gr. 3 up). 1980. PLB 10.89 (*0-440-01349-6*); pap. 6.95 (*0-440-01348-8*) Delacorte.

—Dracula. Farr, Naunerle, ed. Redondo, Nestor, illus. LC 83-5471. 64p. (Orig.). (gr. 5-10). 1973. pap. 2.95 (*0-88301-100-X*); student activity bk. 1.25 (*0-88301-175-1*) Pendulum Pr.

—Dracula. Spinner, Stephanie, adapted by. Spence, Jim, illus. LC 87-235417. 96p. (gr. 3-7). 1982. lib. bdg. 4.99 (*0-394-94828-9*, Bullseye Bks); pap. 2.95 (*0-394-84828-4*, Bullseye Bks) Random Bks Yng Read.

—Dracula. 1992. 3.50 (*0-590-46029-3*, 067, Apple Classics) Scholastic Inc.

Sutcliff, Rosemary. Beowulf. Keeping, Charles, illus. (gr. 5-9). 1984. 22.00 (*0-8446-6165-1*) Peter Smith.

Teitelbaum, Mike. Universal Monsters: Dracula. Ruiz, Art, illus. 96p. (gr. 3-7). 1992. pap. 2.95 (*0-307-22331-0*, 22331, Golden Pr) Western Pub.

Ten Furry Monsters. 1994. 13.27 (*0-8368-0989-0*) Gareth Stevens Inc.

Tester, Sylvia R. Magic Monsters Around the Year. LC 78-23800. (Illus.). (ps-3). 1979. PLB 14.95 (*0-89565-059-2*) Childs World.

—Magic Monsters Learn about Safety. Magine, John, illus. LC 78-24365. (ps-3). 1979. PLB 14.95 (*0-89565-060-6*) Childs World.

—What Is a Monster? Magnuson, Diana, illus. LC 78-23642. (ps-3). 1979. PLB 14.95 (*0-89565-055-X*) Childs World.

Thaler, Mike. King Kong's Underwear. 96p. (Orig.). (gr. 7 up). 1986. pap. 2.50 (*0-380-89823-3*, Camelot) Avon.

Thorne, Ian. The Deadly Mantis. LC 81-22074. (Illus.). 48p. (gr. 3-5). 1982. text ed. 11.95 RSBE (*0-89686-214-3*, Crestwood Hse) Macmillan Child Grp.

—Dracula. LC 76-51145. (Illus.). 48p. (gr. 3-5). 1977. text ed. 11.95 RSBE (*0-913940-67-4*, Crestwood Hse) Macmillan Child Grp.

—Frankenstein. LC 76-51144. (Illus.). 48p. (gr. 3-5). 1977. text ed. 11.95 RSBE (*0-913940-66-6*, Crestwood Hse); cass. 7.95 (*0-685-01269-7*) Macmillan Child Grp.

—Godzilla. LC 76-51148. (Illus.). 48p. (gr. 3 up). 1977. text ed. 11.95 RSBE (*0-913940-68-2*, Crestwood Hse); cass. 7.95 (*0-89686-486-3*) Macmillan Child Grp.

—It Came from Outer Space. LC 81-1419. (Illus.). 48p. (gr. 3-5). 1982. text ed. 11.95 RSBE (*0-89686-213-5*, Crestwood Hse) Macmillan Child Grp.

—King Kong. LC 76-51147. (Illus.). 48p. (gr. 3-5). 1977. text ed. 11.95 RSBE (*0-913940-69-0*, Crestwood Hse) Macmillan Child Grp.

—Mad Scientists. LC 76-51149. (Illus.). 48p. (gr. 3-5). 1977. text ed. 11.95 RSBE (*0-913940-70-4*, Crestwood Hse); cassette o.s.i. 7.95 (*0-89686-487-1*) Macmillan Child Grp.

—The Wolf Man. LC 76-51146. (Illus.). 48p. (gr. 3-5). 1989. text ed. 11.95 RSBE (*0-913940-71-2*, Crestwood Hse); cass. 7.95 (*0-89686-488-X*) Macmillan Child Grp.

Timm, Stephen A. The Dragon & the Mouse: The Dream. Lalo, illus. 45p. 1982. 12.95 (*0-939728-05-2*); pap. 4.95 (*0-939728-06-0*) Steppingstone Ent.

Trumbauer, Lisa. I Swear I Saw a Witch in Washington Square. LC 94-4371. 1994. write for info. (*0-681-00557-2*) Longmeadow Pr.

Van der Meer, Ron & Van der Meer, Atie. Jumping Monsters. (gr. 4 up). 1989. 4.95 (*0-85953-264-X*) Childs Play.

Velde, Vande. Dragon's Bait. 1992. write for info. (*0-15-200726-1*, J Yolen Bks) HarBrace.

Waddell, Martin. Little Dracula's Christmas. Wright, Joseph, illus. 32p. (gr. k up). 1986. pap. 3.95 (*0-14-050658-6*) Viking Child Bks.

—Little Dracula's First Bite. Wright, Joseph, illus. 32p. (gr. k up). 1986. pap. 3.95 (*0-14-050657-8*) Viking Child Bks.

Wahl, Jan. Dracula's Cat. LC 77-27051. (Illus.). (ps-3). 1981. 6.95 (*0-685-03842-4*); pap. 2.50 (*0-685-03843-2*) P-H.

—Dracula's Cat & Frankenstein's Dog. Chorao, Kay, illus. (ps-2). 1990. pap. 13.95 (*0-671-70820-1*) S&S Trade.

Wallace, Daisy, ed. Monster Poems. Chorao, Kay, illus. LC 75-17680. 32p. (ps-3). 1976. reinforced bdg. 13.95 (*0-8234-0268-1*); pap. 4.95 (*0-8234-0848-5*) Holiday.

Weinberg, Michael A. The Horrible Terrible Dragon: A Folktale. Weinberg, Kay, illus. 10p. (gr. 1-3). 1949. pap. 1.00 (*0-9601014-3-8*) Weinberg.

Whitlock, Susan L. Donovan Scares the Monsters. Abolafia, Yossi, illus. LC 86-4783. 24p. (gr. k-3). 1987. 11.75 (*0-688-06438-8*); PLB 11.88 (*0-688-06439-6*) Greenwillow.

Willis, Jeanne. The Monster Bed. Varley, Jeanne, illus. LC 86-10366. 32p. (ps-2). 1987. 14.00 (*0-688-06804-9*); PLB 13.93 (*0-688-06805-7*) Lothrop.

Willoughby, Elaine M. Boris & the Monsters. Munsinger, Lynn, illus. 32p. (gr. k-3). 1986. 13.45 (*0-395-29067-8*) HM.

Wilsdorf, Anne. Philomene. LC 90-24295. 1992. 14.00 (*0-688-10369-3*); PLB 13.93 (*0-688-10370-7*) Greenwillow.

Winthrop, Elizabeth. Maggie & the Monster. De Paola, Tomie, illus. LC 86-19593. 32p. (ps-3). 1987. reinforced bdg. 15.95 (*0-8234-0639-3*); pap. 5.95 (*0-8234-0698-9*) Holiday.

Wolak, Camilla H. Squire Gullible & the Dragon. rev. ed. LC 89-43530. (gr. 3-12). 1985. pap. 6.00 play script (*0-88734-508-5*) Players Pr.

Wylie, Joanne. Sabes Donde Esta Tu Monstruo Esta Noche? Kratky, Lada, tr. Wylie, David, illus. LC 85-31423. (SPA.). 32p. (ps-2). 1986. pap. 3.95 (*0-516-54491-8*) Childrens.

Wylie, Joanne & Wylie, David. The Gumdrop Monster: Learning about Colors. LC 84-12133. (Illus.). 32p. (ps-2). 1984. pap. 3.95 (*0-516-44492-1*) Childrens.

—Has Abrazado Hoy a Tu Monstruo? Un Cuento de los Modales: Have You Hugged Your Monster Today? Learning about Manners. LC 86-21624. (Illus.). 32p. (ps-2). 1986. pap. 3.95 (*0-516-54493-4*) Childrens.

—Little Monster: Learning about Size. LC 85-14988. (Illus.). 32p. (ps-2). 1985. pap. 3.95 (*0-516-44495-6*) Childrens.

—So You Think You Saw a Monster? Learning about Make-Believe. LC 85-16594. (Illus.). 32p. (ps-2). 1985. pap. 3.95 (*0-516-44496-4*) Childrens.

—Y Tu Crees Que Viste un Monstruo? Un Cuento de Fantasia: So You Think You Saw a Monster? A Make Believe Story. LC 86-21604. (Illus.). 32p. (ps-2). 1986. pap. 3.95 (*0-516-54496-9*) Childrens.

Yolen, Jane. Commander Toad in Space. Degen, Bruce, illus. 64p. (gr. 3-5). 1980. (Coward); pap. 6.95 (*0-698-20522-7*) Putnam Pub Group.

—Dragon's Blood. LC 81-69668. 256p. (gr. 7 up). 1982. 14.95 (*0-385-28226-5*) Delacorte.

—Dragon's Blood. (gr. 7 up). 1984. pap. 3.99 (*0-440-91802-2*, LFL) Dell.

Yolen, Jane & Greenberg, Martin H. Vampires. LC 90-27888. 240p. (gr. 5 up). 1993. pap. 3.95 (*0-06-440485-4*, Trophy) HarpC Child Bks.

—Werewolves: A Collection of Stories. 288p. (gr. 5 up). pap. 3.99 (*0-06-107044-0*, Harper Keypoint) HarpC Child Bks.

Los Zapalos Buevos Del Herry. (SPA.). (ps-3). 1993. pap. 4.95 (*0-307-52061-7*, Golden Pr) Western Pub.

Zemach, Harve. The Judge: An Untrue Tale. Zemach, Margot, illus. LC 79-87209. 48p. (ps-3). 1969. 17.00 (*0-374-33960-0*) FS&G.

Ziong, Blia, as told by. Nine-in-One, Grr! Grr! Spagnoli, Cathy, adapted by. (Illus.). 32p. (ps-5). 1993. pap. 5.95 (*0-89239-110-3*) Childrens Book Pr.

Zorn, Steve, retold by. Mostly Monsters. Bradley, John, illus. 56p. 1994. 9.98 (*0-685-71552-3*) Running Pr.

MONSTROSITIES

see Monsters

MONTANA

Amsel, Sheri. Cecils Montana Adventure Activity Book. (Illus.). 32p. (Orig.). (gr. 4-7). 1992. pap. 3.95 (*1-56044-138-0*) Falcon Pr MT.

Carole Marsh Montana Books, 44 bks. 1994. PLB 1027.82 set (*0-7933-1301-5*); pap. 587.80 set (*0-7933-5174-X*) Gallopade Pub Group.

Carpenter, Allan. Montana. new ed. LC 79-683. (Illus.). 96p. (gr. 4 up). 1979. PLB 16.95 (*0-516-04126-6*) Childrens.

Cooper, Myrtle E. From Tent Town to City: A Chronological History of Billings, Montana 1882-1935. Von Vogt, Janice, ed. Hulteng, Lee, illus. Wright, Kathryn, intro. by. (Illus.). 79p. (Orig.). (gr. 6-8). 1982. pap. 5.95 (*0-9613224-0-3*) Parmly Lib.

Fradin, Dennis B. Montana. LC 91-37958. 64p. (gr. 3-5). 1992. PLB 16.45 (*0-516-03826-5*) Childrens.

Heinrichs, Ann. Montana. LC 90-21035. (Illus.). 144p. (gr. 5-8). 1991. PLB 20.55 (*0-516-00472-7*) Childrens.

—Montana. 199p. 1993. text ed. 15.40 (*1-56956-135-4*) W A T Braille.

LaDoux, Rita C. Montana. Lerner Geography Department Staff, ed. (Illus.). 72p. (gr. 4-7). 1992. 17.50 (*0-8225-2714-6*) Lerner Pubns.

Marsh, Carole. Avast, Ye Slobs!: Montana Pirate Trivia. (Illus.). (gr. 3 up). 1994. PLB 24.95 (*0-7933-0715-5*); pap. 14.95 (*0-7933-0714-7*); computer disk 29.95 (*0-7933-0716-3*) Gallopade Pub Group.

—The Beast of the Montana Bed & Breakfast. (Illus.). (gr. 3 up). 1994. PLB 24.95 (*0-7933-1743-6*); pap. 14.95 (*0-7933-1744-4*); computer disk 29.95 (*0-7933-1745-2*) Gallopade Pub Group.

—Bow Wow! Montana Dogs in History, Mystery, Legend, Lore, Humor & More! (Illus.). (gr. 3-12). 1994. PLB 24.95 (*0-7933-3545-0*); pap. 14.95 (*0-7933-3546-9*); computer disk 29.95 (*0-7933-3547-7*) Gallopade Pub Group.

—Chill Out: Scary Montana Tales Based on Frightening Montana Truths. (Illus.). 1994. lib. bdg. 24.95 (*0-7933-4732-7*); pap. 14.95 (*0-7933-4733-5*); disk 29.95 (*0-7933-4734-3*) Gallopade Pub Group.

—Christopher Columbus Comes to Montana! Includes Reproducible Activities for Kids! (Illus.). (gr. 3-12). 1994. PLB 24.95 (*0-7933-3698-8*); pap. 14.95 (*0-7933-3699-6*); computer disk 29.95 (*0-7933-3700-3*) Gallopade Pub Group.

—The Hard-to-Believe-But-True! Book of Montana History, Mystery, Trivia, Legend, Lore, Humor & More. (Illus.). (gr. 3 up). 1994. PLB 24.95 (*0-7933-0712-0*); pap. 14.95 (*0-7933-0711-2*); computer disk 29.95 (*0-7933-0713-9*) Gallopade Pub Group.

—If My Montana Mama Ran the World! (Illus.). (gr. 3 up). 1994. lib. bdg. 24.95 (*0-7933-1746-0*); pap. 14.95 (*0-7933-1747-9*); computer disk 29.95 (*0-7933-1748-7*) Gallopade Pub Group.

—Jurassic Ark! Montana Dinosaurs & Other Prehistoric Creatures. (gr. k-12). 1994. PLB 24.95 (*0-7933-7506-1*); pap. 14.95 (*0-7933-7507-X*); computer disk 29.95 (*0-7933-7508-8*) Gallopade Pub Group.

—Let's Quilt Montana & Stuff It Topographically! (Illus.). (gr. 3 up). 1994. PLB 24.95 (*1-55609-757-3*); pap. 14.95 (*1-55609-131-1*); computer disk 29.95 (*1-55609-759-X*) Gallopade Pub Group.

—Let's Quilt Our Montana County. 1994. lib. bdg. 24.95 (*0-7933-7191-0*); pap. text ed. 14.95 (*0-7933-7192-9*); disk 29.95 (*0-7933-7193-7*) Gallopade Pub Group.

—Let's Quilt Our Montana Town. 1994. lib. bdg. 24.95 (*0-7933-7041-8*); pap. text ed. 14.95 (*0-7933-7042-6*); disk 29.95 (*0-7933-7043-4*) Gallopade Pub Group.

—Meow! Montana Cats in History, Mystery, Legend, Lore, Humor & More! (Illus.). (gr. 3-12). 1994. PLB 24.95 (*0-7933-3392-X*); pap. 14.95 (*0-7933-3393-8*); computer disk 29.95 (*0-7933-3394-6*) Gallopade Pub Group.

—Montana & Other State Greats (Biographies) (Illus.). (gr. 3 up). 1994. PLB 24.95 (*1-55609-772-7*); pap. 14.95 (*1-55609-773-5*); computer disk 29.95 (*1-55609-774-3*) Gallopade Pub Group.

—Montana Bandits, Bushwackers, Outlaws, Crooks, Devils, Ghosts, Desperadoes & Other Assorted & Sundry Characters! (Illus.). (gr. 3 up). 1994. PLB 24.95 (*0-7933-0697-3*); pap. 14.95 (*0-7933-0696-5*); computer disk 29.95 (*0-7933-0698-1*) Gallopade Pub Group.

—Montana Classic Christmas Trivia. (gr. 3 up). 1994. PLB 24.95 (*0-7933-0700-7*); pap. 14.95 (*0-7933-0699-X*); computer disk 29.95 (*0-7933-0701-5*) Gallopade Pub Group.

—Montana Coastales. (Illus.). (gr. 3 up). 1994. PLB 24.95 (*1-55609-766-2*); pap. 14.95 (*1-55609-767-0*); computer disk 29.95 (*1-55609-768-9*) Gallopade Pub Group.

—Montana Coastales! 1994. lib. bdg. 24.95 (*0-7933-7291-7*) Gallopade Pub Group.

—Montana "Crinkum-Crankum" A Funny Word Book about Our State. (Illus.). 1994. lib. bdg. 24.95 (*0-7933-4886-2*); pap. 14.95 (*0-7933-4887-0*); disk 29.95 (*0-7933-4888-9*) Gallopade Pub Group.

—Montana Dingbats! Bk. 1: A Fun Book of Games, Stories, Activities & More about Our State That's All in Code! for You to Decipher. (Illus.). (gr. 3-12). 1994. PLB 24.95 (*0-7933-3851-4*); pap. 14.95 (*0-7933-3852-2*); computer disk 29.95 (*0-7933-3853-0*) Gallopade Pub Group.

—Montana Festival Fun for Kids! (Illus.). (gr. 3-12). 1994. lib. bdg. 24.95 (*0-7933-4004-7*); pap. 14.95 (*0-7933-4005-5*); disk 29.95 (*0-7933-4006-3*) Gallopade Pub Group.
—The Montana Hot Air Balloon Mystery. (Illus.). (gr. 2-9). 1994. 24.95 (*0-7933-2552-8*); pap. 14.95 (*0-7933-2553-6*); computer disk 29.95 (*0-7933-2554-4*) Gallopade Pub Group.
—Montana Jeopardy! Answers & Questions about Our State! (Illus.). (gr. 3-12). 1994. PLB 24.95 (*0-7933-4157-4*); pap. 14.95 (*0-7933-4158-2*); computer disk 29.95 (*0-7933-4159-0*) Gallopade Pub Group.
—Montana "Jography" A Fun Run Thru Our State. (Illus.). (gr. 3 up). 1994. PLB 24.95 (*1-55609-754-9*); pap. 14.95 (*1-55609-755-7*); computer disk 29.95 (*1-55609-756-5*) Gallopade Pub Group.
—Montana Kid's Cookbook: Recipes, How-To, History, Lore & More. (Illus.). (gr. 3 up). 1994. PLB 24.95 (*0-7933-0709-0*); pap. 14.95 (*0-7933-0708-2*); computer disk 29.95 (*0-7933-0710-4*) Gallopade Pub Group.
—The Montana Mystery Van Takes Off! Book 1: Handicapped Montana Kids Sneak Off on a Big Adventure. (Illus.). (gr. 3-12). 1994. 24.95 (*0-7933-5039-5*); pap. 14.95 (*0-7933-5040-9*); computer disk 29.95 (*0-7933-5041-7*) Gallopade Pub Group.
—Montana Quiz Bowl Crash Course! (Illus.). (gr. 3 up). 1994. PLB 24.95 (*1-55609-769-7*); pap. 14.95 (*1-55609-770-0*); computer disk 29.95 (*1-55609-771-9*) Gallopade Pub Group.
—Montana Rollercoasters! (Illus.). (gr. 3-12). 1994. PLB 24.95 (*0-7933-5302-5*); pap. 14.95 (*0-7933-5303-3*); computer disk 29.95 (*0-7933-5304-1*) Gallopade Pub Group.
—Montana School Trivia: An Amazing & Fascinating Look at Our State's Teachers, Schools & Students! (Illus.). (gr. 3 up). 1994. PLB 24.95 (*0-7933-0706-6*); pap. 14.95 (*0-7933-0705-8*); computer disk 29.95 (*0-7933-0707-4*) Gallopade Pub Group.
—Montana Silly Basketball Sportsmysteries, Vol. I. (Illus.). (gr. 3 up). 1994. PLB 24.95 (*0-7933-0703-1*); pap. 14.95 (*0-7933-0702-3*); computer disk 29.95 (*0-7933-0704-X*) Gallopade Pub Group.
—Montana Silly Basketball Sportsmysteries, Vol. II. (Illus.). (gr. 3 up). 1994. PLB 24.95 (*0-7933-1749-5*); pap. 14.95 (*0-7933-1750-9*); computer disk 29.95 (*0-7933-1751-7*) Gallopade Pub Group.
—Montana Silly Football Sportsmysteries, Vol. I. (Illus.). (gr. 3 up). 1994. PLB 24.95 (*1-55609-760-3*); pap. 14.95 (*1-55609-761-1*); computer disk 29.95 (*1-55609-762-X*) Gallopade Pub Group.
—Montana Silly Football Sportsmysteries, Vol. II. (Illus.). (gr. 3 up). 1994. PLB 24.95 (*1-55609-763-8*); pap. 14.95 (*1-55609-764-6*); computer disk 29.95 (*1-55609-765-4*) Gallopade Pub Group.
—Montana Silly Trivia! (Illus.). (gr. 3 up). 1994. PLB 24.95 (*1-55609-751-4*); pap. 14.95 (*1-55609-752-2*); computer disk 29.95 (*1-55609-753-0*) Gallopade Pub Group.
—Montana Timeline: A Chronology of Montana History, Mystery, Trivia, Legend, Lore & More. (Illus.). (gr. 3-12). 1994. PLB 24.95 (*0-7933-5953-8*); pap. 14.95 (*0-7933-5954-6*); computer disk 29.95 (*0-7933-5955-4*) Gallopade Pub Group.
—Montana's (Most Devastating!) Disasters & (Most Calamitous!) Catastrophies! (Illus.). (gr. 3 up). 1994. PLB 24.95 (*0-685-45943-8*); pap. 14.95 (*0-7933-0692-2*); computer disk 29.95 (*0-7933-0695-7*) Gallopade Pub Group.
—Montana's Unsolved Mysteries (& Their "Solutions") Includes Scientific Information & Other Activities for Students. (Illus.). (gr. 3-12). 1994. PLB 24.95 (*0-7933-5800-0*); pap. 14.95 (*0-7933-5801-9*); computer disk 29.95 (*0-7933-5802-7*) Gallopade Pub Group.
—My First Book about Montana. (gr. k-4). 1994. PLB 24.95 (*0-7933-5647-4*); pap. 14.95 (*0-7933-5648-2*); computer disk 29.95 (*0-7933-5649-0*) Gallopade Pub Group.
—The Nebraska Hot Air Balloon Mystery. (Illus.). (gr. 2-9). 1994. 24.95 (*0-7933-2561-7*); pap. 14.95 (*0-7933-2562-5*); computer disk 29.95 (*0-7933-2563-3*) Gallopade Pub Group.
—Patch, the Pirate Dog: A Montana Pet Story. (ps-4). 1994. PLB 24.95 (*0-7933-5494-3*); pap. 14.95 (*0-7933-5495-1*); computer disk 29.95 (*0-7933-5496-X*) Gallopade Pub Group.
—Uncle Rebus: Montana Picture Stories for Computer Kids. (Illus.). (gr. k-3). 1994. PLB 24.95 (*0-7933-4579-0*); pap. 14.95 (*0-7933-4580-4*); disk 29.95 (*0-7933-4581-2*) Gallopade Pub Group.
Shirley, Gayle. M Is for Montana. Bergum, Constance, illus. LC 87-73310. 32p. (Orig.). 1988. pap. 7.95 (*0-937959-32-4*, ABC Press) Falcon Pr MT.
Shirley, Gayle C. Montana Wildlife: A Children's Field Guide to the State's Most Remarkable Animals. Allnock, Sandy, illus. 48p. (Orig.). 1993. pap. 6.95 (*1-56044-154-2*) Falcon Pr MT.
Thompson, Kathleen. Montana. LC 87-26465. 48p. (gr. 3 up). 1988. 19.97 (*0-86514-468-0*) Raintree Steck-V.

MONTANA–FICTION

Corcoran, Barbara. Wolf at the Door. LC 92-45108. 192p. (gr. 3-7). 1993. SBE 14.95 (*0-689-31870-7*, Atheneum Child Bk) Macmillan Child Grp.
Larson, Dorothy W. Bright Shadows. Larson, Dorothy W., illus. LC 92-81679. 96p. (gr. 4-6). 1992. 14.95 (*0-9621779-0-3*) Sandstone Pub.
Lasky, Kathryn. The Bone Wars. LC 88-13426. 378p. (gr. 7 up). 1988. 12.95 (*0-688-07433-2*) Morrow Jr Bks.
Stein, Charlotte M. The Stained Glass Window. Sakurai, Jennifer, ed. Stein, Michele P., illus. LC 88-70883. 150p. (Orig.). 1994. pap. 11.95 incl. wkbk. (*0-916634-12-4*) Double M Pr.

MONTESSORI, MARIA, 1870-1952

O'Connor, Barbara. Mammolina: A Story about Maria Montessori. LC 92-415. 1993. lib. bdg. 14.95 (*0-87614-743-0*); pap. 5.95 (*0-87614-602-7*) Carolrhoda Bks.
Standing, E. M. Maria Montessori: Her Life & Work. McDermott, John J., intro. by. (Illus.). 382p. (gr. 9-12). 1989. pap. 9.95 (*0-452-26090-6*, Plume) NAL-Dutton.

MONTGOMERY, ALABAMA–RACE RELATIONS

Hull, Mary. Rosa Parks: Civil Rights Leader. LC 93-17699. (Illus.). (gr. 5 up). 1994. PLB 18.95 (*0-7910-1881-4*, Am Art Analog); write for info. (*0-7910-1910-1*, Am Art Analog) Chelsea Hse.
Stein, Richard C. The Montgomery Bus Boycott. LC 93-16854. (Illus.). 32p. (gr. 3-6). 1993. PLB 12.30 (*0-516-06671-4*); pap. 3.95 (*0-516-46671-2*) Childrens.

MONTHS

Brown, Marzella. Activities for Cooperative Learning. Rivera, Doreen, et al, illus. 48p. (gr. 2-5). 1990. wkbk. 6.95 (*1-55734-109-5*) Tchr Create Mat.
—All about Cooperative Learning. Wright, Theresa, illus. 48p. (gr. 2-5). 1990. wkbk. 6.95 (*1-55734-107-9*) Tchr Create Mat.
Hale, Janet. April Monthly Activities. Apodaca, Blanqui, illus. 80p. (gr. 1-5). 1990. wkbk. 8.95 (*1-55734-158-3*) Tchr Create Mat.
—February Monthly Activities. Apodaca, Blanqui & Spence, Paula, illus. 80p. (gr. 1-5). 1989. wkbk. 8.95 (*1-55734-156-7*) Tchr Create Mat.
—January Monthly Activities. Apodaca, Blanqui & Spence, Paula, illus. 80p. (gr. 1-5). 1989. wkbk. 8.95 (*1-55734-155-9*) Tchr Create Mat.
—July Monthly Activities. Apodaca, Blanqui, et al, illus. 80p. (gr. 1-5). 1990. wkbk. 8.95 (*1-55734-165-6*) Tchr Create Mat.
—June Monthly Activities. Apodaca, Blanqui & Spence, Paula, illus. 80p. (gr. 1-5). 1990. wkbk. 8.95 (*1-55734-164-8*) Tchr Create Mat.
—March Monthly Activities. Apodaca, Blanqui, et al, illus. 80p. (gr. 1-5). 1990. wkbk. 8.95 (*1-55734-157-5*) Tchr Create Mat.
—May Monthly Activities. Apodaca, Blanqui, et al, illus. 80p. (gr. 1-5). 1990. wkbk. 8.95 (*1-55734-159-1*) Tchr Create Mat.
Halsey, Megan. Jump for Joy: A Book of Months. LC 92-39082. (Illus.). 32p. (ps-1). 1994. SBE 14.95 (*0-02-742040-X*, Bradbury Pr) Macmillan Child Grp.
Leslie, Clare W. Nature All Year Long. LC 90-47866. (Illus.). 56p. (gr. 2 up). 1991. 16.95 (*0-688-09183-0*) Greenwillow.
Lillie, Patricia. When This Box Is Full. Crews, Donald, illus. LC 92-28743. 24p. 1993. 14.00 (*0-688-12016-4*); PLB 13.93 (*0-688-12017-2*) Greenwillow.
Sterling, Mary E. & Nowlin, Susan S. November Monthly Activities. Spence, Paula, et al, illus. 80p. (gr. 1-5). 1989. wkbk. 8.95 (*1-55734-153-2*) Tchr Create Mat.
—October Monthly Activities. Spence, Paula, et al, illus. 80p. (gr. 1-5). 1989. wkbk. 8.95 (*1-55734-152-4*) Tchr Create Mat.
—September Monthly Activities. Spence, Paula, et al, illus. 80p. (gr. 1-5). 1989. wkbk. 8.95 (*1-55734-151-6*) Tchr Create Mat.
Thomas, Jennifer. Masterpiece of the Month. Apodaca, Blanqui & Wright, Theresa, illus. 96p. (gr. k-5). 1990. wkbk. 10.95 (*1-55734-018-8*) Tchr Create Mat.

MONTHS–POETRY

Lewis, J. Patrick. July Is a Mad Mosquito. Hall, Melanie W., illus. LC 93-19743. 32p. (gr. 2-5). 1994. SBE 14.95 (*0-689-31813-8*, Atheneum Child Bk) Macmillan Child Grp.
Sendak, Maurice. Chicken Soup with Rice. Sendak, Maurice, illus. 48p. (ps-3). 1962. PLB 13.89 (*0-06-025535-8*) HarpC Child Bks.
—Chicken Soup with Rice: A Book of Months. Sendak, Maurice, illus. LC 62-13315. 32p. (ps-3). 1991. pap. 3.95 (*0-06-443253-X*, Trophy) HarpC Child Bks.
Singer, Marilyn. Turtle in July. Pinkey, Jerry, illus. LC 93-14430. 32p. (gr. 3-7). 1994. pap. 4.95 (*0-689-71805-5*, Aladdin) Macmillan Child Grp.

MONUMENTS

see also Pyramids

Hallett, Bill & Hallett, Jane. Look up Look down Look All Around Bandelier National Monument. (Illus.). 32p. (Orig.). (gr. 3-8). 1990. pap. 3.95 activity bk. (*1-877827-02-9*) Look & See.
Jessop, Joanne. Big Buildings of the Ancient World. Salariya, David, created by. LC 93-36704. (Illus.). 48p. (gr. 5-8). 1994. write for info. (*0-531-14286-8*); pap. 8.95 (*0-531-15709-1*) Watts.
Martin, Ana. Prehistoric Stone Monuments. LC 93-756. (ENG & SPA., Illus.). 36p. (gr. 3 up). 1993. PLB 14.95 (*0-516-08386-4*); pap. 6.95 (*0-516-48386-2*) Childrens.
Sharp, Margery. The Turret. 144p. (gr. 3 up). 1974. pap. 1.25 (*0-440-48630-0*, YB) Dell.

MONUMENTS, NATURAL

see Natural Monuments

MONUMENTS–U. S.

Ayer, Eleanor. Our National Monuments. LC 91-43230. (Illus.). 48p. (gr. 2-4). 1992. PLB 13.40 (*1-56294-078-3*); pap. 5.95 (*1-56294-816-4*) Millbrook Pr.

MOON

see also Tides

Adler, David. All about the Moon. Burns, Raymond, illus. LC 82-17422. 32p. (gr. 3-6). 1983. PLB 10.59 (*0-89375-886-8*); pap. text ed. 2.95 (*0-89375-887-6*) Troll Assocs.
Asimov, Isaac. Why Does the Moon Change Shape? LC 90-25430. (Illus.). 24p. (gr. 2-3). 1991. PLB 15.93 (*0-8368-0438-4*) Gareth Stevens Inc.
Asimov, Isaac, et al. The Moon. rev. & updated ed. (Illus.). (gr. 3 up). 1994. PLB 17.27 (*0-8368-1131-3*) Gareth Stevens Inc.
Baker, David. Living on the Moon. (Illus.). 48p. (gr. 3-8). 1989. lib. bdg. 18.60 (*0-86592-374-4*); 13.95s.p. (*0-685-58642-1*) Rourke Corp.
Branley, Franklyn M. The Moon Seems to Change. rev. ed. Emberley, Barbara & Emberley, Ed E., illus. LC 86-47747. 32p. (ps-3). 1987. 13.95 (*0-690-04583-2*, Crowell Jr Bks) HarpC Child Bks.
—The Moon Seems to Change. rev. ed. Emberley, Barbara & Emberley, Ed E., illus. LC 86-27097. 32p. (ps-3). 1987. pap. 4.50 (*0-06-445065-1*, Trophy) HarpC Child Bks.
—What the Moon Is Like. rev. ed. Kelley, True, illus. LC 85-47904. 32p. (ps-3). 1986. PLB 14.89 (*0-690-04512-3*, Crowell Jr Bks) HarpC Child Bks.
—What the Moon Is Like. Kelley, True, illus. LC 85-45400. 32p. (gr. k-3). 1987. Book & Cassette Set. 7.95 (*0-694-00205-4*, Trophy); pap. 4.95 (*0-06-445052-X*, Trophy) HarpC Child Bks.
British Museum, Geological Department Staff. Moon, Mars & Meteorites. (Illus.). 36p. (gr. 7 up). 1986. pap. 5.95 (*0-521-32414-9*) Cambridge U Pr.
Dunant, Caroline. What Is the Moon? Loveless, Liz, illus. 32p. (ps-k). 1994. 18.95 (*0-370-31811-0*, Pub. by Bodley Head UK) Trafalgar.
Ehlert, Lois. Moon Rope: Un Lazo a la Luna. 1992. 14.95 (*0-15-255343-6*, HB Juv Bks) HarBrace.
Estalella, Robert. Our Satellite: The Moon. Ferron, Miquel, illus. LC 93-19897. (gr. 4-8). 1994. 12.95 (*0-8120-6369-4*); pap. 6.95 (*0-8120-1740-4*) Barron.
Fowler, Allan. So That's How the Moon Changes Shape. LC 91-3142. 32p. (ps-2). 1991. PLB 10.75 (*0-516-04917-8*); PLB 22.95 big bk. (*0-516-49477-5*); pap. 3.95 (*0-516-44917-6*) Childrens.
George, Michael. The Moon. LC 92-8411. (SPA & ENG.). (gr. 2-6). 1992. PLB 15.95 (*0-89565-853-4*) Childs World.
—The Moon. (gr. 5 up). 1993. PLB 18.95 (*0-88682-436-2*) Creative Ed.
—Moon. 40p. (gr. 4-7). 1993. 15.95 (*1-56846-056-2*) Creat Editions.
Goldish, Meish. Does the Moon Change Shape? (Illus.). 32p. (gr. 1-4). 1989. PLB 18.99 (*0-8172-3518-3*); pap. 3.95 (*0-8114-6718-X*) Raintree Steck-V.
Greenberg, Judith E. & Carey, Helen H. The Moon. Corvi, Donna, illus. 32p. (gr. 2-4). 1990. PLB 10.95 (*0-8172-3752-6*) Raintree Steck-V.
A Kid's Guide to Living on the Moon. 48p. (gr. 4-5). 1991. PLB 11.95 (*1-56065-015-X*) Capstone Pr.
Krupp, E. C. The Moon & You. Krupp, Robin R., illus. LC 92-16231. 48p. (gr. k-4). 1993. RSBE 13.95 (*0-02-751142-1*, Macmillan Child Bk) Macmillan Child Grp.
Mora, Francisco X. The Legend of the Two Moons. Mora, Francisco X., illus. LC 92-31552. 32p. (ps-k). 1993. PLB 15.00 (*0-917846-15-X*, 95517) Highsmith Pr.
Nicoll, Helen & Pienkowski, Jan. Meg on the Moon. (Illus.). 32p. (ps). 1980. 15.95 (*0-434-95424-1*, Pub. by W Heinemann Ltd) Trafalgar.
Santrey, Laurence. Moon. Schindler, S. D., illus. LC 84-8441. 32p. (gr. 3-6). 1985. PLB 9.49 (*0-8167-0252-7*); pap. text ed. 2.95 (*0-8167-0253-5*) Troll Assocs.
Simon, Seymour. The Moon. LC 84-28753. (Illus.). 32p. (gr. k-3). 1984. RSBE 14.95 (*0-02-782840-9*, Four Winds) Macmillan Child Grp.
Sims, Lesley. The Moon. LC 93-28659. 1994. PLB 18.99 (*0-8114-5504-1*) Raintree Steck-V.
Sneider, Cary I. Earth, Moon, & Stars. Bergman, Lincoln & Fairwell, Kay, eds. Baker, Lisa H. & Bevilacqua, Carol, illus. Sneider, Cary I., photos by. 50p. (Orig.). (gr. 5-9). 1986. pap. 10.00 (*0-912511-18-4*) Lawrence Science.
Sorensen, Lynda. Moon. LC 93-14875. (ps-6). 1993. 12.67 (*0-86593-273-5*); 9.50s.p. (*0-685-66589-5*) Rourke Corp.
Witcomb, Gerald, illus. The Moon. 32p. (gr. 3-5). 1985. 7.95x (*0-86685-448-7*) Intl Bk Ctr.

MOON–EXPLORATION

Fowler, Allan. When You Look up at the Moon. LC 93-38589. (Illus.). 32p. (ps-2). 1994. PLB 10.75 (*0-516-06025-2*) Childrens.
Furniss, Tim. The First Men on the Moon. Bull, Peter, illus. LC 88-24166. 32p. (gr. 4-6). 1989. PLB 11.90 (*0-531-18240-1*, Pub. by Bookwright Pr) Watts.
Gold, Susan D. Countdown to the Moon. LC 91-30360. (Illus.). 48p. (gr. 5-6). 1992. text ed. 12.95 RSBE (*0-89686-689-0*, Crestwood Hse) Macmillan Child Grp.
Sullivan, George. The Day We Walked on the Moon. 1990. 5.95 (*0-590-45587-7*, 064) Scholastic Inc.

MOON–EXPLORATION–FICTION

Herge. Explorers on the Moon. (gr. k up). 1976. pap. 7.95 (*0-316-35846-0*, Joy St Bks) Little.

—Objectif Lune. (FRE., Illus.). (gr. 7-9). looseleaf bdg. 19.95 (*0-8288-5051-8*) Fr & Eur.

—On a Marche Sur la Lune. (FRE., Illus.). (gr. 7-9). looseleaf bdg. 19.95 (*0-8288-5053-4*) Fr & Eur.

MOON–FICTION

Addison-Wesley Staff. How the Moon Got in the Sky Little Book. (Illus.). 16p. (gr. k-3). 1989. pap. text ed. 4.50 (*0-201-19359-0*) Addison-Wesley.

Akkerman, Dinie & Van Loon, Paul J. To Catch the Moon. (Illus.). 24p. (ps-1). 1993. 12.95 (*0-8120-6341-4*); pap. 5.95 (*0-8120-1559-2*) Barron.

Alexander, Martha. Maggie's Moon. Alexander, Martha, illus. LC 82-1575. 32p. (ps-2). 1982. Dial Bks Young.

Asch, Frank. Happy Birthday Moon. Asch, Frank, illus. 32p. (ps-1). 1988. Bk. & cassette. pap. 7.95 (*0-671-67145-6*, Little Simon) S&S Trade.

—Happy Birthday, Moon. LC 88-6569. (Illus.). 32p. (gr. k-4). 1985. pap. 14.00 jacketed (*0-671-66454-9*, Little Simon); pap. 4.95 (*0-671-66455-7*, Little Simon) S&S Trade.

—Mooncake. Asch, Frank, illus. 32p. 1986. pap. 4.95 (*0-671-66451-4*) S&S Trade.

Atwell, David L. Sleeping Moon. Atwell, Debby, illus. LC 94-270. 1994. 14.95 (*0-395-68677-6*) HM.

Babcock, Chris. No Moon, No Milk! Teague, Mark, illus. LC 92-40697. 32p. (ps-2). 1993. 12.00 (*0-517-58779-3*); PLB 12.99 (*0-517-58780-7*) Crown Bks Yng Read.

Bates, Betty. The Great Male Conspiracy. (gr. k-6). 1990. pap. 2.95 (*0-440-40247-6*, YB) Dell.

Bess, Clayton. The Truth about the Moon. Hoffman, Rosekrans, illus. 48p. (gr. k-3). 1983. 13.45 (*0-395-34551-0*) HM.

—Truth about the Moon. (ps-3). 1992. pap. 4.95 (*0-395-64371-6*) HM.

Blocksma, Mary. Yoo Hoo, Moon! 1991. pap. 9.99 (*0-553-07094-0*) Bantam.

—Yoo Hoo, Moon! 1992. pap. 3.99 (*0-553-35212-1*) Bantam.

Carle, Eric. Papa, Please Get the Moon for Me. LC 85-29785. (Illus.). 32p. (ps up). 1991. pap. 17.95 (*0-88708-026-X*) Picture Bk Studio.

—Papa, Please Get the Moon for Me. LC 91-14561. (Illus.). 28p. (gr. k up). 1991. pap. 5.95 (*0-88708-177-0*) Picture Bk Studio.

Chadwick, Tim. Cabbage Moon. Harper, Piers, illus. LC 93-28952. 1994. 14.95 (*0-531-06827-7*); lib. bdg. write for info. (*0-531-08677-1*) Orchard Bks Watts.

Daly, Niki. Why the Sun & Moon Live in the Sky. LC 93-47304. (Illus.). 1994. 15.00 (*0-688-13331-2*); lib. bdg. 14.93 (*0-688-13332-0*) Lothrop.

Danziger, Paula. This Place Has No Atmosphere. LC 85-46070. 128p. (gr. 7 up). 1986. pap. 15.00 (*0-385-29489-1*) Delacorte.

Davis, Jenny. Checking on the Moon. 1993. pap. 3.50 (*0-440-21491-2*) Dell.

De Paola, Tomie. The Unicorn & the Moon. LC 94-20297. (Illus.). 1994. 12.95 (*0-382-24659-4*); PLB 14.95 (*0-382-24658-6*); pap. 4.95 (*0-382-24660-8*) Silver Burdett Pr.

DiBlasi, Ric. The Foolish Moon. Nave, Clarence, illus. 27p. 1993. pap. 7.95 (*0-910303-46-0*) Writers Pub Serv.

Duncan, Lois. Birthday Moon. Davis, Susan, illus. 32p. (ps-3). 1989. 13.95 (*0-670-82238-8*) Viking Child Bks.

Dunster, Mark. Moon. 10p. (Orig.). 1993. pap. 4.00 (*0-89642-220-8*) Linden Pubs.

Edens, Cooper. Now Is the Moon's Eyebrow. (Orig.). (gr. 7-12). 1991. pap. 4.95 (*0-88138-070-9*, Green Tiger) S&S Trade.

Elzbieta. Dikou & the Mysterious Moon Sheep. Elzbieta, illus. LC 87-13587. 32p. (ps-3). 1988. (Crowell Jr Bks) HarpC Child Bks.

Farmer, Tony & Farmer, Lynne. How HIGH Is the Moon? LC 91-19350. (gr. 4 up). 1991. 3.95 (*0-85953-517-7*) Childs Play.

Fowler, Susi G. I'll See You When the Moon Is Full. Fowler, Jim, illus. LC 91-47667. 24p. (ps up). 1994. 14.00 (*0-688-10830-X*); PLB 13.93 (*0-688-10831-8*) Greenwillow.

Gantschev, Ivan. Good Morning, Good Night. Clements, Andrew, tr. Gantschev, Ivan, illus. LC 91-3603. 28p. (gr. k up). 1991. pap. 14.95 (*0-88708-183-5*) Picture Bk Studio.

—The Moon Lake. (Illus.). 28p. (gr. k). 1993. Repr. Mini-bk. 4.95 (*0-88708-304-8*) Picture Bk Studio.

Gollub, Matthew. The Moon Was at a Fiesta. Martinez, Leovigildo, illus. LC 93-14750. 32p. 1994. 15.00 (*0-688-11637-X*, Tambourine Bks); PLB 14.93 (*0-688-11638-8*) Morrow.

Green, Timothy. Mystery of Navajo Moon. Green, Timothy, illus. LC 91-52600. 48p. (ps-4). 1991. pap. 7.95 (*0-87358-577-1*) Northland AZ.

Guest, Elissa H. Over the Moon. LC 85-28505. 160p. (gr. 7 up). 1986. 12.95 (*0-688-04148-5*) Morrow Jr Bks.

Hadley, Eric & Hadley, Tessa. Legends of the Sun & Moon. LC 82-17720. (Illus.). 32p. (gr. 3-7). 1989. 14.95 (*0-521-25227-X*); pap. 10.95 (*0-521-37912-1*) Cambridge U Pr.

Harris, Rosemary. Moon in the Cloud. 176p. (gr. 3-6). 1990. pap. 4.95 (*0-571-15338-0*) Faber & Faber.

Helldorfer, M. C. Moon Trouble. Hunt, Jonathan, illus. LC 92-22233. 32p. (gr. k-5). 1994. RSBE 15.95 (*0-02-743517-2*, Bradbury Pr) Macmillan Child Grp.

Hines, Anna G. Moon's Wish. Hines, Anna G., illus. 32p. (ps-1). 1992. 14.45 (*0-395-58114-1*, Clarion Bks) HM.

Hughes, Meredith. Gunther Van Winkle & the Half Moon. Hughes, Meredith, illus. 60p. (Orig.). (gr. 5-7). 1994. pap. 9.95 (*0-910746-75-3*) Hope Farm.

Ikeda, Daisaku. The Princess & the Moon. McCaughrean, Geraldine, tr. from JPN. Wildsmith, Brian, illus. LC 92-148. 32p. (ps-3). 1992. 15.00 (*0-679-83620-9*); PLB 15.99 (*0-679-93620-3*) Knopf Bks Yng Read.

Lankford, Mary D. Is It Dark? Is It Light? Schuett, Stacey, illus. LC 90-21492. 32p. (ps-2). 1991. 13.00 (*0-679-81579-1*); lib. bdg. 13.99 (*0-679-91579-6*) Knopf Bks Yng Read.

L'Engle, Madeleine. The Moon by Night. 256p. (gr. 6 up). 1981. pap. 3.99 (*0-440-95776-1*, LE) Dell.

Norman, Jane & Beazley, Frank. The Night the Moon Fell. 24p. (ps-3). 1993. pap. write for info. (*1-883585-06-6*) Pixanne Ent.

O'Dell, Scott. Sing down the Moon. large type ed. 176p. (gr. 9-12). 1989. Repr. of 1970 ed. lib. bdg. 15.95 (*1-55736-142-8*, Crnrstn Bks) BDD LT Grp.

Ormerod, Jan. Moonlight. Ormerod, Jan, illus. LC 81-8290. 32p. (ps-1). 1982. 15.00 (*0-688-00846-1*); PLB 14.93 (*0-688-00847-X*) Lothrop.

Pacovska, Kveta. The Midnight Play. Clements, Andrew, adapted by. LC 93-16258. (Illus.). (ps-8). 1993. 15.95 (*0-88708-317-X*) Picture Bk Studio.

Peppe, Rodney. Mice on the Moon. (gr. 4 up). 1993. pap. 13.95 (*0-385-30839-6*) Doubleday.

Perlwitz, Ellen C. Charlie's Little Moon Trip. (Illus.). 32p. (gr. k-3). 1992. 7.95 (*1-880851-01-6*) Greene Bark Pr.

Pfister, Marcus. Sun & Moon. (gr. 4-7). 1993. pap. 4.95 (*0-590-44490-5*) Scholastic Inc.

Pittman, Helena C. The Moon's Party. LC 92-40866. 1994. 15.95 (*0-399-22541-2*, Putnam) Putnam Pub Group.

Pyle, Howard. The Garden Behind the Moon. (Illus.). 192p. (gr. 6-8). 1988. Repr. of 1895 ed. 14.95 (*0-930407-06-7*) Parabola Bks.

Rowe, John. Rabbit Moon. Rowe, John, illus. LC 92-6047. 28p. 1992. pap. 14.95 (*0-88708-246-7*) Picture Bk Studio.

Salter, Mary J. The Moon Comes Home. Schuett, Stacey, illus. LC 88-31735. 40p. (ps-2). 1989. 12.95 (*0-394-89983-0*); lib. bdg. 13.99 (*0-394-99983-5*) Knopf Bks Yng Read.

Scheidl, Gerda M. The Moon Man: A Story. adpt. ed. James, J. Alison, adapted by. & tr. Wilkon, Jozef, illus. LC 93-39759. 32p. (gr. k-3). 1994. 14.95 (*1-55858-271-1*); PLB 14.88 (*1-55858-272-X*) North-South Bks NYC.

Seeley, Laura L. The Magical Moonballs. LC 92-16698. (Illus.). 1992. 16.95 (*1-56145-063-4*) Peachtree Pubs.

Speed, Toby. Two Cool Cows. Root, Barry, illus. LC 93-34258. 1995. 14.95 (*0-399-22647-8*, Putnam) Putnam Pub Group.

Tibo, Gilles. Simon Au Clair De Lune. Tibo, Gilles, illus. LC 93-60333. 24p. (gr. k up). 1993. 10.95 (*0-88776-317-0*) Tundra Bks.

—Simon in the Moonlight. Tibo, Gilles, illus. LC 93-60334. 24p. (gr. k up). 1993. 10.95 (*0-88776-316-2*) Tundra Bks.

Turner, Charles. The Turtle & the Moon. Mathis, Melissa B., illus. LC 90-43841. 32p. (ps-2). 1991. 14.00 (*0-525-44659-1*, DCB) Dutton Child Bks.

Vander Els, Betty. The Bombers Moon. LC 85-47591. 129p. (gr. 4 up). 1985. 14.00 (*0-374-30864-0*) FS&G.

Van Loon, Paul. Agarrar la Luna. Akkerman, Dinie, illus. LC 92-43067. 1993. 5.95 (*0-8120-1676-9*) Barron.

Volpe, Joseph & Volpe, Tracey. The Moon & the Mistypips. (Illus.). 32p. (ps-4). 1991. pap. write for info. (*0-9631215-1-0*); write for info. tchr's. ed. (*0-9631215-2-9*) Hopewell Stories.

Whitcher, Susan. Moonfall. (ps-3). 1993. 14.00 (*0-374-35056-6*) FS&G.

Wildsmith, Brian. What the Moon Saw. Wildsmith, Brian, illus. 32p. (ps-3). 1978. 16.00 (*0-19-279724-7*); pap. 7.50 (*0-19-272157-7*) OUP.

Willard, Nancy. The Nightgown of the Sullen Moon. McPhail, David, illus. LC 83-8472. (ps-3). 1983. 14.95 (*0-15-257429-8*, HB Juv Bks) HarBrace.

Wynne-Jones, Tim. Builder of the Moon. Wallace, Ian, illus. LC 88-12703. (ps-3). 1989. SBE 14.95 (*0-689-50472-1*, M K McElderry) Macmillan Child Grp.

Yong, Ed. Let's Go to the Moon with Marty. 1994. pap. 7.95 (*0-533-10689-3*) Vantage.

Zalben, Jane B. Water from the Moon. LC 86-46439. 160p. (gr. 8 up). 1987. 15.00 (*0-374-38238-7*) FS&G.

MOON, VOYAGES TO

see Space Flight to the Moon

MOORE, HENRY SPENCER, 1898-

Gardner, Jane M. Henry Moore: From Bones & Stones to Sketches & Sculptures. (Illus.). 32p. (gr. k-2). 1993. RSBE 15.95 (*0-02-735812-7*, Four Winds) Macmillan Child Grp.

MOORS–FICTION

Rogers, Jean. The Secret Moose. LC 84-12897. (Illus.). 64p. (gr. 3-5). 1985. 15.00 (*0-688-04248-1*); PLB 14.93 (*0-688-04249-X*) Greenwillow.

MOOSE

Ahlstrom, Mark E. The Moose. LC 85-26931. (Illus.). 48p. (gr. 5). 1985. text ed. 12.95 RSBE (*0-89686-279-8*, Crestwood Hse) Macmillan Child Grp.

Fair, Jeff. Moose for Kids. (ps-3). 1992. 14.95 (*1-55971-187-6*); pap. 6.95 (*0-685-74444-2*) NorthWord.

Hassett, Ann & Hassett, John. Moose on the Loose. Hassett, John, illus. 48p. (Orig.). (ps-4). 1987. pap. 7.95 (*0-89272-245-2*) Down East.

Markert, Jenny. Moose. 32p. 1991. 15.95 (*0-89565-713-9*) Childs World.

Petersen, David. Moose. LC 94-10948. (Illus.). 48p. (gr. k-4). 1994. PLB 17.20 (*0-516-01069-7*); pap. 4.95 (*0-516-41069-5*) Childrens.

MOOSE–FICTION

Allen, Jonathan. Mucky Moose. Allen, Jonathan, illus. LC 90-6363. 32p. (ps-3). 1991. SBE 13.95 (*0-02-700251-9*, Macmillan Child Bk) Macmillan Child Grp.

Baker, Marybeth. Maynard's Allagash Friends. 1989. pap. 7.95 (*0-929906-25-X*) G Gannett.

Bernier, Evariste. Baxter Bear & Moses Moose. Peterson, Dawn, illus. LC 90-61408. 48p. (gr. 1-4). 1990. 12.95 (*0-89272-287-8*) Down East.

Brennan, Gale. Toulouse the Mouse. Flint, Russ, illus. 16p. (Orig.). (gr. k-6). 1981. pap. 1.25 (*0-685-02458-X*) Brennan Bks.

DeVries, Douglas. Muscles, the Moose Calf. Parker, Patricia, illus. LC 89-84651. 32p. (Orig.). (ps-3). 1989. 8.00 (*1-877721-00-X*) Jade Ram Pub.

—Muscles Visits Anchorage. Parker, Patricia, illus. LC 90-61154. 32p. (Orig.). (ps-3). 1990. pap. text ed. 8.00 (*1-877721-01-8*) Jade Ram Pub.

Dr. Seuss. Thidwick, the Big-Hearted Moose. Dr. Seuss, illus. (gr. k-3). 1948. 14.00 (*0-394-80086-9*); lib. bdg. 11.99 (*0-394-90086-3*) Random Bks Yng Read.

—Thidwick the Big-Hearted Moose. Dr. Seuss, illus. 48p. (ps-6). 1993. incl. cass. 12.00 (*0-679-84338-8*) Random Bks Yng Read.

Kennedy, William & Kennedy, Brendan. Charlie Malarkey & the Singing Moose. Schindler, S. D., illus. LC 93-41483. 32p. 1994. 14.99 (*0-670-84605-8*) Viking Child Bks.

Latimer, Jim. Moose & Friends. Ewing, Carolyn, illus. LC 91-14047. 32p. (gr. 1-3). 1993. SBE 14.95 (*0-684-19335-3*, Scribners Young Read) Macmillan Child Grp.

—When Moose Was Young. Carrick, Donald, illus. LC 89-10059. 32p. (gr. 1-3). 1990. SBE 13.95 (*0-684-18932-1*, Scribners Young Read) Macmillan Child Grp.

Matthews, Morgan. The Big Race. Schindler, S. D., illus. LC 88-1287. 48p. (Orig.). (gr. 1-4). 1989. PLB 10.59 (*0-8167-1329-4*); pap. text ed. 3.50 (*0-8167-1330-8*) Troll Assocs.

May, D. J. Mr. Marble's Moose. LC 93-1494. 1993. 9.99 (*0-8499-1068-4*) Word Pub.

Numeroff, Laura J. If You Give a Moose a Muffin. Bond, Felicia, illus. LC 91-2207. 32p. (ps-2). 1991. 14.00 (*0-06-024405-4*); PLB 13.89 (*0-06-024406-2*) HarpC Child Bks.

—If You Give a Moose a Muffin Big Book. Bond, Felicia, illus. LC 91-2207. 32p. (ps-2). 1994. pap. 19.95 (*0-06-443366-8*, Trophy) HarpC Child Bks.

Ochs, Carol P. Moose on the Loose. Mitchell, Anastasia, illus. 32p. (ps-4). 1991. PLB 18.95 (*0-87614-448-2*) Carolrhoda Bks.

Pinkwater, Daniel M. Blue Moose, & Return of the Moose. Pinkwater, Daniel M., illus. LC 93-22614. 112p. (Orig.). (gr. 2-7). 1993. pap. 3.99 (*0-679-84717-0*, Bullseye Bks) Random Bks Yng Read.

Proysen, Alf. Mrs. Pepperpot & the Moose. Fisher, Richard E., tr. Berg, Bjorn, illus. 28p. (ps up). 1991. bds. 13.95 (*91-29-59924-5*, Pub. by R & S Bks) FS&G.

Reese, Bob. Mickey Moose. Reese, Bob, illus. (gr. k-6). 1986. 7.95 (*0-89868-171-5*); pap. 2.95 (*0-89868-172-3*) ARO Pub.

Segal. Flying Moose. 1993. 14.95 (*0-8050-1591-4*) H Holt & Co.

Slepian, Jan. Lost Moose. Lewin, Ted, illus. LC 94-6738. 1995. 15.95 (*0-399-22749-0*, Philomel Bks) Putnam Pub Group.

Stapler, Sarah. Spruce the Moose Cuts Loose. (Illus.). 32p. (ps-3). 1992. 14.95 (*0-399-21861-0*, Putnam) Putnam Pub Group.

Wakefield, Pat A. & Carrara, Larry. A Moose for Jessica. Carrara, Larry, photos by. LC 87-13663. (Illus.). 32p. (gr. k up). 1987. 14.95 (*0-525-44342-8*, DCB) Dutton Child Bks.

—A Moose for Jessica. Carrara, Larry, photos by. (Illus.). 64p. (ps up). 1992. pap. 5.99 (*0-14-036134-0*, Puff Unicorn) Puffin Bks.

Milford did save that night. Order from: Milford Production Enterprise, P.O. Box 131, Lewistown, MT 59457.
Publisher Provided Annotation.

Wells, Rosemary. Morris's Disappearing Bag. Wells, Rosemary, illus. 1975. 9.95 (*0-8037-5441-8*) Dial Bks Young.
Wickstrom, Thor. The Big Night Out. Wickstrom, Thor, illus. LC 91-46563. 32p. (ps-3). 1993. 13.99 (*0-8037-1170-0*); PLB 13.89 (*0-8037-1171-9*) Dial Bks Young.
Wiseman, Bernard. Morris Goes to School. Wiseman, Bernard, illus. LC 75-77944. 64p. (gr. k-3). 1970. PLB 13.89 (*0-06-026548-5*) HarpC Child Bks.
—Morris the Moose. rev. ed. Wiseman, Bernard, illus. LC 87-33485. 32p. (ps-2). 1989. PLB 13.89 (*0-06-026476-4*) HarpC Child Bks.
—Morris the Moose. rev. ed. Wiseman, Bernard, illus. LC 87-33485. 32p. (ps-2). 1991. pap. 3.50 (*0-06-444146-6*, Trophy) HarpC Child Bks.

MORAL EDUCATION
see Character Education
MORAL PHILOSOPHY
see Ethics
MORALITY
see Ethics
MORALS
see Behavior; Ethics
MORE, SIR THOMAS, SAINT, 1478-1535
Smith, Dorothy. Thomas More: The King's Good Servant. Broomfield, Robert, illus. 1990. 2.95 (*0-8091-6595-3*) Paulist Pr.
MORGAN, HENRY, 1635?-1688
Featherstone, Vaughn J. The Aaronic Priesthood & You. LC 87-15731. 99p. (gr. 8-12). 1993. pap. 8.95 (*0-87579-755-5*) Deseret Bk.
MORMONS AND MORMONISM
Bernotas, Bob. Brigham Young. (Illus.). 112p. (gr. 5 up). 1993. PLB 17.95 (*0-7910-1642-0*) Chelsea Hse.
Brower, Bob, illus. Latter-Day Saints Temple Coloring Book. 80p. (Orig.). (gr. 2-6). 1993. pap. 5.95 (*0-910523-22-3*) Grandin Bk Co.
—Presidents of the LDS Church Coloring Book. 50p. (Orig.). (gr. 2-6). 1993. pap. 5.95 (*0-910523-21-5*) Grandin Bk Co.
Cannon, Elaine. Turning Twelve or More: Living by the Articles of Faith. 9.95 (*0-88494-732-7*) Bookcraft Inc.
Chadwick, Valerie A., illus. Book of Mormon Story & Coloring Book. (Orig.). (gr. 3-6). 1993. pap. 4.95 (*0-87579-702-4*) Deseret Bk.
Crowther, Jean D. Book of Mormon Puzzles & Pictures for Young Latter-Day Saints. LC 77-74495. (Illus.). 56p. (gr. 3 up). 1977. pap. 5.98 (*0-88290-080-3*) Horizon Utah.
Dean, Bessie. Let's Learn of God's Love. LC 79-89367. (Illus.). 64p. (ps-3). 1979. pap. 3.98 (*0-88290-124-9*) Horizon Utah.
—Let's Learn the First Principles. LC 78-70366. (Illus.). 64p. (ps-3). 1993. pap. 3.98 (*0-88290-104-4*) Horizon Utah.
—Let's Love One Another. LC 77-74492. (Illus.). 64p. (ps-3). 1993. pap. 3.98 (*0-88290-077-3*) Horizon Utah.
—Living the Articles of Faith. Dean, Bessie, illus. 88p. (gr. k-4). 1988. pap. 6.98 (*0-88290-336-5*) Horizon Utah.
Doubleday, Veronica. Salt Lake City. LC 93-32738. (Illus.). 48p. (gr. 5 up). 1994. text ed. 13.95 RSBE (*0-87518-574-6*, Dillon) Macmillan Child Grp.
Edwards, Paul M. Our Legacy of Faith: A Brief History of the Reorganized Church of Jesus Christ of Latter Day Saints. 360p. 1991. text ed. 27.50 (*0-8309-0594-4*) Herald Hse.
England, Kathleen. Why We Are Baptized. LC 78-19180. (Illus.). 27p. (gr. 2-5). 1978. pap. 5.95 (*0-87747-893-7*) Deseret Bk.
Featherstone, Vaughn J. The Aaronic Priesthood & You. LC 87-15731. 99p. (gr. 8-12). 1993. pap. 8.95 (*0-87579-755-5*) Deseret Bk.
Halverson, Sandy. Book of Mormon Activity Book: Creative Scripture Learning Experiences for Children 4-12. Halverson, Sandy, illus. 80p. (gr. 3-8). 1982. pap. 5.98 (*0-88290-188-5*, 4521) Horizon Utah.
Hughes, Dean & Hughes, Tom. Great Stories from Mormon History. LC 94-8988. 1994. 12.95 (*0-87579-849-7*) Deseret Bk.
McCloud, Susan E. Joseph Smith: A Photobiography. LC 91-76005. (Illus.). 169p. (gr. 4-12). 1992. 12.95 (*1-56236-400-6*) Aspen Bks.
Madsen, Susan A. I Walked to Zion: True Stories of Youth Who Walked the Mormon Trail. LC 94-404. (gr. 6-12). 1994. 12.95 (*0-87579-848-9*) Deseret Bk.
—The Lord Needed a Prophet. LC 90-81829. (Illus.). 234p. (gr. 3-6). 1990. 10.95 (*0-87579-276-6*) Deseret Bk.
Neeley, Deta P. A Child's Story of the Book of Mormon. LC 87-19903. 382p. (gr. 1-6). 1987. 12.95 (*0-87579-101-8*) Deseret Bk.
Serving with Strength Around the World: Favorite Talks from Especially for Youth. LC 93-50934. (gr. 8-12). 1994. pap. 7.95 (*0-87579-836-5*) Deseret Bk.
Sharing the Light in the Wilderness: Favorite Talks from Especially for Youth. LC 93-2985. x, 193p. (Orig.). (gr. 8-12). 1993. pap. 5.95 (*0-87579-717-2*) Deseret Bk.
Why Say No When the World Says Yes. iii, 204p. (gr. 8-12). 1993. 12.95 (*0-87579-736-9*) Deseret Bk.

MORMONS AND MORMONISM–FICTION
Bowen, Annette P. Get a Life, Jennifer Parker. LC 93-24538. vi, 201p. (Orig.). (gr. 8-12). 1993. pap. 8.95 (*0-87579-756-3*) Deseret Bk.
Brigham Young & the Robin Soup. 12p. (Orig.). 1988. pap. text ed. 1.95 (*0-929985-01-X*) Jackman Pubng.
Hughes, Dean. Lucky Fights Back. LC 91-31416. 150p. (Orig.). (gr. 3-6). 1991. pap. text ed. 4.95 (*0-87579-559-5*) Deseret Bk.
—Lucky in Love. LC 93-33301. 161p. (Orig.). (gr. 3-7). 1993. pap. 4.95 (*0-87579-805-5*) Deseret Bk.
—Lucky's Cool Club. LC 93-28534. 141p. (gr. 3-7). 1993. pap. 4.95 (*0-87579-786-5*) Deseret Bk.
—Lucky's Gold Mine. LC 90-31072. 132p. (Orig.). (gr. 3-6). 1990. pap. 4.95 (*0-87579-350-9*) Deseret Bk.
Johnson, Marjorie. Book of Mormon Stories for Little Children. LC 76-3991. (Illus.). 96p. (Orig.). (ps-7). 1976. pap. 7.98 (*0-88290-063-3*) Horizon Utah.
Johnson, Sherrie. The Broken Bow. 1994. pap. 4.95 (*0-87579-253-7*) Deseret Bk.
Littke, Lael. Star of the Show. LC 93-27258. 162p. (Orig.). (gr. 5-9). 1993. pap. 4.95 (*0-87579-785-7*) Deseret Bk.
—There's a Snake at Girls' Camp. LC 94-751. (Orig.). (gr. 3-7). 1994. pap. 4.95 (*0-87579-845-4*) Deseret Bk.
Lundberg, Joy S. Book of Mormon Summer. (gr. 5-8). 1991. 6.95 (*0-915029-00-6*) Cherished Bks.
Sealy, Shirley. I, Jason. pap. 6.95 (*1-55503-247-8*, 29004721) Covenant Comms.
Searle, Don L. Light in the Harbor. LC 91-17827. viii, 245p. (Orig.). 1991. pap. 8.95 (*0-87579-528-5*) Deseret Bk.
Weyland, Jack. If Talent Were Pizza. LC 86-16210. 118p. (gr. 8-12). 1993. pap. 6.95 (*0-87579-696-6*) Deseret Bk.
Yates, Alma J. Ghosts in the Baker Mine. LC 91-45230. 197p. (Orig.). (gr. 3-7). 1992. pap. 4.95 (*0-87579-581-1*) Deseret Bk.
MOROCCO
Harmes, Jules. The Children of Morocco. LC 94-12709. (gr. 3 up). 1994. 19.95 (*0-87614-857-7*) Carolrhoda Bks.
Hintz, Martin. Morocco. LC 84-23269. (Illus.). 128p. (gr. 5-9). 1985. PLB 20.55 (*0-516-02774-3*) Childrens.
Lerner Publications, Department of Geography Staff, ed. Morocco in Pictures. (Illus.). 64p. (gr. 5 up). 1988. 17. 50 (*0-8225-1843-0*) Lerner Pubns.
Nelson, Harold D., ed. Morocco: A Country Study. LC 85-600265. (Illus.). 476p. (gr. 9-12). 1986. 15.00 (*0-16-001640-1*, S/N 008-020-01072-3) USGPO.
Wilkins, Frances. Morocco. (Illus.). 96p. (gr. 5 up). 1988. 14.95 (*1-55546-186-7*) Chelsea Hse.
MOROCCO–FICTION
Sales, Francesc. Ibrahim. Simont, Marc, tr. from CAT. Sariola, Eulalia, illus. LC 87-29382. 32p. (gr. k-3). 1989. (Lipp Jr Bks) HarpC Child Bks.
MORONS
see Mentally Handicapped
MORPHOLOGY
see Anatomy; Anatomy, Comparative; Biology; Botany–Anatomy
MORRIS, ROBERT, 1734-1806
Loftin, T. L. Contest for a Capital. (Illus.). 352p. (gr. 9-12). 1989. pap. 19.95 (*0-934812-04-7*) Tee Loftin.
MORSE, SAMUEL FINLEY BREESE, 1791-1872
Kerby, Mona. Samuel Morse. LC 90-13109. (Illus.). 64p. (gr. 3-5). 1991. PLB 12.90 (*0-531-20023-X*) Watts.
Latham, Jean L. Samuel F. B. Morse. (Illus.). 80p. (gr. 2-6). 1991. Repr. of 1961 ed. lib. bdg. 12.95 (*0-7910-1447-9*) Chelsea Hse.
Tiner, John H. Samuel F. B. Morse: Artist with a Message. (Illus.). (gr. 3-6). 1987. pap. 6.95 (*0-88062-137-0*) Mott Media.
MORTUARY CUSTOMS
see Funeral Rites and Ceremonies
MOSAICS
Avi-Yonah, Avi. Piece by Piece! Mosaics of the Ancient World. LC 93-10746. 1993. write for info. (*0-8225-3204-2*) Lerner Pubns.
Boutan, Mila. Mosaiques. (Illus.). (ps-1). 1992. 4.50 (*1-56021-195-4*) W J Fantasy.
MOSBY, JOHN SINGLETON, 1833-1916
Beller, Susan P. Mosby & His Rangers: Adventures of the Gray Ghost. LC 92-17475. (Illus.). 96p. (Orig.). (gr. 3-7). 1992. pap. 6.95 (*1-55870-265-2*, 70154) Shoe Tree Pr.
MOSCOW
Davis, James E. & Hawke, Sharryl D. Moscow. (Illus.). 64p. (gr. 4-9). 1990. PLB 11.95 (*0-8172-3030-0*) Raintree Steck-V.
MOSES
Frank, Penny. Let My People Go! Morris, Tony, et al, illus. 24p. (ps-3). 3.99 (*0-85648-735-X*) Lion USA.
—The Princess & the Baby. (ps-3). 1988. 3.99 (*0-85648-734-1*) Lion USA.
Hodges. Moses & the Ten Plagues. 24p. (Orig.). (gr. k-4). 1985. pap. 1.99 (*0-570-06190-3*, 59-1291) Concordia.
Hutton, Warwick, retold by. & illus. Moses in the Bulrushes. LC 91-13971. 32p. (gr. k-3). 1992. pap. 4.95 (*0-689-71553-6*, Aladdin) Macmillan Child Grp.
Johnson, Sylvia A. Mosses. Izawa, Masana, illus. LC 83-17488. 48p. (gr. 4 up). 1983. PLB 19.95 (*0-8225-1482-6*) Lerner Pubns.
Lashbrook, Marilyn. Who Needs a Boat? The Story of Moses. Britt, Stephanie M., illus. LC 87-83295. 32p. (ps). 1988. 5.95 (*0-86606-431-1*, 862) Roper Pr.

Lehmann, Asher. Young Moses, Crown Prince of Egypt. 150p. (gr. 9-12). 1987. 10.95 (*0-910818-64-9*); pap. 7.95 (*0-685-18059-X*) Judaica Pr.
Moses. (ps-2). 3.95 (*0-7214-5066-0*) Ladybird Bks.
Moses: Leader & Lawgiver. (Illus.). 32p. (gr. 2-12). 1982. incl. audiocassette 9.95 (*0-87510-161-5*) Christian Sci.
Overholtzer, Ruth. Moses, Vol. II. Andreasen, Norma, illus. 50p. (gr. k-6). 1967. pap. text ed. 9.45 (*1-55976-008-7*) CEF Press.
Parry, Alan & Parry, Linda. Baby Moses. Parry, Alan, illus. 24p. (ps). 1990. pap. 0.99 (*0-8066-2477-9*, 9-2477) Augsburg Fortress.
Parry, Linda & Parry, Alan. Miriam & Moses. Parry, Linda & Parry, Alan, illus. LC 90-80556. 24p. (Orig.). (ps-2). 1990. pap. 1.95 (*0-8066-2489-2*, 9-2489, Augsburg) Augsburg Fortress.
Russell, Jim, illus. Moses of the Bullrushes: Retold by Catherine Storr. 32p. (gr. k-4). 1984. 14.65 (*0-8172-1990-0*, Raintree Children's Books Belitha Press Ltd. - London) Raintree Steck-V.
Sanders, Nancy I. Moses. (ps). 1994. pap. 6.99 (*0-8423-7096-X*) Tyndale.
Simon, Mary M. Hide the Baby: The Birth of Moses. Jones, Dennis, illus. 24p. (Orig.). (ps-1). 1991. pap. 2.49 (*0-570-04702-1*) Concordia.
—The No-Go King: Exodus 5-15: The Exodus. Jones, Dennis, illus. LC 92-31888. 32p. (Orig.). (gr. 1-3). 1993. pap. 3.99 (*0-570-04732-3*) Concordia.
Tanvald, Christine H. The Big Big Big Boat, & Other Bible Stories about Obedience. Girouard, Patrick, illus. LC 93-9234. 1993. 7.99 (*0-7814-0926-8*, Chariot Bks) Chariot Family.
Truitt, Gloria A. Noah & God's Promise. 24p. (Orig.). (gr. k-4). 1985. pap. 1.99 (*0-570-06193-8*, 59-1294) Concordia.
Vos Wezeman, Phyllis & Wiessner, Colleen A. On the Move with Moses. 33p. (Orig.). (gr. 1-6). 1988. pap. 5.95 (*0-940754-60-6*) Ed Ministries.
Winder, Linda. Moses. (ps). 1993. 5.99 (*0-7814-0123-2*, Chariot Bks) Chariot Family.
Yenne, Bill, retold by. The Story of Moses. LC 93-37476. 1994. write for info. (*0-7852-8329-3*); pap. write for info. (*0-7852-8325-0*) Nelson.
MOSES, GRANDMA (MRS. ANNA MARY ROBERTSON MOSES) 1860-1961
Laing, Martha. Grandma Moses: The Grand Old Lady of American Art. Rahmas, D. Steve, ed. LC 71-190231. 32p. (Orig.). (gr. 7-9). 1972. lib. bdg. 4.95 incl. catalog cards (*0-87157-513-2*) SamHar Pr.
O'Neal, Zibby. Grandma Moses: Painter of Rural. Ruff, Donna & Moses, Grandma, illus. LC 86-4071. 64p. (gr. 2-6). 1986. pap. 10.95 (*0-670-80664-1*) Viking Child Bks.
MOSQUITOES
Patent, Dorothy H. Mosquitoes. LC 86-45387. (Illus.). 40p. (gr. 3-7). 1986. reinforced bdg. 12.95 (*0-8234-0627-X*) Holiday.
MOSSES
Greenaway, Theresa. Mosses & Liverworts. LC 91-14936. (Illus.). 48p. (gr. 5-9). 1992. PLB 21.34 (*0-8114-2738-2*) Raintree Steck-V.
Johnson, Sylvia. Mosses. Izawa, Masana, photos by. (Illus.). 48p. (gr. 4 up). pap. 5.95g (*0-8225-9563-X*) Lerner Pubns.
MOTHER GOOSE
Anglund, Joan W. A Mother Goose Book. Van Doren, Liz, ed. Anglund, Joan W., illus. 32p. (ps up). 1991. 7.95 (*0-15-200529-3*, Gulliver Bks) HarBrace.
Atkinson, Allen. Old King Cole & Other Favorites. (Illus.). 64p. (Orig.). 1986. pap. 2.50 (*0-553-15355-2*) Bantam.
Barrett, John E. & View-Master International, photos by. Big Bird's Mother Goose. LC 83-63404. (Illus.). 28p. (ps). 1984. bds. 3.25 (*0-394-86745-9*) Random Bks Yng Read.
Battaglia, Aurelius, ed. Mother Goose. (ps-1). 1973. 2.25 (*0-394-82661-2*) Random Bks Yng Read.
Delcher, Eden, compiled by. Mother Goose Counting Rhymes. 1993. 2.98 (*1-55521-832-6*) Bk Sales Inc.
—Mother Goose Rhymes about Children. 1993. 2.98 (*1-55521-833-4*) Bk Sales Inc.
Edens, Cooper, selected by. The Glorious Mother Goose. LC 87-35491. (Illus.). 96p. 1988. SBE 16.95 (*0-689-31434-5*, Atheneum Child Bk) Macmillan Child Grp.
Forsse, Ken & Hughes, Margaret. The Little Red Hen. Becker, Mary, ed. (Illus.). 26p. (ps). 1986. packaged with pre-programmed audio cass. tape 9.95 (*0-934323-22-4*) Alchemy Comms.
—The Tortoise & the Hare. Becker, Mary, ed. (Illus.). 26p. (ps). 1986. incl. pre-programmed audio cass. tape 9.95 (*0-934323-21-6*) Alchemy Comms.
Greenaway, Kate, illus. Mother Goose. 12p. (ps-5). 1973. pap. 3.25 (*0-914510-04-5*) Evergreen.
Halpern, Shari, illus. Little Robin Redbreast: A Mother Goose Rhyme. LC 93-38760. 32p. (ps-k). 1994. 14.95 (*1-55858-247-9*); PLB 14.88 (*1-55858-248-7*) North-South Bks NYC.
Hennessy, B. G. The Missing Tarts. Pearson, Tracey C., illus. 32p. (ps-3). 1989. pap. 12.95 (*0-670-82039-3*) Viking Child Bks.
Hickey. Mother Goose & More: Classic Nursery Rhymes with Added Lines. Moss, Marissa, illus. 48p. (ps-3). 1990. 7.77 (*0-9623940-0-9*); lib. bdg. 7.00 (*0-685-45370-7*); text ed. 12.95 (*0-685-45371-5*); tchr's. ed. 9.00 (*0-685-45372-3*) Additions Pr.
Hopkins, Lee B. Animals from Mother Goose. 11p. (ps-k). 1989. 6.95 (*0-15-200406-8*) HarBrace.

—People from Mother Goose. 18p. (ps-k). 1989. 6.95 (*0-15-200558-7*) HarBrace.

Kearns, Kimberly & O'Brien, Marie. Barney's Farm Animals. Hartley, Linda, ed. Malzeke-McDonald, Karen, illus. 24p. (ps). 1993. bds. 3.95 (*0-7829-0370-3*) Lyons Group.

Lansky, Bruce. The New Adventures of Mother Goose: Gentle Rhymes for Happy Times. Carpenter, Stephen, illus. LC 93-11129. 32p. 1993. 15.00 (*1-88166-201-2*) Meadowbrook.
This children's classic has been updated with a kinder, gentler, yet highly entertaining "sequel." The sometimes meanspirited & frightening versions of the past have been replaced with upbeat & contemporary nursery rhymes that will tickle a child's funny bone. The all-new poems still have the familiar characters & rhyme patterns kids love, but the violence, sexism & meanness are gone. In the old version, "The Old Woman Who Lived In A Shoe" beat her children for no apparent reason before sending them to bed. In the new version, when "the strong summer sun was too hot to handle," the old woman who lives in a shoe "packed up her things & moved to a sandal." #7 on the New York Times Children's Best Sellers list. Complimented by more than 40 full-color illustrations by Stephen Carrpenter. "Long overdue! A kinder, gentler Mother Goose--& funny too!" (Humpty Dumpty Magazine). "Chock full of chuckles!" (Shari Lewis & Lamb Chop). "Now Mother Goose isn't scary anymore." (Pat Gardner, Minneapolis Star Tribune). "An instant classic. Move over, Mother Goose!" (Peggy Gisler, "Dear Teacher", syndicated columnist).
Publisher Provided Annotation.

Lobel, Arnold, illus. The Just Right Mother Goose: Just Right for 3's & 4's. LC 88-43156. 32p. (ps). 1989. PLB 5.99 (*0-394-92860-1*) Random Bks Yng Read.

Loomans, Diane, et al. Positively Mother Goose. Kramer, Linda, ed. Henrichsen, Ronda, illus. LC 90-52634. 32p. (ps-2). 1991. 14.95 (*0-915811-24-3*) H J Kramer Inc.

Marshall, James, illus. James Marshall's Mother Goose. LC 79-2574. 40p. (ps-3). 1979. 15.00 (*0-374-33653-9*) FS&G.

The Mother Goose Book. (ps-1). 1990. write for info. (*0-307-10092-8*, 10092) Western Pub.

Mother Goose-Coloring Book. 1985. pap. 3.95 (*0-88388-012-1*) Bellerophon Bks.

Mother Goose Rhymes. (Illus.). 6p. (gr. k-2). 1991. bds. 17.95 (*1-56144-027-2*, Honey Bear Bks) Modern Pub NYC.

Mother Goose Staff. Little Red Riding Hood. Facsimile ed. LC 86-11772. (Illus.). 56p. (gr. k-5). 1986. Repr. of 1924 ed. 11.95 (*0-916410-35-8*) A D Bragdon.

Mountain, Lee, et al. Mother Goose Tea Party. (Illus.). 16p. (gr. k-1). 1993. pap. 14.75 (*0-89061-741-4*) Jamestown Pubs.

—Mother Goose Tea Party. (Illus.). 16p. (gr. k-1). 1991. pap. 18.75 (*0-89061-944-1*) Jamestown Pubs.

Nudelman, Edward D., frwd. by. The Jessie Willcox Smith Mother Goose. LC 90-19903. (Illus.). 192p. (gr. k up). 1991. 24.95 (*0-88289-844-2*); deluxe ed. 75.00 (*0-88289-830-2*) Pelican.

Officer, Robyn, illus. Mother Goose's Nursery Rhymes. 32p. (ps-3). 1992. 6.95 (*0-8362-4907-0*) Andrews & McMeel.

Provensen, Alice & Provensen, Martin. The Mother Goose Book. reissue ed. Provensen, Alice & Provensen, Martin, illus. LC 76-8548. 64p. (gr. 1 up). 1976. 10.00 (*0-394-82122-X*) Random Bks Yng Read.

Richardson, Frederick, illus. Mother Goose. Grover, Eulalie O., intro. by. LC 72-161577. (Illus.). 160p. (ps-4). 1915. 12.95 (*1-56288-254-6*) Checkerboard.

Scarry, Richard, illus. Richard Scarry's Best Mother Goose Ever. (ps-1). 1970. write for info. (*0-307-15578-1*, Golden Bks) Western Pub.

Sesame Street Staff. The Sesame Street Mother Goose. Jones, Randy, illus. LC 75-39341. (ps-3). 1976. 8.95 (*0-394-83256-6*) Random Bks Yng Read.

Tripp, Wallace. Granfa' Grig Had a Pig & Other Rhymes Without Reason from Mother Goose. Tripp, Wallace, illus. 96p. (gr. 4-12). 1976. 19.95 (*0-316-85282-1*); pap. 10.95 (*0-316-85284-8*) Little.

Tudor, Tasha. Mother Goose. Tudor, Tasha, illus. LC 58-58523. (gr. k-3). 1980. 9.95 (*0-8098-1901-5*) McKay.

—Mother Goose. LC 88-30674. (Illus.). 96p. (ps-2). 1989. 12.00 (*0-394-84407-6*) Random Bks Yng Read.

Walz, Richard, illus. The Pudgy Book of Mother Goose. 16p. (gr. k). 1984. 2.95 (*0-448-10212-9*, G&D) Putnam Pub Group.

White, Stephen. Barney's Favorite Mother Goose Rhymes, Vol. 1. Hartley, Linda, ed. Eubank, Mary G., illus. 32p. (ps-k). 1993. 7.95g (*0-7829-0336-3*) Lyons Group.

MOTHER GOOSE–SONGS AND MUSIC

Lancaster, Francine. Mother Goose & Other Nursery Songs: From the Collection of the Museum of Fine Arts, Boston. (ps up). 1987. incl. cassette 16.95 (*0-930647-03-3*) Lancaster Prodns.

MOTHERS

Aitkens, Maggi. Kerry: A Teenage Mother. Levine, Rob, photos by. LC 94-897. (Illus.). 48p. (gr. 4-8). 1994. PLB 18.95 (*0-8225-2556-9*) Lerner Pubns.

Alvarez Del Real, Maria E., ed. Guia Practica para la Mujer. (SPA., Illus.). 320p. (Orig.). 1989. pap. 4.00x (*0-944499-37-6*) Editorial Amer.

Duggan, Maureen H. Mommy Doesn't Live Here Anymore. Liberman, Jane, illus. 48p. (Orig.). (ps-7). 1987. pap. 8.95 (*0-944453-01-5*) B Brae.

Lasker, Joe. Mothers Can Do Anything. Lasker, Joe, illus. LC 72-83684. 40p. (gr. k-2). 1972. PLB 13.95 (*0-8075-5287-9*) A Whitman.

Parkinson, Carolyn S. My Mommy Has Cancer. Verstraete, Elaine, illus. 20p. (Orig.). (ps-4). 1992. pap. 8.95 (*0-9630287-0-7*) Solace Pub.
MY MOMMY HAS CANCER is a caring, informative & beautifully written book by Carolyn Stearns Parkinson to help young children understand what cancer is. The exceptional, warm, four-color illustrations by Elaine Verstraete are original water paintings of REAL people. The combination of the story & the illustrations help adults & children talk about this difficult subject & what their unique needs & concerns are. This book meets a crucial need for young children & their families, as one parent said, "It helped us to say the words we could not find to say." The book is being used in hospitals, schools, libraries & homes. "Carolyn Stearns Parkinson's book MY MOMMY HAS CANCER provides an excellent & necessary addition to the children's literature explaining illness. The beauty & sensitivity of both Carolyn Parkinson's words & Elaine Verstraete's color illustrations create a gentle ambiance in which children, from their own perspective, can learn about cancer, its emotional impact & its treatment. This is a superb book for parents to read with their children," by Michael H. Henrichs, Ph.D., Founder & Director of Kids Adjusting Through Support, Inc., Clinical, Child & School Psychologist, Cl. Assoc. Professor of Psychiatry & Oncology. To order, contact: Solace Publishing Inc., P.O. Box 567, Folsom, CA 95763-0567; 916-984-9015.
Publisher Provided Annotation.

Polisar, Barry L. Juggling Babies. (ps-6). 1989. incl. cassette 9.95 (*0-9615696-2-X*) Rainbow Morn.

Sirimarco, Elizabeth. Motherhood. LC 91-11169. 64p. (gr. 6-12). 1991. 12.95s.p. (*0-86593-121-6*); lib. bdg. 17.27 (*0-685-59204-9*) Rourke Corp.

MOTHERS–FICTION

Ackerman, Karen. By the Dawn's Early Light: Al Amanecer. Ada, Alma F., tr. Stock, Catherine, illus. LC 93-34815. (ENG & SPA.). 40p. (ps-3). 1994. English ed. SBE 14.95 (*0-689-31788-3*, Atheneum Child Bk); Spanish ed. SBE 14.95 (*0-689-31917-7*) Macmillan Child Grp.

Ada, Alma F. The Kite - El Papalote. Escriva, Vivi, illus. (SPA & ENG.). 23p. (gr. k-2). 1992. English ed. 6.95 (*1-56014-228-6*); Spanish ed. 6.95 (*1-56014-227-8*) Santillana.
A resourceful mother helps her children make & fly a kite in this entertaining selection. A surprise ending adds to the reading experience. Predictable language patterns help young readers to decode the text easily. English & Spanish versions are available to delight children in both languages. To order: Santillana, 901 West Walnut, Compton, CA 90220. Telephone 1-800-245-8584.
Publisher Provided Annotation.

Alden, Laura. Something for Mother. Hohag, Linda, illus. LC 93-37096. 32p. (ps-2). 1994. PLB 12.30 (*0-516-00690-8*) Childrens.

Andrews, Jan. Pumpkin Time. LaFave, Kim, illus. 32p. (ps-3). 1991. 12.95 (*0-88899-112-6*, Pub. by Groundwood-Douglas & McIntyre CN) Firefly Bks Ltd.

Auch, Mary J. Kidnapping Kevin Kowalski. LC 89-46065. 128p. (gr. 3-7). 1990. 14.95 (*0-8234-0815-9*) Holiday.

—Mom Is Dating Weird Wayne. (gr. 4-7). 1991. pap. 2.99 (*0-553-15916-X*) Bantam.

Balian, Lorna. Mother's, Mother's Day. Balian, Lorna, illus. 32p. (ps-3). 1987. Repr. of 1982 ed. 7.50 (*0-687-37097-3*) Humbug Bks.

Balter, Lawrence. A. J.'s Mom Gets a New Job. Schanzer, Roz, illus. 40p. (gr. 3-7). 1990. 5.95 (*0-8120-6151-9*) Barron.

Barber, Barbara E. Saturday at The New You. Rich, Anna, illus. LC 93-5165. 1994. 14.95 (*1-880000-06-7*) Lee & Low Bks.

Bat-Ami, Miriam. When the Frost Is Gone. Ramsey, Marcy D., illus. LC 92-26181. 80p. (gr. 5 up). 1994. SBE 13.95 (*0-02-708497-3*, Macmillan Child Bk) Macmillan Child Grp.

Bauer, Caroline Feller. My Mom Travels a Lot. Parker, Nancy W., illus. (gr. k-3). 1982. incl. cassette 19.95 (*0-941078-23-X*); pap. 12.95 incl. cassette (*0-941078-21-3*); pap. 27.95 4 bks., cassette & guide (*0-941078-22-1*); sound filmstrip 22.95 (*0-941078-24-8*) Live Oak Media.

Baum, Louis. After Dark. Varley, Susan, illus. LC 89-16123. 32p. (ps-3). 1990. 11.95 (*0-87951-382-9*) Overlook Pr.

Berry, Christine. Mama Went Walking. Brusca, Maria C., illus. LC 89-39789. 32p. (ps-2). 1990. 14.95 (*0-8050-1261-3*, Bks Young Read) H Holt & Co.

Black, J. R. Good Night, Mummy. LC 93-84908. 132p. (Orig.). (gr. 3-7). 1994. pap. 3.50 (*0-679-85409-6*) Random Bks Yng Read.

Blackman, Malorie. Girl Wonder & the Terrific Twins. Toft, Lis, illus. LC 92-27667. (gr. 2-5). 1993. 12.99 (*0-525-45065-3*, DCB) Dutton Child Bks.

Boulden, Jim & Boulden, Joan. Mom & Me. Winter, Peter, illus. 32p. (Orig.). (gr. 1-6). 1993. pap. 4.95 (*1-878076-25-6*) Boulden Pub.

Butterworth, Nick. My Mom is Excellent! Butterworth, Nick, illus. LC 92-43769. 32p. (ps up). 1994. 4.99 (*1-56402-289-7*) Candlewick Pr.

Calvert, Patricia. Yesterday's Daughter. LC 86-13753. 144p. (gr. 7 up). 1986. SBE 13.95 (*0-684-18746-9*, Scribners Young Read) Macmillan Child Grp.

Chaffin, Lillie D. Tommy's Big Problem. Petie, Haris, illus. (ps-2). PLB 7.19 (*0-8313-0016-7*) Lantern.

Chapman, Christina. Treasure in the Attic. Hoggan, Pat, illus. LC 92-35814. 32p. (gr. 4-6). 1992. PLB 19.97 (*0-8114-3582-2*) Raintree Steck-V.

Chevalier, Christa. Spence Isn't Spence Anymore. Levine, Abby, ed. Chevalier, Christa, illus. LC 84-29195. 32p. (ps-1). 1985. 11.95 (*0-8075-7565-8*) A Whitman.

Cleary, Beverly. Ramona & Her Mother. LC 79-10323. (Illus.). 208p. (gr. 4-6). 1979. 13.95 (*0-688-22195-5*); PLB 13.88 (*0-688-32195-X*) Morrow Jr Bks.

Clymer, Eleanor. My Mother Is the Smartest Woman in the World. Kincade, Nancy, illus. LC 82-1685. 96p. (gr. 4-6). 1982. SBE 13.95 (*0-689-30916-3*, Atheneum Child Bk) Macmillan Child Grp.

Cole, Babette. The Trouble with Mom. Cole, Babette, illus. 32p. (gr. 5-8). 1984. 13.95 (*0-698-20597-9*, Putnam); pap. 5.95 (*0-698-20681-9*, Sandcastle Bks) Putnam Pub Group.

—Trouble with Mom. LC 83-7750. (ps-3). 1986. pap. 5.95 (*0-698-20624-X*) Putnam Pub Group.

Coman, Carolyn. Tell Me Everything. 1993. 15.00 (*0-374-37390-6*) FS&G.

Corey, Dorothy. Will There Be a Lap for Me? Levine, Abby, ed. Poydar, Nancy, illus. LC 91-20324. 24p. (ps-1). 1992. PLB 11.95 (*0-8075-9109-2*) A Whitman.

Cowen-Fletcher, Jane. Mama Zooms. (ps-3). pap. 19.95 (*0-590-72848-2*) Scholastic Inc.

Daly, Niki. Ben's Gingerbread Man. LC 85-3327. (Illus.). 24p. (ps-1). 1985. 4.95 (*0-670-80806-7*) Viking Child Bks.

Dannhaus, Diane. My Mom, the Professional. McQueen, Don, illus. 24p. (Orig.). (gr. k-4). 1994. pap. 7.95 (*0-89896-104-1*) Larksdale.

Deem, James M. Three NBs of Julian Drew. LC 93-39306. 1994. 14.95 (*0-395-69453-1*) HM.

Delton, Judy. Angel's Mother's Boyfriend. Apple, Margot, illus. LC 82-27054. 176p. (gr. 2-5). 1986. 14. 95 (*0-395-39968-8*) HM.
—Angel's Mother's Boyfriend. (gr. k-6). 1990. pap. 2.95 (*0-440-40275-1*, YB) Dell.
—Angel's Mother's Wedding. (gr. k-6). 1990. pap. 2.95 (*0-440-40281-6*, YB) Dell.
—Bad, Bad Bunnies. (gr. k-6). 1990. pap. 3.25 (*0-440-40278-6*, YB) Dell.
Doherty, Berlie. Dear Nobody. large type ed. LC 93-13531. (gr. 6 up). 1993. Alk. paper. 15.95 (*1-56054-769-3*) Thorndike Pr.
Doman, Bruce K. Goodbye, Mommy. Melton, David, illus. LC 77-79632. 86p. (ps-2). 1982. 8.95 (*0-936676-00-0*) Better Baby.
Dorer, Ann. Mother Makes a Mistake. LC 89-42638. 32p. (gr. 1-2). 1991. PLB 18.60 (*0-8368-0109-1*) Gareth Stevens Inc.
Drescher, Joan. My Mother's Getting Married. Drescher, Joan, illus. LC 84-18642. 32p. (ps-3). 1989. pap. 4.95 (*0-8037-0642-1*) Dial Bks Young.
—My Mother's Getting Married. (ps-3). 1989. pap. 4.99 (*0-14-054667-7*, Puff Pied Piper) Puffin Bks.
Eastman, P. D. Are You My Mother? - Eres Tu Mi Mama? Eastman, P. D., illus. (ENG & SPA.). 64p. (ps-3). 1993. incl. cass. 6.95 (*0-679-84330-2*) Random Bks Yng Read.
Ehrlich, Amy. Where It Stops, Nobody Knows. 224p. (gr. 6 up). 1990. pap. 3.95 (*0-14-034266-4*, Puffin) Puffin Bks.
Eisenberg, Phyllis R. You're My Nikki. Kastner, Jill, illus. LC 91-2670. 32p. (ps-3). 1992. 14.00 (*0-8037-1127-1*); PLB 13.89 (*0-8037-1129-8*) Dial Bks Young.
Ellis, Sarah. Pick-up Sticks. Chan, Harvey, contrib. by. LC 91-26585. 128p. (gr. 7 up). 1992. SBE 13.95 (*0-689-50550-7*, M K McElderry) Macmillan Child Grp.
Farrell, Sue. To the Post Office with Mama. Lewis, Robin B., illus. 24p. (ps-1). 1994. 14.95 (*1-55037-359-5*, Pub. by Annick CN); pap. 4.95 (*1-55037-358-7*, Pub. by Annick CN) Firefly Bks Ltd.
Filichia, Peter. The Most Embarrassing Mother in the World. 192p. 1991. pap. 3.50 (*0-380-76084-3*, Flare) Avon.
Finley, Martha. Elsie's Motherhood. 243p. 1981. Repr. PLB 25.95x (*0-89966-335-4*) Buccaneer Bks.
Fletcher, Susan. The Stuttgart Nanny Mafia. LC 90-23225. 160p. (gr. 3-7). 1991. SBE 14.95 (*0-689-31709-3*, Atheneum Child Bk) Macmillan Child Grp.
Fox, Mem. Koala Lou. 28p. (ps-1). 1989. 13.95 (*0-15-200502-1*) HarBrace.
Fran, Renee & Freshman, Floris, illus. What Happened to Mommy? 32p. (Orig.). (ps-6). 1994. pap. 5.95 (*0-9640250-0-0*) Eastman NY.
Gilchrist, Jan S. Indigo & Moonlight Gold. Gilchrist, Jan S., illus. 32p. 1992. 13.95 (*0-86316-210-X*) Writers & Readers.
Glassman, Peter. My Working Mom. Arnold, Tedd, illus. LC 93-22036. 1994. 15.00g (*0-688-12259-0*); PLB 14. 93 (*0-688-12260-4*) Morrow Jr Bks.
Goode, Diane. Where's Our Mama? Goode, Diane, illus. LC 91-2158. 32p. (ps-2). 1991. 13.95 (*0-525-44770-9*, DCB) Dutton Child Bks.
Grancell-Frank, Barbara. The Oldest Mommy in the Park. Frank, Barbara, illus. Thomas, R. David, frwd. by. (Illus.). 64p. (Orig.). (gr. 6-12). 1993. pap. 8.95 (*1-56883-022-X*) Colonial Pr AL.
Greene, Constance C. Star Shine. (gr. k-6). 1987. pap. 2.75 (*0-440-47920-7*, YB) Dell.
Griffin, Sandra U. Earth Circles. Griffin, Sandra U., illus. 32p. (ps-3). 1989. 12.95 (*0-8027-6843-1*); PLB 13.85 (*0-8027-6845-8*) Walker & Co.
Hamilton, Dorothy. Joel's Other Mother. Graber, Esther R., illus. 120p. (gr. 3-7). 1984. pap. 3.95 (*0-8361-3355-2*) Herald Pr.
Harris, Lois J. Big Mama. (Illus.). 16p. 1994. saddle-stitch 5.95 (*0-8059-3483-9*) Dorrance.
Hathorn, Libby. The Surprise Box. Cutter, Priscilla, illus. LC 93-28957. 1994. 4.25 (*0-383-03778-6*) SRA Schl Grp.
Hautzig, Esther. A Gift for Mama. (gr. 1-4). 1992. 16.50 (*0-8446-6570-3*) Peter Smith.
Hay, John. Mama, Were You Ever Young? (Illus.). 32p. (gr. k-4). 1991. 13.95 (*0-88138-134-9*, Green Tiger) S&S Trade.
Haynes, Betsy. Great Mom Swap. 160p. (Orig.). 1986. pap. 2.50 (*0-553-15398-6*, Skylark) Bantam.
—The Great Mom Swap. 1994. pap. 3.50 (*0-553-15675-6*) Bantam.
Hazen, Barbara S. Even If I Did Something Awful? Kincade, Nancy, illus. LC 81-1907. 32p. (ps-2). 1981. SBE 13.95 (*0-689-30843-4*, Atheneum Child Bk) Macmillan Child Grp.
—Mommy's Office. Soman, David, illus. LC 91-25013. 32p. (ps-1). 1992. SBE 13.95 (*0-689-31601-1*, Atheneum Child Bk) Macmillan Child Grp.
Hest, Amy. The Mommy Exchange. DiSalvo-Ryan, Dyanne, illus. LC 90-40596. 32p. (ps-2). 1991. pap. 3.95 (*0-689-71450-5*, Aladdin) Macmillan Child Grp.
Hines, Anna G. It's Just Me, Emily. Hines, Anna G., illus. (ps-1). 1987. 12.95 (*0-89919-487-7*, Clarion Bks) HM.
Holabird, Katharine. Alexander & the Magic Boat. Craig, Helen, illus. 24p. (ps-2). 1990. 11.95 (*0-517-58142-6*); PLB 12.99 (*0-517-58149-3*) Crown Bks Yng Read.
Holland, Alex N. Ironing with Mother. Holland, Alex N., illus. 20p. (gr. k-3). 1994. pap. 12.95 (*1-895583-71-3*) MAYA Pubs.
Howard, Megan. I'm Going to Meet My Mother. LC 93-85682. 144p. (Orig.). (gr. 3-9). 1994. pap. 3.99 (*0-679-85702-8*) Random Bks Yng Read.
Howe, Quincy. Streetsmart. LC 93-1397. 112p. (gr. 6-12). 1993. pap. 6.95 (*0-932765-42-4*, 1325-93); tchr's. guide 5.95 (*0-685-70875-6*, 1326-93) Close Up.
Jacoby, Alice. My Mother's Boyfriend & Me. (gr. 9 up). 1988. pap. 2.95 (*0-449-70311-8*, Juniper) Fawcett.
Jenks, Graham. Every Mom Is Special. Burris, Priscilla, illus. 1994. 4.99 (*0-7852-8215-7*) Nelson.
Johnson, Angela. Mama Bird, Baby Birds. Mitchell, Rhonda, illus. LC 93-46415. 12p. (ps). 1994. 4.95 (*0-531-06848-X*) Orchard Bks Watts.
—Tell Me a Story, Mama. Soman, David, illus. LC 88-17917. 32p. (ps-1). 1992. pap. 4.95 (*0-531-07032-8*) Orchard Bks Watts.
Johnson, Dolores. What Will Mommy Do When I'm at School? Johnson, Dolores, illus. LC 90-5559. 32p. (ps-1). 1990. RSBE 13.95 (*0-02-747845-9*, Macmillan Child Bk) Macmillan Child Grp.
Joosse, Barbara M. Dinah's Mad, Bad Wishes. McCully, Emily A., illus. LC 88-884. 32p. (gr. k-3). 1989. PLB 12.89 (*0-06-023099-1*) HarpC Child Bks.
Kandoian, Ellen. Maybe She Forgot. LC 89-25271. (Illus.). (ps). 1990. 12.95 (*0-525-65031-8*, Cobblehill Bks) Dutton Child Bks.
Kasza, Keiko. A Mother for Choco. Kasza, Keiko, illus. 32p. (ps-1). 1992. PLB 14.95 (*0-399-21841-6*, Putnam) Putnam Pub Group.
Kennaley, Lucinda H. My Mom Is Pregnant! Kennaley, Lucinda H., illus. 60p. (Orig.). (ps). 1990. pap. text ed. 9.95 (*0-9628067-0-6*) Thoth MO.
Killion, Bette. Think of It. Saldutti, Denise, illus. LC 89-26878. 32p. (ps-1). 1993. 12.00 (*0-06-023257-9*); PLB 11.89 (*0-06-023258-7*) HarpC Child Bks.
Klevin, Jill R. Turtles Together Forever! Edwards, Linda S., illus. LC 82-70313. 160p. (gr. 4-6). 1982. pap. 9.95 (*0-385-29045-4*); pap. 9.89 (*0-385-29046-2*) Delacorte.
Kohlenberg, Sherry. Sammy's Mommy Has Cancer. Crow, Lauri, illus. LC 93-22773. 32p. (ps-3). 1993. 16. 95 (*0-945354-56-8*); pap. 8.95 (*0-945354-55-X*) Magination Pr.
Kotter, Deborah. Arnold Always Answers. Conteh-Morgan, Jane, illus. LC 92-18578. 1993. 14.95 (*0-385-30905-8*, Zephyr-BFYR) Doubleday.
Leach, Norman. My Wicked Stepmother. Browne, Jane, illus. LC 92-19674. 32p. (ps-3). 1993. SBE 13.95 (*0-02-754700-0*, Macmillan Child Bk) Macmillan Child Grp.
Levine, Abby. What Did Mommy Do Before You? (ps-3). 1990. pap. 3.95 (*0-14-054215-9*, Puffin) Puffin Bks.
Levy, Elizabeth. The Case of the Mind-Reading Mommies. Eagle, Ellen, illus. 1990. pap. 2.95 (*0-671-69435-9*) S&S Trade.
Lewin, Hugh. Jafta's Mother. Kopper, Lisa, illus. 24p. (ps-3). 1989. pap. 4.95 (*0-87614-495-4*, First Ave Edns) Lerner Pubns.
—Jafta's Mother. LC 82-12863. (ps-3). 1988. 15.95 (*0-87614-208-0*) Carolrhoda Bks.
Loh, Morag. Tucking Mommy In. LC 87-16740. (Illus.). 40p. (ps-2). 1991. pap. 4.95 (*0-531-07025-5*) Orchard Bks Watts.
Lyon, George E. Mama is a Miner. Catalanotto, Peter, illus. LC 93-49398. 32p. (gr. k-3). 1994. 15.95 (*0-531-06853-6*); PLB 15.99 (*0-531-08703-4*) Orchard Bks Watts.
Ma Maman: My Mom. (FRE.). 14p. (ps). 1992. 4.95 (*1-55037-267-X*, Pub. by Annick Pr) Firefly Bks Ltd.
McDaniel, Lurlene. Mother, Help Me Live: One Last Wish. 1992. pap. 3.50 (*0-553-29811-9*) Bantam.
MacDonald, Caroline. Speaking to Miranda. LC 91-47901. 256p. (gr. 7 up). 1992. 14.00 (*0-06-021102-4*); PLB 13.89 (*0-06-021103-2*) HarpC Child Bks.
McKenna, Colleen O. Mother Murphy. 160p. (gr. 4-7). 1993. 13.95 (*0-590-44820-X*, Scholastic Hardcover); pap. 3.25 (*0-590-44856-0*, Scholastic Hardcover) Scholastic Inc.
Mandrell, Louise. All in a Day's Work: A Story about the Meaning of Mother's Day. (ps-3). 1993. 12.95 (*1-56530-036-X*) Summit TX.
—All in a Day's Work: A Story about the Meaning of Mother's Day. (gr. 4-7). 1993. 12.95 (*1-56540-036-4*) Impact Photograph.
Marsh, Carole. If My Mama Ran the World. 1994. 24.95 (*1-55609-287-3*); pap. 14.95 (*0-318-37385-8*) Gallopade Pub Group.
Martin, Ann M. Karen's Stepmother. (gr. 4-7). 1994. pap. 2.95 (*0-590-47047-7*) Scholastic Inc.
—Kristy & the Mother's Day Surprise. (gr. 4-7). 1989. pap. 3.50 (*0-590-43506-X*) Scholastic Inc.
Marton, Jirina. Flowers for Mom. Marton, Jirina, illus. 24p. (ps-3). 1991. PLB 15.95 (*1-55037-155-X*, Pub. by Annick CN); pap. 5.95 (*1-55037-158-4*, Pub. by Annick CN) Firefly Bks Ltd.
May, Robert E. Poppa & Elizabeth: A Bobtail Romance. McQueen, Don, illus. 32p. (Orig.). (ps-3). 1988. PLB 11.89 (*0-87397-314-3*); pap. 5.95 (*0-87397-313-5*) Strode.
Mazer, Harry. Someone's Mother Is Missing. 1991. pap. 3.50 (*0-440-21097-6*, YB) Dell.
Melmed, Laura K. I Love You As Much... Sorensen, Henri, illus. LC 92-27677. 1993. write for info. (*0-688-11718-X*); PLB write for info. (*0-688-11719-8*) Lothrop.
Merriam, Eve. Mommies at Work. (ps-3). 1991. pap. 2.95 (*0-671-73275-7*, Little Simon) S&S Trade.
Mi Mama: My Mother. (SPA.). 14p. (ps). 1992. bds. 4.95 (*1-55037-264-5*, Pub. by Annick Pr) Firefly Bks Ltd.
Miller, Mary J. Upside Down. 128p. (gr. 3-7). 1992. 13. 00 (*0-670-83648-6*) Viking Child Bks.
Mire, Betty. It's Funny How Things Change. LC 84-1164. 155p. (gr. 5-10). 1985. 12.95 (*0-88289-431-5*) Pelican.
Mori, Kyoko. Shizuko's Daughter. LC 92-26956. 256p. (gr. 7 up). 1993. 15.95 (*0-8050-2557-X*, Bks Young Read) H Holt & Co.
Moulton, Deborah. Summer Girl. LC 91-15790. 128p. (gr. 5-9). 1992. 15.00 (*0-8037-1153-0*) Dial Bks Young.
My Mother. 22p. (gr. k-3). 1980. pap. 3.00 (*0-89744-215-6*, Pub. by Children's Bk India) Auromere.
Nahum-Valensi, Maya. Mom's Sore Throat. (Illus.). 48p. (gr. 3-8). 1990. 8.95 (*0-89565-807-0*) Childs World.
Nixon, Joan L. Star Baby. (gr. 7 up). 1989. 14.95 (*0-553-05838-X*, Starfire) Bantam.
O'Connor, Frank. My Oedipus Complex. Delessert, Etienne, illus. LC 85-32526. 40p. (gr. 4 up). 1986. PLB 13.95 (*0-88682-062-6*) Creative Ed.
O'Neal, Zibby. A Formal Feeling. LC 82-2018. (Illus.). 168p. (gr. 7 up). 1982. pap. 12.95 (*0-670-32488-4*) Viking Child Bks.
Ormerod, Jan. Mom's Home. Ormerod, Jan, illus. LC 87-2712. 24p. (ps). 1987. 5.95 (*0-688-07274-7*) Lothrop.
Owens, Vivian W. Nadanda, the Wordmaker: Hide the Doll. Maxwell, Carolyn, ed. Watson, Richard J., illus. LC 93-74671. 248p. 1994. 16.95 (*0-9623839-3-7*) Eschar Pubns.
Phillips, Wanda C. My Mother Doesn't Like to Cook. Claycamp, Micah, illus. 28p. (Orig.). (ps-5). 1993. pap. 6.95 (*0-936981-20-2*) ISHA Enterprises.
Pirotta, Saviour. Little Bird. Butler, Stephen, illus. LC 91-25413. 32p. (ps-3). 1992. 14.00 (*0-688-11289-7*, Tambourine Bks); PLB 13.93 (*0-688-11290-0*, Tambourine Bks) Morrow.
Porte, Barbara A. Harry's Mom. Abolafia, Yossi, illus. LC 84-25955. 48p. (gr. 1-4). 1985. 10.25 (*0-688-04817-X*); lib. bdg. 10.88 (*0-688-04818-8*) Greenwillow.
Porter, Connie. Addy's Surprise: A Christmas Story. Rosales, Melodye, illus. Graef, Renee, contrib. by. LC 93-5162. (Illus.). 1993. 12.95 (*1-56247-080-9*); pap. 5.95 (*1-56247-079-5*) Pleasant Co.
Porter, Gene S. Girl of the Limberlost. (Illus.). 496p. 1992. 8.99 (*0-517-07235-1*, Pub. by Gramercy) Random Hse Value.
—A Girl of the Limberlost. 432p. (gr. 5 up). 1992. pap. 3.99 (*0-14-035143-4*) Puffin Bks.
Porter-Gaylord, Laurel. I Love My Mommy Because... Wolff, Ashley, illus. LC 90-2792. 24p. (ps). 1991. 5.95 (*0-525-44625-7*, DCB) Dutton Child Bks.
Poulin, Stephane. My Mother's Love. Poulin, Stephane, illus. 32p. (ps-1). 1990. 15.95 (*1-55037-149-5*, Pub. by Annick CN); pap. 5.95 (*1-55037-148-7*, Pub. by Annick CN) Firefly Bks Ltd.
Pulver, Robin. Nobody's Mother Is in Second Grade. Karas, G. Brian, illus. LC 91-16395. 32p. (gr. k-3). 1992. 13.50 (*0-8037-1210-3*); PLB 13.89 (*0-8037-1211-1*) Dial Bks Young.
Riskind, Mary. Follow That Mom. LC 86-20049. (gr. 4-6). 1987. 13.45 (*0-395-41553-5*) HM.
Robinson. Mom, You're Fired! 1992. pap. 2.75 (*0-590-44903-6*, Apple Paperbacks) Scholastic Inc.
Robinson, Mary. Give It up, Mom. 144p. (gr. 4). 1992. pap. 2.99 (*0-380-71126-5*, Camelot) Avon.
Rose, Deborah L. Meredith's Mother Takes the Train. Levine, Abby, ed. Trivas, Irene, illus. LC 90-12756. 24p. (ps-k). 1991. 11.95 (*0-8075-5061-2*) A Whitman.
Rosenberg, Liz. Monster Mama. Gammell, Stephen, illus. 32p. (ps-3). 1993. PLB 14.95 (*0-399-21989-7*, Philomel Bks) Putnam Pub Group.
Ruckman, Ivy. Who Invited the Undertaker? LC 89-1865. 192p. (gr. 3-7). 1989. (Crowell Jr Bks); PLB 13.89 (*0-690-04834-3*, Crowell Jr Bks) HarpC Child Bks.

Salem, Lynn & Stewart, Josie. Notes from Mom. (Illus.). 16p. (ps-2). 1992. pap. 3.50 (*1-880612-01-1*) Seedling Pubns.
This book is part of the SEEDLINGS SERIES, designed by primary educators to meet the needs of young readers who are beyond board books, but not quite ready for independent readers or early chapter books. Other delightful titles include: WHAT'S FOR DINNER?, THE CAT WHO LOVED RED, MY PET, STAYING WITH GRANDMA NORMA, & WHAT A SCHOOL. These 8, 12 & 16 page books range from 14 to 164 words. For preschoolers, just starting to explore print, to young readers needing many opportunities to practice, these books are the perfect building blocks. This series includes a beautifully illustrated display with 56 books (4 copies of 14

different titles). The floor model display stands 20" high & has cubbies holding multiple copies of each title. Identical unit also available in a tabletop version. "...early readers find them fun & luring. Children are sure to enjoy the easy text & superb drawings. "--Children's Librarian. Display unit (table-top or floor) & 56 books...$229. 00, plus 8% shipping. Add-on packs (5 additional titles, 4 copies/each) $70.00, plus shipping. ISBN 1-880612-33-X (floor display/series), ISBN 1-880612-34-8 (table top display/series) Seedling Publications, Inc., 4097 Overlook Drive East, Columbus, OH 43214-2931. Phone & FAX 614-451-2412.
Publisher Provided Annotation.

—Recados de Mama. (Illus.). 16p. (gr. 1). 1993. pap. 3.50 (*1-880612-22-4*) Seedling Pubns.

Sawicki, Norma J. Something for Mom. Weston, Martha, illus. LC 86-34421. 32p. (ps-1). 1987. PLB 12.93 (*0-688-05590-7*) Lothrop.

Say, Allen. Tree of Cranes. Say, Allen, illus. 32p. (gr. k-3). 1991. 16.45 (*0-395-52024-X*, Sandpiper) HM.

Schlein, Miriam. The Way Mothers Are: Thirtieth Anniversary Edition. rev. ed. Tucker, Kathy, ed. Lasker, Joe, illus. LC 92-21516. 32p. (ps-k). 1993. PLB 13.95 (*0-8075-8691-9*) A Whitman.

Shannon, George. The Surprise. Aruego, Jose & Dewey, Ariane, illus. LC 83-1434. 32p. (gr. k-3). 1983. 13.95 (*0-688-02313-4*) Greenwillow.

Sharmat, Marjorie W. Hooray for Mother's Day! Wallner, John, illus. LC 85-14146. 32p. (ps-3). 1986. reinforced bdg. 14.95 (*0-8234-0588-5*) Holiday.

Shine, Michael. Mama Llama's Pajamas. Villegas, Carene, illus. 45p. (Orig.). (ps-3). 1990. pap. 8.95 (*0-945265-32-8*) Accord Comm.

Smalls-Hector, Irene. Jonathan & His Mommy. (ps-3). 1992. 14.95 (*0-316-79870-3*) Little.

Smith, Matthew V. Wake Up, Mommy. Smith, Matthew V., illus. 15p. (gr. 1-3). 1992. pap. 10.95 (*1-56606-009-5*) Bradley Mann.

Stanek, Muriel. I Speak English for My Mom. Tucker, Kathleen, ed. Friedman, Judith, illus. LC 88-20546. 32p. (gr. 2-5). 1989. 11.95 (*0-8075-3659-8*) A Whitman.

Turner, Ann. Stars for Sarah. Teichman, Mary, illus. LC 89-26908. 32p. (ps-3). 1991. PLB 13.89 (*0-06-026187-0*) HarpC Child Bks.

Ungerer, Tomi. No Kiss for Mother. 1993. pap. 4.99 (*0-440-40886-5*) Dell.

Van Laan, Nancy. Country Lullaby: All Around the World. Meade, Holly, illus. LC 93-44484. (gr. 1-4). 1995. 14.95 (*0-316-89732-9*) Little.

Van Leeuwen, Jean. Dear Mom You're Ruining My Life. (gr. 4 up). 1990. pap. 3.99 (*0-14-034386-5*, Puffin) Puffin Bks.

Vigna, Judith. When Eric's Mom Fought Cancer. (ps-3). 1993. 13.95 (*0-8075-8883-0*) A Whitman.

Waber, Bernard. Lyle Finds His Mother. LC 74-5336. (Illus.). 48p. (gr. k-3). 1974. 14.95 (*0-395-19489-X*) HM.

Walker-Blondell, Becky. In My Mother's Arms. LC 93-60918. 186p. (gr. 6-12). 1994. 9.95 (*1-55523-647-2*) Winston-Derek.

Wardlaw, Lee. Operation Rhinoceros. Stouffer, Deborah, illus. LC 92-15933. 120p. (Orig.). (gr. 3-6). 1992. pap. 3.50 (*0-931093-14-7*) Red Hen Pr.

Wells, Rosemary. Hazel's Amazing Mother. Wells, Rosemary, illus. LC 85-1447. (ps-2). 1989. 3.95 (*0-8037-0703-7*) Dial Bks Young.

—Hazel's Amazing Mother. LC 85-1447. (Illus.). 32p. (ps-2). 1992. pap. 17.99 giant size (*0-14-054538-7*, Puff Pied Piper) Puffin Bks.

Williams, Suzanne. Mommy Doesn't Know My Name. Shachat, Andrew, illus. 48p. (ps). 1990. 13.45 (*0-395-54228-6*) HM.

Williams, Vera. A Chair for My Mother. Marcuse, Aida, tr. from ENG. Williams, Vera, illus. (SPA.). 32p. (ps up). 1994. pap. 4.95 (*0-688-13200-6*, Mulberry) Morrow.

Williams, Vera B. A Chair for My Mother. LC 81-7010. (Illus.). 32p. (ps up). 1988. pap. 4.95 (*0-688-04074-8*, Mulberry) Morrow.

—A Chair for My Mother: Big Book Edition. Williams, Vera B., illus. 32p. (ps up). 1993. pap. 18.95 (*0-688-12612-X*, Mulberry) Morrow.

Winthrop, Elizabeth. A Very Noisy Girl. LC 90-39175. (Illus.). 32p. (ps-3). 1991. reinforced 14.95 (*0-8234-0858-2*) Holiday.

Wright, Betty R. My New Mom & Me. (ps-3). 1993. pap. 3.95 (*0-8114-7154-3*) Raintree Steck-V.

Wynot, Jillian. The Mother's Day Sandwich. Chambliss, Maxie, illus. LC 89-35649. 32p. (ps-2). 1990. 14.95 (*0-531-05857-3*); PLB 14.99 (*0-531-08457-4*) Orchard Bks Watts.

Zakhoder's, Boris. The Good Stepmother. Rudolph, Marguerita, retold by. May, Darcy, illus. LC 90-10063. 40p. (ps-2). 1992. pap. 14.00 jacketed (*0-671-68270-9*, S&S BFYR) S&S Trade.

Zeder, Suzan. Mother Hicks. 68p. (Orig.). (gr. k-3). 1986. pap. 5.50 playscript (*0-87602-263-8*) Anchorage.

Zindel, Paul & Zindel, Bonnie. A Star for the Latecomer. 160p. (gr. 6 up). 1985. pap. 2.50 (*0-553-25578-9*) Bantam.

Zolotow, Charlotte. Say It! Stevenson, James, illus. LC 79-25115. 24p. (gr. k-3). 1980. PLB 14.88 (*0-688-84276-3*) Greenwillow.

MOTHERS–POETRY

Leah Komaiko & Kids. A Million Moms & Mine. (Illus.). 28p. 1992. 11.95 (*0-9634893-0-5*); pap. 5.95 (*0-9634893-1-3*) L Claiborne.

Schlein, Miriam. Way Mothers Are. Lasker, Joe, illus. LC 63-13332. (ps-2). 1963. PLB 13.95 (*0-8075-8692-7*) A Whitman.

MOTHER'S DAY

Gore, Willma W. Mother's Day. LC 92-32675. (Illus.). 48p. (gr. 1-4). 1993. lib. bdg. 14.95 (*0-89490-404-3*) Enslow Pubs.

Moncure, Jane B. Our Mother's Day Book. Rev. ed. Lexa, Susan, illus. LC 86-29980. (ps-3). 1987. PLB 13.95 (*0-89565-346-X*) Childs World.

MOTHS

see also Butterflies; Caterpillars; Silkworms

Beaty, Dave. Moths & Butterflies. LC 92-29741. (Illus.). (gr. 2-6). 1993. 15.95 (*1-56766-001-0*) Childs World.

Butterflies. (Illus.). 32p. (ps-1). 1986. pap. 1.25 (*0-8431-1523-8*) Price Stern.

Butterflies & Moths. 8.95 (*1-56458-038-5*) Dorling Kindersley.

Cox & Cork. Butterflies & Moths. (gr. 2-5). 1980. PLB 11.96 (*0-88110-073-0*); pap. 3.95 (*0-86020-477-4*) EDC.

Feltwell, John. Butterflies & Moths. LC 92-54313. (Illus.). 64p. (gr. 3 up). 1993. 9.95 (*1-56458-227-2*) Dorling Kindersley.

Fichter, George S. Butterflies & Moths. Kest, Kristin, illus. 36p. (gr. k-3). 1993. 4.95 (*0-307-11435-X*, 11435, Golden Pr) Western Pub.

Gattis, L. S., III. Butterflies & Moths for Pathfinders: A Basic Youth Enrichment Skill Honor Packet. (Illus.). 20p. (Orig.). (gr. 5 up). 1987. pap. 5.00 tchr's. ed. (*0-936241-31-4*) Cheetah Pub.

Julivert, Maria A. The Fascinating World of Butterflies & Moths. Marcel Socias Studio Staff & Arridondo, F., illus. 32p. (gr. 3-7). 11.95 (*0-8120-6282-5*) Barron.

Kendall, Cindy. Butterflies. Bennish, Gracia, illus. Dudley, Dick. LC 93-3117. (ps). 1994. pap. 3.95 (*0-8037-1275-8*) Dial Bks Young.

Mattern, Joanne. A Picture Book of Butterflies & Moths. Pistolesi, Roseanna, illus. LC 92-5225. 24p. (gr. 1-4). 1992. PLB 9.59 (*0-8167-2796-1*); pap. 2.50 (*0-8167-2797-X*) Troll Assocs.

Mitchell, Robert & Zim, Herbert S. Butterflies & Moths. Durenceau, Andre, illus. (gr. 5 up). 1964. PLB write for info. (*0-307-24052-5*); pap. write for info. (Golden Pr) Western Pub.

Morris, Dean. Butterflies & Moths. rev. ed. LC 87-16666. (Illus.). 48p. (gr. 2-6). 1987. PLB 10.95 (*0-8172-3204-4*) Raintree Steck-V.

Porter, Keith. Discovering Butterflies & Moths. (Illus.). 48p. (gr. 2 up). 1990. pap. 4.95 (*0-531-18364-5*, Pub. by Bookwright Pr) Watts.

Ring, Elizabeth. Night Flier. Kuhn, Dwight, photos by. LC 93-40115. (Illus.). 32p. (gr. k-3). 1994. PLB 15.40 (*1-56294-467-3*) Millbrook Pr.

Robson, Denny. Butterflies & Moths. (Illus.). 32p. (gr. 4-6). 1991. 13.95 (*0-237-60170-2*, Pub. by Evans Bros Ltd) Trafalgar.

Rowan, James P. Butterflies & Moths. LC 83-7216. (Illus.). 48p. (gr. k-4). 1983. PLB 12.85 (*0-516-01692-X*); pap. 4.95 (*0-516-41692-8*) Childrens.

Sabin, Louis. Amazing World of Butterflies & Moths. Helmer, Jean C., illus. LC 81-7504. 32p. (gr. 2-4). 1982. PLB 11.59 (*0-89375-560-5*); pap. text ed. 2.95 (*0-89375-561-3*); cassette 9.95 (*0-685-04943-4*) Troll Assocs.

Still, John. Amazing Butterflies & Moths. Young, Jerry, photos by. LC 90-19234. (Illus.). 32p. (Orig.). (gr. 1-5). 1991. PLB 9.99 (*0-679-91515-X*); pap. 7.99 (*0-679-81515-5*) Knopf Bks Yng Read.

Stone, Lynn M. Moths. LC 93-15695. (gr. 4 up). 1993. 12.67 (*0-86593-297-2*); 9.50s.p. (*0-685-66590-9*) Rourke Corp.

Watts, Barrie. Butterflies & Moths. LC 90-46301. (Illus.). 32p. (gr. k-4). 1991. PLB 11.40 (*0-531-14160-8*); pap. 4.95 (*0-531-15617-6*) Watts.

—Moth. (Illus.). 25p. (gr. k-4). 1991. 5.95 (*0-382-24220-3*); PLB 7.95 (*0-382-24218-1*); pap. 3.95 (*0-382-24241-6*) Silver Burdett Pr.

MOTION

see also Force and Energy; Mechanics

Althea. What Makes Things Move? Green, Robina, illus. LC 90-10924. 32p. (gr. k-3). 1991. PLB 11.59 (*0-8167-2124-6*); pap. text ed. 3.95 (*0-8167-2125-4*) Troll Assocs.

Ardley, Neil. Muscles to Machines: Projects with Movement. LC 89-81569. 1990. PLB 12.40 (*0-531-17200-7*) Watts.

—The Science Book of Motion. 1992. 9.95 (*0-15-200622-2*, Gulliver Bks) HarBrace.

Boyd, Liz. Baby Wiggles - Bunny Hop. LC 92-50279. (ps). 1992. 8.95 (*1-56305-308-X*) Workman Pub.

Cardona, Jose, illus. Disney's Pop-up Book of Things That Go. LC 92-56160. 12p. (ps-k). 1993. 7.95 (*1-56282-509-7*) Disney Pr.

Cobb, Vicki. Why Doesn't the Earth Fall Up? And Other Not Such Dumb Questions about Motion. Enik, Ted, illus. LC 88-11108. 40p. (gr. 2-5). 1989. 13.00 (*0-525-67253-2*, Lodestar Bks) Dutton Child Bks.

Devonshire, Hilary. Movement. LC 92-7837. (Illus.). 32p. (gr. 5-8). 1993. PLB 12.40 (*0-531-14229-9*) Watts.

Jennings, Terry. Bouncing & Rolling. Franklin Watts Ltd., ed. Anstey, David, illus. LC 87-82971. 24p. (gr. k-3). 1988. PLB 10.90 (*0-531-17085-3*, Gloucester Pr) Watts.

Morgan, Sally & Morgan, Adrian. Movement. LC 93-20162. 1993. write for info. (*0-8160-2979-2*) Facts on File.

Morris, Neil. Jump Along: A Fun Book of Movement. Stevenson, Peter, illus. 32p. (ps-2). 1991. PLB 13.50 (*0-87614-671-X*) Carolrhoda Bks.

Motion. (Illus.). 88p. (gr. 7-12). 1990. 15.70 (*0-941008-98-3*) Tops Learning.

Murphy, Bryan. Experiment with Movement. 32p. (gr. 2-5). 1991. PLB 17.50 (*0-8225-2451-1*) Lerner Pubns.

Ross, Michael E. What Makes Everything Go? 94p. (gr. k-2). 1979. pap. 3.95 (*0-939666-19-7*) Yosemite Assn.

Sauvain, Philip. Motion. LC 91-24480. (Illus.). 48p. (gr. 6 up). 1992. text ed. 13.95 RSBE (*0-02-781077-1*, New Discovery) Macmillan Child Grp.

Taylor, Barbara. Get It in Gear! The Science of Movement. Bull, Peter, et al, illus. LC 90-42617. 40p. (Orig.). (gr. 2-5). 1991. pap. 4.95 (*0-679-80812-4*) Random Bks Yng Read.

Watson, Philip. Super Motion. Scruton, Clive & Falconer, Elizabeth, illus. LC 82-80990. 48p. (gr. 3-6). 1983. PLB 11.93 (*0-688-00971-9*) Lothrop.

MOTION–POETRY

McCracken, Elizabeth, ed. To Mother: An Anthology of Mother Verse. Wiggin, Kate D., intro. by. LC 17-13752. (Illus.). (gr. 7-12). 1976. Repr. of 1917 ed. 17.50x (*0-89609-051-5*) Roth Pub Inc.

MOTION PICTURE CARTOONS

Beck, Jerry. I Tawt I Taw a Puddy Tat: Tweety & Sylvester's Golden Jubilee. 192p. 1991. 35.00 (*0-8050-1644-9*) H Holt & Co.

Disney, Walt, Productions Staff. The Sorcerer's Apprentice. LC 73-9891. (Illus.). 48p. (ps-2). 1974. 6.95 (*0-394-82551-9*); lib. bdg. 4.99 (*0-394-92551-3*) Random Bks Yng Read.

Geis, Darlene, ed. Walt Disney's Treasury of Children's Classics. (Illus.). (gr. 5 up). 1978. 29.95 (*0-8109-0812-3*) Abrams.

Gray, Milton. Cartoon Animation: Introduction to a Career. LC 90-63934. (Illus.). 124p. 1991. pap. 12.95 (*0-9628444-5-4*) Lion's Den.
An up-to-date guide to securing employment in the Hollywood animation industry, at the entry & advanced levels, where production is presently booming & the studios are actively seeking new qualified artists. The author is currently an animator/ producer who has worked at the Walt Disney Studio, Warner Bros. & other Hollywood studios for 25 years. This book is also a uniquely insightful how-to on animation, direction, writing & producing cartoon animation films, with special emphasis on high quality production. Illustrated, with bibliography & index. "A major step forward in learning how to animate & make cartoon films. I highly recommend it!"--Eddie Fitzgerald, Instructor, Animation Department, California Institute of the Arts, & Director, Warner Bros. Cartoons. Available through: Lion's Den Publications, Inc., P.O. Box 7368-W, Northridge, CA 91327-7368. Telephone: (818) 772-7234.
Publisher Provided Annotation.

Italia, Robert. Mickey Mouse. Wallner, Rosemary, ed. LC 91-73048. 202p. 1991. 13.95 (*1-56239-053-8*) Abdo & Dghtrs.

Nardo, Don. Animation: Drawings Spring to Life. LC 92-5151. (Illus.). 96p. (gr. 5-8). 1992. PLB 15.95 (*1-56006-218-5*) Lucent Bks.

Nottridge, Rhoda. Animated Films. LC 91-36041. (Illus.). 32p. (gr. 5). 1992. text ed. 13.95 RSBE (*0-89686-717-X*, Crestwood Hse) Macmillan Child Grp.

Rozakis, Laurie. Hanna & Barbera: Yabba-Dabba-Doo! (Illus.). 48p. (gr. 2-5). 1994. PLB 12.95 (*1-56711-065-7*) Blackbirch.

MOTION PICTURE INDUSTRY
Belgrano, Giovanni. Let's Make a Movie. LC 72-90235. (Illus.). 48p. (gr. 4-9). 1973. 9.95 (*0-87592-028-4*) Scroll Pr.
Borie, Marcia & Wilkerson, Tichi. Hollywood Legends: The Golden Years of the Hollywood Reporter. 2nd ed. (Illus.). 350p. (gr. 7 up). 1988. pap. 14.95 (*0-942139-03-8*) Tale Weaver.
Ruth, Marianne & Locke, Raymond F. Cruel City. LC 90-52813. (Illus.). 240p. 1991. 19.95 (*0-915677-48-2*) Roundtable Pub.
Serrian, Michael. Now Hiring: Film. LC 93-2018. 1994. text ed. 14.95 (*0-89686-784-6*, Crestwood Hse) Macmillan Child Grp.
MOTION PICTURE INDUSTRY–FICTION
French, Michael. Split Image. (gr. 7 up). 1990. 14.95 (*0-553-07021-5*, Starfire) Bantam.
Nixon, Joan L. Encore: Hollywood Daughters: A Family Trilogy, Bk. 3. (gr. 7 up). 1990. 14.95 (*0-553-07024-X*, Starfire) Bantam.
Sharmat, Marjorie W. Genghis Khan: A Dog Star Is Born. Rigie, Mitchell, illus. 80p. (Orig.). (gr. 1-4). 1994. PLB 9.99 (*0-679-95406-6*); pap. 2.99 (*0-679-85406-1*) Random Bks Yng Read.
MOTION PICTURE PLAYS
Friedland, Joyce. From Books to Film: A Study Guide. (gr. 6-10). 1991. pap. text ed. 14.95 (*0-88122-690-4*) LRN Links.
Givens, Bill. Film Flubs: Not-So-Great Moments from the Movies. 1990. pap. 6.95 (*0-8065-1161-3*, Citadel Pr) Carol Pub Group.
Walt Disney's Classic Movie Treasury. (ps-3). 1991. write for info. (*0-307-15508-0*, Golden Pr) Western Pub.
MOTION PICTURES
Arginteanu, Judy. The Movies of Alfred Hitchcock. LC 93-23990. (Illus.). 80p. (gr. 5 up). 1994. PLB 18.95 (*0-8225-1642-X*) Lerner Pubns.
Balcziak, B. Movies. (Illus.). 48p. (gr. 4-8). 1989. lib. bdg. 17.27 (*0-86592-058-3*); 12.95 (*0-685-58623-5*) Rourke Corp.
Bliss, Sands & Co. Staff. The Magic Moving Picture Book. 32p. (gr. 4 up). 1975. pap. 3.95 (*0-486-23224-7*) Dover.
Brode, Douglas. Lost Films of the Fifties. (Illus.). 288p. (Orig.). 1988. pap. 15.95 (*0-8065-1092-7*, Citadel Pr) Carol Pub Group.
Cherrell, Gwen. How Movies Are Made. (Illus.). 32p. 1989. 12.95x (*0-8160-2039-6*) Facts on File.
Dowd, Ned. That's a Wrap: How Movies Are Made. Horenstein, Henry, photos by. Mamet, David, frwd. by. LC 91-6435. (Illus.). 64p. (gr. 3-7). 1991. pap. 15.00 jacketed (*0-671-70972-0*, S&S BFYR) S&S Trade.
Gibbons, Gail. Lights! Camera! Action!: How a Movie Is Made. Gibbons, Gail, illus. LC 85-47536. 32p. (gr. 1-4). 1985. (Crowell Jr Bks); PLB 14.89 (*0-690-04477-1*) HarpC Child Bks.
—Lights! Camera! Action! How a Movie Is Made. Gibbons, Gail, illus. LC 85-47536. 32p. (gr. 1-4). 1989. pap. 4.95 (*0-06-446088-6*, Trophy) HarpC Child Bks.
Gleasner, Diana. The Movies. (Illus.). (gr. 4-6). 1983. lib. bdg. 8.85 (*0-8027-6483-5*) Walker & Co.
Haycock, Kate. Science Fiction Films. LC 91-31672. (Illus.). 32p. (gr. 5). 1992. text ed. 13.95 RSBE (*0-89686-716-1*, Crestwood Hse) Macmillan Child Grp.
Hitzeroth, Deborah & Heerboth, Sharon. Movies: The World on Film. LC 91-16712. (Illus.). 96p. (gr. 5-8). 1991. PLB 15.95 (*1-56006-210-X*) Lucent Bks.
Horowitz, Jordan. Behind the Scenes of Home Alone 2: Lost in New York. 1992. 3.95 (*0-590-45720-9*) Scholastic Inc.
Hunter, Nigel. The Movies. LC 90-9937. (Illus.). 48p. (gr. 6-12). 1990. PLB 11.95 (*0-8114-2363-8*) Raintree Steck-V.
Knight, Arthur. The Liveliest Art: A Panoramic History of the Movies. rev. ed. (Illus.). 384p. (gr. 9-12). 1979. pap. 5.99 (*0-451-62652-4*, Ment) NAL-Dutton.
Lackmann, Ron. Let's Make a Movie. (Illus.). 80p. (gr. 5-8). 1994. pap. 12.95 (*0-9640925-0-6*) Pleasant Mt.
Levine, Evan. Kids Pick the Best Videos for Kids. LC 93-43784. 1994. pap. 9.95 (*0-8065-1498-1*, Citdel Pr) Carol Pub Group.
Limousin, Odile & Neumann, Daniele. TV & Films: Behind the Scenes. Vincent, Francois, illus. 40p. (gr. k-5). 1993. PLB 9.95 (*1-56674-073-8*, HTS Bks) Forest Hse.
Merrison, Tim. Movies. Stefoff, Rebecca, ed. LC 90-3964. (Illus.). 32p. (gr. 4-8). 1991. PLB 17.26 (*0-944483-94-1*) Garrett Ed Corp.
Moore, Douglas. Entertainment: Movies. Baker, Syd, illus. 50p. (Orig.). (gr. 7 up). 1986. incl. cass. 22.00 (*0-939990-48-2*) Intl Linguistics.
Morley, Jacqueline. Entertainment: Screen, Stage & Stars. (Illus.). 48p. (gr. 5-8). 1994. pap. 7.95 (*0-531-15710-5*) Watts.
Nottridge, Rhoda. Adventure Films. LC 91-25839. (Illus.). 32p. (gr. 5). 1992. text ed. 13.95 RSBE (*0-89686-718-8*, Crestwood Hse) Macmillan Child Grp.
—Horror Films. LC 91-23328. (Illus.). 32p. (gr. 5). 1992. text ed. 13.95 RSBE (*0-89686-719-6*, Crestwood Hse) Macmillan Child Grp.
Perlman, Marc. Movie Classics. LC 92-30909. 1993. 18.95 (*0-8225-1641-1*) Lerner Pubns.
—Youth Rebellion Movies. LC 92-5534. 1993. 18.95 (*0-8225-1640-3*) Lerner Pubns.
Platt, Richard. Film. King, Dave, photos by. LC 91-53133. (Illus.). 64p. (gr. 5 up). 1992. 16.00 (*0-679-81679-8*); PLB 16.99 (*0-679-91679-2*) Knopf Bks Yng Read.
Powers, Tom. Horror Movies. (Illus.). 80p. (gr. 5 up). pap. 7.95 (*0-8225-9570-2*) Lerner Pubns.
—Movie Monsters. (Illus.). 80p. (gr. 5 up). Repr. of 1989 ed. 7.95 (*0-8225-9571-0*) Lerner Pubns.
Schwartz, Perry. How to Make Your Own Video. 1991. pap. 8.95 (*0-8225-9588-5*) Lerner Pubns.
Scott, Elaine. From Microchips to Moviestars: The Making of Super Mario Brothers. LC 92-55046. (Illus.). 64p. (Orig.). (gr. 2-6). 1993. pap. 6.95 (*1-56282-472-4*) Hyprn Child.
—Look Alive: Behind the Scenes of an Animated Film. Hewett, Richard, photos by. LC 91-36220. (Illus.). 80p. (gr. 3 up). 1992. 14.00 (*0-688-09936-X*); PLB 13.93 (*0-688-09937-8*) Morrow Jr Bks.
Staskowski, Andrea. Movie Musicals. (Illus.). 80p. (gr. 5-12). 1992. PLB 18.95 (*0-8225-1639-X*) Lerner Pubns.
Yeck, Joanne L. & McGreevey, Tom. Movie Westerns. LC 93-38301. (Illus.). 80p. (gr. 5 up). 1994. PLB 18.95 (*0-8225-1643-8*) Lerner Pubns.
MOTION PICTURES–BIOGRAPHY
see also Actors and Actresses
Bach, Julie. Tom Cruise. LC 93-1981. (gr. 4 up). 1993. 12.94 (*1-56239-228-X*) Abdo & Dghtrs.
Bernotas, Bob. Spike Lee: Filmmaker. LC 92-41234. (Illus.). 112p. (gr. 6 up). 1993. lib. bdg. 17.95 (*0-89490-416-7*) Enslow Pubs.
Collins, Tom. Steven Spielberg: Creator of E. T. LC 83-21068. (Illus.). 64p. (gr. 3 up). 1983. text ed. 13.95 RSBE (*0-87518-249-6*, Dillon) Macmillan Child Grp.
Conklin, Thomas. Meet Steven Spielberg. LC 93-4315. (Illus.). 112p. (gr. 2-7). 1994. pap. 2.99 (*0-679-85445-2*) Random Bks Yng Read.
Hargrove, Jim. Steven Spielberg: Amazing Filmmaker. LC 87-13249. (Illus.). 128p. (gr. 4-8). 1988. PLB 14.40 (*0-516-03263-1*) Childrens.
McAllister. Steven Spielberg, Reading Level 2. (Illus.). 24p. (gr. 1-4). 1989. PLB 14.60 (*0-86592-427-9*); 10.95s.p. (*0-685-58803-3*) Rourke Corp.
MOTION PICTURES–FICTION
Bond, Michael. Paddington on Screen. Macey, Barry, illus. (gr. 2-5). 1982. 14.45 (*0-395-32950-7*) HM.
Byars, Betsy C. The Two-Thousand-Pound Goldfish. LC 81-48652. 160p. (gr. 5 up). 1982. PLB 14.89 (*0-06-020890-2*) HarpC Child Bks.
Cooper, Ilene. Lights, Camera, Attitude. 144p. (gr. 3-7). 1993. pap. 3.25 (*0-14-036155-3*) Puffin Bks.
—My Co-Star, My Enemy. 144p. (gr. 3-7). 1993. pap. 3.25 (*0-14-036156-1*) Puffin Bks.
DeGroat, Diane. Annie Pitts, Swamp Monster. LC 93-2474. 1994. pap. 13.00 (*0-671-87004-1*, S&S BFYR) S&S Trade.
Delton, Judy. Lights, Action, Land-Ho! Tiegreen, Alan, illus. 80p. (Orig.). (gr. 1-4). 1992. pap. 3.25 (*0-440-40732-X*, YB) Dell.
Hale, Hanna. Zelda Orangutan. Hale, Hanna, illus. 64p. (gr. 4-6). 1994. Perfect bdg. pap. 12.95 (*0-9638724-0-0*) Cando Pubng.
Handy. My Poppa Loves Old Movies. 1993. pap. 28.67 (*0-590-50152-6*) Scholastic Inc.
Hughes, Dean. Nutty, the Movie Star. LC 88-36614. 144p. (gr. 3-7). 1989. SBE 13.95 (*0-689-31509-0*, Atheneum Child Bk) Macmillan Child Grp.
Kendall, Jane. Miranda & the Movies. Kendall, Jane, illus. LC 89-1515. 224p. (gr. 6 up). 1989. PLB 14.99 (*0-517-57357-1*) Crown Bks Yng Read.
Korman, Gordon. Macdonald Hall Goes Hollywood. 176p. (gr. 3-7). 1991. 12.95 (*0-590-43940-5*, Scholastic Hardcover) Scholastic Inc.
Lobel, Arnold. Martha the Movie Mouse. Lobel, Arnold, illus. LC 66-18654. 32p. (ps-3). 1993. pap. 4.95 (*0-06-443318-8*, Trophy) HarpC Child Bks.
Mike, Jan. La Zariguerya y el Gran Creador de Fuego - Opossum & the Great Filmmaker: Una Leyenda Mexicana. LC 92-36459. (gr. 4-7). 1993. PLB 11.89 (*0-8167-3125-X*); pap. 3.95 (*0-8167-3073-3*) Troll Assocs.
Myers, Bill. My Life As Alien Monster Bait. (gr. 3-7). 1993. pap. 4.99 (*0-8499-3403-6*) Word Inc.
Nickelodeon Staff. Postcards over the Edge. 1992. pap. 5.95 (*0-448-40502-4*, G&D) Putnam Pub Group.
Schwartz, Henry. Albert Goes Hollywood. Schwartz, Amy, illus. LC 91-18495. 32p. (ps-2). 1992. 14.95 (*0-531-05980-4*); lib. bdg. 14.99 (*0-531-08580-5*) Orchard Bks Watts.
Strasser, Todd & Rifkin, Mark. Disney's the Villains Collection: Stories from the Films. DiCicco, Gil, illus. LC 93-70882. 80p. 1993. 14.95 (*1-56282-500-3*); PLB 14.89 (*1-56282-501-1*) Disney Pr.
Streatfeild, Noel. Movie Shoes. 288p. (Orig.). (gr. 4-7). pap. 3.25 (*0-440-45815-3*, YB) Dell.
Weaver, Lydia. Child Star: When Talkies Came to Hollywood. Laporte, Michele, illus. 64p. (gr. 2-6). 1992. PLB 12.00 (*0-670-84039-4*) Viking Child Bks.
Wolfe, Elle. Palm Beach Prep, No. 4: Screen Test. (gr. 4-7). 1990. pap. 2.95 (*0-8125-1062-3*) Tor Bks.
MOTION PICTURES–PLAY WRITING
see Motion Picture Plays
MOTOR BOATS
see Motorboats
MOTOR BUSES
see Buses
MOTOR CARS
see Automobiles
MOTOR CYCLES
see Motorcycles
MOTOR TRUCKS
see Trucks
MOTORBOATS
Andersen, T. J. Power Boat Racing. LC 87-30502. (Illus.). 48p. (gr. 5-6). 1988. text ed. 11.95 RSBE (*0-89686-359-X*, Crestwood Hse) Macmillan Child Grp.
Jackson, Al & Tardy, Gene. Drag Boat Racing: The National Championships. (Illus.). 48p. (gr. 3-7). 1973. PLB 6.89x (*0-914844-05-9*); pap. 3.95 (*0-914844-06-7*) J Alden.
MOTORCYCLES
Barrett, Norman S. Bicicross. LC 90-70885. (SPA., Illus.). 32p. (gr. k-4). 1990. PLB 11.90 (*0-531-07904-X*) Watts.
BMX Photo Fact Book. (Illus.). (gr. k-9). 1989. pap. 1.95 (*0-318-36480-8*) Scholastic Inc.
Carser, S. X. Motocross Cycles. (Illus.). 48p. (gr. 3-6). 1992. PLB 12.95 (*1-56065-069-9*) Capstone Pr.
Chirinian, Alain. Motorcycles. (Illus.). 64p. (gr. 5-9). 1989. lib. bdg. 10.98 (*0-671-68029-3*, J Messner); PLB 8.24s.p. (*0-685-47093-8*); pap. 3.71s.p. (*0-685-47094-6*) S&S Trade.
Cooper, J. Motocicletas (Motorcycles) 1991. 8.95s.p. (*0-86592-508-9*) Rourke Enter.
—Motorcycles. 1991. 8.95s.p. (*0-86592-494-5*) Rourke Enter.
Dregni, Michael. Motorcycle Racing. LC 93-44569. 1994. write for info. (*1-56065-207-1*) Capstone Pr.
Estrem, Paul. ATV's. LC 87-19900. (Illus.). 48p. (gr. 5-6). 1987. text ed. 11.95 RSBE (*0-89686-348-4*, Crestwood Hse) Macmillan Child Grp.
—BMX's. LC 87-15554. (Illus.). 48p. (gr. 5-6). 1987. text ed. 11.95 RSBE (*0-89686-349-2*, Crestwood Hse) Macmillan Child Grp.
—Motocross Cycles. LC 87-16115. (Illus.). 48p. (gr. 5-6). 1987. text ed. 11.95 RSBE (*0-89686-354-9*, Crestwood Hse) Macmillan Child Grp.
Evans, Jeremy. Motocross & Trials. LC 93-9385. (Illus.). 48p. (gr. 5-6). 1994. text ed. 13.95 RSBE (*0-89686-821-4*, Crestwood Hse) Macmillan Child Grp.
Holder, William G. Monster 4-Wheelers. LC 87-15733. (Illus.). 48p. (gr. 5-6). 1987. text ed. 11.95 RSBE (*0-89686-353-0*, Crestwood Hse) Macmillan Child Grp.
Italia, Bob. Motocross. LC 93-19140. 32p. 1992. PLB 9.95 (*1-56239-233-6*) Abdo & Dghtrs.
Kahaner, Ellen. Motorcycles. 48p. (gr. 3-4). 1991. PLB 11.95 (*1-56065-070-2*) Capstone Pr.
Lord, Trevor. Amazing Bikes. Downs, Peter, photos by. LC 92-911. (Illus.). 32p. (Orig.). (gr. 1-5). 1992. PLB 9.99 (*0-679-92772-7*); pap. 7.99 (*0-679-82772-2*) Knopf Bks Yng Read.
Martin, John. The World's Fastest Motorcycles. 48p. (gr. 3-10). 1994. PLB 17.27 (*1-56065-208-X*) Capstone Pr.
Naden, C. J. Cycle Chase. LC 79-64638. (Illus.). 32p. (gr. 4-9). 1980. PLB 10.79 (*0-89375-249-5*); pap. 2.95 (*0-89375-263-0*) Troll Assocs.
—I Can Read About Motorcycles. LC 78-74657. (Illus.). (gr. 3-6). 1979. pap. 2.50 (*0-89375-212-6*) Troll Assocs.
—Motorcycle Challenge, Trials & Races. LC 79-52178. (Illus.). 32p. (gr. 4-9). 1980. PLB 10.79 (*0-89375-252-5*); pap. 2.95 (*0-89375-253-3*) Troll Assocs.
—Rough Rider. LC 79-52177. (Illus.). 32p. (gr. 4-9). 1980. PLB 10.79 (*0-89375-250-9*); pap. 2.95 (*0-89375-251-7*) Troll Assocs.
Scarborough, Kate. How It Goes: Motorcycles. Tegg, Simon & Thompson, Ian, illus. LC 94-1801. 32p. (gr. 3-7). 1994. 10.95 (*0-8120-6456-9*); pap. 4.95 (*0-8120-1994-6*) Barron.
Smith, Don. The Baja Run: Racing Fury. LC 75-23412. (Illus.). 32p. (gr. 5-10). 1976. PLB 10.79 (*0-89375-000-X*) Troll Assocs.
Stewart, Gail. Motorcycle Racing. LC 87-33198. (Illus.). 48p. (gr. 5-6). 1988. text ed. 11.95 RSBE (*0-89686-360-3*, Crestwood Hse) Macmillan Child Grp.
Tardy, Gene & Jackson, Al. Motorcycle: Cross-Country Racing. (Illus.). (gr. 3-7). 1974. PLB 6.89x (*0-914844-00-8*) J Alden.
—Motorcycle: Grand Prix Racing. (Illus.). (gr. 3-7). 1974. PLB 6.89x (*0-914844-01-6*) J Alden.
MOTORCYCLES–FICTION
Aunt Zinnia & the Ogre. (Illus.). 32p. (gr. k-3). 1992. PLB 17.27 (*0-8368-0910-6*); PLB 17.27 s.p. (*0-685-61497-2*) Gareth Stevens Inc.
Christopher, Matt. Dirt Bike Racer. Bomzer, Barry, illus. LC 79-745. (gr. 4-6). 1986. 15.95 (*0-316-13977-7*); pap. 3.95 (*0-316-14053-8*) Little.
Frances, Marian. Witch on a Motorcycle. new ed. (Illus.). (gr. 3-4). 1972. pap. 1.95 (*0-89375-047-6*) Troll Assocs.
Hewett, Joan. Motorcycle on Patrol. LC 86-2689. (gr. 4-7). 1990. pap. 6.95 (*0-395-54789-X*, Clarion Bks) HM.
St. George, Mark. The Wolfpack. 210p. (Orig.). 1990. 14.95 (*0-9620541-2-7*); pap. 4.95 (*0-9620541-3-5*) Proteus LA.
MOTORING
see Automobiles–Touring
MOTORS
see Engines

MOTT, LUCRETIA (COFFIN) 1793-1880
Sawyer, Kem K. Lucretia Mott: Friend of Justice. Carter, Rosalyn & Carter, Rosalynncontrib. by. LC 91-70822. (Illus.). 48p. (gr. 4-8). 1991. 14.95g (*1-878668-04-8*); pap. 7.95 (*1-878668-08-0*) Disc Enter Ltd.
MOUNDS AND MOUND BUILDERS
see also Excavations (Archeology)
Silverberg, Robert. The Mound Builders. LC 85-25953. 276p. 1986. pap. 7.95 (*0-8214-0839-9*) Ohio U Pr.
MOUNT RUSHMORE, SOUTH DAKOTA
St. George, Judith. The Mount Rushmore Story. LC 84-24963. (Illus.). 128p. (gr. 5 up). 1985. 13.95 (*0-399-21117-9*, Putnam) Putnam Pub Group.
Sorensen, Lynda. Mount Rushmore. LC 94-7053. 1994. write for info. (*1-55916-047-0*) Rourke Bk Co.
MOUNT VERNON, VIRGINIA
Heymsfeld, Carla. Where Was George Washington? Koury, Jennifer, illus. LC 92-17341. 1992. 14.95 (*0-931917-20-4*); pap. write for info. (*0-931917-21-2*) Mt Vernon Ladies.
Reef, Catherine. Mount Vernon. LC 91-33494. (Illus.). 72p. (gr. 4 up). 1992. text ed. 14.95 RSBE (*0-87518-474-X*, Dillon) Macmillan Child Grp.
MOUNTAIN CLIMBING
see Mountaineering
MOUNTAIN LIFE–SOUTHERN STATES–FICTION
Dragonwagon, Crescent. The Itch Book. Mahler, Joseph, illus. LC 89-2695. 32p. (gr. k-3). 1990. RSBE 13.95 (*0-02-733121-0*, Macmillan Child Bk) Macmillan Child Grp.
Green, Michelle Y. Willie Pearl: Under the Mountain. McCracken, Steve, illus. Green, Oliver W., contrib. by. (Illus., Orig.). (gr. 4-6). 1992. pap. 9.95 (*0-9627697-1-1*) W Ruth Co.
Lewis, J. Patrick. The Moonbow of Mr. B. Bones. Zimmer, Dirk, illus. LC 88-37107. 40p. (ps-4). 1992. 16.00 (*0-394-85365-2*); PLB 16.99 (*0-394-95365-7*) Knopf Bks Yng Read.
Murray, Cleitus O. Stories of the Southern Mountains & Swamps. Murray, Cleitus O., illus. 192p. (Orig.). 1992. pap. 9.95 (*0-9632132-0-2*) Murray Pubns.
O'Dell, Scott. Thunder Rolling in the Mountains. 1993. pap. 3.99 (*0-440-40879-2*) Dell.
Smyers, Jacquelyn. The Time a Cloud Came into the Cabin (A Mountain Tale for Boys) Smyers, Carrie M., illus. LC 86-50627. 12p. (Orig.). (ps-6). 1986. pap. 3.98 (*0-9615130-3-9*) Very Idea.
—The Time a Cloud Came into the Cabin (A Mountain Tale for Girls) Smyers, Carrie M., illus. LC 86-50626. 12p. (Orig.). (ps-6). 1986. pap. 3.98 (*0-9615130-4-7*) Very Idea.
White, Alana. Come Next Spring. LC 89-37156. 170p. (gr. 6 up). 1990. 13.95 (*0-395-52593-4*, Clarion Bks) HM.
MOUNTAINEERING
Allen, Linda B. High Mountain Challenge: A Guide for Young Mountaineers. Trafton, Mary, illus. LC 89-16. 224p. (Orig.). (gr. 6-12). 1989. pap. 9.95 (*0-910146-98-5*) AMC Books.
Bradley, Catherine. Life in the Mountains. (gr. 4-7). 1993. pap. 4.95 (*0-590-47608-4*) Scholastic Inc.
Evans, Jeremy. Hiking & Climbing. LC 91-4061. (Illus.). 48p. (gr. 5-6). 1992. text ed. 13.95 RSBE (*0-89686-684-X*, Crestwood Hse) Macmillan Child Grp.
Gleasner. Rock Climbing. 1980. 7.95 (*0-679-20925-5*) McKay.
Gonzales, Rod & Faurot, Chip. To the Summit. McDonald, Mike, ed. Gonzales, Rod, illus. 32p. (Orig.). (gr. 5-10). 1993. pap. 3.95 (*1-882724-00-3*) Alaska Comics.
Jones, Michael P. & Boldt, Jeanine, eds. The Mountaineer, Vol. 1, No. 1. (Illus.). 42p. 1984. pap. text ed. 4.00 (*0-89904-017-9*) Crumb Elbow Pub.
McMurtry, Ken. Survival! in the Mountains. 112p. (Orig.). 1993. pap. 3.50 (*0-380-76602-7*, Camelot) Avon.
MOUNTAINEERING–BIOGRAPHY
Moerbeek, Kees. Four Courageous Climbers. (Illus.). 12p. (ps up). 1992. 4.95 (*0-8431-3448-8*) Price Stern.
MOUNTAINEERING–FICTION
Burch, Robert. Ida Early Comes over the Mountain. 152p. (gr. 3-7). 1982. pap. 2.50 (*0-380-57091-2*, Camelot) Avon.
Catchpole, Clive. Mountains. McIntyre, Brian, illus. LC 83-25273. 32p. (gr. k-4). 1985. pap. 4.95 (*0-8037-0087-3*, 0481-140) Dial Bks Young.
Chetwin, Grace. Gom on Windy Mountain. 1990. pap. 3.50 (*0-440-20543-3*, LFL) Dell.
George, Jean C. My Side of the Mountain. George, Jean C., illus. LC 87-27556. 176p. (gr. 3-7). 1988. 15.00 (*0-525-44392-4*, 01258-370, DCB); pap. 4.95 (*0-525-44395-9*, 0481-140, DCB) Dutton Child Bks.
Gerstein, Mordicai. The Mountains of Tibet. Gerstein, Mordicai, illus. LC 85-45684. 32p. (gr. 2 up). 1987. 14.00 (*0-06-022144-5*) HarpC Child Bks.
Gouffe, Marie A. Treasures Beyond the Snows. Sellon, Michael B., illus. LC 77-95392. (gr. 3-9). 1970. 3.75 (*0-8356-0026-2*, Quest) Theos Pub Hse.
Gutman, Bill. Over the Rugged Mountain. (gr. 4-7). 1994. pap. 3.50 (*0-06-106171-9*, Harp PBks) HarpC.
Harshman, Marc & Collins, Bonnie. Rocks in My Pocket. LC 90-32122. (Illus.). 32p. (ps-3). 1991. 13.95 (*0-525-65055-5*, Cobblehill Bks) Dutton Child Bks.
Herz, Roger J. The Old Man of the Mountain. Aldworth, Susan, illus. 1989. pap. text ed. 3.95 (*0-9619560-1-1*) TGNW Pr.
Lobel, Arnold. Ming Lo Moves the Mountain. Lobel, Arnold, illus. LC 81-13327. 32p. (gr. k-3). 1982. PLB 14.93 (*0-688-00611-6*) Greenwillow.
—Ming Lo Moves the Mountain. (ps-3). 1986. pap. 3.95 (*0-590-42902-7*) Scholastic Inc.
Loredo, Betsy. Avalanche in the Alps. LC 93-11175. (Illus.). 80p. (Orig.). (gr. 4-6). 1993. PLB 12.95 (*1-881889-12-2*); pap. cancelled (*1-881889-13-0*) Silver Moon.
Mountain Adventure. (Illus.). (ps-5). 3.50 (*0-7214-0024-8*) Ladybird Bks.
Myers, Edward. Climb or Die. LC 93-44861. 192p. (gr. 5-9). 1994. 14.95 (*0-7868-0026-7*); PLB 14.89 (*0-7868-2021-7*) Hyprn Child.
Ramsay, Marjorie B. Nyra. Ramsay, Marjorie B., illus. (gr. 4-7). 1979. 4.95 (*0-917182-10-3*) Triumph Pub.
Rispin, Karen. Anika's Mountain. LC 93-31345. (Illus.). 1994. pap. 4.99 (*0-8423-1219-6*) Tyndale.
Rylant, Cynthia. When I Was Young in the Mountains. LC 81-5359. (Illus.). 32p. (ps-3). 1982. 14.00 (*0-525-42525-X*, 0966-290, DCB); pap. 3.99 (*0-525-44198-0*, DCB) Dutton Child Bks.
Tomkins, Jasper. The Catalog. (Illus.). 56p. (gr. k up). 1991. pap. 5.95 (*0-671-74972-2*, Green Tiger) S&S Trade.
—The Mountains Crack Up! (Illus.). 60p. (gr. k-6). 1991. pap. 5.95 (*0-671-75273-1*, Green Tiger) S&S Trade.
Ullman, James R. Banner in the Sky. (gr. 7-9). 1980. 2.95 (*0-685-00477-5*, Archway) PB.
—Banner in the Sky. LC 54-7296. 256p. (gr. 7 up). 1988. (Lipp Jr Bks); (Lipp Jr Bks) HarpC Child Bks.
Warner, Gertrude C. Mountain Top Mystery. Cunningham, David, illus. LC 64-7722. 128p. (gr. 2-7). 1964. PLB 10.95 (*0-8075-5292-5*); pap. 3.50 (*0-8075-5293-3*) A Whitman.
MOUNTAINS
see also Mountaineering; Volcanoes;
also names of mountain ranges, e.g. Rocky Mountains; etc.
Arnold, Caroline. A Walk up a Mountain. Brook, Bonnie, ed. Tanz, Freya, illus. 32p. (ps-1). 1990. 4.95 (*0-671-68667-4*); lib. bdg. 6.95 (*0-671-68663-1*) Silver Pr.
Arvetis, Chris & Palmer, Carole. Mountains. LC 93-501. (Illus.). 1993. write for info. (*0-528-83571-8*) Rand McNally.
Ask about the Mountains & the Sea. 64p. (gr. 4-5). 1987. PLB 11.95 (*0-8172-2877-2*) Raintree Steck-V.
Baker, Susan. First Look at Mountains. LC 91-9420. (Illus.). 32p. (gr. 1-2). 1991. PLB 17.27 (*0-8368-0703-0*) Gareth Stevens Inc.
Barnes-Svarney, Patricia L. Born of Heat & Pressure: Mountains & Metamorphic Rocks. LC 89-25856. (Illus.). 64p. (gr. 6 up). 1991. lib. bdg. 15.95 (*0-89490-276-8*) Enslow Pubs.
Barrett, Norman S. Montanas. LC 90-71419. (SPA., Illus.). 32p. (gr. k-4). 1991. PLB 11.90 (*0-531-07923-6*) Watts.
Behm, Barbara J. Exploring Mountains. LC 93-37059. 1994. 17.27 (*0-8368-1066-X*) Gareth Stevens Inc.
Bender, Lionel. Mountain. LC 88-50370. (Illus.). 32p. (gr. 3-5). 1989. PLB 11.90 (*0-531-10646-2*) Watts.
Bramwell, Martyn. Mountains. (Illus.). 32p. (gr. 5-8). 1994. PLB write for info. (*0-531-14303-1*) Watts.
Brandt, Keith. Mountains. Cumings, Art, illus. LC 84-2577. 32p. (gr. 3-6). 1985. PLB 9.49 (*0-8167-0154-7*); pap. text ed. 2.95 (*0-8167-0155-5*) Troll Assocs.
Catchpole, Clive. Mountains. McIntyre, Brian, illus. LC 83-25273. 32p. (gr. k-4). 1985. pap. 4.95 (*0-8037-0087-3*, 0481-140) Dial Bks Young.
Collinson, Allan. Mountains. LC 91-34171. (Illus.). 48p. (gr. 5 up). 1992. text ed. 13.95 RSBE (*0-87518-493-6*, Dillon) Macmillan Child Grp.
Curran, Eileen. Mountains & Volcanoes. Watling, James, illus. LC 84-8638. 32p. (gr. k-2). 1985. PLB 11.59 (*0-8167-0347-7*); pap. text ed. 2.95 (*0-8167-0348-5*) Troll Assocs.
Field, Nancy & Maehlis, Sally. Discovering Mount Rainier. rev. ed. Maehlis, Sally, illus. 32p. (gr. 1-6). 1992. pap. 3.95 (*0-941042-13-8*) Dog Eared Pubns.
George, Jean C. One Day in the Alpine Tundra. Gaffney-Kessell, Walter, illus. LC 82-45590. 48p. (gr. 5-7). 1984. (Crowell Jr Bks); PLB 13.89 (*0-690-04326-0*, Crowell Jr Bks) HarpC Child Bks.
Hogan, Paula. Fragile Mountains. LC 91-2019. (Illus.). 32p. (gr. 3-4). 1991. PLB 17.27 (*0-8368-0475-9*) Gareth Stevens Inc.
Lye, Keith. Mountains. (Illus.). 48p. (gr. 5-8). 1987. PLB 12.95 (*0-382-09498-0*) Silver Burdett Pr.
—Mountains. LC 92-31815. (Illus.). 32p. (gr. 2-3). 1992. PLB 18.99 (*0-8114-3410-9*) Raintree Steck-V.
Magley, Beverly. The Fire Mountains: The Story of the Cascade Volcanos. Dowden, D. D., illus. LC 88-83884. 32p. (Orig.). (gr. 3-6). 1989. pap. 5.95 (*0-937959-57-X*) Falcon Pr MT.
Marcus, Elizabeth. All about Mountains & Volcanoes. Veno, Joseph, illus. LC 83-4834. 32p. (gr. 3-6). 1984. lib. bdg. 10.59 (*0-89375-969-4*); pap. text ed. 2.95 (*0-89375-970-8*) Troll Assocs.
Mariner, Tom. Mountains. LC 89-17280. (Illus.). 32p. (gr. 3-8). 1990. PLB 9.95 (*1-85435-193-1*) Marshall Cavendish.
Merk, Ann & Merk, Jim. Studying Weather. LC 94-13320. (gr. 3 up). 1994. write for info. (*0-86593-385-5*) Rourke Corp.
Morgan, Patricia G. A Mountain Adventure. Herde, Tom, illus. LC 87-3486. 32p. (gr. 3-6). 1988. PLB 10.79 (*0-8167-1173-9*); pap. text ed. 2.95 (*0-8167-1174-7*) Troll Assocs.
Mountains. 32p. (gr. 3-5). 1985. 7.95x (*0-86685-455-X*) Intl Bk Ctr.
Rius, Maria & Parramon, J. M. The Mountains. (ps). 1986. 6.95 (*0-8120-5746-5*); 6.95 (*0-8120-3698-0*) Barron.
Rotter, Charles M. Mountains. LC 92-41340. 1994. 18.95 (*0-88682-596-2*) Creative Ed.
Russell, William. Mountains & Canyons. LC 94-505. (gr. 3 up). 1994. write for info. (*0-86593-360-X*) Rourke Corp.
Sanchez, Isidro & Peris, Carme. Mountain Sports. 32p. (ps-1). 1992. pap. 5.95 (*0-8120-4867-9*) Barron.
Simon, Seymour. Mountains. LC 93-11398. (Illus.). 40p. (gr. k up). 1994. 15.00g (*0-688-11040-1*); PLB 14.93 (*0-688-11041-X*) Morrow Jr Bks.
Steele, Philip. Astronomy. LC 90-20633. (Illus.). 32p. (gr. 5-6). 1991. text ed. 11.95 RSBE (*0-89686-586-X*, Crestwood Hse) Macmillan Child Grp.
Stewart, G. In the Mountains. (Illus.). 32p. (gr. 3-8). 1989. lib. bdg. 15.74 (*0-86592-107-5*); 11.95s.p. (*0-685-58598-0*) Rourke Corp.
Stone, L. Mountains. (Illus.). 48p. (gr. 4-8). 1989. lib. bdg. 15.94 (*0-86592-448-1*); 11.95s.p. (*0-685-67721-4*) Rourke Corp.
Stone, Lynn M. Mountains. LC 83-7276. (Illus.). 48p. (gr. k-4). 1983. PLB 12.85 (*0-516-01698-9*); pap. 4.95 (*0-516-41698-7*) Childrens.
Taylor, Barbara. Mountains & Volcanoes. LC 92-23374. (Illus.). 32p. (gr. 1-4). 1993. 10.95 (*1-85697-874-5*, Kingfisher LKC); pap. 5.95 (*1-85697-938-5*) LKC.
Uba, Gregory. Is a Mountain Just a Rock. Mitchell, Joanie, illus. LC 83-61882. 260p. (gr. 6-9). 1984. pap. 3.95 (*0-942610-03-2*) Mina Pr.
Wilkes. Mountains. 24p. (gr. 4-6). 1980. (Usborne-Hayes); PLB 11.96 (*0-88110-682-8*); pap. 4.50 (*0-7460-0755-8*) EDC.
Williams, Lawrence. Mountains. LC 89-25349. (Illus.). 48p. (gr. 4-8). 1990. PLB 12.95 (*1-85435-173-7*) Marshall Cavendish.
Zoehfeld, Kathleen W. How Mountains Are Made. Hale, James G., illus. LC 93-45436. 1995. 15.00 (*0-06-024509-3*); PLB 14.89 (*0-06-024510-7*) HarpC Child Bks.
MOUNTAINS–POETRY
Curtis, Donald A. Fantasy on Sunset Mountain. LC 82-74122. 44p. (Orig.). (gr. 3-12). 1982. pap. 3.50 (*0-9610284-0-8*) D A Curtis.
MOURNING CUSTOMS
see Funeral Rites and Ceremonies
MOUSE
see Mice
MOUTH-ORGAN–FICTION
McCloskey, Robert. Lentil. McCloskey, Robert, illus. (gr. k-3). 1940. pap. 14.95 (*0-670-42357-2*) Viking Child Bks.
MOVIES
see Motion Pictures
MOVING, HOUSEHOLD–FICTION
Ackerman, Karen. The Sleeping Porch. Sayles, Liz, illus. LC 94-16645. (ps-3). Date not set. write for info. (*0-688-12822-X*); PLB write for info. (*0-688-12823-8*) Morrow Jr Bks.
Amdur, Nikki. One of Us. Sanderson, Ruth, illus. LC 81-65847. (gr. 3-6). 1981. Dial Bks Young.
Anderson, Peggy. First Day Blues. Strecker, Rebekah, illus. LC 91-67808. 64p. (Orig.). (gr. 3-6). 1992. PLB 16.95 (*0-943990-73-4*); pap. 5.95 (*0-943990-72-6*) Parenting Pr.
Ballard, Robin. Good-bye, House. LC 93-252. (Illus.). 24p. (ps up). 1994. 14.00 (*0-688-12525-5*); PLB 13.93 (*0-688-12526-3*) Greenwillow.
Banks, Lynne R. The Mystery of the Cupboard. Newsom, Tom, illus. LC 92-39295. 256p. (gr. 5 up). 1993. 13.95 (*0-688-12138-1*); PLB 13.88 (*0-688-12635-9*) Morrow Jr Bks.
Berenstain, Stan & Berenstain, Jan. Los Osos Berenstain dia de Mudanza. Guibert, Rita, tr. LC 93-37312. (SPA., Illus.). 32p. (ps-3). 1994. pap. 2.50 (*0-679-85430-4*) Random Bks Yng Read.
Bontemps, Arna W. & Hughes, Langston. Popo & Fifina. Campbell, E. Simms, illus. Rampersad, Arnold & Rampersad, Arnoldintro. by. (Illus.). 120p. 1993. jacketed 14.95 (*0-19-508765-8*) OUP.
Bulla, Clyde R. A Lion to Guard Us. Chessare, Michele, illus. LC 80-2455. (gr. 2-5). 1981. (Crowell Jr Bks); PLB 13.89 (*0-690-04097-0*, Crowell Jr Bks) HarpC Child Bks.
Carlstrom, Nancy W. I'm Not Moving, Mama! Wickstrom, Thor, illus. LC 89-38151. 32p. (ps-1). 1990. RSBE 13.95 (*0-02-717286-4*, Macmillan Child Bk) Macmillan Child Grp.
Cartwright, Stephen, illus. Moving House. 16p. (ps up). 1986. PLB write for info. EDC.
Caseley, Judith. Hurricane Harry. LC 90-13809. (Illus.). 128p. (gr. 1 up). 1991. 13.95 (*0-688-10027-9*) Greenwillow.
—Hurricane Harry. Caseley, Judith, illus. LC 93-6991. 112p. (gr. 3 up). 1994. pap. 4.95 (*0-688-12549-2*, Pub. by Beech Tree Bks) Morrow.
—Starring Dorothy Kane. LC 90-24172. (gr. 1 up). 1992. 13.00 (*0-688-10182-8*) Greenwillow.
—Starring Dorothy Kane. Caseley, Judith, illus. LC 93-6992. 160p. (gr. 3 up). 1994. pap. 4.95 (*0-688-12548-4*, Pub. by Beech Tree Bks) Morrow.

Clark, Emma C. Across the Blue Mountains. LC 93-12118. 1993. 14.95 (*0-15-201220-6*) HarBrace.
Clough, Brenda W. An Impossumble Summer. 160p. (gr. 3-6). 1992. 14.95 (*0-8027-8150-0*) Walker & Co.
Craig, Lynn. New Friends in New Places. LC 94-1929. 1994. pap. 4.99 (*0-8407-9239-5*) Nelson.
Danziger, Paula. Amber Brown Is Not a Crayon. Ross, Tony, illus. LC 92-34678. 80p. (gr. 1-4). 1994. 11.95 (*0-399-22509-9*, Putnam) Putnam Pub Group.
Devlin, Harry & Devlin, Wende. Cranberry Moving Day. LC 93-36279. (ps-1). 1994. pap. 2.95 (*0-689-71777-6*) MacMillan Child Grp.
Doherty, Berlie. Willa & Old Miss Annie. Lewis, Kim, illus. LC 93-970. 96p. (gr. 3-6). 1994. 14.95 (*1-56402-331-1*) Candlewick Pr.
Dowling, Paul. Meg & Jack Are Moving. Dowling, Paul, illus. 32p. (ps-3). 1990. 10.70 (*0-395-53514-X*) HM.
Duncan, Lois. Wonder Kid Meets the Evil Lunch Snatcher. Sanfilippo, Margaret, illus. LC 87-26490. 76p. (gr. 7-10). 1988. 12.95 (*0-316-19558-8*) Little.
Ellis, Sarah. Pick-up Sticks. Chan, Harvey, contrib. by. LC 91-26585. 128p. (gr. 7 up). 1992. SBE 13.95 (*0-689-50550-7*, M K McElderry) Macmillan Child Grp.
—Pick-Up Sticks. LC 93-7759. 128p. (gr. 5 up). 1993. pap. 3.99 (*0-14-036340-8*, Puffin) Puffin Bks.
Fakih, Kimberly O. High on the Hog. LC 93-34214. 1994. 16.00 (*0-374-33209-6*) FS&G.
Family Moving Day. (Illus.). 32p. (gr. k-3). 1992. PLB 17.27 (*0-8368-0911-4*); PLB 17.27 s.p. (*0-685-61499-9*) Gareth Stevens Inc.
Giffard, Hannah. Red Fox on the Move. Giffard, Hannah, illus. LC 90-25646. 36p. (ps-3). 1992. 14.00 (*0-8037-1057-7*) Dial Bks Young.
Greenwald, Dorothy. Coping with Moving. Rosen, Ruth, ed. 128p. (gr. 7 up). 1987. PLB 14.95 (*0-8239-0683-3*) Rosen Group.
Greenwald, Sheila. My Fabulous New Life. LC 92-44928. 160p. (gr. 3-7). 1993. 10.95 (*0-15-277693-1*, Browndeer Pr); pap. 3.95 (*0-15-276716-9*, Browndeer Pr) HarBrace.
Griffith, Connie. Mysterious Rescuer. LC 93-8421. 128p. (Orig.). 1994. pap. 4.99 (*0-8010-3865-0*) Baker Bk.
Haas, Jessie. Skipping School. LC 91-37642. (gr. 6-12). 1992. 14.00 (*0-688-10179-8*) Greenwillow.
Hamm, Diane J. Second Family. LC 91-42968. 128p. (gr. 5-7). 1992. SBE 13.95 (*0-684-19436-8*, Scribners Young Read) Macmillan Child Grp.
Harshman, Marc. Moving Days. Popp, Wendy, illus. 32p. (gr. k-4). 1994. 13.99 (*0-525-65135-7*, Cobblehill Bks) Dutton Child Bks.
Harvey, Jayne. Great-Uncle Dracula. Carter, Abby, illus. LC 91-31460. 80p. (Orig.). (gr. 2-4). 1992. PLB 6.99 (*0-679-92448-5*); pap. 2.50 (*0-679-82448-0*) Random Bks Yng Read.
Haywood, Carolyn. Eddie's Valuable Property. Haywood, Carolyn, illus. LC 74-17499. 192p. (gr. 3-7). 1975. PLB 12.88 (*0-688-32014-7*) Morrow Jr Bks.
Hazen, Barbara. Goodbye Hello. 1995. 15.00 (*0-689-31665-8*, Athemeum) Macmillan Child Grp.
Hendry, Diana. Not Anywhere House. (Illus.). (ps-3). 1991. 10.95 (*0-688-10194-1*) Lothrop.
Hilton, Nette. Andrew Jessup. Wilcox, Cathy, illus. LC 92-39799. 32p. (ps-2). 1993. PLB 13.95 (*0-395-66900-6*) Ticknor & Flds Bks Yng Read.
Hofmann, Ginnie. The Bear Next Door: Story & Pictures. LC 93-616. (Illus.). (ps-3). 1994. 2.50 (*0-679-83957-7*) Random Bks Yng Read.
Jacobson, Jane. City, Sing, for Me: A Country Child Moves to the City. Rowen, Amy, illus. LC 77-11130. 32p. (gr. 1-5). 1978. 16.95 (*0-87705-358-8*) Human Sci Pr.
Johnson, Angela. The Leaving Morning. Soman, David, illus. LC 91-21123. 32p. (ps-2). 1992. 14.95 (*0-531-05992-8*); PLB 14.99 (*0-531-08592-9*) Orchard Bks Watts.
Kehret, Peg. The Richest Kids in Town. LC 93-47271. 128p. (gr. 4 up). 1994. 13.99 (*0-525-65166-7*, Cobblehill Bks) Dutton Child Bks.
Keller, Beverly. Desdemona Moves On. LC 92-7127. 176p. (gr. 3-7). 1992. SBE 13.95 (*0-02-749751-8*, Bradbury Pr) Macmillan Child Grp.
Kiser, SuAnn. Hazel Saves the Day. Day, Betsy, illus. LC 92-34782. 1994. write for info. (*0-8037-1488-2*); PLB write for info. (*0-8037-1489-0*) Dial Bks Young.
Koller, Jackie F. The Last Voyage of the Misty Day. LC 91-17482. 160p. (gr. 4-8). 1992. SBE 13.95 (*0-689-31731-X*, Atheneum Child Bk) Macmillan Child Grp.
Lamb, Nancy. The Great Mosquito, Bull, & Coffin Caper. Remkiewicz, Frank, illus. LC 91-31125. 160p. (gr. 3 up). 1992. reinforced bdg. 12.00 (*0-688-10933-0*) Lothrop.
LeMieux, A. C. Fruit Flies, Fish & Fortune Cookies. DeGroat, Diane, illus. LC 93-29606. 1994. write for info. (*0-688-13299-5*, Tambourine Bks) Morrow.
Levitin, Sonia. The Golem & the Dragon Girl. LC 92-27665. 176p. (gr. 3-7). 1993. 14.99 (*0-8037-1280-4*); PLB 14.89 (*0-8037-1281-2*) Dial Bks Young.
Levitt, Sidney. The Mighty Movers. Levitt, Sidney, illus. LC 92-54869. 48p. (gr. k-3). 1994. 10.95 (*1-56282-421-X*); PLB 10.89 (*1-56282-422-8*) Hyprn Child.
Little, Mary E. Old Cat & the Kitten. LC 93-30376. 128p. (gr. 3-7). 1994. pap. 3.95 (*0-689-71800-4*, Aladdin) Macmillan Child Grp.
Lobel, Arnold. Ming Lo Moves the Mountain. Lobel, Arnold, illus. (gr. k-4). 1993. 14.95 (*0-685-64815-X*); audio cass. 11.00 (*1-882869-76-1*) Read Advent.
Lowry, Lois. Anastasia Again! De Groat, Diane, illus. 160p. (gr. 3-6). 1981. 14.45 (*0-395-31147-0*) HM.
McGeorge, Constance W. Boomer's Big Day. Whyte, Mary, illus. LC 93-27273. 1994. 12.95 (*0-8118-0526-3*) Chronicle Bks.
McGuire, Leslie. Big Dan's Moving Van. Mathieu, Joe, illus. LC 90-4417. 32p. (Orig.). (ps-1). 1993. pap. 2.25 (*0-679-80565-6*) Random Bks Yng Read.
McKend, H. Moving Gives Me a Stomach Ache. (Illus.). 32p. (ps-8). 1988. pap. 4.95 (*0-88753-178-4*, Pub. by Black Moss Pr CN) Firefly Bks Ltd.
McLerran, Alice. I Want to Go Home. Kastner, Jill, illus. LC 91-9599. 32p. (ps-3). 1992. 15.00 (*0-688-10144-5*, Tambourine Bks); PLB 14.93 (*0-688-10145-3*, Tambourine Bks) Morrow.
Mahy, Margaret. The Good Fortunes Gang. Young, Marion, illus. LC 92-38784. (gr. 5 up). 1993. 13.95 (*0-385-31015-3*) Delacorte.
Martin, Ann M. Dawn's Big Move. (gr. 4-7). 1993. pap. 3.50 (*0-590-47005-1*) Scholastic Inc.
—Good-Bye, Stacy, Good-Bye. large type ed. LC 93-4345. 176p. (gr. 4 up). 1993. PLB 15.93 (*0-8368-1017-1*) Gareth Stevens Inc.
—Goodbye Stacey, Goodbye. 1993. pap. 3.25 (*0-590-43386-5*) Scholastic Inc.
Mohr, Nicholas. Jaime & the Conch Shell. LC 93-30403. 1995. 13.95 (*0-590-47110-4*) Scholastic Inc.
Monson, A. M. The Deer Stand. Pearson, Susan, ed. LC 91-32122. 160p. (gr. 4 up). 1992. reinforced bdg. 13.00 (*0-688-11057-6*) Lothrop.
Moving Day. (Illus.). 32p. (ps). 1990. 2.99 (*0-517-69195-7*) Random Hse Value.
Mulford, Philippa G. The World Is My Eggshell. LC 85-16198. (gr. 7 up). 1986. pap. 14.95 (*0-385-29432-8*) Delacorte.
Myers, Laurie. Guinea Pigs Don't Talk. Taylor, Cheryl, illus. LC 93-39642. 1994. 13.95 (*0-395-68967-8*, Clarion Bks) HM.
Namioka, Lensey. Yang the Youngest & His Terrible Ear. De Kiefte, Kees, illus. 112p. (gr. 3-7). 1992. 15.95 (*0-316-59701-5*, Joy St Bks) Little.
Nesbit, Jeffrey A. Crosscourt Winner. 132p. 1991. pap. 4.99 (*0-89693-129-3*) SP Pubns.
O'Connor, Jane. Corrie's Secret Pal. Long, Laurie S., illus. LC 92-35602. 64p. (gr. 1-4). 1993. 7.99 (*0-448-40161-4*, G&D); pap. 3.95 (*0-448-40160-6*, G&D) Putnam Pub Group.
O'Kelley, Mattie L. Moving to Town. (Illus.). (ps-3). 1991. 15.95 (*0-316-63805-6*) Little.
Pascal, Francine. Steven's Bride. large type ed. LC 93-1350. 1993. 15.95 (*1-56054-756-1*) Thorndike Pr.
Paterson, Katherine. Flip-Flop Girl. 128p. (gr. 3-7). 1994. 13.99 (*0-525-67480-2*, Lodestar Bks) Dutton Child Bks.
Patron, Susan. Maybe Yes, Maybe No, Maybe Maybe. Donahue, Dorothy, illus. LC 92-34067. 96p. (gr. 3-5). 1993. 14.95 (*0-531-05482-9*); PLB 14.99 (*0-531-08632-1*) Orchard Bks Watts.
Peck, Richard. Bel-Air Bambi & the Mall Rats. LC 92-29377. 1993. 15.95 (*0-385-30823-X*) Delacorte.
Pevsner, Stella. Jon, Flora, & the Odd-Eyed Cat. LC 93-41218. 1994. 13.95 (*0-395-67021-7*, Clarion Bks) HM.
Potok, Chaim. The Tree of Here. Auth, Tony, illus. LC 92-28412. (gr. k-4). 1993. 13.00 (*0-679-84010-9*); PLB 13.99 (*0-679-94010-3*) Knopf Bks Yng Read.
Precek, Katherine W. The Keepsake Chest. LC 91-14808. 160p. (gr. 3-7). 1992. SBE 13.95 (*0-02-775045-0*, Macmillan Child Bk) Macmillan Child Grp.
Pryor, Bonnie. Horses in the Garage. LC 92-7287. 160p. (gr. 4 up). 1992. 14.00 (*0-688-10567-X*) Morrow Jr Bks.
—The House on Maple Street. ALC Staff, ed. Peck, Beth, illus. LC 86-14628. 32p. (gr. k up). 1992. pap. 4.95 (*0-688-12031-8*, Mulberry) Morrow.
Pulver, Robin. Homer & the House Next Door. Levin, Arnie, illus. LC 93-4377. 32p. (ps-2). 1994. RSBE 14.95 (*0-02-775457-X*, Four Winds) Macmillan Child Grp.
Randle, Kristen D. The Only Alien on the Planet. LC 93-34594. 1994. 13.95 (*0-590-46309-8*) Scholastic Inc.
Reiss, Kathryn. Time Windows. 260p. (gr. 5 up). 1991. 15.95 (*0-15-288205-7*, HB Juv Bks) HarBrace.
Repp, Gloria. Noodle Soup. Roberts, John, illus. LC 93-42417. 1994. write for info. (*0-89084-582-4*) Bob Jones Univ Pr.
Rocklin, Joanne. Jace the Ace. De Groat, Diane, illus. LC 90-34095. 112p. (gr. 2-6). 1990. SBE 13.95 (*0-02-777445-7*, Macmillan Child Bk) Macmillan Child Grp.
Rogers, Mary. Moving. 32p. (ps-k). 1992. pap. text ed. 23.00 big bk. (*1-56843-001-9*); pap. text ed. 4.50 (*1-56843-051-5*) BGR Pub.
Rosen, Michael J. Moving. Williams, Sophy, illus. 32p. (ps-1). 1993. 12.99 (*0-670-84865-4*) Viking Child Bks.
Scherer, Bonnie. Benjy's New Home. McCracken, Bill, illus. LC 89-60806. 7p. 1989. pap. 1.50 (*0-9622421-0-1*) B Scherer.
Schulte, Elaine L. Melanie & the Modeling Mess. LC 93-45377. 1994. 4.99 (*1-55661-254-0*) Bethany Hse.
Shannon, George. Seeds. Bjorkman, George, illus. LC 92-40738. 1994. 13.95 (*0-395-66990-1*) HM.
Spinelli, Eileen. Lizzie Logan Wears Purple Sunglasses. Durrell, Julie, illus. LC 93-29104. 1995. 13.00 (*0-671-74685-5*, S&S BFYR) S&S Trade.
Stahl, Hilda. Chelsea & the Outrageous Phone Bill. 160p. (gr. 4-7). 1992. pap. 3.99 (*0-89107-657-3*) Crossway Bks.
Stolz, Mary. King Emmett the Second. Williams, Garth, illus. LC 89-77506. 56p. (gr. 2 up). 1991. 12.95 (*0-688-09520-8*) Greenwillow.
Stowe, Cynthia M. Home Sweet Home, Good-Bye. (gr. 4-7). 1993. pap. 2.95 (*0-590-42759-8*) Scholastic Inc.
Szekeres, Cyndy. Moving Day. (Illus.). 24p. (ps-k). 1989. pap. write for info. (*0-307-11997-1*, Pub. by Golden Bks) Western Pub.
Thesman, Jean. Nothing Grows Here. LC 93-45739. 208p. (gr. 4 up). 1994. 14.00 (*0-06-024457-7*); PLB 13.89 (*0-06-024458-5*) HarpC Child Bks.
Thomas, Abagail. Lily. Low, William, illus. LC 93-14199. (gr. 5 up). 1994. 14.95 (*0-8050-2690-8*) H Holt & Co.
Thomas, Jane R. Courage at Indian Deep. LC 83-14404. (Illus.). 128p. (gr. 3-7). 1984. 13.95 (*0-89919-181-9*, Clarion Bks) HM.
Turner, Ann. Stars for Sarah. Teichman, Mary, illus. LC 89-26908. 32p. (ps-3). 1991. PLB 13.89 (*0-06-026187-0*) HarpC Child Bks.
Vigna, Judith. Black Like Kyra, White Like Me. Tucker, Kathleen, ed. Vigna, Judith, illus. LC 92-1203. 32p. (gr. 2-6). 1992. 13.95g (*0-8075-0778-4*) A Whitman.
Wallace-Brodeur, Ruth. The Godmother Tree. LC 91-17951. 128p. (gr. 3-7). 1992. PLB 12.89 (*0-06-022458-4*) HarpC Child Bks.
Weisman, Joan. The Storyteller. Bradley, David, illus. LC 93-20460. 32p. 1993. 15.95 (*0-8478-1742-3*) Rizzoli Intl.
Williams, Vera B. Scooter. LC 90-38489. (Illus.). 160p. (gr. 4-7). 1993. 15.00 (*0-688-09376-0*); PLB 14.93 (*0-688-09377-9*) Greenwillow.
Wright, Betty R. Ghost Witch. LC 92-55055. 72p. (gr. 4-7). 1993. 13.95 (*0-8234-1036-6*) Holiday.
Yep, Laurence. The Star Fisher. LC 90-23785. 150p. (gr. 3 up). 1991. 12.95 (*0-688-09365-5*) Morrow Jr Bks.

MOZART, JOHANN CHRYSOSTROM WOLFGANG AMADEUS, 1756-1791

Blakely, Roger K. Wolfgang Amadeus Mozart. LC 92-41357. (Illus.). 111p. (gr. 5-8). 1993. PLB 14.95 (*1-56006-028-X*) Lucent Bks.
Brighton, Catherine. Mozart: Scenes from the Childhood of the Great Composer. (ps-3). 1990. PLB 15.99 (*0-385-41538-9*) Doubleday.
Downing, Julie. Mozart Tonight. Downing, Julie, illus. LC 90-34479. 40p. 1991. RSBE 15.95 (*0-02-732881-3*, Bradbury Pr) Macmillan Child Grp.
—Mozart Tonight. LC 93-27445. (Illus.). 40p. 1994. pap. 5.95 (*0-689-71808-X*, Aladdin) Macmillan Child Grp.
Gallez, Christophe. Mozart. 32p. (gr. 4). 1990. PLB 14.95 (*0-88682-322-6*) Creative Ed.
Greene, Carol. Wolfgang Amadeus Mozart: Musical Genius. LC 92-36879. (Illus.). 48p. (gr. k-3). 1993. PLB 12.85 (*0-516-04256-4*); pap. 4.95 (*0-516-44256-2*) Childrens.
—Wolfgang Amadeus Mozart: Musician. LC 87-13824. (Illus.). 152p. (gr. 4 up). 1987. PLB 14.40 (*0-516-03261-5*) Childrens.
Lepscky, Ibi. Amadeus Mozart. Cardoni, Paolo, illus. 24p. (gr. k-3). 1992. pap. 4.95 (*0-8120-1493-6*) Barron.
Loewen, L. Mozart. (Illus.). 112p. (gr. 5 up). 1989. lib. bdg. 18.60 (*0-86592-605-0*); 13.95 (*0-685-58618-9*) Rourke Corp.
Neidorf, Mary. Operantics with Wolfgang Amadeus Mozart. LC 86-14435. 32p. (Orig.). (gr. 3-6). 1987. pap. 4.95 (*0-86534-092-7*) Sunstone Pr.
Patton, Barbara W. Introducing Wolfgang Amadeus Mozart. (Illus.). 48p. (Orig.). (gr. 3-9). 1991. pap. 6.95 (*1-878636-03-0*) Soundboard Bks.
Rachlin, Ann. Mozart. Hellard, Susan, illus. LC 92-10302. 1992. 5.95 (*0-8120-4989-6*) Barron.
Sabin, Francene. Mozart, Young Music Genius. Miyake, Yoshi, illus. LC 89-33980. 48p. (gr. 4-6). 1990. lib. bdg. 10.79 (*0-8167-1773-7*); pap. text ed. 3.50 (*0-8167-1774-5*) Troll Assocs.
Sage, Alison. Play Mozart. Gabby, Terry, illus. Bunting, Janet, contrib. by. (Illus.). 32p. (gr. 1-4). 1988. Incl. built-in 22-note electronic keyboard. 13.95 (*0-8120-5924-7*) Barron.
Switzer, Ellen. Mozart, the Magic Flute, & the Salzburg Marionettes. Costas, photos by. LC 93-47890. 1995. 17.00 (*0-689-31851-0*, Atheneum) Macmillan.
Tames, Richard. Wolfgang Amadeus Mozart. LC 90-32378. (Illus.). 32p. 1991. PLB 12.40 (*0-531-14107-1*) Watts.
Thompson, Wendy. Wolfgang Amadeus Mozart. (Illus.). 48p. (gr. 7up). 1991. 17.95 (*0-670-83679-6*) Viking Child Bks.
Weil, Lisl. Wolferl: The First Six Years in the Life of Wolfgang Amadeus Mozart. Weil, Lisl, illus. LC 90-47684. 32p. (ps-3). 1991. reinforced 14.95 (*0-8234-0876-0*) Holiday.
Willson, Robina B. Mozart's Story. Lewis, Anthony, illus. 48p. (gr. 3 up). 1991. 14.95 (*0-7136-3311-5*, Pub. by A&C Black UK) Talman.

MUHAMMAD ALI, 1942-

Conklin, Tom. Muhammad Ali: The Fight for Respect. LC 91-25950. (Illus.). 104p. (gr. 7 up). 1992. PLB 15.40 (*1-56294-112-7*); pap. 5.95 (*1-56294-832-6*) Millbrook Pr.
Denenberg, Barry. The Story of Muhammad Ali, Heavyweight Champion of the World. (Illus.). 96p. (gr. 3-5). 1990. pap. 3.50 (*0-440-40259-X*, YB) Dell.
Diamond, Arthur. Muhammad Ali. LC 93-47623. (Illus.). 112p. (gr. 5-8). 1994. 14.95 (*1-56006-060-3*) Lucent Bks.

Epes, William. Muhammad Ali. (Illus.). 80p. (gr. 3-5). 1993. PLB 12.95 (*0-7910-1760-5*); pap. write for info. (*0-7910-1966-7*) Chelsea Hse.

Rummel, Jack. Muhammad Ali. King, Coretta Scott, intro. by. (Illus.). 112p. (Orig.). (gr. 5 up). 1988. 17.95 (*1-55546-569-2*); pap. 9.95 (*0-7910-0210-1*) Chelsea Hse.

MUIR, JOHN, 1838-1914

Force, Eden. John Muir. Gallin, Richard, ed. (Illus.). 144p. (gr. 5-9). 1990. PLB 10.95 (*0-382-09965-6*); pap. 6.95 (*0-382-09970-2*) Silver Burdett Pr.

Greene, Carol. John Muir: Man of the Wild Places. Dobson, Steven, illus. LC 90-19993. 48p. (gr. k-3). 1991. PLB 12.85 (*0-516-04220-3*); pap. 4.95 (*0-516-44220-1*) Childrens.

Ledbetter, Cynthia E. & Jones, Richard C. John Muir. LC 92-46763. 1993. 19.93 (*0-86625-494-3*); 14.95s.p. (*0-685-67774-5*) Rourke Pubns.

Naden, Corinne J. John Muir: Saving the Wilderness. (gr. 4-7). 1992. pap. 4.95 (*0-395-63569-1*) HM.

Naden, Corinne J. & Blue, Rose. John Muir: Saving the Wilderness. LC 91-18106. (Illus.). 48p. (gr. 2-4). 1992. PLB 12.90 (*1-56294-110-0*); pap. 4.95 (*1-56294-797-4*) Millbrook Pr.

Talmadge, Katherine S. John Muir: At Home in the Wild. Castro, Antonio, illus. LC 92-36292. 80p. (gr. 4-7). 1993. PLB 14.95 (*0-8050-2123-X*) TFC Bks NY.

Tolan, Sally. John Muir: Naturalist, Writer & Guardian of the North American Wilderness. LC 89-4367. (Illus.). 64p. (gr. 5-6). 1989. PLB 19.93 (*0-8368-0099-0*) Gareth Stevens Inc.

Wadsworth, Ginger. John Muir: Wilderness Protector. (Illus.). 144p. (gr. 4-7). 1992. 21.50 (*0-8225-4912-3*) Lerner Pubns.

Weitzman, David. The Mountain Man & the President. Shaw, Charles, illus. LC 92-23040. 40p. (gr. 2-5). 1992. PLB 19.97 (*0-8114-7224-8*) Raintree Steck-V.

MUMMIES

Aliki. Mummies Made in Egypt. Aliki, illus. LC 77-26603. 32p. (gr. 2-6). 1979. 14.00 (*0-690-03858-5*, Crowell Jr Bks); PLB 13.89 (*0-690-03859-3*, Crowell Jr Bks) HarpC Child Bks.

—Mummies Made in Egypt. Aliki, illus. LC 85-42746. 32p. (gr. 2-6). 1985. pap. 5.95 (*0-06-446011-8*, Trophy) HarpC Child Bks.

Deem, James M. How to Make A Mummy Talk. Kelley, True, illus. LC 94-2186. 1995. write for info. (*0-395-62427-4*) HM.

Getz, David. The Frozen Man. 1994. write for info. (*0-8050-3261-4*) H Holt & Co.

Harris. One Hundred One Wacky Facts about Mummies. 1992. pap. 1.95 (*0-590-44889-7*) Scholastic Inc.

Lauber, Patricia. Tales Mummies Tell. LC 83-46172. (Illus.). 128p. (gr. 5-9). 1985. (Crowell Jr Bks); PLB 15.89 (*0-690-04389-9*, Crowell Jr Bks) HarpC Child Bks.

Perl, Lila. Mummies, Tombs, & Treasure: Secrets of Ancient Egypt. Weihs, Erika, illus. LC 86-17646. 128p. (gr. 4 up). 1987. 15.45 (*0-89919-407-9*, Clarion Bks) HM.

Putnam, Jim. Mummy. LC 92-1591. 64p. (gr. 5 up). 1993. 15.00 (*0-679-83881-3*); PLB 15.99 (*0-679-93881-8*) Knopf Bks Yng Read.

Spinner, Stephanie. The Mummy's Tomb. 64p. (gr. 2 up). 1985. pap. 2.25 (*0-553-15439-7*) Bantam.

Vornholt, John. Mummies. 96p. 1991. pap. 3.50 (*0-380-76317-6*, Camelot) Avon.

Wilcox, Charlotte. Mummies & Their Mysteries. LC 92-32160. 64p. 1993. 22.95 (*0-87614-767-8*) Carolrhoda Bks.

MUNICIPAL ENGINEERING

see also Refuse and Refuse Disposal; Water Supply

MUNICIPAL GOVERNMENT

see also Cities and Towns

also names of cities with the subdivision Politics and Government, e.g. New York (City)–Politics and Government; etc.

MUNICIPALITIES

see Cities and Towns

MURAL PAINTING AND DECORATION

see Cave Drawings; Mosaics

MURDER–FICTION

Arrick, Fran. Where'd You Get the Gun, Billy? (gr. 7 up). 1991. 16.00 (*0-553-07135-1*, Starfire) Bantam.

Duncan, Lois. Killing Mr. Griffin. (gr. 7 up). 1978. 15.95 (*0-316-19549-9*) Little.

Fowler, Zinita. The Last Innocent Summer. LC 89-20417. 144p. (gr. 6-9). 1990. pap. 11.95 (*0-87565-045-7*) Tex Christian.

Hall, Lynn. A Killing Freeze. LC 88-5143. 128p. (gr. 7 up). 1988. 12.95 (*0-688-07867-2*) Morrow Jr Bks.

Harrell, Janice. Dead Girls Can't Scream. 1993. pap. 3.50 (*0-06-106790-3*, Harp PBks) HarpC.

Haynes, Betsy. Deadly Deception. LC 93-39011. 1994. 14.95 (*0-385-32067-1*) Delacorte.

Hilgartner, Beth. Murder for Her Majesty. (gr. 4-7). 1992. pap. 4.80 (*0-395-61619-0*) HM.

Newman, Robert. The Case of the Vanishing Corpse. LC 79-22078. 228p. (gr. 4-6). 1985. pap. 4.95 (*0-689-71037-2*, Aladdin) Macmillan Child Grp.

Nixon, Joan L. The Name of the Game Was Murder. LC 92-8392. 1993. 15.00 (*0-385-30864-7*) Delacorte.

Springer, Nancy. Toughing It. LC 93-42231. (gr. 7 up). 1994. 10.95 (*0-15-200008-9*); pap. 4.95 (*0-15-200011-9*) Harbrace.

Thorburn, James W. Murder at Sun Valley. Witte, Sue, illus. LC 86-50305. 304p. (Orig.). (gr. 6). 1986. 8.99 (*0-938191-00-4*) Woodside Pr ID.

Tolliver, Ruby C. Have Gun - Need Bullets. Washington, Burl, illus. LC 90-49363. 120p. (gr. 4 up). 1991. 15.95 (*0-87565-085-6*); pap. 10.95 (*0-87565-089-9*) Tex Christian.

Wagner, John. Button Man: The Killing Game. Ranson, Arthur, illus. 96p. 1994. pap. 15.95 (*0-87816-276-3*) Kitchen Sink.

Waters, Gaby & Round, Graham. Murder on the Midnight Plane. (Illus.). 48p. (gr. 4-9). 1987. PLB 11.96 (*0-88110-389-6*); pap. 4.95 (*0-86020-952-0*) EDC.

MURROW, EDWARD ROSCOE, 1908-1965

Vonier, Sprague. Edward R. Murrow. LC 89-4344. (Illus.). 64p. (gr. 5-6). 1989. PLB 19.93 (*0-8368-0100-8*) Gareth Stevens Inc.

MUSCLES

Ardley, Neil. Muscles to Machines: Projects with Movement. LC 89-81569. 1990. PLB 12.40 (*0-531-17200-7*) Watts.

Feinberg, Brian. The Musculoskeletal System. Garell, Dale C. & Snyder, Solomon H., eds. (Illus.). 112p. (gr. 7-12). 1994. 19.95 (*0-7910-0028-1*, Am Art Analog) Chelsea Hse.

Ganeri, Anita. Moving. (Illus.). 32p. (gr. 2-4). 1994. PLB 18.99 (*0-8114-5521-1*) Raintree Steck-V.

Harrington, William F. Theories of Muscle Contraction. Head, J. J., ed. LC 77-94953. (Illus.). 32p. (gr. 10 up). 1981. pap. 3.00 (*0-89278-314-1*, 45-9714) Carolina Biological.

Koomar, Jane & Friedman, Barbara. Your Muscle Senses. Wolf, Elizabeth, illus. 16p. (ps-3). 1992. pap. text ed. 11.00 (*0-910317-89-5*) Am Occup Therapy.

Nelson, JoAnne. Nose to Toes. Keith, Doug, illus. LC 91-34706. 24p. (Orig.). (gr. k-2). 1993. pap. 5.95 (*0-935529-16-0*) Comprehen Health Educ.

Saunderson, Jane. Muscles & Bones. Farmer, Andrew & Green, Robina, illus. LC 90-42882. 32p. (gr. 4-6). 1992. lib. bdg. 11.89 (*0-8167-2088-6*); pap. text ed. 3.95 (*0-8167-2089-4*) Troll Assocs.

Silverstein, Alvin & Silverstein, Virginia. Muscular System. (Illus.). 96p. (gr. 5-8). 1994. bds. 16.95 (*0-8050-2836-6*) TFC Bks NY.

Skeleton & Movement. 48p. (gr. 5-8). 1988. PLB 10.95 (*0-382-09702-5*) Silver Burdett Pr.

MUSEUMS

see also Art–Galleries and Museums;

also names of countries, cities, etc. with the subdivision Galleries and Museums (e.g. U. S.–Galleries and Museums; etc.); and names of galleries and museums, e.g. New York Metropolitan Museum of Art

Adams, P., illus. The Child's Play Museum. LC 90-46592. (ps-2). 1976. 9.95 (*0-85953-094-9*, Pub. by Childs's Play England) Childs Play.

Belloli, Andrea P. Make Your Own Museum. Godard, Keith, designed by. (Illus.). 36p. (ps up). 1994. spiral bdg. 29.95 (*0-395-69450-7*) Ticknor & Flds Bks Yng Read.

Hellman, Nina & Brouwer, Norman. A Mariner's Fancy: The Whaleman's Art of Scrimshaw. LC 92-20865. (Illus.). 96p. 1992. pap. 22.50 (*0-295-97212-2*) U of Wash Pr.

Papajani, Janet. Museums. LC 82-23621. (Illus.). 48p. (gr. k-4). 1983. pap. 4.95 (*0-516-41682-0*) Childrens.

Reist, Linnaeus L. The Colorful Landis Brothers: Founders of the Landis Valley Museum. Severs, Susan B., ed. & illus. LC 87-90447. 100p. (Orig.). (gr. 11-12). 1987. pap. write for info. (*0-9618501-0-8*) S R Severs.

Richardson, Joy. Inside the Museum: A Children's Guide to the Metropolitan Museum of Art. (Illus.). 72p. 1993. pap. 12.95 (*0-8109-2561-3*) Abrams.

Suarez, Diana. Color & Discover: A Children's Guide to the North Carolina Museum of Art. Fender, Susan, illus. LC 87-62986. 40p. (Orig.). (ps-6). 1987. pap. 3.50 (*0-88259-956-9*) NCMA.

Weil, Lisl. Let's Go to the Museum. Weil, Lisl, illus. LC 89-2078. 32p. (ps-3). 1989. reinforced 13.95 (*0-8234-0784-5*) Holiday.

MUSEUMS–FICTION

Butterworth, Nick. School Trip. 1990. 13.95 (*0-385-30242-8*) Delacorte.

Freeman, Don. Norman the Doorman. Freeman, Don, illus. (ps-2). 1959. pap. 15.95 (*0-670-51515-9*) Viking Child Bks.

Greenwald, Sheila. The Secret Museum. Greenwald, Sheila, illus. 128p. (gr. k-6). 1989. pap. 2.95 (*0-440-40148-8*, YB) Dell.

Hickle, Victoria. A Big Day for Brum. Mones, Isidre, illus. LC 92-45105. 32p. (ps-1). 1993. pap. 2.25 (*0-679-84494-5*) Random Bks Yng Read.

Mayhew, James. Katie & the Dinosaurs. Mayhew, James, illus. (ps-3). 1992. 15.00 (*0-553-08129-2*, Little Rooster) Bantam.

Ploetz, Craig T. Milo's Trip to the Museum with Grandpa. (ps-3). 1994. 11.95 (*1-882172-01-9*) Milo Prods.

Rohmann, Eric. Time Flies. LC 93-28200. (Illus.). 32p. (ps-4). 1994. 15.00 (*0-517-59598-2*); lib. bdg. 15.99 (*0-517-59599-0*) Crown Bks Yng Read.

Ross, Pat. M & M & the Mummy Mess. Hafner, Marylin, illus. 48p. (gr. 1-4). 1986. pap. 3.95 (*0-14-032084-9*, Puffin) Puffin Bks.

Stanley, Diane. The Gentleman & the Kitchen Maid. Nolan, Dennis, illus. LC 93-157. 1994. 13.99 (*0-8037-1320-7*); lib. bdg. 13.89 (*0-8037-1321-5*) Dial Bks Young.

Wandelmaier, Roy. Secret of the Old Museum. Smolinski, Dick, illus. LC 85-2533. 112p. (gr. 3-6). 1985. lib. bdg. 9.49 (*0-8167-0531-3*); pap. text ed. 2.95 (*0-8167-0532-1*) Troll Assocs.

MUSHROOMS

see also Fungi

Cooper, J. Mushrooms. 1991. 8.95s.p. (*0-86592-623-9*) Rourke Enter.

—Setas y Hongos (Mushrooms) 1991. 8.95s.p. (*0-86592-499-6*) Rourke Enter.

Johnson, Sylvia A. Mushrooms. Izawa, Masana, illus. LC 82-212. 48p. (gr. 4 up). 1982. PLB 19.95 (*0-8225-1473-7*) Lerner Pubns.

Peissel, Michel & Allen, Missy. Dangerous Plants & Mushrooms. (Illus.). 112p. (gr. 5 up). 1993. PLB 19.95 (*0-7910-1787-7*, Am Art Analog) Chelsea Hse.

Selsam, Millicent E. Mushrooms. Wexler, Jerome, photos by. LC 85-18953. (Illus.). 48p. (gr. 2-5). 1986. 12.95 (*0-688-06248-2*); (Morrow Jr Bks) Morrow Jr Bks.

Watts, Barrie. Mushroom. LC 86-6659. (Illus.). 25p. (gr. k-4). 1986. 5.95 (*0-382-09301-1*); PLB 7.95 (*0-382-09287-2*); pap. 3.95 (*0-382-24017-0*) Silver Burdett Pr.

MUSIAL, STANLEY FRANK, 1920-

Grabowski, John F. Stan Musial. (Illus.). 1994. 14.95 (*0-7910-1184-4*, Am Art Analog) Chelsea Hse.

MUSIC

see also Church Music; Jazz Music; Musicians; Sound also Orchestral Music; Organ Music; Piano music; etc. and headings beginning with the words Music and Musical

Boy Scouts of America. Cub Scout Songbook. (Illus.). 80p. (gr. 3-5). 1969. pap. 2.40x (*0-8395-3222-9*, 33222) BSA.

Boy Scouts of America Staff. Cub Scout Academics: Music. (Illus.). 40p. 1991. pap. 1.35 (*0-8395-3034-X*, 33034) BSA.

Clark, Frances & Goss, Louise. Music Maker, Pt. A. (Illus.). 56p. (gr. 2 up). 1986. pap. text ed. 6.95 wkbk. (*0-913277-20-7*) New Schl Mus Study.

Douillard, Jeanne, ed. Chansons de Chez-Nous. Snow, Suzanne. Blais, Lise M. Albert, Julie D., illus. (FRE.). 61p. (gr. k-6). 1978. pap. text ed. 1.00 (*0-911409-01-7*) Natl Mat Dev.

Evans, David & Williams, Claudette. Sound & Music. LC 92-53481. (Illus.). 24p. (gr. k-3). 1993. 9.95 (*1-56458-206-X*) Dorling Kindersley.

Feierabend, John M. Music for Very Little People. Kramer, Gary M., illus. 74p. (ps). 1986. pap. 14.95 (*0-685-14607-3*); pap. write for info. incl. tape (*0-913932-13-2*); cassette avail. Boosey & Hawkes.

Ferguson, Kathleen M. Musical Mysteries. Melton, Gerald, illus. 144p. (gr. 4-8). 1985. wkbk. 12.95 (*0-86653-282-X*, GA 684) Good Apple.

Francis, Carolyn. Music Reading & Theory Skills, Level 1 & 2: A Sequential Method for Practice & Mastery. 226p. (gr. 4-12). 1986. incl. reproducible curriculum pkg. 179.95 (*0-931303-04-4*); 3-ring binder, black line masters avail. (*0-931303-02-8*) Innovative Learn.

Friou, Deborah. Rodgers & Hammerstein for the Harp. 48p. (Orig.). 1990. pap. 15.95 (*0-9628120-0-5*) Friou Music.

Grasmick, Alta C. U'n I Read a Note. Rust, Thomas O., illus. 68p. (gr. k-1). 1989. pap. 15.95 (*0-9621909-0-X*) A C Grasmick.

Hamman, Marc. Hamman Jammin' Music. (Illus.). 18p. (Orig.). (gr. k-6). 1990. pap. 12.95 (*1-56516-062-2*) Houston IN.

Hart, Avery & Mantell, Paul. Kids Make Music! Clapping & Tapping from Bach to Rock. Trezzo-Braren Studio Staff, illus. 160p. (Orig.). (ps-6). 1993. pap. 12.95 (*0-913589-69-1*) Williamson Pub Co.

Kaplan, Don. See with Your Ears: The Creative Music Book. Hoburg, Maryanne R., illus. LC 82-81463. 128p. (Orig.). (gr. 1-7). 1982. pap. 6.95 (*0-938530-09-7*, 09-7); tchr's guide cancelled 2.00 (*0-938530-20-8*, 20-8) Lexikos.

Keener, Joseph. Music Series. (gr. 1-7). 1982. pap. write for info. (*0-686-37780-X*) Rod & Staff.

Laurencin, Genevieve. Music! Bogard, Vicki, tr. from FRE. Millet, Claude & Millet, Denise, illus. LC 89-8892. (gr. k-5). 1989. 5.95 (*0-944589-25-1*, 025) Young Discovery Lib.

Line, Lorie. Selections from Sharing the Season, Vol. 2. Maybery, Paul, ed. Hinman, Jim, illus. 36p. 1993. pap. text ed. 9.95 (*0-9638000-0-0*) Time Line Prods.

Marshall, Mary A. Music: Careers in Music. LC 93-14832. (Illus.). 48p. (gr. 5-6). 1994. text ed. 14.95 RSBE (*0-89686-793-5*, Crestwood Hse) Macmillan Child Grp.

Menotti, Gian-Carlo. Amahl & the Night Visitors. Lemieux, Michele, illus. LC 84-27196. 64p. (ps up). 1986. 15.00 (*0-688-05426-9*); lib. bdg. 14.88 (*0-688-05427-7*, Morrow Jr Bks) Morrow Jr Bks.

Mercuri, Carmela. Toot-in-Time Band: Introducing Children to the World of Music. Smith, Robin A., illus. (Orig.). (gr. 1-6). 1993. pap. 10.95 (*0-935474-21-8*) Carousel Pubns Ltd.

Miles, J. C. First Book of the Keyboard. (Illus.). 64p. (gr. 2 up). 1993. PLB 14.96 (*0-88110-622-4*); pap. 8.95 (*0-7460-0962-3*) EDC.

Music & Bugling. (Illus.). 56p. (gr. 6-12). 1990. pap. 1.85 (*0-8395-3336-5*, 33336) BSA.

Nelson, Lisa M. Bright Smiles & Blue Skies: Positive Music for Today's Kids. (Illus.). 16p. (Orig.). (gr. k-6). 1990. pap. 9.95 incl. audio tape (*0-9627863-0-6*) Brght Ideas CA.

Paker, Josephine. Music from Strings. LC 92-5162. (Illus.). 48p. (gr. 2-6). 1992. PLB 13.90 (*1-56294-283-2*) Millbrook Pr.

Patella, Chris & Oddo, Eileen. Makin Music! Schoonover, Kevin, illus. 75p. (Orig.). (gr. k-2). 1989. write for info. tchrs. ed. (*0-944333-02-8*); LP or Cassette avail. Musical Munchkins.
Pearce, Elvina T. Solo Flight. Clark, Frances & Goss, Louise, eds. (gr. 2 up). 1986. pap. text ed. 3.50 (*0-913277-18-5*) New Schl Mus Study.
Polette, Nancy. Concert Reading. expanded ed. (Illus.). 48p. (gr. k-3). 1992. pap. 5.95 (*1-879287-07-2*) Bk Lures.
—Reading with Music. expanded ed. (Illus.). 48p. (gr. 4-7). 1992. pap. 5.95 (*1-879287-04-8*) Bk Lures.
Reynolds, Malvina. There's Music in the Air. Simmons, Elly, illus. LC 76-19261. 96p. (gr. 1-12). 1976. pap. 5.00 (*0-915620-05-7*) Schroder Music.
Rhoton, Jessian L. The Magic Treble Tree. Erickson, Cindy R., illus. 48p. 1989. PLB write for info. Happy Music Pub.
—The Magic Treble Tree. Erickson, Cindy R., illus. 48p. 1990. write for info. (*0-9624162-9-0*) Happy Music Pub.
Rosenholtz, Stephen. Move Like the Animals. Yoshiko, Fujita, illus. LC 91-66970. 32p. (ps-3). 1992. incl. cassette 19.95 (*0-9630979-1-1*); pap. 14.95 incl. cassette (*0-9630979-0-3*) Rosewd Pubns.
Santrey, Laurence. Music. Croll, Carolyn, illus. LC 84-2648. 32p. (gr. 3-6). 1985. PLB 9.49 (*0-8167-0218-7*); pap. text ed. 2.95 (*0-8167-0219-5*) Troll Assocs.
Sommer, Elyse. The Kids' World Almanac of Music: From Rock to Bach & Back Again. Lane, John, illus. 288p. (Orig.). 1992. 14.95 (*0-88687-522-6*); pap. 7.95 (*0-88687-521-8*) Wrld Almnc.
Susen, Phyllis B., ed. Sound All Around. ps-4 ed. Blake, Amy, illus. 40p. (Orig.). 1992. pap. 8.50 (*0-9635667-0-9*) Phila Orchestra.
Swan, Susan E., illus. The Twelve Days of Christmas. LC 80-28097. 32p. (gr. k-4). 1981. PLB 9.79 (*0-89375-474-9*); pap. text ed. 1.95 (*0-89375-475-7*) Troll Assocs.
Taylor, Ann. Chamber Music Primer: Four Piano Trio Pieces. Bryant, Larkin, illus. (Orig.). (gr. 1-6). 1983. pap. 6.75 (*0-943644-01-1*); cassette 5.98 (*0-685-06794-7*) Ivory Pal.
Taylor, Barbara. Sound & Music. LC 91-8740. (Illus.). 32p. (gr. 5-8). 1991. PLB 12.40 (*0-531-14185-3*) Watts.
Tomei, Joseph A. Music Notation - How to Read & Write: Learning to Read Notes Step by Step. Tomei, Jeri & Steeves, Margo, eds. 80p. (Orig.). 1994. pap. text ed. 14.95 (*0-9629973-1-5*) Minich Pubns.
Weil, Lisl. The Magic of Music. Weil, Lisl, illus. LC 88-21362. 32p. (ps-3). 1989. reinforced bdg. 13.95 (*0-8234-0735-7*) Holiday.
Wojcio, Michael D. & Gustason, Gerilee. Music in Motion: Twenty Two Songs in Signing Exact English, for Children. Norris, Carolyn, illus. 112p. (Orig.). 1982. 12.95 (*0-916708-07-1*) Modern Signs.

MUSIC–ACOUSTICS AND PHYSICS

see also Sound

Ardley, Neil. Science Book of Sound. 29p. (gr. 2-5). 1991. 9.95 (*0-15-200579-X*, HB Juv Bks) HarBrace.
—Sound Waves to Music: Projects with Sound. LC 90-3249. (Illus.). 32p. (gr. 5-8). 1990. PLB 12.40 (*0-531-17236-8*, Gloucester Pr) Watts.
Balcziak, B. Music. (Illus.). 48p. (gr. 4-8). 1989. lib. bdg. 17.27 (*0-86592-056-7*); 12.95s.p. (*0-685-58627-8*) Rourke Corp.
Berger, Melvin. The Science of Music. Buchanan, Yvonne, illus. LC 87-24921. 160p. (gr. 5-9). 1989. (Crowell Jr Bks); PLB 14.89 (*0-690-04647-2*, Crowell Jr Bks) HarpC Child Bks.
Hewitt, Sally. Puff & Blow. LC 94-16910. (Illus.). 24p. (ps-3). 1994. PLB 14.40 (*0-516-07993-X*); pap. 4.95 (*0-516-47993-8*) Childrens.
Kerrod, Robin. Sounds & Music. LC 90-25543. (Illus.). 32p. (gr. 3-8). 1991. PLB 9.95 (*1-85435-270-9*) Marshall Cavendish.

MUSIC, AMERICAN

Axelrod, Alan, commentary by. Songs of the Wild West. Fox, Dan, contrib. by. (Illus.). 128p. 1991. pap. 19.95 jacketed (*0-671-74775-4*, S&S BFYR) S&S Trade.
Saunders, Susan. Dolly Parton: Country Goin' to Town. Pate, Rodney, illus. 64p. (gr. 2-6). 1986. pap. 3.95 (*0-14-032162-4*, Puffin) Puffin Bks.
Waring, Diana. History Alive Through Music America: The Heart of a New Land. (Illus.). 78p. (Orig.). (gr. 3-8). 1991. pap. 17.95 incl. cassette (*1-879459-01-9*); pap. 9.95 (*1-879459-00-0*); cassette 9.95 (*1-879459-02-7*) Hear & Learn Pubns.
—History Alive Through Music Westward Ho! The Heart of the Old West. (Illus.). 66p. (Orig.). (gr. 6-10). 1991. pap. 17.95 incl. cassette (*1-879459-03-5*); pap. 9.95 (*1-879459-04-3*); cassette 9.95 (*1-879459-05-1*) Hear & Learn Pubns.

MUSIC–ANALYSIS, APPRECIATION

Bernstein, Leonard. Leonard Bernstein's Young People's Concerts. 1992. pap. 15.00 (*0-385-42435-3*, Anchor NY) Doubleday.
Copland, Aaron. What to Listen for in Music. rev. ed. Schuman, William. 192p. (RL 9). 1953. pap. 5.50 (*0-451-62735-0*, Ment) NAL-Dutton.
—What to Listen for in Music. rev. ed. 192p. (gr. 9-12). 1989. pap. 4.95 (*0-451-62687-7*, Ment) NAL-Dutton.
Ensor, Wendy-Ann. Heroes & Heroines in Music. (Illus.). (gr. 1-4). 1981. cassette 18.00x (*0-685-06116-7*) OUP.
Luck, Oliver W. Music Is Math. Luck, Oliver W., illus. (Orig.). (gr. 4-12). 1987. pap. 7.00 (*0-9626686-0-5*) Owl Pub CA.
Sharma, Elizabeth. Voice. LC 93-1093. (Illus.). 32p. (gr. 4-6). 1993. 14.95 (*1-56847-116-5*) Thomson Lrning.
Sharp, Vera. Little Princess' Symphony Adventures. Armstrong, M. J., illus. 76p. (ps-6). 1985. incl. 2 cassettes 49.00 (*0-9616987-0-5*) V Sharp.
Tatchell, J. Understanding Music. (Illus.). 64p. (gr. 4 up). 1990. lib. bdg. 13.96 (*0-88110-382-9*, Usborne); pap. 7.95 (*0-7460-0302-1*, Usborne) EDC.

MUSIC–APPRECIATION

see Music–Analysis, Appreciation

MUSIC–BIOGRAPHY

see Musicians

MUSIC, DRAMATIC

see Opera

MUSIC–FICTION

Agnes' Cardboard Piano. (Illus.). 40p. (gr. k-5). 1994. pap. 4.95 (*0-685-71584-1*, 520) W Gladden Found.
Bottner, Barbara. Hurricane Music. Yalowitz, Paul, illus. LC 92-43697. 1994. 15.95 (*0-399-22544-7*, Putnam) Putnam Pub Group.
Brook, Ruth. Play It Again, Rosie! Kondo, Vala, illus. LC 86-30749. 32p. (gr. k-3). 1988. PLB 11.89 (*0-8167-0904-1*); pap. text ed. 2.95 (*0-8167-0905-X*) Troll Assocs.
Burningham, John. Trubloff: The Mouse Who Wanted to Play the Balalaika. Burningham, John, illus. LC 93-13279. (ps-2). 1994. pap. 4.99 (*0-517-59435-8*) Crown Bks Yng Read.
Carlson, Nancy. Harriet's Recital. LC 81-18135. (Illus.). 32p. (ps-3). 1982. lib. bdg. 13.50 (*0-87614-181-5*) Carolrhoda Bks.
—Loudmouth George & the Cornet. LC 82-22171. (Illus.). 32p. (ps-3). 1983. PLB 13.50 (*0-87614-214-5*) Carolrhoda Bks.

Carter, Donna R. Music in the Family. Harris, Cortrell J., illus. 32p. (gr. k-3). 1994. pap. write for info. (*1-885242-01-8*) Lindsey Pubng. Growing up with music Oliver had one wish--to play in his family's band. He strives to become a good musician but discovers it will take much more than talent. This story helps us learn about different instruments & musical styles like gospel, blues, jazz & reggae. This is a story about perseverance & one boy's triumph to make his dream come true.
Publisher Provided Annotation.

Claverie, Jean. Little Lou. Claverie, Jean, illus. 48p. (gr. 3 up). 1990. PLB 17.95 (*0-88682-329-3*) Creative Ed.
Clement, Claude. The Voice of the Wood. Clement, Frederic, photos by. LC 88-22892. (Illus.). 32p. (gr. k up). 1989. 14.95 (*0-8037-0635-9*) Dial Bks Young.
Clymer, Eleanor. The Horse in the Attic. 96p. (gr. 4-6). 1985. pap. 2.50 (*0-440-43798-9*, YB) Dell.
Cooney, Caroline B. Don't Blame the Music. LC 85-21727. 172p. (gr. 8 up). 1986. 14.95 (*0-448-47778-5*, G&D) Putnam Pub Group.
Corbett, W. J. The Song Pentecost. (gr. k-6). 1985. pap. 3.25 (*0-440-48092-2*, YB) Dell.
Davis, Terry. If Rock & Roll Were a Machine. 1994. pap. 3.99 (*0-440-21908-6*) Dell.
Disher, Garry. The Bamboo Flute. LC 92-39787. 96p. (gr. 3-6). 1993. 10.95 (*0-395-66595-7*) Ticknor & Flds Bks Yng Read.
Escovito, Pete. Viva la Musica. (gr. 4-7). 1991. pap. 9.95 (*0-930647-09-2*) Lancaster Prodns.
Feltenberger, Myles. Mr. Everybody's Musical Apartment, Bk. 1. Dominiak, Dana M., et al, illus. LC 92-96919. 40p. 1993. pap. 9.95 (*0-9634218-0-8*) Myles Music.
Finkelstein, Chaim. The Cheery Bim Band, No. 3. LC 93-73854. 176p. (gr. 5-6). Date not set. 10.95 (*1-56062-218-0*) CIS Comm.
Fowler, Susi G. Fog. Fowler, Jim, illus. LC 91-28509. 32p. (ps-8). 1992. 14.00 (*0-688-10593-9*); PLB 13.93 (*0-688-10594-7*) Greenwillow.
Frank, Elizabeth B. Cooder Cutlas. LC 85-45822. 320p. (gr. 7 up). 1987. 13.95i (*0-685-17655-X*) HarpC Child Bks.
Friesel, Uwe. Tim, the Peacemaker. Wilkon, Jozef, illus. LC 72-145822. 32p. (ps-3). 8.95 (*0-87592-052-7*) Scroll Pr.
Gaff, Sha. Bunny Butz Sings the Blues. Geurts, Kelly, illus. LC 91-67753. 70p. 1993. pap. 7.00 (*1-56002-161-6*, Univ Edtns) Aegina Pr.
Greenfield, Eloise. I Make Music. Gilchrist, Jan S., illus. 12p. (ps-1). 1991. bds. 4.95 (*0-86316-205-3*) Writers & Readers.
Gregorich, Barbara. A Different Tune. Hoffman, Joan, ed. (Illus.). 16p. (Orig.). (gr. k-2). 1991. pap. 2.25 (*0-88743-028-7*, 06028) Sch Zone Pub Co.
Griffith, Helen. Georgia Music. Stevenson, James, illus. LC 85-24918. 24p. (gr. k-3). 1986. 13.95 (*0-688-06071-4*); PLB 13.88 (*0-688-06072-2*) Greenwillow.
Haseley, Dennis. The Old Banjo. Gammell, Stephen, illus. LC 89-36796. 32p. (gr. 1-5). 1990. pap. 3.95 (*0-689-71380-0*, Aladdin) Macmillan Child Grp.
Hill, Stephanie. Donald's Wild Adventure. Disney Studios Staff, illus. 24p. (Orig.). (ps-7). 1992. pap. 8.98 incl. cassette (*0-943351-55-3*, XD 1002) Astor Bks.
—Mickey's Marching Band. Disney Studios Staff, illus. 24p. (Orig.). (ps-7). 1992. pap. 8.98 incl. cassette (*0-943351-54-5*, XD 1001) Astor Bks.
Johnston, Tony. Pages of Music. De Paola, Tomie, illus. 32p. (gr. k-3). 1988. PLB 13.95 (*0-399-21436-4*, Putnam) Putnam Pub Group.
Kasperitis, Brian G. Grandad's Old Tuba. (gr. 4 up). 1993. 7.95 (*0-8062-4726-6*) Carlton.
Keats, Ezra J. Louie's Search. Keats, Ezra J., illus. LC 89-15128. 32p. (gr. k-3). 1989. pap. 4.95 (*0-689-71354-1*, Aladdin) Macmillan Child Grp.
Kidd, Ronald. Meet Maximum Clyde. 80p. (gr. 3-6). 1992. pap. 2.99 (*0-14-034989-8*, Puffin) Puffin Bks.
Komaiko, Leah. I Like the Music. Westman, Barbara, illus. LC 87-170. 32p. (ps-3). 1987. HarpC Child Bks.
—I Like the Music. Westman, Barbara, illus. LC 87-170. 32p. (ps-3). 1989. pap. 5.95 (*0-06-443189-4*, Trophy) HarpC Child Bks.
Kraus, Robert. Musical Max. Aruego, Jose & Dewey, Ariane, illus. LC 89-77079. 40p. 1990. pap. 13.95 jacketed (*0-671-68681-X*, Little Simon) S&S Trade.
Le Clezio, J. M. Lullaby. Lemoine, Georges, illus. (FRE.). (gr. 5-10). 1995. pap. 6.95 (*2-07-033448-1*) Schoenhof.
L'Engle, Madeleine. The Small Rain: A Novel. LC 84-47839. 371p. (gr. 7 up). 1984. 14.95 (*0-374-26637-9*) FS&G.
Levy, Elizabeth. Something Queer in Rock N' Roll. Gerstein, Mordicai, illus. LC 86-19772. 48p. (gr. k-3). 1987. pap. 12.95 (*0-385-29547-2*) Delacorte.
Lewis, Richard. All of You Was Singing. Young, Ed, illus. LC 89-18263. 32p. 1991. SBE 13.95 (*0-689-31596-1*, Atheneum Child Bk) Macmillan Child Grp.
Linscott, Jody. The Worthy Wonders Lost at Sea. Holland, Claudia P., illus. LC 92-43367. 1993. pap. 15.00 (*0-385-47053-3*) Doubleday.
Locke, Robert. Tracks. (gr. 5 up). 1986. 12.70 (*0-395-40571-8*) HM.
Locker, Thomas. Anna & the Bagpiper. Locker, Thomas, illus. LC 92-42350. 32p. (ps). 1994. 15.95 (*0-399-22546-3*, Philomel Bks) Putnam Pub Group.
Lynch, Patricia. Brogeen Follows the Magic Flute. 191p. (ps-8). 1988. pap. 6.95 (*1-85371-022-9*, Pub. by Poolbeg Press Ltd Eire) Dufour.
McLerran, Alice. Dreamsong. Vasiliev, Valery, illus. LC 91-32622. 32p. (gr. k up). 1992. 14.00 (*0-688-10105-4*, Tambourine Bks); PLB 13.93 (*0-688-10106-2*, Tambourine Bks) Morrow.
McMillion, Mac. Who'll Sing For Me. LC 87-91267. 130p. (Orig.). 1987. pap. 10.00 (*0-9619399-0-7*) M McMillion Pub.
Magorian, James. The Beautiful Music. LC 88-71142. (Illus.). 12p. (gr. 2-5). 1988. pap. 3.00 (*0-930674-25-1*) Black Oak.
Manson, Christopher. A Farmyard Song. Manson, Christopher, illus. LC 91-46238. 32p. (gr. k). 1992. 14.95 (*1-55858-169-3*); PLB 14.88 (*1-55858-170-7*) North-South Bks NYC.
Melmed, Laura K. First Song Ever Sung. LC 91-28528. (ps-3). 1993. 15.00 (*0-688-08230-0*); PLB 14.93 (*0-688-08231-9*) Lothrop.
Micucci, Charles. A Little Night Music. Micucci, Charles, illus. LC 88-505. 32p. (ps-3). 1989. 10.95 (*0-688-07900-8*); PLB 10.88 (*0-688-07901-6*, Morrow Jr Bks) Morrow Jr Bks.
Moss, Lloyd. Zin! Zin! Zin! A Violin. Priceman, Marjorie, illus. LC 93-37902. 1995. 14.00 (*0-671-88239-2*, S&S BFYR) S&S Trade.
Newberger-Speregen, Devra. Hip Hop Till You Drop. 1994. pap. 3.50 (*0-671-88291-0*, Minstrel Bks) PB.
Nichol, B. P. Once: A Lullaby. Lobel, Anita, illus. LC 85-9942. 24p. (ps up). 1992. pap. 4.95 (*0-688-04286-4*, Mulberry) Morrow.
Ossorio, Nelson A. & Salvadeo, Michele B. The Song No One Liked. (Illus.). 48p. (gr. 3-5). 1994. pap. 6.95 (*1-56721-050-3*) Twenty-Fifth Cent Pr.
Paulsen, Gary. Woodsong. 144p. (gr. 7 up). 1991. pap. 3.99 (*0-14-034905-7*, Puffin) Puffin Bks.
Perkins, Mary. Percival the Piano. Thomas, Wendy, illus. (Orig.). (gr. k-4). 1990. pap. 5.75 (*0-85398-287-2*) G Ronald Pub.
Redhead, Janet S. Something Special for Miss Margery. Forss, Ian, illus. LC 93-6632. 1994. write for info (*0-383-03673-9*) SRA Schl Grp.
Rehnman, Mats. The Clay Flute. Bibb, Eric, tr. Rehnman, Mats, illus. (ps-4). 1989. 12.95 (*91-29-59184-8*, Pub. by R & S Bks) FS&G.
Roalf, Peggy. Musicians. LC 93-15555. (Illus.). 48p. (gr. 3-7). 1993. PLB 14.89 (*1-56282-533-X*); pap. 6.95 (*1-56282-532-1*) Hyprn Ppbks.
Sage, James. The Little Band. Narahashi, Keiko, illus. LC 90-40089. 32p. (ps-3). 1991. SBE 13.95 (*0-689-50516-7*, M K McElderry) Macmillan Child Grp.
Saltzman, Mark. Woodchuck Nation. Buller, Jon, illus. LC 93-4641. 1994. 15.00 (*0-679-85107-0*) Knopf Bks Yng Read.
Schroeder, Alan. Ragtime Tumpie. (ps-3). 1993. pap. 4.95 (*0-316-77504-5*, AMP) Little.
Sharmat, Marjorie W. Nate the Great & the Musical Note. (ps-3). 1991. pap. 3.50 (*0-440-40466-5*) Dell.
Snyder, Zilpha K. Song of the Gargoyle. (gr. 4-7). 1994. pap. 3.99 (*0-440-40898-9*) Dell.
Strasser, Todd. Rock 'n Roll Nights. 224p. (gr. 7 up). 1983. pap. 2.95 (*0-440-97318-X*, LFL) Dell.

Thesman, Jean. Cattail Moon. LC 93-6814. (gr. 4-7). 1994. write for info. (*0-395-67409-3*) HM.
Tusa, Tricia. Miranda. LC 85-26769. (Illus.). 32p. (gr. k up). 1986. pap. 3.95 (*0-689-71064-X*, Aladdin) Macmillan Child Grp.
Vaughan, Marcia. He-De-Hi. 16p. (ps-1). 1994. text ed. 3.95 (*0-673-36197-7*) GdYrBks.
Walter, Mildred P. Ty's One-Man Band. Tomes, Margot, illus. 48p. (gr. k-3). 1984. pap. 3.95 (*0-590-40178-5*) Scholastic Inc.
Wayland, April H. It's Not My Turn to Look for Grandma. Booth, George, illus. LC 93-7018. 1994. 15.00 (*0-679-84491-0*); lib. bdg. 15.99 (*0-679-94491-5*) Knopf.
Yorke, Malcolm. Ritchie F. Dweebly Thunders On. Chamberlain, Margaret, illus. LC 93-5003. 32p. (gr. 1-4). 1994. 10.95 (*1-56458-199-3*) Dorling Kindersley.
Zolotow, Charlotte. Everything Glistens & Everything Sings. Tomes, Margot, illus. LC 86-31917. 96p. (ps-3). 1987. 11.95 (*0-15-226488-4*, HB Juv Bks) HarBrace.

MUSIC–HISTORY AND CRITICISM

Abell. Bib & Tucker. Abell, et al, illus. 50p. (Orig.). (gr. 1-3). 1994. 23.00 (*1-56611-087-4*); pap. 15.00 (*1-56611-088-2*) Jonas.
Adair, Audrey J. Great Composers & Their Music History, Unit 5: Fifty Ready to Use Activities. 112p. (gr. 3-9). 1987. pap. text ed. 18.95 (*0-13-363797-2*, Parker Publishing Co.) P-H.
—Special Days Throughout the Year: Fifty Ready-to-Use Activities, Unit 6. 112p. (gr. 3-9). 1987. pap. 12.95 (*0-13-826421-X*, Parker Publishing Co) P-H.
Carlin, Richard. European Classical Music, 1600-1855. (Illus.). 144p. 1988. 17.95x (*0-8160-1382-9*) Facts on File.
Currie, Stephen. Music in the Civil War. LC 92-18102. (Illus.). 112p. (Orig.). (gr. 3-7). 1992. pap. 8.95 (*1-55870-263-6*, 70155) Shoe Tree Pr.
Jones, K. Maurice. Say It Loud! The Story of Rap Music. LC 93-1939. (Illus.). 128p. (gr. 7 up). 1994. PLB 19.90 (*1-56294-386-3*) Millbrook Pr.
—Say It Loud: The Story of Rap Music. 1994. pap. 12.95 (*1-56294-724-9*) Millbrook Pr.
Kendall, Catherine W. Stories of Women Composers for Young Musicians. large type ed. (Illus.). 212p. (Orig.). (gr. 1-12). 1993. pap. 12.95 (*0-9610878-2-X*) Toadwood Pubs.
Kennedy, Rosemary G. Bach to Rock: An Introduction to Famous Composers & Their Music. 6th, rev. ed. Ronniger, Mary S., illus. 161p. (gr. 4-9). 1989. pap. 14.95 (*0-685-45404-5*); audio cassette 16.95 (*0-685-45405-3*) Rosemary Corp.
Mundy. Story of Music. (gr. 6-9). 1980. (Usborne-Hayes); PLB 13.96 (*0-88110-031-5*); pap. 6.95 (*0-86020-443-X*) EDC.
Shipton, Alyn. Singing. LC 93-20006. (Illus.). 32p. (gr. 1-8). 1993. PLB 19.97 (*0-8114-2315-8*) Raintree Steck-V.
Waring, Diana. History Alive Through Music America: The Heart of a New Land. (Illus.). 78p. (Orig.). (gr. 3-8). 1991. pap. 17.95 incl. cassette (*1-879459-01-9*); pap. 9.95 (*1-879459-00-0*); cassette 9.95 (*1-879459-02-7*) Hear & Learn Pubns.
—History Alive Through Music Westward Ho! The Heart of the Old West. (Illus.). 66p. (Orig.). (gr. 6-10). 1991. pap. 17.95 incl. cassette (*1-879459-03-5*); pap. 9.95 (*1-879459-04-3*); cassette 9.95 (*1-879459-05-1*) Hear & Learn Pubns.

MUSIC, INDIAN
see Indians of North America–Music

MUSIC–INSTRUCTION AND STUDY
see Music–Study and Teaching

MUSIC–NOTATION
see Musical Notation

MUSIC, POPULAR (SONGS, ETC.)

Feierabend, John. Music for Little People. Kramer, Gary, illus. 74p. (Orig.). (ps). 1989. pap. 11.95 (*0-913932-46-9*); pap. 14.95 incl. tape (*0-913932-48-5*) Boosey & Hawkes.
Peeples, Jerome. Hammer: What's Hot. 48p. (gr. 4-7). 1992. pap. 1.49 (*0-440-21380-0*) Dell.
Ramsey, Marjorie E., ed. It's Music! LC 84-435. (Illus.). 56p. (ps-9). 1984. 7.50 (*0-87173-104-5*) ACEI.
Suschitzky, A. More Easy Recorder Tunes. (Illus.). 64p. (gr. 2 up). 1993. pap. 8.95 (*0-7460-1393-0*) EDC.
Warner, Laverne & Craycraft, Kenneth. Fun with Familiar Tunes. Filkins, Vanessa, illus. 128p. (ps-3). 1987. pap. 11.95 (*0-86653-414-8*, GA1014) Good Apple.

MUSIC, POPULAR (SONGS, ETC.)–BIOGRAPHY

Krulik, Nancy E. M. C. Hammer & Vanilla Ice. 1991. pap. 2.95 (*0-590-44980-X*) Scholastic Inc.

MUSIC, SACRED
see Church Music

MUSIC–STUDY AND TEACHING
see also Musical Form

Anderson, Tom. Sing Choral Music at Sight. Blakeslee, Michael, ed. (Illus.). 128p. (Orig.). (gr. 1-12). 1992. pap. 36.00 tchr's. ed. (*1-56545-007-8*) Music Ed Natl.
Beauty & the Beast: Recorder Fun Pack. (Illus.). 1991. incl. instruction bk., songbk., recorder & cass. 14.95 (*0-7935-1179-8*, HL00710351) H Leonard.
Brown, Robert. Stand Alone Blues. 32p. pap. 9.95 (*0-88284-543-8*, 4428) Alfred Pub.
Dillon, Jacquelyn, et al. Strictly Strings: A Comprehensive String Method, Bk. 1: Bass. (Illus.). 40p. (Orig.). (gr. 4-6). 1992. pap. 4.95 (*0-88284-533-0*, 5296) Alfred Pub.
—Strictly Strings: A Comprehensive String Method, Bk. 1: Cello. (Illus.). 40p. (Orig.). (gr. 4-6). 1992. pap. 4.95 (*0-88284-532-2*, 5295) Alfred Pub.
—Strictly Strings: A Comprehensive String Method, Bk. 1: Violin. (Illus.). 40p. (Orig.). (gr. 4-6). 1992. pap. 4.95 (*0-88284-530-6*, 5293) Alfred Pub.
—Strictly Strings: A Comprehensive String Method, Bk. 1: Viola. (Illus.). 40p. (Orig.). (gr. 4-6). 1992. pap. 4.95 (*0-88284-531-4*, 5294) Alfred Pub.
Duna, Bill & Duna, Lois. Let's Play--Right Away with Play-Along Tape, Bk. 1. Guthrie, Ruth, illus. 32p. (Orig.). (gr. k up). 1981. pap. 12.95 (*0-942928-00-8*) Duna Studios.
Easy Keyboard Tunes. (Illus.). 64p. 1992. PLB 14.96 (*0-88110-583-X*); pap. 8.95 (*0-7460-0960-7*) EDC.
Epstein, Melvin H. The Young Musician's Series. Darrell, Gail O., illus. LC 92-80357. (Orig.). (gr. 4-9). 1992. Five vol. set. pap. text ed. 65.00 (*1-881136-00-0*) Vol. 1: The Basics of Music (*1-881136-01-9*) Vol. 2: Melody. pap. text ed. 14.95 (*1-881136-02-7*); Vol. 3: Harmony. pap. text ed. 14.94 (*1-881136-03-5*); Vol. 4: Time & Rhythm. pap. text ed. 12.95 (*1-881136-04-3*); Vol. 5: Special Effects. pap. text ed. 12.95 (*1-881136-05-1*) Word Hse.
Fiarotta, Noel & Fiarotta, Phyllis. Music Crafts for Kids: The How-to Book of Music Dicovery. LC 93-24114. (Illus.). 160p. (gr. 3 up). 1993. 17.95 (*0-8069-0406-2*) Sterling.
Hale, Beverly M. A Rainbow Book of Song: Key of "C" 2nd ed. Hale, Beverly M., illus. 57p. (ps up). 1993. Blue spine bdg. pap. text ed. 13.95 (*0-9634305-1-3*) E-Z Keys Method.
Harp, David. Make Me Musical: Instant Harmonica Education for Kids. 2nd, rev. ed. (Illus.). (ps-4). 1989. pap. 19.95 (*0-918321-15-8*); cassette & harmonica incl. Musical Idiot.
Hellden, Daniel. Hi! Said the Blackbird: And Twelve Other American Folk Songs to Sing & Play. 24p. (gr. 1-4). 1981. pap. 6.00 (*0-918812-17-8*, SE 0743) MMB Music.
Hittler, Louis. Clarinet Primer. 1993. 3.50 (*0-87166-371-6*, 93406) Mel Bay.
Hunka, Alison & Bunting, Philippa. Violin & Stringed Instruments. (Illus.). 32p. (gr. 4-7). 1993. PLB 12.40 (*0-531-17424-7*, Gloucester Pr) Watts.
Keyboard Magic: A Band in a Book. 1992. 19.95 (*0-938971-89-1*) JTG Nashville.
Krosnick, Teresa A. Scales & Arpeggios in Letter Format: One Octave, Bk. 1. 32p. (Orig.). 1992. pap. text ed. 10.00 GVC bdg. (*1-882176-00-6*) Theory Aids Keybd.
Landon, Joseph W. Music Lab. (Illus.). 182p. (Orig.). (gr. 3-8). 1982. pap. 10.95x packet & guide (*0-943988-00-4*) Music Educ Pubns.
Leanza, Frank. Music Book for Kids of Any Age, Bk. 1. rev. ed. (Illus.). 32p. (gr. 1-4). 1988. pap. 3.45 (*0-934687-02-1*) Crystal Pubs.
—Music Book for Kids of Any Age, Vol. 2. rev. ed. (Illus.). 60p. (gr. 1-4). 1988. pap. 3.45 (*0-934687-03-X*) Crystal Pubs.
McClintock, Lorene. The McClintock Piano Course: A New Experience in Learning, 11 vols. 2198p. 1992. Set, incl. keyboard concealer & interval keyblocks. wire-o bdg., slipcased 388.00 (*1-880556-70-7*) McClintock Ent.
Moncomble, Gerard. Octave & His Flute. (Illus.). 275p. (Orig.). (gr. 1-5). 1994. pap. 19.95 (*0-572-01965-3*, Pub. by W Foulsham UK) Trans-Atl Phila.
Preucil, Doris. Suzuki Viola School: Piano Accompaniments, Vol. 3. Suzuki, Shinichi, ed. 32p. (gr. k-12). 1983. pap. text ed. 6.50 (*0-87487-246-4*, Suzuki Method) Summy-Birchard.
Ransom, L. Children As Music Makers. 78p. (gr. k-3). 1979. pap. 8.00 (*0-685-51018-2*) High-Scope.
Ronnholm, Ursula O. Mi Libro de Palabras: Oraciones y Cuentos. rev. ed. Rabell, Edda, ed. & tr. Montero, Miguel, illus. (SPA.). 100p. (gr. k-6). 1989. pap. 7.00 (*0-941911-08-X*) Two Way Bilingual.
—Writing Through Music. rev. ed. Ronnholm, Paul, ed. Montero, Miguel, tr. from SPA. (Illus.). 74p. (gr. k-3). 1989. pap. text ed. 4.00 (*0-941911-09-8*) Two Way Bilingual.
Sharma, Elizabeth. Brass. LC 93-20398. (Illus.). 32p. (gr. 4-6). 1993. 14.95 (*1-56847-114-9*) Thomson Lrning.
Spieler, Benjamin D. The Student Clarinetist: A Method for Class Instruction, 3 bks. rev. ed. (Illus.). (gr. 4-9). 1989. pap. Bk. I, 56p. pap. 2.80 (*0-685-74121-4*); Bk. II, 64p. pap. 2.80 (*0-685-74122-2*); Bk. III, 36 p. pap. 2.80 (*0-685-74123-0*) Player Pr.
Suzuki, Shinichi. Note Reading for Violin. Selden, Kyoko, tr. from JPN. 112p. (gr. 1-6). 1985. pap. text ed. 14.95 (*0-87487-213-8*, Suzuki Method) Summy-Birchard.
—Suzuki Viola School: Viola Part, Vol. 3. Preucil, Doris, ed. 24p. (gr. k-12). 1983. pap. text ed. 6.50 (*0-87487-243-X*, Suzuki Method) Summy-Birchard.
—Suzuki Viola School: Viola Part, Vol. 4. Preucil, Doris, ed. 32p. (gr. k-12). 1983. pap. text ed. 6.50 (*0-87487-244-8*, Suzuki Method) Summy-Birchard.
Time-Life Inc. Editors. Art & Music. Crawford, Jean, ed. (Illus.). 88p. (gr. k-3). 1994. write for info. (*0-8094-9474-4*); PLB write for info. (*0-8094-9475-2*) Time-Life.
Vahila, Michael. Teaching Guitar to Children: A Complete Guide for Ages 5 to 12. LC 88-63797. (Illus.). 100p. (Orig.). (gr. k-7). 1988. pap. 9.95 (*0-942253-01-9*); book & cassette pkg. 18.95 (*0-942253-02-7*) PAZ Pub.

MUSIC–THEORY
see also Musical Form

Lennon, Rebecca D. Keyboard Capers: Music Theory for Children. 143p. 1993. pap. text ed. 18.95 (*1-884098-01-0*) Elijah Co.
Mercuri, Carmela. My First Theory Book: Note Names for Coloring. Smith, R. A., illus. 32p. (Orig.). (gr. 1-6). 1987. pap. text ed. 4.95 (*0-935474-20-X*) Carousel Pubns Ltd.
O'Neal, Scott. Theory on the Major Scales. (Illus.). 64p. (Orig.). 1993. pap. 6.95 (*0-8059-3414-6*) Dorrance.

MUSIC APPRECIATION
see Music–Analysis, Appreciation

MUSIC CONDUCTORS
see Conductors (Music)

MUSICAL APPRECIATION
see Music–Analysis, Appreciation

MUSICAL COMEDIES
see Musical Revues, Comedies, Etc.

MUSICAL CRITICISM
see Music–History and Criticism

MUSICAL EDUCATION
see Music–Study and Teaching

MUSICAL FORM
see also Opera

Meyer, Carolyn & Pickens, Kel. Sing & Learn. Hayes, Steve, illus. 144p. (ps-3). 1989. wkbk. 12.95 (*0-86653-476-8*, GA1078) Good Apple.

MUSICAL INSTRUCTION
see Music–Study and Teaching

MUSICAL INSTRUMENTS
see also Orchestra;
also groups of instruments, e.g. Percussion Instruments; Stringed Instruments; Wind Instruments; etc.; also names of musical instruments, e.g. Drum; etc.

ABC: Musical Instruments from the Metropolitan Museum of Art. 32p. (gr. 2 up). 1988. 12.95 (*0-8109-1878-1*) Abrams.
Ada, Alam F. A Strange Visitor - Una Extrana Visita. Escriva, Vivi, illus. (SPA & ENG.). 26p. (Orig.). (gr. k-2). 1989. English ed. 3.95 (*0-88272-802-4*); Spanish Ed. 3.95 (*0-88272-793-1*) Santillana.
Ardley, Neil. Music. King, Dave, et al, photos by. LC 88-13394. (Illus.). 64p. (gr. 5 up). 1989. 16.00 (*0-394-82259-5*); lib. bdg. 16.99 (*0-394-92259-X*) Knopf Bks Yng Read.
Bouchard, Robert. Let's Play the Recorder. (gr. 6 up). 9.95 (*0-8283-1471-3*) Branden Pub Co.
Delafosse, Claude. Musical Instruments. Grant, Donald, illus. 24p. (ps-2). 1994. 11.95 (*0-590-47729-3*, Cartwheel) Scholastic Inc.
Drew, Helen. My First Music Book. (Illus.). 48p. (gr. k-3). 1993. 12.95 (*1-56458-215-9*) Dorling Kindersley.
Elliott, Donald. Alligators & Music. Arrowood, Clinton, illus. LC 84-13862. (gr. 8). 1984. (Pub. by Gambit); pap. 8.95 (*0-87645-118-0*, Pub. by Gambit) Harvard Common Pr.
Fiarotta, Noel & Fiarotta, Phyllis. Music Crafts for Kids: The How-to Book of Music Dicovery. LC 93-24114. (Illus.). 160p. (gr. 3 up). 1993. 17.95 (*0-8069-0406-2*) Sterling.
Fichter, George S. American Indian Music & Musical Instruments. (gr. 5-10). 1978. 8.95 (*0-679-20443-1*) McKay.
Hausherr, Rosmarie. What Instrument Is This? (Illus.). 1992. 14.95 (*0-590-44644-4*, Scholastic Hardcover) Scholastic Inc.
Hawthorn, P. First Book of the Recorder. (Illus.). 64p. (gr. 2-6). 1987. pap. 8.95 (*0-7460-0069-3*) EDC.
Hewitt, Sally. Pluck & Scrape. LC 94-16939. (Illus.). 24p. (ps-3). 1994. PLB 14.40 (*0-516-07991-3*); pap. 4.95 (*0-516-47991-1*) Childrens.
Isadora, Rachel. Ben's Trumpet. Isadora, Rachel, illus. LC 78-12885. 32p. (gr. k-3). 1979. 14.00 (*0-688-80194-3*) Greenwillow.
Jackson, Michael. Making Music: Shake, Rattle & Roll with Instruments You Make Yourself. (gr. 4-7). 1993. pap. 3.95 (*0-207-17175-0*, Pub. by Angus & Robertson AT) HarpC.
Leanza, Frank. How to Get Started with the Bassoon. (Illus.). 24p. 1993. pap. 3.95 (*0-934687-10-2*) Crystal Pubs.
—How to Get Started with the Cello. (Illus.). 24p. 1993. pap. 3.95 (*0-934687-21-8*) Crystal Pubs.
—How to Get Started with the Clarinet. (Illus.). 24p. 1993. pap. 3.95 (*0-934687-09-9*) Crystal Pubs.
—How to Get Started with the Flute. (Illus.). 24p. 1993. pap. 3.95 (*0-934687-07-2*) Crystal Pubs.
—How to Get Started with the Oboe. (Illus.). 1993. pap. 3.95 (*0-934687-08-0*) Crystal Pubs.
—How to Get Started with the Saxophone. (Illus.). 24p. 1993. pap. 3.95 (*0-934687-11-0*) Crystal Pubs.
—How to Get Started with the String Bass. (Illus.). 24p. 1993. pap. 3.95 (*0-934687-22-6*) Crystal Pubs.
—How to Get Started with the Trombone. (Illus.). 28p. 1993. pap. 3.95 (*0-934687-13-7*) Crystal Pubs.
—How to Get Started with the Trumpet. (Illus.). 32p. 1993. pap. 3.95 (*0-934687-12-9*) Crystal Pubs.
—How to Get Started with the Tuba. (Illus.). 28p. 1993. pap. 3.95 (*0-934687-16-1*) Crystal Pubs.
—How to Get Started with the Viola. (Illus.). 24p. 1993. pap. 3.95 (*0-934687-20-X*) Crystal Pubs.
—How to Get Started with the Violin. (Illus.). 24p. 1993. pap. 3.95 (*0-934687-19-6*) Crystal Pubs.
Lillegard, Dee. Brass. LC 87-32990. (Illus.). 32p. (ps-3). 1988. PLB 11.80 (*0-516-02218-0*); pap. 3.95 (*0-516-42218-9*) Childrens.
—Percussion. LC 87-18217. (Illus.). 32p. (ps-3). 1987. PLB 11.80 (*0-516-02216-4*); pap. 3.95 (*0-516-42216-2*) Childrens.

—Strings. LC 87-32994. (Illus.). 32p. (ps-3). 1988. PLB 11.80 (*0-516-02219-9*); pap. 3.95 (*0-516-42219-7*) Childrens.

—Woodwinds. LC 87-18232. (Illus.). 32p. (ps-3). 1987. PLB 11.80 (*0-516-02217-2*); pap. 3.95 (*0-516-42217-0*) Childrens.

McLaughlin, Patrick F. The Practical Musical Instrument Owner's Guide Series, 4 bks. (Illus.). 40p. (gr. 7 up). 1992. Set. pap. text ed. write for info. (*1-881158-04-7*); A Practical Owner's Guide to the B flat Clarinet. pap. text ed. 5.95 (*1-881158-00-4*); A Practical Owner's Guide to the Saxophone. pap. text ed. 5.95 (*1-881158-02-0*); A Practical Owner's Guide to the Flute. pap. text ed. 5.95 (*1-881158-01-2*); A Practical Owner's Guide to the Brasswinds. pap. text ed. 5.95 (*1-881158-03-9*) Instrument Pr.

McLean, Margaret. Make Your Own Musical Instruments. Stott, Ken, illus. 32p. (gr. 4-7). 1988. PLB 14.95 (*0-8225-0895-8*, First Ave Edns); pap. 4.95 (*0-8225-9558-3*, First Ave Edns) Lerner Pubns.

Morris, Ting & Morris, Neil. Music. LC 93-20424. (Illus.). 32p. (gr. 2-4). 1993. PLB 12.40 (*0-531-14269-8*) Watts.

Music & Bugling. (Illus.). 56p. (gr. 6-12). 1990. pap. 1.85 (*0-8395-3336-5*, 33336) BSA.

Musical Instruments: From Flutes Carved of Bone, to Lutes, to Modern Electric Guitars. LC 94-9150. (gr. 4 up). 1994. write for info. (*0-590-47638-6*) Scholastic Inc.

Oates, Eddie. Garden Hose Trumpet: and 5 Other Musical Instruments You Can Make. Koelsch, Michael, illus. LC 92-20060. 32p. (gr. 2-5). 1995. 15.00 (*0-06-021478-3*); PLB 14.89 (*0-06-021479-1*) HarpC Child Bks.

Pagliaro, Michael J. The Violin. (Illus.). 60p. (gr. 4-8). 1993. wkbk. 6.95 (*1-884417-00-0*) Ardsley Pr.

Pillar, Marjorie. Join the Band! Pillar, Marjorie, illus. LC 90-23261. 32p. (gr. 1-3). 1992. PLB 14.89 (*0-06-021829-0*) HarpC Child Bks.

Poffenberger, Nancy. Instant Recorder Fun: Book One. 32p. (gr. 4). 1986. pap. 4.95 (*0-938293-14-1*) Fun Pub OH.

—Instant Recorder Fun Package 1 (recorder & book) 32p. (ps-3). 1986. Repr. of 1983 ed. blister-pak pkg. 10.95 (*0-938293-15-X*) Fun Pub OH.

Recorder Fun with Disney Favorites. (ps-3). 1990. pap. 14.95 (*0-7935-0295-0*, HL660210) H Leonard.

Sharma, Elizabeth. Keyboards. LC 93-12819. (Illus.). 32p. (gr. 4-6). 1993. 14.95 (*1-56847-117-3*) Thomson Lrning.

Shipton, Alyn. Keyboards. LC 93-16637. (Illus.). 32p. (gr. 5-8). 1993. PLB 19.97 (*0-8114-2318-2*) Raintree Steck-V.

Staples, Danny & Mahoney, Carole. Flutes, Reeds, & Trumpets. LC 92-5165. (Illus.). 48p. (gr. 2-6). 1992. PLB 14.40 (*1-56294-092-9*) Millbrook Pr.

Suzuki, Shinichi. Suzuki Cello School: Piano Accompaniment, Vol. 5. 24p. (gr. k-12). 1983. pap. text ed. 6.50 (*0-87487-270-7*, Suzuki Method) Summy-Birchard.

—Suzuki Cello School, Vol. 4: Cello Part. 16p. (gr. k-12). 1983. pap. text ed. 6.50 (*0-87487-266-9*, Suzuki Method) Summy-Birchard.

—Suzuki Cello School, Vol. 4: Piano Accompaniment. 24p. (gr. k-12). 1983. pap. text ed. 6.50 (*0-87487-269-3*, Suzuki Method) Summy-Birchard.

—Suzuki Cello School, Vol. 5: Cello Part. 24p. (gr. k-12). 1983. pap. text ed. 6.50 (*0-87487-267-7*, Suzuki Method) Summy-Birchard.

—Suzuki Cello School, Vol 6: Cello Part. 16p. (gr. k-12). 1984. pap. text ed. 6.50 (*0-87487-268-5*, Suzuki Method) Summy-Birchard.

—Suzuki Cello School, Vol. 6: Piano Accompaniments. 24p. (Orig.). (gr. 6-12). 1984. pap. text ed. 6.50 (*0-87487-271-5*, Suzuki Method) Summy-Birchard.

—Suzuki Viola School: Piano Accompaniments, Vol. 4. Preucil, Doris, ed. 64p. (gr. k-12). 1983. pap. text ed. 10.95 (*0-87487-275-8*, Suzuki Method) Summy-Birchard.

Walther, Tom. Make Mine Music. Walther, Tom, illus. 128p. (Orig.). (gr. 3 up). 1981. pap. 10.95 (*0-316-92112-2*) Little.

Ward, Alan. Sound & Music. LC 92-370. 1993. 11.40 (*0-531-14237-X*) Watts.

Wiseman, Ann. Making Musical Things: Improvised Instruments. Wiseman, Ann, illus. LC 79-4474. 64p. (gr. 3 up). 1979. SBE 14.95 (*0-684-16114-1*, Scribners Young Read) Macmillan Child Grp.

MUSICAL NOTATION

Hoenack, Peg. Let's Sing & Play: Easy-to-Learn Letter Notation Method for Recorder, "Flutes," Keyboard. 4th ed. Morris, Alix & Hayden, Marilyn, illus. 64p. (gr. 2-7). 1991. student easel book, wire binding 5.50 (*0-913500-43-7*, L-1); Set 1, for teaching 32 songs. transparencies for overhead projector 64.00 (*0-913500-40-2*, L-8) Peg Hoenack MusicWorks.

Hoenack, Peg & Jones, Kay. Let's Sing & Play Carols & Holiday Songs: Thanksgiving, Hanukkah, Christmas, New Year's: Easy-to-Read Letter Notation for Recorder, "Flutes," Piano, any Melody Instrument. 2nd ed. Morris, Alix & Hayden, Marilyn, illus. 48p. (gr. 2-7). 1978. pap. text ed. 4.95 (*0-913500-18-6*, L-3) Peg Hoenack MusicWorks.

—Let's Sing & Play While Learning Rhythm Notation, Bk. 2-R: Easy Transition from Letter Notes to Rhythm Symbols. 2nd ed. Morris, Alix & Hayden, Marilyn, illus. 32p. (gr. 2-7). 1992. A-frame easel book with wire binding 5.50 (*0-913500-44-5*, L-2R) Peg Hoenack MusicWorks.

MUSICAL REVUES, COMEDIES, ETC.

Brooks, Hindi. Captain Noah. (Illus.). 36p. (Orig.). (gr. 1 up). 1989. pap. 4.00 bk. (*0-88680-317-9*); Piano-Vocal Score 15.00 (*0-88680-318-7*); royalty on application 60.00 (*0-685-58559-X*) I E Clark.

Carey, Karla. Julie & Jackie at the Circus: The Play & Musical Play (with Music Book, Story-&-Song Cassette & Piano Cassette) Nolan, Dennis, illus. LC 88-12910. 44p. 1990. pap. 35.00 complete pkg. (*1-55768-152-X*); pap. 25.00 book only (*1-55768-177-5*); story-&-song or piano cass. 8.00 (*1-55768-027-2*) LC Pub.

Church, Jeff. Dick Whittington & His Cat: A Musical Play Based on an English Folk Tale. (Illus.). 56p. (Orig.). (ps-7). 1990. pap. 4.00 (*0-88680-340-3*); piano/vocal score 10.00 (*0-88680-341-1*); royalty on application 50.00 (*0-685-58895-5*) I E Clark.

Crabtree, Paul. I Sincerely Doubt That This Old House Is Very Haunted: Musical. 1968. 4.50 (*0-87602-142-9*) Anchorage.

Daniel, Rebecca & Jones, Kathy. Night of Wonder Musical. (Illus.). 48p. (ps-7). 1992. incl. tape 16.95 (*0-685-50800-5*, SS2841, Shining Star Pubns); 7.95 (*0-86653-705-8*, SS2841, Shining Star Pubns); tape 10.95 (*0-685-50801-3*, SS2842, Shining Star Pubns) Good Apple.

—Noah & Company Musical. (Illus.). 48p. (ps-7). 1992. incl. tape 16.95 (*0-685-50798-X*, SS2839, Shining Star Pubns); 7.95 (*0-86653-704-X*, SS2839, Shining Star Pubns); tape 10.95 (*0-685-50799-8*, SS2840, Shining Star Pubns) Good Apple.

Downey, Michael. Tall Boys: The Rock-n-Roll Musical That Explores Teen-Age Drinking & Driving. Schultz, Paul, contrib. by. (Illus.). 68p. (Orig.). (gr. 7-12). 1990. pap. 4.50 (*0-88680-338-1*); guitar/percussion/vocal score 15.00 (*0-88680-339-X*); royalty on application 75.00 (*0-685-58902-1*) I E Clark.

Egner, Thorbjorn. People & Robbers of Cardemon Town: Musical. 1968. 4.50 (*0-87602-172-0*) Anchorage.

Graczyk, Ed. Aesop's Falables: Musical. 1969. 4.50 (*0-87602-100-3*) Anchorage.

—Runaway: Musical. (gr. 7-12). 1973. 4.50 (*0-87602-196-8*) Anchorage.

Harder, Eleanor & Harder, Ray. Good Grief, a Griffin: Musical. 1968. 4.50 (*0-87602-131-3*) Anchorage.

Harris, Aurand. Just So Stories: Musical. 1971. 4.50 (*0-87602-145-3*) Anchorage.

—The Plain Princess: Musical. 1955. 4.50 (*0-87602-176-3*) Anchorage.

—Steal Away Home: Musical. (gr. 1-9). 1972. 4.50 (*0-87602-206-9*) Anchorage.

—Yankee Doodle: Musical. (gr. 1-7). 1975. 4.50 (*0-87602-223-9*) Anchorage.

Mueller, Tobin J. Danger, Dinosaurs! A Musical Comedy about the Evolution & Extinction of the Dinosaurs. Heller, Joe, illus. (ps-8). 1990. Audio tape incl. pap. 14.95 (*1-56213-003-X*) Ctr Stage Prodns.

—Music of the Planet: A Musical Journey about the World & Wonders of Our Solar System. (ps-8). 1990. pap. 14.95 (*1-56213-017-X*) Ctr Stage Prodns.

—Say Yes! to Life: A Musical Drama about the Dangers Drugs Pose to the Joys of Living. Patros, Ann & Patros, Dan, photos by. (Illus.). (gr. 4-9). 1990. Audio tape incl. pap. 14.95 (*1-56213-045-5*) Ctr Stage Prodns.

—The Sound of Money: A Musical Adventure about Economics & the Building of Community. Vanderlinden, Kathy, illus. (ps-8). Audio tape incl. pap. 14.95 (*1-56213-031-5*) Ctr Stage Prodns.

—To Save the Planet: A Musical Fable about the Global Environment & What We Can Do to Help. Heller, Joe, illus. 54p. (gr. 4-9). 1991. Inc. audio cass. pap. 14.95 (*1-56213-078-1*) Ctr Stage Prodns.

Pickering, Ken, et al. The Inside Story. 24p. (Orig.). 1992. pap. 4.00 (*0-88680-371-3*) I E Clark.

Pulaski High School Drama Club Staff & Mueller, Tobin J. I Want to Know! A Musical Time Line about the History of Science & Invention. Heller, Joe, et al, illus. 55p. (gr. 4-12). 1991. 14.95 (*1-56213-059-5*) Ctr Stage Prodns.

Staskowski, Andrea. Movie Musicals. (Illus.). 80p. (gr. 5-12). 1992. PLB 18.95 (*0-8225-1639-X*) Lerner Pubns.

Wright, Carol L. Pegora the Witch: Musical. (gr. 1-7). 1966. 4.50 (*0-87602-171-2*) Anchorage.

MUSICIANS

see also Black Musicians; Composers; Conductors (Music); Pianists; Singers; Violinists, Violoncellists, Etc.

Andres Segovia. (ps-3). 1993. 18.95 (*0-7910-1697-8*) Chelsea Hse.

Barboza, Ronald, ed. A Salute to Cape Verdean Musicians & Their Music. (Illus.). 48p. (gr. 9-12). 1989. pap. 10.00 (*0-9627637-0-5*) D&C Cape Verdeans.

Bradman, Tony. John Lennon. (Illus.). 64p. (gr. 5-9). 1991. 11.95 (*0-237-60021-8*, Pub. by Evans Bros Ltd) Trafalgar.

Brewer, Chris. Musicians. rev. ed. 96p. (gr. 2-6). 1992. pap. text ed. 14.95 (*0-913705-37-3*) Zephyr Pr AZ.

Clinton, Susan. Live Aid. LC 92-33423. (Illus.). 32p. (gr. 3-6). 1993. PLB 12.30 (*0-516-06665-X*); pap. 3.95 (*0-516-46665-8*) Childrens.

Conord, Bruce W. John Lennon. LC 92-39113. (Illus.). 1994. 18.95 (*0-7910-1739-7*, Am Art Analog); pap. 7.95 (*0-7910-1740-0*, Am Art Analog) Chelsea Hse.

Cunningham, Elaine. Haldor Lillenas: The Marvelous Music Maker. (Illus.). 72p. (Orig.). (gr. 5-6). 1992. pap. 4.95 (*0-8341-1443-7*) Beacon Hill.

Danwick, Chad. Marky Mark: Who's Hot! 48p. (gr. 4-7). 1992. pap. 1.49 (*0-440-21379-7*) Dell.

Gourse, Leslie. Dizzy Gillespie & the Birth of Bebop. LC 93-30222. (Illus.). 160p. (gr. 7 up). 1994. SBE 14.95 (*0-689-31869-3*, Atheneum Child Bk) Macmillan Child Grp.

Grey, Charlotte. Bob Geldof: Champion of Africa's Hungry People. Adrian-Vallance, D'Arcy, adapted by. LC 89-77588. (Illus.). 64p. (gr. 3-4). 1990. PLB 19.93 (*0-8368-0391-4*) Gareth Stevens Inc.

Hamilton, Sue. The Killing of a Rock Star: John Lennon. Hamilton, John, ed. LC 89-84907. (Illus.). 32p. (gr. 4). 1989. PLB 11.96 (*0-939179-59-8*) Abdo & Dghtrs.

Hargrove, Jim. Pablo Casals: Cellist of Conscience. LC 90-21047. (Illus.). 152p. (gr. 4 up). 1991. PLB 14.40 (*0-516-03272-0*); pap. 5.95 (*0-516-43272-9*) Childrens.

Jones, Davy & Green, Alan. Monkees, Memories & Media Madness. Kirshner, Don, frwd. by. (Illus.). 176p. (gr. 9 up). 1992. 39.95 (*0-9631235-1-3*); pap. 29.95 (*0-9631235-0-5*) Click Pub.

Loewen, Nancy. Profiles in Music, 6 bks, Reading Level 6. (Illus.). 602p. (gr. 5 up). 1989. Set. PLB 111.60 (*0-86592-604-2*); 83.70s.p. (*0-685-58764-9*) Rourke Corp.

Mabery, D L. Prince. (Illus.). 48p. (gr. 4-9). 1985. PLB 13.50 (*0-8225-1603-9*) Lerner Pubns.

May, Chris. Bob Geldof. (Illus.). 64p. (gr. 5-9). 1991. 11.95 (*0-237-60031-5*, Pub. by Evans Bros Ltd) Trafalgar.

Medearis, Angela S. Little Louis & the Jazz Band: The Story of Louis "Satchmo" Armstrong. Rich, Ann, illus. LC 93-23596. 1994. write for info. (*0-525-67424-1*, Lodestar Bks) Dutton Child Bks.

Monceaux, Morgan. Jazz: My Music, My People. Monceaux, Morgan, illus. Marsalis, Wynton, intro. by. (Illus.). 64p. (gr. 4 up). 1994. 18.00 (*0-679-85618-8*) Knopf Bks Yng Read.

Moriarty, Mary & Sweeney, Catherine. Bob Geldof. LC 89-50965. (Illus.). 80p. (Orig.). (gr. 9-12). 1990. pap. 8.95 (*0-86278-163-9*, Pub. by O'Brien Press Ltd Eire) Dufour.

New Kids on the Block Trivia Quiz Book. 64p. (gr. 4-7). 1990. pap. 1.95 (*0-8167-2227-7*) Troll Assocs.

Oleksy, Walter. Musicians. (Illus.). 128p. (gr. 3-6). Date not set. 19.95 (*0-685-57489-X*) Capstone Pr.

Paige, David. A Day in the Life of a Rock Musician. Ruhlin, Roger, photos by. LC 78-68808. (Illus.). 32p. (gr. 4-8). 1980. PLB 11.79 (*0-89375-225-8*); pap. 2.95 (*0-89375-229-0*) Troll Assocs.

Raschka, Chris. Charlie Parker Played Be Bop. LC 91-38420. (Illus.). 32p. (ps-1). 1992. 13.95 (*0-531-05999-5*); PLB 13.99 (*0-531-08599-6*) Orchard Bks Watts.

Rowley, Kay. Rock Stars. LC 91-15077. (Illus.). 32p. (gr. 5). 1992. text ed. 13.95 RSBE (*0-89686-713-7*, Crestwood Hse) Macmillan Child Grp.

Saunders, Susan. Dolly Parton: Country Goin' to Town. LC 85-40440. (Illus.). 56p. (gr. 2-6). 1985. pap. 10.95 (*0-670-80787-7*) Viking Child Bks.

Scott, Ricardo. Reggae - the Man Who Named the Music: Why Do the Heathen Rage. (Illus.). 73p. (Orig.). Date not set. pap. write for info. (*1-883427-25-8*) Crnerstone GA.

MUSICIANS, AMERICAN

Bernotas, Bob. Branford Marsalis: Jazz Musician. LC 93-47358. (Illus.). 112p. (gr. 6 up). 1994. lib. bdg. 17.95 (*0-89490-495-7*) Enslow Pubs.

Crocker, Chris. Cyndi Lauper. Arico, Diane, ed. (Illus.). 64p. (gr. 3-7). 1985. 9.29 (*0-685-09958-X*) S&S Trade.

Frankl, Ron. Bruce Springsteen. LC 93-1850. (gr. 7 up). 1994. 18.95 (*0-7910-2327-3*, Am Art Analog); pap. write for info. (*0-7910-2352-4*, Am Art Analog) Chelsea Hse.

Greenberg, Keith E. Madonna. LC 85-18030. (Illus.). 40p. (gr. 4-9). 1986. lib. bdg. 13.50 (*0-8225-1606-3*) Lerner Pubns.

Stefoff, Rebecca. Gloria Estefan. (Illus.). 104p. (gr. 5 up). 1991. lib. bdg. 17.95 (*0-7910-1244-1*) Chelsea Hse.

Tallman, Edward. Garth Brooks: Straight from the Heart. LC 93-10214. (Illus.). 72p. (gr. 3 up). 1993. text ed. 13.95 RSBE (*0-87518-595-9*, Dillon) Macmillan Child Grp.

Wallner, Rosemary. Wynonna Judd. LC 91-73037. 202p. 1991. 12.94 (*1-56239-056-2*) Abdo & Dghtrs.

MUSICIANS, BLACK

see Black Musicians

MUSICIANS–FICTION

Bell, Mary S. Sonata for Mind & Heart. LC 91-20588. 224p. (gr. 7 up). 1992. SBE 14.95 (*0-689-31734-4*, Atheneum Child Bk) Macmillan Child Grp.

Brett, Jan. Berlioz the Bear. LC 90-37634. (Illus.). 32p. 1991. 14.95 (*0-399-22248-0*, Putnam) Putnam Pub Group.

Carlson, Nancy. Harriet's Recital. Carlson, Nancy, illus. (gr. k-3). 1985. bk. & cassette 19.95 (*0-941078-69-8*); pap. 12.95 bk. & cassette (*0-941078-67-1*); cassette, 4 paperbacks & guide 27.95 (*0-941078-68-X*) Live Oak Media.

Cartwright, Pauline. Jimmy Parker's New Job. Hunnam, Lucinda, illus. LC 93-20029. 1994. pap. write for info. (*0-383-03679-8*) SRA Schl Grp.

Coco, Eugene B. The Fiddler's Son. Sabuda, Robert, illus. 32p. 1991. pap. 5.95 (*0-88138-111-X*, Green Tiger) S&S Trade.
Day, Betsy. Stefan & Olga. Day, Betsy, illus. LC 89-23647. 32p. (ps-3). 1991. 12.95 (*0-8037-0816-5*); PLB 12.89 (*0-8037-0817-3*) Dial Bks Young.
Goodman, Joan E. Songs from Home. LC 93-46248. (gr. 5 up). 1994. 10.95 (*0-15-203590-7*); pap. 4.95 (*0-15-203591-5*) HarBrace.
Greenwald, Sheila. Here's Hermione: A Rosy Cole Production. (Illus.). (gr. 3-7). 1991. 13.95 (*0-316-32715-8*) Little.
Griffith, Helen V. Alex & the Cat. Low, Joseph, illus. LC 81-11608. 64p. (gr. 1-3). 1982. 13.95 (*0-688-00420-2*); PLB 13.88 (*0-688-00421-0*) Greenwillow.
Gross, Ruth B. The Bremen-Town Musicians. Kent, Jack, illus. 32p. (Orig.). (ps-2). 1985. pap. 2.50 (*0-590-42364-9*) Scholastic Inc.
Haas, Jessie. Keeping Barney. LC 81-7029. 160p. (gr. 5-9). 1982. reinforced bdg. 11.75 (*0-688-00859-3*) Greenwillow.
Hill, Elizabeth S. The Banjo Player. 160p. (gr. 5-9). 1993. 14.99 (*0-670-84967-7*) Viking Child Bks.
Keller, Holly. Cromwell's Glasses. Keller, Holly, illus. LC 81-6644. 32p. (gr. k-3). 1982. 14.95 (*0-688-00834-8*) Greenwillow.
Kovacs, Deborah. Brewster's Courage. Mathieu, Joe, illus. LC 91-21481. 112p. (gr. 2-6). 1992. pap. 14.00 jacketed, 3-pc. bdg. (*0-671-74016-4*, S&S BFYR) S&S Trade.
Kraus, Robert. Musical Max. LC 89-7707. (ps-3). 1992. pap. 5.95 (*0-671-79250-4*, S&S BFYR) S&S Trade.
Krementz, Jill. Very Young Musician. LC 90-1001. 48p. (gr. 4-7). 1992. pap. 5.95 (*0-671-79251-2*, S&S BFYR) S&S Trade.
Kuskin, Karla. The Philharmonic Gets Dressed. LC 81-48658. (Illus.). 48p. (gr. k-3). 1982. 14.00 (*0-06-023622-1*); PLB 13.89 (*0-06-023623-X*) HarpC Child Bks.
Landis, James D. The Band Never Dances. LC 88-28401. 288p. (gr. 7 up). 1989. PLB 13.89 (*0-06-023722-8*) HarpC Child Bks.
Lawlor, Laurie. George on His Own. Tucker, Kathleen, ed. Gowing, Toby, illus. 144p. (gr. 3-7). 1993. 11.95g (*0-8075-2823-4*) A Whitman.
Levoy, Myron. Kelly 'n' Me. LC 91-35807. 208p. (gr. 7 up). 1992. 15.00 (*0-06-020838-4*); PLB 14.89 (*0-06-020839-2*) HarpC Child Bks.
London, Jonathan. Hip Cat. Hubbard, Woodleigh, illus. LC 93-1179. 1993. 13.95 (*0-8118-0315-5*) Chronicle Bks.
McKee, David. The Sad Story of Veronica Who Played the Violin. (Illus.). 32p. (gr. k-4). 1991. 10.95 (*0-916291-37-5*) Kane-Miller Bk.
Major, Kevin. Dear Bruce Springsteen. (gr. k-12). 1989. pap. 3.25 (*0-440-20410-0*) Dell.
Marino, Jan. The Day That Elvis Came to Town. 208p. (gr. 5). 1993. pap. 3.50 (*0-380-71672-0*, Camelot) Avon.
Okimoto, Jean D. Talent Night. LC 93-34591. 1995. 13.95 (*0-590-47809-5*) Scholastic Inc.
Plemons, Marti. Scott & the Ogre. (Illus.). 128p. (gr. 3-6). 1992. pap. 4.99 (*0-87403-688-7*, 24-03728) Standard Pub.
Rayner, Mary. Garth Pig Steals the Show. Rayner, Mary, illus. LC 92-24508. (ps-3). 1993. 13.99 (*0-525-45023-8*, DCB) Dutton Child Bks.
Schroeder, Alan. Satchmo's Blues. Cooper, Floyd, illus. LC 93-41082. 1995. write for info. (*0-385-32046-9*) Doubleday.
Sebastian, John. J.B.'s Harmonica. LC 91-35841. (ps-3). 1993. 13.95 (*0-15-240091-5*) HarBrace.
Tornqvist, Rita. The Old Musician. Tornqvist, Marit, illus. LC 93-664. 1993. Repr. 13.00 (*91-29-62244-1*, Pub. by R & S Bks) FS&G.
Trist, Alan. The Water of Life: A Tale of the Grateful Dead. Carpenter, Jim, illus. 52p. (gr. 2-12). 1990. PLB 12.95 (*0-938493-12-4*) Hulogosi Inc.
Voigt, Cynthia. Orfe. LC 91-46058. 128p. (gr. 9 up). 1992. SBE 12.95 (*0-689-31771-9*, Atheneum Child Bk) Macmillan Child Grp.
Weik, Mary H. The Jazz Man. 2nd ed. Grifalconi, Ann, illus. LC 93-9965. 48p. (gr. 3-7). 1993. pap. 3.95 (*0-689-71767-9*, Aladdin) Macmillan Child Grp.
Wolff, Virginia E. The Mozart Season. LC 90-23635. 208p. (gr. 6 up). 1991. 15.95 (*0-8050-1571-X*, Bks Young Read) H Holt & Co.

MUSICIANS, NEGRO
see Black Musicians

MUSK-OX
George, Michael. Musk-Oxen. 32p. 1991. 15.95 (*0-89565-721-X*) Childs World.

MUSKRATS
Arnosky, Jim. Come out, Muskrats. Arnosky, Jim, illus. LC 88-26611. 40p. (ps-3). 1989. 12.95 (*0-688-05457-9*); PLB 12.88 (*0-688-05458-7*) Lothrop.

MUSKRATS–FICTION
Burgess, Thornton. Jerry Muskrat at Home. 1986. Repr. lib. bdg. 17.95 (*0-89966-527-6*) Buccaneer Bks.
Burgess, Thornton W. Jerry Muskrat at Home. 18.95 (*0-8488-0399-X*) Amereon Ltd.
Oana, Katherine. Minnie Muskrat. Baird, Tate, ed. Butrick, Lyn M., illus. LC 88-51856. 16p. (Orig.). (ps-k). 1989. pap. 4.52 (*0-914127-10-1*) Univ Class.

MUSLIMS, BLACK
see Black Muslims

MUSLIMS–FICTION
Clyde, Ahmad. Cheng Ho's Voyage. Durkee, Noura, illus. LC 81-66951. 32p. (Orig.). (gr. 3-7). 1981. pap. 2.00 (*0-89259-021-1*) Am Trust Pubns.

MUSSOLINI, BENITO, 1883-1945
Italia, Bob. Benito Mussolini. Walner, Rosemary, ed. LC 90-82618. (Illus.). 32p. (gr. 4). 1990. PLB 11.96 (*0-939179-81-4*) Abdo & Dghtrs.
Mulvihill, Margaret. Mussolini: And Italian Fascism. (Illus.). 64p. (gr. 5-8). 1990. PLB 12.40 (*0-531-17253-8*) Watts.

MUTATION (BIOLOGY)
see Evolution

MYCOLOGY
see Fungi

MYSTERIES AND MIRACLE PLAYS
Bonica, Diane. Biblical Easter & Spring Performances. (Illus.). 96p. (ps-2). 1989. 10.95 (*0-86653-478-4*, SS1869, Shining Star Pubns) Good Apple.
Cheasebro, Margaret. The Prodigal Son & Other Parables As Plays. LC 92-7232. (gr. 5 up). 1993. 6.99 (*0-8054-6065-9*) Broadman.
Daniel, Rebecca. Three-Minute Bible Skits & Songs. 96p. (gr. 1-7). 1991. 10.95 (*0-86653-628-0*, SS1885, Shining Star Pubns) Good Apple.
Daniel, Rebecca, compiled by. Biblical Christmas Performances. 96p. (ps-8). 1988. 10.95 (*0-86653-461-X*, SS1868, Shining Star Pubns) Good Apple.
—Biblical Christmas Plays & Musicals. 96p. (ps-8). 1989. 10.95 (*0-86653-513-6*, SS1871, Shining Star Pubns) Good Apple.
—Biblical Performances for Early Childhood. 96p. (ps-1). 1990. 10.95 (*0-86653-548-9*, SS1872, Shining Star Pubns) Good Apple.
Davidson, Josephine. The Old Testament: Ten Plays for Readers' Theater. Starr, Fiona, illus. LC 92-90957. 189p. (Orig.). (gr. 6-8). 1992. pap. text ed. write for info. (*0-9628252-1-2*) Right Bk.
Glavich, Mary K. Gospel Plays for Students: Thirty-Six Scripts for Education & Worship. LC 89-50562. (Illus.). 112p. 1989. 12.95 (*0-89622-407-4*) Twenty-Third.
Keene, Carolyn. Deadly Intent. 155p. (gr. 5-8). 1991. pap. 3.75 (*0-671-74611-1*, Archway) PB.
Schera, Judith, et al. Biblical Performances for Vacation Bible School. 96p. (gr. 1-8). 1991. 10.95 (*0-86653-578-0*, Shining Star Pubns) Good Apple.
Scherra, J., et al. Biblical Puppet Performances. 96p. (ps-8). 1990. 10.95 (*0-86653-549-7*, SS1873, Shining Star Pubns) Good Apple.
Steiger, Brad. Beyond Belief: Strange, True Mysteries of the Unknown. 176p. (gr. 5 up). 1992. pap. 2.95 (*0-590-44252-X*) Scholastic Inc.
Williams, Guy. The Burning Fiery Furnace: Shadrach, Meshach, & Abednego. LC 91-52608. (Orig.). 1991. pap. 5.00 play script (*0-88734-413-5*) Players Pr.

MYSTERY AND DETECTIVE STORIES
Ables. Mystery on the Delta. (gr. 7 up). PLB 7.19 (*0-8313-0001-9*) Lantern.
Adams, Laurie & Coudert, Allison. Alice Investigates. 96p. (Orig.). 1987. pap. 2.75 (*0-553-15485-0*, Skylark) Bantam.
—Alice Whipple, Fifth Grade Detective. (ps-7). 1987. pap. 2.25 (*0-317-64197-2*, Skylark) Bantam.
Adkins, Jan. Solstice: A Mystery of the Season. Adkins, Jan, illus. 128p. 1990. 12.95 (*0-8027-6970-5*); lib. bdg. 13.85 reinforced (*0-8027-6971-3*) Walker & Co.
Adler, C. S. Footsteps on the Stairs. LC 81-15146. 160p. (gr. 4-6). 1982. pap. 12.95 (*0-385-28303-2*) Delacorte.
—Footsteps on the Stairs. 160p. (gr. 5-9). 1984. pap. 2.25 (*0-440-42654-5*, YB) Dell.
Adler, David A. Cam Jansen & the Mystery at the Haunted House. Natti, Susanna, illus. 64p. (gr. 2-5). 1992. PLB 11.00 (*0-670-83419-X*) Viking Child Bks.
—Cam Jansen & the Mystery at the Monkey House. Natti, Susanna, illus. LC 85-40443. 56p. (gr. 2-4). 1985. pap. 10.95 (*0-670-80782-6*) Viking Child Bks.
—Cam Jansen & the Mystery at the Monkey House. Natti, Susanna, illus. LC 93-13047. 64p. (gr. 2-5). 1993. pap. 3.99 (*0-14-036023-9*, Puffin) Puffin Bks.
—Cam Jansen & the Mystery Corn Popper. Natti, Susanna, illus. 64p. (gr. 2-5). 1986. pap. 10.95 (*0-670-81118-1*) Viking Child Bks.
—Cam Jansen & the Mystery Monster Movie. Natti, Susanna, illus. LC 83-16693. 64p. (gr. 2-5). 1984. pap. 10.95 (*0-670-20035-2*) Viking Child Bks.
—Cam Jansen & the Mystery of Flight 54. Natti, Susanna, illus. 64p. (gr. 2-5). 1989. pap. 10.95 (*0-670-81841-0*) Viking Child Bks.
—Cam Jansen & the Mystery of Flight 54. Natti, Susanna, illus. 64p. (gr. 2-5). 1992. pap. 3.99 (*0-14-036104-9*, Puffin) Puffin Bks.
—Cam Jansen & the Mystery of the Babe Ruth Baseball. Natti, Susanna, illus. LC 82-2621. 64p. (gr. 2-5). 1982. pap. 11.00 (*0-670-20037-9*) Viking Child Bks.
—Cam Jansen & the Mystery of the Babe Ruth Baseball. (gr. 4-7). 1991. pap. 3.99 (*0-14-034895-6*, Puffin) Puffin Bks.
—Cam Jansen & the Mystery of the Carnival Prize. (gr. k-6). 1987. pap. 2.99 (*0-440-41202-1*, YB) Dell.
—Cam Jansen & the Mystery of the Carnival Prize. Natti, Susanna, illus. 64p. (gr. 2-5). 1992. pap. 3.99 (*0-14-036022-0*) Puffin Bks.
—Cam Jansen & the Mystery of the Circus Clown. Natti, Susanna, illus. LC 82-50363. 64p. (gr. 2-4). 1983. pap. 10.95 (*0-670-20036-0*) Viking Child Bks.
—Cam Jansen & the Mystery of the Circus Clown. Natti, Susanna, illus. 64p. (gr. 1-4). 1985. pap. 2.75 (*0-440-41021-5*, YB) Dell.
—Cam Jansen & the Mystery of the Circus Clown. (gr. 4-7). 1991. pap. 3.99 (*0-14-034897-2*, Puffin) Puffin Bks.
—Cam Jansen & the Mystery of the Dinosaur Bones. Natti, Susanna, illus. LC 80-25132. 64p. (gr. 2-5). 1981. pap. 11.99 (*0-670-20040-9*) Viking Child Bks.
—Cam Jansen & the Mystery of the Dinosaur Bones. Natti, Susanna, illus. (gr. 1-4). 1983. pap. 2.75 (*0-440-41199-8*, YB) Dell.
—Cam Jansen & the Mystery of the Dinosaur Bones. Natti, Susanna, illus. 64p. (gr. 2-5). 1991. pap. 3.99 (*0-14-034674-0*, Puffin) Puffin Bks.
—Cam Jansen & the Mystery of the Gold Coins. Natti, Susanna, illus. LC 81-16158. 64p. (gr. 2-5). 1982. pap. 10.95 (*0-670-20038-7*) Viking Child Bks.
—Cam Jansen & the Mystery of the Gold Coins. (gr. 4-7). 1991. pap. 3.99 (*0-14-034896-4*, Puffin) Puffin Bks.
—Cam Jansen & the Mystery of the Haunted House, No. 13. Natti, Susanna, illus. 64p. (gr. 2-5). 1994. pap. 3.99 (*0-14-034478-0*) Puffin Bks.
—Cam Jansen & the Mystery of the Monster Movie. Natti, Susanna, illus. 64p. (gr. 2-5). 1992. pap. 3.99 (*0-14-036021-2*) Puffin Bks.
—Cam Jansen & the Mystery of the Stolen Corn Popper. Natti, Susanna, illus. 64p. (gr. 2-5). 1992. pap. 3.99 (*0-14-036103-0*, Puffin) Puffin Bks.
—Cam Jansen & the Mystery of the Stolen Diamonds. Natti, Susanna, illus. LC 79-20695. 64p. (gr. 2-5). 1980. pap. 10.95 (*0-670-20039-5*) Viking Child Bks.
—Cam Jansen & the Mystery of the Stolen Diamonds. Natti, Susanna, illus. (gr. 1-4). 1982. pap. 2.75 (*0-440-41111-4*, YB) Dell.
—Cam Jansen & the Mystery of the Stolen Diamonds. Natti, Susanna, illus. 64p. (gr. 2-5). 1991. pap. 3.99 (*0-14-034670-8*, Puffin) Puffin Bks.
—Cam Jansen & the Mystery of the Television Dog. Natti, Susanna, illus. LC 81-2207. 64p. (gr. 2-5). 1981. pap. 10.95 (*0-670-20042-5*) Viking Child Bks.
—Cam Jansen & the Mystery of the Television Dog. Natti, Susanna, illus. 64p. (gr. 1-4). 1983. pap. 2.75 (*0-440-41196-3*, YB) Dell.
—Cam Jansen & the Mystery of the Television Dog. Natti, Susanna, illus. 64p. (gr. 2-5). 1991. pap. 3.99 (*0-14-034676-7*, Puffin) Puffin Bks.
—Cam Jansen & the Mystery of the U. F. O. Natti, Susanna, illus. LC 80-15580. 64p. (gr. 7-10). 1980. pap. 10.95 (*0-670-20041-7*) Viking Child Bks.
—Cam Jansen & the Mystery of the U. F. O. Natti, Susanna, illus. 64p. (gr. 2-5). 1991. pap. 3.99 (*0-14-034672-4*, Puffin) Puffin Bks.
—The Cam Jansen Fun Book. Natti, Susanna, illus. 32p. (gr. 2-5). 1992. pap. 3.99 (*0-14-034490-X*, Puffin) Puffin Bks.
—The Fourth Floor Twins & the Fish Snitch Mystery. Trivas, Irene, illus. 64p. (gr. 1-4). 1986. pap. 3.99 (*0-14-032082-2*, Puffin) Puffin Bks.
—The Fourth Floor Twins & the Fortune Cookie Chase. Trivas, Irene, illus. 64p. (gr. 1-4). 1986. pap. 3.95 (*0-14-032083-0*, Puffin) Puffin Bks.
—The Fourth Floor Twins & the Silver Ghost Express. Trivas, Irene, illus. (gr. 2-5). 1987. pap. 4.99 (*0-14-032215-9*, Puffin) Puffin Bks.
—Onion Sundaes: A Houdini Club Magic Mystery. Malone, Heather H., illus. LC 93-5878. 80p. (Orig.). (gr. 1-4). 1994. PLB 9.99 (*0-679-94697-7*); pap. 2.99 (*0-679-84697-2*) Random Bks Yng Read.
—T. F. Benson & the Detective Dog Mystery. (gr. 4-7). 1993. pap. 3.25 (*0-553-15982-8*) Bantam.
—T. F. Benson & the Dinosaur Madness Mystery. (gr. 4-7). 1992. pap. 2.99 (*0-553-15980-1*) Bantam.
—T. F. Benson & the Eye Spy Mystery. (gr. 4-7). 1993. pap. 3.25 (*0-553-15981-X*) Bantam.
—T. F. Benson & the Funny Money Mystery. (gr. 4-7). 1992. pap. 2.99 (*0-553-15979-8*) Bantam.
—Wacky Jacks: A Houdini Club Magic Mystery. Malone, Heather H., illus. LC 93-51259. 80p. (Orig.). (gr. 1-4). 1994. PLB 2.99 (*0-679-84696-4*); pap. 9.99 (*0-679-94696-9*) Random.
Adorjan, Carol. The Copy Cat Mystery. 128p. 1990. pap. 2.95 (*0-380-75743-5*, Camelot) Avon.
Adrian, Mary. The Fireball Mystery. Lonette, Reisie, illus. LC 77-17151. (gr. 2-6). 1977. 8.95 (*0-8038-2325-8*) Hastings.
Ahlberg, Allan. Mystery Tour. LC 90-2942. (Illus.). 24p. (ps up). 1991. 12.95 (*0-688-09957-2*); PLB 12.88 (*0-688-09958-0*) Greenwillow.
Aiken, Joan. Died on a Rainy Sunday. (gr. k-12). 1988. pap. 2.95 (*0-440-20097-0*, LFL) Dell.
—Night Fall. (gr. 5 up). 1988. pap. 2.95 (*0-440-20054-7*, LFL) Dell.
—A Whisper in the Night: Tales of Terror & Suspense. (gr. k-12). 1988. pap. 3.25 (*0-440-20185-3*, LE) Dell.
Albrecht, Peggy. Secret of the Old House. (gr. 6-8). 1983. pap. 3.95 (*0-87508-653-5*) Chr Lit.
Alcock, Vivian. The Mysterious Mr. Ross. large type ed. (gr. 1-8). 1990. 16.95 (*0-7451-0759-1*, Galaxy Child Lrg Print) Chivers N Amer.
Alcock, Vivien. The Mysterious Mr. Ross. LC 87-5455. 160p. (gr. 5-9). 1987. pap. 14.95 (*0-385-29581-2*) Delacorte.
—The Stonewalkers. LC 82-13956. 192p. (gr. 4-6). 1983. pap. 12.95 (*0-385-29233-3*) Delacorte.
Alessandrini, Jean. Mystery & Chocolate. (Illus.). (gr. 3-8). 1992. PLB 8.95 (*0-89565-898-4*) Childs World.

Alexander, Lloyd. Castle of Llyr. 192p. (gr. k-6). 1969. pap. 3.99 (*0-440-41125-4*, YB) Dell.
—Westmark. LC 80-22242. (gr. 5 up). 1981. 15.95 (*0-525-42335-4*, DCB) Dutton Child Bks.
Alexander, Sue. World Famous Muriel & the Magic Mystery. Frazee, Marla, illus. LC 89-22396. 32p. (gr. k-3). 1990. (Crowell Jr Bks); PLB 12.89 (*0-690-04789-4*, Crowell Jr Bks) HarpC Child Bks.
Alexander, William. The Case of the Funny Money Man. Ewers, Joe, illus. LC 89-36358. 96p. (gr. 4-7). 1990. PLB 9.89 (*0-8167-1692-7*); pap. text ed. 2.95 (*0-8167-1693-5*) Troll Assocs.
—The Case of the Gumball Bandits. Ewers, Joe, illus. LC 89-36558. 96p. (gr. 4-7). 1990. PLB 9.89 (*0-8167-1696-X*); pap. text ed. 2.95 (*0-8167-1697-8*) Troll Assocs.
—The Ghost of Shockly Manor. Ewers, Joe, illus. LC 89-36544. 96p. (gr. 4-7). 1990. PLB 9.89 (*0-8167-1694-3*); pap. text ed. 2.95 (*0-8167-1695-1*) Troll Assocs.
Allard, Harry. Miss Nelson Is Missing. (ps-3). 1993. pap. 7.95 incl. cass. (*0-395-45737-8*) HM.
Allen, Laura J. Rollo & Tweedy & the Ghost at Dougal Castle. LC 89-26921. (Illus.). 64p. (gr. k-3). 1992. 13.00 (*0-06-020106-1*); PLB 13.89 (*0-06-020107-X*) HarpC Child Bks.
Alman, Mickey. Scene of the Crime. 1990. pap. 3.50 (*0-8041-0600-2*) Ivy Books.
Amoss, Berthe. Secret Lives. 192p. (gr. 1-9). 1981. pap. 2.95 (*0-440-47904-5*, YB) Dell.
Anastasio, Dina. The Case of the Glacier Park Swallow. Saflund, Birgitta, illus. LC 94-65091. 96p. (Orig.). (gr. 4 up). 1994. pap. 8.95 (*1-879373-85-8*) R Rinehart.
—The Case of the Grand Canyon Eagle. Saflund, Birgitta, illus. LC 94-65090. 96p. (Orig.). (gr. 6 up). 1994. pap. 8.95 (*1-879373-84-X*) R Rinehart.
—Ghostwriter: Courting Danger & Other Stories. (ps-3). 1992. pap. 3.50 (*0-553-48070-7*) Bantam.
Anderson, Sanna. The Stormy Night. (Illus.). (ps-2). 1991. 12.99 (*0-8423-6772-1*) Tyndale.
Apablasa, Bill & Thiesing, Lisa. Rhymin' Simon & the Mystery of the Fake Snake. (Illus.). 64p. (gr. 2-5). 1993. 11.99 (*0-525-44977-9*, DCB) Dutton Child Bks.
Appleton, Victor. The Black Dragon. Greenberg, Anne, ed. 176p. (Orig.). 1991. pap. 2.95 (*0-671-67823-X*, Archway) PB.
Arden, William. The Mystery of the Headless Horse. Hitchcock, Alfred, ed. LC 80-29259. 160p. (gr. 4-7). 1985. pap. 3.95 (*0-679-83042-1*) Random Bks Yng Read.
—The Mystery of the Smashing Glass. LC 83-26984. (Illus.). 192p. (gr. 4-7). 1984. pap. 3.95 (*0-394-86550-2*) Random Bks Yng Read.
Artes, Dorothy B. Rick & Po: Village Detectives, Bk. 2. LC 86-50878. (Illus.). 98p. (Orig.). (gr. 4-6). 1987. pap. 4.00 (*0-932433-28-6*) Windswept Hse.
Ashley, Bernard. Bad Blood. large type ed. (gr. 1-8). 1990. 16.95 (*0-7451-1424-5*, Galaxy Child Lrg Print) Chivers N Amer.
—Running Scared. large type ed. 352p. (gr. 1-8). 1990. 16.95 (*0-7451-1099-1*, Galaxy Child Lrg Print) Chivers N Amer.
Asimov, Janet & Asimov, Isaac. Norby & the Court Jester. 128p. (gr. 3-7). 1991. 14.95 (*0-8027-8131-4*); PLB 15.85 (*0-8027-8132-2*) Walker & Co.
—Norby Down to Earth. (Illus.). (gr. 4-9). 1989. 12.95 (*0-8027-6866-0*); PLB 13.85 (*0-8027-6867-9*) Walker & Co.
Avery, Louisia. The Risks of RO - Episode 4: Child's Play. Wimberly, Potice & Andrews, Dianne, eds. Smith, Pauline, illus. 110p. (Orig.). 1988. pap. text ed. 5.95 (*0-945779-03-8*) Ethnic Role Model.
Avi. The Man Who Was Poe. 224p. 1991. pap. 3.99 (*0-380-71192-3*, Flare) Avon.
—Windcatcher. LC 90-40574. 128p. (gr. 3-7). 1991. SBE 13.95 (*0-02-707761-6*, Bradbury Pr) Macmillan Child Grp.
—Wolf Rider: A Tale of Terror. LC 86-13607. 224p. (gr. 7 up). 1986. SBE 14.95 (*0-02-707760-8*, Bradbury Pr) Macmillan Child Grp.
—Wolf Rider: A Tale of Terror. 2nd ed. 224p. (gr. 7 up). 1993. pap. 3.95 (*0-02-041513-3*, Collier Young Ad) Macmillan Child Grp.
Babbitt, Natalie. The Eyes of the Amaryllis. LC 77-11862. 160p. (gr. 3 up). 1977. 14.00 (*0-374-32241-4*) FS&G.
—Goody Hall. (Illus.). 176p. (gr. 4 up). 1986. pap. 3.50 (*0-374-42767-4*) FS&G.
Babisch, Donald. Who Is That Peeking in My Windows. Caroland, Mary, ed. LC 90-83590. (Illus.). 44p. 1991. pap. 4.95 (*1-55523-374-0*) Winston-Derek.
Bach, Alice. Parrot Woman. (Orig.). (gr. k-6). 1987. pap. 2.95 (*0-440-46987-2*, YB) Dell.
Bagley, Pat. Where Have All the Nephites Gone? Bagley, Pat, illus. (gr. 3-12). 1993. 12.95 (*0-87579-757-1*) Deseret Bk.
Baker, Eugene. At the Scene of the Crime. Axeman, Lois, illus. LC 80-14091. 32p. (gr. 2-6). 1980. PLB 12.95 (*0-89565-151-3*) Childs World.
—In the Detective's Lab. Axeman, Linda, illus. LC 80-17787. 32p. (gr. 2-5). 1980. PLB 12.95 (*0-89565-154-8*) Childs World.
—Master of Disguise. Axeman, Lois, illus. LC 80-11297. 32p. (gr. 2-5). 1980. PLB 12.95 (*0-89565-149-1*) Childs World.
Baker, Tom. High School Highways, 5 novels in ea. set, 48p.ea, Sets 1 & 2. (Illus.). (gr. 2-7). 1988. Set 1. pap. 15.00 (*0-87879-536-7*); Set 2. pap. 15.00 (*0-87879-582-0*) High Noon Bks.
Balian, Lorna. The Socksnatchers. Balian, Lorna, illus. 32p. (ps-3). 1988. PLB 12.95 (*0-687-39047-8*) Humbug Bks.
Balouet, Jean-Christopher & Behm, Barb. In Peril, 4 vols, Set. (Illus.). (gr. 3 up). Date not set. PLB 74.40 (*0-8368-1076-7*) Gareth Stevens Inc.
Banim, Lisa. A Spy in the King's Colony. (Illus.). 80p. (gr. 4-6). 1994. PLB 12.95 (*1-881889-54-8*) Silver Moon.
Banks, Lynne R. Melusine: A Mystery. LC 88-32798. 224p. (gr. 7 up). 1991. pap. 3.95 (*0-06-447054-7*, Trophy) HarpC Child Bks.
Bannatyne-Cugnet, Jo. Estelle & the Self-Esteem Machine. (Illus.). (gr. 4-7). 1993. 2.95 (*0-88995-097-0*, Pub. by Red Deer CN) Empire Pub Srvs.
Bannister, Ned. Cadets: Code Name: Snowball, No. 1. (gr. 3 up). 1988. pap. 2.95 (*0-345-35115-0*) Ballantine.
Barklem, Jill. The Secret Staircase. 32p. (ps-3). 1992. 10.95 (*0-399-21865-3*, Philomel Bks) Putnam Pub Group.
Barzun, Jacques & Taylor, Wendell H. A Catalogue of Crime: A Reader's Guide to the Literature of Mystery, Detection, & Related Genres. LC 88-45884. 864p. (gr. 7 up). 1989. 50.00 (*0-06-010263-2*, HarpT) HarpC.
Base, Graeme. The Eleventh Hour: A Curious Mystery. (Illus.). 32p. 1989. 17.95 (*0-8109-0851-4*) Abrams.
—The Eleventh Hour: A Curious Mystery. (Illus.). 32p. 1993. 11.95 (*0-8109-3265-2*) Abrams.
Bates, Betty. Call Me Friday the Thirteenth. Edwards, Linda S., illus. 112p. (gr. 3-7). 1985. pap. 2.50 (*0-440-40984-5*, LFL) Dell.
Bauer, Marion D. Face to Face. 1993. pap. 3.99 (*0-440-40791-5*) Dell.
Bawden, Nina. A Handful of Thieves. 192p. (gr. 3-7). 1991. 13.45 (*0-395-58634-8*, Clarion Bks) HM.
—The Witch's Daughter. 192p. (gr. 3-7). 1991. 13.45 (*0-395-58635-6*, Clarion Bks) HM.
Bechard, Margaret. Tory & Me & the Spirit of True Love. LC 92-5821. 156p. (gr. 3-7). 1992. 14.00 (*0-670-84688-0*) Viking Child Bks.
Belbin, David. Deadly Secrets. 1994. pap. 3.50 (*0-590-48318-8*) Scholastic Inc.
Bellairs, John. Chessman of Doom. 1989. 13.95 (*0-8037-0729-0*) Dial Bks Young.
—The Curse of the Blue Figurine. 208p. (gr. 4-6). 1984. pap. 3.50 (*0-553-15540-7*, RL6IL4, Skylark) Bantam.
—The Dark Secret of Weatherend. 192p. 1986. pap. 2.50 (*0-553-15375-7*, Skylark) Bantam.
—The Drum, the Doll, & the Zombie. Gorey, Edward, illus. Stickland, Brad, contrib. by. LC 93-43964. (gr. 2 up). 1994. 14.99 (*0-8037-1462-9*); PLB 14.89 (*0-8037-1463-7*) Dial Bks Young.
—The Letter, the Witch & the Ring. 192p. (gr. 3-6). 1977. pap. 3.25 (*0-440-44722-4*, YB) Dell.
—The Mansion in the Mist. LC 91-29639. 176p. (gr. 5 up). 1992. 15.00 (*0-8037-0845-9*); PLB 14.89 (*0-8037-0846-7*) Dial Bks Young.
—The Mummy, the Will & the Crypt. 176p. (gr. 6). 1985. pap. 2.75 (*0-553-15498-2*) Bantam.
—Secret of the Underground Room. (Illus.). 160p. (ps-3). 1990. 14.00 (*0-8037-0863-7*); PLB 13.89 (*0-8037-0864-5*) Dial Bks Young.
—The Secret of the Underground Room. LC 92-17304. 128p. (gr. 5 up). 1992. pap. 3.99 (*0-14-034932-4*, Puffin) Puffin Bks.
Bellem, Robert L. Dan Turner, Hollywood Detective: Lights! Camera! Murder! Mason, Tom, ed. Wilber, Ron, illus. 62p. 1990. pap. 7.95 (*0-944735-65-7*) Malibu Graphics.
Bennett, Jay. Coverup. LC 87-13716. 144p. (gr. 9-12). 1991. PLB 14.40 (*0-531-11091-5*) Watts.
—Coverup. 1992. pap. 3.99 (*0-449-70409-2*, Juniper) Fawcett.
—The Dark Corridor. (gr. 6 up). 1990. pap. 3.50 (*0-449-70337-1*, Juniper) Fawcett.
—Say Hello to the Hit Man. 144p. (gr. 7 up). 1981. pap. 1.95 (*0-440-97618-9*, LFL) Dell.
—Sing Me a Death Song. 144p. (gr. 7 up). 1990. pap. 3.99 (*0-449-70369-X*, Juniper) Fawcett.
—Skinhead. LC 90-13087. 144p. (gr. 7-12). 1991. 13.95 (*0-531-15218-9*); PLB 14.40 (*0-531-11001-X*) Watts.
Benson, Mildred W. Mystery at Lilac Inn. 1994. 12.95 (*1-55709-158-7*) Applewood.
—Secret at Shadow Ranch. 1994. 12.95 (*1-55709-159-5*) Applewood.
Ben-Uri, Galila. Dark Island. LC 93-72271. 172p. (gr. 5-8). 1993. write for info. (*1-56062-206-7*); pap. write for info. (*1-56062-207-5*) CIS Comm.
—The Missing Crown. Hinlicky, Gregg, illus. 223p. (gr. 5-7). 1988. 13.95 (*0-935063-41-2*); pap. 8.95 (*0-935063-42-0*) CIS Comm.
—The Mysterious Cargo. Hinlicky, Gregg, illus. 285p. (gr. 5-7). 1989. 13.95 (*1-56062-006-4*); pap. 10.95 (*1-56062-007-2*) CIS Comm.
Berenstain, Stan & Berenstain, Jan. The Berenstain Bears & the Drug Free Zone. Berenstain, Stan & Berenstain, Jan, illus. LC 92-31604. 112p. (Orig.). (gr. 2-6). 1993. PLB 7.99 (*0-679-93612-2*); pap. 3.50 (*0-679-83612-8*) Random Bks Yng Read.
Bibee, John. The Perfect Star. LC 92-5686. (Illus.). 192p. (Orig.). (gr. 5-12). 1992. pap. 6.99 (*0-8308-1206-7*, 1206) InterVarsity.
Biernot, Michele M. Mystery at Loon Lake. LC 91-67496. 44p. (gr. 4-7). 1992. 6.95 (*1-55523-495-X*) Winston-Derek.
Biggar, Joan R. High Desert Secrets. 160p. (Orig.). (gr. 5-8). 1992. pap. 3.99 (*0-570-04711-0*) Concordia.
Bilezikian, Gary. While I Slept. Bilezikian, Gary, illus. LC 90-52514. 32p. (ps-1). 1990. 12.95 (*0-531-05875-1*); PLB 12.99 (*0-531-08475-2*) Orchard Bks Watts.
Binnamin, Vivian. The Case of the Anteater's Missing Lunch. Brook, Bonnie, ed. Nelsen, Jeffrey S., illus. 32p. (gr. k-3). 1990. PLB 4.95 (*0-671-68816-2*); pap. 2.95 (*0-671-68820-0*) Silver Pr.
—The Case of the Planetarium Puzzle. Brook, Bonnie, ed. Nelsen, Jeffrey S., illus. 32p. (gr. k-3). 1990. PLB 4.95 (*0-671-68819-7*); pap. 2.95 (*0-671-68823-5*) Silver Pr.
Birch, Claire. Collision Course. (gr. 4-7). 1991. pap. 2.99 (*0-440-40512-2*, YB) Dell.
—Double Danger. (gr. 4-7). 1991. pap. 2.99 (*0-440-40525-4*, YB) Dell.
—False Lead. (gr. 4-7). 1991. pap. 2.99 (*0-440-40550-5*, YB) Dell.
—High Stakes. (gr. 4-7). 1992. pap. 2.99 (*0-440-40583-1*) Dell.
Black, Auguste R. The Shelby Avenue Gang. Black, Candice N., illus. 66p. (Orig.). (gr. 2-5). 1990. pap. 3.95 (*0-9628010-0-3*) A R Black.
Blaine, John. The Magic Talisman. Frolich, Dany, illus. Goodwin, Hal, afterword by. (Illus.). 213p. (gr. 8-12). 1989. 25.00 (*0-936414-06-5*) Manuscript Pr.
Blair, Cynthia. The Hot Fudge Sunday Affair. 1985. pap. 3.99 (*0-449-70158-1*, Juniper) Fawcett.
—The Rebellion. 1993. pap. 3.99 (*0-06-106160-3*, Harp PBks) HarpC.
Blake, Olive. The Grape Jelly Mystery. Goodman, Joan E., illus. LC 78-18040. 48p. (gr. 2-4). 1979. PLB 10.89 (*0-89375-096-4*); pap. 3.50 (*0-89375-084-0*) Troll Assocs.
—Mystery of the Lost Letter. Kossin, Sanford, illus. LC 78-18037. 48p. (gr. 2-4). 1979. PLB 10.89 (*0-89375-093-X*); pap. 3.50 (*0-89375-081-6*) Troll Assocs.
—Mystery of the Lost Pearl. Parker, Ed, illus. LC 78-60121. 48p. (gr. 2-4). 1979. PLB 10.89 (*0-89375-086-7*); pap. 3.50 (*0-89375-074-3*) Troll Assocs.
Blundell, Judy. Disappearing Act. 1994. pap. 3.50 (*0-553-37308-0*) Bantam.
Boateng, Yaw A. Young Detectives. (gr. 4-7). 1992. pap. 3.95 (*0-7910-2918-2*) Chelsea Hse.
Bodie, Idella. The Secret of Telfair Inn. Yancy, Louise, illus. LC 79-177909. 98p. (gr. 4-6). 1983. pap. 6.95 (*0-87844-050-X*) Sandlapper Pub Co.
Bolton, Elizabeth. Case of the Wacky Cat. Harvey, Paul, illus. LC 84-8725. 48p. (gr. 2-4). 1985. PLB 10.89 (*0-8167-0400-7*); pap. text ed. 3.50 (*0-8167-0401-5*) Troll Assocs.
—Ghost in the House. Burns, Ray, illus. LC 84-20530. 48p. (gr. 2-4). 1985. PLB 10.89 (*0-8167-0418-X*); pap. 3.50 (*0-8167-0419-8*) Troll Assocs.
—Secret of the Ghost Piano. Fiammenghi, Gioia, illus. LC 84-8745. 48p. (gr. 2-4). 1985. PLB 10.89 (*0-8167-0410-4*); pap. text ed. 3.50 (*0-8167-0411-2*) Troll Assocs.
—The Tree House Detective Club. Schindler, S. D., illus. LC 84-8762. 48p. (gr. 2-4). 1985. PLB 10.89 (*0-8167-0404-X*); pap. text ed. 3.50 (*0-8167-0405-8*) Troll Assocs.
Bolton, Judy. Vanishing Shadow. 1994. 12.95 (*1-55709-250-8*) Applewood.
Bones on Black Spruce Mountain. 128p. (gr. 4-6). 1984. pap. text ed. 2.50 (*0-553-15443-5*, Skylark) Bantam.
Bonsall, Crosby N. Case of the Cat's Meow. Bonsall, Crosby N., illus. LC 65-11451. 64p. (gr. k-3). 1965. PLB 13.89 (*0-06-020561-X*) HarpC Child Bks.
—The Case of the Cat's Meow. Bonsall, Crosby N., illus. LC 65-11451. 64p. (gr. k-3). 1978. pap. 3.50 (*0-06-444017-6*, Trophy) HarpC Child Bks.
—The Case of the Double Cross. LC 80-7768. (Illus.). 64p. (gr. k-3). 1980. PLB 13.89 (*0-06-020603-9*) HarpC Child Bks.
—The Case of the Double Cross. Bonsall, Crosby N., illus. LC 80-7768. 64p. (gr. k-3). 1982. pap. 3.50 (*0-06-444029-X*, Trophy) HarpC Child Bks.
—Case of the Dumb Bells. Bonsall, Crosby N., illus. LC 66-8267. 64p. (gr. k-3). 1966. PLB 13.89 (*0-06-020624-1*) HarpC Child Bks.
—The Case of the Dumb Bells. LC 66-8267. (Illus.). 64p. (gr. k-3). 1982. pap. 3.50 (*0-06-444030-3*, Trophy) HarpC Child Bks.
—Case of the Hungry Stranger. Bonsall, Crosby N., illus. LC 91-13345. 64p. (gr. k-3). 1963. 13.00 (*0-06-020570-9*); PLB 12.89 (*0-06-020571-7*) HarpC Child Bks.
—The Case of the Hungry Stranger. Bonsall, Crosby N., illus. LC 91-14365. 64p. (gr. k-3). 1980. pap. 3.50 (*0-06-444026-5*, Trophy) HarpC Child Bks.
—Case of the Scaredy Cats. LC 75-159039. (Illus.). 64p. (gr. k-3). 1971. PLB 13.89 (*0-06-020566-0*) HarpC Child Bks.
Boyd, Candy D. Circle of Gold. 128p. (Orig.). (gr. 4-6). 1984. pap. 2.95 (*0-590-43266-4*, Apple Paperbacks) Scholastic Inc.
Bradford, Ann & Gezi, Kal. The Mystery of the Midget Clown. McLean, Mina G., illus. LC 80-72513. 32p. (gr. k-4). 1980. PLB 12.95 (*0-89565-146-7*) Childs World.
—The Mystery of the Missing Dogs. McLean, Mina G., illus. LC 80-10436. 32p. (gr. k-4). 1980. PLB 12.95 (*0-89565-143-2*) Childs World.

Bradman, Tony. The Bluebeards: Mystery at Musket Bay. Murphy, Rowan B., illus. 64p. (gr. 3-6). 1990. pap. 2.95 (*0-8120-4422-3*) Barron.
Brady, Esther W. Toliver's Secret. Cuffari, Richard, illus. LC 76-15997. 176p. (Orig.). (gr. 3-7). 1993. pap. 3.99 (*0-679-84804-5*) Random Bks Yng Read.
Brennan, J. H. The Castle of Darkness. 192p. (Orig.). (gr. 6 up). 1986. pap. 2.50 (*0-440-91120-6*, LFL) Dell.
—Voyage of Terror. (Orig.). (gr. k-12). 1987. pap. 2.50 (*0-440-99324-5*, LFL) Dell.
Bricker, Sandra D. Freeze Frame. Parker, Liz, ed. Taylor, Marjorie, illus. 45p. (Orig.). (gr. 6-12). 1992. pap. text ed. 2.95 (*1-56254-050-5*) Saddleback Pubns.
Bridges, Laurie. The Ashton Horror. 160p. (gr. 7 up). 1984. pap. 2.50 (*0-553-26609-8*) Bantam.
Brightfield, Richard. Murder Comes to Life. LC 89-36329. 96p. (gr. 7 up). 1990. PLB 9.89 (*0-8167-1686-2*); pap. text ed. 2.95 (*0-8167-1687-0*) Troll Assocs.
Brink, Carol R. The Pink Motel. Greenwald, Sheila, illus. LC 92-17953. 224p. (gr. 3-7). 1993. pap. 3.95 (*0-689-71677-X*, Aladdin) Macmillan Child Grp.
Brittain, Bill. My Buddy, the King. LC 88-35704. 144p. (gr. 5-8). 1992. pap. 3.95 (*0-06-440339-4*, Trophy) HarpC Child Bks.
Brod, Alexandra. Who Stole Travada? Lucke, Peggy, ed. Stotz, Gunther, illus. 128p. (gr. 3-6). 1987. pap. 4.95 (*0-940589-00-1*) Adventure Pr.
Bronte, Charlotte. Jane Eyre. 448p. (gr. 5 up). 1992. pap. 2.95 (*0-14-035131-0*, Puffin) Puffin Bks.
Bronte, Emily. Wuthering Heights. 1992. 3.50 (*0-590-46030-7*, Apple Classics) Scholastic Inc.
Brooks, Bruce. Midnight Hour Encores. LC 86-45035. 288p. (gr. 7 up). 1988. pap. 3.95 (*0-06-447021-0*, Trophy) HarpC Child Bks.
Brouwer, Sigmund. The Downtown Desperadoes. 132p. 1991. pap. 4.99 (*0-89693-860-3*) SP Pubns.
—Madness at Moonshiner's Bay. 132p. (gr. 5-8). 1992. pap. 4.99 (*0-89693-056-4*) SP Pubns.
—Short Cuts. LC 93-26411. 132p. (Orig.). (gr. 3-7). 1993. pap. 4.99 (*1-56476-158-4*, Victor Books) SP Pubns.
Brown, Janice. Missing! 192p. 1990. pap. 4.99 (*0-7459-1876-X*) Lion USA.
Brown, Ruth. A Dark Dark Tale. Brown, Ruth, illus. LC 81-66798. 32p. (ps-3). 1984. pap. 3.95 (*0-8037-0093-8*) Dial Bks Young.
Bryant, Bonnie. Ghost Rider. (gr. 4-7). 1992. pap. 3.50 (*0-553-48067-7*) Bantam.
Buffie, Margaret. Warnings. 1994. pap. 3.25 (*0-590-43666-X*) Scholastic Inc.
Bunn, T. Davis. Florian's Gate. 400p. 1992. pap. 9.99 (*1-55661-244-3*) Bethany Hse.
Bunting, Eve. Coffin on a Case. LC 92-855. 112p. (gr. 4-7). 1992. 13.00 (*0-06-020273-4*); PLB 12.89 (*0-06-020274-2*) HarpC Child Bks.
—Coffin on a Case. LC 92-855. 112p. (gr. 4-7). 1993. pap. 3.95 (*0-06-440461-7*, Trophy) HarpC Child Bks.
—The Ghosts of Departure Point. LC 81-48602. 113p. (gr. 6 up). 1982. (Lipp Jr Bks); (Lipp Jr Bks) HarpC Child Bks.
—Is Anybody There? LC 87-45881. 176p. (gr. 4-7). 1990. (Trophy); PLB 13.89x (*0-397-32303-4*, Trophy); pap. 3.95 (*0-06-440347-5*, Trophy) HarpC Child Bks.
—The Skate Patrol. Tucker, Kathleen, ed. LC 80-18640. (Illus.). 40p. (gr. 2-5). 1980. PLB 8.95 (*0-8075-7393-0*) A Whitman.
—Someone Is Hiding on Alcatraz Island. 144p. 1986. pap. 3.50 (*0-425-10294-7*, Berkley-Pacer) Berkley Pub.
Burgess, Barbara H. The Fred Field. LC 93-14260. 1994. 14.95 (*0-385-31070-6*) Delacorte.
Burla, Oded. El Nombre Secreto. Writer, C. C. & Nielsen, Lisa C., trs. Elchanan, illus. (SPA.). 24p. (Orig.). (ps). 1992. pap. text ed. 3.00x (*1-56134-156-8*) Dushkin Pub.
—The Secret Name. Kriss, David, tr. from HEB. Elchanan, illus. 24p. (Orig.). (ps). 1992. pap. text ed. 3.00x (*1-56134-146-0*) Dushkin Pub.
Cadwallader, Sharon. Cookie McCorkle & the Case of the King's Ghost. 112p. (Orig.). 1991. pap. 2.99 (*0-380-76350-8*, Camelot) Avon.
—Cookie McCorkle & the Case of the Mystery Map. 128p. (Orig.). 1993. pap. 3.50 (*0-380-76895-X*, Camelot Young) Avon.
—Cookie McCorkle & the Case of the Emerald Earrings. 128p. (Orig.). (gr. 3-4). 1991. pap. 2.95 (*0-380-76098-3*, Camelot Young) Avon.
—Cookie McCorkle & the Case of the Missing Castle. 128p. 1991. pap. 2.99 (*0-380-76348-6*, Camelot) Avon.
—Cookie McCorkle & the Case of the Polka-Dot Safecracker. 128p. (Orig.). (gr. 3-4). 1991. pap. 2.95 (*0-380-76099-1*, Camelot Young) Avon.
Cameron, Eleanor. The Court of the Stone Children. 192p. (gr. 4 up). 1990. pap. 4.99 (*0-14-034289-3*, Puffin) Puffin Bks.
Carey, Mary V. The Mystery of the Blazing Cliffs. Hitchcock, Alfred, ed. LC 80-10954. 192p. (gr. 4-7). 1981. lib. bdg. 6.99 (*0-394-94504-2*); pap. 2.95 (*0-394-84504-8*) Random Bks Yng Read.
Carris, Joan D. Aunt Morbelia & the Screaming Skulls. MacDonald, Pat, ed. Cushman, Doug, illus. 144p. (gr. 3-6). 1992. pap. 2.99 (*0-671-74784-3*, Minstrel Bks) PB.
—Stolen Bones: A Novel. LC 92-36479. 1993. 14.95 (*0-316-13018-4*) Little.
The Case of the Missing Lettuce. (Illus.). 64p. (gr. k-2). 1989. 6.95 (*0-87449-508-3*) Modern Pub NYC.
The Case of the Vanishing House. (Illus.). 64p. (gr. k-2). 1989. 6.95 (*0-87449-510-5*) Modern Pub NYC.
Cassedy, Sylvia. Behind the Attic Wall. 320p. (gr. 4 up). 1985. pap. 3.99 (*0-380-69843-9*, Camelot) Avon.
Cates, Emily. The Ghost Ferry. (gr. 4-7). 1991. pap. 2.95 (*0-553-15863-5*) Bantam.
—The Mystery of Misty Island Inn. 1990. pap. 2.95 (*0-553-15858-9*) Bantam.
Chant, Barry. Spindles & the Mystery of the Missing Numbat. 1991. PLB 3.99 (*0-8423-6213-4*) Tyndale.
Chardiet, Bernice. The Great Carrot Top Mystery. Hartelius, Margaret A., illus. 24p. (ps-1). 1994. pap. 3.50 (*0-590-33426-3*, Cartwheel) Scholastic Inc.
Christian, Mary B. Determined Detectives. (gr. 2-4). 1988. pap. Maltese Feline, 64p. pap. 2.50 (*0-8167-1369-3*); Merger on the Orient Expressway, 48p. pap. 2.50 (*0-8167-1313-8*); Mysterious Case Case, 64p. pap. 2.50 (*0-8167-1311-1*); Phantom of the Operetta, 64p. pap. 2.50 (*0-8167-1312-X*) Troll Assocs.
—The Doggone Mystery. Fay, Ann, ed. LC 80-10448. (Illus.). (gr. 1-3). 1980. PLB 8.95 (*0-8075-1656-2*) A Whitman.
—The Mystery of the Fallen Tree. Boddy, Joe, illus. (ps-8). 1991. 8.95 (*0-88335-274-5*, AH56); pap. 4.95 (*0-88335-288-5*, AS56) Milliken Pub Co.
—The Mystery of the Message from the Sky. Boddy, Joe, illus. (ps-8). 1991. 8.95 (*0-88335-298-2*, AH57); pap. 4.95 (*0-88335-289-3*, AS57) Milliken Pub Co.
—The Mystery of the Midnight Raider. Boddy, Joe, illus. (ps-8). 1991. 8.95 (*0-88335-271-0*, AH53); pap. 4.95 (*0-88335-285-0*, AS53) Milliken Pub Co.
—The Mystery of the Missing Red Wagon. Boddy, Joe, illus. (ps-8). 8.95 (*0-88335-286-9*, AH54); pap. 4.95 (*0-88335-272-9*, AS54) Milliken Pub Co.
—The Mystery of the Missing Scarf. Bolinske, Janet L., ed. Boddy, Joe, illus. LC 88-60630. 32p. (Orig.). (gr. 1-3). 1989. text ed. 8.95 (*0-88335-596-5*); pap. text ed. 4.95 (*0-88335-549-3*) Milliken Pub Co.
—The Mystery of the Polluted Stream. Boddy, Joe, illus. (ps-8). 1991. 8.95 (*0-88335-299-0*, AH58); pap. 4.95 (*0-88335-290-7*, AS58) Milliken Pub Co.
—The Mystery of the Unsigned Valentine. Boddy, Joe, illus. (ps-8). 1991. 8.95 (*0-88335-273-7*, AH55); pap. 4.95 (*0-88335-287-7*, AS55) Milliken Pub Co.
—The North Pole Mystery. Bolinske, Janet L., ed. Boddy, Joe, illus. LC 88-60633. 32p. (Orig.). (gr. 1-3). 1989. text ed. 8.95 (*0-88335-593-0*); pap. text ed. 4.95 (*0-88335-597-3*) Milliken Pub Co.
—The Pet Day Mystery. Bolinske, Janet L., ed. Boddy, Joe, illus. LC 88-60631. 32p. (Orig.). (gr. 1-3). 1989. text ed. 8.95 (*0-88335-595-7*); pap. text ed. 4.95 (*0-88335-599-X*) Milliken Pub Co.
—Sebastian & the Bone to Pick Mystery. 64p. 1986. pap. 2.25 (*0-553-15385-4*, Skylark) Bantam.
—Sebastian (Super Sleuth) & the Baffling Bigfoot. McCue, Lisa, illus. LC 89-13049. 64p. (gr. 2-6). 1990. SBE 11.95 (*0-02-718215-0*, Macmillan Child Bk) Macmillan Child Grp.
—Sebastian (Super Sleuth) & the Bone to Pick Mystery. McCue, Lisa, illus. LC 83-5406. 64p. (gr. 2-5). 1983. RSBE 11.95 (*0-02-718440-4*, Macmillan Child Bk) Macmillan Child Grp.
—Sebastian (Super Sleuth) & the Clumsy Cowboy. McCue, Lisa, illus. LC 84-21758. 64p. (gr. 2-5). 1985. RSBE 11.95 (*0-02-718480-3*, Macmillan Child Bk) Macmillan Child Grp.
—Sebastian (Super Sleuth) & the Copycat Crime. McCue, Lisa, illus. LC 93-7038. 64p. (gr. 2-6). 1993. SBE 11. 95 (*0-02-718211-8*, Macmillan Child Bk) Macmillan Child Grp.
—Sebastian (Super Sleuth) & the Egyptian Connection. McCue, Lisa, illus. 64p. (gr. 3-7). 1991. pap. 3.95 (*0-689-71514-5*, Aladdin) Macmillan Child Grp.
—Sebastian, Super-Sleuth, & the Flying Elephant. McCue, Lisa, illus. LC 94-14434. (gr. 2-6). 1994. 11. 95 (*0-02-718252-5*) Macmillan.
—Sebastian (Super Sleuth) & the Impossible Crime. McCue, Lisa, illus. LC 91-28633. 64p. (gr. 2-6). 1992. SBE 11.95 (*0-02-718435-8*, Macmillan Child Bk) Macmillan Child Grp.
—Sebastian (Super Sleuth) & the Mystery Patient. McCue, Lisa, illus. LC 90-45092. 64p. (gr. 2-6). 1991. SBE 10.95 (*0-02-718571-0*, Macmillan Child Bk) Macmillan Child Grp.
—Sebastian (Super Sleuth) & the Secret of the Skewered Skier. McCue, Lisa, illus. LC 83-19569. 64p. (gr. 2-5). 1984. RSBE 11.95 (*0-02-718450-1*, Macmillan Child Bk) Macmillan Child Grp.
—Sebastian (Super Sleuth) & the Time Capsule Caper. McCue, Lisa, illus. LC 88-29295. 64p. (gr. 2-6). 1989. SBE 10.95 (*0-02-718570-2*, Macmillan Child Bk) Macmillan Child Grp.
—Sebastian (SuperSleuth) & the Crummy Yummies Caper. 64p. (gr. 6 up). 1985. pap. 2.25 (*0-553-15293-9*) Bantam.
—The Sherlock Street Detectives Package. Bolinske, Janet L., ed. Boddy, Joe, illus. (Orig.). (gr. 1-3). 1989. Set of 4 books, 32 pp. ea. text ed. 32.00 (*0-88335-591-4*); Set of 4 books. pap. text ed. 18.00 (*0-88335-592-2*) Milliken Pub Co.
—The UFO Mystery. Bolinske, Janet L., ed. Boddy, Joe, illus. LC 88-60632. 32p. (Orig.). (gr. 1-3). 1989. text ed. 8.95 (*0-88335-594-9*); pap. text ed. 4.95 (*0-88335-598-1*) Milliken Pub Co.
Christie, Agatha. Best Detective Stories of Agatha Christie. 136p. (Orig.). 1986. pap. text ed. 5.95 (*0-582-54087-9*) Longman.
Christopher, Matt. Lefty's Lost Pitch. (Illus.). 13p. (gr. 3-6). 1991. incls. puzzle 12.95 (*0-922242-18-6*) Lombard Mktg.
—Pressure Play. LC 92-37276. 1993. 15.95 (*0-316-14098-8*) Little.
—Top Wing. (Illus.). (gr. 8-12). 1994. 14.95 (*0-316-14099-6*) Little.
Clapp, Patricia. Jane-Emily. 160p. (gr. 5 up). 1971. pap. 1.75 (*0-440-94185-7*, LFL) Dell.
Clarke. Torment of Mr. Gully. 1991. 11.95 (*0-8050-1554-X*) H Holt & Co.
Cleary, Beverly. Ralph S. Mouse. Zelinsky, Paul O., illus. 144p. (gr. 2-6). 1983. pap. 3.25 (*0-440-47582-1*, YB) Dell.
Clifford, Eth. The Dastardly Murder of Dirty Pete. Hughes, George, illus. 128p. (gr. 2-5). 1981. 13.45 (*0-395-31671-5*) HM.
—Flatfoot Fox & the Case of the Bashful Beaver. Lies, Brian, illus. LC 94-14761. 1995. write for info. (*0-395-70560-6*) HM.
—Flatfoot Fox & the Case of the Missing Whoooo. Lies, Brian, illus. LC 92-21903. 1993. 13.95 (*0-395-65364-9*) HM.
—Flatfoot Fox & the Case of the Missing Eye. (gr. 4-7). 1992. pap. 2.95 (*0-590-45812-4*) Scholastic Inc.
—Flatfoot Fox & the Case of the Nosy Otter. Lies, Brian, illus. LC 91-26930. 48p. (gr. 2-5). 1992. 13.45 (*0-395-60289-0*) HM.
—Harvey's Marvelous Monkey Mystery. (gr. 3-7). 1990. pap. 2.95 (*0-671-70927-5*) PB.
—Harvey's Mystifying Raccoon Mix-Up. LC 93-27471. 1994. 13.95 (*0-395-68714-4*) HM.
Cole, Bruce. The Pumpkinville Mystery. Gwynne, Fred, narrated by. (Illus.). 32p. (gr. 1-4). 1988. Incl. cassettes. pap. 6.95 (*0-671-67147-2*) S&S Trade.
Coleman, Mary A. Secret Passageway. Nix, Harriet, illus. 48p. (Orig.). (gr. 1-6). 1989. pap. 8.50 (*0-685-28398-4*) Agee Pub.
Coleman, William. Chesapeake Charlie & the Bay Bank Robbers. LC 80-66638. 112p. (Orig.). (gr. 2-6). 1980. pap. 3.99 (*0-87123-113-1*) Bethany Hse.
Coleman, William L. Chesapeake Charlie & the Haunted Ship. LC 82-73912. 112p. (Orig.). (gr. 2-6). 1983. pap. 3.99 (*0-87123-282-0*) Bethany Hse.
—Chesapeake Charlie & the Stolen Diamonds. LC 81-68077. 112p. (Orig.). (gr. 5-8). 1981. pap. 3.99 (*0-87123-170-0*) Bethany Hse.
Collier, James L. & Collier, Christopher. War Comes to Willy Freeman. LC 82-70317. 192p. (gr. 4-6). 1983. pap. 13.95 (*0-385-29235-X*) Delacorte.
Collins, William W. Moonstone. Lane, L., Jr., intro. by. (gr. 10 up). 1965. pap. 2.95 (*0-8049-0076-0*, CL-76) Airmont.
Conaway, Judith. Detective Tricks You Can Do. Barto, Renzo, illus. LC 85-28881. 48p. (gr. 1-5). 1986. PLB 11.89 (*0-8167-0672-7*); pap. text ed. 3.50 (*0-8167-0673-5*) Troll Assocs.
Conford, Ellen. A Case for Jenny Archer. Palmisciano, Diane, illus. LC 88-14169. (gr. 2-4). 1988. 12.95 (*0-316-15266-8*) Little.
—A Case for Jenny Archer. (ps-3). 1990. pap. 3.95 (*0-316-15352-4*) Little.
Conklin. Ten Great Mysteries of Edgar Allan Poe. 1993. pap. 2.95 (*0-590-43344-X*) Scholastic Inc.
Connell & Thurman. The Case of the Mystery Weekend. 64p. 1994. text ed. write for info. (*0-7167-6554-3*); pap. text ed. write for info. (*0-7167-6555-1*) W H Freeman.
—The Case of the Smart Dummy. 64p. 1994. text ed. write for info. (*0-7167-6556-X*); pap. text ed. write for info. (*0-7167-6557-8*) W H Freeman.
Connell, David D. & Thurman, Jim. The Case of the Willing Parrot: Mathnet, the Book. 1994. text ed. write for info. (*0-7167-6528-4*); pap. text ed. write for info. (*0-7167-6522-5*) W H Freeman.
—Despair in Monterey Bay: A Mathnet Casebook. LC 93-183351. (gr. 4-7). 1993. text ed. write for info. (*0-7167-6505-5*, Sci Am Yng Rdrs); pap. text ed. write for info. (*0-7167-6502-0*) W H Freeman.
—The Map With a Gap. LC 93-37779. 1994. text ed. write for info. (*0-7167-6527-6*); pap. text ed. write for info. (*0-7167-6523-3*) W H Freeman.
—The Unnatural: A Mathnet Casebook. LC 93-18352. (gr. 4-7). 1993. text ed. write for info. (*0-7167-6506-3*, Sci Am Yng Rdrs) W H Freeman.
Conrad, Joseph & Snyder, John K., III. The Secret Agent. (Illus.). 52p. Date not set. pap. 4.95 (*1-57209-017-0*) Classics Int Ent.
Cook, Bernadine. Looking for Susie. Scull, Marie-Louise, illus. LC 90-41001. 32p. (gr. 1-3). 1991. lib. bdg. 14.50 (*0-208-02241-4*, Pub. by Linnet) Shoe String.
Coombs, Charles. Young Atom Detective. (Illus.). (gr. 4-7). PLB 7.19 (*0-8313-0021-3*) Lantern.
Cooper, Ilene. Hollywood Wars, No. 4: Trouble in Paradise. 144p. (gr. 3-7). 1993. pap. 3.25 (*0-14-036158-8*, Puffin) Puffin Bks.
Cooper, Susan. Greenwitch. Heslop, Michael, illus. LC 73-85319. 148p. (gr. 4-7). 1985. SBE 14.95 (*0-689-30426-9*, M K McElderry) Macmillan Child Grp.
Cooper, Susan L. Over Sea, Under Stone. Gill, Margery, illus. LC 66-11199. (gr. 5 up). 1966. 14.95 (*0-15-259034-X*, HB Juv Bks) HarBrace.
Corcoran, Barbara. Which Witch is Which? LC 91-45452. 128p. (gr. 3-7). 1992. pap. 3.95 (*0-689-71572-2*, Aladdin) Macmillan Child Grp.
Cormier, Robert. After the First Death. 1991. pap. 3.99 (*0-440-20835-1*, LFL) Dell.

—Now & at the Hour. 1991. pap. 3.99 (*0-440-20882-3*) Dell.
Costikyan, Greg. Another Day, Another Dungeon. 1990. pap. 3.95 (*0-8125-0140-3*) Tor Bks.
Courtney, Dayle. The Great UFO Chase. rev. ed. 160p. (gr. 6-9). 1991. pap. 4.99 (*0-87403-833-2*, 24-03883) Standard Pub.
—The House That Ate People. rev. ed. 160p. (gr. 6-9). 1991. pap. 4.99 (*0-87403-832-4*, 24-03882) Standard Pub.
—Jaws of Terror. rev. ed. 160p. (gr. 6-9). 1991. pap. 4.99 (*0-87403-831-6*, 24-03881) Standard Pub.
Coville, Bruce. Waiting Spirits. 160p. (Orig.). (gr. 8-10). 1984. pap. text ed. 2.25 (*0-553-26004-9*) Bantam.
Cowan, Dale. Deadly Sleep. 176p. (gr. 7 up). 1992. pap. 3.50 (*0-440-91961-4*, LFL) Dell.
Cox, Phil R. Ghost Train to Nowhere. (Illus.). 48p. (gr. 5 up). 1994. PLB 11.96 (*0-88110-519-8*, Usborne); pap. 4.95 (*0-7460-0677-2*, Usborne) EDC.
Crew, Gary. Strange Objects. LC 92-30519. 224p. (gr. 5-9). 1993. pap. 14.00 JR3 (*0-671-79759-X*, S&S BFYR) S&S Trade.
Cross, Gilbert B. Mystery at Loon Lake. LC 92-42351. 144p. (gr. 3-7). 1993. pap. 3.95 (*0-689-71729-6*, Aladdin) Macmillan Child Grp.
—Terror Train! LC 93-25735. 128p. (gr. 3-7). 1994. pap. 3.95 (*0-689-71765-2*, Aladdin) Macmillan Child Grp.
Cross, Gillian. The Dark Behind the Curtain. 160p. (Orig.). (gr. k-12). 1988. pap. 2.95 (*0-440-20207-8*, LFL) Dell.
—The Dark Behind the Curtain. (Illus.). 160p. (gr. 1-5). 1987. 12.95 (*0-19-271457-0*) OUP.
—On the Edge. LC 84-48741. 176p. (gr. 7 up). 1985. 14. 95 (*0-8234-0559-1*) Holiday.
Cross Your Heart, Hope to Die. (gr. 7 up). 1991. pap. 3.50 (*0-14-034888-3*) Puffin Bks.
Curry, Jane L. The Great Smith House Hustle. LC 92-33073. 192p. (gr. 4-7). 1993. SBE 14.95 (*0-689-50580-9*, M K McElderry) Macmillan Child Grp.
—Mindy's Mysterious Miniature. (gr. 4-7). 19.75 (*0-8446-6433-2*) Peter Smith.
Cushman, Doug. ABC Mystery. Cushman, Doug, illus. LC 92-9621. 32p. (ps-2). 1993. 14.00 (*0-06-021226-8*); PLB 13.89 (*0-06-021227-6*) HarpC Child Bks.
—Aunt Eater Loves a Mystery. Cushman, Doug, illus. LC 87-73. 64p. (gr. k-3). 1987. PLB 13.89 (*0-06-021327-2*) HarpC Child Bks.
—Aunt Eater Loves a Mystery. Cushman, Doug, illus. LC 87-73. 64p. (ps-3). 1989. pap. 3.50 (*0-06-444126-1*, Trophy) HarpC Child Bks.
—Aunt Eater Loves a Mystery. 15p. 1991. text ed. 1.20 (*1-56956-189-3*) W A T Braille.
—Aunt Eater's Mystery Vacation. Cushman, Doug, illus. LC 91-25059. 64p. (gr. k-3). 1992. 13.00 (*0-06-020513-X*); PLB 13.89 (*0-06-020514-8*) HarpC Child Bks.
—Aunt Eater's Mystery Vacation. Cushman, Doug, illus. LC 91-25059. 64p. (gr. k-3). 1993. pap. 3.50 (*0-06-444169-5*, Trophy) HarpC Child Bks.
Cusick, Richie T. Evil on the Bayou. 160p. (gr. 7 up). 1992. pap. 3.50 (*0-440-92431-6*, LFL) Dell.
—The Mall. MacDonald, Pat, ed. 224p. (Orig.). 1992. pap. 3.99 (*0-671-70958-5*, Archway) PB.
Czerkas, Stephen & Czerkas, Sylvia J. My Life with the Dinosaurs. (Orig.). (gr. 4-6). 1989. pap. 2.75 (*0-671-63454-2*, Minstrel Bks) PB.
Damon, Laura. Secret Valentine. Kennedy, Anne, illus. LC 87-13736. 32p. (gr. k-2). 1988. PLB 11.59 (*0-8167-1101-1*); pap. text ed. 2.95 (*0-8167-1102-X*) Troll Assocs.
Daniel, Jennifer. Spin-a-Story, the Haunted Banana & Other Wacky Mysteries. Brown, Jean, illus. 24p. (Orig.). (gr. 4-7). 1990. pap. 2.95 (*1-878890-02-6*) Palisades Prodns.
Danziger, Paula. The Pistachio Prescription. 160p. (gr. 5 up). 1978. pap. 3.99 (*0-440-96895-X*, LFL) Dell.
Davidson, Nicole. Winterkill. 192p. (Orig.). 1991. pap. 3.99 (*0-380-75965-9*, Flare) Avon.
Davis, Doris. The Mystery of Briar Rose Manor. LC 89-82583. (Illus.). 208p. (Orig.). 1990. pap. 3.95 (*0-88243-652-X*, 02-0652) Gospel Pub.
Davis, Jim. Garfield's Tales of Mystery. (ps-3). 1994. pap. 6.95 (*0-8167-3436-4*) Troll Assocs.
Davoll, Barbara. Dusty Mole Private Eye. Hockerman, Dennis, illus. (gr. 2-6). 1992. pap. 5.99 (*0-8024-2700-6*) Moody.
—Foul Play at Moler Park. (gr. 4-7). 1993. pap. 6.99 (*0-8024-2703-0*) Moody.
—Secret at Mossy Root Mansion. Hockerman, Dennis, illus. (gr. 2-7). 1992. 5.99 (*0-8024-2701-4*) Moody.
DeFelice, Cynthia. Devil's Bridge. 96p. (gr. 5 up). 1994. pap. 3.50 (*0-380-72117-1*) Avon.
—Weasel. 128p. (gr. 5). 1991. pap. 3.50 (*0-380-71358-6*, Camelot) Avon.
Delton, Judy. Brimhall Turns Detective. LC 82-9582. (Illus.). 48p. (gr. k-4). 1983. 14.95 (*0-87614-203-X*) Carolrhoda Bks.
—The Mystery of the Haunted Cabin. O'Brien, Anne S., illus. LC 86-7723. 128p. (gr. 2-5). 1986. 13.45 (*0-395-41917-4*) HM.
—Sonny's Secret. (ps-3). 1991. pap. 3.25 (*0-440-40429-0*) Dell.
De Maupassant, Guy. The Necklace. rev. ed. Weissenhorn, Mathilde, tr. from FRE. (gr. 9-12). 1989. Repr. of 1907 ed. multi-media kit 35.00 (*0-685-31124-4*) Balance Pub.
Devlin, Wende & Devlin, Harry. Cranberry Halloween. Devlin, Wende & Devlin, Harry, illus. LC 89-18666. 40p. (gr. k-3). 1990. pap. 3.95 (*0-689-71428-9*, Aladdin) Macmillan Child Grp.
—Cranberry Mystery. LC 85-16015. (Illus.). 40p. (ps-3). 1984. Repr. of 1978 ed. RSBE 13.95 (*0-02-729920-1*, Four Winds) Macmillan Child Grp.
De Weese, Gene. The Dandelion Caper. (gr. k-6). 1989. pap. 2.95 (*0-440-40202-6*, YB) Dell.
Dhondy, Farrukh. Black Swan. LC 92-30425. 208p. (gr. 6 up). 1993. 14.95 (*0-395-66076-9*) HM.
Dickens, Charles. Mystery of Edwin Drood. Budgey, N. F., intro. by. (gr. 10 up). 1966. pap. 1.50 (*0-8049-0114-7*, CL-114) Airmont.
Dickinson, Peter. Seventh Raven. 1991. pap. 3.50 (*0-440-20836-X*, LFL) Dell.
Dicks, Terrance. Goliath & the Cub Scouts. Littlewood, Valerie, illus. 64p. (gr. 2-4). 1990. pap. 2.95 (*0-8120-4493-2*) Barron.
Dixon, Franklin W. The Alien Factor. Greenberg, Anne, ed. 224p. (Orig.). 1993. pap. 3.99 (*0-671-79532-5*, Archway) PB.
—Bad Rap. Greenberg, Ann, ed. 160p. (Orig.). (gr. 6 up). 1993. pap. 3.99 (*0-671-73109-2*, Archway) PB.
—The Baseball Card Conspiracy. Winkler, Ellen, ed. 160p. (Orig.). (gr. 3-6). 1992. pap. 3.99 (*0-671-73064-9*, Minstrel Bks) PB.
—Beyond the Law. Greenberg, Anne, ed. 160p. (Orig.). 1991. pap. 3.50 (*0-671-73091-6*, Archway) PB.
—Blood Money. 160p. (Orig.). 1991. pap. 3.50 (*0-671-74665-0*, Archway) PB.
—The Borgia Dagger. 160p. (Orig.). (gr. 7 up). 1991. pap. 3.50 (*0-671-73676-0*, Archway) PB.
—The Case of the Cosmic Kidnapping. Winkler, Ellen, ed. 160p. (Orig.). 1993. pap. 3.99 (*0-671-79310-1*, Minstrel Bks) PB.
—Case of the Counterfeit Criminals. Winkler, Ellen, ed. 160p. (Orig.). 1992. pap. 3.99 (*0-671-73061-4*, Minstrel Bks) PB.
—Cast of Criminals. (Orig.). (gr. 7 up). 1989. pap. 3.50 (*0-671-66307-0*, Minstrel Bks) PB.
—Castle Fear. Greenberg, Ann, ed. 160p. (Orig.). (gr. 7 up). 1991. pap. 3.75 (*0-671-74615-4*, Archway) PB.
—Cold Sweat. Greenberg, Anne, ed. 160p. (Orig.). 1992. pap. 3.75 (*0-671-73099-1*) PB.
—Collision Course. 160p. 1991. pap. 3.50 (*0-671-74666-9*, Archway) PB.
—The Crowning Terror. 160p. (Orig.). (gr. 7 up). 1991. pap. 3.50 (*0-671-73670-1*, Archway) PB.
—The Crowning Terror: Casefiles Six. large type ed. 154p. (gr. 5-10). 1988. Repr. of 1987 ed. 9.50 (*0-942545-47-8*); PLB 10.50 (*0-942545-57-5*, Dist. by Gareth Stevens) Grey Castle.
—Cult of Crime. (gr. 7 up). 1989. pap. 3.75 (*0-671-68726-3*, Archway) PB.
—Cult of Crime: Casefiles Three. large type ed. LC 88-21493. 151p. (gr. 5-10). 1988. Repr. of 1987 ed. 9.50 (*0-942545-44-3*); PLB 10.50 (*0-942545-54-0*, Dist. by Gareth Stevens) Grey Castle.
—Danger on the Air. (Orig.). (gr. 3-7). 1989. pap. 3.50 (*0-671-66305-4*, Minstrel Bks) PB.
—Danger on the Diamond. Greenberg, Anne, ed. 160p. (gr. 3-6). 1988. pap. 3.99 (*0-671-63425-9*, Minstrel Bks) PB.
—Danger Unlimited. Greenberg, Anne, ed. 160p. (Orig.). (gr. 6 up). 1993. pap. 3.99 (*0-671-79463-9*, Archway) PB.
—Dead on Target: Casefiles One. large type ed. 153p. (gr. 5-10). 1988. Repr. of 1987 ed. 9.50 (*0-942545-42-7*); PLB 10.50 (*0-942545-52-4*, Dist. by Gareth Stevens) Grey Castle.
—The Dead Season. 160p. 1991. pap. 3.50 (*0-671-74105-5*, Archway) PB.
—Deadfall. 160p. (Orig.). 1992. pap. 3.75 (*0-671-73096-7*) PB.
—The Deadliest Dare. (Orig.). (gr. 7 up). 1991. pap. 3.50 (*0-671-74613-8*, Archway) PB.
—Deathgame. 160p. (Orig.). (gr. 7 up). 1991. pap. 3.99 (*0-671-73672-8*, Archway) PB.
—Deathgame: Casefiles Seven. large type ed. 151p. (gr. 7-10). 1988. Repr. of 1987 ed. 9.50 (*0-942545-48-6*); PLB 10.50 (*0-942545-58-3*, Dist. by Gareth Stevens) Grey Castle.
—Deep Trouble. Greenberg, Anne, ed. 160p. (Orig.). 1991. pap. 3.99 (*0-671-73090-8*, Archway) PB.
—The Demolition Mission. Greenberg, Ann, ed. 160p. (Orig.). 1992. pap. 3.99 (*0-671-73058-4*) PB.
—Edge of Destruction. 160p. (Orig.). (gr. 7 up). 1991. pap. 3.99 (*0-671-73669-8*, Archway) PB.
—Edge of Destruction: Casefiles Five. large type ed. LC 88-21492. 153p. (gr. 5-10). 1988. Repr. 9.50 (*0-942545-46-X*); PLB 10.50 (*0-942545-56-7*, Dist. by Gareth Stevens) Grey Castle.
—Evil, Inc. (gr. 7 up). 1991. pap. 3.75 (*0-671-73668-X*, Archway) PB.
—Evil, Inc. Casefiles Two. large type ed. 153p. (gr. 5-10). 1988. Repr. of 1987 ed. 9.50 (*0-942545-43-5*); PLB 10.50 (*0-942545-53-2*, Dist. by Gareth Stevens) Grey Castle.
—Fear on Wheels. Greenberg, Anne, ed. 160p. (Orig.). 1991. pap. 3.99 (*0-671-69277-1*, Minstrel Bks) PB.
—Final Gambit. Greenberg, Anne, ed. 160p. (Orig.). 1992. pap. 3.75 (*0-671-73098-3*) PB.
—Flight into Danger. Greenberg, Ann, ed. 160p. (Orig.). 1991. pap. 3.99 (*0-671-70044-8*, Archway) PB.
—Foul Play. Greenberg, Ann, ed. 160p. (Orig.). (gr. 7 up). 1990. pap. 3.75 (*0-671-70043-X*, Archway) PB.
—The Four-Headed Dragon. 176p. (ps). 1988. pap. 3.50 (*0-671-65797-6*, Minstrel Bks) PB.
—The Genius Thieves. 1991. pap. 3.50 (*0-671-73674-4*, Archway) PB.
—The Genius Thieves: Casefiles Nine. large type ed. 153p. (gr. 5-10). 1988. Repr. of 1987 ed. 9.50 (*0-942545-50-8*); PLB 10.50 (*0-942545-60-5*, Dist. by Gareth Stevens) Grey Castle.
—The Hardy Boys Casefiles, No. 80: Dead of the Night. 160p. (Orig.). (gr. 6 up). 1993. pap. 3.99 (*0-671-79464-7*, Archway) PB.
—The Hardy Boys: Demon's Den. Barish, Wendy, ed. Frame, Paul, illus. 208p. (gr. 3 up). 1984. 9.95 (*0-685-09177-5*) S&S Trade.
—The Hardy Boys Gift Set, 3 vols. Boxed Set. pap. 8.55 (*0-317-12424-2*) S&S Trade.
—Hardy Boys, No. 1: Tower Treasure. LC 91-46833. 1991. 12.95 (*1-55709-144-7*) Applewood.
—The Hardy Boys, No. 122: Carnival of Crime. 160p. (Orig.). (gr. 3-7). 1993. pap. 3.99 (*0-671-79312-8*, Minstrel Bks) PB.
—Hardy Boys, No. 2: The House on the Cliff. LC 91-46733. 1991. pap. 12.95 (*1-55709-145-5*) Applewood.
—Hardy Boys, No. 3: The Secret of the Old Mill. LC 91-46349. 1991. 12.95 (*1-55709-146-3*) Applewood.
—Hardy Boys: The Demon's Den. 1984. 8.95 (*0-685-08794-8*); pap. 2.95 (*0-685-08795-6*) S&S Trade.
—Height of Danger. Greenberg, Anne, ed. 160p. (Orig.). 1991. pap. 3.99 (*0-671-73092-4*, Archway) PB.
—Highway Robbery. Greenberg, Ann, ed. 160p. (Orig.). 1990. pap. 3.75 (*0-671-70038-3*, Archway) PB.
—Hostage of Hate: Casefiles Ten. large type ed. 153p. (gr. 5-10). 1988. Repr. of 1987 ed. 9.50 (*0-942545-51-6*); PLB 10.50 (*0-942545-61-3*, Dist. by Gareth Stevens) Grey Castle.
—In Self-Defense. Greenberg, Ann, ed. 160p. (Orig.). (gr. 7 up). 1990. pap. 3.75 (*0-671-70042-1*, Archway) PB.
—Last Laugh. Greenberg, Ann, ed. 160p. (gr. 7 up). 1991. pap. 3.50 (*0-671-74614-6*, Archway) PB.
—The Lazarus Plot: Casefiles Four. large type ed. 152p. (gr. 5-10). 1988. Repr. of 1987 ed. 9.50 (*0-942545-45-1*); PLB 10.50 (*0-942545-55-9*, Dist. by Gareth Stevens) Grey Castle.
—Lethal Cargo. Greenberg, Anne, ed. 160p. (Orig.). 1992. pap. 3.75 (*0-671-73103-3*, Archway) PB.
—Mayhem in Motion. Greenberg, Anne, ed. 160p. (Orig.). (gr. 7 up). 1992. pap. 3.75 (*0-671-73105-X*, Archway) PB.
—The Million Dollar Nightmare. Greenberg, Ann, ed. 160p. (Orig.). (gr. 4-7). 1990. pap. 3.99 (*0-671-69272-0*, Minstrel Bks) PB.
—Mission: Mayhem. Ashby, Ruth, ed. 160p. (Orig.). 1994. pap. 3.99 (*0-671-88204-X*, Archway) PB.
—The Money Hunt. Greenberg, Ann, ed. 160p. 1990. pap. 3.99 (*0-671-69451-0*, Minstrel Bks) PB.
—The Mummy Case. 192p. (gr. 3-6). 1987. pap. 3.99 (*0-671-64289-8*, Minstrel Bks) PB.
—The Mystery in the Old Mine. 160p. (Orig.). (gr. 5 up). 1993. pap. 3.99 (*0-671-79311-X*, Minstrel Bks) PB.
—Mystery of Smugglers Cove. 176p. (Orig.). (gr. 3-6). 1988. pap. 3.50 (*0-671-66229-5*, Minstrel Bks) PB.
—Mystery of the Samurai Sword. (gr. 2-7). 1984. 8.85 (*0-685-09393-X*) S&S Trade.
—Mystery of the Samurai Sword. 192p. (gr. 3-7). 1988. pap. 3.99 (*0-671-67302-5*, Minstrel Bks) PB.
—The Mystery of the Silver Star. (gr. 3-6). 1987. pap. 3.50 (*0-671-64374-6*, Minstrel Bks) PB.
—Mystery on Makatunk Island. 1994. pap. 3.99 (*0-671-79315-2*, Minstrel Bks) PB.
—Night of the Werewolf. (gr. 2-7). 1984. 8.85 (*0-685-09390-5*, Little Simon) S&S Trade.
—Night of the Werewolf. Greenberg, Ann, ed. 192p. 1990. pap. 3.99 (*0-671-70993-3*, Minstrel Bks) PB.
—No Mercy. Greenberg, Anne, ed. 160p. (Orig.). 1992. pap. 3.99 (*0-671-73101-7*, Archway) PB.
—No Way Out. Greenberg, Anne, ed. 160p. (Orig.). 1993. pap. 3.99 (*0-671-73111-4*, Archway) PB.
—The Pentagon Spy. (gr. 2-7). 1984. 8.85 (*0-685-42775-7*) S&S Trade.
—The Pentagon Spy. reissued ed. Greenberg, Anne, ed. 192p. (gr. 3-7). 1988. pap. 3.99 (*0-671-67221-5*, Minstrel Bks) PB.
—The Phoenix Equation. Greenberg, Anne, ed. 160p. (Orig.). 1992. pap. 3.99 (*0-671-73102-5*, Archway) PB.
—Poisoned Paradise. Greenberg, Anne, ed. 160p. (Orig.). 1993. pap. 3.99 (*0-671-79466-3*, Archway) PB.
—Power Play. Greenberg, Anne, ed. 160p. (Orig.). (gr. 6 up). 1991. pap. 3.99 (*0-671-70047-2*, Archway) PB.
—Program for Destruction. Greenberg, Ann, ed. (gr. 3-6). 1987. pap. 3.99 (*0-671-64895-0*, Minstrel Bks) PB.
—Racing with Disaster. 160p. (Orig.). 1994. pap. 3.99 (*0-671-87210-9*, Minstrel Bks) PB.
—Radical Moves. Winkler, Ellen, ed. 160p. (Orig.). 1992. pap. 3.99 (*0-671-73060-6*) PB.
—Real Horror. Greenberg, Anne, ed. 160p. (Orig.). 1993. pap. 3.99 (*0-671-73107-6*, Archway) PB.
—Rigged for Revenge. Greenberg, Anne, ed. 160p. (Orig.). (gr. 7 up). 1992. pap. 3.75 (*0-671-73106-8*, Archway) PB.
—The Ring of Evil, No. 1: Tagged for Terror. Greenberg, Anne, ed. 160p. (Orig.). 1993. pap. 3.99 (*0-671-73112-2*, Archway) PB.
—The Ring of Evil, No. 2: Survival Run. Greenberg, Ann, ed. 160p. (Orig.). 1993. pap. 3.99 (*0-671-79461-2*, Archway) PB.
—The Ring of Evil, No. 3: The Pacific Conspiracy. 160p. (Orig.). 1993. pap. 3.99 (*0-671-79462-0*, Archway) PB.

—The Roaring River Mystery. Schwartz, Betty, ed. (Orig.). (gr. 3-7). 1991. pap. 3.50 (*0-671-73004-5*) S&S Trade.
—The Robot's Revenge. Winkler, Ellen, ed. 160p. (Orig.). 1993. pap. 3.99 (*0-671-79313-6*, Minstrel Bks) PB.
—Rock 'n' Roll Renegades. Winkler, Ellen, ed. 160p. (Orig.). 1992. pap. 3.99 (*0-671-73063-0*, Minstrel Bks) PB.
—Rough Riding. Greenberg, Anne, ed. 160p. (Orig.). 1992. pap. 3.75 (*0-671-73104-1*, Archway) PB.
—Sabotage at Sports City. Winkler, Ellen, ed. 160p. (Orig.). 1992. pap. 3.99 (*0-671-73062-2*, Minstrel Bks) PB.
—Scene of the Crime. (gr. 7 up). 1989. pap. 2.95 (*0-671-69377-8*, Archway) PB.
—Screamers. Greenberg, Anne, ed. 160p. (Orig.). 1993. pap. 3.75 (*0-671-73108-4*, Archway) PB.
—The Secret of Sigma Seven. 160p. (Orig.). 1991. pap. 3.99 (*0-671-72717-6*, Minstrel Bks) PB.
—See No Evil. (gr. 7 up). 1991. pap. 3.50 (*0-671-73673-6*, Archway) PB.
—See No Evil: Casefiles Eight. large type ed. 152p. (gr. 5-10). 1988. Repr. of 1987 ed. 9.50 (*0-942545-49-4*); PLB 10.50 (*0-942545-59-1*, Dist. by Gareth Stevens) Grey Castle.
—The Serpent's Tooth Mystery. (Orig.). (gr. 3-7). 1988. pap. 3.99 (*0-671-66310-0*, Minstrel Bks) PB.
—The Shadow Killers. 1988. pap. 3.99 (*0-671-66309-7*, Minstrel Bks) PB.
—Sheer Terror. Greenberg, Anne, ed. 160p. (Orig.). 1993. pap. 3.99 (*0-671-79465-5*, Archway) PB.
—Shield of Fear. Greenberg, Ann, ed. 160p. 1988. pap. 3.99 (*0-671-66308-9*, Minstrel Bks) PB.
—The Sky Blue Frame. 160p. (Orig.). (gr. 3-6). 1988. pap. 3.99 (*0-671-64974-4*, Minstrel Bks) PB.
—The Smoke Screen Mystery. Greenberg, Ann, ed. 160p. (Orig.). (gr. 3-6). 1990. pap. 3.99 (*0-671-69274-7*, Minstrel Bks) PB.
—Spark of Suspicion. Greenberg, Ann, ed. 160p. (Orig.). 1989. pap. 3.99 (*0-671-66304-6*, Minstrel Bks) PB.
—Spiked! Greenberg, Anne, ed. 160p. (Orig.). 1991. pap. 3.50 (*0-671-73094-0*, Archway) PB.
—Terminal Shock. Greenberg, Ann, ed. 160p. (gr. 6 up). 1990. pap. 3.99 (*0-671-69288-7*, Minstrel) PB.
—Thick As Thieves. (Orig.). (gr. 7 up). 1991. pap. 3.50 (*0-671-74663-4*, Archway) PB.
—Three-Ring Terror. Greenberg, Anne, ed. 160p. (Orig.). 1991. pap. 3.99 (*0-671-73057-6*, Minstrel Bks) PB.
—Time Bomb. Greenberg, Anne, ed. 224p. (Orig.). 1992. pap. 3.75 (*0-671-75661-3*, Archway) PB.
—Too Many Traitors. 160p. (Orig.). (gr. 7 up). 1991. pap. 3.50 (*0-671-73677-9*, Archway) PB.
—Toxic Revenge. 1994. pap. 3.99 (*0-671-79467-1*, Archway) PB.
—Track of the Zombie. 1986. pap. 3.50 (*0-671-62623-X*) PB.
—Tricky Business. Greenberg, Ann, ed. 160p. (gr. 3-6). 1988. pap. 3.99 (*0-671-64973-6*, Minstrel Bks) PB.
—Uncivil War. Greenberg, Anne, ed. 160p. (Orig.). 1991. pap. 3.50 (*0-671-70049-9*, Archway) PB.
—Virtual Villainy. 1994. pap. 3.99 (*0-671-79470-1*, Archway) PB.
—Web of Horror. Greenberg, Ann, ed. 160p. (Orig.). 1991. pap. 3.99 (*0-671-73089-4*, Archway) PB.
—Wipeout. Ashby, Ruth, ed. 160p. (Orig.). (gr. 7 up). 1989. pap. 3.99 (*0-671-66306-2*, Minstrel Bks) PB.
Dixon, Franklin W. & Greenberg, Anne. Terror on Track. 160p. (Orig.). 1991. pap. 3.99 (*0-671-73093-2*, Archway) PB.
Dixon, S. The Vanishing Village. (Illus.). 48p. 1990. PLB 11.96 (*0-88110-405-1*); pap. 4.95 (*0-7460-0330-7*) EDC.
Djolete, Amu. Frightened Thief. (ps-3). 1992. pap. 2.95 (*0-7910-2902-6*) Chelsea Hse.
Docekal, Eileen M. Nature Detective: How to Solve Outdoor Mysteries. LC 89-31387. (Illus.). 128p. (gr. 4-12). 1989. 14.95 (*0-8069-6844-3*) Sterling.
Dolby, K. The Ghost in the Mirror. (Illus.). 48p. 1989. PLB 11.96 (*0-88110-369-1*); pap. 4.95 (*0-7460-0334-X*) EDC.
Doyle, Arthur Conan. The Adventure of the Solitary Cyclist. 1991. PLB 13.95 (*0-88682-472-9*) Creative Ed.
—The Adventure of the Speckled Band. 64p. (gr. 6). 1990. PLB 13.95 (*0-88682-301-3*) Creative Ed.
—Adventures of Sherlock Holmes. 272p. (gr. 9-12). 1989. pap. 2.50 (*0-8125-0424-0*) Tor Bks.
—The Adventures of Sherlock Holmes, Bk. 1. Glass, Andrew, illus. Sadler, Catherine E., adapted by. (Illus.). 140p. (Orig.). (gr. 4-7). 1981. pap. 3.50 (*0-380-78089-5*, Camelot) Avon.
—The Adventures of Sherlock Holmes, Bk. 2. Glass, Andrew, illus. Sadler, Catherine E., adapted by. (Illus.). 156p. (Orig.). (gr. 4-7). 1981. pap. 2.95 (*0-380-78097-6*, Camelot) Avon.
—The Adventures of Sherlock Holmes, Bk. 3. Glass, Andrew, illus. Sadler, Catherine E., frwd. by. (Illus.). 112p. (Orig.). (gr. 4-7). 1981. pap. 2.95 (*0-380-78105-0*, Camelot) Avon.
—The Adventures of Sherlock Holmes, Bk. 4. Glass, Andrew, illus. Sadler, Catherine E., adapted by. (Illus.). 112p. (Orig.). (gr. 4-7). 1988. pap. 3.50 (*0-380-78113-1*, Camelot) Avon.
—Complete Sherlock Holmes. LC 65-6074. 1960. Two vols. 19.95 (*0-385-04591-3*); pap. 25.00 (*0-385-00689-6*) Doubleday.
—The Great Adventures of Sherlock Holmes. (Illus.). 256p. (gr. 5 up). 1991. pap. 2.95 (*0-14-035116-7*, Puffin) Puffin Bks.
—Great Stories of Sherlock Holmes. 287p. (gr. 5 up). 1962. pap. 1.75 (*0-440-93190-8*, LFL) Dell.
—Hound of the Baskervilles. (gr. 8 up). 1965. pap. 2.50 (*0-8049-0062-0*, CL-62) Airmont.
—Hound of the Baskervilles. new & abr. ed. Fago, John N., ed. Cruz, E. R., illus. (gr. 4-12). 1977. pap. text ed. 2.95 (*0-88301-264-2*) Pendulum Pr.
—The Hound of the Baskervilles. (gr. 10 up). 1983. pap. 3.50 (*0-425-10405-2*) Berkley Pub.
—The Hound of the Baskervilles. (gr. 4-6). 1986. pap. 2.25 (*0-14-035064-0*, Puffin) Puffin Bks.
—The Hound of the Baskervilles. Martinez, Sergio & Paget, Sidney, illus. 272p. (gr. 4 up). 1992. 12.99 (*0-517-07770-1*, Child Classics) Random Hse Value.
—The Hound of the Baskervilles. (Illus.). 272p. 1991. 9.99 (*0-517-67028-3*) Random Hse Value.
—Memoirs of Sherlock Holmes. (gr. 10 up). 1984. pap. 2.75 (*0-425-10402-8*) Berkley Pub.
—Mysteries of Sherlock Holmes. Conaway, Judith, ed. LC 81-15751. (Illus.). 96p. (gr. 3-7). 1982. PLB 4.99 (*0-394-95086-0*); pap. 3.50 (*0-394-85086-6*) Random Bks Yng Read.
—Mysteries of Sherlock Holmes. reissued ed. Conaway, Judith, adapted by. Miller, Lyle, illus. 96p. (gr. 2-6). 1994. pap. 3.50 (*0-679-85086-4*, Bullseye Bks) Random Bks Yng Read.
—Reader's Digest Best Loved Books for Young Readers: Great Cases of Sherlock Holmes. Ogburn, Jackie, ed. Deel, Guy, illus. 184p. (gr. 4-12). 1989. 3.99 (*0-945260-22-9*) Choice Pub NY.
—The Red-Headed League. 64p. (gr. 6). 1990. PLB 13.95 (*0-88682-300-5*) Creative Ed.
—Sherlock Holmes. Toht, Don, illus. Stewart, Diana, adapted by. LC 79-24106. (Illus.). 48p. (gr. 4 up). 1983. PLB 20.70 (*0-8172-1657-X*) Raintree Steck-V.
—Sherlock Holmes Reader. 224p. 1994. 5.98 (*1-56138-429-1*) Running Pr.
—Silver Blaze. 64p. (gr. 6). 1990. PLB 13.95 (*0-88682-302-1*) Creative Ed.
Duffy, James. The Christmas Gang. McClintock, Barbara, illus. LC 88-32762. 80p. (gr. 3-6). 1989. SBE 12.95 (*0-684-19008-7*, Scribners Young Read) Macmillan Child Grp.
—The Christmas Gang. 80p. 1991. pap. 2.99 (*0-380-71149-4*, Camelot) Avon.
—The Graveyard Gang. LC 92-30990. 192p. (gr. 5-7). 1993. SBE 14.95 (*0-684-19449-X*, Scribners Young Read) Macmillan Child Grp.
—The Man in the River. LC 89-10200. 176p. (gr. 5-7). 1990. SBE 13.95 (*0-684-19161-X*, Scribners Young Read) Macmillan Child Grp.
Duncan, Lois. Don't Look Behind You. 1990. pap. 3.99 (*0-440-20729-0*, LFL) Dell.
—Down a Dark Hall. 192p. (gr. 7 up). 1974. 15.95 (*0-316-19547-2*) Little.
—Down a Dark Hall. 192p. (gr. 5-9). 1990. pap. 3.99 (*0-440-91805-7*, LFL) Dell.
—Killing Mr. Griffin. 224p. (gr. 7 up). 1990. pap. 3.99 (*0-440-94515-1*, LFL) Dell.
—Ransom. 144p. (gr. 7-12). 1990. pap. 3.99 (*0-440-97292-2*, LFL) Dell.
—The Twisted Window. LC 86-29054. 192p. (gr. 7 up). 1987. pap. 14.95 (*0-385-29566-9*) Delacorte.
—The Twisted Window. 192p. (gr. k-12). 1988. pap. 3.99 (*0-440-20184-5*, LFL) Dell.
Dunlop, Eileen. Green Willow. LC 92-33402. 160p. (gr. 5-9). 1993. 14.95 (*0-8234-1021-8*) Holiday.
—The House on the Hill. LC 87-388. 160p. (gr. 4 up). 1987. 14.95 (*0-8234-0658-X*) Holiday.
Dunmire, Marj. Not Even Footprints. Dunmire, Marj, illus. 72p. (Orig.). (gr. 2-7). 1987. pap. 4.95 (*0-942559-04-5*) Pegasus Graphics.
Duplex, Mary H. Mystery at Maple Street Park. LC 93-28466. 1994. 7.95 (*0-8163-1187-0*) Pacific Pr Pub Assn.
Dying to Win. (gr. 7 up). 1991. pap. 3.50 (*0-14-034887-5*) Puffin Bks.
Eastman, David, adapted by. Sherlock Holmes: The Adventure of the Empty House. Eitzen, Allan, illus. LC 81-11673. 32p. (gr. 5-9). 1982. PLB 10.79 (*0-89375-616-4*); pap. 2.95 (*0-89375-617-2*) Troll Assocs.
—Sherlock Holmes: The Adventure of the Speckled Band. Eitzen, David, illus. LC 81-11694. 32p. (gr. 5-9). 1982. PLB 10.79 (*0-89375-618-0*); pap. 2.95 (*0-89375-619-9*) Troll Assocs.
—Sherlock Holmes: The Final Problem. Eitzen, Allan, illus. LC 81-11609. 32p. (gr. 5-9). 1982. PLB 10.79 (*0-89375-612-1*); pap. 2.95 (*0-89375-613-X*) Troll Assocs.
—Sherlock Holmes: The Red-Headed League. Eitzen, Allan, illus. LC 81-11619. 32p. (gr. 5-9). 1982. PLB 10.79 (*0-89375-614-8*); pap. 2.95 (*0-89375-615-6*) Troll Assocs.
Ehrlich, Amy. The Dark Card. 1991. 13.95 (*0-670-83733-4*) Viking Child Bks.
Eisenberg, Lisa. Mystery at Camp Windingo. 144p. (gr. 4-7). 1991. 14.95 (*0-8037-0950-1*) Dial Bks Young.
—Mystery at Snowshoe Mountain Lodge. LC 86-11535. 176p. (gr. 5 up). 1987. 12.95 (*0-8037-0359-7*) Dial Bks Young.
—Mystery at Snowshoe Mountain Lodge. 176p. (gr. 2-9). 1988. pap. 2.95 (*0-8167-1322-7*) Troll Assocs.
Ekwensi, Cyprian. Masquerade Time. (ps-3). 1992. pap. 2.95 (*0-7910-2911-5*) Chelsea Hse.
Elam, Richard M., ed. Teen-Age Suspense Stories. (gr. 6-10). 1963. PLB 7.19 (*0-8313-0047-7*) Lantern.
Ellis, Carol. Silent Witness. 1994. pap. 3.25 (*0-590-47101-5*) Scholastic Inc.
Elmore, Patricia. Susannah & the Poison Green Halloween. Schick, Joel, illus. LC 82-2493. 128p. (gr. 4-7). 1982. 9.95 (*0-525-44019-4*, DCB) Dutton Child Bks.
—Susannah & the Purple Mongoose Mystery. LC 91-43643. (Illus.). 120p. (gr. 3-7). 1992. 15.00 (*0-525-44907-8*, DCB) Dutton Child Bks.
Elwood, Roger. The Frankenstein Project. (gr. 3-7). 1991. pap. 4.99 (*0-8499-3303-X*) Word Inc.
Emerson, Kathy L. The Mystery of the Missing Bagpipes. 128p. (Orig.). (gr. 5). 1991. pap. 2.95 (*0-380-76138-6*, Camelot) Avon.
Enright, Elizabeth. Spiderweb for Two. (gr. k-6). 1987. pap. 2.95 (*0-440-48203-8*, YB) Dell.
Erickson, John R. Hank the Cowdog: Faded Love. (gr. 3 up). 1985. 9.95 (*0-916941-11-6*); pap. 6.95 (*0-916941-10-8*); 13.95 (*0-916941-12-4*) Maverick Bks.
—Hank the Cowdog: Murder in the Middle Pasture. Holmes, Gerald L., illus. 91p. (Orig.). (gr. 3 up). 1985. 9.95 (*0-916941-08-6*); pap. 6.95 (*0-916941-07-8*); talking book 13.95 (*0-916941-09-4*) Maverick Bks.
—Hank the Cowdog, Vol. 19: The Case of the Midnight Rustler. Holmes, Gerald, illus. 116p. (Orig.). (gr. 4-6). 1992. 11.95 (*0-87719-219-7*); pap. 6.95 (*0-87719-218-9*); tape 15.95 (*0-87719-220-0*) Gulf Pub.
Erwin, Vicki B. Mystery of the Secret Dolls. (gr. 4-7). 1993. pap. 2.95 (*0-590-44412-3*) Scholastic Inc.
Escott, John. Crime Is a Five Letter Word: A Detective Puzzle. (Illus.). 64p. (gr. 2-5). 1994. 5.95 (*0-340-56910-7*, Pub. by Hodder & Stoughton UK) Trafalgar.
Escoula, Yvonne. Six Blue Horses. LC 70-103044. (gr. 5-9). 1970. 21.95 (*0-87599-162-9*) S G Phillips.
Estes, Rose. The Mystery of the Turkish Tattoo. Fanelli, Jenny, ed. Gowing, Toby, illus. LC 85-62805. 128p. (gr. 4-7). 1986. pap. 2.95 (*0-394-86434-4*) Random Bks Yng Read.
Eyles, Heather. Into the Night House. Gon, Adriano, illus. 64p. (gr. 4-7). 1990. pap. 2.95 (*0-8120-4423-1*) Barron.
False Moves: The Nancy Drew Files, Case 9. large type ed. 149p. (gr. 5-10). 1988. Repr. of 1987 ed. 9.50 (*0-942545-40-0*); PLB 10.50 (*0-942545-35-4*, Dist. by Grolier) Grey Castle.
Famous Tales of Mystery & Horror. (gr. 4-7). 1993. pap. 2.95 (*0-89375-369-6*) Troll Assocs.
Farley, Carol. The Case of the Haunted Health Club. 112p. 1991. pap. 2.95 (*0-380-75918-7*, Camelot) Avon.
—The Case of the Lost Lookalike. 112p. 1988. pap. 2.50 (*0-380-75450-9*, Camelot) Avon.
Farley, Walter. The Black Stallion Mystery. (gr. 4-6). 1977. pap. 3.95 (*0-394-83611-1*) Random Bks Yng Read.
—Black Stallion's Ghost. Draper, Angie, illus. (gr. 5-9). 1978. pap. 3.95 (*0-394-83919-6*) Random Bks Yng Read.
Feder, Harriet K. Mystery in Miami Beach: A Vivi Hartman Adventure. 176p. (gr. 5-12). 1992. PLB 17.50 (*0-8225-0733-1*) Lerner Pubns.
Ferguson, Alane. Poison. LC 94-10560. (gr. 7 up). 1994. 16.95 (*0-02-734528-9*) Macmillan Child Grp.
Fischel, E. & Dolby, K. Book of Spinechillers. (Illus.). 144p. (gr. 4 up). 1994. pap. 9.95 (*0-7460-0718-3*, Usborne) EDC.
Fischel, E. & Oliver, M. Whodunnits (Blu) (Illus.). 144p. (gr. 3 up). 1994. pap. 9.95 (*0-7460-0729-9*, Usborne) EDC.
Fischel, Emma. Murder Unlimited. (Illus.). 48p. (gr. 4-7). 1993. PLB 11.96 (*0-88110-522-8*, Usborne); pap. 4.95 (*0-7460-0610-1*, Usborne) EDC.
Fitzgerald, John D. The Great Brain Does It Again. (gr. 3-7). 1976. pap. 3.50 (*0-440-42983-8*, YB) Dell.
—The Return of the Great Brain. Mayer, Mercer, illus. LC 73-15443. 176p. (gr. 4-7). 1985. 12.95 (*0-8037-7403-6*) Dial Bks Young.
Fitzhugh, Louise. Long Secret. Fitzhugh, Louise, illus. LC 65-23370. (gr. 5 up). 1965. PLB 14.89 (*0-06-021411-2*) HarpC Child Bks.
—Sport. LC 78-72861. 250p. (gr. 4-6). 1979. pap. 8.95 (*0-385-28908-1*) Delacorte.
Fleischman, Paul. The Half-a-Moon Inn. Jacobi, Kathy, illus. LC 79-2010. 96p. (gr. 5 up). 1980. PLB 13.89 (*0-06-021918-1*) HarpC Child Bks.
Fleischman, Sid. Jim Ugly. Sewall, Marcia, illus. LC 91-14392. 144p. (gr. 3 up). 1992. 14.00 (*0-688-10886-5*) Greenwillow.
Foley, Louise M. In Search of the Hidden Statue. Miller, Cliff, illus. (gr. 2-6). 1993. incl. puzzle 12.95 (*0-922242-46-1*) Lombard Mktg.
—The Mardi Gras Mystery. 128p. (Orig.). (gr. 4). 1987. pap. 2.25 (*0-553-26291-2*) Bantam.
—The Mystery of Echo Lodge. 128p. (gr. 4 up). 1985. pap. 2.25 (*0-553-26313-7*) Bantam.
—The Mystery of the Highland Crest. (gr. 4 up). 1984. pap. 1.95 (*0-553-24344-6*) Bantam.
—Mystery of the Sacred Stones: Choose Your Own Adventure, No. 79. 128p. (Orig.). (gr. 7 up). 1988. pap. 2.50 (*0-553-26950-X*) Bantam.
Follett, Ken. The Mystery Hideout. Marchesi, Stephen, illus. LC 89-39961. 96p. (gr. 5 up). 1990. Repr. of 1976 ed. 12.95 (*0-688-08721-3*) Morrow Jr Bks.

—Mystery Hideout. (gr. 4-7). 1991. pap. 2.75 (*0-590-42506-4*, Apple Paperbacks) Scholastic Inc.
Foreman, Marcey G. The Russian in the Attic. LC 88-50755. 119p. (gr. 5-8). 1988. 7.95 (*1-55523-160-8*) Winston-Derek.
Foreman, Mary M., tr. from ENG. Investigalo con Ines. King, Ed, illus. (SPA.). 24p. 1992. pap. 3.95 (*1-56288-239-2*) Checkerboard.
Fox, Paula. The Moonlight Man. LC 85-26907. 192p. (gr. 7 up). 1986. SBE 14.95 (*0-02-735480-6*, Bradbury Pr) Macmillan Child Grp.
Fraser, Wynnette. Invasion on Mirror Mountain. Reck, Sue, ed. LC 93-32678. 128p. (gr. 4-6). 1994. pap. 4.99 (*0-7814-0104-6*, Chariot Bks) Cook.
French, Dorothy K. Pioneer Saddle Mystery. LC 75-12428. 192p. (gr. 5-10). 1975. PLB 7.19 (*0-8313-0113-9*) Lantern.
French, Michael. Pursuit. LC 82-70319. 192p. (gr. 7 up). 1982. 9.95 (*0-385-28781-X*) Delacorte.
Friedland, Joyce & Kessler, Rikki. Charlotte's Web: A Study Guide. (gr. 2-5). 1983. tchr's. ed. & wkbk. 14.95 (*0-88122-015-9*) LRN Links.
Frost, Erica. Case of the Missing Chick. new ed. Harvey, Paul, illus. LC 78-18036. 48p. (gr. 2-4). 1979. PLB 10.89 (*0-89375-092-1*); pap. 3.50 (*0-89375-080-8*) Troll Assocs.
—Harold & the Dinosaur Mystery. new ed. Sims, Deborah, illus. LC 78-60123. 48p. (gr. 2-4). 1979. PLB 10.89 (*0-89375-088-3*); pap. 3.50 (*0-89375-076-X*) Troll Assocs.
—Mystery of the Midnight Visitors. Gamache, Ann, illus. LC 78-18038. 48p. (gr. 2-4). 1979. PLB 10.89 (*0-89375-094-8*); pap. 3.50 (*0-89375-082-4*) Troll Assocs.
—Mystery of the Runaway Sled. Grant, Leigh, illus. LC 78-60124. 48p. (gr. 2-4). 1979. PLB 10.89 (*0-89375-089-1*); pap. 3.50 (*0-89375-077-8*) Troll Assocs.
Furman, Abraham L., ed. Everygirls Detective Stories. (Illus.). (gr. 6-10). PLB 7.19 (*0-8313-0060-4*) Lantern.
—More Teen-Age Haunted Stories. (gr. 5-10). 1967. PLB 7.19 (*0-8313-0057-4*) Lantern.
Galbraith, Kathryn O. Something Suspicious. 128p. (gr. 3 up). 1987. pap. 2.50 (*0-380-70253-3*, Camelot) Avon.
Garden, Nancy. Mystery of the Night Raiders. MacDonald, Patricia, ed. 176p. 1991. pap. 2.99 (*0-671-76064-5*, Minstrel Bks) PB.
Gardiner, John R. General Butterfingers. Smith, Catherine B., illus. 96p. (gr. 3-7). 1986. 13.45 (*0-395-41853-4*) HM.
Garfield, Leon. Devil in the Fog. (gr. k-6). 1988. pap. 3.25 (*0-440-40095-3*, YB) Dell.
Garner, Alan. The Owl Service. 160p. (gr. 5 up). 1992. pap. 3.50 (*0-440-40735-4*, YB) Dell.
Garrett, Sandra G. & Williams, Philip C. The Haunted Barn. LC 93-38341. Date not set. write for info. (*0-86625-505-2*) Rourke Pubns.
—The Pirate's Treasure. LC 93-33877. 1994. write for info. (*0-86625-506-0*) Rourke Pubns.
—The Rainbow Monster. LC 93-38342. 1994. write for info. (*0-86625-504-4*) Rourke Pubns.
Gasperini, Jim. Sail with Pirates. Pierard, John & Nino, Alex, illus. 144p. (gr. 4 up). 1984. pap. 2.50 (*0-553-26497-4*) Bantam.
Gee, Maurice. The Fire-Raiser. LC 92-8017. 150p. (gr. 5-9). 1992. 13.45 (*0-395-62428-2*) HM.
—The Fire-Raiser. large type ed. LC 93-31871. (gr. 9-12). 1993. 15.95 (*0-7862-0065-0*) Thorndike Pr.
Geehan, Wayne. Captain Blackwell's Treasure. Geehan, Wayne, illus. (gr. 2-6). 1993. incl. puzzle 12.95 (*0-922242-47-X*) Lombard Mktg.
—ComputerSleuths. Sullivan, Suzanne, illus. (gr. 2-6). 1993. incl. puzzle 12.95 (*0-922242-45-3*) Lombard Mktg.
George, Jean C. The Fire Bug Connection: An Ecological Mystery. LC 92-18005. 160p. (gr. 3-7). 1993. 14.00 (*0-06-021490-2*); PLB 13.89 (*0-06-021491-0*) HarpC Child Bks.
Gersbach, Jo R. The Case of the Buried Money Bags. (gr. 5-8). 1978. 6.50 (*0-87881-065-X*) Mojave Bks.
Gezi, Kal & Bradford, Ann. The Mystery at Misty Falls. McLean, Mina G., illus. LC 80-15708. 32p. (gr. k-4). 1980. PLB 12.95 (*0-89565-147-5*) Childs World.
—The Mystery in the Secret Club House. McLean, Mina G., illus. LC 78-6418. (gr. k-3). 1978. PLB 12.95 (*0-89565-027-4*) Childs World.
—The Mystery of the Blind Writer. McLean, Mina G., illus. LC 80-12395. 32p. (gr. k-4). 1980. PLB 12.95 (*0-89565-145-9*) Childs World.
—The Mystery of the Square Footprints. McLean, Mina G., illus. LC 80-10437. 32p. (gr. k-4). 1980. PLB 12.95 (*0-89565-144-0*) Childs World.
Gibson, Eva. Marty. LC 86-72529. 176p. (Orig.). (gr. 6-9). 1987. pap. 3.99 (*0-87123-915-9*) Bethany Hse.
Giff, Patricia R. Have You Seen Hyacinth Macaw: A Mystery. Kramer, Anthony, illus. LC 80-68729. 128p. (gr. 4-7). 1981. 9.95 (*0-440-03467-1*); PLB 9.89 (*0-440-03472-8*) Delacorte.
—Loretta P. Sweeny, Where Are You? Kramer, Anthony, illus. 144p. (gr. 4-8). 1990. pap. 3.25 (*0-440-44926-X*, YB) Dell.
—The Mystery of the Blue Ring. (Orig.). (gr. k-6). 1987. pap. 3.50 (*0-440-45998-2*, YB) Dell.
—The Mystery of the Blue Ring. (gr. 1-4). 16.25 (*0-8446-6375-1*) Peter Smith.
—The Powder Puff Puzzle. (Orig.). (gr. k-6). 1987. pap. 3.50 (*0-440-47180-X*, YB) Dell.
—The Riddle of the Red Purse. (Orig.). (gr. k-6). 1987. pap. 3.50 (*0-440-47534-1*, YB) Dell.
—The Riddle of the Red Purse. (gr. 1-4). 16.75 (*0-8446-6374-3*) Peter Smith.
—The Secret at the Polk Street School. (Orig.). (gr. k-6). 1987. pap. 3.50 (*0-440-47696-8*, YB) Dell.
Giff, Patricia R. & Kramer, Anthony. Loretta P. Sweeny, Where Are You? LC 83-5164. (Illus.). 144p. (gr. 4-6). 1983. 11.95 (*0-385-29298-8*); PLB 11.95 (*0-385-29299-6*) Delacorte.
Gillet, David. Mystery Rider at Thunder Ridge. LC 87-27846. (gr. 3-7). 1988. pap. 4.99 (*1-55513-398-3*, Chariot Bks) Chariot Family.
Gilligan, Shannon. The Case of the Missing Formula. (gr. 4-7). 1991. pap. 2.95 (*0-553-15864-3*) Bantam.
—The Clue in the Clock Tower. (gr. 4-7). 1991. pap. 2.95 (*0-553-15855-4*) Bantam.
—The Haunted Swamp. (gr. 4-7). 1991. pap. 2.95 (*0-553-15856-2*) Bantam.
—The Locker Thief. (gr. 4-7). 1991. pap. 2.99 (*0-553-15895-3*) Bantam.
—Mona Is Missing. 64p. (Orig.). 1984. pap. 2.25 (*0-553-15441-9*) Bantam.
—The Mystery of Ura Senke. 128p. (Orig.). (gr. 5). 1985. pap. 2.25 (*0-553-25499-5*) Bantam.
—Our Secret Gang, No. 6. 1992. pap. 2.99 (*0-553-15994-1*) Bantam.
—Science Lab Sabotage. (gr. 4-7). 1991. pap. 2.99 (*0-553-15913-5*) Bantam.
Gilson, Jamie. Soccer Circus. LC 92-9716. 1993. 12.00 (*0-688-12021-0*) Lothrop.
Goddard, Jerome. Mystery at Eastport Cove. LC 91-61636. 130p. (gr. 4-8). 1991. pap. 3.50 (*0-9630609-0-2*) Robins Cliff.
Godden, Rumer. The Rocking Horse Secret. (gr. 2-6). 1992. 16.75 (*0-8446-6568-1*) Peter Smith.
Gold, Avner. The Impostor. Reinman, Y. Y., ed. LC 85-72405. 192p. (gr. 5 up). 1985. 9.95 (*0-935063-14-5*); pap. 7.95 (*0-935063-13-7*) CIS Comm.
Goldman, Kelly & Davidson, Ronnie. Sherlick Hound & the Valentine Mystery. Levine, Abby, ed. Madden, Don, illus. LC 88-20561. 32p. (gr. 1-4). 1989. 8.95 (*0-8075-7335-3*) A Whitman.
Gondosch, Linda. The Witches of Hopper Street. (Illus.). (gr. 3-6). 1990. pap. 2.99 (*0-671-72468-1*, Archway) PB.
Gonzalez, Gloria. A Deadly Rhyme. (Orig.). (gr. 5-8). 1986. pap. 2.50 (*0-440-91866-9*, LFL) Dell.
Goodman, Burton. More Surprises. 144p. (gr. 4). 1990. pap. 8.75 (*0-89061-676-0*) Jamestown Pubs.
—Surprises. 144p. (gr. 4). 1990. pap. 7.75 (*0-89061-675-2*) Jamestown Pubs.
Gorman, Carol. Jennifer the Jerk Is Missing. LC 93-11474. 1994. 15.00 (*0-671-86578-1*, S&S BFYR) S&S Trade.
Grant, Charles L. Fire Mask. (gr. 7 up). 1991. 14.95 (*0-553-07167-X*, Starfire) Bantam.
Great Tales of Suspense. (gr. 4-7). 1993. pap. 2.95 (*0-8167-1466-5*) Troll Assocs.
Greene, Bette. Drowning of Stephan Jones. 1992. pap. 3.99 (*0-553-29793-7*) Bantam.
Greene, Constance C. Double-Dare O'Toole. 176p. (gr. 4-7). 1983. pap. 3.25 (*0-440-41982-4*, YB) Dell.
Griffin, Peni R. The Brick House Burglars. LC 93-22914. 144p. (gr. 4-7). 1994. SBE 14.95 (*0-689-50579-5*, M K McElderry) Macmillan Child Grp.
—Otto from Otherwhere. LC 89-38026. (ps). 1990. SBE 14.95 (*0-689-50500-0*, M K McElderry) Macmillan Child Grp.
Guglielmino, Terese. The Red Tag Mystery. Weinberger, Jane, ed. 160p. (gr. 4-8). 1993. pap. 9.95 (*0-932433-19-7*) Windswept Hse.
Gunning, Thomas G. Strange Mysteries. 96p. (gr. 4-7). 1992. pap. 2.95 (*0-8167-1371-5*) Troll Assocs.
Guy, Rosa. And I Heard a Bird Sing. LC 86-19907. 240p. (gr. 7 up). 1987. pap. 14.95 (*0-385-29563-4*) Delacorte.
—The Disappearance. 256p. (gr. 7 up). 1992. pap. 3.50 (*0-440-92064-7*, LFL) Dell.
—New Guys Around the Block. LC 82-72818. 192p. (gr. 7 up). 1983. pap. 11.95 (*0-385-29247-3*) Delacorte.
Haggard, H. Rider. King Solomon's Mines. Gemme, F. R., intro. by. (gr. 8 up). 1967. pap. 1.95 (*0-8049-0140-6*, CL-140) Airmont.
—She. Wollheim, D., intro. by. (gr. 8 up). 1967. pap. 1.95 (*0-8049-0146-5*, CL-146) Airmont.
Hahn, Mary D. The Dead Man in Indian Creek. 160p. (gr. 4-8). 1990. 14.95 (*0-395-52397-4*, Clarion Bks) HM.
—Following the Mystery Man. 192p. (gr. 4 up). 1989. pap. 3.99 (*0-380-70677-6*, Camelot) Avon.
Hale, Anna. Mystery on Mackinac Island. McLane, Lois, illus. LC 89-35484. 184p. (Orig.). (gr. 3-5). 1989. pap. 9.95 (*0-943173-34-5*) Harbinger AZ.
Hall, Lynn. Murder at the Spaniel Show. LC 88-18244. 128p. (gr. 7 up). 1988. SBE 13.95 (*0-684-18961-5*, Scribners Young Read) Macmillan Child Grp.
—Murder in a Pig's Eye. (gr. 7 up). 1990. 14.95 (*0-15-256268-0*) HarBrace.
—Murder in a Pig's Eye. (gr. 4-7). 1992. pap. 4.95 (*0-15-256269-9*) HarBrace.
—The Mystery of Pony Hollow. Sanderson, Ruth, illus. LC 91-29861. 64p. (Orig.). (gr. 2-4). 1992. PLB 6.99 (*0-679-93052-3*); pap. 2.50 (*0-679-83052-9*) Random Bks Yng Read.
—The Tormentors. 319p. (gr. 3-7). 1990. 14.95 (*0-15-289470-5*) HarBrace.
—Tormentors. LC 90-4805. (gr. 4-7). 1993. pap. 4.95 (*0-15-289471-3*) HarBrace.
Hamilton, Virginia. The House of Dies Drear. reissued ed. Keith, Eros, illus. LC 68-23059. 256p. (gr. 6-9). 1984. SBE 15.95 (*0-02-742500-2*, Macmillan Child Bk); pap. 3.95 (*0-02-043520-7*, Collier) Macmillan Child Grp.
—The Mystery of Drear House. LC 86-9829. 224p. (gr. 5 up). 1987. 13.95 (*0-688-04026-8*) Greenwillow.
Hamley, Dennis. Pageants of Despair. LC 74-10841. 180p. (gr. 7-10). 1974. 21.95 (*0-87599-205-6*) S G Phillips.
Hammer, Jeff. Dying to Know. 176p. (Orig.). 1991. pap. 3.50 (*0-380-76143-2*, Flare) Avon.
Hansen, Joyce. Home Boy. 160p. (gr. 6 up). 1982. 13.95 (*0-89919-114-2*, Clarion Bks) HM.
Hardy, Robin. The Killer's Club. (gr. 7 up). 1994. pap. 3.50 (*0-553-29829-1*) Bantam.
Harnett, Cynthia. The Great House. Harnett, Cynthia, illus. LC 83-24880. 180p. (gr. 5 up). 1984. 13.50 (*0-8225-0893-1*) Lerner Pubns.
—The Sign of the Green Falcon. Harnett, Cynthia, illus. LC 83-24831. 288p. (gr. 5 up). 1984. 13.50 (*0-8225-0888-5*) Lerner Pubns.
Harris, Betsy. Here in My Heart. LC 89-20419. 128p. (gr. 5-9). 1989. pap. text ed. 2.95 (*0-8167-1911-X*) Troll Assocs.
—Only Friends. LC 89-20371. 128p. (gr. 5-9). 1990. pap. text ed. 2.95 (*0-8167-1912-8*) Troll Assocs.
Hartelius, Margaret A. The Great Egg Mystery. Hartelius, Margaret A., illus. 16p. (Orig.). (ps-2). 1994. pap. 2.95 (*0-590-33427-1*, Cartwheel) Scholastic Inc.
Hass, E. A. Incognito Mosquito, Private Insective. Hass, E. A., illus. LC 82-205. 96p. (gr. 2-5). 1982. PLB 13.88 (*0-688-01434-8*) Lothrop.
Hastings, Beverly. Watcher in the Dark. 160p. 1986. pap. 3.99 (*0-425-10131-2*, Berkley-Pacer) Berkley Pub.
Hawthorne, Nathaniel. The House of the Seven Gables. abr. ed. Farr, Naunerle, ed. Trinidad, Angel & Guitierez, Domy, illus. (gr. 4-12). 1977. pap. text ed. 2.95 (*0-88301-265-0*) Pendulum Pr.
Hayes, Geoffrey. The Curse of the Cobweb Queen. LC 92-37272. 48p. (gr. 1-3). 1994. 7.99 (*0-679-93878-8*); pap. 3.50 (*0-679-83878-3*) Random Bks Yng Read.
—The Mystery of the Pirate Ghost: An Otto & Uncle Tooth Adventure. Hayes, Geoffrey, illus. LC 84-18228. 48p. (gr. 2-3). 1985. 3.50 (*0-394-87220-7*) Random Bks Yng Read.
—The Secret of Foghorn Island. Hayes, Geoffrey, illus. LC 87-16095. 48p. (Orig.). (gr. 2-3). 1988. lib. bdg. 7.99 (*0-394-99614-3*); pap. 3.50 (*0-394-89614-9*) Random Bks Yng Read.
Hayes, Sheila. Zoe's Gift. LC 93-42621. 144p. 1994. 14.99 (*0-525-67484-5*, Lodestar Bks) Dutton Child Bks.
Haynes, Betsy. Deadly Deception. LC 93-39011. 1994. 14.95 (*0-385-32067-1*) Delacorte.
Heide, Florence P. The Day of Ahmed's Secret. 32p. 1990. 13.95 (*0-688-08894-5*); PLB 13.88 (*0-688-08895-3*) Lothrop.
Heimann, Rolf. For Eagle Eyes Only. (gr. 4-7). 1990. pap. 3.95 (*0-8167-2202-1*) Troll Assocs.
Herberman, Ethan. The Great Butterfly Hunt: The Mystery of the Migrating Monarchs. (Illus.). (gr. 5 up). 1990. (Little Simon); (Little Simon) S&S Trade.
Herge. Affaire Tournesol. (FRE., Illus.). 64p. (gr. 7-9). 1992. Repr. write for info. (*0-7859-4692-6*) Fr & Eur.
—The Crab with the Golden Claws. LC 73-21249. (Illus.). 64p. (Orig.). (gr. k up). 1974. pap. 7.95 (*0-316-35833-9*, Joy St Bks) Little.
—Ile Noire. (FRE., Illus.). (gr. 7-9). looseleaf bdg. 19.95 (*0-8288-5039-9*) Fr & Eur.
—Objectif Lune. (FRE., Illus.). (gr. 7-9). looseleaf bdg. 19.95 (*0-8288-5051-8*) Fr & Eur.
—Red Rackham's Treasure. LC 73-21253. (Illus.). 64p. (Orig.). (gr. k up). 1974. pap. 7.95 (*0-316-35834-7*, Joy St Bks) Little.
—The Secret of the Unicorn. LC 73-21250. (Illus.). 64p. (Orig.). (gr. k up). 1974. pap. 7.95 (*0-316-35832-0*, Joy St Bks) Little.
—Sept Boules de Cristal. (FRE., Illus.). (gr. 7-9). 19.95 (*0-8288-5069-0*) Fr & Eur.
Hermes, Patricia. Nobody's Fault. 112p. (gr. 5 up). 1983. pap. 2.75 (*0-440-46523-0*, YB) Dell.
Herzig, Alison C. & Mali, Jane L. Mystery on October Road. LC 93-7487. 64p. (gr. 3-7). 1993. pap. 3.99 (*0-14-034614-7*, Puffin) Puffin Bks.
Hess, Debra. Escape from Earth. Newsom, Carol, illus. 128p. (gr. 3-7). 1994. pap. 3.50 (*1-56282-682-4*) Hyprn Child.
—Spies, Incorporated. Newsom, Carol, illus. LC 93-34116. 128p. (gr. 3-6). 1994. pap. 3.50 (*1-56282-683-2*) Hyprn Ppbks.
Heyer, Marilee. The Forbidden Door. 32p. (ps-3). 1988. pap. 14.95 (*0-670-81740-6*) Viking Child Bks.
Highlights for Children Staff. The Ghostly Bell Ringer: And Other Mysteries. LC 90-85915. (Illus.). 96p. (gr. 3-7). 1992. pap. 2.95 (*1-878093-39-8*) Boyds Mills Pr.
Hildick, E. W. The Case of the Desperate Drummer: A McGurk Mystery. LC 92-22726. 144p. (gr. 3-7). 1993. SBE 13.95 (*0-02-743961-5*, Macmillan Child Bk) Macmillan Child Grp.
—The Case of the Fantastic Footprints: A McGurk Mystery. LC 93-28735. 144p. (gr. 3-7). 1994. SBE 14.95 (*0-02-743967-4*, Macmillan Child Bk) Macmillan Child Grp.

—The Case of the Muttering Mummy: A McGurk Mystery. LC 85-23747. (Illus.). 144p. (gr. 3-6). 1986. SBE 13.95 (*0-02-743960-7*, Macmillan Child Bk) Macmillan Child Grp.
—The Case of the Nervous Newsboy. Lane, John, illus. 112p. (gr. 3-6). 1991. pap. 2.95 (*0-88741-807-4*, 01304) Sundance Pubs.
—The Case of the Purloined Parrot: A McGurk Mystery. LC 89-37924. 144p. (gr. 3-7). 1990. SBE 13.95 (*0-02-743965-8*, Macmillan Child Bk) Macmillan Child Grp.
—Case of the Wandering Weathervanes. 160p. (gr. 4-7). 1992. pap. 2.95 (*0-8167-1790-7*) Troll Assocs.
Hill, Susan. Beware, Beware. Barrett, Angela, illus. LC 92-54960. 32p. (ps up). 1993. 14.95 (*1-56402-245-5*) Candlewick Pr.
Hills, Peter B. Inspector Hare & the Black Pearls. Hills, Stephen, illus. LC 93-28977. 1994. 4.25 (*0-383-03751-4*) SRA Schl Grp.
—Inspector Hare & the Locked Room. Hills, Stephen, illus. LC 93-11734. 1994. 4.25 (*0-383-03752-2*) SRA Schl Grp.
Hiser, Constance. Critter Sitters. Smith, Cat B., illus. LC 91-23002. 96p. (gr. 3-7). 1992. 13.95 (*0-8234-0928-7*) Holiday.
—Scoop Snoops. Smith, Cat B., illus. LC 92-25922. 112p. (gr. 3-7). 1993. 13.95 (*0-8234-1011-0*) Holiday.
Hitchcock, Alfred. Alfred Hitchcock's Spellbinders in Suspense. Isen, Harold, illus. (gr. 7-11). 1982. 4.99 (*0-394-84900-0*) Random Bks Yng Read.
Hitchcock, Alfred, ed. Alfred Hitchcock's Daring Detectives. Shilstone, Arthur, illus. LC 76-79077. (gr. 5 up). 1982. pap. 4.99 (*0-394-84902-7*) Random Bks Yng Read.
—Alfred Hitchcock's Haunted Houseful. LC 84-15949. (Illus.). 272p. (gr. 4-9). 1985. pap. 4.99 (*0-394-87041-7*, Random Juv) Random Bks Yng Read.
—Alfred Hitchcock's Monster Museum. LC 81-13883. (Illus.). 224p. (gr. 5 up). 1982. pap. 4.99 (*0-394-84899-3*) Random Bks Yng Read.
—Alfred Hitchcock's Solve-Them-Yourself Mysteries. LC 63-7818. (Illus.). 256p. (gr. 6-9). 1986. (Random Juv); pap. 4.99 (*0-394-88240-7*, Random Juv) Random Bks Yng Read.
Hoban, Lillian. The Case of the Two Masked Robbers. Hoban, Lillian, illus. LC 85-45819. 64p. (gr. k-3). 1988. pap. 3.50 (*0-06-444121-0*, Trophy) HarpC Child Bks.
Holiday Camp Mystery. (Illus.). (ps-5). 3.50 (*0-7214-0012-4*); o.p. (*0-317-04000-6*) Ladybird Bks.
Hope, Laura L. Bobbsey Twins: Camp Fire Mystery. Speirs, John, illus. 128p. (gr. 3-8). 1982. (Little Simon) S&S Trade.
—The Bobbsey Twins on a Houseboat. Gonzalez, Pepe, illus. 120p. 1990. 4.50 (*0-448-09099-6*, G&D) Putnam Pub Group.
—The Bobbsey Twins: The Music Box Mystery. Barish, Wendy, ed. Speirs, John, illus. 128p. (gr. 2-5). 1983. 8.95 (*0-671-43588-4*) S&S Trade.
—The Case of the Close Encounter. Jennis, Paul, illus. 96p. (gr. 2-3). 1988. pap. 2.95 (*0-671-62656-6*, Minstrel Bks) PB.
—The Case of the Goofy Game Show. Greenberg, Anne, ed. Barrett, Randy, illus. 96p. (Orig.). 1991. pap. 2.95 (*0-671-69296-8*, Minstrel Bks) PB.
—The Case of the Runaway Money. (gr. 2-4). 1987. pap. 2.95 (*0-671-62652-3*, Minstrel Bks) PB.
—The Case of the Tricky Trickster. Greenberg, Anne, ed. Henderson, David F., illus. 96p. (Orig.). 1992. pap. 2.99 (*0-671-73041-X*) PB.
—The Case of the Vanishing Video. Greenberg, Ann, ed. Henderson, David F., illus. 96p. (Orig.). 1992. pap. 2.99 (*0-671-73040-1*) PB.
—The Clue at Casper Creek. Greenberg, Anne, ed. Henderson, David F., illus. 96p. (Orig.). 1991. pap. 2.99 (*0-671-73038-X*, Minstrel Bks) PB.
—The Monster Mouse Mystery. Greenberg, Ann, ed. Barrett, Randy, illus. 96p. (Orig.). 1991. pap. 2.95 (*0-671-69295-X*, Minstrel Bks) PB.
—Mystery at Meadowbrook. Gonzalez, Pepe, illus. 120p. 1990. 4.50 (*0-448-09100-3*, G&D) Putnam Pub Group.
—Mystery at School. Gonzalez, Pepe, illus. 120p. (gr. 2-5). 1989. 5.95 (*0-448-09074-0*, G&D) Putnam Pub Group.
—Mystery on the Mississippi. Jennis, Paul, illus. 96p. (Orig.). (gr. 2-4). 1988. pap. 2.95 (*0-671-62657-4*, Minstrel Bks) PB.
—The Secret of Jungle Park. Tsui, George, illus. (gr. 2-4). 1987. pap. 2.95 (*0-671-62651-5*, Minstrel Bks) PB.
Hostetler, Marian. Mystery at the Mall. Stamm, Gwen, illus. LC 85-13951. 88p. (Orig.). (gr. 5-6). 1985. pap. 3.95 (*0-8361-3401-X*) Herald Pr.
The Hound of the Baskervilles. 1993. pap. text ed. 6.50 (*0-582-09679-0*, 79819) Longman.
Howard, John. Backyard Mystery. (Illus.). (gr. 2-3). 1972. pap. 1.95 (*0-89375-046-8*) Troll Assocs.
Howard, Milly. The Treasure of Pelican Cove. (Illus.). 112p. (Orig.). 1988. pap. 4.95 (*0-89084-464-X*) Bob Jones Univ Pr.
Howe, James. Dew Drop Dead. 128p. 1991. pap. 3.99 (*0-380-71301-2*, Camelot) Avon.
—Dew Drop Dead: A Sebastian Barth Mystery. LC 89-34697. 160p. (gr. 3-7). 1990. SBE 14.00 (*0-689-31425-6*, Atheneum Child Bk) Macmillan Child Grp.
—Eat Your Poison, Dear. LC 86-3582. 144p. (gr. 4-7). 1986. SBE 13.95 (*0-689-31206-7*, Atheneum Child Bk) Macmillan Child Grp.
—Howliday Inn. Munsinger, Lynn, illus. LC 81-10886. 208p. (gr. 4-6). 1982. SBE 13.95 (*0-689-30846-9*, Atheneum Child Bk) Macmillan Child Grp.
—Return to Howliday Inn. Daniels, Alan, illus. LC 91-29505. 176p. (gr. 3-7). 1992. SBE 13.95 (*0-689-31661-5*, Atheneum Child Bk) Macmillan Child Grp.
—Stage Fright. 144p. 1991. pap. 3.99 (*0-380-71331-4*, Camelot) Avon.
—Stage Fright: A Sebastian Barth Mystery. 2nd ed. LC 85-20025. 160p. (gr. 3-7). 1990. SBE 13.95 (*0-689-31701-8*, Atheneum Child Bk) Macmillan Child Grp.
—What Eric Knew. 128p. 1991. pap. 3.99 (*0-380-71330-6*, Camelot) Avon.
—What Eric Knew: A Sebastian Barth Mystery. LC 85-7418. 156p. (gr. 4-6). 1990. SBE 13.95 (*0-689-31702-6*, Atheneum Child Bk) Macmillan Child Grp.
Hughes, Dean. Nutty & the Case of the Mastermind Thief. 128p. 1986. pap. 2.75 (*0-553-15414-1*, Skylark) Bantam.
—Nutty & the Case of the Ski-Slope Spy. LC 85-7962. 144p. (gr. 4-6). 1985. SBE 13.95 (*0-689-31126-5*, Atheneum Child Bk) Macmillan Child Grp.
Hunt, Angela E. The Case of the Counterfeit Cash. (Orig.). (gr. 4-7). 1992. pap. 4.99 (*0-8407-4412-9*) Nelson.
—The Case of the Haunting of Lowell Lanes. (Orig.). (gr. 4-7). 1992. pap. 4.99 (*0-8407-4421-8*) Nelson.
—The Case of the Terrified Track Star. (Orig.). (gr. 4-7). 1992. pap. 4.99 (*0-8407-4422-6*) Nelson.
—The Secret of Cravenhill Castle. LC 93-11181. Date not set. pap. 4.99 (*0-8407-6305-0*) Nelson.
Hunt, Nan. Whistle up the Chimney. (ps-3). 1994. pap. 7.00 (*0-207-17606-X*, Pub. by Angus & Robertson AT) HarpC.
Hunter, Mollie. A Stranger Came Ashore. LC 75-10814. 176p. (gr. 5-8). 1975. PLB 14.89 (*0-06-022652-8*) HarpC Child Bks.
Hurd, Thacher. Mystery on the Docks. Hurd, Thacher, illus. LC 82-48261. 32p. (ps-3). 1983. PLB 14.89 (*0-06-022702-8*) HarpC Child Bks.
Hutchens, Paul. The Case of the Missing Calf. (gr. 2-7). 1988. pap. text ed. 3.99 (*0-8024-4837-2*) Moody.
—Locked in the Attic. 128p. (gr. 2-7). 1973. pap. 4.99 (*0-8024-4831-3*) Moody.
—The Mystery Cave. rev. ed. (gr. 2-7). 1989. pap. 4.99 (*0-8024-4807-0*) Moody.
—The Sugar Creek Gang & Blue Cow. (Illus.). 128p. (gr. 3-7). 1971. pap. 4.99 (*0-8024-4822-4*) Moody.
—Sugar Creek Gang & Screams in the Night. (gr. 3-7). 1967. pap. 4.99 (*0-8024-4812-7*) Moody.
—Sugar Creek Gang & the Brown Box Mystery. (gr. 3-7). 1970. pap. 4.99 (*0-8024-4834-8*) Moody.
—The Sugar Creek Gang & the Bull Fighter. (gr. 3-7). pap. 4.99 (*0-8024-4820-8*) Moody.
—Sugar Creek Gang & the Ghost Dog. (gr. 3-7). 1968. pap. 4.99 (*0-8024-4832-1*) Moody.
—The Sugar Creek Gang & the Green Tent Mystery. (gr. 3-7). pap. 4.99 (*0-8024-4819-4*) Moody.
—Sugar Creek Gang & the Haunted House. (gr. 3-7). 1967. pap. 4.99 (*0-8024-4816-X*) Moody.
—The Sugar Creek Gang & the Killer Bear. (gr. 3-7). pap. 4.99 (*0-8024-4802-X*) Moody.
—Sugar Creek Gang & the Killer Cat. (gr. 3-7). 1966. pap. 4.99 (*0-8024-4825-9*) Moody.
—Sugar Creek Gang & the Lost Campers. (gr. 3-7). 1968. pap. 4.99 (*0-8024-4804-6*) Moody.
—The Sugar Creek Gang & the Mystery Thief. (gr. 3-7). pap. 4.99 (*0-8024-4809-7*) Moody.
—Sugar Creek Gang & the Palm Tree Manhunt. (gr. 3-7). 1969. pap. 4.99 (*0-8024-4808-9*) Moody.
—Sugar Creek Gang & the Runaway Rescue. 96p. (gr. 3-7). 1973. pap. 4.99 (*0-8024-4828-3*) Moody.
—Sugar Creek Gang & the Secret Hideout. (gr. 3-7). 1968. pap. 4.99 (*0-8024-4806-2*) Moody.
—The Swamp Robber. (gr. 2-7). 1966. pap. 4.99 (*0-8024-4801-1*) Moody.
—The Timber Wolf. (gr. 3-7). 1965. pap. 4.99 (*0-8024-4823-2*) Moody.
—The Trapline Thief. 128p. (gr. 2-7). 1971. pap. 4.99 (*0-8024-4821-6*) Moody.
—The Treasure Hunt. (gr. 2-7). 1967. pap. 4.99 (*0-8024-4814-3*) Moody.
—The Tree House Mystery. (gr. 2-7). 1972. pap. 4.99 (*0-8024-4835-6*) Moody.
—The Watermelon Mystery. (Illus.). 128p. (gr. 2-7). 1971. pap. 4.99 (*0-8024-4826-7*) Moody.
If Looks Could Kill. (gr. 7 up). 1991. pap. 3.50 (*0-14-034889-1*) Puffin Bks.
Irving, Washington. Legend of Sleepy Hollow. 1991. pap. 2.50 (*0-8125-0475-5*) Tor Bks.
—The Legend of Sleepy Hollow. 1991. pap. 7.00 (*0-385-41929-5*) Doubleday.
Jackson, Dave. Trial by Poison. (gr. 4-7). 1994. pap. 4.99 (*1-55661-274-5*) Bethany Hse.
Jackson, Dave & Jackson, Neta. The Hidden Jewel. 128p. (Orig.). (gr. 3-7). 1992. pap. 4.99 (*1-55661-245-1*) Bethany Hse.
—Spy for the Night Riders. 128p. (gr. 3-7). 1992. pap. 4.99 (*1-55661-237-0*) Bethany Hse.
Jailbird. (gr. 7 up). 1992. pap. 3.50 (*0-14-034890-5*) Puffin Bks.
Janney, Rebecca P. The Cryptic Clue. 1993. pap. 3.99 (*0-8499-3834-1*) Word Inc.
—The Eerie Echo. (gr. 5-9). 1993. pap. 4.99 (*0-8499-3400-1*) Word Inc.
—The Exchange Student's Secret. (gr. 4-7). 1994. pap. 4.99 (*0-8499-3536-9*) Word Inc.
—The Major League Mystery. LC 93-45633. 1994. 4.99 (*0-8499-3535-0*) Word Pub.
—Model Mystery. (gr. 4-7). 1993. pap. 4.99 (*0-8499-3835-X*) Word Inc.
—The Toxic Secret. (gr. 5-9). 1993. pap. 4.99 (*0-8499-3401-X*) Word Inc.
Jenkins, Jerry B. Dallas O'Neil Mysteries Ser, 8 bks. (gr. 2-7). Set. pap. 39.92 (*0-8024-8389-5*) Moody.
—Mystery of the Golden Palomino. (Orig.). 1989. pap. 4.99 (*0-8024-8386-0*) Moody.
—Mystery of the Kidnapped Kid. (gr. 2-7). 1988. pap. 4.99 (*0-8024-8376-3*) Moody.
—Mystery of the Missing Sister. (gr. 2-7). 1988. pap. 4.99 (*0-8024-8378-X*) Moody.
—Mystery of the Mixed-Up Teacher. (Orig.). (gr. 2-7). 1988. pap. 4.99 (*0-8024-8377-1*) Moody.
—Mystery of the Phony Murder. 1989. pap. 4.99 (*0-8024-8388-7*) Moody.
—Mystery of the Scorpion Threat. (gr. 9-12). 1988. pap. 4.99 (*0-8024-8379-8*) Moody.
—Mystery of the Skinny Sophomore. (Orig.). 1989. pap. 4.99 (*0-8024-8387-9*) Moody.
—Mystery on the Midway. (Orig.). 1989. pap. 4.99 (*0-8024-8385-2*) Moody.
Johnson, Lois W. The Creeping Shadows. 144p. (Orig.). (gr. 2-8). 1990. pap. 5.99 (*1-55661-102-1*) Bethany Hse.
—Mystery of the Missing Map. (gr. 4-7). 1994. pap. 5.99 (*1-55661-241-9*) Bethany Hse.
Jonas, Ann. The Thirteenth Clue. 1993. pap. 4.99 (*0-440-40887-3*) Dell.
Jones, Martha T. The Ghost at the Old Stone Fort. LaFreniere, Annette, ed. Loughran, Donna, illus. LC 90-4087. 104p. (gr. 4 up). 1990. lib. bdg. 11.95 (*0-937460-61-3*); pap. 6.95 (*0-937460-87-7*) Hendrick-Long.
Joosse, Barbara M. The Losers Fight Back. Truesdell, Sue, illus. LC 92-40783. 1994. 13.95 (*0-395-62335-9*, Clarion Bks) HM.
Jordan, Cathleen & Manson, Cynthia, eds. Tales from Alfred Hitchcock's Mystery Magazine. Jordan, Cathleen, intro. by. LC 88-9013. 320p. (gr. 7 up). 1988. 12.95 (*0-688-08176-2*) Morrow Jr Bks.
Jukes, Mavis. Blackberries in the Dark. (gr. k-6). 1987. pap. 2.99 (*0-440-40647-1*, YB) Dell.
Kahrimanis, Leola. Blue Hills Robbery. Roberts, M., ed. (Illus.). 128p. (gr. 6-8). 1991. 10.95 (*0-89015-753-7*) Sunbelt Media.
Karl, Jean E. Strange Tomorrow. (gr. 7 up). 1988. pap. 2.95 (*0-440-20052-0*, LFL) Dell.
Kaye, Marilyn. Camp Sunnyside Friends, No. 14: Megan's Ghost. 128p. (Orig.). (gr. 5). 1991. pap. 2.99 (*0-380-76552-7*, Camelot) Avon.
Keene, Carolyn. Bad Medicine. (Orig.). (gr. 7 up). 1989. pap. 2.95 (*0-671-64702-4*, Archway) PB.
—Best of Enemies. Greenberg, Ann, ed. 224p. (Orig.). 1991. pap. 3.99 (*0-671-67465-X*, Archway) PB.
—The Bluebeard Room. 1988. pap. 3.50 (*0-671-66857-9*, Minstrel Bks) PB.
—Broken Anchor. 1991. pap. 3.50 (*0-671-74228-0*) PB.
—Buried In Time. Greenberg, Ann, ed. 224p. (gr. 7 up). 1990. pap. 3.99 (*0-671-67463-3*, Archway) PB.
—Buried Secrets. (gr. 7 up). 1991. pap. 3.50 (*0-671-73664-7*, Archway) PB.
—Buried Secrets: The Nancy Drew Files, Case 10. large type ed. 151p. (gr. 7-10). 1988. Repr. of 1987 ed. 9.50 (*0-942545-41-9*); PLB 10.50 (*0-942545-36-2*, Dist. by Grolier) Grey Castle.
—The Case of the Artful Crime. Winkler, Ellen, ed. 160p. (Orig.). 1992. pap. 3.99 (*0-671-73052-5*) PB.
—The Case of the Disappearing Deejay. (Orig.). (gr. 7 up). 1989. pap. 3.99 (*0-671-66314-3*, Minstrel Bks) PB.
—The Case of the Disappearing Diamonds. (gr. 3-6). 1987. pap. 3.99 (*0-671-64896-9*, Minstrel Bks) PB.
—The Case of the Photo Finish. Greenberg, Ann, ed. 160p. (Orig.). (gr. 3-6). 1990. pap. 3.99 (*0-671-69281-X*, Minstrel Bks) PB.
—The Case of the Rising Stars. Greenberg, Anne, ed. 160p. (gr. 3-7). 1989. pap. 3.99 (*0-671-66312-7*, Minstrel Bks) PB.
—The Case of the Safecracker's Secret. 160p. 1990. pap. 3.99 (*0-671-66318-6*, Minstrel Bks) PB.
—The Case of the Twin Teddy Bears. Winkler, Ellen, ed. 160p. (Orig.). 1993. pap. 3.99 (*0-671-79302-0*, Minstrel Bks) PB.
—The Case of the Vanishing Veil. Greenberg, Anne, ed. 160p. (Orig.). (gr. 3-6). 1988. pap. 3.99 (*0-671-63413-5*, Minstrel Bks) PB.
—Choosing Sides. Greenberg, Anne, ed. 160p. (Orig.). 1993. pap. 3.99 (*0-671-73088-6*, Archway) PB.
—The Clue in the Antique Trunk. Greenberg, Ann, ed. 160p. (Orig.). 1992. pap. 3.99 (*0-671-73051-7*) PB.
—The Clue in the Camera. Greenberg, Ann, ed. 160p. (gr. 3-6). 1988. pap. 3.99 (*0-671-64962-0*, Minstrel Bks) PB.
—Cold As Ice. Greenberg, Ann, ed. 160p. (Orig.). (gr. 7 up). 1990. pap. 3.75 (*0-671-70031-6*, Archway) PB.
—A Crime for Christmas. (gr. 7 up). 1991. pap. 3.99 (*0-671-74617-0*, Archway) PB.
—Crosscurrents. Greenberg, Ann, ed. 160p. (Orig.). 1992. pap. 3.75 (*0-671-73072-X*) PB.
—Cutting Edge. Greenberg, Anne, ed. 160p. (Orig.). 1992. pap. 3.75 (*0-671-73074-6*) PB.

—Danger on Parade. Greenberg, Anne, ed. 160p. (Orig.). (gr. 7 up). 1992. pap. 3.75 (*0-671-73081-9*, Archway) PB.
—Deadly Doubles. (gr. 7 up). 1991. pap. 3.50 (*0-671-73662-0*, Archway) PB.
—Deadly Doubles: The Nancy Drew Files, Case 7. large type ed. 147p. (gr. 5-10). 1988. Repr. of 1987 ed. 9.50 (*0-942545-38-9*); PLB 10.50 (*0-942545-33-8*, Dist. by Grolier) Grey Castle.
—Deadly Intent. large type ed. (gr. 5-10). 1988. 9.50 (*0-942545-23-0*); PLB 10.50 (*0-942545-28-1*, Dist. by Grolier) Grey Castle.
—Deep Secrets. Greenberg, Ann, ed. 160p. (gr. 7 up). 1991. pap. 3.50 (*0-671-74525-5*, Archway) PB.
—Designs in Crime. Greenberg, Anne, ed. 160p. (Orig.). 1993. pap. 3.99 (*0-671-79481-7*, Archway) PB.
—Diamond Deceit. Greenberg, Anne, ed. 160p. (Orig.). 1993. pap. 3.99 (*0-671-73087-8*, Archway) PB.
—Don't Look Twice. Greenberg, Ann, ed. 160p. (Orig.). 1991. pap. 3.75 (*0-671-70032-4*, Archway) PB.
—Double Crossing. 224p. (Orig.). (gr. 7 up). 1991. pap. 3.99 (*0-671-74616-2*, Archway) PB.
—The Double Horror of Fenley Place. Greenberg, Ann, ed. (gr. 3-6). 1987. pap. 3.99 (*0-671-64387-8*, Minstrel Bks) PB.
—Easy Marks. Greenberg, Anne, ed. 160p. (Orig.). 1991. pap. 3.50 (*0-671-73066-5*, Archway) PB.
—The Emerald Eyed Cat Mystery. 1987. pap. 3.50 (*0-671-64282-0*) PB.
—Enemy Match. 192p. (gr. 3-6). 1987. pap. 3.50 (*0-671-64283-9*, Minstrel Bks) PB.
—Eskimo Secret. 1991. pap. 3.50 (*0-671-73003-7*) PB.
—Evil in Amsterdam. Greenberg, Ann, ed. 224p. (Orig.). 1993. pap. 3.99 (*0-671-78173-1*, Archway) PB.
—False Impressions. 160p. 1991. pap. 3.50 (*0-671-74392-9*, Archway) PB.
—False Moves. (gr. 7 up). 1989. pap. 3.75 (*0-671-70493-1*, Archway) PB.
—Final Notes. Greenberg, Anne, ed. 160p. (Orig.). 1991. pap. 3.75 (*0-671-73069-X*, Archway) PB.
—The Ghost of Craven Cove. Greenberg, Anne, ed. 160p. 1989. pap. 3.99 (*0-671-66317-8*, Minstrel Bks) PB.
—The Girl Who Couldn't Remember. Greenberg, Ann, ed. 160p. (Orig.). 1989. pap. 3.99 (*0-671-66316-X*, Minstrel Bks) PB.
—The Greek Symbol Mystery. (gr. 2-7). 1984. 8.50 (*0-685-09397-2*) S&S Trade.
—Guilty Secrets. 160p. (gr. 6 up). 1989. pap. 2.95 (*0-671-67760-8*, Archway) PB.
—The Haunted Carousel. 192p. (gr. 7). 1988. pap. 3.99 (*0-671-66227-9*, Minstrel Bks) PB.
—The Haunting of Horse Island. Greenberg, Ann, ed. 160p. (Orig.). (gr. 3-6). 1990. pap. 3.99 (*0-671-69284-4*, Minstrel Bks) PB.
—High Risk. Greenberg, Anne, ed. 160p. (Orig.). 1991. pap. 3.99 (*0-671-70036-7*, Archway) PB.
—High Survival. Greenberg, Ann, ed. 224p. (Orig.). 1991. pap. 3.99 (*0-671-67466-8*, Archway) PB.
—Hit & Run Holiday. large type ed. (gr. 5-10). 1989. 9.50 (*0-942545-25-7*); lib. bdg. 10.50 (*0-942545-31-1*, Dist. by Grolier) Grey Castle.
—Hits & Misses. Greenberg, Ann, ed. 224p. (Orig.). 1993. pap. 3.99 (*0-671-78169-3*, Archway) PB.
—Hot Pursuit. Greenberg, Anne, ed. 160p. (Orig.). 1991. pap. 3.99 (*0-671-70035-9*, Archway) PB.
—Hot Tracks. Greenberg, Anne, ed. 160p. (Orig.). 1992. pap. 3.75 (*0-671-73075-4*) PB.
—Illusions of Evil. 1994. pap. 3.99 (*0-671-79486-8*, Archway) PB.
—The Joker's Revenge. Greenberg, Ann, ed. 1988. pap. 3.99 (*0-671-63414-3*, Minstrel Bks) PB.
—The Joker's Revenge. (Orig.). (gr. 7 up). 1988. pap. 3.50 (*0-671-63426-7*, Minstrel Bks) PB.
—The Kachina Doll Mystery. (gr. 3-7). 1988. pap. 3.99 (*0-671-67220-7*, Minstrel Bks) PB.
—Last Dance. (Orig.). (gr. 7 up). 1991. pap. 3.50 (*0-671-74657-X*, Archway) PB.
—The Last Resort: A Nancy Drew & Hardy Boys Supermystery. 224p. (gr. 7 up). 1990. pap. 3.99 (*0-671-67461-7*, Archway) PB.
—The Legend of Miner's Creek. Greenberg, Anne, ed. 160p. (Orig.). 1992. pap. 3.99 (*0-671-73053-3*, Minstrel Bks) PB.
—Let's Talk Terror. 160p. (Orig.). 1993. pap. 3.99 (*0-671-79478-7*, Archway) PB.
—Looks Could Kill. 1994. pap. 3.99 (*0-671-79483-3*, Archway) PB.
—Making Waves. Greenberg, Ann, ed. 160p. (Orig.). (gr. 6 up). 1993. pap. 3.99 (*0-671-73085-1*, Archway) PB.
—The Mardi Gras Mystery. Greenberg, Ann, ed. 160p. (gr. 3-6). 1988. pap. 3.99 (*0-671-64961-2*, Minstrel Bks) PB.
—Mixed Signals. Greenberg, Anne, ed. 160p. (Orig.). 1991. pap. 3.50 (*0-671-73067-3*, Archway) PB.
—A Model Crime. Greenberg, Ann, ed. 160p. (Orig.). (gr. 7 up). 1990. pap. 3.75 (*0-671-70028-6*, Archway) PB.
—Moving Target. Greenberg, Anne, ed. 160p. (Orig.). (gr. 6 up). 1993. pap. 3.99 (*0-671-79479-5*, Archway) PB.
—Murder on Ice. (gr. 7 up). 1989. pap. 3.75 (*0-671-68729-8*, Archway) PB.
—Murder on Ice. large type ed. (gr. 5-10). 1988. 9.50 (*0-942545-24-9*); PLB 10.50 (*0-942545-29-X*, Dist. by Grolier) Grey Castle.
—The Mystery at Magnolia Mansion. Greenberg, Ann, ed. 160p. (Orig.). (gr. 3-6). 1990. pap. 3.99 (*0-671-69282-8*, Minstrel Bks) PB.
—The Mystery of Misty Canyon. (gr. 3-7). 1988. pap. 3.99 (*0-671-63417-8*, Minstrel Bks) PB.
—The Mystery of the Jade Tiger. Greenberg, Anne, ed. 160p. (Orig.). 1991. pap. 3.99 (*0-671-73050-9*, Minstrel Bks) PB.
—The Mystery of the Masked Rider. Winkler, Ellen, ed. 160p. (Orig.). 1992. pap. 3.99 (*0-671-73055-X*, Minstrel Bks) PB.
—The Mystery of the Missing Mascot. Greenberg, Anne, ed. 160p. (Orig.). 1994. pap. 3.99 (*0-671-87202-8*, Minstrel Bks) PB.
—The Mystery of the Missing Millionairess. Greenberg, Anne, ed. 160p. (Orig.). 1991. pap. 3.99 (*0-671-69287-9*, Minstrel Bks) PB.
—Mystery of the Winged Lion. (gr. 7 up). 1989. pap. 3.50 (*0-318-41224-1*, Minstrel Bks) PB.
—Mystery Train. Greenberg, Ann, ed. 224p. (Orig.). (gr. 7 up). 1990. pap. 3.99 (*0-671-67464-1*, Archway) PB.
—Nancy Drew & the Flying Saucer Mystery, No. 58. (gr. 4-7). 1990. pap. 3.99 (*0-671-72320-0*) S&S Trade.
—Nancy Drew Digest. 1987. Boxed. pap. 14.00 (*0-671-91515-0*, Minstrel Bks) PB.
—Nancy Drew Files, 5 vols. 1991. Set. pap. 17.50 (*0-671-96785-1*) PB.
—The Nancy Drew Files, No. 6: White Water Terror. 1991. pap. 3.50 (*0-671-73661-2*) PB.
—The Nancy Drew Files, No. 88: False Pretenses. 160p. (Orig.). (gr. 6 up). 1993. pap. 3.99 (*0-671-79480-9*, Archway) PB.
—Nancy Drew Files, No.1: Ghost Stories. 1983. pap. 3.50 (*0-671-46468-X*) S&S Trade.
—The Nancy Drew Ghost Stories. Schneider, Meg F., ed. Frame, Paul, illus. (gr. 3-7). 1983. 8.95 (*0-685-06733-5*); pap. 3.50 (*0-685-42561-4*) S&S Trade.
—Nancy Drew Ghost Stories. Frame, Paul, illus. 160p. 1983. 8.50 (*0-685-06755-6*); pap. 2.85 (*0-685-06756-4*) S&S Trade.
—Nancy Drew Gift Set, 3 vols. Boxed Set. pap. 8.55 (*0-317-12425-0*) S&S Trade.
—Nancy Drew Mystery Stories: Back-to-Back Edition. (gr. 3-7). 1987. 7.95 (*0-448-09570-X*, G&D) Putnam Pub Group.
—Nancy Drew, No. 114: The Suspect in Smoke. 160p. (Orig.). (gr. 3-7). 1993. pap. 3.99 (*0-671-79301-2*, Minstrel Bks) PB.
—Nancy Drew, No. 2: The Hidden Staircase. LC 91-46734. 1991. 12.95 (*1-55709-156-0*) Applewood.
—Nancy Drew, No. 3: The Bungalow Mystery. LC 91-46732. 1991. 12.95 (*1-55709-157-9*) Applewood.
—Nancy Drew: The Bluebeard Room. Barish, Wendy & LeVert, Suzanne, eds. 160p. (Orig.). (gr. 3-7). 1985. write for info. S&S Trade.
—Nancy Drew: The Ghost in the Gondola. Barish, Wendy & LeVert, Suzanne, eds. 160p. (Orig.). (gr. 3-7). 1985. write for info. S&S Trade.
—Nancy Drew: The Sinister Omen. Frame, Paul, illus. 192p. (gr. 3-7). 1991. (Little Simon); pap. 3.50 (*0-671-73938-7*) S&S Trade.
—Nancy Hardy Desperate Measures. 1994. pap. 3.99 (*0-671-78174-X*, Archway) PB.
—Nancy's Mysterious Letter. (gr. 4-7). 1963. 4.95 (*0-448-09508-4*, G&D) Putnam Pub Group.
—Never Say Die. (gr. 7 up). 1991. pap. 3.50 (*0-671-73666-3*, Archway) PB.
—New Year's Evil. Greenberg, Anne, ed. 224p. (Orig.). 1991. pap. 3.99 (*0-671-67467-6*, Archway) PB.
—No Laughing Matter. Greenberg, Anne, ed. 160p. (Orig.). 1993. pap. 3.99 (*0-671-73083-5*, Archway) PB.
—The Nutcracker Ballet Mystery. Winkler, Ellen, ed. 160p. (Orig.). (gr. 3-6). 1992. pap. 3.99 (*0-671-73056-8*, Minstrel Bks) PB.
—Out of Bounds. 160p. 1991. pap. 3.50 (*0-671-73911-5*, Archway) PB.
—Over the Edge. (Orig.). (gr. 7 up). 1991. pap. 3.50 (*0-671-74656-1*, Archway) PB.
—The Paris Connection: A Nancy Drew & Hardy Boys Supermystery. 224p. 1991. pap. 3.99 (*0-671-74675-8*, Archway) PB.
—The Perfect Plot. Greenberg, Anne, ed. 160p. (Orig.). 1992. pap. 3.75 (*0-671-73080-0*, Archway) PB.
—Picture of Guilt. Ashby, Ruth, ed. 160p. (Orig.). 1994. pap. 3.99 (*0-671-88192-2*, Archway) PB.
—The Picture Perfect Mystery. 160p. 1990. pap. 3.99 (*0-671-66319-4*, Minstrel Bks) PB.
—Poison Pen. Greenberg, Ann, ed. 160p. (Orig.). 1991. pap. 3.50 (*0-671-70037-5*, Archway) PB.
—Portrait in Crime. Greenberg, Ann, ed. 160p. (Orig.). 1991. pap. 3.50 (*0-671-73996-4*, Archway) PB.
—Power of Suggestion. Greenberg, Anne, ed. 160p. (Orig.). 1993. pap. 3.75 (*0-671-73084-3*, Archway) PB.
—The Puzzle at Pineview School. Greenberg, Ann, ed. (Orig.). (gr. 7 up). 1989. pap. 3.99 (*0-671-66315-1*, Minstrel Bks) PB.
—Sea of Suspicion. Greenberg, Ann, ed. 160p. (Orig.). 1993. pap. 3.99 (*0-671-79477-9*, Archway) PB.
—The Search for Cindy Austin. (Orig.). (gr. 3-7). 1989. pap. 3.50 (*0-671-66313-5*, Minstrel Bks) PB.
—The Search for the Silver Persian. 160p. (Orig.). (gr. 3-7). 1993. pap. 3.99 (*0-671-79300-4*, Minstrel Bks) PB.
—The Secret of Shady Glen. Greenberg, Ann, ed. 160p. (gr. 5 up). 1988. pap. 3.99 (*0-671-63416-X*, Minstrel Bks) PB.
—Secret of the Tibetan Treasure. Winkler, Ellen, ed. 160p. (Orig.). 1992. pap. 3.99 (*0-671-73054-1*, Minstrel Bks) PB.
—Secrets Can Kill. large type ed. (gr. 5-10). 1988. 9.50 (*0-942545-22-2*); PLB 10.50 (*0-942545-27-3*, Dist. by Grolier) Grey Castle.
—Shock Waves. (gr. 7 up). 1991. pap. 3.99 (*0-671-74393-7*, Archway) PB.
—The Silver Cobweb. Schneider, Meg F., ed. Frame, Paul, illus. 192p. (Orig.). (gr. 3-7). 1983. 9.95 (*0-685-06731-9*) S&S Trade.
—The Silver Cobweb. Frame, Paul, illus. 192p. 1983. 8.95 (*0-685-06757-2*); pap. 3.50 (*0-685-42563-0*) S&S Trade.
—Sisters in Crime. 160p. (Orig.). (gr. 7 up). 1988. pap. 3.75 (*0-671-67957-0*, Archway) PB.
—Smile & Say Murder. (gr. 7 up). 1991. pap. 3.75 (*0-671-73659-0*, Archway) PB.
—Smile & Say Murder. large type ed. (gr. 5-10). 1988. 9.50 (*0-942545-26-5*); PLB 10.50 (*0-942545-30-3*, Dist. by Grolier) Grey Castle.
—Something to Hide. 160p. 1991. pap. 3.50 (*0-671-74659-6*, Archway) PB.
—Spies & Lies. Greenberg, Anne, ed. 224p. 1992. pap. 3.99 (*0-671-73125-4*, Archway) PB.
—Stage Fright. Greenberg, Anne, ed. 160p. (Orig.). 1993. pap. 3.99 (*0-671-79482-5*, Archway) PB.
—Stay Tuned for Danger. 160p. (Orig.). (gr. 7 up). 1991. pap. 3.50 (*0-671-73667-1*, Archway) PB.
—The Stranger in the Shadows. Greenberg, Anne, ed. 160p. (Orig.). 1991. pap. 3.99 (*0-671-73049-5*, Minstrel Bks) PB.
—The Suspect Next Door. (Orig.). (gr. 7 up). 1991. pap. 3.50 (*0-671-74612-X*, Archway) PB.
—Sweet Revenge. Greenberg, Ann, ed. 160p. (Orig.). 1991. pap. 3.50 (*0-671-73065-7*, Archway) PB.
—A Talent for Murder. Greenberg, Anne, ed. 160p. (Orig.). 1992. pap. 3.99 (*0-671-73079-7*, Archway) PB.
—Tall, Dark & Deadly. Greenberg, Ann, ed. 160p. (Orig.). 1991. pap. 3.99 (*0-671-73070-3*, Archway) PB.
—Till Death Do Us Part. 1988. pap. 2.95 (*0-318-35168-4*) PB.
—Tour of Danger. Greenberg, Anne, ed. 224p. (Orig.). 1992. pap. 3.99 (*0-671-67468-4*) PB.
—Trail of Lies. Greenberg, Ann, ed. 160p. (Orig.). (gr. 7 up). 1990. pap. 3.75 (*0-671-70030-8*, Archway) PB.
—The Triple Hoax. (gr. 2-7). 1984. 8.85 (*0-685-09396-4*) S&S Trade.
—Tropic of Fear. Greenberg, Anne, ed. 224p. (Orig.). (gr. 7 up). 1992. pap. 3.99 (*0-671-73126-2*, Archway) PB.
—Trouble at Tahoe. 1994. pap. 3.99 (*0-671-79304-7*, Minstrel Bks) PB.
—The Twin Dilemma. (gr. 3-7). 1988. pap. 3.99 (*0-671-67301-7*, Minstrel Bks) PB.
—Two Points to Murder. (gr. 7 up). 1991. pap. 3.50 (*0-671-73663-9*, Archway) PB.
—Two Points to Murder: The Nancy Drew Files, Case 8. large type ed. 151p. (gr. 5-10). 1988. Repr. of 1987 ed. 9.50 (*0-942545-39-7*); PLB 10.50 (*0-942545-34-6*, Dist. by Grolier) Grey Castle.
—Update on Crime. Greenberg, Anne, ed. 160p. (Orig.). (gr. 7 up). 1992. pap. 3.75 (*0-671-73082-7*, Archway) PB.
—White Water Terror: The Nancy Drew Files, Case 6. large type ed. 149p. (gr. 5-10). 1988. Repr. of 1986 ed. 9.50 (*0-942545-37-0*); PLB 10.50 (*0-942545-32-X*, Dist. by Grolier) Grey Castle.
—Win, Place or Die. 160p. 1990. pap. 3.50 (*0-671-67498-6*, Archway) PB.
—The Wrong Track. Greenberg, Anne, ed. 160p. (Orig.). 1991. pap. 3.99 (*0-671-73068-1*, Archway) PB.
Keene, Carolyn & Dixon, Franklin W. Nancy Drew & the Hardy Boys. Barish, Wendy, ed. Frame, Paul, illus. 192p. (Orig.). (gr. 3 up). 1984. pap. 2.95 (*0-685-09176-7*) S&S Trade.
—Nancy Drew & the Hardy Boys Be a Detective Mystery Stories: Ticket to Intrigue. Arico, Diane, ed. Frame, Paul, illus. 128p. (Orig.). (gr. 3-7). 1985. pap. 2.95 (*0-671-55735-1*) S&S Trade.
—Nancy Drew & the Hardy Boys: Jungle of Evil. Arico, Diane, ed. Frame, Paul, illus. 128p. (Orig.). (gr. 3-7). 1985. pap. 2.95 (*0-671-55734-3*) S&S Trade.
—The Nancy Drew & the Hardy Boys Super Sleuths: Seven New Mysteries. (Illus.). 192p. (Orig.). (gr. 3-7). 1982. (Little Simon) S&S Trade.
—Super Sleuths, No. 2. Frame, Paul, illus. (gr. 2-7). 1984. 3.50 (*0-685-09395-6*) S&S Trade.
Kehret, Peg. Deadly Stranger. 176p. (gr. 2-9). 1988. pap. 2.95 (*0-8167-1308-1*) Troll Assocs.
—Terror at the Zoo. 160p. (gr. 5 up). 1992. 14.00 (*0-525-65083-0*, Cobblehill Bks) Dutton Child Bks.
Keller, Rosanne. Stormy Night Stories: Reading Level 3-4, 10 bks. Kempster, Teddy, ed. (Illus.). 160p. (gr. 8-12). 1993. Boxed Set. incl. tchr's. guide 18.50 (*0-88336-992-3*); tchr's. guide 1.75 (*0-88336-991-5*) New Readers.
Kellogg, Steven. The Mystery of the Flying Orange Pumpkin. Kellogg, Steven, illus. LC 80-11748. 32p. (ps-2). 1983. pap. 3.50 (*0-8037-0019-9*) Dial Bks Young.
—The Mystery of the Missing Red Mitten. LC 73-15439. (Illus.). (gr. k-2). 1979. pap. 3.50 (*0-8037-5749-2*) Dial Bks Young.
—The Mystery of the Stolen Blue Paint. Kellogg, Steven, illus. LC 81-15314. 32p. (ps-2). 1982. PLB 8.89 (*0-8037-5659-3*) Dial Bks Young.

—Mystery of the Stolen Blue Paint. Kellogg, Steven, illus. LC 81-15314. 32p. (ps-2). 1986. pap. 3.95 (*0-8037-0285-X*) Dial Bks Young.

—Prehistoric Pinkerton. Kellogg, Steven, illus. LC 86-2201. 32p. (ps-3). 1987. 12.95 (*0-8037-0322-8*); PLB 12.89 (*0-8037-0323-6*) Dial Bks Young.

—Prehistoric Pinkerton. (ps-3). 1991. pap. 4.95 (*0-8037-1053-4*, Puff Pied Piper) Puffin Bks.

Kelso, Mary J. Abducted! Kelso, Mary J., illus. 144p. (Orig.). (gr. 6 up). 1987. pap. 6.95 (*0-9621406-0-0*) MarKel Pr.

—A Virginia City Mystery. (Illus.). 120p. (Orig.). (gr. 6 up). 1992. pap. 9.95 (*0-9621406-2-7*) MarKel Pr.

Kendall, Carol. The Whisper of Glocken. (gr. 3 up). 1992. 17.50 (*0-8446-6574-6*) Peter Smith.

Kerr, M. E. Fell Back. LC 88-35762. 192p. (gr. 7 up). 1991. pap. 3.95 (*0-06-447057-1*, Trophy) HarpC Child Bks.

—Fell Down. LC 90-49921. 208p. (gr. 7 up). 1991. 15.00 (*0-06-021763-4*); PLB 14.89 (*0-06-021764-2*) HarpC Child Bks.

Kidd, Ronald. Danny Dorfman's Dream Band, No. 3: The Case of the Missing Case. Jones, Bob, illus. LC 92-17208. 80p. (gr. 2-6). 1992. pap. 2.99 (*0-14-034988-X*) Puffin Bks.

Kidney, Dorothy. The Mystery of the Old Clock Shop. 112p. (Orig.). (gr. 4-6). 1981. pap. 4.95 (*0-8341-0728-7*) Beacon Hill.

Killien, Christi. Putting on an Act. (gr. 4-9). 1988. pap. 2.95 (*0-440-20186-1*, LFL) Dell.

King, Christopher. The Case of the Missing Links. 11p. 1990. pap. 17.95 incls. puzzle (*0-922242-15-1*) Lombard Mktg.

Kinyon, Jeannette. Over Home. LC 92-71059. 244p. (gr. 4-8). 1992. PLB 24.95 (*1-880531-01-1*); pap. 13.95 (*1-880531-02-X*) East Eagle.
Set in the 1920s in Huron, South Dakota, OVER HOME captures the essence of small-town rural America through the eyes of an 11-year old girl. It is a story of family relationships & rituals brought to life by a richly detailed cast of characters caught up in a real-life murder mystery. The estranged wife of one of Grandpa & Grandma Weise's boarders has been murdered & Scharmann can't keep her nose out of it. The inquisitive Scharmann is both horrified & fascinated. An active imagination leads Scharmann through a series of colorful adventures which sometimes are nothing but trouble. Mamma & Daddy say it's none of her business, but, for Scharmann, secrets are to be discovered & mysteries are to be solved. Like Laura Ingalls Wilder, Jeannette Kinyon writes with a depth of vivid descripion. OVER HOME reverberates with the customs & fashions of days gone by, yet the lessons of family & adolescence are strikingly familiar for all time. Hardback (ISBN 1-880531-01-1) & paperback (ISBN 1-880531-02-X). Call or write for information to order, East Eagle Company, P.O. Box 812, Huron, SD 57350, 605-352-5875.
Publisher Provided Annotation.

Kjelgaard, Jim. A Nose for Trouble. 1984. pap. 3.50 (*0-553-15578-4*) Bantam.

Klause, Annette C. Alien Secrets. LC 92-31326. 1993. 15.95 (*0-385-30928-7*) Delacorte.

Klaveness, Jan O. Beyond the Cellar Door. (gr. 4-7). 1993. pap. 2.95 (*0-590-43022-X*) Scholastic Inc.

—Keeper of the Light. LC 90-38530. 224p. (gr. 7 up). 1990. 12.95g (*0-688-06996-7*) Morrow Jr Bks.

Kline, Suzy. Herbie Jones & the Class Gift. Williams, Richard, illus. 96p. (gr. 2-6). 1987. 12.95 (*0-399-21452-6*, Putnam) Putnam Pub Group.

—Horrible Harry's Secret. LC 90-32482. (gr. 4-7). 1990. 11.00 (*0-670-82470-4*) Viking Child Bks.

Konigsburg, E. L. The Dragon in the Ghetto Caper. 128p. (gr. 5-6). 1985. pap. 2.75 (*0-440-42148-9*, YB) Dell.

—Father's Arcane Daughter. LC 76-5495. 128p. (gr. 4-8). 1976. SBE 13.95 (*0-689-30524-9*, Atheneum Child Bk) Macmillan Child Grp.

—From the Mixed-Up Files of Mrs. Basil E. Frankweiler. (Illus.). 168p. 1992. Repr. PLB 16.95x (*0-89966-942-5*) Buccaneer Bks.

Kotzwinkle, William. The Empty Notebook. Servello, Joe, illus. LC 89-46198. 96p. (gr. 4). Date not set. 13.95 (*0-87923-826-7*) Godine.

Krayer, Christina, ed. Mystery Express, 88 titles. (Illus.). (gr. 6-10). Date not set. Set. pap. 379.00 (*1-882869-07-9*) Read Advent.

Kwitz, Mary D. Gumshoe Goose, Private Eye. (ps-3). 1991. pap. 3.95 (*0-8037-0923-4*, Dial Easy to Read) Puffin Bks.

Lakin, Patricia. The Birthday Mystery. (Illus.). 13p. (gr. 3-6). 1991. incls. puzzle 12.95 (*0-922242-21-6*) Lombard Mktg.

—The Case of the Missing Ribbons. (Illus.). 14p. (gr. 3-6). 1991. incls. puzzle 12.95 (*0-922242-20-8*) Lombard Mktg.

—The Case of the Stolen Jewels: Puzzling Pen Pal Mysteries Ser. (Illus.). 24p. (gr. 3-4). 1992. bklt., incl. puzzle & pouch 12.95 (*0-922242-33-X*) Lombard Mktg.

Lakin, Patty. Menace or Tennis: A Tennis Twins Mystery. (Illus.). 24p. (gr. 4-8). 1992. bklt., incl. puzzle & pouch 12.95 (*0-922242-35-6*) Lombard Mktg.

Lamb, Nancy. The Great Mosquito, Bull, & Coffin Caper. Remkiewicz, Frank, illus. LC 91-31125. 128p. (gr. 5 up). 1994. pap. 4.95 (*0-688-12944-7*, Pub. by Beech Tree Bks) Morrow.

Landis, Mary M. The Missing Popcorn & Other Stories. (gr. 3-6). 1976. 6.55 (*0-686-15480-0*) Rod & Staff.

Landon, Lucinda. Meg MacKintosh & the Case of the Missing Babe Ruth Baseball: A Solve-It-Yourself Mystery. Landon, Lucinda, illus. LC 85-20055. 48p. (gr. 2-5). 1986. 13.95 (*0-316-51318-0*, 513180, Joy St Bks) Little.

—Meg Mackintosh & the Mystery at the Medieval Castle. (ps-3). 1993. pap. 4.95 (*0-316-51376-8*) Little.

—Meg MacKintosh & the Mystery in the Locked Library: A Solve-It-Yourself Mystery. LC 92-19948. 1993. 13.95 (*0-316-51374-1*, Joy St Bks) Little.

Langton, Jane. The Diamond in the Window. Blegvad, Erik, illus. LC 62-7312. 256p. (gr. 5 up). 1973. pap. 3.95 (*0-06-440042-5*, Trophy) HarpC Child Bks.

Lansdown, Andrew. Beyond the Open Door. (gr. 4-7). 1993. pap. 2.95 (*0-590-47160-0*) Scholastic Inc.

Larkin, Barbara. The Secret of the Stolen Mandolin. 160p. (Orig.). 1987. pap. 3.75 (*1-85168-003-9*) OneWrld Pubns.

Lasky, Kathryn. Double Trouble Squared. (gr. 3 up). 1991. 14.95 (*0-15-224126-4*, HB Juv Bks) HarBrace.

—Double Trouble Squared. (gr. 4-7). 1991. pap. 5.95 (*0-15-224127-2*) HarBrace.

Lavelle, Sheila. The Disappearing Granny. Kopper, Lisa, illus. 42p. (gr. 2-4). 1989. 3.95 (*0-8120-6134-9*) Barron.

Lawrence, James. Binky Brothers, Detectives. Kessler, Leonard, illus. LC 68-10374. 64p. (ps-3). 1985. incl. cassette 5.98 (*0-694-00018-3*, Trophy) HarpC Child Bks.

Lawson, Robert. Captain Kidd's Cat. (Illus.). (gr. 2-4). 1984. pap. 7.95 (*0-316-51735-6*) Little.

Leigh, S. Journey to the Lost Temple. (Illus.). 48p. 1989. PLB 11.96 (*0-88110-406-X*); pap. 4.95 (*0-7460-0308-0*) EDC.

The Lemonade Mystery. (Illus.). 64p. (gr. k-2). 1989. 6.95 (*0-87449-509-1*) Modern Pub NYC.

L'Engle, Madeleine. Dragons in the Waters. LC 76-2477. 304p. (gr. 7 up). 1976. 17.00 (*0-374-31868-9*) FS&G.

—Troubling a Star. LC 93-50956. (gr. 7 up). 1994. 15.00 (*0-374-37783-9*) FS&G.

—The Young Unicorns. LC 68-13682. 256p. (gr. 7 up). 1968. 16.95 (*0-374-38778-8*) FS&G.

Leppard, Lois G. Mandie & the Cherokee Legend, Bk. 2. LC 83-70894. 144p. (Orig.). (gr. 4-7). 1983. pap. 3.99 (*0-87123-321-5*) Bethany Hse.

—Mandie & the Forbidden Attic, Bk. 4. LC 84-72710. 144p. (Orig.). (gr. 4-7). 1985. pap. 3.99 (*0-87123-822-5*) Bethany Hse.

—Mandie & the Midnight Journey. 160p. (Orig.). (gr. 1-6). 1989. pap. 3.99 (*1-55661-084-X*) Bethany Hse.

—Mandie & the Secret Tunnel, Bk. 1. LC 82-74053. 144p. (Orig.). (gr. 4-7). 1983. pap. 3.99 (*0-87123-320-7*) Bethany Hse.

—Mandie & the Shipboard Mystery, Bk. 14. 160p. (Orig.). (gr. 3-8). 1990. 3.99 (*1-55661-120-X*) Bethany Hse.

—Mandie & the Trunk's Secret, Bk. 5. LC 85-71474. 144p. (Orig.). (gr. 3-7). 1985. pap. 3.99 (*0-87123-839-X*) Bethany Hse.

—Mandie & the Washington Nightmare, Bk. 12. LC 88-63464. 160p. (Orig.). (gr. 4-8). 1989. pap. 3.99 (*1-55661-065-3*) Bethany Hse.

Lerangis, Peter. Foul Play. LC 89-39459. 144p. (Orig.). (gr. 5 up). 1990. pap. 2.95 (*0-679-80090-5*) Knopf Bks Yng Read.

Levin, Betty. The Keeping Room. LC 80-23931. (Illus.). 248p. 1989. Repr. of 1981 ed. 11.95 (*0-688-80300-8*) Greenwillow.

Levy, Elizabeth. The Case of the Gobbling Squash. Eagle, Ellen, illus. (gr. 2-4). 1989. pap. 10.95 jacketed (*0-671-63655-3*, S&S BFYR); pap. 2.95 (*0-671-68873-1*, S&S BFYR) S&S Trade.

—Cold As Ice. LC 88-12898. 176p. (gr. 7 up). 1988. 12.95 (*0-688-06579-1*) Morrow Jr Bks.

—Nasty Competition. (gr. 4-7). 1991. pap. 2.75 (*0-590-43833-6*) Scholastic Inc.

—School Spirit Sabotage: A Brian & Pea Brain Mystery. Ulrich, George, illus. LC 93-23029. 96p. 1994. 14.00 (*0-06-023407-5*); PLB 13.89 (*0-06-023408-3*) HarpC Child Bks.

—Something Queer at the Ball Park. Gerstein, Mordicai, illus. 48p. (gr. 1-4). 1984. pap. 3.50 (*0-440-48116-3*, YB) Dell.

—Something Queer at the Haunted School. Gerstein, Mordicai, illus. LC 81-1940. 48p. (gr. 1-3). 1982. 8.95 (*0-440-08349-4*); pap. 9.95 (*0-385-28992-8*) Delacorte.

—Something Queer at the Haunted School. Gerstein, Mordicai, illus. 48p. (gr. 1-4). 1983. pap. 3.25 (*0-440-48461-8*, YB) Dell.

—Something Queer at the Lemonade Stand. Gerstein, Mordicai, tr. LC 81-69666. (Illus.). 48p. (gr. 1-3). 1982. 7.95 (*0-440-07859-8*); pap. 10.95 (*0-385-28901-4*) Delacorte.

—Something Queer at the Library. Gerstein, Mordicai, illus. 48p. (gr. 1-4). 1989. pap. 3.25 (*0-440-48120-1*, YB) Dell.

Lewis, Cass. Dead Man's Confession. LC 93-71557. 232p. 1993. pap. 3.95 (*1-56969-150-9*) FamilyVision.

—Deadly Nightshade. 225p. (gr. 6-12). 1993. pap. 3.95 (*1-56969-155-X*) FamilyVision.

—Till Death Do Us Part. 225p. (gr. 6-12). 1993. pap. 3.95 (*1-56969-153-3*) FamilyVision.

Lexau, Joan M. The Dog Food Caper. Hafner, Marylin, illus. LC 84-1904. 48p. (ps-3). 1985. 8.95 (*0-8037-0107-1*) Dial Bks Young.

—Rooftop Mystery. Hoff, Syd, illus. LC 68-16821. 64p. (gr. k-3). 1968. PLB 13.89 (*0-06-023865-8*) HarpC Child Bks.

Lillington, Kenneth. The Mad Detective. 160p. (gr. 7 up). 1992. 15.95 (*0-571-16593-1*) Faber & Faber.

Lindbergh, Anne M. The Prisoner of Pineapple Place. 192p. 1990. pap. 2.95 (*0-380-70765-9*, Camelot) Avon.

—The Shadow on the Dial. (gr. 3-7). 1988. pap. 2.75 (*0-380-70545-1*, Camelot) Avon.

Lipman, Michel & Furniss, Cathy. Legal Eagle Series, 5 novels. Kratoville, Betty L., ed. (Illus.). 240p. (Orig.). (gr. 4-12). 1988. Set. pap. 15.00 (*0-87879-594-4*) High Noon Bks.

Lisle, Janet T. Sirens & Spies. LC 90-185. 176p. (gr. 7 up). 1990. pap. 3.95 (*0-02-044341-2*, Collier Young Ad) Macmillan Child Grp.

Littke, Lael. Watcher. 1994. pap. 3.50 (*0-590-47088-4*) Scholastic Inc.

Little, Jack. Moon of Isis. LC 76-8728. (gr. 5 up). 1976. pap. 4.00 (*0-934768-00-5*) Altair Pr.

Locke, Joseph. Kiss of Death. 1992. pap. 3.50 (*0-553-29653-1*) Bantam.

—One-Nine-Hundred-Killer. 1994. pap. 3.50 (*0-553-56079-4*) Bantam.

—Vendetta. (gr. 9-12). 1994. pap. 3.50 (*0-553-56080-8*) Bantam.

Logue, Mary. The Haunting of Hunter House. (gr. 3-8). 1992. PLB 8.95 (*0-89565-877-1*) Childs World.

—The Missing Statue of Minnehaha. (gr. 3-8). 1992. PLB 8.95 (*0-89565-902-6*) Childs World.

Longmeyer, Carole M. Clemson Football Mystery. Rhodes, Priscilla, illus. (Orig.). (gr. 3 up). 1994. PLB 24.95 (*1-55609-164-8*); pap. 14.95 (*0-935326-28-6*) Gallopade Pub Group.

—Deadly Duke Football Mystery. Rhodes, Priscilla, illus. (Orig.). (gr. 3 up). 1994. pap. 14.95 (*0-935326-31-6*) Gallopade Pub Group.

—Georgia Tech Football Mystery. Rhodes, Priscilla, illus. (Orig.). (gr. 3 up). 1994. pap. 14.95 (*0-935326-30-8*) Gallopade Pub Group.

—Maryland Football Mystery. Rhodes, Priscilla, illus. 80p. (Orig.). (gr. 3 up). 1994. pap. 14.95 (*0-935326-32-4*) Gallopade Pub Group.

—NC State Football Mystery. Rhodes, Priscilla, illus. (Orig.). (gr. 3 up). 1994. pap. 14.95 (*0-935326-33-2*) Gallopade Pub Group.

—Virginia Football Mystery. Rhodes, Priscilla, illus. 80p. (Orig.). (gr. 3 up). 1994. pap. 24.95 (*0-935326-35-9*) Gallopade Pub Group.

—Wake Forest Football Mystery. Rhodes, Priscilla, illus. (Orig.). (gr. 3 up). 1994. pap. 14.95 (*0-935326-34-0*) Gallopade Pub Group.

Loredo, Betsy. Mystery on the Mississippi. Moran, Michael, illus. 80p. (gr. 4-6). 1994. PLB 12.95 (*1-881889-35-1*) Silver Moon.

Lowenstein, Christina. Fair Play. LC 93-37746. 1994. text ed. write for info. (*0-7167-6520-9*); pap. text ed. write for info. (*0-7167-6531-4*) Spr-Verlag.

Lunn, Janet. Shadow in Hawthorn Bay. 192p. (gr. 5-9). 1988. pap. 3.95 (*0-14-032436-4*, Puffin) Puffin Bks.

Lurie, Susan. Ghostwriter Detective Guide: Tools & Tricks of the Trade. (ps-3). 1992. pap. 3.50 (*0-553-48069-3*) Bantam.

Lutz, John. Double Cross. 4p. (Orig.). 1989. pap. 19.95 incls. puzzle (*0-922242-14-3*) Lombard Mktg.

McBrier, Page. Secret of the Old Garage. Sims, Blanche, illus. LC 85-16505. 96p. (gr. 3-6). 1986. PLB 9.89 (*0-8167-0543-7*); pap. text ed. 2.95 (*0-8167-0544-5*) Troll Assocs.

McCall, Barbara. The Three Investigator's Book of Mystery Puzzles. Rao, Anthony, illus. 64p. (gr. 3-7). 1982. pap. 1.50 (*0-394-85107-2*) Random Bks Yng Read.

McCay, William. Shoot the Works. LC 89-37749. 144p. (gr. 5 up). 1990. pap. 2.95 (*0-679-80157-X*) Random Bks Yng Read.

McCoy, Lois, et al. The Byte Brothers Input an Investigation. Morrill, Leslie H., illus. 1983. pap. 2.25 (*0-380-85571-2*, 85571, Camelot) Avon.

McDaniel, Lurlene. If I Should Die Before I Wake. 128p. (gr. 5-8). 1992. pap. 2.99 (*0-87406-486-4*) Willowisp Pr.
McDonald, Collin. The Chilling Hour. 160p. (gr. 3-7). 1994. pap. 3.95 (*0-06-440493-5*, Trophy) HarpC Child Bks.
MacDonald, Reby E. The Ghosts of Austwick Manor. LC 91-22122. 160p. (gr. 3-7). 1991. pap. 3.95 (*0-689-71533-1*, Aladdin) Macmillan Child Grp.
McEvoy, Seth. Mission to Microworld. 1984. pap. 1.95 (*0-553-24521-X*) Bantam.
McGovern, Ann. Drop Everything, It's D. E. A. R. Time! (ps-3). 1993. pap. 3.95 (*0-590-45802-7*) Scholastic Inc.
McGraw, Eloise. The Seventeenth Swap. 160p. (gr. 4-8). 1987. pap. 2.95 (*0-8167-1050-3*) Troll Assocs.
—Tangled Webb. LC 92-27911. 160p. (gr. 5 up). 1993. SBE 13.95 (*0-689-50573-6*, M K McElderry) Macmillan Child Grp.
McGraw, Eloise J. The Golden Goblet. 248p. (gr. 5-9). 1986. pap. 4.99 (*0-14-030335-9*, Puffin) Puffin Bks.
McHargue, Georgess. The Horseman's Word. (gr. k-12). 1988. pap. 2.95 (*0-440-20126-8*, LFL) Dell.
—The Turquoise Toad Mystery. LC 81-69664. 160p. (gr. 4-6). 1982. 9.95 (*0-385-29057-8*) Delacorte.
McKean, Thomas. Secret of the Seven Willows. LC 91-4447. 160p. (gr. 4-7). 1993. pap. 2.95 (*0-671-86690-7*, Half Moon Bks) S&S Trade.
McKee, Chuck & McKee, David. The Mystery of the Blue Arrows. (Illus.). 32p. (ps-1). 1991. 15.95 (*0-86264-267-1*, Pub. by Andersen Pr UK) Trafalgar.
McKenna, Colleen O. Murphy's Island. 208p. 1991. pap. 2.95 (*0-590-43553-1*, Apple Paperbacks) Scholastic Inc.
McMullan, Kate. Under the Mummy's Spell. 176p. (gr. 5 up). 1992. 16.00 (*0-374-38033-3*) FS&G.
McMurtry, Ken. Manhunt. 1992. pap. 3.25 (*0-553-29841-0*) Bantam.
—Mystery on the Trans-Siberian Express. 1992. pap. 3.25 (*0-553-29686-8*) Bantam.
McNear, Robert & Glassman, Bruce. The Marathon Race Mystery. Rogers, Jackie, illus. LC 84-16395. 128p. (gr. 3-7). 1985. lib. bdg. 9.49 (*0-8167-0444-9*) Troll Assocs.
McOmber, Rachel B., ed. McOmber Phonics Storybooks: The Cove of Gloom. rev. ed. (Illus.). write for info. (*0-944991-83-1*) Swift Lrn Res.
McVey, R. Parker. The Missing Rock Star Caper. Rogers, Jackie, illus. LC 84-8721. 128p. (gr. 3-7). 1985. lib. bdg. 9.49 (*0-8167-0398-1*); pap. text ed. 2.95 (*0-8167-0399-X*) Troll Assocs.
—Mystery at the Ball Game. Rogers, Jackie, illus. LC 84-8486. 128p. (gr. 3-7). 1985. lib. bdg. 9.49 (*0-8167-0336-1*); pap. text ed. 2.95 (*0-8167-0337-X*) Troll Assocs.
Mahy, Margaret. The Changeover. 224p. (gr. 7 up). 1994. pap. 3.99 (*0-14-036599-0*) Puffin Bks.
—Dangerous Spaces. 1991. 12.95 (*0-670-83734-2*) Viking Child Bks.
—Underrunners. 192p. (gr. 5-9). 1992. 14.00 (*0-670-84179-X*) Viking Child Bks.
Maifair, Linda L. The Case of the Angry Actress. 64p. (gr. 2-5). 1994. pap. 2.99 (*0-310-43301-0*) Zondervan.
—The Case of the Bashful Bully. 64p. (gr. 2-5). 1994. pap. 2.99 (*0-310-43281-2*) Zondervan.
—The Case of the Choosey Cheater. 64p. (gr. 2-5). 1993. pap. 2.99 (*0-310-57901-5*, Pub. by Youth Spec) Zondervan.
—The Case of the Creepy Campout. 64p. (gr. 2-5). 1994. pap. 2.99 (*0-310-43271-5*) Zondervan.
—The Case of the Giggling Ghost. 64p. (gr. 2-5). 1993. pap. 2.99 (*0-310-57911-2*, Pub. by Youth Spec) Zondervan.
—The Case of the Missing Max. 64p. (gr. 2-5). 1994. pap. 2.99 (*0-310-43311-8*) Zondervan.
—The Case of the Mixed-up Monsters. 64p. 1993. pap. 0.99 (*0-310-57921-X*, Pub. by Youth Spec) Zondervan.
—The Case of the Pampered Poodler. 64p. (gr. 2-5). 1993. pap. 2.99 (*0-310-57891-4*, Pub. by Youth Spec) Zondervan.
Mallett, Jerry & Bartch, Marian. The Mystery at Chung's Chinese Restaurant. Smith, Mark D., illus. 61p. (gr. 4-7). 1987. PLB 7.80 (*0-8000-1699-8*, 207909) Perma-Bound.
—Mystery at Madame Darkle's Wax Museum. Smith, Mark D., illus. 57p. (gr. 4-7). 1987. PLB 7.80 (*0-8000-0506-6*, 207916) Perma-Bound.
—Mystery at the Hollender Hotel. Smith, Mark D., illus. 57p. (gr. 4-7). 1987. PLB 7.80 (*0-8000-0507-4*, 207918) Perma-Bound.
—Mystery at the Laff-a-Lott Amusement Park. Smith, Mark D., illus. 59p. (gr. 4-7). 1987. PLB 7.80 (*0-8000-0509-0*, 207923) Perma-Bound.
—Mystery at the Seesaw Cinema Company. Smith, Mark D., illus. 60p. (gr. 4-7). 1987. PLB 7.80 (*0-8000-0508-2*, 207922) Perma-Bound.
Manes, Stephen. The Hooples' Haunted House. Weston, Martha, illus. 112p. (gr. 3-7). 1983. pap. 2.25 (*0-440-43794-6*, YB) Dell.
Markham, Marion M. The April Fool's Day Mystery. 64p. 1993. pap. 3.50 (*0-380-71716-6*, Camelot Young) Avon.
—The Birthday Party Mystery. Estrada, Pau, illus. (gr. 2 up). 1989. 13.45 (*0-395-49698-5*) HM.
—The Birthday Party Mystery. 64p. (gr. 1-4). 1990. pap. 2.95 (*0-380-70968-6*, Camelot Young) Avon.
—The Christmas Present Mystery. McCully, Emily A., illus. LC 84-4557. 48p. (gr. 2-5). 13.45 (*0-395-36383-7*) HM.
—The Halloween Candy Mystery. 64p. (gr. 1-4). 1990. pap. 2.95 (*0-380-70965-1*, Camelot Young) Avon.
—The Thanksgiving Day Parade Mystery. Cassidy, Dianne, illus. LC 86-4618. 48p. (gr. 2-5). 1986. 10.95 (*0-395-41855-0*) HM.
Marsh, Carole. Bat Cave Mystery. (Orig.). (gr. 3-8). 1994. PLB 24.95 (*1-55609-154-0*); pap. 14.95 (*0-935326-72-3*) Gallopade Pub Group.
—Blackbeard the Pirate's Missing Head Mystery Spook Kit. (Illus.). (ps-6). 1994. PLB 24.95 (*0-935326-19-7*) Gallopade Pub Group.
—The Haunt of Hope Plantation. Marsh, Carole, illus. (Orig.). (gr. 3-9). 1994. 24.95 (*1-55609-170-2*); pap. 14.95 (*0-935326-03-0*) Gallopade Pub Group.
—Mystery of Old Salem Activity Book. 12p. (Orig.). (gr. 4-8). 1994. pap. 12.00 (*0-935326-67-7*) Gallopade Pub Group.
—Mystery of Old Salem Gamebook. (Orig.). (gr. 4-8). 1994. pap. 19.95 (*0-935326-66-9*) Gallopade Pub Group.
—Mystery of Old Salem S. P. A. R. K. Kit. (Illus., Orig.). (gr. 3-9). 1994. pap. 24.95 (*0-935326-74-X*) Gallopade Pub Group.
—Mystery of Stone Mountain. (Orig.). (gr. 3-7). 1994. PLB 24.95 (*1-55609-180-X*); pap. 14.95 (*0-935326-25-1*) Gallopade Pub Group.
—Mystery of the Lost Colony. (Illus.). (gr. 4-9). 1994. PLB 24.95 (*1-55609-182-6*); pap. 14.95 (*0-935326-05-7*) Gallopade Pub Group.
—Mystery of Tryon Palace Activity Book. (Orig.). (gr. 3-6). 1994. pap. 14.95 (*0-935326-69-3*) Gallopade Pub Group.
—Mystery of Tryon Palace Gamebook. (Orig.). (gr. 2-6). 1994. pap. 14.95 (*0-935326-70-7*) Gallopade Pub Group.
—Mystery of Tryon Palace S. P. A. R. K. Kit. (Illus., Orig.). (gr. 3-8). 1994. pap. 24.95 (*0-317-44654-1*) Gallopade Pub Group.
—Old Salem Mystery. (Orig.). (gr. 3-12). 1994. 24.95 (*1-55609-184-2*); pap. 14.95 (*0-935326-59-6*) Gallopade Pub Group.
—Tryon Palace Mystery. (Orig.). (gr. 3-12). 1994. 24.95 (*1-55609-193-1*); pap. 14.95 (*0-935326-58-8*) Gallopade Pub Group.
Martin, Ann M. Beware Dawn! 160p. 1991. pap. 3.25 (*0-590-44085-3*) Scholastic Inc.
—Claudia & the Mystery at the Museum. 1993. pap. 3.50 (*0-590-47049-3*) Scholastic Inc.
—Dawn & the Disappearing Dogs. (gr. 4-7). 1993. pap. 3.50 (*0-590-44960-5*) Scholastic Inc.
—Jessi and the Jewel Thieves: Baby-sitters Club Mystery Ser. (gr. 4-7). 1993. pap. 3.50 (*0-590-44959-1*) Scholastic Inc.
—Karen's Mystery. 144p. 1991. pap. 2.95 (*0-590-44827-7*) Scholastic Inc.
—Kristy & the Missing Child: Baby-Sitters Club Mystery, No. 4. 160p. 1992. pap. 3.25 (*0-590-44800-5*) Scholastic Inc.
—Mallory & the Ghost Cat. 160p. 1992. pap. 3.25 (*0-590-44799-8*) Scholastic Inc.
—Mary Anne & the Library Mystery. (gr. 4-7). 1994. pap. 3.50 (*0-590-47051-5*) Scholastic Inc.
—Mary Anne's Bad Luck Mystery. 144p. (gr. 3-7). 1988. 3.50 (*0-590-43659-7*) Scholastic Inc.
—Missing since Monday. 176p. (gr. 7 up). 1987. pap. 2.95 (*0-590-43136-6*) Scholastic Inc.
—The Mystery at Claudia's House. 1992. 3.25 (*0-590-44961-3*) Scholastic Inc.
—Stacey & the Mystery at the Mall. (gr. 4-7). 1994. pap. 3.50 (*0-590-47052-3*) Scholastic Inc.
—Stacey & the Mystery Money. (gr. 4-7). 1993. pap. 3.50 (*0-590-45696-2*) Scholastic Inc.
Marvin, Isabel R. Green Fire. Whitaker, Kate, ed. 72p. (gr. 5-8). 1994. pap. 7.95 (*0-932433-15-4*) Windswept Hse.
—Mystery of the Ice Cream House. Whitaker, Kate, ed. LC 93-61532. 64p. (gr. 5-8). 1994. pap. 7.95 (*0-685-72258-9*) Windswept Hse.
Masefield, John. The Midnight Folk. (gr. k-6). 1985. pap. 4.95 (*0-440-45631-2*, Pub. by Yearling Classics) Dell.
Masterman-Smith, Virginia. The Treasure Trap. Litzinger, Roseanne, illus. LC 91-45217. 208p. (gr. 3-7). 1992. pap. 3.95 (*0-689-71578-1*, Aladdin) Macmillan Child Grp.
Masters, Anthony. Klondyker. LC 92-351. 1992. pap. 15. 00 (*0-671-79173-7*, S&S BFYR) S&S Trade.
Matas, Carol. Code Name Kris. LC 90-32656. 160p. (gr. 7 up). 1990. SBE 13.95 (*0-684-19208-X*, Scribners Young Read) Macmillan Child Grp.
Mauser, Pat R. Rip-Off. LC 90-31543. 160p. (gr. 7 up). 1990. pap. 3.95 (*0-02-044471-0*, Collier Young Ad) Macmillan Child Grp.
Mayer, Albert I. Mystery at Seabreeze. (gr. 6-10). 1965. PLB 7.19 (*0-8313-0077-9*) Lantern.
Mazzio, Joann. The One Who Came Back. 208p. (gr. 5-9). 1992. 13.45 (*0-395-59506-1*) HM.
Meacham, Margaret. The Secret of Heron Creek. LC 90-50373. 136p. (Orig.). (gr. 5-8). 1991. pap. 7.95 (*0-87033-414-X*) Tidewater.
Michaels, Ski. Mystery of the Missing Fuzzy. Smolinski, Dick, illus. LC 85-14084. 48p. (Orig.). (gr. 1-3). 1986. PLB 10.59 (*0-8167-0646-8*); pap. text ed. 3.50 (*0-8167-0647-6*) Troll Assocs.
—Mystery of the Windy Meadow. Atkinson, Allen, illus. LC 85-14019. 48p. (Orig.). (gr. 1-3). 1986. PLB 10.59 (*0-8167-0630-1*); pap. text ed. 3.50 (*0-8167-0631-X*) Troll Assocs.
Miller, Marvin. You Be the Detective. (gr. 4-7). 1991. pap. 2.50 (*0-590-42731-8*) Scholastic Inc.
—You Be the Detective, No. II. 1992. 2.50 (*0-590-45690-3*) Scholastic Inc.
—You Be the Jury: Courtroom Three. 96p. (gr. 4 up). 1992. pap. 2.50 (*0-590-45724-1*) Scholastic Inc.
Miller, W. Wesley. Connections, 5 novels. Kratoville, Betty L., ed. Heidinger, Herbert H., illus. 240p. (Orig.). (gr. 4-12). 1988. Set. pap. 15.00 (*0-87879-556-1*) High Noon Bks.
Mills. Secret Carousel. (ps-7). 1987. pap. 2.50 (*0-553-15499-0*, Skylark) Bantam.
Milne, Teddy. The Candy Puzzle: An Alexa Powell Mystery. LC 89-60248. 172p. (gr. 6-8). 1988. pap. 6.95 (*0-938875-16-7*) Pittenbruach Pr.
Monjo, F. N. The Secret of the Sachem's Tree. Tomes, Margot, illus. 64p. (gr. 1-5). 1973. pap. 0.75 (*0-440-47634-8*, Yearling) Dell.
Monsell, Mary E. Crackle Creek. McCord, Kathleen G., illus. LC 89-15105. 64p. (gr. 2-4). 1990. SBE 12.95 (*0-689-31564-3*, Atheneum Child Bk) Macmillan Child Grp.
—A Fish Named Yum: Mr. Spin, Vol. IV. Christelow, Eileen, illus. LC 93-25731. 64p. (gr. 1-4). 1994. SBE 13.95 (*0-689-31882-0*, Atheneum Child Bk) Macmillan Child Grp.
—Mr. Pin: The Chocolate Files. Christelow, Eileen, illus. LC 89-78228. 64p. (gr. 2-5). 1990. SBE 12.95 (*0-689-31639-9*, Atheneum Child Bk) Macmillan Child Grp.
—The Spy Who Came North from the Pole: Mr. Pin, Vol. III. Christelow, Eileen, illus. LC 92-24646. 64p. (gr. 1-4). 1993. SBE 12.95 (*0-689-31754-9*, Atheneum Child Bk) Macmillan Child Grp.
Monson, A. M. The Secret of Sanctuary Island. LC 90-6479. 128p. (gr. 4-7). 1991. 12.95 (*0-688-10111-9*) Lothrop.
The Monster Mystery. (Illus.). 64p. (gr. k-2). 1989. 6.95 (*0-87449-511-3*) Modern Pub NYC.
Montgomery, Lucy M. Among the Shadows. 1991. pap. 4.50 (*0-553-28959-4*) Bantam.
Montgomery, Raymond A. Mystery of the Maya. large type ed. Anderson, Richard, illus. 134p. (gr. 3-7). 1987. Repr. of 1977 ed. 8.95 (*0-942545-00-1*); PLB 9.95 (*0-942545-06-0*, Dist. by Grolier) Grey Castle.
Moore, Ruth N. Danger in the Pines. LC 82-15770. 160p. (gr. 4-9). 1983. text ed. 7.95 (*0-8361-3313-7*); pap. 4.95 (*0-8361-3314-5*) Herald Pr.
—Mystery at Camp Ichthus. Gerig, Sibyl G., illus. LC 86-25637. 128p. (Orig.). (gr. 3-9). 1986. pap. 5.95 (*0-8361-3421-4*) Herald Pr.
—Mystery at Captain's Cove. 160p. (Orig.). (gr. 4-7). 1992. pap. 5.95 (*0-8361-3581-4*) Herald Pr.
—Mystery at Indian Rocks. Bond, Magi, illus. LC 80-25803. 192p. (gr. 5-10). 1981. pap. 4.95 (*0-8361-1944-4*) Herald Pr.
—Mystery at the Spanish Castle. 112p. (Orig.). (gr. 4-8). 1990. pap. 5.95 (*0-8361-3515-6*) Herald Pr.
—Mystery of the Lost Heirloom. Converse, James, illus. LC 85-27334. 152p. (Orig.). (gr. 6-9). 1985. pap. 5.95 (*0-8361-3408-7*) Herald Pr.
—Mystery of the Secret Code. Converse, James, illus. LC 85-5441. 128p. (Orig.). (gr. 7-9). 1985. pap. 5.95 (*0-8361-3394-3*) Herald Pr.
Mooser, Stephen. The Case of the Slippery Sharks. Morrill, Leslie, illus. LC 87-3490. 96p. (gr. 3-6). 1988. PLB 9.89 (*0-8167-1177-1*); pap. text ed. 2.95 (*0-8167-1178-X*) Troll Assocs.
—The Secret Gold Mine. Morrill, Leslie, illus. LC 87-16151. 96p. (gr. 3-6). 1988. PLB 9.89 (*0-8167-1179-8*); pap. text ed. 2.95 (*0-8167-1180-1*) Troll Assocs.
—Secret in the Old Mansion. Morrill, Leslie, illus. LC 87-15456. 96p. (gr. 3-6). 1988. PLB 9.89 (*0-8167-1175-5*); pap. text ed. 2.95 (*0-8167-1176-3*) Troll Assocs.
—The Things Upstairs. LC 93-50676. (Illus.). 144p. (gr. 3-6). 1994. pap. 2.95 (*0-8167-3421-6*) Troll Assocs.
Morris, Gilbert. The Rustlers of Panther Gap. LC 94-7128. (gr. 3-7). 1994. pap. 4.99 (*0-8423-4393-8*) Tyndale.
Moseley, Keith. It Was a Dark & Stormy Night: A Pop-up Mystery Whodunit. Birkinshaw, Linda, illus. 14p. (gr. 1-4). 1991. 12.95 (*0-8037-1021-6*) Dial Bks Young.
Mott, Michael. Master Entrick. (gr. 3-6). 1986. pap. 2.95 (*0-440-45818-8*, YB) Dell.
Murail, Marie-Aude. Mystere. Bloch, Serge, illus. (FRE.). 64p. (gr. 1-5). 1987. pap. 9.95 (*2-07-031217-8*) Schoenhof.
Murphy, Elspeth C. Becky Garcia. Kenyon, Tony, illus. LC 86-8877. 108p. (gr. 3-7). 1986. pap. 4.99 (*1-55513-029-1*, Chariot Bks) Chariot Family.
—The Mystery of the Carousel Horse. LC 87-16722. (gr. 2-4). 1988. pap. 3.99 (*1-55513-163-8*, Chariot Bks) Chariot Family.
—The Mystery of the Double Trouble. LC 87-26461. (gr. 2-4). 1988. pap. 3.99 (*1-55513-545-5*, Chariot Bks) Chariot Family.
—The Mystery of the Gravestone Riddle. LC 87-16721. (gr. 2-4). 1988. pap. 3.99 (*1-55513-800-4*, Chariot Bks) Chariot Family.

—The Mystery of the Laughing Cat. LC 87-16719. (gr. 2-4). 1988. pap. 3.99 (*1-55513-649-4*, Chariot Bks) Chariot Family.
—Mystery of the Messed-Up Wedding. LC 87-16720. (gr. 2-4). 1988. pap. 3.99 (*1-55513-687-7*, Chariot Bks) Chariot Family.
—The Mystery of the Second Map. LC 87-24919. (gr. 2-4). 1988. pap. 3.99 (*1-55513-526-9*, Chariot Bks) Chariot Family.
—The Mystery of the Silent Idol. LC 87-24285. (gr. 2-4). 1988. pap. 3.99 (*1-55513-527-7*, Chariot Bks) Chariot Family.
—The Mystery of the Silver Dolphin. LC 87-24285. (gr. 2-4). 1988. pap. 3.99 (*1-55513-515-3*, Chariot Bks) Chariot Family.
—Mystery of the Tattletale Parrot. LC 87-26460. (gr. 2-4). 1988. pap. 3.99 (*1-55513-528-5*, Chariot Bks) Chariot Family.
—The Mystery of the Vanishing Present. LC 87-20852. (gr. 2-4). 1988. pap. 3.99 (*1-55513-364-9*, Chariot Bks) Chariot Family.
Murrow, Liza K. Fire in the Heart. LC 88-45864. 264p. 1989. 15.95 (*0-8234-0750-0*) Holiday.
—The Ghost of Lost Island. MacDonald, Pat, ed. 176p. (gr. 3-6). 1993. pap. 2.99 (*0-671-75368-1*, Minstrel Bks) PB.
Mysterious Mr. Ross. 1987. pap. 14.95 (*0-440-50235-7*) Dell.
Mystery at Morgan Manor. (gr. 4-8). 1989. PLB 8.49 (*0-87386-060-8*); pap. 1.95 (*0-87386-064-0*) Jan Prods.
The Mystery of Sara Beth. (Illus.). (ps-2). 1991. PLB 6.95 (*0-8136-5116-6*, TK2264); pap. 3.50 (*0-8136-5616-8*, TK2265) Modern Curr.
The Mystery of the Railroad Bell. (gr. 4-6). 1990. 1.55 (*0-89636-115-2*, JB 4B) Accent CO.
Mystery on the Island. (Illus.). (ps-5). 3.50 (*0-7214-0011-6*); o.p. (*0-317-03998-9*) Ladybird Bks.
Naylor, Phyllis R. Bernie & the Bessledorf Ghost. LC 88-29389. 144p. (gr. 3-7). 1990. SBE 13.95 (*0-689-31499-X*, Atheneum Child Bk) Macmillan Child Grp.
—The Bodies in the Bessledorf Hotel. LC 86-3602. 144p. (gr. 3-7). 1986. SBE 13.95 (*0-689-31304-7*, Atheneum Child Bk) Macmillan Child Grp.
—The Mad Gasser of Bessledorf Street. 112p. 1992. pap. 3.50 (*0-380-71350-0*, Camelot) Avon.
—Witch Weed. Burleson, Joe, illus. 192p. (gr. 4-7). 1992. pap. 3.50 (*0-440-40708-7*, YB) Dell.
Nelson, Peter. Deadly Games. 240p. 1992. pap. 2.99 (*0-671-74890-4*, Archway) PB.
—Death Threat. (gr. 9-12). 1993. pap. 3.50 (*0-06-106104-2*, Harp PBks) HarpC.
—Double Dose. 1992. pap. 3.50 (*0-06-106101-8*, Harp PBks) HarpC.
—Scarface. MacDonald, Patricia, ed. 224p. (Orig.). 1991. pap. 2.99 (*0-671-70585-7*, Archway) PB.
—Third Degree. 1992. pap. 3.50 (*0-06-106102-6*, Harp PBks) HarpC.
Nevfield, Len. Skystalker. Rivoche, Paul & Humphrey, Brian, illus. 128p. (Orig.). 1985. pap. 1.95 (*0-553-24894-4*) Bantam.
Nicholson, Peggy & Warner, John F. The Case of the Furtive Firebug. 120p. (gr. 4-7). 1994. RTB 14.95 (*0-8225-0709-9*) Lerner Pubns.
—The Case of the Lighthouse Ghost. 120p. (gr. 4-7). 1994. RTB 14.95 (*0-8225-0710-2*) Lerner Pubns.
—The Case of the Mysterious Codes. 120p. (gr. 4-7). 1994. RTB 14.95 (*0-8225-0712-9*) Lerner Pubns.
—The Case of the Squeaky Thief. 120p. (gr. 4-7). 1994. RTB 14.95 (*0-8225-0711-0*) Lerner Pubns.
Nickell, Joe. The Magic Detectives: Join Them in Solving Strange Mysteries. (Illus.). 115p. (gr. 4-9). 1989. 9.95 (*0-87975-547-4*) Prometheus Bks.
Nixon, Joan L. Candidate for Murder. 1992. pap. 3.99 (*0-440-21212-X*) Dell.
—The Dark & Deadly Pool. LC 87-6723. 192p. (gr. 7 up). 1987. 14.95 (*0-385-29585-5*) Delacorte.
—The Dark & Deadly Pool. 196p. (gr. 6 up). 1989. pap. 3.99 (*0-440-20348-1*, LFL) Dell.
—Deadly Promise. 1993. pap. 3.50 (*0-553-56177-4*) Bantam.
—The Happy Birthday Mystery. Ann, Fay, ed. Cummins, Jim, illus. LC 79-18362. 32p. (gr. 1-3). 1980. PLB 8.95 (*0-8075-3150-2*) A Whitman.
—The Kidnapping of Christina Lattimore. 196p. (gr. 7 up). 1992. pap. 3.99 (*0-440-94520-8*, LFL) Dell.
—The Name of the Game Was Murder. LC 92-8392. 1993. 15.00 (*0-385-30864-7*) Delacorte.
—The New Year's Mystery. Pacini, Kathy, ed. Cummins, Jim, illus. LC 79-172. 32p. (gr. 1-3). 1979. PLB 8.95 (*0-8075-5592-4*) A Whitman.
—The Other Side of Dark. 1987. pap. 3.99 (*0-440-96638-8*, LFL) Dell.
—The Seance. 176p. (gr. 7 up). 1981. pap. 3.99 (*0-440-97937-4*, LFL) Dell.
—Secret Silent Screams. (gr. k-8). 1990. pap. 3.99 (*0-440-20539-5*, LFL) Dell.
—The Stalker. LC 84-16962. (gr. 7 up). 1985. 14.95 (*0-385-29376-3*) Delacorte.
—The Thanksgiving Mystery. Fay, Ann, ed. Cummins, Jim, illus. LC 79-27346. 32p. (gr. 1-3). 1979. PLB 8.95 (*0-8075-7820-7*) A Whitman.
—The Valentine Mystery. Tucker, Kathleen, ed. Cummins, Jim, illus. LC 79-17055. 32p. (gr. 1-3). 1979. PLB 8.95 (*0-8075-8450-9*) A Whitman.
—The Weekend Was Murder. 1992. 15.00 (*0-385-30531-1*) Doubleday.
—Whispers from the Dead. 192p. 1991. pap. 3.50 (*0-440-20809-2*, LFL) Dell.
Norman, Jane & Beazley, Frank. The Case of the Missing Shoes. 24p. (ps-3). 1993. pap. write for info. (*1-883585-07-4*) Pixanne Ent.
—The Mumble Mystery. 24p. (ps-3). 1993. pap. write for info. (*1-883585-12-0*) Pixanne Ent.
—The Mysterious Light. 24p. (ps-3). 1993. pap. write for info. (*1-883585-05-8*) Pixanne Ent.
—The Voice from Nowhere. 24p. (ps-3). 1993. pap. write for info. (*1-883585-10-4*) Pixanne Ent.
—Who Lives There? 24p. (ps-3). 1993. pap. write for info. (*1-883585-13-9*) Pixanne Ent.
Numeroff, Laura J. Why a Disguise? McPhail, David M., illus. LC 93-19025. 1997. pap. 14.00 (*0-671-87006-8*, S&S BFYR) S&S Trade.
O'Brien, Robert C. The Silver Crown. LC 88-2837. 272p. (gr. 7 up). 1988. pap. 3.95 (*0-02-044651-9*, Collier Young Ad) Macmillan Child Grp.
O'Hare, Jeff, ed. Cat & Dog Mysteries: Fourteen Exciting Mini-Mysteries with Hidden Pictures. Palan, R. Michael, illus. 32p. (Orig.). (gr. 2-7). 1993. pap. 4.95 (*1-56397-291-3*) Boyds Mills Pr.
Oliver, M. Search for the Sunken City. (Illus.). 48p. 1989. PLB 11.96 (*0-88110-409-4*); pap. 4.95 (*0-7460-0304-8*) EDC.
Oliver, M. & Waters, G. Agent Arthur's Puzzle Adventures. (Illus.). 1990. pap. 9.95 (*0-7460-0147-9*) EDC.
O'Malley, Kevin. Who Killed Cock Robin? LC 92-40340. (Illus.). (gr. k-3). 1993. 15.00 (*0-688-12430-5*); PLB 14.93 (*0-688-12431-3*) Lothrop.
Oram, Hiawyn. In the Attic. Kitamura, Satoshi, illus. LC 84-15570. 32p. (Orig.). (ps-2). 1988. pap. 4.95 (*0-8050-0780-6*, Bks Young Read) H Holt & Co.
Osborne, Mary P. Spider Kane & the Mystery at Jumbo Nightcrawler's. Chess, Victoria, illus. LC 91-10983. 128p. (gr. 1-5). 1993. 14.00 (*0-679-80856-6*) Knopf Bks Yng Read.
—Spider Kane & the Mystery at Jumbo Nightcrawler's. Chess, Victoria, illus. LC 91-10983. 128p. (gr. 1-5). 1994. pap. 3.50 (*0-679-85393-6*) Random Bks Yng Read.
—Spider Kane & the Mystery under the May-Apple. Chess, Victoria, illus. LC 90-33524. 128p. (gr. 1-7). 1992. 13.00 (*0-679-80855-8*); PLB 13.99 (*0-679-90855-2*) Knopf Bks Yng Read.
—Spider Kane & the Mystery under the May-Apple. Chess, Victoria, illus. LC 90-33524. 128p. (gr. 1-7). 1993. pap. 3.50 (*0-679-84174-1*, Bullseye Bks) Knopf Bks Yng Read.
O'Shea, Brandy. The Black Cat Inn. O'Shea, Bronwyn C., illus. LC 91-67920. Date not set. pap. 8.00 (*1-56002-180-2*, Univ Edtns) Aegina Pr.
Ostheeren, Ingrid. Jonathan Mouse, Detective. Mathieu, Agnes, illus. Lanning, Rosemary, tr. from GER. LC 92-29023. (Illus.). 32p. (gr. k-3). 1993. 14.95 (*1-55858-164-2*); pap. 14.95 (*1-55858-141-3*) North-South Bks NYC.
Packard, Edward. Who Killed Harlowe Thrombey, No. 9. large type ed. Granger, Paul, illus. 121p. (gr. 3-7). 1987. Repr. of 1981 ed. 8.95 (*0-942545-13-3*); PLB 9.95 (*0-942545-18-4*, Dist. by Grolier) Grey Castle.
Pageler, Elaine. Numero Uno Gang Mysteries, 5 novels. (Illus.). 240p. (Orig.). (gr. 3-9). 1988. Set. pap. 15.00 (*0-87879-550-2*) High Noon Bks.

—The Riddle Street Mystery Series, 5 bks. Kratoville, B L, ed. (Illus.). 48p. (gr. 1 up). 1994. pap. 15.00 Set (*0-87879-983-4*) Acad Therapy. Set of five books: The Wrong Robber Mystery, The Market Stake-Out Mystery, The Haunted Apartment House Mystery, The Book Party Mystery, The Radio Station Mystery. Fiction written at a first grade reading level, yet appealing to older youngsters with reading difficulties & to those in literary programs is historically hard to come by. It takes a very special talent to depart from the hackneyed "Dick & Jane" approach yet come up with colorful characters, exciting plots & realistic dialogue all bound together skillfully written first grade level prose. The photographer Brad & the reporter Meg have been assigned the Riddle Street beat by their city editor. Of course, they stumble onto mysteries &, of course, they are on hand to solve them. Plots involving a crooked giveaway, haunted elevator, supermarket scam, bank robbery & book autograph party are all well paced & eminently readable.
Publisher Provided Annotation.

Palazzo-Craig, Janet. Mystery of the Missing Wigs. Harvey, Paul, illus. LC 81-7615. 48p. (gr. 2-4). 1982. PLB 10.89 (*0-89375-592-3*); pap. text ed. 3.50 (*0-89375-593-1*) Troll Assocs.

Papagapitos, Karen. Socorro, Daughter of the Desert. Kleinman, Estelle, ed. Collete, Rondi, illus. 64p. (gr. 1-4). 1993. 6.95 (*0-9637328-0-3*) Kapa Hse Pr.
SOCORRO, DAUGHTER OF THE DESERT is the story of a young girl who knows the answer to a mystery that nobody else seems to see. It is through the eyes of Socorro Hernandez that we find out who the mysterious phantom of the desert road is & why he wants to warn people of any danger that might lie in their path. Socorro's family is going through a difficult period at the same time, & through this young girl's hard work & perseverance, they manage to weather the father's bout with malaria. This book profiles the resourcefulness, courage, & hope women historically have exhibited in trying times. Young readers should enjoy the several appearances of the mysterious phantom & still come away from the conclusion with a strong respect for women & their strength in an often unsettled world. Distributed by Baker & Taylor Books, 652 E. Main St., P.O. Box 6920, Bridgewater, NJ 08807-0920; 908-218-0400.
Publisher Provided Annotation.

Park, Ruth. Things in Corners. (gr. 5-9). 1991. 12.95 (*0-670-82225-6*) Viking Child Bks.
Parker, A. E. Midnight Phone Calls. (gr. 4-7). 1994. pap. 3.25 (*0-590-47804-4*) Scholastic Inc.
—Mystery at the Masked Ball. (gr. 4-7). 1993. pap. 2.95 (*0-590-45633-4*) Scholastic Inc.
Parker, A. E., created by. Who Killed Mr. Boddy? 160p. (gr. 4 up). 1992. pap. 2.95 (*0-590-46110-9*, Apple Paperbacks) Scholastic Inc.
Pascal, Francine. The Case of the Hidden Treasure. (gr. 1-3). 1993. pap. 3.25 (*0-553-48064-2*) Bantam.
—The Case of the Magic Christmas Bell. (ps-3). 1991. pap. 3.25 (*0-553-15964-X*) Bantam.
—The Case of the Million-Dollar Diamonds. (ps-3). 1993. pap. 3.25 (*0-553-48115-0*) Bantam.
—The Case of the Secret Santa. (gr. k-3). 1990. pap. 3.50 (*0-553-15860-0*) Bantam.
—The Charm School Mystery. (gr. 4-7). 1992. pap. 3.25 (*0-553-48050-2*) Bantam.
—The Curse of the Ruby Necklace. (gr. 4-7). 1993. pap. 3.99 (*0-553-15949-6*) Bantam.
—Deadly Summer. 1989. pap. 3.99 (*0-553-28010-4*) Bantam.
—Jessica's Christmas Carol. (gr. 4-6). 1989. pap. 3.50 (*0-553-15767-1*) Bantam.
—The Missing Tea Set. (gr. 1-3). 1993. pap. 2.99 (*0-553-48015-4*) Bantam.
—Murder on the Line. 1992. pap. 3.50 (*0-553-29308-7*) Bantam.
Paterson, Cynthia. The Foxwood Kidnap. Paterson, Brian, illus. 32p. (ps-3). 1986. 6.95 (*0-8120-5771-6*) Barron.
Paterson, Katherine. Sign of the Chrysanthemum. LC 72-7553. 128p. (gr. 7 up). 1991. PLB 14.89 (*0-690-04913-7*, Crowell Jr Bks) HarpC Child Bks.
Patience, John. Dragon Tales. (Illus.). 32p. (gr. k-6). 1991. 3.99 (*0-517-02329-6*) Random Hse Value.
—Hubble Bubble. (Illus.). 32p. (gr. k-6). 1991. 3.99 (*0-517-02333-4*) Random Hse Value.
—The Little People. (Illus.). 32p. (gr. k-6). 1991. 3.99 (*0-517-02334-2*) Random Hse Value.
—Tall Stories. (Illus.). 32p. (gr. k-6). 1991. 3.99 (*0-517-02327-X*) Random Hse Value.
Patneaude, David. Someone Was Watching. Mathews, Judith, ed. LC 92-39130. 240p. (gr. 6-9). 1993. PLB 13.95 (*0-8075-7531-3*) A Whitman.
Paul, Paula. Sarah, Sissy Weed, & the Ships of the Desert. (Illus.). 112p. (gr. 5-6). 1985. 9.95 (*0-89015-504-6*); pap. 5.95 (*0-89015-552-6*) Sunbelt Media.
Paulsen, Gary. Culpepper's Cannon. 96p. (gr. 3-7). 1992. pap. 3.50 (*0-440-40617-X*, YB) Dell.
—Dunc's Undercover. 1993. pap. 3.50 (*0-440-40874-1*) Dell.
Pearson, Susan. The Bogeyman Caper. Fiammenghi, Gioia, illus. 80p. (gr. 1-3). 1990. pap. 11.95 (*0-671-70565-2*, S&S BFYR); (S&S BFYR) S&S Trade.

—The Campfire Ghosts. Fiammenghi, Gioia, illus. 96p. (gr. 1-3). 1990. pap. 11.95 jacketed (*0-671-70567-9*, S&S BFYR); pap. 2.95 (*0-671-70571-7*, S&S BFYR) S&S Trade.
—Eagle-Eye Ernie Comes to Town. Fiammenghi, Gioia, illus. 80p. (gr. 1-3). 1990. pap. 11.95 jacketed (*0-671-70564-4*, S&S BFYR); pap. 2.95 (*0-671-70568-7*, S&S BFYR) S&S Trade.
—The Green Magician Puzzle. Fiammenghi, Gioia, illus. LC 90-22436. 1991. pap. 11.95 (*0-671-74054-7*, S&S BFYR); pap. 2.95 (*0-671-74053-9*, S&S BFYR) S&S Trade.
—The Spooky Sleepover. Fiammenghi, Gioia, illus. 64p. (gr. 1-3). 1991. pap. 12.00 jacketed (*0-671-74070-9*, S&S BFYR); pap. 3.00 (*0-671-74069-5*, S&S BFYR) S&S Trade.
—The Spy Code Caper. Fiammenghi, Gioia, illus. 64p. (gr. 1-3). 1991. pap. 12.00 jacketed (*0-671-74071-7*, S&S BFYR); pap. 3.00 (*0-671-74072-5*, S&S BFYR) S&S Trade.
—The Tap Dance Mystery. Fiammenghi, Gioia, illus. 96p. (gr. 1-3). 1990. (S&S BFYR); pap. 2.95 (*0-671-70570-9*, S&S BFYR) S&S Trade.
Peck, Richard. Blossom Culp & the Sleep of Death. (gr. k-6). 1994. pap. 3.99 (*0-440-40676-5*, YB) Dell.
—The Dreadful Future of Blossom Culp. (gr. k-6). 1994. pap. 3.99 (*0-440-42154-3*, YB) Dell.
—Voices after Midnight. (gr. 5-9). 1989. 14.95 (*0-385-29779-3*) Delacorte.
—Voices after Midnight. 1990. pap. 3.99 (*0-440-40378-2*, Pub. by Yearling Classics) Dell.
Pedersen, Kristin. The Shadow Shop. Thatch, Nancy R., ed. Pedersen, Kristin, illus. Melton, David, intro. by. (Illus.). 29p. (gr. 3-6). 1994. PLB 14.95 (*0-933849-53-2*) Landmark Edns.
Peel, John. Foul Play: Simon Says. 144p. (gr. 3-7). 1993. pap. 2.99 (*0-14-036055-7*, Puffin) Puffin Bks.
—Hangman. LC 92-19940. 128p. (gr. 3-7). 1992. pap. 2.99 (*0-14-036052-2*) Puffin Bks.
—Hide & Seek. LC 92-3757000005. 128p. (gr. 3-7). 1993. pap. 2.99 (*0-14-036054-9*) Puffin Bks.
—Where in Space Is Carmen Sandiego? (gr. 4-7). 1993. pap. 3.25 (*0-307-22207-1*, Golden Pr) Western Pub.
—Where in Space Is Carmen Sandiego? A Mark & See Book with Marker. (gr. 4-7). 1993. pap. 3.95 (*0-307-22305-1*, Golden Pr) Western Pub.
—Where in the World Is Carmen San Diego? 48p. (gr. 4-7). 1991. pap. 3.95 (*0-307-22301-9*, 22301) Western Pub.
—Where in Time Is Carmen San Diego? 48p. (gr. 4-7). 1991. pap. 3.95 (*0-307-22302-7*, 22302) Western Pub.
—Where in Time Is Carmen Sandiego, Pt. II. Nez, John, illus. 96p. (gr. 3-7). 1993. pap. 3.25 (*0-307-22206-3*, 22206-00, Golden Pr) Western Pub.
Peters, Sharon. The Marching Band Mystery. Trivas, Irene, illus. LC 84-8783. 48p. (gr. 2-4). 1985. PLB 10.89 (*0-8167-0406-6*); pap. text ed. 3.50 (*0-8167-0407-4*) Troll Assocs.
Petersen, P. J. Liars. LC 91-28490. 176p. (gr. 5-9). 1992. pap. 15.00 jacketed, 3-pc. bdg. (*0-671-75035-6*, S&S BFYR) S&S Trade.
Pfoutz, Sally. Missing Person. 176p. (gr. 7 up). 1993. 14.99 (*0-670-84663-5*) Viking Child Bks.
Pike, Christopher. Bury Me Deep. MacDonald, Patricia, ed. 224p. (Orig.). 1991. pap. 3.99 (*0-671-69057-4*, Archway) PB.
—Die Softly. MacDonald, Patricia, ed. 224p. (Orig.). 1991. pap. 3.99 (*0-671-69056-6*, Archway) PB.
Pinkwater, Daniel. The Muffin Fiend. LC 85-10944. (Illus.). 48p. (gr. 3-7). 1986. 13.00 (*0-688-04274-0*); PLB 12.93 (*0-688-04275-9*) Lothrop.
Platt, Kin. Big Max. Lopshire, Robert, illus. LC 91-14742. 64p. (gr. k-3). 1965. 13.00 (*0-06-024750-9*); PLB 12.89 (*0-06-024751-7*) HarpC Child Bks.
—Dracula, Go Home. Mayo, Frank, illus. 96p. (gr. 7 up). 1981. pap. 1.25 (*0-440-92022-1*, LE) Dell.
—The Ghost of Hellsfire Street. LC 80-10446. 256p. (gr. 4-6). 1980. 12.95 (*0-385-28317-2*) Delacorte.
Poe, Edgar Allan. The Gold-Bug. 80p. (gr. 6). 1990. PLB 13.95 (*0-88682-303-X*) Creative Ed.
—The Purloined Letter. LC 86-4156. 48p. (gr. 9 up). 1986. PLB 13.95 (*0-88682-061-8*) Creative Ed.
—The Tell-Tale Heart. rev. ed. (gr. 9-12). 1989. Repr. of 1902 ed. multi-media kit 35.00 (*0-685-31131-7*) Balance Pub.
Pokeberry, P. J. The Secret of Hilhouse: An Adult Book for Teens. Mueller, Peggy, illus. Urie, Luanna, frwd. by. LC 93-60940. (Illus.). 96p. (Orig.). (gr. 4 up). 1993. pap. 8.95 (*0-943962-02-1*) Viewpoint Pr.
Porte, Barbara A. Fat Fanny, Beanpole Bertha, & the Boys. Chambliss, Maxie, illus. LC 90-7686. 112p. (gr. 3-5). 1991. 14.95 (*0-531-05928-6*); PLB 14.99 (*0-531-08528-7*) Orchard Bks Watts.
Prince, Steve. The Skylight Cave Mystery. LC 93-79312. 187p. (Orig.). (gr. 9 up). 1993. pap. 9.95 (*0-939116-36-7*) Frontier OR.
Pritts, Kim D. The Mystery of Sadler Marsh. Archambault, Matthew, illus. 112p. (Orig.). (gr. 3-7). 1993. pap. 4.95 (*0-8361-3618-7*) Herald Pr.
Pryor, Bonnie. Marvelous Marvin & the Wolfman Mystery. Sweet, Melissa, illus. 128p. (gr. 7 up). 1994. 14.00 (*0-688-12866-1*) Morrow Jr Bks.
—The Twenty-Four Hour Lipstick Mystery. Hamanaka, Sheila, illus. LC 89-34483. 128p. (gr. 3 up). 1989. 11.95 (*0-688-08198-3*) Morrow Jr Bks.
—The Twenty-Four Hour Lipstick Mystery. Hamanaka, Sheila, illus. 144p. (gr. 4-7). 1992. pap. 3.50 (*0-440-40736-2*, YB) Dell.
Pullman, Philip. The Ruby in the Smoke. LC 86-20983. 240p. (gr. 7 up). 1988. pap. 3.99 (*0-394-89589-4*) Knopf Bks Yng Read.
Quackenbush, Robert. Bicycle to Treachery. 48p. (gr. 1-5). 1991. pap. 2.95 (*0-671-73346-X*, S&S BFYR) S&S Trade.
—Danger in Tibet: A Miss Mallard Mystery. Quackenbush, Robert, illus. 32p. (gr. 1-4). 1989. 14.95 (*0-945912-03-X*) Pippin Pr.
—Evil Under the Sea: A Miss Mallard Mystery. Quackenbush, Robert, illus. 32p. (gr. 1-4). 1992. 14.95 (*0-945912-16-1*) Pippin Pr.
—Sherlock Chick's First Case. Quackenbush, Robert, illus. LC 86-9398. 48p. (ps-3). 1986. 5.95 (*0-8193-1148-0*) Parents.
—Stage Door to Terror. 48p. (gr. 1-5). 1991. pap. 2.95 (*0-671-73347-8*, S&S BFYR) S&S Trade.
—Stairway to Doom. LC 82-21484. (Illus.). 48p. (gr. 2-6). 1998. pap. 5.95 (*0-671-67053-0*, S&S BFYR) S&S Trade.
—Surfboard to Peril. LC 85-24430. (gr. 4-7). 1991. pap. 2.95 (*0-671-73344-3*, S&S BFYR) S&S Trade.
Raphael, Neil & Raphael, Ray. Comic Cops. 182p. (Orig.). (gr. 4-8). 1992. pap. 6.95 (*1-881102-13-0*) Real Bks.
Raskin, Ellen. The Mysterious Disappearance of Leon (I Mean Noel) (Illus.). 160p. (gr. 5-9). 1989. pap. 4.95 (*0-14-032945-5*, Puffin) Puffin Bks.
—Tattooed Potato & Other Clues. (gr. 4-7). 1975. 15.95 (*0-525-40805-3*, 01451-440, DCB) Dutton Child Bks.
—The Westing Game. Raskin, Ellen, illus. 192p. (gr. 7 up). 1984. pap. 3.50 (*0-380-67991-4*, Flare) Avon.
—The Westing Game. (gr. 5-9). 1978. 15.95 (*0-525-42320-6*, DCB) Dutton Child Bks.
—The Westing Game. 192p. (gr. 5 up). 1992. pap. 3.99 (*0-14-034991-X*) Puffin Bks.
Rathjen, Carl H. Mystery at Smoke River. LC 68-23986. (gr. 6-10). 1968. PLB 7.19 (*0-8313-0083-3*) Lantern.
Razzi, Jim & Razzi, Mary. The Search for King Pup's Tomb. 64p. (gr. 3). 1985. pap. 2.25 (*0-553-15312-9*) Bantam.
—Sherluck Bones Mystery, No. 3. (gr. 2-4). 1987. pap. 2.25 (*0-553-15440-0*, Skylark) Bantam.
—The Sherluck Bones Mystery-Detective Book, No. 6. 64p. (Orig.). (gr. 1-3). 1984. pap. text ed. 2.25 (*0-553-15412-5*, Skylark) Bantam.
Razzi, Mary & Razzi, Jim. Sherluck Bones Mystery, No. 2. (gr. 2-4). 1987. pap. 1.95 (*0-685-19144-3*, Skylark) Dell.
Reaves, Michael. Sword of the Samurai. Perry, Steve, illus. 144p. (gr. 4 up). 1984. pap. 2.75 (*0-553-26427-3*) Bantam.
Rebecca. 1993. pap. text ed. 6.50 (*0-582-08486-5*, 79825) Longman.
Repp, Gloria. Secret of the Golden Cowrie. (Illus.). 199p. (Orig.). (gr. 4-6). 1988. pap. 4.95 (*0-89084-459-3*) Bob Jones Univ Pr.
Reynolds, James. Top Secret. 1987. pap. 3.50 (*0-553-15733-7*) Bantam.
Reynolds-Naylor, Phyllis. Night Cry. (gr. 4-7). 1993. pap. 3.50 (*0-440-40017-1*, YB) Dell.
Robbins, Alan. Heading for Trouble: A Soccer Sleuths Mystery. (Illus.). 20p. (gr. 5-7). 1992. bklt., incl. puzzle & pouch 12.95 (*0-922242-34-8*) Lombard Mktg.
Robert, Adrian. The Awful Mess Mystery. Harvey, Paul, illus. LC 84-8724. 48p. (gr. 2-4). 1985. PLB 10.89 (*0-8167-0402-3*); pap. text ed. 3.50 (*0-8167-0403-1*) Troll Assocs.
—Ellen Ross, Private Detective. Garcia, T. R., illus. LC 84-8744. 48p. (gr. 2-4). 1985. PLB 10.89 (*0-8167-0414-7*); pap. text ed. 3.50 (*0-8167-0415-5*) Troll Assocs.
—Secret of the Haunted Chimney. Trivas, Irene, illus. LC 84-8763. 48p. (gr. 2-4). 1985. PLB 10.89 (*0-8167-0408-2*); pap. text ed. 3.50 (*0-8167-0409-0*) Troll Assocs.
—Secret of the Old Barn. Carter, Penny, illus. LC 84-8743. 48p. (gr. 2-4). 1985. PLB 10.89 (*0-8167-0412-0*); pap. text ed. 3.50 (*0-8167-0413-9*) Troll Assocs.
Roberts, Willo D. Dark Secrets. 1991. pap. 3.50 (*0-449-70395-9*) Fawcett.
—Megan's Island. LC 89-18457. 192p. (gr. 4-7). 1990. pap. 3.95 (*0-689-71387-8*, Aladdin) Macmillan Child Grp.
—The Minden Curse. LC 89-18336. 224p. (gr. 4-7). 1990. pap. 3.95 (*0-689-71378-9*, Aladdin) Macmillan Child Grp.
—More Minden Curses. LC 90-31674. 240p. (gr. 3-7). 1990. pap. 3.95 (*0-689-71412-2*, Aladdin) Macmillan Child Grp.
—Nightmare. LC 91-26831. 224p. (gr. 7 up). 1992. pap. 3.95 (*0-02-044938-0*, Collier Young Ad) Macmillan Child Grp.
—No Monsters in the Closet. LC 91-46059. 128p. (gr. 3-7). 1992. pap. 3.95 (*0-689-71577-3*, Aladdin) Macmillan Child Grp.
—The Pet-Sitting Peril. 2nd ed. LC 89-77696. 176p. (gr. 3-7). 1990. pap. 3.95 (*0-689-71427-0*, Aladdin) Macmillan Child Grp.
—Scared Stiff. LC 90-37732. 192p. (gr. 3-7). 1991. SBE 14.95 (*0-689-31692-5*, Atheneum Child Bk) Macmillan Child Grp.
—To Grandmother's House We Go. LC 89-34972. 192p. (gr. 3-7). 1990. SBE 14.95 (*0-689-31594-5*, Atheneum Child Bk) Macmillan Child Grp.
—The View from the Cherry Tree. LC 75-6759. 192p. (gr. 5 up). 1975. SBE 15.95 (*0-689-30483-8*, Atheneum Child Bk) Macmillan Child Grp.
—The View from the Cherry Tree. 3rd ed. LC 93-31170. 192p. (gr. 3-7). 1994. pap. 3.95 (*0-689-71784-9*, Aladdin) Macmillan Child Grp.
—What Could Go Wrong? LC 92-26177. 176p. (gr. 3-6). 1993. pap. 3.95 (*0-689-71690-7*, Aladdin) Macmillan Child Grp.
Robinson, Mary. The Amazing Valvano & the Mystery of the Hooded Rat. LC 87-26179. 168p. (gr. 3-7). 1988. 13.95 (*0-395-44314-8*) HM.
—The Amazing Valvano & the Mystery of the Hooded Rat. 160p. (gr. 5). 1990. pap. 2.75 (*0-380-70713-6*, Camelot) Avon.
Roddy, Lee. The Mystery of the Black Hole Mine. 132p. (gr. 3-7). 1987. pap. 4.99 (*0-89693-320-2*, Victor Books) SP Pubns.
Rodger, Elizabeth. Ollie Solves a Messy Mystery. (Illus.). 32p. (ps-2). 1993. pap. 2.50 (*0-590-44885-4*) Scholastic Inc.
Roland, Timothy. Detective Dan & the Flying Frog Mystery. 48p. (gr. 2-5). 1993. pap. 3.99 (*0-310-38121-5*, Pub. by Youth Spec) Zondervan.
—Detective Dan & the Gooey Gumdrop Mystery. 48p. (gr. 2-5). 1993. pap. 3.99 (*0-310-38111-8*, Pub. by Youth Spec) Zondervan.
—Detective Dan & the Missing Marble Mystery. 2nd, abr., & rev. ed. 48p. (gr. 2-5). 1993. pap. 3.99 (*0-310-38091-X*, Pub. by Youth Spec) Zondervan.
—Detective Dan & the Puzzling Pizza Mystery. 48p. (gr. 2-5). 1993. pap. 3.99 (*0-310-38101-0*, Pub. by Youth Spec) Zondervan.
Roper, Gayle. The Case of the Missing Melody. LC 92-39317. (Illus.). 1993. pap. 4.99 (*1-55513-702-4*, Chariot Bks) Chariot Family.
Rose, M. The Highest Form of Killing. 1992. 16.95 (*0-15-234270-2*, HB Juv Bks) HarBrace.
Rosen, Michael. The Deadman Tapes. 160p. (gr. 7-9). 1989. pap. NOP (*0-233-98443-7*, Pub. by A Deutsch England) Trafalgar.
Ross, Harriet, compiled by. Great Mystery Stories. Bolle, Frank, illus. 160p. (gr. 3-9). 1993. pap. 10.95 (*0-87460-194-0*) Lion Bks.
Ross, Jean. The Martlet Box. 160p. (gr. 5-8). 1990. pap. 6.95 (*0-86241-280-3*, Pub. by Cnngt Pub Ltd) Trafalgar.
Ruckman, Ivy. What's an Average Kid Like Me Doing Way up Here? 144p. (gr. k-6). 1984. pap. 2.75 (*0-440-49448-6*, YB) Dell.
Rushford, Patricia. Silent Witness. 1993. pap. 3.99 (*1-55661-332-6*) Bethany Hse.
—Too Many Secrets. 1993. pap. 3.99 (*1-55661-331-8*) Bethany Hse.
Ryan, John. Pugwash Aloft. (Illus.). 32p. (gr. k-2). 1994. 19.95 (*0-370-00692-5*, Pub. by Bodley Head UK) Trafalgar.
—Pugwash the Smuggler. (Illus.). 32p. (gr. k-2). 1994. 19.95 (*0-370-10786-1*, Pub. by Bodley Head UK) Trafalgar.
Ryan, Mary C. The Voice from the Mendelsohns Maple. Roman, Irena, illus. LC 89-31569. 132p. (gr. 5-7). 1990. 13.95 (*0-316-76360-8*) Little.
Sabin, Fran & Sabin, Lou. The Great Santa Claus Mystery. Trivas, Irene, illus. LC 81-7530. 48p. (gr. 2-4). 1982. PLB 10.89 (*0-89375-602-4*); pap. text ed. 3.50 (*0-89375-603-2*) Troll Assocs.
—Mystery at the Jellybean Factory. Trivas, Irene, illus. LC 81-10388. 48p. (gr. 2-4). 1982. PLB 10.89 (*0-89375-600-8*); pap. text ed. 3.50 (*0-89375-601-6*) Troll Assocs.
Sadler, Mike. Mystery of Mister E. (gr. 4-7). 1992. pap. 4.95 (*0-7910-2924-7*) Chelsea Hse.
St. Antoine, Sara. Ghostwriter: Dress Code Mess. (gr. 4-7). 1992. pap. 2.99 (*0-553-48071-5*) Bantam.
St. John, Patricia M. The Tanglewood's Secret. (gr. 5-8). 1951. pap. 4.99 (*0-8024-0007-8*) Moody.
St. Laurent, Fred. The Heavy House. Soule, Jean, et al, eds. (Illus.). 250p. (Orig.). (gr. 8 up). 1987. pap. 4.95 perfect bdg (*0-938447-02-5*) Rendezvous Pubns.
Samet, Peggy. The Secret on Volcano Hill. LC 89-51672. 44p. (ps). 1989. pap. 5.95 (*1-55523-269-8*) Winston-Derek.
Sanborn, Laura & Sanborn, Jane. The Mystery of Horseshoe Mountain. Wallace, Joan, illus. 108p. (Orig.). (gr. 4-12). 1983. pap. 4.95x (*0-910715-01-7*) Search Public.
Sands, AnnaMaria. Annie Wilkins Mystery Series, 5 novels. Heidinger, Herbert, illus. 240p. (Orig.). (gr. 2-7). 1988. Set. pap. 15.00 (*0-87879-571-5*) High Noon Bks.
Santos, Elsie S. The Mystery at Shawme Pond. Alvaro, Albert M., ed. Santos, Duarte, illus. 20p. (Orig.). (ps-1). 1983. pap. 4.95 (*0-914151-01-0*) E S Santos.
Sargent, Sarah. Between Two Worlds. LC 93-24533. 1995. 13.95g (*0-395-66425-X*) Ticknor & Flds Bks Yng Read.
Sauer, Julia L. The Light at Tern Rock. Schrieber, Georges, illus. 64p. (gr. 3-7). 1994. pap. 3.99 (*0-14-036857-4*) Puffin Bks.
Saunders, Susan. The Creature from Miller's Pond. (Illus.). (gr. 4-8). 1983. pap. 2.25 (*0-553-15424-9*) Bantam.
—Mystery Cat & the Monkey Business. 96p. (Orig.). 1986. pap. 2.25 (*0-553-15452-4*) Bantam.

—The Mystery of the Hard Luck Rodeo. Rosales, Melodye, illus. LC 88-37896. 64p. (Orig.). (gr. 2-4). 1989. PLB 6.99 (*0-394-92344-8*) Random Bks Yng Read.

Schlee, Ann. The Vandal. large type ed. 296p. (gr. 5 up). 1988. 16.95 (*0-7451-0658-7*, Galaxy Child Lrg Print) Chivers N Amer.

Schoch, Tim. Flash Fry, Private Eye. 96p. (Orig.). (gr. 3-7). 1986. pap. 2.50 (*0-380-75108-9*, Camelot) Avon.

Schoolcraft, Robert. Murder on a One-Man Island. Limited ed. Menendez, Manuela, ed. 86p. (Orig.). (gr. 8 up). 1995. pap. 7.50 (*0-9640414-1-3*) MS Bks Pubng.
I spot the speeding boat with two men on board. It's cutting across the Cockenoe Harbor, going full throttle past the flat grassy island. "What are those two fools doing?" I look at Susann who is shouting, flailing one arm, & gesturing to the dive float with the other. "They're coming too close!" Susann is up on the gunwale. "This is a dive site, you creeps. Slow down!" When I look at the speedboat a second later, it's veered straight for Pecks Ledge, & coming towards us. We're in the dinghy which is tied to the anchored sloop, some twenty-five yards from Pecks Ledge Light in Cockenoe Harbor. The aluminized hull shimmers like an unsheathed sword in the sun & the boat splits the water into massive waves as it keeps coming toward us... Thus begins for Marissa Torres (first introduced in ALL CATS ARE GRAY IN THE DARK, 0-9640414-0-5) a three-day sailing trip that becomes a journey of self-discovery.
Publisher Provided Annotation.

Schraff, Anne. Nobody Lives in Apartment N-2. Parker, Liz, ed. Taylor, Marjorie, illus. 45p. (Orig.). (gr. 6-12). 1992. pap. text ed. 2.95 (*1-56254-057-2*) Saddleback Pubns.

Schultz, Irene. The Woodland Gang & the Dark Old House. (Illus.). 128p. (gr. 3 up). 1984. pap. 4.95 (*0-318-40971-2*) Addison-Wesley.

—The Woodland Gang & the Dinosaur Bones. Cahoun, Cindy, illus. 128p. (gr. 3 up). 1988. pap. 4.95 (*0-201-50056-6*) Addison-Wesley.

—The Woodland Gang & the Ghost Cat. Kahoun, Cindy, illus. 128p. (gr. 3 up). 1988. pap. 4.95 (*0-201-50054-X*) Addison-Wesley.

—The Woodland Gang & the Indian Cave. Kahoun, Cindy, illus. 128p. (gr. 3 up). 1988. pap. 4.95 (*0-201-50055-8*) Addison-Wesley.

—The Woodland Gang & the Museum Robbery. Kahoun, Cindy, illus. 128p. (Orig.). (gr. 3 up). 1988. pap. 4.95 (*0-201-50053-1*) Addison-Wesley.

—The Woodland Gang & the Mystery Quilt. Kahoun, Cindy, illus. 128p. (gr. 3 up). 1988. pap. 4.95 (*0-201-50051-5*) Addison-Wesley.

—The Woodland Gang & the Secret Spy Code. Cahoun, Cindy, illus. 128p. (Orig.). (gr. 3 up). 1988. pap. 4.95 (*0-201-50052-3*) Addison-Wesley.

Schuyler, Royce. Jessie J: Red Rock Ranch Detective: A Literary Adventure for Gifted Students. Kester, Ellen S., ed. Turner, Joseph R., III, illus. 190p. (Orig.). (gr. 3-6). 1989. pap. 6.95 (*0-685-26280-4*); tchr's. manual 35.00 (*0-685-26281-2*) Pickwick Pubs.

Schwartz, Alvin. In a Dark, Dark Room & Other Scary Stories. Zimmer, Dirk, illus. LC 83-47699. 64p. (gr. k-3). 1984. 14.00 (*0-06-025271-5*); PLB 13.89 (*0-06-025274-X*) HarpC Child Bks.

Scoppettone, Sandra. Playing Murder. LC 83-47707. 224p. (gr. 7 up). 1987. pap. 2.75 (*0-06-447046-6*, Trophy) HarpC Child Bks.

Scott, Bill. Many Kinds of Magic: Tales of Mystery, Myth & Enchantment. (gr. 4-7). 1990. 14.95 (*0-670-82971-4*) Viking Child Bks.

Scott, Michael. October Moon. LC 93-8693. 160p. (gr. 7 up). 1994. 14.95 (*0-8234-1110-9*) Holiday.

Scott, R. C. Blood Sport. (gr. 7 up). 1984. pap. 2.25 (*0-553-23866-3*) Bantam.

Sefton, Catherine. Along a Lonely Road. large type ed. 1993. 16.95 (*0-7451-1909-3*, Galaxy Child Lrg Print) Chivers N Amer.

Senn, Steve. The Double Disappearance of Walter Fozbek. new ed. 128p. (gr. 2-4). 1980. 9.95 (*0-8038-1571-9*) Hastings.

Service, Pamela F. Phantom Victory. LC 93-37904. 128p. (gr. 5-7). 1994. SBE 14.95 (*0-684-19441-4*, Scribners Young Read) Macmillan Child Grp.

Sharmat, Marjorie W. Mysteriously Yours, Maggie Marmelstein. Shecter, Ben, illus. LC 81-48656. 160p. (gr. 3-6). 1984. pap. 3.95 (*0-06-440145-6*, Trophy) HarpC Child Bks.

—Nate the Great. 64p. (gr. 1-4). 1977. pap. 3.50 (*0-440-46126-X*, YB) Dell.

—Nate the Great & the Boring Beach Bag. Simont, Marc, illus. 48p. (gr. 1-4). 1987. 13.95 (*0-698-20631-2*, Coward) Putnam Pub Group.

—Nate the Great & the Halloween Hunt. (Illus.). 48p. (gr. 1-4). 1989. 12.95 (*0-698-20635-5*, Coward) Putnam Pub Group.

—Nate the Great & the Lost List. Simont, Marc, illus. 48p. 1981. pap. 3.50 (*0-440-46282-7*, YB) Dell.

—Nate the Great & the Mushy Valentine. Simont, Marc, illus. LC 93-15488. 1994. 12.95 (*0-385-31166-4*) Delacorte.

—Nate the Great & the Phony Clue. Simont, Marc, illus. 48p. (gr. k-6). 1981. pap. 3.50 (*0-440-46300-9*, YB) Dell.

—Nate the Great & the Sticky Case. Simont, Marc, illus. (gr. k-6). 1981. pap. 3.50 (*0-440-46289-4*) Dell.

—Nate the Great: And the Stolen Base. Simont, Marc, illus. 48p. (gr. 1-4). 1992. 12.95 (*0-698-20708-4*, Coward) Putnam Pub Group.

—Nate the Great Goes Down in the Dumps. Simont, Marc, illus. 48p. (gr. 1-4). 1989. 13.95 (*0-698-20636-3*, Coward) Putnam Pub Group.

—Nate the Great Goes Undercover. 48p. 1978. pap. 3.50 (*0-440-46302-5*, YB) Dell.

—Nate the Great Goes Undercover. Simont, Marc, illus. 48p. (gr. 1-4). 1989. 13.95 (*0-698-20643-6*, Coward); (Coward) Putnam Pub Group.

—The Princess of the Fillmore Street School. (gr. 4-7). 1991. pap. 2.75 (*0-440-40415-0*) Dell.

Sharmat, Marjorie W. & Sharmat, Mitchell. The Princess of the Fillmore Street School. Brunkus, Denise, illus. LC 89-1106. (gr. 2-4). 1989. 12.95 (*0-385-29811-0*) Delacorte.

Sharmat, Marjorie W. & Weinman, Rosalind. Nate the Great & the Pillowcase. Simont, Marc, illus. LC 92-34405. 1993. 12.95 (*0-385-31051-X*) Delacorte.

Shaw, Diana. Lessons in Fear: A Carter Colborn Mystery. (gr. 7 up). 1987. 12.95 (*0-316-78341-2*, Joy St Bks) Little.

Shaw, Murray. Match Wits with Sherlock Holmes, Vol. 1. (gr. 4-7). 1991. pap. 4.95 (*0-87614-528-4*) Carolrhoda Bks.

—Match Wits with Sherlock Holmes, Vol. 2. (gr. 4-7). 1991. pap. 4.95 (*0-87614-529-2*) Carolrhoda Bks.

—Match Wits with Sherlock Holmes, Vol. 3. (gr. 4-7). 1991. pap. 4.95 (*0-87614-530-6*) Carolrhoda Bks.

—Match Wits with Sherlock Holmes, Vol. 4. (gr. 4-7). 1991. pap. 4.95 (*0-87614-531-4*) Carolrhoda Bks.

—Match Wits with Sherlock Holmes, Vol. 5: The Adventure of the Speckled Band, the Sussex Vampire. (gr. 4-7). 1992. pap. 4.95 (*0-87614-549-7*) Carolrhoda Bks.

—Match Wits with Sherlock Holmes, Vol. 6: The Adventure of the Abbey Grange, the Boscombe Valley. (gr. 4-7). 1992. pap. 4.95 (*0-87614-550-0*) Carolrhoda Bks.

Shaw, Murray, adapted by. The Adventure of Black Peter & The 'Gloria Scott, Vol. I. Overlie, George, illus. (gr. 4-6). 1990. PLB 14.95 (*0-87614-385-0*) Carolrhoda Bks.

—The Adventure of the Cardboard Box & Scandal in Bohemia, Vol. II. Overlie, George, illus. (gr. 4-6). 1990. PLB 14.95 (*0-87614-386-9*) Carolrhoda Bks.

—The Adventure of the Copper Beeches & The Redheaded League, Vol. IV. Overlie, George, illus. (gr. 4-6). 1990. PLB 14.95 (*0-87614-388-5*) Carolrhoda Bks.

—The Adventure of the Six Napoleons & the Blue Carbuncle, Vol. III. Overlie, George, illus. (gr. 4-6). 1990. PLB 14.95 (*0-87614-387-7*) Carolrhoda Bks.

Sheldon, Ann. Linda Craig: Search for Scorpio. Barish, Wendy, ed. 160p. (Orig.). (gr. 3 up). 1984. pap. 3.95 (*0-671-53237-5*) S&S Trade.

Sherlock Chick & the Giant Egg Mystery. (Illus.). 42p. (ps-3). 1993. PLB 13.27 (*0-8368-0897-5*) Gareth Stevens Inc.

Sherlock Chick's First Case. 42p. (ps-3). 1993. PLB 13.27 (*0-8368-0892-4*) Gareth Stevens Inc.

Sherlock Holmes Short Stories. 1993. pap. text ed. 6.50 (*0-582-09676-6*, 79827) Longman.

Shulevitz, Uri. Secret Room. 1993. 15.00 (*0-374-34169-9*) FS&G.

Shura, Mary F. The Josie Gambit. 128p. (gr. 3-7). 1988. pap. 2.50 (*0-380-70497-8*, Camelot) Avon.

Shusterman, Neal. The Scorpian Shard. 1994. 14.95 (*0-312-85506-0*) Forge NYC.

Singer, Marilyn. The Case of the Fixed Election: A Sam & Dave Mystery. Williams, Richard, illus. LC 88-21178. 80p. (gr. 3-7). 1989. HarpC Child Bks.

—A Clue in Code: A Sam & Dave Mystery. Glasser, Judy, illus. LC 84-48335. 64p. (gr. 3-7). 1988. pap. 3.95 (*0-06-440244-4*, Trophy) HarpC Child Bks.

Sisson, Pamla A. Kasandra's Mystery in Mazatlan. 64p. 1993. pap. 5.99 (*0-9638328-0-8*) P A Sisson.

Skulavik, Mary A. Bert. Kostrko, Zofia, illus. 32p. (ps-3). 1990. 13.95 (*0-8027-6962-4*); lib. bdg. 14.85 (*0-8027-6963-2*) Walker & Co.

Sleator, William. Spirit House. LC 91-2131. 144p. (gr. 5-11). 1991. 13.95 (*0-525-44814-4*, DCB) Dutton Child Bks.

—The Spirit House. LC 93-7485. 144p. (gr. 7 up). 1993. pap. 3.99 (*0-14-036483-8*, Puffin) Puffin Bks.

Smath, Jerry. Investigator in the Mystery at Camp Crump. Smath, Jerry, illus. LC 94-20115. 32p. (gr. k-2). 1994. PLB 9.89 (*0-8167-3588-3*, Whistlestop); pap. text ed. 2.25 (*0-8167-3422-4*, Whistlestop) Troll Assocs.

Smith, Doris B. A Taste of Blackberries. Robinson, Charles, illus. LC 72-7558. 64p. (gr. 3-6). 1973. PLB 12.89 (*0-690-80512-8*, Crowell Jr Bks) HarpC Child Bks.

Smith, L. J. The Captive. 1992. pap. 3.99 (*0-06-106715-6*, Harp PBks) HarpC.

—The Power. 1992. pap. 3.99 (*0-06-106719-9*, Harp PBks) HarpC.

—Secret Circle: The Initiation, Vol. 1. 1992. pap. 3.99 (*0-06-106712-1*, Harp PBks) HarpC.

Smith, Matthew V. Where Are All the Children. Smith, Matthew V., illus. 10p. (gr. 1-2). 1992. pap. 12.95 (*1-56606-002-8*) Bradley Mann.

Smith, T. H. Cry to the Night Wind. (gr. 5-9). 1988. pap. 4.95 (*0-14-031931-X*, Puffin) Puffin Bks.

Snyder, Zilpha K. The Famous Stanley Kidnapping Case. (gr. 4-6). 1985. pap. 3.50 (*0-440-42485-2*, YB) Dell.

—Janie's Private Eyes. (gr. 5-7). 1989. 14.95 (*0-440-50123-7*) Delacorte.

—The Truth About Stone Hollow. (gr. k-6). 1986. pap. 3.25 (*0-440-48846-X*, YB) Dell.

—The Velvet Room. (gr. 4-6). 16.75 (*0-8446-6419-7*) Peter Smith.

Sobol, Donald. Encyclopedia Brown & the Case of the Dead Eagle. Sobol, Donald, illus. 1994. pap. 3.50 (*0-553-48167-3*, Skylark) Bantam.

Sobol, Donald J. Encyclopedia Brown. 1982. pap. 3.50 (*0-553-15722-1*) Bantam.

—Encyclopedia Brown - Pitches. 1982. pap. 3.50 (*0-553-15736-1*) Bantam.

—Encyclopedia Brown - Saves. 1982. pap. 3.50 (*0-553-15734-5*) Bantam.

—Encyclopedia Brown - Tracks. 1982. pap. 3.50 (*0-553-15721-3*) Bantam.

—Encyclopedia Brown & the Case of the Dead Eagles. Shortall, Leonard & Brandi, Lillian, illus. LC 75-15911. 96p. (gr. 3-5). 1979. 12.50 (*0-525-67220-6*, Lodestar Bks) Dutton Child Bks.

—Encyclopedia Brown & the Case of the Mysterious Handprints. Owens, Gail, illus. LC 85-8798. 96p. (gr. 3-7). 1985. 12.95 (*0-688-04626-6*) Morrow Jr Bks.

—Encyclopedia Brown & the Case of the Midnight Visitor. Brandi, Lillian & Shortall, Leonard, illus. LC 77-22159. 96p. (gr. 3-5). 1979. 12.50 (*0-525-67221-4*, Lodestar Bks) Dutton Child Bks.

—Encyclopedia Brown & the Case of the Secret Pitch. (gr. 4-8). 1978. pap. 2.25 (*0-553-15587-3*, Skylark Bks) Bantam.

—Encyclopedia Brown & the Case of the Secret Pitch. Shortall, Leonard & Brandi, Lillian, illus. LC 65-199640. 96p. (gr. 3-5). 1979. 12.50 (*0-525-67202-8*, Lodestar Bks) Dutton Child Bks.

—Encyclopedia Brown Boy Detective. (gr. 4-8). 1985. pap. 3.50 (*0-553-15724-8*) Bantam.

—Encyclopedia Brown, Boy Detective. Shortall, Leonard & Brandi, Lillian, illus. LC 63-9632. 96p. (gr. 3-5). 1979. 12.95 (*0-525-67200-1*, Lodestar Bks) Dutton Child Bks.

—Encyclopedia Brown Carries On. Ohlsson, Ib, illus. LC 79-6340. 80p. (gr. 3-7). 1984. SBE 13.95 (*0-02-786190-2*, Four Winds) Macmillan Child Grp.

—Encyclopedia Brown Finds the Clues. (gr. 4-8). 1982. pap. 3.50 (*0-553-15725-6*) Bantam.

—Encyclopedia Brown Finds the Clues. Shortall, Leonard & Brandi, Lillian, illus. LC 66-10230. 96p. (gr. 3-5). 1979. 12.95 (*0-525-67204-4*, Lodestar Bks) Dutton Child Bks.

—Encyclopedia Brown Gets His Man. Shortall, Leonard & Brandi, Lillian, illus. LC 67-24666. 96p. (gr. 3-5). 1979. 12.50 (*0-525-67206-0*, Lodestar Bks) Dutton Child Bks.

—Encyclopedia Brown Gets His Man, No. 4. LC 67-24666. (gr. 4-8). 1982. pap. 2.50 (*0-553-15526-1*, Skylark Bks) Bantam.

—Encyclopedia Brown Keeps the Peace. Shortall, Leonard & Brandi, Lillian, illus. LC 73-82912. 96p. (gr. 3-5). 1979. 12.50 (*0-525-67208-7*, Lodestar Bks) Dutton Child Bks.

—Encyclopedia Brown Keeps the Peace, No. 6. 1982. pap. 3.25 (*0-553-15735-3*, Skylark Bks) Bantam.

—Encyclopedia Brown Lends a Hand. Shortall, Leonard & Brandi, Lillian, illus. LC 74-10281. 96p. (gr. 3-5). 1979. 13.00 (*0-525-67218-4*, Lodestar Bks) Dutton Child Bks.

—Encyclopedia Brown Lends a Hand. (gr. 4-6). 1993. pap. 3.25 (*0-553-48133-9*) Bantam.

—Encyclopedia Brown Saves the Day. Shortall, Leonard & Brandi, Lillian, illus. LC 71-117149. 96p. (gr. 3-5). 1979. 12.50 (*0-525-67210-9*, Lodestar Bks) Dutton Child Bks.

—Encyclopedia Brown Saves the Day, No. 7. (gr. 4-8). 1982. pap. 2.50 (*0-553-15539-3*, Skylark Bks) Bantam.

—Encyclopedia Brown Sets the Pace. Ohlsson, Ib, illus. LC 81-69511. 96p. (gr. 3-7). 1984. SBE 13.95 (*0-02-786200-3*, Four Winds) Macmillan Child Grp.

—Encyclopedia Brown Sets the Pace. 96p. (gr. 3-7). 1991. pap. 2.95 (*0-590-44577-4*, Apple Paperbacks) Scholastic Inc.

—Encyclopedia Brown Shows the Way. Shortall, Leonard & Brandi, Shortall, illus. LC 72-2911. 96p. (gr. 3-5). 1979. 12.50 (*0-525-67216-8*, Lodestar Bks) Dutton Child Bks.

—Encyclopedia Brown Shows the Way, No. 9. 96p. (gr. 3-6). 1982. pap. 3.50 (0-553-15737-X) Bantam.

—Encyclopedia Brown Solves Them All. Shortall, Leonard & Brandi, Lillian, illus. LC 68-22746. 96p. (gr. 3-5). 1979. 12.50 (0-525-67212-5, Lodestar Bks) Dutton Child Bks.

—Encyclopedia Brown Solves Them All. (gr. 4-7). 1993. pap. 3.25 (0-553-48080-4) Bantam.

—Encyclopedia Brown Takes a Case. 1982. pap. 3.50 (0-553-15723-X) Bantam.

—Encyclopedia Brown Takes the Cake. (gr. 4-7). 1991. pap. 2.95 (0-590-44576-6) Scholastic Inc.

—Encyclopedia Brown Takes the Case. Shortall, Leonard & Brandi, Leonard, illus. LC 73-6443. 96p. (gr. 3-5). 1979. 12.50 (0-525-66318-5, Lodestar Bks) Dutton Child Bks.

—Encyclopedia Brown Takes the Case, No. 10. (gr. 8-12). 1982. pap. 2.50 (0-553-15528-8) Bantam.

—Encyclopedia Brown Tracks Them Down. Shortall, Leonard & Brandi, Lillian, illus. LC 77-160147. 96p. (gr. 3-5). 1979. 12.95 (0-525-67214-1, Lodestar Bks) Dutton Child Bks.

—Encyclopedia Brown's Book of Wacky Crimes. Enik, Ted, illus. LC 82-9683. 128p. (gr. 3-5). 1982. 12.95 (0-525-66786-5, Lodestar Bks) Dutton Child Bks.

—Encyclopedia Brown's Book of Wacky Crimes. Enik, Ted, illus. 1983. pap. 2.25 (0-553-15358-7) Bantam.

—Encyclopedia Brown's Book of Wacky Spies. Enik, Ted, illus. LC 83-17179. 128p. (gr. 3-7). 1984. 13.95 (0-688-02744-X) Morrow Jr Bks.

—Encyclopedia Brown's Third Record Book of Weird & Wonderful Facts. Murdocca, Sal, illus. LC 85-11613. 144p. (gr. 3-7). 1985. 11.95 (0-688-05705-5) Morrow Jr Bks.

—Finds The Clues. (gr. 4-7). 1987. pap. 2.50 (0-553-15570-9) Bantam.

—The Secret Case of the Disgusting Sneakers. (gr. 4-7). 1991. pap. 3.50 (0-553-15851-1) Bantam.

—Still More Two-Minute Mysteries. 1993. pap. 2.75 (0-590-44786-6) Scholastic Inc.

—Two-Minute Mysteries. 160p. (Orig.). (gr. 5-8). 1986. pap. 2.50 (0-590-41292-2, Apple Paperbacks) Scholastic Inc.

—Two-Minute Mysteries. 160p. 1991. pap. 2.95 (0-590-44787-4, Apple Paperbacks) Scholastic Inc.

Sobol, Donald J. & Andrews, Glenn. Encyclopedia Brown Takes the Cake! A Cook & Case Book. Ohlsson, Ib, illus. LC 82-84250. 128p. (gr. 3-7). 1984. SBE 13.95 (0-02-786210-0, Four Winds) Macmillan Child Grp.

Sobol, Donald J. & Velasquez, Eric. Encyclopedia Brown & the Case of the Two Spies. LC 93-14350. 1994. 13.95 (0-385-32036-1) Delacorte.

Southall, Ivan. The Long Night Watch. LC 83-48702. 160p. (gr. 7 up). 1984. 14.00 (0-374-34644-5) FS&G.

Spektor, Zev. Shadows in the Night. (Illus.). 150p. (gr. 5-6). 1991. 11.95 (1-56062-100-1); pap. 8.95 (0-685-52958-4) CIS Comm.

Spicer, Dorothy. Humming Top. LC 68-31176. (gr. 7-11). 1968. 21.95 (0-87599-147-5) S G Phillips.

Spirn, Michele. What's in the Trunk? (ps-1). 1988. 8.49 (0-87386-057-8); incl. cassette 16.99 (0-685-25202-7); pap. 1.95 (0-87386-053-5); pap. 9.95 incl. cassette (0-685-25203-5) Jan Prods.

Springstubb, Tricia. Two Plus One Makes Trouble. (ps-3). 1991. pap. 2.50 (0-590-44648-7) Scholastic Inc.

Stahl, Hilda. Elizabeth Gail & the Mystery at the Johnson Farm, No. 1. 128p. (gr. 5 up). 1988. 4.99 (0-8423-0739-7) Tyndale.

—Elizabeth Gail & the Secret Box, No. 2. 128p. (gr. 5 up). 1988. 4.99 (0-8423-0740-0) Tyndale.

—Elizabeth Gail & the Teddy Bear Mystery. (gr. 3-9). 1979. pap. 4.99 (0-8423-0722-2) Tyndale.

—Elizabeth Gail & the Teddy Bear Mystery, No. 3. 128p. (gr. 5 up). 1988. 4.99 (0-8423-0811-3) Tyndale.

—Hannah & the Daring Escape. LC 92-43994. 160p. (gr. 4-7). 1993. pap. 3.99 (0-89107-714-6) Crossway Bks.

—The Missing Newspaper Caper. LC 86-71178. 128p. (gr. 4-6). 1987. pap. 3.99 (0-89636-221-3, Chariot Bks) Chariot Family.

—Mystery at Bellwood Estate. LC 92-41738. 160p. (gr. 4-7). 1993. pap. 3.99 (0-89107-713-8) Crossway Bks.

—Roxie & the Red Rose Mystery. LC 92-4851. 160p. (gr. 4-7). 1992. pap. 3.99 (0-89107-681-6) Crossway Bks.

—Sendi Lee Mason & the Milk Carton Kids. LC 89-81253. 126p. (gr. 2-5). 1990. pap. 4.95 (0-89107-547-X) Crossway Bks.

Stamper, Judith B. More Tales for the Midnight Hour. 1992. pap. 2.95 (0-590-45344-0, Point) Scholastic Inc.

Stanish, Bob. Mindanderings. (Illus.). 112p. (gr. 4-9). 1990. 9.95 (0-86653-526-8, GA1140) Good Apple.

Stanley, George E. Codebreaker Kids. 112p. (gr. 3-7). 1987. pap. 2.95 (0-380-75228-X, Camelot) Avon.

—The Codebreaker Kids Return. 128p. (gr. 3-7). 1989. pap. 2.50 (0-380-75608-0, Camelot) Avon.

—The Italian Spaghetti Mystery. 112p. (gr. 3 up). 1987. pap. 2.50 (0-380-75166-6, Camelot) Avon.

Steffens, J. & Carr, J. Mystery & Suspense. (gr. 7-12). 1983. 9.95 (0-88160-096-2, LW 1006) Learning Wks.

Steig, William. Real Thief. LC 73-77910. (Illus.). 64p. (ps up). 1984. pap. 3.50 (0-374-46208-9, Sunburst) FS&G.

Steiner, Barbara. Deathline. 176p. (Orig.). (gr. 5). 1993. pap. 3.50 (0-380-77066-0, Flare) Avon.

—Oliver Dibbs to the Rescue! Christelow, Eileen, illus. 128p. 1988. pap. 2.50 (0-380-70465-X, Camelot) Avon.

—The Photographer Two: The Dark Room. 176p. (Orig.). 1993. pap. 3.50 (0-380-77064-4, Flare) Avon.

Stevenson, Drew. Toying with Danger: A Sarah Capshaw Mystery. Ramsey, Marcy D., illus. LC 92-19325. (gr. 4-6). 1993. 14.00 (0-525-65115-2, Cobblehill Bks) Dutton Child Bks.

Stevenson, Robert Louis. Dr. Jekyll & Mr. Hyde. new ed. Platt, Kin, ed. Redondo, Nestor, illus. LC 73-75457. 64p. (Orig.). (gr. 5-10). 1973. pap. 2.95 (0-88301-096-8); student activity bk. 1.25 (0-88301-176-X) Pendulum Pr.

—Dr. Jekyll & Mr. Hyde. reissue ed. McMullan, Kate, adapted by. Van Munching, Paul, illus. LC 83-15972. 96p. (gr. 2-6). 1984. pap. 3.50 (0-394-86365-8) Random Bks Yng Read.

—Kidnapped. 1991. pap. 2.50 (0-8125-0473-9) Tor Bks.

Stevenson, Robert Louis & Snyder, John K., III. Dr. Jekyll & Mr. Hyde. (Illus.). 52p. Date not set. pap. 4.95 (1-57209-008-1) Classics Int Ent.

Stewart, Linda. Sam the Cat Detective. (gr. 4-7). 1993. pap. 2.95 (0-590-46145-1) Scholastic Inc.

Stine, Megan & Stine, H. William. Long Shot, Bk. 10. LC 89-24355. 144p. (gr. 5 up). 1990. lib. bdg. 7.99 (0-679-90526-X) Random Bks Yng Read.

—Murder to Go. LC 88-14693. 144p. (Orig.). (gr. 5 up). 1989. pap. 2.95 (0-394-89980-6) Knopf Bks Yng Read.

—Thriller Diller. LC 88-45881. (Illus.). 144p. (Orig.). (gr. 5 up). 1989. pap. 2.95 (0-394-82936-0) Knopf Bks Yng Read.

Stine, Megan & Stine, H. William, eds. The Mummy's Curse. LC 91-53167. (Illus.). 136p. (Orig.). (gr. 4-8). 1992. PLB cancelled (0-679-92774-3); pap. 3.50 (0-679-82774-9) Random Bks Yng Read.

Stine, R. L. Curtains. MacDonald, Patricia, ed. 160p. (Orig.). (gr. 7 up). 1990. pap. 3.50 (0-671-69498-7, Archway) PB.

—Fear Street, 10 vols, Set. large type ed. (gr. 6 up). Date not set. PLB 146.00 (0-8368-1156-9) Gareth Stevens Inc.

—The Knife. 176p. (Orig.). 1992. pap. 3.99 (0-671-72484-3, Archway) PB.

—Lights Out. MacDonald, Patricia, ed. 176p. (Orig.). 1991. pap. 3.99 (0-671-72482-7, Archway) PB.

—Missing. 224p. (gr. 6-9). 1990. pap. 3.99 (0-671-69410-3, Archway) PB.

—Missing. large type ed. (gr. 6 up). Date not set. PLB 14.60 (0-8368-1164-X) Gareth Stevens Inc.

—Party Summer. MacDonald, Patricia, ed. 176p. (Orig.). 1991. pap. 3.99 (0-671-72920-9, Archway) PB.

—Piano Lessons Can Be Murder. (gr. 4-7). 1993. pap. 2.95 (0-590-49448-1) Scholastic Inc.

—The Secret Bedroom. MacDonald, Patricia, ed. 176p. (Orig.). 1991. pap. 3.99 (0-671-72483-5, Archway) PB.

—The Secret Bedroom. large type ed. (gr. 6 up). Date not set. PLB 14.60 (0-8368-1165-8) Gareth Stevens Inc.

—Silent Night. MacDonald, Patricia, ed. 224p. (Orig.). 1991. pap. 3.99 (0-671-73822-4, Archway) PB.

—Ski Weekend. MacDonald, Patricia, ed. 160p. 1991. pap. 3.99 (0-671-72480-0, Archway) PB.

—The Sleepwalker. 160p. (Orig.). (gr. 6-9). 1991. pap. 3.99 (0-671-74652-9, Archway) PB.

—The Sleepwalker. large type ed. (gr. 6 up). Date not set. PLB 14.60 (0-8368-1160-7) Gareth Stevens Inc.

—The Stepsister. MacDonald, Patricia, ed. 176p. (Orig.). (gr. 7 up). 1990. pap. 3.99 (0-671-70244-0, Archway) PB.

Stolz, Mary. Deputy Shep. Johnson, Pamela, illus. LC 90-38664. 96p. (gr. 2-5). 1991. HarpC Child Bks.

Stories of Detection & Mystery. 1993. pap. text ed. 6.50 (0-582-08465-2, 79828) Longman.

Striker, Susan. The Mystery-Anti-Coloring Book. (Illus.). 64p. (Orig.). (gr. 1 up). 1991. pap. 5.95 (0-8050-1600-7, Owl) H Holt & Co.

Sullivan, George. Unsolved! 1992. pap. 2.75 (0-590-42990-6, Point) Scholastic Inc.

Supraner, Robyn. Case of the Missing Canary. new ed. Stillerman, Robbie, illus. LC 78-60122. 48p. (gr. 2-4). 1979. PLB 10.89 (0-89375-087-5); pap. 3.50 (0-89375-075-1) Troll Assocs.

—Case of the Missing Rattles. Goodman, Joan E., illus. LC 81-10378. 48p. (gr. 2-4). 1982. PLB 10.89 (0-89375-590-7); pap. text ed. 3.50 (0-89375-591-5) Troll Assocs.

—Mystery at the Zoo. new ed. Dodson, Bert, illus. LC 78-60126. (gr. 2-4). 1979. PLB 10.89 (0-89375-091-3); pap. 3.50 (0-89375-079-4) Troll Assocs.

—Mystery of the Lost Ring (with Two Hearts) Winborn, Marsha, illus. LC 81-7520. 48p. (gr. 2-4). 1982. PLB 10.89 (0-89375-596-6); pap. text ed. 3.50 (0-89375-597-4); cassette 9.95 (0-685-04951-5) Troll Assocs.

—Mystery of the Witch's Shoes. new ed. Apple, Margot, illus. LC 78-60125. 48p. (gr. 2-4). 1979. PLB 10.89 (0-89375-090-5); pap. 3.50 (0-89375-078-6) Troll Assocs.

Svedberg, Ulf. Nicky the Nature Detective. Anderson, Lena, illus. Selberg, Ingrid, tr. (Illus.). 52p. (gr. 5 up). 1988. 12.95 (91-29-58786-7, R & S Bks) FS&G.

Swanson, Steve. The Mystery of the Gun in the Garbage. LC 93-50925. (gr. 3-7). 1994. pap. 5.99 (0-310-39801-0) Zondervan.

—The Mystery of the Headless Tiger. LC 94-1602. 128p. (gr. 3-7). 1994. pap. 5.99 (0-310-39811-8) Zondervan.

Swift, Carolyn. Bugsy Goes to Limerick. 170p. 1990. pap. 6.95 (1-85371-014-8, Pub. by Poolbeg Pr ER) Dufour.

Swinford, Betty. Mystery at Pier Fourteen. LC 87-82753. (Illus.). 144p. (gr. 7-11). 1988. 3.50 (0-88243-654-6, 02-0654) Gospel Pub.

Tales of Mystery & Imagination. 1993. pap. text ed. 6.50 (0-582-08483-0, 79831) Longman.

Tallent, Mary M. The Secret at Robert's Roost. 168p. (Orig.). (gr. 4-8). 1988. pap. 3.95 (0-941711-05-6) Wyrick & Co.

Talney, Ronald. The Ghost of Deadman's Hollow. LC 93-93785. 112p. 1994. pap. 8.00 (1-56002-320-1, Univ Edtns) Aegina Pr.

Tanya Tinker & the Gizmo Gang: A Lift-the-Flap Book about How Things Work. LC 92-20859. 1992. write for info. (0-8094-9315-2); PLB write for info. (0-8094-9316-0) Time-Life.

Taste & Other Tales. 1993. pap. text ed. 6.50 (0-582-08478-4, 79833) Longman.

Tate, Eleanora E. The Secret of Gumbo Grove. (Orig.). (gr. 7 up). 1988. pap. 3.99 (0-553-27226-8, Pub. by Starfire) Bantam.

Taylor, Andrew. The Coal House. large type ed. (gr. 1-8). 1991. 16.95 (0-7451-0761-3, Galaxy Child Lrg Print) Chivers N Amer.

—The Private Nose. Schongut, Emanuel, illus. LC 92-53016. 96p. (gr. k-4). 1993. 13.95 (1-56402-135-1) Candlewick Pr.

Taylor, Theodore. Sniper. 240p. 1991. pap. 3.99 (0-380-71193-1, Flare) Avon.

—Teetoncey. Cuffari, Richard, illus. (gr. 3-7). 1991. pap. 3.50 (0-380-71024-2, Camelot) Avon.

Tedrow, Carla. Beach Blanket Burglary. (gr. 2-6). 1993. pap. 3.95 (1-56969-178-9) FamilyVision.

—Monster Tag. 150p. (gr. 2-6). 1993. pap. 3.95 (1-56969-180-0) FamilyVision.

—Trouble at the Cave. LC 93-71558. 150p. 1993. pap. 3.95 (1-56969-175-4) FamilyVision.

Thayne. The Day That Arnold J. Crumpet Did Just Disappear. LC 93-61295. (Illus.). 44p. (gr. k-3). 1994. 7.95 (1-55523-663-4) Winston-Derek.

Thesman, Jean. Appointment with a Stranger. (gr. 5-9). 1989. 13.45 (0-395-49215-7) HM.

Thirty-Nine Steps. 1993. pap. text ed. 6.50 (0-582-08467-9, 79834) Longman.

Thomas, Frances. Zak. large type ed. 200p. (gr. 5 up). 1988. 16.95 (0-7451-0727-3, Galaxy Child Lrg Print) Chivers N Amer.

Thomas, Jerry D. Detective Zack & the Mystery at Thunder Mountain. LC 93-41480. (gr. 4 up). 1994. 5.95 (0-8163-1212-5) Pacific Pr Pub Assn.

Thompson, Julian F. Discontinued. 304p. (gr. 7 up). 1986. 12.95 (0-590-33321-6); pap. 3.50 (0-590-42464-5) Scholastic Inc.

Thompson, R. Zoe & the Mysterious X. (Illus.). 24p. (ps-8). 1989. 14.95 (1-55037-081-2, Pub. by Annick CN); pap. 5.95 (1-55037-080-4, Pub. by Annick CN) Firefly Bks Ltd.

Tibo, Gilles. Pikolo: Le Secret du Garde-Robe (Paper Nights in French) Tibo, Gilles, illus. (FRE.). 32p. (Orig.). (ps-6). 1992. PLB 15.95 (1-55037-227-0, Pub. by Annick CN); pap. 5.95 (1-55037-226-2, Pub. by Annick CN) Firefly Bks Ltd.

Tichnor, Richard & Smith, Jenny. A Spark in the Dark. (Illus.). 32p. (ps-4). 1994. 14.95 (1-883220-25-4) Dawn CA.

Time-Life Books Editors. The Bumbletown Detectives: A Critical-Thinking Book. Kagan, Neil, ed. (Illus.). 64p. (gr. 3-7). 1991. write for info. (0-8094-9270-9); PLB write for info. (0-8094-9271-7) Time-Life.

Tintin et la Mystere de la Toison d'Or. (gr. 7-9). 15.95 (0-685-33970-X) Fr & Eur.

Titus, Eve. Basil & the Pygmy Cats: A Basil of Baker Street Mystery. (Illus.). (gr. 3-6). 1989. pap. 2.75 (0-671-64119-0, Minstrel Bks) PB.

—Basil in Mexico: A Basil of Baker Street Mystery. Galdone, Paul, illus. 96p. (gr. 3-6). 1990. pap. 2.75 (0-671-64117-4, Minstrel Bks) PB.

Titus, Eve & Galdone, Paul. Basil of Baker Street. (gr. 3-6). 1958. PLB 8.95 (0-07-064907-3) McGraw.

Topper, Frank. Mystery at the Bike Race. Rogers, Jackie, illus. LC 84-16452. 128p. (gr. 3-7). 1985. lib. bdg. 9.49 (0-8167-0454-6); pap. text ed. 2.95 (0-8167-0455-4) Troll Assocs.

Tournier, Michel. Pierrot ou les Secrets de la Nuit. Bour, Daniele, illus. (FRE.). 56p. (gr. 3-7). 1989. pap. 8.95 (2-07-031205-4) Schoenhof.

Travis, Falcon. Great Book of Whodunit Puzzles: Mini-Mysteries for You to Solve. LC 92-43853. (Illus.). 128p. (gr. 5 up). 1993. pap. 4.95 (0-8069-0348-1) Sterling.

—Super Sleuth: Mini-Mysteries for You to Solve. LC 84-26814. (Illus.). 128p. (gr. 5 up). 1985. 12.95 (0-8069-4700-4) Sterling.

Trease, Geoffrey. A Flight of Angels. 120p. (gr. 4-8). 1989. PLB 14.95 (0-8225-0731-5) Lerner Pubns.

Treat, Lawrence. You're the Detective! Twenty-Four Solve-Them-Yourself Picture Mysteries. Borowik, Kathleen, illus. LC 82-49346. 80p. (Orig.). (gr. 3-6). 1983. pap. 7.95 (0-87923-478-4) Godine.

The Triple Hoax. 192p. 1989. pap. 3.99 (0-671-69153-8, Minstrel Bks) PB.

Turkle, Brinton. Do Not Open. Turkle, Brinton, illus. LC 80-10289. 32p. (ps-2). 1985. pap. 3.95 (0-525-44224-3, DCB) Dutton Child Bks.

—Do Not Open. (ps-3). 1993. pap. 4.99 (0-14-054747-9) Puffin Bks.

Twain, Mark. Tom Sawyer, Abroad & Tom Sawyer, Detective. Busch, Frederick, afterword by. 224p. (ps-8). 1985. pap. 1.95 (0-451-51961-2, Sig Classics) NAL-Dutton.

Tyler, J. Who's Making That Mess? (Illus.). 16p. (ps up). 1994. pap. 6.95 (0-7460-0848-1, Usborne) EDC.

Tyler, J. & Waters, G. Mystery Stories. (Illus.). 144p. (gr. 3-8). 1987. pap. 9.95 (0-7460-0014-6, Usborne) EDC.

Uchida, Yoshiko. The Best Bad Thing. LC 83-2833. 132p. (gr. 4-7). 1983. SBE 13.95 (*0-689-50290-7*, M K McElderry) Macmillan Child Grp.
Ure, Jean. One Green Leaf. (gr. 7 up). 1989. 14.95 (*0-385-29751-3*) Delacorte.
Utz. The Houndstooth Check. LC 79-190268. (Illus.). 32p. (gr. 2-3). 1972. PLB 9.95 (*0-87783-057-6*); pap. 3.94 deluxe ed. (*0-87783-095-9*) Oddo.
Valin, Jonathan. Fire Lake. 1989. pap. 4.99 (*0-440-20145-4*) Dell.
Van Allsburg, Chris. The Mysteries of Harris Burdick. LC 84-9006. (Illus.). 32p. (gr. 5 up). 1984. 16.95 (*0-395-35393-9*) HM.
—The Stranger. Van Allsburg, Chris, illus. LC 86-15235. 32p. (gr. 2-4). 1986. 16.45 (*0-395-42331-7*) HM.
Vandersteen, Willy. The Zincshrinker. Lahey, Nicholas J., tr. from FLE. LC 76-49379. (Illus., Orig.). (gr. 3-8). 1977. pap. 2.50 (*0-915560-03-8*, 03) Hiddigeigei.
Van Hook, Beverly. Supergranny, No. 1: The Mystery of the Shrunken Heads. Wayson, Catherine, illus. 96p. (gr. 3-7). 1985. lib. bdg. 7.95 (*0-916761-11-8*); pap. 2.95 (*0-916761-10-X*) Holderby & Bierce.
—Supergranny, No. 2: The Case of the Riverboat Riverbelle. Wayson, Catherine, illus. 112p. (gr. 3-7). 1986. lib. bdg. 7.95 (*0-916761-09-6*); pap. 2.95 (*0-916761-08-8*) Holderby & Bierce.
—Supergranny, No. 3: The Ghost of Heidelberg Castle. Wayson, Catherine, illus. 112p. (gr. 3-7). 1987. lib. bdg. 7.95 (*0-916761-07-X*); pap. 2.95 (*0-916761-06-1*) Holderby & Bierce.
—Supergranny, No. 5: Character Who Came to Life. Nelken, Andrea, ed. Wayson, Catherine, illus. 112p. (Orig.). (gr. 3-6). 1989. lib. bdg. 7.95 (*0-916761-13-4*); pap. 2.95 (*0-916761-12-6*) Holderby & Bierce.
—Supergranny: Secret of Devil Mountain. Nelken, Andrea, ed. Wayson, Catherine, illus. 112p. (Orig.). (gr. 3-6). 1988. lib. bdg. 7.95 (*0-916761-05-3*); pap. 2.95 (*0-916761-04-5*) Holderby & Bierce.
—Supergranny 6: The Great College Caper, 6 bks. Nelken, Andrea, ed. Wayson, Catherine, illus. 112p. (gr. 3-7). 1991. Set. 53.00 (*0-916761-15-0*) Set. pap. 17.70 (*0-916761-14-2*) Holderby & Bierce.
Vigor, John. Danger, Dolphins, & Ginger Beer. LC 92-26182. (Illus.). 192p. (gr. 3-7). 1993. SBE 14.95 (*0-689-31817-0*, Atheneum Child Bk) Macmillan Child Grp.
Vivelo, Jackie. Super Sleuth. 96p. (gr. 4-7). 1992. pap. 2.95 (*0-8167-1547-5*) Troll Assocs.
Voigt, Cynthia. The Callender Papers. LC 82-13797. 224p. (gr. 4-8). 1983. SBE 15.95 (*0-689-30971-6*, Atheneum Child Bk) Macmillan Child Grp.
—The Callender Papers. (gr. 6 up). 1994. pap. 3.95 (*0-449-70184-0*, Juniper) Fawcett.
—Come a Stranger. LC 86-3610. 208p. (gr. 6 up). 1986. SBE 15.95 (*0-689-31289-X*, Atheneum Child Bk) Macmillan Child Grp.
Wagner, Archibald C. Some Brief Cases of Inspector Alec Stuart of Scotland Yard. Wagner, Jane T., illus. 69p. (Orig.). 1992. pap. 12.95 (*1-880664-01-1*) E M Pr.
Wakan, Naomi. One Day a Stranger Came. Volz, Tatjana K., tr. (Illus.). 32p. (gr. k-2). 1994. 14.95 (*1-55037-354-4*, Pub. by Annick CN); pap. 4.95 (*1-55037-353-6*, Pub. by Annick CN) Firefly Bks Ltd.
Walker, Paul R. The Sluggers Club: A Sports Mystery. LC 92-28201. 1993. 13.95 (*0-15-276163-2*) HarBrace.
Wallace, Barbara B. The Twin in the Tavern. LC 92-36429. 192p. (gr. 3-7). 1993. SBE 14.95 (*0-689-31846-4*, Atheneum Child Bk) Macmillan Child Grp.
Wallace, Bill. Blackwater Swamp. LC 93-28439. 208p. 1994. 15.95 (*0-8234-1120-6*) Holiday.
—Trapped in Death Cave. LC 83-48962. 176p. (gr. 4-7). 1984. 14.95 (*0-8234-0516-8*) Holiday.
Wallace, Pamela. Partners in Crime. 1990. pap. 4.50 (*0-553-28472-X*) Bantam.
Walter, Mildred P. Mariah Loves Rock. 128p. (gr. 3-9). 1989. pap. 2.95 (*0-8167-1838-5*) Troll Assocs.
Wandelmaier, Roy. The Great Rock 'n' Roll Mystery. Burns, Raymond, illus. LC 84-8753. 48p. (gr. 2-4). 1985. PLB 10.89 (*0-8167-0416-3*); pap. text ed. 3.50 (*0-8167-0417-1*) Troll Assocs.
Wardlaw, Lee. Don't Look Back. 160p. (Orig.). (gr. 5). 1993. pap. 3.50 (*0-380-76419-9*) Avon.
Warhola, James, illus. The Pumpkinville Mystery. LC 87-2533. 32p. (gr. 1-4). 1987. PLB 10.95 (*0-671-66905-2*); pap. 5.95 (*0-671-66906-0*) S&S Trade.
Warner, Gertrude C. Benny Uncovers a Mystery. (gr. 2-7). 1991. 10.95 (*0-8075-0644-3*); pap. 3.50 (*0-8075-0645-1*) A Whitman.
—Bicycle Mystery. Cunningham, David, illus. LC 79-126428. 128p. (gr. 2-7). 1971. PLB 10.95 (*0-8075-0708-3*); pap. 3.50 (*0-8075-0709-1*) A Whitman.
—Blue Bay Mystery. LC 61-15230. (Illus.). (gr. 2-7). 1961. PLB 10.95 (*0-8075-0793-8*); pap. 3.50 (*0-8075-0794-6*) A Whitman.
—The Boxcar Children. (Illus.). 158p. 1992. Repr. PLB 14.95x (*0-89966-902-6*) Buccaneer Bks.
—Bus Station Mystery. Cunningham, David, illus. LC 74-8293. 128p. (gr. 2-7). 1974. PLB 10.95 (*0-8075-0975-2*); pap. 3.50 (*0-8075-0976-0*) A Whitman.
—Caboose Mystery. LC 66-10791. (Illus.). 128p. (gr. 2-7). 1966. PLB 10.95 (*0-8075-1008-4*); pap. 3.50 (*0-8075-1009-2*) A Whitman.
—The Canoe Trip Mystery. (gr. 4-7). 1994. 10.95 (*0-8075-1058-0*); pap. 3.50 (*0-8075-1059-9*) A Whitman.
—The Castle Mystery. (gr. 4-7). 1993. 10.95 (*0-8075-1078-5*); pap. 3.50 (*0-8075-1079-3*) A Whitman.
—The Ghost Ship Mystery. Tang, Charles, illus. LC 93-40889. (gr. 4-7). 1994. 10.95 (*0-8075-2856-0*); pap. 3.95 (*0-8075-2855-2*) A Whitman.
—Houseboat Mystery. Cunningham, David, illus. LC 67-26521. 128p. (gr. 2-7). 1966. PLB 10.95 (*0-8075-3412-9*); pap. 3.50 (*0-8075-3413-7*) A Whitman.
—Lighthouse Mystery. Cunningham, David, illus. LC 63-20354. 128p. (gr. 2-7). 1963. PLB 10.95 (*0-8075-4545-7*); pap. 3.50 (*0-8075-4546-5*) A Whitman.
—Mike's Mystery. LC 60-8428. (Illus.). 128p. (gr. 2-7). 1960. PLB 10.95 (*0-8075-5140-6*); pap. 3.50 (*0-8075-5141-4*) A Whitman.
—Mountain Top Mystery. Cunningham, David, illus. LC 64-7722. 128p. (gr. 2-7). 1964. PLB 10.95 (*0-8075-5292-5*); pap. 3.50 (*0-8075-5293-3*) A Whitman.
—Mystery at the Dog Show. (Illus.). 128p. (gr. 2-7). 1993. PLB 10.95 (*0-8075-5395-6*); pap. 3.50 (*0-8075-5394-8*) A Whitman.
—Mystery Behind the Wall. Cunningham, David, illus. LC 72-13356. 128p. (gr. 2-7). 1973. PLB 10.95 (*0-8075-5364-6*); pap. 3.50 (*0-8075-5367-0*) A Whitman.
—The Mystery Horse. (Illus.). 128p. (gr. 2-7). 1993. PLB 10.95 (*0-8075-5338-7*); pap. 3.50 (*0-8075-5339-5*) A Whitman.
—Mystery in the Sand. Cunningham, David, illus. LC 70-165823. 128p. (gr. 2-7). 1971. PLB 10.95 (*0-8075-5373-5*); pap. 3.50 (*0-8075-5372-7*) A Whitman.
—The Mystery in Washington, D.C. (gr. 4-7). 1994. 10.95 (*0-8075-5409-X*); pap. 3.75 (*0-8075-5410-3*) A Whitman.
—The Mystery of the Hidden Beach. (gr. 4-7). 1994. 10.95 (*0-8075-5403-0*); pap. 3.50 (*0-8075-5404-9*) A Whitman.
—The Mystery of the Lost Village. (gr. 4-7). 1993. 10.95 (*0-8075-5400-6*); pap. 3.50 (*0-8075-5401-4*) A Whitman.
—The Mystery of the Purple Pool. (gr. 4-7). 1994. pap. 3.50 (*0-8075-5408-1*) A Whitman.
—The Mystery of the Purple Pool. (gr. 4-7). 1993. 10.95 (*0-8075-5407-3*) A Whitman.
—The Mystery on the Ice. (gr. 4-7). 1993. 10.95 (*0-8075-5414-6*); pap. 3.50 (*0-8075-5413-8*) A Whitman.
—Mystery Ranch. Gringhuis, Dirk, illus. LC 58-9953. 128p. (gr. 2-7). 1958. PLB 10.95 (*0-8075-5390-5*); pap. 3.50 (*0-8075-5391-3*) A Whitman.
—Schoolhouse Mystery. Cunningham, David, illus. LC 65-23889. 128p. (gr. 2-7). 1965. PLB 10.95 (*0-8075-7262-4*); pap. 3.50 (*0-8075-7263-2*) A Whitman.
—Snowbound Mystery. Cunningham, David, illus. LC 68-9124. (gr. 2-7). 1968. PLB 10.95 (*0-8075-7517-8*); pap. 3.50 (*0-8075-7516-X*) A Whitman.
—Surprise Island. Gehr, Mary, illus. LC 49-49618. (gr. 2-7). 1949. PLB 10.95 (*0-8075-7673-5*); pap. 3.50 (*0-8075-7674-3*) A Whitman.
—Tree House Mystery. Cunningham, David, illus. LC 77-91744. 128p. (gr. 2-7). 1969. PLB 10.95 (*0-8075-8086-4*); pap. 3.50 (*0-8075-8087-2*) A Whitman.
—Woodshed Mystery. LC 62-19726. (Illus.). 128p. (gr. 2-7). 1962. PLB 10.95 (*0-8075-9206-4*); pap. 3.50 (*0-8075-9207-2*) A Whitman.
—Yellow House Mystery. LC 53-13243. (Illus.). 128p. (gr. 2-7). 1953. PLB 10.95 (*0-8075-9365-6*); pap. 3.50 (*0-8075-9366-4*) A Whitman.
Warner, Gertrude C., created by. The Animal Shelter Mystery. (Illus.). (gr. 2-7). 1991. 10.95 (*0-8075-0368-1*); pap. 3.50g (*0-8075-0367-3*) A Whitman.
—The Camp-Out Mystery. (Illus.). 192p. (gr. 2-7). 1992. PLB 10.95 (*0-8075-1053-X*); pap. 3.50 (*0-8075-1052-1*) A Whitman.
—The Deserted Library Mystery. (Illus.). (gr. 2-7). 1991. 10.95g (*0-8075-1561-2*); pap. 3.50g (*0-8075-1560-4*) A Whitman.
—The Disappearing Friend Mystery. 192p. (gr. 2-7). 1992. 10.95g (*0-8075-1627-9*); pap. 3.50 (*0-8075-1628-7*) A Whitman.
—The Mystery Cruise. (Illus.). 192p. (gr. 2-7). 1992. PLB 10.95 (*0-8075-5362-X*); pap. 3.50 (*0-8075-5368-9*) A Whitman.
—The Mystery Girl. (Illus.). 192p. (gr. 2-7). 1992. PLB 10.95 (*0-8075-5370-0*); pap. 3.50 (*0-8075-5371-9*) A Whitman.
—The Mystery in the Snow. (Illus.). 192p. (gr. 2-7). 1992. 10.95g (*0-8075-5392-1*); pap. 3.50 (*0-8075-5393-X*) A Whitman.
—The Mystery of the Mixed-Up Zoo. (Illus.). 192p. (gr. 2-7). 1992. PLB 10.95 (*0-8075-5386-7*); pap. 3.50 (*0-8075-5385-9*) A Whitman.
—The Mystery of the Singing Ghost. (Illus.). 192p. (gr. 2-7). 1992. 10.95g (*0-8075-5397-2*); pap. 3.50 (*0-8075-5398-0*) A Whitman.
—The Pizza Mystery. Tang, Charles, illus. LC 92-32263. 128p. (gr. 2-7). 1993. PLB 10.95 (*0-8075-6534-2*); pap. 3.50 (*0-8075-6535-0*) A Whitman.
Wartski, Maureen. Dark Silence. (Orig.). (gr. 9-12). 1993. pap. 3.99 (*0-449-70418-1*, Juniper) Fawcett.
Waters, G. Agent Arthur on the Stormy Seas. (Illus.). 48p. 1990. PLB 11.96 (*0-88110-407-8*); pap. 4.95 (*0-7460-0143-6*) EDC.
—Deckchair Detectives. (Illus.). 48p. (gr. 4 up). 1993. PLB 11.96 (*0-88110-524-4*, Usborne); pap. 4.95 (*0-7460-0716-7*, Usborne) EDC.
—Haunted Tower. (gr. 4-7). 1989. pap. 4.95 (*0-7460-0332-3*, Usborne) EDC.
—Missing Clue. (Illus.). 48p. (gr. 4 up). PLB 10.96 (*0-88110-523-6*, Usborne); pap. 4.50 (*0-7460-0598-9*, Usborne) EDC.
Weber, Ken. Kidz Five-Minute Mysteries: The Sleuth. 64p. (gr. 1 up). 1994. incl. audiocassette 9.95 (*1-56138-402-X*) Running Pr.
Weinberg, Larry. The Curse. (gr. 7 up). 1984. pap. 2.50 (*0-553-26549-0*) Bantam.
Weiner, Eric. Ghostwriter: A Match of Wills. (ps-3). 1992. pap. 3.50 (*0-553-29934-4*) Bantam.
Wells, Colin. Stick Like Glue. Parker, Liz, ed. Taylor, Marjorie, illus. 45p. (Orig.). (gr. 6-12). 1992. pap. text ed. 2.95 (*1-56254-058-0*) Saddleback Pubns.
Wells, Rosemary. The Man in the Woods. 232p. (gr. 7 up). 1991. pap. 2.95 (*0-590-43826-3*) Scholastic Inc.
—Morris's Disappearing Bag. LC 75-9202. (ps-3). 1990. 17.99 (*0-8037-0839-4*) Dial Bks Young.
—Through the Hidden Door. LC 86-24273. 256p. (gr. 5 up). 1987. 14.95 (*0-8037-0276-0*) Dial Bks Young.
West, Cindy. The Superkids & the Singing Dog. Mathieu, Joe, illus. LC 81-50042. 48p. (gr. 1-4). 1982. lib. bdg. 4.99 (*0-394-94924-2*) Random Bks Yng Read.
West, Pamela. Yours Truly, Jack the Ripper. 1989. pap. 3.50 (*0-440-20259-0*) Dell.
Westall, Robert. Stormsearch. (gr. 4-7). 1992. 14.00 (*0-374-37272-1*) FS&G.
—Yaxley's Cat. 208p. 1992. 13.95 (*0-590-45175-8*, Scholastic Hardcover) Scholastic Inc.
What If They Knew? 1983. pap. 2.25 (*0-440-79515-X*) Dell.
White, Ellen E. Friends for Life. 176p. (gr. 7 up). 1983. pap. 2.95 (*0-380-82578-3*, Flare) Avon.
Wilde, Nicholas. Death Knell. (Illus.). 160p. (gr. 7 up). 1991. 14.95 (*0-8050-1851-4*, Bks Young Read) H Holt & Co.
Wilhelm, Doug. Scene of the Crime. (gr. 4-7). 1993. pap. 3.25 (*0-553-56004-2*) Bantam.
—The Secret of Mystery Hill, No. 141. 1993. pap. 3.50 (*0-553-56001-8*) Bantam.
Wilkes. Catching Crooks. (gr. 2-5). 1979. (Usborne-Hayes); pap. 4.50 (*0-86020-229-1*) EDC.
Wilkes, Marilyn Z. C.L.U.T.Z. (gr. 2-3). 1983. pap. 2.50 (*0-553-15515-6*) Bantam.
Willard, Nancy. Night Story. Plume, Ilse, illus. LC 85-17677. 32p. (ps-3). 1986. 13.95 (*0-15-257348-8*, HB Juv Bks) HarBrace.
Willis, Val. El Secreto en la Caja de Fostoros: The Secret in the Matchbox. (ps-3). 1993. 16.00 (*0-374-36701-9*, Mirasol) FS&G.
Wilsdon, Christin. Blast with the Past: Puzzling History Mysteries. (gr. 4-7). 1994. pap. 1.99 (*0-553-37285-8*) Bantam.
Windsor, Patricia. The Christmas Killer. 192p. 1991. 13.95 (*0-590-43311-3*, Scholastic Hardcover) Scholastic Inc.
—The Sandman's Eyes. LC 84-19888. 280p. (gr. 7 up). 1985. 15.95 (*0-385-29381-X*) Delacorte.
Winfield, Arthur. The Rover Boys at College. 312p. 1980. Repr. PLB 12.95x (*0-89967-008-3*) Harmony Raine.
—The Rover Boys at School. 302p. 1980. Repr. PLB 12.95x (*0-89967-009-1*) Harmony Raine.
Winkler, Gershon. The Secret of Sambatyon. Goldman, Bonnie, ed. Bloom, Lloyd, illus. 132p. (gr. 4 up). 1987. 6.95 (*0-910818-68-1*); pap. 5.95 (*0-910818-69-X*) Judaica Pr.
Winterfeld, Henry. Detectives in Togas. 249p. (gr. 3-7). 1990. pap. 3.95 (*0-15-223415-2*, Odyssey) HarBrace.
—Mystery of the Roman Ransom. 217p. (gr. 3-7). 1990. pap. 3.95 (*0-15-256614-7*, Odyssey) HarBrace.
Winthrop, Elizabeth. Castle in the Attic. 1986. pap. 3.99 (*0-553-15601-2*) Bantam.
Wolf, Jill. Teddy Bear's Are Special Friends: Little Treasure Book. Wilson-Heaney, Kathyrn, illus. 24p. (gr. 3-7). 1985. pap. 2.50 (*0-89954-466-5*) Antioch Pub Co.
Wolfe, L. E. Case of the Sneaker Snatcher & Other Mysteries. (gr. 4-7). 1991. pap. 3.50 (*0-316-95097-1*, Spts Illus Kids) Little.
Woodruff, Elvira. Ghosts Don't Get Goosebumps. LC 92-56589. 96p. (gr. 4-7). 1993. 13.95 (*0-8234-1035-8*) Holiday.
Woolgar, Jack. Missing Gold Mystery. (gr. 7 up). 1977. PLB 7.19 (*0-8313-0111-2*) Lantern.
—Mystery in the Desert. (gr. 6-8). 1967. 7.19 (*0-8313-0107-4*); PLB 7.19 (*0-685-13778-3*) Lantern.
Wright, Betty R. Christina's Ghost. LC 85-42880. 128p. (gr. 3-7). 1985. 14.95 (*0-8234-0581-8*) Holiday.
—The Dollhouse Murders. LC 83-6147. 160p. (gr. 3-7). 1983. 14.95 (*0-8234-0497-8*) Holiday.
—Dollhouse Murders. 160p. (gr. 3-7). 1985. pap. 2.75 (*0-590-43461-6*) Scholastic Inc.
—The Ghosts of Mercy Manor. LC 92-21557. 1993. 13.95 (*0-590-43601-5*) Scholastic Inc.
—The Midnight Mystery. 144p. (gr. 4-7). 1991. pap. 3.25 (*0-590-43758-5*, Apple Paperbacks) Scholastic Inc.
—The Secret Window. 1993. pap. 2.95 (*0-590-42749-0*) Scholastic Inc.

Wright, Bob. Falling Star Mystery. bilingual ed. Bourne, Phyllis & Tusquets, Eugenia, trs. (SPA & ENG., Illus.). 96p. (gr. 1-5). 1989. pap. text ed. 4.95 (0-87879-663-0) High Noon Bks.

Wulffson, Don. Five Minute Mysteries. Long, Laurel, illus. 96p. (gr. 3 up). 1994. pap. 4.95 (1-56565-169-3) Lowell Hse Juvenile.

Yeo. The Stranger at Winifield House. 1993. pap. 2.75 (0-590-43912-X) Scholastic Inc.

Yep, Lawrence. The Mark Twain Murders. LC 81-69510. 160p. (gr. 7 up). 1984. SBE 14.95 (0-02-793670-8, Four Winds) Macmillan Child Grp.

Yin-lien C. Chin & Center, Y. The Stone Lion & Other Chinese Detective Stories: The Wisdom of Lord Bau. Lu Wang, illus. LC 91-46520. 192p. (gr. 8-12). 1992. 35.00 (0-87332-634-2); pap. 16.95 (0-87332-635-0) M E Sharpe.

Yolen, Jane. Piggins & the Royal Wedding. Dyer, Jane, illus. 32p. (ps-3). 1989. 13.95 (0-15-261687-X) HarBrace.

York. The Secret House. 1992. pap. 2.75 (0-590-45051-4) Scholastic Inc.

Young Sherlock Holmes. 1986. pap. 1.95 (0-440-82039-1) Dell.

Zambreno, Mary F. Journeyman Wizard: A Magical Mystery. LC 93-37449. 1994. 16.95 (0-15-200022-4, Yolen Bks) HarBrace.

Zeplin, Zeno. Clowns to the Rescue. Brown, Bernice, illus. 48p. (gr. k-3). 1993. 9.95 (1-877740-12-8); pap. 5.50 (1-877740-13-6) Nel-Mar Pub.

—Clowns to the Rescue: A Katy & Beth Mystery. (gr. 4-7). 1993. 9.95 (0-87774-012-7) Schoenhof.

—Popcorn Is Missing. Jones, Judy, illus. 48p. (gr. 2-4). 1990. lib. bdg. 9.95 casebound (1-877740-01-2); pap. text ed. 5.50 (1-877740-02-0) Nel-Mar Pub.

Zeplin, Zeon. Clowns to the Rescue: A Katy & Beth Mystery. (gr. 4-7). 1993. pap. 5.50 (0-87774-013-5) Schoenhof.

Zimmerman, R. D. Bomb. 4p. 1987. incl. puzzle 17.95 (0-922242-01-1) Lombard Mktg.

Zindel, Paul. The Undertaker's Gone Bananas. LC 78-54606. 256p. (gr. 7 up). 1978. PLB 16.89 (0-06-026846-8) HarpC Child Bks.

MYTHICAL ANIMALS

see Animals, Mythical

MYTHOLOGY

see also Animals, Mythical; Folklore; Heroes; Indians of North America–Religion and Mythology; Totems and Totemism

Bailey, John, et al, eds. Gods & Men: Myths & Legends from the World's Religions. (Illus.). 144p. 1993. pap. 10.95 (0-19-274145-4) OUP.

Bellingham, David, et al. Goddesses, Heroes, & Shamans: The Young People's Guide to World Mythology. LC 94-1374. (Illus.). 160p. (gr. 5 up). 1994. 19.95 (1-85697-999-7, Kingfisher LKC) LKC.

Birch, Cyril, ed. Chinese Myths & Fantasies. Kiddell-Monroe, Joan, illus. 144p. 1993. pap. 10.95 (0-19-274152-7) OUP.

Briais, Bernard. Celts. LC 91-15842. (Illus.). 48p. (gr. 4-8). 1991. PLB 13.95 (1-85435-266-0) Marshall Cavendish.

Chatterjee, Debjani. The Elephant-Headed God & Other Hindu Tales. LC 92-20454. 1992. 13.00 (0-19-508112-9) OUP.

Child's Book of Myths & Enchantments. LC 89-15905. (gr. 4-7). 12.95 (1-56288-395-X) Checkerboard.

Climo, Shirley, retold by. Atalanta's Race: A Greek Myth. Koshkin, Alexander, illus. LC 93-26734. 1995. write for info. (0-395-67322-4, Clarion Bks) HM.

Colum, Padraic. The Children of Odin: The Book of Northern Myths. Pogany, Willy, illus. LC 83-20368. 280p. (gr. 5up). 1984. SBE 15.95 (0-02-722890-8, Macmillan Child Bk); pap. 8.95 (0-02-042100-1, Collier Young Ad) Macmillan Child Grp.

Coomaraswamy, Ananda K. & Nivedita, Sr. Myths of the Hindus & Buddhists. (Illus.). 400p. (gr. 4-8). pap. 8.95 (0-486-21759-0) Dover.

Cruse, Amy. The Book of Myths. LC 93-17341. 1993. 9.99 (0-517-09335-9, Pub. by Gramercy) Random Hse Value.

Downing, Charles. Armenian Folk-Tales & Fables. Papas, William, illus. 240p. 1993. pap. 10.95 (0-19-274155-1) OUP.

Evslin, Bernard. Heroes, Gods & Monsters of Greek Myths. (ps-7). 1984. pap. 4.99 (0-553-25920-2) Bantam.

Famous Myths & Legends. 1991. 8.99 (0-517-03762-9) Random Hse Value.

Farrell, William R. Characters in Mythology. Chapman, Bettina B., illus. 60p. (gr. k-10). 1992. spiral bdg. 9.25 (0-939507-38-2, B423) Amer Classical.

Fisher, Leonard E. Jason & the Golden Fleece. Fisher, Leonard E., illus. LC 89-20074. 32p. (gr. k-4). 1990. reinforced bdg. 14.95 (0-8234-0794-2) Holiday.

Fisher, Leonard E., retold by. & illus. Theseus & the Minotaur. LC 88-1970. 32p. (gr. 1-4). 1988. reinforced bdg. 15.95 (0-8234-0703-9); pap. 5.95 (0-8234-0954-6) Holiday.

Frost, Abigail. The Wolf. LC 89-17445. (Illus.). 48p. (gr. 4-8). 1990. PLB 13.95 (1-85435-237-7) Marshall Cavendish.

Graves, Robert. Greek Gods & Heroes. 125p. 1965. pap. 4.50 (0-440-93221-1, LFL) Dell.

Green, R. L. The Tale of Thebes. LC 76-22979. (Illus.). 1977. Cambridge U Pr.

Green, Roger L. Tales of Greek Heroes. (Orig.). (gr. 5-7). 1989. pap. 2.99 (0-14-035099-3, Puffin) Puffin Bks.

Hadley, Eric & Hadley, Tessa. Legends of Earth, Air, Fire & Water. (Illus.). 32p. 1985. 14.95 (0-521-26311-5) Cambridge U Pr.

Harrison, Michael. Doom of the Gods. Humphries, Tudor, illus. 80p. (gr. 3 up). 1987. 20.00 (0-19-274128-4) OUP.

Hawthorne, Nathaniel. Tanglewood Tales for Girls & Boys. 1992. Repr. of 1853 ed. lib. bdg. 75.00 (0-7812-3046-2) Rprt Serv.

—Wonder Book. Hogan, A. H., intro. by. (gr. 5 up). 1966. pap. 2.25 (0-8049-0118-X, CL-118) Airmont.

—A Wonder Book for Girls & Boys. 1992. Repr. of 1852 ed. lib. bdg. 75.00 (0-7812-3045-4) Rprt Serv.

Hollander, P. Scott. Herne's Promise. Hollander, P. Scott, illus. 61p. (gr. k-4). 1992. pap. write for info. (0-9630657-2-6) Godolphin Hse.

Homer. Odysseus & the Giants. Richardson, I. M., adapted by. Frenck, Hal, illus. LC 83-14233. 32p. (gr. 4-8). 1984. PLB 11.79 (0-8167-0009-5); pap. text ed. 2.95 (0-8167-0010-9) Troll Assocs.

Hwa-I Publishing Co., Staff. Chinese Children's Stories, Vol. 61: Pan Koo Creates the World, A Hole in the Sky. Ching, Emily, et al, eds. Wonder Kids Publications Staff, tr. from CHI. (Illus.). 28p. (gr. 3-6). 1991. Repr. of 1988 ed. 7.95 (1-56162-061-0) Wonder Kids.

Knappert, Jan. Kings, Gods & Spirits from African Mythology. Pelizzoli, Francesca, illus. LC 93-12903. 88p. (gr. 6 up). 1993. 22.50 (0-87226-916-7); pap. 12.95 sewn (0-87226-917-5) P Bedrick Bks.

Larungu, Rute. African-American Cultures: Myths & Legends from Ghana for Children. Turechek, Lou, illus. LC 92-81116. 96p. (gr. 3 up). 1992. lib. bdg. 14.95 (1-878893-21-1); pap. 8.95 (1-878893-20-3) Telcraft Bks. KIRKUS REVIEWS: "A story, a story, let it go, let it come.' Three Hausa & five Ashanti tales...one can almost hear the teller's voice." BOOKLIST: "In an insightful, interactive manner, this collection provides a range of fast-paced tales... these stories should be read aloud, perhaps even dramatized, to be fully appreciated." SCHOOL LIBRARY JOURNAL: "...free verse...a fuller background to West African folklore than single-story books." To order: Quality Books, Inc. (libraries); Baker & Taylor (all).
Publisher Provided Annotation.

Lattimore, Deborah N. The Prince & the Golden Ax: A Minoan Tale. Lattimore, Deborah N., illus. LC 87-21193. 40p. (gr. k-3). 1988. PLB 12.89 (0-06-023716-3) HarpC Child Bks.

Li, Xiao M., tr. from CHI. The Mending of the Sky & Other Chinese Myths. Wu, Shan M., illus. Buckley, Cicely, intro. by. (Illus.). 54p. (Orig.). (gr. 5 up). 1989. pap. 9.00 (0-9617481-3-3) Oyster River Pr.

Lindgren, Astrid. Brothers Lionheart. Tate, Joan, tr. Lambert, J. K., illus. LC 85-573. 184p. (gr. 4-6). 1985. pap. 4.95 (0-14-031955-7, Puffin) Puffin Bks.

McKissack, Patricia & McKissack, Fredrick. King Midas & His Gold. Dunnington, Tom, illus. LC 86-11744. 32p. (ps-2). 1986. PLB 10.25 (0-516-03984-9); pap. 3.95 (0-516-43984-7) Childrens.

Magee, James E. Your Place in the Cosmos, Vol. I: A Layman's Book of Astronomy & the Mythology of the Eighty-Eight Celestial Constellations & Registry. Hevelius, Johannes, illus. 530p. 1985. text ed. 34.45 (0-9614354-0-2) Mosele & Assocs.

—Your Place in the Cosmos, Vol. II: A Layman's Book of Astronomy & the Mythology of the Eighty-Eight Celestial Constellations & Registry. Hevelius, Johannes, illus. 508p. 1988. text ed. 34.45 (0-9614354-1-0) Mosele & Assocs.

—Your Place in the Cosmos, Vol. III: A Layman's Book of Astronomy & the Mythology of the Eighty-Eight Celestial Constellations & Registry. Hevelius, Johannes, illus. 388p. 1992. text ed. 49.45 (0-9614354-2-9) Mosele & Assocs.

Metaxas, Eric. King Midas & the Golden Touch. Prato, Rodica, illus. LC 91-40670. 40p. (gr. k up). 1992. pap. 14.95 (0-88708-234-3, Rabbit Ears); incl. cass. 19.95 (0-88708-235-1, Rabbit Ears) Picture Bk Studio.

Middleton, Haydn. Island of the Mighty. 80p. (gr. 5-8). 1987. 20.00 (0-19-274133-0) OUP.

Mikolaycak, Charles. Orpheus. 1992. write for info. (0-15-258804-3, HB Juv Bks) HarBrace.

Mystic Jhamon Publishers Staff, ed. Is Man a Free Agent? (Illus.). 128p. (gr. 6 up). 1985. pap. 9.95 (0-933961-01-4) Mystic Jhamom.

Myths & Legends Series, 4 vols. (Illus.). 192p. (gr. 3-8). 1990. Set. PLB 55.80 (1-85435-233-4) Marshall Cavendish.

Myths & Legends Series: Group 2, 4 vols. (Illus.). 192p. (gr. 3-8). 1991. Set. PLB 55.80 (1-85435-263-6) Marshall Cavendish.

Osborne, Mary P. Favorite Greek Myths. Howell, Troy, illus. (gr. 2-6). 1989. pap. 15.95 (0-590-41338-4) Scholastic Inc.

Passes, David. Dragons: Truth, Myth, & Legend. Anderson, Wayne, illus. LC 92-44745. (gr. 7 up). 1993. 14.95 (0-307-17500-6, Artsts & Writers Guild) Western Pub.

Ragache, Claude-Catherine. Creation of the World. LC 90-25263. (Illus.). 48p. (gr. 4-8). 1991. PLB 13.95 (0-685-52829-4) Marshall Cavendish.

Ragache, Gilles. Dragons. LC 90-25902. (Illus.). 48p. (gr. 4-8). 1991. PLB 13.95 (1-85435-265-2) Marshall Cavendish.

Richardson, I. M. The Adventures of Eros & Psyche. Baxter, Robert, illus. LC 82-16057. 32p. (gr. 4-8). 1983. PLB 11.79 (0-89375-861-2); pap. text ed. 2.95 (0-89375-862-0) Troll Assocs.

Riordan, James & Lewis, Brenda R. An Illustrated Treasury of Myths & Legends. Ambrus, Victor, illus. 152p. (gr. 7 up). 1991. 12.95 (0-87226-349-5) P Bedrick Bks.

Rungachary, Santha. Tales for All Times. Khemraj, P., illus. (gr. 1-9). 1979. pap. 2.50 (0-89744-187-7) Auromere.

Shepard, Aaron. Savitri: A Tale of Ancient India. Mathews, Judith, ed. Rosenberry, Vera, illus. LC 91-16591. 40p. (gr. 1-6). 1992. PLB 15.95 (0-8075-7251-9) A Whitman.

Simon, Seymour. Hidden Worlds: Pictures of the Invisible. LC 83-5407. (Illus.). 48p. (gr. 3up). 1983. 13.95 (0-688-02464-5); lib. bdg. 13.88 (0-688-02465-3, Morrow Jr Bks) Morrow Jr Bks.

Simons, Scott & Simons, Jamie. Why Dolphins Call: A Story of Dionysus. Winograd, Deborah, illus. 32p. (gr. 2-5). 1992. 8.95 (0-671-69125-2); PLB 10.95 (0-671-69121-X) Silver Pr.

—Why Spiders Spin: A Story of Arachne. Winograd, Deborah, illus. 32p. (gr. 2-5). 1992. 8.95 (0-671-69124-4); PLB 10.95 (0-671-69120-1) Silver Pr.

Song Nan Zhang. The Five Heavenly Emperors & Other Chinese Myths from the Creation. Song Nan Zhang, illus. LC 93-61794. 32p. (gr. 1-6). 1994. 16.95t (0-88776-338-3) Tundra Bks.

Steffens, J. & Carr, J. Myths & Fables. (gr. 7-12). 1984. 9.95 (0-88160-113-6, LW 1008) Learning Wks.

Stephanides Brothers Staff. Greek Mythology, 6 Vols. (gr. 5-10). Set. 60.00 (0-916634-26-4) Double M Pr.

Swift, Carolyn. European Myths & Tales. 116p. (gr. 5 up). 1993. pap. 8.95 (1-85371-203-5, Pub. by Poolbeg Pr ER) Dufour.

—World Myths & Tales. (Illus.). 123p. (gr. 4-7). 1994. pap. 8.95 (1-85371-295-7, Pub. by Poolbeg Pr ER) Dufour.

Sylvester, Diane & Wiemann, Mary. Mythology, Archeology, Architecture. 112p. (gr. 4-6). 1982. 9.95 (0-88160-081-4, LW 901) Learning Wks.

Tchudi, Stephen. Probing the Unknown: From Myth to Science. LC 89-35938. (Illus.). 160p. (gr. 7 up). 1990. SBE 14.95 (0-684-19086-9, Scribners Young Read) Macmillan Child Grp.

Waite, Mitchell. The Lost Dutchman & Superstition Mountain Who's Who. Waite, Mitchell, illus. LC 93-83367. 150p. (Orig.). 1993. pap. text ed. 9.95 (1-881260-07-0) Southwest Pubns.

Wonder Kids Publications Group Staff (USA) & Hwa-I Publishing Co., Staff. Mythology: Chinese Children's Stories, Vols. 61-65. Ching, Emily, et al, eds. Wonder Kids Publications Staff, tr. from CHI. Hwa-I Publishing Co., Staff, illus. LC 90-60804. (gr. 3-6). 1991. Repr. of 1988 ed. Five vol. set, 28p. ea. bk. 39.75 (0-685-58712-6) Wonder Kids.

Zimmerman. Dictionary of Classical Mythology. (gr. 9 up). 1983. pap. 5.99 (0-553-25776-5) Bantam.

MYTHOLOGY, CLASSICAL

Asimov, Isaac. Words from the Myths. Barss, William, illus. 224p. (gr. 5-10). 1961. 14.95 (0-395-06568-2) HM.

—Words from the Myths. (Illus.). 144p. (gr. 6). 1969. pap. 2.50 (0-451-14097-4, Sig) NAL-Dutton.

Brazouski, Antoinette & Klatt, Mary J., eds. Children's Books on Ancient Greek & Roman Mythology: An Annotated Bibliography. 1993. 49.95 (0-313-28973-5, Greenwood Pr) Greenwood.

Britt, Helen. Ye Gods. 1987. pap. text ed. 11.16 (0-88334-196-4, 76161) Longman.

Brooks. Heracles. Date not set. 16.00 (0-06-023592-6); PLB 15.89 (0-06-023593-4) HarpC Child Bks.

Connolly, Peter. The Legend of Odysseus. (Illus.). 80p. (gr. 7-12). 1988. 19.95 (0-19-917065-7) OUP.

Coolidge, Olivia E. Greek Myths. Sandoz, E., illus. 256p. (gr. 7 up). 1949. 14.95 (0-395-06721-9) HM.

Daly, Kathleen. Greek & Roman Mythology A to Z: A Young Reader's Companion. (Illus.). 128p. (gr. 4-10). 1992. lib. bdg. 19.95x (0-8160-2151-1) Facts on File.

D'Aulaire, Ingri. D'Aulaire's Book of Greek Myths. (ps-3). 1992. pap. 15.95 (0-440-40694-3, YB) Dell.

D'Aulaire, Ingri & D'Aulaire, Edgar P. D'Aulaires' Book of Greek Myths. D'Aulaire, Ingri & D'Aulaire, Edgar P., illus. LC 62-15877. 1980. 20.00 (0-385-01583-6, Zephyr-BFYR); PLB 19.99 (0-385-07108-6); (Zephyr-BFYR) Doubleday.

Edmondson, Elizabeth. The Trojan War. LC 91-31860. (Illus.). 32p. (gr. 6 up). 1992. text ed. 13.95 RSBE (*0-02-733273-X*, New Discovery) Macmillan Child Grp.

Evans & Millard. Greek Myths & Legends. (Illus.). 64p. (gr. 6-10). 1986. PLB 14.96 (*0-88110-224-5*); pap. 8.95 (*0-86020-946-6*) EDC.

Evans, C. & Millard, A. Greek & Norse Legends. (Illus.). 112p. (gr. 6-10). 1987. pap. 12.95 (*0-7460-0240-8*) EDC.

Evslin, Bernard. Greek Gods. (gr. 4-7). 1984. pap. 2.95 (*0-590-44110-8*) Scholastic Inc.

Evslin, Bernard, et al. Heroes & Monsters of Greek Myth. (gr. 4 up). pap. 2.95 (*0-590-43440-3*) Scholastic Inc.

Fisher, Leonard E. Cyclops. Fisher, Leonard E., illus. LC 90-29317. 32p. (ps-3). 1991. reinforced bdg. 15.95 (*0-8234-0891-4*) Holiday.

Gottlieb, Gerald. The Adventures of Ulysses. Savage, Steele, illus. LC 88-19232. xii, 170p. (gr. 6-12). 1988. Repr. of 1959 ed. lib. bdg. 16.50 (*0-208-02222-8*, Linnet) Shoe String.

Hamilton, Edith. Mythology. Savage, Steele, illus. (gr. 7 up). 1942. 22.95 (*0-316-34114-2*) Little.

Hawthorne, Nathaniel. Tanglewood Tales. (Illus.). (gr. 7 up). 1968. pap. 2.50 (*0-8049-0175-9*, CL-175) Airmont.

—A Wonder Book & Tanglewood Tales. Charvat, William, et al, eds. LC 77-150221. (Illus.). 476p. (gr. 5 up). 1972. 55.00 (*0-8142-0158-X*) Ohio St U Pr.

—A Wonder Book for Girls & Boys. LC 87-50436. 362p. (gr. 3-7). 1987. pap. 12.95 (*0-940561-07-7*) White Rose Pr.

—A Wonder Book for Girls & Boys. LC 94-7352. (gr. 2 up). 1994. 13.95 (*0-679-43643-X*) Knopf.

Hewitt, Kathryn. King Midas & the Golden Touch. Hewitt, Kathryn, illus. LC 86-7681. 29p. (ps-3). 1987. 12.95 (*0-15-242800-3*) HarBrace.

Hodges, Margaret. The Arrow & the Lamp: The Story of Psyche. Diamond, Donna, illus. LC 86-2728. (gr. 4-8). 1989. 14.95 (*0-316-36790-7*) Little.

Homer. Odysseus & the Cyclops. Richardson, I. M., adapted by. Frenck, Hal, illus. LC 83-14236. 32p. (gr. 4-8). 1984. lib. bdg. 11.79 (*0-8167-0007-9*); pap. text ed. 2.95 (*0-8167-0008-7*) Troll Assocs.

—Odysseus & the Great Challenge. Richardson, I. M., adapted by. Frenck, Hal, illus. LC 83-14232. 32p. (gr. 4-8). 1984. lib. bdg. 11.79 (*0-8167-0013-3*); pap. text ed. 2.95 (*0-8167-0014-1*) Troll Assocs.

—Odysseus & the Magic of Circe. Richardson, I. M., adapted by. Frenck, Hal, illus. LC 83-14237. 32p. (gr. 4-8). 1984. lib. bdg. 11.79 (*0-8167-0011-7*); pap. text ed. 2.95 (*0-8167-0012-5*) Troll Assocs.

—The Voyage of Odysseus. Richardson, I. M., adapted by. Frenck, Hal, illus. LC 83-14235. 32p. (gr. 4-8). 1984. lib. bdg. 11.79 (*0-8167-0005-2*); pap. text ed. 2.95 (*0-8167-0006-0*) Troll Assocs.

—The Wooden Horse. Richardson, I. M., adapted by. Frenck, Hal, illus. LC 83-18061. 32p. (gr. 4-8). 1984. PLB 11.79 (*0-8167-0057-5*); pap. text ed. 2.95 (*0-8167-0058-3*) Troll Assocs.

Hutton, Warwick. Persephone. Hutton, Warwick, illus. LC 93-20590. 32p. (gr. 2 up). 1994. SBE 14.95 (*0-689-50600-7*, M K McElderry) Macmillan Child Grp.

—Perseus. Hutton, Warwick, illus. LC 92-7639. 32p. (gr. 2 up). 1993. SBE 14.95 (*0-689-50565-5*, M K McElderry) Macmillan Child Grp.

Lister, Robin, retold by. The Odyssey. Baker, Alan, illus. LC 93-49856. 96p. (gr. 5 up). 1994. pap. 10.95 (*1-85697-522-3*, Kingfisher LKC) LKC.

Low, Alice. The Macmillan Book of Greek Gods & Heroes. Stewart, Arvis, illus. LC 94-3198. (gr. 3-7). 1994. pap. 12.95 (*0-689-71874-8*, Aladdin) Macmillan Child Grp.

McCaughrean, Geraldine, retold by. Greek Myths. LC 92-61748. (Illus.). 96p. (gr. 4 up). 1993. SBE 18.95 (*0-689-50583-3*, M K McElderry) Macmillan Child Grp.

McDermott, Gerald. Daughter of Earth: A Roman Myth. McDermott, Gerald, illus. LC 82-23585. 32p. (ps-3). 1984. pap. 15.00 (*0-385-29294-5*) Delacorte.

McLean, Mollie & Wiseman, Anne. The Adventures of Greek Heroes. Mars, Witold T., illus. LC 61-10628. 192p. (ps-3). 1973. 15.45 (*0-395-06913-0*, Sandpiper); pap. 5.95 (*0-685-42189-9*, Sandpiper) HM.

Martin, Claire. The Race of the Golden Apples. Dillon, Leo D. & Dillon, Diane, illus. LC 85-16290. 32p. (ps-3). 1991. 14.95 (*0-8037-0248-5*); PLB 14.89 (*0-8037-0249-3*) Dial Bks Young.

Naden, C. J., adapted by. Jason & the Golden Fleece. Baxter, Robert, illus. LC 80-50068. 32p. (gr. 4-8). 1980. PLB 11.79 (*0-89375-360-2*); pap. 2.95 (*0-89375-364-5*) Troll Assocs.

—Pegasus, the Winged Horse. new ed. LC 80-50069. (Illus.). 32p. (gr. 4-8). 1980. PLB 11.79 (*0-89375-361-0*); pap. 2.95 (*0-89375-365-3*) Troll Assocs.

—Perseus & Medusa. Baxter, Robert, illus. LC 80-50083. 32p. (gr. 4-8). 1980. PLB 11.79 (*0-89375-362-9*); pap. 2.95 (*0-89375-366-1*) Troll Assocs.

—Theseus & the Minotaur. Baxter, Robert, illus. LC 80-50067. 32p. (gr. 4-8). 1980. PLB 11.79 (*0-89375-363-7*); pap. 2.95 (*0-89375-367-X*) Troll Assocs.

Newby, Robert. King Midas: With Selected Sentences in American Sign Language. Majewski, Dawn & Cozzolino, Sandra, illus. LC 90-4908. 72p. (gr. 1-5). 1990. 14.95 (*0-930323-75-0*, Pub. by K Green Pubns); incl. video 38.20 (*0-930323-77-7*, Pub. by K Green Pubns); video 29.00 (*0-930323-71-8*) Gallaudet Univ Pr.

Picard, Barbara L. Tales of Ancient Persia. Ambrus, Victor G., illus. 176p. 1993. pap. 10.95 (*0-19-274154-3*) OUP.

Richardson, I. M. Demeter & Persephone: The Seasons of Time. Baxter, Robert, illus. LC 82-16023. 32p. (gr. 4-8). 1983. PLB 11.79 (*0-89375-863-9*); pap. text ed. 2.95 (*0-89375-864-7*) Troll Assocs.

—Prometheus & the Story of Fire. Baxter, Robert, illus. LC 82-15979. 32p. (gr. 4-8). 1983. PLB 11.79 (*0-89375-859-0*); pap. text ed. 2.95 (*0-89375-860-4*) Troll Assocs.

Rockwell, Anne. The Robber Baby: Stories from the Greek Myths. LC 90-39560. (Illus.). 80p. (gr. k up). 1994. 18.00 (*0-688-09740-5*); PLB 17.93 (*0-688-09741-3*) Greenwillow.

Sands, Stella. Odyssea. Wolff, Barbara M., illus. 32p. (gr. k-4). 1991. PLB 13.95 (*1-879567-04-0*, Valeria Bks); pap. text ed. 7.95 (*1-879567-03-2*) Wonder Well.

Simons, Scott & Simons, Jamie. Why Seashells Sing. Winograd, Deborah, illus. 32p. (gr. 2-5). 1992. incl. jacket 13.95 (*0-382-69122-9*); PLB 14.98 (*0-382-69118-0*) Silver.

Stephanides Brothers Staff. Greek Mythology, 6 vols. (gr. 5-10). Set. 60.00x (*0-916634-25-6*) Double M Pr.

Stevens, Janet. Androcles & the Lion. Stevens, Janet, illus. LC 89-1953. 32p. (ps-3). 1989. reinforced bdg. 14.95 (*0-8234-0768-3*); pap. 5.95 (*0-8234-0906-6*) Holiday.

Storr, Catherine. King Midas. Codd, Mike, illus. LC 84-18307. 32p. (gr. 2-5). 1985. PLB 19.97 (*0-8172-2112-3*) Raintree Steck-V.

Storr, Catherine, as told by. Theseus & the Minotaur. (Illus.). 32p. (gr. k-5). 1985. PLB 19.97 (*0-8172-2506-4*) Raintree Steck-V.

Sutcliff, Rosemary. Black Ships Before Troy. Lee, Alan, illus. LC 92-38782. (gr. 4 up). 1993. 19.95 (*0-385-31069-2*) Delacorte.

Switzer, Ellen & Costas. Greek Myths: Gods, Heroes & Monsters - Their Sources, Their Stories & Their Meanings. LC 87-22690. (Illus.). 224p. (gr. 6 up). 1988. SBE 17.95 (*0-689-31253-9*, Atheneum Child Bk) Macmillan Child Grp.

Usher, Kerry. Heroes, Gods & Emperors from Roman Mythology. Sibbick, John, illus. 132p. (gr. 6 up). 1992. 22.50 (*0-87226-909-4*) P Bedrick Bks.

Waldherr, Kris. Persephone & the Pomegranate: A Myth from Greece. Waldherr, Kris, illus. LC 92-21349. 32p. (ps-3). 1993. 14.99 (*0-8037-1191-3*); PLB 14.89 (*0-8037-1192-1*) Dial Bks Young.

Williams, Marcia. Greek Myths for Young Children. Williams, Marcia, illus. LC 91-58733. 40p. (ps up). 1992. 17.95 (*1-56402-115-7*) Candlewick Pr.

Woodbridge, F. J. The Son of Apollo: Themes of Plato. 272p. (gr. 7 up). 1972. Repr. of 1929 ed. 24.00 (*0-8196-0278-7*) Biblo.

Yolen, J. & Nolan, D. Wings. 32p. (ps up). 1991. 15.95 (*0-15-297850-X*, HB Juv Bks) HarBrace.

Zorn, Steven, retold by. Start Exploring Bulfinch's Mythology: Classic Tales of Heroes, Gods, & Magic. (Illus.). 128p. (Orig.). (gr. 2 up). 1989. pap. 8.95 (*0-89471-710-3*) Running Pr.

MYTHOLOGY, EGYPTIAN

Frost, Abigail. Ancient Egypt. LC 89-25410. (Illus.). 48p. (gr. 4-8). 1990. PLB 13.95 (*1-85435-234-2*) Marshall Cavendish.

Harris, Geraldine. Gods & Pharaohs from Egyptian Mythology. O'Connor, David & Sibbick, John, illus. LC 90-23455. 132p. (gr. 6 up). 1992. 22.50 (*0-87226-907-8*) P Bedrick Bks.

McDermott, Gerald, as told by. & illus. The Voyage of Osiris: A Myth of Ancient Egypt. LC 94-7067. 1995. write for info. (*0-15-200216-2*); pap. write for info. (*0-15-294446-X*) HarBrace.

Wallace, Zara & Cook, Elizabeth, eds. Gesar! The Wondrous Adventures of King Gesar of Tibet. Witwer, Julia, illus. LC 91-35260. 190p. (Orig.). (gr. 10-12). 1991. pap. 11.95 (*0-89800-223-0*) Dharma Pub.

MYTHOLOGY, INDIAN

see Indians of North America–Religion and Mythology

MYTHOLOGY, NORSE

Branston, Brian. Gods & Heroes from Viking Mythology. Caselli, Giovanni, illus. LC 92-29705. 152p. 1994. 22.50 (*0-87226-905-1*); pap. 14.95 (*0-87226-906-X*) P Bedrick Bks.

Climo, Shirley. Stolen Thunder: A Norse Myth. Koshkin, Alexander, illus. LC 93-24627. (gr. 1-5). 1994. 15.95 (*0-395-64368-6*, Clarion Bks) HM.

Daly, Kathleen N. Norse Mythology A to Z. (Illus.). 128p. 1990. 19.95x (*0-8160-2150-3*) Facts on File.

Green, Richard L. Myths of the Norsemen. Wildsmith, Brian, illus. (gr. 4-6). 1970. pap. 3.50 (*0-14-030464-9*) Viking Child Bks.

Green, Roger L. Myths of the Norsemen. (gr. 5 up). 1970. pap. 3.50 (*0-14-035098-5*) Puffin Bks.

Hull, Robert. Norse Stories. Heap, Johnathan & Stower, Adam, illus. LC 93-30731. 48p. (gr. 5-9). 1993. 15.95 (*1-56847-131-9*) Thomson Lrning.

McNeil, M. E. The Magic Storysinger: From the Finnish Epic Kalevala. (Illus.). 96p. (gr. 4-8). 1993. 16.95 (*0-88045-128-9*) Stemmer Hse.

Mayer, Marianna. Iduna & the Magic Apples. Gal, Laszlo, illus. LC 88-2494. 40p. (gr. k-4). 1988. RSBE 16.95 (*0-02-765120-7*, Macmillan Child Bk) Macmillan Child Grp.

Norse Myths & Legends. (Illus.). 48p. (gr. 6-10). 1986. PLB 14.96 (*0-88110-249-0*); pap. 7.95 (*0-7460-0010-3*) EDC.

MYTHS

see Mythology

N

NADER, RALPH, 1934-

Celsi, Teresa. Ralph Nader: The Consumer Revolution. (Illus.). 104p. (gr. 7 up). 1991. PLB 15.40 (*1-56294-044-9*); pap. 5.95 (*1-56294-834-2*) Millbrook Pr.

Peduzzi, Kelli. Ralph Nader: Crusader for Safe Consumer Products. Tolan, Mary, adapted by. LC 90-9924. (Illus.). 64p. (gr. 3-4). 1991. PLB 19.93 (*0-8368-0455-4*) Gareth Stevens Inc.

—Ralph Nader: Crusader for Safe Consumer Products & Lawyer for Public Interest. LC 89-4282. (Illus.). 68p. (gr. 5-6). 1990. PLB 19.93 (*0-8368-0098-2*) Gareth Stevens Inc.

NAMATH, JOSEPH WILLIAM, 1943-

Chadwick, Bruce. Joe Namath. LC 94-1351. 1994. 14.95 (*0-7910-2454-7*) Chelsea Hse.

NAMES–DICTIONARIES

Heifetz, Jeanne. Colorful Names. (gr. 6 up). 1994. 14.95 (*0-8050-3178-2*) H Holt & Co.

NAMES–FICTION

De Paola, Tomie. Andy: That's My Name. 32p. (ps-2). 1991. (S&S BFYR); pap. 6.00 (*0-671-66465-4*, S&S BFYR) S&S Trade.

Filichia, Peter. What's in a Name? 224p. (gr. 7 up). 1988. pap. 2.75 (*0-380-75536-X*, Flare) Avon.

Larios, Julie. On the Stairs. Hofstrand, Mary, illus. LC 93-20588. 1995. 13.95 (*0-689-31643-7*, Atheneum) Macmillan Child Grp.

Shute, Linda. How I Named the Baby. Grant, Christy, ed. Shute, Linda, illus. LC 92-33292. 32p. (ps-3). 1993. PLB 13.95 (*0-8075-3417-X*) A Whitman.

NAMES, GEOGRAPHICAL

Gerberg, Mort. Geographunny: A Book of Global Riddles. Gerberg, Mort, illus. 64p. (gr. 3 up). 1991. 14.45 (*0-395-52449-0*, Clarion Bks); pap. 7.70 (*0-395-60312-9*, Clarion Bks) HM.

NAMES, PERSONAL

Freeman, J. W. Discovering Surnames: Their Origins & Meanings. 4th ed. 72p. (gr. 6 up). 1979. pap. 4.95 (*0-913714-36-4*) Legacy Bks.

Lee, Mary P. & Lee, Richard S. Last Names First..& Some First Names too. Weber, Debora, illus. LC 84-20860. 119p. (gr. 5-9). 1985. 12.00 (*0-664-32719-2*, Westminster) Westminster John Knox.

Meltzer, Milton. A Book about Names. Richter, Mischa, illus. LC 83-45241. 128p. (gr. 7 up). 1984. (Crowell Jr Bks); PLB 13.89 (*0-690-04381-3*, Crowell Jr Bks) HarpC Child Bks.

Les Nombres. (FRE., Illus.). 3.50 (*0-7214-1427-3*) Ladybird Bks.

Obaba, Al-Imam & Chisa. The Name Book: The One You've Been Waiting For. 48p. (Orig.). 1977. pap. 3.95 (*0-916157-12-1*) African Islam Miss Pubns.

Silverstein, Alvin, et al. Michael: Fun & Facts about a Popular Name & the People Who Made It Great. LC 90-80673. (Illus.). 64p. (gr. 5 up). 1990. 11.95 (*0-9623653-6-X*); pap. 4.95 (*0-9623653-7-8*) Avstar Pub.

Twenty Names Series: Group 2, 6 vols. (Illus.). 288p. (gr. 3-8). 1990. Set. PLB 77.70 (*1-85435-251-2*) Marshall Cavendish.

NAMES, PERSONAL–FICTION

Arnold, Marsha D. Heart of a Tiger. Henterly, Jamichael, illus. LC 94-17126. (gr. 1-8). 1995. write for info. (*0-8037-1695-8*); PLB write for info. (*0-8037-1696-6*) Dial Bks Young.

Engel, Diana. Josephina Hates Her Name. Engel, Diana, illus. LC 88-1500. 32p. (ps-2). 1989. 13.95 (*0-688-07795-1*); PLB 13.88 (*0-688-07796-X*, Morrow Jr Bks) Morrow Jr Bks.

Epstein, June. The Name. Power, Margaret, illus. LC 92-34161. 1993. 3.75 (*0-383-03643-7*) SRA Schl Grp.

Grant, Eva. I Hate My Name. (ps-3). 1993. pap. 3.95 (*0-8114-5204-2*) Raintree Steck-V.

Greene, Constance C. A Girl Called Al. large type ed. 1989. Repr. of 1969 ed. lib. bdg. 15.95 (*1-55736-145-2*, Crnrstn Bks) BDD LT Grp.

Henkes, Kevin. Chrysanthemum. LC 90-39803. (Illus.). 32p. (ps up). 1991. 13.95 (*0-688-09699-9*); PLB 13.88 (*0-688-09700-6*) Greenwillow.

Hinton, S. E. Big David, Little David. Daniel, Alan, illus. LC 93-32307. 1995. 14.95 (*0-385-31093-5*) Doubleday.

Jacobs, Shannon K. Boy Who Loved Morning. (ps-3). 1993. 15.95 (*0-316-45556-3*) Little.

Rochelle, Belinda. When Jo Louis Won the Title. Johnson, Larry, illus. LC 93-34317. (gr. 4 up). 1994. 14.95 (*0-395-66614-7*) HM.

Rogers, Mary. Funny Names. 35p. (gr. 1). 1992. pap. text ed. 23.00 big bk. (*1-56843-016-7*); pap. text ed. 4.50 (*1-56843-066-3*) BGR Pub.

Waber, Bernard. But Names Will Never Hurt Me. Waber, Bernard, illus. LC 75-40473. 32p. (gr. k-3). 1976. 14. 95 (*0-395-24383-1*) HM.
Yamate, Sandra S. Ashok by Any Other Name. (Illus.). 36p. (gr. k-4). 1992. 12.95 (*1-879965-01-1*) Polychrome Pub.

NANSEN, FRIDTJOF, 1861-1930

Jacobs, Francine. A Passion for Danger: Nansen's Arctic Adventures. LC 93-5674. 160p. (gr. 5-9). 1994. 17.95 (*0-399-22674-5*) Putnam Pub Group.

NANTUCKET, MASSACHUSETTS–FICTION

Finley, Martha. Elsie at Nantucket. 301p. 1981. Repr. PLB 25.95x (*0-89966-333-8*) Buccaneer Bks.
—Elsie at Nantucket. 302p. 1980. Repr. PLB 17.95x (*0-89967-011-3*) Harmony Raine.
Miles, Mary. What's So Special about Nantucket? Locke, Barbara K., illus. LC 98-71418. 36p. (ps up). 1993. PLB 17.00 (*0-9636885-0-2*) Faraway Pub.
Turkle, Brinton. Rachel & Obadiah. Turkle, Brinton, illus. LC 77-15661. (gr. k-3). 1978. 15.00 (*0-525-38020-5*, DCB) Dutton Child Bks.
—Rachel & Obadiah. Turkle, Brinton, illus. (gr. 1-3). 1987. pap. 4.95 (*0-525-44303-7*, DCB) Dutton Child Bks.

NAPOLEON 1ST, EMPEROR OF THE FRENCH, 1769-1821

Carroll, Bob. Napoleon. LC 93-17852. (gr. 5-8). 1994. 14. 95 (*1-56006-021-2*) Lucent Bks.
Harris, Nathaniel. Napoleon. (Illus.). 64p. (gr. 6-9). 1989. 19.95 (*0-7134-5730-9*, Pub. by Batsford UK) Trafalgar.
Marrin, Albert. Napoleon & the Napoleonic Wars. 1991. 14.95 (*0-670-83480-7*) Viking Child Bks.
—Napoleon & the Napoleonic Wars. LC 93-13067. 288p. (gr. 7 up). 1993. pap. 5.99 (*0-14-036479-X*, Puffin) Puffin Bks.
Weidhorn, Manfred. Napoleon. LC 86-3352. (Illus.). 224p. (gr. 7 up). 1986. SBE 16.95 (*0-689-31163-X*, Atheneum Child Bk) Macmillan Child Grp.

NAPOLEONIC WARS

see France–History–Revolution, 1789-1799

NARCOTIC HABIT

Adint, Victor. Drugs & Crime. LC 93-41862. 1994. 14.95 (*0-8239-1539-5*) Rosen Group.
—Drugs & Prison. LC 94-1025. 1994. 14.95 (*0-8239-1705-3*) Rosen Group.
August, Paul N. Drugs & Women. (Illus.). 32p. (gr. 5 up). 1991. pap. 4.49 (*0-7910-0002-8*) Chelsea Hse.
Ball, Jacqueline. Everything You Need to Know about Drug Abuse. rev. ed. (gr. 4-7). 1992. 14.95 (*0-8239-1944-7*) Rosen Group.
Benton, John W. New Hope Series, 10 bks. 2004p. (gr. 3-12). Date not set. Set. ten pack 35.00 (*0-9635411-1-0*) J Benton Bks.
Berger, Gilda. Joey's Story: Straight Talk about Drugs. Kirk, Barbara, photos by. (Illus.). 64p. (gr. 7 up). 1991. PLB 13.40 (*1-56294-003-1*); pap. 4.95 (*1-56294-803-2*) Millbrook Pr.
—Joey's Story: Straight Talk about Drugs. 1992. pap. 4.95 (*0-395-63559-4*) HM.
—Meg's Story: Straight Talk about Drugs. LC 91-21515. (Illus.). 64p. (gr. 7 up). 1992. PLB 13.40 (*1-56294-102-X*); pap. 4.95 (*1-56294-804-0*) Millbrook Pr.
—Meg's Story: Straight Talk about Drugs. 1992. pap. 4.95 (*0-395-63557-8*) HM.
—Patty's Story: Straight Talk about Drugs. 1992. pap. 4.95 (*0-395-63558-6*) HM.
Bernards, Neal. The War on Drugs: Examining Cause & Effect Relationships. LC 91-22021. (Illus.). 32p. (gr. 4-7). 1991. PLB 10.95 (*0-89908-612-8*) Greenhaven.
Bernards, Neal, ed. The War on Drugs: Opposing Viewpoints. LC 90-39795. (Illus.). 240p. (gr. 10 up). 1990. PLB 17.95 (*0-89908-483-4*); pap. text ed. 9.95 (*0-89908-458-3*) Greenhaven.
Berry, Joy. About Substance Abuse. Bartholomew, illus. 48p. (gr. 3 up). 1990. PLB 12.30 (*0-516-02956-8*) Childrens.
Bosworth, et al. Alcohol & Other Drugs. (gr. 7-12). Date not set. incl. software 120.00 (*0-912899-59-X*) Lrning Multi-Systs.
Brady, Janeen. Safety Kids Play It Smart, Vol. 2: Stay Safe from Drugs. Twede, Evan, illus. (Orig.). (gr. k-6). 1985. pap. text ed. 6.95 songbook (*0-944803-21-0*); pap. text ed. 1.50 dialogue bk., 1985, 16p. (*0-944803-24-5*); act. bk. 2.50 (*0-944803-22-9*); cassette & bk. 10.95 (*0-944803-23-7*); video 19.95 (*0-944803-72-5*) Brite Music.
Buckalew, M. Walker. Drugs & Stress. Rosen, Ruth, ed. (gr. 7-12). 1993. 14.95 (*0-8239-1418-6*) Rosen Group.
Campbell, Chris. No Guarantees: A Young Woman's Fight to Overcome Drug & Alcohol Addiction. LC 92-25183. (Illus.). 192p. (gr. 6 up). 1993. text ed. 14. 95 RSBE (*0-02-716445-4*, New Discovery) Macmillan Child Grp.
Carroll, Marilyn. Cocaine & Crack. LC 93-43451. (Illus.). 112p. (gr. 6 up). 1994. lib. bdg. 17.95 (*0-89490-472-8*) Enslow Pubs.
Chatt, Andy. Cocaine the Silent Killer: Self Help Manual. (Orig.). (gr. 7 up). 1991. pap. text ed. 8.95 (*0-9626964-0-4*) Nocaine.
Clayton, Lawrence. Amphetamines & Other Stimulants. Rosen, Ruth, ed. (gr. 7-12). 1994. 14.95 (*0-8239-1534-4*) Rosen Group.
—Barbiturates & Other Depressants. Rosen, Ruth, ed. (gr. 7-12). 1994. 14.95 (*0-8239-1535-2*) Rosen Group.
—Designer Drugs. Rosen, Ruth, ed. (gr. 7-12). 1993. 14. 95 (*0-8239-1519-0*) Rosen Group.
Community Intervention, Inc. Staff. Saying Yes, Saying No: You & Drugs--A Positive Approach to Staying Drug Free. 24p. (Orig.). (gr. 8-12). 1986. pap. 3.95 (*0-9613416-4-5*) Comm Intervention.
Crack. rev. ed. 64p. (gr. 7-12). 1994. PLB 14.95 (*0-8239-1753-3*) Rosen Group.
De La Martre, Audrey, ed. Chemical Abuse Assessment Workbook for Adolescents. rev. ed. Payne, William J., intro. by. 34p. (gr. 6-12). 1989. Repr. of 1981 ed. wkbk. 7.00 (*0-317-92294-7*) New Connect Pub.
Dickson, Charles. Beating the Chemical Cop-Out. Nelson, Becky, ed. 22p. (Orig.). (gr. 7-12). 1992. pap. text ed. 1.95 (*1-56309-036-8*, Wrld Changers Res) Womans Mission Union.
Di Silvestro, Frank. Kid Wise Talks to Kids about Drugs. Berlin, Rosemary, illus. 22p. (gr. 1-8). 1990. pap. write for info. (*0-934591-02-4*) Songs & Stories.
Draimin, Barbara H. Drugs & AIDS. LC 94-2331. 1994. 14.95 (*0-8239-1702-9*) Rosen Group.
Las Drogas y Nuestro Mundo (Drugs & Our World) (SPA., Illus.). 48p. (ps-3). 1991. PLB 16.40 (*0-516-37371-4*) Childrens.
Drugs & Drinking. 48p. (gr. 6-8). 1990. pap. 8.99 (*1-55945-118-1*) Group Pub.
Edwards, Gabrielle I. Coping with Drug Abuse. rev. ed. Rosen, Roger, ed. (gr. 7 up). 1990. PLB 14.95 (*0-8239-1144-6*) Rosen Group.
Engelmann, Jeanne. My Body Is My House: A Coloring Book about Alcohol, Drugs & Health. Barton, Patrice, illus. 16p. (gr. k-5). 1990. pap. 1.75 (*0-89486-735-0*, 5100B) Hazelden.
—Rule of the Szak King: A Smoke-Free Adventure on the Planet Quark. Hanson, Eric, illus. 23p. (gr. 5-9). 1991. pap. 1.75 (*0-89486-748-2*, 5359B) Hazelden.
—The Sweet Air of Starship Orr: Rescue from the Inhalant Planet. Hanson, Eric, illus. 27p. (gr. 5-9). 1991. pap. 1.75 (*0-89486-749-0*, 5358B) Hazelden.
Enns, Peter. Drugs - a Dead End Street: The Dangers of Substance Abuse. Wolverton, Lock, illus. 40p. (Orig.). (ps-6). 1992. pap. 5.98 incl. cassette (*0-943593-98-0*) Kids Intl Inc.
Focus on Cocaine & Crack. (Illus.). 64p. (gr. 3-7). 1990. PLB 15.40 (*0-516-07352-4*) Childrens.
Fradin, Dennis B. Drug Abuse. LC 87-33789. (Illus.). 48p. (gr. k-4). 1988. PLB 12.85 (*0-516-01212-6*); pap. 4.95 (*0-516-41212-4*) Childrens.
Frisch, Carlienne. Drugs & Music. LC 94-1026. 1994. 14. 95 (*0-8239-1707-X*) Rosen Group.
Gaetano, Ronald J. & Masterson, James J. Teenage Drug Abusers: One Hundred Most Commonly Asked Questions about Adolescent Substance Abuse. 128p. (gr. 9 up). 1988. write for info. Union Hosp Found.
Gibson, Christine R. & Hargrave, J. Michael. The Tator Tales: A Guide to Substance Abuse Prevention for Youth & Adults. Majewski, Chuck, illus. (Orig.). (gr. 4-8). 1989. pap. write for info. Tator Enterprises.
Gross, Cheryl & Werz, Ed. The Sock Club: Drugs Make You Do Bad Things. 16p. (gr. k-4). 1992. 0.95 (*1-56688-050-5*) Bur For At-Risk.
—The Sock Club: How to Say No to Drugs! 16p. (gr. k-4). 1992. 0.95 (*1-56688-052-1*) Bur For At-Risk.
Grosshandler, Janet. Drugs & the Law. Rosen, Ruth, ed. (gr. 7-12). 1993. 14.95 (*0-8239-1463-1*) Rosen Group.
Hallinan, P. K. Easy Does It. Hallinan, P. K., illus. 32p. 1992. pap. 5.00 (*0-89486-673-7*, 5107B) Hazelden.
—Live & Let Live. Hallinan, P. K., illus. 32p. 1990. pap. 5.00 (*0-89486-650-8*, 5120B) Hazelden.
—One Day At a Time. Hallinan, P. K., illus. 28p. 1990. pap. 5.00 (*0-89486-640-0*, 5084B) Hazelden.
Harris, Jacqueline L. Drugs & Disease. (Illus.). 64p. (gr. 5-8). 1993. PLB 14.95 (*0-8050-2602-9*) TFC Bks NY.
Harris, Jonathan. Drugged Athletes: The Crisis in American Sports. LC 86-29396. 204p. (gr. 5-9). 1987. SBE 14.95 (*0-02-742740-4*, Four Winds) Macmillan Child Grp.
Hawley, Richard. Drugs & Society. rev. ed. 160p. (gr. 7 up). 1992. PLB 15.85 (*0-8027-8114-4*); pap. 9.95 (*0-8027-7366-4*) Walker & Co.
Hawley, Richard A. Think about Drugs & Society: Responding to an Epidemic. LC 87-21681. 157p. 1988. 14.85 (*0-8027-6749-4*); pap. 5.95 (*0-8027-6750-8*) Walker & Co.
Heegaard, Marge. When a Family Is in Trouble: Children Can Cope with Grief from Drug & Alcohol Addictions. (gr. 4-7). 1993. pap. 6.95 (*0-9620502-7-X*) Woodland Pr.
Hipp, Earl. The Second Step - Hope. Yencho, Mike, illus. 28p. (gr. 9-12). 1992. pap. 2.50 (*0-89486-642-7*, 5228B) Hazelden.
—The Third Step - POWER. Yencho, Mike, illus. 35p. (gr. 9-12). 1992. pap. 2.50 (*0-89486-643-5*, 5249B) Hazelden.
Jones, Penny. The Brown Bottle. 40p. (gr. 4 up). 1983. text ed. 4.00 (*0-89486-170-0*, 1162A) Hazelden.
Kendall, Sarita. Cocaine. LC 91-27815. (Illus.). 64p. (gr. 6-12). 1991. PLB 22.80 (*0-8114-3200-9*) Raintree Steck-V.
Kronenwetter, Michael. Drugs in America. (Illus.). 144p. (gr. 7 up). 1990. lib. bdg. 13.98 (*0-671-70557-1*, J Messner) S&S Trade.
Langone, John. Tough Choices: A Book about Substance Abuse. LC 94-17580. (gr. 7 up). 1995. 14.95 (*0-316-51407-1*) Little.
Lee, Essie E. Breaking the Connection: How Young People Achieve Drug-Free Lives. LC 87-18586. (Illus.). 160p. (gr. 7 up). 1988. (J Messner); pap. 5.95 (*0-671-67059-X*) S&S Trade.
Lee, Richard S. & Lee, Mary P. Caffeine & Nicotine. LC 94-2279. (gr. 7 up). 1994. write for info. (*0-8239-1701-0*) Rosen Group.
McCormick, Michele. Designer-Drug Abuse. LC 88-30450. (Illus.). 128p. (gr. 7-12). 1990. 13.40 (*0-531-10660-8*) Watts.
McFarland, Rhoda. Coping with Substance Abuse. rev. ed. Rosen, Ruth, ed. 144p. (gr. 7 up). 1990. PLB 14.95 (*0-8239-1135-7*) Rosen Group.
—Drugs & Your Brothers & Sisters. rev. ed. (gr. 7-12). 1993. PLB 14.95 (*0-8239-1754-1*) Rosen Group.
McMillan, Daniel. Winning the Battle Against Drugs: Rehabilitation Programs. LC 91-16344. (Illus.). 160p. (gr. 9-12). 1991. PLB 14.40 (*0-531-11063-X*) Watts.
Malerba-Foran, Joan. When You Look in the Mirror, What Do You See? 20p. (Orig.). (gr. 7 up). 1985. pap. 2.50 (*0-89486-262-6*) Hazelden.
Marijuana. rev. ed. (Illus.). 64p. (gr. 7-12). 1993. PLB 14. 95 (*0-8239-1683-9*) Rosen Group.
Meer, Jeff. Drugs & Sports. (Illus.). 32p. (gr. 5 up). 1991. pap. 4.49 (*1-55546-996-5*) Chelsea Hse.
Messina, Kathlyn & Dacquino, Vinny. Proud That I'm Still Me. Maley, Matthew & Benjamin, Ann, illus. LC 92-70002. 21p. (Orig.). (ps-5). 1992. pap. 7.95 shrinkwrapped (*0-910569-05-3*) Hampton Court Pub.
Morris-Vann, Artie M. My Parents Are Drug Abusers. 40p. (Orig.). (ps-5). pap. 6.50 (*0-317-02490-6*) Aid-U Pub.
Nardo, Don. Drugs & Sports. LC 90-6686. (Illus.). 112p. (gr. 5-8). 1990. PLB 14.95 (*1-56006-112-X*) Lucent Bks.
Orlandi, Mario & Prue, Donald. Substance Abuse. (gr. 5 up). 1989. 18.95x (*0-8160-1669-0*) Facts On File.
Parker, Steve. The Drug War. LC 90-3213. (Illus.). 32p. (gr. 5-8). 1990. PLB 12.40 (*0-531-17241-4*, Gloucester Pr) Watts.
Phillips, Lynn. Drug Abuse. LC 93-44346. 1994. 14.95 (*1-85435-617-8*) Marshall Cavendish.
Pownall, Mark. Heroin. LC 91-27815. (Illus.). 64p. (gr. 6-12). 1991. PLB 22.80 (*0-8114-3201-7*) Raintree Steck-V.
Pringle, Mary L. & Ellis, Joseph. Sis & Chris & the Knowbots in "We Don't Need Drugs to Be O. K." Educational Coloring Book. (gr. k-5). 1987. pap. 1.95 (*0-935847-03-0*) Inst Subs Abuse Res.
Rawls, Bea O. & Johnson, Gwen. Drugs & Where to Turn. Rosen, Ruth, ed. (gr. 7-12). 1993. 14.95 (*0-8239-1466-6*) Rosen Group.
Read, Edward M. & Daley, Dennis C. You've Got the Power: A Recovery Guide for Young People with Drug & Alcohol Problems. Butler, Ralph, illus. Gondles, James A., Jr., frwd. by. (Illus.). 98p. (Orig.). 1993. pap. 10.00 (*0-929310-87-X*, 349) Am Correctional.
Reiners, Kenneth G. Addicted to the Addict: From Codependency to Recovery. LC 87-50843. 64p. (Orig.). (gr. 9-12). 1987. pap. 4.95 (*0-934104-06-9*) Woodland.
Rico, Armando B. There's a Rock in Your Coke. 47p. (Orig.). 1987. pap. 2.50 (*1-879219-02-6*) Veracruz Pubs.
Rosenberg, Maxine B. On the Mend: Getting Away from Drugs. LC 91-11202. (Illus.). 128p. (gr. 4 up). 1991. SBE 14.95 (*0-02-777914-9*, Bradbury Pr) Macmillan Child Grp.
Rundquist, Thomas J. & Parent, Frederick. Horse Is Boss: Drug Culture Education & Prevention Game. 2nd ed. Randquist, Thomas J, illus. 42p. (Orig.). (gr. 7-12). 1988. pap. text ed. 30.50x (*0-9618567-1-8*) Nova Media.
Ryan, Elizabeth A. Straight Talk about Drugs & Alcohol. 160p. 1989. 16.95x (*0-8160-1525-2*) Facts on File.
Salak, John. Drugs in Society: Are They Our Suicide Pill? (Illus.). 64p. (gr. 5-8). 1993. PLB 15.95 (*0-8050-2572-3*) TFC Bks NY.
Santamaria, Peggy. Drugs & Politics. LC 94-1024. 1994. 14.95 (*0-8239-1703-7*) Rosen Group.
Scherling, Donald. Better All the Time: A Young Person's Recovery Workbook. 30p. (Orig.). 1989. pap. 7.95 wkbk. (*0-942421-12-4*) Hazelden.
Seixas, Judith S. Drugs: What They Are, What They Do. Huffman, Tom, illus. LC 86-33624. 48p. (gr. k up). 1991. pap. 4.95 (*0-688-10487-8*, Mulberry) Morrow.
—Living with a Parent Who Takes Drugs. LC 89-1995. 96p. 1989. 13.95 (*0-688-08627-6*) Greenwillow.
Sherry, Clifford. Inhalants. LC 94-572. 1994. 14.95 (*0-8239-1704-5*) Rosen Group.
Shniderman, Nancy & Hurwitz, Sue. Drugs & Birth Defects. Rosen, Ruth, ed. (gr. 7-12). 1994. 14.95 (*0-8239-1419-4*) Rosen Group.
Shoker, Nancy. Substance Abuse. Koop, C. Everett, intro. by. (Illus.). 112p. (gr. 6-12). 1993. 18.95 (*0-7910-0078-8*) Chelsea Hse.
Shuker-Haines, Frances. Everything You Need to Know about a Drug-Abusing Parent. Rosen, Ruth, ed. (gr. 7-12). 1993. PLB 14.95 (*0-8239-1529-8*) Rosen Group.
Silverstein, Alvin, et al. The Addictions Handbook. LC 90-14093. 192p. (gr. 6 up). 1991. lib. bdg. 18.95 (*0-89490-205-9*) Enslow Pubs.
Sinberg, Janet & Daley, Dennis. I Can Talk about What Hurts: A Book for Kids in Homes Where There's Chemical Dependency. Hartman, Tim, illus. 48p. (Orig.). (gr. 3 up). 1991. pap. 7.00 (*0-89486-641-9*, 5762A) Hazelden.
Smith, Sandra L. Drugs & Your Friends. rev. ed. (Illus.). 64p. (gr. 7-12). 1993. PLB 14.95 (*0-8239-1657-X*) Rosen Group.

—Drugs & Your Parents. rev. ed. (Illus.). 64p. (gr. 7-12). 1993. lib. bdg. 14.95 (*0-8239-1684-7*) Rosen Group.
—Heroin. rev. ed. (gr. 7-12). 1993. PLB 14.95 (*0-8239-1685-5*) Rosen Group.
—Peyote & Magic Mushrooms. LC 94-2268. 1994. 14.95 (*0-8239-1700-2*) Rosen Group.
Stamper, Laura. Getting Help, Gaining Hope: The Second & Third Steps for Teens. 20p. 1990. pap. 1.75 (*0-925190-10-1*, F911021 C) Deaconess Pr.
—Searching & Sharing: The Fourth & Fifth Steps for Teens. 30p. 1991. pap. 1.75 (*0-925190-19-5*, F911124 C) Deaconess Pr.
—Taking the First Step: Being Honest with Yourself. 14p. pap. 1.75 (*0-925190-03-9*, F911007 C) Deaconess Pr.
Starbuck, Marnie. The Gladden Book about Drugs. (gr. 1-4). 1994. 0.75 (*0-685-71637-6*, 656) W Gladden Found.
—The Gladimals Learn about Drugs. (Illus.). 16p. 1990. 0.75 (*1-56456-202-6*, 472) W Gladden Found.
Super, Gretchen. Drugs & Our World. (Illus.). 48p. (gr. k-3). 1990. PLB 14.95 (*0-8050-2888-9*) TFC Bks NY.
—Tu Puedes Decirles "No" A las Drogas! You Can Say "No" to Drugs! Sims, Blanche, illus. (SPA.). 48p. (gr. k-4). 1991. PLB 16.40 (*0-516-37372-2*) Childrens.
—What Are Drugs? (Illus.). 48p. (gr. k-3). 1990. PLB 14.95 (*0-8050-2549-9*) TFC Bks NY.
—You Can Say "No" to Drugs! (Illus.). 48p. (gr. k-3). 1990. PLB 14.95 (*0-8050-2628-2*) TFC Bks NY.
Swisher, Karin L. & DeKoster, Katie, eds. Drug Abuse: Opposing Viewpoints. LC 93-12375. 1994. lib. bdg. 17.95 (*1-56510-060-3*); pap. 9.95 (*1-56510-059-X*) Greenhaven.
Tate, Albert J., III. Dad: Are People Using Alcohol & Drugs As an Alternative to Problem Solving? Design in Demand Staff, illus. 68p. (Orig.). (gr. 10). 1992. pap. 12.95 (*0-9622996-9-3*) Unique Memphis.
Taylor, Clark. The House That Crack Built. Pritchard, Michael, afterword by. (Illus.). 40p. 1992. 11.95 (*0-8118-0133-0*); pap. 5.95 (*0-8118-0123-3*) Chronicle Bks.
Troll Associates Staff. Focus on Cocaine & Crack. (gr. 4-7). 1991. pap. 4.95 (*0-8167-2446-6*) Troll Assocs.
—Focus on Drugs & the Brain. (gr. 4-7). 1991. pap. 4.95 (*0-8167-2447-4*) Troll Assocs.
—Focus on Marijuana. (gr. 4-7). 1991. pap. 4.95 (*0-8167-2449-0*) Troll Assocs.
Wax, Wendy. Say No & Know Why: Kids Learn About Drugs. 64p. (gr. 2-5). 1992. 12.95 (*0-8027-8140-3*); PLB 13.85 (*0-8027-8141-1*) Walker & Co.
Weikel, Ann T. The Very Best Me: Growing up Drug Free. John, Joseph, Jr., illus. Christian, Cora L., contrib. by. (Illus.). 60p. (Orig.). (gr. k-3). 1991. pap. 3.95 (*0-935357-11-4*) CRIC Prod.
Westfall, Tanja & Miles, Patrick. Decisions, 5 Vols. Karch, Cheri, ed. Tully, Carol & Rizzuto, Joe, illus. 160p. (gr. 4-7). 1989. Set. text ed. 38.95 (*1-877618-00-4*) APIX Intl.
—Decisions: Building Bricks - Crystal, Vol 3. Karch, Cherl, ed. Tully, Carol & Rizzuto, Joe, illus. 32p. (gr. 4-7). 1989. text ed. 7.79 (*1-877618-03-9*) APIX Intl.
—Decisions: Struggle in the Willow Tree, Vol. 1. Karch, Cheri, ed. Tully, Carol & Rizzuto, Joe, illus. 32p. (gr. 4-7). 1989. text ed. 7.79 (*1-877618-01-2*) APIX Intl.
—Decisions: The Edge - LSD, Vol. 5. Karch, Cheri, ed. Tully, Carol & Rizzuto, Joe, illus. 32p. (gr. 4-7). 1989. text ed. 7.79 (*1-877618-05-5*) APIX Intl.
—Decisions: The Pit, Vol. 2. Karch, Cheri, ed. Tully, Carol & Rizzuto, Joe, illus. 32p. (gr. 4-7). 1989. text ed. 7.79 (*1-877618-02-0*) APIX Intl.
—Decisions: The Survivor, Vol. 4. Karch, Cheri, ed. Tully, Carol & Rizzuto, Joe, illus. 32p. (gr. 4-7). 1989. text ed. 7.84 (*1-877618-04-7*) APIX Intl.
Williams, Richard N. Handbook of Substance Abuse. 2nd ed. LC 91-60152. (Illus.). 120p. (gr. 6-12). 1991. text ed. 39.50 (*1-879278-00-6*) Pharmaco-Video Pubns.
Wise, Francis H. Youth & Drugs. Wise, Joyce M., illus. (gr. 10 up). Date not set. 4.95 (*0-686-86911-7*) Wise Pub.
Wood, Judy, et al. Sunakorn Drug Prevention Teaching Curriculum. LC 89-50139. 184p. (gr. k-5). 1989. 22.95 (*0-938021-42-7*) Turner Pub KY.
Woolley, Merle E. Say No to Drugs Color & Learn Book. Frising, Nic, illus. 20p. (gr. k-6). 1988. wkbk. 1.50 (*0-9623773-0-9*) Mapakam Inc.
Yoslow, Mark. Drugs in the Body: Effects of Abuse. LC 91-39030. (Illus.). 144p. (gr. 9-12). 1992. PLB 14.40 (*0-531-12507-6*) Watts.
Young, Patrick. Drugs & Pregnancy. (Illus.). 32p. (gr. 5 up). 1991. pap. 4.49 (*0-7910-0001-X*) Chelsea Hse.

NARCOTIC HABIT–FICTION

Allen, Stephen D. Reality: Drugs & Guns--No-Win Solutions. LC 92-64322. 126p. (gr. k-8). 1992. pap. 14.95 (*0-9634084-7-X*) S D A Pub.
Angell, Judie. Yours Truly: A Novel. LC 92-29472. 192p. (gr. 7-12). 1993. 14.95 (*0-531-05472-1*); PLB 14.99 (*0-531-08622-4*) Orchard Bks Watts.
Berenstain, Stan & Berenstain, Jan. The Berenstain Bears & the Drug Free Zone. Berenstain, Stan & Berenstain, Jan, illus. LC 92-31604. 112p. (Orig.). (gr. 2-6). 1993. PLB 7.99 (*0-679-93612-2*); pap. 3.50 (*0-679-83612-8*) Random Bks Yng Read.
Cadnum, Michael. Calling Home. 144p. (gr. 7 up). 1993. pap. 3.99 (*0-14-034569-8*, Puffin) Puffin Bks.
Childress, Alice. A Hero Ain't Nothin but a Sandwich. 128p. (gr. 7 up). 1977. pap. 3.99 (*0-380-00132-2*, Flare) Avon.
Cook, John M. Inside Four Ninety-Five. Haye, Caroline, ed. (Illus.). 128p. 1989. write for info. J M Cook Pub.
Elwood, Roger. Forbidden River. (gr. 3-7). 1991. pap. 4.99 (*0-8499-3304-8*) Word Inc.
Go Ask Alice. LC 74-159446. 160p. (gr. 6 up). 1971. pap. 15.00 jacketed (*0-671-66458-1*, Little Simon) S&S Trade.
Irwin, Hadley. Can't Hear You Listening. LC 90-32675. 208p. (gr. 7 up). 1990. SBE 14.95 (*0-689-50513-2*, M K McElderry) Macmillan Child Grp.
Miklowitz, Gloria D. Anything to Win. 1989. pap. 14.95 (*0-440-50142-3*) Dell.
Milam, June M. The Short Cut. Gilmer, Chris, ed. McIntosh, Chuck, illus. 20p. (ps). 1994. pap. text ed. 42.95 (*1-884307-05-1*); student ed. 4.95 (*1-884307-06-X*) Dev Res Educ.

Slaughter, Rachel. Roxie's Mirage: Featuring the Original Boys & Girls from the Hood. 65p. (gr. 8-12). 1994. pap. 7.95 (*0-9639858-0-9*) Fruits for Knowldge.
LSD is back! Many teens today are adopting some bad habits from the Sixties. They don't know what a ride they are in for. It seems that teens have been dipping in LSD ever since the first particle was invented. In ROXIE'S MIRAGE, you meet a young teen whose foundation is so shaky that she easily falls into the abyss of drugs. From the first page to the last, your mind will intertwine with the thoughts of several urban teens who will never escape the clutches of their dismal fates. And no matter how hard you try... you will never forget them. Signed copies available by calling (610) 323-2982 or writing 1474 Heather Place, Pottstown, PA 19464.
Publisher Provided Annotation.

Starkman, Neal. The Boy & the Hat. LC 91-16798. 32p. (Orig.). (gr. 3). 1991. pap. text ed. 8.00 (*0-935529-27-6*) Comprehen Health Educ.
Sutton, Elizabeth H. Racing for Keeneland. LC 93-43385. (gr. 5-12). 1994. 14.95 (*1-56566-051-X*) Thomasson-Grant.
Voigt, Cynthia. Orfe. LC 91-46058. 128p. (gr. 9 up). 1992. SBE 12.95 (*0-689-31771-9*, Atheneum Child Bk) Macmillan Child Grp.

NARCOTICS

Appalachee Center for Human Services Staff. Choosing for Yourself 6-8. (Illus.). 208p. (gr. 6-8). 1988. Repr. of 1984 ed. 3-ring binder 200.00 (*1-8776670-2-1*) Innovat Lrning Grp.
—Choosing for Yourself 9-12. (Illus.). 222p. 1988. Repr. of 1984 ed. 3-ring binder 200.00 (*1-8776670-3-X*) Innovat Lrning Grp.
Bernards, Neal, ed. The War on Drugs: Opposing Viewpoints. LC 90-39795. (Illus.). 240p. (gr. 10 up). 1990. PLB 17.95 (*0-89908-483-4*); pap. text ed. 9.95 (*0-89908-458-3*) Greenhaven.
Chapman, Dorothy. My Body Is Where I Live. (gr. k-4). 1989. text ed. 17.95 (*0-88671-297-1*, 5102) Am Guidance.
Chiles, John. Teenage Depression & Drugs. updated ed. (Illus.). (gr. 5 up). 1992. lib. bdg. 19.95 (*0-685-52254-7*); pap. 9.95 (*0-685-52255-5*) Chelsea Hse.
Encyclopedia of Psychoactive Drugs, 12 vols. (Illus.). 384p. (gr. 5 up). 1991. pap. 49.95 (*0-7910-0093-1*) Chelsea Hse.
Focus on Drugs & the Brain. (Illus.). 64p. (gr. 3-7). 1990. PLB 15.40 (*0-516-07353-2*) Childrens.
Hafford, Jeannette N. Run Children Run: Tiny Warns Children about the Dangers of Drugs. (Illus.). (ps-8). 1989. pap. text ed. write for info. (*0-9616549-2-9*) Tinys Self Help Bks.
Harris, Jonathan. Drugged America. LC 90-47649. 192p. (gr. 7 up). 1991. SBE 14.95 (*0-02-742745-5*, Four Winds) Macmillan Child Grp.
Hawkes, N. International Drug Trade. (Illus.). 48p. (gr. 5 up). 1988. PLB 18.60 (*0-86592-280-2*); 13.95 (*0-685-58317-1*) Rourke Corp.
Hyde, Margaret O. Drug Wars. (Illus.). 112p. (gr. 6 up). 1990. 11.95 (*0-8027-6900-4*); lib. bdg. 12.85 (*0-8027-6901-2*) Walker & Co.
King, Jesse J., Sr. You Can Say No to Drugs. King, Linda L., ed. King, Jesse J., Sr., illus. 24p. (Orig.). (gr. k-5). 1989. pap. text ed. 1.25 (*0-685-25956-0*) J Lynn Pub.
—You Can Say No to Drugs: For Fifth Grade. King, Linda L., ed. King, Jesse J., Sr., illus. 24p. (Orig.). (gr. 5). 1990. pap. text ed. 1.25 (*0-685-25962-5*) J Lynn Pub.
—You Can Say No to Drugs: For First Grade. King, Linda L., ed. King, Jesse J., Sr., illus. 24p. (Orig.). (gr. 1). 1989. pap. text ed. 1.25 (*0-685-25958-7*) J Lynn Pub.
—You Can Say No to Drugs: For Fourth Grade. King, Linda L., ed. King, Jesse J., Sr., illus. 24p. (Orig.). (gr. 4). 1990. pap. text ed. 1.25 (*0-685-25961-7*) J Lynn Pub.
—You Can Say No to Drugs: For Kindergarten. King, Linda L., ed. King, Jesse J., Sr., illus. 24p. (Orig.). (gr. k). 1989. pap. text ed. 1.25 (*0-685-25957-9*) J Lynn Pub.
—You Can Say No to Drugs: For Second Grade. King, Linda L., ed. King, Jesse J., Sr., illus. 24p. (Orig.). (gr. 2). 1989. pap. text ed. 1.25 (*0-685-25959-5*) J Lynn Pub.
—You Can Say No to Drugs: For Third Grade. King, Linda L., ed. King, Jesse J., Sr., illus. 24p. (Orig.). (gr. 3). 1990. pap. text ed. 1.25 (*0-685-25960-9*) J Lynn Pub.
Klass, David. Wrestling with Honor. LC 88-16147. 208p. (gr. 7 up). 1989. 14.95 (*0-525-67268-0*, Lodestar Bks) Dutton Child Bks.
Knox, Jean M. Drinking, Driving & Drugs. (Illus.). 32p. (gr. 5 up). 1991. pap. 4.49 (*1-55546-997-3*) Chelsea Hse.
Madison, Arnold. Drugs & You. rev. ed. Steltenpohl, Jane, ed. (Illus.). 128p. (gr. 4-6). 1990. PLB 13.98 (*0-671-69147-3*, J Messner); pap. 5.95 (*0-671-69148-1*) S&S Trade.
Pearce, Jenny. Colombia: The Drug War. (Illus.). 40p. (gr. 6-8). 1990. PLB 12.90 (*0-531-17237-6*, Gloucester Pr) Watts.
Rico, Armando B. A Sound Mind in a Sound Body. 23p. (Orig.). 1990. pap. 16.00 (*1-879219-03-4*) Veracruz Pubs.
Schenkerman, Rona D. Growing up with Drugs in Your Neighborhood. 16p. (gr. 3-8). 1993. 1.95 (*1-56688-120-X*) Bur For At-Risk.
Swisher, Karin, ed. Drug Trafficking. LC 91-22022. 200p. (gr. 10 up). 1991. PLB 16.95 (*0-89908-576-8*); pap. text ed. 9.95 (*0-89908-582-2*) Greenhaven.
Terkel, Susan N. Should Drugs Be Legalized? (Illus.). 160p. (gr. 9-12). 1990. 14.45 (*0-531-15182-4*) Watts.
Washton, Arnold M. & Boundy, Donna. Cocaine & Crack: What You Need to Know. LC 88-16814. (Illus.). 96p. (gr. 6 up). 1989. lib. bdg. 16.95 (*0-89490-162-1*) Enslow Pubs.
Zackon, Fred & McAulyfe, William E. Heroin: The Street Narcotic. (Illus.). 32p. (gr. 5 up). 1991. pap. 4.49 (*1-55546-999-X*) Chelsea Hse.

NASCIMENTO, EDSON ARANTES DO, 1940-

Arnold, Caroline. Pele: The King of Soccer. Mathews, V., ed. LC 91-33557. (Illus.). 64p. (gr. 3-6). 1992. PLB 12.90 (*0-531-20077-9*) Watts.

NATION OF ISLAM

see Black Muslims

NATIONAL ANTHEMS

see National Songs

NATIONAL DANCES

see Folk Dancing

NATIONAL DEFENSES

see names of countries with the subdivision Defenses, e.g. U. S.–Defenses

NATIONAL FOOTBALL LEAGUE

Potts, Steve. Buffalo Bills. (gr. 4 up). 1991. PLB 14.95 (*0-88682-360-9*) Creative Ed.
Rambeck, Richard. Detroit Lions. 48p. (gr. 4 up). 1991. PLB 14.95 (*0-88682-366-8*) Creative Ed.

NATIONAL GUARD (U. S.)

see U. S.–National Guard

NATIONAL HOLIDAYS

see Holidays;
see names of national holidays, e. g. Fourth of July

NATIONAL HYMNS

see National Songs

NATIONAL MONUMENTS

see National Parks and Reserves; Natural Monuments

NATIONAL PARKS AND RESERVES

see also Natural Monuments;
also names of national parks, e.g. Yellowstone National park

Acadia National Park Coloring Book. (Illus.). 24p. (ps-6). 1991. pap. 3.00 (*0-934745-20-X*) Acadia Pub Co.
Brown, Richard, illus. A Kid's Guide to National Parks. 160p. (gr. 1 up). 1989. pap. 6.95 (*0-318-37140-5*, Gulliver Bks) HarBrace.
Crump, Donald J., ed. Adventures in Your National Parks. (gr. 3-8). 1989. 8.95 (*0-87044-702-5*); PLB 12.50 (*0-87044-707-6*) Natl Geog.
—Pathways to Discovery: Exploring America's National Trails. (Illus.). 1990. 12.95 (*0-87044-792-0*) Natl Geog.
Diamond, Lynnell. Let's Discover Capitol Reef, Arches, & Canyonlands National Parks: A Children's Activity Book for Ages 6-11. (Illus.). 32p. (gr. 1-6). 1991. pap. 4.95 (*0-89886-285-X*) Mountaineers.
—Let's Discover Petrified Forest National Park: A Children's Activity Book for Ages 6-11. (Illus.). 32p. (gr. 1-6). 1991. pap. 4.95 (*0-89886-286-8*) Mountaineers.
Dolan, Edward F. The American Wilderness & Its Future: Conservation Versus Use. LC 91-33440. (Illus.). 160p. (gr. 9-12). 1992. PLB 14.40 (*0-531-11062-1*) Watts.
Gartner, Bob. Exploring Careers in the National Park Service. Rosen, Ruth, ed. (gr. 7-12). 1993. 14.95 (*0-8239-1414-3*); pap. 9.95 (*0-8239-1726-6*) Rosen Group.
Lee, Michelle. Estes Park Souvenir Coloring Book. 48p. (ps-8). 1993. 4.50 (*0-9637687-0-0*) Vacation Color.

Markert, Jenny. Glacier National Park. (SPA & ENG.). (gr. 2-6). 1992. PLB 15.95 (*0-89565-858-5*) Childs World.
Naranjo, Rafael S. Great Animal Refuges. LC 93-3437. (Illus.). 36p. (gr. 3 up). 1993. PLB 14.95 (*0-516-08385-6*); pap. 6.95 (*0-516-48385-4*) Childrens.
Patent, Dorothy H. Places of Refuge: Our National Wildlife Refuge System. Munoz, William, illus. 80p. (gr. 4-9). 1992. 15.95 (*0-89919-846-5*, Clarion Bks) HM.
Peters, Lisa W. Serengeti. LC 89-7859. (Illus.). 48p. (gr. 4-5). 1989. text ed. 13.95 RSBE (*0-89686-433-2*, Crestwood Hse) Macmillan Child Grp.
Petersen, David. Grand Canyon National Park. LC 92-11343. (Illus.). 48p. (gr. k-4). 1992. PLB 12.85 (*0-516-02197-4*) Childrens.
—Grand Canyon National Park. LC 92-11343. (Illus.). 48p. (gr. k-4). 1993. pap. 4.95 (*0-516-42197-2*) Childrens.
—Grand Teton National Park. LC 92-9209. (Illus.). 48p. (gr. k-4). 1992. PLB 12.85 (*0-516-01948-1*) Childrens.
—Grand Teton National Park. LC 92-9209. (Illus.). 48p. (gr. k-4). 1993. pap. 4.95 (*0-516-41948-X*) Childrens.
—Waterton - Glacier International Peace Park. LC 92-9208. (Illus.). 48p. (gr. k-4). 1992. PLB 12.85 (*0-516-01946-5*) Childrens.
—Waterton-Glacier International Peace Park. LC 92-9208. (Illus.). 48p. (gr. k-4). 1993. pap. 4.95 (*0-516-41946-3*) Childrens.
Powzyk, Joyce. Madagascar Journey. LC 94-21053. (gr. 9-12). 1995. write for info. (*0-688-09487-2*); pap. write for info. (*0-688-13964-7*) Lothrop.
Radlauer, Ruth. Acadia National Park. Radlauer, Ed & Radlauer, Ruth, illus. LC 77-18056. 48p. (gr. 3 up). 1978. (Elk Grove Bks); pap. 4.95 (*0-516-47495-2*) Childrens.
Rudig, Doug. Zion Adventure Guide. LC 77-78309. (Illus.). 32p. (gr. 2-7). 1978. pap. 1.95 (*0-915630-07-9*) Zion.
Sateren, Shelley S. Banff. LC 89-33152. (Illus.). 48p. (gr. 4-5). 1989. text ed. 13.95 RSBE (*0-89686-431-6*, Crestwood Hse) Macmillan Child Grp.
Weber, Michael. Our National Parks. (Illus.). 48p. (gr. 2-4). 1994. 13.40 (*1-56294-438-X*) Millbrook Pr.
Worth, Bonnie. Pretty Park. (ps-3). 1993. pap. 1.95 (*0-307-10555-5*, Golden Pr) Western Pub.

NATIONAL PARKS AND RESERVES–U. S.

Beach-Balthis, Judy. Ano Nuevo: A Children's Guide. Balthis, Frank S., ed. Beach-Balthis, Judy, illus. 24p. (Orig.). (gr. k-8). 1985. pap. 2.95 (*0-918355-02-8*) Firehole Pr.
—Point Reyes: A Children's Guide. Balthis, Frank S., ed. Beach-Balthis, Judy, illus. 24p. (Orig.). (gr. k-8). 1983. pap. 2.95 (*0-685-53258-5*) Firehole Pr.
Diamond, Lynell. Let's Discover Bryce & Zion National Parks. (Illus.). 32p. (gr. 1-6). 1990. pap. 4.95 (*0-89886-253-1*) Mountaineers.
Gilmore, Jackie. Welcome to Grand Teton: An Explosion of Life & Color. NPS Staff, ed. Wordmill Staff, tr. Stark, Jack, intro. by. 24p. 1991. German. pap. 4.95 (*0-931895-15-4*) Spanish. pap. 4.95 (*0-931895-18-9*) Japanese (*0-931895-16-2*) French. pap. 4.95 (*0-931895-17-0*) Grand Teton NHA.
—Welcome to Grand Teton National Park: An Explosion of Life & Color. NPS Staff, ed. (Illus.). 24p. 1991. pap. 4.95 (*0-931895-19-7*) Grand Teton NHA.
Lovett, Sarah. Kidding Around the National Parks of the Southwest: A Young Person's Guide. Strock, Glen, illus. 108p. (Orig.). (gr. 3 up). 1990. pap. 12.95 (*0-945465-72-6*) John Muir.
Mead, Robin, et al. Our National Parks. LC 92-9460. (Illus.). 64p. (gr. 2-6). 1993. 7.98 (*0-8317-2314-9*) Smithmark.
Petersen, David. Canyonlands National Park. LC 91-35274. (Illus.). 48p. (gr. k-4). 1992. PLB 12.85 (*0-516-01132-4*); pap. 4.95 (*0-516-41132-2*) Childrens.
—Carlsbad Caverns National Park. LC 93-36997. (Illus.). 48p. (gr. k-4). 1994. PLB 12.85 (*0-516-01051-4*) Childrens.
—Great Smoky Mountains National Park. LC 92-35049. (Illus.). 48p. (gr. k-4). 1993. PLB 12.85 (*0-516-01332-7*); pap. 4.95 (*0-516-41332-5*) Childrens.
—Mesa Verde National Park. LC 91-35275. (Illus.). 48p. (gr. k-4). 1992. PLB 12.85 (*0-516-01136-7*); pap. 4.95 (*0-516-41136-5*) Childrens.
—Rocky Mountain National Park. LC 93-798. (Illus.). 48p. (gr. k-4). 1993. PLB 12.85 (*0-516-01196-0*); pap. 4.95 (*0-516-41196-9*) Childrens.
—Zion National Park. LC 92-35048. (Illus.). 48p. (gr. k-4). 1993. PLB 12.85 (*0-516-01336-X*); pap. 4.95 (*0-516-41336-8*) Childrens.
Radlauer, Ruth. Bryce Canyon National Park. updated ed. Radlauer, Ed & Radlauer, Ruth, illus. LC 79-22722. 48p. (gr. 3 up). 1987. (Elk Grove Bks.); pap. 4.95 (*0-516-47484-7*) Childrens.
—Haleakala National Park. updated ed. Zillmer, Rolf, illus. LC 79-10500. 48p. (gr. 3 up). 1987. pap. 4.95 (*0-516-47499-5*) Childrens.
—Mammoth Cave National Park. updated ed. Radlauer, Ed, illus. LC 77-26764. 48p. (gr. 3 up). 1987. (Elk Grove Bks); pap. 4.95 (*0-516-47496-0*) Childrens.
—Mesa Verde National Park. updated ed. Zillmer, Rolf, photos by. LC 76-27350. (Illus.). 48p. (gr. 3 up). 1984. pap. 4.95 (*0-516-47490-1*) Childrens.
Root, Phyllis & McCormick, Maxine. Great Basin. LC 88-18645. (Illus.). 48p. (gr. 4-5). 1988. text ed. 13.95 RSBE (*0-89686-410-3*, Crestwood Hse) Macmillan Child Grp.
Salts, Bobbi. Discover Grand Teton National Park. NPS Staff, ed. Parker, Steve, illus. 32p. 1992. pap. 3.95 (*0-931895-22-7*) Grand Teton NHA.
Wade, L. Badlands: Beauty Carved from Nature. 1991. 11.95s.p. (*0-86592-471-6*) Rourke Enter.

NATIONAL PLANNING

see names of countries with the subdivision Economic Policy; Social Policy; e.g. U. S.–Economic Policy; U. S. –Social Policy

NATIONAL RESOURCES

see Natural Resources;
see names of countries with the subdivision Economic Conditions, e.g. U.S.–Economic Conditions

NATIONAL SOCIALISM

Bornstein, Jerry. The Neo-Nazis. LC 85-5363. (Illus.). 192p. (gr. 7 up). 1986. lib. bdg. 11.98 (*0-671-50238-7*, J Messner) S&S Trade.
Chrisp, Peter. The Rise of Fascism. LC 90-46774. (Illus.). 64p. (gr. 9-12). 1991. 13.40 (*0-531-18438-2*, Pub. by Bookwright Pr) Watts.
Heyes, Eileen. Adolf Hitler. LC 93-31269. (gr. 7 up). 1994. PLB 16.90 (*1-56294-343-X*) Millbrook Pr.
Life in the Third Reich. (gr. 7-12). 1992. 19.95 (*0-7134-6542-5*, Pub. by Batsford UK) Trafalgar.
Marrin, Albert. Hitler. LC 93-13057. 256p. (gr. 7 up). 1993. pap. 5.99 (*0-14-036526-5*, Puffin) Puffin Bks.
Racism in the Third Reich. (gr. 7-12). 1992. 19.95 (*0-7134-6600-6*, Pub. by Batsford UK) Trafalgar.
Stewart, Gail B. Hitler's Reich. LC 93-17098. (gr. 6-9). 1994. 14.95 (*1-56006-235-5*) Lucent Bks.

NATIONAL SOCIALISM–FICTION

Kerr, M. E. Gentlehands. LC 77-11860. (gr. 7-9). 1978. PLB 16.89 (*0-06-023177-7*) HarpC Child Bks.
Wuorio, Eva-Lis. Detour to Danger: A Novel. LC 81-65501. 192p. (gr. 7 up). 1981. 12.95 (*0-385-28206-0*) Delacorte.

NATIONAL SONGS

see also Folk Songs

Guthrie, Kari H. National Anthems, Bk. 1. Nichols, Brooke & Guthrie, Kari H., illus. Guthrie, Kari H., intro. by. 36p. (Orig.). (gr. 2-8). 1992. pap. 6.95 (*0-9631333-0-6*) Hi I Que Pub.

—National Anthems: Western & Middle Europe, 4 bks. (Illus.). 163p. (Orig.). (gr. 4-9). 1993. Set. pap. 24.95 (*0-9631333-4-9*) Hi I Que Pub. NATIONAL ANTHEMS--WESTERN & MIDDLE EUROPE is an integrated learning book series. Each anthem includes a map of the individual country & surrounding countries, form of government, language spoken, capital, currency, & national holidays. The cover displays the flags of the included countries in vibrant color. Also included are the words in the original language & English translations. Music is in piano score, arranged for easy to intermediate abilities. This book is suitable for all ages, but is specifically formatted to appeal to grades 4-9. These books provide a wonderful aspect of cultural, historical & heritage information. Ideal reference for schools, teachers, & libraries; also as gifts to young students of history or music. Since these anthems are not easily accessible it is important to note that college age students studying culture, history, music or language may be interested in this series. NATIONAL ANTHEMS (WESTERN & MIDDLE EUROPE) is a series of 4 books. Book 1 (0-9631333-0-6) includes France, Iceland, Ireland, Portugal, Spain. Book 2 (0-9631333-1-4), Andorra, Belgium, Denmark, Germany, Lichtenstein, Luxembourg, Monaco, Netherlands, Norway, Switzerland. Book 3 (0-9631333-2-2), Albania, Austria, Czechoslovakia (1918-1993), Hungary, Italy, Malta, San Marino, Sweden. Book 4 (0-9631333-0-0), Bulgaria, Finland, Greece, Poland, Romania, the former U.S.S.R., Yugoslavia. Each book also available separately at $6.95 each. Order directly from: Hi. I. Que Publishing, P.O. Box 508, Claremont, CA 91711-0508. (909) 622-7501, or your local distributor.
Publisher Provided Annotation.

Hefley, Lynn C. Purple Mountain Majesty. Brummett, Nancy P., ed. Harness, Cheryl, illus. LC 93-84708. 24p. (Orig.). (gr. 3-6). 1993. pap. text ed. write for info. (*0-944943-42-X*) Current Inc.
St. Pierre, Stephanie. Our National Anthem. LC 91-38891. (Illus.). 48p. (gr. 2-4). 1992. PLB 13.40 (*1-56294-106-2*); pap. 5.95 (*1-878841-89-0*) Millbrook Pr.
Spier, Peter. The Star-Spangled Banner. Spier, Peter, illus. LC 73-79112. 48p. (gr. 1 up). 1973. pap. 11.95 (*0-385-07746-7*) Doubleday.
Young, Woody. Song Wise, Three: Battle Hymn of the Republic. White, Craig, illus. 24p. (Orig.). 1986. pap. text ed. 2.95 (*0-939513-13-7*) Joy Pub SJC.
—Song Wise, Vol. Four: America. White, Craig, illus. 24p. (Orig.). 1986. pap. text ed. 2.95 (*0-939513-14-5*) Joy Pub SJC.
—Song Wise, Vol. One: The Star Spangled Banner. White, Craig, illus. 24p. (Orig.). 1986. pap. text ed. 2.95 (*0-939513-11-0*) Joy Pub SJC.
—Song Wise, Vol. Two: America the Beautiful. White, Craig, illus. 24p. (Orig.). 1986. pap. text ed. 2.95 (*0-939513-12-9*) Joy Pub SJC.

NATIONALITY (CITIZENSHIP)

see Citizenship

NATIVITY OF CHRIST

see Jesus Christ–Nativity

NATURAL DISASTERS

see Disasters

NATURAL HISTORY

Here are entered popular works describing animals, plants, minerals and nature in general. Handbooks on the detailed study of birds, flowers, etc. are entered under Nature Study.
see also Aquariums; Biology; Botany; Fossils; Fresh-Water Biology; Geographical Distribution of Animals and Plants; Geology; Marine Biology; Mineralogy; Zoology

Allen, Eugenie. The Best Ever Kids' Book of Lists. 128p. (Orig.). 1991. pap. 2.95 (*0-380-76357-5*, Camelot) Avon.
Allison, Linda. The Sierra Club Summer Book. Allison, Linda, illus. LC 93-41481. 1994. 7.99 (*0-517-10082-7*, Pub. by Wings Bks) Random Hse Value.
Arnosky, Jim. Secrets of a Wildlife Watcher. LC 82-24920. (Illus.). 64p. (gr. 5 up). 1983. 15.00 (*0-688-02079-8*); lib. bdg. 14.93 (*0-688-02081-X*) Lothrop.
Barr, George. Outdoor Science Projects for Young People. (Illus.). 160p. pap. 3.95 (*0-486-26855-1*) Dover.
Benson, Laura. This Is Our Earth. (Illus.). 32p. (ps-4). 1994. 14.95 (*0-88106-445-9*); PLB 15.88 (*0-88106-446-7*) Charlesbridge Pub.
Blashfield, Jean F. Galapagos Islands. LC 94-3030. (Illus.). 64p. (gr. 5-8). 1994. PLB write for info. (*0-8114-6362-1*) Raintree Steck-V.
Brownstone, David M. & Franck, Irene M. Natural Wonders of America. LC 88-32707. (Illus.). 64p. (gr. 3-7). 1989. pap. 7.95 (*0-689-71229-4*, Aladdin) Macmillan Child Grp.
Burnie, David A. How Nature Works: One Hundred Ways Parents & Kids Can Share the Secrets of Nature. LC 91-12432. (Illus.). 192p. (gr. 3 up). 1991. 24.00 (*0-89577-391-0*, Dist. by Random) RD Assn.
Burton, Virginia L. Life Story. (Illus.). (gr. k-3). 1989. 15.45 (*0-395-16030-8*); pap. 6.70 (*0-395-52017-7*) HM.
De Larramendi Ruis, Alberto. Tropical Rain Forests of Central America. LC 92-35062. (Illus.). 36p. (gr. 3 up). 1993. PLB 14.95 (*0-516-08383-X*); pap. 6.75 (*0-516-48383-8*) Childrens.
Dixon, Douglas. Be a Fossil Detective. 40p. (gr. 2 up). 1989. 3.99 (*0-517-68022-X*) Random Hse Value.
Field, Nancy, et al. Nature Discovery Library. Machlis, Sally & Torvik, Sharon, illus. (gr. 3-6). 1990. Set. pap. text ed. 42.50 (*0-941042-15-4*) Dog Eared Pubns.
Ganeri, Anita & Butterfield, Maira. Natural World. Bull, Peter & Johnson, Paul, illus. LC 89-11349. 48p. (gr. 4-5). 1989. PLB 17.27 (*0-8368-0133-4*) Gareth Stevens Inc.
Graham-Barber, Lynda. Toad or Frog, Swamp or Bog? A Big Book of Nature's Confusables. Gillman, Alec, illus. LC 92-35398. 48p. (gr. k-5). 1994. SBE 15.95 (*0-02-736931-5*, Four Winds) Macmillan Child Grp.
Higgins, Deck, photos by. A Walk Through Walden Woods. Henley, Don, afterword by. LC 94-1802. 1994. 14.95 (*0-590-48505-9*) Scholastic Inc.
Hirschi, Ron. Fall. Mangelsen, Thomas D., photos by. LC 90-19595. (Illus.). 32p. (ps-3). 1991. 14.00 (*0-525-65053-9*, Cobblehill Bks) Dutton Child Bks.
Hoban, Tana. Animal, Vegetable, or Mineral? LC 94-20904. (Illus.). 1995. write for info. (*0-688-12746-0*); PLB write for info. (*0-688-12747-9*) Greenwillow.
McGovern, Ann. Swimming with Sea Lions. 48p. 1992. 13.95 (*0-590-45282-7*, Scholastic Hardcover) Scholastic Inc.
McMillan, Bruce. Summer Ice, Antarctic Life. McMillan, Bruce, illus. LC 93-38831. 1994. write for info. (*0-395-66561-2*) HM.
Magley, Beverly. The Fire Mountains: The Story of the Cascade Volcanos. Dowden, D. D., illus. LC 88-83884. 32p. (Orig.). (gr. 3-6). 1989. pap. 5.95 (*0-937959-57-X*) Falcon Pr MT.

Martin, Bill, Jr. Little Nature Books. Incl. Poppies Afield; Frogs in a Pond; Butterflies Becoming; Germination; Ants Underground; A Mushroom Is Growing; A Hydra Goes Walking; Moon Cycle; Messenger Bee; June Bugs. (Illus.). (gr. 1-6). 1975. 149.00 (*0-87827-196-1*); tchr's. guide incl. (*0-685-55948-3*); cassettes incl. Ency Brit Ed.

Middleton, Nick. Atlas of the Natural World. (Illus.). 64p. 1990. 16.95x (*0-8160-2131-7*) Facts on File.

National Geographical Society Staff, ed. Books for Young Explorers, 4 vols, Set 1. Incl. Dinosaurs. LC 72-91418; Treasures in the Sea. LC 72-91421; Dogs Working for People. LC 72-91419; Lion Cubs. LC 72-91420. (ps-3). 1972. PLB 16.95 avail. only from Natl Geog (*0-87044-300-3*) Natl Geog.

Natural History Activity Book. (Illus.). (ps-6). pap. 2.95 (*0-565-00857-9*, Pub. by Natural Hist Mus) Parkwest Pubns.

Nature. 112p. (gr. 4-9). 1989. 18.95 (*1-85435-074-9*) Marshall Cavendish.

Pandell, Karen. Land of Dark, Land of Light: The Arctic National Wildlife Refuge. Bruemmer, Fred, photos by. LC 92-40405. (Illus.). 32p. (ps-3). 1993. 14.99 (*0-525-45094-7*, DCB) Dutton Child Bks.

Parker, Steve. Eyewitness Guide to the Natural World. (Illus.). 192p. (gr. 7 up). 1994. 29.95 (*1-56458-719-3*) Dorling Kindersley.

Pearce, Q. L. Tell Me About Nature Dictionary. 1990. 5.99 (*0-517-03567-7*) Random Hse Value.

Richards, John. Hidden Country: Nature on Your Doorstep. LC 72-12745. (Illus.). 144p. (gr. 5-8). 1973. PLB 21.95 (*0-87599-195-5*) S G Phillips.

Ross, Michael E. Cycles, Cycles, Cycles. (Illus.). 88p. (gr. 1-3). 1979. pap. 3.95 (*0-939666-01-4*) Yosemite Assn.

Stidworthy, John. Naturalist. LC 91-2660. (Illus.). 32p. (gr. 5-8). 1991. PLB 12.40 (*0-531-17356-9*, Gloucester Pr) Watts.

Stine, Megan, et al. Hands-On Science: Things That Grow. Taback, Simms, illus. LC 92-56894. 1993. PLB 18.60 (*0-8368-0959-9*) Gareth Stevens Inc.

Stone, Lynn M. Wildlife of Alaska. LC 93-42649. 1994. write for info. (*1-55916-026-8*) Rourke Bk Co.

Time-Life Books Editors. The Secret Forest: A Lift-the-Flap Nature Book. Kagan, Neil, ed. (Illus.). 20p. (gr. 3-7). 1991. write for info. (*0-8094-9275-X*); PLB write for info. (*0-8094-9276-8*) Time-Life.

Time Life Inc. Editors. Why Is the Grass Green? First Questions & Answers about Nature. Kagan, Neil, ed. (Illus.). 48p. (ps). 1993. write for info. (*0-7835-0858-1*); lib. bdg. write for info. (*0-7835-0859-X*) Time-Life.

Wyler, Rose. Wonderful Woods. Petruccio, Steven, illus. 32p. (gr. k-3). 1990. (J Messner); pap. 4.95 (*0-671-69166-X*) S&S Trade.

NATURAL HISTORY–AFRICA

Brandenburg, Jim. Sand & Fog: Adventures in Southern Africa. Guernsey, JoAnn B., ed. LC 93-30425. (Illus.). 48p. 1994. 16.95 (*0-8027-8232-9*); PLB 17.85 (*0-8027-8233-7*) Walker & Co.

NATURAL HISTORY–AUSTRALIA

Crump, Donald J., ed. Wonderful Animals of Australia, Bk. 1. (Illus.). (ps-3). 1990. Set. 21.95 (*0-87044-809-9*) Natl Geog.

De Larramendi Ruis, Alberto. Australia: Land of Natural Wonders. LC 94-17017. (Illus.). 36p. (gr. 3 up). 1994. PLB 20.00 (*0-516-08390-2*); pap. 6.95 (*0-516-48390-0*) Childrens.

NATURAL HISTORY, BIBLICAL

see Bible–Natural History

NATURAL HISTORY–FICTION

Carlstrom, Nancy W. Wild Wild Sunflower Child Anna. Pinkney, Jerry, illus. LC 90-40679. 32p. (ps-1). 1991. pap. 4.95 (*0-689-71445-9*, Aladdin) Macmillan Child Grp.

Kelly, Karla, et al. Tales of Terratopia: The Secret of the Dragonfly & the Daring Dino Rescue. (Illus.). 36p. (gr. 1-6). 1993. 6.95 (*1-883871-00-X*) Nature Co.

Myers, Christopher A. & Myers, Lynne B. McCrephy's Field. Chartier, Normand, illus. 32p. (gr. 2-5). 1991. 14.45 (*0-395-53807-6*, Sandpiper) HM.

Say, Allen. The Lost Lake. Say, Allen, illus. 32p. (gr. k-3). 1992. pap. 4.80 (*0-395-63036-3*, Sandpiper) HM.

Taylor, C. J. Little Water & the Gift of the Animals. Taylor, C. J., illus. LC 92-8413. 24p. (gr. 1-5). 1992. PLB 13.95 (*0-88776-285-9*) Tundra Bks.

Ziefert, Harriet. On Our Way to the Water! Taback, Simms, illus. 16p. (ps-1). 1993. pap. 4.95 (*0-694-00459-6*, Festival) HarpC Child Bks.

NATURAL HISTORY–NORTH AMERICA

Burns, Diane. Rocky Mountain Seasons: From Valley to Mountaintop. Dannen, Kent & Dannen, Donna, photos by. LC 92-22833. (Illus.). 32p. (gr. 1-5). 1993. RSBE 14.95 (*0-02-716142-0*, Macmillan Child Bk) Macmillan Child Grp.

Hamerstrom, Frances. Walk When the Moon Is Full. Katona, Robert, illus. LC 75-33878. 64p. (gr. 3-8). 1975. 15.95 (*0-912278-69-2*); pap. 6.95 (*0-912278-84-6*) Crossing Pr.

NATURAL HISTORY–OUTDOOR BOOKS

see Nature Study

NATURAL HISTORY–SOUTH AMERICA

Litteral, Linda L. Boobies, Iguanas, & Other Critters: Nature's Story in the Galapagos. (Illus.). 72p. (gr. 5-9). 1994. 23.00 (*1-883966-01-9*) Am Kestrel Pr.

NATURAL HISTORY–SOUTHWEST, NEW

Baylor, Byrd. I'm in Charge of Celebrations. Parnall, Peter, illus. LC 85-19633. 32p. (gr. 1-4). 1986. SBE 14.95 (*0-684-18579-2*, Scribners Young Read) Macmillan Child Grp.

NATURAL HISTORY–U. S.

Cohen, Richard, et al. Snail Trails & Tadpole Tails: Nature Education for Young Children. Seaberg, Kurt, illus. Peterson, Roger T., intro. by. LC 93-5850. (Illus.). 96p. (Orig.). (ps-1). 1993. pap. text ed. 12.95 (*0-934140-78-2*) Redleaf Pr.

Freeman, Marie E. & Davis, Maria H. Alpine to Alkali. Delany, Dan & Walker, Jan, illus. LC 83-80807. 150p. (Orig.). (gr. 7-12). 1983. pap. text ed. 7.95 (*0-913205-01-X*) Grace Dangberg.

George, Jean C. The Everglades. Minor, Wendell, illus. LC 92-9517. Date not set. 15.00 (*0-06-021228-4*); PLB 14.89 (*0-06-021229-2*) HarpC Child Bks.

Michio Hoshino. The Grizzly Bear Family Book. Colligan-Taylor, Karen, tr. from JPN. (Illus.). 52p. (gr. 2 up). 1993. 15.95 (*0-88708-309-9*) Picture Bk Studio.

Perenyi, Constance. Wild Wild West: Wildlife Habitats of Western North America. Pevenyi, Constance, illus. LC 92-46995. 32p. (gr. 1 up). 1993. text ed. 14.95 (*0-912365-82-X*); pap. 8.95 (*0-912365-90-0*) Sasquatch Bks.

Petersen, David. Great Smoky Mountains National Park. LC 92-35049. (Illus.). 48p. (gr. k-4). 1993. PLB 12.85 (*0-516-01332-7*); pap. 4.95 (*0-516-41332-5*) Childrens.

—Yosemite National Park. LC 92-39156. (Illus.). 48p. (gr. k-4). 1993. PLB 12.85 (*0-516-01335-1*); pap. 4.95 (*0-516-41335-X*) Childrens.

—Zion National Park. LC 92-35048. (Illus.). 48p. (gr. k-4). 1993. PLB 12.85 (*0-516-01336-X*); pap. 4.95 (*0-516-41336-8*) Childrens.

Roth, Charles E. The Amateur Naturalist: Explorations & Investigations. LC 93-13390. (Illus.). 144p. (gr. 6-9). 1993. PLB 12.90 (*0-531-11002-8*) Watts.

NATURAL HISTORY MUSEUMS

Gibbons, Gail. Dinosaurs, Dragonflies & Diamonds: All About Natural History Museums. Gibbons, Gail, illus. LC 88-38831. 32p. (gr. k-3). 1988. RSBE 13.95 (*0-02-737240-5*, Four Winds) Macmillan Child Grp.

Ziegler, Sandra. A Visit to the Natural History Museum. LC 88-23268. 32p. (ps-3). 1988. PLB 11.45 (*0-516-01489-7*); pap. 3.95 (*0-516-41489-5*) Childrens.

NATURAL LAW

see Civil Rights; Ethics; Liberty

NATURAL MONUMENTS

King, Celia. The Seven Natural Wonders of the World: A Pop-up Book. King, Celia, illus. 7p. (ps up). 1991. 8.95 (*0-8118-0001-6*) Chronicle Bks.

NATURAL RESOURCES

see also Conservation of Natural Resources; Fisheries; Forests and Forestry; Marine Resources; Mines and Mineral Resources; Power Resources; Soil Conservation; Water Power; Water Supply

Bittinger, Gayle. Our World. McKinnon, Elizabeth, ed. Jones, Kathy, illus. LC 89-52145. 80p. (Orig.). (ps-1). 1990. pap. 8.95 (*0-911019-30-8*) Warren Pub Hse.

Blashfield, Jean F. & Black, Wallace B. Too Many People? LC 91-34603. 128p. (gr. 4-8). 1992. PLB 20.55 (*0-516-05513-5*) Childrens.

Earth Resources Series, 3 bks. (Illus.). (gr. 6 up). Set. lib. bdg. 48.85 (*0-89490-349-7*) Enslow Pubs.

Friend, Mari. Discovering Nature's Secrets: An All-Year-Round Activity Book. (Illus.). 80p. (gr. 3-7). 1992. 15.95 (*0-87663-638-5*) Universe.

Green, I. Conservation from A to Z. LC 66-11443. (Illus.). 64p. (gr. 4 up). 1968. PLB 10.95 (*0-87783-009-6*); pap. 3.94 deluxe ed. (*0-87783-088-6*) Oddo.

It's a Big Big World. (gr. 1-6). 1992. English ed., incl. audio cass. & crayons. 16.98 (*2-89429-007-1*); Spanish ed., incl. audio cass. & crayons. 16.98 (*2-89429-009-8*) Rincon Rodanthe.

Jackman, Wayne. Gas. LC 93-7256. 32p. (gr. 3-6). 1993. 13.95 (*1-56847-049-5*) Thomson Lrning.

Kalman, Bobbie. Natural Resources. (Illus.). 32p. (gr. 2-3). 1987. 15.95 (*0-86505-077-5*); pap. 7.95 (*0-86505-099-6*) Crabtree Pub Co.

Krull, Kathleen. It's My Earth Too: How I Can Help the Earth Stay Alive. Greenberg, Melanie H., illus. (ps-2). 1992. 13.50 (*0-385-42088-9*) Doubleday.

Peckham, Alexander. Changing Landscapes. LC 90-45656. (Illus.). 40p. (gr. 6-9). 1991. PLB 12.90 (*0-531-17289-9*, Gloucester Pr) Watts.

—Resources Control. LC 90-3202. (Illus.). 40p. (gr. 5-8). 1990. PLB 12.90 (*0-531-17234-1*, Gloucester Pr) Watts.

Randle, Damian. Natural Resources. LC 93-25195. (Illus.). 32p. (gr. 4-6). 1993. 14.95 (*1-56847-056-8*) Thomson Lrning.

Wood, John N. Nature Hide & Seek: Jungles. Schulman, Janet, ed. Dean, Kevin, illus. LC 86-21450. 24p. (ps-4). 1987. 11.95 (*0-394-87802-7*) Knopf Bks Yng Read.

NATURAL RESOURCES–U. S.

see also U. S.–Economic Conditions

NATURAL SELECTION

see also Evolution

NATURALISTS

Anker, Debby & De Graff, John. David Brower: Friend of the Earth. (Illus.). 80p. (gr. 4-7). 1993. PLB 14.95 (*0-8050-2124-8*, TFC Bks NY) H Holt & Co.

Bryant, Jennifer. Margaret Murie: A Wilderness Life. Castro, Antonio, illus. 80p. (gr. 4-7). 1993. PLB 14.95 (*0-8050-2220-1*) TFC Bks NY.

Caras, Roger. A World Full of Animals: The Roger Caras Story. LC 93-31009. 1994. 12.95 (*0-8118-0654-5*); pap. 6.95 (*0-8118-0682-0*) Chronicle Bks.

Dunlap, Julie. Aldo Leopold: Living with the Land. (Illus.). 80p. (gr. 4-7). 1993. PLB 14.95 (*0-8050-2501-4*) TFC Bks NY.

Fleischman, Paul. Townsend's Warbler. LC 91-26836. (Illus.). 64p. (gr. 3-7). 1992. PLB 12.89 (*0-06-021875-4*) HarpC Child Bks.

Greene, Carol. John Muir: Man of the Wild Places. Dobson, Steven, illus. LC 90-19993. 48p. (gr. k-3). 1991. PLB 12.85 (*0-516-04220-3*); pap. 4.95 (*0-516-44220-1*) Childrens.

Keene, Ann T. Earthkeepers: Observers & Protectors of Nature. (Illus.). 224p. 1994. 30.00 (*0-19-507867-5*) OUP.

Lorbiecki, Marybeth. Of Things Natural, Wild, & Free: A Story about Aldo Leopold. Maguire, Kerry, illus. LC 92-44049. 1993. 14.95 (*0-87614-797-X*) Carolrhoda Bks.

Lucas, Eileen. Jane Goodall: Friend of the Chimps. (gr. 4-7). 1992. pap. 4.95 (*0-395-63570-5*) HM.

Mitchell, A. The Young Naturalist. (Illus.). 32p. (gr. 5-10). 1984. PLB 13.96 (*0-88110-235-0*); pap. 6.95 (*0-86020-653-X*) EDC.

Roth, Charles. The Amateur Naturalist: Explorations & Investigations. (Illus.). (gr. 5-8). 1994. pap. 6.95 (*0-531-15697-4*) Watts.

Tolan, Sally. John Muir: Naturalist, Writer & Guardian of the North American Wilderness. LC 89-4367. (Illus.). 64p. (gr. 5-6). 1989. PLB 19.93 (*0-8368-0099-0*) Gareth Stevens Inc.

Warren, Betsy. Wilderness Walkers: Naturalists in Early Texas. La Freniere, Annette, ed. Warren, Betsy, illus. LC 55-7501. 112p. (gr. 4-8). 1987. PLB 12.95 (*0-937460-26-5*) Hendrick-Long.

Westrup, Hugh. Maurice Strong: Working for Planet Earth. LC 93-41528. (Illus.). 48p. (gr. 2-4). 1994. PLB 12.90 (*1-56294-414-2*) Millbrook Pr.

NATURE

Bailey, Jill & Felts, Shirley. Naturescapes. LC 88-50187. (ps up). 1988. pap. 15.95 (*0-670-82038-5*) Viking Child Bks.

Benedict, Kitty. My First Nature Book Series, 12 bks. Delessert, Etienne, illus. 32p. (Orig.). (gr. 1-4). 1993. Set. pap. 35.40 (*1-56189-149-5*) Amer Educ Pub.

Booth, Eugene. In the Air. LC 77-7984. (Illus.). 24p. (gr. k-3). 1977. PLB 13.32 (*0-8393-0105-7*) Raintree Steck-V.

British Museum, Geological Department Staff. Nature at Work: Introducing Ecology. LC 78-66795. (Illus.). (gr. 7 up). 1978. pap. 12.95 (*0-521-29469-X*) Cambridge U Pr.

Bryant-Mole, K. Dot to Dot Nature. (Illus.). 24p. (ps-4). 1993. pap. 3.50 (*0-7460-1375-2*, Usborne) EDC.

Childrens First Nature Encyclopedia. 1991. pap. 19.95 (*0-671-08189-6*) S&S Trade.

Cochrane, Jennifer. Nature. LC 92-53091. (Illus.). 48p. (Orig.). (gr. 3-8). 1992. pap. 5.95 (*1-85697-813-3*, Kingfisher LKC) LKC.

Cork, Barbara & Morris, R. Mysteries & Marvels of Nature. Jackson, Ian & Quinn, David, illus. 192p. (gr. 3-6). 1983. 21.95 (*0-7460-0421-4*) EDC.

Cox & Cork. Flowers. (gr. 2-5). 1980. (Usborne-Hayes); PLB 11.96 (*0-88110-074-9*); pap. 3.95 (*0-86020-479-0*) EDC.

Doris, Ellen. Woods, Ponds, & Fields. Rubenstein, Len, photos by. LC 93-61889. (Illus.). 63p. 1994. 15.95 (*0-500-19006-2*) Thames Hudson.

Duncan. Nature Search. 1995. 15.00 (*0-06-023596-9*); PLB 14.89 (*0-06-023597-7*) HarpC Child Bks.

Emert, Phyllis R. Mysteries of Bizarre Animals & Freaks of Nature. 128p. (Orig.). 1994. pap. 2.99 (*0-8125-3630-4*) Tor Bks.

Explore the World of Forces of Nature. (gr. 3-6). 1991. write for info. (*0-307-15602-8*, Golden Pr) Western Pub.

Faber, Doris & Faber, Harold. Great Lives: Nature & the Environment. LC 90-8847. (Illus.). 304p. (gr. 4-6). 1991. SBE 22.95 (*0-684-19047-8*, Scribners Young Read) Macmillan Child Grp.

Feldman, Judy. The Alphabet in Nature. LC 90-22315. (Illus.). 32p. (ps-2). 1991. PLB 13.35 (*0-516-05101-6*) Childrens.

—Shapes in Nature. LC 90-23091. (Illus.). 32p. (ps-2). 1991. PLB 13.35 (*0-516-05102-4*) Childrens.

Field, Nancy & Machlas, Sally. Discovering Endangered Species. (Illus.). 40p. (Orig.). (gr. 3-6). 1990. pap. 4.95 (*0-941042-09-X*) Dog Eared Pubns.

Field, Nancy, et al. Nature Discovery Library. Machlis, Sally & Torvik, Sharon, illus. (gr. 3-6). 1990. Set. pap. text ed. 42.50 (*0-941042-15-4*) Dog Eared Pubns.

Hamerstrom, Frances. Walk When the Moon Is Full. Katona, Robert, illus. LC 75-33878. 64p. (gr. 3-8). 1975. 15.95 (*0-912278-69-2*); pap. 6.95 (*0-912278-84-6*) Crossing Pr.

Hayes, Dympna & Lehman, Melanie. Fun with Nature. Kelly, Teri, ed. Davis, Annelies, illus. 32p. (gr. 2). 1987. PLB 14.97 (*0-88625-154-0*); pap. 2.95 (*0-685-30766-2*) Durkin Hayes Pub.

Heller, Ruth. The Reason for a Flower. Heller, Ruth, illus. 48p. (ps-3). 1992. pap. 5.95 (*0-448-41091-5*, Sandcastle Bks) Putnam Pub Group.

Henry, Lucia K. Nature Study. (Illus.). 48p. (gr. k-2). 1987. wkbk. 6.95 (*1-55734-219-9*) Tchr Create Mat.

Hiller, Ilo. Young Naturalist: From Texas Parks & Wildlife Magazine. LC 83-45107. (Illus.). 176p. (gr. 2-8). 1983. 15.95 (*0-89096-163-8*) Tex A&M Univ Pr.

Howard, Jean G. Bound by the Sea: A Summer Diary. LC 86-50255. (Illus.). 96p. (gr. 6-12). 1986. text ed. 15.00 (*0-930954-25-4*); pap. 10.00 (*0-930954-26-2*) Tidal Pr.

Hoy, Ken. Land Life. (Illus.). 12p. (gr. k-4). 1990. 11.95 (*0-8249-8472-2*, Ideals Child) Hambleton-Hill.

Jones, Michael P., ed. Oregon River Watch: A Contemporary History of Oregon's Waterways, Vol. 1. Bachmann, Mark, et al, illus. 48p. (Orig.). 1985. text ed. 9.95 (*0-89904-143-4*); pap. text ed. 5.00 (*0-89904-144-2*); composition 8.00 (*0-89904-145-0*) Crumb Elbow Pub.

—Oregon River Watch: A Contemporary History of Oregon's Waterways, Vol. 2. Bachmann, Mark, et al, illus. 50p. (Orig.). 1985. text ed. 9.95 (*0-89904-146-9*); pap. text ed. 5.00 (*0-89904-147-7*); composition 8.00 (*0-89904-148-5*) Crumb Elbow Pub.

Jones, Teri C. Little Book of Questions & Answers: Nature. Marsh, T. F., illus. 32p. (gr. k-3). 1992. PLB 10.95 (*1-56674-014-2*, HTS Bks) Forest Hse.

Kalman, Bobbie & Schaub, Janine. I Am a Part of Nature. (Illus.). 32p. (gr. k-8). 1992. PLB 15.95 (*0-86505-552-1*); pap. 7.95 (*0-86505-578-5*) Crabtree Pub Co.

Kelley, Colleen. Kids' Stuff: Simple Science & Nature Projects for Children. Kelley, Colleen, illus. 96p. (gr. k-6). 1989. pap. text ed. 4.95 (*0-9618052-2-6*) Daily Hampshire.

Kidman-Cox, R., et al. First Book of Nature. (Illus.). 168p. (gr. k-6). 1993. pap. 14.95 (*0-7460-0563-6*, Usborne) EDC.

Kilpatrick. Creepy Crawlies. (gr. 2-5). 1982. (Usborne-Hayes); PLB 11.96 (*0-88110-076-5*); pap. 3.95 (*0-86020-630-0*) EDC.

Kirkman, Will. Nature Crafts Workshop. LC 80-84186. (gr. 3-8). 1981. pap. 10.95 (*0-8224-9781-6*) Fearon Teach Aids.

Lampton, Christopher. Science of Chaos: Complexity in the Natural World. LC 91-40896. (Illus.). 128p. (gr. 7-12). 1992. PLB 13.40 (*0-531-12513-0*) Watts.

Langley, Andrew. Wetlands. LC 92-6255. (Illus.). 32p. (gr. 4-7). 1993. 14.00 (*0-89577-482-8*, Dist. by Random) RD Assn.

Lhommedieu, Arthur J. Metamorphoses: Egg, Tadpole, Frog. (ps-3). 1993. 5.95 (*0-85953-169-4*) Childs Play.

Little People Big Book about Nature. 64p. (ps-1). 1990. write for info. (*0-8094-7512-X*); PLB write for info. (*0-8094-7513-8*) Time-Life.

Lohf, Sabine. Things I Can Make with Leaves. (Illus.). 32p. (ps-2). 1990. 6.95 (*0-87701-763-8*) Chronicle Bks.

Lynn, Sara & James, Diane. Rain & Shine. Wright, Joe, illus. LC 93-36420. 32p. (gr. k-2). 1994. 14.95 (*1-56847-142-4*) Thomson Lrning.

Morris, Neil. Where Do Ants Live? Questions Kids Ask about Backyard Nature. Lewis, Jan, illus. LC 94-14122. 1994. write for info. (*0-89577-607-3*, Readers Digest Kids) RD Assn.

Nature Close-Ups. (Illus.). (gr. 3-7). 1986. Set of 40 titles, 32 pp. ea. PLB write for info. (*0-8172-2724-5*); Set of 40 titles, 32 pp. ea. pap. 370.80 (*0-8172-2725-3*) Raintree Steck-V.

Neill, Robert H. Beware the Barking Bumblebees: And Forty-Three More Nature Talks. Rolfes, Ellen, ed. 96p. (gr. k-6). 1993. spiral top-bound 5.95 (*1-879958-18-X*) Tradery Hse.

North Carolina Wildlife Resources Commission Staff. North Carolina Wild Places: A Closer Look. Earley, Lawrence S., ed. Runyon, Anne M. & Brown, Jim, illus. LC 92-81998. 82p. (Orig.). (gr. 2-6). 1994. pap. 10.00 (*0-9628949-1-5*) NC Wildlife.

Oliver, Stephen, photos by. Nature. LC 90-23568. (Illus.). 24p. (ps-k). 1991. 8.00 (*0-679-81805-7*) Random Bks Yng Read.

Pearce, Q. L. Quicksand & Other Earthly Wonders. Steltenpohl, Jane, ed. Fraser, Mary A., illus. 64p. (gr. 4-6). 1989. PLB 12.98 (*0-671-68530-9*, J Messner); pap. 5.95 (*0-671-68646-1*) S&S Trade.

Podendorf, Illa. Jungles. LC 82-4454. (gr. k-4). 1982. 12. 85 (*0-516-01631-8*) Childrens.

Rainis, Kenneth G. Nature Projects for Young Scientists. 1989. pap. 6.95 (*0-531-15135-2*) Watts.

Rankin, William. Come Hibernate with Me. Camphouse, Marylyn J., frwd. by. (Illus.). 214p. (Orig.). (gr. 9 up). 1989. 30.00 (*0-9623948-0-7*) M Camphouse.

Ricciuti, Edward. Patterns in Nature. (Illus.). 64p. (gr. 4-8). 1994. PLB 16.95 (*1-56711-058-4*) Blackbirch.

Robbins, Robin. Looking at Nature. (Illus.). 48p. (gr. 7-9). 1992. 13.95 (*0-563-34498-9*, BBC-Parkwest); pap. 6.95 (*0-563-34499-7*, BBC-Parkwest) Parkwest Pubns.

Rotner, Shelley & Kreisler, Ken. Nature Spy. LC 91-38430. (Illus.). 32p. (ps-1). 1992. RSBE 14.95 (*0-02-777885-1*, Macmillan Child Bk) Macmillan Child Grp.

San Diego County School Children. San Diego County's Special Species: Nature Essays Written by & for Children. Moran, Barbara, ed. 44p. (gr. 1-12). 1993. pap. 4.95 (*0-9634474-1-6*) Ms B Bks.

—Special Species: An Anthology Written by & for the Children of San Diego County. Moran, Barbara, ed. (Illus.). 40p. (Orig.). (gr. 1-12). 1992. pap. 3.95 (*0-9634474-0-8*) Ms B Bks.

Schnieper, Claudia. On the Trail of the Fox. Scherer, Elise, tr. (GER., Illus.). 48p. (gr. 2-5). 1986. lib. bdg. 19.95 (*0-87614-287-0*) Carolrhoda Bks.

Schweninger, Ann. Summertime. Schweninger, Ann, illus. 32p. (ps-3). 1992. RB 13.50 (*0-670-83610-9*) Viking Child Bks.

—Wintertime. LC 93-16685. 32p. (ps-3). 1993. pap. 4.50 (*0-14-054286-8*, Puffin) Puffin Bks.

Seamans, Andy. Who, What, When, Where, Why? In the World of Nature. (Illus.). 300p. (Orig.). (gr. 6 up). 1992. pap. 5.95 (*0-8120-4699-4*) Barron.

Silver, Donald M. The Checkerboard Press Nature Encyclopedia. Wynne, Patricia J., illus. LC 89-48801. 128p. (gr. 3-7). 1990. 12.95 (*1-56288-001-2*) Checkerboard.

Strange Nature. (Illus.). 48p. (gr. 3-4). 1992. PLB 22.80 (*0-8114-3157-6*) Raintree Steck-V.

Swamp, Jake. Giving Thanks: A Native American Good Morning Message. Printup, Erwin, Jr., illus. LC 94-5955. Date not set. 14.95 (*1-880000-15-6*) Lee & Low Bks.

Temple, Lannis, ed. Dear World: How Children Around the World Feel about Our Environment. LC 92-29929. (Illus.). 152p. (gr. k up). 1993. pap. 15.00 (*0-679-84403-1*) Random Bks Yng Read.

Thoreau, Henry David. Walden. Langmack, F., intro. by. Bd. with On Civil Disobedience. (gr. 10 up). pap. 1.50 (*0-8049-0083-3*, CL-83) Airmont.

—Walden. Sherman, Paul, ed. Bd. with Civil Disobedience. LC 60-16148. (gr. 9 up). 1960. pap. 9.96 (*0-395-05113-4*, RivEd) HM.

Time Life Inc. Editors. Why Is the Grass Green? First Questions & Answers about Nature. Kagan, Neil, ed. (Illus.). 48p. (ps). 1993. write for info. (*0-7835-0858-1*); lib. bdg. write for info. (*0-7835-0859-X*) Time-Life.

Unwin, M. Why Do Tigers Have Stripes? (Illus.). 24p. (gr. 1 up). 1993. PLB 11.96 (*0-88110-625-9*); pap. 3.95 (*0-7460-1300-0*) EDC.

Veith, Jan T. Natural Wonders. 64p. (gr. 3-6). 1987. 9.95 (*0-912107-56-1*) Monday Morning Bks.

Ward, Lorraine. A Walk in the Wild. 32p. 1993. PLB 16. 88 (*0-88106-480-7*); pap. 7.95 (*0-88106-478-5*) Charlesbridge Pub.

Waters, Sarah A. Growing Up. (ps-3). 1992. 9.95 (*0-89577-461-5*, Dist. by Random) RD Assn.

Wheeler. Fishes. (gr. 2-5). 1982. (Usborne-Hayes); PLB 11.96 (*0-88110-075-7*); pap. 3.95 (*0-86020-626-2*) EDC.

Williams, Brian. The Living World. LC 92-41309. (Illus.). 96p. (Orig.). (gr. 5 up). 1993. 15.95 (*1-85697-846-X*, Kingfisher LKC); pap. 9.95 (*1-85697-817-6*) LKC.

The Wonders of Nature Take-along Library, 5 vols. (Illus.). 30p. (gr. 2-7). 1991. Set. incl. carrycase 5.99 (*0-517-05454-X*) Random Hse Value.

Wood, Jenny. Wonderworks of Nature, 8 vols. (Illus.). 32p. (gr. 3-4). 1991. Set. PLB 138.16 (*0-8368-0757-X*) Gareth Stevens Inc.

NATURE (ESTHETICS)

Richardson, Wendy & Richardson, Jack. The Natural World: Through the Eyes of Artists. LC 90-34281. (Illus.). 48p. (gr. 4 up). 1991. pap. 7.95 (*0-516-49285-3*) Childrens.

NATURE, EFFECT OF MAN ON

see Man–Influence on Nature

NATURE IN LITERATURE

see also Nature in Poetry

NATURE IN POETRY

Alexander, Cecil. All Things Bright & Beautiful. Heyer, Carol, illus. LC 91-28428. 32p. (ps-2). 1992. 11.95 (*0-8249-8544-3*, Ideals Child) Hambleton-Hill.

Brenner, Barbara, ed. The Earth Is Painted Green: A Garden of Poems about Our Planet. Schindler, S. D., illus. LC 93-21466. 96p. 1993. 16.95 (*0-590-45134-0*) Scholastic Inc.

Carlstrom, Nancy. Northern Lullaby. Dillon, Leo & Dillon, Diane, illus. 32p. (ps-3). 1992. PLB 15.95 (*0-399-21806-8*, Philomel Bks) Putnam Pub Group.

Cowden, Frances B. & Hatchett, Eve B. Of Butterflies & Unicorns: And Other Wonders of the Earth. Grove, Eric, illus. 52p. (gr. 7-12). 1993. pap. 7.95 (*1-884289-02-9*) Grandmother Erth.

Demi, selected by. & illus. In the Eyes of the Cat. Tze-Si Huang, tr. from JPN. LC 91-27729. 80p. (gr. 1-3). 1992. 15.95 (*0-8050-1955-3*, Bks Young Read) H Holt & Co.

Esbensen, Barbara J. Echoes for the Eye. Davie, Helen K., illus. LC 94-623. 1995. 15.00 (*0-06-024398-8*, HarpT); PLB 14.89 (*0-06-024399-6*) HarpC.

Farjeon, Eleanor. Between the Earth & Sun. Date not set. 15.00 (*0-06-020795-7*, HarpT) HarpC.

Ferra, Lorraine. A Crow Doesn't Need a Shadow: A Guide to Writing Poetry from Nature. Boardman, Diane, illus. LC 93-34991. 1994. pap. 9.95 (*0-87905-600-2*) Gibbs Smith Pub.

Fletcher, Ralph. Water Planet. 2nd ed. 34p. (Orig.). (gr. 2-10). 1991. pap. 8.00x (*0-9628238-5-6*) Arrowhead Bks. A poetry collection about water arranged in two parts. The poems in Part One (Water Songs) are humorous & rhythmic as in "H2O": "The recipe /for water is/ the same as/ it's always been/ two parts/ hydrogen/ one part/ oxygen." These playful poems will encourage young readers to wade into Part Two (Deeper Water) which includes "A Writing Kind of Day": "Each word hits the page/ like a drop in a puddle/ and starts off a tiny circle/ of trembling feeling/ that expands from the source/ & slowly fades away..." Essential collection for teachers doing theme units on water or the water cycle. "Ralph Fletcher's WATER PLANET, like water itself, refreshes & laves the reader into new ways of feeling & looking. These poems rescue the young from drowning in the sea of mediocre verse, the false metaphors & tired cliches which threaten to become the standard of our time. This is an important collection with its variety of forms & felicitous images." (Myra Cohn Livingston). To order, write to: Arrowhead Books, 3 Gerrish Drive, Durham, NH 03824. Or call 603-868-7145.

Publisher Provided Annotation.

Ghigna, Charles. Tickle Day: Poems from Father Goose. Moore, Cyd, illus. LC 93-40847. 40p. (ps-2). 1994. 14. 95 (*0-7868-0015-1*); PLB 14.89 (*0-7868-2010-1*) Hyprn Child.

Larrick, Nancy, selected by. Room for Me & a Mountain Lion: Poetry of Open Spaces. LC 73-77810. (Illus.). 192p. (gr. 5 up). 1989. pap. 6.95 (*0-87131-569-6*) M Evans.

Levy, Constance. A Tree Place: And Other Poems. Sabuda, Robert, illus. LC 93-20586. 48p. (gr. k-5). 1994. SBE 12.95 (*0-689-50599-X*, M K McElderry) Macmillan Child Grp.

Lewis, Richard, ed. In a Spring Garden. Keats, Ezra J., illus. LC 65-23965. 32p. (ps up). 1989. Repr. of 1965 ed. 13.95 (*0-8037-4024-7*) Dial Bks Young.

Moon, Pat. Earth Lines: Poems for the Green Age. LC 92-27570. 64p. (gr. 5 up). 1993. 14.00 (*0-688-11853-4*) Greenwillow.

Moore, Lilian. Adam Mouse's Book of Poems. McCord, Kathleen G., illus. LC 91-42223. 64p. (ps-5). 1992. SBE 12.95 (*0-689-31765-4*, Atheneum Child Bk) Macmillan Child Grp.

Paladino, Catherine. Land, Sea, & Sky: Poems to Celebrate the Earth. (ps-3). 1993. 15.95 (*0-316-68892-4*, AMP) Little.

Ryder, Joanne. Under Your Feet. Nolan, Dennis, illus. LC 89-33897. 32p. (gr. k-3). 1990. RSBE 14.95 (*0-02-777955-6*, Four Winds) Macmillan Child Grp.

Sheehan, William. Nature's Wonderful World in Rhyme. Maeno, Itoko, illus. LC 93-15247. 1993. 14.95 (*0-911655-47-6*) Advocacy Pr.

Turner, Ann. A Moon for Seasons. Norieka, Robert, illus. LC 92-36857. 40p. (gr. 1-5). 1994. RSBE 14.95 (*0-02-789513-0*, Macmillan Child Bk) Macmillan Child Grp.

NATURE PHOTOGRAPHY

see also Photography of Animals

Baker, Howard, text by. & photos by Big South Fork Country. LC 93-28260. (Illus.). 120p. (gr. 9 up). 1993. 29.95 (*1-55853-258-7*) Rutledge Hill Pr.

Lasky, Kathryn. Think Like an Eagle: At Work with a Wildlife Photographer. Knight, Christopher G. & Swedberg, Jack, photos by. (Illus.). 48p. (gr. 3 up). 1992. 15.95 (*0-316-51519-1*, Joy St Bks) Little.

NATURE POETRY

see Nature in Poetry

NATURE STUDY

see also Animals–Habits and Behavior; Botany; Nature Photography; Zoology

Allison, Linda. The Reasons for Seasons: The Great Cosmic Megagalactic Trip Without Moving from Your Chair. Allison, Linda, illus. 128p. (gr. 4 up). 1975. pap. 9.95 (*0-316-03440-1*) Little.

Arnosky, Jim. Crinkleroot's Book of Animal Tracking. Arnosky, Jim, illus. LC 88-15353. 48p. (gr. k-5). 1989. RSBE 14.95 (*0-02-705851-4*, Bradbury Pr) Macmillan Child Grp.

—I Was Born in a Tree & Raised by Bees. Arnosky, Jim, illus. LC 88-6121. 48p. (gr. k-5). 1988. Repr. of 1977 ed. RSBE 13.95 (*0-02-705841-7*, Bradbury Pr) Macmillan Child Grp.

Bank Street College of Education Editors. Let's Explore Land, Water, Air. (gr. 1-2). 1986. pap. 2.95 (*0-8120-3624-7*) Barron.

Barlowe, Dot & Barlowe, Sy. Who Lives Here? Barlowe, Dot & Barlowe, Sy, illus. LC 79-27494. 32p. (ps-3). 1980. pap. 2.25 (*0-394-83740-1*) Random Bks Yng Read.

Bennett, Paul. Changing Shape. LC 93-49798. 32p. (gr. 1-5). 1994. 14.95 (*1-56847-205-6*) Thomson Lrning.

Benton, Allen H. & Bunting, Richard L. Young People's Nature Guide. De Santo, Rita, et al, illus. 177p. (gr. 2-4). 1978. pap. text ed. 3.00 (*0-942788-05-2*) Iris Visual.

Binnamin, Vivian. Field Trip Mysteries Series, 4 vols. Nelsen, Jeffrey S., illus. 128p. (gr. k-3). 1990. Set. PLB 19.80 (*0-671-94436-3*) Set. pap. 11.80 (*0-671-94437-1*) Silver Pr.

Border, Rosy. A "Spot-It" Guide to Nature. Banazi, Pauline, illus. 48p. (gr. 3-6). 1992. pap. 2.95 (*1-56680-012-9*) Mad Hatter Pub.

Bowen, Betsy. Antler, Bear, Canoe: A Northwoods Alphabet Year. Bowen, Betsy, illus. 32p. (ps-3). 1991. 15.95 (*0-316-10376-4*, Joy St Bks) Little.

Boy Scouts of America. Nature. (Illus.). 48p. (gr. 6-12). 1973. pap. 1.85 (*0-8395-3285-7*, 33285) BSA.

Brooks, Bruce. Nature by Design. 1994. 8.95 (*0-374-35495-2*) FS&G.

Brown, Tom, Jr. Tom Brown's Field Guide to Nature & Survival for Children. 1989. pap. 9.50 (*0-425-11106-7*, Berkley Trade) Berkley Pub.

Bruce, Jill. Who Did That? Wade, Jan, illus. 48p. (Orig.). (gr. 2-6). 1994. pap. text ed. 7.95 (*0-86417-575-2*, Pub. by Kangaroo Pr AT) Seven Hills Bk Dists.

Burnie, David A. How Nature Works: One Hundred Ways Parents & Kids Can Share the Secrets of Nature. LC 91-12432. (Illus.). 192p. (gr. 3 up). 1991. 24.00 (*0-89577-391-0*, Dist. by Random) RD Assn.

Busch, Phyllis S. Science Safaris to the Nearest Wilderness: Your Own Back Yard. LC 93-48410. (Illus.). 1995. 16.00 (*0-02-715655-9*) Macmillan Child Grp.

Carpenter, Mimi G. What the Sea Left Behind. Carpenter, Mimi G., illus. LC 81-66251. 32p. (gr. 1-4). 1981. pap. 7.95 (*0-89272-123-5*) Down East.

Cooper, Ursula. Mini Walks on the Mesa. Harroun, Dorothy, illus. LC 89-4448. 32p. (Orig.). (gr. 3-6). 1989. pap. 6.95 (*0-86534-133-8*) Sunstone Pr.

Cornell, Joseph & Deranja, Michael. Journey to the Heart of Nature: A Guided Exploration. (Illus.). 128p. (gr. 7-12). 1994. pap. 9.95 wkbk. (*1-883220-06-8*) Dawn CA.

Crump, Donald J., ed. Adventures in Your National Parks. (gr. 3-8). 1989. 8.95 (*0-87044-702-5*); PLB 12.50 (*0-87044-707-6*) Natl Geog.

Diamond, Lynnell. Let's Discover Capitol Reef, Arches, & Canyonlands National Parks: A Children's Activity Book for Ages 6-11. (Illus.). 32p. (gr. 1-6). 1991. pap. 4.95 (*0-89886-285-X*) Mountaineers.

—Let's Discover Petrified Forest National Park: A Children's Activity Book for Ages 6-11. (Illus.). 32p. (gr. 1-6). 1991. pap. 4.95 (*0-89886-286-8*) Mountaineers.

Evelyn-Marie. Pick Your Own Strawberries. rev. ed. Evelyn-Marie, illus. 32p. (gr. k-3). 1983. pap. 3.00 (*0-9614746-3-7*) Berry Bks.

Field, Nancy & Machlis, Sally. Discovering Crater Lake. Machlis, Sally, illus. 32p. (Orig.). (gr. 1-6). 1989. pap. 3.95 (*0-941042-08-1*) Dog Eared Pubns.

Florian, Douglas. Nature Walk. LC 88-39430. (Illus.). 32p. (ps up). 1989. 12.95 (*0-688-08266-1*); PLB 12.88 (*0-688-08269-6*) Greenwillow.

Hamerstrom, Frances. Walk When the Moon Is Full. Katona, Robert, illus. LC 75-33878. 64p. (gr. 3-8). 1975. 15.95 (*0-912278-69-2*); pap. 6.95 (*0-912278-84-6*) Crossing Pr.

Harlow, Rosie & Morgan, Gareth. One Hundred Seventy-Five Amazing Nature Experiments. Kuo Kang Chen, et al, illus. LC 91-21113. 176p. (Orig.). (gr. 4-7). 1992. pap. 12.00 (*0-679-82043-4*) Random Bks Yng Read.

Herridge, Douglas & Hughes, Susan. The Environmental Detective Kit. LC 90-48247. (Illus.). 80p. (gr. 3 up). 1991. pap. 4.00 (*0-06-107408-X*) HarpC Child Bks.

Holing, Dwight. EarthTrips: A Guide to Nature Travel on a Fragile Planet. (Illus.). 224p. (Orig.). 1991. pap. 12.95 (*1-879326-05-1*) Living Planet Pr.

Janssen, Lawrence H. Earth Care a Mandate: Nature Study Guide Keyed to the Black Hills. Janssen, Lawrence H., illus. LC 85-73644. 80p. (Orig.). (gr. 7-12). 1985. pap. 3.95 (*0-917575-03-2*) Cedars WI.

—Horsethief Lake Old Baldy Trail Guides. Janssen, Lawrence H., illus. (Orig.). (gr. 7-12). 1986. pap. 1.00 (*0-917575-04-0*) Cedars WI.

Jenkins, Christine L. Loving Our Neighbor the Earth: Creation Spirituality Activities for 9-11 Year Olds. LC 91-10968. (Illus.). 120p. (Orig.). (gr. 4-6). 1991. pap. 14.95 wkbk. (*0-89390-204-7*) Resource Pubns.

Jorgensen, Eric, et al. Manure, Meadows & Milkshakes. Hone, Elizabeth, ed. Hendrick, Andrea, illus. 132p. (Orig.). (ps-8). 1986. pap. text ed. 9.95 tchrs. ed. (*0-318-20228-X*) Trust Hidden Villa.

Kerrod, Robin. Let's Investigate Science. (Illus.). (gr. 5 up). 1994. Group 1, The Solar System, Animal Life, Force & Motion, Communications, The Environment. PLB write for info.; Group 2, Electricity & Magnetism, Plant Life, Natural Resources, Transportation, Weather. PLB write for info. (*1-85435-688-7*) Marshall Cavendish.

Kuebler, Sharon. Noon to Night. Kirkeeide, Deborah, illus. 32p. (ps-2). Date not set. 11.95 (*1-56065-161-X*) Capstone Pr.

Kurjian, Judi. En Mi Propio Jardin. Wagner, David P., illus. (SPA.). 32p. (Orig.). (ps-4). 1993. PLB 15.88 (*0-88106-644-3*); pap. 6.95 (*0-88106-811-X*) Charlesbridge Pub.

Lawlor, Elizabeth P. Discover Nature Close to Home: Things to Know & Things to Do. Archer, Pat, illus. 224p. (Orig.). (gr. 8 up). 1993. pap. 14.95 (*0-8117-3077-8*) Stackpole.

Leslie, Clare W. Nature All Year Long. LC 90-47866. (Illus.). 56p. (gr. 2 up). 1991. 16.95 (*0-688-09183-0*) Greenwillow.

Lohf, Sabine. Nature Crafts. LC 89-49552. (Illus.). 64p. 1990. pap. 8.95 (*0-516-49257-8*) Childrens.

Lovett, Sarah. Extremely Weird Micro Monsters. (Illus.). 48p. (Orig.). (gr. 3 up). 1993. pap. 9.95 (*1-56261-120-8*) John Muir.

McConnell-Celi, Sue. Making Friends with Nature. (ps). 1993. pap. 7.95 (*0-9636909-1-4*) Lavender Crystal.

Markle, Sandra. Exploring Autumn: A Season of Science Activities, Puzzlers, & Games. Markle, Sandra, illus. LC 90-24209. 160p. (gr. 3-7). 1991. SBE 14.95 (*0-689-31620-8*, Atheneum Child Bk) Macmillan Child Grp.

Milord, Susan. The Kids' Nature Book: Three Hundred Sixty-Five Indoor - Outdoor Activities & Experiences. Williamson, Susan, ed. LC 89-14724. (Illus.). 160p. (Orig.). (ps-3). 1989. pap. 12.95 (*0-913589-42-X*) Williamson Pub Co.

Moran, Barbara, intro. by. Special Species by California Kids. 4th ed. (Illus.). 90p. (gr. k-12). 1994. pap. 14.95 (*0-9634474-2-4*) Ms B Bks.

O'Rourke, Robert. What God Did for Zeke the Fuzzy Caterpillar. Loman, Roberta K., illus. 32p. (gr. k-2). 1991. pasted 2.50 (*0-87403-824-3*, 24-03924) Standard Pub.

Pearce, Q. L. & Pearce, W. J. Nature's Footprints Series, 4 vols. Bettoli, Delana, illus. 96p. (ps-1). 1990. Set. 19.80 (*0-671-94431-2*); Set. PLB 27.80 (*0-671-94430-4*) Silver Pr.

Plattner, Sandra S. Connecting with Nature. (ps-k). 1991. pap. 10.95 (*0-86653-976-X*) Fearon Teach Aids.

Rights, Mollie. Beastly Neighbors: All About Wild Things in the City or Why Earwigs Make Good Mothers. (Illus.). 128p. (Orig.). (gr. 3 up). 1981. pap. 9.95 (*0-316-74577-4*) Little.

Roberts, Allene. The Curiosity Club: Kids' Nature Activity Book. 192p. 1992. text ed. cancelled (*0-471-55590-8*); pap. text ed. 14.95 (*0-471-55589-4*) Wiley.

Scheid, Margaret. Discovering Acadia: A Guide for Young Naturalists. Scheid, Margaret, illus. LC 86-71350. 80p. (ps-12). 1988. pap. 12.95 (*0-934745-04-8*) Acadia Pub Co.

Schnieper, Claudia. An Apple Tree Through the Year. Baumli, Othmar, photos by. (Illus.). 48p. (gr. 2-5). 1987. PLB 19.95 (*0-87614-248-X*); pap. 6.95 (*0-87614-483-0*) Carolrhoda Bks.

Schweininger, Ann. Autumn Days. LC 93-16684. 32p. (ps-3). 1993. pap. 4.50 (*0-14-054055-5*, Puffin) Puffin Bks.

Schweninger, Ann. Springtime. LC 92-22204. (Illus.). 32p. 1993. 13.50 (*0-670-82757-6*) Viking Child Bks.

Silver, Donald M. One Small Square Backyard. Wynne, Patricia J., illus. LC 93-18353. (gr. 4 up). 1993. text ed. write for info. (*0-7167-6510-1*, Sci Am Yng Rdrs) W H Freeman.

Smith, Gina H. Blooming Mother Nature: Fun Language Activities to Unfold the Wonders of Nature Based on Bloom's Taxonomy. (Illus.). 80p. (ps-4). 1990. pap. 15.95 perfect bdg. (*1-55999-119-4*) LinguiSystems.

Stidworthy, John. Naturalist. LC 91-2660. (Illus.). 32p. (gr. 5-8). 1991. PLB 12.40 (*0-531-17356-9*, Gloucester Pr) Watts.

Swanson, Diane. Toothy Tongue & One Long Foot: Nature Activities for Kids. (gr. 2 up). 1994. pap. 6.95 (*1-55850-379-X*) Adams Inc MA.

Time Life Inc Staff. Right in Your Own Backyard: Nature Math. Ward, Elizabeth, et al, eds. LC 92-27222. (Illus.). 64p. (gr. k-4). 1992. write for info. (*0-8094-9962-2*); PLB write for info. (*0-8094-9963-0*) Time-Life.

Ward, Alan. Experimenting with Nature Study. Flax, Zena, illus. 48p. (gr. 2-7). 1991. lib. bdg. 12.95 (*0-7910-1515-7*) Chelsea Hse.

Webster, David. Exploring Nature Around the Year Series, 4 bks. (Illus.). 96p. (gr. 2-4). 1989. Set. PLB write for info. (*0-671-94109-7*, J Messner); Set. pap. write for info. (*0-671-94110-0*) S&S Trade.

—Spring. Steadman, Barbara, illus. 48p. (gr. 2-4). 1990. PLB 10.98 (*0-671-65858-1*, J Messner); pap. 5.95 (*0-671-65983-9*) S&S Trade.

Weiss, Ellen. Off to the Woods! (ps-3). 1993. pap. 1.95 (*0-307-10553-9*, Golden Pr) Western Pub.

Wexler, Jerome. Jack-in-the-Pulpit. Wexler, Jerome, illus. 40p. (gr. 2-6). 1993. 14.99 (*0-525-45073-4*, DCB) Dutton Child Bks.

Wilkes, Angela. My First Activity Book. LC 89-2640. (Illus.). 48p. (gr. 1-5). 1990. 13.00 (*0-394-86583-9*); PLB 13.99 (*0-394-96583-3*) Knopf Bks Yng Read.

—My First Nature Book. LC 89-8019. (Illus.). 48p. (gr. 1-5). 1990. 13.00 (*0-394-86610-X*); PLB 13.99 (*0-394-96610-4*) Knopf Bks Yng Read.

Williams, H. Crazy Creatures. (Illus.). 32p. (gr. 1-4). 1989. pap. 2.95 (*0-88625-222-9*) Durkin Hayes Pub.

Wong, Herbert H. The Backyard Detective: A Guide for Beginning Naturalists. Greer, Deborah, illus. LC 92-63342. 64p. (Orig.). (gr. k-5). 1993. pap. 7.95 (*1-882489-00-4*) NatureVision.

THE BACKYARD DETECTIVE provides children with a headstart in science while they have fun exploring their own environment. This book & nature kit invite children to study nature by direct observation in easily accessible environments. With this fully-illustrated guide as an outdoor companion, they use simple science tools & basic comparison charts to investigate nature's clues & uncover their own areas of interest. Young Backyard Detectives will have the opportunity to examine, identify, measure, grow, feed, & collect organisms. They will learn how to keep their own nature journal. This book encourages children to enjoy & respect their natural environment. Dr. Herbert H. Wong, the author, is a zoologist & science educator whose children's science books have become standard favorites among children & their teachers. The ecological concepts he uses to form the framework for THE BACKYARD DETECTIVE are diversity, interrelationships, adaptations & change. THE BACKYARD DETECTIVE is available in book form only, & also with the complete exploration kit (carrying case, magnifier, observation jar, pencil & measuring tape). AVAILABLE THROUGH BOOKPEOPLE & QUALITY BOOKS.

Publisher Provided Annotation.

Wyler, Rose. Outdoor Science Series, 6 Bks. (Illus.). 64p. (gr. k-2). 1989. Set. PLB write for info. (*0-671-94099-6*, J Messner); Set. pap. write for info. (*0-671-94100-3*) S&S Trade.

Zim, Herbert S. & Ingle, Lester. Seashores. Barlowe, Dorothea & Barlowe, Sy, illus. (gr. 5 up). 1955. pap. write for info. (*0-307-24496-2*, Golden Pr) Western Pub.

NATURE STUDY–DICTIONARIES

Moore, Leonard. Enciclopedia Juvenil De la Naturaleza. 2nd ed. (SPA.). 256p. 1982. write for info. (*0-7859-5097-4*) Fr & Eur.

NATURE STUDY–FICTION

Allen, Marjorie N. & Rotner, Shelley. Changes. Rotner, Shelley, photos by. LC 90-6601. (Illus.). 32p. (ps-1). 1991. RSBE 13.95 (*0-02-700252-7*, Macmillan Child Bk) Macmillan Child Grp.

Allen, Wynell. Nature Stories for Children. 1993. 6.95 (*0-8062-4454-2*) Carlton.

Asch, Frank. The Earth & I. LC 93-237. (ps-2). 1994. 13.95 (*0-15-200443-2*, Gulliver Bks) HarBrace.

Baker. Where the Forest Meets the Sea. 1993. pap. 28.67 (*0-590-72453-3*) Scholastic Inc.

Baker, Marybeth. Maynard's Allagash Friends. 1989. pap. 7.95 (*0-929906-25-X*) G Gannett.

Bandes, Hanna. Sleepy River. Winter, Jeanette, illus. LC 92-26198. 32p. (ps). 1993. 14.95 (*0-399-22349-5*, Philomel Bks) Putnam Pub Group.

Bastin, Marjolein. Vera's Special Hobbies. (Illus.). 28p. (ps-2). 1985. 2.95 (*0-8120-5692-2*) Barron.

Baylor, Byrd. The Table Where Rich People Sit. Parnall, Peter, illus. LC 93-1251. 1994. 14.95 (*0-684-19653-0*, Scribners Young Read) Macmillan Child Grp.

Benjamin, Alan. Let's Take a Walk: Vamos a Caminar. (ENG & SPA.). (ps). 1992. pap. 2.95 (*0-671-76929-4*, Little Simon) S&S Trade.

Blake, Robert J. The Perfect Spot. Blake, Robert J., illus. 32p. (ps-8). 1992. PLB 14.95 (*0-399-22132-8*, Philomel Bks) Putnam Pub Group.

Blatchford, Claire. Down the Path. Eagle, Mike, illus. 24p. (Orig.). (ps). 1992. pap. text ed. 3.00x (*1-56134-142-8*) Dushkin Pub.

Bodsworth, Nan. A Nice Walk in the Jungle. (Illus.). 32p. (ps-2). 1990. pap. 12.95 (*0-670-82476-3*) Viking Child Bks.

Brown, Ruth. Ladybug, Ladybug. LC 88-14852. (Illus.). 32p. (ps-1). 1992. pap. 3.99 (*0-14-054543-3*, Puff Unicorn) Puffin Bks.

Bruchac, Joseph. Fox Song. Morin, Paul, illus. LC 92-24815. 32p. (ps). 1993. 14.95 (*0-399-22346-0*, Philomel Bks) Putnam Pub Group.

Bryant, Bonnie. Autumn Trail, No. 30. 1993. pap. 3.50 (*0-553-48077-4*) Bantam.

Burgess, Thornton W. Mother West Wind's Children. rev. ed. (Illus.). (gr. 1-3). 1962. 16.95 (*0-316-11645-9*) Little.

—Old Mother West Wind. 16.95 (*0-8488-0385-X*) Amereon Ltd.

—Old Mother West Wind's Children. 18.95 (*0-8488-0386-8*) Amereon Ltd.

—Old Mother West Wind's "When" Stories. 18.95 (*0-8488-0387-6*) Amereon Ltd.

—Old Mother West Wind's "Where" Stories. 18.95 (*0-8488-0388-4*) Amereon Ltd.

Canfield, Dorothy. The Bent Twig. 340p. 1981. Repr. PLB 13.95x (*0-89967-018-0*) Harmony Raine.
Capucilli, Alyssa S. Good Morning, Frog. LC 93-29311. (Illus.). 32p. (ps-2). 1994. 13.95 (*1-56282-674-3*); PLB 13.89 (*1-56282-675-1*) Hyprn Child.
—Good Morning, Pond. Jabar, Cynthia, illus. 32p. 1994. 13.95 (*0-685-70785-7*); lib. bdg. 13.89 (*0-685-70786-5*) Hyprn Child.
Couture, Cristin. Walk in the Woods. 1993. 15.00 (*0-374-38227-1*) FS&G.

Curtis, Chara M. How Far to Heaven? Currier, Alfred, illus. 28p. 1993. 15.95 (*0-935699-06-6*) Illum Arts. HOW FAR TO HEAVEN? is the question Little One asks of her grandmother. To find the answer, they slip out the back gate into the woods & begin exploring the many signs of heaven found in nature. This moving story is greatly enhanced by Currier's museum-quality impressionistic paintings. Although designed as a children's book, this story is meant for readers of all ages. "The beauty & sensitivity of the illustrations & words will touch the very center of the heart of everyone who reads this book." - Gerald G. Jampolsky, M.D., Founder, The Center for Attitudinal Healing. "This wonderful little book is about enlightenment - waking up what is all around us. What could be more important?" - Larry Dossey, M.D., author. To order, call Atrium 1-800-275-2606. *Publisher Provided Annotation.*

De Brunhoff, Laurent. Babar's Little Library: Stories About Earth, About Fire, About Air, About Water, 4 bks. De Brunhoff, Laurent, illus. (ps-2). 1992. Set of mini-bks. in slipcase incls. Air, Water, 48 pgs. ea. & Earth & Fire, 32 pgs. ea. 8.99 (*0-394-84365-7*) Random Bks Yng Read.
Dexter, Catherine. Gertie's Green Thumb. Eagle, Ellen, illus. Cohn, Amy, ed. LC 94-20854. (Illus.). (gr. 4 up). 1995. pap. 4.95 (*0-688-13090-9*, Pub. by Beech Tree Bks) Morrow.
Dunbar, Joyce. Why Is the Sky Up? Dunbar, James, illus. 32p. (ps). 1991. 13.45 (*0-395-57580-X*, Sandpiper) HM.
Elsemann, Henry. Hump-Free: The Wrong Way Whale. (Illus., Orig.). (gr. k-6). 1985. pap. 6.95 (*0-938129-00-7*) Emprise Pubns.
Fife, Dale H. The Empty Lot. Arnosky, Jim, illus. 32p. (gr. k-4). 1991. 14.95 (*0-316-28167-0*) Sierra.
Foreman, Mary M., tr. from ENG. Paseate con Paco. King, Ed, illus. (SPA.). 24p. 1929. pap. 3.95 (*1-56288-240-6*) Checkerboard.
George, Jean C. Dear Rebecca, Winter Is Here. Krupinski, Loretta, illus. LC 92-9515. 32p. (ps-3). 1993. 15.00 (*0-06-021139-3*); PLB 14.89 (*0-06-021140-7*) HarpC Child Bks.
George, William T. Christmas at Long Pond. George, Lindsay B., illus. LC 91-31475. 32p. (ps-8). 1992. 14.00 (*0-688-09214-4*); PLB 13.93 (*0-688-09215-2*) Greenwillow.
Gove, Doris. One Rainy Night. Krudop, Walter L., illus. LC 93-13900. 32p. (gr. 2-5). 1994. SBE 14.95 (*0-689-31800-6*, Atheneum Child Bk) Macmillan Child Grp.
Gunn, Robin J. God's Mountains, Meadows, & More: A Book about Places God Has Made. Lauck, Dawn, illus. LC 93-9990. 1994. 5.99 (*0-7814-0101-1*, Chariot Bks) Chariot Family.
Hague & Burgess. Old Mother West Wind. (gr. 4 up). 1991. pap. 18.95 (*0-8050-1426-8*) H Holt & Co.
Harper-Deiters, Cyndi. Jonathan Michael & Mother Nature's Fury. Ruggles, Robert & Ruggles, Grace, eds. Bowers, Helen M., illus. 36p. (Orig.). (gr. 2-4). 1993. pap. text ed. 4.95x (*0-9632513-2-5*) Cntry Home.
Hodgson-Burnett, Frances. The Land of the Blue Flower. Griffith, Judith A., illus. LC 93-19968. 48p. (ps-5). 1993. Repr. of 1938 ed. 15.95 (*0-915811-46-4*) H J Kramer Inc.
Hudson, Jan. Sweetgrass. 160p. (gr. 3-7). 1989. 13.95 (*0-399-21721-5*, Philomel Bks) Putnam Pub Group.
Hughes, Shirley. Hiding. LC 93-47254. (Illus.). 24p. (ps up). 1994. 13.95 (*1-56402-342-7*) Candlewick Pr.
Iverson, Diane. I Celebrate the World. (Illus.). 32p. (Orig.). 1989. pap. 5.95 (*0-9623349-0-1*) MS Pub.
Johnson, Emily R. A House Full of Strangers. 160p. (gr. 5 up). 1992. 14.00 (*0-525-65091-1*, Cobblehill Bks) Dutton Child Bks.
Katherine, Sharon. Sugar Princess. Wood, Paul, ed. Tolley, Lynn & Olds, Tom, illus. 31p. 1989. pap. 8.95 (*0-685-68779-1*) Jungle Pr.
Keats, Ezra J. Over in the Meadow. (gr. 5 up). pap. 19.95 (*0-590-72809-1*) Scholastic Inc.
Kitchen, Bert. Tenrec's Twigs. Kitchen, Bert, illus. 32p. (gr. k-4). 1989. 14.95 (*0-399-21720-7*, Philomel Bks) Putnam Pub Group.
Kroll, Virginia. Wood-Hoopoe Willie. (Illus.). 32p. (ps-4). 1993. 15.88 (*0-88106-409-2*); PLB 15.00 (*0-88106-410-6*) Charlesbridge Pub.
Lindbergh, Reeve. What Is the Sun? Lambert, Stephen, illus. LC 93-3557. 32p. (ps up). 1994. 14.95 (*1-56402-146-7*) Candlewick Pr.
Lockwood, Barbara & McAuley, Marilyn. Good Gifts from God. LC 87-71383. (ps). 1988. bds. 4.99 (*1-55513-366-5*, Chariot Bks) Chariot Family.
Lynch. Walk. 1995. 14.00 (*0-06-023584-5*); PLB 13.89 (*0-06-023585-3*) HarpC Child Bks.
McAllister, Angela. One Breeze-Scented, Sun-Sparkling Morning. Jenkin-Pearce, Susie, illus. 32p. (ps-1). 1993. 17.95 (*0-09-176363-0*, Pub. by Hutchinson UK) Trafalgar.
McLaughlin, Molly. Earthworms, Dirt, & Rotten Leaves. Shetterly, Robert, illus. 96p. 1990. pap. 3.50 (*0-380-71074-9*, Camelot) Avon.
Major, Beverly. Over Back. Allen, Thomas B., illus. LC 91-19696. 32p. (gr. k-4). 1993. 15.00 (*0-06-020286-6*); PLB 14.89 (*0-06-020287-4*) HarpC Child Bks.
Mazer, Anne. The Salamander Room. Johnson, Steve, illus. 32p. (ps-3). 1994. pap. 5.99 (*0-679-86187-4*) Knopf Bks Yng Read.
Meredith, Susan H. Nature Walk. 2nd ed. Meredith, Susan H., illus. 25p. 1993. pap. text ed. 4.95 (*1-880666-09-X*) Oughten Hse.
—Wonder Walk. Meredith, Susan H., illus. 25p. (Orig.). 1993. pap. text ed. 4.95 (*1-880666-02-2*) Oughten Hse.
Merriam, Eve. Shhh! Hamanaka, Sheila, illus. LC 92-44110. (gr. 4 up). 1993. pap. 14.00 (*0-671-79816-2*, S&S BFYR) S&S Trade.
The Old Meadow. (gr. k-6). 1989. pap. 3.25 (*0-440-40238-7*, YB) Dell.
Pascoe, Gwen. The Sea Where I Swim. Wilson, Mark, illus. LC 93-6647. 1994. write for info. (*0-383-03712-3*) SRA Schl Grp.
Pizzo, Joan E. Little Crumb: Tales of the Back Bay. Geronimi, Clyde, illus. 29p. (Orig.). (gr. k-6). 1980. PLB 10.95 (*0-939126-00-1*); pap. 7.95 (*0-939126-01-X*); tchr's manual, 35p 8.95 (*0-939126-03-6*) Back Bay.
Plum, Carol T. The Butterfly Secret: I Am Special Childrens Story Books. 32p. (ps-3). 1989. lib. bdg. 9.95 (*0-87973-017-X*, 17); pap. text ed. 5.95 (*0-87973-014-5*, 14) Our Sunday Visitor.
—The Swinging Tree: I Am Special Childrens Story Books. 32p. (gr. 3-8). 1989. lib. bdg. 9.95 (*0-87973-016-1*, 16); pap. text ed. 5.95 (*0-87973-013-7*, 13) Our Sunday Visitor.
Rand, Gloria. The Cabin Key. Rand, Ted, illus. LC 93-10398. (ps-3). 1994. 14.95 (*0-15-213884-6*) HarBrace.
Rosen, Michael J. All Eyes on the Pond. LC 93-11743. (Illus.). 32p. (ps-2). 1994. 14.95 (*1-56282-475-9*); PLB 14.89 (*1-56282-476-7*) Hyprn Child.
Rylant, Cynthia. All I See. Catalanotto, Peter, illus. LC 88-42547. 32p. (gr. k-2). 1994. pap. 5.95 (*0-531-07048-4*) Orchard Bks Watts.
Seldon, George. Tucker's Countryside. (gr. k-6). 1989. pap. 3.99 (*0-440-40248-4*, YB) Dell.
Selsam, Millicent E. Greg's Microscope. Lobel, Arnold, illus. LC 63-8002. 64p. (gr. k-3). 1990. pap. 3.50 (*0-06-444144-X*, Trophy) HarpC Child Bks.
Sharfstein, Chana. The Little Leaf. Rosenfeld, Dina, ed. Blumenfeld, Rochelle, illus. 32p. (gr. k-4). 1989. 8.95 (*0-922613-18-4*); pap. 6.95 (*0-922613-19-2*) Hachai Pubns.
Shigezawa, Ruth. Celeste: A Fable for All Ages. Altman, Robin W., illus. LC 93-72194. 28p. (gr. 2 up). 1993. 16.95 (*0-9637101-0-9*); pap. 7.95 (*0-9637101-1-7*) Cndlelght Pr.
Showers, Paul. The Listening Walk. Aliki, illus. LC 90-30526. 32p. (ps-2). 1993. pap. 4.95 (*0-06-443322-6*, Trophy) HarpC Child Bks.
Shulevitz, Uri. Dawn. Shulevitz, Uri, illus. LC 74-9761. 32p. (ps up). 1974. 16.00 (*0-374-31707-0*) FS&G.
Spohn, David. Nate's Treasure. (Illus.). (ps-3). 1991. 9.95 (*0-688-10092-9*) Lothrop.
Talbert, Marc. Pillow of Clouds. LC 90-34264. 208p. (gr. 5-9). 1991. 15.00 (*0-8037-0901-3*) Dial Bks Young.
Whelan, Gloria. That Wild Berries Should Grow: The Story of a Summer. LC 93-41106. 122p. (gr. 4-6). 1994. 13.99 (*0-8028-3754-9*); pap. 4.99 (*0-8028-5091-X*) Eerdmans.
Woods, Becky. Beneath the Mask. Weinberger, Jane, ed. Woods, Sarah, illus. 60p. (gr. 4-8). 1994. 12.95 (*1-883650-07-0*) Windswept Hse.
Wright, Lynn F. Just One Blade. Waters, Tony, illus. 32p. (gr. 1-5). 1993. 12.95 (*1-881519-00-7*) WorryWart.
Yep, Laurence. Sweetwater. Noonan, Julia, illus. LC 72-9867. 224p. (gr. 5 up). 1983. pap. 3.50 (*0-06-440135-9*, Trophy) HarpC Child Bks.

NAVAL ADMINISTRATION
see names of countries with the subhead Navy, e.g. U. S. Navy
NAVAL AERONAUTICS
see Aeronautics, Military
NAVAL AIRPLANES
see Airplanes, Military
NAVAL ARCHITECTURE
see also Boatbuilding; Ships; Steamboats; Warships
NAVAL ART AND SCIENCE
see also Military Art and Science; Navigation; Sea Power; Seamen; Signals and Signaling; Submarine Warfare; Submarines; Warships
NAVAL BATTLES
see also Battles; Naval History;
also names of countries with the subdivision History, Naval, e.g. U. S.–History, Naval, etc.; and names of battles
NAVAL BIOGRAPHY
see also Seamen
also names of navies with the subdivision Biography, e.g. U. S. Navy–Biography
NAVAL HISTORY
see also Military History; Pirates
also names of countries with the subhead Navy or the subdivision History, naval, e.g. U. S. Navy; U. S.–History, Naval
Van Orden, M. D. U. S. Navy Ships & Coast Guard Cutters: A Naval Institute Book for Young Readers. Burke, Arleigh, frwd. by. LC 89-13539. (Illus.). 96p. (gr. 5-11). 1990. PLB 17.95 (*0-87021-212-5*) Naval Inst Pr.
NAVAL SIGNALING
see Signals and Signaling
NAVAL UNIFORMS
see Uniforms, Military
NAVAL WARFARE
see Submarine Warfare
NAVIGATION
see also Harbors; Knots and Splices; Lighthouses; Pilots and Pilotage; Radar; Shipwrecks; Signals and Signaling; Tides; Winds
Berenstain, Michael. The Ship Book. (Illus.). (gr. k-3). 1978. 6.95 (*0-679-20449-0*) McKay.
Blanchard, Anne. Navigation: A Three-Dimensional Exploration. Peacock, Irvine, illus. LC 92-80434. 12p. (gr. 2-6). 1992. 15.95 (*0-531-05455-1*) Orchard Bks Watts.
Grady, Sean M. Ships: Crossing the World's Oceans. LC 92-9162. (Illus.). 96p. (gr. 5-8). 1992. 15.95 (*1-56006-220-7*) Lucent Bks.
Stoff, Joshua. From Canoes to Cruisers: The Maritime Heritage of Long Island. Stoff, Joshua, illus. LC 93-40844. 112p. (Orig.). 1994. 18.00 (*1-55787-110-8*, Empire State Bks); pap. 10.00 (*1-55787-111-6*, Empire State Bks) Heart of the Lakes.
NAVIGATORS
see Discoveries (In Geography); Explorers; Seamen
NAVY
see Sea Power
see names of countries with the subhead Navy, e.g. U. S. Navy
NAZI MOVEMENT
see National Socialism
NEAR EAST
Benin. (Illus.). (gr. 5 up). 1989. 14.95 (*0-7910-0143-1*) Chelsea Hse.
Fairbanks, Ellen & Bodman, D. Middle East Master Map Kit: Their Lands & Ours. 39p. (gr. 5 up). 1989. 14.95 (*0-930141-25-3*) World Eagle.
Fox, Mary V. Bahrain. LC 92-8892. (Illus.). 128p. (gr. 5-9). 1992. PLB 20.55 (*0-516-02608-9*) Childrens.
Hassall, S. Bahrain. (Illus.). 96p. (gr. 5 up). 1988. 14.95 (*0-222-01093-2*) Chelsea Hse.
Johnson, Julia. United Arab Emirates. (Illus.). 96p. (gr. 5 up). 1988. 14.95 (*1-55546-178-6*) Chelsea Hse.
Kublin, Hyman. The Middle East: Regional Study. rev. ed. LC 72-6696. (Illus.). 258p. (gr. 9-12). 1973. pap. 20.56 (*0-395-13931-7*) HM.
Mason, Antony. Middle East. LC 88-18312. (Illus.). 48p. (gr. 4-8). 1988. PLB 14.95 (*0-382-09514-6*) Silver Burdett pr.
Morrison, Ian A. Middle East. LC 90-24433. (Illus.). 96p. (gr. 6-12). 1991. PLB 22.80 (*0-8114-2440-5*) Raintree Steck-V.
Stefoff, Rebecca. West Bank-Gaza Strip. (Illus.). 104p. (gr. 5 up). 1988. lib. bdg. 14.95 (*1-55546-782-2*) Chelsea Hse.
Walko, Ann & Fakhro, B. Customs of the Arabian Gulf: Drawings & Paintings by School Children in Bahrain & Dubai. (Illus.). 49p. (ps-8). 1978. 10.95 (*1-882443-01-2*) Bosphorus Bks.
NEAR EAST–ANTIQUITIES
Tubb, Jonathan. Bible Lands. Hills, Alan, photos by. LC 91-2388. (Illus.). 64p. (gr. 5 up). 1991. 16.00 (*0-679-81457-4*); lib. bdg. 16.99 (*0-679-91457-9*) Knopf Bks Yng Read.
NEAR EAST–FICTION
Italia, Robert. Armed Forces. Wallner, Rosemary, ed. LC 91-73075. 202p. (gr. 4 up). 1991. 13.99 (*1-56239-026-0*) Abdo & Dghtrs.
Laird, Elizabeth. Kiss the Dust. LC 91-43517. 284p. (gr. 5 up). 1992. 15.00 (*0-525-44893-4*, DCB) Dutton Child Bks.
—Kiss the Dust. 288p. (gr. 5 up). 1994. pap. 4.50 (*0-14-036855-8*) Puffin Bks.
Schami, Rafik. A Hand Full of Stars. Lesser, Rika, tr. from GER. LC 89-25991. 224p. (gr. 7 up). 1990. 14.95 (*0-525-44535-8*, DCB) Dutton Child Bks.
—A Hand Full of Stars. Lesser, Rika, tr. from GER. 224p. (gr. 7 up). 1992. pap. 4.50 (*0-14-036073-5*, Puffin) Puffin Bks.
Staples, Suzanne F. Haveli. LC 92-29054. (Illus.). 272p. (gr. 7 up). 1993. 18.00 (*0-679-84157-1*) Knopf Bks Yng Read.

NEAR EAST–HISTORY

Civilizations of the Middle East. (Illus.). 80p. (gr. 4 up). 1988. PLB 25.67 (0-8172-3303-2) Raintree Steck-V.

Deegan, Paul J. The Arab-Israeli Conflict. LC 91-73073. 202p. (gr. 4 up). 1991. 13.99 (1-56239-028-7) Abdo & Dghtrs.

—Operation Desert Storm. LC 91-73078. (gr. 4 up). 1991. 13.99 (1-56239-023-6) Abdo & Dghtrs.

—Persian Gulf Nations. LC 91-73072. (gr. 4 up). 1991. 13.99 (1-56239-029-5) Abdo & Dghtrs.

Hall, George. Hot Wings of Desert Storm. (Illus.). 32p. 1991. pap. 2.50 (1-56156-025-1) Kidsbks.

King, John. Kurds. LC 93-35568. (Illus.). 48p. (gr. 6-10). 1994. 16.95 (1-56847-149-1) Thomson Lrning.

Operation Desert Shield. LC 91-730. (gr. 4 up). 13.99 (0-685-65289-0) Abdo & Dghtrs.

Steins, Richard. The Mideast after the Gulf War. LC 91-29944. (Illus.). 64p. (gr. 5-8). 1992. PLB 15.90 (1-56294-156-9) Millbrook Pr.

NEAR EAST–POLITICS

Abodaher, David J. Youth in the Middle East: Voices of Despair. (Illus.). 112p. (gr. 9-12). 1990. PLB 13.40 (0-531-10961-5) Watts.

Dudley, William, ed. The Middle East: Opposing Viewpoints. LC 91-43280. (Illus.). 264p. (gr. 10 up). 1992. PLB 17.95 (0-89908-185-1); pap. text ed. 9.95 (0-89908-160-6) Greenhaven.

Foster, Leila M. The Story of the Persian Gulf War. LC 91-4037. (Illus.). 32p. (gr. 3-6). 1991. PLB 12.30 (0-516-04762-0); pap. 3.95 (0-516-44762-9) Childrens.

Long, Cathryn J. Middle East in Search of Peace. LC 93-42274. (Illus.). 64p. (gr. 5-8). 1994. PLB 15.90 (1-56294-510-6) Millbrook Pr.

Nardo, Don. The Persian Gulf War. LC 91-23064. (Illus.). 112p. (gr. 5-8). 1991. PLB 17.95 (1-56006-411-0) Lucent Bks.

Steins, Richard. Mideast after the Gulf War. 1992. pap. 4.95 (0-395-62471-1) HM.

NEBRASKA

Carole Marsh Nebraska Books, 44 bks. 1994. PLB 1027.80 set (0-7933-1302-3); pap. 587.80 set (0-7933-5176-6) Gallopade Pub Group.

Carpenter, Allan. Nebraska. LC 78-10480. (Illus.). 96p. (gr. 4 up). 1979. PLB 16.95 (0-516-04127-4) Childrens.

Fradin, Dennis. Nebraska: In Words & Pictures. LC 79-19456. (Illus.). 48p. (gr. 2-5). 1980. PLB 12.95 (0-516-03927-X) Childrens.

Hargrove, Jim. Nebraska. LC 88-11746. (Illus.). 144p. (gr. 4 up). 1988. PLB 20.55 (0-516-00473-5) Childrens.

—Nebraska. 177p. 1993. text ed. 15.40 (1-56956-140-0) W A T Braille.

Hutchinson, Duane. A Storyteller's Hometown. LC 88-82706. (Illus.). 316p. (Orig.). (gr. 7 up). 1989. pap. 9.95 (0-934988-19-6) Foun Bks.

Manley, Robert N. Nebraska: Our Pioneer Heritage. Warp, Eric & Elley, Charles, illus. 197p. (gr. 4-6). 1981. text ed. 7.50 (0-939644-00-2); tchr's. guide 50 pgs. 4.00 (0-939644-01-0) Media Pub.

Marsh, Carole. Avast, Ye Slobs!: Nebraska Pirate Trivia. (Illus.). (gr. 3 up). 1994. PLB 24.95 (0-7933-0739-2); pap. 14.95 (0-7933-0738-4); computer disk 29.95 (0-7933-0740-6) Gallopade Pub Group.

—The Beast of the Nebraska Bed & Breakfast. (Illus.). (gr. 3 up). 1994. PLB 24.95 (0-7933-1752-5); pap. 14.95 (0-7933-1753-3); computer disk 29.95 (0-7933-1754-1) Gallopade Pub Group.

—Bow Wow! Nebraska Dogs in History, Mystery, Legend, Lore, Humor & More! (Illus.). (gr. 3-12). 1994. PLB 24.95 (0-7933-3548-5); pap. 14.95 (0-7933-3549-3); computer disk 29.95 (0-7933-3550-7) Gallopade Pub Group.

—Chill Out: Scary Nebraska Tales Based on Frightening Nebraska Truths. (Illus.). 1994. lib. bdg. 24.95 (0-7933-4735-1); pap. 14.95 (0-7933-4736-X); disk 29.95 (0-7933-4737-8) Gallopade Pub Group.

—Christopher Columbus Comes to Nebraska! Includes Reproducible Activities for Kids! (Illus.). (gr. 3-12). 1994. PLB 24.95 (0-7933-3701-1); pap. 14.95 (0-7933-3702-X); computer disk 29.95 (0-7933-3703-8) Gallopade Pub Group.

—The Hard-to-Believe-But-True! Book of Nebraska History, Mystery, Trivia, Legend, Lore, Humor & More. (Illus.). (gr. 3 up). 1994. PLB 24.95 (0-7933-0736-8); pap. 14.95 (0-7933-0735-X); computer disk 29.95 (0-7933-0737-6) Gallopade Pub Group.

—If My Nebraska Mama Ran the World! (Illus.). (gr. 3 up). 1994. PLB 24.95 (0-7933-1755-X); pap. 14.95 (0-7933-1756-8); computer disk 29.95 (0-7933-1757-6) Gallopade Pub Group.

—Jurassic Ark! Nebraska Dinosaurs & Other Prehistoric Creatures. (gr. k-12). 1994. PLB 24.95 (0-7933-7509-6); pap. 14.95 (0-7933-7510-X); computer disk 29.95 (0-7933-7511-8) Gallopade Pub Group.

—Let's Quilt Nebraska & Stuff It Topographically! (Illus.). (gr. 3 up). 1994. PLB 24.95 (1-55609-781-6); pap. 14.95 (1-55609-779-4); computer disk 29.95 (1-55609-783-2) Gallopade Pub Group.

—Let's Quilt Our Nebraska County. 1994. lib. bdg. 24.95 (0-7933-7194-5); pap. text ed. 14.95 (0-7933-7195-3); disk 29.95 (0-7933-7196-1) Gallopade Pub Group.

—Let's Quilt Our Nebraska Town. 1994. lib. bdg. 24.95 (0-7933-7044-2); pap. text ed. 14.95 (0-7933-7045-0); disk 29.95 (0-7933-7046-9) Gallopade Pub Group.

—Meow! Nebraska Cats in History, Mystery, Legend, Lore, Humor & More! (Illus.). (gr. 3-12). 1994. PLB 24.95 (0-7933-3395-4); pap. 14.95 (0-7933-3396-2); computer disk 29.95 (0-7933-3397-0) Gallopade Pub Group.

—My First Book about Nebraska. (gr. k-4). 1994. PLB 24.95 (0-7933-5650-4); pap. 14.95 (0-7933-5651-2); computer disk 29.95 (0-7933-5652-0) Gallopade Pub Group.

—Nebraska & Other State Greats (Biographies) (Illus.). (gr. 3 up). 1994. PLB 24.95 (1-55609-796-4); pap. 14.95 (1-55609-797-2); computer disk 29.95 (1-55609-798-0) Gallopade Pub Group.

—Nebraska Bandits, Bushwackers, Outlaws, Crooks, Devils, Ghosts, Desperadoes & Other Assorted & Sundry Characters! (Illus.). (gr. 3 up). 1994. PLB 24.95 (0-7933-0721-X); pap. 14.95 (0-7933-0720-1); computer disk 29.95 (0-7933-0722-8) Gallopade Pub Group.

—Nebraska Bandits, Bushwackers, Outlaws, Crooks, Devils, Ghosts, Desperadoes & Other Assorted & Sundry Characters. 1994. wkbk. 6.95 (0-7933-6811-1) Gallopade Pub Group.

—Nebraska Classic Christmas Trivia: Stories, Recipes, Activities, Legends, Lore & More! (Illus.). (gr. 3 up). 1994. PLB 24.95 (0-7933-0724-4); pap. 14.95 (0-7933-0723-6); computer disk 29.95 (0-7933-0725-2) Gallopade Pub Group.

—Nebraska Coastales. (Illus.). (gr. 3 up). 1994. PLB 24.95 (1-55609-790-5); pap. 14.95 (1-55609-791-3); computer disk 29.95 (1-55609-792-1) Gallopade Pub Group.

—Nebraska Coastales. 1994. lib. bdg. 24.95 (0-7933-7292-5) Gallopade Pub Group.

—Nebraska "Crinkum-Crankum" A Funny Word Book about Our State. (Illus.). 1994. lib. bdg. 24.95 (0-7933-4889-7); pap. 14.95 (0-7933-4890-0); disk 29.95 (0-7933-4891-9) Gallopade Pub Group.

—Nebraska Dingbats! Bk. 1: A Fun Book of Games, Stories, Activities & More about Our State That's All in Code! for You to Decipher. (Illus.). (gr. 3-12). 1994. PLB 24.95 (0-7933-3854-9); pap. 14.95 (0-7933-3855-7); computer disk 29.95 (0-7933-3856-5) Gallopade Pub Group.

—Nebraska Festival Fun for Kids! (Illus.). (gr. 3-12). 1994. lib. bdg. 24.95 (0-7933-4007-1); pap. 14.95 (0-7933-4008-X); disk 29.95 (0-7933-4009-8) Gallopade Pub Group.

—Nebraska Jeopardy! Answers & Questions about Our State! (Illus.). (gr. 3-12). 1994. PLB 24.95 (0-7933-4160-4); pap. 14.95 (0-7933-4161-2); computer disk 29.95 (0-7933-4162-0) Gallopade Pub Group.

—Nebraska "Jography" A Fun Run thru Our State. (Illus.). (gr. 3 up). 1994. PLB 24.95 (1-55609-778-6); pap. 14.95 (0-685-45948-9); computer disk 29.95 (1-55609-780-8) Gallopade Pub Group.

—Nebraska Jography: Answers & Questions about Our State. 1994. wkbk. 6.95 (0-7933-6810-3) Gallopade Pub Group.

—Nebraska Kid's Cookbook: Recipes, How-To, History, Lore & More! (Illus.). (gr. 3 up). 1994. PLB 24.95 (0-7933-0733-3); pap. 14.95 (0-7933-0732-5); computer disk 29.95 (0-7933-0734-1) Gallopade Pub Group.

—The Nebraska Mystery Van Takes Off! Book 1: Handicapped Nebraska Kids Sneak off on a Big Adventure. (Illus.). (gr. 3-12). 1994. 24.95 (0-7933-5042-5); pap. 14.95 (0-7933-5043-3); computer disk 29.95 (0-7933-5044-1) Gallopade Pub Group.

—Nebraska Quiz Bowl Crash Course! (Illus.). (gr. 3 up). 1994. PLB 24.95 (1-55609-793-X); pap. 14.95 (1-55609-794-8); computer disk 29.95 (1-55609-795-6) Gallopade Pub Group.

—Nebraska Rollercoasters! (Illus.). (gr. 3-12). 1994. PLB 24.95 (0-7933-5305-X); pap. 14.95 (0-7933-5306-8); computer disk 29.95 (0-7933-5307-6) Gallopade Pub Group.

—Nebraska School Trivia: An Amazing & Fascinating Look at Our State's Teachers, Schools & Students! (Illus.). (gr. 3 up). 1994. PLB 24.95 (0-7933-0730-9); pap. 14.95 (0-7933-0729-5); computer disk 29.95 (0-7933-0731-7) Gallopade Pub Group.

—Nebraska Silly Basketball Sportsmysteries, Vol. I. (Illus.). (gr. 3 up). 1994. PLB 24.95 (0-7933-0727-9); pap. 14.95 (0-7933-0726-0); computer disk 29.95 (0-7933-0728-7) Gallopade Pub Group.

—Nebraska Silly Basketball Sportsmysteries, Vol. II. (Illus.). (gr. 3 up). 1994. PLB 24.95 (0-7933-1758-4); pap. 14.95 (0-7933-1759-2); computer disk 29.95 (0-7933-1760-6) Gallopade Pub Group.

—Nebraska Silly Football Sportsmysteries, Vol. I. (Illus.). (gr. 3 up). 1994. PLB 24.95 (1-55609-784-0); pap. 14.95 (1-55609-785-9); computer disk 29.95 (1-55609-786-7) Gallopade Pub Group.

—Nebraska Silly Football Sportsmysteries, Vol. II. (Illus.). (gr. 3 up). 1994. PLB 24.95 (1-55609-787-5); pap. 14.95 (1-55609-788-3); computer disk 29.95 (1-55609-789-1) Gallopade Pub Group.

—Nebraska Silly Trivia! (Illus.). (gr. 3 up). 1994. PLB 24.95 (1-55609-775-1); pap. 14.95 (1-55609-776-X); computer disk 29.95 (1-55609-777-8) Gallopade Pub Group.

—Nebraska Silly Trivia. 1994. wkbk. 6.95 (0-7933-6809-X) Gallopade Pub Group.

—Nebraska Timeline: A Chronology of Nebraska History, Mystery, Trivia, Legend, Lore & More. (Illus.). (gr. 3-12). 1994. PLB 24.95 (0-7933-5956-2); pap. 14.95 (0-7933-5957-0); computer disk 29.95 (0-7933-5958-9) Gallopade Pub Group.

—Nebraska's (Most Devastating!) Disasters & (Most Calamitous!) Catastrophies! (Illus.). (gr. 3 up). 1994. PLB 24.95 (0-7933-0718-X); pap. 14.95 (0-7933-0717-1) (0-7933-0719-8) Gallopade Pub Group.

—Nebraska's Unsolved Mysteries (& Their "Solutions") Includes Scientific Information & Other Activities for Students. (Illus.). (gr. 3-12). 1994. PLB 24.95 (0-7933-5803-5); pap. 14.95 (0-7933-5804-3); computer disk 29.95 (0-7933-5805-1) Gallopade Pub Group.

—Patch, the Pirate Dog: A Nebraska Pet Story. (ps-4). 1994. PLB 24.95 (0-7933-5497-8); pap. 14.95 (0-7933-5498-6); computer disk 29.95 (0-7933-5499-4) Gallopade Pub Group.

—Uncle Rebus: Nebraska Picture Stories for Computer Kids. (Illus.). (gr. k-3). 1994. PLB 24.95 (0-7933-4582-0); pap. 14.95 (0-7933-4583-9); disk 29.95 (0-7933-4584-7) Gallopade Pub Group.

Murray, Eleanor H. Growing up in Aunt Molly's Omaha, 1920-1965: And Facing the World Beyond. (Illus.). 140p. (Orig.). (gr. 9-12). 1990. pap. 8.95 (1-879313-00-6) Murrays Leprechaun Bks.

Prairie-Plains Resource Institute Staff & Whitney, William S. Microcosm of the Platte: A Guide to Bader Memorial Park Natural Area. Whitney, Jan & Twedt, Curt, eds. Whitney, William S., illus. 140p. (Orig.). (gr. 10-12). 1988. pap. text ed. 10.00 (0-945614-00-4) Prairie Plains Res Inst.

Thompson, Kathleen. Nebraska. LC 87-264855. 48p. (gr. 3 up). 1988. 19.97 (0-86514-473-7) Raintree Steck-V.

NEBRASKA–FICTION

Cavanaugh, Kate. Pete & His Elves Series. Kiner, K. C., illus. 28p. 1992. Set. pap. write for info. (0-9622353-4-2) KAC.

Cross, Gillian. The Great American Elephant Chase. LC 92-54492. 160p. (gr. 4-7). 1993. 14.95 (0-8234-1016-1) Holiday.

—The Great American Elephant Chase. 208p. (gr. 5 up). 1994. pap. 3.99 (0-14-037014-5) Puffin Bks.

Morris, Gilbert. The Union Belle. 302p. (Orig.). 1992. pap. 8.99 (1-55661-186-2) Bethany Hse.

Richardson, Arleta. Whistle-Stop West. LC 92-46260. 1993. pap. 4.99 (0-7814-0922-5, Chariot Bks) Chariot Family.

Saban, Vera. Jennie Barnes: Right Now Forever. Mills, Janie, illus. LC 90-39763. 130p. (Orig.). (gr. 4-6). 1990. pap. 6.95 (0-914565-34-6, Timbertrails) Capstan Pubns.

Stahl, Hilda. Sadie Rose & the Mysterious Stranger. 128p. (Orig.). (gr. 6-9). 1993. pap. 4.99 (0-89107-747-2) Crossway Bks.

NECROMANCY

see Divination; Witchcraft

NEEDLEWORK

see also names of needlework; e.g. Dressmaking; Embroidery; Sewing; Tapestry

Castor, H. Starting Needlecraft. (Illus.). 32p. (ps-2). 1994. PLB 12.96 (0-88110-206-7, Usborne); pap. 4.95 (0-7460-1664-6, Usborne) EDC.

Hall, Dorthea. Needlecraft. Harrison, Harry, illus. Forrester, Paul & Wilder, Chas, photos by. (Illus.). 48p. (gr. 9 up). 1994. incl. components 19.95 (0-8431-3665-0) Price Stern.

Messent, Jan. Wool 'n Magic: Creative Uses of Yarn... Knitting, Crochet, Embroidery. Dawson, Pam, ed. Search Press Studios Staff, illus. 144p. 1989. 32.95 (0-85532-614-X, Pub. by Search Pr UK) A Schwartz & Co.

O'Reilly, Susie. Needle Craft. Mukhida, Zul, photos by. (Illus.). 32p. (gr. 4-6). 1994. 14.95 (1-56847-220-X) Thomson Lrning.

NEFERTITI, QUEEN OF EGYPT, 14TH CENTURY B.C.

Holmes, Burnham. Nefertiti: The Mystery Queen. LC 77-10445. (Illus.). 48p. (gr. 4-5). 1983. PLB 20.70 (0-8172-1056-3) Raintree Steck-V.

NEGRO ARTISTS

see Black Artists

NEGRO ATHLETES

see Black Athletes

NEGRO AUTHORS

see Black Authors

NEGRO FOLKLORE

see Black Folklore

NEGRO MUSICIANS

see Black Musicians

NEGRO NATIONALISM

see Black Muslims

NEGRO POETRY

see Black Poetry

NEGROES

see Blacks

NEGROES IN ART

see Blacks in Literature and Art

NEGRO RACE

see Blacks

NEGRO SPIRITUALS

see Spirituals

NEGROES IN BUSINESS

see Blacks–Employment

NEIGHBORHOOD

see Community Life

NEIGHBORHOOD SCHOOLS
see Schools
NEO-IMPRESSIONISM (ART)
see Impressionism (Art)
NEOLITHIC PERIOD
see Stone Age
NEPAL
Burbank, Jonathan. Nepal. LC 91-15866. (Illus.). 128p. (gr. 5-9). 1991. PLB 21.95 (*1-85435-401-9*) Marshall Cavendish.
Lerner Publications, Department of Geography Staff, ed. Nepal in Pictures. (Illus.). 64p. (gr. 5 up). 1989. 17.50 (*0-8225-1851-1*) Lerner Pubns.
Margolies, Barbara A. Kanu of Kathmandu: A Journey to Nepal. Margolies, Barbara, illus. LC 92-12482. 40p. (gr. 1-4). 1992. RSBE 14.95 (*0-02-762282-7*, Four Winds) Macmillan Child Grp.
San Suu Kyi Sung. Nepal. (Illus.). 96p. (gr. 5 up). 1988. 14.95 (*0-222-00981-0*) Chelsea Hse.
Turkovich, Marilyn, et al. Nepal: From Kathmandu to Mt. Everest. 180p. (gr. 6-12). 1983. pap. 10.95 (*0-685-55243-8*, 5116) World Eagle.
NERVOUS SYSTEM
see also Brain; Psychology, Pathological
Brain & Nervous System. 48p. (gr. 5-8). 1988. PLB 10.95 (*0-382-09703-3*) Silver Burdett Pr.
Edelson, Edward. Nervous System. (Illus.). 112p. (gr. 6-12). 1989. 18.95 (*0-7910-0023-0*) Chelsea Hse.
LeMaster, Leslie J. Your Brain & Nervous System. LC 84-7635. (Illus.). 48p. (gr. k-4). 1984. PLB 12.85 (*0-516-01931-7*); pap. 4.95 (*0-516-41931-5*) Childrens.
Parker, Steve. Brain & Nervous System. rev. ed. (gr. 5-7). 1990. PLB 12.90 (*0-531-14026-1*) Watts.
—The Brain & Nervous System. rev. ed. (Illus.). 48p. (gr. 5-8). 1991. pap. 6.95 (*0-531-24600-0*) Watts.
—Nerves to Senses: Projects with Biology. LC 91-8737. (Illus.). 32p. (gr. 5-8). 1991. PLB 12.40 (*0-531-17295-3*, Gloucester Pr) Watts.
Ralston, Diane D. & Ralston, Henry J., III. The Nerve Cell. Head, J. J., ed. Imrick, Ann T., illus. LC 84-45836. 16p. (Orig.). (gr. 10 up). 1988. pap. text ed. 2.75 (*0-89278-357-5*, 45-9757) Carolina Biological.
Silverstein, Alvin & Silverstein, Virginia. Nervous System. (Illus.). 96p. (gr. 5-8). 1994. bds. 16.95 (*0-8050-2835-8*) TFC Bks NY.
NESTS
see Birds–Eggs and Nests
NETHERLANDS
Bailey, Donna. Netherlands. LC 91-20188. (Illus.). 32p. (gr. 1-4). 1992. PLB 18.99 (*0-8114-2565-7*) Raintree Steck-V.
Cumming, David. The Netherlands. LC 91-40478. (Illus.). 32p. (gr. k-4). 1992. PLB 12.40 (*0-531-18423-4*, Pub. by Bookwright Pr) Watts.
Fradin, Dennis B. The Netherlands. LC 82-17896. (Illus.). 128p. (gr. 5-9). 1983. PLB 20.55 (*0-516-02779-4*) Childrens.
Hunt, Christopher. Holland. (Illus.). 32p. (gr. 4-6). 1991. 17.95 (*0-237-60188-5*, Pub. by Evans Bros Ltd) Trafalgar.
Jacobsen, Karen. The Netherlands. LC 91-37974. (Illus.). 48p. (gr. k-4). 1992. PLB 20.55 (*0-516-01137-5*); pap. 4.95 (*0-516-41137-3*) Childrens.
James, Ian. The Netherlands. LC 89-49504. (Illus.). 32p. (gr. 5-8). 1990. PLB 11.90 (*0-531-14044-X*) Watts.
Netherlands in Pictures. 64p. (gr. 5 up). 1991. PLB 17.50 (*0-8225-1893-7*) Lerner Pubns.
Ozer, Steven. Netherlands. (Illus.). 104p. (gr. 5 up). 1990. 14.95 (*0-7910-1107-0*) Chelsea Hse.
Van Stegeren, Theo. The Land & People of the Netherlands. LC 90-47650. (Illus.). 256p. (gr. 6 up). 1992. 17.95 (*0-06-022537-8*); PLB 17.89 (*0-06-022538-6*) HarpC Child Bks.
NETHERLANDS–FICTION
Andersen, Hans Christian. The Tinderbox. Hutton, Warwick, adapted by. & illus. LC 88-9206. 32p. (gr. 1 up). 1988. SBE 14.95 (*0-689-50458-6*, M K McElderry) Macmillan Child Grp.
—Tinderbox, Vol. 1. (ps-9). 1990. 14.95 (*0-316-03938-1*) Little.
Birchman, David F. A Tale of Tulips, a Tale of Onions. Hunt, Jonathan, illus. LC 92-31240. 40p. (gr. 1-4). 1994. RSBE 15.95 (*0-02-710112-6*, Four Winds) Macmillan Child Grp.
DeJong, Meindert. Shadrach. Sendak, Maurice, illus. LC 53-5250. 192p. (gr. 3-6). 1953. PLB 14.89 (*0-06-021546-1*) HarpC Child Bks.
—Wheel on the School. Sendak, Maurice, illus. LC 54-8945. 256p. (gr. 4-7). 1954. 15.00 (*0-06-021585-2*); PLB 14.89 (*0-06-021586-0*) HarpC Child Bks.
Dodge, Mary M. Hans Brinker or The Silver Skates. 1993. pap. 2.50 (*0-8125-3342-9*) Tor Bks.
—Hans Brinker: The Silver Skates. LC 54-14472. (gr. 5 up). 1966. pap. 1.50 (*0-8049-0099-X*, CL-99) Airmont.
Green, Norma. The Hole in the Dyke. Carle, Eric, illus. LC 74-23562. 32p. (gr. k-3). 1975. (Crowell Jr Bks); PLB 15.89 (*0-690-00676-4*) HarpC Child Bks.
Green, Norma, retold by. The Hole in the Dike. Carle, Eric, illus. 32p. (ps-2). 1993. pap. 4.95 (*0-590-46146-X*) Scholastic Inc.
Krasilovsky, Phyllis. Cow Who Fell in the Canal. Spier, Peter, illus. LC 56-8236. 38p. (gr. k-1). 1985. pap. 11. 95 (*0-385-07585-5*) Doubleday.
Noble, Trinka H. Hansy's Mermaid. Noble, Trinka H., illus. LC 82-45509. 32p. (ps-2). 1983. PLB 10.89 (*0-8037-3606-1*) Dial Bks Young.
Shemin, Margaretha. The Little Riders. Spier, Peter, illus. 80p. (gr. 4 up). 1993. pap. 3.95 (*0-688-12499-2*, Pub. by Beech Tree Bks) Morrow.
Spier, Peter. Father, May I Come? LC 92-31328. 1993. 13.95 (*0-385-30935-X*) Doubleday.
Vos, Ida. Anna Is Still Here. Edelstein, Terese & Smidt, Inez, trs. from DUT. LC 92-1618. 144p. (gr. 3-7). 1993. 13.45 (*0-395-65368-1*) HM.
NETHERLANDS–HISTORY–GERMAN OCCUPATION, 1940-1945
Tames, Richard. Anne Frank. (Illus.). 32p. (gr. 5 up). 1991. pap. 5.95 (*0-531-24608-6*) Watts.
NEUROLOGY
see Nervous System
NEVADA
Aylesworth, Thomas G. & Aylesworth, Virginia L. The West (Arizona, Nevada, Utah) (Illus.). 64p. (gr. 3 up). 1992. PLB 16.95 (*0-7910-1049-X*) Chelsea Hse.
Carole Marsh Nevada Books, 44 bks. 1994. PLB 1027.80 set (*0-7933-1303-1*); pap. 587.80 set (*0-7933-5178-2*) Gallopade Pub Group.
Carpenter, Allan. Nevada. LC 79-4355. (Illus.). 96p. (gr. 4 up). 1979. PLB 16.95 (*0-516-04128-2*) Childrens.
Lillegard, Dee. Nevada. 195p. 1993. text ed. 15.40 (*1-56956-139-7*) W A T Braille.
Lillegard, Dee & Stoker, Wayne. Nevada. LC 90-34665. (Illus.). 144p. (gr. 4 up). 1990. PLB 20.55 (*0-516-00474-3*) Childrens.
Lynch, Don & Thompson, David. Battleborn Nevada: Its People, History & Stories. Bean, James H., ed. Horton, Verne, illus. LC 93-79470. 360p. (gr. 6 up). 1994. 31.00 (*0-913205-20-6*) Grace Dangberg.
Marsh, Carole. Avast, Ye Slobs! Nevada Pirate Trivia. (Illus.). 1994. PLB 24.95 (*0-7933-0763-5*); pap. 14.95 (*0-7933-0762-7*); computer disk 29.95 (*0-7933-0764-3*) Gallopade Pub Group.
—The Beast of the Nevada Bed & Breakfast. (Illus.). 1994. PLB 24.95 (*0-7933-1761-4*); pap. 14.95 (*0-7933-1762-2*); computer disk 29.95 (*0-7933-1763-0*) Gallopade Pub Group.
—Bow Wow! Nevada Dogs in History, Mystery, Legend, Lore, Humor & More! (Illus.). (gr. 3-12). 1994. PLB 24.95 (*0-7933-3551-5*); pap. 14.95 (*0-7933-3552-3*); computer disk 29.95 (*0-7933-3553-1*) Gallopade Pub Group.
—Chill Out: Scary Nevada Tales Based on Frightening Nevada Truths. (Illus.). 1994. lib. bdg. 24.95 (*0-7933-4738-6*); pap. 14.95 (*0-7933-4739-4*); disk 29. 95 (*0-7933-4740-8*) Gallopade Pub Group.
—Christopher Columbus Comes to Nevada! Includes Reproducible Activities for Kids! (Illus.). (gr. 3-12). 1994. PLB 24.95 (*0-7933-3704-6*); pap. 14.95 (*0-7933-3705-4*); computer disk 29.95 (*0-7933-3706-2*) Gallopade Pub Group.
—The Hard-to-Believe-But-True! Book of Nevada History, Mystery, Trivia, Legend, Lore, Humor & More. (Illus.). 1994. PLB 24.95 (*0-7933-0760-0*); pap. 14.95 (*0-7933-0759-7*); computer disk 29.95 (*0-7933-0761-9*) Gallopade Pub Group.
—If My Nevada Mama Ran the World! (Illus.). 1994. lib. bdg. 24.95 (*0-7933-1764-9*); pap. 14.95 (*0-7933-1765-7*); computer disk 29.95 (*0-7933-1766-5*) Gallopade Pub Group.
—Jurassic Ark! Nevada Dinosaurs & Other Prehistoric Creatures. (gr. k-12). 1994. PLB 24.95 (*0-7933-7512-6*); pap. 14.95 (*0-7933-7513-4*); computer disk 29.95 (*0-7933-7514-2*) Gallopade Pub Group.
—Let's Quilt Nevada & Stuff It Topographically! (Illus.). 1994. PLB 24.95 (*1-55609-805-7*); pap. 14.95 (*1-55609-130-3*); computer disk 29.95 (*1-55609-807-3*) Gallopade Pub Group.
—Let's Quilt Our Nevada County. 1994. lib. bdg. 24.95 (*0-7933-7197-X*); pap. text ed. 14.95 (*0-7933-7198-8*); disk 29.95 (*0-7933-7199-6*) Gallopade Pub Group.
—Let's Quilt Our Nevada Town. 1994. lib. bdg. 24.95 (*0-7933-7047-7*); pap. text ed. 14.95 (*0-7933-7048-5*); disk 29.95 (*0-7933-7049-3*) Gallopade Pub Group.
—Meow! Nevada Cats in History, Mystery, Legend, Lore, Humor & More! (Illus.). (gr. 3-12). 1994. PLB 24.95 (*0-7933-3398-9*); pap. 14.95 (*0-7933-3399-7*); computer disk 29.95 (*0-685-41935-5*) Gallopade Pub Group.
—My First Book about Nevada. (gr. k-4). 1994. PLB 24. 95 (*0-7933-5653-9*); pap. 14.95 (*0-7933-5654-7*); computer disk 29.95 (*0-7933-5655-5*) Gallopade Pub Group.
—Nevada & Other State Greats (Biographies) (Illus.). 1994. PLB 24.95 (*1-55609-820-0*); pap. 14.95 (*1-55609-821-9*); computer disk 29.95 (*1-55609-822-7*) Gallopade Pub Group.
—Nevada Bandits, Bushwackers, Outlaws, Crooks, Devils, Ghosts, Desperadoes & Other Assorted & Sundry Characters! (Illus.). 1994. PLB 24.95 (*0-7933-0745-7*); pap. 14.95 (*0-7933-0744-9*); computer disk 29.95 (*0-7933-0746-5*) Gallopade Pub Group.
—Nevada Classic Christmas Trivia: Stories, Recipes, Activities, Legends, Lore & More! (Illus.). 1994. PLB 24.95 (*0-7933-0748-1*); pap. 14.95 (*0-7933-0747-3*); computer disk 29.95 (*0-7933-0749-X*) Gallopade Pub Group.
—Nevada Coastales. (Illus.). 1994. PLB 24.95 (*1-55609-814-6*); pap. 14.95 (*1-55609-815-4*); computer disk 29.95 (*1-55609-816-2*) Gallopade Pub Group.
—Nevada Coastales! 1994. lib. bdg. 24.95 (*0-7933-7293-3*) Gallopade Pub Group.
—Nevada "Crinkum-Crankum" A Funny Word Book about Our State. (Illus.). 1994. lib. bdg. 24.95 (*0-7933-4892-7*); pap. 14.95 (*0-7933-4893-5*); disk 29. 95 (*0-7933-4894-3*) Gallopade Pub Group.
—Nevada Dingbats! Bk. 1: A Fun Book of Games, Stories, Activities & More about Our State That's All in Code! for You to Decipher. (Illus.). (gr. 3-12). 1994. PLB 24.95 (*0-7933-3857-3*); pap. 14.95 (*0-7933-3858-1*); computer disk 29.95 (*0-7933-3859-X*) Gallopade Pub Group.
—Nevada Festival Fun for Kids! (Illus.). (gr. 3-12). 1994. lib. bdg. 24.95 (*0-7933-4010-1*); pap. 14.95 (*0-7933-4011-X*); disk 29.95 (*0-7933-4012-8*) Gallopade Pub Group.
—The Nevada Hot Air Balloon Mystery. (Illus.). (gr. 2-9). 1994. 24.95 (*0-7933-2570-6*); pap. 14.95 (*0-7933-2571-4*); computer disk 29.95 (*0-7933-2572-2*) Gallopade Pub Group.
—Nevada Jeopardy! Answers & Questions about Our State! (Illus.). (gr. 3-12). 1994. PLB 24.95 (*0-7933-4163-9*); pap. 14.95 (*0-7933-4164-7*); computer disk 29.95 (*0-7933-4165-5*) Gallopade Pub Group.
—Nevada "Jography" A Fun Run Thru Our State! (Illus.). 1994. PLB 24.95 (*1-55609-802-2*); pap. 14.95 (*1-55609-803-0*); computer disk 29.95 (*1-55609-804-9*) Gallopade Pub Group.
—Nevada Kid's Cookbook: Recipes, How-to, History, Lore & More! (Illus.). 1994. PLB 24.95 (*0-7933-0757-0*); pap. 14.95 (*0-7933-0756-2*); computer disk 29.95 (*0-7933-0758-9*) Gallopade Pub Group.
—The Nevada Mystery Van Takes Off! Book 1: Handicapped Nevada Kids Sneak Off on a Big Adventure. (Illus.). (gr. 3-12). 1994. 24.95 (*0-7933-5045-X*); pap. 14.95 (*0-7933-5046-8*); computer disk 29.95 (*0-7933-5047-6*) Gallopade Pub Group.
—Nevada Quiz Bowl Crash Course! (Illus.). 1994. PLB 24.95 (*1-55609-817-0*); pap. 14.95 (*1-55609-818-9*); computer disk 29.95 (*1-55609-819-7*) Gallopade Pub Group.
—Nevada Rollercoasters! (Illus.). (gr. 3-12). 1994. PLB 24.95 (*0-7933-5308-4*); pap. 14.95 (*0-7933-5309-2*); computer disk 29.95 (*0-7933-5310-6*) Gallopade Pub Group.
—Nevada School Trivia: An Amazing & Fascinating Look at Our State's Teachers, Schools & Students! (Illus.). 1994. PLB 24.95 (*0-7933-0754-6*); pap. 14.95 (*0-7933-0753-8*); computer disk 29.95 (*0-7933-0755-4*) Gallopade Pub Group.
—Nevada Silly Basketball Sportsmystereis, Vol. 2. (Illus.). 1994. PLB 24.95 (*0-7933-1767-3*); pap. 14.95 (*0-7933-1768-1*); computer disk 29.95 (*0-7933-1769-X*) Gallopade Pub Group.
—Nevada Silly Basketball Sportsmysteries, Vol. 1. (Illus.). 1994. PLB 24.95 (*0-7933-0751-1*); pap. 14.95 (*0-7933-0750-3*); computer disk 29.95 (*0-7933-0752-X*) Gallopade Pub Group.
—Nevada Silly Football Sportsmysteries, Vol. 1. (Illus.). 1994. PLB 24.95 (*1-55609-808-1*); pap. 14.95 (*1-55609-809-X*); computer disk 29.95 (*1-55609-810-3*) Gallopade Pub Group.
—Nevada Silly Football Sportsmysteries, Vol. 2. (Illus.). 1994. PLB 24.95 (*1-55609-811-1*); pap. 14.95 (*1-55609-812-X*); computer disk 29.95 (*1-55609-813-8*) Gallopade Pub Group.
—Nevada Silly Trivia! (Illus.). 1994. PLB 24.95 (*1-55609-799-9*); pap. 14.95 (*1-55609-800-6*); computer disk 29.95 (*1-55609-801-4*) Gallopade Pub Group.
—Nevada Timeline: A Chronology of Nevada History, Mystery, Trivia, Legend, Lore & More. (Illus.). (gr. 3-12). 1994. PLB 24.95 (*0-7933-5959-7*); pap. 14.95 (*0-7933-5960-0*); computer disk 29.95 (*0-7933-5961-9*) Gallopade Pub Group.
—Nevada's (Most Devastating!) Disasters & (Most Calamitous!) Castastrophies! (Illus.). 1994. PLB 24.95 (*0-7933-0742-2*); pap. 14.95 (*0-7933-0741-4*); computer disk 29.95 (*0-7933-0743-0*) Gallopade Pub Group.
—Nevada's Unsolved Mysteries (& Their "Solutions") Includes Scientific Information & Other Activities for Students. (Illus.). (gr. 3-12). 1994. PLB 24.95 (*0-7933-5806-X*); pap. 14.95 (*0-7933-5807-8*); computer disk 29.95 (*0-7933-5808-6*) Gallopade Pub Group.
—Patch, the Pirate Dog: A Nevada Pet Story. (ps-4). 1994. PLB 24.95 (*0-7933-5500-1*); pap. 14.95 (*0-7933-5501-X*); computer disk 29.95 (*0-7933-5502-8*) Gallopade Pub Group.
—Uncle Rebus: Nevada Picture Stories for Computer Kids. (Illus.). (gr. k-3). 1994. PLB 24.95 (*0-7933-4585-5*); pap. 14.95 (*0-7933-4586-3*); disk 29. 95 (*0-7933-4587-1*) Gallopade Pub Group.
Miluck, Nancy B. Nevada: This Is Our Land. rev. & updated ed. Miluck, Mary G. & Miluck, Nancy C., illus. 200p. (gr. 7 up). 1994. pap. 15.00 (*0-9606382-7-X*) Dragon Ent.
Root, Phyllis & McCormick, Maxine. Great Basin. LC 88-18645. (Illus.). 48p. (gr. 4-5). 1988. text ed. 13.95 RSBE (*0-89686-410-3*, Crestwood Hse) Macmillan Child Grp.
Sitvaitis, Karen. Nevada. Lerner Geography Department Staff, ed. (Illus.). 72p. (gr. 4-7). 1992. 17.50 (*0-8225-2719-7*) Lerner Pubns.

Thompson, David. Nevada: A History of Changes. Dickerson, Donald, ed. Barker, Bill, illus. Thompson, David, intro. by. LC 86-82332. (Illus.). 232p. (Orig.). (ps-6). 1986. pap. text ed. 17.50 (*0-913205-09-5*); special price 10.50 (*0-685-73849-3*) Grace Dangberg.
Thompson, Kathleen. Nevada. 48p. (gr. 3 up). 1985. PLB 19.97 (*0-86514-437-0*); pap. text ed. 9.27 (*0-86514-512-1*) Raintree Steck-V.

NEVADA–FICTION

Bly, Stephen. Coyote True. LC 92-8224. 128p. 1992. pap. 4.99 (*0-89107-680-8*) Crossway Bks.
—You Can Always Trust a Spotted Horse. LC 92-46667. 128p. (Orig.). (gr. 4-7). 1993. pap. 4.99 (*0-89107-716-2*) Crossway Bks.
Kelso, Mary J. Sierra Summer. Kelso, Mary J., illus. 120p. (Orig.). (gr. 6 up). 1992. pap. 6.95 (*0-9621406-3-5*) Markel Pr.

NEW ENGLAND

Aylesworth, Thomas G. & Aylesworth, Virginia L. Northern New England: Maine - Vermont - New Hampshire. (Illus.). 64p. (gr. 3 up). 1990. lib. bdg. 16.95 (*0-7910-1037-6*) Chelsea Hse.
—Southern New England: Connecticut - Massachusetts - Rhode Island. (Illus.). 64p. (gr. 3 up). 1990. lib. bdg. 16.95 (*0-7910-1038-4*) Chelsea Hse.
—Southern New England (Connecticut, Massachusetts, Rhode Island) LC 87-17880. (Illus.). 64p. (Orig.). (gr. 3 up). 1988. lib. bdg. 16.95 (*1-55546-552-8*); pap. 6.95 (*0-7910-0544-5*) Chelsea Hse.
Crump, Donald J., ed. New England: Land of Scenic Splendor. (Illus.). 1989. 9.95 (*0-87044-715-7*); lib. bdg. 12.95 (*0-87044-720-3*) Natl Geog.
Frost, Ed & Frost, Roon. Just for Kids: The New England Guide & Activity Book for Young Travelers. Leach, Carol, illus. 150p. (Orig.). (ps-5). 1989. pap. 7.95 (*0-9618806-2-7*) Glove Compart Bks.
Mathieu, Joe. The Olden Days. Mathieu, Joe, illus. 32p. (ps-3). 1981. lib. bdg. 4.99 (*0-394-94085-7*) Random Bks Yng Read.
Norris, Joan D. & Forsberg, Barbara. New England. LC 93-49006. 1994. write for info. (*0-86625-510-9*) Rourke Pubns.
Stone, Lynn M. Old New England. LC 93-22881. 1993. write for info. (*0-86593-303-0*) Rourke Corp.

NEW ENGLAND–FICTION

Alcott, Louisa May. Eight Cousins. (gr. 7 up). 1974. 19.95 (*0-316-03091-0*) Little.
—Jack & Jill. (gr. 5 up). 1979. 17.95 (*0-316-03092-9*) Little.
—Little Men. Brich, Reginald, illus. (gr. 7 up). 1971. 19.95 (*0-316-03094-5*) Little.
—Little Women. (Illus.). (gr. 6 up). 1966. pap. 2.95 (*0-8049-0106-6*, CL-106) Airmont.
—Little Women. Magagna, Anna M. & Jambor, Louis, illus. (gr. 4-6). 1981. (G&D); deluxe ed. 15.95 (*0-448-06019-1*) Putnam Pub Group.
—Little Women. (gr. 6 up). 1974. 250.00 (*0-8490-0547-7*) Gordon Pr.
—Little Women. Smith, Jessie W., illus. (gr. 7 up). 1968. 19.95 (*0-316-03095-3*) Little.
—Little Women. 320p. (gr. 3-7). 1983. pap. 2.25 (*0-14-035008-X*, Puffin) Puffin Bks.
—Little Women. (gr. 5 up). 1963. 37.50 (*0-685-20188-0*, 144-7) Saphrograph.
—Little Women. (gr. 6 up). 1983. Repr. lib. bdg. 18.95x (*0-89966-408-3*) Buccaneer Bks.
—Little Women. Douglas, Ann, intro. by. 480p. (gr. 3 up). 1983. pap. 3.95 (*0-451-52341-5*, Sig Classic) NAL-Dutton.
—Little Women. Edwards, Gunvor, illus. Gliberry, Lysbeth, retold by. (Illus.). 48p. (gr. 7-12). 1975. pap. text ed. 3.25x (*0-19-421804-X*) OUP.
—Little Women. LC 62-20197. (gr. 4 up). 1986. pap. 5.00 (*0-02-041240-1*, Collier Young Ad) Macmillan Child Grp.
—Little Women. Smith, Jessie W. & Merrill, Frank, illus. 400p. (gr. 2 up). 1988. 12.99 (*0-517-63489-9*) Random Hse Value.
—Little Women. (Orig.). (gr. k-6). 1987. pap. 6.95 (*0-440-44768-2*, Pub. by Yearling Classics) Dell.
—Little Women. Showalter, Elaine, intro. by. 608p. 1989. pap. 5.95 (*0-14-039069-3*, Penguin Classics) Viking Penguin.
—Little Women. 1989. Repr. of 1867 ed. lib. bdg. 79.00 (*0-7812-1627-3*) Rprt Serv.
—Little Women. Auerbach, Nina, afterword by. 480p. 1983. pap. 3.95 (*0-553-21275-3*, Bantam Classics Spectra) Bantam.
—Little Women. large type ed. 336p. 1987. 15.95 (*0-7089-8384-7*, Charnwood) Ulverscroft.
—Little Women. 1986. pap. 3.25 (*0-590-43797-6*, Apple Paperbacks) Scholastic Inc.
—Little Women. 1988. 2.98 (*0-671-09222-7*) S&S Trade.
—Little Women. Kulling, Monica, adapted by. LC 93-38237. 108p. (gr. 2-6). 1994. pap. 3.50 (*0-679-86175-0*, Bullseye Bks) Random Bks Yng Read.
—Little Women. LC 94-5865. 1994. 15.95 (*0-679-43642-1*, Evrymans Lib Childs) Knopf.
—Little Women, Vol. 1: Four Funny Sisters. Lindskoog, Kathryn, ed. (Illus.). (gr. 3-7). 1991. pap. 4.99 (*0-88070-437-3*, Gold & Honey) Questar Pubs.
—Old-Fashioned Girl. Abbot, Elenore, illus. (gr. 7 up). 1969. 19.95 (*0-316-03096-1*) Little.
—An Old Fashioned Thanksgiving. Wheeler, Jody, illus. LC 93-20352. 40p. (ps-3). 1993. 13.95 (*0-8249-8620-2*, Ideals Child); PLB 14.00 (*0-8249-8630-X*) Hambleton-Hill.
—Reader's Digest Best Loved Books for Young Readers: Little Women. Ogburn, Jackie, ed. English, Mark, illus. 176p. (gr. 4-12). 1989. 3.99 (*0-945260-25-3*) Choice Pub NY.
—Rose in Bloom. Price, Hattie L., illus. (gr. 7 up). 1976. 19.95 (*0-316-03098-8*) Little.
—Under the Lilacs. Davis, Marguerite, illus. (gr. 7 up). 1977. 17.95 (*0-316-03099-6*) Little.
Blos, Joan W. A Gathering of Days: A New England Girl's Journal, 1830-32. LC 79-16898. 160p. (gr. 4-7). 1979. SBE 14.00 (*0-684-16340-3*, Scribners Young Read) Macmillan Child Grp.
Brady, Philip. Reluctant Hero: A Snowy Road to Salem in 1802. 144p. (gr. 7 up). 1990. 16.95 (*0-8027-6972-1*); lib. bdg. 17.85 (*0-8027-6974-8*) Walker & Co.
Curtis, Alice T. A Little Maid of New England. 1991. 7.99 (*0-517-06494-4*) Random Hse Value.
Davol, Marguerite W. Papa Alonzo Leatherby: The Best Storyteller in Carroll County. Leer, Rebecca, illus. LC 94-19372. 1995. 14.00 (*0-671-86580-3*, S&S BFYR) S&S Trade.
Drake, Samuel A. Book of New England Legends & Folk Lore. LC 76-157254. (Illus.). 502p. (gr. 9 up). 1971. pap. 14.95 (*0-8048-0990-9*) C E Tuttle.
Garden, Nancy. Fours Crossing. LC 80-21854. 199p. (gr. 5 up). 1981. 15.00 (*0-374-32451-4*) FS&G.
Hale, Edward E. Man Without a Country & Other Stories. (gr. 5 up). 1968. pap. 1.95 (*0-8049-0185-6*, CL-185) Airmont.
Hall, Donald. Ox-Cart Man. Cooney, Barbara, illus. LC 79-14466. (gr. k-3). 1979. pap. 15.00 (*0-670-53328-9*) Viking Child Bks.
—Ox-Cart Man. Cooney, Barbara, illus. 40p. (ps-3). 1983. pap. 4.99 (*0-14-050441-9*, Puffin) Puffin Bks.
Hawthorne, Nathaniel. House of the Seven Gables. (gr. 9 up). 1964. pap. 2.95 (*0-8049-0016-7*, CL-16) Airmont.
—Scarlet Letter. (gr. 9 up). 1964. pap. 2.95 (*0-8049-0007-8*, CL-7) Airmont.
—Scarlet Letter. Levin, Harry T., ed. LC 60-2662. (gr. 9 up). 1960. pap. 8.76 (*0-395-05142-8*, RivEd) HM.
Hawthorne, Nathaniel, et al. The Scarlet Letter. (Illus.). 52p. Date not set. pap. 4.95 (*1-57209-006-5*) Classics Int Ent.
Little Women. Centennial ed. (Illus.). (gr. 3-7). 1968. 19.95 (*0-685-47121-7*) Little.
Lorimer, Janet. Trouble with Buster: A Day in the Life of a Pilgrim Girl. 1990. pap. 2.50 (*0-590-42641-9*) Scholastic Inc.
Richardson, Judith B. David's Landing. Bang, Molly, illus. LC 84-22084. 150p. (gr. 3-7). 1984. write for info. (*0-9611374-1-X*) Woods Hole Hist.
Shetterly, Susan H. The Tinker of Salt Cove. Beckman, Siri, contrib. by. (Illus.). 48p. 1990. 13.95 (*0-88448-080-1*) Tilbury Hse.
Weller, Frances W. Matthew Wheelock's Wall. Lewin, Ted, illus. LC 91-9608. 40p. (gr. k-3). 1992. RSBE 14.95 (*0-02-792612-5*, Macmillan Child Bk) Macmillan Child Grp.
Wiggin, Eric & Wiggin, Kate D. Rebecca of Sunnybrook Farm: The Girl. 256p. (gr. 4-7). 1990. 9.95 (*1-56121-004-8*) Wolgemuth & Hyatt.
Wiggin, Kate D. Rebecca of Sunnybrook Farm. (gr. 5 up). 1967. pap. 1.50 (*0-8049-0144-9*, CL-144) Airmont.
—Rebecca of Sunnybrook Farm. LC 92-38743. 1993. 12.99 (*0-517-09275-1*, Child Classics) Random Hse Value.
—Rebecca of Sunnybrook Farm. Grose, Helen M., illus. Glassman, Peter, afterword by. LC 94-9899. (Illus.). 1994. write for info. (*0-688-13481-5*) Morrow.

NEW ENGLAND–HISTORY

Conover, Marilyn. Hannah Jumper: A Legend of the New England Seacoast. Conover, Marilyn, illus. 149p. (Orig.). (gr. 4 up). 1994. pap. write for info. (*0-9639867-0-8*) Meristem Bks.
Leach, Douglas E. Flintlock & Tomahawk: New England in King Philip's War. Morison, Samuel E., intro. by. LC 58-5467. 320p. 1992. pap. 12.50t (*0-940160-55-2*) Parnassus Imprints.
Sanseri, Gary & Sanseri, Wanda. The New England Primer of 1777. (Illus.). 115p. 1993. Repr. of 1777 ed. 14.95 (*1-88004-510-9*) Back Home Indust.

NEW FRANCE–HISTORY

see Mississippi Valley–History

NEW GUINEA

Fox, Mary V. Papua New Guinea. LC 93-35493. (Illus.). 128p. (gr. 5-8). 1994. PLB 20.55 (*0-516-02621-6*) Childrens.

NEW HAMPSHIRE

Appelbaum, Diana. Giants in the Land. McCurdy, Michael, illus. LC 92-26526. 32p. 1993. 14.95 (*0-395-64720-7*) HM.
Brown, Dottie. New Hampshire. LC 92-28662. (Illus.). 1993. 17.50 (*0-8225-2730-8*) Lerner Pubns.
Carole Marsh New Hampshire Books, 44 bks. 1994. PLB 1027.80 set (*0-7933-1304-X*); pap. 587.80 set (*0-7933-5180-4*) Gallopade Pub Group.
Carpenter, Allan. New Hampshire. LC 79-11454. (Illus.). 96p. (gr. 4 up). 1979. PLB 16.95 (*0-516-04129-0*) Childrens.
Fradin, Dennis. New Hampshire: In Words & Pictures. Wahl, Richard, illus. LC 80-25421. 48p. (gr. 2-5). 1981. PLB 12.95 (*0-516-03929-6*) Childrens.
Fradin, Dennis B. New Hampshire. LC 92-9216. (Illus.). 64p. (gr. 3-5). 1992. PLB 16.45 (*0-516-03829-X*); pap. 5.95 (*0-516-43829-8*) Childrens.
—The New Hampshire Colony. LC 87-14619. (Illus.). 190p. (gr. 4 up). 1987. PLB 17.95 (*0-516-00388-7*) Childrens.
McNair, S. New Hampshire. LC 91-540. 144p. (gr. 4 up). 1991. PLB 20.55 (*0-516-00475-1*) Childrens.
McNair, Sylvia. New Hampshire. 197p. 1993. text ed. 15.40 (*1-56956-156-7*) W A T Braille.
Marsh, Carole. Avast, Ye Slobs! New Hampshire Pirate Trivia. (Illus.). 1994. PLB 24.95 (*0-7933-0787-2*); pap. 14.95 (*0-7933-0786-4*); computer disk 29.95 (*0-7933-0788-0*) Gallopade Pub Group.
—The Beast of the New Hampshire Bed & Breakfast. (Illus.). 1994. PLB 24.95 (*0-7933-1770-3*); pap. 14.95 (*0-7933-1771-1*); computer disk 29.95 (*0-7933-1772-X*) Gallopade Pub Group.
—Bow Wow! New Hampshire Dogs in History, Mystery, Legend, Lore, Humor & More! (Illus.). (gr. 3-12). 1994. PLB 24.95 (*0-7933-3554-X*); pap. 14.95 (*0-7933-3555-8*); computer disk 29.95 (*0-7933-3556-6*) Gallopade Pub Group.
—Christopher Columbus Comes to New Hampshire! Includes Reproducible Activities for Kids! (Illus.). (gr. 3-12). 1994. PLB 24.95 (*0-7933-3707-0*); pap. 14.95 (*0-7933-3708-9*); computer disk 29.95 (*0-7933-3709-7*) Gallopade Pub Group.
—The Hard-to-Believe-But-True! Book of New Hampshire History, Mystery, Trivia, Legend, Lore, Humor & More. (Illus.). 1994. PLB 24.95 (*0-7933-0784-8*); pap. 14.95 (*0-7933-0783-X*); computer disk 29.95 (*0-7933-0785-6*) Gallopade Pub Group.
—If My New Hampshire Mama Ran the World! (Illus.). 1994. lib. bdg. 24.95 (*0-7933-1773-8*); pap. 14.95 (*0-7933-1774-6*); computer disk 29.95 (*0-7933-1775-4*) Gallopade Pub Group.
—Jurassic Ark! New Hampshire Dinosaurs & Other Prehistoric Creatures. (gr. k-12). 1994. PLB 24.95 (*0-7933-7515-0*); pap. 14.95 (*0-7933-7516-9*); computer disk 29.95 (*0-7933-7517-7*) Gallopade Pub Group.
—Let's Quilt New Hampshire & Stuff It Topographically! (Illus.). 1994. PLB 24.95 (*1-55609-829-4*); pap. 14.95 (*1-55609-067-6*); computer disk 29.95 (*1-55609-831-6*) Gallopade Pub Group.
—Let's Quilt Our New Hampshire County. 1994. lib. bdg. 24.95 (*0-7933-7200-3*); pap. text ed. 14.95 (*0-7933-7201-1*); disk 29.95 (*0-685-60853-0*) Gallopade Pub Group.
—Let's Quilt Our New Hampshire Town. 1994. lib. bdg. 24.95 (*0-7933-7050-7*); pap. text ed. 14.95 (*0-7933-7051-5*); disk 29.95 (*0-7933-7052-3*) Gallopade Pub Group.
—Meow! New Hampshire Cats in History, Mystery, Legend, Lore, Humor & More! (Illus.). (gr. 3-12). 1994. PLB 24.95 (*0-7933-3400-4*); pap. 14.95 (*0-7933-3401-2*); computer disk 29.95 (*0-7933-3402-0*) Gallopade Pub Group.
—New Hampshire & Other State Greats (Biographies) (Illus.). 1994. PLB 24.95 (*0-685-45980-2*); pap. 14.95 (*1-55609-845-6*); computer disk 29.95 (*1-55609-846-4*) Gallopade Pub Group.
—New Hampshire Bandits, Bushwackers, Outlaws, Crooks, Devils, Ghosts, Desperadoes & Other Assorted & Sundry Characters! (Illus.). 1994. PLB 24.95 (*0-7933-0769-4*); pap. 14.95 (*0-7933-0768-6*); computer disk 29.95 (*0-7933-0770-8*) Gallopade Pub Group.
—New Hampshire Classic Christmas Trivia: Stories, Recipes, Activities, Legends, Lore & More! (Illus.). 1994. PLB 24.95 (*0-7933-0772-4*); pap. 14.95 (*0-7933-0771-6*); computer disk 29.95 (*0-7933-0773-2*) Gallopade Pub Group.
—New Hampshire Coastales. (Illus.). 1994. PLB 24.95 (*1-55609-838-3*); pap. 14.95 (*1-55609-839-1*); computer disk 29.95 (*1-55609-840-5*) Gallopade Pub Group.
—New Hampshire Coastales! 1994. lib. bdg. 24.95 (*0-7933-7294-1*) Gallopade Pub Group.
—New Hampshire Dingbats! Bk. 1: A Fun Book of Games, Stories, Activities & More about Our State That's All in Code! for You to Decipher. (Illus.). (gr. 3-12). 1994. PLB 24.95 (*0-7933-3860-3*); pap. 14.95 (*0-7933-3861-1*); computer disk 29.95 (*0-7933-3862-X*) Gallopade Pub Group.
—New Hampshire Festival Fun for Kids! (Illus.). (gr. 3-12). 1994. lib. bdg. 24.95 (*0-7933-4013-6*); pap. 14.95 (*0-7933-4014-4*); disk 29.95 (*0-7933-4015-2*) Gallopade Pub Group.
—The New Hampshire Hot Air Balloon Mystery. (Illus.). (gr. 2-9). 1994. 24.95 (*0-7933-2579-X*); pap. 14.95 (*0-7933-2580-3*); computer disk 29.95 (*0-7933-2581-1*) Gallopade Pub Group.
—New Hampshire Jeopardy! Answers & Questions about Our State! (Illus.). (gr. 3-12). 1994. PLB 24.95 (*0-7933-4166-3*); pap. 14.95 (*0-7933-4167-1*); computer disk 29.95 (*0-7933-4168-X*) Gallopade Pub Group.
—New Hampshire "Jography" A Fun Run Thru Our State! (Illus.). 1994. PLB 24.95 (*1-55609-826-X*); pap. 14.95 (*1-55609-827-8*); computer disk 29.95 (*1-55609-828-6*) Gallopade Pub Group.
—New Hampshire Kid's Cookbook: Recipes, How-to, History, Lore & More! (Illus.). 1994. PLB 24.95 (*0-7933-0781-3*); pap. 14.95 (*0-7933-0780-5*); computer disk 29.95 (*0-7933-0782-1*) Gallopade Pub Group.

—New Hampshire Quiz Bowl Crash Course! (Illus.). 1994. PLB 24.95 (*1-55609-841-3*); pap. 14.95 (*1-55609-842-1*); computer disk 29.95 (*1-55609-843-X*) Gallopade Pub Group.
—New Hampshire Rollercoasters! (Illus.). (gr. 3-12). 1994. PLB 24.95 (*0-7933-5311-4*); pap. 14.95 (*0-7933-5312-2*); computer disk 29.95 (*0-7933-5313-0*) Gallopade Pub Group.
—New Hampshire School Trivia: An Amazing & Fascinating Look at Our State's Teachers, Schools & Students! (Illus.). 1994. PLB 24.95 (*0-7933-0778-3*); pap. 14.95 (*0-7933-0777-5*); computer disk 29.95 (*0-7933-0779-1*) Gallopade Pub Group.
—New Hampshire Silly Basketball Sportsmysteries, Vol. I. (Illus.). 1994. PLB 24.95 (*0-7933-0775-9*); pap. 14. 95 (*0-7933-0774-0*); computer disk 29.95 (*0-7933-0776-7*) Gallopade Pub Group.
—New Hampshire Silly Basketball Sportsmysteries, Vol. II. (Illus.). 1994. PLB 24.95 (*0-7933-1776-2*); pap. 14. 95 (*0-7933-1777-0*); computer disk 29.95 (*0-7933-1778-9*) Gallopade Pub Group.
—New Hampshire Silly Football Sportsmysteries, Vol. 1. (Illus.). 1994. PLB 24.95 (*1-55609-832-4*); pap. 14.95 (*1-55609-833-2*); computer disk 29.95 (*1-55609-834-0*) Gallopade Pub Group.
—New Hampshire Silly Football Sportsmysteries, Vol. 2. (Illus.). 1994. PLB 24.95 (*1-55609-835-9*); pap. 14.95 (*1-55609-836-7*); computer disk 29.95 (*1-55609-837-5*) Gallopade Pub Group.
—New Hampshire Silly Trivia! (Illus.). 1994. PLB 24.95 (*1-55609-823-5*); pap. 14.95 (*1-55609-824-3*); computer disk 29.95 (*1-55609-825-1*) Gallopade Pub Group.
—New Hampshire's (Most Devastating!) Disasters & (Most Calamitous!) Catastrophies! (Illus.). 1994. PLB 24.95 (*0-7933-0766-X*); pap. 14.95 (*0-7933-0765-1*); computer disk 29.95 (*0-7933-0767-8*) Gallopade Pub Group.
—Uncle Rebus: New Hampshire Picture Stories for Computer Kids. (Illus.). (gr. k-3). 1994. PLB 24.95 (*0-7933-4588-X*); pap. 14.95 (*0-7933-4589-8*); disk 29. 95 (*0-7933-4590-1*) Gallopade Pub Group.
Thaxter, Celia. Celia's Island Journal. (ps-3). 1992. 15.95 (*0-316-83921-3*) Little.
Thompson, Kathleen. New Hampshire. LC 87-26480. 48p. (gr. 3 up). 1988. 19.97 (*0-86514-469-9*) Raintree Steck-V.

NEW HAMPSHIRE–FICTION

Bailey, Carolyn S. Miss Hickory. Gannett, Ruth, illus. LC 46-7275. (gr. 4-7). 1977. pap. 3.99 (*0-14-030956-X*, Puffin Bks) Puffin Bks.
—Miss Hickory. Gannett, Ruth, illus. (gr. 4-7). 1946. pap. 14.00 (*0-670-47940-3*) Viking Child Bks.
Corcoran, Barbara. The Sky Is Falling. 192p. 1990. pap. 2.95 (*0-380-70837-X*, Camelot) Avon.
—Stay Tuned. LC 90-1017. 208p. (gr. 3-7). 1991. SBE 14.95 (*0-689-31673-9*, Atheneum Child Bk) Macmillan Child Grp.
Duffy, James. The Graveyard Gang. LC 92-30990. 192p. (gr. 5-7). 1993. SBE 14.95 (*0-684-19449-X*, Scribners Young Read) Macmillan Child Grp.
Fleischman, Paul. Rear-View Mirrors. LC 85-45387. 128p. (gr. 7 up). 1986. 12.95 (*0-06-021866-5*); PLB 12.89 (*0-06-021867-3*) HarpC Child Bks.
Hall, Donald. Lucy's Summer. McCurdy, Michael, illus. LC 93-17130. 1995. write for info. (*0-15-276873-4*, HB Juv Bks) HarBrace.
Hoppe, Joanne. Pretty Penny Farm. LC 86-1516. 224p. (gr. 7 up). 1987. 12.95 (*0-688-07201-1*) Morrow Jr Bks.
Yates, Elizabeth. Hue & Cry. 182p. (gr. 7-12). 1991. pap. 4.95 (*0-89084-536-0*) Bob Jones Univ Pr.

NEW HAMPSHIRE–HISTORY

Marsh, Carole. Chill Out: Scary New Hampshire Tales Based on Frightening New Hampshire Truths. (Illus.). 1994. lib. bdg. 24.95 (*0-7933-4741-6*); pap. 14.95 (*0-7933-4742-4*); disk 29.95 (*0-7933-4743-2*) Gallopade Pub Group.
—My First Book about New Hampshire. (gr. k-4). 1994. PLB 24.95 (*0-7933-5656-3*); pap. 14.95 (*0-7933-5657-1*); computer disk 29.95 (*0-7933-5658-X*) Gallopade Pub Group.
—New Hampshire "Crinkum-Crankum" A Funny Word Book about Our State. (Illus.). 1994. lib. bdg. 24.95 (*0-7933-4895-1*); pap. 14.95 (*0-7933-4896-X*); disk 29. 95 (*0-7933-4897-8*) Gallopade Pub Group.
—The New Hampshire Mystery Van Takes Off! Book 1: Handicapped New Hampshire Kids Sneak Off on a Big Adventure. (Illus.). (gr. 3-12). 1994. 24.95 (*0-7933-5048-4*); pap. 14.95 (*0-7933-5049-2*); computer disk 29.95 (*0-7933-5050-6*) Gallopade Pub Group.
—New Hampshire Timeline: A Chronology of New Hampshire History, Mystery, Trivia, Legend, Lore & More. (Illus.). (gr. 3-12). 1994. PLB 24.95 (*0-7933-5962-7*); pap. 14.95 (*0-7933-5963-5*); computer disk 29.95 (*0-7933-5964-3*) Gallopade Pub Group.
—New Hampshire's Unsolved Mysteries (& Their "Solutions") Includes Scientific Information & Other Activities for Students. (Illus.). (gr. 3-12). 1994. PLB 24.95 (*0-7933-5809-4*); pap. 14.95 (*0-7933-5810-8*); computer disk 29.95 (*0-7933-5811-6*) Gallopade Pub Group.
—Patch, the Pirate Dog: A New Hampshire Pet Story. (ps-4). 1994. PLB 24.95 (*0-7933-5503-6*); pap. 14.95 (*0-7933-5504-4*); computer disk 29.95 (*0-7933-5505-2*) Gallopade Pub Group.
Rosal, Lorenca. The Liberty Key: The Story of the N.H. Constitution. (Illus.). 300p. 1987. 12.95 (*0-685-19456-6*) Equity Pub NH.
Thompson, Dorothea M. Will Stark & Boobear: Ranger Scouts, Vol. 2. 2nd ed. Thompson, Brownlow L., illus. 150p. (gr. 5-10). pap. text ed. 9.95 (*0-931947-52-9*) Thompson Pr.

NEW JERSEY

Aylesworth, Thomas G. & Aylesworth, Virginia L. Upper Atlantic: New Jersey - New York. (Illus.). 64p. (gr. 3 up). 1987. lib. bdg. 16.95 (*1-55546-553-6*); pap. 6.95 (*0-685-35556-X*) Chelsea Hse.
Carole Marsh New Jersey Books, 44 bks. 1994. PLB 1027.80 set (*0-7933-1305-8*); pap. 587.80 set (*0-7933-5182-0*) Gallopade Pub Group.
Carpenter, Allan. New Jersey. LC 78-14891. (Illus.). 96p. (gr. 4 up). 1979. PLB 16.95 (*0-516-04130-4*) Childrens.
Fradin, Dennis. New Jersey: In Words & Pictures. Wahl, Richard, illus. LC 80-19688. 48p. (gr. 2-5). 1980. PLB 12.95 (*0-516-03930-X*) Childrens.
Fradin, Dennis B. New Jersey. LC 92-34601. (Illus.). 64p. (gr. 3-5). 1993. PLB 16.45 (*0-516-03830-3*); pap. 5.95 (*0-516-43830-1*) Childrens.
Fredeen, Charles. New Jersey. LC 92-13363. 1993. PLB 17.50 (*0-8225-2732-4*) Lerner Pubns.
Kent, Deborah. New Jersey. LC 87-9401. (Illus.). 144p. (gr. 4 up). 1987. PLB 20.55 (*0-516-00476-X*) Childrens.
—New Jersey. 191p. 1993. text ed. 15.40 (*1-56956-126-5*) W A T Braille.
Marsh, Carole. Avast, Ye Slobs! New Jersey Pirate Trivia. (Illus.). 1994. PLB 24.95 (*0-7933-1809-2*); pap. 14.95 (*0-7933-1810-6*); computer disk 29.95 (*0-7933-1811-4*) Gallopade Pub Group.
—The Beast of the New Jersey Bed & Breakfast. (Illus.). 1994. PLB 24.95 (*0-7933-1779-7*); pap. 14.95 (*0-7933-1780-0*); computer disk 29.95 (*0-7933-1781-9*) Gallopade Pub Group.
—Bow Wow! New Jersey Dogs in History, Mystery, Legend, Lore, Humor & More! (Illus.). (gr. 3-12). 1994. PLB 24.95 (*0-7933-3557-4*); pap. 14.95 (*0-7933-3558-2*); computer disk 29.95 (*0-7933-3559-0*) Gallopade Pub Group.
—Christopher Columbus Comes to New Jersey! Includes Reproducible Activities for Kids! (Illus.). (gr. 3-12). 1994. PLB 24.95 (*0-7933-3710-0*); pap. 14.95 (*0-7933-3711-9*); computer disk 29.95 (*0-7933-3712-7*) Gallopade Pub Group.
—The Hard-to-Believe-But-True! Book of New Jersey History, Mystery, Trivia, Legend, Lore, Humor & More. (Illus.). 1994. PLB 24.95 (*0-7933-1806-8*); pap. 14.95 (*0-7933-1807-6*); computer disk 29.95 (*0-7933-1808-4*) Gallopade Pub Group.
—If My New Jersey Mama Ran the World! (Illus.). 1994. lib. bdg. 24.95 (*0-7933-1782-7*); pap. 14.95 (*0-7933-1783-5*); computer disk 29.95 (*0-7933-1784-3*) Gallopade Pub Group.
—Jurassic Ark! New Jersey Dinosaurs & Other Prehistoric Creatures. (gr. k-12). 1994. PLB 24.95 (*0-7933-7518-5*); pap. 14.95 (*0-7933-7519-3*); computer disk 29.95 (*0-7933-7520-7*) Gallopade Pub Group.
—Let's Quilt New Jersey & Stuff It Topographically! (Illus.). 1994. PLB 24.95 (*1-55609-853-7*); pap. 14.95 (*1-55609-069-2*); computer disk 29.95 (*1-55609-855-3*) Gallopade Pub Group.
—Let's Quilt Our New Jersey County. 1994. lib. bdg. 24. 95 (*0-7933-7203-8*); pap. text ed. 14.95 (*0-7933-7204-6*); disk 29.95 (*0-7933-7205-4*) Gallopade Pub Group.
—Let's Quilt Our New Jersey Town. 1994. lib. bdg. 24.95 (*0-7933-7053-1*); pap. text ed. 14.95 (*0-7933-7054-X*); disk 29.95 (*0-7933-7055-8*) Gallopade Pub Group.
—Meow! New Jersey Cats in History, Mystery, Legend, Lore, Humor & More! (Illus.). (gr. 3-12). 1994. PLB 24.95 (*0-7933-3404-7*); pap. 14.95 (*0-685-48034-8*); computer disk 29.95 (*0-7933-3406-3*) Gallopade Pub Group.
—New Jersey & Other State Greats (Biographies) (Illus.). 1994. PLB 24.95 (*1-55609-868-5*); pap. 14.95 (*1-55609-869-3*); computer disk 29.95 (*1-55609-870-7*) Gallopade Pub Group.
—New Jersey Bandits, Bushwackers, Outlaws, Crooks, Devils, Ghosts, Desperadoes & Other Assorted & Sundry Characters! (Illus.). 1994. PLB 24.95 (*0-7933-1788-6*); pap. 14.95 (*0-7933-1789-4*); computer disk 29.95 (*0-7933-1790-8*) Gallopade Pub Group.
—New Jersey Classic Christmas Trivia: Stories, Recipes, Activities, Legends, Lore & More! (Illus.). 1994. PLB 24.95 (*0-7933-1791-6*); pap. 14.95 (*0-7933-1792-4*); computer disk 29.95 (*0-7933-1793-2*) Gallopade Pub Group.
—New Jersey Coastales. (Illus.). 1994. PLB 24.95 (*1-55609-862-6*); pap. 14.95 (*1-55609-863-4*); computer disk 29.95 (*1-55609-864-2*) Gallopade Pub Group.
—New Jersey Coastales! 1994. lib. bdg. 24.95 (*0-7933-7295-X*) Gallopade Pub Group.
—New Jersey Dingbats! Bk. 1: A Fun Book of Games, Stories, Activities & More about Our State That's All in Code! for You to Decipher. (Illus.). (gr. 3-12). 1994. PLB 24.95 (*0-7933-3863-8*); pap. 14.95 (*0-7933-3864-6*); computer disk 29.95 (*0-7933-3865-4*) Gallopade Pub Group.
—New Jersey Festival Fun for Kids! (Illus.). (gr. 3-12). 1994. lib. bdg. 24.95 (*0-7933-4016-0*); pap. 14.95 (*0-7933-4017-9*); disk 29.95 (*0-7933-4018-7*) Gallopade Pub Group.
—The New Jersey Hot Air Balloon Mystery. (Illus.). (gr. 2-9). 1994. 24.95 (*0-7933-2588-9*); pap. 14.95 (*0-7933-2589-7*); computer disk 29.95 (*0-7933-2590-0*) Gallopade Pub Group.
—New Jersey Jeopardy! Answers & Questions about Our State! (Illus.). (gr. 3-12). 1994. PLB 24.95 (*0-7933-4169-8*); pap. 14.95 (*0-7933-4170-1*); computer disk 29.95 (*0-7933-4171-X*) Gallopade Pub Group.
—New Jersey "Jography" A Fun Run Thru Our State! (Illus.). 1994. PLB 24.95 (*1-55609-850-2*); pap. 14.95 (*1-55609-851-0*); computer disk 29.95 (*1-55609-852-9*) Gallopade Pub Group.
—New Jersey Kid's Cookbook: Recipes, How-to, History, Lore & More. (Illus.). 1994. PLB 24.95 (*0-7933-1803-3*); pap. 14.95 (*0-7933-1804-1*); computer disk 29.95 (*0-7933-1805-X*) Gallopade Pub Group.
—New Jersey Quiz Bowl Crash Course! (Illus.). 1994. PLB 24.95 (*1-55609-865-0*); pap. 14.95 (*1-55609-866-9*); computer disk 29.95 (*1-55609-867-7*) Gallopade Pub Group.
—New Jersey Rollercoasters! (Illus.). (gr. 3-12). 1994. PLB 24.95 (*0-7933-5314-9*); pap. 14.95 (*0-7933-5315-7*); computer disk 29.95 (*0-7933-5316-5*) Gallopade Pub Group.
—New Jersey School Trivia: An Amazing & Fascinating Look at Our State's Teachers, Schools & Students! (Illus.). 1994. PLB 24.95 (*0-7933-1800-9*); pap. 14.95 (*0-7933-1801-7*); computer disk 29.95 (*0-7933-1802-5*) Gallopade Pub Group.
—New Jersey Silly Basketball Sportsmysteries, Vol. 1. (Illus.). 1994. PLB 24.95 (*0-7933-1794-0*); pap. 14.95 (*0-7933-1795-9*); computer disk 29.95 (*0-7933-1796-7*) Gallopade Pub Group.
—New Jersey Silly Basketball Sportsmysteries, Vol. 2. (Illus.). 1994. PLB 24.95 (*0-7933-1797-5*); pap. 14.95 (*0-7933-1798-3*); computer disk 29.95 (*0-7933-1799-1*) Gallopade Pub Group.
—New Jersey Silly Football Sportsmysteries, Vol. 1. (Illus.). 1994. PLB 24.95 (*1-55609-856-1*); pap. 14.95 (*1-55609-857-X*); computer disk 29.95 (*1-55609-858-8*) Gallopade Pub Group.
—New Jersey Silly Football Sportsmysteries, Vol. 2. (Illus.). 1994. PLB 24.95 (*1-55609-859-6*); pap. 14.95 (*1-55609-860-X*); computer disk 29.95 (*1-55609-861-8*) Gallopade Pub Group.
—New Jersey Silly Trivia! (Illus.). 1994. PLB 24.95 (*1-55609-847-2*); pap. 14.95 (*1-55609-848-0*); computer disk 29.95 (*1-55609-849-9*) Gallopade Pub Group.
—New Jersey Timeline: A Chronology of New Jersey History, Mystery, Trivia, Legend, Lore & More. (Illus.). (gr. 3-12). 1994. PLB 24.95 (*0-7933-5965-1*); pap. 14.95 (*0-7933-5966-X*); computer disk 29.95 (*0-7933-5967-8*) Gallopade Pub Group.
—New Jersey's (Most Devastating!) Disasters & (Most Calamitous!) Catastrophies! (Illus.). 1994. PLB 24.95 (*0-685-45981-0*); pap. 14.95 (*0-7933-1786-X*); computer disk 29.95 (*0-7933-1787-8*) Gallopade Pub Group.
—New Jersey's Unsolved Mysteries (& Their "Solutions") Includes Scientific Information & Other Activities for Students. (Illus.). (gr. 3-12). 1994. PLB 24.95 (*0-7933-5812-4*); pap. 14.95 (*0-7933-5813-2*); computer disk 29.95 (*0-7933-5814-0*) Gallopade Pub Group.
—Uncle Rebus: New Jersey Picture Stories for Computer Kids. (Illus.). (gr. k-3). 1994. PLB 24.95 (*0-7933-4591-X*); pap. 14.95 (*0-7933-4592-8*); disk 29. 95 (*0-7933-4593-6*) Gallopade Pub Group.
Monesson, Harry S. The World's Biggest Tummy. Monesson, Harry S., illus. LC 92-96830. 40p. (Orig.). (gr. k-3). 1992. pap. 6.95 (*0-9633735-0-1*) H S Monesson.
Thompson, Kathleen. New Jersey. LC 85-9981. 48p. (gr. 3 up). 1985. PLB 19.97 (*0-86514-438-9*) Raintree Steck-V.

NEW JERSEY–FICTION

Avi. Captain Grey. LC 92-37643. 160p. 1993. 14.00 (*0-688-12233-7*) Morrow Jr Bks.
Gauch, Patricia L. This Time, Tempe Wick? Tomes, Margot, illus. 48p. (gr. 1-4). 1992. 12.95 (*0-399-21880-7*, Putnam) Putnam Pub Group.
Rinaldi, Ann. A Ride into Morning: The Story of Tempe Wick. Grove, Karen, ed. 289p. (gr. 7 up). 1991. 15.95 (*0-15-200573-0*, Gulliver Bks) HarBrace.
Robertson, Keith. Henry Reed's Baby-Sitting Service. McCloskey, Robert, illus. (gr. 5-8). 1966. pap. 14.95 (*0-670-36825-3*) Viking Child Bks.

NEW JERSEY–HISTORY

Brown, Edward. Just Around the Corner in New Jersey. (Illus.). 112p. (gr. 6 up). 1987. pap. 7.95 (*0-912608-17-X*) Mid Atlantic.
Fradin, Dennis. The New Jersey Colony. LC 90-22437. (Illus.). (gr. 4 up). 1991. PLB 17.95 (*0-516-00395-X*) Childrens.
McCloy, James F. & Miller, Ray, Jr. The Jersey Devil. (Illus.). 121p. (gr. 5 up). 1987. pap. 8.95 (*0-912608-11-0*) Mid Atlantic.
McMahon, William. Pine Barrens Legends, Lore & Lies. (Illus.). 149p. (gr. 6 up). 1986. pap. 8.95 (*0-912608-19-6*) Mid Atlantic.

Marsh, Carole. Chill Out: Scary New Jersey Tales Based on Frightening New Jersey Truths. (Illus.). 1994. lib. bdg. 24.95 (*0-7933-4744-0*); pap. 14.95 (*0-7933-4745-9*); disk 29.95 (*0-7933-4746-7*) Gallopade Pub Group.

—My First Book about New Jersey. (gr. k-4). 1994. PLB 24.95 (*0-7933-5659-8*); pap. 14.95 (*0-7933-5660-1*); computer disk 29.95 (*0-7933-5661-X*) Gallopade Pub Group.

—New Jersey "Crinkum-Crankum" A Funny Word Book about Our State. (Illus.). 1994. lib. bdg. 24.95 (*0-7933-4898-6*); pap. 14.95 (*0-7933-4899-4*); disk 29.95 (*0-7933-4900-1*) Gallopade Pub Group.

—The New Jersey Mystery Van Takes Off! Book 1: Handicapped New Jersey Kids Sneak Off on a Big Adventure. (Illus.). (gr. 3-12). 1994. 24.95 (*0-7933-5051-4*); pap. 14.95 (*0-7933-5052-2*); computer disk 29.95 (*0-7933-5053-0*) Gallopade Pub Group.

—Patch, the Pirate Dog: A New Jersey Pet Story. (ps-4). 1994. PLB 24.95 (*0-7933-5506-0*); pap. 14.95 (*0-7933-5507-9*); computer disk 29.95 (*0-7933-5508-7*) Gallopade Pub Group.

Rabold, Ted & Fair, Phillip. New Jersey: Yesterday & Today. Ferguson, Laurie, illus. 110p. (Orig.). (gr. 4). 1982. 9.95 (*0-931992-41-9*); pap. text ed. 4.95 (*0-931992-43-5*) Penns Valley.

NEW MEXICO

Aylesworth, Thomas G. & Aylesworth, Virginia L. The Southwest (Texas, New Mexico, Colorado) (Illus.). 64p. (gr. 3 up). 1992. lib. bdg. 16.95 (*0-7910-1048-1*) Chelsea Hse.

Carole Marsh New Mexico Books, 44 bks. 1994. PLB 1027.80 set (*0-7933-1306-6*); pap. 587.80 set (*0-7933-5184-7*) Gallopade Pub Group.

Carpenter, Allan. New Mexico. LC 78-2695. (Illus.). 96p. (gr. 4 up). 1978. PLB 16.95 (*0-516-04131-2*) Childrens.

Chapman, Al. Coloring Book of New Mexico Santos. Ortega, Pedro R., tr. Chapman, Al, illus. (SPA & ENG.). 32p. (gr. 1-8). 1982. pap. 3.00 (*0-913270-19-9*) Sunstone Pr.

Early, Theresa S. New Mexico. LC 92-13364. 1993. PLB 17.50 (*0-8225-2748-0*) Lerner Pubns.

Fradin, Dennis. New Mexico: In Words & Pictures. Wahl, Richard, illus. LC 81-298. 48p. (gr. 2-5). 1981. PLB 12.95 (*0-516-03931-8*) Childrens.

Fradin, Dennis B. New Mexico - De Mar A Mar: New Mexico - from Sea to Shining Sea. LC 93-799. (SPA., Illus.). 64p. (gr. 2-5). 1994. PLB 16.45 (*0-516-33831-5*) Childrens.

—New Mexico - From Sea to Shining Sea. LC 93-799. (Illus.). 64p. (gr. 3-5). 1993. PLB 16.45 (*0-516-03831-1*) Childrens.

Hallett, Bill & Hallett, Jane. Look up Look Down Look All Around Chaco Culture National Historical Park. Jackson, Lori, illus. 32p. (Orig.). (gr. 3-8). 1989. pap. 3.45 activity bk. (*0-685-26277-4*) Look & See.

—Look up Look Down Look All Around El Morro National Monument. Chaffee, Dan, illus. 32p. (Orig.). (gr. 3-8). 1988. pap. 3.45 activity bk. (*0-943087-04-X*) Look & See.

Harris, Linda B. Las Cruces: An Illustrated History. Ireland, Joe, et al, illus. Priestley, Lee, intro. by. LC 93-22913. 144p. 1993. 29.95 (*0-9623682-5-3*) Arroyo Pr.

Lavash, Donald R. A Journey Through New Mexico History. rev. ed. Agogino, George A., frwd. by. LC 92-27191. 1993. 24.95 (*0-86534-194-X*) Sunstone Pr.

Marsh, Carole. Avast, Ye Slobs! New Mexico Pirate Trivia. (Illus.). 1994. PLB 24.95 (*0-7933-0811-9*); pap. 14.95 (*0-7933-0810-0*); computer disk 29.95 (*0-7933-0812-7*) Gallopade Pub Group.

—The Beast of the New Mexico Bed & Breakfast. (Illus.). 1994. PLB 24.95 (*0-7933-1812-2*); pap. 14.95 (*0-7933-1813-0*); computer disk 29.95 (*0-7933-1814-9*) Gallopade Pub Group.

—Bow Wow! New Mexico Dogs in History, Mystery, Legend, Lore, Humor & More! (Illus.). (gr. 3-12). 1994. PLB 24.95 (*0-7933-3560-4*); pap. 14.95 (*0-7933-3561-2*); computer disk 29.95 (*0-7933-3562-0*) Gallopade Pub Group.

—Chill Out: Scary New Mexico Tales Based on Frightening New Mexico Truths. (Illus.). 1994. lib. bdg. 24.95 (*0-7933-4747-5*); pap. 14.95 (*0-7933-4748-3*); disk 29.95 (*0-7933-4749-1*) Gallopade Pub Group.

—Christopher Columbus Comes to New Mexico! Includes Reproducible Activities for Kids! (Illus.). (gr. 3-12). 1994. PLB 24.95 (*0-7933-3713-5*); pap. 14.95 (*0-7933-3714-3*); computer disk 29.95 (*0-7933-3715-1*) Gallopade Pub Group.

—The Hard-to-Believe-But-True! Book of New Mexico History, Mystery, Trivia, Legend, Lore, Humor & More. (Illus.). 1994. PLB 24.95 (*0-7933-0808-9*); pap. 14.95 (*0-7933-0807-0*); computer disk 29.95 (*0-7933-0809-7*) Gallopade Pub Group.

—If My New Mexico Mama Ran The World! (Illus.). 1994. lib. bdg. 24.95 (*0-7933-1815-7*); pap. 14.95 (*0-7933-1816-5*); computer disk 29.95 (*0-7933-1817-3*) Gallopade Pub Group.

—Jurassic Ark! New Mexico Dinosaurs & Other Prehistoric Creatures. (gr. k-12). 1994. PLB 24.95 (*0-7933-7521-5*); pap. 14.95 (*0-7933-7522-3*); computer disk 29.95 (*0-7933-7523-1*) Gallopade Pub Group.

—Let's Quilt New Mexico & Stuff It Topographically! (Illus.). 1994. PLB 24.95 (*1-55609-877-4*); pap. 14.95 (*1-55609-127-3*); computer disk 29.95 (*1-55609-879-0*) Gallopade Pub Group.

—Let's Quilt Our New Mexico County. 1994. lib. bdg. 24.95 (*0-7933-7206-2*); pap. text ed. 14.95 (*0-7933-7207-0*); disk 29.95 (*0-7933-7208-9*) Gallopade Pub Group.

—Let's Quilt Our New Mexico Town. 1994. lib. bdg. 24.95 (*0-7933-7056-6*); pap. text ed. 14.95 (*0-7933-7057-4*); disk 29.95 (*0-7933-7058-2*) Gallopade Pub Group.

—Meow! New Mexico Cats in History, Mystery, Legend, Lore, Humor & More! (Illus.). (gr. 3-12). 1994. PLB 24.95 (*0-7933-3407-1*); pap. 14.95 (*0-7933-3408-X*); computer disk 29.95 (*0-7933-3409-8*) Gallopade Pub Group.

—My First Book about New Mexico. (gr. k-4). 1994. PLB 24.95 (*0-7933-5662-8*); pap. 14.95 (*0-7933-5663-6*); computer disk 29.95 (*0-7933-5664-4*) Gallopade Pub Group.

—New Mexico & Other State Greats (Biographies) (Illus.). 1994. PLB 24.95 (*1-55609-892-8*); pap. 14.95 (*1-55609-893-6*); computer disk 29.95 (*1-55609-894-4*) Gallopade Pub Group.

—New Mexico Bandits, Bushwackers, Outlaws, Crooks, Devils, Ghosts, Desperadoes & Other Assorted & Sundry Characters! (Illus.). 1994. PLB 24.95 (*0-7933-0793-7*); pap. 14.95 (*0-7933-0792-9*); computer disk 29.95 (*0-7933-0794-5*) Gallopade Pub Group.

—New Mexico Classic Christmas Trivia: Stories, Recipes, Activities, Legends, Lore & More! (Illus.). 1994. PLB 24.95 (*0-7933-0796-1*); pap. 14.95 (*0-7933-0795-3*); computer disk 29.95 (*0-7933-0797-X*) Gallopade Pub Group.

—New Mexico Coastales. (Illus.). 1994. PLB 24.95 (*1-55609-886-3*); pap. 14.95 (*1-55609-887-1*); computer disk 29.95 (*1-55609-888-X*) Gallopade Pub Group.

—New Mexico Coastales! 1994. lib. bdg. 24.95 (*0-7933-7296-8*) Gallopade Pub Group.

—New Mexico "Crinkum-Crankum" A Funny Word Book about Our State. (Illus.). 1994. lib. bdg. 24.95 (*0-7933-4901-X*); pap. 14.95 (*0-7933-4902-8*); disk 29.95 (*0-7933-4903-6*) Gallopade Pub Group.

—New Mexico Dingbats! Bk. 1: A Fun Book of Games, Stories, Activities & More about Our State That's All in Code! for You to Decipher. (Illus.). (gr. 3-12). 1994. PLB 24.95 (*0-7933-3866-2*); pap. 14.95 (*0-7933-3867-0*); computer disk 29.95 (*0-7933-3868-9*) Gallopade Pub Group.

—New Mexico Festival Fun for Kids! (Illus.). (gr. 3-12). 1994. lib. bdg. 24.95 (*0-7933-4019-5*); pap. 14.95 (*0-7933-4020-9*); disk 29.95 (*0-7933-4021-7*) Gallopade Pub Group.

—The New Mexico Hot Air Balloon Mystery. (Illus.). (gr. 2-9). 1994. 24.95 (*0-7933-2597-8*); pap. 14.95 (*0-7933-2598-6*); computer disk 29.95 (*0-7933-2599-4*) Gallopade Pub Group.

—New Mexico Jeopardy! Answers & Questions about Our State! (Illus.). (gr. 3-12). 1994. PLB 24.95 (*0-7933-4172-8*); pap. 14.95 (*0-7933-4173-6*); computer disk 29.95 (*0-7933-4174-4*) Gallopade Pub Group.

—New Mexico "Jography" A Fun Run Thru Our State! (Illus.). 1994. PLB 24.95 (*1-55609-874-X*); pap. 14.95 (*1-55609-875-8*); computer disk 29.95 (*1-55609-876-6*) Gallopade Pub Group.

—New Mexico Kid's Cookbook: Recipes, How-to, History, Lore & More! (Illus.). 1994. PLB 24.95 (*0-7933-0805-4*); pap. 14.95 (*0-7933-0804-6*); computer disk 29.95 (*0-7933-0806-2*) Gallopade Pub Group.

—The New Mexico Mystery Van Takes Off! Book 1: Handicapped New Mexico Kids Sneak Off on a Big Adventure. (Illus.). (gr. 3-12). 1994. 24.95 (*0-7933-5054-9*); pap. 14.95 (*0-7933-5055-7*); computer disk 29.95 (*0-7933-5056-5*) Gallopade Pub Group.

—New Mexico Quiz Bowl Crash Course! (Illus.). 1994. PLB 24.95 (*1-55609-889-8*); pap. 14.95 (*1-55609-890-1*); computer disk 29.95 (*1-55609-891-X*) Gallopade Pub Group.

—New Mexico Rollercoasters! (Illus.). (gr. 3-12). 1994. PLB 24.95 (*0-7933-5317-3*); pap. 14.95 (*0-7933-5318-1*); computer disk 29.95 (*0-7933-5319-X*) Gallopade Pub Group.

—New Mexico School Trivia: An Amazing & Fascinating Look at Our State's Teachers, Schools & Students! (Illus.). 1994. PLB 24.95 (*0-7933-0802-X*); pap. 14.95 (*0-7933-0801-1*); computer disk 29.95 (*0-7933-0803-8*) Gallopade Pub Group.

—New Mexico Silly Basketball Sportsmystereis, Vol. 1. (Illus.). 1994. PLB 24.95 (*0-7933-0799-6*); pap. 14.95 (*0-7933-0798-8*); computer disk 29.95 (*0-7933-0800-3*) Gallopade Pub Group.

—New Mexico Silly Basketball Sportsmysteries, Vol. 2. (Illus.). 1994. PLB 24.95 (*0-7933-1818-1*); pap. 14.95 (*0-7933-1819-X*); computer disk 29.95 (*0-7933-1820-3*) Gallopade Pub Group.

—New Mexico Silly Football Sportsmysteries. (Illus.). 1994. PLB 24.95 (*1-55609-880-4*); pap. 14.95 (*1-55609-881-2*); computer disk 29.95 (*1-55609-882-0*) Gallopade Pub Group.

—New Mexico Silly Football Sportsmysteries. (Illus.). 1994. pap. 14.95 (*1-55609-884-7*); computer disk 29.95 (*1-55609-885-5*) Gallopade Pub Group.

—New Mexico Silly Trivia! (Illus.). 1994. PLB 24.95 (*1-55609-871-5*); pap. 14.95 (*1-55609-872-3*); computer disk 29.95 (*1-55609-873-1*) Gallopade Pub Group.

—New Mexico Timeline: A Chronology of New Mexico History, Mystery, Trivia, Legend, Lore & More. (Illus.). (gr. 3-12). 1994. PLB 24.95 (*0-7933-5968-6*); pap. 14.95 (*0-7933-5969-4*); computer disk 29.95 (*0-7933-5970-8*) Gallopade Pub Group.

—New Mexico's (Most Devastating!) Disasters & (Most Calamitous!) Catastrophies! (Illus.). 1994. PLB 24.95 (*0-7933-0790-2*); pap. 14.95 (*0-7933-0789-9*); computer disk 29.95 (*0-7933-0791-0*) Gallopade Pub Group.

—New Mexico's Unsolved Mysteries (& Their "Solutions") Includes Scientific Information & Other Activities for Students. (Illus.). (gr. 3-12). 1994. PLB 24.95 (*0-7933-5815-9*); pap. 14.95 (*0-7933-5816-7*); computer disk 29.95 (*0-7933-5817-5*) Gallopade Pub Group.

—Patch, the Pirate Dog: A New Mexico Pet Story. (ps-4). 1994. PLB 24.95 (*0-7933-5509-5*); pap. 14.95 (*0-7933-5510-9*); computer disk 29.95 (*0-7933-5511-7*) Gallopade Pub Group.

—Uncle Rebus: New Mexico Picture Stories for Computer Kids. (Illus.). (gr. k-3). 1994. PLB 24.95 (*0-7933-4594-4*); pap. 14.95 (*0-7933-4595-2*); disk 29.95 (*0-7933-4596-0*) Gallopade Pub Group.

Roberts, Susan & Roberts, Calvin. A History of New Mexico. rev. ed. (Illus.). 400p. (gr. 6-9). 1991. text ed. 45.00 (*0-8263-1264-0*) U of NM Pr.

Salts, Bobbi. New Mexico Is for Kids! An Activity Book. Parker, Steve, illus. 32p. (gr. 1-6). 1989. pap. 2.95 (*0-929526-02-3*) Double B Pubns.

Simmons, Marc. New Mexico! rev. ed. (Illus.). 313p. (gr. 4). 1991. text ed. 45.00 (*0-8263-1265-9*) U of NM Pr.

Smith, MaryLou M. Grandmother's Adobe Dollhouse. Blackstone, Ann, illus. 32p. (gr. k-6). 1988. PLB 12.95 (*0-937206-03-2*); pap. 6.95 (*0-937206-07-5*) New Mexico Mag.

Stein, R. Conrad. New Mexico. 199p. 1993. text ed. 15.40 (*1-56956-129-X*) W A T Braille.

Thompson, Kathleen. New Mexico. LC 85-10832. 48p. (gr. 3 up). 1985. PLB 19.97 (*0-86514-439-7*) Raintree Steck-V.

NEW MEXICO–ANTIQUITIES

Dressman, John. On the Cliffs of Acoma. Ortega, Pedro R., tr. from SPA. LC 83-20177. (Illus.). 32p. (gr. 2-4). 1984. pap. 5.95 (*0-86534-021-8*) Sunstone Pr.

NEW MEXICO–FICTION

Atwood, Marjorie, Jr. Galisteo Legend. Smith, James C., ed. Yamashita, Mina, illus. LC 91-41394. 48p. (Orig.). 1992. pap. 6.95 (*0-86534-154-0*) Sunstone Pr.

Krumgold, Joseph. And Now Miguel. Charlot, Jean, illus. LC 53-8415. 245p. (gr. 5 up). 1987. 16.00 (*0-690-09118-4*, Crowell Jr Bks); PLB 15.89 (*0-690-04696-0*, Crowell Jr Bks) HarpC Child Bks.

Lasky, Kathryn. Voice in the Wind: A Starbuck Family Adventure. (gr. 4-7). 1993. 16.95 (*0-15-294102-9*, HB Juv Bks); pap. 6.95 (*0-15-294103-7*) HarBrace.

Mazzio, Joann. The One Who Came Back. 208p. (gr. 5-9). 1992. 13.45 (*0-395-59506-1*) HM.

Mendel, Kathleen L. Whispering Clay. LC 92-71598. (Illus.). 40p. (Orig.). 1992. pap. 4.50x (*1-878142-29-1*) Telstar TX.

Meyer, Carolyn, compiled by. Rio Grande Stories. LC 93-33639. 1994. write for info. (*0-15-200548-X*); pap. write for info. (*0-15-200066-6*) HarBrace.

NEW ORLEANS

Carvin, Ruth. A Visit to New Orleans: With Pictures to Color & Verses to Read. rev. ed. Dolobowsky, Mena, illus. 32p. (gr. k-4). 1988. coloring bk. 3.50 (*0-9616390-2-4*) Carvin Pub.

Coil, Suzanne M. Mardi Gras! Osborne, Mitchel, illus. LC 92-21166. 48p. (gr. 2 up). 1994. RSBE 15.95 (*0-02-722805-3*, Macmillan Child Bk) Macmillan Child Grp.

Nichols, Joan K. New Orleans. LC 88-35915. (Illus.). 60p. (gr. 3 up). 1989. text ed. 13.95 RSBE (*0-87518-403-0*, Dillon) Macmillan Child Grp.

Vogt, Lloyd. A Young Person's Guide to New Orleans Houses. LC 91-15213. (Illus.). 40p. 1991. pap. 6.95 (*0-88289-829-9*) Pelican.

NEW ORLEANS–FICTION

Couvillon, Alice & Moore, Elizabeth. Mimi's First Mardi Gras. Rougelot, Marilyn C., illus. LC 91-24006. 32p. (gr. 1-3). 1992. 14.95 (*0-88289-840-X*) Pelican.

Dartez, Cecilia C. Jenny Giraffe & the Streetcar Party. Green, Andy, illus. LC 93-9924. 32p. (gr. k-3). 1993. 14.95 (*0-88289-962-7*) Pelican.

—Jenny Giraffe Discovers the French Quarter. Wilson, Shelby, illus. LC 90-48720. 32p. (ps-8). 1991. 12.95 (*0-88289-819-1*) Pelican.

Flettrich, Terry. House in the Bend of Bourbon Street. Lo-An, illus. (gr. 1-6). 1974. pap. 2.95 (*0-88289-015-8*) Pelican.

Hill, Elizabeth S. The Banjo Player. 160p. (gr. 5-9). 1993. 14.99 (*0-670-84967-7*) Viking Child Bks.

Rice, James. Gaston Goes to Mardi Gras. LC 77-13302. (Illus.). 40p. (gr. 1-6). 1977. 12.95 (*0-88289-158-8*) Pelican.

Schroeder, Alan. Satchmo's Blues. Cooper, Floyd, illus. LC 93-41082. 1995. write for info. (*0-385-32046-9*) Doubleday.

NEW ORLEANS–HISTORY
Historic Santa Fe Association Staff, ed. We're So Lucky to Live in Santa Fe: An Activities Book in Historical Preservation. (Illus.). 26p. (gr. 4 up). pap. 4.95 (*0-89013-196-1*) Museum NM Pr.
NEW TESTAMENT
see Bible. New Testament
NEW WORDS
see Words, New
NEW YEAR
Blackwood, Alan. New Year. (Illus.). 48p. (gr. 3-8). 1987. PLB 15.94 (*0-86592-981-5*); 11.95s.p. (*0-685-67597-1*) Rourke Corp.
Chin, Steven A. Dragon Parade: A Chinese New Year Story. Tseng, Mou-Sien, illus. LC 92-18079. 32p. (gr. 2-5). 1992. PLB 18.51 (*0-8114-7215-9*) Raintree Steck-V.
Kalman, Bobbie. We Celebrate New Year. (Illus.). 56p. (gr. 3-4). 1985. 15.95 (*0-86505-041-4*); pap. 7.95 (*0-86505-051-1*) Crabtree Pub Co.
Kelley, Emily. Happy New Year. Kiedrowski, Priscilla, illus. 48p. (gr. k-4). 1984. PLB 14.95 (*0-87614-269-2*) Carolrhoda Bks.
—Happy New Year. Kiedrowski, Priscilla, illus. (gr. k-4). 1987. pap. 3.95 (*0-87614-469-5*, First Ave Edns) Lerner Pubns.
MacMillan, Dianne M. Tet: Vietnamese New Year. LC 93-46184. (Illus.). 48p. (gr. 1-4). 1994. lib. bdg. 14.95 (*0-89490-501-5*) Enslow Pubs.
NEW YEAR–FICTION
Edens, Cooper. Santa Cow Island Vacation. Lane, Daniel, illus. LC 93-30899. (gr. 2 up). 1994. 14.00 (*0-671-88319-4*, Green Tiger) S&S Trade.
Stevenson, James. Un-Happy New Year, Emma! LC 88-18802. (Illus.). 32p. (ps up). 1989. 12.95 (*0-688-08342-0*); PLB 12.88 (*0-688-08343-9*) Greenwillow.
NEW YORK (CITY)
Adams, Barbara Johnston. New York City. LC 88-20245. (Illus.). 60p. (gr. 3 up). 1988. text ed. 13.95 RSBE (*0-87518-384-0*, Dillon) Macmillan Child Grp.
Biemer, Linda. New York City: Our Community. 2nd ed. (Illus.). 100p. (gr. 4). 9.30 (*0-87905-139-6*, Peregrine Smith) Gibbs Smith Pub.
Climo, Shirley. City! New York. Ancona, George, illus. LC 89-13482. 64p. (gr. 3-7). 1990. RSBE 16.95 (*0-02-719020-X*, Macmillan Child Bk) Macmillan Child Grp.
Davis, Jim & Hawke, Sherryl D. New York. (Illus.). 64p. (gr. 4-9). 1990. PLB 11.95 (*0-8172-3031-9*) Raintree Steck-V.
Fisher, Barbara & Spiegel, Richard, eds. Bibliomania Three, Vol. 1. 47p. (Orig.). (gr. k-6). 1993. pap. 3.00 (*0-685-65120-7*) Ten Penny.
—Bibliomania Three, Vol. 2. 47p. (Orig.). (gr. 7-12). 1993. pap. 3.00 (*0-934830-54-1*) Ten Penny.
—Streams Seven. 150p. (Orig.). (gr. 7-12). 1993. pap. 5.00 (*0-934830-53-3*) Ten Penny.
Glassman, Bruce. New York. (Illus.). 64p. (gr. 3-7). PLB 14.95 (*1-56711-024-X*) Blackbirch.
Jakobsen, Kathy. My New York. 1993. 15.95 (*0-316-45653-5*) Little.
Krull, Kathleen. City Within a City: How Kids Live in New York's Chinatown. Hautzig, David, photos by. LC 93-15846. 1994. write for info. (*0-525-67437-3*, Lodestar Bks) Dutton Child Bks.
Mohr, Nicholasa. All for the Better: A Story of el Barrio. Gutierrez, Rudy, illus. LC 92-23639. 56p. (gr. 2-5). 1992. PLB 19.97 (*0-8114-7220-5*) Raintree Steck-V.
Stewart, G. New York. (Illus.). 48p. (gr. 5 up). 1989. lib. bdg. 15.94 (*0-86592-541-0*); 11.95s.p. (*0-685-58586-7*) Rourke Corp.
NEW YORK (CITY)–DESCRIPTION
Brown, Richard, illus. A Kid's Guide to New York City. 138p. (gr. 1 up). 1988. pap. 6.95 (*0-15-200458-0*, Gulliver Bks) HarBrace.
Clinton, Patrick. The Story of the Empire State Building. LC 87-25687. (Illus.). 32p. (gr. 3-6). 1987. pap. 3.95 (*0-516-44730-0*) Childrens.
Kerson, Adrian. Terror in the Towers: Amazing Stories from the World Trade Center Disaster. 80p. (Orig.). (gr. 2-7). 1993. PLB 9.99 (*0-679-95332-9*, Bullseye Bks); pap. 2.99 (*0-679-85332-4*, Bullseye Bks) Random Bks Yng Read.
Lovett, Sarah. Kidding Around New York City: A Young Person's Guide. 2nd ed. Blakemore, Sally, illus. 64p. (gr. 3 up). 1993. pap. 9.95 (*1-56261-095-3*) John Muir.
Munro, Roxie. Christmastime in New York City. (Illus.). 32p. (ps-3). 1994. pap. 5.99 (*0-14-050462-1*) Puffin Bks.
Pearlman, Cari J. Take New York Home. (Illus.). (gr. 9-12). 1988. write for info. (*0-929644-01-8*) MultiMap.
NEW YORK (CITY)–FICTION
Barracca, Debra & Barracca, Sal. Maxi, the Hero. Buehner, Mark, illus. (ps-3). 1991. 12.95 (*0-8037-0939-0*); PLB 12.89 (*0-8037-0940-4*) Dial Bks Young.
Barrie, Barbara. Adam Zigzag. LC 93-8735. 1994. 14.95 (*0-385-31172-9*) Delacorte.
Bartone, Elisa. Peppe the Lamplighter. LC 92-1397. (Illus.). (ps-3). 1993. 14.00 (*0-688-10268-9*); PLB 13.93 (*0-688-10269-7*) Lothrop.

Bennett, Helen S. Jack's Amazing Magic Bed. Hone, Michael J., illus. 32p. (gr. k-3). 1994. pap. 9.95 (*0-9638747-0-5*) Tomac Pubng.

What kid hasn't fantasized about driving around like magic? In JACK'S AMAZING MAGIC BED, Jack has to have a funny-looking hospital bed in his room at home for a little while & starts fooling around - pushing the buttons. Suddenly, the bed moves! "WOW! A magic bed." So he drives on the big, scary highway & goes to see the wonderful sights of New York City. When he gets tired, a helicopter pilot picks Jack up & flies above skyscrapers & Yankee Stadium & so close to the Statue of Liberty Jack can look right in her eyes. From up in the air, New York looks like a gigantic jigsaw puzzle: all the pieces tight together. Awesome! Full & double-page illustrations are fresh, imaginative pen & ink drawings with watercolor, whimsical details tucked in everywhere. First Prize: (Nat'l League Am Pen Women Biennial), Selection (New York Magazine). "Absolutely loved it...a fun trip to New York!" Joan Hambug (WOR-NY). To Order: Baker & Taylor distributor or Tomac Publishing, Box 247, Old Greenwich, CT 06870; 800-829-6133.
Publisher Provided Annotation.

Block, Francesca L. Missing Angel Juan. Braun, Wendy, illus. LC 92-38299. 144p. (gr. 7 up). 1993. 14.00 (*0-06-023004-5*); PLB 13.89 (*0-06-023007-X*) HarpC Child Bks.
Brouwer, Sigmund. The Downtown Desperadoes. 132p. 1991. pap. 4.99 (*0-89693-860-3*) SP Pubns.
Buchan, Stuart. Guys Like Us. (gr. 7 up). 1986. 14.95 (*0-385-29448-4*) Delacorte.
Campbell, Louisa. Gargoyles' Christmas. Taylor, Bridget S., illus. LC 94-4035. 32p. (gr. k-2). 1994. 15.95 (*0-87905-587-1*) Gibbs Smith Pub.
Charnas, Suzy M. The Bronze King. 208p. 1988. pap. 2.95 (*0-553-27104-0*, Starfire) Bantam.
Cohen, Ron. My Dad's Baseball. LC 93-22938. (Illus.). 1994. 15.00 (*0-688-12390-2*); lib. bdg. 14.93 (*0-688-12391-0*) Lothrop.
Cooney, Barbara. Hattie & the Wild Waves. Cooney, Barbara, illus. (ps-3). 1990. 14.95 (*0-670-83056-9*) Viking Child Bks.
Cummings, Pat. C.L.O.U.D.S. LC 85-9719. (Illus.). 32p. (ps-3). 1986. 12.95 (*0-688-04682-7*); PLB 12.88 (*0-688-04683-5*) Lothrop.
Danziger, Paula. Remember Me to Harold Square. LC 87-6844. 168p. (gr. 7 up). 1987. pap. 14.95 (*0-385-29610-X*) Delacorte.
—Remember Me to Harold Square. 144p. (gr. k-12). 1988. pap. 3.99 (*0-440-20153-5*, LFL) Dell.
De Brunhoff, Laurent. Babar a New York. (FRE., Illus.). (gr. 4-6). 1975. bds. 15.95 (*0-7859-5281-0*, 2010025520) Fr & Eur.
Dorros, Arthur. Abuela. Kleven, Elisa, illus. LC 90-21459. 40p. (ps-2). 1991. 14.00 (*0-525-44750-4*, DCB) Dutton Child Bks.
Elish, Dan. The Great Squirrel Uprising. Cazet, Denys, illus. LC 91-27145. 128p. (gr. 4 up). 1992. 14.95 (*0-531-05995-2*); lib. bdg. 14.99 (*0-531-08595-3*) Orchard Bks Watts.
Fitzgerald, Frank. Where's Kevin? LC 92-33058. (gr. 4-7). 1992. pap. 7.99 (*0-553-37199-1*) Bantam.
Fitzhugh, Louise. Sport. 224p. (gr. 7 up). 1980. pap. 1.75 (*0-440-98350-9*, LFL) Dell.
Fox, Paula. Monkey Island. LC 91-7460. 160p. (gr. 5 up). 1991. 14.95 (*0-531-05962-6*); RLB 14.99 (*0-531-08562-7*) Orchard Bks Watts.
French, Fiona. Snow White in New York. (Illus.). 32p. 1990. pap. 6.95 (*0-19-272210-7*) OUP.
Gray, Luli. Falcon's Egg. LC 94-16731. 1995. 10.95 (*0-395-71128-2*) Ticknor & Flds Bks Yng Read.
Greene, Constance C. Al(exandra) the Great. 144p. (gr. 5-9). 1983. pap. 2.95 (*0-440-40350-2*, YB) Dell.
Greenwald, Sheila. My Fabulous New Life. LC 92-44928. 160p. (gr. 3-7). 1993. 10.95 (*0-15-277693-1*, Browndeer Pr); pap. 3.95 (*0-15-276716-9*, Browndeer Pr) HarBrace.
Hamilton, Virginia. The Planet of Junior Brown. LC 71-155264. 240p. (gr. 5-9). 1971. SBE 14.95 (*0-02-742510-X*, Macmillan Child Bk) Macmillan Child Grp.
Happy, Elizabeth. Bailey's Birthday. Chase, Andra, illus. LC 93-32519. 32p. (gr. 1-4). 1994. 16.95 (*1-55942-059-6*, 7658); video, tchr's. guide & storybook 79.95 (*1-55942-062-6*, 9377) Marshfilm.
Herold, Marrie R. A Very Important Day. Stock, Catherine, illus. LC 94-16647. 1995. write for info. (*0-688-13065-8*); PLB write for info. (*0-688-13066-6*) Morrow Jr Bks.
Hest, Amy. Love You, Soldier. LC 90-25161. 48p. (gr. 2-5). 1991. SBE 13.95 (*0-02-743635-7*, Four Winds) Macmillan Child Grp.
—Love You, Soldier. 48p. (gr. 2-6). 1993. pap. 3.99 (*0-14-036174-X*) Puffin Bks.
Hunt, Angela E. Cassie Perkins, No. 7: Star Light, Star Bright. LC 92-18796. 1993. 4.99 (*0-8423-1117-3*) Tyndale.
James, Henry. Washington Square. Tate, E., intro. by. (gr. 10 up). 1969. pap. 1.50 (*0-8049-0210-0*, CL-210) Airmont.
Joosse, Barbara M. The Morning Chair. Sewall, Marcia, illus. LC 93-4870. Date not set. write for info. (*0-395-62337-5*, Clarion Bks) HM.
Konigsburg, E. L. Amy Elizabeth Explores Bloomingdale's. Konigsburg, E. L., illus. LC 91-40132. 32p. (ps-3). 1992. SBE 14.95 (*0-689-31766-2*, Atheneum Child Bk) Macmillan Child Grp.
—From the Mixed-Up Files of Mrs. Basil E. Frankweiler. LC 86-25903. (Illus.). 176p. (gr. 4-7). 1987. pap. 3.95 (*0-689-71181-6*, Aladdin) Macmillan Child Grp.
Kovalski, Maryann. Jingle Bells. Kovalski, Maryann, illus. 32p. (ps-2). 1988. 12.95 (*0-316-50258-8*) Little.
Lebowitz, Fran. Mr. Chas & Lisa Sue Meet the Pandas. Graves, Michael, illus. LC 94-1132. 72p. (gr. 2-7). 1994. 15.00 (*0-679-86052-5*) Knopf Bks Yng Read.
Lehrman, Robert. Separations. LC 92-26782. 224p. (gr. 5-9). 1993. pap. 3.99 (*0-14-032322-8*) Puffin Bks.
L'Engle, Madeleine. The Young Unicorns. LC 68-13682. 256p. (gr. 7 up). 1968. 16.95 (*0-374-38778-8*) FS&G.
Levoy, Myron. Kelly 'n' Me. LC 91-35807. 208p. (gr. 7 up). 1992. 15.00 (*0-06-020838-4*); PLB 14.89 (*0-06-020839-2*) HarpC Child Bks.
Levy, Elizabeth. Gorgonzola Zombies in the Park. Ulrich, George, illus. LC 92-11353. 96p. (gr. 2-5). 1993. 14.00 (*0-06-021461-9*); PLB 13.89 (*0-06-021460-0*) HarpC Child Bks.
Mango, Karin N. Portrait of Miranda. LC 92-8191. 240p. (gr. 7 up). 1993. 16.00 (*0-06-021777-4*); PLB 15.89 (*0-06-021778-2*) HarpC Child Bks.
Marsh, Fabienne. The Moralist of the Alphabet Streets. 252p. (gr. 10 up). 1991. 17.95 (*0-945575-47-5*) Algonquin Bks.
Martin, Ann M. New York, New York. (gr. 4-7). 1991. pap. 3.50 (*0-590-43576-0*) Scholastic Inc.
—Stacey's Mistake. 1993. pap. 3.50 (*0-590-43718-6*) Scholastic Inc.
—Stacey's Mistake. large type ed. LC 93-8086. 176p. (gr. 4 up). 1993. PLB 15.93 (*0-8368-1022-8*) Gareth Stevens Inc.
Miller-Lachmann, Lyn. Hiding Places. 206p. (Orig.). (gr. 9-12). 1987. pap. 4.95 (*0-938961-00-4*, Stamp Out Sheep Pr) Sq One Pubs.
Mohr, Nicholasa. El Bronx Remembered. LC 75-6306. 288p. (gr. 7 up). 1993. pap. 4.95 (*0-06-447100-4*, Trophy) HarpC Child Bks.
Munro, Roxie. The Inside-Outside Book of New York City. (Illus.). 32p. (ps-3). 1994. pap. 4.99 (*0-14-050454-0*) Puffin Bks.
Pinkwater, Jill. Tails of the Bronx: A Tale of the Bronx. LC 90-48914. 176p. (gr. 3-7). 1991. SBE 14.95 (*0-02-774652-6*, Macmillan Child Bk) Macmillan Child Grp.
Roth-Hano, Renee. Safe Harbors. LC 93-10782. 224p. (gr. 12 up). 1993. SBE 16.95 (*0-02-777795-2*, Four Winds) Macmillan Child Grp.
Rush, Ken. Friday's Journey. LC 93-4871. (Illus.). 1994. write for info. (*0-531-06821-8*); lib. bdg. write for info. (*0-531-08671-2*) Orchard Bks Watts.
Rylant, Cynthia. An Angel for Solomon Singer. Catalanotto, Peter, illus. LC 91-15957. 32p. 1992. 14.95 (*0-531-05978-2*); lib. bdg. 14.99 (*0-531-08578-3*) Orchard Bks Watts.
Sachs, Marilyn. Call Me Ruth. LC 94-19695. 1995. write for info. (*0-688-13737-7*, Pub. by Beech Tree Bks) Morrow.
Sawyer, Ruth. Roller Skates. Angelo, Valenti, illus. 184p. (gr. 5-9). 1986. pap. 3.99 (*0-14-030358-8*, Puffin) Puffin Bks.
Selden, George. Cricket in Times Square. Williams, Garth, illus. (gr. 2-7). 1970. pap. 3.99 (*0-440-41563-2*, YB) Dell.
—Un Grillo En Times Square: The Cricket in Times Square. (gr. 4-7). 1994. pap. 4.95 (*0-374-48060-5*, Mirasol) FS&G.
Shreve, Susan. Amy Dunn Quits School. De Groat, Diane, illus. LC 92-41772. 96p. (gr. 3 up). 1993. 13.00 (*0-688-10320-0*, Tambourine Bks) Morrow.
Simon, Carly. The Nightime Chauffeur. Datz, Margot, illus. LC 92-44934. 1993. pap. 16.00 (*0-385-47009-6*) Doubleday.
Slade, Michael. The Horses of Central Park. 96p. 1992. 12.95 (*0-590-44659-2*, Scholastic Hardcover) Scholastic Inc.
Swift, Hildegarde H. & Ward, Lynd. Little Red Lighthouse & the Great Gray Bridge. Ward, Lynd, illus. LC 42-36286. (ps-3). 1942. 15.95 (*0-15-247040-9*, HB Juv Bks) HarBrace.
Taylor, Sydney. All-of-a-Kind Family. John, Helen, illus. 189p. (gr. 3-6). 1988. Repr. of 1951 ed. 11.95 (*0-929093-00-3*) Taylor Prodns.
Thoene, Bodie. Say to This Mountain. 400p. (Orig.). 1993. pap. text ed. 11.99 (*1-55661-191-9*) Bethany Hse.
Twentieth Century Fox Film Corporation Staff. Home Alone Two: Lost in New York. 16p. (ps-2). 1993. write for info. (*1-883366-14-3*) YES Ent.

Vallet, Cedric. Mother, Where Is New York? Vallet, Cedric, illus. 11p. (gr. k-3). 1992. pap. 13.95 (*1-895583-27-6*) MAYA Pubs.

Wersba, Barbara. You'll Never Guess the End. LC 91-24771. 144p. (gr. 7 up). 1992. 14.00 (*0-06-020448-6*); PLB 13.89 (*0-06-020449-4*) HarpC Child Bks.

Wibberley, Leonard. Mouse That Roared. (gr. 6-12). 1971. pap. 3.50 (*0-553-24969-X*) Bantam.

Wood, Marcia. Always, Julia. LC 91-40460. 128p. (gr. 5-9). 1993. SBE 13.95 (*0-689-31728-X*, Atheneum Child Bk) Macmillan Child Grp.

Yektai, Niki. The Secret Room. LC 92-6720. 192p. (gr. 4-7). 1992. 14.95 (*0-531-05456-X*); PLB 14.99 (*0-531-08606-2*) Orchard Bks Watts.

NEW YORK (CITY)–HISTORY

Climo, Shirley. City! New York. Ancona, George, illus. LC 89-13482. 64p. (gr. 3-7). 1990. RSBE 16.95 (*0-02-719020-X*, Macmillan Child Bk) Macmillan Child Grp.

Costabel, Eva D. Jews of New Amsterdam. Costabel, Eva D., illus. LC 87-27873. 32p. (gr. 2-6). 1988. SBE 13.95 (*0-689-31351-9*, Atheneum Child Bk) Macmillan Child Grp.

Diamonstein, Barbaralee. Landmarks: Eighteen Wonders of the New York World. Lorenz, Albert, illus. 160p. 1992. 35.00 (*0-8109-3565-1*) Abrams.

NEW YORK. METROPOLITAN MUSEUM OF ART–FICTION

Konigsburg, E. L. From the Mixed-Up Files of Mrs. Basil E. Frankweiler. Konigsburg, E. L., illus. LC 67-18988. 168p. (gr. 3-7). 1970. SBE 14.95 (*0-689-20586-4*, Atheneum Child Bk) Macmillan Child Grp.

—From the Mixed-Up Files of Mrs. Basil E. Frankweiler. 160p. (gr. 5 up). 1977. pap. 4.50 (*0-440-43180-8*, YB) Dell.

NEW YORK (STATE)

Aylesworth, Thomas G. & Aylesworth, Virginia L. Upper Atlantic: New Jersey - New York. (Illus.). 64p. (gr. 3 up). 1987. lib. bdg. 16.95 (*1-55546-553-6*); pap. 6.95 (*0-685-35556-X*) Chelsea Hse.

Carole Marsh New York Books, 45 bks. 1994. PLB 1052.75 set (*0-7933-1307-4*); pap. 602.75 set (*0-7933-5186-3*) Gallopade Pub Group.

Carpenter, Allan. New York. new ed. LC 78-3395. (Illus.). 96p. (gr. 4 up). 1978. PLB 16.95 (*0-516-04132-0*) Childrens.

Fradin, Dennis. New York: In Words & Pictures. Wahl, Richard, illus. LC 81-28366. 48p. (gr. 2-5). 1981. PLB 12.95 (*0-516-03932-6*) Childrens.

Gelman, Amy. New York. Lerner Geography Department Staff, ed. (Illus.). 72p. (gr. 3-6). 1992. PLB 17.50 (*0-8225-2720-0*) Lerner Pubns.

Higby, Roy C. A Man from the Past. 2nd ed. Lux, Don, illus. McLoughlin, William G., intro. by. (Illus.). (gr. 5-12). pap. 8.00 (*0-914692-02-X*) Big Moose.

McMartin, Barbara. Adventures in Hiking. 110p. 1993. 12.50 (*0-925168-25-4*) North Country.

Marsh, Carole. Avast, Ye Slobs! New York Pirate Trivia. (Illus.). 1994. PLB 24.95 (*0-7933-0835-6*); pap. 14.95 (*0-7933-0834-8*); computer disk 29.95 (*0-7933-0836-4*) Gallopade Pub Group.

—The Beast of the New York Bed & Breakfast. (Illus.). 1994. PLB 24.95 (*0-7933-1821-1*); pap. 14.95 (*0-7933-1822-X*); computer disk 29.95 (*0-7933-1823-8*) Gallopade Pub Group.

—Bow Wow! New York Dogs in History, Mystery, Legend, Lore, Humor & More! (Illus.). (gr. 3-12). 1994. PLB 24.95 (*0-7933-3563-9*); pap. 14.95 (*0-7933-3564-7*); computer disk 29.95 (*0-7933-3565-5*) Gallopade Pub Group.

—Christopher Columbus Comes to New York! Includes Reproducible Activities for Kids! (Illus.). (gr. 3-12). 1994. PLB 24.95 (*0-7933-3716-X*); pap. 14.95 (*0-7933-3717-8*); computer disk 29.95 (*0-7933-3718-6*) Gallopade Pub Group.

—The Hard-to-Believe-But-True! Book of New York History, Mystery, Trivia, Legend, Lore, Humor & More. (Illus.). 1994. PLB 24.95 (*0-7933-0832-1*); pap. 14.95 (*0-7933-0831-3*); computer disk 29.95 (*0-7933-0833-X*) Gallopade Pub Group.

—If My New York Mama Ran the World! (Illus.). 1994. lib. bdg. 24.95 (*0-7933-1827-0*); pap. 14.95 (*0-7933-1828-9*); computer disk 29.95 (*0-7933-1829-7*) Gallopade Pub Group.

—Jurassic Ark! New York Dinosaurs & Other Prehistoric Creatures. (gr. k-12). 1994. PLB 24.95 (*0-7933-7524-X*); pap. 14.95 (*0-7933-7525-8*); computer disk 29.95 (*0-7933-7526-6*) Gallopade Pub Group.

—Let's Quilt New York & Stuff It Topographically! (Illus.). 1994. PLB 24.95 (*1-55609-904-5*); pap. 14.95 (*1-55609-060-9*); computer disk 29.95 (*1-55609-905-3*) Gallopade Pub Group.

—Let's Quilt Our New York County. 1994. lib. bdg. 24.95 (*0-7933-7209-7*); pap. text ed. 14.95 (*0-7933-7210-0*); disk 29.95 (*0-7933-7211-9*) Gallopade Pub Group.

—Let's Quilt Our New York Town. 1994. lib. bdg. 24.95 (*0-7933-7059-0*); pap. text ed. 14.95 (*0-7933-7060-4*); disk 29.95 (*0-7933-7061-2*) Gallopade Pub Group.

—Meow! New York Cats in History, Mystery, Legend, Lore, Humor & More! (Illus.). (gr. 3-12). 1994. PLB 24.95 (*0-7933-3410-1*); pap. 14.95 (*0-7933-3411-X*); computer disk 29.95 (*0-7933-3412-8*) Gallopade Pub Group.

—New York & Other State Greats (Biographies) (Illus.). 1994. PLB 24.95 (*1-55609-918-5*); pap. 14.95 (*1-55609-919-3*); computer disk 29.95 (*1-55609-920-7*) Gallopade Pub Group.

—New York Bandits, Bushwackers, Outlaws, Crooks, Devils, Ghosts, Desperadoes & Other Assorted & Sundry Characters! (Illus.). 1994. PLB 24.95 (*0-7933-0817-8*); pap. 14.95 (*0-7933-0816-X*); computer disk 29.95 (*0-7933-0818-6*) Gallopade Pub Group.

—New York Classic Christmas Trivia: Stories, Recipes, Activities, Legends, Lore & More! (Illus.). 1994. PLB 24.95 (*0-7933-0820-8*); pap. 14.95 (*0-685-45982-9*); computer disk 29.95 (*0-7933-0821-6*) Gallopade Pub Group.

—New York Coastales. (Illus.). 1994. PLB 24.95 (*1-55609-912-6*); pap. 14.95 (*1-55609-913-4*); computer disk 29.95 (*1-55609-914-2*) Gallopade Pub Group.

—New York Coastales! 1994. lib. bdg. 24.95 (*0-7933-7297-6*) Gallopade Pub Group.

—New York Dingbats! Bk. 1: A Fun Book of Games, Stories, Activities & More about Our State That's All in Code! for You to Decipher. (Illus.). (gr. 3-12). 1994. PLB 24.95 (*0-7933-3869-7*); pap. 14.95 (*0-7933-3870-0*); computer disk 29.95 (*0-7933-3871-9*) Gallopade Pub Group.

—New York Festival Fun for Kids! (Illus.). (gr. 3-12). 1994. lib. bdg. 24.95 (*0-7933-4022-5*); pap. 14.95 (*0-7933-4023-3*); disk 29.95 (*0-7933-4024-1*) Gallopade Pub Group.

—The New York Hot Air Balloon Mystery. (Illus.). (gr. 2-9). 1994. 24.95 (*0-7933-2606-0*); pap. 14.95 (*0-7933-2607-9*); computer disk 29.95 (*0-7933-2608-7*) Gallopade Pub Group.

—New York Jeopardy! Answers & Questions about Our State! (Illus.). (gr. 3-12). 1994. PLB 24.95 (*0-7933-4175-2*); pap. 14.95 (*0-7933-4176-0*); computer disk 29.95 (*0-7933-4177-9*) Gallopade Pub Group.

—New York "Jography" A Fun Run Thru Our State! (Illus.). 1994. PLB 24.95 (*1-55609-897-9*); pap. 14.95 (*1-55609-898-7*); computer disk 29.95 (*1-55609-899-5*) Gallopade Pub Group.

—New York Kid's Cookbook: Recipes, How-to, History, Lore & More! (Illus.). 1994. PLB 24.95 (*0-7933-0829-1*); pap. 14.95 (*0-7933-0828-3*); computer disk 29.95 (*0-7933-0830-5*) Gallopade Pub Group.

—New York Quiz Bowl Crash Course! (Illus.). 1994. PLB 24.95 (*1-55609-915-0*); pap. 14.95 (*1-55609-916-9*); computer disk 29.95 (*1-55609-917-7*) Gallopade Pub Group.

—New York Rollercoasters! (Illus.). (gr. 3-12). 1994. PLB 24.95 (*0-7933-5320-3*); pap. 14.95 (*0-7933-5321-1*); computer disk 29.95 (*0-7933-5322-X*) Gallopade Pub Group.

—New York School Trivia: An Amazing & Fascinating Look at Our State's Teachers, Schools & Students! (Illus.). 1994. PLB 24.95 (*0-7933-0826-7*); pap. 14.95 (*0-7933-0825-9*); computer disk 29.95 (*0-7933-0827-5*) Gallopade Pub Group.

—New York Silly Basketball Sportsmysteries, Vol. 1. (Illus.). 1994. PLB 24.95 (*0-7933-0823-2*); pap. 14.95 (*0-7933-0822-4*); computer disk 29.95 (*0-7933-0824-0*) Gallopade Pub Group.

—New York Silly Basketball Sportsmysteries, Vol. 2. (Illus.). 1994. PLB 24.95 (*0-685-45983-7*); pap. 14.95 (*0-7933-1825-4*); computer disk 29.95 (*0-7933-1826-2*) Gallopade Pub Group.

—New York Silly Football Sportsmysteries, Vol. 1. (Illus.). 1994. PLB 24.95 (*1-55609-906-1*); pap. 14.95 (*1-55609-907-X*); computer disk 29.95 (*1-55609-908-8*) Gallopade Pub Group.

—New York Silly Football Sportsmysteries, Vol. 2. (Illus.). 1994. PLB 24.95 (*1-55609-909-6*); pap. 14.95 (*1-55609-910-X*); computer disk 29.95 (*1-55609-911-8*) Gallopade Pub Group.

—New York Silly Trivia! (Illus.). 1994. PLB 24.95 (*1-55609-895-2*); pap. 14.95 (*1-55609-103-6*); computer disk 29.95 (*1-55609-896-0*) Gallopade Pub Group.

—New York's (Most Devasting!) Disasters & (Most Calamitous!) Catastrophies! (Illus.). 1994. PLB 24.95 (*0-7933-0814-3*); pap. 14.95 (*0-7933-0813-5*); computer disk 29.95 (*0-7933-0815-1*) Gallopade Pub Group.

—Uncle Rebus: New York Picture Stories for Computer Kids. (Illus.). (gr. k-3). 1994. PLB 24.95 (*0-7933-4597-9*); pap. 14.95 (*0-7933-4598-7*); disk 29.95 (*0-7933-4599-5*) Gallopade Pub Group.

Perrin, Janet & Howlett, Charles F. A Walk Through History: A Community Named Amityville. (Illus.). 125p. (gr. 7-9). 1993. pap. text ed. write for info. (*1-55787-096-9*) Heart of the Lakes.

Stein, R. Conrad. New York. LC 88-11748. (Illus.). 144p. (gr. 4 up). 1988. PLB 20.55 (*0-516-00478-6*) Childrens.

—New York. 202p. 1993. text ed. 15.40 (*1-56956-158-3*) W A T Braille.

Thompson, Kathleen. New York. LC 87-26481. 48p. (gr. 3 up). 1988. 19.97 (*0-86514-474-5*) Raintree Steck-V.

Turbek, Joan. The Little River & the Big, Big Bridge. LC 93-25968. 48p. 1993. 7.50 (*0-925168-18-1*) North Country.

NEW YORK (STATE)–ANTIQUITIES

Shebar, Judith & Shebar, Sharon S. The Cardiff Giant. Sullivan, Dave, illus. LC 83-13056. 64p. (gr. 7-11). 1983. (J Messner) S&S Trade.

NEW YORK (STATE)–FICTION

Banim, Lisa. Drums at Saratoga. LC 93-16460. 64p. (Orig.). (gr. 4-6). 1993. PLB 12.95 (*1-881889-20-3*) Silver Moon.

Gleiter, Jan. Legend of Sleepy Hollow. (ps-3). 1993. pap. 3.95 (*0-8114-8351-7*) Raintree Steck-V.

Gleiter, Jan, retold by. The Legend of Sleepy Hollow. Thompson, Kathleen, retold by. LC 84-9931. (Illus.). (gr. 2-5). 1984. PLB 19.97 (*0-8172-2117-4*); PLB 29.28 incl. cassette (*0-8172-2239-1*); pap. 23.95 incl. cassette (*0-8172-2270-7*) Raintree Steck-V.

Irving, Washington. The Headless Horseman: A Retelling of The Legend of Sleepy Hollow. Harding, Emma, illus. LC 94-10276. (gr. k-3). 1994. 15.95 (*0-8050-3584-2*) H Holt & Co.

—The Legend of Sleepy Hollow. Flint, Ross, illus. 32p. (gr. k-4). 1992. pap. 4.95 (*0-8249-8574-5*, Ideals Child) Hambleton-Hill.

—The Legend of Sleepy Hollow. Kelley, Gary, illus. (gr. 4-12). 1990. lib. bdg. 19.95 RLB smythe-sewn (*0-88682-328-5*, 97206-098) Creative Ed.

—Legend of Sleepy Hollow & Other Stories. (gr. 6 up). 1964. pap. 2.95 (*0-8049-0050-7*, CL-50) Airmont.

—The Legend of Sleepy Hollow: Minibook Edition. Van Nutt, Robert, illus. LC 93-12153. 1993. incl. cass. 9.95 (*0-88708-321-8*, Rabbit Ears) Picture Bk Studio.

—Rip Van Winkle. Howe, John, retold by. & illus. (ps-3). 1988. 14.95 (*0-316-37578-0*) Little.

—Rip Van Winkle. Rackham, Arthur, illus. LC 92-9843. 128p. (gr. 1). 1992. 19.00 (*0-8037-1264-2*) Dial Bks Young.

—Rip Van Winkle. Kelley, Gary, illus. LC 93-17093. 1993. PLB 21.95 (*0-88682-631-4*) Creative Ed.

—Rip Van Winkle: The Mountain Top Edition. rev. ed. Oakes, Donald T., ed. Wyeth, N. C. & Murtagh, Mark, illus. Hommel, Justine L., contrib. by. LC 89-62869. 92p. (gr. 9). 1989. pap. write for info. (*0-9624216-0-X*) MTH Soc Inc.

Jensen, Patricia A. The Legend of Sleepy Hollow. Barnes-Murphy, Rowan S., illus. LC 93-24803. (gr. k-3). 1993. PLB 11.59 (*0-8167-3168-3*); pap. text ed. 2.95 (*0-8167-3169-1*) Troll Assocs.

Lipsyte, Robert. The Brave. LC 90-25396. 208p. (gr. 7 up). 1991. 15.00 (*0-06-023915-8*); PLB 14.89 (*0-06-023916-6*) HarpC Child Bks.

Standiford, Natalie, retold by. The Headless Horseman. Cook, Donald, illus. LC 90-53228. 48p. (Orig.). (ps-2). 1992. PLB 7.99 (*0-679-91241-X*); pap. 3.50 (*0-679-81241-5*) Random Bks Yng Read.

Storr, Catherine, retold by. Rip Van Winkle. LC 83-26996. (Illus.). 32p. (gr. k-5). 1984. PLB 19.97 (*0-8172-2108-5*); PLB 29.28 incl. cassette (*0-8172-2236-7*) Raintree Steck-V.

West, Tracey. Voyage of the Half Moon. LC 93-16462. 64p. (Orig.). (gr. 4-6). 1993. PLB 12.95 (*1-881889-18-1*) Silver Moon.

Wilder, Laura Ingalls. Farmer Boy. rev. ed. Williams, Garth, illus. LC 52-7527. 372p. (gr. 3-7). 1961. 15.95 (*0-06-026425-X*); PLB 15.89 (*0-06-026421-7*) HarpC Child Bks.

York, Carol B., ed. Ichabod Crane & the Headless Horseman. Irving, Washington. LC 79-66323. (Illus.). 48p. (gr. 3-6). 1980. lib. bdg. 9.89 (*0-89375-316-5*); pap. 2.95 (*0-89375-315-7*) Troll Assocs.

—Rip Van Winkle. new ed. Washington, Irving. LC 79-66314. (Illus.). 48p. (gr. 3-6). 1980. lib. bdg. 9.89 (*0-89375-300-9*); pap. 2.95 (*0-89375-299-1*) Troll Assocs.

NEW YORK (STATE)–HISTORY

Avakian, Monique & Smith, Carter, III. A Historical Album of New York. LC 92-41135. (Illus.). 64p. (gr. 4-8). 1993. PLB 15.90 (*1-56294-005-8*); pap. 6.95 (*1-56294-758-3*) Millbrook Pr.

Fradin, Dennis B. New York - From Sea to Shining Sea. (Illus.). 64p. (gr. 3-5). 1993. PLB 16.45 (*0-516-03832-X*) Childrens.

Marsh, Carole. Chill Out: Scary New York Tales Based on Frightening New York Truths. (Illus.). 1994. lib. bdg. 24.95 (*0-7933-4750-5*); pap. 14.95 (*0-7933-4751-3*); disk 29.95 (*0-7933-4752-1*) Gallopade Pub Group.

—My First Book about New York. (gr. k-4). 1994. PLB 24.95 (*0-7933-5665-2*); pap. 14.95 (*0-7933-5666-0*); computer disk 29.95 (*0-7933-5667-9*) Gallopade Pub Group.

—New York "Crinkum-Crankum" A Funny Word Book about Our State. (Illus.). 1994. lib. bdg. 24.95 (*0-7933-4904-4*); pap. 14.95 (*0-7933-4905-2*); disk 29.95 (*0-7933-4906-0*) Gallopade Pub Group.

—The New York Mystery Van Takes Off! Book 1: Handicapped New York Kids Sneak Off on a Big Adventure. (Illus.). (gr. 3-12). 1994. 24.95 (*0-7933-5057-3*); pap. 14.95 (*0-7933-5058-1*); computer disk 29.95 (*0-7933-5059-X*) Gallopade Pub Group.

—New York Timeline: A Chronology of New York History, Mystery, Trivia, Legend, Lore & More. (Illus.). (gr. 3-12). 1994. PLB 24.95 (*0-7933-5971-6*); pap. 14.95 (*0-7933-5972-4*); computer disk 29.95 (*0-7933-5973-2*) Gallopade Pub Group.

—New York's Unsolved Mysteries (& Their "Solutions") Includes Scientific Information & Other Activities for Students. (Illus.). (gr. 3-12). 1994. PLB 24.95 (*0-7933-5818-3*); pap. 14.95 (*0-7933-5819-1*); computer disk 29.95 (*0-7933-5820-5*) Gallopade Pub Group.
—Patch, the Pirate Dog: A New York Pet Story. (ps-4). 1994. PLB 24.95 (*0-7933-5512-5*); pap. 14.95 (*0-7933-5513-3*); computer disk 29.95 (*0-7933-5514-1*) Gallopade Pub Group.
Ray, Frederic. Old Fort Niagara: An Illustrated History. rev. ed. (Illus.). 16p. 1988. pap. 1.25 (*0-941967-06-9*) Old Fort Niagara Assn.
Schuyler, Doris E. Butlers Bury. 3rd ed. (Illus.). 32p. 1991. pap. text ed. 5.00 (*0-9628208-4-9*) Canal Side Pubs.

Steinberg, Michael. Our Wilderness: How the People of New York Found, Changed, & Preserved the Adirondacks. Burdick, Neal S., ed. LC 91-16550. (Illus.). 112p. (gr. 5 up). 1994. 18.95 (*0-935272-56-9*); pap. 9.95 (*0-935272-57-7*) ADK Mtn Club.
A history of the 6-million-acre Adirondack Park of New York State, which includes towns & farms, businesses & timberlands as well as 1.2 million acres of wilderness. Written for ages 10 & up (Gr. 4 plus). Described by KIRKUS REVIEWS as "a cultural history full of charming, quirky people, plus both funny & sobering anecdotes... Gracefully written with lessons that go far beyond regional interest." APPALACHIA noted that "there is probably no other book available that can provide as thorough an introduction to Adirondack history, particularly with anything close to the brevity & efficiency of this book." Author received award from Adirondack Park Centennial Committee for his contribution to education via OUR WILDERNESS. Historic photographs by Stoddard & Apperson. Publication coincided with the 1992 Centennial of the Adirondack Park. Book carries conservationist message. "The entertaining & informative 'young people's history'... contains plenty of interest the mature mind."--New York's Rochester DEMOCRAT & CHRONICLE.
Publisher Provided Annotation.

Whitman, Bernard. New York State Map Skills Resource Guide. Whitman, Shirley, illus. 85p. (Orig.). (gr. 4-7). 1984. tchr's. ed. 18.00 (*0-918433-00-2*) In Educ.

NEW YORK (STATE)–HISTORY–FICTION
Collier, James L. & Collier, Christopher. Who Is Carrie? LC 83-23947. 192p. (gr. 4-6). 1984. 14.95 (*0-385-29295-3*) Delacorte.
Giff, Patricia R. Columbus Circle. (Orig.). (gr. k-6). 1988. pap. 2.75 (*0-440-40036-8*, YB) Dell.
Irving, Washington. The Legend of Sleepy Hollow. 69p. 1992. text ed. 5.52 (*1-56956-119-2*) W A T Braille.
—Rip Van Winkle. Kelley, Gary, illus. 64p. (gr. 6 up). 1993. 21.95 (*1-56846-082-1*) Creat Editions.
Lonergan, Carroll V. Brave Boys of Old Fort Ticonderoga. LC 87-22144. (gr. 6 up). 1987. write for info., 192 p. (*0-932334-57-1*, Empire State Bks); pap. 7.95, 144 p. (*1-55787-018-7*, NY16028, Empire State Bks) Heart of the Lakes.

NEW YORK METS (BASEBALL TEAM)
Goodman, Michael. New York Mets. 48p. (gr. 4-10). 1992. PLB 14.95 (*0-88682-456-7*) Creative Ed.
Jennings, Jay. Long Shots. 64p. (gr. 5-7). 1991. PLB 10.95 (*0-382-24105-3*); pap. 5.95 (*0-382-24112-6*) Silver Burdett Pr.
New York Mets. (gr. 4-7). 1993. pap. 1.49 (*0-553-56424-2*) Bantam.
Shannon, Bill. The New York Mets. 1991. pap. 2.99 (*0-517-05792-1*) Random Hse Value.

NEW YORK. STOCK EXCHANGE
Davies, Nancy M. The Stock Market Crash of Nineteen Twenty-Nine. LC 92-23310. (Illus.). 96p. (gr. 6 up). 1994. text ed. 14.95 RSBE (*0-02-726221-9*, New Discovery Bks) Macmillan Child Grp.
Kent, Zachary. The Story of the New York Stock Exchange. LC 89-25374. (Illus.). 32p. (gr. 3-6). 1990. pap. 3.95 (*0-516-44748-3*) Childrens.

NEW YORK YANKEES (BASEBALL TEAM)
The New York Yankees. 1991. pap. 2.99 (*0-517-05788-3*) Random Hse Value.
New York Yankees. (gr. 4-7). 1993. pap. 1.49 (*0-553-56412-9*) Bantam.
Rambeck, Richard. New York Yankees. 48p. (gr. 4-10). 1992. PLB 14.95 (*0-88682-445-1*) Creative Ed.

NEW ZEALAND
Fox, Mary V. New Zealand. LC 90-20010. (Illus.). 128p. (gr. 5-9). 1991. PLB 20.55 (*0-516-02728-X*) Childrens.
Keyworth, Valerie. New Zealand: Land of the Long White Cloud. LC 89-11716. (Illus.). 128p. (gr. 5 up). 1990. text ed. 14.95 RSBE (*0-87518-414-6*, Dillon) Macmillan Child Grp.
Lerner Publications, Department of Geography Staff. New Zealand in Pictures. (Illus.). 64p. (gr. 5 up). 1990. PLB 17.50 (*0-8225-1862-7*) Lerner Pubns.

NEW ZEALAND–FICTION
Bond, Nancy. Truth to Tell. LC 93-11248. 336p. (gr. 5 up). 1994. SBE 17.95 (*0-689-50601-5*, M K McElderry) Macmillan Child Grp.
Gee, Maurice. The Champion. LC 92-37670. 1993. pap. 14.00 (*0-671-86561-7*, S&S BFYR) S&S Trade.
—The Fire-Raiser. LC 92-8017. 150p. (gr. 5-9). 1992. 13.45 (*0-395-62428-2*) HM.
Lattimore, Deborah N. Punga: The Goddess of Ugly. LC 92-23191. 32p. 1993. 14.95 (*0-15-292862-6*) HarBrace.
Mahy, Margaret. A Fortunate Name. Young, Marion, illus. LC 93-560. 1993. 13.95 (*0-385-31135-4*) Delacorte.
—A Fortune Branches Out. Young, Marian, illus. LC 93-11441. 1994. 13.95 (*0-385-32037-X*) Delacorte.
—The Good Fortunes Gang. Young, Marion, illus. LC 92-38784. (gr. 5 up). 1993. 13.95 (*0-385-31015-3*) Delacorte.
—The Good Fortunes Gang, Bk. 1: Cousins Quartet. large type ed. (Illus.). (gr. 1-8). 1994. 15.95 (*0-7451-2222-1*, Galaxy etc.) Chivers N Amer.
—Tangled Fortunes. Young, Marian, illus. LC 93-32202. 1994. 14.95 (*0-385-32066-3*) Delacorte.
Mayne, William. Low Tide. LC 92-24717. 1993. 14.00 (*0-385-30904-X*) Delacorte.
Savage, Deborah. A Stranger Calls Me Home. 240p. (gr. 5-9). 1992. 14.45 (*0-395-59424-3*) HM.

NEWBERY MEDAL BOOKS
Newbery Award Treasures, 5 vols, No. 2. (gr. 4-7). 1990. pap. 16.25 boxed set (*0-440-36002-1*) Dell.
Newbery Awards, 5 vols, No. 1. (gr. 4-7). 1990. pap. 16.75 boxed set (*0-440-45963-X*) Dell.

NEWFOUNDLAND–FICTION
Major, Kevin. Thirty-Six Exposures. LC 84-4995. (gr. 7 up). 1984. 14.95 (*0-385-29347-X*) Delacorte.

NEWS BROADCASTS
see Radio Broadcasting; Television Broadcasting

NEWSBOYS
Sant, Thomas. The Amazing Adventures of Albert & His Flying Machine. De Rosa, Dee, illus. 160p. (gr. 4-7). 1990. 13.95 (*0-525-67302-4*, Lodestar Bks) Dutton Child Bks.

NEWSPAPER WORK
see Journalism; Reporters and Reporting

NEWSPAPERS
see also Periodicals; Reporters and Reporting
Abell, J. The Newspaper. (Illus.). 50p. 1994. 25.00 (*1-56611-097-1*); pap. 15.00 (*1-56611-098-X*) Jonas.
Allen, Karen K. & Miller, Margery S. Reading the Newspaper: Advanced Level. 190p. (Orig.). (gr. 9-12). 1989. pap. text ed. 10.95 (*0-89061-500-4*) Jamestown Pubs.
Balcziak, B. Newspapers. (Illus.). 48p. (gr. 4-8). 1989. lib. bdg. 17.27 (*0-86592-069-9*); 12.95s.p. (*0-685-58624-3*) Rourke Corp.
Fleming, Thomas. Behind the Headlines. (gr. 5 up). 1989. 14.95 (*0-8027-6890-3*); PLB 15.85 (*0-8027-6891-1*) Walker & Co.
Gibbons, Gail. Deadline! From News to Newspaper. Gibbons, Gail, illus. LC 86-47654. 32p. (gr. 1-4). 1987. PLB 14.89 (*0-690-04602-2*, Crowell Jr Bks) HarpC Child Bks.
Granfield, Linda. Extra! Extra! The Who, What, Where, When & Why of Newspapers. Slavin, Bill, illus. LC 93-11807. 1994. write for info. (*0-531-06833-1*); lib. bdg. write for info. (*0-531-08683-6*) Orchard Bks Watts.
—Extra! Extra! The Who, What, Where, When & Why of Newspapers. (gr. 4-7). 1994. pap. 7.95 (*0-531-07049-2*) Watts.
Leedy, Loreen. The Furry News - How to Create a Newspaper: A Reading Rainbow Feature Book. Leedy, Loreen, illus. (ps-3). 1993. pap. 5.95 (*0-8234-1026-9*) Holiday.
—The Furry News: How to Make a Newspaper. Leedy, Loreen, illus. LC 89-20094. 32p. (ps-3). 1990. reinforced bdg. 14.95 (*0-8234-0793-4*) Holiday.
Walters, Sarah. How Newspapers Are Made. (Illus.). 32p. 1989. 12.95x (*0-8160-2042-6*) Facts on File.

NEWSPAPERS–FICTION
Grover, Max. Amazing & Incredible Counting Stories. LC 94-17837. 1995. write for info. (*0-15-200090-9*, Browndeer Pr) HarBrace.
Hildick, E. W. The Case of the Nervous Newsboy. Lane, John, illus. 112p. (gr. 3-6). 1991. pap. 2.95 (*0-88741-807-4*, 01304) Sundance Pubs.
Lakin, Patricia. A True Partnership. Cushman, Doug, illus. LC 94-660. (gr. 5 up). 1994. write for info. (*0-8114-3869-4*) Raintree Steck-V.
McBrier, Page. Stinky Business. 128p. (Orig.). 1991. pap. 2.95 (*0-380-76269-2*, Camelot) Avon.
Martin, Ann M. Karen's Newspaper. (gr. 4-7). 1993. pap. 2.95 (*0-590-47040-X*) Scholastic Inc.

NEWTON, SIR ISAAC, 1642-1727
Hitzeroth, Deborah & Leon, Sharon. Isaac Newton. LC 93-38680. (gr. 5-8). 1994. 14.95 (*1-56006-04-68*) Lucent Bks.
Tiner, John H. Isaac Newton: The True Story of His Life. Biel, Bill & Biel, Bill, illus. LC 75-32562. (gr. 3-6). 1976. pap. 6.95 (*0-915134-95-0*) Mott Media.

NEWTS
Gove, Doris. Red-Spotted Newt. Duncan, Beverly, illus. LC 91-34497. (gr. 2 up). 1994. 14.95 (*0-689-31697-6*, Atheneum Child Bk) Macmillan Child Grp.

NIAGARA, FORT, N. Y.–FICTION
Orton, Helen F. The Gold-Laced Coat. rev. ed. Ball, Robert, illus. 226p. (gr. 4-8). 1988. pap. 5.95 (*0-941967-07-7*) Old Fort Niagara Assn.

NIAGARA FALLS–HISTORY
Mooney, Margaret. A Matter of Balance. Kretschmar, Sonia, illus. LC 93-26222. 1994. 4.25 (*0-383-03759-X*) SRA Schl Grp.

NICARAGUA
Ackley, Meredith, et al, eds. Nicaragua. Birmingham, Lucy, et al, photos by. LC 89-43174. (Illus.). (gr. 3-8). PLB 21.26 (*0-8368-0221-7*) Gareth Stevens Inc.
Adams, Faith. Nicaragua: Struggling with Change. LC 86-11608. (Illus.). 152p. (gr. 5 up). 1987. text ed. 14.95 RSBE (*0-87518-340-9*, Dillon) Macmillan Child Grp.
Haverstock, Nathan A. Nicaragua in Pictures. (Illus.). 64p. (gr. 5 up). 1987. PLB 17.50 (*0-8225-1817-1*) Lerner Pubns.

NICHOLAS, SAINT, BISHOP OF MYRA
Seco, Nina S. The Life of St. Nicholas: A Cloud of Witnesses, Vol. 3. Duckworth, Ruch, illus. (Orig.). (gr. k-3). 1993. pap. 6.00 (*0-913026-36-0*) St Nectarios.

NIGERIA
Barker, Carol. A Family in Nigeria. LC 85-6932. (Illus.). 32p. (gr. 2-5). 1985. PLB 13.50 (*0-8225-1659-4*) Lerner Pubns.
Department of Geography, Lerner Publications. Nigeria in Pictures. (Illus.). 64p. (gr. 5 up). 1988. 17.50 (*0-8225-1826-0*) Lerner Pubns.
Johnston, Rhoda O. Iyabo of Nigeria. Samuel, A. Nupo, illus. (gr. 5-12). 1973. pap. 5.00x (*0-914522-01-9*, 163808) Alpha Iota.
Levy, Patricia. Nigeria. LC 92-38754. 1993. 21.95 (*1-85435-574-0*) Marshall Cavendish.

NIGERIA–FICTION
Echewa, T. Obinkaram. The Ancestor Tree. Hale, Christy, illus. 32p. (gr. k-3). 1994. 13.99 (*0-525-67467-5*, Lodestar Bks) Dutton Child Bks.
Emecheta, Buchi. The Moonlight Bride. LC 82-17816. 77p. (gr. 6-10). 1983. pap. 6.95 (*0-8076-1063-1*) Braziller.
—The Wrestling Match. LC 82-17750. 74p. (gr. 6-10). 1983. pap. 6.95 (*0-8076-1061-5*) Braziller.
Hurd, Thacher. The Quiet Evening. LC 90-24179. (ps up). 1992. 15.00 (*0-688-10526-2*) Greenwillow.
Prest, Arthur. Illustrated History of the Nigerian People. LC 73-92798. (gr. 4 up). 1974. write for info. (*0-89388-138-4*) Okpaku Communications.
Rupert, Janet E. The African Mask. LC 93-7726. 1994. write for info. (*0-395-67295-3*, Clarion Bks) HM.
Vesey, Amanda. Duncan's Tree House. LC 92-37334. 1993. 18.95 (*0-87614-784-8*) Carolrhoda Bks.

NIGHT
Butler, Daphne. First Look at Day & Night. LC 90-10246. (Illus.). 32p. (gr. 1-2). 1991. PLB 17.27 (*0-8368-0505-4*) Gareth Stevens Inc.
George, Jean C. The Moon of the Owls. Minor, Wendell, illus. LC 91-2735. 48p. (gr. 3-7). 1993. 15.00 (*0-06-020192-4*); PLB 14.89 (*0-06-020193-2*) HarpC Child Bks.
Hamerstrom, Frances. Walk When the Moon Is Full. Katona, Robert, illus. LC 75-33878. 64p. (gr. 3-8). 1975. 15.95 (*0-912278-69-2*); pap. 6.95 (*0-912278-84-6*) Crossing Pr.
Nayer, Judy. Night Animals. Goldberg, Grace, illus. 10p. (ps-2). 1992. bds. 6.95 (*1-56293-223-3*) McClanahan Bk.
Ryder, Joanne. Step into the Night. Nolan, Dennis, illus. LC 87-37982. 32p. (gr. k-3). 1988. RSBE 14.95 (*0-02-777951-3*, Four Winds) Macmillan Child Grp.
Taylor, David. Nature's Creatures of the Dark: A Pop-up Glow-in-the-Dark Exploration. (Illus.). 14p. (gr. 1-5). 1993. 15.99 (*0-8037-1631-1*) Dial Bks Young.
Time Life Inc. Editors. Where Does the Sun Sleep? First Questions & Answers about Bedtime. Kagan, Neil, ed. (Illus.). 48p. (ps). 1993. write for info. (*0-7835-0866-2*); lib. bdg. write for info. (*0-7835-0867-0*) Time-Life.
Webber, Helen. Good Night, Night. Webber, Helen, illus. (gr. k-6). 1968. 8.95 (*0-8392-3054-0*) Astor-Honor.

NIGHT–FICTION
Ahlberg, Janet. It Was a Dark & Stormy Night. (ps-3). 1994. 13.99 (*0-670-84620-1*, Viking) Viking Penguin.
Aiken, Joan. Midnight Is a Place. (gr. 4-7). 1993. pap. 2.95 (*0-590-45496-X*) Scholastic Inc.
—Past Eight O'Clock. Pienkowski, Jan, illus. 128p. (gr. 2-6). 1991. pap. 4.99 (*0-14-032355-4*, Puffin) Puffin Bks.
Alfredson, Hans. The Night the Moon Came By. Ahlin, Per, illus. Nunnally, Tiina, tr. from SWE. LC 93-663. (Illus.). 1993. Repr. 13.00 (*91-29-62246-8*, Pub. by R & S Bks) FS&G.
Aliki. Overnight at Mary Bloom's. Aliki, illus. LC 86-7719. 32p. (ps-3). 1987. 15.00 (*0-688-06764-6*); lib. bdg. 14.93 (*0-688-06765-4*) Greenwillow.

Allen, Constance. Sesame Street: Sleep Tight! Prebenna, David, illus. (ps-k). 1991. pap. write for info. (*0-307-10026-X*, Golden Pr) Western Pub.

Allen, Valerie. The Night Thief. Soper, Patrick, illus. LC 89-28459. 32p. (gr. k-3). 1990. 14.95 (*0-88289-774-8*) Pelican.

Appelt, Kathi. A Colorful Goodnight Poem to a "Bayou Gal" Waldman, Neil, illus. LC 94-16639. (gr. 4-7). Date not set. write for info. (*0-688-12856-4*); PLB write for info. (*0-688-12857-2*) Morrow Jr Bks.

Babbitt, Natalie. The Something. Babbitt, Natalie, illus. LC 70-125143. 40p. (ps-3). 1987. 11.00 (*0-374-37137-7*) FS&G.

Bandes, Hanna. Sleepy River. Winter, Jeanette, illus. LC 92-26198. 32p. (ps). 1993. 14.95 (*0-399-22349-5*, Philomel Bks) Putnam Pub Group.

Berenstain, Stan & Berenstain, Jan. Los Osos Berenstain en la Oscuridad. Guibert, Rita, tr. from ENG. Berenstain, Stan & Berenstain, Jan, illus. LC 91-51092. (SPA.). 32p. (ps-3). 1992. pap. 2.25 (*0-679-83471-0*) Random Bks Yng Read.

Berger, Barbara H. Grandfather Twilight. Berger, Barbara H., illus. 32p. (ps-3). 1986. 14.95 (*0-399-20996-4*, Philomel) Putnam Pub Group.

—Grandfather Twilight: Mini Edition. (Illus.). 32p. (ps-3). 1992. 5.95 (*0-399-21999-4*, Philomel Bks) Putnam Pub Group.

Blocksma, Mary. Yoo Hoo, Moon! 1991. pap. 9.99 (*0-553-07094-0*) Bantam.

—Yoo Hoo, Moon! 1992. pap. 3.99 (*0-553-35212-1*) Bantam.

Bond, Felicia. Poinsettia & the Firefighters. LC 83-46169. (Illus.). 32p. (ps-3). 1984. PLB 15.89 (*0-690-04401-1*, Crowell Jr Bks) HarpC Child Bks.

Boyd, Lizi. Sweet Dreams, Willy. Boyd, Lizi, illus. 32p. (ps-1). 1992. PLB 12.50 (*0-670-84382-2*) Viking Child Bks.

Bradbury, Ray. Switch on the Night. Dillon, Leo & Dillon, Diane, illus. LC 92-25321. 40p. (ps-2). 1993. 8.99 (*0-394-80486-4*); PLB 9.99 (*0-394-90486-9*) Knopf Bks Yng Read.

Brown, Margaret W. Goodnight Moon. 1993. pap. 19.95 (*0-590-73302-8*) Scholastic Inc.

—Goodnight Moon Board Book. Hurd, Clement, illus. LC 47-30762. 34p. (ps). 1991. 6.95 (*0-694-00361-1*) HarpC Child Bks.

Brown, Ruth. A Dark Dark Tale. Brown, Ruth, illus. LC 81-66798. 32p. (ps-3). 1981. 12.95 (*0-8037-1672-9*); PLB 12.89 (*0-8037-1673-7*) Dial Bks Young.

—One Stormy Night. Brown, Ruth, illus. LC 92-27004. 32p. (ps-1). 1993. 13.99 (*0-525-45091-2*, DCB) Dutton Child Bks.

Carter, Noelle. Where's My Fuzzy Blanket? 14p. 1991. pap. 6.95 (*0-590-44466-2*) Scholastic Inc.

Cazet, Denys. Mother Night. LC 88-36439. (Illus.). 32p. (ps-1). 1989. 14.95 (*0-531-05830-1*); PLB 14.99 (*0-531-08430-2*) Orchard Bks Watts.

Christelow, Eileen. Henry & the Dragon. Christelow, Eileen, illus. LC 83-14405. 32p. (ps-2). 1984. 13.45 (*0-89919-220-3*, Clarion Bks) HM.

Compton, Kenn & Compton, Joanne. Granny Greenteeth & the Noise in the Night. LC 93-18232. (Illus.). 32p. (ps-3). 1993. reinforced bdg. 14.95 (*0-8234-1051-X*) Holiday.

Cramer, Alexander. A Night in Moonbeam County. 208p. (gr. 6-8). 1994. SBE 15.95 (*0-684-19704-9*, Scribners Young Read) Macmillan Child Grp.

Denslow, Sharon P. Night Owls. Kastner, Jill, illus. LC 89-33937. 32p. (ps-2). 1990. RSBE 13.95 (*0-02-728681-9*, Bradbury Pr) Macmillan Child Grp.

Dijs, Carla, illus. Who Sees You? At Night. 12p. (ps). 1993. 5.95 (*0-448-40079-0*, G&D) Putnam Pub Group.

Edmonds, Walter D. Bert Breen's Barn. 280p. 1991. pap. 9.95 (*0-8156-0255-3*) Syracuse U Pr.

Edwards, Frank & Bianchi, John. Melody Mooner Stayed up All Night. (Illus.). 24p. (Orig.). (ps-3). 1991. PLB 14.95 (*0-921285-03-5*, Pub. by Bungalo Bks CN); pap. 4.95 (*0-921285-01-9*, Pub. by Bungalo Bks CN) Firefly Bks Ltd.

Field, Susan. The Sun, the Moon, & the Silver Baboon. Field, Susan, illus. LC 92-44496. 32p. (ps-2). 1993. 14.00 (*0-06-022990-X*); PLB 13.89 (*0-06-022991-8*) HarpC Child Bks.

Fox, Mem. Night Noises. LC 89-216. (ps-3). 1992. pap. 4.95 (*0-15-257421-2*, Voyager Bks) HarBrace.

Gatt, Elizabeth. In the Firefly Night. (ps-3). 1994. 3.99 (*0-89577-574-3*, Readers Digest Kids) RD Assn.

Gerson, Mary-Joan, retold by. How Night Came from the Sea: A Story from Brazil. Golembe, Carla, illus. LC 93-20054. (ps-3). 1994. 15.95 (*0-316-30855-2*, Joy St Bks) Little.

Green, Timothy. Mystery of Navajo Moon. Green, Timothy, illus. LC 91-52600. 48p. (ps-4). 1991. pap. 7.95 (*0-87358-577-1*) Northland AZ.

Greenfield, Eloise. First Pink Light. Gilchrist, Jan S., illus. 32p. (ps-4). 1991. 13.95 (*0-86316-207-X*) Writers & Readers.

Gregorich, Barbara. Noise in the Night. Hoffman, Joan, ed. (Illus.). 16p. (Orig.). (gr. k-2). 1991. pap. 2.25 (*0-88743-027-9*, 06027) Sch Zone Pub Co.

Haseley, Dennis. The Thieves' Market. Desimini, Lisa, illus. LC 90-38440. 32p. (gr. 1-5). 1991. HarpC Child Bks.

Hayes, Sarah. This Is the Bear & the Scary Night. Craig, Helen, illus. (ps-1). 1992. 13.95 (*0-316-35250-0*, Joy St Bks) Little.

Heine, Helme. The Marvelous Journey Through the Night. Manheim, Ralph, tr. (Illus.). 26p. (gr. 4-8). 1990. 15.00 (*0-374-38478-9*) FS&G.

Hindley, Judy. The Sleepy Book: A Lullaby. Aggs, Patrice, illus. LC 91-15787. 32p. (ps-1). 1992. 12.95 (*0-531-05971-5*); lib. bdg. 12.99 (*0-531-08571-6*) Orchard Bks Watts.

Howe, James. A Night Without Stars. 192p. 1993. pap. 3.50 (*0-380-71867-7*, Camelot) Avon.

Isaacs, Gwynne L. While You Are Asleep. Hepworth, Cathi, illus. 32p. (gr. 4-8). 1991. 12.95 (*0-8027-6985-3*); lib. bdg. 13.85 (*0-8027-6986-1*) Walker & Co.

Jewell, Nancy. The Family under the Moon. Kessler, Leonard, illus. LC 76-2344. (ps-3). 1976. PLB 14.89i (*0-06-022827-X*) HarpC Child Bks.

Johnson, Angela. Joshua's Night Whispers. Mitchell, Rhonda, illus. LC 93-46412. 12p. (ps). 1994. 4.95 (*0-531-06847-1*) Orchard Bks Watts.

Johnson, Nancy E. The Magic Blanket That Made All Dreams Happy! Johnson, Nancy E., illus. 42p. (ps-1). 1994. Set incl. blanket, stars 29.95 (*0-9642307-0-4*) TotTales.
THE MAGIC BLANKET THAT MADE ALL DREAMS HAPPY!, first in a series of TotTale(tm) books, is designed not only for enjoyment, but to address fears common to many young children. The lighthearted verse in THE MAGIC BLANKET tells the story of a young prince afraid to go to bed because of frightening dreams. Accompanied by au naturel pictures, a 45" X 60" 100% Polyester OWENS Toddler Blanket, & 20 1/2" glow-in-the-dark gold stars, (& with a little "reader" help!), the story, the magic blanket & the brightly glowing stars offer a warm solution to those youngsters with vivid nocturnal imaginations. The set comes in a sturdy, bright white box with a see-through lid, making it an ideal gift. THE MAGIC BLANKET THAT MADE ALL DREAMS HAPPY! is available through the Tattered Cover Book Store in Denver, Colorado, (303-322-7727). The set is also being made available to child care centers through the distributor, TotTales(tm) (303-797-8722). Nancy E. Johnson is also the author of the popular dog obedience book, EVERYDAY DOG.
Publisher Provided Annotation.

Jonas, Ann. The Quilt. (Illus.). 40p. (ps-3). 1994. pap. 4.99 (*0-14-055308-8*) Puffin Bks.

Kinsey-Warnock, Natalie. On a Starry Night. McPhail, David, illus. LC 93-4878. 1994. write for info. (*0-531-06820-X*); PLB write for info. (*0-531-08670-4*) Orchard Bks Watts.

Krensky, Stephen. Fraidy Cats. Lewin, Betsy, illus. LC 92-35360. (gr. 3 up). 1993. 2.95 (*0-590-46438-8*) Scholastic Inc.

Laden, Nina. The Night I Followed the Dog. LC 93-31008. 1994. 13.95 (*0-8118-0647-2*) Chronicle Bks.

Lesser, Carolyn. The Goodnight Circle. 30p. (ps-3). 1991. pap. 4.95 (*0-15-232159-4*, HB Juv Bks) HarBrace.

Leuck, Laura. Night Is Calling. Eitan, Ora, illus. LC 93-22837. 1994. pap. 15.00 (*0-671-86940-X*, S&S BFYR) S&S Trade.

London, Jonathan. The Owl Who Became the Moon. Rand, Ted, illus. LC 92-14699. (ps-2). 1993. 13.99 (*0-525-45054-8*, DCB) Dutton Child Bks.

McDonald, Megan. Whoo-oo Is It? Schindler, Stephen D., illus. LC 91-18494. 32p. (ps-1). 1992. 14.95 (*0-531-05974-X*); lib. bdg. 14.99 (*0-531-08574-0*) Orchard Bks Watts.

McGilvray, Richard. Don't Climb out of the Window Tonight. Snow, Alan, illus. LC 92-28136. (ps-2). 1993. 13.99 (*0-8037-1373-8*) Dial Bks Young.

McGuire, Richard. Night Becomes Day. McGuire, Richard, illus. LC 94-9923. 32p. (ps up). 1994. PLB 13.99 (*0-670-85547-2*) Viking Child Bks.

Magni, Laura. Goodnight Stories from the Big Tree. (Illus.). 192p. (ps-6). 1990. 9.99 (*0-517-69687-8*) Random Hse Value.

Maiwald, Trudy. Missy & Her Nightlight. 16p. (Orig.). 1994. pap. write for info. (*1-56167-153-3*) Am Literary Pr.

Manushkin, Fran. Peeping & Sleeping. Plecas, Jennifer, illus. LC 93-26297. (ps-3). 1994. 14.95 (*0-395-64339-2*, Clarion Bks) HM.

Mayer, Mercer. There's Something in My Attic. Mayer, Mercer, illus. 32p. (ps-3). 1992. pap. 3.99 (*0-14-054813-0*, Puffin) Puffin Bks.

Mayhew, James. Dare You! LC 92-18862. 1993. 13.45 (*0-395-65013-5*, Clarion Bks) HM.

Mi Libro De Las Buenas Noches. (SPA.). (ps-3). 1993. pap. 4.95 (*0-307-72258-9*, Golden Pr) Western Pub.

Michelson, Richard. Did You Say Ghosts? Baskin, Leonard, illus. LC 92-30134. 32p. (ps up). 1993. RSBE 14.95 (*0-02-766915-7*, Macmillan Child Bk) Macmillan Child Grp.

Mohr, Joseph. Silent Night. LC 84-8113. 1988. pap. 4.95 (*0-685-57131-9*, DCB) Dutton Child Bks.

New, Dorothy. Bedtime Friends. 1994. 8.95 (*0-8062-4873-4*) Carlton.

Nikola-Lisa, W. Night Is Coming. Henterly, Jamichael, illus. LC 90-3806. 32p. (ps-2). 1991. 13.95 (*0-525-44687-7*, DCB) Dutton Child Bks.

Nobisso, Josephine. Shh! The Whale Is Smiling. Hyde, Maureen, illus. LC 91-21521. 40p. (ps-1). 1992. 14.00 (*0-671-74908-0*, Green Tiger) S&S Trade.
In this rhythmic & poetic book by the creators of GRANDPA LOVED & GRANDMA'S SCRAPBOOK, an older sister comforts a little brother frightened by a wind storm. Knowing his love of whales, she comes to his room to comfort him with a fantastic tale that takes him & the reader right out of the bed & into the undersea world of a loving Humpback who "watches us & guides us through the floating, flying freedom of the deep." Children love joining in on the choruses of "Shh!" & will ask to hear it again & again. One librarian told us, "It's my favorite read-aloud!" Order from Simon & Schuster.
Publisher Provided Annotation.

Olofsdotter, Marie. Sofia & the Heartmender. Olofsdotter, Marie, illus. LC 92-46200. 32p. (gr. k up). 1993. 14.95 (*0-915793-50-4*) Free Spirit Pub.

Pank, Rachel. Sonia & Barnie & the Noise in the Night. 1991. pap. 13.95 (*0-590-44657-6*) Scholastic Inc.

Pettigrew, Eileen. Night Time. Kimber, William, illus. 24p. (ps-1). 1992. PLB 14.95 (*1-55037-235-1*, Pub. by Annick Pr); pap. 4.95 (*1-55037-242-4*, Pub. by Annick Pr) Firefly Bks Ltd.

Prater, John. Tim & the Blanket Thief. Prater, John, illus. LC 93-6563. 32p. (ps-1). 1993. SBE 14.95 (*0-689-31881-2*, Atheneum Child Bk) Macmillan Child Grp.

Ray, Stephen & Murdoch, Kathleen. Just Right for the Night. Campbell, Caroline, illus. LC 92-21398. (gr. 4 up). 1993. 4.25 (*0-383-03580-5*) SRA Schl Grp.

Rice, Eve. Goodnight, Goodnight. ALC Staff, ed. LC 79-17253. (Illus.). 32p. (ps up). 1992. pap. 3.95 (*0-688-11707-4*, Mulberry) Morrow.

Robinson, Martha. The Zoo at Night. Fransconi, Antonio, illus. LC 94-12773. 1995. 16.00 (*0-689-50608-2*, M K McElderry) Macmillan Child Grp.

Rydell, Katy. Wind Says Good Night. (ps). 1994. 14.95 (*0-395-60474-5*) HM.

Rylant, Cynthia. Night in the Country. Szilagyi, Mary, illus. LC 90-1043. 32p. (ps-2). 1991. pap. 4.95 (*0-689-71473-4*, Aladdin) Macmillan Child Grp.

Salter, Mary J. The Moon Comes Home. Schuett, Stacey, illus. LC 88-31735. 40p. (ps-2). 1989. 12.95 (*0-394-89983-0*); lib. bdg. 13.99 (*0-394-99983-5*) Knopf Bks Yng Read.

Tibo, Gilles. Paper Nights. Tibo, Gilles, illus. 32p. 1992. PLB 15.95 (*1-55037-225-4*, Pub. by Annick CN); pap. 5.95 (*1-55037-224-6*, Pub. by Annick CN) Firefly Bks Ltd.

Turner, Ann. Through Moon & Stars & Night Skies. Hale, James G., illus. LC 87-35044. 32p. (ps-3). 1992. pap. 4.95 (*0-06-443308-0*, Trophy) HarpC Child Bks.

Wayland, April H. Night Horse. 1991. 12.95 (*0-590-42629-X*, Scholastic Hardcover) Scholastic Inc.

Weiss, Nicki. Where Does the Brown Bear Go? (ps). 1990. pap. 3.95 (*0-14-054181-0*, Puffin) Puffin Bks.

Willard, Nancy. Night Story. LC 85-17677. (ps-3). 1994. pap. 4.95 (*0-15-200075-5*, HB Juv Bks) HarBrace.

Ziefert, Harriet. Dark Night, Sleepy Night. Baruffi, Andrea, illus. (ps-2). 1993. pap. 3.25 (*0-14-036538-9*, Puffin) Puffin Bks.

NIGHT–POETRY

Bierhorst, John, selected by. On the Road of Stars: Native American Night Poems & Sleep Charms. Pedersen, Judy, illus. LC 92-20001. 40p. (gr. 1 up). 1994. RSBE 15.95 (*0-02-709735-8*, Macmillan Child Bk) Macmillan Child Grp.

Clise, Michele D., compiled by. Ophelia's Bedtime Book: A Collection of Poems to Read & Share. LC 93-41485. (Illus.). 32p. (ps-3). 1994. 14.99 (*0-670-85310-0*) Viking Child Bks.
Greenfield, Eloise. Night on Neighborhood Street. (ps-3). 1991. 14.00 (*0-8037-0777-0*); PLB 13.89 (*0-8037-0778-9*) Dial Bks Young.
Harter, Penny. Shadow Play, Night Haiku. Greene, Jeffrey, illus. LC 93-39887. (gr. 1-6). 1994. 15.00 (*0-671-88396-8*, S&S BFYR) S&S Trade.
Larrick, Nancy, ed. Night of the Whippoorwill. Ray, David, illus. 72p. (ps up). 1992. 19.95 (*0-399-21874-2*, Philomel Bks) Putnam Pub Group.
Ver Dorn, Bethea. Moon Glows. Graham, Thomas, illus. 32p. (ps-1). 1990. text ed. 14.95 (*1-55970-073-4*) Arcade Pub Inc.

NIGHTINGALE, FLORENCE, 1820-1910

Brown, Pam. Florence Nightingale: The Founder of Modern Nursing. Tolan, Mary, adapted by. LC 90-9972. (Illus.). 64p. (gr. 3-4). 1991. PLB 19.93 (*0-8368-0456-2*) Gareth Stevens Inc.
Colver, Anne. Florence Nightingale: War Nurse. (Illus.). 80p. (gr. 2-6). 1992. Repr. of 1961 ed. PLB 12.95 (*0-7910-1466-5*) Chelsea Hse.
Gray, Charlotte. Florence Nightingale: The Determined English Woman Who Founded Modern Nursing & Reformed Military Medicine. Sherwood, Rhoda, ed. LC 88-4913. (Illus.). 68p. (gr. 5-6). 1989. PLB 19.93 (*1-55532-860-1*) Gareth Stevens Inc.
Shore, Donna & Renna, Giani. Florence Nightingale. (Illus.). 104p. (gr. 5-8). 1990. 9.95 (*0-382-09978-8*); pap. 5.95 (*0-382-24004-9*) Silver Burdett Pr.
Siegel, Beatrice. Faithful Friend: The Story of Florence Nightingale. 144p. (gr. 3-7). 1991. pap. 2.95 (*0-590-43210-9*) Scholastic Inc.
Tames, Richard. Florence Nightingale. (Illus.). 32p. (gr. 5 up). 1991. pap. 5.95 (*0-531-24611-6*) Watts.

NILE RIVER

De Paola, Tomie. Bill & Pete Go down the Nile. (Illus.). 32p. (ps-3). 1990. pap. 5.95 (*0-399-22003-8*, Sandcastle Bks) Putnam Pub Group.
Mumford, Claire, illus. The Nile. 32p. (gr. 3-5). 1983. 7.95x (*0-86685-447-9*) Intl Bk Ctr.
Waterlow, Julia. The Nile. Waterlow, Julia, photos by. LC 92-39951. (Illus.). 48p. (gr. 5-6). 1993. PLB 22.80 (*0-8114-3100-2*) Raintree Steck-V.

NIXON, RICHARD MILHOUS, PRESIDENT U. S. 1913-

Barr, Roger. Richard Nixon. LC 92-25566. (Illus.). 112p. (gr. 5-8). 1992. PLB 14.95 (*1-56006-035-2*) Lucent Bks.
Dudley, Mark E. United States vs. Nixon, Nineteen Seventy-Four: Presidential Powers. LC 93-40202. 1995. text ed. 14.95 (*0-02-736277-9*, New Discovery Bks) Macmillan Child Grp.
Hargrove, Jim. Richard M. Nixon: The Thirty-Seventh President. LC 84-27416. (Illus.). 128p. (gr. 4 up). 1985. PLB 14.40 (*0-516-03212-7*) Childrens.
Larsen, Rebecca. Richard Nixon: The Rise & Fall of a President. (Illus.). 224p. (gr. 9-12). 1991. PLB 15.40 (*0-531-10997-6*) Watts.
Nadel, Laurie. The Great Stream of History: A Biography of Richard M. Nixon. LC 90-920. (Illus.). 144p. (gr. 5-9). 1991. SBE 14.95 (*0-689-31559-7*, Atheneum Child Bk) Macmillan Child Grp.
Pious, Richard M. Richard Nixon. (gr. 7 up). 1992. lib. bdg. 13.98 (*0-671-72852-0*, J Messner); pap. 7.95 (*0-671-72853-9*, J Messner) S&S Trade.
Randolph, Sallie. Richard M. Nixon, President. 128p. (gr. 5 up). 1989. 13.95 (*0-8027-6848-2*); PLB 14.85 (*0-8027-6849-0*) Walker & Co.
Ripley, C. Peter. Richard Nixon. Schlesinger, Arthur M., Jr., intro. by. (Illus.). 112p. (gr. 5 up). 1988. lib. bdg. 17.95 (*0-87754-585-5*) Chelsea Hse.
Sandak, Cass R. The Nixons. LC 91-40216. (Illus.). 48p. (gr. 5). 1992. text ed. 4.95 RSBE (*0-89686-638-6*, Crestwood Hse) Macmillan Child Grp.
Stefoff, Rebecca. Richard M. Nixon: Thirty-Seventh President of the United States. Young, Richard G., ed. LC 89-39944. (Illus.). 128p. (gr. 5-9). 1990. PLB 17.26 (*0-944483-59-3*) Garrett Ed Corp.

NOAH'S ARK

Abbay, Ellen. Noah Takes Two. LC 85-80406. 1985. 9.95 (*0-9615015-0-2*) Kudzu.
Adams, Pam. Noah's Ark. (gr. 3 up). 1981. 6.95 (*0-85953-267-4*) Childs Play.
All the Animals. (ps-1). 1990. bds. 6.99 (*0-7459-1838-7*) Lion USA.
Amoss, Berthe. Noah. (Illus.). 10p. (ps-7). 1989. pap. 2.95 (*0-922589-10-0*) More Than Card.
Animals Two by Two. (ps-1). 1990. bds. 6.99 (*0-7459-1839-5*) Lion USA.
Arch Books Staff. Story of Noah's Ark: Genesis 6: 5-9: 17. (ps-3). 1993. pap. 1.99 (*0-570-06009-5*) Concordia.
Bible Adventures Staff. Noah's Adventure in the Ark. (Illus.). (ps). 1991. bds. 8.99 (*0-8007-7122-2*) Revell.
Blair, Grandpa. The Gospel Rag: Noah Straight Up. 16p. (gr. 11 up). 1992. 5.95 (*0-930366-69-7*) Northcountry Pub.
Brent, Isabelle. Noah's Ark. 1992. 12.95 (*0-316-10837-5*) Little.
Brown, Christopher, ed. Noah's Ark. Rudegeair, Jean, illus. 24p. (gr. 2-6). 1984. pap. 2.50 (*0-89954-287-5*) Antioch Pub Co.
Brown, Rick, illus. Who Built the Ark? (ps-3). 1994. fold-outs 9.99 (*0-670-85160-4*) Viking Child Bks.
Brown, Rodney. Noah's Great Adventure. (Illus.). 20p. 1993. 15.95 (*1-883909-00-7*) Wisdom Tree.
Clements, Andrew. Noah & the Ark & the Animals. Gantschev, Ivan, illus. 1992. pap. 4.95 (*0-590-44457-3*, Blue Ribbon Bks) Scholastic Inc.
Conteh-Morgan, Jane, illus. Noah's Ark. 18p. (ps). 1994. bds. 3.95 (*0-448-40185-1*, G&D) Putnam Pub Group.
Cousins, Lucy, retold by. & illus. Noah's Ark. LC 92-54589. 40p. (ps up). 1993. 14.95 (*1-56402-213-7*) Candlewick Pr.
Daniel, Rebecca & Hierstein, Judy. Noah's Story. 16p. (ps-3). 1991. 16.95 (*0-86653-576-4*, SS1878, Shining Star Pubns) Good Apple.
Doney. All in the Ark. 1992. 10.99 (*1-55513-766-0*, Chariot Bks) Chariot Family.
Doughty, Bix L. Noah & the Great Auk. (gr. k up). 1978. 5.50 (*0-87602-163-1*) Anchorage.
Emberley, Barbara, adapted by. One Wide River to Cross. Emberley, Ed E., illus. 32p. (ps-3). 1992. pap. 4.95 (*0-316-23445-1*) Little.
Evans, Michael. Noah's Ark: With Press-Out Model Ark, Animals, People & More. Evans, Michael, illus. 20p. (Orig.). (gr. k-4). 1993. pap. 7.95 (*0-8249-8600-8*, Ideals Child) Hambleton-Hill.
Fant, Louie J., Jr. Noah. new ed. Castillo, Romulo & Paul, Frank A., illus. 14p. (gr. 3-4). 1973. pap. text ed. 5.00 (*0-917002-70-9*) Joyce Media.
Faulkner, Keith. Two by Two: The Pop-up Book of Noah's Ark. Lambert, Tony, illus. 16p. (gr. 1-4). 1993. pop-up 12.95 (*0-8431-3477-1*) Price Stern.
Frank, Penny. Noah & the Great Flood. (ps-3). 1988. 3.99 (*0-85648-728-7*) Lion USA.
Fussenegger, Gertrud. Noah's Ark. Fuchshuber, Annegert, illus. LC 87-45153. 32p. (gr. k-3). 1987. (Lipp Jr Bks) HarpC Child Bks.
Gambill, Henrietta G. The First Zoo. Boddy, Joe, illus. 32p. (gr. k-2). 1989. pasted 2.50 (*0-87403-592-9*, 3852) Standard Pub.
Gauch, Patricia L., retold by. Noah. Green, Jonathan, illus. LC 92-44283. 32p. (ps). 1994. 14.95 (*0-399-22548-X*, Philomel Bks) Putnam Pub Group.
Geisert, Arthur. The Building of Noah's Ark. (Illus.). 1988. write for info. HM.
Goetz, Bracha. Noah's Noisy Ark. Zakutinsky, Ruth, ed. Friedman, Aaron, illus. 32p. (gr. 1-4). 1992. PLB 6.95 (*0-911643-13-3*) Aura Bklyn.
Good Little Books for Good Little Children Staff. Noah's Ark. 12p. (ps). 1986. 3.25 (*0-8378-5205-6*) Gibson.
Guernsey, Paul. Noah & the Ark. Lohstoeter, Lori, illus. 40p. (gr. k up). 1993. incl. cass. 19.95 (*0-88708-293-9*, Rabbit Ears); 14.95 (*0-88708-292-0*, Rabbit Ears) Picture Bk Studio.
Hall, Susan T. Noah's Ark: Tickle Giggle Book. (ps). 1990. 7.49 (*1-55513-739-3*, Chariot Bks) Chariot Family.
Hayward, Linda. Noah's Ark. Flynn, Amy, illus. LC 92-64138. 22p. (ps). 1993. 3.25 (*0-679-83600-4*) Random Bks Yng Read.
Hewitt, Kathryn. Two by Two: The Untold Story. Hewitt, Kathryn, illus. LC 84-4579. 32p. (ps-3). 1984. 12.95 (*0-15-291801-9*, HB Juv Bks) HarBrace.
Hughes, Jan. Noah & the Ark. Hughes, Jan, illus. 28p. (Orig.). (gr. 1 up). 1988. 9.95 (*0-914544-97-7*); pap. 6.95 (*0-914544-98-5*) Living Flame Pr.
Jonas, Ann. Aardvarks, Disembark! (Illus.). 40p. (ps-3). 1994. pap. 4.99 (*0-14-055309-6*) Puffin Bks.
Jones, Kathy. Noah's ABC Ark. 48p. (ps-1). 1988. 7.95 (*0-86653-455-5*, SS1805, Shining Star Pubns); tape 10.95 (*0-685-74234-2*) Good Apple.
Kilroy, Sally. Noah & the Rabbits. (Illus.). 20p. (ps-1). 1991. pap. 4.99 (*0-14-054346-5*, Puffin) Puffin Bks.
Kite, Patricia. Noah's Ark: Opposing Viewpoints. LC 89-11635. (Illus.). 112p. (gr. 5-8). 1989. PLB 14.95 (*0-89908-073-1*) Greenhaven.
Kubler, Annie. Noah's Ark. 1985. 4.95 (*0-85953-255-0*) Childs Play.
Lamp Light Press Staff. Noah's Ark: A Story Rhyme. (Illus.). 23p. (ps-6). 1992. pap. text ed. 6.95 (*0-917593-11-1*, Lamp Light Pr) Prosperity & Profits.
Lashbrook, Marilyn. Two by Two: The Story of Noah's Faith. Britt, Stephanie M., illus. LC 87-60263. 32p. (ps). 1987. 5.95 (*0-86606-427-3*, 842) Roper Pr.
Lenski, Lois. Mr. & Mrs. Noah. LC 48-5989. (Illus.). 48p. (ps-1). 1962. PLB 12.89 (*0-690-54562-2*, Crowell Jr Bks) HarpC Child Bks.
Lepon, Shoshana. Noah & the Rainbow. Friedman, Aaron, illus. LC 92-26431. (gr. k-4). 1993. 11.95 (*1-880582-04-X*); pap. 8.95 (*1-880582-05-8*) Judaica Pr.
Lingo, Susan L. & Downey, Melissa C. Noah. Green, Roy, illus. 32p. (ps-7). 1992. wkbk. 3.99 (*0-87403-914-2*, 23-02524) Standard Pub.
Lippman, Peter. Noah's Ark: Mini House Book. (ps). 1994. 9.95 (*1-56305-662-3*) Workman Pub.
Lorimer, Lawrence T., retold by. Noah's Ark. Martin, Charles E., illus. Lerner, Sharon, ed. LC 77-92377. (Illus.). (ps-2). 1978. lib. bdg. 5.99 (*0-394-93861-5*); pap. 2.25 (*0-394-83861-0*) Random Bks Yng Read.
Ludwig, Warren. Old Noah's Elephants. LC 90-35379. (Illus.). 32p. (ps-3). 1991. 14.95 (*0-399-22256-1*, Putnam) Putnam Pub Group.
Morris, John. Noah's Ark & the Ararat Adventure. rev. ed. (Illus.). 64p. (gr. 3-5). 1994. 10.95 (*0-89051-166-7*) Master Bks.
Morton, Jane. Noah's Amazing Ark. (Illus.). 6p. 1994. pop-up bk. 3.99 (*1-56476-170-3*, Victor Books) SP Pubns.
Neilson, Gena, illus. Noah's Ark. (ps-1). 1986. spiral bdg. 9.95 (*0-937763-01-2*) Lauri Inc.
Noah & the Ark. LC 93-14131. 1993. TR. 6.99 (*0-8407-4914-7*); MM. 6.99 (*0-8407-4910-4*) Nelson.
Noah & the Flood. 1992. pap. 9.99 (*0-553-08133-0*) Bantam.
Noah's Ark. (ps-2). 3.95 (*0-7214-5065-2*) Ladybird Bks.
Noah's Ark & Other Old Testament Stories. (ps-2). 1989. 9.99 (*1-55513-812-8*, Chariot Bks) Chariot Family.
Paparone, Pam. Who Built the Ark? LC 93-31383. 1994. 15.00 (*0-671-87129-3*, S&S BFYR) S&S Trade.
Parry, Alan & Parry, Linda. Noah & the Ark. Parry, Alan, illus. 24p. (ps). 1990. pap. 0.99 (*0-8066-2475-2*, 9-2475) Augsburg Fortress.
Paxton, Lenore & Siadi, Phillip. Noah & the Ark: Around the World. (Illus.). 24p. (ps-4). 1993. pap. 7.95 coloring bk.-cassette pkg. (*1-880449-06-4*) Wrldkids Pr.
Pipe, Rhona & Hunt. Where's Noah? An Interactive Bible Storybook. (ps-3). 1993. 7.99 (*1-56507-144-1*) Harvest Hse.
Ray, Jane. Noah's Ark. LC 90-32786. (Illus.). 32p. (ps up). 1990. 14.95 (*0-525-44653-2*, DCB) Dutton Child Bks.
Reid, Barbara. Two by Two. LC 92-9013. (Illus.). 32p. (gr. k-3). 1993. 14.95 (*0-590-45869-8*) Scholastic Inc.
Shely, Patricia. Los Animales Del Arca. Cranberry, Nola, tr. from ENG. Patterson, Ron, illus. (SPA.). 16p. (gr. 1-3). 1987. pap. 1.99 (*0-311-38561-3*, X1982) Casa Bautista.
Simons, John & Ward, Kay. Noah & His Great Ark. Ward, Kay, ed. (Illus.). 16p. (Orig.). (gr. 3-7). 1987. pap. text ed. 2.50 (*0-937039-00-4*) Sun Pr FL.
Singer, Isaac Bashevis. Por Que Noe Eligio la Paloma: Why Noah Chose the Dove. Marcuse, Aida, tr. Carle, Eric, illus. (SPA.). 32p. (ps up). 1992. 16.00 (*0-374-36085-5*, Mirasol) FS&G.
Spier, Peter. Noah's Ark. 1989. incl. audiocassette 17.95 (*0-525-44525-0*, DCB) Dutton Child Bks.
—Noah's Ark. Spier, Peter, illus. 48p. (ps-1). 1992. pap. 4.99 (*0-440-40693-5*, YB) Dell.
Standard Publishing Staff. Noah's Ark Picture Window Book. (ps). 1992. 6.99 (*0-87403-884-7*, 24-03794) Standard Pub.
Stewart, Dana. The Happy Times Players Present - The Story of Noah's Ark. McCallum, Jodie, illus. 12p. (ps). 1993. 4.99 (*0-7847-0128-8*, 23-02220) Standard Pub.
Stirrup Associates, Inc. Staff. My Jesus Pocketbook of Noah & the Floating Zoo. Harvey, Bonnie C. & Phillips, Cheryl M., eds. Fulton, Ginger A., illus. LC 83-51680. 32p. (ps-3). 1984. pap. 0.69 (*0-937420-10-7*) Stirrup Assoc.
The Story of Noah & the Ark. 1992. pap. 4.99 (*0-517-06729-3*) Random Hse Value.
Tanvald, Christine H. The Big Big Big Boat, & Other Bible Stories about Obedience. Girouard, Patrick, illus. LC 93-9234. 1993. 7.99 (*0-7814-0926-8*, Chariot Bks) Chariot Family.
Theobalds, Prue. Noah & the Animals. Theobalds, Prue, illus. LC 92-45630. 34p. (gr. 4 up). 1993. 12.95 (*0-87226-507-2*, Bedrick Blackie) P Bedrick Bks.
Tomaselli, Cecilia. Noah's Family Carousel. (ps). 1993. 14.95 (*0-943706-10-6*) Yllw Brick Rd.
Vos Wezeman, Phyllis & Wiessner, Colleen A. Noah's Noises. 33p. (Orig.). (gr. 1-6). 1988. pap. 5.95 (*0-940754-58-4*) Ed Ministries.
Wilkon, Piotr. Noah's Ark. Wilkon, Jozef, illus. LC 92-2687. 32p. (gr. k-3). 1992. 14.95 (*1-55858-158-8*); PLB 14.88 (*1-55858-159-6*) North-South Bks NYC.
Wilks, Mike. The Ultimate Noah's Ark: Perfect Puzzle for All Ages. Wilks, Mike, illus. LC 93-4021. 80p. (gr. 7 up). 1993. 24.95 (*0-8050-2802-1*) H Holt & Co.
Winder, Linda. Noah. 1993. 5.99 (*0-7814-0122-4*, Chariot Bks) Chariot Family.

NOBEL PRIZES

Aaseng, Nathan. Peace Seekers: The Nobel Peace Prize. (gr. 4-7). 1991. pap. 5.95 (*0-8225-9604-0*) Lerner Pubns.
DeWitt, Lisa F. Nobel Prize Winners: Biographical Sketches for Listening & Reading. (Illus.). 142p. (gr. 8 up). 1991. 12.50x (*0-86647-047-6*); three cassette tapes 27.00x (*0-86647-049-2*) Pro Lingua.
Lazo, Caroline. Rigoberta Menchu. LC 93-8381. (Illus.). 64p. (gr. 4 up). 1994. text ed. 13.95 RSBE (*0-87518-619-X*, Dillon) Macmillan Child Grp.
Schraff, Anne. Women of Peace: Nobel Peace Prize Winners. LC 93-37429. (Illus.). 112p. (gr. 6 up). 1994. lib. bdg. 17.95 (*0-89490-493-0*) Enslow Pubs.

NOISE

Bailey, Donna. What We Can Do about Noise & Fumes. (Illus.). 32p. (gr. k-4). 1992. PLB 11.40 (*0-531-11018-4*) Watts.
MacKinnon, Debbie. What Noise? Sieveking, Anthea, photos by. LC 92-43651. (Illus.). (gr. 4 up). 1994. 10.99 (*0-8037-1510-2*) Dial Bks Young.
Ross, Katharine. The Little Noisy Book. Hirashima, Jean, illus. LC 88-62100. 28p. (ps). 1989. bds. 2.95 (*0-394-82907-7*) Random Bks Yng Read.
Tucker, Sian. Noises. (Illus.). 24p. (ps-k). 1992. pap. 2.95 (*0-671-76906-5*, Little Simon) S&S Trade.

NOISE–FICTION

Boyd, Patti, illus. Oh So Noisy! 12p. (ps). 1993. bds. 4.95 (*0-448-40538-5*, G&D) Putnam Pub Group.
Brodmann, Aliana. Que Ruido! What Noise! Krohn, Hildegard M., tr. from GER. Poppel, Hans, illus. (SPA.). 26p. (gr. 3 up). 1990. 13.95 (*968-6465-08-1*) Hispanic Bk Dist.

Brown, Margaret W. Indoor Noisy Book. new ed. Weisgard, Leonard, illus. LC 92-46879. 48p. (ps-1). 1976. pap. 4.95 (*0-06-443003-0*, Trophy) HarpC Child Bks.
—Summer Noisy Book. new ed. Weisgard, Leonard, illus. LC 92-31435. 40p. (ps-1). 1993. pap. 4.95 (*0-06-443328-5*, Trophy) HarpC Child Bks.
—The Winter Noisy Book. new ed. Shaw, Charles G., illus. LC 92-46880. 48p. (ps-1). 1976. pap. 4.95 (*0-06-443004-9*, Trophy) HarpC Child Bks.
Caseley, Judith. The Noisemakers. LC 90-2806. (Illus.). 24p. (ps-6). 1992. 14.00 (*0-688-09394-9*); PLB 13.93 (*0-688-09395-7*) Greenwillow.
Chislett, G. Whump. (Illus.). 24p. (ps-8). 1989. 12.95 (*1-55037-041-3*, Pub. by Annick CN); pap. 4.95 (*1-55037-040-5*, Pub. by Annick CN) Firefly Bks Ltd.
Coffelt, Nancy. The Dog Who Cried Woof. LC 94-5653. 1994. write for info. (*0-15-200201-4*, Gulliver Bks) HarBrace.
Compton, Kenn & Compton, Joanne. Granny Greenteeth & the Noise in the Night. LC 93-18232. (Illus.). 32p. (ps-3). 1993. reinforced bdg. 14.95 (*0-8234-1051-X*) Holiday.
Cosgrove, Stephen. Wheedle on the Needle. (Illus.). 32p. (Orig.). (gr. 1-4). 1975. pap. 3.95 (*0-8431-0564-X*) Price Stern.
Cowley, Stewart. What's That Noise? (ps). 1994. 2.99 (*0-89577-596-4*, Readers Digest Kids) RD Assn.
Fox, Mem. Night Noises. LC 89-216. (ps-3). 1992. pap. 4.95 (*0-15-257421-2*, Voyager Bks) HarBrace.
Gregorich, Barbara. Noise in the Night. Hoffman, Joan, ed. (Illus.). 16p. (Orig.). (gr. k-2). 1991. pap. 2.25 (*0-88743-027-9*, 06027) Sch Zone Pub Co.
Grossman, Bill. The Banging Book. Zimmerman, Robert, illus. LC 94-18689. 1995. 15.00 (*0-06-024497-6*, Festival); write for info. HarpC Child Bks.
McGovern, Ann. Too Much Noise. (gr. k-3). 1967. 14.45 (*0-395-18110-0*) HM.
—Too Much Noise. Taback, Simms, illus. 48p. (gr. k-3). 1992. pap. 4.80 (*0-395-62985-3*, Sandpiper) HM.
Offen, Hilda. As Quiet As a Mouse. (Illus.). 32p. (ps-2). 1994. 12.99 (*0-525-45309-1*, DCB) Dutton Child Bks.
Olsen, Alfa-Betty & Efron, Marshall. Gabby the Shrew. Chast, Roz, illus. LC 92-31902. 1994. lib. bdg. write for info. (*0-679-94467-2*) Random.
Pank, Rachel. Sonia & Barnie & the Noise in the Night. 1991. pap. 13.95 (*0-590-44657-6*) Scholastic Inc.
Parnall, Peter. Quiet. Parnall, Peter, illus. LC 89-2847. 32p. 1989. 13.95 (*0-688-08204-1*); PLB 13.88 (*0-688-08205-X*, Morrow Jr Bks) Morrow Jr Bks.
Pittman, Helena C. One Quiet Morning: Story & Pictures. LC 93-49596. (Illus.). 1995. write for info. (*0-87614-838-0*) Carolrhoda Bks.
Reiser, Lynn. Night Thunder & the Queen of the Wild Horses. LC 93-25734. 1994. write for info. (*0-688-11791-0*); PLB write for info. (*0-688-11792-9*) Greenwillow.
Rockwell, Anne. Root-a-Toot-Toot. LC 90-46747. (Illus.). 24p. (ps-1). 1991. RSBE 12.95 (*0-02-777272-1*) Macmillan Child Grp.
Sachs, Marilyn. At the Sound of the Beep. LC 89-25655. 128p. (gr. 4-7). 1990. 13.95 (*0-525-44571-4*, DCB) Dutton Child Bks.
Waddell, Martin. Let's Go Home, Little Bear. Firth, Barbara, illus. LC 92-53003. 32p. (ps up). 1993. 14.95 (*1-56402-131-9*) Candlewick Pr.
Wells. Noisy Nora. 1993. pap. 28.67 (*0-590-71436-8*) Scholastic Inc.
Wells, Rosemary. Noisy Nora. Wells, Rosemary, illus. LC 72-6068. 40p. (ps-2). 1973. 10.95 (*0-8037-6638-6*); PLB 10.89 (*0-8037-6639-4*) Dial Bks Young.
Ziefert, Harriet. Andy Toots His Horn. Hoffmann, Sanford, illus. (Orig.). (ps-3). 1988. pap. 3.50 (*0-14-050813-9*, Puffin) Puffin Bks.
—Little Bunny's Noisy Friends. Ernst, Lisa C., illus. 20p. (ps-3). 1990. pap. 4.95 (*0-14-054263-9*, Puffin) Puffin Bks.
—Noisy Barn! Taback, Simms, illus. 16p. (ps-1). 1991. pap. 4.95 (*0-06-107405-5*) HarpC Child Bks.

NOMADS

Halliburton, Warren J. Nomads of the Sahara. LC 91-47153. (Illus.). 48p. (gr. 6). 1992. text ed. 13.95 RSBE (*0-89686-678-5*, Crestwood Hse) Macmillan Child Grp.

NONCONFORMITY

see Dissent

NONSENSE VERSES

see also Limericks

Adams, Pam. There Was an Old Lady Who Swallowed a Fly. LC 90-46921. (ps-3). 1972. 11.95 (*0-85953-021-3*) Childs Play.
Base, Graeme, illus. Jabberwocky: From Lewis Carroll's Through the Looking Glass. 32p. 1989. 16.95 (*0-8109-1150-7*) Abrams.
Brett, Jan & Lear, Edward. Owl & the Pussycat. (Illus.). 32p. (ps-3). 1991. 14.95 (*0-399-21925-0*, Putnam) Putnam Pub Group.
Brown, Marc. Pickle Things. Brown, Marc, illus. LC 80-10540. 48p. (ps-3). 1980. 5.95 (*0-8193-1027-1*) Parents.
Calmenson, Stephanie. Ten Furry Monsters. Chambliss, Maxie, illus. LC 84-4998. 48p. (ps-3). 1984. 5.95 (*0-8193-1128-6*) Parents.
Carroll, Lewis. Humorous Verse of Lewis Carroll. (Illus.). 446p. (gr. 1 up). 1933. pap. 9.95 (*0-486-20654-8*) Dover.
Carryl, Charles E. The Walloping Window-Blind. LaMarche, Jim, illus. LC 92-40338. (gr. k-5). 1993. 15.00 (*0-688-12517-4*); lib. bdg. 14.93 (*0-688-12518-2*) Lothrop.
Chmielewski, Gary. Tongue Twisters. Clark, Ron G., illus. LC 86-17701. (gr. 2-3). 1986. 13.27 (*0-86592-685-9*); 9.95s.p. (*0-685-58366-X*) Rourke Corp.
De Regniers, Beatrice S. May I Bring a Friend? Montresor, Beni, illus. LC 64-19562. 48p. (ps-2). 1971. RSBE 14.95 (*0-689-20615-1*, Atheneum Child Bk) Macmillan Child Grp.
Dr. Seuss. The Butter Battle Book. Dr. Seuss, illus. LC 83-21286. 48p. (gr. 5 up). 1984. 12.00 (*0-394-86580-4*); lib. bdg. 14.99 (*0-394-96580-9*) Random Bks Yng Read.
—Cat in the Hat. Dr. Seuss, illus. LC 56-5470. 72p. (gr. 1-2). 1966. 6.95 (*0-394-80001-X*); lib. bdg. 7.99 (*0-394-90001-4*) Random Bks Yng Read.
—Did I Ever Tell You How Lucky You Are? Dr. Seuss, illus. (ps-4). 1973. 11.00 (*0-394-82719-8*); PLB 11.99 (*0-394-92719-2*) Random Bks Yng Read.
—Dr. Seuss Beginner Book Classics, 5 bks. Dr. Seuss, illus. (ps-3). 1992. Boxed set incls. The Cat in the Hat, Dr. Seuss's ABC, Fox in Socks, Green Eggs & Ham & One Fish Two Fish Red Fish Blue Fish, 72 pgs. ea. 50.00 (*0-679-83846-5*) Random Bks Yng Read.
—Dr. Seuss's ABC. Dr. Seuss, illus. LC 63-9810. 72p. (gr. k-3). 1963. 6.95 (*0-394-80030-3*); lib. bdg. 7.99 (*0-394-90030-8*) Random Bks Yng Read.
—Fox in Socks. Dr. Seuss, illus. LC 65-10484. 72p. (gr. k-3). 1965. 6.95 (*0-394-80038-9*); lib. bdg. 7.99 (*0-394-90038-3*) Random Bks Yng Read.
—Green Eggs & Ham. Dr. Seuss, illus. LC 60-13493. 72p. (gr. 1-2). 1960. 6.95 (*0-394-80016-8*); lib. bdg. 7.99 (*0-394-90016-2*) Random Bks Yng Read.
—Hop on Pop. Dr. Seuss, illus. LC 63-9810. 72p. (gr. 1-2). 1963. 6.95 (*0-394-80029-X*); lib. bdg. 7.99 (*0-394-90029-4*) Random Bks Yng Read.
—Horton Hatches the Egg. Dr. Seuss, illus. (gr. k-3). 1940. 14.00 (*0-394-80077-X*); lib. bdg. 13.99 (*0-394-90077-4*) Random Bks Yng Read.
—Horton Hears a Who. Dr. Seuss, illus. (gr. k-3). 1954. 13.00 (*0-394-80078-8*); PLB 13.99 (*0-394-90078-2*) Random Bks Yng Read.
—How the Grinch Stole Christmas. Dr. Seuss, illus. (gr. k-3). 1957. 11.00 (*0-394-80079-6*); PLB 11.99 (*0-394-90079-0*) Random Bks Yng Read.
—I Can Lick Thirty Tigers Today & Other Stories. Dr. Seuss, illus. (gr. k-3). 1969. 13.00 (*0-394-80094-X*) Random Bks Yng Read.
—If I Ran the Zoo. Dr. Seuss, illus. (gr. k-3). 1950. 13.00 (*0-394-80081-8*); lib. bdg. 13.99 (*0-394-90081-2*) Random Bks Yng Read.
—Lorax. Dr. Seuss, illus. (gr. 2-3). 1971. 13.00 (*0-394-82337-0*); lib. bdg. 12.99 (*0-394-92337-5*) Random Bks Yng Read.
—McElligot's Pool. Dr. Seuss, illus. (gr. k-3). 1947. 11.00 (*0-394-80083-4*); lib. bdg. 11.99 (*0-394-90083-9*) Random Bks Yng Read.
—Oh, Say Can You Say? Dr. Seuss, illus. LC 78-20716. (gr. 1-4). 1979. 6.95 (*0-394-84255-3*, BYR); lib. bdg. 7.99 (*0-394-94255-8*) Beginner.
—On Beyond Zebra. Dr. Seuss, illus. (ps-3). 1955. 12.00 (*0-394-80084-2*); lib. bdg. 13.99 (*0-394-90084-7*) Random Bks Yng Read.
—One Fish Two Fish Red Fish Blue Fish. Dr. Seuss, illus. LC 60-7180. 72p. (gr. 1-2). 1960. 6.95 (*0-394-80013-3*); PLB 7.99 (*0-394-90013-8*) Random Bks Yng Read.
—Scrambled Eggs Super! Dr. Seuss, illus. (gr. k-3). 1953. lib. bdg. 13.99 (*0-394-90085-5*) Random Bks Yng Read.
—Sneetches & Other Stories. Dr. Seuss, illus. (gr. k-4). 1961. 14.00 (*0-394-80089-3*); lib. bdg. 13.99 (*0-394-90089-8*) Random Bks Yng Read.
—There's a Wocket in My Pocket! Dr. Seuss, illus. LC 74-5516. 36p. (ps-1). 1974. 6.95 (*0-394-82920-4*); lib. bdg. 7.99 (*0-394-92920-9*) Random Bks Yng Read.
Hamoy, Carol. What's Wrong? What's Wrong? Hamoy, Carol, illus. (gr. k-3). 1965. 8.95 (*0-685-00564-X*) Astor-Honor.
Heilbroner, Joan. This Is the House Where Jack Lives. Aliki, illus. LC 62-7311. 64p. (gr. k-3). 1962. PLB 13.89 (*0-06-022286-7*) HarpC Child Bks.
Holland, Marion. Big Ball of String. 2nd ed. Mickie, Roy, illus. LC 92-16355. 72p. (gr. 1-2). 1993. 6.95 (*0-394-80005-2*); PLB 7.99 (*0-394-90005-7*) Random Bks Yng Read.
Lear, Edward. A Book of Nonsense. Lear, Edward, illus. LC 92-53176. 240p. 1992. 12.95 (*0-679-41798-2*, Evrymans Lib Childs Class) Knopf.
—The Complete Nonsense of Edward Lear. Lear, Edward, illus. Jackson, H., intro. by. (Illus.). xxix, 287p. (gr. 4-6). pap. 5.95 (*0-486-20167-8*) Dover.
—An Edward Lear Alphabet. Newsom, Carol, illus. LC 82-10037. 32p. (gr. k-3). 1983. PLB 11.88 (*0-688-00965-4*) Lothrop.

—How Pleasant to Know Mr. Lear: Nonsense Poems. Butenko, Bohdan, illus. LC 94-4389. 76p. (gr. 1 up). 1994. 16.95 (*0-88045-126-2*) Stemmer Hse. For the first time, Edward Lear's great nonsense verse is presented for very young readers, who will relate to the charming chalkboard-style illustrations on bright-colored pages more readily than to the elaborate paintings of earlier volumes. Included are four favorite poems: "How Pleasant to Know Mr. Lear," "The Jumblies," "The Dong with a Luminous Nose" & "The Scroobious Pip." The book is square, 9" x 9", enjoyably easy to hold. Short accounts about author & artist are included, & with the title poem, make it easy to introduce biography, as well as poetry & fantasy. Other books in this series of great poetry for young people are I'M NOBODY! WHO ARE YOU?, Emily Dickinson (ISBN 0-916144-21-6, hardbound $21.95; 0-96144-22-4, paper $14.95), A SWINGER OF BIRCHES, Robert Frost (0-919144-92-5, hardbound $21.95; 0-916144-93-3, paper $14.95) & UNDER THE GREENWOOD TREE, William Shakespeare (0-88045-028-2, hardbound $21.95; 0-88045-029-0, paper $14.95). "This irresistible book is its own reason for being." - SLJ. To order, contact Stemmer House Publishers, Inc., 2627 Caves Rd., Owings Mills, MD 21117; tel. 800-676-7511; fax 800-645-6958.
Publisher Provided Annotation.

—Nonsense Poems. LC 93-39193. (Illus.). 96p. (Orig.). 1994. pap. 1.00 (*0-486-28031-4*) Dover.
—The Owl & the Pussy-Cat. Voce, Louise, illus. LC 90-39673. 32p. (ps up). 1991. 13.95 (*0-688-09536-4*); PLB 13.88 (*0-688-09537-2*) Lothrop.
—The Owl & the Pussy Cat. Todd, Justin, illus. 32p. 1992. 15.95 (*0-575-04709-7*, Pub. by Gollancz UK) Trafalgar.
—Owl & the Pussycat. (ps-3). 1991. 3.95 (*0-8037-1044-5*) Dial Bks Young.
—The Table & the Chair. Powers, Tom, illus. LC 91-45538. 32p. (ps-3). 1993. 15.00 (*0-06-020804-X*); PLB 14.89 (*0-06-020805-8*) HarpC Child Bks.
—There Was an Old Man: A Gallery of Nonsense Rhythms, a Selection of Limericks. Lemieux, Michele, illus. LC 93-46492. 1994. write for info. (*0-688-10788-5*); PLB write for info. (*0-688-10789-3*) Morrow Jr Bks.
Lear, Edward & Carroll, Lewis. Owls & Pussycats: Nonsense Verse. Palin, Nicki, illus. LC 93-2714. 64p. (gr. 3 up). 1993. 16.95 (*0-87226-366-5*) P Bedrick Bks.
Lear, Edward & Nash, Ogden. Scroobious Pip. Burkert, Nancy E., illus. LC 68-10373. (gr. 3 up). 1968. HarpC Child Bks.
Le Sieg, Theodore. Maybe You Should Fly a Jet! Maybe You Should Be a Vet. Smollin, Michael J., illus. LC 80-5084. 48p. (ps-3). 1980. lib. bdg. 9.99 (*0-394-94448-8*) Beginner.
Lopshire, Robert. Put Me in the Zoo. LC 60-13494. (Illus.). 72p. (gr. 1-2). 1966. 6.95 (*0-394-80017-6*); lib. bdg. 7.99 (*0-394-90017-0*) Beginner.
Lord, John V. & Burroway, Janet. The Giant Jam Sandwich. Lord, John V., illus. LC 72-13578. 32p. (gr. k-3). 1987. 15.45 (*0-395-16033-2*); pap. 4.80 (*0-395-44237-0*) HM.

McCann, Yvette B. Eddie Pasghetti. Damerest, Nancy & Lea, Judy, eds. Morehiser, Jeanne, illus. 64p. (gr. 4 up). 1994. 14.95 (*0-9639486-5-2*) Rhyme Tyme.
EDDIE PASGHETTI is a whimsical but heartwarming tale of a silly small boy as told by his "hip," self-absorbed, teenaged sister in a unique & sophisticated rhyme. The baby-sitting sister's charge is to get Eddie to eat his greens, but Eddie has other ideas! Kids age nine to ninety-two will laugh at Eddie's antics & at his big sister's growing impatience. "I watched as he ran down the hall with his spoon/ And I thought to myself, 'This kid's like a baboon./ I didn't expect food to ricochet,/ No question about it, I'll ask for more pay!'/ The next thing I knew, Eddie strung his baloney/ On twelve

inches of hard uncooked red rigatoni,/ And he tied it around his small waist, like a child,/ Shouting, 'King Eddie Pasghetti...The King of the Wild!'"/ Parents will readily identify with the struggles of getting a child to eat greens & will greatly appreciate the recipe section containing Eddie's favorite foods. A must read for pasta lovers! Contact: Rhyme Tyme Publications, 214 Presbytere Pkwy., Lafayette, LA 70503-6036 or call (318) 981-4081.
Publisher Provided Annotation.

McClintock, Mike. Stop That Ball! LC 59-9741. (Illus.). (gr. 1-2). 1959. 6.95 (*0-394-80010-9*) Beginner.
Many, Margaret. Non-Stop Nonsense. (gr. k-6). 1991. pap. 3.25 (*0-440-40399-5*, Pub. by Yearling Classics) Dell.
Marshall, James. Pocketful of Nonsense. (Illus.). 24p. (ps-k). 1992. write for info. (*0-307-00140-7*, 312-05, Golden Pr) Western Pub.
Nash, Ogden. Custard the Dragon. Nash, Linell, illus. (gr. k-3). 1973. lib. bdg. 14.95 (*0-316-59841-0*) Little.
Palmer, Michele, ed. Rainy Day Rhymes: A Collection of Chants, Forecasts & Tales. Guerin, Penny, illus. LC 84-60412. 24p. (Orig.). (gr. k up). 1984. pap. 2.95 (*0-932306-02-0*) Rocking Horse.
Pape, D. L. King Robert, the Resting Ruler. LC 68-56823. (Illus.). 48p. (gr. 2-5). 1968. PLB 10.95 (*0-87783-021-5*) Oddo.
—Scientist Sam. LC 68-56826. (Illus.). 48p. (gr. 2-5). 1968. PLB 10.95 (*0-87783-034-7*) Oddo.
Patz, Nancy. Moses Supposes His Toeses Are Roses: And Seven Other Silly Old Rhymes. Patz, Nancy, illus. LC 82-3099. 32p. (ps-3). 1983. 13.95 (*0-15-255690-7*, HB Juv Bks) HarBrace.
Radunsky. Absent-Minded Fellow from Portobello Road. 1993. 14.95 (*0-8050-1131-5*) H Holt & Co.
Raskin, Ellen. Twenty-Two, Twenty-Three. LC 76-5475. (Illus.). 32p. (gr. k-3). 1976. SBE 12.95 (*0-689-30529-X*, Atheneum Childrens Bks) Macmillan Child Grp.
Rounds, Glen, illus. I Know an Old Lady Who Swallowed a Fly. LC 89-46244. 32p. (ps-3). 1991. pap. 5.95 (*0-8234-0908-2*) Holiday.
Stiles, Barbara J. Trinkets & Toads & Other Treasures. LC 91-60705. 48p. 1991. 12.95 (*0-9622057-3-7*); pap. 8.95 (*0-9622057-2-9*) Manzanita Canyon.
Westcott, Nadine B. The Lady with the Alligator Purse. (ps-3). 1990. pap. 4.95 (*0-316-93136-5*) Little.
Westcott, Nadine B., adapted by. & illus. The Lady with the Alligator Purse. LC 87-21368. (ps-3). 1988. 13.95 (*0-316-93135-7*, Joy St Bks) Little.
Wines, James, illus. Edward Lear's Nonsense. LC 93-20461. 32p. 1994. 12.95 (*0-8478-1682-6*) Rizzoli Intl.
Wittels, Harriet & Greisman, Joan. Things I Hate! LC 73-11053. (Illus.). 32p. (ps-3). 1973. 16.95 (*0-87705-096-1*) Human Sci Pr.
Yolen, Jane. Animal Fare: Zoological Nonsense Poems. Street, Janet, illus. LC 92-44931. (gr. 4 up). 1994. 14.95 (*0-15-203550-8*) Harbrace.
Ziegler, Sandra K. Knock-Knocks, Limericks, & Other Silly Sayings. Magnuson, Diana, illus. LC 82-19764. 48p. (gr. 1-5). 1983. pap. 3.95 (*0-516-41872-6*) Childrens.

NONVIOLENCE
Lucas, Eileen. Peace on the Playground: Nonviolent Ways of Problem-Solving. LC 91-12099. (Illus.). 64p. (gr. 5-8). 1991. PLB 12.90 (*0-531-20047-7*) Watts.
Schmidt, Fran & Friedman, Alice. Fighting Fair: Dr. Martin Luther King Jr. for Kids. rev. ed. Heyne, Chris, illus. (gr. 4-9). 1990. Set. pap. text ed. 74.95 69 p., incl. poster, video (*1-878227-02-5*); tchr's. ed., incl. poster 19.95 (*1-878227-07-6*); Set of 5. wkbk., 48p. 11.95 (*1-878227-08-4*) Peace Educ.

NORMANDY, ATTACK ON, 1944
Bliven, Bruce, Jr. Story of D-Day: June 6, 1944. (Illus.). (gr. 6-8). 1963. lib. bdg. 8.99 (*0-394-90362-5*) Random Bks Yng Read.
Miller, Marilyn. D-Day. LC 84-40380. (Illus.). 64p. (gr. 5 up). 1984. PLB 12.95 (*0-382-06825-4*); pap. 7.95 (*0-382-06972-2*) Silver Burdett Pr.
Stein, R. Conrad. D-Day. LC 92-36809. (Illus.). 32p. (gr. 3-6). 1993. PLB 12.30 (*0-516-06661-7*); pap. 3.95 (*0-516-46661-5*) Childrens.

NORMANS
see also Northmen
Martell, Hazel M. The Normans. LC 91-40970. (Illus.). 64p. (gr. 6 up). 1992. text ed. 14.95 RSBE (*0-02-762428-5*, New Discovery) Macmillan Child Grp.

NORSEMEN
see Northmen

NORTH AFRICA
see Africa, North

NORTH AMERICA
Georges, D. V. North America. LC 86-9638. (Illus.). 48p. (gr. k-4). 1986. PLB 12.85 (*0-516-01294-0*); pap. 4.95 (*0-516-41294-9*) Childrens.
Marsh, Carole. Uncle Rebus: North Carolina Picture Stories for Computer Kids. (Illus.). (gr. k-3). 1994. PLB 24.95 (*0-7933-4600-2*); pap. 14.95 (*0-7933-4601-0*); disk 29.95 (*0-7933-4602-9*) Gallopade Pub Group.
Sabin, Louis. North America. Eitzen, Allan, illus. LC 84-8625. 32p. (gr. 3-6). 1985. PLB 9.49 (*0-8167-0240-3*); pap. text ed. 2.95 (*0-8167-0241-1*) Troll Assocs.
Scott, John A. The Story of America. Newhouse, Elizabeth L., ed. LC 84-2018. (Illus.). (gr. 4-8). 1984. 19.95 (*0-87044-508-1*) Natl Geog.
Simon, Seymour. Winter Across America. LC 93-45933. (Illus.). 32p. (ps-5). 1994. 14.95 (*0-7868-0019-4*); PLB 14.89 (*0-7868-2015-2*) Hyprn Child.

NORTH AMERICA–DISCOVERY AND EXPLORATION
see America–Discovery and Exploration

NORTH AMERICA–HISTORY
Andrews, C. L. Story of Sitka. 142p. (gr. 9 up). pap. 9.95 (*0-8466-0094-3*, S94) Shorey.
Shaw, George C. Vancouver's Discovery of Puget Sound. 28p. (gr. 9 up). pap. 1.95 (*0-8466-0102-8*, S102) Shorey.

NORTH AMERICAN INDIANS
see Indians of North America

NORTH CAROLINA
Aylesworth, Thomas G. & Aylesworth, Virginia L. Lower Atlantic (North Carolina, South Carolina) (Illus.). 64p. (gr. 3 up). 1991. lib. bdg. 16.95 (*0-7910-1042-2*) Chelsea Hse.
Campbell, William A. Casting Your Vote in North Carolina. 2nd ed. 25p. (gr. 10-12). 1990. pap. text ed. 5.00 (*1-56011-171-2*) Institute Government.
Carole Marsh North Carolina Books, 55 bks. 1994. PLB 1307.25 set (*0-7933-1308-2*); pap. 767.25 set (*0-7933-5188-X*) Gallopade Pub Group.
Carpenter, Allan. North Carolina. new ed. LC 79-682. (Illus.). 96p. (gr. 4 up). 1979. PLB 16.95 (*0-516-04133-9*) Childrens.
Charlet, James D., et al. North Carolina: Our People, Places, & Past Student Workbook. Charlet, James D., illus. 300p. 1988. wkbk. 49.95 (*0-935911-13-8*) Cornucop Pub.
Fradin, Dennis B. North Carolina. LC 91-35576. 64p. (gr. 3-5). 1992. PLB 16.45 (*0-516-03833-8*); pap. 5.95 (*0-516-43833-6*) Childrens.
Gasque, Pratt. Rum Gully Tales from Tuck'em Inn. (Illus.). 148p. 1990. 14.95 (*0-87844-094-1*); pap. 8.95 (*0-87844-095-X*) Sandlapper Pub Co.
Gravatt, Andrea. The Asheville Alphabet Book. Hall, Kathryn, ed. Grandy, Melody, illus. (Orig.). (ps-9). 1993. pap. 12.95 (*1-56664-058-X*) WorldComm.
Hubbard-Brown, Janet. A History Mystery: The Secret of Roanoke Island. 96p. (Orig.). 1991. pap. 3.50 (*0-380-76223-4*, Camelot) Avon.
Jordan, Louise & Ramsay, Jo. Capital Games: An Activity Book about Raleigh, North Carolina. 32p. (gr. 3-5). 1984. pap. 2.50 (*0-9631710-2-X*) Jr League Raleigh.
Marsh, Carole. Avast, Ye Slobs! North Carolina Pirate Trivia. (Illus.). 1994. PLB 24.95 (*0-7933-0859-3*); pap. 14.95 (*0-7933-0858-5*); computer disk 29.95 (*0-7933-0860-7*) Gallopade Pub Group.
—The Best of the North Carolina Bed & Breakfast. (Illus.). 1994. PLB 24.95 (*0-7933-1830-0*); pap. 14.95 (*0-7933-1831-9*); computer disk 29.95 (*0-7933-1832-7*) Gallopade Pub Group.
—Bow Wow! North Carolina Dogs in History, Mystery, Legend, Lore, Humor & More! (Illus.). (gr. 3-12). 1994. PLB 24.95 (*0-7933-3566-3*); pap. 14.95 (*0-7933-3567-1*); computer disk 29.95 (*0-7933-3568-X*) Gallopade Pub Group.
—Christopher Columbus Comes to North Carolina! Includes Reproducible Activities for Kids! (Illus.). (gr. 3-12). 1994. PLB 24.95 (*0-7933-3719-4*); pap. 14.95 (*0-7933-3720-8*); computer disk 29.95 (*0-7933-3721-6*) Gallopade Pub Group.
—The Hard-to-Believe-But-True! Book of North Carolina History, Mystery, Trivia, Legend, Lore, Humor & More. (Illus.). 1994. PLB 24.95 (*0-7933-0856-9*); pap. 14.95 (*0-7933-0855-0*); computer disk 29.95 (*0-7933-0857-7*) Gallopade Pub Group.
—Hot Shot: Photography for Kids. (Illus., Orig.). (gr. 3-12). 1994. 24.95 (*1-55609-171-0*); pap. 14.95 (*0-935326-79-0*) Gallopade Pub Group.
—If My North Carolina Mama Ran the World! (Illus.). 1994. lib. bdg. 24.95 (*0-7933-1833-5*); pap. 14.95 (*0-7933-1834-3*); computer disk 29.95 (*0-7933-1835-1*) Gallopade Pub Group.
—Jurassic Ark! North Carolina Dinosaurs & Other Prehistoric Creatures. (gr. k-12). 1994. PLB 24.95 (*0-7933-7527-4*); pap. 14.95 (*0-7933-7528-2*); computer disk 29.95 (*0-7933-7529-0*) Gallopade Pub Group.
—Let's Quilt North Carolina & Stuff It Topographically! (Illus.). 1994. PLB 24.95 (*1-55609-925-8*); pap. 14.95 (*1-55609-050-1*); computer disk 29.95 (*1-55609-926-6*) Gallopade Pub Group.
—Let's Quilt Our North Carolina County. 1994. lib. bdg. 24.95 (*0-7933-7212-7*); pap. text ed. 14.95 (*0-7933-7213-5*); disk 29.95 (*0-7933-7214-3*) Gallopade Pub Group.
—Let's Quilt Our North Carolina Town. 1994. lib. bdg. 24.95 (*0-7933-7062-0*); pap. text ed. 14.95 (*0-7933-7063-9*); disk 29.95 (*0-7933-7064-7*) Gallopade Pub Group.
—Meow! North Carolina Cats in History, Mystery, Legend, Lore, Humor & More! (Illus.). (gr. 3-12). 1994. PLB 24.95 (*0-7933-3413-6*); pap. 14.95 (*0-7933-3414-4*); computer disk 29.95 (*0-7933-3415-2*) Gallopade Pub Group.
—North Carolina & Other State Greats (Biographies) (Illus.). 1994. PLB 24.95 (*1-55609-937-1*); pap. 14.95 (*1-55609-938-X*); computer disk 29.95 (*1-55609-939-8*) Gallopade Pub Group.
—North Carolina Bandits, Bushwackers, Outlaws, Crooks, Devils, Ghosts, Desperadoes & Other Assorted & Sundry Characters! (Illus.). 1994. PLB 24.95 (*0-7933-0841-0*); pap. 14.95 (*0-7933-0840-2*); computer disk 29.95 (*0-7933-0842-9*) Gallopade Pub Group.
—North Carolina Classic Christmas Trivia: Stories, Recipes, Activities, Legends, Lore & More. (Illus.). 1994. PLB 24.95 (*0-7933-0844-5*); pap. 14.95 (*0-7933-0843-7*); computer disk 29.95 (*0-7933-0845-3*) Gallopade Pub Group.
—North Carolina Coastales! 1994. lib. bdg. 24.95 (*0-7933-7298-4*) Gallopade Pub Group.
—North Carolina Dingbats! Bk. 1: A Fun Book of Games, Stories, Activities & More about Our State That's All in Code! for You to Decipher. (Illus.). (gr. 3-12). 1994. PLB 24.95 (*0-7933-3872-7*); pap. 14.95 (*0-7933-3873-5*); computer disk 29.95 (*0-7933-3874-3*) Gallopade Pub Group.
—North Carolina Festival Fun for Kids! (Illus.). (gr. 3-12). 1994. lib. bdg. 24.95 (*0-7933-4025-X*); pap. 14.95 (*0-7933-4026-8*); disk 29.95 (*0-7933-4027-6*) Gallopade Pub Group.
—The North Carolina Hot Air Balloon Mystery. (Illus.). (gr. 2-9). 1994. 24.95 (*0-7933-2615-X*); pap. 14.95 (*0-7933-2616-8*); computer disk 29.95 (*0-7933-2617-6*) Gallopade Pub Group.
—North Carolina Jeopardy! Answers & Questions about Our State! (Illus.). (gr. 3-12). 1994. PLB 24.95 (*0-7933-4178-7*); pap. 14.95 (*0-7933-4179-5*); computer disk 29.95 (*0-7933-4180-9*) Gallopade Pub Group.
—North Carolina Jography: A Fun Run Through the Tarheel State. (Illus.). 50p. (Orig.). (gr. 4-8). 1994. pap. 14.95 (*0-935326-81-2*) Gallopade Pub Group.
—North Carolina Kid's Cookbook: Recipes, How-to, History, Lore & More. (Illus.). 1994. PLB 24.95 (*0-7933-0853-4*); pap. 14.95 (*0-7933-0852-6*); computer disk 29.95 (*0-7933-0854-2*) Gallopade Pub Group.
—North Carolina Quiz Bowl Crash Course! (Illus.). 1994. PLB 24.95 (*1-55609-934-7*); pap. 14.95 (*1-55609-935-5*); computer disk 29.95 (*1-55609-936-3*) Gallopade Pub Group.
—North Carolina Rollercoasters! (Illus.). (gr. 3-12). 1994. PLB 24.95 (*0-7933-5323-8*); pap. 14.95 (*0-7933-5324-6*); computer disk 29.95 (*0-7933-5325-4*) Gallopade Pub Group.
—North Carolina School Trivia: An Amazing & Fascinating Look at Our State's Teachers, Schools & Students! (Illus.). 1994. PLB 24.95 (*0-7933-0850-X*); pap. 14.95 (*0-7933-0849-6*); computer disk 29.95 (*0-7933-0851-8*) Gallopade Pub Group.
—North Carolina Silly Basketball Sportsmysteries, Vol. 1. (Illus.). 1994. PLB 24.95 (*0-7933-0847-X*); pap. 14.95 (*0-7933-0846-1*); computer disk 29.95 (*0-7933-0848-8*) Gallopade Pub Group.
—North Carolina Silly Basketball Sportsmysteries, Vol. 2. (Illus.). 1994. PLB 24.95 (*0-7933-1836-X*); pap. 14.95 (*0-7933-1837-8*); computer disk 29.95 (*0-7933-1838-6*) Gallopade Pub Group.
—North Carolina Silly Football Sportmysteries, Vol. 2. (Illus.). 1994. PLB 24.95 (*1-55609-930-4*); pap. 14.95 (*1-55609-931-2*); computer disk 29.95 (*1-55609-932-0*) Gallopade Pub Group.
—North Carolina Silly Football Sportsmysteries, Vol. 1. (Illus.). 1994. PLB 24.95 (*1-55609-927-4*); pap. 14.95 (*1-55609-928-2*); computer disk 29.95 (*1-55609-929-0*) Gallopade Pub Group.
—North Carolina Silly Trivia! (Illus.). 1994. PLB 24.95 (*1-55609-921-5*); pap. 14.95 (*0-685-45984-5*); computer disk 29.95 (*1-55609-922-3*) Gallopade Pub Group.
—North Carolina's (Most Devastating!) Disasters & (Most Calamitous!) Catastrophies! (Illus.). 1994. PLB 24.95 (*0-7933-0838-0*); pap. 14.95 (*0-7933-0837-2*); computer disk 29.95 (*0-7933-0839-9*) Gallopade Pub Group.
—North Carolina's Scariest Swamp: The Great Dismal. (Illus.). (gr. 3 up). 1994. lib. bdg. 24.95 (*0-7933-1270-1*); pap. 14.95 (*0-7933-1271-X*); computer disk 29.95 (*0-7933-1272-8*) Gallopade Pub Group.
North Carolina Wildlife Resources Commission Staff. North Carolina Wild Places: A Closer Look. Earley, Lawrence S., ed. Runyon, Anne M. & Brown, Jim, illus. LC 92-81998. 82p. (Orig.). (gr. 2-6). 1994. pap. 10.00 (*0-9628949-1-5*) NC Wildlife.
Painter, Jacqueline B. The German Invasion of Western North Carolina: A Pictorial History. Bell, John L., frwd. by. LC 92-93524. (Illus.). 128p. (gr. 8 up). 1992. 28.00 (*0-9634256-0-9*) J B Painter.
Stein, R. Conrad. North Carolina. LC 89-17298. 144p. (gr. 4 up). 1989. PLB 20.55 (*0-516-00479-4*) Childrens.
—North Carolina. 190p. 1993. text ed. 15.40 (*1-56956-168-0*) W A T Braille.
Thompson, Kathleen. North Carolina. 48p. (gr. 3 up). 1986. PLB 19.97 (*0-86514-454-0*) Raintree Steck-V.

NORTH CAROLINA–FICTION

Bradfield, Carl. The Sullivans of Little Horsepen Creek: A Tale of Colonial North Carolina's Regulator Era, Circa: 1760s. (Illus.). 350p. (gr. 8-12). Date not set. write for info. (*0-9632319-2-8*) ASDA Pub.

Carris, Joan D. A Ghost of a Chance. Henry, Paul, illus. 160p. (gr. 3-7). 1992. 14.95 (*0-316-13016-8*) Little.

Houston, Gloria. Littlejim. Allen, Thomas B., illus. LC 92-43775. 176p. (gr. 5 up). 1993. pap. 4.95 (*0-688-12112-8*, Pub. by Beech Tree Bks) Morrow.

Klaveness, Jan O. Keeper of the Light. LC 90-38530. 224p. (gr. 7 up). 1990. 12.95g (*0-688-06996-7*) Morrow Jr Bks.

Newton, Suzanne. Where Are You When I Need You? LC 92-31360. 208p. (gr. 7 up). 1993. pap. 3.99 (*0-14-034454-3*) Puffin Bks.

Pinkney, Gloria J. Back Home. Pinkney, Jerry, illus. LC 91-22610. 40p. (gr. k-4). 1992. 15.00 (*0-8037-1168-9*); PLB 14.89 (*0-8037-1169-7*) Dial Bks Young.

Taylor, Theodore. Teetoncey & Ben O'Neal. Cuffari, Richard, illus. 192p. (gr. 5-7). 1991. pap. 3.50 (*0-380-71025-0*, Camelot) Avon.

NORTH CAROLINA–HISTORY

Carriker, S. David. North Carolina Railroads: The Common Carrier Railroads of North Carolina. 66p. 1989. pap. 15.00 (*0-936013-08-7*) Herit Pub NC.

Fradin, Dennis. North Carolina Colony. LC 91-13314. 190p. (gr. 4 up). 1991. PLB 17.95 (*0-516-00396-8*) Childrens.

Johnson, Patricia G. The New River Early Settlement. LC 83-81157. (Illus.). 232p. (gr. 6 up). 1991. Repr. of 1983 ed. 20.00 (*0-9614765-3-2*) Walpa Pub.

Marsh, Carole. Chill Out: Scary North Carolina Tales Based on Frightening North Carolina Truths. (Illus.). 1994. lib. bdg. 24.95 (*0-7933-4753-X*); pap. 14.95 (*0-7933-4754-8*); disk 29.95 (*0-7933-4755-6*) Gallopade Pub Group.

—My First Book about North Carolina. (gr. k-4). 1994. PLB 24.95 (*0-7933-5668-7*); pap. 14.95 (*0-7933-5669-5*); computer disk 29.95 (*0-7933-5670-9*) Gallopade Pub Group.

—North Carolina "Crinkum-Crankum" A Funny Word Book about Our State. (Illus.). (gr. 3-12). 1994. 24.95 (*0-7933-4907-9*); pap. 14.95 (*0-7933-4908-7*); computer disk 29.95 (*0-7933-4909-5*) Gallopade Pub Group.

—The North Carolina Mystery Van Takes Off! Book 1: Handicapped North Carolina Kids Sneak Off on a Big Adventure. (Illus.). (gr. 3-12). 1994. 24.95 (*0-7933-5060-3*); pap. 14.95 (*0-7933-5061-1*); computer disk 29.95 (*0-7933-5062-X*) Gallopade Pub Group.

—North Carolina Timeline: A Chronology of North Carolina History, Mystery, Trivia, Legend, Lore & More. (Illus.). (gr. 3-12). 1994. PLB 24.95 (*0-7933-5974-0*); pap. 14.95 (*0-7933-5975-9*); computer disk 29.95 (*0-7933-5976-7*) Gallopade Pub Group.

—North Carolina's Unsolved Mysteries (& Their "Solutions") Includes Scientific Information & Other Activities for Students. (Illus.). (gr. 3-12). 1994. PLB 24.95 (*0-7933-5821-3*); pap. 14.95 (*0-7933-5822-1*); computer disk 29.95 (*0-7933-5823-X*) Gallopade Pub Group.

—Patch, the Pirate Dog: A North Carolina Pet Story. (ps-4). 1994. PLB 24.95 (*0-7933-5515-X*); pap. 14.95 (*0-7933-5516-8*); computer disk 29.95 (*0-7933-5517-6*) Gallopade Pub Group.

Price, William S., Jr. There Ought to Be a Bill of Rights: North Carolina Enters a New Nation. (Illus.). 19p. (Orig.). (gr. 8-12). 1991. pap. 4.00 (*0-86526-254-3*) NC Archives.

Schouweiler, Thomas. The Lost Colony of Roanoke: Opposing Viewpoints. LC 91-15188. (Illus.). 112p. (gr. 5-8). 1991. PLB 14.95 (*0-89908-093-6*) Greenhaven.

Simmons-Henry, Linda, et al. The Heritage of Blacks in North Carolina. (gr. 6-12). 1990. 60.00 (*0-912081-12-0*) Delmar Co.

Smith, Beth C. Mystery Tour: A Student Guide to North Carolina Ghosts & Legends. (Illus.). 135p. (gr. 4 up). 1992. 12.95 (*0-916107-94-9*) Broadfoot.

NORTH CENTRAL STATES

see Middle West

NORTH DAKOTA

Carole Marsh North Dakota Books, 44 bks. 1994. PLB 1027.80 set (*0-7933-1309-0*); pap. 587.80 set (*0-7933-5190-1*) Gallopade Pub Group.

Carpenter, Allan. North Dakota. new ed. LC 79-11470. (Illus.). 96p. (gr. 4 up). 1979. PLB 16.95 (*0-516-04134-7*) Childrens.

Fradin, Dennis. North Dakota: In Words & Pictures. Wahl, Richard, illus. LC 80-26480. 48p. (gr. 2-5). 1981. PLB 12.95 (*0-516-03934-2*) Childrens.

Fradin, Dennis B. & Fradin, Judith B. North Dakota. LC 94-4871. (Illus.). 64p. (gr. 3-5). 1994. PLB 22.00 (*0-516-03834-6*) Childrens.

Herguth, Margaret S. North Dakota. LC 89-25283. (Illus.). 144p. (gr. 4 up). 1990. PLB 20.55 (*0-516-00480-8*) Childrens.

—North Dakota. 205p. 1993. text ed. 15.40 (*1-56956-142-7*) W A T Braille.

Marsh, Carole. Avast, Ye Slobs! North Dakota Pirate Trivia. (Illus.). 1994. PLB 24.95 (*0-7933-0883-6*); pap. 14.95 (*0-7933-0882-8*); computer disk 29.95 (*0-7933-0884-4*) Gallopade Pub Group.

—The Beast of the North Dakota Bed & Breakfast. (Illus.). 1994. PLB 24.95 (*0-7933-1839-4*); pap. 14.95 (*0-7933-1840-8*); computer disk 29.95 (*0-7933-1841-6*) Gallopade Pub Group.

—Bow Wow! North Dakota Dogs in History, Mystery, Legend, Lore, Humor & More! (Illus.). (gr. 3-12). 1994. PLB 24.95 (*0-7933-3569-8*); pap. 14.95 (*0-7933-3570-1*); computer disk 29.95 (*0-7933-3571-X*) Gallopade Pub Group.

—Chill Out: Scary North Dakota Tales Based on Frightening North Dakota Truths. (Illus.). 1994. lib. bdg. 24.95 (*0-7933-4756-4*); pap. 14.95 (*0-7933-4757-2*); disk 29.95 (*0-7933-4758-0*) Gallopade Pub Group.

—Christopher Columbus Comes to North Dakota! Includes Reproducible Activities for Kids! (Illus.). (gr. 3-12). 1994. PLB 24.95 (*0-7933-3722-4*); pap. 14.95 (*0-7933-3723-2*); computer disk 29.95 (*0-7933-3724-0*) Gallopade Pub Group.

—The Hard-to-Believe-But-True! Book of North Dakota History, Mystery, Trivia, Legend, Lore, Humor & More. (Illus.). 1994. PLB 24.95 (*0-7933-0880-1*); pap. 14.95 (*0-7933-0879-8*); computer disk 29.95 (*0-7933-0881-X*) Gallopade Pub Group.

—If My North Dakota Mama Ran the World! (Illus.). 1994. lib. bdg. 24.95 (*0-7933-1842-4*); pap. 14.95 (*0-7933-1843-2*); computer disk 29.95 (*0-7933-1844-0*) Gallopade Pub Group.

—Jurassic Ark! North Dakota Dinosaurs & Other Prehistoric Creatures. (gr. k-12). 1994. PLB 24.95 (*0-7933-7530-4*); pap. 14.95 (*0-7933-7531-2*); computer disk 29.95 (*0-7933-7532-0*) Gallopade Pub Group.

—Let's Quilt North Dakota & Stuff It Topographically! (Illus.). 1994. PLB 24.95 (*1-55609-946-0*); pap. 14.95 (*1-55609-135-4*); computer disk 29.95 (*1-55609-947-9*) Gallopade Pub Group.

—Let's Quilt Our North Dakota County. 1994. lib. bdg. 24.95 (*0-7933-7215-1*); pap. text ed. 14.95 (*0-7933-7216-X*); disk 29.95 (*0-7933-7217-8*) Gallopade Pub Group.

—Let's Quilt Our North Dakota Town. 1994. lib. bdg. 24.95 (*0-7933-7065-5*); pap. text ed. 14.95 (*0-7933-7066-3*); disk 29.95 (*0-7933-7067-1*) Gallopade Pub Group.

—Meow! North Dakota Cats in History, Mystery, Legend, Lore, Humor & More! (Illus.). (gr. 3-12). 1994. PLB 24.95 (*0-7933-3416-0*); pap. 14.95 (*0-7933-3417-9*); computer disk 29.95 (*0-7933-3418-7*) Gallopade Pub Group.

—My First Book about North Dakota. (gr. k-4). 1994. PLB 24.95 (*0-7933-5671-7*); pap. 14.95 (*0-7933-5672-5*); computer disk 29.95 (*0-7933-5673-3*) Gallopade Pub Group.

—The North Dakota Air Balloon Mystery. (Illus.). (gr. 2-9). 1994. 24.95 (*0-7933-2624-9*); pap. 14.95 (*0-7933-2625-7*); computer disk 29.95 (*0-7933-2626-5*) Gallopade Pub Group.

—North Dakota & Other State Greats (Biographies) (Illus.). 1994. PLB 24.95 (*1-55609-976-2*); pap. 14.95 (*1-55609-977-0*); computer disk 29.95 (*0-685-45973-X*) Gallopade Pub Group.

—North Dakota Bandits, Bushwackers, Outlaws, Crooks, Devils, Ghosts, Desperadoes & Other Assorted & Sundry Characters! (Illus.). 1994. PLB 24.95 (*0-7933-0865-8*); pap. 14.95 (*0-7933-0864-X*); computer disk 29.95 (*0-7933-0866-6*) Gallopade Pub Group.

—North Dakota Classic Christmas Trivia: Stories, Recipes, Activities, Legends, Lore & More! (Illus.). 1994. PLB 24.95 (*0-7933-0868-2*); pap. 14.95 (*0-7933-0867-4*); computer disk 29.95 (*0-7933-0869-0*) Gallopade Pub Group.

—North Dakota Coastales. (Illus.). 1994. PLB 24.95 (*0-685-45972-1*); pap. 14.95 (*1-55609-971-1*); computer disk 29.95 (*1-55609-972-X*) Gallopade Pub Group.

—North Dakota Coastales! 1994. lib. bdg. 24.95 (*0-7933-7299-2*) Gallopade Pub Group.

—North Dakota "Crinkum-Crankum" A Funny Word Book about Our State. (Illus.). (gr. 3-12). 1994. 24.95 (*0-7933-4910-9*); pap. 14.95 (*0-7933-4911-7*); computer disk 29.95 (*0-7933-4912-5*) Gallopade Pub Group.

—North Dakota Dingbats! Bk. 1: A Fun Book of Games, Stories, Activities & More about Our State That's All in Code! for You to Decipher. (Illus.). (gr. 3-12). 1994. PLB 24.95 (*0-7933-3875-1*); pap. 14.95 (*0-7933-3876-X*); computer disk 29.95 (*0-7933-3877-8*) Gallopade Pub Group.

—North Dakota Festival Fun for Kids! (Illus.). (gr. 3-12). 1994. lib. bdg. 24.95 (*0-7933-4028-4*); pap. 14.95 (*0-7933-4029-2*); disk 29.95 (*0-7933-4030-6*) Gallopade Pub Group.

—North Dakota Jeopardy! Answers & Questions about Our State! (Illus.). (gr. 3-12). 1994. PLB 24.95 (*0-7933-4181-7*); pap. 14.95 (*0-7933-4182-5*); computer disk 29.95 (*0-7933-4183-3*) Gallopade Pub Group.

—North Dakota "Jography" A Fun Run Thru Our State! (Illus.). 1994. PLB 24.95 (*1-55609-943-6*); pap. 14.95 (*1-55609-944-4*); computer disk 29.95 (*1-55609-945-2*) Gallopade Pub Group.

—North Dakota Kid's Cookbook: Recipes, How-to, History, Lore & More! (Illus.). 1994. PLB 24.95 (*0-7933-0877-1*); pap. 14.95 (*0-7933-0876-3*); computer disk 29.95 (*0-7933-0878-X*) Gallopade Pub Group.

—The North Dakota Mystery Van Takes Off! Book 1: Handicapped North Dakota Kids Sneak Off on a Big Adventure. (Illus.). (gr. 3-12). 1994. 24.95 (*0-7933-5063-8*); pap. 14.95 (*0-7933-5064-6*); computer disk 29.95 (*0-7933-5065-4*) Gallopade Pub Group.

—North Dakota Quiz Bowl Crash Course! (Illus.). 1994. PLB 24.95 (*1-55609-973-8*); pap. 14.95 (*1-55609-974-6*); computer disk 29.95 (*1-55609-975-4*) Gallopade Pub Group.

—North Dakota Rollercoasters! (Illus.). (gr. 3-12). 1994. PLB 24.95 (*0-7933-5326-2*); pap. 14.95 (*0-7933-5327-0*); computer disk 29.95 (*0-7933-5328-9*) Gallopade Pub Group.

—North Dakota School Trivia: An Amazing & Fascinating Look at Our State's Teachers, Schools & Students! (Illus.). 1994. PLB 24.95 (*0-7933-0874-7*); pap. 14.95 (*0-7933-0873-9*); computer disk 29.95 (*0-7933-0875-5*) Gallopade Pub Group.

—North Dakota Silly Basketball Sportsmysteries, Vol. 1. (Illus.). 1994. PLB 24.95 (*0-7933-0871-2*); pap. 14.95 (*0-7933-0870-4*); computer disk 29.95 (*0-7933-0872-0*) Gallopade Pub Group.

—North Dakota Silly Football Sportsmysteries, Vol. 2. (Illus.). 1994. PLB 24.95 (*1-55609-967-3*); pap. 14.95 (*1-55609-968-1*); computer disk 29.95 (*1-55609-969-X*) Gallopade Pub Group.

—North Dakota Silly Trivia! (Illus.). 1994. PLB 24.95 (*1-55609-940-1*); pap. 14.95 (*1-55609-941-X*); computer disk 29.95 (*1-55609-942-8*) Gallopade Pub Group.

—North Dakota Timeline: A Chronology of North Dakota History, Mystery, Trivia, Legend, Lore & More. (Illus.). (gr. 3-12). 1994. PLB 24.95 (*0-7933-5977-5*); pap. 14.95 (*0-7933-5978-3*); computer disk 29.95 (*0-7933-5979-1*) Gallopade Pub Group.

—North Dakota's (Most Devastating!) Disasters & (Most Calamitous!) Catastrophies! (Illus.). 1994. PLB 24.95 (*0-7933-0862-3*); pap. 14.95 (*0-7933-0861-5*); computer disk 29.95 (*0-7933-0863-1*) Gallopade Pub Group.

—North Dakota's Unsolved Mysteries (& Their "Solutions") Includes Scientific Information & Other Activities for Students. (Illus.). (gr. 3-12). 1994. PLB 24.95 (*0-7933-5824-8*); pap. 14.95 (*0-7933-5825-6*); computer disk 29.95 (*0-7933-5826-4*) Gallopade Pub Group.

—Patch, the Pirate Dog: A North Dakota Pet Story. (ps-4). 1994. PLB 24.95 (*0-7933-5518-4*); pap. 14.95 (*0-7933-5519-2*); computer disk 29.95 (*0-7933-5520-6*) Gallopade Pub Group.

—Uncle Rebus: North Dakota Picture Stories for Computer Kids. (Illus.). (gr. k-3). 1994. PLB 24.95 (*0-7933-4603-7*); pap. 14.95 (*0-7933-4604-5*); disk 29.95 (*0-7933-4605-3*) Gallopade Pub Group.

Thompson, Kathleen. North Dakota. LC 85-9974. 48p. (gr. 3 up). 1985. PLB 19.97 (*0-86514-440-0*) Raintree Steck-V.

Verba, Joan M. North Dakota. Lerner Geography Department Staff, ed. (Illus.). 72p. (gr. 3-6). 1992. PLB 17.50 (*0-8225-2746-4*) Lerner Pubns.

NORTH DAKOTA–FICTION

Marsh, Carole. North Dakota Silly Basketball Sportsmysteries, Vol. 2. (Illus.). 1994. PLB 24.95 (*0-685-45974-8*); pap. 14.95 (*0-7933-1846-7*); computer disk 29.95 (*0-7933-1847-5*) Gallopade Pub Group.

—North Dakota Silly Football Sportsmysteries, Vol. 1. (Illus.). 1994. PLB 24.95 (*1-55609-948-7*); pap. 14.95 (*1-55609-949-5*); computer disk 29.95 (*0-685-45971-3*) Gallopade Pub Group.

Sypher, Lucy J. Cousins & Circuses. Abel, Ray, illus. 250p. (gr. 3-7). 1991. pap. 3.95 (*0-14-034551-5*, Puffin) Puffin Bks.

Wilder, Laura Ingalls. By the Shores of Silver Lake. rev. ed. Williams, Garth, illus. LC 52-7529. 304p. (gr. 3-7). 1961. 15.95 (*0-06-026416-0*); PLB 15.89 (*0-06-026417-9*) HarpC Child Bks.

NORTH POLE

see also Arctic Regions

Anderson, Madelyn K. Robert E. Peary & the Fight for the North Pole. (Illus.). 160p. (gr. 9-12). 1992. PLB 14.40 (*0-531-13004-5*) Watts.

Charleston, Gordon. Peary Reaches the North Pole. LC 92-44500. (Illus.). 32p. (gr. 5 up). 1993. text ed. 13.95 RSBE (*0-87518-535-5*, Dillon) Macmillan Child Grp.

Johnson, LaVerne C. Matthew Henson. Perry, Craig Rex, illus. LC 92-35253. 1992. 3.95 (*0-922162-94-8*) Empak Pub.

Williams, Jean. Matthew Henson: Polar Adventurer. LC 93-6101. (Illus.). 64p. (gr. 5-8). 1994. PLB 12.90 (*0-531-20006-X*) Watts.

NORTH POLE–FICTION

Primavera, Elise. Ralph's Frozen Tale. LC 90-35521. 32p. 1991. 14.95 (*0-399-22252-9*, Putnam) Putnam Pub Group.

Sabin, Tracy. A Visit to the North Pole. (ps up). 1993. 15.95 (*0-8167-3137-3*) BrdgeWater.

Thompson, R. W., Jr. Wow! I Got to Go to the North Pole. Keitz, Roderick K., illus. 16p. (ps-3). 1994. 8.95 (*0-9636442-7-0*) N Pole Chron.

Wynne-Jones, Tim. Zoom Away. Beddows, Eric, illus. LC 92-41171. 32p. (ps-2). 1993. 15.00 (*0-06-022962-4*); PLB 14.89 (*0-06-022963-2*) HarpC.

NORTHMEN

see also Normans

Atkinson, I. The Viking Ships. LC 77-17510. (Illus.). 48p. (gr. 7 up). 1979. pap. 8.95 (*0-521-21951-5*) Cambridge U Pr.
Birkett, Alaric. Vikings. (gr. 5-8). 1985. pap. 10.95 (*0-7175-1321-1*) Dufour.
Bjorke, Drew. Arne the Viking. Bjorke, Drew, illus. (ps). 1993. Gift box set of 4 bks., 12p. ea. incl. viking ship. bds. 14.95 (*1-56828-037-8*) Red Jacket Pr.
Caselli, Giovanni. A Viking Settler. Caselli, Giovanni, illus. LC 86-3302. 32p. (gr. 3-6). 1991. lib. bdg. 12.95 (*0-87226-104-2*) P Bedrick Bks.
Clare, John D., ed. Vikings. (gr. 4-7). 1992. 16.95 (*0-15-200512-9*, Gulliver Bks) HarBrace.
Costumes of the Saxons & Vikings. 72p. (gr. 7-11). 1991. 19.95 (*0-7134-5750-3*, Pub. by Batsford UK) Trafalgar.
Fienberg, Anna. The Hottest Boy Who Ever Lived. Grant, Christy, ed. Gamble, Kim, illus. LC 94-6648. 32p. (gr. k-3). 1994. PLB 14.95 (*0-8075-3387-4*) A Whitman.
Hook, Jason. The Vikings. LC 93-13990. (Illus.). 32p. (gr. 4-6). 1993. 14.95 (*1-56847-060-6*) Thomson Lrning.
Humble, Richard. The Age of Leif Eriksson. Hook, Richard, illus. LC 89-8867. 32p. (gr. 5-8). 1989. PLB 12.40 (*0-531-10741-8*) Watts.
Italia, Bob. The Vikings. Walner, Rosemary, ed. LC 90-82625. (Illus.). 32p. (gr. 4). 1990. PLB 11.96 (*0-939179-93-8*) Abdo & Dghtrs.
MacDonald, Fiona. Vikings. (Illus.). 60p. (gr. 4 up). 1993. 15.95 (*0-8120-6375-9*) Barron.
Margeson, Sue. Viking. LC 93-32593. (Illus.). 64p. (gr. 5 up). 1994. 16.00 (*0-679-86002-9*); PLB 16.99 (*0-679-96002-3*) Knopf Bks Yng Read.
Martell, Hazel M. Everyday Life in Viking Times. LC 93-36128. 1994. write for info. (*0-531-14287-6*) Watts.
—Over Nine Hundred Years Ago: With the Vikings. Payne, Roger, illus. LC 93-2647. 32p. (gr. 6 up). 1993. text ed. 13.95 RSBE (*0-02-726325-8*, New Discovery Bks) Macmillan Child Grp.
—The Vikings. LC 91-507. (Illus.). 64p. (gr. 6 up). 1992. text ed. 14.95 RSBE (*0-02-762427-7*, New Discovery) Macmillan Child Grp.
—The Vikings & Jorvik. LC 92-25215. (Illus.). 32p. (gr. 5 up). 1993. text ed. 13.95 RSBE (*0-87518-541-X*, Dillon) Macmillan Child Grp.
Matthews, Rupert. Viking Explorers. LC 90-178. (Illus.). 24p. (gr. k-4). 1990. PLB 10.90 (*0-531-18346-7*, Pub. by Bookwright Pr) Watts.
Millard, Anne. Eric the Red: The Vikings Sail the Atlantic. LC 93-26113. 1994. PLB 22.80 (*0-8114-7252-3*) Raintree Steck-V.
Morley, Jacqueline. How Would You Survive As a Viking? Bergin, Mark, illus. Salariya, David. LC 94-26161. (gr. 3 up). 1995. lib. bdg. write for info. (*0-531-14344-9*) Watts.
Mulvihill, Margaret. Viking Longboats. Smith, Tony, illus. LC 89-31565. 32p. (gr. 4-6). 1989. PLB 12.40 (*0-531-17168-X*, Gloucester Pr) Watts.
Nicholson, Robert. Vikings. (gr. 4-7). 1994. pap. 6.95 (*0-7910-2733-3*) Chelsea Hse.
Odijk, Pamela. The Vikings. Easton, Emily, ed. (Illus.). 48p. (gr. 5-8). 1990. PLB 12.95 (*0-382-09893-5*); 7.95 (*0-382-24269-6*); tchr's. guide 4.50 (*0-382-24283-1*) Silver Burdett Pr.
Schiller, Barbara. Eric the Red & Leif the Lucky. LC 78-18055. (Illus.). 48p. (gr. 4-7). 1979. PLB 10.59 (*0-89375-174-X*); pap. 3.50 (*0-89375-166-9*) Troll Assocs.
Simon, Charnan. Leif Eriksson & the Vikings: The Norse Discovery of America. LC 90-20804. (Illus.). 128p. (gr. 3 up). 1991. PLB 20.55 (*0-516-03060-4*) Childrens.
Speed, Peter. Harald Hardrada & the Vikings. Hook, Richard, illus. LC 92-5818. 63p. (gr. 6-7). 1992. PLB 24.26 (*0-8114-3353-6*) Raintree Steck-V.
Stainer, Tom & Sutton, Harry. The Vikings. Kesteven, Peter, illus. 32p. (gr. 4-6). 1992. pap. 4.95 (*0-563-21356-6*, BBC-Parkwest) Parkwest Pubns.
Stefoff, Rebecca. The Viking Explorers. Goetzmann, William H., ed. Collins, Michael, intro. by. (Illus.). 112p. (gr. 6-12). 1993. PLB 19.95 (*0-7910-1295-6*, Am Art Analog); pap. write for info. (*0-7910-1520-3*, Am Art Analog) Chelsea Hse.
Triggs, Tony P. Viking Warriors. LC 90-858. (Illus.). 24p. (gr. 2-5). 1991. PLB 10.90 (*0-531-18356-4*, Pub. by Bookwright Pr) Watts.
Tweddle, Dominic. Growing up in Viking Times. McBride, Angus, illus. LC 91-41396. 32p. (gr. 3-5). 1993. PLB 11.89 (*0-8167-2725-2*); pap. text ed. 3.95 (*0-8167-2726-0*) Troll Assocs.
Wilson, David M. The Vikings. (Illus.). (gr. 2-6). pap. 3.95 (*0-7141-0549-X*, Pub. by Brit Mus UK) Parkwest Pubns.
Wright, Rachel. Vikings. LC 92-4618. (Illus.). 32p. (gr. 5-8). 1993. PLB 11.90 (*0-531-14210-8*) Watts.

NORTHMEN–FICTION

Abraham, Norma J. Erik of the Dragon Ships. Steiner, Pat, illus. LC 83-50987. 163p. (Orig.). (gr. 8-11). 1983. pap. 3.95 (*0-912661-00-3*) Woodsong Graph.
Campbell, Civardi. Viking Raiders. (gr. 4-9). 1977. (Usborne-Hayes); PLB 13.96 (*0-88110-102-8*); pap. 6.95 (*0-86020-085-X*) EDC.
De Goscinny, Rene. Le Bouclier Arverne. (FRE.). (gr. 7-9). 1990. 19.95 (*0-8288-5120-4*, FC883) Fr & Eur.
—Le Combat des Chefs. (FRE.). (gr. 7-9). 1990. 19.95 (*0-8288-5121-2*, FC879) Fr & Eur.
—Le Tour de Gaulle. (FRE., Also avail. in Span.). (gr. 3-8). 1990. 19.95 (*0-8288-4909-9*) Fr & Eur.
De Goscinny, Rene & Uderzo, M. Asterix & the Goths. (Illus.). (gr. 7-10). 1990. 19.95 (*0-8288-4919-6*) Fr & Eur.
—Asterix Gladiator. (LAT., Illus.). 1990. 19.95 (*0-8288-4943-9*) Fr & Eur.
—Asterix in Britain. (Illus.). 1990. 19.95 (*0-8288-4944-7*) Fr & Eur.
—Domaine des Dieux. (FRE., Illus.). (gr. 7-9). 1990. 19.95 (*0-8288-5123-9*, FC886) Fr & Eur.
—The Great Crossing. (Illus.). 1990. 19.95 (*0-8288-4971-4*) Fr & Eur.
Hunt, Jonathan. Leif's Saga. LC 94-14233. 1995. 17.95 (*0-02-745780-X*) Macmillan.
Jones, Terry. The Saga of Eric the Viking. large type ed. 248p. (gr. 3 up). 1990. lib. bdg. 16.95x (*0-7451-1152-1*, Lythway Large Print) Hall.
—The Saga of Erik the Viking. Foreman, Michael, illus. 192p. (gr. 3-7). 1993. pap. 3.99 (*0-14-032261-2*, Puffin) Puffin Bks.
Molan, Chris, as told by. The Viking Saga. (Illus.). 32p. (gr. k-5). 1985. PLB 19.97 (*0-8172-2503-X*) Raintree Steck-V.
Packard, Edward. Viking Raiders. (gr. 4-7). 1992. pap. 3.25 (*0-553-29302-8*) Bantam.
Treece, Henry. Road to Miklagard. Price, Christine, illus. LC 57-12280. (gr. 6-10). 1957. 21.95 (*0-87599-118-1*) S G Phillips.
—Viking's Dawn. Price, C., illus. LC 56-9962. (gr. 7-9). 1956. 21.95 (*0-87599-117-3*) S G Phillips.
—Westward to Vinland. Stobbs, William, illus. (gr. 8 up). 1967. 21.95 (*0-87599-136-X*) S G Phillips.

NORTHWEST, OLD

see also Middle West

Connell, Kate. These Lands Are Ours: Tecumseh's Fight for the Old Northwest. Jones, Jan N., illus. LC 92-14417. 96p. (gr. 2-5). 1992. PLB 21.34 (*0-8114-7227-2*) Raintree Steck-V.

NORTHWEST, OLD–FICTION

Silver, Jeffrey H. The Rainier Ice Caves & Other Northwest Stories. Topolski, Diane F., illus. 32p. (gr. 5 up). 1983. pap. 4.00 (*0-910867-01-1*) Silver Seal Bks.

NORTHWEST, PACIFIC

Garrett, Sandra. The Pacific Northwest Coast. LC 94-9098. 1994. write for info. (*0-86625-513-3*) Rourke Pubns.
Parkin, Tom. Green Giants: Rainforests of the Pacific Northwest. (Illus.). 48p. (Orig.). (gr. 8-12). 1992. pap. 7.95 (*1-895565-07-3*) Firefly Bks Ltd.

NORTHWEST, PACIFIC–FICTION

Killingsworth, Monte. Circle Within a Circle. LC 93-17244. 176p. (gr. 7 up). 1994. SBE 14.95 (*0-689-50598-1*, M K McElderry) Macmillan Child Grp.
Tjepkema, Edith R. Lost in Paradise. 125p. (Orig.). (gr. 8-12). 1991. pap. 4.95 (*0-9620280-3-7*) Northland Pr.

NORTHWEST PASSAGE

Brown, Warren. The Search for the Northwest Passage. Goetzmann, William H., ed. Collins, Michael, intro. by. (Illus.). 112p. (gr. 5 up). 1991. lib. bdg. 18.95 (*0-7910-1297-2*) Chelsea Hse.
Chrisp, Peter. Search for a Northern Route. LC 93-30920. (Illus.). 48p. (gr. 4-6). 1993. 14.95 (*1-56847-122-X*) Thomson Lrning.

NORTHWESTERN STATES

Herda, D. J. Environmental America: The Northwestern States. (Illus.). 64p. (gr. 5-8). 1991. PLB 15.40 (*1-878841-10-6*) Millbrook Pr.
—Historical America: The Northwestern States. LC 92-16312. (Illus.). 64p. (gr. 5-8). 1993. PLB 15.40 (*1-56294-122-4*) Millbrook Pr.

NORWAY

Charbonneau, Claudette & Lander, Patricia S. The Land & People of Norway. LC 91-35029. (Illus.). 256p. (gr. 6 up). 1993. 18.00 (*0-06-020573-3*); PLB 17.89 (*0-06-020583-0*) HarpC Child Bks.
Hintz, Martin. Norway. LC 82-9400. (Illus.). (gr. 5-9). 1982. PLB 20.55 (*0-516-02780-8*) Childrens.
Lerner Publications, Department of Geography Staff, ed. Norway in Pictures. (Illus.). 64p. (gr. 5 up). 1990. PLB 17.50 (*0-8225-1871-6*) Lerner Pubns.
St. John, Jetty. A Family in Norway. (Illus.). 32p. (gr. 2-5). 1988. lib. bdg. 13.50 (*0-8225-1681-0*) Lerner Pubns.
Zickgraf, Ralph. Norway. (Illus.). 128p. (gr. 5 up). 1990. 14.95 (*0-7910-1100-3*) Chelsea Hse.

NORWAY–FICTION

Aamundsen, Nina R. Two Short & One Long. 112p. (gr. 4-8). 1990. 13.50 (*0-395-52434-2*) HM.
Bjorke, Drew. Arne & Loki. Bjorke, Drew, illus. 12p. (ps). 1993. 4.95 (*1-56828-033-5*) Red Jacket Pr.
Egner, Thorbjorn. Karius & Baktus. 2nd ed. Sevig, Mike & Olderheim, Turi, trs. from NOR. Egner, Thorbjorn, illus. LC 86-62750. 41p. (gr. 1-3). 1993. 9.95 (*0-9615394-1-0*) Skandisk.
Ibsen, Henrik. Peer Gynt. Canon, R. R., intro. by. (gr. 10 up). 1967. pap. 1.50 (*0-8049-0133-3*, CL-133) Airmont.

NORWAY–HISTORY–FICTION

Emberley, Michael. Welcome Back, Sun. LC 92-9786. (gr. 4 up). 1993. 14.95 (*0-316-23647-0*) Little.

NORWEGIANS IN THE U. S.

Hillbrand, Percie V. The Norwegians in America. rev. ed. LC 67-15683. (Illus.). 80p. (gr. 5 up). PLB 15.95 (*0-8225-0243-7*); pap. 5.95 (*0-8225-1041-3*) Lerner Pubns.

NOTATION, MUSICAL

see Musical Notation

NOVA SCOTIA–FICTION

James, Janet C. Jeremy Gates & the Magic Key. 101p. (gr. 9-12). 1986. 7.95 (*0-920806-32-5*, Pub. by Penumbra Pr CN) U of Toronto Pr.
Wilson, Budge. The Leaving. 208p. (gr. 6 up). 1992. 14.95 (*0-399-21878-5*, Philomel Bks) Putnam Pub Group.

NUCLEAR ENGINEERING

see also Nuclear Reactors

Harwell, Christine C. & Harwell, Mark A. Nuclear Famine. LC 87-70224. (Illus.). 16p. (Orig.). (gr. 10 up). 1990. pap. text ed. 2.75 (*0-89278-185-8*, 45-9785) Carolina Biological.
Lampton, Christopher. Nuclear Accident. LC 91-43564. (Illus.). 48p. (gr. 4-6). 1992. PLB 13.90 (*1-56294-073-2*); pap. 5.95 (*1-56294-782-6*) Millbrook Pr.
Ligou, Jacques P. Elements of Nuclear Engineering. 508p. (gr. 6 up). 1986. text ed. 311.00 (*3-7186-0363-2*, Pub. by Harwood Acad Pubs) Gordon & Breach.

NUCLEAR PHYSICS

see also Nuclear Engineering; Nuclear Reactors; Radioactivity

Newton, David E. Particle Accelerations: From the Cyclotron to the Superconducting Super Collider. LC 88-31375. (Illus.). 128p. (gr. 10-12). 1990. 13.40 (*0-531-10671-3*) Watts.

NUCLEAR POWER

see also Atomic Bomb; Nuclear Engineering; Nuclear Reactors

Asimov, Isaac. How Did We Find Out about Nuclear Power? LC 76-12067. (Illus.). (gr. 4 up). 1976. PLB 12.85 (*0-8027-6266-2*) Walker & Co.
Bernards, Neal. Nuclear Power: Examining Cause & Effect Relationships. LC 90-40412. (Illus.). 32p. (gr. 3-6). 1990. PLB 10.95 (*0-89908-607-1*) Greenhaven.
Boy Scouts of America. Atomic Energy. (Illus.). 80p. (gr. 6-12). 1983. pap. 1.85 (*0-8395-3275-X*, 33275) BSA.
Galperin, Anne L. Nuclear Energy - Nuclear Waste. (Illus.). 112p. (gr. 5 up). 1992. PLB 19.95 (*0-7910-1585-8*) Chelsea Hse.
Hamilton, Sue L. Chernobyl: Nuclear Power Plant Explosion. Hamilton, John C., ed. LC 91-73040. 1991. 11.96 (*1-56239-060-0*) Abdo & Dghtrs.
Kruschke, Earl R. & Jackson, Byron M. Nuclear Energy Policy: A Reference Handbook. 250p. 1989. lib. bdg. 39.50 (*0-87436-238-5*) ABC-CLIO.
Pringle, Laurence. Nuclear Energy: Troubled Past, Uncertain Future. LC 88-28664. (Illus.). 144p. (gr. 7 up). 1989. SBE 14.95 (*0-02-775391-3*, Macmillan Child Bk) Macmillan Child Grp.
Story of Nuclear Power. (ARA., Illus.). (gr. 5-12). 1987. 3.95x (*0-86685-228-X*) Intl Bk Ctr.

NUCLEAR POWER–FICTION

Hesse, Karen. Phoenix Rising. 1994. 15.95 (*0-8050-3108-1*) H Holt & Co.
Krogman, Dane & Holelson, Doug. Skeleton Boy: The Nuclear Hero. (Illus.). 80p. (gr. 6-12). 1982. 8.95 (*0-910519-00-5*) Daneco Pubns.
Moeri, Louise. Downwind. (gr. k-12). 1987. pap. 2.75 (*0-440-92132-5*, LFL) Dell.

NUCLEAR POWER PLANTS

Cheney, Glenn A. Chernobyl: The Ongoing Story of the World's Deadliest Nuclear Disaster. LC 93-17508. (Illus.). 128p. (gr. 6). 1994. text ed. 13.95 RSBE (*0-02-718305-X*, New Discovery) Macmillan Child Grp.
Gosnell, Kelvin. Nuclear Power Stations. LC 91-34406. (Illus.). 32p. (gr. 5-8). 1992. PLB 12.40 (*0-531-17331-3*, Gloucester Pr) Watts.
Hare, Tony. Nuclear Waste Disposal. (Illus.). (gr. 4-8). 1991. PLB 12.40 (*0-531-17291-0*) Watts.
Hawkes, Nigel. Nuclear Power. (Illus.). 48p. (gr. 5 up). 1990. lib. bdg. 18.60 (*0-86592-098-2*); lib. bdg. 13.95s.p. (*0-685-36380-5*) Rourke Corp.

NUCLEAR PROPULSION

see also Nuclear Reactors;

also specific applications; e.g. Atomic Submarines

NUCLEAR REACTORS

Gosnell, Kelvin. Nuclear Power Stations. LC 91-34406. (Illus.). 32p. (gr. 5-8). 1992. PLB 12.40 (*0-531-17331-3*, Gloucester Pr) Watts.

NUCLEAR TEST BAN

see Disarmament

NUCLEAR WARFARE

Brown, Adam. Nuclear Weapons. (Illus.). 48p. (gr. 5 up). 1987. PLB 18.60 (*0-86592-278-0*); 13.95 (*0-685-67572-6*) Rourke Corp.
Cozic, Charles P. & Swisher, Karin L., eds. Nuclear Proliferation: Opposing Viewpoints. LC 92-23065. (Illus.). 240p. (gr. 10 up). 1992. PLB 17.95 (*1-56510-005-0*); pap. text ed. 9.95 (*1-56510-004-2*) Greenhaven.
Martin, Laurence W. Nuclear Warfare. Gibbons, Tony, et al, illus. 48p. (gr. 5 up). 1989. 14.95 (*0-8225-1384-6*) Lerner Pubns.
Sanford, James, Jr. Nuclear War Diary. Alexander, Frank, ed. Sanford, James, Jr. & Bates, Dawn, illus. 186p. (gr. 7-12). 1989. pap. 7.00 (*0-915256-28-2*, 130) Front Row.
Smoke, Richard. Think about Nuclear Arms Control: Understanding the Arms Race. (Illus.). 178p. 1988. PLB 14.85 (*0-8027-6761-3*); pap. 5.95 (*0-8027-6762-1*) Walker & Co.

NUCLEAR WEAPONS AND DISARMAMENT

see Disarmament

NUMBER CONCEPT

Adler, David A. Roman Numerals. Barton, Byron, illus. LC 77-2270. 40p. (gr. 1-4). 1977. PLB 14.89 (*0-690-01302-7*, Crowell Jr Bks) HarpC Child Bks.
Argon, Hilda. Counting Book. (Illus.). 20p. (Orig.). (ps-7). 1981. pap. 3.75 (*0-915347-15-6*) Pueblo Acoma Pr.
Barnes-Murphy, Rowan. Numbers. 16p. (ps). 1992. bds. 3.95 (*0-8249-8531-1*, Ideals Child) Hambleton-Hill.
Bellan Gillen, Patricia. My Signing Book of Numbers. LC 87-28758. (Illus.). 56p. (ps up). 1987. 14.95 (*0-930323-37-8*, Kendall Green Pubns) Gallaudet Univ Pr.
Berenstain, Stan & Berenstain, Janice. Bears on Wheels. LC 72-77840. (Illus.). (ps-1). 1969. 6.95 (*0-394-80967-X*); lib. bdg. 9.99 (*0-394-90967-4*) Random Bks Yng Read.
Bernstein, Bob. Numbers Count. 96p. (gr. 2-7). 1990. 10. 95 (*0-86653-542-X*, GA1151) Good Apple.
Bishop, Roma. Numbers. (Illus.). 14p. (ps-k). 1991. pap. 2.95 (*0-671-74832-7*, Little Simon) S&S Trade.
Boyle, Alison. Playdays Numbers. Johnson, Paul, illus. 32p. (ps-2). 1992. pap. 2.95 (*0-563-20889-9*, BBC-Parkwest) Parkwest Pubns.
Brackenbury, Gill. My Picture Number Book. 1990. 3.99 (*0-517-03206-6*) Random Hse Value.
Brannon, Tom. Flash Cards Get Ready Numbers. (ps). 1986. pap. 3.25 (*0-307-04981-7*, Golden Pr) Western Pub.
Bryant-Mole, K. Numbers. (Illus.). 24p. (ps up). 1992. pap. 3.50 (*0-7460-1042-7*) EDC.
Burningham, John. First Steps: Letters, Numbers, Colors, Opposites. Burningham, John, illus. LC 93-18844. 48p. (ps up). 1994. lib. bdg. 14.95 (*1-56402-205-6*) Candlewick Pr.
Carle, Eric. My Very First Book of Numbers. reissued ed. Carle, Eric, illus. LC 72-83777. 10p. (ps-1). 1985. 4.95 (*0-694-00012-4*, Crowell Jr Bks) HarpC Child Bks.
Challoner, J. The Science Book of Numbers. 1992. 9.95 (*0-15-200623-0*, Gulliver Bks) HarBrace.
Childs, Phyllis, et al. First Book of Numbers. 55p. (ps-k). 1985. wkbk. 4.95 (*0-931749-02-6*) PJC Lrng Mtrls.
Clemson, David & Clemson, Wendy. My First Math Book. LC 93-25425. (Illus.). 48p. (gr. k-4). 1994. write for info. (*1-56458-457-7*) Dorling Kindersley.
Colors, Shapes, Words, & Numbers. 24p. 1989. 5.99 (*0-517-68231-1*) Random Hse Value.
Cook, Marcy. Numbers & Words: A Problem Per Day. (gr. 4-7). 1987. pap. 8.50 (*0-201-48002-6*) Addison-Wesley.
Desputeaux, Helene. Lollypop's Numbers. (Illus.). 8p. (ps). 1993. bath bk. 4.95 (*2-921198-39-8*, Pub. by Les Edits Herit CN) Adams Inc MA.
Disney, Walt, Productions Staff. Adventures with Letters & Numbers. LC 85-43076. 80p. (Orig.). 1985. pap. 5.95 (*0-553-05533-X*) Bantam.
Dreaming Numbers. 1990. text ed. 3.95 cased (*0-7214-5272-8*) Ladybird Bks.
Facklam, Margery & Thomas, Margaret. The Kids' World Almanac of Amazing Facts about Numbers, Math, & Money. (Illus.). 256p. (Orig.). 1992. 14.95 (*0-88687-635-4*); pap. 7.95 (*0-88687-634-6*) Wrld Almnc.
Feelings, Muriel. Moja Means One: A Swahili Counting Book. Feelings, Tom, illus. LC 76-134856. (ps-3). 1987. 13.95 (*0-8037-5776-X*); PLB 13.89 (*0-8037-5777-8*) Dial Bks Young.
Fun with Numbers. 1992. pap. 1.95 (*0-590-45058-1*) Scholastic Inc.
Garcia, Yolanda. Celebremos con Numeros. (SPA., Illus.). 60p. (gr. k-2). 1986. pap. text ed. 7.95 (*0-935303-01-4*) Victory Pub.
Gregorich, Barbara. Contando del 1 al 10: Counting 1 to 10. Hoffman, Joan, ed. Shepherd-Bartram, tr. from ENG. Pape, Richard, illus. (SPA.). 32p. (Orig.). 1987. wkbk. 1.99 (*0-938256-79-3*) Sch Zone Pub Co.
Griffiths, Rose. Numbers. Millard, Peter, photos by. LC 94-7983. (Illus.). 32p. (gr. 1 up). 1994. PLB 17.27 (*0-8368-1112-7*) Gareth Stevens Inc.
Healey, Tim. My Wonderful Number Box. (ps-3). 1994. 16.00 (*0-89577-600-6*, Readers Digest Kids) RD Assn.
Hill, Eric. S. S. Happiness Crew Book of Numbers. (Illus.). 11p. (ps). (*0-915696-65-7*) Determined Prods.
Hyman, Jane. Gumby Book of Numbers. LC 86-6193. (Illus.). 32p. (ps-3). 1986. 5.95 (*0-385-23455-4*); PLB 5.95 (*0-385-23847-9*) Doubleday.
I Know Numbers. (Illus.). 1991. 4.99 (*0-517-05882-0*) Random Hse Value.
Katz, Bobbi. Ten Little Care Bears Counting Book. Barto, Bobbi, illus. LC 83-60084. 14p. (ps-k). 1983. 4.95 (*0-394-86088-8*) Random Bks Yng Read.
Krampe, Leesa. My Number Book. Curlee, Jane, illus. 126p. (ps-1). 1986. pap. text ed. 3.95 (*0-932957-99-4*) Natl School.
—My Number Word Book. Ehrlich, Doris, ed. O'Rourke, Dawn, illus. 100p. (Orig.). (ps-1). 1987. pap. text ed. 3.95 (*0-932957-94-3*) Natl School.
Lambert, Jonathan, illus. Numbers. 18p. (ps-1). 1992. bds. 1.95 (*0-681-41563-0*) Longmeadow Pr.
Learning about Numbers. 1986. pap. 9.95 (*0-394-88315-2*) Random Bks Yng Read.
LeGros, Lucy C. Instant Centers - Numbers 10-20. LeGros, Ivor L., illus. 33p. (gr. k-2). 1988. tchr's ed. 5.95 (*0-937306-07-X*) Creat Res NC.
—Instant Centers: Numbers. (Illus.). 48p. (Orig.). (gr. k-2). 1984. pap. 5.95 (*0-937306-05-3*) Creat Res NC.
Le Sieg, Theodore. Ten Apples up on Top. LC 61-7068. (Illus.). 72p. (gr. 1-2). 1961. 6.95 (*0-394-80019-2*); lib. bdg. 7.99 (*0-394-90019-7*) Beginner.
Lottridge, Celia B. One Watermelon Seed. Patkau, Karen, illus. 24p. (ps up). 1990. pap. 6.95 (*0-19-540735-0*) OUP.
Moncure, Jane B. My Eight Book. Hohag, Linda, illus. LC 85-30962. 32p. (ps-2). 1986. PLB 14.95 (*0-89565-319-2*) Childs World.
—My Five Book. Hohag, Linda, illus. LC 85-9699. 32p. (ps-2). 1985. PLB 14.95 (*0-89565-316-8*) Childs World.
—My Four Book. Hohag, Linda, illus. LC 85-9700. 32p. (ps-2). 1985. PLB 14.95 (*0-89565-315-X*) Childs World.
—My Nine Book. Hohag, Linda, illus. LC 85-30959. 32p. (ps-2). 1986. PLB 14.95 (*0-89565-320-6*) Childs World.
—My One Book. Peltier, Pam, illus. LC 85-5897. 32p. (ps-2). 1985. PLB 14.95 (*0-89565-312-5*) Childs World.
—My Seven Book. Hohag, Linda, illus. LC 86-2594. 32p. (ps-2). 1986. PLB 14.95 (*0-89565-318-4*) Childs World.
—My Six Book. Hohag, Linda, illus. LC 85-30961. 32p. (ps-2). 1986. PLB 14.95 (*0-89565-317-6*) Childs World.
—My Ten Book. Hohag, Linda, illus. LC 86-2293. 32p. (ps-2). 1986. PLB 14.95 (*0-89565-321-4*) Childs World.
—My Three Book. Hohag, Linda, illus. LC 85-5898. 32p. (ps-2). 1985. PLB 14.95 (*0-89565-314-1*) Childs World.
—My Two Book. Peltier, Pam, illus. LC 85-7885. 32p. (ps-2). 1985. PLB 14.95 (*0-89565-313-3*) Childs World.
Morris, Neil. Magic Monkey: A Fun Book of Numbers. Stevenson, Peter, illus. 32p. (ps-2). 1991. PLB 13.50 (*0-87614-677-9*) Carolrhoda Bks.
Moss, David. Numbers. 10p. (ps). 1989. 4.99 (*0-517-69423-9*) Random Hse Value.
My Very First Number Book. LC 93-7623. 1993. write for info. (*1-56458-376-7*) Dorling Kindersley.
Nedobeck, Don. Nedobeck's Numbers Book. 26p. (gr. 1-8). 1988. 9.95 (*0-944314-01-5*) New Wrinkle.
Nelson, Nigel. Writing & Numbers. De Saulles, Tony, illus. LC 93-40963. 32p. (gr. k-2). 1994. 12.95 (*1-56847-158-0*) Thomson Lrning.
Numbers. (Illus.). 10p. (ps-1). 1984. 4.95 (*0-8431-0992-0*) Price Stern.
Numbers. (Illus.). (ps-k). 3.50 (*0-7214-8101-9*) Ladybird Bks.
Numbers One to Twenty Dot-to-Dot. (Illus.). 24p. (ps-k). 1986. 3.98 (*0-86734-063-0*, FS-3055) Schaffer Pubns.
Obrien, Thomas C. Puzzle Tables: Number Problems with Computational Skills. (gr. 4-7). 1980. pap. 8.50 (*0-201-48011-5*) Addison-Wesley.
O'Halloran, Tim. Know Your Numbers. O'Halloran, Tim, illus. 38p. (ps-1). 1983. 10.95 (*0-88625-045-5*) Durkin Hayes Pub.
Oliver, Stephen, photos by. My First Look at Numbers. LC 89-63088. (Illus.). 24p. (ps-k). 1990. 7.00 (*0-679-80533-8*) Random Bks Yng Read.
Oxenbury, Helen. Helen Oxebury's Numbers of Things. Oxenbury, Helen, illus. LC 83-5263. 32p. (ps-3). 1983. pap. 9.95 (*0-385-29288-0*); pap. 9.95 (*0-385-29289-9*) Delacorte.
Pagnucci, Susan. Number Chomp. (Illus.). 48p. (Orig.). (gr. 1-2). 1984. Incl. reproducible math sheets with numbers 0-9 addition & subtraction. 4.50 (*0-929326-04-0*) Bur Oak Pr Inc.
Peppe, Rodney. Circus Numbers. Peppe, Rodney, illus. LC 75-86381. (ps-3). 1969. 5.95 (*0-440-01288-0*); pap. 3.69 (*0-440-01289-9*) Delacorte.
Potter, Beatrix. Peter Rabbit's 1 2 3 Frieze. 1988. 5.00 (*0-7232-5630-6*) Warne.
Ross, Anna. Little Bert's Book of Numbers. Gorbaty, Norman, illus. LC 91-4921. 24p. (ps). 1992. 3.99 (*0-679-82239-9*) Random Bks Yng Read.
Samton, Sheila W. The World from My Window. Samton, Sheila W., illus. LC 90-85732. 28p. (ps-2). 1991. Repr. 14.95 (*1-878093-15-0*) Boyds Mills Pr.
Schaffer, Frank, Publications Staff. Beginning Activities with Numbers. (Illus.). 24p. (ps-k). 1980. 3.98 (*0-86734-014-2*, FS-3027) Schaffer Pubns.
—Getting Ready for Math. (Illus.). 24p. (ps-k). 1980. 3.98 (*0-86734-020-7*, FS-3033) Schaffer Pubns.
—Numbers. (Illus.). 24p. (ps-2). 1978. wkbk. 3.98 (*0-86734-002-9*, FS-3003) Schaffer Pubns.
Schwartz, David M. How Much Is a Million? Kellogg, Steven, illus. LC 84-5736. 40p. (gr. k-5). 1985. PLB 14.88 (*0-688-04050-0*); 15.00 (*0-688-04049-7*) Lothrop.
Shearer, Marilyn J. The Lonely Ten: A Book of Counting for Preschool & Above. Bostic, Alex, illus. 16p. (Orig.). (ps-6). 1989. pap. 19.95 (*0-685-30094-3*) L Ashley & Joshua.
—The Lonely Ten: A Book of Simple Addition for Preschool & Above. Bostic, Alex, illus. 16p. (Orig.). (ps-6). 1989. 19.95 (*0-685-30093-5*) L Ashley & Joshua.
Sitomer, Mindel & Sitomer, Harry. How Did Numbers Begin? LC 75-11756. (Illus.). 40p. (gr. k-3). 1976. PLB 12.89 (*0-690-00794-9*, Crowell Jr Bks) HarpC Child Bks.
Smalley, Guy, illus. My Very Own Book of Numbers. 28p. (ps-2). 1989. 9.95 (*0-929793-00-5*) Camex Bks Inc.
Smart Elephant Peter. Wondering of Little Zero. 1991. write for info. (*1-879789-76-0*) AdRem.
Smith, Doris-Marie. Benjie's Fun Time with Numbers. (Illus.). 16p. (ps-k). pap. 5.95 (*0-8059-3341-7*) Dorrance.
Smoothey, Marion. Numbers. Evans, Ted, illus. 64p. (gr. 4-8). 1992. text ed. 16.95 (*1-85435-457-4*) Marshall Cavendish.
Taulbee, Annette. Numbers. (Illus.). 24p. (ps-k). 1986. 3.98 (*0-86734-061-4*, FS-3053) Schaffer Pubns.
Tucker, Sian. Numbers. (Illus.). 24p. (ps-k). 1992. pap. 2.95 (*0-671-76908-1*, Little Simon) S&S Trade.
Tyler, J. & Round, G. Counting up to Ten. (Illus.). 24p. (ps up). 1987. pap. 3.50 (*0-7460-0217-3*) EDC.
Verkouteren, J. Adrian. A Study of Numbers. 355p. (gr. 5-8). 1981. pap. text ed. 12.95 (*0-685-32862-7*) Longman.
Walsh, Abigail. Exploring the Numbers One to Ten. Dowling, Marilyn, illus. 24p. (ps-2). Date not set. PLB 11.95 (*1-56065-108-3*) Capstone Pr.
Warren, Jean. One-Two-Three Books: Simple Books to Make for Working with Young Children. Bittinger, Gayle, ed. Walker, Cora, illus. LC 89-50120. 80p. (Orig.). (ps-1). 1989. pap. text ed. 7.95 (*0-911019-23-5*) Warren Pub Hse.
Welsh, Patricia A. It's My Number Book. 32p. (gr. k-1). 1979. wkbk. 3.95 (*1-884620-02-7*) PAW Prods.
Wilkes & Zeff. First Book of Numbers. (gr. k-3). 1982. (Usborne-Hayes); pap. 8.95 (*0-7460-0214-9*) EDC.
Zaslavsky, Claudia. Count on Your Fingers African Style. Pinkney, Jerry, illus. LC 77-26586. 32p. (gr. k-3). 1980. (Crowell Jr Bks); (Crowell Jr Bks) HarpC Child Bks.

NUMBERS THEORY

Fisher, Leonard E. Number Art: Thirteen 1 2 3s from Around the World. Fisher, Leonard E., illus. LC 82-5050. 64p. (gr. 3-7). 1984. SBE 16.95 (*0-02-735240-4*, Four Winds) Macmillan Child Grp.
Hershey, Robert L. How to Think with Numbers. 142p. (gr. 7 up). 1987. pap. 7.95 (*0-939765-14-4*, GK108) Janson Pubns.
Hoffman, Joan. Numbers One to Twelve. rev. ed. Cook, Chris, illus. 32p. (ps-1). 1987. wkbk. 1.99 (*0-938256-26-2*) Sch Zone Pub Co.
Richards, Elspeth & Fernyhough, Frances. Fun with Numbers. Kerr, Angela, illus. 24p. (gr. k-3). 1987. pap. 2.95 (*0-385-23844-4*, Zephyr-BFYR) Doubleday.

NUMISMATICS

see also Coins

Counting One, Two, Three. (Illus.). (ps). 1985. bds. 2.98 (*0-517-47338-0*) Random Hse Value.
Davis, Nancy M., et al. Numbers. Davis, Nancy M., illus. 26p. (Orig.). (ps-2). 1986. pap. 4.95 (*0-937103-14-4*) DaNa Pubns.
Hoban, Tana. Twenty-Six Letters & Ninety-Nine Cents. LC 86-11993. (Illus.). 32p. (ps-3). 1987. 15.00 (*0-688-06361-6*); PLB 14.93 (*0-688-06362-4*) Greenwillow.
Hobson, Burton H. Coin Collecting As a Hobby. rev. ed. Obojski, Robert, ed. LC 67-27759. (Illus.). 192p. (gr. 4-10). 1986. 9.95 (*0-8069-4748-9*) Sterling.
Lewis, Brenda R. Coins & Currency. LC 92-46359. (Illus.). 80p. (gr. 5 up). 1993. 13.00 (*0-679-82662-9*); PLB 13.99 (*0-679-92662-3*) Random Bks Yng Read.

NUNEZ CABEZA DE VACA, ALVAR, 16TH CENTURY

Brandt, Keith. Cabeza de Vaca: New World Explorer. Martinez, Sergio, illus. LC 92-36960. 48p. (gr. 4-6). 1993. lib. bdg. 10.79 (*0-8167-2829-1*); 3.50 (*0-8167-2830-5*) Troll Assocs.
Wade, Mary D. Cabeza De Vaca: Conquistador Who Cared. (Illus.). 64p. (gr. 3-5). 1994. 10.95 (*1-882539-14-1*); pap. 4.95 (*1-882539-15-X*); cancelled 5.00 (*1-882539-16-8*) Colophon Hse.

NUNS

see Monasticism and Religious Orders for Women

NURSERY RHYMES

Abby, Tom & Kole, Ted, eds. Katoufs in Nursery Rhymes Chapbook: Mother Goose. Delamer, Gloria T., intro. by. (Illus.). 48p. (Orig.). (gr. 1-4). Date not set. pap. 3.95 (*0-9641381-0-7*) Kreative Character.
—Katoufs in Nursery Rhymes, Ltd, Ed. Mother Goose. Princess Marie, illus. 24p. Date not set. 50.00 (*0-9641381-1-5*) Kreative Character.
Adams, Pam, illus. This Is the House That Jack Built. LC 90-46922. 16p. (Orig.). (ps-2). 1977. pap. 5.95 (*0-85953-075-2*, Pub. by Child's Play England) Childs Play.
—This Old Man. LC 90-34327. 16p. (Orig.). (ps-2). 1974. (Pub. by Child's Play England); pap. 5.95 (*0-85953-026-4*, Pub. by Child's Play England) Childs Play.
Agard, John & Nichols, Grace. No Hickory No Dickory No Dock: A Collection of Nursery Rhymes. Jabar, Cynthia, illus. LC 93-24289. 1994. write for info. (*1-56402-156-4*) Candlewick Pr.
Ahlberg, Janet & Ahlberg, Allan. Each Peach Pear Plum. (Illus.). 32p. (ps-k). 1992. miniature ed. 4.95 (*0-670-84018-1*) Viking Child Bks.
—Peek-A-Boo! LC 81-1925. (Illus.). (ps-1). 1981. pap. 11.95 (*0-670-54598-8*) Viking Child Bks.
Alchemy II, Inc. Staff, illus. The Little Red Hen. 26p. (ps). 1988. incl. cassette 9.95 (*1-55578-905-6*) Worlds Wonder.
Ali-El, Yusuf. Once upon a Ryme Tyme for Growing Minds. Pride, Alexis, et al, illus. LC 83-90101. 90p. (gr. k-5). 1983. pap. 9.95 (*0-912475-09-9*) Natl Res Unltd.

Amoss, Berthe. Mother Goose Rhymes. Amoss, Berthe, illus. 10p. (ps-7). 1989. pap. 2.95 (*0-922589-02-X*) More Than Card.
Anglund, Joan W. In a Pumpkin Shell. Anglund, Joan W., illus. LC 60-10243. 32p. (ps-2). 1977. pap. 3.95 (*0-15-644425-9*, Voyager Bks) HarBrace.
—In a Pumpkin Shell: A Mother Goose ABC. Anglund, Joan W., illus. LC 60-10243. (ps-2). 1960. 10.95 (*0-15-238269-0*, HB Juv Bks) HarBrace.
—A Mother Goose Book. Van Doren, Liz, ed. Anglund, Joan W., illus. 32p. (ps up). 1991. 7.95 (*0-15-200529-3*, Gulliver Bks) HarBrace.
Animal Rhymes. (Illus.). (ps). pap. 1.25 (*0-7214-9549-4*) Ladybird Bks.
Aragon, Hilda, illus. My First Nursery Rhyme Book. 28p. (Orig.). (ps-7). 1981. pap. 3.75 (*0-915347-07-5*) Pueblo Acoma Pr.
Arnold, Tedd, illus. Actions. 16p. (ps). 1992. pap. 3.95 (*0-671-77824-2*, Little Simon) S&S Trade.
—Colors. 16p. (ps). 1992. pap. 3.95 (*0-671-77825-0*, Little Simon) S&S Trade.
—Opposites. 16p. (ps). 1992. pap. 3.95 (*0-671-77823-4*, Little Simon) S&S Trade.
—Sounds. 16p. (ps). 1992. pap. 3.95 (*0-671-77826-9*, Little Simon) S&S Trade.
Arnsteen, Katy K. Mother Goose Rhymes: Hide 'n' Seek. 1990. 3.99 (*0-517-02630-9*) Random Hse Value.
Atkinson, Allen, illus. The Cat & the Fiddle & Other Favorites. 64p. (Orig.). (gr. k). 1985. pap. 2.50 (*0-553-15321-8*) Bantam.
—Humpty Dumpty & Other Favorites. 64p. (Orig.). (gr. k). 1985. pap. 2.50 (*0-553-15340-4*) Bantam.
—Jack & Jill & Other Favorites. 64p. (Orig.). 1986. pap. 2.50 (*0-553-15354-4*) Bantam.
—Little Bo-Peep & Other Favorites. 64p. (Orig.). 1986. pap. 2.50 (*0-553-15353-6*) Bantam.
—Little Boy Blue & Other Favorites. 64p. (Orig.). (gr. k). 1985. pap. 2.50 (*0-553-15320-X*) Bantam.
—Mary Had a Little Lamb & Other Favorites. (Orig.). (gr. k). 1985. pap. 2.50 (*0-553-15319-6*) Bantam.
—Simple Simon & Other Favorites (Mother Goose) 64p. (Orig.). 1986. pap. 2.50 (*0-553-15322-6*) Bantam.
Attinella, Lauren. Muppet Babies Big Book of Nursery Rhymes & Fairy Tales. 1993. 9.99 (*0-307-16752-6*) Western Pub.
Aylesworth, Jim. The Cat & the Fiddle & More. Hull, Richard, illus. LC 91-30956. 32p. (ps-1). 1992. SBE 13.95 (*0-689-31715-8*, Atheneum Child Bk) Macmillan Child Grp.
—The Completed Hickory Dickory Dock. Christelow, Eileen, illus. LC 94-1226. (gr. k-3). 1994. pap. 4.95 (*0-689-71862-4*, Aladdin) Macmillan Child Grp.
Baker, Darrell. Disney Babies Nursery Rhymes. (ps). 1988. 1.95 (*0-307-01137-2*, Golden Pr) Western Pub.
Baker, Keith. Big Fat Hen. LC 93-19160. 1994. 13.95 (*0-15-292869-3*) HarBrace.
Baring-Gould, S. A Book of Nursery Songs & Rhymes. (ps-4). 1972. 59.95 (*0-87968-768-1*) Gordon Pr.
Baron, Michelle. Hey Diddle Diddle. Alchemy II, Inc. Staff, illus. 26p. (ps). 1988. incl. cassette 9.95 (*1-55578-919-6*) Worlds Wonder.
—Hickory Dickory Dock. Alchemy II, Inc. Staff, illus. 26p. (ps). 1988. incl. cassette 9.95 (*1-55578-923-4*) Worlds Wonder.
—Little Boy Blue. Alchemy II, Inc. Staff, illus. 26p. (ps). 1988. incl. cassette 9.95 (*1-55578-918-8*) Worlds Wonder.
Barr, Marilynn G. Mother Goose Caboose. 256p. (ps-2). 1991. 16.95 (*0-86653-618-3*, GA1337) Good Apple.
Baum, L. Frank. Mother Goose in Prose. (gr. k up). 1986. 4.98 (*0-685-16878-6*, 519046) Random Hse Value.
Beall, Pamela C. & Nipp, Susan H. Wee Sing Nursery Rhymes & Lullabies Activity Book. Klein, Nancy, illus. 48p. (ps-2). 1992. pap. 2.95 (*0-8431-1900-4*) Price Stern.
—Wee Sing Nursery Rhymes & Lullabies. (Illus.). 64p. (Orig.). (ps-2). 1985. pap. 2.95 (*0-8431-3811-4*); pap. 9.95 bk. & cass. (*0-8431-3794-0*) Price Stern.
—Wee Sing Pop-up Nursery Rhymes. Bracken, Carolyn, illus. 14p. (ps-2). 1993. 13.95 (*0-8431-3599-9*) Price Stern.
Beck, Ian. Five Little Ducks. LC 92-27193. (Illus.). 32p. (ps-2). 1993. 14.95 (*0-8050-2525-1*, Bks Young Read) H Holt & Co.
Becker, Lois & Stratton, Mark. Little Miss Muffet. Alchemy II, Inc. Staff, illus. 26p. (ps). 1988. incl. cassette 9.95 (*1-55578-922-6*) Worlds Wonder.
Bedtime Rhymes. (Illus.). (ps). pap. 1.25 (*0-7214-9551-6*) Ladybird Bks.
Beers, V. Gilbert. My Sunny Day, & Day Nursery Rhyme Book. O'Connor, Tim, illus. LC 93-17261. 1993. 12.99 (*0-8407-9253-0*) Nelson.
Beisner, Monika. Catch That Cat! A Picture Book of Rhymes & Puzzles. (Illus.). 32p. 1990. 15.00 (*0-374-31226-5*) FS&G.
Berry, Holly, illus. Old MacDonald Had a Farm. 32p. (gr. k-3). 1994. 14.95 (*1-55858-281-9*); lib. bdg. 14.88 (*1-55858-282-7*) North-South Bks NYC.
Beylon, Cathy. The Mulberry Bush. (ps). 1992. 4.95 (*1-56288-282-1*) Checkerboard.
Beylon, Cathy, illus. Wynken, Blynken, & Nod. 24p. (ps). 1992. bds. write for info. (*0-307-06141-8*, 6141, Golden Pr) Western Pub.
Biro, Val. Rub-a-Dub-Dub: Val Biro's Seventy-Seven Favorite Nursery Rhymes. Biro, Val, illus. LC 90-14402. 62p. (ps). 1991. PLB 16.95 (*0-87226-449-1*, Bedrick Blackie) P Bedrick Bks.
The Blue Match the Rhyme Book. (gr. 2-6). 1990. 4.95 (*1-879332-01-9*) XYZ Group.
Boardman, Bob. Red Hot Peppers. Boardman, Diane, illus. 64p. (Orig.). (gr. 3 up). 1993. pap. 12.95 incl. speed rope (*0-912365-78-1*) Sasquatch Bks.
—Red Hot Peppers: The Skookum Book of Jump Rope Games, Rhymes, & Fancy Footwork. Boardman, Diane, illus. 64p. (Orig.). (gr. 3 up). 1993. pap. 8.95 (*0-912365-74-9*) Sasquatch Bks.
Bodger, Lorraine. Great American Cakes. 1990. 7.99 (*0-517-02740-2*) Random Hse Value.
Bolam, Emily, illus. House That Jack Built. LC 91-40927. 32p. (gr. k up). 1993. 14.00 (*0-525-44972-8*, DCB) Dutton Child Bks.
Bornstein, Harry & Saulnier, Karen L. Mother Goose: Nursery Rhymes. Peters, Patricia & Tom, Linda C., illus. 48p. (gr. k-3). 1992. PLB 15.95 (*1-56674-034-7*) Forest Hse.
—Nursery Rhymes from Mother Goose: Told in Signed English. Peters, Patricia & Tom, Linda, illus. 48p. (ps-2). 1992. 14.95 (*0-930323-99-8*, Pub. by K Green Pubns) Gallaudet Univ Pr.
Brannon, Tom. Muppet Babies Giant Book of Rhymes. (ps-3). 1994. pap. 4.95 (*0-307-10362-5*, Golden Pr) Western Pub.
Brinckloe, Julie. Stitch in Time for the Brothers Rhyme. (ps-3). 1993. pap. 4.95 (*0-8114-8400-9*) Raintree Steck-V.
Brooke, L. Leslie. Ring O'Roses. Brooke, L. Leslie, illus. 96p. (ps-3). 1992. 16.95 (*0-395-61304-3*, Clarion Bks) HM.
Brown, Marc T., ed. & illus. Hand Rhymes. LC 84-25918. 32p. (ps-1). 1985. 13.95 (*0-525-44201-4*, DCB) Dutton Child Bks.
Brown, Marc T., compiled by. & illus. Play Rhymes. LC 87-13537. 32p. (ps-1). 1987. 12.95 (*0-525-44336-3*, DCB) Dutton Child Bks.
Brown, Margeret W. Little Donkey Close Your Eyes. Wolff, Ashley, illus. LC 94-16523. (gr. 2-5). 1995. 15.00 (*0-06-024482-8*); PLB 14.89 (*0-06-024483-6*) HarpC.
Brown, Richard, illus. Old MacDonald Had a Farm. (ps-k). 1993. 9.99 (*0-670-85157-4*) Viking Child Bks.
Burke, Dianne O. Itsy-Bitsy Spider. (Illus.). 12p. (ps). 1994. bds. 3.95 (*1-56565-092-1*) Lowell Hse Juvenile.
—Old King Cole. (Illus.). 12p. (ps). 1994. bds. 3.95 (*1-56565-094-8*) Lowell Hse Juvenile.
—There Was an Old Woman. (Illus.). 12p. (ps). 1994. bds. 3.95 (*1-56565-095-6*) Lowell Hse Juvenile.
—Wee Willie Winkle. (Illus.). 12p. (ps) 1994. bds. 3.95 (*1-56565-096-4*) Lowell Hse Juvenile.
Burke, Dianne O., illus. Hush-a-Bye, Baby. 12p. (ps). 1994. bds. 3.95 (*1-56565-093-X*) Lowell Hse Juvenile.
—Rhyme-along Board Books: Hey, Diddle, Diddle. 12p. (ps). 1994. 3.95 (*1-56565-097-2*) Lowell Hse.
Butterworth, Nick. Nick Butterworth's Book of Nursery Rhymes. (ps-3). 1991. 14.95 (*0-670-83551-X*) Viking Child Bks.
Carter, David A. Over in the Meadow. (Illus.). 32p. 1992. 13.95 (*0-590-44498-0*, Scholastic Hardcover) Scholastic Inc.
Cauley, Lorinda B. The Three Little Kittens. (Illus.). 32p. (ps-1). 1982. 3.95 (*0-448-10216-1*, G&D); (G&D) Putnam Pub Group.
Chorao, Kay. The Baby's Bedtime Book. Chorao, Kay, illus. LC 84-6067. 64p. (ps). 1989. 13.95 (*0-525-44149-2*, DCB); bk & cassette 18.95 (*0-525-44506-4*) Dutton Child Bks.
—The Baby's Lap Book. (Illus.). (ps-k). 1977. 12.95 (*0-525-26100-1*, DCB) Dutton Child Bks.
—Baby's Lap Book. Rashad, Phylicia, read by. LC 89-23273. (Illus.). 64p. (ps). 1991. 13.95 (*0-525-44604-4*, DCB); incl. audiocassette 18.95 (*0-525-44628-1*) Dutton Child Bks.
Chorao, Kay, illus. Mother Goose Magic. LC 92-37160. 64p. (ps-k). 1994. 15.99 (*0-525-45064-5*, DCB) Dutton Child Bks.
Chusid, Nancy. Favorite Nursery Songs. Chusid, Nancy, illus. 32p. (Orig.). (gr. 2-6). 1990. pap. 6.95 incl. cassette (*1-878624-05-9*) McClanahan Bk.
The Classic Mother Goose. LC 88-70839. (Illus.). 56p. (gr. k up). 1988. 9.98 (*0-89471-654-9*) Courage Bks.
Cocca-Leffler, Maryann, illus. Hey Diddle Diddle: My First Book of Nursery Rhymes. 18p. (ps). 1991. 3.95 (*0-448-40107-X*, G&D) Putnam Pub Group.
Cole, Joanna & Calmenson, Stephanie, eds. The Read-Aloud Treasury: Favorite Nursery Rhymes, Poems, Stories & More for the Very Young. Schweninger, Ann, illus. 256p. 1988. pap. 18.95 (*0-385-18560-X*) Doubleday.
Conover, Chris. Mother Goose & the Sly Fox. (Illus.). (ps-3). 1989. 15.00 (*0-374-35072-8*) FS&G.
Cope, Wendy. Twiddling Your Thumbs: Hand Rhymes by Wendy Cope. 32p. (ps-3). 1992. pap. 6.95 (*0-571-16537-0*) Faber & Faber.
Counting Rhymes. (ps). 1982. 2.95 (*0-86112-085-X*) Borden.
Courson, Diana. Let's Learn about Fairy Tales & Nursery Rhymes. 64p. (ps-2). 1988. wkbk. 7.95 (*0-86653-437-7*, GA1040) Good Apple.
Craig, Helen. I See the Moon, & the Moon Sees Me. Craig, Helen, illus. LC 92-18996. 48p. (ps-2). 1993. 16.00 (*0-06-021453-8*); PLB 15.89 (*0-06-021454-6*) HarpC Child Bks.
Crane, Walter, illus. Favorite Poems of Childhood. LC 92-42770. 1993. 14.00 (*0-671-86614-1*, Green Tiger) S&S Trade.
Cutts, David, retold by. House That Jack Built. Silverstein, Don, illus. LC 78-18951. 32p. (gr. k-2). 1979. PLB 9.79 (*0-89375-127-8*); pap. 1.95 (*0-89375-105-7*) Troll Assocs.
Dabcovich, Lydia. Keys to My Kingdom: A Poem in Three Languages. LC 90-4040. (Illus.). (ps-3). 1992. 14.00 (*0-688-09774-X*); PLB 13.93 (*0-688-09775-8*) Lothrop.
Daglish, Alice & Rhys, Ernest. Rock-a-Bye Rhymes: Miniature Nursery Rhyme Books, 4 bks. Folkard, Charles, illus. (ps-3). 1993. Repr. of 1932 ed. Set, miniature bks. in rocking-horse slipcase. 16.95 (*0-8118-0537-9*) Chronicle Bks.
De Angeli, Marguerite. Book of Nursery & Mother Goose Rhymes. De Angeli, Marguerite, illus. (gr. k-5). 1954. Doubleday.
—Marguerite De Angeli's Book of Nursery & Mother Goose Rhymes. De Angeli, Marguerite, illus. LC 54-9838. (gr. k-5). 1979. pap. 18.95 (*0-685-01499-1*, Zephyr BFYR); pap. 7.95 (*0-385-15291-4*) Doubleday.
Decker, Marjorie A. Christian Mother Goose Big Book. Sparr, Theanna, et al, illus. LC 92-60502. 304p. (ps-4). 1992. 14.99 (*0-529-07315-3*) World Bible.
—Rock-a-Bye Prayers (Christian Mother Goose) 1990. 7.99 (*0-529-06843-5*) World Bible.
Delacre, Lulu. Arroz Con Leche. Delacre, Lulu, illus. 1992. pap. 3.95 (*0-590-41886-6*, Blue Ribbon Bks); cassette 4.95 (*0-590-60035-4*, Blue Ribbon Bks) Scholastic Inc.
De La Mare, Walter. Rhymes & Verses: Collected Poems for Young People. Blaisdell, Elinore, illus. LC 88-45278. 370p. (gr. 2-4). 1988. 15.95 (*0-8050-0847-0*, Bks Young Read); pap. 7.95 (*0-8050-0848-9*) H Holt & Co.
Delcher, Eden, compiled by. Mother Goose Animal Rhymes. 1993. 2.98 (*1-55521-834-2*) Bk Sales Inc.
—Mother Goose Favorite Rhymes. (gr. k up). 1993. 2.98 (*1-55521-835-0*) Bk Sales Inc.
Demi. Dragon Kites & Dragonflies: A Collection of Chinese Nursery Rhymes. LC 86-7637. (Illus.). 32p. (ps-3). 1986. 14.95 (*0-15-224199-X*, HB Juv Bks) HarBrace.
De Paola, Tomie, selected by. & illus. Tomie de Paola's Favorite Nursery Tales. 128p. (gr. 1 up). 1986. 18.95 (*0-399-21319-8*, Putnam) Putnam Pub Group.
Domanska, Janina. A Was an Angler. LC 88-35589. (Illus.). 32p. (ps up). 1991. 13.95 (*0-688-06990-8*); PLB 13.88 (*0-688-06991-6*) Greenwillow.
Doty, Roy. Fleet of Nursery Rhymes. (Illus.). (ps). 1991. pap. 4.95 punch-outs (*0-671-72843-1*, S&S BFYR) S&S Trade.
Dowell, Ruth I. Move Over, Mother Goose Series. Doolittle, Jerry, et al, illus. (Orig.). (ps-6). 1991. pap. write for info. (*0-945842-24-4*) Pollyanna Prodns.
Dr. Seuss. Mister Brown Can Moo, Can You. Dr. Seuss, illus. (ps-1). 1970. 6.95 (*0-394-80622-0*); lib. bdg. 7.99 (*0-394-90622-5*) Random Bks Yng Read.
Duffield, Francesca, illus. Lullabies. LC 92-75609. (ps-k). 1993. 5.95 (*1-85697-916-4*, Kingfisher LKC) LKC.
—Nursery Rhymes. LC 92-75584. 10p. (ps-k). 1993. 5.95 (*1-85697-917-2*, Kingfisher LKC) LKC.
Duncan, Lois. Birthday Moon. Davis, Susan, illus. 32p. (ps-3). 1989. 13.95 (*0-670-82238-8*) Viking Child Bks.
Dyer, Jane, selected by. & illus. Babyland: A Book for Babies. LC 93-4244. 1995. 17.95 (*0-316-19766-1*) Little.
Emerson, Sally. Nursery Rhyme Songbook: With Easy Music to Play for Piano & Guitar. Maclean, Colin & Maclean, Moira, illus. LC 92-53106. 72p. (ps-k). 1992. 16.95 (*1-85697-823-0*, Kingfisher LKC) LKC.
Emerson, Sally, selected by. ABCs & Other Learning Rhymes. Maclean, Moira & Maclean, Colin, illus. LC 92-32576. 1993. pap. 4.95 (*1-85697-899-0*, Kingfisher LKC) LKC.
Emerson, Sally, compiled by. Nursery Rhymes. Maclean, Moira & Maclean, Colin, illus. LC 92-26446. 32p. (ps-k). 1993. pap. 4.95 (*1-85697-905-9*, Kingfisher LKC) LKC.
Emerson, Sally & Corbett, Pie, eds. Action Rhymes. Maclean, Moira & Maclean, Colin, illus. LC 92-26445. 32p. (ps-k). 1993. pap. 4.95 (*1-85697-900-8*, Kingfisher LKC) LKC.
Falconer, Elizabeth. The House That Jack Built. Falconer, Elizabeth, illus. LC 90-4467. 32p. 1990. 13.95 (*0-8249-8459-5*, Ideals Child) Hambleton-Hill.
Father Gander, pseud. Father Gander Nursery Rhymes. Blattel, Carolyn & Blair, Janice, illus. LC 85-72785. 47p. (ps up). 1985. 15.95 (*0-911655-12-3*, Dist. by Ingram Bookpeople) Advocacy Pr.
Favorite Nursery Rhymes. 1989. 2.98 (*0-517-69216-3*) Random Hse Value.
Fletcher, Cynthia H. My Jesus Pocketbook of Nursery Rhymes. Sherman, Erin, illus. LC 80-52041. 32p. (Orig.). (ps-3). 1980. pap. 0.69 (*0-937420-00-X*) Stirrup Assoc.
Galdone, Paul. Cat Goes Fiddle-i-Fee. Galdone, Paul, illus. LC 85-2686. 32p. (ps-3). 1985. 13.95 (*0-89919-336-6*, Clarion Bks) HM.
—Three Little Kittens. Galdone, Paul, illus. LC 86-2655. 32p. (ps-2). 1988. 13.95 (*0-89919-426-5*, Clarion Bks); pap. 5.95 (*0-89919-796-5*, Clarion Bks) HM.
Galdone, Paul, retold by. & illus. The Gingerbread Boy. LC 74-11461. 40p. (ps-3). 1983. 14.95 (*0-395-28799-5*, Clarion Bks); pap. 5.95 (*0-89919-163-0*, Clarion) HM.
Gerrard, Roy. A Pocket Full of Posies. (Illus.). 32p. 1991. bds. 9.95 (*0-374-36032-4*) FS&G.

Gorsline, Marie, ed. Nursery Rhymes. reissue ed. Gorsline, Douglas, illus. LC 76-24168. 32p. (ps-1). 1992. pap. 2.25 (*0-394-83550-6*) Random Bks Yng Read.

Graham, Bill. My Book of Zoo Rhymes. Horton, Vicki M., illus. 18p. (ps). 1991. 10.95 (*1-879680-10-6*) About You.

Graham, Terry. Let Loose on Mother Goose. LC 81-80248. (Illus.). 96p. (gr. k-1). 1982. pap. text ed. 7.95 (*0-86530-030-5*, IP 30-5) Incentive Pubns.

The Green Match the Rhyme Book. (gr. 2-6). 1990. 4.95 (*1-879332-03-5*) XYZ Group.

Greenaway, Kate. Kate Greenaway Nursery Rhymes. 1993. 9.99 (*0-517-08782-0*) Random Hse Value.

Griego, Margo C., et al. Tortillitas Para Mama: And Other Nursery Rhymes, Spanish & English. LC 81-4823. (Illus.). 32p. (ps-2). 1988. pap. 5.95 (*0-8050-0317-7*, Owlet BYR) H Holt & Co.

—Tortillitas Para Mama: And Other Nursery Rhymes, Spanish & English. Cooney, Barbara, illus. LC 81-4823. 32p. (ps-2). 1981. 14.95 (*0-8050-0285-5*, Bks Young Read) H Holt & Co.

Gutmann, Bessie P. Nursery Poems & Prayers. (Illus.). 32p. 1990. 9.95 (*0-448-23458-0*, G&D) Putnam Pub Group.

—Nursery Poems & Prayers. 32p. 1992. mini ed. 3.95 (*0-448-40259-9*, G&D) Putnam Pub Group.

—Nursery Songs & Lullabies. 32p. 1992. mini ed. 3.95 (*0-448-40260-2*, G&D) Putnam Pub Group.

Hader, Berta & Hader, Elmer, illus. Humpty Dumpty and Other Mother Goose Rhymes. LC 93-38612. 1994. pap. write for info. (*0-486-27488-8*) Dover.

Hague, Michael, illus. Teddy Bear, Teddy Bear: A Classic Action Rhyme. LC 92-17997. 32p. (ps up). 1993. 14.00 (*0-688-10671-4*); PLB 13.93 (*0-688-12085-7*) Morrow Jr Bks.

Hale, Sarah J. Mary Had a Little Lamb. De Paola, Tomie, illus. LC 83-22369. 32p. (ps-3). 1984. reinforced bdg. 15.95 (*0-8234-0509-5*); pap. 5.95 (*0-8234-0519-2*) Holiday.

—Mary Had a Little Lamb. 32p. (ps-1). 1990. 12.95 (*0-590-43773-9*) Scholastic Inc.

Hale, Sarah J., retold by. Mary Had a Little Lamb. Mavor, Salley, illus. LC 94-24847. (gr. 1-8). 1995. write for info. (*0-531-06875-7*); PLB write for info. (*0-531-08725-5*) Orchard Bks Watts.

Hall, Douglas. Douglas Hall's Nursery Rhymes. 1989. 4.98 (*0-671-07573-X*) S&S Trade.

Hall, K. Nursery Rhymes. 1990. 3.50 (*0-685-31997-0*, G018) Hansen Ed Mus.

Hannant, Judith S. The Doorknob Collection of Bedtime Rhymes, Vol. 1. Hannant, Judith S., illus. (ps). 1993. 13.95 (*0-316-34366-8*) Little.

—Doorknob Collection of Nursery Rhymes. (ps). 1991. 13.95 (*0-316-34343-9*) Little.

Harding, Emma. Cock-a-Doodle-Doo! LC 93-11030. 1994. 15.95 (*0-8050-3059-X*) H Holt & Co.

Harrison, Michael & Stuart-Clark, Christopher, eds. The Oxford Treasury of Children's Poems. (Illus.). 174p. (gr. k up). 1988. 20.00 (*0-19-276055-6*) OUP.

Hastings, Scott E., Jr. Miss Mary Mac All Dressed in Black: Tongue Twisters, Jump-Rope Rhymes, & Other Children's Lore from New England. 128p. (Orig.). 1990. pap. 8.95 (*0-87483-156-3*) August Hse.

Hayes, Sarah. Clap Your Hands: Finger Rhymes. Goffe, Toni, illus. LC 87-16958. (ps-1). 1988. 13.00 (*0-688-07692-0*); lib. bdg. 12.88 (*0-688-07693-9*) Lothrop.

Heller, Ruth. The Reason for a Flower. Heller, Ruth, illus. (ps-2). 1983. 9.95 (*0-448-14495-6*, G&D) Putnam Pub Group.

Hildebrandt, Mary, illus. I'm a Little Teapot. 48p. (ps). 1993. 5.95 (*0-88101-281-5*) Unicorn Pub.

Hofer, Grace & Day, Rachel. Oyen Ninos, Listen Children. Day, Rachel, tr. Moncus, Stephen, illus. 96p. (gr. 4-7). 1993. 12.95 (*0-89015-865-7*) Sunbelt Media.

Hoguet, Susan R. Solomon Grundy. Hoguet, Susan R., illus. LC 85-20453. 32p. (ps-3). 1986. 13.95 (*0-525-44239-1*, DCB) Dutton Child Bks.

Holmes, Martha. Time to Rhyme. (Illus.). 52p. (gr. k-1). 1990. lib. bdg. 17.95 (*0-89796-042-4*) New Dimens Educ.

Honey Bear Book of Rhymes. (gr. 2-4). 1991. 6.95 (*0-87449-778-7*) Modern Pub NYC.

Hope, Cathy. Who's He & Who's Out. Kelly, Geoff, illus. LC 92-21396. 1993. 4.25 (*0-383-03607-0*) SRA Schl Grp.

Hopkins, Lee B. Animals from Mother Goose. 11p. (ps-k). 1989. 6.95 (*0-15-200406-8*) HarBrace.

—People from Mother Goose. 18p. (ps-k). 1989. 6.95 (*0-15-200558-7*) HarBrace.

Howard, Nina. Barber, Barber, Shave a Pig. Rayl, Eleanor, illus. 16p. (ps-k). 1981. tchr's ed. 4.95 (*0-917206-13-4*) Children Learn Ctr.

Hunter, Emily. My Bedtime Nursery Rhyme Book. (Illus.). (ps-1). 1991. 12.99 (*0-89081-890-8*) Harvest Hse.

Irani, Meheru. Nursery Rhymes in Meher's Time. White, Susan, illus. (gr. 3 up). 1977. pap. text ed. 5.95 (*0-913078-29-8*) Sheriar Pr.

Ivemey, John W. Three Blind Mice. Mark, Steve, illus. LC 92-41175. (gr. k-4). 1995. 15.95 (*1-56766-090-8*) Childs World.

Ivimey, John W. The Complete Story of the Three Blind Mice. LC 87-689. (gr. k-3). 1987. 13.95 (*0-89919-481-8*, Clarion Bks) HM.

Jeffers, Susan. If Wishes Were Horses: Mother Goose Rhymes. Jeffers, Susan, illus. LC 79-9986. 32p. (ps-3). 1979. 13.95 (*0-525-32531-X*, DCB) Dutton Child Bks.

Jerrold, Walter, ed. Mother Goose's Nursery Rhymes. LC 93-22604. 1993. Repr. of 1903 ed. 13.95 (*0-679-42815-1*, Everymans Lib) Knopf.

Jones, Carol, illus. Hickory Dickory Dock. 48p. (gr. k-3). 1992. 10.70 (*0-395-60834-1*) HM.

—Old MacDonald Had a Farm. (ps-3). 1989. 12.70 (*0-395-49212-2*) HM.

Kemp, Moira, illus. Baa, Baa, Black Sheep. 10p. (ps). 1991. bds. 4.95 (*0-525-67331-8*, Lodestar Bks) Dutton Child Bks.

—Baa, Baa, Black Sheep. LC 93-18703. 12p. (ps). 1994. 2.99 (*0-525-67443-8*, Lodestar Bks) Dutton Child Bks.

—Hey Diddle Diddle. 10p. (ps). 1991. bds. 4.95 (*0-525-67329-6*, Lodestar Bks) Dutton Child Bks.

—Hey Diddle Diddle. LC 93-18702. 12p. (ps). 1994. 2.99 (*0-525-67445-4*, Lodestar Bks) Dutton Child Bks.

—Hickory, Dickory, Dock. 10p. (ps). 1991. bds. 4.95 (*0-525-67328-8*, Lodestar Bks) Dutton Child Bks.

—Hickory, Dickory, Dock. LC 93-18704. 12p. (ps). 1994. 2.99 (*0-525-67444-6*, Lodestar Bks) Dutton Child Bks.

—This Little Piggy. 10p. (ps). 1991. bds. 4.95 (*0-525-67326-1*, Lodestar Bks) Dutton Child Bks.

—This Little Piggy. LC 93-18683. 12p. (ps). 1994. 2.99 (*0-525-67446-2*, Lodestar Bks) Dutton Child Bks.

Kempher, Ruth M. Mother Goose on Wheels. Hogan, Wayne, illus. 30p. (Orig.). 1992. pap. 4.95 (*0-934536-51-1*) Rose Shell Pr.

Kennedy, Pamela, compiled by. Nursery Songs & Lap Games. Covell, Joan, illus. LC 90-36506. 32p. 1990. 13.95 (*0-8249-8486-2*, Ideals Child); incl. 50-min. cassette 17.95 (*0-8249-7399-2*) Hambleton-Hill.

Knapp, John, II. My Book of Bible Rhymes. Deckert, Dianne T., illus. LC 86-24254. (ps-1). 1987. 14.99 (*1-55513-161-1*, 51615, Chariot Bks) Chariot Family.

Lacome, Julie. Walking Through the Jungle. Lacome, Julie, illus. LC 92-53018. 32p. (ps). 1993. 13.95 (*1-56402-137-8*) Candlewick Pr.

Land of Nursery Rhymes. 1993. 3.99 (*0-517-08762-6*) Random Hse Value.

Landgren, Le. Old Mother Bear's Book of Hug Rhymes. Cannon, Christy, illus. LC 88-38973. 40p. (Orig.). (ps-9). 1989. pap. 6.95 (*0-943367-02-6*) Princess Pub.

Langley, Jonathan, illus. Rain, Rain, Go Away! A Book of Nursery Rhymes. LC 89-34594. 96p. (ps-1). 1991. 12.95 (*0-8037-0762-2*) Dial Bks Young.

Lansky, Bruce, created by. New Adventures of Mother Goose: Gentle Rhymes for Happy Times. Carpenter, Stephen, illus. LC 93-11129. 32p. 1993. 15.00 (*0-88166-201-1*) Meadowbrook.

Launchberry, Jane. In Nursery Rhyme Land. 1988. 2.98 (*0-671-09597-8*) S&S Trade.

Lehman, Patricia J. & Padzik, Alicja, eds. At Babci's Knee. Zurawiecka, Aska, tr. Knowlton, Barbara W., illus. LC 85-51371. (ENG & POL.). 165p. (Orig.). (ps). 1985. pap. 25.00 (*0-935003-01-0*); cassette incl. (*0-935003-00-2*) Talent Ed.

Levy, Sara G. Mother Goose Rhymes for Jewish Children. Robinson, Jessie B., illus. (ps-2). 1979. pap. 8.95 (*0-8197-0254-4*) Bloch.

Lewison, Wendy, compiled by. Baby's First Mother Goose. Morgan, Mary, illus. 24p. (ps). 1993. bds. 3.50 (*0-307-06143-4*, 6143, Golden Pr) Western Pub.

Lines, Kathleen. Lavender's Blue. Jones, Harold, illus. 180p. (ps-7). 1990. pap. 12.00 (*0-19-272208-5*) OUP.

Lines, Kathleen, ed. Lavender's Blue: A Book of Nursery Rhymes. Jones, Harold, illus. 180p. 1987. 22.00 (*0-19-279537-6*) OUP.

Little Boy Blue. (Illus.). pap. 0.59 (*0-685-74083-8*) Guild Bks.

Little Jack Horner. (Illus.). pap. 0.59 (*0-685-74086-2*) Guild Bks.

Lobel, Arnold. Gregory Griggs: And Other Nursery Rhyme People. LC 77-22209. (Illus.). 48p. (ps up). 1987. pap. 3.95 (*0-688-07042-6*, Mulberry) Morrow.

Lobel, Arnold, selected by. & illus. The Random House Book of Mother Goose: A Treasury of 306 Timeless Nursery Rhymes. LC 86-47532. 176p. (gr. 2-6). 1986. 16.00 (*0-394-86799-8*); lib. bdg. 16.99 (*0-394-96799-2*, Random Juv) Random Bks Yng Read.

Loomans, Diane, et al. Positively Mother Goose. Kramer, Linda, ed. Henrichsen, Ronda, illus. LC 90-52634. 32p. (ps-2). 1991. 14.95 (*0-915811-24-3*) H J Kramer Inc.

Loveless, Liz. One, Two, Buckle My Shoe. Loveless, Liz, illus. LC 92-40947. 32p. (ps). 1993. 13.95 (*1-56282-477-5*); PLB 13.89 (*1-56282-478-3*) Hyprn Child.

Lulla-Rhymes, Nursery Rhymes for Toddlers. (Illus., Orig.). 1992. pap. 19.95 incl. 2 cass. (*0-9637501-1-9*) E Wiggins Ent.

McCloskey, Patty, illus. Find the Real Mother Goose. 32p. (ps-1). 1993. pap. 5.95 (*1-56565-054-9*) Lowell Hse.

Maclean, Colin & Maclean, Moira. King Cole's Castle. Maclean, Colin & Maclean, Moira, illus. LC 92-53098. 24p. (ps-1). 1992. 9.95 (*1-85697-819-2*, Kingfisher LKC) LKC.

—Peter's Pumpkin House. Maclean, Colin & Maclean, Moira, illus. LC 92-53099. 24p. (ps-1). 1992. 9.95 (*1-85697-820-6*, Kingfisher LKC) LKC.

Maclean, Colin & Maclean, Moira, illus. Mother Goose Rhymes. LC 92-26443. 32p. (ps-1). 1993. 9.95 (*1-85697-898-2*, Kingfisher LKC) LKC.

Mcrae, Rodney. Who Killed Cock Robin? 1990. 13.95 (*0-385-30085-9*) Doubleday.

Marks, Alan, ed. & illus. Ring-a-Ring o' Roses & a Ding, Dong Bell: A Collection of Nursery Rhymes. LC 91-15222. 96p. (gr. k up). 1991. pap. 19.95 (*0-88708-187-8*) Picture Bk Studio.

Marks, Burton. Rhymes & Stories. Harvey, Paul, illus. LC 91-3663. 24p. (gr. k-2). 1992. PLB 9.89 (*0-8167-2409-1*); pap. 2.50 (*0-8167-2410-5*) Troll Assocs.

Marshall, James. James Marshall's Mother Goose. Marshall, James, illus. LC 79-2574. 40p. (ps-6). 1986. pap. 5.95 (*0-374-43723-8*) FS&G.

—Old Mother Hubbard & Her Wonderful Dog. (ps-3). 1991. 13.95 (*0-374-35621-1*) FS&G.

Martin, Bill, Jr. Fire! Fire! Said Mrs. McGuire. Egielski, Richard, illus. LC 94-11258. 1995. write for info. (*0-15-227562-2*) HarBrace.

Martin, Jerome. Carrot-Parrot. (ps). 1991. pap. 9.95 (*0-671-69555-X*, S&S BFYR) S&S Trade.

—Mitten-Kitten. (ps). 1991. pap. 9.95 (*0-671-69556-8*, S&S BFYR) S&S Trade.

Mary Had a Little Lamb. (Illus.). pap. 0.59 (*0-685-74085-4*) Guild Bks.

Mary-Mary Quite Contrary. (Illus.). pap. 0.59 (*0-685-74084-6*) Guild Bks.

The "Match the Rhyme" Value Pack: The Blue Match the Rhyme Book; the Red Match the Rhyme Book; the Green Match the Rhyme Book. (gr. 2-6). 1991. 4.95 (*1-879332-04-3*) XYZ Group.

Maxwell, Judith & Maxwell, Jessica. The Feminist Revised Mother Goose: A Twenty-First Century Children's Edition. 2nd ed. Maxwell, Rafe & Krostag, Zi, illus. (Orig.). (gr. 2-8). 1995. pap. text ed. 7.95 (*0-9632698-7-9*) Veda Vangarde.
4-color cover with wondeful, whimsical illustrations makes the 2nd Edition of THE FEMINIST REVISED MOTHER GOOSE RHYMES the best yet. Judith & Jessica, along with Judith's son, Rafe & his best friend Zi, have collaborated to bring this expanded version of these timeless rhymes to readers both young & old. In addition to the original 25 rewritten rhymes, Judith & Jessica have written more & included their original forms in an appendix with much more history of the original rhymes & an annotated bibliography! Also included in a new section called "From the Mouths of Babes" is a series of original rhymes as told by children from Pacific Northwest playgrounds. These new rhymes include THE TASMANIAN DEVIL which reads: "Australia big, Australia wide/ That's where the Tasmanian Devil may hide./ If you go looking for it, WATCH OUT!/ He's got a terribly hungry snout./ And if you happen to get too close,/ You might get nibbled on (I suppose)". And FARLEY "Old man Marley, had a friend named Farley/ And a weird old Farley was he./ He glowed in the dark/ and he sparked & he sparked/ and ran away yelling "yippey!"'
Publisher Provided Annotation.

—The Feminist Revised Mother Goose Rhymes: A 21st Century Children's Edition. LC 92-81770. 32p. (gr. 1-9). 1992. pap. 7.95 (*0-9632698-1-X*) Veda Vangarde.

Min, Kellet I. Modern Informative Nursery Rhymes: American History, Book I. Hansen, Heidi, illus. LC 89-91719. 64p. (Orig.). (gr. 2-5). 1992. pap. 10.95 (*0-9623411-2-6*) Rhyme & Reason.

—Modern Informative Nursery Rhymes: General Science, Book I. Hansen, Heidi, illus. LC 89-91719. 64p. (Orig.). (gr. 2-5). 1993. pap. 10.95 (*0-9623411-4-2*) Rhyme & Reason.

—Modern Informative Nursery Rhymes: Values, Book I. Hansen, Heidi, illus. LC 89-91719. 32p. (ps-3). 1989. pap. 7.95 (*0-9623411-3-4*) Rhyme & Reason.

Morninghouse, Sundaira. Nightfeathers: Black Goose Rhymes. Kim, Jody, illus. LC 89-63264. 32p. (gr. 1-4). 1989. 9.95 (*0-940880-27-X*); pap. text ed. 4.95 (*0-940880-28-8*) Open Hand.

Mother Goose. 1987. pap. 5.95 (*0-440-55849-2*, Dell Trade Pbks) Dell.

Mother Goose. (Illus.). 24p. (ps up). 1992. write for info. incl. long-life batteries (*0-307-74808-1*, 64808, Golden Pr) Western Pub.

The Mother Goose Book. (ps-1). 1990. write for info. (*0-307-10092-8*, 10092) Western Pub.
Mother Goose Nursery Rhymes. 1991. pap. 2.99 (*0-517-05218-0*) Random Hse Value.
Mother Goose Rhymes. rev. ed. 14p. (ps). 1990. write for info. (*0-307-12253-0*, Golden Bks.) Western Pub.
Mother Goose Rhymes. (Illus.). 6p. (gr. k-2). 1991. bds. 17.95 (*1-56144-027-2*, Honey Bear Bks) Modern Pub NYC.
Mother Goose Rhymes. LC 84-72862. (ps up). 1984. 4.95 (*0-671-49878-9*) S&S Trade.
Mother Goose's Nursery Rhymes. 32p. 1992. 4.95 (*0-8362-3024-8*) Andrews & McMeel.
Muldrow, Diane, selected by. My Little Book of Mother Goose Rhymes. Lubin, Leonard, illus. 24p. (ps-k). 1992. pap. write for info. (*0-307-11756-1*, 11756, Pub. by Golden Bks) Western Pub.
My Big Book of Nursery Rhymes. (Illus.). 64p. (ps-1). 1990. 7.99 (*0-517-69683-5*) Random Hse Value.
Myers, Walter D. Somewhere in the Darkness. (gr. 10 up). 1993. pap. 3.25 (*0-590-42412-2*) Scholastic Inc.
Nash, Corey. Little Treasury of Mother Goose, 6 vols. in 1. 1988. boxed 5.99 (*0-517-38571-6*) Random Hse Value.
—Little Treasury of Nursery Rhymes, 6 vols. in 1. 1988. 5.99 (*0-517-49203-2*) Random Hse Value.
Nayer, Judy, ed. Mother Goose. Brodie, Cynthia, illus. 24p. (ps-2). 1992. pap. 0.99 (*1-56293-105-9*) McClanahan Bk.
Neilson, Gena. Favorite Rhymes. (Illus.). (ps-1). 1986. pap. 9.95 (*0-937763-02-0*) Lauri Inc.
Nic Leodhas, Sorche. Always Room for One More. Hogrogian, Nonny, illus. LC 65-12881. 32p. (ps-2). 1972. reinforced bdg. 14.95 (*0-8050-0331-2*, Bks Young Read); pap. 5.95 (*0-8050-0330-4*) H Holt & Co.
Nudelman, Edward D., frwd. by. The Jessie Willcox Smith Mother Goose. LC 90-19903. (Illus.). 192p. (gr. k up). 1991. 24.95 (*0-88289-844-2*); deluxe ed. 75.00 (*0-88289-830-2*) Pelican.
Nursery Rhymes. (Illus.). 10p. (ps-1). 1984. 4.95 (*0-8431-0994-7*) Price Stern.
Nursery Rhymes. (ps-k). 3.95 (*0-7214-5056-3*) Ladybird Bks.
Nursery Rhymes. (Illus.). 24p. (gr. k-2). 1988. 3.95 (*0-87449-499-0*) Modern Pub NYC.
Nursery Rhymes. (gr. k up). 1991. pap. 1.47 (*1-56297-093-3*, GS-32) Lee Pubns KY.
Nursery Rhymes: I'm a Little Tea Pot & Itsy Bitsy Spider. (Illus.). (ps-k). 1991. write for info. (*0-307-06135-3*, Golden Pr) Western Pub.
The Nursery Rhymes Series. (gr. k-2). 1991. Big Bks. pap. 23.00 (*1-56843-036-1*); Little Bks. 4.50 (*0-685-62344-0*) BGR Pub.
Offen, Hilda, illus. My Favorite Nursery Rhymes. (ps-5). 1987. pap. 12.95 (*0-671-64705-9*, S&S BFYR) S&S Trade.
—A Treasury of Mother Goose. (gr. 1 up). 1984. pap. 13.00 (*0-671-50118-6*, S&S BFYR) S&S Trade.
Officer, Robyn, illus. Mother Goose's Nursery Rhymes. 32p. (ps-3). 1992. 6.95 (*0-8362-4907-0*) Andrews & McMeel.
Old King Cole. (Illus.). pap. 0.59 (*0-685-74103-6*) Guild Bks.
The Old Woman Who Lived in a Shoe. (Illus.). pap. 0.59 (*0-685-74082-X*) Guild Bks.
O'Malley, Kevin. Who Killed Cock Robin? LC 92-40340. (Illus.). (gr. k-3). 1993. 15.00 (*0-688-12430-5*); PLB 14.93 (*0-688-12431-3*) Lothrop.
One, Two, Buckle My Shoe. (Illus.). (ps-1). 1990. 3.50 (*0-7214-1265-3*) Ladybird Bks.
Opie, I. & Opie, P. Tail Feathers from Mother Goose: The Opie Rhyme Book. (Illus.). 124p. 1991. 7.99 (*0-517-05555-4*) Random Hse Value.
Opie, Iona & Opie, Peter, eds. Oxford Nursery Rhyme Book. Hassall, Joan, illus. (ps-3). 1955. 29.95x (*0-19-869112-2*) OUP.
Ormerod, Jan. Jan Ormerod's to Baby with Love. LC 93-8093. (Illus.). 1994. 15.00 (*0-688-12558-1*); lib. bdg. 14.93 (*0-688-12559-X*) Lothrop.
Oxenbury, Helen, illus. Tiny Tim. Bennett, Jill, selected by. LC 81-69816. (Illus.). 32p. (ps-3). 1982. PLB 10.95 (*0-685-01402-9*); pap. 10.95 (*0-385-29055-1*) Delacorte.
Palmer, Michele, ed. A Mother Goose Feast: Rhymes & Recipes. LC 79-65819. (Illus.). (ps-12). 1979. pap. 1.95 (*0-932306-01-2*) Rocking Horse.
Patience, J. The Land of Nursery Rhymes. (Illus.). (ps-1). 1985. 1.98 (*0-517-43878-X*) Random Hse Value.
Pearson, Tracey C. Old MacDonald Had a Farm. Pearson, Tracey C., illus. LC 83-18815. 32p. (ps-2). 1986. pap. 4.95 (*0-8037-0274-4*) Dial Bks Young.
Peppe, Rodney. The House That Jack Built. Peppe, Rodney, illus. 32p. (ps-3). 1985. pap. 4.95 (*0-385-28430-6*) Delacorte.
Percy, Graham, illus. Elephants Never Forget: Classic Nursery Rhymes. 48p. (ps-1). 1992. 12.95 (*0-8118-0239-6*) Chronicle Bks.
Petach, Heidi. One, Two, Buckle My Shoe: A Counting Rhyme. (ps). 1994. 3.95 (*0-307-06146-9*, Golden Pr) Western Pub.
Petersham, Maud & Petersham, Miska. The Rooster Crows: A Book of American Rhymes & Jingles. Petersham, Maud & Petersham, Miska, illus. LC 46-446. 64p. (ps-2). 1969. RSBE 14.95 (*0-02-773100-6*, Macmillan Child Bk) Macmillan Child Grp.
—The Rooster Crows: A Book of American Rhymes & Jingles. Petersham, Maud & Petersham, Miska, illus. LC 87-1138. 64p. (ps-3). 1987. pap. 5.95 (*0-689-71153-0*, Aladdin) Macmillan Child Grp.
Playtime Rhymes. (Illus.). (ps). pap. 1.25 (*0-7214-9552-4*) Ladybird Bks.
Polette, Nancy. Mother Goose's Animals. (Illus.). 128p. (gr. 1-4). 1992. pap. 12.95 (*1-879287-13-7*) Bk Lures.
—The Thinker's Mother Goose. (Illus.). 32p. 1983. pap. 3.95 (*0-913839-25-6*) Bk Lures.
Potter, Beatrix. Appley Dapply's Nursery Rhymes. 1987. 5.95 (*0-7232-3481-7*); pap. 2.25 (*0-7232-3506-6*) Warne.
—Beatrix Potter's Nursery Rhyme Book. 56p. (ps-4). 1984. 11.00 (*0-7232-3254-7*) Warne.
—Cecily Parsley's Nursery Rhymes. Atkinson, Allen, illus. 1983. pap. 2.25 (*0-553-15229-7*) Bantam.
—Cecily Parsley's Nursery Rhymes. 1987. 5.95 (*0-7232-3482-5*); pap. 2.25 (*0-7232-3507-4*) Warne.
—Little Treasury of Beatrix Potter Nursery Rhymes. LC 93-8697. (Illus.). 1994. 5.99 (*0-517-10030-4*, Pub. by Derrydale Bks) Random Hse Value.
Prelutsky, Jack. The Mean Old Mean Hyena. Lobel, Arnold, illus. LC 78-2300. 32p. (gr. k-3). 1978. PLB 11.88 (*0-688-84163-5*) Greenwillow.
Provensen, Alice & Provensen, Martin. Old Mother Hubbard. Provensen, Alice & Provensen, Martin, illus. LC 76-24176. 32p. (ps-1). 1992. pap. 2.25 (*0-394-83460-7*) Random Bks Yng Read.
Purnell. Rhyme Time Books: Humpty Dumpty. 1989. 1.98 (*0-671-09369-X*) S&S Trade.
Ra, Carol F. Trot, Trot to Boston. Stock, Catherine, illus. LC 86-7354. 32p. (ps). 1987. 13.00 (*0-688-06190-7*); PLB 12.93 (*0-688-06191-5*) Lothrop.
Rackham, Arthur. Mother Goose, the Old Nursery Rhymes. (Illus.). (ps-6). 1978. Repr. of 1912 ed. lib. bdg. 12.00 luxury ed. (*0-932106-02-1*, Pub by Marathon Pr) S J Durst.
Rader, Laura. Mother Hubbard's Cupboard: A Mother Goose Surprise Book. Rader, Laura, illus. LC 92-45103. 48p. (ps up). 1993. 12.95 (*0-688-12562-X*, Tambourine Bks) Morrow.
Rao, Anthony, illus. Nursery Rhymes. LC 90-85900. 32p. (ps-1). 1991. Repr. 8.95 (*1-878093-24-X*) Boyds Mills Pr.
Rap, Le. Bonjour, Mr. McGrue. 15p. (gr. k-2). 1991. pap. text ed. 23.00 big bk. (*1-56843-040-X*); pap. text ed. 4.50 (*1-56843-087-6*) BGR Pub.
—Little Betty Blue. 15p. (gr. k-2). 1991. pap. text ed. 23.00 big bk. (*1-56843-042-6*); pap. text ed. 4.50 (*1-56843-089-2*) BGR Pub.
—A Lost Little Pig. 15p. (gr. k-2). 1991. pap. text ed. 23.00 big bk. (*1-56843-038-8*); pap. text ed. 4.50 (*1-56843-085-X*) BGR Pub.
—Sherman Be Nimble. 15p. (gr. k-2). 1991. pap. text ed. 23.00 big bk. (*1-56843-044-2*); pap. text ed. 4.50 (*1-56843-091-4*) BGR Pub.
—Who's in the Shoe? 15p. (gr. k-2). 1991. pap. text ed. 23.00 big bk. (*1-56843-041-8*); pap. text ed. 4.50 (*1-56843-088-4*) BGR Pub.
Rawles, Jess, ed. The House That Jack Built. Avery, Bob, illus. 32p. 1994. 3.95 (*1-879384-24-8*) Cypress Hse.
Real Mother Goose. 75th Anniversary ed. (ps). 1991. 19.95 (*1-56288-144-2*) Checkerboard.
Real Mother Goose - Husky Book Blue. (ps). 1991. 4.95 (*1-56288-068-3*) Checkerboard.
Real Mother Goose - Husky Book Green. (ps). 1991. 4.95 (*1-56288-067-5*) Checkerboard.
Real Mother Goose - Husky Book Red. (ps). 1991. 4.95 (*1-56288-065-9*) Checkerboard.
Real Mother Goose: Husky Book Yellow. (ps). 1991. 4.95 (*1-56288-066-7*) Checkerboard.
The Red Match the Rhyme Book. (gr. 2-6). 1991. 4.95 (*1-879332-02-7*) XYZ Group.
Rees, Ennis. Fast Freddie Frog: And Other Tongue-Twister Rhymes. (ps-3). 1993. 14.95 (*1-56397-038-4*) Boyds Mills Pr.
Reid, Francis. Sing a Song of Mother Goose. 1993. pap. 3.95 (*0-590-41699-5*) Scholastic Inc.
—Sing a Song of Mother Goose. 1993. pap. 28.67 (*0-590-71380-9*) Scholastic Inc.
Rhyme Time. 1989. pap. 1.49 (*0-553-18398-2*) Bantam.
Rhyming Rabbit. 1989. text ed. 3.95 cased (*0-7214-5232-9*) Ladybird Bks.
Robinson, Fay. Rhymes We Like. Iosa, Ann W., illus. LC 92-10754. 32p. (ps-2). 1993. PLB 11.60 (*0-516-02375-6*); pap. 3.95 (*0-516-42375-4*) Childrens.
Roffey, Maureen, illus. The Grand Old Duke of York. rev. ed. Lodge, Bernard, contrib. by. LC 92-21339. (Illus.). 32p. (ps-3). 1993. 13.95 (*1-879085-79-8*) Whsprng Coyote Pr.
Rojankovsky, Feodor. Tall Book of Mother Goose. Rojankovsky, Feodor, illus. 120p. (ps up). 1942. 9.95 (*0-06-025055-0*) HarpC Child Bks.
Rosenberg, Amye, illus. Nursery Rhymes. 24p. (ps-1). 1987. pap. 1.25 (*0-7214-9550-8*, S871-6) Ladybird Bks.
Rosenberg, Liz, retold by. Mama Goose: A New Mother Goose. Street, Janet, illus. LC 93-11525. 32p. (ps-3). 1994. PLB 15.95 (*0-399-22348-7*, Philomel Bks) Putnam Pub Group.
Rossetti, Christina G. Sing Song: A Nursery Rhyme Book. Hughes, Arthur, illus. LC 68-55822. x, 130p. (gr. 3-7). 1969. pap. 4.50 (*0-486-22107-5*) Dover.
Sabia, Joe. The Modern Day Nursery Rhymes of Poppa Gander. (Illus., Orig.). 1993. pap. 7.95 (*0-86534-196-6*) Sunstone Pr.
Schenk De Regniers, Beatrice. It Does Not Say Meow & Other Animal Riddle Rhymes. LC 72-75704. 40p. (gr. k-3). 1983. pap. 4.95 (*0-89919-043-X*, Clarion Bks) HM.
Schwartz, Alvin. I Saw You in the Bathtub: And Other Folk Rhymes. Hoff, Syd, illus. LC 88-16111. 64p. (ps-2). 1991. pap. 3.50 (*0-06-444151-2*, Trophy) HarpC Child Bks.
Scott, Louise B. Rhymes for Learning Times. LC 82-73392. 145p. (Orig.). (ps). 1984. pap. 15.95 (*0-513-01763-1*) Denison.
Sendak, Maurice. Hector Protector & As I Went over the Water: Two Nursery Rhymes. Sendak, Maurice, illus. LC 65-21388. 64p. (ps-1). 1990. pap. 5.95 (*0-06-443237-8*, Trophy) HarpC Child Bks.
—We Are All in the Dumps with Jack & Guy. Sendak, Maurice, illus. LC 93-77287. 56p. (gr. k up). 1993. 20.00 (*0-06-205014-1*); limited edition 125.00 (*0-06-205056-7*); PLB 19.89 (*0-06-205015-X*) HarpC Child Bks.
Seven Little Hippos. LC 90-42437. 1991. pap. 13.95 (*0-671-72964-0*, S&S BFYR) S&S Trade.
Sharon, et al. Sharon, Lois & Bram's Mother Goose Songs, Finger Rhymes, Tickling Verses, Games & More. Kovalski, Maryann, illus. 92p. (ps-2). 1986. 16.95. (*0-316-78281-5*, 782815) Little.
Sicard, Gene, et al. Rappin' Mother Goose: Nursery Rhymes. 24p. (ps-3). 1991. incl. cassette 11.45 (*1-879755-00-9*) Recorded Pubns.
Sieveking, Anthea. Mary Had a Little Lamb & Other Animal Rhymes. (ps-3). 1991. bds. 5.95 (*0-8120-6217-5*) Barron.
Sieveking, Anthea, illus. Rub a Dub Dub & Other Water Rhymes. 12p. (ps-3). 1991. bds. 5.95 (*0-8120-6219-1*) Barron.
—Twinkle, Twinkle, Little Star & Other Bedtime Rhymes. 12p. (ps-3). 1991. bds. 5.95 (*0-8120-6220-5*) Barron.
Simpson, Catherine. My Little Book of Nursery Rhymes. Simpson, Catherine, illus. 32p. 1992. 5.95 (*0-87226-502-1*, Bedrick Blackie) P Bedrick Bks.
Slier, Debby, ed. The Real Mother Goose: Book of American Rhymes. McCloskey, Patty, et al, illus. 128p. (ps-5). 1993. 12.95 (*1-56288-399-2*) Checkerboard.
Spier, Peter. And So My Garden Grows. Spier, Peter, illus. 48p. (ps-3). 1992. pap. 3.99 (*0-440-40714-1*, YB) Dell.
—Hurrah, We're Outward Bound! Spier, Peter, illus. 48p. (ps-3). 1992. pap. 3.99 (*0-440-40715-X*, YB) Dell.
—London Bridge Is Falling Down. Spier, Peter, illus. 48p. (ps-3). 1992. pap. 3.99 (*0-440-40710-9*, YB) Dell.
—To Market, to Market. Spier, Peter, illus. LC 67-18664. 52p. (gr. 1-3). 1967. 8.95a (*0-385-08755-1*); pap. 5.95 (*0-385-09081-1*) Doubleday.
—To Market! To Market! Spier, Peter, illus. 48p. (ps-3). 1992. pap. 3.99 (*0-440-40713-3*, YB) Dell.
Stevens, Janet, illus. The House That Jack Built: A Mother Goose Nursery Rhyme. LC 84-15832. 32p. (ps-3). 1985. reinforced bdg. 14.95 (*0-8234-0548-6*) Holiday.
Stories & Rhymes for under Fives. (Illus.). 80p. (ps-1). 1990. 7.99 (*0-517-69420-4*) Random Hse Value.
Story Rhyme Staff. Fish Convention: A Story Rhyme. Doyle, A. C., illus. 36p. (Orig.). (gr. 4-11). 1994. pap. 9.95 (*1-56820-011-0*) Story Time.
Story Time Stories That Rhyme Staff. Bean Sprouts: A How to Story Rhyme. Story Time Stories That Rhyme Staff, illus. 28p. (gr. 4-7). 1992. GBC bdg. 9.95 (*1-56820-009-9*) Story Time.
—Cowboy Boots: A Story Sample & Activity Pages. Story Time Stories That Rhyme Staff, illus. 16p. (gr. 4-7). 1992. GBC bdg. 9.95 (*1-56820-008-0*) Story Time.
—Mushrooms: A Story Sample & Activity Pages. Story Time Stories That Rhyme Staff, illus. 20p. (gr. 4-7). 1992. GBC bdg. 9.95 (*1-56820-010-2*) Story Time.
—Seaweeds: A Story Sample & Activity Pages. Story Time Stories That Rhyme Staff, illus. 17p. (gr. 4-7). 1992. GBC bdg. 9.95 (*1-56820-007-2*) Story Time.
—Tennis Shoes: A Story Rhyme. Story Time Stories That Rhyme Staff, illus. 21p. (gr. 4-7). 1994. pap. 9.95 (*1-56820-012-9*) Story Time.
Stow, Jenny, illus. The House That Jack Built. LC 91-23850. 32p. (ps-2). 1992. 14.00 (*0-8037-1090-9*) Dial Bks Young.
—The House That Jack Built. 32p. (ps-2). 1993. pap. 4.99 (*0-14-054590-5*, Puff Pied Piper) Puffin Bks.
Stryker & Bingham. Mother Nature Nursery Rhymes. Paine, ed. Itoko Maeno, illus. 32p. (ps-6). 1990. 14.95 (*0-911655-01-8*) Advocacy Pr.
Swan, Frances M. Once upon a Rhyme. Criscuolo, Edna, illus. 48p. 1984. pap. 2.00 (*0-9602126-2-0*) F M Swan.
Sweet, Melissa, adapted by. & illus. Fiddle-I-Fee: A Farmyard Song for the Very Young. 32p. (ps-1). 1992. 15.95 (*0-316-82516-6*, Joy St Bks) Little.
Szekeres, Cyndy. Cyndy Szekeres' Favorite Mother Goose Rhymes. (Illus.). 24p. (ps-2). 1992. write for info. (*0-307-12347-2*, 12347) Western Pub.
Tarrant. Nursery Rhymes & Fairy Tales. 1984. 5.98 (*0-671-06535-1*) S&S Trade.
Tate, Carole. Rhymes & Ballads of London. LC 72-90691. (Illus.). 32p. (gr. k-4). 1973. 6.95 (*0-87592-042-X*) Scroll Pr.
Taylor, Jane. Twinkle, Twinkle, Little Star. LC 92-421. 1992. 15.00 (*0-688-11168-8*) Morrow Jr Bks.

Theobalds, Prue. For Teddy & Me. Theobalds, Prue, illus. 30p. (gr. k-3). 1992. 14.95 (*0-87226-470-X*, Bedrick Blackie) P Bedrick Bks.
Thumbelina. (Illus.). (ps-1). 1989. 2.99 (*0-517-69214-7*) Random Hse Value.
Tryon, Leslie. One Gaping Wide-Mouthed Hopping Frog. Tryon, Leslie, illus. LC 92-11368. 32p. (ps-1). 1993. SBE 14.95 (*0-689-31785-9*, Atheneum Child Bk) Macmillan Child Grp.
Voake, Charlotte, illus. Over the Moon: A Book of Nursery Rhymes. LC 91-71826. 128p. (ps up). 1992. 19.95 (*1-56402-038-X*) Candlewick Pr.
Walton, Rick. One Was Named Abel, He Slept on the Table. LC 94-14594. 1995. write for info. (*0-688-13656-7*); PLB write for info. (*0-688-13657-5*) Lothrop.
Warlow, Aidan, ed. Start with Rhymes, Nos. 7-12: Little Miss Muffett; Baa Baa Black Sheep; 1, 2 Buckle My Shoe; Rain; In a Dark Dark Wood & Round the Moon, 6 bks. Smith, Lesley, et al, illus. 48p. (Orig.). (gr. k-1). 1988. Set. pap. text ed. 29.60 (*1-55624-518-1*) Wright Group.
Watson, Clyde. Father Fox's Pennyrhymes. reissued ed. Watson, Wendy, illus. LC 71-146291. 64p. (gr. k-3). 1971. (Crowell Jr Bks); (Crowell Jr Bks) HarpC Child Bks.
Watson, Wendy. A Valentine for You. Briley, Dorothy, ed. Watson, Wendy, illus. 32p. (ps-1). 1991. 14.45 (*0-395-53625-1*, Clarion Bks) HM.
Weinberg, Larry. Guess a Rhyme: Poems to Complete! Riddles to Solve! reissued ed. McKie, Roy, illus. LC 81-15689. 32p. (ps-1). 1993. 2.25 (*0-394-85062-9*) Random Bks Yng Read.
Weissman, Jackie. Higglety Pigglety Pop: Two Hundred Thirty-Three Playful Rhymes & Chants for Your Baby. (ps). 1991. pap. 9.95 (*0-939514-29-X*) Miss Jackie.
Westcott, Nadine B. House That Jack Built: Pop-up, Pull-tab, Playtime Book. (ps-3). 1991. 14.95 (*0-316-93138-1*) Little.
—Peanut Butter & Jelly: A Play Rhyme. (Illus.). 24p. (ps-k). 1992. pap. 3.99 (*0-14-054852-1*) Puffin Bks.
Westcott, Nadine B., illus. Peanut Butter & Jelly: A Play Rhyme. LC 86-32889. 32p. (ps-k). 1987. 13.00 (*0-525-44317-7*, DCB) Dutton Child Bks.
—Peanut Butter & Jelly: A Play Rhyme. giant ed. 24p. (ps-k). 1993. pap. 17.99 (*0-14-054850-5*) Puffin Bks.
—Peanut Butter & Jelly Read-Aloud Set. (ps-k). 1993. Set incls. 1 Giant copy, 6 paperbacks, giant-sized bookmark & tchr's. guide in a free- standing easel. pap. 41.93 (*0-14-778975-3*) Puffin Bks.
White, Stephen. Barney's Favorite Mother Goose Rhymes. Hartley, Linda, ed. Eubank, Mary G., illus. LC 93-77864. 32p. (ps-k). 1994. 7.95 (*1-57064-012-2*) Barney Pub.
—Barney's Favorite Mother Goose Rhymes. Hartley, Linda, ed. Eubank, Mary G., illus. LC 92-76136. 32p. (ps-k). 1993. 7.95 (*1-57064-001-7*) Barney Pub.
—Barney's Favorite Mother Goose Rhymes, Vol. 2. Hartley, Linda, ed. Eubank, Mary G., illus. 32p. (ps-k). 1993. 7.95 (*0-7829-0380-0*) Lyons Group.
Wiggin, Kate D., et al, eds. Pinafore Palace: A Book of Rhymes for the Nursery. LC 72-8290. (ps-1). Repr. of 1907 ed. 21.00 (*0-8369-6399-7*) Ayer.
Wilcox, Cathy. In the Old Gum Tree: Nursery Rhymes & Verse for Little Kids. Wilcox, Cathy, illus. 48p. (Orig.). (ps-3). 1993. pap. 6.95 (*0-04-442216-4*, Pub. by Allen & Unwin Aust Pty AT) IPG Chicago.
Wildsmith, Brian. Cat on the Mat. (Illus.). 16p. 1987. pap. 2.95 (*0-19-272123-2*) OUP.
—Mother Goose: Nursery Rhymes. (Illus.). 80p. (ps up). 1987. 16.00 (*0-19-279611-9*); pap. 10.00 (*0-19-272180-1*) OUP.
Wilkes, Angela, compiled by. Animal Nursery Rhymes. LC 92-52818. (Illus.). 32p. (ps-k). 1992. 13.95 (*1-56458-122-5*) Dorling Kindersley.
Wilkin, Eloise, illus. Nursery Rhymes. LC 78-64606. (ps). 1979. bds. 3.95 (*0-394-84129-8*) Random Bks Yng Read.
Withers, Carl. Eenie-Meenie-Minie-Mo & Other Counting-Out Rhymes. Ripley, Elizabeth, illus. 44p. (ps up). 1970. pap. 2.50 (*0-486-22414-7*) Dover.
Wood, Jakki. Fiddle-I-Fee: A Noisy Nursery Rhyme. Wood, Jakki, illus. LC 93-23534. 32p. (ps-1). 1994. SBE 14.95 (*0-02-793396-2*, Bradbury Pr) Macmillan Child Grp.
Wood, Jenny. First Songs & Action Rhymes. McEwan, Chris, illus. LC 90-44773. 64p. (ps-k). 1991. pap. 6.95 POB (*0-689-71472-6*, Aladdin) Macmillan Child Grp.
Wright, Blanche F., illus. The Real Mother Goose, 4 bks. 96p. (ps-2). Set Incl. cassettes. pap. 16.98 (*1-55886-018-5*) Smarty Pants.
—The Real Mother Goose, Vol. I. 24p. (ps-2). Incl. cassettes. pap. 5.98 (*1-55886-012-6*) Smarty Pants.
—The Real Mother Goose, Vol. II. 24p. (ps-2). Incl. cassettes. pap. 5.98 (*1-55886-013-4*) Smarty Pants.
—The Real Mother Goose, Vol. III. 24p. (ps-2). Incl. cassettes. pap. 5.98 (*1-55886-014-2*) Smarty Pants.
—The Real Mother Goose, Vol. IV. 24p. (ps-2). Incl. cassettes. pap. 5.98 (*1-55886-015-0*) Smarty Pants.
—Real Mother Goose. 128p. (ps-1). 1991. Repr. 12.95 (*1-56288-041-1*) Checkerboard.
Wyndham, Robert. Chinese Mother Goose Rhymes. Young, Ed, illus. 48p. (ps-k). 1989. (Sandcastle Bks); pap. 5.95 (*0-399-21718-5*) Putnam Pub Group.
Wynken Blynken & Nod. 1991. pap. 2.99 (*0-517-05217-2*) Random Hse Value.
Yolen, Jane, ed. Sleep Rhymes Around the World. (Illus.). 40p. 1994. 16.95 (*1-56397-243-3*, Wordsong) Boyds Mills Pr.
Young, Karen E. Kind Mr. Spider. 15p. (gr. k-2). 1991. pap. text ed. 23.00 big bk. (*1-56843-039-6*); pap. text ed. 4.50 (*1-56843-086-8*) BGR Pub.
Zaslow, David B. & Inada, Lawson F. Hey Diddle Rock. Bullock, Kathleen, illus. 32p. (Orig.). (ps-8). 1986. pap. 7.95 (*0-89411-006-3*) Kids Matter.
—Humpty Dumpty Rock. Bullock, Kathleen, illus. 32p. (Orig.). (ps-8). 1986. pap. 7.95 (*0-89411-007-1*) Kids Matter.
—Rock-a-Doodle-Doo. Bullock, Kathleen, illus. 32p. (Orig.). (ps-8). 1986. pap. 7.95 (*0-89411-005-5*) Kids Matter.
Zemach, Margot. Mother Goose Picture Book. (Illus.). Date not set. 15.00 (*0-06-205046-X*); PLB 14.89 (*0-06-205047-8*) HarpC Child Bks.
Zokeisha. Mother Goose House. Klimo, Kate, ed. Zokeisha, illus. 16p. (ps-k). 1983. pap. 3.50 (*0-671-46127-3*, Little Simon) S&S Trade.

NURSERY RHYMES–DICTIONARIES

Opie, Iona & Opie, Peter, eds. Oxford Dictionary of Nursery Rhymes. (Illus.). (ps-3). 1951. 47.50x (*0-19-869111-4*) OUP.

NURSERY SCHOOLS

see also Kindergarten

Amato, Dolores. Getting Ready for School, No. 2. 80p. (Orig.). (ps-1). 1985. pap. 2.95 (*0-8431-2512-8*) Price Stern.
Ancona, George. Ricardo's Day. Ancona, George, photos by. LC 94-725. 1994. write for info. (*0-590-29257-9*) Scholastic Inc.
Brown, Jerome C. Mother Goose PaperCrafts. (gr. k-5). 1989. pap. 8.95 (*0-8224-3154-8*) Fearon Teach Aids.
Preschool Early Learner Workbook II. 192p. (ps). 1991. pap. 4.95 (*1-56144-046-9*) Modern Pub NYC.
Quinn, Kaye. Preschool Skills. 80p. (Orig.). (ps). pap. 2.95 (*0-8431-2508-X*) Price Stern.
Tyler, Sydney B. Young Think Program Two. 90p. (Orig.). (gr. k-1). 1988. pap. text ed. 25.00 report cover (*0-912781-13-0*) Thomas Geale.

NURSERY SCHOOLS–FICTION

Breinburg, Petronella. Shawn Goes to School. Lloyd, Errol, illus. LC 73-8003. 32p. (ps-2). 1974. PLB 14.89 (*0-690-00277-7*, Crowell Jr Bks) HarpC Child Bks.
Caseley, Judith. Mr. Green Peas. LC 93-24183. 1994. write for info. (*0-688-12859-9*); PLB write for info. (*0-688-12860-2*) Greenwillow.
Chartrand, Micheline. Lollypop at Nursery School. (Illus.). 12p. (ps). 1993. bds. 3.95 (*2-921198-11-8*, Pub. by Les Edits Herit CN) Adams Inc MA.
—Visit for Lollypop. (Illus.). 12p. (ps). 1993. bds. 3.95 (*2-921198-10-X*, Pub. by Les Edits Herit CN) Adams Inc MA.
Rockwell, Harlow. My Nursery School. 32p. (ps). 1984. pap. 3.95 (*0-14-050478-8*, Puffin) Puffin Bks.
Topek, Susan R. A Turn for Noah: A Hanukkah Story. Springer, Sally, illus. LC 92-22958. 1992. 12.95 (*0-929371-37-2*); pap. 4.95 (*0-929371-38-0*) Kar Ben.
Wolde, Gunilla. Betsy's First Day at Nursery School. LC 76-9322. (Illus.). (ps-k). 1982. 1.95 (*0-394-85381-4*) Random Bks Yng Read.

NURSES AND NURSING

see also Children–Care and Hygiene; First Aid; Hospitals

Bauer, Judith. What's It Like to Be a Nurse. Pellaton, Karen E., illus. LC 89-34387. 32p. (gr. k-3). 1990. lib. bdg. 10.89 (*0-8167-1809-1*); pap. text ed. 2.95 (*0-8167-1810-5*) Troll Assocs.
Behrens, June. I Can Be a Nurse. LC 85-29086. (Illus.). 32p. (gr. k-3). 1986. PLB 11.80 (*0-516-01893-0*) Childrens.
Collins, David. Florence Nightingale. (gr. 3-6). 1985. pap. 6.95 (*0-88062-126-5*) Mott Media.
Cosner, Shaaron. War Nurses. (gr. 7 up). 1988. 16.95 (*0-8027-6826-1*); 17.85 (*0-8027-6828-8*) Walker & Co.
Everygirls Nurse Stories. (gr. 6-10). PLB 7.19 (*0-8313-0054-X*) Lantern.
Heron, Jackie. Exploring Careers in Nursing. rev. ed. 144p. (gr. 7-12). 1990. 14.95 (*0-8239-1136-5*) Rosen Group.
Witty, Margot. A Day in the Life of an Emergency Room Nurse. Lewis, Sarah, photos by. LC 78-68842. (Illus.). 32p. (gr. 4-8). 1980. PLB 11.79 (*0-89375-226-6*); pap. 2.95 (*0-89375-230-4*) Troll Assocs.

NURSES AND NURSING–FICTION

Belloc, Hilaire. Jim, Who Ran Away from His Nurse, & Was Eaten by a Lion. Chess, Victoria, illus. (gr. 2 up). 1987. pap. 4.95 (*0-316-13816-9*) Little.
Carlyle, Carolyn. Mercy Hospital: Crisis! 128p. (Orig.). (gr. 5). 1993. pap. 3.50 (*0-380-76846-1*, Camelot) Avon.
—Mercy Hospital: Dr. Cute. 128p. (Orig.). 1993. pap. 3.50 (*0-380-76849-6*, Camelot) Avon.
—Mercy Hospital: Don't Tell Mrs. Harris. 128p. (Orig.). 1993. pap. 3.50 (*0-380-76848-8*, Camelot) Avon.
—Mercy Hospital: The Best Medicine. 128p. (Orig.). 1993. pap. 3.50 (*0-380-76847-X*, Camelot) Avon.
Davidson, Martine. Kevin & the School Nurse. Hafner, Marylin, illus. LC 91-30194. 32p. (Orig.). (ps-2). 1992. PLB 5.99 (*0-679-91821-3*); pap. 2.25 (*0-679-81821-9*) Random Bks Yng Read.
Ellis, Joyce. Tiffany. LC 86-70910. 160p. (Orig.). (gr. 9-12). 1986. pap. 3.99 (*0-87123-893-4*) Bethany Hse.
Lakin, Patricia. The Mystery Illness. Cushman, Doug, illus. LC 93-49843. 1994. write for info. (*0-8114-3867-8*) Raintree Steck-V.
Lyon, George E. Here & Then. LC 94-6921. 128p. (gr. 5-7). 1994. 14.95 (*0-531-06866-8*); PLB 14.99 (*0-531-08716-6*) Orchard Bks Watts.

NURSING

see Nurses and Nursing

NUTRITION

see also Diet; Digestion; Food; Vitamins

Adams, Marylou. Brighten up at Breakfast: Helpful Tips for Heavenly Bodies. Adams, Marylou, illus. LC 81-51601. 120p. (gr. 2-7). 1981. plastic comb 7.95 (*0-9606248-0-5*) Starbright.
American Health Foundation Staff. Great Meals, Great Snacks, Great Kids. 1990. pap. 4.95 (*0-590-43382-2*) Scholastic Inc.
Austin, Trina K. All Aboard the S. S. Nutrient. (Illus.). 26p. (Orig.). (gr. k-4). 1986. pap. 6.50 (*0-9615840-0-9*) Trinas Pr.
Bailey, Donna. Energy for Our Bodies. LC 90-39295. (Illus.). 48p. (gr. 2-6). 1990. PLB 19.97 (*0-8114-2521-5*) Raintree Steck-V.
Berger, Melvin. An Apple a Day. (Illus.). 16p. (ps-2). 1993. pap. text ed. 14.95 (*1-56784-011-6*) Newbridge Comms.
Bodily, Jolene & Kreiswirth, Kinny. The Lunch Book & Bag: A Fit Kid's Guide to Making Delicious (& Nutritious) Lunches. Kreiswirth, Kinny, illus. LC 92-2815. 56p. (gr. 2-6). 1992. pap. 12.95 (*0-688-11624-8*, Tambourine Bks) Morrow.
Carratello, Patricia. Food & Nutrition. Carratello, Patricia, illus. 40p. (gr. 1-4). 1980. wkbk. 6.95 (*1-55734-212-1*) Tchr Create Mat.
Carratello, Patty. Nutrition & Me. Wright, Theresa, illus. 48p. (gr. 1-5). 1987. wkbk. 6.95 (*1-55734-222-9*) Tchr Create Mat.
Epstein, Rachel. Eating Habits & Disorders. (Illus.). 112p. (gr. 6-12). 1990. 18.95 (*0-7910-0048-6*) Chelsea Hse.
Figtree, Dale. Eat Smart: A Guide to Good Health for Kids. LC 92-4550. 128p. 1992. 10.95 (*0-8329-0465-1*) New Win Pub.
Food & Digestion. 48p. (gr. 5-8). 1988. PLB 10.95 (*0-382-09704-1*) (*0-685-24612-4*) Silver Burdett Pr.
Francis, Lynnrae & Francis, Steven. The Shape of Good Nutrition. Nick, Christopher, illus. Birch, Gail, intro. by. (Illus.). 20p. (Orig.). 1993. saddlestitched 2.50 (*0-9638754-0-X*) Providers Pr.
Galperin, Anne. Nutrition. (Illus.). 120p. (gr. 6-12). 1991. 18.95 (*0-7910-0024-9*) Chelsea Hse.
Glyman, Caroline A. Learning Your ABCs of Nutrition. Biser, Dee, illus. LC 92-7862. 32p. (gr. k-3). 1992. PLB 12.95 (*1-878363-75-1*) Forest Hse.
Greenbaum, David & Wasser, Edward. My First Health & Nutrition Coloring Book: Mr. Carrots Coloring Book. Puglisi, Lou, illus. 40p. (Orig.). (gr. 2). 1988. pap. 0.99 (*0-9621833-0-X*) D Greenbaum.
Griscom, Laura & Griscom, Pam. Who Would Want Those Apples Anyway? Halpin, Scot, illus. 24p. (Orig.). (ps-5). 1993. pap. 4.95 (*0-9633705-3-7*) Share Pub CA.
Hamm, Anita M. Lisa in Sugarland, a Child's Book on Nutrition to Be Digested Before Eating. (gr. 1-4). 1978. 3.50x (*0-935513-02-7*) Samara Pubns.
Inglis, Jane. Protein. LC 92-26759. 1993. PLB 14.95 (*0-87614-780-5*); pap. 5.95 (*0-87614-607-8*) Carolrhoda Bks.
Isphording, Julie. Food Fun For Kids: A Recipe Coloring Book. Wolterman, Jan, ed. (Illus.). 48p. (gr. 1-6). 1991. pap. 6.95 spiral bdg. (*0-9629589-0-5*) Kids Kitchen.
Jacobson, Michael & Hill, Laura. Kitchen Fun for Kids: Healthy Recipes & Nutrition Facts for 7-12 Year Old Cooks. 128p. (gr. 2-7). 1991. 14.95 (*0-8050-1609-0*, Bks Young Read) H Holt & Co.
Jacobson, Michael F., et al. Safe Food: Eating Wisely in a Risky World. (Illus.). 252p. (Orig.). 1991. pap. 9.95 (*1-879326-01-9*) Living Planet Pr.
Jennings, Terry. Food. LC 88-22866. (Illus.). 32p. (gr. 3-6). 1989. pap. 4.95 (*0-516-48402-8*) Childrens.
Kamen, Betty. New Facts about Fiber: Health Builder Disease Fighter Vital Nutrient. (Illus.). 152p. (Orig.). 1991. pap. 8.95 (*0-944501-04-4*) Nutrition Encounter.
LeMaster, Leslie J. Nutrition. LC 85-7728. (Illus.). 45p. (gr. k-3). 1985. PLB 12.85 (*0-516-01271-1*) Childrens.
Maloney, Michael & Kranz, Rachel. Straight Talk about Eating Disorders. 128p. (gr. 7-12). 1991. 16.95x (*0-8160-2414-6*) Facts on File.
Marbach, Ellen S., et al. Nutrition in a Changing World: A Curriculum for Primary Level. LC 79-11776. (Illus., Orig.). (gr. 1-3). 1979. pap. 8.95 (*0-8425-1660-3*) BYU Scholarly.
Mayfield, Barbara J. Nutrition Notes: Musical Nutrition Education to Sing & Color. (Illus.). 80p. (ps-2). 1992. pap. 12.00 incl. cass. tape (*1-883983-02-9*) Noteworthy Creat.
Moncure, Jane B. The Health kin Food Train. Endres, Helen, illus. LC 82-14710. 32p. (ps-2). 1982. PLB 13.95 (*0-89565-240-4*) Childs World.
Montgomery, Paul J. Nutritional Analysis of Ready-to-Eat Cereal. rev. ed. 274p. (gr. 7 up). 1989. pap. text ed. 19.95 (*0-9621865-0-3*) Prod Info Analysis.
—Nutritional Cereal Counter. (Illus.). 92p. (Orig.). (gr. 9 up). 1989. pap. 2.95 (*0-9621865-1-1*) Prod Info Analysis.
Moss, Miriam. Eat Well. LC 92-28738. (Illus.). 32p. (gr. 6). 1993. text ed. 13.95 RSBE (*0-89686-785-4*, Crestwood Hse) Macmillan Child Grp.
National Dairy Council Staff. Food...Early Choices Program. rev. ed. (ps-k). 1979. write for info. (*1-55647-491-1*) Natl Dairy Coun.

Needham, Kate. Why Do People Eat? (Illus.). 24p. (gr. 1-5). 1993. lib. bdg. 11.96 (*0-88110-638-0*, Usborne); pap. 3.95 (*0-7460-1302-7*, Usborne) EDC.
Nelson, JoAnne. Feeling Fit, That's It! McKinnell, Michael, illus. LC 92-37719. 1994. pap. 5.95 (*0-935529-58-6*) Comprehen Health Educ.
Noffs, David & Noffs, Laurie. Kindergarten - Introductory, Bk. K: The Happy Healthy Harold. Noffs, Laurie, illus. 24p. (Orig.). (gr. k). 1987. wkbk. 2.50 (*0-929875-01-X*) Noffs Assocs.
Nottridge, Rhoda. Fats. LC 92-26758. 1993. 14.95 (*0-87614-779-1*); pap. 5.95 (*0-87614-606-X*) Carolrhoda Bks.
O'Connell, Lily H., et al. Nutrition in a Changing World: Grade Five. (Illus.). 152p. (Orig.). (gr. 5). 1981. pap. text ed. 11.95 (*0-8425-1916-5*) BYU Scholarly.
Orlandi, Mario, et al. Nutrition. (Illus.). 128p. 1988. 18. 95x (*0-8160-1670-4*) Facts on File.
Parker, Steve. Eating a Meal: How You Eat, Drink & Digest. LC 90-77856. (Illus.). 32p. (gr. k-4). 1991. PLB 11.40 (*0-531-14086-5*) Watts.
Peavy, Linda & Smith, Ursula. Food, Nutrition, & You. LC 82-5694. (Illus.). 192p. (gr. 6 up). 1982. SBE 14.95 (*0-684-17461-8*, Scribners Young Read) Macmillan Child Grp.
Perry, Susan. The Body Bandits. (Illus.). (gr. 2-6). 1992. PLB 14.95 (*0-89565-875-5*) Childs World.
Rubin, Laurie. Food First Curriculum. (Illus.). 146p. (gr. 3-8). 1984. 12.00 (*0-935028-17-X*) Inst Food & Develop.
Salter, Charles A. Food Risks & Controversies: Minimizing the Dangers in Your Diet. LC 92-37442. (Illus.). 112p. (gr. 7 up). 1993. PLB 15.90 (*1-56294-259-X*) Millbrook Pr.
—Looking Good, Eating Right: A Sensible Guide to Proper Nutrition & Weight Loss for Teens. (Illus.). 144p. (gr. 7 up). 1991. PLB 15.90 (*1-56294-047-3*) Millbrook Pr.
—The Nutrition-Fitness Link: How Diet Can Help Your Body & Mind. LC 92-35146. (Illus.). 96p. (gr. 7 up). 1993. PLB 15.90 (*1-56294-260-3*) Millbrook Pr.
—The Vegetarian Teen. (Illus.). 112p. (gr. 7 up). 1991. PLB 15.90 (*1-56294-048-1*) Millbrook Pr.
Sanders, Peter A., Jr. Food & Hygiene. LC 90-3246. (Illus.). 32p. (gr. 2-5). 1990. PLB 11.40 (*0-531-17243-0*, Gloucester Pr) Watts.
Schwarzenegger, Arnold & Gaines, Charles. Arnold's Fitness for Kids: A Guide to Health, Exercise, & Nutrition. LC 92-28577. (gr. 1-5). 1993. 15.00 (*0-385-42267-9*) Doubleday.
—Arnold's Fitness for Kids Ages Birth to Five: A Guide to Health, Exercise, & Nutrition. LC 92-26209. (ps-k). 1993. 15.00 (*0-385-42266-0*) Doubleday.
—Arnold's Fitness for Kids Ages Eleven to Fourteen: A Guide to Health, Exercise, & Nutrition. LC 92-26786. (gr. 6-8). 1993. 15.00 (*0-385-42268-7*) Doubleday.
Seixas, Judith S. Junk Food--What It Is, What It Does. Huffman, Tom, illus. LC 83-14135. 48p. (gr. 1-3). 1984. 12.95 (*0-688-02559-5*); PLB 12.88 (*0-688-02560-9*) Greenwillow.
Singer, Marcia. Eating for a Fresh Start: A P.L.A.Y. Book. Rendal, Camille, illus. LC 90-91969. 64p. (Orig.). (gr. 1-7). 1990. pap. write for info. (*0-9622543-1-2*) PLAY House.
Starbuck, Marnie. Eat the Healthy Way with the Gladimals. (Illus.). 16p. 1990. 0.75 (*1-56456-204-2*, 474) W Gladden Found.
Tatchell, J. & Fraser, K. Food Fitness & Health. (Illus.). 96p. (gr. 6-10). 1987. 12.95 (*0-7460-0079-0*) EDC.
Ward, Brian. Diet: And Health. LC 90-31200. (Illus.). 32p. 1991. PLB 12.40 (*0-531-14095-4*) Watts.
Warren, Jean. Super Snacks. Mulvey, Glen, illus. 48p. 1992. 6.95 (*0-911019-49-9*, WPH 1601) Warren Pub Hse.
Wisconsin Potato Growers Auxiliary Staff, ed. Team up to Unmask Potato Secrets. 14p. 1992. pap. 50.00 (*0-9635149-0-3*) WI Potato Grow.
Woodworth, Viki. Would You Spread a Turtle on Toast? Woodworth, Viki, illus. (ps-2). 1992. PLB 12.95 (*0-89565-823-2*) Childs World.
Zak, Victoria & Vash, Peter. The Dieter's Dictionary & Problem Solver: An A to Z Guide to Nutrition, Health, & Fitness. LC 92-11242. (Illus.). 352p. 1992. 19.95 (*1-55853-172-6*) Rutledge Hill Pr.
Zonderman, Jon & Shader, Laurel. Nutritional Diseases. (Illus.). 64p. (gr. 5-8). 1993. PLB 14.95 (*0-8050-2601-0*) TFC Bks NY.

NUTS

Langham, Barbara A. The Pecan Tree: A True Friend. LC 94-96074. (Illus.). 32p. (gr. k-3). 1994. PLB 12.95 (*0-9640804-0-0*) B A Langham.

O

OAK

Benedict, Kitty. The Oak: My First Nature Books. Felix, Monique, illus. 32p. (gr. k-2). 1993. pap. 2.95 (*1-56189-170-3*) Amer Educ Pub.
Hogan, Paula Z. The Oak Tree. LC 78-21183. (Illus.). 32p. (gr. 1-4). 1979. PLB 19.97 (*0-8172-1251-5*) Raintree Steck-V.
—The Oak Tree. LC 78-21183. (Illus.). 32p. (gr. 1-4). 1984. PLB 29.28 incl. cassette (*0-8172-2230-8*) Raintree Steck-V.

OAK–FICTION

Edwards, Richard. Ten Tall Oaktrees. Crossland, Caroline, illus. LC 92-41771. 32p. (ps up). 1993. 15.00 (*0-688-04620-7*, Tambourine Bks); PLB 14.93 (*0-688-04621-5*, Tambourine Bks) Morrow.
Muller, Gerda. Around the Oak. LC 93-32310. (gr. 3 up). 1994. write for info. (*0-525-45239-7*, DCB) Dutton Child Bks.

OAKLAND ATHLETICS (BASEBALL TEAM)

Oakland Athletics. (gr. 4-7). 1993. pap. 1.49 (*0-553-56418-8*) Bantam.
Rambeck, Richard. Oakland A's. 48p. (gr. 4-10). 1992. PLB 14.95 (*0-88682-444-3*) Creative Ed.

OAKLEY, ANNIE, 1860-1926

Annie Oakley. (Illus.). (gr. 2-5). 1989. 29.28 (*0-8172-2955-8*) Raintree Steck-V.
Gleiter, Jan & Thompson, Kathleen. Annie Oakley. Miyake, Yoshi, illus. 32p. (gr. 2-5). 1986. PLB 19.97 (*0-8172-2641-9*) Raintree Steck-V.
Graves, Charles P. Annie Oakley: The Shooting Star. (Illus.). 80p. (gr. 2-6). 1991. Repr. of 1961 ed. lib. bdg. 12.95 (*0-7910-1448-7*) Chelsea Hse.
Levine, Ellen. Ready, Aim, Fire! The Real Adventures of Annie Oakley. (gr. 5-7). 1989. pap. 2.95 (*0-590-41877-7*) Scholastic Inc.
Wilson, Ellen. Annie Oakley. (Illus.). 192p. (gr. 2-6). 1989. pap. 3.95 (*0-689-71346-0*, Aladdin) Macmillan Child Grp.

OAKLEY, ANNIE, 1860-1926–FICTION

Fontes, Ron & Korman, Justine. Annie Oakley in the Wild West Extravaganza! Shaw, Charlie, illus. LC 93-70937. 80p. (gr. 1-4). 1993. PLB 12.89 (*1-56282-492-9*); pap. 3.50 (*1-56282-491-0*) Disney Pr.
Kunstler, James H. Annie Oakley. Warter, Fred, illus. LC 93-19246. 1993. 14.95 (*0-88708-338-2*, Rabbit Ears); pap. 19.95 incl. cassette (*0-88708-337-4*, Rabbit Ears) Picture Bk Studio.

OBESITY

see Weight Control

OBSTETRICS

see Childbirth

OCCULT SCIENCES

see also Astrology; Clairvoyance; Divination; Fortune Telling; Magic; Medicine Man; Superstition; Witchcraft

Deem, James M. How to Read Your Mother's Mind. Kelley, True, illus. LC 92-41351. 1994. 15.95 (*0-395-62426-6*) HM.
Hunt, Roderick. Ghosts, Witches & Things Like That. 144p. 1990. pap. 10.95 (*0-19-278130-8*) OUP.
Singer, Marcia. Crystal Kids: PLAYBook. Rendal, Camille, illus. LC 89-90988. 64p. (Orig.). 1989. pap. 9.95 (*0-9622543-0-4*) PLAY House.
Sutphen, Dick. The Nasty Dragon Who Became a Nice Puppy: Reincarnation for Young People. (Illus.). 32p. (Orig.). (ps-3). 1992. pap. 10.98 incl. tape (*0-87554-528-9*) Valley Sun.
Wilcox, Tamara. Mysterious Detectives: Psychics. LC 77-14315. (Illus.). 48p. (gr. 4 up). 1983. PLB 20.70 (*0-8172-1061-X*) Raintree Steck-V.

OCCULT SCIENCES–FICTION

Bellairs, John. The Figure in the Shadows. Mayer, Mercer, illus. LC 74-2885. 168p. (gr. 4-7). 1975. Dial Bks Young.
Bennett, Geraldine M. Katrina & Elishia Teach about the Aura. Rider, Tracy & Sheil, Audrey, eds. Poe, Ty, illus. LC 92-83809. 32p. (gr. 3 up). 1994. pap. 7.98 (*0-9630718-9-0*) New Dawn NY.
—Katrina Tells Jamie about John's Invisible Lesson. rev. ed. Rider, Tracy & Sheil, Audrey, eds. Poe, Ti, illus. LC 92-83745. 32p. (gr. 3 up). 1994. pap. 7.98 (*0-9630718-8-2*) New Dawn NY.
—Rebecca Tells of a Miracle of Life: A Special Belief in the Healing Power of Love. Rider, Tracy & Sheil, Audrey, eds. Poe, Ty, illus. LC 92-83744. 42p. (Orig.). (gr. 3-8). 1994. pap. 7.98 (*0-9630718-4-X*) New Dawn NY.
Blair, Cynthia. The Curse. 1993. pap. 3.99 (*0-06-106158-1*, Harp PBks) HarpC.
Blair, Grandpa. Ziggy the Zombie from Zumbrota. 14p. (gr. 10 up). 1991. 5.75 (*0-930366-62-X*) Northcountry Pub.
Clifton, Lucille. The Lucky Stone. (gr. 1-4). 1992. 16.75 (*0-8446-6592-4*) Peter Smith.
DeFelice, Cynthia. The Strange Night Writing of Jessamine Colter. LC 88-4325. 56p. (gr. 5 up). 1988. SBE 13.95 (*0-02-726451-3*, Macmillan Child Bk) Macmillan Child Grp.
Duane, Diane E. High Wizardry. 272p. (gr. 5-9). 1992. pap. 3.50 (*0-440-40680-3*, YB) Dell.
Gifaldi, David. Yours Till Forever. LC 88-35725. 96p. (gr. 7 up). 1989. (Lipp Jr Bks); (Lipp Jr Bks) HarpC Child Bks.
Shute, Linda. Clever Tom & the Leprechaun. Shute, Linda, illus. LC 87-29671. 32p. (gr. k-3). 1988. 14.95 (*0-688-07488-X*); PLB 14.88 (*0-688-07489-8*) Lothrop.
Zalben, Jane B. Fortune Teller in Five B. (gr. 4-7). 1993. pap. 2.95 (*0-590-46041-2*) Scholastic Inc.

OCCUPATION, CHOICE OF

see Vocational Guidance

OCCUPATIONAL THERAPY–VOCATIONAL GUIDANCE

Brown, Margaret F. Careers in Occupational Therapy. Rosen, Ruth, ed. (gr. 7-12). 1989. PLB 14.95 (*0-8239-0981-6*) Rosen Group.
The Livelong Day: Working in the World. (Illus.). (gr. 8 up). 1992. PLB 16.95 (*0-8239-1361-9*); pap. 8.95 (*0-8239-1362-7*) Rosen Group.

OCCUPATIONS

see also Professions; Vocational Guidance; also names of countries, cities, etc. with the subdivision Occupations (e.g. U. S.–Occupations); also such headings as Law–Vocational Guidance

Barkin, Carol & James, Elizabeth. Jobs for Kids. Doty, Roy, illus. LC 89-45900. 128p. (gr. 5 up). 1991. pap. 6.95 (*0-688-09323-X*, Pub. by Beech Tree Bks) Morrow.
Brill, M. I Can Be a Lawyer. LC 87-13227. (Illus.). 32p. (gr. k-3). 1987. PLB 11.80 (*0-516-01911-2*); pap. 3.95 (*0-516-41911-0*) Childrens.
Career Connections Series, 6 vols. 288p. (gr. 6-9). 1993. Set. 84.75 (*0-8103-9384-0*, 102102, UXL) Gale.
Civardi, Anne. Things People Do. Cartwright, Stephen, illus. 38p. (ps-4). 1986. 10.95 (*0-86020-864-8*, Pub. by Usborne); PLB 12.96 (*0-88110-236-9*) EDC.
Downes, Paul, ed. Career Profile Guide. 186p. (gr. 7-10). 1992. pap. text ed. 29.95 (*1-55631-199-0*) Chron Guide.
Eubank, Mary G. & Hollingsworth, Mary. King's Workers. 1990. write for info. (*0-8499-0827-2*) Word Inc.
Farr, J. Michael & Amore, JoAnn. Exploring Careers: The World of Work & You. Reader, Spring D., photos by. (Illus.). 32p. (gr. 6-12). 1989. wkbk. 1.95 (*0-942784-28-6*, EXPAB) JIST Works.
Florian, Douglas. An Auto Mechanic. Florian, Douglas, illus. LC 93-28802. 24p. (ps up). 1994. pap. 4.95 (*0-688-13104-2*, Mulberry) Morrow.
—A Carpenter. LC 90-30752. (Illus.). 24p. (ps up). 1991. 13.95 (*0-688-09760-X*); PLB 13.88 (*0-688-09761-8*) Greenwillow.
—A Chef. LC 91-29545. (Illus.). 32p. (ps-3). 1992. 14.00 (*0-688-11108-4*); PLB 13.93 (*0-688-11109-2*) Greenwillow.
—A Fisher. LC 93-26515. 32p. 1994. 15.00 (*0-688-13129-8*); PLB 14.93 (*0-688-13130-1*) Greenwillow.
—A Painter. LC 92-29583. (Illus.). 32p. (ps up). 1993. 14. 00 (*0-688-11872-0*); PLB 13.93 (*0-688-11873-9*) Greenwillow.
Fry, Ron. Your First Resume: The Essential, Comprehensive Guide for Anyone Entering or Reentering the Job Market. 3rd ed. LC 92-13494. 160p. (gr. 9 up). 1992. pap. 8.95 (*1-56414-018-0*) Career Pr Inc.
Frydenborg, Kay. They Dreamed of Horses: Careers for Horse Lovers. Wood, Tanya, photos by. LC 93-33023. (Illus.). 128p. (gr. 4-6). 1994. 15.95 (*0-8027-8283-3*); PLB 16.85 (*0-8027-8284-1*) Walker & Co.
Funes, Marilyn & Lazarus, Alan. Popular Careers. Piltch, Benjamin, ed. Bartick, Robert, illus. 64p. (gr. 7 up). 1980. 3.95 (*0-934618-01-1*) Learning Well.
Gibbons, Gail. Say Woof! The Day of a Country Veterinarian. Gibbons, Gail, illus. LC 91-48270. 32p. (gr. k-3). 1992. RSBE 13.95 (*0-02-736781-9*, Macmillan Child Bk) Macmillan Child Grp.
Giblin, James C. Chimney Sweeps: Yesterday & Today. Tomes, Margot, illus. LC 81-43878. 64p. (gr. 4-7). 1987. pap. 5.95 (*0-06-446061-4*, Trophy) HarpC Child Bks.
Gilabert, Frank. Business Career Planning Series, 5 bks. (Orig.). (gr. 12). Date not set. Set. pap. 55.00 (*1-884194-05-2*); The Biz Careers Finance Guide: How to Improve Your Business Knowledge about Finance, 100p. pap. 14.95 (*1-884194-02-8*); The Biz Careers Accounting Guide: How to Improve Your Business Knowledge about Accounting, 100p. pap. 14. 95 (*1-884194-01-X*); The Biz Careers Planning Guide: How to Prepare for Your Business Career, 70p. pap. 9.95 (*1-884194-00-1*); The Business Careers Information Systems Guide: How to Improve Your Business Knowledge about Information Systems, 100p. pap. 14.95 (*1-884194-03-6*); The Biz Careers Marketing Guide: How to Improve Your Business Knowledge about Marketing, 100p. pap. 14.95 (*1-884194-04-4*) Biz Careers.
Greene, Carol. I Can Be a Salesperson. LC 89-15848. 32p. (gr. k-3). 1989. pap. 3.95 (*0-516-41959-5*) Childrens.
Hechler, Ellen. Simulated Real Life Experiences Using Classified Ads in the Classroom. (Illus.). 54p. (Orig.). (gr. 6-10). 1991. pap. 10.00 (*0-9638483-3-X*) Midmath.
Hefter, Richard. Bears at Work. Hefter, Richard, illus. LC 83-2192. 32p. (ps-1). 1983. 5.95 (*0-911787-00-3*) Optimum Res Inc.
—Jobs for Bears. Hefter, Richard, illus. LC 83-2197. 32p. (ps-1). 1983. 5.95 (*0-911787-02-X*) Optimum Res Inc.
Higginson, Mel. Scientists Who Study Fossils. LC 94-6995. 1994. write for info. (*0-86593-375-8*) Rourke Corp.
—Scientists Who Study Ocean Life. LC 94-6999. 1994. write for info. (*0-86593-371-5*) Rourke Corp.
—Scientists Who Study Plants. LC 94-6998. 1994. write for info. (*0-86593-373-1*) Rourke Corp.
—Scientists Who Study the Earth. LC 94-7000. (gr. 4 up). 1994. write for info. (*0-86593-372-3*) Rourke Corp.
—Scientists Who Study Wild Animals. LC 94-6997. 1994. write for info. (*0-86593-374-X*) Rourke Corp.
Hurwitz, Sue. Careers Inside the World of Entrepreneurs. LC 94-16192. 1994. 14.95 (*0-8239-1900-5*) Rosen Group.

Imershein, Betsy. The Work People Do, 3 bks. (Illus.). 1989. Set, 32p. ea. lib. bdg. 29.94 (*0-671-94097-X*, J Messner); Set, 32p. ea. pap. 14.85 (*0-671-94098-8*) S&S Trade.

Jill, Jodi. Childrens Money Making Jobs. 32p. 1993. pap. 6.95 (*1-883438-04-7*) J J Features.

Keran, Shirley. Underwater Specialists. LC 88-14890. (Illus.). 48p. (gr. 5-6). 1988. text ed. 11.95 RSBE (*0-89686-400-6*, Crestwood Hse) Macmillan Child Grp.

Letch, Rachael. Special People. LC 90-48944. (gr. 4 up). 1990. 7.95 (*0-85953-360-3*); pap. 3.95 (*0-85953-350-6*) Childs Play.

Lillegard, Dee. I Can Be a Beautician. LC 87-13835. (Illus.). 32p. (gr. k-3). 1987. pap. 3.95 (*0-516-41910-2*) Childrens.

McGee, William & Kabes, Todd. The Basic Guide to Resume Writing & Job Interviews. 75p. (Orig.). 1989. pap. 6.50 (*0-9622594-0-3*) Advantage Video.

Matthias, Catherine. Puedo Ser un Policia (I Can Be a Police Officer) LC 84-12106. (SPA., Illus.). 32p. (gr. k-3). 1987. pap. 3.95 (*0-516-51840-2*) Childrens.

Mendelsohn, A. Pocket Guide to Job Interviewing. rev. ed. Chavez, Joseph, ed. 45p. (gr. 8 up). 1981. text ed. 1.50 (*0-918443-00-8*, AJDBI101) Job Data.

Merriam, Eve. Daddies at Work. Fernandes, Eugenie, illus. (ps-2). 1989. pap. 5.95 (*0-671-64873-X*, S&S BFYR) S&S Trade.

—Mommies at Work. Fernandes, Eugenie, illus. (ps-2). 1989. pap. 5.95 (*0-671-64386-X*, S&S BFYR) S&S Trade.

Miller, Louise. Career Portraits. LC 93-49056. 1995. 13. 95 (*0-8442-4359-0*, VGM Career Bks) NTC Pub Grp.

Mills, Charles. My Talents for Jesus; When I Grow Up. LC 92-26393. 1993. 8.95 (*0-8163-1115-3*) Pacific Pr Pub Assn.

Moncure, Jane B. What Can We Play Today? Hohag, Linda, illus. LC 87-32565. (SPA & ENG.). 32p. (ps-2). 1987. PLB 14.95 (*0-89565-412-1*); PLB 14. 95s.p. (*0-685-55940-8*) Childs World.

—Word Bird's Hats. Gohman, Vera, illus. LC 81-18065. (ps-2). 1982. PLB 14.95 (*0-89565-221-8*) Childs World.

Parramore, Barbara & Hopke, Bill. Activities for the Children's Dictionary of Occupations. rev. ed. Jones, Scott, illus. 20p. (gr. 3-4). 1992. wkbk. 12.95 (*1-56191-191-7*) Meridian Educ.

—Activities for the Children's Dictionary of Occupations. rev. ed. Jones, Scott, illus. 20p. (gr. 5-6). 1992. wkbk. 12.95 (*1-56191-192-5*) Meridian Educ.

—The Children's Dictionary of Occupations. rev. ed. Jones, Scott, illus. 130p. (gr. 3-8). 1992. pap. text ed. 12.95 (*1-56191-190-9*) Meridian Educ.

Pickering, R. I Can Be an Archaeologist. LC 87-14683. (Illus.). 32p. (gr. k-3). 1987. PLB 11.80 (*0-516-01909-0*); pap. 3.95 (*0-516-41909-9*) Childrens.

Richardson, Peter & Richardson, Bob. Great Careers for People Interested in Math & Computers, 6 vols. LC 93-78079. (Illus.). 48p. (gr. 6-9). 1993. 16.95 (*0-8103-9385-9*, 102103, UXL) Gale.

Rigby, Julie. Career Portraits: Sports. LC 94-15315. 1994. 12.95 (*0-8442-4361-2*, VGM Career Bks) NTC Pub Grp.

Rockwell, Anne. When We Grow Up. Rockwell, Anne, illus. LC 80-21768. (ps-1). 1981. 10.95 (*0-525-42575-6*, Dutton) NAL-Dutton.

Russell, William. Pilots. LC 93-45009. 1994. write for info. (*1-57103-059-X*) Rourke Pr.

Scarry, Richard. Richard Scarry's What Do People Do All Day? (Illus.). (ps-3). 1968. 12.00 (*0-394-81823-7*) Random Bks Yng Read.

Sigel, Lois S. New Careers in Hospitals. rev. ed. (Illus.). (gr. 7-12). 1990. PLB 14.95 (*0-8239-1172-1*) Rosen Group.

Sipiera, Paul. I Can Be a Chemist. LC 92-5807. (Illus.). 32p. (gr. k-3). 1992. PLB 11.80 (*0-516-01965-1*) Childrens.

—I Can Be a Physicist. LC 90-20886. (Illus.). 32p. (gr. k-3). 1991. PLB 11.80 (*0-516-01964-3*); pap. 3.95 (*0-516-41964-1*) Childrens.

Stewart, David. Fathering & Career: Keeping a Healthy Balance. 2nd ed. LC 87-63156. 16p. (gr. 7 up). 1987. pap. 1.95 (*0-934426-16-3*) NAPSAC Reprods.

Stewart, Gail. Off-Shore Oil Rig Workers. LC 88-12006. (Illus.). 48p. (gr. 5-6). 1988. text ed. 11.95 RSBE (*0-89686-397-2*, Crestwood Hse) Macmillan Child Grp.

—Smokejumpers & Forest Firefighters. LC 88-12008. (Illus.). 48p. (gr. 5-6). 1988. text ed. 11.95 RSBE (*0-89686-398-0*, Crestwood Hse) Macmillan Child Grp.

—Stuntpeople. LC 88-14946. (Illus.). 48p. (gr. 5-6). 1988. text ed. 11.95 RSBE (*0-89686-396-4*, Crestwood Hse) Macmillan Child Grp.

Summerfield, C. J., ed. Career Discovery Encyclopedia, 6 vols. (Illus.). (gr. 3 up). 1993. 129.95 (*0-89434-144-8*) Ferguson.

What People Do. (Illus.). 80p. (gr. k-6). 1986. per set 199.00 (*0-8172-2588-9*); 14.95 ea. Raintree Steck-V.

White, Dana. High-Rise Workers. LC 88-11991. (Illus.). 48p. (gr. 5-6). 1988. text ed. 11.95 RSBE (*0-89686-402-2*, Crestwood Hse) Macmillan Child Grp.

Winefordner, David. Activities for Individualized Career Exploration & Planning. rev. ed. 48p. (gr. 9-12). 1993. wkbk. pkg. of 10 24.95 (*1-56191-196-8*) Meridian Educ.

Zink, Richard M. California Jobs - The New Employment Manual. 2nd ed. (Illus.). 50p. (Orig.). (gr. 9 up). 1993. pap. text ed. 14.95x (*0-939469-30-8*) Zinks Career Guide.

—Computer Jobs Worldwide: The Employment Manual. (Illus.). 50p. (Orig.). (gr. 9 up). 1993. pap. text ed. 14. 95x (*0-939469-32-4*) Zinks Career Guide.

—Nevada Jobs - The New Employment Manual. (Illus.). 50p. (Orig.). (gr. 9 up). 1993. pap. 14.95x (*0-939469-31-6*) Zinks Career Guide.

—Resumes for Overseas & Stateside Jobs. (Illus.). 50p. (gr. 9 up). 1993. pap. 14.95x (*0-939469-29-4*) Zinks Career Guide.

OCCUPATIONS–FICTION

Bourque, Nina. The Best Trade of All. Urbanovic, Jackie, illus. LC 83-7352. 32p. (gr. 3-6). 1983. 14.65 (*0-940742-33-0*) Raintree Steck-V.

Butterworth, Nick. Busy People. Butterworth, Nick, illus. LC 91-58719. 32p. (ps). 1992. 9.95 (*1-56402-056-8*) Candlewick Pr.

—Busy People. LC 91-58719. (Illus.). 32p. (ps). 1994. pap. 3.99 (*1-56402-365-6*) Candlewick Pr.

Cartwright, Pauline. Jimmy Parker's New Job. Hunnam, Lucinda, illus. LC 93-20029. 1994. pap. write for info. (*0-383-03679-8*) SRA Schl Grp.

Conford, Ellen. A Job for Jenny Archer. (gr. 2-4). 1990. pap. 2.95 (*0-316-15349-4*) Little.

Drew, David. Collections. Davy, Mary, illus. LC 93-16141. 1994. write for info. (*0-383-03683-6*) SRA Schl Grp.

Edwards, Michelle. Chicken Man. (Illus.). (gr. k-3). 1991. 13.95 (*0-688-09708-1*); PLB 13.88 (*0-688-09709-X*) Lothrop.

—Chicken Man. Edwards, Michelle, illus. LC 93-11728. 32p. (ps up). 1994. pap. 4.95 (*0-688-13106-9*, Mulberry) Morrow.

Fitzpatrick, Blanche. Getting A Living, Getting A Life: After the Senior Prom. LC 94-66196. 110p. (Orig.). 1994. pap. 9.95 (*0-9627397-2-3*) Pemberton Pubs.

Grossman, Patricia. The Night Ones. D'Andrade, Diane, ed. Dabcovich, Lydia, illus. 32p. (ps-3). 1991. 13.95 (*0-15-257438-7*) HarBrace.

Hill, Eric. Who Does What? 20p. (ps-k). 1982. 4.95 (*0-8431-0909-2*) Price Stern.

Isaacs, Gwynne L. While You Are Asleep. Hepworth, Cathi, illus. 32p. (gr. 4-8). 1991. 12.95 (*0-8027-6985-3*); lib. bdg. 13.85 (*0-8027-6986-1*) Walker & Co.

Joslin, Sesyle. What Do You Do, Dear? Sendak, Maurice, illus. LC 84-43139. 48p. 1958. 13.95 (*0-201-09387-1*); PLB 13.89 (*0-06-023075-4*) HarpC Child Bks.

Kubler, Annie. The Street Cleaner. LC 90-25105. 1991. 3.95 (*0-85953-530-4*) Childs Play.

—When I Grow Up. LC 91-27125. 1992. 5.95 (*0-85953-505-3*) Childs Play.

Miller, Margaret. Guess Who? LC 93-26704. (Illus.). 40p. 1994. 15.00 (*0-688-12783-5*); PLB 14.93 (*0-688-12784-3*) Greenwillow.

Park, Barbara. Junie B. Jones & Her Big Fat Mouth. Brunkus, Denise, illus. LC 92-50957. 80p. (Orig.). (gr. 1-4). 1993. PLB 9.99 (*0-679-94407-9*); pap. 2.99 (*0-679-84407-4*) Random Bks Yng Read.

Rodriquez, Doris. Diego Wants to Be - Diego Quiere Ser. (Illus.). 32p. (ps-2). 1994. PLB 15.00 (*0-917846-35-4*, 95611) Highsmith Pr.

Scariano, Margaret & Cunningham, Marilyn. Nine to Five Series. (Illus.). (gr. 3-9). 1985. Set. pap. 15.00 (*0-87879-502-2*) High Noon Bks.

Scarry, Richard. Richard Scarry's Busiest People Ever. LC 76-8123. (Illus.). (ps-2). 1976. PLB 11.00 (*0-394-83293-0*) Random Bks Yng Read.

—Richard Scarry's Postman Pig & His Busy Neighbors. LC 77-91646. (Illus.). (ps-2). 1978. lib. bdg. 5.99 (*0-394-93898-4*) Random Bks Yng Read.

Spinelli, Eileen. Boy, Can He Dance! Yalowitz, Paul, illus. LC 92-12929. 32p. (ps-2). 1993. RSBE 14.95 (*0-02-786350-6*, Four Winds) Macmillan Child Grp.

Trella, Phyllis. A Peek at Occupations. Trella, Phyllis, illus. LC 82-73692. 48p. (gr. 2-6). write for info. (*0-914201-03-4*) Cheeruppet.

Wittmann, Patricia. Go Ask Giorgio! Hillenbrand, Will, illus. LC 91-2808. 32p. (gr. k-4). 1992. RSBE 14.95 (*0-02-793221-4*, Macmillan Child Bk) Macmillan Child Grp.

OCEAN

see also Icebergs; Oceanography; Seashore; Storms; Tides

Adams, Pam. The Ocean. 32p. (ps). 1984. 8.95 (*0-85953-193-7*, Child's Play England) Childs Play.

Adler, David. Our Amazing Ocean. Veno, Joseph, illus. LC 82-17373. 32p. (gr. 3-6). 1983. PLB 10.59 (*0-89375-882-5*); pap. text ed. 2.95 (*0-89375-883-3*) Troll Assocs.

Amery. At the Seaside. Cartwright, illus. 20p. (ps). 1985. 3.95 (*0-7460-1540-2*, Pub. by Usborne) EDC.

Arvetis, Chris & Palmer, Carole. Oceans & Seas. Buckley, James, illus. LC 93-33674. 1994. write for info. (*0-528-83675-7*) Rand McNally.

Bendick. Explore an Ocean. 1994. pap. 4.95 (*0-8050-3273-8*) H Holt & Co.

Bendick, Jeanne. Exploring an Ocean Tide Pool. Telander, Todd, illus. LC 91-34572. 64p. (gr. 2-4). 1992. 14.95 (*0-8050-2043-8*, Bks Young Read) H Holt & Co.

Bramwell, Martyn. Oceans. (Illus.). 32p. (gr. 5-8). 1994. PLB write for info. Watts.

—The Oceans. rev. ed. LC 93-40312. 1994. write for info. (*0-531-14304-X*) Watts.

Bright, Michael. The Dying Sea. LC 88-50523. (Illus.). 32p. (gr. 5-8). 1992. PLB 12.40 (*0-531-17385-2*, Gloucester Pr) Watts.

Butterfield, Moira. Undersea World. Johnson, Paul, illus. 16p. (gr. 1-5). 1992. pap. 6.95 (*0-8249-8589-3*, Ideals Child) Hambleton-Hill.

Carter, Katharine J. Oceans. LC 81-17093. (Illus.). 48p. (gr. k-4). 1982. PLB 12.85 (*0-516-01639-3*); pap. 4.95 (*0-516-41639-1*) Childrens.

Collins, Elizabeth. The Living Ocean. Train, Russell E., intro. by. LC 93-26205. 1994. write for info. (*0-7910-1586-6*); pap. write for info. (*0-7910-1611-0*) Chelsea Hse.

De Beauregard, Diane C. The Blue Planet: Seas & Oceans. Bogard, Vicki, tr. from FRE. Lepagnol, Cyril, illus. LC 89-8912. 38p. (gr. k-5). 1989. 5.95 (*0-944589-22-7*, 022) Young Discovery Lib.

Frahm, Randy. Ocean. LC 93-46807. 40p. 1994. 18.95 (*0-88682-705-1*) Creative Ed.

Frame, Jeron A. Discovering Oceans, Lakes, Ponds & Puddles. (gr. 4-7). 1994. pap. 8.99 (*0-7459-2621-5*) Lion USA.

Ganeri, Anita. The Oceans Atlas. Corbella, Luciano, illus. LC 93-28724. (gr. k up). 1994. 19.95 (*1-56458-475-5*) Dorling Kindersley.

Gibbs, B. Ocean Facts. (Illus.). 48p. (gr. 3-7). 1991. lib. bdg. 12.96 (*0-88110-531-7*, Usborne); pap. 5.95 (*0-7460-0621-7*, Usborne) EDC.

Heinrichs, Susan. The Atlantic Ocean. LC 86-9578. (Illus.). 48p. (gr. k-4). 1986. PLB 12.85 (*0-516-01289-4*) Childrens.

—The Indian Ocean. LC 86-9579. (Illus.). 48p. (gr. k-4). 1986. PLB 12.85 (*0-516-01293-2*) Childrens.

Heller, Ruth. How to Hide an Octopus: And Other Sea Creatures. Heller, Ruth, illus. 32p. (ps-3). 1992. pap. 2.25 (*0-448-40478-8*, Platt & Munk Pubs) Putnam Pub Group.

Hirschi, E. & Bauer, Erwin A. Save Our Oceans & Coasts. (gr. 4 up). 1993. pap. 9.95 (*0-385-31126-5*) Dell.

Hirschi, Ron. Save Our Oceans & Coasts. Bauer, Erwin A. & Bauer, Peggy, photos by. LC 92-37384. (gr. 5 up). 1993. write for info. (*0-553-09520-X*) Bantam.

Hoff, Mary. Oceans: Our Endangered Planet. (gr. 4-7). 1993. pap. 8.95 (*0-8225-9628-8*) Lerner Pubns.

Hopkins, Lee B. The Sea Is Calling Me. Gaffney-Kessell, Walter, illus. LC 85-16412. 32p. (gr. 3-7). 1986. 14.95 (*0-15-271155-4*, HB Juv Bks) HarBrace.

Illustrated World Oceans. 1991. pap. 12.95 (*0-671-74128-4*, S&S BFYR) S&S Trade.

In the Sea. 32p. (ps-3). 1994. 4.95 (*1-56458-733-9*) Dorling Kindersley.

Jablonsky, Alice. Descubre La Vida En el Oceano. University of Mexico City Staff, tr. from SPA. O'Neill, Pablo M. & Robare, Lorie, illus. 48p. (gr. 3-8). 1993. PLB 16.95 (*1-56674-050-9*, HTS Bks) Forest Hse.

—Discover Ocean Life. (Illus.). 48p. (gr. 3-6). 1992. PLB 14.95 (*1-878363-69-7*, HTS Bks) Forest Hse.

Lambert, David. Seas & Oceans. Salariya, David, created by. Scrace, Carolyn & Bergin, Mark, illus. LC 93-6352. 1994. PLB 19.97 (*0-8114-9245-1*) Raintree Steck-V.

Lambert, David & McConnell, Anita. Seas & Oceans. LC 84-1654. (Illus.). 64p. (gr. 7 up). 1985. 15.95x (*0-8160-1064-1*) Facts on File.

Little People Big Book about the Sea. 64p. (ps-1). 1989. write for info. (*0-8094-7475-1*); PLB write for info. (*0-8094-7476-X*) Time-Life.

Matthews, Rupert. Record Breakers of the Sea. LC 89-35503. (Illus.). 32p. (gr. 2-6). 1990. PLB 9.59 (*0-8167-1925-X*); pap. text ed. 2.50 (*0-8167-1926-8*) Troll Assocs.

Mattson, Robert A. The Living Ocean. LC 89-25791. (Illus.). 64p. (gr. 6 up). 1991. lib. bdg. 15.95 (*0-89490-277-6*) Enslow Pubs.

Mitgutsch, Ali. From Sea to Salt. Mitgutsch, Ali, illus. LC 84-17466. 24p. (ps-3). 1985. PLB 10.95 (*0-87614-232-3*) Carolrhoda Bks.

Moche. What's Down There? Questions & Answers about the Oceans. 1993. pap. 2.50 (*0-590-42855-1*) Scholastic Inc.

Morgan, Nina. The Sea. LC 94-9084. (Illus.). 128p. (gr. k-4). 1994. pap. 5.95 (*1-85697-526-6*, Kingfisher LKC) LKC.

Myerson, A. Lee. Seawater: A Delicate Balance. LC 88-10961. (Illus.). 64p. (gr. 6 up). 1988. lib. bdg. 15.95 (*0-89490-157-5*) Enslow Pubs.

National Wildlife Federation Staff. Diving into Oceans. (gr. k-8). 1991. pap. 7.95 (*0-945051-36-0*, 75042) Natl Wildlife.

Neal, Philip. The Oceans. (Illus.). 64p. (gr. 6-9). 1993. 24. 95 (*0-7134-6712-6*, Pub. by Batsford UK) Trafalgar.

Oldershaw, Callie. Oceans. Burns, Robert, illus. LC 91-45079. 32p. (gr. 4-6). 1993. PLB 11.59 (*0-8167-2753-8*); pap. text ed. 3.95 (*0-8167-2754-6*) Troll Assocs.

Palmer, Joy. Oceans. LC 92-12409. (Illus.). 32p. (gr. 2-3). 1992. PLB 18.99 (*0-8114-3401-X*) Raintree Steck-V.

Pearce, Q. L. Ocean. (Illus.). 48p. 1991. wkbk. 2.95 (*0-8431-2912-3*) Price Stern.

Petty, Kate. Under the Sea. Wood, Jakki, illus. 32p. (gr. 2-4). 1993. pap. 5.95 (*0-8120-1759-5*) Barron.

Pifer, Joanne. EarthWise: Earth's Oceans. (Illus.). 48p. (gr. 5-8). 1992. pap. text ed. 7.95 (*0-9633019-2-6*) WP Pr.

Pomeroy, Johanna P. Content Area Reading Skills Oceans: Main Idea. (Illus.). (gr. 4). 1987. pap. text ed. 3.25 (*0-89525-857-9*) Ed Activities.

Rice, Tony. Ocean World. (Illus.). 64p. (gr. 4-6). 1991. 15.40 (*1-56294-027-9*) Millbrook Pr.

Robinson, W. Wright. Incredible Facts about the Ocean, Vol. 3: How We Use It, How We Abuse It. (Illus.). 128p. (gr. 4 up). 1990. text ed. 13.95 RSBE (*0-87518-435-9*, Dillon) Macmillan Child Grp.

Rodgers, Mary M. & Hoff, Mary. Our Endangered Planet: Oceans. (Illus.). 72p. (gr. 4-6). 1991. PLB 21.50 (*0-8225-2505-4*) Lerner Pubns.

Sabin, Francene. Oceans. Goldsborough, June, illus. LC 84-8590. 32p. (gr. 3-6). 1985. PLB 9.49 (*0-8167-0216-0*); pap. text ed. 2.95 (*0-8167-0217-9*) Troll Assocs.

Sabin, Louis. Wonders of the Sea. Dodson, Bert, illus. LC 81-3334. 32p. (gr. 2-4). 1982. PLB 11.59 (*0-89375-578-8*); pap. text ed. 2.95 (*0-89375-579-6*) Troll Assocs.

The Sea. (Illus.). 80p. (gr. k-6). 1986. PLB 14.95 (*0-8172-2586-2*) Raintree Steck-V.

Sea Life. (Illus.). 96p. (ps-4). 1994. write for info. (*1-56458-795-9*) Dorling Kindersley.

Seymour, Peter. What's in the Deep Blue Sea? Carter, David A., illus. LC 90-80884. 18p. (ps-2). 1990. 10.95 (*0-8050-1449-7*, Bks Young Read) H Holt & Co.

Simon, Seymour. Oceans. LC 89-28452. (Illus.). 32p. (gr. k up). 1990. 13.95 (*0-688-09453-8*); PLB 13.88 (*0-688-09454-6*, Morrow Jr Bks) Morrow Jr Bks.

Stover, Marjorie F. When the Dolls Woke. 1993. pap. 2.95 (*0-590-44624-X*) Scholastic Inc.

Taylor, Barbara. Rivers & Oceans: Geography Facts & Experiments. LC 92-28421. (Illus.). 32p. (gr. 1-4). 1993. 10.95 (*1-85697-876-1*, Kingfisher LKC); pap. 5.95 (*1-85697-939-3*) LKC.

Taylor, Barbara, et al. Sea Life. (Illus.). 80p. (gr. 1-7). 1994. write for info. (*1-56458-775-4*) Dorling Kindersley.

Tesar, Jenny. Threatened Oceans. (Illus.). 128p. (gr. 7-12). 1992. lib. bdg. 18.95x (*0-8160-2494-4*) Facts on File.

Thompson, Brenda & Overbeck, Cynthia. Under the Sea. Beisner, Monica, illus. LC 76-22470. 24p. (gr. k-3). 1977. PLB 7.95 (*0-8225-1363-3*) Lerner Pubns.

Twist, Clint. Seas & Oceans. LC 91-18086. (Illus.). 48p. (gr. 4-6). 1991. text ed. 13.95 RSBE (*0-87518-491-X*, Dillon) Macmillan Child Grp.

Tyler. The Seas. (gr. 3-6). 1976. pap. 6.95 (*0-86020-064-7*, Usborne-Hayes) EDC.

Wells, Susan. Explore the World of Mighty Oceans. Quigley, Sebastian, illus. 48p. (gr. 3-7). 1992. write for info. (*0-307-15609-5*, 15609, Golden Pr) Western Pub.

Williams, Brian. The Sea. LC 91-10570. (Illus.). 48p. (gr. 5-8). 1991. PLB 13.90 (*0-531-19146-X*, Warwick) Watts.

—The Sea. LC 92-53090. (Illus.). 48p. (Orig.). (gr. 3-8). 1992. pap. 5.95 (*1-85697-815-X*, Kingfisher LKC) LKC.

Williams, Lawrence. Oceans. LC 89-17341. (Illus.). 48p. (gr. 4-8). 1990. PLB 12.95 (*1-85435-172-9*) Marshall Cavendish.

Wood, Jenny. Under the Sea. Livingstone, Malcolm, illus. LC 91-7484. 32p. (gr. k-3). 1991. pap. 5.95 (*0-689-71488-2*, Aladdin) Macmillan Child Grp.

Yardley, Thompson. Make a Splash! Care about the Ocean. LC 91-22963. (Illus.). 40p. (gr. 2-6). 1992. PLB 13.40 (*1-56294-147-X*) Millbrook Pr.

OCEAN–ECONOMIC ASPECTS

see Marine Resources

OCEAN–FICTION

Bozanich, Tony L. Captain Flounder, His Sole Brothers & Friends. Isaksen, Lisa A., ed. Isaksen, Patricia, illus. 16p. (ps-4). 1984. pap. 4.95 (*0-930655-00-1*) Antarctic Pr.

Bush, Timothy. Three at Sea. LC 93-3677. (Illus.). 32p. (ps-2). 1994. 14.00 (*0-517-59299-1*) Crown Bks Yng Read.

Champlin, Dale, illus. Down by the Bay Big Book. (ps-2). 1988. pap. text ed. 14.00 (*0-922053-02-2*) N Edge Res.

Cosgrove, Stephen. Serendipity. James, Robin, illus. LC 94-25575. 1995. write for info. (*0-8431-3819-X*) Price Stern.

Greene, Jacqueline D. Out of Many Waters. 208p. (Orig.). (gr. 5 up). 1993. pap. 8.95 (*0-8027-7401-6*) Walker & Co.

Guiberson, Brenda. Into the Sea. 1994. 15.95 (*0-8050-2263-5*) H Holt & Co.

Huddy, Delia. Puffin at Sea. Heap, Sue, illus. 32p. (ps-1). 1993. 13.95 (*1-85681-161-1*, Pub. by J MacRae UK) Trafalgar.

Jordan, Polly, illus. In the Ocean. 24p. (ps-2). 1993. pap. text ed. 2.95 (*1-56293-319-1*) McClanahan Bk.

Kalan, Robert. Blue Sea. Crews, Donald, illus. LC 78-18396. 24p. (ps up). 1992. pap. 3.95 (*0-688-11509-8*, Mulberry) Morrow.

Levinson, Riki. Our Home Is the Sea. Luzak, Dennis, illus. LC 87-36419. 32p. (gr. k-3). 1988. pap. 13.95 (*0-525-44406-8*, DCB) Dutton Child Bks.

—Our Home Is the Sea. Luzak, Dennis, illus. 32p. (gr. k-3). 1992. pap. 4.99 (*0-14-054552-2*, Puff Unicorn) Puffin Bks.

Page, P. K. A Flask of Sea Water. Gal, Laszlo, illus. 34p. (gr. 2 up). 1989. bds. 17.00 laminated (*0-19-540704-0*) OUP.

Patkau, Karen. In the Sea. Patkau, Karen, illus. 24p. (ps). 1990. 15.95 (*1-55037-067-7*, Pub. by Annick CN); pap. 5.95 (*1-55037-066-9*, Pub. by Annick CN) Firefly Bks Ltd.

Patrick, Denise L. Disney's The Little Mermaid: Ariel's Secret. DiCicco, Sue, illus. 14p. (ps-k). 1992. bds. write for info. (*0-307-12393-6*, 12393, Golden Pr) Western Pub.

Pechter, Alese. What's in the Deep: An Underwater Adventure for Children. rev. ed. 1991. 14.95 (*0-87491-983-5*) Acropolis.

Peretti, Frank E. Trapped at the Bottom of the Sea. (gr. 4-7). 1990. pap. 4.99 (*0-89107-594-1*) Crossway Bks.

Pratt, Kristin J. A Swim Through the Sea. Pratt, Kristin J., illus. 44p. (Orig.). (ps-5). 1994. 14.95 (*1-883220-03-3*); pap. 6.95 (*1-883220-04-1*) Dawn CA.

Sadler, Marilyn. Alistair Underwater. LC 89-3658. (ps-3). 1992. pap. 5.95 (*0-671-79246-6*, S&S BFYR) S&S Trade.

Salisbury, Graham. Blue Skin of the Sea. 1994. pap. 3.99 (*0-440-21905-1*) Dell.

Sargent, Ruth. The Tunnel Beneath the Sea. Weinberger, Jane, ed. Gorski, Paul & Devito, Pam, illus. 120p. (gr. 3-6). 1993. pap. 9.95 (*0-932433-11-1*) Windswept Hse.

Tomkins, Jasper. The Hole in the Ocean. (Illus.). 60p. 1991. pap. 7.95 (*0-671-74974-9*, Green Tiger) S&S Trade.

Ziefert, Harriet. Under the Water. Mandel, Suzy, illus. (gr. k-3). 1993. pap. 3.25 (*0-14-036535-4*, Puffin) Puffin Bks.

OCEAN BOTTOM

Cole, Joanna. The Magic School Bus on the Ocean Floor. (Illus.). (ps up). 1992. 14.95 (*0-590-41430-5*, 003, Scholastic Hardcover) Scholastic Inc.

OCEAN CABLES

see Cables, Submarine

OCEAN LIFE

see Marine Biology

OCEAN ROUTES

see Trade Routes

OCEAN TRAVEL–FICTION

Demarest, Chris. Kitman & Willy at Sea. LC 90-46837. (Illus.). 32p. (ps-1). 1993. pap. 7.95 (*0-671-79849-9*, S&S BYR) S&S Trade.

Quinlan, Patricia. Emma's Sea Journey. Marton, Jirina, illus. 24p. (ps-3). 1991. PLB 15.95 (*1-55037-179-7*, Pub. by Annick CN); pap. 5.95 (*1-55037-177-0*, Pub. by Annick CN) Firefly Bks Ltd.

Stevenson, James. The Stowaway. LC 89-25861. (Illus.). 32p. (ps up). 1990. 12.95 (*0-688-08619-5*); PLB 12.88 (*0-688-08620-9*) Greenwillow.

OCEAN WAVES

Lampton, Christopher. Tidal Wave. LC 91-21518. (Illus.). 64p. (gr. 4-6). 1992. PLB 13.90 (*1-56294-124-0*) Millbrook Pr.

—Tidal Wave: A Disaster Book. (gr. 4-7). 1992. pap. 5.95 (*0-395-62464-9*) HM.

Souza, D. M. Powerful Waves. (ps-3). 1992. 17.50 (*0-87614-661-2*) Carolrhoda Bks.

Walker, Jane. Tidal Waves & Flooding. LC 91-31099. (Illus.). 32p. (gr. 5-9). 1992. PLB 12.40 (*0-531-17361-5*, Gloucester Pr) Watts.

OCEANIA

see Islands of the Pacific

OCEANOGRAPHY

see also Marine Biology; Marine Resources; Navigation; Ocean Waves; Submarine Geology

Asimov, Isaac. How Did We Find Out about Life in the Deep Sea? Wool, David, illus. (gr. 4-7). 1981. lib. bdg. 10.85 (*0-8027-6428-2*) Walker & Co.

Boyer, Robert E. Oceanography. 2nd ed. LC 74-1649. (Illus.). 48p. (gr. 7-12). 1987. pap. 7.50 (*0-8331-6611-5*, 6611) Hubbard Sci.

Center for Environmental Education Staff. The Ocean: Consider the Connections. Maraniss, Linda & Bierce, Rose, eds. Perry, Jill, illus. Asimov, Isaac, frwd. by. (Illus.). 104p. (Orig.). (gr. 2-6). 1985. pap. 8.95 wkbk. (*0-9615294-0-7*) Ctr Env Educ.

Conway, Lorraine. Oceanography. 64p. (gr. 5 up). 1982. 7.95 (*0-86653-066-5*, GA401) Good Apple.

Embry, Lynn. Scientific Encounters of the Mysterious Sea. McClure, Nancee, illus. 64p. (gr. 4-7). 1987. pap. 8.95 (*0-86653-407-5*, GA1013) Good Apple.

Fine, John C. Oceans in Peril. Fine, John C., illus. LC 86-26546. 128p. (gr. 5 up). 1987. SBE 15.95 (*0-689-31328-4*, Atheneum Child Bk) Macmillan Child Grp.

Fitzpatrick, Julie. On the Water. (Illus.). 30p. (gr. 3-5). 1991. 13.95 (*0-237-60210-5*, Pub. by Evans Bros Ltd) Trafalgar.

Fodor, R. V. The Strange World of Deep-Sea Vents. LC 89-71442. (Illus.). 64p. (gr. 6 up). 1991. lib. bdg. 15.95 (*0-89490-249-0*) Enslow Pubs.

Franks, Sharon & Cohen, Judith. Tu Puedos Sor Una Oceanografa. Yanez, Juan, tr. Katz, David, illus. (SPA.). 40p. (gr. 3-6). 1994. pap. 6.00 (*1-880599-15-5*) Cascade Pass.

—You Can Be a Woman Oceanographer. Katz, David, illus. 40p. (gr. 3-6). 1994. pap. 6.00 (*1-880599-14-7*) Cascade Pass.

Kraske, Robert. The Voyager's Stone: The Adventures of a Message-Carrying Bottle Adrift on the Ocean Sea. Floca, Brian, illus. LC 94-21049. (gr. 1-8). 1995. write for info. (*0-531-06890-0*); lib. bdg. write for info. (*0-531-08740-9*) Orchard Bks Watts.

Life in the Water. 88p. (ps-3). 1989. 15.93 (*0-8094-4853-X*); lib. bdg. 21.27 (*0-8094-4854-8*) Time-Life.

Lye, Keith. The Ocean Floor. LC 90-549. (Illus.). 32p. (gr. 4-7). 1991. PLB 12.40 (*0-531-18369-6*, Pub. by Bookwright Pr) Watts.

McGovern, Ann. Desert Beneath the Sea. (gr. 4-7). 1991. 13.95 (*0-590-42638-9*, Scholastic Hardcover) Scholastic Inc.

Mariner, Tom. Oceans. LC 89-9823. (Illus.). 32p. (gr. 3-8). 1990. PLB 9.95 (*1-85435-190-7*) Marshall Cavendish.

Markle, Sandra. Pioneering Ocean Depths. LC 93-33555. 1995. 15.95 (*0-689-31823-5*, Antheneum) Macmillan.

Morris, R. Ocean Life. Jackson, Ian, et al, illus. 32p. (gr. 3-6). 1983. (Usborne-Haynes); PLB 13.96 (*0-88110-149-4*, Usborne-Haynes); pap. 5.95 (*0-86020-753-6*, Usborne-Haynes) EDC.

Oceanography. (Illus.). 72p. (gr. 6-12). 1983. pap. 1.85 (*0-8395-3306-3*, 33306) BSA.

Pearce, Q. L. Tidal Waves & Other Ocean Wonders. Steltenpohl, Jane, ed. Fraser, Mary A., illus. 64p. (gr. 4-6). 1989. lib. bdg. 12.98 (*0-671-68532-5*, J Messner); pap. 5.95 (*0-671-68647-X*) S&S Trade.

Robinson, W. Wright. Incredible Facts about the Ocean: The Land Below, the Life Within, Vol. 2. LC 85-25430. (Illus.). 120p. (gr. 4 up). 1987. text ed. 13.95 RSBE (*0-87518-358-1*, Dillon) Macmillan Child Grp.

Sibbald, Jean. Strange Eating Habits of Sea Creatures. LC 85-11621. (Illus.). 112p. (gr. 4 up). 1987. text ed. 13.95 RSBE (*0-87518-349-2*, Dillon) Macmillan Child Grp.

Simon, Seymour. How to Be an Ocean Scientist in Your Own Home. Carter, David A., illus. LC 87-45988. 144p. (gr. 5-9). 1988. (Lipp Jr Bks); PLB 13.89 (*0-397-32292-5*, Lipp Jr Bks) HarpC Child Bks.

Waters, John F. Deep-Sea Vents: Living Worlds Without Sun. LC 92-41111. (Illus.). 48p. (gr. 5 up). 1994. 14.99 (*0-525-65145-4*, Cobblehill Bks) Dutton Child Bks.

Wells, Susan. The Illustrated World of Oceans. LC 90-27361. (Illus.). 64p. (gr. 3-7). 1993. pap. 7.95 (*0-671-77027-6*, S&S BFYR) S&S Trade.

OCEANOGRAPHY–BIOGRAPHY

Archbold, Rick. Deep Sea Explorer: The Story of Robert Ballard, Discoverer of the Titanic. LC 93-1983. 160p. (gr. 3-7). 1994. 13.95 (*0-590-47232-1*) Scholastic Inc.

OCEANOGRAPHY–FICTION

Olsen, E. A. Mystery at Salvage Rock. LC 68-16401. (Illus.). 48p. (gr. 3 up). 1970. PLB 10.95 (*0-87783-027-4*); pap. 3.94 deluxe ed. (*0-87783-101-7*); cassette 10.60x (*0-87783-195-5*) Oddo.

Reese, Bob. Coral Reef. LC 82-23610. (Illus.). 24p. (ps-2). 1983. pap. 2.95 (*0-516-42312-6*) Childrens.

Russomanno, Diane. Beneath the Deep Blue Sea. 32p. 1991. pap. text ed. write for info. (*1-880501-02-3*) Know Booster.

OCEANOGRAPHY–RESEARCH

see also Skin Diving; Underwater Exploration

OCEANOLOGY

see Oceanography

OCELOTS–FICTION

Bunny. Tigger: Story of a Mayan Ocelot. LC 66-12746. (Illus.). (gr. k-2). 1974. 6.95 (*0-87208-009-9*) Island Pr Pubs.

Wicker, Ireene. How the Ocelots Got Their Spots. Perrot, Catherine, illus. 32p. (gr. 2-4). 1976. 6.95 (*0-8184-0231-8*) Carol Pub Group.

OCTOPUS

Carrick, Carol. Octopus. Carrick, Donald, illus. 32p. (ps-3). 1991. pap. 5.70 (*0-395-59759-5*, Clarion Bks) HM.

Kite, Patricia. Down in the Sea: The Octopus. Levine, Abby, ed. LC 92-12284. (Illus.). 24p. 1993. 13.95g (*0-8075-1715-1*) A Whitman.

Lauber, Patricia. An Octopus Is Amazing. Keller, Holly, illus. LC 89-29300. 32p. (ps-1). 1990. 15.00 (*0-690-04801-7*, Crowell Jr Bks); PLB 14.89 (*0-690-04803-3*, Crowell Jr Bks) HarpC Child Bks.

Markert, Jenny. Octopuses. (gr. 2-6). 1992. PLB 15.95 (*0-89565-836-4*) Childs World.

Schultz, Ellen. I Can Read About the Octopus. LC 78-73715. (gr. 2-4). 1979. pap. 2.50 (*0-89375-213-4*) Troll Assocs.

OCTOPUS–FICTION

Barrett, John. Oscar, the Selfish Octopus. Servello, Joseph, illus. LC 78-18760. 32p. (ps-3). 1978. 16.95 (*0-87705-335-9*) Human Sci Pr.

Beak, Barbara. Octavia Warms Up. LC 91-31644. 1992. 3.95 (*0-85953-786-2*) Childs Play.

Brandenberg, Franz. Otto Is Different. Stevenson, James, illus. LC 84-13654. 24p. (gr. k-3). 1985. 11.75 (*0-688-04253-8*); PLB 11.88 (*0-688-04254-6*) Greenwillow.

Most, Bernard. My Very Own Octopus. D'Andrade, Diane, ed. (Illus.). 32p. (Orig.). (ps-3). 1991. pap. 4.95 (*0-15-256345-8*, Voyager Bks) HarBrace.

Terris, Susan. Octopus Pie. LC 83-11517. 166p. (gr. 5 up). 1983. 14.00 (*0-374-35571-1*) FS&G.

Tomkins, Jasper. My Cousin Has Eight Legs. Tomkins, Jasper, illus. 40p. (Orig.). (ps up). 1992. pap. 9.95 (*0-912365-68-4*) Sasquatch Bks.

Waber, Bernard. I Was All Thumbs. Waber, Bernard, illus. LC 75-11689. 48p. (gr. k-3). 1975. pap. 4.80 (*0-395-53969-2*) HM.

OFFICE WORK–TRAINING

see Business Education

OFFICIALS

see names of countries, cities, etc. and organizations with subdivision Officials and Employees, e.g. U. S.–Officials and Employees

OHIO

Brown, Dottie. Ohio. Lerner Geography Department Staff, ed. (Illus.). 72p. (gr. 3-6). 1992. PLB 17.50 (*0-8225-2725-1*) Lerner Pubns.

Burke, James L. & Davison, Kenneth E. Ohio's Heritage. rev. ed. LC 83-20091. (Illus.). 340p. (gr. 7). 1994. text ed. 19.50 (*0-87905-403-4*, Peregrine Smith) Gibbs Smith Pub.

Carole Marsh Ohio Books, 44 bks. 1994. PLB 1027.80 set (*0-7933-1310-4*); pap. 587.80 set (*0-7933-5192-8*) Gallopade Pub Group.

Carpenter, Allan. Ohio. new ed. LC 78-16162. (Illus.). 96p. (gr. 4 up). 1979. PLB 16.95 (*0-516-04135-5*) Childrens.

Cockley, David H. Over the Falls: A Child's Guide to Chagrin Falls. Ascherman, Herbert, Jr., photos by. (Illus.). 24p. (Orig.). (gr. 1-6). 1981. pap. 2.25 (*0-940900-00-9*) Aschley Pr.

Fradin, Dennis. Ohio: In Words & Pictures. Ulm, Robert, illus. LC 76-46941. 48p. (gr. 2-5). 1977. pap. 4.95 (*0-516-43935-9*) Childrens.

Fradin, Dennis B. Ohio. (Illus.). 64p. (gr. 3-5). 1993. PLB 16.45 (*0-516-03835-4*); pap. 5.95 (*0-516-43835-2*) Childrens.

Garrison, Webb. A Treasury of Ohio Tales. LC 93-29073. (Illus.). 192p. (gr. 9 up). 1993. 9.95 (*1-55853-249-8*) Rutledge Hill Pr.

Hall, Betty L. Ohio Survival. rev. ed. 160p. (gr. 10-12). 1986. pap. text ed. 5.84 (*0-936159-00-6*) Westwood Pr.

Howe, Robert T. Ohio: Our State. (Illus.). 408p. (gr. 7). 1992. text ed. 24.00 (*0-9631313-0-3*); tchr's. hdbk. 12.00 (*0-9631313-1-1*) Roblen Pub.

Kent, Deborah. Ohio. LC 88-38401. (Illus.). 144p. (gr. 4 up). 1989. PLB 20.55 (*0-516-00481-6*) Childrens.

—Ohio. 196p. 1993. text ed. 15.40 (*1-56956-164-8*) W A T Braille.

League of Women Voters of Cleveland Educational Fund, Inc. Staff. Ohio: From Territory to Statehood - From Ordinance to Constitution. 99p. (gr. 7-8). 1987. pap. text ed. 10.00 (*1-880746-04-2*) LOWV Cleve Educ.

—Ohio: From Wilderness to Territory - The Law of the Land. (gr. 3-6). 1987. pap. text ed. 10.00 (*1-880746-03-4*) LOWV Cleve Educ.

Lewis, Lois F. Carlin School, A History Book: The Story of a School in Ravenna, Ohio, U. S. A. Lewis, William B., illus. 28p. (Orig.). (gr. 5). 1989. pap. text ed. write for info. (*0-9620136-3-3*) L F Lewis.

—Tappan School, a History Book: The Story of a School in Ravenna, Ohio, U. S. A. Lewis, William B., illus. 28p. (Orig.). (gr. 5). 1989. pap. text ed. write for info. (*0-9620136-1-7*) L F Lewis.

Marsh, Carole. Avast, Ye Slobs! Ohio Pirate Trivia. (Illus.). 1994. PLB 24.95 (*0-7933-0908-5*); pap. 14.95 (*0-7933-0907-7*); computer disk 29.95 (*0-7933-0909-3*) Gallopade Pub Group.

—The Beast of the Ohio Bed & Breakfast. (Illus.). 1994. PLB 24.95 (*0-7933-0905-0*); pap. 14.95 (*0-7933-1848-3*); computer disk 29.95 (*0-7933-1849-1*) Gallopade Pub Group.

—Bow Wow! Ohio Dogs in History, Mystery, Legend, Lore, Humor & More! (Illus.). (gr. 3-12). 1994. PLB 24.95 (*0-7933-3572-8*); pap. 14.95 (*0-7933-3573-6*); computer disk 29.95 (*0-7933-3574-4*) Gallopade Pub Group.

—Chill Out: Scary Ohio Tales Based on Frightening Ohio Truths. (Illus.). 1994. lib. bdg. 24.95 (*0-7933-4759-9*); pap. 14.95 (*0-7933-4760-2*); disk 29.95 (*0-7933-4761-0*) Gallopade Pub Group.

—Christopher Columbus Comes to Ohio! Includes Reproducible Activities for Kids! (Illus.). (gr. 3-12). 1994. PLB 24.95 (*0-7933-3725-9*); pap. 14.95 (*0-7933-3726-7*); computer disk 29.95 (*0-7933-3727-5*) Gallopade Pub Group.

—The Hard-to-Believe-But-True! Book of Ohio History, Mystery, Trivia, Legend, Lore, Humor & More. (Illus.). 1994. PLB 24.95 (*0-7933-0904-2*); pap. 14.95 (*0-7933-0903-4*); computer disk 29.95 (*0-7933-0906-9*) Gallopade Pub Group.

—If My Ohio Mama Ran the World! (Illus.). 1994. lib. bdg. 24.95 (*0-7933-1850-5*); pap. 14.95 (*0-7933-1851-3*); computer disk 29.95 (*0-7933-1852-1*) Gallopade Pub Group.

—Jurassic Ark! Ohio Dinosaurs & Other Prehistoric Creatures. (gr. k-12). 1994. PLB 24.95 (*0-7933-7533-9*); pap. 14.95 (*0-7933-7534-7*); computer disk 29.95 (*0-7933-7535-5*) Gallopade Pub Group.

—Let's Quilt Ohio & Stuff It Topographically! (Illus.). 1994. PLB 24.95 (*0-685-45975-6*); pap. 14.95 (*1-55609-095-1*); computer disk 29.95 (*1-55609-985-1*) Gallopade Pub Group.

—Let's Quilt Our Ohio County. 1994. lib. bdg. 24.95 (*0-7933-7218-6*); pap. text ed. 14.95 (*0-7933-7219-4*); disk 29.95 (*0-7933-7220-8*) Gallopade Pub Group.

—Let's Quilt Our Ohio Town. 1994. lib. bdg. 24.95 (*0-7933-7068-X*); pap. text ed. 14.95 (*0-7933-7069-8*); disk 29.95 (*0-7933-7070-1*) Gallopade Pub Group.

—Meow! Ohio Cats in History, Mystery, Legend, Lore, Humor & More! (Illus.). (gr. 3-12). 1994. PLB 24.95 (*0-7933-3419-5*); pap. 14.95 (*0-7933-3420-9*); computer disk 29.95 (*0-7933-3421-7*) Gallopade Pub Group.

—My First Book about Ohio. (gr. k-4). 1994. PLB 24.95 (*0-7933-5674-1*); pap. 14.95 (*0-7933-5675-X*); computer disk 29.95 (*0-7933-5676-8*) Gallopade Pub Group.

—Ohio & Other State Greats (Biographies) (Illus.). 1994. PLB 24.95 (*1-55609-998-3*); pap. 14.95 (*1-55609-999-1*); computer disk 29.95 (*1-55609-854-5*) Gallopade Pub Group.

—Ohio Bandits, Bushwackers, Outlaws, Crooks, Devils, Ghosts, Desperadoes & Other Assorted & Sundry Characters! (Illus.). 1994. PLB 24.95 (*0-7933-0889-5*); pap. 14.95 (*0-7933-0888-7*); computer disk 29.95 (*0-7933-0890-9*) Gallopade Pub Group.

—Ohio Classic Christmas Trivia: Stories, Recipes, Activities, Legends, Lore & More! (Illus.). 1994. PLB 24.95 (*0-7933-0892-5*); pap. 14.95 (*0-7933-0891-7*); computer disk 29.95 (*0-7933-0893-3*) Gallopade Pub Group.

—Ohio Coastales. (Illus.). 1994. PLB 24.95 (*1-55609-992-4*); pap. 14.95 (*1-55609-993-2*); computer disk 29.95 (*1-55609-994-0*) Gallopade Pub Group.

—Ohio Coastales! 1994. lib. bdg. 24.95 (*0-7933-7300-X*) Gallopade Pub Group.

—Ohio "Crinkum-Crankum" A Funny Word Book about Our State. (Illus.). (gr. 3-12). 1994. 24.95 (*0-7933-4913-3*); pap. 14.95 (*0-7933-4914-1*); computer disk 29.95 (*0-7933-4915-X*) Gallopade Pub Group.

—Ohio Dingbats! Bk. 1: A Fun Book of Games, Stories, Activities & More about Our State That's All in Code! for You to Decipher. (Illus.). (gr. 3-12). 1994. PLB 24.95 (*0-7933-3878-6*); pap. 14.95 (*0-7933-3879-4*); computer disk 29.95 (*0-7933-3880-8*) Gallopade Pub Group.

—Ohio Festival Fun for Kids! (Illus.). (gr. 3-12). 1994. lib. bdg. 24.95 (*0-7933-4031-4*); pap. 14.95 (*0-7933-4032-2*); disk 29.95 (*0-7933-4033-0*) Gallopade Pub Group.

—The Ohio Hot Air Balloon Mystery. (Illus.). (gr. 2-9). 1994. 24.95 (*0-7933-2633-8*); pap. 14.95 (*0-7933-2634-6*); computer disk 29.95 (*0-7933-2635-4*) Gallopade Pub Group.

—Ohio Jeopardy! Answers & Questions about Our State! (Illus.). (gr. 3-12). 1994. PLB 24.95 (*0-7933-4184-1*); pap. 14.95 (*0-7933-4185-X*); computer disk 29.95 (*0-7933-4186-8*) Gallopade Pub Group.

—Ohio "Jography" A Fun Run Thru Our State! (Illus.). 1994. PLB 24.95 (*1-55609-981-9*); pap. 14.95 (*1-55609-982-7*); computer disk 29.95 (*1-55609-983-5*) Gallopade Pub Group.

—Ohio Kid's Cookbook: Recipes, How-to, History, Lore & More! (Illus.). 1994. PLB 24.95 (*0-7933-0901-8*); pap. 14.95 (*0-7933-0900-X*); computer disk 29.95 (*0-7933-0902-6*) Gallopade Pub Group.

—The Ohio Mystery Van Takes Off! Book 1: Handicapped Ohio Kids Sneak Off on a Big Adventure. (Illus.). (gr. 3-12). 1994. 24.95 (*0-7933-5066-2*); pap. 14.95 (*0-7933-5067-0*); computer disk 29.95 (*0-7933-5068-9*) Gallopade Pub Group.

—Ohio Quiz Crash Course! (Illus.). 1994. PLB 24.95 (*1-55609-995-9*); pap. 14.95 (*1-55609-996-7*); computer disk 29.95 (*1-55609-997-5*) Gallopade Pub Group.

—Ohio Rollercoasters! (Illus.). (gr. 3-12). 1994. PLB 24.95 (*0-7933-5329-7*); pap. 14.95 (*0-7933-5330-0*); computer disk 29.95 (*0-7933-5331-9*) Gallopade Pub Group.

—Ohio School Trivia: An Amazing & Fascinating Look at Our State's Teachers, Schools & Students! (Illus.). 1994. PLB 24.95 (*0-7933-0898-4*); pap. 14.95 (*0-7933-0897-6*); computer disk 29.95 (*0-7933-0899-2*) Gallopade Pub Group.

—Ohio Silly Basketball Sportsmysteries, Vol. 1. (Illus.). 1994. PLB 24.95 (*0-7933-0895-X*); pap. 14.95 (*0-7933-0894-1*); computer disk 29.95 (*0-7933-0896-8*) Gallopade Pub Group.

—Ohio Silly Basketball Sportsmysteries, Vol. 2. (Illus.). 1994. PLB 24.95 (*0-685-45976-4*); pap. 14.95 (*0-7933-1854-8*); computer disk 29.95 (*0-7933-1855-6*) Gallopade Pub Group.

—Ohio Silly Football Sportsmysteries, Vol. 1. (Illus.). 1994. PLB 24.95 (*1-55609-986-X*); pap. 14.95 (*1-55609-987-8*); computer disk 29.95 (*1-55609-988-6*) Gallopade Pub Group.

—Ohio Silly Football Sportsmysteries, Vol. 2. (Illus.). 1994. PLB 24.95 (*1-55609-989-4*); pap. 14.95 (*1-55609-990-8*); computer disk 29.95 (*1-55609-991-6*) Gallopade Pub Group.

—Ohio Silly Trivia1. (Illus.). 1994. PLB 24.95 (*1-55609-979-7*); pap. 14.95 (*1-55609-112-5*); computer disk 29.95 (*1-55609-980-0*) Gallopade Pub Group.

—Ohio Timeline: A Chronology of Ohio History, Mystery, Trivia, Legend, Lore & More. (Illus.). (gr. 3-12). 1994. PLB 24.95 (*0-7933-5980-5*); pap. 14.95 (*0-7933-5981-3*); computer disk 29.95 (*0-7933-5982-1*) Gallopade Pub Group.

—Ohio's (Most Devastating!) Disasters & (Most Calamitous!) Catastrophies! (Illus.). 1994. PLB 24.95 (*0-7933-0886-0*); pap. 14.95 (*0-7933-0885-2*); computer disk 29.95 (*0-7933-0887-9*) Gallopade Pub Group.

—Ohio's Unsolved Mysteries (& Their "Solutions") Includes Scientific Information & Other Activities for Students. (Illus.). (gr. 3-12). 1994. PLB 24.95 (*0-7933-5827-2*); pap. 14.95 (*0-7933-5828-0*); computer disk 29.95 (*0-7933-5829-9*) Gallopade Pub Group.

—Patch, the Pirate Dog: A Ohio Pet Story. (ps-4). 1994. PLB 24.95 (*0-7933-5521-4*); pap. 14.95 (*0-7933-5522-2*); computer disk 29.95 (*0-7933-5523-0*) Gallopade Pub Group.

—Uncle Rebus: Ohio Picture Stories for Computer Kids. (Illus.). (gr. k-3). 1994. PLB 24.95 (*0-7933-4606-1*); pap. 14.95 (*0-7933-4607-X*); disk 29.95 (*0-7933-4608-8*) Gallopade Pub Group.

Regina, Karen & Rhodes, Gregory L., eds. Cincinnati: An Urban History Sourcebook, Bk. 1. LC 87-72186. (Illus.). 88p. (Orig.). (gr. 4-6). 1988. pap. text ed. 6.95 (*0-911497-01-3*) Cinc Hist Soc.

—Cincinnati: An Urban History Sourcebook, Bk. II. LC 87-72186. (Illus.). 88p. (Orig.). (gr. 7-8). 1988. pap. text ed. 6.95 (*0-911497-02-1*) Cinc Hist Soc.

Stith, Bari O. Lake County, Ohio: One Hundred Fifty Years of Tradition: An Illustrated History. (Illus.). 128p. (gr. 7 up). 1988. 25.95 (*0-89781-249-2*) Preferred Mktg.

Thompson, Kathleen. Ohio. LC 87-26482. 48p. (gr. 3 up). 1988. 19.97 (*0-86514-455-9*) Raintree Steck-V.

OHIO–FICTION

Christopher, Debbonnaire. The Day the Ohio Canal Turned Eerie. Christopher, Debbonnaire, illus. LC 93-6614. 1993. 3.00 (*1-880443-10-4*) Roscoe Village.

Fleischman, Paul. The Borning Room. LC 91-4432. 80p. (gr. 6 up). 1991. 14.00 (*0-06-023762-7*); PLB 13.89 (*0-06-023785-6*) HarpC Child Bks.

Greegor, Katherine. Trouble - of the Northwest Territory. Cummins, Lisa, illus. LC 92-61031. 100p. (Orig.). (gr. 3-8). 1992. pap. 5.95 (*0-9633091-7-X*) Promise Land Pubs.

Hamilton, Virginia. The House of Dies Drear. reissued ed. Keith, Eros, illus. LC 68-23059. 256p. (gr. 6-9). 1984. SBE 15.95 (*0-02-742500-2*, Macmillan Child Bk); pap. 3.95 (*0-02-043520-7*, Collier) Macmillan Child Grp.

Krieger, Michael T. Melvin Howard's Fireside Chats. Mills, Tiffany, illus. 149p. (Orig.). (gr. 7 up). 1992. pap. 9.00 (*0-9634329-0-7*) M T Krieger.

McCloskey, Robert. Lentil. (ps-3). 1978. pap. 3.95 (*0-14-050287-4*, Puffin) Puffin Bks.

Sanders, Scott R. Warm As Wool. LC 91-34987. (Illus.). 32p. (gr. k-5). 1992. RSBE 14.95 (*0-02-778139-9*, Bradbury Pr) Macmillan Child Grp.

Willis, Patricia. Out of the Storm. LC 94-2133. Date not set. write for info. (*0-395-68708-X*, Clarion Bks) HM.

Woodyard, Chris. Haunted Ohio: Ghostly Tales from the Buckeye State. LC 91-75343. 224p. (Orig.). (gr. 6 up). 1991. pap. 9.95 (*0-9628472-0-8*) Kestrel Pubns.

OHIO–HISTORY–FICTION

Fradin, Dennis. Ohio: In Words & Pictures. Ulm, Robert, illus. LC 76-46941. 48p. (gr. 2-5). 1977. pap. 4.95 (*0-516-43935-9*) Childrens.

OIL

see Petroleum

OIL ENGINES

see Gas and Oil Engines

OIL WELLS

see Petroleum

OKLAHOMA

Aylesworth, Thomas G. & Aylesworth, Virginia L. South Central (Louisiana, Arkansas, Missouri, Kansas, Oklahoma) (Illus.). 64p. (gr. 3 up). 1992. PLB 16.95 (*0-7910-1047-3*) Chelsea Hse.

Carole Marsh Oklahoma Books, 44 bks. 1994. PLB 1027.86 set (*0-7933-1311-2*); pap. 587.80 set (*0-7933-5194-4*) Gallopade Pub Group.

Ferguson, Elva S. They Carried the Torch: The Story of Oklahoma's Pioneer Newspapers. Griffis, Molly L., ed. Ferguson, Benton, illus. Johnson, Edith, intro. by. LC 89-80349. (Illus.). 84p. (gr. 8 up). 1989. pap. 5.00 (*0-9618634-8-X*) Levite Apache.

Fradin, Dennis. Oklahoma: In Words & Pictures. Wahl, Richard, illus. LC 80-26961. 48p. (gr. 2-5). 1981. PLB 12.95 (*0-516-03936-9*) Childrens.

Hardin, Thurman, et al. Oklahoma Treasure Trails: Adventure Fun Pack. (gr. 3 up). 1993. Incl. audio cass. & map. 14.95 (*0-9638173-0-2*) MythicMedia.

Heinrichs, Ann. Oklahoma. LC 88-11743. (Illus.). 144p. (gr. 4 up). 1988. PLB 20.55 (*0-516-00482-4*) Childrens.

Heinrichs, Ann A. Oklahoma. 196p. 1993. text ed. 15.40 (*1-56956-131-1*) W A T Braille.

Kirschstein, Carolyn V. Hooray for Oklahoma (1889) Merrell, David, illus. 48p. (gr. k-4). 1989. write for info. B C Pub Inc.

LaDoux, Rita C. Oklahoma. Lerner Geography Department Staff, ed. (Illus.). 72p. (gr. 3-6). 1992. PLB 17.50 (*0-8225-2717-0*) Lerner Pubns.

Marsh, Carole. Avast, Ye Slobs! Oklahoma Pirate Trivia. (Illus.). 1994. PLB 24.95 (*0-7933-0932-8*); pap. 14.95 (*0-7933-0931-X*); computer disk 29.95 (*0-7933-0933-6*) Gallopade Pub Group.

—The Beast of the Oklahoma Bed & Breakfast. (Illus.). 1994. PLB 24.95 (*0-7933-1869-6*); pap. 14.95 (*0-7933-1870-X*); computer disk 29.95 (*0-7933-1871-8*) Gallopade Pub Group.

—Bow Wow! Oklahoma Dogs in History, Mystery, Legend, Lore, Humor & More! (Illus.). (gr. 3-12). 1994. PLB 24.95 (*0-7933-3575-2*); pap. 14.95 (*0-7933-3576-0*); computer disk 29.95 (*0-7933-3577-9*) Gallopade Pub Group.

—Christopher Columbus Comes to Oklahoma! Includes Reproducible Activities for Kids! (Illus.). (gr. 3-12). 1994. PLB 24.95 (*0-7933-3728-3*); pap. 14.95 (*0-7933-3729-1*); computer disk 29.95 (*0-7933-3730-5*) Gallopade Pub Group.

—The Hard-to-Believe-But-True! Book of Oklahoma History, Mystery, Trivia, Legend, Lore, Humor & More. (Illus.). 1994. PLB 24.95 (*0-7933-0929-8*); pap. 14.95 (*0-7933-0928-X*); computer disk 29.95 (*0-7933-0930-1*) Gallopade Pub Group.

—If My Oklahoma Mama Ran the World! (Illus.). 1994. lib. bdg. 24.95 (*0-7933-1875-0*); pap. 14.95 (*0-7933-1876-9*); computer disk 29.95 (*0-7933-1877-7*) Gallopade Pub Group.

—Jurassic Ark! Oklahoma Dinosaurs & Other Prehistoric Creatures. (gr. k-12). 1994. PLB 24.95 (*0-7933-7536-3*); pap. 14.95 (*0-7933-7537-1*); computer disk 29.95 (*0-7933-7538-X*) Gallopade Pub Group.

—Let's Quilt Oklahoma & Stuff It Topographically! (Illus.). 1994. PLB 24.95 (*0-7933-1860-2*); pap. 14.95 (*0-7933-1861-0*); computer disk 29.95 (*0-7933-1862-9*) Gallopade Pub Group.

—Let's Quilt Our Oklahoma County. 1994. lib. bdg. 24. 95 (*0-7933-7221-6*); pap. text ed. 14.95 (*0-7933-7222-4*); disk 29.95 (*0-7933-7223-2*) Gallopade Pub Group.

—Let's Quilt Our Oklahoma Town. 1994. lib. bdg. 24.95 (*0-7933-7071-X*); pap. text ed. 14.95 (*0-7933-7072-8*); disk 29.95 (*0-7933-7073-6*) Gallopade Pub Group.

—Meow! Oklahoma Cats in History, Mystery, Legend, Lore, Humor & More! (Illus.). (gr. 3-12). 1994. PLB 24.95 (*0-7933-3422-5*); pap. 14.95 (*0-7933-3423-3*); computer disk 29.95 (*0-7933-3424-1*) Gallopade Pub Group.

—Oklahoma & Other State Greats (Biographies) (Illus.). 1994. PLB 24.95 (*0-7933-1878-5*); pap. 14.95 (*0-7933-1879-3*); computer disk 29.95 (*0-7933-1880-7*) Gallopade Pub Group.

—Oklahoma Bandits, Bushwackers, Outlaws, Crooks, Devils, Ghosts, Desperadoes & Other Assorted & Sundry Characters! (Illus.). 1994. PLB 24.95 (*0-7933-0914-X*); pap. 14.95 (*0-7933-0913-1*); computer disk 29.95 (*0-7933-0915-8*) Gallopade Pub Group.

—Oklahoma Classic Christmas Trivia: Stories, Recipes, Activities, Legends, Lore & More! (Illus.). 1994. PLB 24.95 (*0-7933-0917-4*); pap. 14.95 (*0-7933-0916-6*); computer disk 29.95 (*0-7933-0918-2*) Gallopade Pub Group.

—Oklahoma Coastales. (Illus.). 1994. PLB 24.95 (*0-7933-1872-6*); pap. 14.95 (*0-7933-1873-4*); computer disk 29.95 (*0-7933-1874-2*) Gallopade Pub Group.

—Oklahoma Coastales. 1994. lib. bdg. 24.95 (*0-7933-7301-8*) Gallopade Pub Group.

—Oklahoma Dingbats! Bk. 1: A Fun Book of Games, Stories, Activities & More about Our State That's All in Code! for You to Decipher. (Illus.). (gr. 3-12). 1994. PLB 24.95 (*0-7933-3881-6*); pap. 14.95 (*0-7933-3882-4*); computer disk 29.95 (*0-7933-3883-2*) Gallopade Pub Group.

—Oklahoma Festival Fun for Kids! (Illus.). (gr. 3-12). 1994. lib. bdg. 24.95 (*0-7933-4034-9*); pap. 14.95 (*0-7933-4035-7*); disk 29.95 (*0-7933-4036-5*) Gallopade Pub Group.

—The Oklahoma Hot Air Balloon Mystery. (Illus.). (gr. 2-9). 1994. 24.95 (*0-7933-2642-7*); pap. 14.95 (*0-7933-2643-5*); computer disk 29.95 (*0-7933-2644-3*) Gallopade Pub Group.

—Oklahoma Jeopardy! Answers & Questions about Our State! (Illus.). (gr. 3-12). 1994. PLB 24.95 (*0-7933-4187-6*); pap. 14.95 (*0-7933-4188-4*); computer disk 29.95 (*0-7933-4189-2*) Gallopade Pub Group.

—Oklahoma "Jography" A Fun Run Thru Our State! (Illus.). 1994. PLB 24.95 (*0-7933-1858-0*); pap. 14.95 (*1-55609-086-2*); computer disk 29.95 (*0-7933-1859-9*) Gallopade Pub Group.

—Oklahoma Kid's Cookbook: Recipes, How-to, History, Lore & More! (Illus.). 1994. PLB 24.95 (*0-7933-0926-3*); pap. 14.95 (*0-7933-0925-5*); computer disk 29.95 (*0-7933-0927-1*) Gallopade Pub Group.

—Oklahoma Quiz Bowl Crash Course! (Illus.). 1994. PLB 24.95 (*0-7933-1881-5*); pap. 14.95 (*0-7933-1882-3*); computer disk 29.95 (*0-7933-1883-1*) Gallopade Pub Group.

—Oklahoma Rollercoasters! (Illus.). (gr. 3-12). 1994. PLB 24.95 (*0-7933-5332-7*); pap. 14.95 (*0-7933-5333-5*); computer disk 29.95 (*0-7933-5334-3*) Gallopade Pub Group.

—Oklahoma School Trivia: An Amazing & Fascinating Look at Our State's Teachers, Schools & Students! (Illus.). 1994. PLB 24.95 (*0-7933-0923-9*); pap. 14.95 (*0-7933-0922-0*); computer disk 29.95 (*0-7933-0924-7*) Gallopade Pub Group.

—Oklahoma Silly Basketball Sportsmysteries, Vol. 1. (Illus.). 1994. PLB 24.95 (*0-7933-0920-4*); pap. 14.95 (*0-7933-0919-0*); computer disk 29.95 (*0-7933-0921-2*) Gallopade Pub Group.

—Oklahoma Silly Basketball Sportsmysteries, Vol. 2. (Illus.). 1994. PLB 24.95 (*0-7933-1884-X*); pap. 14.95 (*0-7933-1885-8*); computer disk 29.95 (*0-7933-1886-6*) Gallopade Pub Group.

—Oklahoma Silly Football Sportsmysteries, Vol. 1. (Illus.). 1994. PLB 24.95 (*0-7933-1863-7*); pap. 14.95 (*0-7933-1864-5*); computer disk 29.95 (*0-7933-1865-3*) Gallopade Pub Group.

—Oklahoma Silly Football Sportsmysteries, Vol. 2. (Illus.). 1994. PLB 24.95 (*0-7933-1866-1*); pap. 14.95 (*0-7933-1867-X*); computer disk 29.95 (*0-7933-1868-8*) Gallopade Pub Group.

—Oklahoma Silly Trivia! (Illus.). 1994. PLB 24.95 (*0-685-45977-2*); pap. 14.95 (*1-55609-082-X*); computer disk 29.95 (*0-7933-1857-2*) Gallopade Pub Group.

—Oklahoma's (Most Devastating!) Disasters & (Most Calamitous!) Catastrophies! (Illus.). 1994. PLB 24.95 (*0-7933-0911-5*); pap. 14.95 (*0-7933-0910-7*); computer disk 29.95 (*0-7933-0912-3*) Gallopade Pub Group.

—Patch, the Pirate Dog: A Oklahoma Pet Story. (ps-4). 1994. PLB 24.95 (*0-7933-5524-9*); pap. 14.95 (*0-7933-5525-7*); computer disk 29.95 (*0-7933-5526-5*) Gallopade Pub Group.

Thompson, Kathleen. Oklahoma. 48p. (gr. 3 up). 1986. text ed. 19.97 (*0-86514-456-7*) Raintree Steck-V.

OKLAHOMA–FICTION

Antle, Nancy. Hard Times: A Story of the Great Depression. Watling, James, illus. 64p. (gr. 2-6). 1993. RB 12.99 (*0-670-84665-1*) Viking Child Bks.

Heck, Bessie H. Danger on the Homestead. rev. ed. Anderson, Peggy P., illus. LC 93-71892. 160p. (gr. 3-6). 1993. Repr. of 1991 ed. 14.95 (*0-9637259-0-4*) Dinosaur Pr.

Hinton, Susie E. Outsiders. (gr. 7 up). 1967. 13.00 (*0-670-53257-6*) Viking Child Bks.

Hurmence, Belinda. Dixie in the Big Pasture. LC 93-9983. (gr. 4 up). 1994. write for info. (*0-395-52002-9*, Clarion) HM.

Myers, Anna. Red-Dirt Jessie. 107p. 1992. 13.95 (*0-8027-8172-1*) Walker & Co.

—Rosie's Tiger. LC 94-50814. 1994. write for info. (*0-8027-8305-8*) Walker & Co.

Thomas, Joyce C. Marked by Fire. 160p. (gr. 7 up). 1982. pap. 3.99 (*0-380-79327-X*, Flare) Avon.

OKLAHOMA–HISTORY

Baird, W. David & Goble, Danney. The Story of Oklahoma. LC 93-47075. (Illus.). 528p. 1994. text ed. 28.95x (*0-8061-2650-7*) U of Okla Pr.

Marsh, Carole. Chill Out: Scary Oklahoma Tales Based on Frightening Oklahoma Truths. (Illus.). 1994. lib. bdg. 24.95 (*0-7933-4762-9*); pap. 14.95 (*0-7933-4763-7*); disk 29.95 (*0-7933-4764-5*) Gallopade Pub Group.

—My First Book about Oklahoma. (gr. k-4). 1994. PLB 24.95 (*0-7933-5677-6*); pap. 14.95 (*0-7933-5678-4*); computer disk 29.95 (*0-7933-5679-2*) Gallopade Pub Group.

—Oklahoma "Crinkum-Crankum" A Funny Word Book about Our State. (Illus.). (gr. 3-12). 1994. 24.95 (*0-7933-4916-8*); pap. 14.95 (*0-7933-4917-6*); computer disk 29.95 (*0-7933-4918-4*) Gallopade Pub Group.

—The Oklahoma Mystery Van Takes Off! Book 1: Handicapped Oklahoma Kids Sneak Off on a Big Adventure. (Illus.). (gr. 3-12). 1994. 24.95 (*0-7933-5069-7*); pap. 14.95 (*0-7933-5070-0*); computer disk 29.95 (*0-7933-5071-9*) Gallopade Pub Group.

—Oklahoma Timeline: A Chronology of Oklahoma History, Mystery, Trivia, Legend, Lore & More. (Illus.). (gr. 3-12). 1994. PLB 24.95 (*0-7933-5983-X*); pap. 14.95 (*0-7933-5984-8*); computer disk 29.95 (*0-7933-5985-6*) Gallopade Pub Group.

—Oklahoma's Unsolved Mysteries (& Their "Solutions") Includes Scientific Information & Other Activities for Students. (Illus.). (gr. 3-12). 1994. PLB 24.95 (*0-7933-5830-2*); pap. 14.95 (*0-7933-5831-0*); computer disk 29.95 (*0-7933-5832-9*) Gallopade Pub Group.

—Uncle Rebus: Oklahoma Picture Stories for Computer Kids. (Illus.). (gr. k-3). 1994. PLB 24.95 (*0-7933-4609-6*); pap. 14.95 (*0-7933-4610-X*); disk 29. 95 (*0-7933-4611-8*) Gallopade Pub Group.

Meinders, LaDonna K. Leaves in the Wind. Loftin, Beth, illus. Wheeler, J. Clyde, intro. by. LC 89-81374. (Illus.). 152p. 1989. 15.95 (*0-934188-31-9*) Evans Pubns.

Newsom, D. Earl. The Birth of Oklahoma. (Illus.). 178p. (gr. 5-12). 1983. 14.95 (*0-934188-08-4*) Evans Pubns.

Speer, Bonnie. Hillback to Boggy: A Family Struggles for Survival During the Great Depression, in a Tent in the Hills of Oklahoma. Speer, Jess W., as told by. LC 89-64193. (Illus.). 200p. (gr. 6-12). 1992. PLB 20.95 (*0-9619639-7-2*); pap. 11.95 (*0-9619639-5-6*) Reliance Pr.

Wagoner, Jay J. Oklahoma! Boutas, Nora, illus. LC 89-90110. 229p. 1989. lib. bdg. 20.00 (*0-9622361-0-1*) Thunderbird Bks.

Wise, Lu C. Oklahoma's First Ladies. LC 83-82947. (Illus.). 88p. (gr. 5-12). 1984. 14.95 (*0-934188-10-6*) Evans Pubns.

OKLAHOMA–HISTORY–FICTION

Antle, Nancy. Beautiful Land: A Story of the Oklahoma Land Rush. Gampert, John, illus. 64p. (gr. 2-6). 1994. 12.99 (*0-670-85304-6*) Viking Child Bks.

Keith, Harold. The Obstinate Land: Cherokee Strip Run of 1893. 2nd ed. LC 77-1826. 214p. (gr. 4 up). pap. 12.95 (*0-927562-15-4*) Levite Apache.

Kirschstein, Carolyn. Hooray for Oklahoma Eighteen Eighty-Nine. (Illus.). 72p. (gr. k-4). 1989. 9.95 (*0-926521-00-4*) B C Pub Inc.

Vogt, Esther L. A Race for Land. 112p. (Orig.). (gr. 4-7). 1992. pap. 4.95 (*0-8361-3575-X*) Herald Pr.

OLD AGE

see also Aged

Adams, Pam. Elderly People. LC 90-45702. (gr. 4 up). 1990. 7.95 (*0-85953-362-X*); pap. 3.95 (*0-85953-352-2*) Childs Play.

Bliss. Aging. 1991. 12.95s.p. (*0-86593-114-3*) Rourke Corp.

Darling, David. Could You Ever Live Forever? (Illus.). 60p. (gr. 5 up). 1991. text ed. 14.95 RSBE (*0-87518-457-X*, Dillon) Macmillan Child Grp.

Farber, Norma. How Does It Feel to Be Old? Hyman, Trina S., illus. LC 79-11516. 32p. (ps-3). 1988. (DCB); pap. 4.99 (*0-525-44367-3*, DCB) Dutton Child Bks.

Kibbey, Marsha. My Grammy: A Book about Alzheimer's Disease. (ps-3). 1991. pap. 4.95 (*0-87614-544-6*) Carolrhoda Bks.

OLD AGE–FICTION

Ackerman, Karen. Walking with Clara Belle. Mason, Debbie, illus. 40p. (gr. k-3). Date not set. 9.95 (*0-8198-8243-7*) St Paul Bks.
Ages 5-8. How old is "old?" Children are brought to a special appreciation of the elderly through this charming treatment of friendship. The child who goes "walking with Clara Belle" can develop positive attitudes towards aging - & loving relationships with the aged. "This charming experience of a little girl with her elderly next-door neighbor can be an eye-opener in helping children to develop positive attitudes toward aging. The story encourages love & deep regard for the aged in a world that seems to do its best to downplay the goodness of getting old. This book can help parents & teachers explore attitudes toward aging & the aged with children in kindergarten through third grade. The illustrations lend themselves to questions." - Ruth Charlesworth, THE VERMONT CATHOLIC TRIBUNE. To order, please call (800) 876-4463.
Publisher Provided Annotation.

Althaus, Anne-Marie. A Touch of Sepia. LC 93-26299. (Illus.). 1994. 4.25 (*0-383-03781-6*) SRA Schl Grp.

Arkin, Alan. Some Fine Grampa! Zimmer, Dirk, illus. LC 92-24436. 32p. (gr. k-3). 1995. 14.00 (*0-06-021533-X*); PLB 13.89 (*0-06-021534-8*) HarpC Child Bks.

Bawden, Nina. Humbug. 144p. (gr. 4-7). 1992. 13.45 (*0-395-62149-6*, Clarion Bks) HM.

Blake, Robert J. Dog. Blake, Robert J., illus. LC 92-39313. 32p. (ps-3). 1994. 14.95 (*0-399-22019-4*, Philomel Bks) Putnam Pub Group.

Bunting, Eve. Sunshine Home. De Groat, Diane, illus. LC 93-570. (gr. k-3). 1994. 14.95 (*0-395-63309-5*, Clarion Bks) HM.

Coleman, Evelyn. Cymbals. Brown, Sterling, illus. LC 93-8690. 1995. 15.95 (*0-02-722817-7*) Macmillan.

Cormier, Michael J. A Second Thought. Milone, Karen, illus. LC 91-41619. 32p. (gr. 2-6). 1992. PLB 19.97 (*0-8114-3578-4*) Raintree Steck-V.

Doherty, Berlie. Willa & Old Miss Annie. Lewis, Kim, illus. LC 93-970. 96p. (gr. 3-6). 1994. 14.95 (*1-56402-331-1*) Candlewick Pr.

Dugan, Barbara. Loop the Loop. Stevenson, James P., illus. LC 92-40168. 32p. (ps-3). 1993. pap. 4.99 (*0-14-054904-8*, Puffin) Puffin Bks.

Fair, Sylvia. The Bedspread. Fair, Sylvia, illus. LC 81-11152. 32p. (gr. k-3). 1982. 14.95 (*0-688-00877-1*) Morrow Jr Bks.

Fox, Mem. Night Noises. 30p. (ps-2). 1989. 13.95 (*0-15-200543-9*) HarBrace.

Franklin, Kristine L. The Old, Old Man & the Very Little Boy. Shaffer, Terea, illus. LC 91-2611. 32p. (ps-1). 1992. SBE 14.95 (*0-689-31735-2*, Atheneum Child Bk) Macmillan Child Grp.

Gardiner, John R. General Butterfingers. Smith, Cat B., illus. LC 92-44487. 96p. (gr. 3-7). 1993. pap. 3.99 (*0-14-036355-6*, Puffin) Puffin Bks.

Griffith, Helen V. Dream Meadow. Barnet, Nancy, illus. LC 93-18175. 24p. (ps up). 1994. 14.00 (*0-688-12293-0*); PLB 13.93 (*0-688-12294-9*) Greenwillow.

Hager, Betty. Miss Tilly & the Haunted Mansion. 112p. (gr. 3-7). 1994. pap. 4.99 (*0-310-38411-7*) Zondervan.

Hamm, Diane J. Second Family. LC 91-42968. 128p. (gr. 5-7). 1992. SBE 13.95 (*0-684-19436-8*, Scribners Young Read) Macmillan Child Grp.

Heckert, Connie. Dribbles. Sayles, Elizabeth, illus. LC 92-24846. 1993. 14.45 (*0-395-62336-7*, Clarion Bks) HM.

Howe, James. Pinky & Rex & the Mean Old Witch. Sweet, Melissa, illus. LC 89-78204. 48p. (gr. k-3). 1991. SBE 12.95 (*0-689-31617-8*, Atheneum Child Bk) Macmillan Child Grp.

Johnston, Tony. Grandpa's Song. Sneed, Brad, illus. LC 90-43836. 32p. (ps-3). 1991. 12.95 (*0-8037-0801-7*); lib. bdg. 12.89 (*0-8037-0802-5*) Dial Bks Young.

Jones, Rebecca C. Great Aunt Martha. Jackson, Shelley, illus. LC 93-43958. 1994. write for info. (*0-525-45257-5*) Dutton Child Bks.

Jung, Minna. William's Ninth Life. Rosenberry, Vera, illus. LC 92-44520. 32p. (ps-2). 1993. 14.95 (*0-531-05492-6*); PLB 14.99 (*0-531-08642-9*) Orchard Bks Watts.

Krasilovsky, Phyllis. The Woman Who Saved Things. Cymerman, John E., illus. LC 92-5126. 32p. (gr. k up). 1993. 14.00 (*0-688-11162-9*, Tambourine Bks); PLB 13.93 (*0-688-11163-7*, Tambourine Bks) Morrow.

Lisle, Janet T. Looking for Juliette. LC 94-6922. 128p. (gr. 3-5). 1994. 14.95 (*0-531-06870-6*); PLB 14.99 (*0-531-08720-4*) Orchard Bks Watts.

Logue, Mary. The Haunting of Hunter House. (gr. 3-8). 1992. PLB 8.95 (*0-89565-877-1*) Childs World.

McEwan, Elaine K. Murphy's Mansion. Norton, LoraBeth, ed. 96p. (gr. 3-6). Date not set. pap. 4.99 (*0-7814-0160-7*, Chariot Bks) Chariot Family.

Martin, C. L. The Dragon Nanny. Rayevsky, Robert, illus. LC 90-39985. 32p. (gr. k-3). 1991. pap. 3.95 (*0-689-71451-3*, Aladdin) Macmillan Child Grp.

Mills, Claudia. Dinah for President. LC 93-44668. (gr. 3-7). 1994. pap. 3.95 (*0-689-71854-3*, Aladdin) Macmillan Child Grp.

Nordqvist, Sven. Festus & Mercury Go Camping. LC 92-43181. 1993. 18.95 (*0-87614-802-X*) Carolrhoda Bks.

The Old Man & the Afternoon Cat. 42p. (ps-3). 1992. PLB 13.27 (*0-8368-0886-X*) Gareth Stevens Inc.

Pochocki, Ethel. Wildflower Tea. Essley, Roger, illus. LC 92-29872. 1993. 14.00 (*0-671-78115-4*, Green Tiger) S&S Trade.

Radley, Gail. The Golden Days. LC 90-46935. 144p. (gr. 3-7). 1991. SBE 13.95 (*0-02-775652-1*) Macmillan Child Grp.

—The Golden Days. LC 92-19526. 160p. (gr. 5 up). 1992. pap. 3.99 (*0-14-036002-6*) Puffin Bks.

Roberts, Mary. The Creeper. Stewart, Chantal, illus. LC 93-134. 1994. write for info. (*0-383-03684-4*) SRA Schl Grp.

Ryan, Cheryl. Sally Arnold. Farnsworth, Bill, illus. LC 94-6455. 1995. write for info. (*0-525-65176-4*, Cobblehill Bks) Dutton Child Bks.

Ryan, Mary C. The Voice from the Mendelsohns Maple. Roman, Irena, illus. LC 89-31569. 132p. (gr. 5-7). 1990. 13.95 (*0-316-76360-8*) Little.

Rylant, Cynthia. Miss Maggie. DiGrazia, Thomas, illus. LC 82-18206. 32p. (gr. k-3). 1983. 12.95 (*0-525-44048-8*, DCB) Dutton Child Bks.

—Mr. Putter & Tabby Pick the Pears. Howard, Arthur, illus. LC 94-11259. 1995. write for info. (*0-15-200245-6*) HarBrace.

—Mr. Putter & Tabby Pour the Tea. Howard, Arthur, illus. LC 93-21470. (ps-6). 1994. 10.95 (*0-15-256255-9*) HarBrace.

—Mr. Putter & Tabby Walk the Dog. Howard, Arthur, illus. LC 93-21467. (ps-6). 1994. 10.95 (*0-15-256259-1*) HarBrace.

—The Old Woman Who Named Things. Brown, Kathryn, illus. LC 93-40537. 1994. write for info. (*0-15-257809-9*) HarBrace.

Sakai, Kimiko. Sachiko Means Happiness. Arai, Tomie, illus. LC 90-2248. 32p. (gr. k-5). 1990. 13.95 (*0-89239-065-4*) Childrens Book Pr.

Smith, Doris B. Remember the Red-Shouldered Hawk. LC 93-14405. 160p. (gr. 5-9). 1994. 14.95 (*0-399-22443-2*, Putnam) Putnam Pub Group.

Stahl, Hilda. Hannah & the Snowy Hideaway. LC 93-8295. 160p. (Orig.). (gr. 6-9). 1993. pap. 3.99 (*0-89107-748-0*) Crossway Bks.

Stolz, Mary. Stealing Home. LC 92-5226. 160p. (gr. 3-6). 1992. 14.00 (*0-06-021154-7*); PLB 13.89 (*0-06-021157-1*) HarpC Child Bks.

—The Weeds & the Weather. Watson, N. Cameron, illus. LC 93-240. 40p. (gr. k up). 1994. 14.00 (*0-688-12289-2*); PLB 13.93 (*0-688-12290-6*) Greenwillow.

Strangis, Joel. Grandfather's Rock. Recht, Ruth, illus. LC 92-26525. 1993. 14.95 (*0-395-65367-3*) HM.

Tharlet, Eve. Archibald the Great. Clements, Andrew, tr. from FRE. Tharlet, Eve, illus. 28p. (gr. k up). 1993. 14.95 (*0-88708-267-X*) Picture Bk Studio.

Toretta-Fuentes, June. Maria's Secret. Machlin, Mikki, illus. LC 92-9866. 32p. 1992. pap. 3.95 (*0-8091-6606-2*) Paulist Pr.

Trevaskis, Ian. Periwinkle's Ride. Crossett, Warren, illus. LC 93-18049. 1994. write for info. (*0-383-03708-5*) SRA Schl Grp.

Wahl, Jan. I Remember, Cried Grandma Pinky. Johnson, Arden, illus. LC 93-33806. 32p. (gr. k-2). 1994. PLB 14.95 (*0-8167-3456-9*); pap. text ed. 3.95 (*0-8167-3457-7*) BrdgeWater.

Weisman, Joan. The Storyteller. Bradley, David, illus. LC 93-20460. 32p. 1993. 15.95 (*0-8478-1742-3*) Rizzoli Intl.

Williams, Karen L. Applebaum's Garage. LC 92-31336. 1993. 13.95 (*0-395-65227-8*, Clarion Bks) HM.

Zolotow, Charlotte. I Know a Lady. Stevenson, James, illus. LC 83-25361. 24p. (gr. k-3). 1984. 14.95 (*0-688-03837-9*); PLB 14.88 (*0-688-03838-7*) Greenwillow.

Zolotow, Charlotte & Stevenson, James P. I Know a Lady. (Illus.). 32p. (ps-3). 1986. pap. 3.99 (*0-14-050550-4*, Puffin) Puffin Bks.

OLD TESTAMENT

see Bible. Old Testament

OLMSTED, FREDERICK LAW, 1822-1903

Dunlap, Julie. Parks for the People: A Story about Frederick Law Olmsted. Lieber, Susan F., illus. LC 93-40988. 1994. write for info. (*0-87614-824-0*) Carolrhoda Bks.

OLYMPIC GAMES

Arnold, Caroline. The Olympic Summer Games. LC 91-4666. (Illus.). 64p. (gr. 5-8). 1991. PLB 12.90 (*0-531-20052-3*) Watts.

—The Olympic Winter Games. LC 91-4667. (Illus.). 64p. (gr. 5-8). 1991. PLB 12.90 (*0-531-20053-1*) Watts.

Duden, Jane. The Olympics. (Illus.). 48p. (gr. 5). 1991. text ed. 11.95 RSBE (*0-89686-624-6*, Crestwood Hse) Macmillan Child Grp.

Duder, Tessa. Journey to Olympia, the Story of the Ancient Olympics. (Illus.). 1992. pap. 3.95 (*0-590-45796-9*) Scholastic Inc.

Fradin, Dennis B. Olympics. LC 83-7214. (Illus.). 48p. (gr. k-4). 1983. PLB 12.85 (*0-516-01703-9*); pap. 4.95 (*0-516-41703-7*) Childrens.

Glubok, Shirley & Tamarin, Alfred. Olympic Games in Ancient Greece. LC 75-25408. (Illus.). 128p. (gr. 5-9). 1976. PLB 15.89 (*0-06-022048-1*) HarpC Child Bks.

Haycock, Kate. Gymnastics. LC 91-16118. (Illus.). 48p. (gr. 6). 1991. text ed. 13.95 RSBE (*0-89686-666-1*, Crestwood Hse) Macmillan Child Grp.

—Skiing. LC 91-670. (Illus.). 48p. (gr. 6). 1991. text ed. 13.95 RSBE (*0-89686-669-6*, Crestwood Hse) Macmillan Child Grp.

Jarrett, William. Timetables of Sports History: The Olympic Games. (Illus.). 96p. 1990. 17.95x (*0-8160-1921-5*) Facts on File.

Kent, Zachary. U. S. Olympians. LC 92-4812. 32p. (gr. 3-6). 1992. PLB 12.30 (*0-516-06659-5*) Childrens.

Knight, Theodore. The Olympic Games. LC 91-15562. (Illus.). 112p. (gr. 5-8). 1991. PLB 14.95 (*1-56006-119-7*) Lucent Bks.

Kristy, Davida. Coubertin's Olympics: How the Games Began. LC 94-12889. 1994. 21.50 (*0-8225-3327-8*) Lerner Pubns.

Lambert, David. Seas & Oceans. (Illus.). 48p. (gr. 5-8). 1987. PLB 12.95 (*0-382-09503-0*) Silver Burdett Pr.

McGuire, William. The Summer Olympics. 32p. (gr. 4). 1990. PLB 14.95 (*0-88682-318-8*) Creative Ed.

Malley, Stephen. A Kid's Guide to the Nineteen Ninety-Four Winter Olympics. (Illus.). (gr. 4-7). 1994. pap. 9.99 (*0-553-48159-2*) Bantam.

—The Kids' Guide to the Nineteen Ninety-Two Summer Olympics. (Illus.). 80p. (gr. 3-7). 1992. pap. 12.95 (*0-316-54534-1*, Spts Illus Kids) Little.

Mariotti, Mario. Hand Games. (Illus.). 32p. (ps-4). 1992. 11.95 (*0-916291-43-X*) Kane-Miller Bk.

Marsh, Carole. A Fun Book of Olympic Trivia A-Z: 1886-1996! 1994. lib. bdg. 24.95 (*0-7933-6876-6*); pap. text ed. 14.95 (*0-7933-6875-8*); disk 29.95 (*0-7933-6877-4*) Gallopade Pub Group.

Merrison, Tim. Field Athletics. LC 90-27451. (Illus.). 48p. (gr. 6). 1991. text ed. 13.95 RSBE (*0-89686-665-3*, Crestwood Hse) Macmillan Child Grp.

Sandelson, Robert. Ball Sports. LC 91-21804. (Illus.). 48p. (gr. 6). 1991. text ed. 13.95 RSBE (*0-89686-664-5*, Crestwood Hse) Macmillan Child Grp.

—Ice Sports. LC 91-3881. (Illus.). 48p. (gr. 6). 1991. text ed. 13.95 RSBE (*0-89686-667-X*, Crestwood Hse) Macmillan Child Grp.

—Swimming & Diving. LC 91-16117. (Illus.). 48p. (gr. 6). 1991. text ed. 13.95 RSBE (*0-89686-670-X*, Crestwood Hse) Macmillan Child Grp.

—Track Athletics. LC 90-27449. (Illus.). 48p. (gr. 6). 1991. text ed. 13.95 RSBE (*0-89686-671-8*, Crestwood Hse) Macmillan Child Grp.

Sandelson, Robert & Merrison, Tim. Olympic Sports, 8 Bks. (Illus.). (gr. 6). 1991. Set. RSBE 89.28 (*0-89686-754-4*, Crestwood Hse) Macmillan Child Grp.

Trella, Phyllis. Les Duit at the Olympics...& Be a Strong. Trella, Phyllis, illus. 48p. (gr. 2-6). write for info. (*0-914201-01-8*) Cheeruppet.

OLYMPIC GAMES–FICTION

Baglio, Ben. The First Olympics, No. 77. 176p. (Orig.). (gr. 7 up). 1988. pap. 3.25 (*0-553-27063-X*) Bantam.

Bell, Clarisa. En Las Olimpidas. Sanchez, Jose R., illus. (SPA.). 24p. (Orig.). (gr. 2-6). 1992. PLB 9.95x (*1-56492-051-8*) Laredo.

Birenbaum, Barbara. The Olympic Glow. Sapp, Pat, illus. LC 93-34122. 56p. (gr. 3-6). 1994. 12.95 (*0-935343-45-8*); pap. 5.95 (*0-935343-46-6*) Peartree.
THE OLYMPIC GLOW, nominated GOLD INK AWARD, PARENT'S CHOICE AWARD; CONSORTIUM OF LATIN AMERICAN STUDIES PROGRAMS (CLASP) CHILDREN'S LITERATURE AWARD. New edition & ninth Kindl historical adventure, story of the Olympic torch. Kindl, THE SYMBOL OF LIGHT, wears trunks, tank shirt & tennis shoes as he meets Olympic torchbearers of today. He learns about Zeus & the original torchbearers of 776 B.C. He travels through the modern history of the torch from its invention to design, the motto, formal protocol of how to hold & pass it, & the Olympic oath. THE OLYMPIC GLOW includes sporting events & meaning of Olympic symbols - interlacing rings, flame & relay. Travels to Summer & Winter Games by swimmers, boaters, the handicapped in wheelchairs & by laser. Thousands train as torchbearers between Olympiads. The torch bears a special message as told by runners to Kindl, "The torch is passed from person to person as it travels from Greece to the host country. Though we are each different, we share a very special unity between the ancient & modern people & the youth of today." Listed in Curriculum Guide for Teachers, Vol. II, 1994, (ACOG) Atlanta Centennial Olympic Games): RESEARCHED WITH (USOC) UNITED STATES OLYMPIC COMMITTEE. Considered for UNICEF & Peace awards due to cultural diversity. Order from distributors including Baker & Taylor, Ingram, Brodart, Quality Books Inc. & The Learning Plant or directly from Peartree, Box 14533, Clearwater, FL 34629-4533.
Publisher Provided Annotation.

Davis, Gibbs. Olympics Otis. (ps-3). 1993. pap. 3.25 (*0-553-48078-2*) Bantam.

Drake, Ann. Quigby Captures His Dream. Caroland, Mary, ed. LC 90-71142. 79p. (gr. 4-8). 1991. 6.95 (*1-55523-368-6*) Winston-Derek.

Duder, Tessa. Alex in Rome. LC 91-41275. 166p. (gr. 6 up). 1992. 13.95 (*0-395-62879-2*) HM.

Wojciechowska, Maia. Dreams of Winter Gold. Karsky, A. K., illus. 52p. 1993. 14.50 (*1-883740-04-5*) Pebble Bch Pr Ltd.

ONASSIS, JACQUELINE BOUVIER, 1929-

Capeci, Anne. Meet Jacqueline Kennedy Onassis. 112p. (Orig.). (gr. 2-6). 1995. pap. 3.50 (*0-679-87184-5*) Random Bks Yng Read.

ONE-ACT PLAYS

Jones, Michael P. Land of the Animal Spirits: A One Act Play. Willis, Kathy & Boldt, Jeaninefrwd. by. (Illus.). 132p. (Orig.). 1985. text ed. 15.00 (*0-89904-113-2*); pap. text ed. 9.99 (*0-89904-114-0*) Crumb Elbow Pub.

OPERA

see also Ballet

Biscardi, Cyrus H. The Storybook of Opera, Vol. II. Blythe, Anne, frwd. by. LC 86-81155. (Illus.). 224p. (gr. 7 up). 1987. lib. bdg. 23.95 (*0-918452-99-6*); pap. 23.95 (*1-55691-006-1*) Learning Pubns.

Brooks, Clifford, et al. Music! Words! Opera, 4 vols, Level 2. Vogelsang, Johanna, illus. Fowler, Charles, frwd. by. LC 91-45210. (Illus.). (gr. 3-5). 1991. One vol., 460p. tchr's. manual 82.50 (*0-918812-66-6*, SE 0706); Three vols., 48p. ea. wkbk. 4.95 (*0-918812-68-2*, SE 0707, SE 0708, SE 0709) MMB Music.

Englander, Roger. Opera! What's All the Screaming About? LC 82-23742. (Illus.). 192p. (gr. 6 up). 1983. 12.95 (*0-8027-6491-6*) Walker & Co.

Hill, Stephanie. Now, That's Opera Doc. Warner Bros. Studios Staff, illus. 24p. 1993. pap. 7.98 (*0-943351-59-6*, XL1002) Astor Bks.

John, Nicholas. Opera. 48p. (gr. 4-7). 1986. pap. 9.95 (*0-19-321335-4*) OUP.

Neidorf, Mary. Operantics with Wolfgang Amadeus Mozart. LC 86-14435. 32p. (Orig.). (gr. 3-6). 1987. pap. 4.95 (*0-86534-092-7*) Sunstone Pr.

Purrington, Sandra, et al. Music! Words! Opera, 4 vols, Level 1. Vogelsang, Johanna & Roth, Roger, illus. Fowler, Charles, frwd. by. LC 90-19274. 264p. (gr. k-2). 1990. One vol., 264p. tchr's. manual 65.00 (*0-918812-65-8*, SE0694); Three vols., 24p. ea. wkbk. 3.50 (*0-918812-67-4*, SE0695, SE0696, SE0697) MMB Music.

Williams, Sylvia. Leontyne Price: Opera Superstar. rev. ed. LC 84-7617. (Illus.). 32p. (gr. 2-5). 1990. PLB 11. 80 (*0-516-03531-2*); pap. 3.95 (*0-516-43531-0*) Childrens.

OPERA–FICTION

Mayhew, James. Madame Nightingale Will Sing. (ps-3). 1991. 13.95 (*0-553-07100-9*) Bantam.

Sparks, Richard W. A Candle Opera. Acheson, Robert B., illus. 54p. (gr. 1-10). 1983. pap. 5.95 (*0-9614185-0-8*) S J F Co.

OPERA HOUSES

see Theaters

OPERETTA
see also Musical Revues, Comedies, etc.
OPIATES
see Narcotics
OPINION, PUBLIC
see Public Opinion
OPOSSUMS
Crofford, Emily. Opossum. LC 89-28269. (Illus.). 48p. (gr. 5). 1990. text ed. 12.95 RSBE (*0-89686-518-5*, Crestwood Hse) Macmillan Child Grp.
Lepthien, Emilie U. Opossums. LC 93-33516. (Illus.). 48p. (gr. k-4). 1994. PLB 12.85 (*0-516-01055-7*) Childrens.
Stone, Lynn M. Opossums. LC 93-10724. 1993. write for info. (*0-86593-295-6*) Rourke Corp.
Wilmot, Zoe. Opossum. LC 93-77344. (Illus.). (ps). 1993. 3.99 (*0-89577-511-5*, Dist. by Random) RD Assn.
OPOSSUMS-FICTION
Burgess, Thornton W. Adventures of Unc' Billy Possum. 18.95 (*0-8488-0382-5*) Amereon Ltd.
Clough, Brenda W. An Impossumble Summer. 160p. (gr. 3-6). 1992. 14.95 (*0-8027-8150-0*) Walker & Co.
Fox, Mem. Possum Magic. Vivas, Julie, illus. 32p. (ps-2). 1990. 13.95 (*0-15-200572-2*, Gulliver Bks) HarBrace.
Jensen, Kiersten. Possum in the House. Sherwood, Rhoda, ed. Olliver, Tony, illus. LC 88-42910. 32p. (gr. 1-2). 1988. PLB 18.60 (*1-55532-933-0*) Gareth Stevens Inc.
Pellowski, Michael J. Professor Possum's Great Adventure. Durrell, Julie, illus. LC 88-1281. 48p. (Orig.). (gr. 1-4). 1988. PLB 10.59 (*0-8167-1341-3*); pap. text ed. 3.50 (*0-8167-1342-1*) Troll Assocs.
Sargent, Dave & Sargent, Pat. Pokey Opossum. Sapaugh, Blaine, illus. 48p. (Orig.). (gr. k-8). 1993. text ed. 11. 95 (*1-56763-042-1*); pap. text ed. 5.95 (*1-56763-043-X*) Ozark Pub.
Swartzentruber, Mrs. James. God Made the Opossum. 1976. 2.50 (*0-686-18187-5*) Rod & Staff.
OPPENHEIMER, J. ROBERT, 1904-1967
Driemen, J. E. Robert Oppenheimer: Atomic Dawn: A Biography of Robert Oppenheimer. LC 88-18968. (Illus.). 160p. (gr. 5 up). 1988. text ed. 13.95 RSBE (*0-87518-397-2*, Dillon) Macmillan Child Grp.
Rummel, Jack. Robert Oppenheimer: Dark Prince. (Illus.). 144p. (gr. 7-12). 1992. lib. bdg. 16.95x (*0-8160-2598-3*) Facts on File.
OPTICAL ILLUSIONS
Baum, Arline & Baum, Joseph. Opt: An Illusionary Tale. (Illus.). 32p. (ps-3). 1989. pap. 3.99 (*0-14-050573-3*, Puffin) Puffin Bks.
Brandes, Louis G. Can You Believe What You See? Illusions. Laycock, Mary, ed. Brandes, Louis G., illus. 96p. (Orig.). (gr. 4-10). 1988. pap. 12.50 (*0-918932-92-0*) Activity Resources.
Brandreth, Gyles. The Great Book of Optical Illusions. Murphy, Rowan B. & Murphy, Albert, illus. LC 85-9898. 96p. (Orig.). (gr. 2 up). 1985. pap. 4.95 (*0-8069-6258-5*) Sterling.
Carini, E. Take Another Look. (ps-3). 1969. pap. 1.50 (*0-685-03910-2*) P-H.
Churchill, E. Richard. How to Make Optical Illusion Tricks & Toys. LC 89-26169. (Illus.). 128p. (Orig.). 1990. pap. 4.95 (*0-8069-6869-9*) Sterling.
Gardner, Robert. Experimenting with Illusions. LC 89-24780. (gr. 7-12). 1990. PLB 13.40 (*0-531-10909-7*) Watts.
Joyce, Katherine. Astounding Optical Illusions. LC 93-43911. 1994. 12.95 (*0-8069-0431-3*) Sterling.
Paraquin, Charles H. Eye Teasers: Optical Illusion Puzzles. Kuttner, Paul, tr. LC 76-21844. (Illus.). (gr. 3 up). 1976. 7.95 (*0-8069-4538-9*); PLB 9.99 (*0-8069-4539-7*) Sterling.
—World's Best Optical Illusions. Kuttner, Paul, tr. LC 87-13885. (Illus.). 96p. (Orig.). (gr. 4-12). 1987. pap. 4.95 (*0-8069-6644-0*) Sterling.
Powers, Tom. Special Effects in the Movies. LC 89-12703. (Illus.). 96p. (gr. 5-8). 1989. PLB 14.95 (*1-56006-102-2*) Lucent Bks.
Supraner, Robyn. Stop & Look! Illusions. Barto, Renzo, illus. LC 80-23799. 48p. (gr. 1-5). 1981. pap. 3.50 (*0-89375-435-8*) Troll Assocs.
Visual Magic. 64p. 1991. 14.95 (*0-8037-1118-2*) Dial Bks Young.
Westray, Kathleen. Picture Puzzler. Westray, Kathleen, illus. LC 94-4066. 32p. (gr. k-3). 1994. PLB 13.95g (*0-395-70130-9*) Ticknor & Flds Bks Yng Read.
White, Lawrence B. & Brockel, Ray. Optical Illusions. Green, Anne C., illus. LC 86-10986. (gr. 4-9). 1986. PLB 10.90 (*0-531-10220-3*) Watts.
OPTICAL MASERS
see Lasers
OPTICS
see also Color; Light; Vision
Cobb, Vicki & Cobb, Joshua. Light Action! Amazing Experiments with Optics. Cobb, Theo, illus. LC 92-25528. 208p. (gr. 6 up). 1993. 15.00 (*0-06-021436-8*); PLB 14.89 (*0-06-021437-6*) HarpC Child Bks.
Darling, David. Making Light Work: The Science of Optics. LC 91-3999. (Illus.). 60p. (gr. 4-6). 1991. text ed. 13.95 RSBE (*0-87518-476-6*, Dillon) Macmillan Child Grp.
Gardner, Robert. Optics. (Illus.). 96p. (gr. 5-8). 1994. bds. 16.95 (*0-8050-2852-8*) TFC Bks NY.
Hecht, Jeff. Optics: Light for a New Age. LC 87-23398. (Illus.). 44p. (gr. 5-9). 1988. SBE 15.95 (*0-684-18879-1*, Scribners Young Read) Macmillan Child Grp.
Joval, Nomi. El Color de la Luz. Kubinyi, Laszlo, illus. (SPA.). 16p. (ps-4). 1993. PLB 13.95 (*1-879567-20-2*, Valeria Bks) Wonder Well.
—Color of Light. Kubinyi, Laszlo, illus. 16p. (ps-4). 1993. PLB 13.95 (*1-879567-19-9*, Valeria Bks) Wonder Well.
—Power of Glass. Kubinyi, Laszlo, illus. 16p. (ps-4). 1993. PLB 13.95 (*1-879567-21-0*, Valeria Bks) Wonder Well.
—Room of Mirrors. Kubinyi, Laszlo, illus. 16p. (gr. k-4). 1991. PLB 13.95 (*1-879567-06-7*, Valeria Bks) Wonder Well.
Robson, Pam. Light, Color & Optics Lenses. LC 92-37097. (Illus.). 32p. (gr. 4-7). 1993. PLB 12.40 (*0-531-17407-7*, Gloucester Pr) Watts.
Wood, Robert W. Physics For Kids: 49 Easy Experiments with Optics. (Illus.). 176p. 1990. 16.95 (*0-8306-8402-6*, 3402); pap. 9.95 (*0-8306-3402-9*) TAB Bks.
OPTICS-EXPERIMENTS
Ardley, Neil. Science Book of Light. 29p. (gr. 2-5). 1991. 9.95 (*0-15-200577-3*) HarBrace.
OPTIONS
see Stock Exchange
OPTOMETRY
see also Eye
Silverstein, Alvin & Silverstein, Virginia B. Glasses & Contact Lenses: Your Guide to Eyes, Eyewear, & Eye Care. LC 88-13026. (Illus.). 144p. (gr. 7 up). 1989. (Lipp Jr Bks); PLB 13.89 (*0-397-32185-6*, Lipp Jr Bks) HarpC Child Bks.
ORANGE
Cleaver, Vera & Cleaver, Bill. Hazel Rye. LC 81-48603. 160p. (gr. 5-8). 1983. (Lipp Jr Bks); PLB 13.89 (*0-397-31952-5*, Lipp Jr Bks) HarpC Child Bks.
Moncure, Jane B. What Was It Before It Was Orange Juice? Lexa, Susan, illus. LC 85-11396. 32p. (ps-2). 1985. PLB 14.95 (*0-89565-322-2*) Childs World.
Western Promotional Books Staff. Orange. (ps). 1994. 0.95 (*0-307-13463-6*) Western Pub.
ORATORY
see Public Speaking
ORBITING VEHICLES
see Artificial Satellites
ORCHARDS
see Fruit Culture
ORCHESTRA
see also Bands (Music)
Blackwood, Alan. The Orchestra: An Introduction to the World of Classical Music. LC 92-18412. (Illus.). 96p. (gr. 3-6). 1993. PLB 16.90 (*1-56294-202-6*); pap. 9.95 (*1-56294-708-7*) Millbrook Pr.
Elliott, Donald. Alligators & Music. Arrowood, Clinton, illus. LC 84-13862. (gr. 8). 1984. (Pub. by Gambit); pap. 8.95 (*0-87645-118-0*, Pub. by Gambit) Harvard Common Pr.
Hayes, Ann. Meet the Orchestra. D'Andrade, Diane, ed. Thompson, Karmen, illus. 32p. (ps-3). 1991. 13.95 (*0-15-200526-9*, Gulliver Bks) HarBrace.
Hill, Stephanie. Special Delivery Symphony. Warner Bros. Studios Staff, illus. 24p. 1993. pap. 7.98 incl. 20 min. cassette (*0-943351-58-8*, XL1001) Astor Bks.
Rubin, Mark. The Orchestra. Daniel, Alan, illus. 48p. (gr. k-3). 1992. pap. 7.95 (*0-920668-99-2*) Firefly Bks Ltd.
Swalin, Benjamin. Hard Circus Road: The Odyssey of the North Carolina Symphony. McVaugh, Julia A., ed. (Illus.). 158p. Date not set. 24.95 (*0-9618952-0-9*) NC Symphony.
ORCHESTRA-FICTION
Van Kampen, Vlasta. Orchestranimals. 1990. pap. 12.95 (*0-590-43149-8*) Scholastic Inc.
ORCHIDS
Bown, Deni. Orchids. LC 91-14937. (Illus.). 48p. (gr. 5-9). 1992. PLB 21.34 (*0-8114-2736-6*) Raintree Steck-V.
ORDNANCE
see also names of general and specific military ordnance, e.g. Atomic Weapons; also names of armies with the subdivision Ordnance and Ordnance Stores, e.g. U. S. Army-Ordnance and Ordnance Stores
Culver, Bruce & Feist, Uwe. Tiger I & Stormtiger in Detail. (Illus.). Date not set. 40.00 (*0-9633824-0-3*) Ryton Pub.
OREGON
Bratvold, Gretchen. Oregon. (Illus.). 72p. (gr. 3-6). 1991. PLB 17.50 (*0-8225-2704-9*) Lerner Pubns.
Carole Marsh Oregon Books, 44 bks. 1994. PLB 1027.80 set (*0-7933-1312-0*); pap. 587.80 set (*0-7933-5196-0*) Gallopade Pub Group.
Cloutier, James. This Day in Oregon. Cloutier, James, illus. LC 80-83719. 128p. 1981. pap. 6.95 (*0-918966-06-X*) Image West.
Dodson, Benjamin C. The Promise of Oregon. Dodson, O. Ray, intro. by. 118p. (Orig.). (gr. 7-12). 1989. pap. 6.75 (*0-9620550-3-4*) Dodson Assocs.
Fradin, Dennis. Oregon: In Words & Pictures. Wahl, Richard, illus. LC 80-15183. 48p. (gr. 3-8). 1980. PLB 12.95 (*0-516-03937-7*) Childrens.
Jones, Michael P., ed. Oregon River Watch: A Contemporary History of Oregon's Waterways, Vol. 1. Bachmann, Mark, et al, illus. 48p. (Orig.). 1985. text ed. 9.95 (*0-89904-143-4*); pap. text ed. 5.00 (*0-89904-144-2*); composition 8.00 (*0-89904-145-0*) Crumb Elbow Pub.
—Oregon River Watch: A Contemporary History of Oregon's Waterways, Vol. 2. Bachmann, Mark, et al, illus. 50p. (Orig.). 1985. text ed. 9.95 (*0-89904-146-9*); pap. text ed. 5.00 (*0-89904-147-7*); composition 8.00 (*0-89904-148-5*) Crumb Elbow Pub.
Marsh, Carole. Avast, Ye Slobs! Oregon Pirate Trivia. (Illus.). 1994. PLB 24.95 (*0-7933-0956-5*); pap. 14.95 (*0-7933-0955-7*); computer disk 29.95 (*0-685-45979-9*) Gallopade Pub Group.
—The Beast of the Oregon Bed & Breakfast. (Illus.). 1994. PLB 24.95 (*0-7933-1901-3*); pap. 14.95 (*0-7933-1902-1*); computer disk 29.95 (*0-7933-1903-X*) Gallopade Pub Group.
—Bow Wow! Oregon Dogs in History, Mystery, Legend, Lore, Humor & More! (Illus.). (gr. 3-12). 1994. PLB 24.95 (*0-7933-3578-7*); pap. 14.95 (*0-7933-3579-5*); computer disk 29.95 (*0-7933-3580-9*) Gallopade Pub Group.
—Christopher Columbus Comes to Oregon! Includes Reproducible Activities for Kids! (Illus.). (gr. 3-12). 1994. PLB 24.95 (*0-7933-3731-3*); pap. 14.95 (*0-7933-3732-1*); computer disk 29.95 (*0-7933-3733-X*) Gallopade Pub Group.
—The Hard-to-Believe-But-True! Book of Oregon History, Mystery, Trivia, Legend, Lore, Humor & More. (Illus.). 1994. PLB 24.95 (*0-7933-0953-0*); pap. 14.95 (*0-7933-0952-2*); computer disk 29.95 (*0-7933-0954-9*) Gallopade Pub Group.
—If My Oregon Mama Ran the World! (Illus.). 1994. lib. bdg. 24.95 (*0-7933-1910-2*); pap. 14.95 (*0-7933-1911-0*); computer disk 29.95 (*0-7933-1912-9*) Gallopade Pub Group.
—Jurassic Ark! Oregon Dinosaurs & Other Prehistoric Creatures. (gr. k-12). 1994. PLB 24.95 (*0-7933-7539-8*); pap. 14.95 (*0-7933-7540-1*); computer disk 29.95 (*0-7933-7541-X*) Gallopade Pub Group.
—Let's Quilt Oregon & Stuff It Topographically! (Illus.). 1994. PLB 24.95 (*0-7933-1893-9*); pap. 14.95 (*1-55609-132-X*); computer disk 29.95 (*0-7933-1894-7*) Gallopade Pub Group.
—Let's Quilt Our Oregon County. 1994. lib. bdg. 24.95 (*0-7933-7224-0*); pap. text ed. 14.95 (*0-7933-7225-9*); disk 29.95 (*0-7933-7226-7*) Gallopade Pub Group.
—Let's Quilt Our Oregon Town. 1994. lib. bdg. 24.95 (*0-7933-7074-4*); pap. text ed. 14.95 (*0-7933-7075-2*); disk 29.95 (*0-7933-7076-0*) Gallopade Pub Group.
—Meow! Oregon Cats in History, Mystery, Legend, Lore, Humor & More! (Illus.). (gr. 3-12). 1994. PLB 24.95 (*0-7933-3425-X*); pap. 14.95 (*0-7933-3426-8*); computer disk 29.95 (*0-7933-3427-6*) Gallopade Pub Group.
—My First Book about Oregon. (gr. k-4). 1994. PLB 24. 95 (*0-7933-5680-6*); pap. 14.95 (*0-7933-5681-4*); computer disk 29.95 (*0-7933-5682-2*) Gallopade Pub Group.
—Oregon & Other State Greats (Biographies) (Illus.). 1994. PLB 24.95 (*0-7933-1913-7*); pap. 14.95 (*0-7933-1914-5*); computer disk 29.95 (*0-7933-1915-3*) Gallopade Pub Group.
—Oregon Bandits, Bushwackers, Outlaws, Crooks, Devils, Ghosts, Desperadoes & Other Assorted & Sundry Characters! (Illus.). 1994. PLB 24.95 (*0-7933-0938-7*); pap. 14.95 (*0-7933-0937-9*); computer disk 29.95 (*0-7933-0939-5*) Gallopade Pub Group.
—Oregon Classic Christmas Trivia: Stories, Recipes, Activities, Legends, Lore & More! (Illus.). 1994. PLB 24.95 (*0-7933-0941-7*); pap. 14.95 (*0-7933-0940-9*); computer disk 29.95 (*0-7933-0942-5*) Gallopade Pub Group.
—Oregon Coastales. (Illus.). 1994. PLB 24.95 (*0-7933-1907-2*); pap. 14.95 (*0-685-45978-0*) Gallopade Pub Group.
—Oregon Coastales! 1994. lib. bdg. 24.95 (*0-7933-7302-6*) Gallopade Pub Group.
—Oregon Dingbats! Bk. 1: A Fun Book of Games, Stories, Activities & More about Our State That's All in Code! for You to Decipher. (Illus.). (gr. 3-12). 1994. PLB 24.95 (*0-7933-3884-0*); pap. 14.95 (*0-7933-3885-9*); computer disk 29.95 (*0-7933-3886-7*) Gallopade Pub Group.
—Oregon Festival Fun for Kids! (Illus.). (gr. 3-12). 1994. lib. bdg. 24.95 (*0-7933-4037-3*); pap. 14.95 (*0-7933-4038-1*); disk 29.95 (*0-7933-4039-X*) Gallopade Pub Group.
—The Oregon Hot Air Balloon Mystery. (Illus.). (gr. 2-9). 1994. 24.95 (*0-7933-2651-6*); pap. 14.95 (*0-7933-2652-4*); computer disk 29.95 (*0-7933-2653-2*) Gallopade Pub Group.
—Oregon Jeopardy! Answers & Questions about Our State! (Illus.). (gr. 3-12). 1994. PLB 24.95 (*0-7933-4190-6*); pap. 14.95 (*0-7933-4191-4*); computer disk 29.95 (*0-7933-4192-2*) Gallopade Pub Group.
—Oregon "Jography" A Fun Run Thru Our State. (Illus.). 1994. PLB 24.95 (*0-7933-1890-4*); pap. 14.95 (*0-7933-1891-2*); computer disk 29.95 (*0-7933-1892-0*) Gallopade Pub Group.
—Oregon Kid's Cookbook: Recipes, How-to, History, Lore & More! (Illus.). 1994. PLB 24.95 (*0-7933-0950-6*); pap. 14.95 (*0-7933-0949-2*); computer disk 29.95 (*0-7933-0951-4*) Gallopade Pub Group.
—Oregon Quiz Bowl Crash Course! (Illus.). 1994. PLB 24.95 (*0-7933-1904-8*); pap. 14.95 (*0-7933-1905-6*); computer disk 29.95 (*0-7933-1906-4*) Gallopade Pub Group.
—Oregon Rollercoasters! (Illus.). (gr. 3-12). 1994. PLB 24.95 (*0-7933-5335-1*); pap. 14.95 (*0-7933-5336-X*); computer disk 29.95 (*0-7933-5337-8*) Gallopade Pub Group.

—Oregon School Trivia: An Amazing & Fascinating Look at Our State's Teachers, Schools & Students. (Illus.). 1994. PLB 24.95 (*0-7933-0947-6*); pap. 14.95 (*0-7933-0946-8*); computer disk 29.95 (*0-7933-0948-4*) Gallopade Pub Group.
—Oregon Silly Basketball Sportsmysteries, Vol. 1. (Illus.). 1994. PLB 24.95 (*0-7933-0944-1*); pap. 14.95 (*0-7933-0943-3*); computer disk 29.95 (*0-7933-0945-X*) Gallopade Pub Group.
—Oregon Silly Basketball Sportsmysteries, Vol. 2. (Illus.). 1994. PLB 24.95 (*0-7933-1916-1*); pap. 14.95 (*0-7933-1917-X*); computer disk 29.95 (*0-7933-1918-8*) Gallopade Pub Group.
—Oregon Silly Football Sportsmysteries, Vol. 1. (Illus.). 1994. PLB 24.95 (*0-7933-1895-5*); pap. 14.95 (*0-7933-1896-3*); computer disk 29.95 (*0-7933-1897-1*) Gallopade Pub Group.
—Oregon Silly Football Sportsmysteries, Vol. 2. (Illus.). 1994. PLB 24.95 (*0-7933-1898-X*); pap. 14.95 (*0-7933-1899-8*); computer disk 29.95 (*0-7933-1900-5*) Gallopade Pub Group.
—Oregon Silly Trivia! (Illus.). 1994. PLB 24.95 (*0-7933-1887-4*); pap. 14.95 (*0-7933-1888-2*); computer disk 29.95 (*0-7933-1889-0*) Gallopade Pub Group.
—Oregon's (Most Devastating!) Disasters & (Most Calamitous!) Catastrophies! (Illus.). 1994. PLB 24.95 (*0-7933-0935-2*); pap. 14.95 (*0-7933-0934-4*); computer disk 29.95 (*0-7933-0936-0*) Gallopade Pub Group.
—Patch, the Pirate Dog: A Oregon Pet Story. (ps-4). 1994. PLB 24.95 (*0-7933-5527-3*); pap. 14.95 (*0-7933-5528-1*); computer disk 29.95 (*0-7933-5529-X*) Gallopade Pub Group.
Riegel, Martin P. Ghost Ports of the Pacific, Vol. II: Oregon. LC 89-90772. (Illus.). 52p. (Orig.). 1989. 11.00 (*0-944871-20-8*); pap. 4.95 (*0-944871-21-6*) Riegel Pub.
Sanders, Richard S. Government in Oregon. LC 91-62149. (Orig.). (gr. 6 up). 1991. pap. 19.95 (*1-880118-02-5*) MESD Pr.
Stein, R. Conrad. Oregon. LC 88-38528. (Illus.). 144p. (gr. 4 up). 1989. PLB 20.55 (*0-516-00483-2*) Childrens.
—Oregon. 189p. 1993. text ed. 15.40 (*1-56956-128-1*) W A T Braille.
Stewart, Judi & Weit, Kathryn. Around Portland with Kids. rev. ed. (Illus.). 205p. (ps-7). 1987. pap. 9.95 (*0-9614261-2-8*) Discovery Pr.
Thompson, Kathleen. Oregon. LC 85-9973. 48p. (gr. 3 up). 1985. PLB 19.97 (*0-86514-441-9*) Raintree Steck-V.
Wood, Sharon. The Portland Bridge Book. Alley, Joy D., illus. (Orig.). (ps-7). 1989. pap. 12.95 (*0-87595-211-9*) Oregon Hist.

OREGON–FICTION

Biggar, Joan R. High Desert Secrets. 160p. (Orig.). (gr. 5-8). 1992. pap. 3.99 (*0-570-04711-0*) Concordia.
Cleary, Beverly. Emily's Runaway Imagination. Krush, Joe & Krush, Beth, illus. LC 61-10939. 224p. (gr. 3-7). 1961. 12.95 (*0-688-21267-0*); PLB 12.88 (*0-688-31267-5*, Morrow Jr Bks) Morrow Jr Bks.
Crew, Linda. Nekomah Creek Christmas. Robinson, Charles, illus. LC 94-478. 1994. 14.95 (*0-385-32047-7*) Delacorte.
Killingsworth, Monte. Eli's Songs. LC 91-6452. 144p. (gr. 5 up). 1991. SBE 13.95 (*0-689-50527-2*, M K McElderry) Macmillan Child Grp.
Kimmel, Eric A. One Good Tern Deserves Another. LC 94-4505. 160p. (gr. 5-7). 1994. 14.95 (*0-8234-1138-9*) Holiday.
Love, Glen A., ed. The World Begins Here: An Anthology of Oregon Short Fiction. LC 92-43642. (Illus.). 320p. (Orig.). 1993. text ed. 35.95x (*0-87071-369-8*); pap. 21.95t (*0-87071-370-1*) Oreg St U Pr.

OREGON–HISTORY

Barklow, Irene. From Trails to Rails: The Post Offices, Stage Stops, & Wagon Roads of Union County, Oregon. Evans, Jack, ed. (Illus.). 306p. (Orig.). (gr. 8up). 1987. 24.95 (*0-9618185-2-2*); pap. 18.95 (*0-9618185-0-6*) Enchant Pub Oregon.
Braly, David. Cattle Barons of Early Oregon. LC 78-105220. (Illus.). 44p. (gr. 7-12). 1982. pap. 4.50 (*0-942206-00-2*) Mediaor Co.
Long, James A. Oregon Firsts: Oregon's Trailblazing Past & Present. O'Neal, Lauren, illus. 224p. (Orig.). 1993. pap. 24.95 (*1-8826350-0-0*) Pumpkin Ridge.
Marsh, Carole. Chill Out: Scary Oregon Tales Based on Frightening Oregon Truths. (Illus.). 1994. lib. bdg. 24.95 (*0-7933-4765-3*); pap. 14.95 (*0-7933-4766-1*); disk 29.95 (*0-7933-4767-X*) Gallopade Pub Group.
—Oregon "Crinkum-Crankum" A Funny Word Book about Our State. (Illus.). (gr. 3-12). 1994. 24.95 (*0-7933-4919-2*); pap. 14.95 (*0-7933-4920-6*); computer disk 29.95 (*0-7933-4921-4*) Gallopade Pub Group.
—The Oregon Mystery Van Takes Off! Book 1: Handicapped Oregon Kids Sneak Off on a Big Adventure. (Illus.). (gr. 3-12). 1994. 24.95 (*0-7933-5072-7*); pap. 14.95 (*0-7933-5073-5*); computer disk 29.95 (*0-7933-5074-3*) Gallopade Pub Group.
—Oregon Timeline: A Chronology of Oregon History, Mystery, Trivia, Legend, Lore & More. (Illus.). (gr. 3-12). 1994. PLB 24.95 (*0-7933-5986-4*); pap. 14.95 (*0-7933-5987-2*); computer disk 29.95 (*0-7933-5988-0*) Gallopade Pub Group.
—Oregon's Unsolved Mysteries (& Their "Solutions") Includes Scientific Information & Other Activities for Students. (Illus.). (gr. 3-12). 1994. PLB 24.95 (*0-7933-5833-7*); pap. 14.95 (*0-7933-5834-5*); computer disk 29.95 (*0-7933-5835-3*) Gallopade Pub Group.
—Uncle Rebus: Oregon Picture Stories for Computer Kids. (Illus.). (gr. k-3). 1994. PLB 24.95 (*0-7933-4612-6*); pap. 14.95 (*0-7933-4613-4*); disk 29.95 (*0-7933-4614-2*) Gallopade Pub Group.

OREGON TRAIL

Fisher, Leonard E. The Oregon Trail. LC 90-55103. (Illus.). 64p. (gr. 3-7). 1990. reinforced 14.95 (*0-8234-0833-7*) Holiday.
Gildemeister, Jerry. A Letter Home. Gildemeister, Jerry & Gray, Don, illus. LC 87-1151. 120p. (gr. 4-12). 1987. 24.50 (*0-936376-04-X*) Bear Wallow Pub.
Hill, William E. & Hill, Jan C. Heading West: An Activity Book for Children. Hill, William E. & Hill, Jan C., illus. 32p. (Orig.). (gr. k-4). 1992. pap. 3.95 (*0-9636071-0-3*) HillHouse Pub.
Parkman, Francis. Oregon Trail. (gr. 6 up). 1964. pap. 1.50 (*0-8049-0037-X*, CL-37) Airmont.
Salts, Bobbi. Discover the Oregon Trail. Parker, Steve, illus. 32p. (Orig.). (gr. 4-6). 1992. pap. 3.95 (*0-931056-06-3*) Jefferson Natl.
Santrey, Laurence. Oregon Trail. Livingston, Francis, illus. LC 84-2643. 32p. (gr. 3-6). 1985. PLB 9.49 (*0-8167-0196-2*); pap. text ed. 2.95 (*0-8167-0197-0*) Troll Assocs.
Steedman, Scott. A Frontier Fort on the Oregon Trail. Bergin, Mark, illus. 48p. 1994. 17.95 (*0-87226-371-1*); pap. 8.95 (*0-87226-264-2*) P Bedrick Bks.
Stein, R. Conrad. The Oregon Trail. LC 93-36994. (Illus.). 32p. (gr. 3-6). 1994. PLB 12.30 (*0-516-06674-9*) Childrens.
Stein, R. Conrad, III. The Story of the Oregon Trail. LC 83-23997. (Illus.). 31p. (gr. 3-5). 1984. pap. 3.95 (*0-516-44668-1*) Childrens.
Stickney, Joy. Native Americans along the Oregon Trail. Stickney, Joy, illus. 24p. (Orig.). (gr. 4-6). 1993. pap. 4.50 (*1-884563-02-3*) Canyon Creat.
—Young Pioneers on the Oregon Trail. Stickney, Joy, illus. 20p. (gr. 4-6). 1992. pap. 4.50 (*1-884563-01-5*) Canyon Creat.

OREGON TRAIL–FICTION

Arntson, Herbert E. Caravan to Oregon. LC 57-13207. (Illus.). (gr. 7-11). 1957. 8.95 (*0-8323-0164-7*) Binford Mort.
Kudlinski, Kathleen V. Facing West: A Story of the Oregon Trail. Watling, James, illus. LC 93-41349. 64p. (gr. 2-6). 1994. 12.99 (*0-670-85451-4*) Viking Child Bks.
Morrow, Honore. On to Oregon. Shenton, Edward, illus. LC 90-19554. 240p. (gr. 5 up). 1991. pap. 4.95 (*0-688-10494-0*, Pub. by Beech Tree Bks) Morrow.
Nolan, Cecile A. Journey West, on the Oregon Trail. (gr. 5 up). 1993. 16.95 (*0-9633168-2-6*) Rain Dance Pub.
Van Leeuwen, Jean. Bound for Oregon. LC 93-26709. (gr. 4 up). 1994. 14.99 (*0-8037-1526-9*); PLB 14.89 (*0-8037-1527-7*) Dial Bks Young.

ORELLANA, FRANCISCO DE, 1500?-1549?

Bernhard, Brendan. Pizarro, Orellana, & the Exploration of the Amazon. Goetzmann, William H., ed. Collins, Michael, intro. by. (Illus.). 112p. (gr. 5 up). 1991. lib. bdg. 18.95 (*0-7910-1305-7*) Chelsea Hse.

ORGANIC FARMING

see Organiculture

ORGANIC GARDENING

see Organiculture

ORGANICULTURE

Condon, Judith. Farming. LC 92-32910. Date not set. write for info. (*0-531-14251-5*) Watts.

ORGANIZATION, INTERNATIONAL

see International Organization

ORGANIZED LABOR

see Labor Unions

ORIENT

see East (Far East)

ORIENTALS IN THE U. S.

Marvis, Barbara J. Contemporary American Success Stories, Vol. 4: Famous People of Asian Ancestry. LC 93-78991. (Illus.). 96p. (gr. 5 up). 1994. 15.95 (*1-883845-03-3*); pap. 8.95 (*1-883845-09-2*) M Lane Pubs.
—Contemporary American Success Stories, Vol. 5: Famous People of Asian Ancestry. LC 93-78991. (Illus.). 96p. (gr. 5 up). 1994. 15.95 (*1-883845-12-2*); pap. 8.95 (*1-883845-11-4*) M Lane Pubs.

ORIENTATION

Fowler, Allan. North, South, East, & West. LC 92-39261. (Illus.). 32p. (ps-2). 1993. big bk. 22.95 (*0-516-49642-5*); PLB 10.75 (*0-516-06011-2*); pap. 3.95 (*0-516-46011-0*) Childrens.
Gorbaty, Norman, illus. Kitty in & Out. 12p. (ps). 1991. pap. 3.95 (*0-671-74437-2*, Little Simon) S&S Trade.
—Turtle Count. 12p. (ps). 1991. pap. 3.95 (*0-671-74434-8*, Little Simon) S&S Trade.
Lieberman, Lillian. Following Directions. 64p. (gr. 2-5). 1989. 6.95 (*0-912107-87-1*, MM1904) Monday Morning Bks.
McMillan, Bruce. Beach Ball - Left, Right. McMillan, Bruce, illus. LC 91-32802. 32p. (ps-3). 1992. reinforced bdg. 14.95 (*0-8234-0946-5*) Holiday.
Orienteering. (Illus.). 32p. (gr. 6-12). 1992. pap. 1.85 (*0-8395-3385-3*, 33385) BSA.

ORIGAMI

see also Paper Crafts

Araki, Chiyo. Origami in the Classroom, 2 vols. LC 65-13412. (Illus.). (gr. 1 up). 1965-68. bds. Vol. 1. bds. 14.95 (*0-8048-0452-4*); Vol. 2. bds. 14.95 (*0-8048-0453-2*) C E Tuttle.
Biddle, Steve. Amazing Origami for Children. 1993. 8.95 (*1-55521-944-6*) Bk Sales Inc.
Biddle, Steve & Biddle, Megumi. Origami Safari. (Illus.). 80p. (gr. 3 up). 1994. pap. 8.95 (*0-688-13570-6*, Tupelo Bks) Morrow.
Huber, Joanna & Claudius, Christel. Easy & Fun Paper Folding. LC 90-9829. (Illus.). 128p. (gr. 2-8). 1990. 12.95 (*0-8069-7444-3*) Sterling.
Kasahara, Kunihiko. Creative Origami. LC 67-87040. (Illus.). 1977. pap. 22.00 (*0-87040-411-3*) Japan Pubns USA.
Kitamura, Keiji. Origami Treasure Chest. (Illus.). 80p. (Orig.). 1991. pap. 17.00 (*0-87040-868-2*) Japan Pubns USA.
Kneissler, Irmgard. Origami for Children. Jonas, Dieter, illus. LC 92-453. 64p. (ps up). 1993. pap. 8.95 (*0-516-49261-6*) Childrens.
Medvene, Mark. Foilrigami. (Illus.). (gr. 4-7). 1968. 10.95 (*0-685-06619-3*) Astor-Honor.
Montroll, John. African Animals in Origami. Montroll, John, illus. LC 91-76400. 160p. (Orig.). 1993. pap. 9.95 (*1-877656-09-7*) Antroll Pub.
—Origami American Style. 32p. (gr. 2 up). 1990. pap. 6.00 (*0-9627254-0-4*) Zenagraf.
—Origami Inside-Out. Montroll, John, illus. LC 95-90214. 120p. (Orig.). 1993. pap. 9.95 (*1-877656-08-9*) Antroll Pub.
—Origami Sculptures. 2nd ed. Montroll, Andrew, ed. Montroll, John, illus. 144p. 1990. pap. text ed. 9.95 (*1-877656-02-X*) Antroll Pub.
Morris, Campbell. Fold Your Own Dinosaurs. Jackson, Paul, illus. LC 92-32894. 48p. (Orig.). 1993. pap. 7.95 (*0-399-51794-4*, Perigee Bks) Berkley Pub.
Murray, William D. & Rigney, Francis J. Paper Folding for Beginners. (Illus.). (gr. 1 up). pap. 2.95 (*0-486-20713-7*) Dover.
My First Origami, No. 1: Airplanes, Penguin, Ivy & Pinwheel. (gr. 1-3). 1989. bds. 3.50 incl. origami paper (*0-89346-317-5*) Heian Intl.
My First Origami, No. 2: Waterbird, Hat, Bat & Turtle. (gr. 1-3). 1989. bds. 3.50 incl. origami paper (*0-89346-318-3*) Heian Intl.
My First Origami, No. 3: Cap, Piano, Pigeon & Snake. (gr. 1-3). 1989. bds. 3.50 incl. origami paper (*0-89346-319-1*) Heian Intl.
My First Origami, No. 4: Grasshopper, Cat, Fish & Boat. (gr. 1-3). 1989. bds. 3.50 incl. origami paper (*0-89346-320-5*) Heian Intl.
My First Origami, No. 5: Crow, Flower, Cicada & Boots. (gr. 1-3). 1989. bds. 3.50 incl. origami paper (*0-89346-321-3*) Heian Intl.
My First Origami, No. 6: Box, Sailboat, Table & Chair, & Angelfish. (gr. 1-3). 1989. bds. 3.50 incl. origami paper (*0-89346-322-1*) Heian Intl.
Nakano, Dokuihtei. Easy Origami. Kenneway, Eric, tr. Nakano, Dokuihtei, illus. LC 85-40644. 64p. (gr. k-12). 1986. pap. 13.00 (*0-670-80382-0*) Viking Child Bks.
—Easy Origami. Kenneway, Eric, tr. (Illus.). 64p. (gr. 2-5). 1994. pap. 4.99 (*0-14-036525-7*) Puffin Bks.
Origami, No. 13. 16p. (Orig.). (gr. 1-9). 1992. pap. 4.50 (*0-89346-379-5*) Heian Intl.
Origami, No. 14. 16p. (Orig.). (gr. 1-9). 1992. pap. 4.50 (*0-89346-380-9*) Heian Intl.
Origami, No. 15. 16p. (Orig.). (gr. 1-9). 1992. pap. 4.50 (*0-89346-381-7*) Heian Intl.
Origami, No. 16. 16p. (Orig.). (gr. 1-9). 1992. pap. 4.50 (*0-89346-382-5*) Heian Intl.
Origami Playtime, Bk. 1: Animals. (Illus.). 32p. (Orig.). (gr. 2-8). 1992. pap. 4.95 (*0-8048-1726-X*) C E Tuttle.
Origami Playtime, Bk. 2: Toys & Knick-Knacks. (Illus.). 32p. (Orig.). (gr. 2-8). 1992. pap. 4.95 (*0-8048-1727-8*) C E Tuttle.
Rojas, Hector. Origami Animals. LC 92-18266. (Illus.). 160p. (gr. 3-9). 1992. 24.95 (*0-8069-8648-4*) Sterling.
—Origami Animals. LC 91-18266. (Illus.). 160p. (gr. 7 up). 1993. pap. 12.95 (*0-8069-8649-2*) Sterling.
Sakade, Florence. Origami: Japanese Paper Folding, 3 Vols. LC 57-10685. (Illus., Orig.). (gr. 2 up). 1957. pap. Vol. 1. pap. 5.95 (*0-8048-0454-0*); Vol. 2. pap. 5.95 (*0-8048-0455-9*); Vol. 3. pap. 5.95 (*0-8048-0456-7*) C E Tuttle.
Sarasas, Claude. ABCs of Origami: Paper Folding for Children. Sarasas, Claude, illus. LC 64-17160. (gr. 3-8). 1964. bds. 12.95 (*0-8048-0000-6*) C E Tuttle.
Saunders, Richard & Mackness, Brian. Horrorgami! LC 91-20005. (Illus.). 64p. (gr. 1-7). 1991. 14.95 (*0-8069-8480-5*) Sterling.
Somerville, L. How to Do Origami. (Illus.). 32p. (gr. 3-7). 1991. PLB 12.96 (*0-88110-628-3*, Usborne); pap. 5.95 (*0-7460-1489-9*, Usborne) EDC.
Takahama, Toshie. Happy Origami. (Illus.). 60p. (Orig.). 1989. pap. 19.00 boxed set incl. 96 sheets origami paper (*0-87040-830-5*) Japan Pubns USA.
—Joy of Origami: Ten Basic Folds Which Create Many Forms. (Illus.). 128p. (Orig.). 1985. pap. 13.00 (*0-87040-603-5*) Japan Pubns USA.
Temko, Florence. Jewish Origami. (Illus.). 12p. (Orig.). (gr. 1-9). 1991. pap. 5.95 (*0-89346-335-3*) Heian Intl.
—Jewish Origami II. (Illus.). 16p. (Orig.). (gr. 1-9). 1992. pap. 5.95 (*0-89346-375-2*) Heian Intl.
—Origami Magic. (gr. 4-7). 1993. pap. 7.95 (*0-590-47124-4*) Scholastic Inc.

Trodglen, James E., Jr. Super Origami: Book One. (Illus.). 44p. 1991. pap. 9.95 (1-879610-01-9) Origami Intl.

Urton, Andrea. Fifty Nifty Origami Crafts. Staunton, James, illus. 80p. (Orig.). (gr. 3-7). 1993. pap. 3.95 (1-56565-011-5) Lowell Hse.

ORIGIN OF MAN

see Man–Origin and Antiquity

ORIGIN OF SPECIES

see Evolution

ORNAMENT

see Decoration and Ornament

ORNAMENTAL ALPHABETS

see Lettering

ORNITHOLOGY

see Birds

ORPHANS AND ORPHANS' HOMES–FICTION

Alder, Elizabeth. The King's Shadow. 1994. 17.00 (0-374-34182-6) FS&G.

Atwell, David L. Sleeping Moon. Atwell, Debby, illus. LC 94-270. 1994. 14.95 (0-395-68677-6) HM.

Avery, Gillian. Maria Escapes. Snow, Scott, illus. LC 91-36730. 272p. (gr. 4-8). 1992. pap. 15.00 jacketed, 3-pc. bdg. (0-671-77074-8, S&S BFYR) S&S Trade.

Bradley, Virginia. Wait & See. 1994. write for info. (0-525-65158-6, Cobblehill Bks) Dutton Child Bks.

Bronte, Charlotte. Jane Eyre. Mitchell, Kathy, illus. (gr. 4 up). 1983. deluxe ed. 15.95 (0-448-06031-0, G&D) Putnam Pub Group.

Burch, Robert. Skinny. LC 89-28225. 128p. (gr. 4-6). 1990. Repr. of 1964 ed. 19.95 (0-8203-1223-1) U of Ga Pr.

Burnett, Frances H. Little Princess. (gr. 3 up). 1993. pap. 4.99 (0-88070-527-2, Gold & Honey) Questar Pubs.

—A Little Princess. Dubowski, Cathy E., adapted by. 108p. (Orig.). (gr. 2-6). 1994. pap. 2.99 (0-685-71036-X) Random Bks Yng Read.

—Little Princess. 14.95 (0-8488-1253-0) Amereon Ltd.

—The Secret Garden. 302p. 1981. Repr. PLB 21.95x (0-89966-326-5) Buccaneer Bks.

—Secret Garden. (gr. k-6). 1990. pap. 3.50 (0-440-47709-3, Pub. by Yearling Classics); pap. 3.50 (0-440-97709-6, Dell Trade Pbks) Dell.

—The Secret Garden. (gr. 4-6). 1987. pap. 2.95 (0-14-035004-7, Puffin) Puffin Bks.

—The Secret Garden. Mitchell, Kathy, illus. 320p. (gr. 4 up). 1987. 13.95 (0-448-06029-9, G&D) Putnam Pub Group.

—The Secret Garden. Tudor, Tasha, illus. LC 62-17457. 256p. (gr. 4-8). 1987. pap. 3.50 (0-06-440188-X, Trophy) HarpC Child Bks.

—The Secret Garden. McNulty, Faith, afterword by. 1987. pap. 2.95 (0-451-52417-9, Sig Classics) NAL-Dutton.

—The Secret Garden. Allen, Thomas B., illus. Howe, James, adapted by. LC 86-17788. (Illus.). 72p. (gr. k-5). 1993. 13.95 (0-394-86467-0) Random Bks Yng Read.

—The Secret Garden. Howell, Troy, illus. 288p. (gr. k-6). 12.99 (0-517-63225-X) Random Hse Value.

—The Secret Garden. Hague, Michael, illus. LC 86-22780. 240p. (gr. 4-6). 1987. 19.95 (0-8050-0277-4, Bks Young Read) H Holt & Co.

—The Secret Garden. Lowry, Lois, intro. by. 256p. 1987. pap. 3.50 (0-553-21201-X, Bantam Classics) Bantam.

—The Secret Garden. Betts, Louise, adapted by. LC 87-15490. (Illus.). (gr. 3-6). 1988. PLB 12.89 (0-8167-1203-4); pap. 3.95 (0-8167-1204-2) Troll Assocs.

—The Secret Garden. 360p. 1987. pap. 4.95 (0-19-281772-8) OUP.

—The Secret Garden. Sanderson, Ruth, illus. LC 86-46002. 240p. 1988. 18.95 (0-394-55431-0) Knopf Bks Yng Read.

—The Secret Garden. (gr. 5 up). 1989. pap. 2.50 (0-451-52080-7) NAL-Dutton.

—The Secret Garden. 304p. (gr. 4-7). 1987. pap. 2.95 (0-590-43346-6) Scholastic Inc.

—The Secret Garden. 1987. pap. 3.50 (0-440-40055-4) Dell.

—Secret Garden. 288p. 1990. pap. 2.50 (0-8125-0501-8) Tor Bks.

—The Secret Garden. 1991. pap. 3.99 (0-8125-1910-8) Tor Bks.

—The Secret Garden. 1979. pap. 3.25 (0-440-77706-2) Dell.

—The Secret Garden. 288p. (gr. 5-8). 1991. pap. 2.99 (0-87406-575-5) Willowisp Pr.

—The Secret Garden. 1993. 14.95 (0-679-42309-5, Everymans Lib) Knopf.

—The Secret Garden. Howe, James, adapted by. Allen, Thomas B., illus. LC 93-18509. 128p. (Orig.). (gr. 2-6). 1993. pap. 3.50 (0-679-84751-0, Bullseye Bks) Random Bks Yng Read.

—The Secret Garden. Bauman, Jill, illus. LC 94-17836. 1994. 10.95 (0-681-00646-3) Longmeadow Pr.

Burnett, Frances Hodgson. The Secret Garden. (Illus.). 96p. (Orig.). (gr. 4-7). 1994. pap. 1.00 (0-486-28024-1) Dover.

Burnett, Francis H. The Secret Garden: A Young Reader's Edition of the Classic Story. Abr. ed. Crawford, Dale, illus. LC 90-80198. 56p. (gr. 1 up). 1990. 9.98 (0-89471-860-6) Courage Bks.

Byrum, Isabel. How John Became a Man. 64p. (gr. 7 up). pap. 0.75 (0-686-29118-2) Faith Pub Hse.

Cassedy, Sylvia. Lucie Babbidge's House. LC 89-1296. 256p. (gr. 4-7). 1989. (Crowell Jr Bks); PLB 13.89 (0-690-04798-3, Crowell Jr Bks) HarpC Child Bks.

Cleaver, Vera & Cleaver, Bill. Where the Lilies Bloom. LC 75-82402. (Illus.). 176p. (gr. 7 up). 1991. PLB 14.89 (0-397-32500-2, Lipp Jr Bks) HarpC Child Bks.

Cohen, Barbara. The Orphan Game. (gr. 3-7). 1989. pap. 2.75 (0-553-15706-X, Skylark) Bantam.

Cross, Gillian. The Great American Elephant Chase. 208p. (gr. 5 up). 1994. pap. 3.99 (0-14-037014-5) Puffin Bks.

Dahl, Roald. The BFG. LC 93-22605. 1993. 13.95 (0-679-42813-5, Everymans Lib) Knopf.

Dickens, Charles. Great Expectations. (Illus.). 48p. (gr. 4 up). 1988. PLB 20.70 (0-8172-2762-8) Raintree Steck-V.

—Oliver Twist. (gr. 9 up). 1964. pap. 3.50 (0-8049-0009-4, CL-9) Airmont.

—Oliver Twist. Martin, Les, adapted by. Zallinger, Jean, illus. LC 89-24279. 96p. (gr. 2-6). 1990. PLB 5.99 (0-679-90391-7); pap. 2.99 (0-679-80391-2) Random Bks Yng Read.

Disher, Garry. Ratface. LC 93-48131. 128p. (gr. 5 up). 1994. 10.95g (0-395-69451-5) Ticknor & Flds Bks Yng Read.

Doherty, Berlie. Street Child. LC 94-5020. 160p. (gr. 3-7). 1994. 14.95 (0-531-06864-1); PLB 14.99 (0-531-08714-X) Orchard Bks Watts.

Eckles, Melita Z. The Horse That Blew Up. LC 89-52188. (Illus.). 35p. (gr. 2-5). 1990. pap. 4.95 (1-55523-319-8) Winston-Derek.

Edwards, Julie. Mandy. Brown, Judith G., illus. LC 76-157901. 224p. (gr. 3-6). 1989. pap. 3.95 (0-06-440296-7, Trophy) HarpC Child Bks.

Eliot, George. Silas Marner. (gr. 9 up). 1964. pap. 2.50 (0-8049-0014-0, CL-14) Airmont.

Farmer, Penelope. Thicker Than Water. LC 92-53133. 32p. (gr. 6-10). 1993. 14.95 (1-56402-178-5) Candlewick Pr.

Fisher, Dorothy C. Understood Betsy. (gr. 4-7). 1994. pap. 3.25 (0-590-48005-7) Scholastic Inc.

Gabel, Susan L. Where the Sun Kisses the Sea. Bowring, Joanne, illus. LC 89-16296. 32p. (ps-5). 1989. 12.95 (0-944934-00-5) Perspect Indiana.

Garland, Sherry. The Silent Storm. LC 92-33690. 1992. write for info. (0-15-274170-4) HarBrace.

Godden, Rumer. Listen to the Nightingale. 192p. (gr. 5 up). 1992. 15.00 (0-670-84517-5) Viking Child Bks.

—The Story of Holly & Ivy. Cooney, Barbara, illus. LC 84-25799. 32p. (ps-5). 1985. pap. 15.00 (0-670-80622-6) Viking Child Bks.

Gruelle, Johnny. Orphant Annie Story Book. 2nd ed. LC 89-80852. 100p. (gr. k-5). 1989. Repr. of 1921 ed. 14.95 (0-9617367-9-8) Guild Pr IN.

Hardy, Thomas. Tess of the D'Urbervilles. Hogan, A. H., intro. by. (gr. 11 up). 1965. pap. 3.50 (0-8049-0082-5, CL-82) Airmont.

Hill, Elizabeth S. The Banjo Player. 160p. (gr. 5-9). 1993. 14.99 (0-670-84967-7) Viking Child Bks.

Howard, Ellen. Edith Herself. LC 93-28061. (Illus.). 144p. (gr. 3-7). 1994. pap. 3.95 (0-689-71795-4, Aladdin) Macmillan Child Grp.

Kosman, Miriam. Family for a While. LC 93-72272. 176p. (gr. 6-10). 1993. write for info. (1-56062-202-4); pap. write for info. (1-56062-203-2) CIS Comm.

Levin, Betty. Brother Moose. LC 89-34437. (gr. 5 up). 1990. 12.95 (0-688-09266-7) Greenwillow.

Lindbergh, Anne M. Nobody's Orphan. (gr. 3-7). 1987. pap. 2.95 (0-380-70395-5, Camelot) Avon.

Lyon, David. The Crumbly Coast. LC 93-41083. 1995. write for info. (0-385-32079-5) Doubleday.

McCully, Emily A. Little Kit, or, the Industrious Flea Circus Girl. LC 93-40658. 1995. write for info. (0-8037-1671-0); PLB write for info. (0-8037-1674-5) Dial Bks Young.

Macken, Walter. Flight of the Doves. LC 91-3922. 1992. pap. 14.00 (0-671-73801-1, S&S BFYR) S&S Trade.

Maguire, Gregory. Missing Sisters. LC 93-8300. 160p. (gr. 5-9). 1994. SBE 14.95 (0-689-50590-6, M K McElderry) Macmillan Child Grp.

Mazer, Harry. Who Is Eddie Leonard? LC 93-22114. (gr. 4 up). 1993. 14.95 (0-385-31136-2) Delacorte.

Mollel, Tololwa M. The Orphan Boy. Morin, Paul, illus. 1991. 14.95 (0-685-53587-8, Clarion Bks) HM.

Montgomery, L. M. Anne of Green Gables. Moore, Inga, illus. (gr. 4-8). 1994. 14.95 (0-8050-3126-X) H Holt & Co.

—Anne of Green Gables. Felder, Deborah, adapted by. LC 93-36331. 108p. (Orig.). (gr. 2-6). 1994. pap. 2.99 (0-679-85467-3) Random Bks Yng Read.

Montgomery, Lucy M. Anne of Avonlea. (gr. 4-7). 1991. pap. 3.25 (0-590-44556-1, Apple Classics) Scholastic Inc.

—Anne of Avonlea. 1992. pap. 3.25 (0-553-15114-2) Bantam.

—Anne of Green Gables. 1982. pap. 2.95 (0-553-21313-X, Bantam Classics) Bantam.

—Anne of Green Gables. Mattern, Joanne, ed. Graef, Renee, illus. LC 92-12703. 48p. (gr. 3-6). 1992. PLB 12.89 (0-8167-2866-6); pap. text ed. 3.95 (0-8167-2867-4) Troll Assocs.

—Anne of Green Gables. facsimile ed. 352p. 1992. Repr. of 1908 ed. 16.95 (1-55109-013-9, Pub. by Nimbus Publishing Ltd CN) Chelsea Green Pub.

—Anne of Green Gables. Atwood, Margaret, afterword by. 338p. 1993. pap. 4.95 (0-7710-9883-9) Firefly Bks Ltd.

—Anne of Green Gables. LC 93-70551. 240p. (gr. 4 up). 1993. 5.98 (1-56138-324-4) Courage Bks.

—Anne of Green Gables. 256p. (gr. 5 up). 1994. pap. 2.99 (0-14-035148-5) Puffin Bks.

—Anne of Green Gables, Vol. 1. (gr. 4-7). 1984. pap. 3.50 (0-553-15327-7) Bantam.

—Anne's House of Dreams. 1983. pap. 2.95 (0-553-21318-0, Bantam Classics) Bantam.

Newton, Suzanne. M. V. Sexton Speaking. 198p. (ps up). 1990. pap. 3.95 (0-14-032356-2, Puffin) Puffin Bks.

Nixon, Joan L. In the Face of Danger. (gr. 7 up). 1989. pap. 3.99 (0-553-28196-8, Starfire) Bantam.

—In the Face of Danger: The Orphan Train Quartet, No. 3. 160p. (gr. 7 up). 1988. 16.00 (0-553-05490-2, Starfire) Bantam.

—The Specter. LC 82-70322. 160p. (gr. 7 up). 1982. pap. 12.95 (0-385-28948-0) Delacorte.

Peck, Robert N. Arly. 160p. 1991. pap. 2.95 (0-590-43469-1, Point) Scholastic Inc.

—Arly's Run. 160p. (gr. 5-9). 1991. 16.95 (0-8027-8120-9) Walker & Co.

Pennypacker, Sara. Dumbstruck. Auch, Mary J., illus. 112p. (gr. 4-7). 1994. 14.95 (0-8234-1123-0) Holiday.

Pfeffer, Susan B. Nobody's Daughter. LC 94-19681. 1995. 14.95 (0-385-32106-6) Delacorte.

—The Ring of Truth. LC 92-25272. 1993. 15.95 (0-553-09224-3) Bantam.

—Ring of Truth. 1994. pap. 3.99 (0-440-21911-6) Dell.

Porter, Gene S. Freckles. 272p. (gr. 5 up). 1992. pap. 2.99 (0-14-035144-2) Puffin Bks.

—Freckles. LC 93-42393. 1994. 7.99 (0-517-10126-2, Pub. by Gramercy) Random Hse Value.

Reeder, Carolyn. Shades of Gray. LC 89-31976. 176p. (gr. 3-7). 1989. SBE 13.95 (0-02-775810-9, Macmillan Child Bk) Macmillan Child Grp.

Richardson, Arleta. Looking for Home. LC 92-46259. 1993. pap. 4.99 (0-7814-0921-7, Chariot Bks) Chariot Family.

—Whistle-Stop West. LC 92-46260. 1993. pap. 4.99 (0-7814-0922-5, Chariot Bks) Chariot Family.

Roberts, Willo D. Eddie & the Fairy Godpuppy. Morrill, Leslie, illus. LC 83-15678. 136p. (gr. 3-5). 1984. SBE 13.95 (0-689-31021-8, Atheneum Child Bk) Macmillan Child Grp.

—Eddie & the Fairy Godpuppy. Morrill, Leslie, illus. LC 91-28003. 128p. (gr. 3-7). 1992. pap. 3.95 (0-689-71602-8, Aladdin) Macmillan Child Grp.

Ross, Ramon R. Harper & Moon. LC 92-17216. (Illus.). 192p. (gr. 4 up). 1993. SBE 14.95 (0-689-31803-0, Atheneum Child Bk) Macmillan Child Grp.

Sherman, Josepha. Windleaf. LC 93-615. 128p. (gr. 7 up). 1993. 14.95 (0-8027-8259-0); cancelled (0-8027-8260-4) Walker & Co.

Snyder, Vern W. For the Lov'va Winkie. 135p. 1988. write for info.; pap. write for info. V W Snyder.

—For the Lov'va Winkie. 90p. (gr. 3 up). 1989. pap. 8.95 (0-926366-00-9) V W Snyder.

Spyri, Johanna. Heidi. (gr. k-1). 1986. 8.98 (0-685-16841-7, 618141) Random Hse Value.

—Heidi. Dole, Helen B., tr. Sharp, William, illus. LC 93-50908. 1994. write for info. (0-448-40563-6, G&D) Putnam Pub Group.

Stahl, Hilda. Kayla O'Brian & the Runaway Orphans. 128p. (gr. 4-7). 1991. pap. 4.95 (0-89107-631-X) Crossway Bks.

—Sadie Rose & the Cottonwood Creek Orphan. LC 88-71808. 128p. (gr. 4-7). 1989. pap. 4.99 (0-89107-513-5) Crossway Bks.

Streatfield, Noel. Dancing Shoes. 276p. (gr. 4-9). 1994. pap. 3.99 (0-679-85428-2) Random Bks Yng Read.

Talbot, Charlene J. An Orphan for Nebraska. Brown, Judith G., illus. LC 78-12179. 216p. (gr. 4-6). 1979. SBE 14.95 (0-689-30698-9, Atheneum Childrens Bks) Macmillan Child Grp.

Taylor, Theodore. Walking up a Rainbow: Being the True Version of the Long & Hazardous Journey of Susan D. Carlisle, Mrs. Myrtle Dessery, Drover Bert Pettit & Cowboy Clay Carmer & Others. LC 94-16548. (gr. 7 up). 1994. 14.95 (0-15-294512-1) HarBrace.

Thomas, Joyce C. When the Nightingale Sings. LC 92-6045. 160p. (gr. 7 up). 1992. 14.00 (0-06-020294-7); PLB 13.89 (0-06-020295-5) HarpC Child Bks.

Tolliver, Ruby C. Have Gun - Need Bullets. Washington, Burl, illus. LC 90-49363. 120p. (gr. 4 up). 1991. 15.95 (0-87565-085-6); pap. 10.95 (0-87565-089-9) Tex Christian.

Von Tempski, Armine. Bright Spurs. Brown, Paul, illus. LC 92-24540. x, 284p. 1992. pap. 14.95 (0-918024-95-1) Ox Bow.

Wallace, Barbara B. The Twin in the Tavern. LC 92-36429. 192p. (gr. 3-7). 1993. SBE 14.95 (0-689-31846-4, Atheneum Child Bk) Macmillan Child Grp.

Walt Disney Staff. The Rescuers. (gr. 5-8). 1989. 6.98 (0-8317-7388-X) Viking Child Bks.

Warner, Gertrude C. Boxcar Children. LC 42-1418. (gr. 2-7). 1942. PLB 10.95 (0-8075-0851-9); pap. 3.50 (0-8075-0852-7); Set of 4, Nos. 1-4. pap. 14.00 boxed (0-8075-0854-3); Set of 4, Nos. 5-8. pap. 14.00 boxed (0-8075-0857-8) A Whitman.

—The Boxcar Children. (Illus.). 158p. 1992. Repr. PLB 14.95x (0-89966-902-6) Buccaneer Bks.

Webster, Jean. Daddy-Long-Legs. (Orig.). (gr. k-6). 1987. pap. 4.95 (0-440-41673-6, Pub. by Yearling Classics) Dell.

—Daddy-Long-Legs. Hearn, Michael P., afterword by. 1988. pap. 2.50 (0-451-52187-0, Sig Classics) NAL-Dutton.

—Daddy-Long-Legs. 256p. (gr. 5 up). 1989. pap. 3.95 (0-14-035111-6, Puffin) Puffin Bks.

—Daddy-Long-Legs. 176p. (gr. 5-8). 1988. pap. 3.25 (0-590-44094-2) Scholastic Inc.

Wicke, Ed. The Screeps. LC 92-12259. (Illus.). 180p. 1992. pap. 5.99 (*0-8308-1352-7*, 1352) InterVarsity.

Wickstrom, Lois. Oliver: A Story about Adoption. (Illus.). 32p. 1991. 14.95 (*0-9611872-5-5*) Our Child Pr.

Woodruff, Elvira. The Secret Funeral of Slim Jim the Snake. LC 92-54419. 144p. (gr. 3-7). 1993. 13.95 (*0-8234-1014-5*) Holiday.

Wright, Betty R. The Ghosts of Mercy Manor. LC 92-21557. 1993. 13.95 (*0-590-43601-5*) Scholastic Inc.

Zistel, Era. Orphan. Coombs, Christine, illus. 64p. (Orig.). (gr. 4 up). 1990. pap. 11.95 (*0-9617426-5-8*) J N Townsend.

ORWELL, GEORGE, 1903-1950

Flynn, Nigel. Orwell. (Illus.). 112p. (gr. 7 up). 1990. lib. bdg. 19.94 (*0-86593-018-X*); lib. bdg. 14.95s.p. (*0-685-46452-0*) Rourke Corp.

Manovrier, Lynne. Animal Farm: A Study Guide. (gr. 6-10). 1983. tchr's. ed. & wkbk. 14.95 (*0-88122-021-3*) LRN Links.

OSCEOLA, SEMINOLE CHIEF, 1800?-1838

Jumper, Moses & Sonder, Ben. Osceola, Patriot & Warrior. Soper, Patrick, illus. LC 92-25209. 76p. (gr. 2-5). 1992. PLB 19.97 (*0-8114-7225-6*) Raintree Steck-V.

Oppenheim, Joanne. Osceola, Seminole Warrior. LC 78-60116. (Illus.). 48p. (gr. 4-6). 1979. PLB 10.59 (*0-89375-158-8*); pap. 3.50 (*0-89375-148-0*) Troll Assocs.

Zadra, Dan. Indians of America: Osceola. rev. ed. (gr. 2-4). 1987. PLB 14.95 (*0-88682-162-2*) Creative Ed.

Zane, Alex. Osceola: Seminole Rebel. Baird, W. David, ed. LC 93-21750. (Illus.). (gr. 5 up). 1994. PLB 18.95 (*0-7910-1716-8*, Am Art Analog); pap. write for info. (*0-7910-1993-4*, Am Art Analog) Chelsea hse.

OSTEOLOGY

see Bones

OSTRICHES

Arnold, Caroline. Ostriches & Other Flightless Birds. Hewett, Richard R., illus. 48p. (gr. 2-5). 1990. PLB 19.95 (*0-87614-377-X*) Carolrhoda Bks.

Fowler, Allan. Podria Sr un Pajaro - Libro Grande: (It Could Still Be a Bird Big Book) LC 90-2206. (SPA., Illus.). 32p. (ps-2). 1993. 22.95 (*0-516-59461-3*) Childrens.

Green, Carl R. & Sanford, William R. The Ostrich. LC 87-20175. (Illus.). 48p. (gr. 5). 1987. text ed. 12.95 RSBE (*0-89686-336-0*, Crestwood Hse) Macmillan Child Grp.

Lepthien, Emilie U. Ostriches. LC 93-3407. (Illus.). 48p. (gr. k-4). 1993. PLB 12.85 (*0-516-01193-6*); pap. 4.95 (*0-516-41193-4*) Childrens.

Ostrich. 1989. 3.50 (*1-87865-736-4*) Blue Q.

Stone, L. Ostriches. (Illus.). 24p. (gr. k-5). 1989. lib. bdg. 11.94 (*0-86592-323-X*) Rourke Corp.

OSTRICHES–FICTION

Brown, Kent. Why Can't I Fly? 1990. 13.95 (*0-385-41208-8*) Doubleday.

Erickson, Gina C. & Foster, Kelli C. Pip & Kip. Russell, Kerri G., illus. LC 92-29864. 24p. (ps-2). 1993. pap. 3.50 (*0-8120-1454-5*) Barron.

OTTERS

Cousteau Society Staff. Otters. LC 92-34177. (ps-1). 1993. pap. 3.95 POB (*0-671-86567-6*, Little Simon) S&S Trade.

Esbensen, Barbara J. Playful Slider: The North American River Otter. Brown, Mary B., illus. LC 92-13783. 1993. 15.95 (*0-316-24977-7*) Little.

Goodall, Jane. Jane Goodall's Animal World: Sea Otters. LC 89-78133. (Illus.). 32p. (gr. 3-7). 1990. pap. 3.95 (*0-689-71394-0*, Aladdin) Macmillan Child Grp.

Graves, Jack A. What Is a California Sea Otter? Cooke, Ralph W., illus. (gr. 3 up). 1977. pap. 3.95 (*0-910286-61-2*) Boxwood.

Greene, Carol. Reading about the River Otter. LC 92-26801. (Illus.). 32p. (gr. k-3). 1993. lib. bdg. 13.95 (*0-89490-425-6*) Enslow Pubs.

Hurd, Edith T. Song of the Sea Otter. Dewey, Jennifer, illus. LC 83-4675. 48p. (gr. 2-7). 1983. (Pant Bks Young); PLB 9.95 (*0-394-86191-4*) Pantheon.

Leon, Vicki. A Raft of Sea Otters. rev. ed. LC 93-15418. (Illus.). 48p. (Orig.). (gr. 5 up). 1993. perfect bdg. 9.95 (*0-918303-34-6*) Blake Pub.

Lepthien, Emilie U. Otters. LC 93-33515. (Illus.). 48p. (gr. k-4). 1994. PLB 12.85 (*0-516-01056-5*) Childrens.

Murray, Peter. Sea Otters. LC 93-42. (gr. 2-6). 1993. 15. 95 (*1-56766-007-X*) Childs World.

Palmer, S. Nutrias de Mar (Sea Otters) 1991. 8.95s.p. (*0-86592-681-6*) Rourke Enter.

Robinson, Sandra C. Sea Otters, River Otters: A Story & Activity Book. Opsahl, Gail K., illus. LC 92-62078. 64p. (Orig.). (gr. 1-6). 1993. pap. 7.95 (*1-879373-41-6*) R Rinehart.

Ryder, Joanne, ed. Sea Elf. Rothman, Michael, illus. LC 92-27608. 32p. (gr. k up). 1993. 15.00 (*0-688-10060-0*); PLB 14.93 (*0-688-10061-9*) Morrow Jr Bks.

Schneider, Jeff. My Friend the Sea Otter: An Ocean Magic Book. Spoon, Wilfred, illus. LC 90-61578. 12p. (ps). 1991. 4.95g (*1-877779-10-5*) Schneider Educational.

Sea Otters. 1991. PLB 14.95 (*0-88682-415-X*) Creative Ed.

Storms, John. Sammy the Sea Otter. Storms, Robert, illus. 24p. (gr. k-4). 1993. 4.95 (*0-89346-528-3*) Heian Intl.

OTTERS–FICTION

Bailey, Jill. Otter Rescue. Baum, Ann, illus. LC 91-19277. 48p. (gr. 3-7). 1992. PLB 21.34 (*0-8114-2710-2*); pap. 4.95 (*0-8114-6548-9*) Raintree Steck-V.

Benchley, Nathaniel. Oscar Otter. Lobel, Arnold, illus. LC 66-11499. 64p. (gr. k-3). 1966. PLB 13.89 (*0-06-020472-9*) HarpC Child Bks.

—Oscar Otter. Lobel, Arnold, illus. LC 66-11499. 64p. (gr. k-3). 1980. pap. 3.50 (*0-06-444025-7*, Trophy) HarpC Child Bks.

Burgess, Thornton. Little Joe Otter. 103p. 1981. Repr. PLB 17.95x (*0-89966-353-2*) Buccaneer Bks.

—Little Joe Otter. 169p. 1981. Repr. PLB 17.95 (*0-89967-027-X*) Harmony Raine.

Burgess, Thornton W. Little Joe Otter. 18.95 (*0-8488-0398-1*) Amereon Ltd.

Carlstrom, Nancy W. Swim the Silver Sea, Joshie Otter. (Illus.). 40p. (ps-3). 1993. PLB 14.95 (*0-399-21872-6*, Philomel Bks) Putnam Pub Group.

Chandrasekhar, Aruna. Oliver & the Oil Spill. Thatch, Nancy R., ed. Chandrasekhar, Aruna, illus. Melton, David, intro. by. LC 91-3340. (Illus.). 26p. (gr. k-4). 1991. PLB 14.95 (*0-933849-33-8*) Landmark Edns.

Craft, Mary. Sea Otters Cruz & Slick. Craft, Mary, illus. 24p. (Orig.). (ps-4). 1991. pap. write for info. (*0-9624842-2-9*) M Craft.

Craft, Mary L. Little Orphan Otter. Craft, Mary L., illus. 20p. (Orig.). (gr. k-12). 1989. pap. text ed. 5.25 (*0-9624842-0-2*) M Craft.

Hanks, Jacqueline. Splash! A Little Otter in Big Trouble. (Illus.). 24p. (gr. k-3). 1992. pap. 1.99 (*0-87406-600-X*) Willowisp Pr.

Hoban, Russell. Emmet Otter's Jug Band Christmas. (Illus.). 42p. 1992. Repr. PLB 11.95x (*0-89966-951-4*) Buccaneer Bks.

Prince, Michael. Oscar the Otter. 1992. 10.95 (*0-533-10235-9*) Vantage.

Savage, Deborah. A Rumour of Otters. 160p. (gr. 6 up). 1993. pap. 3.80 (*0-395-65748-2*) HM.

Williamson, Henry. Tarka the Otter: His Joyful Water-Life & Death in the Country of the Two Rivers. Finch, Robert, intro. by. LC 90-55169. (Illus.). 276p. 1990. pap. 9.95 (*0-8070-8507-3*) Beacon Pr.

OUTBOARD MOTORS

see Motorboats

OUTDOOR COOKERY

Boy Scouts of America. Cooking. LC 19-600. (Illus.). 80p. (gr. 6-12). 1986. pap. 1.85 (*0-8395-3257-1*, 33257) BSA.

OUTDOOR LIFE

see also Camping; Country Life; Hiking; Mountaineering; Nature Study; Sports; Wilderness Survival

Allison, Linda. The Wild Inside: Sierra Club's Guide to Great Outdoors. Allison, Linda, illus. 144p. (gr. 3-7). 1988. pap. 7.95 (*0-316-03434-7*) Little.

Beame, Rona. Backyard Explorer Kit. LC 88-51582. (Illus.). 64p. (gr. k-5). 1989. pap. 10.95 (*0-89480-343-3*, 1343) Workman Pub.

Henckel, Mark. Outdoors Just for Kids. Potter, John, illus. 128p. (Orig.). (gr. 1-8). 1992. pap. 8.95 spiral bdg. (*0-9627618-3-4*) Billings Gazette.

Humberstone, Eliot. Things Outdoors. (gr. 2-5). 1981. (Usborne-Hayes); pap. 4.50 (*0-86020-464-2*) EDC.

Jenny, Gerri. Outdoor Projects for Children. 1992. pap. 10.95 (*1-878767-55-0*) Murdoch Bks.

Kaplan, Andrew. Careers for Outdoor Types. (Illus.). 64p. (gr. 7 up). 1991. PLB 14.40 (*1-56294-022-8*); pap. 4.95 (*1-56294-770-2*) Millbrook Pr.

Klingel, Fitterer. Outdoor Safety. (Illus.). 32p. (ps up). 1986. PLB 12.95 (*0-88682-082-0*) Creative Ed.

Mason, Helen. Great Careers for People Who Like Being Outdoors, 6 vols. LC 93-78075. (Illus.). 48p. (gr. 6-9). 1993. 16.95 (*0-8103-9390-5*, 102108, UXL) Gale.

Nelson, JoAnne. Play It Safe. Meier, Melissa, illus. LC 93-12173. 1994. 5.95 (*0-935529-62-4*) Comprehen Health Educ.

Oakland, Don. Wildwoods Dad. Schley, Cynthia, illus. 220p. (Orig.). (gr. 5 up). 1987. pap. 6.95 (*0-9615242-1-9*) Oak Pr.

Olsen, Larry D. Outdoor Survival Skills. rev. ed. (Illus.). (gr. 6 up). 1988. pap. 9.95 (*0-9620429-0-0*) Salmon Falls Pub.

Paulsen, Gary. Woodsong. Paulsen, Ruth W., illus. LC 89-70835. 160p. (gr. 7 up). 1990. SBE 15.00 (*0-02-770221-9*, Bradbury Pr) Macmillan Child Grp.

Sobol, Donald J. Encyclopedia Brown's Book of the Wacky Outdoors. Enik, Ted, illus. LC 87-7851. 112p. (gr. 3-7). 1987. 12.95 (*0-688-06635-6*) Morrow Jr Bks.

Sun Bear. At Home in the Wilderness. Rev. ed. (Illus.). 90p. (gr. 4 up). 1973. pap. 6.95 (*0-87961-004-2*) Naturegraph.

OUTDOOR LIFE–FICTION

Christopher, John. The White Mountains. LC 67-10362. 192p. (gr. 5-9). 1970. SBE 14.95 (*0-02-718360-2*, Macmillan Child Bk); (Collier Young Ad) Macmillan Child Grp.

Hawkins, Colin & Hawkins, Jacqui. Crocodile Creek. 1989. 9.95 (*0-385-24979-9*); PLB 10.99 (*0-385-24980-2*) Doubleday.

Kjelgaard, Jim. Big Red. Kuhn, Bob, illus. 254p. (gr. 6 up). 1956. 16.95 (*0-8234-0007-7*) Holiday.

Mayne, William. Drift. 1990. pap. 3.25 (*0-440-40381-2*, Pub. by Yearling Classics) Dell.

Montgomery, Rutherford G. Pekan the Shadow. Nenninger, Jerome D., illus. LC 78-84779. (gr. 8-12). 1970. 3.95 (*0-87004-132-0*) Caxton.

Seton, Ernest T. Two Little Savages. (Illus.). 286p. (gr. 4-8). 1903. pap. 6.95 (*0-486-20985-7*) Dover.

OUTDOOR SURVIVAL

see Wilderness Survival

OUTER BANKS–NORTH CAROLINA–HISTORY–ANECDOTES, FACETIAE, SATIRE, ETC.

Preston, Judy J. The Outer Banks Story. Preston, Judy J., illus. 117p. (Orig.). (gr. 5 up). 1985. pap. 3.49 (*0-9613824-0-6*) Seabright.

OUTER SPACE

Alter, Anna. Destination Outer Space. (gr. 6 up). 1988. 4.95 (*0-8120-3839-8*) Barron.

Asimov, Isaac. How Did We Find Out about Outer Space? 64p. (gr. 5 up). 1977. PLB 11.85 (*0-8027-6284-0*) Walker & Co.

Asimov, Isaac, et al. Exploring Outer Space: Rockets, Probes, & Satellites. rev. & updated ed. (Illus.). (gr. 3 up). 1995. PLB 17.27 (*0-8368-1193-3*) Gareth Stevens Inc.

—Our Vast Home: The Milky Way. rev. & updated ed. (Illus.). (gr. 3 up). 1995. PLB 17.27 (*0-8368-1195-X*) Gareth Stevens Inc.

—Pollution in Space. rev. & updated ed. (Illus.). (gr. 3 up). 1995. PLB 17.27 (*0-8368-1196-8*) Gareth Stevens Inc.

Attalides, Stephanos. Journey into Space: Adventure Box IV. Attalides, Stephanos, illus. 12p. (ps up). 1988. 4.95 (*0-694-00266-6*) HarpC Child Bks.

Bailey, Donna. Far Out in Space. LC 90-40083. (Illus.). 48p. (gr. 2-6). 1990. PLB 19.97 (*0-8114-2525-8*) Raintree Steck-V.

Baker, D. Today's World in Space, 6 bks, Set I, Reading Level 5. (Illus.). 288p. (gr. 3-8). 1988. Set. PLB 111.60 (*0-86592-403-1*); PLB 83.70s.p. (*0-685-58830-0*) Rourke Corp.

Baker, David. Believe It Or Not Space Facts, Reading Level 5. (Illus.). 48p. (gr. 3-8). 1988. 18.60 (*0-86592-407-4*) Rourke Corp.

—Living in Space. (Illus.). 48p. (gr. 3-8). 1989. lib. bdg. 18.60 (*0-86592-401-5*); 13.95s.p. (*0-685-58639-1*) Rourke Corp.

—Today's World in Space, 6 bks, Set II, Reading Level 5. (Illus.). 288p. (gr. 3-8). 1989. Set. PLB 111.60 (*0-86592-370-1*); PLB 83.70s.p. (*0-685-58762-2*) Rourke Corp.

Be a Space Detective. 1992. pap. 3.99 (*0-517-06727-7*) Random Hse Value.

Berger, Joan. The Outer Space Tracing Fun Book. 1992. pap. 1.95 (*0-590-45133-2*) Scholastic Inc.

Bernards, Neal. Living in Space: Opposing Viewpoints. LC 90-3727. (Illus.). 112p. (gr. 5-8). 1990. PLB 14.95 (*0-89908-075-8*) Greenhaven.

Billingsley, Berry-Anne. Space. (Illus.). 48p. (Orig.). (gr. 4 up). 1992. pap. 6.95 (*0-563-34789-9*, BBC-Parkwest) Parkwest Pubns.

Boney, Lesley, illus. Space. 48p. (gr. k-5). 1988. pap. 2.95 (*0-8431-2247-1*) Price Stern.

Brenner, Barbara A. Planetarium. LC 91-6629. (ps-3). 1993. pap. 9.95 (*0-553-35428-0*) Bantam.

Butterfield, Moira. Space. Lipscombe, illus. 32p. (gr. 1-4). 1994. 5.95 (*1-56458-682-0*) Dorling Kindersley.

Carrie, Christopher. Mission to the Space Station. (Illus.). 40p. (gr. k up). 1990. 1.59 (*0-86696-247-6*) Binney & Smith.

Cleeve, Roger. Outer Space. Steltenpohl, Jane, ed. (Illus.). 32p. (gr. 3-5). 1990. PLB 10.98 (*0-671-68628-3*, J Messner) S&S Trade.

Cole, Norma. Blast Off! A Space Counting Book. Peck, Marshall, III, illus. LC 93-28794. 32p. (ps-4). 1994. 14.95 (*0-88106-499-8*); PLB 15.88 (*0-88106-493-9*); pap. 6.95 (*0-88106-498-X*) Charlesbridge Pub.

Couper, H. & Henbest, Nigel. The Space Atlas: A Pictorial Guide to our Universe. 1992. 16.95 (*0-15-200598-6*, HB Juv Bks) HarBrace.

Daniels, Patricia, ed. Let's Discover Outer Space. (Illus.). 80p. (gr. k-6). 1986. per set 199.00 (*0-8172-2595-1*); 14.95 ea. Raintree Steck-V.

Dolan, Edward F. Space. 1995. PLB write for info. (*0-8050-2864-1*) H Holt & Co.

Donnelly, Judy & Kramer, Sydelle. Space Junk: Pollution Beyond the Earth. LC 89-13544. (Illus.). 112p. (gr. 4-7). 1990. 12.95 (*0-688-08678-0*); PLB 12.88 (*0-688-08679-9*, Morrow Jr Bks) Morrow Jr Bks.

Furniss, Tim. Exploitation of Space. (Illus.). 48p. (gr. 5 up). 1990. lib. bdg. 18.60 (*0-86592-097-4*); lib. bdg. 13. 95s.p. (*0-685-36377-5*) Rourke Corp.

Gardner, Robert. Space. (Illus.). 96p. (gr. 5-8). 1994. bds. 16.95 (*0-8050-2851-X*) TFC Bks NY.

Greenberg, Judith E. & Carey, Helen H. Space. Karpinski, Rick, illus. 32p. (gr. 2-4). 1990. 10.95 (*0-8172-3754-2*) Raintree Steck-V.

Heathcote, Nick, et al. The New Discovery Book of Space. (Illus.). 96p. (gr. 6 up). 1994. text ed. 15.95 RSBE (*0-02-743506-7*, New Discovery Bks) Macmillan Child Grp.

Jones, Brian. Space: A Three-Dimensional Journey. Clifton-Dey, Richard, illus. 14p. (gr. k-4). 1991. 15.95 (*0-8037-0759-2*) Dial Bks Young.

Kay, Jerry. Living in Space. Allison, Linda & Wells, William S., illus. 22p. (Orig.). (gr. 3-7). 1988. 9.95 (*0-929201-06-X*) Kay Productions.

Kerrod, Robin. The Children's Space Atlas. LC 91-30148. (Illus.). 96p. (gr. 2-6). 1992. 16.95 (*1-56294-721-4*); PLB 18.90 (*1-56294-164-X*); pap. 10.95 (*0-685-72514-6*) Millbrook Pr.

—The Story of Space Exploration. Smith, Guy & Jobson, Ron, illus. 11p. 1994. 14.99 (*0-525-67487-X*, Lodestar Bks) Dutton Child Bks.

Kohler, Pierre. Earth & the Conquest of Space. (gr. 6 up). 1988. 4.95 (*0-8120-3831-2*) Barron.

Little People Big Book about Space. 64p. (ps-1). 1990. write for info. (*0-8094-7500-6*); lib. bdg. write for info. (*0-8094-7501-4*) Time-Life.

Marsh, Carole. Kids & Space: Look Forward, Plan, Prepare, Go! (Illus.). (gr. 3-8). 1994. PLB 24.95 (*0-7933-0003-7*); pap. 14.95 (*0-7933-0004-5*); computer disk 29.95 (*0-7933-0005-3*) Gallopade Pub Group.

Mayes, S. What's Out in Space? (Illus.). 24p. (gr. 1-4). 1990. lib. bdg. 11.96 (*0-88110-443-4*, Usborne); pap. 3.95 (*0-7460-0430-3*, Usborne) EDC.

Maynard, Chris. I Wonder Why Stars Twinkle & Other Questions about Space: And Other Questions about Space. Forsey, Chris & Kenyon, Tony, illus. LC 92-44259. 32p. (gr. k-3). 1993. 8.95 (*1-85697-881-8*, Kingfisher LKC) LKC.

Moncure, Jane B. Magic Monsters Learn about Space. Sommers, Linda, illus. LC 79-25765. (ps-3). 1980. PLB 14.95 (*0-89565-119-X*) Childs World.

Montgomery, Raymond A. Space & Beyond. large type ed. Granger, Paul, illus. 117p. (gr. 3-7). 1987. Repr. of 1979 ed. 8.95 (*0-942545-11-7*); PLB 9.95 (*0-942545-16-8*, Dist. by Grolier) Grey Castle.

Morris, Ting & Morris, Neil. Space. Levy, Ruth, illus. LC 93-24435. 32p. (gr. 2-4). 1994. PLB 12.90 (*0-531-14282-5*) Watts.

Nayer, Judy. Space. Goldberg, Grace, illus. 12p. (ps-2). 1993. bds. 6.95 (*1-56293-338-8*) McClanahan Bk.

Podendorf, Illa. Space. LC 82-4507. (gr. k-4). 1982. 12.85 (*0-516-01650-4*); pap. 4.95 (*0-516-41650-2*) Childrens.

Quinn, Kaye. Mission: Space. Quinn, Kaye, illus. 40p. (Orig.). (ps-4). 1986. pap. 2.95 (*0-8431-1894-6*) Price Stern.

Reid, S. Space Facts. (Illus.). 48p. (gr. 3-7). 1987. PLB 12.96 (*0-88110-240-7*); pap. 5.95 (*0-7460-0024-3*) EDC.

Richardson, James. Science Dictionary of Space. Hunt, Joseph, illus. LC 91-16551. 48p. (gr. 3-7). 1992. lib. bdg. 11.59 (*0-8167-2524-1*); pap. 3.95 (*0-8167-2443-1*) Troll Assocs.

Rickard, Graham. Homes in Space. (Illus.). 32p. (gr. 2-5). 1989. 13.50 (*0-8225-2125-3*) Lerner Pubns.

Ridpath, Ian. Space. LC 91-7455. (Illus.). 48p. (gr. 5-8). 1991. PLB 13.90 (*0-531-19144-3*, Warwick) Watts.

—Space. LC 92-53096. (Illus.). 48p. (Orig.). (gr. 3-8). 1992. pap. 5.95 (*1-85697-814-1*, Kingfisher LKC) LKC.

Seevers, James. Space. rev. ed. LC 87-20801. (Illus.). 48p. (gr. 2-6). 1987. PLB 10.95 (*0-8172-3260-5*) Raintree Steck-V.

Siegel, Mark A., et al, eds. Space: New Frontiers. (Illus.). 48p. (gr. 6-9). 1992. pap. text ed. 11.95 (*1-878623-44-3*) Info Plus Tx.

Simon, Seymour. Space Words: A Dictionary. Chewning, Randy, illus. LC 90-37402. 48p. (gr. 2-5). 1991. 15.00 (*0-06-022532-7*); PLB 14.89 (*0-06-022533-5*) HarpC Child Bks.

Space. (Illus.). 96p. (ps-4). 1994. write for info. (*1-56458-796-7*) Dorling Kindersley.

Spangenberg, Ray & Moser, Diane. Living & Working in Space. (Illus.). 136p. 1989. 22.95x (*0-8160-1849-9*) Facts on File.

Spizzirri Publishing Co. Staff. Space Explorers: An Educational Coloring Book. Spizzirri, Linda, ed. Spizzirri, Peter M., illus. 32p. (gr. 1-8). 1981. pap. 1.75 (*0-86545-037-4*) Spizzirri.

Weissman, Paul & Harris, Alan. The Great Voyager Adventure. (Illus.). 64p. (gr. 5-9). 1990. 14.95 (*0-671-72539-4*, J Messner); lib. bdg. 16.98 (*0-671-72538-6*) S&S Trade.

Wells, Susan. The Illustrated World of Space. LC 90-20263. (Illus.). 64p. (gr. 3-7). 1993. pap. 7.95 (*0-671-77033-0*, S&S BFYR) S&S Trade.

OUTER SPACE–COMMUNICATION

see Interstellar Communication

OUTER SPACE–EXPLORATION

Apfel, Necia H. Voyager to the Planets. Briley, Dorothy, ed. (Illus.). 48p. (gr. 3 up). 1991. 15.45 (*0-395-55209-5*, Clarion Bks) HM.

Arno, Roger. The Story of Space & Rockets. (Illus.). (gr. 5). 1978. pap. 3.95 (*0-88388-063-6*) Bellerophon Bks.

Baker, David. Factories in Space. LC 87-16689. (Illus.). 48p. (gr. 3-8). 1987. PLB 18.60 (*0-86592-409-0*); lib. bdg. 13.95s.p. (*0-685-67602-1*) Rourke Corp.

—I Want to Fly the Shuttle. LC 87-20467. (Illus.). 48p. (gr. 3-8). 1987. PLB 18.60 (*0-86592-406-6*); 13.95s.p. (*0-685-67600-5*) Rourke Corp.

—Journey to the Outer Planets. LC 87-19888. (Illus.). 48p. 1987. PLB 18.60 (*0-86592-405-8*); 13.95 (*0-685-67599-8*) Rourke Corp.

—Peace in Space. LC 87-19885. (Illus.). 48p. (gr. 3-8). 1987. PLB 18.60 (*0-86592-408-2*); 13.95s.p. (*0-685-67601-3*) Rourke Corp.

Barrett, Norman S. The Picture World of Space Voyages. (Illus.). 32p. (gr. k-4). 1990. PLB 12.40 (*0-531-14057-1*) Watts.

Branley, Franklyn M. Journey into a Black Hole. Simont, Marc, illus. LC 85-48249. 32p. (ps-3). 1986. PLB 13.89 (*0-690-04544-1*, Crowell Jr Bks) HarpC Child Bks.

—Neptune: Voyager's Final Target. LC 91-2469. (Illus.). 64p. (gr. 3-6). 1992. 15.00 (*0-06-022519-X*); PLB 14.89 (*0-06-022520-3*) HarpC Child Bks.

Burrows, William E. Mission to Deep Space: Voyager's Interplanetary Odyssey. LC 92-29746. 1993. text ed. write for info. (*0-7167-6500-4*) W H Freeman.

Cohen, Lynn. Air & Space. 64p. (ps-2). 1988. 6.95 (*0-912107-80-4*, MM984) Monday Morning Bks.

Cole, Joanna. The Magic School Bus Lost in the Solar System. Degen, Bruce, illus. (ps-3). 1990. 14.95 (*0-590-41428-3*, Scholastic Hardcover) Scholastic Inc.

Cozic, Charles P., ed. Space Exploration: Opposing Viewpoints. LC 92-8149. (Illus.). 240p. (gr. 10 up). 1992. PLB 17.95 (*0-89908-197-5*); pap. text ed. 9.95 (*0-89908-172-X*) Greenhaven.

Cromie, William. Skylab: The Story of Man's First Station in Space. LC 74-25983. (Illus.). 192p. (gr. 7 up). 1976. pap. 10.95 (*0-679-20300-1*) McKay.

Dolan, Terrance. Probing Deep Space. Goetzmann, William H., ed. Collins, Michael, intro. by. (Illus.). 112p. (gr. 6-12). 1993. PLB 19.95 (*0-7910-1326-X*, Am Art Analog); pap. write for info. (*0-7910-1550-5*, Am Art Analog) Chelsea Hse.

Donnelly, Judy. Moonwalk: The First Trip to the Moon. Davidson, Dennis, illus. LC 88-23668. 48p. (Orig.). (gr. 2-4). 1989. PLB 7.99 (*0-394-92457-6*); pap. 3.50 (*0-394-82457-1*) Random Bks Yng Read.

Dudley, Mark. An Eye to the Sky. LC 91-33880. (Illus.). 48p. (gr. 5-6). 1992. text ed. 12.95 RSBE (*0-89686-691-2*, Crestwood Hse) Macmillan Child Grp.

Exploring Space: From Ancient Legends to the Telescope to Modern Space Missions. LC 94-9646. (Illus.). 48p. (gr. 3 up). 1994. 19.95 (*0-590-47615-7*) Scholastic Inc.

Fradin, Dennis B. Space Colonies. LC 85-7722. (Illus.). 48p. (gr. k-4). 1985. pap. 4.95 (*0-516-41273-6*) Childrens.

Gentry, Linnea & Liptak, Karen. The Glass Ark. 80p. (gr. 3-7). 1991. 7.95 (*0-14-034928-6*) Puffin Bks.

—The Glass Ark: The Story of Biosphere Two. LC 81-25328. (Illus.). 94p. (gr. 5-8). 1991. 15.95 (*0-670-84173-0*) Viking Child Bks.

George, Michael. Space Exploration. (gr. 5 up). 1993. PLB 18.95 (*0-88682-481-8*) Creative Ed.

—Space Exploration. (gr. 4-7). 1993. 15.95 (*1-56846-058-9*) Creat Editions.

Gold, Susan D. To Space & Back: The Story of the Shuttle. LC 91-42565. (Illus.). 48p. (gr. 5-6). 1992. text ed. 12.95 RSBE (*0-89686-688-2*, Crestwood Hse) Macmillan Child Grp.

Graham, Ian. Space Science. LC 92-18319. 48p. (gr. 5). 1992. PLB 22.80 (*0-8114-2806-0*) Raintree Steck-V.

Halliday, Ian. Saturn. 48p. 1989. 13.95 (*0-8160-2049-3*) Facts on File.

Hawkes, Nigel. Into Space. LC 93-13468. (Illus.). 32p. (gr. 5-8). 1993. PLB 12.40 (*0-531-17416-6*, Gloucester Pr) Watts.

Kennedy, Gregory P. The First Men in Space. Goetzmann, William H., ed. Collins, Michael, intro. by. (Illus.). 112p. (gr. 5 up). 1991. PLB 18.95 (*0-7910-1324-3*) Chelsea Hse.

McCormick, Anita L. Space Exploration. LC 93-1830. (gr. 4 up). 1994. 14.95 (*1-56006-149-9*) Lucent Bks.

Mammana, Dennis. Start Exploring Space: A Fact-Filled Coloring Book. Driggs, Helen, illus. 128p. (Orig.). (gr. 3 up). 1991. pap. 8.95 (*0-89471-864-9*) Running Pr.

Markle, Sandra. Pioneering Space. LC 91-24936. (Illus.). 40p. (gr. 3-7). 1992. SBE 14.95 (*0-689-31748-4*, Atheneum Child Bk) Macmillan Child Grp.

Maurer, Richard. The NOVA Space Explorer's Guide: Where to Go & What to See. NASA Staff, photos by. LC 90-20074. (Illus.). 128p. (gr. 3-7). 1991. 20.00 (*0-517-57758-5*, Clarkson Potter) Crown Bks Yng Read.

Maynard, Christopher. Space. LC 92-32266. (Illus.). 32p. (gr. 1-4). 1993. 3.95 (*1-85697-897-4*, Kingfisher LKC) LKC.

—The Space Shuttle. LC 93-41941. 1994. 8.95 (*1-85697-512-6*, Kingfisher LKC) LKC.

Maynard, Christopher & Verdet, Jean-Pierre. The Universe. LC 94-9085. (Illus.). 128p. (gr. k-4). 1994. pap. 5.95 (*1-85697-527-4*, Kingfisher LKC) LKC.

Nicolson, Iain. Explore the World of Space & the Universe. Quigley, Sebastian, illus. 48p. (gr. 3-7). 1992. write for info. (*0-307-15608-7*, 15608, Golden Pr) Western Pub.

Petty, Kate. Into Space. Wood, Jakki, illus. 32p. (gr. 2-4). 1993. pap. 5.95 (*0-8120-1761-7*) Barron.

Ride, Sally. Voyager: An Adventure to the Edge of the Solar System. NASA Staff, photos by. LC 91-32495. (Illus.). 36p. (gr. 2-6). 1992. 14.00 (*0-517-58157-4*); PLB 14.99 (*0-517-58158-2*) Crown Bks Yng Read.

Ride, Sally & Okie, Susan. To Space & Back. LC 85-23757. (Illus.). 96p. (gr. 1 up). 1989. Repr. of 1985 ed. 17.00 (*0-688-06159-1*) Lothrop.

Ridpath, Ian. Space. LC 91-7455. (Illus.). 48p. (gr. 5-8). 1991. PLB 13.90 (*0-531-19144-3*, Warwick) Watts.

Sabin, Louis. Space Exploration & Travel. Moylan, Holly, illus. LC 84-2698. 32p. (gr. 3-6). 1985. PLB 9.49 (*0-8167-0258-6*); pap. text ed. 2.95 (*0-8167-0259-4*) Troll Assocs.

Scott, Elaine. Adventure in Space: The Flight to Fix the Hubble. Miller, Margaret, photos by. LC 94-7756. 1994. write for info. (*0-7868-0038-0*); lib. bdg. write for info. (*0-7868-2031-4*) Hyprn Child.

Sims, Lesley. Exploring Space. LC 93-28858. 1994. PLB 18.99 (*0-8114-5507-6*) Raintree Steck-V.

Souza, D. M. Space Sailing. LC 92-45176. 1993. 19.95 (*0-8225-2850-9*) Lerner Pubns.

Space. (Illus.). 112p. (gr. 4-9). 1989. 18.95 (*1-85435-072-2*) Marshall Cavendish.

Spangenberg, Ray & Moser, Diane. Living & Working in Space. (Illus.). 136p. 1989. 22.95x (*0-8160-1849-9*) Facts on File.

—Opening the Space Frontier. (Illus.). 136p. 1989. 22.95x (*0-8160-1848-0*) Facts on File.

Steele, Philip. Space Travel. LC 90-20735. (Illus.). 32p. (gr. 5-6). 1991. text ed. 3.95 RSBE (*0-89686-585-1*, Crestwood Hse) Macmillan Child Grp.

Verba, Joan M. Voyager: Exploring the Outer Planets. 64p. (gr. 5 up). 1991. PLB 19.95 (*0-8225-1597-0*) Lerner Pubns.

Vogt, Gregory. Apollo & the Moon Landing. (Illus.). 112p. (gr. 4-6). 1991. PLB 15.90 (*1-878841-31-9*); pap. 4.95 (*1-878841-37-8*) Millbrook Pr.

—Voyager. (Illus.). 112p. (gr. 4-6). 1991. PLB 15.90 (*1-56294-050-3*) Millbrook Pr.

OUTER SPACE–FICTION

Bailey, Donna. Facts About: Space. (gr. 4-7). 1993. pap. 4.95 (*0-8114-6628-0*) Raintree Steck-V.

Bowser, Milton & Haramilio, Alyce, eds. Saucer Sam. Cantrell, Ray, illus. 72p. 1992. 10.00 (*0-940178-38-9*) Sitare.

Coffelt, Nancy. Dogs in Space. (Illus.). 32p. (ps-3). 1993. 14.95 (*0-15-200440-8*) HarBrace.

Davis, Natalie L. The Space Twin. Taylor, Neil, illus. 112p. (gr. 4-8). 1987. 7.95 (*1-55523-037-7*) Winston-Derek.

Etra, Jon & Spinner, Stephanie. Aliens for Lunch. Bjorkman, Steve, illus. LC 90-39417. 64p. (Orig.). (gr. 2-4). 1991. PLB 6.99 (*0-679-91056-5*); pap. 2.50 (*0-679-81056-0*) Random Bks Yng Read.

Etra, Jonathan & Spinner, Stephanie. Aliens for Breakfast. Bjorkman, Steve, illus. LC 88-6653. 64p. (Orig.). (gr. 2-4). 1988. lib. bdg. 6.99 (*0-394-92093-7*); pap. 2.50 (*0-394-82093-2*) Random Bks Yng Read.

Fletcher, Bill & Fletcher, Sally. The Universe is My Home: A Children's Adventure Story. Fletcher, Bill & Fletcher, Sally, illus. 34p. (gr. k-5). 1993. 14.95 (*0-9634622-0-2*) Sci & Art Prods.

Freeman, Mae B. & Freeman, Ira M. The Sun, the Moon, & the Stars. rev. ed. Martin, Rene, illus. LC 78-64604. (gr. 2-4). 1979. 8.95 (*0-394-80110-5*) Random Bks Yng Read.

Friedman & DeLancie. The Best of Star Trek: The Next Generation. Kahan, B., ed. Marcos, et al, illus. 192p. 1994. pap. 19.95 collected ed. (*1-56389-125-5*) DC Comics.

George, Maureen. The Neighbor from Outer Space. 96p. (gr. 2-5). 1992. pap. 2.75 (*0-590-44583-9*, Little Apple) Scholastic Inc.

Gibson, Andrew. Jemima, Grandma & the Great Lost Zone. Riddell, Chris, illus. 128p. (gr. 3-7). 1992. pap. 6.95 (*0-571-16737-3*) Faber & Faber.

Good, Sharon. Alpha, Beta & Gamma: A Small Story. LC 90-86292. (Illus.). 48p. 1991. pap. 6.95 (*0-9627226-1-8*) Excalibur Publishing.

Gormley, Beatrice. Wanted: UFO. LC 89-26017. (Illus.). 128p. (gr. 3-6). 1990. 12.95 (*0-525-44593-5*, DCB) Dutton Child Bks.

Greer, Gery & Ruddick, Robert. Let Me off This Spaceship! Sims, Blanche C., illus. LC 90-32045. 64p. (gr. 2-5). 1991. 12.95 (*0-06-021605-0*); PLB 12.89 (*0-06-021606-9*) HarpC Child Bks.

Heinlein, Robert A. Tunnel in the Sky. reissued ed. LC 55-10142. 288p. (gr. 7 up). 1988. SBE 15.95 (*0-684-18916-X*, Scribners Young Read) Macmillan Child Grp.

Hess, Debra. Too Many Spies. Newsom, Carol, illus. LC 95-529. 128p. (gr. 3-6). 1993. pap. 3.50 (*1-56282-569-0*) Hyprn Ppbks.

Johnson, Crockett. Harold's Trip to the Sky. Johnson, Crockett, illus. LC 57-9262. (gr. k-3). 1957. PLB 13.89 (*0-06-022986-1*) HarpC Child Bks.

L'Engle, Madeleine. A Swiftly Tilting Planet. (gr. 7 up). 1979. pap. 4.50 (*0-440-90158-8*, LFL) Dell.

Levy, Elizabeth. Something Queer in Outer Space. Gerstein, Mordicai, illus. LC 92-54870. 48p. (gr. 2-5). 1993. pap. 4.95 (*1-56282-279-9*) Hyprn Ppbks.

—Something Queer in Outer Space. Gerstein, Mordicai, illus. LC 92-54870. 48p. (gr. 2-5). 1993. 12.95 (*1-56282-566-6*); PLB cancelled (*1-56282-280-2*) Hyprn Child.

Lorian, D. D. The Adventures of Zeb-Roo & Weeboo. 16p. 1994. pap. 6.00 (*0-8059-3585-1*) Dorrance.

Marshall, Edward. Space Case. Marshall, James, illus. LC 80-13369. 32p. (ps-3). 1980. 14.00 (*0-8037-8005-2*); PLB 12.89 (*0-8037-8007-9*) Dial Bks Young.

Marzollo, Jean & Marzollo, Claudio. Jed's Junior Space Patrol. Rose, David, illus. LC 81-12483. 56p. (ps-3). 1982. Dial Bks Young.

Mullin, Penn. Message from Outer Space. Kratoville, Betty L., ed. (Illus.). 64p. (gr. 3-9). 1989. PLB 4.95 (*0-87879-616-9*) High Noon Bks.

O'Neill, Mary. Power Failure. Bindon, John, illus. LC 90-11148. 32p. (gr. 3-6). 1991. PLB 12.89 (*0-8167-2288-9*); pap. text ed. 3.95 (*0-8167-2289-7*) Troll Assocs.

Ossorio, Joseph D. & Salvadeo, Michele B. Mikey's Walk in Space. (Illus.). 60p. (gr. 4-6). 1994. pap. 6.95 (*1-56721-053-8*) Twnty-Fifth Cent Pr.

Paton Walsh, Jill. The Green Book. Bloom, Lloyd, illus. LC 81-12620. 80p. (gr. 5 up). 1982. 13.00 (*0-374-32778-5*) FS&G.

Peel, John. Where in Space Is Carmen Sandiego? (gr. 4-7). 1993. pap. 3.25 (*0-307-22207-1*, Golden Pr) Western Pub.

—Where in Space Is Carmen Sandiego? A Mark & See Book with Marker. (gr. 4-7). 1993. pap. 3.95 (*0-307-22305-1*, Golden Pr) Western Pub.

Peterson, Melvin N. David's Star Studded Adventures. (Illus.). 58p. (gr. 1-4). 1988. spiral binding 48.00 (*0-938880-07-1*) MNP Star.
Polacco, Patricia. Meteor! (Illus.). 32p. (ps-3). 1992. pap. 5.95 (*0-399-22407-6*, Sandcastle Bks) Putnam Pub Group.
Rauch, Sidney J. Barnaby Brown: Home from Erehwon. Keating, Pam, illus. 80p. (Orig.). (gr. 2-4). 1990. pap. 4.95 (*1-55743-162-0*) Berrent Pubns.
—The Further Adventures of Barnaby Brown. Keating, Pam, illus. 63p. (Orig.). (gr. 2-4). 1990. pap. 4.95 (*1-55743-159-0*) Berrent Pubns.
—The Return of B. B. Keating, Pam, illus. 48p. (Orig.). (gr. 2-4). 1989. pap. 4.95 (*1-55743-153-1*) Berrent Pubns.
—A Visit to B. B.'s Planet. Keating, Pam, illus. 64p. (Orig.). (gr. 2-4). 1989. pap. 4.95 (*1-55743-156-6*) Berrent Pubns.
—The Visitor from Outer Space. Keating, Pam, illus. 48p. (Orig.). (gr. 2-4). 1989. pap. 4.95 (*1-55743-150-7*) Berrent Pubns.
Rays First Spaceship Ride. 60p. (gr. 3-4). pap. write for info. Rapcom Enter.
Rotsler, William. The Star Trek II Gift Set, 3 vols. Boxed Set. pap. 9.50 (*0-317-12429-3*) S&S Trade.
Sadler, Marilyn. Alistair in Outer Space. LC 84-4896. 1989. pap. 13.95 jacketed (*0-671-66678-9*, S&S BFYR); pap. 5.95 (*0-671-67938-4*, S&S BFYR) S&S Trade.
Schade, Susan, ed. Space Rock. Buller, Jon, illus. LC 87-12762. 48p. (Orig.). (gr. 2-3). 1988. lib. bdg. 7.99 (*0-394-99384-5*); pap. 3.50 (*0-394-89384-0*) Random Bks Yng Read.
Siracusa, Catherine. The Banana Split from Outer Space. LC 94-6917. 1995. 12.95 (*0-7868-0040-2*); 12.89 (*0-7868-2033-0*) Hyprn Child.
Spinelli, Jerry. Space Station Seventh Grade. LC 82-47915. 192p. (gr. 7 up). 1982. 15.95 (*0-316-80709-5*) Little.
—Space Station Seventh Grade. (gr. 7-12). 1984. pap. 2.95 (*0-440-96165-3*, LFL) Dell.
Stern, Leonard & Price, Roger. Mad Libs from Outer Space. 48p. (Orig.). (gr. 2 up). 1989. pap. 2.95 incl. chipboard (*0-8431-2443-1*) Price Stern.
Stine, R. L. Losers in Space. 144p. 1991. pap. 2.75 (*0-590-44746-7*, Apple Paperbacks) Scholastic Inc.
Trip to the Lost Planet. (Illus.). 48p. (Orig.). (gr. k-3). 1989. pap. 2.95 (*0-8431-2708-2*) Price Stern.
Williams, Lawrence. Space. LC 89-17338. (Illus.). 48p. (gr. 4-8). 1990. PLB 12.95 (*1-85435-174-5*) Marshall Cavendish.
Yolen, Jane. Commander Toad & the Big Black Hole. Degen, Bruce, illus. LC 82-23524. (gr. 1-4). 1983. (Coward); pap. 6.95 (*0-698-20594-4*) Putnam Pub Group.

OUTLAWS

see Robbers and Outlaws

OVERLAND JOURNEYS TO THE PACIFIC

Erickson, Paul. Daily Life in Covered Wagon. (gr. 4 up). 1994. write for info. (*0-89133-245-6*) Preservation Pr.
Fleischman, Paul. Townsend's Warbler. LC 91-26836. (Illus.). 64p. (gr. 3-7). 1992. PLB 12.89 (*0-06-021875-4*) HarpC Child Bks.
Parkman, Francis. Oregon Trail. (gr. 6 up). 1964. pap. 1.50 (*0-8049-0037-X*, CL-37) Airmont.
Stein, R. Conrad. The Oregon Trail. LC 93-36994. (Illus.). 32p. (gr. 3-6). 1994. PLB 12.30 (*0-516-06674-9*) Childrens.
Wright, Courtni C. Wagon Train: A Black Family's Westward Journey in 1865. Griffith, Gershom, illus. LC 94-18975. Date not set. write for info. (*0-8234-1152-4*) Holiday.

OVERLAND JOURNEYS TO THE PACIFIC–FICTION

Coerr, Eleanor. The Josefina Story Quilt. Degen, Bruce, illus. LC 85-45260. 64p. (gr. k-3). 1986. 14.00 (*0-06-021348-5*); PLB 13.89 (*0-06-021349-3*) HarpC Child Bks.
Kudlinski, Kathleen V. Facing West: A Story of the Oregon Trail. Watling, James, illus. LC 93-41349. 64p. (gr. 2-6). 1994. 12.99 (*0-670-85451-4*) Viking Child Bks.
Morris, Neil. Wagon Wheels Roll West. LC 89-988. (Illus.). 32p. (gr. 3-8). 1989. PLB 9.95 (*1-85435-167-2*) Marshall Cavendish.
Paulsen, Gary. Mr. Tucket. LC 93-31180. 1994. 14.95 (*0-385-31169-9*) Delacorte.
Ray, Mary L. Alvah & Arvilla. Root, Barry, illus. LC 93-31874. (gr. k-3). 1994. 14.95 (*0-15-202655-X*) HarBrace.
Taylor, Theodore. Walking up a Rainbow: Being the True Version of the Long & Hazardous Journey of Susan D. Carlisle, Mrs. Myrtle Dessery, Drover Bert Pettit & Cowboy Clay Carmer & Others. LC 94-16548. (gr. 7 up). 1994. 14.95 (*0-15-294512-1*) HarBrace.
Van Leeuwen, Jean. Bound for Oregon. LC 93-26709. (gr. 4 up). 1994. 14.99 (*0-8037-1526-9*); PLB 14.89 (*0-8037-1527-7*) Dial Bks Young.
Woodruff, Elvira. Dear Levi: Letters from the Overland Trail. Peck, Beth, illus. LC 93-5315. (gr. 3-7). 1994. 14.00 (*0-679-84641-7*); PLB 14.99 (*0-679-94641-1*) Knopf Bks Yng Read.

OVERWEIGHT

see Weight Control

OWENS, JESSE, 1913-

Coffey, Wayne. Jesse Owens. (Illus.). 64p. (gr. 3-7). 1992. PLB 14.95 (*1-56711-000-2*) Blackbirch.
Gentry, Tony. Jesse Owens. King, Coretta Scott, intro. by. (Illus.). (gr. 5 up). 1990. 17.95 (*1-55546-603-6*); pap. 9.95 (*0-7910-0247-0*) Chelsea Hse.
Green, Carl R. & Sanford, William R. Jesse Owens. LC 91-27185. (Illus.). 48p. (gr. 5). 1992. text ed. 11.95 RSBE (*0-89686-742-0*, Crestwood Hse) Macmillan Child Grp.
McKissack, Patricia & McKissack, Fredrick. Jesse Owens: Olympic Star. LC 92-3584. (Illus.). 32p. (gr. 1-4). 1992. lib. bdg. 12.95 (*0-89490-312-8*) Enslow Pubs.
Rennert, Richard S. Jesse Owens. (Illus.). 72p. (gr. 3-5). 1991. lib. bdg. 12.95 (*0-7910-1570-X*) Chelsea Hse.
Sabin, Francene. Jesse Owens, Olympic Hero. Frenck, Hal, illus. LC 85-1101. 48p. (gr. 4-6). 1986. lib. bdg. 10.79 (*0-8167-0551-8*); pap. text ed. 3.50 (*0-8167-0552-6*) Troll Assocs.

OWLS

Bailey, Jill. Life Cycle of an Owl. (ps-3). 1990. PLB 11.90 (*0-531-18315-7*, Pub. by Bookwright Pr) Watts.
Brown, Fern G. Owls. Perrotta, Mary, ed. LC 90-13093. (Illus.). 64p. (gr. 3-5). 1991. PLB 12.90 (*0-531-20008-6*) Watts.
Butterworth, Christine & Bailey, Donna. Owls. LC 90-37529. (Illus.). 32p. (gr. 1-4). 1990. PLB 18.99 (*0-8114-2643-2*) Raintree Steck-V.
Coldrey, Jennifer. The Owl in the Tree. Oxford Scientific Film Staff, illus. LC 87-9915. 32p. (gr. 4-6). 1987. PLB 17.27 (*1-55532-272-7*) Gareth Stevens Inc.
Cooper, Ann. Owls: On Silent Wings. Bruchac, Joseph, intro. by. LC 94-65092. (Illus.). 64p. (Orig.). 1994. pap. 7.95 (*1-879373-78-5*) R Rinehart.
Epple, Wolfgang. Barn Owls. Rogl, Manfred, photos by. (Illus.). 48p. (gr. 2-5). 1992. 19.95 (*0-87614-742-2*) Carolrhoda Bks.
Esbensen, Barbara J. Tiger with Wings: The Great Horned Owl. Brown, Mary B., illus. LC 90-23034. 32p. (gr. 2-4). 1991. 14.95 (*0-531-05940-5*); RLB 14.99 (*0-531-08540-6*) Orchard Bks Watts.
George, Jean George Spotted Owl. Date not set. 15.00 (*0-06-023641-8*); PLB 14.89 (*0-06-023640-X*) HarpC Child Bks.
George, Jean C. The Moon of the Owls. Minor, Wendell, illus. LC 91-2735. 48p. (gr. 3-7). 1993. 15.00 (*0-06-020192-4*); PLB 14.89 (*0-06-020193-2*) HarpC Child Bks.
George, Michael. Owls. (gr. 2-6). 1992. PLB 15.95 (*0-89565-837-2*) Childs World.
Guiberson, Brenda Z. Spotted Owl. (gr. 2-4). 1994. 14.95 (*0-8050-3171-5*) H Holt & Co.
Hawcock, David. Owl. Bampton, Bob, illus. 5p. (ps). 1994. 3.95 (*0-307-17303-8*, Artsts Writrs) Western Pub.
Kalman, Bobbie. Owls. Loates, Glen, illus. 56p. (gr. 3-4). 1987. 15.95 (*0-86505-164-X*); pap. 7.95 (*0-86505-184-4*) Crabtree Pub Co.
Kappeler, Markus. Owls. (Illus.). 32p. (gr. 4-6). 1991. PLB 18.60 (*0-8368-0687-5*) Gareth Stevens Inc.
Ling, Mary. Owl. LC 92-52811. (Illus.). 24p. (ps-1). 1992. 7.95 (*1-56458-115-2*) Dorling Kindersley.
McKeever, Catherine. A Place for Owls. Kassian, Olena, illus. 96p. (gr. 3 up). 1992. pap. 7.95 (*0-920775-24-1*, Pub. by Greey de Pencier CN) Firefly Bks Ltd.
Saintsing, David. The World of Owls. Oxford Scientific Films Staff, illus. LC 87-6537. 32p. (gr. 2-3). 1987. PLB 17.27 (*1-55532-301-4*) Gareth Stevens Inc.
Selsam, Millicent E. & Hunt, Joyce. A First Look at Owls, Eagles, & Other Hunters of the Sky. Springer, Harriet, illus. 32p. (gr. 6-9). 1986. 10.95 (*0-8027-6625-0*); PLB 10.85 (*0-8027-6642-0*) Walker & Co.
Silverstein, Alvin, et al. The Spotted Owl. LC 93-42624. (Illus.). 48p. (gr. 4-6). 1994. PLB 13.40 (*1-56294-415-0*) Millbrook Pr.
Stone, Lynn M. The Great Horned Owl. LC 87-570. (Illus.). 48p. (gr. 5). 1987. text ed. 12.95 RSBE (*0-89686-325-5*, Crestwood Hse) Macmillan Child Grp.
Wexo, John B. Owls. 24p. (gr. 4). 1989. PLB 14.95 (*0-88682-268-8*) Creative Ed.
Wildlife Education, Ltd. Staff. Owls. Boyer, Trevor, et al, illus. 20p. (Orig.). (gr. 5 up). 1985. pap. 2.75 (*0-937934-32-1*) Wildlife Educ.

OWLS–FICTION

Alden, Laura. Owl's Adventure in Alphabet Town. McCallum, Jodie, illus. LC 92-4091. 32p. (ps-2). 1992. PLB 11.80 (*0-516-05415-5*) Childrens.
Bunting, Eve. The Man Who Could Call Down Owls. Mikolaycak, Charles, illus. LC 83-17568. 32p. (gr. k-3). 1984. RSBE 14.95 (*0-02-715380-0*, Macmillan Child Bk) Macmillan Child Grp.
—The Man Who Could Call Down Owls. Mikolaycak, Charles, illus. LC 93-23706. (gr. k-3). 1994. pap. 4.95 (*0-689-71837-3*, Atheneum) Macmillan.
Crebbin, June. Fly by Night. Lambert, Stephen, illus. LC 92-53140. 32p. (ps up). 1993. 14.95 (*1-56402-149-1*) Candlewick Pr.
Dowling, Paul. Happy Birthday, Owl. Dowling, Paul, illus. LC 91-45660. 32p. (ps-k). 1992. 9.95 (*1-56282-253-5*) Hyprn Child.
Edmiston, Jim. Little Eagle Lots of Owls. Ross, Jane, illus. LC 92-22683. 32p. (gr. k-3). 1993. 13.95 (*0-395-65564-1*) HM.
Erickson, Russell E. A Toad for Tuesday. Di Fiori, Lawrence, photos by. LC 92-24595. (Illus.). 64p. (gr. 3 up). 1993. pap. 3.95 (*0-688-12276-0*, Pub. by Beech Tree Bks) Morrow.
Gallop, Louise. Owl's Secret. 1994. pap. 8.95 (*0-934007-21-7*) Paws Four Pub.
Gregorich, Barbara. Mouse & Owl. Hoffman, Joan, ed. (Illus.). 16p. (Orig.). (gr. k-2). 1991. pap. 2.25 (*0-88743-025-2*, 06025) Sch Zone Pub Co.
Gullander, Elizabeth. Oswald Hoot: The Owl Who Was Scared of the Dark. Youra, Dan, illus. 64p. (ps-6). 1982. PLB 7.95 (*0-940828-06-5*); pap. 4.95 (*0-940828-05-7*) Olympic Pub.
Hale, Janet C. The Owl's Song. (gr. 5 up). 1991. pap. 2.95 (*0-553-28829-6*, Starfire) Bantam.
Harris, Nicholas. Owlbert. Horvat, Karl J., illus. LC 89-4445. 32p. (gr. 2-3). 1989. PLB 18.60 (*0-8368-0110-5*) Gareth Stevens Inc.
Hooper, Lyn L. My Own Home. Richardson, Ruth, illus. LC 90-4386. 32p. (gr. k-3). 1991. HarpC Child Bks.
Hutchins, Pat. Good-Night, Owl! Hutchins, Pat, illus. LC 72-186355. 32p. (ps-2). 1972. RSBE 14.95 (*0-02-745900-4*, Macmillan Child Bk) Macmillan Child Grp.
—Good Night, Owl. LC 89-17708. 32p. (ps-3). 1990. pap. 3.95 (*0-689-71371-1*, Aladdin) Macmillan Child Grp.
—Good-Night, Owl! Hutchins, Pat, illus. LC 91-8172. 36p. (gr. k-3). 1991. pap. 16.95 big book ed. (*0-689-71541-2*, Aladdin) Macmillan Child Grp.
Johansen, Hanna. Duck & the Owl. Bhend-Zaugg, Kathi, illus. LC 91-33011. 64p. (gr. 2-5). 1992. 12.95 (*0-525-44828-4*, DCB) Dutton Child Bks.
Jones, Donna J. Oolik: The Owl Who Couldn't Whoo. Grove, Jason, illus. 29p. (Orig.). (gr. k-5). 1987. pap. 3.50 (*0-9617382-0-0*) Glacier Pub.
Joubert, Jean. White Owl & Blue Mouse. Levertov, Denise, tr. from FRE. Gay, Michel, illus. LC 90-70710. 64p. (gr. 1-3). 1990. 13.95 (*0-944072-13-5*) Zoland Bks.
Kindl, Patrice. Owl in Love. LC 92-26952. 1993. 13.95 (*0-395-66162-5*) HM.
—Owl in Love. 208p. (gr. 7 up). 1994. pap. 3.99 (*0-14-037129-X*) Puffin Bks.
Kraus, Robert. The Adventures of Wise Old Owl. Kraus, Robert, illus. LC 92-20436. 32p. (ps-3). 1992. PLB 10.89 (*0-8167-2943-3*); pap. text ed. 2.95 (*0-8167-2944-1*) Troll Assocs.
—Owliver. Aruego, Jose & Dewey, Ariane, illus. LC 80-13664. (ps). 1987. pap. 13.95 jacketed (*0-671-66523-5*, S&S BFYR) S&S Trade.
—Wise Old Owl's Christmas Adventure. LC 93-25544. (Illus.). 32p. (ps-3). 1993. PLB 10.89 (*0-8167-2945-X*); pap. text ed. 2.95 (*0-8167-2946-8*) Troll Assocs.
—Wise Old Owl's Halloween Adventure. LC 93-18686. (Illus.). 32p. (gr. k-3). 1993. PLB 10.89 (*0-8167-2949-2*); pap. text ed. 2.95 (*0-8167-2950-6*) Troll Assocs.
Kraus, Robert, ed. & illus. Wise Old Owl's Canoe Trip Adventure. LC 91-39014. 32p. (ps-3). 1993. text ed. 10.89 (*0-8167-2947-6*); 2.95 (*0-8167-2948-4*) Troll Assocs.
Lear, Edward. The Owl & the Pussycat. (ps-1). 1989. 13.95 (*0-89919-505-9*, Clarion Bks); pap. 4.95 (*0-89919-854-6*, Clarion Bks) HM.
Lehman, James H. The Owl & the Tuba. Raschka, Christopher, illus. LC 91-73880. 32p. 1991. 13.95 (*1-878925-02-4*) Brotherstone Pubs.
Leonard, Marcia. Little Owl Leaves the Nest. Newson, Carol, illus. 32p. 1984. pap. 2.75 (*0-553-15460-5*) Bantam.
Lobel, Arnold. Owl at Home. Lobel, Arnold, illus. LC 74-2630. 64p. (gr. k-3). 1975. PLB 13.89 (*0-06-023949-2*) HarpC Child Bks.
—Owl at Home. Lobel, Arnold, illus. LC 74-2630. 64p. (gr. k-3). 1987. (Trophy); pap. 3.50 (*0-06-444034-6*, Trophy) HarpC Child Bks.
McDonald, Megan. Whoo-oo Is It? Schindler, Stephen D., illus. LC 91-18494. 32p. (ps-1). 1992. 14.95 (*0-531-05974-X*); lib. bdg. 14.99 (*0-531-08574-0*) Orchard Bks Watts.
Matthews, Morgan. Whoo's Too Tired? Kolding, Richard M., illus. LC 88-1285. 48p. (Orig.). (gr. 1-4). 1988. PLB 10.59 (*0-8167-1331-6*); pap. text ed. 3.50 (*0-8167-1332-4*) Troll Assocs.
Mowat, Farley. Owls in the Family. (gr. 4-7). 1985. pap. 3.50 (*0-553-15585-7*) Bantam.
Nicoll, Helen & Pienkowski, Jan. Owl at School. (Illus.). 32p. (ps). 1984. 15.95 (*0-434-95434-9*, Pub. by W Heinemann Ltd) Trafalgar.
Ollie the Owl. (Illus.). (ps-1). 2.98 (*0-517-46984-7*) Random Hse Value.
Plemons, Marti. Megan & the Owl Tree. (Illus.). 128p. (gr. 3-6). 1992. pap. 4.99 (*0-87403-685-2*, 24-03725) Standard Pub.
Provensen, Alice & Provensen, Martin. An Owl & Three Pussycats. LC 93-44747. (gr. k-3). 1994. 16.95 (*0-15-200183-2*, Browndeer Pr) HarBrace.

Shles, Larry. The Adventure of the Squib Owl: Squib Ser. Shles, Larry, illus. 1988. pap. 7.95 (*0-915190-85-0*) Jalmar Pr.

Squib the Owl series, written & whimsically illustrated by Larry Shles, teaches self-esteem & personal & social responsibility as it entertains. The author uses the name Squib to personify the small vulnerable part of us all that struggles & at times feels helpless in an enormous world filled

with emotions. This Series, five volumes, traces the adventures of this tiny owl as he struggles with his feelings searching at least for understanding. Each of the five titles explores a different vulnerability. MOTHS & MOTHERS, FEATHERS & FATHERS (explores feelings); HOOTS & TOOTS & HAIRY BRUTES (explores disabilities); ALIENS IN MY NEST (explores adolescent behavior); HUGS & SHRUGS (explores inner peace). The latest volume DO I HAVE TO GO TO SCHOOL TODAY? is great for the young reader who needs encouragement from teachers who accept him "just as he is". Brilliantly simple, yet realistically complex, Squib personifies each & every one of us. He is a reflection of what we are, & what we can become. Every reader who has struggled with life's limitations will recognize his own struggles & triumphs in the microcosm of Squib's forest world - in Squib we find a parable for all ages from 8-80.
Publisher Provided Annotation.

—Hoots & Toots & Hairy Brutes, Vol. 2: The Continuing Adventures of Squib. 2nd ed. Shles, Larry, illus. LC 89-83466. 72p. (gr. k-8). 1989. pap. 7.95 (*0-915190-56-7*, JP9056-7) Jalmar Pr.
—Moths & Mothers, Feathers & Fathers, Vol. 1: A Story about a Tiny Owl Named Squib. 2nd ed. Winch, Bradley, ed. Shles, Larry, illus. LC 89-83467. 72p. (gr. k-8). 1989. pap. 7.95 (*0-915190-57-5*, JP9057-5) Jalmar Pr.
—Scooter's Tail of Terror: A Fable of Addiction & Hope. Ciconte, Marie, ed. (Illus.). 80p. (Orig.). (gr. 2 up). 1992. pap. 9.95 (*0-915190-89-3*, JP9089-3) Jalmar Pr.
Shles, Lawrence. Hoots & Toots & Hairy Brutes: Squib the Owl Saves the Day. Shles, Lawrence, illus. 70p. (gr. k-3). 1984. 10.95 (*0-685-42996-2*); pap. 4.95 (*0-685-42997-0*) HM.
Simmons, Dawn L. The Great White Owl of Sissinghurst. Schindler, S. D., illus. LC 91-17490. 32p. (ps-3). 1993. SBE 14.95 (*0-689-50522-1*, M K McElderry) Macmillan Child Grp.
Tomlinson, Jill. The Owl Who Was Afraid of the Dark. large type ed. (gr. 1-8). 1994. sewn 16.95 (*0-7451-2038-5*, Galaxy Child Lrg Print) Chivers N Amer.

Waddell, Martin. Las Lechucitas: Owl Babies. Benson, Patrick, illus. (SPA.). 14p. (gr. k-1). 1994. 14.95 (*0-88272-137-2*) Santillana. Adorable baby owls are alone in a dark forest, wondering where their mother could be. Beautiful illustrations depict the spooky forest & the many moods of these endearing owls. To order: Santillana, 901 West Walnut, Compton, CA 90220. 1-800-245-8584.
Publisher Provided Annotation.

—Owl Babies. Benson, Patrick & Benson, Patrick, illus. LC 91-58750. 32p. (ps up). 1992. 14.95 (*1-56402-101-7*) Candlewick Pr.
Wahl, Jan. Mrs. Owl & Mr. Pig. Christelow, Eileen, illus. 32p. (gr. k-3). 1991. 13.95 (*0-525-67311-3*, Lodestar Bks) Dutton Child Bks.
Wildsmith, Brian. The Owl & the Woodpecker. (Illus.). 32p. 1992. pap. 7.50 (*0-19-272255-7*) OUP.

OWLS–POETRY
Livingston, Myra C. If the Owl Calls Again: A Collection of Owl Poems. Frasconi, Antonio, illus. LC 89-27659. 128p. (gr. 5 up). 1990. SBE 13.95 (*0-689-50501-9*, M K McElderry) Macmillan Child Grp.

OZARK MOUNTAINS–FICTION
MacBride, Roger L. Little Farm in the Ozarks. Gilleece, David, illus. 256p. (gr. 3-7). 1994. 14.95 (*0-06-024245-0*); PLB 14.89 (*0-06-024246-9*) HarpC Child Bks.

P

PACIFIC CABLE
see Cables, Submarine

PACIFIC ISLANDS
see Islands of the Pacific

PACIFIC NORTHWEST
see Northwest, Pacific

PACIFIC OCEAN
Heinrichs, Susan. The Pacific Ocean. LC 86-9653. (Illus.). 48p. (gr. k-4). 1986. PLB 12.85 (*0-516-01295-9*); pap. 4.95 (*0-516-41295-7*) Childrens.

PACIFIC STATES
Riegel, Martin P. Ghost Ports of the Pacific, Vol. III: Washington. LC 89-90772. (Illus.). 52p. (Orig.). 1989. 11.00 (*0-944871-22-4*); pap. 4.95 (*0-944871-23-2*) Riegel Pub.
Yocom, Charles & Dasmann, Raymond. Pacific Coastal Wildlife Region. rev. ed. (Illus.). 120p. (gr. 4 up). 1965. 15.95 (*0-911010-05-X*); pap. 7.95 (*0-911010-04-1*) Naturegraph.

PACKAGING–FICTION
Bonfils, Bolette. Peter's Package. Mogensen, Jan, illus. 24p. (ps-2). 1994. 9.95 (*1-56656-155-8*, Crocodile Bks) Interlink Pub.

PAGEANTS
see also Mysteries and Miracle Plays
Randolph, Sallie G. Putting on Perfect Proms, Programs, & Pageants. LC 91-18527. (Illus.). 144p. (gr. 9-12). 1991. PLB 13.90 (*0-531-11061-3*) Watts.

PAIGE, LEROY, 1906-
McKissack, Patricia & McKissack, Fredrick. Satchel Paige: The Best Arm in Baseball. LC 92-3583. (Illus.). 32p. (gr. 1-4). 1992. lib. bdg. 12.95 (*0-89490-317-9*) Enslow Pubs.

PAINE, THOMAS, 1737-1809
Farley, Karin C. Thomas Paine. LC 92-17662. (Illus.). 128p. (gr. 7-10). 1992. PLB 22.80 (*0-8114-2329-8*) Raintree Steck-V.
Vail, John. Thomas Paine. Schlesinger, Arthur M., Jr., intro. by. (Illus.). 112p. (gr. 5 up). 1990. 17.95 (*1-55546-819-5*) Chelsea Hse.

PAINTED GLASS
see Glass Painting and Staining

PAINTERS
see also Artists;
also names of individual painters
Beauzile, Anthony L. & Beauzile, Gerard, Jr. Kartik Trivedi, Contemporary Impressionist. Fairhall, Winnifred, ed. Trivedi, Kartik, illus. (Orig.). (gr. 10-12). 1992. 59.95g (*0-9633124-1-3*); pap. 34.95g (*0-685-62455-2*) T&T Dyno-Srvs.
Frazier, Nancy. Frida Kahlo: Mysterious Painter. (Illus.). 64p. (gr. 3-7). 1992. PLB 14.95 (*1-56711-012-6*) Blackbirch.
Howard, Nancy S. William Sidney Mount: Painter of Rural America. Siegel, Martha, ed. LC 93-72834. (Illus.). 48p. (gr. 2-8). 1994. 14.95 (*0-87192-275-4*, 275-7) Davis Mass.
Jones, Jane A. The Arts - Frida Kahlo. LC 92-44758. 1993. 19.93 (*0-86625-485-4*); 14.95s.p. (*0-685-66535-6*) Rourke Pubns.
Loughery, John. John Sloan. (gr. 6 up). 1994. write for info. (*0-8050-2878-1*) H Holt & Co.
Turner, Robyn M. Frida Kahlo: Portraits of Women Artists for Children. (gr. 4-7). 1993. 15.95 (*0-316-85651-7*) Little.
Venezia, Mike. Diego Rivera. LC 94-11650. (Illus.). 48p. (gr. 4 up). 1994. PLB 17.20 (*0-516-02299-7*); pap. 4.95 (*0-516-42299-5*) Childrens.

PAINTERS, AMERICAN
Goldstein, Ernest. Grant Wood: American Gothic. (Illus.). 52p. (gr. 9-12). 1984. pap. 9.95 (*0-317-02721-2*) NAL-Dutton.
Lyons, Mary E. Starting Home: The Story of Horace Pippin, Painter. LC 92-26990. (Illus.). 48p. (gr. 3-6). 1993. SBE 15.95 (*0-684-19534-8*, Scribners Young Read) Macmillan Child Grp.
Meyer, Susan E. Mary Cassatt. (Illus.). 80p. (gr. 7 up). 1990. 19.95 (*0-8109-3154-0*) Abrams.
Reef, Pat D. William Thon, Painter. (Illus.). 56p. (gr. 4-7). 1991. pap. 12.95 (*0-933858-28-0*) Kennebec River.
Shuman, R. Baird. The Arts - Georgia O'Keeffe. LC 92-44759. 1993. 19.93 (*0-86625-487-0*); 14.95s.p. (*0-685-67773-7*) Rourke Pubns.
Willoughby, Bebe & Mass, Wendy, eds. Norman Rockwell: Self-Portrait of My Early Years. LC 94-14874. 1994. 12.95 (*0-681-00733-8*) Longmeadow Pr.

PAINTERS, FRENCH
Muhlberger, Richard, text by. What Makes a Monet a Monet? (Illus.). 48p. (gr. 5 up). 1993. 9.95 (*0-670-85200-7*) Viking Child Bks.

PAINTERS' MATERIALS
see Artists' Materials

PAINTING
see also Animal Painting and Illustration; Color; Flower Painting and Illustration; Impressionism (Art); Landscape Painting; Paintings; Stencil Work; Water Color Painting
Armstrong, Carole. My Art Museum: A Sticker Book of Paintings. LC 93-50786. (Illus.). 16p. (ps-3). 1994. pap. 9.95 (*0-399-22791-1*, Philomel Bks) Putnam Pub Group.
Blizzard, Gladys S. Come Look with Me: Animals in Art. LC 92-5357. 32p. (gr. 1-8). 1992. 13.95 (*1-56566-013-7*) Thomasson-Grant.
Butterfield, Moira. Fun with Paint. Venus, Joanna & Kerr, Elizabeth, illus. 48p. (gr. 1-5). 1993. PLB 9.99 (*0-679-93492-8*); pap. 6.99 (*0-679-83492-3*) Random Bks Yng Read.
Canady, Robert & Annis, Scott. Color in Iowa Coloring Album. (Illus.). 32p. (Orig.). (gr. 1-5). 1984. pap. 3.95 (*0-9615584-0-7*) Little Gnome.
Capek, Michael. Artistic Trickery: The Tradition of Trompe l'Oeil Art. LC 94-13902. 1994. 21.50 (*0-8225-2064-8*) Lerner Pubns.
Chaudron, Chris & Childs, Caro. Face Painting. (Illus.). 32p. (gr. 2-6). 1993. PLB 12.96 (*0-88110-649-6*, Usborne); pap. 5.95 (*0-7460-1445-7*) EDC.
Chinese Brush Painting. (Illus.). 48p. (gr. 9 up). 1994. 19.95 (*0-8431-3753-3*) Price Stern.
Emert, Phyllis. Fun with Paints: Little Crafters. 1992. pap. 3.99 (*0-517-08276-4*) Random Hse Value.
Foster, P. Painting. (Illus.). 32p. (gr. 5-10). 1981. PLB 13.96 (*0-88110-026-9*); pap. 6.95 (*0-86020-546-0*) EDC.
Haldane, Suzanne. Painting Faces. LC 88-3706. (Illus.). 32p. (gr. 3 up). 1988. 13.95 (*0-525-44408-4*, DCB) Dutton Child Bks.
Hodge, Anthony & Kline, Marjory. Painting. LC 90-45004. (Illus.). 32p. (gr. 5-7). 1991. PLB 12.40 (*0-531-17299-6*, Gloucester Pr) Watts.
Hughes, Andrew. Van Gogh. (Illus.). 32p. (gr. 5 up). 1994. 10.95 (*0-8120-6462-3*); pap. 5.95 (*0-8120-1999-7*) Barron.
James, Diane. Playing with Paint. Lynn, Sara, photos by. (Illus.). 24p. (ps-1). 1992. pap. 3.95 (*0-590-45739-X*, Cartwheel) Scholastic Inc.
Lynn, Sara & James, Diane. Play with Paint. (Illus.). 24p. (ps-2). 1993. 18.95 (*0-87614-755-4*) Carolrhoda Bks.
Martin, Judy. Painting & Drawing. (Illus.). 96p. (gr. 3-6). 1993. PLB 16.90 (*0-685-72619-3*); pap. 9.95 (*1-56294-709-5*) Millbrook Pr.
Mason, Antony. Leonardo Da Vinci. (Illus.). 32p. (gr. 5 up). 1994. 10.95 (*0-8120-6460-7*); pap. 5.95 (*0-8120-1997-0*) Barron.
Micklethwait, Lucy, selected by. I Spy a Lion: Animals in Art. LC 93-30017. 48p. 1994. 19.00 (*0-688-13230-8*); PLB 18.93 (*0-688-13231-6*) Greenwillow.
—I Spy: An Alphabet in Art. LC 91-42212. (Illus.). 64p. 1992. 19.00 (*0-688-11679-5*) Greenwillow.
Muhlberger, Richard, text by. What Makes a Degas a Degas? (Illus.). 48p. (gr. 5 up). 1993. 9.95 (*0-670-85205-8*) Viking Child Bks.
—What Makes a Raphael a Raphael? (Illus.). 48p. (gr. 5 up). 1993. 9.95 (*0-670-85204-X*) Viking Child Bks.
—What Makes a Rembrandt a Rembrandt? (Illus.). 48p. (gr. 5 up). 1993. 9.95 (*0-670-85199-X*) Viking Child Bks.
—What Makes a van Gogh a van Gogh? (Illus.). 48p. (gr. 5 up). 1993. 9.95 (*0-670-85198-1*) Viking Child Bks.
Oil Painting. (Illus.). 48p. (gr. 9 up). 1994. 19.95 (*0-8431-3754-1*) Price Stern.
Richmond, Robin. Animals in Art. Richmond, Robin, illus. LC 93-9766. 48p. (gr. 2-5). 1993. PLB 16.00 (*0-8249-8626-1*, Ideals Child); text ed. 15.95 (*0-8249-8613-X*) Hambleton-Hill.
—Children in Art. Richmond, Robin, illus. LC 92-7184. 48p. (gr. 2-5). 1992. 15.95 (*0-8249-8552-4*, Ideals Child); PLB 16.00 (*0-8249-8588-5*) Hambleton-Hill.
Russon, Jacqueline. Face Painting. Mukhida, Zul, photos by. (Illus.). 32p. (gr. 2-4). 1994. 14.95 (*1-56847-197-1*) Thomson Lrning.
—Making Faces. LC 94-25632. 1995. write for info. (*0-8069-0929-3*) Sterling.
Shuman, R. Baird. The Arts - Georgia O'Keeffe. LC 92-44759. 1993. 19.93 (*0-86625-487-0*); 14.95s.p. (*0-685-67773-7*) Rourke Pubns.
Sirett, Dawn. My First Painting Book. (Illus.). 48p. (gr. k-5). 1994. 12.95 (*1-56458-466-6*) Dorling Kindersley.
Stocks, Sue. Painting. Fairclough, Chris, photos by. LC 93-44582. (Illus.). 32p. (gr. 1-4). 1994. 14.95 (*1-56847-162-9*) Thomson Lrning.
Triado, Juan-Ramon. The Key to Painting. (Illus.). 80p. (gr. 8 up). 1990. PLB 21.50 (*0-8225-2050-8*) Lerner Pubns.
Venezia, Mike. Jackson Pollock. Moss, Meg, contrib. by. LC 93-36699. (Illus.). 32p. (ps-4). 1994. PLB 12.85 (*0-516-02298-9*) Childrens.
—Michelangelo. Venezia, Mike, illus. LC 91-555. 32p. (ps-4). 1991. PLB 12.85 (*0-516-02293-8*); pap. 4.95 (*0-516-42293-6*) Childrens.
—Paul Klee. Venezia, Mike, illus. LC 91-12554. 32p. (gr. 4). 1991. PLB 12.85 (*0-516-02294-6*); pap. 4.95 (*0-516-42294-4*) Childrens.
—Salvador Dali. Venezia, Mike, illus. LC 92-35053. 32p. (ps-4). 1993. PLB 12.85 (*0-516-02296-2*); pap. 4.95 (*0-516-42296-0*) Childrens.
Young Artists Painting Pack. (gr. 3-6). 1992. pap. 7.95 (*1-56680-501-5*) Mad Hatter Pub.
A Young Painter: The Life & Paintings of Wang Yani - China's Extraordinary Young Artist. 80p. 1991. 17.95 (*0-590-44906-0*, Scholastic Hardcover) Scholastic Inc.

PAINTING–FICTION
Agee, Jon. Incredible Painting of Felix Clousseau. (gr. 4-8). 1990. pap. 4.95 (*0-374-43582-0*, Sunburst) FS&G.
Alcorn, Johnny. Rembrandt's Beret. Alcorn, Stephen, illus. LC 90-42330. 32p. (gr. 1 up). 1991. 13.95 (*0-688-10206-9*, Tambourine Bks); PLB 13.88 (*0-688-10207-7*, Tambourine Bks) Morrow.
Asch, Frank. Bread & Honey. Asch, Frank, illus. LC 81-16893. 48p. (ps-3). 1982. 5.95 (*0-8193-1077-8*); PLB 5.95 (*0-8193-1078-6*) Parents.
Ayme, Marcel. Boites de Peinture. Sabatier, Roland, illus. (FRE.). 72p. (gr. 1-5). 1990. pap. 9.95 (*2-07-031199-6*) Schoenhof.

Berman, Linda. The Goodbye Painting. Hannon, Mark, illus. LC 81-20217. 32p. (ps-3). 1982. 16.95 (*0-89885-074-6*) Human Sci Pr.

Bread & Honey. (Illus.). 42p. (ps-3). 1992. PLB 13.26 (*0-8368-0880-0*); PLB 13.27 s.p. (*0-685-61512-X*) Gareth Stevens Inc.

Butenhoff, Lisa K. Nina's Magic. Thatch, Nancy R., ed. Butenhoff, Lisa K., illus. Melton, David, intro. by. LC 92-18293. (Illus.). 26p. (gr. 3-4). 1992. PLB 14.95 (*0-933849-40-0*) Landmark Edns.

Clement, Claude. The Painter & the Wild Swans. Clement, Frederic, illus. LC 86-2154. 32p. (gr. k up). 1986. 13.95 (*0-8037-0268-X*) Dial Bks Young.

Demi. Liang & the Magic Paintbrush. Demi, illus. LC 80-11351. 32p. (ps-2). 1988. pap. 5.95 (*0-8050-0801-2*, Bks Young Read) H Holt & Co.

Dunrea, Olivier. The Painter Who Loved Chickens. LC 94-4243. 1995. 14.95 (*0-02-733209-8*) Macmillan.

—The Painter Who Loved Chickens. LC 94-27562. 1995. 15.00 (*0-374-35729-3*) FS&G.

Hewetson, Sarah. I Can Paint. (ps-3). 1994. pap. 9.95 (*0-89577-598-0*, Readers Digest Kids) RD Assn.

Johnson, Jane. The Princess & the Painter. LC 93-39987. (ps-3). 1994. 15.00 (*0-374-36118-5*) FS&G.

Johnston, Fay. The Painting Day. Macallan, Heather, illus. LC 93-112. 1994. write for info. (*0-383-03706-9*) SRA Schl Grp.

Liang & the Magic Paintbrush. LC 80-11351. (Illus.). 32p. (ps-2). 1980. 14.95 (*0-8050-0220-0*, Bks Young Read) H Holt & Co.

Markun, Patricia M. The Little Painter of Sabana Grande. Casilla, Robert, illus. LC 91-35230. 32p. (ps-2). 1993. RSBE 14.95 (*0-02-762205-3*, Bradbury Pr) Macmillan Child Grp.

Mathers, Petra. Victor & Christabel. Mathers, Petra, illus. LC 92-33468. 40p. (ps-3). 1993. 15.00 (*0-679-83060-X*); PLB 15.99 (*0-679-93060-4*) Knopf Bks Yng Read.

Peck, Richard. Unfinished Portrait. 1993. pap. 3.99 (*0-440-21886-1*) Dell.

Percy, Graham. Max and the Orange Door. LC 92-45563. (Illus.). (ps-3). 1993. 15.95 (*1-56766-076-2*) Childs World.

Reiner, Annie. Visit to the Art Galaxy. LC 91-16989. (Illus.). (gr. 1 up). 1991. 15.95 (*0-671-74957-9*, Green Tiger) S&S Trade.

Rinder, Lenore. A Big Mistake. Horn, Susan, illus. LC 94-7028. 32p. (ps up). Date not set. PLB 18.60 (*0-8368-0674-3*) Gareth Stevens Inc.

Rockwell, Anne. Mr. Panda's Painting. Rockwell, Anne, illus. LC 92-9220. 32p. (ps-1). 1993. RSBE 14.95 (*0-02-777451-1*, Macmillan Child Bk) Macmillan Child Grp.

Schwartz, Amy. Begin at the Beginning. Schwartz, Amy, illus. LC 82-48257. 32p. (ps-3). 1983. PLB 12.89 (*0-06-025228-6*) HarpC Child Bks.

Spier, Peter. Oh, Were They Ever Happy. Spier, Peter, illus. LC 77-78144. 48p. (gr. k-3). 1978. 12.95 (*0-385-13175-5*); pap. 10.95 (*0-385-13176-3*) Doubleday.

Stanley, Diane. The Gentleman & the Kitchen Maid. Nolan, Dennis, illus. LC 93-157. 1994. 13.99 (*0-8037-1320-7*); lib. bdg. 13.89 (*0-8037-1321-5*) Dial Bks Young.

Stolz, Mary. Say Something. rev. ed. Koshkin, Alexander, illus. LC 92-8317. 32p. (ps-3). 1993. 15.00 (*0-06-021158-X*); PLB 14.89 (*0-06-021159-8*) HarpC Child Bks.

Sugar & Garrison. Josiah True & the Art Maker. 1995. 14.00 (*0-671-88354-2*, S&S BFYR) S&S Trade.

Thomas, Abigail. Pearl Paints. (ps-2). 1994. 15.95 (*0-8050-2976-1*) H Holt & Co.

Ventura, Piero & Ventura, Marisa. The Painter's Trick. Ventura, Piero & Ventura, Marisa, illus. LC 76-54411. (gr. k-2). 1977. lib. bdg. 6.99 (*0-394-93320-6*) Random Bks Yng Read.

Yamaka, Sara. The Gift of Driscoll Lipscomb. Kim, Joung U., illus. LC 93-43207. 1995. 16.00 (*0-02-793599-X*, Four Winds) Macmillan Child Grp.

PAINTING, FLEMISH

Muhlberger, Richard, text by. What Makes a Bruegel a Bruegel? (Illus.). 48p. (gr. 5 up). 1993. 9.95 (*0-670-85203-1*) Viking Child Bks.

PAINTING–HISTORY

Peppin. Story of Painting. (Illus.). 32p. 1980. PLB 13.96 (*0-88110-030-7*); pap. 6.95 (*0-86020-441-3*) EDC.

PAINTING, RELIGIOUS

see Christian Art and Symbolism

PAINTING–TECHNIQUE

Craig, Diana. How to Draw & Paint Pets. 1991. 12.98 (*1-55521-716-8*) Bk Sales Inc.

Gair, Angela. How to Draw & Paint People. 1991. 12.98 (*1-55521-717-6*) Bk Sales Inc.

Gibson, R. & Gee, R. Paint Fun. (Illus.). 32p. (ps-3). 1992. PLB 13.96 (*0-88110-285-7*); pap. 5.95 (*0-7460-1085-0*) EDC.

Momiyama, Nanae. Sumi-E: An Introduction to Ink Painting. LC 67-15320. (Illus.). 1967. pap. 6.95 (*0-8048-0554-7*) C E Tuttle.

Monahan, Patricia. Beginner's Guides: Painting in Acrylics. (Illus.). 96p. (gr. 10-12). 1993. pap. 17.95 (*0-289-80072-2*, Pub. by Cassell UK) Sterling.

Morgan, Judith. An Art Text-Workbook: Painting (Introduction) Wallace, Dorathye, ed. (Illus.). 127p. (Orig.). (gr. 8-10). 1990. pap. 13.27 (*0-914127-57-8*); tchr's. ed. avail. Univ Class.

Muller, Brunhild. Painting with Children. 1988. pap. 8.50 (*0-86315-052-7*, 20240) Gryphon Hse.

Robb, Tom. First Steps in Paint: A New & Simple Way to Learn How to Paint. (Illus.). 64p. (ps up). 1992. 12.95 (*0-87663-619-9*) Universe.

Rodwell, Jenny. Beginner's Guides: Painting in Pastels. (Illus.). 96p. (gr. 10-12). 1993. pap. 17.95 (*0-289-80073-0*, Pub. by Cassell UK) Sterling.

Savage-Hubbard, Kathy & Speicher, Rose C. Paint Adventures! (Illus.). 48p. 1993. 11.95 (*0-89134-508-6*, 30524) North Light Bks.

Thomson, Ruth. Painting. LC 94-16938. (Illus.). 24p. (ps-3). 1994. PLB 14.40 (*0-516-07990-5*); pap. 4.95 (*0-516-47990-3*) Childrens.

Tofts, Hannah. Paint Book. (gr. 1 up). 1990. pap. 11.95 (*0-671-70364-1*, S&S BFYR); (S&S BFYR) S&S Trade.

PAINTINGS

see also Portraits

Adams, Henry. Handbook of American Paintings in the Nelson - Atkins Museum of Art, Kansas City, Missouri. LC 91-29780. (Illus.). 208p. (Orig.). 1991. pap. 4.00 (*0-942614-17-8*) Nelson-Atkins.

Everett, Gwen & National Museum of American Art Staff. Li'l Sis & Uncle Willie: A Story Based on the Life & Paintings of William H. Johnson. Johnson, William H., illus. LC 91-14800. 32p. (ps-3). 1992. Repr. of 1991 ed. 13.95 (*0-8478-1462-9*) Rizzoli Intl.

Levine, Bobbie, et al. A Child's Walk Through Twentieth Century American Painting & Sculpture. (Illus.). 29p. (gr. 2-6). 1986. spiral bdg. 1.50 (*0-912303-37-9*) Michigan Mus.

Martin, Mary & Zorn, Steven. Start Exploring Masterpieces: A Fact-Filled Coloring Book. rev. ed. (Illus.). 128p. (gr. 2 up). 1990. pap. 8.95 (*0-89471-801-0*) Running Pr.

Pekarik, Andrew. Painting. LC 92-52987. (Illus.). 64p. (gr. 3-7). 1992. 18.95 (*1-56282-296-9*); PLB 18.89 (*1-56282-297-7*) Hyprn Child.

Roalf, Peggy. Children. LC 92-52982. (Illus.). 48p. (Orig.). (gr. 3-7). 1993. PLB 14.89 (*1-56282-308-6*); pap. 6.95 (*1-56282-309-4*) Hyprn Ppbks.

—Circus. LC 92-52983. (Illus.). 48p. (Orig.). (gr. 3-7). 1993. PLB 14.89 (*1-56282-304-3*); pap. 6.95 (*1-56282-305-1*) Hyprn Ppbks.

—Dogs. LC 93-10585. (Illus.). (gr. 3-7). 1993. PLB 14.89 (*1-56282-531-3*) Hyprn Child.

—Flowers. LC 92-72015. (Illus.). 48p. (gr. 3-7). 1993. PLB 14.89 (*1-56282-359-0*); pap. 6.95 (*1-56282-358-2*) Hyprn Ppbks.

—Horses. LC 92-52979. (Illus.). 48p. (Orig.). (gr. 3-7). 1993. PLB 14.89 (*1-56282-306-X*); pap. 6.95 (*1-56282-307-8*) Hyprn Ppbks.

—Landscapes. LC 92-52980. (Illus.). 48p. (Orig.). (gr. 3-6). 1992. PLB 14.89 (*1-56282-302-7*); pap. 6.95 (*1-56282-303-5*) Hyprn Ppbks.

—Self-Portraits. LC 92-72042. (Illus.). 48p. (gr. 3-7). 1993. PLB 14.89 (*1-56282-357-4*); pap. 6.95 (*1-56282-356-6*) Hyprn Ppbks.

Welton, Jude. Looking at Paintings. LC 93-38299. (Illus.). 64p. 1994. 16.95 (*1-56458-494-1*) Dorling Kindersley.

Yenawine, Philip. Stories. (Illus.). (gr. 2-5). 1991. 14.95 (*0-385-30256-8*); PLB 14.99 (*0-385-30316-5*) Delacorte.

PAINTINGS–FICTION

Wilde, Oscar. Picture of Dorian Gray. (gr. 9 up). 1964. pap. 2.50 (*0-8049-0039-6*, CL-39) Airmont.

PAKISTAN

Hughes, Libby. From Prison to Prime Minister: A Biography of Benazir Bhutto. (Illus.). 128p. (gr. 5 up). 1990. text ed. 13.95 RSBE (*0-87518-438-3*, Dillon) Macmillan Child Grp.

Nugent, Nicholas. Pakistan & Bangladesh. LC 92-10765. 96p. 1992. lib. bdg. 22.80 (*0-8114-2456-1*) Raintree Steck-V.

Rumalshah, Mano. Pakistan. (Illus.). 32p. (gr. 7-10). 1991. 17.95 (*0-237-60193-1*, Pub. by Evans Bros Ltd) Trafalgar.

Sansevere-Dreher, Diane. Benazir Bhutto. (gr. 4-7). 1991. pap. 3.50 (*0-553-15857-0*) Bantam.

Scarsbrook, Ailsa & Scarsbrook, Alan. A Family in Pakistan. LC 85-6886. (Illus.). 32p. (gr. 2-5). 1985. PLB 13.50 (*0-8225-1662-4*) Lerner Pubns.

Shaw, Denis J. Pakistani Twins. Spence, Geraldine, illus. (gr. 6-9). 1965. 12.95 (*0-8023-1094-X*) Dufour.

Sheehan, Sean. Pakistan. LC 93-4379. (gr. 5 up). 1993. write for info. (*1-85435-583-X*) Marshall Cavendish.

Yusufali, Jabeen. Pakistan: An Islamic Treasure. (Illus.). 128p. (gr. 5 up). 1990. text ed. 14.95 RSBE (*0-87518-433-2*, Dillon) Macmillan Child Grp.

PALEOBOTANY

see Plants, Fossil

PALEOLITHIC PERIOD

see Stone Age

PALEONTOLOGISTS

Higginson, Mel. Scientists Who Study Fossils. LC 94-6995. 1994. write for info. (*0-86593-375-8*) Rourke Corp.

PALEONTOLOGY

see Fossils

PALESTINE

Reische, Diana. Arafat & the Palestine Liberation Organization. LC 90-46868. (Illus.). 160p. (gr. 9-12). 1991. PLB 14.40 (*0-531-11000-1*) Watts.

PALESTINE–FICTION

Abdul-Baki, Kathryn K. Fields of Fig & Olive: Ameera & Other Stories of the Middle East. Stone, Ellen, intro. by. 208p. (Orig.). (gr. 10 up). 1991. 20.00 (*0-89410-725-9*); pap. 14.00 (*0-89410-726-7*) Three Continents.

Speare, Elizabeth G. Bronze Bow. 256p. (gr. 6 up). 1961. 13.45 (*0-395-07113-5*) HM.

—The Bronze Bow. LC 61-10640. (Illus.). 272p. (gr. 6 up). 1973. pap. 7.95 (*0-395-13719-5*, Sandpiper) HM.

Stewart, Dana. Friends from Galilee: A Bible-Times Visit with Micah & Hannah. Couri, Kathy, illus. 28p. (ps). 1994. 4.99 (*0-7847-0003-6*, 24-03869) Standard Pub.

Thoene, Bodie. The Key to Zion. LC 88-7439. 352p. (Orig.). (gr. 11 up). 1988. pap. 9.99 (*1-55661-034-3*) Bethany Hse.

Travis, Lucille. Tirzah. Garber, S. David, ed. LC 90-23580. 160p. (Orig.). (gr. 3-7). 1991. pap. 5.95 (*0-8361-3546-6*) Herald Pr.

PALESTINE–HISTORY

Britton, Colleen. Palestine Thirty A. D. You Are There. Britton, Colleen, illus. 73p. (Orig.). (ps-6). 1987. pap. 12.95 (*0-940754-38-X*) Ed Ministries.

Jones, Graham. How They Lived in Bible Times. Deverell, Richard & Deverell, Christine, illus. LC 91-30420. 48p. (gr. 1-8). 1992. 12.99 (*0-8307-1574-6*, 5112125) Regal.

PALSY, CEREBRAL

see Cerebral Palsy

PANAMA

Griffiths, John. Take a Trip to Panama. LC 89-8929. (Illus.). 32p. (gr. 3-5). 1989. PLB 10.90 (*0-531-10736-1*) Watts.

Lerner Publications, Department of Geography Staff. Panama in Pictures. (Illus.). 64p. (gr. 5 up). 1987. PLB 17.50 (*0-8225-1818-X*) Lerner Pubns.

Stewart, Gail B. Panama. LC 90-36249. (Illus.). 48p. (gr. 6-7). 1990. text ed. 4.95 RSBE (*0-89686-536-3*, Crestwood Hse) Macmillan Child Grp.

Vazquez, Ana M. Panama. LC 91-12667. 128p. (gr. 5-9). 1991. PLB 20.55 (*0-516-02604-6*) Childrens.

PANAMA–FICTION

Markun, Patricia M. The Little Painter of Sabana Grande. Casilla, Robert, illus. LC 91-35230. 32p. (ps-2). 1993. RSBE 14.95 (*0-02-762205-3*, Bradbury Pr) Macmillan Child Grp.

Palacios, Argentina. A Christmas Surprise for Chabelita. Lohstoeter, Lori, photos by. LC 93-22336. (Illus.). 32p. (gr. k-4). 1993. PLB 14.95 (*0-8167-3131-4*); pap. 3.95 (*0-8167-3132-2*) Brdgewater.

PANAMA CANAL

St. George, Judith. The Panama Canal: Gateway to the World. 144p. (gr. 5 up). 1989. 16.95 (*0-399-21637-5*, Putnam) Putnam Pub Group.

PANDAS

Bailey, Jill. Project Panda. LC 90-9802. (Illus.). 48p. (gr. 3-7). 1990. PLB 21.34 (*0-8114-2704-8*); pap. 4.95 (*0-8114-6552-7*) Raintree Steck-V.

Bright, Michael. Giant Panda. LC 88-83104. (Illus.). 32p. (gr. 5-6). 1989. PLB 12.40 (*0-531-17140-X*, Gloucester Pr) Watts.

Buxton, Jane H., ed. Playful Pandas, Bk. 1 of 2. (Illus.). (ps-3). 1991. Set. 24.50 (*0-87044-840-4*) Natl Geog.

Crozat, Francois. I Am a Little Panda. LC 92-30962. 28p. (ps-k). 1993. 8.95 (*0-8120-6311-2*); Miniature. 3.50 (*0-8120-6312-0*) Barron.

Gambill, Henrietta, ed. Little Panda. (Illus.). 18p. 1994. 7.99 (*0-7847-0233-0*, 24-03119) Standard Pub.

Green, Carl R. & Sanford, William R. The Giant Panda. LC 87-14002. (Illus.). 48p. (gr. 5). 1987. text ed. 12.95 RSBE (*0-89686-331-X*, Crestwood Hse) Macmillan Child Grp.

Greenaway, Theresa. Amazing Bears. King, Dave, photos by. LC 92-910. (Illus.). 32p. (Orig.). (gr. 1-5). 1992. PLB 9.99 (*0-679-92769-7*); pap. 7.99 (*0-679-82769-2*) Knopf Bks Yng Read.

Gross, Ruth B. A Book about Pandas. (Illus.). 32p. (gr. k-3). 1991. pap. 2.50 (*0-590-43492-6*) Scholastic Inc.

Highlights for Children Editors. Pandas. (Illus.). 32p. (Orig.). (gr. 2-5). 1993. pap. 3.95 (*1-56397-285-9*) Boyds Mills Pr.

Hoffman, Mary. Panda. LC 84-15882. (Illus.). 24p. (gr. k-5). 1985. PLB 9.95 (*0-8172-2407-6*); pap. 3.95 (*0-8114-6884-4*) Raintree Steck-V.

Kim, Melissa. The Giant Panda. Felts, Shirley, illus. LC 94-10158. 32p. (gr. 1-5). 1994. lib. bdg. 12.00 (*1-57102-024-1*, Ideals Child); pap. 5.95 (*1-57102-008-X*) Hambleton-Hill.

Lee, Sandra. Giant Pandas. LC 92-35066. (gr. 2-6). 1993. 15.95 (*1-56766-009-6*) Childs World.

MacClintock, Dorcas. Red Pandas: A Natural History. Young, Ellan, illus. LC 88-3528. 112p. (gr. 7 up). 1988. SBE 14.95 (*0-684-18677-2*, Scribners Young Read) Macmillan Child Grp.

Martin, L. Panda. (Illus.). 24p. (gr. k-5). 1988. PLB 11.94 (*0-86592-996-3*) Rourke Corp.

Masui, Mitsuko. Pandas of the World. Ooka, Diane, tr. (Illus.). 32p. (gr. k-2). 1989. 11.95 (*0-89346-314-0*) Heian Intl.

The Panda. (Illus.). 28p. (gr. 2-5). 1988. pap. 3.50 (*0-8167-1573-4*) Troll Assocs.

Panda. 1989. 3.50 (*1-87865-735-6*) Blue Q.

Petty, Kate. Baby Animals: Pandas. (Illus.). 24p. (ps-3). 1992. pap. 3.95 (*0-8120-4968-3*) Barron.

—Pandas. LC 90-45005. (Illus.). 24p. (gr. k-3). 1991. PLB 10.90 (*0-531-17287-2*, Gloucester Pr) Watts.

Propper. Panda, Reading Level 3-4. (Illus.). 28p. (gr. 2-5). 1983. PLB 16.67 (*0-86592-851-7*); 12.50 (*0-685-58822-X*) Rourke Corp.

Rothaus, Jim. Giant Pandas. 24p. (gr. 3). 1988. PLB 14.95s.p. (*0-88682-228-9*) Creative Ed.

Schmidt, Annemarie & Schmidt, Christian R. Bears & Their Forest Cousins. LC 91-9428. (Illus.). 32p. (gr. 4-6). 1991. PLB 18.60 (*0-8368-0684-0*) Gareth Stevens Inc.

Standring, Gillian. Pandas. LC 90-21969. (Illus.). 32p. (gr. k-4). 1991. 12.40 (*0-531-18397-1*, Pub. by Bookwright Pr) Watts.

Steele, Philip. The Giant Panda. LC 93-41689. 24p. (gr. 2-5). 1994. pap. 8.95 (*1-856975-11-8*, Kingfisher LKC) LKC.

Whittaker, Bibby. Bears & Pandas. (Illus.). 32p. (gr. 4-6). 1991. 13.95 (*0-237-60171-0*, Pub. by Evans Bros Ltd) Trafalgar.

Winograd, Deborah. My Color Is Panda. Winograd, Deborah, illus. LC 92-17423. 32p. (ps-1). 1993. JRT 13.00 (*0-671-79152-4*, Green Tiger) S&S Trade.

Wong, Ovid. Giant Pandas. LC 87-10717. (Illus.). 48p. (gr. k-4). 1987. PLB 12.85 (*0-516-01241-X*); pap. 4.95 (*0-516-41241-8*) Childrens.

PANDAS–FICTION

Bushell, Isobel & Bushell, John. Tales of Alexander Panda. (Illus.). (ps). 1994. Set (4) slipcased. bds. 9.95 (*0-8120-8124-2*) Barron.

Calmenson, Stephanie. Dinner at the Panda Palace. Westcott, Nadine B., illus. LC 90-33720. 32p. (ps-3). 1991. 15.00 (*0-06-021010-9*); PLB 14.89 (*0-06-021011-7*) HarpC Child Bks.

Conover, Chris. Sam Panda & Thunder Dragon. (ps-3). 1992. 16.00 (*0-374-36393-5*) FS&G.

Cosgrove, Stephen. Ming Ling. James, Robin, illus. 32p. (Orig.). (gr. 1-4). 1978. pap. 2.95 (*0-8431-0592-5*) Price Stern.

Dowell, Olivia S. The First Adventure of Peter Nelson Panda. West, Linnea F., illus. 16p. (gr. 2-4). 1986. pap. 5.95 (*0-9617624-0-3*) Bear Tracks Pub.

Eisemann, Henry. Su-Su, the Fremont School Panda. Steinberg, Chris, illus. 22p. (Orig.). (gr. k-6). 1987. pap. 6.95 (*0-938129-03-1*) Emprise Pubns.

Erickson, Gina K. Bat's Surprise. (ps-3). 1993. pap. 3.95 (*0-8120-1735-8*) Barron.

Gackenbach, Dick. Poppy the Panda. Gackenbach, Dick, illus. LC 84-4952. 32p. (ps-3). 1984. (Pub. by Clarion); pap. 4.80 (*0-89919-492-3*, Pub. by Clarion) HM.

Gelman, Rita G. Panda Grows Up. (ps-3). 1993. pap. 3.95 (*0-590-43612-0*) Scholastic Inc.

Hoban, Tana. Panda, Panda. Hoban, Tana, illus. LC 86-3088. 12p. (ps). 1986. pap. 4.95 (*0-688-06564-3*) Greenwillow.

Johnson, Debra A. I Dreamed I Was--a Panda. LC 94-5654. (gr. k up). 1994. write for info. (*1-56239-301-4*) Abdo & Dghtrs.

Kim, Joy. You Look Funny! Boyd, Patti, illus. LC 86-30839. 32p. (gr. k-2). 1988. PLB 7.89 (*0-8167-0976-9*); pap. text ed. 1.95 (*0-8167-0977-7*) Troll Assocs.

Kraus, Robert. Milton the Early Riser. Aruego, Jose & Dewey, Ariane, illus. LC 81-9460. (ps). 1987. pap. 13.95 jacketed (*0-671-66272-4*, S&S BFYR); pap. 5.95 (*0-671-66911-7*, S&S BFYR) S&S Trade.

Lebowitz, Fran. Mr. Chas & Lisa Sue Meet the Pandas. Graves, Michael, illus. LC 94-1132. 72p. (gr. 2-7). 1994. 15.00 (*0-679-86052-5*) Knopf Bks Yng Read.

Leonard, Marcia & Schmidt, Karen L. Little Panda Gets Lost. 32p. (Orig.). (gr. 1). 1985. pap. 2.50 (*0-553-15302-1*) Bantam.

Liu Qian. Panda Bear Goes Visiting. (Illus.). 22p. (gr. 3-4). 1982. 3.95 (*0-8351-1108-3*); pap. 2.95 (*0-8351-1139-3*) China Bks.

McClung, Robert M. Lili: A Giant Panda of Sichuan. Brady, Irene, illus. LC 87-28271. 96p. (gr. 3-7). 1988. 12.95 (*0-688-06942-8*); PLB 12.88 (*0-688-06943-6*, Morrow Jr Bks) Morrow Jr Bks.

Ono, Koichi. Little Panda Bear. McClain, Mary, illus. 12p. (ps-2). 1982. 4.95 (*0-671-42549-8*, Little Simon) S&S Trade.

Owen, Annie. Hungry Panda. Owen, Annie, illus. LC 93-79580. 14p. (ps). 1994. bds. 4.95 (*1-85697-946-6*, Kingfisher LKC) LKC.

Plum, Carol T. Pandy's Rainbow. Schneck, Susan, illus. 32p. (gr. k-3). 1991. 9.95 (*0-87973-008-0*, 8); pap. 5.95 (*0-87973-009-9*, 9) Our Sunday Visitor.

Schlein, Miriam. The Year of the Panda. Mak, Kam, illus. LC 89-71307. 96p. (gr. 2-5). 1992. pap. 3.95 (*0-06-440366-1*, Trophy) HarpC Child Bks.

Stimson, Joan. Big Panda, Little Panda. Rutherford, Meg, illus. LC 93-36235. 32p. (ps-2). 1994. 12.95 (*0-8120-6404-6*); pap. 4.95 (*0-8120-1691-2*) Barron.

Temko, Florence. Paper Pandas & Jumping Frogs. Jackson, Paul, illus. Petersen, Richard, et al, photos by. LC 86-70960. (Illus.). 135p. (gr. 3-6). 1986. pap. 11.95 (*0-8351-1770-7*) China Bks.

Willard, Nancy. Papa's Panda. Hoban, Lillian, illus. LC 78-31787. (ps-2). 1979. 5.95 (*0-15-259462-0*, HB Juv Bks) HarBrace.

PANEUROPEAN FEDERATION

see European Federation

PANICS

see Depressions

PANKHURST, EMMELINE (GOULDEN) 1858-1928

Hoy, Linda. Emmeline Pankhurst. (Illus.). 64p. (gr. 5-9). 1991. 11.95 (*0-237-60019-6*, Pub. by Evans Bros Ltd) Trafalgar.

PANTHERS

Kappeler, Markus. Big Cats. (Illus.). 32p. (gr. 4-6). 1991. PLB 18.60 (*0-8368-0685-9*) Gareth Stevens Inc.

Sateren, Shelley S. Black Panther. LC 89-28267. (Illus.). 48p. (gr. 5). 1990. text ed. 12.95 RSBE (*0-89686-519-3*, Crestwood Hse) Macmillan Child Grp.

PANTHERS–FICTION

Ayme, Marcel. Canard et la Panthere. Sabatier, C. & Sabatier, R., illus. (FRE.). 63p. (gr. 1-5). 1991. pap. 9.95 (*2-07-031128-7*) Schoenhof.

Sampson, Fay. Josh's Panther. (Illus.). 96p. (gr. 3-5). 1988. 13.95 (*0-575-03914-0*, Pub. by Gollancz England) Trafalgar.

PANTOMIMES

see also Shadow Pantomimes and Plays

Stolzenberg, Mark. Be a Mime! Moore, Jim, photos by. LC 91-18171. (Illus.). 128p. (gr. 4-12). 1991. pap. 10.95 (*0-8069-8394-9*) Sterling.

PAPER

Daniel, Jamie & Bonar, Veronica. Coping with - Paper Trash. Kenyon, Tony, illus. LC 93-37688. 32p. (gr. 2 up). 1994. PLB 17.27 (*0-8368-1059-7*) Gareth Stevens Inc.

Dixon, Annabelle. Paper. Stefoff, Rebecca, ed. Barber, Ed, photos by. LC 91-18188. (Illus.). 32p. (gr. 3-5). 1991. PLB 15.93 (*1-56074-003-5*) Garrett Ed Corp.

Limousin, Odile. The Story of Paper. Matthews, Sarah, tr. from FRE. Brusch, Beat, illus. LC 87-31752. 38p. (gr. k-5). 1988. 5.95 (*0-944589-16-2*, 162) Young Discovery Lib.

Sneider, Cary I. & Barber, Jacqueline. Paper Towel Testing. Bergman, Lincoln & Fairwell, Kay, eds. Bevilacqua, Carol, illus. Hoyt, Richard, photos by. (Illus.). 29p. (Orig.). (gr. 5-9). 1987. pap. 8.50 (*0-912511-65-6*) Lawrence Science.

Witcombmsia, Gerald, illus. Paper. 32p. (gr. 3-5). 1985. 7.95x (*0-86685-450-9*) Intl Bk Ctr.

PAPER–HISTORY

Smith, Elizabeth S. Paper. LC 84-7271. (Illus.). 64p. (gr. 4 up). 1984. PLB 10.85 (*0-8027-6569-6*) Walker & Co.

PAPER CRAFTS

see also names of paper crafts, e.g. Origami

Amery, Heather. Fun with Paper. LC 92-51071. 1993. lib. bdg. 6.99 (*0-679-83493-1*); pap. 9.99 (*0-679-93493-6*) Random.

Ancona, George. The Pinatamaker: El Pinatero. LC 93-2389. (gr. 5 up). 1994. 16.95 (*0-15-261875-9*) HarBrace.

Araki, Chiyo. Origami in the Classroom, 2 vols. LC 65-13412. (Illus.). (gr. 1 up). 1965-68. bds. Vol. 1. bds. 14.95 (*0-8048-0452-4*); Vol. 2. bds. 14.95 (*0-8048-0453-2*) C E Tuttle.

Barr, Marilynn G. Paper Plates. (Illus.). 64p. (ps-k). 1989. 6.95 (*0-912107-98-7*, MM1916) Monday Morning Bks.

—Paper Rolls. (Illus.). 64p. (ps-k). 1989. 6.95 (*1-878279-00-9*, MM1917) Monday Morning Bks.

Bawden, Juliet. One Hundred One Things to Make: Fun Craft Projects with Everyday Materials. Pang, Alex, illus. LC 93-29633. 104p. 1994. 14.95 (*0-8069-0596-4*) Sterling.

Bemelmans, Ludwig. Madeline Paper Dolls. Wheeler, Jody, designed by. (Illus.). (ps up). 1994. 5.99 (*0-670-85601-0*) Viking Child Bks.

Bennett, Andrew. The Paper Hat Book: Six Incredible Hats to Assemble & Wear. (Illus.). 64p. (Orig.). (gr. 3 up). 1993. pap. 19.95 (*1-56138-256-6*) Running Pr.

Birmingham, Duncan. Fantasy Mobiles. (Illus.). 32p. (Orig.). (gr. 3-5). 1990. pap. 4.95 (*0-906212-52-9*, Pub. by Tarquin UK) Parkwest Pubns.

Boden, Arthur & Woodside, John. Boden's Beasts. Boden, Art, illus. (gr. 1-5). 1964. 8.95 (*0-8392-3045-1*) Astor-Honor.

Borja, Corinne & Borja, Robert. Making Chinese Paper Cuts. Tucker, Kathleen, ed. Borja, Corinne & Borja, Robert, illus. LC 79-18358. (gr. 3-8). 1980. PLB 13.95 (*0-8075-4948-7*) A Whitman.

Bottomley, Jim. Paper Projects for Creative Kids of All Ages. 160p. (gr. 5 up). 1983. pap. 12.95 (*0-316-10349-7*) Little.

Bradley, Susannah. Paper Fun Pack. (Illus.). (gr. 3-6). 1992. pap. 7.95 (*1-56680-504-X*) Mad Hatter Pub.

Brown, Jerome C. Fables & Tales PaperCrafts. (gr. k-5). 1989. pap. 8.95 (*0-8224-3155-6*) Fearon Teach Aids.

—Holiday Crafts & Greeting Cards. (gr. 3-6). 1982. pap. 6.95 (*0-8224-5194-8*) Fearon Teach Aids.

—Paper Designs. (gr. 1-6). 1982. pap. 6.95 (*0-8224-5193-X*) Fearon Teach Aids.

Burt, Erica. Paper. (Illus.). 32p. (gr. 2-6). 1990. lib. bdg. 15.94 (*0-86592-488-0*); lib. bdg. 11.95s.p. (*0-685-46443-1*) Rourke Corp.

Caldecott, Barrie. Papier Mache. LC 92-6259. (Illus.). 48p. (gr. 4-6). 1993. PLB 12.40 (*0-531-14217-5*) Watts.

Chernoff, Goldie T. Easy Costumes You Don't Have to Sew. LC 76-46428. (Illus.). 48p. (gr. 1-3). 1984. RSBE 13.95 (*0-02-718230-4*, Four Winds) Macmillan Child Grp.

Churchill, E. Richard. Building with Paper. LC 89-26220. (Illus.). 128p. 1990. 14.95 (*0-8069-5772-7*) Sterling.

—Fabulous Paper Airplanes. Michaels, James, illus. LC 91-10490. 128p. (gr. 5 up). 1992. pap. 7.95 (*0-8069-8343-4*) Sterling.

—Fantastic Flying Paper Toys. LC 90-39007. (Illus.). 96p. (Orig.). (gr. 4-10). 1990. pap. 3.95 (*0-8069-7460-5*) Sterling.

—Holiday Paper Projects. Michaels, James, illus. LC 92-12100. 128p. (gr. 3-9). 1992. 14.95 (*0-8069-8512-7*) Sterling.

—Holiday Paper Projects. Michaels, James, illus. 128p. (gr. 6 up). 1993. pap. 7.95 (*0-8069-8513-5*) Sterling.

—Paper Tricks & Toys. LC 91-38789. 128p. 1992. 14.95 (*0-8069-8416-3*) Sterling.

—Paper Tricks & Toys. Michaels, James, illus. 128p. (gr. 2-8). 1993. pap. 7.95 (*0-8069-8417-1*) Sterling.

—Terrific Paper Toys. LC 90-24115. (Illus.). 128p. (gr. 7-12). 1992. pap. 7.95 (*0-8069-7497-4*) Sterling.

Chwast, Seymour. Paper Pets: Make Your Own Three Dogs, 2 Cats, 1 Parrot, 1 Rabbit, 1 Monkey. LC 92-23609. (Illus.). 24p. 1993. pap. 19.95 (*0-8109-2531-1*) Abrams.

Clemens, Peter & Delgado, Jose. Super Wings: The Step-by-Step Paper Airplane Book. 64p. (ps-3). 1992. pap. 4.95 (*0-929923-87-1*) Lowell Hse.

Cobb, Vicki. Vicki Cobb's Papermaking Book & Kit. Bloom, Tom, illus. 32p. (gr. 2-6). 1993. 16.95 (*0-694-00467-7*, Festival) HarpC Child Bks.

Corwin, Judith H. Papercrafts. Corwin, Judith H., illus. IRosoff, ed. LC 87-21611. (Illus.). 72p. (gr. 2-4). 1988. PLB 12.90 (*0-531-10465-6*) Watts.

Curtis, Annabelle. Paper People. (Illus.). 32p. (Orig.). (gr. 3-4). 1991. pap. text ed. 6.95 (*0-906212-61-8*, Pub. by Tarquin UK) Parkwest Pubns.

D'Amato, Janet & D'Amato, Alex. Cardboard Carpentry. D'Amato, Jane & D'Amato, Alex, illus. Thompson, Morton, intro. by. (gr. 2-5). PLB 13.95 (*0-87460-085-5*) Lion Bks.

Davidson, Patricia S. & Willcutt, Robert E. Spatial Problem Solving with Paper Folding & Cutting. 64p. (gr. 4-12). 1984. pap. text ed. 8.50 (*0-914040-36-7*) Cuisenaire.

DeRosemond, Peggy. A Royal Romance Paper Dolls. (gr. 8-12). 1984. pap. 4.00 (*0-914510-14-2*) Evergreen.

Devonshire, Hilary. Moving Art. LC 90-31637. (Illus.). 48p. (gr. 5-8). 1990. PLB 12.40 (*0-531-14076-8*) Watts.

Emert, Phyllis. Fun with Paper: Little Crafters. 1992. pap. 3.99 (*0-517-08277-2*) Random Hse Value.

Fiarotta, Phyllis & Fiarotta, Noel. Cups & Cans & Paper Plate Fans: Craft Projects from Recycled Materials. (Illus.). 200p. (gr. 2 up). 1993. pap. 9.95 (*0-8069-8529-1*) Sterling.

Forte, Imogene. Paper Capers. LC 84-62932. (Illus.). 80p. (gr. k-6). 1985. 3.95 (*0-86530-097-6*, IP 91-1) Incentive Pubns.

Gibson, R. Paperplay. (Illus.). 32p. (ps-3). 1989. lib. bdg. 13.96 (*0-88110-422-1*, Usborne); pap. 5.95 (*0-7460-0466-4*) EDC.

Grant, Elaine. Critter Crafts. Grant, Elaine, illus. 30p. (gr. 4-7). 1991. pap. 9.95 spiral bdg. (*0-9632722-0-9*) Arteg Creations.

Grater, Michael. Make It in Paper: Creative Three-Dimensional Paper Projects. (Illus.). 96p. (gr. 5 up). 1983. pap. 4.95 (*0-486-24468-7*) Dover.

—Puppets, Jumping Jacks, & Other Paper People. LC 94-9546. 1994. write for info. (*0-486-28175-2*) Dover.

Green, Jen. Making Crazy Animals. LC 91-33868. (Illus.). 32p. (gr. 2-4). 1992. PLB 12.40 (*0-531-17324-0*, Gloucester Pr) Watts.

Grummer, Arnold E. Tin Can Papermaking: Recycle for Earth & Art. Grummer, Arnold & Rotzel, Spencer, illus. 80p. (Orig.). (gr. 1 up). 1992. pap. 7.95 (*0-938251-01-5*) G Markim.

Hall, Andy. Famous Balloon Mobiles. (Illus.). 32p. (Orig.). (gr. 3-5). 1990. pap. 4.95 (*0-906212-19-7*, Pub. by Tarquin UK) Parkwest Pubns.

Hough, Judith. Mary Mack - A Paper Doll Circa 1895: Color Decorate Authentic Fashions & Ethnic Costumes. Hough, Judith, illus. 26p. (gr. 2-6). 1992. pap. 7.95 (*0-9633769-1-8*) Touch The Sky.

Hughes, Phyllis. Indian Children Paper Dolls. LC 91-60334. (Illus.). 12p. 1991. pap. 5.95 perforated (*1-878610-05-8*) Red Crane Bks.

James, Diane. Playing with Paper. Lynn, Sara, photos by. (Illus.). 24p. (ps-1). 1992. pap. 3.95 (*0-590-45738-1*, Cartwheel) Scholastic Inc.

Jenkins, Gerald & Wild, Anne. The Gift Box Book. (Illus.). 32p. (Orig.). 1991. pap. 6.95 (*0-906212-36-7*, Pub. by Tarquin UK) Parkwest Pubns.

—More Gift Boxes. (Illus.). 32p. (Orig.). 1992. pap. 6.95 (*0-685-70552-8*, Pub. by Tarquin UK) Parkwest Pubns.

Johnston, Mary G. Paper Sculpture. rev. & enl. ed. LC 64-24721. (Illus.). 88p. (gr. 4-12). 1965. 9.95 (*0-87192-019-0*) Davis Mass.

Joslin, Margaret. See What I Can Do Today: A Year's Worth of Fascinating Fun for Your Pre-Schooler. 366p. (Orig.). (ps). 1992. spiral bdg. 8.50 (*1-882835-07-7*) STA-Kris.

Klettenheimer, Ingrid. Great Paper Craft Projects. LC 91-43519. (Illus.). 64p. (gr. 8-12). 1992. 14.95 (*0-8069-8556-9*) Sterling.

—Great Paper Folding Projects. LC 91-46524. (Illus.). 64p. (gr. 8-12). 1992. 14.95 (*0-8069-8554-2*) Sterling.

Knight, Brian. Space Mobiles. (Illus.). 32p. (Orig.). (gr. 3-5). 1990. pap. 4.95 (*0-906212-38-3*, Pub. by Tarquin UK) Parkwest Pubns.

Leonard, Kay. Paper Kaleidoscopes. (Illus.). 40p. (gr. k-12). 1989. pap. 5.95 (*0-685-26430-0*) Pelona Pr.

Levine, Shar. The Paper Book & Paper Maker. Weissmann, Joe, illus. LC 92-72021. 32p. (gr. k-5). 1993. 12.95 (*1-56282-235-7*) Hyprn Child.

Lohf, Sabine. Things I Can Make with Paper. (Illus.). 32p. (ps-3). 1989. 6.95 (*0-87701-671-2*) Chronicle Bks.

McGill, Ormond. Paper Magic: Creating Fantasies & Performing Tricks with Paper. LC 91-20996. (Illus.). 64p. (gr. 4-6). 1992. PLB 13.40 (*1-56294-136-4*) Millbrook Pr.

Mah, Ronald. Predator Prey Puppets & Toys: Eight Paper Animal Projects to Make. Mah, Ronald, illus. 32p. (ps-3). 1986. pap. 3.95 (*0-9615903-1-9*) Symbiosis Bks.

Medvene, Mark. Foilrigami. (Illus.). (gr. 4-7). 1968. 10.95 (*0-685-06619-3*) Astor-Honor.

Miescke, Lori. Christian Crafts from Construction Paper. 64p. (ps-5). 1992. 8.95 (*0-86653-707-4*, SS2843, Shining Star Pubns) Good Apple.

Moxley, Susan. Play with Papier-Mache. LC 94-14247. (gr. 1 up). 1994. write for info. (*0-87614-865-8*) Carolrhoda Bks.

Murray, Peter. World's Greatest Paper Airplanes. (Illus.). (gr. 2-6). 1992. PLB 14.95 (*0-89565-963-8*) Childs World.

Murray, William D. & Rigney, Francis J. Paper Folding for Beginners. (Illus.). (gr. 1 up). pap. 2.95 (*0-486-20713-7*) Dover.

Oldfield, Margaret J. Tell & Draw Paper Cut-Outs. Oldfield, Margaret J., illus. (Orig.). (gr. k-2). 1988. pap. 3.50 (*0-934876-23-1*, 23) Creative Storytime.

Olson, Margaret J. Tell & Draw Animal Cut-outs. 3rd ed. (gr. k-2). 1963. pap. 3.00 (*0-934876-15-0*) Creative Storytime.

O'Reilly, Susie. Papermaking. LC 93-24397. (Illus.). 32p. (gr. 4-6). 1994. 14.95 (*1-56847-069-X*) Thomson Lrning.

Roberts, Ray. Paper Airplanes from Around the World, Vol. I. 3rd, rev. & enl. ed. Roberts, Ken G., illus. 240p. (gr. 6 up). 1992. Repr. of 1988 ed. lib. bdg. 19.95 (*0-929995-00-7*) AIR Burbank.

Robins, Deri. Papier Mache. LC 92-41102. (Illus.). 40p. (gr. 3-7). 1993. 10.95 (*1-85697-927-X*, Kingfisher LKC); pap. 5.95 (*1-85697-926-1*) LKC.

Robson, Denny A. Paper Craft: Arts & Crafts. LC 93-8580. (Illus.). 32p. 1993. PLB 11.90 (*0-531-17428-X*, Gloucester Pr) Watts.

Sakade, Florence. Origami: Japanese Paper Folding, 3 Vols. LC 57-10685. (Illus., Orig.). (gr. 2 up). 1957. pap. Vol. 1. pap. 5.95 (*0-8048-0454-0*); Vol. 2. pap. 5.95 (*0-8048-0455-9*); Vol. 3. pap. 5.95 (*0-8048-0456-7*) C E Tuttle.

Sarasas, Claude. ABCs of Origami: Paper Folding for Children. Sarasas, Claude, illus. LC 64-17160. (gr. 3-8). 1964. bds. 12.95 (*0-8048-0000-6*) C E Tuttle.

Saunders, Richard & Mackness, Brian. Horrorgami: Spooky Paperfolding Just for Fun. LC 91-20005. (Illus.). 64p. (gr. 2-7). 1992. pap. 5.95 (*0-8069-8481-3*) Sterling.

Schmidt, Norman. Best Ever Paper Airplanes. LC 93-39122. (Illus.). 96p. (gr. 4 up). 1994. 17.95 (*1-895569-20-6*, Pub. by Tamos Bks CN) Sterling.

Simon, Seymour. The Paper Airplane Book. (gr. 4-6). 1976. pap. 3.99 (*0-14-030925-X*, Puffin) Puffin Bks.

Simpson, Lane. The Easy to Make Paper Airplane Book. 46p. (gr. 1-7). 1989. pap. 4.00 (*1-880892-00-6*) Fam Lrng Ctr.

Smith, Bob. Stunt Flying with Paper Airplanes. (Illus.). 32p. (gr. 3 up). 1992. pap. 2.50 (*0-87406-625-5*) Willowisp Pr.

Supraner, Robyn. Fun with Paper. Barto, Renzo, illus. LC 80-19859. 48p. (gr. 1-5). 1981. PLB 11.89 (*0-89375-430-7*); pap. 3.50 (*0-89375-431-5*) Troll Assocs.

Swanberg, Nancie. Great Ballet Paper Dolls. (Illus.). 32p. (Orig.). (gr. k-6). 1981. pap. 4.50 (*0-8431-1702-8*, Troubador) Price Stern.

Thomas, Meredith. Paper Shapes. Thomas, Meredith, illus. LC 93-27994. 1994. 4.25 (*0-383-03767-0*) SRA Schl Grp.

Tofts, Hannah. Paper Book. 1990. pap. 11.95 (*0-671-70366-8*); pap. 4.95 (*0-671-70367-6*) S&S Trade.

—Three-D. LC 89-27416. (ps-3). 1990. pap. 11.95 (*0-671-70370-6*, S&S BFYR); pap. 4.95 (*0-671-70371-4*, S&S BFYR) S&S Trade.

Using Paper & Paint. LC 91-17038. (Illus.). 48p. (gr. 4-8). 1991. PLB 14.95 (*1-85435-406-X*) Marshall Cavendish.

Walter, F. Virginia. Great Newspaper Crafts. LC 90-20731. 80p. (gr. 4 up). 1993. pap. 9.95 (*0-920534-79-1*, Pub. by Tamos Bks CN) Sterling.

Walton, Stewart & Walton, Sally. Dinosaur Paper Chains. (Illus.). 32p. (gr. 3 up). 1994. pap. 6.95 (*0-688-13413-0*, Tupelo Bks) Morrow.

Webb, Dave. Adventures with the Santa Fe Trail: An Activity Book for Kids & Teachers. rev. ed. Buntin, Phillip R., illus. 76p. (gr. 4 up). 1993. pap. 7.95 (*1-882404-05-X*) KS Herit Ctr.

Westphal, Arnold C. Paper & Scissors Truth Talks, No. 5. 1971. perfect bdg. 4.95 (*0-915398-04-4*) Visual Evangels.

Wild, Anne. Animal Mobiles. (Illus.). 32p. (Orig.). (gr. 3-5). 1990. pap. 4.95 (*0-685-70551-X*, Pub. by Tarquin UK) Parkwest Pubns.

—Dinosaur Mobiles. (Illus.). 32p. (Orig.). (gr. 2 up). 1990. pap. 4.95 (*0-906212-18-9*, Pub. by Tarquin UK) Parkwest Pubns.

—Dragon Mobiles. (Illus.). 32p. (Orig.). (gr. 3-5). 1990. pap. 4.95 (*0-906212-10-3*, Pub. by Tarquin UK) Parkwest Pubns.

Zubrowski, Bernie. Messing Around with Drinking Straw Construction: A Children's Museum Activity Book. Fleischer, Stephanie, illus. 64p. (gr. 3-7). 1981. 9.95 (*0-316-98875-8*); pap. 7.95 (*0-685-57751-1*) Little.

PAPER FOLDING

see Paper Crafts

PAPER MAKING AND TRADE

see also Book Industries and Trade

Asimov, Isaac. How Is Paper Made? (Illus.). 24p. (gr. 1-8). 1992. PLB 15.93 (*0-8368-0803-7*); PLB 15.93 s.p. (*0-685-61489-1*) Gareth Stevens Inc.

Bourgeois, Paulette. Amazing Paper Book. (gr. 4-8). 1990. pap. 6.68 (*0-201-52377-9*) Addison-Wesley.

Boy Scouts of America. Pulp & Paper. (Illus.). 40p. (gr. 6-12). 1974. pap. 1.85 (*0-8395-3343-8*, 33343) BSA.

Churchill, E. Richard. Paper Action Toys. Michaels, James, illus. LC 93-23860. 128p. (gr. 6 up). 1993. 14.95 (*0-8069-0368-6*) Sterling.

Curtis, Neil & Greenland, Peter. How Paper Is Made. (Illus.). 24p. (gr. 1-3). 1992. PLB 13.50 (*0-8225-2376-0*) Lerner Pubns.

Gibbons, Gail. Paper, Paper Everywhere. Gibbons, Gail, illus. LC 82-3109. 32p. (gr. 1-5). 1983. 10.95 (*0-15-259488-4*, HB Juv Bks) HarBrace.

Grummer, Arnold E. Paper by Kids. rev. ed. LC 79-22904. (Illus.). 116p. (gr. 5 up). 1990. text ed. 12.95 RSBE (*0-87518-191-0*, Dillon) Macmillan Child Grp.

Langley, Andrew. Paper. LC 93-6818. (Illus.). 32p. (gr. 3-5). 1993. 13.95 (*1-56847-047-9*) Thomson Lrning.

The Manufacture of Pulp & Paper: Science & Engineering Concepts. 113p. 1988. pap. 12.00 (*0-89852-448-2*, 0101R148) TAPPI.

Mitgutsch, Ali. From Wood to Paper. Lerner, Mark, tr. from GER. Mitgutsch, Ali, illus. 24p. (ps-3). 1986. lib. bdg. 10.95 (*0-87614-296-X*) Carolrhoda Bks.

PAPER MONEY

Parker. U. S. Currency. 1995. 15.00 (*0-06-023411-3*); PLB 14.89 (*0-06-023412-1*) HarpC Child Bks.

PAPER SCULPTURE

see Paper Crafts

PAPER WORK

see Paper Crafts

PAPIER-MACHE

see Paper Crafts

PARABLES

see also Allegories; Fables; Jesus Christ–Parables

Castagnola, Lawrence. Parables for Little People. Muren, Nancy LaBerge, illus. Quinn, Francis A. LC 86-60029. (Illus.). 104p. (Orig.). (gr. 4 up). 1982. pap. 7.95 (*0-89390-034-6*) Resource Pubns.

Dodds, Bill. Bedtime Parables, Vol. 1. LC 92-61549. (Illus.). 32p. (gr. 5-6). 1993. 9.95 (*0-87973-570-8*, 570); pap. 7.95 (*0-87973-569-4*, 569) Our Sunday Visitor.

Glavich, Mary K. A Child's Book of Parables. LC 94-2383. 1994. 2.50 (*0-8294-0801-0*) Loyola.

Lane, Christopher. King Leonard's Great Grape Harvest. Dahl, Sharon, illus. 32p. 1991. text ed. 7.99 (*0-89693-268-0*, Victor Books) SP Pubns.

—Mrs. Beaver & the Wolf at the Door. Dahl, Sharon, illus. 32p. 1991. text ed. 7.99 (*0-89693-269-9*, Victor Books) SP Pubns.

Lippman, Peter. From Here to There. Lippman, Peter, illus. LC 75-19947. 48p. (gr. 1 up). 1975. pap. 5.00 (*0-912846-11-9*) Bookstore Pr.

Mitchell, Darby. Blue Eye of a Pond. Harris, Andrew S., illus. 10p. (ps-5). 1991. 8.00 (*0-9631809-0-8*) Castle MI.

O'Neal, Debbie T. & Rosato, Amelia. The Lost Coin. Rosato, Amelia, illus. LC 92-46610. 14p. 1993. 7.00 (*0-8170-1194-3*) Judson.

—The Lost Sheep. Rosato, Amelia, illus. LC 92-46612. 14p. 1993. 7.00 (*0-8170-1193-5*) Judson.

Reid, John C. Bird Life in Wington: Practical Parables for Young People. Weidenaar, Reynold H., illus. 142p. (gr. 1-4). 1990. pap. 7.99 (*0-8028-4062-0*) Eerdmans.

Silverstein, Shel. The Giving Tree Gift Edition. Silverstein, Shel, illus. 56p. (gr. 2 up). 1994. 13.00 (*0-06-024419-4*) HarpC Child Bks.

PARADES–FICTION

Baker, Eugene. Shadowing the Suspect. Axeman, Lois, illus. LC 80-13982. 32p. (gr. 2-5). 1980. PLB 12.95 (*0-89565-152-1*) Childs World.

—Spotting the Fakes-Forgeries & Counterfeits. Axeman, Lois, illus. LC 80-15998. 32p. (gr. 2-5). 1980. PLB 12.95 (*0-89565-153-X*) Childs World.

Bunting, Eve. St. Patrick's Day in the Morning. Brett, Jan, illus. LC 79-15934. 32p. (ps-3). 1983. 13.95 (*0-395-29098-8*, Clarion Bks); pap. 5.95 (*0-89919-162-2*, Clarion Bks) HM.

Crews, Donald. Parade. LC 82-20927. (Illus.). (ps up). 1986. 3.95 (*0-688-06520-1*, Mulberry) Morrow.

Herman, Emmi S. The Dress-up Parade. Learner, Vickie, illus. 24p. (ps-2). 1992. pap. 0.99 (*1-56293-112-1*) McClanahan Bk.

How I Saw the Parade (EV, Unit 4. (gr. 1). 1991. 5-pack 21.25 (*0-88106-732-6*) Charlesbridge Pub.

Mock, Dorothy K. The Thanksgiving Parade: The Good News Kids Learn about Faithfulness. Mitter, Kathy, illus. LC 93-2988. 32p. (Orig.). (ps-2). 1993. pap. 3.99 (*0-570-04743-9*) Concordia.

Mockrin, Ida. The Big Parade. Brodsky, Harry, illus. 16p. (ps-1). 1983. pap. 2.00 (*0-9612244-0-1*) Honeycomb Pr.

O'Donnell, Elizabeth L. Patrick's Day. Rogers, Jacqueline, illus. LC 92-27421. 32p. (gr. k up). 1994. 15.00g (*0-688-07853-2*); PLB 14.93 (*0-688-07854-0*) Morrow Jr Bks.

Roberts, Bethany. Cat Parade! Greenseid, Diane, illus. LC 93-26726. 1995. write for info. (*0-395-67893-5*, Clarion Bks) HM.

Ziefert, Harriet. Parade. 1990. 9.95 (*0-553-05862-2*, Little Rooster) Bantam.

PARAGUAY

Haverstock, Nathan A. Paraguay in Pictures. (Illus.). 64p. (gr. 5 up). 1987. PLB 17.50 (*0-8225-1819-8*) Lerner Pubns.

Morrison, Marion. Paraguay. LC 93-754. (Illus.). 128p. (gr. 5-9). 1993. PLB 20.55 (*0-516-02619-4*) Childrens.

PARASITES

see also Bacteriology; Insects, Injurious and Beneficial

Facklam, Howard. Parasites. (Illus.). 64p. (gr. 5-8). 1994. bds. 15.95 (*0-8050-2858-7*) TFC Bks NY.

PARCEL POST

see Postal Service

PAREJA, JUAN DE, 1606-1670–FICTION

De Trevino, Elizabeth B. I, Juan De Pareja. LC 65-19330. 192p. (gr. 7 up). 1965. 16.00 (*0-374-33531-1*); pap. 3.95, 1987 (*0-374-43525-1*, Sunburst) FS&G.

PARENT AND CHILD

see also Children–Management; Fathers; Mothers

Adoff, Arnold. Black Is Brown Is Tan. McCully, Emily A., illus. LC 73-9855. 32p. (ps-3). 1973. 15.00i (*0-06-020083-9*); PLB 14.89 (*0-06-020084-7*) HarpC Child Bks.

Bailey, Marilyn. Single-Parent Families. LC 89-1415. (Illus.). 48p. (gr. 5-6). 1989. text ed. 4.95 RSBE (*0-89686-437-5*, Crestwood Hse) Macmillan Child Grp.

NATION THROUGH REAL PARENTING, by Michael Mayer (0-88247-929-6); WHAT IS HAPPENING TO OUR CHILDREN: HOW TO RAISE THEM RIGHT, by Michael Gustafson (1-56875-044-7); TAKE CHARGE NOW!: SURVIVING THE CLASSROOM (1-56875-069-2).
Publisher Provided Annotation.

Berry, Joy. Every Kid's Guide to Laws That Relate to Parents & Children. Bartholomew, illus. 48p. (gr. 3-7). 1987. 4.95 (*0-516-21411-X*) Childrens.
Berry, Joy W. Teach Me About Mommies & Daddies. Dickey, Kate, ed. LC 85-45078. (Illus.). 36p. (ps). 1986. 4.98 (*0-685-10717-5*) Grolier Inc.
Beyer, Kay. Coping with Teen Parenting. rev. ed. Rosen, Ruth, ed. (gr. 7-12). 1992. PLB 14.95 (*0-8239-1525-5*) Rosen Group.
Bradley, R. C. Teaching for "Self-Directed" Living & Learning in Students - How to Help Students Get in Charge of Their Lives: "Self-Directed" Living & Learning. LC 90-85800. 224p. 1991. text ed. 19.95 (*0-9628624-0-1*) Bassi Bk.
Bratman, Fred. Everything You Need to Know When a Parent Dies. (gr. 7-12). 1992. PLB 14.95 (*0-8239-1324-4*) Rosen Group.
Brown, Fern G. Teen Guide to Caring for Your Unborn Baby. LC 88-51487. (Illus.). 62p. (gr. 7-12). 1989. PLB 13.40 (*0-531-10668-3*) Watts.
Cain, V. M. Steps of Love: Single Adoptive Parenting. 133p. (Orig.). 1988. text ed. write for info. V M H Cain.
Chapian, Marie. Mothers & Daughters. LC 88-4199. 176p. (Orig.). (gr. 8 up). 1988. pap. 8.99 (*1-55661-007-6*) Bethany Hse.
Clinton, Patrick. I Can Be a Father. LC 88-11749. (Illus.). 32p. (gr. k-3). 1988. pap. 3.95 (*0-516-41904-8*) Childrens.
Cochran, Vicki. My Daddy Is a Stranger. Johnson, Joy, ed. Aitken, Susan, illus. 24p. (Orig.). (gr. 1-5). 1992. pap. 3.85 (*1-56123-049-9*) Centering Corp.
Coleman, William L. What You Should Know about Living with One Parent. LC 93-31851. 1993. 5.99 (*0-8066-2636-4*) Augsburg Fortress.
Corey, Dorothy. You Go Away. Rubin, Caroline & Axeman, Lois, illus. LC 75-33015. 32p. (ps-1). 1976. PLB 10.95 (*0-8075-9441-5*) A Whitman.
Craven, Linda. Stepfamilies: New Patterns of Harmony. LC 82-60652. (Illus.). 192p. (gr. 7 up). 1983. (J Messner) S&S Trade.
Davis, Ken. How to Live with Your Parents Without Losing Your Mind. (gr. 7 up). 1988. pap. 7.99 (*0-310-32331-2*, 11791P, Pub. by Youth Spec) Zondervan.
Dinkmeyer, Don, Sr., et al. PREP for Effective Family Living. (gr. 7 up). 1985. 129.95 (*0-88671-225-4*, 6400) Am Guidance.
Duggan, Maureen H. Mommy Doesn't Live Here Anymore. Liberman, Jane, illus. 48p. (Orig.). (ps-7). 1987. pap. 8.95 (*0-944453-01-5*) B Brae.
Elovson, Allana. The Kindergarten Survival Handbook: The Before School Checklist & a Guide for Parents. rev. ed. Elovson, Andrea K., illus. 96p. (Orig.). (gr. k). 1993. Spanish ed. pap. text ed. 12.95 perfect bdg. (*1-879888-07-6*); English ed. pap. text ed. 12.95 (*1-879888-06-8*) Parent Ed.
Evans, Marla D. This Is Me & My Single Parent: A Discovery Workbook for Children & Single Parents. (Illus.). 88p. (Orig.). (gr. 2-6). 1989. pap. 13.95 (*0-945354-17-7*) Magination Pr.
Fitz-Gerald, Christine M. I Can Be a Mother. LC 87-35189. (Illus.). 32p. (gr. k-3). 1988. pap. 3.95 (*0-516-41914-5*) Childrens.
Gardner, Richard A. The Boys & Girls Book about One-Parent Families. LC 78-18388. (Illus.). 122p. (gr. k-8). 1983. pap. 4.99 (*0-933812-16-7*) Creative Therapeutics.
Gilbert, Sara. How to Live with a Single Parent. LC 81-12413. 128p. (gr. 7 up). 1982. PLB 12.88 (*0-688-00633-7*) Lothrop.
Havens, Ami. Now You're Talking. Richey, Donald, illus. LC 90-10764. 128p. (gr. 5-9). 1991. lib. bdg. 10.89 (*0-8167-2142-4*); pap. text ed. 2.95 (*0-8167-2143-2*) Troll Assocs.
Holden, Sue. My Daddy Died & It's All God's Fault. (Illus.). (gr. 4-7). 1991. 8.99 (*0-8499-0879-5*) Word Inc.

Hyde, Sharon K. Babies Looking Book: Stimulation for the Newborn to Six Month Old Infant. (Illus.). 36p. (ps). 1992. 12.95 (*0-9624349-0-6*) S K Hyde. Babies tend to orient to faces more than other things around them. Using the technique of preferential looking, preferences have been ordered. For the newborn...color or pattern over grey... high contrast pattern over color... moderate complexity over high complexity...symmetrical over random. Interest in specific stimuli decreases over time & with the number of exposures. Visual stimulation is more effective when combined with auditory & tactile stimuli. Cognitive skills can be enhanced by appropriate stimulation. Also the nature of the interaction between the parent & the baby is developed. The baby is provided a safe, supportive & sensitive environment in which to see & learn. Reading to the baby allows focusing of attention, change of material as often as necessary, develops habit which remains valuable to relationship for years.
Publisher Provided Annotation.

Jester, Harold D. Pulling Together: Crisis Prevention for Teens & Their Parents. LC 91-41371. 155p. (Orig.). 1992. pap. 9.95 (*0-938179-30-6*) Mills Sanderson.
Lash, Michele, et al. My Kind of Family: A Book for Kids in Single-Parent Homes. LC 90-31471. (Illus.). 208p. (ps-6). 1990. plastic comb spiral bdg. 16.95 (*0-914525-13-1*); pap. 16.95 plastic comb spiral (*0-914525-12-3*) Waterfront Bks.
LeShan, Eda. When Grownups Drive You Crazy. LC 87-22005. 128p. (gr. 3-7). 1988. SBE 13.95 (*0-02-756340-5*, Macmillan Child Bk) Macmillan Child Grp.
Lindsay, Jeanne W. Do I Have a Daddy? A Story about a Single-Parent Child. 2nd ed. Boeller, Cheryl, illus. LC 90-49676. 48p. 1991. 12.95 (*0-930934-45-8*); pap. 5.95 (*0-930934-44-X*) Morning Glory.
—Teen Dads: Rights, Responsibilities & Joys. Crawford, David, photos by. (Illus.). 192p. (Orig.). (gr. 7 up). 1993. 15.95 (*0-930934-77-6*); pap. 9.95 (*0-930934-78-4*); tchr's. guide 2.50 (*0-930934-80-6*); wkbk. 2.50 (*0-930934-79-2*) Morning Glory.
Making Parents Proud. 48p. (gr. 6-8). 1990. pap. 8.99 (*1-55945-107-6*) Group Pub.
Marsh, Carole. Meet in the Middle: The Parents Test - The Kids Test. (Illus.). (gr. 4 up). 1994. 24.95 (*0-935326-24-3*) Gallopade Pub Group.
Mathes, Patricia G. & Irby, Beverly J. Teen Pregnancy & Parenting Handbook. LC 92-85264. 440p. (Orig.). 1993. pap. text ed. 19.95 (*0-87822-333-9*, 4660) Res Press.
Mayle, Peter. Why Are We Getting a Divorce? Robins, Arthur, illus. LC 87-12105. 32p. (gr. k-3). 1988. 15.00 (*0-517-56527-7*, Harmony) Crown Pub Group.
Mazer, Norma F. D, My Name Is Danita. (gr. 7 up). 1991. 13.95 (*0-590-43655-4*) Scholastic Inc.
Moutoussamy-Ashe, Jeanne. Daddy & Me. Moutoussamy-Ashe, Jeanne, photos by. LC 93-11513. (Illus.). 40p. (ps-3). 1993. 13.00 (*0-679-85096-1*); PLB 14.99 (*0-679-95096-6*) Knopf Bks Yng Read.
Packer, Alex J. Bringing up Parents, the Teenager's Handbook. 264p. 1994. 12.95 (*0-685-71613-9*, 752) W Gladden Found.
Parramon, J. M., et al. Parents. 32p. (gr. 3-5). 1987. Eng. ed. pap. 6.95 (*0-8120-3852-5*); Span. ed.: Los Padres. pap. 6.95 (*0-8120-3856-8*) Barron.
Powell, Richard. How to Deal with Parents. Snow, Alan, illus. LC 91-14997. 24p. (gr. k-3). 1992. lib. bdg. 9.59 (*0-8167-2418-0*); pap. text ed. 2.95 (*0-8167-2419-9*) Troll Assocs.
Rashkis, Harold A. & Tashjian, Levon D. Understanding Your Parents. LC 78-60444. (Illus.). 154p. (gr. 9-12). 1978. 6.95 (*0-397-53067-6*) Lippincott.
Reynolds, Moira. Coping with An Immigrant Parent. Rosen, Ruth, ed. (gr. 7-12). 1992. 14.95 (*0-8239-1462-3*) Rosen Group.
Roop, Peter & Roop, Connie. Keep the Lights Burning, Abbie. Hanson, Peter E., illus. LC 84-27446. 40p. (gr. k-4). 1985. lib. bdg. 14.95 (*0-87614-275-7*); pap. 5.95 (*0-87614-454-7*) Carolrhoda Bks.
Rosenberg, Maxine B. Living with a Single Parent. LC 92-3883. (Illus.). 128p. (gr. 4 up). 1992. SBE 14.95 (*0-02-777915-7*, Bradbury Pr) Macmillan Child Grp.
Ryan, Elizabeth A. Straight Talk about Parents. 144p. 1989. 16.95x (*0-8160-1526-0*) Facts on File.
—Straight Talk about Parents. 132p. (gr. 7 up). 1992. pap. 3.99 (*0-440-21300-2*, LFL) Dell.
Schenkerman, Rona D. Growing up with a Single Parent. 16p. (gr. 3-8). 1993. 1.95 (*1-56688-118-8*) Bur For At-Risk.
Seixas, Judith S. Living with a Parent Who Drinks Too Much. LC 78-11108. 128p. (gr. 5 up). 1991. pap. 3.95 (*0-688-10493-2*, Pub. by Beech Tree Bks) Morrow.
Sexias, Judith S. Living with a Parent Who Takes Drugs. LC 89-1995. 112p. (gr. 5 up). 1991. pap. 3.95 (*0-688-10492-4*, Pub. by Beech Tree Bks) Morrow.
Siegel, Eli. Children's Guide to Parents & Other Matters: Little Essays for Children & Others. Koppelman, Dorothy, illus. LC 78-171393. 77p. (gr. 1-6). 1971. text ed. 7.50 (*0-910492-16-6*) Definition.
Silverstein, Herma. Teen Guide to Single Parenting. LC 88-51486. (Illus.). 62p. (gr. 7-12). 1989. PLB 13.40 (*0-531-10669-1*) Watts.
Waring, Shirley B. What Happened to Benjamin: A True Story. Bergstrom, Lucy, illus. LC 92-83949. 38p. (Orig.). (gr. k-6). 1993. PLB 13.95g (*0-9622808-2-8*); Audio cass. 9.98 (*0-9622808-3-6*) S&T Waring.
Webb, Margot. Coping with Parents Who Are Activists. Rosen, Ruth, ed. (gr. 7-12). 1992. 14.95 (*0-8239-1416-X*) Rosen Group.
Wijnberg, Ellen. Parental Unemployment. LC 93-25154. (Illus.). 80p. (gr. 6-9). 1993. PLB 21.34 (*0-8114-3525-3*) Raintree Steck-V.

PARENT AND CHILD–FICTION

Adler, C. S. Daddy's Climbing Tree. 144p. (gr. 4-7). 1993. 13.95 (*0-395-63032-0*, Clarion Bks) HM.
Adshead, Paul. The Secret Hedgehog. LC 91-38897. (gr. 4 up). 1991. 7.95 (*0-85953-510-X*) Childs Play.
Agell, Charlotte. I Wear Long Green Hair in Summer. Agell, Charlotte, illus. LC 93-33612. 32p. (ps up). 1994. 7.95 (*0-88448-113-1*) Tilbury Hse.
Alexander, Martha. When the New Baby Comes, I'm Moving Out. Alexander, Martha, illus. LC 79-4275. (ps-2). 1979. PLB 9.89 (*0-8037-9558-0*) Dial Bks Young.
Anderson, Joan. Sally's Submarine. Ancona, George, contrib. by. LC 94-16644. (gr. 4-7). Date not set. write for info. (*0-688-12690-1*); PLB write for info. (*0-688-12691-X*) Morrow Jr Bks.
Anderson, Rachel. Paper Faces. 128p. (gr. 4-7). 1993. 14.95 (*0-8050-2527-8*, Bks Young Read) H Holt & Co.
Angell, Judie. Yours Truly: A Novel. LC 92-29472. 192p. (gr. 7-12). 1993. 14.95 (*0-531-05472-1*); PLB 14.99 (*0-531-08622-4*) Orchard Bks Watts.
Asch, Frank. Bread & Honey. Asch, Frank, illus. LC 81-16893. 48p. (ps-3). 1982. 5.95 (*0-8193-1077-8*); PLB 5.95 (*0-8193-1078-6*) Parents.
Auch, Mary J. Out of Step. LC 92-4704. 96p. (gr. 4-7). 1992. 13.95 (*0-8234-0985-6*) Holiday.
Avi. The Barn. LC 94-6920. 112p. (gr. 4-6). 1994. 13.95 (*0-531-06861-7*); PLB 13.99 (*0-531-08711-5*) Orchard Bks Watts.
Baillie, Allan. Adrift. 128p. (gr. 3-7). 1992. 14.00 (*0-670-84474-8*) Viking Child Bks.
Baker, Alan. Where's Mouse? Baker, Alan, illus. LC 92-53117. 16p. (ps-k). 1992. 12.95 (*1-85697-821-4*, Kingfisher LKC) LKC.
Ballard, Robin. My Father Is Far Away. LC 91-29580. (Illus.). 32p. (ps-6). 1992. 14.00 (*0-688-10953-5*); PLB 13.93 (*0-688-10954-3*) Greenwillow.
Barrett, John. Daniel Discovers Daniel. Servello, Joe, illus. LC 79-17897. 32p. (gr. k-5). 1980. 16.95 (*0-87705-423-1*) Human Sci Pr.
Barron, T. A. The Merlin Effect. LC 93-36234. 280p. (gr. 5-9). 1994. 16.95 (*0-399-22689-3*, Philomel Bks) Putnam Pub Group.
Bartone, Elisa. Peppe the Lamplighter. LC 92-1397. (Illus.). (ps-3). 1993. 14.00 (*0-688-10268-9*); PLB 13.93 (*0-688-10269-7*) Lothrop.
Bawden, Nina. Humbug. 144p. (gr. 4-7). 1992. 13.45 (*0-395-62149-6*, Clarion Bks) HM.
Bennett, Cherie. The Fall of the the Perfect Girl. 224p. (gr. 7 up). 1993. pap. 3.50 (*0-14-036319-X*, Puffin) Puffin Bks.
Berenstain, Stan & Berenstain, Jan. The Berenstain Bears & the Trouble with Grownups. Berenstain, Stan & Berenstain, Jan, illus. LC 91-27430. 32p. (Orig.). (ps-1). 1992. PLB 5.99 (*0-679-93000-0*); pap. 2.25 (*0-679-83000-6*) Random Bks Yng Read.
Berry, Liz. Mel. LC 93-7484. 224p. (gr. 7 up). 1993. pap. 3.99 (*0-14-036534-6*, Puffin) Puffin Bks.
Best, Cari. Taxi! Taxi! Gottlieb, Dale, illus. LC 92-32249. 1994. 14.95 (*0-316-09259-2*) Little.
Bishop, Roma. Mommy & Baby. (ps). 1992. pap. 2.95 (*0-671-79119-2*, Little Simon) S&S Trade.
Block, Francesca L. The Hanged Man. LC 94-720. 128p. (gr. 7 up). 1994. 14.00 (*0-06-024536-0*); PLB 13.89 (*0-06-024537-9*) HarpC Child Bks.
Blue, Rose. Wishful Lying. Hartman, Laura, illus. LC 79-21806. 32p. (ps-3). 1980. 16.95 (*0-87705-473-8*) Human Sci Pr.
Boelts, Meribeth. With My Mom - with My Dad. 32p. 1992. pap. 5.95 (*0-8163-1060-2*) Pacific Pr Pub Assn.
Bond, Nancy. Truth to Tell. LC 93-11248. 336p. (gr. 5 up). 1994. SBE 17.95 (*0-689-50601-5*, M K McElderry) Macmillan Child Grp.
Bread & Honey. (Illus.). 42p. (ps-3). 1992. PLB 13.26 (*0-8368-0880-0*); PLB 13.27 s.p. (*0-685-61512-X*) Gareth Stevens Inc.
Brown, Margaret W. The Runaway Bunny Board Book. Hurd, Clement, illus. LC 71-183168. 32p. (ps). 1991. pap. 6.95 (*0-06-107429-2*) HarpC Child Bks.
Buffie, Margaret. Someone Else's Ghost. LC 93-48015. (gr. 6 up). 1994. write for info. (*0-590-46922-3*) Scholastic Inc.
Bunn, Scott. Just Hold On. LC 82-70316. 160p. (gr. 7 up). 1982. pap. 9.95 (*0-385-28490-X*) Delacorte.
Bunting, Eve. Flower Garden. Hewitt, Kathryn, illus. LC 92-25766. 1994. 13.95 (*0-15-228776-0*) HarBrace.
—A Part of the Dream. (Illus.). 64p. (gr. 3-8). 1992. 8.95 (*0-89565-771-6*) Childs World.
—Sharing Susan. LC 90-27097. 128p. (gr. 4-7). 1991. 14.00 (*0-06-021693-X*); PLB 13.89 (*0-06-021694-8*) HarpC Child Bks.
—Spying on Miss Muller. LC 94-15003. (gr. 1-8). 1995. write for info. (*0-395-69172-9*, Clarion Bks) HM.
Burnett, Frances H. A Little Princess. 1990. pap. 3.50 (*0-440-40386-3*, Pub. by Yearling Classics) Dell.
—A Little Princess. Dubowski, Cathy E., ed. LC 93-14000. 1994. 2.99 (*0-679-85090-2*) Random.

Burningham, John. Come Away from the Water, Shirley. Burningham, John, illus. LC 77-483. 32p. (gr. 1-2). 1977. (Crowell Jr Bks); PLB 14.89 (*0-690-01361-2*) HarpC Child Bks.
Burstein, Fred. The Dancer. Auclair, Joan, illus. LC 91-41429. 40p. (ps-3). 1993. RSBE 14.95 (*0-02-715625-7*, Bradbury Pr) Macmillan Child Grp.
Caines, Jeannette. Abby. Kellogg, Steven, illus. LC 73-5480. 32p. (ps-3). 1973. PLB 12.89 (*0-06-020922-4*) HarpC Child Bks.
Caisley, Raewyn. Hannah & Her Dad. Thomas, Meredith, illus. LC 93-28997. 1994. 4.25 (*0-383-03787-5*) SRA Schl Grp.
Calvert, Patricia. Bigger. LC 93-14415. 144p. (gr. 4-6). 1994. SBE 14.95 (*0-684-19685-9*, Scribners Young Read) Macmillan Child Grp.
Carlstrom, Nancy. Goodbye Geese. Young, Ed, illus. 32p. (ps-3). 1991. 14.95 (*0-399-21832-7*, Philomel) Putnam Pub Group.
Carrick, Carol. Valentine. Bouma, Paddy, illus. LC 93-35911. 1995. write for info. (*0-395-66554-X*, Clarion Bks) HM.
Caseley, Judith. Mama, Coming & Going. LC 92-29402. (Illus.). 32p. (ps up). 1994. 14.00 (*0-688-11441-5*); PLB 13.93 (*0-688-11442-3*) Greenwillow.
Cazet, Denys. Are There Any Questions? LC 91-42977. (Illus.). 32p. (ps-2). 1992. 14.95 (*0-531-05451-9*); PLB 14.99 (*0-531-08601-1*) Orchard Bks Watts.
—Born in the Gravy. Cazet, Denys, illus. LC 92-44523. 32p. (ps-1). 1993. 14.95 (*0-531-05488-8*); PLB 14.99 (*0-531-08638-0*) Orchard Bks Watts.
Chetwin, Grace. Jason's Seven Magical Night Rides. Chetwin, Grace, illus. LC 93-21125. 128p. (gr. 2-6). 1994. SBE 14.95 (*0-02-718221-5*, Bradbury Pr) Macmillan Child Grp.
Christopher, Matt. Centerfield Ballhawk. Beier, Ellen, illus. 64p. (gr. 2-4). 1992. 13.95 (*0-316-14079-1*) Little.
Cleary, Beverly. Dear Mr. Henshaw. large type ed. Zelinsky, Paul O., illus. 141p. (gr. 2-6). 1987. Repr. of 1983 ed. lib. bdg. 14.95 (*1-55736-001-4*, Crnrstn Bks) BDD LT Grp.
—Ramona & Her Father. Tiegreen, Alan, illus. LC 77-1614. 192p. (gr. 3-7). 1977. 13.95 (*0-688-22114-9*); PLB 13.88 (*0-688-32114-3*) Morrow Jr Bks.
Clifton, Lucille. Everett Anderson's 1-2-3. Grifalconi, Ann, illus. LC 92-8031. 32p. (ps-2). 1992. 14.95 (*0-8050-2310-0*, Bks Young Read) H Holt & Co.
Cohen, Barbara. Make a Wish, Molly. Jones, Jan N., illus. LC 93-17901. 1994. 14.95 (*0-385-31079-X*) Delacorte.
Cohen, Ron. My Dad's Baseball. LC 92-22938. (Illus.). 1994. 15.00 (*0-688-12390-2*); lib. bdg. 14.93 (*0-688-12391-0*) Lothrop.
Collins, H. When You Were Little & I Was Big. (Illus.). 32p. (ps-8). 1984. 12.95 (*0-920236-84-7*, Pub. by Annick CN); pap. 4.95 (*0-920236-71-5*, Pub. by Annick CN) Firefly Bks Ltd.
Colman, Hila. Weekend Sisters. LC 85-5665. 176p. (gr. 7 up). 1985. 11.95 (*0-688-05785-3*) Morrow Jr Bks.
Cooney, Caroline B. Whatever Happened to Janie? LC 92-32334. 208p. 1993. 15.95 (*0-385-31035-8*) Delacorte.
Cottonwood, Joe. Danny Ain't. (gr. 7 up). 1992. 13.95 (*0-590-45067-0*, 026, Scholastic Hardcover) Scholastic Inc.
Cummings, Pat. Carousel. Cummings, Pat, illus. LC 93-8708. 32p. (ps-3). 1994. RSBE 14.95 (*0-02-725512-3*, Bradbury Pr) Macmillan Child Grp.
Danis, Naomi. Walk with Me. Rogers, Jacqueline, illus. LC 94-16973. (gr. 1-8). 1995. 6.95 (*0-590-45855-8*, Cartwheel) Scholastic Inc.
Danziger, Paula. The Divorce Express. 160p. (gr. 7 up). 1983. pap. 3.99 (*0-440-92062-0*, LFL) Dell.
—Everyone Else's Parents Said Yes. (gr. k-6). 1990. pap. 3.99 (*0-440-40333-2*, YB) Dell.
Davol, Marguerite. Black, White, Just Right. Trivas, Irene, illus. LC 93-19932. 1993. write for info. (*0-8075-0785-7*) A Whitman.
Deaver, Julie R. You Bet Your Life. LC 92-28211. 224p. (gr. 7 up). 1993. 15.00 (*0-06-021516-X*); PLB 14.89 (*0-06-021517-8*) HarpC Child Bks.
De Balzac, Honore. Pere Goriot. Canon, R. R., intro. by. (gr. 10 up). 1965. pap. 1.50 (*0-8049-0084-1*, CL-84) Airmont.
DenBoer, Helen. Please Don't Cry, Mom. Goldstein, Janice G., illus. LC 93-14699. 1993. 13.50 (*0-87614-805-4*) Carolrhoda Bks.
Devore, Cynthia D. Breakfast for Dinner. LC 93-13066. 32p. (gr. 5 up). 1993. 14.96 (*1-56239-245-X*) Abdo & Dghtrs.
—The Wind Before It Blows. LC 93-7723. (Illus.). 1993. 14.96 (*1-56239-247-6*) Abdo & Dghtrs.
Doherty, Berlie. Dear Nobody. 192p. (gr. 6-12). 1992. 14.95 (*0-531-05461-6*); PLB 14.99 (*0-531-08611-9*) Orchard Bks Watts.
—Dear Nobody. LC 93-9626. 192p. (gr. 8 up). 1994. pap. 4.95 (*0-688-12764-9*, Pub. by Beech Tree Bks) Morrow.
Dumond, Michael. Dad Is Leaving Home. 196p. (gr. 7-12). 1987. PLB 12.95 (*0-8239-0699-X*) Rosen Group.
Dunlop, Eileen. Finn's Island. LC 91-55027. 128p. (gr. 5-9). 1992. 13.95 (*0-8234-0910-4*) Holiday.
Edwards, Michelle. Meera's Blanket. LC 94-14825. 1995. write for info. (*0-688-09710-3*); PLB write for info. (*0-688-09711-1*) Lothrop.
Eisenberg, Phyllis R. You're My Nikki. Kastner, Jill, illus. LC 91-2670. 32p. (ps-3). 1992. 14.00 (*0-8037-1127-1*); PLB 13.89 (*0-8037-1129-8*) Dial Bks Young.
Ellis, Sarah. Pick-Up Sticks. LC 93-7759. 128p. (gr. 5 up). 1993. pap. 3.99 (*0-14-036340-8*, Puffin) Puffin Bks.
Eyles, Heather. Well, I Never! Ross, Tony, illus. 32p. (ps-3). 1990. 11.95 (*0-87951-383-7*) Overlook Pr.
Falwell, Cathryn. Nicky Loves Daddy. Falwell, Cathryn, illus. 32p. (ps). 1992. 5.70 (*0-395-60820-1*, Clarion Bks) HM.
Farmer, Patti. Bartholomew's Dream. Wummer, Amy, illus. 32p. (ps-2). 1994. 12.95 (*0-8120-6403-8*); pap. 4.95 (*0-8120-1991-1*) Barron.
Fenner, Carol. A Summer of Horses. LC 88-45878. 144p. (Orig.). (gr. 3-6). 1989. lib. bdg. 7.99 (*0-394-90480-X*); pap. 2.95 (*0-394-80480-5*) Knopf Bks Yng Read.
Ferguson, Virginia & Durkin, Peter. Tell Me a Story, Dad. Vane, Mitch, illus. LC 93-6629. 1994. write for info. (*0-383-03717-4*) SRA Schl Grp.
Feuer, Elizabeth. Camp Bugaboo. LC 93-34212. 1994. 15.00 (*0-374-31020-3*) FS&G.
Fine, Anne. Alias Madame Doubtfire. 1990. pap. 3.99 (*0-553-56615-6*) Bantam.
—Flour Babies & the Boys of Room 8. LC 93-35698. 1994. Repr. of 1992 ed. 14.95 (*0-316-28319-3*) Little.
—Madame Doubtfire. Pena, Flora, tr. (SPA.). 165p. (gr. 5-8). 1992. pap. write for info. (*84-204-4680-7*) Santillana.
—Poor Monty. Vulliamy, Clara, illus. 32p. (ps-1). 1992. 14.45 (*0-395-60472-9*, Clarion Bks) HM.
Fowler, Susi G. I'll See You When the Moon Is Full. Fowler, Jim, illus. LC 91-47667. 24p. (ps up). 1994. 14.00 (*0-688-10830-X*); PLB 13.93 (*0-688-10831-8*) Greenwillow.
French, Simon. Change the Locks. LC 92-30194. 112p. (gr. 3-7). 1993. 13.95 (*0-590-45593-1*) Scholastic Inc.
Friedman, Aileen. A Cloak for the Dreamer. Howard, Kim, illus. LC 94-11274. 1994. write for info. (*0-590-48987-9*) Scholastic Inc.
Friend, David. Baseball, Football, Daddy & Me. Brown, Richard, illus. 32p. (ps-3). 1992. pap. 3.99 (*0-14-050914-3*) Puffin Bks.
Gardella, Tricia. Just Like My Dad. Apple, Margot, illus. LC 90-4403. 32p. (ps-3). 1993. 15.00 (*0-06-021937-8*); PLB 14.89 (*0-06-021938-6*) HarpC Child Bks.
Geisert, Arthur. Oink, Oink. Geisert, Arthur, illus. LC 92-31778. 32p. (gr. k-3). 1993. 13.45 (*0-395-64048-2*) HM.
George, William T. Christmas at Long Pond. George, Lindsay B., illus. LC 91-31475. 32p. (ps-8). 1992. 14.00 (*0-688-09214-4*); PLB 13.93 (*0-688-09215-2*) Greenwillow.
Glassman, Peter. My Working Mom. Arnold, Tedd, illus. LC 93-22036. 1994. 15.00g (*0-688-12259-0*); PLB 14.93 (*0-688-12260-4*) Morrow Jr Bks.
Gleitzman, Morris. Misery Guts. LC 92-22570. 1993. 12.95 (*0-15-254768-1*) HarBrace.
Goodman, Joan E. Songs from Home. LC 93-46248. (gr. 5 up). 1994. 10.95 (*0-15-203590-7*); pap. 4.95 (*0-15-203591-5*) HarBrace.
Gove, Doris. One Rainy Night. Krudop, Walter L., illus. LC 93-13900. 32p. (gr. 2-5). 1994. SBE 14.95 (*0-689-31800-6*, Atheneum Child Bk) Macmillan Child Grp.
Gray, Luli. Falcon's Egg. LC 94-16731. 1995. 10.95 (*0-395-71128-2*) Ticknor & Flds Bks Yng Read.
Green, Phyllis. A New Mother for Martha. Luks, Margaret. LC 78-16731. (Illus.). 32p. (gr. k-3). 1978. 16.95 (*0-87705-330-8*) Human Sci Pr.
Greenberg, Melanie H. My Father's Luncheonette. Greenberg, Melanie H., illus. LC 90-45586. 32p. (ps-2). 1991. 12.95 (*0-525-44725-3*, DCB) Dutton Child Bks.
Greenwood, Pamela D. I Found Mouse. Plecas, Jennifer, illus. LC 93-46427. (ps). 1994. 14.95 (*0-395-65478-5*, Clarion Bks) HM.
Guy, Rosa. Billy the Great. Binch, Caroline, illus. LC 92-34704. 32p. (gr. k-3). 1992. 15.00 (*0-385-30666-0*) Delacorte.
Hafen, Lyman. Over the Joshua Slope. LC 93-30712. 160p. (gr. 4-8). 1994. SBE 14.95 (*0-02-741100-1*, Bradbury Pr) Macmillan Child Grp.
Hahn, Mary D. The Wind Blows Backwards. large type ed. LC 93-31870. (gr. 9-12). 1993. 15.95 (*0-7862-0064-2*) Thorndike Pr.
Hamilton, Virginia. Plain City. LC 93-19910. 176p. (gr. 3-7). 1993. 13.95 (*0-590-47364-6*) Scholastic Inc.
Hanson, Regina. The Tangerine Tree. Stevenson, Harvey, illus. LC 93-40530. 1995. write for info. (*0-395-68963-5*, Clarion Bks) HM.
Harshman, Marc. Moving Days. Popp, Wendy, illus. 32p. (gr. k-4). 1994. 13.99 (*0-525-65135-7*, Cobblehill Bks) Dutton Child Bks.
Haseley, Dennis. Kite Flier. Wiesner, David, illus. LC 92-22721. 32p. (ps-3). 1993. pap. 4.95 (*0-689-71668-0*, Aladdin) Macmillan Child Grp.
Hathorn, Libby. Looking for Felix. Culio, Ned, illus. LC 92-34259. 1993. 4.25 (*0-383-03638-0*) SRA Schl Grp.
—The Surprise Box. Cutter, Priscilla, illus. LC 93-28957. 1994. 4.25 (*0-383-03778-6*) SRA Schl Grp.
Haugen, Tormod. Zeppelin. Diamond, Donna, illus. Jacobs, David R., tr. from NOR. LC 92-8319. (Illus.). 128p. (gr. 4-7). 1994. 15.00 (*0-06-020881-3*); PLB 14.89 (*0-06-020882-1*) HarpC Child Bks.
Haynes, Betsy. Fabulous Five Parent Game. (ps-1). 1989. pap. 2.75 (*0-553-15670-5*, #06) Bantam.
Hazen, Barbara S. Even If I Did Something Awful? Kincade, Nancy, illus. LC 91-23143. 32p. (ps-2). 1992. pap. 3.95 (*0-689-71600-1*, Aladdin) Macmillan Child Grp.
Hendry, Diana, ed. Back Soon. Thompson, Carol, illus. LC 93-45590. 32p. (gr. k-3). 1994. PLB 13.95 (*0-8167-3487-9*); pap. text ed. 3.95 (*0-8167-3488-7*) BrdgeWater.
Henkes, Kevin. Protecting Marie. LC 94-16387. 1995. write for info. (*0-688-13958-2*) Greenwillow.
—Words of Stone. LC 91-28543. (gr. 5-12). 1992. 13.00 (*0-688-11356-7*) Greenwillow.
—Words of Stone. LC 93-7488. 160p. (gr. 4-7). 1993. pap. 3.99 (*0-14-036601-6*, Puffin) Puffin Bks.
Hermes, Patricia. Mama, Let's Dance. (gr. 4-7). 1993. pap. 2.95 (*0-590-46633-X*) Scholastic Inc.
—Someone to Count On. LC 93-13502. (ps-6). 1993. 14.95 (*0-316-35925-4*) Little.
—Take Care of My Girl: A Novel. LC 92-9819. 1992. 14.95 (*0-316-35913-0*) Little.
Himmelman, John. Wanted: Perfect Parents. LC 93-22201. (Illus.). 32p. (ps-3). 1993. PLB 13.95 (*0-8167-3028-8*); pap. write for info. (*0-8167-3029-6*) BrdgeWater.
Hines, Anna G. Even If I Spill My Milk? (ps-3). 1994. 13.95 (*0-395-65010-0*, Clarion Bks) HM.
Hinton, S. E. Big David, Little David. Daniel, Alan, illus. LC 93-32307. 1995. 14.95 (*0-385-31093-5*) Doubleday.
Hoban, Julia. Amy Loves the Rain. Hoban, Lillian, illus. LC 88-45851. 32p. (ps). 1989. PLB 9.89 (*0-06-022358-8*) HarpC Child Bks.
—Amy Loves the Snow. Hoban, Lillian, illus. LC 76-45852. 24p. (ps). 1989. PLB 10.89 (*0-06-022395-2*) HarpC Child Bks.
Hoffius, Stephen. Winners & Losers. LC 92-42394. 123p. (gr. 6 up). 1993. pap. 15.00 (*0-671-79194-X*, S&S BFYR) S&S Trade.
Hopkins, Lee B. Mama. Marchesi, Stephen, illus. LC 91-24712. 112p. (gr. 2-8). 1992. pap. 13.00 jacketed, 3-pc. bdg. (*0-671-74985-4*, S&S BFYR) S&S Trade.
—Mama & Her Boys. Marchesi, Stephen, illus. LC 91-23399. 176p. (gr. 5 up). 1993. pap. 13.00 JRT (*0-671-74986-2*, S&S BFYR) S&S Trade.
Horton, Barbara S. What Comes in Spring? Young, Ed, illus. LC 89-39695. 40p. (ps-1). 1992. 14.00 (*0-679-80268-1*); PLB 14.99 (*0-679-90268-6*) Knopf Bks Yng Read.
Houston, Gloria. Littlejim. Allen, Thomas B., illus. LC 92-43775. 176p. (gr. 5 up). 1993. pap. 4.95 (*0-688-12112-8*, Pub. by Beech Tree Bks) Morrow.
—Littlejim's Gift: An Appalachian Christmas Story. Allen, Thomas B., illus. LC 93-41736. 32p. (gr. 1-5). 1994. PLB 15.95 (*0-399-22696-6*, Philomel Bks) Putnam Pub Group.
Howard, Elizabeth F. Papa Tells Chita a Story. Cooper, Floyd, illus. LC 93-1252. 40p. (ps-2). 1995. RSBE 15.00 (*0-02-744623-9*, Four Winds) Macmillan Child Grp.
Howard, Ellen. Gilly's Secret. LC 92-44896. 128p. (gr. 3-7). 1993. pap. 3.95 (*0-689-71746-6*, Aladdin) Macmillan Child Grp.
—The Tower Room. LC 92-39240. 160p. (gr. 3-7). 1993. SBE 13.95 (*0-689-31856-1*, Atheneum Child Bk) Macmillan Child Grp.
Howe, James. Pinky & Rex & the Double-Dad Weekend. Sweet, Melissa, illus. LC 94-9384. 1995. 14.00 (*0-689-31871-5*, Atheneum) Macmillan.
Hughes, Dean. Quarterback Hero. Stroud, Steve, illus. LC 93-8039. 112p. (Orig.). 1994. pap. 3.99 (*0-679-84360-4*, Bullseye Bks) Random Bks Yng Read.
—The Trophy. LC 93-42234. 128p. (gr. 3-7). 1994. 13.00 (*0-679-84368-X*); lib. bdg. cancelled (*0-679-94368-4*) Knopf Bks Yng Read.
Hwa-I Publishing Co., Staff. Chinese Children's Stories, Vol. 51: Moginlin Saves His Mother, Hwang Shun & His Father. Ching, Emily, et al, eds. Wonder Kids Publications Staff, tr. from CHI. (Illus.). 28p. (gr. 3-6). 1991. Repr. of 1988 ed. 7.95 (*1-56162-051-3*) Wonder Kids.
James, Mary. Frankenlouse. LC 93-39651. (gr. 6 up). 1994. 13.95 (*0-590-46528-7*) Scholastic Inc.
Javernick, Ellen. Where's Brooke? Hackney, Richard, illus. LC 92-11097. 32p. (ps-2). 1992. PLB 10.27 (*0-516-02012-9*) Childrens.
Jennings, Dana A. Me, Dad & No. 6. Sasaki, Goro, illus. LC 93-43640. 1995. write for info. (*0-15-200085-2*, Gulliver Bks) HarBrace.
Johnson, Angela. Joshua's Night Whispers. Mitchell, Rhonda, illus. LC 93-46412. 12p. (ps). 1994. 4.95 (*0-531-06847-1*) Orchard Bks Watts.
—Tell Me a Story, Mama. Soman, David, illus. LC 88-17917. 32p. (ps-1). 1989. 14.95 (*0-531-05794-1*); PLB 14.99 (*0-531-08394-2*) Orchard Bks Watts.
Johnson, Dolores. Papa's Stories. Johnson, Dolores, illus. LC 93-17534. 32p. (gr. k-3). 1994. RSBE 14.95 (*0-02-747847-5*, Macmillan Child Bk) Macmillan Child Grp.
—Your Dad Was Just Like You. Johnson, Dolores, illus. LC 92-6347. 32p. (gr. k-3). 1993. RSBE 13.95 (*0-02-747838-6*, Macmillan Child Bk) Macmillan Child Grp.
Joosse, Barbara M. Mama, Do You Love Me? Lavallee, Barbara, illus. 32p. (ps-1). 1991. 13.95 (*0-87701-759-X*) Chronicle Bks.
Karr, Kathleen. Gideon & the Mummy Professor. 1993. 16.00 (*0-374-32563-4*) FS&G.
Kaye, Marilyn. Camp Sunnyside Friends, No. 11: The Problem with Parents. 128p. 1991. pap. 2.95 (*0-380-76183-1*, Camelot) Avon.

Kenkes, Kevin. Owen. LC 92-30084. 24p. (ps up). 1993. 14.00 (*0-688-11449-0*); lib. bdg. 13.93 (*0-688-11450-4*) Greenwillow.

Kimmel, Eric A. One Good Tern Deserves Another. LC 94-4505. 160p. (gr. 5-7). 1994. 14.95 (*0-8234-1138-9*) Holiday.

Kinsey-Warnock, Natalie. On a Starry Night. McPhail, David, illus. LC 93-4878. 1994. write for info. (*0-531-06820-X*); PLB write for info. (*0-531-08670-4*) Orchard Bks Watts.

Komaiko, Leah. Just My Dad & Me. Greene, Jeffrey, illus. LC 94-18688. 1995. 15.00 (*0-06-024573-5*, Festival); PLB 14.89 (*0-06-024574-3*) HarpC Child Bks.

Krisher, Trudy. Spite Fences. LC 94-8665. 1994. 14.95 (*0-385-32088-4*) Delacorte.

Lakin, Patricia. Dad & Me in the Morning. Steele, Robert, illus. LC 93-36169. (ps-3). 1994. 14.95 (*0-8075-1419-5*) A Whitman.

La Mann, Angela. Mom Is Going to Stop It. 27p. (gr. k). 1992. pap. text ed. 23.00 big bk. (*1-56843-014-0*); pap. text ed. 4.50 (*1-56843-064-7*) BGR Pub.

Lee, Joanna. I Want to Keep My Baby! 176p. (Orig.). (gr. 9-12). 1977. pap. 3.50 (*0-451-15733-8*, Sig) NAL-Dutton.

Leeka, M. C. Just Like Mommy, Just Like Daddy. Borgo, Deborah, illus. 24p. (ps-2). 1993. pap. text ed. 0.99 (*1-56293-345-0*) McClanahan Bk.

Lehne, Judith L. When the Ragman Sings. LC 93-20346. 128p. (gr. 3-7). 1993. 14.00 (*0-06-023316-8*); PLB 13.89 (*0-06-023317-6*) HarpC Child Bks.

Leuck, Laura. Night Is Calling. Eitan, Ora, illus. LC 93-22837. 1994. pap. 15.00 (*0-671-86940-X*, S&S BFYR) S&S Trade.

Lewin, Hugh. Jafta: The Homecoming. Kopper, Lisa, illus. LC 93-12945. 32p. (ps-2). 1994. 8.99 (*0-679-84722-7*); PLB 9.99 (*0-679-94722-1*) Knopf Bks Yng Read.

—Jafta's Father. Kopper, Lisa, illus. 24p. (ps-3). 1983. pap. 4.95 (*0-87614-209-9*) Carolrhoda Bks.

Lewis, Beverly. Secret Summer Heart. 160p. (gr. 6-9). 1993. pap. 4.99 (*0-310-38061-8*, Pub. by Youth Spec) Zondervan.

Limmer, Milly J. Where Do Little Girls Grow? Levine, Abby, ed. Hoffman, Rosekrans, illus. LC 92-22936. 32p. (ps-2). 1993. PLB 14.95 (*0-8075-8924-1*) A Whitman.

Lisle, Janet T. The Gold Dust Letters. LC 93-11806. 128p. (gr. 3-5). 1994. 14.95 (*0-531-06830-7*); lib. bdg. 14.99 RLB (*0-531-08680-1*) Orchard Bks Watts.

London, Jonathan. A Koala for Katie. Jabar, Cynthia, illus. LC 93-16085. 1993. write for info. (*0-8075-4209-1*) A Whitman.

—Let's Go, Froggy! Remkiewicz, Frank, illus. LC 93-24059. 32p. (ps-3). 1994. PLB 12.99 (*0-670-85055-1*) Viking Child Bks.

Lutzeier, Elizabeth. The Wall. LC 92-52712. 160p. (gr. 5-9). 1992. 14.95 (*0-8234-0987-2*) Holiday.

Lynch, Chris. Gypsy Davey. 160p. (gr. 7 up). 1994. 14.00 (*0-06-023586-1*); PLB 13.89 (*0-06-023587-X*) HarpC Child Bks.

—Iceman. LC 93-7776. 160p. (gr. 7 up). 1994. 15.00 (*0-06-023340-0*); PLB 14.89 (*0-06-023341-9*) HarpC Child Bks.

—Shadow Boxer. LC 92-47490. 224p. (gr. 5 up). 1993. 14.00 (*0-06-023027-4*); PLB 13.89 (*0-06-023028-2*) HarpC Child Bks.

Lyon, George-Ella. Who Came Down That Road? Catalanotto, Peter, illus. LC 91-20742. 32p. (ps-2). 1992. 15.95 (*0-531-05987-1*); PLB 15.99 (*0-531-08587-2*) Orchard Bks Watts.

Macaulay, David. Black & White. Macaulay, David, illus. 32p. 1990. 14.45 (*0-395-52151-3*) HM.

McCully, Emily A. My Real Family. LC 92-46290. 1994. 13.95 (*0-15-277698-2*, Browndeer Pr) HarBrace.

McDonald, Megan. The Bridge to Nowhere. LC 92-50844. 160p. (gr. 6 up). 1993. 14.95 (*0-531-05478-0*); PLB 14.99 (*0-531-08628-3*) Orchard Bks Watts.

McKenzie, Ellen K. The King, the Princess, & the Tinker. Low, William, illus. LC 91-31316. 80p. (gr. 2-4). 1993. 14.95 (*0-8050-1773-9*, Redfeather BYR) H Holt & Co.

McOmber, Rachel B., ed. McOmber Phonics Storybooks: Mom & Dad Hop-Jig. rev. ed. (Illus.). write for info. (*0-944991-16-5*) Swift Lrn Res.

Madenski, Melissa. In My Mother's Garden. Speidel, Sandra, illus. LC 93-40112. 1995. 15.95 (*0-316-54326-8*) Little.

Mahy, Margaret. The Catalogue of the Universe. LC 85-72262. 192p. (gr. 9 up). 1986. SBE 15.95 (*0-689-50391-1*, M K McElderry) Macmillan Child Grp.

Manushkin, Fran. The Best Toy of All. LC 91-34589. (Illus.). 24p. (ps-1). 1992. 11.00 (*0-525-44897-7*, DCB) Dutton Child Bks.

—Peeping & Sleeping. Plecas, Jennifer, illus. LC 93-26297. (ps-3). 1994. 14.95 (*0-395-64339-2*, Clarion Bks) HM.

Marcus, Irene W. & Marcus, Paul. Into the Great Forest: A Story for Children Away from Parents for the First Time. LC 91-37636. (Illus.). 32p. (ps-3). 1992. pap. 6.95 (*0-945354-40-1*); 16.95 (*0-945354-39-8*) Magination Pr.

—Into the Great Forest: A Story for Children Away from Parents for the First Time. Jeschke, Susan, illus. LC 92-56871. 1993. PLB 17.27 (*0-8368-0932-7*) Gareth Stevens Inc.

Marino, Jan. For the Love of Pete: A Novel. LC 92-36465. 1993. 14.95 (*0-316-54627-5*) Little.

Marshall, Linda D. What Is a Step? Marshall, Linda D. & Johnson, Daphane, illus. LC 91-67511. 48p. (Orig.). (ps-5). 1992. pap. 8.00 (*1-879289-00-8*) Native Sun Pubs. "If you are looking for a mind-strengthening fun gift to get a special little one..., then we recommend Linda D. Marshall's WHAT IS A STEP? Our children are faced with the reality of such unfortunate words as 'bastard,' 'half-brother,' 'half-sister,' 'separation,' 'divorce,' & the like; & they need a way out of the confusion & sickness produced by the manifestations of those terms. This is especially true for children of Afrikan descent whose LONGER historical & cultural reality preclude such terms. Told with good humor, maternal caring, & a child's splendid wonder, WHAT IS A STEP? is a book useful to all parents who read to & communicate with their young." - THE RICHMOND NEWS LEADER. To be sure, here is a children's book whose integrity is not compromised by both its widespread & its specific appeal: it has mainstream, multicultural, & Afrikan-centered relevance, all genuine as the warm adults & enthusiastic children who will enjoy & learn from this story of Whobee & his family. Indeed, once we open this book's bright seven-color covers, we will learn how Whobee's overhearing his mother on the phone confuses him, the lessons he will learn, & the nature of his summer's special gift to him. A book of life-long value. *Publisher Provided Annotation.*

Martin, C. L. The Blueberry Train. Thomas, Angela T., illus. LC 93-31014. 1995. 14.00 (*0-02-762441-2*) Macmillan Child Grp.

Matthews, Cecily. Why Not? Culic, Ned, illus. LC 93-9280. 1994. write for info. (*0-383-03727-1*) SRA Schl Grp.

Mazer, Norma F. Up in Seth's Room. LC 79-2102. 208p. (gr. 7 up). 1979. pap. 7.95 (*0-385-29058-6*) Delacorte.

Mennen, Ingrid. One Round Moon & a Star for Me. Daly, Niki, illus. LC 93-9628. 32p. (ps-2). 1994. 14.95 (*0-531-06804-8*); PLB 14.99 (*0-531-08654-2*) Orchard Bks Watts.

Mills, Claudia. Boardwalk with Hotel. 144p. (gr. 7-12). 1986. pap. 2.50 (*0-553-15397-8*, Skylark) Bantam.

Minarik, Else H. Am I Beautiful? Abolafia, Yossi, illus. LC 91-32562. 24p. (ps-4). 1992. 14.00 (*0-688-09911-4*); PLB 13.93 (*0-688-09912-2*) Greenwillow.

Miyamoto, Tadao. Papa & Me. LC 94-1563. 1994. 18.95 (*0-87614-843-7*) Carolrhoda Bks.

Modesitt, Jeanne. Mama, If You Had a Wish. Spowart, Robin, illus. LC 91-31354. 40p. (ps-1). 1993. JRT 14.00 (*0-671-75437-8*, Green Tiger) S&S Trade.

Moessinger, Pierre. Socrates. Boix, Manuel, illus. LC 92-44060. 1993. 14.95 (*0-88682-606-3*) Creative Ed.

Morris-Vann, Artie M. My Mom Keeps Hitting Me...But. Orlowski, Dennis, illus. 32p. (Orig.). (ps-5). 1981. pap. 6.50x (*0-940370-02-6*); counseling activity guide-abused children 6.50 (*0-940370-06-9*) Aid-U Pub.

Murphy, Barbara B. Eagles in Their Flight. LC 93-11438. 1994. 14.95 (*0-385-32035-3*) Delacorte.

Myers, Walter D. Mop, Moondance, & the Nagasaki Knights. LC 91-36824. 160p. (gr. 3-7). 1992. 14.00 (*0-385-30687-3*) Delacorte.

Nasaw, Jonathan. Shakedown Street. LC 92-43046. 1993. 14.95 (*0-385-31071-4*) Delacorte.

Nelson, Theresa. Earthshine: A Novel. LC 94-8793. 192p. (gr. 6-9). 1994. 15.95 (*0-531-06867-6*); PLB 15.99 (*0-531-08717-4*) Orchard Bks Watts.

Newton-John, Olivia & Hurst, Brian S. A Pig Tale. Murdocca, Sal, illus. LC 92-44116. 1993. pap. 12.00 (*0-671-78778-0*, S&S BFYR) S&S Trade.

Nichols, Janet. Casey Wooster's Pet Care Service. LC 93-7041. 128p. (gr. 4-7). 1993. SBE 12.95 (*0-689-31879-0*, Atheneum Child Bk) Macmillan Child Grp.

Numeroff. Fathers & Mothers. 1993. 15.95 (*0-8050-2056-X*) H Holt & Co.

Olsen, Ib S. The Grown-up Trap. LC 91-35251. (Illus.). 32p. (ps-4). 1990. 6.98 (*0-934738-96-3*) Thomasson-Grant.

Oram, Hiawyn. Reckless Ruby. Ross, Tony, illus. LC 91-20124. 32p. (ps-2). 1992. 12.00 (*0-517-58744-0*) Crown Bks Yng Read.

Palacios, Argentina. A Christmas Surprise for Chabelita. Lohstoeter, Lori, photos by. LC 93-22336. (Illus.). 32p. (gr. k-4). 1993. PLB 14.95 (*0-8167-3131-4*); pap. 3.95 (*0-8167-3132-2*) Brdgewater.

Parton, Dolly. Coat of Many Colors. Sutton, Judith, illus. LC 93-3866. 32p. (gr. 1 up). 1994. 14.00 (*0-06-023413-X*); PLB 13.89 (*0-06-023414-8*) HarpC Child Bks.

Pascal, Francine. Sarah's Dad & Sophia's Mom. 1992. pap. 3.25 (*0-553-15944-5*) Bantam.

Patron, Susan. Maybe Yes, Maybe No, Maybe Maybe. Donahue, Dorothy, illus. LC 92-34067. 96p. (gr. 3-5). 1993. 14.95 (*0-531-05482-9*); PLB 14.99 (*0-531-08632-1*) Orchard Bks Watts.

Peck, Sylvia. Kelsey's Raven. 240p. (gr. 5 up). 1992. 14.00 (*0-688-09583-6*) Morrow Jr Bks.

Petersen, P. J. Liars. LC 91-28490. 176p. (gr. 5-9). 1992. pap. 15.00 jacketed, 3-pc. bdg. (*0-671-75035-6*, S&S BFYR) S&S Trade.

Peterson, Jeanne W. My Mama Sings. Speidel, Sandra, illus. LC 91-72. 32p. (ps-3). 1994. 15.00 (*0-06-023854-2*); PLB 14.89 (*0-06-023859-3*) HarpC Child Bks.

Pfeffer, Susan B. Family of Strangers. 1992. 16.00 (*0-553-08364-3*) Bantam.

Pfoutz, Sally. Missing Person. 176p. (gr. 7 up). 1993. 14.99 (*0-670-84663-5*) Viking Child Bks.

Phillips, Louis. How to Tell if Your Parents Are Aliens. 80p. 1994. pap. 3.50 (*0-380-77387-2*, Camelot) Avon.

Pomerantz, Charlotte. Chalk Doll. Lessac, Frane, illus. LC 88-872. 32p. (ps-3). 1993. pap. 4.95 (*0-06-443333-1*, Trophy) HarpC Child Bks.

Porte, Barbara A. Something Terrible Happened: A Novel. LC 94-6923. 224p. (gr. 6-9). 1994. 16.95 (*0-531-06869-2*); PLB 16.99 (*0-531-08719-0*) Orchard Bks Watts.

Porter, Gene S. Girl of the Limberlost. (Illus.). 496p. 1992. 8.99 (*0-517-07235-1*, Pub. by Gramercy) Random Hse Value.

—A Girl of the Limberlost. 432p. (gr. 5 up). 1992. pap. 3.99 (*0-14-035143-4*) Puffin Bks.

Porter, Penny. The Keymaker: Born to Steal. (Illus.). 144p. (Orig.). (gr. 7-12). 1994. pap. 10.95 (*0-943173-99-X*) Harbinger AZ.

Ransom, Candice. The Big Green Pocketbook. Bond, Felicia, illus. LC 92-29393. 32p. (ps-2). 1993. 14.00 (*0-06-020848-1*); PLB 13.89 (*0-06-020849-X*) HarpC Child Bks.

—The Man on Stilts. Bowman, Leslie, illus. LC 92-39358. 1994. write for info. (*0-399-22537-4*, Philomel Bks) Putnam Pub Group.

Reynolds, Marilyn. Too Soon for Jeff. 224p. (Orig.). (gr. 7 up). 1994. 15.95 (*0-930934-90-3*); pap. 8.95 (*0-930934-91-1*) Morning Glory.

Roberts, Willo D. Don't Hurt Laurie! Sanderson, Ruth, illus. LC 76-46569. 176p. (gr. 4-6). 1977. SBE 14.95 (*0-689-30571-0*, Atheneum Child Bk) Macmillan Child Grp.

Robinson, Fay. Pizza Soup. Iosa, Ann W., illus. LC 92-10756. 32p. (ps-2). 1993. PLB 11.60 (*0-516-02373-X*); pap. 3.95 (*0-516-42373-8*) Childrens.

Rockwell, Anne. Ducklings & Polliwogs. Rockwell, Lizzy, illus. LC 93-16600. (ps-2). 1994. 14.95 (*0-02-777452-X*) Macmillan Child Grp.

Rodgers, Mary. Freaky Friday. LC 74-183158. 156p. (gr. 5 up). 1973. pap. 3.95 (*0-06-440046-8*, Trophy) HarpC Child Bks.

Rodowsky, Colby. Hannah in Between. (gr. 5 up). 1994. 15.00 (*0-374-32837-4*) FS&G.

Rosselson, Leon. Where's My Mom? Lamont, Priscilla, illus. LC 93-32383. 32p. (ps up). 1994. 13.95 (*1-56402-392-3*) Candlewick Pr.

Roy, J. Soul Daddy. 1992. 16.95 (*0-15-277193-X*, HB Juv Bks) HarBrace.

Roybal, Laura. Billy. LC 93-4837. 1994. write for info. (*0-395-67649-5*) HM.

Rush, Ken. Friday's Journey. LC 93-4871. (Illus.). 1994. write for info. (*0-531-06821-8*); lib. bdg. write for info. (*0-531-08671-2*) Orchard Bks Watts.

Russo, Marisabina. Time to Wake Up! LC 93-18185. (Illus.). 24p. (ps up). 1994. 14.00 (*0-688-04599-5*); PLB 13.93 (*0-688-04600-2*) Greenwillow.

Rylant, Cynthia. Birthday Presents. Stevenson, Sucie, illus. LC 87-5485. 32p. (ps-1). 1987. 13.95 (*0-531-05705-4*); PLB 13.99 (*0-531-08305-5*) Orchard Bks Watts.

—Henry & Mudge & the Forever Sea: The Sixth Book of Their Adventures. Stevenson, Sucie, illus. LC 92-28646. 48p. (gr. 1-3). 1993. pap. 3.95 (*0-689-71701-6*, Aladdin) Macmillan Child Grp.

Sachs, Marilyn. Call Me Ruth. LC 94-19695. 1995. write for info. (*0-688-13737-7*, Pub. by Beech Tree Bks) Morrow.

Sacks, Margaret. Themba. Clay, Wil, illus. LC 92-9754. 48p. (gr. 2-5). 1992. 12.00 (*0-525-67414-4*, Lodestar Bks) Dutton Child Bks.

Salisbury, Graham. Blue Skin of the Sea: A Novel in Stories. (gr. 4-7). 1992. 15.95 (*0-385-30596-6*) Doubleday.

Saltzburg, Barney. Show & Tell. LC 93-47365. (Illus.). 32p. (gr. k-3). 1994. 14.95 (*0-7868-0020-8*); PLB 14.89 (*0-7868-2016-0*) Hyprn Child.

Schertle, Alice. Down the Road. Date not set. 14.95 (*0-06-020057-X*, HarpT) HarpC.

—Down the Road. Lewis, E. B., illus. LC 94-9901. 1995. write for info. (*0-15-276622-7*, Browndeer Pr) HarBrace.

Schreier, Joshua. Hank's Work. LC 92-15205. (ps-2). 1993. 13.50 (*0-525-44970-1*, DCB) Dutton Child Bks.

Sebastian, John. J.B.'s Harmonica. LC 91-35841. (ps-3). 1993. 13.95 (*0-15-240091-5*) HarBrace.

Seymour, Tres. I Love My Buzzard. Schindler, Stephen D., illus. LC 93-4877. 1994. write for info. (*0-531-06819-6*); lib. bdg. write for info. (*0-531-08669-0*) Orchard Bks Watts.

Shannon, George. Climbing Kansas Mountains. Allen, Thomas B., illus. LC 89-38197. 32p. (ps-2). 1993. RSBE 15.95 (*0-02-782181-1*, Bradbury Pr) Macmillan Child Grp.

Sharratt, Nick. My Mom & Dad Make Me Laugh. Sharratt, Nick, illus. LC 93-3558. 1994. 12.95 (*1-56402-250-1*) Candlewick Pr.

Shields, Carol D. I Am Really a Princess. Meisel, Paul, illus. LC 92-37161. 32p. (ps-3). 1993. 13.99 (*0-525-45138-2*, DCB) Dutton Child Bks.

Shreve, Susan. Amy Dunn Quits School. De Groat, Diane, illus. LC 92-41772. 96p. (gr. 3 up). 1993. 13.00 (*0-688-10320-0*, Tambourine Bks) Morrow.

Skinner, David. You Must Kiss a Whale. LC 91-30352. 104p. (gr. 6 up). 1992. pap. 14.00 3-pc. bdg. (*0-671-74781-9*, S&S BFYR) S&S Trade.

Skofield, James. Round & Round. Hale, James G., illus. LC 90-32831. 32p. (ps-2). 1993. 15.00 (*0-06-025746-6*); PLB 14.89 (*0-06-025747-4*) HarpC Child Bks.

Slepian, Jan. Pinocchio's Sister. LC 94-1361. 1995. 14.95 (*0-399-22811-X*, Philomel Bks) Putnam Pub Group.

Smith, Doris B. Best Girl. LC 92-25931. 144p. (gr. 3-7). 1993. 13.99 (*0-670-83752-0*) Viking Child Bks.

Smith, Roland. Thunder Cave. LC 9-19714. 1995. 14.95 (*0-7868-0068-2*); 14.89 (*0-7868-2055-1*) Hyprn Child.

Snider, Catherine. Mommy Loves Jesus. Arnsteen, Katy K., illus. LC 93-13354. 24p. (Orig.). (ps-6). 1993. pap. 3.95 (*0-8198-4731-3*) St Paul Bks.

Soto, Gary. The Mustache. Hinojosa, Celina, illus. LC 93-42395. 1995. 14.95 (*0-399-22617-6*, Putnam) Putnam Pub Group.

Staples, Donna. Arena Beach. LC 92-36302. 1993. 14.95 (*0-395-65366-5*) HM.

Starry Night. LC 93-15030. write for info. (*1-56179-163-6*) Focus Family.

Steiner, Barbara. Tessa. LC 87-31524. 224p. (gr. 7 up). 1988. 12.95 (*0-688-07232-1*) Morrow Jr Bks.

Stock, Catherine. Christmas Time. Stock, Catherine, illus. LC 89-71249. 32p. (ps-1). 1990. SBE 11.95 (*0-02-788403-1*, Bradbury Pr) Macmillan Child Grp.

—Christmas Time. Stock, Catherine, illus. LC 92-42225. 32p. (ps-1). 1993. pap. 3.95 (*0-689-71725-3*, Aladdin) Macmillan Child Grp.

Tate, Eleanore E. A Blessing in Disguise. LC 94-13073. 1995. 14.95 (*0-385-32103-1*) Delacorte.

Taylor, Theodore. Sweet Friday Island. LC 93-32435. (gr. 7 up). 1994. write for info. (*0-15-200009-7*); pap. write for info. (*0-15-200012-7*) HarBrace.

Thesman, Jean. Cattail Moon. LC 93-6814. (gr. 4-7). 1994. write for info. (*0-395-67409-3*) HM.

Thomson, Pat. The Best Thing of All. Chamberlain, Margaret, illus. 32p. (ps-1). 1993. pap. 6.95 (*0-575-05159-0*, Pub. by Gollancz UK) Trafalgar.

Thureen, Faythe D. Jenna's Big Jump. Sandeen, Eileen, illus. 112p. (gr. 2-5). 1993. SBE 12.95 (*0-689-31834-0*, Atheneum Child Bk) Macmillan Child Grp.

Udry, Janice M. Is Susan Here? Gundersheimer, Karen, illus. LC 90-32044. 24p. (gr. k-3). 1993. 14.00 (*0-06-026142-0*); PLB 13.89 (*0-06-026143-9*) HarpC Child Bks.

—What Mary Jo Shared. Sayles, Elizabeth, illus. 32p. (ps-3). 1991. pap. 3.95 (*0-590-43757-7*) Scholastic Inc.

Vail, Rachel. Do-Over. LC 92-6717. 160p. (gr. 6-12). 1992. 14.95 (*0-531-05460-8*); PLB 14.99 (*0-531-08610-0*) Orchard Bks Watts.

Valens, Amy. Jesse's Day Care. Brown, Richard, illus. 32p. (ps-2). 1990. 13.45 (*0-395-53357-0*) HM.

Vertreace, Martha. Kelly in the Mirror. Speidel, Sandra, illus. LC 92-22655. 1993. 13.95 (*0-8075-4152-4*) A Whitman.

Vigna, Judith. Eric's Mom Has Cancer. LC 93-6533. (Illus.). 1993. write for info. (*0-8075-2133-7*) A Whitman.

Voigt, Cynthia. If She Hollers. LC 93-43519. (gr. 7 up). 1994. 14.95 (*0-590-46714-X*) Scholastic Inc.

Waddell, Martin. The Big, Big Sea. Eachus, Jennifer, illus. LC 93-33228. 32p. 1994. 15.95 (*1-56402-066-5*) Candlewick Pr.

—Las Lechucitas: Owl Babies. Benson, Patrick, illus. (SPA.). 14p. (gr. k-1). 1994. 14.95 (*0-88272-137-2*) Santillana. Adorable baby owls are alone in a dark forest, wondering where their mother could be. Beautiful illustrations depict the spooky forest & the many moods of these endearing owls. To order: Santillana, 901 West Walnut, Compton, CA 90220. 1-800-245-8584.
Publisher Provided Annotation.

Wallace, Bill. Buffalo Gal. LC 91-28243. 192p. (gr. 5 up). 1992. 14.95 (*0-8234-0943-0*) Holiday.

Walton, Rick. Will You Still Love Me? Teare, Brad, illus. LC 92-341. 32p. (ps). 1992. 11.95 (*0-87579-582-X*) Deseret Bk.

Weaver, Will. Striking Out. LC 93-565. 288p. (gr. 5 up). 1993. 15.00 (*0-06-023346-X*); PLB 14.89 (*0-06-023347-8*) HarpC Child Bks.

Weiss, E. & Friedman, M. The Poof Point. (gr. 3-7). 1992. 14.00 (*0-679-83257-2*) Knopf Bks Yng Read.

Weiss, Nicki. On a Hot, Hot Day. Weiss, Nicki, illus. 32p. (ps-1). 1992. PLB 13.95 (*0-399-22119-0*, Putnam) Putnam Pub Group.

Westall, Robert. A Place to Hide. 208p. (gr. 7 up). 1994. 13.95 (*0-590-47748-X*, Scholastic Hardcover) Scholastic Inc.

Weyn, Suzanne. Ashley's Big Mistake. LC 93-43505. (Illus.). 128p. (gr. 4-8). 1994. PLB 9.89 (*0-8167-3231-0*); pap. text ed. 2.95 (*0-8167-3232-9*) Troll Assocs.

—Tracey's Tough Choice. LC 93-25185. (Illus.). 128p. (gr. 4-8). 1993. PLB 9.89 (*0-8167-3237-X*); pap. 2.95 (*0-8167-3238-8*) Troll Assocs.

Williams, Karen L. Tap-Tap. Stock, Catherine, illus. LC 93-13006. (gr. 1-4). 1994. 14.95 (*0-395-65617-6*, Clarion Bks) HM.

Williams, Vera B. Scooter. LC 90-38489. (Illus.). 160p. (gr. 4-7). 1993. 15.00 (*0-688-09376-0*); PLB 14.93 (*0-688-09377-9*) Greenwillow.

Winthrop, Elizabeth. Sloppy Kisses. Burgess, Anne, illus. (ps-3). 1983. pap. 3.95 (*0-14-050433-8*, Puffin) Puffin Bks.

Wood, Audrey. Weird Parents. Fogelman, Phyllis J., ed. Wood, Audrey, illus. LC 88-25742. 32p. (ps-3). 1990. 12.99 (*0-8037-0648-0*); PLB 11.89 (*0-8037-0649-9*) Dial Bks Young.

Wood, Jakki. Dads Are Such Fun. Bonner, Rog, illus. LC 91-21517. 32p. (ps). 1992. pap. 12.00 jacketed (*0-671-75342-8*, S&S BFYR) S&S Trade.

Woodson, Jacqueline. From the Notebooks of MelaninSun. (gr. 4 up). 1995. 13.95 (*0-590-45880-9*) Scholastic Inc.

Wright, Betty R. My New Mom & Me. Day, Betsy, illus. Silverman, Manuel S. LC 80-25529. (Illus.). (gr. k-6). 1981. PLB 16.67 (*0-8172-1368-6*) Raintree Steck-V.

Yolen, Jane. All Those Secrets of the World. (ps-3). 1991. 14.95 (*0-316-96891-9*) Little.

Zolotow, Charlotte. The Quiet Mother & the Noisy Little Boy. Simont, Marc, illus. LC 88-936. 32p. (ps-3). 1989. 13.00 (*0-06-026978-2*); PLB 12.89 (*0-06-026979-0*) HarpC Child Bks.

PARENTS AND TEACHERS

see Home and School

PARIS

Aaseng, Nathan. Paris. LC 92-709. (Illus.). 96p. (gr. 6 up). 1992. text ed. 14.95 RSBE (*0-02-700010-9*, New Discovery) Macmillan Child Grp.

Clay, Rebecca. Kidding Around Paris: A Young Person's Guide to the City. Lambert, Mary, illus. 64p. (Orig.). (gr. 3 up). 1991. pap. 9.95 (*0-945465-82-3*) John Muir.

Munro, Roxie. The Inside-Outside Book of Paris. Munro, Roxie, illus. LC 91-29318. 48p. (ps up). 1992. 15.00 (*0-525-44863-2*, DCB) Dutton Child Bks.

PARIS–FICTION

Bemelmans, Ludwig. Mad about Madeline. Quindlen, Anna, intro. by. (Illus.). 352p. 1993. 35.00 (*0-670-85187-6*) Viking Child Bks.

—Madeline. (Illus.). 1993. pap. 6.99 incl. cassette (*0-14-095120-2*, Puffin) Puffin Bks.

—Madeline's Rescue. Bemelmans, Ludwig, illus. 64p. (gr. k-3). 1977. pap. 4.50 (*0-14-050207-6*, Puffin) Puffin Bks.

—Madeline's Rescue. (Illus.). 1993. pap. 6.99 incl. cassette (*0-14-095122-9*, Puffin) Puffin Bks.

Carlson, Natalie S. Family under the Bridge. Williams, Garth, illus. LC 58-5292. 112p. (gr. 3-7). 1958. PLB 14.89 (*0-06-020991-7*) HarpC Child Bks.

Devlin, Wende & Devlin, Harry. The Trouble with Henriette. 1995. 15.00 (*0-02-729937-6*, Four Winds) Macmillan Child Grp.

Dragonwagon, Crescent. Winter Holding Spring. Himler, Ronald, illus. LC 88-13747. 32p. (gr. 2-5). 1990. RSBE 12.95 (*0-02-733122-9*, Macmillan Child Bk) Macmillan Child Grp.

Fender, Kay. Odette: A Springtime in Paris. Dumas, Philippe, illus. 32p. (ps-3). 1991. 10.95 (*0-916291-33-2*) Kane-Miller Bk.

Goode, Diane. Where's Our Mama? Goode, Diane, illus. LC 91-2158. 32p. (ps-2). 1991. 13.95 (*0-525-44770-9*, DCB) Dutton Child Bks.

Hugo, Victor. Hunchback of Notre Dame. Canon, R. R., intro. by. (gr. 11 up). 1968. pap. 2.25 (*0-8049-0162-7*, CL-162) Airmont.

Knight, Joan. Bon Appetit, Bertie! Winter, Susan, illus. LC 92-54319. 32p. (ps-1). 1993. 13.95 (*1-56458-195-0*) Dorling Kindersley.

Lamerisse, Albert. The Red Balloon. 32p. (gr. 6). 1990. PLB 13.95 (*0-88682-304-8*) Creative Ed.

Lamorisse, Albert. Red Balloon. Lamorisse, Albert, photos by. LC 57-9229. (Illus.). 45p. (gr. 3-7). 1967. 13.95 (*0-685-01494-0*) Doubleday.

Poulet, Virginia. Blue Bug Goes to Paris. Anderson, Peggy P., illus. LC 85-31390. 32p. (ps-3). 1986. pap. 3.95 (*0-516-43480-2*) Childrens.

Schotter, Roni. That Extraordinary Pig of Paris. Catalano, Dominic, illus. LC 92-26223. 32p. (ps-3). 1994. 14.95 (*0-399-22023-2*, Philomel Bks) Putnam Pub Group.

Thompson, Kay. Eloise in Paris. (Illus.). 66p. 1991. Repr. PLB 21.95x (*0-89966-834-8*) Buccaneer Bks.

Vallet, Cedric. A Trip to Paris. Vallet, Cedric, illus. 17p. (gr. k-3). 1992. pap. 15.95 (*1-895583-26-8*) MAYA Pubs.

Woodman, Allen & Kirby, David. The Cows Are Going to Paris. Demarest, Chris L., illus. LC 90-85733. 32p. (ps-3). 1991. 15.95 (*1-878093-11-8*) Boyds Mills Pr.

PARIS–POETRY

Bemelmans, Ludwig. Madeline. Bemelmans, Ludwig, illus. LC 39-21791. (gr. k-3). 1977. pap. 4.99 incl. cassette (*0-14-050198-3*, Puffin) Puffin Bks.

—Madeline & the Bad Hat. Bemelmans, Ludwig, illus. LC 57-62. (gr. k-3). 1977. pap. 4.99 (*0-14-050206-8*, Puffin) Puffin Bks.

—Madeline & the Gypsies. Bemelmans, Ludwig, illus. (gr. k-3). 1959. pap. 14.99 (*0-670-44682-3*) Viking Child Bks.

—Madeline's Rescue. Bemelmans, Ludwig, illus. LC 53-8709. 56p. (gr. k-3). 1953. pap. 14.00 (*0-670-44716-1*) Viking Child Bks.

Bemmelmans, Ludwig. Madeline. Bemelmans, Ludwig, illus. LC 68-666. (gr. k-3). 1958. pap. 15.00 (*0-670-44580-0*) Viking Child Bks.

—Madeline & the Bad Hat. Bemelmans, Ludwig, illus. (gr. k-3). 1957. pap. 14.00 (*0-670-44614-9*) Viking Child Bks.

PARKER, QUANAH, COMANCHE INDIAN, 1854-1911

Hilts, Len. Quanah Parker: Warrior for Freedom, Ambassador for Peace. (gr. 4-7). 1992. pap. 4.95 (*0-15-264447-4*) HarBrace.

Sanford, William R. Quanah Parker, Comanche Warrior. LC 93-42258. (Illus.). 48p. (gr. 4-10). 1994. lib. bdg. 14.95 (*0-89490-512-0*) Enslow Pubs.

Wilson, Claire. Quanah Parker. (Illus.). 112p. (gr. 5 up). 1992. lib. bdg. 17.95 (*0-7910-1702-8*) Chelsea Hse.

PARKS, GORDON ALEXANDER BUCHANON, 1912-

Berry, Skip. Gordon Parks. King, Coretta Scott, intro. by. (Illus.). 112p. (gr. 5 up). 1991. lib. bdg. 17.95 (*1-55546-604-4*) Chelsea Hse.

PARKS, ROSA, 1903-

Adler, David A. A Picture Book of Rosa Parks. Casilla, Robert, illus. LC 92-41826. 32p. (ps-3). 1993. reinforced bdg. 15.95 (*0-8234-1041-2*) Holiday.

Brandt, Keith. Rosa Parks: Fight for Freedom. Griffith, Gershom, illus. LC 91-34939. 48p. (gr. 4-6). 1993. lib. bdg. 10.79 (*0-8167-2831-3*); pap. text ed. 3.50 (*0-8167-2832-1*) Troll Assocs.

Celsi, Teresa. Rosa Parks & the Montgomery Bus Boycott. (Illus.). 32p. (gr. 2-4). 1991. PLB 12.90 (*1-878841-14-9*); pap. 4.95 (*1-878841-34-3*) Millbrook Pr.

Did You Know Publishings Staff. Rosa Parks. LC 92-71756. 32p. 1992. text ed. 8.50 (*0-9633151-0-2*) Did You Know Pub.

Friese, Kai J. Rosa Parks: The Movement Organizes. Gallin, Richard, ed. Young, Andrew, intro. by. (Illus.). 128p. (gr. 5 up). 1990. lib. bdg. 12.95 (*0-382-09927-3*); pap. 7.95 (*0-382-24065-0*) Silver Burdett Pr.

Greenfield, Eloise. Rosa Parks. Marlow, Eric, illus. LC 72-83787. 40p. (gr. 1-5). 1973. PLB 14.89 (*0-690-71211-1*, Crowell Jr Bks) HarpC Child Bks.

Hull, Mary. Rosa Parks: Civil Rights Leader. LC 93-17699. (Illus.). (gr. 5 up). 1994. PLB 18.95 (*0-7910-1881-4*, Am Art Analog); write for info. (*0-7910-1910-1*, Am Art Analog) Chelsea Hse.

Jackson, Garnet N. Rosa Parks: Hero of Our Time. Wade, Tony, illus. LC 92-28583. 1992. write for info. (*0-8136-5232-4*); pap. write for info. (*0-8136-5705-9*) Modern Curr.

Parks, Rosa. Rosa Parks: Mother to a Movement. Haskins, Jim, contrib. by. LC 89-1124. (Illus.). 200p. 1992. 17.00 (*0-8037-0673-1*) Dial Bks Young.

Siegel, Beatrice. The Year They Walked: Rosa Parks & the Montgomery Bus Boycott. LC 91-14078. (Illus.). 128p. (gr. 4-7). 1992. SBE 13.95 (*0-02-782631-7*, Four Winds) Macmillan Child Grp.

PARKS–FICTION

Breeze, Lynn, illus. This Little Baby Goes Out. Morris, Ann, text by. LC 92-30880. (Illus.). (ps). 1993. 5.95 (*0-316-10854-5*) Little.

Bryant. Zoe McCully: Park Ranger. 1991. 0.85 (*0-8050-2016-0*) H Holt & Co.

Compton, Sara. Daredevil Park. 1991. pap. 3.50 (*0-553-28795-8*) Bantam.

Day, Alexandra. Carl's Afternoon in the Park. (Illus.). 32p. 1991. bds. 12.95 (*0-374-31109-9*) FS&G.

Derby, Janice. Are You My Friend? Keenan, Joy D., illus. 40p. (ps-3). 1993. 12.95 (*0-8361-3609-8*) Herald Pr. The expressive watercolors of Joy Dunn Keenan dance across these pages as a boy & his grandfather spend a day at the park. Throughout the day they meet many people & the boy observes how they are different from him. He also notices that they are like him in the things they enjoy seeing & doing. He asks each one, "Are you my friend?" At the end, all the friends

gather at the carousel. This book written by Janice Derby allows children to acknowledge characteristics such as language, skin color, being physically or mentally challenged, or having a different economic status that can separate us. By observing that others enjoy the same kinds of activities, children learn that the differences are minor compared to the many similarities we share. For children ages 4-to-8 & the adults who love them.
Publisher Provided Annotation.

Hamilton, Dorothy. Busboys at Big Bend. Ponter, James, illus. LC 74-8689. 112p. (gr. 8-12). 1974. o. p. 4.95 (*0-8361-1744-1*); pap. 3.95 (*0-8361-1745-X*) Herald Pr.
Hendry, Diana. Camel Called April. (ps-3). 1991. 10.95 (*0-688-10193-3*) Lothrop.
Lowry, Lois. Taking Care of Terrific. LC 82-23331. 160p. (gr. 5 up). 1983. 14.95 (*0-395-34070-5*) HM.
McAllister, Angela. Paradise Park. (Illus.). 32p. (ps-2). 1992. 16.95 (*0-370-31576-6*, Pub. by Bodley Head UK) Trafalgar.
Matthias, Catherine. Over-Under. Sharp, Gene, illus. LC 83-21005. 32p. (ps-2). 1984. lib. bdg. 10.25 (*0-516-02048-X*); pap. 2.95 (*0-516-42048-8*) Childrens.
Reiser, Lynn. Margaret & Margarita, Margarita y Margaret. LC 92-29012. 32p. (ps up). 1993. 14.00 (*0-688-12239-6*); lib. bdg. 13.93 (*0-688-12240-X*) Greenwillow.
Rockwell, Anne. Hugo at the Park. Rockwell, Anne, illus. LC 89-2417. 32p. (ps-k). 1990. RSBE 13.95 (*0-02-777301-9*, Macmillan Child Bk) Macmillan Child Grp.
Sanders, Lawrence. The Great Coaster Ride. Block, Lori, illus. Sargent, Dave, intro. by. (Illus.). 135p. (Orig.). (gr. k-8). 1993. text ed. 11.95 (*1-56763-099-5*); pap. text ed. 5.95 (*1-56763-100-2*) Ozark Pub.
Silverstre, Ruth. Stranger Who Lived in a Merry-Go-Round. (gr. 4-7). 1993. pap. 2.75 (*0-590-45573-7*) Scholastic Inc.
Su, Lucy. Ten Little Teddies. LC 93-24148. 24p. (ps up). 1994. 3.99 (*1-56402-251-X*) Candlewick Pr.
Takeshita, Fumiko. The Park Bench. Kanagy, Ruth A., tr. from JPN. Suzuki, Mamoru, illus. 40p. (ps-3). 1988. 13.95 (*0-916291-15-4*) Kane-Miller Bk.
—The Park Bench. Kanagy, Ruth A., tr. from JPN. Suzuki, Mamoru, illus. 40p. (gr. 3-8). 1989. pap. 6.95 (*0-916291-21-9*) Kane-Miller Bk.
Vulliamy, Clara. Yum Yum. LC 93-28124. (Illus.). 14p. (ps). 1994. 4.95 (*1-56402-408-3*) Candlewick Pr.
Wolff, Ashley. Stella & Roy. Wolff, Ashley, illus. LC 92-27005. 32p. (ps-k). 1993. 12.99 (*0-525-45081-5*, DCB) Dutton Child Bks.
Zolotow, Charlotte. Park Book. Rey, H. A., illus. LC 44-9471. 32p. (ps-1). 1986. PLB 13.89 (*0-06-026973-1*) HarpC Child Bks.

PARLIAMENTARY PRACTICE

Jones, O. Garfield. Parliamentary Procedure at a Glance. (gr. 9 up). 1971. pap. 4.95 (*0-8015-5766-6*, 0481-140, Dutton) NAL-Dutton.
Russell, Kenneth L., ed. How in Parliamentary Procedure. 5th ed. (Illus.). 74p. (gr. 9-12). 1990. pap. text ed. 2.50 (*0-8134-2871-8*, 2171) Interstate.

PARROTS

Dunnahoo, Terry. The Lost Parrots of America. LC 89-7846. (Illus.). 48p. (gr. 5-6). 1989. text ed. 12.95 RSBE (*0-89686-461-8*, Crestwood Hse) Macmillan Child Grp.
Frisch. Parrots. 1991. 11.95s.p. (*0-86625-190-1*) Rourke Pubns.
Gabin, Martin. Your First Parrot. (Illus.). 36p. (Orig.). 1991. pap. 1.95 (*0-86622-070-4*, YF-113) TFH Pubns.
Gnam, Rosemarie. Let's Get to Know the Bahama Parrot. (Illus.). 20p. (gr. 1-3). 1991. write for info. (*0-9629613-0-2*) Isld Conser Effort.
Houk, Randy. Ruffle, Coo & Hoo Doo. Houk, Randy, illus. 32p. (gr. k-3). 1993. 14.95 (*1-882728-02-5*); read-along cass. 7.95 (*1-882728-05-X*) Benefactory.
Murray, Peter. Parrots. LC 92-44265. (Illus.). (gr. 2-6). 1993. 15.95 (*1-56766-015-0*) Childs World.
Parrots. 1991. PLB 14.95 (*0-88682-408-7*) Creative Ed.
Serventy, Vincent. Parrot. (Illus.). 24p. (gr. k-5). 1986. PLB 9.95 (*0-8172-2705-9*); pap. 3.95 (*0-8114-6885-2*) Raintree Steck-V.
Stone, Lynn M. Parrots. LC 93-7461. 1993. 12.67 (*0-86593-280-8*); 9.50s.p. (*0-685-66584-4*) Rourke Corp.
Wildlife Education, Ltd. Staff. Parrots. Boyer, Trevor, illus. 20p. (gr. 5 up). 1984. pap. text ed. 2.75 (*0-937934-27-5*) Wildlife Educ.
—Parrots. Boyer, Trevor, illus. 24p. 1992. 13.95 (*0-937934-84-4*) Wildlife Educ.
Wolter, Annette. African Gray Parrots. (Illus.). 64p. (gr. 4 up). 1987. pap. 5.95 (*0-8120-3773-1*) Barron.

PARROTS–FICTION

Benitez, Mirna. Super Parrot. (Illus.). 32p. (gr. 1-4). 1989. PLB 18.99 (*0-8172-3503-5*); pap. 3.95 (*0-8114-6704-X*) Raintree Steck-V.
Bennett, Penelope. Town Parrot. Heap, Sue, illus. LC 94-6409. 1995. 14.95 (*1-56402-484-9*) Candlewick Pr.
Connell, David D. & Thurman, Jim. The Case of the Willing Parrot: Mathnet, the Book. 1994. text ed. write for info. (*0-7167-6528-4*); pap. text ed. write for info. (*0-7167-6522-5*) W H Freeman.
Cutler, Ivor. Doris. Munoz, Claudio, illus. LC 92-5923. 32p. (gr. k-3). 1992. PLB 14.00 (*0-688-11939-5*, Tambourine Bks) Morrow.
Demuth, Patricia B. Max, the Bad-Talking Parrot. Zaunders, Bo, illus. LC 89-26015. 32p. (gr. k-4). 1990. 12.95 (*0-525-44613-3*, DCB); pap. 3.95 (*0-525-44595-1*, DCB) Dutton Child Bks.
Griffin, Peni R. The Treasure Bird. Gowing, Toby, illus. LC 91-42773. 144p. (gr. 4-7). 1992. SBE 13.95 (*0-689-50554-X*, M K McElderry) Macmillan Child Grp.
—The Treasure Bird. 144p. (gr. 3-7). 1994. pap. 3.99 (*0-14-036653-9*) Puffin Bks.
Hills, Peter B. Inspector Hare & the Black Pearls. Hills, Stephen, illus. LC 93-28977. 1994. 4.25 (*0-383-03751-4*) SRA Schl Grp.
Johnston, Terry C. Lorenzo the Naughty Parrot. Politi, L., illus. 1992. write for info. (*0-15-249350-6*, HB Juv Bks) HarBrace.
McDermott, Gerald. Papagayo: The Mischief Maker. LC 91-4036. (ps-3). 1992. write for info. (*0-15-259465-5*, HB Juv Bks); pap. write for info. (*0-15-259464-7*, HB Juv Bks) HarBrace.
Ossorio, Nelson A. & Salvadeo, Michele B. Puppy & the Parrot. (Illus.). 60p. (gr. 4-6). 1994. pap. 6.95 (*1-56721-059-7*) Twnty-Fifth Cent Pr.
Remkiewicz, Frank. The Last Time I Saw Harris. LC 90-40263. (Illus.). 32p. (gr. k up). 1991. 13.95 (*0-688-10291-3*); PLB 13.88 (*0-688-10292-1*) Lothrop.
—There's Only One Harris. LC 92-44163. (Illus.). (gr. 3-6). 1993. 14.00 (*0-688-11827-5*); PLB 13.93 (*0-688-11828-3*) Lothrop.
Robinson, Ronald W. Stanley, the Talking Parrot. Todd, Thomas, illus. LC 89-60801. 22p. (Orig.). (gr. 3-4). 1989. Incl. cassette & filmstrip pkg. 12.95 (*0-9622692-2-0*); Incl. cassette pkg. 8.95 (*0-9622692-1-2*); pap. 4.95 (*0-9622692-0-4*) R W Robinson.
Siracusa, Catherine. The Parrot Problem. (Illus.). 48p. (gr. 3 up). 1994. 10.95 (*1-56282-626-3*); PLB 10.89 (*1-56282-627-1*) Hyprn Child.
Slaughter, Hope. Plato's Fine Feathers. Shearer, Hope, illus. LC 84-4830. 32p. (ps-3). 1984. PLB 7.95 (*0-931093-00-7*); pap. 3.95 (*0-685-15364-9*) Red Hen Pr.
Swan, Walter. Stick 'em up! I've Got You Covered! Swan, Deloris, ed. Asch, Connie, illus. 16p. (Orig.). (ps-8). 1989. pap. 1.50 (*0-927176-03-3*) Swan Enterp.
Weber, Kathryn. Molly Moonshine & Timothy. Downey, Jane, illus. 44p. (gr. 2-4). 1990. pap. 2.95 (*1-878438-01-8*) Ranch House Pr.
Wiggins, VeraLee. Julius, the Perfectly Pesky Pet Parrot. LC 93-14254. 1994. 7.95 (*0-8163-1173-0*) Pacific Pr Pub Assn.
Woolf, Virginia. The Widow & the Parrot. Bell, Julian, illus. Bell, Quentin, afterword by. (Illus.). 26p. (ps up). 1988. 12.95 (*0-15-296783-4*) HarBrace.
Zacharias, Thomas. Where Is the Green Parrot? 1990. 12. 95 (*0-385-30091-3*) Doubleday.

PARTICLES (NUCLEAR PHYSICS)

Newton, David E. Particle Accelerations: From the Cyclotron to the Superconducting Super Collider. LC 88-31375. (Illus.). 128p. (gr. 10-12). 1990. 13.40 (*0-531-10671-3*) Watts.

PARTIES, POLITICAL

see Political Parties

PASADENA TOURNAMENT OF ROSES–FICTION

Lampton, Christopher F. Particle Physics: The New View of the Universe. LC 90-48049. (Illus.). 64p. (gr. 6 up). 1991. lib. bdg. 15.95 (*0-89490-328-4*) Enslow Pubs.

PASCAL (COMPUTER PROGRAM LANGUAGE)

Nance, Douglas W. Pascal: Introduction to Programming & Problem Solving. (Illus.). 639p. (gr. 9-12). 1989. Repr. of 1986 ed. text ed. 34.25 (*0-314-93206-2*) West Pub.

PASSIONS

see Emotions

PASSIVE RESISTANCE

see also Nonviolence

PASSOVER

Adler, David A. Passover Fun Book: Puzzles, Riddles, Magic & More. (Illus.). (gr. k-5). 1978. saddlewire bdg. 3.95 (*0-88482-759-3*, Bonim Bks) Hebrew Pub.
—A Picture Book of Passover. Heller, Linda, illus. LC 81-6983. 32p. (ps-3). 1982. reinforced bdg. 14.95 (*0-8234-0439-0*); pap. 5.95 (*0-8234-0609-1*) Holiday.
Atlas, Susan. Passover Passage. (gr. 4-7). 1991. 5.95 (*0-933873-46-8*) Torah Aura.
Bin-Nun, Judy & Cooper, Nancy. Pesach: A Holiday Funtext. Steinberger, Heidi, illus. 32p. (Orig.). (gr. 1-3). 1983. pap. text ed. 5.00 (*0-8074-0161-7*, 101310) UAHC.
Chaikin, Miriam. Ask Another Question: The Story & Meaning of Passover. Friedman, Marvin, illus. LC 84-12744. 96p. (gr. 3-6). 1985. (Clarion Bks); pap. 4.95 (*0-89919-423-0*, Clarion Bks) HM.
Chanover, Hyman & Chanover, Alice. Pesah Is Coming. Kessler, Leonard, illus. (gr. k-2). 1956. 5.95 (*0-8381-0713-3*, 10-713) United Syn Bk.
—Pesah Is Here. Kessler, Leonard, illus. (gr. k-2). 1956. 5.95 (*0-8381-0714-1*) United Syn Bk.
De Paola, Tomie. My First Passover. (Illus.). 12p. 1991. 5.95 (*0-399-21784-3*, Putnam) Putnam Pub Group.
Fishman, Cathy. On Passover. Baskin, Leonard, illus. LC 91-43110. 32p. (gr. k up). 1995. RSBE 14.95 (*0-02-735320-6*, Macmillan Child Bk) Macmillan Child Grp.
Freedland, Sara. Passover! A Three-Dimensional Celebration. Clarke, Sue, illus. LC 93-34026. 8p. (ps-3). 1994. 15.99 (*0-670-85111-6*) Viking Child Bks.
Gikow, Louise. A Sesame Street Passover: Kippi & the Missing Matzah. Brannon, Tom, illus. 36p. 1994. pap. 5.95 (*1-884857-02-7*) Comet Intl.
Goldin, Barbara D. The Passover Journey: A Seder Companion. Waldman, Neil, illus. LC 93-5133. 64p. 1994. 15.99 (*0-670-82421-6*) Viking Child Bks.
Groner, Judye & Wikler, Madeline. Where is the Afikomen. Schanzer, Roz, illus. LC 89-63254. 12p. (ps). 1989. bds. 4.95 (*0-929371-06-2*) Kar Ben.
Halper, Roe. Passover Haggadah. Halper, Roe, illus. 40p. (Orig.). 1986. pap. 5.00 (*0-916326-03-9*) Bayberry Pr.
Kahn, Katherine J. Passover Fun: For Little Hands. Kahn, Katherine J., illus. 32p. (ps-2). 1991. wkbk. 3.95 (*0-929371-56-9*) Kar Ben.
Miller, Deborah U. Only Nine Chairs-A Tall Tale for Passover. LC 82-80035. (Illus.). 40p. (ps-3). 1982. pap. 4.95 (*0-930494-13-X*) Kar Ben.
Nerlove, Miriam. Passover. Levine, Abby, ed. Nerlove, Miriam, illus. LC 89-35393. 24p. (ps-1). 1989. 11.95 (*0-8075-6360-9*); pap. 4.95 (*0-8075-6361-7*) A Whitman.
Oren, Rony. The Animated Haggadah (1990 Edition) (Illus.). 54p. 1990. 14.95 (*0-944007-43-0*) Shapolsky Pubs.
Panas, Peter, illus. The Shalom Sesame Players Present: The Story of Passover. 32p. 1994. 12.95 (*1-884857-00-0*); incl. audiocassette 14.95 (*1-884857-01-9*) Comet Intl.
Pliskin, Jacqueline. My Animated Haggadah & Story of Passover. (Illus.). 48p. (gr. 5-8). 1989. pap. 5.95 (*0-933503-28-8*) Shapolsky Pubs.
Pushker, Gloria T. Toby Belfer's Seder: A Passover Story Retold. Hierstein, Judith, illus. LC 93-5585. 1994. 14. 95 (*0-88289-987-2*) Pelican.
Roekard, Karen. The Santa Cruz Haggadah Kids Passover Fun Book. Paley, Nina, illus. 56p. (Orig.). (ps-10). 1994. pap. 4.95 (*0-9628913-0-4*) Hineni Concisus.
Rosen, Anne, et al. Family Passover. Salzmann, Laurence, photos by. LC 79-89298. 64p. (gr. 2 up). 1980. 8.95 (*0-8276-0169-7*) JPS Phila.
Rubenstein, Howard S. & Rubenstein, Judith S. Becoming Free: A Biblically Oriented Haggadah for Passover: The Permanent Relevance of the Ancient Lesson. LC 93-73663. 200p. 1993. pap. 9.95 (*0-9638886-0-9*) Granite Hills Pr.
Rudin, Jacob. Haggadah for Children. (gr. 3 up). 1973. 2. 95x (*0-8197-0032-0*) Bloch.
Schreiner, Elissa, et al. Let's Celebrate Passover! 16p. 1993. pap. 5.98 incl. 28 min. cassette (*0-943351-57-X*, XS2200) Astor Bks.
Schwartz, Lynne S. The Four Questions. Sherman, Ori, illus. LC 88-18881. 40p. (ps up). 1989. 15.95 (*0-8037-0600-6*); PLB 15.89 (*0-8037-0601-4*) Dial Bks Young.
Silberg, Francis B. The Story of Passover for Children. Britt, Stephanie, illus. 24p. (ps-2). 1989. pap. 3.95 (*0-8249-8309-2*, Ideals Child) Hambleton-Hill.
Silverman, Maida. Festival of Freedom: The Story of Passover. Ewing, Carolyn S., illus. (gr. 1-5). 1988. pap. 8.95 (*0-671-64567-6*, S&S BFYR); pap. 3.95 (*0-671-66340-2*, S&S BFYR) S&S Trade.
Simon, Norma. My Family Seder. Weiss, Harvey, illus. (ps-k). 1961. plastic cover 4.50 (*0-8381-0710-9*, 10-710) United Syn Bk.
Stuhlman, Daniel D. My Own Pesah Story. Klugman, Micha, illus. (Orig.). (gr. 1-6). 1981. Personalized Version. pap. 3.95x (*0-934402-09-4*); Trade Version. pap. 3.00 (*0-934402-10-8*); Seder cards 1.50 (*0-934402-11-6*) BYLS Pr.
Swartz, Leslie. First Passover. (ps-3). 1994. pap. 4.95 (*0-671-88025-X*, Half Moon Bks.) S&S Trade.
Wark, Mary A. We Tell It to Our Children: The Story of Passover: A Haggadah for Seders with Young Children. 2nd ed. Oskow, Craig, illus. Lerner, Leigh D., frwd. by. LC 88-92282. (Illus.). 126p. (Orig.). (ps-6). 1988. pap. 5.95 wire bdg. (*0-9619880-8-8*) Mensch Makers Pr.

Wark, MaryAnn B. We Tell It to Our Children: The Story of Passover: A Haggadah for Seders with Young Children. Oskow, Craig, illus. Lerner, Leigh D., frwd. by. LC 87-63604. (Illus.). 150p. (Orig.). (ps-6). 1988. Leader's Edition with Puppets. pap. 11. 95 wire-o bdg. (*0-9619880-9-6*) Mensch Makers Pr.
Children's active participatory Haggadah makes the Passover story into an engaging drama of the Exodus story. A complete guide, including multi-national recipes, for putting on the traditional Seder meal for Passover. Text is a musical puppet

show with Judaically-meaningful lyrics set to simple American folk tunes. Everyone participates in singing throughout the service. This Leader's edition has 9 cut-out puppets who are the "guests" from the past, who in a "you-are-there" style tell the story of the Exodus. Parts for non-readers & early readers. Guest edition - no puppets with full text also available. Endorsed by rabbis, religious educators (Jewish & Christian), children's book store owners, preschool teachers, parents & grandparents nationwide. For home or model seders. Authentically Jewish; easy for non-Jews. Developmentally appropriate for children. Downright fun for adults. Other unique features include the Passover food symbols, like matzoh, explained at the appropriate time in the story; special sections to personalize & teach about world Jewry. Difficult concepts like slavery are taught through action, songs, & pictures. Lyrics respond to children's thinking while tackling complicated issues surrounding freedom. Plentiful, detailed drawings emphasize immediacy of ideas & illustrate every idea & ceremonial symbol.
Publisher Provided Annotation.

Wengrov, Charles. The Story of Passover. (Illus.). (gr. k-7). 1965. pap. 2.50 (*0-914080-54-7*) Shulsinger Sales.
Wikler, Madeline & Groner, Judye. I Have Four Questions. Radin, Chari M., illus. LC 88-83570. 12p. (ps). 1989. bds. 4.95 (*0-930494-90-3*) Kar Ben.
Ziefert, Harriet. What Is Passover? James, Lillie, illus. 16p. (ps-2). 1994. 5.95 (*0-694-00482-0*, Festival) HarpC Child Bks.
Zwebner, Janet. The Animated Haggadah Activity Book. 48p. (ps-8). 1990. pap. 5.95 (*0-944007-46-5*) Shapolsky Pubs.

PASTEL DRAWING
Birker, Stefan. Drawing & Painting with Colored Pencils. LC 92-41349. (Illus.). 128p. (gr. 9-12). 1993. pap. 16. 95 (*0-8069-0312-0*) Sterling.

PASTEUR, LOUIS, 1822-1895
Angel, Ann. Louis Pasteur. LC 91-19552. (Illus.). 68p. (gr. 3-4). 1992. PLB 19.93 (*0-8368-0625-5*) Gareth Stevens Inc.
Bains, Rae. Louis Pasteur. Smolinski, Dick, illus. LC 84-2748. 32p. (gr. 3-6). 1985. PLB 9.49 (*0-8167-0148-2*); pap. text ed. 2.95 (*0-8167-0149-0*) Troll Assocs.
Greene, Carol. Louis Pasteur: Enemy of Disease. Dobson, Steven, illus. LC 90-2197. 48p. (gr. k-3). 1990. PLB 12.85 (*0-516-04216-5*); pap. 4.95 (*0-516-44216-3*) Childrens.
Morgan, Nina. Louis Pasteur. LC 91-16935. (Illus.). 48p. (gr. 5-7). 1992. PLB 12.40 (*0-531-18459-5*, Pub. by Bookwright Pr) Watts.
Newfield, Marcia. The Life of Louis Pasteur. Castro, Antonio, illus. 84p. (gr. 4-7). 1991. PLB 13.95 (*0-941477-67-3*) TFC Bks NY.
Rich, Beverly. Louis Pasteur: The Scientist Who Found the Cause of Infectious Disease & Invented Pasteurization. LC 88-24867. (Illus.). 64p. (gr. 5-6). 1989. PLB 19.93 (*1-55532-839-3*) Gareth Stevens Inc.
Sabin, Francene. Louis Pasteur: Young Scientist. Swan, Susan, illus. LC 82-15924. 48p. (gr. 4-6). 1983. PLB 10.79 (*0-89375-853-1*); pap. text ed. 3.50 (*0-89375-854-X*) Troll Assocs.
Tames, Richard. Louis Pasteur. LC 89-29278. (Illus.). 32p. (gr. 4-6). 1990. PLB 12.40 (*0-531-14025-3*) Watts.
Tiner, John H. Louis Pasteur. (gr. 3-6). 1991. pap. 6.95 (*0-88062-159-1*) Mott Media.
Yount, Lisa. Louis Pasteur. LC 93-49486. (Illus.). 112p. (gr. 5-8). 1994. 14.95 (*1-56006-051-4*) Lucent Bks.

PASTIMES
see Amusements; Games; Recreation; Sports

PASTORS
see Clergy

PATHOLOGICAL PSYCHOLOGY
see Psychology, Pathological

PATHOLOGY
see also Bacteriology; Immunity; Medicine
Guthrie, Donna W. Grandpa Doesn't Know It's Me: A Family Adjusts to Alzheimer's Disease. Arnsteen, Katy, illus. Aronson, Miriam, intro. by. (Illus.). (ps-5). 1986. 14.95 (*0-89885-302-8*); pap. 9.95 (*0-89885-308-7*) Human Sci Pr.
Harris, Jacqueline L. Drugs & Disease. (Illus.). 64p. (gr. 5-8). 1993. PLB 14.95 (*0-8050-2602-9*) TFC Bks NY.
—Hereditary Diseases. (Illus.). 64p. (gr. 5-8). 1993. PLB 14.95 (*0-8050-2603-7*) TFC Bks NY.
Smith, Patty. Mango Days: A Teenager Facing Eternity Reflects on the Beauty of Life. Smith, Patty, illus. Smith, Kit, intro. by. LC 92-10039. (Illus.). 135p. (Orig.). (gr. 9-12). 1992. lib. bdg. 17.95 (*0-932727-59-X*); pap. 11.95 (*0-932727-77-8*) Hope Pub Hse.
Zonderman, Jon & Shader, Laurel. Environmental Diseases. (Illus.). 64p. (gr. 5-8). 1993. PLB 14.95 (*0-8050-2600-2*) TFC Bks NY.

PATRICK, SAINT, 373?-463?
De Paola, Tomie. Patrick: Patron Saint of Ireland. De Paola, Tomie, illus. LC 91-19417. 32p. (ps-3). 1992. reinforced bdg. 15.95 (*0-8234-0924-4*) Holiday.
DePaola, Tomie. Patrick: Patron Saint of Ireland. DePaola, Tomie, illus. 1994. pap. 5.95 (*0-8234-1077-3*) Holiday.
Hodges, Margaret. Saint Patrick & the Peddler. Johnson, Paul B., illus. LC 92-44522. 40p. (gr. k-3). 1993. 15.95 (*0-531-05489-6*); PLB 15.99 (*0-531-08639-9*) Orchard Bks Watts.
Simms, George O. St. Patrick: The Real Story of Patrick Who Became Ireland's Patron Saint. (Illus.). 93p. (gr. 5 up). 1994. pap. 9.95 (*0-86278-347-X*, Pub. by OBrien Pr ER) Dufour.
Turcotte, Mary C. The Wind at My Back: The Life of St. Patrick. Bliss, Bob, illus. LC 88-13763. 115p. (gr. 3 up). 1991. 4.95 (*0-8198-8236-4*) St Paul Bks.

PATRIOTIC SONGS
see National Songs

PATRIOTISM
Brady, Janeen. Take Your Hat Off When the Flag Goes By. Perry, Scott & Hulet, Grant, illus. 22p. (Orig.). (gr. k-6). 1987. activity bk. 2.95 (*0-944803-31-8*); Set of 20. wkbk. 15.00 (*0-944803-34-2*); cassette & bk. 10. 95 (*0-944803-32-6*); dialogue bk. 1.50 (*0-944803-33-4*); songbk. 8.95 (*0-944803-29-6*) Brite Music.
Davis, Nancy M., et al. Patriotism. Davis, Nancy M., illus. 34p. (Orig.). (ps-5). 1986. pap. 4.95 (*0-937103-19-5*) DaNa Pubns.
Johnson, Linda C. Patriotism. rev. ed. (Illus.). 64p. (gr. 7-12,RL 4-6). 1993. PLB 14.95 (*0-8239-1507-7*) Rosen Group.
Szumski, Bonnie. Patriotism: Recognizing Stereotypes. LC 89-37555. (Illus.). 32p. (gr. 3-6). 1990. PLB 10.95 (*0-89908-640-3*) Greenhaven.
The Value of Patriotism. (gr. 7-12). 1993. PLB 15.95 (*0-8239-1288-4*) Rosen Group.

PATTON, GEORGE SMITH, 1885-1945
Finke, Blythe F. General Patton: Fearless Military Leader. Rahmas, D. Steve, ed. LC 76-190251. 32p. (gr. 7-12). 1972. lib. bdg. 4.95 incl. catalog cards (*0-87157-534-5*) SamHar Pr.
Peifer, Charles, Jr. George Patton: Soldier of Destiny: A Biography of George Patton. LC 88-20265. (Illus.). 128p. (gr. 5 up). 1988. text ed. 13.95 RSBE (*0-87518-395-6*, Dillon) Macmillan Child Grp.

PAUL, SAINT, APOSTLE
Dean, Bessie. Paul, God's Special Missionary. 72p. (Orig.). (gr. k-5). 1980. pap. 5.98 (*0-88290-152-4*) Horizon Utah.
Ham, Wayne. Paul's First Missionary Journey. (Illus.). 24p. 1989. pap. 4.00 (*0-8309-0538-3*) Herald Hse.
Lysne, Mary E. Paul. Gambill, Henrietta, ed. Patterson, Kathleen, illus. 24p. (ps-3). 1993. wkbk. 2.39 (*0-7847-0106-7*, 23-02586) Standard Pub.
Parry, Alan & Parry, Linda. Paul Meets Jesus. Parry, Alan, illus. 24p. (ps). 1990. pap. 0.99 (*0-8066-2480-9*, 9-2480) Augsburg Fortress.
Paul. (gr. 3 up). pap. 2.50 perfect bdg. (*1-55748-135-0*) Barbour & Co.
Tangvald, Christine H. Swish, Swish, Went the Giant Fish: And Other Bible Stories about Prayer. Griego, Tony, illus. LC 94-6709. Date not set. write for info. (*0-7814-0929-2*, Chariot Bks) Chariot Family.
Vos Wezeman, Phyllis & Wiessner, Colleen A. Saul to Paul: Enlightened to Serve. 32p. (Orig.). (gr. 1-6). 1989. pap. 5.95 (*0-940754-74-6*) Ed Ministries.
Whalin, Terry. A Strange Place to Sing. LC 94-7171. (gr. 4 up). 1994. write for info. (*0-7847-0273-X*) Standard Pub.
Woods, Paul. Advice to Young Christians: Exploring Paul's Letters. (Illus.). 48p. (gr. 6-8). 1992. pap. 8.99 (*1-55945-146-7*) Group Pub.

PAUL, SAINT, APOSTLE–FICTION
Hostetler, Marian. We Knew Paul. 128p. (Orig.). (gr. 4-8). 1992. pap. 4.95 (*0-8361-3589-X*) Herald Pr.

PEACE
see also Disarmament; War
Aaseng, Nathan. The Peace Seekers: The Nobel Peace Prize. (Illus.). 80p. (gr. 5 up). 1987. PLB 17.50 (*0-8225-0654-8*) Lerner Pubns.
Blue, Rose & Naden, Corinne J. People of Peace. LC 93-30547. (Illus.). 80p. (gr. 4-6). 1994. PLB 18.90 (*1-56294-409-6*) Millbrook Pr.
Brody, Ed, et al, eds. Spinning Tales, Weaving Hope: Stories, Storytelling & Activities for Peace, Justice, & the Environment. Bond, Lahki, illus. 288p. (Orig.). 1992. lib. bdg. 49.95 (*0-86571-228-X*); pap. 22.95 (*0-86571-229-8*) New Soc Pubs.
Carter, Jimmy. Talking Peace. (Illus.). 168p. (gr. 7 up). 1993. 16.99 (*0-525-44959-0*, DCB) Dutton Child Bks.
Durell, Ann & Sachs, Marilyn, eds. The Big Book for Peace. LC 89-37595. (Illus.). 128p. (gr. 7-12). 1990. 17.50 (*0-525-44605-2*, DCB) Dutton Child Bks.
Goffe, Toni. War & Peace. LC 91-18197. (gr. 4 up). 1991. 7.95 (*0-85953-366-2*); pap. 3.95 (*0-85953-356-5*) Childs Play.
Griscom, Bailey & Griscom, Pam. Why Can't I Be the Leader? (Illus.). 24p. (Orig.). (ps up). 1992. pap. 4.95 (*0-9633705-2-9*) Share Pub CA.
Kronenwetter, Michael. The Peace Commandos: Nonviolent Heroes in the Struggle Against War & Injustice. LC 93-31204. (Illus.). 160p. (gr. 4-6). 1994. text ed. 13.95 RSBE (*0-02-751051-4*, New Discovery Bks) Macmillan Child Grp.
Obold, Ruth. Prepare for Peace, Pt. I. (Illus.). 40p. (gr. 1-3). 1986. 6.25 (*0-87303-116-4*) Faith & Life.
—Prepare for Peace, Pt. II. (Illus.). 48p. (gr. 4-6). 1986. 6.25 (*0-87303-117-2*) Faith & Life.
—Prepare for Peace, Pt. III. (Illus.). 55p. (gr. 7-8). 1986. 6.25 (*0-87303-118-0*) Faith & Life.
Parolini, Stephen & Young, Christine. Peace & War. (Illus.). 48p. (gr. 6-8). 1991. pap. 8.99 (*1-55945-123-8*) Group Pub.
Perkins, Mary. Growing into Peace: A Manual for Peace-Builders in the 1990s & Beyond. (gr. 9-12). 1991. pap. 10.95 (*0-85398-323-2*) G Ronald Pub.
Scholes, Katherine. Peace Begins with You. Ingpen, Robert, illus. 40p. (gr. 1-5). 1990. 13.95 (*0-316-77436-7*) Sierra.
—Peace Begins with You. (ps-3). 1994. pap. 5.95 (*0-316-77440-5*) Little.
Webster-Doyle, Terrence. Fighting the Invisible Enemy: Understanding the Effects of Conditioning. (Illus.). 164p. (gr. 5-12). 1990. 17.95 (*0-942941-19-5*); pap. 12. 95 (*0-942941-18-7*) Atrium Soc Pubns.
—Peace, the Enemy of Freedom: The Myth of Non-Violence. (Illus.). 157p. (gr. 5-12). 1991. pap. 9.95 (*0-942941-12-8*) Atrium Soc Pubns.
—Tug of War: Peace Through Understanding Conflict. (Illus.). 106p. (gr. 5-12). 1990. 17.95 (*0-942941-21-7*); pap. 12.95 (*0-942941-20-9*) Atrium Soc Pubns.
Whitman, Edmund S. Little Pax. Ely, Gladys, illus. LC 74-182528. 120p. (gr. 5-9). 1972. 3.75 (*0-8356-0428-4*, Quest) Theos Pub Hse.

PEACE–FICTION
Douglis, Marjie. Peace Porridge. Peterson, Pete, ed. French, Ed, illus. 122p. (gr. 3-6). 1986. pap. 3.99 (*0-934998-22-1*) Bethel Pub.
Webster-Doyle, Terrence. Flight of the Golden Eagle: Tales of the Empty-Handed Masters. (Illus.). 112p. (gr. 5-12). 1992. 17.95 (*0-942941-29-2*); pap. 12.95 (*0-942941-28-4*) Atrium Soc Pubns.
—Maze of the Fire Dragon: Tales of the Empty-Handed Masters. (Illus.). 112p. (gr. 5-12). 1992. 17.95 (*0-942941-27-6*); pap. 12.95 (*0-942941-26-8*) Atrium Soc Pubns.

PEAFOWL
Kalbacken, Joan. Peacocks & Peahens. LC 94-10946. (Illus.). 48p. (gr. k-4). 1994. PLB 17.20 (*0-516-01070-0*); pap. 4.95 (*0-516-41070-9*) Childrens.

PEAFOWL–FICTION
Lehman, Bob & Lehman, Elaine. Petey the Peacock Breaks a Leg. LC 93-60914. (Illus.). 44p. (gr. k-3). 1994. 7.95 (*1-55523-649-9*) Winston-Derek.
Peet, Bill. The Spooky Tail of Prewitt Peacock. (Illus.). (gr. k-3). 1979. pap. 4.80 (*0-395-28159-8*) HM.
—The Spooky Tail of Prewitt Peacock. Peet, Bill, illus. LC 72-7930. 32p. (gr. k-3). 1973. 13.95 (*0-395-15494-4*) HM.

PEALE, CHARLES WILLSON, 1741-1827
Tunnell, Michael O. The Joke's on George. Osborn, Kathy, illus. LC 92-33312. 32p. (gr. k up). 1993. 14.00 (*0-688-11758-9*, Tambourine Bks); PLB 13.93 (*0-688-11759-7*, Tambourine Bks) Morrow.

PEANUT
Berger, Melvin. From Peanuts to Peanut Butter. (Illus.). 16p. (ps-2). 1992. pap. text ed. 14.95 (*1-56784-001-9*) Newbridge Comms.
Erlbach, Arlene. Peanut Butter. LC 93-20217. (gr. 3-7). 1993. 17.50 (*0-8225-2387-6*) Lerner Pubns.
Robbins, Ken. Make Me a Peanut Butter Sandwich & a Glass of Milk. (Illus.). (ps up). 1992. 14.95 (*0-590-43550-7*, 023, Scholastic Hardcover) Scholastic Inc.

PEANUTS–FICTION
Asher, Sandy. Teddy Teaberry's Peanutty Problem. (gr. k-6). 1989. pap. 2.95 (*0-440-40229-8*, YB) Dell.

PEARL FISHERIES–FICTION
O'Dell, Scott. Black Pearl. Johnson, Milton, illus. LC 67-23311. 160p. (gr. 7 up). 1967. 13.45 (*0-395-06961-0*) HM.

PEARL HARBOR, ATTACK ON, 1941
Bachrach, Deborah. Pearl Harbor: Opposing Viewpoints. LC 88-24288. (Illus.). 112p. (gr. 5-8). 1989. PLB 14.95 (*0-89908-059-6*) Greenhaven.
Black, Wallace B. & Blashfield, Jean F. Pearl Harbor! LC 90-45621. (Illus.). 48p. (gr. 5-6). 1991. text ed. 4.95 RSBE (*0-89686-555-X*, Crestwood Hse) Macmillan Child Grp.
Dunnahoo, Terry. Pearl Harbor: America Enters the War. LC 90-13035. (Illus.). 144p. (gr. 7-12). 1991. PLB 13. 90 (*0-531-11010-9*) Watts.
Hamilton, Elizabeth L. Remember Pearl Harbor. Kaser, Robert, illus. 29p. (gr. 3). 1981. pap. 2.95 (*0-685-63557-0*) AZ Mem Mus.
Hamilton, Sue L. Pearl Harbor. Hamilton, John C., ed. LC 91-73041. 1991. 11.96 (*1-56239-059-7*) Abdo & Dghtrs.
Harris, Nathan. Pearl Harbor. (Illus.). 64p. (gr. 6-8). 1987. 19.95 (*0-85219-669-5*, Pub. by Batsford UK) Trafalgar.
Lord, Walter. Day of Infamy. (gr. 8 up). 1991. pap. 4.99 (*0-553-26777-9*, Falcon) Bantam.

—Day of Infamy. (Illus.). (gr. 9 up). 1991. Repr. of 1957 ed. 15.00 (*0-03-027620-9*) Adm Nimitz Foun.
Nicholson, Dorinda M. Pearl Harbor Child: A Child's View of Pearl Harbor-From Attack to Peace. Nicholson, Larry, illus. 60p. 1993. pap. write for info. (*0-9631388-6-3*) AZ Mem Mus.
Stein, R. Conrad. The USS Arizona. LC 91-44646. (Illus.). 32p. (gr. 3-6). 1992. PLB 12.30 (*0-516-06656-0*) Childrens.
Sullivan, George. The Day Pearl Harbor Was Bombed. 96p. 1991. pap. 5.95 (*0-590-43449-7*) Scholastic Inc.
Taylor, Theodore. Air Raid: Pearl Harbor. 179p. (gr. 3-7). 1991. pap. 4.95 (*0-15-201655-4*, Odyssey) HarBrace.
Thompson, Richard W. The First Star: The Pearl Harbor Attack Comes Alive. 80p. (gr. 10-12). 1991. pap. text ed. 9.95 (*0-9631097-0-7*) Barriclyn.
Wills, Charles. Pearl Harbor. (Illus.). 64p. (gr. 5 up). 1991. PLB 12.95 (*0-382-24125-8*); pap. 7.95 (*0-382-24119-3*) Silver Burdett Pr.

PEARL HARBOR, ATTACK ON, 1941–FICTION
Hoobler, Dorothy & Hoobler, Thomas. Aloha Means Come Back: The Story of a World War II Girl. Bleck, Cathie, illus. 64p. (gr. 4-6). 1992. 5.95 (*0-382-24156-8*); PLB 7.95 (*0-382-24148-7*); pap. 3.95 (*0-382-24349-8*) Silver Burdett Pr.
Kudlinski, Kathleen V. Pearl Harbor is Burning! A Story of World War II. Himler, Ronald, illus. LC 93-15135. 64p. (gr. 2-6). 1993. pap. 3.99 (*0-14-034509-4*, Puffin) Puffin Bks.
Salisbury, Graham. Under the Blood Red Sun. LC 94-444. 1994. 15.95 (*0-385-32099-X*) Delacorte.

PEARLS–FICTION
Heine, Helme. The Pearl. Heine, Helme, illus. LC 84-72404. 32p. (gr. k-4). 1985. SBE 14.95 (*0-689-50321-0*, M K McElderry) Macmillan Child Grp.
Lawson, Julie. The Dragon's Pearl. Morin, Paul, illus. 32p. (gr. k-3). 1993. 15.45 (*0-395-63623-X*, Clarion Bks) HM.

PEARY, ROBERT EDWIN, 1856-1920
Anderson, Madelyn K. Robert E. Peary & the Fight for the North Pole. (Illus.). 160p. (gr. 9-12). 1992. PLB 14.40 (*0-531-13004-5*) Watts.
Kent, Zachary. The Story of Admiral Peary at the North Pole. LC 88-11824. (Illus.). 32p. (gr. 3-6). 1988. pap. 3.95 (*0-516-44738-6*) Childrens.
Rozakis, Laurie. Henson & Peary: The Race for the North Pole. (Illus.). 48p. (gr. 2-5). 1994. PLB 12.95 (*1-56711-066-5*) Blackbirch.

PEASANT ART
see Art Industries and Trade; Folk Art

PEASANTRY
see also Agricultural Laborers

PEBBLES
see Rocks

PECCARIES
George, Jean C. The Moon of the Wild Pigs. Mirocha, Paul, illus. LC 91-3495. 48p. (gr. 3-7). 1992. 15.00 (*0-06-020263-7*); PLB 14.89 (*0-06-020264-5*) HarpC Child Bks.

PECOS BILL
Anderson, J. I. I Can Read About Pecos Bill. Killgrew, John, illus. LC 76-54575. (gr. 2-5). 1977. pap. 2.50 (*0-89375-042-5*) Troll Assocs.
Dewey, Ariane. Pecos Bill. Dewey, Ariane, illus. LC 93-11731. 56p. (gr. 1 up). 1994. pap. 4.95 (*0-688-13108-5*, Mulberry) Morrow.
Jensen, Patricia A. Pecos Bill, the Roughest, Toughest Best. Mahan, Benton, illus. LC 93-2217. 32p. (gr. k-2). 1993. PLB 11.59 (*0-8167-3165-9*); pap. text ed. 2.95 (*0-8167-3166-7*) Troll Assocs.
Kellogg, Steven. Pecos Bill. ALC Staff, ed. LC 86-784. (Illus.). 32p. (gr. k up). 1992. pap. 4.95 (*0-688-09924-6*, Mulberry) Morrow.

PEDAGOGY
see Education; Teaching

PEDDLERS AND PEDDLING–FICTION
Haley, Gail E. Dream Peddler. Haley, Gail E., illus. LC 92-42074. 32p. (ps-3). 1993. 14.99 (*0-525-45153-6*, DCB) Dutton Child Bks.
Lewis, J. Patrick. The Moonbow of Mr. B. Bones. Zimmer, Dirk, illus. LC 88-37107. 40p. (ps-4). 1992. 16.00 (*0-394-85365-2*); PLB 16.99 (*0-394-95365-7*) Knopf Bks Yng Read.
McDonald, Megan. The Potato Man. Lewin, Ted, illus. LC 90-7758. 32p. (ps-2). 1991. 14.95 (*0-531-05914-6*); PLB 14.99 (*0-531-08514-7*) Orchard Bks Watts.
Sanders, Scott R. Here Comes the Mystery Man. Cogancherry, Helen, illus. LC 92-24572. 32p. (gr. k-5). 1993. RSBE 15.95 (*0-02-778145-3*, Bradbury Pr) Macmillan Child Grp.
Shannon, George. The Piney Woods Peddler. Tafuri, Nancy, illus. LC 81-2219. 32p. (gr. k-3). 1981. PLB 14.88 (*0-688-84304-2*) Greenwillow.
Shelby, Anne. We Keep a Store. Ward, John, illus. LC 89-35105. 32p. (ps-2). 1990. 14.95 (*0-531-05856-5*); PLB 14.99 (*0-531-08456-6*) Orchard Bks Watts.
Valens, Amy. Danilo the Fruit Man. Valens, Amy, illus. LC 91-46893. 32p. (ps-3). 1993. 12.99 (*0-8037-1151-4*); PLB 12.89 (*0-8037-1152-2*) Dial Bks Young.
Waller, Barrett. New Feet for Old. Stevenson, Harvey, illus. LC 90-21339. 32p. (gr. k-3). 1992. RSBE 13.95 (*0-02-792371-1*, Four Winds) Macmillan Child Grp.

PEDIATRICS
see Children–Care and Hygiene; Children–Diseases

PEDIGREES
see Heraldry

PELE
see Nascimento, Edson Arantes Do, 1940-

PELICANS
Ciardi, John. The Reason for the Pelican. Catalano, Dominic, illus. LC 93-61163. 64p. (gr. 1 up). 1994. 13.95 (*1-56397-370-7*) Boyds Mills Pr.
Fowler, Allan. Podria Sr un Pajaro - Libro Grande: (It Could Still Be a Bird Big Book) LC 90-2206. (SPA., Illus.). 32p. (ps-2). 1993. 22.95 (*0-516-59461-3*) Childrens.
Frith, Julia. Pelican Sketchbook. Frith, Julia, illus. LC 93-29013. 1994. 4.25 (*0-383-03769-7*) SRA Schl Grp.
Green, Carl R. & Sanford, William R. The Pelicans. LC 87-22251. (Illus.). 48p. (gr. 5). 1987. text ed. 12.95 RSBE (*0-89686-337-9*, Crestwood Hse) Macmillan Child Grp.
Patent, Dorothy H. Pelicans. Munoz, William, illus. 64p. (gr. 4-7). 1992. 14.45 (*0-395-57224-X*, Clarion Bks) HM.
Stone, Lynn. The Pelican. LC 89-26049. (Illus.). 60p. (gr. 3 up). 1990. text ed. 13.95 RSBE (*0-87518-430-8*, Dillon) Macmillan Child Grp.
Stone, Lynn M. Pelicans. LC 88-26428. (Illus.). (gr. 2-4). 1989. PLB 11.94 (*0-86592-322-1*) Rourke Corp.

PELICANS–FICTION
Cumpiano, Ina. Pan, Pan, Gran Pan (Small Book) Murdocca, Sal, illus. (SPA.). 16p. (Orig.). (gr. k-3). 1992. pap. text ed. 6.00 (*1-56334-085-2*) Hampton-Brown.
Hamilton, Wanda W. Peter Pelican's Pouch Problem. Hamilton, Wanda W., illus. 22p. (Orig.). (gr. k-6). 1986. pap. 3.95 (*0-935357-01-7*) CRIC Prod.
O'Reilly, Edward. Brown Pelican at the Pond. Strange, Florence, illus. LC 78-58689. (gr. k-4). 1979. 7.95 (*0-931644-01-1*) Manzanita Pr.
Pizzo, Joan. Pelican Bill. Geronimi, Clyde, illus. (gr. k-6). 1990. PLB 11.95 (*0-939126-10-9*) Back Bay.
Reese, Bob. Wellington Pelican. LC 82-23587. (Illus.). 24p. (ps-2). 1983. pap. 2.95 (*0-516-42316-9*) Childrens.
Roa, Annia. Peter Pelican-Pedro Pelicano. Henry, William, illus. LC 64-22715. (SPA & ENG.). (gr. k-4). 1974. 8.95 (*0-87208-006-4*) Island Pr Pubs.
Wildsmith, Brian. Pelican. Wildsmith, Brian, illus. LC 82-12431. 64p. (ps-2). 1983. lib. bdg. 10.99 (*0-394-95668-0*) Pantheon.

PEN DRAWING–STUDY AND TEACHING
Evans, Lee. Basic Pen & Ink Sketching for Pathfinders III: A Y. E. S. Book. Gattis, L. S., ed. (Illus.). 20p. (Orig.). (gr. 5-6). 1987. tchrs. ed 5.00 (*0-936241-34-9*) Cheetah Pub.

PENAL CODES
see Criminal Law

PENAL INSTITUTIONS
see Prisons

PENAL LAW
see Criminal Law

PENCIL DRAWING–STUDY AND TEACHING
Birker, Stefan. Drawing & Painting with Colored Pencils. LC 92-41349. (Illus.). 128p. (gr. 9-12). 1993. pap. 16.95 (*0-8069-0312-0*) Sterling.
Hobbis, Charles I. Pencil Drawing for the Architect. (gr. 10-12). 1954. 9.95 (*0-85458-100-6*); pap. 7.95 (*0-85458-101-4*) Transatl Arts.
Mitgutsch, Ali. From Graphite to Pencil. Mitgutsch, Ali, illus. LC 84-17469. 24p. (ps-3). 1985. PLB 10.95 (*0-87614-231-5*) Carolrhoda Bks.

PENGUINS
Allen, Douglas. The Penguin in the Snow. Oxford Scientific Film Staff, illus. LC 87-9968. 32p. (gr. 4-6). 1987. PLB 17.27 (*1-55532-270-0*) Gareth Stevens Inc.
Arnold, Caroline. Penguin. Hewett, Richard, photos by. LC 87-31458. (Illus.). 48p. (gr. 2-5). 1988. 12.95 (*0-688-07706-4*); PLB 12.88 (*0-688-07707-2*) Morrow Jr Bks.
Barkhausen, Annette. Penguins. LC 93-13050. (gr. 3 up). 1994. 18.60 (*0-8368-1002-3*) Gareth Stevens Inc.
Barrett, Norman S. Penguins. LC 90-32151. (Illus.). 32p. (gr. k-4). 1991. PLB 11.90 (*0-531-14114-4*) Watts.
—Penguins. (Illus.). 32p. (gr. k-4). 1991. pap. 4.95 (*0-531-15613-3*) Watts.
Bonners, Susan. A Penguin Year. Bonners, Susan, illus. LC 79-53595. 48p. (ps-3). 1981. 11.95 (*0-685-01398-7*); PLB 12.95 (*0-385-28022-X*) Delacorte.
Cousteau Society Staff. Penguins. LC 91-35229. (Illus.). 24p. (ps-1). 1992. pap. 3.95 (*0-671-77058-6*, Little Simon) S&S Trade.
Cowcher, Helen. Antarctica. Cowcher, Helen, illus. Grammer, Red, contrib. by. (Illus.). 32p. (gr. k-3). 1990. incl. audiocassette 19.95 (*0-924483-24-5*); incl. audio cass. tape & stuffed penguin toy 44.95 (*0-924483-65-2*) Soundprints.
Dalmais. Penguin, Reading Level 3-4. (Illus.). 28p. (gr. 2-5). 1983. PLB 16.67 (*0-86592-854-1*); 12.50 (*0-685-58823-8*) Rourke Corp.
Davis, Lloyd S., photos by & text by. Penguin: A Season in the Life of the Adelie Penguin. LC 93-36407. (gr. 3 up). 1994. 18.95 (*0-15-200070-4*, HB Juv Bks) HarBrace.
Dewey, Jennifer O. The Adelie Penguin. Dewey, Jennifer O., illus. LC 88-13010. 48p. (gr. 3-6). 1989. 15.95 (*0-316-18207-9*) Little.
Fontanel, Beatrice & Tracqui, Valerie. The Penguin: Animal Close-Ups. (Illus.). 28p. (ps-3). 1992. pap. 6.95 (*0-88106-426-2*) Charlesbridge Pub.
Fowler, Allan. Podria Sr un Pajaro - Libro Grande: (It Could Still Be a Bird Big Book) LC 90-2206. (SPA., Illus.). 32p. (ps-2). 1993. 22.95 (*0-516-59461-3*) Childrens.
Hawcock, David. Penguin. Bampton, Bob, illus. 5p. (ps). 1994. 3.95 (*0-307-17304-6*, Artsts Writrs) Western Pub.
Hogan, Paula Z. The Penguin. Strigenz, Geri K., illus. LC 78-21225. 32p. (gr. 1-4). 1979. PLB 19.97 (*0-8172-1257-4*) Raintree Steck-V.
—The Penguin. LC 78-21225. (Illus.). 32p. (gr. 1-4). 1984. PLB 29.28 incl. cassette (*0-8172-2231-6*) Raintree Steck-V.
Johnson, Sylvia A. Penguins. LC 80-28180. (Illus.). 48p. (gr. 4 up). 1981. PLB 19.95 (*0-8225-1453-2*) Lerner Pubns.
Kessler, Ethel. Is There a Penguin at Your Party? (ps). 1994. pap. 4.95 (*0-671-88302-X*, Little Simon) S&S Trade.
Lepthien, Emilie U. Penguins. LC 82-17911. (Illus.). 48p. (gr. k-4). 1983. PLB 12.85 (*0-516-01683-0*); pap. 4.95 (*0-516-41683-9*) Childrens.
Ling, Mary. Penguin. LC 93-22105. (Illus.). 24p. (ps-3). 1993. 7.95 (*1-56458-312-0*) Dorling Kindersley.
Linley, Mike. The Penguin: The Fastest Flightless Birds. Stefoff, Rebecca, ed. LC 92-10245. (Illus.). 31p. (gr. 3-6). 1992. PLB 17.26 (*1-56074-052-3*) Garrett Ed Corp.
McMillan, Bruce. Penguins at Home: Gentoos of Antarctica. McMillan, Bruce, illus. LC 92-34769. 1993. 15.95 (*0-395-66560-4*) HM.
Markert, Jenny. Penguins. 32p. 1991. 15.95 (*0-89565-709-0*) Childs World.
Paladino, Catherine. Pomona: The Birth of a Penguin. (Illus.). (gr. 2-4). 1991. PLB 12.90 (*0-531-10988-7*) Watts.
Patent, Dorothy H. Looking at Penguins. Robertson, Graham, illus. LC 92-37673. 40p. (ps-4). 1993. reinforced bdg. 15.95 (*0-8234-1037-4*) Holiday.
The Penguin. 28p. (gr. 2-5). 1988. pap. 3.50 (*0-8167-1572-6*) Troll Assocs.
Robinson, Clarie. Penguin. Hargreaves, Angela, illus. LC 91-44727. 32p. (gr. 4-6). 1993. text ed. 11.59 (*0-8167-2771-6*); tchr's. ed. 3.95 (*0-8167-2772-4*) Troll Assocs.
Saintsing, David. The World of Penguins. Oxford Scientific Films Staff, illus. LC 87-6536. 32p. (gr. 2-3). 1987. PLB 17.27 (*1-55532-274-3*) Gareth Stevens Inc.
Schneider, Jeff. My Friend the Penguin: An Ocean Magic Book. Spoon, Wilfred, illus. LC 90-61577. 12p. (ps). 1991. 4.95g (*1-877779-09-1*) Schneider Educational.
Serventy, Vincent. Penguin. LC 84-18045. (Illus.). 24p. (gr. k-5). 1985. PLB 9.95 (*0-8172-2415-7*); pap. 3.95 (*0-8114-6886-0*) Raintree Steck-V.
Stone, Lynn M. Penguin. (Illus.). 48p. (gr. 5). 1987. text ed. 12.95 RSBE (*0-89686-326-3*, Crestwood Hse) Macmillan Child Grp.
—Penguins. LC 88-31606. (Illus.). (gr. 2-4). 1989. PLB 11.94 (*0-86592-325-6*) Rourke Corp.
Todd, Frank S. Sea World Book of Penguins. LC 86-25588. (Illus.). 96p. (gr. 4-7). 1981. 12.95 (*0-15-271949-0*, HB Juv Bks) HarBrace.
—The Sea World Book of Penguins. Todd, Frank S., photos by. LC 80-25588. (Illus.). 96p. (gr. 4-7). 1984. pap. 9.95 (*0-15-271951-2*, Voyager Bks) HarBrace.
Wexo, John B. Penguins. 24p. (gr. 4). 1989. PLB 14.95 (*0-88682-263-7*) Creative Ed.
Wildlife Education, Ltd. Staff. Penguins. Stuart, Walter & Boyer, Trevor, illus. 20p. (gr. 5 up). 1983. pap. 2.75 (*0-937934-17-8*) Wildlife Educ.
Yee, Patrick. Baby Penguin. (Illus.). 12p. (ps). 1994. bds. 3.99 (*0-670-85291-0*) Viking Child Bks.

PENGUINS–FICTION
Alborough, Jez. Cuddly Dudley. Alborough, Jez, illus. LC 92-52994. 32p. (ps up). 1993. 14.95 (*1-56402-095-9*) Candlewick Pr.
Alden, Laura. Penguin's Adventure in Alphabet Town. Williams, Jenny, illus. LC 92-1068. 32p. (ps-2). 1992. PLB 11.80 (*0-516-05416-3*) Childrens.
Atwater, Richard. Mr. Popper's Penguins. (gr. 4-7). 1992. pap. 1.99 (*0-440-21370-3*) Dell.
Atwater, Richard & Atwater, Florence. Mr. Popper's Penguins. (Illus.). 144p. (gr. 3-6). 1978. 3.50 (*0-440-45934-6*, YB) Dell.
—Mr. Popper's Penguins. Lawson, Robert, illus. (gr. 3 up). 1938. 15.95 (*0-316-05842-4*) Little.
—Mr. Popper's Penguins: A Pop-Up Book. Williams, Karin, illus. LC 92-53195. 1993. 16.95 (*0-316-05844-0*) Little.
Benson, Patrick. Little Penguin. (Illus.). 32p. (ps-2). 1991. 14.95 (*0-399-21757-6*, Philomel Bks) Putnam Pub Group.
Bianchi, John. Penelope Penguin: The Incredibly Good Baby. Bianchi, John, illus. 24p. (ps-3). 1992. PLB 14.95 (*0-921285-13-2*, Pub. by Bungalo Bks CN); pap. 4.95 (*0-921285-11-6*, Pub. by Bungalo Bks CN) Firefly Bks Ltd.
Breathed, Berkeley. Goodnight Opus. (Illus.). 1993. 15.95 (*0-316-10853-7*) Little.
—The Last Basselope: One Ferocious Story. LC 92-14467. (Illus.). 1992. 14.95 (*0-316-10761-1*) Little.
—A Wish for Wings That Work: An Opus Christmas Story. Breathed, Berkeley, illus. 32p. 1991. 14.95 (*0-316-10758-1*) Little.
Gravois, Jeanne M. Quickly, Quigley. Hill, Alison, illus. LC 93-1990. 32p. 1994. 14.00 (*0-688-13047-X*, Tambourine Bks); PLB 13.93 (*0-688-13048-8*, Tambourine Bks) Morrow.

Inkpen, Mick. Penguin Small. (ps-3). 1993. pap. 14.95 (*0-15-200567-6*) HarBrace.
Lester, Helen. Tacky the Penguin. Munsinger, Lynn, illus. LC 87-30684. 32p. (ps-3). 1988. 13.45 (*0-395-45536-7*) HM.
—Tacky the Penguin. Munsinger, Lynn, illus. 32p. (gr. k-3). 1990. pap. 4.80 (*0-395-56233-3*) HM.
—Three Cheers for Tacky. Munsinger, Lynn, illus. LC 93-14342. 1994. 13.95 (*0-395-66841-7*) HM.
Little, Karen E. Penguin Partners. (Illus.). (ps-1). 1981. 4.50 (*0-913545-05-8*) Moonlight FL.
The Littlest Penguin, Unit 3. (gr. 1). 1991. 5-pack 21.25 (*0-88106-725-3*) Charlesbridge Pub.
McEwan, Chris. The Little Penguin. 1989. pap. 12.95 (*0-385-24977-2*) Doubleday.
Marks, Burton. Penguin's Plane. (Illus.). 10p. (ps). 1993. 4.99 (*0-89577-517-4*, Dist. by Random) RD Assn.
Monsell, Mary E. A Fish Named Yum: Mr. Spin, Vol. IV. Christelow, Eileen, illus. LC 93-25731. 64p. (gr. 1-4). 1994. SBE 13.95 (*0-689-31882-0*, Atheneum Child Bk) Macmillan Child Grp.
—The Spy Who Came North from the Pole: Mr. Pin, Vol. III. Christelow, Eileen, illus. LC 92-24646. 64p. (gr. 1-4). 1993. SBE 12.95 (*0-689-31754-9*, Atheneum Child Bk) Macmillan Child Grp.
Obedin, Harry. Peter Penguin & the Polar Sea. Strecker, Rebekah J., illus. LC 88-63171. 32p. (Orig.). (ps-4). 1989. pap. 4.95 (*0-943990-54-8*) Parenting Pr.
O'Donnell, Peter. Pinkie Leaves Home. 1992. 13.95 (*0-590-45485-4*, Scholastic Hardcover) Scholastic Inc.
Ollason, Robert J. Penguin Parade. Thomson, Alan R., illus. LC 94-6433. 40p. (gr. 4-6). 1994. PLB 19.95 (*0-8225-1491-5*) Lerner Pubns.
Perlman, Janet. Cinderella Penguin. (Illus.). 32p. (ps-3). 1993. 13.00 (*0-670-84753-4*) Viking Child Bks.
Peter Penguin. (Illus.). (ps). 1.79 (*0-517-46419-5*) Random Hse Value.
Pfister, Marcus. Les Nouveaux Amis De Pit. Pfister, Marcus, illus. (FRE.). 32p. (gr. k-3). 1992. 13.95 (*3-85539-632-9*) North-South Bks NYC.
—Penguin Pete. Pfister, Marcus, illus. LC 87-1627. 32p. (gr. k-3). 1987. 13.95 (*1-55858-018-2*) North-South Bks NYC.
—Penguin Pete & Pat. Pfister, Marcus, illus. Bell, Anthea, tr. from GER. LC 88-25296. (Illus.). 32p. (gr. k-3). 1989. 14.95 (*1-55858-003-4*) North-South Bks NYC.
—Penguin Pete's New Friends. Pfister, Marcus, illus. LC 87-72037. 32p. (gr. k-3). 1988. 13.95 (*1-55858-025-5*) North-South Bks NYC.
—Pinguin Pit. Pfister, Marcus, illus. (GER.). 32p. (gr. k-3). 1992. 13.95 (*3-314-00297-1*) North-South Bks NYC.
—Pit et Pat. Pfister, Marcus, illus. (FRE.). 32p. (gr. k-3). 1992. 13.95 (*3-85539-657-4*) North-South Bks NYC.
—Pit, le Petit Pingouin. Pfister, Marcus, illus. (FRE.). 32p. (gr. k-3). 1992. 13.95 (*3-314-20627-5*) North-South Bks NYC.
—Pit und Pat. Pfister, Marcus, illus. (GER.). 32p. (gr. k-3). 1992. 13.95 (*3-314-00327-7*) North-South Bks NYC.
—Pit's Neue Freunde. Pfister, Marcus, illus. (GER.). 32p. (gr. k-3). 1992. 13.95 (*3-85825-301-4*) North-South Bks NYC.
Playful Penguins, EV Unit 3. (gr. 1). 1991. 5-pack 21.25 (*0-88106-723-7*) Charlesbridge Pub.
Reilly, Pauline. The Penguin That Walks at Night. Rolland, Will, illus. 32p. (Orig.). 1993. pap. 6.95 (*0-86417-034-3*, Pub. by Kangaroo Pr AT) Seven Hills Bk Dists.
Rigby, Rodney. Hello, This Is Your Penguin Speaking. Rigby, Rodney, illus. LC 91-39501. 32p. (ps-2). 1992. 13.95 (*1-56282-231-4*); PLB 13.89 (*1-56282-232-2*) Hyprn Child.
Tripp, Valerie. Los Pinguinos Se Ponen a Pintar (The Penguins Paint) Martin, Sandra K., illus. LC 87-14081. (SPA.). 24p. (ps-2). 1990. PLB 9.75 (*0-516-31567-6*); pap. 3.95 (*0-516-51567-5*) Childrens.
Voelzke, Daryl E. Pierre Penguin: Finds a New Home. 24p. (ps-5). 1991. 11.95 (*0-9630803-0-X*) D E Voelzke.
Wood, Audrey. Little Penguin's Tale. 32p. (ps-1). 1989. 13.95 (*0-15-246475-1*) HarBrace.
—Little Penguin's Tale. (gr. k up). 1993. Repr. 5.95 (*0-15-247476-5*, Voyager Bks) HarBrace.

PENITENTIARIES

see Prisons

PENN, WILLIAM, 1644-1718

Aliki. The Story of William Penn. Aliki, illus. LC 93-26289. (Orig.). 1994. pap. 14.00 (*0-671-88558-8*, S&S BFYR) S&S Trade.
—Story of William Penn. LC 93-26289. 1994. pap. 5.95 (*0-671-88646-0*, Half Moon Bks) S&S Trade.

PENNSYLVANIA

Carole Marsh Pennsylvania Books, 44 bks. 1994. PLB 1027.80 set (*0-7933-1313-9*); pap. 587.80 set (*0-7933-5198-7*) Gallopade Pub Group.
Carpenter, Allan. Pennsylvania. new ed. LC 78-5089. (Illus.). 96p. (gr. 4 up). 1978. PLB 16.95 (*0-516-04138-X*) Childrens.
Cooper, Richard & Crary, Ryland. The Politics of Progress. (gr. 7-12). 1982. 9.95 (*0-931992-42-7*) Penns Valley.
Fradin, Dennis. Pennsylvania: In Words & Pictures. LC 79-24942. (Illus.). 48p. (gr. 2-5). 1980. pap. 4.95 (*0-516-43938-3*) Childrens.
Fradin, Dennis B. Pennsylvania - From Sea to Shining Sea. LC 93-32757. (Illus.). 64p. (gr. 3-5). 1994. PLB 16.45 (*0-516-03838-9*) Childrens.
Kent, Deborah. Pennsylvania. 201p. 1993. text ed. 15.40 (*1-56956-141-9*) W A T Braille.
McGough, Michael R. Pennsylvania from Wilderness Colony to National Leader. (Illus.). 44p. (gr. 4-6). 1989. pap. text ed. 5.95 (*0-939631-15-6*) Thomas Publications.
Marsh, Carole. Avast, Ye Slobs! Pennsylvania Pirate Trivia. (Illus.). 1994. PLB 24.95 (*0-7933-0980-8*); pap. 14.95 (*0-7933-0979-4*); computer disk 29.95 (*0-7933-0981-6*) Gallopade Pub Group.
—The Beast of the Pennsylvania Bed & Breakfast. (Illus.). 1994. PLB 24.95 (*0-7933-1933-1*); pap. 14.95 (*0-7933-1934-X*); computer disk 29.95 (*0-7933-1935-8*) Gallopade Pub Group.
—Bow Wow! Pennsylvania Dogs in History, Mystery, Legend, Lore, Humor & More! (Illus.). (gr. 3-12). 1994. PLB 24.95 (*0-7933-3581-7*); pap. 14.95 (*0-7933-3582-5*); computer disk 29.95 (*0-7933-3583-3*) Gallopade Pub Group.
—Christopher Columbus Comes to Pennsylvania! Includes Reproducible Activities for Kids! (Illus.). (gr. 3-12). 1994. PLB 24.95 (*0-7933-3734-8*); pap. 14.95 (*0-7933-3735-6*); computer disk 29.95 (*0-7933-3736-4*) Gallopade Pub Group.
—The Hard-to-Believe-But-True! Book of Pennsylvania History, Mystery, Trivia, Legend, Lore. Humor & More. (Illus.). 1994. PLB 24.95 (*0-7933-0977-8*); pap. 14.95 (*0-7933-0976-X*); computer disk 29.95 (*0-7933-0978-6*) Gallopade Pub Group.
—If My Pennsylvania Mama Ran the World! (Illus.). 1994. lib. bdg. 24.95 (*0-7933-1939-0*); pap. 14.95 (*0-7933-1940-4*); computer disk 29.95 (*0-7933-1941-2*) Gallopade Pub Group.
—Jurassic Ark! Pennsylvania Dinosaurs & Other Prehistoric Creatures. (gr. k-12). 1994. PLB 24.95 (*0-7933-7542-8*); pap. 14.95 (*0-7933-7543-6*); computer disk 29.95 (*0-7933-7544-4*) Gallopade Pub Group.
—Let's Quilt Our Pennsylvania County. 1994. lib. bdg. 24.95 (*0-7933-7227-5*); pap. text ed. 14.95 (*0-7933-7228-3*); disk 29.95 (*0-7933-7229-1*) Gallopade Pub Group.
—Let's Quilt Our Pennsylvania Town. 1994. lib. bdg. 24.95 (*0-7933-7077-9*); pap. text ed. 14.95 (*0-7933-7078-7*); disk 29.95 (*0-7933-7079-5*) Gallopade Pub Group.
—Let's Quilt Pennsylvania & Stuff It Topographically! (Illus.). 1994. PLB 24.95 (*0-7933-1925-0*); pap. 14.95 (*1-55609-059-5*); computer disk 29.95 (*0-7933-1926-9*) Gallopade Pub Group.
—Meow! Pennsylvania Cats in History, Mystery, Legend, Lore, Humor & More! (Illus.). (gr. 3-12). 1994. PLB 24.95 (*0-7933-3428-4*); pap. 14.95 (*0-7933-3429-2*); computer disk 29.95 (*0-7933-3430-6*) Gallopade Pub Group.
—My First Book about Pennsylvania. (gr. k-4). 1994. PLB 24.95 (*0-7933-5683-0*); pap. 14.95 (*0-7933-5684-9*); computer disk 29.95 (*0-7933-5685-7*) Gallopade Pub Group.
—Patch, the Pirate Dog: A Pennsylvania Pet Story. (ps-4). 1994. PLB 24.95 (*0-7933-5530-3*); pap. 14.95 (*0-7933-5531-1*); computer disk 29.95 (*0-7933-5532-X*) Gallopade Pub Group.
—Pennsylvania & Other State Greats (Biographies) (Illus.). 1994. PLB 24.95 (*0-7933-1942-0*); pap. 14.95 (*0-7933-1943-9*); computer disk 29.95 (*0-7933-1944-7*) Gallopade Pub Group.
—Pennsylvania Bandits, Bushwackers, Outlaws, Crooks, Devils, Ghosts, Desperadoes & Other Assorted & Sundry Characters! (Illus.). 1994. PLB 24.95 (*0-7933-0962-X*); pap. 14.95 (*0-7933-0961-1*); computer disk 29.95 (*0-7933-0963-8*) Gallopade Pub Group.
—Pennsylvania Classic Christmas Trivia: Stories, Recipes, Activities, Legends, Lore & More! (Illus.). 1994. PLB 24.95 (*0-7933-0965-4*); pap. 14.95 (*0-7933-0964-6*); computer disk 29.95 (*0-7933-0966-2*) Gallopade Pub Group.
—Pennsylvania Coastales. (Illus.). 1994. PLB 24.95 (*0-7933-1936-6*); pap. 14.95 (*0-7933-1937-4*); computer disk 29.95 (*0-7933-1938-2*) Gallopade Pub Group.
—Pennsylvania Coastales. 1994. lib. bdg. 24.95 (*0-7933-7303-4*) Gallopade Pub Group.
—Pennsylvania Dingbats! Bk. 1: A Fun Book of Games, Stories, Activities & More about Our State That's All in Code! for You to Decipher. (Illus.). (gr. 3-12). 1994. PLB 24.95 (*0-7933-3887-5*); pap. 14.95 (*0-7933-3888-3*); computer disk 29.95 (*0-7933-3889-1*) Gallopade Pub Group.
—Pennsylvania Festival Fun for Kids! (Illus.). (gr. 3-12). 1994. lib. bdg. 24.95 (*0-7933-4040-3*); pap. 14.95 (*0-7933-4041-1*); disk 29.95 (*0-7933-4042-X*) Gallopade Pub Group.
—The Pennsylvania Hot Air Balloon Mystery. (Illus.). (gr. 2-9). 1994. 24.95 (*0-7933-2660-5*); pap. 14.95 (*0-7933-2661-3*); computer disk 29.95 (*0-7933-2662-1*) Gallopade Pub Group.
—Pennsylvania Jeopardy! Answers & Questions about Our State! (Illus.). (gr. 3-12). 1994. PLB 24.95 (*0-7933-4193-0*); pap. 14.95 (*0-7933-4194-9*); computer disk 29.95 (*0-7933-4195-7*) Gallopade Pub Group.
—Pennsylvania "Jography" A Fun Run Thru Our State! (Illus.). 1994. PLB 24.95 (*0-7933-1922-6*); pap. 14.95 (*0-7933-1923-4*); computer disk 29.95 (*0-7933-1924-2*) Gallopade Pub Group.
—Pennsylvania Kid's Cookbook: Recipes, How-to, History, Lore & More! (Illus.). 1994. PLB 24.95 (*0-7933-0974-3*); pap. 14.95 (*0-7933-0973-5*); computer disk 29.95 (*0-7933-0975-1*) Gallopade Pub Group.
—Pennsylvania Quiz Bowl Crash Course! (Illus.). 1994. PLB 24.95 (*0-7933-1945-5*); pap. 14.95 (*0-7933-1946-3*); computer disk 29.95 (*0-7933-1947-1*) Gallopade Pub Group.
—Pennsylvania Rollercoasters! (Illus.). (gr. 3-12). 1994. PLB 24.95 (*0-7933-5338-6*); pap. 14.95 (*0-7933-5339-4*); computer disk 29.95 (*0-7933-5340-8*) Gallopade Pub Group.
—Pennsylvania School Trivia: An Amazing & Fascinating Look at Ou State's Teachers, Schools & Students! (Illus.). 1994. PLB 24.95 (*0-7933-0971-9*); pap. 14.95 (*0-7933-0970-0*); computer disk 29.95 (*0-7933-0972-7*) Gallopade Pub Group.
—Pennsylvania Silly Basketball Sportsmysteries, Vol. 1. (Illus.). 1994. PLB 24.95 (*0-7933-0968-9*); pap. 14.95 (*0-7933-0967-0*); computer disk 29.95 (*0-7933-0969-7*) Gallopade Pub Group.
—Pennsylvania Silly Basketball Sportsmysteries, Vol. 2. (Illus.). 1994. PLB 24.95 (*0-7933-1948-X*); pap. 14.95 (*0-7933-1949-8*); computer disk 29.95 (*0-7933-1950-1*) Gallopade Pub Group.
—Pennsylvania Silly Football Sportsmysteries, Vol. 1. (Illus.). 1994. PLB 24.95 (*0-7933-1927-7*); pap. 14.95 (*0-7933-1928-5*); computer disk 29.95 (*0-7933-1929-3*) Gallopade Pub Group.
—Pennsylvania Silly Football Sportsmysteries, Vol. 2. (Illus.). 1994. PLB 24.95 (*0-7933-1930-7*); pap. 14.95 (*0-7933-1931-5*); computer disk 29.95 (*0-7933-1932-3*) Gallopade Pub Group.
—Pennsylvania Silly Trivia! (Illus.). 1994. PLB 24.95 (*0-7933-1919-6*); pap. 14.95 (*0-7933-1920-X*); computer disk 29.95 (*0-7933-1921-8*) Gallopade Pub Group.
—Pennsylvania's (Most Devastating!) Disasters & (Most Calamitous!) Catastrophies! (Illus.). 1994. PLB 24.95 (*0-7933-0959-X*); pap. 14.95 (*0-7933-0958-1*); computer disk 29.95 (*0-7933-0960-3*) Gallopade Pub Group.
Shires, H. Bess & March, Rita N. Adventures in Pennsylvania. (gr. 5-6). 1984. pap. 4.95 (*0-931992-12-5*) Penns Valley.
Stone, Lynn M. Pennsylvania Dutch Country. LC 93-13976. 1993. write for info. (*0-86593-301-4*) Rourke Corp.
Swain, Gwenyth. Pennsylvania. LC 93-12333. 1993. write for info. (*0-8225-2727-8*) Lerner Pubns.
Thompson, Kathleen. Pennsylvania. LC 85-9972. 48p. (gr. 3 up). 1985. PLB 19.97 (*0-86514-442-7*) Raintree Steck-V.
Wallower, Lucille. All about Pennsylvania. Wholey, Ellen J., ed. Wallower, Lucille, illus. (gr. 3-4). 1984. pap. 4.55 (*0-931992-05-2*) Penns Valley.
—Your Pennsylvania. Brebner, Daphne B. & Stevens, S. K., eds. (gr. 4-6). 1959. 6.35 (*0-931992-07-9*) Penns Valley.
—Your State: Pennsylvania. Gump, Patricia L., ed. (gr. 3-4). 1984. pap. 4.90 (*0-931992-09-5*) Penns Valley.
Wallower, Lucille & Wier, Bernice. The New Pennsylvania Primer. (gr. 3-4). 1984. 9.45 (*0-931992-04-4*) Penns Valley.

PENNSYLVANIA–FICTION

Avi. Encounter at Easton. Cohn, Amy, ed. LC 94-81. 144p. (gr. 5 up). 1994. pap. 4.95 (*0-688-05296-7*, Pub. by Beech Tree Bks) Morrow.
—Night Journeys. Cohn, Amy, ed. LC 93-50233. 160p. (gr. 5 up). 1994. write for info. (*0-688-05298-3*, Pub. by Beech Tree Bks); pap. 4.95 (*0-688-13628-1*, Pub. by Beech Tree Bks) Morrow.

uncle, William Miller, agonized over registering his whiskey still & facing retribution from neighbor "Tom the Tinker," or ignoring the law & facing the consequences in a far-off Philadelphia courtroom. Increasingly pressured to take a stand, he finds himself--& his family--overtaken by events. This dramatic story is seen through Janie's eyes. Pioneer crafts & activities are woven into the story. "1794" is suitable for older children & young adults but can be enjoyed by all ages. L. C. Zajdel, 203 Old Oak Rd., McMurray, PA 15317 (412) 941-2160. *Publisher Provided Annotation.*

Davis, Jenny. Checking on the Moon. LC 91-8284. 224p. (gr. 6 up). 1991. 14.95 (*0-531-05960-X*); RLB 14.99 (*0-531-08560-0*) Orchard Bks Watts.

Fritz, Jean. The Cabin Faced West. Rojankovsky, Feodor, illus. (gr. 4-7). 1958. 13.95 (*0-698-20016-0*, Coward) Putnam Pub Group.

—The Cabin Faced West. Rojanovsky, Feodor, illus. (gr. 1-7). 1987. pap. 3.99 (*0-14-032256-6*, Puffin) Puffin Bks.

Jensen, Dorothea. Riddle of Penncroft Farm. 242p. (gr. 3-7). 1991. pap. 4.95 (*0-15-266908-6*, Odyssey) HarBrace.

Kerr, M. E. Linger. LC 92-30988. 224p. (gr. 7 up). 1993. 15.00 (*0-06-022879-2*); PLB 14.89 (*0-06-022882-2*) HarpC Child Bks.

Knight, James E. The Farm, Life in Colonial Pennsylvania. Milone, Karen, illus. LC 81-23083. 32p. (gr. 5-9). 1982. PLB 11.59 (*0-89375-730-6*); pap. text ed. 2.95 (*0-89375-731-4*) Troll Assocs.

Miller, Shirley J. Billy. Casey, Marjorie, illus. 60p. (Orig.). (gr. 2-6). 1993. pap. 6.95 (*1-878580-92-2*) Asylum Arts.

Skurzynski, Gloria. Good Bye, Billy Radish. LC 92-7577. (Illus.). 144p. (gr. 5 up). 1992. SBE 14.95 (*0-02-782921-9*, Bradbury Pr) Macmillan Child Grp.

Smith, Helene & Swetnam, George. Hannah's Town. LC 73-84564. (Illus.). 113p. 1973. 7.95 (*0-913228-06-0*) MacDonald-Sward.

PENNSYLVANIA–HISTORY

Aliki. Story of William Penn. LC 93-26289. 1994. pap. 5.95 (*0-671-88646-0*, Half Moon Bks) S&S Trade.

Cooper, Richard & Crary, Ryland. The Politics of Progress. (gr. 7-12). 1982. 9.95 (*0-931992-42-7*) Penns Valley.

Cornell, William A. & Altland, Millard. Our Pennsylvania Heritage. LC 78-50430. (gr. 7-12). 1983. 15.95 (*0-931992-21-4*) Penns Valley.

Fradin, Dennis B. The Pennsylvania Colony. LC 88-11975. 160p. (gr. 4 up). 1988. PLB 17.95 (*0-516-00390-9*) Childrens.

McElroy, Janice H., ed. Our Hidden Heritage: Pennsylvania Women in History. LC 83-71272. (Illus.). 440p. (gr. 7-8). 1983. pap. 12.00 (*0-9611476-0-1*) Am Assoc U Women.

Marsh, Carole. Chill Out: Scary Pennsylvania Tales Based on Frightening Pennsylvania Truths. (Illus.). 1994. lib. bdg. 24.95 (*0-7933-4768-8*); pap. 14.95 (*0-7933-4769-6*); disk 29.95 (*0-7933-4770-X*) Gallopade Pub Group.

—Pennsylvania "Crinkum-Crankum" A Funny Word Book about Our State. (Illus.). (gr. 3-12). 1994. 24.95 (*0-7933-4922-2*); pap. 14.95 (*0-7933-4923-0*); computer disk 29.95 (*0-7933-4924-9*) Gallopade Pub Group.

—The Pennsylvania Mystery Van Takes Off! Book 1: Handicapped Pennsylvania Kids Sneak Off on a Big Adventure. (Illus.). (gr. 3-12). 1994. 24.95 (*0-7933-5075-1*); pap. 14.95 (*0-7933-5076-X*); computer disk 29.95 (*0-7933-5077-8*) Gallopade Pub Group.

—Pennsylvania Timeline: A Chronology of Pennsylvania History, Mystery, Trivia, Legend, Lore & More. (Illus.). (gr. 3-12). 1994. PLB 24.95 (*0-7933-5989-9*); pap. 14.95 (*0-7933-5990-2*); computer disk 29.95 (*0-7933-5991-0*) Gallopade Pub Group.

—Pennsylvania's Unsolved Mysteries (& Their "Solutions") Includes Scientific Information & Other Activities for Students. (Illus.). (gr. 3-12). 1994. PLB 24.95 (*0-7933-5836-1*); pap. 14.95 (*0-7933-5837-X*); computer disk 29.95 (*0-7933-5838-8*) Gallopade Pub Group.

—Uncle Rebus: Pennsylvania Picture Stories for Computer Kids. (Illus.). (gr. k-3). 1994. PLB 24.95 (*0-7933-4615-0*); pap. 14.95 (*0-7933-4616-9*); disk 29.95 (*0-7933-4617-7*) Gallopade Pub Group.

Wallower, Lucille. Indians of Pennsylvania Workshop. LC 76-12651. (gr. 3-4). 1985. pap. 4.90 (*0-931992-53-2*) Penns Valley.

PENNSYLVANIA DUTCH

Ammon, Richard. Growing up Amish. LC 88-27493. (Illus.). 80p. (gr. 3-7). 1989. SBE 13.95 (*0-689-31387-X*, Atheneum Child Bk) Macmillan Child Grp.

Aylesworth, Jim. The Folks in the Valley: A Pennsylvania Dutch ABC. Vitale, Stefano, illus. LC 91-12451. 32p. (ps-3). 1992. 15.00 (*0-06-021672-7*); PLB 14.89 (*0-06-021929-7*) HarpC Child Bks.

Smucker, Barbara. Amish Adventure. Price, Caroline, illus. LC 83-80892. 144p. (Orig.). (gr. 6-9). 1983. pap. 6.95 (*0-8361-3339-0*) Herald Pr.

Stone, Lynn M. Pennsylvania Dutch Country. LC 93-13976. 1993. write for info. (*0-86593-301-4*) Rourke Corp.

Troyer, Terry L. Amish Life Style Illustrated. Smith, Tilman R., intro. by. LC 82-90105. (Illus.). 96p. (gr. 6-12). 1982. 19.95 (*0-943314-00-3*) TLT.

Wallower, Lucille. The Pennsylvania Dutch. Gump, Patricia L., ed. (gr. 3-4). 1971. pap. 3.75 (*0-931992-31-1*) Penns Valley.

PENNSYLVANIA DUTCH–FICTION

Milhous, Katherine. The Egg Tree. Milhous, Katherine, illus. LC 50-6817. 32p. (gr. 1-4). 1971. RSBE 13.95 (*0-684-12716-4*, Scribners Young Read) Macmillan Child Grp.

—The Egg Tree. LC 91-15854. (Illus.). 32p. (gr. k-3). 1992. pap. 4.95 (*0-689-71568-4*, Aladdin) Macmillan Child Grp.

PENNSYLVANIA GERMANS

see Pennsylvania Dutch

PENOLOGY

see Prisons

PEOPLE'S DEMOCRACIES

see Communist Countries

PEOPLE'S REPUBLIC OF CHINA

see China (People'S Republic of China)

PERCEPTION

Allington, Richard L. Opposites. Conner, Eulala, illus. LC 79-20525. 32p. (gr. k-3). 1985. PLB 9.95 (*0-685-73419-6*); pap. 3.95 (*0-8114-8237-5*) Raintree Steck-V.

Brooks. Each a Piece. Date not set. 16.00 (*0-06-023594-2*); PLB 14.89 (*0-06-023595-0*) HarpC Child Bks.

Hoban, Tana. Black on White. LC 92-18897. (Illus.). 12p. (ps up). 1993. bds. 4.95 (*0-688-11918-2*) Greenwillow.

—Is It Rough? Is It Smooth? Is It Shiny? Hoban, Tana, illus. LC 83-25460. 32p. (ps-1). 1984. 15.95 (*0-688-03823-9*); PLB 15.88 (*0-688-03824-7*) Greenwillow.

—Look up, Look Down. LC 91-12613. 32p. (ps up). 1992. 14.00 (*0-688-10577-7*); lib. bdg. 13.93 (*0-688-10578-5*) Greenwillow.

Joyce, Katherine. Astounding Optical Illusions. LC 93-43911. 1994. 12.95 (*0-8069-0431-3*) Sterling.

Mind & Perception: The Marshall Cavendish Guide to Projects & Experiments, 6 vols. (Illus.). (gr. 4-9). 1990. Set. PLB 89.95 (*1-85435-307-1*) Marshall Cavendish.

Pesiri, Evelyn. Learn to See. Pesiri, Evelyn, illus. 64p. (gr. k-3). 1985. wkbk. 7.95 (*0-86653-286-2*, GA 674) Good Apple.

Tyler, J. & Round, G. Opposites. (Illus.). 24p. (ps up). 1987. pap. 3.50 (*0-7460-0219-X*) EDC.

Tytla, Milan & Crystal, Nancy. You Won't Believe Your Eyes. Eldridge, Susan, illus. 88p. (gr. 2-8). 1992. pap. 9.95 (*1-55037-218-1*, Pub. by Annick CN) Firefly Bks Ltd.

Wassermann, Selma & Wassermann, Jack. The Book of Comparing. Smith, Dennis, illus. 32p. (gr. k-3). 1990. lib. bdg. 12.85 (*0-8027-6944-6*); pap. 4.95 (*0-8027-9451-3*) Walker & Co.

Watkins, Dawn L. Wait & See. Altizer, Suzanne R., photos by. (Illus.). 46p. (Orig.). (ps-1). 1991. pap. 4.95 (*0-89084-576-X*) Bob Jones Univ Pr.

PERCUSSION INSTRUMENTS

see also names of percussion instruments, e.g. Drums

Hewitt, Sally. Bang & Rattle. LC 94-16948. (Illus.). 24p. (ps-3). 1994. PLB 14.40 (*0-516-07987-5*); pap. 4.95 (*0-516-47987-3*) Childrens.

Sharma, Elizabeth. Percussion. LC 93-710. (Illus.). 32p. (gr. 4-6). 1993. 14.95 (*1-56847-113-0*) Thomson Lrning.

Shipton, Alyn. Percussion. LC 93-20013. (Illus.). 32p. (gr. 5-8). 1993. PLB 19.97 (*0-8114-2316-6*) Raintree Steck-V.

PERFORMING ARTS

see also Theater;

also art forms performed on stage or screen, e.g. Ballet

Exploring the Arts Series, 4 vols. (Illus.). (gr. 4-8). 1990. Set. 55.80 (*1-85435-101-X*) Marshall Cavendish.

Let's Discover Sport & Entertainment. (Illus.). 80p. (gr. k-6). 1981. per set 199.00 (*0-8172-1768-1*) Raintree Steck-V.

Morley, Jacqueline. Entertainment. LC 93-4826. 1993. write for info. (*0-531-15264-2*) Watts.

—Entertainment: Screen, Stage & Stars. (Illus.). 48p. (gr. 5-8). 1994. PLB 13.90 (*0-531-14311-2*) Watts.

Morris, Ann. On with the Show. (Illus.). 25p. (gr. 2-4). 1991. 12.95 (*0-237-60144-3*, Pub. by Evans Bros Ltd) Trafalgar.

Shorto, Russell. Careers for People Who Like to Perform. LC 91-27660. (Illus.). 64p. (gr. 7 up). 1992. PLB 14.40 (*1-56294-158-5*); pap. 4.95 (*1-56294-772-9*) Millbrook Pr.

—Careers for People Who Like to Perform. 1992. pap. 4.95 (*0-395-63574-8*) HM.

Straub, Cindie & Straub, Matthew. Mime: Basic for Beginners. (Illus., Orig.). (gr. 7-12). 1984. pap. 13.95 (*0-8238-0263-9*) Plays.

PERIODICALS

see also Newspapers

Garcia, John. Hispanic Magazine: A Publishing Success Story. (gr. 4-7). 1994. 14.95 (*0-8027-8309-0*); PLB 15.85 (*0-8027-8310-4*) Walker & Co.

Merrison, Tim. Comics & Magazines. Stefoff, Rebecca, ed. LC 90-13985. (Illus.). 32p. (gr. 4-8). 1991. PLB 17.26 (*0-944483-97-6*) Garrett Ed Corp.

Taylor, Barbara. Create Your Own Magazine. LC 92-46352. (Illus.). 46p. (gr. 2-10). 1993. 12.95 (*0-8069-0425-9*) Sterling.

PERRY, MATTHEW CALBRAITH, 1794-1858

Kuhn, Ferdinand. Commodore Perry & the Opening of Japan. (Illus.). (gr. 4-6). 1955. 2.95 (*0-394-80356-6*) Random Bks Yng Read.

PERSONAL APPEARANCE

see Beauty, Personal

PERSONAL DEVELOPMENT

see Personality; Success

PERSONAL FINANCE

see Finance, Personal

PERSONAL GROOMING

see Beauty, Personal

PERSONAL LIBERTY

see Liberty

PERSONALITY

see also Individuality

Ask about Who I Am. 64p. (gr. 4-5). 1987. PLB 11.95 (*0-8172-2883-7*) Raintree Steck-V.

Beckman, Jean E. Why? There Is More to You Than Meets the Eye. (Illus.). 50p. (Orig.). (gr. 9-12). 1981. pap. 4.25 (*0-941992-00-4*) Los Arboles Pub.

Brady, Janeen. Someone Special - You! Clarkson & Twede, illus. 26p. (gr. k-9). 1991. activity bk. 2.50 (*0-944803-76-8*); cassette & bklt. 10.95 (*0-944803-74-1*) Brite Music.

Brown, Tricia. Someone Special, Just Like You. Ortiz, Fran, photos by. LC 83-18377. (Illus.). 64p. (ps-2). 1984. 15.95 (*0-8050-0481-5*, Bks Young Read) H Holt & Co.

Carr, Jan. I Am Curious about Me. Campana, Manny, illus. 48p. (ps-2). 1990. pap. 1.95 (*0-590-44032-2*) Scholastic Inc.

Carroll, Jeri. Let's Learn about Magnificent Me. Foster, Tom, illus. 64p. (ps-2). 1987. pap. 7.95 (*0-86653-384-2*, GA1010) Good Apple.

Cox, W. Miles. The Addictive Personality. (Illus.). 32p. (gr. 5 up). 1991. pap. 4.49 (*0-7910-0006-0*) Chelsea Hse.

Ets, Marie H. Just Me. Ets, Marie H., illus. (gr. k-3). 1985. bk. & cassette 19.95 (*0-941078-75-2*); pap. 12.95 bk. & cassette (*0-941078-73-6*); cassette, 4 paperbacks & guide 27.95 (*0-941078-74-4*) Live Oak Media.

Fass, Bernie & Caggiano, Rosemary. The Power Is You. 48p. (gr. 2-12). 1979. pap. 14.95 (*0-86704-005-X*) Clarus Music.

Hallinan, P. K. I Know Who I Am. Hallinan, P. K., illus. 28p. 1991. pap. 5.00 (*0-89486-781-4*, 5442B) Hazelden.

Peebles, Catherine & Edge, Denzil. A Natural Curiosity: Taffy's Search for Self. LC 87-36882. (Illus., Orig.). 1988. pap. 6.95 (*0-939991-01-2*) Learning KY.

Schwartz, Linda. The Month-To-Month Me. 48p. (gr. 3-7). 1976. 5.95 (*0-88160-021-0*, LW 205) Learning Wks.

Smith, Sandra L. Discovering Your Own Space. (gr. 7-12). 1992. PLB 14.95 (*0-8239-1279-5*) Rosen Group.

Spier, Peter. People. Spier, Peter, illus. LC 78-19832. 48p. (gr. 1-3). 1980. PLB 15.95 (*0-385-13181-X*) Doubleday.

PERSONALITY–FICTION

American Etiquette Institute Staff. Eddycat & Buddy Entertain a Guest, Bk. 5. (Illus.). 32p. (gr. k-3). 1991. 13.95 (*1-879322-14-5*) Amer Etiquette Inst.

—Eddycat & Gabby Gorilla Babysit, Bk. 9. (Illus.). 32p. (gr. k-3). 1991. 13.95 (*1-879322-18-8*) Amer Etiquette Inst.

—Eddycat Attends Sunshine's Birthday Party, Bk. 3. (Illus.). 32p. (gr. k-3). 1991. 13.95 (*1-879322-12-9*) Amer Etiquette Inst.

—Eddycat Brings Soccer to Mannersville, Bk. 8. (Illus.). 32p. (gr. k-3). 1991. 13.95 (*1-879322-17-X*) Amer Etiquette Inst.

—Eddycat Goes on Vacation with the Ducks, Bk. 11. (Illus.). 32p. (gr. k-3). 1991. 13.95 (*1-879322-20-X*) Amer Etiquette Inst.

—Eddycat Goes Shopping with Becky Bunny, Bk. 6. (Illus.). 32p. (gr. k-3). 1991. 13.95 (*1-879322-15-3*) Amer Etiquette Inst.

—Eddycat Helps Sunshine Plan Her Party, Bk. 2. (Illus.). 32p. (gr. k-3). 1991. 13.95 (*1-879322-11-0*) Amer Etiquette Inst.

—Eddycat Introduces Leonardo Lion, Bk. 12. (Illus.). 32p. (gr. k-3). 1991. 13.95 (*1-879322-21-8*) Amer Etiquette Inst.

—Eddycat Introduces Mannersville, USA, Bk. 1. (Illus.). 32p. (gr. k-3). 1991. 13.95 (*1-879322-10-2*) Amer Etiquette Inst.

—Eddycat Serves Grandma's Birthday Brunch, Bk. 10. (Illus.). 32p. (gr. k-3). 1991. 13.95 (*1-879322-19-6*) Amer Etiquette Inst.

—Eddycat Teaches Telephone Skills, Bk. 4. (Illus.). 32p. (gr. k-3). 1991. 13.95 (*1-879322-13-7*) Amer Etiquette Inst.

—Eddycat Visits Wright Street School, Bk. 7. (Illus.). 32p. (gr. k-3). 1991. 13.95 (*1-879322-16-1*) Amer Etiquette Inst.

Anderson, Wayne. Dragon. LC 91-4790. (ps-3). 1992. 15.00 (*0-671-78397-1*, Green Tiger) S&S Trade.

Angell, Judie. Secret Selves. 192p. (gr. 7 up). 1981. pap. 2.25 (*0-440-97716-9*, LE) Dell.

Aver, Kate. Joey's Way. Himler, Ronald, illus. LC 92-7830. 48p. (gr. 1-4). 1992. SBE 13.95 (*0-689-50552-3*, M K McElderry) Macmillan Child Grp.

Barkan, Joanne. That Fat Hat. Swanson, Maggie, illus. LC 92-7414. 1992. 2.95 (*0-590-45643-1*) Scholastic Inc.

Bawden, Nina. The Real Plato Jones. LC 92-43873. 1993. 13.95 (*0-395-66972-3*, Clarion Bks) HM.

Breitmeyer, Lois & Leithauser, Gladys. Who Should I Be? (gr. 4 up). 1991. pap. 2.95 (*0-8091-6599-6*) Paulist Pr.

Bunting, Eve. Just Like Everyone Else. LC 92-11455. (Illus.). (gr. 3-8). 1992. PLB 8.95 (*0-89565-972-7*) Childs World.

Charaleone. All I See Is Part of Me. Aldrich, Cynthia, illus. 56p. (gr. 2-8). 1989. 14.95 (*0-935699-03-1*) Illum Arts.

Conford, Ellen. Why Me? 156p. (gr. 5 up). 1985. 14.95 (*0-316-15326-5*) Little.

Cooney, Caroline B. Party's Over. 1991. 13.95 (*0-590-42552-8*, Scholastic Hardcover) Scholastic Inc.

—The Party's Over. 192p. (gr. 7 up). 1992. pap. 3.25 (*0-590-42553-6*, Point) Scholastic Inc.

Cosgrove, Stephen. Leo the Lop. James, Robin, illus. LC 94-21448. 1995. write for info. (*0-8431-3820-3*) Price Stern.

Dyer, T. A. Way of His Own. 1990. pap. 4.80 (*0-395-54969-8*) HM.

Evans, Mari. I Look at Me. (ps-2). 1974. pap. 2.50 (*0-88378-038-0*) Third World.

Fox, Mem. Guess What? Goodman, Vivienne, illus. LC 90-4127. 28p. (ps up). 1990. 13.95 (*0-15-200452-1*, Gulliver Bks) HarBrace.

Grant, Eva. I Hate My Name. Mayo, Gretchen, illus. Hollingsworth, Charles, intro. by. LC 80-14428. (Illus.). 32p. (gr. k-6). 1980. PLB 19.97 (*0-8172-1362-7*) Raintree Steck-V.

Grejniec, Michael. What Do You Like? Grejniec, Michael, illus. LC 92-3481. 32p. (gr. k). 1992. 14.95 (*1-55858-175-8*); PLB 14.88 (*1-55858-176-6*) North-South Bks NYC.

Hargreaves, Roger. Mr. Nonsense. 32p. (ps up). 1978. PLB 9.95 (*0-87191-820-X*) Creative Ed.

Hazen, Barbara S. To Be Me. Hook, Frances, illus. LC 75-12960. (ps-2). 1975. PLB 14.95 (*0-913778-09-5*) Childs World.

Kennedy, Fiona & Noakes, Polly. The Last Little Duckling. LC 92-21695. (Illus.). 28p. (ps-1). 1993. 12.95 (*0-8120-6326-0*); pap. 4.95 (*0-8120-1355-7*) Barron.

Krauss, Ruth. I'll Be You-You Be Me. Sendak, Maurice, illus. (gr. k-5). 1973. pap. 8.00 (*0-912846-14-3*) Bookstore Pr.

Kuyper, Vicki J. I'm the Greatest Me There Could Ever Be! Gress, Jonna, ed. LC 92-72843. (Illus.). 14p. (ps-1). 1992. pap. text ed. 14.25 (*0-944943-12-8*, CODE 19710-6) Current Inc.

Landa, Norbert. How Does It Feel? Littlewood, Karin, illus. LC 92-39238. 26p. (ps-1). 1993. 14.95 (*1-56566-032-3*) Thomasson-Grant.

Lester, Alison. Clive Eats Alligators. LC 85-17213. (ps-3). 1986. 13.95 (*0-395-40775-3*) HM.

Lionni, Leo. Mr. McMouse. Lionni, Leo, illus. LC 92-8963. 40p. (ps-1). 1992. 15.00 (*0-679-83890-2*); PLB 15.99 (*0-679-93890-7*) Knopf Bks Yng Read.

Lovelace, Maud H. Betsy in Spite of Herself. Neville, Vera, illus. LC 46-11995. 288p. (gr. 4-7). 1980. pap. 3.95 (*0-06-440111-1*, Trophy) HarpC Child Bks.

McDonnell, Janet & Ziegler, Sandra. What's So Special about Me? I'm One of a Kind. Friedman, Joy, illus. LC 88-2872. 32p. (ps-2). 1988. PLB 14.95 (*0-89565-419-9*) Childs World.

McPhail, David. Something Special. McPhail, David, illus. 32p. (ps-3). 1988. 12.95 (*0-316-56324-2*) Little.

Merriam, Eve. Fighting Words. Small, David, illus. 32p. (gr. k up). 1992. 15.00 (*0-688-09676-X*); PLB 14.93 (*0-688-09677-8*) Morrow Jr Bks.

Nordlicht, Lillian. I Love to Laugh. Davis, Allen, illus. Silverman, Manuel, intro. by. LC 80-14399. (Illus.). 32p. 1980. 19.97 (*0-8172-1364-3*) Raintree Steck-V.

Plum, Carol T. Where the Big River Runs. Most, Richard, illus. 32p. (gr. k-3). 1991. 5.95 (*0-87973-011-0*, 11); pap. 9.95 (*0-87973-010-2*, 10) Our Sunday Visitor.

Rana, Indi. The Roller Birds of Rampur. 272p. (gr. 7 up). 1993. 15.95 (*0-8050-2670-3*, Bks Young Read) H Holt & Co.

Roe, Eileen. All I Am. LC 88-30510. (Illus.). 32p. (ps-1). 1990. RSBE 13.95 (*0-02-777372-8*, Bradbury Pr) Macmillan Child Grp.

Shannon, Margaret, text by. & illus. Elvira. LC 92-39784. 32p. (ps-2). 1993. PLB 13.95 (*0-395-66597-3*) Ticknor & Flds Bks Yng Read.

Sharmat, Marjorie W. I'm Terrific. Chorao, Kay, illus. LC 76-9094. 32p. (ps-3). 1992. pap. 4.95 (*0-8234-0955-4*) Holiday.

Vail, Rachel. Ever After. LC 93-29802. 176p. (gr. 6-9). 1993. 14.95 (*0-531-06838-2*); lib. bdg. 14.99 RLB (*0-531-08688-7*) Orchard Bks Watts.

Wyman, Andrea. Faith, Hope & Chicken Feathers. LC 93-26293. 1994. 15.95 (*0-8234-1117-6*) Holiday.

PERSONNEL SERVICE IN EDUCATION

see also Counseling; Dropouts; Vocational Guidance

PERSPECTIVE

see also Drawing

PERSUASION (RHETORIC)

see Public Speaking; Rhetoric

PERU

Lepthein, Emilie U. Peru. LC 92-4813. (Illus.). 128p. (gr. 5-9). 1992. PLB 20.55 (*0-516-02610-0*) Childrens.

Lerner Publications, Department of Geography Staff. Peru in Pictures. (Illus.). 64p. (gr. 5 up). 1987. PLB 17.50 (*0-8225-1820-1*) Lerner Pubns.

Peru. LC 89-43183. (Illus.). 64p. (gr. 3-8). 1992. PLB 21.26 (*0-8368-0235-7*) Gareth Stevens Inc.

Peru Is My Home. 48p. (gr. 2-8). 1992. PLB 18.60 (*0-8368-0903-3*) Gareth Stevens Inc.

St. John, Jetty. A Family in Peru. (Illus.). 32p. (gr. 2-5). 1987. PLB 13.50 (*0-8225-1669-1*) Lerner Pubns.

PERU–ANTIQUITIES

McMullen, David. Mystery in Peru: The Lines of Nazca. LC 77-10456. (Illus.). 48p. (gr. 4 up). 1983. PLB 20.70 (*0-8172-1058-X*) Raintree Steck-V.

PERU–FICTION

Clark, Ann N. Secret of the Andes. Charlot, Jean, illus. (gr. 4-8). 1952. pap. 14.99 (*0-670-62975-8*) Viking Child Bks.

PESTS

see Fungi; Insects, Injurious and Beneficial; Parasites

PESTICIDE POLLUTION

see Pesticides and the Environment

PESTICIDES AND THE ENVIRONMENT

Billings, Charlene W. Pesticides: Necessary Risk. LC 92-30394. (Illus.). 112p. (gr. 6 up). 1993. lib. bdg. 17.95 (*0-89490-299-7*) Enslow Pubs.

Gay, Kathlyn. Cleaning Nature Naturally. 144p. (gr. 7-9). 1991. 15.95 (*0-8027-8118-7*); PLB 16.85 (*0-8027-8119-5*) Walker & Co.

Griscom, Laura & Griscom, Pam. Who Would Want Those Apples Anyway? Halpin, Scot, illus. 24p. (Orig.). (ps-5). 1993. pap. 4.95 (*0-9633705-3-7*) Share Pub CA.

Lee, Sally. Pesticides. LC 90-46839. (Illus.). 144p. (gr. 7-12). 1991. PLB 13.90 (*0-531-13017-7*) Watts.

Yount, Lisa. Pesticides. (Illus.). (gr. 5-8). 1994. 14.95 (*1-56006-156-1*) Lucent Bks.

PETER, SAINT, APOSTLE

Lysne, Mary E. Peter. Gambill, Henrietta, ed. Patterson, Kathleen, illus. 24p. (ps-3). 1993. wkbk. 2.39 (*0-7847-0105-9*, 23-02585) Standard Pub.

PETER 1ST, EMPEROR AND TSAR OF RUSSIA, 1672-1725

Stanley, Diane. Peter the Great. Stanley, Diane, illus. LC 85-13060. 32p. (gr. k-3). 1986. RSBE 15.95 (*0-02-786790-0*, Four Winds) Macmillan Child Grp.

—Peter the Great. Stanley, Diane, illus. LC 91-20089. 32p. (gr. 1-4). 1992. pap. 4.95 (*0-689-71548-X*, Aladdin) Macmillan Child Grp.

PETROLEUM

Ardley, Neil. Oil Rigs. Stefoff, Rebecca, ed. LC 90-40246. (Illus.). 48p. (gr. 4-7). 1990. PLB 17.26 (*0-944483-76-3*) Garrett Ed Corp.

Asimov, Isaac. How Did We Find Out about Oil? Wool, David, illus. 64p. (gr. 5-8). 1980. PLB 10.85 (*0-8027-6381-2*) Walker & Co.

—Why Are Some Beaches Oily? LC 92-5345. 1992. PLB 15.93 (*0-8368-0796-0*) Gareth Stevens Inc.

Bailey, Donna. Energy from Oil & Gas. LC 90-39300. (Illus.). 48p. (gr. 2-6). 1990. PLB 19.97 (*0-8114-2518-5*) Raintree Steck-V.

Blashfield, Jean & Black, Wallace. Oil Spills. LC 91-25861. 128p. (gr. 4-8). 1991. PLB 20.55 (*0-516-05508-9*) Childrens.

Cast, C. Vance. Where Does Oil Come From? Wilkinson, Sue, illus. 40p. (ps-2). 1993. pap. 4.95 (*0-8120-1467-7*) Barron.

Lampton, Christopher. Oil Spill. LC 91-43565. (Illus.). 48p. (gr. 4-6). 1992. PLB 13.90 (*1-56294-071-6*); pap. 5.95 (*1-56294-783-4*) Millbrook Pr.

Mitgutsch, Ali. From Oil to Gasoline. Mitgutsch, Ali, illus. LC 80-29562. 24p. (ps-3). 1981. PLB 10.95 (*0-87614-160-2*) Carolrhoda Bks.

Rickard, Graham. Oil. LC 93-18304. 32p. (gr. 3-5). 1993. 13.95 (*1-56847-045-2*) Thomson Lrning.

Robson, Pat, illus. Oil. 32p. (gr. 3-5). 1985. 7.95x (*0-86685-449-5*) Intl Bk Ctr.

Walker, Jane. Oil Spills. LC 92-37095. (Illus.). 32p. (gr. 5-8). 1993. PLB 12.40 (*0-531-17406-9*, Gloucester Pr) Watts.

PETROLEUM–FICTION

Hawthorne, Dorothy. Chocolate Wildcat. Washington, Bill, illus. LC 87-72602. (gr. 4-6). 1988. pap. 5.95 (*0-931722-65-9*) Corona Pub.

Rice, James. Gaston Drills an Offshore Oil Well. Rice, James, illus. LC 82-11240. 48p. (gr. 1-6). 1982. 12.95 (*0-88289-289-4*) Pelican.

PETROLEUM ENGINES

see Gas and Oil Engines

PETROLEUM INDUSTRY AND TRADE

Cast, C. Vance. Where Does Oil Come From? Wilkinson, Sue, illus. 40p. (ps-2). 1993. pap. 4.95 (*0-8120-1467-7*) Barron.

Lynch, Michael. How Oil Rigs Are Made. (Illus.). 32p. (gr. 7 up). 1986. 12.95x (*0-8160-0041-7*) Facts on File.

Mitgutsch, Ali. From Oil to Gasoline. Mitgutsch, Ali, illus. LC 80-29562. 24p. (ps-3). 1981. PLB 10.95 (*0-87614-160-2*) Carolrhoda Bks.

Schouweiler, Thomas. The Exxon-Valdez Oil Spill. LC 91-29499. (Illus.). 96p. (gr. 5-8). 1991. PLB 11.95 (*1-56006-016-6*) Lucent Bks.

PETROLEUM PRODUCTS

Brice, Raphaelle. From Oil to Plastic. Matthews, Sarah, tr. from FRE. Kniffke, Sophie, illus. LC 87-31753. 38p. (gr. k-5). 1988. 5.95 (*0-944589-17-0*, 170) Young Discovery Lib.

PETS

see also Domestic Animals;

also names of animals, e.g. Cats; Dogs

Animal Friends. 88p. (ps-3). 1989. 15.93 (*0-8094-4849-1*); lib. bdg. 21.27 (*0-8094-4850-5*) Time-Life.

Arnold, Caroline. Pets Without Homes. Hewett, Richard, illus. LC 83-2106. 48p. (gr. k-3). 1983. 14.95 (*0-89919-191-6*, Clarion Bks) HM.

Baby Pet Animals. (Illus.). (ps). pap. 1.25 (*0-7214-9547-8*) Ladybird Bks.

Berry, Joy W. Teach Me about Pets. Dickey, Kate, ed. LC 85-45081. (Illus.). 36p. (ps). 1986. 4.98 (*0-685-10720-5*) Grolier Inc.

Broekel, Ray. Gerbil Pets & Other Small Rodents. LC 82-23501. (Illus.). 48p. (gr. k-4). 1983. PLB 12.85 (*0-516-01679-2*) Childrens.

Carpentier, Marcel. Your First Puppy. (Illus.). 34p. (Orig.). (gr. 1-6). 1991. pap. 1.95 (*0-86622-064-X*, YF-119) TFH Pubns.

Caulkins, Janet. Pets of the Presidents. LC 91-33179. (Illus.). 72p. (gr. 3-6). 1992. PLB 15.40 (*1-56294-060-0*) Millbrook Pr.

Cousins, Lucy. Pet Animals. Cousins, Lucy, illus. LC 90-36260. (ps). 1991. bds. 3.95 (*0-688-10073-2*, Tambourine Bks) Morrow.

Cowing, Renee. The Complete Book of Pet Names. LC 90-81851. 112p. 1990. 9.95 (*0-9626950-2-5*) Fireplug CA.

Dupont, Marie. Your First Kitten. (Illus.). 36p. (Orig.). 1991. pap. 1.95 (*0-86622-061-5*, YF-118) TFH Pubns.

Felder, Deborah G. The Kids' World Almanac of Animals & Pets. Lane, John, illus. 1990. 14.95 (*0-88687-556-0*); pap. 6.95 (*0-88687-555-2*) Wrld Almnc.

Frisch. Ducks. 1981. 11.95s.p. (*0-86625-192-8*) Rourke Pubns.

—Responsible Pet Care Series, 6 bks, Set II. 1991. s.p. 71.70 (*0-86625-195-2*) Rourke Pubns.

—Turtles. 1991. 11.95s.p. (*0-86625-194-4*) Rourke Pubns.

Hains, Harriet. My New Puppy. LC 91-58200. (Illus.). 24p. (ps-3). 1992. 9.95 (*1-879431-77-7*) Dorling Kindersley.

Holmes, Jean E. Norah's Ark. Woolsey, Raymond H., ed. 128p. 1989. pap. 4.95 (*0-8280-0417-X*) Review & Herald.

James, Robin. Baby Pets. (Illus.). 8p. (ps-1). 1983. 3.95 (*0-8431-0740-5*) Price Stern.

Jameson, Pam & Hearne, Tina. Responsible Pet Care, 6 bks, Reading Level 3. (Illus.). 192p. (gr. 2-5). 1989. Set. PLB 95.64 (*0-86625-188-X*); 71.70s.p. (*0-685-58765-7*) Rourke Corp.

Kelly, Michael. Your First Lovebird. (Illus.). 34p. (Orig.). 1991. pap. 1.95 (*0-86622-069-0*, YF-112) TFH Pubns.

Kindersley. Pets. LC 90-49259. (Illus.). 24p. (ps-k). 1991. pap. 6.95 (*0-689-71404-1*, Aladdin) Macmillan Child Grp.

Kneidel, Sally. Pet Bugs: A Kid's Guide to Catching & Keeping Touchable Insects. LC 93-39403. 1994. pap. text ed. 10.95 (*0-471-31188-X*) Wiley.

Kotes, F. F. A Puppy to Love: A Child's Guide to Dog Care. LC 91-67328. 40p. (Orig.). (gr. 3-8). 1991. pap. 9.95 (*1-878500-00-7*, Valley Hse Bk) Martin Mgmt.

Lohr, J. E. Your First Cockatiel. (Illus.). 36p. (Orig.). 1991. pap. 1.95 (*0-86622-060-7*, YF-104) TFH Pubns.

McPherson, Mark. Choosing Your Pet. Bernstein, Dianne, illus. LC 84-226. 48p. (gr. 3-7). 1985. PLB 9.89 (*0-8167-0111-3*) Troll Assocs.

Mitchell, Victor. Pets. Mitchell, Victor, illus. 16p. (gr. k up). 1988. pap. 1.99 (*0-7459-1469-1*) Lion USA.

Moore, Jo E. My Pets. (Illus.). 48p. (ps-1). 1988. pap. 9.95 (*1-55799-131-6*) Evan-Moor Corp.

My Book of Baby Pet Animals. (ps-2). 3.95 (*0-7214-5151-9*) Ladybird Bks.

Noreen, George W. Your First Finch. (Illus.). 36p. (Orig.). 1991. pap. 1.95 (*0-86622-062-3*, YF-106) TFH Pubns.

Nutkins, Terry & Corwin, Marshall. Pets. (Illus.). 48p. (gr. 7-9). 1992. 13.95 (*0-563-34523-3*, BBC-Parkwest); pap. 6.95 (*0-563-34524-1*, BBC-Parkwest) Parkwest Pubns.

Pasca, Sue-Rhee. Your First Canary. (Illus.). 36p. (Orig.). 1991. pap. 1.95 (*0-86622-059-3*, YF-103) TFH Pubns.

Petersen-Fleming, Judy & Fleming, Bill. Kitten Care & Critters, Too! Reingold-Reiss, Debra, photos by. LC 93-24200. (Illus.). 40p. 1994. 15.00 (*0-688-12563-8*, Tambourine Bks); PLB 14.93 (*0-688-12564-6*, Tambourine Bks) Morrow.

—Puppy Care & Critters, Too! Ringold-Reiss, Debra, photos by. LC 93-23129. (Illus.). 40p. 1993. 15.00 (*0-688-12565-4*, Tambourine Bks); PLB 14.93 (*0-688-12566-2*, Tambourine Bks) Morrow.

Pets. (Illus.). 64p. (gr. 6-12). 1984. pap. 1.85 (*0-8395-3281-4*, 33281) BSA.

Pets. (Illus.). 32p. (ps-1). 1986. pap. 1.25 (*0-8431-1519-X*) Price Stern.

Petty, Kate. Gatos. Thompson, George, illus. LC 90-71414. (SPA.). 24p. (gr. k-4). 1991. PLB 10.90 (*0-531-07916-3*) Watts.

—Guinea Pigs. Thompson, George, illus. LC 94-26050. (gr. 1-4). 1995. write for info. (*0-8120-9080-2*) Barron.

—Perros. Thompson, George, illus. LC 90-71411. (SPA.). 24p. (gr. k-4). 1991. PLB 10.90 (*0-531-07915-5*) Watts.

Pienkowski, Jan. Pets. Pienkowski, Jan, illus. 24p. (ps). 1992. pap. 2.95 (*0-671-74518-2*, Little Simon) S&S Trade.

Piers, Helen. Taking Care of Your Cat. (Illus.). 32p. 1992. pap. 4.95 (*0-8120-4873-3*) Barron.

—Taking Care of Your Dog. (Illus.). 32p. 1992. pap. 4.95 (*0-8120-4874-1*) Barron.
—Taking Care of Your Gerbils: Young Pet Owner's Guides Ser. Vriends, Matthew M., ed. LC 92-26959. 32p. 1993. pap. 4.95 (*0-8120-1369-7*) Barron.
—Taking Care of Your Goldfish. Vriends, Matthew M., ed. LC 92-32170. 32p. 1993. pap. 4.95 (*0-8120-1368-9*) Barron.
Podendorf, Illa. Pets. LC 81-7679. (Illus.). 48p. (gr. k-4). 1981. PLB 12.85 (*0-516-01641-5*) Childrens.
Pope, Joyce. Taking Care of Your Gerbil. 1990. pap. 3. 95_o.s. (*0-531-15168-9*) Watts.
—Taking Care of Your Guinea Pig. (Illus.). 32p. (gr. 4-9). 1990. pap. 3.95 o.s. (*0-531-15169-7*) Watts.
Seltzer, Meyer. Petcetera: The Pet Riddle Book. Fay, Ann, ed. LC 88-21. (Illus.). 32p. (gr. 1-5). 1988. PLB 8.95 (*0-8075-6515-6*) A Whitman.
Simon, Seymour. Pets in a Jar: Collecting & Caring for Small Animals. Fraser, Betty, illus. (gr. 4-8). 1979. pap. 5.99 (*0-14-049186-4*, Puffin) Puffin Bks.
Smith, Lane. The Big Pets. Smith, Lane, illus. 32p. (ps-3). 1991. 14.95 (*0-670-83378-9*) Viking Child Bks.
Spizzirri, Peter M. Pets: Alphabet Dot to Dot: Educational Activity-Coloring Book. Spizzirri, Linda, ed. (Illus.). 32p. (gr. k-3). 1992. pap. 1.00 (*0-86545-209-1*) Spizzirri.
Stuart, Jesse. Andy Finds a Way. rev. ed. Herndon, Jerry A., ed. & intro. by. LC 91-41495. (Illus.). 96p. (gr. 3-6). 1992. 12.00 (*0-945084-25-0*); pap. 6.00 (*0-945084-26-9*) J Stuart Found.
Taylor, Nigel. Going Live! Pet Book. (Illus.). 112p. 1992. pap. 3.95 (*0-563-20733-7*, BBC-Parkwest) Parkwest Pubns.
Vrbova, Zuza. Junior Pet Care Koi for Ponds. McAulay, Robert, illus. 48p. (gr. 1-6). 1990. PLB 9.95 (*0-685-45484-3*, J-008) TFH Pubns.
Warren, Dean. Small Animal Care & Management. LC 94-17075. 1994. write for info. (*0-8273-4557-7*) Delmar.
Watts, Barrie. Stick Insects. Kline, Marjory, ed. Watts, Barrie, photos by. (Illus.). 32p. (gr. k-4). 1992. PLB 11.40 (*0-531-14220-5*) Watts.
—Wood Lice & Millipedes. Kline, Marjory, ed. Watts, Barrie, photos by. LC 91-16539. (Illus.). 32p. (gr. k-4). 1992. PLB 11.40 (*0-531-14162-4*) Watts.
Wexler, Jerome. Pet Mice. Tucker, Kathleen, ed. LC 88-2. (Illus.). 48p. (gr. 2-8). 1989. PLB 14.95 (*0-8075-6524-5*) A Whitman.
World Book Editors. Pets & Other Animals: Childcraft Annual, 1992. LC 65-25105. (Illus.). 256p. (gr. 1-7). 1992. lib. bdg. write for info. (*0-7166-0692-5*) World Bk.
Ziefert, Harriet. Let's Get a Pet. Smith, Mavis, illus. 40p. (ps-5). 1993. PLB 13.50 (*0-670-84550-7*) Viking Child Bks.

PETS–FICTION

Armstrong, Jennifer. Too Many Pets. (gr. 4-7). 1990. pap. 2.75 (*0-553-15804-X*) Bantam.
Baehr, Patricia. Mouse in the House. Lydecker, Laura, illus. LC 93-4068. 32p. (ps-3). 1994. reinforced bdg. 15.95 (*0-8234-1102-8*) Holiday.
Barasch, Marc I. No Plain Pets! Drescher, Henrik, illus. LC 90-22518. 40p. (ps-3). 1991. PLB 14.89 (*0-06-022473-8*) HarpC Child Bks.
—No Plain Pets! Drescher, Henrik, illus. LC 90-22518. 40p. (ps-3). 1994. pap. 5.95 (*0-06-443375-7*, Trophy) HarpC Child Bks.
Beuth, Eugene. We Love Our New Home. Beuth, Eugene, illus. LC 93-77946. 34p. (Orig.). (ps). 1993. pap. 12.95 (*0-9636417-2-7*) Make-Hawk Pub.
Beveridge, Barbara. Honey, My Rabbit. Love, Judith D., illus. LC 92-34272. 1993. 2.50 (*0-383-03630-5*) SRA Schl Grp.
Boughton, Richard. Rent-a-Puppy, Inc. LC 93-41688. 1995. pap. 3.95 (*0-689-71836-5*, Atheneum) Macmillan.
Bragg, Ruth. Mrs. Muggle's Sparkle. Bragg, Ruth, illus. LC 89-31371. 28p. (ps up). 1991. pap. 15.95 (*0-88708-106-1*) Picture Bk Studio.
Brown, Marc T. Arthur's Pet Business. (ps-3). 1993. pap. 4.95 (*0-316-11316-6*) Little.
—Arthur's Puppy. LC 92-46342. (gr. 1-8). 1993. 14.95 (*0-316-11355-7*, Joy St Bks) Little.
But No Elephants. (Illus.). 42p. (ps-3). 1992. PLB 13.26 (*0-8368-0875-4*); PLB 13.26 s.p. (*0-685-61510-3*) Gareth Stevens Inc.
Carlson, Natalie S. A Pet for the Orphelines. (gr. k-6). 1988. pap. 2.75 (*0-440-46838-8*, YB) Dell.
—A Pet for the Orphelines. (gr. 1-4). 1988. 2.75 (*0-440-40014-7*, Pub. by Yearling Classics) Dell.
Carris, Joan D. Pets, Vets, & Marty Howard. (gr. k-6). 1987. pap. 2.95 (*0-440-46855-8*, Yearling) Dell.
Caseley, Judith. Mr. Green Peas. LC 93-24183. 1994. write for info. (*0-688-12859-9*); PLB write for info. (*0-688-12860-2*) Greenwillow.
Cebulash, Mel. Willie's Wonderful Pet. Ford, George, illus. 32p. (ps-2). 1993. pap. 2.95 (*0-590-45787-X*) Scholastic Inc.
Cottrill, Peter. Anteater on the Stairs. LC 93-41505. 32p. (gr. 1-3). 1994. 12.95 (*1-85697-976-8*, Kingfisher LKC) LKC.
Cresswell, Helen. Meet Posy Bates. Aldous, Kate, illus. LC 91-24481. 96p. (gr. 1-4). 1992. SBE 13.95 (*0-02-725375-9*, Macmillan Child Bk) Macmillan Child Grp.
Davies, Andrew & Davies, Diana. Poonam's Pets. Dowling, Paul, illus. 32p. (ps-2). 1990. pap. 12.95 (*0-670-83321-5*) Viking Child Bks.
De Hamel, Joan. Hemi's Pet. LC 86-26905. (ps-2). 1987. 13.95 (*0-395-43665-6*) HM.
Delton, Judy. Piles of Pets. (ps-3). 1993. pap. 3.25 (*0-440-40792-3*) Dell.
De Paola, Tomie. Little Grunt & the Big Egg: A Prehistoric Fairy Tale. De Paola, Tomie, illus. LC 88-17009. 32p. (ps-3). 1990. reinforced bdg. 14.95 (*0-8234-0730-6*) Holiday.
Dorman, N. B. Petey & Miss Magic. LC 92-11265. (Illus.). 99p. (gr. 2-6). 1992. lib. bdg. 14.95 (*0-208-02345-3*, Pub. by Linnet) Shoe String.
Duffey, Betsy. Throw-Away Pets. Natti, Susanna, illus. 80p. (gr. 2-6). 1993. 12.99 (*0-670-84348-2*) Viking Child Bks.
Erickson, Gina C. & Foster, Kelli C. The Best Pets Yet. Gifford-Russell, Kerri, illus. 24p. (ps-2). 1992. pap. 3.50 (*0-8120-4857-1*) Barron.
Ernst, Lisa C. Nattie Parsons' Good-Luck Lamb. (Illus.). 32p. (ps-3). 1990. pap. 3.95 (*0-14-050772-8*, Puffin) Puffin Bks.
Freeman, Lydia & Freeman, Don. Pet of the Met. (Illus.). 64p. (ps-3). 1953. pap. 13.95 (*0-670-54875-8*) Viking Child Bks.
Garland, Sarah. Billy & Belle. Garland, Sarah, illus. 32p. (ps-3). 1992. 13.00 (*0-670-84396-2*) Viking Child Bks.
Gaynor, Brigid. The Home Zoo. Rollins, Nancy O., illus. 12p. (ps). 1992. 4.95 (*1-56828-017-3*) Red Jacket Pr.
Graham, Amanda. Who Wants Arthur? Gynell, Donna, illus. LC 86-42812. 32p. (gr. 2-3). 1987. PLB 18.60 (*1-55532-868-7*) Gareth Stevens Inc.
Gregorich, Barbara. I Want a Pet. Hoffman, Joan, ed. Schneider, Rex, illus. 16p. (Orig.). (gr. k-2). 1984. pap. 2.25 (*0-88743-003-1*, 06003) Sch Zone Pub Co.
—I Want a Pet. Hoffman, Joan, ed. (Illus.). 32p. (gr. k-2). 1992. pap. 3.95 (*0-88743-401-0*, 06053) Sch Zone Pub Co.
Greydanus, Rose. Let's Get a Pet. Sweat, Lynn, illus. LC 87-10938. 32p. (gr. k-2). 1988. PLB 7.89 (*0-8167-0986-6*); pap. text ed. 1.95 (*0-8167-0987-4*) Troll Assocs.
Griffith, Helen V. Mine Will, Said John. Smith, J. A., illus. LC 91-32476. 32p. (ps-8). 1992. 14.00 (*0-688-10957-8*); PLB 13.93 (*0-688-10958-6*) Greenwillow.
Haywood, Carolyn. Eddie's Menagerie. Fetz, Ingrid, illus. LC 78-6519. (gr. 4-6). 1978. PLB 12.88 (*0-688-32158-5*) Morrow Jr Bks.
Helpern, Shari. I Have a Pet! LC 93-40892. (ps-1). 1994. 14.95 (*0-02-741982-7*) Macmillan.
Hessell, Jenny. Troublesome Snout. Axelsen, Stephen, illus. LC 92-34274. 1993. 14.00 (*0-383-03662-3*) SRA Schl Grp.
Hiser, Constance. Critter Sitters. Smith, Cat B., illus. LC 91-23002. 96p. (gr. 3-7). 1992. 13.95 (*0-8234-0928-7*) Holiday.
Howard, Jean G. Half a Cage. Howard, Jean G., illus. LC 78-62962. 319p. (gr. 4-12). 1978. 5.50 (*0-930954-07-6*) Tidal Pr.
Howe, James. Return to Howliday Inn. 128p. 1993. pap. 3.99 (*0-380-71972-X*, Camelot) Avon.
Johnson, Angela. The Girl Who Wore Snakes. Ransome, James E., illus. LC 92-44521. 32p. (ps-2). 1993. 14.95 (*0-531-05491-8*); PLB 14.99 (*0-531-08641-0*) Orchard Bks Watts.
Keats, Ezra J. Pet Show! Keats, Ezra J., illus. LC 86-17225. 40p. (gr. k-3). 1987. pap. 4.95 (*0-689-71159-X*, Aladdin) Macmillan Child Grp.
Keller, Holly. Furry. LC 90-24645. (Illus.). 24p. 1992. 14. 00 (*0-688-10519-X*); PLB 13.93 (*0-688-10520-3*) Greenwillow.
Kellogg, Steven. Can I Keep Him? Kellogg, Steven, illus. LC 72-142453. (ps-3). 1971. 13.99 (*0-8037-0988-9*); PLB 12.89 (*0-8037-0989-7*) Dial Bks Young.
—The Mysterious Tadpole. LC 77-71517. (Illus.). (ps-3). 1987. 14.99 (*0-8037-6245-3*); PLB 13.89 (*0-8037-6246-1*) Dial Bks Young.
—Pinkerton, Behave. giant ed. (ps-3). 1990. 17.99 (*0-8037-0841-6*) Dial Bks Young.
—Tallyho, Pinkerton! Kellogg, Steven, illus. LC 82-2341. 32p. (ps-3). 1985. 4.95 (*0-8037-0166-7*) Dial Bks Young.
Kimmel, Eric A. I Took My Frog to the Library. Sims, Blanche, illus. 32p. (ps-3). 1990. pap. 13.00 (*0-670-82418-6*) Viking Child Bks.
—I Took My Frog to the Library. Sims, Blanche, illus. 32p. (ps-3). 1992. pap. 3.99 (*0-14-050916-X*) Puffin Bks.
King-Smith, Dick. Pretty Polly. Peck, Marshall, illus. LC 91-42449. 128p. (gr. 2-7). 1992. o.s.i 14.00 (*0-517-58606-1*); PLB 14.99 (*0-517-58607-X*) Crown Bks Yng Read.
Kline, Suzy. Herbie Jones & Hamburger Head. Williams, Richard, illus. 112p. (gr. 2-6). 1989. 13.95 (*0-399-21748-7*, Putnam) Putnam Pub Group.
Lakin, Patricia. Up a Tree. Cushman, Doug, illus. LC 93-49847. 1994. write for info. (*0-8114-3868-6*) Raintree Steck-V.
Lee, Rebecca. The Perfect Pet. 1994. 7.95 (*0-8062-4878-5*) Carlton.
Little, Mary E. Old Cat & the Kitten. LC 93-30376. 128p. (gr. 3-7). 1994. pap. 3.95 (*0-689-71800-4*, Aladdin) Macmillan Child Grp.

Loder, Ann. The Wet Hat: And Other Stories from Beyond the Black Stump. Peters, Terry, illus. 102p. (Orig.). (gr. 4 up). 1993. pap. write for info. (*0-9636643-0-1*) A L Loder. THE WET HAT, & OTHER STORIES FROM BEYOND THE BLACK STUMP is a collection of Australian short stories taken from the author's childhood & family album growing up on an Australian sheep ranch. The stories concern family pets; a gutsy pony, two heroic dogs; a kookaburra, (a native Australian bird), a chicken, & a tale about a tiny silkworm. There is a mystery story about a lost ring. Lastly, there is a humorous one. Each story is based on fact & is suitable for children from fourth to eighth grade, up. A dog is featured on the full color cover & there is a black & white illustration with each story. Order from: American Business Communications, 251 Michelle Ct., South San Francisco, CA 94080. FAX: (415) 952-3716 (att: Noel Loder). 415-952-8700.
Publisher Provided Annotation.

Long, Olivia. Diary of a Dog. Long, Olivia, illus. 32p. (ps-4). Date not set. 9.95 (*1-880042-06-1*, SL12456) Shelf-Life Bks.
Luttrell, Ida. Mattie's Little Possum Pet. Lewin, Betsy, illus. LC 91-47709. 40p. (ps-3). 1993. SBE 14.95 (*0-689-31786-7*, Atheneum Child Bk) Macmillan Child Grp.
McBrier, Michael. Oliver & the Runaway Alligator. Sims, Blanche, illus. LC 86-7120. 96p. (Orig.). (gr. 3-6). 1987. PLB 9.89 (*0-8167-0818-5*); pap. text ed. 2.95 (*0-8167-0819-3*) Troll Assocs.
—Oliver's Back-Yard Circus. Sims, Blanche, illus. LC 86-40378. 96p. (Orig.). (gr. 3-6). 1987. PLB 9.89 (*0-8167-0822-3*); pap. text ed. 2.95 (*0-8167-0823-1*) Troll Assocs.
—Oliver's High-Flying Adventure. Sims, Blanche, illus. LC 86-16038. 96p. (Orig.). (gr. 3-6). 1987. PLB 9.89 (*0-8167-0820-7*); pap. text ed. 2.95 (*0-8167-0821-5*) Troll Assocs.
McBrier, Page. Oliver's Lucky Day. Sims, Blanche, illus. LC 85-8437. 96p. (gr. 3-6). 1986. lib. bdg. 9.89 (*0-8167-0537-2*); pap. text ed. 2.95 (*0-8167-0538-0*) Troll Assocs.
—Secret of the Missing Camel. Sims, Blanche, illus. LC 86-887. 96p. (Orig.). (gr. 3-6). 1987. PLB 9.89 (*0-8167-0816-9*); pap. text ed. 2.95 (*0-8167-0817-7*) Troll Assocs.
McOmber, Rachel B., ed. McOmber Phonics Storybooks: Ben Has a Pet. rev. ed. (Illus.). write for info. (*0-944991-26-2*) Swift Lrn Res.
McPhail, David. Emma's Pet. McPhail, David, illus. LC 85-4414. 24p. (ps-k). 1985. 9.95 (*0-525-44210-3*, DCB) Dutton Child Bks.
—Emma's Pet. McPhail, David, illus. LC 85-4414. 24p. (ps-k). 1988. pap. 3.95 (*0-525-44430-0*, DCB) Dutton Child Bks.
McPhail, Mac. Emma's Pet. (ps). 1988. pap. 4.50 (*0-14-054749-5*, DCB) Dutton Child Bks.
Manes, Stephen. The Great Gerbil Roundup. McKinley, John, illus. LC 88-2266. 112p. (gr. 3-7). 1991. pap. 3.95 (*0-06-440375-0*, Trophy) HarpC Child Bks.
Mayer, Mercer. These Are My Pets, Level 2. Mayer, Mercer, illus. 32p. (gr. 1-2). 1992. pap. 3.00 (*0-307-15962-0*, 15962, Golden Pr) Western Pub.
My Pet's First Book. (ps-3). 1993. pap. 2.50 (*0-8167-3138-1*, Pub. by Watermill Pr) Troll Assocs.
Oke, Janette. A Cote of Many Colors. Mann, Brenda, illus. 128p. (Orig.). (gr. 3 up). 1987. pap. 4.99 (*0-934998-27-2*) Bethel Pub.
Oram, Hiawyn. A Boy Wants a Dinosaur. (ps-3). 1991. bds. 13.95 jacketed (*0-374-30939-6*) FS&G.
Packard, Mary. The Pet That I Want. Magino, John, illus. LC 94-16976. 1995. 3.95 (*0-590-48512-1*) Scholastic Inc.
Parish, Peggy. No More Monsters for Me. Simont, Marc, illus. LC 81-47111. 64p. (gr. k-3). 1981. PLB 13.89 (*0-06-024658-8*) HarpC Child Bks.
Peteraf, Nancy J. A Plant Called Spot. Hoban, Lillian, illus. LC 92-27474. 1994. 13.95 (*0-385-30885-X*) Doubleday.
Peters, Lisa W. The Room. Sneed, Brad, illus. LC 92-39807. (gr. 3 up). 1994. 14.99 (*0-8037-1431-9*); PLB 14.89 (*0-8037-1432-7*) Dial Bks Young.
Pets I Wouldn't Pick. (Illus.). 42p. (ps-3). 1993. PLB 13. 27 (*0-8368-0896-7*) Gareth Stevens Inc.
Polacco, Patricia. Mrs. Katz & Tush. (ps-3). 1994. pap. 4.99 (*0-440-40936-5*) Dell.
Primavera, Elise. Plantpet. Primavera, Elise, illus. LC 93-36526. 32p. (ps-3). 1994. PLB 15.95 (*0-399-22627-3*, Putnam) Putnam Pub Group.
Roos, Stephen. Crocodile Christmas: The Pet Lovers Club. Rogers, Jacqueline, illus. LC 91-47079. 128p. (gr. 3-6). 1992. 14.00 (*0-385-30681-4*) Delacorte.
Rutman, Shereen. Cat Man. Jarka, Jeff, illus. 16p. (ps). 1993. wkbk. 2.25 (*1-56293-327-2*) McClanahan Bk.

—Hug a Cub. Silverstein, Cindy, illus. 16p. (ps). 1993. wkbk. 2.25 (*1-56293-323-X*) McClanahan Bk.

Rylant, Cynthia. The Everyday Books: Everyday Pets. Rylant, Cynthia, illus. LC 92-40934. 14p. (ps-k). 1993. pap. 4.95 with rounded corners (*0-02-778025-2*, Bradbury Pr) Macmillan Child Grp.

—Mr. Putter & Tabby Row the Boat. Howard, Arthur, illus. LC 93-41832. 1995. write for info. (*0-15-256257-5*) HarBrace.

Sachar, Louis. Marvin Redpost: Alone in His Teacher's House. Sullivan, Barbara, illus. LC 93-19791. 96p. (Orig.). (gr. 1-4). 1994. 2.99 (*0-679-81949-5*); PLB 2.99 (*0-679-91949-X*) Random Bks Yng Read.

Salem, Lynn & Stewart, Josie. My Pet. Graham, Jennifer, illus. 8p. (gr. 1). 1992. pap. 3.50 (*1-880612-11-9*) Seedling Pubns.

Schmeltz, Susan A. Pets I Wouldn't Pick. Appleby, Ellen, illus. LC 81-11071. 48p. (ps-3). 1982. 5.95 (*0-8193-1073-5*); PLB 5.95 (*0-8193-1074-3*) Parents.

Seidel, Jennifer R. Jaeger Finds a Family. 40p. (gr. 3-4). 1992. 7.95 (*1-880851-03-2*) Greene Bark Pr.

Selden, George. Harry Cat's Pet Puppy. 176p. (gr. 2-6). 1975. pap. 3.99 (*0-440-45647-9*, YB) Dell.

—Harry Cat's Pet Puppy. Williams, Garth, illus. LC 74-12436. 160p. (gr. 3 up). 1974. 15.00 (*0-374-32856-0*) FS&G.

Sesame Street Pet Parade. (Illus.). 24p. (ps-2). 1991. write for info. (*0-307-74007-2*, Golden Pr) Western Pub.

Seymour, Tres. I Love My Buzzard. Schindler, Stephen D., illus. LC 93-4877. 1994. write for info. (*0-531-06819-6*); lib. bdg. write for info. (*0-531-08669-0*) Orchard Bks Watts.

Smith, Lane. The Big Pets. LC 93-18608. (Illus.). 32p. (ps-3). 1993. pap. 4.99 (*0-14-054265-5*, Puffin) Puffin Bks.

Spinelli, Jerry. Bathwater Gang Gets down to Business. (ps-3). 1992. 12.95 (*0-316-80808-3*) Little.

Springstubb, Tricia. Pet-Sitters Plus Five. (gr. 4-7). 1993. pap. 2.75 (*0-590-46127-3*) Scholastic Inc.

Squire, Ann. One Hundred & One Questions & Answers about Pets & People. Karas, Brian, illus. LC 87-36457. 96p. (gr. 3-7). 1988. SBE 13.95 (*0-02-786580-0*, Macmillan Child Bk) Macmillan Child Grp.

Stanley, Carol. Dog Walkers Club. (gr. 4 up). 1990. pap. 2.95 (*0-380-75916-0*, Camelot) Avon.

Stoddard, Sando. Turtle Time. Munsinger, Lynn, illus. LC 93-39192. (gr. 3 up). 1994. write for info. (*0-395-56754-8*) HM.

Swanson, Harry. Pets & Pathos. rev. ed. Swanson, Harry, illus. 52p. (gr. 9-12). 1989. pap. 5.00 (*1-878200-03-8*) SwanMark Bks.

Thaler, Mike. Uses for Mooses & Other Popular Pets. Smath, Jerry, illus. LC 93-25542. 32p. (ps-3). 1993. PLB 9.89 (*0-8167-3301-5*); pap. text ed. 2.50 (*0-8167-3302-3*) Troll Assocs.

Vaughan, Marsha K. Whistling Dixie. Date not set. 15.00 (*0-06-021030-3*, HarpT); 14.89 (*0-06-021029-X*, HarpT) HarpC.

Whayne, Susanne S. Watch the House. Morrill, Leslie, illus. LC 91-28071. 80p. (gr. k-3). 1992. pap. 12.00 jacketed (*0-671-75886-1*, S&S BFYR) S&S Trade.

White, James E. The Triumphs of Trisha & Tripod: Tripod Finds a Home. Senf, Richard L., illus. 22p. 1991. pap. 7.95 (*0-9629102-0-1*) Pyramid TX.

Wiggins, VeraLee. Julius, the Perfectly Pesky Pet Parrot. LC 93-14254. 1994. 7.95 (*0-8163-1173-0*) Pacific Pr Pub Assn.

Wilcox, Cathy, text by. & illus. Enzo the Wonderfish. LC 93-11021. 32p. (ps-2). 1994. PLB 12.95 (*0-395-68382-3*) Ticknor & Flds Bks Yng Read.

Yashima, Mitsu & Yashima, Taro. Momo's Kitten. Yashima, Taro, illus. (gr. k-2). 1977. pap. 4.99 (*0-14-050200-9*, Puffin) Puffin Bks.

Zahn, Ellsworth E. Dudley. Zahn, Ellsworth E., illus. 40p. (Orig.). Date not set. pap. text ed. 14.95 (*0-9637308-0-0*) L E Zahn.

Ziefert, Harriet. Pet Day (Mr. Rose's Class) Brown, Richard, illus. 64p. 1988. pap. 2.50 (*0-553-15620-9*, Skylark) Bantam.

Zolotow, Charlotte. The Old Dog. rev. ed. Ransome, James, illus. LC 93-41081. 1995. 15.00 (*0-06-024409-7*); PLB 14.89 (*0-06-024412-7*) HarpC.

PHANTOMS

see Apparitions; Ghosts

PHARMACY

see also Botany, Medical; Drugs

Monroe, Judy. Prescription Drugs. LC 88-22911. (Illus.). 48p. (gr. 5-6). 1988. text ed. 12.95 RSBE (*0-89686-414-6*, Crestwood Hse) Macmillan Child Grp.

PHEASANTS

Endo, Kimio. The Pheasant. Pohl, Kathy, ed. LC 85-28207. (Illus.). 32p. (gr. 3-7). 1986. PLB 10.95 (*0-8172-2549-8*) Raintree Steck-V.

Holmgren, Virginia. The Pheasant. LC 82-23672. (Illus.). 48p. (gr. 5). 1983. text ed. 12.95 RSBE (*0-89686-222-4*, Crestwood Hse) Macmillan Child Grp.

PHILADELPHIA

Balcer, Bernadette & O'Byrne-Pelham, Fran. Philadelphia. LC 88-20198. (Illus.). 60p. (gr. 3 up). 1988. text ed. 13.95 RSBE (*0-87518-388-3*, Dillon) Macmillan Child Grp.

Clay, Rebecca. Kidding Around Philadelphia: A Young Person's Guide to the City. (Illus.). 64p. (gr. 3 up). 1990. pap. 9.95 (*0-945465-71-8*) John Muir.

Loewen, N. Philadelphia. (Illus.). (gr. 5 up). 1989. lib. bdg. 15.94 (*0-86592-542-9*); 11.95s.p. (*0-685-58593-X*) Rourke Corp.

PHILADELPHIA–FICTION

Alexander, Lloyd. Philadelphia Adventure. (gr. 4-7). 1992. pap. 3.50 (*0-440-40605-6*) Dell.

Rinaldi, Ann. Finishing Becca: A Story of Peggy Shippen & Benedict Arnold. (gr. 7 up). 1994. pap. 3.95 (*0-15-200879-9*); 10.95 (*0-15-200880-2*) HarBrace.

PHILADELPHIA–HISTORY–FICTION

Knight, James E. Seventh & Walnut, Life in Colonial Philadelphia. Guzzi, George, illus. LC 81-24036. 32p. (gr. 5-9). 1982. PLB 11.59 (*0-89375-740-3*); pap. text ed. 2.95 (*0-89375-741-1*) Troll Assocs.

Ratner-Gantshar, Barbara. Philadelphia: The City & the Bell. Miller, Wynne, ed. LC 76-43573. (Illus.). (gr. 4-8). 1976. 3.98 (*0-686-16319-2*); tchr's. & research guide 3.48 (*0-686-16320-6*) Artistic Endeavors.

PHILADELPHIA. INDEPENDENCE HALL

Steen, Sandra & Steen, Susan. Independence Hall. LC 93-5365. (Illus.). 72p. (gr. 4 up). 1994. text ed. 14.95 RSBE (*0-87518-603-3*, Dillon) Macmillan Child Grp.

PHILADELPHIA PHILLIES (BASEBALL TEAM)

Goodman, Michael. Philadelphia Phillies. 48p. (gr. 4-10). 1992. PLB 14.95 (*0-88682-455-9*) Creative Ed.

Philadelphia Phillies. (gr. 4-7). 1993. pap. 1.49 (*0-553-56425-0*) Bantam.

PHILANTHROPY

see Gifts; Social Work

PHILIP, DUKE OF EDINBRUGH, 1921-

Hamilton, Alan. Prince Philip. (Illus.). 64p. (gr. 5-9). 1991. 11.95 (*0-237-60012-9*, Pub. by Evans Bros Ltd) Trafalgar.

PHILIP, KING (METACOMET) SACHEM OF THE WAMPANOAGS, d. 1676

Fradin, Dennis B. King Philip: Indian Leader. LC 88-31344. (Illus.). 48p. (gr. 3-6). 1990. lib. bdg. 14.95 (*0-89490-231-8*) Enslow Pubs.

Roman, Joseph. King Philip. (Illus.). 112p. (gr. 5 up). 1992. lib. bdg. 17.95 (*0-7910-1704-4*) Chelsea Hse.

PHILIPPINE ISLANDS

Bailey, Donna & Sproule, Anna. Philippines. LC 90-9547. (Illus.). 32p. (gr. 1-4). 1990. PLB 18.99 (*0-8114-2564-9*); pap. 3.95 (*0-8114-7185-3*) Raintree Steck-V.

Harper, Peter & Peplow, Evelyn. Philippines Handbook. (Illus.). 596p. (Orig.). 1991. pap. 12.95 (*0-918373-62-X*) Moon Pubns CA.

Haskins, James. Corazon Aquino: Leader of the Philippines. LC 87-24440. (Illus.). 128p. (gr. 6 up). 1988. lib. bdg. 17.95 (*0-89490-152-4*) Enslow Pubs.

Lepthien, Emilie U. The Philippines. LC 83-23152. (Illus.). 128p. (gr. 5-9). 1986. PLB 20.55 (*0-516-02782-4*) Childrens.

—The Philippines. LC 93-15017. (Illus.). 48p. (gr. k-4). 1993. PLB 12.85 (*0-516-01195-2*); pap. 4.95 (*0-516-41195-0*) Childrens.

Lerner Publications, Department of Geography Staff, ed. Phillipines in Pictures. (Illus.). 64p. (gr. 5 up). 1989. PLB 17.50 (*0-8225-1863-5*) Lerner Pubns.

Nadel, Laurie. Corazon Aquino: Journey to Power. LC 86-33266. 93p. (gr. 6 up). 1987. lib. bdg. 13.98 (*0-671-63950-1*, J Messner) S&S Trade.

Nance, John. Lobo of the Tasaday: A Stone Age Boy Meets the Modern World. Nance, John, illus. LC 81-14113. 56p. (gr. 3-7). 1982. 9.95 (*0-394-85077-7*) Pantheon.

Ramos, Teresita V. & Clausen, Josie. Filipino Word Book. Betco, Boboy, illus. (ENG & ILO & TAG.). 112p. (gr. k-6). 1993. pap. 11.95 (*1-880188-44-9*) Bess Pr.

Stewart, Gail B. The Philippines. LC 91-11143. (Illus.). 48p. (gr. 6-7). 1991. text ed. 12.95 RSBE (*0-89686-659-9*, Crestwood Hse) Macmillan Child Grp.

Sullivan, Margaret. The Philippines: Pacific Crossroads. LC 92-37093. (Illus.). 128p. (gr. 4 up). 1993. text ed. 14.95 RSBE (*0-87518-548-7*, Dillon) Macmillan Child Grp.

Tope, Lily R. Philippines. LC 91-15855. (Illus.). 128p. (gr. 5-9). 1991. PLB 21.95 (*1-85435-403-5*) Marshall Cavendish.

Wheeler, Jill. Corazon Aquino. LC 91-73025. 202p. 1991. 12.94 (*1-56239-082-1*) Abdo & Dghtrs.

Willis, Doris. Teacher's Guide to Pearl Makers. Lansdale, Paul, illus. 64p. (Orig.). 1989. pap. 5.95 (*0-377-00194-5*) Friendship Pr.

PHILIPPINE ISLANDS–FICTION

Fuentes, Vilma M. Pearl Makers: Six Stories about Children in the Philippines. (Illus., Orig.). (gr. 1-6). 1989. 4.95 (*0-377-00191-0*) Friendship Pr.

Richardson, Arleta. Andrew's Secret. Payne, Peggy & Yoder, Tamra, eds. Secaur, Emiline, illus. 30p. (Orig.). (gr. 1-3). 1989. pap. 3.00 (*0-89367-143-6*) Light & Life.

PHILOLOGY

see Language and Languages

PHILOLOGY, COMPARATIVE

Here are entered comparative studies of languages. General works on the history, philosophy, origin, etc. of languages are entered under Language and Languages.

see also Language and Languages

PHILOSOPHERS

Ozmon, H. Twelve Great Western Philosophers. Steinbauer, S., illus. LC 68-16403. 48p. (gr. 4 up). 1967. PLB 9.95 (*0-87783-046-0*); pap. 3.94 deluxe ed (*0-87783-115-7*) Oddo.

Parker, Steve. Aristotle & Scientific Thought. LC 94-8263. 1994. write for info. (*0-7910-3004-0*) Chelsea Hse.

Roets, Lois. Philosophy & Philosophers. 52p. (gr. 5-12). 1994. pap. 8.00 tchr's. manual & text in 1 vol. (*0-911943-37-4*) Leadership Pub.

Russell, Bertrand. Bertrand Russell. Redpath, Ann, ed. Delessert, Etienne, illus. 32p. (gr. 9 up). 1986. PLB 12.95 (*0-88682-012-X*) Creative Ed.

PHILOSOPHY

see also Belief and Doubt; Ethics; God; Knowledge, Theory of; Logic; Mind and Body; Psychology; Universe also general subjects with the subdivision Philosophy, e.g. History–Philosophy, etc.

Bender, David L., ed. Constructing a Life Philosophy: Opposing Viewpoints. (Illus.). 264p. (gr. 10 up). 1993. PLB 17.95 (*0-89908-198-3*); pap. text ed. 9.95 (*0-89908-173-8*) Greenhaven.

Falcone, Vincent J. Great Thinkers, Great Ideas: An Introduction to Western Thought. 2nd ed. LC 92-7554. 288p. (gr. 12 up). 1992. pap. text ed. 9.95 (*0-9629323-1-0*) Cranbury Pubns.

Franco, Eloise. The Young Look. (Illus.). (gr. 3-7). 1979. pap. 5.95 (*0-87516-294-0*) DeVorss.

Lipman, Matthew. Kio & Gus. LC 79-9315. 77p. (gr. 3-4). 1982. pap. 9.00 (*0-916834-19-0*, TX942-173) Inst Advncmnt Philos Child.

—Pixie. LC 81-67706. 98p. (Orig.). (gr. 3-4). 1981. pap. 9.00 (*0-916834-17-4*, TX782-682) Inst Advncmnt Philos Child.

Provost, C. Antonio. Modern Renaissance Poetry & Philosophy. Kroll, William, ed. Forster, Maria, frwd. by. LC 92-96848. (Illus.). 148p. (gr. 9-12). 1992. 14.00 (*0-317-05253-5*); pap. 10.00 (*0-317-05254-3*) Provost.

Roets, Lois. Philosophy & Philosophers. 52p. (gr. 5-12). 1994. pap. 8.00 tchr's. manual & text in 1 vol. (*0-911943-37-4*) Leadership Pub.

Thayer, Eva. Adventures in the Land of Me. (Illus.). 65p. (Orig.). (gr. 4-8). 1989. pap. 5.95 wkbk. (*0-9616432-4-2*) TES Pub.

—Me Esteem Creates We Esteem. (Illus.). 70p. (Orig.). (gr. 7-12). 1990. pap. 5.95 wkbk. (*0-9616432-3-4*) TES Pub.

PHILOSOPHY–DICTIONARIES

Goodman, Florence J. A Young Person's Philosophical Dictionary. (gr. 5-12). 1978. pap. 9.95x (*0-917232-06-2*) Gee Tee Bee.

PHILOSOPHY, MODERN

see also Evolution; Existentialism

Hansen, Ellen, intro. by. The New England Transcendentalists: Life of the Mind & of the Spirit. (Illus.). 64p. (Orig.). (gr. 5-12). 1993. pap. 4.95 (*1-878668-22-6*) Disc Enter Ltd.

PHILOSOPHY, MORAL

see Ethics

PHILOSOPHY AND RELIGION

see also Religion–Philosophy

PHONETICS

see also Speech; Voice

Auld, Janice L. Cut & Paste Phonics: Extra Help for Troublesome Letter Combinations. (gr. 1-3). 1985. pap. 8.95 (*0-8224-5540-4*) Fearon Teach Aids.

Bachman, Barbara. Frisky Phonics Fun I. Bachman, Barbara, illus. 152p. (gr. 1-3). 1984. wkbk. 12.95 (*0-86653-195-5*, GA 548) Good Apple.

—Frisky Phonics Fun II. Bachman, Barbara, illus. 152p. (gr. 1-3). 1984. wkbk. 12.95 (*0-86653-212-9*, GA 549) Good Apple.

Block, Arlene. Phonics Consonants. Nayer, Judith E., ed. Schanzer, Roz, illus. 32p. (gr. k-1). 1991. wkbk. 1.95 (*1-878624-64-4*) McClanahan Bk.

Fields, Harriette. Phonics for the New Reader: Step-by-Step. Cox, Anne, illus. LC 90-70334. 128p. (Orig.). (ps-2). 1991. 17.95x (*0-9625802-0-1*); pap. 8.95 (*0-9625802-1-X*) Words Pub CO. "The author provides a ready-to-use blueprint for helping young children understand phonics & provides the necessary tools for that understanding," says former President of the National Association of State Boards of Education, Roseann Bentley. "This book provides clear, well-organized directions, & I think this would be an excellent book for people striving to learn English as a second language." TABLE OF CONTENTS: Lesson 1- Letter Names, Shapes & Sounds; Lesson 2- Short Vowels; Lesson 3- Long Vowels; Lesson 4- Special Words & Letters; Lesson 5- Reading Consonant Combinations; Lesson 6- Reading Vowel Combinations; Lesson 7- Special Vowel Combinations; Lesson 8- Reading Vowel-Consonant Combinations.

Publisher Provided Annotation.

Foltzer, Monica. Professor Phonics Gives Sound Advice. 12th ed. Hoffmann, Jo-Ann, illus. 1990. pap. text ed. 6.80 (*0-9607918-0-9*, A 505419) St Ursula. PROFESSOR PHONICS GIVES SOUND ADVICE, the primary book, is unique in that it has the only totally organized phonics system. All of the consonant sounds are taught around four categories of vowels. It is so streamlined that all 42 basic sounds are taught on 23 pages interspersed with practice pages. Sounds arranged in more difficult spelling patterns follow. A SOUND TRACK TO READING has exactly the same format but starts with two-syllable words. All the basic sounds are taught on 14 pages. This advanced book is not geared for intermediate grades & up. Phonics is NOT reading. It is reading's only sure foundation for unlocking unknown words. The system also contains 38 PICTURE KEY WORD CARDS, MANUALS & a SPELLING WORD LIST. At the end of the year, first graders can spell 1500 words without memorizing. Taking regular spelling first helps greatly. The ten percent of non-phonetic words then fall into place. Systematic, intensive phonics should be taught first & fast before sight words are introduced because all one does is slide sounds together. Anyone can teach another to read in this manner if one has an organized system. As Mary Pride says in her New Big Book Of Home Learning, "The program author really knows her stuff."
Publisher Provided Annotation.

—Spelling Phonics Gives Sound Advice. 5th ed. 16p. 1984. pap. text ed. 1.20x (*0-9607918-2-5*, 801878) St Ursula.

Hilderbrand, Karen M. & Thompson, Kim M. Rhythm, Rhyme & Read: Phonics. 64p. (gr. 3). 1992. wkbk. 6.99 (*0-9632249-0-5*) Twin Sisters.

Hill, Charlotte M. Wee Folks Moving Up: A Phonetic Approach to Beginning Reading. Shortridge, Cleona, intro. by. Jefferson, Sharon & Fields, Theodore, illus. LC 91-70303. (Orig.). (gr. k-3). 1991. pap. text ed. 7.95 (*0-9620182-5-2*) Charill Pubs.

—Wee Folks Readers: A Phonetic Approach to Beginning Reading, 5 vols. Shortridge, Cleona, ed. Fields, Theodore, et al, illus. LC 90-832256. 70p. (Orig.). (gr. k-5). 1992. Set. pap. write for info. (*0-9620182-9-5*) Charill Pubs.
This five volume reading series is an eclectic approach to beginning reading. Phonics is introduced in story form, lending itself to building comprehension, skills & simultaneously, sight words to build vocabulary as well. Each sound is introduced with illustrations that represent that sound. Books One through Four teach the vowel sounds & this teaching of sounds in context allows for the immediate application of phonetic skills learned. This approach follows the principle of use & reinforcement. Book Five, "Wee Folks on Top" (Adventures in Reading), contains stories, fables & poetry with follow-up questions to improve comprehension. A bookstore owner & mother of a six year old daughter who lives in San Antonio, Texas, wrote, "My daughter was reading the first hour after I started her in Book I. I called relatives all over the country to tell them that she was reading." A director of a Prep School in Seattle, Washington, writes, "Your reading series is excellent. I am an experienced teacher & have always believed that a phonics based reading program is the best way to teach reading."
Publisher Provided Annotation.

—Wee Folks Soaring High: A Phonetic Approach to Beginning Reading. Shortridge, Cleona, ed. LC 91-73581. (Illus.). 101p. (Orig.). (gr. k-3). 1992. pap. text ed. 7.95 (*0-9620182-6-0*) Charill Pubs.

Kirsten, Suzanne. Begin with Phonics. Kahn, Betsey, ed. LC 81-85695. (Illus.). 80p. (Orig.). (gr. 1-4). 1982. pap. 4.95 (*0-89709-033-0*) Liberty Pub.

Lockhart, Charlotte F. Discover Intensive Phonics for Yourself. rev. ed. Griffin, Glen C., frwd. by. LC 83-71502. 452p. 1983. tchrs. ed. 49.95 (*0-9605654-1-8*) Char-L.

Messick, Linda S. Through My Day with the 'L' Sound. (Illus.). 120p. (Orig.). (gr. k-6). 1975. pap. text ed. 7.95x (*0-87015-212-2*) Pacific Bks.

—Through My Day with the 'S' Sound. (Illus.). 120p. (Orig.). (gr. k-6). 1975. pap. text ed. 7.95x (*0-87015-214-9*) Pacific Bks.

—Through My Day with the 'SH' Sound. (Illus.). 112p. (Orig.). (gr. k-6). 1975. pap. text ed. 7.95x (*0-87015-215-7*) Pacific Bks.

Moncure, Jane B. Word Bird Makes Words with Pig. LC 83-23945. (Illus.). 32p. (gr. k-2). 1984. PLB 14.95 (*0-89565-262-5*) Childs World.

Reichenberg, Monte. Sam, Old Kate & I. Brasch, Susan, illus. 32p. (Orig.). (ps-4). 1994. pap. 3.00 (*0-9640260-2-3*) MM & I Ink.
"Learning should be fun," says author Monte Reichenberg, "and that is precisely why I wrote SAM, OLD KATE & I & its companion book CHEATING CHET." SAM, OLD KATE & I is a delightfully illustrated children's story & activity book which uses various rhyming "A" words in a humorous story line. This whole language concept allows beginning readers to actually see the difference between words with long & short "A" sounds & the second rhyming word has blanks with a starter letter to encourage student creativity & develop rhyming skills. The author, who is approved as an Artist-in-the-Schools in Nebraska & Kansas, has successfully used SAM, OLD KATE & I at all grade levels, not only to get students excited about reading & writing poetry & stories, but also to demonstrate the ease with which they can be written. Fast paced & entertaining, SAM, OLD KATE & I will encourage & excite even the most ardent anti-readers. Wholesale discount rates are available to Teachers/schools making volume purchases. Dealer/distributor inquiries welcome. SAM, OLD KATE & I, 32 pages with illustrations. $3.00 each to M M & I Ink, Rt. 1, Box 432, Bayard, NE 69334.
Publisher Provided Annotation.

Schaffer, Frank, Publications Staff. Getting Ready for Phonics. (Illus.). 24p. (ps-k). 1980. wkbk. 3.98 (*0-86734-018-5*, FS-3031) Schaffer Pubns.

—Phonics: Consonants. (Illus.). 24p. (ps-2). 1978. wkbk. 3.98 (*0-86734-003-7*, FS-3004) Schaffer Pubns.

—Phonics: Vowels. (Illus.). 24p. (gr. 1-3). 1978. wkbk. 3.98 (*0-86734-004-5*, FS-3005) Schaffer Pubns.

Sunrise Phonics. (gr. k-2). 1992. pap. write for info. Charlesbridge Pub.

Taulbee, Annette. Phonics. (Illus.). 24p. (ps-k). 1986. 3.98 (*0-86734-066-5*, FS-3058) Schaffer Pubns.

Thompson, Kim M. & Hilderbrand, Karen M. Phonics. Kuzjak, Goran, illus. 24p. (gr. k-3). 1993. wkbk. incl. audiocassette 9.98 (*1-882331-23-0*, TWIN 405) Twin Sisters.

—Rhythm, Rhyme & Read Twinset: Rhonics. Kuzjak, Goran, illus. 64p. (gr. k-3). 1993. pap. 14.99 wkbk. incl. audiocassette & poster (*1-882331-07-9*, TWIN 305) Twin Sisters.

Welsh, Patricia A. It's My Phonics Book. 72p. (gr. 1-2). 1981. wkbk. 4.95 (*1-884620-03-5*) PAW Prods.

Wise, Beth A. Letters & Sounds. Nayer, Judith E., ed. Regan, Dana & DeMarco, Susanne, illus. 32p. (gr. k-1). 1991. wkbk. 1.95 (*1-878624-60-1*) McClanahan Bk.

Wise, Beth A. & Block, Arlene. Phonics Vowels. Nayer, Judith E., ed. Sims, Deborah & Lustig, Loretta, illus. 32p. (gr. k-1). 1991. wkbk. 1.95 (*1-878624-65-2*) McClanahan Bk.

Wise, Beth A. & Sokoloff, Myka-Lynne. Key Words to Reading. Nayer, Judith E., ed. Beckes, Shirley, illus. 32p. (gr. k-1). 1991. wkbk. 1.95 (*1-878624-61-X*) McClanahan Bk.

PHONICS
see Phonetics

PHONOGRAPH
see also Sound–Recording and Reproducing

Laufer, Diana. Hide 'n' Seek Friends. Laufer, Diana, illus. 12p. (ps-2). 1994. lift-the-flap 10.95 (*0-8431-3591-3*) Price Stern.

Steffens, Bradley. Phonograph: Sound on Disk. LC 92-27850. (Illus.). 96p. (gr. 5-8). 1992. PLB 15.95 (*1-56006-222-3*) Lucent Bks.

PHONOLOGY
see Phonetics

PHOTOGRAPHERS

Cech, John. Jacques-Henri Lartigue: Boy with a Camera. LC 94-10210. (gr. 1-4). 1994. 15.95 (*0-02-718136-7*, Four Winds) Macmillan Child Grp.

Freedman, Russell. Kids at Work: Lewis Hine & the Crusade Against Child Labor. Hine, Lewis, photos by. LC 93-5989. (Illus.). 1994. 16.95 (*0-395-58703-4*, Clarion Bks) HM.

Gherman, Beverly. Georgia O'Keefe: The "Wideness & Wonder" of Her World. LC 85-26860. (Illus.). 144p. (gr. 4 up). 1986. SBE 13.95 (*0-689-31164-8*, Atheneum Child Bk) Macmillan Child Grp.

Jann, Gayle. A Day in the Life of a Photographer. Jann, Gayle, illus. LC 87-13751. 32p. (gr. 4-8). 1988. PLB 11.79 (*0-8167-1123-2*); pap. text ed. 2.95 (*0-8167-1124-0*) Troll Assocs.

Keller, Emily. Margaret Bourke-White: A Photographer's Life. LC 92-44382. (gr. 4-9). 1993. 21.50 (*0-8225-4916-6*) Lerner Pubns.

Lawlor, Laurie. Shadow Catcher: The Life & Work of Edward Sherriff Curtis. LC 93-40272. 1994. 16.95 (*0-8027-8288-4*); PLB 17.85 (*0-8027-8289-2*) Walker & Co.

Turner, Robyn M. Dorothea Lange. LC 93-42573. (gr. 1-5). 1994. 15.95 (*0-316-85656-8*) Little.

Wolf, Sylvia. Focus: Five Women Photographers. Levine, Abby, ed. LC 94-1416. (Illus.). 64p. (gr. 4 up). 1994. PLB 18.95 (*0-8075-2531-6*) A Whitman.

PHOTOGRAPHY
see also Cameras; Nature Study

Ancona, George. My Camera. LC 91-2288. (Illus.). 48p. (Orig.). (gr. 2-7). 1992. PLB 15.99 (*0-517-58280-5*); pap. 8.99 (*0-517-58279-1*) Crown Bks Yng Read.

Collins, Kevin & Collins, Betty. Experimenting with Science Photography. LC 93-31074. (Illus.). (gr. 9-12). 1994. PLB 13.90 (*0-531-11166-0*) Watts.

Czaja, Paul C. Writing with Light: A Simple Workshop in Basic Photography. LC 72-93261. 96p. (gr. 6 up). 1973. 12.95 (*0-85699-068-X*) Chatham Pr.

Eastman Kodak Company Staff, ed. Hot Shots (AC-210) LC 91-71095. 48p. (Orig.). (gr. 7-12). text ed. 2.00 (*0-87985-745-5*) Saunders Photo.

Evans, Art. First Photos: How Kids Can Take Great Pictures. LC 92-50482. (Illus.). 64p. (Orig.). (gr. 3-12). 1993. pap. 9.95 perfect bdg. (*0-9626508-7-0*) Photo Data Res.

Gleason, Roger. Seeing for Yourself: Techniques & Projects for Beginning Photographers. (Illus.). 176p. (gr. 9-12). 1992. pap. 14.95 (*1-55652-159-6*) Chicago Review.

Jeunesse, Gallimard, et al, eds. The Camera: Snapshots, Movies, Videos, & Cartoons. Valat, Pierre-Marie, illus. LC 92-41412. 1993. 11.95 (*0-590-47129-5*) Scholastic Inc.

Kohn, Eugene. Photography: A Manual for Shutterbugs. Plasencia, Peter P., illus. Noa, Pedro A., photos by. (Illus.). (gr. 3-7). 1965. pap. 1.25 (*0-685-03891-2*) P-H.

Langford, Michael. Starting Photography. 2nd ed. LC 93-17759. (Illus.). 160p. (gr. 7 up). 1993. pap. 19.95 (*0-240-51348-7*, Focal) Buttrwrth-Heinemann.

Mitchell, Barbara. Click! A Story about George Eastman. Hosking-Smith, Jan, illus. 64p. (gr. 3-6). 1986. PLB 14.95 (*0-87614-289-7*) Carolrhoda Bks.

Morgan, Terri. Photography: Terri Morgan. 1991. pap. 8.95 (*0-8225-9605-9*) Lerner Pubns.

Morgan, Terri & Thaler, Shmuel. Photography: Take Your Best Shot. 80p. (gr. 5 up). 1991. PLB 19.95 (*0-8225-2302-7*) Lerner Pubns.

Moss, Miriam. Fashion Photographer. LC 90-15059. (Illus.). 32p. (gr. 5-6). 1991. text ed. 13.95 RSBE (*0-89686-608-4*, Crestwood Hse) Macmillan Child Grp.

Noonan, Diana. Shooting It Straight. LC 93-21248. 1994. 4.25 (*0-383-03731-X*) SRA Schl Grp.

Peach, S. & Butterfield, M. Photography. (Illus.). 48p. (gr. 6 up). 1987. PLB 14.96 (*0-88110-292-X*); pap. 7.95 (*0-7460-0107-X*) EDC.

Photography. (Illus.). 64p. (gr. 6-12). 1983. pap. 1.85 (*0-8395-3334-9*, 33334) BSA.
Steffens, Bradley. Photography: Preserving the Past. LC 91-15570. (Illus.). 96p. (gr. 5-8). 1991. PLB 15.95 (*1-56006-212-6*) Lucent Bks.
Stokes. The Photography Book. 1992. 5.95 (*0-590-45257-6*) Scholastic Inc.
Wilson, Keith. Photography. LC 93-11574. (Illus.). 80p. (gr. 5 up). 1994. 15.00 (*0-679-83443-5*) Random Bks Yng Read.
Yee, Kal. Perfect Face. 96p. 1994. 45.00 (*0-9631574-1-8*) Sec Glance.

PHOTOGRAPHY, ARTISTIC

Avery, Charles. Everybody Has Feelings - Todos Tenemos Sentimientos: The Moods of Children As Photographed by Charles E. Avery. Marulanda, Sandra, tr. (ENG & SPA., Illus.). 48p. (gr. k-8). 1992. 14.95 (*0-940880-33-4*) Open Hand.
Hoban, Tana. Shadows & Reflections. LC 89-30461. (Illus.). 32p. (ps up). 1990. 12.95 (*0-688-07089-2*); lib. bdg. 12.88 (*0-688-07090-6*) Greenwillow.
Lynch, Marietta & Perry, Patricia. No More Monkeys: A Photographic Version of the Children's Finger Game. (Orig.). (ps-3). pap. 2.95 (*0-9610962-0-9*) M Lynch.
Sodeika, Zita. Caged-In. Kezys, Algimantas, photos by. 94p. (Orig.). 1992. pap. 15.00 (*0-685-59569-2*) Galerija.

PHOTOGRAPHY–ESTHETICS

see Photography, Artistic

PHOTOGRAPHY–FICTION

Calvert, Patricia. Yesterday's Daughter. LC 86-13753. 144p. (gr. 7 up). 1986. SBE 13.95 (*0-684-18746-9*, Scribners Young Read) Macmillan Child Grp.
Cartwright, Pauline. Taking Our Photo. Strahan, Heather, illus. LC 92-31950. 1993. 3.75 (*0-383-03595-3*) SRA Schl Grp.
Castle, Caroline. Grandpa Baxter & the Photographs. Bowman, Peter, illus. LC 92-44192. 32p. (ps-1). 1993. 14.95 (*0-531-05487-X*); PLB 14.99 (*0-531-08637-2*) Orchard Bks Watts.
Essley, Roger. Paul's Fantastic Photos. LC 93-12035. (ps-6). 1994. 16.00 (*0-671-86722-9*, S&S BFYR) S&S Trade.
LeMieux, A. C. The TV Guidance Counselor. LC 92-33664. 240p. (gr. 7 up). 1993. 13.00 (*0-688-12402-X*, Tambourine Bks) Morrow.
Levoy, Myron. Pictures of Adam. LC 92-24598. 224p. (gr. 7 up). 1993. pap. 4.95 (*0-688-11941-7*, Pub. by Beech Tree Bks) Morrow.
Light, John. Snap Happy. LC 91-36610. (gr. 4 up). 1991. 3.95 (*0-85953-504-5*) Childs Play.
Weiss, Monica. Snap! Charlie Gets the Whole Picture: Getting the Main Idea. Berlin, Rosemary, illus. LC 91-16499. (gr. k-2). 1992. PLB 10.59 (*0-8167-2494-6*); pap. 2.95 (*0-8167-2495-4*) Troll Assocs.
Willard, Nancy. Simple Pictures Are Best. De Paola, Tomie, illus. LC 78-6424. 32p. (ps-3). 1978. pap. 3.95 (*0-15-682625-9*, Voyager Bks) HarBrace.

PHOTOGRAPHY–HISTORY

Wakin, Edward & Wakin, Daniel. Photos That Made U. S. History: From the Cold War to the Space Age, Vol. II. (Illus.). 59p. (gr. 4-7). 1993. 12.95 (*0-8027-8270-1*); PLB 13.85 (*0-8027-8272-8*) Walker & Co.
—Photos That Made U. S. History: From the Civil War to the Atomic Age, Vol. I. (Illus.). 64p. (gr. 4-7). 1993. 12.95 (*0-8027-8230-2*); PLB 13.85 (*0-8027-8231-0*) Walker & Co.

PHOTOGRAPHY–VOCATIONAL GUIDANCE

Henderson, Kathy. Market Guide for Young Artists & Photographers. LC 90-39084. (Illus.). 176p. (Orig.). (gr. 3 up). 1990. pap. 12.95 (*1-55870-176-1*, 70068) Shoe Tree Pr.

PHOTOGRAPHY OF ANIMALS

see also Animal Painting and Illustration

Arrabito, James. Cameras at the Zoo. Glaser, Mary J., illus. 16p. (Orig.). (gr. 3-10). 1991. pap. 4.95 (*0-9622596-0-8*) Arraster Pub.
Baruch, Jacques-Olivier. Incredibly Fast. LC 93-462. (Illus.). 48p. (gr. 6 up). 1993. text ed. 14.95 RSBE (*0-02-708435-3*, New Discovery Bks) Macmillan Child Grp.
Campbell, John C. Two Dogs Plus. Cunningham, Imogen & Richardson, David, illus. 95p. (Orig.). (gr. 8 up). 1984. pap. text ed. 9.95 (*0-9613596-0-9*); pap. 7.95 (*0-685-09160-0*) Deer Creek Pr.
Lasky, Kathryn. Think Like an Eagle: At Work with a Wildlife Photographer. Knight, Christopher G. & Swedberg, Jack, photos by. (Illus.). 48p. (gr. 3 up). 1992. 15.95 (*0-316-51519-1*, Joy St Bks) Little.

PHOTOGRAPHY OF NATURE

see Nature Photography

PHOTOSYNTHESIS

Asimov, Isaac. How Did We Find out about Photosynthesis. Kors, Erika, illus. 32p. (gr. 1-4). 1989. 11.95 (*0-8027-6899-7*); PLB 12.85 (*0-8027-6886-5*) Walker & Co.
Nakatani, Herbert Y. Photosynthesis. Head, J. J., ed. Steffen, Ann T., illus. LC 84-45838. 16p. (Orig.). (gr. 10 up). 1988. pap. text ed. 2.75 (*0-89278-109-2*, 45-9793) Carolina Biological.

PHYSICAL CULTURE

see Physical Education and Training

PHYSICAL EDUCATION AND TRAINING

see also Athletics; Coaching (Athletics); Exercise; Games; Gymnastics; Health Education; Physical Fitness; Sports; also names of kinds of exercises, e.g. Fencing; Judo

Black, John & Evans, Patrick. John Black Presents Power Build. (Illus.). 92p. 1990. pap. 9.95 (*0-929994-05-1*) Crains Muscle.
Heron, Jackie. Careers in Health & Fitness. rev. ed. Rosen, Ruth, ed. (Illus.). 160p. (gr. 7 up). 1990. 14.95 (*0-8239-1162-4*) Rosen Group.
Isberg, Emily. Peak Performance. (gr. 3 up). 1989. (S&S BFYR); pap. 5.95 (*0-671-67745-4*, S&S BFYR) S&S Trade.
Jarrell, Steve. Working Out with Weights. LC 77-1919. (gr. 8 up). 1984. P-H.
Ponce, Omar. Educate para una Mejor Condicion Fisica: Guia Basica para el Desarrollo de un Programa de Eficiencia Fisica. Figueroa, Ivelisse, illus. (SPA.). 75p. (Orig.). 1986. write for info. B Ponce.
Savage, Jeff. Weight Lifting. LC 93-27211. (gr. 6 up). 1995. text ed. 13.95 (*0-89686-856-7*) MacMillan Child Grp.
Shiffer, Eric. Pumping Iron for Teenage Guys. (Orig.). 1987. pap. 6.95 (*0-449-90187-4*, Columbine) Fawcett.
Stillwell, Jim. The Perceptual-Motor Activities Book. Gimlin, Rick & Kamiya, Artie, illus. 96p. (Orig.). (gr. k-6). 1990. pap. 10.00 (*0-945872-05-4*) Great Activities Pub Co.

PHYSICAL FITNESS

Crelinsten, J. To the Limit. 1992. write for info. (*0-15-200616-8*, Gulliver Bks) HarBrace.
Diet & Exercise. (Illus.). (gr. 5 up). 1987. lib. bdg. 15.94 (*0-86625-280-0*); 11.95s.p. (*0-685-73926-0*) Rourke Corp.
Erson, Tim. Courageous Pacers: The Complete Guide to Running, Walking & Fitness for Kids (Ages 8-108) Diaz, Michael A., illus. 264p. (Orig.). (gr. 2 up). 1993. Incl. logbook & journal. 18.95 (*0-9636547-0-5*) PRO-ACTIV Pubns.
Fraser, K. & Tatchell, J. Fitness & Health. (Illus.). 48p. (gr. 6-10). 1987. PLB 13.96 (*0-88110-234-2*); pap. 6.95 (*0-7460-0004-9*) EDC.
Grubbs, J. Muscle Building. Abel, J., illus. 36p. 1992. pap. 15.00 (*1-56611-010-6*) Jonas.
Hyman, Jane & Millen-Posner, Barbara. The Fitness Book: The Diet & Exercise Book. Barish, Wendy, ed. (Illus.). 192p. (Orig.). (gr. 5 up). 1984. PLB 9.49 (*0-685-09179-1*) S&S Trade.
Maitland, William J. Weight Training for Gifted Athletes. Mollen, Art, intro. by. LC 89-90833. (Illus.). 147p. (Orig.). (gr. 8 up). 1990. pap. 17.95 (*0-936759-01-1*) Maitland Enter.
Martinez, Alicia. Feeling Fit. Richey, Donald, illus. LC 90-10864. 128p. (gr. 5-9). 1991. PLB 10.89 (*0-8167-2140-8*); pap. text ed. 2.95 (*0-8167-2141-6*) Troll Assocs.
Nelson, JoAnne. Feeling Fit, That's It! McKinnell, Michael, illus. LC 92-37719. 1994. pap. 5.95 (*0-935529-58-6*) Comprehen Health Educ.
Perry, Susan. Getting in Step. (Illus.). (gr. 2-6). 1992. PLB 14.95 (*0-89565-872-0*) Childs World.
Personal Fitness. (Illus.). 64p. (gr. 6-12). 1990. pap. 1.85 (*0-8395-3286-5*, 33286) BSA.
Reef, Catherine. Stay Fit: Build a Strong Body. LC 93-19349. 64p. (gr. 4-7). 1993. 15.95 (*0-8050-2441-7*) TFC Bks NY.
Roberts, Alison J. Fun with Fitness. Hayes, Dympna, ed. Mansfield, Renee & Pawczuk, Eugene, illus. 32p. (gr. 2). 1987. PLB 14.97 (*0-88625-167-2*); pap. 2.95 (*0-88625-157-5*) Durkin Hayes Pub.
Rosenholtz, Stephen. Move Like the Animals. Yoshiko, Fujita, illus. LC 91-66970. 32p. (ps-3). 1992. incl. cassette 19.95 (*0-9630979-1-1*); pap. 14.95 incl. cassette (*0-9630979-0-3*) Rosewd Pubns.
Savage, Jeff. Aerobics. LC 93-37296. 1995. text ed. 13.95 (*0-89686-853-2*, Crestwood Hse) Macmillan Child Grp.
Schade, Charlene. Move with Me One Two Three. Ziebarth, Pat, ed. Pileggi, Steve, illus. Senter, Sheri, intro. by. (Illus.). 58p. (Orig.). (ps-1). 1988. Includes audio cassette. 16.90 (*0-924860-00-6*) Exer Fun Pub.
Schwarzenegger, Arnold & Gaines, Charles. Arnold's Fitness for Kids: A Guide to Health, Exercise, & Nutrition. LC 92-28577. (gr. 1-5). 1993. 15.00 (*0-385-42267-9*) Doubleday.
—Arnold's Fitness for Kids Ages Eleven to Fourteen: A Guide to Health, Exercise, & Nutrition. LC 92-26786. (gr. 6-8). 1993. 15.00 (*0-385-42268-7*) Doubleday.
Sheehan, Angela, ed. Encyclopedia of Health, 14 vols. LC 89-17336. (Illus.). 900p. (gr. 4-8). 1991. PLB 299.95x (*1-85435-203-2*) Marshall Cavendish.

Silkwood, Chris & Levicki, Nancy. Awesome Teen. Schwarzenegger, Arnold, frwd. by. (Illus.). 140p. (Orig.). (gr. 8-12). 1991. pap. 11.95 (*0-9631318-0-X*) NJL Interests. The topic on a recent TV show was obese children. The startling statistic, 1 out of 5 children are obese children, was over-shadowed by the alarming increase in obese children (54% over the last ten years). AWESOME TEEN is a fitness guide that teenagers can read & use to make positive changes in their life style. Arnold Schwarzenegger wrote the foreword for this book for boys & girls ages 12-18. Arnold has this to say: "This book is an excellent example of the grassroots effort & support that is so needed in this country if we are to reverse the decline in youth fitness." AWESOME TEEN is candidly written in teen vernacular. The authors' use of photographs of teens exercising along with charts the readers can use to plan their fitness routine make this book "user friendly." A section on food choices includes "smart choice" recipes, simple in preparation & written so the teen can prepare the recipes. Linda Johnson, a high school teacher in the Houston Independent School District, has this to say about AWESOME TEEN: "I've taught nutrition & exercise to students & had to obtain information from several sources. Now I have it all in one book! The point system is a great motivator." To order, please contact NJL Interests 713-780-1268.
Publisher Provided Annotation.

Simon, Nissa. Good Sports: Plain Talk about Health & Fitness for Teens. Tobin, Patricia, illus. LC 89-78556. 128p. (gr. 7 up). 1990. 13.95 (*0-690-04902-1*, Crowell Jr Bks); PLB 13.89 (*0-690-04904-8*, Crowell Jr Bks) HarpC Child Bks.
Time-Life Books Editors. Super Firm: Tough Workouts. (Illus.). 144p. 1989. 17.27 (*0-8094-6134-X*); lib. bdg. 23.27 (*0-8094-6135-8*) Time-Life.
—Walking & Running. (Illus.). 144p. 1989. 17.27 (*0-8094-6130-7*); lib. bdg. 23.27 (*0-8094-6131-5*) Time-Life.
Vitkus, Jessica. Beauty & Fitness with "Saved by the Bell" LC 91-42583. (Illus.). 64p. (Orig.). (gr. 5 up). 1992. pap. 6.95 (*0-02-045425-2*, Collier Young Ad) Macmillan Child Grp.
Wood, Bill. Marty the Marathon Bear. Kaluza, Mary K. & Carreiro, Bob, illus. Kauffman, Helen, photos by. 136p. (Orig.). (gr. 3-7). 1988. pap. text ed. 6.95 (*0-317-93376-0*) Rallysport Video Prodns.
Zeldis, Yona. Coping with Beauty, Fitness & Fashion. Rosen, Ruth, ed. Daven, Douglas, illus. LC 86-24850. 128p. (gr. 7 up). 1987. PLB 14.95 (*0-8239-0731-7*) Rosen Group.

PHYSICAL GEOGRAPHY

see also Climate; Earth; Earthquakes; Geophysics; Glaciers; Ice; Icebergs; Lakes; Meteorology; Mountains; Ocean; Rivers; Tides; Volcanoes; Winds

Jessop, Joanne. Planet Earth. Wood, Gerald, illus. LC 93-28339. 1994. PLB 19.97 (*0-8114-9244-3*) Raintree Steck-V.

McNeil, Mary. Earth Sciences Reference. 709p. (gr. 6 up). 1991. 55.00 (*0-938905-00-7*); pap. 49.00 (*0-938905-01-5*) Flamingo Pr. CHOICE notes that, "There is no other single volume that combines the wealth of knowledge found in this work...Definitions are concise but informative & they are indexed geographically & by subject... Appropriate...especially for those libraries with small earth science collections or tight budgets." October, 1991. LIBRARY JOURNAL: "McNeil's bibliography of books & journal articles published through 1990 is exhaustive. Special emphasis has been given to the Southern Hemisphere since it has often been underrepresented. Appropriate for large public or academic library reference collections...More detailed coverage of earth science than a multi-volume encyclopedia." June 1, 1991. The reference has been found useful for curriculum development from middle school to college level. To order: Flamingo Press, 2956 Roosevelt St., Carlsbad, CA 92008; 619-471-8705 or FAX 619-279-0357.
Publisher Provided Annotation.

Morris, Scott, ed. The Physical World. De Blij, Harm J., intro. by. LC 92-22285. (Illus.). 1993. 15.95 (*0-7910-1801-6*, Am Art Analog); pap. write for info. (*0-7910-1814-8*, Am Art Analog) Chelsea Hse.

Seddon, Tony & Bailey, Jill. Physical World. LC 87-6855. (Illus.). 160p. (gr. 3 up). 1987. 12.95 (*0-385-24179-8*) Doubleday.

PHYSICAL STAMINA

see Physical Fitness

PHYSICAL THERAPY–VOCATIONAL GUIDANCE

Paige, David. A Day in the Life of a Sports Therapist. Ruhlin, Roger, illus. LC 84-2433. 32p. (gr. 4-8). 1985. PLB 11.79 (*0-8167-0099-0*); pap. text ed. 2.95 (*0-8167-0100-8*) Troll Assocs.

PHYSICAL TRAINING

see Physical Education and Training

PHYSICALLY HANDICAPPED

see also Blind; Deaf

Alexander, Sally. Mom Can't See Me. Ancona, George, illus. LC 89-13241. 48p. (gr. 1-5). 1990. RSBE 14.95 (*0-02-700401-5*, Macmillan Child Bk) Macmillan Child Grp.

Alexander, Sally H. Taking Hold: My Journey into Blindness. LC 94-12302. (gr. 5 up). 1994. 13.95 (*0-02-700402-3*) Macmillan Child Grp.

Bergman, Thomas. On Our Own Terms: Children Living with Physical Handicaps. LC 88-42973. (Illus.). 48p. (gr. 4-5). 1989. PLB 18.60 (*1-55532-942-X*) Gareth Stevens Inc.

Bernstein, Joanne E. & Fireside, Bryna. Special Parents, Special Children. Mathews, Judith, ed. Bernstein, Michael, photos by. LC 90-42442. (Illus.). 64p. (gr. 3-7). 1991. 11.95 (*0-8075-7559-3*) A Whitman.

Berry, Joy. About Physical Disabilities. Bartholomew, illus. 48p. (gr. 3 up). 1990. PLB 12.30 (*0-516-02954-1*) Childrens.

Boy Scouts of America. Handicap Awareness. (Illus.). 48p. (gr. 6-12). 1981. pap. 1.85 (*0-8395-3370-5*, 33370) BSA.

Brearley, Sue. Adventure Holiday. Mathews, Jenny, photos by. (Illus.). 28p. (gr. 1-4). 1991. 12.95 (*0-7136-3382-4*, Pub. by A&C Black UK) Talman.

Buckman, Mary. Ben. Morgan, Connie, illus. 32p. (gr. k-5). 1992. pap. 8.95 (*1-879414-09-0*) Mary Bee Creat.

Chaney, Sky & Fisher, Pam, eds. The Discovery Book: A Helpful Guide for the World Written by Children with Disabilities. rev. ed. (Illus.). 100p. (gr. 3-10). 1989. pap. 7.95 (*0-9616891-1-0*) UCPANB.

Craymer, Sally. There's a Blue Square on My Brother's School Bus. LC 92-61768. (Illus.). 59p. (Orig.). (gr. k-2). 1992. pap. 4.95x (*0-931563-12-7*) Wishing Rm.

Exley, Helen. What It's Like to Be Me. 2nd ed. (Illus.). 127p. (gr. 4-11). 1984. pap. 10.95 (*0-377-00144-9*) Friendship Pr.

Fox, C. Lynn. Handicapped...How Does It Feel: Activity Packet. Lovelady, Janet, ed. Button, Mary, illus. 48p. (gr. k-12). 1982. pap. 5.95 (*0-935266-13-5*, BW6613-5) B L Winch.

Hunter, Edith F. Child of the Silent Night. Holmes, Bea, illus. LC 94-26217. 1995. pap. write for info. (*0-688-13794-6*) Morrow.

Miller, Mark S. The Physically Handicapped. (Illus.). (gr. 6-12). 1994. 19.95 (*0-7910-0073-7*, Am Art Analog); pap. write for info. (*0-7910-0500-3*) Chelsea Hse.

Peterson, Jeanne W. I Have a Sister, My Sister Is Deaf. Ray, Deborah K., illus. LC 76-24306. (gr. k-3). 1977. PLB 13.89 (*0-06-024702-9*) HarpC Child Bks.

Powers, Mary E. Our Teacher's in a Wheelchair. Tucker, Kathleen, ed. Powers, Mary E., illus. LC 86-1623. 32p. (ps-3). 1986. 11.95 (*0-8075-6240-8*) A Whitman.

Richmond, Sandra. Wheels for Walking. Kroupa, Melanie, ed. LC 85-70855. 196p. (gr. 6 up). 1985. 13.95 (*0-316-74439-5*, Joy St Bks) Little.

Sirof, Harriet. The Road Back: Living with a Physical Disability. LC 92-43581. 160p. (gr. 6 up). 1993. text ed. 13.95 RSBE (*0-02-782885-9*, New Discovery Bks) Macmillan Child Grp.

Stein, Sara B. About Handicaps. LC 73-15270. (Illus.). 48p. (ps-8). 1984. pap. 8.95 (*0-8027-7225-0*) Walker & Co.

—About Handicaps. LC 73-15270. (Illus.). 48p. (gr. 1 up). 1974. 12.95 (*0-8027-6174-7*) Walker & Co.

PHYSICALLY HANDICAPPED–BIOGRAPHY

Gibson, William. The Miracle Worker. (gr. 6-9). 1984. pap. 4.50 (*0-553-24778-6*) Bantam.

Greene, Carol. Margarete Steiff: Toy Maker. LC 93-16855. (Illus.). 48p. (gr. k-3). 1993. PLB 12.85 (*0-516-04257-2*); pap. 4.95 (*0-516-44257-0*) Childrens.

Hafford, Jeannette N. Tiny Goes to the Doctor. 48p. (Orig.). (gr. 3-8). 1990. pap. write for info. Tinys Self Help Bks.

McDaniel, Melissa. Stephen Hawking: Physicist. (Illus.). 1994. 18.95 (*0-7910-2078-9*, Am Art Analog) Chelsea Hse.

MacDonald, W. Scott & Oden, Chester W., Jr. Moose: The Story of a Very Special Person. 2nd ed. 200p. (Orig.). (gr. 8 up). 1978. pap. 10.95 (*0-03-043936-1*) Brookline Bks.

Martin, Patricia S. Ted Kennedy Jr. He Faced His Challenge. (Illus.). 24p. (gr. 1-4). 1987. PLB 14.60 (*0-86592-174-1*); 10.95s.p. (*0-685-58129-2*) Rourke Corp.

Moss, Nathaniel. Ron Kovic: Antiwar Activist. LC 93-16373. (Illus.). 1994. 18.95 (*0-7910-2076-2*, Am Art Analog); pap. write for info. (*0-7910-2089-4*, Am Art Analog) Chelsea Hse.

Rosenberg, Maxine B. My Friend Leslie: The Story of a Handicapped Child. Ancona, George, photos by. LC 82-12734. (Illus.). (gr. 1-3). 1983. 16.00 (*0-688-01690-1*); PLB 15.93 (*0-688-01691-X*) Lothrop.

PHYSICALLY HANDICAPPED–EDUCATION

Miller, Mary Beth & Ancona, George. Handtalk School. LC 90-24030. (Illus.). 32p. (gr. k-6). 1991. RSBE 14.95 (*0-02-700912-2*, Four Winds) Macmillan Child Grp.

PHYSICALLY HANDICAPPED–FICTION

Andrews, Jean F. Hasta Luego, San Diego. LC 90-27125. 104p. (Orig.). (gr. 3-6). 1991. pap. 4.95 (*0-930323-83-1*, Pub. by K Green Pubns) Gallaudet Univ Pr.

Berenstain, Stan & Berenstain, Jan. The Berenstain Bears & the Wheelchair Commando. Berenstain, Stan & Berenstain, Jan, illus. 112p. (Orig.). (gr. 2-6). 1993. PLB 7.99 (*0-679-94034-0*); pap. 3.50 (*0-679-84034-6*) Random Bks Yng Read.

Booth, Barbara D. Mandy. LaMarche, Jim, illus. LC 90-19989. 32p. (gr. 1 up). 1991. 14.95 (*0-688-10338-3*); PLB 14.88 (*0-688-10339-1*) Lothrop.

Brown, Irene B. Before the Lark. Milam, Larry, illus. 180p. (gr. 4 up). 1992. pap. 7.95 (*0-936085-22-3*) Blue Heron OR.

Burnett, Frances H. The Secret Garden. 302p. 1981. Repr. PLB 21.95x (*0-89966-326-5*) Buccaneer Bks.

—Secret Garden. (gr. k-6). 1990. pap. 3.50 (*0-440-47709-3*, Pub. by Yearling Classics); pap. 3.50 (*0-440-97709-6*, Dell Trade Pbks) Dell.

—The Secret Garden. (gr. 4-6). 1987. pap. 2.95 (*0-14-035004-7*, Puffin) Puffin Bks.

—The Secret Garden. Mitchell, Kathy, illus. 320p. (gr. 4 up). 1987. 13.95 (*0-448-06029-9*, G&D) Putnam Pub Group.

—The Secret Garden. Tudor, Tasha, illus. LC 62-17457. 256p. (gr. 4-8). 1987. pap. 3.50 (*0-06-440188-X*, Trophy) HarpC Child Bks.

—The Secret Garden. McNulty, Faith, afterword by. 1987. pap. 2.95 (*0-451-52417-9*, Sig Classics) NAL-Dutton.

—The Secret Garden. Allen, Thomas B., illus. Howe, James, adapted by. LC 86-17788. (Illus.). 72p. (gr. k-5). 1993. 13.95 (*0-394-86467-0*) Random Bks Yng Read.

—The Secret Garden. Howell, Troy, illus. 288p. (gr. k-6). 12.99 (*0-517-63225-X*) Random Hse Value.

—The Secret Garden. Hague, Michael, illus. LC 86-22780. 240p. (gr. 4-6). 1987. 19.95 (*0-8050-0277-4*, Bks Young Read) H Holt & Co.

—The Secret Garden. Lowry, Lois, intro. by. 256p. 1987. pap. 3.50 (*0-553-21201-X*, Bantam Classics) Bantam.

—The Secret Garden. Betts, Louise, adapted by. LC 87-15490. (Illus.). (gr. 3-6). 1988. PLB 12.89 (*0-8167-1203-4*); pap. 3.95 (*0-8167-1204-2*) Troll Assocs.

—The Secret Garden. 360p. 1987. pap. 4.95 (*0-19-281772-8*) OUP.

—The Secret Garden. Sanderson, Ruth, illus. LC 86-46002. 240p. 1988. 18.95 (*0-394-55431-0*) Knopf Bks Yng Read.

—The Secret Garden. Hughes, Shirley, illus. 240p. (gr. 5 up). 1989. pap. 18.95 (*0-670-82571-9*) Viking Child Bks.

—The Secret Garden. (gr. 5 up). 1989. pap. 2.50 (*0-451-52080-7*) NAL-Dutton.

—The Secret Garden. 304p. (gr. 4-7). 1987. pap. 2.95 (*0-590-43346-6*) Scholastic Inc.

—The Secret Garden. 1987. pap. 3.50 (*0-440-40055-4*) Dell.

—Secret Garden. 288p. 1990. pap. 2.50 (*0-8125-0501-8*) Tor Bks.

—The Secret Garden. 1991. pap. 3.99 (*0-8125-1910-8*) Tor Bks.

—The Secret Garden. 1979. pap. 3.25 (*0-440-77706-2*) Dell.

—The Secret Garden. 288p. (gr. 5-8). 1991. pap. 2.99 (*0-87406-575-5*) Willowisp Pr.

—The Secret Garden. 1993. 14.95 (*0-679-42309-5*, Everymans Lib) Knopf.

—The Secret Garden. Howe, James, adapted by. Allen, Thomas B., illus. LC 93-18509. 128p. (Orig.). (gr. 2-6). 1993. pap. 3.50 (*0-679-84751-0*, Bullseye Bks) Random Bks Yng Read.

—The Secret Garden. Bishop, Michael, illus. 200p. 1993. 25.00 (*0-88363-202-0*) H L Levin.

—The Secret Garden. Bauman, Jill, illus. LC 94-17836. 1994. 10.95 (*0-681-00646-3*) Longmeadow Pr.

Burnett, Frances Hodgson. The Secret Garden. (Illus.). 96p. (Orig.). (gr. 4-7). 1994. pap. 1.00 (*0-486-28024-1*) Dover.

Burnett, Francis H. The Secret Garden: A Young Reader's Edition of the Classic Story. Abr. ed. Crawford, Dale, illus. LC 90-80198. 56p. (gr. 1 up). 1990. 9.98 (*0-89471-860-6*) Courage Bks.

Butler, Beverly. Witch's Fire. LC 93-44. 144p. (gr. 5 up). 1993. 14.99 (*0-525-65132-2*, Cobblehill Bks) Dutton Child Bks.

Calvert, Patricia. Picking up the Pieces. LC 92-27909. 192p. (gr. 7 up). 1993. SBE 14.95 (*0-684-19558-5*, Scribner's Young Read) Macmillan Child Grp.

Carlson, Judy. Here Comes Kate! (Illus.). 32p. (gr. 1-4). 1989. PLB 18.99 (*0-8172-3515-9*); pap. 3.95 (*0-8114-6713-9*) Raintree Steck-V.

Carlson, Nancy. Arnie & the New Kid. (Illus.). 32p. (ps-2). 1990. pap. 12.00 (*0-670-82499-2*) Viking Child Bks.

—Arnie & the New Kid. (Illus.). 32p. (ps-3). 1992. pap. 3.99 (*0-14-050945-3*, Puffin) Puffin Bks.

Dobkin, Bonnie. Just a Little Different. Martin, Clovis, illus. LC 93-13024. 32p. (ps-2). 1994. PLB 13.80 (*0-516-02018-8*); pap. 2.95 (*0-516-42018-6*) Childrens.

Dunlap, Hope. The Little Lame Prince. Dunlap, Hope, illus. LC 92-37665. 1993. 8.99 (*0-517-08484-8*, Pub. by Derrydale Bks) Random Hse Value.

Garfield, Leon. Empty Sleeve. 1988. 14.95 (*0-385-29817-X*) Delacorte.

Gerson, Corinne. Passing Through. 208p. (gr. 8 up). 1980. pap. 1.50 (*0-440-96958-1*, LFL) Dell.

Good, Janis. Summer of the Lost Limb. Cates, Elizabeth, illus. 110p. (Orig.). 1994. pap. 7.95 (*0-9640365-5-X*) Christ Recollect.

Readers will step back 90 years in time to horse & buggy days. Young Mary & her people are of a religious sect similar to the Amish who live yet today as years ago. A tragic farm accident changes Mary's life, dashing her dreams of walking the half mile to her community school with other children. Readers follow Mary through a country operation on her own kitchen table, a trip to Washington, D.C., for an artificial limb, adjustments & struggles. They will feel with the limitations of the handicapped & even learn some valuable lessons & bits of history. Who believes teddy bears always existed? This book tells two stories behind the beginning of teddy bears. Then there are two strangers on horseback who meet Mary. Will she allow horses to cross the narrow swinging bridge that spans the river? Will she be able to perform a difficult duty on her wooden leg? Her faith makes all the difference. Christian Recollections, Rt. 1, Box 351, Mt. Solon, VA 22821.

Publisher Provided Annotation.

Hager, Betty. Marcie & the Monster of the Bayou. LC 93-44490. 112p. (gr. 3-7). 1994. pap. 4.99 (*0-310-38431-1*) Zondervan.

Halvorson, Marilyn. Hold on, Geronimo. LC 87-25656. 240p. (gr. 7 up). 1988. pap. 14.95 (*0-385-29665-7*) Delacorte.

Harshman, Marc. The Storm. Mohr, Mark, illus. LC 94-4894. 1995. write for info. (*0-525-65150-0*, Cobblehill Bks) Dutton Child Bks.

Helfman, Elizabeth. On Being Sarah. Mathews, Judith, ed. Saffioti, Lino, illus. 144p. (gr. 5-9). 1992. 11.95g (*0-8075-6068-5*) A Whitman.

Henriod, Lorraine. Grandma's Wheelchair. Tucker, Kathy, ed. LC 81-12918. (Illus.). 32p. (ps-1). 1982. PLB 13.95 (*0-8075-3035-2*) A Whitman.

Hill, David. See Ya, Simon. LC 93-39870. 120p. 1994. 14.99 (*0-525-45247-8*, DCB) Dutton Child Bks.

Holcomb, Nan. A Smile from Andy. Yoder, Dot, illus. 32p. (ps-2). 1989. pap. 6.95 (*0-944727-04-2*) Jason & Nordic Pubs.

Howard, Ellen. Circle of Giving. LC 83-15631. 112p. (gr. 4-6). 1984. SBE 13.95 (*0-689-31027-7*, Atheneum Child Bk) Macmillan Child Grp.

Howe, James. A Night Without Stars. LC 82-16278. 192p. (gr. 4-7). 1983. SBE 13.95 (*0-689-30957-0*, Atheneum Child Bk) Macmillan Child Grp.

Johnston, Julie. Hero of Lesser Causes. LC 92-37268. 1993. 15.95 (*0-316-46988-2*, Joy St Bks) Little.

—Hero of Lesser Causes. 192p. (gr. 5 up). 1994. pap. 3.99 (*0-14-036998-8*) Puffin Bks.

Kadish, Sharona. Discovering Friendship. Scribner, Joanne, illus. LC 93-34500. 1994. PLB 19.97 (*0-8114-4458-9*) Raintree Steck-V.

Klusmeyer, Joann. Shelly from Rockytop Farm. Taylor, Neil, illus. 65p. (gr. 3-6). 1986. 5.95 (*1-55523-014-8*) Winston-Derek.

Kneeland, Linda C. Cookie. Fargo, Todd, illus. 32p. (ps-2). 1989. pap. 6.95 (*0-944727-05-0*) Jason & Nordic Pubs.

Kroll, Virginia. Pink Paper Swans. Clouse, Nancy L., illus. LC 93-41093. 32p. (gr. k-3). 1994. 14.99 (*0-8028-5081-2*) Eerdmans.

Lasker, Joe. Nick Joins In. Tucker, Kathleen, ed. Lasker, Joe, illus. LC 79-29637. 32p. (gr. 1-3). 1980. PLB 13.95 (*0-8075-5612-2*) A Whitman.

Lee, Jeanne. Silent Lotus. (Illus.). 32p. (gr. k-3). 1991. 14.95 (*0-374-36911-9*) FS&G.

Levene, Nancy S. Crocodile Meatloaf. LC 92-32615. (ps-6). 1993. pap. 4.99 (*0-7814-0000-7*, Chariot Bks) Chariot Family.

Levin, Betty. Away to Me, Moss. LC 93-48136. 192p. 1994. write for info. (*0-688-13439-4*) Greenwillow.

Little, Jean. Listen for the Singing. LC 90-40019. 272p. (gr. 4-7). 1991. PLB 14.89 (*0-06-023910-7*) HarpC Child Bks.

Maguire, Gregory. Missing Sisters. LC 93-8300. 160p. (gr. 5-9). 1994. SBE 14.95 (*0-689-50590-6*, M K McElderry) Macmillan Child Grp.

Metzger, Lois. Barry's Sister. LC 93-7760. 240p. (gr. 5 up). 1993. pap. 4.50 (*0-14-036484-6*, Puffin) Puffin Bks.

Miller, Mary B. & Charlip, Remy. Handtalk Birthday: A Number & Story Book in Sign Language. Ancona, George, illus. LC 91-1967. 48p. (ps-3). 1991. pap. 4.95 (*0-689-71531-5*, Aladdin) Macmillan Child Grp.

Nelson, JoAnne. Friends All Around. DuCharme, Tracy, illus. LC 92-4657. 24p. (Orig.). (gr. k-2). 1993. pap. 5.95 (*0-935529-17-9*) Comprehen Health Educ.

Perske, Robert. Don't Stop the Music. LC 86-17426. (gr. 12 up). 1986. pap. 9.95 (*0-687-11060-2*) Abingdon.

—Show Me No Mercy: A Compelling Story of Remarkable Courage. LC 83-21384. 144p. (Orig.). (gr. 12 up). 1984. pap. 9.95 (*0-687-38435-4*) Abingdon.

Philbrick, W. R. Freak the Mighty. LC 93-19913. 176p. (gr. 5-9). 1993. 13.95 (*0-590-47412-X*) Scholastic Inc.

Porter, Gene S. Freckles. 272p. (gr. 5 up). 1992. pap. 2.99 (*0-14-035144-2*) Puffin Bks.

—Freckles. LC 93-42393. 1994. 7.99 (*0-517-10126-2*, Pub. by Gramercy) Random Hse Value.

Rabe, Berniece. The Balancing Girl. Hoban, Lillian, illus. LC 80-22100. (ps-2). 1981. 12.95 (*0-525-26160-5*, 0995-300, DCB) Dutton Child Bks.

Richmond, Sandra. Wheels for Walking. (Illus.). 176p. (gr. 9-12). 1988. pap. 2.50 (*0-451-15235-2*, Sig) NAL-Dutton.

Ripslinger, Jon. Triangle. (gr. 7 up). 1994. write for info. (*0-15-200048-8*); pap. write for info. (*0-15-200049-6*) HarBrace.

Rosofsky, Iris. My Aunt Ruth. LC 90-4940. 224p. (gr. 7 up). 1991. HarpC Child Bks.

Russo, Marisabina. Alex Is My Friend. LC 90-24643. 32p. 1992. 14.00 (*0-688-10418-5*); PLB 13.93 (*0-688-10419-3*) Greenwillow.

Sanford, Agnes. Melissa & the Little Red Book. Heinen, Sandy, illus. (gr. 1-6). pap. 2.25 (*0-910924-81-3*) Macalester.

Smith, Elizabeth S. A Service Dog Goes to School: The Story of a Dog Trained to Help the Disabled. Petruccio, Steven, illus. LC 88-17598. 64p. (gr. 1-4). 1988. 12.95 (*0-688-07648-3*); PLB 12.88 (*0-688-07649-1*, Morrow Jr Bks) Morrow Jr Bks.

Springer, Nancy. Colt. (gr. 4-7). 1991. 13.95 (*0-8037-1022-4*) Dial Bks Young.

Strachan, Ian. Flawed Glass. (gr. 9-12). 1990. 14.95 (*0-316-81813-5*) Little.

Tada, Joni E. & Jensen, Steve. Darcy & the Meanest Teacher in the World. LC 92-33075. (gr. 3-7). 1993. pap. 4.99 (*0-7814-0885-7*, Chariot Bks) Chariot Family.

—Darcy's Dog Dilemma. Norton, LoraBeth, ed. LC 93-36330. 128p. (gr. 4-8). 1994. pap. 4.99 (*0-7814-0167-4*, Chariot Bks) Cook.

Thesman, Jean. When the Road Ends. 192p. (gr. 5-9). 1992. 13.45 (*0-395-59507-X*) HM.

Thomasma, Kenneth. Moho Wat: Sheepeater Boy Attempts A Rescue. Brouwer, Jack, illus. 184p. 1994. 10.95 (*1-880114-14-3*); pap. 6.95 (*1-880114-13-5*) Grandview. Moho Wat is a Sheepeater Indian boy living in what is now Yellowstone National Park. In a violent encounter with a mountain lion, the boy loses his left hand. Although devastated, Moho Wat struggles to overcome his loss & teaches himself to hunt using his feet to hold his bow & arrow. After a trip to the sacred Medicine Wheel, his courage & strength are tested when he makes a dangerous attempt to rescue the beautiful girl, Wind Flower, who was taken captive by a large enemy tribe. He does eveything he can to prove he is as good as any other boy. One day his father will say, "You have shown your bravery & skill. I am proud of my son, Moho Wat. To order call: 1-800-525-7344. Grandview Publishing, Box 2863, Jackson, WY 83001.
Publisher Provided Annotation.

Turner, Bonnie. Haunted Igloo. 160p. (gr. 3-7). 1991. 13.45 (*0-395-57037-9*, Sandpiper) HM.

Van Raven, Pieter. The Great Man's Secret. (Illus.). 176p. (gr. 5-9). 1991. pap. 3.95 (*0-14-034390-3*, Puffin) Puffin Bks.

Voigt, Cynthia. Izzy, Willy-Nilly. 1987. pap. 3.99 (*0-449-70214-6*, Juniper) Fawcett.

Wallace, Bill. True Friends. LC 94-6449. 160p. (gr. 4-6). 1994. 14.95 (*0-8234-1141-9*) Holiday.

Weissman, Jackie. My Toes are Starting to Wiggle. (ps-5). 1991. pap. 12.95 (*0-939514-12-5*) Miss Jackie.

Werlin, Nancy. Are You Alone on Purpose? 1994. 14.95 (*0-395-67350-X*) HM.

White, James E. The Triumphs of Trisha & Tripod: Tripod Finds a Home. Senf, Richard L., illus. 22p. 1991. pap. 7.95 (*0-9629102-0-1*) Pyramid TX.

Winthrop, Elizabeth. Marathon Miranda. (gr. 4 up). 1990. pap. 3.95 (*0-14-034391-1*, Puffin) Puffin Bks.

Wright, Betty R. Out of the Dark. LC 93-48025. (gr. 3-7). 1995. 13.95 (*0-590-43598-1*) Scholastic Inc.

Yates, Elizabeth. Hue & Cry. 182p. (gr. 7-12). 1991. pap. 4.95 (*0-89084-536-0*) Bob Jones Univ Pr.

Zeier, Joan T. Stick Boy. LC 92-23326. 144p. (gr. 2-6). 1993. SBE 13.95 (*0-689-31835-9*, Atheneum Child Bk) Macmillan Child Grp.

Zelonky, Joy. I Can't Always Hear You. Bejna, Barbara & Jensen, Shirlee, illus. Geist, Chris, intro. by. LC 79-23891. 32p. (gr. k-6). 1980. PLB 19.97 (*0-8172-1355-4*) Raintree Steck-V.

PHYSICIANS

see also Women As Physicians;
also names of specialists, e.g. Surgeons

Baldwin, Joyce Y. To Heal the Heart of a Child: Helen Taussig, M.D. 128p. 1992. 14.95 (*0-8027-8166-7*); lib. bdg. 15.85 (*0-8027-8167-5*) Walker & Co.

Bauer, Judith. What's It Like to Be a Doctor. Burns, Raymond, illus. LC 89-34398. 32p. (gr. k-3). 1990. lib. bdg. 10.89 (*0-8167-1801-6*); pap. text ed. 2.95 (*0-8167-1802-4*) Troll Assocs.

Berry, Joy W. Teach Me about the Doctor. Dickey, Kate, ed. (Illus.). 36p. (ps). 1986. 4.98 (*0-685-10723-X*) Grolier Inc.

Bianchi, Anne. C. Everett Koop: The Health of a Nation. LC 92-1230. (Illus.). 104p. (gr. 7 up). 1992. PLB 15.40 (*1-56294-103-8*) Millbrook Pr.

Brew, Lydia E. & Brew, Annie S. Dr. Edith Irby Jones: A Story of Triumph. 58p. (gr. k-2). 1992. pap. text ed. 3.50 (*0-9635351-0-2*) Lydias Educ.

Drescher, Joan. Your Doctor, My Doctor. 32p. (gr. 1-3). 1987. 10.95 (*0-8027-6668-4*); PLB 11.85 (*0-8027-6669-2*) Walker & Co.

Ferris, Jeri. Native American Doctor: The Story of Susan LaFlesche Picotte. (Illus.). 80p. (gr. 3-6). 1991. PLB 17.50 (*0-87614-443-1*) Carolrhoda Bks.

—Native American Doctor: The Story of Susan Laflesche Picotte. (gr. 4-7). 1991. pap. 6.95 (*0-87614-548-9*) Carolrhoda Bks.

Hankin, Rebecca. I Can Be a Doctor. LC 84-23304. (Illus.). 32p. (gr. k-3). 1985. PLB 11.80 (*0-516-01846-9*); pap. 3.95 (*0-516-41846-7*) Childrens.

Hayden, Robert C. Eleven African-American Doctors. rev. ed. (Illus.). 208p. (gr. 5-8). 1992. Repr. of 1976 ed. PLB 14.95 (*0-8050-2135-3*) TFC Bks NY.

Monroe, Betsy. My Visit to My Doctor: A Coloring Book for Kids. Monroe, Betsy, illus. 24p. (Orig.). (gr. k-4). 1989. pap. write for info. (*1-878083-01-5*) Color Me Well.

Nunis, Doyce B., Jr. Great Doctors. Conkle, Nancy, illus. 64p. (Orig.). (gr. 8). 1991. pap. 3.95 (*0-88388-144-6*) Bellerophon Bks.

Rockwell, Harlow. My Doctor. Rockwell, Harlow, illus. LC 72-92442. 24p. (ps-1). 1973. SBE 13.95 (*0-02-777480-5*, Macmillan Child Bk) Macmillan Child Grp.

Thompson-Peters, Flossie E. Daniel Hale Williams: Surgeon. Wilson, Lillian, illus. 32p. (Orig.). (gr. 3-9). 1988. pap. 4.70 (*1-880784-05-X*) Atlas Pr.

Watson, Jane W., et al. My Friend the Doctor: A Read-Together Book for Parents & Children. rev. & updated ed. Smith, Catherine B., illus. 32p. (ps up). 1987. pap. 3.50 (*0-517-56485-8*) Crown Bks Yng Read.

PHYSICIANS–FICTION

Allen, Julia. My First Doctor Visit. Reese, Bob, illus. (gr. k-3). 1987. 7.95 (*0-89868-187-1*); pap. 2.95 (*0-89868-188-X*) ARO Pub.

Carr, M. J. Cabbage Patch Kids Visit the Doctor. (ps-3). 1993. pap. 2.50 (*0-685-64929-6*) Scholastic Inc.

The Citadel. 1993. pap. text ed. 6.50 (*0-582-09673-1*, 79817) Longman.

Cole, Joanna. Doctor Change. Carrick, Donald, illus. LC 86-881. 32p. (ps-3). 1986. 12.95 (*0-688-06135-4*); lib. bdg. 12.88 (*0-688-06136-2*, Morrow Jr Bks) Morrow Jr Bks.

Cronin, A. J. The Citadel. 1983. 16.45 (*0-316-16158-6*); pap. 10.95i (*0-316-16183-7*) Little.

De Brunhoff, Laurent. Babar Chez le Docteur. (FRE.). (gr. 2-3). 15.95 (*0-685-28425-5*) Fr & Eur.

Fine, Anne. Poor Monty. Vulliamy, Clara, illus. 32p. (ps-1). 1992. 14.45 (*0-395-60472-9*, Clarion Bks) HM.

Freeman, Don. Corduroy's Busy Street & Corduroy Goes to the Doctor, 2 bks. McCue, Lisa, illus. (ps-k). 1989. Repr. of 1987 ed. bds. 12.95 incl. cass. (*0-87499-133-1*) Live Oak Media.

Gordon, Nayvin. A Family Visits the Doctor. LC 93-60740. 140p. (gr. 2-8). 1993. pap. 5.95 (*1-55523-631-6*) Winston-Derek.

I Want to Be a Doctor. (Illus.). (ps-k). 1991. write for info. (*0-307-12625-0*, Golden Pr) Western Pub.

Kroll, Steven. Doctor on an Elephant. (gr. 1-5). 1994. 14.95 (*0-8050-2876-5*) H Holt & Co.

Kuklin, Susan. When I See My Doctor. LC 87-25621. (Illus.). 32p. (ps-k). 1988. RSBE 13.95 (*0-02-751232-0*, Bradbury Pr) Macmillan Child Grp.

Lowry, Lois. Anastasia, Ask Your Analyst. 128p. (Orig.). (gr. 4-6). 1992. pap. 3.50 (*0-440-40289-1*, YB) Dell.

McCue, Lisa. Corduroy Goes to the Doctor. (Illus.). (ps). 1987. pap. 3.99 (*0-670-81495-4*) Viking Child Bks.

Medearis, Mary. Big Doc's Girl. LC 84-45641. 142p. (gr. 7-12). 1985. pap. 7.95 (*0-87483-105-9*) August Hse.

Montgomery, Lucy M. Doctor's Sweetheart. 1993. pap. 4.50 (*0-553-56330-0*) Bantam.

Peters, Tim, ed. Toby Turtle Takes a Tumble. (Illus.). (ps-2). pap. 4.95 (*1-879874-29-6*) T Peters & Co.

Revich, S. J. Ezra the Physician. Hinlicky, Gregg, illus. 126p. (gr. 5-7). 1988. 9.95 (*0-935063-63-3*); pap. 7.95 (*0-935063-64-1*) CIS Comm.

Roessler, Mark. The Last Magician in Blue Haven. Hundgen, Donald, illus. 52p. (Orig.). (gr. 4-8). 1994. pap. 12.95 (*0-9638293-0-0*) Hundelrut Studio. THE LAST MAGICIAN is an imaginative tale for children & adults, filled with numerous delicate pen drawings by Donald Hundgen. A sophisticated city doctor comes to Blue Haven to serve the rural community but ends up becoming a thorn in their side. The simple villagers love magic. The doctor, Fortunamus Gengeloof, drives off all the magicians by revealing their secrets, until one comes along who is a match for the doctor. For prepublication order & general information: Write: Hundelrut Studio, 10 Hawthorne Street, Plymouth, NH 03264. USA. Phone: 603-536-4396.
Publisher Provided Annotation.

Schwartz, Joel L. Shrink. (Orig.). (gr. 3-6). 1986. pap. 2.75 (*0-440-47687-9*, YB) Dell.

Sirken, Michael L. Mr. Fine Goes to the Eye Doctor. 28p. (ps-4). 1993. pap. 1.25 (*0-9635483-0-1*) Sirken Pubns.

Steel, Danielle. Freddie & the Doctor. Rogers, Jacqueline, illus. 32p. (Orig.). (gr. 1-3). 1992. pap. 2.99 (*0-440-40575-0*, YB) Dell.

Steig, William. Doctor de Soto. LC 82-15701. (ps-3). 1982. 16.00 (*0-374-31803-4*) FS&G.

PHYSICISTS

Ferguson, Kitty. Stephen Hawking: Quest for a Theory of the Universe. (Illus.). 240p. (gr. 9-12). 1991. PLB 15.40 (*0-531-11067-2*) Watts.

McDaniel, Melissa. Stephen Hawking: Physicist. (Illus.). 1994. 18.95 (*0-7910-2078-9*, Am Art Analog) Chelsea Hse.

McPartland, Scott. Gordon Gould. LC 93-2819. 1993. 15.93 (*0-86592-079-6*); 11.95s.p. (*0-685-66585-2*) Rourke Enter.

Parker, Steve. Isaac Newton & Gravity. LC 94-8260. 1994. write for info. (*0-7910-3010-5*) Chelsea Hse.

Simon, Sheridan. Stephen Hawking: Unlocking the Universe. (Illus.). 112p. (gr. 5 up). 1991. text ed. 13.95 (*0-87518-455-3*, Dillon) Macmillan Child Grp.

Sipiera, Paul. I Can Be a Physicist. LC 90-20886. (Illus.). 32p. (gr. k-3). 1991. PLB 11.80 (*0-516-01964-3*); pap. 3.95 (*0-516-41964-1*) Childrens.

PHYSICS

see also Astrophysics; Dynamics; Electricity; Electronics; Geophysics; Gravitation; Hydrostatics; Light; Liquids; Magnetism; Matter; Mechanics; Music–Acoustics and Physics; Nuclear Physics; Optics; Radioactivity; Relativity (Physics); Sound; Thermodynamics

Barber, Jacqueline & Willard, Carolyn. Bubble Festival. Bergman, Lincoln & Babcock, Carl, eds. (Illus.). 184p. (gr. k-6). 1992. pap. 12.50 (*0-912511-80-X*) Lawrence Science.

Barr, George. Sports Science for Young People. 1990. pap. 3.95 (*0-486-26527-7*) Dover.

Burchard, Elizabeth & Soroka, Matthew. Physics: In a Flash. 476p. (gr. 7-12). 1994. pap. 9.95 (*1-881374-02-5*) Flash Blasters.

Crump, Donald J., ed. Fun with Physics. LC 86-8501. (Illus.). 104p. (gr. 5 up). 1986. 8.95 (*0-87044-576-6*); lib. bdg. 12.50 (*0-87044-581-2*) Natl Geog.

—How Things Work. LC 81-47894. (Illus.). 104p. (gr. 7 up). 1983. 8.95 (*0-87044-425-5*); PLB 12.50 (*0-87044-430-1*) Natl Geog.

Dunn, Andrew. Lifting by Levers. Carr, Ed, illus. LC 93-6828. 32p. (gr. 3-6). 1993. 13.95 (*1-56847-016-9*) Thomson Lrning.

—Simple Slopes. Carr, Ed, illus. LC 93-6836. 32p. (gr. 3-6). 1993. 13.95 (*1-56847-017-7*) Thomson Lrning.

Ehrlich, Robert. The Cosmological Milkshake: A Semi-Serious Look at the Size of Things. Ehrlich, Gary, illus. LC 93-28135. 1994. 24.00 (*0-8135-2045-2*) Rutgers U Pr.

Evans, David & Williams, Claudette. Make It Balance. LC 92-52814. (Illus.). 32p. (gr. k-3). 1992. 9.95 (*1-56458-118-7*) Dorling Kindersley.

Golden, Michael. Traveling Through Time & Space: A Study Guide. (gr. 5-8). 1991. pap. text ed. 19.95 (*0-88122-563-0*) LRN Links.

Hoover, Evalyn, et al. Primariamente Fisica. Hillen, J., ed. Sands, Iso, tr. (SPA & ENG., Illus.). 155p. (Orig.). (gr. k-3). 1992. pap. 16.95 (*1-881431-34-7*, 1404) AIMS Educ Fnd.
Hoyt, Marie A. Kitchen Chemistry & Front Porch Physics. Finkler, C. Etana, illus. 60p. (Orig.). (gr. 3-8). 1983. pap. 5.00 (*0-914911-00-7*) Educ Serv Pr.
—Workbook Game Sheets for Kitchen Chemistry & Front Porch Physics. Green, Victor D. & Loor, Robin, illus. 44p. (Orig.). (gr. 3-8). 1983. pap. text ed. 4.00 (*0-914911-02-3*) Educ Serv Pr.
Koenig, Herbert G., et al. Physical Science: A Concise Competency Review. rev. ed. Gamsey, Wayne, ed. Fairbanks, Eugene B., illus. 96p. (gr. 7-12). 1991. pap. text ed. 4.11 (*0-935487-46-8*) N & N Pub Co.
Kraul, Walter. Earth, Water, Fire & Air: Playful Explorations in the Four Elements. (Illus.). 120p. (gr. 4-8). pap. 12.95 (*0-86315-090-X*, Pub. by Floris Bks UK) Gryphon Hse.
Lafferty, Peter. The World of Science. LC 94-20019. 1994. write for info. (*0-8160-3219-X*) Facts on File.
Lampton, Christopher. Sailboats, Flag Poles, Cranes: Using Pulleys as Simple Machines. (Illus.). 32p. (gr. 2-4). 1991. PLB 12.90 (*1-56294-026-0*) Millbrook Pr.
Marsh, Carole. Phyzzics for Kids. (gr. 4-9). 1994. 24.95 (*1-55609-258-X*); pap. 14.95 (*1-55609-245-8*); computer disk 29.95 (*1-55609-340-3*) Gallopade Pub Group.
Pendulums. (gr. 7-12). 1992. pap. 8.80 (*0-941008-71-1*) Tops Learning.
Pressure. (gr. 7-12). 1992. pap. 14.00 (*0-941008-86-X*) Tops Learning.
Saxon. Physics: An Incremental Development. (gr. 9-12). 1993. student ed. 45.00 (*1-56577-005-6*); lab manual 20.00 (*1-56577-009-9*); testmasters 39.00 (*1-56577-006-4*); solution manual 17.00 (*1-56577-007-2*) Saxon Pubs OK.
Sipiera, Paul. I Can Be a Physicist. LC 90-20886. (Illus.). 32p. (gr. k-3). 1991. PLB 11.80 (*0-516-01964-3*); pap. 3.95 (*0-516-41964-1*) Childrens.
Stacy, Tom. Earth, Sea & Sky. Forsey, Chris, illus. LC 90-12974. 40p. (gr. 4-5). 1991. PLB 12.40 (*0-531-19106-0*) Watts.
Stockley, C. Dictionary of Physics. (Illus.). 128p. (gr. 6 up). 1988. PLB 15.96 (*0-88110-308-X*); pap. 9.95 (*0-86020-987-3*) EDC.
Time Life Books Staff. Physical Forces. 1992. 18.95 (*0-8094-9675-5*) Time-Life.
Wingate, P. Essential Physics. (Illus.). 64p. 1992. lib. bdg. 12.96 (*0-88110-507-4*, Usborne); pap. 5.95 (*0-7460-0703-5*) EDC.
Wood, Robert W. Physics for Kids: Forty-Nine Easy Experiments with Electricity & Magnetism. (Illus.). 192p. 1990. 16.95 (*0-685-32939-9*, 3412); pap. 9.95 (*0-8306-3412-6*) TAB Bks.

PHYSICS, ASTRONOMICAL

see Astrophysics

PHYSICS–EXPERIMENTS

Breckenridge, Judy. Simple Physics Experiments with Everyday Materials. Zweifel, Frances, illus. LC 92-25312. 128p. (gr. 4 up). 1993. 12.95 (*0-8069-8606-9*) Sterling.
Cash, Terry. One Hundred One Physics Tricks: Fun Experiments with Everyday Materials. LC 92-21859. (Illus.). 104p. (gr. 3-9). 1992. 14.95 (*0-685-60095-5*) Sterling.
Challand, Helen J. Activities in the Physical Sciences. LC 83-26224. (Illus.). 96p. (gr. 5 up). 1984. PLB 13.95 (*0-516-00504-9*) Childrens.
Gardner, Robert. Famous Experiments You Can Do. LC 90-34043. (Illus.). 144p. (gr. 9-12). 1990. PLB 13.90 (*0-531-10883-X*) Watts.
Goodwin, Peter. Physics Projects for Young Scientists. LC 91-17822. (Illus.). 128p. (gr. 9-12). 1991. PLB 13.90 (*0-531-11070-2*) Watts.
Lyon, Sue & Lyon, Sue, eds. Science in Action: Experiments in Physics. Berman, Paul, designed by. LC 92-34427. 1993. write for info. (*0-86307-342-5*) Marshall Cavendish.
Mandell, Muriel. Physics Experiments for Children. Matsuda, S., illus. LC 68-9308. (gr. 3-10). 1968. pap. 2.95 (*0-486-22033-8*) Dover.
Vancleave, Janice P. Physics for Every Kid: One Hundred One Easy Experiments in Motion, Heat, Light, Machines & Sound. 1991. pap. text ed. 10.95 (*0-471-52505-7*) Wiley.
Ward, Alan. Experimenting with Surface Tension & Bubbles. Flax, Zena, illus. 48p. (gr. 2-7). 1991. lib. bdg. 12.95 (*0-7910-1513-0*) Chelsea Hse.
Wellnitz, William R. Be a Kid Physicist. LC 92-40506. 1993. 17.95 (*0-8306-4091-6*); pap. 9.95 (*0-8306-4092-4*) TAB Bks.

PHYSICS, TERRESTIAL

see Geophysics

PHYSIOGRAPHY

see Physical Geography

PHYSIOLOGICAL CHEMISTRY

see also Biochemistry; Cells; Digestion; Poisons; Vitamins

PHYSIOLOGY

see also Anatomy; Blood; Bones; Cells; Digestion; Growth; Nervous System; Nutrition; Old Age; Reproduction; Respiration; Senses and Sensation
also names of organs, e.g. Heart

Asimov, Isaac & Dierks, Carrie. How Does a Cut Heal? LC 93-18271. 1993. PLB 15.93 (*0-8368-0805-3*) Gareth Stevens Inc.
Cole, Joanna. The Magic School Bus Inside the Human Body. Degen, Bruce, illus. 1992. pap. 3.95 (*0-685-53602-5*) Scholastic Inc.
—Your Insides. Meisel, Paul, illus. 40p. (ps-1). 1992. 14.95 (*0-399-22123-9*, Putnam) Putnam Pub Group.
Day, Trevor. The Random House Book of One Thousand One Questions & Answers about the Human Body. LC 93-6386. 160p. (gr. 4-7). 1994. pap. 13.00 (*0-679-85432-0*) Random Bks Yng Read.
Demuth, Patricia. Inside Your Busy Body. Billin-Frye, Paige, illus. LC 92-44173. 32p. (ps-3). 1993. pap. 2.25 (*0-448-40189-4*, G&D) Putnam Pub Group.
Gabb, Michael. The Human Body. LC 91-2560. (Illus.). 48p. (gr. 3-5). 1991. PLB 13.90 (*0-531-19145-1*, Warwick) Watts.
Gakken Co. Ltd., Staff, ed. Our Bodies. Time-Life Books Inc., Staff, tr. (Illus.). 90p. (gr. k-3). 1991. write for info. (*0-8094-9450-7*); lib. bdg. write for info. (*0-8094-9451-5*); text ed. write for info. (*0-8094-9452-3*); pap. write for info. (*0-8094-9453-1*) Time-Life.
Ganeri, Anita. What's Inside Us? LC 94-19406. (gr. 1 up). 1995. write for info. (*0-8114-3885-6*) Raintree Steck V.
Gardner, Robert. Science Projects about the Human Body. LC 92-43802. (Illus.). 104p. (gr. 6 up). 1993. lib. bdg. 17.95 (*0-89490-443-4*) Enslow Pubs.
How Our Bodies Work Series, 8 vols. (Illus.). 384p. (gr. 5-8). 1988. Set. 87.60g (*0-382-09733-5*) Silver Burdett Pr.
Human Body: A Prentice Hall Illustrated Dictionary. LC 92-22213. (Illus.). 160p. 1993. 19.00 (*0-671-84693-0*) P-H Gen Ref & Trav.
Kolkmeyer, Alexandra. The Clear Red Stone: A Myth & the Meaning of Menstruation. Goldstein, Lynn, ed. Kirby, Thomas, illus. LC 82-2956. 64p. (gr. 3-12). 1982. text ed. 9.50 (*0-942524-01-2*) In Sight Pr NM.
Lauber, Patricia. Your Body & How It Works. (Illus.). (gr. 3-5). 1966. PLB 12.99 (*0-394-90125-8*) Random Bks Yng Read.
Little, Marjorie. The Endocrine System. (Illus.). 112p. (gr. 6-12). 1990. 18.95 (*0-7910-0016-8*) Chelsea Hse.
Marzollo, Jean. Getting Your Period. (gr. 4-7). 1993. pap. 6.99 (*0-14-036193-6*) Puffin Bks.
Morris, Neil. Where Does My Spaghetti go When I Eat It? Questions Kids Ask about the Human Body. Brown, Mik, illus. LC 94-14121. 1994. write for info. (*0-89577-608-1*, Readers Digest Kids) RD Assn.
My Body. LC 91-60535. (Illus.). 24p. (ps-3). 1991. 8.95 (*1-879431-07-6*) Dorling Kindersley.
Olivier, Pierre & Wessels, Florence. My Body. (Illus.). 128p. (ps-3). 1993. 7.00 (*0-679-84160-1*); PLB 11.99 (*0-679-94160-6*) Random Bks Yng Read.
Parker, Steve. Human Body. LC 93-31076. (Illus.). 64p. (gr. k-5). 1994. 9.95 (*1-56458-322-8*) Dorling Kindersley.
Rojany, Lisa & Strong, Stacie. Exploring the Human Body. Griffith, Linda, illus. Haber, Jon Z. & Smith, Rodgerconcept by. LC 92-7514. (Illus.). (gr. 4-7). 1992. 13.95 (*0-8120-6298-1*) Barron.
Royston, Angela. You & Your Body. LC 94-16304. 1994. write for info. (*0-8160-3217-3*) Facts on File.
Settel, Joanne & Baggett, Nancy. Why Does My Nose Run? (And Other Questions Kids Ask about Their Bodies) Tunney, Linda, illus. LC 84-21549. 80p. (gr. 4-6). 1985. SBE 13.95 (*0-689-31078-1*, Atheneum Child Bk) Macmillan Child Grp.
Skin, Hair & Teeth. 48p. (gr. 5-8). 1988. PLB 10.95 (*0-382-09706-8*) Silver Burdett Pr.
Stein, Sara. The Body Book. LC 91-50957. (Illus.). (gr. 4-7). 1992. 19.95 (*1-56305-298-9*, 3298); pap. 11.95 (*0-89480-805-2*, 1805) Workman Pub.
Time Life Book Editors. What Is a Bellybutton? First Questions & Answers about the Human Body. Kagan, Neil, ed. (Illus.). 48p. (ps). 1993. write for info. (*0-7835-0854-9*); lib. bdg. write for info. (*0-7835-0855-7*) Time-Life.
VanCleave, Janice P. Janice VanCleave's Human Body Book for Every Kid: Easy Activities that Make Learning Science Fun. LC 94-20862. (gr. k up). 1995. write for info. (*0-471-02413-9*); pap. write for info. (*0-471-02408-2*) Wiley.
You & Your Body. (Illus.). 80p. (gr. k-6). 1986. per set 199.00 (*0-8172-2589-7*) Raintree Steck-V.

PHYSIOLOGY OF PLANTS

see Plant Physiology

PIANISTS

Guerry, Jack. Silvio Scionti: Remembering a Master Pianist & Teacher. LC 91-10498. (Illus.). 240p. 1991. 25.00 (*0-929398-27-0*) UNTX Pr.
Kidd, Leonice T. They All Sat Down: Pianists in Profile. (Illus.). viii, 133p. (Orig.). (gr. 8-12). 1986. pap. 9.95 (*0-9619974-0-0*) Chrlstn SC.
—They All Sat Down: Pianists in Profile. 2nd ed. (Illus.). 151p. (Orig.). (gr. 8 up). 1989. pap. write for info. (*0-9619974-1-9*) Chrlstn SC.

PIANISTS–FICTION

Bailey, Bobbi M. Emma's Happy Birthday Piano. DeFazio, Deborah, illus. 36p. (gr. k-4). 1991. pap. 7.95 (*0-9625005-1-8*) Wee Pr.
Barrett, Mary B. Sing to the Stars. Speidel, Sandra, illus. LC 92-41773. 1994. 15.95 (*0-316-08224-4*) Little.
Delton, Judy. My Mom Made Me Take Piano Lessons. LC 92-45661. (gr. 4 up). 1994. 13.95 (*0-385-31091-9*) Doubleday.
Pascal, Francine. Elizabeth's Piano Lessons. (ps-3). 1994. pap. 2.99 (*0-553-48102-9*) Bantam.
Ray, Mary L. Pianna. LC 91-14609. (ps-3). 1994. 14.95 (*0-15-261357-9*, HB Juv Bks) HarBrace.
Sweeney, Joyce. Piano Man. 1994. pap. 3.99 (*0-440-21915-9*) Dell.

PIANO

Beirne, Barbara. A Pianist's Debut: Preparing for the Concert Stage. Beirne, Barbara, photos by. (Illus.). 56p. (gr. 2-5). 1990. PLB 21.50 (*0-87614-432-6*) Carolrhoda Bks.
Blackwood, Alan. Piano & Keyboards. (Illus.). 32p. (gr. 4-7). 1993. PLB 12.40 (*0-531-17422-0*, Gloucester Pr) Watts.
Bock, Fred. Charlie Brown's Favorite Sunday School Songs. Schulz, Charles, illus. 24p. (Orig.). (gr. 1-6). 1992. pap. 7.95 (*1-56516-012-6*) Houston IN.
Brimhall, John. Children's Piano Method. (Illus.). 64p. (Orig.). (gr. 1-6). 1984. pap. text ed. 5.95 (*0-8494-2887-4*, T430) Hansen Ed Mus.
Bubniuk, Irena. Preliminary Piano Work for the Student of Music, Vol. 1. (Illus.). (gr. k up). 1992. Set; Incl. music wkbk. & text bk. 75.00 (*1-882596-00-5*); Text bk., 159p. write for info. (*1-882596-01-3*); Music wkbk., spiral bdg., 200p. write for info. (*1-882596-02-1*) BML.
Czerny, Carl. School of Velocity for Piano, Op. 299, Complete Edition. 101p. 1903. pap. 7.50 (*0-8258-0108-7*, L 338) Fischer Inc NY.
Danes, E. More Easy Piano Classics. (Illus.). 64p. (gr. 2-9). 1994. PLB 17.96 (*0-88110-703-4*, Usborne); pap. 8.95 (*0-7460-1698-0*, Usborne) EDC.
Edison, June. Clavinova Sampler Pack Software. Schulz, Charles, illus. 12p. (Orig.). (gr. 1-6). 1992. pap. 19.95 (*1-56516-014-2*) Houston IN.
—Peanuts, Bk. 1. Schulz, Charles, illus. 40p. (Orig.). (gr. 1-6). 1989. pap. 5.50 (*1-56516-038-X*) Houston IN.
—Peanuts, Bk. 2. Schulz, Charles, illus. 38p. (Orig.). (gr. 1-6). 1989. pap. 5.50 (*1-56516-039-8*) Houston IN.
—Peanuts, Bk. 3. Schulz, Charles, illus. 40p. (Orig.). (gr. 1-6). 1989. pap. 5.50 (*1-56516-040-1*) Houston IN.
—Peanuts, Bk. 4. Schulz, Charles, illus. 40p. (Orig.). (gr. 1-6). 1989. pap. 5.50 (*1-56516-041-X*) Houston IN.
—Peanuts, Bk. 5. Schulz, Charles, illus. 40p. (Orig.). (gr. 1-6). 1989. pap. 5.50 (*1-56516-042-8*) Houston IN.
—Peanuts, Bk. 6. Schulz, Charles, illus. 38p. (Orig.). (gr. 1-6). 1989. pap. 5.50 (*1-56516-043-6*) Houston IN.
—Peanuts Christmas Album. Schulz, Charles, illus. 38p. (Orig.). (gr. 1-6). 1989. pap. 5.50 (*1-56516-049-5*) Houston IN.
—Peanuts First Program Book. Schultz, Charles, illus. 30p. (Orig.). (gr. 1-6). 1989. pap. 5.50 (*1-56516-044-4*) Houston IN.
—Peanuts First Program Book: Clavinova Software. Schulz, Charles, illus. 30p. (Orig.). (gr. 1-6). 1992. pap. 34.95 (*1-56516-018-5*) Houston IN.
—Peanuts Piano, Bk. 1: Clavinova Software. Schulz, Charles, illus. 40p. (Orig.). (gr. 1-6). 1992. pap. 34.95 (*1-56516-015-0*) Houston IN.
—Peanuts Piano, Bk. 2: Clavinova Software. Schulz, Charles, illus. 38p. (Orig.). (gr. 1-6). 1992. pap. 34.95 (*1-56516-016-9*) Houston IN.
—Peanuts Second Program Book. Schulz, Charles, illus. 36p. (Orig.). (gr. 1-6). 1989. pap. 5.50 (*1-56516-045-2*) Houston IN.
—Snoopy's Very First Christmas Songs. Schulz, Charles, illus. 32p. (Orig.). (gr. 1-6). 1989. pap. 5.50 (*1-56516-046-0*) Houston IN.
—Snoopy's Very First Christmas Songs: Clavinova Software. Schulz, Charles, illus. 32p. (Orig.). (gr. 1-6). 1992. pap. 34.95 (*1-56516-020-7*) Houston IN.
Kochevitsky, George. Art of Piano Playing: A Scientific Approach. (Illus.). 80p. (gr. 9 up). 1967. pap. text ed. 11.95 (*0-87487-068-2*) Summy-Birchard.
Leanza, Frank. How to Get Started with the Piano. (Illus.). 24p. 1993. pap. 3.95 (*0-934687-23-4*) Crystal Pubs.
Lubin, Ernest. A Start at the Piano. LC 78-110975. (Orig.). (gr. 5-8). 1977. pap. 9.95 (*0-8256-2149-6*) Music Sales.
Moncomble, Gerard. Octave & His Piano. (Illus.). 275p. (gr. 1-5). 1993. pap. 19.95 (*0-572-01966-1*, Pub. by W Foulsham UK) Trans-Atl Phila.
Patrick, Ann. Let's Make Piano Music with Marvin, Bk. 3. 40p. (Orig.). (gr. k-7). 1987. pap. 6.95 (*0-685-17364-X*) Centerstream Pub.
Philipp, Lillie H. Piano Technique: Tone, Touch, Phrasing & Dynamics. (Illus.). 90p. (gr. 7 up). 1982. pap. 5.95 (*0-486-24272-2*) Dover.
Phipps, C. & Hawthorne, P. Piano Classics (Blu) (Illus.). 128p. (gr. 2-9). 1994. pap. 16.95 (*0-7460-1967-X*, Usborne) EDC.
Poffenberger, Nancy. Instant Piano Fun: Book One. 34p. (gr. 4). 1985. pap. 9.95 (*0-938293-25-7*) Fun Pub OH.
—Now! Instant Keyboard Fun I. 32p. (gr. 4 up). 1985. pap. 4.95 (*0-938293-39-7*) Fun Pub OH.
Storr, Catherine. The Nutcracker. Tchaikovsky, contrib. by. (Illus.). 32p. (ps up). 1988. pap. 9.95 (*0-571-10080-5*) Faber & Faber.
Thomas, A. First Book of the Piano. (Illus.). 64p. (gr. 2-6). 1988. PLB 14.96 (*0-88110-332-2*); pap. 8.95 (*0-7460-0197-5*) EDC.
Welch, John. Charlie Brown's Piano Album. Schulz, Charles, illus. 38p. (Orig.). (gr. 1-6). 1989. pap. 5.50 (*1-56516-054-1*) Houston IN.
—Snoopy's Easy Piano Album. Schulz, Charles, illus. 38p. (Orig.). (gr. 1-6). 1989. pap. 5.50 (*1-56516-052-5*) Houston IN.

—Snoopy's Favorite Piano Solos. Schulz, Charles, illus. 38p. (Orig.). (gr. 1-6). 1989. pap. 5.50 (*1-56516-053-3*) Houston IN.
Welch, John, ed. Schroeder's Favorite Classics, Vol. 1. Schulz, Charles, illus. 38p. (Orig.). (gr. 1-6). 1989. pap. 5.50 (*1-56516-047-9*) Houston IN.
—Schroeder's Favorite Classics, Vol. 2. Schulz, Charles, illus. 38p. (Orig.). (gr. 1-6). 1989. pap. 5.50 (*1-56516-048-7*) Houston IN.
—Schroeder's Favorite Classics, Vol. 1: Clavinova Software. Schulz, Charles, illus. 38p. (Orig.). (gr. 1-6). 1992. pap. 34.95 (*1-56516-021-5*) Houston IN.
—Schroeder's First Recital. Schulz, Charles, illus. 38p. (Orig.). (gr. 1-6). 1989. pap. 5.50 (*1-56516-050-9*) Houston IN.
—Schroeder's First Recital Encores. Schulz, Charles, illus. 38p. (Orig.). (gr. 1-6). 1989. pap. 5.50 (*1-56516-051-7*) Houston IN.

PIANO MUSIC

Abbey, Randall. Octahedral: Eight Intermediate Piano Solos. 20p. (gr. 6-12). 1993. 3.95 (*0-9636777-6-4*) Aplomb Pub.
Aladdin. (Illus.). 16p. (Orig.). 1993. pap. 19.95 (*0-7935-2809-7*, HL00826003) H Leonard.
Brimhall, John. My Favorite Easy Classics, Bk. 5. 128p. (Orig.). (gr. 1-3). 1984. pap. text ed. 10.95 (*0-8494-2182-9*, 0116) Hansen Ed Mus.
Bryansky, Faina. The Key to Music Making, Pt. I: Piano Method for Beginners. Squillace, Albert & Kuznetsov, Eugene, illus. LC 88-50726. 48p. (gr. 1-5). 1988. pap. 8.00 (*0-929571-00-2*) White Lilac Pr.
Clark, Frances. Look & Listen, Pt. A. Goss, Louise & Kraehenbuehl, Davidcontrib. by. 48p. (Orig.). (gr. k-6). 1962. pap. text ed. 6.95 (*0-87487-176-X*) Summy-Birchard.
—Look & Listen, Pt. B. Goss, Louise & Kraehenbuehl, Davidcontrib. by. 48p. (Orig.). (gr. k-12). 1962. pap. text ed. 6.95 (*0-87487-177-8*) Summy-Birchard.
—Look & Listen, Pt. C. Goss, Louise & Kraehenbuehl, Davidcontrib. by. 48p. (Orig.). (gr. k-12). 1962. pap. text ed. 6.95 (*0-87487-178-6*) Summy-Birchard.
—Look & Listen, Pt. D. Goss, Louise & Kraehenbuehl, Davidcontrib. by. 48p. (Orig.). (gr. k-12). 1962. pap. text ed. 6.95 (*0-87487-179-4*) Summy-Birchard.
Clark, Frances & Goss, Louise. Write & Play Time, Pt. A. 64p. (Orig.). (gr. k-6). 1974. pap. text ed. 9.95 (*0-87487-196-4*) Summy-Birchard.
Collins, Ann & Clary, Linda. Sing & Play--Preschool Piano Book One. (Illus.). 60p. (ps). 1987. spiral bdg. 5.00 (*0-87563-307-2*) Stipes.
Cramer, J. B. Fifty Selected Studies for Piano. Von Bulow, Hans, ed. 116p. 1946. pap. 12.00 (*0-8258-0138-9*, L 525) Fischer Inc NY.
Czerny, Carl. One Hundred Practical Exercises for Piano, Op. 139. 76p. 1905. pap. 8.95 (*0-8258-0134-6*) Fischer Inc NY.
—Thirty New Studies in Technique for Piano, Op. 849. 56p. 1907. pap. 6.75 (*0-8258-0127-3*, L 487) Fischer Inc NY.
Dittenhaver, Sarah L., et al. Tune Time, 2 pts. rev. ed. Goss, Louise, ed. 48p. (gr. k-6). 1973. pap. text ed. 6.95 pt. A (*0-87487-194-8*); pap. text ed. 6.95 pt. B (*0-87487-195-6*) Summy-Birchard.
Durnin, Michael. Learn to Play Mozart. (Illus.). 64p. (gr. 5-12). 1993. pap. 8.95 (*0-7460-0964-X*, Usborne) EDC.
Eckstein, Maxwell, ed. Let Us Have Music for Piano: Seventy-Four Famous Melodies, Vol. 2. 111p. pap. 9.95 (*0-8258-0048-X*, 03127) Fischer Inc NY.
—Let Us Have Music for Piano: Seventy-Four Melodies, Vol. 1. 112p. pap. 9.95 (*0-8258-0047-1*, 02942) Fischer Inc NY.
Faber, Nancy & Faber, Randall. ChordTime Piano Hymns: Level 2 - I, IV, V7 Chords in Keys of C,G & F. McLean, Edwin, ed. Terpstra, Gwen, illus. 24p. (gr. 2-4). 1988. pap. 4.95 (*0-929666-03-8*) FJH Music Co Inc.
—PlayTime Piano Christmas: Level 1 - Five Finger Melodies. McLean, Edwin, ed. Terpstra, Gwen, illus. 24p. (gr. 1-3). 1988. pap. 4.95 (*0-929666-02-X*) FJH Music Co Inc.
—PlayTime Piano Hymns: Level One - Five Finger Melodies. McLean, Edwin, ed. Terpstra, Gwen, illus. 24p. (gr. 1-3). 1988. pap. 4.95 (*0-929666-00-3*) FJH Music Co Inc.
—PlayTime Piano Popular: Level One - Five Finger Melodies. McLean, Edwin, ed. Terpstra, Gwen, illus. 24p. (gr. 1-3). 1988. pap. 4.95 (*0-929666-01-1*) FJH Music Co Inc.
Goss, Louise & McArtot, Marion. Technic Time, Pt. A. 48p. (Orig.). (gr. k-6). 1974. pap. text ed. 6.95 (*0-87487-189-1*) Summy-Birchard.
Goss, Louise, ed. Themes from Masterworks, 3 bks. 16p. (Orig.). (gr. k-12). 1970. pap. text ed. 5.95 Bk. 1 (*0-87487-191-3*); pap. text ed. 5.95 Bk. 2 (*0-87487-192-1*); pap. text ed. 5.95 Bk. 3 (*0-87487-193-X*) Summy-Birchard.
Grove, Roger. Riches of Rag. 16p. (Orig.). (gr. k-12). 1976. pap. text ed. 5.95 (*0-87487-188-3*) Summy-Birchard.

Guthrie, Kari H. National Anthems: Western & Middle Europe, 4 bks. (Illus.). 163p. (Orig.). (gr. 4-9). 1993. Set. pap. 24.95 (*0-9631333-4-9*) Hi I Que Pub.

NATIONAL ANTHEMS--WESTERN & MIDDLE EUROPE is an integrated learning book series. Each anthem includes a map of the individual country & surrounding countries, form of government, language spoken, capital, currency, & national holidays. The cover displays the flags of the included countries in vibrant color. Also included are the words in the original language & English translations. Music is in piano score, arranged for easy to intermediate abilities. This book is suitable for all ages, but is specifically formatted to appeal to grades 4-9. These books provide a wonderful aspect of cultural, historical & heritage information. Ideal reference for schools, teachers, & libraries; also as gifts to young students of history or music. Since these anthems are not easily accessible it is important to note that college age students studying culture, history, music or language may be interested in this series. NATIONAL ANTHEMS (WESTERN & MIDDLE EUROPE) is a series of 4 books. Book 1 (0-9631333-0-6) includes France, Iceland, Ireland, Portugal, Spain. Book 2 (0-9631333-1-4), Andorra, Belgium, Denmark, Germany, Lichtenstein, Luxembourg, Monaco, Netherlands, Norway, Switzerland. Book 3 (0-9631333-2-2), Albania, Austria, Czechoslovakia (1918-1993), Hungary, Italy, Malta, San Marino, Sweden. Book 4 (0-9631333-0-0), Bulgaria, Finland, Greece, Poland, Romania, the former U.S.S.R., Yugoslavia. Each book also available separately at $6.95 each. Order directly from: Hi. I. Que Publishing, P.O. Box 508, Claremont, CA 91711-0508. (909) 622-7501, or your local distributor.
Publisher Provided Annotation.

Hammond, Vicky L. & Dalby, Judy N. Primary Passages Plus: Favorite Songs & Hymns Arranged for Newcomers to the Piano. Waller, Nancy G., illus. 32p. (Orig.). 1989. pap. 5.95 (*0-9624262-3-7*) Hammond Dalby Music.
Hammond, Vicky L. & Smith, Jerry. Accent on Youth: Piano Solos of Favorite Songs & Hymns. 24p. (Orig.). 1989. pap. 6.95 (*0-9624262-7-X*) Hammond Dalby Music.
Hanon & Lindquist, A. Technical Variants. 32p. (Orig.). (gr. k-12). 1929. pap. text ed. 5.95 (*0-87487-657-5*) Summy-Birchard.
Hawthorn, P. Easy Piano Classics. (Illus.). 64p. (gr. 2-6). 1991. PLB 14.96 (*0-88110-424-8*, Usborne); pap. 8.95 (*0-7460-0643-8*, Usborne) EDC.
Hawthorn, P. & Armstrong, S. Easy Piano Tunes. (Illus.). 64p. (gr. 2-6). 1989. PLB 14.96 (*0-88110-410-8*, Usborne); pap. 8.95 (*0-7460-0459-1*, Usborne) EDC.
Kidsongs: An Easy Book of Musical Fun for Children. 80p. 1992. pap. 9.95 stay-open bdg. (*0-7935-0233-0*, 00001102) H Leonard.
Kraehenbuehl, David, et al. Supplementary Solos: Level 1. Clark, Frances & Goss, Louise, eds. 32p. (gr. k-12). 1979. pap. text ed. 5.95 (*0-87487-105-0*) Summy-Birchard.
—Supplementary Solos: Level 2. Clark, Frances & Goss, Louise, eds. 32p. (gr. k-12). 1980. pap. text ed. 5.95 (*0-87487-106-9*) Summy-Birchard.
Lemoine, H. Etudes Enfantines for Piano, Op. 37. 52p. 1904. pap. 7.00 (*0-8258-0106-0*, L 323) Fischer Inc NY.
Singing Keys Omnibus. 64p. (Orig.). (gr. 6-12). 1946. pap. text ed. 9.95 (*0-87487-651-6*) Summy-Birchard.
Storr, Catherine. Hansel & Gretel. Humperdinck, Engelbert, contrib. by. (Illus.). 32p. (ps up). 1988. pap. 9.95 (*0-571-10083-X*) Faber & Faber.
—The Nutcracker. Tchaikovsky, contrib. by. (Illus.). 32p. (ps up). 1988. pap. 9.95 (*0-571-10080-5*) Faber & Faber.
Summy Piano Solo Package: Advanced, No. 501. 32p. (gr. 10-12). 1976. pap. text ed. 5.95 (*0-87487-656-7*) Summy-Birchard.
Summy Piano Solo Package: Elementary, No. 101. (Illus.). 32p. (Orig.). (gr. k-2). 1976. pap. text ed. 5.95 (*0-87487-652-4*) Summy-Birchard.
Summy Piano Solo Package: Intermediate, No.301. 32p. (Orig.). (gr. 5-8). 1976. pap. text ed. 5.95 (*0-87487-654-0*) Summy-Birchard.
Summy Piano Solo Package: Late Elementary, No.201. 32p. (Orig.). (gr. 2-6). 1976. pap. text ed. 5.95 (*0-87487-653-2*) Summy-Birchard.
Summy Piano Solo Package: Late Intermediate, No.401. 32p. (Orig.). (gr. 8-10). 1976. pap. text ed. 5.95 (*0-87487-655-9*) Summy-Birchard.
Suschitsky, Anya. More Easy Piano Tunes. (Illus.). 64p. (gr. 3 up). 1993. pap. 8.95 (*0-7460-1390-6*, Usborne) EDC.
Wolff, B. The Little Pischna: Forty-Eight Preparatory Exercises for Piano. (ENG & GER.). 1907. pap. 4.00 (*0-8258-0122-2*, L 475) Fischer Inc NY.

PICASSO, PABLO, 1881-1972

Beardsley, John. Pablo Picasso. (Illus.). 92p. 1991. 19.95 (*0-8109-3713-1*) Abrams.
Giraudy, Daniele, text by. Pablo Picasso: The Minotaur, An Art Play Book. (Illus.). 32p. (gr. 2 up). 1988. 17.95 (*0-8109-1471-9*) Abrams.
Hart, Tony. Picasso. Hellard, Susan, illus. LC 93-8750. 24p. (ps-3). 1994. pap. 5.95 (*0-8120-1826-5*) Barron.
Heslewood, Juliet. Introducing Picasso: Painter, Sculptor. LC 92-29653. 1993. 15.95 (*0-316-35917-3*) Little.
Lepscky, Ibi. Pablo Picasso. Cardoni, Paolo, illus. 24p. (gr. k-3). pap. 4.95 (*0-8120-1450-2*) Barron.
Lyttle, Richard B. Pablo Picasso: The Man & the Image. LC 89-6561. (Illus.). 192p. (gr. 7 up). 1989. SBE 15.95 (*0-689-31393-4*, Atheneum Child Bk) Macmillan Child Grp.
Raboff, Ernest. Pablo Picasso. 1987. pap. 7.95 (*0-06-446067-3*) HarpC Child Bks.
Rollyson, Carl. The Arts - Pablo Picasso. LC 92-44757. 1992. 19.93 (*0-86625-488-9*); 14.95s.p. (*0-685-67772-9*) Rourke Pubns.
Selfridge, John W. Pablo Picasso: Spanish Painter. LC 93-19205. (Illus.). (ps-3). 1993. PLB 18.95 (*0-7910-1777-X*, Am Art Analog); pap. write for info. (*0-7910-1996-9*) Chelsea Hse.
Sommer, Robin L. & MacDonald, Patricia. Pablo Picasso. (Illus.). 128p. (gr. 7-9). 1990. 9.95 (*0-382-24031-6*); lib. bdg. 12.95 (*0-382-09903-6*) Silver Burdett Pr.
Swisher, Clarice. Pablo Picasso. LC 94-8475. (Illus.). 112p. (gr. 5-8). 1995. 14.95 (*1-56006-062-X*) Lucent Bks.
Venezia, Mike. Picasso. Venezia, Mike, illus. LC 87-33023. 32p. (ps-4). 1988. PLB 12.85 (*0-516-02271-7*); pap. 4.95 (*0-516-42271-5*) Childrens.
Vila, Carmen. Tracy Knows Picasso: Children's Art History Read-Along Book. (Illus.). 24p. (gr. 1-3). Date not set. write for info. incl. tape (*0-9635047-0-3*) VILA Grp.

PICKLING

see Canning and Preserving

PICKNICKING

Darling, Abigail. Teddy Bears' Picnic Cookbook. Day, Alexandra, illus. LC 92-28174. 1993. 4.99 (*0-14-054157-8*) Puffin Bks.
Kennedy, Jimmy. The Teddy Bears' Picnic. Hague, Michael, illus. LC 91-27709. 32p. (ps-2). 1992. 16.95 (*0-8050-1008-4*, Bks Young Read); poster avail. H Holt & Co.

PICTOGRAPHS

see Picture Writing

PICTORIAL WORKS

see Pictures

PICTURE BOOKS

Aardema, Verna. Oh, Kojo! How Could You? Brown, Marc T., illus. LC 84-1710. 32p. (ps-3). 1984. 14.00 (*0-8037-0006-7*); PLB 12.89 (*0-8037-0007-5*) Dial Bks Young.
ABC Colouring Book. (Illus.). (ps-6). pap. 2.95 (*0-565-00834-X*, Pub. by Natural Hist Mus) Parkwest Pubns.
Ada, Alam F. In the Cow's Backyard - La Hamaca de la Vaca. Escriva, Vivi, illus. (SPA & ENG.). 23p. (gr. k-2). 1991. English ed. 6.95 (*1-56014-275-8*); Spanish ed. 6.95 (*1-56014-219-7*) Santillana.
Ada, Alma F. Pregones. Torrecilla, Pablo, illus. (SPA.). 24p. (gr. 3-8). 1993. 16.95x (*1-56492-110-7*) Laredo.
Adams, David. The Three Little Pigs Go to Greasy Pete's. Holland, Janet, illus. 40p. (ps-3). 1994. PLB 14.95 (*0-9638421-9-6*); pap. 5.95 (*0-9638421-8-8*) Flatland Tales.
Adams, Pam. The Fairground. (Illus.). 32p. (ps). 1984. 8.95 (*0-85953-194-5*, Child's Play England) Childs Play.
—Tingaling. (gr. 4 up). 1981. 9.95 (*0-85953-328-X*) Childs Play.
Adams, Pam, illus. How Many? 16p. (Orig.). (ps-2). 1975. pap. 3.95 (*0-85953-045-0*, Pub. by Child's Play England) Childs Play.
—Same & Different. 16p. (Orig.). (ps-2). 1975. pap. 3.95 (*0-85953-043-4*, Pub. by Child's Play England) Childs Play.
Add It Up! 1989. pap. 1.49 (*0-553-18396-6*) Bantam.
Addison-Wesley Staff. The Farmer & the Beet. (Illus.). (gr. k-2). 1988. text ed. 31.75 (*0-201-19318-3*); pap. text ed. 12.95 (*0-201-19059-1*) Addison-Wesley.
—The Gingerbread Man. (Illus.). 16p. (gr. k-2). 1989. text ed. 31.75 (*0-201-19320-5*); pap. text ed. 12.95 (*0-201-19064-8*) Addison-Wesley.
—Goldilocks & the Three Bears. (Illus.). (gr. k-2). 1988. pap. text ed. 31.75 (*0-201-19319-1*) Addison-Wesley.

—Goldilocks & the Three Bears Little Book. (Illus.). 16p. (gr. k-3). 1989. text ed. 12.95 (0-201-19065-6); pap. text ed. 4.50 (0-201-19055-9) Addison-Wesley.
—The Hare & the Tortoise. (Illus.). 16p. (gr. k-2). 1989. 31.75 (0-201-19324-8); pap. text ed. 12.95 (0-201-19369-8) Addison-Wesley.
—How the Moon Got in the Sky. (Illus.). (gr. k-2). 1989. 31.75 (0-201-19325-6); pap. text ed. 12.95 (0-201-19366-3) Addison-Wesley.
—The Little Red Hen. (Illus.). 16p. (gr. k-2). 1989. text ed. 31.75 (0-201-19323-X); pap. text ed. 12.95 (0-201-19368-X) Addison-Wesley.
—The Three Little Pigs. 16p. (gr. k-2). 1988. text ed. 31.75 (0-201-19322-1); pap. 12.95 (0-201-19066-4) Addison-Wesley.
Addy, Sharon H. A Visit with Great-Grandma. Fay, Ann, ed. LC 88-20867. (Illus.). 32p. (gr. 1-3). 1989. 13.95g (0-8075-8497-5) A Whitman.
Adler, David A. A Picture Book of George Washington. Wallner, John & Wallner, Alexandra, illus. LC 88-16384. 32p. (ps-3). 1989. reinforced bdg. 15.95 (0-8234-0732-2); pap. 5.95 (0-8234-0800-0) Holiday.
—A Picture Book of Jewish Holidays. Heller, Linda, illus. LC 81-2765. 32p. (ps-3). 1981. reinforced bdg. 14.95 (0-8234-0396-3); pap. 5.95 (0-8234-0756-X) Holiday.
Adoff, Arnold. Black Is Brown Is Tan. McCully, Emily A., illus. LC 73-9855. 32p. (ps-3). 1992. pap. 3.95 (0-06-443269-6, Trophy) HarpC Child Bks.
—Hard to Be Six. Hanna, Cheryl, illus. LC 89-45903. 32p. (gr. k-3). 1990. 12.95 (0-688-09013-3); lib. bdg. 12.88 (0-688-09579-8) Lothrop.
Agee, Jon. Flapstick! Agee, Jon, illus. 24p. 1993. 10.99 (0-525-45124-2, DCB) Dutton Child Bks.
Agell, Charlotte. The Sailor's Book. Agell, Charlotte, illus. 32p. (gr. 3-6). 1991. PLB 14.95 (0-920668-90-9); pap. 4.95 (0-920668-91-7) Firefly Bks Ltd.
Ahlberg, Janet. Peek-A-Boo. (ps). 1990. 4.95 (0-670-83283-9) Viking Child Bks.
Ahlberg, Janet & Ahlberg, Allan. The Baby's Catalogue. Ahlberg, Janet & Ahlberg, Allan, illus. 32p. (gr. k up). 1986. pap. 5.95 (0-316-02038-9) Little.
—Each Peach Pear Plum. Ahlberg, Janet & Ahlberg, Allan, illus. 32p. (ps-1). 1986. pap. 3.99 (0-14-050639-X, Puffin) Puffin Bks.
—Each Peach Pear Plum: An I-Spy Story. LC 79-16726. (Illus.). 32p. (gr. k-3). 1979. pap. 12.95 (0-670-28705-9) Viking Child Bks.
—Peek-A-Boo. (Illus.). 32p. (ps-k). 1984. pap. 4.50 (0-14-050107-X, Puffin) Puffin Bks.
Albertsen, June. Two Are Twins. Anton, Karen, illus. LC 86-70195. 31p. (ps-3). 1987. pap. 5.95 (0-9615839-0-8) Double Talk.
Alcott, Louisa May. Little Men. 240p. (gr. 4-6). 1984. pap. 2.99 (0-14-035018-7, Puffin) Puffin Bks.
Aldis, Dorothy. Hiding. Collins, Heather, illus. 32p. (ps-k). 1994. 11.99 (0-670-85410-7) Viking Child Bks.
Aleichem, Sholem. Hanukah Money. Shulevitz, Uri & Shub, Elizabeth, trs. Shulevitz, Uri, illus. LC 77-26693. 32p. (ps up). 1991. pap. 3.95 (0-688-10993-4, Mulberry) Morrow.
Alexander, Cecil F. All Things Bright & Beautiful. Morgan, Mary, illus. 32p. (Orig.). (ps-2). 1989. pap. 1.95 (0-448-34304-5, Platt & Munk Pubs) Putnam Pub Group.
Alexander, Liza. I Want to Be a Cowboy. Ewers, Joe, illus. 24p. (ps-k). 1992. write for info. (0-307-13117-3) Western Pub.
—Sesame Street: Ernie & Twiddlebug Town Fair. 1990. pap. write for info. (0-307-10030-8, Golden Pr) Western Pub.
—Sesame Street: Splish Splashy Day. (Illus.). 24p. (ps-k). 1989. pap. write for info. (0-307-10064-2, Pub. by Golden Bks) Western Pub.
—A Visit to the Sesame Street Museum. Mathiew, Joe, illus. LC 87-1685. 32p. (gr. 3-6). 1987. lib. bdg. 5.99 (0-394-98715-2); pap. 2.25 (0-394-88715-8) Random Bks Yng Read.
Alexander, Lloyd. The Kestrel. 256p. (gr. 7 up). 1983. pap. 3.99 (0-440-94393-0, LFL) Dell.
Alexander, Martha. I'll Protect You from the Jungle Beasts. Alexander, Martha, illus. LC 73-6015. 32p. (ps-2). 1983. PLB 8.89 (0-8037-4309-2) Dial Bks Young.
—The Magic Box. (Illus.). 64p. (ps-3). 1994. pap. 1.99 (0-14-050504-0, Puff Pied Piper) Puffin Bks.
—The Magic Hat. (Illus.). 64p. (ps-3). 1994. pap. 1.99 (0-14-050471-0, Puff Pied Piper) Puffin Bks.
—The Magic Picture. (Illus.). 64p. (ps-3). 1994. pap. 1.99 (0-14-050505-9, Puff Pied Piper) Puffin Bks.
—Maybe a Monster. Alexander, Martha, illus. LC 68-28732. 32p. (ps-2). 1985. PLB 8.89 (0-8037-5513-9) Dial Bks Young.
—Out, Out, Out. Alexander, Martha, illus. LC 68-15251. (gr. k-3). 1968. PLB 6.95 (0-685-01457-6) Dial Bks Young.
Alexander, Sue. Small Plays for Special Days. Huffman, Tom, illus. LC 76-28424. 64p. (ps-1). 1988. pap. 4.95 (0-89919-798-1, Clarion Bks) HM.
Aliki. The Two of Them. LC 79-10161. 32p. (ps up). 1987. pap. 4.95 (0-688-07337-9, Mulberry) Morrow.
Allard, Harry. Miss Nelson Has a Field Day. Marshall, James, illus. 32p. (gr. k-3). 1988. pap. 4.80 (0-395-48654-8, Sandpiper) HM.
—Miss Nelson Is Back. Marshall, James, illus. 1988. pap. 7.70 incl. cass. (0-395-48872-9) HM.
Allard, Harry & Marshall, James. The Stupids Take Off. Allard, Harry & Marshall, James, illus. 32p. (gr. k-3). 1989. 13.45 (0-395-50068-0) HM.
Allen, Constance. Grover's Book of Cute Things to Touch. (ps). 1990. write for info. (0-307-12320-0, Golden Pr) Western Pub.
Allen, Judy. Panda. Humphries, Tudor, illus. LC 92-54411. 32p. (ps up). 1993. 14.95 (1-56402-142-4) Candlewick Pr.
Allert, Kathy. Kate Greenaway Paper Dolls in Full Color. 1981. pap. 3.50 (0-486-24153-X) Dover.
Alley, R. W., illus. Busy Farm Trucks. 12p. (ps up). 1986. 6.95 (0-448-09883-0, G&D) Putnam Pub Group.
Almaraz, Humberto. Santa Will Love My Tree (Play Format) Almaraz, Humberto, illus. & intro. by. 12p. (Orig.). (ps-3). 1982. pap. 5.00 incl. 45 rpm record (0-9616528-1-0) Alpha Beto Music.
—Santa Will Love My Tree (Story Format) Almaraz, Humberto, illus. & intro. by. 12p. (Orig.). (ps-2). 1982. pap. 5.00 incl. 45 rpm record (0-9616528-0-2) Alpha Beto Music.
Alonso, Fernando. Little Red Hen - La Gallina Paulina. Gimeno, J. M., illus. (SPA & ENG.). 26p. (gr. k-2). 1989. Spanish ed. 5.25 (0-88272-467-3); English ed. 5.25 (0-88272-468-1) Santillana.
Alvin S. White Studio Staff, illus. Walt Disney's Pinocchio. LC 91-58612. 12p. (ps-3). 1992. 11.95 (1-56282-172-5) Disney Pr.
American Colortype Co., Staff. Cut & Assemble Paper Dollhouse Furniture. 1981. pap. 4.95 (0-486-24150-5) Dover.
Amerikaner, Susan. My Silly Book of ABCs. Brook, Bonnie, ed. Ziegler, Judy, illus. 32p. (ps-1). 1989. 4.95 (0-671-68119-2); PLB 6.95 (0-671-68363-2) Silver Pr.
—My Silly Book of Colors. Brook, Bonnie, ed. Ziegler, Judy, illus. 32p. (ps-1). 1989. 4.95 (0-671-68120-6); PLB 6.95 (0-671-68364-0) Silver Pr.
—My Silly Book of Counting. Brook, Bonnie, ed. Ziegler, Judy, illus. 32p. (ps-1). 1989. 4.95 (0-671-68121-4); PLB 6.95 (0-671-68365-9) Silver Pr.
—My Silly Book of Opposites. Brook, Bonnie, ed. Ziegler, Judy, illus. 32p. (ps-1). 1989. 4.95 (0-671-68122-2); PLB 6.95 (0-671-68366-7) Silver Pr.
—Silly Me! Books, 4 bks. Ziegler, Judy, illus. (ps-1). 1990. Set, 24p. ea. 19.80 (0-671-93116-4, J Messner); Set, 24p. ea. lib. bdg. 35.92 (0-671-93137-7) S&S Trade.
Amery. On the Farm. Cartwright, Stephen, illus. 20p. (ps). 1984. 3.95 (0-86020-853-2, Pub. by Usborne) EDC.
Amery, H. At the Zoo. (Illus.). 16p. (ps-1). 1984. (Usborne); pap. 3.95 (0-7460-1542-9) EDC.
Ancona, George & Miller, Mary B. Handtalk Zoo. Ancona, George, illus. LC 88-36861. 32p. (ps up). 1989. RSBE 14.95 (0-02-700801-0, Four Winds) Macmillan Child Grp.
Andersen, Hans Christian. The Emperor & the Nightingale. Van Nutt, Robert, illus. Tuber, Joel, adapted by. LC 88-11541. (Illus.). 44p. (ps up). 1991. pap. 14.95 (0-88708-082-0, Rabbit Ears); bk. & cass. pkg. 19.95 (0-88708-087-1, Rabbit Ears) Picture Bk Studio.
—The Little Mermaid. Iwasaki, Chihiro, illus. LC 84-9490. 32p. (gr. 2 up). 1991. pap. 15.95 (0-907234-59-3) Picture Bk Studio.
—The Nightingale. Le Gallienne, Eva, tr. from DAN. Burkert, Nancy E., illus. LC 64-18574. 48p. (gr. 2-6). 1985. pap. 7.95 (0-06-443070-7, Trophy) HarpC Child Bks.
—Thumbelina. Roberts, Tom, adapted by. Johnson, David, illus. LC 89-8484. 32p. (gr. 1 up). 1991. pap. 14.95 (0-88708-113-4, Rabbit Ears); incl. cassette 19.95 (0-88708-114-2, Rabbit Ears) Picture Bk Studio.
—Thumbeline. Zwerger, Lisbeth, illus. LC 85-12062. 28p. (gr. 1 up). 1991. pap. 14.95 (0-88708-006-5) Picture Bk Studio.
—The Ugly Duckling. Van Nutt, Robert, illus. LC 86-185. 48p. (gr. k up). 1986. 12.95 (0-394-88403-5); incl. cassette 15.95 (0-394-88298-9) Knopf Bks Yng Read.
—The Ugly Duckling. Bell, Anthea, tr. Marks, Alan, illus. LC 89-3975. 42p. (gr. k up). 1991. pap. 14.95 (0-88708-116-9) Picture Bk Studio.
Anderson, Carol J. Alphabet Soup. Harding, Trish T., illus. 60p. (gr. k-4). 1989. 12.95 (0-935317-26-0) Blue Heron WA.
Anderson, Debby. Here & There, Everywhere! LC 87-72709. (Illus.). 18p. (ps). 1988. bds. 4.99 (1-55513-643-5, Chariot Bks) Chariot Family.
—Jesus Loves Me. LC 87-72711. (Illus.). 18p. (ps). 1988. bds. 4.99 (1-55513-647-8, Chariot Bks) Chariot Family.
—My Friend Noah. LC 87-72710. (Illus.). 18p. (ps). 1988. bds. 4.99 (1-55513-665-6, Chariot Bks) Chariot Family.
Anderson, Kathleen. Old Mission San Luis Obispo de Tolosa: A Miniature Cut-Out & Color Model. Fast, Marti, illus. 8p. (Orig.). (gr. 4). 1990. pap. 3.95 (0-945092-12-1) EZ Nature.
Anderson, Paul S. Storytelling with the Flannel Board, 3 Bks, Bk. 1. Francis, Irene, illus. LC 21-650. 270p. (ps). 1963. 15.95 (0-513-00105-0) Denison.
—Storytelling with the Flannel Board, 3 Bks, Bk. 2. Arms, William, illus. LC 21-650. 260p. (ps). 1970. 15.95 (0-513-00137-9) Denison.
Anderson, Peggy P. Time for Bed, the Babysitter Said. LC 86-27388. (ps). 1987. 13.45 (0-395-41851-8) HM.
Andrews, Jan. Very Last First Time. Wallace, Ian, illus. LC 85-71606. 32p. (gr. k-4). 1986. SBE 14.95 (0-689-50388-1, M K McElderry) Macmillan Child Grp.
Anglo-Saxon Helmet. (Illus.). (gr. 2-6). cut-out model, incl. instructions 4.95 (0-7141-1673-4, Pub. by Brit Mus UK) Parkwest Pubns.
Anglund, Joan W. Baby's First Book. Anglund, Joan W., illus. 12p. (ps). 1985. 4.99 (0-394-87470-6) Random Bks Yng Read.
—How Many Days Has Baby To Play? Anglund, Joan W., illus. LC 87-19665. 21p. (ps-k). 1988. 7.95 (0-15-200460-2, Gulliver Bks) HarBrace.
—Morning Is a Little Child. Anglund, Joan W., illus. LC 69-11592. (gr. 4-6). 1969. 7.95 (0-15-255652-4, HB Juv Bks) HarBrace.
Animal Families. 8p. (ps). 1991. bds. 1.99 (0-517-66919-6) Random Hse Value.
Animal Fun. 1986. 1.98 (0-685-16868-9, 614979) Random Hse Value.
Animals. (Illus.). (ps-k). 1986. 0.75 (0-8091-6542-2) Paulist Pr.
Animals. 5p. (ps). 1991. soft fabric 3.95 (0-681-41091-4) Longmeadow Pr.
Animals' ABC's. (Illus.). (ps-3). 1988. 9.95 (0-8167-1443-6) Troll Assocs.
Anno, Mitsumasa. Anno's Alphabet: An Adventure in Imagination. Anno, Mitsumasa, illus. LC 73-21652. 64p. (ps up). 1988. pap. 7.95 (0-06-443190-8, Trophy) HarpC Child Bks.
—Anno's Counting Book. LC 76-28977. (Illus.). 32p. (ps-3). 1986. pap. 5.95 (0-06-443123-1, Trophy) HarpC Child Bks.
—Anno's Peekaboo. (Illus.). 32p. (ps-k). 1988. 10.95 (0-399-21520-4, Philomel Bks) Putnam Pub Group.
Appelbaum, Neil. Is There a Hole in Your Head? Appelbaum, Neil, illus. (gr. k-3). 1963. 8.95 (0-8392-3012-5) Astor-Honor.
Appleby, Ellen. Delicious Garden: Yummy Board Book. 1994. 3.98 (0-8317-9652-9) Smithmark.
—Happy Birthday: Yummy Board Book. 1994. 3.98 (0-8317-9659-6) Smithmark.
—I Love You: Yummy Board Book. 1994. 3.98 (0-8317-9651-0) Smithmark.
—Perfect Pizza: Yummy Board Book. 1994. 3.98 (0-8317-9653-7) Smithmark.
Appleby, Ellen, illus. Peek-A-Boo. 16p. (ps-k). 1990. pap. 3.95 casebound (0-671-70722-1, Little Simon) S&S Trade.
Apps, Roy. Trouble Next Door. White, Lorrain, illus. 80p. (ps-2). 1992. 13.95 (0-09-173975-6, Pub. by Hutchinson UK) Trafalgar.
Apy, Deborah, retold by. Beauty & the Beast. Hague, Michael, illus. LC 83-5495. 80p. (gr. 2-4). 1988. pap. 6.95 (0-8050-0948-5, Bks Young Read) H Holt & Co.
Archambault, John. Counting Sheep. Rombola, John, illus. LC 89-11163. 32p. (ps-2). 1989. 14.95 (0-8050-1135-8, Bks Young Read) H Holt & Co.
Argent, Kerry & Trinca, Rod. One Woolly Wombat. LC 84-21854. (Illus.). 32p. (ps-1). 1985. 12.95 (0-916291-00-6) Kane Miller Bk.
Ariev, Lauren. What Can Baby Do? Morgan, Mary, illus. 24p. (ps). 1992. bds. write for info. (0-307-06140-X, 6140) Western Pub.
Arnold, Arnold. Antique Paper Dolls, 1915-1920. 1976. pap. 3.95 (0-486-23176-3) Dover.
Arnosky, Jim. Come Out, Muskrats. LC 88-26611. (Illus.). 32p. (ps up). 1991. pap. 3.95 (0-688-10490-8, Mulberry) Morrow.
—Deer at the Brook. LC 84-12239. (Illus.). 32p. (ps up). 1991. pap. 4.95 (0-688-10488-6, Mulberry) Morrow.
—Raccoons & Ripe Corn. LC 87-4243. (Illus.). 32p. (ps up). 1991. pap. 4.95 (0-688-10489-4, Mulberry) Morrow.
Aronin, Ben. The Secret of the Sabbath Fish. Rieger, Shay, illus. LC 78-63437. (gr. k-4). 1979. 8.95 (0-8276-0110-7) JPS Phila.
The Artist, the Book & the Child: An Exhibition of Original Art for Children's Books. (Illus.). 60p. 1989. pap. 17.00 (0-89792-120-8) Ill St Museum.
Aruego, Jose. Look What I Can Do! Aruego, Jose, illus. LC 87-21743. 32p. (ps-1). 1988. pap. 3.95 (0-689-71205-7, Aladdin) Macmillan Child Grp.
Aruego, Jose & Dewey, Ariane. We Hide, You Seek. LC 78-13638. (Illus.). 32p. (ps up). 1988. pap. 4.95 (0-688-07815-X, Mulberry) Morrow.
Aryai, Sia. Baby Bright Board Books: ABC's. Aryai, Sia, photos by. (Illus.). 1993. 5.95 (1-56565-049-2) Lowell Hse.
—Baby Bright Board Books: Colors. Aryai, Sia, photos by. (Illus.). 1993. 5.95 (1-56565-050-6) Lowell Hse.
—Baby Bright Board Books: Shapes. Aryai, Sia, photos by. (Illus.). 1993. 5.95 (1-56565-051-4) Lowell Hse.
Asch, Frank. Moongame. (Illus.). 32p. (gr. k-4). 1987. pap. 14.00 (0-671-66452-2, S&S BFYR); pap. 4.95 (0-671-66453-0, S&S BFYR) S&S Trade.
Aseltine, Lorraine. First Grade Can Wait. Tucker, Kathleen, ed. LC 87-26457. (Illus.). 32p. (ps-2). 1988. PLB 11.95 (0-8075-2451-4) A Whitman.
Aseltine, Lorraine, et al. I'm Deaf, & It's Okay. LC 85-26446. (Illus.). 40p. (gr. 1-4). 1986. 11.95 (0-8075-3472-2) A Whitman.
Ashton, Elizabeth A. An Old-Fashioned ABC Book. Smith, Jessie W., illus. 32p. (ps-3). 1990. pap. 14.95 (0-670-83048-8) Viking Child Bks.
Averill, Esther. Jenny's Birthday Book. Averill, Esther, illus. LC 54-6589. 32p. (gr. k-3). 1954. PLB 14.89 (0-06-020251-3) HarpC Child Bks.
Awdry, W. Catch Me, Catch Me! A Thomas the Tank Engine Story. Bell, Owain, illus. LC 89-37547. 24p. (Orig.). (ps-2). 1990. pap. 2.25 (0-679-80485-4) Random Bks Yng Read.

—Choo-Choo, Peek-a-Boo. Bell, Owain, illus. LC 91-61250. 14p. (ps). 1992. 3.99 (*0-679-82262-3*) Random Bks Yng Read.
—Good Morning, James. Bell, Owain, illus. 12p. (ps). 1992. 3.99 (*0-679-82707-2*) Random Bks Yng Read.
—Thomas the Tank Engine ABC: (Just Right for 2's & 3's) McArthur, Kenny, photos by. LC 89-10605. (Illus.). 24p. (ps). 1990. 5.99 (*0-679-80362-9*) Random Bks Yng Read.
—Thomas the Tank Engine Starter Library, 4 bks. Dalby, C. Reginald, illus. (gr. 1-5). 1990. Repr. of 1945 ed. boxed set 19.95 (*0-679-80792-6*) Random Bks Yng Read.
Aylesworth, Jim. The Good-Night Kiss. Krudop, Walter L., illus. LC 91-40952. 32p. (ps-1). 1993. SBE 14.95 (*0-689-31515-5*, Atheneum Child Bk) Macmillan Child Grp.
—Mr. McGill Goes to Town. Graham, Thomas, illus. LC 89-31111. 32p. (ps-2). 1989. 13.95 (*0-8050-0772-5*, Owlet BYR) H Holt & Co.
—Mother Halverson's New Cat. Goffe, Toni, illus. LC 88-29279. 32p. (gr. k-3). 1989. SBE 13.95 (*0-689-31465-5*, Atheneum Child Bk) Macmillan Child Grp.
—Two Terrible Frights. Christelow, Eileen, illus. LC 86-25859. 32p. (ps-2). 1987. SBE 13.95 (*0-689-31327-6*, Atheneum Child Bk) Macmillan Child Grp.
Ayrai, Sia. Baby Bright Board Books: 123's. Ayrai, Sia, photos by. (Illus.). 1993. 5.95 (*1-56565-048-4*) Lowell Hse.
Ayres, Pam. Guess What. 2nd ed. Lacome, Julie, illus. LC 93-22356. 32p. (ps up). 1994. 3.99 (*1-56402-346-X*) Candlewick Pr.
—Guess Who. 2nd ed. Lacome, Julie, illus. LC 93-22357. 32p. (ps up). 1994. 3.99 (*1-56402-345-1*) Candlewick Pr.
Babbitt, Natalie. Bub or The Very Best Thing. Babbitt, Natalie, illus. LC 93-78758. 32p. (gr. k up). 1994. 15.00 (*0-06-205044-3*); PLB 14.89 (*0-06-205045-1*) HarpC Child Bks.
—The Something. (Illus.). (ps-3). 1987. pap. 2.95 (*0-374-46464-2*) FS&G.
Baby. (Illus.). (ps). 3.50 (*0-7214-1121-5*) Ladybird Bks.
Baby Animals. 8p. (ps). 1988. bds. 1.99 (*0-517-66917-X*) Random Hse Value.
Baby Bear Learns Numbers. 1988. 3.99 (*0-517-65510-1*) Random Hse Value.
Baby Bear Learns Opposites. 1988. 2.99 (*0-517-65511-X*) Random Hse Value.
The Baby Born in a Stable: The Christmas Story. Bd. with The Secret Journey: Mary & Joseph.. (ps-3). 1979. bk. & cassette 6.99 (*0-570-08054-1*, 59-2105) Concordia.
Baby Daisy's Good Idea. write for info. (*1-56326-321-1*, 032201) Disney Bks By Mail.
Baby Daisy's Walk. (Illus.). 10p. (ps). 1986. write for info (*0-307-06095-0*, Pub. by Golden Bks) Western Pub.
Baby Dino's Busy Day. (Illus.). 24p. (ps-1). 1988. 6.95 (*0-8431-4730-X*) Price Stern.
Baby Donald at the Playground. (Illus.). 10p. (ps). 1986. write for info (*0-307-06096-9*, Pub. by Golden Bks.) Western Pub.
Baby Donald Goes to Playland. write for info. (*1-56326-317-3*, 031807) Disney Bks By Mail.
Baby Donald Makes a Sandwich. write for info. (*1-56326-309-2*, 031005) Disney Bks By Mail.
Baby Donald Makes a Snowfriend. write for info. (*1-56326-301-7*, 030205) Disney Bks By Mail.
Baby Donald's Day at the Beach. write for info. (*1-56326-318-1*, 031906) Disney Bks By Mail.
Baby Goofy Catches a Fish. write for info. (*1-56326-302-5*, 030304) Disney Bks By Mail.
Baby Goofy's Missing Mitten. write for info. (*1-56326-316-5*, 031708) Disney Bks By Mail.
Baby Jesus. 12p. (ps). 1986. 3.25 (*0-8378-5089-4*) Gibson.
Baby Mickey Finds a Friend. write for info. (*1-56326-312-2*, 031302) Disney Bks By Mail.
Baby Mickey Plays Hide & Seek. (Illus.). 10p. (ps). 1986. write for info (*0-307-06097-7*, Pub. by Golden Bks) Western Pub.
Baby Mickey's Nap. write for info. (*1-56326-319-X*, 032003) Disney Bks By Mail.
Baby Mickey's Toys. (Illus.). 10p. (ps). 1986. write for info (*0-307-06098-5*, Pub. by Golden Bks.) Western Pub.
Baby Minnie - Do You Know? write for info. (*1-56326-320-3*, 032102) Disney Bks By Mail.
Baby Minnie Come & Play. write for info. (*1-56326-326-2*, 032706) Disney Bks By Mail.
Baby Minnie's Busy Day. write for info. (*1-56326-314-9*, 031500) Disney Bks By Mail.
Baby Minnie's Treat. write for info. (*1-56326-304-1*, 030502) Disney Bks By Mail.
Baby's Animal Sounds. 8p. 1989. 3.95 (*0-448-02786-0*, G&D) Putnam Pub Group.
Baby's Blue Picture Book. (Illus.). (ps). 3.50 (*0-7214-1089-8*) Ladybird Bks.
Baby's Favorite Foods. (Illus.). (ps-k). 1991. write for info. (*0-307-06138-8*, Golden Pr) Western Pub.
Baby's Favorite Toys. (Illus.). (ps-k). 1991. write for info. (*0-307-06137-X*, Golden Pr) Western Pub.
Baby's First Book. (Illus.). (ps). 3.50 (*0-7214-1082-0*) Ladybird Bks.
Baby's First Rattle. (ps). 1984. pap. 3.95 vinyl (*0-671-47668-8*, Little Simom) S&S Trade.
Baby's Green Picture Book. (Illus.). (ps). 3.50 (*0-7214-1101-0*) Ladybird Bks.
Baby's Little Engine That Could. 8p. 1989. 3.95 (*0-448-02785-2*, G&D) Putnam Pub Group.
Baby's Mother Goose. 8p. 1989. 3.95 (*0-448-02790-9*, G&D) Putnam Pub Group.
Baby's Peek-a-Boo. 8p. 1989. 3.95 (*0-448-02789-5*, G&D) Putnam Pub Group.
Baby's Red Picture Book. (Illus.). (ps). 3.50 (*0-7214-1088-X*) Ladybird Bks.
Baby's Yellow Picture Book. (Illus.). (ps). 3.50 (*0-7214-1100-2*) Ladybird Bks.
Baer, Gene. Thump, Thump, Rat-a-Tat-Tat Big Book. Ehlert, Lois, illus. LC 88-28469. 32p. (ps-1). 1992. 19.95 (*0-694-00386-7*) HarpC Child Bks.
Bailey, Debbie. The Talk-about-Books Series, 6 vols. Huszar, Susan, photos by. (Illus.). 14p. (ps-k). 1991. (Pub. by Annick CN); Toys. 4.95 (*1-55037-165-7*); Hats. 4.95 (*1-55037-159-2*); Shoes. 4.95 (*1-55037-161-4*); Clothes. 4.95 (*1-55037-167-3*); My Mom. 4.95 (*1-55037-163-0*); My Dad. 4.95 (*1-55037-164-9*) Firefly Bks Ltd.
Baker, Alan. Two Tiny Mice. Baker, Alan, illus. LC 90-13939. 32p. (ps-1). 1991. 12.95 (*0-8037-0973-0*) Dial Bks Young.
Baker, Arthur. Cut & Assemble Paper Airplanes That Fly. 1982. pap. 3.95 (*0-486-24302-8*) Dover.
Baker, Barbara. Digby & Kate. Winborn, Marsha, illus. LC 87-24455. 48p. (ps-2). 1988. 9.95 (*0-525-44370-3*, 0966-290, DCB) Dutton Child Bks.
Baker, Darrell, illus. Baby Donald's Busy Play Group. LC 87-81947. 14p. (ps-1). 1988. write for info. (*0-307-12316-2*) Western Pub.
—Disney Babies Nursery Rhymes. LC 87-83006. 12p. (ps). 1988. write for info. (*0-307-06082-9*) Western Pub.
—Disney Babies Rock-a-Bye. LC 87-83007. 12p. (ps). 1988. write for info. (*0-307-06084-5*) Western Pub.
—Disney Babies What's up High? LC 87-83009. 12p. (ps). 1988. write for info. (*0-307-06100-0*) Western Pub.
Baker, Pamela J. My First Book of Sign. Bellan Gillen, Patricia, illus. LC 86-14937. iv, 80p. (ps-3). 1986. 14.95 (*0-930323-20-3*, Kendall Green Pubns) Gallaudet Univ Pr.
Balducci, Rita. Disney's Beauty & the Beast. Cardona, Jose, illus. 24p. (ps-k). 1992. write for info. (*0-307-10021-9*, 10021) Western Pub.
Balestrino, Philip. The Skeleton Inside You. Bolognese, Don, illus. LC 85-42982. 40p. (ps-3). 1986. pap. 4.95 (*0-06-445039-2*, Trophy) HarpC Child Bks.
Ball, Jacqueline. Riddles about Baby Animals. Brook, Bonnie, ed. (Illus.). 32p. (ps-3). 1989. 4.95 (*0-671-68577-5*); PLB 6.95 (*0-671-68576-7*); 2.50 (*0-382-24385-4*) Silver Pr.
—Riddles about Our Bodies. Brook, Bonnie, ed. (Illus.). 32p. (ps-3). 1989. 4.95 (*0-671-68579-1*); PLB 6.95 (*0-671-68578-3*) Silver Pr.
—Riddles about the Seasons. Brook, Bonnie, ed. (Illus.). 32p. (ps-3). 1989. 4.95 (*0-671-68583-X*); PLB 6.95 (*0-671-68582-1*) Silver Pr.
—Riddles about the Senses. Brook, Bonnie, ed. (Illus.). 32p. (ps-3). 1989. 4.95 (*0-671-68581-3*); PLB 6.95 (*0-671-68580-5*) Silver Pr.
Ball, Jacqueline A. What Can It Be, 8 bks. (Illus.). (gr. k-3). 1990. Set, 32p. ea. 19.80 (*0-671-94104-6*); Set, 32p. ea. lib. bdg. 27.80 (*0-671-94103-8*) Silver Pr.
Balzola, Asun. Munia & the Day Things Went Wrong. (Illus.). 24p. (gr. k-2). 1988. 11.95 (*0-521-35643-1*) Cambridge U Pr.
Bang, Molly. Dawn. LC 83-886. (Illus.). 32p. (gr. k up). 1991. pap. 3.95 (*0-688-10989-6*, Mulberry) Morrow.
—The Grey Lady & the Strawberry Snatcher. LC 85-29224. (Illus.). 48p. (ps-3). 1984. RSBE 14.95 (*0-02-708140-0*, Four Winds) Macmillan Child Grp.
—The Paper Crane. LC 84-13546. 32p. (gr. k up). 1987. pap. 4.95 (*0-688-07333-6*, Mulberry) Morrow.
—Ten, Nine, Eight. LC 81-20106. (Illus.). 24p. (ps up). 1991. pap. 3.95 (*0-688-10480-0*, Mulberry) Morrow.
Bank Street College of Education Editors. ABC Come Play with Me. (Illus.). 64p. (ps-k). 1985. 3.95 (*0-8120-3617-4*) Barron.
—All Around the House. (Illus.). 64p. (ps-k). 1985. 2.95 (*0-8120-3613-1*) Barron.
—All Around the Neighborhood. (Illus.). 64p. (ps-k). 1985. 2.95 (*0-8120-3612-3*) Barron.
—Get Ready to Read. (Illus.). 64p. (ps-k). 1985. 3.95 (*0-8120-3616-6*) Barron.
—Let's Take a Ride. (gr. 1-2). 1986. pap. 2.95 (*0-8120-3623-9*) Barron.
Banner, Angela. Ant & Bee: Alphabetical Story for Tiny Tots. Ward, Bryan, illus. 96p. (ps-1). 1991. 6.95 (*0-434-92966-2*, Pub. by W Heinemann Ltd) Trafalgar.
—Ant & Bee & the ABC. (Illus.). 96p. (ps-1). 1989. 6.95 (*0-434-92967-0*, Pub. by W Heinemann Ltd) Trafalgar.
—Ant & Bee & the Doctor. Ward, Bryan, illus. 96p. (ps-1). 1992. 6.95 (*0-434-92968-9*, Pub. by W. Heinemann Ltd) Trafalgar.
—Ant & Bee & the Rainbow. Ward, Bryan, illus. 96p. (ps-1). 1992. 6.95 (*0-434-92972-7*, Pub. by W. Heinemann Ltd) Trafalgar.
—Ant & Bee & the Secret. (Illus.). 96p. (ps-1). 1989. 6.95 (*0-434-92959-X*, Pub. by W Heinemann Ltd) Trafalgar.
—Ant & Bee Go Shopping. Ward, Bryan, illus. 96p. (ps-1). 1992. 6.95 (*0-434-92970-0*, Pub. by W Heinemann Ltd) Trafalgar.
—Ant & Bee Time. (Illus.). 94p. (ps-3). 1988. 6.95 (*0-434-92961-1*, Pub. by W Heinemann Ltd) Trafalgar.
—Around the World with Ant & Bee. (Illus.). 96p. (ps-1). 1989. 6.95 (*0-434-92958-1*, Pub. by W Heinemann Ltd) Trafalgar.
—Happy Birthday with Ant & Bee. (Illus.). 96p. (ps-1). 1989. 6.95 (*0-434-92963-8*, Pub. by W Heinemann Ltd) Trafalgar.
—More & More Ant & Bee. (Illus.). 96p. (ps-1). 1989. 6.95 (*0-434-92962-X*, Pub. by W Heinemann Ltd) Trafalgar.
—More Ant & Bee. (Illus.). 96p. (ps-1). 1989. 6.95 (*0-434-92965-4*, Pub. by W Heinemann Ltd) Trafalgar.
—One, Two, Three with Ant & Bee. (Illus.). 96p. (ps-1). 1989. 6.95 (*0-434-92964-6*, Pub. by W Heinemann Ltd) Trafalgar.
Bannerman, Helen. The Story of Little Black Mingo. (Illus.). 72p. (ps-4). 1990. Repr. of 1901 ed. 12.95 (*0-9616844-5-3*) Greenhouse Pub.
Bantock, Nick. Kubla Khan: A Pop-up Version of Coleridge's Classic. (Illus.). 19p. 1994. 12.95 (*0-670-85242-2*, Viking) Viking Penguin.
Bantock, Nick & Strong, Stacie. Runners, Sliders, Bouncers, Climbers: A Pop-up Look at Animals in Motion. Bantock, Nick, illus. 15p. (gr. 1-5). 1992. 14.95 (*1-56282-219-5*) Hyprn Child.
Bantock, Nick, retold by. & illus. Solomon Grundy: A Pop-up Rhyme. 12p. 1992. 8.95 (*0-670-84319-9*) Viking Child Bks.
—There Was an Old Lady. (gr. 4 up). 1990. pap. 8.95 (*0-670-83194-8*) Viking Child Bks.
Barcos, Barcos, Barcos (Boats, Boats, Boats) (SPA., Illus.). 28p. (ps-2). 1991. PLB 11.55 (*0-516-35351-9*); pap. 3.95 (*0-516-55351-8*) Childrens.
Barkan, Joanne. Boxcar. Walz, Richard, illus. 12p. (ps-k). 1992. pap. 3.50 POB (*0-689-71573-0*, Aladdin) Macmillan Child Grp.
—Whiskerville Firehouse. Schmidt, Karen L., illus. 12p. (ps-k). 1990. bds. 3.50 (*0-448-19468-6*, G&D) Putnam Pub Group.
Barks, Carl. Walt Disney's Donald & Daisy Comic Album. Barks, Carl, illus. Blum, Geoffrey, intro. by. (Illus.). 48p. (Orig.). (ps up). 1988. pap. 5.95 (*0-944599-11-7*) Gladstone Pub.
—Walt Disney's Donald Duck Adventures Album. Barks, Carl, illus. Blum, Geoffrey, intro. by. (Illus.). 48p. (Orig.). (ps up). 1988. pap. 5.95 (*0-944599-13-3*) Gladstone Pub.
—Walt Disney's Donald Duck Adventures Album. Barks, Carl, illus. Blum, Geoffrey, intro. by. (Illus.). 48p. (Orig.). (ps up). 1989. pap. 5.95 (*0-944599-15-X*) Gladstone Pub.
—Walt Disney's Uncle Scrooge Album. Barks, Carl, illus. Blum, Geoffrey, intro. by. (Illus.). 48p. (Orig.). (ps up). 1988. pap. 5.95 (*0-944599-14-1*) Gladstone Pub.
—Walt Disney's Uncle Scrooge Comic Album. Barks, Carl, illus. Blum, Geoffrey, intro. by. (Illus.). 48p. (Orig.). (ps up). 1988. pap. 5.95 (*0-944599-10-9*) Gladstone Pub.
Barlass, Gail. Dinosquares: A Modern Dinosaur Book for Imaginative Children. Hansen, Ron, ed. & illus. LC 87-62124. 24p. (ps-3). 1988. pap. 3.95 (*0-943925-07-X*) Purple Turtle Bks.
Barnyard Animals. 8p. (ps). 1991. bds. 1.99 (*0-517-66918-8*) Random Hse Value.
Baron, Michelle. Safe at Home with Teddy Ruxpin. Armstrong, Julie, et al, illus. 34p. (ps). 1988. write for info. incl. audio tape (*0-934323-70-4*) Alchemy Comms.
—Water Safety with Teddy Ruxpin. Armstrong, Julie, et al, illus. 34p. (ps). 1988. incl. audio tape 9.95 (*0-934323-74-7*) Alchemy Comms.
Baron, Phil. Fire Safety with Teddy Ruxpin. Armstrong, Julie, et al, illus. 22p. (ps). 1988. write for info. incl. pre-programmed audiotape (*0-934323-75-5*) Alchemy Comms.
—Gizmos & Gadgets. (Illus.). 34p. (ps). 1987. packaged with pre-programmed audio cass. tape 9.95 (*0-934323-45-3*) Alchemy Comms.
—Quiet Please. Hicks, Russell, et al, illus. 34p. (ps). 1987. incl. pre-programmed audio cass. 9.95 (*0-934323-40-2*) Alchemy Comms.
—Wooly & the Giant Snowzos. Hicks, Russell, et al, illus. 34p. (ps). 1987. incl. pre-programmed audio cass. 9.95 (*0-934323-42-9*) Alchemy Comms.
Barone, Shirley A. Bugs - Bugs - Bugs, Vol. 10. Coleman, Debbie, illus. 44p. (Orig.). (ps-2). 1989. pap. write for info. Toad Hse Bks.
—Easter Parade, Vol. 6. Coleman, Debbie, illus. 44p. (Orig.). (ps-2). 1990. pap. write for info. Toad Hse Bks.
—Funny Dinosaurs, Vol. 4. Coleman, Debbie, illus. 44p. (Orig.). (ps-2). 1989. pap. write for info. Toad Hse Bks.
—Halloween Fun for Everyone, Vol. 1. Coleman, Debbie, illus. 44p. (Orig.). (ps-2). 1989. pap. 1.69 (*0-685-30447-7*) Toad Hse Bks.
—Happy Valentines, Vol. 5. Coleman, Debbie, illus. 44p. (Orig.). (ps-2). 1990. pap. text ed. write for info. Toad Hse Bks.
—I Know My ABC's, Vol. 13. Coleman, Debbie, illus. 44p. (Orig.). (ps-2). 1989. pap. write for info. Toad Hse Bks.
—I Know My Numbers, Vol. 14. Coleman, Debbie, illus. 44p. (Orig.). (ps-2). 1989. pap. write for info. Toad Hse Bks.
—I Like Monsters, Vol. 9. Coleman, Debbie, illus. 44p. (Orig.). (ps-2). 1989. pap. write for info. Toad Hse Bks.
—In My Toy Box, Vol. 8. Coleman, Debbie, illus. 44p. (Orig.). (ps-2). 1989. pap. write for info. Toad Hse Bks.

—Kittens & Puppies, Vol. 11. Coleman, Debbie, illus. 44p. (Orig.). (ps-2). 1989. pap. write for info. Toad Hse Bks.
—Let's Give Thanks, Vol. 2. Coleman, Debbie, illus. 44p. (Orig.). (ps-2). 1989. pap. 1.75 (*0-685-30448-5*) Toad Hse Bks.
—Meet My Friends: Children of the World, Vol. 15. Coleman, Debbie, illus. 44p. (Orig.). (ps-2). 1989. pap. write for info. Toad Hse Bks.
—My Teddy Bears, Vol. 12. Coleman, Debbie, illus. 44p. (Orig.). (ps-2). 1989. pap. write for info. Toad Hse Bks.
—A Shoe for You, Vol. 7. Coleman, Debbie, illus. 44p. (Orig.). (ps-2). 1989. pap. write for info. Toad Hse Bks.
—A Time for Joy (Christmas, Vol. 3. Coleman, Debbie, illus. 44p. (Orig.). (ps-2). 1989. pap. write for info. Toad Hse Bks.
Barr, Marilynn G. Pop-up Theater. (gr. 4-6). 1991. pap. 14.95 (*0-8224-5586-2*) Fearon Teach Aids.
Barrett, John E., photos by. Big Bird Is Yellow: A Sesame Street Book of Colors. LC 89-63996. (Illus.). 14p. (ps). 1990. bds. 3.95 (*0-679-80752-7*) Random Bks Yng Read.
Barrett, Judi. Animals Should Definitely Not Act Like People. Barrett, Ron, illus. 32p. (ps-1). 1988. pap. 3.95 (*0-689-71287-1*, Aladdin) Macmillan Child Grp.
—Animals Should Definitely Not Wear Clothing. Barrett, Ron, illus. 32p. (ps-1). 1988. pap. 3.95 (*0-689-70807-6*, Aladdin) Macmillan Child Grp.
—Pickles Have Pimples: And Other Silly Statements. Johnson, Lonnie S., illus. LC 85-20073. 32p. (ps-2). 1986. SBE 13.95 (*0-689-31187-7*, Atheneum Child Bk) Macmillan Child Grp.
Barrett, Judith. A Snake Is Totally Tail. Johnson, Lonni S., illus. LC 87-1123. 32p. (ps-1). 1987. pap. 3.95 (*0-689-71148-4*, Aladdin) Macmillan Child Grp.
Bartlett, Jaye. Caterpillar Had a Dream: A Poetic Story about Dreams Coming True. (Illus.). 1991. 8.95 (*1-878064-02-9*) TLC Bks.
—Caterpillar Had a Dream: A Story about Dreams Coming True. Dubina, Alan, illus. 38p. (Orig.). (ps up). 1990. PLB 11.95 incl. cassette (*1-878064-00-2*) New Age CT.
—Freddy the Elephant: The Story of a Sensitive Leader. Dubina, Alan, illus. 45p. (Orig.). (ps up). 1991. pap. 11.95 incl. cassette (*1-878064-01-0*) New Age CT.
Barton, Byron. I Want to Be an Astronaut. Barton, Byron, illus. LC 87-24311. 32p. (ps-1). 1992. pap. 4.95 (*0-06-443280-7*, Trophy) HarpC Child Bks.
—Where's Al? LC 78-171866. (Illus.). 32p. (ps). 1989. pap. 5.70 (*0-395-51582-3*, Clarion Bks) HM.
Bastin, Marjolein. Vera the Mouse. (ps-k). 1986. Four-bk. boxed set. 11.95 (*0-8120-7391-6*) Barron.
Battistella, B. The Legend of Little White Hood. (gr. 1 up). 1988. pap. 1.75 (*0-8198-4405-5*) St Paul Bks.
Bauer, Caroline F. Midnight Snowman. Stock, Catherine, illus. LC 86-26540. 32p. (ps-2). 1987. SBE 13.95 (*0-689-31294-6*, Atheneum Child Bk) Macmillan Child Grp.
Baum, L. Frank. Adventures in Oz: Wonderful Wizard of Oz Pop-Ups. 1991. 2.99 (*0-517-05267-9*) Random Hse Value.
—Cyclone. 6p. 1991. 2.99 (*0-517-05269-5*) Random Hse Value.
—Emerald City. (Illus.). 6p. 1991. 2.99 (*0-517-05266-0*) Random Hse Value.
—Wonderful Wizard of Oz Pop Ups. 1991. slipcased 12. 99 (*0-517-06094-9*) Random Hse Value.
—Yellow Brick Road. (Illus.). 6p. 1991. 2.99 (*0-517-05268-7*) Random Hse Value.
Baum, Louis. I Want to See the Moon. Daly, Niki, illus. LC 88-33061. 32p. (ps-3). 1989. cloth 11.95 (*0-87951-367-5*) Overlook Pr.
Bauman, A. F. Guess Where You're Going, Guess What You'll Do. Kelley, True, illus. 32p. (ps-k). 1989. 13.45 (*0-395-50211-X*) HM.
Bazaldua, Barbara. Disney's Beauty & the Beast Word Book. Baker, Darrell, illus. 14p. (ps-k). 1992. write for info. (*0-307-12391-X*, 12391) Western Pub.
Beall, Pamela C. & Nipp, Susan H. King Cole's Party. Klein, Nancy, illus. (ps-2). 1987. incl. videocassette 14.95 (*0-8431-4714-8*) Price Stern.
—Wee Sing & Play Activity Book. (Illus.). 48p. (ps-2). 1992. pap. 2.95 (*0-8431-1240-9*) Price Stern.
Beasley, Roberta, illus. Baby's Cradle Songs. 12p. (ps). 1986. 4.99 (*0-394-88242-3*) Random Bks Yng Read.
Beckmann, Beverly. Numbers in God's World. (ps). 1983. 6.99 (*0-570-04083-3*, 56-1438) Concordia.
Bedtime. (Illus.). (ps). 3.50 (*0-7214-1087-1*) Ladybird Bks.
Beisner, Monika. Topsy Turvy. LC 87-45751. (Illus.). 32p. (ps up). 1988. 15.00 (*0-374-37679-4*) FS&G.
Bell, Anthea. Swan Lake. Iwasaki, Chihiro, illus. LC 86-9509. 28p. (gr. 1 up). 1991. pap. 15.95 (*0-88708-028-6*) Picture Bk Studio.
Bell, Clarisa. El Circo. Sanchez, Jose R., illus. (SPA.). 24p. (Orig.). (gr. 2-6). 1992. PLB 9.95x (*1-56492-078-X*) Laredo.
—En Las Olimpidas. Sanchez, Jose R., illus. (SPA.). 24p. (Orig.). (gr. 2-6). 1992. PLB 9.95x (*1-56492-051-8*) Laredo.
Bell, Owain, illus. Thomas the Tank Engine Says Goodnight. 12p. (ps-k). 1990. sponge filled 4.99 (*0-679-80791-8*) Random Bks Yng Read.
Bell, Robert. My First Book of Space Coloring & Activity Book. Epstein, Len, et al, illus. 160p. (gr. 1 up). 1986. pap. 6.95 (*0-671-62407-5*, Little Simon) S&S Trade.
Bellamy, David. Our Changing World: The Rock Pool. Dow, Jill, illus. 32p. (gr. 1-5). 1988. 9.95 (*0-517-56977-9*, Clarkson Potter) Crown Bks Yng Read.
Bemelmans, Ludwig. Madeline. Bemelmans, Ludwig, illus. LC 39-21791. (gr. k-3). 1977. pap. 4.99 incl. cassette (*0-14-050198-3*, Puffin) Puffin Bks.
—Madeline & the Bad Hat. Bemelmans, Ludwig, illus. LC 57-62. (gr. k-3). 1977. pap. 4.99 (*0-14-050206-8*, Puffin) Puffin Bks.
—Madeline & the Gypsies. Bemelmans, Ludwig, illus. (gr. k-3). 1959. pap. 14.99 (*0-670-44682-3*) Viking Child Bks.
—Madeline Book & Toy Box. (ps-3). 1991. pap. 19.95 (*0-14-034880-8*, Puffin) Puffin Bks.
—Madeline's Christmas. (ps-3). 1988. pap. 4.50 (*0-14-050666-7*, Puffin) Puffin Bks.
—Madeline's Rescue. Bemelmans, Ludwig, illus. LC 53-8709. 56p. (gr. k-3). 1953. pap. 14.00 (*0-670-44716-1*) Viking Child Bks.
Bemmelmans, Ludwig. Madeline. Bemelmans, Ludwig, illus. LC 68-666. (gr. k-3). 1958. pap. 15.00 (*0-670-44580-0*) Viking Child Bks.
—Madeline & the Bad Hat. Bemelmans, Ludwig, illus. (gr. k-3). 1957. pap. 14.00 (*0-670-44614-9*) Viking Child Bks.
—Madeline in London. Bemelmans, Ludwig, illus. (gr. k-3). 1961. pap. 15.00 (*0-670-44648-3*) Viking Child Bks.
Benchley, Nathaniel. Oscar Otter. Lobel, Arnold, illus. LC 66-11499. 64p. (gr. k-3). 1966. PLB 13.89 (*0-06-020472-9*) HarpC Child Bks.
—Red Fox & His Canoe. Lobel, Arnold, illus. LC 64-16650. 64p. (gr. k-3). 1985. pap. 3.50 (*0-06-444075-3*, Trophy) HarpC Child Bks.
—Sam the Minuteman. Lobel, Arnold, illus. LC 68-10211. 64p. (gr. k-3). 1987. pap. 3.50 (*0-06-444107-5*, Trophy) HarpC Child Bks.
Benjamin, A. What's up the Coconut Tree? Biro, Val, illus. 32p. (ps up). 1992. laminated boards 11.95 (*0-19-279896-0*) OUP.
Benjamin, Alan. Busy Bunnies. Santoro, Christopher, illus. 16p. (ps). 1988. pap. 3.95 (*0-671-64807-1*, Little Simon) S&S Trade.
—Ducky's Easter Surprise. Santoro, Christopher, illus. 16p. 1988. pap. 3.95 (*0-671-64808-X*, Little Simon) S&S Trade.
Bennett, David. Fire. Kightley, Rosalinda, illus. 1989. 3.95 (*0-553-05813-4*) Bantam.
Bennett, Nancy & Bennett, Pearl. My ABC Book. Bennett, Pearl, illus. 54p. (ps-1). 1988. wkbk. 12.00 (*0-9622242-0-0*) Red Baron Pub Co.
Berenstain, Michael. The Biggest Dinosaurs. (Illus.). 24p. (ps-k). 1989. pap. write for info. (*0-307-11977-7*, Pub. by Golden Bks) Western Pub.
—The Horned Dinosaur: Triceratops. (Illus.). 24p. (ps-k). 1989. pap. write for info. (*0-307-11979-3*, Pub. by Golden Bks) Western Pub.
—King of the Dinosaurs: Tyrannosaurus Rex. (Illus.). 24p. (ps-k). 1989. pap. write for info. (*0-307-11976-9*, Pub. by Golden Bks) Western Pub.
Berenstain, Stan & Berenstain, Janice. Bears' Picnic. LC 66-10156. (Illus.). 72p. (gr. k-3). 1966. 6.95 (*0-394-80041-9*); lib. bdg. 7.99 (*0-394-90041-3*) Beginner.
—El Bebe de los Osos Berenstain: (The Berenstain Bears' New Baby) De Cuenca, Pilar & Alvarez, Ines, trs. from ENG. Berenstain, Stan & Berenstain, Janice, illus. LC 81-12193. (SPA.). 32p. (Orig.). (ps-3). 1982. lib. bdg. 5.99 (*0-394-95144-1*); pap. 2.50 (*0-394-85144-7*) Random Bks Yng Read.
—The Berenstain Bears & the In-Crowd. LC 88-32095. (Illus.). 32p. (Orig.). (ps-1). 1989. pap. 2.25 (*0-394-83013-X*) Random Bks Yng Read.
—The Berenstain Bears & Too Much Vacation. LC 88-32094. (Illus.). 32p. (Orig.). (ps-1). 1989. pap. 2.25 (*0-394-83014-8*) Random Bks Yng Read.
—The Berenstain Bears Go Out for the Team. LC 85-30164. (Illus.). 32p. (ps-1). 1987. 2.50 (*0-394-87338-6*) Random Bks Yng Read.
—The Berenstain Bears' Make & Do Book. Berenstain, Stan & Berenstain, Jan, illus. 64p. (ps-3). 1984. pap. 3.95 (*0-394-86895-1*) Random Bks Yng Read.
—The Berenstain Bears Meet Santa Bear. Berenstain, Stan & Berenstain, Jan, illus. LC 84-4829. 32p. (ps-1). 1984. Random Bks Yng Read.
—The Day of the Dinosaur. Berenstain, Michael, illus. LC 87-9828. 32p. (gr. k-3). 1987. lib. bdg. 5.99 (*0-394-99130-3*); pap. 2.25 (*0-394-89130-9*) Random Bks Yng Read.
—Old Hat, New Hat. (Illus.). (ps-1). 1970. 6.95 (*0-394-80669-7*); lib. bdg. 7.99 (*0-394-90669-1*) Random Bks Yng Read.
Berenzy, Alix. A Frog Prince. Berenzy, Alix, illus. 32p. (ps up). 1989. 14.95 (*0-8050-0426-2*, Bks Young Read) H Holt & Co.
Bergstrom, Gunilla. Who's Scaring Alfie Atkins? Sandin, Joan, tr. from SWE. Bergstrom, Gunilla, illus. 32p. (ps up). 1987. 6.95 (*91-29-58318-7*, Pub. by R & S Bks) FS&G.
Bernstein, Sharon C. A Family That Fights. Levine, Abby, ed. Ritz, Karen, illus. LC 90-29889. 32p. (gr. k-4). 1991. 11.95 (*0-8075-2248-1*) A Whitman.
Berry, Joy W. Teach Me about Looking. Dickey, Kate, ed. LC 85-45086. (Illus.). 36p. (ps). 1986. 4.98 (*0-685-10725-6*) Grolier Inc.
Beskow, Elsa. Around the Year. (Illus.). (ps-2). 1988. 14. 95 (*0-86315-075-6*, 20245) Gryphon Hse.
—Pelle's New Suit. Beskow, Elsa, illus. 16p. (ps-1). 1929. PLB 13.89 (*0-06-020496-6*) HarpC Child Bks.
—Peter in Blueberry Land. (ps-2). 1988. 14.95 (*0-86315-050-0*, 20237) Gryphon Hse.
—The Tale of the Little, Little Old Woman. Beskow, Elsa, illus. (ps). 1989. 10.95 (*0-86315-079-9*, 20246) Gryphon Hse.
Beyl, Judith. Sunshine, Rainbows & Friends. Sydlik, Danilea & Campbell, Elisa L., illus. LC 80-50828. 83p. (Orig.). (ps-k). 1980. pap. 5.95 (*0-933308-01-9*) Harper SF.
Bible Promises. 32p. (ps-1). 1988. pap. 0.69 (*1-55513-337-1*, Chariot Bks) Chariot Family.
Big & Little. (ps-k). 1990. bds. 3.50 (*0-7214-9120-0*) Ladybird Bks.
The Big Storm. write for info. (*1-56326-323-8*, 032409) Disney Bks By Mail.
Billout, Guy. By Camel or by Car: A Look at Transportation. Billout, Guy, illus. 32p. 1983. (Pub. by Treehouse) P-H.
—Journey. (Illus.). 32p. (gr. 6 up). 1993. 16.95 (*1-56846-081-3*) Creat Editions.
Birch, David. The King's Chessboard. Grebu, Devis, illus. LC 87-20164. 32p. (gr. k up). 1988. PLB 10.89 (*0-8037-0367-8*) Dial Bks Young.
Bird, E. J. Chuck Wagon Stew. (Illus.). 72p. (gr. 2-6). 1988. 14.95 (*0-87614-313-3*); pap. 4.95 (*0-87614-498-9*) Carolrhoda Bks.
—How Do Bears Sleep? (Illus.). 32p. (ps-3). 1989. PLB 18.95 (*0-87614-384-2*) Carolrhoda Bks.
Birds Activity Book. (Illus.). (ps-6). pap. 2.95 (*0-565-01030-1*, Pub. by Natural Hist Mus) Parkwest Pubns.
Black, Donald O. Lama's SuperAmerican Coloring Book. (Illus.). 7p. (gr. 3). 1991. pap. write for info. (*0-9625753-1-3*) SuperAmerican Bks.
Black, Irma S. Little Old Man Who Could Not Read. Fleishman, Seymour, illus. LC 68-9115. (gr. k-2). 1968. PLB 11.95 (*0-8075-4621-6*) A Whitman.
Blegvad, Lenore. Anna Banana & Me. Blegvad, Erik, illus. (gr. 1-3). 1988. bk. & cassette 19.95 (*0-87499-104-8*); bk. & cassette 12.95 (*0-87499-103-X*); 4 cassettes & guide 27.95 (*0-87499-105-6*) Live Oak Media.
Blocksma, Mary. All My Toys Are on the Floor. Kalthoff, Sandra C., illus. LC 85-27000. 24p. (ps-2). 1986. pap. 3.95 (*0-516-41579-4*) Childrens.
—Apple Tree! Apple Tree! Big Book. 24p. (ps-2). 1990. PLB 22.95 (*0-516-49514-3*) Childrens.
—Rub-a-Dub-Dub - What's in the Tub? Kalthoff, Sandra C., illus. LC 84-12139. 24p. (ps-2). 1984. pap. 3.95 (*0-516-41586-7*) Childrens.
—Rub-a-dub-dub-What's in the Tub? Big Book. 24p. (ps-2). 1987. PLB 22.95 (*0-516-49505-4*) Childrens.
Blonder. Wee Wonders of Nature. (gr. 2 up). 1988. 2.50 (*0-448-09254-9*, G&D) Putnam Pub Group.
Blonder, Ellen. illus. My Very First Things. (ps). 1988. bds. 2.50 (*0-448-09253-0*, G&D) Putnam Pub Group.
Blume, Judy. Freckle Juice. Lisker, Sonia O., illus. LC 85-280. 40p. (gr. 1-3). 1984. Repr. of 1971 ed. 13.95 (*0-02-711690-5*, Four Winds) Macmillan Child Grp.
Blumenthal, Nancy. Count-a-Saurus. Kaufman, Robert, illus. LC 88-21320. 24p. (ps-3). 1989. RSBE 13.95 (*0-02-749391-1*, Four Winds) Macmillan Child Grp.
Boccaccio, Giovanni. Chichibo & the Crane. Luzatti, Lele, illus. (gr. 1-6). 1961. 8.95 (*0-8392-3004-4*) Astor-Honor.
Bohlke, Dorothee. Mr. Chang & the Yellow Robe. Bradford, Elizabeth, ed. Verlag, Mangold, tr. from GER. Bohlke, Dorothee, illus. LC 91-21303. 32p. (gr. k-3). 1991. PLB 14.60 (*1-56074-029-9*) Garrett Ed Corp.
Boholm-Olsson, Eva. Tuan. Van Don, Pham, illus. Jonasson, Dianne, tr. (Illus.). 32p. (ps up). 1988. 11.95 (*91-29-58766-2*, R & S Bks) FS&G.
Bond, Felicia. Four Valentines in a Rainstorm. Bond, Felicia, illus. LC 82-45586. 32p. (gr. k-3). 1990. pap. 3.95 (*0-06-443216-5*, Trophy) HarpC Child Bks.
—The Halloween Performance. Bond, Felicia, illus. LC 82-45920. 32p. (ps-3). 1987. pap. 4.95 (*0-06-443155-X*, Trophy) HarpC Child Bks.
Bonsall, Crosby N. The Day I Had to Play with My Sister. Bonsall, Crosby N., illus. LC 72-76507. 32p. (ps-2). 1988. pap. 3.50 (*0-06-444117-2*, Trophy) HarpC Child Bks.
—It's Mine: A Greedy Book. Bonsall, Crosby N., illus. LC 64-11839. 32p. (gr. k-3). 1964. PLB 13.89 (*0-06-020586-5*) HarpC Child Bks.
—Who's Afraid of the Dark? Bonsall, Crosby N., illus. LC 79-2700. 32p. (ps-2). 1985. pap. 3.50 (*0-06-444071-0*, Trophy) HarpC Child Bks.
Books, Emma. Jingle Bells. Conner, Rachel, illus. 12p. (ps). 1994. 5.95 (*0-694-00656-4*, Festival) HarpC Child Bks.
Books, Emma K. Frosty the Snowman. Bushell, Isobel, illus. 12p. (ps). 1994. 5.95 (*0-694-00655-6*, Festival) HarpC Child Bks.
Boola's Secrets. (Illus.). 26p. (ps-1). 1988. pap. 2.95 incl. sticker pgs. (*0-671-66867-6*, Little Simon) S&S Trade.
Boone, Debby. Bedtime Hugs for Little Ones. Ferrer, Gabriel, illus. LC 87-81035. 64p. (ps-1). 1988. 11.99 (*0-89081-616-6*) Harvest Hse.
Bourgeois, Paulette. Amazing Potato Book. LC 91-23847. 1991. pap. 7.64 (*0-201-56761-X*) Addison-Wesley.
Bowman, Pete. A Surprise for Easter: A Revolving Picture Book. (Illus.). 12p. (Orig.). (ps-2). 1992. pap. 11.95 POB (*0-689-71552-8*, Aladdin) Macmillan Child Grp.

Boyd, Patti. My Doctor Bag. Boyd, Patti, illus. 12p. (ps). 1994. bds. 3.95 (*0-8431-3741-X*) Price Stern.
—My Lunch Box. Boyd, Patti, illus. 12p. (ps). 1994. bds. 3.95 (*0-8431-3742-8*) Price Stern.
—My Tool Kit. Boyd, Patti, illus. 12p. (ps). 1994. bds. 3.95 (*0-8431-3743-6*) Price Stern.
Boyle, Alison. Playdays Letters & Words. Johnson, Paul, illus. 32p. (ps-2). 1992. pap. 2.95 (*0-563-20890-2*, BBC-Parkwest) Parkwest Pubns.
—Playdays Out & About. Johnson, Paul, illus. 32p. (ps-2). 1992. pap. 2.95 (*0-563-20888-0*, BBC-Parkwest) Parkwest Pubns.
Boynton, Sandra. But Not the Hippopotamus. Klimo, Kate, ed. Boynton, Sandra, illus. 14p. (ps-k). 1982. 3.95 (*0-671-44904-4*, Little Simon) S&S Trade.
—Opposites. Klimo, Kate, ed. Boynton, Sandra, illus. (ps-k). 1982. 3.95 (*0-671-44903-6*, Little Simon) S&S Trade.
Bracken, Carolyn. Peter Rabbit's Pockets. Bracken, Carolyn, illus. 8p. (ps). 1982. pap. 3.95 (*0-671-44528-6*, Little Simon) S&S Trade.
Bracken, Carolyn, illus. The Busy School Bus. 12p. (ps up). 1986. 6.95 (*0-448-09880-6*, G&D) Putnam Pub Group.
Bracken, Carolyn & Barbaresi, Nina, illus. Baby Seal. (ps). 1984. pap. 2.95 vinyl (*0-671-50031-7*, Little Simon) S&S Trade.
—Duckling. (ps). 1984. pap. 2.95 vinyl (*0-671-50030-9*, Little Simon) S&S Trade.
Bradman, Tony. The Bad Babies' Counting Book. Van Der Beek, Debbie, illus. LC 86-71. 32p. (ps-2). 1986. Set. 4.95 (*0-394-88352-7*) Knopf Bks Yng Read.
Brady, Esther W. Toliver's Secret. Cuffari, Richard, illus. 176p. (gr. 3-7). 1988. pap. 4.99 (*0-517-56910-8*) Crown Bks Yng Read.
Brady, Susan. Find My Blanket. Brady, Susan, illus. LC 87-45310. 32p. (ps-1). 1988. (Lipp Jr Bks) HarpC Child Bks.
Bragg, Michael, illus. Monday's Child. 32p. (ps-1). 1989. 15.95 (*0-575-04097-1*, Pub. by Gollancz England) Trafalgar.
Brandenberg, Franz. Nice New Neighbors. Aliki, illus. LC 77-1651. 56p. (ps up). 1991. pap. 4.95 (*0-688-10997-7*, Mulberry) Morrow.
Branley, Franklyn M. Flash, Crash, Rumble & Roll. Emberley, Barbara & Emberley, Ed E., illus. LC 84-48532. 32p. (ps-3). 1987. (Trophy); pap. 4.95 (*0-06-445012-0*, Trophy) HarpC Child Bks.
—Snow Is Falling. rev. ed. Keller, Holly, illus. LC 85-48256. 32p. (ps-3). 1986. pap. 4.95 (*0-06-445058-9*, Trophy) HarpC Child Bks.
Braumiller, Tanya. Visiting Gig Harbor. Hamer, Bonnie, illus. (Orig.). (gr. 1-4). 1983. pap. 2.75 (*0-933992-28-9*) Coffee Break.
Bravo, Olga. Olga's Cup & Saucer. 1995. write for info. (*0-8050-3301-7*) H Holt & Co.
Brenner, Barbara A. Wagon Wheels. newly illustrated ed. Bolognese, Don, illus. LC 92-18780. 64p. (gr. k-3). 1984. pap. 3.50 (*0-06-444052-4*, Trophy) HarpC Child Bks.
Briggs, Raymond. The Snowman. Briggs, Raymond, illus. LC 78-55904. 32p. (Orig.). (ps-2). 1986. pap. 4.95 book & doll pkg. (*0-394-88466-3*) Random Bks Yng Read.
Bright, Robert. Georgie. Bright, Robert, illus. 44p. (gr. k-1). 1944. pap. 7.95 (*0-385-07307-0*) Doubleday.
—Georgie & the Robbers. Bright, Robert, illus. LC 63-11384. 28p. (ps-1). 1963. pap. 5.95 (*0-385-04483-6*); pap. 2.50 (*0-385-13341-3*) Doubleday.
—My Red Umbrella. LC 59-7928. (Illus.). 32p. (ps-1). 1985. 8.95 (*0-688-05249-5*); pap. 3.95 (*0-688-05250-9*) Morrow Jr Bks.
Briscoe, Stuart & Briscoe, Jill. Danny D Books, 4 vols. Marinin, Sally, illus. 12p. (gr. 2-5). 1993. Set. pap. 9.99 (*0-8010-1061-6*) Baker Bk.
Brown, Forman. The Generous Jefferson Bartleby Jones. (Illus.). 32p. (Orig.). (gr. 1-5). 1991. pap. 7.95 (*1-55583-198-2*) Alyson Pubns.
Brown, Jeff. Flat Stanley. Ungerer, Tomi, illus. LC 63-17525. 64p. (gr. 1-5). 1964. PLB 13.89 (*0-06-020681-0*) HarpC Child Bks.
Brown, Jerome C. Dinosaur Color & Pattern Book. (gr. k-3). 1989. pap. 9.95 (*0-8224-2322-7*) Fearon Teach Aids.
Brown, Laurene K. & Brown, Marc T. Visiting the Art Museum. LC 85-32552. (Illus.). 32p. (ps-1). 1986. 14. 99 (*0-525-44233-2*, DCB); (DCB) Dutton Child Bks.
Brown, Lynn. All about Me. MacCombie, Lynn, illus. 92p. (ps-1). 1993. 14.95 (*0-9640001-0-5*) Jikani Pr.
Brown, Marc. The Silly Tail Book. Brown, Marc, illus. LC 83-2250. 48p. (ps-3). 1983. 5.95 (*0-8193-1109-X*); pap. 2.95 (*0-8193-1158-8*) Parents.
Brown, Marc T. Arthur's Eyes. Brown, Marc T., illus. 32p. (ps-3). 1986. pap. 4.95 (*0-316-11069-8*, Joy St Bks) Little.
—Arthur's Valentine. Brown, Marc T., illus. 32p. (ps-3). 1988. pap. 4.95 (*0-316-11187-2*, Joy St Bks) Little.
—D. W. All Wet. (ps-3). 1991. pap. 4.95 (*0-316-11268-2*) Little.
—D. W. Flips. Brown, Marc T., illus. (ps-2). 1987. 12.95 (*0-316-11239-9*, Joy St Bks) Little.
—D. W. Flips. (ps-3). 1991. write for info.; pap. 4.95 (*0-316-11269-0*) Little.
Brown, Marc T., illus. One, Two Buckle My Shoe. 8p. (ps-k). 1989. 5.95 (*0-525-44462-9*, DCB) Dutton Child Bks.
Brown, Marcia. Dick Whittington & His Cat. Brown, Marcia, illus. LC 50-9157. 32p. (gr. k-3). 1988. Repr. of 1950 ed. RSBE 14.95 (*0-684-18998-4*, Scribners Young Read) Macmillan Child Grp.
—Once a Mouse. Brown, Marcia, illus. LC 89-32057. 32p. (gr. k-4). 1989. pap. 3.95 (*0-689-71343-6*, Aladdin) Macmillan Child Grp.
—Stone Soup. Brown, Marcia, illus. (gr. 1-4). 1987. incl. cassette 19.95 (*0-87499-053-X*); pap. 12.95 incl. cassette (*0-87499-052-1*); 4 paperbacks, cassette & guide 27.95 (*0-87499-054-8*) Live Oak Media.
Brown, Margaret W. A Child's Good Night Book. Charlot, Jean, illus. LC 84-43123. 32p. (ps-2). 1986. pap. 4.95 (*0-06-443114-2*, Trophy) HarpC Child Bks.
—Christmas in the Barn. Cooney, Barbara, illus. LC 85-42738. 32p. (ps-3). 1985. pap. 5.95 (*0-06-443082-0*, Trophy) HarpC Child Bks.
—Goodnight Moon. Hurd, Clement, illus. LC 47-30762. 36p. (ps-1). 1947. 13.00 (*0-06-020705-1*); PLB 12.89 (*0-06-020706-X*) HarpC Child Bks.
—Goodnight Moon. (gr. k-3). 1984. incl. cassette 19.95 (*0-941078-30-2*); pap. 12.95 incl. cassette (*0-941078-28-0*); incl. 4 bks., cassette, & guide 27.95 (*0-317-07120-3*) Live Oak Media.
—Goodnight Moon Bedtime Box. Hurd, Clement, illus. 32p. (ps-3). 1992. incl. bunny 19.95 (*0-694-00373-5*) HarpC Child Bks.
—The Goodnight Moon Room: A Pop-Up Book. Hurd, Clement, illus. LC 83-48169. 10p. (ps-1). 1985. 10.95 (*0-694-00003-5*) HarpC Child Bks.
—Important Book. Weisgard, Leonard, illus. LC 49-9133. 22p. (ps-1). 1949. 14.00 (*0-06-020720-5*); PLB 13.89 (*0-06-020721-3*) HarpC Child Bks.
—The Important Book. Weisgard, Leonard, illus. LC 49-9133. 24p. (gr. k-3). 1990. pap. 4.95 (*0-06-443227-0*, Trophy) HarpC Child Bks.
—The Little Fir Tree. Cooney, Barbara, illus. LC 85-42743. 40p. (ps-3). 1985. pap. 5.95 (*0-06-443083-9*, Trophy) HarpC Child Bks.
—The Quiet Noisy Book. new ed. Weisgard, Leonard, illus. LC 92-8320. 40p. (ps-1). 1993. 15.00 (*0-06-020845-7*); PLB 14.89 (*0-06-021220-9*) HarpC Child Bks.
—Sleepy Little Lion. Ylla, photos by. LC 47-11482. (Illus.). 24p. (gr. k-3). 1947. PLB 12.89 (*0-06-020771-X*) HarpC Child Bks.
—Wait till the Moon Is Full. Williams, Garth, illus. LC 48-9278. 32p. (ps-1). 1948. 15.00 (*0-06-020800-7*); PLB 14.89 (*0-06-020801-5*) HarpC Child Bks.
Brown, Richard. Cookie Monster's Good Time to Eat! (Illus.). 14p. (ps-k). 1989. write for info. (*0-307-12259-X*, Pub. by Golden Bks) Western Pub.
—One Hundred Words about Animals. Brown, Richard, illus. LC 86-22774. 27p. (ps-k). 1987. 5.95 (*0-15-200550-1*, Gulliver Bks) HarBrace.
—One Hundred Words about My House. LC 87-7574. (Illus.). 28p. (ps-k). 1988. 6.95 (*0-15-200552-8*, Gulliver Bks) HarBrace.
Brown, Richard, illus. Sesame Street, Cookie Monster's Book of Cookie Shapes. 24p. (ps-k). 1979. pap. write for info (*0-307-10074-X*, Pub. by Golden Bks) Western Pub.
Brown, Ruth. Our Cat Flossie. Brown, Ruth, illus. LC 86-19895. 32p. (ps-1). 1986. 10.95 (*0-525-44256-1*, DCB) Dutton Child Bks.
Browne, Anthony. Piggybook. Browne, Anthony, illus. LC 86-3008. 32p. (ps-3). 1986. 14.95 (*0-394-88416-7*); lib. bdg. 14.99 (*0-394-98416-1*) Knopf Bks Yng Read.
Browne, Gerard & Browne, Gerard, illus. The Car & Truck Lift-the-Flap Book. LC 88-29994. 18p. (gr. 2-5). 1989. 12.95 (*0-525-67273-7*, Lodestar Bks) Dutton Child Bks.
Bruce, Linda. Al Phillip Bettle. Bruce, Linda, illus. (gr. k-3). 1965. 8.95 (*0-8392-3050-8*) Astor-Honor.
Bruna, Dick. Dick Bruna's Picture Wordbook. (Illus.). 64p. 1991. 5.99 (*0-517-05662-3*) Random Hse Value.
Bryan, Ashley. Turtle Knows Your Name. Bryan, Ashley, illus. LC 89-2. 32p. (ps-2). 1989. SBE 14.95 (*0-689-31578-3*, Atheneum Child Bk) Macmillan Child Grp.
Buckley, Richard & Williams, Alex. The Bird Who Couldn't Fly. (Illus.). 32p. (ps-1). 1989. 15.95 (*0-340-41990-3*, Pub. by Hodder & Stoughton UK) Trafalgar.
Buckman, Mary. Ben. Morgan, Connie, illus. 32p. (gr. k-5). 1992. pap. 8.95 (*1-879414-09-0*) Mary Bee Creat.
Buell, Ellen L., ed. Treasury of Little Golden Books. 120p. (ps-2). 1989. write for info. (*0-307-86540-1*, Golden Bks) Western Pub.
Buenas Noches, Gatito (Good Night, Little Kitten) (SPA., Illus.). 28p. (ps-2). 1991. PLB 11.55 (*0-516-35354-3*); pap. 3.95 (*0-516-55354-2*) Childrens.
Bulla, Clyde R. Singing Sam. Magurn, Susan, illus. LC 88-19758. 48p. (Orig.). (gr. 1-3). 1989. PLB 7.99 (*0-394-91977-7*); pap. 3.50 (*0-394-81977-2*) Random Bks Yng Read.
Bullock, Gloria S. & Crocitto, Jane B. Shopping at the Ani-Mall. Weinberger, Jane, ed. DeVito, Pam, illus. LC 90-70475. 44p. (ps-3). 1991. pap. 9.95 (*0-932433-72-3*) Windswept Hse.
Bunsen, Rick, ed. Golden Christmas Treasury. rev. & enl. ed. LC 84-72934. (Illus.). 96p. (gr. k-12). 1989. write for info. (*0-307-95585-0*, Pub. by Golden Bks) Western Pub.
Bunting, Eve. Ghost's Hour, Spook's Hour. Carrick, Donald, illus. LC 86-31674. 32p. (ps). 1989. pap. 4.95 (*0-395-51583-1*, Clarion Bks) HM.
—No Nap. Meddaugh, Susan, illus. LC 88-35256. 32p. (ps-k). 1989. 15.45 (*0-89919-813-9*, Clarion Bks) HM.
Burditt, Faraday & Holley, Cynthia. Every Day in Every Way. (ps). 1989. pap. 12.95 (*0-8224-2507-6*) Fearon Teach Aids.
Burgess, Thornton W. The Adventures of Jimmy Skunk. Cady, Harrison, illus. 128p. (ps-3). 1987. pap. 2.95 (*0-316-11662-9*) Little.
Burnnett, Carroll. Kikko's Tracks. Burnnett, Carroll, illus. 28p. (Orig.). (ps up). 1988. pap. 6.95 (*0-9619414-1-3*) Foto Fantasi Pr.
Burton, Marilee R. Tail Toes Eyes Ears Nose. Burton, Marilee R., illus. LC 87-32276. 32p. (ps-1). 1992. pap. 4.95 (*0-06-443260-2*, Trophy) HarpC Child Bks.
Burton, Virginia L. Choo Choo. (Illus.). 48p. (gr. k-3). 1973. 14.45 (*0-395-17684-0*) HM.
—The Little House. (Illus.). (gr. k-3). 1978. 13.95 (*0-395-18156-9*); pap. 4.95 (*0-395-25938-X*) HM.
—Mike Mulligan & His Steam Shovel. (Illus.). (gr. k-3). 1939. PLB 11.95 (*0-395-06681-6*) HM.
A Bus Ride with Bernie. (Illus.). 6p. (gr. k-2). 1991. bds. 17.95 (*1-56144-029-9*, Honey Bear Bks) Modern Pub NYC.
Busch, Laura C. Ant Books. 180p. (ps-1). 1990. 13.95 (*1-880642-01-8*) Little Read.
—Bunny Books. (ps-2). 1990. 13.95 (*1-880642-06-9*) Little Read.
—Butterfly Books. (ps-2). 1989. 13.95 (*1-880642-03-4*) Little Read.
—Canary Books. (ps-2). 1990. 13.95 (*1-880642-04-2*) Little Read.
—Caterpillar Books. 180p. (ps-1). 1990. 13.95 (*1-880642-02-6*) Little Read.
—Kitty Books. (ps-2). 1991. 13.95 (*1-880642-07-7*) Little Read.
—Letter Sound Books. (ps-2). 1991. pap. 13.95 (*1-880642-00-X*) Little Read.
—Turtle Books, 12 bks. (ps-2). 1990. Set. 13.95 (*1-880642-05-0*) Little Read.
Butterworth, Oliver. The Enormous Egg. Darling, Louis, illus. (gr. 4-6). 1956. 14.95 (*0-316-11904-0*, Pub. by Atlantic Monthly Pr) Little.
Bye, Bye Bottle. (ps). 1991. bds. 3.50 (*0-307-12328-6*, Golden Pr) Western Pub.
Bye, Bye Crib. (ps). 1991. bds. 3.50 (*0-307-12325-1*, Golden Pr) Western Pub.
Bye, Bye, Diaper. (ps-k). 1991. bds. 3.50 (*0-307-12326-X*, Golden Pr) Western Pub.
Bye, Bye High Chair. (ps-k). 1991. bds. 3.50 (*0-307-12327-8*, Golden Pr) Western Pub.
Cahill, Chris. Bear Magic. Young, Ruth & Rose, Mitchell, illus. LC 89-61636. 12p. (ps-1). 1990. bds. 5.95 incl. finger puppet (*1-877779-00-8*) Schneider Educational.
—Bunny Magic. Young, Ruth & Rose, Mitchell, illus. LC 89-61633. 12p. (ps-1). 1990. bds. 5.95 incl. finger puppet (*1-877779-02-4*) Schneider Educational.
Caines, Jeannette. Abby. Kellogg, Steven, illus. LC 73-5480. 32p. (ps-3). 1984. pap. 4.95 (*0-06-443049-9*, Trophy) HarpC Child Bks.
—I Need a Lunch Box. Cummings, Pat, illus. LC 85-45829. 32p. (ps-1). 1993. pap. 4.95 (*0-06-443341-2*, Trophy) HarpC Child Bks.
—Just Us Women. Cummings, Pat, illus. LC 81-48655. 32p. (gr. k-3). 1984. pap. 4.95 (*0-06-443056-1*, Trophy) HarpC Child Bks.
Calder, S. J. If You Were a Bird. Brook, Bonnie, ed. Van Wright, Cornelius, illus. 32p. (ps-1). 1989. 6.95 (*0-671-68599-6*); PLB 6.95 (*0-671-68595-3*) Silver Pr.
—If You Were a Cat. Brook, Bonnie, ed. Van Wright, Cornelius, illus. 32p. (ps-1). 1989. 2.95 (*0-382-24405-2*); PLB 6.95 (*0-671-68598-8*) Silver Pr.
—If You Were a Fish. Brook, Bonnie, ed. (Illus.). 32p. (ps-1). 1989. 2.95 (*0-382-24406-0*); PLB 6.95 (*0-671-68596-1*) Silver Pr.
—If You Were an Ant. Brook, Bonnie, ed. Van Wright, Cornelius, illus. 32p. (ps-1). 1989. 2.95 (*0-382-24403-6*); PLB 6.95 (*0-671-68597-X*) Silver Pr.
Calders, Pere. Brush. Feitlowitz, Marguerite, tr. from SPA. Vendrell, Carme S., illus. LC 85-23873. 32p. (ps-3). 1986. 10.95 (*0-916291-05-7*) Kane-Miller Bk.
Calhoun, Mary. Hungry Leprechaun. Duvoisin, Roger, illus. LC 62-7214. 32p. (gr. k-3). 1962. PLB 12.88 (*0-688-31713-8*) Morrow Jr Bks.
Calmenson, Stephanie. Babies. Wilburn, Kathy, illus. LC 86-81490. 22p. (ps). 1987. write for info. (*0-307-12118-6*, Golden Bks) Western Pub.
—Little Bunny. (ps-1). 1985. pap. 3.50 (*0-671-53110-7*, Little Simon) S&S Trade.
—The Little Bunny. Chambliss, Maxie, illus. (gr. 2-6). 1986. 4.95 (*0-671-62079-7*, Little Simon) S&S Trade.
—Little Chick. (ps-1). 1985. 3.50 (*0-671-53111-5*, Little Simon) S&S Trade.
—What Am I? Very First Riddles. Gundersheimer, Karen, illus. LC 87-22959. 32p. (ps-2). 1992. pap. 4.95 (*0-06-443291-2*, Trophy) HarpC Child Bks.
Camel. 1989. 3.50 (*1-87865-733-X*) Blue Q.
Campbell, Louise A. & Bowers, Grace A. Muffin, The Maine Puffin. Mason, MacAdam L., illus. 40p. (Orig.). (gr. k-3). 1988. pap. 9.95 (*0-9621949-0-5*) Muffin Enter.
Campbell, Rod. Buster Gets Dressed. (gr. 1-3). 1988. 4.95 (*0-8120-5922-0*) Barron.
—Buster Keeps Warm. (gr. 1-3). 1988. 4.95 (*0-8120-5923-9*) Barron.
—Dear Zoo. Campbell, Rod, illus. LC 82-83224. 22p. (ps-1). 1986. pap. 10.95 (*0-02-716440-3*, Four Winds) Macmillan Child Grp.

—Dear Zoo. (ps-k). 1987. pap. 4.95 (*0-317-62180-7*, Puffin) Puffin Bks.
—Dear Zoo. Campbell, Rod, illus. 24p. (ps-1). 1988. pap. 3.95 (*0-689-71230-8*, Aladdin) Macmillan Child Grp.
—I'm a Mechanic. 12p. (ps-2). 1986. bds. 6.95 (*0-8120-5768-6*) Barron.
—I'm a Nurse. 12p. (ps-2). 1986. bds. 6.95 (*0-8120-5769-4*) Barron.
—It's Mine. (Illus.). 24p. (ps). 1988. 8.95 (*0-8120-5921-2*) Barron.
—Oh Dear! Campbell, Rod, illus. LC 84-3993. 20p. (ps-1). 1986. pap. 9.95 (*0-02-716430-6*, Four Winds) Macmillan Child Grp.
—Oh Dear! Campbell, Rod, illus. 20p. (ps-k). 1994. pap. 4.95 (*0-689-71774-1*, Aladdin) Macmillan Child Grp.
Cannon, Frances A. A Picture Book. Petz, Rita K., ed. Carr, Linda, illus. (gr. 4-6). write for info. Rapcom Enter.
Caple, Kathy. Harry's Smile. Caple, Kathy, illus. LC 87-5094. 32p. (gr. k-3). 1987. 13.95 (*0-395-43417-3*) HM.
Carey, Karla. Julie & Jackie at Christmas-Time: The Play & Musical Play (with Music Book, Story-&-Song Cassette & Piano Cassette) Nolan, Dennis, illus. LC 88-12909. 39p. 1990. pap. 35.00 complete pkg. (*1-55768-151-1*); pap. 25.00 book only (*1-55768-026-4*); story-&-song or piano cass. 8.00 (*0-685-19710-7*) LC Pub.
—Julie & Jackie Go a'Journeying: The Play & Musical Play (with Music Book, Story-&-Song Cassette & Piano Cassette) Nolan, Dennis, illus. LC 88-9171. 73p. 1990. pap. 35.00 complete pkg. (*1-55768-153-8*); pap. 25.00 book only (*1-55768-028-0*); story-&-song or piano cass. 8.00 (*0-685-19711-5*) LC Pub.
—Julie & Jackie on the Ranch: The Play & Musical Play (with Music Book, Story-&-Song Cassette & Piano Cassette) Nolan, Dennis, illus. LC 88-12911. 46p. 1990. pap. 35.00 complete pkg. (*1-55768-154-6*); pap. 25.00 book only (*1-55768-029-9*); story-&-song or piano cass. 8.00 (*0-685-19712-3*) LC Pub.
Carle, Eric. All Around Us. Carle, Eric, illus. LC 86-9354. (ps up). 1991. bds. 11.95 3 friezes, incl. carry case (*0-88708-016-2*) Picture Bk Studio.
—Do You Want to Be My Friend? Carle, Eric, illus. LC 70-140643. 32p. (ps-2). 1971. 15.00 (*0-690-24276-X*, Crowell Jr Bks); PLB 14.89 (*0-690-01137-7*, Crowell Jr Bks) HarpC Child Bks.
—Do You Want to Be My Friend? Carle, Eric, illus. LC 70-140643. 32p. (ps-2). 1987. pap. 5.95 (*0-06-443127-4*, Trophy) HarpC Child Bks.
—The Grouchy Ladybug. LC 77-3170. (Illus.). 48p. (ps-2). 1986. pap. 5.95 (*0-06-443116-9*, Trophy) HarpC Child Bks.
—A House for Hermit Crab. LC 87-29261. (Illus.). 32p. (ps up). 1991. pap. 15.95 (*0-88708-056-1*) Picture Bk Studio.
—La Mariquita Malhumorada. Carle, Eric, illus. LC 91-28582. 48p. (gr. k-3). 1992. pap. 5.95 (*0-06-443301-3*, Trophy) HarpC Child Bks.
—The Mixed-up Chameleon. rev. ed. LC 83-45950. (Illus.). 32p. (ps-3). 1988. pap. 5.95 (*0-06-443162-2*, Trophy) HarpC Child Bks.
—My Very First Book of Food. Carle, Eric, illus. LC 85-45259. 10p. (ps-k). 1986. 2.95 (*0-694-00130-9*, Crowell Jr Bks) HarpC Child Bks.
—My Very First Book of Heads & Tails. Carle, Eric, illus. LC 85-45260. 10p. (ps-k). 1986. 2.95 (*0-694-00128-7*, Crowell Jr Bks) HarpC Child Bks.
—My Very First Book of Tools. Carle, Eric, illus. LC 85-45258. 10p. (ps-k). 1986. 2.95 (*0-694-00129-5*, Crowell Jr Bks) HarpC Child Bks.
—My Very First Book of Touch. Carle, Eric, illus. LC 84-47894. 10p. (ps-k). 1986. 2.95 (*0-694-00095-7*, Crowell Jr Bks) HarpC Child Bks.
—One, Two, Three to the Zoo. (Illus.). 34p. (ps-2). 1990. pap. 5.95 (*0-399-21970-6*, Sandcastle Bks) Putnam Pub Group.
—La Oruga Muy Hambrienta. Carle, Eric, illus. (SPA.). 32p. (ps up). 1990. 16.95 (*0-399-21933-1*, Philomel Bks) Putnam Pub Group.
—Rooster's Off to See the World. LC 86-25509. (Illus.). 28p. (ps up). 1991. pap. 15.95 (*0-88708-042-1*) Picture Bk Studio.
—Secret Birthday Message. Carle, Eric, illus. LC 75-168726. 26p. (ps-3). 1972. 15.00 (*0-690-72347-4*, Crowell Jr Bks); PLB 14.89 (*0-690-72348-2*) HarpC Child Bks.
—Secret Birthday Message. Carle, Eric, illus. LC 85-45403. 26p. (ps-3). 1986. pap. 5.95 (*0-06-443099-5*, Trophy) HarpC Child Bks.
—The Tiny Seed. Carle, Eric, illus. LC 86-2534. 32p. (gr. k up). 1991. pap. 15.95 (*0-88708-015-4*) Picture Bk Studio.
—The Very Busy Spider. Carle, Eric, illus. 32p. (ps-2). 1989. 16.95 (*0-399-21166-7*, Philomel Bks); mini ed. 5.95 (*0-399-21592-1*) Putnam Pub Group.
Carlson, George. I Can Draw, 8 vols. in 1. 1988. 5.99 (*0-517-62540-7*) Random Hse Value.
Carlson, Nancy. Louanne Pig in Making the Team. Carlson, Nancy, illus. (gr. k-3). 1987. 19.95 (*0-685-18332-7*); pap. 12.95 (*0-87499-038-6*); 4 paperbacks, cassette & guide 27.95 (*0-87499-036-X*) Live Oak Media.
—Louanne Pig in the Mysterious Valentine. Carlson, Nancy, illus. (gr. 1-3). 1988. bk. & cassette 19.95 (*0-87499-087-4*); bk. & cassette 12.95 (*0-87499-086-6*); 4 cassettes & guide 27.95 (*0-87499-088-2*) Live Oak Media.
—Louanne Pig in The Perfect Family. Carlson, Nancy, illus. (gr. k-3). 1987. incl. cassette 19.95 (*0-87499-037-8*); pap. 12.95 incl. cassette (*0-87499-035-1*); 4 paperbacks, cassette & guide 27.95 (*0-685-18333-5*) Live Oak Media.
—Loudmouth George & The Big Race. Carlson, Nancy, illus. (gr. k-3). 1986. incl. cassette 19.95 (*0-317-59227-0*); pap. 12.95 incl. cassette (*0-87499-029-7*); 4 paperbacks, cassette & guide 27.95 (*0-87499-031-9*) Live Oak Media.
Carlstorm, Nancy W. How Does the Wind Walk? Ray, Deborah K., illus. LC 90-25958. 32p. (ps-2). 1993. RSBE 14.95 (*0-02-717275-9*, Macmillan Child Bk) Macmillan Child Grp.
Carlstrom, Nancy W. Jesse Bear, What Will You Wear? Degen, Bruce, illus. LC 85-10610. 32p. (ps-k). 1986. RSBE 15.00 (*0-02-717350-X*, Macmillan Child Bk) Macmillan Child Grp.
—Wild Wild Sunflower Child Anna. Pinkney, Jerry, illus. LC 86-18226. 32p. (ps-1). 1987. RSBE 14.95 (*0-02-717360-7*, Macmillan Child Bk) Macmillan Child Grp.
Carmichael, Hoagy. Raffles & Other Singing Stories. Stearns, Helen M., ed. Urbahn, Clara, illus. 44p. (ps up). 1989. incl. cass. 25.00 (*0-9614281-5-5*, Cricketfld Pr) Picton Pr.
Carr, Jo. Trouble with Tikki. Petie, Haris, illus. LC 71-115459. (gr. k-2). 1970. 7.19 (*0-8313-0013-2*) Lantern.
Carratello, Patricia. My Body. Carratello, Patricia, illus. 38p. (gr. 1-4). 1980. wkbk. 6.95 (*1-55734-211-3*) Tchr Create Mat.
Carratello, Patty. Brett, My Pet. Spivak, Darlene, ed. Spence, Paula, illus. 16p. (gr. k-2). 1988. wkbk. 1.95 (*1-55734-387-X*) Tchr Create Mat.
—My Cap. Spivak, Darlene, ed. Smythe, Linda, illus. 16p. (gr. k-2). 1988. wkbk. 1.95 (*1-55734-386-1*) Tchr Create Mat.
Carrick, Carol. Ben & the Porcupine. Carrick, Donald, illus. LC 80-214020. 32p. (ps-3). 1985. pap. 6.95 (*0-89919-348-X*, Clarion Bks) HM.
—Left Behind. Carrick, Donald, illus. LC 88-1040. 32p. (gr. k-3). 1988. 13.95 (*0-89919-535-0*, Clarion Bks) HM.
—Patrick's Dinosaurs. Carrick, Donald, illus. LC 83-2049. (gr. k-3). 1985. pap. 5.95 (*0-89919-402-8*, Clarion Bks) HM.
—What Happened to Patrick's Dinosaurs? Carrick, Donald, illus. 1988. pap. 7.70 incl. cass. (*0-89919-838-4*, Clarion Bks) HM.
Carrick, Donald. Patrick's Dinosaurs. (ps-3). 1987. incl. cass. 6.95 (*0-317-64570-6*, Clarion Bks) HM.
Carrie, Christopher. Astronauts to Diving Ducks. (Illus.). 40p. (Orig.). (gr. k up). 1989. pap. 1.49 (*0-86696-219-0*) Binney & Smith.
—Elephants to Haunted Houses. (Illus.). 40p. (Orig.). (gr. k up). 1989. pap. 1.49 (*0-86696-225-5*) Binney & Smith.
—Everything Has a Shape. (Illus.). 40p. (Orig.). (ps up). 1989. pap. 1.99 (*0-86696-222-0*) Binney & Smith.
—Going Places. (Illus.). 40p. (Orig.). (ps up). 1989. pap. 1.99 (*0-86696-221-2*) Binney & Smith.
—Growing Up. (Illus.). 40p. (Orig.). (ps up). 1989. pap. 1.99 (*0-86696-220-4*) Binney & Smith.
—Icebergs to Lazy Lizards. (Illus.). 40p. (Orig.). (gr. k up). 1989. pap. 1.49 (*0-86696-226-3*) Binney & Smith.
—Measurement. (Illus.). 12p. (Orig.). (gr. 3-6). 1987. pap. 4.70 (*0-86696-206-9*) Binney & Smith.
—Monsters to Playful Penquins. (Illus.). 40p. (Orig.). (gr. k up). 1989. pap. 1.49 (*0-86696-227-1*) Binney & Smith.
—My Perfect Pet. (Illus.). 40p. (Orig.). (ps up). 1989. pap. 1.99 (*0-86696-218-2*) Binney & Smith.
—Quilts to Unusual Unicorns. (Illus.). 40p. (Orig.). (gr. k up). 1989. pap. 1.49 (*0-86696-229-8*) Binney & Smith.
—Smiles, Giggles & Frowns. (Illus.). 40p. (Orig.). (ps up). 1989. pap. 1.99 (*0-86696-223-9*) Binney & Smith.
—So Big. (Illus.). 32p. 1988. 2.70 (*0-86696-205-0*) Binney & Smith.
—Time. (Illus.). 12p. (Orig.). (gr. 3-6). 1987. pap. 4.70 (*0-86696-207-7*) Binney & Smith.
—Volcanoes to Zany Zebras. (Illus.). 40p. (Orig.). (gr. k up). 1989. pap. 1.49 (*0-86696-230-1*) Binney & Smith.
Carrier, Lark. Do Not Touch. LC 87-32730. (Illus.). (ps-12). 1991. pap. 15.95 (*0-88708-061-8*) Picture Bk Studio.
—A Perfect Spring. Carrier, Lark, illus. LC 89-49262. 32p. (ps up). 1991. pap. 14.95 (*0-88708-131-2*) Picture Bk Studio.
—Scout & Cody. Carrier, Lark, illus. LC 86-883. 28p. (ps up). 1991. pap. 14.95 (*0-88708-013-8*) Picture Bk Studio.
—Snowy Path: A Christmas Journey. Carrier, Lark, illus. LC 89-8449. 28p. (ps up). 1991. pap. 15.95 (*0-88708-121-5*) Picture Bk Studio.
—There Was a Hill... Carrier, Lark, illus. LC 84-25536. 40p. (ps up). 1991. pap. 15.95 (*0-907234-70-4*) Picture Bk Studio.
Carrier, Roch. The Hockey Sweater. Fischman, Sheila, tr. from FRE. Cohen, Sheldon, illus. 24p. (gr. 1 up). 1984. text ed. 14.95 (*0-88776-169-0*, Dist. by U of Toronto Pr); pap. 6.95 (*0-88776-174-7*) Tundra Bks.
Carroll, Lewis. Alice in Wonderland Pop-up Book. (ps-3). 1991. 14.00 (*0-440-40540-8*, YB) Dell.
Carter, David A. How Many Bugs in a Box? (ps-1). 1988. pap. 12.95 (*0-671-64965-5*, S&S BFYR) S&S Trade.
—Jingle Bugs. (ps). 1992. pap. 16.00 (*0-671-72924-1*, S&S BFYR) S&S Trade.
—What's in My Pocket? A Pop-up & Peek-in Book. Carter, David A., illus. 10p. (ps-k). 1989. 8.95 (*0-399-21685-5*, Putnam) Putnam Pub Group.
Carter, Noelle. Where's My Squishy Ball? A Lift & Touch Book. Carter, Noelle, illus. 14p. (ps). 1993. 6.95 (*0-590-47385-9*, Cartwheel) Scholastic Inc.
Cartlidge, Michelle. Baby Mice at Home. Cartlidge, Michelle, illus. 24p. (ps). 1992. bds. 2.95 (*0-525-44840-3*, DCB) Dutton Child Bks.
—Bears on the Go. Cartlidge, Michelle, illus. 24p. (ps). 1992. bds. 2.95 (*0-525-44841-1*, DCB) Dutton Child Bks.
—Bunny's Birthday. Cartlidge, Michelle, illus. 24p. (ps). 1992. bds. 2.95 (*0-525-44843-8*, DCB) Dutton Child Bks.
—Doggy Days. Cartlidge, Michelle, illus. 24p. (ps). 1992. bds. 2.95 (*0-525-44844-6*, DCB) Dutton Child Bks.
Cartwright, Stephen. Find the Bird. Cartwright, Stephen, illus. Zeff, C. (Illus.). 12p. (ps). 1984. bds. 3.95 (*0-86020-719-6*, Pub. by Usborne) EDC.
—Find the Duck. Cartwright, Stephen, illus. Zeff, C. (Illus.). 12p. (ps). 1984. bds. 3.95 (*0-86020-714-5*, Pub. by Usborne) EDC.
—Find the Kitten. Cartwright, Stephen, illus. Zeff, C. (Illus.). 12p. (ps). 1984. bds. 3.95 (*0-86020-718-8*, Pub. by Usborne) EDC.
—Find the Piglet. Cartwright, Stephen, illus. Zeff, C. (Illus.). 12p. (ps). 1984. bds. 3.95 (*0-86020-716-1*, Pub. by Usborne) EDC.
—Find the Puppy. Cartwright, Stephen, illus. Zeff, C. (Illus.). 12p. (ps). 1984. bds. 3.95 (*0-86020-717-X*, Pub. by Usborne) EDC.
—Find the Teddy. Cartwright, Stephen, illus. Zeff, C. (Illus.). 12p. (ps). 1984. bds. 3.95 (*0-86020-715-3*, Pub. by Usborne) EDC.
Case, Elinor. Humphrey, Wimsey & Doo. Taylor, Marie, illus. 48p. (Orig.). (ps-6). 1984. pap. 5.95 (*0-910781-02-8*) G Whittell Mem.
Caseley, Judith. Silly Baby. LC 87-4097. (Illus.). 24p. (ps-3). 1988. 11.95 (*0-688-07355-7*); lib. bdg. 11.88 (*0-688-07356-5*) Greenwillow.
The Caterpillar Who Turned into a Butterfly. 16p. (ps-k). 1980. pap. 3.95 (*0-671-41347-3*, Little Simon) S&S Trade.
Catley, Alison. The Party in the Sky. (Illus.). 32p. (ps-2). 1992. 17.95 (*0-09-174036-3*, Pub. by Hutchinson UK) Trafalgar.
Cauley, Lorinda B. The Ugly Duckling. Canley, Lorinda B., illus. LC 79-12340. 40p. (gr. k-3). 1979. pap. 4.95 (*0-15-692528-1*, Voyager Bks) HarBrace.
Cazet, Denys. December Twenty-Fourth. Cazet, Denys, illus. LC 86-8247. 32p. (ps-2). 1986. RSBE 13.95 (*0-02-717950-8*, Bradbury Pr) Macmillan Child Grp.
—Frosted Glass. Cazet, Denys, illus. LC 86-26822. 32p. (ps-2). 1987. RSBE 13.95 (*0-02-717960-5*, Bradbury Pr) Macmillan Child Grp.
Cecil, Laura. Listen to This. Clark, Emma C., illus. LC 87-8556. 96p. (ps-3). 1988. 15.00 (*0-688-07617-3*) Greenwillow.
Cecotti, Loralie. Seattle Center. Hamer, Bonnie, illus. 24p. (Orig.). (gr. 1-4). 1983. pap. 2.75 (*0-933992-30-0*) Coffee Break.
Chadwick, Kenneth E. A Hear Do'n Sing Book: Little Bitty You Little Bitty Me. Boss, Jackie, illus. (ps). 1979. 4.25 (*0-9603698-0-5*) Bet-Ken Prods.
Chalmers, Mary. Easter Parade. Chalmers, Mary, illus. LC 87-45277. 32p. (ps-1). 1990. pap. 4.95 (*0-06-443219-X*, Trophy) HarpC Child Bks.
Chaplin, Susan. I Can Sign My ABC's. McCaul, Laura, illus. LC 86-22890. 56p. (ps-1). 1986. 9.95 (*0-930323-19-X*, Kendall Green Pubns) Gallaudet Univ Pr.
Chapman, Carol. Barney Bipple's Magic Dandelions. Kellogg, Steven, illus. LC 77-5747. 32p. (gr. k-3). 1988. 13.95 (*0-525-44449-1*, DCB) Dutton Child Bks.
Charaleone. All I See Is Part of Me. Aldrich, Cynthia, illus. 56p. (gr. 2-8). 1989. 14.95 (*0-935699-03-1*) Illum Arts.
Chardiet, Bernice. I Help Daddy. Cote, Pamela, illus. 20p. (ps-1). 1994. pap. 4.99 (*0-14-054999-4*) Puffin Bks.
—I Help Mommy. Cote, Pamela, illus. 20p. (ps-1). 1994. pap. 4.99 (*0-14-054998-6*) Puffin Bks.
Charles, Donald. Gordito, Gordon Gato Galano: (Fat, Fat Calico Cat) Charles, Donald, illus. LC 77-7154. (SPA.). 32p. (ps-2). 1988. PLB 11.80 (*0-516-33456-5*); pap. 3.95 (*0-516-53456-4*) Childrens.
Charles, Oz. How Is a Crayon Made? LC 87-11436. (Illus.). 32p. (gr. 1-5). 1990. (S&S BFYR); pap. 3.95 (*0-671-69437-5*, S&S BFYR) S&S Trade.
Charlip, Remy. Fortunately. Charlip, Remy, illus. LC 80-36956. 48p. (ps-3). 1984. Repr. of 1964 ed. RSBE 14.95 (*0-02-718100-6*, Four Winds) Macmillan Child Grp.
Charlip, Remy & Joyner, Jerry. Thirteen. LC 75-8875. (Illus.). 40p. (ps up). 1984. Repr. of 1975 ed. RSBE 14.95 (*0-02-718120-0*, Four Winds) Macmillan Child Grp.
Chartier, Normand. Jingle Bells. 16p. 1989. pap. 3.95 (*0-671-68269-5*, Little Simon) S&S Trade.
Chartrand, Micheline. Lollypop Knows How. (Illus.). 12p. (ps). 1993. bds. 3.95 (*2-921198-08-8*, Pub. by Les Edits Herit CN) Adams Inc MA.
Chauhan, Manhar, illus. Muppet Babies Take a Bath. 10p. (ps). 1992. vinyl 3.95 (*0-394-86362-3*) Random Bks Yng Read.

Chevalier, Christa. Spence & the Mean Old Bear. Levine, Abby, ed. LC 86-1570. (Illus.). 32p. (ps-1). 1986. 11.95 (*0-8075-7572-0*) A Whitman.
—Spence Is Small. Levine, Abby, ed. Chevalier, Christa, illus. LC 87-2054. (ps-1). 1987. PLB 11.95 (*0-8075-7567-4*) A Whitman.
Children's Television Workshop Staff. Who's Hiding? Cooke, Tom, illus. LC 84-81602. 14p. (ps-k). 1986. write for info. (*0-307-12157-7*, Pub. by Golden Bks) Western Pub.
Childress, Alice. A Hero Ain't Nothin' but a Sandwich. 100p. (gr. 5-9). 1973. 14.95 (*0-698-20278-3*, Coward) Putnam Pub Group.
Chochola, Frantisek. The Forest. (Illus.). (ps). 1988. bds. 5.50 (*0-86315-073-X*, 20234) Gryphon Hse.
—On the Farm. (ps). 1988. bds. 5.50 (*0-86315-051-9*, 20235) Gryphon Hse.
Chorao, Kay, illus. Baby's Good Morning Book. Collins, Judy, contrib. by. LC 86-6415. (Illus.). 64p. (ps). 1990. 13.95 (*0-525-44257-X*, DCB); incl. audio cass. 17.95 (*0-525-44627-3*, DCB) Dutton Child Bks.
Christensen, Nancy. Easy As ABC - A Wipe Clean Activity Book. (ps). 1994. 2.24 (*1-884270-00-X*) Nancy Hall.
—Easy As One Two Three - (A Wipe Clean Book) (ps). 1994. 2.24 (*1-884270-01-8*) Nancy Hall.
Christian, Cheryl, ed. What Happens Next? Dwight, Laura, illus. 12p. (ps). 1991. 4.95 (*1-56288-131-0*) Checkerboard.
—Where's the Baby? Dwight, Laura, illus. 12p. (ps). 1992. 4.95 (*1-56288-128-0*) Checkerboard.
—Where's the Kitten? Dwight, Laura, illus. 12p. (ps). 1992. 4.95 (*1-56288-130-2*) Checkerboard.
—Where's the Puppy? Dwight, Laura, illus. 12p. (ps). 1992. 4.95 (*1-56288-129-9*) Checkerboard.
Christiansen, C. B. My Mother's House, My Father's House. Trivas, Irene, illus. LC 88-16802. 32p. (gr. k-3). 1989. SBE 13.95 (*0-689-31394-2*, Atheneum Child Bk) Macmillan Child Grp.
Chubby Bear. 1984. pap. 2.95 (*0-671-50949-7*, Little Simon) S&S Trade.
Chubby Engine. 1984. pap. 2.95 (*0-671-50951-9*, Little Simon) S&S Trade.
Chubby Snowman. 1984. pap. 2.95 (*0-671-50948-9*, Little Simon) S&S Trade.
Chubby Tugboat. 1984. pap. 3.50 (*0-671-50950-0*, Little Simon) S&S Trade.
Cleary, Beverly. The Real Hole. rev. ed. Stevens, Mary, illus. LC 85-18815. 32p. (ps-1). 1986. 11.95 (*0-688-05850-7*); PLB 11.88 (*0-688-05851-5*) Morrow Jr Bks.
—Ribsy. Darling, Louis, illus. 192p. (gr. 3-7). 1982. pap. 3.50 (*0-440-47456-6*, YB) Dell.
Clements, Andrew. Big Al. Yoshi, illus. LC 88-15129. 28p. (ps up). 1991. pap. 14.95 (*0-88708-075-8*) Picture Bk Studio.
—Noah & the Ark & the Animals. Gantschev, Ivan, illus. LC 84-9438. 28p. (gr. 1 up). 1991. pap. 14.95 (*0-907234-58-5*) Picture Bk Studio.
Clements, Jehan. Alfred the Ant, An Ant Who Lives & Has Fun in Central Park: The First Storytelling "Flip Over" Picture Book. Clements, Jehan, illus. LC 89-61138. 48p. (gr. k-3). 1991. 19.95 (*0-9622500-0-7*) Strytllr Co.
Climo, Shirley. The Cobweb Christmas. Lasker, Joe, illus. LC 81-43879. 32p. (ps-3). 1986. pap. 4.50 (*0-06-443110-X*, Trophy) HarpC Child Bks.
—The Egyptian Cinderella. Heller, Ruth, illus. LC 88-37547. 32p. (gr. k-3). 1992. pap. 4.95 (*0-06-443279-3*, Trophy) HarpC Child Bks.
Coats, Laura J. Mr. Jordan in the Park. Coats, Laura J., illus. LC 88-13295. 32p. (gr. k-3). 1989. RSBE 14.95 (*0-02-719053-6*, Macmillan Child Bk) Macmillan Child Grp.
Cocca-Leffler, Maryann. Grandma & Me. Cocca-Leffler, Maryann, illus. LC 90-61044. 28p. (ps). 1991. bds. 2.95 (*0-679-80758-6*) Random Bks Yng Read.
Coerr, Eleanor. Big Balloon Race. Croll, Carolyn, illus. LC 91-13607. 64p. (gr. k-3). 1984. pap. 3.50 (*0-06-444053-2*, Trophy) HarpC Child Bks.
Cohen, Barbara. Molly's Pilgrim. Deraney, Michael J., illus. LC 83-797. 32p. (gr. 2-5). 1983. 14.00 (*0-688-02103-4*); PLB 13.93 (*0-688-02104-2*) Lothrop.
Cohen, Marsha, illus. Baby's Favorite Things. 12p. (ps). 1986. 3.99 (*0-394-88243-1*) Random Bks Yng Read.
Cohen, Miriam. Best Friends. Hoban, Lillian, illus. 32p. (ps-1). 1989. pap. 3.95 (*0-689-71334-7*, Aladdin) Macmillan Child Grp.
—It's George! Hoban, Lillian, illus. LC 86-19384. 24p. (ps-2). 1988. 15.00 (*0-688-06812-X*); lib. bdg. 14.93 (*0-688-06813-8*) Greenwillow.
—The New Teacher. Hoban, Lillian, illus. LC 78-163239. 32p. (ps-1). 1989. pap. 3.95 (*0-689-71332-0*, Aladdin) Macmillan Child Grp.
—Will I Have a Friend? Hoban, Lillian, illus. LC 67-10127. 32p. (ps-1). 1967. RSBE 13.95 (*0-02-722790-1*, Macmillan Child Bk) Macmillan Child Grp.
—Will I Have a Friend? Hoban, Lillian, illus. LC 89-31340. 32p. (ps-1). 1989. pap. 3.95 (*0-689-71333-9*, Aladdin) Macmillan Child Grp.
Colby, J. Disney's the Little Mermaid: Sebastian's Story. Kurtz, John, illus. 24p. (ps-k). 1992. write for info. (*0-307-10020-0*, 10020) Western Pub.
Cole, Betsy. Green Creatures Ten to One. Happe, Cary, illus. LC 88-71429. 32p. (Orig.). (gr. k-3). 1988. pap. 4.95 (*0-9620606-0-7*) Adventure VA.
Cole, Brock. The Giant's Toe. (Illus.). 32p. (ps up). 1988. pap. 3.95 (*0-374-42557-4*) FS&G.
Cole, Joann. Norma Jean, Jumping Bean. Munsinger, Lynn, illus. LC 86-15588. 48p. (gr. 1-3). 1987. 3.50 (*0-394-88668-2*); lib. bdg. 7.99 (*0-394-98668-7*) Random Bks Yng Read.
Cole, Joanna. The Clown-Arounds. Smath, Jerry, illus. LC 81-4662. 48p. (ps-3). 1981. 5.95 (*0-8193-1059-X*); PLB 5.95 (*0-8193-1060-3*) Parents.
—Don't Tell the Whole World! Duke, Kate, illus. LC 89-29283. 32p. (gr. k-3). 1992. pap. 4.95 (*0-06-443292-0*, Trophy) HarpC Child Bks.
Colladi, Carlo. The Adventures of Pinocchio: The Ultimate Illustrated Edition. (Illus.). 160p. (ps up). write for info. Bantam.
Collier, Jaunell & Hill, Marie. I Love You. Collier, Jaunell, illus. 27p. (Orig.). 1983. write for info. (*0-918464-58-7*) Irresistible.
Collins, Crystal. Teddy Bear Paper Dolls. 1983. pap. 3.50 (*0-486-24550-0*) Dover.
Collins, Doris. Fun Times Growing Up. Walsh, Janice, illus. 24p. (Orig.). (gr. k-3). 1988. pap. 7.95 (*0-9621650-0-X*) Periwinkle MA.
Collins, Grace. Willy, Zilly & the Little Bantams. LC 88-51662. (Illus.). 32p. (gr. 1-3). 1988. 10.25x (*0-943864-54-2*) Davenport.
Collins, Pat L. Waiting for Baby Joe. Tucker, Kathy, ed. Dunn, Joan W., illus. LC 89-21457. 48p. (ps-2). 1990. PLB 11.95 (*0-8075-8625-0*) A Whitman.
Collins, Sterling C. Doll-Victorian Mouse Paper Dolls in Full Color. 1986. pap. 3.95 (*0-486-25045-8*) Dover.
Collins-Sterling, Crystal. Panda-Paper Dolls. 1989. pap. 2.95 (*0-486-25929-3*) Dover.
Colossal Book of Dinosaurs. 240p. (gr. k-2). 1989. 19.95 (*0-87449-649-7*) Modern Pub NYC.
Come to the Circus. 16p. (ps-k). 1980. pap. 2.95 (*0-671-41479-8*, Little Simon) S&S Trade.
A Concert in the Woods. (Illus.). 6p. (gr. k-2). 1991. bds. 17.95 (*1-56144-030-2*, Honey Bear Bks) Modern Pub NYC.
Conejito (Bunny, Bunny) (SPA., Illus.). 28p. (ps-2). 1991. PLB 10.50 (*0-516-35352-7*); pap. 3.95 (*0-516-55352-6*) Childrens.
Conkle, Nancy E. Terrific Bee on Terrific Me. Blackard, Sandy, illus. 32p. (Orig.). (ps-1). 1993. pap. 9.50 (*0-9639061-0-0*) N Conkle.
Conrad, Lynn. All Aboard Trucks. Courtney, Richard, illus. 32p. (Orig.). (ps-2). 1989. pap. 2.25 (*0-448-19094-X*, Platt & Munk Pubs) Putnam Pub Group.
Conrad, Pam. The Tub People. Egielski, Richard, illus. LC 88-32804. 32p. (gr. k-3). 1995. pap. 4.95 (*0-06-443306-4*, Trophy) HarpC Child Bks.
Conservation at Home Activity Book. (Illus.). (ps-6). pap. 2.95 (*0-565-01098-0*, Pub. by Natural Hist Mus) Parkwest Pubns.
Cooke, Tom, illus. Grover's Adventure under the Sea. LC 88-61629. 14p. (ps). 1989. bds. 3.99 (*0-394-81951-9*) Random Bks Yng Read.
—Sesame Street Hide-&-Seek Safari. LC 87-61638. 14p. (ps). 1988. bds. 3.99 (*0-394-89474-X*) Random Bks Yng Read.
Cooper, Susan. The Selkie Girl. Hutton, Warwick, illus. LC 86-70147. 32p. (gr. k-4). 1986. SBE 14.95 (*0-689-50390-3*, M K McElderry) Macmillan Child Grp.
Corey, Dorothy. Will It Ever Be My Birthday? Fay, Ann, ed. LC 86-1565. (Illus.). 32p. (ps-3). 1986. PLB 13.95 (*0-8075-9106-8*) A Whitman.
Cornell, Donald. Ice Told Tales. Rosoff, Barbara, tr. Cornell, Donald, illus. (ENG & FRE.). 58p. (Orig.). (ps-2). 1991. pap. 4.00 (*0-9620738-1-4*) D Cornell.
Corpening, Gene S. I Love to Hear the Cold Wind Howl. James, Linda & Corpening, Gene S., illus. 40p. (Orig.). (gr. 2 up). 1993. pap. 7.95g (*0-9636775-9-4*) Alice Pub.
Corrigan, Dorothy D. Watch Out for the Golly Whompers. McBride, Michael, illus. LC 88-50754. 35p. (gr. k-3). 1988. 6.95 (*1-55523-149-7*) Winston-Derek.
Corrin, Sara & Corrin, Stephen, eds. Stories for Eight-Year-Olds. Hughes, Shirley, illus. 192p. (gr. 2-4). 1984. pap. 9.95 (*0-571-12969-2*) Faber & Faber.
—Stories for Six-Year-Olds. Hughes, Shirley, illus. 198p. (gr. k-2). 1984. pap. 9.95 (*0-571-12959-5*) Faber & Faber.
Corwin, Judith H. Patriotic Fun. Corwin, Judith H., illus. LC 85-18730. 64p. (gr. 3 up). 1985. lib. bdg. 10.98 (*0-671-50799-0*, J Messner); PLB 7.71s.p. (*0-685-47060-1*); pap. 3.71s.p. (*0-685-47061-X*) S&S Trade.
Cosgrove, Stephen. Balderdash. Gedrose, E. D., illus. 32p. (gr. 3-6). 1991. 14.95 (*1-55868-045-4*) Gr Arts Ctr Pub.
—The Dream Stealer. Heyer, Carol, illus. LC 89-83843. 48p. (gr. 1-4). 1990. 16.95 (*1-55868-009-8*); pap. 5.95 (*1-55868-021-7*); pap. 12.95 incl. audio (*1-55868-042-X*) Gr Arts Ctr Pub.
—Harmony. Casad, Michael, illus. LC 89-83842. 72p. (gr. 7 up). 1991. 24.95 (*1-55868-008-X*) Gr Arts Ctr Pub.
—Heidi's Rose. Edelson, Wendy, illus. LC 90-71079. 32p. (gr. 3-6). 1991. 14.95 (*1-55868-033-0*) Gr Arts Ctr Pub.
—Leo the Lop: Tail Two. James, Robin, illus. 32p. (Orig.). (gr. 1-4). 1978. pap. 2.95 (*0-8431-0572-0*) Price Stern.
—Maui-Maui. James, Robin, illus. 32p. (Orig.). (gr. 1-4). 1979. pap. 3.95 (*0-8431-0573-9*) Price Stern.
—Prancer. Heyer, Carol, illus. LC 89-83843. 32p. (gr. k-7). 1990. 14.95 (*1-55868-019-5*); pap. 5.95 (*1-55868-020-9*); pap. 12.95 incl. audio (*1-55868-041-1*) Gr Arts Ctr Pub.
—Read Aloud Topsy-Turvy Library, 26 vols. Reasoner, Charles, illus. (ps-3). 1988. Set. 155.48 (*0-87475-600-6*) Stuttman.
Cosgrove, Stephen E. Gigglesnitcher. James, Robin, illus. 48p. (gr. k-9). 1991. 12.95 (*1-55868-034-9*) Gr Arts Ctr Pub.
Costa, Nicoletta. My Poke & Look Busy Book. (Illus.). 44p. (ps-2). 1990. bds. 14.95 (*0-448-21034-7*, G&D) Putnam Pub Group.
Counting One, Two, Three. (Illus.). (ps). 1985. bds. 2.98 (*0-517-47338-0*) Random Hse Value.
Cousins, Lucy. Maisy Goes to Bed. Cousins, Luch, illus. (ps). 1990. 12.95 (*0-316-15832-1*) Little.
Coville, Bruce. The Foolish Giant. Coville, Katherine, illus. LC 77-18522. 48p. (ps-2). 1990. pap. 4.95 (*0-06-443229-7*, Trophy) HarpC Child Bks.
Coville, Bruce & Coville, Katherine. Sarah's Unicorn. Coville, Bruce & Coville, Katherine, illus. LC 85-42749. 48p. (gr. 1-4). 1985. pap. 4.95 (*0-06-443084-7*, Trophy) HarpC Child Bks.
Cow. 1989. 3.50 (*1-87865-729-1*) Blue Q.
Coxe, Molly. Louella & the Yellow Balloon. Coxe, Molly, illus. LC 87-30379. 32p. (ps-2). 1988. (Crowell Jr Bks) HarpC Child Bks.
Crews, Donald. Harbor. LC 81-6607. (ps up). 1987. pap. 3.95 (*0-688-07332-8*, Mulberry) Morrow.
—Parade. Crews, Donald, illus. LC 82-20927. 32p. (gr. k-3). 1983. 14.00 (*0-688-01995-1*); PLB 13.93 (*0-688-01996-X*) Greenwillow.
—Truck. LC 79-19031. (Illus.). 32p. (ps-2). 1980. 14.00 (*0-688-80244-3*); PLB 13.93 (*0-688-84244-5*) Greenwillow.
—Truck. LC 79-19031. (Illus.). 32p. (ps up). 1991. pap. 3.95 (*0-688-10481-9*, Mulberry) Morrow.
Crillis, Carla, illus. I Can Help. 14p. (ps). 1991. Repr. bds. 5.50 (*0-86315-123-X*) Gryphon Hse.
Cristini, Ermanno & Puricelli, Luigi. In My Garden. Cristini, Ermanno & Puricelli, Luigi, illus. LC 85-9402. 28p. (ps up). 1991. pap. 12.95 (*0-907234-05-4*) Picture Bk Studio.
—In the Pond. Cristini, Ermanno & Puricelli, Luigi, illus. LC 84-972. 28p. (ps up). 1991. pap. 12.95 (*0-907234-43-7*) Picture Bk Studio.
—In the Woods. Cristini, Ermanno & Puricelli, Luigi, illus. LC 83-8153. 28p. (ps up). 1991. pap. 12.95 (*0-907234-31-3*) Picture Bk Studio.
Crocodile. 1989. 3.50 (*1-87865-726-7*) Blue Q.
Cross, Molly. Wait for Me! Mathieu, Joe, illus. LC 87-12926. 40p. (ps-3). 1987. 4.95 (*0-394-89135-X*) Random Bks Yng Read.
Cross, Verda. Great-Grandma Tells of Threshing Day. Tucker, Kathleen, ed. Owens, Gail, illus. LC 90-28442. 40p. (gr. 1-6). 1992. 15.95 (*0-8075-3042-5*) A Whitman.
Crowe, Robert L. Clyde Monster. Chorao, Kay, illus. LC 76-10733. 32p. (ps-3). 1987. (DCB); pap. 3.95 (*0-525-44289-8*, DCB) Dutton Child Bks.
—Tyler Toad & the Thunder. Chorao, Kay, illus. LC 80-347. 32p. (ps-1). 1986. pap. 4.95 (*0-525-44243-X*, DCB) Dutton Child Bks.
Crowther, Robert. Most Amazing Hide & Seek Opposites Book. Crowther, Robert, illus. LC 85-42757. 12p. (ps-3). 1985. pap. 12.95 pop-up (*0-670-80121-6*) Viking Child Bks.
—Pop Goes the Weasel! Twenty-Five Pop-Up Nursery Rhymes. (Illus.). (ps-3). 1987. Pop-Up ed. pap. 14.95 (*0-670-81815-1*) Viking Child Bks.
—Robert Crowther's Most Amazing Pop-Up Book of Machines. (ps-3). 1988. pap. 14.95 (*0-670-82339-2*) Viking Child Bks.
Crozat, Francois. I Am a Little Bear. (Illus.). 24p. (ps). 1989. 8.95 (*0-8120-5903-4*); Miniature, 1990. 2.95 (*0-8120-6191-8*) Barron.
—I Am a Little Dog. (Illus.). 28p. (ps-k). 1992. 8.95 (*0-8120-6276-0*); miniature version o.p. 2.95 (*0-8120-6286-8*) Barron.
—I Am a Little Rabbit. (Illus.). 24p. (ps). 1989. 8.95 (*0-8120-5905-0*); Miniature. 3.50 (*0-8120-6194-2*) Barron.
Cuddle's Bathtime. (ps). 1977. 3.50 (*0-86112-275-5*, Pub. by Brimax Bks) Borden.
Cuddle's Bedtime. (ps). 1977. 3.50 (*0-86112-278-X*, Pub. by Brimax Bks) Borden.
Cuddle's Mealtime. (ps). 1977. 3.50 (*0-86112-276-3*, Pub. by Brimax Bks) Borden.
Cuddle's Playtime. (ps). 1977. 3.50 (*0-86112-277-1*, Pub. by Brimax Bks) Borden.
Cuddly Casey. 12p. (ps-1). 1989. bds. 5.95 (*0-87449-710-8*) Modern Pub NYC.
Cunningham, Dru. The Most Wonderful Place to Live. LC 93-85310. (Illus.). 40p. (gr. k-3). 1994. pap. 5.95 (*1-55523-644-8*) Winston-Derek.
Curran, Eileen. Hello, Farm Animals. Goldsborough, June, illus. LC 84-8657. 32p. (gr. k-2). 1985. PLB 11.59 (*0-8167-0345-0*); pap. text ed. 2.95 (*0-8167-0346-9*) Troll Assocs.
—Life in the Meadow. Watling, James, illus. LC 84-12384. 32p. (gr. k-2). 1985. PLB 11.59 (*0-8167-0343-4*); pap. 2.95 (*0-8167-0344-2*) Troll Assocs.
—Little Christmas Elf. Page, Don, illus. LC 84-8628. 32p. (gr. k-2). 1985. PLB 11.59 (*0-8167-0352-3*); pap. text ed. 2.95 (*0-8167-0432-5*) Troll Assocs.

—Look at a Tree. Goldsborough, June, illus. LC 84-8843. 32p. (gr. k-2). 1985. PLB 11.59 (*0-8167-0349-3*); pap. text ed. 2.95 (*0-8167-0350-7*) Troll Assocs.

Curtis, Chara M. All I See Is Part of Me. rev. ed. Aldrich, Cynthia, illus. 48p. 1994. 15.95 (*0-935699-07-4*) Illum Arts.
In ALL I SEE IS PART OF ME a child discovers his universal connection with all of life. Illuminating answers to life's questions are discovered on an enchanting journey of awakening. The conclusion brings reassurance & comfort from knowing that for each of us, "there can be no end." "This warm, gentle, tender, trusting book is just what the world needs." - Gerald G. Jampolsky, M.D., author. "You will be warmed by its love - as I have - over & over." - NAPRA Trade News. "The child in this world shines forth with vibrancy & warmth," - Montessori Life. To order, call Atrium 1-800-275-2606.
Publisher Provided Annotation.

Dabney, Joy, illus. A Book about Me. 32p. (gr. k-3). 1987. wkbk. 2.50 (*0-939985-00-4*) Creative Dimensions.
Daly, Niki. Not So Fast, Songololo. Daly, Niki, illus. LC 85-70134. 32p. (gr. k-3). 1986. SBE 14.95 (*0-689-50367-9*, M K McElderry) Macmillan Child Grp.
—Not So Fast, Songololo. (ps-3). 1987. pap. 3.99 (*0-14-050715-9*, Puffin) Puffin Bks.
D'Andrea, Deborah. If I Were a Firefighter: Or a Doctor, or an Astronaut, or... Ayers, Michael B., illus. 12p. (ps-k). 1991. 4.99 (*1-878338-04-8*) Picture Me Bks.
—If I Were a Reindeer. (Illus.). (ps-k). 1991. write for info. (*1-878338-03-X*) Picture Me Bks.
—Learn Letters with Me ABC. Ayers, Michael B., illus. 12p. (ps-k). 1991. 4.99 (*1-878338-06-4*) Picture Me Bks.
D'Andrea, Deborah B. If I Were a Bunny, Or a Panda, Or a Monkey, Or... Ayers, Michael B., illus. 12p. (ps-1). 1989. bds. 4.99 (*1-878338-00-5*) Picture Me Bks.
—If I Were a Fairy, Or a Ballerina, Or a Witch, Or... Ayers, Michael B., illus. 12p. (ps-1). 1989. bds. 4.99 (*1-878338-01-3*) Picture Me Bks.
—If I Were a Pirate, Or a Cowboy, Or a Knight, Or... Ayers, Michael B., illus. 12p. (ps-1). 1989. bds. 4.99 (*1-878338-02-1*) Picture Me Bks.
Daugherty, James. Andy & the Lion. Daugherty, James, illus. LC 38-27390. 80p. (gr. 1-4). 1938. pap. 13.95 (*0-670-12433-8*) Viking Child Bks.
Davis, Inez T. Modestita's Gift - El Regalo de Modestita. LC 91-71032. (ENG & SPA.). 32p. (ps-3). 1991. pap. 4.99 (*0-8066-2532-5*, 9-2532) Augsburg Fortress.
Davis, Kerry. The Swetsville Zoo. (Illus.). 44p. (gr. 1-6). 1994. 8.95 (*0-9635263-1-6*); It's More Than A Tree That You See, Bk. 1. pap. 4.95 (*0-9635263-0-8*); Set. 12.95 (*0-9635263-2-4*) Kerry Tales.
Davis, Robert C. The E-waa, Vol. 1. Tremblay, Martin, illus. LC 91-61838. 28p. (Orig.). 1991. pap. 5.50g (*0-9629949-0-1*) Across the Road.
Davoll, Barbara. A Sunday Surprise. Hockerman, Dennis, illus. 24p. 1988. 6.99 (*0-89693-405-5*, Victor Books); cassette 9.99 (*0-89693-616-3*) SP Pubns.
A Day at the Zoo. write for info. (*1-56326-310-6*, 031104) Disney Bks By Mail.
Day, O. M. ABCs of Bugs & Beasts. Day, O. M., illus. 31p. (Orig.). (gr. 3-12). 1991. pap. 11.95 (*0-9629795-1-1*) Klar-Iden Pub.
Daytime Words. (Illus.). 1991. 4.99 (*0-517-05885-5*) Random Hse Value.
DC Comics Staff. Batman: The Animated Series Pop-up Playbook. (Illus.). (ps-3). 1994. 16.95 (*0-316-17788-1*) Little.
De Beaumont, Madame. Beauty & the Beast. Shumate, Mark, adapted by. Hicks, Russell, illus. 26p. (ps). 1987. Packaged with pre-programmed audio cass. tape. 9.95 (*0-934323-66-6*) Alchemy Comms.
De Brunhoff, Jean. Babar & His Children. Haas, Merle, tr. (Illus.). (ps). 1969. 11.00 (*0-394-80577-1*); lib. bdg. 11.99 (*0-394-90577-6*) Random Bks Yng Read.
—The Pop-up Travels of Babar. De Brunhoff, Laurent, illus. LC 91-60192. 12p. (ps-1). 1991. 13.00 (*0-679-82151-1*) Random Bks Yng Read.
—The Story of Babar. (Illus.). (ps). 1937. 9.95 (*0-394-80575-5*); PLB 10.99 (*0-394-90575-X*) Random Bks Yng Read.
—Travels of Babar. (Illus.). (ps). 1967. 11.00 (*0-394-80576-3*); lib. bdg. 11.99 (*0-394-90576-8*) Random Bks Yng Read.
De Brunhoff, Laurent. Babar's French Lessons. (Illus.). (ps). 1963. 11.00 (*0-394-80587-9*); lib. bdg. 5.99 (*0-394-90587-3*) Random Bks Yng Read.
De Brunhoff, Laurent, illus. Babar's Busy Week. LC 89-64400. 22p. (ps). 1990. bds. 2.95 (*0-679-80664-4*) Random Bks Yng Read.
Decker, Marjorie. Christian Mother Goose Pop-up Bedtime Animal Friends. (ps). 1989. 6.99 (*0-529-06689-0*) World Bible.
De Cuenca, Pilar. Cinco Ciento Palabras Nuevas Para Ti. Alvarez, Ines, tr. McNaught, Harry, illus. LC 81-13766. 32p. (ps-3). 1982. pap. 2.25 (*0-394-85145-5*) Random Bks Yng Read.
DeFelice, Cynthia C. The Dancing Skeleton. Parker, Robert Andrew, illus. LC 88-30245. 32p. (gr. k-3). 1989. RSBE 14.95 (*0-02-726452-1*, Macmillan Child Bk) Macmillan Child Grp.
Degen, Bruce. Jamberry. Degen, Bruce, illus. (gr. k-3). 1986. incl. cassette 19.95 (*0-87499-028-9*); pap. 12.95 incl. cassette (*0-87499-026-2*); 4 paperbacks, cassette & guide 27.95 (*0-87499-027-0*) Live Oak Media.
De Gerez, Toni, retold by. Louhi, Witch of North Farm: A Finnish Tale. Cooney, Barbara, illus. (ps-3). 1988. pap. 4.99 (*0-14-050529-6*, Puffin) Puffin Bks.
De Goscinny, Rene. Le Devin. (FRE.). (gr. 7-9). 1990. 19.95 (*0-8288-5122-0*, FC890) Fr & Eur.
De Hieronymis, Elve F. A Night at the Circus. (Illus.). 16p. 1989. 8.95 (*0-8120-5995-6*) Barron.
Delessert, Etienne. A Long Long Song. LC 87-73491. (Illus.). 32p. (ps up). 1988. 13.95 (*0-374-34638-0*) FS&G.
Delton, Judy. I'll Never Love Anything Ever Again. Fay, Ann, ed. Daniel, Alan, illus. LC 84-17271. 32p. (gr. k-3). 1985. PLB 11.95 (*0-8075-3521-4*) A Whitman.
Delton, Judy & Tucker, Dorothy. My Grandma's in a Nursing Home. Tucker, Kathleen, ed. Robinson, Charles, illus. LC 86-1640. 32p. (gr. 2-5). 1986. PLB 11.95 (*0-8075-5333-6*) A Whitman.
Demi. Cuddly Chick. Demi, illus. 12p. (ps). 1987. bds. 6.95 (*0-448-19154-7*, G&D) Putnam Pub Group.
—Demi's Find the Animal A B C. (Illus.). 48p. 1990. pap. 5.95 (*0-448-19165-2*, G&D) Putnam Pub Group.
—Downy Duckling. Demi, illus. 12p. (ps). 1987. bds. 6.95 (*0-448-19153-9*, G&D) Putnam Pub Group.
—Fleecy Lamb. Demi, illus. 12p. (gr. 4 up). 1987. 6.95 (*0-448-19152-0*, G&D) Putnam Pub Group.
—Sequel to Empty Pot. 1994. write for info. (*0-8050-3243-6*) H Holt & Co.
—So Soft Kitty. Demi, illus. 12p. (ps). 1986. pap. 6.95 (*0-448-18986-0*, G&D) Putnam Pub Group.
Deming, A. G. Who Is Tapping at My Window? Wellington, Monica, illus. 24p. (ps). 1994. pap. 4.99 (*0-14-054553-0*, Puff Unicorn) Puffin Bks.
—Who Is Tapping at My Window? Wellington, Monica, illus. 24p. (ps). 1994. pap. 17.99 giant format (*0-14-050303-X*) Puffin Bks.
De Paola, Tomie. Baby's First Christmas. (Illus.). 12p. (ps). 1988. bds. 4.95 (*0-399-21591-3*, Putnam) Putnam Pub Group.
—Big Anthony & the Magic Ring. De Paola, Tomie, illus. LC 78-23631. 32p. (gr. k up). 1979. 14.95 (*0-15-207124-5*); pap. 4.95 (*0-15-611907-2*) HarBrace.
—The Comic Adventures of Old Mother Hubbard & Her Dog. LC 80-19270. (Illus.). 32p. (ps-3). 1981. 13.95 (*0-15-219541-6*, HB Juv Bks); pap. 3.95 (*0-15-219542-4*, PL) HarBrace.
—Haircuts for the Woolseys. De Paola, Tomie, illus. 24p. (ps-1). 1989. 5.95 (*0-399-21662-6*, Putnam) Putnam Pub Group.
Depaola, Tomie. El Libro de las Arenas Movedizas. 32p. (ps-3). 1993. reinforced bdg. 15.95 (*0-8234-1056-0*); pap. 5.95 (*0-8234-1057-9*) Holiday.
—El Libro de las Nubes. 32p. (ps-3). 1993. reinforced bdg. 15.95 (*0-8234-1054-4*); pap. 5.95 (*0-8234-1055-2*) Holiday.
—El Libro de las Palomitas de Maiz. 32p. (ps-3). 1993. reinforced bdg. 15.95 (*0-8234-1058-7*); pap. 5.95 (*0-8234-1059-5*) Holiday.
De Paola, Tomie. Nana Upstairs & Nana Downstairs. (Illus.). (gr. 1-3). 1978. pap. 4.99 (*0-14-050290-4*, Puffin) Puffin Bks.
—Oliver Button Is a Sissy. De Paola, Tomie, illus. LC 78-12624. 48p. (gr. k-3). 1979. 11.95 (*0-15-257852-8*, HB Juv Bks) HarBrace.
—Sing, Pierrot, Sing. LC 83-8403. (Illus.). 32p. (Orig.). (ps-3). 1987. pap. 3.95 (*0-15-274989-6*, Voyager Bks) HarBrace.
—Sing, Pierrot, Sing: A Picture Book in Mime. De Paola, Tomie, illus. LC 83-8403. 32p. (ps-3). 1983. 12.95 (*0-15-274988-8*, HB Juv Bks) HarBrace.
De Paola, Tomie, illus. Hey Diddle Diddle: And Other Mother Goose Rhymes. (gr. 1 up). 1988. pap. 5.95 (*0-399-21589-1*, Putnam) Putnam Pub Group.
De Poix, Carol. Jo, Flo & Yolanda. (SPA & ENG., Illus.). 35p. (Orig.). (ps-1). 1973. pap. 4.95 (*0-914996-04-5*) Lollipop Power.
De Regniers, Beatrice S. May I Bring a Friend? Montresor, Beni, illus. LC 64-19562. 48p. (ps-2). 1971. RSBE 14.95 (*0-689-20615-1*, Atheneum Child Bk) Macmillan Child Grp.
—May I Bring a Friend? Montresor, Beni, illus. LC 89-15087. 48p. (gr. k-3). 1989. pap. 4.95 (*0-689-71353-3*, Aladdin) Macmillan Child Grp.
—The Snow Party. Myers, Bernice, illus. LC 88-13332. 32p. (ps-3). 1989. 12.95 (*0-688-08570-9*) Lothrop.
De Regniers, Beatrice S. & Haas, Irene. Little House of Your Own. Haas, Irene, illus. LC 86-27013. 32p. (ps-3). 1955. 9.95 (*0-15-245787-9*, HB Juv Bks) HarBrace.
Derrydale. Animals. 1989. 2.49 (*0-517-67588-9*) Random Hse Value.
—Machines. (ps-1). 1989. 2.49 (*0-517-67587-0*) Random Hse Value.
Deverell, Catherine. Grandpa Told Me So. Petach, Heidi, illus. LC 87-62600. 20p. (ps). 1988. pap. 1.59 (*0-87403-387-X*, 24-02017) Standard Pub.
DeVito, Pam. Lydia & the Purple Paint. Weinberger, Jane, ed. DeVito, Pam, illus. LC 89-50681. 52p. (ps-4). 1989. pap. 5.95 (*0-932433-59-6*) Windswept Hse.
Dewey, Ariane. The Tea Squall. LC 87-14868. (Illus.). 40p. (gr. 1-4). 1988. 11.95 (*0-688-07492-8*); lib. bdg. 11.88 (*0-688-07493-6*) Greenwillow.
Dickens, Charles. A Christmas Carol. Zwerger, Lisbeth, illus. LC 88-15161. 60p. (gr. 5 up). 1991. pap. 19.95 (*0-88708-069-3*) Picture Bk Studio.
—A Christmas Carol: A Changing Picture & Lift-the-Flap Book. Taylerson, Kareen, illus. 32p. (ps-3). 1989. pap. 14.95 (*0-670-82694-4*) Viking Child Bks.
DiFiori, Lawrence. The Truck Book. DiFiori, Lawrence, illus. LC 83-83106. (ps). 1984. write for info. (*0-307-12299-9*, Golden Bks) Western Pub.
Dijs, Carla. Are You My Daddy? Dijs, Carla, illus. 12p. (ps). 1990. pap. 6.95 casebound, pop-up (*0-671-70227-0*, Little Simon) S&S Trade.
—Are You My Mommy? Dijs, Carla, illus. 12p. (ps). 1990. pap. 6.95 casebound, pop-up (*0-671-70226-2*, Little Simon) S&S Trade.
—Hansel & Gretel Pop-up Book. (ps). 1991. 4.99 (*0-440-40538-6*, YB) Dell.
—How Many Fingers? Pop-up Book. (Illus.). 20p. (ps-1). 1994. 5.99 (*0-679-85074-0*) Random Bks Yng Read.
—Who Sees You? at the Ocean. (ps-2). 1987. 5.95 (*0-448-34350-9*, G&D) Putnam Pub Group.
—Who Sees You? at the Zoo. (ps-2). 1987. 5.95 (*0-448-34353-3*, G&D) Putnam Pub Group.
—Who Sees You? in the Forest. (ps-2). 1987. 5.95 (*0-448-34351-7*, G&D) Putnam Pub Group.
—Who Sees You? on the Farm. (ps-3). 1987. 5.95 (*0-448-34352-5*, G&D) Putnam Pub Group.
Dijs, Carla & Moerbeek, Kees. Let's Play. (gr. 3 up). 1990. 9.95 (*0-85953-224-0*) Childs Play.
Dillow, John, illus. Baby's Toys: Little Ladybird Board Book. 8p. (ps). 1991. bds. 3.50 (*0-7214-9137-5*, S851-15) Ladybird Bks.
Dinosaur. (Illus.). 288p. 1991. pap. 2.99 (*0-517-67870-5*) Random Hse Value.
Dinosaur Creatures & More. (Illus.). 5p. (gr. k-3). 1993. bds. 3.50 (*1-56144-355-7*, Honey Bear Bks) Modern Pub NYC.
Dinosaur Giants & More. (Illus.). 5p. (gr. k-3). 1993. bds. 3.50 (*1-56144-356-5*, Honey Bear Bks) Modern Pub NYC.
Dinosaur Monsters & More. (Illus.). 5p. (gr. k-3). 1993. bds. 3.50 (*1-56144-357-3*, Honey Bear Bks) Modern Pub NYC.
Dinosaur Titans & More. (Illus.). 5p. (gr. k-3). 1993. bds. 3.50 (*1-56144-358-1*, Honey Bear Bks) Modern Pub NYC.
Dinosaurs Activity Book. (Illus.). (ps-6). pap. 2.95 (*0-565-01078-6*, Pub. by Natural Hist Mus) Parkwest Pubns.
Dinosaurs Colouring Book. (Illus.). (ps-6). pap. 2.95 (*0-565-00825-0*, Pub. by Natural Hist Mus) Parkwest Pubns.
Dinosaurs: Pop-Up. (ps-3). 1993. pap. 4.95 (*0-8167-2925-5*) Troll Assocs.
DiPrima, Daniel. The Extra Nose. Persche, Beth & Persche, Todd, illus. 32p. (ps-3). 1994. 14.95 (*1-55933-151-8*) Know Unltd.
Discovering Dragons Activity Book. (Illus.). (ps-6). pap. 2.95 (*0-565-01005-0*, Pub. by Natural Hist Mus) Parkwest Pubns.
Disney Babies at the Big Circus. write for info. (*1-56326-300-9*, 030106) Disney Bks By Mail.
Disney Babies at the Farm. write for info. (*1-56326-325-4*, 032607) Disney Bks By Mail.
Disney Babies, Baby Mickey's Word Book. (Illus.). 24p. (ps-k). 1987. pap. write for info. (*0-307-10088-X*, Pub. by Golden Bks) Western Pub.
Disney Babies First Words. LC 86-72424. (Illus.). 12p. (ps). 1988. pap. write for info. (*0-307-06058-6*, Pub. by Golden Bks) Western Pub.
Disney Babies Good Night. LC 87-81754. (Illus.). 12p. (ps). 1988. write for info. (*0-307-06067-5*, Pub. by Golden Bks) Western Pub.
Disney Babies Have a Beach Party. write for info. (*1-56326-327-0*, 032805) Disney Bks By Mail.
Disney Babies One to Ten. (Illus.). (ps-k). 1991. write for info. (*0-307-12324-3*, Golden Pr) Western Pub.
Disney Classics: A Treasury of Best-loved Tales. (ps-3). 1990. write for info. (*0-307-15536-6*) Western Pub.
Disney, Walt. Aladdin: The Genie Gets Wet Bath Book. (ps). 1993. 5.98 (*0-453-03169-2*) Mouse Works.
—Beauty & the Beast: Be Our Guest Bath Book. (ps). 1993. 5.98 (*0-453-03171-4*) Mouse Works.
—The Little Mermaid: Makes a Splash Bath Book. (ps). 1993. 5.98 (*0-453-03172-2*) Mouse Works.
—Meet Mickey Mouse & Friends. (ps). 1993. 6.98 (*0-453-03126-9*) Mouse Works.
—One Hundred & One Dalmatians: Spotless Puppies Bath Book. (ps). 1993. 5.98 (*0-453-03173-0*) Mouse Works.
—Speak up, Patch! With One Hundred & One Dalmations. (ps). 1993. 6.98 (*0-453-03131-5*) Mouse Works.
Disney, Walt, Productions Staff. Colors, Shapes, & Sizes. LC 85-43077. 80p. (Orig.). 1985. pap. 5.95 (*0-553-05534-8*) Bantam.

—How It Works in the City. (gr. 4-6). 1982. write for info. (*0-89434-046-8*) Ferguson.
—How It Works in the Country. (gr. 4-6). 1982. write for info. (*0-89434-047-6*) Ferguson.
—How It Works in the Home. (gr. 4-6). 1982. write for info. (*0-89434-048-4*) Ferguson.
Disney, Walt, Studios Staff. The Pop-up Mickey Mouse: Story & Illustrations. facsimile ed. LC 93-31910. (Illus.). 32p. 1994. Repr. of 1933 ed. 9.95 (*1-55709-210-9*); collector's ed. 100.00 (*1-55709-215-X*) Applewood.
Disney's Snow White & the Seven Dwarfs: A Book of Opposites. (Illus.). (ps-k). 1991. write for info. (*0-307-12323-5*, Golden Pr) Western Pub.
Disney's Two-Minute Stories: Mickey Mouse & Friends. (ps-1). 1991. 4.25 (*0-307-12193-3*, Golden Pr) Western Pub.
Dodd, Lynley. Dragon in a Wagon. Sherwood, Rhoda, ed. Dodd, Lynley, illus. LC 88-42925. 32p. (gr. 1-2). 1988. PLB 17.27 (*1-55532-911-X*) Gareth Stevens Inc.
—Find Me a Tiger. LC 91-50553. (Illus.). 32p. (gr. 1-2). 1992. PLB 17.27 (*0-8368-0762-6*) Gareth Stevens Inc.
—Hairy Maclary-Scattercat. Dodd, Lynley, illus. LC 86-42797. 32p. (gr. 1-2). 1988. PLB 17.27 (*1-55532-123-2*) Gareth Stevens Inc.
—Hairy Maclary's Caterwaul Caper. Dodd, Lynley, illus. LC 88-42926. 32p. (ps-2). 1989. PLB 17.27 (*1-55532-910-1*) Gareth Stevens Inc.
Dollhouse. 16p. (ps). 1984. pap. 2.95 (*0-671-49718-9*, Little Simon) S&S Trade.
Dolson, Gina, ed. Lisa & the Magic Doll: Russian & Ukrainian Fairy Tales. Mandeville, Jerry & Brodsky, Anna, trs. from RUS & UKR. Mawolski, Stanley M., illus. 56p. (Orig.). (gr. 4-10). 1986. pap. 4.50x (*0-914265-07-5*) New Eng Pub MA.
Domanska, Janina, illus. If All the Seas Were One Sea. reissued ed. LC 73-146621. 32p. (ps-2). 1987. SBE 14. 95 (*0-02-732540-7*, Macmillan Child Bk) Macmillan Child Grp.
Donahue, Marilyn. A Place to Belong. LC 88-14808. 1988. pap. 4.49 (*1-55513-757-1*, Chariot Bks) Chariot Family.
Donde Esta Jake? (Where Is Jake?) (SPA., Illus.). 28p. (ps-2). 1991. PLB 11.55 (*0-516-35361-6*); pap. 3.95 (*0-516-55361-5*) Childrens.
Donovan, Melanie, selected by. The Mother Goose Word Book. Schweninger, Ann, illus. LC 86-81489. 22p. (ps). 1987. write for info. (*0-307-12119-4*, Pub. by Golden Bks) Western Pub.
Dot to Dot Animals. (Illus.). 24p. (ps-2). 1991. pap. 3.50 (*0-7460-0616-0*, Usborne) EDC.
Douglas-Hamilton, Oria. The Elephant Family Book. Douglas-Hamilton, Iain, photos by. LC 89-77319. (Illus.). 56p. (ps up). 1991. pap. 15.95 (*0-88708-126-6*) Picture Bk Studio.
Down by the Station. 24p. 1987. pap. 2.95 (*0-553-15575-X*) Bantam.
Downie, Jill. Follow the Wind. (Illus.). 32p. (ps-2). 1992. 15.95 (*0-86264-287-6*, Pub. by Andersen Pr UK) Trafalgar.
Doyle, A. C. Story Rhyme Journal. 60p. (Orig.). (gr. 6-9). 1991. pap. text ed. 15.95 (*0-317-04222-X*, Pub. by Biblio Pr GA) Prosperity & Profits.
Dragonwagon, Crescent. Alligator Arrived with Apples: A Potluck Alphabet Feast. Aruego, Jose & Dewey, Ariane, illus. LC 86-37. 40p. (gr. k-3). 1987. RSBE 15. 95 (*0-02-733090-7*, Macmillan Child Bk) Macmillan Child Grp.
—Half a Moon & One Whole Star. Pinkney, Jerry, illus. LC 85-13818. 32p. (gr. k-3). 1986. RSBE 14.95 (*0-02-733120-2*, Macmillan Child Bk) Macmillan Child Grp.
—I Hate My Sister Maggie. Morrill, Leslie, illus. LC 88-8197. 32p. (gr. k-3). 1989. RSBE 13.95 (*0-02-733150-4*, Macmillan Child Bk) Macmillan Child Grp.
—This Is the Bread I Baked for Ned. Seltzer, Isadore, illus. LC 88-22619. 32p. (gr. k-3). 1989. RSBE 14.95 (*0-02-733220-9*, Macmillan Child Bk) Macmillan Child Grp.
Drayton, Grace G. Adventures of Dolly Dingle Paper Dolls. 1985. pap. 3.95 (*0-486-24809-7*) Dover.
Drescher, Henrik. Simon's Book. LC 82-24931. (Illus.). 32p. (gr. k-3). 1983. 16.00 (*0-688-02085-2*); lib. bdg. 15.93 (*0-688-02086-0*) Lothrop.
—Whose Furry Nose? Drescher, Henrik, illus. LC 87-45151. 32p. (gr. k-3). 1987. (Lipp Jr Bks) HarpC Child Bks.
Drescher, Joan. My Mother's Getting Married. Drescher, Joan, illus. LC 84-18642. 32p. (ps-3). 1986. PLB 10.89 (*0-8037-0176-4*) Dial Bks Young.
—Your Family, My Family. Drescher, Joan, illus. 32p. (gr. 2-5). 1980. PLB 13.85 (*0-8027-6383-9*) Walker & Co.
Dr. Seuss. Dr. Seuss's ABC. (Illus.). 64p. (ps-1). 1988. pap. 7.95 bk. & cassette pkg. (*0-394-89784-6*) Random Bks Yng Read.
—Dr. Seuss's Sleep Book. Dr. Seuss, illus. (gr. 3-7). 1962. 13.00 (*0-394-80091-5*); lib. bdg. 13.99 (*0-394-90091-X*) Random Bks Yng Read.
—Fox in Socks. Dr. Seuss, illus. LC 65-10484. 72p. (gr. k-3). 1965. 6.95 (*0-394-80038-9*); lib. bdg. 7.99 (*0-394-90038-3*) Random Bks Yng Read.
—Hop on Pop. Dr. Seuss, illus. 64p. (ps-1). 1987. pap. 6.95 incl. cassette (*0-394-89222-4*) Random Bks Yng Read.
—Horton Hears a Who. Dr. Seuss, illus. (gr. k-3). 1954. 13.00 (*0-394-80078-8*); PLB 13.99 (*0-394-90078-2*) Random Bks Yng Read.
—I Am Not Going to Get up Today! Stevenson, James, illus. LC 87-11466. 48p. (gr. k-3). 1987. 6.95 (*0-394-89217-8*); lib. bdg. 7.99 (*0-394-99217-2*) Random Bks Yng Read.
—I Am Not Going to Get up Today! Stevenson, James, illus. 32p. (ps-1). 1990. Includes audio cassette. pap. 6.95 (*0-679-80307-6*) Random Bks Yng Read.
—I Can Lick Thirty Tigers Today & Other Stories. Dr. Seuss, illus. (gr. k-3). 1969. 13.00 (*0-394-80094-X*) Random Bks Yng Read.
—I Can Read with My Eyes Shut! Dr. Seuss, illus. 40p. (ps-1). 1987. Incl. cassette. pap. 7.95 (*0-394-88767-0*) Random Bks Yng Read.
—If I Ran the Zoo. Dr. Seuss, illus. (gr. k-3). 1950. 13.00 (*0-394-80081-8*); lib. bdg. 13.99 (*0-394-90081-2*) Random Bks Yng Read.
—King's Stilts. Dr. Seuss, illus. (gr. k-3). 1939. 9.95 (*0-394-80082-6*); lib. bdg. 9.99 (*0-394-90082-0*) Random Bks Yng Read.
—McElligot's Pool. Dr. Seuss, illus. (gr. k-3). 1947. 11.00 (*0-394-80083-4*); lib. bdg. 11.99 (*0-394-90083-9*) Random Bks Yng Read.
—Marvin K. Mooney, Will You Please Go Now. Dr. Seuss, illus. (ps-2). 1972. 6.95 (*0-394-82490-3*); lib. bdg. 7.99 (*0-394-92490-8*) Random Bks Yng Read.
—Oh Say Can You Say? Dr. Seuss, illus. 40p. (ps-1). 1987. Incl. cassette. 6.95 (*0-394-88769-7*) Random Bks Yng Read.
—Oh, the Places You'll Go! LC 89-36892. (gr. k-3). 1990. 14.00 (*0-679-80527-3*); PLB 13.99 (*0-679-90527-8*) Random Bks Yng Read.
—There's a Wocket in My Pocket & Marvin K. Mooney Will You Please Go Now! Dr. Seuss, illus. (ps-1). 1989. bk. & cassette 7.95 (*0-394-82954-9*) Random Bks Yng Read.
Dubanevich, Arlene. Pigs at Christmas. Dubanevich, Arlene, illus. LC 86-6891. 32p. (ps-2). 1986. RSBE 14. 95 (*0-02-733160-1*, Bradbury Pr) Macmillan Child Grp.
—Pigs at Christmas. Dubanevich, Arlene, illus. LC 89-32229. 32p. (ps-3). 1989. pap. 3.95 (*0-689-71344-4*, Aladdin) Macmillan Child Grp.
Du Bois, William P. Bear Party. (ps-1). 1987. pap. 3.99 (*0-14-050793-0*, Puffin) Puffin Bks.
Duchess of York. Budgie at Bendick's Point. Richardson, John, illus. (ps-1). 1989. pap. 11.95 jacketed (*0-671-67684-9*, S&S BFYR) S&S Trade.
—Budgie the Little Helicopter. Richardson, John, illus. (ps-1). 1989. pap. 11.95 jacketed (*0-671-67683-0*, S&S BFYR) S&S Trade.
Dudko, Mary A. & Larsen, Margie. Baby Bop Pretends. Dowdy, Linda C., ed. Valentine, June, illus. LC 93-74289. 24p. (ps-k). 1994. pap. 2.25 (*1-57064-022-X*) Barney Pub.
Duffy, Deborah. Barnyard Tracks. Marshall, Janet P., illus. LC 91-72973. 32p. (ps up). 1992. 12.95 (*1-878093-66-5*) Boyds Mills Pr.
Duke, Kate. Bedtime. Duke, Kate, illus. LC 84-73140. 12p. (ps). 1986. bds. 2.95 (*0-525-44207-3*, DCB) Dutton Child Bks.
—Clean-Up Day. Duke, Kate, illus. LC 84-73139. 12p. (ps). 1986. bds. 2.95 (*0-525-44208-1*, DCB) Dutton Child Bks.
—The Playground. Duke, Kate, illus. LC 84-73141. 12p. (ps). 1986. bds. 2.95 (*0-525-44206-5*, DCB) Dutton Child Bks.
—What Bounces? Duke, Kate, illus. LC 84-73138. 12p. (ps). 1986. 2.95 (*0-525-44209-X*, DCB) Dutton Child Bks.
Dumond, Val. Visiting Olympia. Ballman, Jean, illus. 24p. (Orig.). (gr. 1-4). 1983. pap. 2.75 (*0-933992-39-4*) Coffee Break.
Duncan, Riana. When Emily Woke up Angry. Duncan, Riana, illus. 32p. (ps-1). 1989. incl. dust jacket 12.95 (*0-8120-5985-9*) Barron.
Dunn, Joyce E. Riding on a School Bus. rev. ed. Dunn, Joyce E., illus. Doyle, James M., intro. by. (Illus.). 56p. (gr. k-1). 1989. pap. 4.95 (*0-9624280-0-0*) SPI Pub.
Dunn, Judy. The Little Duck. Dunn, Phoebe, photos by. LC 75-36467. (Illus.). 32p. (ps-1). 1976. pap. 2.25 (*0-394-83247-7*) Random Bks Yng Read.
Dunn, Phoebe. Baby's Busy Year. LC 89-51127. (Illus.). 28p. (ps). 1990. 2.95 (*0-679-80260-6*) Random Bks Yng Read.
—Busy Busy Toddlers. LC 86-62247. (Illus.). 14p. (ps). 1987. 2.99 (*0-394-88604-6*) Random Bks Yng Read.
Dunn, Phoebe, photos by. Baby's Animal Friends. LC 87-61462. (Illus.). 28p. (ps). 1988. bds. 2.95 (*0-394-89583-5*) Random Bks Yng Read.
—I'm a Baby! LC 86-61904. (Illus.). 14p. 1987. 2.99 (*0-394-88605-4*) Random Bks Yng Read.
Dunrea, Olivier. Deep Down Underground. Dunrea, Olivier, illus. LC 88-13534. 32p. (ps-2). 1989. RSBE 14.95 (*0-02-732861-9*, Macmillan Child Bk) Macmillan Child Grp.
Durhan, Robert. My Giant Picture Dictionary. (Illus.). 1988. 5.99 (*0-517-65715-5*) Random Hse Value.
Durrell, Julie. Peek-a-Boo. Bahr, Amy C. & Klimo, Kate, eds. Durrell, Julie, illus. 8p. (ps). 1982. pap. 3.95 (*0-671-45546-X*, Little Simon) S&S Trade.
Duvoisin, Roger. Petunia. Duvoisin, Roger, illus. (gr. k-3). 1962. lib. bdg. 10.99 (*0-394-90865-1*) Knopf Bks Yng Read.
—Petunia, Beware! Duvoisin, Roger, illus. (gr. 1-3). 1964. lib. bdg. 12.99 (*0-394-90867-8*) Knopf Bks Yng Read.
—Petunia, Beware! Duvoisin, Roger, illus. LC 72-580009. 32p. (ps-2). 1990. pap. 3.95 (*0-679-80334-3*) Knopf Bks Yng Read.
Dwight, Laura, photos by. All My Things. (Illus.). 28p. (ps). 1992. bds. 2.95 (*1-56288-185-X*) Checkerboard.
—Babies All Around. (Illus.). 28p. (ps). 1992. bds. 2.95 (*1-56288-184-1*) Checkerboard.
Dyer, Jane. Moo, Moo Peekaboo. Dyer, Jane, illus. LC 85-61530. (ps). 1986. 3.99 (*0-394-87883-3*) Random Bks Yng Read.
Eager, George B. See & Do. (Illus.). 128p. (gr. 3-6). 1993. pap. 4.95 (*1-879224-14-3*) Mailbox.
Eastman, P. D. Flap Your Wings. (Illus.). 32p. (ps-6). 1991. pap. 2.99 incl. cass. (*0-517-05445-0*) Random Hse Value.
Eastman, Patricia. Sometimes Things Change Big Book. (Illus.). 32p. (ps-2). 1988. PLB 22.95 (*0-516-49509-7*) Childrens.
Eastman, Philip D. Sam & the Firefly. LC 58-11966. (Illus.). 72p. (gr. 1-2). 1958. 6.95 (*0-394-80006-0*); lib. bdg. 7.99 (*0-394-90006-5*) Beginner.
Easy As ABC. 1989. pap. 1.49 (*0-553-18380-X*) Bantam.
Eberle, Irmengarde. Picture Stories for Children. (gr. k-6). 1988. pap. 2.95 (*0-440-40031-7*, YB) Dell.
Eberts, Marjorie & Gisler, Margaret. Pancakes, Crackers & Pizza: A Book of Shapes. Hayes, Steven, illus. LC 84-7699. 32p. (ps-2). 1984. lib. bdg. 10.25 (*0-516-02063-3*); pap. 2.95 (*0-516-42063-1*) Childrens.
Eccles, Anne M. New Mexico Activity & Coloring Book. (Illus.). 32p. (ps-8). 1987. activity & coloring book 2.95 (*0-9618555-1-7*) Anne M Eccles.
Edens, Cooper. Caretakers of Wonder. 2nd ed. (Illus.). 40p. (ps up). 1991. pap. 4.95 (*0-671-76052-1*, Green Tiger) S&S Trade.
Edens, Cooper & Day, Alexandra. Children of Wonder. 14p. (Orig.). (ps-2). 1991. pap. 3.95 (*0-88138-083-0*, Green Tiger) S&S Trade.
Egyptian Funeral Boat. (Illus.). (gr. 2-6). cut-out model, incl. instructions 4.95 (*0-7141-1675-0*, Pub. by Brit Mus UK) Parkwest Pubns.
Egyptian Mummy Case. (Illus.). (gr. 2-6). cut-out model, incl. instructions 4.95 (*0-7141-1672-6*, Pub. by Brit Mus UK) Parkwest Pubns.
Ehrlich, Doris. Animal Alphabet. 2nd ed. O'Rourke, Dawn M., illus. 36p. (ps-k). 1988. pap. text ed. 80.00 classroom pack (*0-932957-90-0*); tchr's. ed. 4.50 (*0-932957-91-9*); wkbk. 3.90 (*0-932957-89-7*); wall posters 17.50 (*0-932957-96-X*) Natl School.
Eisenberg, Ann. I Can Celebrate. Schanzer, Roz, illus. LC 88-83567. 12p. (ps). 1989. bds. 4.95 (*0-930494-93-8*) Kar Ben.
Elephant. 1989. 3.50 (*1-87865-728-3*) Blue Q.
Elliott, Dan. The Adventures of Ernie & Bert at the South Pole. Cooke, Tom, illus. LC 84-60187. 32p. (ps-3). 1984. pap. 1.50 (*0-394-86299-6*) Random Bks Yng Read.
Elzbieta. Dikou & the Baby Star. Elzbieta, illus. LC 88-302. 32p. (ps-3). 1989. (Crowell Jr Bks) HarpC Child Bks.
Emberley, Barbara. Drummer Hoff. Emberley, Ed E., illus. LC 74-8201. 32p. (gr. k-4). 1985. pap. 12.95 jacketed (*0-671-66682-7*, S&S BFYR); pap. 5.95 (*0-671-66745-9*, S&S BFYR) S&S Trade.
Emberley, Ed E. & Emberley, Rebecca. Ed Emberley's Big Red Drawing Book, Vol. 1. Emberley, Ed E. & Emberley, Rebecca, illus. 96p. (gr. 1-5). 1987. 14.95 (*0-316-23434-6*); pap. 9.95 (*0-316-23435-4*) Little.
Emberley, Ed E., illus. First Words: Cars, Boats, & Planes. (ps). 1987. pap. 3.50 (*0-316-23430-3*) Little.
—First Words: Home. (ps). 1987. pap. 3.50 (*0-316-23433-8*) Little.
Emerson, Sally, compiled by. The Nursery Treasury: A Collection of Rhymes, Poems, Lullabies & Games. Maclean, Moira & Maclean, Colin, illus. 128p. 1988. pap. 18.95 (*0-385-24650-1*) Doubleday.
Emmert, Michelle. I'm the Big Sister Now. Levine, Abby, ed. Owens, Gail, illus. LC 89-5584. 32p. (gr. 2-6). 1989. PLB 13.95 (*0-8075-3458-7*) A Whitman.
Endersby, Frank. Jasmine & the Cat. (Illus.). 12p. (ps). 1984. 3.95 (*0-85953-183-X*, Child's Play England) Childs Play.
—Jasmine & the Flowers. 12p. (ps). 1984. 3.95 (*0-85953-184-8*, Child's Play England) Childs Play.
—Jasmine's Bath Time. 12p. (ps). 1984. 3.95 (*0-85953-185-6*, Child's Play England) Childs Play.
—Jasmine's Bed Time. 12p. (ps). 1984. 3.95 (*0-85953-186-4*, Child's Play England) Childs Play.
Erickson, Mary. Six Busy Days. LC 88-11803. (Illus.). 32p. (ps-2). 1988. 9.99 (*1-55513-699-0*, Chariot Bks) Chariot Family.
Erie Art Museum Staff. Commodore Perry & Other Paper Dolls of the Flagship Niagara. Macie, Edward, illus. 10p. (Orig.). (gr. 1-3). 1988. pap. 6.00 (*0-9616623-4-4*) Erie Art Mus.
Ernst, Kathryn F. Danny & His Thumb. De Paola, Tomie, illus. (ps-3). 1975. (Pub. by Treehouse) P-H.
Ernst, Lisa C. Sam Johnson & the Blue Ribbon Quilt. LC 82-9980. (Illus.). 32p. (gr. k-3). 1983. lib. bdg. 13.93 (*0-688-01517-4*) Lothrop.
—When Bluebell Sang. Ernst, Lisa C., illus. LC 88-22262. 32p. (ps-1). 1989. RSBE 14.95 (*0-02-733561-5*, Bradbury Pr) Macmillan Child Grp.
Escudie, Rene. Paul & Sebastian. Townley, Roderick, tr. Wensell, Ulises, illus. (FRE.). 32p. (ps-3). 1994. pap. 6.95 (*0-916291-49-9*) Kane-Miller Bk.

Estep, Don. Cat & Kittens. Dubin, Jill, illus. 28p. (ps). 1990. 2.95 (*0-02-689487-4*) Checkerboard.
—Lucy's Early Day. Dubin, Jill, illus. 28p. (ps). 1990. 2.95 (*0-02-689485-8*) Checkerboard.
Estes, Eleanor. Hundred Dresses. Slobodkin, Louis, illus. LC 44-8963. 32p. (gr. 1-5). 1944. 14.95 (*0-15-237374-8*, HB Juv Bks) HarBrace.
Etow, Carole, illus. What Goes Inside? 10p. (ps). 1992. 5.95 (*0-8431-2998-0*) Price Stern.
—Where Does It Come From? 10p. (ps-1). 1992. 5.95 (*0-8431-2999-9*) Price Stern.
Ets, Marie H. Gilberto & the Wind. Ets, Marie H., illus. (ps-1). 1963. pap. 14.00 (*0-670-34025-1*) Viking Child Bks.
—Just Me. Ets, Marie H., illus. (ps-2). 1965. pap. 14.95 (*0-670-41109-4*) Viking Child Bks.
Evans, Larry. Invisibles Two. (Illus.). 40p. (Orig.). (gr. 1 up). 1981. pap. 3.50 (*0-8431-1711-7*, Troubador) Price Stern.
Evans, Michael. Animals. (Illus.). 24p. (ps). 1992. bds. 2.95 (*0-8249-8525-7*, Ideals Child) Hambleton-Hill.
—My Day. (Illus.). 24p. (ps-2). 1992. bds. 2.95 (*0-8249-8526-5*, Ideals Child) Hambleton-Hill.
—Peek-a-Boo! (Illus.). 24p. (ps-2). 1992. bds. 2.95 (*0-8249-8528-1*, Ideals Child) Hambleton-Hill.
—Wheels. (Illus.). 24p. (ps-2). 1992. bds. 2.95 (*0-8249-8527-3*, Ideals Child) Hambleton-Hill.
Evans, Phillip. Doing. (ps). 1990. 9.95 (*0-8172-3651-1*) Raintree Steck-V.
Faces in Places, Famous Faces, Funny Faces & Happy Faces. (Illus.). (gr. k-2). 1989. Faces in Places. bds. 4.95 (*0-87449-727-2*) Famous Faces. bds. 4.95 (*0-87449-728-0*); Funny Faces. bds. 4.95 (*0-87449-729-9*); Happy Faces. bds. 4.95 (*0-87449-730-2*) Modern Pub NYC.
Facklam, Margery. I Eat Dinner. Riggio, Anita, illus. LC 91-76020. 6p. (ps). 1992. bds. 3.95 (*1-56397-031-7*) Boyds Mills Pr.
—I Go to Sleep. Riggio, Anita, illus. LC 91-76018. 6p. (ps). 1992. bds. 3.95 (*1-56397-030-9*) Boyds Mills Pr.
—So Can I. Bassett, Jeni, illus. LC 86-33720. 28p. (ps-k). 1988. 6.95 (*0-15-200419-X*, Gulliver Bks) HarBrace.
Fairy Tales. (Illus.). 400p. (Orig.). (gr. k-2). 1993. pap. 7.95 (*1-56144-333-6*, Honey Bear Bks) Modern Pub NYC.
Farm Sounds: A Cozy Cloth Book. (Illus.). 6p. (ps-1). 1987. pap. 2.95 (*0-553-18349-4*) Bantam.
Farmyard Animals. 8p. (ps). 1991. bds. 1.99 (*0-517-66920-X*) Random Hse Value.
Fassler, Joan. Howie Helps Himself. Lasker, Joe, illus. LC 74-12284. 32p. (gr. 1-3). 1975. PLB 13.95 (*0-8075-3422-6*) A Whitman.
Faulkner, Keith. Good Night, Tom. Lambert, Jonathan, illus. LC 92-82912. 20p. (ps). 1993. 4.95 (*0-590-46924-X*, Cartwheel) Scholastic Inc.
—Oh No! A Giant Flap Book. Lambert, Jonathan, illus. 16p. (ps-1). 1991. pap. 14.95 (*0-671-74747-9*, S&S BFYR) S&S Trade.
—Tom's Friends. Lambert, Jonathan, illus. LC 92-82910. 20p. (ps). 1993. 4.95 (*0-590-46949-5*, Cartwheel) Scholastic Inc.
—Tom's Picnic. Lambert, Jonathan, illus. LC 92-82911. 20p. (ps). 1993. 4.95 (*0-590-46947-9*, Cartwheel) Scholastic Inc.
—Tom's School Day. Lambert, Jonathan, illus. LC 92-82909. 20p. (ps). 1993. 4.95 (*0-590-46948-7*, Cartwheel) Scholastic Inc.
Favorite. (Illus.). 400p. (Orig.). (gr. k-2). 1993. pap. 7.95 (*1-56144-332-8*, Honey Bear Bks) Modern Pub NYC.
Feczko, Kathy. Three Little Chicks. Harvey, Paul, illus. LC 84-8629. 32p. (gr. k-2). 1985. PLB 11.59 (*0-8167-0355-8*); pap. text ed. 2.95 (*0-8167-0435-X*) Troll Assocs.
—Umbrella Parade. Borgo, Deborah C., illus. LC 84-8650. 32p. (gr. k-2). 1985. PLB 11.59 (*0-8167-0356-6*); pap. text ed. 2.95 (*0-8167-0436-8*) Troll Assocs.
Feeling Afraid. (ps-k). 1986. 0.75 (*0-8091-6544-9*) Paulist Pr.
Fehlner, Paul. The Story of Christmas. (Illus.). 24p. (ps-3). 1989. pap. write for info. (*0-307-11710-3*, Pub. by Golden Bks) Western Pub.
Felix, Monique. Mouse Book Series, 6 bks. Felix, Monique, illus. 32p. (Orig.). (ps-k). 1993. Set. pap. 17.70 (*1-56189-077-4*) Amer Educ Pub.
Fern, Eugene. Pepito's Story. Fern, Eugene, illus. LC 90-23639. 52p. (ps-3). 1991. Repr. of 1960 ed. smythe sewn 14.95 (*1-878274-04-X*) Yarrow Pr.
Fernandes, Eugenie, illus. One Light, One Sun. 32p. (ps-2). 1988. PLB 9.95 (*0-517-56785-7*) Crown Bks Yng Read.
Ferraro, Bonita R., ed. Snoopy's ABC's. Schulz, Charles M., illus. 20p. (ps). 1994. bds. 3.95 (*1-56189-258-0*) Amer Educ Pub.
—Snoopy's Counts to Ten. Schulz, Charles M., illus. 20p. (ps). 1994. bds. 3.95 (*1-56189-257-2*) Amer Educ Pub.
—Snoopy's Crayons. Schulz, Charles M., illus. 20p. (ps). 1994. bds. 3.95 (*1-56189-259-9*) Amer Educ Pub.
Field, Rachel. General Store. Parker, Nancy W., illus. LC 87-21641. 24p. (ps-1). 1988. 11.95 (*0-688-07353-0*); lib. bdg. 11.88 (*0-688-07354-9*) Greenwillow.
Firmin, Peter. Boastful Mr. Bear. Firmin, Peter, illus. (ps-1). 1989. 8.95 (*0-440-50083-4*) Delacorte.
—Foolish Miss Crow. Firmin, Peter, illus. (ps-1). 1989. 8.95 (*0-440-50082-6*) Delacorte.
—Happy Miss Rat. Firmin, Peter, illus. (ps-1). 1989. 8.95 (*0-440-50081-8*) Delacorte.
—Hungry Mr. Fox. Firmin, Peter, illus. (ps-1). 1989. 8.95 (*0-440-50034-6*) Delacorte.
First Graders of A. R. Shepherd Washington, D. C. A Caterpillar's Wish. (Illus.). 24p. (Orig.). (ps-2). 1988. pap. 3.50 (*0-87406-307-8*) Willowisp Pr.
Fisher, Barbara. Linkups. (Illus., Orig.). (ps-3). 1977. pap. 2.00 slipcased (*0-934830-05-3*) Ten Penny.
Fitzhugh, Louise. I Am Five. Fitzhugh, Louise, illus. LC 78-50404. (ps-2). 1978. PLB 5.47 (*0-440-03953-3*); pap. 5.95 (*0-440-03952-5*) Delacorte.
Flack, Marjorie. Ask Mr. Bear. LC 58-8370. (Illus.). 32p. (gr. k-1). 1968. RSBE 12.95 (*0-02-735390-7*, Macmillan Child Bk) Macmillan Child Grp.
Floppy Ears Puppy. 22p. (ps). 1993. 3.25 (*0-679-85105-4*) Random Bks Yng Read.
Florian, Douglas. A Winter Day. LC 86-33524. (Illus.). 24p. (ps-1). 1987. 11.75 (*0-688-07351-4*); lib. bdg. 11.88 (*0-688-07352-2*) Greenwillow.
Flournoy, Valerie. The Best Time of Day. Ford, George, illus. LC 77-91641. 32p. (ps-1). 1992. 2.25 (*0-394-83799-1*) Random Bks Yng Read.
—The Patchwork Quilt. Pinkey, Jerry, illus. LC 84-1711. (gr. 4-8). 1985. 14.00 (*0-8037-0097-0*); PLB 13.89 (*0-8037-0098-9*) Dial Bks Young.
Floyd, James C. Some Gentle Moving Thing. 2nd ed. McBride, Michael, illus. LC 82-60198. 70p. (gr. 7-9). 1982. 6.95 (*0-938232-11-8*) Winston-Derek.
Fluffy Bunny. 12p. (ps up). 1987. 6.95 (*0-448-19151-2*, G&D) Putnam Pub Group.
Follow Your Nose, Baby Pluto. write for info. (*1-56326-315-7*, 031609) Disney Bks By Mail.
Fontane, Theodor. Nick Ribbeck of Ribbeck of Havelland. Bell, Anthea, tr. from GER. Koci, Marta, illus. LC 90-7164. 32p. (gr. k up). 1991. pap. 14.95 (*0-88708-149-5*) Picture Bk Studio.
Ford, George. Baby's First Picture Book. Ford, George, illus. LC 79-62941. (ps). 1979. 3.50 (*0-394-84245-6*) Random Bks Yng Read.
Foreman, Mark. Scraps. (Illus.). 32p. (ps-2). 1991. 15.95 (*0-86264-306-6*, Pub. by Andersen Pr UK) Trafalgar.
Foreman, Michael & Gray, Nigel. I'll Take You to Mrs. Cole. (Illus.). 32p. (gr. k-3). 1986. 11.95 (*0-930267-21-4*) Bergh Pub.
Foreman, Michael, illus. Over in the Meadow. 20p. (ps). 1992. pap. 13.00 casebound, pop-up (*0-671-75109-3*, S&S BFYR) S&S Trade.
Forsse, Ken. Teddy Ruxpin Lullabies II. Hicks, Russell, et al, illus. 26p. (ps). 1988. Incl. pre-programmed audiocassette. 21.00 (*0-934323-68-2*) Alchemy Comms.
Forte, Imogene. Dinosaur Learning Fun. (Illus.). 48p. (ps-3). 1987. pap. 2.95 (*0-86530-145-X*, IP 100-6) Incentive Pubns.
—Fairy Tale Learning Fun. (Illus.). 48p. (ps-3). 1987. pap. 2.95 (*0-86530-146-8*, IP 100-7) Incentive Pubns.
—Monster Learning Fun. (Illus.). 48p. (ps-3). 1987. pap. 2.95 (*0-86530-147-6*, IP 100-8) Incentive Pubns.
—Mother Goose Learning Fun. (Illus.). 48p. (ps-3). 1987. pap. 2.95 (*0-86530-148-4*, IP 100-5) Incentive Pubns.
Fowler, Allan. Feeling Things Big Book. 32p. (ps-2). 1991. PLB 22.95 (*0-516-49468-6*) Childrens.
Fowler, Richard. Let's Make It Go from Side to Side. Fowler, Richard, illus. 8p. (ps). 1990. Repr. of 1985 ed. bds. 4.95 (*0-88335-898-0*, AT03) Milliken Pub Co.
—Let's Make It Go In & Out. Fowler, Richard, illus. 8p. (ps). 1990. Repr. of 1984 ed. bds. 4.95 (*0-88335-737-2*, AT01) Milliken Pub Co.
—Let's Make It Go Round. Fowler, Richard, illus. 8p. (ps). 1990. Repr. of 1984 ed. bds. 4.95 (*0-88335-738-0*, AT02) Milliken Pub Co.
—Mr. Little's Noisy Truck: A Life-the-Flap Book. Fowler, Richard, illus. 20p. (ps-1). 1989. 11.95 (*0-448-19021-4*, G&D) Putnam Pub Group.
Fox, Mem. Hattie & the Fox. Mullins, Patricia, illus. LC 86-18849. 32p. (ps-2). 1988. RSBE 14.95 (*0-02-735470-9*, Bradbury Pr); pap. 16.95 big book (*0-02-735471-7*) Macmillan Child Grp.
—Shoes from Grandpa. Mullins, Patricia, illus. LC 89-35401. 32p. (ps-1). 1990. 13.95 (*0-531-05848-4*); PLB 13.99 (*0-531-08448-5*) Orchard Bks Watts.
Fraidy Cat's Halloween Pop-Up Storybook. 12p. (ps-3). 1990. pap. 2.95 (*0-8167-2194-7*) Troll Assocs.
Frankel, Alona. Mi Bacinica y Yo (Once upon a Potty) (SPA.). 36p. (ps). 1986. Hers. 5.50 (*0-8120-5751-1*); His. (*0-8120-5750-3*) Barron.
Frascino, Edward. Nanny Noony & the Magic Spell. Frascino, Edward, illus. 32p. (gr. k-3). 1988. 14.95 (*0-945912-00-5*) Pippin Pr.
Fraser, Betty. First Things First. Fraser, Betty, illus. LC 86-42993. 32p. (gr. k-3). 1994. pap. 4.95 (*0-06-443300-5*, Trophy) HarpC Child Bks.
Freedman, Sally. Devin's New Bed. Levine, Abby, ed. LC 86-15823. (Illus.). 32p. (ps-k). 1986. PLB 13.95 (*0-8075-1565-5*) A Whitman.
Freeman, Don. Beady Bear. Freeman, Don, illus. LC 54-12295. 48p. (ps-1). 1954. 13.95 (*0-670-15056-8*) Viking Child Bks.
—Corduroy. Freeman, Don, illus. LC 68-16068. 32p. 1968. 12.99 (*0-670-24133-4*) Viking Child Bks.
—Corduroy, Edicion Espanola. Freeman, Don, illus. (SPA.). 32p. (ps-3). 1988. 11.95 (*0-670-82265-5*) Viking Child Bks.
—Dandelion. Freeman, Don, illus. LC 64-21472. 48p. (ps-2). 1964. pap. 14.00 (*0-670-25532-7*) Viking Child Bks.
—Mop Top. Freeman, Don, illus. (ps-1). 1955. pap. 13.95 (*0-670-48882-8*) Viking Child Bks.
—Norman the Doorman. Freeman, Don, illus. (ps-3). 1989. pap. 4.99 (*0-14-050288-2*, Puffin) Puffin Bks.
—A Pocket for Corduroy. LC 77-16123. (Illus.). (gr. 3-5). 1978. 11.95 (*0-670-56172-X*) Viking Child Bks.
—A Rainbow of My Own. 32p. (ps-2). 1978. pap. 3.95 (*0-14-050328-5*, Puffin) Puffin Bks.
—Rainbow of My Own. (Illus.). (gr. k-3). 1966. pap. 13.95 (*0-670-58928-4*) Viking Child Bks.
Frere Jacques. 12p. (ps). 1994. 5.95 (*0-694-00574-6*, Festival) HarpC Child Bks.
Friskey, Margaret. Seven Diving Ducks. Morey, Jean, illus. LC 65-20889. 32p. (gr. k-3). 1965. PLB 11.45 (*0-516-03605-X*) Childrens.
Fuchshuber, Annegert. The Cuckoo-Clock Cuckoo. 32p. (gr. k-4). 1988. lib. bdg. 18.95 (*0-87614-320-6*) Carolrhoda Bks.
—The Cuckoo-Clock Cuckoo. (Illus.). 32p. (gr. k-4). 1989. pap. 5.95 (*0-87614-499-7*, First Ave Edns) Lerner Pubns.
—Giant Story - Mouse Tale: A Half Picture Book. (Illus.). 32p. (ps-3). 1988. lib. bdg. 18.95 (*0-87614-319-2*) Carolrhoda Bks.
Fujikawa, Gyo. Babes of the Wild. Fujikawa, Gyo, illus. 16p. (ps). 1989. Repr. bds. 6.95 (*1-55987-008-7*, Sunny Bks) J B Comns.
—Betty Bear's Birthday. Fujikawa, Gyo, illus. 16p. (ps). 1989. Repr. bds. 6.95 (*1-55987-011-7*, Sunny Bks) J B Comns.
—Can You Count? Fujikawa, Gyo, illus. 16p. (ps). 1989. Repr. of 1977 ed. bds. 6.95 (*1-55987-003-6*, Sunny Bks) J B Comns.
—Gyo Fujikawa's Oh, What a Busy Day! Fujikawa, Gyo, illus. 80p. 1989. 13.95 (*0-448-04304-1*, G&D) Putnam Pub Group.
—Let's Eat. Fujikawa, Gyo, illus. 16p. (ps). 1989. Repr. of 1975 ed. bds. 6.95 (*1-55987-005-2*, Sunny Bks) J B Comns.
—Let's Grow a Garden. Fujikawa, Gyo, illus. 16p. (ps). 1989. Repr. bds. 6.95 (*1-55987-010-9*, Sunny Bks) J B Comns.
—Let's Play. Fujikawa, Gyo, illus. 16p. (ps). 1989. Repr. of 1975 ed. bds. 6.95 (*0-317-93045-1*, Sunny Bks) J B Comns.
—Millie's Secret. Fujikawa, Gyo, illus. 16p. (ps). 1989. bds. 6.95 (*1-55987-006-0*, Sunny Bks) J B Comns.
—My Favorite Thing. Fujikawa, Gyo, illus. 16p. (ps). 1989. Repr. of 1978 ed. bds. 6.95 (*1-55987-004-4*, Sunny Bks) J B Comns.
—Our Best Friends. Fujikawa, Gyo, illus. 16p. (ps). 1989. Repr. bds. 6.95 (*1-55987-009-5*, Sunny Bks) J B Comns.
—Puppies, Pussycats & Other Friends. Fujikawa, Gyo, illus. 16p. (ps). 1989. Repr. of 1977 ed. bds. 6.95 (*1-55987-000-1*, Sunny Bks) J B Comns.
—Sleepy Time. Fujikawa, Gyo, illus. 16p. (ps). 1989. Repr. of 1975 ed. bds. 6.95 (*1-55987-001-X*, Sunny Bks) J B Comns.
—Sunny Books - Four-Favorite Tales, 4 bks, No. 1. Fujikawa, Gyo, illus. (ps). 1989. Repr. of 1975 ed. Boxed set, 4 books, 16 pgs. ea. bds. write for info. (*1-55987-040-0*, Sunny Bks) J B Comns.
—Sunny Books - Four-Favorite Tales, 4 bks, No. 2. Fujikawa, Gyo, illus. (ps). 1989. Repr. Boxed set, four bks., 16 pgs. ea. bds. write for info. (*1-55987-041-9*, Sunny Bks) J B Comns.
—Sunny Books - Four-Favorite Tales, 4 bks, No. 3. Fujikawa, Gyo, illus. (ps). Repr. Boxed set, four bks., 16 pgs. ea. bds. write for info. (*1-55987-042-7*, Sunny Bks) J B Comns.
—Surprise! Surprise! Fujikawa, Gyo, illus. 16p. (ps). 1989. Repr. bds. 6.95 (*1-55987-007-9*, Sunny Bks) J B Comns.
Fujikawa, Gyo, illus. Babies. (ps). 1963. bds. 4.95 (*0-448-03084-5*, G&D) Putnam Pub Group.
—Good Night, Sleep Tight, Shh... 22p. (ps). 1990. bds. 2.95 (*0-679-80845-0*) Random Bks Yng Read.
Fuller, Bob. God Made Big & Little Things. 12p. 1992. bds. 2.99 (*0-89693-139-0*) SP Pubns.
—God Made Quiet & Loud Things. 12p. 1992. bds. 2.99 (*0-89693-140-4*) SP Pubns.
—God Made Warm & Cool Things. 12p. 1992. bds. 2.99 (*0-89693-142-0*) SP Pubns.
—God Made Wild & Tame Things. 12p. 1992. bds. 2.99 (*0-89693-141-2*) SP Pubns.
Funakoshi, Canna. One Morning. LC 86-91538. (Illus.). 34p. (ps-3). 1991. pap. 11.95 (*0-88708-033-2*) Picture Bk Studio.
Fusako Ishinabe. Hiro's Pillow. Young, Richard G., ed. Kaisei - Sha, tr. LC 89-11768. (Illus.). 32p. (gr. 1-3). 1989. PLB 14.60 (*0-944483-44-5*) Garrett Ed Corp.
Fyleman, Rose. Fairy Went A-Marketing. Henterly, Jamichael, illus. LC 86-4468. 24p. (ps-1). 1986. 11.95 (*0-525-44258-8*, DCB) Dutton Child Bks.
Gaban, Jesus. Harry the Hippo, 4 vols. Colorado, Nani, illus. 16p. (ps-1). 1992. Set. PLB 53.08 (*0-8368-0714-6*) Gareth Stevens Inc.
—Tub Time for Harry. Colorado, Nani, illus. 16p. (ps-1). 1992. PLB 13.27 (*0-8368-0718-9*) Gareth Stevens Inc.
Gackenbach, Dick. Timid Timothy's Tongue Twisters. Gackenbach, Dick, illus. (gr. k-3). 1989. bk. & cassette 19.95 (*0-87499-128-5*); bk. & cassette 12.95 (*0-87499-127-7*); 4 cassettes & guide 27.95 (*0-87499-129-3*) Live Oak Media.
Gage, Wilson, pseud. Mrs. Gaddy & the Ghost. Hafner, Marilyn, illus. LC 78-16366. 56p. (gr. k up). 1991. pap. 4.95 (*0-688-10996-9*, Mulberry) Morrow.

Gaines, M. C., ed. Picture Stories from the Bible: The New Testament in Full-Color Comic-Strip Form. Cameron, Don, illus. LC 80-51593. 144p. (gr. 3-10). 1980. Repr. of 1946 ed. 12.95 (*0-934386-02-1*) Scarf Pr.

Galdone, Paul. Henny Penny. Galdone, Paul, illus. LC 68-24735. 32p. (ps-3). 1984. pap. 4.95 (*0-89919-225-4*, Clarion Bks) HM.

—The Little Red Hen. LC 84-4311. (Illus.). 48p. (ps-3). 1985. pap. 4.95 (*0-89919-349-8*, Clarion Bks) HM.

Galvin, Matthew R. Clouds & Clocks: A Story for Children Who Soil. Ferraro, Sandra, illus. LC 89-12278. 48p. 1989. 16.95 (*0-945354-18-5*); pap. 6.95 (*0-945354-15-0*) Magination Pr.

Gamboli, Mario. What Else Could It Be? Gamboli, Mario, illus. LC 91-70423. 12p. (ps-k). 1991. bds. 3.95 (*1-878093-72-X*) Boyds Mills Pr.

—What Is Hiding? Gamboli, Mario, illus. LC 91-70422. 12p. (ps-k). 1991. bds. 3.95 (*1-878093-71-1*) Boyds Mills Pr.

—What Is Missing? Gamboli, Mario, illus. LC 91-70414. 10p. (ps-k). 1991. bds. 3.95 (*1-878093-70-3*); Set of 3 bks. bds. 11.85 (*0-685-72462-X*) Boyds Mills Pr.

—What Will It Be? Gamboli, Mario, illus. LC 91-70413. 12p. (ps-k). 1991. bds. 3.95 (*1-878093-73-8*) Boyds Mills Pr.

Gantos, Jack. Rotten Ralph. Rubel, Nicole, illus. 1988. Incl. cass. pap. 7.70 (*0-395-48873-7*) HM.

—Rotten Ralph's Trick or Treat. Rubel, Nicole, illus. 32p. (gr. k-3). 1988. pap. 4.95 (*0-395-48655-6*, Sandpiper) HM.

Gantschev, Ivan. Where Is Mr. Mole? Clements, Andrew, tr. Gantschev, Ivan, illus. LC 89-8778. 28p. (ps up). 1991. pap. 15.95 (*0-88708-109-6*) Picture Bk Studio.

Gapper, Joe, illus. Colors. 12p. (ps). 1993. bds. 5.95 (*0-8431-3624-3*) Price Stern.

—Mommy & Baby. 12p. (ps). 1993. bds. 5.95 (*0-8431-3625-1*) Price Stern.

—Opposites. 12p. (ps). 1993. bds. 5.95 (*0-8431-3626-X*) Price Stern.

—Togethers. 12p. (ps). 1993. bds. 5.95 (*0-8431-3627-8*) Price Stern.

Garcia, Gloria. Be My Friend. LC 90-49243. (ps). 1990. 9.95 (*0-85953-421-9*) Childs Play.

—Flying High. LC 90-49238. 1990. 9.95 (*0-85953-424-3*) Childs Play.

—I Can't Stop Now. LC 90-49239. (ps). 1990. 9.95 (*0-85953-423-5*) Childs Play.

—Life on the Ocean Wave. LC 90-49237. (ps). 1990. 9.95 (*0-85953-422-7*) Childs Play.

Garcia, Richard. My Aunt Otilia's Spirits: Los espiritus de mi Tia Otilia. Guerrero Rea, Jesus, tr. Cherin, Robin & Reyes, Roger I., illus. LC 86-17129. (ENG & SPA.). 24p. (gr. 2-9). 1987. 13.95 (*0-89239-029-8*) Childrens Book Pr.

Gardner, Karen A. My Life As a Hand. rev. ed. (Illus.). 37p. (ps-2). 1984. Set of 1-4. PLB 1.70 (*0-931421-03-9*) Psychol Educ Pubns.

—My Life As a Nose. rev. ed. (Illus.). 37p. (ps-2). 1984. Set of 1-4. PLB 1.70 (*0-931421-04-7*) Psychol Educ Pubns.

—My Life As a Tongue. rev. ed. (Illus.). 37p. (ps-2). 1984. Set of 1-4. PLB 1.70 (*0-931421-05-5*) Psychol Educ Pubns.

—My Life As an Eye. rev. ed. (Illus.). 37p. (ps-2). 1984. Set of 1-4. PLB 1.70 (*0-931421-02-0*) Psychol Educ Pubns.

Garland, Sarah. All Gone! (ps). 1991. pap. 3.95 (*0-14-054409-7*, Puffin) Puffin Bks.

—Going to Playschool. (Illus.). 32p. (gr. k-2). 1992. 13.95 (*0-370-31539-1*, Pub. by Bodley Head UK) Trafalgar.

—Oh, No! (Illus.). 32p. (ps-1). 1990. pap. 8.95 (*0-670-83075-5*) Viking Child Bks.

—Oh, No! (ps). 1991. pap. 3.95 (*0-14-054411-9*, Puffin) Puffin Bks.

Gay, Marie-Louise. Rainy Day Magic. Tucker, Kathy, ed. Gay, Marie-Louise, illus. LC 89-5380. 32p. (ps-2). 1989. PLB 13.95 (*0-8075-6767-1*) A Whitman.

Gee, John. Hidden Pictures: Favorites by John Gee. (Illus.). 32p. (Orig.). (gr. 1-6). 1981. pap. 2.95 (*0-87534-230-2*) Highlights.

Geisert, Arthur. The Ark. Geisert, Arthur, illus. LC 88-15889. 48p. (ps up). 1988. 15.45 (*0-395-43078-X*) HM.

Gelbert, Ofra. Something Else. Kriss, David, tr. from HEB. Elchanan, illus. 24p. (Orig.). (ps). 1992. pap. text ed. 3.00x (*1-56134-165-7*) Dushkin Pub.

Gellman, Ellie. Tamar's Sukkah. Kahn, Katherine J., illus. LC 88-23388. 32p. (ps-2). 1988. pap. 4.95 (*0-930494-79-2*) Kar Ben.

Gelman, Rita G. Cats & Mice. Gurney, Eric, illus. 48p. (gr. k-3). 1989. Big Book. 28.67 (*0-590-64644-3*); pap. 1.95 (*0-590-71593-3*) Scholastic Inc.

Genet, Barbara. Ta-Poo-Ach Means Apple. Genet, Barbara, illus. LC 85-60009. 46p. (ps-3). 1985. 8.00 (*0-86705-015-2*) A R E Pub.

Gentle Friends. 12p. (ps-1). 1988. bds. 5.95 (*0-87449-628-4*) Modern Pub NYC.

Georgiady, Nicholas P. & Romano, Louis G. Trudi La Cane. Thorne, Patrice, tr. Wilson, Dagmar W., illus. 32p. (gr. 1-4). 1982. pap. 5.00 (*0-317-05572-0*) Argee Pubs.

Geraghty, Paul. The Great Knitting Needle Hunt. (Illus.). 32p. (ps-2). 1992. 14.95 (*0-09-173749-4*, Pub. by Hutchinson UK) Trafalgar.

Gere, Bill. The Truck Book. LaPadula, Tom, illus. 24p. (ps-k). 1987. pap. write for info. (*0-307-10051-0*, Pub. by Golden Bks) Western Pub.

Geringer, Laura. A Three Hat Day. Lobel, Arnold, illus. LC 85-42640. 32p. (ps-3). 1987. pap. 4.95 (*0-06-443157-6*, Trophy) HarpC Child Bks.

Gerrard, Roy. The Favershams. (Illus.). 32p. (gr. 2 up). 1987. pap. 3.95 (*0-374-42293-1*) FS&G.

Gerstein, Mordicai. The Seal Mother. Gerstein, Mordicai, illus. LC 82-29295. 32p. (ps-3). 1986. PLB 10.89 (*0-8037-0303-1*) Dial Bks Young.

Gerver, Jane E. Happy Bear, Christmas Star. Barto, Bobbi, illus. LC 90-60174. 32p. (Orig.). (ps-3). 1990. pap. 2.25 (*0-679-80858-2*) Random Bks Yng Read.

Gibbons, Gail. The Milk Makers. Gibbons, Gail, illus. LC 86-22148. 32p. (gr. k-3). 1987. pap. 3.95 (*0-689-71116-6*, Aladdin) Macmillan Child Grp.

—The Pottery Place. Gibbons, Gail, illus. LC 86-32790. 32p. (ps-3). 1987. 12.95 (*0-15-263265-4*, HB Juv Bks) HarBrace.

—Sun up, Sun Down. LC 82-23420. (Illus.). 32p. (Orig.). (ps-3). 1987. pap. 4.95 (*0-15-282782-X*, Voyager Bks) HarBrace.

—Trucks. Gibbons, Gail, illus. LC 81-43039. 32p. (ps-1). 1985. pap. 4.95 (*0-06-443069-3*, Trophy) HarpC Child Bks.

Giff, Patricia R. The Almost Awful Play. Natti, Susanna, illus. (gr. 2-4). 1989. bk. & cassette 19.95 (*0-87499-116-1*); bk. & cassette 12.95 (*0-87499-115-3*); pap. 27.95 4 cassettes & guide (*0-87499-117-X*) Live Oak Media.

—Happy Birthday, Ronald Morgan! Natti, Susanna, illus. LC 85-32303. 32p. (ps-4). 1986. pap. 10.95 (*0-670-80741-9*) Viking Child Bks.

—Happy Birthday, Ronald Morgan. Natti, Susanna, illus. (gr. 2-4). 1989. bk. & cassette 19.95 (*0-87499-122-6*); bk. & cassette 12.95 (*0-87499-121-8*); 4 cassettes & guide 27.95 (*0-87499-123-4*) Live Oak Media.

—Have You Seen Hyacinth Macaw? 128p. (gr. k-6). 1982. pap. 3.25 (*0-440-43450-5*, YB) Dell.

The Giggle Book. 1994. 13.27 (*0-8368-0987-4*) Gareth Stevens Inc.

Gilchrist, Guy. Tiny Dinos Fun at the Beach: A Book of Actions. Gilchrist, Guy, illus. LC 87-40337. (ps-1). 1988. 4.95 (*1-55782-013-9*, Pub. by Warner Juvenile Bks) Little.

Giles, Lucille. Color Me Brown. rev. ed. Holmes, Louis F., illus. 47p. (gr. k-6). 1974. pap. 5.00 (*0-87485-017-7*) Johnson Chi.

Gill, Bob. What Color Is Your World. Gill, Bob, illus. (gr. k-3). 1963. 10.95 (*0-8392-3042-7*) Astor-Honor.

Gillon, Edmund. Cut & Assemble a Western Frontier Town. 1950. pap. 5.95 (*0-486-23736-2*) Dover.

—Cut & Assemble an Early New England Village. 1950. pap. 5.95 (*0-486-23536-X*) Dover.

Gillon, Edmund V. Cut & Assemble-Victorian Houses. 1980. pap. 5.95 (*0-486-23849-0*) Dover.

—Cut & Assemble Victorian Seaside Resort. 1986. pap. 5.95 (*0-486-25097-0*) Dover.

Gilson, Jamie. Can't Catch Me, I'm the Gingerbread Man. 128p. (gr. 4-7). 1989. pap. 2.75 (*0-671-69160-0*, Minstrel Bks) PB.

Ginsburg, Mirra. Across the Stream. Tafuri, Nancy, illus. LC 81-20306. 24p. (ps up). 1991. pap. 3.95 (*0-688-10477-0*, Mulberry) Morrow.

—The Chick & the Duckling. Aruego, Jose & Dewey, Ariane, illus. 32p. (ps-1). 1988. pap. 4.95 (*0-689-71226-X*, Aladdin) Macmillan Child Grp.

—Where Does the Sun Go at Night? Aruego, Jose & Dewey, Ariane, illus. LC 79-16151. 32p. (ps up). 1987. pap. 4.95 (*0-688-07041-8*, Mulberry) Morrow.

Giovanni, Nikki. Spin a Soft Black Song. rev. ed. Martins, George, illus. LC 84-19287. 64p. (gr. 2 up). 1985. 11.95 (*0-8090-8796-0*) Hill & Wang.

—Spin a Soft Black Song. rev. ed. Martins, George, illus. (gr. k up). 1987. pap. 3.95 (*0-374-46469-3*, Sunburst) FS&G.

Girard, Linda W. Adoption Is for Always. Levine, Abby, ed. LC 86-15843. (Illus.). 32p. (gr. 1-5). 1986. PLB 11.95 (*0-8075-0185-9*); pap. 4.95 (*0-8075-0187-5*) A Whitman.

—At Daddy's on Saturdays. Levine, Abby, ed. LC 87-2126. (Illus.). 32p. (gr. k-3). 1987. PLB 13.95 (*0-8075-0475-0*); pap. 5.95 (*0-8075-0473-4*) A Whitman.

—We Adopted You, Benjamin Koo. Levine, Abby, ed. LC 88-23653. (Illus.). 32p. (gr. 2-6). 1989. 13.95 (*0-8075-8694-3*); pap. 5.95 (*0-8075-8695-1*) A Whitman.

Gleeson, Brian, as told by. Pecos Bill. Raglin, Tim, illus. LC 88-11581. 36p. (ps up). 1991. pap. 14.95 (*0-88708-081-2*, Rabbit Ears); bk. & cass. pkg. 19.95 (*0-88708-086-3*, Rabbit Ears) Picture Bk Studio.

Glover, Susanne, et al. A Bulletin Board Book for All Seasons. 64p. (gr. k-6). 1980. 7.95 (*0-916456-79-X*, GA 160) Good Apple.

Glugg, Professor. The Blue Skidoo Crew. Glugg, Professor, illus. LC 92-75278. 32p. (Orig.). (ps up). 1993. pap. 3.95 (*1-881905-03-9*) Glue Bks.

—Flip & the Magic Wando Whip. Glugg, Professor, illus. LC 92-73552. 32p. (Orig.). (ps up). 1993. pap. 3.95 (*1-881905-01-2*) Glue Bks.

—Who Took Apple Frapple's Cookbook? Glugg, Professor, illus. LC 92-73242. 32p. (Orig.). (ps up). 1992. pap. 3.95 (*1-881905-00-4*) Glue Bks.

Goble, Paul. Beyond the Ridge. Goble, Paul, illus. LC 87-33113. 32p. (ps-3). 1989. RSBE 14.95 (*0-02-736581-6*, Bradbury Pr) Macmillan Child Grp.

—Dream Wolf. Goble, Paul, illus. LC 89-687. 32p. (gr. 3 up). 1990. RSBE 14.95 (*0-02-736585-9*, Bradbury Pr) Macmillan Child Grp.

—The Great Race. LC 85-4202. (Illus.). 32p. (ps-2). 1985. RSBE 14.95 (*0-02-736950-1*, Bradbury Pr) Macmillan Child Grp.

—Star Boy. Goble, Paul, illus. LC 82-20599. 32p. (gr. k up). 1983. SBE 14.95 (*0-02-722660-3*, Bradbury Pr) Macmillan Child Grp.

God Gives Me Animals. (ps). 1991. vinyl 4.99 (*1-55513-471-8*, 64717, Chariot Bks) Chariot Family.

God Gives Me Baby Animals. (ps). 1991. vinyl 4.99 (*1-55513-472-6*, 64725, Chariot Bks) Chariot Family.

God Gives Me Fun Times. (ps). 1991. vinyl 4.99 (*1-55513-470-X*, 64709, Chariot Bks) Chariot Family.

God Gives Me Good Food. (ps). 1991. vinyl 4.99 (*1-55513-469-6*, 64691, Chariot Bks) Chariot Family.

God Made Pears. (Illus.). (ps). 1990. bds. 0.99 (*0-8007-7105-2*) Revell.

Goffin, Josse, illus. Silent Christmas. LC 90-83430. 32p. (ps-k). 1991. 14.95 (*1-878093-08-8*) Boyds Mills Pr.

Golden, Silvia. The King's Forest. Eichenauer, Gabriele G., illus. 1988. 14.95 (*0-86315-085-3*, 20247) Gryphon Hse.

Goldman, Ronald & Lynch, Martha E. High Hat Story: Book Two. (ps-1). 1986. 24.49 (*0-88671-245-9*, 7942); lesson guide 7.95 (*0-88671-248-3*, 7932); wkbk. 7.00 (*0-88671-249-1*) Am Guidance.

Gomboli, Mario. What Are You Touching? Gomboli, Mario, illus. 10p. (ps-k). 1992. bds. 3.95 (*1-56397-150-X*) Boyds Mills Pr.

—What Shape Is This? Gomboli, Mario, illus. 10p. (ps-k). 1992. bds. 3.95 (*1-56397-149-6*) Boyds Mills Pr.

—What's in Disguise? Gomboli, Mario, illus. 10p. (ps-k). 1992. bds. 3.95 (*1-56397-151-8*); Set of 3 bks. bds. 11.85 (*1-56397-156-9*) Boyds Mills Pr.

Gomi, Taro. The Big Book of Boxes. Gomi, Taro, illus. 12p. (ps up). 1991. pap. 14.95 (*0-8118-0067-9*) Chronicle Bks.

—Guess What? A Peek-a-Boo Book. Chronicle Books, tr. from JPN. Gomi, Taro, illus. 16p. (ps-k). 1992. bds. 4.95 (*0-8118-0015-6*) Chronicle Bks.

—Guess Who? A Peek-A-Boo Book. Gomi, Taro, illus. 16p. (ps-k). 1991. bds. 4.95 (*0-8118-0021-0*) Chronicle Bks.

—There's a Mouse in the House. Chronicle Books, tr. from JPN. Gomi, Taro, illus. 16p. (ps-k). 1991. bds. 4.95 (*0-8118-0024-5*) Chronicle Bks.

—Who Ate It? (Illus.). 24p. (ps). 1991. 6.95 (*1-56294-706-0*); PLB 8.90 (*1-56294-010-4*); pap. 4.95 (*1-56294-842-3*) Millbrook Pr.

Good, Elaine W. That's What Happens When It's Spring. Shenks, Susie, illus. LC 87-14964. 32p. (ps-1). 1987. 12.95 (*0-934672-53-9*) Good Bks PA.

Good, Merle. Amos & Susie: An Amish Story. Benner, Cheryl A., illus. LC 93-11483. 24p. (ps-3). 1993. 12.95 (*1-561480-88-6*); pap. 4.95 (*0-934672-46-6*) Good Bks PA.

Good Morning, Sunshine. 32p. (ps-1). 1985. 4.95 (*0-671-54733-X*, Little Simon) S&S Trade.

Good Night, Baby Donald. write for info. (*1-56326-305-X*, 030601) Disney Bks By Mail.

Good Night Stars. (ps-1). 1985. 4.95 (*0-671-54734-8*, Little Simon) S&S Trade.

Goodall, John S. Great Days of a Country House. Goodall, John S., illus. LC 91-62147. 64p. (ps up). 1992. SBE 15.95 (*0-689-50545-0*, M K McElderry) Macmillan Child Grp.

—Lavinia's Cottage: A Pop-Up Story. LC 82-71160. (Illus.). 16p. (gr. 1-4). 1983. SBE 14.95 (*0-689-50257-5*, M K McElderry) Macmillan Child Grp.

Goode, Diane. I Hear a Noise. Goode, Diane, illus. LC 87-3060. 32p. (ps-1). 1988. 12.95 (*0-525-44353-3*, DCB) Dutton Child Bks.

Goodman, Billy. Taking Care of the Earth. Gleeson, Kate, illus. 24p. (ps-k). 1992. write for info. (*0-307-11532-1*, 11532) Western Pub.

Goodman, Michael E. Cars & Trucks. (Illus.). 24p. (ps-k). 1989. pap. write for info. (*0-307-11753-7*, Pub. by Golden Bks) Western Pub.

Goodspeed, Peter. A Rhinoceros Wakes Me up in the Morning. Panek, Dennis, illus. 32p. (ps-k). 1984. pap. 3.95 (*0-14-050455-9*, Puffin) Puffin Bks.

Gorbaty, Norman. Dump Truck. Gorbaty, Norman, illus. 12p. (ps). 1993. bds. 6.95 (*0-448-40594-6*, G&D) Putnam Pub Group.

—Good Morning, Little Bert. 1987. 1.10 (*0-394-88504-X*) Random Bks Yng Read.

—Little Dinosaur. Gorbaty, Norman, illus. LC 87-61420. 24p. (ps-1). 1988. bk. & doll pkg. 5.95 (*0-394-89575-4*) Random Bks Yng Read.

—Little Ernie's Animal Friends. 1987. 1.10 (*0-394-88508-2*) Random Bks Yng Read.

—Sesame Street: At the Playground. 1987. 1.10 (*0-394-88503-1*) Random Bks Yng Read.

—Sesame Street: Goodnight Little Grover. 1987. 1.10 (*0-394-88506-6*) Random Bks Yng Read.

—Sesame Street: Playtime with Bigbird. 1987. 1.10 (*0-394-88507-4*) Random Bks Yng Read.

—Sesame Street: Tubbie Time with Little Ernie. 1987. 1.10 (*0-394-88505-8*) Random Bks Yng Read.

Gorbaty, Norman, tr. Baby in the Park. (Illus.). 12p. (ps). 1988. 2.95 (*0-394-81925-X*) Random Bks Yng Read.

Gorbaty, Norman, illus. Baby Animals Say Hello. 12p. (ps). 1986. 4.99 (*0-394-88241-5*) Random Bks Yng Read.

—Baby at Home. 12p. (ps). 1988. 2.95 (*0-394-81924-1*) Random Bks Yng Read.

—Fire Engine. 12p. (ps). 1993. bds. 6.95 (*0-448-40595-4*, G&D) Putnam Pub Group.

—Get up & Go, Little Dinosaur! LC 89-64282. 22p. (ps). 1990. bds. 2.95 (*0-679-80693-8*) Random Bks Yng Read.
—What Do You See on Sesame Street? 12p. (ps). 1988. 4.99 (*0-394-80594-1*) Random Bks Yng Read.
Gordon, Jeffie R. Six Sleepy Sheep. O'Brien, John, illus. LC 90-85728. 24p. (ps-1). 1991. 12.95 (*1-878093-06-1*) Boyds Mills Pr.
—Two Badd Babies. Demarest, Chris L., illus. LC 91-72869. 32p. (ps-3). 1992. 14.95 (*1-878093-85-1*) Boyds Mills Pr.
Gorey, Edward. Cat E Gory. LC 86-10938. (ps up). 1986. 8.95 (*0-915361-55-8*) Modan-Adama Bks.
—The Wuggly Ump. Gorey, Edward, illus. LC 86-11273. (ps up). 1986. 6.95 (*0-915361-56-6*, Dist. by Watts) Modan-Adama Bks.
Gould, Deborah. Aaron's Shirt. Harness, Cheryl, illus. LC 88-10414. 32p. (ps-2). 1989. SBE 13.95 (*0-02-736351-1*, Bradbury Pr) Macmillan Child Grp.
Gould, Toni. Fun with the Fumble Families. LC 83-5928. (Illus.). (gr. 1-3). 1984. pap. 12.95x (*0-8027-9191-3*) Walker & Co.
—Fun with Water & Ice. LC 83-5938. (Illus.). (gr. 1-3). 1984. pap. text ed. 12.95x (*0-8027-9194-8*) Walker & Co.
Grafton, Carol B. Cut & Use Stencil Alphabet. 1984. pap. 4.95 (*0-486-24623-X*) Dover.
Gramatky, Hardie. Little Toot. Long, Laurie, illus. 12p. (ps). 1993. bds. 4.95 (*0-448-40585-7*, G&D) Putnam Pub Group.
Grambling, Lois G. Hundred Million Reasons for Owning an Elephant: Or at Least a Dozen That I Can Think of Right Now. Learner, Vickie M., illus. 32p. (ps). 1990. 6.95 (*0-8120-6189-6*) Barron.
Grand et Petit. (FRE., Illus.). 3.50 (*0-7214-1431-1*) Ladybird Bks.
Grater, Michael. Cut & Fold Extraterrestrial Invaders That Fly. 1983. pap. 2.95 (*0-486-24478-4*) Dover.
—Cut & Fold Paper Spaceships. 1981. pap. 2.95 (*0-486-23978-0*) Dover.
—Cut & Make Monster Masks in Full Color. 1978. pap. 4.95 (*0-486-23576-9*) Dover.
Gray, Catherine. One, Two, Three & Four: No More? Moss, Marissa, illus. 32p. (gr. k-3). 1988. 13.45 (*0-395-48293-3*) HM.
Gray, Nigel. The One & Only Robin Hood. Craig, Helen, illus. LC 87-2680. 32p. (ps-3). 1987. 12.95 (*0-316-32578-3*, Joy St Bks) Little.
Green, Cecile. Tale of Theodore Bear. LC 68-56812. (Illus.). 32p. (gr. 1-2). 1968. PLB 9.95 (*0-87783-038-X*) Oddo.
Green, Ivah. Splash & Trickle. LC 68-56818. (Illus.). 32p. (gr. 2-3). 1968. PLB 9.95 (*0-87783-037-1*); pap. 3.94 deluxe ed. (*0-87783-109-2*); cassette o.s.i. 7.94x (*0-87783-226-9*) Oddo.
Greenaway, Elizabeth. Cat Nap. Greenaway, Elizabeth, illus. 14p. (ps). 1994. bds. 2.99 (*0-679-83958-5*) Random Bks Yng Read.
—Rabbit Food. Greenaway, Elizabeth, illus. 14p. (ps). 1994. bds. 2.99 (*0-679-83959-3*) Random Bks Yng Read.
Greenberg, Kenneth R. The Adventures of Tusky & His Friends Series, Bk. I. Pearson, Allison K., illus. (gr. k-3). 1992. PLB write for info. (*1-879100-49-5*) Tusky Enterprises.
Greene, Carol. Ice Is...Whee! Sharp, Paul, illus. LC 82-19855. 32p. (ps-2). 1983. PLB 10.25 (*0-516-02037-4*); pap. 2.95 (*0-516-42037-2*) Childrens.
—The Pilgrims Are Marching. Dunnington, Tom, illus. LC 88-20219. 32p. (ps-2). 1988. PLB 11.80 (*0-516-08234-5*); pap. 3.95 (*0-516-48234-3*) Childrens.
Greenfield, Eloise. Me & Neesie. Barnett, Moneta, illus. LC 74-23078. 40p. (gr. k-3). 1984. pap. 4.95 (*0-06-443057-X*, Trophy) HarpC Child Bks.
—She Come Bringing Me That Little Baby Girl. Steptoe, John, illus. LC 74-8104. 32p. (gr. k-3). 1990. 16.00 (*0-397-31586-4*, Lipp Jr Bks); PLB 15.89 (*0-397-32478-2*) HarpC Child Bks.
—Sweet Baby Coming. Cilchrist, Jan S., illus. 14p. (ps). 1994. 4.95 (*0-694-00578-9*, Festival) HarpC Child Bks.
—Under the Sunday Tree. Ferguson, Amos, illus. LC 87-29373. 48p. (gr. 1 up). 1991. pap. 5.95 (*0-06-443257-2*, Trophy) HarpC Child Bks.
Greenfield, Monica. Baby. Gilchrist, Jan S., illus. 14p. (ps). 1994. 4.95 (*0-694-00577-0*, Festival) HarpC Child Bks.
Greenleaf, E. Who Wants to Nap? LC 68-56820. (Illus.). 32p. (gr. 2-3). PLB 9.95 (*0-87783-050-9*) Oddo.
Greeson, Janet. The Stingy Baker. LaRochelle, David, illus. 32p. (ps-3). 1989. PLB 18.95 (*0-87614-378-8*) Carolrhoda Bks.
Gregorich, Barbara. Hidden Pictures. Hoffman, Joan, ed. Pape, Richard, illus. 32p. (Orig.). (ps). 1983. wkbk. 1.99 (*0-938256-50-5*) Sch Zone Pub Co.
—Jace, Mace, & the Big Race. Hoffman, Joan, ed. (Illus.). 16p. (Orig.). (gr. k-2). 1985. pap. 2.25 (*0-88743-018-X*, 06018) Sch Zone Pub Co.
—Rhyming Pictures. Hoffman, Joan, ed. Pape, Richard, illus. 32p. (ps). 1983. wkbk. 1.99 (*0-938256-53-X*) Sch Zone Pub Co.
Gretz, Susanna & Sage, Alison. Teddy Bears at the Seaside. Gretz, Susanna, illus. LC 88-11280. 32p. (gr. k-3). 1989. SBE 13.95 (*0-02-738141-2*, Four Winds) Macmillan Child Grp.
Grey, J. The Turtle Who Wanted to Run. LC 68-56813. (Illus.). 32p. (gr. 1-3). 1968. PLB 9.95 (*0-87783-045-2*) Oddo.
Griffith, Helen V. Grandaddy's Place. Stevenson, James, illus. LC 86-19573. 40p. (gr. k up). 1991. pap. 4.95 (*0-688-10491-6*, Mulberry) Morrow.
Grillis, Carla. Animals. (Illus.). (ps). 1988. bds. 5.50 (*0-86315-072-1*, 20232) Gryphon Hse.
Grimes, Nikki. Something on My Mind. Feelings, Tom, illus. LC 77-86266. 32p. (gr. k up). 1986. pap. 4.95 (*0-8037-0273-6*) Dial Bks Young.
Grimm, Jacob & Grimm, Wilhelm K. The Brave Little Tailor. Bell, Anthea, tr. Tharlet, Eve, illus. LC 88-33367. 28p. (ps up). 1991. pap. 14.95 (*0-88708-091-X*) Picture Bk Studio.
—Bremen Town Musicians. Bell, Anthea, tr. Palecek, Josef, illus. LC 88-15179. 32p. (ps up). 1991. pap. 13.95 (*0-88708-071-5*) Picture Bk Studio.
—The Fisherman & His Wife. Bell, Anthea, tr. Marks, Alan, illus. LC 88-15165. 28p. (ps up). 1991. pap. 14.95 (*0-88708-072-3*) Picture Bk Studio.
—The Fisherman & His Wife. Metaxas, Eric, tr. from GER. Bryan, Diana, illus. LC 89-28445. 32p. (ps up). 1991. pap. 14.95 (*0-88708-122-3*, Rabbit Ears); includes cassette 19.95 (*0-88708-123-1*) Picture Bk Studio.
—Hansel & Gretel. Becker, Lois & Stratton, Mark, eds. (Illus.). 26p. (ps). 1987. Packaged with pre-programmed audio cass. tape. 9.95 (*0-934323-64-X*) Alchemy Comms.
—Hansel & Gretel. LC 87-32833. 1991. pap. 14.95 (*0-88708-068-5*) Picture Bk Studio.
—The Seven Ravens. Zwerger, Lisbeth, illus. LC 83-61777. 28p. (gr. k up). 1991. pap. 14.95 (*0-88708-092-8*); pap. 5.95 (*0-685-24951-4*) Picture Bk Studio.
—Snow White & the Seven Dwarfs. Iwasaki, Chihiro, illus. LC 85-12158. 40p. (gr. 1 up). 1991. pap. 15.95 (*0-88708-012-X*) Picture Bk Studio.
Grindley, Sally. Knock, Knock! Who's There? Browne, Anthony, illus. LC 86-112. 32p. (ps-2). 1986. PLB 7.95 (*0-394-88400-0*) Knopf Bks Yng Read.
Griscom, Laura & Griscom, Pam. Who Would Want Those Apples Anyway? Halpin, Scot, illus. 24p. (Orig.). (ps-5). 1993. pap. 4.95 (*0-9633705-3-7*) Share Pub CA.
Groner, Judye & Wikler, Madeline. Shabbat Shalom. Yaffa, illus. LC 88-83568. 12p. (ps). 1989. bds. 4.95 (*0-930494-91-1*) Kar Ben.
Grossman, Bill. Tommy at the Grocery Store Big Book. Chess, Victoria, illus. LC 88-35756. 32p. (ps-1). 1992. 19.95 (*0-694-00387-5*) HarpC Child Bks.
Guell, Fernando, illus. Disney's Pop-up Book of Places to Go. 12p. (ps-k). 1994. 7.95 (*1-56282-507-0*) Disney Pr.
Gullette, Margaret M. The Lost Bellybutton. Udry, Leslie, illus. LC 76-26377. 32p. (Orig.). (ps-2). 1976. pap. 4.95 (*0-914996-11-8*) Lollipop Power.
Gunn, Robin J. When I Celebrate His Birthday. Acquistapace, David & Gary, N. C., illus. LC 88-70837. (ps). 1988. bds. 4.99 (*1-55513-567-6*, Chariot Bks) Chariot Family.
—When I Go to the Park. Acquistapace, David & Gary, N. C., illus. LC 88-70836. (ps). 1988. bds. 4.99 (*1-55513-589-7*, Chariot Bks) Chariot Family.
—When I Have a Babysitter. Acquistapace, David & Gary, N. C., illus. LC 88-70838. (ps). 1988. bds. 4.99 (*1-55513-573-0*, Chariot Bks) Chariot Family.
—When I Help My Mommy. Acquistapace, David & Gary, N. C., illus. LC 88-70835. (ps). 1988. 4.99 (*1-55513-566-8*, Chariot Bks) Chariot Family.
Gurney, Nancy & Gurney, Eric. King, the Mice & the Cheese. Vallier, Jean, illus. LC 89-8463. 72p. (gr. k-3). 1965. 6.95 (*0-394-80039-7*); lib. bdg. 7.99 (*0-394-90039-1*) Random Bks Yng Read.
Haddock, Peter. Fairy Tale Shape Board Book: Cinderella. 1988. 2.49 (*0-671-09409-2*) S&S Trade.
—Hansel & Gretel. 1988. 2.49 (*0-671-09408-4*) S&S Trade.
Hadithi, Mwenye. Crafty Chameleon. Kennaway, Adrienne, illus. 32p. (ps-3). 1987. 15.95 (*0-316-33723-4*) Little.
Hague, Michael, illus. Magic Moments: A Book of Days. 96p. 1990. 14.95 (*1-55970-069-6*) Arcade Pub Inc.
—A Unicorn Journal. 64p. 1990. 12.95 (*1-55970-068-8*) Arcade Pub Inc.
Haidle, Elizabeth. Elmer the Grump. Thatch, Nancy R., ed. Haidle, Elizabeth, illus. Melton, David, intro. by. LC 89-31872. (Illus.). 26p. (gr. k-5). 1989. PLB 14.95 (*0-933849-20-6*) Landmark Edns.
Hale, Janet. Spring & Summer Think & Do Shape Books. Hale, Janet, illus. 48p. (gr. k-2). 1989. wkbk. 5.95 (*1-55734-129-X*) Tchr Create Mat.
Hale, Sarah J. Mary Had a Little Lamb. De Paola, Tomie, illus. (ps-2). 1989. bk. & cassette 19.95 (*0-87499-125-0*); pap. 12.95 bk. & cassette (*0-87499-124-2*); pap. 27.95 4 cassettes & guide (*0-87499-126-9*) Live Oak Media.
Haley, Gail E. A Story, a Story. Haley, Gail E., illus. LC 87-17412. 36p. (ps-3). 1988. pap. 4.95 (*0-689-71201-4*, Aladdin) Macmillan Child Grp.
Hall, Katy & Eisenberg, Lisa. Buggy Riddles. Taback, Simms, illus. (gr. 2-5). 1989. bk. & cassette 19.95 (*0-87499-118-8*); bk. & cassette 12.95 (*0-87499-119-6*); 4 cassettes & guide 27.95 (*0-87499-120-X*) Live Oak Media.
Hall, Kirsten. Kittens: Pop up Book. (ps). 1994. 3.28 (*1-884270-03-4*) Nancy Hall.
—Puppies - A Pop up Book. (ps). 1994. 3.28 (*1-884270-02-6*) Nancy Hall.
Hall, Susan T. Creation. (Illus.). 10p. (ps). 1991. bds. 7.49 (*1-55513-482-3*, 63230, Chariot Bks) Chariot Family.
—Noah's Ark. Hall, Susan T., illus. 12p. (ps). 1990. pap. text ed. 5.95 (*0-927106-03-5*) Prod Concept.
—Perfect Pals. Hall, Susan T., illus. 12p. (ps). 1989. pap. text ed. 5.95 (*0-927106-00-0*) Prod Concept.
—So Sleepy. Hall, Susan T., illus. 12p. (ps). 1989. pap. text ed. 5.95 (*0-927106-01-9*) Prod Concept.
—So Sleepy Fuzzy Book. 10p. (ps). 1989. pap. 7.49 (*1-55513-280-4*, Chariot Bks) Chariot Family.
—Thank You, God, for Peanut Butter & Jelly. (Illus.). 10p. (ps). 1991. bds. 5.99 (*1-55513-487-4*, 63248, Chariot Bks) Chariot Family.
—Thank You, God, for Watermelon. (Illus.). 10p. (ps). 1991. bds. 5.99 (*1-55513-486-6*, 63255, Chariot Bks) Chariot Family.
Hallinan, P. K. We're Very Good Friends, My Grandma & I. Hallinan, Patrick, illus. 24p. (ps-2). 1989. pap. 4.95 perfect bdg. (*0-8249-8548-6*, Ideals Child) Hambleton-Hill.
—We're Very Good Friends, My Grandpa & I. Hallinan, Patrick, illus. 24p. (ps-2). 1989. pap. 4.95 perfect bdg. (*0-8249-8549-4*, Ideals Child) Hambleton-Hill.
Halloween Night. 1994. pap. 6.99 (*0-553-45909-0*) Bantam.
Halverson, Sandy. Book of Mormon Activity Book: Creative Scripture Learning Experiences for Children 4-12. Halverson, Sandy, illus. 80p. (gr. 3-8). 1982. pap. 5.98 (*0-88290-188-5*, 4521) Horizon Utah.
Hamilton, Virginia. Dustland. LC 79-19003. 192p. (gr. 7 up). 1980. 13.00 (*0-688-80228-1*); PLB 12.88 (*0-688-84228-3*) Greenwillow.
Hamsa, Bobbie. Fast Draw Freddie Big Book. 32p. (ps-2). 1990. PLB 22.95 (*0-516-49453-8*) Childrens.
—Polly Wants a Cracker. Warshaw, Jerry, illus. LC 85-30000. 32p. (ps-2). 1986. PLB 10.25 (*0-516-02071-4*); pap. 2.95 (*0-516-42071-2*) Childrens.
Handford, Martin. Find Waldo Now. Handford, Martin, illus. (ps up). 1988. 14.95 (*0-316-34292-0*) Little.
—The Great Waldo Search. Handford, Martin, illus. (ps up). 1989. 14.95 (*0-316-34282-3*) Little.
—Where's Waldo? (ps up). 1987. 14.95 (*0-316-34293-9*) Little.
Handy, Libby. Boss for a Week. 32p. (gr. k-3). Big Book. 28.67 (*0-590-64641-9*) Scholastic Inc.
Hansel & Gretel. (Illus.). (ps-k). 1991. write for info. (*0-307-11516-X*, Golden Pr) Western Pub.
Hansen, Kathleen. A New Sibling. 2nd ed. Silverthorn, Tina, illus. 16p. (ps). 1989. color book 1.95x (*0-685-29408-0*) Time Grow Co.
Harada, Joyce. It's the 0-1-2-3 Book. Harada, Joyce, illus. 32p. (ps-3). 1985. pap. 7.95 (*0-89346-252-7*) Heian Intl.
Harchy, Philippe, illus. Disney's the Lion King Pop-up Book. 12p. (ps-3). 1994. 11.95 (*0-7868-3005-0*) Disney Pr.
Harding, Mary. All Aboard Trains. Courtney, Richard, illus. 32p. (Orig.). (ps-2). 1989. pap. 2.25 (*0-448-19111-3*, Platt & Munk Pubs) Putnam Pub Group.
Hargreaves, Roger. Mr. Skinny. 32p. (ps up). 1978. PLB 9.95 (*0-87191-823-4*) Creative Ed.
—Mr. Small. 32p. (ps up). 1972. PLB 9.95 (*0-87191-824-2*) Creative Ed.
—Mr. Snow. 32p. (ps up). 1971. PLB 9.95 (*0-87191-915-X*) Creative Ed.
Harper-Deiters, Cyndi. The Jonathan Michael Series. Ruggles, Robert & Ruggles, Grace, eds. Bowers, Helen M., illus. (Orig.). (gr. 2-5). 1993. pap. text ed. write for info. (*0-9632513-4-1*) Cntry Home.
Harriman, Marinell & Harriman, Robert. A Myriad of Minstrels. Harriman, Marinell & Harriman, Robert, illus. 32p. (Orig.). (gr. 5-7). pap. 3.50 (*0-940920-00-X*) Drollery Pr.
Harris, Denise, illus. The Kitten Pop-up Book. Costello, Linda, contrib. by. LC 90-85726. (Illus.). 12p. (ps-3). 1991. 9.95 (*1-878093-04-5*) Boyds Mills Pr.
Harris, Jack C. Big Boats, Little Boats. (Illus.). 24p. (ps). 1990. pap. write for info. (*0-307-11667-0*, Pub. by Golden Bks) Western Pub.
—My First Book of Fire Trucks. (Illus.). 24p. (ps). 1990. pap. write for info. (*0-307-11666-2*, Pub. by Golden Bks) Western Pub.
Hart, Marj. Fold-&-Cut Stories & Fingerplays. (ps-3). 1987. pap. 9.95 (*0-8224-3150-5*) Fearon Teach Aids.
Harte, Cheryl, illus. Bunny Rattle. 12p. (ps). 1989. sponge-filled cloth 5.99 (*0-394-89956-3*) Random Bks Yng Read.
—Ducky Squeak. 12p. (ps). 1989. sponge-filled cloth 6.99 (*0-394-89955-5*) Random Bks Yng Read.
—My Chalkboard Book: Green Ladder Books for Kids Through 6 Years. 14p. (ps-1). 1988. bds. 6.95 (*0-394-89401-4*) Random Bks Yng Read.
Hartelius, Margaret A., illus. Over in the Meadow. 1987. pap. 6.99 incl. audiocassette (*0-553-45900-7*) Bantam.
—The Twelve Days of Christmas. 1994. pap. 6.99 incl. audiocassette (*0-553-45906-6*) Bantam.
Hartley, Al. Family Fun. Hartley, Al, illus. (gr. 1). 1988. pap. text ed. 1.29 (*1-55748-004-4*) Barbour & Co.
—Flying Colors. Hartley, Al, illus. 32p. (gr. 1). 1988. pap. text ed. 1.29 (*1-55748-000-1*) Barbour & Co.
—Fun in the Car. Hartley, Al, illus. 32p. (gr. 1). 1988. pap. text ed. 1.29 (*1-55748-001-X*) Barbour & Co.
—Happy Home. Hartley, Al, illus. (gr. 1). 1988. pap. text ed. 1.29 (*1-55748-005-2*) Barbour & Co.
—School Fun. Hartley, Al, illus. (gr. 1). 1988. pap. text ed. 1.29 (*1-55748-003-6*) Barbour & Co.

Hartley, David, ed. Freaky Fillins, No. 3. 48p. (Orig.). (gr. 3-5). 1980. pap. 1.50 (*0-937518-02-6*) Hartley Hse.
Hartley, Deborah. Up North in Winter. Dabcovich, Lydia, illus. 32p. (ps-3). 1986. 11.95 (*0-525-44268-5*, DCB) Dutton Child Bks.
Hartley, Melissa, ed. Freaky Fillins, No. 4. 48p. (Orig.). (gr. 3-5). 1980. pap. 1.50 (*0-937518-03-4*) Hartley Hse.
Haseley, Dennis. The Pirate Who Tried to Capture the Moon. new ed. Truesdell, Sue, illus. LC 82-47734. 64p. (gr. k-4). 1992. pap. 3.95 (*0-06-440420-X*, Trophy) HarpC Child Bks.
Haskins, Jim. Count Your Way Through China. Skoro, Martin, illus. 24p. (gr. 1-4). 1988. pap. 5.95 (*0-87614-486-5*, First Ave Edns) Lerner Pubns.
—Count Your Way Through Japan. (Illus.). 24p. (gr. 1-4). 1987. lib. bdg. 17.50 (*0-87614-301-X*); pap. 4.95 (*0-87614-485-7*) Carolrhoda Bks.
—Count Your Way Through Russia. (Illus.). 24p. (gr. 1-4). 1987. lib. bdg. 17.50 (*0-87614-303-6*); pap. 5.95 (*0-87614-488-1*) Carolrhoda Bks.
—Count Your Way Through the Arab World. Skoro, Martin, illus. 24p. (gr. 1-4). 1988. pap. 5.95 (*0-87614-487-3*, First Ave Edns) Lerner Pubns.
Hathon, Elizabeth. We Go to School. LC 92-80390. (Illus.). 14p. (ps). 1992. bds. 2.99 (*0-679-83377-3*) Random Bks Yng Read.
—We Go to the Zoo. LC 92-80391. (Illus.). 14p. (ps). 1992. bds. 2.99 (*0-679-83376-5*) Random Bks Yng Read.
Hathon, Elizabeth, illus. Sleepy Time. 18p. (ps). 1993. bds. 2.95 (*0-448-40524-5*, G&D) Putnam Pub Group.
Hathon, Elizabeth, photos by. Sharing & Caring. LC 91-62663. (Illus.). 14p. (ps). 1992. bds. 2.99 (*0-679-82226-7*) Random Bks Yng Read.
Haus, Felice. Big Bird Flies Alone. Fritz, Ron, illus. LC 88-62523. 32p. (Orig.). (ps-3). 1989. pap. 1.50 (*0-394-83932-3*) Random Bks Yng Read.
—Happy Birthday, Cookie Monster! A Step One Book. Nicklaus, Carol, illus. LC 85-25639. 32p. (ps-1). 1986. lib. bdg. 7.99 (*0-394-98182-0*); pap. 3.50 (*0-394-88182-6*) Random Bks Yng Read.
Hautzig, Deborah. Big Bird at the Beach. Nicklaus, Carol, illus. LC 89-61613. 32p. (Orig.). (ps-3). 1990. pap. 1.50 (*0-679-80159-6*) Random Bks Yng Read.
—Get Well, Granny Bird. Mathieu, Joe, illus. LC 88-18446. 40p. (ps-3). 1989. 4.95 (*0-394-82247-1*); PLB 6.99 (*0-394-92247-6*) Random Bks Yng Read.
—Happy Mother's Day. Chartler, Normand, illus. LC 88-14002. 32p. (Orig.). (ps-1). 1989. pap. 3.50 (*0-394-82204-8*) Random Bks Yng Read.
—It's a Secret! Leigh, Tom, illus. LC 87-20542. 40p. (ps-3). 1988. 4.95 (*0-394-89672-6*); lib. bdg. 6.99 (*0-394-99672-0*) Random Bks Yng Read.
—It's Easy! Mathieu, Joe, illus. LC 88-6441. 40p. (ps-3). 1988. 4.95 (*0-394-81376-6*) Random Bks Yng Read.
—A Visit to the Sesame Street Library. Mathieu, Joe, illus. LC 85-18312. 32p. (ps-1). 1986. 2.50 (*0-394-87744-6*); lib. bdg. 5.99 (*0-394-97744-0*) Random Bks Yng Read.
Hautzig, Esther. Make It Special: Cards, Decorations, & Party Favors for Holiday & Other Celebrations. Weston, Martha, illus. LC 86-8616. 96p. (gr. 3-7). 1986. SBE 13.95 (*0-02-743370-6*, Macmillan Child Bk) Macmillan Child Grp.
Hawkins, Colin & Hawkins, Jacqui. The Numberlies: Number Nine. (Illus.). 32p. (ps-k). 1993. 8.95 (*0-370-31514-6*, Pub. by Bodley Head UK) Trafalgar.
Hawkins, Colin & Hawkins, Jacqui, eds. I Know an Old Lady Who Swallowed a Fly. Hawkins, Colin & Hawkins, Jacqui, illus. 24p. (ps-1). 1987. 12.95 (*0-399-21484-4*, Putnam) Putnam Pub Group.
Hawthorne, Nathaniel & Andersen, Hans Christian. King Midas & The Emperor's New Clothes. (Illus.). 48p. (ps-3). 1985. 5.95 (*0-88110-253-9*) EDC.
Hayes, Geoffrey. Patrick & Ted Ride the Train: (Just Right for 4's & 5's) Hayes, Geoffrey, illus. LC 88-3084. 32p. (Orig.). (ps-k). 1988. 4.95 (*0-394-89872-9*) Random Bks Yng Read.
—Patrick Goes to Bed. Hayes, Geoffrey, illus. LC 84-6099. 40p. (ps-1). 1985. 4.95 (*0-394-87264-9*) Knopf Bks Yng Read.
Hayes, Sarah. Blancanieves y los Siete Enanitos (Snow White & the Seven Dwarfs) Puncel, Maria, tr. from ENG. Anestey, Caroline, illus. (SPA.). 32p. (gr. 2-4). 1990. Incl. cass. 11.95 (*84-372-8053-2*) Santillana.
—Cenicienta (Cinderella) Puncel, Maria, tr. from ENG. Tomblin, Gill, illus. (SPA.). 32p. (gr. 2-4). 1990. Incl. cass. 11.95 (*84-372-8055-9*) Santillana.
Hayward, Linda. Baby Moses. LC 88-25917. (Illus.). 32p. (Orig.). (ps-1). 1989. PLB 7.99 (*0-394-99410-8*); pap. 3.50 (*0-394-89410-3*) Random Bks Yng Read.
—Elmo Goes to Day Camp. Nicklaus, Carol, illus. LC 89-61614. 32p. (Orig.). 1990. pap. 1.25 (*0-679-80158-8*) Random Bks Yng Read.
—Grover's Summer Vacation. Fritz, Ron, illus. LC 88-62524. 32p. (Orig.). (ps-3). 1989. pap. 1.50 (*0-394-83969-2*) Random Bks Yng Read.
—Hello, House! Munsinger, Lynn, illus. LC 86-22080. 32p. (Orig.). (ps-1). 1988. lib. bdg. 6.99 (*0-394-98864-7*); pap. 3.50 (*0-394-88864-2*) Random Bks Yng Read.
—Mine! A Sesame Street Book about Sharing: (Just Right for 2's & 3's) Gorbaty, Norman, illus. LC 87-42810. 24p. (ps). 1988. 6.00 (*0-394-89599-1*) Random Bks Yng Read.
—Noah's Ark. Wright, Freire, illus. LC 86-17790. 32p. (ps-1). 1987. lib. bdg. 6.99 (*0-394-98716-0*); pap. 3.50 (*0-394-88716-6*) Random Bks Yng Read.
Haywood, Carolyn. Primrose Day. Haywood, Carolyn, illus. LC 86-4620. 200p. (gr. k-3). 1986. pap. 4.95 (*0-15-263510-6*, Voyager Bks) HarBrace.
—Two & Two Are Four. Haywood, Carolyn, illus. LC 86-4619. 171p. (gr. k-3). 1986. pap. 4.95 (*0-15-291771-3*, Voyager Bks) HarBrace.
Hazen, Barbara S. Fang. Morrill, Leslie, illus. LC 86-28697. 32p. (ps-2). 1987. SBE 13.95 (*0-689-31307-1*, Atheneum Child Bk) Macmillan Child Grp.
—The Gorilla Did It. LC 87-23589. (Illus.). 32p. (ps-1). 1988. pap. 3.95 (*0-689-71214-6*, Aladdin) Macmillan Child Grp.
Heap, Sue. Fraser's Grump. (Illus.). 32p. (ps-k). 1994. 17.95 (*1-85681-015-1*, Pub. by J MacRae UK) Trafalgar.
Heesakkers, Wim. My Little Rooster Woodbook. (ps). 1985. 9.95 (*0-8120-5628-0*) Barron.
Hegg, Tom. The Mark of the Maker. Hanson, Warren, illus. 46p. (gr. 4 up). 1991. 10.95 (*0-931674-18-2*) Waldman Hse Pr.
Heine, Helme. The Most Wonderful Egg in the World. Heine, Helme, illus. LC 82-22251. 32p. (gr. k-3). 1987. pap. 4.95 (*0-689-71117-4*, Aladdin) Macmillan Child Grp.
Held, E. R., illus. My Adventure Pack. 12p. (ps-k). 1994. 8.95 (*0-448-40442-7*, G&D) Putnam Pub Group.
—My Little Pocketbook. 12p. (ps). 1994. 8.95 (*0-448-40443-5*, G&D) Putnam Pub Group.
Helldorfer, M. C. Daniel's Gift. Downing, Julie, illus. LC 87-5160. 32p. (ps-3). 1987. RSBE 14.95 (*0-02-743511-3*, Bradbury Pr) Macmillan Child Grp.
Hello God. 8p. (ps). 1985. bds. 3.99 (*0-85648-863-1*) Lion USA.
Hellsing, Lennart. Cantankerous Crow. Stroyer, Paul, illus. (gr. k-3). 1962. 9.95 (*0-8392-3002-8*) Astor-Honor.
Helstrom, David C. My Tacoma Dome. Hamer, Bonnie, illus. 24p. (Orig.). (gr. 1-4). 1983. pap. 2.75 (*0-933992-29-7*) Coffee Break.
—Visiting Mt. Rainier. Harder, Arvid & Hamer, Bonnie, illus. 28p. (Orig.). (gr. 1-4). 1984. pap. 2.75 (*0-933992-37-8*) Coffee Break.
Henderson, Angela. JoJo Meets Scrappy. (Illus.). (ps-3). 1992. write for info. (*1-882185-07-2*) Crnrstone Pub.
Henkes, Kevin. Bailey Goes Camping. (Illus.). 24p. (ps-1). 1989. pap. 3.95 (*0-14-050979-8*, Puffin) Puffin Bks.
—A Weekend with Wendell. (ps-3). 1987. pap. 3.99 (*0-14-050728-0*, Puffin) Puffin Bks.
Hennessy, B. G. The Dinosaur Who Lived in My Backyard. Davis, Susan, illus. LC 87-19867. 32p. (ps-1). 1988. pap. 12.95 (*0-670-81685-X*) Viking Child Bks.
Henny Penny. 24p. (ps-3). 1988. 2.25 (*1-56288-157-4*) Checkerboard.
Henry, Gilson. Animal Squares: An Animal Picture & Rhyme Book for Imaginative Children. Hansen, Ronnie, ed. & illus. LC 87-62123. 24p. (ps-4). 1987. pap. 3.95 (*0-943925-01-0*) Purple Turtle Bks.
—How the Tooth Fairy Got Her Job. Eide, Joyce, illus. LC 87-62126. 24p. (ps-5). 1987. pap. 3.95 (*0-943925-03-7*) Purple Turtle Bks.
Hens. 1989. 3.50 (*0-685-49867-0*) Blue Q.
Hest, Amy. The Crack of Dawn Walkers. Schwartz, Amy, illus. LC 83-19597. 32p. (ps-2). 1984. RSBE 13.95 (*0-02-743710-8*, Macmillan Child Bk) Macmillan Child Grp.
Heuninck, Ronald. A New Day. (Illus.). (ps). 1988. bds. 5.50 (*0-685-25277-9*, 20233) Gryphon Hse.
—Rain or Shine. (Illus.). 12p. (ps). 1990. bds. 5.95 (*0-86315-089-6*, 1361, Pub. by Floris Bks UK) Anthroposophic.
Highlights Editors. Hidden Pictures & Other Challengers. (Illus.). 32p. (Orig.). (gr. 1-6). 1981. pap. 2.95 (*0-87534-227-2*) Highlights.
—Hidden Pictures & Other Fun. (Illus.). 32p. (Orig.). (gr. 1-6). 1981. pap. 2.95 (*0-87534-178-0*) Highlights.
—Hidden Pictures & Other Puzzlers. (Illus.). 32p. (Orig.). (gr. 1-6). 1981. pap. 2.95 (*0-87534-180-2*) Highlights.
Highlights for Children Editors. Rebus Treasury: Forty-Four Stories Kids Can Read by Following the Pictures. LC 90-85899. (Illus.). 48p. (ps-2). 1991. 9.95 (*1-878093-23-1*) Boyds Mills Pr.
Highlights for Children Editors, compiled by. The Jumbo Book of Hidden Pictures. LC 91-72975. (Illus.). 96p. (ps-5). 1992. pap. 4.95 (*1-56397-021-X*) Boyds Mills Pr.
Hill, Eric. Animals. (Illus.). 8p. (ps). 1993. 4.95 (*0-399-22524-2*, Putnam) Putnam Pub Group.
—Ayna Boby. (ARA., Illus.). 24p. (ps-2). 1988. 10.95 (*0-940793-01-6*, Pub. by Crocodile Bks.) Interlink Pub.
—Boby Yath'hab Ilal Madrasa. (ARA., Illus.). 24p. (ps-2). 1988. 10.95 (*0-940793-03-2*, Pub. by Crocodile Bks) Interlink Pub.
—Clothes. (Illus.). 8p. (ps). 1993. 4.95 (*0-399-22521-8*, Putnam) Putnam Pub Group.
—Home. (Illus.). 8p. (ps). 1993. 4.95 (*0-399-22522-6*, Putnam) Putnam Pub Group.
—Khatawat Boby Al- Oula. (ARA., Illus.). 22p. (ps-2). 1988. 10.95 (*0-940793-02-4*, Pub. by Crocodile Bks.) Interlink Pub.
—My Very Own Spot Book: A Special Book to Fill in & Keep. Hill, Eric, illus. 28p. (ps). 1993. 9.95 (*0-399-22601-X*, Putnam) Putnam Pub Group.
—Play. (Illus.). 8p. (ps). 1993. 4.95 (*0-399-22523-4*, Putnam) Putnam Pub Group.
—Spot Counts from One to Ten. Hill, Eric, illus. 14p. (ps-k). 1989. bds. 3.95 (*0-399-21672-3*, Putnam) Putnam Pub Group.
—Spot Goes to School. (ARA & ENG., Illus.). 24p. (ps-2). 1988. 11.95 (*0-940793-06-7*, Pub. by Crocodile Bks.) Interlink Pub.
—Spot Goes to the Circus. Hill, Eric, illus. LC 85-24471. 22p. (ps). 1986. 11.95 (*0-399-21317-1*, Putnam) Putnam Pub Group.
—Spot Learns to Count. Hill, Eric, illus. (ps-2). 1983. 1.95 (*0-399-20985-9*, Putnam) Putnam Pub Group.
—Spot Looks at Colors. Hill, Eric, illus. 14p. (ps-k). 1986. 3.95 (*0-399-21349-X*, Putnam) Putnam Pub Group.
—Spot Looks at Opposites. Hill, Eric, illus. 14p. (ps-k). 1989. bds. 3.75 (*0-399-21681-2*, Putnam) Putnam Pub Group.
—Spot Looks at Shapes. Hill, Eric, illus. 14p. (ps-1). 1986. 3.95 (*0-399-21350-3*, Putnam) Putnam Pub Group.
—Spot Looks at the Weather. Hill, Eric, illus. 14p. (ps-k). 1989. bds. 3.75 (*0-399-21673-1*, Putnam) Putnam Pub Group.
—Spot Va a la Circo (Spot Goes to the Circus) Hill, Eric, illus. (SPA.). 22p. (ps). 1986. 11.95 (*0-399-21318-X*, Putnam) Putnam Pub Group.
—Spot Va a la Granja. (SPA., Illus.). 22p. (ps-1). 1987. 12.95 (*0-399-21463-1*, Putnam) Putnam Pub Group.
—Spot's Alphabet. Hill, Eric, illus. (ps-2). 1983. pap. 1.95 (*0-399-20984-0*, Putnam) Putnam Pub Group.
—Spot's Big Book of Colors, Shapes & Numbers. Hill, Eric, illus. 32p. (ps-k). 1994. 10.95 (*0-399-22679-6*) Putnam Pub Group.
—Spot's Big Book of Words - El Libro Grande de las Palabras de Spot. Hill, Eric, illus. (SPA & ENG.). 32p. (ps-1). 1989. 11.95 (*0-399-21689-8*, Putnam) Putnam Pub Group.
—Spot's Busy Year. Hill, Eric, illus. (ps-2). 1983. pap. 1.95 (*0-399-20987-5*, Putnam) Putnam Pub Group.
—Spot's First Christmas. Hill, Eric, illus. LC 82-23073. (ps-2). 1983. 11.95 (*0-399-20963-8*, Putnam) Putnam Pub Group.
—Spot's First Walk. (ARA & ENG., Illus.). 24p. (ps-2). 1988. 11.95 (*0-940793-05-9*, Pub. by Crocodile Bks) Interlink Pub.
—Spot's First Words. Hill, Eric, illus. 14p. 1986. 3.95 (*0-399-21348-1*, Putnam) Putnam Pub Group.
—Spot's Toy Box. Hill, Eric, illus. (ps-k). 1991. bds. 3.95 (*0-399-21773-8*) Putnam Pub Group.
—Where's Spot? (ENG & ARA., Illus.). 24p. (ps-2). 1988. 11.95 (*0-940793-04-0*, Pub. by Crocodile Bks) Interlink Pub.
—Where's Spot? (Illus.). 22p. (ps-1). 1980. 11.95 (*0-399-20758-9*, Putnam) Putnam Pub Group.
—Where's Spot? A Lift-the-Flap Book Miniature Edition. Hill, Eric, illus. 22p. (ps-k). 1990. 4.95 (*0-399-21822-X*, Putnam) Putnam Pub Group.
Hill, Tom & Friedman, Donna. Pat the Stimpy: A Nitty Gritty Touchy Smelly Book. Reccardi, Chris, illus. 14p. (gr. 3 up). 1993. 9.95 (*0-448-40199-1*, G&D) Putnam Pub Group.
Hilleary, Jane K. Fletcher & the Great Big Dog. Brown, Richard, illus. 32p. (gr. k-3). 1988. 13.45 (*0-395-46761-6*) HM.
Hillert, Margaret. Guess, Guess. O'Connell, Ruth, illus. 24p. (gr. k-1). 1988. 4.99 (*0-87403-456-6*, 24-03695) Standard Pub.
—Jesus Grows Up. Endres, Helen, illus. 24p. (gr. k-1). 1988. 4.99 (*0-87403-459-0*, 24-03698) Standard Pub.
Himmelman, John. Amanda & the Witch Switch. (ps-3). 1987. pap. 4.99 (*0-14-050635-7*, Puffin) Puffin Bks.
Hindley, Judy & Reyes, Gregg. Once There Was a Knight & You Can Be One too! Bartelt, Robert, illus. LC 87-20485. 32p. (ps-2). 1988. lib. bdg. 5.99 (*0-394-99007-2*) Random Bks Yng Read.
Hines, Anna G. I'll Tell You What They Say. Hines, Anna G., illus. LC 86-4743. 24p. (ps-1). 1987. 11.75 (*0-688-06486-8*); PLB 11.88 (*0-688-06487-6*) Greenwillow.
Hippo. 1989. 3.50 (*1-87865-732-1*) Blue Q.
Hirashima, Jean. The ABC Block Book. Hirashima, Jean, illus. 22p. (ps). 1994. 3.25 (*0-679-83712-4*) Random Bks Yng Read.
Hirsh, Marilyn. Joseph Who Loved the Sabbath. Grebu, Devis, illus. 32p. (ps-3). 1988. pap. 3.95 (*0-14-050670-5*, Puffin) Puffin Bks.
Hissey, Jane. The Jane Hissey Collection, 3 bks. (Illus.). 96p. 1991. Set. slipcase 14.95 (*0-399-21758-4*, Philomel Bks) Putnam Pub Group.
—Little Bear Lost. Hissey, Jane, illus. 32p. (ps-1). 1989. 14.95 (*0-399-21743-6*, Philomel Bks) Putnam Pub Group.
—Old Bear Birthday Book. 128p. (gr. 1 up). 1990. 9.95 (*0-8120-6154-3*) Barron.
Hoban, Julia. Amy Loves the Sun. Hoban, Lillian, illus. LC 87-45987. 24p. (ps). 1988. HarpC Child Bks.
Hoban, Lillian. Arthur's Christmas Cookies. Hoban, Lillian, illus. LC 72-76596. 64p. (gr. k-3). 1986. incl. cassette 5.98 (*0-694-00160-0*, Trophy); pap. 3.50 (*0-06-444055-9*, Trophy) HarpC Child Bks.
—Arthur's Funny Money. Hoban, Lillian, illus. LC 80-7903. 64p. (gr. k-3). 1987. incl. cassette 5.98 (*0-694-00173-2*, Trophy); pap. 3.50 (*0-06-444048-6*, Trophy) HarpC Child Bks.
—Arthur's Honey Bear. Hoban, Lillian, illus. LC 73-14324. 64p. (gr. k-3). 1986. incl. cassette 5.98 (*0-694-00116-3*, Trophy); pap. 3.50 (*0-06-444033-8*, Trophy) HarpC Child Bks.

Hoban, Russell. Baby Sister for Frances. Hoban, Lillian, illus. LC 92-32603. 32p. (ps-3). 1964. 15.00 (*0-06-022335-9*); PLB 14.89 (*0-06-022336-7*) HarpC Child Bks.
—Bargain for Frances. Hoban, Lillian, illus. LC 91-12265. 64p. (gr. k-3). 1970. 14.00 (*0-06-022329-4*); PLB 13.89 (*0-06-022330-8*) HarpC Child Bks.
—Bedtime for Frances. Williams, Garth, illus. LC 60-8347. 32p. (gr. k-3). 1960. 14.00 (*0-06-022350-2*); PLB 13.89 (*0-06-022351-0*) HarpC Child Bks.
—Best Friends for Frances. Hoban, Lillian, illus. LC 92-38401. 32p. (ps-3). 1969. 15.00 (*0-06-022327-8*); PLB 14.89 (*0-06-022328-6*) HarpC Child Bks.
—Birthday for Frances. Hoban, Lillian, illus. LC 68-24321. 32p. (gr. k-3). 1968. 15.00 (*0-06-022338-3*); PLB 14.89 (*0-06-022339-1*) HarpC Child Bks.
—Bread & Jam for Frances. Hoban, Lillian, illus. LC 92-13622. 32p. (ps-3). 1965. 15.00 (*0-06-022359-6*); PLB 14.89 (*0-06-022360-X*) HarpC Child Bks.
Hoban, Tana. A Children's Zoo. Hoban, Tana, illus. LC 84-25318. 24p. (ps-1). 1985. 15.00 (*0-688-05202-9*); lib. bdg. 14.93 (*0-688-05204-5*) Greenwillow.
—A Children's Zoo. LC 84-25318. (Illus.). 24p. (ps up). 1987. pap. text ed. 4.95 (*0-688-07044-2*, Mulberry) Morrow.
—Dots, Spots, Speckles, & Stripes. (ps-3). 1987. 14.00 (*0-688-06862-6*); PLB 13.93 (*0-688-06863-4*) Greenwillow.
—I Read Signs. LC 83-1482. (Illus.). 32p. (ps up). 1987. pap. 4.95 (*0-688-07331-X*, Mulberry) Morrow.
—Is It Red? Is It Yellow? Is It Blue? LC 78-2549. (Illus.). 32p. (ps up). 1987. pap. 4.95 (*0-688-07034-5*, Mulberry) Morrow.
—Look Again! LC 72-127469. 40p. (ps-1). 1971. SBE 13.95 (*0-02-744050-8*, Macmillan Child Bk) Macmillan Child Grp.
—Look! Look! Look! Hoban, Tana, illus. LC 87-25655. 40p. (ps-1). 1988. 15.00 (*0-688-07239-9*); lib. bdg. 14.93 (*0-688-07240-2*) Greenwillow.
—Take Another Look. LC 80-21342. (Illus.). 32p. (ps-3). 1981. PLB 15.93 (*0-688-84298-4*) Greenwillow.
—Tana Hoban's Red, Blue, Yellow Shoe. (Illus.). 8p. (ps up). 1994. bath bk. 3.95 (*0-688-13492-0*, Tupelo Bks) Morrow.
—Tana Hoban's What Is It? (Illus.). 8p. (ps up). 1994. bath bk. 3.95 (*0-688-13493-9*, Tupelo Bks) Morrow.
—What Is It? Hoban, Tana, illus. LC 84-13483. 12p. (ps). 1985. bds. 4.95 (*0-688-02577-3*) Greenwillow.
Hoban, Tana, illus. Shapes & Things. LC 70-102965. 32p. (ps-2). 1970. 13.95 (*0-02-744060-5*, Macmillan Child Bk) Macmillan Child Grp.
Hoberman, Mary A. A House Is a House for Me. Fraser, Betty, illus. LC 77-15518. (gr. k-3). 1978. pap. 14.00 (*0-670-38016-4*) Viking Child Bks.
Hofer, Angelika. The Lion Family Book. Ziesler, Gunter, illus. LC 88-15139. 52p. (gr. k up). 1991. pap. 15.95 (*0-88708-070-7*) Picture Bk Studio.
Hoff, Syd. Grizzwold. LC 63-14366. (Illus.). 64p. (gr. k-3). 1984. pap. 3.50 (*0-06-444057-5*, Trophy) HarpC Child Bks.
—Little Chief. Hoff, Syd, illus. LC 61-12098. 64p. (gr. k-3). 1990. pap. 3.50 (*0-06-444135-0*, Trophy) HarpC Child Bks.
—Who Will Be My Friends? Hoff, Syd, illus. LC 60-14096. 32p. (ps-2). 1985. pap. 3.50 (*0-06-444072-9*, Trophy) HarpC Child Bks.
Hoffman, Phyllis. We Play. Wilson, Sarah, illus. LC 89-36381. 32p. (ps). 1990. HarpC Child Bks.
Hoffmann, E. T. The Strange Child. Zweger, Lisbeth, illus. LC 84-8404. 28p. (gr. 3 up). 1991. pap. 16.95 (*0-907234-60-7*) Picture Bk Studio.
Hofman, Ginnie. The Runaway Teddy Bear. Hofman, Ginnie, illus. LC 84-23740. 32p. (ps-3). 1986. pap. 2.25 (*0-394-86286-4*) Random Bks Yng Read.
Hogrogian, Nonny. One Fine Day. Hogrogian, Nonny, illus. LC 75-119834. 32p. (gr. k-3). 1974. pap. 4.95 (*0-02-043620-3*, Aladdin) Macmillan Child Grp.
—One Fine Day. LC 75-119834. (Illus.). 32p. (gr. k-3). 1971. RSBE 14.95 (*0-02-744000-1*, Macmillan Child Bk) Macmillan Child Grp.
Holcomb, Nan. Andy Finds a Turtle. Yoder, Dot, illus. 32p. (Orig.). (ps-2). 1988. pap. 6.95 (*0-944727-02-6*) Jason & Nordic Pubs.
—Danny & the Merry-Go-Round. Lucia, Virginia, illus. 32p. (Orig.). 1988. pap. 6.95 (*0-944727-00-X*) Jason & Nordic Pubs.
—How About A Hug. Taggart, Tricia, illus. 32p. (Orig.). (ps). 1988. pap. 6.95 (*0-944727-01-8*) Jason & Nordic Pubs.
Holden, L. Dwight. Gran-Gran's Best Trick: A Story for Children Who Have Lost Someone They Love. Chesworth, Michael, illus. LC 89-8336. 48p. 1989. 16.95 (*0-945354-19-3*); pap. 6.95 (*0-945354-16-9*) Magination Pr.
Holden, Queen. Best Friends-Paper Dolls in Full Color. 1985. pap. 3.50 (*0-486-24973-5*) Dover.
Holder, Heidi, illus. Crows: An Old Rhyme. LC 87-45364. 32p. (ps up). 1987. 14.95 (*0-374-31660-0*) FS&G.
Holl, Adelaide. Rain Puddle. Duvoisin, Roger, illus. LC 65-22026. 32p. (gr. k-3). 1965. PLB 15.93 (*0-688-51096-5*) Lothrop.
Hollow, Fern. All in a Day. (Illus.). (ps-1). 1985. 2.98 (*0-517-48288-6*) Random Hse Value.
Holmes, Efner T. Amy's Goose. Tudor, Tasha, illus. LC 85-45391. 32p. (ps-3). 1986. pap. 5.95 (*0-06-443091-X*, Trophy) HarpC Child Bks.
Home. (Illus.). (ps). 3.50 (*0-7214-1097-9*) Ladybird Bks.
Hooks, William A., et al. Let's Get Dressed! Bank Street College Media Group, ed. Schick, Joel, illus. 32p. (Orig.). (ps). 1986. write for info. (*0-9617460-0-9*) Levi Strauss.
Hooks, William H. The Three Little Pigs & the Fox. Schindler, S. D., illus. LC 88-29296. 32p. (gr. k-3). 1989. RSBE 14.95 (*0-02-744431-7*, Macmillan Child Bk) Macmillan Child Grp.
Hooper, Meredith. Seven Eggs. reissued ed. McKenna, Terry, illus. 24p. (ps-1). 1986. 5.95 (*0-694-00144-9*) HarpC Child Bks.
Hoopes, Lyn L. Mommy, Daddy, Me. Bornstein, Ruth L., illus. LC 87-45286. 32p. (ps-2). 1988. HarpC Child Bks.
Hopkins, Lee B. Surprises. Lloyd, Megan, illus. LC 83-47712. 64p. (gr. k-3). 1986. pap. 3.50 (*0-06-444105-9*, Trophy) HarpC Child Bks.
La Hora de la Comida. (SPA., Illus.). 12p. (ps). 1992. bds. 4.95 (*0-525-44855-1*, DCB) Dutton Child Bks.
La Hora del Bano. (SPA., Illus.). 12p. (ps). 1992. bds. 4.95 (*0-525-44857-8*, DCB) Dutton Child Bks.
Horan, Stephen F., Sr. Baby Boo. 1994. 7.95 (*0-533-10753-9*) Vantage.
Horning, Robert, illus. My Pop-up Photo Book. Costello, Linda, contrib. by. LC 90-85727. (Illus.). 8p. (ps-1). 1991. 10.95 (*1-878093-05-3*) Boyds Mills Pr.
How to Make Bubbles. 1992. pap. 9.99 (*0-553-07887-9*) Bantam.
Howard, Elizabeth F. Chita's Christmas Tree. Cooper, Floyd, illus. LC 88-26250. 32p. (ps-2). 1989. RSBE 14.95 (*0-02-744621-2*, Bradbury Pr) Macmillan Child Grp.
Howl-Oween Party Pop-up Storybook. 10p. (ps-3). 1990. 3.95 (*0-8167-2186-6*) Troll Assocs.
Huang, Benrei, illus. Boo! Guess Who? LC 89-61374. 14p. (ps). 1990. bds. 3.99 (*0-679-80278-9*) Random Bks Yng Read.
Hudson, Cheryl W. Afro-Bets A B C Book. Hudson, Cheryl W., illus. LC 87-81580. 24p. (ps-3). 1987. pap. 3.95 (*0-940975-00-9*) Just Us Bks.
—Afro-Bets 1 2 3 Book. Hudson, Cheryl W., illus. LC 87-82952. 24p. (ps-3). 1988. pap. 3.95 (*0-940975-01-7*) Just Us Bks.
—Good Morning Baby. (Illus.). 1992. bds. 5.95 (*0-590-45760-8*, Cartwheel) Scholastic Inc.
—Good Night Baby. Ford, George, illus. 1992. bds. 5.95 (*0-590-45761-6*, Cartwheel) Scholastic Inc.
Hugh Pine. 96p. (ps-1). 1983. pap. 2.50 (*0-553-15558-X*, Skylark) Bantam.
Hughes, Barbara & Dwiggins, Gwen. God Loves Children. Dow, Bonnie, illus. (ps-3). 1987. 0.99 (*0-8091-6562-7*) Paulist Pr.
—God Loves Colors. Dow, Bonnie, illus. (ps-3). 1987. 0.99 (*0-8091-6566-X*) Paulist Pr.
—God Loves Fun. Dow, Bonnie, illus. (ps-3). 1987. 0.99 (*0-8091-6564-3*) Paulist Pr.
—God Loves Love. Dow, Bonnie, illus. (ps-3). 1987. 0.99 (*0-8091-6565-1*) Paulist Pr.
—God Loves Seasons. Dow, Bonnie, illus. (ps-3). 1987. 0.99 (*0-8091-6563-5*) Paulist Pr.
Hughes, Shirley. Alfie Gives a Hand. Hughes, Shirley, illus. LC 83-14883. 32p. (ps-1). 1984. 12.95 (*0-688-02386-X*); PLB 14.88 (*0-688-02387-8*) Lothrop.
—Alfie's Feet. LC 82-13012. (Illus.). 32p. (ps up). 1988. pap. 3.95 (*0-688-07812-5*, Mulberry) Morrow.
—All Shapes & Sizes. LC 86-2734. (Illus.). 24p. (ps). 1986. 4.95 (*0-688-04205-8*) Lothrop.
—Angel Mae: A Tale of Trotter Street. Hughes, Shirley, illus. LC 89-45288. 32p. (ps-1). 1989. 12.95 (*0-688-08538-5*); PLB 12.88 (*0-688-08539-3*) Lothrop.
—Colors. LC 86-2732. (Illus.). 24p. (ps). 1986. 4.95 (*0-688-04206-6*) Lothrop.
—Lucy & Tom's Christmas. (ps-1). 1987. pap. 4.95 (*0-14-050698-5*, Puffin) Puffin Bks.
—Two Shoes, New Shoes. LC 86-2733. (Illus.). 24p. (ps). 1986. 4.95 (*0-688-04207-4*) Lothrop.
Hulbert, Jay. The Bedtime Beast. (Illus.). 32p. (gr. 1-4). 1989. PLB 18.99 (*0-8172-3516-7*); pap. 3.95 (*0-8114-6712-0*) Raintree Steck-V.
Hurd, Edith T. Day the Sun Danced. Hurd, Clement, illus. LC 64-16641. 32p. (gr. k-3). 1966. PLB 13.89 (*0-06-022692-7*) HarpC Child Bks.
—Johnny Lion's Book. Hurd, Clement, illus. LC 65-14490. 64p. (gr. k-3). 1965. PLB 13.89 (*0-06-022706-0*) HarpC Child Bks.
Hurd, Thacher. Axle the Freeway Cat. Hurd, Thacher, illus. LC 80-8432. 32p. (ps-3). 1988. pap. 3.95 (*0-06-443173-8*, Trophy) HarpC Child Bks.
—Mama Don't Allow. Hurd, Thacher, illus. LC 83-47703. 40p. (ps-3). 1985. pap. 4.95 (*0-06-443078-2*, Trophy) HarpC Child Bks.
—Mystery on the Docks. Hurd, Thacher, illus. LC 82-48261. 32p. (gr. k-3). 1984. pap. 4.95 (*0-06-443058-8*, Trophy) HarpC Child Bks.
Hutchins, Pat. Changes, Changes. Hutchins, Pat, illus. LC 86-22331. 32p. (ps-1). 1987. pap. 4.95 (*0-689-71137-9*, Aladdin) Macmillan Child Grp.
—Good-Night, Owl! Hutchins, Pat, illus. LC 72-186355. 32p. (ps-2). 1972. RSBE 14.95 (*0-02-745900-4*, Macmillan Child Bk) Macmillan Child Grp.
—Rosie's Walk. Hutchins, Pat, illus. LC 68-12090. 32p. (ps-1). 1968. RSBE 14.95 (*0-02-745850-4*, Macmillan Child Bk) Macmillan Child Grp.
—The Surprise Party. reissued ed. LC 86-7255. (Illus.). 32p. (ps-3). 1986. RSBE 14.95 (*0-02-745930-6*, Macmillan Child Bk) Macmillan Child Grp.
—The Very Worst Monster. LC 84-5928. (Illus.). 32p. (gr. k up). 1988. pap. 3.95 (*0-688-07816-8*, Mulberry) Morrow.
Hutton, Warwick. Theseus & the Minotaur. Hutton, Warwick, illus. LC 88-26875. 32p. (gr. 1-5). 1989. SBE 14.95 (*0-689-50473-X*, M K McElderry) Macmillan Child Grp.
Hutton, Warwick, retold by. & illus. The Trojan Horse. LC 91-21590. 32p. (gr. 2 up). 1992. SBE 14.95 (*0-689-50542-6*, M K McElderry) Macmillan Child Grp.
Hyman, Jane. Gumby Book of Colors. LC 86-6222. (Illus.). 32p. (ps-3). 1986. 5.95 (*0-385-23454-6*); PLB 5.95 (*0-385-23845-2*) Doubleday.
—Gumby Book of Letters. LC 86-6216. (Illus.). 32p. (ps-3). 1986. 5.95 (*0-685-38408-X*); PLB 5.97 (*0-685-38409-8*) Doubleday.
—Gumby Book of Shapes. LC 86-6194. (Illus.). 32p. (ps-3). 1986. 5.95 (*0-385-23453-8*); PLB 5.95 (*0-385-23848-7*) Doubleday.
I Am an Owl. 24p. (ps-k). 1989. 9.95 (*0-448-21027-4*, G&D) Putnam Pub Group.
I Can See, Hear, Smell, Taste & Touch. (Illus.). (ps). 1985. bds. 3.98 (*0-517-47340-2*) Random Hse Value.
I Learn Letters: A Jumbo Board Book. (Illus.). 16p. (ps-1). 1987. pap. 5.95 (*0-553-18351-6*) Bantam.
I Learn Numbers: A Jumbo Board Book. (Illus.). 16p. (ps-1). 1987. 5.95 (*0-553-18350-8*) Bantam.
I'm a Little Baby. (ps). 1982. pap. 2.95 vinyl (*0-671-44567-7*, Little Simon) S&S Trade.
I'm a Little Choo-Choo. (ps). 1982. pap. 3.95 vinyl (*0-671-44568-5*, Little Simon) S&S Trade.
Immel, Mary B. No Longer Sings the Brown Thrush. 208p. (Orig.). (gr. 4-8). 1988. pap. 7.99 (*0-8272-2509-1*) Chalice Pr.
In the Yard, What Can You Find? (ps). 1993. bds. 4.95 (*1-56458-267-1*) Dorling Kindersley.
Indoor Things. (ps-k). 3.95 (*0-7214-5141-1*) Ladybird Bks.
Ingle, Annie. Don't Wake the Animals. Barrett, Peter, illus. LC 91-67720. 14p. (ps-k). 1992. bds. 3.99 (*0-679-83433-8*) Random Bks Yng Read.
—Zoo Animals. LC 91-66561. (Illus.). 28p. (ps). 1992. 3.25 (*0-679-83070-7*) Random Bks Yng Read.
Ingoglia, Gina. Disney's the Lion King Mask Book. (Illus.). 26p. 1994. pap. 12.95 (*0-7868-4007-2*) Disney Pr.
—Those Mysterious Dinosaurs. (Illus.). 24p. (ps-k). 1989. pap. write for info. (*0-307-11747-2*, Pub. by Golden Bks) Western Pub.
Insects & Other Arthropods Activity Book. (Illus.). (ps-6). pap. 2.95 (*0-565-01099-9*, Pub. by Natural Hist Mus) Parkwest Pubns.
Inspector Gadget: Coloring-Activity Book. (ps-3). 1993. pap. 2.50 (*0-8167-3034-2*) Troll Assocs.
Intervisional Communications Staff. Viking Circus Block Books: Circus Parade Zoo-A Book in-a-Box with a Performing Picture, 3 vols. LC 83-80225. (Illus.). (gr. 1-5). 1983. Set. 10.95 (*0-685-42583-5*) Viking Child Bks.
Isaak, Betty. Perception Panda. Armstrong, Bev, illus. 24p. (ps). 1982. wkbk. 2.95 (*0-88160-088-1*, LW 122) Learning Wks.
Isadora, Rachel. Ben's Trumpet. Isadora, Rachel, illus. LC 78-12885. 32p. (gr. k-3). 1979. 14.00 (*0-688-80194-3*) Greenwillow.
—Ben's Trumpet. LC 79-12885. (Illus.). 32p. (ps up). 1991. pap. 4.95 (*0-688-10988-8*, Mulberry) Morrow.
—I Touch. Isadora, Rachel, illus. LC 84-13673. 32p. (ps). 1985. 15.00 (*0-688-04255-4*); lib. bdg. 14.93 (*0-688-04256-2*) Greenwillow.
Isami, Ikuyo. The Fox's Egg. Isami, Ikuyo, illus. 40p. (ps-2). 1989. 18.95 (*0-87614-339-7*) Carolrhoda Bks.
Ishikawa, Eiko, illus. Mother Goose. 16p. (ps). 1992. pap. 4.95 (*0-671-77012-8*, Little Simon) S&S Trade.
—What's Inside? 16p. (ps). 1992. pap. 4.95 (*0-671-77017-9*, Little Simon) S&S Trade.
—Where Is Kitty? 16p. (ps). 1992. pap. 4.95 (*0-671-77018-7*, Little Simon) S&S Trade.
—Who Lives Here? 16p. (ps). 1992. pap. 4.95 (*0-671-77023-3*, Little Simon) S&S Trade.
Ivanovsky, Elisabeth. Things in My House. (Illus.). (ps). 1985. bds. 3.98 (*0-517-47341-0*) Random Hse Value.
—What Color Is It. (Illus.). (ps). 1985. bds. 3.98 (*0-517-47342-9*) Random Hse Value.
—What Time Is It? (Illus.). (ps). 1985. bds. 3.98 (*0-517-47343-7*) Random Hse Value.
Ives, Penny. My Nursery Book. (Illus.). 64p. 1991. 6.99 (*0-517-05399-3*) Random Hse Value.
Ivimey, John W. The Complete Story of the Three Blind Mice. Galdone, Paul, illus. LC 87-689. 32p. (ps). 1989. pap. 5.95 (*0-395-51585-8*, Clarion Bks) HM.
Jabar, Cynthia. Party Day! Jabar, Cynthia, illus. (ps-1). 1987. 11.95 (*0-316-43456-6*, Joy St Bks) Little.
Jackson, Bobby L. Pops, Chops, & Crops. 2nd ed. King, Kevin, illus. LC 89-51297. 32p. (gr. k-4). 1994. 9.95g (*0-9634932-4-8*); pap. 5.95g (*0-9634932-5-6*) Multicult Pubns.
Jacob, Ellen. Great Skaters Learn-by-Coloring Book: Famous Figures of the Sport & Their Inspiring Stories. (Illus.). 48p. (ps-7). 1991. pap. 4.95 (*0-937180-07-6*) Variety Arts.
—Nutcracker Learn-by-Coloring Book: Scenes from the Best Loved Ballet of All Times. (Illus.). 48p. (Orig.). (ps-7). 1991. pap. 4.95 (*0-937180-09-2*) Variety Arts.
—Stars of the Ballet. (Illus.). 48p. (ps-7). 1991. pap. 4.95 (*0-937180-06-8*) Variety Arts.

—Story of Gymnastics. (Illus.). 48p. (ps-7). 1991. pap. 4.95 (*0-937180-08-4*) Variety Arts.

Jaffrey, Madhur. Seasons of Splendor. Foreman, Michael, illus. (ps up). pap. 7.95 (*0-317-62172-6*, Puffin) Puffin Bks.

James, Betsy. The Dream Stair. Watson, Richard J., illus. LC 89-36420. 32p. (gr. k-2). 1990. PLB 13.89 (*0-06-022788-5*) HarpC Child Bks.

James, Robin. Baby Farm Animals. 8p. (ps-1). 1983. 3.95 (*0-8431-0739-1*) Price Stern.

—Baby Forest Animals. 8p. (ps-1). 1983. bds. 3.95 (*0-8431-0738-3*) Price Stern.

James, Sara. Boots Loses a Tooth. Barcita, Pamela, illus. 7p. 1993. 4.98 (*1-56156-126-6*) Kidsbks.

—Boots Plays Hide & Seek. Barcita, Pamela, illus. 7p. 1993. 4.98 (*1-56156-127-4*) Kidsbks.

—Boots Plays Hide & Seek. Barcita, Pamela, illus. 14p. (ps-k). 1993. 4.98 (*0-8317-0607-4*) Smithmark.

—What Does Boots Hear? Barcita, Pamela, illus. 6p. 1993. 2.98 (*1-56156-129-0*) Kidsbks.

—What Does Boots Hear? Barcita, Pamela, illus. 12p. (ps). 1993. 2.98 (*0-8317-9606-5*) Smithmark.

—What Does Boots See? Barcita, Pamela, illus. 6p. 1993. 2.98 (*1-56156-128-2*) Kidsbks.

—What Does Boots See? Barcita, Pamela, illus. 12p. (ps). 1993. 2.98 (*0-8317-9605-7*) Smithmark.

—What Does Boots Smell? Barcita, Pamela, illus. 6p. 1993. PLB 2.98 (*1-56156-130-4*) Kidsbks.

—What Does Boots Smell? Barcita, Pamela, illus. 12p. (ps). 1993. 2.98 (*0-8317-9607-3*) Smithmark.

—What Does Boots Touch? Barcita, Pamela, illus. 6p. 1993. PLB 2.98 (*1-56156-131-2*) Kidsbks.

—What Does Boots Touch? Barcita, Pamela, illus. 12p. (ps). 1993. 2.98 (*0-8317-9608-1*) Smithmark.

Janovitz, Marilyn. Hey Diddle Diddle. LC 91-26483. (Illus.). 32p. (ps-k). 1992. 6.95 (*1-56282-168-7*); PLB 6.89 (*1-56282-169-5*) Hyprn Child.

—Look Out, Bird! LC 93-38765. (Illus.). 32p. (ps-k). 1994. 14.95 (*1-55858-249-5*); PLB 14.88 (*1-55858-250-9*) North-South Bks NYC.

—Pat-a-Cake. Janovitz, Marilyn, adapted by. LC 91-26950. (Illus.). 32p. (ps-k). 1992. 6.95 (*1-56282-170-9*); PLB 6.89 (*1-56282-171-7*) Hyprn Child.

Javernick, Ellen. What If Everybody Did That? Hackney, Richard, illus. LC 89-28625. 32p. (ps-3). 1990. PLB 11.45 (*0-516-03669-6*); pap. 3.95 (*0-516-43669-4*) Childrens.

Jean, Priscilla. Pattie Round & Wally Square. Jean, Priscilla, illus. (gr. k-3). 1965. 8.95 (*0-8392-3048-6*) Astor-Honor.

Jeffers, Susan. The Three Jovial Huntsmen. Jeffers, Susan, illus. LC 88-32708. 32p. (ps-2). 1989. pap. 3.95 (*0-689-71309-6*, Aladdin) Macmillan Child Grp.

Jemima Puddle-Duck. (Illus.). (ps-2). 1989. 1.95 (*0-7214-5218-3*) Ladybird Bks.

Jensen, Kent W. Slippers & Wraparound Wraps. Traba, Henry & Faigin, Cecilia, illus. 41p. (ps-2). 1988. pap. 7.95 (*0-9621024-0-7*) K Jensen.

Jeschke, Susan. Perfect the Pig. Jeschke, Susan, illus. LC 80-39998. 48p. (ps-2). 1981. 14.95 (*0-8050-0704-0*, Bks Young Read) H Holt & Co.

Jessie Willcox Smith Mother Goose. (ps up). 1986. 7.98 (*0-685-16881-6*, 603578) Random Hse Value.

Johnson, Allen, Jr. Picker McClikker. Hanson, Stephen, illus. (gr. k-3). 1993. 16.95 (*1-878561-20-0*) Seacoast AL.

Johnson, B. J. Baa Baa Book. (Illus.). 12p. (ps). 1993. pap. 3.50 (*0-671-86530-7*, Little Simon) S&S Trade.

—Baby Bubbles. (ps). 1994. pap. 3.50 (*0-671-88606-1*, Little Simon) S&S Trade.

—Baby Giggles. (ps). 1994. pap. 3.50 (*0-671-88605-3*, Little Simon) S&S Trade.

—Beddy Bye. (Illus.). 12p. (ps). 1993. pap. 3.50 (*0-671-86533-1*, Little Simon) S&S Trade.

—I Twirl. (Illus.). 12p. (ps). 1993. pap. 3.50 (*0-671-86531-5*, Little Simon) S&S Trade.

—On a Blossom. (Illus.). 12p. (ps). 1993. pap. 3.50 (*0-671-86532-3*, Little Simon) S&S Trade.

—Teeney Poppers: Baby Hugs. (ps). 1994. pap. 3.50 (*0-671-88604-5*, Little Simon) S&S Trade.

—Teeney Poppers: Baby Joys. (ps). 1994. pap. 3.50 (*0-671-88603-7*, Little Simon) S&S Trade.

Johnson, Crockett. Harold & the Purple Crayon. Johnson, Crockett, illus. LC 55-7683. (gr. k-3). 1958. 12.00 (*0-06-022935-7*); PLB 11.89 (*0-06-022936-5*) HarpC Child Bks.

—Harold's Trip to the Sky. Johnson, Crockett, illus. LC 57-9262. (gr. k-3). 1957. PLB 13.89 (*0-06-022986-1*) HarpC Child Bks.

—Will Spring Be Early or Will Spring Be Late? Johnson, Crockett, illus. LC 59-9424. 48p. (gr. k-3). 1961. PLB 13.89 (*0-690-89423-6*, Crowell Jr Bks) HarpC Child Bks.

Johnson, George C., illus. Baby's First Words. 20p. (ps-1). 1986. bds. 4.95 (*0-448-03093-4*, G&D) Putnam Pub Group.

Johnson, Odette & Johnson, Bruce. One Prickly Porcupine. (Illus.). 32p. (ps up). 1992. laminated boards 13.95 (*0-19-540834-9*) OUP.

Johnson, Ryerson. Why Is Baby Crying? Tucker, Kathy, ed. DiSalvo-Ryan, DyAnne, illus. LC 89-5380. 32p. (ps-2). 1989. PLB 13.95 (*0-8075-9084-3*) A Whitman.

Johnson, Sue. Popsicles Are Cold: Storybook for Young Children in Sign Languages. Herigstad, Joni, illus. 30p. (Orig.). (ps-3). 1984. pap. 4.75 (*0-916708-12-8*) Modern Signs.

Johnson, Susan. Erte Fashion Paper Dolls of the Twenties. 1979. pap. 3.95 (*0-486-23627-7*) Dover.

Johnson, William R. Color Monkeys. Johnson, Pauline, ed. (Illus.). 48p. (ps-2). 1989. write for info. (*0-936917-05-9*, B608) Blip Prods.

—Dinosaurs & Other Prehistorics. Johnson, Pauline D., ed. Johnson, William R., illus. 48p. (gr. 3-6). 1986. pap. 4.95 (*0-936917-02-4*, B606) Blip Prods.

—Kids of the World: Cursive. Johnson, Pauline D., ed. Johnson, William R., illus. 48p. (gr. 3-6). 1986. pap. 4.95 (*0-936917-01-6*, B604) Blip Prods.

—Kids of the World: Manuscript. Johnson, Pauline D., ed. Johnson, William R., illus. 48p. (Orig.). (ps-2). 1986. pap. 4.95 (*0-936917-00-8*, B603) Blip Prods.

—Monthly Calendars. Johnson, Pauline, ed. (Illus.). 48p. (gr. k-4). 1989. write for info. (*0-936917-04-0*, B607) Blip Prods.

—Numbers One to Twenty: The Circus & the Bees. Johnson, Pauline D., ed. Johnson, William R., illus. 48p. (ps-2). 1986. pap. 4.95 (*0-936917-03-2*, B605) Blip Prods.

Johnston, Norma. The Delphic Choice. LC 88-24570. 208p. (gr. 7 up). 1989. SBE 14.95 (*0-02-747711-8*, Four Winds) Macmillan Child Grp.

Johnston, S. Paper Doll-Godey Fashion. 1979. pap. 3.95 (*0-486-23511-4*) Dover.

Jolly, Christopher. The Animal Jiglets. Stephen, Lib, illus. (ps-1). 1994. 11.95 (*1-870946-33-2*, Pub. by Jolly Lrning UK) Am Intl Dist.

—The Stencilets. Stephen, Lib, illus. (ps-1). 1994. 14.95 (*1-870946-35-9*, Pub. by Jolly Lrning UK) Am Intl Dist.

—The Vehicle Jiglets. Stephen, Lib, illus. (ps-1). 1994. 11. 95 (*1-870946-34-0*, Pub. by Jolly Lrning UK) Am Intl Dist.

Jonas, Ann. Reflections. LC 86-33545. (Illus.). 24p. (gr. k-3). 1987. 15.00 (*0-688-06140-0*); lib. bdg. 14.93 (*0-688-06141-9*) Greenwillow.

Jones, Carolyn E. The Lottie Moon Storybook. Ellis, Debbie, illus. 20p. (Orig.). (gr. k-4). 1984. pap. 1.25x (*0-9616996-0-4*) Honor Pub.

Jones, Kathleen I. I Am This & More, Bk. 1. Jones, Kert, illus. 12p. (ps-5). 1989. write for info. (*0-9624790-0-4*) Kindle Bks.

Jones, Malcolm. Jump! An HBJ Book & Musical Cassette. Goldberg, Whoopi, narrated by. Parks, Van D., contrib. by. (Illus.). 32p. (gr. 1-5). 1990. 19.95 (*0-15-241351-0*) HarBrace.

Jones, Rebecca. The Biggest (& Best) Flag That Ever Flew. Geer, Charles, illus. LC 87-40609. 32p. (gr. k-4). 1988. 8.95 (*0-87033-381-X*) Tidewater.

Jones, Rebecca C. Down at the Bottom of the Deep Dark Sea. Wright-Frierson, Virginia, illus. LC 90-33981. 40p. (ps-k). 1991. RSBE 14.95 (*0-02-747901-3*, Bradbury Pr) Macmillan Child Grp.

Jones, Sally L. The Hippo's Adventure. Weissman, Bari, illus. 8p. (ps). 1993. vinyl 8.49 (*0-7847-0049-4*, 24-03687) Standard Pub.

—The Whale's Tale. Weissman, Bari, illus. 8p. (ps). 1993. vinyl 8.49 (*0-7847-0048-6*, 24-03686) Standard Pub.

Joos, Francoise & Joos, Frederic. Sarah & the Stone Man. (Illus.). 32p. (gr. k-2). 1989. 13.95 (*0-86264-202-7*, Pub. by Anderson Pr UK) Trafalgar.

Jordan, MaryKate. Losing Uncle Tim. Levine, Abby, ed. Wennekes, Ron, illus. LC 89-5280. 32p. (gr. 2-6). 1989. PLB 13.95 (*0-8075-4756-5*); pap. 5.95 (*0-8075-4758-1*) A Whitman.

Jorgensen, Gail. Crocodile Beat. Mullins, Patricia, illus. LC 89-578. 32p. (ps-1). 1989. RSBE 14.95 (*0-02-748010-0*, Bradbury Pr) Macmillan Child Grp.

Joseph, Lorraine F. My Island: A Picture Storybook. Washington, Helen, illus. 23p. (Orig.). (gr. k-3). 1985. pap. 2.95 (*0-935357-00-9*) Cric Prod.

Josiah, the Boy King. (ps-1). 1988. pap. 0.79 (*1-55513-918-3*, Chariot Bks) Chariot Family.

Joslin, Sesyle. What Do You Do, Dear? Sendak, Maurice, illus. LC 84-43139. 48p. (ps-3). 1986. pap. 4.95 (*0-06-443113-4*, Trophy) HarpC Child Bks.

—What Do You Say, Dear? Sendak, Maurice, illus. LC 84-43140. 48p. (ps-3). 1986. pap. 4.95 (*0-06-443112-6*, Trophy) HarpC Child Bks.

Joyce, Susan. Post Card Passages. DuBosque, Doug, illus. 1994. 13.95 (*0-939217-27-9*) Peel Prod.

Joyce, William. George Shrinks. Joyce, William, illus. LC 83-47697. 32p. (ps-2). 1985. 15.00 (*0-06-023070-3*); PLB 14.89 (*0-06-023071-1*) HarpC Child Bks.

A Jugar! (SPA., Illus.). 12p. (ps). 1992. bds. 4.95 (*0-525-44854-3*, DCB) Dutton Child Bks.

Juster, Norton. As: A Surfeit of Similes. Small, David, illus. LC 88-8449. 80p. 1989. 9.95 (*0-688-08139-8*); PLB 9.88 (*0-688-08140-1*, Morrow Jr Bks) Morrow Jr Bks.

Kachenmeister, Cherryl. On Monday When It Rained. Berthiaume, Tom, photos by. (Illus.). 40p. (gr. k-3). 1989. 11.95 (*0-395-51940-3*) HM.

Kahalewai, Marilyn. Whose Slippers Are Those? Kahalewai, Marilyn, illus. LC 87-92272. 16p. (ps-6). 1988. 7.95 (*0-935848-58-4*) Bess Pr.

Kahalewai, Marilyn & Poepoe, Karen. Too Many Curls. Kahalewai, Marilyn & Poepoe, Karen, illus. LC 89-82131. 16p. (ps-2). 1992. 12.95 (*0-935848-83-5*); pap. 5.95 (*1-880188-20-1*) Bess Pr.

Kalin, Robert. Jump, Frog, Jump! Barton, Byron, illus. 32p. (gr. k-3). Big Book. 19.95 (*0-590-71722-7*); pap. 2.95 (*0-590-71723-5*) Scholastic Inc.

Kalmenoff, Matthew. Dinosaur Dioramas to Cut & Assemble. 1983. pap. 4.95 (*0-486-24541-1*) Dover.

Kamen, Gloria. Paddle, Said the Swan. Kamen, Gloria, illus. LC 88-16749. 32p. (ps-1). 1989. SBE 13.95 (*0-689-31330-6*, Atheneum Child Bk) Macmillan Child Grp.

Kanao, Keiko. Kitten up a Tree. Spinner, Stephanie, ed. Greenstein, Mina, designed by. LC 86-21075. (Illus.). 24p. (ps-1). 1987. 7.95 (*0-394-88817-0*) Knopf Bks Yng Read.

Kantrowitz, Mildred. Willy Bear. Parker, Nancy W., illus. LC 89-31868. 32p. (ps-1). 1989. pap. 3.95 (*0-689-71345-2*, Aladdin) Macmillan Child Grp.

Kaplan, Carol B. The Brown Bear Who Wasn't. Bolinske, Janet L., ed. Quenell, Midge, illus. LC 87-63000. (ps-k). 1988. 17.95 (*0-88335-753-4*); pap. 4.95 (*0-88335-076-9*) Milliken Pub Co.

—The Underground Tea Party. Bolinske, Janet L., ed. Quenell, Midge, illus. LC 87-62996. 24p. (Orig.). (ps-k). 1988. spiral-bound Big Book 17.95 (*0-88335-758-5*); pap. 4.95 (*0-88335-080-7*) Milliken Pub Co.

Karlin, Nurit. The Tooth Witch. Karlin, Nurit, illus. LC 84-62553. 32p. (ps-2). 1985. pap. 4.95 (*0-06-443079-0*, Trophy) HarpC Child Bks.

Katherine, Sharon. Sugar Princess. Wood, Paul, ed. Tolley, Lynn & Olds, Tom, illus. 31p. 1989. pap. 8.95 (*0-685-68779-1*) Jungle Pr.

Katz, Bobbi. Tick Tock, Let's Read the Clock: Green Ladder Books for Kids Through 6 Years. Nicklaus, Carol, illus. 16p. (ps-1). 1988. incl. clock 7.99 (*0-394-89399-9*) Random Bks Yng Read.

Katz, David. You Can Be a Winner Today: Reading Rap. 40p. (Orig.). (gr. k-4). 1991. pap. 6.00 (*1-880599-00-7*) Cascade Pass.

Katz, Illana & Ritvo, Edward. Joey & Sam: A Heartwarming Storybook about Autism, a Family, & a Brother's Love. Borowitz, Franz, illus. LC 92-38812. 40p. (gr. k-6). 1993. smythe sewn 16.95 (*1-882388-00-3*) Real Life Strybks.

Kaufman, Curt & Kaufman, Gita. Hotel Boy. Curt, Kaufman, illus. LC 86-25925. 40p. (gr. k-3). 1987. SBE 12.95 (*0-689-31287-3*, Atheneum Child Bk) Macmillan Child Grp.

Kawami, David. Cut & Assemble Paper Dragons That Fly. 1989. pap. 3.50 (*0-486-25325-2*) Dover.

Keathley, Jean. Pennies, Nickels, & Dreams. Graves, Helen, ed. LC 88-50117. 44p. (gr. k-3). 1988. 7.95 (*1-55523-137-3*) Winston-Derek.

Keats, Ezra J. Dreams. 2nd ed. LC 91-25572. (Illus.). 32p. (gr. 1-3). 1992. pap. 4.95 (*0-689-71599-4*, Aladdin) Macmillan Child Grp.

—Dreams. Keats, Ezra J., illus. LC 73-15857. 32p. (gr. 1-3). 1992. RSBE 14.95 (*0-02-749611-2*, Macmillan Child Bk) Macmillan Child Grp.

—Jennie's Hat. Keats, Ezra J., illus. LC 66-15683. 32p. (gr. k-3). 1966. 15.00i (*0-06-023113-0*); PLB 14.89 (*0-06-023114-9*) HarpC Child Bks.

—Jennie's Hat. Keats, Ezra J., illus. LC 66-15683. 32p. (ps-3). 1985. pap. 5.95 (*0-06-443072-3*, Trophy) HarpC Child Bks.

—Letter to Amy. Keats, Ezra J., illus. LC 68-24329. (gr. k-3). 1968. 15.00 (*0-06-023108-4*); PLB 14.89 (*0-06-023109-2*) HarpC Child Bks.

—Regards to the Man in the Moon. Keats, Ezra J., illus. LC 86-28774. 32p. (gr. k-3). 1987. pap. 3.95 (*0-689-71160-3*, Aladdin Bks) Macmillan Child Grp.

—The Snowy Day. Keats, Ezra J., illus. LC 62-15441. 40p. (ps-1). 1962. pap. 13.00 (*0-670-65400-0*) Viking Child Bks.

—The Trip. LC 77-24907. (ps up). 1987. pap. 4.95 (*0-688-07328-X*, Mulberry) Morrow.

—Whistle for Willie. Keats, Ezra J., illus. LC 64-13595. (ps-1). 1977. pap. 4.50 (*0-14-050202-5*, Puffin) Puffin Bks.

—Whistle for Willie. Keats, Ezra J., illus. (ps-1). 1964. pap. 14.00 (*0-670-76240-7*) Viking Child Bks.

Keller, Holly. Geraldine's Blanket. LC 83-14062. (Illus.). 32p. (ps up). 1988. pap. 3.95 (*0-688-07810-9*, Mulberry) Morrow.

Keller, Irene. The Thingumajig Book of Manners. Keller, Dick, illus. 32p. (ps-3). 1989. pap. 4.95 (*0-8249-8346-7*, Ideals Child) Hambleton-Hill.

Kelley, True. Look Baby! Listen Baby! Do Baby! Kelley, True, illus. LC 87-6800. 32p. (ps). 1987. 9.95 (*0-525-44320-7*, DCB) Dutton Child Bks.

Kellogg, Steven. Aster Aardvark's Alphabet Adventures. Kellogg, Steven, illus. LC 87-5715. 40p. (gr. k up). 1987. 13.95 (*0-688-07256-9*); lib. bdg. 13.88 (*0-688-07257-7*, Morrow Jr Bks) Morrow Jr Bks.

—Aster Aardvark's Alphabet Adventures. LC 87-5715. (Illus.). 40p. (gr. 1 up). 1992. pap. 3.95 (*0-688-11571-3*, Mulberry) Morrow.

Kemp, Moira, illus. I'm a Little Teapot. 12p. (ps). 1992. bds. 2.50 (*0-525-67394-6*, Lodestar Bks) Dutton Child Bks.

—Knock at the Door. 12p. (ps). 1992. bds. 2.50 (*0-525-67396-2*, Lodestar Bks) Dutton Child Bks.

—Pat-a-Cake. 12p. (ps). 1992. bds. 2.50 (*0-525-67393-8*, Lodestar Bks) Dutton Child Bks.

—Round & Round the Garden. 12p. (ps). 1992. bds. 2.50 (*0-525-67395-4*, Lodestar Bks) Dutton Child Bks.

Kent, Jack. Ice Cream Soup. Herman, Gail, retold by. Alley, R. W., illus. LC 89-43680. 24p. (Orig.). (ps-2). 1990. pap. 2.25 (*0-679-80790-X*) Random Bks Yng Read.

—Little Peep. Kent, Jack, illus. 32p. (ps up). 1989. pap. 12.95 jacketed (*0-671-67051-4*, S&S BFYR); pap. 5.95 (*0-671-67052-2*, S&S BFYR) S&S Trade.

—The Wizard. rev. ed. Kent, Jack, illus. 32p. (gr. k-3). 1989. pap. 5.95 (*0-927370-00-X*) WW Pr.
Kent, Richard. Play On! 2nd ed. LC 85-50588. 124p. (gr. 9-12). 1989. 5.95 (*0-932433-04-9*) Windswept Hse.
Kepes, Juliet. Cock-A-Doodle-Doo. Kepes, Juliet, illus. LC 76-44433. (ps-2). 1978. 6.95 (*0-394-83867-X*) Pantheon.
—Frogs Merry. Kepes, Juliet, illus. (ps-2). 1963. lib. bdg. 6.99 (*0-394-91176-8*) Pantheon.
Kessler, Ethel & Kessler, Leonard. Are There Seals in the Sandbox? Kessler, Leonard, illus. 24p. (ps). 1990. pap. 4.95 casebound, padded cover (*0-671-70539-3*, Little Simon) S&S Trade.
—Is There a Horse in Your House? Kessler, Leonard, illus. 22p. (ps). 1990. pap. 4.95 casebound with padded cov (*0-671-70540-7*, Little Simon) S&S Trade.
Khalsa, Dayal K. Sleepers. (Illus.). 24p. (ps-1). 1988. PLB 7.95 (*0-517-56917-5*, Clarkson Potter) Crown Bks Yng Read.
Kidner, Maria C. ABC Come See Wyoming. Campbell, Loreen, illus. 56p. (Orig.). (gr. k-3). 1990. pap. 4.95 (*0-9625920-0-5*) Rainbow Rhapsody.
Kightley, Lynn, et al. One Two Three. (Illus.). 32p. (ps-1). 1986. pap. 6.95 (*0-316-54004-8*) Little.
—Opposites. (Illus.). 32p. (ps-1). 1986. pap. 6.95 (*0-316-49931-5*) Little.
Kile, Joan. God's Mustard Seed, Vol. 1. Ragland, Teresa, illus. 32p. (ps-5). 1993. PLB 15.00 (*0-9636314-0-3*) Musty the Mustard.
Kindergarteners of Paul Mort Elementary. Looking for a Rainbow. (Illus.). 24p. (gr. k-3). 1987. 3.50 (*0-87406-227-6*) Willowisp Pr.
Kindersley, Dorling. Baby Animals. LC 91-27723. (Illus.). 24p. (ps-k). 1992. pap. 7.95 POB (*0-689-71563-3*, Aladdin) Macmillan Child Grp.
—Sea Animals. LC 91-27724. (Illus.). 24p. (ps-k). 1992. pap. 7.95 POB (*0-689-71565-X*, Aladdin) Macmillan Child Grp.
—Ships & Boats. LC 91-25687. (Illus.). 24p. (ps-k). 1992. pap. 7.95 POB (*0-689-71566-8*, Aladdin) Macmillan Child Grp.
King, Celia. Seven Ancient Wonders: A Pop-up Book. (Illus.). 7p. 1990. text ed. 8.95 (*0-87701-707-7*) Chronicle Bks.
—Seven Modern Wonders of the World: A Pop-up Book. King, Celia, illus. 7p. (gr. 3 up). 1992. 9.95 (*0-8118-0159-4*) Chronicle Bks.
King, Ed, illus. Gus Is Gone. LC 90-28634. 24p. (ps up). 1991. pap. 3.95 (*1-56288-008-X*) Checkerboard.
—Lucy is Lost. LC 90-27675. 24p. 1991. pap. 3.95 (*1-56288-009-8*) Checkerboard.
—William Wanders Off. LC 90-27677. 24p. 1991. pap. 3.95 (*1-56288-011-X*) Checkerboard.
King, P. E. Down on the Funny Farm: A Step Two Book. Graham, Alastair, illus. LC 85-11893. 48p. (gr. 1-3). 1986. PLB 7.99 (*0-394-97460-3*); pap. 3.50 (*0-394-87460-9*) Random Bks Yng Read.
Kingshead Corporation Staff. Cut-Color & Create: Make Your Own: Dinosaur Playmates. (Illus.). 24p. (ps-8). 1989. pap. write for info. (*1-55941-041-8*) Kingshead Corp.
—Cut-Color & Create: Make Your Own: Fashions of the Ages. (Illus.). 24p. (ps-8). 1989. pap. write for info. (*1-55941-028-0*) Kingshead Corp.
—Cut-Color & Create: Make Your Own: Land of the Dinosaurs. (Illus.). 24p. (ps-8). 1989. pap. write for info. (*1-55941-040-X*) Kingshead Corp.
—Cut-Color & Create: Make Your Own: Space Settlers. (Illus.). 24p. (ps-8). 1989. pap. write for info. (*1-55941-042-6*) Kingshead Corp.
Kingsley, Emily P. Sesame Street Big Bird & Little Bird's Book of Big & Little. Delaney, A., illus. 24p. (ps-k). 1977. pap. write for info (*0-307-10073-1*, Pub. by Golden Bks) Western Pub.
Kipling, Rudyard. How the Camel Got His Hump. Raglin, Tim, illus. LC 88-33366. 32p. (ps up). 1991. pap. 14.95 (*0-88708-096-0*, Rabbit Ears); incl. cassette 19.95 (*0-88708-097-9*, Rabbit Ears) Picture Bk Studio.
—How the Rhinoceros Got His Skin. Raglin, Tim, illus. LC 88-11439. 28p. (ps up). 1991. pap. 14.95 (*0-88708-078-2*, Rabbit Ears); bk. & cass. pkg. 19.95 (*0-88708-083-9*, Rabbit Ears) Picture Bk Studio.
Kitamura, Satoshi. What's Inside? Kitamura, Satoshi, illus. 32p. (ps up). 1987. pap. 4.95 (*0-374-48324-8*) FS&G.
—When Sheep Cannot Sleep. (Illus.). 32p. (ps up). 1988. pap. 3.95 (*0-374-48359-0*) FS&G.
Kitchen, Bert. Pig in a Barrow. Kitchen, Bert, illus. LC 90-43413. 32p. (ps-3). 1991. 13.95 (*0-8037-0943-9*) Dial Bks Young.
Kline, Suzy. Ooops! Fay, Ann, ed. Leder, Dora, illus. LC 87-25429. 32p. (ps-2). 1988. PLB 13.95 (*0-8075-6122-3*) A Whitman.
—Ooops! Leder, Dora, illus. 32p. (ps). 1989. pap. 3.95 (*0-14-050986-0*, Puffin) Puffin Bks.
Knight, Hilary. Hilary Knight's the Owl & the Pussycat. LC 89-31667. (Illus.). 32p. (ps-3). 1989. pap. 3.95 (*0-689-71331-2*, Aladdin) Macmillan Child Grp.
—Where's Wallace? Knight, Hilary, illus. LC 64-19717. (ps-3). 1964. 15.00 (*0-06-023170-X*); PLB 14.89 (*0-06-023171-8*) HarpC Child Bks.
—Where's Wallace? Knight, Hilary, illus. LC 64-19717. 48p. (ps-3). 1986. pap. 5.95 (*0-06-443094-4*, Trophy) HarpC Child Bks.
Knight, Joan. The Baby Who Would Not Come Down. Santini, Debrah, illus. LC 89-3987. 28p. (ps up). 1991. pap. 14.95 (*0-88708-107-X*) Picture Bk Studio.
Know an Old Lady. 24p. 1987. pap. 2.95 (*0-553-15574-1*) Bantam.
Kobayashi, Yuji. Miss Josephine's Secret Walk. (Illus.). 32p. (ps-2). 1991. 12.95 (*0-88138-096-2*, Green Tiger) S&S Trade.
Kohen, Clarita. El Agua y Tu. Barath, Judith, illus. (SPA.). 16p. (gr. k-5). 1993. PLB 7.50x (*1-56492-101-8*) Laredo.
—El Conejo y el Coyote. Menicucci, Gina, illus. (SPA.). 16p. (Orig.). (gr. k-5). 1993. PLB 7.50x (*1-56492-100-X*) Laredo.
Komaiko, Leah. Earl's Too Cool for Me. Cornell, Laura, illus. LC 87-30803. 40p. (gr. k-3). 1990. pap. 5.95 (*0-06-443245-9*, Trophy) HarpC Child Bks.
Kontoyiannaki, Elizabeth. Bozo Is a Dog. Kontoyiannaki, Elizabeth, illus. 17p. (gr. k-3). 1992. pap. 8.95 (*1-895583-44-6*) MAYA Pubs.
—Plants Grow in Gardens. Kontoyiannaki, Elizabeth, illus. 18p. (gr. k-3). 1992. pap. 10.95 (*1-895583-43-8*) MAYA Pubs.
—Where Does the World End? Kontoyiannaki, Elizabeth, illus. 14p. (gr. k-3). 1992. pap. 12.95 (*1-895583-45-4*) MAYA Pubs.
Kopper, Lisa, illus. Hush-a-Bye Baby. 18p. (ps). 1992. bds. 4.95 (*0-448-40266-1*, G&D) Putnam Pub Group.
—Peek-a-Boo Baby. 12p. (ps). 1993. bds. 3.95 (*0-448-40197-5*, G&D) Putnam Pub Group.
—Peek-a-Boo Kitty. 12p. (ps). 1993. bds. 3.95 (*0-448-40196-7*, G&D) Putnam Pub Group.
—Peek-a-Boo Teddy. 12p. (ps). 1993. bds. 3.95 (*0-448-40195-9*, G&D) Putnam Pub Group.
Koralek, Jenny. The Cobweb Curtain: A Christmas Story. Baynes, Pauline, illus. LC 88-27035. 32p. (ps-2). 1989. 13.95 (*0-8050-1051-3*, Bks Young Read) H Holt & Co.
Korschunow, Irina. Small Fur. Skofield, James, tr. from GER. Michl, Reinhard, illus. LC 87-45289. 80p. (gr. 1-4). 1988. HarpC Child Bks.
Kovacs, Deborah. Woody's First Dictionary. Rose, Eve, illus. 24p. (ps-2). 1988. 3.95 (*0-448-09287-5*, G&D) Putnam Pub Group.
Kovalski, Maryann. The Wheels on the Bus. Kovalski, Maryann, illus. 32p. (ps-k). 1987. 14.95 (*0-316-50256-1*, Joy St Bks) Little.
Kowalczyk, Carolyn. El Morado Es Parte del Arco Iris (Purple Is Part of a Rainbow) Sharp, Gene, illus. LC 85-11693. (SPA.). 32p. (ps-2). 1988. pap. 2.95 (*0-516-52068-7*) Childrens.
Krahn, Fernando. Amanda & the Mysterious Carpet. Krahn, Fernando, illus. LC 84-14201. 32p. (ps-3). 1985. 13.45 (*0-89919-258-0*, Clarion Bks) HM.
Kraul, Edward G. & Beatty, Judith. Little Herman Meets la Llorona at the Santa Fe Fiestas: A Story-Color Book in English & Spanish. Gomez, Jose, illus. (ENG & SPA.). 24p. (gr. 3-6). 1989. story-color book 2.95 (*0-945937-03-2*) Word Process.
Kraus, Robert. Buggy Bear Cleans Up. Brook, Bonnie, ed. Kraus, Robert, illus. 48p. (ps-3). 1989. PLB 5.95 (*0-671-68608-9*); pap. 3.95 (*0-671-68612-7*) Silver Pr.
—Bunny's Nutshell Library, 4 bks. Kraus, Robert, illus. Incl. The First Robin (*0-06-023285-4*); Juniper (*0-06-023295-1*); The Silver Dandelion (*0-06-023300-1*); Springfellow's Parade. LC 65-11450. (gr. 1 up). 1965. Set. 10.95 (*0-06-023225-0*) HarpC Child Bks.
—Ella the Bad Speller. Brook, Bonnie, ed. Kraus, Robert, illus. 48p. (ps-3). 1989. PLB 5.95 (*0-671-68606-2*); pap. 3.95 (*0-671-68610-0*) Silver Pr.
—Good Morning, Miss Gator. Brook, Bonnie, ed. Kraus, Robert, illus. 48p. (ps-3). 1989. PLB 5.95 (*0-671-68605-4*); pap. 3.95 (*0-671-68609-7*) Silver Pr.
—Here Comes Tardy Toad. Brook, Bonnie, ed. Kraus, Robert, illus. 48p. (ps-3). 1989. PLB 5.95 (*0-671-68607-0*); pap. 3.95 (*0-671-68611-9*) Silver Pr.
Krauss, Ruth. Birthday Party. Sendak, Maurice, illus. (gr. k-3). 1978. PLB 11.89 (*0-06-023330-3*) HarpC Child Bks.
—Carrot Seed. Johnson, Crockett, illus. LC 45-4530. 24p. (gr. k-3). 1945. 13.00 (*0-06-023350-8*); PLB 12.89 (*0-06-023351-6*) HarpC Child Bks.
—The Carrot Seed. Johnson, Crockett, illus. (ps-3). 1990. incl. cass. 19.95 (*0-87499-177-3*); pap. 12.95 incl. cass. (*0-87499-176-5*); Set; incl. 4 bks., guide, & cass. pap. 27.95 (*0-685-38538-8*) Live Oak Media.
—Growing Story. Rowand, Phyllis, illus. LC 47-30688. (gr. k-3). 1947. 11.95i (*0-06-023380-X*) HarpC Child Bks.
—The Happy Day. Simont, Marc, illus. LC 49-10568. 36p. (gr. k-3). 1989. pap. 4.95 (*0-06-443191-6*, Trophy) HarpC Child Bks.
—A Hole Is to Dig: A First Book of Definitions. Sendak, Maurice, illus. LC 52-7731. 48p. (ps up). 1989. pap. 3.95 (*0-06-443205-X*, Trophy) HarpC Child Bks.
—Hole Is to Dig: A First Book of First Definitions. Sendak, Maurice, illus. LC 52-7731. (ps-1). 1952. 14.00 (*0-06-023405-9*); PLB 13.89 (*0-06-023406-7*) HarpC Child Bks.
—I'll Be You & You Be Me. Sendak, Maurice, illus. LC 54-9214. (gr. k-3). 1954. PLB 12.89 (*0-06-023431-8*) HarpC Child Bks.
—Very Special House. Sendak, Maurice, illus. LC 53-7115. (ps-1). 1953. PLB 15.89 (*0-06-023456-3*) HarpC Child Bks.
Krensky, Stephen. Lionel at Large. Natti, Susanna, illus. LC 85-1450. 56p. (ps-3). 1986. 9.95 (*0-8037-0240-X*) Dial Bks Young.
Kroeber, Theodora. Green Christmas. Larrecq, John M., illus. LC 67-26304. (gr. k-2). 1967. 6.95 (*0-87466-047-5*, Pub. by Parnassus) HM.
Kroll, Steven. Pigs in the House. Kirk, Tim, illus. LC 83-13310. 48p. (ps-3). 1983. 5.95 (*0-8193-1111-1*) Parents.
Krueger, Ron, et al. Bearly There at All. French, Marty, illus. 26p. (ps up). 1986. Incl. cass. 7.95 (*1-55578-106-3*) Worlds Wonder.
Krulik, Nancy E. My Picture Book of the Planets. (ps-3). 1991. pap. 2.50 (*0-590-43907-3*) Scholastic Inc.
Kubick, Dana. Pop-Up Ballerina Bear. Kubick, Dana, illus. 16p. (ps up). 1993. Incl. 4 1/2" doll. 12.95 (*0-590-46753-0*, Cartwheel) Scholastic Inc.
Kudrna, C. Imbior. To Bathe a Boa. Kudrna, C. Imbiore., illus. 32p. (ps-4). 1986. PLB 18.50 (*0-87614-306-0*); pap. 5.95 (*0-87614-490-3*) Carolrhoda Bks.
Kuklin, Susan. Going to My Ballet Class. Kuklin, Susan, illus. LC 88-37556. 32p. (ps-2). 1989. RSBE 13.95 (*0-02-751235-5*, Bradbury Pr) Macmillan Child Grp.
—Taking My Cat to the Vet. Kuklin, Susan, illus. LC 88-5052. 32p. (ps-k). 1988. RSBE 13.95 (*0-02-751233-9*, Bradbury Pr) Macmillan Child Grp.
—Taking My Dog to the Vet. Kuklin, Susan, illus. LC 88-5047. 32p. (ps-k). 1988. RSBE 13.95 (*0-02-751234-7*, Bradbury Pr) Macmillan Child Grp.
Kunhardt, Dorothy. Pat the Bunny. Kunhardt, Dorothy, illus. (ps). 1988. Includes Touch & Feel Book with Plush Doll. pap. write for info. (*0-307-14000-8*, Pub. by Golden Bks) Western Pub.
Kunhardt, Edith. The Airplane Book. Bracken, Carolyn, illus. 24p. (ps-k). 1987. pap. write for info. (*0-307-10083-9*, Pub. by Golden Bks) Western Pub.
—Pat the Cat. Kunhardt, Edith, illus. LC 83-83106. (ps-3). 1984. write for info. comb. bdg. (*0-307-12001-5*, 12001, Golden Bks) Western Pub.
Kurz, Ann. Cranberries from A to Z: An Educational Picture Book. Kurz, Ann, illus. LC 89-61059. 32p. (gr. k-8). 1989. PLB 13.95 (*0-9622784-0-8*) Cranberry Origs.
Kuskin, Karla. The Dallas Titans Get Ready for Bed. Simont, Marc, illus. LC 83-49470. 48p. (ps-3). 1988. pap. 4.95 (*0-06-443180-0*, Trophy) HarpC Child Bks.
—Jerusalem, Shining Still. Frampton, David, illus. LC 86-25841. 32p. (gr. 1 up). 1990. pap. 5.50 (*0-06-443243-2*, Trophy) HarpC Child Bks.
—The Philharmonic Gets Dressed. Simont, Marc, illus. LC 81-48658. 48p. (ps-3). 1986. pap. 4.95 (*0-06-443124-X*, Trophy) HarpC Child Bks.
—Roar & More. rev. ed. Kuskin, Karla, illus. LC 89-15650. 48p. (ps-1). 1990. pap. 4.95 (*0-06-443244-0*, Trophy) HarpC Child Bks.
Kvasnosky, Laura M. One, Two, Three, Play with Me! (Illus.). 12p. (ps). 1994. 3.99 (*0-525-45234-6*) Dutton Child Bks.
—Pink, Red, Blue, What Are You? (Illus.). 12p. (ps). 1994. 3.99 (*0-525-45233-8*) Dutton Child Bks.
LaBelle, Susan. Flopsy, Mopsy & Cottontail: A Little Book of Paper Dolls in Full Color. (Illus.). 48p. (gr. 1 up). 1983. pap. 2.95 (*0-486-24376-1*) Dover.
Labrosse, Darcia. Greg's My Egg! (Illus.). 32p. (ps-1). 1994. 15.95 (*0-86264-411-9*, Pub. by Andersen Pr UK) Trafalgar.
Lambert, Jonathan. Giant Jungle Pop-up Book: Animals of the Endangered Rain Forest. Lambert, Jonathan, illus. (ps-3). 1992. 28.00 (*1-56021-183-0*) W J Fantasy.
Lamont, Priscilla. Our Mammoth Goes to School. Lamont, Pricilla, illus. LC 86-26939. 32p. (ps-3). 1988. 11.95 (*0-15-258837-X*, HB Juv Bks) HarBrace.
Landa, Norbert. Rabbit & Chicken Find a Box. Turk, Hanne, illus. LC 90-33379. (ps). 1992. bds. 4.95 (*0-688-09968-8*, Tambourine Bks) Morrow.
Langenscheidt Staff. Langenscheidt Picture Dictionary. (gr. 4-7). 1993. English. 19.95 (*0-88729-850-8*) FRE-ENG. 19.95 (*0-88729-851-6*); GER-ENG. 19.95 (*0-88729-852-4*); ITA-ENG. 19.95 (*0-88729-853-2*); SPA-ENG. 19.95 (*0-88729-854-0*); JPN-ENG. 24.95 (*0-88729-855-9*); GRE-ENG. 19.95 (*0-88729-862-1*); HEB-ENG. 19.95 (*0-88729-863-X*) Langenscheidt.
Langstaff, John & Rojankovsky, Feodor. Over in the Meadow. Rojankovsky, Feodor, illus. LC 57-8587. 32p. (ps-3). 1973. pap. 3.95 (*0-15-670500-1*, Voyager Bks) HarBrace.
Lansky, Vicki. Koko Bear's Big Earache: Preparing for Ear Tube Surgery. 32p. (Orig.). (ps). 1990. pap. 4.95 (*0-916773-26-4*) Book Peddlers.
—Koko Bear's New Babysitter. 32p. (Orig.). (ps). 1989. pap. 3.95 (*0-916773-24-8*) Book Peddlers.
—Koko Bear's New Potty, No. 1. Prince, Jane L., illus. 32p. 1986. pap. 3.50 (*0-553-34243-6*) Bantam.
La Pierre, Keith C. The Wanna Beezzz. La Pierre, Keith C., illus. LC 93-78057. 34p. (ps-3). 1993. 8.95 (*0-9631513-1-2*); PLB write for info. (*0-9631513-2-0*) Lee Pub NY.
Large Mammals Activity Book. (Illus.). (ps-6). pap. 2.95 (*0-565-01014-X*, Pub. by Natural Hist Mus) Parkwest Pubns.
La Rochelle, David. A Christmas Guest. Skoro, Martin, illus. 32p. (ps-3). 1988. PLB 18.95 (*0-87614-325-7*); pap. 5.95 (*0-87614-506-3*) Carolrhoda Bks.
LaRochelle, David. A Christmas Guest. Skoro, Martin, illus. 32p. (ps-3). 1989. pap. 5.95 (*0-685-25636-7*, First Ave Edns) Lerner Pubns.
Lasker, Joe. He's My Brother. Lasker, Joe, illus. LC 73-7318. 40p. (gr. 1-3). 1974. PLB 13.95 (*0-8075-3218-5*) A Whitman.
—A Tournament of Knights. Lasker, Joe, illus. LC 85-48075. 32p. (gr. 3 up). 1989. pap. 5.95 (*0-06-443192-4*, Trophy) HarpC Child Bks.

Lattimore, Eleanor F. Little Pear. Lattimore, Eleanor F., illus. LC 31-22069. (gr. 2-5). 1968. pap. 3.95 (*0-15-652799-5*, Voyager Bks) HarBrace.

Lauber, Patricia. The News about Dinosaurs. reissued ed. Gurche, John, et al, illus. LC 88-24140. 48p. (gr. 1-5). 1989. RSBE 16.95 (*0-02-754520-2*, Bradbury Pr) Macmillan Child Grp.

Laufer, Diana. Peek-a-Boo Family: My First Photo Album. Laufer, Diana, illus. 12p. (ps-1). 1994. life-the-flap 10.95 (*0-8431-3386-4*) Price Stern.

Laurin, Anne. Perfect Crane. Mikolaycak, Charles, illus. LC 80-7912. 32p. (gr. 1-4). 1987. pap. 4.95 (*0-06-443154-1*, Trophy) HarpC Child Bks.

Lavie, Arlette. Half a World Away. LC 90-49096. (ps-3). 1990. 7.95 (*0-85953-335-2*); pap. 3.95 (*0-85953-334-4*) Childs Play.

Leaf, Munro. The Story of Ferdinand. Lawson, Robert, illus. (ps-3). 1988. pap. 9.95 (*0-14-095075-3*, Puffin); bk. & t-shirt 9.95 (*0-318-37105-7*, Puffin); bk. & cassette 6.95 (*0-318-37106-5*, Puffin) Puffin Bks.

Lear, Edward. The Owl & the Pussycat. Falconer, Elizabeth, illus. 16p. (ps-2). 1993. pop-up bk. 12.95 (*0-8249-8571-0*, Ideals Child) Hambleton-Hill.

Learning: Little Friends Board Book. 1992. bds. 2.49 (*0-517-07283-1*) Random Hse Value.

LeCain, Errol. Thorn Rose. (Illus.). (ps-3). 1978. pap. 3.95 (*0-14-050222-X*, Puffin) Puffin Bks.

Leder, Dora, illus. Let's Peek in Santa's Pack. LC 89-61375. 14p. (ps). 1990. bds. 3.99 (*0-679-80277-0*) Random Bks Yng Read.

Lee, Jeanne M., retold by. & illus. Toad Is the Uncle of Heaven: A Vietnamese Folk Tale. LC 85-5639. 32p. (ps-2). 1989. pap. 5.95 (*0-8050-1147-1*, Owlet BYR) H Holt & Co.

Leedy, Loreen. Big, Small, Short, Tall. Leedy, Loreen, illus. LC 86-46203. 32p. (ps-3). 1987. reinforced bdg. 12.95 (*0-8234-0645-8*) Holiday.

—Pingo the Plaid Panda. Leedy, Loreen, illus. LC 88-17005. 32p. (ps-3). 1989. reinforced bdg. 13.95 (*0-8234-0727-6*) Holiday.

Leffler, Maryann C. My A B C's at Home. (Illus.). 24p. (ps). 1990. bds. 2.50 (*0-448-02257-5*, G&D) Putnam Pub Group.

Le Guin, Ursula K. Fire & Stone. LC 88-16799. (Illus.). 32p. (gr. 1-3). 1989. SBE 13.95 (*0-689-31408-6*, Atheneum Child Bk) Macmillan Child Grp.

Lehman, James H. The Owl & the Tuba. Raschka, Christopher, illus. LC 91-73880. 32p. 1991. 13.95 (*1-878925-02-4*) Brotherstone Pubs.

—The Saga of Shakespeare Pintlewood & the Great Silver Fountain Pen. Raschka, Christopher, illus. LC 90-82303. 32p. (gr. k-3). 1990. PLB 13.95 (*1-878925-00-8*) Brotherstone Pubs.

Lehmann, Terry & Nobisso, Joi. How to Fill an Empty Lap. Greenberg, Melanie, illus. 32p. (Orig.). (ps). 1980. pap. text ed. 3.00 (*0-940112-00-0*) Little Feat.

Leigh, Tom, illus. The Sesame Street Word Book. 72p. (ps). 1983. write for info. (*0-307-15549-8*, 15818, Golden Bks) Western Pub.

Lemke, Horst, illus. Places & Faces. LC 78-160446. 32p. (ps-k). 8.95 (*0-87592-041-1*) Scroll Pr.

Lenski, Lois. Cowboy Small. LC 60-12094. (Illus.). (gr. k-3). 1980. 5.25 (*0-8098-1021-2*) McKay.

—Little Airplane. Lenski, Lois, illus. LC 59-12487. (gr. k-3). 1980. 5.25 (*0-8098-1004-2*) McKay.

—Little Auto. Lenski, Lois, illus. LC 58-14239. (gr. k-3). 1980. 5.25 (*0-8098-1001-8*) McKay.

—Little Farm. Lenski, Lois, illus. LC 58-12902. (gr. k-3). 1980. 5.25 (*0-8098-1009-3*) McKay.

—Lois Lenski's Big Big Book of Mr. Small. (Illus.). 300p. (ps-1). 1985. 5.98 (*0-517-46307-5*) Random Hse Value.

—More Mr. Small. (ps-3). 1980. 9.95 (*0-8098-6300-6*, Walk) McKay.

Lentz, Pam. My Camera. (ps). 1993. 3.99 (*0-307-15903-5*, Golden Pr) Western Pub.

—My Flightbag. (ps). 1993. 3.99 (*0-307-15902-7*, Golden Pr) Western Pub.

—My Purse. (ps). 1993. 3.99 (*0-307-15901-9*, Golden Pr) Western Pub.

—My Schoolbag. (ps). 1993. 3.99 (*0-307-15900-0*, Golden Pr) Western Pub.

Leonard, Alain. Theodore's Superheroes. Tambourine Books Staff, tr. from FRE. Leonard, Alain, illus. LC 92-82140. 32p. (ps up). 1993. 15.00 (*0-688-12766-5*, Tambourine Bks); PLB 14.93 (*0-688-12767-3*, Tambourine Bks) Morrow.

Leonard, Marcia. Birthday in a Bathtub. Brook, Bonnie, ed. Wallner, John, illus. 24p. (ps-1). 1989. 4.95 (*0-671-68592-9*); PLB 6.95 (*0-671-68588-0*) Silver Pr.

—Counting Kangaroos, A Book about Numbers. Palmisciano, Diane, illus. LC 89-4960. 24p. (gr. k-2). 1990. PLB 9.59 (*0-8167-1722-2*); pap. text ed. 2.50 (*0-8167-1723-0*) Troll Assocs.

—Follow Me. 1988. pap. 4.95 (*0-553-05477-5*, Little Rooster) Bantam.

—The Kitten Twins: A Book about Opposites. Cocca-Leffler, Maryann, illus. LC 89-4945. 24p. (gr. k-2). 1990. PLB 9.59 (*0-8167-1724-9*); pap. text ed. 2.50 (*0-8167-1725-7*) Troll Assocs.

—Noisy Neighbors: A Book about Animal Sounds. Weissman, Bari, illus. LC 89-4959. 24p. (gr. k-2). 1990. PLB 9.59 (*0-8167-1726-5*); pap. text ed. 2.50 (*0-8167-1727-3*) Troll Assocs.

—Paintbox Penguins, A Book about Colors. Palmisciano, Diane, illus. LC 89-4979. 24p. (gr. k-2). 1990. lib. bdg. 9.59 (*0-8167-1716-8*); pap. text ed. 2.50 (*0-8167-1717-6*) Troll Assocs.

—Rainboots for Breakfast. Brook, Bonnie, ed. Himmelman, John, illus. 24p. (ps-1). 1989. 4.95 (*0-671-68591-0*); PLB 6.95 (*0-671-68587-2*) Silver Pr.

—Shopping for Snowflakes. Brook, Bonnie, ed. Himmelman, John, illus. 24p. (ps-1). 1989. 4.95 (*0-671-68594-5*); PLB 6.95 (*0-671-68590-2*) Silver Pr.

—Swimming in the Sand. Brook, Bonnie, ed. Wallner, John, illus. 24p. (ps-1). 1989. 4.95 (*0-671-68593-7*); PLB 6.95 (*0-671-68589-9*) Silver Pr.

—What Next, 4 bks. Himmelman, John & Wallner, John, illus. (ps-1). 1990. Set, 24p. ea. 19.80 (*0-671-94102-X*, J Messner); Set, 24p. ea. lib. bdg. 39.92 (*0-671-94101-1*) S&S Trade.

—What's Missing? Ser, 4 vols. Cushman, Doug & Banek, Yvette, illus. 96p. (ps-1). 1990. Set. 19.80 (*0-671-94433-9*); Set. PLB 27.80 (*0-671-94432-0*) Silver Pr.

Lesch, Christiane. A Farmyard Morning. Lawson, Polly, tr. from GER. (Illus.). 24p. (ps-k). 1990. Repr. lib. bdg. 12.95 (*0-86315-117-5*) Gryphon Hse.

LeSieg, Theo. The Pop-up Mice of Mr. Brice. McKie, Roy, illus. LC 89-60507. 20p. (ps-3). 1989. 10.00 (*0-679-80132-4*) Random Bks Yng Read.

Le Sieg, Theodore. Ten Apples up on Top. LC 61-7068. (Illus.). 72p. (gr. 1-2). 1961. 6.95 (*0-394-80019-2*); lib. bdg. 7.99 (*0-394-90019-7*) Beginner.

—Wacky Wednesday. Booth, George, illus. LC 74-5520. 48p. (gr. k-4). 1974. 6.95 (*0-394-82912-3*); lib. bdg. 7.99 (*0-394-92912-8*) Beginner.

Lessac, Frane. My Little Island. Lessac, Frane, illus. LC 84-48355. 48p. (ps-3). 1987. pap. 4.95 (*0-06-443146-0*, Trophy) HarpC Child Bks.

Lester, Alison. Rosie Sips Spiders. Lester, Alison, illus. 32p. (ps-k). 1989. 13.45 (*0-395-51526-2*) HM.

Lester, Helen. Pookins Gets Her Way. Munsinger, Lynn, illus. (ps-3). 1987. 13.95 (*0-395-42636-7*); pap. 4.80 (*0-395-53965-X*) HM.

Let's Be Friends. 1989. 4.99 (*0-517-66936-6*) Random Hse Value.

Let's Feed the Animals: A Lift-the-Flap Book. (Illus.). 24p. (ps-1). 1987. pap. 5.95 (*0-553-18352-4*) Bantam.

Let's Go: Panda's First Word Book. 1989. 0.99 (*0-517-66937-4*) Random Hse Value.

Let's Have Fun. 1989. 4.99 (*0-517-66939-0*) Random Hse Value.

Let's See & Do. 1989. 4.99 (*0-517-66938-2*) Random Hse Value.

LeValley, Norma. A Tree for Me. Darcy, Tom, illus. LC 87-70974. 50p. (ps-2). 1987. pap. 5.95 (*0-9618740-0-7*) Caring Tree.

Levine, Abby. Too Much Mush! Tucker, Kathy, ed. Parkinson, Kathy, illus. LC 88-33906. 32p. (ps-2). 1989. PLB 13.95 (*0-8075-8025-2*) A Whitman.

—What Did Mommy Do Before You? Fay, Ann, ed. LC 87-27908. (Illus.). 32p. (ps-3). 1988. PLB 13.95 (*0-8075-8819-9*) A Whitman.

—You Push, I Ride. Tucker, Kathleen, ed. Apple, Margot, illus. LC 87-36852. 32p. (ps-k). 1989. PLB 13.95 (*0-8075-9444-X*) A Whitman.

Levinson, Nancy S. Clara & the Bookwagon. Croll, Carolyn, illus. LC 86-45773. 64p. (gr. k-3). 1988. PLB 13.89 (*0-06-023838-0*) HarpC Child Bks.

Levinson, Riki. I Go with My Family to Grandma's. Goode, Diane, illus. LC 86-4490. 32p. (ps-1). 1986. 14.00 (*0-525-44261-8*, DCB); pap. 3.95 (*0-525-44557-9*, DCB) Dutton Child Bks.

Levy, Nathan & Levy, Janet. There Are Those. Edwards, Joan, illus. LC 82-81111. 32p. (ps up). 1990. 21.95 (*0-9608240-0-6*) NL Assoc Inc.

Lewis, Glenn A. Dinner at Mario's. Lewis, Glenn A., illus. 19p. (gr. k-3). 1992. pap. 5.95 (*1-895583-53-5*) MAYA Pubs.

Lewis, Naomi, ed. The Twelve Dancing Princesses & Other Tales from Grimm. Postma, Lidia, illus. LC 85-6964. 100p. (ps up). 1986. 14.95 (*0-8037-0237-X*) Dial Bks Young.

Lewis, Paul O. Davy's Dream. (Illus.). 64p. (ps-6). 1988. 14.95 (*0-941831-32-9*); pap. 9.95 (*0-941831-28-0*) Beyond Words Pub.

—Ever Wondered. Lewis, Paul O., illus. 36p. (gr. 3-6). 1991. pap. 4.95 (*0-941831-67-1*) Beyond Words Pub.

—P. Bear's New Years Party - A Counting Book. (Illus.). 24p. (ps-1). 1989. 12.95 (*0-941831-21-3*); pap. 8.95 (*0-941831-29-9*) Beyond Words Pub.

—The Starlight Bride. (Illus.). 40p. (ps-6). 1988. cloth 14.95 (*0-941831-33-7*); pap. 9.95 (*0-941831-25-6*) Beyond Words Pub.

Lewis, Shari. One-Minute Bedtime Stories. (ps). 1991. pap. 3.99 (*0-440-40626-9*, YB) Dell.

—One-Minute Greek Myths. Ewing, Carolyn S., illus. 48p. (ps-3). 1987. 6.95 (*0-385-23849-5*); pap. 9.95 (*0-385-23423-6*) Doubleday.

Lexau, Joan M. Don't Be My Valentine. Hoff, Syd, illus. LC 85-42621. 64p. (gr. k-3). 1988. pap. 3.50 (*0-06-444115-6*, Trophy) HarpC Child Bks.

Lightbody, Nancy K. & Malley, Sarah H. Observa-Story: Portland to Cut & Color. Malley, Sarah H., illus. LC 76-54460. (gr. 1-4). 1976. pap. 1.25 (*0-9600612-5-8*) Greater Portland.

Lillegard, Dee. Where Is It? Sharp, Gene, illus. LC 84-7005. 32p. (ps-2). 1984. lib. bdg. 10.25 (*0-516-02065-X*); pap. 2.95 (*0-516-42065-8*) Childrens.

Lillington, Kenneth, text by. A Christmas Carol. Dickens, Charles, contrib. by. (Illus.). 32p. (Orig.). (gr. k up). 1988. pap. 9.95 (*0-571-10093-7*) Faber & Faber.

—The Mikado: Easy Piano Picture Book. Sullivan, Arthur, contrib. by. (Illus.). 32p. (gr. k up). 1988. pap. 9.95 (*0-571-10085-6*) Faber & Faber.

Linda's Late: A Fun Book of Time. (ps). 1992. pap. 6.95 (*0-87614-573-X*) Carolrhoda Bks.

Lindberg, Becky T. Speak up, Chelsea Martin! Tucker, Kathleen, ed. Poydar, Nancy, illus. LC 91-313. 128p. (gr. 2-4). 1991. 11.95 (*0-8075-7552-6*) A Whitman.

Lindgren, Astrid. I Don't Want to Go to Bed. Lucas, Barbara, tr. from SWE. Wikland, Ilon, illus. 32p. (ps up). 1988. 12.95 (*91-29-59066-3*, R & S Bks) FS&G.

—I Want a Brother or Sister. Wikland, Ilon, illus. Bibb, Eric, tr. (Illus.). 32p. (ps up). 1988. 10.95 (*91-29-58778-6*, R & S Bks) FS&G.

—The Tomten. Wiberg, Harald, illus. LC 61-10658. (gr. 1-3). 1979. 14.95 (*0-698-20147-7*, Coward); (Coward) Putnam Pub Group.

Lindsey, Marilyn L. The Little Lost Sheep. O'Connell, Ruth, illus. LC 87-91993. (gr. k-2). 1988. 2.50 (*0-87403-398-5*, 24-03808) Standard Pub.

Linn, Margot. A Trip to the Dentist. Siracusa, Catherine, illus. LC 87-14884. 20p. (ps-k). 1988. HarpC Child Bks.

—A Trip to the Doctor. Siracusa, Catherine, illus. LC 87-15004. 20p. (ps-k). 1988. HarpC Child Bks.

Lion. 1989. 3.50 (*1-87865-730-5*) Blue Q.

Lion. (Illus.). 288p. 1991. pap. 2.99 (*0-517-67868-3*) Random Hse Value.

Lionni, Leo. Alexander & the Wind-up Mouse. Lionni, Leo, illus. LC 76-77423. 32p. (ps-2). 1969. 15.00 (*0-394-80914-9*); lib. bdg. 15.99 (*0-394-90914-3*) Knopf Bks Yng Read.

—Frederick. Lionni, Leo, illus. LC 66-10355. 40p. (ps-2). 1967. 16.00 (*0-394-81040-6*); PLB 16.99 (*0-394-91040-0*) Knopf Bks Yng Read.

—Frederick. Lionni, Leo, illus. LC 66-10355. 32p. (gr. k-3). 1973. pap. 4.99 (*0-394-82614-0*) Knopf Bks Yng Read.

—Inch by Inch. (Illus.). (gr. k-1). 1962. 10.95 (*0-8392-3010-9*) Astor-Honor.

—Let's Play. Lionni, Leo, illus. 28p. (ps). 1993. 3.25 (*0-679-84030-3*) Random Bks Yng Read.

—Little Blue & Little Yellow. (Illus.). (gr. k-1). 1959. 10.95 (*0-8392-3018-4*) Astor-Honor.

—On My Beach There Are Many Pebbles. (Illus.). (gr. k-1). 1961. 10.95 (*0-8392-3024-9*) Astor-Honor.

—Pouce par Pouce. (FRE., Illus.). (gr. k-1). 1961. 10.95 (*0-8392-3028-1*) Astor-Honor.

—Swimmy. reissued ed. Lionni, Leo, illus. LC 63-8504. 40p. (ps-2). 1963. 14.95 (*0-394-81713-3*); lib. bdg. 15.99 (*0-394-91713-8*) Knopf Bks Yng Read.

Little Bear Paints a Picture. 1988. 1.98 (*0-671-09562-5*) S&S Trade.

Little Bears Go Visiting the Hawaiian Islands, Bk. 23. (ps-1). write for info. (*0-931363-23-3*) Celia Totus Enter.

Little Bears Visit the Ocean Beach, Bk. 22. (ps-1). write for info. (*0-931363-21-7*) Celia Totus Enter.

A Little Book of Numbers. 16p. (ps-k). 1980. pap. 3.95 (*0-671-41346-5*, Little) S&S Trade.

Little Kids at Home. (Illus.). 48p. (gr. k-2). 1989. 5.95 (*0-87449-680-2*) Modern Pub NYC.

Little Kids at Play. (Illus.). 48p. (gr. k-2). 1989. 5.95 (*0-87449-679-9*) Modern Pub NYC.

Little Kids at School. (Illus.). 48p. (gr. k-2). 1989. 5.95 (*0-87449-677-2*) Modern Pub NYC.

Little Kids in the Neighborhood. (Illus.). 48p. (gr. k-2). 1989. 5.95 (*0-87449-678-0*) Modern Pub NYC.

Little Mermaid: Pop-Up. (ps-3). 1993. 4.95 (*0-8167-2927-1*) Troll Assocs.

Little Mouse Around the House. (Illus.). 24p. (ps-2). 1988. 5.95 (*0-8431-4731-8*) Price Stern.

Little Pioneer Bears, Bk. 21. (ps-1). write for info. (*0-931363-20-9*) Celia Totus Enter.

Little Puppy Learns to Share. (Illus.). (ps-k). 1991. write for info. (*0-307-11519-4*, Golden Pr) Western Pub.

Little Treasury of Walt Disney. 1986. 5.98 (*0-685-16883-2*, 616300) Random Hse Value.

Littledale, Freya. Peter & the North Wind. Howell, Troy, illus. 32p. (gr. k-3). 1989. pap. 2.50 (*0-590-40629-9*) Scholastic Inc.

Littlejohn, Claire, illus. Aesop's Fables: A Pull-the-Tab-Pop-Up-Book. LC 87-24478. 14p. (ps up). 1988. 13.95 (*0-8037-0487-9*) Dial Bks Young.

Lobato, Arcadio. Just One Wish. Clements, Andrew, tr. from GER. Lobato, Arcadio, illus. LC 89-49263. 32p. (ps up). 1991. pap. 14.95 (*0-88708-134-7*) Picture Bk Studio.

Lobel, Arnold. The Book of Pigericks (Pig Limericks) Lobel, Arnold, illus. LC 82-47730. 48p. (ps up). 1988. pap. 5.95 (*0-06-443163-0*, Trophy) HarpC Child Bks.

—Days with Frog & Toad. Lobel, Arnold, illus. LC 78-21786. 64p. (ps-3). 1985. (Trophy); pap. 3.50 (*0-06-444058-3*, Trophy) HarpC Child Bks.

—Frog & Toad All Year. Lobel, Arnold, illus. LC 76-2343. 64p. (ps-3). 1985. (Trophy); pap. 3.50 (*0-06-444059-1*, Trophy) HarpC Child Bks.

—Frog & Toad Are Friends. Lobel, Arnold, illus. LC 73-105492. 64p. (ps-3). 1985. (Trophy); pap. 3.50 (*0-06-444020-6*, Trophy) HarpC Child Bks.

—Frog & Toad Together. Lobel, Arnold, illus. LC 73-183163. 64p. (ps-3). 1985. (Trophy); pap. 3.50 (*0-06-444021-4*, Trophy) HarpC Child Bks.

—Giant John. Lobel, Arnold, illus. LC 64-16639. 32p. (gr. k-3). 1964. PLB 14.89 (*0-06-022946-2*) HarpC Child Bks.

—Grasshopper on the Road. Lobel, Arnold, illus. LC 77-25653. 64p. (gr. k-3). 1986. pap. 3.50 (*0-06-444094-X*, Trophy) HarpC Child Bks.

—Holiday for Mister Muster. Lobel, Arnold, illus. LC 63-15323. 32p. (gr. k-3). 1963. PLB 12.89 (*0-06-023956-5*) HarpC Child Bks.
—Mouse Soup. Lobel, Arnold, illus. LC 76-41517. 64p. (gr. k-3). 1986. (Trophy); pap. 3.50 (*0-06-444041-9*, Trophy) HarpC Child Bks.
—On the Day Peter Stuyvesant Sailed into Town. Lobel, Arnold, illus. LC 75-148420. 48p. (ps-3). 1987. pap. 4.95 (*0-06-443144-4*, Trophy) HarpC Child Bks.
—Prince Bertram the Bad. Lobel, Arnold, illus. LC 63-8741. 32p. (gr. k-3). 1963. PLB 13.89 (*0-06-023976-X*) HarpC Child Bks.
—Small Pig. Lobel, Arnold, illus. LC 69-10213. 64p. (gr. k-3). 1988. pap. 3.50 (*0-06-444120-2*, Trophy) HarpC Child Bks.
—The Turnaround Wind. Lobel, Arnold, illus. LC 87-45293. 32p. (ps-3). 1988. PLB 12.89 (*0-06-023988-3*) HarpC Child Bks.
Locker, Thomas. Family Farm. Locker, Thomas, illus. LC 87-19645. 32p. (ps up). 1988. 16.99 (*0-8037-0489-5*); PLB 14.89 (*0-8037-0490-9*) Dial Bks Young.
Loehr, Mallory. The Little Country Book. Miller, Edward, illus. 28p. (ps). 1994. 3.25 (*0-679-85289-1*) Random Bks Yng Read.
—Trucks. McNaught, Harry, illus. LC 91-75344. 22p. (ps). 1992. 3.25 (*0-679-83061-8*) Random Bks Yng Read.
Loelling, Carol. Whose House Is This? (Illus.). 24p. (gr. 3-6). 1978. 5.95 (*0-8431-0444-9*) Price Stern.
Logan, Les. The Game. 160p. (Orig.). (gr. 7-12). 1986. pap. 2.25 (*0-553-25211-9*) Bantam.
Look What I Found! 14p. (ps). 1993. bds. 2.99 (*0-679-84909-2*) Random Bks Yng Read.
Loomans, Diane. Lovables in the Kingdom of Self-Esteem. Carleton, Nancy, ed. Howard, Kim, illus. LC 90-52633. 32p. (ps-5). 1991. 14.95 (*0-915811-25-1*) H J Kramer Inc.
Lorenzen, Anna L. Tiger. Craft, Mary, illus. 22p. (Orig.). (gr. 1-2). 1989. pap. text ed. 2.95 (*0-9626133-0-4*) ALL Ventura Pub.
Love, Marsha L. The Vitamin Parade. LC 89-51346. (Illus.). 44p. (gr. k-3). 1989. 5.95 (*1-55523-264-7*) Winston-Derek.
Loving: Little Friends Board Book. 1992. bds. 2.49 (*0-517-07284-X*) Random Hse Value.
Lowrey, Janette S. The Poky Little Puppy. Tenggren, Gustaf, illus. 24p. (ps-k). 1992. Repr. of 1942 ed. write for info. (*0-307-10394-3*, 10394, Pub. by Golden Bks) Western Pub.
Lowry, Lois. All about Sam. (Illus.). 144p. (gr. 1-5). 1988. 13.45 (*0-395-48662-9*) HM.
Lukas, Noah. Tiny Trolls' ABC. Schindler, S. D., illus. LC 92-62940. 24p. (Orig.). (ps-k). 1993. pap. 1.50 (*0-679-84797-9*) Random Bks Yng Read.
—Tiny Trolls' 1, 2, 3. Schindler, S. D., illus. LC 92-62939. 24p. (Orig.). (ps-k). 1993. pap. 1.50 (*0-679-84792-8*) Random Bks Yng Read.
Lundell, Margaretta. The Land of Colors. Pazzaglia, Nadia, illus. LC 84-81410. 24p. (ps-k). 1989. 9.95 (*0-448-21028-2*, G&D) Putnam Pub Group.
Lundell, Margo. What Does Baby See? Pagnoni, Roberta, illus. 24p. (ps-k). 1990. bds. 9.95 (*0-448-19098-2*, G&D) Putnam Pub Group.
—Woody, Be Good! A First Book of Manners. Rose, Eve, illus. 24p. (ps-2). 1988. 3.95 (*0-448-09288-3*, G&D) Putnam Pub Group.
Lunn, Carolyn. Spiders & Webs. Dunnington, Tom, illus. LC 89-34665. 32p. (ps-2). 1989. PLB 10.25 (*0-516-02093-5*); pap. 2.95 (*0-516-42093-3*) Childrens.
Lurie, Morris. The Story of Imelda, Who Was Small. Denton, Terry, illus. 32p. (gr. k-3). 1988. 13.45 (*0-395-48663-7*) HM.
Lustig, Loretta, illus. The Pop-up Book of Trucks. LC 73-19318. (ps-2). 1974. 8.99 (*0-394-82826-7*) Random Bks Yng Read.
Lydon, Kerry R. A Birthday for Blue. Levine, Abby, ed. Hays, Michael, illus. LC 88-21697. 32p. (gr. k-3). 1989. 13.95g (*0-8075-0774-1*) A Whitman.
Lynn, Sara. Clothes. Lynn, Sara, illus. 14p. (ps). 1986. pap. 2.95 (*0-689-71095-X*, Aladdin Bks) Macmillan Child Grp.
Lyon, David. The Runaway Duck. LC 84-5677. (Illus.). 32p. (ps up). 1987. pap. 3.95 (*0-688-07334-4*, Mulberry) Morrow.
McAllister, Angela. The King Who Sneezed. Henwood, Simon, illus. LC 88-6858. 32p. (gr. k-3). 1988. 12.95 (*0-688-08327-7*); PLB 12.88 (*0-688-08328-5*, Morrow Jr Bks) Morrow Jr Bks.
McCay, Winsor. Complete Little Nemo in Slumberland, Vol. II. Marschall, Richard, ed. & intro. by. (Illus.). 96p. (gr. 6 up). 1989. 34.95 (*0-924359-02-1*) Remco Wrldserv Bks.
McClain, Mary. Baby's Pockets. McClain, Mary, illus. 8p. (ps). 1981. pap. 3.95 (*0-671-43204-4*, Little Simon) S&S Trade.
McCloskey, Robert. Blueberries for Sal. McCloskey, Robert, illus. LC 48-4955. (ps-1). 1976. pap. 3.99 (*0-14-050169-X*, Puffin) Puffin Bks.
—Blueberries for Sal. McCloskey, Robert, illus. LC 48-4955. 56p. (ps-1). 1948. pap. 14.95 (*0-670-17591-9*) Viking Child Bks.
—Lentil. McCloskey, Robert, illus. (gr. k-3). 1940. pap. 14.95 (*0-670-42357-2*) Viking Child Bks.
—Make Way for Ducklings. McCloskey, Robert, illus. (gr. k-3). 1941. pap. 13.99 (*0-670-45149-5*) Viking Child Bks.
—Time of Wonder. McCloskey, Robert, illus. 64p. (gr. k-3). 1989. pap. 4.99 (*0-14-050201-7*, Puffin) Puffin Bks.
McCue, Dick. Baby Elephant's Bedtime. McCue, Lisa, illus. 24p. (ps). 1985. pap. 2.95 (*0-671-55853-6*, Little Simon) S&S Trade.
—Bunny's Numbers. McCue, Lisa, illus. 24p. (ps). 1984. pap. 2.95 (*0-671-50944-6*, Little Simon) S&S Trade.
—Panda's Playtime. McCue, Lisa, illus. 12p. (ps). 1985. 2.95 (*0-671-55850-1*, Little Simon) S&S Trade.
—Raccoon's Hide & Seek. McCue, Lisa, illus. 12p. (ps). 1985. 2.95 (*0-671-55854-4*, Little Simon) S&S Trade.
McCue, Dick & McCue, Lisa. Puppy's Day. (ps). 1984. pap. 2.95 (*0-671-50945-4*, Little Simon) S&S Trade.
McCue, Lisa. Fuzzytail Bunny. McCue, Lisa, illus. 22p. (ps). 1992. bds. 3.25 (*0-679-81721-2*) Random Bks Yng Read.
—Fuzzytail Lamb. McCue, Lisa, illus. 22p. (ps). 1992. bds. 3.25 (*0-679-81720-4*) Random Bks Yng Read.
—Fuzzytall Bunny Book & Bunny Set. McCue, Lisa, illus. 22p. (ps). 1994. incl. stuffed animal 10.00 (*0-679-85103-8*) Random Bks Yng Read.
—Kittens Love. McCue, Lisa, illus. LC 89-61137. 24p. (ps-1). 1990. 4.95 (*0-394-82876-3*) Random Bks Yng Read.
—The Little Chick. McCue, Lisa, illus. LC 85-63658. 7p. (ps). 1993. bds. 3.95 (*0-394-88017-X*) Random Bks Yng Read.
—Nighty-Night, Little One. McCue, Lisa, illus. LC 87-42786. 28p. (ps). 1988. bds. 2.95 (*0-394-89476-6*) Random Bks Yng Read.
—Puppies Love. McCue, Lisa, illus. LC 89-61140. 24p. (ps-1). 1990. 4.95 (*0-394-82875-5*) Random Bks Yng Read.
McCue, Lisa, illus. Kitten's Christmas. 1985. pap. 2.95 (*0-671-55851-X*, Little Simon) S&S Trade.
—Puppy Peek-a-Boo. LC 88-60759. 14p. (ps). 1989. bds. 3.99 (*0-394-81950-0*) Random Bks Yng Read.
McCully, Emily A. First Snow. McCully, Emily A., illus. LC 84-43244. 32p. (ps-1). 1985. PLB 14.89 (*0-06-024129-2*) HarpC Child Bks.
—First Snow. McCully, Emily A., illus. LC 84-43244. 32p. (ps-1). 1988. pap. 4.95 (*0-06-443181-9*, Trophy) HarpC Child Bks.
—Picnic. McCully, Emily A., illus. LC 83-47913. 32p. (ps-1). 1989. pap. 3.95 (*0-06-443199-1*, Trophy) HarpC Child Bks.
—School. McCully, Emily A., illus. LC 87-156. 32p. (ps-2). 1987. PLB 14.89 (*0-06-024133-0*) HarpC Child Bks.
—School. McCully, Emily A., illus. LC 87-156. 32p. (ps-1). 1990. pap. 4.95 (*0-06-443233-5*, Trophy) HarpC Child Bks.
McCurdy, Michael. The Devils Who Learned to Be Good. McCurdy, Michael, illus. 32p. (gr. 2-5). 1987. 13.95 (*0-316-55527-4*, Joy St Bks) Little.
McDaniel, Becky B. Katie Can. Axeman, Lois, illus. LC 87-5190. 32p. (ps-2). 1987. PLB 10.25 (*0-516-02082-X*); pap. 2.95 (*0-516-42082-8*) Childrens.
McDermott, Gerald. Daniel O'Rourke. McDermott, Gerald, illus. LC 85-20188. 32p. (ps-3). 1986. pap. 12.95 (*0-670-80924-1*) Viking Child Bks.
—The Stonecutter. (Illus.). (gr. 1-3). 1978. pap. 4.99 (*0-14-050289-0*, Puffin) Puffin Bks.
MacDonald, Amy. Let's Pretend. Roffey, Maureen, illus. 12p. (ps). 1994. 5.95 (*1-56402-201-3*) Candlewick Pr.
MacDonald, George. The Christmas Stories of George MacDonald. LC 81-68187. (gr. 3-7). 1981. 12.99 (*0-89191-491-9*, 54916, Chariot Bks) Chariot Family.
MacDonald, Sharon. We Learn All about Community Helpers. (ps-1). 1988. pap. 6.95 (*0-8224-4599-9*) Fearon Teach Aids.
—We Learn All about Dinosaurs. (ps-1). 1988. pap. 6.95 (*0-8224-4595-6*) Fearon Teach Aids.
—We Learn All about Fall. (ps-1). 1988. pap. 6.95 (*0-8224-4596-4*) Fearon Teach Aids.
—We Learn All about Farms. (ps-1). 1988. pap. 6.95 (*0-8224-4594-8*) Fearon Teach Aids.
—We Learn all about the Circus. (ps-1). 1988. pap. 6.95 (*0-8224-4598-0*) Fearon Teach Aids.
—We Learn All about Winter. (ps-1). 1988. pap. 6.95 (*0-8224-4597-2*) Fearon Teach Aids.
MacDonald, Suse. Alphabatics. LC 85-31429. (Illus.). 64p. (ps up). 1986. SBE 16.95 (*0-02-761520-0*, Bradbury Pr) Macmillan Child Grp.
McDowell, Josh & McDowell, Dottie. Katie's Adventure at Blueberry Pond. LC 88-14039. (Illus.). 32p. (ps-2). 1988. 8.99 (*1-55513-598-6*, Chariot Bks) Chariot Family.
—Pizza for Everyone. LC 88-14041. (Illus.). 32p. (ps-2). 1988. 8.99 (*1-55513-596-X*, Chariot Bks) Chariot Family.
McDowell, Margaret & Trottier, Maxine. The Big Heart. Trottier, Maxine, illus. 32p. (ps-2). 1991. pap. 29.50 (*1-55037-186-X*, Pub. by Annick CN) Firefly Bks Ltd.
McFarland, Kathleen & Larkin, Judy. Colleen Marie. (Illus.). 56p. (Orig.). (ps). 1985. pap. write for info. (*0-9621691-1-0*, TX 1-705-162) B Bumpers Inc.
MacFarlane, Kee & Cunningham, Carolyn. Steps to Healthy Touching. Mortenson, Bob, illus. 144p. (Orig.). (gr. k-7). 1988. wkbk. 19.95 (*0-685-20041-8*, 1400) Kidsrights.
McGrath, Meggan. My Grapes. McGrath, Meggan, illus. LC 93-24057. 48p. (Orig.). 1993. pap. 16.95 (*0-938586-99-8*) Pfeifer-Hamilton.
MacKay, Judy F. Tales of a Nuf in the Land of Doon. Langley, William A., illus. 84p. (Orig.). (gr. 4-7). 1992. pap. 9.95 perfect bdg. (*1-882748-00-X*) MacKay-Langley.
McKee, David. Elmer. McKee, David, illus. LC 89-2285. 32p. (ps-2). 1989. Repr. of 1968 ed. 12.95 (*0-688-09171-7*); PLB 12.88 (*0-688-09172-5*) Lothrop.
—King Rollo's Letter: And Other Stories. (Illus.). 28p. (gr. k-3). 1989. 16.95 (*0-86264-076-8*, Pub. by Anderson Pr UK) Trafalgar.
Mackenzie, Jill W. The Golden Fairy. LC 90-70311. (Illus.). 44p. (gr. 1-6). 1990. 6.95 (*1-55523-336-8*) Winston-Derek.
MacKenzie, Joy. Bible Read-to-Me: ABC. LC 87-18337. 48p. (ps-1). 1988. 9.99 (*1-55513-861-6*, Chariot Bks) Chariot Family.
—Bible Read-to-Me: 1-2-3. LC 87-18334. 48p. (ps-1). 1988. 9.99 (*1-55513-480-7*, Chariot Bks) Chariot Family.
McKie, Roy & Eastman, Philip D. Snow. LC 62-15114. (Illus.). 72p. (gr. 1-2). 1962. 6.95 (*0-394-80027-3*); lib. bdg. 7.99 (*0-394-90027-8*) Beginner.
MacKinnon, Christy. Silent Observer. (Illus.). 48p. 1993. 15.95 (*1-56368-022-X*, Pub. by K Green Pubns) Gallaudet Univ Pr.
McKissack, Patricia. Quien Viene? (Who Is Coming?) Martin, Clovis, illus. LC 86-11805. (SPA & ENG.). 32p. (ps-2). 1989. pap. 2.95 (*0-516-52073-3*) Childrens.
McKissack, Patricia & McKissack, Fredrick. Constance Stumbles. Dunnington, Tom, illus. 32p. (ps-2). 1988. PLB 10.25 (*0-516-02086-2*); pap. 2.95 (*0-516-42086-0*) Childrens.
—The King's New Clothes. Connelly, Gwen, illus. LC 86-33422. 32p. (ps-3). 1987. pap. 3.95 (*0-516-42365-7*) Childrens.
—Messy Bessey. LC 87-15079. (Illus.). (ps-2). 1987. PLB 10.25 (*0-516-02083-8*); pap. 2.95 (*0-516-42083-6*) Childrens.
—Three Billy Goats Gruff. Dunnington, Tom, illus. LC 86-33450. 32p. (ps-2). 1987. PLB 10.25 (*0-516-02366-7*); pap. 3.95 (*0-516-42366-5*) Childrens.
—El Traje Nuevo del Emperador: (The King's New Clothes) LC 86-33422. (ENG & SPA., Illus.). 32p. (ps-2). 1989. PLB 10.75 (*0-516-32365-2*); pap. 3.95 (*0-516-52365-1*) Childrens.
McKissack, Patricia C. Quien Es Quien? (Who Is Who?) Allen, Elizabeth M., illus. LC 83-7361. (SPA.). 32p. (ps-2). 1989. pap. 2.95 (*0-516-52042-3*) Childrens.
McKissack, Patricia C. & McKissack, Fredrick. Messy Bessey's Closet. Hackney, Rick, illus. LC 89-34667. 32p. (ps-2). 1989. PLB 10.25 (*0-516-02091-9*); pap. 2.95 (*0-516-42091-7*) Childrens.
McLeod, Emilie W. The Bear's Bicycle. McPhail, David, illus. (gr. 1-3). 1986. incl. cassette 19.95 (*0-87499-025-4*); pap. 12.95 incl. cassette (*0-87499-023-8*); 4 paperbacks, cassette & guide 27.95 (*0-87499-024-6*) Live Oak Media.
McLerran, Alice. The Mountain That Loved a Bird. Carle, Eric, illus. LC 85-9391. 32p. (ps up). 1991. pap. 15.95 (*0-88708-000-6*) Picture Bk Studio.
McMillan, Bruce. The Alphabet Symphony. (Illus.). 32p. (gr. k-2). 1989. 15.00 (*0-317-93064-8*) Apple Isl Bks.
—Becca Backward, Becca Frontward: A Book of Concept Pairs. LC 86-7221. (Illus.). 32p. (ps-1). 1986. 12.95 (*0-688-06282-2*); PLB 12.88 (*0-688-06283-0*) Lothrop.
—Step by Step. (Illus.). 28p. (ps-2). 1990. PLB 15.00 (*0-685-35118-1*) Apple Isl Bks.
McMillan, Naomi. Wish You Were Here. LC 90-85435. (Illus.). 32p. (gr. k-3). 1991. 5.95 (*1-56282-036-2*) Disney Pr.
McNaught, Harry, illus. Words to Grow On. LC 84-6880. 24p. (ps-1). 1984. 3.95 (*0-394-86103-5*) Random Bks Yng Read.
McNulty, Faith. How to Dig a Hole to the Other Side of the World. Simont, Marc, illus. LC 78-22479. 32p. (gr. k-3). 1990. pap. 4.95 (*0-06-443218-1*, Trophy) HarpC Child Bks.
—The Lady & the Spider. Marstall, Bob, illus. LC 85-5427. 48p. (gr. 1-4). 1987. pap. 4.95 (*0-06-443152-5*, Trophy) HarpC Child Bks.
McPartland, Suzy. Good Morning, Sun. Neeper, William, illus. 12p. (ps-k). 1994. pap. 4.95 (*0-689-71747-4*, Aladdin) Macmillan Child Grp.
—Sleepy-Time Moon. Neeper, William, illus. 12p. (ps-k). 1994. pap. 4.95 (*0-689-71748-2*, Aladdin) Macmillan Child Grp.
—Toy-Shop Surprise. Neeper, William, illus. 12p. (ps-k). 1994. pap. 4.95 (*0-689-71749-0*, Aladdin) Macmillan Child Grp.
—Zoom, Car, Zoom. Neeper, William, illus. 12p. (ps-k). 1994. pap. 4.95 (*0-689-71750-4*, Aladdin) Macmillan Child Grp.
McPhail, David. The Bear's Toothache. McPhail, David, illus. (gr. k-2). 1986. incl. cassette 19.95 (*0-87499-081-5*); pap. 12.95 incl. cassette (*0-87499-080-7*); 4 paperbacks, cassette & guide 27.95 (*0-87499-082-3*) Live Oak Media.
—Emma's Pet. McPhail, David, illus. (ps-2). 1988. bk. & cassette 19.95 (*0-87499-107-2*); bk. & cassette 12.95 (*0-87499-106-4*); 4 cassettes & guide 27.95 (*0-87499-108-0*) Live Oak Media.
—Farm Boy's Year. McPhail, David, illus. LC 91-4982. 32p. (gr. k-3). 1992. SBE 13.95 (*0-689-31679-8*, Atheneum Child Bk) Macmillan Child Grp.

—Fix-It. McPhail, David, illus. (gr. k-3). 1988. bk. & cassette 19.95 (*0-87499-084-X*); bk. & cassette 12.95 (*0-87499-083-1*); 4 cassettes & guide 27.95 (*0-87499-085-8*) Live Oak Media.
—Fix-It. McPhail, David, illus. LC 83-16459. 24p. (ps-k). 1987. pap. 3.95 (*0-525-44323-1*, 0383-120, DCB) Dutton Child Bks.
—Great Cat. LC 81-12654. (Illus.). 32p. (gr. k up). 1986. pap. 4.95 (*0-525-44273-1*, DCB) Dutton Child Bks.
—Pig Pig & the Magic Photo Album. McPhail, David, illus. LC 85-20459. 24p. (ps-3). 1986. 10.95 (*0-525-44238-3*, DCB) Dutton Child Bks.
—Pig Pig Rides. McPhail, David, illus. (gr. 1-3). 1988. bk. & cassette 19.95 (*0-87499-090-4*); bk. & cassette 12.95 (*0-87499-089-0*); 4 cassettes & guide 27.95 (*0-87499-091-2*) Live Oak Media.
McPherson, Betty. A Mayflower Adventure. Stefano, Nancy Di, illus. 32p. (ps-1). 1985. 6.00 (*0-918823-00-5*) Boyce-Pubns.
—The Small Patriot. (Illus.). 32p. (ps-1). 1987. 6.00 (*0-918823-01-3*) Boyce-Pubns.
McQueen. What Does Sunny Bunny Love? (gr. 2 up). 1988. 2.50 (*0-448-09252-2*, G&D) Putnam Pub Group.
McQueen, Lucinda. Counting Bears. (Illus.). 24p. (gr. 1-3). 1990. bds. 2.50 (*0-448-02263-X*, G&D) Putnam Pub Group.
McQueen, Lucinda, illus. Pudgy Zoo Babies. 16p. 1989. bds. 2.95 (*0-448-02256-7*, G&D) Putnam Pub Group.
Maddern, Eric. Life Story. Duff, Leo, illus. LC 87-73253. 32p. (gr. 1 up). 1988. 11.95 (*0-8120-5941-7*) Barron.
Madinaveitia, Horacio. Sir Robert's Little Outing. Madinaveitia, Horacio, illus. 32p. (gr. k-4). 1991. PLB 13.95 (*1-879567-01-6*, Valeria Bks); pap. text ed. 7.95 (*1-879567-00-8*) Wonder Well.
Magical Moments. (gr. 3 up). 1991. pap. 1.97 (*1-56297-119-0*, WD-180M) Lee Pubns KY.
Magni, Laura. Come to the Park. Cluet, Jaume, illus. 16p. (ps up). 1989. 8.95 (*0-8120-5994-8*) Barron.
—Two Little Monkeys. Bosni, Nella, illus. 18p. (ps-k). 1992. bds. 3.95 (*1-56397-154-2*) Boyds Mills Pr.
Magorian, James. Fimperings & Torples. LC 81-69872. (Illus.). 44p. (gr. 4-6). 1981. pap. 3.00 (*0-930674-06-5*) Black Oak.
—Imaginary Radishes. LC 79-53857. (Illus.). 32p. (gr. 3-5). 1980. 5.00 (*0-930674-03-0*) Black Oak.
Mahoney, Ellen V. Animals. Smith, Terry, illus. 8p. (ps). 1994. vinyl 3.95 (*0-8431-3545-X*) Price Stern.
—Buttontales: Fluffy Gets Dressed. Mahoney, Ellen, illus. 8p. (ps). 1993. 6.95 (*0-8431-3543-3*) Price Stern.
—Food. Smith, Terry, illus. 8p. (ps). 1994. vinyl 3.95 (*0-8431-3546-8*) Price Stern.
—Pocketales: In My Pocket. Mahoney, Ellen, illus. 8p. (ps). 1993. 6.95 (*0-8431-3544-1*) Price Stern.
—The Sea. Smith, Terry, illus. 8p. (ps). 1994. vinyl 3.95 (*0-8431-3547-6*) Price Stern.
—Toys. Smith, Terry, illus. 8p. (ps). 1994. vinyl 3.95 (*0-8431-3548-4*) Price Stern.
Mahy, Margaret. Boy Who Was Followed Home. Kellogg, Steven, illus. LC 75-2866. 32p. (ps-3). 1986. 13.95 (*0-8037-0286-8*) Dial Bks Young.
—Seventeen Kings & Forty-Two Elephants. MacCarthy, Patricia, illus. LC 87-5311. 32p. (ps-3). 1987. 13.99 (*0-8037-0458-5*) Dial Bks Young.
Make-Believe Moon. 12p. (ps-1). 1988. bds. 5.95 (*0-87449-627-6*) Modern Pub NYC.
Mammoth Book of Dinosaurs. 240p. (gr. k-2). 1989. 19.95 (*0-87449-650-0*) Modern Pub NYC.
Mandel, Peter. Ballerina Bunny Loves to Dance. 1987. pap. 2.50 (*0-89954-674-9*) Antioch Pub Co.
Mandelbaum, Pili. You Be Me, I'll Be You. (Illus.). 40p. (ps-3). pap. 6.95 (*0-916291-47-2*) Kane-Miller Bk.
Mann, Marek. Annie's City Adventures. Max, Jill, ed. Verlag, Mangold, tr. from GER. Mann, Marek, illus. LC 91-21302. 24p. (gr. k-3). 1991. PLB 14.60 (*1-56074-031-0*) Garrett Ed Corp.
—Annie's High Sea Adventure. Max, Jill & Bradford, Elizabeth, eds. Verlag, Mangold, tr. from GER. Mann, Marek, illus. LC 91-21305. 24p. (gr. k-3). 1991. PLB 14.60 (*1-56074-027-2*) Garrett Ed Corp.
—Dino, the Star Keeper. Max, Jill, ed. Verlag, Mangold, tr. from GER. Mann, Marek, illus. LC 91-21304. 24p. (gr. k-3). 1991. PLB 14.60 (*1-56074-028-0*) Garrett Ed Corp.
Mannino, Marc P. & Mannino, Angelica L. Marjorie's Magical Tail. LC 93-86041. (Illus.). 32p. (Orig.). (ps-5). 1993. pap. 7.95 (*0-9638340-0-2*) Sugar Sand.
Mantegazza, Giovanna. The Cat. Mesturini, Cristina, illus. LC 91-73872. 12p. (ps-1). 1992. 6.95 (*1-56397-032-5*) Boyds Mills Pr.
—The Hippopotamus. Mesturini, Cristina, illus. LC 91-73871. 12p. (ps-1). 1992. 6.95 (*1-56397-033-3*) Boyds Mills Pr.
Manton, Denis. Tigers in the Park. (Illus.). 32p. (ps-2). 1992. 15.95 (*0-09-174525-X*, Pub. by Hutchinson UK) Trafalgar.
Manushkin, Fran. Baby, Come Out! Himler, Ronald, illus. LC 78-183159. 32p. (ps-3). 1984. pap. 4.95 (*0-06-443050-2*, Trophy) HarpC Child Bks.
—Puppies & Kittens. (Illus.). 24p. (ps-k). 1989. pap. write for info. (*0-307-11806-1*, Pub. by Golden Bks) Western Pub.
Marcellino. Picture Book 2. (Illus.). Date not set. 15.00 (*0-06-205064-8*); PLB 14.89 (*0-06-205065-6*) HarpC Child Bks.
—Picture Book 3. (Illus.). Date not set. 15.00 (*0-06-205066-4*); PLB 14.89 (*0-06-205067-2*) HarpC Child Bks.
Marcuse, Aida E. Caperucita Roja y la Luna de Papel. Torrecilla, Pablo, illus. (SPA.). 24p. (Orig.). (gr. k-6). 1993. PLB 7.50x (*1-56492-103-4*) Laredo.
Mariotti, Mario. Hanimations. (Illus.). 40p. (ps-4). 1989. 10.95 (*0-916291-22-7*) Kane-Miller Bk.
—Humages. Marchiori, Roberto, illus. (Orig.). 1991. pap. 8.95 (*0-671-75233-2*, Green Tiger) S&S Trade.
Maris, Ron. Are You There, Bear? Maris, Ron, illus. 32p. (ps-1). 1986. pap. 3.50 (*0-14-050524-5*, Puffin) Puffin Bks.
—Hold Tight, Bear! (ps-1). 1989. 12.95 (*0-440-50152-0*) Delacorte.
—I Wish I Could Fly. Maris, Ron, illus. LC 86-9797. 32p. (ps-1). 1987. 13.95 (*0-688-06654-2*); PLB 13.88 (*0-688-06655-0*) Greenwillow.
Marks, Alan. Nowhere to be Found. Marks, Alan, illus. LC 87-32729. 28p. (ps up). 1991. pap. 14.95 (*0-88708-062-6*) Picture Bk Studio.
Marksbury, Tina, illus. Nighty-Night, Teddy Beddy Bear. 12p. (ps). 1986. 4.99 (*0-394-88244-X*) Random Bks Yng Read.
Marsh, Carole. Snowshoe & Earmuff Go West. (Illus.). (ps-3). 1994. 24.95 (*1-55609-304-7*); pap. 14.95 (*1-55609-303-9*) Gallopade Pub Group.
Marshall, James. Fox on the Job. Marshall, James, illus. LC 87-15589. 48p. (gr. k-3). 1988. 10.99 (*0-8037-0350-3*); PLB 9.89 (*0-8037-0351-1*) Dial Bks Young.
—George & Martha Round & Round. Marshall, James, illus. LC 88-14739. 48p. (gr. k-3). 1988. 13.45 (*0-395-46763-2*) HM.
—Goldilocks & the Three Bears. Marshall, James, illus. LC 87-32983. 32p. (ps-3). 1988. 14.00 (*0-8037-0542-5*); PLB 13.89 (*0-8037-0543-3*) Dial Bks Young.
—Red Riding Hood. LC 86-16722. (Illus.). 32p. (ps-3). 1987. 13.99 (*0-8037-0344-9*); PLB 10.89 (*0-8037-0345-7*) Dial Bks Young.
—Willis. Marshall, James, illus. LC 74-5259. (gr. k-3). 1974. 13.95 (*0-395-19494-6*) HM.
—Yummers! Marshall, James, illus. LC 72-5400. 32p. (gr. k-3). 1973. 13.45 (*0-395-14757-3*) HM.
—Yummers Too. Marshall, James, illus. LC 86-10667. 32p. (gr. k-3). 1986. 12.95 (*0-395-38990-9*) HM.
Martin, Bill, Jr. & Archambault, John. Chicka Chicka Boom Boom. Ehlert, Lois, illus. (gr. 2-6). 1989. pap. 13.95 jacketed (*0-671-67949-X*, S&S BFYR) S&S Trade.
—Here Are My Hands. Rand, Ted, illus. LC 86-25842. 32p. (ps-2). 1987. 14.95 (*0-8050-0328-2*, Bks Young Read) H Holt & Co.
—Here Are My Hands. Rand, Ted, illus. LC 86-25842. 32p. (ps-2). 1989. pap. 5.95 (*0-8050-1168-4*, Owlet BYR) H Holt & Co.
—Listen to the Rain. Endicott, James, illus. LC 88-6502. 32p. (ps-2). 1988. 15.95 (*0-8050-0682-6*, Bks Young Read) H Holt & Co.
—Up & down on the Merry-Go-Round. Rand, Ted, illus. LC 87-28836. 32p. (ps-2). 1988. 12.95 (*0-8050-0681-8*, Bks Young Read) H Holt & Co.
Martin, Dick. Cut & Assemble the Emerald City. 1980. pap. 5.95 (*0-486-24053-3*) Dover.
—Cut & Assemble Wizard of Oz Theatre. 1985. pap. 4.95 (*0-486-24799-6*) Dover.
Martin, Jacqueline B. Bizzy Bones & the Lost Quilt. Qrmai, Stella, illus. LC 87-13577. (ps-3). 1988. 12.95 (*0-688-07407-3*); PLB 12.88 (*0-688-07408-1*) Lothrop.
Martin, Kerry & Wakeman, Diana, illus. Walt Disney's Sleeping Beauty. LC 92-53435. 12p. (ps-k). 1993. 11.95 (*1-56282-369-8*) Disney Pr.
Martin, Rodney. The Making of a Picture Book. Siow, John, illus. LC 88-42911. 32p. (gr. 3-4). 1989. PLB 18.60 (*1-55532-958-6*) Gareth Stevens Inc.
Marvin, Fred, illus. Walt Disney's Pinocchio: Geppetto's Surprise. LC 92-54877. 10p. (ps-k). 1993. 4.95 (*1-56282-397-3*) Disney Pr.
Marzollo, Jean. The Rebus Treasury. Carson, Carol D., illus. LC 85-16133. 64p. (ps up). 1986. Dial Bks Young.
Maslen, Bobby L. Bob Books, Beginning Readers, 12 bks, Set I. (Illus.). 144p. (ps). 1983. pap. 14.95 (*0-9612104-0-0*) Bob Bks.
Mason, Margo C. Go Away, Crows! Prebenna, David, illus. 32p. (ps-1). 1989. 3.50 (*0-553-34725-X*) Bantam.
—Rover. Hoffman, Sandy, illus. 32p. (ps-1). write for info. Bantam.
—Winter Coats. (ps-k). 1989. 8.95 (*0-553-05818-5*) Bantam.
Massi, Jeri. Crown & Jewel. (Illus.). 160p. (Orig.). (gr. 5). 1987. pap. 4.95 (*0-89084-390-2*) Bob Jones Univ Pr.
Matarasso, Janet. Why Can't You Grow Up? Chambers, Margaret, illus. LC 85-25539. 24p. (ps-2). 1986. 11.95 (*0-521-32125-5*) Cambridge U Pr.
Mateu, Franc, illus. Disney's Snow White & the Seven Dwarfs Whistle While You Work: A Musical Pop-up Book. 10p. (ps-1). 1994. 11.95 (*1-56282-514-3*) Disney Pr.
—Walt Disney's the Jungle Book: Mowgli's Journey. LC 92-53438. 18p. (ps-1). 1993. 9.95 (*1-56282-374-4*) Disney Pr.
Mateu, Franc & Mateo, Franc, illus. Walt Disney's Snow White & the Seven Dwarfs. LC 92-53432. 12p. (ps-k). 1993. 11.95 (*1-56282-365-5*) Disney Pr.
Mathiesen, Egon. Jungle in the Wheat Field. (Illus.). (gr. k-3). 1960. 9.95 (*0-8392-3014-1*) Astor-Honor.
—Oswald the Monkey. (Illus.). (gr. k-3). 1959. 9.95 (*0-8392-3025-7*) Astor-Honor.
Mathieu, Joe. Big Bird's Big Book. Mathieu, Joe, illus. 12p. (ps-1). 1987. 29.95 (*0-394-89128-7*) Random Bks Yng Read.
—Elmo Wants a Bath. Mathieu, Joe, illus. 10p. (ps). 1992. vinyl 3.95 (*0-679-83066-9*) Random Bks Yng Read.
Mathieu, Joe, illus. Sesame Street Fire Trucks. 14p. (ps-k). 1988. bds. 3.99 (*0-394-89952-0*) Random Bks Yng Read.
—Trucks in Your Neighborhood. 14p. (ps-k). 1988. bds. 4.99 (*0-394-89951-2*) Random Bks Yng Read.
Matthias, Catherine. Arriba y Abajo (Over-Under) Sharp, Gene, illus. LC 83-21005. (SPA.). 32p. (ps-2). 1989. PLB 10.25 (*0-516-32048-3*); pap. 2.95 (*0-516-52048-2*) Childrens.
—Sal y Entra (Out the Door) Neill, Eileen M., illus. LC 81-17060. (SPA.). 32p. (ps-2). 1989. pap. 2.95 (*0-516-53560-9*) Childrens.
Mattox, Cheryl. My Play a Tune Book: Shake It to the One That You Love the Best. 1991. 15.95 (*0-938971-11-5*) JTG Nashville.
Mayer, Andy & Becker. Let's Look at Animals. Witt, Dick, illus. 12p. 1993. 5.95 (*0-590-45700-4*) Scholastic Inc.
—Let's Look at My World. Witt, Dick, illus. 12p. 1993. 5.95 (*0-590-45699-7*) Scholastic Inc.
Mayer, Gina & Mayer, Mercer. The New Potty. (Illus.). 24p. (ps-k). 1992. write for info. (*0-307-11523-2*, 11523) Western Pub.
Mayer, Marianna. The Little Jewel Box. Torres, Margot, illus. (ps-3). 1990. pap. 3.95 (*0-8037-0737-1*, Puff Pied Piper) Puffin Bks.
Mayer, Marianna & McDermott, Gerald. The Brambleberrys Animal Alphabet. LC 91-70420. (Illus.). 32p. (ps up). 1991. 3.95 (*1-878093-78-9*) Boyds Mills Pr.
—The Brambleberrys Animal Book of Colors. LC 91-70418. (Illus.). 32p. (ps up). 1991. 3.95 (*1-878093-76-2*) Boyds Mills Pr.
—The Brambleberrys Animal Book of Counting. LC 91-70419. (Illus.). 32p. (ps up). 1991. 3.95 (*1-878093-75-4*) Boyds Mills Pr.
—The Brambleberrys Animal Book of Shapes. LC 91-70421. (Illus.). 32p. (ps up). 1991. 3.95 (*1-878093-77-0*) Boyds Mills Pr.
Mayer, Mercer. Appelard & Liverwurst. Kellogg, Steven, illus. LC 89-13803. 40p. (gr. k up). 1990. 13.95 (*0-688-09659-X*); PLB 13.88 (*0-688-09660-3*, Morrow Jr Bks) Morrow Jr Bks.
—Baby Sister Says No. Mayer, Mercer, illus. LC 86-82368. 24p. (gr. 4-8). 1987. pap. write for info. (*0-307-11949-1*, Pub. by Golden Bks) Western Pub.
—A Boy, a Dog, a Frog & a Friend. LC 70-134857. (ps-2). 1978. 8.95 (*0-8037-0754-1*); PLB 8.89 (*0-8037-0755-X*); pap. 2.95 (*0-8037-0804-1*) Dial Bks Young.
—Hiccup. LC 76-2284. (Illus.). (ps-2). 1978. pap. 3.95 (*0-8037-3590-1*, 0383-120) Dial Bks Young.
—I Just Forgot. Mayer, Mercer, illus. LC 87-81779. 24p. (Orig.). (ps-3). 1988. pap. write for info. (*0-307-11975-0*) Western Pub.
—Just a Daydream. (Illus.). 24p. (ps-3). 1989. pap. write for info. (*0-307-11973-4*, Pub. by Golden Bks) Western Pub.
—Just a Mess. Mayer, Mercer, illus. LC 86-82369. 24p. (gr. 4-8). 1987. pap. write for info. (*0-307-11948-3*, Pub. by Golden Bks) Western Pub.
—Just a Nap. (Illus.). 24p. (ps-k). 1989. pap. write for info. (*0-307-11713-8*, Pub. by Golden Bks) Western Pub.
—Just a Snowy Day. (Illus.). 20p. (gr. k). 1983. write for info. comb. bdg. (*0-307-12156-9*, 12156, Golden Bks) Western Pub.
—Just Camping Out. (Illus.). 24p. (ps-k). 1989. pap. write for info. (*0-307-11714-6*, Pub. by Golden Bks) Western Pub.
—Just for You. Mayer, Mercer, illus. 24p. (ps-3). 1975. pap. write for info. (*0-307-11838-X*, Golden Bks.) Western Pub.
—Just Go to Bed. rev. ed. Mayer, Mercer, illus. 24p. (ps-3). 1985. pap. write for info. (*0-307-11940-8*, 11940, Pub. by Golden Bks) Western Pub.
—Just Grandma & Me. (Illus.). 24p. (ps-3). 1985. pap. write for info. (*0-307-11893-2*, Golden Bks) Western Pub.
—Just Grandpa & Me. Mayer, Mercer, illus. 24p. (ps-3). 1985. pap. write for info. (*0-307-11936-X*, Pub. by Golden Bks) Western Pub.
—Just Me & My Babysitter. Mayer, Mercer, illus. 24p. (Orig.). (ps-3). 1986. pap. write for info. (*0-307-11945-9*, Pub. by Golden Bks) Western Pub.
—Just Me & My Little Sister. Mayer, Mercer, illus. 24p. (Orig.). (ps-3). 1986. pap. write for info. (*0-307-11946-7*, Pub. by Golden Bks) Western Pub.
—Just Me & My Puppy. Mayer, Mercer, illus. 24p. (ps-3). 1985. pap. write for info. (*0-307-11937-8*, Pub. by Golden Bks) Western Pub.
—Just My Friend & Me. Mayer, Mercer, illus. 1988. write for info. (*0-307-11947-5*, 11947, Pub. by Golden Bks) Western Pub.
—Just Shopping with Mom. (Illus.). 24p. (ps-3). 1989. pap. write for info. (*0-307-11972-6*, Pub. by Golden Bks) Western Pub.
—Me Too! Mayer, Mercer, illus. 24p. (ps-3). 1985. pap. write for info. (*0-307-11941-6*, Pub. by Golden Bks) Western Pub.

—The New Baby. Mayer, Mercer, illus. 24p. (ps-3). 1985. pap. write for info. (*0-307-11942-4*, Pub. by Golden Bks) Western Pub.
—A Silly Story: Nothing Less Nothing More. Mayer, Mercer, illus. 48p. 1992. pap. 5.95 (*1-879920-02-6*) Rain Bird Prods.
—Terrible Troll. Mayer, Mercer, illus. LC 68-28730. (gr. k-3). 1968. Dial Bks Young.
—There's a Nightmare in My Closet. Mayer, Mercer, illus. LC 68-15250. (ps-3). 1985. 12.95 (*0-8037-8682-4*); PLB 12.89 (*0-8037-8683-2*); pap. 4.95 (*0-8037-8574-7*); guide 17.99 (*0-8037-0843-2*) Dial Bks Young.
—There's Something in My Attic. Mayer, Mercer, illus. LC 86-32875. 32p. (ps-3). 1988. 11.95 (*0-8037-0414-3*); PLB 11.89 (*0-8037-0415-1*) Dial Bks Young.
—When I Get Bigger. Mayer, Mercer, illus. 24p. (ps-3). 1985. pap. write for info. (*0-307-11943-2*, Pub. by Golden Bks) Western Pub.
Mayer, Mercer & Mayer, Marianna. One Frog Too Many. Mayer, Mercer, illus. LC 75-6325. 32p. (ps-2). 1985. 9.95 (*0-8037-4838-8*); PLB 9.89 (*0-8037-4858-2*) Dial Bks Young.
Mayer-Skumanz, Lene. Caroline Moves In. Sklenitzka, Franz S., illus. 96p. (gr. 1-3). 1988. pap. 2.95 (*0-8120-3938-6*) Barron.
Meggendorfer, Lothar. The Doll's House: A Reproduction of the Antique Pop-up Book. Meggendorfer, Lothar, illus. Shiller, Justin G., notes by. LC 79-5072. (Illus.). (gr. k-3). 1989. pap. 8.95 (*0-670-27761-4*) Viking Child Bks.
Meltzer, Lisa. One-Two-Three Look at Me. Gilchrest, Mary, illus. 28p. (ps). 1990. 2.95 (*0-02-689486-6*) Checkerboard.
Mendel, Kathleen L., ed. Lions, Lizards & Ladybugs. Harrison, Judy A., illus. LC 89-51485. 80p. (gr. k-6). 1989. pap. 9.95g (*0-9624384-2-1*) Telstar TX.
Mendoza, George. Hunter I Might Have Been. (Illus.). (gr. 3-5). 1968. 10.95 (*0-8392-3064-8*) Astor-Honor.
Menten, Ted. Cut & Use Stencil Bunny Rabbit. 1985. pap. 5.95 (*0-486-24909-3*) Dover.
—Folk Art Cut & Use Stencils. 1985. pap. 4.95 (*0-486-24838-0*) Dover.
—Ships & Boats Punch Out Stencils. 1986. pap. 3.50 (*0-486-25049-0*) Dover.
—Teddy Bear-Cut & Use Stencils. 1983. pap. 5.95 (*0-486-24595-0*) Dover.
—Teddy Bear Punch Out Stencils. 1985. pap. 3.50 (*0-486-24832-1*) Dover.
Menten, Theodore. Art Deco Cut & Use Stencils. 1977. pap. 4.95 (*0-486-23551-3*) Dover.
—Victorian Fashion Paper Dolls from Harper's Bazar, 1867-1898. 1979. pap. 3.95 (*0-486-23453-3*) Dover.
Merriam, Eve. Goodnight to Annie. Schwartz, Carol, illus. LC 92-7111. 32p. (ps-1). 1992. 14.95 (*1-56282-205-5*); PLB 14.89 (*1-56282-206-3*) Hyprn Child.
—Halloween ABC. Smith, Lane, illus. LC 86-23772. 32p. (gr. k up). 1987. RSBE 14.95 (*0-02-766870-3*, Macmillan Child Bk) Macmillan Child Grp.
Meryl, Debra. Baby's Peek-a-Boo Album. Kelley, True, illus. 24p. (ps). 1989. 11.95 (*0-448-15375-0*, G&D) Putnam Pub Group.
Messenger, Jannat. Lullaby & Goodnight: A Bedtime Book with Music. Messenger, Jannat, illus. 12p. (ps-1). 1988. pap. 10.95 POB (*0-689-71268-5*, Aladdin) Macmillan Child Grp.
—Twinkle Twinkle Little Star: A Lullaby Book with Lights & Music. Messenger, Jannat, illus. 12p. (ps-1). 1987. pap. 11.95 (*0-689-71136-0*, Aladdin) Macmillan Child Grp.
Meyrick, Kathryn. Musical Life of Gustav Mole. LC 90-49100. (ps-3). 1990. 11.95 (*0-85953-303-4*); pap. 5.95 (*0-85953-347-6*) Childs Play.
Mi Casa (My House) (SPA., Illus.). 28p. (ps-2). 1991. PLB 10.50 (*0-516-35359-4*); pap. 3.95 (*0-516-55359-3*) Childrens.
Michels, Tilde. Sophie the Rag Picker. Michels, Tilde, illus. (gr. k-1). 1962. 10.95 (*0-8392-3036-2*) Astor-Honor.
—Who's That Knocking at My Door? Michl, Reinhard, illus. 28p. (ps-3). 1986. 10.95 (*0-8120-5732-5*) Barron.
Mike, Jan & Lowmiller, Cathie. Bizagolaa; Apache Cut & Color Book. Lowmiller, Cathie, illus. 32p. (Orig.). (gr. k-6). 1989. pap. 3.95 (*0-918080-46-0*) Treasure Chest.
Mike, Jan M. Desert Seasons. Mike, Samuel A., illus. 32p. (gr. k-8). 1991. pap. 7.95 (*0-918080-49-5*) Treasure Chest.
Miles, Sally. Alfi & the Dark. Le Cain, Errol, illus. LC 88-1043. 32p. (ps-1). 1988. 13.95 (*0-87701-527-9*) Chronicle Bks.
Milios, Rita. Bears, Bears Everywhere. (ps-2). 1988. PLB 10.25 (*0-516-02085-4*); pap. 2.95 (*0-516-42085-2*) Childrens.
—I Am. Martin, Clovis, illus. LC 87-5163. 32p. (ps-2). 1987. PLB 10.25 (*0-516-02081-1*); pap. 2.95 (*0-516-42081-X*) Childrens.
—Osos, osos, aqui y alli: (Bears, Bears, Everywhere) Dunnington, Tom, illus. LC 87-33780. (ENG & SPA.). 32p. (ps-2). 1989. pap. 2.95 (*0-516-52085-7*) Childrens.
—Yo Soy (I Am) Martin, Clovis, illus. LC 87-5163. (SPA.). 32p. (ps-2). 1990. pap. 2.95 (*0-516-52081-4*) Childrens.
Miller, Albert G. Sesame Street Storybook. 1986. pap. 6.95 (*0-394-88301-2*) Random Bks Yng Read.
Miller, Edna. Mousekin Finds a Friend. Miller, Edna, illus. (ps-3). 1971. (Pub. by Treehouse) P-H.
Miller, His Son & the Donkey Pop up Book. 10p. (gr. 4-7). 1991. 8.95 (*0-8167-2200-5*) Troll Assocs.
Miller, J. P. Good Night, Little Rabbit. Miller, J. P., illus. LC 85-62017. 7p. (ps). 1993. bds. 3.95 (*0-394-87992-9*) Random Bks Yng Read.
Miller, M. L. Dizzy from Fools. Tharlet, Eve, illus. LC 85-9390. 32p. (gr. 1 up). 1991. pap. 13.95 (*0-88708-004-9*) Picture Bk Studio.
Milne, A. A. House at Pooh Corner: A Pop-Up Book. (Illus.). 12p. (ps up). 1986. 12.95 (*0-525-44245-6*, DCB) Dutton Child Bks.
—Now We Are Six. Shepard, Ernest H., illus. 112p. (ps up). 1988. 9.95 (*0-525-44446-7*, DCB) Dutton Child Bks.
—Pooh's Adventures with Eeyore & Tigger. (Illus.). 18p. (ps-4). 1986. 2.98 (*0-525-44263-4*, DCB) Dutton Child Bks.
—Pooh's Adventures with Piglet. (Illus.). 18p. (ps-4). 1986. 2.98 (*0-525-44264-2*, DCB) Dutton Child Bks.
—When We Were Very Young. Shepard, Ernest H., illus. 112p. (ps up). 1988. 9.95 (*0-525-44445-9*, DCB) Dutton Child Bks.
—Winnie the Pooh & Some Bees Storybooks. 128p. (ps-2). 1993. (DCB); pap. 4.99 (*0-525-45033-5*, DCB) Dutton Child Bks.
—Winnie-the-Pooh Goes Exploring. (ps-4). 1986. 2.98 (*0-525-44269-3*, DCB) Dutton Child Bks.
—Winnie-the-Pooh Lift-the-Flap Rebus Book. (Illus.). 16p. (ps-3). 1992. 12.95 (*0-525-44987-6*, DCB) Dutton Child Bks.
—Winnie-the-Pooh's Calendar Book 1987. Shepard, Ernest H., illus. (ps up). 1986. 4.95 (*0-525-44235-9*, Dutton) NAL-Dutton.
—Winnie the Pooh's Pop-up Theater Book. (Illus.). 12p. 1993. 15.95 (*0-525-44990-6*, DCB) Dutton Child Bks.
—Winnie-the-Pooh's Revolving Picture Book. (Illus.). 12p. (ps up). 1990. 13.00 (*0-525-44645-1*, DCB) Dutton Child Bks.
Minarik, Else H. Kiss for Little Bear. Sendak, Maurice, illus. LC 57-9263. 32p. (gr. k-3). 1968. 14.00 (*0-06-024298-1*); PLB 13.89 (*0-06-024299-X*) HarpC Child Bks.
—Little Bear. LC 57-9263. (Illus.). 64p. (gr. k-3). 1986. (Trophy); pap. 3.50 (*0-06-444004-4*, Trophy) HarpC Child Bks.
Mirame! (SPA., Illus.). 12p. (ps). 1992. bds. 4.95 (*0-525-44853-5*, DCB) Dutton Child Bks.
Miranda, Anne. Baby Talk. Stott, Dorothy, illus. 16p. (ps). 1987. 9.95 (*0-525-44319-3*, 0772-230, DCB) Dutton Child Bks.
—Baby Walk. Stott, Dorothy, illus. 14p. (ps). 1988. 8.95 (*0-525-44421-1*, DCB) Dutton Child Bks.
Miss Lori. Shapeless & the Magic Box, Bk. 1. White, Lori G., ed. Miss Lori, illus. 18p. (Orig.). (ps-1). 1990. pap. 11.99 (*0-9623368-3-1*) Shapeless Enterprises.
—Shapeless & the Magic Box, Bk. 2. White, Lori G., ed. Miss Lori, illus. 18p. (Orig.). (ps-1). 1991. pap. 11.99 (*0-9623368-8-2*) Shapeless Enterprises.
Mitchell, Cindy. Happy Hands & Feet. LC 88-82903. (Illus.). 80p. (ps-3). 1989. pap. text ed. 7.95 (*0-86530-062-3*, IP 166-0) Incentive Pubns.
Mitchell, Darby. Blue Eye of a Pond. Harris, Andrew S., illus. 10p. (ps-5). 1991. 8.00 (*0-9631809-0-8*) Castle MI.
Mitchell, Kathy. Silent Night: A Christmas Book with Lights & Music. Mitchell, Kathy, illus. 12p. (ps-3). 1989. pap. 11.95 (*0-689-71330-4*, Aladdin) Macmillan Child Grp.
Mitchell, Lyn, illus. Animals. 10p. (ps). 1992. 4.95 (*0-448-40304-8*, G&D) Putnam Pub Group.
—Clothes. 10p. (ps). 1992. 4.95 (*0-448-40307-2*, G&D) Putnam Pub Group.
—Eating. 10p. (ps). 1992. 4.95 (*0-448-40305-6*, G&D) Putnam Pub Group.
—Playing. 10p. (ps). 1992. 4.95 (*0-448-40306-4*, G&D) Putnam Pub Group.
Miyazaki, Hayao. Tokuma's Magical Adventure Series. Zimmerman, Maureen, ed. Saburi, Eugene, tr. from JPN. Miyazaki, Hayao, illus. 112p. (gr. 3-6). 1992. PLB 44.85 (*4-19-086974-0*) Tokuma Pub.
Modan, Shula. Why Jonathan Doesn't Cry. Leon, Yael, illus. (ps-2). 1988. 7.95 (*1-55774-022-4*, Dist. by Watts) Modan-Adama Bks.
Modell, Frank. One Zillion Valentines. LC 81-2215. 32p. (ps up). 1987. pap. 3.95 (*0-688-07329-8*, Mulberry) Morrow.
Modesitt, Jeanne. Night Call. (ps). 1991. pap. 3.95 (*0-14-050944-5*, Puffin) Puffin Bks.
Moerbeek, Kees. Boo Whoo? Moorbeek, Kees, illus. 10p. (ps up). 1993. 9.95 (*0-8431-3623-5*) Price Stern.
—Four Courageous Climbers. (Illus.). 12p. (ps up). 1991. 9.95 (*0-8431-2915-8*) Price Stern.
—New at the Zoo: A Mix-&-Match Pop-up Book. Moerbeek, Kees, illus. LC 89-60077. 10p. (ps-1). 1989. bds. 8.99 (*0-679-80076-X*) Random Bks Yng Read.
—New at the Zoo Two: A Mix-&-Match Pop-up Book. Moerbeek, Kees, illus. LC 92-60763. 10p. (ps-1). 1993. 8.99 (*0-679-83711-6*) Random Bks Yng Read.
—Oh No, Santa! (Illus.). 12p. (ps up). 1991. 10.95 (*0-8431-2984-0*) Price Stern.
—Who's Peeking at Me? Moerbeek, Kees, illus. 12p. (ps-3). 1994. 9.95 (*0-8431-2410-5*) Price Stern.
Mogensen, Jan. The Forty-Six Little Men. LC 90-36470. (Illus.). 28p. (ps up). 1991. 13.95 (*0-688-09283-7*); PLB 13.88 (*0-688-09284-5*) Greenwillow.
Mohr, Joseph. Silent Night. Jeffers, Susan, illus. LC 84-8113. 32p. (ps up). 1984. 14.95 (*0-525-44144-1*, DCB); pap. 4.95 (*0-8037-4443-9*, DCB) Dutton Child Bks.
Molnar, Dorothy E. & Fenton, Stephen H. Who Will Pick Me up When I Fall? Mathews, Judith, ed. Trivas, Irene, illus. LC 90-28250. 32p. (ps-2). 1991. 13.95 (*0-8075-9072-X*) A Whitman.
Moncure, Jane B. Apes Find Shapes. Freidman, Joy, illus. LC 87-11747. (ENG & SPA.). 32p. (ps-2). 1987. PLB 14.95 (*0-89565-364-8*) Childs World.
—Away Went the Farmer's Hat. Hohag, Linda, illus. LC 87-11742. (ENG & SPA.). 32p. (ps-2). 1987. PLB 14.95 (*0-89565-367-2*) Childs World.
—The Bears Upstairs. Knipper, Sue, illus. LC 87-11715. (ENG & SPA.). 32p. (ps-2). 1987. PLB 14.95 (*0-89565-373-7*) Childs World.
—A Color Clown Comes to Town. Hohag, Linda, illus. LC 87-11605. (ENG & SPA.). 32p. (ps-2). 1987. PLB 14.95 (*0-89565-369-9*) Childs World.
—A Dragon in a Wagon. Hohag, Linda, illus. LC 87-11755. (ENG & SPA.). 32p. (ps-2). 1987. PLB 14.95 (*0-89565-400-8*) Childs World.
—Hop-skip-jump-a-roo Zoo. Hohag, Linda, illus. LC 87-11743. (ENG & SPA.). 32p. (ps-2). 1987. PLB 14.95 (*0-89565-371-0*) Childs World.
—Let's Take a Walk in the Zoo. Axeman, Lois, illus. LC 86-20744. 32p. (ps-2). 1986. PLB 14.95 (*0-89565-356-7*) Childs World.
—Little Too-Tall. Hohag, Linda, illus. LC 87-11632. (ENG & SPA.). 32p. (ps-2). 1987. PLB 14.95 (*0-89565-374-5*) Childs World.
—Magic Monsters Learn about Manners. Sommers, Linda, illus. LC 79-24528. (ps-3). 1980. PLB 14.95 (*0-89565-118-1*) Childs World.
—Mousekin's Special Day. Williams, Jenny, illus. LC 87-11750. (SPA & ENG.). 32p. (ps-2). 1987. PLB 14.95 (*0-89565-366-4*) Childs World.
—My First Book. Hutton, Kathryn, illus. LC 84-17455. 32p. (ps-2). 1984. PLB 14.95 (*0-89565-271-4*) Childs World.
—One Tricky Monkey Up on Top. Freidman, Joy, illus. LC 87-11612. 32p. (ps-2). 1987. PLB 14.95 (*0-89565-365-6*) Childs World.
—A Pocketful of Pets. Hohag, Linda, illus. LC 87-11748. (SPA & ENG.). 32p. (ps-2). 1987. PLB 14.95 (*0-89565-370-2*) Childs World.
—What Do You Do with a Grumpy Kangaroo? Hohag, Linda, illus. LC 87-11731. (SPA & ENG.). 32p. (ps-2). 1987. PLB 14.95 (*0-89565-372-9*) Childs World.
—What Do You Say When a Monkey Acts This Way? Super, Terri, illus. LC 87-11736. (SPA & ENG.). 32p. (ps-2). 1987. PLB 14.95 (*0-89565-368-0*) Childs world.
—Where? Axeman, Lois, illus. LC 83-7307. 32p. (gr. k-2). 1983. pap. 3.95 (*0-516-46593-7*) Childrens.
—Word Bird's Christmas Words. Gohman, Vera, illus. LC 86-31666. 32p. (gr. k-2). 1987. PLB 14.95 (*0-89565-361-3*) Childs World.
—Word Bird's Easter Words. Axeman, Lois, illus. 32p. (gr. k-2). 1987. PLB 14.95 (*0-89565-363-X*) Childs World.
—Word Bird's Halloween Words. Gohman, Vera, illus. LC 86-31024. 32p. (gr. k-2). 1987. PLB 14.95 (*0-89565-359-1*) Childs World.
—Word Bird's Thanksgiving Words. Hohag, Linda, illus. LC 86-32639. 32p. (gr. k-2). 1987. PLB 14.95 (*0-89565-360-5*) Childs World.
—Word Bird's Valentine Day Words. Fullam, Sue M., illus. 32p. (gr. k-2). 1987. PLB 14.95 (*0-89565-362-1*) Childs World.
Monesson, Harry S. The World's Biggest Tummy. Monesson, Harry S., illus. LC 92-96830. 40p. (Orig.). (gr. k-3). 1992. pap. 6.95 (*0-9633735-0-1*) H S Monesson.
Monsell, Mary E. Underwear! Levine, Abby, ed. Munsinger, Lynn, illus. LC 87-25419. 24p. (ps-2). 1988. PLB 11.95 (*0-8075-8308-1*) A Whitman.
Monster Pop-Up. (ps-3). 1988. 9.95 (*0-8167-1445-2*) Troll Assocs.
Monsters: Pop-Up. (Illus.). (ps-3). 1993. 4.95 (*0-8167-2926-3*) Troll Assocs.
Monstruos! (Monsters!) (SPA., Illus.). 28p. (ps-2). 1991. PLB 11.55 (*0-516-35358-6*); pap. 3.95 (*0-516-55358-5*) Childrens.
Montgomery, H. Mongoose Magoo. LC 68-56822. (Illus.). 64p. (gr. 2-5). 1968. PLB 10.95 (*0-87783-026-6*); pap. 3.94 deluxe ed. (*0-87783-100-9*) Oddo.
Moorbeek, Kees. Museum of Unnatural History. Moorbeek, Kees, illus. 6p. (ps up). 1993. 14.95 (*0-8431-3541-7*) Price Stern.
Moore, Beverly. Echo's Song. Moore, Beverly, illus. 40p. (gr. k-3). 1993. PLB 13.95g (*0-9637288-7-3*) River Walker Bks.
Moore, Clement C. The Night Before Christmas: A Revolving Picture & Lift-the-Flap Book. Ives, Penny, illus. 14p. 1988. 14.95 (*0-399-21544-1*, Putnam) Putnam Pub Group.
Moore, Dessie. Good Morning. Moore, Chevelle, illus. 16p. (ps). 1994. 5.95 (*0-694-00593-2*, Festival) HarpC Child Bks.
—Good Night. Moore, Chevelle, illus. 16p. (ps). 1994. 5.95 (*0-694-00592-4*, HarpT) HarpC Child Bks.
—Let's Pretend. Moore, Chevelle, illus. 16p. (ps). 1994. 5.95 (*0-694-00591-6*, HarpT) HarpC Child Bks.

Moore, Frank J. The Incredible Moving Picture Book. 32p. (gr. 1 up). 1987. pap. 3.95 (0-486-25374-0) Dover.

Moore, Lilian. Junk Day on Easy Street & Other Easy-To-Read Stories. Lobel, Arnold, illus. (gr. 1-4). 1991. pap. 2.75 (0-553-15627-6, Skylark) Bantam.

Mooser, Stephen & Oliver, Lin. Tad & Dad. Day, Susan, illus. LC 87-40340. (ps-2). 1990. 4.95 (1-55782-023-6, Pub. by Warner Juvenile Bks) Little.

Mora, Pat. Agua, Agua, Agua. 16p. (ps-1). 1994. text ed. 3.95 (0-673-36195-0) GdYrBks.

Morehead, Ruth J. The Christmas Story with Holly Babes. Morehead, Ruth J., illus. LC 85-32305. 32p. (ps-1). 1987. 2.25 (0-394-88051-X); cassette pkg. 5.95 (0-394-89058-2) Random Bks Yng Read.

Morgan, Mary. Wee Seasons. (Illus.). 24p. (ps). 1990. bds. 2.50 (0-448-02261-3, G&D) Putnam Pub Group.

Morgan, Mary, illus. The Pudgy Merry Christmas Book. 16p. 1989. bds. 2.95 (0-448-02262-1, G&D) Putnam Pub Group.

—Sleepy Time. LC 89-63997. 14p. (ps). 1990. bds. 3.95 (0-679-80753-5) Random Bks Yng Read.

Morris, Ann. The Cinderella Rebus Book. Rylands, Ljiljana, illus. LC 88-1451. 32p. (ps-3). 1989. 13.95 (0-531-05761-5); PLB 13.99 (0-531-08361-6) Orchard Bks Watts.

Morris, Neil. Feel! A Fun Book of Touch. (ps). 1992. pap. 6.95 (0-87614-569-1) Carolrhoda Bks.

—Holly & Harry: A Fun Book of Sizes. (ps). 1992. pap. 6.95 (0-87614-570-5) Carolrhoda Bks.

—I'm Big: A Fun Book of Opposites. (ps). 1992. pap. 6.95 (0-87614-571-3) Carolrhoda Bks.

—Magic Monkey: A Fun Book of Shapes & Colors. (ps). 1992. pap. 6.95 (0-87614-574-8) Carolrhoda Bks.

—Rummage Sale: A Fun Book of Shapes & Colors. (ps). 1992. pap. 6.95 (0-87614-575-6) Carolrhoda Bks.

—What a Noise: A Fun Book of Sounds. (ps). 1992. pap. 6.95 (0-87614-576-4) Carolrhoda Bks.

Morrison, Blake. The Yellow House. Craig, Helen, illus. 32p. (ps-3). 1987. 12.95 (0-15-299820-9, HB Juv Bks) HarBrace.

Mosel, Arlene. Tikki Tikki Tembo. Lent, Blair, illus. LC 68-11839. 32p. (ps-2). 1968. 14.95 (0-8050-0662-1, Bks Young Read) H Holt & Co.

Mosel, Arlene, retold by. Tikki Tikki Tembo. Lent, Blair, illus. LC 68-11839. 32p. (ps-2). 1989. pap. 5.95 (0-8050-1166-8, Bks Young Read) H Holt & Co.

Moseley, Keith & Everitt-Stewart, Andy. The Door under the Stairs. (Illus.). 12p. 1990. 8.95 (0-448-40044-8, G&D) Putnam Pub Group.

Moss, Marissa. Who Was It? Moss, Marissa, illus. (gr. k-3). 1989. 13.45 (0-395-49699-3) HM.

Most, Bernard. Whatever Happened to the Dinosaurs? LC 84-37795. (Illus.). 32p. (Orig.). (ps-3). 1987. pap. 4.95 (0-15-295296-9, Voyager Bks) HarBrace.

Moulton, Dwayne. The Mystery of the Pink Waterfall. Headley, Adriane M., illus. LC 80-84116. 192p. (gr. 3-8). 1980. 14.95 (0-9605236-0-X) Pandoras Treasures.

Mountain, Lee, et al. Goldilocks & the Three Bears. (Illus.). 16p. (gr. k-1). 1993. pap. 14.75 (0-89061-739-2) Jamestown Pubs.

MPI, Bk. 5. (gr. 3 up). 1991. pap. 1.68 (1-56297-082-8) Lee Pubns KY.

MPI, Bk. 6. (gr. 3 up). 1991. pap. 1.68 (1-56297-083-6) Lee Pubns KY.

Mueller, Virginia. A Halloween Mask for Monster. Fay, Ann, ed. Munsinger, Lynn, illus. LC 86-1569. 24p. (ps-1). 1986. 11.95 (0-8075-3134-0) A Whitman.

—A Halloween Mask for Monster. Munsinger, Lynn, illus. (ps-1). 1988. pap. 3.95 (0-14-050879-1, Puffin) Puffin Bks.

—Monster & the Baby. Munsinger, Lynn, illus. (ps-1). 1988. pap. 3.95 (0-14-050880-5, Puffin) Puffin Bks.

—Monster Can't Sleep. Fay, Ann, ed. Munsinger, Lynn, illus. LC 86-1568. 24p. (ps-1). 1986. PLB 11.95 (0-8075-5261-5) A Whitman.

—Monster Goes to School. Levine, Abby, ed. Munsinger, Lynn, illus. LC 90-29873. 24p. (ps-1). 1991. 11.95 (0-8075-5264-X) A Whitman.

—Monster's Birthday Hiccups. Levine, Abby, ed. Munsinger, Lynn, illus. LC 91-2118. 24p. (ps-1). 1991. 11.95 (0-8075-5267-4) A Whitman.

Muldoon, Kathleen M. Princess Pooh. Mathews, Judith, ed. Shute, Linda, illus. LC 88-33978. 32p. (gr. 2-5). 1989. PLB 13.95 (0-8075-6627-6) A Whitman.

Munger, Carol V. Billy Groat. Decker, Tim, illus. LC 87-71679. 23p. (Orig.). 1990. pap. 4.00 (0-916383-45-8) Aegina Pr.

Munsch, Robert. The Dark. Suomalainen, Sami, illus. 24p. (ps-1). 1987. pap. 0.99 (0-920303-47-1, Pub. by Annick CN) Firefly Bks Ltd.

—I Have to Go! Martchenko, Michael, illus. 24p. (ps-1). 1987. pap. 0.99 (0-920303-51-X, Pub. by Annick CN) Firefly Bks Ltd.

—Mud Puddle. Suomalainen, Sami, illus. 24p. (ps-1). 1986. pap. 0.99 (0-920236-23-5, Pub. by Annick CN) Firefly Bks Ltd.

Muntean, Michaela. The Little Engine That Could & the Big Chase. Graham, Florence, illus. 32p. (ps-2). 1988. pap. 1.95 (0-448-19095-8, Platt & Munk Pubs) Putnam Pub Group.

Muppet Babies Invisible. (gr. 3 up). 1991. pap. 1.97 (1-56297-126-3, MB-450) Lee Pubns KY.

Muppet Babies Invisible. (gr. 3 up). 1991. pap. 1.97 (1-56297-128-X, MUP-401) Lee Pubns KY.

Muppet Babies Magic Pen. (gr. 3 up). 1991. pap. 1.97 (1-56297-127-1, MB-450) Lee Pubns KY.

Muppet Babies Magic Pen. (gr. 3 up). 1991. pap. 1.97 (1-56297-129-8, MUP-401) Lee Pubns KY.

Muppet Babies Two in One. (gr. 3 up). 1991. pap. 1.97 (1-56297-157-3) Lee Pubns KY.

Muppet Two in One Books. (gr. 3 up). 1991. pap. 1.97 (1-56297-156-5) Lee Pubns KY.

Murphy, Elspeth C. Barney Wigglesworth & the Birthday Surprise. Yakovetic, illus. LC 88-4346. 32p. (ps-2). 1988. 9.99 (1-55513-696-6, Chariot Bks) Chariot Family.

—Barney Wigglesworth & the Church Flood. Yakovetic, illus. LC 88-5008. 32p. (ps-2). 1988. 9.99 (1-55513-685-0, Chariot Bks) Chariot Family.

—Barney Wigglesworth & the Party That Almost Wasn't. Yakovetic, illus. LC 88-4342. 32p. (ps-2). 1988. 9.99 (1-55513-684-2, Chariot Bks) Chariot Family.

—Barney Wigglesworth & the Smallest Christmas Pageant. Yakovetic, illus. LC 88-5009. 32p. (ps-2). 1989. 9.99 (1-55513-686-9, Chariot Bks) Chariot Family.

—Kids Can Be Wise Too. LC 87-35539. 24p. (ps-2). 1988. pap. 4.99 (1-55513-893-4, Chariot Bks) Chariot Family.

—Sometimes I Get Scared. Nelson, Jane E., illus. (ps-2). 1980. pap. 3.99 (0-89191-275-4, 52753, Chariot Bks) Chariot Family.

—What Can I Say to You, God? Nelson, Jane E., illus. (ps-2). 1980. pap. 3.99 (0-89191-276-2, Chariot Bks) Chariot Family.

Murphy, Jim. The Last Dinosaur. Weatherby, Mark A., illus. LC 87-3008. 32p. (gr. 1-3). 1988. pap. 14.95 (0-590-41097-0, Scholastic Hardcover) Scholastic Inc.

Murrow, Liza K. Good-Bye, Sammy. Owens, Gail, illus. LC 88-17011. 32p. (ps-3). 1989. reinforced bdg. 13.95 (0-8234-0726-8) Holiday.

My Big Book of Fairy Tales: A Treasury of Favorite Stories for Children. 1987. 8.98 (0-671-08503-4) S&S Trade.

My Biggest Playtime Book Ever. 1987. 8.98 (0-671-07933-6) S&S Trade.

My Book of One Minute Stories & Verses. 1987. 3.98 (0-671-08500-X) S&S Trade.

My Castle. (Illus.). (ps-1). 1991. 25.00 (1-56021-098-2) W J Fantasy.

My Day. 16p. (ps-k). 1980. pap. 2.95 (0-671-41344-9, Little) S&S Trade.

My First Book of Bible Devotions. LC 90-37714. 80p. (ps). 1991. 6.99 (1-55513-416-5, 64162, Chariot Bks) Chariot Family.

My First Picture Dictionary. (ps-1). 1985. 5.98 (0-517-44379-1) Random Hse Value.

My First Picture Word Book. (Illus.). (ps-1). 1985. 3.98 (0-517-46373-3) Random Hse Value.

My First Sticker Book Atlas. (Illus.). 12p. (ps-2). 1994. 6.95 (1-56458-714-2) Dorling Kindersley.

My Little Bible Picture Book. LC 88-4575. (Illus.). 80p. (ps). 1988. 5.99 (1-55513-513-7, Chariot Bks) Chariot Family.

My Little Duck Woodbook. 8p. (ps). 1986. bds. 15.95 (0-8120-5694-9) Barron.

My Mini Rooster Woodbook. 8p. (ps). 1986. bds. 5.95 (0-8120-5702-3) Barron.

My Name Is Bert. (Illus.). (ps-k). 1991. write for info. (0-307-11517-8, Golden Pr) Western Pub.

My Plane Bath Book. (Illus.). (ps). 1989. vinyl 4.95 (0-8167-1607-2) Troll Assocs.

My Rocket Bath Book. (Illus.). (ps). 1989. vinyl 4.95 (0-8167-1604-8) Troll Assocs.

My Sensational Sticker Set. (Illus.). (ps-3). 1993. pap. 2.95 (0-8167-3098-9) Troll Assocs.

My Stand up Baby Animals. (Illus.). (ps-k). 1993. 6.00 (1-56021-199-7) W J Fantasy.

My Stand up Farm Animals. (Illus.). (ps-k). 1993. 6.00 (1-56021-200-4) W J Fantasy.

My Submarine Bath Book. (Illus.). (ps). 1989. 4.95 (0-8167-1606-4) Troll Assocs.

My Super Duper Sticker Set. (ps-3). 1993. pap. 2.95 (0-8167-3099-7) Troll Assocs.

My Train Bath Book. (ps). 1989. vinyl 4.95 (0-8167-1605-6) Troll Assocs.

Myers, Tim. Let's Call Him Lau-Wili-Wili-Humu-Humu-Nukuauku-Nukuanukai-Apuaa-Oioi. Arakaki, Daryl, illus. LC 93-72767. 24p. (ps-3). 1993. 12.95 (1-880188-67-8); pap. 5.95 (0-685-68878-X) Bess Pr.

Nash, Ogden. Custard the Dragon. Nash, Linell, illus. (gr. k-3). 1973. lib. bdg. 14.95 (0-316-59841-0) Little.

Natural History Activity Book. (Illus.). (ps-6). pap. 2.95 (0-565-00857-9, Pub. by Natural Hist Mus) Parkwest Pubns.

La Navidad de Azulin. LC 87-15793. (SPA., Illus.). 32p. (gr. k-3). 1987. PLB 11.80 (0-516-33483-2); pap. 3.95 (0-516-53483-1) Childrens.

Naylor, Phyllis R. Keeping a Christmas Secret. Shiffman, Lena, illus. LC 88-29277. 32p. (ps-2). 1989. RSBE 13.95 (0-689-31447-7, Atheneum Child Bk) Macmillan Child Grp.

Neasi, Barbara. Just Like Me Big Book. (Illus.). 32p. (ps-2). 1988. PLB 22.95 (0-516-49506-2) Childrens.

—Listen To Me Big Book. (Illus.). 32p. (ps-2). 1988. PLB 22.95 (0-516-49507-0) Childrens.

—Sweet Dreams. Martin, Clovis, illus. LC 87-15083. 32p. (ps-2). 1987. PLB 10.25 (0-516-02084-6); pap. 2.95 (0-516-42084-4) Childrens.

Neasi, Barbara J. A Minute Is a Minute. Martin, Clovis, illus. 32p. (ps-3). 1988. pap. 3.95 (0-516-43491-8) Childrens.

Nerlove, Miriam. Halloween. Levine, Abby, ed. Nerlove, Miriam, illus. LC 88-36858. 24p. (ps-1). 1989. PLB 11.95 (0-8075-3131-6); pap. 4.95 (0-8075-3130-8) A Whitman.

—Hanukkah. Levine, Abby, ed. Nerlove, Miriam, illus. LC 88-36648. 24p. (ps-1). 1989. PLB 11.95 (0-8075-3143-X); pap. 4.95 (0-8075-3142-1) A Whitman.

—I Made a Mistake. Nerlove, Miriam, illus. LC 85-6018. 32p. (ps-2). 1985. SBE 13.95 (0-689-50327-X, M K McElderry) Macmillan Child Grp.

Nesbit, Edith. The Deliverers of Their Country. Zwerger, Lisbeth, illus. LC 85-9389. 32p. (gr. 3-5). 1991. pap. 15.95 (0-88708-005-7) Picture Bk Studio.

Ness, Evaline. Sam, Bangs & Moonshine. Ness, Evaline, illus. LC 66-10113. 48p. (ps-2). 1971. 14.95 (0-8050-0314-2, Bks Young Read); pap. 5.95 (0-8050-0315-0) H Holt & Co.

Nevins, Kathy. Dot-to-Dot Dinos. (Illus.). 48p. (Orig.). (gr. 2 up). 1989. pap. 2.95 incl. chipboard (0-8431-2338-9) Price Stern.

A New Doll for Baby Daisy. write for info. (1-56326-308-4, 030908) Disney Bks By Mail.

Newberry, Clare T. April's Kittens. Newberry, Clare T., illus. LC 40-32442. 32p. (gr. k-3). 1940. 17.00 (0-06-024400-3); PLB 16.89 (0-06-024401-1) HarpC Child Bks.

Newell, Peter. The Hole Book. LC 84-52396. (Illus.). 50p. (gr. k-4). 1985. Repr. of 1902 ed. 14.95 (0-8048-1498-8) C E Tuttle.

Newell, Peter S. Topsys & Turvys. LC 87-51208. (gr. k-4). 1988. 12.95 (0-8048-1551-8) C E Tuttle.

—Topsys & Turvys, No. 2. LC 87-51208. (gr. k-4). 1988. 12.95 (0-8048-1552-6) C E Tuttle.

Newman, Leslea. Belinda's Bouquet. Willhoite, Michael, illus. 24p. (gr. k-3). 1991. pamphlet 6.95 (1-55583-154-0) Alyson Pubns.

Newton, Laura. Me & My Aunts. Fay, Ann, ed. Oz, Robin, illus. LC 86-15950. 32p. (gr. 2-5). 1986. PLB 13.95 (0-8075-5029-9) A Whitman.

Newton, Laura P. William the Vehicle King. Rogers, Jackie, illus. LC 86-33412. 32p. (ps-2). 1987. RSBE 13.95 (0-02-768230-7, Bradbury Pr) Macmillan Child Grp.

Nichol, B. P. Once: A Lullaby. Lobel, Anita, illus. LC 85-9942. 24p. (ps-1). 1986. 11.95 (0-688-04284-8); PLB 11.88 (0-688-04285-6) Greenwillow.

Nic Leodhas, Sorche. Always Room for One More. Hogrogian, Nonny, illus. LC 65-12881. 32p. (ps-2). 1972. reinforced bdg. 14.95 (0-8050-0331-2, Bks Young Read); pap. 5.95 (0-8050-0330-4) H Holt & Co.

Nicoll, Helen & Pienkowski, Jan. Meg & Mog. (Illus.). (ps-2). 1976. pap. 3.50 (0-14-050117-7, Puffin) Puffin Bks.

—Mog's Box. (Illus.). 32p. (ps-k). 1987. 15.95 (0-434-95658-9, Pub. by W Heinemann Ltd) Trafalgar.

The Night Before Christmas. (Illus.). (ps-k). 1991. write for info. (0-307-10038-3, Golden Pr) Western Pub.

Nikola-Lisa, W. One, Two, Three Thanksgiving! Levine, Abby, ed. Kramer, Robin, illus. LC 90-28638. 32p. (ps-1). 1991. 13.95 (0-8075-6109-6) A Whitman.

Nims, Bonnie L. Where Is the Bear? Fay, Ann, ed. Wallner, John, illus. LC 87-25321. 24p. (ps-2). 1988. PLB 11.95 (0-8075-8933-0) A Whitman.

Nister, Ernest. The Children's Picture Book. Nister, Ernest, illus. LC 80-7613. 18p. (ps-3). 1980. pop-up bk. 9.95 (0-385-28173-0) Delacorte.

—Christmas Toys. (Illus.). 10p. (ps up). 1992. 4.95 (0-399-21995-1, Philomel Bks) Putnam Pub Group.

—Darling Babies. Nister, Ernest, illus. 10p. 1994. 4.95 (0-399-22722-9, Philomel) Putnam Pub Group.

—Good Friends. (Illus.). 1989. 5.95 (0-399-21729-0, Philomel Bks) Putnam Pub Group.

—The Great Panorama Picture Book. Nister, Ernest, illus. LC 82-70305. 18p. (ps-3). 1982. pop-up bk. 8.95 (0-385-28327-X) Delacorte.

—Land of Sweet Surprises: An Antique Revolving Picture Books. Nister, Ernest, illus. (gr. k up). 1983. 12.95 (0-399-20993-X, Philomel) Putnam Pub Group.

—Magic Windows: An Antique Revolving Picture Book. (Illus.). 14p. (ps up). 1981. 12.95 (0-399-20773-2, Philomel) Putnam Pub Group.

—Our Baby. (Illus.). 32p. 1991. 15.95 (0-399-21856-4, Philomel Bks) Putnam Pub Group.

—Pop up Mother Goose Favorites. (Illus.). 18p. (ps up). 1989. 13.50 (0-525-44504-8, DCB) Dutton Child Bks.

—Santa's Surprises. (Illus.). 10p. (ps up). 1992. 4.95 (0-399-21996-X, Philomel Bks) Putnam Pub Group.

—Snowy Days. (Illus.). 10p. (ps up). 1992. 4.95 (0-399-21997-8, Philomel Bks) Putnam Pub Group.

—Spring Gardens. Nister, Ernest, illus. 10p. 1994. 4.95 (0-399-22723-7, Philomel) Putnam Pub Group.

—Sunny Days. Nister, Ernest, illus. 10p. 1994. 4.95 (0-399-22721-0, Philomel) Putnam Pub Group.

—Tiny Tots. Intervisual Staff, illus. 10p. (ps up). 1991. 4.95 (0-399-22108-5, Philomel) Putnam Pub Group.

—Token of Love. Nister, Ernest, illus. 10p. 1994. 4.95 (0-399-22720-2, Philomel) Putnam Pub Group.

—Yuletide Delights. (Illus.). 10p. (ps up). 1992. 4.95 (0-399-21998-6, Philomel Bks) Putnam Pub Group.

Nister, Ernest, illus. Moving Pictures: An Antique Picture Book. 12p. (ps up). 1985. 11.95 (0-399-21272-8, Philomel) Putnam Pub Group.

Nixon, Joan L. Beats Me, Claude. Pearson, Tracey C., illus. (ps-3). 1988. pap. 4.99 (0-14-050847-3, Puffin) Puffin Bks.

Noble, Kate. Bubble Gum. Bass, Rachel, illus. 32p. (ps-3). 1992. 14.95 (*0-9631798-0-2*) Silver Seahorse.
Nodset, Joan L. Go Away, Dog. Bonsall, Crosby H., illus. LC 63-11162. 32p. (ps-3). 1963. PLB 9.89 (*0-06-024556-5*) HarpC Child Bks.
—Who Took the Farmer's Hat? Siebel, Fritz, illus. LC 62-17964. 32p. (gr. k-3). 1963. PLB 14.89 (*0-06-024566-2*) HarpC Child Bks.
—Who Took the Farmer's Hat? Siebel, Fritz, illus. LC 62-17964. 32p. (ps-2). 1988. pap. 5.95 (*0-06-443174-6*, Trophy) HarpC Child Bks.
Noll, Sally. Jiggle Wiggle Prance. Noll, Sally, illus. LC 86-18322. 24p. (ps-1). 1987. 11.75 (*0-688-06760-3*); PLB 11.88 (*0-688-06761-1*) Greenwillow.
Nordtvedt, Matilda. Ladybugs Bees & Butterfly Trees. LC 84-24343. 160p. (Orig.). (ps). 1985. pap. 5.99 (*0-87123-820-9*) Bethany Hse.
Norton, Mary. Borrowers. Krush, Beth & Krush, Joe, illus. LC 53-7870. 180p. (gr. 3 up). 1953. 13.95 (*0-15-209987-5*, HB Juv Bks) HarBrace.
—Borrowers Afield. Krush, Beth & Krush, Joe, illus. LC 55-11011. 215p. (gr. 3 up). 1955. 13.95 (*0-15-210166-7*, HB Juv Bks) HarBrace.
—Borrowers Aloft. Krush, Beth & Krush, Joe, illus. LC 61-11751. 192p. (gr. 3 up). 1961. 12.95 (*0-15-210524-7*, HB Juv Bks) HarBrace.
Now I'm Sleepy: A Cozy Cloth Book. (Illus.). 6p. (ps). 1987. pap. 2.95 (*0-553-18331-1*) Bantam.
Nunes, Susan. Tiddalick the Frog. Chen, Ju-Hong, illus. LC 89-1. 32p. (gr. k-3). 1989. SBE 13.95 (*0-689-31502-3*, Atheneum Child Bk) Macmillan Child Grp.
Nygren, Tord. The Red Thread. (Illus.). 32p. (ps up). 1988. 12.95 (*91-29-59005-1*, R & S Bks) FS&G.
Obligado, Lilian. Guess the Animal! 1990. pap. write for info. (*0-307-12165-8*, Golden Pr) Western Pub.
O'Brien, Theresa. Little Fish in a Big Pond. LC 90-46519. (ps-3). 1990. 7.95 (*0-85953-390-5*); pap. 3.95 (*0-85953-391-3*) Childs Play.
O'Connor, Jane. The Care Bears' Party Cookbook. Sustendal, Pat, illus. LC 84-18252. 48p. (gr. k-3). 1985. pap. 3.50 (*0-394-87305-X*) Random Bks Yng Read.
Oda, Stephanie C. My Nighttime Book. 12p. (ps). 1986. 3.25 (*0-8378-5091-6*) Gibson.
Oechsle, Robert. Ducky, Ucky & Mucky. (Illus.). 40p. (ps). 1985. pap. 7.95 (*0-9603376-0-1*) Flourtown Pub.
Ogle, Lucille & Thoburn, Tina. The Golden Picture Dictionary. Knight, Hilary, illus. (ps-3). 1989. write for info. (*0-307-17861-7*, Pub. by Golden Bks) Western Pub.
O'Halloran, Tim. Words Around Us. O'Halloran, Tim, illus. 48p. (ps-k). 1985. 10.95 (*0-88625-124-9*) Durkin Hayes Pub.
O'Hare, Jeff. Searchin' Safari: Looking for Camouflaged Creatures. Nadel, Marc, illus. LC 91-72974. 32p. (ps-3). 1992. 8.95 (*1-56397-016-3*) Boyds Mills Pr.
Oivardi, Anne & Philpot, Graham. My First Picture Dictionary. (Illus.). 64p. (gr. 1-3). 1989. incl. dust jacket 7.95 (*0-8120-5961-1*) Barron.
Oliver, Stephen, photos by. Home. LC 89-63092. (Illus.). 24p. (ps-k). 1990. 7.00 (*0-679-80622-9*) Random Bks Yng Read.
—Seasons. LC 89-63094. (Illus.). 24p. (ps-k). 1990. 7.00 (*0-679-80621-0*) Random Bks Yng Read.
—Touch. LC 89-63095. (Illus.). (ps-k). 1990. 6.95 (*0-679-80623-7*) Random Bks Yng Read.
Olson, Arielle N. The Lighthouse Keeper's Daughter. Wentworth, Elaine, illus. 32p. (ps-3). 1987. 14.95 (*0-316-65057-9*) Little.
On the Beach, What Can You Find? (ps). 1993. bds. 4.95 (*1-56458-270-1*) Dorling Kindersley.
On the Farm, What Can You Find? (ps). 1993. bds. 4.95 (*1-56458-269-8*) Dorling Kindersley.
One Green Frog. 24p. (ps-k). 1989. 9.95 (*0-448-21031-2*, G&D) Putnam Pub Group.
One Hundred Color & Activity Book: Tom & Jerry. 56p. (ps-3). Date not set. pap. write for info. (*1-57041-000-3*) Rose Art Indust.
One, Two, Three Board Shape Book. (Illus.). (ps). 1985. bds. 1.69 (*0-517-46320-2*) Random Hse Value.
O'Neill, Catharine. Mrs. Dunphy's Dog. (Illus.). 32p. (ps-3). 1989. pap. 3.95 (*0-14-050622-5*, Puffin) Puffin Bks.
Oomen, Francine. Come Outside. Oomen, Francine, illus. 8p. (ps). 1993. 4.95 (*0-8431-3535-2*) Price Stern.
—I Can Do It, Too! Oomen, Francine, illus. 8p. (ps). 1993. 4.95 (*0-8431-3534-4*) Price Stern.
—Moo, Says the Cow. Oomen, Francine, illus. 8p. (ps). 1993. 4.95 (*0-8431-3532-8*) Price Stern.
—My Day. Oomen, Francine, illus. 8p. (ps). 1993. 4.95 (*0-8431-3533-6*) Price Stern.
Oppenheim, Joanne. Have You Seen Birds? Reid, Barbara, illus. (ps-2). 1988. pap. 2.95 (*0-590-40890-9*) Scholastic Inc.
—Wake Up, Baby. (ps-3). 1990. PLB 9.99 (*0-685-54065-0*, Little Rooster); pap. 3.50 (*0-685-46039-8*) Bantam.
Oppenheim, Joanne F. You Can't Catch Me! Shachat, Andrew, illus. LC 86-7211. 32p. (gr. k). 1986. 15.95 (*0-395-41452-0*) HM.
Oram, Hiawyn. Mine! Rees, Mary, illus. 16p. (ps-k). 1992. with dust jacket 12.95 (*0-8120-6303-1*); pap. 5.95 (*0-8120-4905-5*) Barron.
Oram, Hiawyn & Ross, Tony. Anyone Seen Harry Lately? (Illus.). 32p. (gr. 1-4). 1989. 13.95 (*0-86264-198-5*, Pub. by Anderson Pr UK) Trafalgar.
Ormerod, Jan. Kitten Day. Ormerod, Jan, illus. LC 88-26687. 22p. (ps-1). 1989. 11.95 (*0-688-08536-9*) Lothrop.
—One Hundred One Things to Do with a Baby. Ormerod, Jan, illus. 32p. (ps-3). 1986. pap. 3.50 (*0-14-050447-8*, Puffin) Puffin Bks.
—Sunshine. (Illus.). 32p. (ps-k). 1984. pap. 3.50 (*0-14-050362-5*, Puffin) Puffin Bks.
Ormondroyd, Edward. Broderick. Larrecq, John M., illus. LC 77-83752. (gr. k-3). 1969. (Pub. by Parnassus); PLB 4.77 (*0-686-86580-4*) HM.
—Theodore's Rival. Larrecq, John M., illus. LC 76-156876. 40p. (ps-3). 1971. (Pub. by Parnassus); PLB 4.59 (*0-87466-001-7*) HM.
O'Rourke, Page, illus. Rub-a-Dub-Dub. 9p. (ps-1). 1993. bds. 4.95 (*0-448-40521-0*, G&D) Putnam Pub Group.
Osito (Little Bear) (SPA., Illus.). 28p. (ps-2). 1991. PLB 15.40 (*0-516-35356-X*); pap. 3.95 (*0-516-55356-9*) Childrens.
Ostarch, Judy. I Love Pets. Nex, Anthony, illus. 10p. (ps). 1993. pap. 4.95 (*0-8431-3656-1*) Price Stern.
Ostarch, Judy & Nex, Anthony. Let's Get Dressed. (Illus.). 10p. (ps). 1993. bds. 4.95 (*0-8431-3654-5*) Price Stern.
—My Family. (Illus.). 10p. (ps). 1993. bds. 4.95 (*0-8431-3655-3*) Price Stern.
—Playtime. (Illus.). 10p. (ps). 1993. bds. 4.95 (*0-8431-3657-X*) Price Stern.
Ostheeren, Ingrid. Jonathan Mouse at the Circus. Lanning, Rosemary, tr. from GER. Mathieu, Agnes, illus. LC 87-42980. 32p. (gr. k-3). 1988. 12.95 (*1-55858-055-7*) North-South Bks NYC.
Ostrich. 1989. 3.50 (*1-87865-736-4*) Blue Q.
Otto, Carolyn B. That Sky, That Rain. Lloyd, Megan, illus. LC 89-36582. 32p. (ps-3). 1992. pap. 4.95 (*0-06-443290-4*, Trophy) HarpC Child Bks.
Outdoor Things. (ps-k). 3.95 (*0-7214-5142-X*) Ladybird Bks.
Outlet Staff. At the Zoo. 1991. bds. 3.99 (*0-517-05402-7*) Random Hse Value.
Oxenbury, Helen. All Fall Down. Oxenbury, Helen, illus. 10p. (ps-k). 1987. pap. 6.95 (*0-02-769040-7*, Aladdin) Macmillan Child Grp.
—Clap Hands. Oxenbury, Helen, illus. 10p. (ps). 1987. pap. 6.95 (*0-02-769030-X*, Aladdin) Macmillan Child Grp.
—Pippo Gets Lost. Oxenbury, Helen, illus. LC 89-340. 14p. (ps-k). 1989. pap. 5.95 (*0-689-71336-3*, Aladdin) Macmillan Child Grp.
—Say Goodnight. Oxenbury, Helen, illus. 10p. (ps). 1987. pap. 6.95 (*0-02-769010-5*, Aladdin) Macmillan Child Grp.
—Tickle, Tickle. Oxenbury, Helen, illus. 10p. (ps). 1987. pap. 6.95 (*0-02-769020-2*, Aladdin) Macmillan Child Grp.
—Tom & Pippo & the Dog. Oxenbury, Helen, illus. LC 89-341. 14p. (ps-k). 1989. pap. 5.95 (*0-689-71338-X*, Aladdin) Macmillan Child Grp.
—Tom & Pippo Go Shopping. Oxenbury, Helen, illus. LC 88-10497. 14p. (ps-1). 1989. pap. 5.95 (*0-689-71278-2*, Aladdin) Macmillan Child Grp.
—Tom & Pippo in the Garden. Oxenbury, Helen, illus. LC 88-9145. 14p. (ps-1). 1989. pap. 5.95 (*0-689-71275-8*, Aladdin) Macmillan Child Grp.
—Tom & Pippo in the Snow. Oxenbury, Helen, illus. LC 89-336. 14p. (ps-k). 1989. pap. 5.95 (*0-689-71337-1*, Aladdin) Macmillan Child Grp.
—Tom & Pippo Make a Friend. Oxenbury, Helen, illus. LC 89-337. 14p. (ps-k). 1989. pap. 5.95 (*0-689-71339-8*, Aladdin) Macmillan Child Grp.
—Tom & Pippo See the Moon. Oxenbury, Helen, illus. 14p. (ps-1). 1989. pap. 5.95 (*0-689-71277-4*, Aladdin) Macmillan Child Grp.
—Tom & Pippo's Day. Oxenbury, Helen, illus. 14p. (ps-1). 1989. pap. 5.95 (*0-689-71276-6*, Aladdin) Macmillan Child Grp.
—Working. Oxenbury, Helen, illus. 7p. (ps). 1981. 3.95 (*0-671-42112-3*, Little Simon) S&S Trade.
Oxendine, Bess H. Miriam. LC 93-61292. (Illus.). 44p. (gr. 2-6). 1994. 6.95 (*1-55523-665-0*) Winston-Derek.
Pace, Betty. Chris Gets Ear Tubes. Hutton, Kathryn, illus. LC 87-26759. 48p. (ps-2). 1987. 7.95 (*0-930323-36-X*, Kendall Green Pubns) Gallaudet Univ Pr.
Palazzo, Tony. The Biggest & the Littlest Animals. Palazzo, Tony, illus. LC 77-112374. 40p. (gr. k-3). 1973. PLB 13.95 (*0-87460-225-4*) Lion Bks.
Palmer, Bernard & Palmer, Marjorie. Who Helps. Webb, Gary A., illus. 32p. (Orig.). (ps-k). 1982. pap. 3.99 (*0-934998-08-6*) Bethel Pub.
Palmer, Mary R. As Clean As a Whistle. LC 90-70148. 48p. (gr. 1-4). 1990. pap. 5.95 (*0-932433-66-9*) Windswept Hse.
Panda. 1989. 3.50 (*1-87865-735-6*) Blue Q.
El Papalote (The Kite) (SPA., Illus.). 28p. (ps-2). 1991. PLB 11.55 (*0-516-35355-1*); pap. 3.95 (*0-516-55355-0*) Childrens.
Pape, D. L. Liz Dearly's Silly Glasses. LC 68-56824. (Illus.). 48p. (gr. 2-5). 1968. PLB 10.95 (*0-87783-023-1*) Oddo.
—Professor Fred & the Fid Fuddlephone. LC 68-56825. (Illus.). 48p. (gr. 2-5). 1968. PLB 10.95 (*0-87783-032-0*) Oddo.
—Scientist Sam. LC 68-56826. (Illus.). 48p. (gr. 2-5). 1968. PLB 10.95 (*0-87783-034-7*) Oddo.
—Shoemaker Fooze. Frank, Lola E., illus. LC 68-56827. 48p. (gr. 2-5). 1969. PLB 10.95 (*0-87783-036-3*) Oddo.
—Three Thinkers of Thay-Lee. LC 68-56828. (Illus.). 48p. (gr. 2-5). 1968. PLB 10.95 (*0-87783-040-1*) Oddo.
Parachute Press Staff. The Twelve Days of Christmas. 24p. 1988. pap. 2.50 (*0-553-15638-1*, Bantam Aud Pub) Bantam.
Paris, Pat. On a Rainy Day: A Playtime Pop-Up. (Illus.). 10p. (ps). 1992. pap. 4.95 casebound (*0-671-74175-6*, Little Simon) S&S Trade.
—On a Windy Day: A Playtime Pop-Up. (Illus.). 10p. (ps). 1992. pap. 4.95 casebound (*0-671-74174-8*, Little Simon) S&S Trade.
Paris, Pat, illus. Bear Cubs. 10p. (ps). 1989. 4.95 (*0-8120-5987-5*) Barron.
—Bunnies. 10p. (ps). 1989. 4.95 (*0-8120-5990-5*) Barron.
—Kittens. 10p. (ps). 1989. 4.95 (*0-8120-5989-1*) Barron.
—Puppies. 10p. (ps). 1989. 4.95 (*0-8120-5988-3*) Barron.
Parish, Peggy. Amelia Bedelia & the Surprise Shower. Siebel, Fritz, illus. LC 66-18655. 64p. (gr. k-3). 1966. 14.00 (*0-06-024642-1*); PLB 13.89 (*0-06-024643-X*) HarpC Child Bks.
—Amelia Bedelia & the Surprise Shower. Siebel, Fritz, illus. LC 66-18655. 64p. (gr. k-3). 1986. incl. cassette 5.98 (*0-694-00161-9*, Trophy) HarpC Child Bks.
—Come Back, Amelia Bedelia. Tripp, Wallace, illus. LC 73-121799. 64p. (gr. k-3). 1986. incl. cassette 5.98 (*0-694-00112-0*, Trophy); pap. 3.50 (*0-06-444016-8*, Trophy) HarpC Child Bks.
—Scruffy. Oechsli, Kelly, illus. LC 87-45564. 64p. (gr. k-3). 1988. 14.00 (*0-06-024659-6*); PLB 13.89 (*0-06-024660-X*) HarpC Child Bks.
—Scruffy. Oechsli, Kelly, illus. LC 87-45564. 64p. (gr. k-3). 1990. pap. 3.50 (*0-06-444137-7*, Trophy) HarpC Child Bks.
—Willy Is My Brother. Rogers, Jacqueline, illus. (ps up). 1989. 12.95 (*0-385-29723-8*) Delacorte.
Park, Ruth. Playing Beatie Bow. 200p. (gr. 5-9). 1984. pap. 3.99 (*0-14-031460-1*, Puffin) Puffin Bks.
Parke, Sara. No Fair Peeking. LC 90-85436. (Illus.). 32p. (gr. k-3). 1991. 5.95 (*1-56282-037-0*) Disney Pr.
Parkhurst, Carole. Visiting Tacoma. Hamer, Bonnie, illus. 24p. (Orig.). (gr. 1-4). 1983. pap. 2.75 (*0-933992-38-6*) Coffee Break.
Parkinson, Kathy, illus. The Enormous Turnip. LC 85-14432. 32p. (ps-1). 1985. 13.95 (*0-8075-2062-4*) A Whitman.
—The Farmer in the Dell. LC 87-25322. 32p. (ps-2). 1988. PLB 13.95 (*0-8075-2271-6*) A Whitman.
Parramon, J. M. Los Arboles Frutales. (ps-3). 1991. pap. 6.95 (*0-8120-4714-1*) Barron.
—El Bosque. (ps-3). 1991. pap. 6.95 (*0-8120-4712-5*) Barron.
—El Jardin. (ps-3). 1991. pap. 6.95 (*0-8120-4713-3*) Barron.
—Mi Primeros Colores. (SPA.). (ps-3). 1991. pap. 6.95 (*0-8120-4726-5*) Barron.
—Mi Primeros Formas. (SPA.). (ps-3). 1991. pap. 6.95 (*0-8120-4728-1*) Barron.
—Mi Primeros Numeros. (SPA.). (ps-3). 1991. pap. 6.95 (*0-8120-4727-3*) Barron.
Parry, Alan & Parry, Linda. Bruno Helps Out. Parry, Alan & Parry, Linda, illus. LC 91-70401. 16p. (ps-k). 1991. bds. 1.49 (*0-8066-2528-7*, 9-2528, Augsburg) Augsburg Fortress.
—Bruno Is Sorry. Parry, Alan & Parry, Linda, illus. LC 91-70402. 16p. (ps-k). 1991. bds. 1.49 (*0-8066-2529-5*, 9-2529, Augsburg) Augsburg Fortress.
—Bruno Makes Friends. Parry, Alan & Parry, Linda, illus. LC 91-70402. 16p. (ps-k). 1991. bds. 1.49 (*0-685-59565-X*, 9-2530, Augsburg) Augsburg Fortress.
Parry, Linda & Parry, Alan. Wonderful Jesus! A Pop-up Activity Book. (Illus.). 12p. 1993. 15.99 (*0-7847-0045-1*, 24-03643) Standard Pub.
Partin, Charlotte C. Daydreams & Sunbeams: An Album of Framable Word Pictures. Partin, Robin C., illus. 18p. (Orig.). (gr. 7 up). 1987. pap. 4.00 (*0-9619816-0-1*) C C Partin.
Pashuk, Lauren. Fun with Colors. Pashuk, Lauren, illus. 32p. (ps-k). 1985. pap. 2.95 (*0-88625-106-0*) Durkin Hayes Pub.
Paterson, Bettina. Scaredy-Ghost. (Illus.). 12p. (ps). 1993. bds. 2.50 (*0-448-40574-1*, G&D) Putnam Pub Group.
Paterson, Bettina, illus. Baby's ABC. 18p. 1992. bds. 4.95 (*0-448-40130-4*, G&D) Putnam Pub Group.
—Baby's 1, 2, 3. 18p. (ps). 1992. bds. 4.95 (*0-448-40265-3*, G&D) Putnam Pub Group.
—Busy Witch. 12p. (ps). 1993. bds. 2.50 (*0-448-40573-3*, G&D) Putnam Pub Group.
—Jolly Snowman. 12p. (ps). 1992. bds. 2.50 (*0-448-40575-X*, G&D) Putnam Pub Group.
—Merry Christmas, Santa! 12p. (ps). 1992. bds. 2.50 (*0-448-40576-8*, G&D) Putnam Pub Group.
—Potty Time. 12p. (ps). 1993. bds. 4.95 (*0-448-40539-3*, G&D) Putnam Pub Group.
Paterson, Cynthia & Paterson, Brian. The Foxwood Smugglers. (Illus.). 32p. (ps-3). 1988. incl. dust jacket 6.95 (*0-8120-5984-0*) Barron.
Patience, John. Who's Afraid of Tigers? Patience, John, illus. 12p. (ps up). 1994. 14.99 (*0-8431-3542-5*) Price Stern.
Patrick, Denice. Look Inside a House. (Illus.). 16p. (ps-1). 1989. 11.95 (*0-448-19351-5*, G&D) Putnam Pub Group.
—Look Inside a Ship. (Illus.). 16p. (ps-1). 1989. 11.95 (*0-448-19352-3*, G&D) Putnam Pub Group.
—Look Inside Your Body. (Illus.). 16p. (ps-1). 1989. bds. 11.95 (*0-448-21033-9*, G&D) Putnam Pub Group.

Patrick, Denise L. Disney's Peek-a-Boo Bambi. Pacheco, Dave & Wakeman, Diana, illus. 14p. (ps-k). 1992. write for info. (*0-307-12392-8*, 12392) Western Pub.

Patterson, Francine. Koko's Story. Cohn, Ronald H., photos by. (Illus.). 40p. 1988. pap. 5.95 (*0-590-41364-3*) Scholastic Inc.

Patty Cake. 12p. (ps-1). 1989. bds. 5.95 (*0-87449-713-2*) Modern Pub NYC.

Patz, Nancy. No Thumping No Bumping No Rumpus Tonight! Patz, Nancy, illus. LC 88-7717. 32p. (gr. k-3). 1990. RSBE 13.95 (*0-689-31510-4*, Atheneum Child Bk) Macmillan Child Grp.

—Sarah Bear & Sweet Sidney. Patz, Nancy, illus. LC 88-21300. 32p. (ps-2). 1989. RSBE 13.95 (*0-02-770270-7*, Four Winds) Macmillan Child Grp.

Paulsen, Gary. Hatchet. (gr. 5-9). 1988. pap. 4.50 (*0-14-032724-X*, Puffin) Puffin Bks.

—Hatchet Rack Trim. (gr. 4-7). 1989. pap. 4.50 (*0-14-034371-7*, Puffin) Puffin Bks.

Paxton, Lenore & Siadi, Phillip. Going to Grandma's: A Sing, Color 'n Say Coloring Book Package. Farago, Julius, illus. (ps-3). 1991. Includes cassette tape. pap. 6.95 (*1-880449-00-5*) Wrldkids Pr.

Payne, Emmy. Katy No-Pocket. (gr. 1-3). 1973. reinforced bdg. 13.95 (*0-395-17104-0*) HM.

Pearce, Colin. The Monkey & the Crocodile. (Illus.). (ps-2). 1990. 12.99 (*0-8423-4537-X*) Tyndale.

Pearse, Patricia. See How You Grow. Riddell, Edwina, illus. LC 87-33268. 32p. (gr. 1-4). 1988. 13.95 (*0-8120-5936-0*) Barron.

Pearson, Susan. The Baby & the Bear. Carlson, Nancy, illus. (ps-k). 1987. pap. 3.95 (*0-670-81299-4*) Viking Child Bks.

—The Day Porkchop Climbed the Christmas Tree. Brown, Richard, illus. (gr. k-3). 9.95 (*0-317-62031-2*) P-H.

—My Favorite Time of Year. Wallner, John, illus. LC 87-45296. 32p. (ps-3). 1988. PLB 12.89 (*0-06-024682-0*) HarpC Child Bks.

Pearson, Tracey C. Sing a Song of Sixpence. Pearson, Tracey C., illus. LC 84-14206. 32p. (ps-2). 1988. Dial Bks Young.

Peaslee, Ann & De Witt, Sorena. Guess What Day It Is? Clayson, David N., illus. 216p. (gr. 3-6). 1988. pap. 14.50 (*0-89346-305-1*) Heian Intl.

Peet, Bill. Big Bad Bruce. (gr. 3 up). 1987. Incl. cass. pap. 7.70 (*0-395-45741-6*) HM.

—Chester the Worldly Pig. (Illus.). 48p. (gr. k-3). 1980. 13.45 (*0-395-18470-3*) HM.

—Eli. Peet, Bill, illus. LC 77-17500. 48p. (gr. k-3). 1984. pap. 5.95 (*0-395-36611-9*) HM.

—Farewell to Shady Glade. Peet, Bill, illus. 48p. (gr. k-3). 1991. 14.95 (*0-395-18975-6*); pap. 7.95 incl. cassette (*0-395-60166-5*) HM.

—Hubert's Hair-Raising Adventure. (Illus.). 36p. (gr. k-3). 1959. 14.95 (*0-395-15083-3*) HM.

—Kermit the Hermit. (Illus.). (gr. k-3). 1980. 14.95 (*0-395-15084-1*); pap. 5.95 (*0-395-29607-2*) HM.

—The Kweeks of Kookatumdee. Peet, Bill, illus. 32p. (gr. k-3). 1988. pap. 5.95 (*0-395-48656-4*, Sandpiper) HM.

—Smokey. (Illus.). (gr. k-3). 1962. 14.45 (*0-395-15992-X*) HM.

Peifer, Jane & Nolt, Marilyn. Good Thoughts about Me. (Illus.). 24p. (Orig.). (ps-2). 1985. pap. 2.95 (*0-8361-3389-7*) Herald Pr.

—Good Thoughts at Bedtime. (Illus.). 24p. (Orig.). (ps-2). 1985. pap. 2.95 (*0-8361-3388-9*) Herald Pr.

People - Neighbor. 1989. pap. 1.49 (*0-553-18397-4*) Bantam.

Peppe, Rodney. Circus Numbers. Peppe, Rodney, illus. LC 75-86381. (ps-3). 1969. 5.95 (*0-440-01288-0*); pap. 3.69 (*0-440-01289-9*) Delacorte.

—Circus Numbers: A Counting Book. (Illus.). 32p. (ps-2). 1985. 11.95 (*0-385-29424-7*) Delacorte.

—Thumbprint Circus. Peppe, Rodney, illus. (ps-1). 1989. 12.95 (*0-440-50154-7*) Delacorte.

Perkins, Al. Nose Book. McKie, Roy, illus. LC 71-117540. (ps-1). 1970. 6.95 (*0-394-80623-9*); lib. bdg. 7.99 (*0-394-90623-3*) Random Bks Yng Read.

Perkins, Anne T. Little Eddy Elephant. Lomax, James & Perkins, Anne T., illus. 8p. (ps-k). 1993. 12.00 (*1-884204-06-6*) Teach Nxt Door.

—My Name Is Jack. Lomax, James, illus. 8p. (ps-k). 1993. 12.00 (*1-884204-05-8*) Teach Nxt Door.

Perkins, Myrna. What Does A Spider Do? Perkins, William C. & Perkins, Lori L., illus. 20p. (Orig.). (ps-3). 1985. pap. 3.95 (*0-937729-00-0*) Markins Enter.

—What Is This? Perkins, William C. & Perkins, Lori L., illus. 36p. (Orig.). (ps-3). 1986. pap. 4.95 (*0-937729-01-9*) Markins Enter.

—What Makes Honey? Perkins, William C. & Perkins, Lori L., illus. 32p. (Orig.). (ps-3). pap. 3.95 (*0-937729-03-5*) Markins Enter.

Perrault, Charles. The Pancake That Ran Away & Toads & Diamonds. (Illus.). 48p. (ps-3). 1985. 5.95 (*0-88110-254-7*) EDC.

Perrine, Mary. Nannabah's Friend. Weisgard, Leonard, illus. 32p. (gr. k-3). 1989. pap. 4.80 (*0-395-52020-7*) HM.

Perugini, Donna. Don't Hug a Grudge. (Orig.). (gr. k-3). 1987. 3.98 (*0-89274-433-2*) Harrison Hse.

Pesiri, Evelyn. Learn to Hear. Pesiri, Evelyn, illus. 64p. (gr. k-3). 1986. wkbk. 7.95 (*0-86653-337-0*, GA 675) Good Apple.

—Learn to Think. Pesiri, Evelyn, illus. 64p. (gr. k-3). 1986. wkbk. 7.95 (*0-86653-343-5*, GA 676) Good Apple.

Pesiri, Evelyn, ed. & illus. Learn to Write. 64p. (gr. k-3). 1986. wkbk. 7.95 (*0-86653-342-7*, GA 791) Good Apple.

Peters, Lisa W. The Sun, the Wind & the Rain. Rand, Ted, illus. LC 87-23808. 48p. (ps-2). 1988. 13.95 (*0-8050-0699-0*, Bks Young Read) H Holt & Co.

Peters, Sharon. Pussycat Kite. Hall, Susan T., illus. LC 84-8632. 32p. (gr. k-2). 1985. PLB 11.59 (*0-8167-0358-2*); pap. text ed. 2.95 (*0-8167-0438-4*) Troll Assocs.

Petersham, Maud & Petersham, Miska. Circus Baby. Petersham, Maud & Petersham, Miska, illus. LC 50-9295. 32p. (ps-1). 1968. RSBE 13.95 (*0-02-771670-8*, Macmillan Child Bk) Macmillan Child Grp.

Peterson, Elizabeth J. Christina & the Little Red Bird. Mcknight, C. D., illus. 23p. (Orig.). (ps-1). pap. 5.95 (*0-938911-02-3*) Indiv Educ Syst.

Peterson, Jeanne W. I Have a Sister, My Sister Is Deaf. Ray, Deborah K., illus. LC 76-24306. 32p. (ps-3). 1984. pap. 4.95 (*0-06-443059-6*, Trophy) HarpC Child Bks.

Pevsner, Stella. How Could You Do It, Diane? LC 88-35923. 192p. (gr. 5-9). 1989. 13.45 (*0-395-51041-4*, Clarion Bks) HM.

Pfeffer, Susan B. What Do You Do When Your Mouth Won't Open? 128p. (gr. 4-8). 1982. pap. 2.75 (*0-440-49320-X*, YB) Dell.

Pfloog, Jan. The Farm Book. (Illus.). 24p. (ps-k). 1989. pap. write for info. (*0-307-58117-9*, Pub. by Golden Bks) Western Pub.

—The Kitten Book. (Illus.). 24p. (ps-k). 1968. pap. write for info. (*0-307-10079-0*, Pub. by Golden Bks) Western Pub.

—The Puppy Book. (Illus.). 24p. (ps-k). 1968. pap. write for info (*0-307-10078-2*, Pub. by Golden Bks) Western Pub.

—The Zoo Book. (Illus.). 24p. (ps-k). 1989. pap. write for info. (*0-307-58118-7*, Pub. by Golden Bks) Western Pub.

Phillips, Joan. Peek-a-Boo! I See You! Wilburn, Kathy, illus. (ps). 1983. 4.95 (*0-448-03092-6*, G&D) Putnam Pub Group.

—Tiger Is a Scaredy Cat: A Step One Book. Gorbaty, Norman, illus. LC 85-19673. 32p. (ps-1). 1986. pap. 3.50 (*0-394-88056-0*) Random Bks Yng Read.

Phillips, Tamara. Day Care ABC. Levine, Abby, ed. Leder, Dora, illus. LC 88-33911. (ps-2). 1989. PLB 13. 95 (*0-8075-1483-7*) A Whitman.

Pickart, Joan E. Mixed Signals. 1990. pap. 2.50 (*0-553-44018-7*, Loveswept) Bantam.

Pickle Things. 1994. 13.27 (*0-8368-0985-8*) Gareth Stevens Inc.

Picture Book for Baby. (Illus.). (ps). 3.50 (*0-7214-0749-8*) Ladybird Bks.

Picture-Book One in Arabic. (ARA., Illus.). (gr. 1-3). 1987. 3.95x (*0-86685-214-X*) Intl Bk Ctr.

Picture-Book Two in Arabic. (ARA., Illus.). (gr. 1-3). 1987. 3.95x (*0-86685-215-8*) Intl Bk Ctr.

Piemontes, Grayce. Classic Shirley Temple-Paperdolls. 1989. pap. 3.95 (*0-486-25193-4*) Dover.

Pienkowski, Jan. Casa Embrujada. (SPA., Illus.). 12p. (ps-6). 1992. 14.95 (*0-525-45002-5*, DCB) Dutton Child Bks.

—Faces. Pienkowski, Jan, illus. 24p. (ps-k). 1991. pap. 2.95 (*0-671-72846-6*, Little Simon) S&S Trade.

—Farm. 14p. 1990. pap. 2.95 (*0-671-70476-1*, S&S BFYR) S&S Trade.

—Homes. 14p. (ps). 1990. pap. 2.95 (*0-671-70478-8*, Little Simon) S&S Trade.

—Oh My, a Fly! Pienkowski, Jan, illus. 10p. (ps up). 1989. 9.95 (*0-8431-2765-1*) Price Stern.

—Phone Book. (Illus.). 10p. (ps up). 1991. incl. sound chip 13.95 (*0-8431-2967-0*) Price Stern.

—Road Hog. Peinkowski, Jan, illus. 10p. (ps up). 1993. incl. sound chip 13.95 (*0-8431-3586-7*) Price Stern.

—Sizes. Pienkowski, Jan, illus. 24p. (ps-k). 1991. pap. 2.95 (*0-671-72844-X*, Little Simon) S&S Trade.

—Stop Go. Pienkowski, Jan, illus. 24p. (ps). 1992. pap. 2.95 (*0-671-74519-0*, Little Simon) S&S Trade.

—Time. Pienkowski, Jan, illus. 24p. (ps-k). 1991. pap. 2.95 (*0-671-72847-4*, Little Simon) S&S Trade.

—Weather - Nursery Board Book. (ps). 1990. pap. 2.95 (*0-671-70479-6*, Little Simon) S&S Trade.

—Wheels. Pienkowski, Jan, illus. 24p. (ps). 1992. pap. 2.95 (*0-671-74517-4*, Little Simon) S&S Trade.

—Yes No. Pienkowski, Jan, illus. 24p. (ps). 1992. pap. 2.95 (*0-671-74520-4*, Little Simon) S&S Trade.

—Zoo - Nursery Board Book. (ps). 1990. pap. 2.95 (*0-671-70477-X*, Little Simon) S&S Trade.

Pig. 1989. 3.50 (*1-87865-725-9*) Blue Q.

Pinkwater, Daniel. Guys from Space. Pinkwater, Daniel, illus. LC 88-13485. 32p. (gr. k-3). 1989. RSBE 13.95 (*0-02-774672-0*, Macmillan Child Bk) Macmillan Child Grp.

Piper, Watty. The Little Engine That Could. Walz, Richard, illus. LC 99-44044. 12p. (ps-2). 1984. 8.95 (*0-448-18963-1*, Platt & Munk) Putnam Pub Group.

Pittman, Helena C. The Gift of the Willows. Pittman, Helena C., illus. 32p. (gr. k-4). 1988. 18.95 (*0-87614-354-0*) Carolrhoda Bks.

—Miss Hindy's Cats. Pittman, Helena C., illus. LC 89-22214. 32p. (ps-3). 1990. pap. 18.95 (*0-87614-368-0*) Carolrhoda Bks.

Piumini, Roberto. Store. (ps). 1992. 4.50 (*1-56397-203-4*) Boyds Mills Pr.

Planes. LC 91-25688. (Illus.). 24p. (ps-k). 1992. pap. 7.95 POB (*0-689-71564-1*, Aladdin) Macmillan Child Grp.

Play Ball Baby Minnie. write for info. (*1-56326-328-9*, 032904) Disney Bks By Mail.

Playing: Little Friends Board Book. 1992. bds. 2.49 (*0-517-07282-3*) Random Hse Value.

Playtime Words. (Illus.). 1991. 4.99 (*0-517-05884-7*) Random Hse Value.

Plume, Ilse. The Bremen-Town Musicians. Plume, Ilse, illus. LC 86-42990. 32p. (ps-3). 1987. pap. 5.95 (*0-06-443141-X*, Trophy) HarpC Child Bks.

Poelker, Kathy. At the Firehouse. Judge, Matt, ed. Hedran, Susan, illus. 8p. (Orig.). (ps-3). 1988. pap. text ed. 15.00 (*0-929842-00-6*) Hawthorne Pubs.

—One Little Drop of Sunshine. Judge, Matt, ed. Hedran, Susan, illus. 8p. (Orig.). (ps-3). 1988. pap. text ed. 15. 00 (*0-929842-01-4*) Hawthorne Pubs.

Poky Little Puppy's Day at the Fair. 1990. pap. write for info. (*0-307-12162-3*, Pub. by Golden Bks) Western Pub.

Polette, Nancy. E Is for Everybody: A Manual for Bringing Fine Picture Books into the Hands & Hearts of Children. 2nd ed. LC 82-10508. 194p. (gr. 1-7). 1982. 20.00 (*0-8108-1579-6*) Scarecrow.

Polka Dot Pony. 12p. (ps-1). 1988. bds. 5.95 (*0-87449-626-8*) Modern Pub NYC.

Polushkin, Maria. Who Said Meow? Weiss, Ellen, illus. LC 87-28073. 32p. (ps). 1988. RSBE 13.95 (*0-02-774770-0*, Bradbury Pr) Macmillan Child Grp.

Pomaska, Anna. Cut & Assemble a Peter Rabbit. 1984. pap. 4.95 (*0-486-24713-9*) Dover.

—Easy Mazes Activity Book. (Illus.). (ps up). 1988. pap. 1.00 (*0-486-25531-X*) Dover.

—The Little Alphabet Follow-the-Dots Book. (ps up). 1988. pap. 1.00 (*0-486-25623-5*) Dover.

—The Little Dinosaur Activity Book. (ps up). 1987. pap. 1.00 (*0-486-25344-9*) Dover.

—The Little Follow the Dots Book. 1986. pap. 1.00 (*0-486-25157-8*) Dover.

—The Little Seashore Activity Book. (ps up). 1988. pap. 1.00 (*0-486-25608-1*) Dover.

Pomerantz, Charlotte. How Many Trucks Can a Tow Truck Tow. Alley, R. W., illus. LC 89-3657. 24p. (ps-k). 1987. pap. 6.00 (*0-394-88775-1*) Random Bks Yng Read.

—The Piggy in the Puddle. Marshall, James, illus. LC 88-8368. 32p. (ps-1). 1989. pap. 4.95 (*0-689-71293-6*, Aladdin) Macmillan Child Grp.

—Where's the Bear. Barton, Byron, illus. LC 83-1697. 32p. (ps up). 1991. pap. 3.95 (*0-688-10999-3*, Mulberry) Morrow.

Pop up Book, No. 1. (ps). 1993. pap. 13.00 (*0-671-72923-3*, S&S BYR) S&S Trade.

Pop up Book, No. 3. (ps). 1993. pap. 7.95 (*0-671-72925-X*) S&S Trade.

The Pop-up Minnie Mouse. (Illus.). 32p. 1994. Repr. of 1933 ed. 9.95 (*1-55709-211-7*) Applewood.

Potter, Beatrix. Beatrix Potter's Peter Rabbit: A Lift-the-Flap Rebus Book. (ps-3). 1991. 11.95 (*0-7232-3798-0*) Warne.

—Jemima Puddle-Duck Bath Book. (Illus.). 8p. (ps). 1988. pap. 3.99 waterproof (*0-7232-3512-0*) Warne.

—The Jemima Puddle-Duck Pop-up Book. (Illus.). 6p. (ps-3). 1993. 13.00 (*0-7232-4122-8*) Viking Child Bks.

—Jemima Puddleduck Pop-Up. 1988. 3.99 (*0-517-67097-6*) Random Hse Value.

—Jeremy Fisher Bath Book. (Illus.). 8p. (ps). 1989. 2.95 (*0-7232-3513-9*) Warne.

—Letters to Children. (Illus.). 48p. (gr. 2 up). 1986. pap. 5.95 (*0-8027-7293-5*) Walker & Co.

—Meet Hunca Munca. Potter, Beatrix, illus. 12p. (ps). 1986. bds. 2.95 (*0-7232-3421-3*) Warne.

—Meet Jemima Puddle-Duck. Potter, Beatrix, illus. 12p. (ps). 1986. bds. 3.50 (*0-7232-3420-5*) Warne.

—Meet Peter Rabbit. Potter, Beatrix, illus. 12p. (ps). 1986. bds. 3.50 (*0-7232-3418-3*) Warne.

—Meet Tom Kitten. Potter, Beatrix, illus. 12p. (ps). 1986. bds. 3.50 (*0-7232-3419-1*) Warne.

—My First Peter Rabbit Book & Toy. (ps-3). 1991. 14.95 (*0-7232-4014-0*) Warne.

—My Peter Rabbit Learning Box: Peter Rabbit's 123 & Peter Rabbit's ABC. (ps-3). 1988. Boxed Set. 13.95 (*0-7232-5168-1*) Warne.

—The Original Peter Rabbit Miniature Collection, No. I. Potter, Beatrix, illus. (ps-3). 1991. pap. 5.95 (*0-7232-3982-7*) Warne.

—Peter Rabbit Diary for Any Year. 1991. 6.95 (*0-7232-3993-2*) Warne.

—The Tailor of Gloucester. Jorgensen, David, illus. LC 88-11510. 44p. (ps up). 1991. pap. 14.95 (*0-88708-080-4*, Rabbit Ears); bk. & cass. pkg. 19.95 (*0-88708-085-5*, Rabbit Ears) Picture Bk Studio.

—The Tale of Benjamin Bunny. Leach, Rosemary, read by. Davis, Carl, contrib. by. (Illus.). (ps-3). 1989. pap. 6.95 incl. tape (*0-7232-3628-3*) Warne.

—Tale of Benjamin Bunny Pop Up. 1988. 3.99 (*0-517-67096-8*) Random Hse Value.

—The Tale of Jemima Puddle-Duck. West, Timothy, read by. Davis, Carl, contrib. by. (Illus.). (ps-3). 1989. pap. 6.95 incl. tape (*0-7232-3630-5*) Warne.

—The Tale of Mr. Jeremy Fisher. LC 74-75269. (Illus.). 59p. (gr. 2-4). 1974. pap. 1.75 (*0-486-23066-X*) Dover.

—The Tale of Mr. Jeremy Fisher. Jorgensen, David, illus. LC 88-34668. 32p. (ps up). 1991. pap. 14.95 (*0-88708-094-4*, Rabbit Ears); incl. cassette 19.95 (*0-88708-095-2*, Rabbit Ears) Picture Bk Studio.

—The Tale of Mrs. Tiggy-Winkle. Routledge, Patricia, read by. Davis, Carl, contrib. by. (Illus.). (ps-3). 1989. pap. 6.95 incl. tape (*0-7232-3629-1*) Warne.

—The Tale of Peter Rabbit. Jorgensen, David, illus. LC 88-11509. 36p. (ps up). 1991. 14.95 (*0-317-89758-6*, Rabbit Ears); bk. & cass. pkg. 19.95 (*0-88708-084-7*, Rabbit Ears) Picture Bk Studio.
—Tale of Peter Rabbit Pop Up. 1988. 3.99 (*0-517-67098-4*) Random Hse Value.
—Tale of Tom Kitten Pop-Up. 1988. 3.99 (*0-517-67099-2*) Random Hse Value.
—The Two Bad Mice Pop-Up Book. Potter, Beatrix, illus. (ps-3). 1986. 11.95 (*0-7232-3360-8*) Warne.
—Where's Tom Kitten? 24p. (ps-3). 1990. 6.95 (*0-7232-3597-X*) Warne.
—The World of Peter Rabbit Postcard Book. (Illus.). 1990. pap. 6.95 (*0-7232-3647-X*) Warne.
—The World of Peter Rabbit Sticker Book. Twinn, Colin, illus. 32p. (ps-3). 1990. pap. 6.95 (*0-7232-3645-3*) Warne.
Poulet, Virginia. Blue Bug's Christmas. LC 87-15793. (Illus.). 32p. (ps-3). 1987. PLB 11.80 (*0-516-03483-9*) Childrens.
—El Tesoro de Azulin (Blue Bug's Treasure) Maloney, M. & Fleming, S., illus. LC 75-40352. (SPA.). 32p. (ps-2). 1988. pap. 3.95 (*0-516-53424-6*) Childrens.
Powell, Patricia. Diddle Diddle Red Hot Fiddle. Metrejean, Nikki N., illus. 32p. (gr. 1-8). 1990. pap. text ed. 6.95 (*0-944512-01-1*) Radiant LA.
Pragoff, Fiona. Fiona Pragoff Board Books. (Illus.). (ps). 1988. pap. 4.95 (*0-318-32999-9*) Doubleday.
—Growing. LC 87-5239. (Illus.). 20p. (gr. k-3). 1987. 6.95 (*0-385-24174-7*) Doubleday.
—How Many? From Zero to Twenty. LC 87-5053. (Illus.). 28p. (gr. k-3). 1987. pap. 6.95 (*0-385-24172-0*) Doubleday.
—It's Fun to Be One. Pragoff, Fiona, illus. 24p. (ps). 1994. pap. 6.95 (*0-689-71813-6*, Aladdin) Macmillan Child Grp.
Precek, Katharine W. Penny in the Road. Cullen-Clark, Patricia, illus. LC 88-13331. 32p. (gr. k-3). 1989. RSBE 14.95 (*0-02-774970-3*, Macmillan Child Bk) Macmillan Child Grp.
Precious Moments: What a Wonderful World. 24p. (ps-k). 1992. write for info. (*0-307-10022-7*, 10022) Western Pub.
Prelutsky, Jack. Circus! Lobel, Arnold, illus. 32p. (ps-2). 1989. pap. 4.95 (*0-689-70806-8*, Aladdin) Macmillan Child Grp.
—The Terrible Tiger. Lobel, Arnold, illus. LC 88-7901. 32p. (ps-2). 1989. pap. 3.95 (*0-689-71300-2*, Aladdin) Macmillan Child Grp.
Preschool ABC: Step Ahead Plus Workbook. (ps-3). 1993. pap. 3.50 (*0-307-03669-3*, Pub. by Golden Bks) Western Pub.
Preschool Playtime Pals, Bks. 1-4. (24 pgs. ea. bk.). (ps-1). 1992. Bk. 1. pap. 0.99 (*1-56144-219-4*, Honey Bear Bks) Bk. 2. pap. 0.99 (*1-56144-220-8*); Bk. 3. pap. 0.99 (*1-56144-221-6*); Bk. 4. pap. 0.99 (*1-56144-222-4*) Modern Pub NYC.
Price, Donna. Greenberg's LGB Coloring Book. (Illus.). 32p. (Orig.). (gr. k-5). 1987. pap. 3.50 (*0-89778-093-0*, 10-7020) Greenberg Bks.
Price, Donna W. Greenberg's LGB Malbuch. (Illus.). 32p. (Orig.). (gr. k-5). 1988. text ed. 3.50 (*0-89778-085-X*, 10-7020G) Greenberg Bks.
Price, Mathew. Peekaboo! Claverie, Jean, illus. 24p. (ps). 1993. 5.99 (*0-679-84031-1*) Knopf Bks Yng Read.
Prince, Pamela. Once upon a Time. Smith, Jesse W., illus. LC 87-33359. 48p. (ps up). 1988. 12.95 (*0-517-56832-2*, Harmony) Crown Pub Group.
Provensen, Alice & Provensen, Martin. The Glorious Flight Across the Channel with Louis Bleriot. LC 82-7034. (Illus.). 40p. (gr. 5-8). 1983. pap. 14.95 (*0-670-34259-9*) Viking Child Bks.
—El Libro de las Estaciones. Cuenca, Pilar de & Alvarez, Ines, trs. LC 81-13821. (SPA., Illus.). 32p. (ps-3). 1982. lib. bdg. 5.99 (*0-394-95143-3*); pap. 2.25 (*0-394-85143-9*) Random Bks Yng Read.
Provensen, Alice & Provensen, Martin, illus. A Peaceable Kingdom: The Shaker Abecedarius. Barsam, Richard M., afterword by. (gr. k-3). 1981. pap. 5.99 (*0-14-050370-6*, Puffin) Puffin Bks.
Proysen, Alf. Mrs. Pepperpot in the Magic Wood. Berg, Bjorn, illus. 128p. (gr. 1-4). 1988. pap. 3.95 (*0-14-030538-6*, Puffin) Puffin Bks.
Pryor, Ainslie. The Baby Blue Cat Who Said No. Pryor, Ainslie, illus. LC 87-21026. 32p. (ps-k). 1988. 11.95 (*0-670-81780-5*) Viking Child Bks.
Put It Together. 1989. pap. 1.49 (*0-553-18392-3*) Bantam.
Quackenbush, Robert. Henry Babysits. Quackenbush, Robert, illus. LC 83-2247. 48p. (ps-3). 1983. 5.95 (*0-8193-1107-3*); lib. bdg. 5.95 (*0-8193-1108-1*) Parents.
—Mouse Feathers. Quackenbush, Robert, illus. LC 87-15690. 40p. (gr. k-3). 1988. 12.95 (*0-89919-527-X*, Clarion Bks) HM.
Quality Family Entertainment, Inc. Staff. Shining Time Station: Station House. 2p. (ps-2). 1993. write for info. (*1-883366-10-0*) YES Ent.
Que Sorpresa! (Surprise!) (SPA., Illus.). 28p. (ps-2). 1991. PLB 11.55 (*0-516-35360-8*); pap. 3.95 (*0-516-55360-7*) Childrens.
Quien Dice? (Who Says?) (SPA., Illus.). 28p. (ps-2). 1991. PLB 11.55 (*0-516-35362-4*); pap. 3.95 (*0-516-55362-3*) Childrens.
Quinn, Kaye. Under the Big Top. (Illus.). 48p. (Orig.). (ps-2). 1989. pap. 2.95 (*0-8431-2729-5*) Price Stern.
Rabe, Berniece. A Smooth Move. Tucker, Kathleen, ed. Sims, Blanche, illus. LC 87-2099. (gr. 1-4). 1987. PLB 11.95 (*0-8075-7486-4*) A Whitman.
Rabe, Tish. My Name Is Grover. Swanson, Maggie, illus. 24p. (ps-k). 1992. pap. write for info. (*0-307-11534-8*, 11534, Golden Pr) Western Pub.
Rackham, Arthur, illus. Sixty Fairy Tales of the Brothers Grimm. (gr. 2-7). 8.98 (*0-517-28525-8*) Random Hse Value.
Rader, Laura, illus. The Pudgy Where Is Your Nose? Book. 16p. 1989. bds. 2.95 (*0-448-02258-3*, G&D) Putnam Pub Group.
Radin, Ruth Y. High in the Mountains. Young, Ed, illus. LC 88-13395. 32p. (gr. k-4). 1989. RSBE 13.95 (*0-02-775650-5*, Macmillan Child Bk) Macmillan Child Grp.
Raffi. Down by the Bay. Westcott, Nadine B., illus. 32p. (ps-2). 1988. PLB 14.00 (*0-517-56644-3*) Crown Bks Yng Read.
—Down by the Bay. Westcott, Nadine B., illus. LC 87-750291. 32p. (ps-2). 1988. pap. 3.99 (*0-517-56645-1*) Crown Bks Yng Read.
—One Light, One Sun. Fernandes, Eugenie, illus. LC 87-22256. 32p. (ps-2). 1990. pap. 4.99 (*0-517-57644-9*) Crown Bks Yng Read.
—Shake My Sillies Out. Allender, David, illus. LC 87-750478. 32p. (ps-2). 1988. pap. 3.99 (*0-517-56647-8*) Crown Bks Yng Read.
—Wheels on the Bus. Wickstrom, Sylvie K., illus. LC 87-30126. 32p. (ps-2). 1990. pap. 3.99 (*0-517-57645-7*) Crown Bks Yng Read.
Raichert, Lane. D.C. Hopper, the First Starbunny. Raichert, Lane, illus. LC 91-23055. 32p. (gr. 2-6). 1992. 15.95 (*1-880009-81-1*, DC-P1) Blue Zero Pub.
Rao, Anthony. Cut & Make Animal Masks. 1989. pap. 4.95 (*0-486-25199-3*) Dover.
Rappaport, Doreen. The Boston Coffee Party. McCully, Emily A., illus. LC 87-45301. 64p. (gr. k-3). 1988. PLB 13.89 (*0-06-024825-4*) HarpC Child Bks.
Rapp-Hunt, Tawney. The Boo Boo Zoo. 36p. 1993. text ed. 11.95 (*0-9638882-0-X*) Tawney Pubng.
Rasbach, Hubert H. The Dinkywinkies & Snickity Snackety Snort. Ingram, Fred & Jennings, Elkay, illus. LC 79-89378. (ps-4). 1982. 6.95 (*0-934822-05-0*) Plus One Pub.
Raskin, Ellen. Nothing Ever Happens on My Block. Raskin, Ellen, illus. LC 89-31342. 32p. (gr. k-4). 1989. pap. 4.95 (*0-689-71335-5*, Aladdin) Macmillan Child Grp.
Ray, Margaret & Shalleck, Allan J. Curious George Goes to an Ice Cream Shop. (Illus.). 32p. (ps-2). 1989. pap. 2.80 (*0-395-51937-3*) HM.
Rayburn, Cherie. Fee Fiddle Foo What Should We Do? Gress, Jonna, ed. Yalowitz, Paul, illus. LC 92-76154. 14p. (ps-3). 1993. pap. 16.20 (*0-944943-23-3*, CODE 22494-7) Current Inc.
Rayner, Shoo. Cat in a Flap. Rayner, Shoo, illus. 18p. 1992. 12.95 (*0-87226-501-3*, Bedrick Blackie) P Bedrick Bks.
—My First Picture Joke Book. (Illus.). 32p. (ps-1). 1990. pap. 11.95 (*0-670-82450-X*) Viking Child Bks.
Raynor, Mary, illus. Thank You for the Tadpole. LC 87-474. (gr. k-2). 1988. pap. 2.50 (*0-317-69488-X*) Delacorte.
Razzi, Jim. The Very Best Christmas Present. Fernandes, Henry, illus. LC 87-83045. 24p. (Orig.). (ps-3). 1988. pap. write for info. (*0-307-11711-1*) Western Pub.
Real Mother Goose Clock Book. Wright, Blanche F., illus. 22p. (ps-2). 6.95 (*1-56288-095-0*) Checkerboard.
Reasoner, Charles. Chomp, Crunch, Chew! Reasoner, Chuck, illus. 12p. (ps). 1993. bds. 3.95 (*0-8431-3549-2*) Price Stern.
—Who's Peeking? Reasoner, Chuck, illus. 12p. (ps). 1993. 9.95 (*0-8431-3478-X*) Price Stern.
—Who's There? Reasoner, Chuck, illus. 12p. (ps). 1993. 9.95 (*0-8431-3479-8*) Price Stern.
Reasoner, Charles, illus. My First Musical Piggy Bank Book. 6p. (ps-2). 1992. bds. 9.95 (*1-56293-139-3*) McClanahan Bk.
Reeves, Eira, illus. Doing Things. LC 91-76214. 12p. (ps). 1992. bds. 3.99 bds. (*0-8066-2590-2*, 9-2590, Augsburg) Augsburg Fortress.
—Going Places. LC 91-76215. 12p. (ps). 1992. 3.99 (*0-8066-2589-9*, 9-2589) Augsburg Fortress.
—Helping. LC 91-76216. 12p. (ps). 1992. bds. 3.99 (*0-8066-2588-0*, 9-2588, Augsburg) Augsburg Fortress.
—Playing. LC 91-76217. 12p. (ps). 1992. bds. 3.99 (*0-8066-2587-2*, 9-2587, Augsburg) Augsburg Fortress.
Reeves, Mona R. I Had a Cat. Downing, Julie, illus. LC 87-37608. 32p. (ps-1). 1989. RSBE 13.95 (*0-02-775731-5*, Bradbury Pr) Macmillan Child Grp.
Reichmeier, Betty, illus. Potty Time! Yellow Ladder Books for Toddlers Through 4 Years. 10p. 1988. vinyl 7.00 (*0-394-89403-0*) Random Bks Yng Read.
Reid, Saralou L. Mommakitty's Surprise: "Skyler" LC 88-60613. (Illus.). (gr. k-3). write for info. (*0-9620420-0-5*); lib. bdg. write for info. (*0-9620420-1-3*); pap. write for info. (*0-9620420-3-X*) Surge Pub.
Reisberg. Baby Rattlesnake. 32p. (gr. 3-4). 1990. 21.34 (*0-8172-6749-2*) Raintree Steck-V.
Reiss, John J. Colors. Reiss, John J., illus. LC 86-22189. 32p. (ps-2). 1987. pap. 4.95 (*0-689-71119-0*, Aladdin) Macmillan Child Grp.
—Shapes. LC 73-76545. (Illus.). 32p. (ps-2). 1982. RSBE 13.95 (*0-02-776190-8*, Bradbury Pr) Macmillan Child Grp.
—Shapes. Reiss, John J., illus. LC 86-22164. 32p. (ps-2). 1987. pap. 3.95 (*0-689-71121-2*, Aladdin) Macmillan Child Grp.
Rey, H. A. Cecily G. & the Nine Monkeys. Rey, H. A., illus. 32p. (gr. 1-3). 1974. 14.45 (*0-395-18430-4*) HM.
—Curious George. (Illus.). 56p. (gr. k-3). 1973. 12.70 (*0-395-15993-8*) HM.
—Curious George Gets a Medal. (Illus.). 48p. (gr. k-3). 1957. 12.70 (*0-395-16973-9*) HM.
—Curious George Paper Doll. 1982. pap. 3.95 (*0-486-24386-9*) Dover.
—Curious George Rides a Bike. (Illus.). 48p. (gr. k-3). 1952. 12.95 (*0-395-16964-X*) HM.
—Curious George Takes a Job. (Illus.). 48p. (gr. k-3). 1973. 13.45 (*0-395-15086-8*) HM.
Rey, H. A. & Rey, Margaret. Curious George Goes to the Hospital. (Illus.). 48p. (gr. 1-5). 1973. 14.95 (*0-395-18158-5*); pap. 4.80 (*0-395-07062-7*) HM.
Rey, Margaret & Rey, H. A. Curious George Flies a Kite. (Illus.). 80p. (gr. k-3). 1973. 12.70 (*0-395-16965-8*) HM.
Rey, Margaret & Shalleck, Allan J. Curious George & the Dinosaur. (Illus.). 32p. (ps-2). 1989. pap. 3.80 (*0-395-51936-5*) HM.
—Curious George & the Pizza. 1988. pap. 7.70 incl. cass. (*0-395-48874-5*) HM.
—Curious George at the Beach. (Illus.). 32p. (ps-2). 1988. HM.
—Curious George at the Fire Station. 1988. pap. 7.70 incl. cass. (*0-395-48875-3*) HM.
—Curious George Goes to a Restaurant. (Illus.). 32p. (ps-2). 1988. HM.
—Curious George Goes to School. (Illus.). 32p. (ps-2). 1989. 9.70 (*0-395-51944-6*); pap. 3.80 (*0-395-51939-X*) HM.
—Curious George Goes to the Dentist. (Illus.). 32p. (ps-2). 1989. 9.95 (*0-685-26499-8*) HM.
Reynolds, Annette. The Christmas Baby. (Illus.). 12p. (ps-1). 1987. bds. 6.99 (*0-7459-1368-7*) Lion USA.
—The First Christmas Presents. (Illus.). 12p. (ps-1). 1987. bds. 6.99 (*0-7459-1369-5*) Lion USA.
Rice, Eve. Aren't You Coming Too? Parker, Nancy W., illus. LC 86-33506. 32p. (ps-3). 1988. 11.95 (*0-688-06446-9*); lib. bdg. 11.88 (*0-688-06447-7*) Greenwillow.
—Benny Bakes a Cake. LC 92-33053. (Illus.). 32p. (ps up). 1993. pap. 4.95 (*0-688-07814-1*, Mulberry) Morrow.
—City Night. Sis, Peter, illus. 24p. (ps-1). 1987. 11.75 (*0-688-06856-1*); PLB 11.88 (*0-688-06857-X*) Greenwillow.
—Goodnight, Goodnight. LC 79-17253. (Illus.). (ps-1). 1980. 13.95 (*0-688-80254-0*); PLB 13.88 (*0-688-84254-2*) Greenwillow.
—Sam Who Never Forgets. LC 76-30370. (Illus.). 32p. (ps up). 1987. pap. 3.95 (*0-688-07335-2*, Mulberry) Morrow.
Rice, Melanie & Rice, Chris. All About Me. Smith, Lesley, illus. LC 87-15498. 48p. (ps-3). 1988. PLB 11.99 (*0-385-24282-4*); pap. 10.95 (*0-385-24281-6*) Doubleday.
Richards, Selena. Rebecca Goes Out. Dubin, Jill, illus. 18p. (ps). 1992. 3.50 (*1-56288-269-4*) Checkerboard.
—Rebecca Goes to the Country. Dubin, Jill, illus. 18p. (ps). 1992. 3.50 (*1-56288-270-8*) Checkerboard.
—Rebecca Goes to the Park. Dubin, Jill, illus. 18p. (ps). 1992. 3.50 (*1-56288-271-6*) Checkerboard.
—Rebecca's Rainy Day. Dubin, Jill, illus. 18p. (ps). 1992. 3.50 (*1-56288-272-4*) Checkerboard.
Richardson, Gale T. Serenity, Courage & Wisdom. 2p. (ps). 1989. 3.50 (*0-9614337-2-8*) Poetry Unltd.
Richardson, Lee. Sophie's Surprise. 2nd ed. Holt, Shirley, illus. 28p. (gr. 3-8). 1984. 16.95 (*0-9613476-0-0*) Shirlee.
Richardson, Lewis. Come along with Me. Orecchia, Giulia, illus. 16p. (ps-k). 1994. bds. 9.95 (*0-448-40188-6*, G&D) Putnam Pub Group.
Richmond, Gary. Howard the Horrible Gets Even. 32p. 1990. 6.99 (*0-8499-0744-6*) Word Inc.
Ricklen, Neil. Babys Big & Little. 1990. 4.95 (*0-671-69542-8*) S&S Trade.
—Baby's Colors. 1990. 4.95 (*0-671-69539-8*) S&S Trade.
—Baby's Good Morning: A Super Chubby Board Book. (ps). 1992. pap. 4.95 (*0-671-76084-X*, Little Simon) S&S Trade.
—Baby's Good Night: A Super Chubby Board Book. (ps). 1992. pap. 4.95 (*0-671-76085-8*, Little Simon) S&S Trade.
—Baby's School: A Super Chubby Board Book. (ps). 1992. pap. 4.95 (*0-671-76086-6*, Little Simon) S&S Trade.
—Baby's Zoo: A Super Chubby Board Book. (ps). 1992. pap. 4.95 (*0-671-76087-4*, Little Simon) S&S Trade.
—Baby's 1-2-3. 1990. 4.95 (*0-671-69541-X*) S&S Trade.
Ricklen, Neil, photos by. Baby's ABC. (Illus.). 24p. 1990. casebound, padded cover 4.95 (*0-671-69540-1*, Little Simon) S&S Trade.
Ricklin, Neil. Baby's Friends. 1986. 4.95 (*0-671-62076-2*) S&S Trade.
—Baby's Toys. 1986. 4.95 (*0-671-62078-9*) S&S Trade.
Ricklin, Neil, photos by. Daddy & Me. (Illus.). 28p. (ps). 1988. 4.95 (*0-671-64537-4*, Little Simon) S&S Trade.
—Grandma & Me. (Illus.). 28p. (ps-k). 1988. 4.95 (*0-671-64540-4*, S&S BFYR) S&S Trade.
—Grandpa & Me. (Illus.). 28p. (ps-k). 1988. 4.95 (*0-671-64539-0*, S&S BFYR) S&S Trade.
—Mommy & Me. (Illus.). 28p. (ps-k). 1988. 4.95 (*0-671-64538-2*, Little Simon) S&S Trade.
Riddell, Edwina. My First Animal Word Book. (Illus.). 32p. (ps). 1989. 9.95 (*0-8120-6127-6*) Barron.

—One Hundred First Words. (Illus.). 32p. (ps). 1988. 8.95 (*0-8120-5786-4*) Barron.

Riehecky, Janet. Polka-Dot Puppy's Visitor: A Book about Opposites. Hohag, Linda, illus. LC 88-10935. 32p. (ps-2). 1988. PLB 14.95 (*0-89565-378-8*) Childs World.

Ringstad, Muriel. Eye of the Changer. Croly, Donald, illus. LC 83-7121. 96p. (Orig.). (gr. 4 up). 1984. pap. 9.95 (*0-88240-251-X*) Alaska Northwest.

Roberts, Sarah. The Adventures of Grover in Outer Space. McPheeters, Neal, illus. LC 84-60188. 32p. (ps-3). 1984. pap. 1.50 (*0-394-86300-3*) Random Bks Yng Read.

Roberts, Tom. The Three Billy Goats Gruff. Jorgensen, David, illus. LC 89-32138. 32p. (gr. 1 up). 1991. pap. 14.95 (*0-88708-117-7*, Rabbit Ears); incl. cassette 19.95 (*0-88708-118-5*, Rabbit Ears) Picture Bk Studio.

—The Three Little Pigs. Jorgensen, David, illus. LC 89-70097. 32p. (ps up). 1991. pap. 14.95 (*0-88708-132-0*, Rabbit Ears); pap. 19.95 incl. cass. (*0-88708-133-9*, Rabbit Ears) Picture Bk Studio.

Roberts, Willo D. Don't Hurt Laurie! Sanderson, Ruth, illus. LC 87-21742. 176p. (gr. 3-7). 1988. pap. 3.95 (*0-689-71206-5*, Aladdin) Macmillan Child Grp.

Robins, Joan. Addie Meets Max. Truesdell, Sue, illus. LC 84-48329. 32p. (ps-2). 1988. pap. 3.50 (*0-06-444116-4*, Trophy) HarpC Child Bks.

Robinsunne. Nannee. Robinsunne, illus. 36p. (ps). 1993. 15.95 (*0-9636986-0-5*) Robinsunne Pstcrd.

Rockwell, Anne. Apples & Pumpkins. Rockwell, Lizzy, illus. LC 88-22628. 24p. (ps-1). 1989. RSBE 13.95 (*0-02-777270-5*, Macmillan Child Bk) Macmillan Child Grp.

—Big Wheels. Rockwell, Anne, illus. LC 85-16248. 24p. (ps-1). 1986. 12.95 (*0-525-44226-X*, DCB) Dutton Child Bks.

—Bikes. Rockwell, Ann, illus. LC 86-19923. 24p. (ps-1). 1987. 11.95 (*0-525-44287-1*, DCB) Dutton Child Bks.

—My Spring Robin. Rockwell, Harlow & Rockwell, Lizzy, illus. LC 88-13333. 24p. (ps-1). 1989. RSBE 13.95 (*0-02-777611-5*, Macmillan Child Bk) Macmillan Child Grp.

—Things That Go. Rockwell, Anne, illus. LC 86-6199. 24p. (ps-1). 1986. 10.95 (*0-525-44266-9*, DCB) Dutton Child Bks.

—Things to Play With. Rockwell, Anne, illus. LC 87-33399. 24p. (ps-1). 1988. 11.95 (*0-525-44409-2*, DCB) Dutton Child Bks.

—Things to Play With. (Illus.). 24p. (ps-1). 1994. pap. 3.99 (*0-14-050308-0*, Puff Unicorn) Puffin Bks.

—Trains. Rockwell, Anne, illus. LC 87-22180. 24p. (ps-1). 1988. 13.00 (*0-525-44377-0*, 01063-320, DCB) Dutton Child Bks.

Rockwell, Anne & Rockwell, Harlow. Happy Birthday to Me. Rockwell, Anne & Rockwell, Harlow, illus. LC 81-3738. 24p. (ps-k). 1981. RSBE 10.95 (*0-02-777680-8*, Macmillan Child Bk) Macmillan Child Grp.

—I Play in My Room. Rockwell, Anne & Rockwell, Harlow, illus. LC 81-2634. 24p. (ps-k). 1981. RSBE 10.95 (*0-02-777670-0*, Macmillan Child Bk) Macmillan Child Grp.

—My Baby-Sitter. LC 85-5000. (Illus.). 24p. (ps-k). 1985. RSBE 9.95 (*0-02-777780-4*, Macmillan Child Bk) Macmillan Child Grp.

Rodriguez, Ed & Cardona, Jose, illus. Disney's Goofy Pop-up Book. 14p. (ps-3). 1994. 11.95 (*0-7868-3006-9*) Disney Pr.

Roffey, Maureen. I Spy at the Zoo. Roffey, Maureen, illus. LC 87-12116. 32p. (ps-2). 1988. SBE 13.95 (*0-02-777150-4*, Four Winds) Macmillan Child Grp.

—I Spy at the Zoo. Roffey, Maureen, illus. LC 88-19360. 32p. (ps-2). 1989. pap. 3.95 (*0-689-71227-8*, Aladdin) Macmillan Child Grp.

Rogers, Carol A. Just Picture This: My Own Photo Album. (Illus.). 10p. 1993. vinyl 24.95 (*0-9635899-0-3*) New Vision VA.

Rogers, George L. Mac & Zach from Hackensack. Eskander, Stefanie C., illus. 32p. (gr. k-6). 1992. PLB 12.95 (*0-938399-07-1*); pap. 4.95 (*0-938399-06-3*) Acorn Pub MN.

Rogers, Jean. Runaway Mittens. Munoz, Rie, illus. LC 87-12024. 24p. (ps-3). 1988. 15.00 (*0-688-07053-1*); lib. bdg. 14.93 (*0-688-07054-X*) Greenwillow.

Rogers, Marion. Caribbean ABC. Roger, Marion, illus. 26p. (Orig.). (ps-1). 1992. pap. 3.50 (*0-935357-02-5*) CRIC Prod.

A Rooster Reminds Peter. (ps-1). 1988. pap. 0.79 (*1-55513-920-5*, Chariot Bks) Chariot Family.

Rose, Dorothy. Baby Games: Follow Me. (ps). 1994. pap. 3.50 (*0-671-88361-5*, Little Simon) S&S Trade.

—Baby Games: Peek A Boo. (ps). 1994. pap. 3.50 (*0-671-88358-5*, Little Simon) S&S Trade.

—Baby Games: What Do Lambs Say? (ps). 1994. pap. 3.50 (*0-671-88359-3*, Little Simon) S&S Trade.

—Baby Games: Where's Your Nose. (ps). 1994. pap. 3.50 (*0-671-88360-7*, Little Simon) S&S Trade.

Rosen, Michael. We're Going on a Bear Hunt. Oxenbury, Helen, illus. LC 88-13338. 40p. (ps-4). 1989. SBE 15.95 (*0-689-50476-4*, M K McElderry) Macmillan Child Grp.

Rosen, Michael J. Down at the Doctor's: The Sick Book. Blake, Quentin, illus. 24p. (gr. k-4). 1998. 10.95 (*0-13-218942-9*, Little Simon) S&S Trade.

Rosenberg, Amye, illus. The Pudgy Peek-a-Boo Book. 16p. (ps). 1983. pap. 2.95 (*0-448-10205-6*, G&D) Putnam Pub Group.

Rosenholtz, Stephen. Move Like the Animals. Yoshiko, Fujita, illus. LC 91-66970. 32p. (ps-3). 1992. incl. cassette 19.95 (*0-9630979-1-1*); pap. 14.95 incl. cassette (*0-9630979-0-3*) Rosewd Pubns.

Rosentheil, Agnes. Mimi Makes a Splash. Stryker, Sandra & Paine, Penelope, eds. Paine, Penelope, tr. LC 91-11286. (Illus.). 48p. (Orig.). (ps-4). 1991. pap. 6.95 (*0-911655-51-4*) Advocacy Pr.

—Mimi Takes Charge. Stryker, Sandra & Paine, Penelope, eds. Paine, Penelope, tr. LC 91-11285. (Illus.). 48p. (Orig.). (ps-4). 1991. pap. 6.95 (*0-911655-50-6*) Advocacy Pr.

Rosner, Ruth. Arabba, Gah, Zee, Marissa & Me! Fay, Ann, ed. Rosner, Ruth, illus. LC 86-15904. 32p. (ps-3). 1987. PLB 13.95 (*0-8075-0442-4*) A Whitman.

Ross, Alison, illus. Daytime Baby: Baby Books. 8p. (ps). 1992. bds. 3.50 (*0-7214-1515-6*, S9212-4) Ladybird Bks.

—Hello Baby: Baby Books. 8p. (ps). 1992. bds. 3.50 (*0-7214-1497-4*, S9212-3) Ladybird Bks.

—Noisy Baby: Baby Books. 8p. (ps). 1992. bds. 3.50 (*0-7214-1496-6*, S9212-1) Ladybird Bks.

—Playtime Baby: Baby Books. 8p. (ps). 1992. bds. 3.50 (*0-7214-1514-8*, S9212-2) Ladybird Bks.

Ross, Andrea. Chester's Coloring Book. Ross, Andrea, illus. 70p. (Orig.). (gr. k-2). 1992. 7.00 (*1-56002-016-4*, Univ Edtns) Aegina Pr.

—Oscar Crab & Rallo Car. LC 86-72872. 64p. (Orig.). (ps-2). 1987. pap. 5.00 (*0-916383-18-0*) Aegina Pr.

Ross, Anna. Elmo's Big Lift-&-Look Book. Mathieu, Joe, illus. 12p. (ps-k). 1994. 10.00 (*0-679-84468-6*) Random Bks Yng Read.

—Knock, Knock, Who's There? A Sesame Street Book. Mathieu, Joe, illus. 22p. (ps-k). 1994. 3.50 (*0-679-85304-9*) Random Bks Yng Read.

—Not the Monster. Nicklaus, Carol, illus. 12p. (ps). 1994. bds. 3.99 (*0-679-84739-1*) Random Bks Yng Read.

—Open Sesame. Chartier, Normand, illus. LC 91-67671. 14p. (ps-k). 1992. bds. 3.99 (*0-679-83063-4*) Random Bks Yng Read.

—Rock-a-Bye Babies. Nicklaus, Carol, illus. 12p. (ps). 1994. bds. 3.99 (*0-679-84740-5*) Random Bks Yng Read.

—Rubber Duckies Don't Say Quack! Nicklaus, Carol, illus. 12p. (ps). 1994. bds. 3.99 (*0-679-84741-3*) Random Bks Yng Read.

—Say Bye-Bye. Gorbaty, Norman, illus. LC 90-52915. 24p. (ps). 1992. 3.95 (*0-394-85485-3*) Random Bks Yng Read.

—Say Good Night. Gorbaty, Norman, illus. LC 90-52914. 24p. (ps). 1992. 3.95 (*0-394-85491-8*) Random Bks Yng Read.

—Sesame Street Whose Knees Are These? (ps). 1994. 3.99 (*0-679-84742-1*) Random Bks Yng Read.

—Where, Oh, Where? A Sesame Street Book. Mathieu, Joe, illus. 22p. (ps-k). 1994. 3.50 (*0-679-85303-0*) Random Bks Yng Read.

—Whose Knees Are These? Nicklaud, Carol, illus. 12p. (ps). 1994. write for info. Random Bks Yng Read.

Ross, K. K. Bert's Little Bedtime Story: A Sesame Street Book. Wenzel, Rick, illus. LC 89-64283. 28p. (ps). 1991. bds. 3.25 (*0-679-80757-8*) Random Bks Yng Read.

—Cozy in the Woods. Dyer, Jane, illus. LC 88-63931. 28p. (ps). 1990. 2.95 (*0-394-85400-4*) Random Bks Yng Read.

Ross, Katharine. Rainbow Babies. Petach, Heidi, illus. LC 91-66659. 28p. (ps). 1992. 2.95 (*0-679-83068-5*) Random Bks Yng Read.

—Teeny Tiny Farm. Flynn, Amy, illus. LC 91-50647. 22p. (ps). 1992. 3.25 (*0-679-83388-9*) Random Bks Yng Read.

Ross, Katherine. The Fuzzytail Friends' Great Egg Hunt. McCue, Lisa, illus. LC 87-50812. 14p. (ps). 1988. bds. 3.99 (*0-394-89475-8*) Random Bks Yng Read.

Ross, Tony. This Old Man. 12p. (ps-1). 1990. pap. 10.95 POB (*0-689-71386-X*, Aladdin) Macmillan Child Grp.

—Towser & the Haunted House. Ross, Tony, illus. 32p. (ps-1). 1987. 5.95 (*0-86264-079-2*, Pub. by Anderson Pr UK) Trafalgar.

—Towser & the Magic Apple. Ross, Tony, illus. 32p. (ps-1). 1987. 5.95 (*0-86264-078-4*, Pub. by Anderson Pr UK) Trafalgar.

Roving Rosie Reports. LC 90-27867. 24p. 1991. pap. 3.95 (*1-56288-010-1*) Checkerboard.

Rowe, William. Viu's Night Book. (Illus.). 55p. (gr. 3-6). 1995. pap. 7.95 (*0-9641330-0-8*) Portunus Pubng.

Roy, Cal. Time Is Day. (Illus.). (gr. k-3). 1968. 9.95 (*0-8392-3065-6*) Astor-Honor.

Rudner, Barry. The Bumblebee & the Ram. Fahsbender, Thomas, illus. LC 89-81585. 32p. (Orig.). 1989. pap. 5.95 (*0-925928-03-8*) Tiny Thought.

—The Handstand. Fahsbender, Thomas, illus. 32p. 1991. pap. 5.95 (*0-925928-05-4*) Tiny Thought.

—Nonsense. Fahsbender, Thomas, illus. (gr. k-6). 1991. 5.95 (*0-925928-04-6*) Tiny Thought.

—Will I Still Have to Make My Bed In The Morning? (Illus.). 32p. 1991. pap. 5.95 (*0-925928-10-0*) Tiny Thought.

Rudolph the Red-Nosed Reindeer: Musical Board Book. 12p. (ps). Date not set. 5.95 (*0-694-00564-9*) HarpC Child Bks.

Rumney, Donna. My Picture Book about Me. (Illus.). 20p. (ps). 1988. write for info. My Picture Bks.

Running Press Staff. The Dinosaurs Postcard Book. (Illus.). 64p. (Orig.). 1987. pap. 7.95 (*0-89471-553-4*) Running Pr.

Ruschak, Lynette. Snack Attack: A Tasty Pop Up Book. Carter, David A., illus. 12p. (ps-3). 1990. pap. 8.95 (*0-671-70448-6*, S&S BFYR) S&S Trade.

—Who's Hiding? (ps). 1991. pap. 8.95 (*0-671-73957-3*, S&S BFYR) S&S Trade.

Russo, Marisabina. The Line-up Book. Russo, Marisabina, illus. LC 85-24907. 24p. (ps-1). 1986. 11.75 (*0-688-06204-0*); PLB 11.88 (*0-688-06205-9*) Greenwillow.

—Only Six More Days. LC 86-19586. (Illus.). 32p. (ps-3). 1988. 11.95 (*0-688-07071-X*); lib. bdg. 11.88 (*0-688-07072-8*) Greenwillow.

Rutman, Shereen G. Observing. Banta, Susan, illus. 16p. (ps). 1992. wkbk. 2.25 (*1-56293-189-X*) McClanahan Bk.

—Sorting. Banta, Susan, illus. 16p. (ps). 1992. wkbk. 2.25 (*1-56293-186-5*) McClanahan Bk.

—What Belongs? Morgado, Richard, illus. 32p. (ps). 1992. wkbk. 1.95 (*1-56293-175-X*) McClanahan Bk.

Ryan, Cheli D. Hildilid's Night. reissued ed. Lobel, Arnold, illus. LC 86-5294. 32p. (ps-2). 1986. RSBE 13.95 (*0-02-777260-8*, Macmillan Child Bk) Macmillan Child Grp.

Ryder, Joanne. Without Words. Sonneborn, Barbara, photos by. (Illus.). 32p. 1995. 15.95 (*0-87156-580-3*) Sierra.

Ryder, Joanne, adapted by. Hardie Gramatky's Little Toot. Ross, Larry, illus. 32p. (ps-2). 1988. pap. 2.25 (*0-448-34301-0*, Platt & Munk Pubs) Putnam Pub Group.

Rylant, Cynthia. Everyday Town. Rylant, Cynthia, illus. LC 92-40541. 14p. (ps-k). 1993. pap. 4.95 with rounded corners (*0-02-778026-0*, Bradbury Pr) Macmillan Child Grp.

—Henry & Mudge Get the Cold Shivers: The Seventh Book of Their Adventures. Stevenson, Sucie, illus. LC 88-18854. 48p. (gr. 1-3). 1989. RSBE 12.95 (*0-02-778011-2*, Bradbury Pr) Macmillan Child Grp.

—Henry & Mudge in Puddle Trouble: The Second Book of Their Adventures. Stevenson, Sucie, illus. LC 86-13616. 48p. (gr. 1-3). 1987. RSBE 12.95 (*0-02-778002-3*, Bradbury Pr) Macmillan Child Grp.

—Henry & Mudge in the Green Time: The Third Book of Their Adventures. Stevenson, Sucie, illus. LC 86-26386. 48p. (gr. 1-3). 1987. RSBE 12.95 (*0-02-778003-1*, Bradbury Pr) Macmillan Child Grp.

—Henry & Mudge under the Yellow Moon: The Fourth Book of Their Adventures. Stevenson, Sucie, illus. LC 86-26390. 48p. (gr. 1-3). 1987. RSBE 12.95 (*0-02-778004-X*, Bradbury Pr) Macmillan Child Grp.

—Mr. Griggs' Work. Downing, Julie, illus. LC 88-1484. 32p. (ps-2). 1989. 14.95 (*0-531-05769-0*); PLB 14.99 (*0-531-08369-1*) Orchard Bks Watts.

Sadler, Marilyn. Knock, Knock, It's P. J. Funnybunny! Bollen, Roger, illus. 24p. (ps-1). 1992. 8.00 (*0-679-81733-6*) Random Bks Yng Read.

Safari Adventure. (ps-3). 1988. 9.95 (*0-8167-1444-4*) Troll Assocs.

Sage, Margaret A. Wee Taste & See: A Story Book - Cook Book - Coloring Book. Tusken, Dee, illus. 32p. (Orig.). (gr. 1-3). 1992. pap. 9.95 (*0-9631988-1-5*) Taste & See.

St. John, Patricia. Star of Light. (gr. 5-8). 1953. pap. 4.99 (*0-8024-0004-3*) Moody.

Sainz, Frances. La Caja de Botones. 23p. (ps-1). 1992. pap. text ed. 23.00 big bk. (*1-56843-045-0*); pap. text ed. 4.50 (*1-56843-092-2*) BGR Pub.

—Nubecitas. 23p. (ps-1). 1992. pap. text ed. 23.00 big bk. (*1-56843-046-9*); pap. text ed. 4.50 (*1-56843-093-0*) BGR Pub.

Salazar, Yolanda L. The Beestys' Journey, 20 Vols, Vol. 1. Kelley, Midorie, illus. 36p. (gr. 3 up). 1989. write for info. ADAPT Pub Co.

—The Beestys' What Color Is... Kelley, Midorie, illus. 10p. (ps). 1989. 7.95 (*0-317-94002-3*) ADAPT Pub Co.

—The Beesty's What Shape Is... Kelley, Midorie, illus. 10p. (ps). 1989. 7.95 (*0-317-94001-5*) ADAPT Pub Co.

—The Beestys' What Time Is... Kelley, Midorie, illus. 10p. (ps). 1989. 7.95 (*0-317-94003-1*) ADAPT Pub Co.

Salem, Lynn & Stewart, Josie. Cuidando a Rosita. (Illus.). 8p. (gr. 1). 1993. 3.50 (*1-880612-23-2*) Seedling Pubns.

—Espero Que No. (Illus.). 8p. (gr. 1). 1993. pap. 3.50 (*1-880612-15-1*) Seedling Pubns.

—Here's Skipper. (Illus.). 8p. (gr. 1). 1993. pap. 3.50 (*1-880612-14-3*) Seedling Pubns.

—I Suficiente. (Illus.). 12p. (gr. 1). 1993. pap. 3.50 (*1-880612-28-3*) Seedling Pubns.

—Mi Mascota. (Illus.). 8p. (gr. 1). 1993. pap. 3.50 (*1-880612-24-0*) Seedling Pubns.

—Nunca. (Illus.). 8p. (gr. 1). 1993. pap. 3.50 (*1-880612-25-9*) Seedling Pubns.

—Que Escuela. (Illus.). 16p. (gr. 1). 1993. pap. 3.50 (*1-880612-21-6*) Seedling Pubns.

—Que Hay para Cenar. (Illus.). 12p. (gr. 1). 1993. pap. 3.50 (*1-880612-20-8*) Seedling Pubns.

—Sopa Marciana. (Illus.). 8p. (gr. 1). 1993. pap. 3.50 (*1-880612-17-8*) Seedling Pubns.

Salter-Mathieson, Nigel. Little Chief Mischief. Gruen, Chuck, illus. (gr. 2-7). 1962. 10.95 (*0-8392-3020-6*) Astor-Honor.

Salzman, Yuri, retold by. & illus. The Three Little Pigs. LC 87-81773. 24p. (ps-k). 1988. pap. write for info. (*0-307-10099-5*, Pub. by Golden Bks) Western Pub.

Samson, Smadar. Ophir. (Illus.). 32p. (gr. k-2). 1993. 16. 95 (*0-370-31740-8*, Pub. by Bodley Head UK) Trafalgar.
—Through the Glass Door. (Illus.). 32p. (ps-2). 1992. 16. 95 (*0-370-31573-1*, Pub. by Bodley Head UK) Trafalgar.
Samton, Sheila W. Moon to Sun: An Adding Book. Samton, Sheila W., illus. LC 90-85729. 24p. (ps-1). 1991. 9.95 (*1-878093-13-4*) Boyds Mills Pr.
—My Haunted House: A Lift-the-Flap Book. Samton, Sheila W., illus. 24p. (ps-k). 1992. bds. 12.95 (*1-56397-093-7*) Boyds Mills Pr.
—On the River: An Adding Book. Samton, Sheila W., illus. LC 90-85730. 24p. (ps-1). 1991. 9.95 (*1-878093-14-2*) Boyds Mills Pr.
—The World from My Window. Samton, Sheila W., illus. LC 90-85732. 28p. (ps-2). 1991. Repr. 14.95 (*1-878093-15-0*) Boyds Mills Pr.
Samuels, Vyanne. Carry Go Bring Come. Northway, Jennifer, illus. LC 89-1528. 32p. (ps-2). 1989. SBE 13. 95 (*0-02-778121-6*, Four Winds) Macmillan Child Grp.
Sanchez, Isidro & Peris, Carme. La Ciudad. 32p. (ps-1). 1992. pap. 6.95 (*0-8120-4871-7*) Barron.
—El Mar. 32p. (ps-1). 1992. pap. 6.95 (*0-8120-4869-5*) Barron.
—La Montana. 32p. (ps-1). 1992. pap. 6.95 (*0-8120-4872-5*) Barron.
—La Nieve. 32p. (ps-1). 1992. pap. 6.95 (*0-8120-4870-9*) Barron.
Sandberg, Inger. Dusty Wants to Borrow Everything. Sandberg, Lasse, illus. Maurer, Judy A., tr. (Illus.). 32p. (ps up). 1988. 6.95 (*91-29-58782-4*, R & S Bks) FS&G.
Sanders, Scott R. Aurora Means Dawn. Kastner, Jill, illus. LC 88-24127. 32p. (gr. 1-5). 1989. 13.95 (*0-02-778270-0*, Bradbury Pr) Macmillan Child Grp.
San Souci, Daniel, illus. The Bedtime Book. LC 85-12898. 48p. (gr. k-3). 1985. PLB 11.79 (*0-685-42987-3*, J Messner) S&S Trade.
Santacruz, Daniel, tr. Dentro Fuera: Un Libro Disney de Opuestos. Duerrstein, Richard, illus. (SPA.). 12p. 1993. 5.95 (*1-56282-458-9*) Disney Pr.
Sawyer, Ruth. Roller Skates. Angelo, Valenti, illus. 192p. (gr. 4-7). 1969. pap. 1.50 (*0-440-47499-X*, YB) Dell.
Say, Allen. A River Dream. Say, Allen, illus. 32p. (gr. k-3). 1988. 14.45 (*0-395-48294-1*) HM.
Scarry, Huck, illus. My First Picture Dictionary. LC 76-24174. (ps-2). 1978. lib. bdg. 5.99 (*0-394-93486-5*); pap. 2.25 (*0-394-83486-0*) Random Bks Yng Read.
Scarry, Richard. The Best Mistake Ever! A Step Two Book. Scarry, Richard, illus. LC 84-2029. 48p. (ps-2). 1984. pap. 3.50 (*0-394-86816-1*) Random Bks Yng Read.
—The Bunny Book. (Illus.). 24p. (ps-k). 1987. pap. write for info (*0-307-10048-0*, Pub. by Golden Bks) Western Pub.
—I Am a Bunny. Scarry, Richard, illus. 22p. (gr. k-2). 1967. write for info. (*0-307-12125-9*, Golden Bks.) Western Pub.
—Richard Scarry's Bedtime Stories. reissue ed. LC 86-484. (Illus.). 32p. (ps-1). 1989. pap. 2.25 (*0-394-88269-5*) Random Bks Yng Read.
—Richard Scarry's Best Busy Year Ever. Scarry, Richard, illus. (ps-1). 1991. 5.25 (*0-307-15748-2*, Golden Pr) Western Pub.
—Richard Scarry's Best Friend Ever. (Illus.). 24p. (ps-k). 1989. pap. write for info. (*0-307-11715-4*, Pub. by Golden Bks) Western Pub.
—Richard Scarry's Best Word Book Ever. Scarry, Richard, illus. (ps-3). 1963. write for info. (*0-307-15510-2*, Golden Bks) Western Pub.
—Richard Scarry's Busy Busy World. Scarry, Richard, illus. (gr. k-5). write for info. (*0-307-15511-0*, Golden Bks) Western Pub.
—Richard Scarry's Counting Book. (Illus.). 24p. (ps). 1990. pap. write for info. (*0-307-11659-X*, Pub. by Golden Bks) Western Pub.
—Richard Scarry's Great Big Schoolhouse. Scarry, Richard, illus. (ps-2). 1969. 12.00 (*0-394-80874-6*) Random Bks Yng Read.
—Richard Scarry's Just Right Word Book: (Just Right for 2's & 3's) Scarry, Richard, illus. LC 89-42839. 24p. (ps). 1990. 6.00 (*0-679-80073-5*) Random Bks Yng Read.
Scheer, Julian. Rain Makes Applesauce. Bileck, Marvin, illus. 36p. (ps-3). 1964. 15.95 (*0-8234-0091-3*) Holiday.
Scheffler, Ursel. Stop Your Crowing, Kasimir! Brix-Henker, Silke, illus. 32p. (gr. k-3). 1988. lib. bdg. 18. 95 (*0-87614-323-0*) Carolrhoda Bks.
Scheidl, Gerda M. Flowers for the Snowman. Lanning, Rosemary, tr. Wilkon, Jozef, illus. LC 88-42532. 32p. (gr. k-3). 1988. 13.95 (*1-55858-068-9*) North-South Bks NYC.
Schmidt, Karen L., illus. Down by the Station. 1987. pap. 6.99 incl. audiocassette (*0-553-45902-3*) Bantam.
Schneider, Howie & Seligson, Susan. Amos: The Story of an Old Dog & His Couch. Schneider, Howie, illus. LC 87-2813. 32p. (ps-3). 1987. 14.95 (*0-316-77404-9*) Little.
Schoepfer, G. R. River of Miracles. Schoepfer, Virginia B., ed. Brenes, Irma M., illus. (gr. 1-11). 1978. pap. text ed. 2.75x (*0-931436-01-X*, Children's Books) G R Schoepfer.
Schoolhouse. 8p. (ps). 1984. pap. 3.50 (*0-671-49717-0*, Little Simon) S&S Trade.
Schroeder, Ruth. The Adventure of Fifi's Honey Bee Bears & the Big Bee Hive. Dixon, David, illus. 28p. (gr. k-5). 1987. PLB 8.95 (*0-935087-24-9*) R & D Bks.
Schwager, Istar. What's Different? Siede, George & Preis, Donna, photos by. (Illus.). 24p. (ps-3). 1993. PLB 12. 95 (*1-56674-070-3*, HTS Bks) Forest Hse.
Schwartz, Alvin. In a Dark, Dark Room. LC 83-47699. (Illus.). 64p. (gr. k-3). 1986. incl. cassette 5.98 (*0-694-00163-5*, Trophy); pap. 3.50 (*0-06-444090-7*, Trophy) HarpC Child Bks.
—Ten Copycats in a Boat & Other Riddles. Simont, Marc, illus. LC 79-2811. 64p. (gr. k-3). 1985. pap. 3.50 (*0-06-444076-1*, Trophy) HarpC Child Bks.
Schwartz, Amy. Bea & Mr. Jones. Schwartz, Amy, illus. LC 81-18041. 32p. (ps-2). 1982. SBE 13.95 (*0-02-781430-0*, Bradbury Pr) Macmillan Child Grp.
—Begin at the Beginning. Scwartz, Amy, illus. LC 82-48257. 32p. (gr. k-3). 1984. pap. 4.95 (*0-06-443060-X*, Trophy) HarpC Child Bks.
Schwartz, David M. How Much Is a Million? Kellogg, Steven, illus. 40p. (gr. k-3). 1987. Big Book. 28.67 (*0-590-71767-7*) Scholastic Inc.
—How Much Is a Million? Kellogg, Steven, illus. 40p. (gr. 1-4). 1986. pap. 3.95 (*0-590-43614-7*) Scholastic Inc.
Schwartz, Henry. How I Captured a Dinosaur. Schwartz, Amy, illus. LC 88-1482. 32p. (ps-2). 1989. 14.95 (*0-531-05770-4*); PLB 14.99 (*0-531-08370-5*) Orchard Bks Watts.
Schweninger, Ann. Off to School! (Illus.). 32p. (ps-3). 1989. pap. 3.99 (*0-14-050661-6*, Puffin) Puffin Bks.
—Valentine Friends. LC 87-22326. 32p. (ps-1). 1988. pap. 10.95 (*0-670-81448-2*) Viking Child Bks.
Schweninger, Ann, illus. Mary Had a Little Lamb. 24p. (ps). 1992. bds. write for info. (*0-307-06139-6*, 6139) Western Pub.
Sclavi, Tiziano. Touch & Read. Michelini, Carlo A., illus. 1994. 14.85 (*1-56397-344-8*) Boyds Mills Pr.
—Wiggle Your Fingers. Michelini, Carlo A., illus. 1994. 14.85 (*1-56397-342-1*) Boyds Mills Pr.
Scott, Ann H. Someday Rider. Himler, Ronald, illus. LC 88-35255. 32p. (ps-1). 1989. 13.45 (*0-89919-792-2*, Clarion Bks) HM.
Scribner, Toni, illus. The Glo Friends' Good Night Book. LC 85-60757. 28p. (ps). 1986. 2.95 (*0-394-87797-7*) Random Bks Yng Read.
—Where's Baby? LC 86-43148. 14p. (ps). 1987. bds. 3.99 (*0-394-89071-X*) Random Bks Yng Read.
Seablom, Seth H. Seattle Coloring Guide. Seablom, Seth H., illus. (gr. 4-6). 1977. pap. 2.50 (*0-918800-01-3*) Seablom.
Seaman, Rosie. Discovering Plants & Animals. (ps-k). 1987. pap. 6.95 (*0-8224-1928-9*) Fearon Teach Aids.
Sebarg, R. & Zakutinsky, Adina. Torah Shapes. Feld, Goldie, illus. 12p. (ps). 1987. 4.95 (*0-911643-08-7*) Aura Bklyn.
Seeley, Laura L. The Book of Shadowboxes: A Story of the ABC's. Seeley, Laura L., illus. 64p. (ps-3). 1993. pap. 8.95 (*1-56145-072-3*) Peachtree Pubs.
—Coloring the Book of the Shadowboxes: A Story of the ABC's. Seeley, Laura L., illus. 64p. (Orig.). (ps-3). 1993. pap. 4.95 (*1-56145-037-5*) Peachtree Pubs.
Segal, Lore. All the Way Home. Marshall, James, illus. 32p. (ps up). 1988. pap. 3.95 (*0-374-40355-4*) FS&G.
Selsam, Millicent E. & Hunt, Joyce. Keep Looking! Chartier, Normand, illus. LC 88-1416. 32p. (gr. k-3). 1989. RSBE 14.95 (*0-02-781840-3*, Macmillan Child Bk) Macmillan Child Grp.
Sendak, Maurice. Chicken Soup with Rice. Sendak, Maurice, illus. 32p. (gr. k-3). 1986. Big book. 19.95 (*0-590-64645-1*); pap. 2.50 (*0-590-41033-4*) Scholastic Inc.
—Hector Protector & As I Went over the Water: Two Nursery Rhymes. Sendak, Maurice, illus. LC 65-21388. 64p. (ps-1). 1990. pap. 5.95 (*0-06-443237-8*, Trophy) HarpC Child Bks.
—Higglety Pigglety Pop! Or There Must be More to Life. LC 67-18553. (Illus.). 80p. (gr. k-4). 1979. pap. 5.95 (*0-06-443021-9*, Trophy) HarpC Child Bks.
—Higglety Pigglety Pop! or There Must be More to Life. (ps-3). 1967. PLB 14.89 (*0-06-025488-2*) HarpC Child Bks.
—In the Night Kitchen. Sendak, Maurice, illus. LC 70-105483. 48p. (ps-3). 1970. 16.00 (*0-06-025489-0*); PLB 15.89 (*0-06-025490-4*) HarpC Child Bks.
—In the Night Kitchen. Sendak, Maurice, illus. LC 70-105483. 48p. (ps-3). 1985. pap. 5.95 (*0-06-443086-3*, Trophy) HarpC Child Bks.
—Kenny's Window. LC 56-5148. (Illus.). 64p. (gr. k-3). 1956. 13.00 (*0-06-025494-7*); PLB 12.89 (*0-06-025495-5*) HarpC Child Bks.
—Maurice Sendak's Really Rosie. (Illus.). 48p. (gr. k-4). 1986. pap. 10.95 (*0-06-443138-X*, Trophy) HarpC Child Bks.
—Outside Over There. Sendak, Maurice, illus. LC 79-2682. 40p. (ps up). 1989. pap. 8.95 (*0-06-443185-1*, Trophy) HarpC Child Bks.
—Pierre: A Cautionary Tale in Five Chapters & a Prologue. Sendak, Maurice, illus. 48p. (ps-3). 1962. PLB 13.89 (*0-06-025965-5*) HarpC Child Bks.
—Sign on Rosie's Door. Sendak, Maurice, illus. LC 60-9451. 48p. (gr. k-3). 1960. 14.00 (*0-06-025505-6*); PLB 13.89 (*0-06-025506-4*) HarpC Child Bks.
—Very Far Away. Sendak, Maurice, illus. LC 57-5356. (gr. k-3). 1962. 13.00 (*0-06-025514-5*); PLB 12.89 (*0-06-025515-3*) HarpC Child Bks.
—Where the Wild Things Are. new ed. Sendak, Maurice, illus. LC 63-21253. 48p. (ps up). 1988. pap. 4.95 (*0-06-443178-9*, Trophy) HarpC Child Bks.
Sereno, Paul C. How Tough Was a Tyrannosaurus? More Fascinating Facts about Dinosaurs. Coutney, Richard, illus. 32p. (ps-7). 1989. pap. 2.25 (*0-448-19116-4*, Platt & Munk Pubs) Putnam Pub Group.
Serfozo, Mary. Who Said Red? Narahashi, Keiko, illus. LC 88-9345. 32p. (ps-1). 1988. RSBE 13.95 (*0-689-50455-1*, M K McElderry) Macmillan Child Grp.
—Who Wants One? Narahashi, Keiko, illus. LC 88-26614. 32p. (ps-1). 1989. SBE 13.95 (*0-689-50474-8*, M K McElderry) Macmillan Child Grp.
Sesame Street Editors. The Sesame Street ABC Book of Words. McNaught, Harry, illus. LC 86-62405. 48p. (ps-k). 1988. pap. 11.00 (*0-394-88880-4*) Random Bks Yng Read.
Sesame Street Favorites. (ps-3). 1990. write for info. (*0-307-15537-4*) Western Pub.
Sesame Street Golden Books, 10 vols. (ps-3). 1993. Set. boxed 12.95 (*0-307-95534-6*, Golden Pr) Western Pub.
Sesame Street Staff. Ernie & Bert Can...Can You. Smollin, Michael J., illus. LC 81-83696. 28p. (ps). 1982. 2.95 (*0-394-85150-1*) Random Bks Yng Read.
Sewall, Marcia. Animal Song. Sewall, Marcia, illus. LC 87-4092. (ps-1). 1988. 14.95 (*0-316-78191-6*, Joy Street Bks) Little.
Seymour, Peter. If Pigs Could Fly: A Pull & Push Pop-up Book. (Illus.). 12p. (ps up). 1989. pop-up 9.95 (*0-8431-2411-3*) Price Stern.
—What's in the Jungle. Carter, David A., illus. LC 87-81818. 18p. (ps-2). 1988. 10.95 (*0-8050-0688-5*, Bks Young Read) H Holt & Co.
Shannon, George. Dance Away. Aruego, Jose & Dewey, Ariane, illus. LC 81-6391. 32p. (ps up). 1991. pap. 3.95 (*0-688-10483-5*, Mulberry) Morrow.
Shapes. (Illus.). 12p. (gr. k-2). 1982. bds. 3.95 (*0-87449-179-7*) Modern Pub NYC.
Shapiro, Mary S. My Playbook, One, Bk. 4. Hinchberger, William D., illus. 12p. (ps-k). 1985. wkbk. 3.95x (*0-934361-04-5*) Kinder Read.
—Play. Wisniewski, Dennis, photos by. (Illus.). 14p. (ps-k). 1985. 3.95 (*0-934361-02-9*); Set. write for info. Kinder Read.
—Red, Green, Yellow. Hron, Debi, illus. 12p. (ps-k). 1985. 3.95 (*0-934361-01-0*); Set. write for info. Kinder Read.
—Stop, Start. Hron, Debi, illus. 14p. (ps-k). 1985. 3.95 (*0-934361-03-7*) Set. Kinder Read.
Sharing: Little Friends Board Book. 1992. bds. 2.49 (*0-517-07281-5*) Random Hse Value.
Sharks-Sticker Book. 1989. pap. 2.50 (*0-89954-129-1*) Antioch Pub Co.
Sharmat, Marjorie W. My Mother Never Listens to Me. Tucker, Kathleen, ed. Munsinger, Lynn, illus. LC 84-17201. 32p. (ps-3). 1984. 11.95 (*0-8075-5347-6*) A Whitman.
Shaw, Charles G. It Looked Like Spilt Milk. Shaw, Charles G., illus. LC 47-30767. 30p. (ps-2). 1947. 13. 00 (*0-06-025566-8*); PLB 12.89 (*0-06-025565-X*) HarpC Child Bks.
—It Looked Like Spilt Milk. Shaw, Charles G., illus. LC 47-30767. 32p. (ps-2). 1988. pap. 4.95 (*0-06-443159-2*, Trophy) HarpC Child Bks.
—It Looked Like Spilt Milk. Shaw, Charles G., illus. (ps-2). 1988. pap. 19.95 incl. cassette (*0-87499-110-2*); bk. & cassette 12.95 (*0-87499-109-9*); 4 cassettes & guide 27.95 (*0-87499-111-0*) Live Oak Media.
—It Looked Like Spilt Milk Big Book. Shaw, Charles G., illus. LC 47-30767. 32p. (ps-3). 1992. pap. 19.95 (*0-06-443312-9*, Trophy) HarpC Child Bks.
Shaw, Nancy. Sheep in a Jeep. Apple, Margot, illus. 32p. (ps-k). 1991. pap. 3.80 (*0-395-47030-7*, Sandpiper); pap. 7.70 incl. cassette (*0-395-60167-3*, Sandpiper) HM.
Shearer, Marilyn J. The Adventures of Curious Eric: Learning Concepts. Roberts, Tom, illus. LC 90-60397. 16p. (ps-6). 1990. 19.95 (*0-685-33064-8*); pap. 10.95 (*1-878389-01-7*) L Ashley & Joshua.
Sheppard, Jeff. The Right Number of Elephants. Bond, Felicia, illus. LC 90-4148. 32p. (ps-3). 1992. pap. 4.95 (*0-06-443299-8*, Trophy) HarpC Child Bks.
Shepperson, Bob. The Sandman. Shepperson, Bob, illus. 32p. (ps-3). 1989. 13.95 (*0-374-36405-2*) FS&G.
Shine, Deborah. The Little Engine That Could Pudgy Word Book. Ong, Christina, illus. 18p. (ps). 1988. bds. 2.95 (*0-448-19054-0*, G&D) Putnam Pub Group.
Shott, Stephen, photos by. El Mundo del Bebe. (SPA., Illus.). 48p. (ps). 1992. 14.95 (*0-525-44846-2*, DCB) Dutton Child Bks.
Showers, Paul. A Drop of Blood. rev. ed. Madden, Paul, illus. LC 85-43021. 32p. (gr. k-4). 1989. pap. 4.50 (*0-06-445090-2*, Trophy) HarpC Child Bks.
—What Happens to a Hamburger? rev. ed. Rockwell, Anne, illus. LC 84-48784. 32p. (gr. k-3). 1985. pap. 4.95 (*0-06-445013-9*, Trophy) HarpC Child Bks.
Shulevitz, Uri. Dawn. Shulevitz, Uri, illus. 32p. (ps up). 1988. 5.95 (*0-374-41689-3*) FS&G.
—One Monday Morning. Shulevitz, Uri, illus. LC 66-24483. 48p. (ps-4). 1974. SBE 14.95 (*0-684-13195-1*, Scribners Young Read) Macmillan Child Grp.
—Rain Rain Rivers. (Illus.). 32p. 1988. pap. 3.95 (*0-374-46195-3*) FS&G.
Sibbett, Ed. American Indian Cut & Use Stencils. pap. 5.95 (*0-486-24183-1*) Dover.
—Cut & Make Christmas Decorations. 1985. pap. 3.95 (*0-486-24912-3*) Dover.

—Decorative Americana Cut & Use Stencils. 1985. pap. 4.95 (*0-486-24970-0*) Dover.
—Decorative Cut & Use Stencils. 1988. pap. 4.95 (*0-486-23880-6*) Dover.
—Holidays & Special Occasions, Cut & Use Stencils. 1986. pap. 4.95 (*0-486-25052-0*) Dover.
—Messages & Greetings Cut & Use Stencils. 1985. pap. 4.95 (*0-486-24965-4*) Dover.
Siebert, Diane. Mojave. Minor, Wendell, illus. LC 86-24329. 32p. (ps up). 1988. 15.00 (*0-690-04567-0*, Crowell Jr Bks); PLB 14.89 (*0-690-04569-7*, Crowell Jr Bks) HarpC Child Bks.
—Mojave. Minor, Wendell, illus. LC 86-24329. 32p. (gr. k-3). 1992. pap. 4.95 (*0-06-443283-1*, Trophy) HarpC Child Bks.
—Truck Song. LC 83-46173. (Illus.). 32p. (ps-3). 1987. pap. 4.95 (*0-06-443134-7*, Trophy) HarpC Child Bks.
—Truck Song. Barton, Byron, illus. (gr. k-3). 1988. bk. & cassette 19.95 (*0-87499-093-9*); bk. & cassette 12.95 (*0-87499-092-0*); 4 cassettes & guide 27.95 (*0-87499-094-7*) Live Oak Media.
Silbert, Linda P. & Silbert, Alvin J. My Own Book of Wishes. (Illus.). (gr. k-6). 1976. wkbk. 4.98 (*0-89544-016-4*) Silbert Bress.
Silent Night. (ps-3). 1991. pap. 2.50 (*0-89954-406-1*) Antioch Pub Co.
A Silly Day at Willy's. (Illus.). 6p. (gr. k-2). 1991. bds. 17.95 (*1-56144-028-0*, Honey Bear Bks) Modern Pub NYC.
Silverman, Erica. Warm in Winter. Deraney, Michael J., illus. LC 88-22691. 32p. (gr. k-3). 1989. RSBE 13.95 (*0-02-782661-9*, Macmillan Child Bk) Macmillan Child Grp.
Silverman, Maida. Baby's First Body Book. Kramer, Robin, illus. (ps-1). 1987. 3.95 (*0-448-10554-3*, G&D) Putnam Pub Group.
—Bunny's ABC Box. Blonder, Ellen, illus. 24p. (ps-1). 1986. pap. 3.95 (*0-448-01464-5*, G&D) Putnam Pub Group.
Silverstein, Shel. Lafcadio, the Lion Who Shot Back. Silverstein, Shel, illus. LC 62-13320. 112p. (gr. 3-6). 1963. 15.00 (*0-06-025675-3*); PLB 14.89 (*0-06-025676-1*) HarpC Child Bks.
—A Light in the Attic. Silverstein, Shel, illus. LC 80-8453. 176p. 1981. 15.95 (*0-06-025673-7*); PLB 15.89 (*0-06-025674-5*) HarpC Child Bks.
—Where the Sidewalk Ends: Poems & Drawings. Silverstein, Shel, illus. LC 70-105486. 176p. (gr. 4 up). 1974. 15.95 (*0-06-025667-2*); PLB 15.89 (*0-06-025668-0*) HarpC Child Bks.
Simon, Norma. Cats Do, Dogs Don't. Levine, Abby, ed. LC 86-5618. (Illus.). 32p. (ps-2). 1986. 13.95 (*0-8075-1102-1*) A Whitman.
—Children Do, Grownups Don't. Tucker, Kathleen, ed. Cogancherry, Helen, illus. LC 87-2205. (ps-3). 1987. PLB 13.95 (*0-8075-1144-7*) A Whitman.
—I Am Not a Crybaby! Tucker, Kathleen, ed. Cogancherry, Helen, illus. LC 88-21698. 40p. (gr. k-4). 1989. 13.95 (*0-8075-3447-1*) A Whitman.
—I'm Busy, Too. Tucker, Kathleen, ed. Leder, Dora, illus. LC 79-18374. (ps-1). 1980. PLB 11.95 (*0-8075-3464-1*) A Whitman.
—Nobody's Perfect, Not Even My Mother. Tucker, Kathleen, ed. Leder, Dora, illus. LC 81-520. 32p. (gr. k-3). 1981. PLB 11.95 (*0-8075-5707-2*) A Whitman.
—The Saddest Time. (Illus.). 40p. (gr. 1-4). 1986. 11.95 (*0-8075-7203-9*); pap. 4.95 (*0-8075-7204-7*) A Whitman.
—Wedding Days. Tucker, Kathleen, ed. (Illus.). 32p. (ps-4). 1988. PLB 13.95 (*0-8075-8703-6*) A Whitman.
—What Do I Do: English - Spanish Edition. Lasker, Joe, illus. LC 74-79544. 40p. (ps-2). 1969. PLB 13.95 (*0-8075-8823-7*) A Whitman.
—What Do I Say. Lasker, Joe, illus. LC 67-17420. (ENG & SPA.). (ps-2). 1967. 13.95 (*0-8075-8828-8*); PLB 13.95 (*0-8075-8826-1*) A Whitman.
Simpson, Bert & Simpson, Bonnie. Shake My Sillies Out. Allender, David, illus. 32p. (ps-2). 1988. PLB 11.00 (*0-517-56646-X*) Crown Bks Yng Read.
Singer, Marilyn. Turtle in July. Pinkney, Jerry, illus. LC 89-2745. 32p. (gr. k-3). 1989. RSBE 14.95 (*0-02-782881-6*, Macmillan Child Bk) Macmillan Child Grp.
Sipherd, Ray. When Is My Birthday? Cooke, Tom, illus. LC 88-80284. 32p. (ps-1). 1988. write for info. (*0-307-12028-7*) Western Pub.
Sis, Peter. Waving. LC 86-25762. (Illus.). 24p. (ps-1). 1988. 11.95 (*0-688-07159-7*); lib. bdg. 11.88 (*0-688-07160-0*) Greenwillow.
Six Blind Men & the Elephant Pop up Book. 10p. (gr. 4-7). 1991. 8.95 (*0-8167-2199-8*) Troll Assocs.
Sklenitzka, Franz S. The Red Sports Car. (Illus.). 96p. (gr. 1-3). 1988. pap. 2.95 (*0-8120-3937-8*) Barron.
Skurzynski, Gloria. The Minstrel in the Tower. Heller, Julek, illus. LC 87-26614. 64p. (Orig.). (gr. 2-4). 1988. pap. 2.50 (*0-394-89598-3*) Random Bks Yng Read.
Slater, Teddy. Molly's Monsters. Morgan, Mary, illus. 32p. (ps-2). 1988. pap. 2.25 (*0-448-19099-0*, Platt & Munk Pubs) Putnam Pub Group.
Slater, Teddy, adapted by. Walt Disney's Dumbo. Dias, Ron, illus. LC 88-80740. 24p. (ps-1). 1988. write for info. (*0-307-11994-7*) Western Pub.
Sleator, William. The Duplicate. LC 87-30562. 160p. (gr. 5-11). 1988. 13.95 (*0-525-44390-8*, 01258-370, DCB) Dutton Child Bks.
Slegers, Guusje. Toys. (ps). 1987. 1.95 (*0-8120-5802-X*) Barron.
Slier, Debby. Baby's Places. 12p. (ps). 1989. 2.95 (*1-56288-149-3*) Checkerboard.
—More Baby Animals. (Illus.). 18p. (ps). 1992. bds. 4.50 (*1-56288-308-9*) Checkerboard.
—Words I Know. 12p. (ps). 1989. 2.95 (*1-56288-145-0*) Checkerboard.
Slier, Debby, ed. Baby's Words. 12p. (ps). 1988. bds. 2.95 (*1-56288-085-3*) Checkerboard.
—Busy Baby. 12p. (ps). 1988. bds. 2.95 (*1-56288-086-1*) Checkerboard.
—Hello Baby. (Illus.). 12p. (ps). 1988. bds. 2.95 (*1-56288-087-X*) Checkerboard.
—Hello School. Dwight, Laura, illus. 28p. (ps). 1990. 2.95 (*0-02-689483-1*) Checkerboard.
—I Can Do It. (Illus.). 28p. (ps). 1990. 2.95 (*1-56288-378-X*) Checkerboard.
—Me & My Dad. Dwight, Laura, illus. 28p. (ps). 1990. 2.95 (*1-56288-380-1*) Checkerboard.
—Me & My Grandma. Dwight, Laura, photos by. (Illus.). 28p. (ps). 1992. bds. 2.95 (*1-56288-183-3*) Checkerboard.
—Me & My Grandpa. Dwight, Laura, photos by. (Illus.). 28p. (ps). 1992. bds. 2.95 (*1-56288-182-5*) Checkerboard.
—Me & My Mom. Dwight, Laura, illus. 28p. (ps). 1990. 2.95 (*1-56288-379-8*) Checkerboard.
Slier, Deborah, ed. Farm Animals. (Illus.). 12p. (ps). 1988. 2.95 (*1-56288-084-5*) Checkerboard.
Slobodkina, Esphyr. Caps for Sale. Slobodkina, Esphyr, illus. LC 84-43122. 48p. (ps-2). 1987. pap. 3.95 (*0-06-443143-6*, Trophy) HarpC Child Bks.
—Caps for Sale. Slobodkina, Esphyr, illus. (gr. k-3). 1987. incl. cassette 19.95 (*0-87499-059-9*); pap. 12.95 incl. cassette (*0-87499-058-0*); 4 paperbacks, cassette & guide 27.95 (*0-87499-060-2*) Live Oak Media.
Smallman, Clare & Riddell, Edwina. Outside In. (Illus.). 32p. (ps-2). 1986. 13.95 (*0-8120-5760-0*) Barron.
Smath, Jerry, illus. Helicopters. 12p. (ps). 1992. bds. 3.95 (*0-448-41093-1*, G&D) Putnam Pub Group.
—Jumbo Jet. 12p. (ps). 1992. bds. 3.95 (*0-448-41094-X*, G&D) Putnam Pub Group.
—Peek-a-Bug. LC 89-61381. 14p. (ps). 1990. pap. 3.99 (*0-679-80139-1*) Random Bks Yng Read.
—Space Shuttle. 12p. (ps). 1992. bds. 3.95 (*0-448-41095-8*, G&D) Putnam Pub Group.
Smee, Nicola. Noah's Ark Board Books, 6 vols. (ps). 1993. Boxed set. 14.95 (*0-316-79895-9*) Little.
Smiling Sandy. 12p. (ps-1). 1989. bds. 5.95 (*0-87449-712-4*) Modern Pub NYC.
Smith, A. G. Civil War Paper Soldiers in Full Color. 1985. pap. 4.95 (*0-486-24987-5*) Dover.
—Cut & Assemble a Medieval Castle. 1984. pap. 5.95 (*0-486-24663-9*) Dover.
—Cut & Assemble an Early American Seaport. 1984. pap. 5.95 (*0-486-24754-6*) Dover.
—Cut & Assemble an Old Fashioned Carousel in Full Color. 1985. pap. 5.95 (*0-486-24992-1*) Dover.
—Cut & Assemble an Old-Fashioned Train. 1989. pap. 5.95 (*0-486-25324-4*) Dover.
—Cut & Assemble Circus Parade. 1985. pap. 5.95 (*0-486-24861-5*) Dover.
—Cut & Assemble New York Harbor. 1986. pap. 4.95 (*0-486-25026-1*) Dover.
—Cut & Assemble 3-D Geometric Shapes. 1986. plastic comb bdg. 5.95 (*0-486-25093-8*) Dover.
—Dinosaur Punch out Stencils. 1989. pap. 3.50 (*0-486-25305-8*) Dover.
—Easy-to-Make Playtime Castle. 1989. pap. 2.95 (*0-486-25469-0*) Dover.
—Easy-to-Make Playtime Farm. 1989. pap. 2.95 (*0-486-25585-9*) Dover.
—Easy-to-Make Playtime Village. 1989. pap. 2.95 (*0-486-25478-X*) Dover.
—Fun with Dinosaur Stencils. 1989. pap. 1.00 (*0-486-25450-X*) Dover.
—Fun with Favorite Pets Stencils. 1989. pap. 1.00 (*0-486-25451-8*) Dover.
Smith, Barry. Cumberland Road. Smith, Barry, illus. 32p. (gr. k-3). 1989. 9.70 (*0-395-51739-7*) HM.
Smith, Jennifer. Grover & the New Kid. Cooke, Tom, illus. LC 86-42965. 40p. (ps-3). 1987. 4.95 (*0-394-88519-8*) Random Bks Yng Read.
Smith, Jessie. Sesame Street: Going Places. Ewers, Joseph, illus. LC 87-81768. 24p. (ps-k). 1988. pap. write for info. (*0-307-10057-X*, Pub. by Golden Bks) Western Pub.
Smith, Josephine A. Hickle the Pickle. rev. ed. Dowley, May, illus. LC 92-96864. 40p. 1992. pap. 2.99 (*1-881958-00-0*, TX2-116-470) Hickle Pickle.
Smith, Matthew V. Fun Time with Bonzo. Smith, Matthew V., illus. 12p. (gr. k-3). 1992. pap. 11.95 (*1-895583-32-2*) MAYA Pubs.
—What's a Right Turn. Smith, Matthew V., illus. 13p. (gr. k-3). 1993. pap. 12.95 (*1-895583-56-X*) MAYA Pubs.
—Where Do We Go from Here? Smith, Matthew V., illus. 15p. (gr. k-3). 1992. pap. 11.95 (*1-895583-35-7*) MAYA Pubs.
—Where Is All the Honey? Smith, Matthew V., illus. 17p. (gr. k-3). 1992. pap. 13.95 (*1-895583-31-4*) MAYA Pubs.
Smith, Mavis. Look Out! (ps-3). 1991. pap. 5.95 (*0-14-054433-X*, Puffin) Puffin Bks.
Smith, Robert K. Jelly Belly. 160p. (gr. 4-9). 1982. pap. 3.50 (*0-440-44207-9*, YB) Dell.
Smith, Wendy. Think Hippo! (Illus.). 28p. (ps-2). 1989. PLB 17.50 (*0-87614-372-9*) Carolrhoda Bks.
—Twice Mice. (Illus.). 28p. (ps-2). 1989. PLB 17.50 (*0-87614-371-0*) Carolrhoda Bks.
Smithson, Colin. Blunty. (Illus.). 32p. (ps-1). 1994. 15.95 (*1-85681-025-9*, Pub. by J MacRae UK) Trafalgar.
Snolo, Allen. Baby Bear Learns Colors. 1988. 3.99 (*0-517-65509-8*) Random Hse Value.
Snow, Pegeen. Come los Guisantes, Cuanto Antes: (Eat Your Peas, Louise!) Venezia, Mike, illus. LC 84-27445. (ENG & SPA.). 32p. (ps-2). 1989. PLB 10.25 (*0-516-32067-X*); pap. 2.95 (*0-516-52067-9*) Childrens.
Snuggle Uppy Puppy. 22p. (ps). 1993. 3.25 (*0-679-85104-6*) Random Bks Yng Read.
Somme, Lauritz & Kalas, Sybille. The Penguin Family Book. LC 87-32830. (Illus.). (ps-12). 1991. pap. 15.95 (*0-88708-057-X*) Picture Bk Studio.
Sommer, Ann. Youngest Shepherd. (ps-2). 1989. 12.99 (*1-55513-602-8*, Chariot Bks) Chariot Family.
Spar, J. Willy, a Story of Water. LC 68-56819. (Illus.). 32p. (gr. 2-3). 1968. PLB 9.95 (*0-87783-051-7*); pap. 3.94 deluxe ed (*0-87783-117-3*) Oddo.
Spier, Peter. Dreams. Spier, Peter, illus. LC 85-13130. 32p. (ps-3). 1986. Doubleday.
—Fast-Slow High-Low: A Book of Opposites. Spier, Peter, illus. LC 72-76207. 48p. (gr. k-3). 1972. pap. 10.95 (*0-385-06781-X*); pap. 10.95 (*0-385-02876-8*); pap. 2.95 (*0-685-01490-8*) Doubleday.
—Fox Went Out on a Chilly Night. Spier, Peter, illus. LC 60-7139. 42p. (gr. k-3). 1961. pap. 11.95 (*0-385-07990-7*) Doubleday.
—Oh, Were They Ever Happy! LC 77-78144. (Illus.). 48p. (ps-3). 1988. pap. 6.95 (*0-385-24477-0*, Zephyr-BFYR) Doubleday.
—Peter Spier's Rain. Spier, Peter, illus. LC 81-43506. 40p. (ps-3). 1982. PLB 12.95 (*0-385-15485-2*, Zephyr-BFYR) Doubleday.
—Star-Spangled Banner. Spier, Peter, illus. LC 73-79112. 48p. (gr. 1 up). 1986. pap. 8.00 (*0-385-23401-5*, Pub. by Zephyr-BFYR) Doubleday.
Spires, Elizabeth. The Falling Star. Michelini, Carlo A., illus. LC 84-80288. 24p. (ps-k). 1989. 9.95 (*0-448-21026-6*, G&D) Putnam Pub Group.
Spirit, Bonnie. It's Fun to Read Coloring, Vol. 1. Lightfoot, Patricia, illus. 10p. (Orig.). (ps up). 1988. pap. text ed. 3.95 (*0-9614089-1-X*) Avitar Bks.
—Pink Rose Bush. Lightfoot, Patricia, illus. 64p. (ps up). 1985. text ed. 9.95 (*0-9614089-0-1*) Avitar Bks.
Spivak, Darlene. My Favorite Things. Olsen, Shirley, illus. 48p. (gr. k-2). 1988. wkbk. 6.95 (*1-55734-375-6*) Tchr Create Mat.
Spizzirri Publishing Co. Staff. Animal Alphabet: An Educational Coloring Book. Spizzirri, Linda, ed. (Illus.). 32p. (gr. 1-8). 1982. pap. 1.75 (*0-86545-042-0*) Spizzirri.
—Cats of the Wild: An Educational Coloring Book. Spizzirri, Linda, ed. (Illus.). 32p. (gr. 1-8). 1982. pap. 1.75 (*0-86545-045-5*) Spizzirri.
—Counting & Coloring Dinosaurs: An Educational Coloring Book. Spizzirri, Linda, ed. (Illus.). 32p. (gr. 1-8). 1982. pap. 1.75 (*0-86545-044-7*) Spizzirri.
—Endangered Species: An Educational Coloring Book. Spizzirri, Linda, ed. (Illus.). 32p. (gr. 1-8). 1982. pap. 1.75 (*0-86545-041-2*) Spizzirri.
—Kachina Dolls: An Educational Coloring Book. Spizzirri, Linda, ed. (Illus.). 32p. (gr. 1-8). 1982. pap. 1.75 (*0-86545-046-3*) Spizzirri.
—Picture Dictionary: An Educational Coloring Book. Spizzirri, Linda, ed. (Illus.). 32p. (gr. 1-8). 1982. pap. 1.75 (*0-86545-049-8*) Spizzirri.
—Planets: An Educational Coloring Book. Spizzirri, Linda, ed. (Illus.). 32p. (gr. 1-8). 1982. pap. 1.75 (*0-86545-043-9*) Spizzirri.
—Whales: An Educational Coloring Book. Spizzirri, Linda, ed. (Illus.). 32p. (gr. 1-8). 1982. pap. 1.75 (*0-86545-039-0*) Spizzirri.
Spizzirri Publishing Inc Staff. Atlantic Fish: An Educational Coloring Book. Spizzirri, Linda, ed. (Illus.). 32p. (gr. 1-8). 1989. pap. 1.75 (*0-86545-135-4*) Spizzirri.
—Butterfly Mazes: An Educational-Activity Coloring Book. Spizzirri, Linda, ed. (Illus.). 32p. (gr. 1-8). 1989. pap. 1.00 (*0-86545-146-X*) Spizzirri.
—Eskimos: An Educational Coloring Book. Spizzirri, Linda, ed. (Illus.). 32p. (gr. 1-8). 1989. pap. 1.75 (*0-86545-140-0*) Spizzirri.
—Farm Animals: An Educational Coloring Book. Spizzirri, Linda, ed. (Illus.). 32p. (gr. 1-8). 1989. pap. 1.75 (*0-86545-141-9*) Spizzirri.
—Mammal Mazes: An Educational-Activity Coloring Book. Spizzirri, Linda, ed. (Illus.). 32p. (gr. 1-8). 1989. pap. 1.00 (*0-86545-144-3*) Spizzirri.
—Pacific Fish: An Educational Coloring Book. Spizzirri, Linda, ed. (Illus.). 32p. (gr. 1-8). 1989. pap. 1.75 (*0-86545-136-2*) Spizzirri.
—Penguins: An Educational Coloring Book. Spizzirri, Linda, ed. (Illus.). 32p. (gr. 1-8). 1989. pap. 1.75 (*0-86545-134-6*) Spizzirri.
—Pioneers: An Educational Coloring Book. Spizzirri, Linda, ed. (Illus.). 32p. (gr. 1-8). 1989. pap. 1.75 (*0-86545-138-9*) Spizzirri.
—Shell Mazes: An Educational-Activity Coloring Book. Spizzirri, Linda, ed. (Illus.). 32p. (gr. 1-8). 1989. pap. 1.00 (*0-86545-145-1*) Spizzirri.
—State Flowers: An Educational Coloring Book. Spizzirri, Linda, ed. (Illus.). 32p. (gr. 1-8). 1989. pap. 1.75 (*0-86545-142-7*) Spizzirri.
—Tree Mazes: An Educational-Activity Coloring Book. Spizzirri, Linda, ed. (Illus.). 32p. (gr. 1-8). 1989. pap. 1.00 (*0-86545-143-5*) Spizzirri.

Spot Va a la Escuela (Spot Goes to School) (SPA.). 22p. (gr. 3-7). 1985. 12.95 (*0-399-21223-X*, Putnam) Putnam Pub Group.
Springer, Margaret. A Royal Ball. O'Sullivan, Tom, illus. 32p. (gr. k-3). 1992. bds. 9.95 (*1-878093-64-9*) Boyds Mills Pr.
Stadler, John. Cat at Bat. Stadler, John, illus. LC 87-36400. 32p. (ps-2). 1988. 9.95 (*0-525-44416-5*, DCB) Dutton Child Bks.
Standiford, Natalie. The Best Little Monkeys in the World. Knight, Hilary, illus. LC 86-15425. 48p. (gr. 1-3). 1987. lib. bdg. 7.99 (*0-394-98616-4*); 3.50 (*0-394-88616-X*) Random Bks Yng Read.
Stanek, Muriel. All Alone after School. Fay, Ann, ed. Owens, Gay, illus. LC 84-17243. 32p. (gr. 1-4). 1985. PLB 11.95 (*0-8075-0278-2*) A Whitman.
—My Mom Can't Read. Levine, Abby, ed. Rogers, Jacqueline, illus. LC 86-1637. 32p. (gr. 1-4). 1986. 11.95 (*0-8075-5343-3*) A Whitman.
—Starting School. Fay, Ann, ed. De Luna, Tony & De Luna, Betty, illus. LC 81-297. 32p. (ps-1). 1981. PLB 10.95 (*0-8075-7617-4*) A Whitman.
Stanton, Elizabeth & Stanton, Henry. Sometimes I Like to Cry. Rubin, Caroline, ed. Leyden, Richard, illus. LC 77-19131. 32p. (ps-2). 1978. PLB 13.95 (*0-8075-7537-2*) A Whitman.
Stanton, P. The Yellow Star Sticker. Moser, Jeanie W., illus. (gr. k-3). Bk. & cassette 4.95 (*0-932715-08-7*) Evans FL.
Starting School. (Illus.). (ps). 3.50 (*0-7214-1086-3*) Ladybird Bks.
Stearns, Helen M. The Space Cadet & the Marionette. Urbahn, Clara, illus. 36p. 1986. 8.95 (*0-9614281-2-0*, Cricketfld Pr); cassette 4.95 (*0-685-73739-X*) Picton Pr.
Steig, William. Roland the Minstrel Pig. (Illus.). (gr. k-3). 1968. 12.95 (*0-06-025761-X*) HarpC Child Bks.
—Solomon the Rusty Nail. Steig, William, illus. 32p. (ps up). 1985. 16.00 (*0-374-37131-8*) FS&G.
—Solomon the Rusty Nail. (Illus.). 32p. (ps up). 1987. pap. 4.95 (*0-374-46903-2*) FS&G.
—Yellow & Pink. LC 84-80503. 32p. (ps up). 1988. pap. 3.95 (*0-374-48735-9*) FS&G.
Stelson, Caren B. Safari. Stelson, Kim A., illus. 40p. (gr. k-4). 1988. PLB 19.95 (*0-87614-324-9*) Carolrhoda Bks.
Steptoe, John. Stevie. Steptoe, John, illus. (gr. 1-4). 1987. incl. cassette 19.95 (*0-87499-050-5*); pap. 12.95 incl. cassette (*0-87499-049-1*); 4 paperbacks, cassette & guide 27.95 (*0-87499-051-3*) Live Oak Media.
Steptoe, John L. Stevie. Steptoe, John L., illus. LC 69-16700. 32p. (ps-3). 1969. PLB 12.89 (*0-06-025764-4*) HarpC Child Bks.
—Stevie. LC 69-16700. (Illus.). 32p. (ps-3). 1986. pap. 4.95 (*0-06-443122-3*, Trophy) HarpC Child Bks.
Stevens, Kathleen. The Beast in the Bathtub. Bowler, Ray, illus. LC 86-45074. 32p. (ps-3). 1987. pap. 5.95 (*0-06-443121-5*, Trophy) HarpC Child Bks.
Stevenson, James. Could Be Worse! LC 76-28534. (Illus.). 32p. (gr. k up). 1987. pap. 3.95 (*0-688-07035-3*, Mulberry) Morrow.
—Emma. LC 84-4141. (gr. k up). 1987. pap. 3.95 (*0-688-07336-0*, Mulberry) Morrow.
—Grandpa's Great City Tour: An Alphabet Book. Stevenson, James, illus. LC 83-1459. 48p. (gr. k-3). 1983. PLB 12.95 (*0-688-02324-X*); 12.88 (*0-688-02323-1*) Greenwillow.
—We Hate Rain! LC 87-21204. (Illus.). 32p. (gr. k-3). 1988. 11.95 (*0-688-07786-2*); lib. bdg. 11.88 (*0-688-07787-0*) Greenwillow.
—The Wish Card Ran Out! Stevenson, James, illus. LC 80-22139. 32p. (gr. k-4). 1981. 11.75 (*0-688-80305-9*) Greenwillow.
Stiles, Norman. Sesame Street, the Ernie & Bert Book. Mathieu, Joe, illus. 24p. (ps-k). 1977. pap. write for info. (*0-307-10072-3*, Pub. by Golden Bks) Western Pub.
Stiles, Norman & Wilcox, Daniel. Grover & the Everything in the Whole Wide World Museum. Mathieo, Joe, illus. LC 73-18736. 32p. (ps-k). 1974. pap. 2.25 (*0-394-82707-4*) Random Bks Yng Read.
Stinga, Frank, illus. The Carousel Fantasy Gift Box & Mobile, 3 bks. 36p. (ps). Date not set. bds. 13.95 Set (*1-56828-067-X*) Red Jacket Pr.
Stinson, Kathy. Big Or Little. Baird Lewis, Robin, illus. 32p. (gr. k-2). 1983. PLB 14.95 (*0-920236-30-8*, Pub. by Annick CN); pap. 4.95 (*0-920236-32-4*, Pub. by Annick CN) Firefly Bks Ltd.
—Red Is Best. Baird, Robin L., illus. 32p. (gr. k-3). 1982. PLB 14.95 (*0-920236-24-3*, Pub. by Annick CN); pap. 4.95 (*0-920236-26-X*, Pub. by Annick CN) Firefly Bks Ltd.
Stock, Catherine. The Birthday Present. Stock, Catherine, illus. LC 90-1914. 32p. (ps-1). 1991. SBE 11.95 (*0-02-788401-5*, Bradbury Pr) Macmillan Child Grp.
—Sophie's Knapsack. LC 87-3103. (Illus.). (ps-2). 1988. 12.95 (*0-688-06457-4*); 12.88 (*0-688-06458-2*) Lothrop.
Stockton, Frank R. The Griffin & the Minor Canon. Sendak, Maurice, illus. LC 85-45827. 56p. (gr. 2 up). 1987. pap. 4.95 (*0-06-443126-6*, Trophy) HarpC Child Bks.
Stolz, Mary. Storm in the Night. Cummings, Pat, illus. LC 85-45838. 32p. (gr. k-3). 1990. pap. 4.95 (*0-06-443256-4*, Trophy) HarpC Child Bks.
Stone, Erika, illus. Baby Talk. 18p. (ps). 1992. bds. 2.95 (*0-448-40312-9*, G&D) Putnam Pub Group.
Stone, Jon. Big Bird in China. (Illus.). (gr. 4-8). 1983. lib. bdg. 7.99 (*0-394-95645-1*) Random Bks Yng Read.
Stoneback, Jean C. Pup Pup & Murray Find a New Home. Weisbecker, Gene, illus. 45p. (Orig.). (ps). 1984. pap. 4.00 (*0-931440-09-2*) Stoneback Pub.
Stortz, Diane M. Where Does the Puppy Live? Hackney, richard, illus. LC 87-62602. (ps). 1988. 1.59 (*0-87403-389-6*, 24-02019) Standard Pub.
—Who Tells the Wind? Rigo, Christian, tr. LC 87-62603. 20p. (ps). 1988. 1.59 (*0-87403-390-X*, 24-02020) Standard Pub.
Stover, Jo Ann. If Everybody Did. Stover, Jo Ann, illus. 48p. (Orig.). (gr. k-1). 1989. pap. 3.95 (*0-89084-487-9*) Bob Jones Univ Pr.
Stowell, Gordon. Little Fish Surprise Picture Books. Roe, Earl O., ed. Incl. Noah's Big Boat. pap. 0.89 (*0-8307-1129-5*, 5608701); Joseph & His Dreams (*0-8307-1130-9*, 5608702); David the Shepherd Boy (*0-8307-1131-7*, 5608703); Christmas in Bethlehem. pap. 0.89 (*0-8307-1132-5*, 5608704); The Wise Men Find Jesus. pap. 0.89 (*0-8307-1133-3*, 5608705); The Little Man's Happy Day. pap. 0.89 (*0-8307-1134-1*, 5608706); The Great Big Picnic (*0-8307-1136-8*, 5608707); The First Easter (*0-8307-1137-6*, 5608708). (Illus.). 16p. (Orig.). (gr. 1 up). 1986. (*0-685-14585-9*) Regal.
Strain, Jim. Bingo. (ps). 1991. 14.95 (*1-55868-077-2*) Gr Arts Ctr Pub.
Strand, Mark. Rembrandt Takes a Walk. Grooms, Red, illus. (gr. 3 up). 1987. 14.95 (*0-517-56293-6*) Crown Bks Yng Read.
Stuart, Alexander & Vendrell, Carme S. Joe, Jo-Jo & the Monkey Masks. (Illus.). 32p. (gr. 1-4). 1989. 13.95 (*0-86264-199-3*, Pub. by Anderson Pr UK) Trafalgar.
Suire, Diane D. Polka-Dot Puppy's Birthday: A Book about Colors. Hohag, Linda, illus. LC 88-10937. 32p. (ps-2). 1988. PLB 14.95 (*0-89565-381-8*) Childs World.
Sullivan, Dianna. Make Your Own Adventure Books. Ecker, Beverly, illus. 48p. (gr. 1-4). 1988. wkbk. 6.95 (*1-55734-395-0*) Tchr Create Mat.
—Make Your Own Fable & Fairy Tale Books. Ecker, Beverly, illus. 48p. (gr. 1-4). 1988. wkbk. 6.95 (*1-55734-392-6*) Tchr Create Mat.
—Make Your Own Happy Times Books. Ecker, Beverly, illus. 48p. (gr. 1-4). 1988. wkbk. 6.95 (*1-55734-394-2*) Tchr Create Mat.
—Make Your Own Holiday Books. Ecker, Beverly, illus. 48p. (gr. 1-4). 1988. wkbk. 6.95 (*1-55734-393-4*) Tchr Create Mat.
Sun, Ming-Ju. Japanese Kimono-Paper Dolls. 1986. pap. 3.95 (*0-486-25094-6*) Dover.
Super, Terri, illus. The Pudgy Pat-a-Cake. 16p. (ps). 1983. pap. 2.95 (*0-448-10204-8*, G&D) Putnam Pub Group.
—The Three Little Pigs. 16p. (ps-1). 1984. 3.95 (*0-448-10214-5*, G&D) Putnam Pub Group.
Surowiecki, Sandra L. Joshua's Day. 2nd ed. LC 77-20479. (Illus.). 27p. (ps-1). 1977. pap. 5.00 (*0-914996-18-5*) Lollipop Power.
Sutcliff, Rosemary. Flame-Colored Taffeta. 120p. (gr. 5 up). 1986. 14.00 (*0-374-32344-5*) FS&G.
Sutton, Scott E. Oh No! More Wizard Lessons! Sutton, Scott E., illus. 35p. (gr. 2-4). 1986. 13.95x (*0-9617199-2-3*) Sutton Pubns.
Swanson, Harry. Oscar Otter Meets the Mayor. Swanson, Harry, illus. 48p. (Orig.). (ps-6). 1989. pap. 5.00 (*1-878200-02-X*) SwanMark Bks.
Sweet Dreams. 12p. (ps-1). 1988. bds. 5.95 (*0-87449-625-X*) Modern Pub NYC.
Szekeres, Cyndy. Cyndy Szekeres' Nice Animals. 1990. pap. write for info. (*0-307-06109-4*, Golden Pr) Western Pub.
—Fluffy Duckling. (Illus.). 14p. (ps-k). 1992. write for info. (*0-307-12390-1*, 12390) Western Pub.
—Good Night, Sweet Mouse. Szekeres, Cyndy, illus. LC 87-81789. 20p. (ps). 1988. write for info. (*0-307-12159-3*) Western Pub.
—Puppy Too Small. Szekeres, Cyndy, illus. LC 83-83353. 18p. (ps-k). 1992. bds. write for info. (*0-307-12201-8*, 12231, Golden Pr) Western Pub.
—Sammy's Special Day. Szekeres, Cyndy, illus. LC 85-81986. 18p. (ps-k). 1992. bds. write for info. (*0-307-12288-3*, 12296, Golden Pr) Western Pub.
—Thumpity Thump Gets Dressed. Szekeres, Cyndy, illus. LC 83-83284. 16p. (ps-k). 1991. 4.95 (*0-307-12203-4*, 12233, Golden Bks) Western Pub.
Tafuri, Nancy. Have You Seen My Duckling? LC 83-17196. (Illus.). 24p. (ps up). 1991. pap. 3.95 (*0-688-10994-2*, Mulberry) Morrow.
—In a Red House. Tafuri, Nancy, illus. LC 86-27114. (ps). 1987. Board book. pap. 3.95 (*0-688-07185-6*) Greenwillow.
—One Wet Jacket. LC 87-8439. (Illus.). 12p. (ps). 1988. Board Book. pap. 3.95 (*0-688-07465-0*) Greenwillow.
—Spots, Feathers, & Curly Tails. LC 87-15638. (Illus.). 32p. (ps-1). 1988. 15.00 (*0-688-07536-3*); lib. bdg. 14.93 (*0-688-07537-1*) Greenwillow.
Tagel, Peggy. Pop-up Baby Bunny. (Illus.). 14p. (ps-1). 1991. 3.95 (*0-448-40054-5*, G&D) Putnam Pub Group.
—Pop-up Little Duck. (Illus.). 14p. 1991. 3.95 (*0-448-40056-1*, G&D) Putnam Pub Group.
—Pop-up Tiny Chick. (Illus.). 14p. 1991. 3.95 (*0-448-40055-3*, G&D) Putnam Pub Group.
Taggart, George. Bible Promises for Tiny Tots, II. Coffen, Richard W., ed. 32p. (Orig.). (ps). 1985. pap. 4.50 (*0-8280-0246-0*) Review & Herald.
Tagore, Rabindranath. Paper Boats. Bochak, Grayce, illus. LC 91-72987. 32p. (ps-3). 1992. 14.95 (*1-878093-12-6*) Boyds Mills Pr.
Take It Away. 1989. pap. 1.49 (*0-553-18399-0*) Bantam.
Takihara, Koji. Rolli. LC 87-29262. (Illus.). (ps-12). 1991. pap. 14.95 (*0-88708-058-8*) Picture Bk Studio.
Talbot, John. The Raries. (Illus.). 32p. (gr. k-3). 1989. 13.95 (*0-86264-144-6*, Pub. by Anderson Pr UK) Trafalgar.
Talbott, Hudson. We're Back: A Dinosaur's Story. 32p. (ps-2). 1988. PLB 15.00 (*0-517-56599-4*) Crown Bks Yng Read.
Talkington, Bruce. Disney's Winnie the Pooh & the Perfect Christmas Tree: A Pop-up Book. Vaccaro Associates Staff, illus. 12p. (ps-1). 1994. 11.95 (*1-56282-649-2*) Disney Pr.
Tallarico, Tony. More Preschool Can You Find Picture Book. Tallarico, Tony, illus. (ps). 1991. 3.95 (*0-448-48801-9*, Tuffy) Putnam Pub Group.
—My First All about Cats Jigsaw Puzzle Book. Tallarico, Tony, illus. (ps). 1991. 4.95 (*0-448-48804-3*, Tuffy) Putnam Pub Group.
—My First All about Circus Jigsaw Puzzle Book. Tallarico, Tony, illus. (ps). 1991. 4.95 (*0-448-48805-1*, Tuffy) Putnam Pub Group.
—My First All about Dinosaurs Jigsaw Puzzle Book. Tallarico, Tony, illus. (ps). 1991. 4.95 (*0-448-48802-7*, Tuffy) Putnam Pub Group.
—My First All about Dogs Jigsaw Puzzle Book. Tallarico, Tony, illus. (ps). 1991. 4.95 (*0-448-48803-5*, Tuffy) Putnam Pub Group.
—Preschool Can You Find Picture Book. Tallarico, Tony, illus. (ps). 1991. 3.95 (*0-448-48800-0*, Tuffy) Putnam Pub Group.
—What Can You Find. (Illus.). 28p. (ps). 1992. 2.95 (*0-448-40429-X*, G&D) Putnam Pub Group.
—What's In. (Illus.). 28p. (ps). 1992. 2.95 (*0-448-40427-3*, G&D) Putnam Pub Group.
Tallarico, Tony, illus. At Home. 28p. (ps-1). 1984. bds. 2.95 (*0-448-48818-3*, Tuffy) Putnam Pub Group.
—Colors. 28p. (ps-1). 1988. bds. 2.95 (*0-448-48819-1*, Tuffy) Putnam Pub Group.
—Here We Go. 28p. (ps-1). 1988. bds. 2.95 (*0-448-48821-3*, Tuffy) Putnam Pub Group.
—How Many? 28p. (ps-1). 1984. bds. 2.95 (*0-448-48822-1*, Tuffy) Putnam Pub Group.
—Time To... 28p. (ps-1). 1984. bds. 2.95 (*0-448-48823-X*, Tuffy) Putnam Pub Group.
—What's Opposite? 28p. (ps-1). 1984. bds. 2.95 (*0-448-48824-8*, Tuffy) Putnam Pub Group.
—Who Am I? 28p. (ps-1). 1984. bds. 2.95 (*0-448-48825-6*, Tuffy) Putnam Pub Group.
Tangvald, Christine. Mom & Dad Don't Live Together Anymore. LC 87-34211. 24p. (ps-2). 1988. 7.99 (*1-55513-502-1*, Chariot Bks) Chariot Family.
Tangvald, Christine H. The Bible Is for Me. Nelson, Donna, illus. 24p. (ps-1). 1988. pap. 3.99 (*1-55513-706-7*, Chariot Bks) Chariot Family.
—Christmas Is for Me. Nelson, Donna, illus. LC 88-70665. 24p. (ps-1). 1988. pap. 3.99 (*1-55513-705-9*, Chariot Bks) Chariot Family.
Tanner, Suzy-Jane. Bunnies & Bears Learning Box Set. (Illus.). 32p. (ps-6). 1993. 17.50 (*0-525-44916-7*, DCB) Dutton Child Bks.
Tarsky, Sue. Kiss the Boo-Boo. Ayliffe, Alex, illus. 10p. (ps). 1994. 8.99 (*0-670-85435-2*) Viking Child Bks.
Tauber, Debra. I Don't Care. Wibright, Betsy, illus. 16p. (Orig.). (gr. 1). 1993. pap. write for info. (*1-882225-14-7*) Tott Pubns.
Tax, Meredith. Families. Hafner, Marilyn, illus. 32p. (ps-3). 1981. 15.95 (*0-316-83240-5*, Pub. by Atlantic) Little.
Taylor, Anelise. Lights Off, Lights On. (Illus.). 32p. (ps-k). 1989. pap. 5.95 (*0-19-272193-3*) OUP.
Taylor, Judy. My Cat. Cartwright, Reg, illus. LC 88-22127. 32p. (ps-2). 1989. pap. 3.95 (*0-689-71209-X*, Aladdin) Macmillan Child Grp.
—My Dog. Cartwright, Reg, illus. LC 88-19441. 32p. (ps-2). 1989. pap. 3.95 (*0-689-71210-3*, Aladdin) Macmillan Child Grp.
Taylor, Kenneth. New Testament in Pictures for Little Eyes. (Illus.). 155p. (Orig.). 1989. pap. 6.99 (*0-8024-0682-3*) Moody.
Taylor, Kenneth N. Giant Steps for Little People. 64p. (ps-1). 1985. 10.99 (*0-8423-1023-1*) Tyndale.
Teach Me Now 1. 80p. (ps). 1981. 4.95 (*1-55976-401-5*); 6.99 (*0-685-17899-4*) CEF Press.
Teach Me Now 3. 80p. (ps). 1983. 4.95 (*1-55976-403-1*); 6.99 (*0-685-17902-8*) CEF Press.
Teach Me Now 4. 80p. (ps). 1984. 4.95 (*1-55976-404-X*); 6.99 (*0-685-17903-6*) CEF Press.
Teen Creed Key Lock Diary. 1988. 9.98 (*0-89954-700-1*) Antioch Pub Co.
Teeny Books Staff. Patterns. Davies, Kate, illus. 10p. (ps). 1993. 4.95 (*0-448-40534-2*, G&D) Putnam Pub Group.
—Pictures. Davies, Kate, illus. 10p. (ps). 1993. 4.95 (*0-448-40535-0*, G&D) Putnam Pub Group.
Teitelbaum, Michael. Disney's Duck Tales: Journey to Magic Island. (Illus.). 24p. (ps-k). 1989. pap. write for info. (*0-307-11754-5*, Pub. by Golden Bks) Western Pub.
Tell a Story. 1989. pap. 1.49 (*0-553-18402-4*) Bantam.
Testa, Fulvio. If You Look Around You. LC 83-5310. (Illus.). 32p. (ps-2). 1987. pap. 3.95 (*0-8037-0432-1*) Dial Bks Young.

—Time to Get Out. Testa, Fulvio, illus. LC 93-60218. 32p. (ps up). 1993. 14.00 (*0-688-12907-2*, Tambourine Bks); PLB 13.93 (*0-688-12908-0*, Tambourine Bks) Morrow.
—Wolf's Favor. Testa, Fulvio, illus. LC 85-15934. 32p. (ps-3). 1986. 11.95 (*0-8037-0244-2*) Dial Bks Young.
Thaler, Mike. Pack 109. Chartier, Normand, illus. LC 87-30493. 48p. (ps-2). 1988. 9.95 (*0-525-44393-2*, 0966-290, DCB) Dutton Child Bks.
Things That Go. (ps-k). 3.95 (*0-7214-5140-3*) Ladybird Bks.
Things that Go. 5p. (ps). 1991. soft fabric 3.95 (*0-681-41090-6*) Longmeadow Pr.
Things That Go. 1989. pap. 1.49 (*0-553-18395-8*) Bantam.
Things That Go Board Shape Book. (Illus.). (ps). 1985. bds. 1.69 (*0-517-46322-9*) Random Hse Value.
Things to Play With. (ps-k). 3.95 (*0-7214-5144-6*) Ladybird Bks.
Things to Wear. (ps-k). 3.95 (*0-7214-5143-8*) Ladybird Bks.
This Is Me. Blegvad, Lenore. LC 85-61671. 28p. (ps-k). 1986. bds. 3.25 (*0-394-87816-7*) Random Bks Yng Read.
This Little Piggy. (Illus.). (ps-k). 1991. write for info. (*0-307-06136-1*, Golden Pr) Western Pub.
Thoburn, Tina, compiled by. My First Golden Dictionary. Chandler, Jean, illus. LC 87-81750. 24p. 1988. write for info. (*0-307-11992-0*, Pub. by Golden Bks) Western Pub.
Thomasson, Merry. Hey Look at Me! Baby Days. LC 90-61135. 20p. (ps). 1990. 9.95 (*0-9615407-5-3*) Merrybooks VA.
—Hey Look at Me-Boys. (ps). 1990. 9.95 (*0-9615407-3-7*) Merrybooks VA.
—Hey Look at Me! I Like to Play Book for Girls. (ps-2). 1990. 9.95 (*0-9615407-4-5*) Merrybooks VA.
Thompson, Brian. Puffin First Picture Dictionary. Berridge, Celia, illus. 38p. (ps-3). 1989. pap. 3.95 (*0-14-050777-9*, Puffin) Puffin Bks.
Thompson, Frances M. Miss Circo Comes Apart at the Seams. Holt, Cather C., illus. 18p. (Orig.). (gr. k-3). 1986. pap. 3.95 (*0-9616207-0-6*) Bks By Brooks.
Thomson, Pat. Best Thing of All. Chamberlain, Margaret, illus. 32p. (gr. 1-4). 1990. 13.95 (*0-575-04578-7*, Pub. by Gollancz UK) Trafalgar.
—Dial D for Disaster. Demeyer, Paul, illus. 32p. (gr. 1-4). 1990. 13.95 (*0-575-04572-8*, Pub. by Gollancz UK) Trafalgar.
Three Little Kittens. (Illus.). (ps-k). 1991. write for info. (*0-307-15703-2*, Golden Pr) Western Pub.
Tibo, Gilles. Simon & the Snowflakes. Tibo, Gilles, illus. LC 88-50259. 24p. (ps-4). 1991. pap. 4.95 (*0-88776-274-3*) Tundra Bks.
—Simon & the Wind. Tibo, Gilles, illus. LC 89-50776. 24p. (ps-4). 1991. pap. 4.95 (*0-88776-276-X*) Tundra Bks.
Tierney, Tom. Abraham Lincoln & His Family - Paper Dolls. 1989. pap. 3.95 (*0-486-26024-0*) Dover.
—American Family of the Civil War Era Paper Dolls in Full Color. 1985. pap. 3.95 (*0-486-24833-X*) Dover.
—American Family of the Colonial Era Paper Dolls in Full Color. 1982. pap. 3.95 (*0-486-24394-X*) Dover.
—Carmen Miranda Paper Dolls in Full Color. 1982. pap. 3.95 (*0-486-24285-4*) Dover.
—Chanel Fashions: Review Paper Dolls in Full Color. 1986. pap. 3.95 (*0-486-25105-5*) Dover.
—Diana & Prince Charles Fashion Paper Dolls in Full Color. 1985. pap. 3.95 (*0-486-24961-1*) Dover.
—Great Black Entertainers Paper Dolls. 1984. pap. 3.95 (*0-486-24748-1*) Dover.
—Great Empresses & Queen Paper Dolls. 1982. pap. 3.95 (*0-486-24268-4*) Dover.
—Great Fashion Design of the Fifties, Paper Dolls in Full Color. 1985. pap. 3.95 (*0-486-24960-3*) Dover.
—Great Fashion Designs of the Belle Epoque, Paper Dolls in Full Color. 1983. pap. 3.95 (*0-486-24425-3*) Dover.
—Great Fashion Designs of the 30s Paper Dolls. 1989. pap. 3.95 (*0-486-24724-4*) Dover.
—Greta Garbo Paper Dolls in Full Color. 1985. pap. 3.95 (*0-486-24802-X*) Dover.
—Joan Crawford Paper Dolls in Full Color. 1983. pap. 3.95 (*0-486-24569-1*) Dover.
—Legendary Baseball Stars Paper Dolls. 1985. pap. 3.95 (*0-486-24846-1*) Dover.
—Little Cupid Dolls-Paper Dolls. 1986. pap. 2.50 (*0-486-25028-8*) Dover.
—Marilyn Monroe-Paper Dolls. 1980. pap. 3.95 (*0-486-23769-9*) Dover.
—More Erte Fashion Paper Dolls in Full Color. 1984. pap. 3.95 (*0-486-24630-2*) Dover.
—Paper Doll-Gibson Girl. 1985. pap. 3.95 (*0-486-24980-8*) Dover.
—Paper Doll-Judy Garland. 1982. pap. 3.95 (*0-486-24404-0*) Dover.
—Poiret Fashion Design Paper Dolls in Full Color. 1985. pap. 3.95 (*0-486-24952-2*) Dover.
—Ronald Reagan-Paper Dolls in Full Color. 1984. pap. 3.95 (*0-486-24628-0*) Dover.
—Santa Claus-Paper Dolls in Full Color. 1983. pap. 3.95 (*0-486-24546-2*) Dover.
—Three Little Kittens Paper Dolls in Full Color. 1986. pap. 3.50 (*0-486-25065-2*) Dover.
—Vivien Leigh Paper Dolls in Full Color. pap. 3.95 (*0-486-24207-2*) Dover.
Tiger. 1989. 3.50 (*1-87865-731-3*) Blue Q.
Time-Life Books Editors. The Great ABC Treasure Hunt: A Hidden Picture Alphabet Book. (Illus.). 56p. (ps-2). 1991. write for info. (*0-8094-9254-7*); lib. bdg. write for info. (*0-8094-9255-5*) Time-Life.
—Guess Who? A Lift-the-Flap Animal Book. (Illus.). 20p. (ps-2). 1990. write for info. (*0-8094-9250-4*); lib. bdg. write for info. (*0-8094-9251-2*) Time-Life.
Time Life Inc. Editors. Hound Bee! A Mix-&-Match Imagination Book. Kagan, Neil, ed. (Illus.). 40p. (ps-2). 1991. write for info. Time-Life.
—The Search for the Seven Sisters: A Hidden-Picture Geography Book. (Illus.). 56p. (ps-2). 1991. write for info. (*0-8094-9287-3*); PLB write for info. (*0-8094-9288-1*) Time-Life.
—The Three Storytellers of Or: A Flexible-Thinking Book. Kagan, Neil & Ward, Elizabeth, eds. (Illus.). 64p. (ps-2). 1991. write for info. (*0-8094-9283-0*); PLB write for info. (*0-8094-9284-9*) Time-Life.
—Voyage of the Micronauts: A Book about the Human Body. Fallow, Allan, ed. Cooke, Tom, illus. 64p. (ps-2). 1992. write for info. (*0-8094-9295-4*); PLB write for info. (*0-8094-9296-2*) Time-Life.
Time to Clean. 12p. (ps-1). 1989. bds. 5.95 (*0-87449-620-9*) Modern Pub NYC.
Time to Eat. 12p. (ps-1). 1989. bds. 5.95 (*0-87449-618-7*) Modern Pub NYC.
Time to Go. 12p. (ps-1). 1989. bds. 5.95 (*0-87449-619-5*) Modern Pub NYC.
Titherington, Jeanne. Big World, Small World. Titherington, Jeanne, illus. LC 84-4140. 24p. (ps-1). 1985. 11.75 (*0-688-04022-5*); PLB 11.88 (*0-688-04023-3*) GreenWillow.
Todd, H. E. & Biro, Val. The Sleeping Policeman. (Illus.). 32p. (ps-1). 1989. 13.95 (*0-340-41299-2*, Pub. by Hodder & Stoughton UK) Trafalgar.
Toddler Totes: Animals. 12p. (ps). 1993. 4.99 (*0-525-45129-3*, DCB) Dutton Child Bks.
Toddler Totes: Clothes. 12p. (ps). 1993. 4.99 (*0-525-45130-7*, DCB) Dutton Child Bks.
Toddler Totes: Food. 12p. (ps). 1993. 4.99 (*0-525-45131-5*, DCB) Dutton Child Bks.
Toddler Totes: Toys. 12p. (ps). 1993. 4.99 (*0-525-45132-3*, DCB) Dutton Child Bks.
Toddling Terry. 12p. (ps-1). 1989. bds. 5.95 (*0-87449-711-6*) Modern Pub NYC.
Todo Tirado (The Mess) (SPA., Illus.). 28p. (ps-2). 1991. pap. 3.95 (*0-516-55357-7*) Childrens.
Tompert, Ann. Will You Come Back for Me? Tucker, Kathleen, ed. LC 87-37258. (Illus.). 32p. (ps-k). 1988. PLB 13.95 (*0-8075-9112-2*); pap. 5.95 (*0-8075-9113-0*) A Whitman.
Topek, Susan R. Israel Is... Kahn, Katherine J., illus. LC 88-83569. 12p. (ps). 1989. bds. 4.95 (*0-930494-92-X*) Kar Ben.
Tortoise. 1989. 3.50 (*1-87865-734-8*) Blue Q.
Toussaint, Michael E. The Playland Kids, Featuring Marcus Toussaint, the Recycler. Hamburg, Cary, illus. 24p. (Orig.). (gr. k-6). 1992. pap. 2.95 (*0-9630905-0-X*) Michael T Enter.
Toussant, Eliza. Soddy Bear: The Persian Gulf War. Rasher, Steven, illus. 76p. (Orig.). (gr. 4 up). 1991. pap. 17.95 (*0-9630583-0-4*) E Toussant.
Tracy, Michael S. My Favorite Things to Do. 31p. (ps-k). 1992. pap. text ed. 23.00 big bk. (*1-56843-005-1*); pap. text ed. 4.50 (*1-56843-055-8*) BGR Pub.
Tran-Khan-Tuyet. The Little Weaver of Thai-Yen Village. Hom, Nancy, illus. LC 86-17186. (ENG & VIE.). 24p. (gr. 2-9). 1987. 13.95 (*0-89239-030-1*) Childrens Book Pr.
Trent, Robbie. First Christmas Board Book. Simont, Marc, illus. LC 89-29729. 26p. (ps). 1992. 4.95 (*0-694-00423-5*, Festival) HarpC Child Bks.
Tresselt, Alvin. Hide & Seek Fog. Duvoisin, Roger, illus. LC 65-14087. 32p. (ps up). 1988. pap. 3.95 (*0-688-07813-3*, Mulberry) Morrow.
—The Rabbit Story. Ewing, Carolyn, illus. LC 88-32594. 32p. (ps-2). 1989. 12.95 (*0-688-08650-0*); PLB 12.88 (*0-688-08651-9*) Lothrop.
—White Snow Bright Snow. Duvoisin, Roger, illus. LC 88-10018. 32p. (ps up). 1988. pap. 3.95 (*0-688-08294-7*, Mulberry) Morrow.
Tresselt, Alvin R. Autumn Harvest. Duvoisin, Roger, illus. LC 51-8824. 32p. (gr. k-3). 1951. PLB 15.88 (*0-688-51155-4*) Lothrop.
Tripp, Valerie. Baby Koala Finds a Home. Kalthoff, Sandra C., illus. LC 87-6325. 24p. (ps-2). 1987. pap. 3.95 (*0-516-41577-8*) Childrens.
—Baby Koala Finds a Home Big Book. (Illus.). 24p. (ps-2). 1990. PLB 22.95 (*0-516-49515-1*) Childrens.
—The Penguins Paint. LC 87-14081. (Illus.). 24p. (ps-2). 1987. pap. 3.95 (*0-516-41567-0*) Childrens.
—Pequeno Coala Busca Casa (Baby Koala Finds a Home) Kalthoff, Sandra C., illus. LC 87-6325. (SPA & ENG.). 24p. (ps-2). 1989. pap. 3.95 (*0-516-51577-2*); pap. 22.95 big bk. (*0-516-59515-6*) Childrens.
Tryon, Leslie. Albert's Play. Tryon, Leslie, illus. LC 91-23145. 32p. (gr. k-3). 1992. SBE 13.95 (*0-689-31525-2*, Atheneum Child Bk) Macmillan Child Grp.
Tsuchiya, Yukio. Faithful Elephants. Dykes, Tomoko T., tr. from JPN. Lewin, Ted, illus. 32p. (ps up). 1988. 13.45 (*0-395-46555-9*) HM.
Tsutsui, Yoriko. Anna's Secret Friend. Hayashi, Akiko, illus. 32p. (ps-1). 1989. pap. 3.99 (*0-14-050731-0*, Puffin) Puffin Bks.
Tudor, Tasha. Dolls' Christmas. Tudor, Tasha, illus. LC 59-12744. (gr. k-3). 1979. 6.95 (*0-8098-1026-3*); pap. 4.95 (*0-8098-2912-6*) McKay.
—Tale for Easter. Tudor, Tasha, illus. LC 62-8626. (gr. k-3). 1985. 6.95 (*0-8098-1008-5*); pap. 4.95 (*0-8098-1807-8*) McKay.
Turkle, Brinton. Obadiah the Bold. Turkle, Brinton, illus. LC 65-13350. (gr. k-3). 1977. pap. 3.95 (*0-14-050233-5*, Puffin) Puffin Bks.
Turner, Ann. Hedgehog for Breakfast. McCue, Lisa, illus. LC 88-8228. 32p. (ps-2). 1989. RSBE 13.95 (*0-02-789241-7*, Macmillan Child Bk) Macmillan Child Grp.
—Stars for Sarah. Teichman, Mary, illus. LC 89-36908. 32p. (ps-3). 1993. pap. 4.95 (*0-06-443344-7*, Trophy) HarpC Child Bks.
Twinkle Tots. 1991. pap. 2.99 (*0-517-05215-6*) Random Hse Value.
Twinkle, Twinkle, Little Star. 12p. (ps). 1994. 5.95 (*0-694-00575-4*, Festival) HarpC Child Bks.
Tyler, J. Dot to Dot Machines. (Illus.). 24p. (ps-2). 1991. pap. 3.50 (*0-7460-0606-3*, Usborne) EDC.
Tyler, Jan. Holly Lolly. Mattingly, Jennie, ed. LC 87-50981. (Illus.). 44p. (gr. k-3). 1987. 7.95 (*1-55523-084-9*) Winston-Derek.
Tyler, Linda W. Waiting for Mom. Davis, Susan, illus. 32p. (ps-2). 1989. pap. 3.95 (*0-14-050652-7*, Puffin) Puffin Bks.
Udry, Janice M. Let's Be Enemies. Sendak, Maurice, illus. LC 61-5777. 32p. (ps-1). 1961. 13.00 (*0-06-026130-7*); PLB 13.89 (*0-06-026131-5*) HarpC Child Bks.
—Let's Be Enemies. Sendak, Maurice, illus. LC 61-5777. 32p. (ps-2). 1988. pap. 4.95 (*0-06-443188-6*, Trophy) HarpC Child Bks.
—Moon Jumpers. Sendak, Maurice, illus. 32p. (gr. k-2). 1959. 15.00 (*0-06-026145-5*) HarpC Child Bks.
—Tree Is Nice. Simont, Marc, illus. LC 56-5153. 32p. (ps-1). 1957. 14.00 (*0-06-026155-2*); PLB 13.89 (*0-06-026156-0*) HarpC Child Bks.
—A Tree Is Nice. Simont, Marc, illus. LC 56-5153. 32p. (ps-3). 1987. pap. 4.95 (*0-06-443147-9*, Trophy) HarpC Child Bks.
—What Mary Jo Shared. Mill, Eleanor, illus. LC 66-16082. 40p. (gr. k-2). 1966. PLB 13.95 (*0-8075-8842-3*) A Whitman.
Under the Sea. (Illus.). (ps-k). 1991. write for info. (*0-307-06255-4*, Golden Pr) Western Pub.
Ungerer, Tomi. Adelaide. (ps). 1991. pap. 3.99 (*0-440-40571-8*, YB) Dell.
—The Beast of Monsieur Racine. Ungerer, Tomi, illus. LC 74-149216. 32p. (ps-3). 1971. 15.95 (*0-374-30640-0*) FS&G.
—Crictor. LC 58-5288. (Illus.). 32p. (ps-3). 1983. pap. 4.95 (*0-06-443044-8*, Trophy) HarpC Child Bks.
—Rufus. (ps). 1991. pap. 3.99 (*0-440-40570-X*, YB) Dell.
—The Three Robbers. Ungerer, Tomi, illus. LC 87-11549. 32p. (ps-3). 1987. Repr. of 1962 ed. SBE 14.95 (*0-689-31391-8*, Atheneum Child Bk) Macmillan Child Grp.
UNICEF Staff. Children's Chorus. 32p. (ps up). 1989. 12.95 (*0-525-44545-5*, DCB) Dutton Child Bks.
Unwin, Charlotte. Let's Pretend. Dann, Penny & Kindberg, Sally, illus. LC 87-19963. 24p. (ps-3). 1989. 4.95 (*0-8037-0507-7*) Dial Bks Young.
Updike, David. An Autumn Tale. Parker, Robert A., illus. 40p. (gr. 2 up). 1988. 14.95 (*0-945912-02-1*) Pippin Pr.
—A Spring Story. Parker, Robert A., illus. 40p. (gr. 2 up). 1989. PLB 14.95 (*0-945912-06-4*) Pippin Pr.
Upton, Pat. Who Does This Job? Novak, Matt, illus. LC 90-85722. 32p. (ps-1). 1991. 7.95 (*1-878093-20-7*) Boyds Mills Pr.
—Who Lives in the Woods? Upton, Pat & Schmidt, Karen L., illus. LC 90-85721. 32p. (ps-1). 1991. 7.95 (*1-878093-19-3*) Boyds Mills Pr.
Vallet, Muriel. Chantal Takes Her First Steps. Vallet, Muriel, illus. 11p. (gr. k-3). 1992. pap. 6.95 (*1-895583-50-0*) MAYA Pubs.
—How Many Times? Vallet, Muriel, illus. 13p. (gr. k-3). 1992. pap. 6.95 (*1-895583-47-0*) MAYA Pubs.
—My Turn. Vallet, Muriel, illus. 17p. (gr. k-3). 1992. pap. 12.95 (*1-895583-46-2*) MAYA Pubs.
—Where on Earth Is Jean? Vallet, Muriel, illus. 17p. (gr. k-3). 1992. pap. 8.95 (*1-895583-49-7*) MAYA Pubs.
Vallet, Roxanne. Minochet. Vallet, Roxanne, illus. 19p. (gr. k-3). 1992. pap. 10.95 (*1-895583-36-5*) MAYA Pubs.
—Thinking. Vallet, Roxanne, illus. 14p. 1992. pap. 10.95 (*1-895583-39-X*) MAYA Pubs.
Van Allsburg, Chris. Two Bad Ants. Van Allsburg, Chris, illus. 32p. (ps up). 1988. 17.45 (*0-395-48668-8*) HM.
Van der Meer, Ron. Family Bear Pop-up Book. Rohner, Thomas, illus. 10p. (ps-k). 1994. pap. 9.95 (*0-689-71766-0*, Aladdin) Macmillan Child Grp.
—What Is the Time. (ps-1). 1990. pap. 4.95 (*0-8167-2176-9*) Troll Assocs.
Van der Meer, Ron & Van der Meer, Altie. Funny Shoes. Van der Meer, Ron & Van der Meer, Altie, illus. 14p. (ps-k). 1994. pap. 9.95 (*0-689-71823-3*, Aladdin) Macmillan Child Grp.
Van der Meer, Ron & Van der Meer, Atie. Who Changes into What? (Illus.). 10p. (ps-1). 1986. 5.95 (*0-8431-1558-0*) Price Stern.
—Who Eats What? (Illus.). 10p. (ps-1). 1986. 5.95 (*0-8431-1559-9*) Price Stern.
—Who Is in the Water? (Illus.). 10p. (ps-1). 1986. 5.95 (*0-8431-1560-2*) Price Stern.
—Whose Footprints Are These? (Illus.). 10p. (ps-1). 1992. 5.95 (*0-8431-3358-9*) Price Stern.

Van Leeuwen, Jean. Oliver, Amanda & Grandmother Pig. Schweninger, Ann, illus. LC 86-243326. 56p. (ps-3). 1987. 9.95 (*0-8037-0361-9*); PLB 9.89 (*0-8037-0362-7*) Dial Bks Young.
Van Loon, Joan & Van Loon, John. Jelly, Chips & Caramel Whips. (gr. 1-3). 1988. 13.95 (*0-09-148830-3*, Pub. by Hutchinson UK) Trafalgar.
Varley, Susan. Badger's Parting Gifts. Varley, Susan, illus. LC 83-17500. 32p. (gr. k-3). 1984. 13.95 (*0-688-02699-0*); lib. bdg. 13.88 (*0-688-02703-2*) Lothrop.
Vaughn, Salle W. A Little One's Draw a Story Drawing Book. Vaughn, Jimmy, illus. 120p. (ps-5). 1990. wkbk, incl. protective envelope & rainbow drawing pencil 35. 00 (*0-9625832-0-0*) Crystal TX.
Velcoe Come un Grillo. (ps-3). 5.95 (*0-85953-557-6*) Childs Play.
Velthuijs, Max. A Birthday Cake for Little Bear. Lanning, Rosemary, tr. Velthuijs, Max, illus. LC 87-73270. 32p. (gr. k-3). 1988. 9.95 (*1-55858-046-8*) North-South Bks NYC.
Velveteen Rabbit's Pockets. (ps). 1985. pap. 3.95 (*0-671-52404-6*, Little Simon) S&S Trade.
Velveteen Rabit: Pop-Up. (ps-3). 1993. 4.95 (*0-8167-2928-X*) Troll Assocs.
Vesey, Amanda. Merry Christmas, Thomas! (ps-3). 1988. pap. 3.99 (*0-14-050803-1*, Puffin) Puffin Bks.
Vif Comme un Grillon. (ps-3). pap. 5.95 (*0-85953-467-7*) Childs Play.
Vigna, Judith. Boot Weather. Fay, Ann, ed. Vigna, Judith, illus. LC 88-20563. 32p. (ps-2). 1989. 13.95 (*0-8075-0837-3*) A Whitman.
—Mommy & Me by Ourselves Again. Fay, Ann, ed. Vigna, Judith, illus. LC 87-2059. 32p. (ps-3). 1987. PLB 13.95 (*0-8075-5232-1*) A Whitman.
—Nobody Wants a Nuclear War. Tucker, Kathleen, ed. Vigna, Judith, illus. LC 86-1654. 40p. (gr. 1-4). 1986. 13.95 (*0-8075-5739-0*) A Whitman.
—She's Not My Real Mother. Fay, Ann, ed. Vigna, Judith, illus. LC 80-19073. 32p. (gr. 1-3). 1980. PLB 13.95 (*0-8075-7340-X*) A Whitman.
Viking Ship. (Illus.). (gr. 2-6). cut-out model, incl. instructions 4.95 (*0-7141-1674-2*, Pub. by Brit Mus UK) Parkwest Pubns.
Vincent, Gabrielle. Ernest & Celestine's Patchwork Quilt. Vincent, Gabrielle, illus. LC 84-25891. 16p. (ps-1). 1985. 5.25 (*0-688-04557-X*) Greenwillow.
—Ernest & Celestine's Picnic. LC 82-2909. (Illus.). 24p. (ps up). 1988. pap. 3.95 (*0-688-07809-5*, Mulberry) Morrow.
—Merry Christmas, Ernest & Celestine. LC 83-14155. (ps up). 1987. pap. 3.95 (*0-688-07330-1*, Mulberry) Morrow.
Viorst, Judith. Alexander, Que Era Rico el Domingo Pasado. Ada, Alma F., tr. Cruz, Ray, illus. (SPA.). 32p. (gr. k-4). 1989. pap. 3.95 (*0-689-71351-7*, Aladdin) Macmillan Child Grp.
—Alexander, Que Era Rico el Domingo Pasado. Ada, Alma F., tr. Cruz, Ray, illus. LC 89-6503. (SPA.). 32p. (gr. k-4). 1989. SBE 13.95 (*0-689-31590-2*, Atheneum Child Bk) Macmillan Child Grp.
—Alexander y el Dia Terrible, Horrible, Espantoso, Horroso. Ada, Alma F., tr. Cruz, Ray, illus. (SPA.). 32p. (gr. k-4). 1989. pap. 3.95 (*0-689-71350-9*, Aladdin) Macmillan Child Grp.
—Alexander y el Dia Terrible, Horrible, Espantoso, Horroso. Ada, Alma F., tr. Cruz, Ray, illus. LC 89-33916. (SPA.). 32p. (gr. k-4). 1989. SBE 13.95 (*0-689-31591-0*, Atheneum Child Bk) Macmillan Child Grp.
—The Good-Bye Book. Chorao, Kay, illus. LC 87-1778. 32p. (ps-1). 1988. SBE 13.95 (*0-689-31308-X*, Atheneum Child Bk) Macmillan Child Grp.
—I'll Fix Anthony. Lobel, Arnold, illus. LC 87-18725. 32p. (gr. k-4). 1988. pap. 3.95 (*0-689-71202-2*, Aladdin) Macmillan Child Grp.
—My Mama Says There Aren't Any Zombies, Ghosts, Vampires, Creatures, Demons, Monsters, Fiends, Goblins, or Things. Chorao, Kay, illus. LC 87-18733. 48p. (gr. k-4). 1987. pap. 3.95 (*0-689-71204-9*, Aladdin) Macmillan Child Grp.
—The Tenth Good Thing about Barney. Blegvad, Erik, illus. LC 86-25948. 32p. (gr. k-4). 1987. pap. 3.95 (*0-689-71203-0*, Aladdin) Macmillan Child Grp.
Vita-finzi, Claudio. Planet Earth. 10p. 1989. pap. 13.95 casebound, pop-up (*0-671-67573-7*, S&S BFYR) S&S Trade.
Vonk, Idalee. Storytelling with the Flannel Board, Bk. 3. LC 21-650. 313p. (ps). 1983. 15.95 (*0-513-01762-3*) Denison.
Wabbes, Marie. Happy Birthday, Little Rabbit. Wabbes, Marie, illus. 24p. (ps-k). 1987. pap. 4.95 (*0-87113-129-3*, Joy St Bks) Little.
—It's Snowing, Little Rabbit. Wabbes, Marie, illus. 24p. (ps-k). 1987. pap. 4.95 (*0-87113-128-5*, Joy St Bks) Little.
Waber, Bernard. Anteater Named Arthur. Waber, Bernard, illus. LC 67-20374. 48p. (gr. k-3). 1977. 13. 95 (*0-395-20336-8*); pap. 5.70 (*0-395-25936-3*) HM.
—House on East Eighty-Eighth Street. (Illus.). 48p. (gr. k-3). 1973. 14.95 (*0-395-18157-7*) HM.
—The House on East Eighty-Eighth Street. Waber, Bernard, illus. (ps up). 1993. pap. 7.95 incl. cass. (*0-395-48878-8*) HM.
—Lovable Lyle. LC 69-14728. (Illus.). (gr. k-3). 1977. 14. 95 (*0-395-19858-5*); pap. 5.95 (*0-395-25378-0*) HM.
—Lyle & the Birthday Party. (Illus.). (gr. k-3). 1966. 13. 45 (*0-395-15080-9*) HM.
—Lyle, Lyle, Crocodile. (Illus.). (gr. k-3). 1965. 13.45 (*0-395-16995-X*) HM.
—You Look Ridiculous Said the Rhinoceros to the Hippopotamus. (Illus.). (gr. k-3). 1973. reinforced bdg. 16.95 (*0-395-07156-9*) HM.
Wagner, E. Vernel. Dinosaurs & Prehistoric Animals Coloring Book. Wagner, E. Vernel, illus. 64p. (gr. 3-5). 1988. pap. 3.00 (*0-941875-05-9*) Wolverine Gallery.
Wagner, Karen. Silly Fred. Chartier, Normand, illus. LC 88-22620. 32p. (gr. k-3). 1989. RSBE 14.95 (*0-02-792280-4*, Macmillan Child Bk) Macmillan Child Grp.
Wahl, Jan. Humphrey's Bear. Joyce, William, illus. LC 85-5541. 32p. (ps-2). 1989. pap. 5.95 (*0-8050-1169-2*, Bks Young Read) H Holt & Co.
Waite, Michael. Casey, the Greedy Young Cowboy. LC 37-35512. (Illus.). 32p. (ps-2). 1988. 7.99 (*1-55513-615-X*, Chariot Bks) Chariot Family.
—Sir Maggie, the Mighty. LC 87-35527. (Illus.). 32p. (ps-2). 1988. 7.99 (*1-55513-616-8*, Chariot Bks) Chariot Family.
Waite, Michael P. Boggin, Blizzy, & Sleeter the Cheater. LC 87-35510. (Illus.). 32p. (ps-2). 1988. 7.99 (*1-55513-618-4*, Chariot Bks) Chariot Family.
—Max & the Big Fat Lie. LC 87-35511. (Illus.). 32p. (ps-2). 1988. 7.99 (*1-55513-617-6*, Chariot Bks) Chariot Family.
Wakeman, Diana, illus. Disney's Aladdin. LC 91-58974. 12p. (ps-3). 1993. 11.95 (*1-56282-242-X*) Disney Pr.
Waldman, David K. How Teddy Bears Find Their Homes. Danner, Maggie, illus. LC 92-53786. 32p. (gr. k-2). 1994. casebound 12.95 (*0-945522-02-9*) Rebecca Hse.
Walking in Two Worlds: Paper Doll Book for Girls, Bk. 50. (ps-3). write for info. (*0-931363-50-0*) Celia Totus Enter.
Walking in Two Worlds: Paper Doll Book for Boys, Bk. 51. (ps-3). write for info. (*0-931363-51-9*) Celia Totus Enter.
Waller, John & Wallner, John, illus. Things That Go Zoom! 24p. (ps-2). 1993. 6.95 (*0-8431-3605-7*) Price Stern.
Wallis, Diz. Pip's Adventure. Wallis, Diz, illus. LC 90-85917. 24p. (ps up). 1991. 5.95 (*1-878093-43-6*) Boyds Mills Pr.
Wallner, S. J. Hans & the Golden Stirrup. LC 68-56815. (Illus.). 48p. (gr. 2-3). PLB 10.95 (*0-87783-016-9*); pap. 3.94 deluxe ed. (*0-87783-093-2*) Oddo.
Walt Disney Company Staff. Disney's Adventureland. (Illus.). (ps-1). 1989. Contains "Robin Hood & the Daring Mouse," "The Sword in the Stone: the Wizards' Duel," & "The Aristocats" write for info. (*0-307-15752-0*, Golden Pr) Western Pub.
—Disney's Ducktales: Down the Drain. (Illus.). 24p. (ps-3). 1990. pap. write for info. (*0-307-11726-X*, Pub. by Golden Bks) Western Pub.
—Walt Disney's Peter Pan. (Illus.). 24p. (ps-2). 1989. write for info. (*0-307-12081-3*, Pub. by Golden Bks) Western Pub.
Walt Disney Staff. Disney Babies Bath Books: I Can Spell. 1989. 5.98 (*0-8317-2480-3*) Viking Child Bks.
—Disney Babies Bath Books: I Love Opposites. 1989. 5.98 (*0-8317-2481-1*) Viking Child Bks.
—Meet the Seven Dwarfs: Interlocking Board Books. (ps). 1993. 5.98 (*0-453-03106-4*) NAL-Dutton.
—Rub-a-Dub-Dub Seven Dwarfs & a Tub Bath Book. (ps). 1993. 5.98 (*0-453-03099-8*) NAL-Dutton.
—The Secret of Aladdin's Lamp. (ps-3). 1993. pap. 5.98 (*0-453-03098-X*) Mouse Works.
—Snow White Meets the Dwarves Pop-up Book. (ps). 1993. 6.98 (*0-453-03097-1*) NAL-Dutton.
Walt Disney's Bambi's Fragrant Forest. LC 74-33127. 32p. (ps-2). 1988. write for info. (*0-307-13530-6*) Western Pub.
Walt Disney's Lady & the Tramp: Dinner at Tony's. 10p. (ps-1). 1994. 4.95 (*1-56282-611-5*) Disney Pr.
Walt Disney's Peter Pan to the Rescue. (Illus.). 24p. (ps-3). 1989. pap. write for info. (*0-307-12566-1*, Pub. by Golden Bks) Western Pub.
Walt Disney's Pinocchio. (Illus.). 24p. (ps-k). 1988. pap. write for info. (*0-307-10093-6*, Pub. by Golden Bks) Western Pub.
Walt Disney's the Mickey Mouse Book. (Illus.). 24p. (ps-k). 1965. pap. write for info (*0-307-10077-4*, Pub. by Golden Bks) Western Pub.
Walt Disney's Winnie the Pooh Scratch & Sniff Book. (Illus.). 32p. (ps-2). 1989. write for info. (*0-307-13528-4*, Pub. by Golden Bks) Western Pub.
Walter, Marion. Look at Annette. Haber-Schaim, Navah, illus. LC 77-186592. 32p. (ps-3). 1977. 5.95 (*0-87131-071-6*) M Evans.
—Make a Bigger Puddle, Make a Smaller Worm. Walter, Marion, illus. LC 70-186593. 32p. (ps-3). 1970. 5.95 (*0-87131-073-2*) M Evans.
Walter, Mildred P. Ty's One-Man Band. Tomes, Margot, illus. LC 80-11224. 32p. (gr. k-3). 1987. Repr. of 1980 ed. RSBE 14.95 (*0-02-792300-2*, Pub. by Four Winds Pr) Macmillan Child Grp.
Wang, Mary L. The Ant & the Dove. Walters, Mary C., illus. LC 89-34414. 32p. (ps-2). 1989. PLB 10.25 (*0-516-02367-5*); pap. 3.95 (*0-516-42367-3*) Childrens.
—The Frog Prince. Connelly, Gwen, illus. LC 86-11796. 32p. (ps-2). 1986. PLB 10.25 (*0-516-03983-0*); pap. 3.95 (*0-516-43983-9*) Childrens.
—El Leon y el Raton: The Lion & the Mouse. Dunnington, Tom, illus. LC 85-31441. (SPA.). 32p. (ps-2). 1988. PLB 10.25 (*0-516-33981-8*); pap. 3.95 (*0-516-53981-7*) Childrens.
Ward, Lynd. Biggest Bear. (Illus.). 88p. (gr. k-3). 1952. 14.45 (*0-395-14806-5*) HM.
—The Silver Pony: A Story in Pictures. Ward, Lynd, illus. LC 72-5402. 192p. (gr. k-3). 1973. 17.95 (*0-395-14753-0*) HM.
Ward, Sally G. & Ward, Sally G. The Yawn Goes On. (Illus.). 16p. (ps). 1994. 4.99 (*0-525-45076-9*, DCB) Dutton Child Bks.
Warner, Jerry S. Charlie McTwiddle & the Wobbly-Wheeled Sputter Putter Popper. Telfer, Judy, ed. Conlin, Jim, illus. LC 90-70308. 128p. (gr. 3-7). 1990. PLB 12.95 (*0-9626293-0-8*) Windsor Medallion.
Warren, Jean. Animal Rhymes: Reproducible Pre-Reading Books for Young Children. Bittinger, Gayle, ed. Buskirk, Judith P., illus. 160p. (Orig.). (ps-1). 1990. pap. text ed. 14.95 (*0-911019-34-0*) Warren Pub Hse.
—Everyday Patterns: Multi-Sized Patterns for Making Cut-Outs, Puppets, & Learning Games. Bittinger, Gayle, ed. Mohrmann, Gary, illus. 240p. (Orig.). (ps-1). 1990. pap. text ed. 16.95 (*0-911019-35-9*) Warren Pub Hse.
—Nature Patterns: Multi-Sized Patterns for Making Cut-Outs, Puppets & Learning Games. Bittinger, Gayle, ed. Mohrmann, Gary, illus. 240p. (Orig.). (ps-1). 1990. pap. text ed. 16.95 (*0-911019-36-7*) Warren Pub Hse.
—Object Rhymes: Reproducible Pre-Reading Books for Young Children. Bittinger, Gayle, ed. Tourtillotte, Barb, illus. 160p. (Orig.). (ps-1). 1990. pap. text ed. 14.95 (*0-911019-33-2*) Warren Pub Hse.
Watson, Claire. Big Creatures from the Past: A Pop-up Book. Cremins, Robert, illus. 14p. (gr. k-4). 1990. 14. 95 (*0-399-22159-X*, Putnam) Putnam Pub Group.
Watson, Clyde. Father Fox's Pennyrhymes. Watson, Wendy, illus. LC 71-146291. 56p. (ps-3). 1987. pap. 6.95 (*0-06-443137-1*, Trophy) HarpC Child Bks.
Watson, Jane W., et al. Sometimes a Family Has to Split Up. (Illus.). 32p. (ps-1). 1988. pap. 4.99 (*0-517-56811-X*) Crown Bks Yng Read.
Watson, Wendy. Wendy Watson's Mother Goose. Watson, Wendy, illus. LC 88-37913. (ps-2). 1989. 19. 95 (*0-688-05708-X*) Lothrop.
Wattenberg, Jane. Mrs. Mustard's Baby Faces. (Illus.). 6p. (ps). 1989. 4.95 (*0-87701-659-3*) Chronicle Bks.
—Mrs. Mustard's Beastly Babies. (Illus.). 7p. (ps). 1990. board book 4.95 (*0-87701-683-6*) Chronicle Bks.
Webber, Helen. Good Night, Night. Webber, Helen, illus. (gr. k-6). 1968. 8.95 (*0-8392-3054-0*) Astor-Honor.
—My Kite Is the Magic Me. Webber, Helen, illus. (gr. k-6). 1968. 8.95 (*0-8392-3055-9*) Astor-Honor.
—Sea Is My Blanket. (Illus.). (gr. k-6). 1968. 8.95 (*0-8392-3057-5*) Astor-Honor.
—Summer Sun. Webber, Helen, illus. (gr. k-6). 1968. 8.95 (*0-8392-3056-7*) Astor-Honor.
—Webber Quartet, 4 Vols. (gr. k-6). Set. deluxe slipcase 35.00 (*0-8392-3070-2*) Astor-Honor.
Weber, Bernard. Ira Says Goodbye. Weber, Bernard, illus. 40p. (ps-3). 1988. 13.45 (*0-395-48315-8*) HM.
Weimann, Elaine & Friedman, Rita. The Cotton Candy Caper. (Illus.). 30p. (ps-1). 1985. PLB 12.50 (*0-89796-988-X*) New Dimens Educ.
—A Dozen Delicious Doughnuts. (Illus.). 30p. (ps-1). 1988. PLB 12.50 (*0-89796-803-4*) New Dimens Educ.
—Gooey Gum Is Not for Chewing. (Illus.). 30p. (ps-1). 1985. PLB 12.50 (*0-89796-989-8*) New Dimens Educ.
—The Incredible Inventor. (Illus.). 30p. (ps-1). 1985. PLB 12.50 (*0-89796-985-5*) New Dimens Educ.
—The Inimitable Mr. X. (Illus.). 30p. (ps-1). 1986. PLB 12.50 (*0-89796-992-8*) New Dimens Educ.
—Jingling, Jangling Joggers. (Illus.). 30p. (ps-1). 1986. PLB 12.50 (*0-89796-994-4*) New Dimens Educ.
—The Longest Kick. (Illus.). 30p. (ps-1). 1986. PLB 12. 50 (*0-89796-990-1*) New Dimens Educ.
—Lovely Lemon Lollies. (Illus.). 30p. (ps-1). 1978. PLB 12.50 (*0-89796-802-6*) New Dimens Educ.
—Meet Me at the Market. (Illus.). 30p. (ps-1). 1978. PLB 12.50 (*0-89796-801-8*) New Dimens Educ.
—A Most Unusual Umbrella. (Illus.). 30p. (ps-1). 1986. PLB 12.50 (*0-89796-999-5*) New Dimens Educ.
—The Noisy Nose Nanny. (Illus.). 30p. (ps-1). 1985. PLB 12.50 (*0-89796-986-3*) New Dimens Educ.
—The Optimistic Optimist. (Illus.). 30p. (ps-1). 1986. PLB 12.50 (*0-89796-996-0*) New Dimens Educ.
—Popping Pointy Patches. (Illus.). 30p. (ps-1). 1985. PLB 12.50 (*0-89796-984-7*) New Dimens Educ.
—The Rubberbit Roundup. (Illus.). 30p. (ps-1). 1986. PLB 12.50 (*0-89796-998-7*) New Dimens Educ.
—The Super Sock Sensation. (Illus.). 30p. (ps-1). 1985. PLB 12.50 (*0-89796-987-1*) New Dimens Educ.
—To Be or Not to Be...Quiet. (Illus.). 30p. (ps-1). 1986. PLB 12.50 (*0-89796-997-9*) New Dimens Educ.
—Vanishing Vests. (Illus.). 30p. (ps-1). 1978. PLB 12.50 (*0-89796-804-2*) New Dimens Educ.
—Wonderful Winks & Weather Wishes. (Illus.). 30p. (ps-1). 1986. PLB 12.50 (*0-89796-995-2*) New Dimens Educ.
—The Yawn Maker. (Illus.). 30p. (ps-1). 1986. PLB 12.50 (*0-89796-993-6*) New Dimens Educ.
—Zipping Zippers Save the Zoo. (Illus.). 30p. (ps-1). 1986. PLB 12.50 (*0-89796-991-X*) New Dimens Educ.
Weimann, Elayne & Friedman, Rita. The A-Choo Confusion. Callen, Elizabeth, illus. 30p. (ps-1). 1988. PLB 12.50 (*0-89796-000-9*) New Dimens Educ.
—The Best Quiet Meter. Callen, Elizabeth, illus. 30p. (ps-1). 1989. PLB 12.50 (*0-89796-016-5*) New Dimens Educ.
—Buttonyms for Safety. Callen, Elizabeth, illus. 30p. (ps-1). 1989. PLB 12.50 (*0-89796-001-7*) New Dimens Educ.

—The Cotton Candy Creature. Callen, Elizabeth, illus. 30p. (ps-1). 1989. PLB 12.50 (*0-89796-002-5*) New Dimens Educ.

—The Dictionary Doughnut Shop. Callen, Elizabeth, illus. 30p. (ps-1). 1989. PLB 12.50 (*0-89796-003-3*) New Dimens Educ.

—Exercise Excitement. Callen, Elizabeth, illus. 30p. (ps-1). 1988. PLB 12.50 (*0-89796-004-1*) New Dimens Educ.

—Fantastic Friendship. Callen, Elizabeth, illus. 30p. (ps-1). 1988. PLB 12.50 (*0-89796-005-X*) New Dimens Educ.

—Gooey Gumball Game. Callen, Elizabeth, illus. 30p. (ps-1). 1989. PLB 12.50 (*0-89796-006-8*) New Dimens Educ.

—The Hat House Hotel. Callen, Elizabeth, illus. 30p. (ps-1). 1988. PLB 12.50 (*0-89796-007-6*) New Dimens Educ.

—Inchy the Incredible Inventor. Callen, Elizabeth, illus. 30p. (ps-1). 1988. PLB 12.50 (*0-89796-008-4*) New Dimens Educ.

—The Kazoo Kicker. Callen, Elizabeth, illus. 30p. (ps-1). 1989. PLB 12.50 (*0-89796-010-6*) New Dimens Educ.

—Lemonberry Lollipops. Callen, Elizabeth, illus. 30p. (ps-1). 1989. PLB 12.50 (*0-89796-011-4*) New Dimens Educ.

—Mr. J's Junkyard. Callen, Elizabeth, illus. 30p. (ps-1). 1989. PLB 12.50 (*0-89796-009-2*) New Dimens Educ.

—Mr. X's Mix-ups. Callen, Elizabeth, illus. 30p. (ps-1). 1989. PLB 12.50 (*0-89796-023-8*) New Dimens Educ.

—Munching Magic. Callen, Elizabeth, illus. 30p. (ps-1). 1988. PLB 12.50 (*0-89796-012-2*) New Dimens Educ.

—Ostrich Express. Callen, Elizabeth, illus. 30p. (ps-1). 1988. PLB 12.50 (*0-89796-014-9*) New Dimens Educ.

—Parking Pandemonium. Callen, Elizabeth, illus. 30p. (ps-1). 1989. PLB 12.50 (*0-89796-015-7*) New Dimens Educ.

—The Rubber Band Runner Champion. Callen, Elizabeth, illus. 30p. (ps-1). 1989. PLB 12.50 (*0-89796-017-3*) New Dimens Educ.

—Say No & Fly Away! Callen, Elizabeth, illus. 30p. (ps-1). 1988. PLB 12.50 (*0-89796-013-0*) New Dimens Educ.

—Super Socks for Courage. Callen, Elizabeth, illus. 30p. (ps-1). 1989. PLB 12.50 (*0-89796-018-1*) New Dimens Educ.

—Tall Toothbrush Retires. Callen, Elizabeth, illus. 30p. (ps-1). 1988. PLB 12.50 (*0-89796-019-X*) New Dimens Educ.

—Valuable Volunteers. Callen, Elizabeth, illus. 30p. (ps-1). 1989. PLB 12.50 (*0-89796-021-1*) New Dimens Educ.

—The Worry Machine. Callen, Elizabeth, illus. 30p. (ps-1). 1989. PLB 12.50 (*0-89796-022-X*) New Dimens Educ.

—Yawn-Maker Wanted. Callen, Elizabeth, illus. 30p. (ps-1). 1989. PLB 12.50 (*0-89796-024-6*) New Dimens Educ.

—You Forget Too. Callen, Elizabeth, illus. 30p. (ps-1). 1989. PLB 12.50 (*0-89796-020-3*) New Dimens Educ.

—Zip Codes. Callen, Elizabeth, illus. 30p. (ps-1). 1989. PLB 12.50 (*0-89796-025-4*) New Dimens Educ.

Weinberger, Jane. Wee Peter Puffin. LC 84-51988. (Illus.). 40p. (ps-8). 1984. 9.95 (*0-932433-03-0*) Windswept Hse.

Weingarten, Elaine. Kenny the Caterpillar. Sweeney, Phyllis, illus. 30p. (ps-3). 1988. text ed. 13.50 (*0-89777-702-6*, 97003) Soc Issues.

—One Duck. Sweeney, Phyllis, illus. 56p. (ps-3). 1988. text ed. 13.50 (*0-89777-700-X*, 97001) Soc Issues.

Weiss, Ellen. Oh Beans! Starring Wax Bean. Hall, Susan, illus. LC 88-4902. 32p. (gr. k-3). 1989. PLB 8.79 (*0-8167-1408-8*); pap. text ed. 1.95 (*0-8167-1409-6*) Troll Assocs.

—A Visit to the Sesame Street Zoo. Leigh, Tom, illus. LC 88-3201. 32p. (Orig.). (ps-1). 1988. pap. 2.25 (*0-394-80447-3*, Random Juv) Random Bks Yng Read.

Weiss, Nicki. Barney Is Big. LC 87-8546. (Illus.). 24p. (ps-1). 1988. 11.95 (*0-688-07586-X*); lib. bdg. 11.88 (*0-688-07587-8*) Greenwillow.

—If You're Happy & You Know It. LC 86-753170. (Illus.). 40p. (gr. k-3). 1987. 16.00 (*0-688-06444-2*) Greenwillow.

Welber, Robert. The Winter Picnic. Ray, Deborah K., illus. (ps-3). 1973. pap. 0.95 (*0-394-82621-3*) Pantheon.

Well, Rosemary. Max's Bedtime. Wells, Rosemary, illus. LC 84-14968. 12p. (ps-k). 1985. bds. 3.95 (*0-8037-0160-8*) Dial Bks Young.

Wells, Rosemary. Benjamin & Tulip. Wells, Rosemary, illus. LC 73-6018. 32p. (ps-2). 1977. 12.00 (*0-8037-1808-X*); PLB 9.89 (*0-8037-2057-2*); pap. 4.50 (*0-8037-0545-X*) Dial Bks Young.

—Hooray for Max. Wells, Rosemary, illus. (ps). 1986. Max doll 8.95 (*0-8037-0203-5*) Dial Bks Young.

—Max's Bath. Wells, Rosemary, illus. LC 84-14969. 12p. (ps-k). 1985. bds. 3.95 (*0-8037-0162-4*) Dial Bks Young.

—Max's Birthday. Wells, Rosemary, illus. LC 84-14970. 12p. (ps-k). 1985. bds. 4.50 (*0-8037-0163-2*) Dial Bks Young.

West, Colin. Between the Sun, the Moon & Me. Banyard, Julie, illus. 32p. (ps-2). 1992. 15.95 (*0-09-173644-7*, Pub. by Hutchinson UK) Trafalgar.

—Have You Seen the Crocodile? West, Colin, illus. LC 85-45748. 24p. (ps-2). 1986. pap. 4.95 (*0-06-443101-0*, Trophy) HarpC Child Bks.

—The King's Toothache. Dalton, Anne, illus. LC 87-3713. 32p. (ps-2). 1988. (Lipp Jr Bks) HarpC Child Bks.

—Pardon? Said the Giraffe. West, Colin, illus. LC 85-45747. 24p. (ps-2). 1986. pap. 4.95 (*0-06-443102-9*, Trophy) HarpC Child Bks.

West, Cyndy. I Am Mickey Mouse. DiCicco, Sue, illus. (ps-k). 1991. 3.50 (*0-307-12166-6*, Golden Pr) Western Pub.

Westcott, Nadine B. Going to Bed. Westcott, Nadine B., illus. LC 86-28767. (ps). 1987. pap. 4.95 (*0-316-93132-2*, Joy St Bks) Little.

Western Promotional Books Staff. Clothes: Sarah & Tommy. 1993. 2.49 (*0-307-16277-X*) Western Pub.

—Cowboy Pup Furry Face. 1993. 6.99 (*0-307-16452-7*) Western Pub.

—Farmer Cat Furry Face. 1993. 6.99 (*0-307-16451-9*) Western Pub.

—Fireman Bear Furry Face. 1993. 6.99 (*0-307-16450-0*) Western Pub.

—Food: Sarah & Tommy. 1993. 2.49 (*0-307-16275-3*) Western Pub.

—Friends: Sarah & Tommy. 1993. 2.49 (*0-307-16276-1*) Western Pub.

—Fruits: Tiny Tots. 1993. 2.79 (*0-307-16225-7*) Western Pub.

—Garden Colors: Little Look-In. 1993. 2.99 (*0-307-16702-X*) Western Pub.

—Growing Up: Little Look-In. 1993. 2.99 (*0-307-16705-4*) Western Pub.

—Hello, Hello: Little Look-In. 1993. 2.99 (*0-307-16704-6*) Western Pub.

—Kermit's Ball: Little Look-In. 1993. 2.99 (*0-307-16701-1*) Western Pub.

—Little Pets: Little Look-In. 1993. 2.99 (*0-307-16703-8*) Western Pub.

—Merry Muppet Christmas: A Playtime Window Book. 1993. 5.99 (*0-307-16350-4*) Western Pub.

—Pets: Tiny Tots. 1993. 2.79 (*0-307-16226-5*) Western Pub.

—Piggy's House: Little Look-In. 1993. 2.99 (*0-307-16700-3*) Western Pub.

—Play: Sarah & Tommy. 1993. 2.49 (*0-307-16278-8*) Western Pub.

—Sailor Pig Furry Face. 1993. 6.99 (*0-307-16453-5*) Western Pub.

—Things: Tiny Tots. 1993. 2.79 (*0-307-16227-3*) Western Pub.

—Toys: Tiny Tots. 1993. 2.79 (*0-307-16228-1*) Western Pub.

Wetzel, Rick. What Do You Eat? Wetzel, Rick, illus. LC 92-61623. 6p. (ps-1). 1993. 3.99 (*0-679-83844-9*) Random Bks Yng Read.

—What Do You Say? Wetzel, Rick, illus. LC 91-61624. 6p. (ps-1). 1993. 3.99 (*0-679-83845-7*) Random Bks Yng Read.

Wetzel, Rick & Swanson, Maggie. Big Bird's Bedtime Story. Wetzel, Rick & Swanson, Maggie, illus. LC 87-4764. 32p. (ps-1). 1987. pap. 2.50 (*0-394-89126-0*) Random Bks Yng Read.

What Do Animals Eat Colouring Book. (Illus.). (ps-6). pap. 2.95 (*0-565-00808-0*, Pub. by Natural Hist Mus) Parkwest Pubns.

What Do Babies Do. LC 84-61897. 14p. (ps). 1985. bds. 2.99 (*0-394-87279-7*) Random Bks Yng Read.

What Do Toddlers Do? LC 84-61895. 14p. (ps). 1985. 2.99 (*0-394-87280-0*) Random Bks Yng Read.

What Will We Eat? write for info. (*1-56326-322-X*, 032300) Disney Bks By Mail.

What Will You Do Today? write for info. (*1-56326-313-0*, 031401) Disney Bks By Mail.

What's Missing, Baby Daisy? write for info. (*1-56326-324-6*, 032508) Disney Bks By Mail.

What's That Noise, Baby Daisy? write for info. (*1-56326-307-6*, 030809) Disney Bks By Mail.

What's the Word? 1989. pap. 1.49 (*0-553-18400-8*) Bantam.

What's under My Bed? (ps-k). 1991. write for info. (*0-307-06254-6*, Golden Pr) Western Pub.

Wheeler, Cindy. Rose. Wheeler, Cindy, illus. LC 83-19985. 32p. (ps-1). 1985. lib. bdg. 10.99 (*0-394-96233-8*) Knopf Bks Yng Read.

Wheels Go Round. 24p. (ps-k). 1989. 9.95 (*0-448-21030-4*, G&D) Putnam Pub Group.

Wheels That Work. 16p. (ps-k). 1988. pap. 2.95 (*0-671-64872-1*, Little Simon) S&S Trade.

Whelan, Gloria. A Week of Raccoons. Munsinger, Lynn, illus. LC 87-16800. 40p. (ps-1). 1988. PLB 12.99 (*0-394-98396-3*) Knopf Bks Yng Read.

Whelchel, Sandy. A Day in Blue: Follow Freddy Falcon on a Child's Tour of the U. S. Air Force Academy. Brandt, Bill, illus. 28p. (gr. k-4). 1986. pap. 2.95 (*1-878406-00-0*) Parker Dstb.

When I Grow Up. (Illus.). (ps-k). 1991. write for info. (*0-307-11520-8*, Golden Pr) Western Pub.

Where Are They? Where's the Bunny? (Illus.). 32p. (ps-3). 1993. Repr. 5.98 (*0-8317-7728-1*) Smithmark.

Where Is Baby Donald's Kitten. write for info. (*1-56326-329-7*, 033001) Disney Bks By Mail.

Where Is Baby Mickey's Shoe? write for info. (*1-56326-306-8*, 030700) Disney Bks By Mail.

Where Is Mickey's Red Ball? write for info. (*1-56326-303-3*, 030403) Disney Bks By Mail.

Where's Rufus. 1994. 13.27 (*0-8368-0990-4*) Gareth Stevens Inc.

White, Stephen. What Can It Be? Dowdy, Linda C., ed. Sharp, Chris & McGlothlin, David, illus. LC 94-70489. 32p. (ps-k). 1994. 4.95 (*1-57064-019-X*) Barney Pub.

Whitehead, Patricia. Arnold Plays Baseball. Karas, Brian, illus. LC 84-8827. 32p. (gr. k-2). 1985. PLB 11.59 (*0-8167-0367-1*); pap. text ed. 2.95 (*0-8167-0368-X*) Troll Assocs.

—Best Halloween Book. Britt, Stephanie, illus. LC 84-8828. 32p. (gr. k-2). 1985. PLB 11.59 (*0-8167-0373-6*); pap. text ed. 2.95 (*0-8167-0374-4*) Troll Assocs.

—Best Thanksgiving Book. Hall, Susan T., illus. LC 84-8831. 32p. (gr. k-2). 1985. PLB 11.59 (*0-8167-0371-X*); pap. text ed. 2.95 (*0-8167-0372-8*) Troll Assocs.

—Best Valentine Book. Harvy, Paul, illus. LC 84-8829. 32p. (gr. k-2). 1985. PLB 11.59 (*0-8167-0369-8*); pap. text ed. 2.95 (*0-8167-0370-1*) Troll Assocs.

—Christmas Alphabet Book. Borgo, Deborah C., illus. LC 84-8830. 32p. (gr. k-2). 1985. PLB 11.59 (*0-8167-0365-5*); pap. text ed. 2.95 (*0-8167-0366-3*) Troll Assocs.

—Here Comes Hungry Albert. Karas, G. Brian, illus. LC 84-8835. 32p. (gr. k-2). 1985. PLB 11.59 (*0-8167-0379-5*); pap. text ed. 2.95 (*0-8167-0380-9*) Troll Assocs.

—Let's Go to the Farm. Gold, Ethel, illus. LC 84-8834. 32p. (gr. k-2). 1985. lib. bdg. 11.59 (*0-8167-0377-9*); pap. 2.95 (*0-8167-0378-7*) Troll Assocs.

—Let's Go to the Zoo. Boyd, Patti, illus. LC 84-8832. 32p. (gr. k-2). 1985. PLB 11.59 (*0-8167-0375-2*); pap. text ed. 2.95 (*0-8167-0376-0*) Troll Assocs.

—What a Funny Bunny. Page, Don, illus. LC 84-8833. 32p. (gr. k-2). 1985. PLB 11.59 (*0-8167-0361-2*); pap. text ed. 2.95 (*0-8167-0362-0*) Troll Assocs.

Whitelaw, Nancy. A Beautiful Pearl. Tucker, Kathleen, ed. Friedman, Judith, illus. LC 90-28761. 32p. (gr. 2-5). 1991. 13.95 (*0-8075-0599-4*) A Whitman.

Who Will Baby Mickey Meet? write for info. (*1-56326-311-4*, 031203) Disney Bks By Mail.

Wickstrom, Sylvie K., illus. Wheels on the Bus. 32p. (ps-2). 1988. PLB 13.00 (*0-517-56784-9*) Crown Bks Yng Read.

Wiesner, David. Free Fall. LC 87-22834. (Illus.). 32p. (ps up). 1991. pap. 4.95 (*0-688-10990-X*, Mulberry) Morrow.

Wiggs, Susan. The Canary Who Sailed with Columbus. Roberts, Melissa, ed. Anderson, Sharon, illus. 48p. (ps-2). 1989. 12.95 (*0-89015-719-7*, Pub. by Panda Bks) Sunbelt Media.

Wik, Lars, photos by. Baby's First Words. LC 84-60700. (Illus.). 28p. (ps). 1985. 2.95 (*0-394-86945-1*) Random Bks Yng Read.

Wikler, Madeline & Groner, Judye. I Have Four Questions. Radin, Chari M., illus. LC 88-83570. 12p. (ps). 1989. bds. 4.95 (*0-930494-90-3*) Kar Ben.

Wilburn, Kathy, illus. Pudgy Pals. 16p. (ps). 1983. pap. 2.95 (*0-448-10203-X*, G&D) Putnam Pub Group.

—The Pudgy Rock-a-Bye Book. 16p. (ps). 1983. pap. 2.95 (*0-448-10206-4*, G&D) Putnam Pub Group.

Wild, Anne. The Egyptians Pop-Up. (Illus.). 32p. (gr. 5-9). 1986. pap. 7.95 (*0-906212-44-8*, Pub. by Tarquin UK) Parkwest Pubns.

Wild West Bears, Bk. 24. (ps-1). write for info. (*0-931363-22-5*) Celia Totus Enter.

Wilde, Irma, illus. Baby's Farm Animals. 20p. (ps-1). 1986. bds. 4.95 (*0-448-03094-2*, G&D) Putnam Pub Group.

Wilde, Oscar. The Canterville Ghost. Zwerger, Lisbeth, illus. LC 86-8179. (gr. 4 up). 1991. pap. 15.95 (*0-88708-027-8*) Picture Bk Studio.

Wildsmith, Brian. The Circus. (Illus.). (ps-3). 1970. pap. 7.50x (*0-19-272102-X*) OUP.

—Goat's Trail. Wildsmith, Brian, illus. LC 86-2731. 40p. (gr. k-3). 1986. 10.95 (*0-394-88276-8*); lib. bdg. 12.99 (*0-394-98276-2*) Knopf Bks Yng Read.

Willard, Nancy. The Marzipan Moon. Sewall, Marcia, illus. LC 80-24221. 46p. (gr. 2-5). 1981. pap. 3.95 (*0-15-252963-2*, Voyager Bks) HarBrace.

—The Mountains of Quilt. De Paola, Tomie, illus. LC 86-19577. 32p. (ps-3). 1987. 12.95 (*0-15-256010-6*, HB Juv Bks) HarBrace.

—The Nightgown of the Sullen Moon. McPhail, David, illus. LC 83-8472. 32p. (Orig.). (ps-3). 1987. pap. 4.95 (*0-15-257430-1*, Voyager Bks) HarBrace.

Willhoite, Michael. Daddy's Roommate. Willhoite, Michael, illus. 32p. (ps-2). 1991. pap. 8.95 (*1-55583-118-4*) Alyson Pubns.

Williams, Barbara. Donna Jean's Disaster. Levine, Abby, ed. Apple, Margot, illus. LC 86-15817. 32p. (gr. 1-5). 1986. PLB 11.95 (*0-8075-1682-1*) A Whitman.

Williams, Garth. Rabbits' Wedding. Williams, Garth, illus. LC 58-5285. 30p. (ps-1). 1958. 15.00 (*0-06-026495-0*) HarpC Child Bks.

Williams, Jay. Everyone Knows What a Dragon Looks Like. 32p. (gr. k-3). 1984. pap. 5.95 (*0-02-045600-X*, Aladdin) Macmillan Child Grp.

Williams, Karen L. Galimoto. Stock, Catherine, illus. LC 89-2258. 32p. (ps up). 1991. pap. 4.95 (*0-688-10991-8*, Mulberry) Morrow.

Williams, Karin. Flying. Williams, Karin, illus. LC 93-83000. 12p. (ps-1). 1994. 4.99 (*0-679-84997-1*) Random Bks Yng Read.

—Jumping. Williams, Karin, illus. LC 93-83006. 12p. (ps-1). 1994. 4.99 (*0-679-84998-X*) Random Bks Yng Read.

—Running. Williams, Karin, illus. LC 93-83001. 12p. (ps-1). 1994. 4.99 (*0-679-84999-8*) Random Bks Yng Read.

Williams, Linda. The Little Old Lady Who Was Not Afraid of Anything. Lloyd, Megan, illus. LC 85-48250. 32p. (ps-2). 1986. 15.00 (*0-690-04584-0*, Crowell Jr Bks); PLB 14.89 (*0-690-04586-7*) HarpC Child Bks.

—The Little Old Lady Who Was Not Afraid of Anything. Lloyd, Megan, illus. LC 85-48250. 32p. (ps-2). 1988. pap. 4.95 (*0-06-443183-5*, Trophy) HarpC Child Bks.

Williams, Marcia. The First Christmas. Williams, Marcia, illus. LC 88-1961. 32p. (Orig.). (ps-1). 1988. 4.95 (*0-394-80434-1*) Random Bks Yng Read.

Williams, Margery. The Velveteen Rabbit. Graham, Florence, illus. 32p. (ps-2). 1987. pap. 2.25 (*0-448-19083-4*, Platt & Munk); (Platt & Munk) Putnam Pub Group.

Williams, Rose. What Am I? (ps). 1993. 7.99 (*1-56476-148-7*, Victor Books) SP Pubns.

—What Is It? (ps). 1993. 7.99 (*1-56476-149-5*, Victor Books) SP Pubns.

Williams, Sam. Rock-a-bye Baby Books & Cradle Set. (Illus.). 10p. (ps). 1992. 19.95 (*0-525-44925-6*, DCB) Dutton Child Bks.

Williams, Vera B. Music, Music for Everyone. LC 83-14196. (Illus.). 32p. (ps up). 1988. pap. 3.95 (*0-688-07811-7*, Mulberry) Morrow.

—Three Days on a River in a Red Canoe. LC 80-23893. (Illus.). 32p. (ps up). 1986. pap. 3.95 (*0-688-04072-1*, Mulberry) Morrow.

Wilson, Jean A. Caz & His Cat: Now We Like the Night. Wilson, Richard C., illus. 32p. 1994. 14.95 (*1-884739-00-8*) Wahr.

Winborn, Marsha, illus. Inside Sesame Street. 22p. (ps). 1986. write for info. (*0-307-12142-9*, Pub. by Golden Bks.) Western Pub.

Windsor, Patricia. The Sandman's Eyes. (gr. k-12). 1992. pap. 3.50 (*0-440-97585-9*, LFL) Dell.

Winik, J. T. Fun with Numbers. Winik, J. T., illus. 32p. (ps-k). 1985. pap. 2.95 (*0-88625-104-4*) Durkin Hayes Pub.

Winik, J. T. & Pashuk, Lauren. Fun from A-Z. Winik, J. T. & Pashuk, Lauren, illus. 32p. (ps-k). 1985. pap. 2.95 (*0-88625-105-2*) Durkin Hayes Pub.

Winter, Ginny L. What's in My Tree. Winter, Ginny L., illus. (gr. k-1). 1962. 8.95 (*0-8392-3044-3*) Astor-Honor.

Winthrop, Elizabeth. Grover Sleeps Over. Swanson, Maggie, illus. LC 83-83279. 32p. (ps). 1984. write for info. (*0-307-12010-4*, 12010, Golden Bks) Western Pub.

—Shoes. Joyce, William, illus. LC 85-45841. 32p. (ps-2). 1986. 14.00 (*0-06-026591-4*); PLB 13.89 (*0-06-026592-2*) HarpC Child Bks.

—Shoes. Joyce, William, illus. LC 85-45841. 32p. (ps-3). 1988. pap. 4.95 (*0-06-443171-1*, Trophy) HarpC Child Bks.

—Shoes. Joyce, William, illus. (ps-1). 1988. bk. & cassette 19.95 (*0-87499-113-7*); bk. & cassette 12.95 (*0-87499-112-9*); 4 cassettes & guide 27.95 (*0-87499-114-5*) Live Oak Media.

Wise, Beth A. Follow Directions. Jordan, Polly, illus. 32p. (ps). 1992. wkbk. 1.95 (*1-56293-169-5*) McClanahan Bk.

—Get Ready to Read. Dorr, Mary A., illus. 32p. (ps). 1992. wkbk. 1.95 (*1-56293-173-3*) McClanahan Bk.

Wiskur, Darrell. Mary's Merry Chase. Silver Dollar City, Inc. Staff, ed. Wiskur, Darrell, illus. (ps-1). 1977. 1.99g (*0-686-19126-9*) Silver Dollar.

Witch Who Changed Her Ways Pop-Up. 10p. (ps-3). 1990. 3.95 (*0-8167-2184-X*) Troll Assocs.

Witte, Eve & Witte, Pat. Touch Me Book. Rockwell, Harlow, illus. (ps). 1961. write for info (*0-307-12146-1*, Golden Bks) Western Pub.

Wittman, Sally. A Special Trade. Gundersheimer, Karen, illus. LC 77-25673. 32p. (ps-2). 1985. pap. 5.95 (*0-06-443071-5*, Trophy) HarpC Child Bks.

Wolcott, Patty. Double-Decker Double-Decker Double-Decker Bus. Barner, Bob, illus. LC 91-14210. 32p. (ps-2). 1991. PLB 6.99 (*0-679-91930-9*) Random Bks Yng Read.

Wolde, Gunilla. This Is Betsy. Wolde, Gunilla, illus. LC 75-7566. 24p. (ps). 1990. 4.95 (*0-394-83161-6*) Random Bks Yng Read.

Wolf, Aline D. A Book about Anna: For Children & Their Parents. Rajpar, Shamin & Wolf, Gerald, illus. LC 80-84874. 56p. (Orig.). (ps-k). 1981. 9.95x (*0-685-03953-6*); pap. 5.95x (*0-9601016-4-0*) Parent-Child Pr.

Wolf, Andrea. Valentino. Bradford, Elizabeth, ed. Verlag, Mangold, tr. from GER. Wolf, Alexander, illus. LC 91-21301. 32p. (gr. k-3). 1991. PLB 14.60 (*1-56074-030-2*) Garrett Ed Corp.

Wolf, Jill. Bears in Toyland. 1988. pap. 2.50 (*0-89954-785-0*) Antioch Pub Co.

—Teddy Bear's Easter Picnic. Nelson, Linda K., illus. 24p. (gr. 3-7). 1985. pap. 2.50 (*0-89954-424-X*) Antioch Pub Co.

Wolff, Ashley. Only the Cat Saw. (Illus.). (ps-3). 1988. pap. 3.95 (*0-14-050853-8*, Puffin) Puffin Bks.

—A Year of Beasts. Wolff, Ashley, illus. LC 85-27419. 32p. (ps-1). 1986. 11.95 (*0-525-44240-5*, DCB) Dutton Child Bks.

—A Year of Birds. (ps-3). 1988. pap. 3.95 (*0-14-050854-6*, Puffin) Puffin Bks.

Wolff, Barbara M. Pappa & Me. Wolff, Barbara M., illus. 16p. (ps-1). 1991. PLB 13.95 (*1-879567-11-3*, Valeria Bks) Wonder Well.

Woo, Diane. The Curious Carnival Caper. Yamamoto, Neal, illus. 64p. (Orig.). (gr. 2-6). 1992. pap. 3.95 (*1-56288-217-1*) Checkerboard.

—The Mystery of Cavanaugh's Mansion. Yamamoto, Neal, illus. 64p. (Orig.). (gr. 2-6). 1992. pap. 3.95 (*1-56288-219-8*) Checkerboard.

—The Riddle of Rattlesnake Gulch. Yamamoto, Neal, illus. 64p. (Orig.). (gr. 2-6). 1992. pap. 3.95 (*1-56288-216-3*) Checkerboard.

—The Secret of the S. S. Crimson. Yamamoto, Neal, illus. 64p. (Orig.). (gr. 2-6). 1992. pap. 3.95 (*1-56288-218-X*) Checkerboard.

Wood, A. J. Look! The Ultimate Spot the Difference Book. (gr. 1 up). 1990. 13.00 (*0-8037-0925-0*) Dial Bks Young.

Wood, Audrey. Heckedy Peg. Wood, Don, illus. LC 86-33639. 32p. (ps-3). 1987. 14.95 (*0-15-233678-8*, HB Juv Bks) HarBrace.

—Three Sisters. Hoffman, Rosekrans, illus. LC 85-29392. 48p. (ps-3). 1986. 9.95 (*0-8037-0279-5*); PLB 9.89 (*0-8037-0280-9*) Dial Bks Young.

Wood, Don. Little Mouse, the Red Ripe Strawberry & the Big Hungry Bear. LC 90-46414. (ps-3). 1990. 11.95 (*0-685-56131-3*); pap. 5.95 (*0-85953-012-4*) Childs Play.

—Quick As a Cricket. (ps-3). 1990. 11.95 (*0-85953-151-1*); pap. 5.95 (*0-85953-306-9*) Childs Play.

Wood, Leslie. Bump, Bump, Bump. (Illus.). 16p. 1987. pap. 2.95 (*0-19-272162-3*) OUP.

Woody, Marilyn. God Made My World. John, Joyce, illus. LC 88-70793. 14p. (ps). 1988. bds. 6.99 (*1-55513-320-7*, Chariot Bks) Chariot Family.

Woody, Marilyn J. God Cares for Me. John, Joyce, illus. LC 88-70794. 14p. (ps). 1988. bds. 6.99 (*1-55513-319-3*, Chariot Bks) Chariot Family.

—High Chair Devotions: God Gave Me a Gift. John, Joyce, illus. LC 90-81146. 14p. (ps). 1989. bds. 6.99 spiral bdg. (*1-55513-729-6*, 37325, Chariot Bks) Chariot Family.

—High Chair Devotions: God Is My Friend. John, Joyce, illus. LC 90-81147. 14p. (ps). 1989. bds. 6.99 spiral bdg. (*1-55513-728-8*, 37283, Chariot Bks) Chariot Family.

World Around Us. (Illus.). (ps-7). 1987. 5.95 (*0-553-05411-2*) Bantam.

Worley, Daryl. Billy & the Big Truck. Daab, John, illus. 32p. (ps). 1989. 9.95 (*0-924067-06-3*) Tyke Corp.

—Billy & the Bright Red Ball. Daab, John, illus. 32p. (ps). 1989. 9.95 (*0-924067-05-5*) Tyke Corp.

—Billy & the Chocolate Chip Cookies. Daab, John, illus. 32p. (ps). 1989. 9.95 (*0-924067-02-0*) Tyke Corp.

—Billy & the Department Store. Daab, John, illus. 32p. (ps). 1989. 9.95 (*0-924067-04-7*) Tyke Corp.

—Billy & the Scary Things. Daab, John, illus. (ps). 1989. 9.95 (*0-924067-03-9*) Tyke Corp.

Worsley, Elizabeth. Baby Bunny's Day. (ps). 1992. bds. 2.50 (*0-681-41486-3*) Longmeadow Pr.

—Baby Bunny's Garden. (ps). 1992. bds. 2.50 (*0-681-41488-X*) Longmeadow Pr.

—Baby Bunny's Party. (ps). 1992. bds. 2.50 (*0-681-41487-1*) Longmeadow Pr.

—Baby Bunny's Picnic. (ps). 1992. bds. 2.50 (*0-681-41489-8*) Longmeadow Pr.

Worth, Bonnie. I Can Help. Cooke, Tom, illus. 18p. (ps). 1994. 3.95 (*0-307-12425-8*, Pub. by Golden Bks) Western Pub.

Worthington, Joan & Worthington, Phoebe. Teddy Bear Farmer. (ps-1). pap. 2.95 (*0-317-62188-2*, Puffin) Puffin Bks.

Wouters, Anne. This Book Is Too Small. Wouters, Anne, illus. LC 91-23743. 32p. (ps-1). 1992. 8.95 (*0-525-44881-0*, DCB) Dutton Child Bks.

Wray, Kit, retold by. & illus. Robin Hood: A Hidden Picture Story. LC 91-72976. 32p. (ps-3). 1992. 7.95 (*1-56397-020-1*) Boyds Mills Pr.

Wren & Maile. At the Beach. Wren, illus. (ENG & HAW.). 10p. (ps). 1992. bds. 3.95 (*1-880188-04-X*) Bess Pr.

Wright, Friere & Foreman, Michael. Seven in One Blow. Wright, Friere & Foreman, Michael, illus. 32p. (ps-3). 1981. lib. bdg. 4.99 (*0-394-93805-4*) Random Bks Yng Read.

Wright, Rachel. Why Do I Eat? Trotter, Stuart, illus. LC 91-26683. 32p. (ps-2). 1992. pap. 5.95 (*0-689-71588-9*, Aladdin) Macmillan Child Grp.

Wylie, Joanne. Un Cuento de Peces y Sus Formas (A Fishy Shape Story) Kratky, Lada, tr. Wylie, David, illus. LC 85-23264. (SPA.). 32p. (ps-2). 1986. pap. 3.95 (*0-516-52985-4*) Childrens.

Wylie, Joanne & Wylie, David. Un Cuento Gracioso de Peces (A Funny Fish Story) LC 83-24058. (ENG & SPA., Illus.). 32p. (ps-2). 1989. PLB 11.45 (*0-516-32986-3*); pap. 3.95 (*0-516-52986-2*) Childrens.

Yagyu, Genichiro. The Holes in Your Nose. Stinchecum, Amanda M., tr. from JPN. (Illus.). 32p. (ps). 1994. 11.95 (*0-916291-50-2*, Cranky Nell Pr) Kane-Miller Bk.

Yashima, Taro. Umbrella. Yashima, Taro, illus. (ps-1). 1977. pap. 3.99 (*0-14-050240-8*, Puffin) Puffin Bks.

—Umbrella. Yashima, T., illus. (ps-1). 1958. pap. 15.99 (*0-670-73858-1*) Viking Child Bks.

Yeager, Nancy & Yeager, Doug. A Tiny Little Story. 32p. (ps-k). 1993. pap. write for info. (*1-879911-01-9*) Rams Horn Bks.

—Where's Billy? 32p. (ps-k). 1991. pap. 4.95 (*1-879911-00-0*) Rams Horn Bks.

Yektai, Niki. Bears in Pairs. De Groat, Diane, illus. LC 86-18828. 32p. (ps-k). 1987. RSBE 14.95 (*0-02-793691-0*, Bradbury Pr) Macmillan Child Grp.

—What's Missing. Ryan, Susannah, illus. LC 87-784. 32p. (ps-1). 1989. (Clarion Bks); pap. 4.95 (*0-317-04349-8*, Clarion Bks) HM.

YES Entertainment Corp. Staff. Dino Den. 2p. (ps-2). 1993. write for info. (*1-883366-03-8*) Yes Ent.

—My Doll House. 2p. (ps-2). 1993. write for info. (*1-883366-04-6*) Yes Ent.

—Police & Fire Station. 2p. (ps-2). 1993. write for info. (*1-883366-05-4*) Yes Ent.

YES! Entertainment Corporation Staff. Cinderella: The Fairy Tale. 2p. (ps-2). 1993. write for info. (*1-883366-11-9*) YES Ent.

Yogesvara dosa-Jyotirmayi. Gopal the Invincible. Bhaktivedanta Swami Prabhupado, A. C., tr. Sunita-devi dosa, illus. 15p. (gr. 3 up). 1983. 7.95 (*0-89647-017-2*) Bala Bks.

Yolen, Jane. All in the Woodland Early: An ABC Book. Zalben, Jane B., illus. LC 91-70415. 32p. (ps-3). 1991. Repr. 14.95 (*1-878093-62-2*) Boyds Mills Pr.

—The Emperor & the Kite. Young, Ed, illus. 32p. (ps-2). 1988. 15.95 (*0-399-21499-2*, Philomel Bks) Putnam Pub Group.

—The Girl Who Loved the Wind. reissue ed. Young, Ed, illus. LC 71-171012. 32p. (ps-3). 1987. pap. 5.95 (*0-06-443088-X*, Trophy) HarpC Child Bks.

—An Invitation to the Butterfly Ball: A Counting Rhyme. Zalben, Jane B., illus. LC 91-70416. 32p. (ps-3). 1991. 14.95 (*1-878093-61-4*) Boyds Mills Pr.

—The Three Bears Rhyme Book. Dyer, Jane, illus. LC 86-19514. 32p. (ps-3). 1987. 14.95 (*0-15-286386-9*, HB Juv Bks) HarBrace.

Young, Ruth & Rose, Mitchell, illus. Spider Magic. LC 89-61632. 12p. (ps-1). 1990. bds. 5.95 incl. finger puppet (*1-877779-03-2*) Schneider Educational.

—Turtle Magic. LC 89-61634. 12p. (ps-1). 1990. bds. 5.95 incl. finger puppet (*1-877779-01-6*) Schneider Educational.

Young, Sheila. Betty Bonnet Paper Dolls in Full Color. 1982. pap. 3.95 (*0-486-24415-6*) Dover.

—Lettie Lane Paper Doll. 1981. pap. 3.95 (*0-486-24089-4*) Dover.

Younger, Jesse. The Fire Engine Book. Battaglia, Aurelius, illus. 24p. (ps-k). 1987. pap. write for info (*0-307-10082-0*, Pub. by Golden Bks) Western Pub.

Zakutinsky, Adina. Ha Shem's World of Color. Geld, Goldie, illus. 12p. (ps). 1987. PLB 4.95x (*0-911643-10-9*); board book 4.95 (*0-685-55893-2*) Aura Bklyn.

Zalben, Jane B. Beni's First Chanukah. Zalben, Jane B., illus. LC 86-33634. 32p. (gr. k-3). 1988. 12.95 (*0-8050-0479-3*, Bks Young Read) H Holt & Co.

Zemach, Harve. The Judge: An Untrue Tale. Zemach, Margot, illus. 48p. (ps up). 1988. pap. 5.95 (*0-374-43962-1*, Sunburst) FS&G.

Zemach, Margot. Jake & Honeybunch Go to Heaven. Zemach, Margot, illus. 40p. (ps up). 1987. pap. 4.95 (*0-374-43714-9*, Sunburst) FS&G.

—The Little Red Hen. (ps-3). 1987. pap. 3.95 (*0-14-050567-9*, Puffin) Puffin Bks.

—The Three Wishes: An Old Story. Zemach, Margot, illus. LC 86-80956. 32p. (ps up). 1986. 16.00 (*0-374-37529-1*) FS&G.

Zerner, Jesse, illus. Astro-Dots: Find the Constellations. 64p. (Orig.). (ps-7). 1985. pap. 3.95 (*0-913319-01-5*) Sunstone Pubns.

Ziefert, Harriet. Animal Count. Baum, Susan, illus. 20p. (ps-1). 1989. pap. 4.95 (*0-14-054174-8*, Puffin) Puffin Bks.

—The Big, Red Blanket. Jacobson, David, illus. 24p. (ps-3). 1992. 3.95 (*0-694-00393-X*) HarpC Child Bks.

—Breakfast Time! Ernst, Lisa C., illus. (ps). 1988. pap. 3.95 (*0-670-81579-9*) Viking Child Bks.

—Bye, Bye, Daddy! Ernst, Lisa C., illus. (ps). 1988. pap. 3.95 (*0-670-81581-0*) Viking Child Bks.

—Can You Play. Smith, Mavis, illus. LC 88-24025. 24p. (Orig.). (ps-2). 1989. pap. 2.25 (*0-394-82001-0*) Random Bks Yng Read.

—A Clean House for Mole & Mouse. Prebenna, David, illus. LC 87-25420. 32p. (ps-3). 1988. pap. 8.95 (*0-670-82032-6*) Viking Child Bks.

—Come Visit My House! Three Books Inside: My Mommy; My Daddy; My Puppy, 3 bks. Smith, Mavis, illus. (ps-1). 1992. Set. bds. 12.00 (*0-670-84485-3*) Viking Child Bks.

—Count with Little Bunny. Ernst, Lisa C., illus. (ps-1). 1988. pap. 5.95 (*0-670-82308-2*) Viking Child Bks.

—Daddy, Can You Play with Me? Boon, Emilie, illus. (ps-k). 1988. pap. 5.95 (*0-14-050895-3*, Puffin) Puffin Bks.

—Don't Cry, Baby Sam. Brown, Richard, illus. 20p. (gr. 2-6). 1988. pap. 4.95 (*0-14-050858-9*, Puffin) Puffin Bks.

—Feed Little Bunny. Ernst, Lisa C., illus. (ps-1). 1988. pap. 5.95 (*0-670-82309-0*) Viking Child Bks.

—Follow Me! (Illus.). 32p. (ps-2). 1990. pap. 8.95 (*0-670-83197-2*) Viking Child Bks.

—Going on a Lion Hunt. Smith, Mavis, illus. 20p. (ps). 1989. pap. 5.99 (*0-14-054083-0*, Puffin) Puffin Bks.

—Here Comes a Bus. 20p. (gr. 2-6). 1988. pap. 4.95 (*0-14-050857-0*, Puffin) Puffin Bks.

—How Big Is Big? Baruffi, Andrea, illus. LC 88-612151. 32p. (ps-3). 1989. pap. 3.50 (*0-14-050983-6*, Puffin) Puffin Bks.

—In a Scary Old House. Smith, Mavis, illus. 20p. (ps). 1989. pap. 5.99 (*0-14-054082-2*, Puffin) Puffin Bks.
—Let's Get Dressed. Ernst, Lisa C., illus. (ps). 1988. pap. 3.95 (*0-670-81580-2*) Viking Child Bks.
—Let's Trade. Morgan, Mary, illus. LC 88-62150. 32p. (ps-3). 1989. pap. 3.50 (*0-14-050982-8*, Puffin) Puffin Bks.
—Mommy, Where Are You? Boon, Emilie, illus. (ps-k). 1988. pap. 5.95 (*0-14-050894-5*, Puffin) Puffin Bks.
—My Camera. Rader, Laura, illus. 14p. (ps). 1993. 4.50 (*0-694-00417-0*) HarpC Child Bks.
—A New Coat for Anna. Lobel, Anita, illus. LC 86-2722. 40p. (ps-3). 1986. PLB 12.99 (*0-394-97426-3*) Knopf Bks Yng Read.
—Nicky's Picnic. Brown, Richard, illus. 20p. (Orig.). (ps-k). 1986. pap. 4.95 (*0-14-050584-9*, Puffin) Puffin Bks.
—No More TV, Sleepy Dog. Gorbaty, Norman, illus. LC 88-26316. 24p. (Orig.). (ps-2). 1989. 2.25 (*0-394-81996-9*) Random Bks Yng Read.
—Piggety Pig Books, 6 of ea. title. Prebenna, David, illus. 96p. (ps-k). 1988. 2.95 (*0-316-98758-1*) Little.
—Play with Little Bunny. Ernst, Lisa C., illus. 12p. (ps-1). 1986. pap. text ed. 6.99 (*0-670-80359-6*) Viking Child Bks.
—Please Let It Snow. Brown, Richard, illus. LC 88-62145. 32p. (ps-3). 1989. pap. 3.50 (*0-14-050981-X*, Puffin) Puffin Bks.
—The Prince Has a Boo-Boo. Alley, R. W., illus. LC 88-26322. 24p. (Orig.). (ps-2). 1989. PLB 2.25 (*0-394-81999-3*) Random Bks Yng Read.
—The Princess Needs a Bath. Gradisher, Martha, illus. 24p. (ps-3). 1992. 3.95 (*0-694-00391-3*) HarpC Child Bks.
—So Hungry! Nicklaus, Carol, illus. LC 87-4763. 32p. (ps-1). 1987. 3.50 (*0-394-89127-9*); lib. bdg. 7.99 (*0-394-99127-3*) Random Bks Yng Read.
—Surprise! Morgan, Mary, illus. LC 87-26217. 32p. (ps-3). 1988. pap. 8.95 (*0-670-82036-9*) Viking Child Bks.
—What Is Father's Day? Schumacher, Claire, illus. 16p. (ps-k). 1992. 5.95 (*0-694-00383-2*) HarpC Child Bks.
—What Is Mother's Day? Schumacher, Claire, illus. 16p. (ps-k). 1992. 5.95 (*0-694-00382-4*) HarpC Child Bks.
—What's a Wedding? A Lift-the-Flap Bk. Schumacher, Claire, illus. 16p. (ps-k). 1993. 5.95 (*0-694-00450-2*, Festival) HarpC Child Bks.
—The Wheels on the Bus. Baruffi, Andrea, illus. LC 89-38100. 24p. (Orig.). (ps-2). 1990. pap. 2.25 (*0-394-84870-5*) Random Bks Yng Read.
—Who Spilled the Milk? Gradisher, Martha, illus. 24p. (ps-3). 1992. 3.95 (*0-694-00390-5*) HarpC Child Bks.
Ziefert, Harriet & Brown, Richard. Nicky Upstairs & Down. (ps-2). 1994. pap. 3.25 (*0-14-036852-3*) Puffin Bks.
Zion, Gene. Harry by the Sea. Graham, Margaret B., illus. LC 65-21302. 32p. (gr. k-3). 1965. PLB 14.89 (*0-06-026856-5*) HarpC Child Bks.
—Harry the Dirty Dog. Graham, Margaret B., illus. LC 56-8137. 32p. (gr. k-3). 1956. 15.00 (*0-06-026865-4*); PLB 14.89 (*0-06-026866-2*) HarpC Child Bks.
—No Roses for Harry. Graham, Margaret B., illus. LC 58-7752. (gr. k-3). 1958. 15.00 (*0-06-026890-5*); PLB 14.89 (*0-06-026891-3*) HarpC Child Bks.
Zokeisha. A Little Book of Colors. Klimo, Kate, ed. Zokeisha, illus. 16p. 1982. pap. 2.95 (*0-671-45570-2*, Little Simon) S&S Trade.
—Things I Like to Look At. Zokeisha, illus. 16p. (ps-k). 1981. pap. 3.50 (*0-671-44451-4*, Little Simon) S&S Trade.
Zolotow, Charlotte. Do You Know What I'll Do? Williams, Garth, illus. LC 58-7755. 32p. (ps-1). 1958. PLB 13.89 (*0-06-026940-5*) HarpC Child Bks.
—The Hating Book. Shecter, Ben, illus. LC 69-14444. 32p. (ps-3). 1969. 14.00 (*0-06-026923-5*); PLB 13.89 (*0-06-026924-3*) HarpC Child Bks.
—I Like to Be Little. Blegvad, Erik, illus. LC 83-45056. 32p. (gr. k-4). 1990. pap. 4.95 (*0-06-443248-3*, Trophy) HarpC Child Bks.
—If It Weren't for You. Reissue. ed. Shecter, Ben, illus. LC 66-15682. 32p. (gr. k-3). 1966. HarpC Child Bks.
—Mister Rabbit & the Lovely Present. Sendak, Maurice, illus. LC 62-7590. (gr. k-3). 1962. 14.00 (*0-06-026945-6*); PLB 13.89 (*0-06-026946-4*) HarpC Child Bks.
—Mr. Rabbit & the Lovely Present. Sendak, Maurice, illus. (gr. k-3). 1987. incl. cassette 19.95 (*0-87499-047-5*); pap. 12.95 incl. cassette (*0-87499-046-7*); 4 paperbacks, cassette & guide 27.95 (*0-87499-048-3*) Live Oak Media.
—My Friend John. Shecter, Ben, illus. LC 68-10209. (gr. k-3). 1968. (C Zolotow Bks); PLB 14.89 (*0-06-026948-0*, C Zolotow Bks) HarpC Child Bks.
—Park Book. Rey, H. A., illus. LC 44-9471. 32p. (ps-1). 1986. PLB 13.89 (*0-06-026973-1*) HarpC Child Bks.
—The Quarreling Book. Lobel, Arnold, illus. LC 63-14445. 32p. (gr. k-3). 1963. PLB 12.89 (*0-06-026976-6*) HarpC Child Bks.
—The Quarreling Book. Lobel, Arnold, illus. LC 63-14445. 32p. (gr. k-3). 1982. pap. 3.95 (*0-06-443034-0*, Trophy) HarpC Child Bks.
—The Sky Was Blue. Williams, Garth, illus. LC 62-13328. (gr. k-3). 1963. PLB 14.89 (*0-06-027001-2*) HarpC Child Bks.
—Sleepy Book. Plume, Ilse, illus. LC 87-45861. 32p. (ps-1). 1988. PLB 13.89 (*0-06-026968-5*) HarpC Child Bks.
—Sleepy Book. Plume, Ilse, illus. LC 87-45861. 32p. (ps-1). 1990. pap. 5.95 (*0-06-443239-4*, Trophy) HarpC Child Bks.
—Some Things Go Together. Gundersheimer, Karen, illus. LC 82-48694. 24p. (ps-2). 1987. pap. 4.95 (*0-06-443133-9*, Trophy) HarpC Child Bks.
—Storm Book. Graham, Margaret B., illus. LC 52-7880. (gr. k-3). 1952. PLB 13.89 (*0-06-027026-8*) HarpC Child Bks.
—The Storm Book. Graham, Margaret B., illus. LC 52-7880. 32p. (ps-3). 1989. pap. 4.95 (*0-06-443194-0*, Trophy) HarpC Child Bks.
—When I Have a Little Boy. Knight, Hilary, illus. LC 67-14072. 32p. (ps-3). 1988. pap. 3.95 (*0-06-443176-2*, Trophy) HarpC Child Bks.
—When I Have a Little Girl. Knight, Hilary, illus. LC 65-24656. 32p. (gr. k-3). 1965. HarpC Child Bks.
—When I Have a Little Girl. Knight, Hilary, illus. LC 65-24656. 32p. (ps-3). 1988. pap. 4.95 (*0-06-443175-4*, Trophy) HarpC Child Bks.
—William's Doll. Pene Du Bois, William, illus. LC 70-183173. 32p. (ps-3). 1985. pap. 4.95 (*0-06-443067-7*, Trophy) HarpC Child Bks.
Zoo. 8p. (ps). 1984. pap. 2.95 (*0-671-49716-2*, Little Simon) S&S Trade.

PICTURE GALLERIES
see Art–Galleries and Museums

PICTURE POSTERS
see Posters

PICTURE WRITING
see also Cave Drawings; Hieroglyphics
Hofsinde, Robert. Indian Sign Language. Hofsinde, Robert, illus. LC 56-5178. (gr. 5 up). 1956. PLB 13.88 (*0-688-31610-7*) Morrow Jr Bks.

PICTURES
see also Cartoons and Caricatures; Paintings; Portraits also names of countries, states, etc. with the subdivision Description and Travel, e.g. U. S.–Description and Travel, etc.; and names of cities with the subdivision Description, e.g. New York (City)–Description
Gregorich, Barbara. Alike-Not Alike & Go-Togethers: Kindergarten. Hoffman, Joan, ed. Koontz, Robin M., illus. 32p. (gr. k). 1990. wkbk. 2.29 (*0-88743-176-3*) Sch Zone Pub Co.

PICTURES, HUMOROUS
see Cartoons and Caricatures

PIERCE, FRANKLIN, PRES. U. S., 1804-1869
Brown, Fern G. Franklin Pierce: Fourteenth President of the United States. Young, Richard G., ed. LC 88-30050. (Illus.). (gr. 5-9). 1989. PLB 17.26 (*0-944483-25-9*) Garrett Ed Corp.
Simon, Charnan. Franklin Pierce. LC 88-10883. (Illus.). 100p. (gr. 3 up). 1988. PLB 14.40 (*0-516-01357-2*) Childrens.

PIGEONS
Frisch. Pigeons. 1991. 11.95s.p. (*0-86625-193-6*) Rourke Pubns.
Morrison, Susan D. The Passenger Pigeon. LC 89-31839. (Illus.). 48p. (gr. 5-6). 1989. text ed. 12.95 RSBE (*0-89686-457-X*, Crestwood Hse) Macmillan Child Grp.
Nofsinger, Ray & Hargrove, Jim. Pigeons & Doves. LC 92-12948. (Illus.). 48p. (gr. k-4). 1992. PLB 12.85 (*0-516-02196-6*) Childrens.
—Pigeons & Doves. LC 92-12948. (Illus.). 48p. (gr. k-4). 1993. pap. 4.95 (*0-516-42196-4*) Childrens.
Schlein, Miriam. Pigeons. Miller, Margaret, photos by. LC 88-35286. (Illus.). 48p. (gr. 2-6). 1989. (Crowell Jr Bks); (Crowell Jr Bks) HarpC Child Bks.

PIGEONS–FICTION
Alexander, Martha. Out, Out, Out. Alexander, Martha, illus. LC 68-15251. (gr. k-3). 1968. PLB 6.95 (*0-685-01457-6*) Dial Bks Young.
Baker, Jeannie. Home in the Sky. Baker, Jeannie, illus. LC 83-25379. 32p. (gr. k-3). 1984. 13.00 (*0-688-03841-7*); PLB 11.96 (*0-688-03842-5*) Greenwillow.
Graeber, Charlotte T. Grey Cloud. Bloom, Lloyd, illus. LC 79-14673. 128p. (gr. 3-7). 1984. SBE 13.95 (*0-02-736910-2*, Four Winds) Macmillan Child Grp.
Mukerji, Dhan G. Gay-Neck: The Story of a Pigeon. Artzybasheff, Boris, illus. LC 68-13419. 192p. (gr. 4 up). 1968. 15.00 (*0-525-30400-2*, DCB) Dutton Child Bks.
—Gay-Neck: The Story of a Pigeon. 190p. 1991. text ed. 15.20 (*1-56956-238-5*) W A T Braille.
Ransome, Arthur. Pigeon Post. 372p. 1992. pap. 11.95 (*0-87923-864-X*) Godine.
Renton, Alice. Victoria: The Biography of a Pigeon. (gr. 7 up). 1988. pap. 3.50 (*0-8041-0395-X*) Ivy Books.
Turnbull, Ann. Speedwell. LC 91-58757. 128p. (gr. 5-9). 1994. pap. 3.99 (*1-56402-281-1*) Candlewick Pr.
Zolotow, Charlotte. Peter & the Pigeons. Gourgault, Martine, illus. LC 92-29405. 24p. (ps up). 1993. 14.00 (*0-688-12185-3*); PLB 13.93 (*0-688-12186-1*) Greenwillow.

PIGMENTATION
see Color of Animals; Color of Man

PIGMIES
see Pygmies

PIGS
Ahlstrom, Mark & Schroeder, Howard. The Wild Pigs. LC 86-2282. (Illus.). 48p. (gr. 5). 1986. text ed. 12.95 RSBE (*0-89686-272-0*, Crestwood Hse) Macmillan Child Grp.
Fowler, Allan. Smart, Clean Pigs. LC 92-36365. (Illus.). 32p. (ps-2). 1993. big bk. 22.95 (*0-516-49644-1*); PLB 10.75 (*0-516-06013-9*); pap. 3.95 (*0-516-46013-7*) Childrens.
King-Smith, Dick. All Pigs Are Beautiful. Jeram, Anita, illus. LC 92-53136. 32p. (ps-3). 1993. 14.95 (*1-56402-148-3*) Candlewick Pr.
Ling, Mary. Pig. Ling, Bill, photos by. LC 92-53487. (Illus.). 24p. (ps-1). 1993. 7.95 (*1-56458-204-3*) Dorling Kindersley.
Munsch, Robert. Pigs. Martchenko, Michael, illus. 24p. (gr. k-2). 1989. 12.95 (*1-550370-39-1*, Pub. by Annick CN); pap. 4.95 (*1-550370-38-3*, Pub. by Annick CN) Firefly Bks Ltd.
Pig. 1989. 3.50 (*1-87865-725-9*) Blue Q.
Retan, Walter. Piggies Piggies Piggies. (gr. 3 up). 1993. pap. 15.00 (*0-671-75244-8*, S&S BFYR) S&S Trade.
Royston, Angela. Pig. LC 89-22532. 1990. PLB 10.90 (*0-531-19080-3*, Warwick) Watts.
Schmidt, Annemarie & Schmidt, Christian R. Pigs & Peccaries. LC 93-13051. (gr. 3 up). 1994. 18.60 (*0-8368-1003-1*) Gareth Stevens Inc.
Stone, L. Cerdos (Pigs) 1991. 8.95s.p. (*0-86592-989-0*) Rourke Enter.
Stone, Lynn. Pigs. (Illus.). 24p. (gr. k-5). 1990. lib. bdg. 11.94 (*0-86593-037-6*); lib. bdg. 8.95s.p. (*0-685-36312-0*) Rourke Corp.
Thaler, Mike. Oinkers Away! Pig Riddles, Cartoons & Jokes. (gr. 3-6). 1989. pap. 2.50 (*0-671-67456-0*, Minstrel Bks) PB.

PIGS–FICTION
Adams, David. The Three Little Pigs Go to Greasy Pete's. Holland, Janet, illus. 40p. (ps-3). 1994. PLB 14.95 (*0-9638421-9-6*); pap. 5.95 (*0-9638421-8-8*) Flatland Tales.
Addison-Wesley Staff. The Three Little Pigs Little Book. (Illus.). 16p. (gr. k-3). 1989. pap. text ed. 4.50 (*0-201-19058-3*) Addison-Wesley.
—Los Tres Cerditos - Little Book. (SPA., Illus.). 16p. (gr. k-3). 1989. pap. text ed. 4.50 (*0-201-19710-3*) Addison-Wesley.
—Los Tres Cerditos Big Book. (SPA., Illus.). 16p. (gr. k-3). 1989. pap. text ed. 31.75 (*0-201-19938-6*) Addison-Wesley.
Adler, C. S. Good-Bye Pink Pig. 176p. (gr. 3-7). 1986. pap. 2.75 (*0-380-70175-8*, Camelot) Avon.
—Help, Pink Pig! 160p. 1991. pap. 2.95 (*0-380-71156-7*, Camelot) Avon.
Allard, Harry. Bumps in the Night. Marshall, James, illus. (gr. k-3). 1984. 3.25 (*0-553-15711-6*, Skylark) Bantam.
Allen, Jonathan. Who's at the Door? Allen, Jonathan, illus. LC 92-19618. 32p. (ps up). 1993. 11.95 (*0-688-12257-4*, Tambourine Bks) Morrow.
Amery, H. Pig Gets Lost. (Illus.). 16p. (ps-3). 1992. pap. 3.95 (*0-7460-0590-3*) EDC.
—Pig Gets Stuck. (Illus.). 16p. (ps). 1989. 3.95 (*0-7460-0469-9*, Usborne); PLB 7.96 (*0-88110-374-8*, Usborne) EDC.
Aruego, Jose & Dewey, Ariane. Rockabye Crocodile. LC 92-24587. 32p. (ps up). 1993. pap. 4.95 (*0-688-12333-3*, Mulberry) Morrow.
Ashwill, Beverly. Jeffrey, the Littlest Pig. Ashwill, Betty J., illus. LC 90-83312. 24p. (ps-3). 1990. pap. 3.98 (*0-941381-06-4*) BJO Enterprises.
Axelrod, Amy. Pigs Will Be Pigs. McGinley-Nally, Sharon, illus. LC 93-7640. 40p. (gr. k-3). 1994. RSBE 14.95 (*0-02-765415-X*, Four Winds) Macmillan Child Grp.
Ayres, Pam. Piggo & the Nosebag. Ellis, Andy, illus. 32p. (gr. k-3). 1991. 9.95 (*0-563-20922-4*, BBC-Parkwest) Parkwest Pubns.
—Piggo Has a Train Ride. Ellis, Andy, illus. 32p. (gr. k-3). 1992. 9.95 (*0-563-20921-6*, BBC-Parkwest) Parkwest Pubns.
Battaglia, Aurelius, illus. Three Little Pigs. LC 76-24170. 32p. (ps-2). 1982. lib. bdg. 5.99 (*0-394-93459-8*) Random Bks Yng Read.
Bawden, Nina. The Peppermint Pig. 160p. (gr. 5 up). 1988. pap. 4.95 (*0-440-40122-4*, Pub. by Yearling Classics) Dell.
Bianchi, J. The Swine Snafu. (Illus.). 24p. (ps-8). 1988. 12.95 (*0-921285-14-0*, Pub. by Bungalo Bks CN); pap. 4.95 (*0-921285-12-4*, Pub. by Bungalo Bks CN) Firefly Bks Ltd.
Birney, Betty. Piglet Bakes Half a Haycorn Pie. Baker, Darrell, illus. 24p. (ps-2). 1992. write for info. (*0-307-12338-3*, 12338) Western Pub.
Blake, Jon. Wriggly Pig. Jenkin-Pearce, Susie, illus. LC 91-24171. 32p. (ps-3). 1992. 14.00 (*0-688-11295-1*, Tambourine Bks); PLB 13.93 (*0-688-11296-X*, Tambourine Bks) Morrow.
Bloom, Suzanne. We Keep a Pig in the Parlor. Bloom, Suzanne, illus. 32p. (ps-1). 1988. 13.95 (*0-517-56829-2*, Clarkson Potter) Crown Bks Yng Read.
Bond, Michael. The Tales of Olga da Polga. Helweg, Hans, illus. LC 88-31444. 128p. (gr. 3-7). 1989. Repr. of 1973 ed. SBE 13.95 (*0-02-711731-6*, Macmillan Child Bk) Macmillan Child Grp.
Bonsall, Crosby N. Piggle. Bonsall, Crosby, illus. LC 73-5478. 64p. (gr. k-3). 1973. PLB 13.89 (*0-06-020580-6*) HarpC Child Bks.
Brooks, Walter R. Freddy & the Perilous Adventure. Morrill, Leslie & Wiese, Kurt, illus. LC 85-14653. 256p. (gr. 3-7). 1986. lib. bdg. 9.99 (*0-394-97601-0*) Knopf Bks Yng Read.

—Freddy Goes Camping. Morrill, Leslie & Wiese, Kurt, illus. LC 48-8629. 264p. (gr. 3-7). 1986. lib. bdg. 9.99 (*0-394-97602-9*); pap. 4.95 (*0-394-87602-4*) Knopf Bks Yng Read.

—Freddy Plays Football. 1992. Repr. lib. bdg. 18.95x (*0-89968-302-9*) Lightyear.

—Freddy Rides Again. 1992. Repr. lib. bdg. 18.95x (*0-89968-300-2*) Lightyear.

—Freddy the Cowboy. 1992. Repr. lib. bdg. 18.95x (*0-89968-301-0*) Lightyear.

—Freddy the Politician. Morrill, Leslie, illus. LC 85-14713. 264p. (gr. 3-7). 1986. pap. 3.95 (*0-394-87600-8*) Knopf Bks Yng Read.

Bucknall, Caroline. The Three Little Pigs. Bucknall, Caroline, illus. LC 86-16716. 32p. (ps-2). 1987. 10.95 (*0-8037-0100-4*) Dial Bks Young.

Campbell, Janet, adapted by. Walt Disney's Three Little Pigs. DiCicco, Gil, illus. LC 92-53443. 32p. 1993. 12. 95 (*1-56282-381-7*); PLB 12.89 (*1-56282-382-5*) Disney Pr.

Carlson, Nancy. I Like Me! (Illus.). 32p. (ps-1). 1990. pap. 3.99 (*0-14-050819-8*, Puffin) Puffin Bks.

—I Like Me! Read-Aloud Set. (Illus.). (ps-3). 1993. Set incls. 1 Giant copy, 6 paperbacks, giant-sized bookmark & tchr's. guide in a free- standing easel. pap. 41.93 (*0-14-778977-X*) Puffin Bks.

—Louanne Pig in the Mysterious Valentine. (ps-3). 1987. pap. 3.95 (*0-14-050604-7*, Puffin) Puffin Bks.

—Louanne Pig in the Talent Show. Carlson, Nancy, illus. 32p. (ps-3). 1986. pap. 3.95 (*0-14-050603-9*, Puffin) Puffin Bks.

—Louanne Pig in The Talent Show. Carlson, Nancy, illus. (gr. k-3). 1987. incl. cassette 19.95 (*0-87499-065-3*); pap. 12.95 incl. cassette (*0-87499-064-5*); 4 paperbacks, cassette & guide 27.95 (*0-87499-066-1*) Live Oak Media.

—Louanne Pig in the Witch Lady. Carlson, Nancy, illus. 32p. (ps-3). 1986. pap. 3.95 (*0-14-050602-0*, Puffin) Puffin Bks.

—Louanne Pig in Witch Lady. Carlson, Nancy, illus. (gr. k-3). 1987. incl. cassette 19.95 (*0-87499-068-8*); pap. 12.95 incl. cassette (*0-87499-067-X*); 4 paperbacks, guide & cassette 27.95 (*0-87499-069-6*) Live Oak Media.

Carlson, Nancy L. I Like Me! giant ed. LC 92-25330. 1993. 17.99 (*0-14-054846-7*) Puffin Bks.

Celsi, Teresa. The Fourth Little Pig. Cushman, Doug, illus. 24p. (ps-3). 1990. PLB 17.10 (*0-8172-3577-9*); pap. 10.95 pkg. of 3 (*0-685-67711-7*) Raintree Steck-V.

Chevat, Richard. If You Were Miss Piggy. (ps-3). 1994. pap. 2.25 (*0-307-12815-6*, Golden Pr) Western Pub.

Christelow, Eileen. The Great Pig Escape. LC 93-38788. 1994. 14.95 (*0-395-66973-1*, Clarion Bks) HM.

Cibula, Matt. Slumgullion, the Executive Pig. (Illus.). 32p. Date not set. 14.95 (*1-55933-149-6*) Know Unltd.

Clapman, Arnold. Angel the Pig. LC 94-20302. (Illus.). 1994. pap. 5.95 (*0-382-24662-4*) Silver Burdett Pr.

Claverie, Jean. Die Drei Kleinen Schweinchen. Claverie, Jean, illus. (GER.). 32p. (gr. k-3). 1992. 13.95 (*3-85825-330-8*) North-South Bks NYC.

—The Three Little Pigs. Claverie, Jean, illus. Crawford, Elizabeth, tr. from GER. LC 88-25327. (Illus.). 32p. (gr. k-3). 1989. 13.95 (*1-55858-004-2*) North-South Bks NYC.

Clem, Margaret H. Elbert Ein Swine, Genius Pig. Clem, Margaret H., illus. LC 93-80378. 24p. (Orig.). (gr. k-4). 1994. pap. 6.95 (*1-878044-12-5*) Mayhaven Pub.

Copeland, Colene. Little Prissy & T. C. Harrison, Edith, illus. LC 88-81916. 1992. 8.95 (*0-939810-07-7*); pap. 3.95 (*0-939810-08-5*) Jordan Valley.

—Mystery in the Farrowing Barn. Harrison, Edith, illus. LC 91-62326. 150p. (Orig.). (gr. 3-7). 1991. 9.95 (*0-939810-13-1*); pap. 3.95 (*0-939810-14-X*) Jordan Valley.

—Priscilla. Harrison, Edith, illus. LC 81-80663. 212p. (Orig.). (gr. 3 up). 1981. 8.95 (*0-939810-01-8*); pap. 3.95 (*0-939810-02-6*) Jordan Valley.

—Priscilla. 1992. 8.95 (*0-685-52575-9*); pap. 3.95 (*0-685-52576-7*) Jordan Valley.

Craig, Helen. Susie & Alfred in a Busy Day in Town. Craig, Helen, illus. LC 93-21181. 32p. (Orig.). 1994. pap. 4.99 (*1-56402-380-X*) Candlewick Pr.

Crawford, Thomas. Pig Who Saved the Day. (Illus.). (gr. 3-4). 1972. pap. 1.95 (*0-89375-049-2*) Troll Assocs.

Crozat, Francois. I Am a Little Pig. (Illus.). (ps-3). 1991. large 8.95 (*0-8120-6201-9*); miniature 2.95 (*0-8120-6222-1*) Barron.

De Brunhoff, Laurent. The One Pig with Horns. Howard, Richard, tr. from FRE. De Brunhoff, Laurent, illus. LC 78-4917. (gr. k-3). 1979. Pantheon.

Do Pigs Sit in Trees? (Illus.). (ps-2). 1991. PLB 6.95 (*0-8136-5115-8*, TK2260); pap. 3.50 (*0-8136-5615-X*, TK2261) Modern Curr.

Dubanevich, Arlene. Pig William. LC 85-5776. (Illus.). 32p. (gr. k-3). 1990. pap. 3.95 (*0-689-71372-X*, Aladdin) Macmillan Child Grp.

—Pigs in Hiding. Dubanevich, Arlene, illus. LC 83-1409. 32p. (ps-1). 1984. RSBE 13.95 (*0-02-732140-1*, Four Winds) Macmillan Child Grp.

Dunn, Judy. The Little Pig. Dunn, Phoebe, photos by. LC 86-42956. (Illus.). 32p. (ps-3). 1987. Random Bks Yng Read.

Enderle, Judith R. & Tessler, Stephanie G. Pile of Pigs. 24p. (ps-3). 1993. 10.95 (*1-878093-88-6*) Boyds Mills Pr.

Faber, Roger A. Peter Pig Likes to Dig. Faber, Roger A., illus. 32p. (gr. 1-2). Date not set. 12.00 (*1-880122-05-7*) White Stone.

Frost, Erica. The Littlest Pig. Paterson, Diane, illus. LC 85-14121. 48p. (Orig.). (gr. 1-3). 1986. PLB 10.59 (*0-8167-0654-9*); pap. text ed. 3.50 (*0-8167-0655-7*) Troll Assocs.

Gackenbach, Dick. Harvey the Foolish Pig. Gackenbach, Dick, illus. LC 87-15691. 32p. (gr. k-3). 1988. 13.95 (*0-89919-540-7*, Clarion Bks) HM.

Galdone, Paul. The Amazing Pig. LC 80-16990. (Illus.). 32p. (ps-3). 1981. 14.45 (*0-395-29101-1*, Clarion Bks) HM.

—Three Little Pigs. Galdone, Paul, illus. LC 75-123456. (ps-3). 1979. 13.45 (*0-395-28813-4*, Clarion Bks) HM.

—The Three Little Pigs. Galdone, Paul, illus. LC 75-123456. 40p. (Orig.). (ps-3). 1984. pap. 4.95 (*0-89919-275-0*, Clarion Bks) HM.

—Three Little Pigs. (gr. 1 up). 1987. incl. cass. 6.95 (*0-317-64579-X*, Clarion Bks) HM.

Geisert, Arthur. Oink. Geisert, Arthur, illus. LC 90-46123. 32p. 1991. 13.45 (*0-395-55329-6*) HM.

—Oink, Oink. Geisert, Arthur, illus. LC 92-31778. 32p. (gr. k-3). 1993. 13.45 (*0-395-64048-2*) HM.

—Pa's Balloon & Other Pig Tales. Geisert, Arthur, illus. LC 83-18552. 96p. (gr. k-3). 1984. 13.95 (*0-395-35381-5*, 5-86480) HM.

—Pigs from A to Z. Geisert, Arthur, illus. LC 86-18542. 64p. (gr. 2 up). 1986. 16.45 (*0-395-38509-1*) HM.

—Pigs from One to Ten. Geisert, Arthur, illus. LC 92-5097. 32p. (gr. k-3). 1992. 14.45 (*0-395-58519-8*) HM.

Geoghegan, Adrienne. Six Perfectly Different Pigs. Moseng, Elisabeth, illus. 32p. (gr. k up). Date not set. PLB 18.60 (*0-8368-1148-8*) Gareth Stevens Inc.

Gikow, Louise. Piggy & the Missing Penny. (ps-3). 1993. pap. 3.50 (*0-307-11569-0*, Golden Pr) Western Pub.

Gilman, Phoebe. Wonderful Pigs of Jillian Jiggs. 1989. pap. 2.50 (*0-590-41341-4*) Scholastic Inc.

Grace, Eileen, illus. Three Little Pigs. LC 80-27483. 32p. (gr. k-2). 1981. PLB 9.79 (*0-89375-462-5*); pap. text ed. 1.95 (*0-89375-463-3*) Troll Assocs.

Gray, Nigel. Pigs Can't Fly. Vendrell, Carme S., illus. 32p. (ps-1). 1991. 15.95 (*0-86264-272-8*, Pub. by Andersen Pr UK) Trafalgar.

Greenway, Jennifer, retold by. The Three Little Pigs. Dieneman, Debbie, illus. 1991. 6.95 (*0-8362-4904-6*) Andrews & McMeel.

Griffin, Sandi Z. Curly Pig, Vol. 2: Tails with a Moral. Griffin, Sandi Z., illus. 28p. (ps-2). 1993. write for info. (*1-883838-02-9*) S Z Griffin.

Gustafson, Anita. The Case of the Purloined Pork. Gordon, Melinda, illus. 32p. (gr. 2-3). 1985. 7.95 (*0-88700-004-5*) Natl Live Stock.

Hammar, Asa. Fit for Pigs. Moller, Johanna, illus. 40p. (gr. k-3). 1992. 9.95 (*1-56288-265-1*) Checkerboard.

Heine, Helme. The Pigs' Wedding. reissue ed. Heine, Helme, illus. LC 78-57691. 32p. (ps-3). 1986. SBE 14. 95 (*0-689-50409-8*, M K McElderry) Macmillan Child Grp.

—The Pigs' Wedding. Heine, Helme, illus. LC 90-40996. 32p. (gr. k-3). 1991. pap. 4.95 (*0-689-71478-5*, Aladdin) Macmillan Child Grp.

—Seven Wild Pigs. LC 87-3448. (Illus.). 120p. (gr. k up). 1988. SBE 18.95 (*0-689-50439-X*, M K McElderry) Macmillan Child Grp.

Hessell, Jenny. Troublesome Snout. Axelsen, Stephen, illus. LC 92-34274. 1993. 14.00 (*0-383-03662-3*) SRA Schl Grp.

Hoban, Lillian. Mr. Pig & Sonny Too. LC 76-58731. (Illus.). 64p. (gr. k-3). 1977. PLB 13.89 (*0-06-022341-3*) HarpC Child Bks.

Hoban, Russell. The Marzipan Pig. Blake, Quentin, illus. LC 86-24253. 40p. (gr. 1-4). 1987. 13.00 (*0-374-34859-6*) FS&G.

—The Marzipan Pig. Blake, Quentin, illus. 40p. (gr. 1 up). 1989. pap. 3.50 (*0-374-44750-0*) FS&G.

Hofstrand, Mary. By the Sea. (Illus.). 32p. (ps-3). 1990. pap. 3.95 (*0-14-054208-6*, Puffin) Puffin Bks.

Hulbert, Jay. Pete Pig Cleans Up. (Illus.). 32p. (gr. 1-4). 1989. PLB 18.99 (*0-8172-3504-3*); pap. 3.95 (*0-8114-6703-1*) Raintree Steck-V.

Hutchins, Pat. Little Pink Pig. LC 93-18176. (Illus.). 32p. (ps up). 1994. 14.00 (*0-688-12014-8*); PLB 13.93 (*0-688-12015-6*) Greenwillow.

Inkpen, Mick. Gumboot's Chocolatey Day. 1991. pap. 11. 95 (*0-385-41489-7*) Doubleday.

—If I Had a Pig. (ps). 1992. pap. 3.99 (*0-440-40609-9*, Pub. by Yearling Classics) Dell.

Jerris, Tony. The Littlest Piggy. Lyness, Katy, illus. 20p. (Orig.). (ps up). 1992. pap. 9.95 (*0-9630107-2-7*) Little Spruce.

Jeschke, Susan. Perfect the Pig. Jeschke, Susan, illus. 40p. (gr. k-3). 1985. pap. 3.50 (*0-590-43710-0*) Scholastic Inc.

Johnson, Angela. Julius. Pilkey, Dav, photos by. LC 92-24175. (Illus.). 32p. (ps-1). 1993. 14.95 (*0-531-05465-9*); PLB 14.99 (*0-531-08615-1*) Orchard Bks Watts.

Jose, Eduard, adapted by. The Three Little Pigs: A Classic Tale. McDonnell, Janet, tr. Asensio, Augusti, illus. LC 88-35314. 32p. (gr. k-3). 1988. PLB 13.95 (*0-89565-459-8*) Childs World.

Kanno, Wendy. Elmo Pig. Reese, Bob, illus. (gr. k-2). 1984. 7.95 (*0-89868-161-8*); pap. 2.95 (*0-89868-162-6*) ARO Pub.

—Elmo Pig. Reese, Bob, illus. (gr. k-3). 1984. pap. 20.00 (*0-685-50870-6*) ARO Pub.

Kaplan, Carol B. The Picky Pig. Bolinske, Janet L., ed. Quenell, Midge, illus. LC 87-62998. 24p. (Orig.). (ps-k). 1988. spiral bdg. 17.95 (*0-88335-756-9*); pap. 4.95 (*0-88335-078-5*) Milliken Pub Co.

Kasza, Keiko. The Pigs' Picnic. Kasza, Keiko, illus. 32p. (ps-1). 1988. PLB 13.95 (*0-399-21543-3*, Putnam) Putnam Pub Group.

—The Pigs' Picnic. Kasza, Keiko, illus. 32p. (ps-3). 1992. pap. 5.95 (*0-399-21883-1*, Sandcastle Bks) Putnam Pub Group.

Kerins, Anthony. Tat Rabbit's Treasure. Kerins, Anthony, illus. LC 92-32600. 32p. (ps-1). 1993. SBE 14.95 (*0-689-50553-1*, M K McElderry) Macmillan Child Grp.

King-Smith, Deborah. Ace: The Very Important Pig. 112p. 1990. text ed. 8.96 (*1-56956-178-8*) W A T Braille.

King-Smith, Dick. Ace: The Very Important Pig. Hemmant, Lynette, illus. LC 90-1447. 144p. (gr. 2-7). 1990. 13.00 (*0-517-57832-8*); PLB 13.99 (*0-517-57833-6*) Crown Bks Yng Read.

—Babe: The Gallant Pig. Rayner, Mary, illus. LC 84-11429. 176p. (gr. 3-6). 1993. 13.00 (*0-517-55556-5*) Crown Bks Yng Read.

—Daggie Dogfoot. large type ed. 192p. (gr. 1-7). 1990. 14.95 (*0-7451-1229-3*) G K Hall.

—Pigs Might Fly. (gr. 4 up). 1990. pap. 3.95 (*0-14-034537-X*, Puffin) Puffin Bks.

Kiser, SuAnn. The Hog Call to End All! Gurney, John S., illus. LC 93-49392. 32p. (ps-2). 1994. 14.95 (*0-531-06826-9*); PLB 14.99 (*0-531-08676-3*) Orchard Bks Watts.

Kitchen, Bert. Pig in a Barrow. (Illus.). 32p. (ps-3). 1994. pap. 4.99 (*0-14-050341-2*, Puff Pied Piper) Puffin Bks.

Kohler, Jan. Piggy-T Goes to Town. Van Treese, James B., ed. Ingram, tr. 28p. 1992. 9.95 (*1-880416-30-1*) NW Pub.

Krause, Ute. Pig Surprise. Krause, Ute, illus. LC 88-31108. 32p. (ps-3). 1989. 11.95 (*0-8037-0714-2*) Dial Bks Young.

—Pig Surprise. (Illus.). 32p. (ps-3). 1993. pap. 4.50 (*0-14-054592-1*) Puffin Bks.

Kroll, Steven. The Pigrates Clean Up. Bassett, Jeni, illus. LC 92-21823. 32p. (ps-k). 1993. 14.95 (*0-8050-2368-2*, Bks Young Read) H Holt & Co.

Krull, Kathleen. Songs of Praise. LC 87-751091. 1993. pap. 5.95 (*0-15-277109-3*) HarBrace.

Kujoko. Pig Tales: The Adventures of Arnold the Chinese Potbelly Miniature Pig. Clifford, Sandy, illus. 21p. (Orig.). (ps-8). 1988. pap. 4.95 (*0-9623210-0-1*) Kiyoko & Co.

Laird, Donivee. The Three Little Hawaiian Pigs & the Magic Shark. Jossem, Carol, illus. LC 81-67047. 40p. (ps-3). 1981. 7.95x (*0-940350-19-X*) Barnaby Bks.

Laird, Elizabeth. The Day Sidney Ran Off. Reeder, Colin, illus. LC 90-11154. 32p. (gr. k up). 1991. 11.95 (*0-688-10241-7*, Tambourine Bks); PLB 11.88 (*0-688-10242-5*, Tambourine Bks) Morrow.

Lantz, Frances. Mom, There's a Pig in My Bed! 144p. (Orig.). (gr. 4). 1992. pap. 3.50 (*0-380-76112-2*, Camelot) Avon.

Larke, Joe. Two Pigs in Wigs. (ps-3). 1991. 11.95 (*0-9620112-2-3*) Grin A Bit.

Latta, Richard. This Little Pig Had a Riddle. Fay, Anne, ed. Munsinger, Lynn, illus. LC 83-26112. 32p. (gr. 1-5). 1984. PLB 8.95 (*0-8075-7893-2*) A Whitman.

Lawson, John. If Pigs Could Fly. 144p. (gr. 5-9). 1989. 13.45 (*0-395-50928-9*) HM.

Leonard, Marcia. Little Pig's Birthday. Hockerman, Dennis, illus. 32p. 1984. pap. 2.50 (*0-553-15267-X*) Bantam.

Lester, Helen. Me First. Munsinger, Lynn, illus. LC 91-45808. 32p. (ps up). 1992. 13.45 (*0-395-58706-9*) HM.

Levine, Abby. You Push, I Ride. (ps). 1990. pap. 3.95 (*0-14-054180-2*, Puffin) Puffin Bks.

Lies, Brian. Hamlet & the Enormous Chinese Dragon Kite. LC 93-30726. 1994. 14.95 (*0-395-68391-2*) HM.

Lobel, Arnold. Small Pig. Lobel, Arnold, illus. LC 69-10213. 64p. (gr. k-3). 1969. PLB 13.89 (*0-06-023932-8*) HarpC Child Bks.

—A Treeful of Pigs. Lobel, Anita, illus. 32p. (gr. k-3). 1988. pap. 3.95 (*0-590-41280-9*, Blue Ribbon Bks) Scholastic Inc.

Lorenz, Lee. A Weekend in the Country. Lorenz, Lee, illus. 32p. (gr. k-3). 1985. 11.95 (*0-13-947961-9*) P-H.

Lowell, Susan. The Three Little Javelinas. Harris, Jim, illus. LC 92-14232. 32p. (ps-2). 1992. 14.95 (*0-87358-542-9*) Northland AZ.

Lowry, Lois. Anastasia, Ask Your Analyst. LC 83-26687. 128p. (gr. 3-6). 1984. 13.45 (*0-395-36011-0*, 5-90388) HM.

Luttrell, Ida. Milo's Toothache. Giannini, Enzo, illus. LC 91-24315. 40p. (ps-3). 1992. 11.00 (*0-8037-1034-8*); PLB 10.89 (*0-8037-1035-6*) Dial Bks Young.

McPhail, David. Pig Pig & the Magic Photo Album. LC 85-20459. (Illus.). 24p. (ps-3). 1989. pap. 3.95 (*0-525-44539-0*, DCB) Dutton Child Bks.

—Pig Pig Gets a Job. LC 89-25606. (Illus.). 24p. (ps-3). 1990. 12.95 (*0-525-44619-2*, DCB) Dutton Child Bks.

—Pig Pig Goes to Camp. LC 83-1412. (Illus.). 24p. (ps-3). 1983. 12.95 (*0-525-44064-X*, 0966-290, DCB) Dutton Child Bks.

—Pig Pig Goes to Camp. McPhail, David, illus. LC 83-1412. 24p. (ps-3). 1987. pap. 3.95 (*0-525-44302-9*, DCB) Dutton Child Bks.

—Pig Pig Goes to Camp. (ps-3). 1987. pap. 4.99 (*0-14-054778-9*) Dutton Child Bks.

—Pig Pig Grows Up. LC 80-377. (Illus.). 32p. (ps-2). 1980. 13.95 (*0-525-37027-7*, DCB); pap. 3.95 (*0-525-44195-6*, DCB) Dutton Child Bks.
—Pig Pig Grows Up. McPhail, David, illus. (ps-2). 1985. pap. 12.95 incl. cassette (*0-941078-94-9*); incl. cassette 19.95 (*0-941078-96-5*); incl. cassette 4 paperbacks guide 27.95 (*0-941078-95-7*) Live Oak Media.
—Pig Pig Rides. McPhail, David, illus. LC 82-9777. 24p. (ps-3). 1982. 14.00 (*0-525-44024-0*, DCB) Dutton Child Bks.
—Pig Pig Rides. McPhail, David, illus. LC 82-9777. 24p. (ps-3). 1985. pap. 3.95 (*0-525-44222-7*, DCB) Dutton Child Bks.
—Pigs Aplenty, Pigs Galore. LC 92-27986. (ps-2). 1993. 13.99 (*0-525-45079-3*, DCB) Dutton Child Bks.
Magorian, James. The Three Diminutive Pigs. LC 88-71605. (Illus.). 20p. (gr. 1-4). 1988. pap. 3.00 (*0-930674-30-8*) Black Oak.
Marshall, James, retold by. & illus. The Three Little Pigs. LC 88-33411. (ps-3). 1989. 12.95 (*0-8037-0591-3*); PLB 12.89 (*0-8037-0594-8*) Dial Bks Young.
Mason, Margo C. Go Away, Crows. 1989. pap. 8.95 (*0-553-05817-7*, Little Rooster) Bantam.
Milne, A. A. Piglet Is Entirely Surrounded by Water. Shepard, Ernest H., illus. 16p. (ps up). 1991. 7.95 (*0-525-44784-9*, DCB) Dutton Child Bks.
—Pooh & Piglet Go Hunting. Shepard, Ernest H., illus. 32p. 1993. 4.99 (*0-525-45136-6*, DCB) Dutton Child Bks.
Moller, Linda. The Great Pig Escape. 112p. (gr. 3-5). 1994. pap. 6.95 (*0-86241-408-3*, Pub. by Cnngt UK) Trafalgar.
Moore, Inga. The Truffle Hunter. (Illus.). 32p. (ps-3). 1987. 10.95 (*0-916291-09-X*) Kane-Miller Bk.
Morley, Carol. A Spider & a Pig. LC 92-53215. 1993. 14. 95 (*0-316-58405-3*) Little.
Morton, Christine. The Pig That Barked. (Illus.). 32p. (gr. 2-4). 1994. 11.95 (*0-340-56814-3*, Pub. by Hodder & Stoughton UK); pap. 6.95 (*0-340-58659-1*, Pub. by Hodder & Stoughton UK) Trafalgar.
Munsch, Robert. Los Cochinos: (Pigs) Langer, Shirley, tr. Martchenko, Michael, illus. (SPA.). 32p. 1991. pap. 5.95 (*1-55037-191-6*, Pub. by Annick CN) Firefly Bks Ltd.
—Pigs. (CHI., Illus.). 32p. 1993. pap. 5.95 (*1-55037-304-8*, Pub. by Annick CN) Firefly Bks Ltd.
Murphy, Pat. Pigasus. Percy, Graham, photos by. LC 93-32214. (gr. 3 up). 1995. write for info. (*0-8037-1587-0*); lib. bdg. write for info. (*0-8037-1588-9*) Dial Bks Young.
Nagel, Karen. Two Crazy Pigs. Schatell, Brian, illus. 32p. 1992. pap. 2.95 (*0-590-44972-9*, Cartwheel) Scholastic Inc.
Newton-John, Olivia & Hurst, Brian S. A Pig Tale. Murdocca, Sal, illus. LC 92-44116. 1993. pap. 12.00 (*0-671-78778-0*, S&S BFYR) S&S Trade.
Nightingale, Sandy. Pink Pigs A-Plenty. (ps-3). 1992. pap. 14.95 (*0-15-261882-1*, HB Juv Bks) HarBrace.
Offen, Hilda. Nice Work, Little Wolf! LC 91-23741. (Illus.). 32p. (ps-2). 1992. 14.00 (*0-525-44880-2*, DCB) Dutton Child Bks.
Oke, Janette. This Little Pig. Mann, Brenda, illus. 145p. (Orig.). (gr. 1-6). 1991. pap. 4.99 (*0-934998-43-4*) Bethel Pub.
Ostheeren, Ingrid. Fabian Youngpig Sails the World. Romanelli, Serena, illus. James, Alison, tr. from GER. LC 91-16531. (Illus.). 32p. (gr. k-3). 1992. 14.95 (*1-55858-125-1*); lib. bdg. 14.88 (*1-55858-145-6*) North-South Bks NYC.
Outlet Staff. Go to Sleep Little Pig. 1991. 3.99 (*0-517-05684-4*) Random Hse Value.
Paine, Penelope C. Molly's Magic. Maeno, Itoko, illus. 32p. (gr. 1-4). 1994. 16.95 (*1-55942-068-5*, 7660) Marshfilm.
Peck, Robert N. A Day No Pigs Would Die. 144p. (gr. 7 up). 1979. pap. 3.50 (*0-440-92083-3*, LFL) Dell.
Peet, Bill. Chester the Worldly Pig. (Illus.). 48p. (gr. k-3). 1980. 13.45 (*0-395-18470-3*) HM.
—Chester the Worldly Pig. Peet, Bill, illus. (gr. k-3). 1978. pap. 4.80 (*0-395-27271-8*) HM.
Pennington, Eunice. Perry, the Pet Pig. Pennington, Eunice, illus. (gr. 4-7). 1966. 3.00 (*0-685-19374-8*, 911120-06-8); pap. 1.00 (*0-685-19375-6*) Pennington.
Peppe, Rodney. Here Comes Huxley Pig. (ps-3). 1993. pap. 2.99 (*0-440-40794-X*) Dell.
—Huxley Pig the Clown. 1990. 8.95 (*0-385-29819-6*) Doubleday.
—Huxley Pig the Clown. (ps-3). 1993. pap. 2.99 (*0-440-40795-8*) Dell.
—Huxley Pig's Airplane. Peppe, Rodney, illus. (ps-2). 1990. 8.95 (*0-385-30038-7*) Doubleday.
—Huxley Pig's Model Car. (ps). 1991. pap. 8.95 (*0-385-30238-X*) Doubleday.
Peterkin, Mike, illus. Walt Disney's Three Little Pigs: Pop-up Book. LC 93-70940. 10p. (ps-3). 1993. 11.95 (*1-56282-513-5*) Disney Pr.
Peters, Sharon. Rub-a-Dub Suds. Carter, Penny, illus. LC 86-30856. 32p. (gr. k-2). 1988. PLB 7.89 (*0-8167-0984-X*); pap. text ed. 1.95 (*0-8167-0985-8*) Troll Assocs.
Pigs in the House. (Illus.). 42p. (ps-3). 1992. PLB 13.27 (*0-8368-0879-7*) Gareth Stevens Inc.
Pomerantz, Charlotte. The Piggy in the Puddle. Marshall, James, illus. LC 73-6047. 32p. (ps-1). 1974. RSBE 14. 95 (*0-02-774900-2*, Macmillan Child Bk) Macmillan Child Grp.
Porte, Barbara A. Ruthann & Her Pig. LC 88-31452. (Illus.). 96p. (gr. 2-5). 1989. 14.95 (*0-531-05825-5*); PLB 14.99 (*0-531-08425-6*) Orchard Bks Watts.
Potter, Beatrix. The Tale of Little Pig Robinson. 1987. 5.95 (*0-7232-3478-7*); pap. 2.25 (*0-7232-3503-1*) Warne.
—The Tale of Pigling Bland. (Illus.). (ps-3). 1993. pap. 4.99 (*0-7232-4150-3*) Warne.
Potter, Beatrix, created by. Pigling Bland. Thiewes, Sam & Nelson, Anita, illus. 24p. (gr. 2-4). 1992. PLB 10.95 (*1-56674-021-5*, HTS Bks) Forest Hse.
Ramachander, Akumal. Little Pig. Eidregevicius, Stasys, illus. 32p. 1992. 15.00 (*0-670-84350-4*) Viking Child Bks.
Rayner, Mary. Garth Pig & the IceCream Lady. LC 77-1647. (Illus.). 32p. (gr. k-3). 1978. SBE 14.95 (*0-689-30598-2*, Atheneum Child Bk) Macmillan Child Grp.
—Garth Pig Steals the Show. Rayner, Mary, illus. LC 92-24508. (ps-3). 1993. 13.99 (*0-525-45023-8*, DCB) Dutton Child Bks.
—Mr. & Mrs. Pig's Evening Out. Rayner, Mary, illus. LC 76-4476. 32p. (gr. k-3). 1976. SBE 14.95 (*0-689-30530-3*, Atheneum Child Bk) Macmillan Child Grp.
—Mrs. Pig Gets Cross & Other Stories. Rayner, Mary, illus. LC 86-13433. 64p. (ps-3). 1987. 11.95 (*0-525-44280-4*, DCB) Dutton Child Bks.
—Mrs. Pig Gets Cross & Other Stories. LC 86-13433. (Illus.). 64p. (ps-3). 1991. pap. 5.95 (*0-525-44705-9*, Puffin) Puffin Bks.
—Mrs. Pig's Bulk Buy. Rayner, Mary, illus. LC 80-19875. 32p. (gr. k-3). 1981. SBE 14.95 (*0-689-30831-0*, Atheneum Child Bk) Macmillan Child Grp.
—One by One: Garth Pig's Rain Song. Rayner, Mary, illus. 24p. (ps-1). 1994. 5.99 (*0-525-45240-0*) Dutton Child Bks.
—Ten Pink Piglets: Garth Pig's Wall Song. Rayner, Mary, illus. 24p. (ps-1). 1994. 5.99 (*0-685-70795-4*, DCB) Dutton Child Bks.
Reddix, Valerie. Millie & the Mud Hole. Wickstrom, Thor, illus. LC 90-21147. 32p. (ps-3). 1992. 14.00 (*0-688-10212-3*); PLB 13.93 (*0-688-10213-1*) Lothrop.
Rodda, Emily. The Pigs Are Flying! Young, Noela, illus. LC 88-2449. 160p. (gr. 4-6). 1988. Repr. of 1986 ed. 13.95 (*0-688-08130-4*) Greenwillow.
—The Pigs Are Flying! (Illus.). 144p. (gr. 2 up). 1989. pap. 2.95 (*0-380-70555-9*, Camelot) Avon.
Rodger, Elizabeth. Boo to You, Too. LC 92-40023. 1993. write for info. (*0-671-86765-2*, S&S BFYR); pap. 2.95 (*0-671-86766-0*, S&S BFYR) S&S Trade.
Romanova, Natalia. Once There Was a Tree. 1985. 13.95 (*0-8037-0235-3*) Dial Bks Young.
Ruiter, Barbara & Ruiter, Cindy. Pink Is Perfect for Pigs. (Illus.). 32p. (Orig.). 1993. pap. 5.95 (*1-56883-019-X*) Colonial Pr AL.
Rutman, Shereen. The Thin Pig. Mahan, Ben, illus. 16p. (ps). 1993. wkbk. 2.25 (*1-56293-325-6*) McClanahan Bk.
—Top Hog. Neidigh, Sherry, illus. 16p. (ps). 1993. wkbk. 2.25 (*1-56293-322-1*) McClanahan Bk.
Sanford, Monard G. The Free Pigs. Bookless, George, ed. Skivington, Janice, illus. LC 86-63205. 21p. (ps-5). 1987. PLB 13.00 (*0-940273-00-4*) Mill Creek Ent.
Saunders, Susan. The Daring Rescue of Marlon the Swimming Pig. Owens, Gail, illus. LC 87-4633. 64p. (gr. 2-4). 1987. lib. bdg. 6.99 (*0-394-98293-2*); (Random Juv) Random Bks Yng Read.
Scarffe, Bronwen. Traffic Jam. Kelly, Geoff, illus. LC 92-31956. 1993. 3.75 (*0-383-03599-6*) SRA Schl Grp.
Scarry, Richard. Richard Scarry's The Three Little Pigs. (Illus.). 28p. (ps). 1993. bds. 3.25 (*0-307-12521-1*, 12521, Golden Pr) Western Pub.
Schotter, Roni. That Extraordinary Pig of Paris. Catalano, Dominic, illus. LC 92-26223. 32p. (ps-3). 1994. 14.95 (*0-399-22023-2*, Philomel Bks) Putnam Pub Group.
Schwartz, Mary A. Spiffen: A Tale of a Tidy Pig. Levine, Abby, ed. Munsinger, Lynn, illus. LC 88-15. 32p. (ps-3). 1988. PLB 13.95 (*0-8075-7580-1*) A Whitman.
Scieszka, Jon. The True Story of the Three Little Pigs. Smith, Lane, illus. 32p. (ps up). 1989. pap. 15.00 (*0-670-82759-2*) Viking Child Bks.
Sherrow, Victoria. The Pigs Got Out. Eagle, Mike, illus. 24p. (Orig.). (ps). 1992. pap. text ed. 3.00x (*1-56134-161-4*) Dushkin Pub.
Shufflebotham, Anne. This Little Piggy. (gr. 4 up). 1991. 4.95 (*0-85953-445-6*) Childs Play.
Snowhite. 16p. 1991. write for info. incl. cassette (*1-880459-04-3*) Arrow Trad.
Sprock, Inge & Biser, Len. The Land of Flop-Eared Piggies. Sprock, Inge, illus. 32p. (ps-3). 1992. write for info. (*1-880015-30-7*) Petra Pub Co.
Steig, William. The Amazing Bone. Steig, William, illus. LC 76-26479. 32p. (ps-3). 1983. 17.00 (*0-374-30248-0*) FS&G.
—Roland the Minstrel Pig. (Illus.). (gr. k-3). 1968. 12.95 (*0-06-025761-X*) HarpC Child Bks.
Stepto, Michele. Snuggle Piggy & the Magic Blanket. Himmelman, John, illus. LC 86-23943. 24p. (ps-k). 1990. pap. 3.95 (*0-525-44609-5*, DCB) Dutton Child Bks.
Stevenson, James. All Aboard! LC 94-5825. (Illus.). 32p. 1995. write for info. (*0-688-12438-0*); PLB write for info. (*0-688-12439-9*) Greenwillow.
Stevenson, Sucie. Christmas Eve. Stevenson, Sucie, illus. 32p. (ps-2). 1992. pap. 4.99 (*0-440-40729-X*, YB) Dell.
Stine, Bob. The Pigs' Book of World Records. Lippman, Peter, illus. LC 79-5239. 96p. (gr. 3 up). 1980. pap. 4.99 (*0-394-94402-X*) Random Bks Yng Read.
Stolz, Mary. Emmett's Pig. Williams, Garth, illus. LC 58-7763. 64p. (gr. k-3). 1959. PLB 13.89 (*0-06-025856-X*) HarpC Child Bks.
Taylor, Lisa. Pig Called Shrimp. (ps-3). 1993. pap. 7.00 NOP (*0-00-664291-8*) Collins SF.
Teague, Mark. Pigsty. LC 93-21179. (gr. 1-4). 1994. 13. 95 (*0-590-45915-5*) Scholastic Inc.
Tharlet, Eve. Little Pig, Big Trouble. Clements, Andrew, tr. Tharlet, Eve, illus. LC 89-31369. (ps up). 1991. pap. 14.95 (*0-88708-073-1*) Picture Bk Studio.
—Little Pig, Big Trouble. Clements, Andrew, tr. Tharlet, Eve, illus. LC 91-40637. 28p. (gr. k up). 1992. pap. 4.95 (*0-88708-227-0*) Picture Bk Studio.
—Little Pig, Bigger Trouble. Clements, Andrew, tr. Tharlet, Eve, illus. LC 91-40637. 28p. (gr. k up). 1992. pap. 14.95 (*0-88708-237-8*) Picture Bk Studio.
Thompson, Carol. In My Bathroom. LC 89-31720. 1990. 8.95 (*0-385-29856-0*) Doubleday.
—In My Bedroom. 1990. 8.95 (*0-385-29857-9*) Doubleday.
Three Little Pigs. (FRE.). (gr. k-3). 4.25 (*0-685-28448-4*) Fr & Eur.
Three Little Pigs. Facsimile ed. LC 86-33407. (Illus.). 56p. (gr. k-5). 1987. Repr. of 1924 ed. 11.95 (*0-916410-38-2*) A D Bragdon.
Three Little Pigs. 1989. 2.98 (*0-671-06785-0*) S&S Trade.
Three Little Pigs. 1988. 2.98 (*0-671-10041-6*) S&S Trade.
Three Little Pigs. (ps-2). 3.95 (*0-7214-5059-8*) Ladybird Bks.
The True Story of the Three Little Pigs. 1991. incl. audiocassette 22.50 (*0-453-00768-6*) Viking Child Bks.
Tyler, Linda W. The Sick-in-Bed Birthday. Davis, Susan, illus. 32p. (ps-3). 1990. pap. 3.95 (*0-14-050783-3*, Puffin) Puffin Bks.
Ungerer, Tomi. Christmas Eve at the Mellops. Ungerer, Tomi, illus. 32p. (gr. k-3). 1992. pap. 3.99 (*0-440-40728-1*, YB) Dell.
—The Mellops Go Spelunking. Ungerer, Tomi, illus. 32p. (gr. k-3). 1992. pap. 3.99 (*0-440-40727-3*, YB) Dell.
Van, Leeuwan J. Oliver Pig at School. LC 89-25607. (ps-3). 1990. 11.00 (*0-8037-0812-2*); PLB 10.89 (*0-8037-0813-0*) Dial Bks Young.
Van Horne, Carmon. The Three Big Pigs. Van Horne, Carmon, illus. LC 92-91035. 48p. (Orig.). (ps-3). 1993. incl. computer coloring disk 23.95 (*1-882643-02-X*); pap. 18.95 incl. computer coloring disk (*1-882643-03-8*); 12.95 (*1-882643-00-3*); pap. 7.95 (*1-882643-01-1*) V H Visionarts.
Van Leeuwen, Jean. Amanda Pig & Her Big Brother Oliver. Schweninger, Ann, illus. LC 82-70188. 56p. (ps-3). 1982. pap. 4.95 (*0-8037-0016-4*) Dial Bks Young.
—Amanda Pig & Her Big Brother Oliver. Schweninger, Ann, illus. (gr. k-3). 1994. pap. 3.25 (*0-14-037008-0*) Puffin Bks.
—Amanda Pig & Her Brother Oliver. (ps-3). 1992. pap. 4.99 (*0-14-036176-6*) Viking Child Bks.
—Amanda Pig on her Own. LC 90-3504. (Illus.). (ps-3). 1991. 9.95 (*0-8037-0893-9*); PLB 9.89 (*0-8037-0894-7*) Dial Bks Young.
—Amanda Pig on Her Own. Schweninger, Ann, illus. (gr. k-3). 1994. pap. 3.25 (*0-14-037144-3*) Puffin Bks.
—More Tales of Oliver Pig. Lobel, Arnold, illus. LC 80-23289. (ps-3). 1981. PLB 9.89 (*0-8037-8714-6*); pap. 4.95 (*0-8037-8713-8*) Dial Bks Young.
—More Tales of Oliver Pig. Lobel, Arnold, illus. (gr. k-3). 1993. pap. 3.25 (*0-14-036554-0*, Puffin) Puffin Bks.
—Oliver, Amanda, & Grandmother Pig. 1990. pap. 4.95 (*0-8037-0745-2*, Dial Easy to Read) Puffin Bks.
—Oliver & Amanda & the Big Snow. Schweninger, Ann, illus. LC 93-48598. 1995. write for info. (*0-8037-1762-8*); lib. bdg. write for info. (*0-8037-1763-6*) Dial Bks Young.
—Oliver & Amanda's Halloween. Schweninger, Ann, illus. LC 91-30941. 48p. (ps-3). 1992. 11.00 (*0-8037-1237-5*); PLB 10.89 (*0-8037-1238-3*) Dial Bks Young.
—Tales of Amanda Pig. Schweninger, Ann, illus. LC 82-23545. 56p. (ps-3). 1983. pap. 4.95 (*0-8037-8443-0*) Dial Bks Young.
—Tales of Amanda Pig. Schweninger, Ann, illus. LC 93-25615. (gr. k-3). 1994. pap. 3.25 (*0-14-036840-X*, Puffin) Puffin Bks.
—Tales of Amanda Pig: (Cuentos de la Cerdita Amanda) (SPA.). 6.95 (*84-204-4013-2*) Santillana.
—Tales of Oliver Pig. Lobel, Arnold, illus. LC 79-4276. 64p. (ps-3). 1979. PLB 9.89 (*0-8037-8736-7*); pap. 4.95 (*0-8037-8737-5*) Dial Bks Young.
—Tales of Oliver Pig. Lobel, Arnold, illus. (gr. k-3). 1993. pap. 3.25 (*0-14-036549-4*, Puffin) Puffin Bks.
Wahl, Jan. Mrs. Owl & Mr. Pig. Christelow, Eileen, illus. 32p. (gr. k-3). 1991. 13.95 (*0-525-67311-3*, Lodestar Bks) Dutton Child Bks.
Walker, Alice. To Hell with Dying. LC 86-27122. 1993. pap. 5.95 (*0-15-289074-2*) HarBrace.
Waller, John, illus. Where's That Pig? 24p. (ps-2). 1993. 6.95 (*0-8431-3604-9*) Price Stern.
Weston, Martha. Tuck in the Pool. LC 94-7408. 1995. write for info. (*0-395-65479-3*, Clarion Bks) HM.
White, E. B. Charlotte's Web. Williams, Garth, illus. LC 52-9760. (gr. 2-6). 1952. 13.00 (*0-06-026385-7*); PLB 12.89 (*0-06-026386-5*) HarpC Child Bks.
Winthrop, Elizabeth. Sloppy Kisses. Burgess, Anne, illus. (ps-3). 1983. pap. 3.95 (*0-14-050433-8*, Puffin) Puffin Bks.

Wolf, A. The True Story of the Three Little Pigs Gift Set. Scieszka, Jon & Scieszka, Jon, eds. Smith, Lane, illus. 32p. (ps-3). 1992. incl. cass. 24.95 (*0-670-89779-5*) Viking Child Bks.
Wood, Don. Piggies. 28p. (ps-1). 1991. 13.95 (*0-15-256341-5*) HarBrace.
Yolen, Jane. Picnic with Piggins. Dyer, Jane, illus. 32p. (ps-3). 1988. 14.95 (*0-15-261534-2*) HarBrace.
—Picnic with Piggins. LC 87-13564. (ps-3). 1993. pap. 4.95 (*0-15-261535-0*) HarBrace.
—Piggins. (ps-3). 1992. pap. 4.95 (*0-15-261686-1*) HarBrace.
—Piggins & the Royal Wedding. LC 88-5399. (ps-3). 1994. pap. 4.95 (*0-15-200078-X*, HB Juv Bks) HarBrace.
Zemach, Margot. The Three Little Pigs. (Illus.). 32p. (ps up). 1991. pap. 3.95 (*0-374-47717-5*, Sunburst) FS&G.
Zindel, Paul. The Pigman. LC 68-10784. 192p. (gr. 7 up). 1968. PLB 14.89 (*0-06-026828-X*) HarpC Child Bks.

PIGS–POETRY

Lobel, Arnold. The Book of Pigericks. Lobel, Arnold, illus. LC 82-47730. 48p. (gr. k-3). 1983. PLB 14.89 (*0-06-023983-2*) HarpC Child Bks.

PIKE, ZEBULLON MONTGOMERY, 1779-1813

Sinnott, Susan. Zebulon Pike: Up the Mississippi & Out to the Rockies. LC 90-2221. (Illus.). 128p. (gr. 3 up). 1990. PLB 20.55 (*0-516-03058-2*) Childrens.
Stallones, Jared. Zebulon Pike & the Explorers of the American West. Goetzmann, William H., ed. Collins, Michael, intro. by. (Illus.). 112p. (gr. 5 up). 1992. lib. bdg. 18.95 (*0-7910-1317-0*) Chelsea Hse.

PILGRIM FATHERS

Bains, Rae. Pilgrims & Thanksgiving. Wenzel, David, illus. LC 84-2686. 32p. (gr. 3-6). 1985. PLB 9.49 (*0-8167-0222-5*); pap. text ed. 2.95 (*0-8167-0223-3*) Troll Assocs.
Bolognese, Don & Raphael, Elaine. Drawing America: The Story of the First Thanksgiving. 32p. 1991. 10.95 (*0-590-44373-9*, Scholastic Hardcover) Scholastic Inc.
Bowen, Gary. One Year at Plimoth Plantation 1626. Bowen, Gary, illus. LC 93-31016. 88p. (gr. 3-7). 1994. 19.95 (*0-06-022541-6*); PLB 19.89 (*0-06-022542-4*) HarpC Child Bks.
Boynton, Alice B. Priscilla Alden & the Story of the First Thanksgiving. Brook, Bonnie, ed. Kiefer, Christa, illus. 32p. (gr. k-2). 1990. 4.95 (*0-671-69111-2*); PLB 6.95 (*0-671-69105-8*) Silver Pr.
Brown, Margaret W., ed. Homes in the Wilderness: A Pilgrim's Journal of Plymouth Plantation in 1620, by William Bradford & Others of the Mayflower Company. LC 87-27321. (Illus.). 76p. (gr. 5-12). 1988. PLB 16.00 (*0-208-02197-3*, Linnet); pap. 8.95 (*0-208-02269-4*, Linnet) Shoe String.
Dunnahoo, Terry J. The Plymouth Plantation. LC 93-39625. 1995. text ed. 14.95 (*0-87518-627-0*, Dillon) Macmillan Child Grp.
Felloney, Nanette. Meet Me on the Mayflower. (Illus.). 21p. (gr. 3 up). 1992. pap. 3.95 (*1-882684-00-1*) True Tales.
George, Jean C. First Thanksgiving. Locker, Thomas, illus. LC 91-46643. 32p. (ps up). 1993. PLB 15.95 (*0-399-21991-9*, Philomel Bks) Putnam Pub Group.
Greene, Carol. The Pilgrims Are Marching. Dunnington, Tom, illus. LC 88-20219. 32p. (ps-2). 1988. PLB 11.80 (*0-516-08234-5*); pap. 3.95 (*0-516-48234-3*) Childrens.
Licht, Fred. Shelter the Pilgrim. 48p. (gr. 6). 1990. PLB 13.95 (*0-88682-307-2*) Creative Ed.
McGovern, Ann. The Pilgrim's First Thanksgiving. Lasker, Joe, illus. 48p. (gr. k-5). 1984. pap. 2.50 (*0-590-40617-5*) Scholastic Inc.
Richards, Norman. The Story of the Mayflower Compact. Wiskur, Darrell, illus. LC 67-22901. 32p. (gr. 3-6). 1967. pap. 3.95 (*0-516-44625-8*) Childrens.
San Souci, Robert. N. C. Wyeth's Pilgrims. Wyeth, N. C., illus. 40p. (gr. 3-7). 1991. 13.95 (*0-87701-806-5*) Chronicle Bks.
Sewall, Marcia. The Pilgrims of Plimoth. Sewall, Marcia, illus. LC 86-3362. 48p. (gr. 2 up). 1986. SBE 15.95 (*0-689-31250-4*, Atheneum Child Bk) Macmillan Child Grp.
Siegel, Beatrice. Fur Trappers & Traders: The Indians, the Pilgrims, & the Beaver. Bock, William S., illus. LC 80-7671. 64p. (gr. 3-7). 1987. PLB 11.85 (*0-8027-6397-9*) Walker & Co.
—A New Look at the Pilgrims: Why They Came to America. Morris, Douglas, illus. LC 76-57060. 82p. (gr. 3-7). 1987. Repr. of 1977 ed. 13.85 (*0-8027-6292-1*) Walker & Co.
Wade, L. Plymouth: Pilgrims' Story of Survival. 1991. 11. 95s.p. (*0-86592-469-4*) Rourke Enter.
Waters, Kate. Sarah Morton's Day: A Day in the Life of a Pilgrim Girl. Kendall, Russell, photos by. (Illus.). 32p. 1991. pap. 4.95 (*0-590-44871-4*, Blue Ribbon Bks) Scholastic Inc.
Wisler, G. Clifton. This New Land. LC 87-17749. (gr. 5 up). 1987. 13.95 (*0-8027-6726-5*); PLB 14.85 (*0-8027-6727-3*) Walker & Co.

PILGRIM FATHERS–FICTION

Cauper, Eunice. The Story of the Pilgrims & Their Indian Friends: A Thanksgiving Story for Children. 5th ed. Cauper, David, illus. 15p. (gr. k). 1990. pap. 4.95 (*0-9617551-1-3*) E Cauper.
Daugherty, James. The Landing of the Pilgrims. LC 80-21430. (Illus.). 160p. (gr. 5-9). 1963. PLB 8.99 (*0-394-90302-1*); pap. 3.95 (*0-394-84697-4*) Random Bks Yng Read.
Gay, David. Voyage to Freedom: Story of the Pilgrim Fathers. 149p. 1984. pap. 8.95 (*0-85151-384-0*) Banner of Truth.
Hall, Elvajean. Margaret Pumphrey's Pilgrim Stories. 128p. 1991. pap. 2.95 (*0-590-45202-9*, Apple Paperbacks) Scholastic Inc.
Harness, Cheryl. Three Young Pilgrims. Harness, Cheryl, illus. LC 91-7289. 40p. (gr. k-5). 1992. RSBE 15.95 (*0-02-742643-2*, Bradbury Pr) Macmillan Child Grp.
The Seekers. 1987. pap. 3.95 (*0-14-032320-1*, Puffin) Puffin Bks.
Taylor, Helen L. Little Pilgrim's Progress. (gr. 2-7). pap. 6.99 (*0-8024-4926-3*) Moody.
Waters. Sarah Morton's Day: A Day in the Life of a Pilgrim Girl. 1993. pap. 4.95 (*0-590-47400-6*) Scholastic Inc.

PILOTING (AERONAUTICS)

see Airplanes–Piloting

PILOTS, AIRPLANE

see Air Pilots

PILOTS AND PILOTAGE

see also Navigation

Thompson, Jonathon J., Jr. Air Raiders. (Illus.). 75p. (gr. 6-12). 1992. 4.50 (*0-933479-02-6*) Thompson.
—Air Raiders Two. (Illus.). 70p. (gr. 7-12). 1987. 4.60 (*0-933479-10-7*) Thompson.
—Superflyer: Captain John Champion Flyer. 40p. (gr. 3-6). 1992. 3.95 (*0-933479-08-5*) Thompson.

PING-PONG

Parker, Donald & Hewitt, David. Table Tennis. rev. ed. (Illus.). 80p. (gr. 10-12). 1993. pap. 7.95 (*0-7063-7159-3*, Pub. by Ward Lock UK) Sterling.
—Table Tennis. (Illus.). 80p. (gr. 10-12). 1993. pap. 7.95 (*0-7137-2412-9*, Pub. by Blandford Pr UK) Sterling.

PIONEER LIFE

see Frontier and Pioneer Life

PIRATES

Alwin-Hill, Raymond. Treasure Island. LC 91-52607. (Orig.). 1991. pap. 6.00 (*0-88734-412-7*) Players Pr.
Drechsler, Lawrence. The Pirates. LC 85-52401. (Illus., Orig.). (gr. 6 up). pap. write for info. (*0-935143-01-7*) Treadle Pr.
Gibbons, Gail. Pirates: Robbers of the High Seas. LC 92-18375. 1993. 14.95 (*0-316-30975-3*) Little.
Leonard, Marcia. Violet & the Pirates. Wallner, John, illus. 24p. (ps-1). 1992. 4.95 (*0-671-72976-4*); lib. bdg. 6.95 (*0-671-72975-6*) Silver Pr.
McWilliams, Karen. Pirates. LC 87-23711. (Illus.). 64p. (gr. 3-5). 1989. PLB 12.90 (*0-531-10464-8*) Watts.
Marrin, Albert. The Sea Rovers: Pirates, Privateers & Buccaneers. LC 83-15886. (Illus.). 224p. (gr. 6 up). 1984. SBE 15.95 (*0-689-31029-3*, Atheneum Child Bk) Macmillan Child Grp.
Marsh, Carole. Avast, Ye Slobs! The Book of Silly Pirate Trivia. (Illus., Orig.). (gr. 1-12). 1994. PLB 24.95 (*1-55609-281-4*); pap. 14.95 (*0-935326-82-0*) Gallopade Pub Group.
Wright, Rachel. Pirates. LC 90-46110. (Illus.). 32p. (gr. 4-6). 1991. PLB 11.90 (*0-531-14156-X*) Watts.

PIRATES–FICTION

Allen, Pamela. I Wish I Had a Pirate Suit. LC 92-12295. (gr. 4 up). 1993. 3.99 (*0-14-050988-7*) Puffin Bks.
Ambrus, Victor G. Blackbeard the Pirate. (Illus.). 32p. (gr. 2 up). 1990. pap. 5.95 (*0-19-272220-4*) OUP.
Asch, Frank. Pearl's Pirates. Asch, Frank, illus. LC 86-19621. 160p. (gr. k-3). 1987. pap. 13.95 (*0-385-29546-4*) Delacorte.
—Pearl's Pirates. (gr. k-6). 1989. pap. 3.25 (*0-440-40245-X*, YB) Dell.
Avi. Captain Grey. Mikolaycak, Charles, illus. LC 76-41182. (gr. 5 up). 1977. 5.95 (*0-394-83484-4*) Pantheon.
—Captain Grey. LC 92-37643. 160p. 1993. 14.00 (*0-688-12233-7*) Morrow Jr Bks.
Bashful Bard. Pirates. Bashful Bard, illus. LC 89-84960. 24p. (Orig.). (ps-1). 1989. pap. 3.99 (*1-877906-00-X*) Kenney Pubns.
Binato, Leonardo. What's Hidden in the Pirate's Chest? 12p. (ps-3). 1992. 4.95 (*1-56566-009-9*) Thomasson-Grant.
Bradman, Tony. The Bluebeards: Revenge at Ryan's Reef. Murphy, Rowan B., illus. 52p. (ps-3). 1992. pap. 3.50 (*0-8120-4903-9*) Barron.
Carris, Joan D. A Ghost of a Chance. Henry, Paul, illus. 160p. (gr. 3-7). 1992. 14.95 (*0-316-13016-8*) Little.
Cartwright, Pauline. Jake Was a Pirate. Sofilas, Mark, illus. LC 93-26216. 1994. 4.25 (*0-383-03754-9*) SRA Schl Grp.
Cole, Babette. The Trouble with Uncle. (Illus.). (ps-3). 1992. 14.95 (*0-316-15190-4*) Little.
Cox, David. Captain Ding, the Double-Decker Pirate. Round, Graham, illus. 32p. (ps-1). 1993. 17.95 (*0-09-176365-7*, Pub. by Hutchinson UK) Trafalgar.
Cox, Greg. The Pirate Paradox. 1991. pap. 3.50 (*0-06-106016-X*, Harp PBks) HarpC.
Dadey, Debbie. Pirates Don't Wear Pink Sunglasses. (gr. 4-7). 1994. pap. 2.95 (*0-590-47298-4*) Scholastic Inc.
Dewey, Ariane. Lafitte, the Pirate. LC 92-43787. (Illus.). 48p. (gr. 1 up). 1993. pap. 4.95 (*0-688-04578-2*, Mulberry) Morrow.
Drew, David. Ah, Treasure! Tulloch, Coral, illus. LC 92-21455. 1993. 3.75 (*0-383-03611-9*) SRA Schl Grp.
Dupasquier, Philippe. Andy's Pirate Ship. 1994. 11.95 (*0-8050-3154-5*) H Holt & Co.
Ferguson, Virginia & Durkin, Peter. Yo Ho! Yo Ho! Lau, Yen, illus. LC 93-20018. 1994. write for info. (*0-383-03729-8*) SRA Schl Grp.
Fox, Mem. Boris. Brown, Kathryn, illus. LC 92-8015. 1994. 13.95 (*0-15-289612-0*) HarBrace.
Gale, Cathy. Pirates! Gale, Cathy, illus. 32p. (ps-3). 1994. pap. 2.99 (*1-56402-406-7*) Candlewick Pr.
Giff, Patricia R. The Gift of the Pirate Queen. Rutherford, Jenny, illus. 160p. (gr. 4-8). 1983. pap. 3.25 (*0-440-43046-1*, Pub. by Yearling Classics) Dell.
Homer, Larona. Blackbeard the Pirate & Other Stories of the Pine Barrens. Bock, William S., illus. 96p. (gr. 3-5). 1987. pap. 8.95 (*0-912608-04-8*) Mid Atlantic.
Hutchins, Pat. One-Eyed Jake. Hutchins, Pat, illus. 32p. (ps up). 1994. pap. 4.95 (*0-688-13113-1*, Mulberry) Morrow.
Isadora, Rachel. The Pirates of Bedford Street. LC 84-25904. (Illus.). 32p. (ps-3). 1988. 11.95 (*0-688-05206-1*); lib. bdg. 11.88 (*0-688-05208-8*) Greenwillow.
Kennedy, Richard. Amy's Eyes. Egielski, Richard, illus. LC 82-48841. 448p. (ps up). 1985. 15.00 (*0-06-023219-6*) HarpC Child Bks.
Kroll, Steven. The Pigrates Clean Up. Bassett, Jeni, illus. LC 92-21823. 32p. (ps-k). 1993. 14.95 (*0-8050-2368-2*, Bks Young Read) H Holt & Co.
Leigh, S. Uncle Pete the Pirate. (Illus.). 32p. (ps). 1994. PLB 12.96 (*0-88110-713-1*, Usborne); pap. 4.95 (*0-7460-1529-1*, Usborne) EDC.
Lofgren, Ulf. Alvin the Pirate. Lotfren, Ulf, illus. 32p. (ps-3). 1990. PLB 18.95 (*0-87614-402-4*) Carolrhoda Bks.
—Alvin the Pirate: Picture Book. (ps-3). 1991. pap. 5.95 (*0-87614-551-9*) Carolrhoda Bks.
McAllister, Angela. The Babies of Cockle Bay. Jenkin-Pearce, Susie, illus. 32p. (ps-3). 1994. incl. dust jacket 13.95 (*0-8120-6424-0*); pap. 5.95 (*0-8120-1952-0*) Barron.
MacDonald, Marianne. The Pirate Queen. Smith, Jan, illus. 32p. (ps-3). 1992. incl. dust jacket 12.95 (*0-8120-6288-4*); pap. 5.95 (*0-8120-4952-7*) Barron.
MacGill-Callahan, Sheila. How the Boats Got Their Sails. LC 93-45966. 1995. write for info. (*0-8037-1541-2*); lib. bdg. write for info. (*0-8037-1542-0*) Dial Bks Young.
McNaughton, Colin. Captain Abdul's Pirate School. McNaughton, Colin, illus. LC 93-21293. 40p. (ps up). 1994. 16.95 (*1-56402-429-6*) Candlewick Pr.
Mahy, Margaret. The Horrendous Hullabaloo. MacCarthy, Patricia, illus. 32p. (ps-3). 1992. 13.00 (*0-670-84547-7*) Viking Child Bks.
—The Pirates' Mixed-up Voyage. Chamberlain, Margaret, illus. LC 92-3931. 192p. (gr. 4-8). 1993. 13.99 (*0-8037-1350-9*) Dial Bks Young.
Marston, Elsa. Cynthia & the Runaway Gazebo. Henstra, Friso, illus. LC 91-32548. 32p. (gr. k-4). 1992. 14.00 (*0-688-10282-4*, Tambourine Bks); PLB 13.93 (*0-688-10283-2*, Tambourine Bks) Morrow.
Moerbeek, Kees. When the Wild Pirates Go Sailing. (Illus.). 12p. (ps up). 1992. 4.95 (*0-8431-3450-X*) Price Stern.
Nelson, Ginger K. Pirate's Revenge. Kratoville, Betty L., ed. (Illus.). 64p. (gr. 3-9). 1989. PLB 4.95 (*0-87879-654-1*) High Noon Bks.
Osborne, Mary P. Pirates Past Noon. Murdocca, Sal, illus. LC 93-2039. 80p. (gr. 1-4). 1994. PLB 9.99 (*0-679-92425-6*); pap. 2.99 (*0-679-82425-1*) Random.
Parker, Beth. Thomas Knew There Were Pirates Living in the Bathroom. Mansfield, Renee, illus. 28p. (ps-3). 1990. 12.95 (*0-88753-224-1*, Pub. by Black Moss Pr CN); pap. 4.95 (*0-88753-201-2*, Pub. by Black Moss Pr CN) Firefly Bks Ltd.
Pyle, Howard. Tales of Pirates & Buccaneers. Pyle, Howard, illus. LC 93-44689. 1994. write for info. (*0-517-10162-9*) Random Hse Value.
Ryan, John. Pugwash & the Ghost Ship. Ryan, John, illus. LC 68-23218. (gr. k-3). 1968. 21.95 (*0-87599-146-7*) S G Phillips.
Scarry, Richard. Pie Rats Ahoy! LC 92-50998. 32p. (ps-1). 1994. PLB 7.99 (*0-679-94760-4*); pap. 3.50 (*0-679-84760-X*) Random Bks Yng Read.
Schubert, Ingrid & Schubert, Dieter. Wild Will. LC 93-2484. 1993. 17.50 (*0-87614-816-X*) Carolrhoda Bks.
Scieszka, Jon. The Not-So-Jolly-Roger. Smith, Lane, illus. 64p. (gr. 3-7). 1991. 11.00 (*0-670-83754-7*) Viking Child Bks.
—The Not-So-Jolly Roger. Smith, Lane, illus. 64p. (gr. 2-6). 1993. pap. 2.99 (*0-14-034684-8*, Puffin) Puffin Bks.
Sharrat, Nick. Mrs. Pirate. Sharratt, Nick, illus. LC 93-878. 24p. (ps). 1994. 8.95 (*1-56402-249-8*) Candlewick Pr.
Shub, Elizabeth. Cutlass in the Snow. Isadora, Rachel, illus. LC 85-5442. 48p. (gr. 1-4). 1986. 11.95 (*0-688-05927-9*); PLB 11.88 (*0-688-05928-7*) Greenwillow.
Simons, Scott & Simons, Jamie. Why Dolphins Call: A Story of Dionysus. Winograd, Deborah, illus. 32p. (gr. 2-5). 1992. 8.95 (*0-671-69125-2*); PLB 10.95 (*0-671-69121-X*) Silver Pr.
Slote, Elizabeth. Ana & Bold Berto. LC 93-37534. 1995. write for info. (*0-688-12980-3*, Tambourine Bks); PLB write for info. (*0-688-12981-1*, Tambourine Bks) Morrow.
Sohl, Marcia & Dackerman, Gerald. Treasure Island. 16p. (gr. 4-10). 1976. pap. 2.95 (*0-88301-106-9*); pap. 1.25 student activity bk. (*0-88301-185-9*) Pendulum Pr.
Stevenson, Robert Louis. Reader's Digest Best Loved Books for Young Readers: Treasure Island. Ogburn, Jackie, ed. Glanzman, Louis S., illus. 144p. (gr. 4-12). 1989. 3.99 (*0-945260-23-7*) Choice Pub NY.

—Treasure Island. (gr. 7 up). 1962. pap. 2.95 (*0-8049-0002-7*, CL-2) Airmont.
—Treasure Island. (Illus.). (gr. 1-9). 1947. deluxe ed. 13. 95 (*0-448-06025-6*, G&D) Putnam Pub Group.
—Treasure Island. 224p. (gr. 2-5). 1984. pap. 2.95 (*0-14-035016-0*, Puffin) Puffin Bks.
—Treasure Island. Letley, Emma, ed. (gr. 7-12). 1985. pap. 3.95 (*0-19-281681-0*) OUP.
—Treasure Island. (gr. k-6). 1986. 7.98 (*0-685-16845-X*, 618168) Random Hse Value.
—Treasure Island. reissued ed. Norby, Lisa, adapted by. Fernandez, Fernando, illus. LC 89-70039. 96p. (Orig.). (gr. 2-6). 1990. PLB 5.99 (*0-679-90402-6*, Bullseye Bks); pap. 2.99 (*0-679-80402-1*, Bullseye Bks) Random Bks Yng Read.
—Treasure Island. 272p. 1990. pap. 2.50 (*0-8125-0508-5*) Tor Bks.
—Treasure Island. Wyeth, N. C., illus. 274p. (gr. 5 up). 1992. Repr. of 1911 ed. 24.95 (*1-879329-07-7*) Time Warner Libraries.
—Treasure Island. Peake, Mervyn, illus. LC 92-53174. 240p. 1992. 12.95 (*0-679-41800-8*, Evrymans Lib Childs Class) Knopf.
—Treasure Island. LC 92-29791. 160p. 1993. pap. 1.00 (*0-486-27559-0*) Dover.
—Treasure Island. Wyeth, N. C., illus. LC 89-43034. 274p. (gr. 5 up). 1993. Repr. of 1989 ed. 16.95 (*1-56138-264-7*) Running Pr.
—Treasure Island. McNaughton, Colin, illus. LC 93-18941. 272p. (gr. 4-8). 1993. 15.95 (*0-8050-2773-4*, Bks Young Read) H Holt & Co.
—Treasure Island. (gr. 4-7). 1993. pap. 4.95 (*0-8114-6844-5*) Raintree Steck-V.
—Treasure Island. Price, Norman, illus. LC 93-50905. 1994. write for info. (*0-448-40562-8*, G&D) Putnam Pub Group.
—Treasure Island. (gr. 4 up). 1994. 4.98 (*0-8317-1649-5*) Smithmark.
Townsend, Tom. Powderhorn Passage: Sequel to Where the Pirates Are, Vol. 3. Roberts, Melissa, ed. (gr. 4-7). 1988. 10.95 (*0-89015-642-5*, Pub. by Panda Bks) Sunbelt Media.
Treasure Island. (Illus.). 24p. (Orig.). (gr. k up). 1993. pap. 2.50 (*1-56144-103-1*, Honey Bear Bks) Modern Pub NYC.
Tucker, Kathy. Do Pirates Take Baths? Levine, Abby, ed. Westcott, Nadine B., illus. LC 94-4109. 32p. (ps-1). 1994. PLB 14.95 (*0-8075-1696-1*) A Whitman.
Vinton, Iris. Look Out for Pirates. LC 61-7790. (Illus.). 72p. (gr. 1-2). 1961. lib. bdg. 8.99 (*0-394-90022-7*) Beginner.
Wilhelm, Hans. Pirates Ahoy! Wilhelm, Hans, illus. LC 87-30197. 40p. (ps-3). 1987. 5.95 (*0-8193-1162-6*) Parents.
Wood, A. J. The Treasure Hunt. Downer, Maggie, illus. LC 92-5515. 32p. (ps-4). 1992. 13.95 (*1-56566-018-8*) Thomasson-Grant.
Woychuk, Denis. Pirates! LC 91-3387. (Illus.). (ps-3). 1992. 14.00 (*0-688-10336-7*); PLB 13.93 (*0-688-10337-5*) Lothrop.
Yolen, Jane. The Ballad of the Pirate Queens. Shannon, David, illus. LC 94-7874. 1995. write for info. (*0-15-200710-5*) HarBrace.

PITTSBURGH PIRATES (BASEBALL TEAM)

Goodman, Michael. Pittsburgh Pirates. 48p. (gr. 4-10). 1992. PLB 14.95 (*0-88682-454-0*) Creative Ed.
Pittsburgh Pirates. (gr. 4-7). 1993. pap. 1.49 (*0-553-56426-9*) Bantam.

PIUS 5TH, SAINT, POPE, 1566-1572

Daughters of St. Paul. No Place for Defeat. (gr. 3-9). 1987. 2.00 (*0-8198-5100-0*) St Paul Bks.

PIUS 10TH, SAINT, POPE, 1835-1914

Windeatt, Mary F. St. Pius X. Harmon, Gedge, illus. 32p. (gr. 1-5). 1989. Repr. of 1954 ed. wkbk. 3.00 (*0-89555-371-6*) TAN Bks Pubs.

PIZARRO, FRANCISCO, 1470?-1541

Bernhard, Brendan. Pizarro, Orellana, & the Exploration of the Amazon. Goetzmann, William H., ed. Collins, Michael, intro. by. (Illus.). 112p. (gr. 5 up). 1991. lib. bdg. 18.95 (*0-7910-1305-7*) Chelsea Hse.

PLACE NAMES

see Names, Geographical

PLANE GEOMETRY

see Geometry

PLANE TRIGONOMETRY

see Trigonometry

PLAGUE

Biel, Timothy L. The Black Death. LC 89-112269. (Illus.). 64p. (gr. 5-8). 1989. PLB 11.95 (*1-56006-001-8*) Lucent Bks.
Turner, Derek. The Black Death. Reeves, Marjorie, ed. (Illus.). 96p. (gr. 7-12). 1978. pap. text ed. 10.02 (*0-582-31097-0*, 78068) Longman.

PLANETS

see also Life on Other Planets; Solar System; Stars; also names of planets, e.g. Venus (Planet)

Asimov, Isaac. How Did We Find Out about Neptune? Kors, Erika, illus. 64p. (gr. 5 up). 1990. 12.95 (*0-8027-6981-0*); lib. bdg. 13.85 (*0-8027-6982-9*) Walker & Co.
Asimov, Isaac, et al. A Distant Puzzle: The Planet Uranus. rev. & updated ed. (Illus.). (gr. 3 up). 1994. PLB 17.27 (*0-8368-1136-4*) Gareth Stevens Inc.
Bailey, Donna. Facts About: The Far Planets. (ps-3). 1993. pap. 4.95 (*0-8114-5200-X*) Raintree Steck-V.
—Facts About: The Near Planets. (ps-3). 1993. pap. 4.95 (*0-8114-5201-8*) Raintree Steck-V.
—The Far Planets. LC 90-40081. (Illus.). 48p. (gr. 2-6). 1990. PLB 19.97 (*0-8114-2524-X*) Raintree Steck-V.
—The Near Planets. LC 90-40078. (Illus.). 48p. (gr. 2-6). 1990. PLB 19.97 (*0-8114-2523-1*) Raintree Steck-V.
Barrett, Norman S. The Picture World of Planets. (Illus.). 32p. (gr. k-4). 1990. PLB 12.40 (*0-531-14054-7*) Watts.
Bendick, Jeanne. Moons & Rings: Companions to the Planets. (Illus.). 32p. (gr. k-2). 1991. PLB 12.90 (*1-56294-000-7*); pap. 3.95 (*1-878841-54-8*) Millbrook Pr.
Berger, Melvin. A Tour of the Planets. 16p. (gr. 2-4). 1994. pap. 14.95 (*1-56784-207-0*) Newbridge Comms.
Bergstralh, Jay T., et al, eds. Uranus. LC 90-21185. 1076p. 1991. 75.00x (*0-8165-1208-6*) U of Ariz Pr.
Branley, Franklyn M. The Planets in Our Solar System. rev. ed. Madden, Don, illus. LC 86-47530. 32p. (ps-3). 1987. (Crowell Jr Bks); PLB 14.89 (*0-690-04581-6*) HarpC Child Bks.
—Uranus: The Seventh Planet. Buchanan, Yvonne, illus. LC 87-35046. 64p. (gr. 3-6). 1988. (Crowell Jr Bks); PLB 12.89 (*0-690-04687-1*, Crowell Jr Bks) HarpC Child Bks.
Brewer, Duncan. Planet Guides, 8 vols. (Illus.). 512p. (gr. 5-9). 1992. Set. PLB 127.60 (*1-85435-368-3*) Marshall Cavendish.
Burrows, William E. Mission to Deep Space: Voyager's Interplanetary Odyssey. LC 92-29746. 1993. text ed. write for info. (*0-7167-6500-4*) W H Freeman.
Discovery Atlas of Planets & Stars. LC 93-16805. 1993. write for info. (*0-528-83580-7*) Rand McNally.
Estalella, Robert. Planets & Satellites. (Illus.). 32p. (gr. 4-8). 1993. 12.95 (*0-8120-6372-4*); pap. 6.95 (*0-8120-1737-4*) Barron.
Eugene, Toni. Descubre Estrellas y Planetas. University of Mexico City Staff, tr. from SPA. O'Neill, Pablo M. & Robare, Lorie, illus. 48p. (gr. 3-8). 1993. PLB 16.95 (*1-56674-052-5*, HTS Bks) Forest Hse.
—Discover Stars & Planets. (Illus.). 48p. (gr. 3-6). 1992. PLB 14.95 (*1-878363-71-9*, HTS Bks) Forest Hse.
Fowler, Allan. Los Planetas Del Sol - The Sun's Family of Planets. LC 92-7405. (SPA., Illus.). 32p. (ps-2). 1993. big bk. 22.95 (*0-516-59631-4*); PLB 10.75 (*0-516-36004-3*); pap. 3.95 (*0-516-56004-2*) Childrens.
—The Sun's Family of Planets. LC 92-7405. (Illus.). 32p. (ps-2). 1992. PLB 10.75 (*0-516-06004-X*); big bk. 22. 95 (*0-516-49631-X*) Childrens.
—The Sun's Family of Planets. LC 92-7405. (Illus.). 32p. (ps-2). 1993. pap. 3.95 (*0-516-46004-8*) Childrens.
Fradin, Dennis B. Jupiter. LC 89-9983. 48p. (gr. k-4). 1989. PLB 12.85 (*0-516-01173-1*); pap. 4.95 (*0-516-41173-X*) Childrens.
—Neptune. LC 89-71174. (Illus.). 48p. (gr. k-4). 1990. PLB 12.85 (*0-516-01187-1*); pap. 4.95 (*0-516-41187-X*) Childrens.
—Pluto. LC 89-9925. 48p. (gr. k-4). 1989. PLB 12.85 (*0-516-01175-8*); pap. 4.95 (*0-516-41175-6*) Childrens.
—Saturn. LC 88-39117. (Illus.). 48p. (gr. k-4). 1989. PLB 12.85 (*0-516-01166-9*); pap. 4.95 (*0-516-41166-7*) Childrens.
—Uranus. LC 89-9984. 48p. (gr. k-4). 1989. PLB 12.85 (*0-516-01177-4*); pap. 4.95 (*0-516-41177-2*) Childrens.
Gabriele. Planets. 1986. pap. 1.95 (*0-911211-61-6*) Penny Lane Pubns.
Gibbons, Gail. The Planets. LC 92-44429. (Illus.). 32p. (ps-3). 1993. reinforced bdg. 15.95 (*0-8234-1040-4*); pap. 5.95 (*0-8234-1133-8*) Holiday.
Glyman, Caroline A. What's above the Sky? A Book about the Planets. Biser, Dee, illus. LC 92-10247. 32p. (gr. k-3). 1992. PLB 12.95 (*1-878363-76-X*) Forest Hse.
Greenberg, Judith E. & Carey, Helen H. Space. Karpinski, Rick, illus. 32p. (gr. 2-4). 1990. 10.95 (*0-8172-3754-2*) Raintree Steck-V.
Halliday, Ian. Saturn. 48p. 1989. 13.95 (*0-8160-2049-3*) Facts on File.
Herbst, Judith. The Golden Book of Stars & Planets. LaPadula, Tom, illus. 48p. (gr. 3-7). 1988. write for info. (*0-307-15572-2*) Western Pub.
Jackson, Kim. The Planets. Watling, James, illus. LC 84-16451. 32p. (gr. k-2). 1985. lib. bdg. 11.59 (*0-8167-0450-3*); pap. text ed. 2.95 (*0-8167-0451-1*) Troll Assocs.
Krulik, Nancy E. My Picture Book of the Planets. (ps-3). 1991. pap. 2.50 (*0-590-43907-3*) Scholastic Inc.
Lambert, David. Stars & Planets. Donohoe, Bill & Townsend, Tony, illus. LC 93-28282. 1994. PLB 19.97 (*0-8114-9246-X*) Raintree Steck-V.
Lampton, Christopher. Jupiter. LC 93-31094. 1994. text ed. 13.95 (*0-89686-756-0*, Crestwood Hse) Macmillan Child Grp.
Landau, Elaine. Jupiter. LC 90-13099. (Illus.). 64p. (gr. 3-5). 1991. PLB 12.90 (*0-531-20015-9*) Watts.
—Neptune. LC 90-13098. (Illus.). 64p. (gr. 3-5). 1991. PLB 12.90 (*0-531-20014-0*) Watts.
—Saturn. LC 90-13081. (Illus.). 64p. (gr. 3-5). 1991. PLB 12.90 (*0-531-20013-2*) Watts.
Lauber, Patricia. Journey to the Planets. 2nd, rev. ed. NASA Staff, illus. LC 90-33102. 1990. PLB 16.99 (*0-517-58125-6*) Crown Bks Yng Read.
Leedy, Loreen. Postcards from Pluto: A Tour of the Solar System. LC 92-32658. (Illus.). 32p. (ps-3). 1993. reinforced bdg. 15.95 (*0-8234-1000-5*) Holiday.
McDonald, Mary A. Jupiter. LC 93-3595. (SPA & ENG., Illus.). 1993. 15.95 (*1-56766-022-3*) Childs World.
Maynard. Stars & Planets. (Illus.). 32p. (gr. 4-8). 1976. PLB 13.96 (*0-88110-313-6*); pap. 6.95 (*0-86020-094-9*) EDC.
Morrison, Rob & Morrison, James. Monsters! Just Imagine. Crossett, Warren, illus. LC 93-26927. 1994. 4.25 (*0-383-03763-8*) SRA Schl Grp.
Muirden, James. Planets. LC 93-51250. 32p. (gr. 2-5). 1994. 3.95 (*1-85697-507-X*, Kingfisher LKC) LKC.
Murray, Peter. The Planets. LC 92-20016. (Illus.). (gr. 2-6). 1992. PLB 14.95 (*0-89565-975-1*) Childs World.
—Saturn. LC 92-41542. (ENG & SPA.). (gr. 2-6). 1993. 15.95 (*1-56766-014-2*) Childs World.
Radlauer, Ruth & Stembridge, Charles. Planets. LC 83-21043. (Illus.). 48p. (gr. 3 up). 1984. pap. 4.95 (*0-516-47838-9*) Childrens.
Ride, Sally. Voyager: An Adventure to the Edge of the Solar System. NASA Staff, photos by. LC 91-32495. (Illus.). 36p. (gr. 2-6). 1992. 14.00 (*0-517-58157-4*); PLB 14.99 (*0-517-58158-2*) Crown Bks Yng Read.
Ridpath, Ian. Atlas of Stars & Planets. LC 92-32463. 80p. (gr. 5-10). 1993. 16.95 (*0-8160-2926-1*) Facts on File.
Robinson, Fay. Space Probes to the Planets. Grant, Christy, ed. LC 92-10792. (Illus.). 32p. (gr. k-3). 1993. 14.95g (*0-8075-7548-8*) A Whitman.
Robson, Denny A. The Planets. LC 91-10315. (Illus.). 32p. (gr. k-4). 1991. PLB 11.90 (*0-531-17335-6*, Gloucester Pr) Watts.
Rosen, Sidney. Can You Find a Planet? 40p. (gr. k-2). 1991. lib. bdg. 19.95 (*0-87614-683-3*) Carolrhoda Bks.
Schecter, Darrow. I Can Read About Planets. new ed. LC 78-66272. (Illus.). (gr. 3-6). 1979. pap. 2.50 (*0-89375-215-0*) Troll Assocs.
Shepherd, Donna W. Uranus. LC 93-6097. (Illus.). 64p. (gr. 5-8). 1994. PLB 12.90 (*0-531-20167-8*) Watts.
Simon, Seymour. Uranus. LC 86-31223. (Illus.). 32p. (ps-3). 1987. 13.00 (*0-688-06582-1*); lib. bdg. 12.88 (*0-688-06583-X*, Morrow Jr Bks) Morrow Jr Bks.
—Uranus. LC 86-31223. (Illus.). 32p. (ps up). 1990. pap. 5.95 (*0-688-09929-7*, Mulberry) Morrow.
Sims, Lesley. The Planets. LC 93-28660. 1994. PLB 18. 99 (*0-8114-5506-8*) Raintree Steck-V.
Sorensen, Lynda. Planets. LC 93-14874. (ps-6). 1993. 12. 67 (*0-86593-274-3*); 9.50s.p. (*0-685-66588-7*) Rourke Corp.
Verba, Joan M. Voyager: Exploring the Outer Planets. 64p. (gr. 5 up). 1991. PLB 19.95 (*0-8225-1597-0*) Lerner Pubns.
Vogt, Gregory. Planets. 1995. PLB write for info. (*0-8050-3249-5*); pap. write for info. (*0-8050-3248-7*) H Holt & Co.
Vogt, Gregory L. Jupiter. LC 92-30187. (Illus.). 32p. (gr. 2-4). 1993. PLB 12.90 (*1-56294-329-4*); pap. 6.95 (*1-56294-799-0*) Millbrook Pr.
—Neptune. LC 92-30183. (Illus.). 32p. (gr. 2-4). 1993. PLB 12.90 (*1-56294-331-6*); pap. 6.95 (*1-56294-800-8*) Millbrook Pr.
—Saturn. LC 92-30188. (Illus.). 48p. (gr. 2-4). 1993. PLB 12.90 (*1-56294-332-4*); pap. 6.95 (*1-56294-801-6*) Millbrook Pr.
—Uranus. LC 92-30184. (Illus.). 32p. (gr. 2-4). 1993. PLB 12.90 (*1-56294-330-8*); pap. 6.95 (*1-56294-802-4*) Millbrook Pr.

PLANETS, LIFE ON OTHER

see Life on Other Planets

PLANNED PARENTHOOD

see Birth Control

PLANNING, CITY

see City Planning

PLANNING, ECONOMIC

see Economic Policy
see names of countries, states, etc. with the subdivision Economic Policy, e.g. U. S.–Economic Policy

PLANNING, NATIONAL

see Economic Policy
see names of countries with the subdivision Economic Policy, Social Policy; e.g. U. S.–Economic Policy; U. S. –Social policy

PLANS

see Geometrical Drawing; Map Drawing; Maps; Mechanical Drawing

PLANT ANATOMY

see Botany–Anatomy

PLANT PHYSIOLOGY

see also Growth (Plants)

Julivert, M. Angels. The Life of Plants. (Illus.). 1994. 13. 95 (*0-7910-2129-7*, Am Art Analog) Chelsea Hse.
Wexler, Jerome. Wonderful Pussy Willows. Wexler, Jerome, photos by. LC 91-32262. (Illus.). 32p. (ps-3). 1992. 14.50 (*0-525-44867-5*, DCB) Dutton Child Bks.

PLANT PROPAGATION

see also Seeds

PLANTATION LIFE

McKissack, Patricia C. & McKissack, Frederick. Christmas in the Big House, Christmas in the Quarters. Thompson, John, illus. LC 92-33831. (gr. 3-8). 1994. 15.95 (*0-590-43027-0*) Scholastic Inc.

Stone, Lynn. Plantations. LC 93-771. (ps-6). 1993. 15.93 (*0-86625-446-3*); 11.95s.p. (*0-685-66594-1*) Rourke Pubns.

PLANTING

see Agriculture; Gardening

PLANTS

see also Desert Plants; Flowers; Fresh-Water Plants; Gardening; House Plants; Marine Plants; Shrubs; Weeds also names of plants (e.g. Mosses, etc.)

Aldis, Rodney. Towns & Cities. LC 91-35801. (Illus.). 48p. (gr. 5 up). 1992. text ed. 13.95 RSBE (*0-87518-496-0*, Dillon) Macmillan Child Grp.

Andersen, Honey. Which Comes First? Berry, Ruth, illus. LC 93-18113. 1994. write for info. (*0-383-03726-3*) SRA Schl Grp.

Animals, Birds, Bees, & Flowers. 24p. 1989. 5.99 (*0-517-68230-3*) Random Hse Value.

Arvetis, Chris & Palmer, Carole. Forests. LC 93-500. (Illus.). 1993. write for info. (*0-528-83573-4*) Rand McNally.

Bates, Jeffrey W. Seeds to Plants: Projects with Biology. LC 90-45659. (Illus.). 32p. (gr. 5-9). 1991. PLB 12.40 (*0-531-17292-9*, Gloucester Pr) Watts.

Binato, Leonardo. What Grows in a Flower Pot? 12p. (ps-3). 1992. 4.95 (*1-56566-010-2*) Thomasson-Grant.

Borland, Hal. Plants of Christmas. Dowden, Anne O., illus. LC 87-552. 32p. (gr. 3 up). 1987. Repr. of 1969 ed. (Crowell Jr Bks); (Crowell Jr Bks) HarpC Child Bks.

Burnie, David. Plant & Flower. King, Dave, et al, illus. LC 88-27172. 64p. (gr. 5 up). 1989. 16.00 (*0-394-82252-8*); PLB 16.99 (*0-394-92252-2*) Knopf Bks Yng Read.

Byles, Monica. Experiments with Plants. Anderson, Nancy, illus. LC 92-43117. 1993. 17.50 (*0-8225-2456-2*) Lerner Pubns.

Capon, Brian. Plant Survival: Adapting to a Hostile World. Capon, Brian, illus. LC 93-43342. 144p. 1994. 24.95 (*0-88192-283-8*); pap. 15.95 (*0-88192-287-0*) Timber.

Carle, Eric. The Tiny Seed. 2nd ed. Carle, Eric, illus. LC 86-2534. 36p. (gr. k up). 1991. pap. 4.95 (*0-88708-155-X*) Picture Bk Studio.

Carratello, John & Carratello, Patty. Hands on Science: Plants. Wright, Terry, illus. 32p. (gr. 2-5). 1988. wkbk. 5.95 (*1-55734-224-5*) Tchr Create Mat.

Catherall, Ed. Exploring Plants. LC 91-40544. (Illus.). 48p. (gr. 4-8). 1992. PLB 22.80 (*0-8114-2601-7*) Raintree Steck-V.

Challand, Helen. Plants Without Seeds. LC 85-30935. (Illus.). 48p. (gr. k-4). 1986. PLB 12.85 (*0-516-01286-X*) Childrens.

Clyne, Densey. Plants of Prey. (Illus.). 32p. (Orig.). (gr. 1-5). 1993. pap. 6.95 (*1-86373-132-6*, Pub. by Allen & Unwin Aust Pty AT) IPG Chicago.

Coil, Suzanne M. Poisonous Plants. (Illus.). 64p. (gr. 5-8). 1992. pap. 5.95 (*0-531-15647-8*) Watts.

Conway, Lorraine. Plants. 64p. (gr. 5 up). 1980. 7.95 (*0-916456-69-2*, GA 176) Good Apple.

—Plants & Animals in Nature. Akins, Linda, illus. 64p. (gr. 5 up). 1986. wkbk. 7.95 (*0-86653-356-7*, GA 797) Good Apple.

Cooper, J. Flowers. 1991. 8.95s.p. (*0-86592-620-4*) Rourke Enter.

—Insect-Eating Plants. 1991. 8.95s.p. (*0-86592-624-7*) Rourke Enter.

—Plantas Insectivoras (Insect-Eating Plants) 1991. 8. 95s.p. (*0-86592-548-8*) Rourke Enter.

—Plantas Singulares (Strange Plants) 1991. 8.95s.p. (*0-86592-547-X*) Rourke Enter.

—Strange Plants. 1991. 8.95s.p. (*0-86592-625-5*) Rourke Enter.

Cork, Barbara. Plant Life. Jackson, Ian, illus. 32p. (gr. 6up). 1984. PLB 13.96 (*0-88110-169-9*); pap. 5.95 (*0-86020-755-2*) EDC.

Crowell, Robert L. The Lore & Legends of Flowers. Dowden, Anne O., illus. LC 79-7829. 88p. (gr. 7 up). 1982. (Crowell Jr Bks); (Crowell Jr Bks) HarpC Child Bks.

Davenport, Zoe. Gardens. LC 94-21456. (gr. 1-8). 1995. 4.95 (*0-395-71538-5*) Ticknor & Flds Bks Yng Read.

Dietl, Ulla. The Plant-&-Grow Project Book. LC 93-24788. (Illus.). 48p. (gr. 2-10). 1993. 12.95 (*0-8069-0456-9*) Sterling.

Facklam, Howard & Facklam, Margery. Plants: Extinction or Survival? LC 89-17038. (Illus.). 96p. (gr. 6 up). 1990. lib. bdg. 16.95 (*0-89490-248-2*) Enslow Pubs.

Fustec, Fabienne. Plants. (Illus.). 128p. (ps-3). 1993. 7.00 (*0-679-84161-X*); PLB 11.99 (*0-679-94161-4*) Random Bks Yng Read.

Gale, Frank C. & Gale, Clarice W. Experiences with Plants for Young Children. Solis-Navarro, Kelly, illus. Durett, Mary E., frwd. by. LC 78-88376. (Illus.). (ps-3). 1975. 14.95x (*0-87015-211-4*) Pacific Bks.

Gibbons, Gail. From Seed to Plant. Gibbons, Gail, illus. LC 90-47037. 32p. (ps-3). 1991. reinforced bdg. 15.95 (*0-8234-0872-8*) Holiday.

—From Seed to Plant. Gibbons, Gail, illus. (ps-3). 1993. pap. 5.95 (*0-8234-1025-0*) Holiday.

Goldenberg, Janet. Weird Things You Can Grow. Gloeckner, Phoebe, illus. LC 93-43146. 48p. (Orig.). (gr. 3-7). 1994. pap. 10.00 (*0-679-85298-0*) Random Bks Yng Read.

Goldish, Meish. How Plants Get Food. (Illus.). 32p. (gr. 1-4). 1989. PLB 18.99 (*0-8172-3507-8*); pap. 3.95 (*0-8114-6708-2*) Raintree Steck-V.

Gomez-Navarro, Maria J., et al, eds. Plantas - Plants. Del Carmen Blazquez, Maria, tr. End, Simone & Woodcock, John, illus. (SPA.). 64p. (gr. 5-12). 1993. write for info. (*84-372-4529-X*) Santillana.

Halpern, Robert R. Green Planet Rescue: Saving the Earth's Endangered Plants. LC 93-10583. (Illus.). 56p. (gr. 5-7). 1993. 15.95 (*0-531-15261-8*); PLB 15.90 (*0-531-11095-8*) Watts.

Heller, Ruth. Plants That Never Ever Bloom. Heller, Ruth, illus. 48p. (ps-3). 1992. pap. 5.95 (*0-448-41092-3*, Sandcastle Bks) Putnam Pub Group.

Hershey, David R. Plant Biology Science Projects. LC 94-12934. 1995. write for info. (*0-471-04983-2*) Wiley.

Hickman, Pamela M. Habitats. English, Sarah J., illus. LC 93-12683. 1993. write for info. (*0-201-62651-9*); pap. 9.57 (*0-201-62618-7*) Addison-Wesley.

Holly, Brian. Plants & Flowers. McGee, Martin, illus. 32p. (gr. 3-7). 1985. pap. 3.50 (*0-88625-114-1*) Durkin Hayes Pub.

Holstead, Christy & Linder, Pamela. Learn about Growing Friendships with Little Bud. rev. ed. Arlt, Bob, illus. (ps-3). 1992. activity bk. 3.98 (*1-881037-00-2*) McGreen Wisdom.

Hoover, Evalyn & Mercier, Sheryl. Primariamente Plantas. (SPA & ENG.). 149p. (gr. k-3). 1992. pap. text ed. 16.95 (*1-881431-32-0*) AIMS Educ Fnd.

Jordan, Helene J. How a Seed Grows. Low, Joseph, illus. LC 60-11541. 33p. (gr. k-3). 1972. pap. 4.95 (*0-690-40646-0*, Crowell Jr Bks) HarpC Child Bks.

Kerrod, Robin. Plant Life. Evans, Ted, illus. LC 93-50186. (gr. 2 up). 1994. 16.95 (*1-85435-627-5*) Marshall Cavendish.

Kirkpatrick, Rena K. Look at Seeds & Weeds. rev. ed. King, Debbie, illus. LC 84-26226. 32p. (gr. 2-4). 1985. PLB 10.95 (*0-8172-2357-6*); pap. 4.95 (*0-8114-6903-4*) Raintree Steck-V.

Korman, Justine. All about Plants Activity Book. (ps-3). 1994. pap. 1.95 (*0-590-47590-8*) Scholastic Inc.

Kuchalla, Susan. All about Seeds. McBee, Jane, illus. LC 81-11480. 32p. (gr. k-2). 1982. lib. bdg. 11.59 (*0-89375-658-X*); pap. 2.95 (*0-89375-659-8*) Troll Assocs.

Landau, Elaine. Endangered Plants. (Illus.). 64p. (gr. 5-8). 1992. pap. 5.95 (*0-531-15645-1*) Watts.

Lerner, Carol. Plant Families. Lerner, Carol, illus. LC 88-26653. 32p. (gr. 4 up). 1989. 12.95 (*0-688-07881-8*); PLB 12.88 (*0-688-07882-6*, Morrow Jr Bks) Morrow Jr Bks.

Madgwick, Wendy. Flowering Plants. LC 90-9572. (Illus.). 48p. (gr. 5-9). 1990. PLB 21.34 (*0-8114-2730-7*) Raintree Steck-V.

Marcus, Elizabeth. Amazing World of Plants. Boyd, Patti, illus. LC 83-4836. 32p. (gr. 3-6). 1984. lib. bdg. 10.59 (*0-89375-967-8*); pap. text ed. 2.95 (*0-89375-968-6*) Troll Assocs.

Miner, O. Irene. Plants We Know. LC 81-9929. 48p. (gr. k-4). 1981. PLB 12.85 (*0-516-01642-3*) Childrens.

Moncure, Jane B. What Plants Need: The Rabbit Who Knew. Dunnington, Tom, illus. LC 89-24001. 32p. (ps-2). 1990. PLB 13.95 (*0-89565-559-4*) Childs World.

Morgan, Nina. The Plant Cycle. Yates, John, illus. LC 93-977. 32p. (gr. 2-5). 1993. 12.95 (*1-56847-091-6*) Thomson Lrning.

Nielsen, Nancy J. Carnivorous Plants. LC 91-34422. (Illus.). 64p. (gr. 3-6). 1992. PLB 12.90 (*0-531-20056-6*) Watts.

—Carnivorous Plants. (Illus.). 64p. (gr. 5-8). 1992. pap. 5.95 (*0-531-15644-3*) Watts.

Nussbaum, Hedda. Plants Do Amazing Things. Mathieu, Joe, illus. LC 75-36471. 72p. (gr. 2-3). 1977. 11.00 (*0-394-83232-9*); lib. bdg. 8.99 (*0-394-93232-3*) Random Bks Yng Read.

Overbeck, Cynthia. Carnivorous Plants. LC 81-17234. (Illus.). 48p. (gr. 4 up). 1982. PLB 19.95 (*0-8225-1470-2*, First Ave Edns); pap. 5.95 (*0-8225-9535-4*, First Ave Edns) Lerner Pubns.

Peacock, Graham & Hudson, Terry. Exploring Habitats. Hughes, Jenny, illus. LC 92-29907. 48p. (gr. 4-8). 1992. PLB 22.80 (*0-8114-2608-4*) Raintree Steck-V.

The Picture-Perfect Planet. LC 92-20831. 1992. write for info. (*0-8094-9319-5*); PLB write for info. (*0-8094-9320-9*) Time-Life.

Plant Life. LC 92-34975. 1993. write for info. (*0-8094-9712-3*); PLB write for info. (*0-8094-9713-1*) Time-Life.

Plant Science. (Illus.). 48p. (gr. 6-12). 1983. pap. 1.85 (*0-8395-3396-9*, 33396) BSA.

Plants. (gr. k-3). 1989. 3.95 (*0-7214-5214-0*) Ladybird Bks.

Plants. 1991. pap. 3.95 (*0-7214-5327-9*) Ladybird Bks.

Plants. LC 91-58214. (Illus.). 24p. (ps-3). 1992. 8.95 (*1-56458-005-9*) Dorling Kindersley.

Plants. LC 91-58208. (Illus.). 64p. (gr. 6 up). 1992. 14.95 (*1-56458-016-4*); PLB 15.99 (*1-56458-017-2*) Dorling Kindersley.

Pluckrose, Henry A. Flowers. LC 93-45661. (Illus.). 32p. (ps-3). 1994. PLB 11.95 (*0-516-08117-9*) Childrens.

Pope, Joyce. Plant Partnerships. LC 90-32395. (Illus.). 62p. (gr. 6 up). 1991. PLB 15.95 (*0-8160-2422-7*) Facts on File.

—Plants & Flowers. Pantry, Stuart, illus. LC 91-45378. 32p. (gr. 3-6). 1993. PLB 11.59 (*0-8167-2779-1*); pap. text ed. 3.95 (*0-8167-2780-5*) Troll Assocs.

Rahn, Joan E. Plants Up Close. (Illus.). (gr. 2-5). 1981. 13.45 (*0-395-31677-4*) HM.

Riehecky, Janet. What Plants Give Us: The Gift of Life. Collette, Rondi, illus. LC 90-30374. 32p. (ps-2). 1990. PLB 13.95 (*0-89565-570-5*) Childs World.

Ring, Elizabeth. Tiger Lilies & Other Beastly Plants. Bash, Barbara, illus. LC 84-7499. 32p. (gr. 3 up). 1985. 9.95 (*0-8027-6540-8*) Walker & Co.

Rowe, Julian & Perham, Molly. Watch It Grow! LC 94-12258. (Illus.). 32p. (gr. 1-4). 1994. PLB 18.60 (*0-516-08141-1*); pap. 4.95 (*0-516-48141-X*) Childrens.

Sabin, Louis. Plants, Seeds & Flowers. Moylan, Holly, illus. LC 84-2720. 32p. (gr. 3-6). 1985. PLB 9.49 (*0-8167-0226-8*); pap. text ed. 2.95 (*0-8167-0227-6*) Troll Assocs.

Samson, Suzanne. Fairy Dusters & Blazing Stars: Exploring Wildflowers with Children. Neel, Preston, illus. LC 94-65089. 40p. (Orig.). (gr. k-6). 1994. pap. 9.95 (*1-879373-81-5*) R Rinehart.

Schwartz, Linda. Plants. (Illus.). 48p. (gr. 2-5). 1990. 5.95 (*0-88160-189-6*, LW 148) Learning Wks.

Selsam, Millicent E. & Hunt, Joyce. A First Look at the World of Plants. Springer, Harriett, illus. LC 77-78088. (gr. 1-4). 1978. PLB 9.85 (*0-8027-6299-9*) Walker & Co.

Suzuki, David. Looking at Plants. (Illus.). 96p. 1992. text ed. 22.95 (*0-471-54748-4*); pap. text ed. 9.95 (*0-471-54049-8*) Wiley.

Taylor, Barbara. Green Thumbs Up! The Science of Growing Plants. Bull, Peter, et al, illus. LC 91-4290. 40p. (Orig.). (gr. 2-5). 1992. pap. 4.95 (*0-679-82042-6*) Random Bks Yng Read.

—Growing Plants. LC 91-2568. (Illus.). 40p. (gr. k-4). 1991. PLB 12.90 (*0-531-19128-1*, Warwick) Watts.

Tesar, Jenny. Green Plants. (Illus.). 64p. (gr. 4-8). 1993. PLB 16.95 (*1-56711-039-8*) Blackbirch.

Unwin, M. Science with Plants. (Illus.). 24p. (gr. 1-4). 1993. PLB 12.96 (*0-88110-620-8*); pap. 4.50 (*0-7460-0976-3*) EDC.

Walker, Richard. Plants. LC 93-19075. 1993. 12.95 (*1-56458-383-X*) Dorling Kindersley.

Warren, Elizabeth. I Can Read About Trees & Plants. LC 74-24991. (Illus.). (gr. 2-4). 1975. pap. 2.50 (*0-89375-069-7*) Troll Assocs.

Webster, Vera. Plant Experiments. LC 82-9448. (Illus.). 48p. (gr. k-4). 1982. PLB 12.85 (*0-516-01638-5*); pap. 4.95 (*0-516-41638-3*) Childrens.

Wexler, Jerome. Flowers, Fruits & Seeds. (gr. k-3). 1991. pap. 3.95 (*0-671-73986-7*, Little Simon) S&S Trade.

—Sundew Stranglers: Plants That Eat Insects. (Illus.). 48p. (gr. 2-6). 1994. 14.99 (*0-525-45208-7*) Dutton Child Bks.

Wilson, April, illus. Look Again! The Second Ultimate Spot-the-Difference Book. Wood, A. J., notes by. LC 91-31214. (Illus.). 40p. (gr. 1 up). 1992. 13.00 (*0-8037-0958-7*) Dial Bks Young.

Wood, Robert W. Thirty-Nine Easy Plant Biology Experiments. 160p. 1991. 16.95 (*0-8306-1941-0*, 5003); pap. 9.95 (*0-8306-1935-6*) TAB Bks.

Woodworth, Viki. Can You Grow a Popsicle? Woodworth, Viki, illus. (ps-2). 1992. PLB 12.95 (*0-89565-820-8*) Childs World.

Wren & Maile. Na Mea Kanu: Plants. Wren, illus. (ENG & HAW.). 10p. (ps). 1992. bds. 3.95 (*1-880188-28-7*) Bess Pr.

PLANTS, CULTIVATED

see also House Plants; Plants, Edible

Rahn, Joan E. More Plants That Changed History. LC 84-21563. 136p. (gr. 5 up). 1985. SBE 13.95 (*0-689-31099-4*, Atheneum Child Bk) Macmillan Child Grp.

PLANTS–ECOLOGY

see Botany–Ecology

PLANTS, EDIBLE

Christensen, Bonnie. An Edible Alphabet. LC 93-7799. 1994. write for info. (*0-8037-1404-1*); lib. bdg. write for info. (*0-8037-1406-8*) Dial Bks Young.

Sweet, Muriel. Common Edible & Useful Plants of the West. rev. ed. LC 76-58. (Illus.). 64p. (gr. 4 up). 1976. 13.95 (*0-87961-047-6*); pap. 5.95 (*0-87961-046-8*) Naturegraph.

PLANTS, EXTINCT

see Plants, Fossil

PLANTS–FICTION

Ada, Alma F. Una Semilla Nada Mas (Small Book) Remkiewicz, Frank, illus. (SPA.). 16p. (Orig.). (gr. k-3). 1992. pap. text ed. 6.00 (*1-56334-083-6*) Hampton-Brown.

Cates, Joe W. Carl the Cactus. Cates, Joe W., illus. 64p. (Orig.). (gr. k-6). 1986. PLB 9.95 (*0-942403-03-7*); pap. 7.00 (*0-942403-01-0*) J Barnaby Dist.

Christopher, John. When the Tripods Came. LC 90-1436. 160p. (gr. 7 up). 1990. pap. 3.95 (*0-02-042575-9*, Collier Young Ad) Macmillan Child Grp.

Derby, Sally. Jacob & the Stranger. Gore, Leonid, illus. LC 93-11022. 32p. (ps-3). 1994. 11.95 (*0-395-66897-2*) Ticknor & Flds Bks Yng Read.

Hwa-I Publishing Co., Staff. Chinese Children's Stories, Vol. 6: Miss Gold 'n' Silver, Pearl Rice. Ching, Emily, et al, eds. Wonder Kids Publications Staff, tr. from CHI. (Illus.). 28p. (gr. 3-6). 1991. Repr. of 1988 ed. 7.95 (*1-56162-006-8*) Wonder Kids.

Kerven, Rosalind. The Tree in the Moon & Other Legends of Plants & Trees. (Illus.). 1989. 16.95 (*0-521-34269-4*) Cambridge U Pr.

Kontoyiannaki, Elizabeth. Plants Grow in Gardens. Kontoyiannaki, Elizabeth, illus. 18p. (gr. k-3). 1992. pap. 10.95 (*1-895583-43-8*) MAYA Pubs.

Krauss, Ruth. The Carrot Seed. Johnson, Crockett, illus. LC 45-4530. 32p. (ps-1). 1989. pap. 3.95 (*0-06-443210-6*, Trophy) HarpC Child Bks.

McArthur, Nancy. The Return of the Plant That Ate Dirty Socks. 128p. (Orig.). (gr. 5-6). 1990. pap. 3.50 (*0-380-75873-3*, Camelot) Avon.

McClure, Michael. Acorn Alone. Robertson, Jon, ed. McClure, Nancee J., illus. LC 94-6638. 1994. 16.95 (*0-87604-326-0*) ARE Pr.

Mahy, Margaret. Pumpkin Man & the Crafty Creeper. (ps-3). 1991. 14.95 (*0-688-10347-2*); PLB 14.88 (*0-688-10348-0*) Lothrop.

Marbach, Ethel. The Cabbage Moth & the Shamrock. Hague, Michael, illus. LC 91-575. 32p. (ps-2). 1991. jacketed, reinforced bdg. 9.00 (*0-671-74864-5*, Green Tiger) S&S Trade.

Mark, Jan. Silly Tails. LC 92-38679. (Illus.). 32p. (gr. k-3). 1993. SBE 13.95 (*0-689-31843-X*, Atheneum Child Bk) Macmillan Child Grp.

Peteraf, Nancy J. A Plant Called Spot. Hoban, Lillian, illus. LC 92-27474. 1994. 13.95 (*0-385-30885-X*) Doubleday.

Primavera, Elise. Plantpet. Primavera, Elise, illus. LC 93-36526. 32p. (ps-3). 1994. PLB 15.95 (*0-399-22627-3*, Putnam) Putnam Pub Group.

Quinlan, Patricia. Planting Seeds. Krykorka, Vladyana, illus. 24p. (ps-2). 1988. 12.95 (*1-55037-007-3*, Pub. by Annick CN); pap. 4.95 (*1-55037-006-5*, Pub. by Annick CN) Firefly Bks Ltd.

Reese, Bob. Lactus Cactus. LC 81-3866. (Illus.). 24p. (ps-2). 1981. pap. 2.95 (*0-516-42304-5*) Childrens.

Rey, H. A. Elizabite: Adventures of a Carnivorous Plant. Rey, H. A., illus. LC 90-4834. 32p. (ps-3). 1990. Repr. of 1942 ed. lib. bdg. 17.00 (*0-208-02288-0*, Linnet) Shoe String.

Roberts, Mary. The Creeper. Stewart, Chantal, illus. LC 93-134. 1994. write for info. (*0-383-03684-4*) SRA Schl Grp.

Schwartz, Paula & Schartz, Sara. A Leaf Named Bud. (Illus.). 32p. (ps-1). 1993. 12.95 (*0-87663-795-0*) Universe.

Story Time Stories That Rhyme Staff. Story Habitat: Plant & Animal Stories. Story Time Stories That Rhyme Staff, illus. 40p. (Orig.). (gr. 4-7). 1992. GBC bdg. 19.95 (*1-56820-014-5*) Story Time.

Wildsmith, Brian & Wildsmith, Rebecca. Jack & the Meanstalk. LC 93-30374. 1994. 15.00 (*0-679-85810-5*); pap. 15.99 (*0-679-95810-X*) Knopf Bks Yng Read.

PLANTS, FOSSIL

Garassino, Alessandro. Plants: Origin & Evolution. LC 94-3838. 1994. write for info. (*0-8114-3332-3*) Raintree Steck-V.

Henderson, Douglas. Dinosaur Tree. LC 93-34204. (gr. 1-7). 1994. 15.95 (*0-02-743547-4*, Bradbury Pr) Macmillan Child Grp.

Wexo, John B. Out of the Water. 24p. (gr. 3 up). 1991. PLB 14.95 (*0-88682-391-9*) Creative Ed.

PLANTS–GROWTH

see Growth (Plants)

PLANTS, MEDICINAL

see Botany, Medical

PLANTS, USEFUL

see Plants, Edible

PLASTIC MATERIALS

see Plastics

PLASTICS

Cash, Terry. Plastics. Stefoff, Rebecca, ed. Barber, Ed, photos by. LC 90-40368. (Illus.). 32p. (gr. 3-5). 1990. PLB 15.93 (*0-944483-70-4*) Garrett Ed Corp.

Daniel, Jamie & Bonar, Veronica. Coping with - Plastic Trash. Kenyon, Tony, illus. LC 93-37687. 32p. (gr. 2 up). 1994. PLB 17.27 (*0-8368-1060-0*) Gareth Stevens Inc.

Galas, Judith C. Plastics: Molding the Past, Shaping the Future. (Illus.). (gr. 5-8). 1994. 15.95 (*1-56006-251-7*) Lucent Bks.

Jackman, Wayne. Plastics. LC 92-45669. 32p. (gr. 3-6). 1993. 13.95 (*1-56847-040-1*) Thomson Lrning.

Lambert, M. Plastics. (Illus.). 48p. (gr. 5 up). 1985. PLB 17.27 (*0-86592-269-1*); 12.95s.p. (*0-685-58326-0*) Rourke Corp.

Mebane, Robert & Rybolt, Thomas. Plastics & Polymers. (Illus.). 64p. (gr. 5-8). 1995. bds. 15.95 (*0-8050-2843-9*) TFC Bks NY.

PLATYPUS

Reilly, Pauline. Platypus. Rolland, Will, illus. 32p. (Orig.). (gr. 2-6). 1994. pap. 6.95 (*0-86417-391-1*, Pub. by Kangaroo Pr AT) Seven Hills Bk Dists.

PLAY

see also Amusements; Games; Recreation; Sports

Blizzard, Gladys S. Come Look with Me: World of Play. Barns, Rebecca B., ed. LC 92-36263. (Illus.). 32p. (gr. 1 up). 1993. 13.95 (*1-56566-031-5*) Thomasson-Grant.

Boyd, L. M. Clancy's Treasure Book for Children. Boyd, L. M., illus. 166p. (Orig.). (gr. k-5). 1981. pap. 7.95 (*0-941620-34-4*) Carson Ent.

Chlad, Dorothy. Jugando en el Patio de Recreo (Playing on the Playground) Halverson, Lydia, illus. LC 87-5197. (SPA.). 32p. (ps-2). 1988. pap. 3.95 (*0-516-51989-1*) Childrens.

Costa, Nicoletta, illus. My Poke & Look Busy Book Two. 32p. (ps-2). 1992. bds. 14.95 (*0-448-40390-0*, G&D) Putnam Pub Group.

Heuninck, Ronald. Playtime. Heuninck, Ronald, illus. 14p. (ps). 1991. Repr. bds. 5.50 (*0-86315-124-8*) Gryphon Hse.

Lamb, Sandra & Bellows, Dena. Parties for Home & School: A Piece of Cake. Hyndman, Kathryn, illus. 144p. (ps-4). 1985. wkbk. 12.95 (*0-86653-328-1*, GA 647) Good Apple.

McMillan, Bruce. Play Day: A Book of Terse Verse. McMillan, Bruce, illus. LC 90-29077. 32p. (ps-3). 1991. reinforced 14.95 (*0-8234-0894-9*) Holiday.

Oxenbury, Helen. Playing. Oxenbury, Helen, illus. 14p. (ps-k). 1981. 3.95 (*0-671-42109-3*, Little Simon) S&S Trade.

PLAY–FICTION

Abrams, Rita. Stepping Out. 1991. bds. 12.95 incl. song tape (*0-938971-75-1*) JTG Nashville.

Adorjan, Carol. I Can! Can You? rev. ed. Levine, Abby, ed. Nerlove, Miriam, illus. LC 90-37665. 24p. (ps). 1990. 11.95 (*0-8075-3491-9*) A Whitman.

Alexander, Martha. Lily & Willy. Alexander, Martha, illus. LC 92-53004. 14p. (ps). 1993. 4.95 (*1-56402-163-7*) Candlewick Pr.

Allen, Pamela. I Wish I Had a Pirate Suit. (ps). 1990. 12.95 (*0-670-82475-5*) Viking Child Bks.

—I Wish I Had a Pirate Suit. LC 92-12295. (gr. 4 up). 1993. 3.99 (*0-14-050988-7*) Puffin Bks.

Antonsen, Ray. Memoirs of a Mischievous Kid. Van Treese, James B., ed. 120p. 1993. pap. 7.95 (*1-56901-182-6*) NW Pub.

Baer, Gene. Have You Seen My Finger? Baer, Gene, illus. LC 91-61251. 16p. (ps-k). 1992. 5.99 (*0-679-81382-9*) Random Bks Yng Read.

Baillie, Allan. Drac & the Gremlin. Tanner, Jane, illus. LC 88-20275. 32p. (ps-3). 1989. 11.95 (*0-8037-0628-6*) Dial Bks Young.

Bang, Molly. One Fall Day. LC 93-36490. (Illus.). 24p. 1994. 15.00 (*0-688-07015-9*); PLB 14.93 (*0-688-07016-7*) Greenwillow.

Bebe Donald Juega en Grupo. (SPA.). (ps-3). 1993. pap. 4.95 (*0-307-72316-X*, Golden Pr) Western Pub.

Benjamin, Alan. Let's Play: Vamos a Jugar. (ENG & SPA.). (ps). 1992. pap. 2.95 (*0-671-76928-6*, Little Simon) S&S Trade.

Blass, Jacqueline. My Playhouse. Blass, Jacqueline, illus. 8p. (ps-4). 1989. bds. 6.99 (*1-55037-033-2*, Pub. by Annick CN) Firefly Bks Ltd.

Boivin, Kelly. What's in a Box? Skivington, Janice, illus. LC 91-4062. 32p. (ps-2). 1991. PLB 10.25 (*0-516-02010-2*); pap. 2.95 (*0-516-42010-0*) Childrens.

Boyd, Lizi. Baby Wiggles - Baby Plays. LC 92-50278. (ps). 1992. 8.95 (*1-56305-310-1*) Workman Pub.

Brandenberg, Franz. Leo & Emily's Big Ideas. Aliki, illus. LC 81-6424. 56p. (gr. 1-3). 1982. 13.88 (*0-688-00754-6*); PLB 13.95 (*0-688-00755-4*) Greenwillow.

Breeze, Lynn, illus. This Little Baby's Playtime. Morris, Ann, text by. LC 92-30878. (Illus.). (ps). 1993. 5.95 (*0-316-10855-3*) Little.

Brook, Leeanne. The Great Big, Enormous, Gigantic Cardboard Box. Vanzet, Gaston, illus. LC 92-29957. (gr. 3 up). 1993. 14.00 (*0-383-03571-6*) SRA Schl Grp.

Brown, Laurie K. Rex & Lilly at Play. Brown, Marc, illus. LC 93-25877. 1995. 12.95 (*0-316-11386-7*) Little.

Buckle, Mariette. All Dressed Up. Strahan, Heather, illus. LC 92-21447. 1993. 3.75 (*0-383-03613-5*) SRA Schl Grp.

Carlson, Nancy. Harriet & the Roller Coaster. LC 81-18138. (Illus.). 32p. (ps-3). 1982. lib. bdg. 13.50 (*0-87614-183-1*) Carolrhoda Bks.

Caseley, Judith. The Noisemakers. LC 90-2806. (Illus.). 24p. (ps-6). 1992. 14.00 (*0-688-09394-9*); PLB 13.93 (*0-688-09395-7*) Greenwillow.

Cauley, Lorinda B. Clap Your Hands. Cauley, Lorinda B., illus. 32p. (ps-1). 1992. PLB 14.95 (*0-399-22118-2*, Putnam) Putnam Pub Group.

Chevalier, Christa. Spence Isn't Spence Anymore. Levine, Abby, ed. Chevalier, Christa, illus. LC 84-29195. 32p. (ps-1). 1985. 11.95 (*0-8075-7565-8*) A Whitman.

Chlad, Dorothy. Playing Outdoors in the Winter. Halverson, Lydia, illus. LC 90-22258. 32p. (ps-2). 1991. pap. 3.95 (*0-516-41972-2*) Childrens.

Chorao, Kay. Annie & Cousin Precious. LC 93-32611. 1994. write for info. (*0-525-45238-9*, DCB) Dutton Child Bks.

Clyne, Densey. Catch Me If You Can! 1993. pap. 6.95 (*0-685-63824-3*) Routledge Chapman & Hall.

—Catch Me If You Can! (gr. 4-7). 1993. pap. 6.95 (*1-86373-205-5*, Pub. by Allen & Unwin Aust Pty AT) IPG Chicago.

Cohen, Seth. Baby Safari. Cohen, Helena, illus. 28p. (ps). 1993. 3.25 (*0-679-83608-X*) Random Bks Yng Read.

Coxon, Michelle. Who Will Play with Me? Coxon, Michelle, illus. LC 91-40498. 32p. (gr. k-3). 1992. PLB 12.95 (*0-87226-469-6*, Bedrick Blackie) P Bedrick Bks.

Cuneo, Mary L. How to Grow a Picket Fence. Westcott, Nadine B., illus. LC 91-36444. 32p. (ps-3). 1993. 15.00 (*0-06-020863-5*); PLB 14.89 (*0-06-020864-3*) HarpC Child Bks.

Dale, Penny. All about Alice. Dale, Penny, illus. LC 92-52991. 32p. (ps-3). 1993. 13.95 (*1-56402-171-8*) Candlewick Pr.

Desputeaux, Helene. Lollypop's Playtime. (Illus.). (ps). 1993. bath bk. 4.95 (*2-921198-40-1*, Pub. by Les Edits Herit CN) Adams Inc MA.

Disney Fun. (gr. 3 up). 1991. pap. 1.97 (*1-56297-118-2*, WD-180F) Lee Pubns KY.

Driscoll, Debbie. Three Two One Day. Cravath, Lynne, illus. LC 92-23420. 1994. pap. 14.00 (*0-671-79330-6*, S&S BFYR) S&S Trade.

Dudko, Mary A. & Larsen, Margie. BJ's Fun Week. Full, Dennis, photos by. LC 94-72001. (Illus.). 20p. (ps-k). 1994. bds. 3.95 (*1-57064-015-7*) Barney Pub.

Ets, Marie H. Play with Me. (ps-k). 1976. pap. 3.95 (*0-14-050178-9*, Puffin) Puffin Bks.

Falwell, Cathryn. Nicky & Alex. Falwell, Cathryn, illus. 32p. (ps). 1992. 5.95 (*0-395-56915-X*, Clarion Bks) HM.

—Nicky & Grandpa. Falwell, Cathryn, illus. 32p. (ps). 1991. 5.70 (*0-395-56917-6*, Clarion Bks) HM.

—Where's Nicky? Briley, Cathryn, ed. Falwell, Cathryn, illus. 24p. (ps). 1991. 5.70 (*0-395-56936-2*, Clarion Bks) HM.

Foley, Diane. My Big Box. Quinn, Annie, illus. LC 92-31910. 1993. 3.75 (*0-383-03584-8*) SRA Schl Grp.

Foo-Foo, Where Are You? (Illus.). 24p. (ps-2). 1991. 22.00 (*0-307-74015-3*, Golden Pr) Western Pub.

Gaban, Jesus. Harry's Sandbox Surprise. Colorado, Nani, illus. 16p. (ps-1). 1992. PLB 13.27 (*0-8368-0716-2*) Gareth Stevens Inc.

Gave, Marc. Monkey See, Monkey Do. Rogers, Jacqueline, illus. 32p. (ps-2). 1993. pap. 2.95 (*0-590-45801-9*) Scholastic Inc.

Gaynor, Brigid. Back Yard Attractions. Rollins, Nancy O., illus. (ps). 1992. 15.95 (*1-56828-018-1*) Red Jacket Pr.

—Things to Do. Rollins, Nancy O., illus. 12p. (ps). 1992. 4.95 (*1-56828-015-7*) Red Jacket Pr.

Goffe, Toni. The Monster. LC 93-21862. (ps-3). 1993. 5.95 (*0-85953-406-5*) Childs Play.

Goldish, Meish. The Paper Party. 16p. (ps-2). 1992. pap. 14.95 (*1-56784-054-X*) Newbridge Comms.

Gomi, Taro. Who Hid It? (ps). 1992. pap. 4.80 (*0-395-65835-7*) HM.

Havill, Juanita. Jennifer, Too. LC 93-6319. (Illus.). 56p. (gr. 2-5). 1994. 11.95 (*1-56282-618-2*); PLB 11.89 (*1-56282-619-0*) Hyprn Child.

Heller, Nicholas. Ten Old Pails. Abolafia, Yossi, illus. LC 92-31511. 24p. (ps up). 1994. 14.00 (*0-688-12419-4*); PLB 13.93 (*0-688-12420-8*) Greenwillow.

Henderson, Kathy. Bounce, Bounce, Bounce. Thompson, Carol, illus. LC 93-3556. 24p. (ps up). 1994. 9.95 (*1-56402-311-7*) Candlewick Pr.

Hillert, Margaret. Come Play with Me. (Illus.). (ps-k). 1975. PLB 6.95 (*0-8136-5036-4*, TK2292); pap. 3.50 (*0-8136-5536-6*, TK2293) Modern Curr.

Hines, Anna G. It's Just Me, Emily. Hines, Anna G., illus. (ps-1). 1987. 12.95 (*0-89919-487-7*, Clarion Bks) HM.

Huelsberg, Enid L. Sometimes of Children. (gr. k-2). 1976. pap. 3.00 (*0-89039-172-6*, Ann Arbor Div) Acad Therapy.

Hughes, Shirley. Bouncing. Hughes, Shirley, illus. LC 92-53001. 24p. (ps up). 1993. 12.95 (*1-56402-128-9*) Candlewick Pr.

Kellogg, Steven. Won't Somebody Play with Me? LC 72-708. (Illus.). (gr. k-3). 1976. pap. 4.95 (*0-8037-9612-9*) Dial Bks Young.

Kent, Jack. Joey. LC 84-4694. (Illus.). 32p. (gr. k-4). 1987. jacketed 11.95 (*0-671-66459-X*, S&S BFYR); (S&S BFYR) S&S Trade.

Kingman, Lee. Catch the Baby! (ps). 1990. 12.95 (*0-670-81751-1*) Viking Child Bks.

—Catch the Baby! Natti, Susanna, photos by. LC 92-26588. (Illus.). 1993. pap. 4.99 (*0-14-050762-0*) Puffin Bks.

Knutson, Kimberley. Muddigush. LC 91-15393. (Illus.). 32p. (ps-1). 1992. RSBE 13.95 (*0-02-750843-9*, Macmillan Child Bk) Macmillan Child Grp.
Kornblatt, Marc. Eli & the Dimplemeyers. Ziegler, Jack, illus. LC 92-36793. 32p. (gr. k-3). 1994. RSBE 14.95 (*0-02-750947-8*, Macmillan Child Bk) Macmillan Child Grp.
Kotter, Deborah. Arnold Always Answers. Conteh-Morgan, Jane, illus. LC 92-18578. 1993. 14.95 (*0-385-30905-8*, Zephyr-BFYR) Doubleday.
Kubler, Annie. When I Grow Up. LC 91-27125. 1992. 5.95 (*0-85953-505-3*) Childs Play.
Levert, Mirielle, illus. Tiny Toes. LC 93-40846. 1995. write for info. (*0-7868-0013-5*); PLB write for info. (*0-7868-2009-8*) Hyprn Child.
Light, John. Playing at Home. LC 90-34356. (gr. 4 up). 1991. 3.95 (*0-85953-336-0*) Childs Play.
Lomasney, Eileen. What Do You Do with the Rest of the Day, Mary Ann? 1991. pap. 3.95 (*0-8091-6601-1*) Paulist Pr.
McDaniel, Becky B. Larry & the Cookie. Martin, Clovis, illus. LC 92-37871. 32p. (ps-2). 1993. PLB 10.25 (*0-516-02014-5*); pap. 2.95 (*0-516-42014-3*) Childrens.
MacDonald, Marianne. The Pirate Queen. Smith, Jan, illus. 32p. (ps-3). 1992. incl. dust jacket 12.95 (*0-8120-6288-4*); pap. 5.95 (*0-8120-4952-7*) Barron.
McFann, Julia B. We Can Play. Wibright, Betsy, illus. 13p. (Orig.). (gr. 1). 1993. pap. text ed. write for info. (*1-882225-15-5*) Tott Pubns.
Mclerran, Alice. Roxaboxen. (ps-3). 1991. 14.95 (*0-688-07592-4*); PLB 14.88 (*0-688-07593-2*) Lothrop.
—Roxaboxen. Cooney, Barbara, illus. 32p. (ps-3). 1992. pap. 4.99 (*0-14-054475-5*, Puffin) Puffin Bks.
McOmber, Rachel B., ed. McOmber Phonics Storybooks: A Nifty Ball of String. rev. ed. (Illus.). write for info. (*0-944991-50-5*) Swift Lrn Res.
Martin, David. Lizzie & Her Friend. Gliori, Debi, illus. LC 92-53009. 24p. (ps). 1993. 5.95 (*1-56402-061-4*) Candlewick Pr.
—Lizzie & Her Puppy. Gliori, Debi, illus. LC 92-53008. 24p. (ps). 1993. 5.95 (*1-56402-059-2*) Candlewick Pr.
Martin, Juliet. A Puzzle. Kelly, Geoff, illus. LC 93-18051. 1994. write for info. (*0-383-03710-7*) SRA Schl Grp.
Messenger, Norman. Making Faces. (Illus.). 16p. 1993. 14.95 (*1-56458-111-X*) Dorling Kindersley.
Michaels, Ski. Something New to Do. Palmer, Jan, illus. LC 85-14021. 48p. (Orig.). (gr. 1-3). 1986. PLB 10.59 (*0-8167-0634-4*); pap. text ed. 3.50 (*0-8167-0635-2*) Troll Assocs.
Moss, Marissa. Want to Play? Moss, Marissa, illus. 32p. (ps-3). 1990. 13.45 (*0-395-52022-3*) HM.
Nagel, Karen B. The Three Young Maniacs & the Red Rubber Boots. Gullikson, Sandy, illus. LC 91-30842. 32p. (ps-3). 1993. 15.00 (*0-06-020777-9*); PLB 14.89 (*0-06-020778-7*) HarpC Child Bks.
Offen, Hilda. The Sheep Made a Leap. Offen, Hilda, illus. 32p. (ps-2). 1994. 10.99 (*0-525-45174-9*, DCB) Dutton Child Bks.
Orgel, Doris. Sarah's Room. LC 63-13675. (Illus.). (gr. k-3). 1963. 11.95 (*0-06-024605-7*) HarpC Child Bks.
Palumbo, Nancy. Penelope P'Nutt at Play: Penelope P'Nutt au Jeu. Weaver, Judith, illus. 32p. (Orig.). (gr. k-6). 1989. wkbk. 5.95 (*0-927024-17-9*) Crayons Pubns.
Pare, R. Play Time. (Illus.). 24p. (ps-8). 1988. 12.95 (*1-55037-087-1*, Pub. by Annick CN); pap. 4.95 (*1-55037-086-3*, Pub. by Annick CN) Firefly Bks Ltd.
Pearson, Gayle. One Potato, Tu. (gr. 4-7). 1994. pap. 2.95 (*0-590-47100-7*) Scholastic Inc.
Peck, Robert N. Soup's Hoop. (gr. 4-7). 1992. pap. 3.50 (*0-440-40589-0*, YB) Dell.
Peppe, Rodney. Huxley Pig's Model Car. (ps). 1991. pap. 8.95 (*0-385-30238-X*) Doubleday.
Peters, Lisa W. The Hayloft. Plum, K. D., illus. LC 93-18718. Date not set. write for info. (*0-8037-1490-4*); lib. bdg. write for info. (*0-8037-1491-2*) Dial Bks Young.
Pocock, Rita. Annabelle & the Big Slide. 28p. (ps-k). 1989. 10.95 (*0-15-200407-6*, Gulliver Bks) HarBrace.
Reiser, Lynn. Margaret & Margarita, Margarita y Margaret. LC 92-29012. 32p. (ps up). 1993. 14.00 (*0-688-12239-6*); lib. bdg. 13.93 (*0-688-12240-X*) Greenwillow.
Richardson, John. Where's Jack? A Christmas Pop-up Book. Richardson, John, illus. 24p. (ps-2). 1993. pap. 12.95 POB (*0-689-71713-X*, Aladdin) Macmillan Child Grp.
Rogers, Mary. I Want to Play. 26p. (gr. 1). 1992. pap. text ed. 23.00 big bk. (*1-56843-020-5*); pap. text ed. 4.50 (*1-56843-070-1*) BGR Pub.
Rosenbluth, Rosalyn. The Land of Peek-A-Boo. Mahan, Ben, illus. 24p. (ps-2). 1993. pap. text ed. 0.99 (*1-56293-344-2*) McClanahan Bk.
Ross, Pat. M & M & the Haunted House Game. (gr. 4 up). 1990. pap. 4.50 (*0-14-034577-9*, Puffin) Puffin Bks.
Russo, Marisabina. The Line Up Book. (Illus.). 24p. (ps-3). 1992. pap. 3.99 (*0-14-054471-2*) Puffin Bks.
Rylant, Cynthia. The Everyday Books: Everyday Children. Rylant, Cynthia, illus. LC 92-40932. 14p. (ps-k). 1993. pap. 4.95 with rounded corners (*0-02-778022-8*, Bradbury Pr) Macmillan Child Grp.
Shearer, Marilyn J. I Like to Play. Roberts, Tom, illus. 16p. (Orig.). (ps-6). 1989. 19.95 (*0-685-30097-8*); pap. 10.95 (*0-685-30098-6*) L Ashley & Joshua.
Shott, Stephen, photos by. Playtime. LC 91-2601. (Illus.). 12p. (ps). 1991. bds. 4.95 (*0-525-44757-1*, DCB) Dutton Child Bks.
Shufflebotham, Anne. Round & Round the Garden. LC 91-12964. (gr. 4 up). 1991. 5.99 (*0-85953-426-X*) Childs Play.
Sinnett, Kate. My Five Disguises. Lewis, Anthony, illus. LC 90-44374. 28p. (gr. 4-8). 1991. PLB 12.95 (*0-87226-444-0*, Bedrick Blackie) P Bedrick Bks.
Taylor, Lisa. Beryl's Box. Dann, Penny, illus. LC 92-44990. 32p. (ps-2). 1993. 12.95 (*0-8120-6355-4*); pap. 5.95 (*0-8120-1673-4*) Barron.
Taylor, Lucinda. Mitchell D. Fardle. Young, Karen, illus. LC 93-28987. 1994. 4.25 (*0-383-03761-1*) SRA Schl Grp.
Van Allsburg, Chris. Jumanji. Van Allsburg, Chris, illus. (gr. 3 up). 1981. 15.95 (*0-395-30448-2*) HM.
Vos-Wezeman, Phyllis. Benjamin Brody's Backyard Bag. (Illus.). 32p. (Orig.). 1991. pap. 11.95 (*0-87178-091-7*) Brethren.
Winter, Susan. My Shadow. LC 93-11437. (gr. 4 up). 1994. 14.95 (*0-385-31066-8*) Doubleday.
Wright, Christine. Just Like Emma: How She Has Fun in God's World. LC 92-70792. 32p. (ps-3). 1992. 7.99 (*0-8066-2617-8*, 9-2617) Augsburg Fortress.
Yaccarino, Dan. The House of Fun! 8p. (Orig.). (gr. 4-7). 1993. pap. 12.95 (*1-55550-885-5*) Universe.
Yardley, Joanna. The Red Ball. Yolen, Jane, ed. Yardley, Joanna, illus. 32p. (ps-3). 1991. 14.95 (*0-15-200894-2*, J Yolen Bks) HarBrace.
You Can Go Jump. (Illus.). (ps-2). 1991. PLB 6.95 (*0-8136-5082-8*, TK2392); pap. 3.50 (*0-8136-5582-X*, TK2393) Modern Curr.
Ziefert, Harriet. Come out, Jessie! Smith, Mavis, illus. LC 90-41880. 32p. (ps-1). 1991. pap. 4.95 (*0-06-107414-4*) HarpC Child Bks.
—Playtime for Baby. Baum, Susan, illus. 8p. (ps). 1993. 4.95 (*0-694-00505-3*, Festival) HarpC Child Bks.
Zokeisha. Things I Like to Play With. Zokeisha, illus. 16p. (ps-k). 1981. pap. 2.95 (*0-671-44450-6*, Little Simon) S&S Trade.

PLAY CENTERS
see Playgrounds

PLAY DIRECTION (THEATER)
see Theater–Production and Direction

PLAY PRODUCTION
see Theater–Production and Direction

PLAY WRITING
see Drama–Technique

PLAYGROUNDS

Gibbons, Gail. Playgrounds. Gibbons, Gail, illus. LC 84-19285. 32p. (ps-3). 1985. reinforced bdg. 15.95 (*0-8234-0553-2*) Holiday.

PLAYGROUNDS–FICTION

Barnes, Jill & Kanabe, Junkichi. Road Roller Saves the Day. Rubin, Caroline, ed. Japan Foreign Rights Centre Staff, tr. from JPN. Emu, Namae, illus. LC 90-3841. 40p. (gr. k-3). 1990. PLB 15.93 (*0-944483-81-X*) Garrett Ed Corp.
Collis, Annabel. You Can't Catch Me! LC 92-54486. 1993. 13.95 (*0-316-15237-4*) Little.
Gordon, Sharon. Playground Fun. Karas, G. Brian, illus. LC 86-30854. 32p. (gr. k-2). 1988. lib. bdg. 7.89 (*0-8167-0990-4*); pap. text ed. 1.95 (*0-8167-0991-2*) Troll Assocs.
Naylor, Phyllis R. The King of the Playground. Malone, Nola L., illus. LC 93-25125. 32p. (gr. k-3). 1994. pap. 4.95 (*0-689-71802-0*, Aladdin) Macmillan Child Grp.
Wilmer, Diane. The Playground. rev. ed. Chamberlain, Margaret, illus. 32p. (gr. k-2). 1990. Repr. of 1986 ed. PLB 10.95 (*1-878363-10-7*) Forest Hse.

PLAYHOUSES
see Theaters

PLAYING CARDS
see Cards

PLAYS

Alwin-Hill, Raymond. Treasure Island. LC 91-52607. (Orig.). 1991. pap. 6.00 (*0-88734-412-7*) Players Pr.
Ammann, Herman. The Little Troll Without a Soul. (Illus.). 27p. (Orig.). (gr. 4-9). 1976. pap. 3.00 (*0-88680-117-6*); royalty on application 25.00 (*0-685-59268-5*) I E Clark.
Annable, Toni & Kaspar, Maria H. The Runaway Match, 2 vols. Viola, Amy, tr. 48p. (Orig.). (gr. 2 up). 1992. pap. 8.95 Set (*1-882828-10-0*) Vol. 1: English-Spanish, La Cerrilla Fugitiva. Vol. 2: English-Spanish, L'Allumette Fugutive. Kasan Imprints.
Ashby, Sylvia. Once upon a Broomstick: A Halloween Happening in One Act. (Illus.). 28p. (Orig.). (gr. 1-8). 1990. pap. 2.50 (*0-88680-329-2*); royalty on application 25.00 (*0-685-58901-3*) I E Clark.
Avery, Helen P. The Ghost of Canterville Hall. 1977. 4.50 (*0-87602-112-7*) Anchorage.
Ayckbourn, Alan. Mr. A's Amazing Maze Plays. 96p. 1990. pap. 7.95 (*0-571-14160-9*) Faber & Faber.
Battle of San Pascual: Mini-Play. (gr. 5 up). 1978. 5.00 (*0-89550-308-5*) Stevens & Shea.
Beebe, Hank. The Other Person's Shoes. (Illus.). 20p. (Orig.). (gr. 6-12). 1992. pap. 3.00 (*0-88680-366-7*); piano-vocal score 10.00 (*0-88680-367-5*); royalty on application 35.00 (*0-685-62711-X*) I E Clark.
Behm, Tom. How Things Happen in Three: A Participation Musical. (Orig.). (gr. k-3). 1992. pap. 4.50 playscript (*0-87602-317-0*) Anchorage.
Beiner, Stan J. Sedra Scenes: Skits for Every Torah Portion. LC 82-71282. 225p. (Orig.). (gr. 6-12). 1982. pap. text ed. 9.75 (*0-86705-007-1*) A R E Pub.
Bellville, Cheryl W. Theater Magic: Behind the Scenes at a Children's Theater. Bellville, Cheryl W., illus. LC 86-9757. 48p. (gr. k-4). 1986. PLB 19.95 (*0-87614-278-1*) Carolrhoda Bks.
Bennett, Rowena. Creative Plays & Programs for Holidays. (gr. 2-6). 1989. pap. 15.00 (*0-8238-0005-9*) Plays.
Berger, Sidney. Rapunzel. (Illus.). 32p. (Orig.). (ps up). 1991. pap. 3.00 (*0-88680-359-4*); royalty on application 40.00 (*0-685-59134-4*) I E Clark.
Birch, Beverly, retold by. Shakespeare's Stories: Comedies. Tarrant, Carol, illus. LC 88-16947. 126p. (gr. 7-12). 1988. 12.95 (*0-87226-191-3*) P Bedrick Bks.
—Shakespeare's Stories: Histories. Green, Robina, illus. LC 88-15693. 126p. (gr. 7-12). 1988. 12.95 (*0-87226-192-1*) P Bedrick Bks.
Bland, Joellen. Stage Plays from the Classics. LC 87-14669. (Orig.). (gr. 7-12). 1987. pap. 14.95 (*0-8238-0281-7*) Plays.
Boiko, Claire. Children's Plays for Creative Actors. 384p. (gr. 3-7). 1985. pap. 15.00 (*0-8238-0267-1*) Plays.
Bradley, Alfred & Bond, Michael. Paddington on Stage. Fortnum, Peggy, illus. LC 76-62497. (gr. 2-5). 1977. 14.45 (*0-395-25155-9*) HM.
Brill, Michael E. The Masque of Beauty & the Beast. 1979. 4.50 (*0-87602-156-9*) Anchorage.
Broadhurst, Alan. The Great Cross-Country Race. 1965. 5.50 (*0-87602-133-X*) Anchorage.
—Young Dick Whittington. (gr. 1-7). 1964. 4.50 (*0-87602-224-7*) Anchorage.
Bronstein, Robert & Maxwell, James. Just a Moment, Soldier! LC 93-74141. (Illus.). 207p. (gr. 8-12). 1994. 17.95 (*0-9638960-3-2*); pap. 12.95 (*0-9638960-2-4*) Bronfam Pr.
Brooks, Courtaney. The Case of the Stolen Dinosaur: A Play in Two Versions: Stage & Radio. Way, Merrilee, illus. 26p. (Orig.). (gr. 4 up). 1983. pap. text ed. 4.00x (*0-941274-02-0*) Belnice Bks.
—Eight Steps to Choral Reading. Way, Marrilee, illus. (Orig.). (gr. 1 up). 1983. pap. text ed. 3.00x (*0-941274-01-2*) Belnice Bks.
—Little Red & the Wolf: A Puppet Play. Way, Merrilee, illus. (gr. k up). 1983. pap. text ed. 2.50x (*0-941274-04-7*) Belnice Bks.
—Pardner & Freddie: A Puppet Play. Way, Merrilee, illus. (gr. k up). 1983. pap. text ed. 2.50x (*0-941274-03-9*) Belnice Bks.
—Plays & Puppets &cetera. 7th ed. Runyan, Merrilee, illus. LC 81-68933. 100p. (Orig.). (gr. k up). 1981. pap. text ed. 14.95 (*0-941274-00-4*) Belnice Bks.
Brown, Regina. Play at Your House. Brown, Regina, illus. (gr. 3-7). 1962. 8.95 (*0-8392-3027-3*) Astor-Honor.
Bruestle, Beaumont. The Wonderful Tang. (gr. 1-7). 1952. 4.50 (*0-87602-222-0*) Anchorage.
Bush, Max. The Voyage of the Dragonfly. 1989. Playscript. 4.50 (*0-87602-287-5*) Anchorage.
Campbell, Ken. Skungpoomery. 47p. 1988. pap. text ed. 5.95x (*0-413-33910-6*, A0263, Pub. by Methuen UK) Heinemann.
Carey, Karla. Julie & Jackie at Christmas-Time: The Play & Musical Play (with Music Book, Story-&-Song Cassette & Piano Cassette) Nolan, Dennis, illus. LC 88-12909. 39p. 1990. pap. 35.00 complete pkg. (*1-55768-151-1*); pap. 25.00 book only (*1-55768-026-4*); story-&-song or piano cass. 8.00 (*0-685-19710-7*) LC Pub.
—Julie & Jackie at the Circus: The Play & Musical Play (with Music Book, Story-&-Song Cassette & Piano Cassette) Nolan, Dennis, illus. LC 88-12910. 44p. 1990. pap. 35.00 complete pkg. (*1-55768-152-X*); pap. 25.00 book only (*1-55768-177-5*); story-&-song or piano cass. 8.00 (*1-55768-027-2*) LC Pub.
—Julie & Jackie Go a'Journeying: The Play & Musical Play (with Music Book, Story-&-Song Cassette & Piano Cassette) Nolan, Dennis, illus. LC 88-9171. 73p. 1990. pap. 35.00 complete pkg. (*1-55768-153-8*); pap. 25.00 book only (*1-55768-028-0*); story-&-song or piano cass. 8.00 (*0-685-19711-5*) LC Pub.
—Julie & Jackie on the Ranch: The Play & Musical Play (with Music Book, Story-&-Song Cassette & Piano Cassette) Nolan, Dennis, illus. LC 88-12911. 46p. 1990. pap. 35.00 complete pkg. (*1-55768-154-6*); pap. 25.00 book only (*1-55768-029-9*); story-&-song or piano cass. 8.00 (*0-685-19712-3*) LC Pub.
Caruso, Joseph G. Tom Sawyer, Detective. 34p. (Orig.). (gr. 2 up). 1991. pap. 3.00 (*0-88680-358-6*); royalty on application 35.00 (*0-685-59132-8*) I E Clark.
Charles, Carole. General George at Yorktown. Seible, Bob, illus. LC 75-33158. 32p. (gr. 2-6). 1975. PLB 14.95 (*0-913778-23-0*) Childs World.
—Martha Helps the Rebel. Seible, Bob, illus. LC 75-33126. (gr. 2-6). 1975. PLB 14.95 (*0-913778-22-2*) Childs World.
Charpentier, Aristide-Christian. The Violin of Passing Time. (gr. 1-7). 1972. 4.50 (*0-87602-217-4*) Anchorage.
Cheasebro, Margaret. The Prodigal Son & Other Parables As Plays. LC 92-7232. (gr. 5 up). 1993. 6.99 (*0-8054-6065-9*) Broadman.
Cherokee Removal: Mini-Play. (gr. 5 up). 1982. 6.50 (*0-89550-377-8*) Stevens & Shea.
Chief Joseph: Mini-Play. (gr. 5 up). 1982. 6.50 (*0-89550-378-6*) Stevens & Shea.
Child Labor: Mini-Play. (gr. 5 up). 1978. 6.50 (*0-89550-334-4*) Stevens & Shea.
Chinese in America: Mini-Play. (gr. 5up). 1975. 6.50 (*0-89550-350-6*) Stevens & Shea.
Chokai, M. Sherlock Holmes & the Jewel & Other Short Plays. Biswas, Dolly, illus. 169p. (gr. 6). 1983. pap. 3.95x (*0-86131-330-5*) Apt Bks.
Chorpenning, Charlotte B. Cinderella. (gr. 1-7). 1940. 4.50 (*0-87602-116-X*) Anchorage.

—Jack & the Beanstalk. 1935. 4.50 (*0-87602-143-7*) Anchorage.
—Robinson Crusoe. (gr. 1-9). 1952. 4.50 (*0-87602-192-5*) Anchorage.
—Rumpelstiltskin. (gr. 1-7). 1944. 4.50 (*0-87602-195-X*) Anchorage.
—The Sleeping Beauty. (gr. 1-7). 1947. 4.50 (*0-87602-203-4*) Anchorage.
Church, Jeff. The Pied Piper of New Orleans. (Orig.). 1993. pap. 4.50 playscript (*0-87602-324-3*) Anchorage.
Clark, I. E. The Happy Scarecrow. (Illus.). 17p. (Orig.). (gr. 5-12). 1966. pap. 3.00 (*0-88680-077-3*); director's script 7.50 (*0-88680-078-1*); royalty on application 25.00 (*0-685-59264-2*) I E Clark.
Cockley, Dave. Kids' Country: A Musical Play in Two Acts. Gulick, Lissy, contrib. by. (Illus.). 68p. (Orig.). (gr. 4 up). 1990. pap. 4.25 (*0-88680-331-4*); piano-vocal score 15.00 (*0-88680-332-2*); royalty on application 85.00 (*0-685-58898-X*) I E Clark.
Conradson, Shari. Just Junior High. rev. ed. 52p. (Orig.). (gr. 6-9). 1992. pap. 5.00 (*0-9620445-1-2*) KSJ Publishing.
Cox, Thomas J. Leaflets of the White Rose: A Filmplay. 119p. (Orig.). 1991. pap. 14.50 (*1-879710-02-1*) Riverside FL.
Cullen, Alan. The Beeple. 1968. 4.50 (*0-87602-108-9*) Anchorage.
—The Man in the Moon. 1964. 4.50 (*0-87602-153-4*) Anchorage.
—Trudi & the Minstrel. (gr. 1-9). 1957. 4.50 (*0-87602-214-X*) Anchorage.
Cullen, Allan. Niccolo & Nicolette. (gr. 1-9). 1957. 4.50 (*0-87602-162-3*) Anchorage.
Dahl, Roald. Charlie & the Chocolate Factory. Schindelman, Joseph, illus. (gr. 5 up). 1964. 16.00 (*0-394-81011-2*); PLB 15.99 (*0-394-91011-7*) Knopf Bks Yng Read.
Davenport, May. Two Plays. LC 75-55603. (gr. 5-12). 1977. 2.50x (*0-9603118-0-7*) Davenport.
Davis, Ossie. Langston: A Play. LC 82-70314. 144p. (gr. 7 up). 1982. pap. 11.95 (*0-385-28543-4*) Delacorte.
Dean, Lois. Fox in a Fix. 1959. 4.00 (*0-87602-128-3*) Anchorage.
Dinges, Susan & Thomas, Sue. Curtain II: Creative Drama for Children 9-12. (ps-7). 1986. 15.00 (*0-89824-168-5*) Trillium Pr.
The Donner Party: Mini-Play. (gr. 5 up). 1982. 6.50 (*0-89550-379-4*) Stevens & Shea.
Doyle, Sharon E. In Other Words. 1976. 4.00 (*0-87602-141-0*) Anchorage.
Dubay, Brenda, adapted by. Just So Stories: Adapted from the Book by Rudyard Kipling. Dubay, Bren, contrib. by. (Illus.). 36p. (Orig.). (ps-7). 1990. pap. 3.50 (*0-88680-333-0*); royalty on application 40.00 (*0-685-58897-1*) I E Clark.
Dunster, Mark. Chimney. 14p. (Orig.). 1990. pap. 4.00 (*0-89642-180-5*) Linden Pubs.
Elias, Miriam L. Thanks to You! LC 94-44850. 1994. write for info. (*0-87306-663-4*); pap. write for info. (*0-87306-664-2*) Feldheim.
Elitzig, Francis. Sea Girl. (Orig.). 1993. pap. 4.50 playscript (*0-87602-318-9*) Anchorage.
Enscoe, Lawrence & Enscoe, Andrea. Get a Grip! A Year 'Round Drama-Rama of Scenes & Monologs for Christian Teens. Zapel, Arthur L., ed. LC 91-37422. 128p. (Orig.). (gr. 9-12). 1992. pap. 9.95 (*0-916260-82-8*, B128) Meriwether Pub.
Faber, Roger A. The Return. 64p. (gr. 9-12). 1992. pap. 7.00 (*1-880122-03-0*) White Stone.
Falls, Gregory A. & Beattie, Kurt. The Odyssey. 1978. 5.00 (*0-87602-238-7*) Anchorage.
Fanning, Margaret & Bak, Linda. The Famished Fox. 18p. (Orig.). (gr. k-1). 1992. pap. text ed. 6.00 set of 2 scripts (*1-882063-23-6*) Cottage Pr MA.
—The Greedy Pup. Bak, Linda, illus. 18p. (Orig.). 1992. Set of 2 scripts. pap. text ed. 6.00 (*1-882063-25-2*) Cottage Pr MA.
—The Lad & the Fib. 18p. (Orig.). 1992. pap. text ed. 18.00 set of 6 scripts (*1-882063-24-4*) Cottage Pr MA.
—The Three Little Pigs. 24p. (gr. k-1). 1992. pap. text ed. 18.00 set of 6 scripts (*1-882063-22-8*) Cottage Pr MA.
The Farmworkers: Mini-Play. (gr. 5 up). 1975. 5.00 (*0-89550-307-7*) Stevens & Shea.
Farnagle, A. E. The Not So Goody Gum Drop Shop: A Play in One Act. 32p. (Orig.). (gr. 3-8). 1984. pap. 3.50 (*0-916565-06-8*) Whitehall Pr.
Fauquez, Arthur. Don Quixote of La Mancha. 1967. 4.50 (*0-87602-121-6*) Anchorage.
—The Man Who Killed Time. 1964. 4.50 (*0-87602-154-2*) Anchorage.
—Reynard the Fox. 1962. 5.50 (*0-87602-187-9*) Anchorage.
Fisher, Aileen, ed. Holiday Programs for Boys & Girls. 393p. (gr. 2-6). 1986. pap. 13.95 (*0-8238-0277-9*) Plays.
Flanagan, Mike. Westward Ho! (Orig.). 1992. pap. 4.50 playscript (*0-87602-307-3*) Anchorage.
Gallo, Donald R., ed. Center Stage: One-Act Plays for Teenage Readers & Actors. LC 90-4050. 384p. (gr. 7 up). 1990. PLB 16.89 (*0-06-022171-2*) HarpC Child Bks.
Garfield, Leon, abridged by. Romeo & Juliet. Makarov, Igor, illus. LC 92-14523. 48p. (gr. 5 up). 1993. PLB 11.99 (*0-679-93874-5*); pap. 6.99 (*0-679-83874-0*) Knopf Bks Yng Read.
Giff, Patricia R. Show Time at the Polk Street School: Plays You Can Do Yourself. Sims, Blanche, illus. LC 91-46163. 80p. (gr. 1-4). 1992. 14.00 (*0-385-30794-2*) Delacorte.
Glore, John. Folktales Too. (Illus.). 52p. (Orig.). (ps up). 1991. pap. 3.50 (*0-88680-352-7*); royalty on application 40.00 (*0-685-59140-9*) I E Clark.
Goldberg, Moses. Aladdin: A Participation Play. 1977. 4.50 (*0-87602-101-1*) Anchorage.
—The Analysis of Mineral Number Four. (Orig.). (gr. 4 up). 1982. playscript 4.50 (*0-87602-234-4*) Anchorage.
—The Men's Cottage. (Orig.). (gr. 4 up). 1980. playscript 4.50 (*0-87602-229-8*) Anchorage.
—The Outlaw Robin Hood. 1967. 4.50 (*0-87602-168-2*) Anchorage.
—The Wind in the Willows. (gr. 1-7). 1974. 4.50 (*0-87602-220-4*) Anchorage.
Golden, Joseph. Johnny Moonbeam & the Silver Arrow. 1962. 4.50 (*0-87602-144-5*) Anchorage.
Graczyk, Ed. Appleseed. 1971. 4.50 (*0-87602-106-2*) Anchorage.
—Livin' de Life. 1970. 4.50 (*0-87602-151-8*) Anchorage.
—The Rude Mechanicals. (gr. 4-12). 1970. 4.50 (*0-87602-194-1*) Anchorage.
Grauer, Rita & Urquhart, John. Gold Fever. 46p. (Orig.). 1992. pap. 4.50 playscript (*0-87602-302-2*) Anchorage.
Greidanus, Aad. Two Pails of Water. (gr. 1-7). 1965. 4.50 (*0-87602-215-8*) Anchorage.

Guida, Frank J. Romeo & Juliet - with a Happy Ending, Vol. 1. rev. ed. Guida, Frank J., illus. 20p. 1991. lib. bdg. write for info. (*1-878476-00-9*) Rockmasters Intl.
This children's adaptation of William Shakespeare's classic ROMEO & JULIET is intended to cultivate at an early age some of the most dramatic writing in literature. Wait till you hear your youngster reading, understanding & quoting The Bard! "What a wonderful treasure you have added to the shelves of children's literature in your adaptation of Romeo & Juliet. I thank & applaud you as future generations are certain to do likewise."--Constance F. Zimmerman, Chairperson, Norfolk Reading Council. "The presentation is superb; the art work attractive; & the text very interesting."--James Cullinan, Finnbar Books, Kent, England. "I like your story Mr. Guida because it's with a happy ending. If they're sad, I start to cry & I have bad dreams. But I wonder where you got that name wink milch?"--Crystal (Drew School, 8 years old, Washington, D.C.). "My favorite part is when the two families become friends again & nobody gets killed!"--Brett (Drew School, 9 years old). "In a unique adaptation, Frank Guida has forged a new method of bringing great literary works to young minds."--(Julie Cimino, Educator, Wash., D.C.). "Guida's adaptation incorporates portions of the original in all capital letters, such as Juliet's famous balcony scene."--Philip Walzer (Virginian-Pilot, Norfolk, Va.).
Publisher Provided Annotation.

Gunning, Peter. Alas in Blunderland. Henderson, Catherine, illus. 32p. (Orig.). (gr. 5-7). 1991. pap. 10.95 (*0-86278-271-6*, Pub. by OBrien Pr IE) Dufour.
Hall, Robin. Three Tales from Japan. (gr. 1-9). 1973. 4.50 (*0-87602-209-3*) Anchorage.
Hamlett, Christina. Humorous Plays for Teenagers. LC 86-16916. (Orig.). (gr. 7-12). 1987. pap. 12.95 (*0-8238-0276-0*) Plays.
Harder, Eleanor. Goldilocks & the Christmas Bears. 1981. pap. 3.45 playscript (*0-87129-198-3*, G06) Dramatic Pub.
Harder, Eleanor & Harder, Ray. The Near-Sighted Knight & the Far-Sighted Dragon: Musical. (gr. 1-9). 1977. 4.50 (*0-87602-161-5*) Anchorage.
—Sacramento Fifty Miles: Musical. (gr. 1-7). 1969. 4.50 (*0-87602-198-4*) Anchorage.
Harris, Aurand. Androcles & the Lion: Musical. 1964. 4.50 (*0-87602-105-4*) Anchorage.
—The Arkansaw Bear. (Orig.). (gr. 5 up). 1980. playscript 4.50 (*0-87602-226-3*) Anchorage.
—The Brave Little Tailor. 1961. 4.50 (*0-87602-109-7*) Anchorage.
—A Doctor in Spite of Himself. 1968. 4.50 (*0-87602-120-8*) Anchorage.
—Huck Finn's Story. 42p. 1988. Playscript. 4.50 (*0-87602-280-8*) Anchorage.
—Peck's Bad Boy. (gr. 1-9). 1974. playscript 4.50 (*0-87602-170-4*) Anchorage.
—The Pinballs. 1992. pap. 4.50 playscript (*0-87602-301-4*) Anchorage.
—Pocahontas. 1961. 4.50 (*0-87602-177-1*) Anchorage.
—Punch & Judy: Musical. 47p. (Orig.). 1970. 4.50 (*0-87602-183-6*) Anchorage.
—Rags to Riches: Musical. 1966. 4.50 (*0-87602-185-2*) Anchorage.
—Star Spangled Salute. (gr. 1-12). 1974. 4.50 (*0-87602-205-0*) Anchorage.
Harris, Aurand & Shakespeare, William. Robin Goodfellow. 1977. 4.50 (*0-87602-190-9*) Anchorage.
Haycock, Kate. Plays. Stefoff, Rebecca, ed. LC 90-13937. (Illus.). 32p. (gr. 4-8). 1991. PLB 17.26 (*0-944483-98-4*) Garrett Ed Corp.
Haynes, Harold J. I Just Wanna Tell Somebody. (Illus.). 48p. (Orig.). (gr. 7 up). 1987. pap. 4.00 (*0-88680-285-7*); piano-vocal score 10.00 (*0-88680-286-5*); royalty on application 60.00 (*0-685-58887-4*) I E Clark.
Helen Gahagen Douglas: Mini-Play. (gr. 5 up). 1978. 6.50 (*0-89550-333-6*) Stevens & Shea.
Herbert, Victor. Babes in Toyland: Musical. Holamon, Ken, adapted by. (Orig.). (ps up). 1987. playscript 5.50 (*0-87602-275-1*) Anchorage.
Herlihy, Dirlie. Ludie's Song. 224p. (gr. 4 up). 1990. pap. 4.95 (*0-14-034245-1*, Puffin) Puffin Bks.
Hoban, Gordon. High Jinks: A Play. LC 91-90470. 160p. (Orig.). 1991. pap. 11.95 (*0-944204-13-9*) Omniun.
Holman, David. Whale. 46p. (gr. 6-10). 1990. pap. 7.95 (*0-413-63090-0*, A0470, Pub. by Methuen UK) Heinemann.
Hume, Pat. Dick Whittington & His Amazing Cat. (Orig.). (gr. k up). 1980. 4.50 (*0-87602-230-1*) Anchorage.
Integration: Mini-Play. (gr. 5 up). 1978. 6.50 (*0-89550-329-8*) Stevens & Shea.
Irish Famine: Mini-Play. (gr. 5 up). 1982. 6.50 (*0-89550-376-X*) Stevens & Shea.
Ison, Colleen. Skits That Teach Children: Including "Goliath's Last Stand" & Fifteen Other Short Dramas. rev. ed. Fittro, Pat, ed. 112p. (ps-7). 1993. pap. 5.99 (*0-87403-947-9*, 14-03347) Standard Pub.
—Skits That Teach Teens: Including "Three Ways to Mess up a Relationship" & Nine Other Short Dramas. Fittro, Pat, ed. 112p. (Orig.). 1993. pap. 5.99 (*0-7847-0108-3*, 14-03348) Standard Pub.
Jackson, R. Eugene. Babes in Toyland: Stage Magic Plays for Children's Theatre. Alette, Carl, adapted by. (Illus.). 48p. (Orig.). (ps up). 1987. pap. 4.50 (*0-88680-267-9*); piano-vocal score 15.00 (*0-88680-268-7*); royalty on application 90.00 (*0-685-58886-6*) I E Clark.
—Christmas with the Three Bears. Alette, Carl, contrib. by. (Illus.). 48p. (Orig.). (gr. 1-10). 1990. pap. 4.00 (*0-88680-326-8*); piano-vocal score 10.00 (*0-88680-327-6*); royalty on application 50.00 (*0-685-58893-9*) I E Clark.
—Rock 'n Roll Santa. Alette, Carl, contrib. by. (Illus.). 55p. (Orig.). (gr. 1 up). 1991. pap. 4.25 (*0-88680-346-2*); piano/vocal score 15.00 (*0-88680-347-0*); royalty on application 60.00 (*0-685-59131-X*) I E Clark.
Japanese Relocation: Mini-Play. (gr. 5 up). 1978. 6.50 (*0-89550-328-X*) Stevens & Shea.
Jetsmark, Torben. Peter the Postman. 37p. 1988. Playscript. 4.50 (*0-87602-279-4*) Anchorage.
John Peter Zenger: Mini-Play. (gr. 5 up). 1982. 6.50 (*0-89550-375-1*) Stevens & Shea.
Julian, Faye. A Magic Christmas: A Play for Children in One Act. (Illus.). 28p. (gr. k-12). 1983. pap. 2.00 (*0-88680-121-4*); royalty on application 20.00 (*0-685-57861-5*) I E Clark.
Kamerman, Sylvia E., ed. The Big Book of Dramatized Classics: 25 Adaptations of Favorite Novels, Stories, & Plays for Stage & Round-the-Table Reading. LC 93-3387. 400p. (gr. 1-8). 1993. 18.95 (*0-8238-0299-X*) Plays.
—Children's Plays from Favorite Stories. 583p. (gr. 1-6). 1990. pap. 16.95 (*0-8238-0270-1*) Plays.
—Plays from Favorite Folk Tales. LC 87-12960. (Orig.). (gr. 2 up). 1987. pap. 13.95 (*0-8238-0280-9*) Plays.
Kaplan, Carol B. Holiday Plays. Mitter, Kathy, illus. 37p. (ps). 1989. tchr's. ed. 17.00 (*0-88734-410-0*) Players Pr.
Kehret, Peg. Acting Natural: Monologs, Dialogs, & Playlets for Teens. Zapel, Arthur L., ed. Panowski, James A., frwd. by. LC 91-43552. (Orig.). (gr. 9-12). 1992. pap. text ed. 10.95 (*0-916260-84-4*, B133) Meriwether Pub.
Kelly, Tim. The Lalapalooza Bird. (Illus.). 24p. (Orig.). (gr. 5-12). 1981. pap. 2.50 (*0-88680-105-2*); royalty on application 25.00 (*0-685-59257-X*) I E Clark.
Kern, Phil, et al. When the Hippos Crashed the Dance. (Illus.). 125p. (gr. 1-6). 1991. pap. 69.95 (*1-56516-008-8*) Houston IN.
Kern, Susan & Kern, Phil. Anything Toy. (Illus.). 125p. (gr. 1-6). 1991. pap. 69.95 (*1-56516-009-6*) Houston IN.
—Concerto in A Minor Dispute. (Illus.). 125p. (gr. 2-6). 1991. pap. 79.95 (*1-56516-011-8*) Houston IN.

Kesselman, Wendy. Becca: (Musical) 61p. 1988. playscript 5.50 (*0-87602-277-8*) Anchorage.
King, Martha B. Riddle Me Ree. 1977. 4.50 (*0-87602-188-7*) Anchorage.
Kline, Suzy. The Herbie Jones Reader's Theater. Williams, Richard, illus. 160p. (gr. 2-6). 1992. pap. 8.95 (*0-399-22120-4*, Putnam) Putnam Pub Group.
Kornhauser, Barry. This Is Not a Pipe Dream. (Orig.). 1992. pap. 4.50 playscript (*0-87602-316-2*) Anchorage.
Koste, Virginia G. The Medicine Show. (gr. 4-12). 1975. 4.50 (*0-87602-258-1*) Anchorage.
Kral, Brian. Apologies. 42p. (Orig.). (gr. 9-12). 1988. playscript 5.00 (*0-87602-278-6*) Anchorage.
—East of the Sun, West of the Moon. 56p. (Orig.). (ps up). 1987. playscript 5.50 (*0-87602-273-5*) Anchorage.
—One to Grow On. (Orig.). 1993. pap. 4.50 playscript (*0-87602-320-0*) Anchorage.
—Ransom of Red Chief. (Orig.). (gr. 3 up). 1980. playscript 4.50 (*0-87602-227-1*) Anchorage.
Kraus, Joanna. The Dragon Hammer & the Tale of Oniroku. LC 77-83857. (Illus.). 64p. (gr. 3-5). 1977. pap. 4.95 (*0-932720-17-X*); 7.95 (*0-932720-18-8*) New Plays Inc.
Kraus, Joanna H. The Shaggy Dog Murder Trial. (Orig.). (gr. 4-7). 1988. playscript 4.50 (*0-87602-274-3*) Anchorage.
Krell-Oishi, Mary. Scenes That Happen: Dramatized Snapshots about the Real Life of Highschoolers. Zapel, Theodore O., ed. Glore, John, intro. by. LC 91-26778. 176p. (Orig.). (gr. 9-12). 1991. pap. 10.95 (*0-916260-79-8*, B156) Meriwether Pub.
Laing, John. One Cool Cat. 43p. 1988. pap. 5.95 (*0-413-54220-3*, A0197) Heinemann.
Lamb, Wendy, ed. Ten Out of Ten: Ten Winning Plays Selected from the Young Playwrights Festival 1982-1991. Quinn, Nancy & Wasserstein, Wendyintro. by. LC 92-7944. 320p. (gr. 7 up). 1992. 18.00 (*0-385-30811-6*) Delacorte.
Landes, William-Alan. Aladdin n' His Magic Lamp. rev. ed. LC 89-43679. 52p. (gr. 3-12). 1985. pap. 6.00 play script (*0-88734-102-0*); dir. guide 30.00 (*0-88734-003-2*) Players Pr.
—Jack 'n the Beanstalk. rev. ed. LC 89-43681. (gr. 3-12). 1985. pap. 6.00 play script (*0-88734-101-2*); tchr's. ed. 30.00 (*0-88734-001-6*) Players Pr.
—Jack 'n the Beanstalk: Music & Lyrics. rev. ed. (gr. 3-12). 1985. pap. text ed. 15.00 (*0-88734-000-8*) Players Pr.
—Peter N' the Wolf. rev. ed. LC 89-69871. (gr. 3-12). 1988. pap. 6.00 play script (*0-88734-106-3*); tchr's. ed. 30.00 (*0-88734-013-X*) Players Pr.
—Rapunzel 'N the Witch. rev. ed. LC 89-43682. (gr. 3-12). 1985. pap. 6.00 play script (*0-88734-107-1*); tchr's. ed. 30.00 (*0-88734-007-5*) Players Pr.
—Rapunzel 'N the Witch: Music & Lyrics. rev. ed. (gr. 3-12). 1985. pap. 15.00 play script (*0-88734-006-7*) Players Pr.
—Rhyme Tyme. rev. ed. LC 89-63869. (gr. 3-12). 1985. pap. 6.00 play script (*0-88734-108-X*) Players Pr.
Landes, William-Alan & Rizzo, Jeff. Rhyme Tyme: Music & Lyrics. rev. ed. (gr. 3-12). 1985. pap. text ed. 15.00 (*0-88734-008-3*) Players Pr.
Lavrakas, Paul. The Princess & the Pea. (Orig.). 1993. pap. 4.50 playscript (*0-87602-321-9*) Anchorage.
Lawrence, V. J. Nine Plays for African American Youth: Children's Window to Africa. 45p. (gr. 1-12). 1993. pap. 8.95 (*0-929917-06-5*) Magnolia PA.
Levitt, Saul. Jim Thorpe, All American. (Orig.). (gr. 4 up). 1980. playscript 5.00 (*0-87602-237-9*) Anchorage.
Longmeyer, Carole M. An American Mystery: Script. (Orig.). (gr. 3-12). 1994. pap. 24.95 (*0-935326-50-2*) Gallopade Pub Group.
Love, Douglas. Blame It on the Wolf & Be Kind to Your Mother (Earth): Two Original Plays. Zimmerman, Robert, illus. LC 92-4624. 80p. (gr. 5 up). 1993. PLB 13.89 (*0-06-021106-7*) HarpC Child Bks.
—Holiday in the Rain Forest & Kabuki Gift: Two Plays. Zimmerman, Robert, illus. LC 93-41615. 96p. (gr. 5 up). 1994. PLB 13.89 (*0-06-024276-0*) HarpC Child Bks.
—Holiday in the Rain Forest: Theater Kit. Zimmerman, Robert, illus. (gr. 5 up). 1993. 14.95 (*0-694-00561-4*, Festival) HarpC Child Bks.
—Kabuki Gift. Zimmerman, Robert, illus. 64p. (gr. 3 up). 1994. pap. 3.50 (*0-694-00658-0*, Festival) HarpC Child Bks.
—Kabuki Gift: Theater Kit. Zimmerman, Robert, illus. 32p. (gr. 5 up). 1993. 14.95 (*0-694-00562-2*, Festival) HarpC Child Bks.
McAlvay, Nora & Chorpenning, Charlotte B. The Elves & the Shoemaker. 1946. 4.50 (*0-87602-124-0*) Anchorage.
—Flibbertygibbet. 1952. 4.50 (*0-87602-127-5*) Anchorage.
McCaslin, Nellie. Angel of the Battlefield. LC 93-2604. 20p. 1993. pap. 5.00 (*0-88734-430-5*) Players Pr.
—Bluebonnets. LC 93-5271. 20p. 1993. pap. 5.00 (*0-88734-439-9*) Players Pr.
—Brave New Banner. 20p. 1993. pap. 5.00 (*0-88734-436-4*) Players Pr.
—Cold Face - Warm Heart. LC 93-5273. 20p. 1993. pap. 5.00 (*0-88734-440-2*) Players Pr.
—The Last Horizon. LC 93-5270. 24p. 1993. pap. 5.00 play script (*0-88734-431-3*) Players Pr.
—The Legend of Minna Lamourrie. LC 93-2603. 20p. 1993. pap. 5.00 play script (*0-88734-438-0*) Players Pr.
—Legends in Action: Ten Plays of Ten Lands. Landes, William-Alan, frwd. by. LC 93-22161. 1994. pap. 15.95 (*0-88734-633-2*) Players Pr.
—A Straight Shooter. LC 93-5252. 16p. 1993. pap. 5.00 play script (*0-88734-429-1*) Players Pr.
—Too Many Cooks. LC 93-5250. 20p. 1993. pap. 5.00 play script (*0-88734-434-8*) Players Pr.
McDonough, Jerome. Alky. 40p. (Orig.). (gr. 7-12). 1991. pap. 3.00 (*0-88680-354-3*); royalty on application 35.00 (*0-685-59145-X*) I E Clark.
—It's Sad, So Sad When an Elf Goes Bad. (Illus.). 24p. (Orig.). (gr. k-6). 1979. pap. 2.50 (*0-88680-100-1*); royalty on application 20.00 (*0-685-59260-X*) I E Clark.
—Limbo. 28p. (Orig.). (gr. 7 up). 1984. pap. 3.00 (*0-88680-219-9*); royalty on application 35.00 (*0-685-57920-4*) I E Clark.
—Not Even A. Mouse: A Chris-Mouse Tale. (Illus.). 20p. (Orig.). (gr. k-9). 1984. pap. 2.00 (*0-88680-220-2*) royalty on application 15.00 (*0-685-57922-0*) I E Clark.
McDonough, Jerome, adapted by. Alice: A One-Act Play. (Illus.). 36p. (Orig.). (gr. 4-12). 1990. pap. 3.00 (*0-88680-336-5*); royalty on application 25.00 (*0-685-58889-0*) I E Clark.
McKenna, Helen. Young Hickory. (gr. 1-7). 1940. 4.50 (*0-87602-225-5*) Anchorage.
Martin, Judith & Ashwander, Donald. Christmas All over the Place. 22p. (Orig.). (ps-12). 1977. playscript 3.50 (*0-87602-113-5*) Anchorage.
—The Lost & Found Christmas. 14p. (Orig.). (ps up). 1977. playscript 3.50 (*0-87602-152-6*) Anchorage.
—The Runaway Presents. 16p. (Orig.). (ps up). 1977. playscript 3.50 (*0-87602-197-6*) Anchorage.
—Wiggle Worm's Surprise. 16p. (Orig.). (ps up). 1977. playscript 3.50 (*0-87602-218-2*) Anchorage.
Martin, Judith & Charlip, Remy. The Tree Angel. Charlip, Remy, illus. 40p. (gr. k-3). 1992. pap. 3.25 (*0-440-40725-7*, YB) Dell.
Mathews-Deacon, Saundra. Magic Theatre I: Children's Musical. 1977. playscript 3.75 (*0-87129-230-0*, M12) Dramatic Pub.
May, Bob & Tibbetts, Cristopher. The Andrew Is Dead Story. 26p. (Orig.). (gr. 7-12). 1991. pap. 3.00 (*0-88680-345-4*); royalty on application 35.00 (*0-685-59141-7*) I E Clark.
Melanos, Jack. Rapunzel & the Witch. 1950. 4.50 (*0-87602-186-0*) Anchorage.
Miller, Helen L. First Plays for Children. 295p. (gr. 1-3). 1985. pap. 12.00 (*0-8238-0268-X*) Plays.
—Special Plays for Holidays. LC 86-9332. (Orig.). (gr. 1-6). 1986. pap. 12.00 (*0-8238-0275-2*) Plays.
Miller, Kathryn S. The Shining Moment: (Musical) 1989. Playscript. 4.50 (*0-87602-286-7*) Anchorage.
Miller, Lucille. Heidi. 1936. 4.50 (*0-87602-136-4*) Anchorage.
Miller, Madge. Alice in Wonderland. 1953. 4.50 (*0-87602-104-6*) Anchorage.
—Hansel & Gretel. 1954. 4.50 (*0-87602-135-6*) Anchorage.
—The Land of the Dragon. 1946. 4.50 (*0-87602-148-8*) Anchorage.
—The Pied Piper of Hamelin. 1951. 4.50 (*0-87602-174-7*) Anchorage.
—Pinocchio. 1954. 4.00 (*0-87602-175-5*) Anchorage.
—The Princess & the Swineherd. 1946. 4.50 (*0-87602-181-X*) Anchorage.
—Puss in Boots: Miniature Play. 37p. (Orig.). 1954. 4.00 (*0-87602-184-4*) Anchorage.
—Robinson Crusoe. (gr. 1-9). 1954. 4.00 (*0-87602-193-3*) Anchorage.
—The Unwicked Witch. (gr. 1-7). 1964. 4.50 (*0-87602-216-6*) Anchorage.
Miller, Sarah W. Bible Dramas for Older Boys & Girls. LC 75-95409. (gr. 3-6). 1970. pap. 4.99 (*0-8054-7506-0*) Broadman.
Mofid, Bijan. The Butterfly. 1974. 4.50 (*0-87602-111-9*) Anchorage.
Molyneux, Lynn & Gordner, Brad. Act It Out: Original Plays Plus Crafts for Costumes & Scenery. Marasco, Pam, illus. 192p. (gr. 2-6). 1986. spiral bdg. 12.95 (*0-685-29139-1*) Trellis Bks Inc.
Morris-McKinsey, Jill, ed. Religiously Speaking: Plays & Poems for Children's Church. 48p. (Orig.). 1992. pap. 7.98 (*1-877588-03-2*) Creatively Yours.
Mother Jones: Mini-Play. (gr. 5up). 1975. 6.50 (*0-89550-367-0*) Stevens & Shea.
Murray, John. Mystery Plays for Young Actors. (Orig.). (gr. 5-12). 1984. pap. 13.95 (*0-8238-0265-5*) Plays.
Musil, Rosemary G. The Ghost of Mr. Penny. 1940. 4.50 (*0-87602-129-1*) Anchorage.
Musselman, Don, ed. O Ye Jigs & Juleps! 1992. pap. 5.50 playscript (*0-87602-315-4*) Anchorage.
Norris, James. Aladdin & the Wonderful Lamp. 1940. 4.50 (*0-87602-102-X*) Anchorage.
—Robin Hood. (gr. 1-9). 1952. 4.50 (*0-87602-191-7*) Anchorage.
Nursey-Bray, Rosemary. Through the Looking Glass & What Alice Found There. (Orig.). (ps up). 1987. playscript 5.00 (*0-87602-276-X*) Anchorage.
Okies & the Dustbowl: Mini-Play. (gr. 5 up). 1975. 6.50 (*0-89550-335-2*) Stevens & Shea.
Orton, Stephen A. Pan the Man. 36p. (Orig.). (gr. 7-12). 1991. pap. 3.00 (*0-88680-355-1*); royalty on application 35.00 (*0-685-59135-2*) I E Clark.
Osterberg, Susan S. & Jackson, R. Eugene. Bumper Snickers. 30p. (Orig.). (gr. 6-12). 1978. pap. 2.50 (*0-88680-015-3*); royalty on application 20.00 (*0-685-59247-2*) I E Clark.
Palmer, Greg. The Falcon. (Orig.). 1993. pap. 4.50 playscript (*0-87602-319-7*) Anchorage.
Pearson, Carol L. Don't Count Your Chickens until They Cry Wolf: Musical. 1979. 4.50 (*0-87602-122-4*) Anchorage.
Peter N' the Wolf: Music & Lyrics. rev. ed. (gr. 3-12). 1985. pap. 15.00 (*0-88734-012-1*) Players Pr.
Peterson, Liz. Wind in the Willows: (A Musical) (Orig.). 1993. pap. 4.50 playscript (*0-87602-325-1*) Anchorage.
Pilipski, Mark. Les Belles Lettres, Ser. IV: Four Roles for Three Characters. LC 92-62380. 50p. (gr. k-8). 1993. pap. write for info. (*1-882965-03-5*) Markov Pr.
Porter, Steven. The Prairie Man. LC 89-92532. 62p. (Orig.). 1990. pap. text ed. 6.00 (*0-9625372-0-9*) Phantom Pubns.
Pugh, Shirley. In One Basket. 1972. 4.50 (*0-87602-140-2*) Anchorage.
Rabin, Arnold. The Outing. 53p. (Orig.). 1992. pap. 4.50 playscript (*0-87602-303-0*) Anchorage.
Reed, Roland. The Miser. (gr. 4-12). 1973. 4.50 (*0-87602-158-5*) Anchorage.
Riley, Dorothy W. The Blackburn Affair. 25p. (gr. 4-12). 1986. pap. write for info. (*1-880234-04-1*) Winbush Pub.
—Family Reunion. 25p. 1986. pap. write for info. (*1-880234-02-5*) Winbush Pub.
—It's up to You. 25p. (gr. 4-12). 1986. pap. write for info. (*1-880234-03-3*) Winbush Pub.
Robinette, Joseph. ABC (America Before Columbus) 40p. (gr. k-8). 1984. pap. 4.00 (*0-88680-212-1*); royalty on application (non-musical version) 50.00 (*0-685-57918-2*); (musical version) 60.00 (*0-685-57919-0*) I E Clark.
Rockwell, Thomas. How to Eat Fried Worms: And Other Plays. Schick, Joel, illus. LC 78-72854. (gr. 4-7). 1980. 9.95 (*0-440-03498-1*); PLB 9.89 (*0-440-03499-X*) Delacorte.
Roets, Lois. Readers' Theater, Vol. 1: General Interest. 106p. (Orig.). (gr. 5-12). 1992. pap. text ed. 15.00 (*0-911943-29-3*) Leadership Pub.
—Readers' Theater, Vol. 2: Famous People. 108p. (Orig.). (gr. 5-12). 1992. pap. text ed. 15.00 (*0-911943-30-7*) Leadership Pub.
—Readers' Theater, Vol. 3: Entrepreneurs. 96p. (Orig.). (gr. 5-12). 1992. pap. 15.00 (*0-911943-31-5*) Leadership Pub.
Roger Williams: Mini-Play. (gr. 5 up). 1982. 6.50 (*0-89550-349-2*) Stevens & Shea.
Rogers, June W. Heidi. 1969. pap. 3.75 playscript (*0-87129-200-9*, H14) Dramatic Pub.
Roser, Bill, et al, eds. The Tale of the Frog Prince. 1979. pap. 3.75 playscript (*0-87129-199-1*, T48) Dramatic Pub.
Ross, Monica L. Montana Molly & the Peppermint Kid: (Musical) 1989. Playscript. 4.50 (*0-87602-285-9*) Anchorage.
—Wilma's Revenge. 1989. Playscript. 4.50 (*0-87602-288-3*) Anchorage.
Rostand, Edmond, et al. Cyrano de Bergerac. (Illus.). 52p. Date not set. pap. 4.95 (*1-57209-019-7*) Classics Int Ent.
Rozell, O. B. Nathan the Nervous. (Illus.). 24p. (Orig.). (gr. 6-12). 1977. pap. 2.50 (*0-88680-136-2*); royalty on application 20.00 (*0-685-59271-5*) I E Clark.
Rumble, Patricia B. The Archer & the Princess: A Comedy Based on a Russian Folk Tale. (Illus.). 48p. (Orig.). (gr. 4-10). 1990. pap. 3.00 (*0-88680-334-9*); royalty on application 40.00 (*0-685-58890-4*) I E Clark.
Russell, Willey. Our Day Out. 56p. 1988. pap. 7.95 (*0-413-54870-8*, A0201) Heinemann.
Saunders, Dudley. Dracula's Treasure. 1975. 4.50 (*0-87602-123-2*) Anchorage.
Schoolcraft, Robert. All Cats Are Gray in the Dark: A Graphic Play. Menendez, Manuela, ed. Schoolcraft, Robert, illus. 88p. (Orig.). (gr. 9 up). 1994. pap. 7.50x (*0-9640414-0-5*) MS Bks Pubng.
Schuyler, Royce. Boomerang: A One-Act Play for Grades 7-9. Kester, Ellen S., ed. Omoto, Larry, illus. 50p. (Orig.). 1989. pap. text ed. 6.95 (*0-685-26284-7*) Pickwick Pubs.
—Boomerang: Drama for Study & Performance. Kester, Ellen S., ed. Omoto, Larry, illus. 100p. (Orig.). 1989. pap. text ed. 35.00 (*0-685-26285-5*) Pickwick Pubs.
Schwartz, Yevgeny. Little Red Riding Hood. Shail, George, tr. from RUS. (gr. 4 up). 1992. pap. 3.45 playscript (*0-87129-196-7*, L25) Dramatic Pub.
Seale, Jan E. Texas History Classroom Plays, Vol. 1. (Illus.). 56p. (gr. 4-8). 1986. PLB 4.25 (*0-317-89748-9*) Knowing Pr.
—Texas History Plays Series. (Illus.). (ps-8). 1986. PLB 89.95 (*0-317-89749-7*) Knowing Pr.
Seale, Nancy. The Little Princess, Sara Crewe. (Orig.). 1982. playscript 5.00 (*0-87602-231-X*) Anchorage.
Sexton, Nancy N., et al. My Days As a Youngling, John Jacob Niles. (Orig.). (gr. 4 up). 1982. playscript 5.50 (*0-87602-239-5*) Anchorage.
Shakespeare, William. Hamlet. Mack, Maynard & Boynton, Robert W., eds. 180p. (gr. 9-12). 1990. pap. 4.50 (*0-86709-019-7*, 0019) Boynton Cook Pubs.
—Henry the Fifth for Young People. Davidson, Diane, ed. & illus. LC 91-20093. 64p. (gr. 5-8). 1991. pap. text ed. 4.95 (*0-934048-23-1*) Swan Books.
—Julius Caesar. Mack, Maynard & Boynton, Robert W., eds. 148p. (gr. 9-12). 1990. pap. text ed. 4.50 (*0-86709-023-5*, 0023) Boynton Cook Pubs.
—King Henry IV, Pt. II. Girling, Zoe. (gr. 10 up). 1967. pap. 0.60 (*0-685-42963-6*) Airmont.
—King Henry V. Thomas, Clara. (gr. 10 up). 1967. pap. 0.60 (*0-8049-1017-0*) Airmont.

—Macbeth. Stewart, Diana, adapted by. LC 81-19273. (Illus.). 48p. (gr. 4 up). 1983. PLB 20.70 (*0-8172-1681-2*); pap. 9.27 (*0-8172-2014-3*) Raintree Steck-V.
—Macbeth. Mack, Maynard & Boynton, Robert W., eds. 141p. (gr. 9-12). 1990. pap. text ed. 4.50 (*0-86709-021-9*, 0021) Boynton Cook Pubs.
—A Midsummer Night's Dream. Stewart, Diana, adapted by. LC 81-19272. (Illus.). 48p. (gr. 4 up). 1983. PLB 20.70 (*0-8172-1680-4*) Raintree Steck-V.
—A Midsummer Night's Dream. Pickett, Cecil, adapted by. (Illus.). 32p. (gr. 7 up). 1984. pap. 2.50 (*0-88680-214-8*); royalty on application 20.00 (*0-685-57921-2*) I E Clark.
—Romeo & Juliet. Mack, Maynard & Boynton, Robert W., eds. 159p. (gr. 9-12). 1990. pap. text ed. 4.50 (*0-86709-035-9*, 0035) Boynton Cook Pubs.
—Three Great Plays of Shakespeare. (gr. 4-7). 1991. pap. 6.50 (*0-582-03586-4*, 79122) Longman.
—Twelfth Night. abr. ed. Pickett, Cecil, adapted by. (Illus.). 36p. (gr. 7 up). 1984. pap. 2.50 (*0-88680-213-X*); royalty on application 20.00 (*0-685-57924-7*) I E Clark.
Shakespeare, William, et al. Hamlet. (Illus.). 52p. Date not set. pap. 4.95 (*1-57209-004-9*) Classics Int Ent.
Siks, Geraldine B. The Sandalwood Box. (gr. 1-7). 1954. 4.50 (*0-87602-199-2*) Anchorage.
Sit-In: Mini-Play. (gr. 5 up). 1977. 6.50 (*0-89550-309-3*) Stevens & Shea.
Spencer, Sara. Little Women. 1940. 4.50 (*0-87602-150-X*) Anchorage.
—Tom Sawyer. (gr. 1-9). 1935. 4.50 (*0-87602-211-5*) Anchorage.
Stephenson, R. Rex. The Jack Tales. (Illus.). 66p. (Orig.). (gr. k up). 1991. pap. 4.00 (*0-88680-361-6*); royalty on application 60.00 (*0-685-59137-9*) I E Clark.
Sternberg, Pat & Beechman, Dolly. Sojourner. 46p. 1989. Playscript. 4.50 (*0-87602-283-2*) Anchorage.
Stevens, Lawrence. Black Death: Mini-Play & Activities. (gr. 7 up). 1981. 6.50 (*0-89550-342-5*) Stevens & Shea.
Still, James. The King of the Golden River. (Orig.). 1992. pap. 4.50 playscript (*0-685-61713-0*) Anchorage.
Still, James, adapted by. The Velveteen Rabbit. 33p. (Orig.). 1989. playscript 4.50 (*0-87602-289-1*) Anchorage.
Sturkie, Joan & Cassady, Marsh. Acting It Out Junior. LC 92-29698. 264p. 1992. 15.95 (*0-89390-240-3*) Resource Pubns.
Sunanda. Stories & Plays for Children. 91p. (gr. 3-8). 1984. pap. 3.00 (*0-89071-329-4*, Pub. by Sri Aurobindo Ashram IA) Aurobindo Assn.
Surface, Mary H. Prodigy: Wolfgang Amadeus Mozart: (Musical) 50p. 1988. Playscript. 4.50 (*0-87602-281-6*) Anchorage.
—The Sorcerer's Apprentice. (Orig.). 1993. pap. 4.50 playscript (*0-87602-323-5*) Anchorage.
Swortzell, Lowell. Gulliver's Travels. 84p. (Orig.). 1992. pap. 5.00 playscript (*0-87602-304-9*) Anchorage.
Thane, Adele. Plays from Famous Stories & Fairy Tales. (gr. 4-7). 1989. pap. 15.00 (*0-8238-0060-1*) Plays.
—The Wizard of Oz. (gr. 1-7). 1957. 4.50 (*0-87602-221-2*) Anchorage.
Thomas, Eberle & Redmond, Barbara. Six Canterbury Tales. (Orig.). 1993. pap. 5.50 playscript (*0-87602-305-7*) Anchorage.
Thurston, Cheryl M. A Frog King's Daughter Is Nothing to Sneeze At. LC 88-93068. (Orig.). (gr. k-12). 1990. pap. 10.00 play script (*0-88734-513-1*) Players Pr.
—Melanie & the Trash Can Troll: A Modern-Day Fairy Tale. 67p. (Orig.). (gr. 6-9). 1991. pap. text ed. 5.95 (*1-877673-11-0*) Cottonwood Pr.
Tissot, John & Carlin, Matthew. The Auntiques & the Valentine Card. 16p. (Orig.). (gr. 2 up). 1991. pap. 3.00 (*0-88680-357-8*); royalty on application 25.00 (*0-685-59142-5*) I E Clark.
Triangle Shirtwaist Fire: Mini-Play. (gr. 5 up). 1975. 6.50 (*0-89550-369-7*) Stevens & Shea.
Trifiletti, Don. Spirit Playmates: A Boy's Adventure with Music & Lyrics. 64p. (Orig.). (gr. 3-6). 1990. pap. 8.95 (*1-56167-015-4*) Am Literary Pr.
Turner, Glennette T. Take a Walk in Their Shoes: Biographies of Fourteen Outstanding African Americans - with Skits about Each to Act Out. Fax, Elton C., illus. LC 92-19524. 176p. (gr. 3-7). 1992. pap. 5.99 (*0-14-036250-9*) Puffin Bks.
Urquhart, John, et al. Nightingale (A Participation Play) (Orig.). (gr. k up). 1983. pap. 4.00 (*0-87602-245-X*) Anchorage.
Vos, Eric. Professor Filarsky's Miraculous Invention. 1980. 4.50 (*0-685-45738-9*) Anchorage.
Vos, Erik. The Dancing Donkey: Musical. 1965. 4.50 (*0-87602-117-8*) Anchorage.
Waechter, F. K. & Campbell, Ken. Clown Plays. Stewart, Eve, illus. Eyre, Richard, intro. by. (Illus.). 129p. 1992. pap. 11.95 (*0-413-66550-X*, A0661) Heinemann.
Water for the Angels: Mini-Play. (gr. 5 up). 1978. 6.50 (*0-89550-332-8*) Stevens & Shea.
Wheeler, Jacuqe & Hartsfield, Mariella G. Tall Betsy & the Crackerbarrel Tales. LC 93-5663. 1993. pap. 6.00 (*0-88734-265-5*); music & lyrics 15.00 (*0-88734-036-9*) Players Pr.
Whiting, Frank. Huckleberry Finn. 1948. 4.50 (*0-87602-138-0*) Anchorage.
Whitney, Sharon. Totty - Young Eleanor Roosevelt. (Orig.). 1992. pap. 5.50 playscript (*0-87602-306-5*) Anchorage.
Williams, Guy. Billy Budd. LC 91-50833. 60p. (Orig.). 1992. pap. 5.00 play script (*0-88734-415-1*) Players Pr.
—David & Goliath. LC 90-53572. (Orig.). (gr. 3 up). 1991. pap. 5.00 play script (*0-88734-411-9*) Players Pr.
Wilson, Alice, et al. Flashback! (Orig.). (gr. k up). 1980. pap. 4.50 (*0-87602-259-X*) Anchorage.
Winther, Barbara. Plays from African Tales. (Orig.). 1992. pap. 13.95 (*0-8238-0296-5*) Plays.
Wise, Arthur & Wise, Sarah. Six Christian One-Act Plays for Young Adults. 52p. (gr. 7-12). pap. 5.00 (*0-88680-178-8*) I E Clark.
Woyiwada, Allison, ed. The Little Fir Tree: A Musical for Primary Children Based on a Story by Hans Christian Andersen. LC 93-50820. 1994. write for info. (*0-88734-428-3*) Players Pr.
Zarambouka, Sofia. Irene. Zarambouka, Sofia & Loftin, Tee, trs. (Illus.). 42p. (gr. k-3). 1979. 8.95 (*0-934812-00-4*) Tee Loftin.
Zeder, Susan. Ozma of Oz: A Tale of Time. (Orig.). (gr. 4 up). 1981. playscript 5.00 (*0-87602-233-6*) Anchorage.
Zeder, Suzan. The Play Called Noah's Flood. (Orig.). (gr. 4 up). 1985. pap. 5.00 (*0-87602-247-6*) Anchorage.
—Step on a Crack. (gr. 1-9). 1976. 4.50 (*0-87602-207-7*) Anchorage.
Zeder, Suzan L. An Evening at Versailles. Moliere, J. B., contrib. by. 1989. Playscript. 5.00 (*0-87602-284-0*) Anchorage.
—In a Room Somewhere: (Musical) 60p. 1988. Playscript. 5.00 (*0-87602-282-4*) Anchorage.
Zoot Suit Riot: Mini-Play. (gr. 5 up). 1975. 5.00 (*0-89550-306-9*) Stevens & Shea.

PLAYS, CHRISTMAS
see Christmas Plays

PLAYS FOR CHILDREN
see Plays

PLAYWRIGHTS
see Dramatists

PLAYWRITING
see Drama–Technique

PLUMBING
Plumbing. (Illus.). 48p. (gr. 6-12). 1989. pap. 1.85 (*0-8395-3386-1*, 33386) BSA.

PLUMBING–FICTION
Endersby, Frank. The Plumber. (gr. 4 up). 1981. 3.95 (*0-85953-272-0*) Childs Play.

PLUMBING–VOCATIONAL GUIDANCE
Lillegard, Dee & Stoker, Wayne. I Can Be a Plumber. LC 86-30950. (Illus.). 32p. (gr. k-3). 1987. PLB 11.80 (*0-516-01906-6*) Childrens.

PLUTO (PLANET)
Asimov, Isaac. How Did We Find Out about Pluto? Kors, Erika, illus. 64p. (gr. 5 up). 1991. 12.95 (*0-8027-6991-8*); PLB 13.85 (*0-8027-6992-6*) Walker & Co.
Daily, Bob. Pluto. LC 94-58. 1994. write for info. (*0-531-20166-X*) Watts.
Vogt, Gregory L. Pluto. LC 93-11224. (Illus.). 32p. (gr. 2-4). 1994. PLB 12.90 (*1-56294-393-6*) Millbrook Pr.

PLYMOUTH, MASSACHUSETTS–HISTORY
Fritz, Jean. Who's That Stepping on Plymouth Rock? Handelsman, J. B., illus. LC 74-30593. 32p. (gr. 2-6). 1975. 13.95 (*0-698-20325-9*, Coward) Putnam Pub Group.
Shaffer, Elizabeth. Daughter of the Dawn. 1992. write for info. (*0-936369-72-8*) Son-Rise Pubns.

POCAHONTAS, 1595?-1617
Accorsi, William. My Name Is Pocahontas. Accorsi, William, illus. LC 91-24218. 32p. (ps-3). 1992. reinforced bdg. 14.95 (*0-8234-0932-5*) Holiday.
Benjamin, Anne. Young Pocahontas: Indian Princess. Powers, Christine, illus. LC 91-32654. 32p. (gr. k-2). 1992. PLB 11.59 (*0-8167-2534-9*); pap. text ed. 2.95 (*0-8167-2535-7*) Troll Assocs.
Fritz, Jean. The Double Life of Pocahontas. LC 90-48977. (Illus.). 128p. (gr. 6-10). 1991. PLB 13.95 (*1-55905-092-6*) Marshall Cavendish.
Greene, Carol. Pocahontas: Daughter of a Chief. Dobson, Steven, illus. LC 88-11978. 48p. (gr. k-3). 1988. PLB 12.85 (*0-516-04203-3*); pap. 4.95 (*0-516-44203-1*) Childrens.
Holler, Anne. Chief Powhatan & Pocahontas. (Illus.). 112p. (gr. 5 up). 1993. PLB 17.95 (*0-7910-1705-2*) Chelsea Hse.
—Pocahontas. (gr. 4-7). 1992. pap. 7.95 (*0-7910-1952-7*) Chelsea Hse.
Jassem, Kate. Pocahontas, Girl of Jamestown. LC 78-18045. (Illus.). 48p. (gr. 4-6). 1979. PLB 10.59 (*0-89375-152-9*); pap. 3.50 (*0-89375-142-1*) Troll Assocs.
Penner, Lucille R. The True Story of Pocahontas: A Step 2 Book. Johnson, Pamela, illus. LC 93-45709. 48p. (Orig.). (gr. k-2). 1994. PLB 7.99 (*0-679-96166-6*); pap. 3.50 (*0-679-86166-1*) Random Bks Yng Read.
Richards, Dorothy F. Pocahontas, Child-Princess. Nelson, John, illus. LC 78-7719. (gr. k-4). 1978. PLB 13.95 (*0-89565-035-5*) Childs World.
Santrey, Laurence. Pocahontas. Wenzel, David, illus. LC 84-8443. 32p. (gr. 3-6). 1985. PLB 9.49 (*0-8167-0276-4*); pap. text ed. 2.95 (*0-8167-0277-2*) Troll Assocs.

POCAHONTAS, 1595?-1617–FICTION
Gleiter, Jan & Thompson, Kathleen. Pocahontas. LC 84-9819. (Illus.). 32p. (gr. 2-5). 1984. PLB 19.97 (*0-8172-2118-2*); PLB 29.28 incl. cassette (*0-8172-2240-5*); cassette 14.00 (*0-685-09501-0*) Raintree Steck-V.
O'Dell, Scott. The Serpent Never Sleeps: A Novel of Jamestown & Pocahontas. (gr. 8 up). 1988. pap. 3.99 (*0-449-70328-2*, Juniper) Fawcett.

POE, EDGAR ALLAN, 1809-1849
Anderson, Madelyn K. Edgar Allan Poe, a Mystery. LC 92-43935. (Illus.). 144p. (gr. 7-12). 1993. PLB 14.40 (*0-531-13012-6*) Watts.
—Edgar Allan Poe: A Mystery. (Illus.). 144p. (gr. 7-12). 1993. pap. 6.95 (*0-531-15678-8*) Watts.
Loewen, Nancy. Poe. Mucci, Tina, illus. 64p. (gr. 6-12). 1993. 16.95 (*1-56846-084-8*) Creat Editions.
—Poe. Mucci, Tina, photos by. LC 93-17095. (Illus.). 1993. PLB 16.95 (*0-88682-509-1*) Creative Ed.
Shorto, Russell. Edgar Allan Poe: Dark Poet. Corcoran, Mark, illus. Lemay, Leo, frwd. by. (Illus.). 48p. (gr. 5-8). 1988. Kipling Pr.

POE, EDGAR ALLAN, 1809-1849–FICTION
Avi. The Man Who Was Poe. LC 89-42537. 224p. (gr. 6-8). 1989. 13.95 (*0-531-05833-6*); PLB 13.99 (*0-531-08433-7*) Orchard Bks Watts.

POETICS
Here are entered works on the art and technique of poetry. Works on the appreciation and philosophy of poetry are entered under Poetry.
see also Rhythm
Charpentreau, J. & Jean, G. Dictionnaire des Poetes et de la Poesie. (FRE.). 427p. (gr. 5-10). 1983. 27.95 (*2-07-051019-0*) Schoenhof.
Ferra, Lorraine. A Crow Doesn't Need a Shadow: A Guide to Writing Poetry from Nature. Boardman, Diane, illus. LC 93-34991. 1994. pap. 9.95 (*0-87905-600-2*) Gibbs Smith Pub.
Hardt, Elaine. Writing Poetry. Kruck, Gerry, illus. 32p. (Orig.). (gr. 1-9). 1983. pap. 1.95 (*0-940406-09-8*) Perception Pubns.
Hayes, Dympna. Fun with Rhymes. Davis, Annelies, illus. 32p. (gr. 1). 1987. PLB 14.97 (*0-88625-165-6*); pap. 2.95 (*0-88625-144-3*) Durkin Hayes Pub.
Janeczko, Paul B. The Place My Words Are Looking For: What Poets Say about & Through Their Work. LC 89-39331. 128p. (gr. 4-8). 1990. SBE 14.95 (*0-02-747671-5*, Bradbury Pr) Macmillan Child Grp.
Jean, Georges. Plaisir des Mots: Dictionnaire Poetique Illustre. 352p. (gr. 4-9). 1982. 29.95 (*2-07-039499-9*) Schoenhof.
Jones, Charla. Poetry Patterns. 2nd, expanded ed. (Illus.). 48p. (gr. 3-6). 1992. pap. 5.95 (*1-879287-11-0*) Bk Lures.
Kuskin, Karla. Near the Window Tree: Poems & Notes. Kuskin, Karla, illus. LC 74-20394. 64p. (gr. 2-6). 1975. PLB 13.89 (*0-06-023540-3*) HarpC Child Bks.
Livingston, Myra C. Poem-Making: Ways to Begin Writing Poetry. LC 90-5012. 176p. (gr. 4-8). 1991. 16. 00 (*0-06-024019-9*); PLB 15.89 (*0-06-024020-2*) HarpC Child Bks.
Moore, Jo E. & Evans, Joy. Writing Poetry with Children. (Illus.). 64p. (gr. 1-6). 1988. pap. 6.95 (*1-55799-129-4*) Evan-Moor Corp.
Ottenstein, Claire. The Poetry Fun Book. (Illus.). 40p. (Orig.). 1992. pap. 7.95 (*1-878149-20-2*) Counterpoint Pub.
Provost, C. Antonio. Modern Renaissance Poetry & Philosophy. Kroll, William, ed. Forster, Maria, frwd. by. LC 92-96848. (Illus.). 148p. (gr. 9-12). 1992. 14.00 (*0-317-05253-5*); pap. 10.00 (*0-317-05254-3*) Provost.
Raffel, Burton. How to Read a Poem: Metrics. 260p. (gr. 9-12). 1989. pap. 8.95 (*0-452-00917-0*, Mer) NAL-Dutton.
Ryan, Margaret. How to Read & Write Poems. LC 91-12141. (Illus.). 64p. (gr. 5-8). 1991. PLB 12.90 (*0-531-20043-4*) Watts.
Spellman, Linda. Poetry Party. 48p. (gr. 4-6). 1981. 5.95 (*0-88160-038-5*, LW 223) Learning Wks.
Wainwright, James. Poetivities - Intermediate. 64p. (gr. 4-6). 1989. 8.95 (*0-86653-488-1*, GA1090) Good Apple.
—Poetivities - Primary. 64p. (gr. 1-3). 1989. 8.95 (*0-86653-484-9*, GA1089) Good Apple.
Williams, Jean. Let Me Out! Introducing Poetry to Elementary Students. (gr. 1-6). 1993. 5.95 (*0-929917-08-1*) Magnolia PA.

POETRY
see also Ballads; Hymns; Love Poetry; Nature in Poetry also American Poetry; English Poetry, etc.; and general subjects, names of historical events, places and famous persons with the subdivision Poetry, e.g. Animals–poetry
Abeel, Samantha. Reach for the Moon: What Once was White. Murphy, Charles R., illus. LC 93-46417. 48p. 1994. 17.95 (*1-57025-013-8*) Pfeifer-Hamilton.
Ada, Alma F., et al. A Chorus of Cultures Poetry Anthology: Developing Literacy Through Multicultural Poetry. (Illus.). 304p. (Orig.). (gr. 1-6). 1993. pap. 59.95 (*1-56334-325-8*) Hampton-Brown.
Adoff, Arnold. All the Colors of the Race. Steptoe, John, illus. LC 81-11777. 56p. (gr. 5 up). 1992. pap. 4.95 (*0-688-11496-2*, Pub. by Beech Tree Bks) Morrow.
—Chocolate Dreams. MacCombie, Turi, illus. LC 88-27208. 64p. (gr. 3 up). 1989. 13.95 (*0-688-06822-7*); PLB 13.88 (*0-688-06823-5*) Lothrop.
—In for Winter, Out for Spring. Ingber, Bonnie V., ed. Pinkney, Jerry, illus. 43p. (ps-3). 1991. 14.95 (*0-15-238637-8*) HarBrace.
Agard, John. Life Doesn't Frighten Me at All. LC 89-26766. (Illus.). 96p. (gr. 6 up). 1990. 14.95 (*0-8050-1237-0*, Bks Young Read) H Holt & Co.
Agard, John & Nichols, Grace, eds. A Caribbean Dozen: A Collection of Poems. Felstead, Cathie, illus. LC 93-47272. 96p. (ps up). 1994. 19.95 (*1-56402-339-7*) Candlewick Pr.

Ain, Diantha. What Do You Know about Succotash? Poems & Drawings. Ain, Diantha, illus. 75p. (Orig.). (gr. 1-6). 1991. pap. 7.95 (*0-925360-01-5*) Geste Pub.

Allen, Johann. Verse for Grandchildren, Vol. I. 30p. (gr. k-4). 1992. pap. 5.00 (*0-9633569-0-9*) Home Imag.

Allum, Faith T. Respite. Allum, Lois Saarinen, illus. 48p. (Orig.). (gr. 6 up). 1985. pap. 3.00 (*0-9613349-2-4*) F T Allum.

Alston, Nelson G. Sonnets in the Names of Love: In the Names of Love. Avent, Barbara P., ed. (Illus.). 96p. (Orig.). 1993. pap. 10.95 (*0-9632202-2-5*) Alpha Bk Pr.

Altman, Susan & Lechner, Susan. Followers of the North Star: Rhymes about African American Heroes, Heroines, & Historical Times. Wooden, Bryan, illus. LC 93-797. 48p. (ps-4). 1993. PLB 15.40 (*0-516-05151-2*); pap. 6.95 (*0-516-45151-0*) Childrens.

Amery, H. Children's Poems. (Illus.). 96p. (gr. 2-6). 1992. pap. 12.95 (*0-7460-0482-6*) EDC.

Anglund, Joan W. Peace Is a Circle of Love. LC 92-28855. 1993. 8.95 (*0-15-259922-3*) HarBrace.

Artell, Mike, illus. T'was the Night Before Christmas. LC 93-37281. (ps-1). 1994. pap. 10.95 (*0-689-71801-2*, Aladdin) Macmillan Child Grp.

Ashley, Jill. Riddles about Christmas. Brook, Bonnie, ed. Gray, Rob, illus. 32p. (ps-3). 1990. 4.95 (*0-671-70554-7*); PLB 6.95 (*0-671-70552-0*); 2.50 (*0-382-24383-8*) Silver Pr.

Astley, Neil, ed. Bossy Parrot. LC 87-73294. (Illus.). 64p. (Orig.). (gr. 1 up). 1988. pap. 10.95 (*1-85224-040-7*, Pub. by Bloodaxe Bks) Dufour.

Axeman, Lois, illus. Holidays. LC 84-9429. 32p. (gr. k-3). 1984. PLB 14.95 (*0-89565-266-8*) Childs World.

Bagert, Brod. Chicken Socks: And Other Contagious Poems. Ellis, Tim, illus. 32p. (gr. 3-7). 1994. 15.95 (*1-56397-292-1*, Wordsong) Boyds Mills Pr.

—Let Me Be the Boss. Smith, Gerald, illus. LC 91-91408. 48p. (gr. 3-7). 1992. 14.95 (*1-56397-099-6*, Wordsong) Boyds Mills Pr.

Bantock, Nick. Nick Bantock Boxed Set: Jabberwocky; The Walrus & the Carpenter. (Illus.). 1993. 18.90 (*0-670-77265-8*, Viking) Viking Penguin.

—Nick Bantock Boxed Set: Robin Hood; Solomon Grundy; There Was an Old Lady. (Illus.). 1993. 27.85 (*0-670-77264-X*, Viking) Viking Penguin.

Barker, Cicely M. Flower Fairies of the Garden. Barker, Cicely M., illus. (ps up). 1991. 5.95 (*0-7232-3758-1*) Warne.

Barker, Cicely M., illus. Old Rhymes for All Times. 112p. (gr. 4-7). 1994. 12.99 (*0-7232-3751-4*) Warne.

Bauer, Caroline F., ed. Windy Day: Stories & Poems. Zimmer, Dirk, illus. LC 86-42994. 96p. (gr. 2-5). 1988. (Lipp Jr Bks); PLB 14.89 (*0-397-32208-9*) HarpC Child Bks.

Beck, Ian. Five Little Ducks. LC 92-27193. (Illus.). 32p. (ps-2). 1993. 14.95 (*0-8050-2525-1*, Bks Young Read) H Holt & Co.

Beers, V. Gilbert. My Sunny Day, & Day Nursery Rhyme Book. O'Connor, Tim, illus. LC 93-17261. 1993. 12.99 (*0-8407-9253-0*) Nelson.

Bell, Clarisa. Animales del Circo de Sonora. Sanchez, Jose R., illus. (SPA.). 24p. (Orig.). (gr. k-5). 1993. pap. 9.95x (*1-56492-081-X*) Laredo.

—At the Olympics. Kohen, Gabriela, tr. from SPA. Sanchez, Jose R., illus. 24p. (Orig.). (gr. 2-6). 1992. pap. 9.95x (*1-56492-007-0*) Laredo.

—El Circo. Sanchez, Jose R., illus. (SPA.). 24p. (Orig.). (gr. 2-6). 1992. PLB 9.95x (*1-56492-078-X*) Laredo.

—En Las Olimpidas. Sanchez, Jose R., illus. (SPA.). 24p. (Orig.). (gr. 2-6). 1992. PLB 9.95x (*1-56492-051-8*) Laredo.

—Games People Play. Kohen, Gabriela, tr. from SPA. Sanchez, Jose R., illus. 24p. (gr. 2-6). 1992. PLB 9.95x (*1-56492-004-6*) Laredo.

—Games People Play: Big Book. Kohen, Gabriela, tr. from SPA. Sanchez, Jose R., illus. 24p. (Orig.). (gr. 2-6). 1992. pap. 19.95x (*1-56492-005-4*) Laredo.

—El Teatro. Sanchez, Jose R., illus. (SPA.). 24p. (gr. 2-6). 1992. PLB 9.95x (*1-56492-056-9*) Laredo.

—El Teatro: Big Book. Sanchez, Jose R., illus. (SPA.). 24p. (Orig.). (gr. 2-6). 1992. pap. 19.95x (*1-56492-057-7*) Laredo.

—Vamos a Jugar. Sanchez, Jose R., illus. (SPA.). 24p. (Orig.). (gr. 2-6). 1992. PLB 9.95x (*1-56492-048-8*) Laredo.

—Vamos a Jugar: Big Book. Sanchez, Jose R., illus. (SPA.). 24p. (Orig.). (gr. 2-6). 1992. pap. 19.95x (*1-56492-049-6*) Laredo.

Bennett, Jill, ed. People Poems. Sharratt, Nick, illus. 28p. (gr. k up). 1990. bds. 11.00 laminated (*0-19-276086-6*) OUP.

Berry, James. When I Dance. Ingber, Bonnie V., ed. Barbour, Karen, illus. 120p. (gr. 7 up). 1991. 15.95 (*0-15-295568-2*) HarBrace.

Berry, T. The Day God Came. 44p. (gr. 6 up). 1992. pap. 5.95 (*1-55523-515-8*) Winston-Derek.

Billings, John. My Pet Crocodile: And Other Slightly Outrageous Verse. Todd, Janette, illus. LC 93-72718. 128p. (gr. k-12). 1994. 16.95 (*1-884035-55-8*) Chokecherry.

Blankenship, Judy, illus. Teddy Beddy Bear's Bedtime Songs & Poems. LC 84-4837. 32p. (ps). 1984. pap. 2.25 saddle-stitched (*0-394-86826-9*) Random Bks Yng Read.

Blishen, Edward, ed. Oxford Book of Poetry for Children. Wildsmith, Brian, illus. 168p. (gr. k-5). 1987. 20.00 (*0-19-276031-9*) OUP.

Bodger, Lorraine. Great American Cakes. 1990. 7.99 (*0-517-02740-2*) Random Hse Value.

Bonner, Ann & Bonner, Roger. Earlybirds...Earlywords. LC 72-89449. (Illus.). 32p. (ps-2). 1973. 7.95 (*0-87592-013-6*) Scroll Pr.

Booth, David, selected by. Til All the Stars Have Fallen: A Collection of Poems for Children. Denton, Kady M., illus. 96p. (ps-3). 1994. pap. 6.99 (*0-14-034438-1*) Puffin Bks.

Bordeaux, Michelle, compiled by. Poetry: Friends for a Lifetime. (Illus.). 40p. (gr. 5 up). 1992. pap. 2.99 (*0-87406-633-6*) Willowisp Pr.

Bowman, Crystal. Cracks in the Sidewalk: Children's Daily Adventures. Hartman, Alan G., ed. Williams, Aaron, illus. 128p. (Orig.). (gr. k-8). 1993. 12.00 (*0-9636050-1-1*); pap. 6.00 (*0-9636050-0-3*) Cygnet Pub.
Crystal Bowman is a homemaker, lyricist, & freelance writer. She especially enjoys writing for children & draws from her experience as a mother & former school teacher. When Crystal began sharing her poems with students in the local schools, the response was so positive that she wanted to make her poems available to the students. CRACKS IN THE SIDEWALK is a wonderful collection of these poems that children of all ages & backgrounds will enjoy. These poems address everyday issues such as the hiccups, mosquito bites, vegetables, & bubble gum. The reader will have an opportunity to meet such characters as Charles with snarles, messy Bess, Walter who hates his name, & a unique set of twins named Marilyn May & Mike. CRACKS IN THE SIDEWALK allows the reader to observe life through the eyes of an innocent child. It is warm, sensitive, humorous, & thought provoking. The poems are cleverly written in precise rhythm & rhyme, often with delightful endings. The poems are richly enhanced by outstanding illustrations. The illustrator, a fourteen year old boy, beautifully captures the warmth, humor, & emotions in unique & refreshing drawings. This book will appeal to all children, regardless of age, race or creed. To order: Cygnet Publishing Co., 2153 Wealthy Street, SE #238. East Grand Rapids, MI 49506.
Publisher Provided Annotation.

Brewton, Sara, et al, eds. Of Quarks, Quasars, & Other Quirks: Quizzical Poems for the Supersonic Age. Blake, Quentin, illus. LC 76-54747. 128p. (gr. 5 up). 1990. PLB 13.89 (*0-690-04885-8*, Crowell Jr Bks) HarpC Child Bks.

Brown, Kenneth. Barn House Book: Rhymes, Riddles, & Jokes. Brown, Kenneth, illus. Date not set. 12.95 (*1-56743-046-5*) Amistad Pr.

Brown, Marc T. Party Rhymes. (Illus.). 48p. (ps-3). 1994. pap. 4.99 (*0-14-050318-8*, Puff Unicorn) Puffin Bks.

Brown, Marcia. Shadow. Brown, Marcia, illus. LC 86-3432. 38p. (ps up). 1986. pap. 3.95 (*0-689-71084-4*, Aladdin) Macmillan Child Grp.

Brown, Margaret W. Nibble Nibble: Poems for Children. Weisgard, Leonard, illus. LC 84-43128. 64p. (ps-3). 1959. PLB 13.89 (*0-201-09291-3*) HarpC Child Bks.

Bryan, Ashley. Sing to the Sun. LC 91-38359. (Illus.). 32p. (gr. 2 up). 1992. 15.00 (*0-06-020829-5*); PLB 14.89 (*0-06-020833-3*) HarpC Child Bks.

Buak, Karen. Grandma's Cookies. Kita, Helen M., illus. 40p. (Orig.). (ps-4). 1992. pap. text ed. 6.95 chapbk. (*1-56315-055-7*) Sterling Hse.

Burke, Dianne O. Hey, Diddle, Diddle. (ps). 1994. 3.95 (*1-56565-098-0*) Lowell Hse Juvenile.

Burton, Michael H. In the Light of a Child: Fifty-Two Verses for Children & the Child in Every Human Being. McHenry, Kitsy & Geard, David, illus. 62p. (Orig.). (gr. 4). 1989. pap. text ed. 12.95 (*0-932776-17-5*) Adonis Pr.

Caballito Blanco y Otras Poesias Favoritas. (SPA.). 40p. (Orig.). (gr. 1-4). 1991. pap. text ed. 7.00 (*1-56334-062-3*) Hampton-Brown.

Cantor, Clarence. Good Times in Rhyme. 1993. 7.95 (*0-533-10420-3*) Vantage.

Carson, Jo. Stories I Ain't Told Nobody Yet: Selections from the People Pieces. LC 88-19821. 96p. (gr. 7 up). 1989. 13.95 (*0-531-05808-5*); PLB 13.99 (*0-531-08408-6*) Orchard Bks Watts.

Carter, David A. Over in the Meadow. (Illus.). 32p. 1992. 13.95 (*0-590-44498-0*, Scholastic Hardcover) Scholastic Inc.

Cassedy, Sylvia. Roomrimes. Chessare, Michele, illus. LC 86-4583. 80p. (gr. k-3). 1987. (Crowell Jr Bks); PLB 12.89 (*0-690-04467-4*, Crowell Jr Bks) HarpC Child Bks.

Cendrars, Blaise. Shadow. Brown, Marcia, tr. from FRE. & illus. LC 81-9424. 40p. (gr. 2 up). 1982. SBE 16.95 (*0-684-17226-7*, Scribners Young Read) Macmillan Child Grp.

Cerf, Bennett. Riddle-De-Dee. 144p. (ps-8). 1990. pap. 3.95 (*0-345-36872-X*) Ballantine.

Chandra, Deborah. Balloons: And Other Poems. (gr. 4-7). 1993. pap. 3.95 (*0-374-40492-5*) FS&G.

Christison, Mary Ann. English Through Poetry. Peterson, Kathleen, illus. 130p. (gr. 3-6). 1982. pap. text ed. 8.95 (*0-88084-002-1*) Alemany Pr.

Church, Elmer T. Walk with Me in White. LC 86-81184. 154p. 1986. perfect bdg. 5.98 (*0-318-21723-6*) E T Church.

Ciardi, John. Fast & Slow: Poems for Advanced Children of Beginning Parents. Gaver, Becky, intro. by. LC 74-22405. (Illus.). 68p. (gr. k-3). 1975. 15.95 (*0-395-20282-5*) HM.

—The Monster Den: or Look What Happened at My House - & to It. Gorey, Edward, illus. LC 90-85904. 64p. (gr. k up). 1991. Repr. 13.95 (*1-878093-35-5*, Wordsong) Boyds Mills Pr.

—You Know Who. Gorey, Edward, illus. LC 90-85903. 48p. (gr. k up). 1991. Repr. 13.95 (*1-878093-34-7*, Wordsong) Boyds Mills Pr.

—You Read to Me, I'll Read to You. Gorey, Edward, illus. LC 62-16296. 64p. (gr. k-6). 1961. (Lipp Jr Bks); PLB 12.89 (*0-397-30646-6*) HarpC Child Bks.

—You Read to Me, I'll Read to You. Gorey, Edward, illus. LC 62-16296. 64p. (gr. k-4). 1987. pap. 6.95 (*0-06-446060-6*, Trophy) HarpC Child Bks.

Cinco Pollitos y Otras Poesias Favoritas. (SPA.). 40p. (Orig.). (gr. 1-4). 1991. pap. text ed. 7.00 (*1-56334-061-5*) Hampton-Brown.

Clark, Ann N. In My Mother's House. Herrara, Velino, illus. 64p. (ps up). 1991. 15.95 (*0-670-83917-5*) Viking Child Bks.

Clifford, Eth. The Remembering Box. Diamond, Donna, illus. 64p. (gr. 2-5). 1985. 13.45 (*0-395-38476-1*) HM.

Cohen, Shari. Prime Time Rhyme. (gr. k-6). 1990. 10.95 (*0-9620467-4-4*) Forward March.

Cole, William E. Beastly Boys & Ghastly Girls. (gr. 4 up). 1977. pap. 1.25 (*0-440-40467-3*, YB) Dell.

—Oh, How Silly! Ungerer, Tomi, illus. 80p. (gr. 2 up). 1990. pap. 3.95 (*0-14-034441-1*, Puffin) Puffin Bks.

—Oh, What Nonsense. Ungerer, Tomi, illus. 80p. (gr. 2 up). 1990. pap. 3.95 (*0-14-034442-X*, Puffin) Puffin Bks.

Cole, William E., selected by. Oh, Such Foolishness! Poems Selected by William Cole. De Paola, Tomie, illus. LC 78-1622. 96p. (gr. 4-6). 1991. PLB 13.89 (*0-397-32502-9*, Lipp Jr Bks) HarpC Child Bks.

Cole, William E., ed. Poem Stew. Weinhaus, Karen A., illus. LC 81-47106. 96p. (gr. 3-6). 1981. (Lipp Jr Bks); PLB 13.89 (*0-397-31964-9*) HarpC Child Bks.

Connelly, Gwen, illus. Adventures. LC 83-25212. 32p. (gr. k-3). 1984. PLB 14.95 (*0-89565-265-X*) Childs World.

Corpening, Gene S. I Love to Hear the Cold Wind Howl. James, Linda & Corpening, Gene S., illus. 40p. (Orig.). (gr. 2 up). 1993. pap. 7.95g (*0-9636775-9-4*) Alice Pub.

Cowling, Sue. What Is a Kumquat? And Other Poems. Edwards, Gunvor, illus. 64p. (Orig.). (gr. 2 up). 1991. pap. 6.95 (*0-571-16065-4*) Faber & Faber.

Creedon, Sharon. A Look over the Edge. Waterline, Wendy, illus. 16p. (gr. k-4). 1987. pap. 5.95 (*0-9620446-0-1*) Sunset Mktg.

Cummings, Cynthia H. Christmas Joy. (Illus.). 84p. Repr. of 1986 ed. 8.00 (*1-881811-05-0*) H Peterson Pr.

—Christmas Spirit. (Illus.). 84p. Repr. of 1989 ed. 8.00 (*1-881811-08-5*) H Peterson Pr.

—Christmas Surprise. 2nd ed. (Illus.). 84p. 1990. Repr. of 1985 ed. 8.00 (*1-881811-04-2*) H Peterson Pr.

Cummings, E. E., et al. Spooky Poems. Bennett, Jill, compiled by. Rees, Mary, illus. (ps-3). 1989. 14.95 (*0-316-08987-7*, Joy St Bks) Little.

Da Free, John. I Am Happiness: A Rendering for Children of the Spiritual Adventure of Master Da Free John. Bodha, Daji & Closser, Lynne, eds. (Illus., Orig.). (gr. 2 up). 1982. pap. 8.95 (*0-913922-68-4*) Dawn Horse Pr.

Dahl, Roald. Dirty Beasts. Blake, Quentin, illus. LC 85-594. 32p. (gr. 1 up). 1986. pap. 4.99 (*0-14-050435-4*, Puffin) Puffin Bks.

—Rhyme Stew. Blake, Quentin, illus. 80p. (gr. 4 up). 1990. pap. 14.95 (*0-670-82916-1*) Viking Child Bks.

Dakos, Kalli. If You're Not Here, Please Raise Your Hand: Poems about School. Karas, G. Brian, illus. LC 89-71530. 64p. (gr. 2-6). 1990. SBE 14.00 (*0-02-725581-6*, Four Winds) Macmillan Child Grp.

Daniel, Mark. Child's Treasury of Animal Verse. (ps up). 1989. 16.95 (*0-8037-0606-5*) Dial Bks Young.

Daniel, Mark, ed. A Child's Treasury of Poems. LC 86-2194. (Illus.). 160p. (ps up). 1986. 17.00 (*0-8037-0330-9*) Dial Bks Young.

Davenport, May, ed. Watch Out, the Tide. LC 86-91602. 84p. (Orig.). (gr. 7-12). 1987. Pogosticks by Andrea Ross. pap. 4.95x (*0-943864-27-5*); Ginger: Poof! Bam! Growl! by Andrea Ross. pap. 4.95x (*0-685-73920-1*); Poems by Kay Garrard. pap. 4.95x (*0-685-73921-X*) Davenport.

Davis, Hubert J. What Will the Weather Be?, No. 1: A Folk Weather Calendar. Turner, Erin, illus. LC 88-17869. 40p. (Orig.). (gr. k-12). 1988. pap. 4.95 (*0-936015-11-X*) Pocahontas Pr.

—What Will the Weather Be?, No. 2: Animal Signs. Turner, Erin, illus. LC 90-22327. 56p. (Orig.). (gr. k-12). 1991. pap. 5.95 (*0-936015-12-8*) Pocahontas Pr.

Decker, Marjorie A. Rock-a-Bye-Bible. (Illus.). 96p. (ps-k). 1987. text ed. 7.99 (*0-529-06481-2*) World Bible.

Demi. In the Eyes of the Cat: Japanese Poetry for All Seasons. LC 91-27728. (ps-3). 1994. pap. 5.95 (*0-8050-3383-1*) H Holt & Co.

Der Manuelian, Peter. Hieroglyphs from A to Z: A Rhyming Book with Ancient Egyptian Stencils for Kids. (Illus.). 48p. (gr. 2 up). 1993. 19.95 (*0-8478-1701-6*) Rizzoli Intl.

DeWitt, Jim. Fingernail Souffle. Cole, Bradley, illus. 136p. (Orig.). (gr. 4-12). 1987. pap. 6.00 (*0-915199-03-3*) Pen Dec.

—Jammy Donuts a Season After. LC 83-90481. (Illus.). 64p. (Orig.). (gr. 4-12). 1984. pap. text ed. 5.95 (*0-915199-04-1*) Pen-Dec.

—Quiet-Time Thoughts. LC 83-90474. (Illus.). 64p. (Orig.). (gr. 3-10). 1984. pap. text ed. 5.95 (*0-915199-00-9*) Pen-Dec.

—Sharpshooting at Kinkajous. Cole, Bradley, illus. 136p. (gr. 4-12). 1987. pap. 6.00 (*0-915199-06-8*) Pen Dec.

Dickinson, Emily. A Brighter Garden. Ackerman, Karen, compiled by. Tudor, Tasha, illus. 63p. 1990. 17.95 (*0-399-21490-9*, Philomel Bks) Putnam Pub Group.

Disney Minnie 'N Me: My Favorite Book: A Book of Poems. 48p. (ps). 1992. 5.98 (*0-8317-2349-1*) Viking Child Bks.

Dolce, J. Ellen, illus. Baby's Mother Goose. LC 87-81921. 12p. (ps). 1988. write for info. (*0-307-06066-7*, Pub. by Golden Bks) Western Pub.

Duffield, Francesca, illus. ABC Rhymes. LC 92-75611. 10p. (ps). 1993. bds. 5.95 (*1-85697-941-5*, Kingfisher LKC) LKC.

—One-Two-Three Rhymes. LC 92-75610. 10p. (ps). 1993. bds. 5.95 (*1-85697-942-3*, Kingfisher LKC) LKC.

Dunning, Stephen & Stafford, William. Getting the Knack: Twenty Poetry Writing Exercises. LC 92-36710. 1992. 15.95 (*0-8141-1848-8*) NCTE.

Dunnington, Tom, illus. Animals. LC 83-25213. 32p. (gr. k-3). 1984. PLB 14.95 (*0-89565-264-1*) Childs World.

Eastwick, Ivy O. In & Out the Windows: Happy Poems for Children. Barth, Gillian, illus. Swinger, Marlys. LC 73-90841. (Illus.). 80p. (ps-3). 1969. 8.00 (*0-87486-007-5*) Plough.

Eavey, Louise. Happiness Rhymes for Children. Murphy, Emmy L., illus. (ps-1). 1969. pap. 1.95 (*0-915374-09-9*, 09-0) Rapids Christian.

Edwards, Richard. A Mouse in My Roof. 1990. 13.95 (*0-385-30035-2*) Doubleday.

Eliot, T. S. Growltiger's Last Stand & Other Poems. Le Cain, Errol, illus. 32p. (ps up). 1987. 14.00 (*0-374-32809-9*, Co-pub. by HarBraceJ) FS&G.

Emanuel, James A. Whole Grain: Collected Poems 1958-1989. Anderson, Keith O., illus. LC 90-61082. 400p. (gr. 9-12). 1991. 25.00 (*0-916418-79-0*) Lotus.

Esbensen, Barbara J. Cold Stars & Fireflies: Poems for the Four Seasons. Bonners, Susan, illus. LC 83-45051. 80p. (gr. 3-7). 1984. PLB 14.89 (*0-690-04363-5*, Crowell Jr Bks) HarpC Child Bks.

—Words with Wrinkled Knees. Stadler, John, illus. LC 85-47886. 48p. (gr. 2-7). 1987. (Crowell Jr Bks); PLB 14.89 (*0-690-04505-0*, Crowell Jr Bks) HarpC Child Bks.

Ewart, Gavin. Caterpillar Stew: A Feast of Animal Poems. Ferns, Ronald, illus. 80p. (gr. 3-5). 1992. 15.95 (*0-09-174097-5*, Pub. by Hutchinson UK) Trafalgar.

Falconer, Elizabeth, illus. The House That Jack Built. LC 90-4467. 32p. (ps-2). 1994. pap. 4.95 (*0-8249-8651-2*, Ideals Child) Hambleton-Hill.

Farjeon, Eleanor. Eleanor Farjeon's Poems for Children. LC 51-11164. 256p. (gr. 4 up). 1984. PLB 12.89 (*0-685-17657-6*); PLB 12.89 (*0-397-32091-4*) HarpC Child Bks.

Farley, Margaret M. Little Tots, Big Tots: Poems for Young Children. 1994. pap. 7.95 (*0-533-10759-8*) Vantage.

Fast, Suellen M. Celebrations of Daughterhood. Serman, Gina L., ed. LC 85-72281. 68p. (Orig.). (gr. 1 up). 1985. pap. 8.00 (*0-935281-06-1*) Daughter Cult.

Faust, Naomi F. And I Travel by Rhythms & Words: New & Selected Poems. LC 89-63039. 318p. (gr. 7-12). 1990. pap. 18.00 perfect bdg. (*0-916418-77-4*) Lotus.

Feldman, Jacqueline. The Lavender Box. Hoffman, Nannette, illus. LC 89-85206. 41p. (ps-6). 1992. 11.95 (*0-9623903-0-5*) Ellicott Pr.

A small boy disappears into a very large hat; a child silently shares poignant feelings with a chipmunk; a little girl preaches the rules of etiquette to a bee. Poems dealing with nature & the pleasures of domestic life transform childhood experiences into rhythmic images. And in the final offering, a lavender box becomes a metaphor for the entire book. Although these poems were written for children aged 3 to 11, Ms. Feldman's awareness of & wonder at the workings of a child's mind give readers of all ages an exhilarating & joyous experience. The poems are beautifully complemented by Nannette Hoffman's whimsical black & white drawings. "A resonant voice is gently in tune with the imagination of children in this poetry collection...the imagery reverberates on every page." -- SCHOOL LIBRARY JOURNAL. "In rhythmical, memorable verse, she recreates-- for children & adult readers alike-- a child's sense of wonder." -- Anne Whitehouse, poet & reviewer for THE NEW YORK TIMES. "Quite a treasure box of a book." --THE BOOK READER. THE LAVENDER BOX is now in its second printing.
Publisher Provided Annotation.

Felty, Sherry. Kaboodle of Kidlets. 40p. (gr. k-6). 1993. pap. 2.00 (*1-884801-01-3*) Fun Enter.

—S'more Kidlets. 38p. (gr. k-6). 1993. pap. 2.00 (*1-884801-04-8*) Fun Enter.

Ferris, Helen, ed. Favorite Poems Old & New. Weisgard, Leonard, illus. LC 57-11418. 598p. (gr. 3-7). 1957. pap. 19.95 (*0-385-07696-7*) Doubleday.

Field, Eugene. The Gingham Dog & the Calico Cat. Street, Janet, illus. 32p. 1990. 14.95 (*0-399-22151-4*, Philomel Bks) Putnam Pub Group.

—A Little Book of Western Verse. 1992. Repr. of 1889 ed. lib. bdg. 75.00 (*0-7812-2642-2*) Rprt Serv.

—Love Songs of Children. 1992. Repr. of 1894 ed. lib. bdg. 75.00 (*0-7812-2645-7*) Rprt Serv.

—Lullaby Land. 1992. Repr. of 1897 ed. lib. bdg. 75.00 (*0-7812-2646-5*) Rprt Serv.

—Poems of Childhood. (Illus.). (gr. 4 up). 1969. pap. 2.95 (*0-8049-0211-9*, CL-211) Airmont.

—Second Book of Verse. 1992. Repr. of 1892 ed. lib. bdg. 75.00 (*0-7812-2644-9*) Rprt Serv.

Fields, Richard L. Haiku Animal World. Lam, Fahn, illus. 80p. (Orig.). (gr. 6-12). 1989. pap. 7.95 (*0-927256-00-2*) ELF Assocs.

—Haiku Fin & Fathom World. (Illus.). 86p. (Orig.). (gr. 6-12). 1989. pap. 7.95 (*0-317-93460-0*) ELF Assocs.

—Haiku Wing & Feather World. (Illus.). 108p. (Orig.). (gr. 6-12). 1989. pap. 7.95 (*0-317-93461-9*) ELF Assocs.

—Haiku Zing & Sting World. (Illus.). 70p. (Orig.). (gr. 6-12). 1989. pap. 7.95 (*0-317-93459-7*) ELF Assocs.

Finkelstein, Ruth. Baila Wants a Bicycle Bell. Dinkels, Rochel, illus. 24p. (ps-4). 1992. 8.95 (*0-9628157-1-3*) Feldheim.

Fisher, Aileen. Always Wondering: Some Favorite Poems of Aileen Fisher. Sandin, Joan, illus. LC 90-23069. 96p. (gr. 2-6). 1991. PLB 13.89 (*0-06-022858-X*) HarpC Child Bks.

Fisher, Barbara. Dan. Fisher, Barbara, illus. 20p. (Orig.). (gr. k-5). 1981. pap. 2.00 (*0-934830-19-3*) Ten Penny.

Fisher, Barbara & Spiegel, Richard, eds. In Search of a Song: PS-114, Vol. 1. (Illus.). 90p. (Orig.). (gr. k-6). 1981. pap. 2.00 (*0-934830-25-8*) Ten Penny.

—In Search of a Song: PS-276, Vol. 2. (Illus.). 90p. (Orig.). (gr. k-6). 1981. pap. 2.00 (*0-934830-26-6*) Ten Penny.

—More Poetry Hunter. (Illus.). 92p. (Orig.). (gr. 3 up). 1981. pap. 2.00 (*0-934830-23-1*) Ten Penny.

—Poetry Hunter, No. 1. (Illus.). 92p. (Orig.). (gr. k-6). 1981. pap. 2.00 (*0-934830-21-5*) Ten Penny.

—Still More Poetry Hunter. (Illus.). 36p. (Orig.). (gr. k-6). 1981. pap. 2.00 (*0-934830-24-X*) Ten Penny.

Fisher, Robert, ed. Amazing Monsters: Verses to Thrill & Chill. Allen, Rowena, illus. 96p. (gr. k-5). 1982. pap. 5.95 (*0-571-13925-6*) Faber & Faber.

—Funny Folk: Poems about People. Dann, Penny, illus. 80p. (ps-3). 1992. pap. 5.95 (*0-571-16214-2*) Faber & Faber.

—Minibeasts: Poems about Little Creatures. Widdowson, Kay, illus. 96p. (gr. 2 up). 1992. 13.95 (*0-571-16511-7*) Faber & Faber.

—Witch Words: Poems of Magic & Mystery. Felts, Shirley, illus. 80p. (gr. 3-6). 1987. laminated boards 9.95 (*0-571-14559-0*) Faber & Faber.

Fitch, Marguerite. Samuel Francis Smith: My Country 'tis of Thee. (Illus.). (gr. 3-6). 1987. pap. 6.95 (*0-88062-049-8*) Mott Media.

Fitch, Sheree. Toes in My Nose: And Other Poems. Bobak, Molly, illus. 48p. (gr. 1-5). 1993. pap. 6.95 (*1-56397-127-5*, Wordsong) Boyds Mills Pr.

Flashinski, Linda. Just As We Are. Flashinski, Todd, illus. 120p. (gr. k-8). 1987. spiral bdg. 11.95 (*0-9619625-0-X*); lib. bdg. 14.95 (*0-9619625-1-8*) Lavinia Pub.

Fleischman, Paul. I Am Phoenix: Poems for Two Voices. Nutt, Ken, illus. LC 85-42615. 64p. (gr. 3-8). 1985. 14.00 (*0-06-021881-9*); PLB 13.89 (*0-06-021882-7*) HarpC Child Bks.

—Joyful Noise: Poems for Two Voices. Beddows, Eric, illus. LC 87-45280. 64p. (gr. 3-8). 1988. 14.00 (*0-06-021852-5*); PLB 13.89 (*0-06-021853-3*) HarpC Child Bks.

—Joyful Noise: Poems for Two Voices. Beddows, Eric, illus. LC 87-45280. 64p. (gr. 3 up). 1992. pap. 3.95 (*0-06-446093-2*, Trophy) HarpC Child Bks.

Forelle, Helen. Mortimer Meets Melody. Leih, Janet, ed. Stevens, Barbara, illus. 20p. (gr. 1-3). 1981. pap. 2.00 (*1-877649-02-3*) Tesseract SD.

Foster, John, ed. Dragon Poems. Paul, Corky, illus. 32p. (gr. 1 up). 1992. bds. 14.00 laminated (*0-19-276096-3*); pap. 2.95 (*0-19-916425-8*) OUP.

—Egg Poems. (Illus.). 16p. (gr. 1 up). 1992. pap. 2.95 (*0-19-916422-3*) OUP.

Foster, John, compiled by. A First Poetry Book. Orr, Chris, et al, illus. 128p. (gr. 1-3). 1980. 11.95 (*0-19-918113-6*); pap. 6.95 (*0-19-918112-8*) OUP.

Foster, John, ed. Fox Poems. (Illus.). 16p. (gr. 1 up). 1992. pap. 2.95 (*0-19-916423-1*) OUP.

—Ghost Poems. (Illus.). 16p. (gr. 1 up). 1992. pap. 2.95 (*0-19-916429-0*) OUP.

—Horse Poems. (Illus.). 16p. (gr. 1 up). 1992. pap. 2.95 (*0-19-916421-5*) OUP.

—Mouse Poems. (Illus.). 16p. (gr. 1 up). 1992. pap. 2.95 (*0-19-916430-4*) OUP.

—Pocket Poetry: Horse Poems, Egg Poems, Fox Poems, Sea Poems, Dragon Poems, Seed Poems, Snow Poems, Sports Poems, Ghost Poems, Mouse Poems, 10 vols. (Illus.). (gr. 1 up). 1992. Set. pap. 29.50 (*0-19-501516-9*) OUP.

—Sea Poems. (Illus.). 16p. (gr. 1 up). 1992. pap. 2.95 (*0-19-916424-X*) OUP.

—Seed Poems. (Illus.). 16p. (gr. 1 up). 1992. pap. 2.95 (*0-19-916426-6*) OUP.

—Snow Poems. (Illus.). 16p. (gr. 1 up). 1992. pap. 2.95 (*0-19-916427-4*) OUP.

—Sports Poems. (Illus.). 16p. (gr. 1 up). 1992. pap. 2.95 (*0-19-916428-2*) OUP.

Fowke, Edith. Ring Around the Moon: Two Hundred Songs, Tongue Twisters, Riddles & Rhymes for Children. Brown, Judith G., illus. 160p. (gr. k-5). 1987. pap. 12.95 (*1-55021-006-8*, Pub. by NC Press CN) U of Toronto Pr.

Frank, Josette, selected by. Snow Toward Evening, a Year in a River Valley. Locker, Thomas, illus. LC 89-48307. 32p. 1990. 16.00 (*0-8037-0810-6*); PLB 15.89 (*0-8037-0811-4*) Dial Bks Young.

Frank-Mosenson, Sandra. Earth Day Lessons from Planet Mars. Carlos, Christina, illus. 72p. (Orig.). (gr. 4 up). 1991. Perfect bdg. 10.95 (*0-9629607-3-X*) Wisdom Pr IL.

Frasier, Elizabeth. Wow! What a Wonderful World. Black, Robert, illus. 32p. (Orig.). (gr. k-4). 1990. pap. 4.50 (*1-879253-00-3*) Apex Creat.

Fratti, Mario, et al. Thank You, Gorbachev! 70p. (Orig.). 1990. pap. write for info. (*0-9626427-0-3*) Wall to Wall.

Frost, Robert. Birches. Young, Ed, illus. LC 87-46359. 32p. (gr. 2-4). 1988. 13.95 (*0-8050-0570-6*, Bks Young Read) H Holt & Co.

—Christmas Trees. Rand, Ted, illus. LC 89-48899. 32p. (gr. 2-4). 1990. 14.95 (*0-8050-1208-7*, Bks Young Read) H Holt & Co.

—A Swinger of Birches: Poems of Robert Frost for Young People. Koeppen, Peter, illus. Fadiman, Clifton, intro. by. LC 82-5517. (Illus.). 80p. (gr. 4 up). 1982. 21.95 (*0-916144-92-5*); pap. 14.95 (*0-916144-93-3*); cass. & bk. 23.90 (*0-685-05629-5*, 102-5); cassette only 8.95 (*0-88045-099-1*) Stemmer Hse.

Fukijawa, Gyo, illus. Gyo Fujikawa's a Child's Book of Poems. 80p. (gr. k up). 1989. 13.95 (*0-448-04302-5*, G&D) Putnam Pub Group.

Gaber, Susan. Favorite Poems for Children Coloring Book. (Illus.). 48p. (Orig.). (ps-3). 1980. pap. 2.95 (*0-486-23923-3*) Dover.

Gaige, Amity. We Are a Thunderstorm. Thatch, Nancy R., ed. Melton, David, intro. by. LC 90-5922. (Illus.). 26p. 1990. PLB 14.95 (*0-933849-27-3*) Landmark Edns.

Garcia, Conrad. Thinking in Poetry. 65p. (Orig.). (gr. 10-12). 1988. pap. 7.50 (*0-9621124-0-2*) C Garcia.

Garrett, Beatrice. A Bite of Black History: A Collective of Narrative & Short Poems of Afro-American History for Juveniles & Young Adults. LC 91-74117. 72p. (gr. 6 up). 1991. 14.95 (*0-9629887-1-5*); pap. 9.95 (*0-9629887-0-7*) Bosck Pub Hse.

Gillespie, Bill. Because I Care. 24p. (Orig.). 1985. pap. 5.95 (*0-940859-01-7*) Snd Dollar Pub.

—Boat Ride. Poe, Janice, illus. 24p. 1988. pap. 3.50 (*0-940859-05-X*) Snd Dollar Pub.

—Peter Potter Teeter Totter. Poe, Janice, illus. 22p. (Orig.). 1987. pap. 3.50 (*0-940859-06-8*) Snd Dollar Pub.

—Spotty Spotty Jones. Poe, Janice, illus. 22p. (Orig.). 1986. pap. 3.50 (*0-940859-03-3*) Snd Dollar Pub.

Gillsepie, Bill. Giraffes. Poe, Janice, illus. 12p. (Orig.). 1985. pap. 3.00 (*0-940859-00-9*) Snd Dollar Pub.

Giovanni, Nikki. Vacation Time: Poems for Children. Russo, Marisabina, illus. LC 79-91643. 32p. (gr. 7 up). 1981. pap. 6.00 (*0-688-00507-1*, Quill) Morrow.

Glenn, Mel. Back to Class: Poems by Mel Glenn. Bernstein, Michael J., photos by. LC 88-2835. (Illus.). 112p. (gr. 7 up). 1988. 13.95 (*0-89919-656-X*, Clarion Bks) HM.

—Class Dismissed! High School Poems. Bernstein, Michael J., illus. LC 81-38441. 112p. 1991. pap. 5.70 (*0-395-58111-7*, Clarion Bks) HM.

—Class Dismissed Two: More High School Poems. Bernstein, Michael J., photos by. LC 86-2671. (Illus.). 96p. (gr. 8 up). 1986. 13.95 (*0-89919-443-5*, Clarion Bks) HM.

—My Friend's Got This Problem, Mr. Candler. (gr. 4-7). 1991. 14.95 (*0-89919-833-3*, Clarion Bks) HM.

Glyman, Caroline A. All Around the World: A Bedtime Book. (Illus.). 32p. (gr. k-3). Date not set. PLB 12.95 (*1-878363-77-8*) Forest Hse.

Goldstein, Bobbye S., ed. Inner Chimes: Poems on Poetry. Zalben, Jane B., illus. 32p. (ps-7). 1992. PLB 15.95 (*1-56397-040-6*, Wordsong) Boyds Mills Pr.

Goodrich, Patricia. Barefeet & Bellybuttons: Poems & Activities to Tickle a Child. Boytin, Michael, illus. 46p. (gr. k-4). 1989. pap. 5.00 (*0-9625348-1-1*) P Goodrich.

Goulet, Rosalina M. Poems of Childhood: Mga Tula ng Kabataan. (TAG & ENG., Illus.). 106p. (Orig.). (gr. k-2). 1989. pap. 7.50x (*971-10-0349-X*, Pub. by New Day Pub PI) Cellar.

Granville, Katherine H. Let's Go See. (gr. 4 up). 1981. 6.50 (*0-9623897-1-4*) Catalyst Pr.

Gravel, Fern, pseud. Oh Millersville! Andrews, Clarence A., tr. LC 41-3646. (Illus.). 128p. (gr. 3 up). 1981. PLB 8.95 (*0-934582-01-7*); pap. 5.95 (*0-685-42267-4*) Midwest Heritage.

Greenfield, Eloise. Honey, I Love & Other Love Poems. Dillon, Diane & Dillon, Leo D., illus. LC 85-45398. 48p. (gr. 1-4). 1986. pap. 3.95 (*0-06-443097-9*, Trophy) HarpC Child Bks.

—Nathaniel Talking. Gilchrist, Jan S., illus. 32p. (gr. k-5). 1988. 12.95 (*0-86316-200-2*) Writers & Readers.

Gross, Philip. The All-Nite Cafe. (gr. 4 up). 1993. pap. 5.95 (*0-571-16753-5*) Faber & Faber.

Grossman, John & Dunhill, Priscilla. Nonsense & Commonsense: A Child's Book of Victorian Verse. 128p. 1992. 17.95 (*1-56305-313-6*, 3313) Workman Pub.

Gunning, Monica. Not a Copper Penny in Me House: Poems from the Caribbean. Lessac, Frane, illus. 32p. 1993. 14.95 (*1-56397-050-3*, Wordsong) Boyds Mills Pr.

Gutman, Bessie P., illus. I Love You: Verses & Sweet Sayings. 32p. 1994. 4.95 (*0-448-40258-0*, G&D) Putnam Pub Group.

Hague, Michael, compiled by. & illus. Sleep, Baby, Sleep: Lullabies & Night Poems. LC 93-27119. 1994. PLB write for info. (*0-688-10877-6*) Morrow Jr Bks.

Hall, Steven. Down Came the Sun. Steffan, Leonard, illus. Hall, Mary A. LC 72-176097. (Illus.). 64p. (gr. 3 up). 1972. 8.95 (*0-87929-010-2*) Barlenmir.

Halloran, Phyllis. I'd Like to Hear a Flower Grow. Reynolds, Carol, illus. LC 89-60979. 56p. (gr. k-8). 1989. 12.95 (*0-943867-02-9*) Reading Inc.

Harper, Jo. The Harper's Voices: Caves & Cowboys: Family Song Book. George, R. Jefferson, photos by. Boustany, Robert, illus. (ENG & SPA.). 20p. (Orig.). (gr. 1-5). 1988. pap. 8.95 incl. cassette (*0-929932-00-5*) JCH Pr.

Harrison, Michael & Stuart-Clark, Christopher. The Oxford Book of Story Poems. (Illus.). 176p. (gr. 3 up). 1990. jacketed 17.95 (*0-19-276087-4*) OUP.

Harrison, Ted. Children of the Yukon. LC 77-79543. (Illus.). (gr. 1-4). 1977. pap. 6.95 (*0-88776-163-1*) Tundra Bks.

Hathorn, Libby. There & Back. LC 92-27236. 1993. 4.25 (*0-383-03659-3*) SRA Schl Grp.

Hazard, James. Look Both Ways. 55p. (Orig.). (gr. 4-6). 1987. pap. 4.25 (*0-935399-03-8*) Main St Pub.

Hazeltine, Alice I., compiled by. The Year Around: Poems for Children. Hazeltine, Smith, compiled by. LC 72-11921. (gr. 7 up). 1973. Repr. of 1956 ed. 15. 00 (*0-8369-6403-9*) Ayer.

Heard, Georgia. Creatures of Earth, Sea, & Sky. Dewey, Jennifer O., illus. LC 91-65978. 32p. (gr. 1-4). 1992. 15.95 (*1-56397-013-9*, Wordsong) Boyds Mills Pr.

Hearne, Betsy. Love Lines: Poetry in Person. LC 87-1737. 72p. (gr. 9 up). 1987. SBE 12.95 (*0-689-50437-3*, M K McElderry) Macmillan Child Grp.

Hedge-Cheney, Jacquelyn & Cheney, Roland J. The Little Daisy Girl & Other Poems. Hedge-Cheney, Jacquelyn & Cheny, Roland J., illus. 48p. (Orig.). (gr. 6 up). 1989. pap. write for info (*0-9621283-0-9*) Lil Daisy Bks.

Hegler, Michele & Hegler, Jodi. Faces of the World. Cuthbert, Peter, illus. 79p. (gr. 9-12). 1989. pap. 7.95 (*0-945362-02-1*) Best Sllrs TX.

Higginson, William J., ed. Wind in the Long Grass: A Collection of Haiku. Speidel, Sandra, illus. LC 89-21804. 48p. (gr. 2-5). 1991. pap. 13.95 jacketed (*0-671-67978-3*, S&S BFYR) S&S Trade.

Highwater, Jamake. Songs for the Seasons. Speidel, Sandra, illus. LC 93-8094. 1994. 15.00 (*0-688-10658-7*); PLB 14.93 (*0-688-10659-5*) Lothrop.

Higman, Anita. Willing to Grow. Cuthbert, Peter, illus. 45p. (gr. 9-12). 1988. pap. 4.95 (*0-945362-01-3*) Best Sllrs TX.

Hill, Charlotte M. Poetry for Wee Folks. Hill, Fred D., ed. Young, Elaine, et al, illus. LC 88-70281. 28p. (gr. k-3). 1988. 11.95 (*0-9620182-0-1*); pap. 6.95 (*0-9620182-2-8*) Charill Pubs.

Hillman, Priscilla. Merry Mouse Christmas ABC. Hillman, Priscilla, illus. LC 79-6586. 32p. (ps-1). 1980. pap. 4.95 (*0-385-15596-4*) Doubleday.

Hilton, Kathlyn G. Come, Walk in the Woods with Me. Presutto, Josephine, illus. LC 92-72704. 40p. (gr. 7-9). 1993. 14.95 (*1-880851-04-0*) Greene Bark Pr.

Hirsch, Virginia R. Heart Country Destiny: Twenty Poems by the Heart Country Lady. 28p. (Orig.). 1990. pap. 4.00 (*0-9616334-4-1*) Heart Ctry Pubns.

Hodgson, Harriet W. My First Fourth of July Book. Hohag, Linda, illus. LC 86-30987. 32p. (ps-2). 1987. pap. 3.95 (*0-516-42907-8*) Childrens.

Holbrook, Sara. The Dog Ate My Homework. 44p. (gr. 4-8). 1990. pap. 6.95 (*1-881786-00-5*) Kid Poems.

—Feelings Make Me Real. 46p. (gr. 4-8). 1990. pap. 6.95 (*1-881786-02-1*) Kid Poems.

—I Never Said I Wasn't Difficult. (Orig.). (gr. 4-8). Date not set. pap. 6.95 (*1-881786-04-8*) Kid Poems.

—Kid Poems for the Not-So-Bad, 4 vols. (gr. 4-8). 1992. pap. 24.95 (*1-881786-06-4*) Kid Poems.

—Some Families: I Want to Move Across the Street. 51p. (gr. 4-8). 1990. pap. 6.95 (*1-881786-01-3*) Kid Poems.

Homer. The Iliad. Shaw, Charlie, illus. Stewart, Diana, adapted By. LC 80-15669. (Illus.). 48p. (gr. 4 up). 1983. PLB 20.70 (*0-8172-1663-4*) Raintree Steck-V.

—The Odyssey. Hack, Konrad, illus. Stewart, Diana, adapted by. LC 79-24480. (Illus.). 48p. (gr. 4 up). 1983. PLB 20.70 (*0-8172-1654-5*) Raintree Steck-V.

Hopkins, Lee B. Happy Birthday. Knight, Hilary, illus. LC 90-10086. 40p. (ps-2). 1993. pap. 5.95 (*0-671-79851-0*, S&S BYR) S&S Trade.

—Merrily Comes Our Harvest In: Poems for Thanksgiving. Shecter, Ben, illus. 32p. (gr. 2 up). 1993. 9.95 (*1-878093-57-6*, Wordsong) Boyds Mills Pr.

—Ragged Shadows: Poems of Halloween Night. (ps-3). 1993. 15.95 (*0-316-37276-5*) Little.

—The Sky Is Full of Song. Zimmer, Dirk, illus. LC 82-48263. 48p. (gr. k-3). 1987. pap. 4.95 (*0-06-446064-9*, Trophy) HarpC Child Bks.

Hopkins, Lee B., selected by. Beat the Drum: Independence Day Has Come. De Paola, Tomie, illus. LC 92-85033. 32p. (gr. 1-4). 1993. reinforced 9.95 (*1-878093-60-6*, Wordsong) Boyds Mills Pr.

Hopkins, Lee B., ed. Munching: Poems about Eating. Davis, Nelle, illus. 48p. (gr. 3-6). 1985. 14.95 (*0-316-37269-2*) Little.

Hopkins, Lee B., selected by. Questions. Croll, Carolyn, illus. LC 90-21745. 64p. (gr. k-3). 1992. 13.00 (*0-06-022412-6*); PLB 12.89 (*0-06-022413-4*) HarpC Child Bks.

Hopkins, Lee B., ed. Rainbows Are Made: Poems by Carl Sandburg. Eichenberg, Fritz, illus. LC 82-47934. 82p. (gr. k up). 1982. 17.95 (*0-15-265480-1*, HB Juv Bks) HarBrace.

—Side by Side: Poems to Read Together. Knight, Hilary, illus. LC 87-33025. 96p. (gr. 1 up). 1988. pap. 14.95 (*0-671-63579-4*, S&S BFYR) S&S Trade.

Huff, Barbara A. Once Inside the Library, Vol. 1. (ps-4). 1990. 14.95 (*0-316-37967-0*) Little.

Hulme, Joy N. What If? Just Wondering Poems. Gorbachev, Valeri, illus. LC 90-60863. 32p. (ps-1). 1993. 14.95 (*1-56397-186-0*, Wordsong) Boyds Mills Pr.

Hummel, Berta. The Hummel. Hummel, Berta, illus. 1972. 17.00 (*0-88431-129-5*) IBD Ltd.

Hyman, Ramona. Grandma Jackson's Poetry. Omolade, Kip, illus. 32p. 1992. 16.95 (*0-685-60764-X*); pap. 8.95 (*0-685-60765-8*) Third World.

I Love the World (Small Book) 36p. (gr. 1-6). 1993. 6-pack 42.00 (*1-56334-339-8*) Hampton-Brown.

Jabar, Cynthia. Bored Blue? Think What You Can Do. (ps-3). 1991. 14.95 (*0-316-43458-2*) Little.

Jackson, Bobby. Pops, Chops & Crops. LC 89-51297. 44p. (gr. k-3). 1990. 5.95 (*1-55523-259-0*) Winston-Derek.

James, Henry G. Limericks, Fables & Poems. (Orig.). (gr. 12). 1987. 12.00 (*0-942951-00-X*); PLB 12.00 (*0-942951-01-8*); pap. 12.00 (*0-942951-02-6*) Universal Res LA.

Janeczko, Paul. Poetspeak: In Their Work, About Their Work: A Special Kind of Poetry Anthology. LC 91-15532. 256p. (gr. 7 up). 1991. pap. 9.95 (*0-02-043850-8*, Collier Young Ad) Macmillan Child Grp.

Janeczko, Paul B. Brickyard Summer. Rush, Ken, illus. LC 89-42542. 64p. (gr. 7 up). 1989. 13.95 (*0-531-05846-8*); PLB 13.99 (*0-531-08446-9*) Orchard Bks Watts.

Janeczko, Paul B., selected by. The Music of What Happens: Poems That Tell Stories. LC 87-30791. 208p. (gr. 7 up). 1988. 15.95 (*0-531-05757-7*); PLB 15.99 (*0-531-08357-8*) Orchard Bks Watts.

Janeczko, Paul B., compiled by. This Delicious Day: Sixty-Five Poems. LC 87-7717. 96p. (gr. 4-6). 1987. 11.95 (*0-531-05724-0*); PLB 11.99 (*0-531-08324-1*) Orchard Bks Watts.

Janger, Kathie, ed. Rainbow Collection, 1987: Stories & Poetry by Young People. Ishikawa, Yoko, illus. Johnson, Rafer, intro. by. (Illus.). 160p. (gr. 1-8). 1987. pap. text ed. 6.00 (*0-929889-02-9*) Young Writers Contest Found.

—Rainbow Collection, 1988: Stories & Poetry by Young People. Turtiainen, Tuomas, illus. Valenti, Jack, intro. by. (Illus.). 160p. (gr. 1-8). 1988. pap. 6.00 (*0-929889-03-7*) Young Writers Contest Found.

Janger, Kathie & Korenblit, Joan, eds. Rainbow Collection, 1985: Stories & Poetry by Young People. Allen, Steve, frwd. by. 160p. (gr. 1-8). 1985. pap. 6.00 (*0-929889-00-2*) Young Writers Contest Found.

—Rainbow Collection, 1986: Stories & Poetry by Young People. Scott, Willard, frwd. by. 160p. (gr. 1-8). 1986. pap. 6.00 (*0-929889-01-0*) Young Writers Contest Found.

Jea, Kayla & Gene. The Rain Duck: A First Poem for Preschoolers & Kindergarten. Abell, ed. & illus. 50p. (ps). Date not set. 25.00 (*1-56611-050-5*); pap. 15.00 (*1-56611-051-3*) Jonas.

Jean-Jacques, Tony. Pour Mieux t'Aimer. Jean-Jacques, Tony, illus. (FRE & CRP.). 128p. (gr. 6-12). 1993. text ed. 10.00x (*0-938534-01-7*) Soup Nuts Pr.

Jernigan, Gisela. Sonoran Seasons: A Year in the Desert. Jernigan, E. Wesley, illus. LC 93-38709. 32p. (Orig.). (ps-5). 1994. pap. 10.95 (*0-943173-91-4*) Harbinger AZ.

Johnson, George F. Poems & Things, Vol. 1. 98p. (Orig.). (gr. 9-12). 1989. write for info. G F Johnson.

Johnson, Kristopher K. A Day Without Cartoons: Poetry for Gifted Students. Kester, Ellen S., ed. (Illus.). 50p. (Orig.). (gr. 3-8). 1989. pap. 6.95 (*0-685-26282-0*) Pickwick Pubs.

Joseph, Lynn. Coconut Kind of Day. 32p. 1990. 13.95 (*0-688-09119-9*); PLB 13.88 (*0-688-09120-2*) Lothrop.

Katz, Bobbi. Ghosts & Goose Bumps: Poems to Chill Your Bones. Ray, Deborah K., illus. LC 89-37134. 32p. (Orig.). (ps-3). 1991. pap. 2.25 (*0-679-80372-6*) Random Bks Yng Read.

—Upside Down & Inside Out: Poems for All Your Pockets. Watson, Wendy, illus. 48p. (ps-3). 1992. PLB 14.95 (*1-56397-122-4*, Wordsong) Boyds Mills Pr.

Keck, Carol J. What a Wonderful World: Poems for Nature-Loving Children. 1994. 7.95 (*0-533-10787-3*) Vantage.

Keel-Williams, Mildred. Legacies of a Shopping Bag Lady: Poems of Life. Holmes, Darryl, ed. George, Anthony & Washington, Ruby, photos by. Harewood, Lasana K., frwd. by. LC 84-62520. (Illus.). 72p. (Orig.). (gr. 7 up). 1984. pap. 6.00 (*0-9614084-1-3*) Mus Fed Ink.

Kellogg, Mary G. Doing Things & Happenings. Rytter, Peggy, illus. LC 80-80271. 90p. (gr. 1-6). 1979. 6.95 (*0-9603972-0-5*); pap. 4.95 (*0-9603972-1-3*) Bks by Kellogg.

Kennedy, Dorothy M., et al, eds. I Thought I'd Take My Rat to School: Poems for September to June. Soto, Gary & Kuskin, Karla. Carter, Abby, illus. LC 92-12775. 1993. 15.95 (*0-316-48893-3*) Little.

Kennedy, Joy. Jellybean Dreams. Shaw, Charles, illus. LC 92-46429. 120p. (gr. 6-12). 1993. 14.95 (*0-89015-864-9*) Sunbelt Media.

Kennedy, X. J. Brats. Watts, James, illus. LC 85-20018. 48p. (gr. 3 up). 1986. SBE 12.95 (*0-689-50392-X*, M K McElderry) Macmillan Child Grp.

—The Forgetful Wishing Well: Poems for Young People. Incisa, Monica, illus. LC 84-45977. 96p. (gr. 4 up). 1985. SBE 12.95 (*0-689-50317-2*, M K McElderry) Macmillan Child Grp.

—Fresh Brats. Watts, James, illus. LC 89-38031. 48p. (gr. 3-5). 1990. SBE 12.95 (*0-689-50499-3*, M K McElderry) Macmillan Child Grp.

—The Kite That Braved Old Orchard Beach: Year-Round Poems for Young People. LC 90-20100. (Illus.). 96p. (gr. 4 up). 1991. SBE 13.95 (*0-689-50507-8*, M K McElderry) Macmillan Child Grp.

Kennedy, X. J. & Kennedy, Dorothy M. Knock at a Star: A Child's Introduction to Poetry. Weinhaus, Karen A., illus. 160p. (gr. 2-6). 1985. 15.95 (*0-316-48853-4*); pap. 9.95 (*0-316-48854-2*) Little.

Khayyam, Omar. Rubaiyat of Omar Khayyam. Fitzgerald, Edward, tr. (Illus.). (gr. 9 up). 1969. pap. 1.50 (*0-8049-0204-6*, CL-204) Airmont.

Kherdian, David. Beat Poetry. 1995. write for info. (*0-8050-3315-7*) H Holt & Co.

Kimball, Richard S. A Funny Feeling. Reid, William K., Jr., illus. LC 87-32155. 64p. (Orig.). (gr. 3 up). Date not set. pap. 7.95 (*0-944443-00-1*) Green Timber.
This collection of 41 cleverly illustrated poems explores common feelings & sayings about them for entertainment & enlightenment of youngsters aged eight & above. Eight-year olds will identify with Reginald Botts who was "tied up in knots & couldn't get his thoughts undone." Ten-year olds will enjoy the image of Louise being made small by the weight of the grudge she carries. Twelve-year

olds will sympathize with Annie who has reached the age "when staying in means being left out" & "going out means being in." Everybody will be delighted by "tongue tied" Sid & by the many other characters & poems. With humor, this book allows readers & listeners to think about their own funny feelings & can open the way for discussion with parents, teachers, counselors, church groups, & friends. Paperback, $7.95. Call or write for information to order, Green Timber Publications, P.O. Box 3884, Portland, ME 04104, 207-797-4180.
Publisher Provided Annotation.

Klawitter, P. Poetry Parade. (gr. 4-6). 1987. 5.95 (*0-88160-156-X*, LW 274) Learning Wks.

Knudson, R. R. & Swenson, May, eds. American Sports Poems. LC 87-24384. 240p. (gr. 6 up). 1988. 15.95 (*0-531-05753-4*); PLB 15.99 (*0-531-08353-5*) Orchard Bks Watts.

Koch, Kenneth & Farrell, Kate. Talking to the Sun: An Illustrated Anthology of Poems for Young People. LC 85-15428. 112p. (ps up). 1985. 22.50 (*0-8050-0144-1*, Bks Young Read) H Holt & Co.

Kohen, Clarita. Pajaritos. Torrecilla, Pablo, illus. 24p. (Orig.). (gr. k-3). 1993. PLB 7.50x (*1-56492-104-2*) Laredo.

Kohen, Gabriela. The Circus. Sanchez, Jose R., illus. 24p. (Orig.). (gr. 2-6). 1992. PLB 9.95x (*1-56492-023-2*) Laredo.

—The Circus: Big Book. Sanchez, Jose R., illus. 24p. (gr. 2-6). 1992. pap. 19.95x (*1-56492-024-0*) Laredo.

—The Theatre. Sanchez, Jose R., illus. 24p. (Orig.). (gr. 2-6). 1992. PLB 9.95x (*1-56492-012-7*) Laredo.

—The Theatre: Big Book. Sanchez, Jose R., illus. 24p. (Orig.). (gr. 2-6). 1992. pap. 19.95x (*1-56492-013-5*) Laredo.

Korman, Gordon & Korman, Bernice. The D-Poems of Jeremy Bloom. 1992. pap. 2.95 (*0-590-44819-6*, 059, Apple Paperbacks) Scholastic Inc.

Krauss, Ruth. Monkey Day. Rowand, Phyllis, illus. 23p. (gr. k-5). 1973. pap. 8.00 (*0-912846-05-4*) Bookstore Pr.

Kruss, James & Lewis, Naomi. Johnny Longnose. Eidrigevicius, Stasys, illus. LC 89-42612. 32p. (gr. k-3). 1990. 13.95 (*1-55858-023-9*) North-South Bks NYC.

Kuskin, Karla. Dogs & Dragons, Trees & Dreams: A Collection of Poems. Kuskin, Karla, illus. LC 79-2814. 96p. (gr. 1-6). 1980. PLB 13.89 (*0-06-023544-6*) HarpC Child Bks.

—Dogs & Dragons, Trees & Dreams: A Collection of Poems. Kuskin, Karla, illus. LC 79-2814. 96p. (gr. k-3). 1992. pap. 4.95 (*0-06-446122-X*, Trophy) HarpC Child Bks.

—Patchwork Island. Mathers, Petra, illus. LC 92-10344. 32p. (gr. 3-7). 1994. 15.00 (*0-06-021242-X*, HarpT); PLB 14.89 (*0-06-021284-5*, HarpT) HarpC.

—Soap Soup: And Other Verses. Kuskin, Karla, illus. LC 91-22947. 64p. (gr. k-3). 1992. 14.00 (*0-06-023571-3*); PLB 13.89 (*0-06-023572-1*) HarpC Child Bks.

—Soap Soup: And Other Verses. Kuskin, Karla, illus. LC 91-22947. 64p. (ps-3). 1994. pap. 3.50 (*0-06-444174-1*, Trophy) HarpC Child Bks.

Ladson, Etta M. Strange Land Songs. (Illus.). 146p. (gr. 7-12). 1992. text ed. 14.95 (*0-9630574-0-5*) Jewelgate.

Langill, Ellen. Pompey Poems... Celebrating a Cat. Davenport, May, illus. LC 86-91603. 64p. (Orig.). (gr. 7-12). 1986. 10.25x (*0-943864-28-3*); pap. 3.50x (*0-943864-26-7*) Davenport.

Larke, Joe. Dopie Dope Grin A Bit Poetry Series. Larke, Karol, illus. (gr. k-6). 1992. write for info. (*0-9620112-9-0*) Grin A Bit.

Larrick, Nancy. Crazy to Be Alive in Such a Strange World: Poems about People. Crosby, Alexander L., photos by. LC 76-49667. (Illus.). 192p. (gr. 5 up). 1989. pap. 6.95 (*0-87131-566-1*) M Evans.

—When the Dark Comes Dancing: A Bedtime Poetry Book. Wallner, John, illus. LC 81-428. (ps-2). 1983. 17.95 (*0-399-20807-0*, Philomel) Putnam Pub Group.

Larungu, Rute, as told by. Betty Elizabeth Brown: A Keepsake Book. Ross, Connie, illus. 32p. (ps up). 1992. pap. 2.75 (*1-878893-26-2*) Telcraft Bks.

—Dearie Dot: A Keepsake Book. Ross, Connie, illus. 32p. (ps up). 1992. pap. 2.75 (*1-878893-25-4*) Telcraft Bks.

Lash, Jamie S. Righteous Rhymes, Vol. 1. Jackson, Jeff, illus. 24p. (gr. 2-7). 1983. pap. 2.95 (*0-915775-00-X*, Dist. by Stardust) Love Song Mess Assn.

Lash, Jamie S., ed. Righteous Rhymes, Vol. 2. Jackson, Jeff, illus. 24p. (Orig.). 1987. pap. 2.95 (*0-915775-01-8*) Love Song Mess Assn.

Lawlor, Dorothy. Troubles & Other Poems. 1993. 8.95 (*0-533-10522-6*) Vantage.

Lear, Edward. The Owl & the Pussycat. Littlejohn, Claire, illus. LC 86-46115. 14p. (ps-3). 1987. 6.95 (*0-694-00193-7*) HarpC Child Bks.

LeMair, Henriette. Child's Garden of Verses. (Illus.). 112p. (gr. k up). 1991. 15.95 (*0-399-21818-1*, Philomel Bks) Putnam Pub Group.

Leo, Kathleen R., et al, eds. Waiting for the Apples. LC 82-62746. (Illus.). 100p. (Orig.). (gr. k up). 1983. pap. 6.50 (*0-9606678-2-2*) Sylvan Pubns.

Lesser, Carolyn. Flamingo Knees. 3rd ed. 52p. (gr. 5 up). 1991. pap. 10.00 (*0-9630604-0-6*) Oakwood MO.

—The Knees Knock Again. 2nd ed. 56p. 1991. pap. 10.00 (*0-9630604-1-4*) Oakwood MO.

Levy, Nathan & Levy, Janet. There Are Those. Edwards, Joan, illus. LC 82-81111. 32p. (ps up). 1990. 21.95 (*0-9608240-0-6*) NL Assoc Inc.

Lewis, Claudia L. Long Ago in Oregon. Fontaine, Joel, illus. LC 86-45781. 64p. (gr. 3-7). 1987. HarpC Child Bks.

Lewis, J. Patrick. Earth Verses & Water Rhymes. Sabuda, Robert, illus. LC 90-40709. 32p. (gr. 2-5). 1991. SBE 13.95 (*0-689-31693-3*, Atheneum Child Bk) Macmillan Child Grp.

Lindbloom, James A. Make the Morning. Lindbloom, Nancy, illus. (gr. 3-8). 1977. pap. 3.00 (*0-89409-007-0*) Childrens Art.

Lindo, Howard. Making Dreams Come True. Brand, Jennifer, illus. 1993. 7.95 (*0-533-10406-8*) Vantage.

Lindsay, Vachel. Johnny Appleseed & Other Poems. 129p. 1981. Repr. PLB 23.95x (*0-89966-365-6*) Buccaneer Bks.

—Johnny Appleseed & Other Poems. 138p. 1981. PLB 21.95 (*0-89967-039-3*) Harmony Raine.

Livingston, Myra C. Abraham Lincoln: A Man for All the People: A Ballad. Byrd, Samuel, illus. LC 93-2731. 32p. (ps-3). 1993. reinforced bdg. 15.95 (*0-8234-1049-8*) Holiday.

—Dilly Dilly Piccalilli: Poems for the Very Young. Christelow, Eileen, illus. (gr. 1 up). 1989. SBE 13.95 (*0-689-50466-7*, M K McElderry) Macmillan Child Grp.

—I Like You, If You Like Me: Poems of Friendship. LC 86-21108. 160p. (gr. 5 up). 1987. SBE 14.95 (*0-689-50408-X*, M K McElderry) Macmillan Child Grp.

—Monkey Puzzle & Other Poems. Frasconi, Antonio, illus. LC 84-3050. 64p. (gr. 6 up). 1984. SBE 13.95 (*0-689-50310-5*, M K McElderry) Macmillan Child Grp.

—Poems for Mothers. Ray, Deborah K., illus. LC 87-19629. 32p. (ps-3). 1988. reinforced bdg. 13.95 (*0-8234-0678-4*) Holiday.

—Remembering & Other Poems. LC 89-2654. 64p. (gr. 3-7). 1989. SBE 13.95 (*0-689-50489-6*, M K McElderry) Macmillan Child Grp.

—A Song I Sang to You: A Selection of Poems. Tomes, Margot, illus. LC 84-4585. 84p. (ps-3). 1984. 12.95 (*0-15-277105-0*, HB Juv Bks) HarBrace.

—There Was a Place: And Other Poems. LC 88-12832. 40p. (gr. 3-7). 1988. SBE 12.95 (*0-689-50464-0*, M K McElderry) Macmillan Child Grp.

—Up in the Air. Fisher, Leonard E., illus. LC 88-23293. 32p. (ps-3). 1989. reinforced bdg. 14.95 (*0-8234-0736-5*) Holiday.

—Valentine Poems. Livingston, Myra C., selected by. LC 85-31723. (Illus.). 32p. (ps-3). 1987. reinforced bdg. 14.95 (*0-8234-0587-7*) Holiday.

—Worlds I Know & Other Poems. Arnold, Tim, illus. LC 85-7344. 64p. (gr. 4-7). 1985. SBE 13.95 (*0-689-50332-6*, M K McElderry) Macmillan Child Grp.

Livingston, Myra C., selected by. Halloween Poems. Gammell, Stephen, illus. LC 89-1741. 32p. (ps-3). 1989. reinforced bdg. 13.95 (*0-8234-0762-4*) Holiday.

—Lots of Limericks. Perry, Rebecca, illus. LC 91-329. 144p. (gr. 3 up). 1991. SBE 13.95 (*0-689-50531-0*, M K McElderry) Macmillan Child Grp.

—New Year's Poems. Tomes, Margot, illus. LC 86-22885. 32p. (ps-3). 1987. reinforced bdg. 12.95 (*0-8234-0641-5*) Holiday.

—Poems for Grandmothers. Cullen-Clark, Patricia, illus. LC 90-55102. 32p. (ps-3). 1990. reinforced 12.95 (*0-8234-0830-2*) Holiday.

—Poems for Jewish Holidays. Bloom, Lloyd, illus. LC 85-27179. 32p. (ps-4). 1986. reinforced bdg. 13.95 (*0-8234-0606-7*) Holiday.

Livingston, Myra C., ed. Thanksgiving Poems. Gammell, Stephen, illus. LC 85-762. 32p. (ps-4). 1985. reinforced bdg. 14.95 (*0-8234-0570-2*) Holiday.

Logan, Mike. Little Friends: In Verse & Photography. (ps-3). 1992. pap. 7.95 (*1-56044-139-9*) Falcon Pr MT.

Lomas Garza, Carmen. Family Pictures (Cuadros de familia) Garza, Carmen L., illus. LC 89-27845. (SPA & ENG.). 32p. (gr. 1-7). 1990. 13.95 (*0-89239-050-6*) Childrens Book Pr.

Long, Jeanne & Mallis, Jackie. Pathways to Poetry Series: Kaleidoscope, Mosaics, Visions. Miller, Jo & Monroe, Laura, eds. (gr. 1-12). 1984. Set of 3. pap. text ed. 39.95 (*0-685-62412-9*) Multi Media TX.

Longfellow, Henry Wadsworth. Paul Revere's Ride. Parker, Nancy W., illus. LC 84-4139. 48p. (gr. 1 up). 1985. 14.95 (*0-688-04014-4*); PLB 14.88 (*0-688-04015-2*) Greenwillow.

Lyon, George-Ella. Together. LC 89-2892. (Illus.). 32p. (ps-1). 1989. 14.95 (*0-531-05831-X*); PLB 14.99 (*0-531-08431-0*) Orchard Bks Watts.

McBrown, Gertrude P. Picture Poetry Book. Jones, Lois M., illus. 1990. 4.25 (*0-87498-007-0*) Assoc Pubs DC.

McCann, Yvette B. Eddie Pasghetti. Damerest, Nancy & Lea, Judy, eds. Morehiser, Jeanne, illus. 64p. (gr. 4 up). 1994. 14.95 (*0-9639486-5-2*) Rhyme Tyme.
EDDIE PASGHETTI is a whimsical but heartwarming tale of a silly small boy as told by his "hip," self-absorbed, teenaged sister in a unique & sophisticated rhyme. The baby-sitting sister's charge is to get Eddie to eat his greens, but Eddie has other ideas! Kids age nine to ninety-two will laugh at Eddie's antics & at his big sister's growing impatience. "I watched as he ran down the hall with his spoon/ And I thought to myself, 'This kid's like a baboon./ I didn't expect food to ricochet,/ No question about it, I'll ask for more pay!'/ The next thing I knew, Eddie strung his baloney/ On twelve inches of hard uncooked red rigatoni,/ And he tied it around his small waist, like a child,/ Shouting, 'King Eddie Pasghetti...The King of the Wild!'"/ Parents will readily identify with the struggles of getting a child to eat greens & will greatly appreciate the recipe section containing Eddie's favorite foods. A must read for pasta lovers! Contact: Rhyme Tyme Publications, 214 Presbytere Pkwy., Lafayette, LA 70503-6036 or call (318) 981-4081.
Publisher Provided Annotation.

McCord, Catherine G. Of Butterflies & Buttercups. Scudder, Barbara J., illus. LC 85-61275. 64p. (gr. 5-12). 1985. 12.50 (*0-9614997-0-2*) Buttercup Bks.

McCord, David. One at a Time. Kane, Henry B., illus. (gr. 4 up). 1986. 18.95 (*0-316-55516-9*) Little.

—Speak Up: More Rhymes of the Never Was & Always Is. Simont, Marc, illus. 80p. (gr. 5 up). 1980. 13.95 (*0-316-55517-7*) Little.

McCracken, Lisa. The Lilies' Edge. Taylor, Neil, illus. LC 86-40282. 48p. (gr. 1-3). 1987. 5.95 (*1-55523-036-9*) Winston-Derek.

McCullough, Frances, ed. Love Is Like the Lion's Tooth. LC 77-25659. 96p. (gr. 7 up). 1984. PLB 13.89 (*0-06-024139-X*) HarpC Child Bks.

McDonald, Marilyn. Inspired by a Child of God Called Marilyn. LC 90-71950. 44p. (gr. 9-12). 1991. 5.95 (*1-55523-416-X*) Winston-Derek.

McLoughland, Beverly. Hippo's a Heap: And Other Animal Poems. 32p. (ps-3). 1993. 14.95 (*1-56397-017-1*) Boyds Mills Pr.

McMahon, Sean, ed. Poolbeg Book of Children's Verse. 240p. 1987. pap. 9.95 (*0-905169-88-3*, Pub. by Poolbeg Press Ltd Eire) Dufour.

Mcmillan, Bruce. One Sun: A Book of Terse Verse. Mcmillan, Bruce, illus. LC 89-24625. 32p. (ps-3). reinforced bdg. 15.95 (*0-8234-0810-8*); pap. 5.95 (*0-8234-0951-1*) Holiday.

MacPherson, Jennifer B. To Attempt a Tower. LC 85-90339. 84p. (gr. 9-12). 1985. 16.95 (*0-9614849-0-X*); pap. 8.95 (*0-9614849-1-8*) MacPherson Pub.

Madgett, Naomi L. Octavia & Other Poems. Duskin, Leisia, illus. LC 87-51637. 117p. (Orig.). (gr. 9-12). 1988. pap. 8.00 (*0-88378-121-2*) Third World.

Magorian, James. The Palace of Water. LC 90-81003. (Illus.). 16p. (gr. 2-5). 1990. pap. 3.00 (*0-930674-33-2*) Black Oak.

—Spoonproof Jello & Other Poems. LC 90-81004. (Illus.). 16p. (gr. 2-5). 1990. pap. 3.00 (*0-930674-34-0*) Black Oak.

—The Witches' Olympics. LC 83-71262. 44p. (gr. 4-7). 1983. pap. 5.00 (*0-930674-10-3*) Black Oak.

Maguire, Arlene. Life's Changes. Holtman, Noel, illus. LC 91-9353. 32p. (Orig.). (ps-5). 1991. 6.95 (*0-941992-26-8*) Los Arboles Pub.

Maldonado, Jesus M. Esta Era una Vez: Once upon a Time. Castro, Raul & Lopez, Blas E., illus. LC 94-71028. (ENG & SPA.). 48p. (gr. 2-6). 1994. PLB 14.95x (*0-9636912-1-X*) J M Maldonado.

Manes, Stephen. Some of the Adventures of Rhode Island Red. Joyce, William, illus. LC 89-35397. 128p. (gr. 3-7). 1990. (Lipp Jr Bks); PLB 10.89 (*0-397-32348-4*, Lipp Jr Bks) HarpC Child Bks.

Manushkin, Fran, compiled by. Disney Babies Somebody Loves You: Poems of Friendship & Love. Shelly, Jeff, illus. LC 92-53436. 32p. (ps-k). 1993. 9.95 (*1-56282-370-1*) Disney Pr.

Marrs, Carol R. Pet Cobwebs. Marrs, Greg, illus. 112p. (gr. 1 up). 1988. 12.95 (*0-9621234-0-4*) Funny Farm Pr.

Marsh, James. Bizarre Birds & Beasts: Animal Verses. 1991. 12.95 (*0-8037-1046-1*) Dial Bks Young.

Martin, Prisha. The Poor People of England & Other Works. (Orig.). 1991. pap. write for info. (*1-879019-04-3*) Amer Edit Servs.
Matanah. Love Bones. Ridge, Delores F., ed. 75p. (Orig.). (gr. 9). 1974. pap. text ed. 4.95 (*0-9600978-1-3*) Knees Pbk.
Maxwell, Judith & Maxwell, Jessica. The Feminist Revised Mother Goose Rhymes: A 21st Century Children's Edition. LC 92-81770. 32p. (gr. 1-9). 1992. pap. 7.95 (*0-9632698-1-X*) Veda Vangarde.
Mazer, Norma F. & Lewis, Margorie. Waltzing on Water: Poetry by Women. (Orig.). (gr. k-12). 1989. pap. 3.50 (*0-440-20257-4*, LFL) Dell.
Mendoza, George & Wilson, Gahan. Hairticklers. (Illus.). 128p. (gr. 5 up). 1989. cloth 13.95 (*0-89815-332-8*); pap. 8.95 (*0-89815-330-1*) Ten Speed Pr.
Mennella, Roxanna. Roxanna Mennella, in Search of a Song: Inner Clockwork, Vol. 8. Fisher, Barbara, ed. (Illus.). 10p. (Orig.). (gr. 5-9). 1985. pap. 2.00 (*0-934830-36-3*) Ten Penny.
Merriam, Eve. Chortles: New & Selected Wordplay Poems. Hamanaka, Sheila, illus. LC 88-29129. 64p. (gr. 3-7). 1989. 11.95 (*0-688-08152-5*); PLB 11.88 (*0-688-08153-3*, Morrow Jr Bks) Morrow Jr Bks.
—Fresh Paint: New Poems. Frampton, David, illus. LC 85-23742. 48p. (gr. 5 up). 1986. RSBE 13.95 (*0-02-766860-6*, Macmillan Child Bk) Macmillan Child Grp.
—A Poem for a Pickle: Funnybone Verses. Hamanaka, Sheila, illus. LC 88-22047. 40p. (gr. k up). 1989. 12.95 (*0-688-08137-1*); PLB 12.88 (*0-688-08138-X*, Morrow Jr Bks) Morrow Jr Bks.
—A Sky Full of Poems. Gaffney-Kessell, Walter, illus. (Orig.). (gr. k-6). 1986. pap. 3.25 (*0-440-47986-X*, YB) Dell.
—You Be Good & I'll Be Night: Jump-on-the-Bed-Poems. Schmidt, Karen L., illus. LC 87-24859. 40p. (ps-2). 1988. 13.95 (*0-688-06742-5*); PLB 13.88 (*0-688-06743-3*, Morrow Jr Bks) Morrow Jr Bks.
Miller, May. Collected Poems. LC 88-83172. 235p. (gr. 7-12). 1989. 18.00 (*0-916418-70-7*) Lotus.
—Halfway to the Sun. Pauker, John, intro. by. LC 81-50427. (Illus.). 50p. (Orig.). (gr. 6). 1981. pap. text ed. 7.00 (*0-931846-17-X*) Wash Writers Pub.
Miller, Tom. This Path of Scattered Glass: A Collection of Poems. Miller, Tom, illus. LC 92-84067. 96p. (Orig.). (gr. 7 up). 1993. pap. 6.95 (*1-878893-39-4*) Telcraft Bks.
Miller, Vousette T. Poems by Shining Star: The Voice of Shining Star. 16p. (Orig.). (ps-6). 1990. pap. write for info. wkbk. (*0-9619641-1-1*) Vous Etes Tres Belle.
Milne, A. A. Now We Are Six. Shepard, Ernest H., illus. 112p. (ps up). 1988. 9.95 (*0-525-44446-7*, DCB) Dutton Child Bks.
—The Poems & Hums of Winnie-the-Pooh. Shepard, Ernest H., illus. 10p. (gr. 4-7). 1994. pap. 5.99 (*0-525-45205-2*, DCB) Dutton Child Bks.
—When We Were Very Young. Shepard, Ernest H., illus. 112p. (ps up). 1988. 9.95 (*0-525-44445-9*, DCB) Dutton Child Bks.
Moncure, Jane B. My First Thanksgiving Book. Connelly, Gwen, illus. LC 84-9433. 32p. (ps-2). 1984. PLB 11.45 (*0-516-02903-7*); pap. 3.95 (*0-516-42903-5*) Childrens.
—Wishes, Whispers & Secrets. Hook, Frances, illus. LC 78-31295. (ps-3). 1979. PLB 14.95 (*0-89565-024-X*) Childs World.
Moore, Clement C. The Night Before Christmas. Gorsline, Douglas, illus. LC 75-7511. 32p. (gr. 2-6). 1975. 2.25 (*0-394-83019-9*) Random Bks Yng Read.
—The Night Before Christmas. Wilburn, Kathy, illus. 24p. (ps-1). 1985. write for info. (*0-307-10202-5*, Pub. by Golden Bks) Western Pub.
—The Night Before Christmas: A Reproduction of an Antique Christmas Classic. LC 88-19600. (Illus.). 32p. 1989. 15.95 (*0-399-21614-6*, Philomel Bks) Putnam Pub Group.
Morris-McKinsey, Jill, ed. Religiously Speaking: Plays & Poems for Children's Church. 48p. (Orig.). 1992. pap. 7.98 (*1-877588-03-2*) Creatively Yours.
Morrison, Lillian. Whistling the Morning in New Poems by Lillian Morrison: New Poems. Cook, Joel, illus. 40p. 1992. PLB 16.95 (*1-56397-035-X*, Wordsong) Boyds Mills Pr.
Morrison, Lillian, compiled by. At the Crack of the Bat. Cieslawski, Steve, illus. LC 91-28946. 64p. (gr. 2-5). 1992. 14.95 (*1-56282-176-8*); PLB 14.89 (*1-56282-177-6*) Hyprn Child.
Moss, Graveyard. Graveyard Moss Is Still Alive. 48p. (Orig.). (gr. 9). 1988. pap. 5.00 (*0-945237-00-6*) Morgan Virginia Pub.
Moss, Jeff. Other Side of the Door. (gr. k up). 1991. 15.00 (*0-553-07259-5*) Bantam.
Moss, Jeffrey. The Butterfly Jar. Demarest, Chris, illus. (ps up). 1989. 15.00 (*0-553-05704-9*) Bantam.
Most, Bernard. Four & Twenty Dinosaurs. Most, Bernard, illus. LC 89-34472. 40p. (ps-2). 1990. PLB 13.89 (*0-06-024377-5*) HarpC Child Bks.
Nash, Ogden. The Cruise of the Aardvark. Watson, Wendy, illus. LC 67-27296. 48p. (ps up). 1989. pap. 5.95 (*0-87131-570-X*) M Evans.
—Custard & Company. Blake, Quentin, illus. 128p. (gr. 2-6). 1985. pap. 6.95 (*0-316-59855-0*) Little.
Neville, Mary, ed. If a Poem Bothers You. (Illus.). 64p. (Orig.). (gr. 2-6). 1991. pap. 7.00 (*0-913678-14-7*) New Day Pr.
Newell, Peter. The Slant Book. Newell, Peter, illus. LC 67-12304. 50p. (gr. k-4). 1967. Repr. of 1910 ed. 16.95 (*0-8048-0532-6*) C E Tuttle.
Nicholls, Judith, ed. Sing Freedom! Children's Poetry. (Illus.). 132p. (gr. 3 up). 1992. 16.95 (*0-571-16513-3*); pap. 9.95 (*0-571-16514-1*) Faber & Faber.
—What on Earth? Poems with a Conservation Theme. Baker, Alan, illus. 132p. (gr. 2 up). 1989. pap. 8.95 (*0-571-15262-7*) Faber & Faber.
Nickerson, Betty, ed. All about Us - Nous Autres: Creative Writing & Painting by & for Young People. (ENG & FRE., Illus.). 36p. 1992. pap. 4.95 (*0-685-61052-7*) All About Us.
Nims, Bonnie L. Just Beyond Reach. Anema, George, illus. 48p. 1992. 13.95 (*0-590-44077-2*, Scholastic Hardcover) Scholastic Inc.
Nister, Ernest. A Day in the Country. (Illus.). 10p. 1990. 5.95 (*0-399-21959-5*, Philomel Bks) Putnam Pub Group.
—Favorite Animals. (Illus.). 10p. 1989. 5.95 (*0-399-21728-2*, Philomel Bks) Putnam Pub Group.
—Mother & Me. (Illus.). 10p. 1990. 5.95 (*0-399-21958-7*, Philomel Bks) Putnam Pub Group.
—My Best Friend. (Illus.). 10p. 1990. 5.95 (*0-399-21960-9*, Philomel Bks) Putnam Pub Group.
Nister, Ernest & Bingham, Clifton. Revolving Pictures. LC 79-12438. (Illus.). (ps-4). 1981. 12.95 (*0-399-20802-X*, Philomel) Putnam Pub Group.
Norskog, Howard L. High Country Ballads: Cowboy Poetry. 80p. (Orig.). (gr. 8 up). 1988. pap. 6.99 (*0-685-30409-4*) H L Norskog.
—Yesterdays Trails: Cowboy Poetry. 49p. (gr. 8 up). 1989. pap. 6.99 (*0-685-30410-8*) H L Norskog.
Nye, Robert E. Beowulf. 96p. (gr. 5 up). 1982. pap. 3.99 (*0-440-90560-5*, LFL) Dell.
NYS Waterways Project Child Poet Supplement. (Illus.). 7p. (Orig.). (gr. 1-5). 1979. pap. 0.50 (*0-934830-17-7*) Ten Penny.
Oram, Hiawyn. Out of the Blue: Poems about Color. McKee, David, illus. LC 92-55044. 64p. (gr. 1-5). 1993. 18.95 (*1-56282-469-4*); PLB 18.89 (*1-56282-470-8*) Hyprn Child.
Ormerod, Jan. Jan Ormerod's to Baby with Love. LC 93-8093. (Illus.). 1994. 15.00 (*0-688-12558-1*); lib. bdg. 14.93 (*0-688-12559-X*) Lothrop.
Orska, Kr. Illustrated Poems for Children. (Illus.). 1985. 12.95 (*0-02-689410-6*) Macmillan.
Ottenstein, Claire. Catch a Whiffle-Poofle! Ottenstein, Claire & Cogbill, Catherine, illus. 64p. (Orig.). 1991. lib. bdg. 8.95 (*1-878149-03-2*) Counterpoint Pub.
Oxenbury, Helen & Bennett, Jim. Tiny Tim: Verses for Children. (ps-2). 1992. 3.99 (*0-440-40521-1*, YB) Dell.
Pagliaro, Penny, ed. I Like Poems & Poems Like Me. Kim Chee, Wendy, illus. LC 76-50343. (gr. 1-6). 1977. PLB 8.95 (*0-916630-03-X*) Pr Pacifica.
Pagnucci, Franco. I Never Had a Pet. Pagnucci, Gian, ed. Pagnucci, Susan, illus. 32p. (Orig.). (gr. 1-5). 1992. pap. 5.95 (*0-929326-09-1*) Bur Oak Pr Inc.
Pagnucci, Gianfranco, ed. Face the Poem. (Illus.). 32p. (Orig.). (gr. 2-8). 1979. Incl. animal poems with animal face masks for choral readings. 3.95 (*0-929326-02-4*) Bur Oak Pr Inc.
Paraskevas, Betty. Junior Kroll. Paraskevas, Michael, illus. LC 92-14207. (gr. k up). 1993. 13.95 (*0-15-241497-5*) HarBrace.
Paul, Ted. The Christmas Collie. Kummer, Mary, illus. LC 89-17994. 42p. (ps-7). 1989. 12.95 (*0-89802-548-6*) Beautiful Am.
Penny, Rob. Romance Rhythm & Revolution: New & Selected Poetry. 2nd ed. 100p. (gr. 9-12). 1993. pap. text ed. 9.95 (*0-685-60180-3*) Magnolia PA.
Perinchief, Robert. Drug-Free Word Spree. 58p. (ps-12). 1993. 19.95 (*1-882809-01-7*) Perry Pubns.
Perry, Marion. Dishes. Walsh, Joy, ed. Michael, Linda, illus. 25p. 1988. pap. 5.00 (*0-938838-29-6*) Textile Bridge.
Petersham, Maud & Petersham, Miska. The Rooster Crows: A Book of American Rhymes & Jingles. Petersham, Maud & Petersham, Miska, illus. LC 87-1138. 64p. (ps-3). 1987. pap. 5.95 (*0-689-71153-0*, Aladdin) Macmillan Child Grp.
Pfister, Marcus, selected by. & illus. I See the Moon: Good-Night Poems & Lullabies. LC 91-10841. 32p. (ps-k). 1991. 14.95 (*1-55858-119-7*) North-South Bks NYC.
Philipps, Myra. Smooth As Silk. 2nd ed. Ramon, Estelle, illus. (gr. 3 up). 1979. 1.95 (*0-686-10960-0*) Basin Pub.
Piper, Watty. The Easy-to-Read Little Engine That Could. Mateu, illus. Retan, Walter, adapted by. (Illus.). (ps-2). 1990. pap. 4.95 (*0-448-34344-4*, Platt & Munk Pubs) Putnam Pub Group.
Plath, Sylvia. The Bed Book. McCully, Emily A., illus. LC 76-3825. 40p. (ps-3). 1989. pap. 6.95 (*0-06-443184-3*, Trophy) HarpC Child Bks.
Pomerantz, Charlotte. If I Had a Paka: Poems in Eleven Languages. Tafuri, Nancy, illus. 32p. 1982. 11.75 (*0-688-00836-4*); PLB 11.88 (*0-688-00837-2*) Greenwillow.
Poskanzer, Susan. Riddles about Hannukah. Brook, Bonnie, ed. Gray, Rob, illus. 32p. (ps-3). 1990. 4.95 (*0-671-70555-5*); PLB 6.95 (*0-671-70553-9*) Silver Pr.
Poulin, Stephane. Pourrais-Tu Arreter Josephine? LC 88-50261. (FRE., Illus.). 24p. (ps-3). 1989. 12.95 (*0-88776-217-4*); pap. 6.95 (*0-88776-228-X*) Tundra Bks.
Prelutsky, Jack. The Baby Uggs Are Hatching! Stevenson, James, illus. LC 81-7266. 32p. (gr. k-3). 1982. 15.00 (*0-688-00922-0*); PLB 14.93 (*0-688-00923-9*) Greenwillow.
—The Dragons Are Singing Tonight. Sis, Peter, illus. LC 92-29013. 40p. (ps up). 1993. 15.00 (*0-688-09645-X*); PLB 14.93 (*0-688-12511-5*) Greenwillow.
—The Headless Horseman Rides Tonight. Lobel, Arnold, illus. LC 80-10372. 40p. (gr. 1-4). 1980. 13.95 (*0-688-80273-7*); PLB 13.88 (*0-688-84273-9*) Greenwillow.
—It's Thanksgiving. Hafner, Marylin, illus. LC 81-1929. 48p. (gr. 1-3). 1982. 14.00 (*0-688-00441-5*); lib. bdg. 13.93 (*0-688-00442-3*) Greenwillow.
—My Parents Think I'm Sleeping. Abolafia, Yossi, illus. LC 84-13640. 48p. (gr. 2-4). 1985. 13.95 (*0-688-04018-7*); lib. bdg. 13.88 (*0-688-04019-5*) Greenwillow.
—The New Kid on the Block. Stevenson, James, illus. LC 83-20621. 160p. (gr. 1 up). 1984. 15.95 (*0-688-02271-5*); PLB 15.88 (*0-688-02272-3*) Greenwillow.
—Nightmares: Poems to Trouble Your Sleep. Lobel, Arnold, illus. LC 76-4820. 40p. (gr. 3 up). 1976. 14.00 (*0-688-80053-X*); PLB 13.93 (*0-688-84053-1*) Greenwillow.
—The Queen of Eene. Chess, Victoria, illus. LC 77-17311. 32p. (gr. k-3). 1978. PLB 14.88 (*0-688-84144-9*) Greenwillow.
—Rainy, Rainy Saturday. Hafner, Marilyn, illus. LC 79-22217. 48p. (gr. 1-3). 1980. 15.00 (*0-688-80252-4*); PLB 14.93 (*0-688-84252-6*) Greenwillow.
—Ride a Purple Pelican. Williams, Garth, illus. LC 84-6024. 64p. (ps up). 1986. 15.95 (*0-688-04031-4*) Greenwillow.
—Rolling Harvey Down the Hill. Chess, Victoria, illus. LC 79-18236. 32p. (gr. k-3). 1980. 14.95 (*0-688-80258-3*); PLB 12.88 (*0-688-84258-5*) Greenwillow.
—The Sheriff of Rottenshot. Chess, Victoria, illus. LC 81-6420. 32p. (gr. k-3). 1982. 12.95 (*0-688-00205-6*); PLB 14.93 (*0-688-00198-X*) Greenwillow.
—The Snopp on the Sidewalk & Other Poems. Barton, Byron, illus. LC 76-46323. 32p. (gr. 3 up). 1977. PLB 15.93 (*0-688-84084-1*) Greenwillow.
—Tyrannosaurus Was a Beast. LC 87-25131. (Illus.). 32p. (ps-6). 1988. 13.95 (*0-688-06442-6*); lib. bdg. 13.88 (*0-688-06443-4*) Greenwillow.
—Tyrannosaurus Was a Beast. Lobel, Arnold, illus. LC 87-25131. 32p. (ps up). 1992. pap. 4.95 (*0-688-11569-1*, Mulberry) Morrow.
Prelutsky, Jack, intro. by. Poems of A. Nonny Mouse. Drescher, Henrik, illus. LC 89-31672. 48p. (gr. 1-7). 1989. lib. bdg. 14.99 (*0-394-98711-X*) Knopf Bks Yng Read.
Provensen, Alice & Provensen, Martin, illus. A Peaceable Kingdom: The Shaker Abecedarius. Barsam, Richard M., afterword by. LC 78-125. 42p. (gr. k-2). 1978. pap. 16.00 (*0-670-54500-7*) Viking Child Bks.
Pyle, Howard. The Wonder Clock or, Four & Twenty Marvelous Tales, Being One for Each Hour of the Day. (Illus.). xiv, 319p. (gr. 3-6). pap. 7.95 (*0-486-21446-X*) Dover.
Rabbitts, Muriel J. Thought of Childhood. 1991. 10.95 (*0-533-09371-6*) Vantage.
Radunsky. Absent-Minded Fellow from Portobello Road. 1993. 14.95 (*0-8050-1131-5*) H Holt & Co.
Raemsch, Dorothy C. Spinning with Gold: Poems for Young & Old. Tosti, Selma, illus. 32p. 1991. pap. 7.50 (*0-9605398-2-4*) D C Raemsch.
Reece, Colleen L. My First Christmas Book. Hohag, Linda, illus. LC 84-9431. 32p. (ps-2). 1984. pap. 3.95 (*0-516-42901-9*) Childrens.
—My First Halloween Book. Peltier, Pam, illus. LC 84-9431. 32p. (ps-2). 1984. pap. 3.95 (*0-516-42902-7*) Childrens.
Reichenberg, Monte. Cheating Chet. Dane, Don, illus. 32p. (Orig.). (ps-4). 1992. pap. 3.00 (*0-9640260-1-5*) MM & I Ink.
Rice, James. Texas Night Before Christmas. Rice, James, illus. LC 86-9445. 32p. (gr. 1-6). 1986. 12.95 (*0-88289-603-2*) Pelican.
Ricken, Robert. Love Me When I'm Most Unlovable, Vol. II. 32p. (gr. 6-9). 1987. pap. 4.00 (*0-88210-198-6*) Natl Assn Principals.
Riley, James W. Riley Child Rhymes with Hoosier Pictures. (Illus.). 188p. Repr. 18.95 (*1-878208-17-9*) Guild Pr IN.
Rivlin, Asher E. & Gimmestad, Nancy, eds. Poetry Unfolding Basic Kit. 450p. (gr. 4-12). 1983. pap. 200.00 (*0-915291-05-3*) Know Unltd.
Robson, Tom. Musical Wisdom: Songs & Drawings for the Child in Us All. James, Nancy V., illus. 88p. (Orig.). (gr. k-6). 1992. pap. 16.95 (*0-9633332-0-8*) Laughing Cat.
Rockwell, Harlow. My Kitchen. LC 79-15929. (Illus.). 24p. (ps-2). 1980. 13.95 (*0-688-80236-2*); PLB 15.88 (*0-688-84236-4*) Greenwillow.
Rodriguez, Alejo. Simple Poems for Children: Hey What Kind of World Is This? LC 90-71368. 126p. (gr. 3-9). 1991. pap. 5.95 (*1-55523-393-7*) Winston-Derek.
Rogers, Bruce H. Tales & Declarations. 32p. (Orig.). (gr. 10 up). 1991. pap. 4.00 (*0-916155-13-7*) Trout Creek.
Rogers, Rick. Earth Tales & Bird Song. Hayes, Suzanne, illus. Rogers, Rick, intro. by. (Illus.). 125p. (Orig.). (gr. k-9). 1991. pap. 7.50 (*0-9631017-0-6*) Timberdoodle.
Romain, Trevor. The Little People's Guide to the Big World, Vol. 1. Romain, Trevor, illus. 48p. (ps-5). 1993. 13.95 (*1-880092-04-2*, Dist. by Publishers Distribution Service) Bright Bks TX.

Rosen, Michael. Mind Your Own Business. Blake, Quentin, illus. LC 74-9969. 96p. (gr. 3 up). 1974. 21.95 (0-87599-209-9) S G Phillips.

Ross, Gwendolyn. A Child's Treasure for a Lifetime. 24p. (gr. 2-6). 1988. pap. 2.95 (0-88144-134-1) Christian Pub.

Rossetti, Christina G. The Skylark. LC 91-13112. (Illus.). 24p. 1992. 4.95 (0-8037-1143-3) Dial Bks Young.

Roth Publishing Editorial Board. Core Poetry Collection Index. 1127p. (Orig.). (gr. 9). 1993. pap. text ed. 75.00x (0-89609-325-5) Roth Pub Inc.

Rutherford, Erica. The Owl & the Pussycat. (Illus.). 24p. (gr. 1 up). 1986. text ed. 12.95 (0-88776-181-X, Dist. by Univ. of Toronto Pr) Tundra Bks.

Rylant, Cynthia. Soda Jerk. Catalanotto, Peter, illus. LC 89-35654. 48p. (gr. 7 up). 1990. 14.95 (0-531-05864-6); PLB 14.99 (0-531-08464-7) Orchard Bks Watts.

—This Year's Garden. Szilagyi, Mary, illus. LC 84-10974. 32p. (gr. k-3). 1984. RSBE 13.95 (0-02-777970-X, Bradbury Pr) Macmillan Child Grp.

Saltoon, Diana. Four Hands: Green Gulch Poems. 25p. (Orig.). (gr. 7 up). 1988. pap. 2.95 (0-931191-08-4) Rob Briggs.

Sanchez, Sonia. It's a New Day: Poems for Young Brothas & Sistuhs. Olugebefola, Ademola & Sherman, Ed, illus. LC 72-155311. (gr. 5 up). 1971. pap. 3.00 (0-910296-60-X) Broadside Pr.

Sandburg, Carl. Early Moon. Daugherty, James, illus. LC 77-16488. 136p. (gr. 5 up). 1978. pap. 1.95 (0-15-627326-8, Voyager Bks) HarBrace.

—Sandburg Treasury: Prose & Poetry for Young People. Bacon, Paul, illus. LC 79-120818. 480p. (gr. 7 up). 1970. 24.95 (0-15-270180-X, HB Juv Bks) HarBrace.

Sandcastles & Cucumber Ships Last Forever. LC 78-74555. 48p. (Orig.). (gr. 3-8). 1978. 2.95 (0-916872-06-8) Delafield Pr.

Sanders, Addie M. Alligators, Monsters & Cool School Poems. Sanders, Dave, Jr., illus. 80p. (Orig.). (gr. 3-10). 1994. pap. 9.00 (0-911943-38-2) Leadership Pub.

Scherer, Catharine D. Ladybug. Legman, Linda C., illus. LC 83-70738. 10p. (gr. 6-11). 1983. 2.95 (0-9611024-0-3) Drum Assocs.

Schmidt, Annie. Pink Lemonade. Ten Harmsel, Henrietta, tr. Foley, Timothy, illus. 64p. (ps-6). 1992. 14.99 (0-8028-4050-7) Eerdmans.

Schwartz, Alvin, ed. I Saw You in the Bathtub & Other Folk Rhymes. Hoff, Syd, illus. LC 88-16111. 64p. (gr. k-3). 1989. 14.00 (0-06-025298-7); PLB 13.89 (0-06-025299-5) HarpC Child Bks.

Sclavi, Tiziano. What Animal Is It? Michelini, Carlo A., illus. 10p. (ps). 1994. 4.95 (1-56397-339-1) Boyds Mills Pr.

—What's on the Other Side? Michelini, Carlo A., illus. 10p. (ps). 1994. 4.95 (1-56397-345-6) Boyds Mills Pr.

Scott, Bob. The Backcountry. Arcade, Greg, illus. 24p. (gr. 4-12). 1989. cardstock cover 5.00 (0-9621201-0-3) B Scott Bks.

Scribbles, R. J., pseud. Back to School. Scribbles, R. J., illus. 32p. (Orig.). (gr. 2-5). 1992. pap. 12.95 (0-9632192-0-0) R J Miller.

Seabrooke, Brenda. Judy Scuppernong. LC 90-31583. (Illus.). (gr. 4-7). 1990. 13.00 (0-525-65038-5, Cobblehill Bks) Dutton Child Bks.

Seeley, Laura L. The Book of Shadowboxes: A Story of the ABC's. Seeley, Laura L., illus. 64p. (ps-3). 1990. 16.95 (0-934601-65-8) Peachtree Pubs.

Sendak, Maurice. Seven Little Monsters. Sendak, Maurice, illus. LC 76-18400. (gr. 1 up). 1977. PLB 14.89 (0-06-025478-5) HarpC Child Bks.

Service, Robert. The Cremation of Sam McGee. Harrison, Ted, illus. LC 86-14971. 32p. (ps up). 1987. 15.95 (0-688-06903-7) Greenwillow.

Sesame Street Staff. Big Bird's Rhyming Book. Chartier, Norm, illus. LC 78-68790. (ps-3). 1979. 8.99 (0-394-84140-9) Random Bks Yng Read.

Seven Little Hippos. LC 90-42437. 1991. pap. 13.95 (0-671-72964-0, S&S BFYR) S&S Trade.

Shank, Merna B. Happy Ways: Verses for Children. 1982. pap. 1.95 (0-87813-211-2) Christian Light.

—Thankful Days: Verses for Children. 1982. pap. 1.95 (0-87813-212-0) Christian Light.

Shaw, Alison. Seashore Poems. 1995. write for info. (0-8050-2755-6) H Holt & Co.

Shelley, Percy Bysshe. Love's Philosophy. LC 91-602. (Illus.). 24p. 1992. 4.95 (0-8037-1142-5) Dial Bks Young.

Sherry, Helen J. Splashes. Sherry, Helen J., illus. 36p. (Orig.). 1989. pap. 2.75 (0-922273-00-6) Chocho Bks.

Silverstein, Shel. Where the Sidewalk Ends: Poems & Drawings. Silverstein, Shel, illus. LC 70-105486. 176p. (gr. 4 up). 1974. 15.95 (0-06-025667-2); PLB 15.89 (0-06-025668-0) HarpC Child Bks.

Slater, Teddy. Eloise Wilkin's Babies: A Book of Poems. (ps-3). 1993. 8.95 (0-307-15864-0, Golden Pr) Western Pub.

Smith, Janet A., ed. The Faber Book of Children's Verse. 412p. (gr. 4 up). 1953. pap. 10.95 (0-571-05457-9) Faber & Faber.

Smith, William J. Big & Little. Bolognese, Don, illus. LC 91-66057. 32p. (gr. 5 up). 1992. 15.95 (1-56397-023-6, Wordsong) Boyds Mills Pr.

Smith, William J. & Ra, Carol, eds. Behind the King's Kitchen Door. Hnizdovsky, Jacques, illus. LC 91-66056. 56p. (gr. 5 up). 1992. 18.95 (1-56397-024-4, Wordsong) Boyds Mills Pr.

Soto, Gary. Fire in My Hands. 64p. 1991. 11.95 (0-590-45021-2, Scholastic Hardcover) Scholastic Inc.

—Fire in My Hands: A Book of Poems. 1992. pap. 2.95 (0-590-44579-0) Scholastic Inc.

Spiegel, Richard & Fisher, Barbara, eds. Streams, No. 8. (Illus.). 150p. (Orig.). (gr. 7-12). Date not set. pap. 5.00 (0-934830-56-8) Ten Penny.

Spilka, Arnold. Monkeys Write Terrible Letters: And Other Poems. (Illus.). 32p. (gr. k-5). 1994. 14.95 (1-56397-132-1, Wordsong) Boyds Mills Pr.

Springer, Nancy. Music of Their Hooves: Poems about Horses. Rabinowitz, Sandy, illus. 32p. (gr. 3-7). 1994. 15.95 (1-56397-182-8, Wordsong) Boyds Mills Pr.

Steele, Susanna & Styles, Morag, eds. Mother Gave a Shout: Poems by Women & Girls. Ray, Jane, illus. LC 90-12938. 128p. (gr. 3-8). 1991. 14.95 (0-912078-90-1) Volcano Pr.

Stevenson, Robert Louis. A Child's Garden of Verses. LC 85-12766. (Illus.). (gr. 3-5). 1950. pap. 2.95 (0-14-030022-8, Puffin) Puffin Bks.

—A Child's Garden of Verses. Tudor, Tasha, illus. LC 85-12766. 72p. (ps up). 1992. SBE 13.95 (0-02-788365-5) Macmillan Child Grp.

—A Child's Garden of Verses. Smith, Jessie W., illus. LC 85-12766. 120p. (ps-4). 1905. SBE 18.95 (0-684-20949-7, Scribners Young Read) Macmillan Child Grp.

—A Child's Garden of Verses. Robinson, Charles, illus. (gr. 1 up). 1976. pap. 9.95 (0-85967-313-8, Pub. by Scolar Pr UK) Ashgate Pub Co.

—A Child's Garden of Verses. Wildsmith, Brian, illus. 96p. (gr. 1-4). pap. 10.95 (0-19-276065-3) OUP.

—A Child's Garden of Verses. LC 85-12766. (gr. 5-6). 15.95 (0-89190-739-4, Pub. by Am Repr) Amereon Ltd.

—A Child's Garden of Verses. Foreman, Michael, illus. LC 85-12766. 128p. (ps-3). 1985. 14.95 (0-385-29430-1) Delacorte.

—A Child's Garden of Verses. LC 88-43564. 144p. 1989. 4.95 (0-89471-715-4) Running Pr.

—A Child's Garden of Verses. (Illus.). 128p. 1989. 15.95 (0-87701-608-9) Chronicle Bks.

—Child's Garden of Verses. 1984. 4.98 (0-671-06537-8) S&S Trade.

—A Child's Garden of Verses. Robinson, Charles, illus. LC 93-41101. 1994. 6.00 (1-56957-926-1) Barefoot Bks.

—From a Railway Carriage. Thomas, Llewellyn, illus. 32p. (ps-3). 1993. 14.99 (0-670-84894-8) Viking Child Bks.

—The Moon. Saldutti, Denise, illus. LC 83-47704. 32p. (ps-3). 1986. pap. 4.95 (0-06-443098-7, Trophy) HarpC Child Bks.

—My Shadow. Rand, Ted, illus. 32p. 1990. 14.95 (0-399-22216-2, Putnam) Putnam Pub Group.

Stiles, Barbara J. Cheeky Rubs. Arthur, John, illus. LC 89-164732. 20p. (ps-5). 1989. text ed. 12.95 (0-9622057-1-0); pap. text ed. 7.95 (0-9622057-0-2) Manzanita Canyon.

Stopple, Libby. A Box of Peppermints. Dromgoole, Dick, ed. Bell, Martha, illus. LC 75-20957. 96p. (gr. 2-10). 1975. 12.95 (0-913632-08-2); pap. 7.95 (0-913632-07-4) All Things Pr.

Storytime Stories That Rhyme Staff. Cowboy Boots - a Story Rhyme Plus Twenty Other Stories. (Illus.). 60p. (Orig.). (gr. 6-9). 1992. binder 19.95 (0-317-04687-X, Pub. by Alpha Pyramis) Prosperity & Profits.

Strickland, Michael & Strickland, Dorothy. Families: Poems Celebrating the African American Experience. Ward, John, illus. LC 93-61162. 32p. (ps-3). 1994. 14.95 (1-56397-288-3) Boyds Mills Pr.

Strickland, Michael, ed. Poems That Sing to You. Leiner, Alan, illus. 64p. (gr. 5 up). 1993. 13.95 (1-56397-178-X, Wordsong) Boyds Mills Pr.

Stutson, Caroline. On the River ABC. Crum, Anna M., illus. LC 92-61907. 32p. (gr. k-3). 1993. lib. bdg. 12.95 (1-879373-46-7) R Rinehart.

Suire, Diane D. Seasons. Connelly, Gwen, illus. LC 89-773. 32p. (gr. k-3). 1989. PLB 14.95 (0-89565-503-9) Childs World.

Sullivan, Charles, ed. Imaginary Gardens: American Poetry & Art for Young People. (Illus.). 112p. 1989. 19.95 (0-8109-1130-2) Abrams.

Swann, Brian. A Basket Full of White Eggs: Riddle-Poems. Goembel, Ponder, illus. LC 87-11220. 32p. (gr. k-3). 1988. 14.95 (0-531-05734-8); PLB 14.99 (0-531-08334-9) Orchard Bks Watts.

Thayer, Ernest L. Casey at the Bat. (ps-3). 1993. pap. 4.95 (0-8114-8357-6) Raintree Steck-V.

Thomas, Marlo. Free to Be...You & Me. Hart, Carole, ed. 1987. pap. 9.95 (0-317-62189-0) McGraw.

Thornton, Suzi. Sometimes Childhood Stinks. Thornton, Don, intro. by. Lassalle, Cindy & Logan, Anne, illus. 64p. (Orig.). (gr. k-6). 1994. pap. 15.00 (1-882913-06-X) Thornton LA. SOMETIMES CHILDHOOD STINKS is a compilation of poems & songs about childhood. Characters in the poems/songs are reminiscent of the author as child & as teacher. Many of the poems/songs reflect painful experiences of childhood such as parent unemployment, divorce, or loneliness. Other poem/songs invest in the more humorous side of childhood with selections like Loose Tooth, Lost & Found, & Fried Liver. The poems are records of climatic moments in the lives of children. Songs have been written for fifteen of the thirty-four poems. The music score is included in the book. The spiral binding allows the book to open flat for use on a music stand or piano. The cassette includes all fifteen songs sung by the author. The work is especially appropriate for the elementary level for elocution & for musical presentations. The songs were written about childhood to be sung to children or performed by children. Those who do not read music or are uncomfortable singing alone can use the tape as a sing-along.
Publisher Provided Annotation.

Tobias, Jerry J. Imma Drug. Tobias, Jerry J., illus. 70p. (ps-6). Date not set. pap. write for info. (1-880017-12-1) Teddy Bear Pr.

—Imma Fish: And Other Related Poems. Tobias, Jerry J., illus. (Orig.). (ps-6). 1993. pap. 5.95 (1-880017-13-X) Teddy Bear Pr.

—Imma Insect, No. 8. rev. ed. (Illus.). 90p. (ps-6). 1992. pap. 5.95 (1-880017-07-5) Teddy Bear Pr.

Tolkien, J. R. R. Bilbo's Last Song. Baynes, Pauline, illus. 32p. 1990. 14.45 (0-395-53810-6) HM.

A Treasury of Children's Poetry. LC 93-85533. (Illus.). 136p. 1994. 4.95 (1-56138-362-7) Running Pr.

Treece, Henry. The Magic Wood. Moser, Barry, illus. LC 91-29547. 32p. (gr. 1 up). 1992. 16.00 (0-06-020802-3); PLB 15.89 (0-06-020803-1) HarpC Child Bks.

Tripp, Wallace. A Great Big Ugly Man Came up & Tied His Horse to Me: A Book of Nonsense Verse. (Illus.). 48p. (gr. k-12). 1974. lib. bdg. 14.95 (0-316-85280-5) Little.

Tudor, Tasha, illus. First Poems of Childhood. 32p. (ps-1). 1979. pap. 1.25 (0-448-49611-9, G&D) Putnam Pub Group.

Velez, Jennicel. Poemas. Mendoza, Ester F., pref. by. LC 83-3526. (SPA.). xvii, 51p. (gr. 3-7). 1983. pap. 2.50 (0-8477-0063-1) U of PR Pr.

Villa, Jose G. Parlement of Giraffes: Poems for the World's Children. Cowen, John E., compiled by. Francia, Hilario S., tr. & illus. (TAG.). 150p. (Orig.). (gr. 4-12). 1994. 30.00 (1-884861-03-2); pap. 20.00 (1-884861-04-0) Bravo Edit.

Viorst, Judith. If I Were in Charge of the World & Other Worries: Poems for Children & Their Parents. Cherry, Lynn, illus. LC 81-2342. 64p. (gr. 3 up). 1981. SBE 14.95 (0-689-30863-9, Atheneum Child Bk) Macmillan Child Grp.

Wahl, John & Wahl, Stacey. I Can Count the Petals of a Flower. 2nd, rev. ed. LC 85-13670. (Illus.). 36p. (ps-1). 1985. 10.00 (0-87353-224-4) NCTM.

Wallace, Daisy, ed. Fairy Poems. Hyman, Trina S., illus. LC 79-18763. 32p. (ps-3). 1980. reinforced bdg. 13.95 (0-8234-0371-8) Holiday.

—Ghost Poems. LC 78-11028. (Illus.). 32p. (ps-3). 1979. reinforced bdg. 13.95 (0-8234-0344-0); pap. 4.95 (0-8234-0849-3) Holiday.

—Witch Poems. Hyman, Trina S., illus. LC 76-9036. 32p. (ps-3). 1976. reinforced bdg. 13.95 (0-8234-0281-9); pap. 4.95 (0-8234-0850-7) Holiday.

Walter, Dean S. Pages of My Mind. Teasley, Jamie, ed. 45p. 1990. pap. 4.95 (1-55523-280-9) Winston-Derek.

Wayman, Joseph. If You Promise Not to Tell. Wayman, Joseph, illus. 92p. (gr. k up). 1991. 13.95 (0-945799-04-7); Discussion Guide 5.95 (0-945799-05-5) Pieces of Lrning.

Weissman, Jackie. Higglety Pigglety Pop: Two Hundred Thirty-Three Playful Rhymes & Chants for Your Baby. (ps). 1991. pap. 9.95 (0-939514-29-X) Miss Jackie.

Wells, Carolyn. A Christmas Alphabet. (Illus.). 32p. 1989. 15.95 (0-399-21683-9, Putnam) Putnam Pub Group.

Westcott, Nadine B., illus. Peanut Butter & Jelly: A Play Rhyme. LC 86-32889. 24p. (ps-k). 1992. pap. 3.99 (0-525-44885-3, DCB) Dutton Child Bks.

—Peanut Butter & Jelly: A Play Rhyme. (ps-3). 1994. pap. 6.99 incl. cassette (0-14-095142-3, Puffin) Puffin Bks.

Wheeler, Kim. Loves of the Cat: An Illustrated Anthology of Old & Modern Cat Poems. Wheeler, Kim, ed. LC 85-63189. (Illus.). 101p. (Orig.). (gr. 5 up). 1985. pap. 5.75 (0-9615937-0-9) Star City Pubns.

Whiteley, Opal. Only Opal: The Diary of a Young Girl. Boulton, Jane, adapted by. Cooney, Barbara, illus. 32p. (ps). 1994. 14.95 (0-399-21990-0, Philomel) Putnam Pub Group.

Wiands, Catherine. Positive Strokes for Little Folks, Vols. 1-7. 2nd ed. Ziebarth, Pat, ed. & illus. 32p. (Orig.). (gr. 1-6). 1983. pap. 2.50

(*0-943262-00-3*); Set of 7. pap. write for info. Transitions.
Catherine Wiands' POSITIVE STROKES FOR LITTLE FOLKS are designed to inspire, motivate & stimulate children to creative thinking, positive action & feeling good about themselves. Children love to carry these small, 4 1/2" X 5 1/2" paperbacks wherever they go. They fit in purses, etc. for easy carrying. They are building healthy self-images & feel good. Benefits are many - fun to read to children too! Endorsed by Og Mandino. "Catherine Wiands' POSITIVE STROKES FOR LITTLE FOLKS fills a much needed gap in the field of success literature." What a refreshing change after the usual poop we try to inflict on our young!--Og. Set books (1 & 2) $6.95 ppd. Accompanying cassette available $10.00 if purchased separately. $5.00 with books. Order: Catherine Wiands, P.O. Box 478, 9745 W. Peoria Ave., Peoria, AZ 85345. (602) 972-7504. Check, MO or invoice. Quantity Discounts available.
Publisher Provided Annotation.

Wilkins, Sarah. Sarah Wilkins, in Search of a Song, Vol. 7. Fisher, Barbara, ed. 22p. (Orig.). (gr. 5-8). 1984. pap. 2.00 (*0-934830-35-5*) Ten Penny.

Willard, Nancy. A Visit to William Blake's Inn: Poems for Innocent & Experienced Travelers. Provensen, Alice & Provensen, Martin, illus. LC 80-27403. 44p. (ps-3). 1981. 14.95 (*0-15-293822-2*, HB Juv Bks) HarBrace.

Williams, Selver B. Life's Battles. Lundberg, Louise, ed. Knotts, Richard, illus. 220p. (gr. 8 up). 1991. pap. 10.95 (*0-9626633-0-1*) Taliaferro IN.

Wilner, Isabel. The Poetry Troupe: Poems to Read Aloud. LC 77-9439. (Illus.). 224p. (gr. 3-7). 1977. SBE 14.95 (*0-684-15198-7*, Scribners Young Read) Macmillan Child Grp.

Wilson, Jean A. Come Follow Me. Massmann, Jane H., illus. 26p. (ps-3). 1989. 6.50 (*0-911586-01-6*) Wahr.

Withers, Carl. A Rocket in My Pocket: The Rhymes & Chants of Young Americans. Suba, Sussanne, illus. LC 48-4881. 224p. (gr. 2-4). 1988. 14.95 (*0-8050-0821-7*, Bks Young Read); pap. 8.95 (*0-8050-0804-7*) H Holt & Co.

Wood, Robert W. How to Tell the Birds from the Flowers. (Illus.). 64p. (gr. 4 up). 1959. pap. 1.95 (*0-486-20523-1*) Dover.

Worth, Valerie. All the Small Poems. Babbitt, Natalie, illus. 192p. (gr. 3 up). 1987. pap. 3.95 (*0-374-40344-9*, Sunburst) FS&G.

—Small Poems Again. Babbitt, Natalie, illus. LC 85-47513. 48p. (gr. 3 up). 1986. 11.00 (*0-374-37074-5*) FS&G.

—Still More Small Poems. Babbitt, Natalie, illus. LC 78-11739. 48p. (gr. 3 up). 1978. 11.00 (*0-374-37258-6*) FS&G.

Yolen, Jane. Best Witches. Primavera, Elise, illus. 48p. (gr. k-4). 1989. 14.95 (*0-399-21539-5*, Putnam) Putnam Pub Group.

—Bird Watch. Lewin, Ted, illus. 48p. 1990. 15.95 (*0-399-21612-X*, Philomel Bks) Putnam Pub Group.

—Dinosaur Dances. Degen, Bruce, illus. 40p. 1990. 14.95 (*0-399-21629-4*, Putnam) Putnam Pub Group.

—How Beastly! A Menagerie of Nonsense Poems. Marshall, James, illus. 48p. (gr. 2-6). 1994. 14.95 (*1-56397-086-4*, Wordsong) Boyds Mills Pr.

Yolen, Jane, ed. Street Rhymes Around the World. LC 91-66058. (Illus.). 40p. (ps-5). 1992. 16.95 (*1-878093-53-3*, Wordsong) Boyds Mills Pr.

Young, Ruth. Golden Bear. Isadora, Rachel, illus. 32p. (ps-1). 1994. pap. 4.99 (*0-14-050959-3*) Puffin Bks.

Zaslow, David. A Rose by Any Other Name. (Illus.). 96p. (Orig.). 1980. pap. 4.95 (*0-89411-002-0*) Kids Matter.

—Somedays It Feels Like It Wants to Rain. Fink, Grace, illus. LC 76-46244. (gr. 2-6). 1976. pap. 3.95 (*0-89411-001-2*) Kids Matter.

Zeringue, Dona. I Am I. Thornton, Don, intro. by. Zeringue, Dona, illus. 32p. (Orig.). (gr. 6-12). Date not set. pap. 7.50 (*1-882913-02-7*) Thornton LA.

Zito, Penny. Through My Eyes - A Teenage Look at Life. York, Sherri, ed. LC 87-50257. (Illus.). 152p. (gr. 7 up). 1987. 7.95 (*1-55523-075-X*) Winston-Derek.

POETRY–COLLECTIONS

see also American Poetry–Collections; English Poetry–Collections

Adoff, Arnold. All the Colors of the Race. Steptoe, John, illus. LC 81-11777. 64p. (gr. 5 up). 1982. 13.95 (*0-688-00879-8*); PLB 13.88 (*0-688-00880-1*) Lothrop.

Adoff, Arnold, ed. I Am the Darker Brother: An Anthology of Modern Poems by Negro Americans. LC 68-12077. (Illus.). 128p. (gr. 7 up). 1970. pap. 4.95 (*0-02-041120-0*, Collier Young Ad) Macmillan Child Grp.

—The Poetry of Black America: Anthology of the Twentieth Century. Brooks, Gwendolyn, intro. by. LC 72-76518. 576p. (gr. 7 up). 1973. 25.00 (*0-06-020089-8*); PLB 24.89 (*0-06-020090-1*) HarpC Child Bks.

Ainsworth, Catherine H. Jump Rope Verses Around the United States. LC 75-4827. 24p. (ps-12). 1976. 5.00 (*0-933190-01-8*) Clyde Pr.

Alexander, Martha. Poems & Prayers for the Very Young. (Illus.). (ps-1). 1973. pap. 2.25 (*0-394-82705-8*) Random Bks Yng Read.

Amery, H., compiled by. Creepy Poems. (Illus.). 32p. (gr. 2-6). 1990. (Usborne); pap. 5.95 (*0-7460-0440-0*, Usborne) EDC.

Anglesky, Zoe, ed. Word Up: Hope for Youth Poetry from El Centro de la Raza. (ENG, SPA & TAG.). 1992. 12.95 (*0-9633275-1-8*) El Centro de la Raza.

Antologia de Poesia-Primavera: Anthology of Poetry-Spring. (SPA.). (gr. k-6). 1990. 6.95 (*0-935303-02-2*) Victory Pub.

Archard, Cary, ed. Poetry Wales: Twenty-Five Years. 280p. (Orig.). (gr. 10-12). 1990. pap. 21.00 (*1-85411-031-4*, Pub. by Seren Bks UK) Dufour.

Bassett, Harmon. Children's Daily Verses for Growing up the Easy Way with Fun & Play. LC 88-47545. (Illus.). 150p. (gr. 2-7). 1988. 19.95 (*0-88164-712-8*); pap. 15.95 (*0-88164-713-6*) ABBE Pubs Assn.

Bayer, Jane. A, My Name Is Alice. Kellogg, Steven, illus. LC 84-7059. (gr. k-3). 1984. 15.00 (*0-8037-0123-3*); PLB 14.89 (*0-8037-0124-1*) Dial Bks Young.

Bedtime Bear's Book of Bedtime Poems. Leder, Dora, illus. 40p. (ps-3). 1983. lib. bdg. 4.99 (*0-394-95956-6*) Random Bks Yng Read.

Bell, Bill, illus. Let's Pretend: Poems Collected by Natalie Bober. 72p. (ps-3). 1990. pap. 4.95 (*0-14-032132-2*, Puffin) Puffin Bks.

Bennett, Jill, ed. Machine Poems. Sharratt, Nick, illus. 24p. 1993. pap. 5.95 (*0-19-276114-5*) OUP.

Booth, David, ed. Voices on the Wind: Poems for All Seasons. Lemieux, Michele, illus. LC 90-5566. 48p. (ps up). 1990. 13.95 (*0-688-09554-2*); PLB 13.88 (*0-688-09555-0*, Morrow Jr Bks) Morrow Jr Bks.

Bradford, Gigi & Moos, Michael, eds. Sixteen Toes: Anthology. (Illus.). (gr. 2-7). 1978. pap. 2.50 (*0-930970-00-4*) O'Neill Pr.

Brenner, Barbara, ed. The Earth Is Painted Green: A Garden of Poems about Our Planet. Schindler, S. D., illus. LC 93-21466. 96p. 1993. 16.95 (*0-590-45134-0*) Scholastic Inc.

Brown, Marc T., compiled by. & illus. Play Rhymes. 32p. (ps-1). 1993. pap. 4.99 (*0-14-054936-6*, Puff Unicorn) Puffin Bks.

Caddy, John, ed. A Box of Night Mirrors. Schanilec, Gaylord, illus. 120p. (Orig.). 1980. pap. 5.00 (*0-927663-11-2*) COMPAS.

Carter, Ann, compiled by. Birds, Beasts, & Fishes: A Selection of Animal Poems. Cartwright, Reg, illus. Carter, Ann, intros. by. LC 90-21493. (Illus.). 64p. (ps up). 1991. SBE 16.95 (*0-02-717776-9*, Macmillan Child Bk) Macmillan Child Grp.

Cecil, Laura. Preposterous Pets. Clark, Emma C., photos by. LC 94-6527. (Illus.). 80p. 1995. write for info. RTE (*0-688-13581-1*) Greenwillow.

Chisholm, Louey, ed. The Golden Staircase: Poems & Verses for Children. LC 79-51973. (Illus.). (gr. 3-8). 1980. Repr. of 1906 ed. 23.50x (*0-89609-182-1*) Roth Pub Inc.

Chorao, Kay. The Baby's Bedtime Book. Chorao, Kay, illus. LC 84-6067. 64p. (ps). 1989. 13.95 (*0-525-44149-2*, DCB); bk & cassette 18.95 (*0-525-44506-4*) Dutton Child Bks.

Clise, Michele D., compiled by. Ophelia's Bedtime Book: A Collection of Poems to Read & Share. LC 93-41485. (Illus.). 32p. (ps-3). 1994. 14.99 (*0-670-85310-0*) Viking Child Bks.

Cole, Joanna & Calmenson, Stephanie, eds. The Read-Aloud Treasury: Favorite Nursery Rhymes, Poems, Stories & More for the Very Young. Schweninger, Ann, illus. 256p. 1988. pap. 18.95 (*0-385-18560-X*) Doubleday.

Cole, William E., selected by. A Zooful of Animals. Munsinger, Lynn, illus. 96p. (ps-8). 1992. 17.45 (*0-395-52278-1*) HM.

Collen, Arne. Friends & Fiends. (Illus.). 72p. (Orig.). (gr. 7 up). 1989. pap. write for info. Eagleye Bks Intl.

Cook, Roy J., ed. One Hundred & One Famous Poems. (Illus.). 186p. (gr. 9-12). 1990. Repr. lib. bdg. 21.95x (*0-89966-667-1*) Buccaneer Bks.

Corrin, Sara, et al, eds. Stories for Under-Fives. Hughes, Shirley, illus. 158p. (ps-5). 1974. pap. 9.95 (*0-571-12920-X*) Faber & Faber.

Cowden, Frances B. & Hatchett, Eve B. Of Butterflies & Unicorns: And Other Wonders of the Earth. Grove, Eric, illus. 52p. (gr. 7-12). 1993. pap. 7.95 (*1-884289-02-9*) Grandmother Erth.

Crane, Walter, illus. Favorite Poems of Childhood. LC 92-42770. 1993. 14.00 (*0-671-86614-1*, Green Tiger) S&S Trade.

Cummings, E. E. Hist Whist & Other Poems for Children. Firmage, George J., ed. (Illus.). (gr. 3 up). 1983. 12.95 (*0-87140-640-3*) Liveright.

Dec, Myra & Dec, Sam. Wilderness Tails: A Book to Color, Poetry to Share. 32p. (ps-3). 1993. pap. 3.50 (*0-9638192-0-8*) Quinn Pubng.

Decker, Marjorie A. Christian Mother Goose Big Book. Sparr, Theanna, et al, illus. LC 92-60502. 304p. (ps-4). 1992. 14.99 (*0-529-07315-3*) World Bible.

De la Mare, Walter. Peacock Pie: A Book of Rhymes. Ardizzone, Edward, illus. 128p. (gr. 3-7). 1988. pap. 9.95 (*0-571-14963-4*) Faber & Faber.

Demi, compiled by. & illus. Demi's Secret Garden. LC 92-27204. 50p. (ps-2). 1993. 19.95 (*0-8050-2553-7*, Bks Young Read) H Holt & Co.

De Regniers, Beatrice S., et al, eds. Sing a Song of Popcorn: Every Child's Book of Poems. (Illus.). 160p. (gr. k up). 1988. pap. 18.95 (*0-590-43974-X*, Scholastic Hardcovers) Scholastic Inc.

Dittberner-Jax, Norita, ed. The Ragged Heart. Wood, Marce, illus. 164p. (Orig.). 1989. pap. 8.00 (*0-927663-14-7*) COMPAS.

Dunning, Stephen, et al, eds. Reflections on a Gift of Watermelon Pickle & Other Modern Verse. LC 66-8763. (Illus.). 144p. (gr. 7 up). 1966. 16.00 (*0-688-41231-9*); PLB 15.93 (*0-688-51231-3*) Lothrop.

Dyer, Jane, selected by. & illus. Babyland: A Book for Babies. LC 93-4244. 1995. 17.95 (*0-316-19766-1*) Little.

Egan, Louise B., ed. The Classic Treasury of Children's Poetry. LC 89-83327. (Illus.). 56p. (gr. 1 up). 1990. 9.98 (*0-89471-802-9*) Courage Bks.

Elementary School Children of California. The Poetry Express, Nineteen Eighty-Eight: A Collection of Poetry by the Children of California. Reed, John M. & Gillman, Lillian E., eds. Hayden, Jaime, contrib. by. 192p. (ps-6). 1988. 8.95 (*0-317-93373-6*) Other Eye.

Elementary School Children of Oregon. Rhyme Time, Nineteen Eighty-Eight: A Collection of Poetry by the Children of Oregon. Reed, John M. & Gillman, Lillian E., eds. Hayden, Jaime, contrib. by. 104p. (Orig.). (ps-6). 1988. 6.95 (*0-317-93374-4*) Other Eye.

Elementary School Children of Washington State. A Child's Eye View: A Collection of Poetry by the Children of Washington State, Vol. 1. Reed, John M. & Gillman, Lillian E., eds. Hayden, Jaime, contrib. by. 143p. (ps-6). 1987. 7.95 (*0-317-93371-X*) Other Eye.

—A Child's Eye View: A Collection of Poetry by the Children of Washington State, Vol. 2. Reed, John M. & Gillman, Lillian E., eds. Hayden, Jaime, contrib. by. 200p. (ps-6). 1988. 7.95 (*0-317-93372-8*) Other Eye.

Farber, Norma & Livingston, Myra C., eds. These Small Stones. Livingston, Myra C., intro. by. LC 87-264. 128p. (gr. 3-7). 1987. PLB 12.89 (*0-06-024014-8*) HarpC Child Bks.

Ferris, Helen, ed. Favorite Poems Old & New. Weisgard, Leonard, illus. LC 57-11418. 598p. (gr. 3-7). 1957. pap. 19.95 (*0-385-07696-7*) Doubleday.

Fifty-Two Stories & Poems for Children. (Illus.). 160p. (gr. 2-5). 1987. casebound 7.99 (*0-570-04158-9*, 56-1616) Concordia.

Finger Fun-ics: A Collection of Finger Plays, Action Verses & Songs. (Illus.). 1995. pap. text ed. 9.95 (*0-9635535-1-8*) Kinder Kollege.
FINGER FUN-ICS is a delightful series of fingerplays, action verses, & songs designed to encourage participatory learning & to develop language skills. FINGER FUN-ICS is an invaluable teaching tool for teachers & parents of preschoolers. The daily use of FINGER FUN-ICS strengthens a child's memory & attention span. Through happy play, children learn to follow directions cheerfully while having fun. FINGER FUN-ICS opens up exciting worlds to young children in simple language & catchy rhythms.
Publisher Provided Annotation.

Fisher, Barbara & Spiegel, Richard, eds. Streams. (Illus.). 138p. (Orig.). (gr. 9-12). 1987. pap. 5.00 (*0-934830-39-8*) Ten Penny.

—Streams, No. 2. (Illus.). 142p. (gr. 9-12). 1988. pap. 5.00 (*0-934830-42-8*) Ten Penny.

—Streams, No. 3. (Illus.). (gr. 9-12). 1989. pap. 5.00 (*0-934830-43-6*) Ten Penny.

—Subway Slams. (Illus.). 48p. (Orig.). (gr. k-8). 1981. pap. 2.00 (*0-934830-22-3*) Ten Penny.

Fisher, Robert, ed. Pet Poems. Kindberg, Sally, illus. 96p. (gr. 1 up). 1993. pap. 4.95 (*0-571-16830-2*) Faber & Faber.

Footprints in the Sand. LC 93-130. (gr. 4 up). 1994. pap. write for info. (*0-383-03688-7*) SRA Schl Grp.

Foster, John. Let's Celebrate: Festival Poems. (Illus.). 112p. (gr. 3 up). 1990. 15.00 (*0-19-276083-1*) OUP.

Foster, John & Curless, Alan. A Second Poetry Book. White, Martin & Wright, Joseph, illus. 128p. (gr. 4-6). 1987. 11.95 (*0-19-918137-3*); pap. 6.95 (*0-19-918136-5*) OUP.

Foster, John, compiled by. Another Fifth Poetry Book. (Illus.). 128p. (gr. 5-7). 1989. bds. 11.95 laminated (*0-19-917128-9*); pap. 6.95 (*0-19-917127-0*) OUP.
—Another First Poetry Book. (Illus.). 128p. (ps-6). 1988. pap. 6.95 (*0-19-917119-X*) OUP.
—Another Second Poetry Book. (Illus.). 128p. (ps-6). 1988. pap. 6.95 (*0-19-917121-1*) OUP.
—Another Third Poetry Book. (Illus.). 128p. (ps-6). 1988. pap. 6.95 (*0-19-917123-8*) OUP.
—A Fifth Poetry Book. (Illus.). 128p. 1987. 11.95 (*0-19-916054-6*); pap. 6.96 (*0-19-916053-8*) OUP.
—A Fourth Poetry Book. Benton, Peter, et al, illus. 128p. 1987. 11.95 (*0-19-918152-7*); pap. 6.95 (*0-19-918151-9*) OUP.

Frank, Josette, ed. Poems to Read to the Very Young. Wilkin, Eloise, illus. LC 82-518. 48p. (ps-3). 1982. 10.00 (*0-394-85188-9*) Random Bks Yng Read.
—Poems to Read to the Very Young. Wilson, Dagmar W., illus. LC 87-23234. 32p. (ps-1). 1988. pap. 2.25 (*0-394-89768-4*) Random Bks Yng Read.

Galdone, Paul, adapted by. & illus. Over in the Meadow. (ps-1). 1989. (S&S BFYR); pap. 5.95 (*0-671-67837-X*, S&S BFYR) S&S Trade.

Goldstein, Bobbye S. Birthday Rhymes, Special Times. (ps-3). 1993. 15.00 (*0-385-30419-6*) Doubleday.

Goode, Diane, illus. Diane Goode's Christmas Magic: Poems & Carols. LC 92-6366. 32p. (Orig.). (ps-3). 1992. PLB 5.99 (*0-679-92427-2*); pap. 2.25 (*0-679-82427-8*) Random Bks Yng Read.

Gordon, Ruth, selected by. Peeling the Onion: An Anthology of Poems Selected by Ruth Gordon. LC 92-571. 112p. (gr. 5 up). 1993. 15.00 (*0-06-021727-8*); 14.89 (*0-06-021728-6*) HarpC Child Bks.

Gordon, Ruth, ed. Time Is the Longest Distance. LC 90-4947. 96p. (gr. 7 up). 1991. 13.95 (*0-06-022297-2*); PLB 13.89 (*0-06-022424-X*) HarpC Child Bks.
—Under All Silences: The Many Shades of Love (An Anthology of Poems Selected by Ruth Gordon) LC 85-45845. 128p. (gr. 7 up). 1987. 13.00 (*0-06-022154-2*) HarpC Child Bks.

Harrison, Michael & Stuart-Clark, Christopher, eds. The Oxford Book of Animal Poems. (Illus.). 160p. 1992. 20.00 (*0-19-276105-6*) OUP.

Hoberman, Mary A. The Cozy Book. Fraser, Betty, illus. LC 93-10826. 1995. write for info. (*0-15-276620-0*, Browndeer Pr) HarBrace.

Hoberman, Mary A., selected by. My Song Is Beautiful: A Celebration of Multicultural Poems & Pictures. LC 93-24976. 1994. 15.95 (*0-316-36738-9*) Little.

Hopkins, Lee B. Ring Out, Wild Bells. Baumann, K., ed. 1992. 17.95 (*0-15-267100-5*, HB Juv Bks) HarBrace.

Hopkins, Lee B., selected by. Blast Off! Poems about Space. Sweet, Melissa, illus. LC 93-24536. 1995. 14.00 (*0-06-024260-4*); PLB 13.89 (*0-06-024261-2*) HarpC Child Bks.

Hopkins, Lee B., ed. Click, Rumble, Roar: Poems about Machines. Audette, Anna H., illus. LC 86-47746. 48p. (gr. 2-6). 1987. (Crowell Jr Bks); PLB 13.89 (*0-690-04589-1*, Crowell Jr Bks) HarpC Child Bks.

Hopkins, Lee B., selected by. Extra Innings: Baseball Poems. Medlock, Scott, illus. LC 92-13013. (gr. 4 up). 1993. write for info. (*0-15-226833-2*) HarBrace.

Hopkins, Lee B., ed. Hey-How for Halloween! McGaffrey, Janet, illus. LC 74-5601. 32p. (gr. 1-5). 1974. 12.95 (*0-15-233900-0*, HB Juv Bks) HarBrace.
—More Surprises. Lloyd, Megan, illus. LC 86-45335. 64p. (gr. k-3). 1987. PLB 13.89 (*0-06-022605-6*) HarpC Child Bks.
—Side by Side: Poems to Read Together. (gr. 1 up). 1991. pap. 7.95 (*0-671-73622-1*, S&S BFYR) S&S Trade.
—Surprises. LC 83-47712. (Illus.). 64p. (gr. k-3). 1984. PLB 13.89 (*0-06-022585-8*) HarpC Child Bks.

Huber, Miriam B., et al, eds. The Poetry Book: Vol. 4. Hartwell, Marjorie, illus. LC 79-51968. (gr. 4). 1980. Repr. of 1926 ed. 18.00x (*0-89609-183-X*) Roth Pub Inc.

Huigin, S. O. Scary Poems for Rotten Kids. (Illus.). 32p. (ps-8). 1988. pap. 4.95 (*0-88753-177-6*, Pub. by Black Moss Pr CN) Firefly Bks Ltd.

I Have a News. Philip, Ned, compiled by. LC 93-32620. (gr. 2 up). 1994. 15.00 (*0-688-13367-3*) Lothrop.

Illustrated Poems for Children. 1986. 10.95 (*0-8331-0019-X*) Hubbard Sci.

Janeczko, Paul B. Going over to Your Place: Poems for Each Other. LC 86-26439. 176p. (gr. 7 up). 1987. SBE 14.95 (*0-02-747670-7*, Bradbury Pr) Macmillan Child Grp.
—Strings: A Gathering of Family Poems. LC 83-19033. 144p. (gr. 7 up). 1984. SBE 13.95 (*0-02-747790-8*, Bradbury Pr) Macmillan Child Grp.

Janeczko, Paul B., ed. Pocket Poems. LC 84-21537. 160p. (gr. 7 up). 1985. SBE 13.95 (*0-02-747820-3*, Bradbury Pr) Macmillan Child Grp.

Janeczko, Paul B., selected by. Preposterous: Poems of Youth. LC 90-39644. 144p. (gr. 7 up). 1991. 14.95 (*0-531-05901-4*); PLB 14.99 (*0-531-08501-5*) Orchard Bks Watts.

Janger, Kathie, ed. Rainbow Collection, 1989: Stories & Poetry by Young People. Viorst, Judith, frwd. by. Sarecky, Melody, illus. 176p. (gr. 1-8). 1989. pap. 6.00 (*0-929889-04-5*) Young Writers Contest Found.
—Rainbow Collection, 1990: Stories & Poetry by Young People. Sarecky, Melody, illus. Bush, Barbara, frwd. by. (Illus.). 176p. 1990. pap. 6.00 (*0-929889-06-1*) Young Writers Contest Found.

Katz, Bobbi, ed. Puddle Wonderful: Poems to Welcome Spring. Morgan, Mary, illus. LC 91-8066. 32p. (Orig.). (ps-1). 1992. pap. 2.25 (*0-679-81493-0*) Random Bks Yng Read.

Kennedy, X. J. & Kennedy, Dorothy M., eds. Talking Like the Rain: A First Book of Poems. Dyer, Jane, illus. (ps up). 1992. 18.95 (*0-316-48889-5*) Little.

Kratky, Lada J. Pinta, Pinta, Gregorita (Small Book) Hockerman, Dennis, illus. (SPA.). 16p. (Orig.). (gr. k-3). 1992. pap. text ed. 6.00 (*1-56334-084-4*) Hampton-Brown.

Kroll, Steven. It's April Fools' Day! Bassett, Jeni, illus. LC 88-28434. 32p. (ps-3). 1990. reinforced bdg. 14.95 (*0-8234-0747-0*) Holiday.

Kuskin, Karla. Any Me I Want to Be. Kuskin, Karla, illus. LC 77-105485. 64p. (gr. 1-4). 1972. PLB 11.89 (*0-06-023616-7*) HarpC Child Bks.

Larke, Joe. Can't Reach the Itch. Larke, Karol, illus. 72p. (gr. 1-6). 1988. 10.00x (*0-9620112-1-5*) Grin A Bit.

Larrick, Nancy. Bring Me All of Your Dreams. LC 79-26892. 128p. (gr. 10 up). 1988. pap. 6.95 (*0-87131-550-5*) M Evans.

Larrick, Nancy, compiled by. The Merry-Go-Round Poetry Book. Gundersheimer, Karen, illus. 1989. 14.95 (*0-385-29814-5*) Delacorte.

Larrick, Nancy, ed. Night of the Whippoorwill. Ray, David, illus. 72p. (ps up). 1992. 19.95 (*0-399-21874-2*, Philomel Bks) Putnam Pub Group.

Leary, Lory B. An Alaskan Child's Garden of Verse. Leary, Lory B., illus. 40p. (Orig.). (gr. 6 up). 1989. pap. 6.95x (*0-924663-02-2*) Alaskan Viewpoint.

Lewis, Naomi, ed. Messages: A Book of Poems. LC 85-10326. 255p. (gr. 7 up). 1985. Faber & Faber.

Little Treasury of Love Poems. 1987. 4.99 (*0-517-63752-9*) Random Hse Value.

Livingston, Myra C. Birthday Poems. Tomes, Margot, illus. LC 89-2114. 32p. (ps-3). 1989. reinforced bdg. 13.95 (*0-8234-0783-7*) Holiday.
—Sky Songs. Fisher, Leonard E., illus. LC 83-12955. 32p. (ps-4). 1984. reinforced bdg 14.95 (*0-8234-0502-8*) Holiday.
—A Time to Talk: Poems of Friendship. Pinkney, Brian, illus. LC 91-42234. 128p. (gr. 7 up). 1992. SBE 13.95 (*0-689-50558-2*, M K McElderry) Macmillan Child Grp.

Livingston, Myra C., compiled by. Cat Poems. Hyman, Trina S., illus. LC 86-14810. 32p. (ps-3). 1987. reinforced bdg. 13.95 (*0-8234-0631-8*) Holiday.

Livingston, Myra C., ed. Easter Poems. Wallner, John, illus. LC 84-15866. 32p. (ps-3). 1985. reinforced bdg. 13.95 (*0-8234-0546-X*) Holiday.
—Poems for Fathers. Casilla, Robert, illus. LC 88-17010. 32p. (ps-3). 1989. reinforced bdg. 13.95 (*0-8234-0729-2*) Holiday.

Livingston, Myra C., selected by. Riddle-Me Rhymes. Perry, Rebecca, illus. LC 93-25179. 96p. (gr. 3-7). 1994. SBE 13.95 (*0-689-50602-3*, M K McElderry) Macmillan Child Grp.

Malley, Barbara & Allen, Frances. Poetry with a Purpose. Lawrence, Grace, illus. 128p. (gr. 4-7). 1987. pap. 11.95 (*0-86653-415-6*, GA 1018) Good Apple.

Marshall, James, compiled by. & illus. Pocketful of Nonsense. LC 93-18297. 1993. 12.95 (*0-307-17552-9*, Golden Pr) Western Pub.

Mastrangelo, Judy & Mastrangelo, Judy, illus. The Sandman: And Other Sleepy-Time Rhymes. LC 90-34513. 48p. (ps-2). 1990. 4.95 (*0-88101-105-3*) Unicorn Pub.

Maxwell, Judith & Maxwell, Jessica. The Feminist Revised Mother Goose: A Twenty-First Century Children's Edition. 2nd ed. Maxwell, Rafe & Krostag, Zi, illus. (Orig.). (gr. 2-8). 1995. pap. text ed. 7.95 (*0-9632698-7-9*) Veda Vangarde.
4-color cover with wondeful, whimsical illustrations makes the 2nd Edition of THE FEMINIST REVISED MOTHER GOOSE RHYMES the best yet. Judith & Jessica, along with Judith's son, Rafe & his best friend Zi, have collaborated to bring this expanded version of these timeless rhymes to readers both young & old. In addition to the original 25 rewritten rhymes, Judith & Jessica have written more & included their original forms in an appendix with much more history of the original rhymes & an annotated bibliography! Also included in a new section called "From the Mouths of Babes" is a series of original rhymes as told by children from Pacific Northwest playgrounds. These new rhymes include THE TASMANIAN DEVIL which reads: "Australia big, Australia wide/ That's where the Tasmanian Devil may hide./ If you go looking for it, WATCH OUT!/ He's got a terribly hungry snout./ And if you happen to get too close,/ You might get nibbled on (I suppose)". And FARLEY "Old man Marley, had a friend named Farley/ And a weird old Farley was he./ He glowed in the dark/ and he sparked & he sparked/ and ran away yelling "yippey!"'
Publisher Provided Annotation.

Min, Kellet I. Modern Informative Nursery Rhymes: American History, Book I. Hansen, Heidi, illus. LC 89-91719. 64p. (Orig.). (gr. 2-5). 1992. pap. 10.95 (*0-9623411-2-6*) Rhyme & Reason.
—Modern Informative Nursery Rhymes: General Science, Book I. Hansen, Heidi, illus. LC 89-91719. 64p. (Orig.). (gr. 2-5). 1993. pap. 10.95 (*0-9623411-4-2*) Rhyme & Reason.
—Modern Informative Nursery Rhymes: Values, Book I. Hansen, Heidi, illus. LC 89-91719. 32p. (ps-3). 1989. pap. 7.95 (*0-9623411-3-4*) Rhyme & Reason.

Moore, Peggy S. My Very First book of Poetry & Other Things. Moore, Peggy S., illus. 16p. (gr. 3-5). 1982. pap. 1.98 (*0-9613078-0-3*) Detroit Black.

Nunez, Ana R. Antologia de Poesia Infantil. LC 85-81795. (SPA.). 180p. (Orig.). (gr. 3-12). 1985. pap. 9.95 (*0-89729-369-X*) Ediciones.

Nye, Naomi S. This Same Sky: A Collection of Poems from Around the World. LC 92-11617. (Illus.). 224p. (gr. 5 up). 1992. SBE 15.95 (*0-02-768440-7*, Four Winds) Macmillan Child Grp.

On Top of Strawberry Hill. LC 92-34165. 1993. 14.00 (*0-383-03645-3*) SRA Schl Grp.

Parry, Caroline, compiled by. Zoomerang a Boomerang: Poems to Make Your Belly Laugh. Martchenko, Michael, illus. LC 92-26589. 32p. (ps-3). 1993. pap. 4.99 (*0-14-054869-6*) Puffin Bks.

Paton, Kathleen, ed. Poems to Share. Van Wright, Cornelius & Ying-Hwa Hu, illus. 24p. (ps-3). 1990. 4.95 (*1-56288-050-0*) Checkerboard.

Plume, Ilse, ed. & illus. Lullaby & Goodnight: Songs & Poems for Babies. LC 93-4425. 32p. (ps-1). 1994. 12.00 (*0-06-023501-2*); PLB 11.89 (*0-06-023502-0*) HarpC Child Bks.

Poet's Workshop Staff. Black American History: Rap & Rhyme. 8p. (gr. 6-12). 1989. pap. text ed. 2.50 (*0-913597-53-8*, Pub. by Alpha Pyramis) Prosperity & Profits.

Pollard, Nan. Friends Together. Pollard, Nan, illus. 32p. (ps-3). 1990. 4.95 (*1-56288-048-9*) Checkerboard.

Prelutsky, Jack. Kermit's Garden of Verses. McNally, Bruce, illus. LC 82-480. 64p. (gr. 4-6). 1982. lib. bdg. 5.99 (*0-394-95410-6*) Random Bks Yng Read.
—The Random House Book of Poetry for Children. Lobel, Arnold, illus. LC 81-85940. 248p. (gr. 1-5). 1983. 17.00 (*0-394-85010-6*); lib. bdg. 17.99 (*0-394-95010-0*) Random Bks Yng Read.

Prelutsky, Jack, ed. Read Aloud Rhymes for the Very Young. Brown, Marc, illus. Trelease, Jim, intro. by. LC 86-7147. (Illus.). 112p. (ps-3). 1986. 17.00 (*0-394-87218-5*); PLB 17.99 (*0-394-97218-X*) Knopf Bks Yng Read.

Reed, Ronald, ed. I Wish That I Could Live Outdoors: Mohican Outdoor School Student Poetry Contest Winners & Others. (Illus.). 100p. (Orig.). (gr. 4-7). 1992. pap. 18.95 incl. cass. (*0-685-53268-2*) Mohican Schl.

Reynolds, James J., ed. Modern Poetry for Children, Bk. 8. LC 30-10164. (gr. 4). 1979. Repr. of 1928 ed. 15.00x (*0-89609-167-8*) Roth Pub Inc.

Robb, Laura, compiled by. Music and Drum: Voices of War and Peace, Hope and Dreams. LC 92-39312. 1994. write for info. (*0-399-22024-0*, Philomel Bks) Putnam Pub Group.

Robinson, Fay. A Frog Inside My Hat. Moore, Cyd, photos by. LC 93-22200. (Illus.). 64p. (ps-3). 1993. PLB 16.95 (*0-8167-3129-2*); pap. write for info. (*0-8167-3130-6*) BrdgeWater.

Roche, P. K., selected by. & illus. At Christmas Be Merry. 32p. (ps-1). 1989. pap. 3.95 (*0-14-050680-2*, Puffin) Puffin Bks.

Rodriguez, Alejo. It's Tough Being a Kid These Days. LC 93-85309. 65p. (gr. 6-12). 1994. pap. 5.95 (*1-55523-638-3*) Winston-Derek.

Roes, Mimi. Poems for Young Children. Fuhrman, James, illus. (ps-6). 1979. pap. 1.95x (*0-89780-003-6*) NAR Pubns.

Rosen, Michael, selected by. The Kingfisher Book of Children's Poetry. LC 92-26444. (Illus.). 256p. (gr. 3-9). 1993. 16.95 (*1-85697-910-5*, Kingfisher LKC); pap. 10.95 (*1-85697-909-1*) LKC.

Rosen, Michael, ed. Poems for the Very Young. Graham, Bob, illus. LC 92-45574. 80p. (gr. k-3). 1993. 15.95 (*1-85697-908-3*, Kingfisher LKC) LKC.

Running Press Staff, ed. KIDZ Mother Goose Car Rhyme Book & Audiocassette. (Illus.). 96p. (Orig.). (gr. 1 up). 1991. incl. 60-min. audiocass. 9.95 (*1-56138-019-9*) Running Pr.

Schertle, Alice. How Now, Brown Cow? Schaffer, Amanda, illus. LC 93-24052. (ps up). 1994. 14.95 (*0-15-276648-0*, Browndeer Pr) HarBrace.

Scott, Louise. Quiet Times. 66p. (ps). 1986. saddle stitched 9.95 (*0-513-01785-2*) Denison.
Sloan, Phyllis J., et al. Trembling with Wonder. Knight, Ginny, illus. (gr. 4 up). 1990. 3.00 (*0-940248-80-8*) Guild Pr.
Smith, Philip, ed. Favorite Poems of Childhood. (Illus.). 96p. (Orig.). 1992. pap. 1.00t (*0-486-27089-0*) Dover.
Sneve, Virginia H., ed. Dancing Teepees: Poems of American Indian Youth. Gammell, Stephen, illus. LC 88-11075. 32p. (ps-4). 1989. reinforced bdg. 15.95 (*0-8234-0724-1*) Holiday.
Spiegel, Richard. BiblioMania, Vol. 2. Fisher, Barbara, ed. (Illus.). 52p. (Orig.). (gr. 7-12). 1991. pap. 3.00 (*0-934830-49-5*) Ten Penny.
Spiegel, Richard & Fisher, Barbara, eds. BiblioMania, Vol. 1. (Illus.). 36p. (Orig.). (gr. 2-6). 1991. pap. 3.00 (*0-934830-48-7*) Ten Penny.
Sproxton, Mildred. Children's Treasure House of Poetry. (gr. 7-10). 1986. 30.00x (*0-7223-2073-6*, Pub. by A H Stockwell England) St Mut.
Taylor, Phoebe, ed. Thoughts for the Free Life: Lao Tsu to the Present. 2nd ed. Buckley, Cicely, illus. 110p. (Orig.). (gr. 8 up). 1989. pap. 10.00 (*0-9617481-5-X*) Oyster River Pr.
Turner, Ann. Grass Songs: Poems. Moser, Barry, illus. LC 92-11684. (gr. 4 up). 1993. write for info. (*0-15-136788-4*) HarBrace.
Untermeyer, Louis, ed. Rainbow in the Sky: Golden Anniversary Edition. Birch, Reginald, illus. LC 84-19306. 498p. (gr. 3-7). 1985. 19.95 (*0-15-265479-8*, HB Juv Bks) HarBrace.
Wade, Theodore E., Jr., ed. With Joy, Poems for Children. rev. ed. LC 88-72233. (Illus.). 48p. (gr. k-7). 1988. pap. 2.95 (*0-930192-20-6*) Gazelle Pubns.
Wallace, Daisy, ed. Monster Poems. Chorao, Kay, illus. LC 75-17680. 32p. (ps-3). 1976. reinforced bdg. 13.95 (*0-8234-0268-1*); pap. 4.95 (*0-8234-0848-5*) Holiday.
Walsh, Caroline, selected by. The Little Book of Poems. Marklew, Gilly, illus. LC 92-29126. 1993. 7.95 (*1-85697-887-7*, Kingfisher LKC) LKC.
Waters, Fiona, ed. Whiskers & Paws. Julian-Ottie, Vanessa, illus. LC 89-77349. 32p. 1990. 9.95 (*0-940793-51-2*, Pub. by Crocodile Bks) Interlink Pub.
Webber, Helen. How Long Is Long Ago & Other Poems. Webber, Helen, illus. (gr. k-6). 1968. 8.95 (*0-8392-3068-0*) Astor-Honor.
Wolman, Bernice, compiled by. Taking Turns: Poetry to Share. Stock, Catherine, illus. LC 90-46533. 32p. (gr. 1-4). 1992. SBE 13.95 (*0-689-31677-1*, Atheneum Child Bk) Macmillan Child Grp.
Yolen, Jane. Three Bears Holiday Book. Dyer, Jane, illus. LC 93-17252. 1994. write for info. (*0-15-200932-9*, J Yolen Bks) HarBrace.
Young Folks' Book of Mirth: A Collection of the Best Fun in Prose & Verse. LC 79-51961. (gr. 2-6). 1980. Repr. of 1924 ed. 19.75x (*0-89609-197-X*) Roth Pub Inc.

POETRY–INDEXES

Damon, Valerie H. Grindle Lamfoon & the Procurnious Fleekers. Damon, Dave, ed. Damon, Valerie H., illus. LC 78-64526. (gr. 1-12). 1979. 12.95 (*0-932356-05-2*); fleeker ed. 14.95 (*0-932356-06-0*) Star Pubns MO.

POETS

see also Dramatists

Bernotas, Bob. Amiri Baraka (Le Roi Jones) King, Coretta Scott, intro. by. (Illus.). 112p. (gr. 5 up). 1991. lib. bdg. 17.95 (*0-7910-1117-8*) Chelsea Hse.
Bhatt, H. D. Kalidas. (Illus.). (gr. 3-8). 1979. pap. 3.95 (*0-89744-144-3*) Auromere.
Bodie, Idella. A Hunt for Life's Extras: The Story of Archibald Rutledge. (Illus.). 176p. (gr. 5-12). 1986. pap. 6.95 (*0-87844-073-9*) Sandlapper Pub Co.
Chaney, J. R. Aleksandr Pushkin: Poet for the People. 112p. (gr. 5 up). 1991. PLB 21.50 (*0-8225-4911-5*) Lerner Pubns.
Chapman, Lynne F. Sylvia Plath. LC 93-3354. 1994. PLB 18.95 (*0-88682-614-4*) Creative Ed.
Charpentreau, J. & Jean, G. Dictionnaire des Poetes et de la Poesie. (FRE.). 427p. (gr. 5-10). 1983. 27.95 (*2-07-051019-0*) Schoenhof.
King, Sarah E. Maya Angelou: Greeting the Morning. LC 93-4572. (Illus.). 48p. (gr. 2-4). 1994. PLB 12.90 (*1-56294-431-2*) Millbrook Pr.
Lewis, J. Patrick. Boshblobberbosh: Runcible Poems for Mr. Lear. LC 93-43749. 1995. write for info. (*0-8037-1390-8*); PLB write for info. (*0-8037-1391-6*) Dial Bks Young.
Reef, Catherine. Walt Whitman. LC 94-7405. 1995. write for info. (*0-395-68705-5*, Clarion Bks) HM.
Walker, Alice. Langston Hughes, American Poet. rev. ed. Deeter, Catherine, illus. LC 92-28540. 48p. (gr. 3-6). Date not set. 15.00 (*0-06-021518-6*); PLB 14.89 (*0-06-021519-4*) HarpC Child Bks.
West, Alan. Jose Marti, Man of Poetry, Soldier of Freedom. LC 93-6258. (Illus.). 32p. (gr. 2-4). 1994. PLB 12.90 (*1-56294-408-8*) Millbrook Pr.

POETS–FICTION

Bedard, Michael. Emily. Cooney, Barbara, illus. LC 91-41806. 40p. (gr. k-3). 1992. 16.00 (*0-385-30697-0*) Doubleday.
Cole, William E., ed. Poem Stew. Weinhaus, Karen A., illus. LC 81-47106. 96p. (gr. 2-6). 1983. pap. 4.95 (*0-06-440136-7*, Trophy) HarpC Child Bks.
Siebert, Diane. Heartland. Minor, Wendell, illus. LC 87-29380. 32p. (ps-3). 1989. 16.00 (*0-690-04730-4*, Crowell Jr Bks); PLB 15.89 (*0-690-04732-0*) HarpC Child Bks.

POETRY–PHILOSOPHY

see Poetry

POETRY–SELECTIONS

see Poetry–Collections

POETRY–TECHNIQUE

see Poetics

POETRY FOR CHILDREN

see Nursery Rhymes; Poetry

POETRY OF LOVE

see Love Poetry

POETRY OF NATURE

see Nature in Poetry

POINTE DE SABLE, JEAN BAPTISTE, 1745?-1818

Johnson, LaVerne C. Jean Baptiste DuSable: Writer. Perry, Craig R., illus. LC 92-35252. 1992. 3.95 (*0-922162-93-X*) Empak Pub.

POISONOUS PLANTS

Darlington, Joan R. Is It Poison Ivy? A Field Book on Poisonous Plants & Look-Alikes. Darlington, Joan R., illus. 32p. (Orig.). 1993. pap. 7.50 (*1-882291-53-0*) Oyster River Pr.
Dowden, Anne O. Poisons in Our Path: Plants That Harm & Heal. Dowden, Anne O., illus. LC 92-9518. 64p. 1994. 17.00 (*0-06-020861-9*); PLB 16.89 (*0-06-020862-7*) HarpC Child Bks.
Lerner, Carol. Dumb Cane & Daffodils: Poisonous Plants in the House & Garden. Lerner, Carol, illus. LC 89-33622. 32p. 1990. 13.95 (*0-688-08791-4*); PLB 13.88 (*0-688-08796-5*, Morrow Jr Bks) Morrow Jr Bks.
—Moonseed & Mistletoe: A Book of Poisonous Wild Plants. LC 87-13989. (Illus.). 32p. (ps up). 1988. 12.95 (*0-688-07307-7*); PLB 12.88 (*0-688-07308-5*, Morrow Jr Bks) Morrow Jr Bks.
Peissel, Michel & Allen, Missy. Dangerous Plants & Mushrooms. (Illus.). 112p. (gr. 5 up). 1993. PLB 19.95 (*0-7910-1787-7*, Am Art Analog) Chelsea Hse.

POISONS

Chlad, Dorothy. Poisons Make You Sick. Halverson, Lydia, illus. LC 83-24029. 32p. (ps-2). 1984. pap. 3.95 (*0-516-41976-5*) Childrens.
Deadly Venom. (Illus.). 48p. (gr. 3-4). Date not set. PLB 22.80 (*0-8114-3154-1*) Raintree Steck-V.
Gay, Kathlyn & Kline, Marjory. Silent Killers: Radon & Other Hazards. LC 88-5549. (Illus.). (gr. 6-12). 1988. PLB 13.40 (*0-531-10598-9*) Watts.
Kronenwetter, Michael. Managing Toxic Wastes. Steltenpohl, Jane, ed. (Illus.). 126p. (gr. 7-10). 1989. lib. bdg. 13.98 (*0-671-69051-5*, J Messner) S&S Trade.
Kusinitz, Marc. Poisons & Toxins. (Illus.). (gr. 6-12). 1992. 18.95 (*0-7910-0074-5*) Chelsea Hse.
Szumski, Bonnie. Toxic Wastes: Examining Cause & Effect Relationships. LC 89-16906. (Illus.). 32p. (gr. 3-6). 1990. PLB 10.95 (*0-89908-643-8*) Greenhaven.
Zipko, Stephen J. Toxic Threat: How Hazardous Substances Poison Our Lives. rev. ed. Steltenpohl, Jane, ed. (Illus.). 208p. (gr. 7 up). 1990. lib. bdg. 14.98 (*0-671-69330-1*, J Messner); pap. 5.95 (*0-671-69331-X*) S&S Trade.

POLAND

Angel, Ann. Lech Walesa. LC 91-50539. (Illus.). 68p. (gr. 3-4). 1992. PLB 19.93 (*0-8368-0628-X*) Gareth Stevens Inc.
Craig, Mary. Lech Walesa: The Leader of Solidarity & Campaigner for Freedom & Human Rights in Poland. LC 88-17732. (Illus.). 68p. (gr. 5-6). 1990. PLB 19.93 (*1-55532-821-0*) Gareth Stevens Inc.
Greene, Carol. Poland. LC 82-19737. (Illus.). 128p. (gr. 5-9). 1983. PLB 20.55 (*0-516-02783-2*) Childrens.
Heale, Jay. Poland. LC 93-45744. 1994. write for info. Set (*1-85435-585-6*); 21.95 (*1-85435-589-9*) Marshall Cavendish.
Holland, Gini. Poland. LC 89-43181. (Illus.). 64p. (gr. 5-6). 1992. PLB 21.26 (*0-8368-0233-0*) Gareth Stevens Inc.
Landau, Elaine. The Warsaw Ghetto Uprising. LC 92-15851. (Illus.). 144p. (gr. 6 up). 1992. text ed. 14.95 RSBE (*0-02-751392-0*, New Discovery) Macmillan Child Grp.
Lazo, Caroline E. Lech Walesa. LC 92-39959. (Illus.). 64p. (gr. 4 up). 1993. text ed. 13.95 RSBE (*0-87518-525-8*, Dillon) Macmillan Child Grp.
Pfeiffer, Christine. Poland: Land of Freedom Fighters. LC 90-26093. (Illus.). 144p. (gr. 5 up). 1991. text ed. 14.95 RSBE (*0-87518-464-2*, Dillon) Macmillan Child Grp.
Poland in Pictures. LC 93-10769. 1994. lib. bdg. write for info. (*0-8225-1885-6*) Lerner Pubns.
Poland Is My Home. 48p. (gr. 2-8). 1992. PLB 18.60 (*0-8368-0904-1*) Gareth Stevens Inc.
Stewart, Gail B. Poland. LC 90-35498. (Illus.). 48p. (gr. 6-7). 1990. text ed. 12.95 RSBE (*0-89686-549-5*, Crestwood Hse) Macmillan Child Grp.
Vnenchak, Dennis. Lech Walesa & Poland. LC 92-40266. 1994. write for info. (*0-531-11128-8*) Watts.

POLAND–FICTION

Carey, Valerie S. Tsugele's Broom. Zimmer, Dirk, illus. LC 92-9873. 48p. (gr. k-3). 1993. 15.00 (*0-06-020986-0*); PLB 14.89 (*0-06-020987-9*) HarpC Child Bks.
Drucker, Malka & Halperin, Michael. Jacob's Rescue: A Holocaust Story. LC 92-30523. 128p. (gr. 4-7). 1993. 15.95 (*0-553-08976-5*, Skylark) Bantam.
Kelly, Eric P. The Trumpeter of Krakow. Domanska, Janina, illus. LC 91-26879. 224p. (gr. 3-7). 1992. pap. 3.95 (*0-689-71571-4*, Aladdin) Macmillan Child Grp.
Seidler, Babara. The Legend of King Piast. Kedron, Jane, tr. Rosinski, Grzegorz, illus. (gr. 2-8). 1977. pap. 1.00 (*0-917004-08-6*) Kosciuszko.

Singer, Isaac Bashevis. The Fools of Chelm & Their History. Shub, Elizabeth, tr. from YID. Shulevitz, Uri, illus. LC 73-81500. 64p. (gr. 3 up). 1973. 14.00 (*0-374-32444-1*) FS&G.

POLAR EXPEDITIONS

see Antarctic Regions; Arctic Regions; North Pole; Polar Regions; South Pole

POLAR REGIONS

see also Antarctic Regions; Arctic Regions; North Pole; South Pole

Aldis, Rodney. Polar Lands. LC 91-34170. (Illus.). 48p. (gr. 5 up). 1992. text ed. 13.95 RSBE (*0-87518-494-4*, Dillon) Macmillan Child Grp.
Berger, Melvin. Life in the Polar Regions. 16p. (gr. 2-4). 1994. pap. 14.95 (*1-56784-210-0*) Newbridge Comms.
Byles, Monica. Life in the Polar Lands. (Illus.). (gr. 4-7). 1993. pap. 4.95 (*0-590-46130-3*) Scholastic Inc.
James, Barbara. Conserving the Polar Regions. LC 90-46064. (Illus.). 48p. (gr. 4-9). 1990. PLB 21.34 (*0-8114-2393-X*); pap. 5.95 (*0-8114-3458-3*) Raintree Steck-V.
Johnson, Jinny. Poles & Tundra Wildlife. (Illus.). 24p. (gr. 4-7). 1993. 9.95 (*0-89577-538-7*, Dist. by Random) RD Assn.
Khanduri, K. Polar Wildlife. (Illus.). 32p. (gr. 3-7). 1993. PLB 13.96 (*0-88110-601-1*); pap. 6.95 (*0-7460-0938-0*) EDC.
Lambert, David. Polar Regions. (Illus.). 48p. (gr. 5-8). 1987. PLB 12.95 (*0-382-09502-2*) Silver Burdett Pr.
Palmer, Joy. Polar Lands. LC 92-12405. (Illus.). 32p. (gr. 2-3). 1992. PLB 18.99 (*0-8114-3403-6*) Raintree Steck-V.
Stewart, G. In the Polar Regions. (Illus.). 32p. (gr. 3-8). 1989. lib. bdg. 15.74 (*0-86592-108-3*); 11.95s.p. (*0-685-58596-4*) Rourke Corp.
Stone, L. Arctic Tundra. (Illus.). 48p. (gr. 4-8). 1988. lib. bdg. 15.94 (*0-86592-436-8*); PLB 11.95s.p. (*0-685-58568-9*) Rourke Corp.
Twist, Clint. Ice Caps to Glaciers: Projects with Geography. LC 92-33917. 1993. 12.40 (*0-531-17396-8*, Gloucester Pr) Watts.
Williams, Lawrence. Polar Lands. LC 89-25350. (Illus.). 48p. (gr. 4-8). 1990. PLB 12.95 (*1-85435-170-2*) Marshall Cavendish.

POLAR REGIONS–FICTION

Newton, Jill. Polar Scare. (Illus.). (ps-3). 1992. 15.00 (*0-688-11232-3*); PLB 14.93 (*0-685-75779-X*) Lothrop.

POLES IN THE U. S.

Moscinski, Sharon. Tracing Our Polish Roots. (Illus.). 48p. (gr. 4-7). 1994. 12.95 (*1-56261-161-5*) John Muir.
Toor, Rachel. The Polish Americans. Moynihan, Daniel P., intro. by. 112p. (Orig.). (gr. 5 up). 1988. 17.95 (*0-87754-895-1*); pap. 9.95 (*0-7910-0274-8*) Chelsea Hse.

POLES IN THE U. S.–FICTION

Blos, Joan W. Brooklyn Doesn't Rhyme. Birling, Paul, illus. LC 93-31589. 96p. (gr. 3-6). 1994. SBE 12.95 (*0-684-19694-8*, Scribners Young Read) Macmillan Child Grp.

POLICE

see also Crime and Criminals; Criminal Investigation; Detectives

also names of cities with the subdivision Police, e.g. N. Y. (city)–Police, etc.

Almonte, Paul & Desmond, Theresa. Police, People & Power. LC 91-46951. (Illus.). 48p. (gr. 5-6). 1992. text ed. 12.95 RSBE (*0-89686-748-X*, Crestwood Hse) Macmillan Child Grp.
Anderson, Kelly C. Police Brutality. LC 94-9707. (Illus.). (gr. 5-8). 1994. 14.95 (*1-56006-164-2*) Lucent Bks.
Barrett, Norman S. Picture World of Police Vehicles. LC 90-31020. (Illus.). 32p. (gr. k-4). 1991. PLB 12.40 (*0-531-14092-X*) Watts.
Bornstein, Jerry. Police Brutality: A National Debate. LC 92-42146. (Illus.). 112p. (gr. 6 up). 1993. lib. bdg. 17.95 (*0-89490-430-2*) Enslow Pubs.
Broekel, Ray. Police. LC 81-7693. (Illus.). 48p. (gr. k-4). 1981. PLB 12.85 (*0-516-01643-1*) Childrens.
—La Policia (Police) Kratky, Lada, tr. from ENG. LC 81-7693. (SPA., Illus.). 48p. (gr. k-4). 1984. PLB 12.85 (*0-516-31643-5*); pap. 4.95 (*0-516-51643-4*) Childrens.
Bryant, Eric H. Arrest Me Not: The Common Sense Survival Guide for Teens (& Adults) When Stopped by Police. 41p. (gr. 7 up). 1994. pap. 5.95 (*0-9640336-0-7*) Page One Communs.
Campling, Elizabeth. Timeline: The Police. (Illus.). 64p. (gr. 7-10). 1989. 19.95 (*0-85219-789-6*, Pub. by Batsford UK) Trafalgar.
Dick, Jean. Bomb Squads & SWAT Teams. LC 88-15907. (Illus.). 48p. (gr. 5-6). 1988. text ed. 11.95 RSBE (*0-89686-401-4*, Crestwood Hse) Macmillan Child Grp.
Dumpleton, John. Law & Order: The Story of the Police. (Illus.). (gr. 3-7). 1983. Repr. of 1963 ed. 14.95 (*0-7136-1079-4*) Dufour.
Johnson, Jean. Police Officers: A to Z. (Illus.). 48p. (gr. k-3). 1986. 11.95 (*0-8027-6614-5*); lib. bdg. 12.85 (*0-8027-6615-3*) Walker & Co.
Sobol, David J. Encyclopedia Brown's Book of Strange but True Facts. (gr. 4-7). 1991. 12.95 (*0-590-44147-7*) Scholastic Inc.

POLICE–FICTION

Alexander, Liza. Sesame Street: I Want to Be a Police Officer. (ps-3). 1994. pap. 2.25 (*0-307-13124-6*, Golden Pr) Western Pub.
Bantam. Cop & a Half. (gr. 4-6). 1993. pap. 3.50 (*0-553-48138-X*) Bantam.

Barry, Mark, illus. Sirens & Lights. 12p. (ps). 1992. 3.95 (*1-56828-007-6*) Red Jacket Pr.
Baum, L. Frank. Policeman Bluejay. LC 81-9044. (gr. 1-6). 1981. Repr. of 1907 ed. 50.00x (*0-8201-1367-0*) Schol Facsimiles.
Grubbs, J. & Abell, J. Henry the Cop. Grubbs, J., illus. 50p. (Orig.). (gr. 2-5). 1993. text ed. 18.00 (*1-56611-020-3*); pap. 15.00 (*1-56611-399-7*) Jonas.
Rathmann, Peggy. Officer Buckle & Gloria. LC 93-43887. 1995. write for info. (*0-399-22616-8*, Putnam) Putnam Pub Group.
Rosenbloom, Joseph. Deputy Dan Gets His Man. Raglin, Tim, illus. 48p. (gr. 2-3). 1985. pap. 3.50 (*0-394-87250-9*) Random Bks Yng Read.
Scarry, Richard. Richard Scarry: Sergeant Murphy's Busiest Day Ever. (Illus.). 20p. (ps up). 1992. write for info. incl. long-life batteries (*0-307-74710-7*, 64710, Golden Pr) Western Pub.
Thomson, Andy. Sheriff at Waterstop. (Illus.). 133p. (Orig.). (gr. 4-6). 1987. pap. 4.95 (*0-89084-371-6*) Bob Jones Univ Pr.
Whitman, Ken & Wilkey, Chris. Mutazoids. Sumner, Robert, ed. Radford, Stephan, illus. 98p. (Orig.). (gr. 10-12). 1989. pap. text ed. 12.95 (*0-685-29088-3*) Whit Prodns.

POLICE–VOCATIONAL GUIDANCE

Cohen, Payl & Cohen, Shari. Careers in Law Enforcement & Security. rev. ed. Rosen, Ruth, ed. (gr. 7-12). 1994. PLB 14.95 (*0-8239-1878-5*); pap. 9.95 (*0-8239-1908-0*) Rosen Group.
Martin, John H. A Day in the Life of a Police Cadet. Jann, Gayle, illus. LC 84-2578. 32p. (gr. 4-8). 1985. PLB 11.79 (*0-8167-0103-2*); pap. text ed. 2.95 (*0-8167-0104-0*) Troll Assocs.
Matthias, Catherine. I Can Be a Police Officer. LC 84-12106. (Illus.). 32p. (gr. k-3). 1984. PLB 11.80 (*0-516-01840-X*); pap. 3.95 (*0-516-41840-8*) Childrens.
Pellowski, Michael J. What's It Like to Be a Police Officer. Dolobowsky, Mena, illus. LC 89-34395. 32p. (gr. k-3). 1990. lib. bdg. 10.89 (*0-8167-1811-3*); pap. text ed. 2.95 (*0-8167-1812-1*) Troll Assocs.
Smith, Carter. A Day in the Life of an FBI Agent-in-Training. Jantzen, Franz, illus. LC 90-11150. 32p. (gr. 4-8). 1991. PLB 11.79 (*0-8167-2210-2*); pap. text ed. 2.95 (*0-8167-2211-0*) Troll Assocs.

POLICE DOGS

Emert, Phyllis R. Law Enforcement Dogs. LC 85-21351. (Illus.). 48p. (gr. 5-6). 1985. text ed. 11.95 RSBE (*0-89686-284-4*, Crestwood Hse) Macmillan Child Grp.
McPherson, Jan. The Dog School. LC 90-10085. (Illus.). 24p. (gr. 1-4). 1990. PLB 15.96 (*0-8114-2697-1*) Raintree Steck-V.

POLIO

see Poliomyelitis

POLIOMYELITIS

Tomlinson, Michael. Jonas Salk. LC 92-46284. 1993. 19. 93 (*0-86625-495-1*); 14.95s.p. (*0-685-66537-2*) Rourke Pubns.

POLITENESS

see Courtesy; Etiquette

POLITICAL CRIMES AND OFFENSES

see also Concentration Camps

Steele, Philip. Terrorism. LC 91-39803. (Illus.). 48p. (gr. 6 up). 1992. text ed. 12.95 RSBE (*0-02-735401-6*, New Discovery) Macmillan Child Grp.

POLITICAL CRIMES AND OFFENSES–FICTION

Cormier, Robert. After the First Death. LC 78-11770. (Illus.). (gr. 7-12). 1979. 7.95 (*0-394-84122-0*); lib. bdg. 14.99 (*0-394-94122-5*) Pantheon.
Hale, Edward E. Man Without a Country & Other Stories. (gr. 5 up). 1968. pap. 1.95 (*0-8049-0185-6*, CL-185) Airmont.

POLITICAL ECONOMY

see Economics

POLITICAL PARTIES

see also Politics, Practical
also names of parties, e.g. Democratic Party

Wekesser, Carol, ed. Politics in America: Opposing Viewpoints. LC 91-42803. (Illus.). 264p. (gr. 10 up). 1992. PLB 17.95 (*0-89908-189-4*); pap. text ed. 9.95 (*0-89908-164-9*) Greenhaven.

POLITICAL SCIENCE

see also Church and State; Citizenship; Civil Rights; Communism; Democracy; Government, Resistance to; Kings and Rulers; Law; Liberty; Local Government; Political Parties; Revolutions; State Governments; World Politics

Arab-Israeli Issue. LC 86-20259. (Illus.). (gr. 7 up). 1988. 18.60 (*0-86592-029-X*) Rourke Corp.
Coffey, William E., et al. West Virginia Government. Buckalew, Marshall & Thoenen, Eugenia G., eds. (Illus.). 112p. (Orig.). (gr. 8). 1984. pap. 10.00 (*0-914498-05-3*) WV Hist Ed Found.
DeBiase, Louis A. How to Break into Politics on a Shoestring. Lyon, Lucinda, illus. 61p. (Orig.). (gr. 9-12). 1981. pap. 4.95 (*0-686-31571-5*) Louvin Pub.
Griscom, Bailey & Griscom, Pam. Why Can't I Be the Leader? (Illus.). 24p. (Orig.). (ps up). 1992. pap. 4.95 (*0-9633705-2-9*) Share Pub CA.
Lee, Richard S. & Lee, Mary P. Careers for Women in Politics. Rosen, Ruth, ed. (gr. 7-12). 1989. PLB 14.95 (*0-8239-0966-2*) Rosen Group.
Lewis, Barbara A. A Kid's Guide to Social Action: How to Solve the Social Problems You Choose - & Turn Creative Thinking Into Positive Action. Espeland, Pamela, ed. LC 90-44297. (Illus.). 208p. (Orig.). (gr. 5 up). 1991. pap. 14.95 (*0-915793-29-6*) Free Spirit Pub.
Machiavelli, Niccolo. Prince. Detmold, C. E., intro. by. (gr. 11 up). 1965. pap. 2.25 (*0-8049-0056-6*, CL-56) Airmont.
Plato. Plato's Republic. Jowett, Benjamin, tr. Gemme, F., intro. by. (gr. 11 up). 1968. pap. 2.75 (*0-8049-0172-4*, CL-172) Airmont.
Samuels, Cynthia K. It's a Free Country! A Young Person's Guide to Politics & Elections. LC 87-30857. (Illus.). 144p. (gr. 5 up). 1988. SBE 13.95 (*0-689-31416-7*, Atheneum Child Bk) Macmillan Child Grp.
Sharman, Tim. Rise of Solidarity. LC 86-20276. (Illus.). 78p. (gr. 7 up). 1987. 18.60 (*0-86592-030-3*); 13.95s.p. (*0-685-58242-6*) Rourke Corp.
Silberdick, Barbara F. Words in the News: A Student's Dictionary of American Government & Politics. Huehnergarth, John, illus. LC 93-19373. 144p. 1993. PLB 13.40 (*0-531-11164-4*) Watts.
Suez Crisis. (Illus.). (gr. 7 up). 1988. lib. bdg. 18.60 (*0-86592-026-5*); lib. bdg. 13.95s.p. (*0-685-58243-4*) Rourke Corp.

POLITICS, PRACTICAL

see also Elections

Buhay, Debra. Black & White of Politics. 30p. (gr. 12). 1990. pap. 2.00 (*1-878056-03-4*) D Hockenberry.
Coil, Suzanne M. Campaign Financing: Politics & the Power of Money. (Illus.). 128p. (gr. 7 up). 1994. 15.90 (*1-56294-220-4*) Millbrook Pr.
League of Women Voters of Cleveland Educational Fund, Inc. Staff. New Voter's Guide to Practical Politics. 61p. (gr. 7-12). 1982. pap. 2.00 (*1-880746-02-6*) LOWV Cleve Educ.
Reische, Diana. Electing a U. S. President. LC 91-32339. (Illus.). 144p. (gr. 7-12). 1992. PLB 14.40 (*0-531-11043-5*) Watts.
Sullivan, George. Campaigns & Elections. (Illus.). 128p. (gr. 5 up). 1991. PLB 10.95 (*0-382-24315-3*); pap. 7.95 (*0-382-24321-8*) Silver Burdett Pr.
Wekesser, Carol, ed. Politics in America: Opposing Viewpoints. LC 91-42803. (Illus.). 264p. (gr. 10 up). 1992. PLB 17.95 (*0-89908-189-4*); pap. text ed. 9.95 (*0-89908-164-9*) Greenhaven.

POLITICS, PRACTICAL–FICTION

Fritz, Jean. Shh! We're Writing the Constitution. De Paola, Tomie, illus. 64p. (gr. 3-7). 1987. 14.95 (*0-399-21403-8*, Putnam); pap. 6.95 (*0-399-21404-6*, Putnam) Putnam Pub Group.
Hughes, Dean. Re-elect Nutty. LC 94-12776. 1995. 14.00 (*0-689-31862-6*, Atheneum) Macmillan.
Hunt, Angela E. The Chance of a Lifetime. LC 92-20635. 1993. pap. 4.99 (*0-8423-1118-1*) Tyndale.
Jones, Rebecca C. Germy in Charge. LC 92-42076. 128p. (gr. 4-7). 1993. 13.95 (*0-525-45093-9*, DCB) Dutton Child Bks.
Nixon, Joan L. A Candidate for Murder. large type ed. LC 93-42058. 1994. pap. 15.95 (*0-7862-0142-8*) Thorndike Pr.
Pfeffer, Susan B. The Ring of Truth. LC 92-25272. 1993. 15.95 (*0-553-09224-3*) Bantam.
—Ring of Truth. 1994. pap. 3.99 (*0-440-21911-6*) Dell.

POLLS, ELECTION

see Elections

POLLUTION OF AIR

see Air–Pollution

POLLUTION OF WATER

see Water–Pollution

POLO, MARCO, 1254?-1324?

Graves, Charles P. Marco Polo. (Illus.). 96p. (gr. 3-5). 1991. Repr. of 1963 ed. lib. bdg. 12.95 (*0-7910-1505-X*) Chelsea Hse.
Greene, Carol. Marco Polo: Voyager to the Orient. LC 86-29977. (Illus.). 112p. (gr. 4 up). 1987. PLB 14.40 (*0-516-03229-1*) Childrens.
Hull, Mary. The Travels of Marco Polo. LC 94-2924. (Illus.). 128p. (gr. 6-9). 1994. 14.95 (*1-56006-238-X*) Lucent Bks.
Humble, Richard. Travels of Marco Polo. LC 89-36214. 1990. PLB 12.40 (*0-531-14022-9*) Watts.
Italia, Bob. Marco Polo. Walner, Rosemary, ed. LC 90-82626. (Illus.). 32p. (gr. 4). 1990. PLB 11.96 (*0-939179-92-X*) Abdo & Dghtrs.
Kent, Zachary. Marco Polo: Traveler to Central & Eastern Asia. LC 91-34521. (Illus.). 128p. (gr. 3 up). PLB 20.55 (*0-516-03070-1*); pap. 9.95, Jul. 1992 (*0-516-43070-X*) Childrens.
Noonan, Jon. Marco Polo. LC 91-38219. (Illus.). 48p. (gr. 5). 1993. text ed. 12.95 RSBE (*0-89686-704-8*, Crestwood Hse) Macmillan Child Grp.
Reynolds, Kathy, ed. Marco Polo. Woods, Dan, illus. LC 86-6678. 32p. (gr. 2-5). 1986. PLB 19.97 (*0-8172-2627-3*) Raintree Steck-V.
Rosen, Mike. The Travels of Marco Polo. Bull, Peter, illus. LC 88-23375. 32p. (gr. 4-6). 1989. PLB 11.90 (*0-531-18241-X*, Pub. by Bookwright Pr) Watts.
Stefoff, Rebecca. Marco Polo & the Medieval Explorers. (Illus.). 112p. (gr. 5 up). 1992. lib. bdg. 18.95 (*0-7910-1294-8*) Chelsea Hse.
Twist, Clint. Marco Polo: Overland to Medieval China. LC 93-30744. 1994. PLB 22.80 (*0-8114-7251-5*) Raintree Steck-V.

POLTERGEISTS

see Ghosts

POLYMERS AND POLYMERIZATION

see also Plastics

Mebane, Robert & Rybolt, Thomas. Plastics & Polymers. (Illus.). 64p. (gr. 5-8). 1995. bds. 15.95 (*0-8050-2843-9*) TFC Bks NY.

POLYNESIA–FICTION

Schields, Gretchen. The Water Shell. LC 94-15606. Date not set. write for info. (*0-15-200404-1*, Gulliver Bks) HarBrace.

POMPEII

Andrews, Ian. Pompeii. (Illus.). 48p. (gr. 7 up). 1978. pap. 7.95 (*0-521-20973-0*) Cambridge U Pr.
Biel, Timothy L. Pompeii. LC 89-9395. (Illus.). 64p. (gr. 5-8). 1989. PLB 11.95 (*1-56006-000-X*) Lucent Bks.
Connolly, Peter. Pompeii. (Illus.). 80p. (gr. 6 up). 1990. bds. 19.95 laminated (*0-19-917159-9*) OUP.
Goor, Ron & Goor, Nancy. Pompeii: Exploring a Roman Ghost Town. Goor, Ron & Goor, Nancy, illus. LC 85-47895. 128p. (gr. 5-9). 1986. (Crowell Jr Bks); PLB 14.89 (*0-690-04516-6*, Crowell Jr Bks) HarpC Child Bks.

PONCE DE LEON, JUAN, 1460?-1521

Blassingame, Wyatt. Ponce de Leon. (Illus.). 96p. (gr. 3-5). 1991. Repr. of 1965 ed. lib. bdg. 12.95 (*0-7910-1493-2*) Chelsea Hse.

POND ECOLOGY

see Fresh-Water Biology

PONIES

see also Horses

Baber, Carolyn S. Pony. Fleischman, Luke T., illus. 22p. 1990. pap. 9.95 (*0-9628937-0-6*, TX2910777) Richmond Saddlery.
Brady, Irene. America's Horses & Ponies. Brady, Irene, illus. 202p. (gr. 4 up). 1976. pap. 15.45 (*0-395-24050-6*, Sandpiper) HM.
Burton, Jane. Dizzie the Pony. LC 89-11395. (Illus.). 32p. (gr. 2-3). 1989. PLB 17.27 (*0-8368-0207-1*) Gareth Stevens Inc.
Cockrill, Pamela. Winter Ponies. 160p. (gr. 3-5). 1994. pap. 6.95 (*0-86241-409-1*, Pub. by Cnngt UK) Trafalgar.
Dennis, Wesley. Flip. Dennis, Wesley, illus. (ps-1). 1977. pap. 3.95 (*0-14-050203-3*, Puffin) Puffin Bks.
—Flip & the Morning. Dennis, Wesley, illus. LC 51-13521. (ps-1). 1977. pap. 3.95 (*0-14-050204-1*, Puffin) Puffin Bks.
Folsom, Franklin. Sand Dune Pony. (Illus.). 250p. (gr. 3-6). 1991. pap. 8.95 (*0-911797-99-8*) R Rinehart.
Kidd, Jane, ed. A First Guide to Horse & Pony Care: What Every Young Rider Must Know about Feeding, Grooming & Handling. (Illus.). 208p. (gr. 3-7). 1991. 24.95 (*0-87605-833-0*) Howell Bk.
Ling, Mary. Foal. LC 92-52809. (Illus.). 24p. (ps-1). 1992. 7.95 (*1-56458-113-6*) Dorling Kindersley.
McGowan, E. M. Horses & Ponies, A Photo-Fact Book. (Illus., Orig.). 1988. pap. 1.95 (*0-942025-26-1*) Kidsbks.
Petty, Kate. Ponies & Foals. 24p. (gr. k-3). 1993. pap. 3.95 (*0-8120-1487-1*) Barron.
Rawson, C. & Spector, J. Riding & Pony Care. 32p. (gr. 2 up). 1987. PLB 14.96 (*0-88110-297-0*); pap. 8.95 (*0-7460-0111-8*) EDC.
Royston, Angela. Pony. LC 89-22530. 1990. PLB 10.90 (*0-531-19081-1*, Warwick) Watts.
Spector, Joanna. Horses & Ponies. (Illus.). 64p. (gr. 3 up). 1993. pap. 4.95 (*0-86020-255-0*, Usborne) EDC.

PONIES–FICTION

Anderson, C. W. Billy & Blaze. (Illus.). 56p. 1992. Repr. PLB 11.95x (*0-89966-947-6*) Buccaneer Bks.
—Billy & Blaze: A Boy & His Pony. 2nd ed. LC 91-29882. (Illus.). 56p. (gr. k-3). 1992. pap. 3.95 (*0-689-71608-7*, Aladdin) Macmillan Child Grp.
—Blaze & the Forest Fire: Billy & Blaze Spread the Alarm. 2nd ed. LC 91-26586. (Illus.). 56p. (gr. k-3). 1992. pap. 3.95 (*0-689-71605-2*, Aladdin) Macmillan Child Grp.
—Blaze & the Lost Quarry: Story & Pictures. Anderson, C. W., illus. LC 93-10721. 48p. (gr. k-3). 1994. pap. 3.95 (*0-689-71775-X*, Aladdin) Macmillan Child Grp.
—Blaze & the Mountain Lion: Billy & Blaze to the Rescue. Anderson, C. W., illus. LC 92-27148. 48p. (gr. k-3). 1993. pap. 3.95 (*0-689-71711-3*, Aladdin) Macmillan Child Grp.
Beales, Valerie. Emma & Freckles. Rogers, Jacqueline, illus. LC 91-20751. 208p. (gr. 5-9). 1992. pap. 13.00 jacketed, 3-pc. bdg. (*0-671-74686-3*, S&S BFYR) S&S Trade.
Campbell, John N. Gator: The Cowpony Goes to School. (Illus.). 72p. (gr. 4-7). 1990. 9.95 (*0-89015-699-9*, Pub. by Panda Bks) Sunbelt Media.
Cohen, Caron L. Mud Pony. (ps-3). pap. 19.95 (*0-590-72838-5*) Scholastic Inc.
Cooley, Regina F. The Magic Christmas Pony. Hansen, Han H., illus. LC 91-76342. 36p. (gr. 1-5). 1991. 19.95 (*1-880450-04-6*) Capstone Pub.
Crompton, Anne E. The Snow Pony. 128p. (gr. 4-6). 1991. 14.95 (*0-8050-1573-6*, Bks Young Read) H Holt & Co.
Doren, Marion. A Pony in the Field. 160p. (gr. 3-7). 1991. pap. 2.75 (*0-590-43663-5*, Apple Paperbacks) Scholastic Inc.
Fidler, Kathleen. Haki the Shetland Pony. 142p. (gr. 5-8). 1989. pap. 6.95 (*0-86241-075-4*, Pub. by Cnngt Pub Ltd) Trafalgar.
Hall, Lynn. The Mystery of Pony Hollow. Sanderson, Ruth, illus. LC 91-29861. 64p. (Orig.). (gr. 2-4). 1992. PLB 6.99 (*0-679-93052-3*); pap. 2.50 (*0-679-83052-9*) Random Bks Yng Read.
Hamilton, Dorothy. Cricket. Van Demark, Paul, illus. LC 74-30421. 80p. (gr. 3-7). 1975. pap. 3.95 (*0-8361-1761-1*) Herald Pr.

Henry, Marguerite. Sea Star: Orphan of Chincoteague. LC 49-11474. (Illus.). 176p. (gr. 3-7). 1991. SBE 13.95 (*0-02-743627-6*); pap. 3.95 (*0-689-71530-7*, Aladdin) Macmillan Child Grp.

Hol, Coby. Bela, Etoile du Cirque. Hol, Coby, illus. (FRE.). 32p. (gr. k-3). 1992. 14.95 (*3-314-20724-7*) North-South Bks NYC.

—Bela Wird Zirkuspony. Hol, Coby, illus. (GER.). 32p. (gr. k-3). 1992. 14.95 (*3-314-00533-4*) North-South Bks NYC.

Hurmence, Belinda. Dixie in the Big Pasture. LC 93-9983. (gr. 4 up). 1994. write for info. (*0-395-52002-9*, Clarion) HM.

Kalnay, Francis. Chucaro: Wild Pony of the Pampa. De Miskey, Julian, illus. 115p. 1993. pap. 6.95 (*0-8027-7387-7*) Walker & Co.

Kipling, Rudyard. The Maltese Cat. 1991. PLB 13.95 (*0-88682-475-3*) Creative Ed.

Kirkwood, James. There Must Be a Pony. 1989. pap. 4.50 (*0-440-20238-8*) Dell.

Kuchn, Nora A. Thunder, the Maverick Mustang. 96p. 1991. pap. 6.95 (*0-8163-0932-9*) Pacific Pr Pub Assn.

Penner, Fred & Oberman, Sheldon. Julie Gerond & the Polka Dot Pony. Pakarnyk, Alan, illus. 32p. (gr. 2-6). 1990. pap. 5.95 (*0-920534-70-8*, Pub. by Hyperion Pr Ltd CN) Sterling.

Springer, Nancy. The Great Pony Hassle. Duffy, Daniel M., illus. LC 92-34781. (gr. 3-7). 1993. 12.99 (*0-8037-1306-1*); PLB 13.89 (*0-8037-1308-8*) Dial Bks Young.

Steinbeck, John. The Red Pony. reissue ed. Dennis, Wesley, illus. (gr. 7 up). 1986. pap. 15.95 (*0-670-59184-X*) Viking Child Bks.

Sutton, Elizabeth H. The Pony Champions. LC 92-10518. 48p. (gr. 1-4). 1992. 13.95 (*1-56566-019-6*) Thomasson-Grant.

—Racing for Keeneland. LC 93-43385. (gr. 5-12). 1994. 14.95 (*1-56566-051-X*) Thomasson-Grant.

Ward, Lynd. Silver Pony. (ps-3). 1992. pap. 6.95 (*0-395-64377-5*) HM.

—The Silver Pony: A Story in Pictures. Ward, Lynd, illus. LC 72-5402. 192p. (gr. k-3). 1973. 17.95 (*0-395-14753-0*) HM.

Weber, Kathryn. Midnite & Mark. Hamilton, Sandi, illus. LC 83-8622. 64p. (Orig.). (gr. 4-6). 1983. pap. 3.95 (*0-88100-021-3*) Ranch House Pr.

PONTIAC, OTTAWA CHIEF, d. 1769

Fleischer, Jane. Pontiac, Chief of the Ottawas. LC 78-18050. (Illus.). 48p. (gr. 4-6). 1979. PLB 10.59 (*0-89375-156-1*); pap. 3.50 (*0-89375-146-4*) Troll Assocs.

Wheeler, Jill. The Story of Pontiac. Deegan, Paul, ed. Dodson, Liz, illus. LC 89-84910. 32p. (gr. 4). 1989. PLB 11.96 (*0-939179-69-5*) Abdo & Dghtrs.

Zadra, Dan. Indians of America: Pontiac. rev. ed. (gr. 2-4). 1987. PLB 14.95 (*0-88682-160-6*) Creative Ed.

PONY EXPRESS

DiCerto, Joseph J. The Pony Express: Hoofbeats in the Wilderness. LC 88-34548. (Illus.). 64p. (gr. 3-5). 1989. PLB 12.90 (*0-531-10751-5*) Watts.

Lake, A. L. Pony Express. (Illus.). 32p. (gr. 3-8). 1990. PLB 18.00 (*0-86625-368-8*); 13.50s.p. (*0-685-58648-0*) Rourke Corp.

Van der Linde, Laurel. The Pony Express. LC 92-31756. (Illus.). 72p. (gr. 6 up). 1993. text ed. 14.95 RSBE (*0-02-759056-9*, New Discovery) Macmillan Child Grp.

PONY EXPRESS–FICTION

Coerr, Eleanor. Buffalo Bill & the Pony Express. Bolognese, Don, illus. LC 93-24261. 1995. 14.00 (*0-06-023372-9*); PLB 13.89 (*0-06-023373-7*) HarpC Child Bks.

Fontes, Ron & Korman, Justine. Wild Bill Hickok & the Rebel Raiders. Shaw, Charlie & Bill Smith Studios Staff, illus. LC 92-56159. 80p. (Orig.). (gr. 1-4). 1993. PLB 12.89 (*1-56282-494-5*); pap. 3.50 (*1-56282-493-7*) Disney Pr.

Gould, Arlen. Pony Express. Date not set. write for info. (*0-517-59825-6*); PLB write for info. (*0-517-59826-4*) Crown Pub Group.

Gregory, Kristiana. Jimmy Spoon & the Pony Express. LC 93-47420. (gr. 4-7). 1994. 13.95 (*0-590-46577-5*) Scholastic Inc.

POODLES

Moncure, Jane B. Mr. Doodle Had a Poodle. Hohag, Linda, illus. LC 87-15808. (SPA & ENG.). 32p. (ps-2). 1987. PLB 14.95 (*0-89565-409-1*) Childs World.

POPES

Daughters of St. Paul. Karol from Poland. (gr. 4-9). Date not set. write for info. St Paul Bks.

—No Place for Defeat. (gr. 3-9). 1987. 2.00 (*0-8198-5100-0*) St Paul Bks.

Sullivan, George. Pope John Paul II: The People's Pope. LC 83-40395. (Illus.). 120p. (gr. 7 up). 1984. 11.95 (*0-8027-6523-8*) Walker & Co.

Walch, Timothy. John Paul Second. (Illus.). (gr. 5 up). 1990. 17.95 (*1-55546-839-X*) Chelsea Hse.

POPULAR GOVERNMENT

see Democracy

POPULAR MUSIC

see Music, Popular (Songs, etc.)

POPULARITY

Nardo, Don. Population. LC 90-23525. (Illus.). 112p. (gr. 5-8). 1991. PLB 14.95 (*1-56006-123-5*) Lucent Bks.

POPULATION

see also Birth Control

also names of countries, cities, etc. with the subdivision Population, e.g. U. S.–Population

Aaseng, Nathan. Overpopulation: Crisis or Challenge? LC 90-13121. (Illus.). 160p. (gr. 9-12). 1991. PLB 13.90 (*0-531-11006-0*) Watts.

Becklake, John. Population Explosion. LC 89-81595. 1990. PLB 12.90 (*0-531-17198-1*, Gloucester Pr) Watts.

Blashfield, Jean F. & Black, Wallace B. Too Many People? LC 91-34603. 128p. (gr. 4-8). 1992. PLB 20.55 (*0-516-05513-5*) Childrens.

Gallant, Roy A. The Peopling of Planet Earth: Human Population Growth Through the Ages. LC 89-34575. (Illus.). 128p. (gr. 3-7). 1990. SBE 15.95 (*0-02-735772-4*, Macmillan Child Bk) Macmillan Child Grp.

Hoff, Mary & Rodgers, Mary M. Our Endangered Planet: Population Growth. (Illus.). 64p. 1991. PLB 21.50 (*0-8225-2502-X*) Lerner Pubns.

Lambert, David. The World's Population. LC 93-716. (Illus.). 32p. (gr. 4-6). 1993. 14.95 (*1-56847-050-9*) Thomson Lrning.

Leggett, Dennis. People Trap. LC 90-46400. (Illus.). 48p. (gr. 5-9). 1991. PLB 12.95 (*1-85435-378-0*) Marshall Cavendish.

McGraw, Eric. Population Growth. (Illus.). 48p. (gr. 5 up). 1987. Set. PLB 18.60 (*0-317-60380-9*); 13.95s.p. (*0-86592-276-4*) Rourke Corp.

Morris, Scott, ed. Populations of the World. De Blij, Harm J., intro. by. LC 92-22283. (Illus.). 1993. 15.95 (*0-7910-1805-9*, Am Art Analog) Chelsea Hse.

Newton, David E. Population: Too Many People? LC 92-14306. (Illus.). 128p. (gr. 6 up). 1992. lib. bdg. 18.95 (*0-89490-295-4*) Enslow Pubs.

Stefoff, Rebecca. Overpopulation. (Illus.). (gr. 5 up). 1992. lib. bdg. 19.95 (*0-7910-1581-5*); pap. write for info. (*0-7910-1606-4*) Chelsea Hse.

Wheeler, Jill C. The People We Live With. Kallen, Stuart A., ed. LC 91-73067. 1991. 12.94 (*1-56239-034-1*) Abdo & Dghtrs.

POPULATION, FOREIGN

see Immigration and Emigration

PORCELAIN

Perret, Annick. Painting on Porcelain: Traditional & Contemporary Design. (Illus.). 96p. (Orig.). 1994. pap. 22.50 (*0-85532-766-9*, Pub. by Search Pr UK) A Schwartz & Co.

PORCELAIN ENAMELS

see Enamel and Enameling

PORCUPINES

Dalmais. Porcupine, Reading Level 3-4. (Illus.). 28p. (gr. 2-5). 1983. PLB 16.67 (*0-86592-852-5*); 12.50 (*0-685-58824-6*) Rourke Corp.

Murray, Peter. Porcupines. LC 93-22833. (Illus.). (gr. 2-6). 1993. 15.95 (*1-56766-019-3*) Childs World.

Sherrow, Victoria. The Porcupine. LC 90-3278. (Illus.). 60p. (gr. 3 up). 1991. text ed. 13.95 RSBE (*0-87518-442-1*, Dillon) Macmillan Child Grp.

PORCUPINES–FICTION

Christian, Mary B. Penrod's Pants. Dyer, Jane, illus. LC 85-11545. 56p. (gr. 1-4). 1986. RSBE 11.95 (*0-02-718520-6*, Macmillan Child Bk) Macmillan Child Grp.

—Penrod's Pants. LC 89-32228. (Illus.). 56p. (gr. 1-4). 1989. pap. 3.95 (*0-689-71340-1*, Aladdin) Macmillan Child Grp.

Greenleaf, E. Pricky, a Pet Porcupine. LC 65-22311. (Illus.). 48p. (gr. 2-5). 1968. PLB 10.95 (*0-87783-031-2*); pap. 3.94 deluxe ed. (*0-87783-158-0*) Oddo.

Harshman, Terry W. Porcupine's Pajama Party. Cushman, Doug, illus. LC 87-45681. 64p. (gr. k-3). 1990. pap. 3.50 (*0-06-444140-7*, Trophy) HarpC Child Bks.

Lester, Helen. A Porcupine Named Fluffy. LC 85-24820. 32p. (ps-3). 1989. 14.95 (*0-395-36895-2*); pap. 5.95 (*0-395-52018-5*) HM.

Lies, Brian. Hamlet & the Enormous Chinese Dragon Kite. LC 93-30726. 1994. 14.95 (*0-395-68391-2*) HM.

Morgan, Mary. Benjamin's Bugs. Morgan, Mary, illus. LC 93-22911. 44p. (ps-1). 1994. RSBE 12.95 (*0-02-767450-9*, Bradbury Pr) Macmillan Child Grp.

Thompson-Hoffman, Susan. Little Porcupine's Winter Den. Thomas, Peter, narrated by. Haberstock, Jennifer, illus. LC 92-14295. 32p. (ps-3). 1992. 11.95 (*0-924483-64-4*); incl. audiocass. tape 16.95 (*0-924483-63-6*); incl. audiocass. tape & 9" stuffed porcupine toy 39.95 (*0-924483-62-8*); incl. audiocass. tape & 7 inch stuffed porcupine toy 25.95 (*0-924483-71-7*); write for info. audiocass. tape (*0-924483-73-3*) Soundprints.

Van De Wetering, Janwillem. Hugh Pine & the Good Place. Munsinger, Lynn, illus. LC 86-3108. 80p. (gr. 3 up). 1986. 13.95 (*0-395-40147-X*) HM.

PORPOISES

Carwardine, Mark. Whales, Dolphins, & Porpoises. LC 92-7624. (Illus.). 64p. (gr. 3 up). 1992. 11.95 (*1-56458-144-6*) Dorling Kindersley.

Gordon, Sharon. Dolphins & Porpoises. Goldsborough, June, illus. LC 84-8594. 32p. (gr. k-2). 1985. PLB 11.59 (*0-8167-0340-X*); pap. text ed. 2.95 (*0-8167-0443-0*) Troll Assocs.

Hatherly, Janelle & Nicholls, Delia. Dolphins & Porpoises. 72p. 1990. 17.95 (*0-8160-2272-0*) Facts on File.

Hoyt, Erich. Riding with the Dolphins: The Equinox Guide to Dolphins & Porpoises. Folkens, Pieter, illus. 64p. (gr. 5 up). 1992. PLB 17.95 (*0-921820-55-0*, Pub. by Camden Hse CN); pap. 9.95 (*0-921820-57-7*, Pub. by Camden Hse CN) Firefly Bks Ltd.

Patent, Dorothy H. Dolphins & Porpoises. LC 87-45332. (Illus.). 96p. (gr. 4 up). 1987. reinforced bdg. 15.95 (*0-8234-0663-6*) Holiday.

—Looking at Dolphins & Porpoises. LC 88-39985. (Illus.). 48p. (ps-4). 1989. reinforced bdg. 13.95 (*0-8234-0748-9*) Holiday.

Schneider, Jeff. My Friend the Porpoise: An Ocean Magic Book. Spoon, Wilfred, illus. LC 90-61572. 12p. (ps). 1991. 4.95g (*1-877779-07-5*) Schneider Educational.

Smith, Roland. Whales, Dolphins, & Porpoises in the Zoo. Munoz, William, photos by. LC 93-35425. (Illus.). 64p. (gr. 3-6). 1994. PLB 14.40 (*1-56294-318-9*) Millbrook Pr.

PORPOISES–FICTION

Dominick, Bayard. Joe, a Porpoise. (Illus.). (gr. 3-5). 1968. 10.95 (*0-8392-3067-2*) Astor-Honor.

Sargent, Dave & Sargent, Pat. Peggy Porcupine. Sapaugh, Blaine, illus. 48p. (Orig.). (gr. k-8). 1993. text ed. 11.95 (*1-56763-044-8*); pap. text ed. 5.95 (*1-56763-045-6*) Ozark Pub.

POST OFFICE

see Postal Service

PORTRAIT PAINTING

see also Crayon Drawing; Pastel Drawing

PORTRAITS

see also Cartoons and Caricatures

Yee, Kal. Perfect Face. 96p. 1994. 45.00 (*0-9631574-1-8*) Sec Glance.

PORTS

see Harbors

PORTUGAL

Cross, Esther & Cross, Wilbur. Portugal. LC 85-26991. (Illus.). 127p. (gr. 5-6). 1986. PLB 20.55 (*0-516-02778-6*) Childrens.

Moore, Richard. Portugal. LC 91-26998. (Illus.). 96p. (gr. 6-12). 1992. PLB 22.80 (*0-8114-2451-0*) Raintree Steck-V.

PORTUGAL–FICTION

L'Engle, Madeleine. The Arm of the Starfish. LC 65-10919. 256p. (gr. 7 up). 1965. 18.00 (*0-374-30396-7*) FS&G.

PORTUGUESE LANGUAGE

Goodman, Marlene, illus. Let's Learn Portuguese Picture Dictionary: Elementary. (POR.). 72p. (gr. 4-7). 1993. 11.95 (*0-8442-4699-9*, Natl Textbk) NTC Pub Grp.

POSSUM

see Opossums

POSTAGE STAMPS

Benanti, Carol. World Stamps. (Illus.). 48p. (gr. 3 up). 1994. pap. 10.00 (*0-679-85070-8*) Random Bks Yng Read.

Boy Scouts of America. Stamp Collecting. (Illus.). 48p. (gr. 6-12). 1974. pap. 1.85 (*0-8395-3359-4*, 33296) BSA.

Editorial America, S. A., Staff. Manual Del Filatelista. Del Real, Maria E., ed. (SPA., Illus.). 256p. (Orig.). 1990. pap. 4.95 (*0-944499-51-1*) Editorial Amer.

Frank, Mike. Young Stamp Collector. Benanti, Carol, ed. 48p. (Orig.). (gr. 3-7). 1991. pap. 2.95 (*1-880592-00-2*) Pace Prods.

Hinceman, Glenn, ed. The Junior All American Stamp Album. (Illus.). 80p. (Orig.). (gr. 3-9). 1993. pap. 12.95 (*0-912236-13-2*, Minkus Pubns) Novus Debut.

—The Junior All American Stamp Kit. (Illus.). (gr. 3-9). 1993. boxed 15.95 (*0-912236-31-0*, Minkus Pubns) Novus Debut.

Jacobsen, Karen. Stamps. LC 83-7591. (Illus.). 48p. (gr. k-4). 1983. PLB 12.85 (*0-516-01709-8*) Childrens.

Lewis, Brenda R. Stamps! A Young Collector's Guide. (Illus.). 96p. (gr. 5-9). 1991. 15.00 (*0-525-67341-5*, Lodestar Bks) Dutton Child Bks.

Macdonald, David S., ed. U. S. Liberty Album. (Illus.). 416p. (gr. 6 up). 1984. text ed. 18.95 (*0-937458-29-5*) Harris & Co.

My First Stamp Album Starter Kit. (Orig.). (gr. 3-9). 1988. pap. 9.95 (*0-912236-26-4*, Minkus Pubns) Novus Debut.

Schwarz, Ted. The Beginner's Guide to Stamp Collecting. 192p. (gr. 12 up). 1983. P-H Gen Ref & Trav.

POSTAL SERVICE

see also Pony Express

Barklow, Irene. The Old & the New: History of the Post Offices of Wallowa County. (Illus.). 184p. (Orig.). (gr. 8 up). 1987. pap. 11.95 (*0-9618185-1-4*) Enchant Pub Oregon.

Berger, Melvin & Berger, Gilda. Where Does the Mail Go? A Book about the Postal System. Brittingham, Geoffrey H., illus. LC 94-6254. 1994. lib. bdg. 12.00 (*1-57102-022-5*, Ideals Child); pap. 4.50 (*1-57102-006-3*, Ideals Child) Hambleton-Hill.

Bolger, William F., intro. by. All about Letters. Rev. ed. LC 82-600601. (Illus.). 64p. (gr. 9-12). 1982. pap. 2.50x (*0-685-06202-3*, 01135) USPS.

—P. S. Write Soon! All about Letters. LC 82-600641. (Illus.). 64p. (Orig.). (gr. 4-8). 1982. pap. 2.50x (*0-8141-3796-2*, 37962) USPS.

Bolick, Nancy O. Mail Call! The History of the U.S. Mail Service. LC 94-49. 1994. write for info. (*0-531-20170-8*) Watts.

Gibbons, Gail. The Post Office Book: Mail & How It Moves. Gibbons, Gail, illus. LC 85-45397. 32p. (gr. k-4). 1986. pap. 4.95 (*0-06-446029-0*, Trophy) HarpC Child Bks.

Johnson, Jean. Postal Workers: A to Z. (Illus.). 48p. (gr. 1-3). 1987. 11.95 (*0-8027-6663-3*); PLB 12.85 (*0-8027-6664-1*) Walker & Co.

Matthews, Morgan. What's It Like to Be a Postal Worker. Hicks, Mark A., illus. LC 89-34385. 32p. (gr. k-3). 1990. lib. bdg. 10.89 (*0-8167-1813-X*); pap. text ed. 2.95 (*0-8167-1814-8*) Troll Assocs.

Miller, Robert H. The Story of "Stagecoach" Mary Fields. Hanna, Cheryl, illus. LC 93-46286. 1994. write for info. (*0-382-24394-3*) Silver.

Ziegler, Sandra. A Visit to the Post Office. Holmes, Dave, photos by. LC 89-35061. 32p. (ps-3). 1989. PLB 11.45 (*0-516-01487-0*); pap. 3.95 (*0-516-41487-9*) Childrens.

POSTAL SERVICE–FICTION

Ahlberg, Janet & Ahlberg, Allan. Jolly Christmas Postman. (Illus.). 1991. 17.95 (*0-316-02033-8*) Little.

—The Jolly Postman. Ahlberg, Janet & Ahlberg, Allan, illus. 32p. (gr. k-3). 1986. 16.95 (*0-316-02036-2*) Little.

Anderson, Honey & Reinholdt, Bill. Getting the Mail. Fleming, Leanne, illus. LC 92-34338. 1993. 3.75 (*0-383-03624-0*) SRA Schl Grp.

Boelts, Maribeth. Grace & Joe. Tucker, Kathy, ed. Gourbalt, Martine, illus. LC 93-45920. 32p. (ps-1). 1994. PLB 13.95 (*0-8075-3019-0*) A Whitman.

Corbett. The Mailbox Trick. 1993. pap. 2.75 (*0-590-42750-4*) Scholastic Inc.

Cunliffe, John. Postman Pat & the Mystery Thief. (ps-5). 1993. pap. 2.50 (*0-590-47099-X*) Scholastic Inc.

—Postman Pat to the Rescue. (ps-5). 1993. pap. 2.50 (*0-590-47098-1*) Scholastic Inc.

Enderle, Judith R. & Tessler, Stephanie G. Dear Timothy Tibbitts. Ewing, Carolyn, illus. LC 94-14412. 1995. 13. 95 (*0-02-733384-1*) Macmillan.

Farrell, Sue. To the Post Office with Mama. Lewis, Robin B., illus. 24p. (ps-1). 1994. 14.95 (*1-55037-359-5*, Pub. by Annick CN); pap. 4.95 (*1-55037-358-7*, Pub. by Annick CN) Firefly Bks Ltd.

Gibbons, Gail. The Post Office Book. Gibbons, Gail, illus. LC 81-43888. 32p. (gr. k-3). 1982. (Crowell Jr Bks); PLB 14.89 (*0-690-04199-3*) HarpC Child Bks.

Gormley, Beatrice. Mail-Order Wings. McCully, Emily A., illus. 164p. (gr. 3-7). 1984. pap. 2.95 (*0-380-67421-1*, Camelot) Avon.

Marshak, Samuel. Hail to Mail. Pevear, Richard, tr. from RUS. Radunsky, Vladimir, illus. LC 89-7605. 32p. (ps-2). 1990. 14.95 (*0-8050-1132-3*, Bks Young Read) H Holt & Co.

Maury, Inez. My Mother the Mail Carrier - Mi Mama la Cartera. Alemany, Norah, tr. McCrady, Lady, illus. LC 76-14275. (ENG & SPA.). 32p. (Orig.). (gr. k-4). 1976. pap. 7.95 (*0-935312-23-4*) Feminist Pr.

Pollak, Felix. The Castle & the Flaw. 1963. pap. 4.00 (*0-685-01010-4*) Elizabeth Pr.

Rylant, Cynthia. Mr. Griggs' Work. Downing, Julie, illus. LC 88-1484. 32p. (ps-2). 1993. pap. 5.95 (*0-531-07037-9*) Orchard Bks Watts.

Scott, Ann H. Hi! Coalson, Glo, illus. 32p. (ps-3). 1994. 14.95 (*0-399-21964-1*, Philomel) Putnam Pub Group.

Shulevitz, Uri. Toddlecreek Post Office. (Illus.). 32p. 1990. 14.95 (*0-374-37635-2*) FS&G.

Skurzynski, Gloria. Here Comes the Mail. LC 91-40454. (Illus.). 32p. (ps-3). 1992. RSBE 13.95 (*0-02-782916-2*, Bradbury Pr) Macmillan Child Grp.

Taylor, Linda L. The Lettuce Leaf Birthday Letter. Durrell, Julie, illus. LC 93-16906. 1994. 13.99 (*0-8037-1454-8*); PLB 13.89 (*0-8037-1455-6*) Dial Bks Young.

POSTERS

see also Signs and Signboards

Droscher, Elke. The Victorian Sticker Postcard Book. (Illus.). 64p. (Orig.). pap. 7.95 (*0-89471-384-1*) Running Pr.

POTTER, BEATRIX, 1866-1943

Aldis, Dorothy. Nothing Is Impossible - The Story of Beatrix Potter. Cuffari, Richard, illus. (gr. 4-6). 1988. 18.75 (*0-8446-6359-X*) Peter Smith.

Buchan, Elizabeth. Beatrix Potter. 64p. 1991. 10.95 (*0-7232-3780-8*) Warne.

Collins, David R. The Country Artist: A Story about Beatrix Potter. Wilken, Mark, illus. 56p. (gr. 3-6). 1989. 14.95 (*0-87614-344-3*); pap. 5.95 (*0-87614-509-8*) Carolrhoda Bks.

Durwood, Peter. Beatrix Potter: Peter Rabbit's Creator. Cundiff, L. L., illus. Stickney-Bailey, Susan, frwd. by. (Illus.). 48p. (gr. 5-8). 1988. Kipling Pr.

Taylor, Judy. Beatrix Potter: Artist, Storyteller & Countrywoman. (Illus.). 224p. (gr. 9 up). 1987. 24.95 (*0-7232-3314-4*) Warne.

Taylor, Judy, ed. So I Shall Tell You a Story: The Magic World of Beatrix Potter. Potter, Beatrix, illus. Sendak, Maurice, et al. (Illus.). 224p. 1993. 24.95 (*0-7232-4025-6*) Warne.

Taylor, Judy, et al. Beatrix Potter, 1866-1943: The Artist & Her World. 244p. (gr. 9 up). 1988. pap. 19.95 (*0-7232-3561-9*) Warne.

POTTERY

see also Porcelain

Anderson, Peter. Maria Martinez: Pueblo Potter. LC 92-4807. (Illus.). 32p. (gr. 2-5). 1993. pap. 3.95 (*0-516-44184-1*) Childrens.

Caselli, Giovanni. A Greek Potter. Caselli, Giovanni, illus. LC 85-30637. 32p. (gr. 3-6). 1991. lib. bdg. 12.95 (*0-87226-101-8*) P Bedrick Bks.

Dixon, Annabelle. Clay. Stefoff, Rebecca, ed. Barber, Ed, photos by. LC 90-40369. (Illus.). 22p. (gr. 3-5). 1990. PLB 15.93 (*0-944483-69-0*) Garrett Ed Corp.

Florian, Douglas. A Potter. LC 90-33940. (Illus.). 24p. (ps up). 1991. 13.95 (*0-688-10100-3*); PLB 13.88 (*0-688-10101-1*) Greenwillow.

Gonen, Rivka. Fired Up! How Ancient Pottery Was Made. LC 92-41748. 1993. PLB 22.95 (*0-8225-3202-6*, Runestone Pr) Lerner Pubns.

Leach, Bernard. Potter's Book. 1946. pap. 14.00 (*0-693-01157-2*) Transatl Arts.

Morgan, Judith. An Art Text-Workbook: Ceramics (Introduction) Wallace, Dorathye, ed. (Illus.). 123p. (gr. 8-10). 1990. pap. 13.27 (*0-914127-24-1*); tchr's. ed. avail. Univ Class.

Potter, T. Pottery. (Illus.). 48p. (gr. 6 up). 1986. PLB 14. 96 (*0-88110-319-5*); pap. 7.95 (*0-86020-944-X*) EDC.

Pottery. (Illus.). 64p. (gr. 6-12). 1969. pap. 1.85 (*0-8395-3314-4*, 33314) BSA.

Roussel, Mike. Clay. (Illus.). 32p. (gr. 2-6). 1990. lib. bdg. 15.94 (*0-86592-485-6*); lib. bdg. 11.95s.p. (*0-685-36301-5*) Rourke Corp.

Swentzell, Rina. Children of Clay: A Family of Pueblo Potters: We Are Still Here. (gr. 4-7). 1993. pap. 6.95 (*0-8225-9627-X*) Lerner Pubns.

POTTERY–FICTION

Baylor, Byrd. When Clay Sings. Bahti, Tom, illus. LC 70-180758. (gr. 1-5). 1981. (Scribner) Macmillan.

Pascal, Francine. The Missing Tea Set. (gr. 1-3). 1993. pap. 2.99 (*0-553-48015-4*) Bantam.

POULTRY

see also names of domesticated birds, e.g. Ducks; Geese; Turkeys, etc.

Back, Christine. Chicken & Egg. LC 86-10019. (Illus.). 25p. (gr. k-4). 1991. 5.95 (*0-382-09292-9*); PLB 7.95 (*0-382-09284-8*); pap. 3.95 (*0-382-09959-1*) Silver Burdett.

Bantam Staff. Chick: Baby Animal. (ps). 1994. 4.99 (*0-553-09548-X*) Bantam.

Coldrey, Jennifer. Chicken on the Farm. LC 86-5716. (Illus.). 32p. (gr. 4-6). 1986. PLB 17.27 (*1-55532-067-8*) Gareth Stevens Inc.

Ensminger, M. E. Poultry Science. 3rd ed. (Illus.). (gr. 9-12). 1992. 59.95 (*0-8134-2929-3*, 2087); text ed. 44.95 (*0-685-51895-7*) Interstate.

Hariton, Anca. Egg Story. LC 91-34588. (Illus.). 24p. (gr. k-2). 1992. 12.00 (*0-525-44861-6*, DCB) Dutton Child Bks.

Royston, Angela. Hen. (ps-3). 1990. PLB 10.90 (*0-531-19079-X*, Warwick) Watts.

Selsam, Millicent E. Egg to Chick. rev. ed. Wolff, Barbara, illus. LC 74-85034. 64p. (ps-3). 1970. PLB 13.89 (*0-06-025290-1*) HarpC Child Bks.

—Egg to Chick. Wolff, Barbara, illus. LC 74-85034. 64p. (gr. k-3). 1987. pap. 3.50 (*0-06-444113-X*, Trophy) HarpC Child Bks.

Stone, L. Pollos (Chickens) 1991. 8.95s.p. (*0-86592-949-1*) Rourke Enter.

Stone, Lynn. Chickens. (Illus.). 24p. (gr. k-5). 1990. lib. bdg. 11.94 (*0-86593-034-1*); lib. bdg. 8.95s.p. (*0-685-36308-2*) Rourke Corp.

POULTRY–FICTION

Alexander, Linda. Job Well Done. Petie, Haris, illus. (gr. 1-4). PLB 7.19 (*0-8313-0002-7*) Lantern.

Benchley, Nathaniel. Strange Disappearance of Arthur Cluck. Lobel, Arnold, illus. LC 67-4151. 64p. (gr. k-3). 1967. PLB 13.89 (*0-06-020478-8*) HarpC Child Bks.

POVERTY

see also names of countries with the subdivision Economic Conditions and Social Conditions e.g. U. S. –Economic Conditions; U. S.–Social Conditions

Barrett, John M. It's Hard Not to Worry: Stories for Children about Poverty. (Illus., Orig.). (gr. 1-6). 1988. pap. 4.75 (*0-377-00178-3*) Friendship Pr.

Coil, Suzanne M. The Poor in America. Steltenpohl, Jane, ed. (Illus.). 136p. (gr. 7-10). 1989. lib. bdg. 13.98 (*0-671-69052-3*, J Messner) S&S Trade.

Dando, William A. & Dando, Caroline Z. A Reference Guide to World Hunger. LC 91-10733. 112p. (gr. 6 up). 1991. lib. bdg. 17.95 (*0-89490-326-8*) Enslow Pubs.

Davis, Bertha. Poverty in America: What We Do About It. (Illus.). 144p. (gr. 9-12). 1991. PLB 13.90 (*0-531-13016-9*) Watts.

Jenkins, Curtis J. Homeless: Thirty Days Undercover in America's Exploding Subculture. LC 93-87205. 248p. (Orig.). (gr. 9-12). 1994. pap. 14.95 (*0-9639331-0-8*) Selah Pubng.

Kosof, Anna. Homeless in America. Kline, Marjory, ed. (Illus.). 96p. (gr. 7-12). 1988. PLB 13.40 (*0-531-10519-9*) Watts.

O'Neill, Terry. The Homeless: Distinguishing Between Fact & Opinion. LC 90-45283. (Illus.). 32p. (gr. 3-6). 1990. PLB 10.95 (*0-89908-605-5*) Greenhaven.

Orr, Lisa, ed. The Homeless: Opposing Viewpoints. LC 89-25734. (Illus.). 216p. (gr. 10 up). 1990. lib. bdg. 17. 95 (*0-89908-476-1*); pap. text ed. 9.95 (*0-89908-451-6*) Greenhaven.

O'Sullivan, Carol. Poverty: Locating the Authors Main Idea. LC 89-17069. (Illus.). 32p. (gr. 3-6). 1990. PLB 10.95 (*0-89908-641-1*) Greenhaven.

The Poor in America. (Illus.). 128p. (gr. 7-10). 1989. 11. 96 (*0-382-09578-2*, J Messner) S&S Trade.

Spencer, William. The Challenge of World Hunger. LC 90-49430. (Illus.). 64p. (gr. 6 up). 1991. lib. bdg. 15.95 (*0-89490-283-0*) Enslow Pubs.

Woods, Daniel W. Poverty in the U. S. Problems & Policies. LC 87-25246. 1992. PLB 14.85 (*0-8027-6764-8*); pap. 5.95 (*0-8027-6765-6*) Walker & Co.

POVERTY–FICTION

Burnett, Frances H. A Little Princess. 1990. pap. 3.50 (*0-440-40386-3*, Pub. by Yearling Classics) Dell.

—A Little Princess. Dubowski, Cathy E., ed. LC 93-14000. 1994. 2.99 (*0-679-85090-2*) Random.

Kallstrom, Theresa. Lyndy. York, Sherri, ed. Iarsen, Barbara, illus. LC 87-50259. 44p. (Orig.). (gr. 3 up). 1987. pap. 3.95 (*1-55523-081-4*) Winston-Derek.

McGuigan, Mary A. Cloud Dancer. LC 93-5562. 128p. (gr. 6-8). 1994. SBE 14.95 (*0-684-19632-8*, Scribners Young Read) Macmillan Child Grp.

Meltzer, Milton. Poverty in America. LC 85-31963. 128p. (gr. 7 up). 1986. 12.95 (*0-688-05911-2*) Morrow Jr Bks.

Waters, Mary. The Little Red Blanket. LC 93-61157. (Illus.). 40p. (ps-3). 1993. PLB 6.95 (*0-9638123-0-0*) WAI Pubng.

POWER (MECHANICS)

see also Electric Power; Force and Energy; Machinery; Water Power

Jennings, Terry. Energy Exists? LC 94-20027. 1995. write for info. (*0-8114-3881-3*) Raintree Steck-V.

Neal, Philip. Energy, Power Sources & Electricity. (Illus.). 48p. (gr. 6-9). 1989. 19.95 (*0-85219-776-4*, Pub. by Batsford UK) Trafalgar.

POWER BOATS

see Motorboats

POWER RESOURCES

see also Electric Power; Fuel; Solar Energy; Water Power

Ardley, Neil. Science Book of Energy. (gr. 4-7). 1992. 9.95 (*0-15-200611-7*, HB Juv Bks) HarBrace.

Asimov, Isaac. How Did We Find Out about Solar Power? Wool, David, illus. 64p. (gr. 4-7). 1983. PLB 12.85 (*0-8027-6423-1*) Walker & Co.

Bailey, Donna. Energy All Around Us. LC 90-39294. (Illus.). 48p. (gr. 2-6). 1990. PLB 19.97 (*0-8114-2520-7*) Raintree Steck-V.

Baker, Susan. First Look at Using Energy. LC 91-2372. (Illus.). 32p. (gr. 1-2). 1991. PLB 17.27 (*0-8368-0680-8*) Gareth Stevens Inc.

Brown, Warren. Alternative Sources of Energy. LC 93-7470. (Illus.). 112p. (gr. 5 up). 1993. PLB 19.95 (*0-7910-1588-2*); pap. write for info. (*0-7910-1613-7*) Chelsea Hse.

Carless, Jennifer. Renewable Energy: A Concise Guide to Green Alternatives. LC 92-35137. 224p. 1993. 19.95 (*0-8027-8214-0*) Walker & Co.

Catherall, Ed. Exploring Energy Sources. LC 90-21764. (Illus.). 48p. (gr. 4-8). 1991. PLB 22.80 (*0-8114-2597-5*) Raintree Steck-V.

Challoner, Jack. Energy. LC 92-54479. (Illus.). 64p. (gr. 7 up). 1993. 15.95 (*1-56458-232-9*) Dorling Kindersley.

Collinson, Alan. Renewable Energy. LC 90-19791. (Illus.). 48p. (gr. 5-8). 1991. PLB 22.80 (*0-8114-2802-8*) Raintree Steck-V.

Condon, Judith. Energy. LC 92-32911. Date not set. write for info. (*0-531-14252-3*) Watts.

Diener, Carolyn S., et al. Energy: A Curriculum Unit for Three, Four & Five Year Olds. LC 81-83050. (Illus.). 112p. (ps-k). 1982. pap. 9.95 (*0-89334-069-3*) Humanics Ltd.

Gibson, Michael. The Energy Crisis. (Illus.). 48p. (gr. 5 up). 1987. PLB 18.60 (*0-86592-277-2*); 13.95 (*0-685-67573-4*) Rourke Corp.

Godman, Arthur. Energy Supply A-Z. LC 90-34909. 144p. (gr. 6 up). 1991. lib. bdg. 18.95 (*0-89490-262-8*) Enslow Pubs.

Haines, Gail B. The Challenge of Supplying Energy. LC 89-28498. (Illus.). 64p. (gr. 6 up). 1991. lib. bdg. 15.95 (*0-89490-269-5*) Enslow Pubs.

Hawkes, Nigel. Energy. (Illus.). 32p. (gr. 5-8). PLB 13.95 (*0-8050-3419-6*) TFC Bks NY.

Herda, D. J. & Madden, Margaret L. Energy Resources: Towards a Renewable Future. LC 91-3034. (Illus.). 144p. (gr. 9-12). 1991. PLB 13.90 (*0-531-11005-2*) Watts.

Houghton, Graham & Rickard, Graham. Alternative Energy, 5 vols. (Illus.). 32p. (gr. 4-6). 1991. Set. PLB 86.35 (*0-8368-0712-X*) Gareth Stevens Inc.

Jennings, Terry. Energy. LC 88-36214. (Illus.). 32p. (gr. 3-6). 1989. pap. 4.95 (*0-516-48438-9*) Childrens.

—Energy Exists? LC 94-20027. 1995. write for info. (*0-8114-3881-3*) Raintree Steck-V.

Jones, Norma, et al, eds. Energy: Is There Enough? 76p. 1992. pap. text ed. 12.95 (*1-878623-35-4*) Info Plus TX.

Kerrod, Robin. Energy Resources. LC 93-34611. (Illus.). 32p. (gr. 4-7). 1994. 14.95 (*1-56847-107-6*) Thomson Lrning.

Knowledge Unlimited Staff. Energy: Conserving a Vital Resource. (Illus.). 19p. (Orig.). (gr. 4-12). 1984. tchr's guide 13.00 (*0-915291-22-3*) Know Unltd.

Lambert, Mark. Energy Technology. LC 90-27544. (Illus.). 48p. (gr. 5-7). 1991. 12.90 (*0-531-18457-9*, Pub. by Bookwright Pr) Watts.

Mason, John. Power Station Sun: The Story of Energy. (Illus.). 48p. (gr. 1-4). 1987. 12.95x (*0-8160-1778-6*) Facts on File.

Morgan, Sally & Morgan, Adrian. Using Energy. LC 93-20407. (gr. 4 up). 1993. write for info. (*0-8160-2984-9*) Facts on File.

Pack, Janet. Fueling the Future. LC 91-34602. 128p. (gr. 4-8). 1992. PLB 20.55 (*0-516-05512-7*) Childrens.

Pifer, Joanne. EarthWise: Earth's Energy. (Illus.). 48p. (gr. 5-8). 1993. pap. text ed. 7.95 (*0-9633019-3-4*) WP Pr.

Podendorf, Illa. Energy. LC 81-12309. (Illus.). 48p. (gr. k-4). 1982. PLB 12.85 (*0-516-01625-3*) Childrens.

Polesetsky, Matthew & Cozic, Charles, eds. Energy Alternatives. LC 91-24387. 200p. (gr. 10 up). 1991. PLB 16.95 (*0-89908-577-6*); pap. text ed. 9.95 (*0-89908-583-0*) Greenhaven.

Rising, Trudy & Williams, Peter. Light Magic: And Other Science Activities about Energy. Kurisu, Jane, illus. 64p. (gr. 3-7). 1994. PLB 16.95 (*1-895688-15-9*, Pub. by Greey dePencier CN); pap. 9.95 (*1-895688-16-7*, Pub. by Greey dePencier CN) Firefly Bks Ltd.

Rowe, Julian & Perham, Molly. Using Energy. LC 94-13911. (Illus.). 32p. (gr. 1-4). 1994. PLB 18.60 (*0-516-08140-3*); pap. 4.95 (*0-516-48140-1*) Childrens.

Snyder, Thomas F. Energy Searchbook. Cullinan, Dorothy K., illus. Snyder, Thomas F., intro. by. 56p. (gr. 4-12). 1982. pap. text ed. 8.08 (*0-07-059472-4*) McGraw.

Spence, Margaret. Fossil Fuels. LC 92-33919. (Illus.). (gr. k-4). 1993. PLB 11.90 (*0-531-17394-1*, Gloucester Pr) Watts.

—Solar Power. LC 92-33920. (Illus.). 32p. (gr. k-4). 1993. PLB 11.90 (*0-531-17378-X*, Gloucester Pr) Watts.

Taylor, Barbara. Energy & Power. LC 90-31032. (Illus.). 32p. (gr. 5-8). 1990. PLB 12.40 (*0-531-14080-6*) Watts.

Twist, Clint. Future Sources. LC 92-33918. (Illus.). 32p. (gr. k-4). 1993. PLB 11.90 (*0-531-17395-X*, Gloucester Pr) Watts.

—Wind & Water Power. LC 92-33921. (Illus.). 32p. (gr. k-4). 1993. PLB 11.90 (*0-531-17377-1*, Gloucester Pr) Watts.

Yanda, Bill. Rads, Ergs, & Cheeseburgers: The Kid's Guide to Energy & the Environment. (Illus.). 108p. (Orig.). (gr. 3 up). 1991. pap. 12.95 (*0-945465-75-0*) John Muir.

POWER SUPPLY

see Power Resources

PRACTICAL POLITICS

see Politics, Practical

PRAIRIE DOGS

Beers, Dorothy S. The Prairie Dog. LC 90-3327. (Illus.). 60p. (gr. 3 up). 1990. RSBE 13.95 (*0-87518-444-8*, Dillon) Macmillan Child Grp.

Patent, Dorothy H. Prairie Dogs. Munoz, William, photos by. LC 92-34724. (Illus.). 1993. 15.45 (*0-395-56572-3*, Clarion Bks) HM.

Stone, Lynn M. Prairie Dogs. LC 93-19463. 1993. write for info. (*0-86593-282-4*) Rourke Corp.

PRAIRIE-DOGS–FICTION

Oetting, R. Prairie Dog Town. LC 68-56829. (Illus.). 48p. (gr. 2-5). 1968. PLB 10.95 (*0-87783-030-4*); pap. 3.94 deluxe ed. (*0-87783-157-2*) Oddo.

Oke, Janette. Prairie Dog Town. Mann, Brenda, illus. 140p. (gr. 3 up). 1988. pap. 4.99 (*0-934998-31-0*) Bethel Pub.

PRAIRIES

Amsel, Sheri. Grasslands. Amsel, Sheri, illus. LC 92-8788. 32p. 1992. lib. bdg. 19.24 (*0-8114-6302-8*) Raintree Steck-V.

Bannatyne-Cugnet, Jo. A Prairie Alphabet. Moore, Yvette, illus. LC 92-80414. 32p. (gr. k up). 1992. 19.95 (*0-88776-292-1*) Tundra Bks.

Conrad, Pam. Prairie Visions: The Life & Times of Solomon Butcher. Butcher, Solomon, illus. LC 90-38658. 96p. (gr. 5 up). 1994. pap. 8.95 (*0-06-446135-1*, Trophy) HarpC Child Bks.

Dvorak, David, Jr. A Sea of Grass: The Tallgrass Prairie. Dvorak, David, Jr., illus. LC 93-19507. 32p. (gr. 1-4). 1994. RSBE 14.95 (*0-02-733245-4*, Macmillan Child Bk) Macmillan Child Grp.

Flint, David. The Prairies & Their People. LC 93-30718. (Illus.). 48p. (gr. 5-8). 1994. 15.95 (*1-56847-154-8*) Thomson Lrning.

Harvey, Brett. My Prairie Year. Ray, Deborah K., illus. (ps-3). 1993. pap. 4.95 (*0-8234-1028-5*) Holiday.

Hirschi, Ron. Save Our Prairies & Grasslands. Bauer, Irwin A. & Bauer, Peggy, photos by. LC 93-4985. (Illus.). 1994. 17.95 (*0-385-31149-4*); pap. 9.95 (*0-385-31199-0*) Delacorte.

Knapp, Brian. What Do We Know about the Grasslands? LC 92-7888. (Illus.). 40p. (gr. 4-6). 1992. PLB 15.95 (*0-87226-359-2*) P Bedrick Bks.

Kurelek, William. A Prairie Boy's Winter. Kurelek, William, illus. LC 73-8913. 48p. (gr. k-3). 1984. 14.45 (*0-395-17708-1*); pap. 6.70 (*0-395-36609-7*) HM.

Lawlor, Laurie. Addie Across the Prairie. LC 85-15548. (Illus.). 128p. (gr. 3-6). 1986. 11.95 (*0-8075-0165-4*) A Whitman.

Rotter, Charles M. The Prairie. LC 92-44822. (gr. 4 up). 1994. 18.95 (*0-88682-598-9*) Creative Ed.

Rowan, James P. Prairies & Grasslands. LC 83-7310. (Illus.). 48p. (gr. k-4). 1983. PLB 12.85 (*0-516-01706-3*); pap. 4.95 (*0-516-41706-1*) Childrens.

Siy, Alexandra. Native Grasslands. LC 91-18412. (Illus.). 72p. (gr. 5 up). 1991. text ed. 14.95 RSBE (*0-87518-469-3*, Dillon) Macmillan Child Grp.

Staub, Frank. America's Prairies. LC 93-7841. 1993. 19.95 (*0-87614-781-3*) Carolrhoda Bks.

Stone, L. Prairies. (Illus.). 48p. (gr. 4-8). 1989. lib. bdg. 15.94 (*0-86592-446-5*); 11.95 (*0-685-58573-5*) Rourke Corp.

PRAYER

see also Prayers

Biffi, Inos. Prayer. Vignazia, Franco, illus. LC 93-41090. 48p. (Orig.). 1994. pap. 9.99 (*0-8028-3759-X*) Eerdmans.

Bogot, Howard & Syme, Daniel. Prayer Is Reaching. Ruthen, Marlene L., illus. 32p. (ps). 1982. text ed. 4.00 (*0-8074-0172-2*, 101230) UAHC.

Catholic Children's Prayer Book. 1986. 5.95 (*0-88271-127-X*) Regina Pr.

Center for Learning Network. Praying with Children, Bk. 1. 119p. (gr. 1-3). 1991. pap. text ed. 12.95 (*1-56077-028-7*) Ctr Learning.

—Praying with Children, Bk. 2. 107p. (gr. 4-6). 1991. pap. text ed. 12.95 (*1-56077-029-5*) Ctr Learning.

Chapian, Marie. Am I the Only One Here with Faded Genes? LC 87-11611. (Illus.). 192p. 1987. pap. 7.99 (*0-87123-945-0*) Bethany Hse.

Coleman, William. Friends Forever. LC 87-700. 160p. (Orig.). 1987. pap. 6.99 (*0-87123-959-0*) Bethany Hse.

Cosby, Clair G. Junior High's a Jungle. LC 87-27040. 88p. (Orig.). (gr. 7-9). 1988. pap. 4.95 (*0-8361-3455-9*) Herald Pr.

Gibbons, Ted. Amen! An Interrupted Prayer. 6p. 1990. pap. text ed. 1.95 (*0-929985-00-1*) Jackman Pubng.

Giombi, Gary. Paths of Prayer: A Textbook of Prayer & Meditation. 160p. (Orig.). (gr. 9-12). 1993. pap. text ed. 9.95 (*0-937997-27-7*); tchr's. ed. 23.95 (*0-937997-28-5*) Hi-Time Pub.

Gotta, K. L. Teach Me How to Pray. 72p. (Orig.). 1993. pap. 6.00 (*0-9628819-0-2*) LWMM.

Groth, J. L. Prayer: Learning How to Talk to God. LC 56-1395. (gr. 1 up). 1983. pap. 3.99 (*0-570-07799-0*) Concordia.

Hague, Michael. A Child's Book of Prayers. LC 85-8380. (Illus.). 32p. (ps-2). 1985. 14.95 (*0-8050-0211-1*, Bks Young Read) H Holt & Co.

Halpin, Marlene. At Home with God, Vol. I: A Child's Book of Prayer. 30p. 1992. 4.25 (*0-7829-0361-4*, 22000) Tabor Pub.

Heerey, Frances. My First Prayer Book. 1986. pap. 3.95 (*0-88271-131-8*) Regina Pr.

Hugh, Mitchell. Always Take Time to Pray. (Illus.). (gr. k-6). 1973. visualized song 4.99 (*3-90117-014-6*) CEF Press.

Johnson, Kevin. Can I Be a Christian Without Being Weird? LC 92-15804. 1992. pap. 6.99 (*1-55661-281-8*) Bethany Hse.

Kaukola, Olavi. The Riches of Prayer. Hillila, Bernhard, tr. from FIN. & pref. by. 80p. 1991. pap. 7.95 (*0-8006-1861-0*) Polaris AZ.

Kizer, Kathryn. Tell Me about Prayer. Gross, Karen, ed. 64p. (Orig.). (gr. 1-3). 1993. pap. 4.95 (*1-56309-067-8*, New Hope AL) Womans Mission Union.

L'Engle, Madeleine. Anytime Prayers. Rooney, Maria, photos by. LC 93-46429. (Illus.). 64p. (gr. 1-6). 1994. 14.99 (*0-87788-055-7*) Shaw Pubs.

Littleton, Mark. Tunin' Up: Daily Jammin' for Tight Relationships. Heaney, Liz, ed. 208p. 1992. pap. 8.99 (*0-88070-454-3*, Gold & Honey) Questar Pubs.

Nystrom, Carolyn. What Is Prayer? 32p. (ps-2). 1980. pap. 4.99 (*0-8024-6156-5*) Moody.

O'Connor, Francine M. The ABCs of Prayer...for Children. Boswell, Kathryn, illus. 32p. (gr. 1-5). 1989. pap. 3.95 (*0-89243-317-5*) Liguori Pubns.

Odor, Ruth S. God Answers Prayers. Leisner, Kurt, illus. LC 91-67209. 32p. (gr. 5-7). 1992. saddle-stitch 5.99 (*0-87403-932-0*, 24-03562) Standard Pub.

Peterson, Lorraine. Lord, I Haven't Talked to You since the Last Crisis, But... The Purpose & Power of Prayer. LC 93-40579. 1994. pap. 7.99 (*1-55661-385-7*) Bethany Hse.

Porter, Barbara. All Kinds of Answers. Marsh, Dilleen, illus. LC 92-6976. 29p. (gr. 1-3). 1992. 11.95 (*0-87579-538-2*) Deseret Bk.

Prayer: How to Talk to God. (gr. 1-8). 1970. pap. text ed. 4.50 (*0-86508-153-0*) BCM Pubn.

Silverman, Morris & Silverman, Hillel. Prayer Book for Summer Camps. (gr. 3-12). 8.95x (*0-87677-060-X*); pap. 6.95x (*0-87677-061-8*) Prayer Bk.

Sledge, Sharlande. With My Whole Heart: Knowing God Through Prayer. Gross, Karen, ed. 64p. (gr. 4-6). 1993. pap. text ed. 4.95 (*1-56309-078-3*, New Hope) Womans Mission Union.

Smith, Judy G. Teaching Children about Prayer. 25p. (Orig.). (gr. 4-6). 1988. pap. 6.95 (*0-940754-56-8*) Ed Ministries.

Thompson, Cameron V. Master Secrets of Prayer. 112p. (Orig.). (gr. 8 up). 1990. pap. 5.95 (*0-9627630-0-4*) Light & Living.

Titherington, Jeanne. Child's Prayer. Titherington, Jeanne, illus. LC 88-16566. 24p. (ps up). 1989. 13.95 (*0-688-08317-X*); PLB 13.88 (*0-688-08318-8*) Greenwillow.

Touching Incidents & Remarkable Answers to Prayer. 135p. (gr. k up). pap. 1.00 (*0-686-29172-7*) Faith Pub Hse.

Tudor, Tasha. Give Us This Day: The Lord's Prayer. 32p. (ps-3). 1992. mini ed. 4.95 (*0-399-21891-2*, Philomel Bks) Putnam Pub Group.

—The Lord Is My Shepherd: The Twenty-Third Psalm. 32p. (ps-3). 1992. pap. 4.95 (*0-399-21892-0*, Philomel Bks) Putnam Pub Group.

PRAYERS

see also Prayer

Aiken, Nick. More Prayers for Teenagers. 128p. pap. 4.99 (*0-551-02725-8*, Pub. by Harper Religious UK) Zondervan.

—Prayers for Teenagers. 104p. pap. 3.99 (*0-551-01931-X*, Pub. by Harper Religious UK) Zondervan.

Alberione, James. Queen of Apostles Prayerbook. rev. ed. Daughters of St. Paul Staff, compiled by. 377p. 1991. blue vinyl bdg. 9.95 (*0-8198-6201-0*); black vinyl bdg. 9.95 (*0-8198-6202-9*); white vinyl bdg. o.s.i. 9.95 (*0-8198-6203-7*); pap. 7.95 (*0-8198-6200-2*) St Paul Bks.

Alexander, Martha. Poems & Prayers for the Very Young. (Illus.). (ps-1). 1973. pap. 2.25 (*0-394-82705-8*) Random Bks Yng Read.

Armstrong, William. Health, Happiness, Humor & Holiness. Graves, Helen, ed. LC 86-51342. (Illus.). 86p. (gr. 3-8). 1987. pap. text ed. 5.95 (*1-55523-065-2*) Winston-Derek.

Baehr, Kingsley M. Hope in a Scarlet Rope. LC 94-9000. 1994. 6.99 (*0-8423-1345-1*) Tyndale.

Batchelor, Mary. The Lion Book of Bible Stories & Prayers. (Illus.). 96p. (gr. 1-5). 1989. 11.95 (*0-85648-239-0*) Lion USA.

—Lion Book of Children's Prayers. (Illus.). 96p. 1984. 11.95 (*0-85648-070-3*) Lion USA.

Baynes, Pauline, compiled by. & illus. Thanks Be to God: Prayers from Around the World. LC 89-28622. 32p. (ps up). 1990. 13.95 (*0-02-708541-4*, Macmillan Child Bk) Macmillan Child Grp.

Bernos De Gasztold, Carmen. Prayers from the Ark: Selected Poems. Godden, Rumer, tr. Moser, Barry, illus. 32p. 1992. 16.00 (*0-670-84496-9*) Viking Child Bks.

Boyce, Kim & Abraham, Ken. In Process: Devotions to Help You Develop Your Faith. Reck, Sue, ed. LC 93-32713. 160p. (gr. 7-12). 1994. pap. 7.99 (*0-7814-0822-9*, Chariot Bks) Cook.

Britt, Stephanie M., illus. My Little Prayers. Ward, Brenda C., compiled by. LC 93-578. (Illus.). (gr. 3 up). 1993. pap. 5.99 (*0-8499-1064-1*) Word Pub.

Brown, Angela. Prayers That Avail Much for Children. (Illus.). 32p. (Orig.). (gr. 1-3). 1983. pap. 3.98 (*0-89274-296-8*) Harrison Hse.

Burgess, Beverly C. Prayers for Pre-Schoolers. (Illus., Orig.). (ps-2). 1991. pap. 4.98 (*1-879470-02-0*) Burgess Pub.

Butcher, Sam. Precious Moments Prayers for Boys & Girls. 1989. 10.99 (*0-8407-7230-0*) Nelson.

Carr & Paquet. God, I've Got to Talk to You Again! LC 59-1315. 24p. (Orig.). (gr. k-4). 1985. pap. 1.99 (*0-570-06197-0*, 59-1315) Concordia.

Center for Learning Network Staff. Today Is: An Ecumenical Prayer Journal for Young Teens. rev. ed. 80p. (gr. 6-9). 1992. pap. text ed. 3.95 (*1-56077-217-4*) Ctr Learning.

Costello, Gwen. Prayer Services for Religious Educators: Services for Catechists, Teachers, Parents, Children, Teenagers, & Parish Ministers. LC 88-51811. (Illus.). 80p. 1989. tchr's. ed. 9.95 (*0-89622-390-6*) Twenty-Third.

—Praying With Children: Twenty-Eight Services for Various Occasions. LC 90-70560. 96p. (Orig.). (gr. 2-6). 1990. pap. 9.95 (*0-89622-439-2*) Twenty-Third.

Daughters of St. Paul Staff. I Pray with Jesus. rev. ed. Smolinski, Dick, illus. 177p. (gr. 1-5). 1991. deluxe ed. 8.50 white (*0-8198-3630-3*); deluxe ed. 8.50 black (*0-8198-3631-1*); 4.50 (*0-8198-3629-X*) St Paul Bks.

Daughters of St Paul. My Prayerbook. (gr. 3 up). 1978. pap. 1.95 (*0-8198-0360-X*) St Paul Bks.

Davis, Ken. Jumper Fables. 1994. pap. 8.99 (*0-310-40011-2*) Zondervan.

De Gasztold, Carmen B. Prayers from the Ark. (FRE.). (gr. 3-8). 29.95 (*0-685-11511-9*) Fr & Eur.

Dietz, ed. Prayers for Children. (Illus.). (gr. k-6). 1990. booklet .99 (*0-87509-121-0*) Chr Pubns.

Dixon, Dorothy A. Teaching Young Children to Care: Thirty-Seven Activities for Developing Self-Esteem. LC 90-70418. 88p. (Orig.). (gr. k-3). 1990. pap. 9.95 (*0-89622-436-8*) Twenty-Third.

—Teaching Young Children to Care: Thirty-Seven Activities for Developing Concern for Others. LC 90-70417. (Illus.). 88p. (Orig.). (gr. k-3). 1990. pap. 9.95 (*0-89622-437-6*) Twenty-Third.

Donze, Mary T. I Can Pray the Mass! (Illus.). 48p. 1992. pap. text ed. 2.95 (*0-89243-449-X*) Liguori Pubns.

—I Can Pray the Rosary: Spanish - English Edition. (SPA & ENG.). 48p. (gr. 7-9). 1992. pap. text ed. 2.95 (*0-89243-457-0*) Liguori Pubns.

—I Can Pray with the Saints! (Illus.). 32p. 1992. pap. text ed. 3.95 (*0-89243-441-4*) Liguori Pubns.

—In My Heart Room, Bk. 2: More Love Prayers for Children. LC 90-70810. (Illus.). 80p. (Orig.). (gr. 1-5). 1990. pap. 3.95 (*0-89243-329-9*) Liguori Pubns.

Duplex, Mary H., et al. Quiet Times with Jesus. LC 92-20278. (ps). 1992. pap. 9.95 (*0-8280-0678-4*) Review & Herald.

Edwards, Michelle. Blessed Are You: Traditional Everyday Hebrew Prayers. LC 92-1666. (ps-3). 1993. 15.00 (*0-688-10759-1*); PLB 14.93 (*0-688-10760-5*) Lothrop.

Elkins, Stephen. Stories That End with a Prayer. Menck, Kevin, illus. 32p. (gr. k-8). Date not set. 12.98 (*1-56919-003-8*) Wonder Wkshop.

Everyday Prayers. 8p. (ps-k). 1993. 2.98 (*0-8317-4275-5*) Smithmark.

Field, Rachel. Prayer for a Child. Jones, Elizabeth O., illus. LC 44-47191. 32p. (ps-1). 1968. SBE 12.95 (*0-02-735190-4*, Macmillan Child Bk) Macmillan Child Grp.

Fletcher, Sarah. Prayers for Little People. Kueker, Don, illus. 32p. (gr. 3-7). 1974. pap. 2.89 (*0-570-03429-9*, 56-1184) Concordia.

Foss, Allen J. Walking in God's Truth: Ten Commandments-Lord's Prayer. rev. ed. Rinden, David, intro. by. Heiman, Lori, illus. 276p. (gr. 6-8). 1989. pap. text ed. 5.95 (*0-943167-04-3*) Faith & Fellowship Pr.

Fox, Robert J. A Prayer Book for Young Catholics. LC 82-81318. 168p. (gr. 4-8). 1982. pap. 4.95 leatherette (*0-87973-370-5*, 370) Our Sunday Visitor.

Gates of Wonder: Prayerbook for Young Children. (Illus.). 48p. (ps-8). 1990. 12.95 (*0-88123-009-X*) Central Conf.

Gaudrat, Marie-Agnes. Hello, God. (Illus.). 48p. (ps-4). 1991. 6.99 (*0-7459-1959-6*) Lion USA.

—Here I Am, God. (Illus.). 48p. (ps-4). 1991. 6.99 (*0-7459-1960-X*) Lion USA.

Gockel, Herman W. & Saleska, Edward J., eds. Child's Garden of Prayer. (Illus.). (gr. k-2). 1981. pap. 2.99 (*0-570-03412-4*, 56-1016) Concordia.

Gompertz, Helen. First Prayers. (Illus.). 32p. (ps-3). 1983. 7.00 (*0-8170-1013-0*) Judson.

Gooding, Margaret K. A Growing-up Year. 70p. (gr. 6-7). 1992. 19.95 (*0-933840-34-9*) Unitarian Univ.

Grimes, Nikki. From a Child's Heart. Joysmith, Brenda, illus. LC 93-79000. 32p. (gr. 2-6). 1993. 15.95 (*0-940975-44-0*); pap. 7.95 (*0-940975-43-2*) Just Us Bks.

Groner, Judyth & Wikler, Madeline. Thank You, God: A Jewish Child's Book of Prayers. Haas, Shelly O., illus. LC 93-7550. (HEB & ENG.). 32p. (ps-2). 1993. 14.95 (*0-929371-65-8*) Kar Ben.

Groth, Lynn. Reaching Tender Hearts, 3 vols. Grunze, R., ed. May, Lawrence & Steele, Lawrence, illus. (Orig.). (ps-k). 1988. Set. pap. text ed. write for info. (*0-938272-45-4*) WELS Board.

—Reaching Tender Hearts, Vol. 3. Grunze, R., ed. May, Lawrence & Steele, Lawrence, trs. (Illus.). 163p. (Orig.). (gr. k). 1988. pap. text ed. 8.95 (*0-938272-44-6*) WELS Board.

Group Publishing, Inc. Editors. Fun Group Devotions for Children's Ministry. LC 93-16970. (Illus.). 96p. 1993. pap. 10.99 (*1-55945-161-0*) Group Pub.

Group Publishing, Inc. Staff, ed. Ten-Minute Devotions, Vol. III. LC 93-7811. 1993. 10.99 (*1-55945-171-8*) Group Pub.

Harmer, Juliet. Prayers for Children. (ps-3). 1990. 12.95 (*0-670-83348-7*) Viking Child Bks.

—Prayers for Children. LC 92-10624. (gr. 4 up). 1992. 4.99 (*0-14-054523-9*) Puffin Bks.

Harmon. My Jesus Pocket Book of Prayer. 1992. pap. 0.69 (*1-55513-733-4*, Chariot Bks) Chariot Family.

Harmon, ed. Prayertime Bible Stories. LC 91-35647. 1992. 7.99 (*0-7814-0045-7*, Chariot Bks) Chariot Family.

Harrison House Staff. Prayers That Avail Much, for Children, Bk. 2. 32p. (Orig.). (gr. 1-6). 1990. pap. 3.98 (*0-89274-806-0*, HH806) Harrison Hse.

Hart, Corinne. We Say Thanks: A Young Child's Book for Eucharist. rev. ed. Benner, Patti, illus. 32p. (ps-2). 1991. pap. 1.90 (*1-55944-004-X*) Franciscan Comns.

Hart, Corinne & Shannon, Ellen. We Ask Forgiveness: A Young Child's Book for Reconciliation. rev. ed. Benner, Patti, illus. 32p. (ps-2). 1991. pap. 1.90 (*1-55944-005-8*) Franciscan Comns.

Harvey, Gail. Prayers, Graces, & Hymns for Children. LC 92-39152. (Illus.). (gr. 2 up). 1993. 8.99 (*0-517-09276-X*) Random Hse Value.

Have You Got a Minute, GOD? Prayers by Teens. (Illus.). 30p. (Orig.). (gr. 7-12). 1990. pap. 2.00 (*0-937997-15-3*) Hi-Time Pub.

Hayes, Edward J., et al. Catholicism & Reason. 256p. (gr. 8-12). 1981. pap. 7.95 (*0-913382-23-X*, 103-14); tchr's. manual 3.50 (*0-913382-25-6*, 103-15) Prow Bks-Franciscan.

Heinrich, Annette. Not a Hollywood Family: Realistic Devotions for Teens. 110p. (Orig.). (gr. 7 up). 1989. pap. 5.99 (*0-87788-584-2*) Shaw Pubs.

—One in a Zillion: Realistic Devotions for Teens. 112p. (Orig.). (gr. 9-12). 1990. pap. 5.99 (*0-87788-621-0*) Shaw Pubs.

Henderson, Felicity. My Little Box of Prayers, 4 bks. Goffe, Toni, illus. 32p. (ps-1). 1988. Set. casebound 10.95 (*0-7459-1250-8*) Lion USA.

Hodgson, Joan. Our Father. Ripper, Peter, illus. (ps-3). 1977. pap. 2.95 (*0-85487-040-7*) DeVorss.

Hollingsworth, Mary. My Very First Book of Prayers. Incrocci, Rick, illus. LC 93-7291. 1993. 4.99 (*0-8407-9229-8*) Nelson.

Holmes, Andy. Gerberts Goodnight Prayer. (ps). 1992. 12.99 (*0-929216-75-X*) HSH Edu Media Co.

Hunt, Angela E. Pulling Yourself Together When Your Parents Are Pulling Apart. LC 94-11147. (gr. 3 up). 1995. write for info. (*0-8423-5104-3*) Tyndale.

Jahsmann, Allan H. & Simon, Martin P. Little Visits with God. (gr. k-3). 1957. 12.99 (*0-570-03016-1*, 6-1055); pap. 9.99 (*0-570-03032-3*, 6-1158) Concordia.

Johnson, Lois. Just a Minute, Lord: Prayers for Girls. LC 73-78265. (Illus.). 96p. (Orig.). (gr. 3-8). 1973. pap. 5.99 (*0-8066-1329-7*, 10-3605, Augsburg) Augsburg Fortress.

Johnson, Paul, illus. Christmas Prayers. 16p. (ps). 1993. bds. 2.98 (*0-8317-4277-1*) Smithmark.

—Family Prayers. 16p. (ps). 1993. bds. 2.98 (*0-8317-4278-X*) Smithmark.

Johnson, Ruth I. Devotions for Early Teens. (gr. 7-12). 1974. Vol. 1. pap. 4.50 (*0-8024-2181-4*) Moody.

Jones, Chris. Lord, I Want to Tell You Something: Prayers for Boys. LC 73-78266. (Illus.). 96p. (Orig.). (gr. 5-8). 1973. pap. 5.99 (*0-8066-1330-0*, 10-4100, Augsburg) Augsburg Fortress.

Kelemen, Julie. Prayer Is for Children: Stories, Prayers, Activities. LC 91-66154. 80p. (gr. 4-6). 1992. pap. 2.95 (*0-89243-413-9*) Liguori Pubns.

Kennedy, Pamela. Prayers at Eastertime. Britt, Stephanie, illus. 24p. (ps-k). 1990. pap. 3.95 (*0-8249-8422-6*, Ideals Child) Hambleton-Hill.

Ketcham, Hank. Dennis the Menace: Prayers & Graces. Graham, Ruth, intros. by. LC 92-17186. (Illus.). 64p. (Orig.). 1993. 10.00 (*0-664-21993-4*); pap. 5.99 (*0-664-25252-4*) Westminster John Knox.

Klug, Ron. You Promised, Lord: Prayers for Boys. LC 83-70502. 80p. (Orig.). (gr. 3-7). 1983. pap. 5.99 (*0-8066-2008-0*, 10-7417, Augsburg) Augsburg Fortress.

Koch, Carl, ed. Dreams Alive: Prayers by Teenagers. St. George, Carolyn, illus. 87p. (Orig.). (gr. 9-12). 1991. pap. 4.95 (*0-88489-262-X*) St Marys.

Kramer, William A. Teenagers Pray. LC 55-12193. (gr. 8-12). 1956. 5.99 (*0-570-03018-8*, 6-1054) Concordia.

Laird, Elizabeth. Children's Treasury of Graces, Hymns & Prayers, 3 vols. (Illus.). 1991. 7.99 (*0-517-05384-5*) Random Hse Value.

Leimert, Karen M. Goodnight Blessings. LC 93-41583. (ps-3). 1994. pap. 10.99 (*0-8499-1134-6*) Word Pub.

Le Tord, Bijou. Peace on Earth: A Book of Prayers from Around the World. LC 91-39913. (Illus.). 80p. 1992. 18.00 (*0-385-30692-X*) Doubleday.

Little Folded Hands. rev. ed. LC 59-12074. (gr. 1-5). 1959. 4.99 (*0-570-03417-5*, 56-1038); pap. 1.99 laminated (*0-570-03416-7*, 56-1037) Concordia.

Littleton, Mark. When They Invited Me to Fellowship I Thought They Meant a Cruise. LC 92-81349. 166p. (Orig.). 1992. pap. 7.99 (*0-87509-496-1*) Chr Pubns.

Littleton, Mark R. Beefin' Up: Daily Feed for Amazing Grazing. Heaney, Liz, ed. LC 89-29297. 181p. (Orig.). (gr. 7-12). 1990. pap. 8.99 (*0-88070-317-2*, Gold & Honey) Questar Pubs.

Livingstone Corporation Staff, ed. Baby's First Bible. Galvin, James C., contrib. by. LC 94-9694. (gr. k up). 1995. write for info. (*0-8423-1306-0*) Tyndale.

Loth, Paul J. First Steps. LC 92-11389. 1992. 7.99 (*0-8407-9167-4*) Nelson.

—God's Word in My Heart. LC 93-18774. 1993. 7.99 (*0-8407-9233-6*) Nelson.

Lovasik, L. G. My Picture Prayer Book. (ps-3). 4.75 (*0-89942-134-2*) Catholic Bk Pub.

McEntee, Sean & Breen, Michael. Lectionary for Masses with Children: Cycle A. vi, 216p. (Orig.). (gr. 1-6). 1989. pap. 19.95 (*0-89622-411-2*) Twenty-Third.

McKissack, Patricia & McKissack, Fredrick. When Do You Talk to God? Prayers for Small Children. Gumble, Gary, illus. LC 86-71903. 32p. (Orig.). (gr. 3-8). 1986. pap. 5.99 (*0-8066-2239-3*, 10-7078, Augsburg) Augsburg Fortress.

Moskowitz, Nachama S. Bridge to Prayer: The Jewish Worship Workbook, Vol. II. (Illus.). 144p. (gr. 6-7). 1989. pap. text ed. 6.00 (*0-8074-0432-2*, 123596) UAHC.

My First Box of Prayers, 4 bks. (gr. 2 up). 1988. adhesive board 7.95 (*0-687-27539-3*) Abingdon.

My First Prayer Book. (Illus.). 32p. (ps-2). 1985. 1.95 (*0-225-66387-2*) Harper SF.

Nally, Susan & Lee, Liz. How to Feel Most Excellent! About Who You Are (& Really Enjoy It) LC 93-48685. (gr. 6 up). 1994. 7.99 (*0-8054-4008-9*) Broadman.

Nepstad, Verna. Prayer Adventure for Boys & Girls: A Prayer Soldier's Manual. (Illus.). 80p. (gr. 3-5). 1993. wkbk. 6.95 (*0-88243-338-5*, 02-0338) Gospel Pub.

Nevins, Albert J. My Baptismal Book. 20p. (ps). 1971. pap. 4.95 (*0-87973-360-8*, 360) Our Sunday Visitor.

Newman, Marjorie, ed. My Book of Favorite Prayers. Pasifull, Linda, illus. LC 89-82555. 28p. (ps-2). 1990. pap. 9.99 (*0-8066-2469-8*, 9-2469) Augsburg Fortress.

Noble, Trudy V. God Answers Children's Prayers Too. Carmen, Dave, illus. LC 85-217377. 30p. (ps-4). 1990. write for info. (*0-9620133-0-7*) Joy Deliverance.

The One Year Book of Devotions for Kids. LC 93-15786. 1993. pap. 10.99 (*0-8423-5088-8*) Tyndale.

Paltro, Piera. Angel of God. Daughters of St. Paul Staff, tr. from ITA. Curti, Anna M., illus. 14p. (Orig.). (ps-1). 1981. pap. 2.50 (*0-8198-0739-7*, CH0031P) St Paul Bks.

—Eternal Rest: A Prayer for People Who Have Died. Daughters of St. Paul Staff, tr. from ITA. Curti, Anna M., illus. 15p. (Orig.). (gr. k-3). 1992. pap. 2.50 (*0-8198-2332-5*) St Paul Bks.

—Hail, Holy Queen. Daughters of St. Paul Staff, tr. from ITA. Curti, Anna M., illus. 16p. (Orig.). (gr. k-3). 1992. pap. 2.50 (*0-8198-3365-7*) St Paul Bks.

—Our Father. Daughters of St. Paul Staff, tr. from ITA. Curti, Anna M., illus. 24p. (Orig.). (ps-1). 1991. pap. 2.50 (*0-8198-5416-6*, CH0416P) St Paul Bks.

Pappas, Michael G. Sweet Dreams for Little Ones. Wenz-Vietor, Ilse, illus. 64p. (Orig.). 1985. pap. 10.00 (*0-86683-641-1*, AY8156) Harper SF.

Price, Joyce. A Banged up Angel. Jones, M. L., ed. 192p. (Orig.). 1993. pap. text ed. 6.95 (*1-882270-07-X*) Old Rugged Cross.

Reeves, Eira. Thank You God for Our Day in the Town. (Illus.). 24p. (Orig.). (ps). 1988. pap. 2.00 (*0-8170-1136-6*) Judson.

—Thank You God for Our Day Indoors. (Illus.). 24p. (Orig.). (ps). 1988. pap. 2.00 (*0-8170-1137-4*) Judson.

Richards, H. J. The Creed for Children. 28p. (Orig.). 1991. pap. 2.95 (*0-8146-2037-X*) Liturgical Pr.

Riley, Anne. Help Me. LC 90-82929. (Illus.). 10p. 1990. text ed. 3.99 (*0-8066-2495-7*, 9-2495) Augsburg Fortress.

—I'm Sorry. LC 90-82927. (Illus.). 10p. 1990. text ed. 3.99 (*0-8066-2494-9*, 9-2494) Augsburg Fortress.

—Please God. LC 90-82930. (Illus.). 10p. 1990. text ed. 3.99 (*0-8066-2496-5*, 9-2496) Augsburg Fortress.

—Thank You. LC 90-82928. (Illus.). 10p. 1990. text ed. 3.99 (*0-8066-2493-0*, 9-2493) Augsburg Fortress.

Rogers, M. Dear God. 12p. (ps). 1994. bds. 2.98 (*0-86112-218-6*) Brimax Bks.

—God Bless. 12p. (ps). 1994. bds. 2.98 (*0-86112-195-3*) Brimax Bks.

—God Made. 12p. (ps). 1994. bds. 2.98 (*0-86112-219-4*) Brimax Bks.

—Thank You God. 12p. (ps). 1994. bds. 2.98 (*0-86112-196-1*) Brimax Bks.

Sayler, Mary H. First Days in High School: Devotions to Cheer You On. 208p. 1994. 8.99 (*0-8054-5372-5*, 4253-72) Broadman.

Schaap, James C. Intermission: Breaking Away with God. Treman, Terry, illus. Smith, Harvey A., intro. by. LC 85-4156. (Illus.). 221p. (Orig.). (gr. 9-12). 1987. pap. 11.50 (*0-930265-06-8*, 1701-5000) CRC Pubns.

Schmidt, J. David. Graffiti: Devotions for Girls. new ed. LC 83-3225. (Illus.). 128p. (Orig.). (gr. 8-12). 1983. pap. 7.99 (*0-8007-5115-9*) Revell.

—Graffiti: Devotions for Guys. new ed. LC 83-3191. (Illus.). 128p. (Orig.). (gr. 8-12). 1983. pap. 7.99 (*0-8007-5114-0*) Revell.

Schreivogel, Paul A. Small Prayers for Small Children. Holmgren, George E., illus. LC 76-135226. 32p. (gr. k-4). 1980. pap. 5.99 (*0-8066-1804-3*, 10-5836, Augsburg) Augsburg Fortress.

Shannon, Ellen & Hart, Corinne. Pedimos Perdon: Libro de Reconciliacion para Ninos. Silva, P. Fidencio & Di Raimondo, P. Domenico, trs. from ENG. Benner, Patti, illus. (SPA.). 32p. (ps-2). 1991. pap. 1.90 (*1-55944-007-4*) Franciscan Comns.

Shepherd, Linda E. Kara's Quest. LC 93-26476. Date not set. 7.99 (*0-8407-9680-3*) Nelson.

Singer, C. Gospel Prayers. (Illus.). 64p. (gr. 3-7). 1993. pap. 8.95 (*0-915531-12-7*) OR Catholic.

Smith, Julic, ed. Sleepytime, Anytime with God. LC 94-4610. (Illus.). 384p. (ps-2). Date not set. 15.99 (*0-7814-0174-7*, Chariot Bks) Chariot Family.

Songs & Prayers for Children. 32p. (ps-k). 1993. 3.98 (*0-8317-5184-3*) Smithmark.

Sorensen, David A. It's a Mystery to Me, Lord: Bible Devotions for Boys. LC 85-22993. 112p. (Orig.). (gr. 3-7). 1985. pap. 5.99 (*0-8066-2183-4*, 10-3445, Augsburg) Augsburg Fortress.

Sorenson, Stephen W. Lord, I Want to Know You Better: Story Devotions for Boys. LC 81-52280. 112p. (Orig.). (gr. 3-7). 1982. pap. 5.99 (*0-8066-1912-0*, 10-4103, Augsburg) Augsburg Fortress.

Stephens, Andrea & Stephens, Bill. Prime Time: Devotions for Girls. LC 90-22459. (Orig.). 1992. pap. 7.99 (*0-8007-5390-9*) Revell.

—Prime Time: Devotions for Guys. LC 91-6638. (Orig.). 1992. pap. 7.99 (*0-8007-5391-7*) Revell.

—Ready for Prime Time: Devotions for Girls. LC 92-31717. 176p. (Orig.). 1993. pap. 7.99 (*0-8007-5459-X*) Revell.

—Ready for Prime Time: Devotions for Guys. LC 92-31721. 176p. (Orig.). 1993. pap. 7.99 (*0-8007-5460-3*) Revell.

Stoddard, Sandol, compiled by. Prayers, Praises, & Thanksgivings. Isadora, Rachel, illus. LC 86-32822. 160p. 1992. 18.50 (*0-8037-0421-6*) Dial Bks Young.

Swanson, Steve. Faith Journeys: Youth Devotions by Nine Youth Writers. LC 91-19369. 152p. (gr. 4 up). 1991. pap. 8.99 (*0-8066-2562-7*, 9-2562) Augsburg Fortress.

Taylor, Kenneth N. Stories about Jesus. Munger, Nancy, illus. LC 94-4083. 112p. 1994. 7.99 (*0-8423-6093-X*) Tyndale.

Tirabassi, Becky. Live It. 1991. pap. 7.99 (*0-310-53751-7*) Zondervan.

Titherington, Jeanne. A Child's Prayer: Miniature Edition. (Illus.). 32p. (ps up). 1993. 4.95 (*0-688-12751-7*, Tupelo Bks) Morrow.

Tucker, Jeff & Tucker, Ramona. Life Oughta Come with Directions! Realistic Devotions for Teens. 112p. (Orig.). (gr. 9-12). 1990. pap. 5.99 (*0-87788-496-X*) Shaw Pubs.

Tudor, Tasha. First Graces. Tudor, Tasha, illus. LC 59-12017. (gr. k-3). 1978. pap. 6.95 (*0-8098-1953-8*) McKay.

—First Prayers. Tudor, Tasha, illus. LC 59-9631. (gr. k-3). 1978. protestant ed. 6.95 (*0-8098-1952-X*) McKay.

—Tasha Tudor's Treasure, 3 vols. 144p. (gr. k-4). 1981. 13.95 (*0-679-20983-2*) McKay.

Tudor, Tasha, tr. First Graces. LC 88-30673. (Illus.). 48p. (ps-2). 1989. Repr. of 1955 ed. 9.00 (*0-394-84409-2*) Random Bks Yng Read.

Tyndale Staff. One Year Book of Devotions for Kids. (gr. 4-7). 1993. pap. 10.99 (*0-8423-5087-X*) Tyndale.

Walk Thru the Bible Staff. More Youthwalk: Faith, Dating, Friendship, & Other Topics for Teen Survival. 272p. 1992. pap. 9.99 (*0-310-54591-9*, Pub. by Daybreak) Zondervan.

—Youthwalk Again. 272p. 1993. pap. 9.99 (*0-310-54601-X*, Pub. by Daybreak Bks) Zondervan.

Walsh, Caroline. The Little Book of Prayers. Moore, Inga, illus. LC 92-30860. 1993. 7.95 (*1-85697-888-5*, Kingfisher LKC) LKC.

Wangerin, W., Jr. & Jennings, A. God, I've Gotta Talk to You. (Illus.). 32p. (gr. k-4). 1974. pap. 1.99 (*0-570-06086-9*, 59-1301) Concordia.

Watson, Carol, compiled by. Three Hundred Sixty-Five Children's Prayers. (Illus.). 160p. 1989. text ed. 12.95 (*0-7459-1454-3*); white ed. 24.95 (*0-7459-1721-6*) Lion USA.

Webb, Barbara O. Now What, Lord? Bible Devotions for Girls. LC 85-22884. 112p. (Orig.). (gr. 3-7). 1985. pap. 5.99 (*0-8066-2182-6*, 10-4680, Augsburg) Augsburg Fortress.

Webb, Joan C. Devotions for Little Boys & Girls: New Testament. McCallum, Joanne V., illus. 112p. (ps-k). 1992. pap. 5.99 (*0-87403-682-8*, 12-02822) Standard Pub.

We're in This Together, Lord. LC 92-30987. 112p. (gr. 3-7). 1992. pap. 5.99 (*0-8066-2649-6*, 9-2649) Augsburg Fortress.

Westberg, Barbara. Rhymes, Riddles & Reasons, Vol. I: Genesis, A Devotional Book for Children. Agnew, Tim, illus. LC 90-38218. 224p. (Orig.). (gr. 3-7). 1991. pap. 7.99 (*0-932581-75-7*) Word Aflame.

Wilkes, Paul. My Book of Bedtime Prayers. Shields, Sandra S., illus. LC 92-70386. 32p. (ps-k). 1992. PLB 12.99 (*0-8066-2592-9*, 9-2592, Augsburg) Augsburg Fortress.

Williams, Abbie, illus. Little Talks with God. Dumelle, Grace & Stong, Susantext by. LC 93-2782. (Illus.). 1993. write for info. (*0-937739-17-0*) Roman IL.

Yeatman, Linda, ed. A Child's Book of Prayers. Williamson, Tracey, illus. LC 91-37706. 96p. 1992. 19. 95 (*1-55670-251-5*) Stewart Tabori & Chang.

PRAYING MANTIS

Lavies, Bianca. Backyard Hunter: The Praying Mantis. LC 89-37485. (Illus.). 32p. (gr. 2-5). 1990. 13.95 (*0-525-44547-1*, DCB) Dutton Child Bks.

Pohl, Kathleen. The Praying Mantis. (Illus.). 32p. (gr. 3-7). 1986. PLB 10.95 (*0-8172-2715-6*) Raintree Steck-V.

Watts, Barrie. Stick Insects. Kline, Marjory, ed. Watts, Barrie, photos by. (Illus.). 32p. (gr. k-4). 1992. PLB 11.40 (*0-531-14220-5*) Watts.

PREACHERS

see Clergy

PRECIOUS METALS

see also Gold; Silver

PRECIOUS STONES

see also Gems;

also names of precious stones, e.g. Diamonds

Russell, William. Precious Stones. LC 94-506. (gr. 3 up). 1994. write for info. (*0-86593-361-8*) Rourke Corp.

Symes, R. F. & Harding, Roger. Crystal & Gem. Keates, Colin, photos by. LC 90-4930. (Illus.). 64p. (gr. 5 up). 1991. 16.00 (*0-679-80781-0*); PLB 16.99 (*0-679-90781-5*) Knopf Bks Yng Read.

PREGNANCY

see also Childbirth

Arthur, Shirley M. Surviving Teen Pregnancy: Your Choices, Dreams & Decisions. LC 91-6931. (Illus.). 192p. (Orig.). (gr. 1-8). 1991. pap. 9.95 (*0-930934-47-4*) Morning Glory.

Barr, Linda & Monserrat, Catherine. Student Study Guide for Teenage Pregnancy: A New Beginning. rev. ed. 60p. (gr. 6-12). 1992. wkbk. 4.95 (*0-945886-11-X*) New Futures.

—Teenage Pregnancy: A New Beginning. rev. ed. Behm, Kim, et al, illus. Jones, Lyn, et al, photos by. 112p. (gr. 6-12). 1992. pap. 14.95 (*0-945886-07-1*) New Futures.

Berlfein, Judy. Teen Pregnancy. LC 92-9673. (Illus.). 112p. (gr. 5-8). 1992. PLB 14.95 (*1-56006-130-8*) Lucent Bks.

Bowe-Gutman, Sonia. Teen Pregnancy. 72p. (gr. 6 up). 1987. PLB 15.95 (*0-8225-0039-6*) Lerner Pubns.

Brinkley, Ginny & Sampson, Sherry. Joven y Embarazada: Un Libro Para Usted. Salmon, Otilia & Rodriquez, Judy, trs. from ENG. Cooper, Gail S., illus. Mahan, Charles S., pref. by. (SPA., Illus.). 80p. (gr. 7-12). 1992. pap. text ed. 4.95 (*0-9622585-3-9*) Pink Inc.

—Promises: A Teen's Guide to Pregnancy. Cooper, Gail, illus. Mahan, Charles, pref. by. (Illus.). 48p. (gr. 7-12). 1993. pap. text ed. write for info. (*0-9622585-4-7*) Pink Inc.

—Young & Pregnant: A Book for You. Cooper, Gail S., illus. Mahan, Charles, intro. by. (Illus.). 80p. (Orig.). (gr. 7-12). 1989. pap. text ed. 4.95x (*0-317-93681-6*) Pink Inc.

Cole, Joanna. How You Were Born. rev. ed. Miller, Margaret, photos by. LC 92-23970. (Illus.). 48p. (ps up). 1994. pap. 4.95 (*0-688-12061-X*, Mulberry) Morrow.

—How You Were Born: Illustrated with Photographs. rev. ed. Miller, Margaret, photos by. LC 92-23970. (Illus.). 48p. (ps up). 1993. 15.00 (*0-688-12059-8*); PLB 14.93 (*0-688-12060-1*) Morrow Jr Bks.

Cousins, Linda. Monica Made Me Promise. Webb, Jim, illus. 32p. (gr. 5-8). Date not set. pap. 3.99 (*0-912444-39-8*) DARE Bks.

Cush, Cathie. Pregnancy. LC 93-25155. (Illus.). (gr. 6-9). 1993. PLB 21.34 (*0-8114-3530-X*) Raintree Steck-V.

Glore, John. Teenage Parents. (Illus.). 64p. (gr. 7 up). 1990. lib. bdg. 17.27 (*0-86593-080-5*); lib. bdg. 12. 95s.p. (*0-685-36299-X*) Rourke Corp.

Guernsey, JoAnn B. Teen Pregnancy. LC 89-1384. (Illus.). 48p. (gr. 5-6). 1989. text ed. 12.95 RSBE (*0-89686-435-9*, Crestwood Hse) Macmillan Child Grp.

Hales, Dianne. Pregnancy & Birth. (Illus.). 112p. (gr. 6-12). 1989. 18.95 (*0-7910-0040-0*) Chelsea Hse.

Hughes, Tracy. Everything You Need to Know about Teen Pregnancy. rev. ed. Rosen, Roger, ed. (Illus.). 64p. (gr. 7 up). PLB 14.95 (*0-8239-2038-0*) Rosen Group.

Jakobson, Cathryn. Teenage Pregnancy. rev. ed. 160p. (gr. 7 up). 1992. PLB 15.85 (*0-8027-8128-4*); pap. 9.95 (*0-8027-7372-9*) Walker & Co.

Kuklin, Susan. What Do I Do Now? (Illus.). 1991. 15.95 (*0-399-21843-2*, Putnam); pap. 7.95 (*0-399-22043-7*, Putnam) Putnam Pub Group.

Lindsay, Jeanne W. & Brunelli, Jean. Teens Parenting - Your Pregnancy & Newborn Journey (Easier Reading) How to Take Care of Yourself & Your Newborn When You're a Pregnant Teen - Easy Reading Edition. LC 91-3712. (Illus.). 192p. (Orig.). (gr. 6 up). 1992. text ed. 15.95 (*0-930934-62-8*); pap. text ed. 9.95 (*0-930934-61-X*); tchr's. guide 2.50 (*0-930934-68-7*); wkbk. 2.50 (*0-930934-63-6*) Morning Glory.

—Teens Parenting - Your Pregnancy & Newborn Journey: How to Take Care of Yourself & Your Newborn When You're a Pregnant Teen. LC 91-3712. (Illus.). 192p. (Orig.). (gr. 6 up). 1991. text ed. 15.95 (*0-930934-51-2*); pap. text ed. 9.95 (*0-930934-50-4*); wkbk. 2.50 (*0-930934-60-1*) Morning Glory.

McGuire, Paula. It Won't Happen to Me: Teenagers Talk about Pregnancy. LC 82-72754. 224p. (gr. 7 up). 1983. 14.95 (*0-385-29244-9*); pap. 6.95 (*0-685-06445-X*) Delacorte.

—It Won't Happen to Me: Teenagers Talk about Pregnancy. Ryan, George M., frwd. by. 1923. pap. 6.95 (*0-385-29201-5*, Delta) Dell.

Mathes, Patricia G. & Irby, Beverly J. Teen Pregnancy & Parenting Handbook. LC 92-85264. 440p. (Orig.). 1993. pap. text ed. 19.95 (*0-87822-333-9*, 4660) Res Press.

Meier, Gisela. Teenage Pregnancy. LC 93-14169. 1993. write for info. (*1-85435-611-9*) Marshall Cavendish.

Minor, Nancy & Bradley, Patricia. Coping with School-Age Motherhood. rev. ed. (gr. 7-12). 1988. PLB 14.95 (*0-8239-0923-9*) Rosen Group.

Nilsson, Lennart & Swanberg, Lena K. How Was I Born? James, Clare, tr. LC 94-11908. (Illus.). 1994. 18.95 (*0-385-31357-8*) Delacorte.

Nixon, Joan L. Before You Were Born. McIlrath, James, illus. LC 79-91741. 32p. (ps up). 1980. pap. 5.95 (*0-87973-343-8*) Our Sunday Visitor.

Redpath, Ann. What Happens If You Have a Baby? (Illus.). 48p. (gr. 3-6). Date not set. PLB 12.95 (*1-56065-138-5*) Capstone Pr.

Roggow, Linda M. & Owens, Carolyn. Handbook for Pregnant Teenagers. (Orig.). (gr. 9-12). 1984. pap. 8.99 (*0-310-45821-8*, 12734P) Zondervan.

Rozakis, Laurie. Teen Pregnancy: Why Are Kids Having Babies? (Illus.). 64p. (gr. 5-8). 1993. PLB 15.95 (*0-8050-2569-3*) TFC Bks NY.

Silverstein, Herma. Teenage & Pregnant: What You Can Do. (Illus.). (gr. 7 up). 1989. PLB 13.98 (*0-671-65221-4*, J Messner); pap. 5.95 (*0-671-65222-2*) S&S Trade.

Simpson, Carolyn. Coping with An Unplanned Pregnancy. rev. ed. Rosen, Ruth, ed. (gr. 7-12). 1993. PLB 14.95 (*0-8239-1815-7*) Rosen Group.

—Coping with Teenage Motherhood. Rosen, Ruth, ed. LC 92-8168. (gr. 7-12). 1992. 14.95 (*0-8239-1458-5*) Rosen Group.

Taylor, Laurie. How Could This Happen? Dealing with Crisis Pregnancy. Nelson, Becky, ed. 20p. (Orig.). (gr. 7-12). 1992. pap. text ed. 1.95 (*1-56309-034-1*, Wrld Changers Res) Womans Mission Union.

Vondra, Mary & Vondra, Lisa. This Time It's Me: For Teens Who Have Just Found out They're Pregnant. Borum, Shari, illus. 24p. (Orig.). 1985. pap. 2.85 (*1-56123-042-1*) Centering Corp.

Wabbes, Marie. How I Was Born. LC 91-8336. (Illus.). 32p. (gr. 1 up). 1991. 13.95 (*0-688-10734-6*, Tambourine Bks); PLB 13.88 (*0-688-10735-4*, Tambourine Bks) Morrow.

Young, Patrick. Drugs & Pregnancy. (Illus.). 32p. (gr. 5 up). 1991. pap. 4.49 (*0-7910-0001-X*) Chelsea Hse.

PREHISTORY

see Stone Age

PREJUDICES AND ANTIPATHIES

Blue, Rose & Naden, Corrine J. Working Together Against Hate Groups. LC 94-433. 1994. 14.95 (*0-8239-1776-2*) Rosen Group.

Chin, Steven A. When Justice Failed: The Fred Korematsu Story. Tamura, David, illus. LC 92-18086. 105p. (gr. 2-5). 1992. PLB 21.34 (*0-8114-7236-1*) Raintree Steck-V.

Coleman, Willaim L. What You Should Know about Accepting People Who Aren't Like You. 1994. 5.99 (*0-8066-2637-2*, Augsburg) Augsburg Fortress.

Everything You Need to Know about Discrimination. rev. ed. 1993. lib. bdg. 14.95 (*0-8239-1656-1*) Rosen Group.

Kronenwetter, Michael. Prejudice in America: Causes & Cures. (Illus.). 144p. (gr. 7-12). 1993. PLB 13.40 (*0-531-11163-6*) Watts.

Lang, Susan S. Extremist Groups in America. LC 89-38533. 1990. PLB 14.40 (*0-531-10901-1*) Watts.

Langone, John J. Spreading Poison: A Book about Racism & Prejudice. LC 92-17847. 1993. 15.95 (*0-316-51410-1*) Little.

Lee. Discrimination. 1991. 12.95s.p. (*0-86593-113-5*) Rourke Corp.

Muse, Daphne. Prejudice. 256p. 1995. write for info. Hyprn Child.

Nash, Renea D. Coping with Interracial Dating. LC 93-6895. 1994. 14.95 (*0-8239-1606-5*) Rosen Group.

Osborn, Kevin. Everything You Need to Know about Bias Incidents. Rosen, Ruth, ed. (gr. 7-12). 1993. PLB 14.95 (*0-8239-1530-1*) Rosen Group.

Ryan, Elizabeth A. Straight Talk about Prejudice. 128p. (gr. 5-12). 1992. lib. bdg. 16.95x (*0-8160-2488-X*) Facts on File.

Zeltmann, Walter F. The Roots of Prejudice. LC 93-93974. 93p. 1993. 24.90 (*0-9622705-4-7*) Yellow Hook Pr.

PREJUDICES AND ANTIPATHIES–FICTION

Ada, Alma F. Friends - Amigos. Koch, Barry, illus. (SPA & ENG.). 26p. (gr. k-2). 1989. Spanish ed. 5.25 (*0-88272-501-7*); English ed. 5.25 (*0-88272-500-9*) Santillana.

Alphin, Elaine M. The Proving Ground. LC 92-11356. 192p. (gr. 4-7). 1992. 14.95 (*0-8050-2140-X*, Bks Young Read) H Holt & Co.

Babbitt, Lucy C. Where the Truth Lies: A Novel. LC 92-34061. 208p. (gr. 7 up). 1993. 15.95 (*0-531-05473-X*); PLB 15.99 (*0-531-08623-2*) Orchard Bks Watts.

Berenstain, Stan & Berenstain, Jan. The Berenstain Bears & the New Girl in Town. Berenstain, Jan & Berenstain, Stan, illus. LC 92-32570. 112p. (Orig.). (gr. 2-6). 1993. PLB 7.99 (*0-679-93613-0*); pap. 3.50 (*0-679-83613-6*) Random Bks Yng Read.

Betancourt, Jeanne. More Than Meets the Eye. 1990. 14. 95 (*0-553-05871-1*) Bantam.

Bush, Lawrence. Rooftop Secrets & Other Stories of Anti-Semitism. Vorspan, Albert, commentary by. LC 86-1362. (Illus.). 144p. (Orig.). (gr. 7 up). 1986. pap. text ed. 7.95 (*0-8074-0314-8*, 121720); tchr's. guide 5.00 (*0-8074-0326-1*, 201441) UAHC.

Conly, Jane L. Crazy Lady! LC 92-18348. 192p. (gr. 5 up). 1993. 13.00 (*0-06-021357-4*); PLB 12.89 (*0-06-021360-4*) HarpC Child Bks.

Cormier, Robert. Tunes for Bears to Dance To. LC 92-2734. 112p. (gr. 5 up). 1992. 15.00 (*0-385-30818-3*) Delacorte.

De Gree, Melvin. Brickhouse Dreams: Young Benjamin E. Mays. Davis, Beverly, illus. 140p. (Orig.). (gr. 3-10). 1992. pap. 11.95 (*0-9632895-0-0*) Trail of Success.

Disher, Garry. Ratface. LC 93-48131. 128p. (gr. 5 up). 1994. 10.95g (*0-395-69451-5*) Ticknor & Flds Bks Yng Read.

Doleski, Teddi. Silvester & the Oogaloo Boogaloo. 1990. 2.95 (*0-8091-6596-1*) Paulist Pr.

Gorman, Carol. Nobody's Friend. Nappi, Rudy, illus. LC 92-24936. 60p. (Orig.). (gr. 1-4). 1993. pap. 3.99 (*0-570-04729-3*) Concordia.

Greene, Bette. Drowning of Stephan Jones. 1991. 16.00 (*0-553-07437-7*) Bantam.

Ikeda, Daisaku. Over the Deep Blue Sea. Wildsmith, Brian, illus. McCaughrean, Geraldine, tr. from JPN. LC 92-22557. (Illus.). 32p. (ps-3). 1993. 15.00 (*0-679-84184-9*); PLB 15.99 (*0-679-94184-3*) Knopf Bks Yng Read.

James, Mary. The Shuteyes. LC 92-16170. 176p. (gr. 3-7). 1993. 13.95 (*0-590-45069-7*) Scholastic Inc.

Klein, Robin. Boss of the Pool. 96p. (gr. 3-7). 1992. pap. 3.99 (*0-14-036037-9*) Puffin Bks.

Koller, Jackie F. The Primrose Way. 1992. write for info. (*0-15-256745-3*, Gulliver Bks) HarBrace.

Konigsburg, E. L. T-Backs, T-Shirts, Coat & Suit. LC 94-27288. (gr. 1-8). 1995. pap. write for info. (*0-7868-1027-0*) Hyprn Child.

Lee, Marie G. Finding My Voice. LC 92-2947. 176p. (gr. 6 up). 1992. 13.95 (*0-395-62134-8*) HM.

—Saying Goodbye. LC 93-26092. 1994. write for info. (*0-395-67066-7*) HM.

Levene, Nancy S. Hero for a Season. Reck, Sue, ed. LC 93-21126. 96p. (gr. 3-6). 1994. pap. 4.99 (*0-7814-0702-8*, Chariot Bks) Cook.

Levitin, Sonia. The Return. LC 86-25891. 224p. (gr. 5 up). 1987. SBE 14.95 (*0-689-31309-8*, Atheneum Child Bk) Macmillan Child Grp.

Littleton, Mark. Tree Fort Wars. LC 92-44181. (gr. 4 up). 1993. pap. 5.99 (*1-555-13764-4*, Chariot Bks) Chariot Family.

McClaskey, Marilyn H. What Kind of Name Is Juan? Rosen, Roger, ed. (gr. 7 up). 1989. PLB 12.95 (*0-8239-0830-5*) Rosen Group.

Mazer, Anne. The Oxboy. LC 92-37199. 112p. (gr. 3-7). 1993. 13.00 (*0-679-84191-1*); PLB cancelled (*0-679-94119-3*) Knopf Bks Yng Read.

Means, Florence C. The Moved-Outers. LC 92-13706. 156p. 1993. pap. 6.95 (*0-8027-7386-9*) Walker & Co.

Miller, M. L. Those Bottles! Root, Barry, illus. LC 93-19684. 32p. (ps-3). 1994. 14.95 (*0-399-22607-9*, Putnam) Putnam Pub Group.

Mochizuki, Ken. Baseball Saved Us. Lee, Dom, illus. LC 92-73215. 32p. (gr. k-8). 1993. 14.95 (*1-880000-01-6*) Lee & Low Bks.

Nelson, Vaunda M. Mayfield Crossing. Jenkins, Leonard, illus. LC 92-10564. 96p. (gr. 3-7). 1993. 14.95 (*0-399-22331-2*, Putnam) Putnam Pub Group.

Neville, Emily C. Berries Goodman. LC 65-19485. (gr. 5-9). 1975. pap. 3.95 (*0-06-440072-7*, Trophy) HarpC Child Bks.

Oram, Hiawyn & Baird, Daniel. Just Like Us. (Illus.). 32p. (gr. 2-4). 1988. 11.95 (*0-8192-1472-8*) Morehouse Pub.

Qualey, Marsha. Revolutions of the Heart. LC 92-24528. 192p. (gr. 6 up). 1993. 13.45 (*0-395-64168-3*) HM.

Roper, Gayle. The Puzzle of the Poison Pen. LC 94-6755. 1994. write for info. (*0-7814-1507-1*, Chariot Bks) Chariot Family.

Ruby, Lois. Skin Deep. LC 93-13707. (gr. 7 up). 1994. 14.95 (*0-590-47699-8*) Scholastic Inc.

Swope, Sam. The Araboolies of Liberty Street. Root, Barry, illus. LC 88-12687. 32p. (ps-3). 1989. (Clarkson Potter); PLB 15.99 (*0-517-57411-X*, Clarkson Potter) Crown Bks Yng Read.

Taylor, Mildred D. The Road to Memphis. 304p. (gr. 5-9). 1992. pap. 3.99 (*0-14-036077-8*, Puffin) Puffin Bks.

Tedrow, T. L. Land of Promise. LC 92-28222. 1992. 4.99 (*0-8407-7735-3*) Nelson.

Tolan, Stephanie S. Plague Year. LC 89-13605. (Illus.). 208p. (gr. 7 up). 1990. 12.95 (*0-688-08801-5*) Morrow Jr Bks.

Tunis, John R. All-American. 261p. (gr. 3-7). 1989. pap. 3.95 (*0-15-202292-9*, Odyssey) HarBrace.

Uchida, Yoshiko. A Jar of Dreams. 2nd ed. LC 92-18803. 144p. (gr. 4-7). 1993. pap. 3.95 (*0-689-71672-9*, Aladdin) Macmillan Child Grp.

—Journey Home. 2nd ed. Robinson, Charles, illus. LC 91-40149. 144p. (gr. 3-7). 1992. pap. 3.95 (*0-689-71641-9*, Aladdin) Macmillan Child Grp.

Velthuijs, Max. Frog & the Stranger. Velthuijs, Max, illus. LC 93-26401. 32p. 1994. 14.00 (*0-688-13267-7*, Tambourine Bks); PLB 13.93 (*0-688-13268-5*, Tambourine Bks) Morrow.

Wainwright, Richard M. Montanas Escalar. Crompton, Jack, illus. LC 90-13990. (SPA.). 64p. 1991. 15.00 (*0-9619566-5-8*) Family Life.

—Mountains to Climb. Crompton, Jack, illus. 64p. 1990. 13.95 (*0-9619566-3-1*) Family Life.

Waite, Michael. Sylvester the Jester. LC 91-38875. (ps-3). 1992. pap. 8.99 (*0-7814-0033-3*, Chariot Bks) Chariot Family.

Wyeth, Sharon D. The World of Daughter McGuire. LC 93-15489. 1994. 14.95 (*0-385-31174-5*) Delacorte.

Yamate, Sandra S. The Best of Intentions. Lee, Wendy K., illus. LC 93-45794. 1994. 12.95 (*1-879965-09-7*) Polychrome Pub.

PRESCHOOL EDUCATION
see Nursery Schools

PRESENTS
see Gifts

PRESERVATION OF FORESTS
see Forests and Forestry

PRESERVATION OF NATURAL RESOURCES
see Conservation of Natural Resources

PRESERVATION OF NATURAL SCENERY
see Natural Monuments

PRESERVATION OF WILDLIFE
see Wildlife–Conservation

PRESERVATION OF ZOOLOGICAL SPECIMENS
see Zoological Specimens–Collection and Preservation

PRESERVING
see Canning and Preserving

PRESIDENTS–FRANCE

Sabin, Francene. Young Thomas Jefferson. Baxter, Robert, illus. LC 85-1093. 48p. (gr. 4-6). 1985. lib. bdg. 10.79 (*0-8167-0561-5*); pap. text ed. 3.50 (*0-8167-0562-3*) Troll Assocs.

PRESIDENTS–U. S.

Aten, Jerry. Presidential Leaders. Hierstein, Judy, illus. 64p. (gr. k-4). 1986. wkbk. 7.95 (*0-86653-347-8*, GA 697) Good Apple.

—Presidents. Hyndman, Kathryn, illus. 176p. (gr. 4 up). 1985. wkbk. 13.95 (*0-86653-281-1*, GA 627) Good Apple.

Beard, Charles A. & Vagts, Detlev F. Presidents in American History. 2nd, rev. ed. Steltenpohl, Jane, ed. (Illus.). 240p. (gr. 6-10). 1989. lib. bdg. 14.98 (*0-671-68574-0*, J Messner); pap. 6.95 (*0-671-68575-9*) S&S Trade.

Beckman, Beatrice. I Can Be President. LC 84-12653. (Illus.). 32p. (gr. k-3). 1984. PLB 11.80 (*0-516-01841-8*); pap. 3.95 (*0-516-41841-6*) Childrens.

Bedik. Our President: Bill Clinton. 1993. pap. 2.50 (*0-590-47126-0*) Scholastic Inc.

Behrens, June. George Bush: Forty-First President of the United States. LC 89-693. (Illus.). 32p. (gr. 2-4). 1989. PLB 11.80 (*0-516-04172-X*); pap. 3.95 (*0-516-44172-8*) Childrens.

Blassingame, Wyatt. The Look-It-Up Book of Presidents. rev. & updated ed. LC 89-10519. (Illus.). (gr. 5-9). 1990. 12.00 (*0-679-80353-X*); PLB 12.99 (*0-679-90353-4*); pap. 6.99 (*0-679-80358-0*) Random Bks Yng Read.

Brandt, Keith. President. Dole, Bob, illus. LC 84-2652. 32p. (gr. 3-6). 1985. PLB 9.49 (*0-8167-0268-3*); pap. text ed. 2.95 (*0-8167-0269-1*) Troll Assocs.

Buchman, Dian D. Our Forty-Second President. (gr. 4-7). 1993. pap. 2.95 (*0-590-46572-4*) Scholastic Inc.

Bumann, Joan & Patterson, John. All-New Edition of Our American Presidents. 176p. (gr. 5 up). 1993. pap. 2.99 (*0-87406-644-1*) Willowisp Pr.

Cleveland, Will & Alvarez, Mark. Yo! Millard Fillmore: And All Those Other Presidents You Never Heard Of. Nation, Tate, illus. 112p. (gr. 5). 1992. pap. 7.95 (*0-9632778-0-4*) Goodwood Pr.

—Yo, Millard Fillmore! And All Those Other Presidents You Never Heard Of. 2nd, rev. ed. Nation, Tate, illus. 112p. (Orig.). (gr. 5). 1993. pap. write for info. (*0-9632778-1-2*) Goodwood Pr.

Clinton, Susan. Benjamin Harrison. LC 89-33751. 100p. (ps up). 1989. PLB 14.40 (*0-516-01370-X*) Childrens.

Cwiklik, Robert. Bill Clinton: Our Forty-Second President. (Illus.). 48p. (gr. 2-4). 1993. PLB 12.90 (*1-56294-387-1*); pap. 4.95 (*1-56294-764-8*) Millbrook Pr.

D'Aulaire, Ingri & D'Aulaire, Edgar P. Abraham Lincoln. rev. ed. (gr. k-4). 1957. pap. 10.95 (*0-385-07669-X*) Doubleday.

—George Washington. D'Aulaire, Ingri & D'Aulaire, Edgar P., illus. LC 36-27417. 64p. (gr. 1-4). 1936. pap. 13.95 (*0-385-07306-2*) Doubleday.

Dell Puzzle Magazine Staff. Story of Bill Clinton & Al Gore. (gr. 4-7). 1993. pap. 3.50 (*0-440-40843-1*) Dell.

Eliot, Chip. The Clintons: Meet the First Family. LC 93-14027. (Illus.). 24p. (gr. 2-6). 1993. pap. text ed. 1.95 (*0-8167-3243-4*) Troll Assocs.

Falkof, Lucille. Ulysses S. Grant: 18th President of the United States. Young, Richard G., ed. LC 87-32817. (Illus.). (gr. 5-9). 1988. PLB 17.26 (*0-944483-02-X*) Garrett Ed Corp.

Fisher, Leonard E. The White House. LC 89-1990. (Illus.). 96p. (gr. 3-7). 1989. reinforced bdg. 15.95 (*0-8234-0774-8*) Holiday.

Gamiello, Elvira. America's Presidents Activity & Fun Book. (Illus., Orig.). (gr. 4-6). 1989. pap. 1.95 (*0-942025-51-2*) Kidsbks.

George Bush: The Story of Our Forty-First President. (gr. 2-6). 1989. pap. 2.95 (*0-440-40174-7*, YB) Dell.

Goldman, Phyllis B., ed. Monkeyshines on the United States Presidents: Games, Puzzles, & Trivia. (Illus.). 97p. (gr. 4 up). 1990. pap. 12.95x (*0-9620900-1-8*) NC Learn Inst Fitness.

Green, Carl & Sanford, William. Presidency. (Illus.). 96p. (gr. 7 up). 1990. lib. bdg. 18.60 (*0-86593-084-8*); lib. bdg. 13.95s.p. (*0-685-36360-0*) Rourke Corp.

Greenberg, Keith E. Bill & Hillary: Working Together in the White House. (Illus.). 48p. (gr. 2-5). 1994. PLB 12.95 (*1-56711-067-3*) Blackbirch.

—Bill & Hillary: Working Together in the White House. (Illus.). 48p. (gr. 2-5). 1994. pap. 6.95 (*1-56711-069-X*) Blackbirch.

Greenblatt, Miriam. James K. Polk: 11th President of the United States. Young, Richard G., ed. LC 87-35981. (Illus.). (gr. 5-9). 1988. PLB 17.26 (*0-944483-04-6*) Garrett Ed Corp.

Greene, Carol. Los Presidentes (Presidents) Kratky, Lada, tr. LC 85-31848. (SPA., Illus.). 48p. (gr. k-4). 1986. PLB 12.85 (*0-516-31928-0*); pap. 4.95 (*0-516-51928-X*) Childrens.

—Presidents. LC 84-7719. (Illus.). 48p. (gr. k-4). 1984. PLB 12.85 (*0-516-01928-7*); pap. 4.95 (*0-516-41928-5*) Childrens.

Hample, Stuart & Kovalchik, Sally, eds. Dear Mr. President. (Illus.). 96p. (Orig.). 1993. pap. 6.95 on board (*1-56305-504-X*, 3504) Workman Pub.

Honey, Michael. Records of Impeachment. LC 86-16307. (Illus.). 20p. (Orig.). 1987. pap. text ed. 3.50x (*0-911333-49-5*, 200109) Natl Archives & Records.

Hudson, Wilma J. Harry S. Truman: Missouri Farm Boy. Doremus, Robert, illus. LC 92-7513. 192p. (gr. 3-7). 1992. pap. 3.95 (*0-689-71658-3*, Aladdin) Macmillan Child Grp.

Italia, Bob. Bill Clinton: The 42nd President of the United States. LC 93-24849. 1993. 13.99 (*1-56239-249-2*) Abdo & Dghtrs.

Johnson, Mary O. The President. (Illus.). (gr. 5-6). 1992. PLB 21.34 (*0-8114-7352-X*) Raintree Steck-V.

Kent, Zachary. George Bush. LC 89-33744. 100p. (gr. 3 up). 1989. PLB 14.40 (*0-516-01374-2*); pap. 6.95 (*0-516-41374-0*) Childrens.

—William Jefferson Clinton. (Illus.). 100p. (gr. 3 up). 1993. PLB 14.40 (*0-516-01350-5*) Childrens.

Landau, Elaine. Bill Clinton. LC 92-39174. (Illus.). (gr. 5-8). 1993. PLB 12.40 (*0-531-11143-1*); pap. 5.95 (*0-531-15670-2*) Watts.

Larsen, Rebecca. Ronald Reagan. (Illus.). 128p. (gr. 7-12). 1994. lib. bdg. 14.84 (*0-531-11191-1*) Watts.

Law, Kevin J. Millard Fillmore: Thirteenth President of the United States. Young, Richard G., ed. LC 89-25651. (Illus.). 128p. (gr. 5-9). 1990. PLB 17.26 (*0-944483-61-5*) Garrett Ed Corp.

Lindop, Edmund. Presidents by Accident. LC 91-17056. (Illus.). 208p. (gr. 9-12). 1991. PLB 15.40 (*0-531-11059-1*) Watts.

—Presidents vs. Congress: Conflict & Compromise. LC 93-30784. (Illus.). 168p. (gr. 9-12). 1994. PLB 13.40 (*0-531-11165-2*) Watts.

Martin, Gene L. & Boyd, Aaron. Bill Clinton: President from Arkansas. (Illus.). 104p. (gr. 7-12). 1993. PLB 17.95 (*0-936389-31-1*) Tudor Pubs.

Moncure, Jane B. My First Presidents' Day Book. Halverson, Lydia, illus. LC 87-10309. 32p. (ps-2). 1987. pap. 3.95 (*0-516-42910-8*) Childrens.

Muntean, Michaela. I Want to Be President. Brannon, Tom, illus. 24p. (ps-k). 1993. pap. 1.95 (*0-307-13118-1*, 13118, Golden Pr) Western Pub.

Nardo, Don. The U. S. Presidency. (Illus.). (gr. 5-8). 1994. 14.95 (*1-56006-157-X*) Lucent Bks.

National Archives Staff, ed. Kennedy's Inaugural Address of 1961. LC 86-600367. (Illus.). 30p. (Orig.). 1987. pap. text ed. 3.50x (*0-911333-53-3*, 200110) Natl Archives & Records.

North, Sterling. Abe Lincoln: Log Cabin to White House. LC 87-4654. (Illus.). 160p. (gr. 5-9). 1987. pap. 4.99 (*0-394-89179-1*) Random Bks Yng Read.

Oakley, Ruth. Presidents of the United States: The Illustrated History of the, 8 vols. (Illus.). 512p. 1990. Set. PLB 149.95 (*1-85435-144-3*) Marshall Cavendish.

Our Presidents. 1988. pap. 3.95 (*0-88388-140-3*) Bellerophon Bks.

Parker, Nancy W. The President's Cabinet & How It Grew. LC 89-70851. (Illus.). 40p. (gr. 3-5). 1992. pap. 5.95 (*0-06-446131-9*, Trophy) HarpC Child Bks.

Patrick, Diane. The Executive Branch. LC 94-963. 1994. write for info. (*0-531-20179-1*) Watts.

Phillips, Louis. Ask Me Anything about the Presidents. 144p. (Orig.). 1992. pap. 3.99 (*0-380-76426-1*, Camelot) Avon.

Pious, Richard M. The Presidency. (Illus.). 128p. (gr. 5 up). 1991. PLB 10.95 (*0-382-24316-1*); pap. 7.95 (*0-382-24322-6*) Silver Burdett Pr.

—The Young Oxford Companion to the Presidency of the United States. LC 93-19908. 1993. Alk. paper. 35. 00 (*0-19-507799-7*) OUP.

Presidents of a Divided Nation: A Sourcebook on the U. S. Presidency. LC 93-12753. (Illus.). 96p. (gr. 5-8). 1993. 18.90 (*1-56294-360-X*) Millbrook Pr.

Provensen, Alice. The Buck Stops Here: The Presidents of the United States. LC 88-35036. (Illus.). 56p. (gr. 2 up). 1992. pap. 7.95 (*0-06-446132-7*, Trophy) HarpC Child Bks.

Rubel, David. The Scholastic Encyclopedia of the Presidents & Their Times. LC 93-11810. (Illus.). 224p. (gr. 4 up). 1994. 16.95 (*0-590-49366-3*, Scholastic Ref) Scholastic Inc.

Sandak, Cass A. The Carters: First Families Ser. LC 93-3943. (Illus.). 48p. (gr. 5). 1993. text ed. 4.95 RSBE (*0-89686-652-1*, Crestwood Hse) Macmillan Child Grp.

Sherrow, Victoria. The Big Book of U. S. Presidents: A Young Person's Guide to American History. Prosser, Bill, illus. 56p. 1994. 9.98 (*1-56138-427-5*) Running Pr.

—Bill Clinton. LC 93-1747. (Illus.). 72p. (gr. 4-6). 1993. text ed. 13.95 RSBE (*0-87518-620-3*, Dillon) Macmillan Child Grp.

Simon, Charnan. Chester A. Arthur. LC 89-35386. 100p. (gr. 3 up). 1989. PLB 14.40 (*0-516-01369-6*) Childrens.

Smith, Carter, ed. The Founding Presidents: A Sourcebook on the U. S. Presidency. LC 93-12751. (Illus.). 96p. (gr. 5-8). 1993. PLB 18.90 (*1-56294-357-X*) Millbrook Pr.

—Presidents in a Time of Change: A Sourcebook on the U. S. Presidency. LC 93-15092. (Illus.). 96p. (gr. 5-8). 1993. 18.90 (*1-56294-362-6*) Millbrook Pr.

—Presidents of a Growing Country: A Sourcebook on the U. S. Presidency. LC 93-15090. (Illus.). 96p. (gr. 5-8). 1993. 18.90 (*1-56294-358-8*) Millbrook Pr.

—Presidents of a World Power: A Sourcebook on the U. S. Presidency. LC 93-15091. (Illus.). 96p. (gr. 5-8). 1993. 18.90 (*1-56294-361-8*) Millbrook Pr.

—Presidents of a Young Republic: A Sourcebook on the U. S. Presidency. LC 93-12752. (Illus.). 96p. (gr. 5-8). 1993. 18.90 (*1-56294-359-6*) Millbrook Pr.

Smith, Kathie B. Abraham Lincoln. Seward, James, illus. LC 86-28060. 24p. (gr. 4-6). 1987. (J Messner); PLB 5.99s.p. (*0-685-18829-9*) S&S Trade.

Stevens, Rita. Chester A. Arthur: 21st President of the United States. Young, Richard G., ed. LC 87-36120. (Illus.). (gr. 5-9). 1989. PLB 17.26 (*0-944483-05-4*) Garrett Ed Corp.

Sufrin, Mark. George Bush: The Story of the Forty-First President of the United States. (gr. 5 up). 1989. 12.95 (*0-440-50158-X*) Delacorte.

Suid, Murray. How to Be President of the U. S. A. Barr, Marilynn G., illus. 80p. (Orig.). (gr. 3-8). 1992. pap. text ed. 9.95 (*1-878279-47-5*, MM1963) Monday Morning Bks.

Sullivan, George. Facts & Fun about the Presidents. 96p. (Orig.). (gr. 3-7). 1987. pap. 2.50 (*0-590-44428-X*) Scholastic Inc.

—George Bush. Steltenpohl, Jane, ed. (Illus.). 128p. (gr. 6-10). 1989. lib. bdg. 12.98 (*0-671-64599-4*, J Messner); pap. 5.95 (*0-671-67814-0*) S&S Trade.

—Presidents at Play. LC 94-15002. 1995. write for info. (*0-8027-8333-3*); lib. bdg. write for info. (*0-8027-8334-1*) Walker & Co.

Sullivan, Steve. Mr. President: A Book of U. S. Presidents. 1993. pap. 2.95 (*0-590-46540-6*) Scholastic Inc.

Swerdlick, Harriet & Reiter, Edith. President Games: Puzzles, Quizzes, & Mind Teasers for Every George, Abe, & Lyndon! 48p. (Orig.). (gr. 3 up). 1988. pap. 2.95 incl. chipboard (*0-8431-2240-4*) Putnam Pub Group.

Waters, Kate. The Story of the White House. 1991. 12.95 (*0-590-43335-0*, Scholastic Hardcover) Scholastic Inc.

White, Nancy B. Meet John F. Kennedy. (Illus.). (gr. 2-5). 1965. 7.99 (*0-394-80059-1*) Random Bks Yng Read.

World Book Editors. The World Book of America's Presidents. rev. ed. LC 93-60575. (Illus.). 448p. (gr. 6 up). 1993. PLB write for info. (*0-7166-3694-8*) World Bk.

PRESIDENTS–U. S.–ASSASSINATION

Sullivan, George. They Shot the President: Ten True Stories. (gr. 4-7). 1993. pap. 3.25 (*0-590-46101-X*) Scholastic Inc.

PRESIDENTS–U. S.–ELECTION

Brown, Gene. H. Ross Perot. LC 93-11998. (gr. 1-8). 1993. 15.93 (*0-86592-060-5*); 11.95s.p. (*0-685-66543-7*) Rourke Enter.

—The Nineteen Ninety-Two Election. LC 92-19963. (Illus.). 64p. (gr. 5-8). 1992. PLB 15.90 (*1-56294-080-5*); pap. 5.95 (*1-56294-806-7*) Millbrook Pr.

Gill, Nancy. Electing Our President. rev. ed. (gr. 5-8). 1991. pap. 8.95 (*0-86653-953-0*) Fearon Teach Aids.

Hanneman, Tamara. Election Book: People Pick a President. (gr. 4-7). 1992. pap. 1.95 (*0-590-46414-0*) Scholastic Inc.

Hargrove, Jim. The Story of Presidential Elections. LC 88-1021. (Illus.). 31p. (gr. 2-4). 1988. pap. 3.95 (*0-516-44737-8*) Childrens.

Hewett, Joan. Getting Elected: The Diary of a Campaign. Hewett, Richard, photos by. LC 88-11109. (Illus.). 48p. (gr. 4-7). 1989. 13.95 (*0-525-67259-1*, Lodestar Bks) Dutton Child Bks.

Raber, Thomas R. Presidential Campaign. (Illus.). 88p. (gr. 4 up). 1988. lib. bdg. 14.95 (*0-8225-1750-7*) Lerner Pubns.

Reische, Diana. Electing a U. S. President. LC 91-32339. (Illus.). 144p. (gr. 7-12). 1992. PLB 14.40 (*0-531-11043-5*) Watts.

Sullivan, George. Campaigns & Elections. (Illus.). 128p. (gr. 5 up). 1991. PLB 10.95 (*0-382-24315-3*); pap. 7.95 (*0-382-24321-8*) Silver Burdett Pr.

PRESIDENTS–U. S.–FAMILY

Sandak, Cass R. The Bushes. LC 91-11153. (Illus.). 48p. (gr. 5). 1991. text ed. 4.95 RSBE (*0-89686-632-7*, Crestwood Hse) Macmillan Child Grp.

PRESIDENTS–U. S.–FICTION

Adams, Laurie & Coudert, Allison. Who Wants a Turnip for President, Anyway? 96p. (Orig.). 1990. pap. 2.75 (*0-553-15432-X*) Bantam.

Brown, Marc T. Arthur Meets the President. (ps-3). 1991. 14.95 (*0-316-11265-8*) Little.

Goffe, Toni. The President. LC 92-259. 1992. 7.95 (*0-85953-787-0*); pap. 3.95 (*0-85953-788-9*) Childs Play.

Griest, Lisa. Lost at the White House: A 1909 Easter Story. Shine, Andrea, illus. LC 93-7945. 1993. 14.95 (*0-87614-726-0*) Carolrhoda Bks.

Gross, Virginia. The President Is Dead: A Story of the Kennedy Assassination. Andreasen, Dan, illus. 64p. (gr. 2-6). 1993. reinforced bdg. 12.99 (*0-670-85156-6*) Viking Child Bks.

PRESIDENTS–U. S.–INAUGURATION–FICTION

Sinnott, Trip. President Clinton Visits Hyde Park: Story & Coloring Book. Glass, Eric, illus. 52p. (Orig.). (gr. k-5). 1993. pap. 4.95 (*1-883551-00-5*) Attic Studio.

PRESIDENTS–U. S.–STAFF

Bruce, Preston & Johnson, Katharine. From the Door of the White House. LC 81-23672. (Illus.). 160p. (gr. 6 up). 1984. 12.95 (*0-688-00883-6*) Lothrop.

PRESIDENTS–U. S.–WIVES

Anthony, Carl S. America's Most Influential First Ladies. Ford, Betty, frwd. by. LC 92-18444. (Illus.). 160p. (gr. 5-12). 1992. PLB 14.95 (*1-881508-00-5*) Oliver Pr MN.

Bach, Julie. Hillary Clinton. LC 93-15325. (Illus.). 1993. 12.94 (*1-56239-221-2*) Abdo & Dghtrs.

Behrens, June. Barbara Bush: First Lady of Literacy. LC 90-2201. (Illus.). 32p. (gr. 2-5). 1990. PLB 11.80 (*0-516-04275-0*); pap. 3.95 (*0-516-44275-9*) Childrens.

Blue, Rose & Naden, Corinne J. Barbara Bush: First Lady. LC 90-48318. (Illus.). 104p. (gr. 6 up). 1991. lib. bdg. 17.95 (*0-89490-350-0*) Enslow Pubs.

Boyd, Aaron. First Lady: The Story of Hillary Rodham Clinton. (Illus.). 128p. (gr. 6 up). 1994. PLB 17.95 (*1-883846-02-1*) M Reynolds.

Flynn, Jean. Lady: The Story of Claudia Alta (Lady Bird) Johnson. 144p. (gr. 8-12). 1992. 14.95 (*0-89015-821-5*) Sunbelt Media.

Giblin, James C. Edith Wilson: The Woman Who Ran the United States. Laporte, Michele, illus. 64p. (gr. 2-6). 1992. RB 11.00 (*0-670-83005-4*) Viking Child Bks.

—Edith Wilson: The Woman Who Ran the United States. Laporte, Michele, illus. LC 93-15139. 64p. (gr. 2-5). 1993. pap. 3.99 (*0-14-034249-4*, Puffin) Puffin Bks.

Greenberg, Keith E. Bill & Hillary: Working Together in the White House. (Illus.). 48p. (gr. 2-5). 1994. PLB 12.95 (*1-56711-067-3*) Blackbirch.

—Bill & Hillary: Working Together in the White House. (Illus.). 48p. (gr. 2-5). 1994. pap. 6.95 (*1-56711-069-X*) Blackbirch.

Guernsey, JoAnn B. Hillary Rodham Clinton, a New Kind of First Lady. LC 93-21856. 1993. PLB 13.50 (*0-8225-2875-4*); pap. 6.95 (*0-8225-9650-4*) Lerner Pubns.

Levert, Suzanne. Hillary Rodham Clinton: First Lady. (gr. 4-7). 1994. pap. 6.95 (*1-56294-726-5*) Millbrook Pr.

McGrath-Heiss, Arleen. Barbara Bush. (Illus.). 128p. (gr. 5 up). 1992. lib. bdg. 17.95 (*0-7910-1627-7*) Chelsea Hse.

Sandak, Cass A. The Carters: First Families Ser. LC 93-3943. (Illus.). 48p. (gr. 5). 1993. text ed. 4.95 RSBE (*0-89686-652-1*, Crestwood Hse) Macmillan Child Grp.

Sandak, Cass R. The Trumans. LC 92-6879. (Illus.). 48p. (gr. 5). 1992. text ed. 4.95 RSBE (*0-89686-643-2*, Crestwood Hse) Macmillan Child Grp.

—The Wilsons. LC 93-3503. (Illus.). 48p. (gr. 5). 1993. text ed. 12.95 RSBE (*0-89686-651-3*, Crestwood Hse) Macmillan Child Grp.

Shelley, Mary V. & Munro, Sandra H. Harriet Lane, First Lady of the White House. LC 80-20151. (Illus.). 48p. (gr. 4-6). 1980. 6.95 (*0-915010-29-1*) Sutter House.

Sherrow, Victoria. Hillary Rodham Clinton. LC 93-7806. (Illus.). 72p. (gr. 4-6). 1993. text ed. 13.95 RSBE (*0-87518-621-1*, Dillon) Macmillan Child Grp.

Spain, Valerie. Meet Hillary Rodham Clinton. LC 93-29194. (Illus.). 112p. (Orig.). (gr. 2-7). 1994. PLB 9.99 (*0-679-95089-3*); pap. 2.99 (*0-679-85089-9*) Random Bks Yng Read.

Spies, Karen B. Barbara Bush: Helping America Read. LC 91-17725. (Illus.). 72p. (gr. 4-6). 1991. text ed. 13.95 RSBE (*0-87518-488-X*, Dillon) Macmillan Child Grp.

Wallner, Rosemary. Barbara Bush. LC 91-73028. 32p. 1991. 12.94 (*1-56239-079-1*) Abdo & Dghtrs.

Wheeler, Jill C. & Stone, Judith A. Nancy R. Reagan. LC 91-73027. 202p. 1991. 12.94 (*1-56239-080-5*) Abdo & Dghtrs.

Wilkie, Katharine E. Mary Todd Lincoln, Girl of the Bluegrass. Goldstein, Leslie, illus. LC 92-9782. 192p. (gr. 3-7). 1992. pap. 3.95 (*0-689-71655-9*, Aladdin) Macmillan Child Grp.

Winner, David. Eleanor Roosevelt: Defender of Human Rights & Democracy. LC 91-291. (Illus.). 68p. (gr. 5-6). 1992. PLB 19.93 (*0-8368-0218-7*) Gareth Stevens Inc.

PRESIDENTS' WIVES

see Presidents–U. S.–Wives

PRESLEY, ELVIS ARON, 1935-1977

Alico, Stella H. Elvis Presley - The Beatles. Cruz, E. R. & Guanlao, Ernie, illus. (gr. 4-12). 1979. pap. text ed. 2.95 (*0-88301-352-5*); wkbk 1.25 (*0-88301-376-2*) Pendulum Pr.

Krohn, Katherine E. Elvis Presley: The King. LC 93-23905. (gr. 4 up). 1993. 29.95 (*0-8225-2877-0*) Lerner Pubns.

—Elvis Presley: The King. (gr. 4-7). 1994. pap. 4.95 (*0-8225-9654-7*) Lerner Pubns.

Loewen, L. Elvis. (Illus.). 112p. (gr. 5 up). 1989. lib. bdg. 18.60 (*0-86592-606-9*); 13.95 (*0-685-58614-6*) Rourke Corp.

Rubel, David. Elvis Presely: The Rise of Rock & Roll. 1992. pap. 5.95 (*0-395-63566-7*) HM.

—Elvis Presley: The Rise of Rock & Roll. (Illus.). 96p. (gr. 7 up). 1991. PLB 14.90 (*1-878841-18-1*); pap. 5.95 (*1-56294-829-6*) Millbrook Pr.

PRESS

see Journalism; Newspapers; Periodicals

PREVENTION OF ACCIDENTS

see Accidents–Prevention

PREVENTION OF CRUELTY TO ANIMALS

see Animals–Treatment

PREVENTION OF FIRE

see Fire Prevention

PREVENTIVE MEDICINE

see Bacteriology; Hygiene; Immunity; Public Health

PRIMARY EDUCATION

see Education, Elementary

PRIMATES

see also Man; Monkeys

Ashby, Ruth. The Orangutan. LC 93-5754. (Illus.). 60p. (gr. 5 up). 1994. text ed. 13.95 RSBE (*0-87518-600-9*, Dillon) Macmillan Child Grp.

Beaty, Dave. Primates. (gr. 2-6). 1992. PLB 15.95 (*0-89565-851-8*) Childs World.

Bogard, Vicki, tr. from FRE. Monkeys, Apes & Other Primates. Wallis, Diz, illus. LC 89-5378. 38p. (gr. k-5). 1989. 5.95 (*0-944589-26-X*, 026) Young Discovery Lib.

Gallardo, Evelyn. Among the Orangutans: The Birute Galdikas Story. (gr. 4-7). 1993. pap. 6.95 (*0-8118-0408-9*) Chronicle Bks.

Green, Carl R. & Sanford, William R. The Orangutan. LC 87-19811. (Illus.). 48p. (gr. 5). 1987. text ed. 12.95 RSBE (*0-89686-335-2*, Crestwood Hse) Macmillan Child Grp.

Harrison, Virginia. How Mountain Gorillas Live. Nichols, Michael, illus. LC 91-2022. 32p. (gr. 2-3). 1991. PLB 17.27 (*0-8368-0446-5*) Gareth Stevens Inc.

—Mountain Gorillas & Their Young. Nichols, Michael, illus. LC 91-7600. 32p. (gr. 2-3). 1991. PLB 17.27 (*0-8368-0445-7*) Gareth Stevens Inc.

Hogan, Paula Z. The Gorilla. LC 79-13602. (Illus.). 32p. (gr. 1-4). 1981. PLB 29.28 incl cassette (*0-8172-1845-9*) Raintree Steck-V.

Maynard, Thane. Primates: Apes, Monkeys, Prosimians. (Illus.). 56p. (gr. 2 up). 1994. PLB 14.91 (*0-531-11169-5*) Watts.

Ritchie, Rita. Mountain Gorillas in Danger. Nichols, Michael, photos by. LC 91-10831. (Illus.). 32p. (gr. 2-3). 1991. PLB 17.27 (*0-8368-0447-3*) Gareth Stevens Inc.

Selsam, Millicent E. & Hunt, Joyce. A First Look at Monkeys & Apes. Springer, Harriett, illus. LC 78-74164. (gr. 1-4). 1979. 7.95 (*0-8027-6358-8*); lib. bdg. 9.85 (*0-8027-6359-6*) Walker & Co.

Smith, Roland. Primates in the Zoo. Munoz, William, illus. LC 91-46968. 64p. (gr. 3-6). 1992. PLB 14.40 (*1-56294-210-7*) Millbrook Pr.

Spizzirri Publishing Co. Staff. Primates: An Educational Coloring Book. Spizzirri, Linda, ed. Fuller, Glenn, et al, illus. 32p. (gr. 1-8). 1981. pap. 1.75 (*0-86545-030-7*) Spizzirri.

Wilmot, Zoe. Lemur. LC 93-77343. (ps). 1993. 3.99 (*0-89577-508-5*, Dist. by Random) RD Assn.

PRIME MINISTERS–GREAT BRITAIN

Hole, Dorothy. Margaret Thatcher: Britain's Prime Minister. LC 89-16996. (Illus.). 128p. (gr. 6 up). 1990. lib. bdg. 17.95 (*0-89490-246-6*) Enslow Pubs.

PRIMERS

see also Alphabet Books

Bank Street College of Education Editors. It's about Time: Play Time - Work Time - Learning Time. (Illus.). 64p. (ps-k). 1985. 2.95 (*0-8120-3611-5*) Barron.

—One to Ten More Counting Fun. (Illus.). 64p. (ps-k). 1985. 3.95 (*0-8120-3614-X*) Barron.

—One, Two, Three Come Count with Me. (Illus.). 64p. (ps-k). 1985. 3.95 (*0-8120-3615-8*) Barron.

Berenstain, Stan & Berenstain, Janice. The Bear Detectives. Berenstain, Stan & Berenstain, Janice, illus. LC 75-1603. 48p. (gr. k-3). 1975. 6.95 (*0-394-83127-6*); lib. bdg. 7.99 (*0-394-93127-0*) Beginner.

—Bears' Christmas. LC 79-117542. (Illus.). 72p. (gr. k-3). 1987. 6.95 (*0-394-80090-7*) Beginner.

Gackenbach, Dick. Hattie Rabbit. LC 75-37018. (Illus.). 32p. (ps-3). 1976. PLB 13.89 (*0-06-021940-8*) HarpC Child Bks.

Hall, K. & Flaxman, J. Who Says? (Illus.). 28p. (ps-2). 1990. 10.50 (*0-516-05362-0*); pap. 3.95 (*0-516-45362-9*) Childrens.

Harding, Jacqueline. Building: First Readers. Trotter, Stuart, illus. 28p. (ps-k). 1992. 3.50 (*0-7214-1491-5*) Ladybird Bks.

—Wheels: First Readers. Chapman, Gaynor, illus. 28p. (ps-k). 1992. 3.50 (*0-7214-1483-4*) Ladybird Bks.

—Zoo: First Readers. Hallahan, Maureen, illus. 28p. (ps-k). 1992. 3.50 (*0-7214-1490-7*) Ladybird Bks.

Harker, Jillian. Best Friends: Toddler's. Russell, Chris, illus. 26p. (ps). 1992. 3.50 (*0-7214-1504-0*) Ladybird Bks.

Hoff, Syd. Albert the Albatross. Hoff, Syd, illus. LC 61-5767. 32p. (gr. k-3). 1961. PLB 13.89 (*0-06-022446-0*) HarpC Child Bks.

—Barkley. Hoff, Syd, illus. LC 75-6290. 32p. (gr. k-3). 1975. PLB 13.89 (*0-06-022448-7*) HarpC Child Bks.

Hurd, Edith T. Come & Have Fun. Hurd, Clement, illus. LC 62-13324. 32p. (gr. k-3). 1962. PLB 13.89 (*0-06-022681-1*) HarpC Child Bks.

Jensen, P. The Mess. (Illus.). 28p. (ps-2). 1990. 10.50 (*0-516-05357-4*); pap. 3.95 (*0-516-45357-2*) Childrens.

Kalb, Jonah. The Easy Baseball Book. Kossin, Sandy, illus. LC 75-44085. 64p. (gr. 2-5). 1976. 14.45 (*0-395-24385-8*) HM.

McKissack, Patricia. Who Is Coming? Martin, Clovis, illus. LC 86-11805. 32p. (ps-3). 1990. PLB 10.25 (*0-516-02073-0*); pap. 2.95 (*0-516-42073-9*); pap. 22.95 big bk. (*0-516-49458-9*) Childrens.

Minarik, Else H. Cat & Dog. Siebel, Fritz, illus. LC 60-14998. 32p. (gr. k-2). 1960. PLB 13.89 (*0-06-024221-3*) HarpC Child Bks.

Moncure, Jane B. My "a" Sound Box. Peltier, Pam, illus. LC 84-17024. 32p. (ps-2). 1984. PLB 14.95 (*0-89565-296-X*) Childs World.

—Watch Out! Word Bird. Hohag, Linda S., illus. (ps-2). 1982. PLB 14.95 (*0-89565-219-6*) Childs World.

Packard, M. Surprise! (Illus.). 28p. (ps-2). 1990. PLB 10.50 (*0-516-05360-4*); pap. 3.95 (*0-516-45360-2*) Childrens.

Parish, Peggy. Good Work, Amelia Bedelia. Sweat, Lynn, illus. LC 75-20360. 56p. (gr. 1-4). 1976. 14.00 (*0-688-80022-X*); PLB 13.93 (*0-688-84022-1*) Greenwillow.

Prather, Gloria A. & Prather, Alfred G. My First Reader & Skills Book: One Hundred Words Plus. Prather, Arden C., ed. Hafer, Dick, illus. 36p. (Orig.). (gr. 1-3). 1988. pap. write for info. (*0-9619655-2-5*) Academic Parks Co.

Prather, Gloria M. & Prather, Alfred G. Especially for Special Children: The A-B-C's of Super Stars. Prather, Arden C., ed. Hafer, Dick, illus. 30p. (Orig.). 1988. Picture bk. PLB write for info. (*0-9619655-3-3*) Academic Parks Co.

Schreckhise, Roseva. What Was It Before It Was My Chair? McLean, Mina G., illus. LC 85-13238. 32p. (ps-2). 1985. PLB 14.95 (*0-89565-326-5*) Childs World.

—What Was It Before It Was My Sweater? Endres, Helen, illus. LC 85-11401. 32p. (ps-2). 1985. PLB 14.95 (*0-89565-324-9*) Childs World.

Schulman, Janet. The Big Hello. Hoban, Lillian, illus. LC 75-33672. (gr. 1-4). 1976. 13.95 (*0-688-80036-X*) Greenwillow.

Spizman, Robyn. Bulletin Boards: For Reading, Spelling & Language Skills. Pesiri, Evelyn, illus. 64p. (gr. k-6). 1984. wkbk. 7.95 (*0-86653-210-2*, GA 574) Good Apple.

A Whisper Is Quiet Big Book. (Illus.). 32p. (ps-3). 1990. pap. 22.95 (*0-516-49457-0*) Childrens.

Wise, Francis H. & Wise, Joyce M. Fun in the Sun. Wise, Joyce M., illus. 21p. (ps-1). 1975. pap. 1.50 (*0-915766-30-2*) Wise Pub.

—Jay's Fat Cat. Wise, Joyce M., illus. 20p. (ps-1). 1974. pap. text ed. 1.50 (*0-915766-29-9*) Wise Pub.

PRIMITIVE ART

see Art, Primitive

PRINCE EDWARD ISLAND–FICTION

Conkie, Heather. Dreamer of Dreams. (gr. 4-6). 1993. pap. 3.99 (*0-553-48044-8*) Bantam.

—Old Quarrels, Old Love. (gr. 4-6). 1993. pap. 3.99 (*0-553-48041-3*) Bantam.

Montgomery, L. M. Anne of Green Gables. Moore, Inga, illus. (gr. 4-8). 1994. 14.95 (0-8050-3126-X) H Holt & Co.

—Anne of Green Gables. Felder, Deborah, adapted by. LC 93-36331. 108p. (Orig.). (gr. 2-6). 1994. pap. 2.99 (0-679-85467-3) Random Bks Yng Read.

—Anne of the Island. large type ed. LC 94-1765. 377p. 1994. lib. bdg. 17.95 (0-7862-0205-X) Thorndike Pr.

Montgomery, Lucy M. Anne of Avonlea. (gr. 4-7). 1991. pap. 3.25 (0-590-44556-1, Apple Classics) Scholastic Inc.

—Anne of Avonlea. 1992. pap. 3.25 (0-553-15114-2) Bantam.

—Anne of Green Gables. 320p. (gr. 7-12). 1976. pap. 2.95 (0-553-24295-4) Bantam.

—Anne of Green Gables. 1987. Boxed set. pap. 8.95 (0-553-33306-2) Bantam.

—Anne of Green Gables. 1982. pap. 2.95 (0-553-21313-X, Bantam Classics) Bantam.

—Anne of Green Gables. Mattern, Joanne, ed. Graef, Renee, illus. LC 92-12703. 48p. (gr. 3-6). 1992. PLB 12.89 (0-8167-2866-6); pap. text ed. 3.95 (0-8167-2867-4) Troll Assocs.

—Anne of Green Gables. facsimile ed. 352p. 1992. Repr. of 1908 ed. 16.95 (1-55109-013-9, Pub. by Nimbus Publishing Ltd CN) Chelsea Green Pub.

—Anne of Green Gables. Atwood, Margaret, afterword by. 338p. 1993. pap. 4.95 (0-7710-9883-9) Firefly Bks Ltd.

—Anne of Green Gables. LC 93-70551. 240p. (gr. 4 up). 1993. 5.98 (1-56138-324-4) Courage Bks.

—Anne of Green Gables. 256p. (gr. 5 up). 1994. pap. 2.99 (0-14-035148-5) Puffin Bks.

—Anne of Green Gables, Vol. 1. (gr. 4-7). 1984. pap. 3.50 (0-553-15327-7) Bantam.

—Anne of Ingleside, No. 6. 1984. pap. 2.95 (0-553-21315-6, Bantam Classics) Bantam.

—Anne of the Island. 1983. pap. 2.95 (0-553-21317-2, Bantam Classics) Bantam.

—Anne of the Island. (gr. 3-7). 1992. pap. 3.50 (0-553-48066-9) Bantam.

—Anne of the Island. Graham, Mark, illus. 288p. (gr. 4 up). 1992. 14.95 (0-448-40311-0, G&D) Putnam Pub Group.

—Anne of the Island. (gr. 4-7). 1993. pap. 3.25 (0-590-46163-X) Scholastic Inc.

—Anne of Windy Poplars. (gr. 3-7). 1992. pap. 3.50 (0-553-48065-0) Bantam.

—Anne's House of Dreams. 1983. pap. 2.95 (0-553-21318-0, Bantam Classics) Bantam.

—Chronicles of Avonlea. 1988. pap. 2.95 (0-553-21378-4, Bantam Classics) Bantam.

—Rainbow Valley. 1976. 19.95 (0-8488-0591-7) Amereon Ltd.

—Rilla of Ingleside. 1985. pap. 3.50 (0-553-26922-4) Bantam.

—Rilla of Ingleside. 1976. 21.95 (0-8488-0592-5) Amereon Ltd.

Quarantine at Alexander Abraham's. (gr. 3-7). 1992. pap. 3.99 (0-553-48031-6) Bantam.

PRINCES AND PRINCESSES–FICTION

Andersen, Hans Christian. The Princess & the Pea. Bell, Anthea, tr. Tharlet, Eve, illus. LC 87-13913. (ps up). 1991. pap. 13.95 (0-88708-052-9) Picture Bk Studio.

Ashby, Sylvia. Shining Princess of the Slender Bamboo. (Illus.). 44p. (Orig.). (gr. 6 up). 1987. pap. 3.50 (0-88680-266-0); royalty on application 50.00 (0-685-67658-7) I E Clark.

Barkan, Joanne. Krystal Princess: Krystal Princess & the Grand Contest. (ps-3). 1994. pap. 2.50 (0-590-47875-3) Scholastic Inc.

Bianchi, J. Princess Frownsalot. (Illus.). 24p. (ps-8). 1987. 12.95 (0-921285-06-X, Pub. by Bungalo Bks CN); pap. 4.95 (0-921285-04-3, Pub. by Bungalo Bks CN) Firefly Bks Ltd.

Birrer, Cynthia & Birrer, William. The Lady & the Unicorn. Birrer, Cynthia & Birrer, William, illus. LC 86-20872. 32p. (ps-3). 1987. 12.95 (0-688-04037-3) Lothrop.

Bos, Burny. Le Prince Ferdinand. De Beer, Hans, illus. (FRE.). 32p. (gr. k-3). 1992. 13.95 (3-85539-703-1) North-South Bks NYC.

—Prince Valentino. De Beer, Hans, illus. LC 89-43247. 32p. (gr. k-3). 1990. 13.95 (1-55858-089-1) North-South Bks NYC.

Bradshaw, Gillian. The Land of Gold. LC 91-31810. 160p. (gr. 5 up). 1992. 14.00 (0-688-10576-9) Greenwillow.

Braybrooks, Ann. The Disney's the Princesses Collection: Stories from the Films. Thompkins, Kenny, illus. LC 92-56163. 80p. 1993. 14.95 (1-56282-497-X); PLB 14.89 (1-56282-498-8) Disney Pr.

Brentano, Clemens. The Legend of Rosepetal. Zwerger, Lisbeth, illus. LC 84-27386. 32p. (gr. 2-6). 1991. pap. 16.95 (0-907234-71-2) Picture Bk Studio.

Brooks, Jennifer. Princess Jessica Rescues a Prince. Flores, Lennie, illus. Ridley, Chas, ed. LC 93-92628. (Illus.). 40p. (ps-2). 1994. 15.95 (0-9636335-0-3) Nadja Pub.

Burnett, Frances H. A Little Princess. 232p. 1981. Repr. PLB 15.95 (0-89966-327-3) Buccaneer Bks.

—A Little Princess. 300p. 1977. PLB 15.95x (0-89967-005-9) Harmony Raine.

—A Little Princess. 256p. (Orig.). (gr. 4-6). 1987. pap. 3.25 (0-590-40719-8, Apple Classics) Scholastic Inc.

—A Little Princess. Adorjan, Carol M., adapted by. Marvin, Frederic, illus. LC 87-15485. 48p. (gr. 3-6). 1988. PLB 12.89 (0-8167-1201-8); pap. text ed. 3.95 (0-8167-1202-6) Troll Assocs.

—A Little Princess. Henterly, Jamichael, illus. 288p. (gr. 4 up). 1989. 13.95 (0-448-09299-9, G&D) Putnam Pub Group.

—A Little Princess. Schwartz, Lynne S., intro. by. 240p. 1990. pap. 2.95 (0-451-52509-4, Sig Classics) NAL-Dutton.

—A Little Princess. 1990. pap. 3.50 (0-440-40386-3, Pub. by Yearling Classics) Dell.

—The Lost Prince. (gr. 4-6). 1986. pap. 2.95 (0-14-035071-3, Puffin) Puffin Bks.

—Lost Prince. 23.95 (0-8488-0691-3) Amereon Ltd.

Cardinal, Catherine S. Mud Grape Pie. 29p. (gr. k-6). 1991. pap. 6.00 (0-9630655-0-5) Garden Gate.

Coville, Bruce. The Dragonslayers. MacDonald, Pat, ed. Coville, Katherine, illus. LC 93-40194. 128p. (gr. 7 up). 1994. 14.00 (0-671-89036-0, Minstrel Bks) PB.

Curtis, Dorris. Skammy: Prince of Troy. Curtis, Dorris, illus. 231p. (gr. 5-9). 1988. lib. bdg. 18.50 (0-944436-04-8) Univ Central AR Pr.

Davis, Michael. The Flower Princess. Luongo, Aldo, illus. 32p. (gr. k-12). 1989. write for info.; PLB write for info. R Bane Ltd.

De Camp, L. Sprague. The Undesired Princess & the Enchanted Bunny. 1990. pap. 4.99 (0-671-69875-3) Baen Bks.

De Paola, Tomie. The Prince of the Dolomites. De Paola, Tomie, illus. LC 79-18524. 46p. (gr. 1-5). 1980. pap. 4.50 (0-15-674432-5, Voyager Bks) HarBrace.

De Saint-Exupery, Antoine. The Little Prince. 1992. Repr. lib. bdg. 18.95x (0-89968-299-5) Lightyear.

—Petit Prince. (FRE.). 123p. (gr. 5-10). 1987. pap. 9.95 (2-07-033453-8) Schoenhof.

—Petit Prince. (FRE.). 93p. (gr. 5-10). 1988. pap. 29.95 incl. cassette (2-07-032267-X) Schoenhof.

Gal, Laszlo. Prince Ivan & the Firebird. Gal, Laszlo, illus. 40p. 1992. text ed. 14.95 (0-920668-98-4) Firefly Bks Ltd.

Gold, Auner. The Marrano Prince. Hinlicky, Gregg, illus. 286p. (gr. 9-12). 1988. 13.95 (0-935063-39-0); text ed. 10.95 (0-935063-40-4) CIS Comm.

Gouffe, Marie A. Treasures Beyond the Snows. Sellon, Michael B., illus. LC 77-95392. (gr. 3-9). 1970. 3.75 (0-8356-0026-2, Quest) Theos Pub Hse.

Greaves, Margaret. Sarah's Lion. (ps-3). 1992. 13.95 (0-8120-6279-5) Barron.

Gregory, Philippa. Florizella & the Wolves. Aggs, Patrice, illus. LC 92-52998. 80p. (gr. 3-6). 1993. 13.95 (1-56402-126-2) Candlewick Pr.

Grimm, Jacob & Grimm, Wilhelm K. Le Prince Grenouille. Schroeder, Binette, illus. (FRE.). 32p. (gr. k-3). 1992. 15.95 (3-314-20666-6) North-South Bks NYC.

Harris, Aurand. The Flying Prince. (Orig.). (gr. k up). 1985. 4.50 (0-87602-262-X) Anchorage.

Hellman-Hurpoil, Odile. Prince Oliver Doesn't Want to Take a Bath. (Illus.). (gr. 3-8). 1992. PLB 8.95 (0-89565-887-9) Childs World.

Helprin, Mark, as told by. Swan Lake. Van Allsburg, Chris, illus. (gr. 1-8). 1989. 19.45 (0-395-49858-9) HM.

Hunt, Angela E. True Princess. LC 92-828. (ps-3). 1992. 13.99 (1-55513-760-1, Chariot Bks) Chariot Family.

Ikeda, Daisaku. The Snow Country Prince. McCaughrean, Geraldine, tr. Wildsmith, Brian, illus. LC 90-24908. 32p. (ps-3). 1991. 15.00 (0-679-81965-7) Knopf Bks Yng Read.

Johnson, Crockett. Frowning Prince. Johnson, Crockett, illus. (gr. 1-4). 1974. Repr. 15.00 (0-912846-09-7) Bookstore Pr.

Johnson, Jane. The Princess & the Painter. LC 93-39987. (ps-3). 1994. 15.00 (0-374-36118-5) FS&G.

Kaye, M. M. Ordinary Princess. 1993. pap. 3.50 (0-440-40880-6) Dell.

Keens-Douglas, Richardo. El Misterio De la Isla De las Especies: The Nutmeg Princess. Galouchko, Annouchka, illus. (SPA.). 32p. (ps-2). 1992. pap. 6.95 (1-55037-260-2, Pub. by Annick Pr) Firefly Bks Ltd.

—Le Mystere de l'Iles aux Epices: The Nutmeg Princess. Galouchko, Annouchka, illus. (FRE.). 32p. (ps-2). 1992. PLB 15.95 (1-55037-249-1, Pub. by Annick Pr); pap. 6.95 (1-55037-250-5, Pub. by Annick Pr) Firefly Bks Ltd.

—The Nutmeg Princess. Galouchko, Annouchka, illus. 32p. (ps-2). 1992. PLB 15.95 (1-55037-239-4, Pub. by Annick Pr); pap. 5.95 (1-55037-236-X, Pub. by Annick Pr) Firefly Bks Ltd.

Kleven, Elisa. The Paper Princess. LC 93-32612. (Illus.). (ps-3). 1994. 14.99 (0-525-45231-1, DCB) Dutton Child Bks.

Korman, Justine. Krystal Princess: Krystal Princesses Shake up the Day. (ps-3). 1994. pap. 2.50 (0-590-47881-8) Scholastic Inc.

Kurtz, Jane. Miro in the Kingdom of the Sun. (Illus.). 32p. (ps-2). 1995. 14.95g (0-395-69181-8) Ticknor & Flds Bks Yng Read.

Latella, Lisa. A Song for the Prince. Latella, Lisa, illus. 36p. (Orig.). (gr. k up). 1984. pap. write for info. (0-9608592-1-7) Gallery Arts.

LeCain, Errol. Twelve Dancing Princesses. 32p. (ps-k). 1981. pap. 3.95 (0-14-050322-6, Puffin) Puffin Bks.

Lewis, Paul O. The Starlight Bride. (Illus.). 40p. (ps-6). 1988. cloth 14.95 (0-941831-33-7); pap. 9.95 (0-941831-25-6) Beyond Words Pub.

Lewison, Wendy C. The Princess & the Potty. Brown, Richard, illus. LC 93-7853. (gr. 2 up). 1994. pap. 14.00 (0-671-87284-2, S&S BFYR) S&S Trade.

Littke, Lael. Prom Dress. 176p. (Orig.). (gr. 6-10). 1989. pap. 3.25 (0-590-44237-6) Scholastic Inc.

A Little Princess. 1994. write for info. (0-8050-3128-6) H Holt & Co.

Lowry, Lois. Anastasia. write for info. HM.

Luth, Sophie A. The Special Princess. McColgan, Susie, illus. 36p. 1990. glossy cover 5.95 (0-9626153-0-7) Luth & Assocs.

Lynch, Patricia. Brogeen & the Princess of Sheen. (gr. 1 up). 1986. pap. 11.95 (0-85105-905-8, Pub. by Colin Smythe Ltd Britain) Dufour.

MacDonald, George. The Light Princess & Other Tales. (Illus.). 288p. (gr. 5-8). 1989. pap. 7.95 (0-86241-164-5, Pub. by Cnngt Pub Ltd) Trafalgar.

—Little Daylight. Ingraham, Erick, adapted by. & illus. LC 85-29769. 40p. (gr. 2 up). 1988. 12.95 (0-688-06300-4); PLB 12.88 (0-688-06301-2, Morrow Jr Bks) Morrow Jr Bks.

—The Princess & Curdie. 306p. 1989. Repr. lib. bdg. 26.95x (0-89966-591-8) Buccaneer Bks.

—The Princess & The Goblin. 1986. pap. 4.95 (0-440-47189-3, Yearling Classics) Dell.

—The Princess & the Goblin. Smith, Jesse W., illus. Glassman, Peter, afterword by. LC 86-2532. (Illus.). 208p. (ps up). 1986. 17.95 (0-688-06604-6) Morrow Jr Bks.

—The Princess & the Goblin. 1989. Repr. lib. bdg. 26.95x (0-89966-598-5) Buccaneer Bks.

—The Princess & the Goblin. (gr. 4-7). 1991. pap. 2.95 (0-590-44025-X) Scholastic Inc.

—The Princess & the Goblin, The Princess & Curdie. McGillis, Roderick, intro. by. 400p. 1990. pap. 5.95 (0-19-282579-8) OUP.

Manson, Frank A. The Adventures of Prince Albert & the Royal Dinosaurs. Henley, Joan, illus. 144p. (gr. 2-7). 1990. 11.95 (0-918339-17-0) Vandamere.

Marvin, Fred, illus. Walt Disney's Snow White & the Seven Dwarfs: Suppertime. LC 93-71376. 10p. (ps-k). 1994. 4.95 (1-56282-600-X) Disney Pr.

Mayer, Marianna. Twelve Dancing Princess. Craft, Kinuko Y., illus. LC 83-1034. 40p. (ps up). 1989. 14.95 (0-688-08051-0); PLB 14.88 (0-688-02026-7, Morrow Jr Bks) Morrow Jr Bks.

Merrill, Linda & Ridley, Sarah. The Princess & the Peacocks: Or, the Story of the Room. Dixon, Tennessee, illus. LC 92-72019. 32p. (gr. k-4). 1993. 14.95 (1-56282-327-2); PLB 14.89 (1-56282-328-0) Hyprn Child.

Moodie, Fiona. The Sugar Prince. (Illus.). (ps-3). 1987. 12.95 (1-55774-005-4) Modan-Adama Bks.

Mulock, Dinah M. Little Lame Prince, Adventures of Brownie. 1976. 18.95 (0-8488-1109-7) Amereon Ltd.

Munsch, Robert. Paper Bag Princess. Martchenko, Michael, illus. 32p. (gr. k-3). 1980. PLB 14.95 (0-920236-82-0, Pub. by Annick CN); pap. 4.95 (0-920236-16-2, Pub. by Annick CN) Firefly Bks Ltd.

—The Paper Bag Princess. Martchenko, Michael, illus. 24p. (ps-1). 1986. pap. 0.99 (0-920236-25-1, Pub. by Annick CN) Firefly Bks Ltd.

—La Princesa Vestida Con Una Bolsa De Papel: The Paperbag Princess. Martchenko, Michael, illus. (SPA.). 32p. (ps-2). 1991. pap. 5.95 (1-55037-098-7, Pub. by Annick CN) Firefly Bks Ltd.

Nikolai. Frog Princess Tales. 1988. 12.95 (0-385-24624-2) Doubleday.

Peck, Richard. Princess Ashley. (gr. k-12). 1988. pap. 3.50 (0-440-20206-X, LFL) Dell.

Robbins, Neal. The Neglected Princess. 72p. 1992. pap. 4.00 (1-884993-00-1) Koldarana.

Ross, Tony. I Want My Potty. (Illus.). 24p. (ps-k). 1988. pap. 6.95 (0-916291-14-6) Kane-Miller Bk.

—I Want to Be. LC 92-41527. (Illus.). 32p. (ps-1). 1993. 11.95 (0-916291-46-4) Kane-Miller Bk.

Roth, Susan L. Princess. Roth, Susan, illus. LC 92-55042. 32p. (ps-3). 1993. 13.95 (1-56282-465-1); PLB 13.89 (1-56282-466-X) Hyprn Child.

Saint-Exupery, Antoine de. The Little Prince. Woods, Katherine, tr. LC 67-1144. (Illus.). 111p. (gr. 3-7). 1968. pap. 3.95 (0-15-652820-7) HarBrace.

—Petit Prince. (FRE.). (gr. 3-8). write for info. Fr & Eur.

Sampson, Fay. Pangur Ban. (Illus.). 128p. (Orig.). (gr. 4-8). 1989. pap. 4.99 (0-85648-580-2) Lion USA.

Sanderson, Ruth, retold by. The Twelve Dancing Princesses. (Illus.). (gr. 4-8). 1993. pap. 5.95 (0-316-77062-0, Joy St Bks) Little.

Scieszka, Jon. The Frog Prince, Continued. Johnson, Steve, illus. 32p. (ps-3). 1991. 14.95 (0-670-83421-1) Viking Child Bks.

Sharmat, Marjorie W. The Princess of the Fillmore Street School. (gr. 4-7). 1991. pap. 2.75 (0-440-40415-0) Dell.

Shearer, Marilyn J. The Nubian Princess. Walker, Larry, illus. 16p. (Orig.). (ps-6). 1989. 19.95 (0-685-30091-9); pap. 10.95 (0-685-30092-7) L Ashley & Joshua.

Shields, Carol D. I Am Really a Princess. Meisel, Paul, illus. LC 92-37161. 32p. (ps-3). 1993. 13.99 (0-525-45138-2, DCB) Dutton Child Bks.

Simpson, Juwairiah J. L. The Princess Who Wanted to Be Poor. American Trust Publications, ed. (Illus.). 52p. 1987. pap. 4.75 (0-89259-104-8) Am Trust Pubns.

Slater, Teddy, adapted by. Disney's the Prince & the Pauper. Wilson, Phil, illus. LC 92-56165. 48p. 1993. 12.95 (1-56282-511-9); PLB 12.89 (1-56282-512-7) Disney Pr.

Swiderska, Barbara. The Fisherman's Bride. Swiderska, Barbara, illus. LC 78-148051. 32p. (ps-3). 8.95 (*0-87592-018-7*) Scroll Pr.
Thomas, Frances. The Prince & the Cave. 1992. pap. 35.00x (*0-86383-768-9*, Pub. by Gomer Pr UK) St Mut.
Thomas, Jane R. The Princess in the Pigpen. LC 89-856. 128p. (gr. 3-7). 1989. 13.95 (*0-395-51587-4*, Clarion Bks) HM.
Thurber, James. Many Moons. Simont, Marac, illus. LC 89-36465. 48p. (gr. 3-7). 1990. 14.95 (*0-15-251872-X*) HarBrace.
Trenholm, Harriet. How the Princess Returned Color to Her Kingdom. 60p. (gr. k-8). 1994. pap. 13.95 (*0-9633876-0-X*) Inner Child Play.
Trussell-Cullen, Alan. The Real Cinderella Rap. Webb, Philip, illus. LC 93-24528. 1994. 4.25 (*0-383-03771-9*) SRA Schl Grp.
Twain, Mark. The Prince & the Pauper. 256p. (gr. 3-7). 1983. pap. 2.95 (*0-14-035017-9*, Puffin) Puffin Bks.
—The Prince & the Pauper. (gr. k-6). 1985. pap. 4.95 (*0-440-47186-9*, Pub. by Yearling Classics) Dell.
—The Prince & the Pauper. (Illus.). 304p. 1991. 9.99 (*0-517-66845-9*) Random Hse Value.
Tyler, Anne. Tumble Tower. Modarressi, Mitra, illus. LC 92-44524. 32p. (ps-2). 1993. 14.95 (*0-531-05497-7*); PLB 14.99 (*0-531-08647-X*) Orchard Bks Watts.
Vesey, Amanda. The Princess & the Frog. Vesey, A., illus. 32p. (ps-3). 1985. 14.95 (*0-316-90036-2*, 900362, Joy St Bks) Little.
Walker, Nicholas. Ice Princess. (gr. 4-7). 1994. pap. 2.95 (*0-590-47727-7*) Scholastic Inc.
Wein, Elizabeth. The Winter Prince. LC 91-39129. 208p. (gr. 7 up). 1993. SBE 14.95 (*0-689-31747-6*, Atheneum Child Bk) Macmillan Child Grp.
White, John. The Sword Bearer. LC 86-2860. (Illus.). 295p. (Orig.). (gr. 4 up). 1986. pap. 10.99 (*0-87784-590-5*, 590) InterVarsity.

Wixom, Tedi T. A Princess, Dragon & Baker. Hale, Leon & May, Mike, illus. 40p. (ps-8). 1994. Saddlestitch bdg. 6.95 (*1-885227-33-7*) TNT Bks.
A PRINCESS, DRAGON & BAKER by Tedi Tuttle Wixom (Author of "To Heal A Heart", adult non-fiction, by Northwest Pub. Inc.). Illustrated by Leon Hale & Mike May; TNT Books. A fast-paced NEW fairy tale set high in a mystical kingdom in Europe! Princess Catherine, a vivacious young girl with an attitude, wants to have everything her way. The people of the town realize she has no friends, except for 10 white rabbits. A blue dragon, who is flying around looking for adventure, crashes through the palace window when he smells his favorite food, carrots, inside the castle walls. His crash landing terrifies Princess Catherine & her maid. The rotund village baker, upon hearing her screaming, sprints to the castle to save Princess Catherine from a watery grave when she falls into the shark infested moat. Herein lies action & adventure no child will want to miss. This will be the future classic fairy tale your children will want to tell & retell to their children & grandchildren. 40 pages. 8 1/2 X 11. Exquisite illustrations by experts. Artists utilize magnificent perspectives done in watercolor washes/four-color. $6.95 saddlestitched. ISBN 1-885227-33-7.
Publisher Provided Annotation.

Wood, Audrey. Princess & the Dragon. Wood, Audrey, illus. LC 90-49098. 32p. (ps-2). 1989. 7.95 (*0-85953-150-3*); pap. 3.95 (*0-85953-013-2*) Childs Play.
Ziefert, Harriet. The Prince's Tooth Is Loose. Alley, R. W., illus. LC 89-36433. 24p. (Orig.). (ps-2). 1990. pap. 2.25 (*0-394-84840-3*) Random Bks Yng Read.

PRINTING
see also Books
Brommer, Gerald F. Relief Printmaking. LC 77-113860. (Illus.). 148p. (gr. 7-12). 1970. 15.95 (*0-87192-034-4*) Davis Mass.
Cross, Jeanne. Simple Printing Methods. Cross, Jeanne, illus. LC 72-39812. 48p. (gr. 6 up). 1972. 21.95 (*0-87599-192-0*) S G Phillips.
Falwell, Cathryn. The Letter Jesters. Falwell, Cathryn, illus. LC 93-22739. 48p. (gr. k-3). 1994. 14.95g (*0-395-66898-0*) Ticknor & Flds Bks Yng Read.
Graphic Arts. (Illus.). 64p. (gr. 6-12). 1988. pap. 1.85 (*0-8395-3374-8*, 3374) BSA.
Harrison, Steve & Harrison, Patricia. Writing & Printing. 48p. (Orig.). (gr. 4 up). 1992. pap. 6.95 (*0-563-34787-2*, BBC-Parkwest) Parkwest Pubns.
Lynn, Sara & James, Diane. Play with Paint. (Illus.). 24p. (ps-2). 1993. 18.95 (*0-87614-755-4*) Carolrhoda Bks.
Morgan, Judith. An Art Text-Workbook: Printmaking (Introduction) Wallace, Dorathye, ed. (Illus.). 124p. (Orig.). (gr. 8-10). 1990. pap. 13.27 (*0-914127-27-6*); tchr's. ed. avail. Univ Class.
O'Neill, Catherine. Let's Visit a Printing Plant. Parker, James W., illus. LC 87-3484. 32p. (gr. 2-4). 1988. PLB 10.79 (*0-8167-1163-1*); pap. text ed. 2.95 (*0-8167-1164-X*) Troll Assocs.
O'Reilly, Susie. Block Printing. Mukhida, Zul, photos by. LC 92-43263. 32p. (gr. 4-6). 1993. 14.95 (*1-56847-065-7*) Thomson Lrning.
Robins, Deri. Making Prints. LC 92-40216. 40p. (gr. 3-7). 1993. 10.95 (*1-85697-925-3*, Kingfisher LKC); pap. 5.95 (*1-85697-924-5*) LKC.
Stocks, Sue. Printing. LC 94-2661. (Illus.). 32p. (gr. 1-4). 1994. 14.95 (*1-56847-210-2*) Thomson Lrning.
Thomson, Ruth. Printing. LC 94-16913. (Illus.). 24p. (ps-3). 1994. PLB 14.40 (*0-516-07992-1*); pap. 4.95 (*0-516-47992-X*) Childrens.
Tofts, Hannah. Print Book. (ps-3). 1990. pap. 11.95 (*0-671-70368-4*, S&S BFYR); pap. 4.95 (*0-671-70369-2*, S&S BFYR) S&S Trade.
Turner, Herschel. The Black West Print Set. (gr. 4-6). 1992. 75.00 (*1-882205-25-1*) All Media Prods.
Using Paper & Paint. LC 91-17038. (Illus.). 48p. (gr. 4-8). 1991. PLB 14.95 (*1-85435-406-X*) Marshall Cavendish.

PRINTING–HISTORY
Fisher, Leonard E. Gutenberg. Fisher, Leonard E., illus. LC 92-26991. 32p. (gr. 2-6). 1993. SBE 14.95 (*0-02-735238-2*, Macmillan Child Bk) Macmillan Child Grp.

PRISON ESCAPES
see Escapes

PRISONS
see also Crime and Criminals; Criminal Law; Escapes
Adint, Victor. Drugs & Prison. LC 94-1025. 1994. 14.95 (*0-8239-1705-3*) Rosen Group.
Barden. Prisons. 1991. 12.95s.p. (*0-86593-110-0*); 17.27 (*0-685-59207-3*) Rourke Corp.
Bernards, Neal & Szumski, Bonnie. Prisons: Detecting Bias. LC 90-45284. (Illus.). 32p. (gr. 3-6). 1990. PLB 10.95 (*0-89908-604-7*) Greenhaven.
Gordon, Vivian V. & Smith-Owens, Lois. Prisons & the Criminal Justice System. 160p. (gr. 7 up). 1992. PLB 15.85 (*0-8027-8121-7*); pap. 9.95 (*0-8027-7370-2*) Walker & Co.
Hjelmeland, Andy. Kids in Jail. Wolf, Dennis, photos by. (Illus.). 40p. (gr. 4-8). 1992. PLB 17.50 (*0-8225-2552-6*) Lerner Pubns.
O'Neill, Judith. Transported to Van Diemen's Land. (Illus.). 48p. (gr. 7 up). 1977. pap. 7.95 (*0-521-21231-6*) Cambridge U Pr.
Redpath, Ann. What Happens If You Go to Jail? (Illus.). 48p. (gr. 3-6). Date not set. PLB 12.95 (*1-56065-135-0*) Capstone Pr.
St. Pierre, Stephanie. Everything You Need to Know When a Parent Is in Jail. Rosen, Ruth, ed. (gr. 7-12). 1993. PLB 14.95 (*0-8239-1526-3*) Rosen Group.
Warburton, Lois. Prisons. LC 92-43246. (Illus.). 112p. (gr. 5-8). 1993. PLB 14.95 (*1-56006-138-3*) Lucent Bks.
Weiss, Ann E. Prisons: A System in Trouble. LC 88-431. 160p. (gr. 6 up). 1988. lib. bdg. 18.95 (*0-89490-165-6*) Enslow Pubs.

PRISONS–FICTION
Butterworth, Oliver. Visitng the Big House. Cohn, Amy, ed. Avishai, Susan, illus. LC 94-20844. 48p. 1995. pap. 3.95 (*0-688-13303-7*, Pub. by Beech Tree Bks) Morrow.
De Jenkins, Lyll B. The Honorable Prison. 208p. (gr. 7 up). 1989. pap. 3.95 (*0-14-032952-8*, Puffin) Puffin Bks.
Koranteng, Kwasi. Innocent Prisoner. (gr. 4-7). 1992. pap. 4.95 (*0-7910-2920-4*) Chelsea Hse.
Myers, Walter D. Somewhere in the Darkness. 224p. 1992. 14.95 (*0-590-42411-4*, Scholastic Hardcover) Scholastic Inc.
Sebestyen, Ouida. The Girl in the Box: The Diary of Anne Frank. 160p. (gr. 7 up). 1988. 12.95 (*0-316-77935-0*, Joy St Bks) Little.
Takashima, Shizuye. A Child in Prison Camp. (Illus.). 100p. (gr. 4 up). 1991. pap. 7.95 (*0-88776-241-7*) Tundra Bks.

PRIZE FIGHTING
see Boxing

PROBABILITIES
Cushman, Jean. Do You Wanna Bet? Your Chance to Find Out about Probability. Weston, Martha, illus. 112p. (gr. 3-7). 1991. 14.45 (*0-395-56516-2*, Clarion Bks) HM.
Lovell, Robert. Probability Activities. 308p. (gr. 9-12). 1993. pap. 18.95 (*1-55953-067-7*) Key Curr Pr.
Wyler, Rose & Elting, Mary. Math Fun: Test Your Luck. LC 91-3919. (Illus.). 64p. (gr. 4-7). 1992. lib. bdg. 10.98 (*0-671-74311-2*, J Messner); pap. 5.95 (*0-671-74312-0*, J Messner) S&S Trade.

PROBES, SPACE
see Space Probes

PROBLEM CHILDREN
see also Juvenile Delinquency
Shapiro, Lawrence E. Sometimes I Drive My Mom Crazy, but I Know She's Crazy about Me: A Self-Esteem Book for Overactive & Impulsive Children. Shore, Hennie M., ed. Parrotte, Timothy, illus. 80p. (gr. k-6). 1993. 9.95 (*1-882732-03-0*) Ctr Applied Psy.

PROBLEM CHILDREN–FICTION
Fassler, Joan. The Boy with a Problem: Johnny Learns to Share His Troubles. LC 78-147125. (Illus.). 32p. (ps-3). 1971. 16.95 (*0-87705-054-6*) Human Sci Pr.
—Don't Worry Dear. Kranz, Stewart, illus. LC 74-147124. 32p. (ps-3). 1971. 16.95 (*0-87705-055-4*) Human Sci Pr.
McCoy, Diana L. A Special Place: A Child's Story about Entering Counseling for Children Ages 4 Through 6. Brown, Wynne, illus. 24p. (Orig.). (ps-1). 1988. pap. 5.50 (*0-9619250-2-7*) Magic Lantrn.
—A Special Place: A Child's Story about Entering Counseling for Children Ages 7 Through 10. Brown, Wynne, illus. 32p. (gr. 2-5). 1988. pap. text ed. 5.50 (*0-9619250-3-5*) Magic Lantrn.
Schwier, Karin M. Keith Edward's Different Day. Schwier, Karin M., illus. LC 92-22010. 36p. (Orig.). (gr. k-4). 1992. pap. 4.95 (*0-915166-74-7*) Impact Pubs Cal.

PROBLEM SOLVING–DATA PROCESSING
Youngs, Bettie B. Problem Solving Skills for Children. 69p. (gr. k-6). 1989. pap. text ed. 9.95 (*0-940221-01-2*); tchr's. ed. 10.00 (*0-685-25381-3*); wkbk. 10.00 (*0-685-25382-1*); lab manual 10.00 (*0-685-25383-X*) Lrng Tools-Bilicki Pubns.

PRODUCTION
see Economics; Industry

PRODUCTS, DAIRY
see Dairy Products

PRODUCTS, WASTE
see Waste Products

PROFESSION, CHOICE OF
see Vocational Guidance

PROFESSIONS
see also Occupations; Vocational Guidance; also names of professions (e.g. Law; Medicine); also Law–Vocational Guidance; music–Vocational guidance
Barkin, Carol & James, Elizabeth. Jobs for Kids. Doty, Roy, illus. LC 89-45900. 128p. (gr. 5 up). 1991. pap. 6.95 (*0-688-09323-X*, Pub. by Beech Tree Bks) Morrow.
Lock, Robert D. Student Activities for Taking Charge of Your Career Direction & Job Search: Career Planning Guide, Bk. 3. 2nd ed. 136p. 1992. pap. 14.95 (*0-534-13659-1*) Brooks-Cole.
Stern, Benjamin J. Opportunities in Machines Shop Trades. (gr. 8 up). 1986. 13.95 (*0-8442-6147-5*, VGM Career Bks); pap. 10.95 (*0-8442-6148-3*, VGM Career Bks) NTC Pub Grp.

PROFESSORS
see Teachers

PROGRAMMING (ELECTRONIC COMPUTERS)
Baumann, Susan K. & Mandell, Steven L. QBASIC. Perlee, Clyde, ed. 450p. 1992. text ed. 40.50 (*0-314-78351-2*) West Pub.
Blanc, Iris. Learning WordPerfect 5.0 & 5.1: Through Step-by-Step Exercises & Applications. (gr. 9-12). 1991. pap. 20.00 comb bdg. (*1-56243-046-7*, W-9); tchr's. ed. 10.00 (*1-56243-047-5*, W-106); transparencies of exercises 250.00 (*1-56243-049-1*, PW-1); cancelled (*1-56243-050-5*, PW-2); answer key on diskette 65.00 (*1-56243-048-3*, SW-25) DDC Pub.
Kennedy, Sandra & MacDonald, James. Adventures in SeeLogo: Course Code 192-2. Schroeder, Bonnie, ed. Anastasia, Karyn & Knapp, William, illus. 91p. (Orig.). (gr. 4). 1989. wkbk. 6.95 (*0-917531-44-2*) CES Compu-Tech.
Leonard, Michael. Learning BASIC: Answers & Notes. 38p. (gr. 4-8). 1988. pap. text ed. 2.95 (*0-913684-14-7*) Key Curr Pr.
—Learning BASIC, Bk. 1: PRINT & GO TO. 44p. (gr. 4-8). 1988. pap. text ed. 2.30 (*0-913684-10-4*) Key Curr Pr.
—Learning BASIC, Bk. 2: INPUT & IF-THEN. 44p. (gr. 4-8). 1988. pap. text ed. 2.30 (*0-913684-11-2*) Key Curr Pr.
—Learning BASIC, Bk. 3: LET & FOR-NEXT. 52p. (gr. 4-8). 1988. pap. text ed. 2.30 (*0-913684-12-0*) Key Curr Pr.
Muller, Jim. One-Two-Three My Computer & Me: A LOGO Funbook for Kids. (gr. 3 up). 1984. (Reston); Commodore 64. pap. 15.95 (*0-8359-5244-4*) P-H.
Nance, Douglas W. Pascal: Introduction to Programming & Problem Solving. (Illus.). 639p. (gr. 9-12). 1989. Repr. of 1986 ed. text ed. 34.25 (*0-314-93206-2*) West Pub.
Resnick, Kathleen. Kermit Learns Windows. 48p. (Orig.). (gr. 5 up). 1993. 9.95 (*1-55958-366-5*) Prima Pub.
Wagner, Roger. Assembly Lines the Book. rev., 2nd ed. (Illus.). 273p. (Orig.). pap. 19.95 (*0-927796-99-6*); Apple format disk 15.95 (*0-927796-24-4*) R Wagner Pub.

PROGRAMMING (ELECTRONIC COMPUTERS) –VOCATIONAL GUIDANCE
Kaplan, Andrew. Careers for Computer Buffs. (Illus.). 64p. (gr. 7 up). 1991. PLB 14.40 (*1-56294-021-X*); pap. 4.95 (*1-56294-768-0*) Millbrook Pr.

PROGRESS
see also Civilization; Science and Civilization; Social Change

PROHIBITION–FICTION
Reaver, Chap. Bill. 1994. 14.95 (*0-385-31175-3*) Delacorte.

PROJECT APOLLO
see Apollo Project
PROJECT MARINER
see Mariner Project
PROPAGANDA
see also Advertising
PROPHETS
Hashim, A. S. Stories of Some of the Prophets, Vol. I. pap. 5.95 (0-933511-61-2) Kazi Pubns.
—Stories of Some of the Prophets, Vol II. pap. 5.95 (0-933511-64-7) Kazi Pubns.
Overholtzer, Ruth. Elisha. Biel, Bill, illus. 33p. (gr. k-6). 1967. pap. text ed. 9.45 (1-55976-010-9) CEF Press.
PROSPECTING
Gintzler, A. S. Rough & Ready Prospectors. 48p. (gr. 4-7). 1994. text ed. 12.95 (1-56261-153-4) John Muir.
Petralia, Joseph F. Gold! Gold! A Beginner's Handbook & Recreational Guide: How & Where to Prospect for Gold. 5th, rev. ed. Applegate, Jill, ed. Neri, Susan, illus. LC 81-126200. 144p. 1992. pap. 9.95 (0-9605890-5-8, AB92) Sierra Trading.
Rynerson, Fred. Exploring & Mining for Gems & Gold in the West. (Illus.). 204p. (gr. 4 up). 1970. 16.95 (0-911010-61-0); pap. 8.95 (0-911010-60-2) Naturegraph.
PROSPECTING–FICTION
Coombs, Charles. Young Atom Detective. (Illus.). (gr. 4-7). PLB 7.19 (0-8313-0021-3) Lantern.
PROTECTION OF ANIMALS
see Animals–Treatment
PROTECTION OF BIRDS
see Birds–Protection
PROTECTION OF CHILDREN
see Child Welfare
PROTECTION OF ENVIRONMENT
see Environmental Protection
PROTECTION OF NATURAL SCENERY
see Natural Monuments
PROTECTION OF WILDLIFE
see Wildlife–Conservation
PROTEST
see Dissent
PROTESTANT REFORMATION
see Reformation
PROTESTANTISM
see also Reformation
Olsen, Warren & Rinden, David. Explanation of Luther's Small Catachism. 128p. (gr. 7-8). 1988. text ed. 7.95 (0-943167-12-4) Faith & Fellowship Pr.
PROVERBS
see also Epigrams
Burgest, David R. Proverbs for the Young...& the Not So Young. Burgest, David R., II, illus. 75p. (Orig.). (gr. 7-12). 1989. pap. write for info. Self-Taught Pubs.
Davidson, Alice J. Alice in Bibleland Storybooks: Psalms & Proverbs. Marshall, Victoria, illus. 32p. (gr. 3 up). 1984. 5.50 (0-8378-5069-X) Gibson.
Fraser, Betty. First Things First: An Illustrated Collection of Sayings Useful & Familiar for Children. Fraser, Betty, illus. LC 86-42993. 32p. (gr. k-3). 1990. PLB 12.89 (0-06-021855-X) HarpC Child Bks.
Fulton, Ginger A. When I'm a Mommy: A Little Girl's Paraphrase of Proverbs 31. (Illus.). (gr. 1-4). 1984. pap. 3.25 (0-8024-0367-0) Moody.
Hurwite, Johanna, compiled by. A Word to the Wise: And Other Proverbs. Rayevsky, Robert, illus. LC 93-26836. 40p. (ps up). 1994. 15.00 (0-688-12065-2); PLB 14.93 (0-688-12066-0) Morrow Jr Bks.
Schwartz, Linda. Fun With Proverbs. LC 91-77042. (Illus.). 40p. (gr. 2-6). 1991. 5.95 (0-88160-208-6, LW 298) Learning Wks.
Taylor, Phoebe, ed. Thoughts for the Free Life: Lao Tsu to the Present. 2nd ed. Buckley, Cicely, illus. 110p. (Orig.). (gr. 8 up). 1989. pap. 10.00 (0-9617481-5-X) Oyster River Pr.
White, Kathy. Proverbs for Children. Haynes, Betty B., ed. Haynes, Rebecca, illus. 64p. (ps-3). 1985. pap. 6.95 (0-9616130-0-9) Naftaolh Pubns.
PSALMODY
see Church Music; Hymns
PSYCHIATRISTS
Scariano, Margaret M. Dr. Ruth Westheimer. LC 91-40923. (Illus.). 128p. (gr. 6 up). 1992. lib. bdg. 17.95 (0-89490-333-0) Enslow Pubs.
PSYCHIATRISTS–FICTION
Galvin, Matthew R. Ignatius Finds Help: A Story About Psychotherapy for Children. Ferraro, Sandra, illus. LC 87-34899. 48p. (ps-6). 1988. 16.95 (0-945354-01-0); pap. 6.95 (0-945354-00-2) Magination Pr.
Lowry, Lois. Anastasia, Ask Your Analyst. large type ed. 176p. 1989. Repr. of 1984 ed. lib. bdg. 15.95 (1-55736-133-9, Crnrstn Bks) BDD LT Grp.
PSYCHIATRY
see also Psychotherapy
Sanders, Corine & Turner, Cynthia. Coping. Villalpando, Eleanor, illus. 64p. (gr. 2-8). 1983. wkbk. 8.95 (0-9607366-2-X, GA 494) Good Apple.
PSYCHICAL RESEARCH
see also Apparitions; Clairvoyance; Dreams; Extrasensory Perception; Ghosts; Hypnotism; Mind and Body; Thought Transference
Green, Carl R. & Sanford, William R. Recalling Past Lives. Robinson, Keith, illus. LC 93-74. 48p. (gr. 4-10). 1993. lib. bdg. 14.95 (0-89490-458-2) Enslow Pubs.
Nash, Bruce & Zullo, Allan. Spooky Kids: Strange but True Tales. LC 93-44029. (Illus.). 128p. (gr. 1-6). 1994. pap. 2.95 (0-8167-3447-X, Pub. by Watermill Pr) Troll Assocs.
O'Neill, Terry, ed. Paranormal Phenomena: Opposing Viewpoints. LC 90-24081. (Illus.). 240p. (gr. 10 up). 1991. PLB 17.95 (0-89908-487-7); pap. 9.95 (0-89908-462-1) Greenhaven.
PSYCHICAL RESEARCH–FICTION
Kassem, Lou. A Summer for Secrets. 112p. 1989. pap. 2.95 (0-380-75759-1, Camelot) Avon.
Nordic, Rolla. Let's Talk about the Tarot: A Story for Children & the Young at Heart. 1992. 12.95 (0-533-09686-3) Vantage.
Rose, Mary K. The Children's Tarot: The Road Is a River. Rose, Mary K., illus. 52p. (Orig.). (gr. k-6). 1993. pap. 18.95 incl. audio cass. & set of 24 cards (0-9636234-0-0) Wild Rose CO.
Zalben. Fortune Teller in 5B. 1991. 14.95 (0-8050-1924-3) H Holt & Co.
PSYCHOANALYSIS
see also Dreams; Hypnotism; Mind and Body; Psychology; Psychology, Pathological
Stwertka, Eve. Psychoanalysis: From Freud to the Age of Therapy. Kline, Marjory, ed. LC 87-7357. (Illus.). 96p. (gr. 7-9). 1988. PLB 10.90 (0-531-10481-8) Watts.
PSYCHOLOGY
see also Attitude (Psychology); Emotions; Imagination; Individuality; Intellect; Perception; Personality; Psychical Research; Psychoanalysis; Reasoning; Senses and Sensation; Thought and Thinking
Anderson, Jill. Thinking, Changing, Rearranging: Improving Self Esteem in Young People. LC 88-2289. (Illus.). 80p. (gr. 2). 1990. Repr. of 1981 ed. wkbk. 7.50 (0-943920-30-2) Metamorphous Pr.
Baines, Gwendolyn L. People in the Web of Life. 2nd ed. (gr. 7 up). 1992. pap. 9.95 (0-9614505-1-7) Nevada Pub.
Barden, Renardo. Fears & Phobias. LC 89-1340. (Illus.). 48p. (gr. 5-6). 1989. text ed. 12.95 RSBE (0-89686-441-3, Crestwood Hse) Macmillan Child Grp.
Cohen, Daniel & Cohen, Susan. Teenage Stress: Understanding the Tensions You Feel at Home, at School & among Your Friends. LC 83-16477. 160p. (gr. 5 up). 1984. 13.95 (0-87131-423-1) M Evans.
Cox, W. Miles. Addictive Personality. updated ed. (Illus.). (gr. 5 up). 1992. lib. bdg. 19.95 (0-685-52233-4) Chelsea Hse.
Diebert, Linda. Motivational Magic. (Illus.). 128p. (ps-2). 1990. 11.95 (0-86653-535-7, GA1137) Good Apple.
Dinkmeyer, Don, Sr. & Dinkmeyer, Don, Jr. Developing Understanding of Self & Others (DUSO) Storybook, No. 1. (gr. k-4). 1982. pap. text ed. 42.75 (0-88671-278-5, 5505) Am Guidance.
Freed, Alvyn M. & Freed, Margaret. TA for Kids (& Grownups Too) 3rd rev ed. Hackney, Rick, illus. LC 77-81761. (gr. 4-7). 1977. pap. 9.95 (0-915190-09-5, JP9009-5) Jalmar Pr.
Garell, Dale C. & Snyder, Solomon H., eds. Psychological Disorders & Their Treatment, 13 vols. (Illus.). 1248p. (gr. 6-12). 1994. Set. 246.35x (0-7910-0010-9, Am Art Analog) Chelsea Hse.
Goley, Elaine. Believing in Yourself, Reading Level 2. (Illus.). 32p. (gr. 1-4). 1989. PLB 15.94 (0-86592-398-1); 11.95s.p. (0-685-58777-0) Rourke Corp.
Gordon, James. Stress Management. (Illus.). 112p. (gr. 6-12). 1990. 18.95 (0-7910-0042-7) Chelsea Hse.
Gordon, Michael. I Would If I Could: A Teenager's Guide to ADHD-Hyperactivity. Jimco, Janet, illus. 34p. (Orig.). (gr. 6-12). 1992. pap. 12.50 (0-9627701-3-2) GSI Pubns.
Greenberg, Harvey R. Hanging In: What You Should Know about Psychotherapy. LC 94-1894. 1995. 16.95 (0-02-736765-7) Macmillan.
Grewe, Georgeann & Glover, Susanne. Motivational Units for Spring. (Illus.). 144p. (gr. 2-6). 1990. 12.95 (0-86653-524-1, GA1145) Good Apple.
Hayes, Marnell L. The Tuned-In, Turned-on Book about Learning Problems. rev. & expanded ed. Rarey, Damon, illus. LC 94-3474. 132p. 1994. pap. text ed. 10.00 (1-57128-090-1, 090-1) Acad Therapy.
Kerr, M. E. Me Me Me Me Me: Not a Novel. LC 82-48521. 224p. (gr. 7 up). 1983. PLB 16.89 (0-06-023193-9) HarpC Child Bks.
Kincher, Jonni. Psychology for Kids: Forty Fun Tests That Help You Learn about Yourself. Bach, Julie, ed. Maclean & Tuminell, illus. Elliott, Thomas, frwd. by. LC 90-47742. 160p. (Orig.). (gr. 4 up). 1990. pap. 11.95 (0-915793-23-7) Free Spirit Pub.
Knox, Jean. Learning Disabilities. (Illus.). (gr. 6-12). 1989. 18.95 (0-7910-0049-4); pap. 9.95 (0-7910-0529-1) Chelsea Hse.
Kubersky, Rachel. Everything You Need to Know about Eating Disorders. (gr. 7-12). 1992. PLB 14.95 (0-8239-1321-X) Rosen Group.
Lawless, Joann A. Mysteries of the Mind. LC 77-10726. (Illus.). 48p. (gr. 4 up). 1983. PLB 20.70 (0-8172-1066-0) Raintree Steck-V.
LeShan, Eda. What Makes You So Special? LC 91-16925. 160p. (gr. 3-7). 1992. 15.00 (0-8037-1155-7) Dial Bks Young.
Mahoney, Bateman & Mahoney, Bill. Macho: Is This What I Really Want? 1986. pap. 6.00 (0-87738-024-4) Youth Ed.
Palmer, Pat. I Wish I Could Hold Your Hand: A Child's Guide to Grief & Loss. Burke, Dianne O., illus. 32p. (ps-6). 1994. pap. 6.95 (0-915166-82-8) Impact Pubs Cal.
Schenkerman, Rona D. Growing up with Stress. 16p. (gr. 3-8). 1993. 1.95 (1-56688-121-8) Bur For At-Risk.
Septien, Al. Everything You Need to Know about Codependency. Rosen, Ruth, ed. (gr. 7-12). 1993. PLB 14.95 (0-8239-1527-1) Rosen Group.
Sylvester, Sandra. Living with Stress - Middle School. 64p. (gr. 5-9). 1991. 7.95 (0-86653-594-2, GA1313) Good Apple.
—Living with Stress - Primary. 64p. (gr. 1-4). 1991. 7.95 (0-86653-593-4, GA1312) Good Apple.
Walter, Nancy L. Inside of Me I Feel... 48p. (ps-3). 1993. pap. 10.95 (0-9635127-3-0) Naturally By Nan.
Walter, Nancy T. Inside of Me I Have Feelings. 48p. (ps-3). 1992. pap. 10.95 (0-9635127-0-6) Naturally by Nan.
Wayman, Joe. Let's Talk about It! Wayman, Joe, illus. 96p. (gr. 1-8). 1986. wkbk. 10.95 (0-86653-372-9, GA 799) Good Apple.
Wilson, Marie M. Nellie's Girl Two. (Illus.). 156p. (ps up). 1988. PLB 11.00 (0-9615259-1-6) Wilson Oregon.
Wingfield, Jack & Wingfield, Angela. Growing up Now. (Illus.). 48p. (gr. 4-8). 1992. 14.95 (0-7459-1537-X) Lion USA.
PSYCHOLOGY, ABNORMAL
see Psychology, Pathological
PSYCHOLOGY, APPLIED
see also Counseling; Human Relations
Elchoness, Monte. Why Can't Anyone Hear Me? A Guide for Surviving Adolescence. 2nd, rev. ed. Elchoness, Monte, illus. LC 86-737. 200p. (gr. 6-12). 1989. pap. 10.95 (0-936781-06-8, Dist. by Publishers Group West) Monroe Pr.
Herzfeld, Gerald & Powell, Robin. Coping for Kids: A Complete Stress-Control Program for Students Ages 8-18. 202p. (gr. 3-12). 1985. pap. 47.95x (0-87628-234-6); wkbk. 6.95x (0-317-43482-9) Ctr Appl Res.
Kalb, Jonah & Viscott, David. What Every Kid Should Know. LC 75-45123. (Illus.). 128p. (gr. 5-9). 1976. 14.45 (0-395-24386-6) HM.
LeShan, Eda. What Makes Me Feel This Way? Growing up with Human Emotions. Weil, Lisl, illus. LC 71-165573. 128p. (gr. 3-6). 1974. (Macmillan Child Bk); pap. 4.95 (0-02-044340-4, Aladdin) Macmillan Child Grp.
Silbert, Linda P. & Silbert, Alvin. My Own Book of Feelings. (Illus.). (gr. k-8). 1977. 4.98 (0-89544-017-2, 017) Silbert Bress.
PSYCHOLOGY, CHILD
see Child Study
PSYCHOLOGY, INDUSTRIAL
see Psychology, Applied
PSYCHOLOGY, MEDICAL
see Psychology, Pathological
PSYCHOLOGY, PATHOLOGICAL
see also Mental Illness; Psychiatry; Psychoanalysis
Friedland, Bruce. Personality Disorders. (Illus.). 112p. (gr. 6-12). 1991. 18.95 (0-7910-0051-6) Chelsea Hse.
PSYCHOLOGY, PRACTICAL
see Psychology, Applied
PSYCHOPATHOLOGISTS
see Psychiatrists
PSYCHOPATHOLOGY
see Psychology, Pathological
PSYCHOPATHY
see Psychology, Pathological
PSYCHOSES
see Mental Illness
PSYCHOTHERAPY
Freed, Alvyn M. TA for Tots Coloring Book. (ps-3). 1976. pap. 1.95 (0-915190-33-8, JP9033-8) Jalmar Pr.
Greenberg, Harvey R. Hanging In: What You Should Know about Psychotherapy. LC 94-1894. 1995. 16.95 (0-02-736765-7) Macmillan.
Koplow, Lesley. Tanya & the Tobo Man: A Story for Children Entering Therapy. LC 91-85. (SPA & ENG., Illus.). 32p. (ps-4). 1991. 16.95 (0-945354-34-7); pap. 6.95 (0-945354-33-9) Magination Pr.
—Tanya & the Tobo Man: A Story for Children Entering Therapy. Velasquez, Eric, illus. LC 92-56875. 1993. PLB 17.27 (0-8368-0936-X) Gareth Stevens Inc.
Nemiroff, Marc A. & Annunziata, Jane. A Child's First Book about Play Therapy. Scott, Margaret, illus. LC 90-49954. 60p. (Orig.). 1990. 19.95 (1-55798-112-4); pap. text ed. write for info. (1-55798-089-6) Am Psychol.
PTOMAINE POISONING
see Food Poisoning
PUBLIC FINANCE
see Finance
PUBLIC HEALTH
see also Cemeteries; Communicable Diseases; Hospitals; Noise; Refuse and Refuse Disposal; Sanitation; Sewage Disposal; Vaccination; Water-Pollution; Water Supply
Hampton, J. World Health. (Illus.). 48p. (gr. 5 up). 1988. PLB 18.60 (0-86592-281-0); PLB 13.95s.p. (0-685-58318-X) Rourke Corp.
Hurwitz, Sue & Hurwitz, Jane. Staying Healthy. Rosen, Ruth, ed. (gr. 7-12). 1993. 13.95 (0-8239-1471-2) Rosen Group.
Nardo, Don. Hygiene. Koop, C. Everett, intro. by. LC 92-32086. 1993. pap. write for info. (0-7910-0460-0) Chelsea Hse.

Public Health. (Illus.). 56p. (gr. 6-12). 1985. pap. 1.85 (*0-8395-3251-2*, 33251) BSA.

PUBLIC OPINION

see also Attitude (Psychology)

also names of countries with the subdivision Foreign Opinion, u. s.–Foreign Opinion

Roets, Lois F. Survey & Public Opinion Research: Grades Five to Twelve. 2nd ed. 120p. (gr. 3 up). 1988. 14.00 (*0-911943-14-5*) Leadership Pub.

PUBLIC PLAYGROUNDS

see Playgrounds

PUBLIC SCHOOLS

Leinwand, Gerald. Public Education. 128p. (gr. 7-12). 1992. lib. bdg. 16.95x (*0-8160-2100-7*) Facts on File.

Wygant, Foster. School Art in American Culture, 1820-1970. (Illus.). 240p. (Orig.). 1993. pap. 21.95 (*0-9610376-1-X*) Interwood Pr.

PUBLIC SPEAKING

see also Acting; Debates and Debating

Carratello, Patricia. I Can Give a Speech. Chacon, Rick, illus. 32p. (gr. 3-6). 1981. 5.95 (*1-55734-327-6*) Tchr Create Mat.

Cocetti, Robert A. & Snyder, Lee. Talk That Matters: An Introduction to Public Speaking. rev. ed. 338p. (gr. 10 up). 1992. 18.00 (*1-878276-44-1*) Educ Systs Assocs Inc.

Detz, Joan. You Mean I Have to Stand Up & Say Something? Marshall, David, illus. LC 86-3611. 96p. (gr. 5-9). 1986. SBE 13.95 (*0-689-31221-0*, Atheneum Child Bk) Macmillan Child Grp.

McCutcheon, Randall, et al. Communication Matters. LC 93-10452. 1993. text ed. 43.75 (*0-314-01390-3*) West Pub.

Public Speaking. (Illus.). 44p. (gr. 6-12). 1969. pap. 1.85 (*0-8395-3373-X*, 33373) BSA.

PUBLIC UTILITIES

see also Railroads; Telephone; Water Supply

PUBLISHERS AND PUBLISHING

see also Book Industries and Trade; Books; Printing

Bold, Mary. Publish Your Own Book: A Resource Book for Young Authors. Small, Carol B., illus. LC 86-91615. 36p. (Orig.). (gr. 5 up). 1986. pap. 6.95 (*0-938267-02-7*) Bold Prodns.

Chapman, Gillian & Robson, Pam. Making Books: A Step-by-Step Guide to Your Own Publishing. (Illus.). 32p. (gr. 3-6). 1992. PLB 13.40 (*1-56294-154-2*) Millbrook Pr.

Freed, Judith M. Freed's Guide to Student Contests & Publishing. 5th, rev. ed. (Illus.). 128p. (gr. k-12). pap. 13.95 (*0-9621647-3-9*) Fountainpen Pr.

Greenberg, Keith E. John Johnson. LC 92-41751. (gr. 3 up). 1993. 15.93 (*0-86592-033-8*); 11.95s.p. (*0-685-66329-9*) Rourke Enter.

Lent, Penny. Young Writer's Manuscript Manual: A Students Guide on How to Submit Their Work for Publication. LC 93-78340. 64p. (Orig.). 1993. pap. 7.95 (*1-877882-07-0*) Kldoscope Pr.

—Young Writer's Market Manual: A Students Guide on Where to Send Their Work for Publication. LC 93-78343. (Orig.). 1993. pap. 7.95 (*1-877882-08-9*) Kldoscope Pr.

Publish-A-Book Complete Book & Cassette Set, 15 titles. (gr. 1-6). 1992. Set. write for info. (*0-8172-2522-6*) Raintree Steck-V.

PUBLISHING

see Publishers and Publishing

PUERTO RICANS IN THE U. S.

Larsen, Ronald J. The Puerto Ricans in America. (Illus.). 80p. (gr. 5 up). 1989. PLB 15.95 (*0-8225-0238-0*); pap. 5.95 (*0-8225-1036-7*) Lerner Pubns.

Mohr, Nicholasa. All for the Better: A Story of el Barrio. Gutierrez, Rudy, illus. LC 92-23639. 56p. (gr. 2-5). 1992. PLB 19.97 (*0-8114-7220-5*) Raintree Steck-V.

PUERTO RICANS IN THE U. S.–FICTION

Mohr, Nicholasa. Going Home. LC 85-20621. 176p. (gr. 5-8). 1986. 14.95 (*0-8037-0269-8*); PLB 13.89 (*0-8037-0338-4*) Dial Bks Young.

Simon, Norma. What Do I Do: English - Spanish Edition. Lasker, Joe, illus. LC 74-79544. 40p. (ps-2). 1969. PLB 13.95 (*0-8075-8823-7*) A Whitman.

PUERTO RICO

Fontanez, Edwin. The Vejigante & the Folk Festivals of Puerto Rico. Fontanez, Edwin, illus. (SPA & ENG.). 24p. (Orig.). (gr. 4-6). 1994. pap. 5.99 (*0-9640868-0-8*) Exit Studio.

Johnston, Joyce. Puerto Rico. (SPA., Illus.). 72p. (gr. 3-6). 1994. 17.50 (*0-8225-2753-7*) Lerner Pubns.

Kent, Deborah. Puerto Rico. LC 91-543. 144p. (gr. 4 up). 1991. PLB 20.55 (*0-516-00498-0*) Childrens.

—Puerto Rico. 190p. 1993. text ed. 15.40 (*1-56956-154-0*) W A T Braille.

Lerner Publications, Department of Geography Staff. Puerto Rico in Pictures. (Illus.). 64p. (gr. 5 up). 1987. PLB 17.50 (*0-8225-1821-X*) Lerner Pubns.

Thompson, Kathleen. Puerto Rico. 48p. (gr. 3 up). 1985. PLB 19.97 (*0-86514-443-5*) Raintree Steck-V.

PUERTO RICO–BIOGRAPHY

Luis Munoz Marin. (Illus.). 32p. (gr. 3-6). 1988. PLB 19.97 (*0-8172-2907-8*); pap. 4.95 (*0-8114-6760-0*) Raintree Steck-V.

PUERTO RICO–FICTION

Barsy, Kalman. Del Nacimiento de la Isla de Boriken. Quintero, Nora, illus. LC 82-83288. (SPA.). 76p. (gr. 6). 1982. pap. 7.95 (*0-940238-01-2*) Ediciones Huracan.

London, Jonathan. Island Hurricane. Sorensen, Henri, illus. LC 94-14518. 1994. write for info. (*0-688-08117-7*); PLB write for info. (*0-688-08118-5*) Lothrop.

Misla, Victor M. Little Anabo from Boriken. Misla, Victor M., illus. 28p. (Orig.). (gr. 6-7). 1987. pap. 5.00 (*0-9626870-0-6*) NW Monarch Pr.

Nodar, Carmen M. Abuelita's Paradise. Mathews, Judith, ed. Paterson, Diane, illus. LC 91-42330. 32p. (gr. k-3). 1992. 13.95g (*0-8075-0129-8*) A Whitman.

—El Paraiso de Abuelita. Mathews, Judith, ed. Mlawer, Teresa, tr. Paterson, Diane, illus. LC 92-3767. (SPA.). 32p. (gr. k-3). 1992. 13.95g (*0-8075-6346-3*) A Whitman.

Pomerantz, Charlotte. The Outside Dog. Plecas, Jennifer, illus. LC 91-6351. 64p. (gr. k-3). 1993. 14.00 (*0-06-024782-7*); PLB 13.89 (*0-06-024783-5*) HarpC Child Bks.

PUERTO RICO–HISTORY

Abodaher, David J. Puerto Rico: America's Fifty-First State. LC 92-39474. (Illus.). 112p. (gr. 9-12). 1993. PLB 13.40 (*0-531-13024-X*) Watts.

Hauptly, Denis J. Puerto Rico: An Unfinished Story. LC 90-37953. (Illus.). 160p. (gr. 5 up). 1991. SBE 14.95 (*0-689-31431-0*, Atheneum Child Bk) Macmillan Child Grp.

Luis Munoz Marin. (Illus.). 32p. (gr. 3-6). 1988. PLB 19.97 (*0-8172-2907-8*); pap. 4.95 (*0-8114-6760-0*) Raintree Steck-V.

Pico, Fernando & Izcoa, Carmen R. Puerto Rico, Tierra Adentro y Mar Afuera: Historia y Cultura de los Puertorriquenos. LC 91-71358. (SPA.). 304p. (gr. 7). 1991. text ed. 23.50 (*0-929157-12-5*) Ediciones Huracan.

PUFFINS

Gibbons, Gail. The Puffins Are Back! Gibbons, Gail, illus. LC 90-30525. 32p. (gr. 3-5). 1991. 15.00 (*0-06-021603-4*); PLB 14.89 (*0-06-021604-2*) HarpC Child Bks.

McMillan, Bruce. Nights of the Pufflings. McMillan, Bruce, illus. LC 94-14808. (ps-3). Date not set. write for info. (*0-395-70810-9*) HM.

PUGILISM

see Boxing

PUMAS

Farentinos, Robert. Winter's Orphans: The Search for a Family of Mountain Lion Cubs, a True Story. (Illus.). 64p. (gr. 4-6). 1993. 19.95 (*1-879373-54-8*); pap. 13.95 (*1-879373-53-X*) R Rinehart.

Funston, Sylvia. Eastern Cougar. Kassian, Elena, illus. 32p. (gr. 1-5). 1992. 4.95 (*0-920775-95-0*, Pub. by Greey de Pencier CN) Firefly Bks Ltd.

George, Jean C. The Moon of the Mountain Lions. new ed. Parker, Ron, illus. LC 90-39451. 48p. (gr. 3-7). 1991. 15.00 (*0-06-022429-0*); PLB 14.89 (*0-06-022438-X*) HarpC Child Bks.

Gouck, Maura M. Mountain Lions. LC 93-16250. (Illus.). (gr. 2-6). 1993. 15.95 (*1-56766-057-6*) Childs World.

Robinson, Sandra C. Mountain Lion: Puma, Panther, Painter, Cougar. (Illus.). 64p. (gr. 4-6). 1991. pap. 7.95 (*1-879373-00-9*) R Rinehart.

Stone, L. Cougars. (Illus.). 24p. (gr. k-5). 1989. lib. bdg. 11.94 (*0-86592-505-4*) Rourke Corp.

—Jaguars. (Illus.). 24p. (gr. k-5). 1989. lib. bdg. 11.94 (*0-86592-506-2*); 8.95s.p. (*0-685-58631-6*) Rourke Corp.

PUMAS–FICTION

Harris, Marian. Goose & the Mountain Lion. 1st ed. Harris, Jim, illus. LC 93-45424. 32p. (gr. k up). 1994. 14.95 (*0-87358-576-3*) Northland AZ.

London, Jonathon. Master Elk & the Mountain Lion. McLoughlin, Wayne, illus. LC 94-1754. 1995. write for info. (*0-517-59917-1*, Crown); deluxe ed. write for info. (*0-517-59918-X*) Crown Pub Group.

Nesbit, Jeff. Cougar Chase. LC 93-40145. 1994. pap. 4.99 (*0-8407-9255-7*) Nelson.

PUMPKIN–FICTION

Bauer, Joan. Squashed. LC 91-44905. 192p. (gr. 7 up). 1992. 15.95 (*0-385-30793-4*) Delacorte.

Cole, Bruce. The Pumpkinville Mystery. Warhola, James, illus. (gr. 1-4). 1987. 10.95 (*0-13-741620-2*) P-H.

The Dancing Pumpkin. 1992. write for info. (*0-9634270-0-8*) Dancing Pumpkin.

Deich, Joy. J. P.'s Pumpkin Patch: Too Many Pumpkins. 32p. (gr. k-4). 1993. pap. 2.95 (*0-9629698-5-0*) Aaron Lake Pub.

Dillon, Jana. Jeb Scarecrow's Pumpkin Patch. Dillon, Jana, illus. LC 91-16423. 32p. (ps-3). 1992. 14.45 (*0-395-57578-8*) HM.

Friskey, Margaret. The Perky Little Pumpkin. Dunnington, Tom, illus. LC 90-38376. 32p. (ps-3). 1990. PLB 11.45 (*0-516-03564-9*); pap. 4.95 (*0-516-43564-7*) Childrens.

Gale, Wendy, illus. Jack-O-Faces Big Book. (ps-2). 1988. pap. text ed. 14.00 (*0-922053-23-5*) N Edge Res.

Greenleaf, Ann G. The Goblins Did It! LC 93-19746. (Illus.). 1993. 4.99 (*0-517-09157-7*) Random Hse Value.

Haas, James. Paco Pumpkin. Kendzia, Mary C., ed. Meyer, Mary A., illus. 32p. (Orig.). 1992. pap. 4.95 (*0-89622-529-1*) Twenty-Third.

Hall, Zoe. It's Pumpkin Time! Halpern, Shari, illus. LC 93-35909. (ps-2). 1994. 14.95 (*0-590-47833-8*) Scholastic Inc.

Kaslow, Florence R. The Puzzled Pumpkin. Phillips, Jennifer, illus. LC 91-60798. 24p. (Orig.). (gr. k-4). 1991. pap. 4.95 (*0-9628321-0-3*) Pumpkin Patch Pubs.

King, Elizabeth. Pumpkin Patch. LC 89-25938. (Illus.). 40p. (ps-3). 1990. 14.00 (*0-525-44640-0*, DCB) Dutton Child Bks.

Kroll, Steven. The Biggest Pumpkin Ever. Bassett, Jeni, illus. 32p. (gr. k-3). 1985. pap. 2.50 (*0-590-41113-6*) Scholastic Inc.

—The Biggest Pumpkin Ever. Bassett, Jeni, illus. 32p. (ps-1). 1993. pap. 2.50 (*0-590-46463-9*, Cartwheel) Scholastic Inc.

McDonald, Megan. The Great Pumpkin Switch. Lewin, Ted, illus. LC 91-39660. 32p. (ps-2). 1992. 14.95 (*0-531-05450-0*); PLB 14.99 (*0-531-08600-3*) Orchard Bks Watts.

Ray, M. L. Pumpkins. Root, Barry, ed. 1992. 13.95 (*0-15-252252-2*, Gulliver Bks) HarBrace.

Silverman, Erica. Big Pumpkin. Schindler, S. D., illus. LC 91-14053. 32p. (ps-3). 1992. RSBE 14.95 (*0-02-782683-X*, Macmillan Child Bk) Macmillan Child Grp.

Somerville, Sheila, illus. Five Little Pumpkins Big Book. (ps-2). 1988. pap. text ed. 14.00 (*0-922053-18-9*) N Edge Res.

Titherington, Jeanne. Pumpkin, Pumpkin. Titherington, Jeanne, illus. LC 84-25334. 24p. (ps-1). 1986. 13.95 (*0-688-05695-4*); PLB 13.88 (*0-688-05696-2*) Greenwillow.

Zagwyn, Deborah T. Pumpkin Blanket. (ps-5). 1991. 14.95 (*0-89087-637-1*) Celestial Arts.

PUNCH AND JUDY

see Puppets and Puppet Plays

PUNCHED CARD SYSTEMS

see Information Storage and Retrieval Systems

PUNCTUATION

Alward, Edgar C. & Dale, E. Up Your Punctuation! An Almost Non-Grammatical Approach to Punctuation. 112p. (Orig.). (gr. 9-12). 1988. pap. 12.95 (*0-9620092-0-2*) Pine Isl Pr.

Armstrong, Beverly. Punctuation Passport. 38p. (gr. 4-6). 1979. 6.95 (*0-88160-029-6*, LW 214) Learning Wks.

Carratello, Patricia. I Can Capitalize. Chacon, Rick, illus. 32p. (gr. 3-6). 1983. wkbk. 5.95 (*1-55734-331-4*) Tchr Create Mat.

—I Can Punctuate. Chacon, Rick, illus. 32p. (gr. 3-6). 1983. wkbk. 5.95 (*1-55734-332-2*) Tchr Create Mat.

Carratello, Patty. It's Easy to Capitalize. Wright, Theresa, illus. 32p. (gr. 1-4). 1988. 5.95 (*1-55734-322-5*) Tchr Create Mat.

—It's Easy to Punctuate. Spence, Paula & Wright, Theresa, illus. 32p. (gr. 1-4). 1988. wkbk. 5.95 (*1-55734-321-7*) Tchr Create Mat.

Cushman, Jack L. Punctuation & Capitalization Flipper. (Illus.). 49p. (gr. 5 up). 1989. Repr. of 1974 ed. trade edition 5.95 (*1-878383-00-0*) C Lee Pubns.

Gregorich, Barbara. Apostrophe, Colon, Hyphen. Pape, Richard, illus. 24p. (gr. 3-4). 1980. wkbk. 2.95 (*0-89403-593-2*) EDC.

—Comma. Pape, Richard, illus. 24p. (gr. 3-4). 1980. wkbk. 2.95 (*0-89403-595-9*) EDC.

—Period, Question Mark, Exclamation Mark. Pape, Richard, illus. 24p. (gr. 3-4). 1980. wkbk. 2.95 (*0-89403-592-4*) EDC.

Sebranek, Patrick & Meyer, Verne. Punctuation Pockets: A Student Folder. (Illus.). (gr. 7-12). 1984. pap. text ed. 0.95x (*0-9605312-8-9*) Write Source.

Spellman, Linda. More Creative Investigations. 48p. (gr. 4-8). 1984. 5.95 (*0-88160-114-4*, LW 246) Learning Wks.

Tilkin, Sheldon. Quotation Marks & Underlining. Pape, Richard, illus. 24p. (gr. 3-4). 1980. 2.95 (*0-89403-594-0*) EDC.

Tyler, J. & Gee, R. Punctuation Puzzles. (Illus.). 32p. (gr. 2-6). 1993. pap. 4.95 (*0-7460-1054-0*) EDC.

PUPPETS AND PUPPET PLAYS

Bailey, Vanessa. Puppets: Games & Projects. LC 90-44841. (Illus.). 32p. (gr. 2-4). 1991. PLB 11.90 (*0-531-17269-4*, Gloucester Pr) Watts.

Baird, Bil. Art of the Puppet. (Illus.). (gr. 9 up). 1966. 35.00 (*0-8238-0067-9*) Plays.

Bivens, Ruth. Aunt Ruth's Puppet Scripts, Bk. I. (Orig.). (gr. 1-8). 1986. Incl. cassette narration. pap. 19.95 (*0-89265-096-6*) Randall Hse.

—Aunt Ruth's Puppet Scripts, Bk. III. 55p. (gr. 1-6). 1987. 19.95 (*0-89265-119-9*); cassette incl. Randall Hse.

Brannon, Tom, illus. Jim Henson's Muppet Babies' Christmas Book. 48p. (ps-2). 1992. 6.95 (*0-307-15955-8*, 15955, Golden Pr) Western Pub.

Brooks, Courtaney. How to Teach Children Kindness & Manners with Puppets: Including Stories, Plays, Puppets & Props. Brooks, Courtaney & Runyan, Merrilee, illus. 100p. (Orig.). 1994. pap. 14.95 (*0-941274-06-3*) Belnice Bks. HOW TO TEACH CHILDREN KINDNESS & MANNERS WITH PUPPETS shows parents & teachers how to help children be kind & mannerly, by using puppet characters in stories, plays & exercises. Through puppets, children can experience the way characters feel & act. Everything

in the book enables children to suggest & use their own ways of expressing kindness & manners. Part I explains & shows through illustrations & patterns: 1) how to make simple hand or glove puppets, sock & stick puppets; 2) how to find or make simple props: a sausage, a basket of cookies; 3) how to get acquainted with your puppet as he walks, talks, picks up a spoon. Part II presents the stories & plays with puppet patterns & props. The plays & stories are short, usually two pages each, with many animal characters. You can prepare & present them easily, change the characters, add characters, have children change parts. You do not need a puppet stage; just the puppets, props & children. For more information or to order, write or call: Courtaney Brooks, Belnice Books, 337 8th St., Manhattan Beach, CA 90266; (310) 379-5405.
Publisher Provided Annotation.

—Plays & Puppets &cetera. 7th ed. Runyan, Merrilee, illus. LC 81-68933. 100p. (Orig.). (gr. k up). 1981. pap. text ed. 14.95 (*0-941274-00-4*) Belnice Bks.

Buchwald, Claire. The Puppet Book: How to Make & Operate Puppets & Stage a Puppet-Play. Jakubiszyn, Audrey, illus. LC 90-38080. 134p. (Orig.). 1990. pap. 13.95 (*0-8238-0293-0*) Plays.

Collodi, Carlo. Pinocchio. (gr. 4-6). 1985. pap. 2.99 (*0-14-035037-3*, Puffin) Puffin Bks.

Duch, Mabel. Easy-to-Make Puppets: Step-by-Step Instructions. Mohrmann, Gary, illus. LC 93-15320. 64p. (gr. 3-8). 1993. pap. 8.95 (*0-8238-0300-7*) Plays.

Forte, Imogene. Puppets. LC 84-62934. (Illus.). 80p. (gr. k-6). 1985. pap. text ed. 3.95 (*0-86530-101-8*, IP 91-5) Incentive Pubns.

Galdston, Olive. Play with Puppets. rev. ed. Galdston, Olive, illus. 52p. (Orig.). (ps up). 1971. pap. 1.50x (*0-686-01100-7*); pap. text ed. 1.50x (*0-936426-07-1*) Play Schs.

Hart, Marj & Shelly, Walt. Pom-Pom Puppets, Stories, & Stages. (gr. 5-8). 1989. pap. 13.95 (*0-8224-5596-X*) Fearon Teach Aids.

Italia, Robert. The Muppets. Wallner, Rosemary, ed. LC 91-73049. 202p. 1991. 13.95 (*1-56239-052-X*) Abdo & Dghtrs.

Keefe, Betty. Fingerpuppets, Fingerplays & Holidays. (Illus.). 136p. (ps-3). 1984. spiral bdg. 17.95 (*0-938594-05-2*) Spec Lit Pr.

King, Virginia. Hello, Puppet. Mancini, Rob, illus. LC 92-21392. 1993. 2.50 (*0-383-03572-4*) SRA Schl Grp.

Kingshead Corporation Staff. Cut, Color & Create: Make Your Own: Paperplate Puppets. Kingshead Corporation Staff, illus. 24p. (ps-3). 1987. pap. 2.97 (*1-55941-002-7*) Kingshead Corp.

McKay, Sindy. Something's Fishy. Alchemy II, Inc., illus. 26p. (ps up). 1986. 12.95 (*1-55578-610-3*) Worlds Wonder.

Mehrens, Gloria & Wick, Karen. Bagging It with Puppets. (gr. k-2). 1988. pap. 16.95 (*0-8224-0677-2*) Fearon Teach Aids.

Oldfield, Margaret J. Finger Puppets & Finger Plays. (Illus.). (ps-3). 1982. pap. 3.00 (*0-934876-18-5*) Creative Storytime.

—Tell & Draw Paper Bag Puppet Book. 2nd ed. Oldfield, Margaret J., illus. (gr. k-2). 1981. pap. 5.95 (*0-934876-16-9*) Creative Storytime.

Olson, Margaret J. Tell & Draw Animal Cut-outs. 3rd ed. (gr. k-2). 1963. pap. 3.00 (*0-934876-15-0*) Creative Storytime.

Philpott, V. & McNeil, M. J. Puppets: A Simple Guide to Making & Working Puppets. (Illus.). 32p. (gr. 3-6). 1977. pap. 6.95 (*0-86020-003-5*) EDC.

Poskanzer, Susan C. Puppeteer. Paterson, Diane, illus. LC 88-10042. 32p. (gr. 1-3). 1989. PLB 10.89 (*0-8167-1432-0*); pap. text ed. 2.95 (*0-8167-1433-9*) Troll Assocs.

Quick & Easy Puppets - Seasonal Book. 1993. write for info. (*1-884376-01-0*) Clever Creat.

Quick & Easy Puppets, Bk. 1: Craft Pattern Book. 1993. write for info. (*1-884376-00-2*) Clever Creat.

Renfro, Nancy. Puppet Shows Made Easy! Cromack, Celeste, ed. Renfro, Nancy, illus. 96p. (Orig.). (gr. 2-12). pap. 14.95 (*0-931044-13-8*) Renfro Studios.

Renfro, Nancy & Armstrong, Beverly. Make Amazing Puppets. 32p. (gr. 1-6). 1979. 3.95 (*0-88160-007-5*, LW 109) Learning Wks.

River, Chatham. Make a Pinocchio String Puppet. 1990. 4.99 (*0-517-69513-8*) Random Hse Value.

Sierra, Judy. Fantastic Theater: Puppets & Plays for Young Performers & Young Audiences. 250p. (gr. 3-7). 1991. 40.00 (*0-8242-0809-9*) Wilson.

Sims, J. Puppets for Dreaming & Scheming. (gr. 1-6). 1988. 15.95 (*0-88160-167-5*, LW 277) Learning Wks.

Supraner, Robyn & Supraner, Lauren. Plenty of Puppets to Make. Barto, Renzo, illus. LC 80-23785. 48p. (gr. 1-5). 1981. PLB 11.89 (*0-89375-432-3*); pap. 3.50 (*0-89375-433-1*) Troll Assocs.

Warshawsky, Gale. Creative Puppetry for Jewish Kids. LC 85-70544. 192p. (Orig.). (gr. 4-7). 1985. pap. text ed. 13.75 (*0-86705-017-9*) A R E Pub.

Watson, N. Cameron. Little Pigs Puppet Book. (gr. 4-8). 1990. 14.95 (*0-316-92468-7*) Little.

Wright, Lyndie. Puppets. Fairclough, Chris, photos by. LC 88-50373. (Illus.). 48p. (gr. 3-6). 1989. PLB 12.40 (*0-531-10635-7*) Watts.

PUPPETS AND PUPPET PLAYS–FICTION

Alexander, Liza, et al. The Sesame Street Treasury: Featuring Jim Henson's Sesame Street Muppets. Chartier, Normand, et al, illus. LC 93-8326. Date not set. write for info. (*0-679-84655-7*); PLB write for info. (*0-679-94655-1*) Random.

Avi. Judy with Punch. LC 92-27157. (Illus.). 176p. (gr. 5-9). 1993. SBE 14.95 (*0-02-707755-1*, Bradbury Pr) Macmillan Child Grp.

Baron, Michelle. Nanny Piggy. Alchemy II, Inc, illus. 26p. (ps up). 1987. 12.95 (*1-55578-602-2*) Worlds Wonder.

Becker, Lois & Stratton, Mark. Muppet Babies on Twinkledink. Alchemy II, Inc., illus. 26p. (ps up). 1987. 12.95 (*1-55578-606-5*) Worlds Wonder.

Bedard, Michael. Painted Devil. LC 92-35637. 224p. (gr. 5-9). 1994. SBE 15.95 (*0-689-31827-8*, Atheneum Child Bk) Macmillan Child Grp.

Bond, Michael. The Caravan Puppets. Julian-Ottie, Vanessa, illus. LC 85-109047. 130p. (gr. 3 up). 1983. write for info. (*0-00-184135-1*) Harper SF.

Bove, Linda. Sesame Street Sign Language ABC with Linda Bove. Cooke, Tom, illus. Shevett, Anita & Shevett, Anita, photos by. LC 85-1845. (Illus.). 32p. (gr. 3-8). 1985. lib. bdg. 5.99 (*0-394-97516-2*); 2.25 (*0-394-87516-8*) Random Bks Yng Read.

Brandenberg, Franz. Aunt Nina's Visit. Aliki, illus. LC 83-16531. 32p. (gr. k-3). 1984. 15.00 (*0-688-01764-9*); PLB 14.93 (*0-688-01766-5*) Greenwillow.

Bridwell, Norman. Hello, Clifford: A Puppet Book. (ps-3). 1991. 7.95 (*0-590-44673-8*) Scholastic Inc.

Brown, Jane Clark, illus. George Washington's Ghost. LC 93-39194. 1994. 13.95 (*0-395-69452-3*, HM) HM.

Chaney, Steve. The Puppet in the Big Black Box. Katz, Richard, illus. 32p. (gr. k-3). 1989. write for info. Stiff Lip.

Collodi, C. The Adventures of Pinocchio. Chiesa, Carol D., tr. from ITA. Mussino, Attilio, illus. LC 88-26684. 320p. (gr. 3 up). 1989. SBE 24.95 (*0-02-722821-5*, Macmillan Child Bk) Macmillan Child Grp.

Collodi, Carlo. Adventures of Pinocchio. (Illus.). (gr. 4 up). 1966. pap. 1.75 (*0-8049-0101-5*, CL-101) Airmont.

—Adventures of Pinocchio. Kredel, Fritz, illus. (gr. 4-6). 1982. 12.95 (*0-448-06001-9*, G&D) Putnam Pub Group.

—The Adventures of Pinocchio. Kassirer, Sue, adapted by. Haverfield, Mary, illus. LC 92-2503. 32p. (Orig.). (ps-2). 1992. pap. 2.25 (*0-679-83466-4*) Random Bks Yng Read.

—Pinocchio. Mattotti, Lorenzo, illus. LC 92-44161. (ENG.). (gr. 2 up). 1993. 15.00 (*0-688-12450-X*); lib. bdg. 14.93 (*0-688-12451-8*) Lothrop.

—Pinocchio: A Classic Tale. Jose, Eduard, adapted by. Moncure, Jane B., tr. from SPA. Asensio, Augusti, illus. LC 88-35308. 32p. (gr. k-2). 1988. PLB 13.95 (*0-89565-458-X*) Childs World.

Cooke, Tom, illus. Bert & Ernie on the Go. LC 80-54574. 16p. (ps-2). 1981. 8.99 (*0-394-84869-1*) Random Bks Yng Read.

Disney, Walt. Pinocchio. (ps-3). 1986. 2.95 (*0-307-10381-1*) Western Pub.

Disney, Walt, Productions Staff. Walt Disney's Pinocchio. (Illus.). (ps-3). 1973. lib. bdg. 4.99 (*0-394-92626-9*) Random Bks Yng Read.

Elliott, Dan. Ernie's Little Lie. Mathieu, Joe, illus. LC 82-7574. 40p. (ps-3). 1992. 4.95 (*0-394-85440-3*); pap. 2.99 (*0-679-82401-4*) Random Bks Yng Read.

—Grover Goes to School. Chartier, Normand, illus. LC 81-15398. 40p. (ps-3). 1992. pap. 2.99 (*0-679-82397-2*) Random Bks Yng Read.

—Grover Learns to Read. Chartier, Normand, illus. LC 84-27692. 40p. (ps-3). 1985. 4.95 (*0-394-87498-6*) Random Bks Yng Read.

—Oscar's Rotten Birthday. Chartier, Normand, illus. LC 81-2398. 40p. (ps-3). 1992. pap. 2.99 (*0-679-82400-6*) Random Bks Yng Read.

—Two Wheels for Grover. Mathieu, Joe, illus. LC 84-4732. 40p. (ps-3). 1984. 4.95 (*0-394-86586-3*); lib. bdg. 6.99 (*0-394-96586-8*) Random Bks Yng Read.

Fleischman, Paul. Shadow Play. Beddows, Eric, illus. LC 89-26874. 48p. (gr. 2 up). 1990. PLB 14.89 (*0-06-021865-7*) HarpC Child Bks.

Freudberg, Judy & Geiss, Tony. Susan & Gordon Adopt a Baby. Mathieu, Joe, illus. LC 86-2951. 24p. (ps-2). 1986. 8.99 (*0-394-88341-1*) Random Bks Yng Read.

Gikow, Louise. Baby Kermit & the Magic Trunk. Spahr, Kathy, illus. 26p. (ps up). 1987. 12.95 (*1-55578-601-4*) Worlds Wonder.

—Baby Rowlf & the Boomtown Bandits. Cooke, Tom, illus. 26p. (ps up). 1987. 12.95 (*1-55578-600-6*) Worlds Wonder.

—Muppet Babies & the Magic Garden. Attinello, Lauren, illus. 26p. (ps up). 1987. 12.95 (*1-55578-608-1*) Worlds Wonder.

—What's A Fraggle? McClintock, Barbara, illus. 32p. (gr. k-2). 1985. 5.95 (*0-03-071086-3*, Bks Young Read); pap. 1.95 (*0-03-071889-9*) H Holt & Co.

Gilchrist, Ellen. Muppets, No. 3: Froggy Mountain Breakdown. 1988. pap. 2.50 (*0-8125-7380-3*) Tor Bks.

—Muppets, No. 4: Chickens Are People Too. 128p. (Orig.). 1985. pap. 1.95 (*0-8125-7369-2*) Tor Bks.

—Muppets, No. 5: On the Town. 128p. (Orig.). 1986. pap. 1.95 (*0-8125-7371-4*) Tor Bks.

Gilchrist, Guy & Gilchrist, Brad. Muppets, No. 3: Froggy Mountain Breakdown. 128p. (Orig.). 1985. pap. 1.95 (*0-8125-7367-6*, Dist. by Warner Pub Services & St. Martin's Press) Tor Bks.

Gondosch, Linda. The Monsters of Marble Avenue. (Illus.). (gr. 2-4). 1988. 10.95 (*0-316-31991-0*) Little.

Hautzig, Deborah. Why Are You So Mean to Me? Cooke, Tom, illus. LC 85-18434. 40p. (ps-3). 1992. pap. 2.99 (*0-679-82402-2*) Random Bks Yng Read.

Hillert, Margaret. Pinocchio. (Illus.). (ps-k). 1981. PLB 6.95 (*0-8136-5103-4*, TK2172); pap. 3.50 (*0-8136-5603-6*, TK2173) Modern Curr.

Ingoglia, Gina. Walt Disney's Pinocchio & the Whale. Ortiz, Phil & Wakeman, Diana, illus. 40p. (ps-1). 1992. write for info. (*0-307-11583-6*, 11583, Golden Pr) Western Pub.

—Walt Disney's Pinocchio & the Whale. Ortiz, Phil & Wakeman, Diana, illus. 32p. (ps-1). 1993. pap. 3.25 (*0-307-15975-2*, 15975, Golden Pr) Western Pub.

Lewis, Shari. Lamb Chop's Fables: The Lamb Who Could Featuring Aesop's The Tortoise & the Hare. Doyle, Robert A., ed. Campana, Manny & Pidgeon, Jean, illus. 32p. Date not set. write for info. (*0-8094-7804-8*) Time-Life.

Lichtenstein, Judy. Dinosaur Cowboys Puppet Theatre. (ps-3). 1994. 10.95 (*1-55550-882-0*) Universe.

McKay, Sindy. Color Crazy. Alchemy II, Inc., illus. 26p. (ps up). 1987. 12.95 (*1-55578-609-X*) Worlds Wonder.

McKay, Sindy & Swerdlove, Larry. Radio Station K-E-R-M. Alchemy II, Inc., illus. 26p. (ps up). 1987. 12.95 (*1-55578-607-3*) Worlds Wonder.

McNaught, Harry. Muppets in My Neighborhood. McNaught, Harry, illus. LC 77-74472. (ps-k). 1977. bds. 3.95 (*0-394-83593-X*) Random Bks Yng Read.

Muldrow, Diane, adapted by. Walt Disney's Pinocchio. Marvin, Fred, illus. 28p. (ps). 1992. bds. write for info. (*0-307-12532-7*, 12532, Golden Pr) Western Pub.

Muntean, Michaela. Baby Fozzie Goes Camping. Wilson, Ann, illus. 26p. (ps up). 1987. 12.95 (*1-55578-604-9*) Worlds Wonder.

Muppets, Muppets, Muppets. (ps-2). 1986. 6.98 (*0-685-16866-2*, 618109) Random Hse Value.

Paterson, Katherine. The Master Puppeteer. Wells, Haru, illus. 180p. (gr. 5 up). 1981. pap. 2.95 (*0-380-53322-7*, Camelot) Avon.

—The Master Puppeteer. Wells, Haru, illus. LC 75-8614. 192p. (gr. 6 up). 1976. 15.00 (*0-690-00913-5*, Crowell Jr Bks) HarpC Child Bks.

—The Master Puppeteer. Wells, Haru, illus. LC 75-8614. 192p. (gr. 4 up). 1989. pap. 3.95 (*0-06-440281-9*, Trophy) HarpC Child Bks.

—The Master Puppeteer. LC 75-8614. 192p. (gr. 7 up). 1991. PLB 14.89 (*0-690-04905-6*, Crowell Jr Bks) HarpC Child Bks.

Peters, Sharon. Una Funcion De Titeres. Lee, Alana, illus. (SPA.). 32p. (gr. k-2). 1981. PLB 7.89 (*0-89375-551-6*); pap. 1.95 (*0-685-42387-5*) Troll Assocs.

Pinocchio. (FRE.). 6.25 (*0-685-33974-2*) Fr & Eur.

Pinocchio. (Illus.). (ps-3). 1985. 2.98 (*0-517-28809-5*) Random Hse Value.

Pinocchio. 1991. 1.00 (*1-880459-06-X*) Arrow Trad.

Pinocho. (SPA.). (gr. 2). 1990. casebound 3.50 (*0-7214-1412-5*) Ladybird Bks.

Prady, Bill. Muppet Babies & the Time Machine. Brannon, Tom, illus. 26p. (ps up). 1987. 12.95 (*1-55578-605-7*) Worlds Wonder.

Riordan, James. Pinocchio. Ambrus, Victor G., illus. 96p. (gr. 3 up). 1988. 18.95 (*0-19-279855-3*) OUP.

Rivlin, Elizabeth. Elmo's Little Glowworm. Mathieu, Joe, illus. LC 93-38193. 16p. (ps-1). 1994. pap. 5.99 (*0-679-85402-9*) Random Bks Yng Read.

Roberts, Sarah. Ernie's Big Mess. Mathieu, Joe, illus. LC 81-2464. 40p. (ps-3). 1992. 4.95 (*0-394-84847-0*); pap. 2.99 (*0-679-82398-0*) Random Bks Yng Read.

—I Want to Go Home. Mathieu, Joe, illus. LC 84-11725. 40p. (ps-3). 1985. 4.95 (*0-394-87027-1*) Random Bks Yng Read.

—Nobody Cares about Me! Mathieu, Joe, illus. LC 81-15913. 40p. (ps-3). 1992. 4.95 (*0-394-85177-3*); pap. 2.99 (*0-679-82399-9*) Random Bks Yng Read.

Ross, Anna. I Did It! Gorbaty, Norman, illus. LC 89-34543. 24p. (ps). 1990. 3.95 (*0-394-86019-5*) Random Bks Yng Read.

—I Have to Go. Gorbaty, Norman, illus. LC 89-34542. 24p. (ps). 1990. 3.95 (*0-394-86051-9*) Random Bks Yng Read.

—Naptime. Gorbaty, Norman, illus. LC 89-34545. 24p. (ps). 1990. 3.95 (*0-394-85828-X*) Random Bks Yng Read.

—Quiet Time. Gorbaty, Norman, illus. LC 89-24354. 24p. (ps). 1991. 3.95 (*0-394-85495-0*) Random Bks Yng Read.

—Say Bye-Bye. Gorbaty, Norman, illus. LC 90-52915. 24p. (ps). 1992. 3.95 (*0-394-85485-3*) Random Bks Yng Read.

—Say Good Night. Gorbaty, Norman, illus. LC 90-52914. 24p. (ps). 1992. 3.95 (*0-394-85491-8*) Random Bks Yng Read.

—Say the Magic Word, Please. Gorbaty, Norman, illus. LC 89-34544. 24p. (ps). 1990. 3.95 (0-394-85857-3) Random Bks Yng Read.

Scarffe, Bronwen. You're So Clever. Hunnam, Lucinda, illus. LC 92-34339. 1993. 3.75 (0-383-03669-0) SRA Schl Grp.

Sesame Street Babies. Date not set. 23.70 (0-679-86351-6) Random Bks Yng Read.

Sesame Street Staff. Cookie Monster, Where Are You? Jones, Randy, illus. LC 75-39342. (ps-3). 1976. 8.99 (0-394-83257-4) Random Bks Yng Read.

—Your Friends from Sesame Street. Smollin, Michael J., illus. (ps). 1979. 3.50 (0-394-84137-9) Random Bks Yng Read.

Stevenson, Jocelyn. The Great Muppet Caper. LC 81-4583. (Illus.). 64p. (gr. 4-7). 1981. lib. bdg. 6.99 (0-394-94874-2) Random Bks Yng Read.

Stone, Jon. Would You Like to Play Hide & Seek in This Book with Lovable, Furry Old Grover? Smollin, Michael J., illus. LC 76-8120. (ps-1). 1976. pap. 2.25 (0-394-83292-2) Random Bks Yng Read.

Sustendal, Pat, illus. Sesame Street Farm Friends. 12p. (ps). 1985. 4.99 (0-394-87466-8) Random Bks Yng Read.

Walt Disney Staff. Pinocchio. (ps-3). 1992. 6.98 (0-453-03026-2) Viking-Penguin.

—Pinocchio Bath Book. (ps). 1992. 5.98 (0-453-03028-9) Viking-Penguin.

—Pinocchio Little Library. (ps-3). 1992. 5.98 (0-453-03027-0) Viking-Penguin.

Walt Disney's Pinocchio. (Illus.). 24p. (ps up). 1992. deluxe ed. write for info. incl. long-life batteries (0-307-74025-0, 64025, Golden Pr) Western Pub.

Weiss, Ellen. Baby Gonzo in Backwardsland. DiCicco, Sue, illus. 26p. (ps up). 1987. 12.95 (1-55578-603-0) Worlds Wonder.

PURCHASING

see Shopping

PURIM (FEAST OF ESTHER)

Chaikin, Miriam. Make Noise, Make Merry: The Story & Meaning of Purim. Demi, illus. LC 82-12926. 96p. (gr. 3-6). 1986. pap. 4.95 (0-89919-424-9, Clarion Bks) HM.

Gottlieb, Yaffa L. The Shushan Chronicle: The Story of Purim. Barkman, Aidel, illus. 56p. (gr. k-4). 1991. 11.95 (0-922613-39-7); pap. 9.95 (0-922613-40-0) Hachai Pubns.

Nerlove, Miriam. Purim. Levine, Abby, ed. Nerlove, Miriam, illus. LC 91-19516. 24p. (ps-1). 1992. PLB 11.95 (0-8075-6682-9) A Whitman.

Silberman, Shoshana. The Whole Megillah. Kahn, Katherine, illus. LC 90-5137. 40p. (gr. k-6). 1991. pap. 3.95 (0-929371-23-2) Kar Ben.

Silverman, Maida. Festival of Esther: The Story of Purim. Ewing, Carolyn S., illus. (gr. 1-5). 1988. (Little Simon) S&S Trade.

Simon, Norma. Happy Purim Night. Gordon, Ayala, illus. (ps-k). plastic cover 4.50 (0-8381-0706-0, 10-706) United Syn Bk.

—Purim Party. Gordon, Ayala, illus. (ps-k). 1959. plastic cover 4.50 (0-8381-0707-9) United Syn Bk.

Wengrov, Charles. The Story of Purim. (Illus.). (gr. k-7). 1965. pap. 2.50 (0-914080-53-9) Shulsinger Sales.

Zwerm, Raymond A. & Marcus, Audrey F. Purim Album. (Illus.). 32p. (gr. k-3). 1981. 10.95 (0-8074-0154-4, 101250) UAHC.

PURITANS–FICTION

Hawthorne, Nathaniel. Scarlet Letter. Levin, Harry T., ed. LC 60-2662. (gr. 9 up). 1960. pap. 8.76 (0-395-05142-8, RivEd) HM.

Hawthorne, Nathaniel, et al. The Scarlet Letter. (Illus.). 52p. Date not set. pap. 4.95 (1-57209-006-5) Classics Int Ent.

Speare, Elizabeth G. Witch of Blackbird Pond. (Illus.). 256p. (gr. 7 up). 1958. 14.95 (0-395-07114-3) HM.

PUZZLES

Accorsi, William. Billy's Button. LC 91-37742. (Illus.). 24p. (ps-3). 1992. 14.00 (0-688-10686-2); PLB 13.93 (0-688-10687-0) Greenwillow.

Adamo, Adam. Babysitters Club Trivia & Puzzle Fun Book. (gr. 4-7). 1992. pap. 3.50 (0-590-47314-X) Scholastic Inc.

Adler, David A. Bible Fun Book: Puzzles, Riddles, Magic, & More. (Illus., Orig.). (gr. 1-5). 1979. pap. 3.95 (0-88482-769-0) Hebrew Pub.

Adshead, Paul. Puzzle Island. LC 91-33416. (Illus.). (gr. k-7). 1991. 11.95 (0-85953-402-2); pap. 5.95 (0-85953-403-0) Childs Play.

Anderson, Karen C. Disney's Big Book of Puzzlers: Picture Puzzles, Brainteasers, Games, Mazes, & More. LC 91-73805. (Illus.). 176p. (gr. 2-7). 1992. pap. 9.95 (1-56282-067-2) Disney Pr.

Animals Sticker Jigsaw Book. (gr. 3-6). 1992. pap. 3.95 (1-56680-510-4) Mad Hatter Pub.

Apelbaum, Shiffy. Moshe Mendel the Mitzva Maven & His Amazing Mitzva Quest. LC 94-4118. 1994. 12.95 (0-87306-662-6) Feldheim.

Arboleda, Alba, et al. Outer Space Adventures. (Illus.). 32p. (gr. 3 up). 1986. incl. hand held Decoder 5.95 (0-88679-462-5) Educ Insights.

Ashbach, Dawn & Veal, Janice. Adventures in Greater Puget Sound: An Educational Guide Exploring the Marine Environment of Greater Puget Sound. Veal, Janice, illus. 56p. (Orig.). (gr. 3-9). 1991. 7.95 (*0-9629778-0-2*) NW Island.

ADVENTURES IN GREATER PUGET SOUND captures the magic of marine life in this unique region. An educational guide & activity book, it is designed for 8 to 12 year olds, but adults will be tempted to try their hands at a variety of challenges ranging from hidden pictures to crossword puzzles & decoding the "Captain's Secret Message." The rich green waters of Greater Puget Sound are the hub for a multitude of marine activities. Colorful sea anemones & shy octopuses undulate their tentacles on the sea floor, while orca whales breach & yachts & ferry boats wend their watery ways at the surface. ADVENTURES IN GREATER PUGET SOUND includes concise & definitive information on a host of creatures & boats from wrinkled whelks to eagles to oil freighters. The activities are designed to reinforce text information. The book is illustrated with more than 150 pen & ink drawings. To order: Northwest Island Associates, 444 Guemes Island Road, Anacortes, WA 98221; (206) 293-3721.

Publisher Provided Annotation.

Ayres, Pam. Guess Where? Lacome, Julie, illus. LC 93-24336. 32p. (gr. 2 up). 1994. 3.99 (1-56402-314-1) Candlewick Pr.

—Guess Why. Lacome, Julie, illus. LC 93-24337. 32p. (gr. 2 up). 1994. 3.99 (1-56402-315-X) Candlewick Pr.

Baker & Boyington. Down East Puzzles & Word Games. Hassett, John, illus. 80p. (Orig.). 1989. pap. 3.95 (0-89272-272-X) Down East.

Ball, Jacqueline A. A Puzzle for Apatosaurus. (gr. 4-7). 1990. pap. 2.95 (0-06-106002-X, PL) HarpC.

Barry, Mark. Car Books & Puzzle. Barry, Mark, illus. (ps). 1993. Gift box set of 4 bks., 12p. ea. bds. 14.95 (1-56828-039-4) Red Jacket Pr.

Barry, Sheila A. Super-Colossal Book of Puzzles, Tricks & Games. (Illus.). 640p. 1992. Repr. of 1978 ed. 9.99 (0-517-07769-8, Pub. by Wings Bks) Random Hse Value.

Beisner, Monika. Catch That Cat! A Picture Book of Rhymes & Puzzles. (Illus.). 32p. 1990. 15.00 (0-374-31226-5) FS&G.

Birds Sticker Jigsaw Book. (gr. 3-6). 1992. pap. 3.95 (1-56680-511-2) Mad Hatter Pub.

Birminham, Duncan. M Is for Mirror. (Illus.). 33p. (gr. 2-5). 1989. pap. 6.95 (0-906212-66-9, Pub. by Tarquin UK) Parkwest Pubns.

Black, Sonia. Full House Trivia & Puzzle Fun Book. (gr. 4-7). 1993. pap. 2.95 (0-590-47145-7) Scholastic Inc.

Blazing Mazes. (Illus.). 24p. (gr. 4-7). 1994. pap. 3.95 (1-56144-384-0, Honey Bear Bks) Modern Pub NYC.

Blundell, Kim & Tyler, Jenny. Animal Mazes. (Illus.). 24p. (gr. k-2). 1993. pap. 3.95 (0-7460-1323-X, Usborne) EDC.

Bolton, Linda. Hidden Pictures. LC 92-10528. 1993. 14.99 (0-8037-1378-9) Dial Bks Young.

Book, David L. Problems for Puzzlebusters. LC 92-90284. (Illus.). 358p. (gr. 7-12). 1992. 24.95 (0-9633217-0-6) Enigmatics.

Brain-Bending Mazes. (gr. 2-5). 1987. pap. 1.99 (0-671-64357-6, Little Simon) S&S Trade.

Brandreth, Gyles. Super Silly Riddles. 1991. 3.99 (0-517-07352-8) Random Hse Value.

Brenner, Barbara & Chardiet, Bernice. Where's That Cat. Schwartz, Carol, illus. LC 93-40722. 1994. write for info. (0-590-45216-9) Scholastic Inc.

Brenner, Barbara A. & Chardiet, Bernice. Hide & Seek Science: Where's That Reptile? Schwartz, Carol, illus. LC 92-20905. 1993. 10.95 (0-590-45212-6) Scholastic Inc.

—Where's That Insect? Hide & Seek Science. Schwartz, Carol, illus. LC 92-20906. 32p. 1993. 10.95 (0-590-45210-X) Scholastic Inc.

Bright, Leonard D. The Gifted Kids Guide to Puzzles & Mind Games. (Illus.). 143p. 1985. pap. 7.95 (0-936750-15-4) Paradon Pub Co.

Brown, Marcia. Award Puzzles: Shadow. 1990. 5.95 (0-938971-63-8) JTG Nashville.

Bryant-Mole, K. Second Big Dot to Dot. (Illus.). 96p. (gr. k-4). 1993. pap. 10.95 (0-7460-1377-9, Usborne) EDC.

Bryant-Mole, K. & Tyler, J. Dot to Dot (B - U) (Illus.). 72p. (ps-2). 1992. 7.95 (0-7460-1448-1) EDC.

Bryant-Mole, Karen. Dot-to-Dot Dinosaurs. (Illus.). 24p. (gr. k-1). 1993. pap. 3.50 (0-7460-1374-4, Usborne) EDC.

Bureloff, Morris. Brain-Busting Decode Puzzles. Laycock, Mary, ed. Bureloff, Morris, illus. 64p. (gr. 7-10). 1985. pap. 7.95 (0-918932-86-6) Activity Resources.

Case, Adam. Who Tells the Truth? A Collection of Logical Puzzles to Make You Think. 39p. 1991. 4.95 (0-906212-77-4, Pub. by Tarquin UK) Parkwest Pubns.

Cauley, Lorinda B. Treasure Hunt. Cauley, Lorinda B., illus. LC 93-14043. 32p. (ps-1). 1994. PLB 14.95 (0-399-22447-5, Putnam) Putnam Pub Group.

Chickadee Magazine Editors. The Chickadee Book of Puzzles & Fun. Perna, Debi, ed. & illus. 32p. (ps up). 1992. pap. 4.95 (0-920775-82-9, Pub. by Greey de Pencier CN) Firefly Bks Ltd.

Child, A. What Would It Be? 13p. (gr. k). 1992. pap. text ed. 23.00 big bk. (1-56843-011-6); pap. text ed. 4.50 (1-56843-061-2) BGR Pub.

Code & Cypher Puzzles. (Illus.). 48p. (gr. 5 up). PLB 10.96 (0-88110-526-0, Usborne); pap. 4.50 (0-7460-0675-6, Usborne) EDC.

Construction Machinery Puzzle Book. 12p. (ps). Date not set. 4.95 (1-56828-069-6) Red Jacket Pr.

Crazy Mazes & Other Bamboozlers. (Illus.). 24p. (gr. 4-7). 1994. pap. 3.95 (1-56144-385-9, Honey Bear Bks) Modern Pub NYC.

Crews, Donald. Award Puzzles: Freight Train. 1991. 5.95 (0-938971-70-0) JTG Nashville.

Crossword Puzzle Adventures. (gr. 2-5). 1987. pap. 1.99 (0-671-64356-8, Little Simon) S&S Trade.

Crowther, Jean D. Book of Mormon Puzzles & Pictures for Young Latter-Day Saints. LC 77-74495. (Illus.). 56p. (gr. 3 up). 1977. pap. 5.98 (0-88290-080-3) Horizon Utah.

Deception Destruction Mazes & Puzzles. (Illus.). 64p. (Orig.). (gr. 1-3). 1993. pap. 2.95 (1-56144-379-4, Honey Bear Bks) Modern Pub NYC.

The Dell Book of Cryptograms. 1989. pap. 6.95 (0-440-50091-5) Dell.

Dinosaur Puzzles & Mazes. (Illus.). 64p. (Orig.). (gr. 2-5). 1993. pap. 2.95 (1-56144-301-8, Honey Bear Bks) Modern Pub NYC.

Dinozord's Dynamic Mazes. (Illus.). 24p. (gr. 4-7). 1994. pap. 4.95 (1-56144-470-7, Honey Bear Bks) Modern Pub NYC.

Dixon, S. Advanced Puzzle Adventure. (Illus.). 48p. (gr. 6 up). pap. 9.95 (0-7460-0753-1, Usborne) EDC.

—Cobra Consignment. (Illus.). 48p. (gr. 6 up). PLB 10.96 (0-88110-516-3, Usborne); pap. 4.50 (0-7460-0751-5, Usborne) EDC.

—Codename Quicksilver. (Illus.). 48p. (gr. 6 up). 1992. PLB 11.96 (0-88110-517-1, Usborne); pap. 4.95 (0-7460-0688-8, Usborne) EDC.

—Mystery on Main Street. (Illus.). 48p. (gr. 6 up). PLB 10.96 (0-88110-518-X, Usborne); pap. 4.50 (0-7460-0660-8, Usborne) EDC.

Dixon, Sarah. Map & Maze Puzzles. (Illus.). 48p. (gr. 4-8). 1993. PLB 12.96 (0-88110-525-2, Usborne); pap. 6.95 (0-7460-1579-8, Usborne) EDC.

Dodd, Lynley. Find Me a Tiger. LC 91-50553. (Illus.). 32p. (gr. 1-2). 1992. PLB 17.27 (0-8368-0762-6) Gareth Stevens Inc.

Dolby, K. Ghostly Puzzle Adventures. (gr. 4-7). 1990. pap. 9.95 (0-7460-0336-6, Usborne) EDC.

Dolby, K., et al. Second Usborne Book of Puzzle Adventures. (Illus.). 144p. (gr. 3-8). 1990. pap. 9.95 (0-7460-0310-2, Usborne) EDC.

Drew, David. The Big Brown Box. Ruth, Trevor, illus. LC 92-30673. 1993. 2.50 (0-383-03619-4) SRA Schl Grp.

—Something Silver, Something Blue. Roennfeldt, Robert, illus. LC 92-34256. 1993. 4.25 (0-383-03654-2) SRA Schl Grp.

Edmiston, Margaret C. Merlin Book of Logic Puzzles. Williams, Jack, illus. LC 91-24019. 128p. (gr. 8 up). 1992. pap. 4.95 (0-8069-8221-7) Sterling.

Ehlert, Lois. Award Puzzles: Color Zoo. 1991. 5.95 (0-938971-66-2) JTG Nashville.

Evans, Larry. Three Dimensional Mazes. (Illus.). 40p. (Orig.). (gr. 1 up). 1976. pap. 3.95 (0-8431-1744-3, Troubador) Price Stern.

Famous Places Mazes. (gr. 4-7). 1992. pap. 2.95 (0-8167-2840-2, Pub. by Watermill Pr) Troll Assocs.

Fifty Amazing United States Mazes. (gr. 4-7). 1992. pap. 2.95 (0-8167-2795-3, Pub. by Watermill Pr) Troll Assocs.

Find Frosty as He Sings Christmas Carols. 1991. 7.98 (1-56173-162-5) Pubns Intl Ltd.

Find Santa Claus as He Brings Christmas Joy. 1991. 7.98 (1-56173-161-7) Pubns Intl Ltd.

Find the Gifts. (gr. k-3). 1991. 5.98 (0-8317-9729-0) Smithmark.

Find the Gifts on the Twelve Days of Christmas. 1991. 7.98 (1-56173-164-1) Pubns Intl Ltd.

Find the Nutcracker in His Christmas Ballet. 1991. 7.98 (1-56173-163-3) Pubns Intl Ltd.

Fowler, M. Logic Puzzles. (Illus.). 48p. (gr. 4 up). 1994. PLB 10.96 (0-88110-527-9, Usborne); pap. 6.95 (0-7460-0733-7, Usborne) EDC.

Gamiello, Elvira. Hidden Messages You Can Solve. (Illus., Orig.). (gr. 4-6). 1989. pap. 1.95 (0-942025-41-5) Kidsbks.

—More Fun to Find Word Search. (Illus.). 64p. (Orig.). 1991. pap. 1.95 (1-56156-000-6) Kidsbks.

—Search-A-Picture Puzzles. (Illus., Orig.). (gr. 4-6). 1987. pap. 1.95 (0-942025-07-5) Kidsbks.

—Secret Codes & Other Word Games. (Illus., Orig.). (gr. 4-6). 1988. pap. 1.95 (0-942025-45-8) Kidsbks.

—Secret Jokes & Hidden Riddles Activity & Fun Book. (Illus., Orig.). (gr. 4-6). 1989. pap. 1.95 (0-942025-25-3) Kidsbks.

—Sharks Activity & Game Book. (Illus., Orig.). (gr. 4-6). 1988. pap. 1.95 (*0-942025-46-6*) Kidsbks.
—Snowy Days Activity & Game Book. (Illus., Orig.). (gr. 4-6). 1989. pap. 1.95 (*0-942025-36-9*) Kidsbks.
—Spooky Haunted House Puzzles. (Illus.). 64p. (Orig.). (gr. 4-6). 1987. pap. 1.95 (*0-942025-06-7*) Kidsbks.
—Summertime Puzzle & Fun Book. (Illus., Orig.). (gr. 4-6). 1989. pap. 1.95 (*0-942025-62-8*) Kidsbks.
—Sunny Days Word Games & Mazes. (Illus., Orig.). (gr. 4-6). 1988. pap. 1.95 (*0-942025-40-7*) Kidsbks.
—Super Secret Codes & Jokes. (Illus., Orig.). (gr. 4-6). 1990. pap. 1.95 (*0-942025-44-X*) Kidsbks.
—What's Wrong Here. (Illus., Orig.). (gr. 4-6). 1989. pap. 1.95 (*0-942025-91-1*) Kidsbks.
Gammell, Stephen. Award Puzzles: Song & Dance Man. 1991. 5.95 (*0-938971-61-1*) JTG Nashville.
Gardner, Martin. The Snark Puzzle Book. Holiday, Henry & Tenniel, John, illus. 124p. (gr. 3 up). 1990. Repr. of 1973 ed. PLB 16.95 (*0-87975-583-0*) Prometheus Bks.
Geisert, Arthur. Pigs from One to Ten. Geisert, Arthur, illus. LC 92-5097. 32p. (gr. k-3). 1992. 14.45 (*0-395-58519-8*) HM.
Gifted & Talented: Puzzles & Games for Critical & Creative Thinking. 80p. (ps-1). 1994. pap. 3.95 (*1-56565-129-4*) Lowell Hse.
Gifted & Talented: Puzzles & Games for Critical & Creative Thinking. 80p. (gr. 1-3). 1994. pap. 3.95 (*1-56565-139-1*) Lowell Hse.
Ginns, P. C. Ghostwriter: The Big Book of Kid's Puzzles Mystery Issue. (ps-3). 1992. pap. 2.50 (*0-553-37074-X*) Bantam.
Gleason, Norma. Fun with Word Puzzles. 1991. pap. 2.95 (*0-486-26923-X*) Dover.
Goble, Paul. Award Puzzles: The Girl Who Loved Wild Horses. 1991. 5.95 (*0-938971-65-4*) JTG Nashville.
Goldberg, Steve. Pholdit. (gr. 3 up). 1972. 6.50 (*0-918932-67-X*) Activity Resources.
Gomi, Taro. Who Hid It? (Illus.). 24p. (ps). 1992. 6.95 (*1-56294-707-9*); PLB 8.90 (*1-56294-011-2*); pap. 4.95 (*1-56294-841-5*) Millbrook Pr.
Graham, Dennis, et al. Culture Trek. (Illus.). 32p. (gr. 3 up). 1989. incl. hand held Decoder 5.95 (*0-88679-572-9*) Educ Insights.
—Exploring America. (Illus.). 32p. (gr. 3 up). 1989. incl. hand held Decoder 5.95 (*0-88679-573-7*) Educ Insights.
—Prehistoric Life. (Illus.). 32p. (gr. 3 up). 1989. incl. hand held Decoder 5.95 (*0-88679-571-0*) Educ Insights.
—Undersea Adventures. (Illus.). 32p. (gr. 3 up). 1989. incl. hand held Decoder 5.95 (*0-88679-574-5*) Educ Insights.
Griffiths, Rose. Number Puzzles. Millard, Peter, photos by. (Illus.). 32p. (gr. 1 up). 1995. PLB 17.27 (*0-8368-1180-1*) Gareth Stevens Inc.
Guhm, Susan & Guhm, Karl. The Great Bodie Activity Book. (Illus.). 1991. write for info. (*0-9627621-1-3*) Froggy Bywater.
Hall, John. Maze Craze Three. (Illus.). 40p. (Orig.). (gr. 1 up). 1974. pap. 3.50 (*0-8431-1734-6*, Troubador) Price Stern.
—Maze Craze Two. (Illus.). 40p. (Orig.). (gr. 1 up). 1973. pap. 3.50 (*0-8431-1733-8*, Troubador) Price Stern.
Hallett, Bill & Hallett, Jane. National Park Service: Activities & Adventures for Kids. Paltrow, Robert, illus. 32p. (Orig.). (gr. 3-8). 1991. activity bk. 3.95 (*1-877827-07-X*) Look & See.
Handford, Martin. Donde Esta Waldo? LC 92-54399. (Illus.). 32p. (ps up). 1993. PLB 14.88 (*1-56402-228-5*); pap. text ed. cancelled (*1-56402-225-0*) Candlewick Pr.
—Donde Esta Waldo Ahora? LC 92-54507. (Illus.). 32p. (ps up). 1993. PLB 14.88 (*1-56402-229-3*); pap. text ed. cancelled (*1-56402-226-9*) Candlewick Pr.
—Fun with Waldo. (ps-3). 1992. 3.95 (*0-316-34380-3*) Little.
—More Fun with Waldo. (ps-3). 1992. 3.95 (*0-316-34383-8*) Little.
—Waldo y la Gran Busqueda. LC 92-54508. (Illus.). 32p. (ps up). 1993. PLB 14.88 (*1-56402-230-7*); pap. text ed. cancelled (*1-56402-227-7*) Candlewick Pr.
—Where's Waldo? 1993. 5.95 (*0-316-34391-9*) Little.
Harris, Tina, et al. Worldwide Wonders. (Illus.). 32p. (gr. 3 up). 1986. incl. hand held Decoder 5.95 (*0-88679-461-7*) Educ Insights.
—Inventions & Discoveries. (Illus.). 32p. (gr. 3 up). 1989. incl. hand held Decoder 5.95 (*0-88679-458-7*) Educ Insights.
Harvey, Jane. Marvin the Mouse Look & Find Book. (Illus.). 64p. (ps-1). 1991. 6.99 (*0-517-05389-6*) Random Hse Value.
Hawtin, Jeff. Secret Messages: A Collection of Puzzles Using Codes & Ciphers. 48p. 1991. 6.95 (*0-906212-78-2*, Pub. by Tarquin UK) Parkwest Pubns.
Hayes. Picture Puzzles. (Illus.). 32p. (gr. 2-6). 1988. pap. 2.95 (*0-88625-147-8*) Durkin Hayes Pub.
Hayward, Linda. I Spy. Cooke, Tom, illus. 32p. (Orig.). (ps-1). 1993. PLB 7.99 (*0-679-94979-8*); pap. 3.50 (*0-679-84979-3*) Random Bks Yng Read.
Heimann, Rolf. Amazing Mazes. (gr. 4-7). 1990. pap. 3.95 (*0-8167-2201-3*) Troll Assocs.
—Mega Mind-Twisters. (gr. 4-7). 1994. pap. 3.95 (*0-8167-3393-7*) Troll Assocs.
Heller, Ruth. Maze Craze One. (Illus.). 40p. (Orig.). (gr. 1 up). 1971. pap. 3.50 (*0-8431-1732-X*, Troubador) Price Stern.
Herman, Gail. The Fire-Engine Book & Puzzle Set. (Illus.). 18p. (ps-6). 1991. incl. 26-piece puzzle 2.99 (*0-517-05124-9*) Random Hse Value.
Herzog, Brad. Heads Up! Puzzles for Sports Brains. (gr. 4-7). 1994. pap. 2.99 (*0-553-48160-6*) Bantam.
Highlights Editors. Hidden Pictures & Other Puzzlers. (Illus.). 32p. (Orig.). (gr. 1-6). 1981. pap. 2.95 (*0-87534-180-2*) Highlights.
Highlights for Children Editors. Second Jumbo Book of Hidden Pictures. 96p. (ps-3). 1993. pap. 4.95 (*1-56397-185-2*) Boyds Mills Pr.
Highlights for Children Staff. Hidden Pictures & Brain Bogglers. Highlights for Children Staff, illus. 32p. (gr. 1-5). 1992. pap. 2.95 (*0-87534-094-6*) Highlights.
—Hidden Pictures & Brain Twisters. Highlights for Children Staff, illus. 32p. (gr. 1-5). 1992. pap. 2.95 (*0-87534-092-X*) Highlights.
—Hidden Pictures & Mind Boosters. Highlights for Children Staff, illus. 32p. (gr. 1-5). 1992. pap. 2.95 (*0-87534-098-9*) Highlights.
—Hidden Pictures & More Fun. Highlights for Children Staff, illus. 32p. (gr. 1-5). 1992. pap. 2.95 (*0-87534-095-4*) Highlights.
—Hidden Pictures & Thinking Games. Highlights for Children Staff, illus. 32p. (gr. 1-5). 1992. pap. 2.95 (*0-87534-097-0*) Highlights.
—Hidden Pictures & Tricky Teasers. Highlights for Children Staff, illus. 32p. (gr. 1-5). 1992. pap. 2.95 (*0-87534-090-3*) Highlights.
—Hidden Pictures Plus Brain Bafflers. Highlights for Children Staff, illus. 32p. (gr. 1-5). 1992. pap. 2.95 (*0-87534-089-X*) Highlights.
—Hidden Pictures Plus Mind Stretchers. Highlights for Children Staff, illus. 32p. (gr. 1-5). 1992. pap. 2.95 (*0-87534-093-8*) Highlights.
—Hidden Pictures Plus Mind Tanglers. Highlights for Children Staff, illus. 32p. (gr. 1-5). 1992. pap. 2.95 (*0-87534-091-1*) Highlights.
—Hidden Pictures Plus Other Stumpers. Highlights for Children Staff, illus. 32p. (gr. 1-5). 1992. pap. 2.95 (*0-87534-096-2*) Highlights.
—Puzzlemania. Highlights for Children Staff, illus. (gr. 3-7). 1989. pap. 2.98 48p. (*0-87534-701-0*); pap. 2.98 32p. (*0-87534-801-7*) Highlights.
—Puzzlemania. Highlights for Children Staff, illus. (gr. 3-7). 1989. pap. 2.98 48p. (*0-87534-702-9*); pap. 2.98 32p. (*0-87534-802-5*) Highlights.
—Puzzlemania. Highlights for Children Staff, illus. (gr. 3-7). 1989. pap. 2.98 48p. (*0-87534-703-7*); pap. 2.98 32p. (*0-87534-803-3*) Highlights.
—Puzzlemania. Highlights for Children Staff, illus. (gr. 3-7). 1989. pap. 2.98 48p. (*0-87534-704-5*); pap. 2.98 32p. (*0-87534-804-1*) Highlights.
—Puzzlemania. Highlights for Children Staff, illus. (gr. 3-7). 1989. pap. 2.98 48p. (*0-87534-705-3*); pap. 2.98 32p. (*0-87534-805-X*) Highlights.
—Puzzlemania. Highlights for Children Staff, illus. (gr. 3-7). 1989. pap. 2.98 48p. (*0-87534-706-1*); pap. 2.98 32p. (*0-87534-806-8*) Highlights.
—Puzzlemania. Highlights for Children Staff, illus. (gr. 3-7). 1989. pap. 2.98 48p. (*0-87534-707-X*); pap. 2.98 32p. (*0-87534-807-6*) Highlights.
—Puzzlemania. Highlights for Children Staff, illus. (gr. 3-7). 1989. pap. 2.98 48p. (*0-87534-708-8*); pap. 2.98 32p. (*0-87534-808-4*) Highlights.
—Puzzlemania. Highlights for Children Staff, illus. (gr. 3-7). 1989. pap. 2.98 48p. (*0-87534-709-6*); pap. 2.98 32p. (*0-87534-809-2*) Highlights.
—Puzzlemania. Highlights for Children Staff, illus. (gr. 3-7). 1989. pap. 2.98 48p. (*0-87534-710-X*); pap. 2.98 32p. (*0-87534-810-6*) Highlights.
—Puzzlemania. Highlights for Children Staff, illus. 48p. (gr. 3-7). 1990. pap. 2.98 (*0-87534-711-8*) Highlights.
—Puzzlemania. Highlights for Children Staff, illus. 48p. (gr. 3-7). 1990. pap. 2.98 (*0-87534-712-6*) Highlights.
—Puzzlemania. Highlights for Children Staff, illus. 48p. (gr. 3-7). 1990. pap. 2.98 (*0-87534-713-4*) Highlights.
—Puzzlemania. Highlights for Children Staff, illus. 48p. (gr. 3-7). 1990. pap. 2.98 (*0-87534-714-2*) Highlights.
—Puzzlemania. Highlights for Children Staff, illus. 48p. (gr. 3-7). 1990. pap. 2.98 (*0-87534-715-0*) Highlights.
—Puzzlemania. Highlights for Children Staff, illus. 48p. (gr. 3-7). 1990. pap. 2.98 (*0-87534-716-9*) Highlights.
—Puzzlemania. Highlights for Children Staff, illus. 48p. (gr. 3-7). 1990. pap. 2.98 (*0-87534-717-7*) Highlights.
—Puzzlemania. Highlights for Children Staff, illus. 48p. (gr. 3-7). 1990. pap. 2.98 (*0-87534-718-5*) Highlights.
—Puzzlemania. Highlights for Children Staff, illus. 48p. (gr. 3-7). 1990. pap. 2.98 (*0-87534-719-3*) Highlights.
—Puzzlemania. Highlights for Children Staff, illus. 48p. (gr. 3-7). 1990. pap. 2.98 (*0-87534-720-7*) Highlights.
—Puzzlemania. Highlights for Children Staff, illus. 48p. (gr. 3-7). 1990. pap. 2.98 (*0-87534-721-5*) Highlights.
—Puzzlemania. Highlights for Children Staff, illus. 48p. (gr. 3-7). 1990. pap. 2.98 (*0-87534-722-3*) Highlights.
—Puzzlemania. Highlights for Children Staff, illus. 48p. (gr. 3-7). 1991. pap. 2.98 (*0-87534-723-1*) Highlights.
—Puzzlemania. Highlights for Children Staff, illus. 48p. (gr. 3-7). 1991. pap. 2.98 (*0-87534-724-X*) Highlights.
—Puzzlemania. Highlights for Children Staff, illus. 48p. (gr. 3-7). 1991. pap. 2.98 (*0-87534-725-8*) Highlights.
—Puzzlemania. Highlights for Children Staff, illus. 48p. (gr. 3-7). 1991. pap. 2.98 (*0-87534-726-6*) Highlights.
—Puzzlemania. Highlights for Children Staff, illus. 48p. (gr. 3-7). 1991. pap. 2.98 (*0-87534-727-4*) Highlights.
—Puzzlemania. Highlights for Children Staff, illus. 48p. (gr. 3-7). 1991. pap. 2.98 (*0-87534-728-2*) Highlights.
Hite, Nancy. A Pocket Book of Puzzles. 200p. (ps up). 1979. 7.95 (*0-916456-47-1*, GA98) Good Apple.
Hochstatter, Daniel J., illus. Sammy's Excellent Real-Life Adventures. LC 92-40532. (gr. 5 up). 1993. 9.99 (*0-8407-9675-7*) Nelson.
Holland, Penny & Kubota, Carole. Puzzles & Thinking Games. (Illus.). 32p. (gr. 3 up). 1986. incl. hand held Decoder 5.95 (*0-88679-459-5*) Educ Insights.
Home Alone Two - Lost in New York. (80 pgs. ea. bk.). (gr. k-3). 1992. Bk. 1. pap. 2.95 (*1-56144-223-2*, Honey Bear Bks) Bk. 2. pap. 2.95 (*1-56144-224-0*) Modern Pub NYC.
Home Alone Two - Lost in New York: Games & Puzzles. 64p. (gr. k-3). 1992. pap. 2.95 (*1-56144-229-1*, Honey Bear Bks) Modern Pub NYC.
Home Alone Two - Lost in New York: Puzzles & Mazes. 64p. (gr. k-3). 1992. pap. 2.95 (*1-56144-230-5*, Honey Bear Bks) Modern Pub NYC.
Horses & Ponies. 32p. (Orig.). (gr. k-2). 1993. pap. 2.95 (*0-8431-3538-7*) Price Stern.
Howell, Ann C. Tuskegee Airmen: Heroes in Flight for Dignity Inclusion & Citizenship Rights. Chandler, Alton, ed. Johannes, Greg, illus. 24p. (Orig.). (gr. 3-8). 1994. pap. text ed. 1.50 (*0-685-71995-2*) Chandler White.
Hyamm, Trina S. Award Puzzles: Saint George & the Dragon. 1991. 5.95 (*0-938971-68-9*) JTG Nashville.
Ingram, Anne & O'Donnell, Peggy. Family Car Book. Graham, Bob, illus. 48p. (gr. 4 up). 1992. pap. 6.95 (*0-920775-43-8*, Pub. by Greey dePencier CN) Firefly Bks Ltd.
—Rainy Day Book. Peters, Shirley, illus. 48p. (gr. 3 up). 1992. pap. 6.95 (*0-920775-44-6*, Pub. by Greey dePencier CN) Firefly Bks Ltd.
James, Robin, illus. Creole's Clever Collection of Puzzles. 48p. (gr. 2-6). 1983. Repr. wkbk. 2.95 (*0-8431-1403-7*) Price Stern.
Jenkins, Lee. Time & Time Again. Laycock, Mary, ed. Gittings, Elisa, illus. 72p. (Orig.). (gr. 1-6). 1985. pap. text ed. 7.95 (*0-918932-85-8*) Activity Resources.
Johnson, William. Dinosaur Fun Book. (Illus.). 40p. (gr. 1 up). 1979. pap. 3.50 (*0-8431-1704-4*, Troubador) Price Stern.
Jones, Elizabeth. Award Puzzles: Prayer for a Child. 1991. 5.95 (*0-938971-64-6*) JTG Nashville.
Jones, Evelyn. World's Wackiest Riddle Book. 1991. 3.99 (*0-517-07353-6*) Random Hse Value.
Jordan, Polly, illus. In the Jungle. 24p. (ps-2). 1993. pap. text ed. 2.95 (*1-56293-320-5*) McClanahan Bk.
Kightly, Rosalinda. My First Book: Picture Puzzles & Word Fun for the Very Young. Knightly, Rosalinda, et al, illus. LC 91-71831. 64p. (ps up). 1994. pap. 9.99 (*1-56402-370-2*) Candlewick Pr.
King, Christopher. The Case of the Missing Links. 11p. 1990. pap. 17.95 incls. puzzle (*0-922242-15-1*) Lombard Mktg.
King, Colin. Amazing Book of Puzzles & Tricks. 32p. 1990. 3.50 (*0-517-69194-9*) Random Hse Value.
Kisner, R. & Knowles, B. Warm-up Exercises: Calisthenics for the Brain, Bk. III. 107p. (gr. 5-12). pap. 15.00 (*0-930599-77-2*) Thinking Pubns.
Krulik, Nancy E. All about the Fifty States: A Picture Puzzle Book. 1992. pap. 1.95 (*0-590-45223-1*) Scholastic Inc.
Lasley, Mary. A Day at the Beach. 4p. (ps-2). 1990. incl. 24 puzzle pieces 9.95 (*0-88679-843-4*) Educ Insights.
—A Day at the Park. 4p. (ps-2). 1990. incl. 24 puzzle pieces 9.95 (*0-88679-841-8*) Educ Insights.
—Do-It-Yourself Story Puzzle Book. Brown, Amy L., illus. 2p. (ps). 1988. 9.95 (*0-9622406-0-5*) MOL Bks.
Lattimore, Deborah. Digging into the Past. (Illus.). 32p. (gr. 3 up). 1986. incl. hand held Decoder 5.95 (*0-88679-460-9*) Educ Insights.
Leigh, S. The Haunted Tower. (Illus.). 48p. 1989. PLB 11.96 (*0-88110-367-5*, Usborne) EDC.
—Puzzle Castle. (Illus.). 32p. (ps up). 1993. PLB 13.96 (*0-88110-624-0*); pap. 5.95 (*0-7460-1284-5*) EDC.
—Puzzle Farm. (Illus.). 32p. (ps up). 1992. PLB 13.96 (*0-88110-555-4*, Usborne); pap. 5.95 (*0-7460-0712-4*, Usborne) EDC.
—Puzzle Island. (Illus.). 32p. (ps up). 1991. lib. bdg. 13.96 (*0-88110-558-9*, Usborne); pap. 5.95 (*0-7460-0596-2*, Usborne) EDC.
—Puzzle Town. (Illus.). 32p. (ps up). 1991. PLB 13.96 (*0-88110-554-6*, Usborne); pap. 5.95 (*0-7460-0681-0*, Usborne) EDC.
—Puzzle World (B - U) (Illus.). 96p. (ps up). 1992. pap. 9.95 (*0-7460-0731-0*) EDC.
Leigh, Susannah. Puzzle Planet. (Illus.). 32p. (gr. k-5). 1993. lib. bdg. 13.96 (*0-88110-646-1*, Usborne); pap. 5.95 (*0-7460-1286-1*, Usborne) EDC.
Levy, Nathan. Stories with Holes, Vol. VIII. 20p. (gr. 3 up). 1992. pap. 6.00 (*1-878347-11-X*) NL Assocs.
—Stories with Holes, Vol. I. (gr. 3 up). 1987. 6.00 (*0-685-63374-8*) NL Assocs.
—Stories with Holes, Vol. II. (gr. 3 up). 1990. pap. 6.00 (*1-878347-00-4*) NL Assocs.
—Stories with Holes, Vol. III. (gr. 3 up). 1990. pap. 6.00 (*1-878347-01-2*) NL Assocs.
—Stories with Holes, Vol. IV. (gr. 3 up). 1990. pap. 6.00 (*1-878347-02-0*) NL Assocs.
—Stories with Holes, Vol. V. (gr. 3 up). 1990. pap. 6.00 (*1-878347-03-9*) NL Assocs.
—Stories with Holes, Vol. VI. (gr. 3 up). 1991. pap. 6.00 (*1-878347-09-8*) NL Assocs.
—Stories with Holes, Vol. VII. (gr. 3 up). 1992. pap. 6.00 (*1-878347-10-1*) NL Assocs.

—Stories with Holes, Vol. IX. (gr. 3 up). 1992. pap. 6.00 (*1-878347-17-9*) NL Assocs.
—Stories with Holes, Vol. X. (gr. 3 up). 1992. pap. 6.00 (*1-878347-21-7*) NL Assocs.
—Stories with Holes, Vol. XI. (gr. 3 up). 1992. pap. 6.00 (*1-878347-22-5*) NL Assocs.
—Stories with Holes, Vol. XII. (gr. 3 up). 1993. pap. 6.00 (*1-878347-26-8*) NL Assocs.
—Stories with Holes, Vols. I-XII. (gr. 3 up). 1993. Set. 70.00 (*0-685-63375-6*, NL1970) NL Assocs.
—Stories with Holes, Vol. XIV. (gr. 3 up). 1993. write for info. (*1-878347-28-4*) NL Assocs.
—Stories with Holes, Vol. XV. (gr. 3 up). 1993. write for info. (*1-878347-29-2*) NL Assocs.
—Stories with Holes, Vol. XVI. (gr. 3 up). 1993. write for info. (*1-878347-30-6*) NL Assocs.
—Stories with Holes, Vol. XVII. (gr. 3 up). 1993. write for info. (*1-878347-31-4*) NL Assocs.
—Stories with Holes, Vol. XVIII. (gr. 3 up). 1993. write for info. (*1-878347-32-2*) NL Assocs.
Longe, Bob. Nutty Challenges & Zany Dares. Longe, Bob, illus. LC 93-32391. 128p. 1994. pap. 4.95 (*0-8069-0454-2*) Sterling.
Lum, Ray J. The Rebus Escape. LC 91-76970. 64p. (Orig.). (gr. 3-5). 1992. pap. 5.95x (*0-943864-63-1*) Davenport.
Lutz, John. Double Cross. 4p. (Orig.). 1989. pap. 19.95 incls. puzzle (*0-922242-14-3*) Lombard Mktg.
Macdonald, Suse. Puzzlers. LC 88-33392. 1989. 13.89 (*0-8037-0690-1*); PLB 13.95 (*0-8037-0689-8*) Dial Bks Young.
Madcap Mazes. (Illus.). 24p. (gr. 4-7). 1994. pap. 3.95 (*1-56144-386-7*, Honey Bear Bks) Modern Pub NYC.
Madgwick, Wendy. Animaze! A Collection of Amazing Nature Mazes. Hussey, Lorna, illus. LC 91-46892. 40p. (ps-3). 1992. 13.00 (*0-679-82665-3*); PLB 13.99 (*0-679-92665-8*) Knopf Bks Yng Read.
—Behold! Spot-the-Difference Bible Stories. Alles, Hemesh, illus. LC 93-5506. 48p. (gr. k-3). 1994. 12.00 (*0-679-85333-2*) Random Bks Yng Read.
Maleska, Eugene T., ed. Children's Word Games & Puzzles. 2nd ed. LC 86-886. 80p. (gr. 3 up). 1986. pap. 7.00 (*0-8129-1308-6*) Random.
Mallett, Jerry J. Library Skills Activity Puzzles Series, 5 bks. Incl. Book Bafflers. 1982; Dictionary Puzzlers. 1982; Lively Locators. 1982; Reading Incentives. 1982; Resource Rousers. 1982. (gr. 2-6). 1988. pap. text ed. write for info. (*0-87628-537-X*) Ctr Appl Res.
Marzollo, Jean. I Spy Fantasy: A Book of Picture Riddles. Wick, Walter, photos by. LC 93-44814. (ps-3). 1994. 12.95 (*0-590-46295-4*) Scholastic Inc.
Marzollo, Jean & Carson, Carol D. I Spy: A Book of Picture Riddles. Wick, Walter, illus. 48p. 1992. 12.95 (*0-590-45087-5*, Cartwheel) Scholastic Inc.
Marzollo, Jean & Wick, Walter. I Spy Christmas. 1992. bds. 12.95 (*0-590-45846-9*, Cartwheel) Scholastic Inc.
Maschke, Ruby. Bible Puzzles for Children, Vol. 2. 64p. 1991. pap. 9.00 (*0-8170-1165-X*) Judson.
Maschke, Ruby A. Bible Puzzles for Children. 64p. (gr. 4-6). 1986. pap. 8.00 (*0-8170-1095-5*) Judson.
Mayorga, Dolores. David Plays Hide-&-Seek in Celebrations: David Juega Al Escondite y Celebra. Mayorga, Dolores, illus. (ENG & SPA.). 24p. (gr. 2-5). 1992. PLB 18.95 (*0-8225-2001-X*) Lerner Pubns.
—David Plays Hide-&-Seek in Folktales: David Juega Al Escondite En Cuentos Folkloricos. Mayorga, Dolores, illus. (ENG & SPA.). 24p. (gr. 2-5). 1992. PLB 18.95 (*0-8225-2003-6*) Lerner Pubns.
—David Plays Hide-&-Seek in the City: David Juega Al Escondite En la Ciudad. Mayorga, Dolores, illus. (ENG & SPA.). 24p. (gr. 2-5). 1992. PLB 18.95 (*0-8225-2002-8*) Lerner Pubns.
—David Plays Hide-&-Seek on Vacation: David Juega Al Escondite En Vacaciones. Mayorga, Dolores, illus. (ENG & SPA.). 24p. (gr. 2-5). 1992. PLB 18.95 (*0-8225-2004-4*) Lerner Pubns.
Megazord's Mighty Mazes. (Illus.). 24p. (gr. 4-7). 1994. pap. 4.95 (*1-56144-469-3*, Honey Bear Bks) Modern Pub NYC.
Mighty Morphin Power Rangers: Puzzles & Mazes. (Illus.). 64p. (gr. k-4). 1994. pap. 2.95 (*1-56144-463-4*, Honey Bear Bks) Modern Pub NYC.
Miller, Gary. Mind Bogglers for Juniors. 38p. 1991. wkbk. 1.95 (*1-882449-00-2*) Messenger Pub.
Mind Teasers. 48p. (Orig.). 1982. pap. 2.95 (*0-8431-0293-4*) Price Stern.
Modern Puzzle Books. (256 pgs. ea. bk.). (gr. 4-8). 1992. Bk. 36. pap. 5.95 (*1-56144-195-3*, Honey Bear Bks) Bk. 37. pap. 5.95 (*1-56144-196-1*); Bk. 38. pap. 5.95 (*1-56144-197-X*); Bk. 39. pap. 5.95 (*1-56144-198-8*) Modern Pub NYC.
Moore, Clement C. The Night Before Christmas Hidden Picture Book. Manning, Maurie J., illus. 32p. 1992. bds. 7.95 (*1-56397-116-X*) Boyds Mills Pr.
Moscovich, Ivan. Puzzling Reflections: Test Your Thinking Powers with Mirror-Cubes. 1991. pap. 6.95 (*0-906212-72-3*, Pub. by Tarquin UK) Parkwest Pubns.
Most, Bernard. Can You Find It? LC 92-33691. (ps-3). 1993. 13.95 (*0-15-292872-3*) HarBrace.
Nichols, V. Hunt for Humphrey. Turkow, E., tr. M. J. Studios Staff, illus. (SPA & ENG.). 32p. (gr. k-6). 1992. pap. 1.95 (*1-879424-23-1*) Nickel Pr.
—Hunt for Humphrey. M. J. Studios Staff, illus. 32p. (gr. k-6). 1992. pap. 1.95 (*1-879424-15-0*) Nickel Pr.
Nims, Bonnie L. Where Is the Bear in the City? Mathews, Judith, ed. Gill, Madelaine, illus. LC 92-3390. 24p. (ps-1). 1992. 11.95g (*0-8075-8937-3*) A Whitman.
Oliver, M. Agent Arthur's Jungle Journey. (Illus.). 48p. 1989. PLB 11.96 (*0-88110-334-9*); pap. 4.95 (*0-7460-0141-X*) EDC.
Owl Magazine Editors. My Summer Book. (Illus.). 64p. (gr. 3 up). 1992. pap. 8.95 (*0-920775-36-5*, Pub. by Greey dePencier CN) Firefly Bks Ltd.
—Nature What's It? Creatures, Plants, Nature's Oddities & More. (Illus.). 32p. (gr. 4 up). 1992. pap. 4.95 (*0-920775-38-1*, Pub. by Greey dePencier CN) Firefly Bks Ltd.
—Puzzles & Puzzlers. (Illus.). 96p. (gr. 3 up). 1992. pap. 3.95 (*0-920775-67-5*, Pub. by Greey dePencier CN) Firefly Bks Ltd.
—Summer Fun. (Illus.). 128p. (gr. 4 up). 1992. pap. 8.95 (*0-919872-87-5*, Pub. by Greey dePencier CN) Firefly Bks Ltd.
—What's It? Gadgets, Objects, Machines & More. (Illus.). 32p. (gr. 3 up). 1992. pap. 4.95 (*0-920775-30-6*, Pub. by Greey dePencier CN) Firefly Bks Ltd.
Owl Magazine Editors & Chickadee Magazine Editors. Party Fun. (Illus.). 32p. (gr. 3 up). 1992. pap. 7.95 (*0-920775-41-1*, Pub. by Greey dePencier CN) Firefly Bks Ltd.
Pack of Puzzle Pads, Bks. 17-20. (80 pgs. ea. bk.). (gr. 4-8). 1993. Bk. 17. pap. 1.50 (*1-56144-191-0*, Honey Bear Bks) Bk. 18. pap. 1.50 (*1-56144-192-9*); Bk. 19. pap. 1.50 (*1-56144-193-7*); Bk. 20. pap. 1.50 (*1-56144-194-5*) Modern Pub NYC.
Pack of Puzzle Pads, Bks. 21-24. (80 pgs. ea. bk.). (gr. 4-8). Date not set. Bk. 21. pap. 1.50 (*1-56144-201-1*, Honey Bear Bks) Bk. 22. pap. 1.50 (*1-56144-202-X*); Bk. 23. pap. 1.50 (*1-56144-203-8*); Bk. 24. pap. 1.50 (*1-56144-204-6*) Modern Pub NYC.
Pape, Donna L. The Children's Arkansas Puzzle Book. Mueller, Virginia & Karle, Carol, illus. 28p. (gr. k up). 1984. pap. 2.00 (*0-914546-55-4*) Rose Pub.
Paraquin, Charles. Optical Illusion Puzzles. Kuttner, Paul, tr. LC 83-18198. (Illus.). 96p. (Orig.). (gr. 7 up). 1984. 12.95 (*0-8069-6868-0*) Sterling.
Patrick, Denise L. Ghostwriter: The Mini Book of Kid's Puzzles Sports Issue. (ps-3). 1992. pap. 1.25 (*0-553-37073-1*) Bantam.
Phillips, Dave. Animal Mazes. (Illus.). 48p. 1991. pap. 2.95 (*0-486-26707-5*) Dover.
Phillips, Dave, illus. Hidden Treasure Maze Book. 48p. (Orig.). (gr. 2 up). 1984. pap. 2.95 (*0-486-24566-7*) Dover.
The Picture-Perfect Planet. LC 92-20831. 1992. write for info. (*0-8094-9319-5*); PLB write for info. (*0-8094-9320-9*) Time-Life.
Power Zords' Puzzles & Mazes. (Illus.). 24p. (gr. 4-7). 1994. pap. 4.95 (*1-56144-467-7*, Honey Bear Bks) Modern Pub NYC.
Pragoff, Fiona. Let's Find Teddy. Pragoff, Fiona, illus. LC 92-2765. 32p. (ps). 1992. 10.00 (*0-679-83501-6*) Random Bks Yng Read.
Puzzle House Staff, ed. Picture Puzzles. (Illus.). 48p. (gr. 3-6). 1992. pap. 2.95 (*1-56680-007-2*) Mad Hatter Pub.
—Pocket Puzzler. (Illus.). 48p. (gr. 3-6). 1992. pap. 2.95 (*1-56680-006-4*) Mad Hatter Pub.
Ranucci, Ernest R. & Rollins, Wilma E. Brain Drain, 2 bks. Klassen, Grace & Nachtigall, Kelly, illus. 70p. (gr. 6-12). Bks. A & B. write for info. incl. tchr's. ed. (*1-878669-09-5*, 4301); 7.50 (*0-685-74212-1*) Bk. A, 1975 (*1-878669-10-9*, 4301) Bk. B, 1978 (4420) Crea Tea Assocs.
Revealing Hidden Pictures. (Illus.). 64p. (gr. 2-5). 1990. pap. 1.99 (*0-671-72336-7*, Little Simon) S&S Trade.
Ripley, Catherine. Two Dozen Dinosaurs: A First Book of Dinosaur Facts & Mysteries, Games & Fun. Louie, Bo-Kim, illus. 32p. (gr. k up). 1992. pap. 7.95 (*0-920775-55-1*, Pub. by Greey dePencier CN) Firefly Bks Ltd.
Ripley, Robert L. Puzzles. Stott, Carol, illus. 48p. (gr. 3-6). Date not set. PLB 12.95 (*1-56065-126-1*) Capstone Pr.
Rojankovsky, Feodor. Award Puzzles: Frog Went a-Courting. 1991. 5.95 (*0-938971-69-7*) JTG Nashville.
Russo, Carol, illus. Three-D Hidden Pictures Activity Book. 16p. 1991. pap. write for info. (*1-56156-012-X*) Kidsbks.
Ryan, Steve. Challenging Pencil Puzzlers. (Illus.). 96p. (gr. 6-10). 1992. pap. 4.95 (*0-8069-8752-9*) Sterling.
—Pencil Puzzlers. (Illus.). 96p. (gr. 7-12). 1992. pap. 4.95 (*0-8069-8542-9*) Sterling.
Sanders, Nancy. Amazing Bible Puzzles: New Testament. (Illus.). 80p. (Orig.). (gr. 3-7). 1993. pap. 4.99 (*0-570-04749-8*) Concordia.
—Amazing Bible Puzzles: Old Testament. (Illus.). 80p. (Orig.). (gr. 3-7). 1993. pap. 4.99 (*0-570-04748-X*) Concordia.
Schanzer, Rosalyn. Ezra on a Quest: A Maze Chase Medieval. LC 93-19537. 1994. 12.95 (*0-385-32262-3*) Doubleday.
Schwartz, Alvin. A Twister of Twists: Tangler of Tongues. LC 72-1434. (Illus.). 128p. (gr. 4 up). 1972. pap. 5.95 (*0-06-446004-5*, Trophy) HarpC Child Bks.
Seattle Arts Commission Staff. Insight: The Seattle Public Art Puzzle Book. (Illus.). 62p. (gr. 5 up). 1994. 17.95 (*0-9617443-5-9*) Seattle Arts.
Selsam, Millicent E. Is This a Baby Dinosaur? & Other Science Picture Puzzles. LC 72-76508. (Illus.). 32p. (gr. k-3). 1984. pap. 4.95 (*0-06-443054-5*, Trophy) HarpC Child Bks.
Sensational Search-a-Words. (Illus.). 64p. (gr. 2-5). 1990. pap. 1.99 (*0-671-72334-0*, Little Simon) S&S Trade.
Shannon, George. Stories to Solve: Folktales from Around the World. Sis, Peter, illus. LC 84-18656. 56p. (gr. 3 up). 1991. pap. 4.95 (*0-688-10496-7*, Pub. by Beech Tree Bks) Morrow.
Silvani, Harold. Famous Athletes Number Puzzles. Sharpsteen, Linda, illus. 28p. (gr. 4-6). 1975. wkbk. 6.95 (*1-878669-23-0*, 4161) Crea Tea Assocs.
—Presidents Number Puzzles, 2 bks. 46p. Bks. A & B. write for info. set (*1-878669-15-X*, 4158) Bk. A, Grades 3-5, 1977. pap. text ed. 6.95 (*0-685-74214-8*, 4158); Bk. B, Grades 4-7, 1973. pap. text ed. 6.95 (*0-685-74215-6*, 4159) Crea Tea Assocs.
Simon & Schuster Staff. Amazing Mazes. (Illus.). 64p. (gr. 2-5). 1990. pap. 1.99 (*0-671-72333-2*, Little Simon) S&S Trade.
Sloane, Paul & MacHale, Des. Logical Thinking Puzzles. Miller, Myron, illus. LC 92-19095. 96p. (gr. 5 up). 1992. 12.95 (*0-8069-8670-0*) Sterling.
Smart, Margaret A. & Laycock, Mary. Create a Cube. Kyzer, Walter & Kyzer, Martha, illus. 64p. (Orig.). (gr. 4-12). 1985. pap. text ed. 7.95 (*0-918932-84-X*) Activity Resources.
Smith, J. C. & McLean, J. Kidworks Series, No. 1. Horine, Billie & Seitz, Connie, illus. (ps-5). 1993. Set. PLB 32.65g (*1-882627-17-2*) KTS Pub.
Smith, T. L. Word Search Puzzles. 34p. (gr. k-6). 1991. saddle stitch bdg. 1.69 (*1-880825-02-3*) Tracey Smith.
Snakes & Lizards. 48p. (gr. k-2). 1993. pap. 2.95 (*0-8431-3539-5*) Price Stern.
Speirs, John. Ghostly Games. LC 91-22407. (Illus.). 32p. (gr. k-6). 1991. 9.95 (*0-89577-393-7*, Dist. by Random) RD Assn.
—The Great Carnival Caper. LC 92-38171. (Illus.). 32p. (gr. k-6). 1993. 9.95 (*0-89577-453-4*, Dist. by Random) RD Assn.
—The Quest for the Golden Mane. Speirs, John, illus. LC 91-33894. 32p. (gr. k-6). 1991. 9.95 (*0-89577-394-5*, Dist. by Random) RD Assn.
—Safari for the Tigrus. LC 92-11328. (Illus.). 32p. (gr. k-6). 1992. 9.95 (*0-89577-452-6*, Dist. by Random) RD Assn.
Spier, Peter. Award Puzzles: Noah's Ark. 1990. 5.95 (*0-938971-62-X*) JTG Nashville.
Spires, Elizabeth, ed. One White Wing: Puzzles in Poems & Pictures. Blegvad, Erik, illus. LC 94-12927. 1995. 16.00 (*0-689-50622-8*, M K McElderry) Macmillan Child Grp.
Spivak, Darlene E. Scrambled Word Puzzles. Spivak, Darlene E., illus. 48p. (gr. 2-5). 1987. wkbk. 6.95 (*1-55734-066-8*) Tchr Create Mat.
Springtime Search & Find. 24p. (gr. k-4). 1992. pap. 2.50 (*0-8167-1853-9*) Troll Assocs.
Steig, William. Award Puzzles: Sylvester & the Magic Pebble. 1990. 5.95 (*0-938971-60-3*) JTG Nashville.
Steptoe, John. Award Puzzles: Mufaro's Beautiful Daughters. 1991. 5.95 (*0-938971-67-0*) JTG Nashville.
Sullivan, Scott. Tough Mazes Three: Historical Monuments, Landmarks & Famous Historical Faces. 40p. (Orig.). (gr. 1 up). 1991. pap. 4.50 (*0-8431-2916-6*, Troubador) Price Stern.
Super Dot to Dot Activity Book 3: Dot-to-Dot. (Illus.). 48p. (Orig.). (gr. k-3). 1990. pap. 2.95 (*0-8431-2786-4*) Price Stern.
Super Outer Space Puzzles & Mazes Activity Book. (Illus.). 48p. (Orig.). (gr. k-3). 1994. 2.95 (*0-8431-3728-2*) Price Stern.
Super Puzzles & Mazes Activity Book 2: Puzzles & Mazes. (Illus.). 48p. (Orig.). (gr. k-3). 1990. pap. 2.95 (*0-8431-2787-2*) Price Stern.
Tailor, Z. Little Red Riding Hood "Puzzle 'n Book" Belli, Fred, illus. 8p. (gr. k up). 1989. PLB write for info. ABC Child Bks.
Tallarico, A. Stop & Find Maze Madness. (Illus.). 14p. 1991. pap. 1.95 (*1-56156-108-8*) Kidsbks.
Tallarico, Anthony. Find Freddie. Tallarico, Anthony, illus. 24p. (gr. 2-6). 1990. lib. bdg. 10.59 (*0-8167-1955-1*); pap. 2.95 (*0-685-44996-3*) Troll Assocs.
—Find Freddie. (Illus.). 24p. (Orig.). 1988. pap. 2.95 (*0-942025-65-2*) Kidsbks.
—Hunt for Hector. Tallarico, Anthony, illus. 24p. (gr. 2-6). 1990. lib. bdg. 10.59 (*0-8167-1956-X*); pap. 2.95 (*0-685-44993-9*) Troll Assocs.
—Hunt for Hector. (Illus.). 24p. (Orig.). 1988. pap. 2.95 (*0-942025-68-7*) Kidsbks.
—Look for Lisa. Tallarico, Anthony, illus. 24p. (gr. 2-6). 1990. lib. bdg. 10.59 (*0-8167-1957-8*); pap. 2.95 (*0-685-44994-7*) Troll Assocs.
—Look for Lisa. (Illus.). 24p. (Orig.). 1988. pap. 2.95 (*0-942025-66-0*) Kidsbks.
—Search for Sam. Tallarico, Anthony, illus. 24p. (gr. 2-6). 1990. lib. bdg. 10.59 (*0-8167-1958-6*); pap. 2.95 (*0-685-44995-5*) Troll Assocs.
—Search for Sam. (Illus.). 24p. (Orig.). 1988. pap. 2.95 (*0-942025-67-9*) Kidsbks.
Tallarico, Tony. Bunny Honey Springtime Search. (Illus.). 24p. 1992. pap. 3.95 (*1-56156-099-5*) Kidsbks.
—Find Frankie & His Monster Friends. (Illus.). 24p. 1992. pap. 2.95 (*1-56156-149-5*) Kidsbks.
—Find Freddie & Lisa in the Haunted House. (Illus.). 32p. 1991. 10.95 (*1-56156-016-2*) Kidsbks.
—Find Freddie & Lisa in the Haunted House. (Illus.). 32p. 1991. pap. 3.95 (*1-56156-041-3*) Kidsbks.
—Find Freddie Around the World. (Illus.). 24p. 1992. 9.95 (*1-56156-066-9*) Kidsbks.
—Freddie's Picture Puzzle Book. (Illus.). 24p. 1991. 3.98 (*1-56156-006-5*) Kidsbks.

—Hector's Picture Puzzle Books. (Illus.). 24p. 1991. 3.98 (*1-56156-008-1*) Kidsbks.
—Hidden Pictures: Crazy Classroom. (Illus.). 32p. 1992. pap. 2.95 (*1-56156-141-X*) Kidsbks.
—Hidden Pictures: Creepy Castles. (Illus.). 24p. 1992. 9.95 (*1-56156-120-7*) Kidsbks.
—Hidden Pictures: Monster Madness. (Illus.). 24p. 1992. 9.95 (*1-56156-121-5*) Kidsbks.
—Hidden Pictures: Santa's Super Surprises. (Illus.). 24p. 1992. 9.95 (*1-56156-118-5*) Kidsbks.
—Hidden Pictures: Twelve Days of Christmas. (Illus.). 24p. 1992. 9.95 (*1-56156-119-3*) Kidsbks.
—Lisa's Picture Puzzle Books. (Illus.). 24p. 1991. 3.98 (*1-56156-007-3*) Kidsbks.
—Look for Lisa: Time Traveller. (Illus.). 24p. 1992. 9.95 (*1-56156-067-7*) Kidsbks.
—Preschool Can You Find ABC Picture Book. (Illus.). 12p. (ps). 1992. 3.95 (*0-448-40426-5*, G&D) Putnam Pub Group.
—Preschool Can You Find Counting Picture Book. (Illus.). 12p. (ps). 1992. 3.95 (*0-448-40425-7*, G&D) Putnam Pub Group.
—Sam's Picture Puzzle Books. (Illus.). 24p. 1991. 3.98 (*1-56156-009-X*) Kidsbks.
—Search for Santa's Helpers. (Illus.). 32p. 1991. 10.95 (*1-56156-015-4*); pap. 3.95 (*1-56156-031-6*) Kidsbks.
—Search for Santa's Helpers. (Illus.). 32p. (Orig.). 1991. pap. 3.95 (*1-56156-042-1*) Kidsbks.
—Search for Sylvester. (Illus.). 24p. 1992. 9.95 (*1-56156-068-5*) Kidsbks.
—What's Wrong Here? At School. (Illus.). 24p. 1991. pap. 2.95 (*1-56156-034-0*) Kidsbks.
—What's Wrong Here? At School. (Illus.). 24p. 1991. 9.95 (*1-56156-005-7*) Kidsbks.
—What's Wrong Here? At the Amusement Park. (Illus.). 32p. 1991. pap. 2.95 (*1-56156-032-4*) Kidsbks.
—What's Wrong Here? At the Amusement Park. (Illus.). 24p. 1991. 9.95 (*1-56156-003-0*) Kidsbks.
—What's Wrong Here? At the Movies. (Illus.). 24p. 1991. pap. 2.95 (*1-56156-035-9*) Kidsbks.
—What's Wrong Here? At the Movies. (Illus.). 24p. 1991. 9.95 (*1-56156-004-9*) Kidsbks.
—What's Wrong Here? In the Haunted House. (Illus.). 24p. 1991. pap. 2.95 (*1-56156-033-2*) Kidsbks.
—What's Wrong Here? In the Haunted House. (Illus.). 24p. 1991. 9.95 (*1-56156-002-2*) Kidsbks.
—Where Are They? (Illus.). 96p. 1992. 14.95 (*1-56156-139-8*) Kidsbks.
—Where's Columbus? (Illus.). 24p. 1992. 9.95 (*1-56156-098-7*) Kidsbks.
—Where's Columbus? (Illus.). 24p. 1992. pap. 2.95 (*1-56156-097-9*) Kidsbks.
—Where's Cupid? (Illus.). 32p. 1991. pap. 3.95 (*1-56156-043-X*) Kidsbks.
—Where's Cupid? (Illus.). 32p. 1991. 10.95 (*1-56156-048-0*) Kidsbks.
—Where's the Bunny? (Illus.). 32p. (Orig.). 1991. pap. 3.95 (*1-56156-011-1*) Kidsbks.
—Where's the Bunny? (Illus.). 28p. 1991. pap. 2.95 (*1-56156-096-0*) Kidsbks.
—Where's the Bunny? (Illus.). 24p. 1992. 10.95 (*1-56156-101-0*) Kidsbks.
—Where's Wendy? (Illus.). 24p. (Orig.). 1991. pap. 2.95 (*1-56156-040-5*) Kidsbks.
—Where's Wendy? (Illus.). 24p. 1992. 9.95 (*1-56156-069-3*) Kidsbks.
Taylor, Jody, ed. Circus Hidden Pictures. 32p. (ps-5). 1994. pap. 4.95 (*1-56397-358-8*) Boyds Mills Pr.
—Sports Hidden Pictures. (Illus.). 32p. (Orig.). (ps-5). 1993. pap. 3.95 (*1-56397-255-7*) Boyds Mills Pr.
Tetz, Rosanne. Nina Can. 32p. 1993. pap. 5.95 (*0-8163-1111-0*) Pacific Pr Pub Assn.
Thompson, Carol. Alphaboo! A Hidden Letter ABC Book. Hartelius, Margaret A., illus. LC 93-26925. 32p. (ps-3). 1994. pap. 2.25 (*0-448-40213-0*, G&D) Putnam Pub Group.
Time Life Inc. Editors. The Search for the Seven Sisters: A Hidden-Picture Geography Book. (Illus.). 56p. (ps-2). 1991. write for info. (*0-8094-9287-3*); PLB write for info. (*0-8094-9288-1*) Time-Life.
—The Three Storytellers of Or: A Flexible-Thinking Book. Kagan, Neil & Ward, Elizabeth, eds. (Illus.). 64p. (ps-2). 1991. write for info. (*0-8094-9283-0*); PLB write for info. (*0-8094-9284-9*) Time-Life.
Tiner, John H. Acts Word Puzzles. (Illus.). 48p. 1986. pap. 2.95 (*1-56794-040-4*, C2300) Star Bible.
Titanus's Braintwisters & Mazes. (Illus.). 24p. (gr. 4-7). 1994. pap. 4.95 (*1-56144-468-5*, Honey Bear Bks) Modern Pub NYC.
Townsend, Charles B. World's Hardest Puzzles. LC 91-41544. (Illus.). 128p. (gr. 10-12). 1992. 12.95 (*0-8069-8516-X*) Sterling.
—World's Most Baffling Puzzles. LC 91-21324. (Illus.). 128p. (gr. 4-11). 1991. 12.95 (*0-8069-5832-4*) Sterling.
—The World's Most Challenging Puzzles. LC 88-19729. (Illus.). 128p. (gr. 3-9). 1989. pap. 4.95 (*0-8069-6731-5*) Sterling.
—World's Most Incredible Puzzles. LC 93-39527. (Illus.). 128p. 1994. 12.95 (*0-8069-0504-2*) Sterling.
—World's Toughest Puzzles. LC 89-49131. (Illus.). 96p. 1990. 12.95 (*0-8069-6962-8*) Sterling.
—World's Toughest Puzzles. LC 89-49131. 96p. (gr. 6-12). 1991. pap. 4.95 (*0-8069-6963-6*) Sterling.
Travis, Falcon. Great Book of Whodunit Puzzles: Mini-Mysteries for You to Solve. LC 92-43853. (Illus.). 128p. (gr. 5 up). 1993. pap. 4.95 (*0-8069-0348-1*) Sterling.
Treat, Lawrence. You're the Detective! Twenty-Four Solve-Them-Yourself Picture Mysteries. Borowik, Kathleen, illus. LC 82-49346. 80p. (Orig.). (gr. 3-6). 1983. pap. 7.95 (*0-87923-478-4*) Godine.
Tricks & Puzzles: Superfacts. 1992. 4.99 (*0-517-07327-7*) Random Hse Value.
Tricky Brain Ticklers & Mazes. (Illus.). 24p. (gr. 4-7). 1994. pap. 3.95 (*1-56144-387-5*, Honey Bear Bks) Modern Pub NYC.
Troll. Brain Teasers & Puzzles for Kids. 32p. (ps-3). 1991. pap. 1.95 (*0-8167-2247-1*) Troll Assocs.
Trolls Activity Book. 64p. (gr. k-3). 1992. pap. 2.95 (*1-56144-218-6*, Honey Bear Bks) Modern Pub NYC.
Trolls Puzzles & Mazes. 64p. (gr. k-3). 1992. pap. 2.95 (*1-56144-217-8*, Honey Bear Bks) Modern Pub NYC.
Tropea, Maria. Look & Look Again: Lost in the Haunted Mansion. Tallarico, A., illus. 24p. 1991. 2.98 (*1-56156-044-8*); pap. 1.95 (*1-56156-050-2*) Kidsbks.
—Look & Look Again: Missing Snowman. Tallarico, A., illus. 24p. 1991. 2.98 (*1-56156-047-2*); pap. 1.95 (*1-56156-053-7*) Kidsbks.
—Look & Look Again: Silly Schoolhouse. Tallarico, A., illus. 24p. 1991. pap. 1.95 (*1-56156-051-0*) Kidsbks.
—Look & Look Again: Silly Schoolhouse. Tallarico, A., illus. 24p. 1991. 2.98 (*1-56156-045-6*) Kidsbks.
—Look & Look Again: Where's Benjy Bunny? Tallarico, A., illus. 24p. 1991. 2.98 (*1-56156-046-4*); pap. 1.95 (*1-56156-052-9*) Kidsbks.
Tyler. Number Puzzles. (gr. 2-5). 1980. PLB 12.96 (*0-88110-050-1*, Usborne-Hayes); pap. 4.50 (*0-86020-435-9*) EDC.
—Picture Puzzles. (gr. 2-5). 1980. (Usborne-Hayes); PLB 12.96 (*0-88110-049-8*); pap. 4.50 (*0-86020-433-2*) EDC.
Tyler, J. Brainbenders. (Illus.). 96p. 1993. pap. 10.95 (*0-7460-1629-8*, Usborne) EDC.
Tyler, J. & Gee, R. Spelling Puzzles. (Illus.). 32p. (gr. 2-5). 1992. pap. 4.95 (*0-7460-1053-2*) EDC.
Usborne Publishing Editors. More Adventures from Puzzle World. (ps-3). 1994. pap. 9.95 (*0-7460-1290-X*, Usborne) EDC.
Valentine's Day Search & Find. 24p. (gr. k-4). 1992. pap. 2.50 (*0-8167-1852-0*) Troll Assocs.
Walt Disney Staff. Aladdin Puzzle Play Book. (ps-3). 1993. pap. 5.98 (*0-453-03062-9*) Mouse Works.
—Beauty & the Beast Puzzle Play Book. (ps-3). 1993. pap. 5.98 (*0-453-03095-5*) Mouse Works.
Walter, Marion. The Mirror Puzzle Book. (Illus.). 32p. (gr. 2 up). 1985. pap. 6.95 (*0-906212-39-1*, Pub. by Tarquin UK) Parkwest Pubns.
Waters, G. Time Train to Ancient Rome. (Illus.). 48p. (gr. 3-5). 1988. PLB 11.96 (*0-88110-302-0*); pap. 4.95 (*0-7460-0153-3*) EDC.
Waters, G., et al. Puzzle Adventures. (Illus.). 144p. (gr. 3-5). 1988. pap. 9.95 (*0-7460-0155-X*) EDC.
Weaver, Charles. Hidden Logic Puzzles. 128p. (gr. 10-12). 1992. 12.95 (*0-8069-8334-5*) Sterling.
Wheeler, Joan & Carter, Sharon. Brain Benders. 48p. (gr. 4-6). 1982. 5.95 (*0-88160-048-2*, LW 234) Learning Wks.
Where's Waldo, Inc. Staff. Where's Waldo? Waldo in Dinoland. 16p. (ps-2). 1993. write for info. (*1-883366-13-5*) YES Ent.
Wild Animal Family Album: Puzzle Book. 12p. (ps). Date not set. 5.95 (*1-56828-068-8*) Red Jacket Pr.
Wood, John N. Nature Hide & Seek: Rivers & Lakes. Wood, John N. & Dean, Kevin, illus. LC 93-22501. (gr. 1-4). 1993. 13.00 (*0-679-83690-X*) Knopf Bks Yng Read.
—Nature Hide & Seek: Woods & Forests. Silver, Maggie, illus. LC 93-22506. 22p. (gr. k-4). 1993. 13.00 (*0-679-83691-8*) Knopf Bks Yng Read.
Woofenden, Louise. Rainbow Colors in the Word: An Activity Book with Puzzles & Pictures to Color. Hill, Betty, ed. Woofenden, Louise, illus. 32p. (Orig.). 1992. pap. text ed. 2.50 (*0-917426-08-8*) Am New Church Sunday.
World Book Staff, ed. Childcraft Supplement, 5 vols. LC 91-65174. (Illus.). (gr. 2-6). 1991. Set. write for info. (*0-7166-0666-6*) Prehistoric Animals, 304p. About Dogs, 304p. The Magic of Words, 304p. The Indian Book, 304p. The Puzzle Book, 304p. World Bk.
Wray, Kit, as told by. & illus. King Arthur: A Hidden Picture Story. LC 91-76019. 32p. (ps-5). 1992. 7.95 (*1-56397-018-X*) Boyds Mills Pr.

PYGMIES

Jones. Pygmies of Central Africa, Reading Level 5. (Illus.). 48p. (gr. 4-8). 1989. PLB 16.67 (*0-86625-268-1*); 12.50s.p. (*0-685-58813-0*) Rourke Corp.
Siy, Alexandra. The Efe: People of the Ituri Rain Forest. LC 93-6717. (Illus.). 80p. (gr. 5 up). 1993. text ed. 14.95 RSBE (*0-87518-551-7*, Dillon) Macmillan Child Grp.

PYRAMIDS

Abels, Harriette S. The Pyramids. LC 87-15455. (Illus.). 48p. (gr. 5-6). 1987. text ed. 12.95 RSBE (*0-89686-345-X*, Crestwood Hse) Macmillan Child Grp.
Horne, Lee. Pyramid Explorer's Kit. (Illus.). 64p. (gr. 3 up). 1991. 17.95 (*1-56138-031-8*) Running Pr.
Millard, Anne. Pyramids. LC 88-83093. (Illus.). 32p. (gr. 4-6). 1989. PLB 12.40 (*0-531-17154-X*, Gloucester Pr) Watts.
Morley, Jacqueline. An Egyptian Pyramid. Bergin, Mark & James, John, illus. 48p. (gr. 5 up). 1993. pap. 8.95 (*0-87226-255-3*) P Bedrick Bks.
Putnam, James. Pyramid. Brightling, Geoff & Hayman, Peter, photos by. LC 94-8804. (Illus.). 64p. (gr. 5 up). 1994. 16.00 (*0-679-86170-X*); PLB 17.99 (*0-679-96170-4*) Knopf Bks Yng Read.
—Pyramid. (Illus.). (gr. 3-7). 1994. 16.95 (*1-56458-684-7*) Dorling Kindersley.

Q

QUAILS–FICTION

Burgess, Thornton. The Adventures of Bob White. 1992. Repr. lib. bdg. 17.95x (*0-89966-994-8*) Buccaneer Bks.

QUAKERS

see Friends, Society of

QUANTUM THEORY

see also Chemistry; Force and Energy; Relativity (Physics); Thermodynamics

QUARANTINE

see Communicable Diseases

QUEBEC, BATTLE OF, 1759

Ochoa, George. The Fall of Quebec & the French & Indian War. (Illus.). 64p. (gr. 5 up). 1990. PLB 12.95 (*0-382-09954-0*); pap. 7.95 (*0-382-09950-8*) Silver Burdett Pr.

QUEBEC (PROVINCE)

LeVert, Suzanne. Quebec. Berton, Pierre, intro. by. (Illus.). 64p. (gr. 3 up). 1991. PLB 16.95 (*0-7910-1030-9*) Chelsea Hse.
Provencher, Jean. Quebec. (Illus.). 144p. (gr. 4 up). 1992. PLB 20.55 (*0-516-06617-X*) Childrens.

QUEENS

see also Kings and Rulers;
also names of countries with the subdivision Kings and Rulers (e.g. Great Britain–Kings and Rulers;); and names of queens, e.g. Elizabeth 2nd, Queen of Great Britain
Harrill, Ronald. Makeda, Queen of Sheba. LC 93-60916. (Illus.). 50p. (gr. 2-8). 1994. pap. 7.95 (*1-55523-651-0*) Winston-Derek.

QUERIES

see Questions and Answers

QUESTIONS AND ANSWERS

Adler, David. All about the Moon. Burns, Raymond, illus. LC 82-17422. 32p. (gr. 3-6). 1983. PLB 10.59 (*0-89375-886-8*); pap. text ed. 2.95 (*0-89375-887-6*) Troll Assocs.
—Amazing Magnets. Lawler, Dan, illus. LC 82-17377. 32p. (gr. 3-6). 1983. PLB 10.59 (*0-89375-894-9*); pap. text ed. 2.95 (*0-89375-895-7*) Troll Assocs.
Alden, Laura. When. Axeman, Lois, illus. LC 83-7305. 32p. (gr. k-2). 1983. pap. 3.95 (*0-516-46592-9*) Childrens.
Amazing Book of Quizzes. 32p. 1990. 3.50 (*0-517-69193-0*) Random Hse Value.
Ardley, Bridget & Ardley, Neil. The Random House Book of 1001 Questions & Answers. LC 88-23200. (Illus.). 176p. (Orig.). (gr. 3-7). 1989. PLB 12.99 (*0-394-99992-4*); 14.00 (*0-394-89992-X*) Random Bks Yng Read.
Asher, Sandy. Where Do You Get Your Ideas? 96p. (Orig.). (gr. 4-7). 1994. pap. 6.95 (*0-8027-7421-0*) Walker & Co.
Buehner, Caralyn & Buehner, Mark. The Courtesy Quiz Book. LC 93-36293. (gr. 5 up). 1994. write for info. (*0-8037-1494-7*); PLB write for info. (*0-8037-1495-5*) Dial Bks Young.
Campbell, John P. Campbell's Middle School Quiz Book No. 1. 326p. (Orig.). (gr. 5-8). 1985. pap. 14.95x (*0-9609412-4-X*) Patricks Pr.
—Campbell's Potpourri III of Quiz Bowl Questions. 288p. (Orig.). (gr. 7-12). 1985. pap. 14.95x (*0-9609412-5-8*) Patricks Pr.
Clark, Roberta. Why? Axeman, Lois, illus. LC 83-7306. 32p. (gr. k-2). 1983. pap. 3.95 (*0-516-46594-5*) Childrens.
Coffen, Ron. K-Zoo News. 128p. 1992. pap. 8.95 (*0-8163-1086-6*) Pacific Pr Pub Assn.
Computer Age. 1992. 18.95 (*0-8094-9670-4*) Time-Life.
Crawford, Jean, ed. Amazing Facts. LC 93-11599. (Illus.). 88p. (gr. k-3). 1994. write for info. (*0-8094-9458-2*); PLB write for info. (*0-8094-9459-0*) Time-Life.
Crystal Clarity Staff. Life's Little Secrets. (gr. 4-7). 1993. 5.95 (*1-56589-601-7*) Crystal Clarity.
Curtis, Neil. How Do We Know the Earth Is Round? LC 94-16253. 1995. write for info. (*0-8114-3879-1*) Raintree Steck-V.
Day, Trevor. The Random House Book of One Thousand One Questions & Answers about the Human Body. LC 93-6386. 160p. (gr. 4-7). 1994. pap. 13.00 (*0-679-85432-0*) Random Bks Yng Read.
Dennard, Deborah. Do Cats Have Nine Lives? The Strange Things People Say about Animals Around the House. Urbanovic, Jackie, illus. LC 92-10353. 1992. 19.95 (*0-87614-773-2*) Carolrhoda Bks.
—How Wise Is an Owl? The Strange Things People Say about Animals in the Woods. Neavill, Michelle, illus. LC 92-10354. 1992. 19.95 (*0-87614-721-X*) Carolrhoda Bks.
Dickinson, Jane. All about Trees. D'Adamo, Anthony, illus. LC 82-17382. 32p. (gr. 3-6). 1983. PLB 10.59 (*0-89375-892-2*); pap. text ed. 2.95 (*0-89375-893-0*) Troll Assocs.
The Dorling Kindersley Q & A Quiz Book. 72p. (gr. 7 up). 1994. 16.95 (*1-56458-678-2*) Dorling Kindersley.

Dr. Seuss. The Cat's Quizzer. LC 92-17409. (Illus.). (gr. k-3). 1993. 6.95 (*0-394-83296-5*) Random Bks Yng Read.
Duffy, Robert. Children's Quiz Book. 132p. 1988. pap. 5.95 (*1-85371-020-2*, Pub. by Poolbeg Pr UK) Dufour.
Eichel, C. & Sanders, E. Question Collection. (gr. 5-12). 1988. 7.95 (*0-88160-153-5*, LW 271) Learning Wks.
Evolution of Life. LC 92-8227. 1992. write for info. (*0-8094-9695-X*); pap. write for info. (*0-8094-9696-8*) Time-Life.
Farndon, John. Eyewitness Question & Answer Book. LC 93-3523. (Illus.). 32p. (gr. 3-6). 1993. 16.95 (*1-56458-347-3*) Dorling Kindersley.
Feder, Chris W. Brain Quest for Threes: Ages Three-Four. (ps-3). 1994. 10.95 (*1-56305-633-X*) Workman Pub.
—My First Brain Quest: Ages Two-Three. (ps). 1994. 10.95 (*1-56305-634-8*) Workman Pub.
Firth, Lesley, ed. When Did It Happen. (Illus.). 128p. (gr. 3-7). 1990. (S&S BFYR); pap. 7.95 (*0-671-72497-5*, S&S BFYR) S&S Trade.
Ford, Michael. One Hundred Questions & Answers about AIDS: What You Need to Know Now. 208p. (gr. 7 up). 1993. pap. 4.95 (*0-688-12697-9*, Pub. by Beech Tree Bks) Morrow.
Ganeri, Anita. Animal Babies. Taylor, Kate, illus. 32p. (ps-1). 1991. 6.95 (*0-8120-6241-8*) Barron.
—Animal Behavior. Taylor, Kate, illus. 32p. (ps-1). 1992. 6.95 (*0-8120-6301-5*) Barron.
—Animal Families. Taylor, Kate, illus. 32p. (ps-1). 1992. 6.95 (*0-8120-6274-4*) Barron.
—Animal Food. Taylor, Kate, illus. 32p. (ps-1). 1992. 6.95 (*0-8120-6302-3*) Barron.
—Animal Movements. Taylor, Kate, illus. 32p. (ps-1). 1991. 6.95 (*0-8120-6238-8*) Barron.
—Animal Science. LC 92-25342. (Illus.). 48p. (gr. 5 up). 1993. text ed. 13.95 RSBE (*0-87518-575-4*, Dillon) Macmillan Child Grp.
—Animal Talk. Taylor, Kate, illus. 32p. (ps-1). 1991. 6.95 (*0-8120-6239-6*) Barron.
—Biggest & Smallest: Questions & Answers about Record Breakers. West, David, illus. LC 92-12497. (ps-3). 1992. 6.95 (*0-8120-6291-4*) Barron.
—Body Science. LC 92-22722. (Illus.). 48p. (gr. 5 up). 1993. text ed. 13.95 RSBE (*0-87518-576-2*, Dillon) Macmillan Child Grp.
—Earth Science. LC 93-16753. (Illus.). 48p. (gr. 5 up). 1993. text ed. 13.95 RSBE (*0-87518-577-0*, Dillon) Macmillan Child Grp.
—Fastest & Slowest: Questions & Answers about Record Breakers. West, David, illus. LC 92-10077. (ps-3). 1992. 6.95 (*0-8120-6290-6*) Barron.
—First & Last: Questions & Answers about Record Breakers. (ps-3). 1992. 6.95 (*0-8120-6292-2*) Barron.
—I Wonder Why the Wind Blows & Other Questions about Our Planet. LC 93-48559. 32p. (gr. k-3). 1994. 8.95 (*1-85697-996-2*, Kingfisher LKC) LKC.
—Longest & Tallest: Questions & Answers about Record Breakers. LC 92-12502. (ps-3). 1992. 6.95 (*0-8120-6293-0*) Barron.
Graham, Ian. Cars, Planes, Ships, & Trains. LC 94-16303. 1994. write for info. (*0-8160-3220-3*) Facts on File.
—How Things Work. LC 94-20013. 1994. write for info. (*0-8160-3218-1*) Facts on File.
Greeley, Valerie. Where's My Share? Greeley, Valerie, illus. LC 89-13299. 32p. (ps-1). 1990. SBE 12.95 (*0-02-736761-4*, Macmillan Child Bk) Macmillan Child Grp.
Greene, Constance C. Ask Anybody. 160p. (gr. k-6). 1984. pap. 2.75 (*0-440-40330-8*, YB) Dell.
Greenway, Shirley. Whose Baby Am I? LC 92-6133. 32p. (ps-2). 1992. 11.00 (*0-8249-8577-X*, Ideals Child); pap. 3.95 (*0-8249-8562-1*) Hambleton-Hill.
Groseclose, Kel. Why Did God Make Bugs & Other Icky Things? Questions Kids Ask. 128p. 1993. Braille. 10.24 (*1-56956-390-X*) W A T Braille.
—Why Did God Make Zits & Other Disgusting Stuff? Questions Preteens Ask. 135p. 1993. Braille. 10.80 (*1-56956-391-8*) W A T Braille.
Guess What. (Illus.). (ps-5). 3.50 (*0-7214-8005-5*); Ser. S50. wkbk. C 1.95 (*0-317-04024-3*) Ladybird Bks.
Harris, Linda K. Kids' Talk. Auth, Tony, illus. LC 93-16169. 96p. 1993. pap. 6.95 (*0-8362-8019-9*) Andrews & McMeel.
Hausherr, Rosmarie. What Food is This? LC 93-17328. (Illus.). 40p. (ps-3). 1994. 14.95 (*0-590-46583-X*) Scholastic Inc.
Hayes. Brain Twisters. (Illus.). 32p. (gr. 2-6). 1988. pap. 2.95 (*0-88625-149-4*) Durkin Hayes Pub.
—Number Mysteries. (Illus.). 32p. (gr. 2-6). 1988. pap. 2.95 (*0-88625-145-1*) Durkin Hayes Pub.
—Word Teasers. (Illus.). 32p. (gr. 2-6). 1988. pap. 2.95 (*0-88625-148-6*) Durkin Hayes Pub.
Hollingsworth, Mary. My Very First Book of Bible Questions. Incrocci, Rick, illus. LC 94-10220. 1994. 4.99 (*0-7852-8023-5*) Nelson.
Human Body. 1992. 18.95 (*0-8094-9654-2*) Time-Life.
Incredible Little Monsters. (Illus.). 32p. (Orig.). (gr. 2-5). 1994. pap. 4.95 (*1-56458-553-0*) Dorling Kindersley.
Incredible Mini-Beasts. (Illus.). 32p. (Orig.). (gr. 2-5). 1994. pap. 4.95 (*1-56458-554-9*) Dorling Kindersley.
Insect World. LC 92-30847. 176p. 1993. 18.60 (*0-8094-9687-9*); lib. bdg. 24.60 (*0-8094-9688-7*) Time-Life.
Jefferies, Lawrence. Air, Air, Air. Johnson, Lewis, illus. LC 82-15808. 32p. (gr. 3-6). 1983. PLB 10.59 (*0-89375-880-9*); pap. text ed. 2.95 (*0-89375-881-7*) Troll Assocs.
—All about Stars. Veno, Joseph, illus. LC 82-20027. 32p. (gr. 3-6). 1983. PLB 10.59 (*0-89375-888-4*); pap. text ed. 2.95 (*0-89375-889-2*) Troll Assocs.
—Amazing World of Animals. D'Adamo, Anthony, illus. LC 82-20061. 32p. (gr. 3-6). 1983. PLB 10.59 (*0-89375-898-1*); pap. text ed. 2.95 (*0-89375-899-X*) Troll Assocs.
Jones, Teri C. Little Book of Questions & Answers: Animals. Marsh, T. F., illus. 32p. (gr. k-3). 1992. PLB 10.95 (*1-56674-012-6*, HTS Bks) Forest Hse.
—Little Book of Questions & Answers: My Home. Marsh, T. F., illus. 32p. (gr. k-3). 1992. PLB 10.95 (*1-56674-013-4*, HTS Bks) Forest Hse.
—Little Book of Questions & Answers: Nature. Marsh, T. F., illus. 32p. (gr. k-3). 1992. PLB 10.95 (*1-56674-014-2*, HTS Bks) Forest Hse.
—Little Book of Questions & Answers: Things That Go. Marsh, T. F., illus. 32p. (gr. k-3). 1992. PLB 10.95 (*1-56674-015-0*, HTS Bks) Forest Hse.
The Julian Messner Color Illustrated Question & Answer Book: What Is It? (Illus.). 128p. (gr. 4 up). 1984. lib. bdg. 11.79 (*0-671-53130-1*, J Messner) S&S Trade.
The Julian Messner Color Illustrated Question & Answer Book: What Is It? 1984. pap. 8.95 (*0-685-09674-2*) S&S Trade.
Jumbo Amazing Question & Answer Book. (Illus.). 278p. 1991. pap. 2.99 (*0-517-02234-6*) Random Hse Value.
Kallen, Stuart A. Funny Answers to Foolish Questions. LC 92-14771. 1992. 12.94 (*1-56239-131-3*) Abdo & Dghtrs.
Kinney, Karin, ed. Geography. LC 93-28237. (Illus.). 88p. (gr. k-3). 1994. write for info. (*0-8094-9462-0*); PLB write for info. (*0-8094-9463-9*) Time-Life.
Knight, David C. All about Sound. Johnson, Lewis, illus. LC 82-17387. 32p. (gr. 3-6). 1983. PLB 10.59 (*0-89375-878-7*); pap. text ed. 2.95 (*0-89375-879-5*) Troll Assocs.
Kolatch, A. J. The Jewish Child's First Book of Why. LC 91-25352. 32p. 1992. 14.95 (*0-8246-0354-0*) Jonathan David.
Lafferty, Peter. The World of Science. LC 94-20019. 1994. write for info. (*0-8160-3219-X*) Facts on File.
Lahey, Richard. Quiz Bowl I. Sellers, Marci, illus. 56p. (Orig.). (gr. 4-12). 1982. tchr's. manual 7.50 (*0-88047-012-7*, 8216) DOK Pubs.
—Quiz Bowl II. Sellers, Marci, illus. 56p. (Orig.). (gr. 4-12). 1984. 7.50 (*0-88047-037-2*, 8408) DOK Pubs.
Levy, Nathan. Nathan Levy's One Hundred Intriguing Questions, Bk. 1. (gr. 3 up). 1993. write for info. (*1-878347-35-7*) NL Assocs.
—Nathan Levy's One Hundred Intriguing Questions, Bk. 2. (gr. 3 up). 1993. write for info. (*1-878347-36-5*) NL Assocs.
—Nathan Levy's One Hundred Intriguing Questions, Bk. 3. (gr. 3 up). 1993. write for info. (*1-878347-37-3*) NL Assocs.
Lindbergh, Reeve. What Is the Sun? Lambert, Stephen, illus. LC 93-3557. 32p. (ps up). 1994. 14.95 (*1-56402-146-7*) Candlewick Pr.

McKaughan, Larry. Why Are Your Fingers Cold? Keenan, Joy D., illus. LC 92-16549. 32p. (Orig.). (ps-1). 1992. 14.95 (*0-8361-3604-7*) Herald Pr. Childlike questions & reassuring answers are complemented by exquisite illustrations. Several family groupings including African American & Caucasian people appear, as children & adults interact. This delightful picture book helps children to become more sensitive to the needs of others. It fosters a strong sense of extended family & community. For children ages 2 to 6 & the adults that love them. *Publisher Provided Annotation.*

Marsh, Carole. Autumn: Silly Trivia. Marsh, Carole, illus. (Orig.). (gr. 2-6). 1994. 24.95 (*1-55609-274-1*); pap. 14.95 (*0-685-14606-5*) Gallopade Pub Group.
—The Crazy Comet Silly Trivia Book. (Illus.). 60p. (Orig.). (gr. 2-12). 1994. pap. 14.95 (*0-935326-64-2*) Gallopade Pub Group.
—Dinosaur Trivia for Kids: I'm Saury! (Illus., Orig.). (gr. 2 up). 1994. PLB 24.95 (*1-55609-162-1*); pap. 14.95 (*0-935326-54-5*) Gallopade Pub Group.
—Quiz Bowl Crash Course. (gr. 5 up). 1994. 24.95 (*1-55609-288-1*); pap. 14.95 (*1-55609-195-8*); computer disk 29.95 (*1-55609-289-X*) Gallopade Pub Group.
—The Secret of Somerset Place S. P. A. R. K. Kit. (Illus., Orig.). (gr. 3-9). 1994. pap. 24.95 (*0-935326-20-0*) Gallopade Pub Group.
—Tyrannosaurus & Other Wrecks: Fossil Trivia for Kids. (Illus., Orig.). (gr. 2 up). 1994. 24.95 (*1-55609-166-4*); pap. 14.95 (*0-935326-56-1*) Gallopade Pub Group.
Maynard, Chris. I Wonder Why Planes Have Wings & Other Questions about Transport. Quigley, Sebastian, illus. LC 92-42373. 32p. (gr. k-3). 1993. 8.95 (*1-85697-877-X*, Kingfisher LKC) LKC.
Maynard, Christopher. Amazing Animal Facts. (Illus.). (gr. 1-5). 1993. 18.00 (*0-679-85085-6*) Knopf Bks Yng Read.
Miller, Margaret. Can You Guess? LC 92-29406. (Illus.). 40p. (ps up). 1993. 14.00 (*0-688-11180-7*); PLB 13.93 (*0-688-11181-5*) Greenwillow.
Milne, A. A. Winnie-The-Pooh's Trivia Quiz Book. Shepard, Ernest H., illus. LC 93-39969. 48p. 1994. 8.99 (*0-525-45265-6*, DCB) Dutton Child Bks.
Minn, Loretta B. Trek for Trivia. Jurgens, Steve, illus. 48p. (gr. 3-8). 1985. wkbk. 6.95 (*0-86653-291-9*, GA 646) Good Apple.
More Big Book of Questions & Answers. 192p. 1990. 14.98 (*1-56173-412-8*) Pubns Intl Ltd.
More Yes & Know. (gr. 3 up). 1991. pap. 2.47 (*1-56297-009-7*, YK-08) Lee Pubns KY.
More Yes & Know. (gr. 3 up). 1991. pap. 2.47 (*1-56297-010-0*, YK-09) Lee Pubns KY.
Morris, Neil. Do Animals Take Baths? Questions Kids Ask about Animals. Goffe, Toni, illus. LC 94-14119. 1994. write for info. (*0-89577-610-3*, Readers Digest Kids) RD Assn.
—What Is My Shadow Made Of? Questions Kids Ask about Everyday Science. Brown, Mik, illus. LC 94-14120. 1994. write for info. (*0-89577-609-X*, Readers Digest Kids) RD Assn.
—Where Do Ants Live? Questions Kids Ask about Backyard Nature. Lewis, Jan, illus. LC 94-14122. 1994. write for info. (*0-89577-607-3*, Readers Digest Kids) RD Assn.
—Where Does My Spaghetti go When I Eat It? Questions Kids Ask about the Human Body. Brown, Mik, illus. LC 94-14121. 1994. write for info. (*0-89577-608-1*, Readers Digest Kids) RD Assn.
My First Book of Questions. (Illus.). 1992. pap. 14.95 (*0-590-44942-7*, 032, Cartwheel) Scholastic Inc.
Myers, Jack. Do Cats Really Have Nine Lives? And Other Questions about Your World. LC 91-77713. (gr. 4-7). 1993. 12.95 (*1-56397-089-9*) Boyds Mills Pr.
—Do Cats Really Have Nine Lives? And Other Questions about Your World. LC 91-77713. (Illus.). 64p. (gr. 1-7). 1994. pap. 7.95 (*1-56397-215-8*) Boyds Mills Pr.
—What Makes Popcorn Pop? And Other Questions about the World Around Us. Gardner, Charles, et al, illus. LC 90-85912. 64p. (gr. 1-5). 1991. 12.95 (*1-878093-33-9*) Boyds Mills Pr.
Myst M31. (gr. 4 up). 1991. pap. 2.47 (*1-56297-015-1*, M-33) Lee Pubns KY.
Myst M32. (gr. 4 up). 1991. pap. 2.47 (*1-56297-016-X*, M-33) Lee Pubns KY.
Neary, Kevin & Smith, Dave. The Ultimate Disney Trivia Book Two. LC 94-2207. (Illus.). 176p. (gr. 2 up). 1994. pap. 9.95 (*0-7868-8024-4*) Hyprn Child.
O'Leary, Sean C. Whizz Quiz: Quiz & Puzzle Book. (Illus.). 92p. (gr. 2-6). 1993. pap. 7.95 (*0-86278-287-2*, Pub. by OBrien Pr IE) Dufour.
Outlet Staff. That's My Hat: Dial the Answer. 1992. 3.99 (*0-517-06617-3*) Random Hse Value.
OWL Magazine Editors. The Kids' Question & Answer Book. (Illus.). 80p. (gr. 3-7). 1988. 11.95 (*0-448-19221-7*, G&D) Putnam Pub Group.
OWL Magazine Editors Staff. The Kids' Question & Answer Book Two. (Illus.). 80p. (gr. 3-7). 1988. 11.95 (*0-448-09276-X*, G&D) Putnam Pub Group.
Pansini, Anna, ed. Great Answer Book. Kinnealy, Janice, illus. LC 90-44452. 48p. (gr. 3-6). 1991. PLB 10.89 (*0-8167-2308-7*); pap. text ed. 2.95 (*0-8167-2309-5*) Troll Assocs.
—I Wonder Why. Barto, Renzo, illus. LC 90-44455. 48p. (gr. k-2). 1991. PLB 10.89 (*0-8167-2304-4*); pap. text ed. 2.95 (*0-8167-2305-2*) Troll Assocs.
—Kids' Question & Answer Book. Barto, Renzo, illus. LC 90-43969. 48p. (gr. 2-4). 1991. PLB 10.89 (*0-8167-2306-0*); pap. text ed. 2.95 (*0-8167-2307-9*) Troll Assocs.
Parker, Steve. Our Planet Earth. LC 94-16302. 1994. write for info. (*0-8160-3216-5*) Facts on File.
Phillips, Louis. How Do You Get a Horse Out of the Bathtub? Profound Answers to Preposterous Questions. Stevenson, James P., illus. 80p. (gr. 1 up). 1983. pap. 10.95 (*0-670-38119-5*) Viking Child Bks.
Plant Life. LC 92-34975. 1993. write for info. (*0-8094-9712-3*); PLB write for info. (*0-8094-9713-1*) Time-Life.
Quinsey, Mary Beth. Why Does That Man Have Such a Big Nose? Chan, Wilson, illus. LC 85-63760. 32p. (Orig.). (ps-1). 1986. lib. bdg. 16.95 (*0-943990-25-4*); pap. 5.95 (*0-943990-24-6*) Parenting Pr.
Reece, Colleen L. What? Axeman, Lois, illus. LC 83-7308. 32p. (gr. k-2). 1983. pap. 3.95 (*0-516-46591-0*) Childrens.
Rolde, Neil. So You Think You Know Maine. LC 84-47758. (Illus.). 216p. (Orig.). (gr. 6-12). 1984. pap. 13.95 (*0-88448-025-9*) Tilbury Hse.
Rosen, Sidney. Can You Find a Planet? 40p. (gr. k-2). 1991. lib. bdg. 19.95 (*0-87614-683-3*) Carolrhoda Bks.
Rowland-Entwistle, Theodore & Cooke, Jean. Factfinder. LC 92-53118. (Illus.). 280p. (Orig.). (gr. 4-8). 1992. pap. 12.95 (*1-85697-835-4*, Kingfisher LKC); 16.95 (*1-85697-803-6*) LKC.
Royston, Angela. You & Your Body. LC 94-16304. 1994. write for info. (*0-8160-3217-3*) Facts on File.
Sanders, Bill. Life, Sex & Everything in Between: Straight on Answers to the Questions That Trouble You Most. LC 90-49951. 160p. (Orig.). 1991. pap. 7.99 (*0-8007-5385-2*) Revell.

Scarry, Richard. Richard Scarry's Things to Know. (ps-3). 1994. pap. 1.95 (*0-307-11616-6*, Golden Pr) Western Pub.
Schwartz, L. Junior Question Collection. (gr. 1-6). 1988. 7.95 (*0-88160-169-1*, LW 279) Learning Wks.
—Trivia Trackdown - Animals & Science. (gr. 4-6). 1985. 3.95 (*0-88160-119-5*, LW 252) Learning Wks.
—Trivia Trackdown - Social Studies & Famous People. (gr. 4-6). 1985. 3.95 (*0-88160-120-9*, LW 253) Learning Wks.
Simon, Seymour. The Dinosaur Is the Biggest Animal That Ever Lived & Other Wrong Ideas You Thought Were True. Maestro, Giulio, illus. LC 83-48960. 64p. (gr. 2-5). 1984. (Lipp Jr Bks); PLB 13.89 (*0-397-32076-0*, Lipp Jr Bks) HarpC Child Bks.
—The Dinosaur Is the Biggest Animal That Ever Lived, & Other Wrong Ideas You Thought Were True. Maestro, Giulio, illus. LC 83-48960. 64p. (gr. 2-5). 1986. pap. 5.95 (*0-06-446053-3*, Trophy) HarpC Child Bks.
—New Questions & Answers about Dinosaurs. Dewey, Jennifer, illus. LC 92-25546. 48p. (gr. 2 up). 1993. pap. 4.95 (*0-688-12271-X*, Mulberry) Morrow.
Souter, John C. Trivia. 96p. (gr. 8-12). 1984. 4.95 (*0-8423-7338-1*) Tyndale.
Stanish, Bob. Mindglow. Stanish, Jon, illus. 96p. (gr. 3-12). 1986. wkbk. 10.95 (*0-86653-346-X*, GA 693) Good Apple.
Stidworthy, John. The World of Dinosaurs. LC 94-16305. 1994. write for info. (*0-8160-3215-7*) Facts on File.
Stock, Gregory. Kids' Book of Questions. LC 88-40230. (gr. 4-7). 1988. pap. 4.95 (*0-89480-631-9*, 1631) Workman Pub.
Stoops, Erik D. & Stone, Debbie L. Alligators & Crocodiles. LC 94-15691. (Illus.). 80p. 1994. 14.95 (*0-8069-0422-4*) Sterling.
Super Treasures of Amazing Knowledge. (Illus.). 278p. 1991. pap. 2.99 (*0-685-50837-4*) Random Hse Value.
Taylor, Barbara. I Wonder Why Soap Makes Bubbles & Other Questions about Science. LC 94-2313. 32p. (gr. k-3). 1994. 8.95 (*1-85697-995-4*, Kingfisher LKC) LKC.
Time Life Book Editors. What Is a Bellybutton? First Questions & Answers about the Human Body. Kagan, Neil, ed. (Illus.). 48p. (ps). 1993. write for info. (*0-7835-0854-9*); lib. bdg. write for info. (*0-7835-0855-7*) Time-Life.
Time-Life Books Staff, ed. Animal Behavior. 144p. 1992. write for info. (*0-8094-9658-5*); lib. bdg. write for info. (*0-8094-9659-3*) Time-Life.
—Space & Planets. 144p. 1991. write for info. (*0-8094-9650-X*); lib. bdg. write for info. (*0-8094-9651-8*) Time-Life.
Time Life Editors. Who Named My Street Magnolia? First Questions & Answers about Neighborhoods. Mark, Sara, ed. (Illus.). 48p. (ps-k). 1995. PLB write for info. (*0-7835-0898-0*) Time-Life.
Time Life Inc. Editors. Do Bears Give Bear Hugs? First Questions & Answers about Animals. Fallow, Allan, ed. (Illus.). 48p. (gr. 2-5). 1994. write for info. (*0-7835-0870-0*); PLB write for info. (*0-7835-0871-9*) Time-Life.
Time-Life Inc. Editors. Do Fish Drink? First Questions & Answers about Water. Kagan, Neil, ed. LC 92-40301. (Illus.). 48p. (ps). 1993. write for info. (*0-7835-0850-6*); PLB write for info. (*0-7835-0851-4*) Time-Life.
—Do Mommies Have Mommies? First Questions & Answers about Families. Fallow, Allan, ed. (Illus.). 48p. (ps-k). 1994. write for info. (*0-7835-0874-3*); PLB write for info. (*0-7835-0875-1*) Time-Life.
—How Big Is the Ocean? First Questions & Answers about the Beach. Fallow, Allan, ed. (Illus.). 48p. (ps-k). 1994. write for info. (*0-7835-0897-2*) Time-Life.
Time Life Inc. Editors. Where Does the Sun Sleep? First Questions & Answers about Bedtime. Kagan, Neil, ed. (Illus.). 48p. (ps). 1993. write for info. (*0-7835-0866-2*); lib. bdg. write for info. (*0-7835-0867-0*) Time-Life.
—Why Is the Grass Green? First Questions & Answers about Nature. Kagan, Neil, ed. (Illus.). 48p. (ps). 1993. write for info. (*0-7835-0858-1*); lib. bdg. write for info. (*0-7835-0859-X*) Time-Life.
Transportation. LC 92-24929. 176p. 1993. 18.60 (*0-8094-9700-X*); lib. bdg. 24.60 (*0-8094-9701-8*) Time-Life.
Tunney, Christopher. Aircraft Carriers. LC 79-64384. (Illus.). 36p. (gr. 3-6). 1980. PLB 13.50 (*0-8225-1176-2*) Lerner Pubns.
Walton, Rick. How Many, How Many, How Many. Jabar, Cynthia, illus. LC 92-54408. 32p. (ps up). 1993. 14.95 (*1-56402-062-2*) Candlewick Pr.
Ward, Elizabeth, ed. What Makes Popcorn Pop? First Questions & Answers about Food. (Illus.). 48p. (ps). 1994. write for info. (*0-7835-0862-X*); PLB write for info. (*0-7835-0863-8*) Time-Life.
West, David. Why Is the Sky Blue? And Answers to Questions You Always Wanted to Ask. (Illus.). 64p. 1992. 14.95 (*0-8120-6284-1*); pap. 8.95 (*0-8120-4884-9*) Barron.
What Is It? (gr. 1 up). 1984. pap. 11.95 (*0-671-53129-8*, Little Simon) S&S Trade.
What Would Happen If. 32p. (gr. 3-7). 1994. 4.95 (*0-685-71578-7*, 514) W Gladden Found.
Wilkins, Mary-Jane. Everyday Things & How They Work. Bull, Peter, illus. LC 90-12999. 40p. (gr. 4-6). 1991. PLB 12.40 (*0-531-19109-5*, Warwick) Watts.
Willis, William M. The Children's Question Book: A Parent Teacher Guide. LC 81-83727. 115p. (Orig.). (gr. 1 up). 1981. pap. text ed. 7.95 (*0-9607028-1-4*) Ocean East.
Winfield, Dave. Ask Dave: Dave Winfield Answers Kids' Questions about Baseball & Life. LC 94-225. 1994. pap. 6.95 (*0-8362-8057-1*) Andrews & McMeel.
Woolger, David, ed. Who Do You Think You Are? (Illus.). 128p. (gr. 6 up). 1990. jacketed 16.95 (*0-19-276074-2*) OUP.
Yes & Know. (gr. 3 up). 1991. pap. 2.47 (*1-56297-001-1*, YK-08) Lee Pubns KY.
Yes & Know. (gr. 4 up). 1991. pap. 2.47 (*1-56297-002-X*, YK-09) Lee Pubns KY.
Yes & Know. (gr. 3 up). 1991. pap. 2.47 (*1-56297-003-8*, YK-14) Lee Pubns KY.
Yes & Know Books. (gr. 3 up). 1991. pap. 1.47 (*1-56297-000-3*, YK-15) Lee Pubns KY.
Yes & Know Line Up. 1991. pap. 2.47 (*1-56297-074-7*, L-18) Lee Pubns KY.
Yes & Know More Line Up. 1991. pap. 2.47 (*1-56297-075-5*, L-18) Lee Pubns KY.

QUILTS
see Coverlets

QUIZ BOOKS
see Questions and Answers

QUOTATIONS
see also Proverbs

Alvarez Del Real, Maria E., ed. Frases Celebres De Todos los Tiempos. (SPA., Illus.). 336p. (Orig.). 1988. pap. 4.00x (*0-944499-40-6*) Editorial Amer.
Riley, Dorothy W. My Soul Looks Back, 'Less I Forget. 332p. 1991. write for info. (*1-880234-06-8*); pap. write for info. (*1-880234-00-9*) Winbush Pub.
—My Soul Looks Back, 'Less I Forget, Vol. 2. 332p. 1992. pap. write for info. (*1-880234-01-7*) Winbush Pub.
Watts, Gayle. Quotes for Kids & Teens: Motivational & Inspirational. 192p. 1992. pap. text ed. 13.95 (*0-945772-03-3*) Clarkston Pub.

R

RABBIS

Goldman, Alex J. The Greatest Rabbis Hall of Fame. (gr. 7 up). 1987. 14.95 (*0-933503-11-3*); pap. 7.95 (*0-933503-14-8*) Shapolsky Pubs.
Karlenstein, Tzira. Reb Aryeh: A Portrait of the Jerusalem Tzaddik Reb Aryeh Levin. (Illus.). (gr. 4-7). 1989. 11.95 (*0-87306-490-9*) Feldheim.
Piontac, Nechemiah. The Arizal: The Life & Times of Rabbi Yitzchak Luria. Weinbach, Shaindel, tr. from HEB. Bardugo, Miriam, illus. 288p. (gr. 5-12). 1988. 12.95 (*0-89906-835-9*); pap. 9.95 (*0-89906-836-7*) Mesorah Pubns.
Rabbi Mindy Avra Portnoy. Ima on the Bima: My Mommy Is a Rabbi. Rubin, Steffi, illus. LC 86-3023. 32p. (ps-4). 1986. 10.95 (*0-930494-55-5*); pap. 4.95 (*0-930494-54-7*) Kar Ben.

RABBIS–VOCATIONAL GUIDANCE

Brenner, Barbara A. Group Soup. Munsinger, Lynn, illus. 32p. (ps-3). 1992. PLB 12.50 (*0-670-82867-X*) Viking Child Bks.
Gottschalk, Alfred. To Learn & to Teach Your Life as a Rabbi. (Illus.). (gr. 7-12). 1988. lib. bdg. 12.95 (*0-8239-0700-7*) Rosen Group.
Hooks, William H. Rough Tough Rowdy. Munsinger, Lynn, illus. 32p. (ps-3). 1992. PLB 12.50 (*0-670-82868-8*) Viking Child Bks.

RABBITS

Bantam Staff. Rabbit: Baby Animal. (ps). 1994. 4.99 (*0-553-09547-1*) Bantam.
Barkhausen, Annette & Geiser, Franz. Rabbits & Hares. Daniel, Jamie, tr. from GER. LC 93-15932. 1994. 17.27 (*0-8368-1004-X*) Gareth Stevens Inc.
Barrett, Norman S. Rabbits. LC 89-21527. (Illus.). 32p. (gr. k-4). 1990. PLB 11.90 (*0-531-14033-4*) Watts.
Brown, Margaret W. The Runaway Bunny. Hurd, Clement, illus. LC 71-183168. 40p. (ps-2). 1942. 13.00 (*0-06-020765-5*); PLB 12.89 (*0-06-020766-3*) HarpC Child Bks.
Bryant, Donna. My Rabbit Roberta. Wood, Jakki, illus. 20p. (ps-3). 1991. 8.95 (*0-8120-6210-8*) Barron.
Coldrey, Jennifer. The Rabbit in the Fields. LC 85-30298. (Illus.). 32p. (gr. 4-6). 1987. 17.27 (*1-55532-061-9*) Gareth Stevens Inc.
—The World of Rabbits. LC 85-28988. (Illus.). 32p. (gr. 2-3). 1986. 17.27 (*1-55532-064-3*) Gareth Stevens Inc.
Drenchko, John D. A True Story about Button. 1989. 6.95 (*0-533-07972-1*) Vantage.
Dunn, Judy. The Little Rabbit. Dunn, Phoebe, illus. LC 79-5241. 32p. (ps). 1980. lib. bdg. 5.99 (*0-394-94377-5*); pap. 2.25 (*0-394-84377-0*) Random Bks Yng Read.
Dunn, Opal. Rabbit Match & Patch Book. (ps). 1992. 4.99 (*0-440-40607-2*) Dell.
Evans, Mark. Rabbit. LC 92-52829. (Illus.). 48p. (gr. 2 up). 1992. 9.95 (*1-56458-128-4*) Dorling Kindersley.
Hall, K. Bunny, Bunny. (Illus.). 28p. (ps-2). 1990. 10.50 (*0-516-05352-3*); pap. 3.95 (*0-516-45352-1*) Childrens.
Hearne, T. Rabbits. (Illus.). 32p. (gr. 2-5). 1989. lib. bdg. 15.94 (*0-86625-187-1*); 11.95s.p. (*0-685-58609-X*) Rourke Corp.
Hoban, Tana. Where Is It? LC 73-8573. (Illus.). 32p. (ps-1). 1974. RSBE 13.95 (*0-02-744070-2*, Macmillan Child Bk) Macmillan Child Grp.
Knutson, Barbara, retold by. & illus. Sungura & Leopard: A Swahili TricksterTale. LC 92-31905. 1993. 15.95 (*0-316-50010-0*) Little.
Lepthien, Emilie U. Rabbits & Hares. LC 93-33514. (Illus.). 48p. (gr. k-4). 1994. PLB 12.85 (*0-516-01058-1*) Childrens.
McCue, Lisa, illus. Bunnies Love. LC 90-61307. 24p. (ps-1). 1991. 4.95 (*0-679-80385-8*) Random Bks Yng Read.
Mayo, Gretchen W., retold by. & illus. Here Comes Tricky Rabbit. LC 93-29763. 48p. (gr. 2-3). 1994. 12.95 (*0-8027-8273-6*); PLB 13.85 (*0-8027-8274-4*) Walker & Co.
Moncure, Jane B. Rabbits' Habits. Peltier, Pam, illus. LC 87-12841. 32p. (ps-2). 1987. PLB 14.95 (*0-89565-406-7*) Childs World.
Peet, Bill. Huge Harold. (Illus.). 48p. (gr. k-3). 1974. 13.45 (*0-395-18449-5*) HM.
Petty, Kate. Rabbits. (Illus.). 24p. (ps-3). 1993. pap. 3.95 (*0-8120-1473-1*) Barron.
Piers, Helen. Taking Care of Your Rabbit. 32p. 1992. pap. 4.95 (*0-8120-4697-8*) Barron.
Potter, Beatrix. The Tale of Peter Rabbit. Potter, Beatrix, illus. 24p. (ps-2). 1991. incl. cassette 5.98 (*1-55886-055-X*) Smarty Pants.
Pouyanne. Hare, Reading Level 3-4. (Illus.). 28p. (gr. 2-5). 1983. PLB 16.67 (*0-86592-853-3*); 12.50s.p. (*0-685-58818-1*) Rourke Corp.
Riehecky, Janet. Saving the Forests: A Rabbit's Story. Hohag, Linda, illus. LC 89-28122. 32p. (ps-2). 1990. PLB 13.95 (*0-89565-561-6*) Childs World.
Spier, Peter. Peter Spier's Rabbits. 1984. pap. 2.50 (*0-385-18198-1*) Doubleday.
Vernier, Louise. Your First Rabbit. (Illus.). 36p. (Orig.). 1991. pap. 1.95 (*0-86622-071-2*, YF-114) TFH Pubns.
Watts, Barrie, photos by. Rabbit. (Illus.). 24p. (gr. k-3). 1992. 6.95 (*0-525-67356-3*, Lodestar Bks) Dutton Child Bks.
Williams, Margery. The Velveteen Rabbit: Or, How Toys Become Real. Hague, Michael, illus. LC 82-15606. 48p. (gr. k up). 1983. 12.95 (*0-8050-0209-X*, Bks Young Read) H Holt & Co.
York, Carol B. Rabbit Magic. 128p. (gr. 2-5). 1991. pap. 2.50 (*0-590-43894-8*) Scholastic Inc.
Zolotow, Charlotte. The Bunny Who Found Easter. Peterson, Betty F., illus. 32p. (gr. k-3). 1983. 14.45 (*0-395-27677-2*); pap. 5.95 (*0-395-34068-3*) HM.

RABBITS–FICTION

Aardema, Verna. Rabbit Makes a Monkey of Lion. Pinkney, Jerry, illus. LC 86-11523. 32p. (ps-3). 1989. 11.95 (*0-8037-0297-3*); PLB 11.89 (*0-8037-0298-1*) Dial Bks Young.
Aardema, Verna, retold by. Who's in Rabbit's House? Dillon, Leo D. & Dillon, Diane, illus. LC 77-71514. 32p. (ps-3). 1979. pap. 4.95 (*0-8037-9549-1*) Dial Bks Young.
Aardema, Verna & Dillon, Leo D., eds. Who's in Rabbit's House? Dillon, Diane, illus. LC 77-71514. 32p. (gr. k-3). 1977. PLB 14.89 (*0-8037-9551-3*) Dial Bks Young.
Ada, Alma F. Serafina's Birthday. Bates, Louise, illus. LC 91-15389. 32p. (ps-2). 1992. SBE 13.95 (*0-689-31516-3*, Atheneum Child Bk) Macmillan Child Grp.
Adams, Adrienne. The Christmas Party. 2nd ed. Adams, Adrienne, illus. LC 91-42159. 32p. (ps-3). 1992. pap. 3.95 (*0-689-71630-3*, Aladdin) Macmillan Child Grp.
—The Easter Egg Artists. Adams, Adrienne, illus. LC 90-1097. 32p. (ps-3). 1991. pap. 4.95 (*0-689-71481-5*, Aladdin) Macmillan Child Grp.
—The Great Valentine's Day Balloon Race. Adams, Adrienne, illus. LC 86-3382. 32p. (ps-3). 1986. pap. 4.95 (*0-689-71085-2*, Aladdin) Macmillan Child Grp.
—The Great Valentine's Day Balloon Race. 2nd ed. LC 93-46114. 1995. pap. 4.95 (*0-689-71847-0*, Aladdin) Macmillan Child Grp.
Addison-Wesley Staff. El Conejo la Tortuga - Big Book. (SPA., Illus.). 16p. (gr. k-3). 1989. pap. text ed. 31.75 (*0-201-19937-8*) Addison-Wesley.
—El Conejo la Tortuga - Little Book. (SPA., Illus.). 16p. (gr. k-3). 1989. pap. text ed. 4.50 (*0-201-19709-X*) Addison-Wesley.
—The Hare & the Tortoise Little Book. (Illus.). 16p. (gr. k-3). 1989. pap. text ed. 4.50 (*0-201-19365-5*) Addison-Wesley.
Adler, David A. Bunny Rabbit Rebus. Linden, Madelaine G., illus. LC 82-45574. 40p. (gr. 1-4). 1983. (Crowell Jr Bks); (Crowell Jr Bks) HarpC Child Bks.
—Bunny Rabbit Rebus. Linden, Madelaine G., illus. (ps-3). 1987. pap. 3.95 (*0-14-050775-2*, Puffin) Puffin Bks.
The Adventures of Jason Jackrabbit. LC 89-2164. 48p. (gr. k-4). 1990. 9.95 (*0-937460-60-5*) Hendrick-Long.
Anderson, Lena. Bunny Bath. Anderson, Lena, illus. LC 89-63049. (ps-k). 1991. bds. 3.95 (*91-29-59652-1*) R & S Books.
—Bunny Box. (Illus.). 20p. (ps). 1991. bds. 3.95 (*91-29-59858-3*, Pub. by R&S Bks) FS&G.
—Bunny Fun. (Illus.). 20p. (ps). 1991. bds. 3.95 (*91-29-59860-5*, Pub. by R&S Bks) FS&G.
—Bunny Surprise. Anderson, Lena, illus. LC 89-63050. (ps-k). 1991. bds. 3.95 (*91-29-59654-8*) R & S Books.
Anderson, Lena, illus. Bunny Party. (ps). 1989. bds. 3.95 (*91-29-59134-1*, Pub. by R & S Bks) FS&G.

—Bunny Story. (ps). 1989. bds. 3.95 (*91-29-59132-5*, Pub. by R & S Bks) FS&G.
Anglund, Joan W. Baby Bunny. (ps). 1994. 3.95 (*0-307-12498-3*, Golden Pr) Western Pub.
Aunt Zinnia & the Ogre. (Illus.). 32p. (gr. k-3). 1992. PLB 17.27 (*0-8368-0910-6*); PLB 17.27 s.p. (*0-685-61497-2*) Gareth Stevens Inc.
Bailey, Carolyn S. The Little Rabbit Who Wanted Red Wings. Santoro, Chris, illus. 32p. (ps-1). 1988. pap. 2.25 (*0-448-19089-3*, Platt & Munk); (Platt & Munk) Putnam Pub Group.
Balian, Lorna. Humbug Rabbit. Balian, Lorna, illus. 32p. (ps-3). 1987. Repr. of 1975 ed. 7.50 (*0-687-37098-1*) Humbug Bks.
Ballman, Wanda. Jack the Jack Rabbit. (Illus.). 16p. (gr. k-4). 1990. 1.95 (*0-8059-3178-3*) Dorrance.
Banks, Kate. The Bunnysitters. Sims, Blanche, illus. LC 90-27441. 80p. (Orig.). (gr. 2-4). 1991. Random Bks Yng Read.
Barasch, Lynne. Rodney's Inside Story. LC 91-24405. (Illus.). 32p. (ps-1). 1992. 13.95 (*0-531-05993-6*); PLB 13.99 (*0-531-08593-7*) Orchard Bks Watts.
Barnett, Ada, et al. Eddycat Goes Shopping with Becky Bunny. Hoffmann, Mark, illus. LC 93-56884. 32p. (gr. 1 up). 1993. Repr. of 1991 ed. PLB 17.27 incl. tchr's. guide (*0-8368-0947-5*) Gareth Stevens Inc.
Barr, Marilynn G. Bunny Days. (Illus.). 48p. (ps-1). 1993. pap. 5.95 (*1-878279-54-8*) Monday Morning Bks.
Barry, Robert. Mr. Willowby's Christmas Tree. Barry, Robert, illus. 32p. (ps-2). 1992. pap. 4.99 (*0-440-40726-5*, YB) Dell.
Bassett, Lisa. The Bunny's Alphabet Eggs. Bassett, Jeni, illus. LC 92-37987. (gr. 2 up). 1993. 3.99 (*0-517-08153-9*) Random Hse Value.
—Ten Little Bunnies. Bassett, Jeni, illus. LC 92-37986. (gr. 2 up). 1993. 3.99 (*0-517-08154-7*) Random Hse Value.
Bate, Lucy. Little Rabbit's Loose Tooth. De Groat, Diane, illus. LC 75-6833. 32p. (gr. k-3). 1988. PLB 16. 00 (*0-517-52240-3*); pap. 4.99 (*0-517-55122-5*) Crown Bks Yng Read.
Becker, John. Seven Little Rabbits. Cooney, Barbara, illus. 32p. 1991. pap. 3.95 (*0-590-44849-8*, Blue Ribbon Bks) Scholastic Inc.
—Seven Little Rabbits. 2nd ed. Cooney, Barbara, tr. (Illus.). 32p. (ps-3). 1994. Repr. of 1974 ed. 5.95 (*0-8027-8311-2*) Walker & Co.
Bemelmans, Ludwig. Rosebud. Bemelmans, Ludwig, illus. LC 92-47046. 40p. (ps-2). 1993. 8.99 (*0-679-84913-0*); PLB 9.99 (*0-679-94913-5*) Knopf Bks Yng Read.
Bergstrom, Gunilla. Is That a Monster, Alfie Atkins? Swindells, Robert, tr. (Illus.). 28p. (ps up). 1989. 6.95 (*91-29-59136-8*, Pub. by R & S Bks) FS&G.
Beveridge, Barbara. Honey, My Rabbit. Love, Judith D., illus. LC 92-34272. 1993. 2.50 (*0-383-03630-5*) SRA Schl Grp.
Billam, Rosemary. Fuzzy Rabbit. Julian-Ottie, Vanessa, illus. LC 83-17637. 32p. (ps-3). 1984. pap. 2.25 (*0-394-86346-1*) Random Bks Yng Read.
Blake, Jon. You're a Hero, Daley B.! Scheffler, Axel & Scheffler, Axel, illus. LC 91-58725. 32p. (ps up). 1994. 13.95 (*1-56402-078-9*); pap. 4.99 (*1-56402-367-2*) Candlewick Pr.
Blau, Judith. Bunny Mitten's Book. Blau, Judith, illus. 7p. (ps). 1991. incl. puppet 5.95 (*0-679-81315-2*) Random Bks Yng Read.
Brickey, Louise. Pouche: The Assistant to the Easter Bunny. rev. ed. (Illus.). 36p. (gr. k-3). 1989. Repr. of 1987 ed. write for info. Cottontail Creations.
Bronstein, Ruth L. Rabbit's Good News. LC 93-30719. (gr. 4 up). Date not set. write for info. (*0-395-68700-4*, Clarion Bks) HM.
Brown, Cathy J. & Paterson, Debi. Bouncy Bunny's Birthday: A Family Story about Bravery. Adams, Kathy R., illus. LC 86-61065. 32p. (Orig.). (gr. 1-3). 1985. pap. 8.75 (*0-9614796-0-4*) C J Brown.
—Bouncy Bunny's Birthday: A Family Story about Bravery. Adams, Kathy R., illus. 32p. (Orig.). (gr. 1-3). 1985. pap. 8.75 (*0-318-19386-8*) Offset Hse.
Brown, Marc. The Bionic Bunny Show. Brown, Laurene K., illus. 32p. (ps-3). 1985. 14.95 (*0-316-11120-1*, Joy St Bks); pap. 5.95 (*0-316-10992-4*, Joy St Bks) Little.
Brown, Marc T. What Do You Call a Dumb Bunny? & Other Rabbit Riddles, Games, Jokes & Cartoons. Brown, Marc T., illus. LC 82-21650. 32p. (ps-3). 1983. (Joy St Bks); pap. 4.95 (*0-316-11119-8*, Joy St Bks) Little.
Brown, Margaret W. Goodnight Moon. Hurd, Clement, illus. LC 47-30762. 36p. (ps-1). 1947. 13.00 (*0-06-020705-1*); PLB 12.89 (*0-06-020706-X*) HarpC Child Bks.
—Goodnight Moon. Hurd, Clement, illus. LC 47-30762. (ps-2). 1977. pap. 3.95 (*0-06-443017-0*, Trophy) HarpC Child Bks.
—My World. LC 94-25755. 1995. 13.00 (*0-06-024798-3*, Festival); PLB 12.89 (*0-06-024799-1*) HarpC Child Bks.
—The Runaway Bunny. Hurd, Clement, illus. LC 71-183168. 40p. (ps-2). 1977. pap. 3.95 (*0-06-443018-9*, Trophy) HarpC Child Bks.
—The Runaway Bunny. Hurd, Clement, illus. (gr. k-3). 1985. incl. cassette 19.95 (*0-941078-78-7*); pap. 12.95 incl. cassette (*0-941078-76-0*); cassette, 4 paperbacks & guide 27.95 (*0-941078-77-9*) Live Oak Media.
—The Runaway Bunny Board Book. Hurd, Clement, illus. LC 71-183168. 32p. (ps). 1991. pap. 6.95 (*0-06-107429-2*) HarpC Child Bks.
—The Whispering Rabbit. Szekeres, Cyndy, illus. 24p. (ps-k). 1992. write for info. (*0-307-00138-5*, 312-03, Golden Pr) Western Pub.
Brutschy, Jennifer. The Winter Fox. Garns, Allen, illus. LC 92-33467. 40p. (ps-3). 1993. 15.00 (*0-679-81524-4*); PLB 15.99 (*0-679-91524-9*) Knopf Bks Yng Read.
Buchwald, Emilie. Gildaen: The Heroic Adventures of a Most Unusual Rabbit. Flynn, Barbara, illus. LC 93-16255. 192p. 1993. 14.95 (*0-915943-38-7*); pap. 6.95 (*0-915943-75-1*) Milkweed Ed.
Bugs Bunny: The Pirate Island. 24p. (ps-3). 1991. write for info. (*0-307-14176-4*, 14176) Western Pub.
Bullock, Kathleen. The Rabbits Are Coming! LC 90-49830. (Illus.). 40p. (ps-1). 1993. pap. 4.95 (*0-671-79609-7*, Little Simon) S&S Trade.
Burgess, Thornton. The Adventures of Peter Cottontail. (Illus.). (ps-8). 1990. Repr. lib. bdg. 18.95x (*0-89966-664-7*) Buccaneer Bks.
Burgess, Thornton W. The Adventures of Peter Cottontail. large type ed. 96p. 1992. pap. 1.00 (*0-486-26929-9*) Dover.
—Adventures of Peter Cottontail. 18.95 (*0-8488-0353-1*) Amereon Ltd.
—Mrs. Peter Rabbit. 18.95 (*0-8488-0390-6*) Amereon Ltd.
Caitlin, Stephen. Busy Bunnies. Mahan, Ben, illus. LC 87-10912. 32p. (gr. k-2). 1988. PLB 11.59 (*0-8167-1083-X*); pap. text ed. 2.95 (*0-8167-1084-8*) Troll Assocs.
Calmenson, Stephanie. Marigold & Grandma on the Town. Chalmers, Mary, illus. LC 89-31147. 64p. (gr. k-3). 1994. 14.00 (*0-06-020812-0*); PLB 13.89 (*0-06-020813-9*) HarpC Child Bks.
Campbell, Alison & Barton, Julia. Are You Asleep, Rabbit? Scriven, Gill, illus. 32p. (ps-3). 1992. pap. 3.99 (*0-14-054495-X*) Puffin Bks.
Capucilli, Alyssa S. Peekaboo Bunny. Melcher, Mary, illus. 24p. (ps). 1994. 6.95 (*0-590-46754-9*, Cartwheel) Scholastic Inc.
Carlson, Nancy. Bunnies & Their Hobbies. Carlson, Nancy, illus. LC 83-23161. 32p. (ps-3). 1984. PLB 13. 50 (*0-87614-257-9*) Carolrhoda Bks.
—Bunnies & Their Hobbies. LC 84-26458. (Illus.). 32p. (ps-3). 1985. pap. 3.99 (*0-14-050538-5*, Puffin) Puffin Bks.
—Bunnies & Their Sports. (Illus.). 32p. (ps-3). 1989. pap. 3.95 (*0-14-050617-9*, Puffin) Puffin Bks.
—Loudmouth George & the Big Race. Carlson, Nancy, illus. 32p. (ps-3). 1986. pap. 3.95 (*0-14-050516-4*, Puffin) Puffin Bks.
Castle, Caroline, retold by. Hare & the Tortoise. Weevers, Peter, illus. LC 84-9569. 32p. (ps-3). 1987. pap. 4.95 (*0-8037-0147-0*) Dial Bks Young.
Catley, Alison. Rabbit. (Illus.). 32p. (ps-1). 1993. 15.95 (*0-09-174408-3*, Pub. by Hutchinson UK) Trafalgar.
Chadwick, Tim. Cabbage Moon. Harper, Piers, illus. LC 93-28952. 1994. 14.95 (*0-531-06827-7*); lib. bdg. write for info. (*0-531-08677-1*) Orchard Bks Watts.
Chardiet, Bernice. Something Is Coming. Cote, Pamela, illus. 20p. (ps-1). 1994. pap. 4.99 (*0-14-054996-X*) Puffin Bks.
Chardiet, Bernice & Maccarone, Grace. Bunny Runs Away. 1992. pap. 2.50 (*0-590-44932-X*) Scholastic Inc.
Christelow, Eileen. Henry & the Dragon. Christelow, Eileen, illus. LC 83-14405. 32p. (ps-2). 1984. 13.45 (*0-89919-220-3*, Clarion Bks) HM.
Cleveland, David. The April Rabbits. Karlin, Nurit, illus. 32p. (gr. k-3). 1986. pap. 2.95 (*0-590-42369-X*) Scholastic Inc.
Cloke, Rene. Br'er Rabbit Stories. 1988. 2.98 (*0-671-06187-9*) S&S Trade.
Colmenson, Stephenie. Hopscotch, the Tiny Bunny. Lanza, Barbara, illus. (ps-3). 1991. pap. 1.75 (*0-307-12617-X*, Golden Pr) Western Pub.
Compton, Kenn & Compton, Joanne. Little Rabbit's Easter Surprise. Compton, Kenn & Compton, Joanne, illus. LC 91-17957. 32p. (ps-3). 1992. reinforced bdg. 14.95 (*0-8234-0920-1*) Holiday.
Cook, Elizabeth, adapted by. Rabbit Who Overcame Fear: A Jataka Tale. Meller, Eric, illus. Tulku, Tarthang, intro. by. (Illus.). 32p. (Orig.). (gr. k-4). 1991. 14.95 (*0-89800-212-5*); pap. 7.95 (*0-89800-211-7*) Dharma Pub.
Cooper, Helen. Ella & the Rabbit. Cooper, Helen, illus. LC 90-34499. 32p. (ps-3). 1990. 12.95 (*0-940793-62-8*, Crocodile Bks) Interlink Pub.
Cornell, S. A. Flying Carrots. Jones, John, illus. LC 85-14093. 48p. (Orig.). (gr. 1-3). 1986. PLB 10.59 (*0-8167-0640-9*); pap. text ed. 3.50 (*0-8167-0641-7*) Troll Assocs.
Cosgrove, Stephen. Buttermilk. James, Robin, illus. 32p. (Orig.). (gr. 1-4). 1986. pap. 2.95 (*0-8431-1565-3*) Price Stern.
—Leo the Lop. James, Robin, illus. LC 94-21448. 1995. write for info. (*0-8431-3820-3*) Price Stern.
—Leo the Lop Mini Book & Plush Toy. James, Robin, illus. 32p. (ps-4). 1994. pap. 9.95 incl. plush toy (*0-8431-3636-7*) Price Stern.
Cosgrove, Stephen E. Derby Downs. Edelson, Wendy, illus. 32p. (ps-3). 1990. PLB 14.95 (*0-89565-659-0*) Childs World.
Cottonpaw. Buns Travels Across America. Love, David, photos by. (Illus.). 48p. (gr. k-5). 1992. pap. 7.95 (*1-881274-01-2*) Cotton Tale.
Cousins, Lucy. What Can Rabbit Hear? LC 90-21212. (Illus.). 16p. (ps up). 1991. 12.95 (*0-688-10455-X*, Tambourine Bks) Morrow.
Cowley, Stewart. Little Lost Rabbit. Slade, Catharine, illus. LC 92-60792. 20p. (ps). 1992. 6.99 (*0-89577-445-3*, Dist. by Random) RD Assn.
Cry Bunny. 1989. text ed. 3.95 cased (*0-7214-5234-5*) Ladybird Bks.
Dahlin, Kari. The Very First Easter Bunny. 16p. 1995. write for info. (*0-944943-57-8*, 247799) Current Inc.
Daniel, Kira. Habits of Rabbits. Pellaton, Karen E., illus. LC 85-14122. 48p. (Orig.). (gr. 1-3). 1986. PLB 10.59 (*0-8167-0632-8*); pap. text ed. 3.50 (*0-8167-0633-6*) Troll Assocs.
Davies, Mark, adapted by. Brer Rabbit. (Illus.). 32p. (gr. 1 up). 1989. Kipling Pr.
De Beer, Hans. Little Polar Bear & the Brave Little Hare. De Beer, Hans, illus. James, J. Alison, tr. from GER. LC 92-9803. (Illus.). 32p. (gr. k-3). 1992. 12.95 (*1-55858-179-0*); PLB 12.88 (*1-55858-180-4*) North-South Bks NYC.
DeJong, Meindert. Shadrach. Sendak, Maurice, illus. LC 53-5250. 192p. (gr. 3-6). 1953. PLB 14.89 (*0-06-021546-1*) HarpC Child Bks.
—Shadrach. Sendak, Maurice, illus. LC 53-5250. 192p. (gr. 3-6). 1980. pap. 3.95 (*0-06-440115-4*, Trophy) HarpC Child Bks.
Delacre, Lulu. Peter Cottontail's Easter Book. Delacre, Lulu, illus. 32p. (ps-1). 1991. 12.95 (*0-590-43338-5*, Scholastic Hardcover) Scholastic Inc.
Delton, Judy. Rabbit's New Rug. Brown, Marc, illus. LC 79-16639. 40p. (ps-3). 1980. 5.95 (*0-8193-1009-3*); PLB 5.95 (*0-8193-1010-7*) Parents.
—Rabbit's New Rug. Brown, Marc, illus. 48p. (ps-2). 1992. pap. 2.95 (*0-448-40318-8*, G&D) Putnam Pub Group.
—Rabbit's New Rug. Brown, Marc, illus. LC 93-15453. 1993. 13.27 (*0-8368-0972-6*) Gareth Stevens Inc.
Denim, Sue. The Dumb Bunnies. Pilkey, Dav, illus. LC 93-2255. 32p. (ps-3). 1994. 12.95 (*0-590-47708-0*, Blue Sky Press) Scholastic Inc.
—The Dumb Bunnies' Easter. Pilkey, Dav, illus. LC 94-15050. (gr. 1-8). 1995. write for info. (*0-590-20241-3*, Blue Sky Press) Scholastic Inc.
Dennis, Martin C. Will Arnold See Christmas? 1993. 7.95 (*0-533-10404-1*) Vantage.
Dickinson, Susan. Brer Rabbit & the Peanut Patch. rev. ed. Frankland, David, illus. 32p. (gr. k-2). 1990. Repr. of 1985 ed. PLB 10.95 (*1-878363-18-2*) Forest Hse.
Dodge, Nancy C. Thumpy's Story: A Story of Love & Grief Shared. Veara, Kevin, illus. LC 84-61293. 24p. (gr. k-12). 1985. pap. 5.95 (*0-918533-00-7*) Prairie Lark.
Dowling, Paul. You Can Do It, Rabbit. Dowling, Paul, illus. LC 91-48352. 32p. (ps-k). 1992. text ed. 9.95 (*1-56282-252-7*) Hyprn Child.
Dunbar, Joyce. Spring Rabbit. (Illus.). (ps-3). 1994. 13.00 (*0-688-13191-3*) Lothrop.
Dyjak, Elisabeth. Bertha's Garden. Wilkins, Janet, illus. LC 93-28594. 1994. write for info. (*0-395-68715-2*) HM.
Eagle, Mike. The Marathon Rabbit. Eagle, Mike, illus. LC 84-27944. 48p. (ps-2). 1986. 12.95 (*0-03-004058-2*, Bks Young Read) H Holt & Co.
The Easter Bunny's Helper. 1989. text ed. 3.95 cased (*0-7214-5233-7*) Ladybird Bks.
Easterling, Bill. Prize in the Snow. Owens, Mary B., illus. LC 92-23411. (ps-3). 1994. 15.95 (*0-316-22489-8*) Little.
Egan, Louise B., retold by. The Easter Bunny. Dieneman, Debbie, illus. LC 92-32435. 1993. 6.95 (*0-8362-4935-6*) Andrews & McMeel.
Ehrlich, Amy. Bunnies All Day Long. Henry, Marie H., illus. LC 84-20031. 32p. (ps-2). 1989. (Puff Pied Piper); (Puff Pied Piper) Puffin Bks.
—Bunnies at Christmastime. Henry, Marie H., illus. LC 86-2202. 32p. (ps-2). 1989. 11.95 (*0-8037-0321-X*) Dial Bks Young.
—Bunnies on Their Own. LC 85-20467. (Illus.). 32p. (ps-2). 1992. pap. 3.99 (*0-8037-1138-7*, Puff Pied Piper) Puffin Bks.
Eldrid, Brenda. Pershey the Rabbit. County Studio Staff, illus. 24p. (ps-2). 1993. pap. text ed. 0.99 (*1-56293-342-6*) McClanahan Bk.
Erickson, Gina C. & Foster, Kelli C. A Mop for Pop. Russell, Kerri G., illus. 24p. (ps-2). 1991. pap. 3.50 (*0-8120-4680-3*) Barron.
Ernst, Lisa C. Miss Penny & Mr. Grubbs. Ernst, Lisa C., illus. LC 90-43175. 40p. (ps-2). 1991. RSBE 14.95 (*0-02-733563-1*, Bradbury Pr) Macmillan Child Grp.
Everett, Louise. Bubble Gum in the Sky. Harvey, Paul, illus. LC 86-30859. 32p. (gr. k-2). 1988. PLB 7.89 (*0-8167-0998-X*); pap. text ed. 1.95 (*0-8167-0999-8*) Troll Assocs.
Family Moving Day. (Illus.). 32p. (gr. k-3). 1992. PLB 17.27 (*0-8368-0911-4*); PLB 17.27 s.p. (*0-685-61499-9*) Gareth Stevens Inc.
Feczko, Kathy. The Great Bunny Race. Jones, John, illus. LC 84-8634. 32p. (gr. k-2). 1985. PLB 11.59 (*0-8167-0357-4*); pap. text ed. 2.95 (*0-8167-0437-6*) Troll Assocs.
Fittro, Charlene C. Hoppy the Easter Bunny. LC 92-71919. (Illus.). 20p. (Orig.). (ps-3). 1992. pap. 7.95 (*0-9633053-4-4*) Child Bks & Mus.
Frenck, Hal, illus. The Tale of Benjamin Bunny. LC 87-40283. (ps up). 1990. incl. audio cassettes 6.95 (*1-55782-016-3*, Pub. by Warner Juvenile Bks) Little.

Gackenbach, Dick. Hattie Be Quiet, Hattie Be Good. LC 76-58697. (Illus.). 32p. (ps-3). 1977. PLB 13.89 (*0-06-021952-1*) HarpC Child Bks.
—Hattie Rabbit. LC 75-37018. (Illus.). 32p. (ps-3). 1976. PLB 13.89 (*0-06-021940-8*) HarpC Child Bks.
—Hattie Rabbit. Gackenbach, Dick, illus. LC 75-37018. 32p. (ps-2). 1990. pap. 3.50 (*0-06-444133-4*, Trophy) HarpC Child Bks.
Gag, Wanda. ABC Bunny. Gag, Wanda, illus. LC 33-27359. (gr. k-2). 1978. 14.95 (*0-698-20000-4*, Sandcastle Bks); (Sandcastle Bks); pap. 6.95 (*0-698-20683-5*, Coward) Putnam Pub Group.
Giff, Patricia R. Monster Rabbit Runs. (gr. 4-7). 1991. pap. 3.25 (*0-440-40424-X*) Dell.
Gill, Madelaine. The Spring Hat. LC 91-30556. (Illus.). 40p. (ps-1). 1993. pap. 13.00 (*0-671-75666-4*, S&S BYR) S&S Trade.
Gleeson, Kate. Kate Gleeson's Bunny's Special Dream. (ps-3). 1994. pap. 1.95 (*0-307-10558-X*, Golden Pr) Western Pub.
Greenway, Jennifer. A Real Little Bunny: A Sequel to The Velveteen Rabbit. Officer, Robyn, illus. LC 92-37149. 40p. 1993. 14.95 (*0-8362-4936-4*) Andrews & McMeel.
Griffin, Sandi Z. Becca Bumbum Bunny, Vol. 3: Tails with a Moral. Griffin, Sandi Z., illus. 28p. (ps-2). 1993. write for info. (*1-883838-03-7*) S Z Griffin.
Grover, Teddi. Buttons: The Foster Bunny. Iverson, Diane, illus. Martone, Frederick M., intro. by. (Illus.). 48p. (Orig.). (ps-5). 1992. pap. 8.95 (*0-9623349-3-6*) MS Pub.
Hardgrove, Nelle. Hurrah for Funny Bunny. Goodman, Joe, ed. (Illus.). 48p. 1987. pap. write for info. (*0-9619227-1-0*) N A Hardegrove.
Harris, Joel C. Jump Again! More Adventures of Brer Rabbit. Moser, Barry, illus. & adapted by. 40p. (ps-3). 1987. 16.95 (*0-15-241352-9*, HB Juv Bks) HarBrace.
—Jump: The Adventures of Brer Rabbit. Parks, Van D. & Jones, Malcolm, eds. Goldberg, Whoopi, read by. LC 86-7654. (Illus.). 40p. (ps-3). 1986. 15.95 (*0-15-241350-2*, HB Juv Bks) HarBrace.
—Little Treasury of Br'er Rabbit, 6 vols. 1988. Set. 5.99 (*0-517-66567-0*) Random Hse Value.
Herford, Oliver. The Most Timid in the Land: A Bunny Romance. Long, Sylvia, illus. 32p. (ps-1). 1992. 12.95 (*0-87701-862-6*) Chronicle Bks.
Heyward, Du Bose. The Country Bunny & the Little Gold Shoes. Flack, Marjorie, illus. 48p. (gr. k-3). 1974. reinforced bdg. 13.45 (*0-395-15990-3*, Sandpiper); pap. 4.80 (*0-395-18557-2*, Sandpiper) HM.
Heyward, DuBose. The Country Bunny & the Little Gold Shoes. Flack, Marjorie, illus. (ps-3). 1989. pap. 7.95 incl. cassette (*0-395-52140-8*) HM.
Hillert, Margaret. The Baby Bunny. (Illus.). (ps-k). 1981. PLB 6.95 (*0-8136-5064-X*, TK2272); pap. 3.50 (*0-8136-5564-1*, TK2273) Modern Curr.
Hogg, Gary. The Half-Hearted Hare. Anderson, Gary, illus. (gr. k-6). 1991. 11.95 (*0-89868-206-1*); pap. 4.95 (*0-89868-207-X*) ARO Pub.
Hooks, William H. & Boegehold, Betty D. The Rainbow Ribbon. Munsinger, Lynn, illus. LC 93-27706. 32p. 1995. pap. 3.99 (*0-14-054092-X*) Puffin Bks.
Hopkins, Margo. Honey Rabbit. Szekeres, Cyndy, illus. 14p. (ps). 1982. write for info. (*0-307-12268-9*, Golden Bks) Western Pub.
Houck, Eric L., Jr. Rabbit Surprise. Catalano, Dominic, illus. LC 92-1318. 32p. (ps-2). 1993. 14.00 (*0-517-58777-7*); PLB 14.99 (*0-517-58778-5*) Crown Bks Yng Read.
Howard, Katherine. Little Bunny Follows His Nose. Miller, J. P., illus. 32p. (ps-2). 1971. write for info. (*0-307-13536-5*, Golden Bks.) Western Pub.
Howe, Deborah & Howe, James. Bunnicula: A Rabbit Tale of Mystery. Daniel, Alan, illus. LC 78-11472. 112p. (gr. 4-6). 1979. SBE 14.00 (*0-689-30700-4*, Atheneum Child Bk) Macmillan Child Grp.
—Bunnicula: A Rabbit-Tale of Mystery. Daniel, Alan, illus. 100p. (gr. 3-7). 1980. pap. 3.99 (*0-380-51094-4*, Camelot) Avon.
Howe, James. The Bunnicula Fun Book. Daniel, Alan, illus. LC 92-34561. 176p. 1993. pap. 9.95 (*0-688-11952-2*) Morrow Jr Bks.
—The Celery Stalks at Midnight. Morrill, Leslie, illus. LC 83-2665. 128p. (gr. 4-6). 1983. SBE 14.00 (*0-689-30987-2*, Atheneum Child Bk) Macmillan Child Grp.
—The Celery Stalks at Midnight. Morrill, Leslie H., illus. 128p. (gr. 3-7). 1984. pap. 3.99 (*0-380-69054-3*, Camelot) Avon.
—Rabbit Cadabra! Daniel, Alan, illus. LC 91-34656. 48p. (gr. k up). 1993. 15.00 (*0-688-10402-9*); PLB 14.93 (*0-688-10403-7*) Morrow Jr Bks.
Huriet, Genevieve. Beechwood Bunny Tales Series, 7 vols. Jouannigot, Loic, illus. (gr. k-2). 1991. Set. PLB 120.89 (*0-8368-0924-6*) Gareth Stevens Inc.
—Dandelion's Vanishing Vegetable Garden. Jouannigot, Loic, illus. LC 90-4857. 32p. (gr. k-2). 1991. lib. bdg. 17.27 (*0-8368-0526-7*) Gareth Stevens Inc.
—Mistletoe & the Baobab Tree. Jouannigot, Loic, illus. LC 90-4856. 32p. (gr. k-2). 1991. PLB 17.27 (*0-8368-0527-5*) Gareth Stevens Inc.
—Perriwinkle at the Full Moon Ball. Jouannigot, Loic, illus. LC 90-4859. 32p. (gr. k-2). 1991. lib. bdg. 17.27 (*0-8368-0525-9*) Gareth Stevens Inc.
—Poppy's Dance. Jouannigot, Loic, illus. LC 90-4858. 32p. (gr. k-2). 1991. PLB 17.27 (*0-8368-0528-3*) Gareth Stevens Inc.
Ikeda, Daisaku. The Princess & the Moon. McCaughrean, Geraldine, tr. from JPN. Wildsmith, Brian, illus. LC 92-148. 32p. (ps-3). 1992. 15.00 (*0-679-83620-9*); PLB 15.99 (*0-679-93620-3*) Knopf Bks Yng Read.
Ingle, Annie. The Rabbits' Carnival. Bratun, Katy, illus. LC 92-29930. 24p. (Orig.). (ps-3). 1995. pap. 2.50 (*0-679-85337-5*) Random Bks Yng Read.
Johnston, Tony. Little Rabbit Goes to Sleep. Stevenson, Harvey, illus. LC 92-8543. 32p. (ps-k). 1994. 15.00 (*0-06-021239-X*); PLB 14.89 (*0-06-021241-1*) HarpC Child Bks.
Kaplan, Carol B. The Not-So-Fast Rabbit. Bolinske, Janet L., ed. Quenell, Midge, illus. LC 87-62997. 24p. (Orig.). (ps-k). 1988. 17.95 (*0-88335-755-0*); pap. 4.95 (*0-88335-079-3*) Milliken Pub Co.
Karin, Nurit. Ten Little Bunnies. Wilhelm, Hans, illus. LC 93-13450. 1994. pap. 14.00 (*0-671-88026-8*, S&S BFYR) S&S Trade.
Karl, Linda & Siegel, Seth M. Daisy Bunny's Teatime. Guell, Fernando & Beelaerts, Marie, illus. 12p. (ps-k). 1994. 3.99 (*0-679-84001-X*) Random Bks Yng Read.
—Rose Bunny's Teatime. Guell, Fernando & Beelaerts, Marie, illus. 12p. (ps-k). 1994. 3.99 (*0-679-84002-8*) Random Bks Yng Read.
—Tulip Bunny's Teatime. Guell, Fernando & Beelaerts, Marie, illus. 12p. (ps-k). 1994. 3.99 (*0-679-84003-6*) Random Bks Yng Read.
—Violet Bunny's Teatime. Guell, Fernando & Beelaerts, Marie, illus. 12p. (ps-k). 1994. 3.99 (*0-679-84004-4*) Random Bks Yng Read.
Karlin, Nurit. Ten Little Bunnies. (ps-3). 1994. pap. 4.95 (*0-671-88601-0*, Little Simon) S&S Trade.
Kass, Kimberly, retold by. The Velveteen Rabbit. abr. ed. Carpenter, Nancy, illus. LC 92-6036. 22p. (ps). 1993. 3.25 (*0-679-83617-9*) Random Bks Yng Read.
Kennedy, Pamela. A, B, C, Bunny. Chartier, Normand, illus. 12p. (ps-k). 1990. bds. 4.99 (*0-929608-69-0*) Focus Family.
—All Mine, Bunny. Chartier, Normand, illus. 12p. (ps-k). 1990. bds. 4.99 (*0-929608-65-8*) Focus Family.
—Night, Night, Bunny. Chartier, Normand, illus. 12p. (ps-k). 1990. bds. 4.99 (*0-929608-70-4*) Focus Family.
—Oh, Oh, Bunny. Chartier, Normand, illus. 12p. (ps-k). 1990. bds. 4.99 (*0-929608-67-4*) Focus Family.
—One, Two, Three, Bunny. Chartier, Normand, illus. 12p. (ps-k). 1990. bds. 4.99 (*0-929608-68-2*) Focus Family.
—Red, Yellow, Blue, Bunny. Chartier, Normand, illus. 12p. (ps-k). 1990. bds. 4.99 (*0-929608-66-6*) Focus Family.
Kerins, Anthony. Tat Rabbit's Treasure. Kerins, Anthony, illus. LC 92-32600. 32p. (ps-1). 1993. SBE 14.95 (*0-689-50553-1*, M K McElderry) Macmillan Child Grp.
Komoda, Beverly. The Winter Day. Komoda, Beverly, illus. LC 91-104. 32p. (ps-1). 1991. PLB 13.89 (*0-06-023302-8*) HarpC Child Bks.
Koontz, Robin M. Chicago & the Cat. Koontz, Robin M., illus. LC 91-34863. 32p. (gr. k-3). 1993. 12.00 (*0-525-65097-0*, Cobblehill Bks) Dutton Child Bks.
—Chicago & the Cat: The Camping Trip. Koontz, Robin M., illus. LC 92-46685. 32p. (gr. k-3). 1994. 12.99 (*0-525-65137-3*, Cobblehill Bks) Dutton Child Bks.
—Chicago & the Cat: The Halloween Party. Koontz, Robin M., illus. LC 93-27043. 32p. (gr. k-3). 1994. 12. 99 (*0-525-65138-1*, Cobblehill Bks) Dutton Child Bks.
Kraus, Robert. Daddy Long Ears Christmas Surprise. 1989. 4.95 (*0-671-68150-8*, Little Simon) S&S Trade.
Kroll, Steven. The Big Bunny & the Easter Eggs. (Illus.). 1992. pap. 2.95 (*0-685-54832-5*) Scholastic Inc.
—The Big Bunny & the Magic Show. Stevens, Janet, illus. LC 85-14147. 32p. (ps-3). 1986. reinforced bdg. 15.95 (*0-8234-0589-3*) Holiday.
—The Big Bunny & the Magic Show. Stevens, Janet, illus. 32p. (ps-2). 1987. pap. 3.95 (*0-590-44633-9*) Scholastic Inc.
Kunhardt, Dorothy. Pat the Bunny. Kunhardt, Dorothy, illus. (ps). 1942. write for info. (*0-307-12000-7*, Golden Bks) Western Pub.
Laird, Rebecca. Robinson Rabbit, What Do You Hear? Boddy, Joe, illus. LC 89-82550. 32p. (ps-k). 1990. pap. 5.99 (*0-8066-2463-9*, 9-2463) Augsburg Fortress.
Langerman, Jean. No Carrots for Harry! Remkiewicz, Frank, illus. 48p. (ps-2). 1992. pap. 2.95 (*0-448-40320-X*, G&D) Putnam Pub Group.
—No Carrots for Harry. (Illus.). 42p. (ps-3). 1992. PLB 13.27 (*0-8368-0876-2*) Gareth Stevens Inc.
Lasky, Kathryn. Lunch Bunnies. Hafner, Marylin, illus. LC 92-31554. 1993. 13.95 (*0-316-51525-6*, Joy St Bks) Little.
Lawson, Robert. Rabbit Hill. (Illus.). (gr. 1-3). 1977. pap. 3.99 (*0-14-031010-X*, Puffin) Puffin Bks.
—Robbut: A Tale of Tails. Lawson, Robert, illus. LC 89-32367. 94p. (gr. 2-6). 1989. Repr. of 1948 ed. lib. bdg. 16.00 (*0-208-02236-8*, Linnet) Shoe String.
Leedy, Loreen. The Bunny Play. Leedy, Loreen, illus. LC 87-17793. 32p. (ps-3). 1988. reinforced bdg. 12.95 (*0-8234-0679-2*) Holiday.
Lester, Julius. The Tales of Uncle Remus: The Adventures of Brer Rabbit, Vol. I. Pinckney, Jerry, illus. LC 85-20449. (ps up). 1987. 16.95 (*0-8037-0271-X*); PLB 16.89 (*0-8037-0272-8*) Dial Bks Young.
Le Tord, Bijou. Rabbit Seeds. (ps-3). 1993. pap. 3.99 (*0-440-40767-2*) Dell.
Levine, Abby. Ollie Knows Everything. Munsinger, Lynn, illus. LC 93-29600. 1994. write for info. (*0-8075-6020-0*) A Whitman.
Lewis, Naomi. Hare & Badger Go to Town. Ross, Tony, illus. 32p. (ps-1). 1987. 9.95 (*0-905478-94-0*, Pub. by Century UK) Trafalgar.
Lian, Ann & Lian, Leslie. The Fourteen Carat Caper. LC 88-51031. (Illus.). 44p. 1988. 5.95 (*1-55523-171-3*) Winston-Derek.
Lionni, Leo. Let's Make Rabbits. (Illus.). 40p. (ps-3). 1992. 4.99 (*0-679-82640-8*) Knopf Bks Yng Read.
Little Bunnies All Through the Year. 1990. text ed. 3.95 cased (*0-7214-5289-2*) Ladybird Bks.
Little Bunnies Around Town. 1990. text ed. 3.95 cased (*0-7214-5290-6*) Ladybird Bks.
Little Bunnies at Home. 1990. text ed. 3.95 cased (*0-7214-5288-4*) Ladybird Bks.
Little Bunnies on the Move. 1990. text ed. 3.95 cased (*0-7214-5291-4*) Ladybird Bks.
Little Bunnies on Vacation. 1990. text ed. 3.95 cased (*0-7214-5292-2*) Ladybird Bks.
Little Bunny Foo Foo. 24p. (ps-3). 1991. write for info. (*0-307-14163-2*, 14163) Western Pub.
Lloyd, Tracey. Old Man & the Rabbit. (gr. 4-7). 1992. pap. 3.95 (*0-7910-2917-4*) Chelsea Hse.
Lo que le Encanta a Conejito. (SPA.). (ps-3). 1993. pap. 5.95 (*0-307-91590-5*, Golden Pr) Western Pub.
London, Jonathan. Jackrabbit. Ray, Deborah K., illus. LC 94-1082. 1995. write for info. (*0-517-59657-1*, Crown); lib. bdg. write for info. (*0-517-59658-X*, Crown) Crown Pub Group.
—Liplap & the Snowbunny. Long, Sylvia, illus. LC 93-31007. 1994. 13.95 (*0-8118-0505-0*) Chronicle Bks.
Long, Jack. Little Treasury of the Velveteen Rabbit. 1988. 5.99 (*0-517-64371-5*) Random Hse Value.
Lord, Wendy. Gorilla on the Midway. LC 93-1051. 1994. pap. 4.99 (*0-7814-0892-X*, Chariot Bks) Chariot Family.
—Pickle Stew. LC 93-19018. 1994. pap. 4.49 (*0-7814-0886-5*, Chariot Bks) Chariot Family.
McCabe, Bernard. Bottle Rabbit. (gr. 4-7). 1992. pap. 3.95 (*0-571-15339-9*) Faber & Faber.
—Bottle Rabbit & Friends. Scheffler, Axel, illus. 136p. (gr. 3-7). 1991. 14.95 (*0-571-15318-6*) Faber & Faber.
MacCombie, Turi, illus. Velveteen Rabbit. 48p. (ps-3). 1991. 9.95 (*0-88101-114-2*) Unicorn Pub.
—Velveteen Rabbit. 48p. (ps-3). 1992. 12.95 (*0-88101-236-X*) Unicorn Pub.
Macdonald, Maryann. Rosie & the Poor Rabbits. Sweet, Melissa, illus. LC 92-42766. 32p. (ps-2). 1994. SBE 13.95 (*0-689-31832-4*, Atheneum Child Bk) Macmillan Child Grp.
—Rosie's Baby Tooth. Sweet, Melissa, illus. LC 90-35923. 32p. (ps-2). 1991. SBE 12.95 (*0-689-31626-7*, Atheneum Child Bk) Macmillan Child Grp.
McNaughton, Colin. Walk Rabbit Walk. McNaughton, Colin, illus. LC 91-32608. 32p. (ps-3). 1992. Repr. of 1977 ed. 13.00 (*0-688-11410-5*, Tambourine Bks) Morrow.
Malinowski, Stanley B. & Melodia, Thomas V. The Easter Bunny Comes to Forgottenville. 48p. (ps-3). 1988. 11.95 (*0-941316-02-5*) TSM Books.
Mangas, Brian. Carrot Delight. 1990. pap. 5.95 (*0-671-67886-8*, S&S BFYR) S&S Trade.
—Carrot Delight. Levitt, Sidney, illus. 32p. (ps-1). 1991. pap. 2.25 (*0-671-73278-1*, Little Simon) S&S Trade.
—A Nice Surprise for Father Rabbit. Levitt, Sidney, illus. 32p. (ps-1). 1991. pap. 2.95 (*0-671-73277-3*, Little Simon) S&S Trade.
—Sshaboom! Bratun, Katy, illus. LC 91-24764. 40p. (ps-1). 1993. pap. 14.00 JRT (*0-671-75538-2*, S&S BFYR) S&S Trade.
—You Don't Get a Carrot Unless You're a Bunny. Levitt, Sidney, illus. 1989. pap. 5.95 (*0-671-67201-0*, Little Simon) S&S Trade.
Mark, Jan. Silly Tails. LC 92-38679. (Illus.). 32p. (gr. k-3). 1993. SBE 13.95 (*0-689-31843-X*, Atheneum Child Bk) Macmillan Child Grp.
Martin, Rafe. Foolish Rabbit's Big Mistake. (Illus.). 32p. (ps-3). 1991. pap. 6.95 (*0-399-21778-9*, Sandcastle Bks) Putnam Pub Group.
Martin, Rafe, rev. by. Foolish Rabbit's Big Mistake. Young, Ed, illus. LC 84-11665. 32p. (gr. k-3). 1985. 14.95 (*0-399-21178-0*, Putnam); pap. 6.95 (*0-685-73728-4*) Putnam Pub Group.
Mastrangelo, Judy. What Do Bunnies Do All Day? (Illus.). 32p. (ps-1). 1991. pap. 4.95 perfect bdg. (*0-8249-8509-5*, Ideals Child) Hambleton-Hill.
Matthews. Bunches & Bunches of Bunnies. 1993. pap. 28. 67 (*0-590-71572-0*) Scholastic Inc.
Matthews, Morgan. Houdini, the Vanishing Hare. Gustafson, Dana, illus. LC 88-1286. 48p. (Orig.). (gr. 1-4). 1989. PLB 10.59 (*0-8167-1343-X*); pap. text ed. 3.50 (*0-8167-1344-8*) Troll Assocs.
May, Robert E. How Billy Joe Bobtail Met Texas Slim. McQueen, Don, illus. 32p. (gr. k-7). 1987. lib. bdg. 11. 89 (*0-87397-303-8*); pap. 5.95 (*0-87397-300-3*) Strode.
Mellen, Stephanie. The Crystal Rabbit. Mellen, Stephanie, illus. LC 93-91632. 52p. (Orig.). 1993. pap. 5.95 (*0-9637414-0-3*) Meltec.
Michaels, Tilde. Rabbit Spring. James, J. Alison & Bhend-Zaugg, Kathi, illus. LC 87-18107. 85p. (gr. 2-6). 1989. 11.95 (*0-15-200568-4*, Gulliver Bks) HarBrace.
Miller, J. P. Little Rabbit Takes a Walk. Miller, J. P., illus. LC 86-61525. 24p. (ps-1). 1987. pap. 5.95 bk. & doll pkg. (*0-394-88667-4*) Random Bks Yng Read.
—Yoo-Hoo Little Rabbit. Miller, J. P., illus. LC 85-61529. (ps). 1986. 3.99 (*0-394-87884-1*) Random Bks Yng Read.

Miller, Minnie T. Why the March Hare Went Mad & Other Stories. 55p. (gr. k-4). 1972. 5.00 (*0-87881-002-1*) Mojave Bks.

Miller, Sherry. The Day Happy E. Bunny Lost His Cotton Tail. Martinez, Jesse, illus. 16p. (Orig.). (gr. k-5). 1983. pap. 0.49 saddle-stitched (*0-685-43303-X*) Double M Pub.

Mills, Elaine. The Cottage at the End of the Lane. LC 93-45748. (Illus.). 32p. (ps-4). 1994. 15.00 (*0-517-59703-9*) Crown Bks Yng Read.

Modesitt, Jeanne. Mama, If You Had a Wish. Spowart, Robin, illus. LC 91-31354. 40p. (ps-1). 1993. JRT 14. 00 (*0-671-75437-8*, Green Tiger) S&S Trade.

—Vegetable Soup. Spowart, Robin, illus. LC 87-11169. 32p. (ps-1). 1988. RSBE 13.95 (*0-02-767630-7*, Macmillan Child Bk) Macmillan Child Grp.

—Vegetable Soup. Spowart, Robin, illus. LC 91-247. 32p. (ps-3). 1991. pap. 4.50 (*0-689-71523-4*, Aladdin) Macmillan Child Grp.

Moore, Inga. A Big Day for Little Jack. LC 93-6272. (Illus.). 32p. 1994. text ed. 14.95 RTE (*1-56402-418-0*) Candlewick Pr.

Mora, Jo. Budgee Budgee Cottontail. Mitchell, Steve, ed. Mora, Jo, illus. (gr. 3). 1994. 24.95 (*0-922029-23-7*) D Stoecklein Photo.

A wonderful story written in verse & gorgeously illustrated by famous artist, sculptor, & writer, Jo Mora. Written in 1936, eleven years before his death, the book contains a multitude of animal sketches & color illustrations by Mora. He was known as a cowboy & author of classic books on the American West, but Mora began as a Boston cartoonist & children's book author at the turn of the century. After sculpting the Will Rogers Memorial, the Father Serra Sarcophagus at the Carmel, California, mission, & the Don Quixote statue in San Francisco's Golden Gate Park, Mora returned to complete the children's book he always wanted to write - BUDGEE BUDGEE COTTONTAIL!

Publisher Provided Annotation.

Mosse, Richard. Bun-Bun's Brook Trout. Sonstegard, Jeff, ed. Mosse, Richard, illus. 32p. (gr. 6-10). 1992. 9.95 (*0-9630328-1-X*) SDPI.

—Bun-Bun's Garden. Sonstegard, Jeff, ed. (Illus.). 24p. (gr. 6-10). 1993. text ed. 12.95 (*0-9630328-4-4*) SDPI.

Murray, Marjorie D. Saturday with Little Rabbit. Britt, Stephanie, illus. LC 91-48362. 48p. (gr. k-3). 1993. RSBE 12.95 (*0-02-767753-2*, Macmillan Child Bk) Macmillan Child Grp.

Nakano, Mei T. Riko Rabbit. LC 82-81737. (gr. 2-5). 1982. pap. 5.95 (*0-942610-00-8*) Mina Pr.

Nash, Corey, retold by. Little Treasury of Peter Rabbit, 6 vols. Potter, Beatrix, illus. (ps). 1983. 5.99 (*0-517-41069-9*, Chatham River Pr) Random Hse Value.

New Boots for Rabbit. 1989. text ed. 3.95 cased (*0-7214-5230-2*) Ladybird Bks.

Newberry, Clare T. Marshmallow. reissued ed. LC 89-20052. (Illus.). 32p. (ps-3). 1990. 17.00 (*0-06-024460-7*) HarpC Child Bks.

Newton, Jill. Polar Scare. (Illus.). (ps-3). 1992. 15.00 (*0-688-11232-3*); PLB 14.93 (*0-685-75779-X*) Lothrop.

Nicklaus, Carol, illus. Bunny Shines. LC 91-68458. 48p. (Orig.). (ps up). 1993. pap. 2.50 (*0-679-83449-4*) Random Bks Yng Read.

Nilsson, Ulf & Nilsson, Eriksson. Little Bunny & Friends. 1993. pap. 2.99 (*0-517-11071-7*) Random Hse Value.

—Little Bunny Gets Lost. 1993. pap. 2.99 (*0-517-11075-X*) Random Hse Value.

Norman, Jane & Beazley, Frank. Tick-i-ty Ted Meets the Rude Rabbits. 24p. (ps-3). 1993. pap. write for info. (*1-883585-09-0*) Pixanne Ent.

Ohanesian, Diane. Let's Pretend Bunny. (Illus.). 12p. (ps). 1993. Incl. bunny. bds. 9.95 (*0-89577-451-8*, Dist. by Random) RD Assn.

Olson, Jim. The Reindeer & the Easter Bunny. Van Vleck, Jane & Olson, Sally, eds. (Illus.). 18p. (Orig.). (gr. 1-4). 1981. pap. 4.95 (*0-943806-00-3*) Neahtawanta Pr.

Parish, Peggy. Too Many Rabbits. (ps-3). 1992. pap. 3.50 (*0-440-40591-2*) Dell.

Parker, Carol. Why Do You Call Me Chocolate Boy? Barter, Nan, illus. LC 93-79098. 28p. (Orig.). (gr. 2-6). 1993. pap. 7.95 (*0-9637267-0-6*) Gull Crest.

Paxton, Tom. Jennifer's Rabbit. Ayers, Donna, illus. LC 87-14113. 32p. (ps-1). 1988. 12.95 (*0-688-07431-6*); lib. bdg. 12.88 (*0-688-07432-4*, Morrow Jr Bks) Morrow Jr Bks.

Peck, Robert N. Little Soup's Bunny. (ps-3). 1993. pap. 2.99 (*0-440-40772-9*) Dell.

Peppe, Rodney. Run Rabbit, Run! A Pop-Up Book. Peppe, Rodney, illus. LC 82-70307. 12p. (ps-3). 1982. pap. 8.95 (*0-385-28851-4*) Delacorte.

Perkins, Anne T. The Bunny. Perkins, Anne T. & Lomax, James, illus. 8p. 1993. 12.00 (*1-884204-02-3*) Teach Nxt Door.

Peter Rabbit. (Illus.). (ps-2). 1989. 1.95 (*0-7214-5138-1*) Ladybird Bks.

Peter Rabbit & His Friends. 1985. pap. 3.95 (*0-671-52698-7*, Little Simon) S&S Trade.

Peters, Tim, ed. Little Hopper Catches a Cold. (Illus.). (ps-2). pap. 4.95 (*1-879874-27-X*) T Peters & Co.

Pitcher, Diana. The Mischief Maker. Dove, Sally, illus. 64p. 1990. pap. 5.95 (*0-86486-106-0*, Pub. by D Philip South Africa) Interlink Pub.

Porter, Sue. My Little Rabbit Tale. LC 93-29765. (Illus.). 32p. (ps-1). 1994. 13.95 (*1-56458-339-2*) Dorling Kindersley.

Potter, Beatrix. Beatrix Potter & Peter Rabbit Classic Treasury. 1988. 9.99 (*0-517-67150-6*) Random Hse Value.

—Beatrix Potter Tale of Baby Da. (gr. k up). 1979. 17.00 (*0-8378-8011-4*) Gibson.

—Benjamin Bunny. (Illus.). 10p. (ps). 1994. 3.99 (*0-7232-0018-1*) Warne.

—Benjamin Bunny: Beatrix Potter Deluxe Pop Up. (Illus.). 1992. 4.99 (*0-517-07001-4*) Random Hse Value.

—Benjamin Bunny's Colors. (Illus.). 24p. (ps). 1994. bds. 2.99 (*0-7232-4118-X*) Warne.

—Birthday Book of Peter Rabbit. (Illus.). 256p. (ps up). 1983. 5.99 (*0-517-40303-X*) Random Hse Value.

—The Complete Adventures of Peter Rabbit. 80p. (ps-3). 1984. pap. 6.95 (*0-14-050444-3*, Puffin) Puffin Bks.

—The Complete Adventures of Peter Rabbit. Potter, Beatrix, illus. 96p. (ps-3). 1987. 12.95 (*0-7232-2951-1*) Warne.

—Complete Tales of Peter Rabbit: And Other Favorite Stories. Santore, Charles, illus. LC 86-10116. 56p. (gr. k up). 1986. 9.98 (*0-89471-460-0*) Courage Bks.

—El Cuento de Pedrito Conejo. Marcuse, Aida, tr. from ENG. McPhail, David, illus. (SPA.). (gr. k-4). 1993. pap. 2.95 (*0-590-46475-2*) Scholastic Inc.

—El Cuento de Pedro, el Conejo - The Tales of Peter Rabbit. (ps-3). 1994. pap. 2.95 (*0-486-27995-2*) Dover.

—El Cuento de Perico, el Conejo Travieso. (SPA., Illus.). 64p. 1988. 5.95 (*0-7232-3556-2*) Warne.

—El Cuento del Conejito Benjamin. (SPA., Illus.). 64p. 1988. 5.95 (*0-7232-3558-9*) Warne.

—Giant Treasury of Peter Rabbit. Wilkins, C., intro. by. (Illus.). 92p. (gr. k-6). 1985. 6.99 (*0-517-31687-0*) Random Hse Value.

—Jeannot Lapin. (FRE.). 58p. 1990. 10.95 (*2-07-056094-5*) Schoenhof.

—Jeannot Lapin. (FRE., Illus.). 58p. 1990. 9.95 (*0-7859-3631-9*, 2070560945) Fr & Eur.

—Little Treasury of Peter Rabbit & His Friends. 1994. 5.95 (*0-517-10084-3*) Random Hse Value.

—Mechant Petit Lapin. (FRE.). (gr. 5-10). 1990. 10.95 (*2-07-056073-2*) Schoenhof.

—Mechant Petit Lapin. (FRE., Illus.). 58p. 1990. 9.95 (*0-7859-3627-0*, 2070560732) Fr & Eur.

—Meet Benjamin Bunny. (Illus.). 12p. (ps). 1987. bds. 2.95 (*0-7232-3451-5*) Warne.

—Meet Peter Rabbit. Potter, Beatrix, illus. 12p. (ps). 1986. bds. 3.50 (*0-7232-3418-3*) Warne.

—Mini Peter Rabbit Bookshop, 23 bks. (Illus.). (ps-3). 1993. Set. 35.00 (*0-7232-3989-4*) Warne.

—My Peter Rabbit Play Box. 1991. bds. 14.95 incl. tape & toy (*0-7232-3794-8*) Warne.

—Original Peter Rabbit Books: 13-23 Presentation Box. 1990. 65.00 (*0-7232-5178-9*) Warne.

—The Original Peter Rabbit Miniature Collection, No. III. (Illus.). (ps-3). 1989. pap. 4.95 set of 4 in slipcase (*0-7232-3984-3*) Warne.

—Original Peter Rabbit Miniature Collection. (Illus.). 1989. Twelve-copy drawer. pap. 18.50 (*0-7232-5173-8*) Warne.

—Original Peter Rabbit Miniature Collection, No. IV. (ps-3). 1990. pap. 4.95 (*0-7232-5076-6*) Warne.

—Original Peter Rabbit Miniature Collection V. (ps-3). 1990. pap. 4.95 (*0-7232-5078-2*) Warne.

—Original Peter Rabbit Miniature Collection VI. (Illus.). (ps-3). 1991. pap. 4.95 (*0-7232-3987-8*) Warne.

—Peter Rabbit. LC 87-24226. (Illus.). 64p. (gr. k-5). 1989. 11.95 (*0-916410-24-2*) A D Bragdon.

—Peter Rabbit. Twinn, Colin, illus. 10p. (ps-5). 1992. 5.99 (*0-7232-3997-5*) Warne.

—Peter Rabbit & Benjamin Bunny Coloring Book. (Illus.). (gr. 1 up). 1987. pap. 1.49 (*0-671-62987-5*, Little Simon) S&S Trade.

—Peter Rabbit & Friends: Three Complete Tales, 3 vols. (Illus.). 178p. (gr. 2 up). 1985. Set. pap. 5.25 (*0-486-24772-4*) Dover.

—Peter Rabbit & His Friends. (Illus.). 24p. (ps). 1994. bds. 2.99 (*0-7232-4093-0*) Warne.

—Peter Rabbit & His Friends Word Book. 1989. 4.99 (*0-517-64156-9*) Random Hse Value.

—Peter Rabbit: Bath Book. 8p. (ps). 1989. 3.99 (*0-7232-3584-8*) Warne.

—Peter Rabbit: Beatrix Potter Deluxe Pop Up. (Illus.). 1992. 4.99 (*0-517-07000-6*) Random Hse Value.

—Peter Rabbit Comes Home. 1988. 2.99 (*0-517-60596-1*) Random Hse Value.

—Peter Rabbit in Mr. McGregor's Garden. 1988. 2.99 (*0-517-60597-X*) Random Hse Value.

—The Peter Rabbit Nursery Frieze. (Illus.). (ps-k). 1989. shrink-wrapped 5.00 (*0-7232-3583-X*) Warne.

—The Peter Rabbit Pop-Up Book. 12p. 1983. 12.99 (*0-7232-2950-3*) Warne.

—The Peter Rabbit Theatre. (Illus.). 16p. (gr. 1). 1992. 6.95 (*0-7232-4006-X*) Warne.

—Peter Rabbit with Many Other Beloved Beatrix Potter Characters Coloring Book. (Illus.). (gr. 1 up). 1987. pap. 1.49 (*0-671-62984-0*, Little Simon) S&S Trade.

—Peter Rabbit's Christmas Book. (ps-3). 1990. pap. 5.95 (*0-7232-3778-6*) Warne.

—Peter Rabbit's Colors. 48p. (ps-k). 1988. 6.95 (*0-7232-3612-7*); frieze 5.00 (*0-7232-3613-5*) Warne.

—Peter Rabbit's One Two Three. (ps-k). 1988. 6.95 (*0-7232-3424-8*) Warne.

—Peter Rabbit's 1 2 3 Frieze. 1988. 5.00 (*0-7232-5630-6*) Warne.

—Pierre Lapin. (FRE.). 62p. 1980. 10.95 (*2-07-056069-4*) Schoenhof.

—Pierre Lapin. (FRE., Illus.). 62p. 1980. 9.95 (*0-7859-3624-6*, 2070560694) Fr & Eur.

—Pierre Lapin: Peter Rabbit. (FRE., Illus.). (gr. 3-7). 1973. 5.00 (*0-7232-0650-3*) Warne.

—The Rabbit's Christmas Party: A. Frieze. (Illus.). 1989. pap. 4.95 (*0-7232-3566-X*) Warne.

—Scenes from the Tale of Peter Rabbit. (Illus.). 1989. 6.95 (*0-7232-3547-3*) Warne.

—The Story of a Fierce Bad Rabbit. 1987. 5.95 (*0-7232-3479-5*); pap. 2.25 (*0-7232-3504-X*) Warne.

—The Story of Miss Moppet. 1987. 5.95 (*0-7232-3480-9*); pap. 2.25 (*0-7232-3505-8*) Warne.

—The Tailor of Gloucester. 1987. 5.95 (*0-7232-3462-0*); pap. 2.25 (*0-7232-3487-6*) Warne.

—The Tale of Benjamin Bunny. Stewart, Pat, illus. LC 74-78812. 59p. (gr. 2 up). 1974. pap. 1.75 (*0-486-21102-9*) Dover.

—The Tale of Benjamin Bunny. Kirk, Tim, illus. LC 80-27468. 32p. (gr. k-3). 1981. PLB 9.79 (*0-89375-484-6*); pap. text ed. 1.95 (*0-89375-485-4*) Troll Assocs.

—The Tale of Benjamin Bunny. Atkinson, Allen, illus. 64p. 1984. pap. 2.25 (*0-553-15203-3*) Bantam.

—The Tale of Benjamin Bunny. (Illus.). 64p. (ps-3). 1986. 3.95 (*0-671-62925-5*, Little Simon) S&S Trade.

—The Tale of Benjamin Bunny. 1987. 5.95 (*0-7232-3463-9*); pap. 2.25 (*0-7232-3488-4*) Warne.

—Tale of Benjamin Bunny. 1988. 2.99 (*0-517-65277-3*) Random Hse Value.

—The Tale of Benjamin Bunny. 1992. 3.99 (*0-517-07240-8*) Random Hse Value.

—The Tale of Benjamin Bunny. (Illus.). 32p. (ps-3). 1994. pap. 3.99 (*0-14-054300-7*) Puffin Bks.

—The Tale of Benjamin Bunny Paint with Water Book. (Illus.). (gr. 1 up). 1987. pap. 1.49 (*0-671-62986-7*, Little Simon) S&S Trade.

—Tale of Benjamin Bunny-Sticker. 1990. pap. 2.95 (*0-671-69254-2*, Little Simon) S&S Trade.

—The Tale of Ginger & Pickles. 1987. 5.95 (*0-7232-3477-9*); pap. 2.25 (*0-7232-3502-3*) Warne.

—The Tale of Johnny Town-Mouse. (ps-3). 1987. 5.95 (*0-7232-3472-8*); pap. 2.25 (*0-7232-3497-3*) Warne.

—The Tale of Little Pig Robinson. 1987. 5.95 (*0-7232-3478-7*); pap. 2.25 (*0-7232-3503-1*) Warne.

—The Tale of Mr. Jeremy Fisher. 1987. 5.95 (*0-7232-3466-3*); pap. 2.25 (*0-7232-3491-4*) Warne.

—The Tale of Mr. Tod. 1987. 5.95 (*0-7232-3473-6*); pap. 2.25 (*0-7232-3498-1*) Warne.

—The Tale of Mrs. Tiggy-Winkle. 1987. 5.95 (*0-7232-3465-5*); pap. 2.25 (*0-7232-3490-6*) Warne.

—The Tale of Mrs. Tittlemouse. 1987. 5.95 (*0-7232-3470-1*); pap. 2.25 (*0-7232-3495-7*) Warne.

—The Tale of Peter Rabbit. (Illus.). 60p. (gr. 1-5). 1972. pap. 1.75 (*0-486-22827-4*) Dover.

—The Tale of Peter Rabbit. Graham, Florence, illus. LC 85-70809. 13p. (ps). 1986. 3.95 (*0-448-10224-2*, G&D) Putnam Pub Group.

—The Tale of Peter Rabbit. McPhail, David, illus. 32p. (Orig.). (gr. k-3). 1986. pap. 2.50 (*0-590-41101-2*); incl. cassette 5.95 (*0-590-63091-1*) Scholastic Inc.

—The Tale of Peter Rabbit. (Illus.). 64p. (ps-3). 1986. 3.95 (*0-671-62924-7*, Little Simon) S&S Trade.

—The Tale of Peter Rabbit. Frenck, Hal, illus. LC 87-40282. 24p. (ps up). 1990. incl. audio cassettes 6.95 (*1-55782-015-5*, Pub. by Warner Juvenile Bks) Little.

—The Tale of Peter Rabbit. Leach, Rosemary, read by. Davis, Carl, contrib. by. (Illus.). (ps-3). 1989. pap. 6.95 incl. tape (*0-7232-3627-5*) Warne.

—The Tale of Peter Rabbit. (ps-3). 1987. 5.95 (*0-7232-3460-4*); pap. 2.25 (*0-7232-3485-X*) Warne.

—Tale of Peter Rabbit. 1988. 2.99 (*0-517-65276-5*) Random Hse Value.

—The Tale of Peter Rabbit. Graham, Florence, illus. 32p. 1991. pap. 2.25 (*0-448-40061-8*, Platt & Munk Pubs) Putnam Pub Group.

—A Tale of Peter Rabbit. Officer, Robyn, illus. 1991. 6.95 (*0-8362-4908-9*) Andrews & McMeel.

—The Tale of Peter Rabbit. (Illus.). 32p. (ps-3). 1992. pap. 3.99 (*0-14-054497-6*, Puffin) Puffin Bks.

—The Tale of Peter Rabbit. 1992. 3.99 (*0-517-07236-X*) Random Hse Value.

—The Tale of Peter Rabbit. deluxe ed. (Illus.). 60p. 1993. 16.00 (*0-7232-4026-4*); Cased set. limited ed. 150.00x (*0-7232-4045-0*) Warne.

—The Tale of Peter Rabbit. Jorgensen, David, illus. LC 92-36655. 64p. 1993. Repr. of 1988 ed. 4.95 (*0-88708-296-3*, Rabbit Ears); incl. cassette 9.95 (*0-88708-297-1*) Picture Bk Studio.

—The Tale of Peter Rabbit. Szekeres, Cyndy, illus. 24p. (ps-3). 1993. 3.50 (*0-307-12349-9*, 12349, Golden Pr) Western Pub.

—The Tale of Peter Rabbit. (Illus.). 24p. (ps-3). 1993. pap. 17.99 (*0-7232-4029-9*) Warne.
—The Tale of Peter Rabbit: A Coloring Book in Signed English. Miller, Ralph R., illus. Roy, Howard L., et al. (Illus.). 64p. (ps-2). 1986. pap. 4.95 (*0-930323-29-7*, Pub. by K Green Pubns) Gallaudet Univ Pr.
—Tale of Peter Rabbit & Other Stories. 1983. pap. 2.25 (*0-553-15202-5*) Bantam.
—The Tale of Peter Rabbit: Die Geschichte Des Peterchen Hase. Werner, Meike, tr. (GER., Illus.). 64p. (Orig.). 1992. pap. 2.75t (*0-486-27014-9*) Dover.
—The Tale of Peter Rabbit: La Storia Del Coniglietto Pietro. Vettori, Alessandro, tr. (ITA., Illus.). 64p. (Orig.). 1992. pap. 2.75t (*0-486-27015-7*) Dover.
—Tale of Peter Rabbit Sticker Book. 1990. pap. 2.95 (*0-671-69255-0*, Little Simon) S&S Trade.
—The Tale of Pigling Bland. 1987. 5.95 (*0-7232-3474-4*); pap. 2.25 (*0-7232-3499-X*) Warne.
—The Tale of Samuel Whiskers. 1987. 5.95 (*0-7232-3475-2*); pap. 2.25 (*0-7232-3500-7*) Warne.
—The Tale of Samuel Whiskers. (Illus.). 32p. (ps-3). 1993. pap. 4.99 (*0-7232-4142-2*) Warne.
—The Tale of Squirrel Nutkin. 1987. 5.95 (*0-7232-3461-2*); pap. 2.25 (*0-7232-3486-8*) Warne.
—The Tale of the Flopsy Bunnies. 64p. (gr. 1 up). 1985. pap. 1.75 (*0-486-24806-2*) Dover.
—The Tale of the Flopsy Bunnies. (Illus.). 64p. (ps-3). 1987. 3.95 (*0-671-63237-X*, Little Simon) S&S Trade.
—The Tale of the Flopsy Bunnies. 1987. 5.95 (*0-7232-3469-8*); pap. 2.25 (*0-7232-3494-9*) Warne.
—The Tale of the Pie & the Patty-Pan. 1987. 5.95 (*0-7232-3476-0*); pap. 2.25 (*0-7232-3501-5*) Warne.
—The Tale of Timmy Tiptoes. 1987. 5.95 (*0-7232-3471-X*); pap. 2.25 (*0-7232-3496-5*) Warne.
—Tales of Peter Rabbit. Santore, Charles, illus. LC 91-52695. 128p. 1991. 4.95 (*1-56138-039-3*) Running Pr.
—Tales of Peter Rabbit & His Friends, 2 vols. in 1. 1988. 7.99 (*0-517-44901-3*) Random Hse Value.
—Tom Kitten: Bath Book. 1989. 3.50 (*0-7232-3585-6*) Warne.
—What Time Is It, Peter Rabbit? (Illus.). (ps-k). 1989. 6.95 (*0-7232-3586-4*); pap. 5.00 (*0-7232-3624-0*) Warne.
—Where's Peter Rabbit? Twinn, Colin, illus. (ps-3). 1988. 6.95 (*0-7232-3519-8*) Warne.
Potter, Beatrix, created by. Benjamin Bunny. Thiewes, Sam, et al, illus. 24p. (gr. 2-4). 1992. PLB 10.95 (*1-56674-006-1*, HTS Bks) Forest Hse.
—The Flopsy Bunnies. Schoonover, pat & Nelson, Anita, illus. 24p. (gr. 2-4). 1992. PLB 10.95 (*1-56674-016-9*, HTS Bks) Forest Hse.
—Peter Rabbit. Schoonover, Pat & Nelson, Anita, illus. 24p. (gr. 2-4). 1992. PLB 10.95 (*1-56674-008-8*, HTS Bks) Forest Hse.
Potter, Beatrix, illus. The Peter Rabbit Sticker Book. rev. ed. 20p. (ps-3). 1991. pap. 6.99 (*0-7232-3979-7*) Warne.
Raichert, Lane. D.C. Hopper, the First Starbunny. Raichert, Lane, illus. LC 91-23055. 32p. (gr. 2-6). 1992. 15.95 (*1-880009-81-1*, DC-P1) Blue Zero Pub.
Ratz De Tagyos, Paul. A Coney Tale. Ratz De Tagyos, Paul, illus. 32p. (gr. k-3). 1992. 14.45 (*0-395-58834-0*, Clarion Bks) HM.
Rees, Ennis. Brer Rabbit & His Tricks. (ps-3). 1990. pap. 5.95 (*0-929077-10-5*) WaterMark Inc.
—Brer Rabbit & His Tricks. LC 93-32674. (Illus.). 56p. (gr. k-5). 1992. Repr. 12.95 (*1-56282-215-2*) Hyprn Child.
—More Brer Rabbit & His Tricks. 1990. pap. 5.95 (*0-929077-11-3*) WaterMark Inc.
—More of Brer Rabbit's Tricks. LC 93-32676. (Illus.). 56p. (gr. k-5). 1992. Repr. 13.95 (*1-56282-217-9*) Hyprn Child.
Reinheimer, Joel. The Adventure of Squeek the Rabbit. 1990. 6.95 (*0-533-08900-X*) Vantage.
Richardson, Jean. Tag-along Timothy Tours Alaska. Eakin, Edwin M., ed. Edington, Jo A., illus. 48p. (gr. 2-3). 1989. 12.95 (*0-89015-706-5*, Pub. by Panda Bks) Sunbelt Media.
Roberts, Bethany. Waiting-for-Christmas Stories. Stapler, Sarah, illus. LC 93-11480. 1994. 13.95 (*0-395-67324-0*) HM.
—Waiting-for-Spring Stories. Joyce, William, illus. LC 83-49486. 32p. (ps-3). 1984. PLB 14.89 (*0-06-025062-3*) HarpC Child Bks.
Roloff, Nan & Flynn, Amy. The Bunnies' Easter Bonnet. Flynn, Amy, illus. LC 94-6728. 1994. 2.25 (*0-448-40739-6*, G&D) Putnam Pub Group.
Ronnie the Rabbit. (Illus.). (ps-1). 2.98 (*0-517-46986-3*) Random Hse Value.
Roos, Stephen. Cottontail Caper: The Pet Lovers Club. (gr. 4-7). 1994. pap. 3.50 (*0-440-40925-X*) Dell.
Rosen, Michael J. Little Rabbit Foo Foo. LC 90-9598. (Illus.). 32p. (ps-1). 1990. pap. 12.95 jacketed (*0-671-70968-2*, S&S BFYR) S&S Trade.
—Little Rabbit Foo Foo. Robins, Arthur, illus. LC 90-9598. 32p. (ps-1). 1993. pap. 4.95 (*0-671-79604-6*, Little Simon) S&S Trade.
Rosenberg, Amye. Good Job, Jelly Bean! (Illus.). 24p. (ps-1). 1992. pap. 2.95 (*0-671-75512-9*, Little Simon) S&S Trade.
—Ten Treats for Ginger. (Illus.). 24p. (ps-1). 1992. pap. 2.95 (*0-671-75511-0*, Little Simon) S&S Trade.
Ross, Katharine. Bunnies' Ball. Bratun, Katy, illus. LC 92-29930. 1994. 2.50 (*0-679-83503-2*); lib. bdg. cancelled (*0-679-93503-7*) Random Bks Yng Read.
Rotunno, Rocco & Rotunno, Betsy. A Trick for Magic Bunny. Rotunno, Betsy, illus. 12p. (gr. 2-6). 1992. Mixed Media Pkg. incls. stamp pad, stamps & box of 4 crayons. 7.00 (*1-881980-02-2*) Noteworthy.
Rowe, John. Rabbit Moon. Rowe, John, illus. LC 92-6047. 28p. 1992. pap. 14.95 (*0-88708-246-7*) Picture Bk Studio.
Ryder, Joanne. Hello, First Grade. Lewin, Betsy, illus. LC 93-9041. 32p. (ps-2). 1993. PLB 9.79 (*0-8167-3008-3*); pap. text ed. 2.95 (*0-8167-3009-1*) Troll Assocs.
Sadler, Marilyn. Bedtime for Bunnies. Bollen, Roger, illus. 14p. (ps). 1994. bds. 3.99 (*0-679-83868-6*) Random Bks Yng Read.
—The Very Bad Bunny. LC 84-3319. (Illus.). 48p. (ps-3). 1984. 6.95 (*0-394-86861-7*); lib. bdg. 7.99 (*0-394-96861-1*) Beginner.
Sanderson, Ruth, illus. The Pudgy Bunny Book. 16p. (gr. k). 1984. 2.95 (*0-448-10210-2*, G&D) Putnam Pub Group.
Sargent, Dave & Sargent, Pat. Chrissy Cottontail. 64p. (gr. 2-6). 1992. pap. write for info. (*1-56763-009-X*) Ozark Pub.
Scarry, Richard. I Am a Bunny. Scarry, Richard, illus. 22p. (gr. k-2). 1967. write for info. (*0-307-12125-9*, Golden Bks.) Western Pub.
—Richard Scarry's Naughty Bunny. (Illus.). 24p. (ps-2). 1989. write for info. (*0-307-12092-9*, Pub. by Golden Bks) Western Pub.
—Watch Your Step, Mr. Rabbit! Scarry, Richard, illus. LC 90-34336. 24p. (Orig.). (ps-2). 1991. pap. 2.25 (*0-679-81072-2*) Random Bks Yng Read.
Scherer, Bonnie. Benjy's New Home. McCracken, Bill, illus. LC 89-60806. 7p. 1989. pap. 1.50 (*0-9622421-0-1*) B Scherer.
Scherer, Bonnie L. The Rescue of Rusty Rabbit. Roberts, Mary & Hendricks, Janie, eds. Thayer, Carolyn, illus. LC 90-63373. 12p. (Orig.). (gr. 1-6). 1991. pap. text ed. write for info. (*0-9622421-1-X*) B Scherer.
Schlachter, Rita. Winter Fun. Swan, Susan, illus. LC 85-14008. 48p. (Orig.). (gr. 1-3). 1986. PLB 10.59 (*0-8167-0584-4*); pap. text ed. 3.50 (*0-8167-0585-2*) Troll Assocs.
Schlein, Miriam. Just Like Me. Janovitz, Marilyn, illus. LC 91-40019. 32p. (ps-2). 1993. 12.95 (*1-56282-233-0*); PLB 12.89 (*1-56282-234-9*) Hyprn Child.
Schoder, Judy. Funny Bunny. Wasserman, Dan, ed. Reese, Bob, illus. (gr. k-1). 1979. 7.95 (*0-89868-069-7*); pap. 2.95 (*0-89868-080-8*) ARO Pub.
Schotter, Roni. Warm at Home. Goldman, Dara, illus. LC 91-48145. 32p. (gr. k-3). 1993. RSBE 14.95 (*0-02-781295-2*, Macmillan Child Bk) Macmillan Child Grp.
Schweninger, Ann. Christmas Secrets. Schweninger, Ann, illus. 32p. (ps-1). 1986. pap. 4.99 (*0-14-050577-6*, Puffin) Puffin Bks.
—Halloween Surprises. Schweninger, Ann, illus. 32p. (ps-1). 1986. pap. 3.99 (*0-14-050634-9*, Puffin) Puffin Bks.
Shetterly, Susan H. Muwin & the Magic Hare. Shetterly, Robert, illus. LC 91-2170. 32p. (gr. 1-5). 1993. SBE 14.95 (*0-689-31699-2*, Atheneum Child Bk) Macmillan Child Grp.
Siegenthaler, Kathrin & Pfister, Marcus. Hopper's Easter Surprise. Pfister, Marcus, illus. Lanning, Rosemary, tr. from GER. LC 92-29117. (Illus.). 32p. (gr. k-3). 1993. 14.95 (*1-55858-199-5*); PLB 14.88 (*1-55858-200-2*) North-South Bks NYC.
Singer, Muff. Bunny's Hungry. LC 93-85485. (ps). 1994. 4.99 (*0-89577-566-2*) RD Assn.
Slater, Helen. Fuzzy Friends: Snuggle the Bunny. (Illus.). 10p. 1993. 3.95 (*0-681-41809-5*) Longmeadow Pr.
Slater, Teddy. The Bunny Hop. Difiori, Larry, illus. 32p. 1992. pap. 2.95 (*0-590-45354-8*, Cartwheel) Scholastic Inc.
—Dining with Prunella. Hearn, Diane D., illus. 24p. (ps-1). 1991. 4.95 (*0-671-72982-9*); PLB 6.95 (*0-671-72981-0*) Silver Pr.
Smath, Jerry. Pretzel & Pop's Closetful of Stories. Smath, Jerry, illus. 64p. (gr. 1-3). 1991. 5.95 (*0-671-72232-8*); PLB 7.95 (*0-671-72231-X*) Silver Pr.
Smee, Nicola. Three Little Bunnies. (Illus.). 10p. (ps). 1994. bds. 6.95 (*0-590-48078-2*, Cartwheel) Scholastic Inc.
Solotaroff, Gregoire. Don't Call Me Little Bunny. LC 88-45430. (Illus.). 32p. (ps up). 1988. 13.95 (*0-374-35012-4*) FS&G.
Sonnenschein, Harriet. Harold's Hideaway Thumb. Obrist, Jurg, illus. 32p. (ps-k). 1993. pap. 2.25 (*0-671-79602-X*, Little Simon) S&S Trade.
—Harold's Hideway Thumb. Obrist, Jurg, illus. LC 91-6486. 40p. (ps-k). 1991. pap. 12.95 jacketed (*0-671-73568-3*, S&S BFYR) S&S Trade.
Stephens, Amanda. Peter Cottontail. Santoro, Christopher, illus. 32p. (ps-3). 1994. pap. 2.50 (*0-590-47761-7*, Cartwheel) Scholastic Inc.
Stevenson, James. The Great Big Especially Beautiful Easter Egg. LC 82-11731. (Illus.). (ps up). 1990. 4.95 (*0-688-09355-8*, Mulberry) Morrow.
Stinson, Kathy. Teddy Rabbit. Poulin, Stephane, illus. 32p. (gr. k-3). 1988. 12.95 (*1-550370-17-0*, Pub. by Annick CN); pap. 4.95 (*1-550370-16-2*, Pub. by Annick CN) Firefly Bks Ltd.
Sundeen, Poppy. Rosie, the Rosedown Rabbit: A Storybook to Color. West, Joanne, ed. & illus. 26p. (Orig.). 1988. pap. text ed. 5.95 (*0-929317-00-9*) Rosedown Plantation.
Supraner, Robyn. Mrs. Wigglesworth's Secret. Harvey, Paul, illus. LC 78-18041. 48p. (gr. 2-4). 1979. 10.89 (*0-89375-097-2*); pap. 3.50 (*0-89375-085-9*) Troll Assocs.
Sweet, Melissa, illus. Hippity-Hop. 18p. (ps). 1992. bds. 2.95 (*0-448-40314-5*) Putnam Pub Group.
Szekeres, Cyndy. Things Bunny Sees. (ps-3). 1990. write for info. (*0-307-11591-7*) Western Pub.
—What Bunny Loves. (ps-3). 1990. write for info. (*0-307-11590-9*) Western Pub.
—What Bunny Loves. Szekeres, Cyndy, illus. (ps-1). 1990. write for info. (Golden Pr) Western Pub.
Tafuri, Nancy. Rabbit's Morning. Tafuri, Nancy, illus. LC 84-10229. 24p. (ps-1). 1985. 13.95 (*0-688-04063-2*); PLB 13.88 (*0-688-04064-0*) Greenwillow.
Tanner, Suzy-Jane. Bunnies & Bear Nature Box. (Illus.). 32p. (ps). 1992. 17.50 (*0-525-44924-8*, DCB) Dutton Child Bks.
Tate, Susan. Bonnie Bunnie's Bicycle. Henium, Marian, illus. 40p. (gr. k-3). 1993. pap. 3.99 (*1-884395-01-5*) Clear Blue Sky.
Taylor, Judy. That Naughty Rabbit. 96p. (ps up). 1987. 15.95 (*0-7232-3442-6*) Warne.
Taylor, Linda L. The Lettuce Leaf Birthday Letter. Durrell, Julie, illus. LC 93-16906. 1994. 13.99 (*0-8037-1454-8*); PLB 13.89 (*0-8037-1455-6*) Dial Bks Young.
Teitelbaum, Michael, retold by. Little Bunny's Magic Nose. Macombi, Turi, illus. (ps-2). 1991. 5.25 (*0-307-15701-6*, Golden Pr) Western Pub.
Thomas, Patricia. Stand Back, Said the Elephant, I'm Going to Sneeze! Tripp, Wallace, illus. LC 89-43215. 32p. (ps-2). 1990. 16.00 (*0-688-09338-8*); lib. bdg. 15.93 (*0-688-09339-6*) Lothrop.
A Tiny Tale of Peter Rabbit. 1985. pap. 2.95 (*0-671-52695-2*, Little Simon) S&S Trade.
Turtle & Rabbit. (Illus.). (ps-2). 1991. PLB 6.95 (*0-8136-5086-0*, TK2374); pap. 3.50 (*0-8136-5586-2*, TK2375) Modern Curr.
Unruh, John. Bright Eyes: The Life of a Baby Jack Rabbit. LC 80-18667. (Illus.). 112p. (Orig.). (gr. 4 up). 1980. pap. 4.95 (*0-914598-02-3*) Padre Prods.
Valloglise, P. Luc. The Search for the Rabbit. 138p. (gr. 7 up). 1988. pap. 10.00 (*0-934852-55-3*) Lorien Hse.
Vanemst, Charlotte. Little Rabbit's Big Day, Vol. 1. (ps-3). 1990. 12.95 (*0-316-89623-3*, Joy St Bks) Little.
Van Leeuwen, Jean. Emma Bean. Wijngaard, Juan, illus. LC 92-29035. 40p. (ps-3). 1993. 13.99 (*0-8037-1392-4*); PLB 13.89 (*0-8037-1393-2*) Dial Bks Young.
Varley, M. C. White Rabbits Can't Jump. LC 93-71350. (gr. 4-7). 1993. pap. 3.95 (*1-56282-516-X*) Disney Pr.
Venturi-Pickett, Stacy. Here Comes Peter Cottontail. Venturi-Pickett, Stacy, illus. 20p. (Orig.). (ps-3). 1994. pap. 7.95 (*0-8249-8656-3*, Ideals Child) Hambleton-Hill.
Violette's Daring Adventure. (Illus.). 32p. (gr. k-3). 1992. PLB 17.27 (*0-8368-0912-2*) Gareth Stevens Inc.
Wahl, Jan. Doctor Rabbit's Foundling. 1990. pap. 3.95 (*0-671-69008-6*, Little Simon) S&S Trade.
—Doctor Rabbit's Lost Scout. 1990. pap. 3.95 (*0-671-69007-8*, Little Simon) S&S Trade.
Waldrop, Ruth. Bunny Rabbits in Mother Gooseland. Hendrix, Hurston H., illus. LC 86-61389. (Orig.). (ps-3). 1987. pap. 4.95 (*0-317-59032-4*); cassette 4.95 (*0-317-59033-2*) RuSk Inc.
Walters, Jennie. Gardening with Peter Rabbit. Potter, Beatrix, illus. 48p. (gr. k-4). 1992. 9.00 (*0-7232-3998-3*) Warne.
Warrener. Bunnykins in the Kitchen. 1987. 4.95 (*0-670-80569-6*) Viking Child Bks.
Wayland, April H. To Rabbittown. Spowart, Robin, illus. (gr. 2-5). 1989. pap. 12.95 (*0-590-40852-6*) Scholastic Inc.
—To Rabbittown. Spowart, Robin, illus. 32p. 1992. pap. 3.95 (*0-590-44777-7*, Blue Ribbon Bks) Scholastic Inc.
Weedn, Flavia. Flavia & the Velveteen Rabbit. (Illus.). 52p. 1990. 16.00 (*0-929632-10-9*) Applause Inc.
Weiss, Jaqueline S. Young Brer Rabbit & Other Trickster Tales from the Americas. Arrowood, Clinton, illus. Pellowski, Anne, intro. by. (Illus.). 80p. (gr. 3-7). 1985. 14.95 (*0-88045-037-1*) Stemmer Hse.
Wells, Rosemary. First Tomato. Wells, Rosemary, illus. LC 91-41599. 32p. (ps-3). 1992. PLB 12.89 (*0-8037-1175-1*) Dial Bks Young.
—The Island Light. Wells, Rosemary, illus. LC 91-41598. 32p. (ps-3). 1992. PLB 12.89 (*0-8037-1178-6*) Dial Bks Young.
—Max & Ruby's First Greek Myth. Wells, Rosemary, illus. LC 92-30332. 32p. (ps-3). 1993. 11.99 (*0-8037-1524-2*); PLB 11.89 (*0-8037-1525-0*) Dial Bks Young.
—Max & Ruby's Midas: Another Greek Myth. LC 94-11181. Date not set. write for info. (*0-8037-1782-2*); PLB write for info. (*0-8037-1783-0*) Dial Bks Young.
—Moss Pillows. Wells, Rosemary, illus. LC 91-41600. 32p. (ps-3). 1992. PLB 12.89 (*0-8037-1177-8*) Dial Bks Young.
—Voyage to the Bunny Planet: First Tomato, Moss Pillows, The Island Light, 3 bks. Wells, Rosemary, illus. 32p. (ps-3). 1992. Boxed Set, 32p. ea. 13.00 (*0-8037-1174-3*) Dial Bks Young.
Where Is Grandma Rabbit? 1989. text ed. 3.95 cased (*0-7214-5231-0*) Ladybird Bks.
Where's Benji Bunny. 1991. pap. 3.99 (*0-517-06141-4*) Random Hse Value.
Wilhelm, Hans. Bad, Bad Bunny Trouble. (ps-3). 1994. 3.95 (*0-590-47916-4*) Scholastic Inc.

—Bunny Trouble. (Illus.). 40p. (Orig.). (ps-3). 1991. 3.95 (*0-590-45042-5*); pap. 6.95 (*0-590-63198-5*); Book & cassette. 6.95 (*0-590-63153-5*) Scholastic Inc.
Willard, Nancy. Starlit Somersault Downhill. (ps-3). 1993. 15.95 (*0-316-94113-1*) Little.
Williams, Garth. Rabbits' Wedding. Williams, Garth, illus. LC 58-5285. 30p. (ps-1). 1958. 15.00 (*0-06-026495-0*) HarpC Child Bks.
Williams, Margery. Classic Tale of the Velveteen Rabbit. 1991. 5.98 (*1-56138-069-5*) Courage Bks.
—Margery Williams "The Velveteen Rabbit" Eastman, David, ed. Schindler, S. D., illus. LC 87-11269. 32p. (gr. k-4). 1988. PLB 9.79 (*0-8167-1061-9*); pap. text ed. 1.95 (*0-8167-1062-7*) Troll Assocs.
—The Velveteen Rabbit. (Illus.). 40p. (gr. 1-9). 1982. pap. 2.95 (*0-380-58156-6*, Flare) Avon.
—Velveteen Rabbit. Nicholson, William, illus. 47p. (gr. 3-5). 1958. PLB (*0-385-07748-3*); pap. 9.95 (*0-385-07725-4*); pap. 15.95 slipcased (*0-385-00913-5*) Doubleday.
—Velveteen Rabbit. Klimo, Kate, ed. Ho, Tien, illus. 48p. 1983. pap. 8.95 (*0-671-44498-0*) S&S Trade.
—The Velveteen Rabbit. Nicholson, William, illus. 40p. (gr. k up). 1979. pap. 2.99 (*0-380-00255-8*, Camelot) Avon.
—The Velveteen Rabbit. LC 81-1454. (Illus.). (ps up). deluxe ed. 7.95 (*0-89471-153-9*); pap. 3.95 (*0-89471-128-8*) Running Pr.
—The Velveteen Rabbit. Jorgensen, David, illus. 48p. (ps up). 1985. with cassette 15.95 (*0-394-87712-8*); 12.00 (*0-394-87711-X*) Knopf Bks Yng Read.
—The Velveteen Rabbit. Green, Michael, illus. LC 89-42996. 88p. (gr. 1-8). 1989. 4.95 (*0-89471-755-3*) Running Pr.
—Velveteen Rabbit. 1988. 5.99 (*0-517-61813-3*) Random Hse Value.
—The Velveteen Rabbit. Jorgensen, David, illus. LC 85-4257. 48p. (ps-2). 1990. pap. 4.99 (*0-679-80333-5*) Knopf Bks Yng Read.
—The Velveteen Rabbit. Chandler, Jean, illus. 1991. Incl. book, cass. & toy rabbit. 14.99 (*0-517-66810-6*) Random Hse Value.
—The Velveteen Rabbit. 40p. 1992. 4.95 (*0-8362-3022-1*) Andrews & McMeel.
—The Velveteen Rabbit: A Board Book. Jorgensen, David, illus. LC 89-63161. 10p. (ps). 1990. bds. 3.95 (*0-679-80644-X*) Random Bks Yng Read.
—The Velveteen Rabbit: Or How Toys Become Real. Green, Michael, illus. LC 81-1454. 48p. (Orig.). (gr. k-12). 1984. 9.98 (*0-89471-266-7*) Courage Bks.
Williams, Marjorie & Culbertson, Roger. The Velveteen Rabbit. Adams, Michael, illus. 12p. 1994. 12.95 (*1-56138-448-8*) Running Pr.
Wise, Francis H. & Wise, Joyce M. Jack, the Rabbit. (Illus.). 21p. (gr. 1). 1976. pap. 1.50 (*0-685-42418-9*) Wise Pub.
Wood, A. J. The Tale of the Napkin Rabbit. Downer, Maggie, illus. LC 93-9864. (gr. 3 up). 1993. 14.95 (*0-307-17603-7*, Artsts Writrs) Western Pub.
Woods, Becky. A Rocky Mountain Rabbit. LC 90-70093. (Illus.). 86p. (gr. 4-8). 1991. 12.95 (*0-932433-65-0*) Windswept Hse.
The World of Peter Rabbit & Friends: Posters. (Illus.). 1993. Set. shrinkwrapped 7.95 (*0-7232-4129-5*) Warne.
Worth, Bonnie. Peter Cottontail's Surprise. Hildebrandt, Greg, illus. LC 84-28031. 48p. (ps-2). 1985. 4.95 (*0-88101-015-4*) Unicorn Pub.
Yazaki, Setsuo. Little Bunny's Christmas Present. Ooka, D. T., tr. from JPN. Kuroi, Ken, illus. 32p. (ps-8). 1983. 11.95 (*0-89346-225-X*) Heian Intl.
Yee, Patrick. Little Buddy Goes Shopping. LC 92-16432. (ps). 1993. 10.95 (*0-670-84804-2*) Viking Child Bks.
—Winter Rabbit. (Illus.). 32p. (ps-1). 1994. 13.99 (*0-670-85383-6*) Viking Child Bks.
Yost, Carolyn K. Mother Rabbit Knew. Gardner, Katherine L., tr. (Illus.). 32p. (gr. k-2). 1989. pasted 2.50 (*0-87403-595-3*, 3855) Standard Pub.
Ziefert, Harriet. Little Bunny's Melon Patch. Ernst, Lisa C., illus. 20p. (ps-3). 1990. pap. 4.95 (*0-14-054262-0*, Puffin) Puffin Bks.
Zolotow, Charlotte. Mister Rabbit & the Lovely Present. Sendak, Maurice, illus. LC 62-7590. (gr. k-3). 1962. 14.00 (*0-06-026945-6*); PLB 13.89 (*0-06-026946-4*) HarpC Child Bks.
—Mr. Rabbit & the Lovely Present. Sendak, Maurice, illus. LC 62-7590. 32p. (ps-3). 1977. pap. 4.95 (*0-06-443020-0*, Trophy) HarpC Child Bks.

RACCOONS

Fair, Jeff. Raccoons for Kids. LC 93-47298. (Illus.). 48p. (gr. k-8). 1994. pap. 6.95 (*1-55971-229-5*) NorthWord.
Hawthorne, Sadie H. Racky. (Illus.). 60p. (gr. k-7). 1992. 10.00 (*0-931647-03-7*) S & B Pubs.
Holmgren, Virginia C. Raccoons: In Folklore, History & Today's Backyards. LC 89-48704. (Illus.). 174p. (Orig.). 1990. pap. 10.95 (*0-88496-312-8*) Capra Pr.
Kostyal, Karen. Raccoons. Crump, Donald J., ed. (Illus.). 32p. (ps-3). 1987. Set. 13.95 (*0-87044-677-0*); Set. lib. bdg. 16.95 (*0-87044-682-7*) Natl Geog.
Nentl, Jerolyn. Raccoon. LC 83-21072. (Illus.). 48p. (gr. 5). 1984. text ed. 12.95 RSBE (*0-89686-246-1*, Crestwood Hse) Macmillan Child Grp.
North, Sterling. Rascal: A Memoir of a Better Era. Shoenherr, John, illus. LC 63-13882. (gr. 4 up). 1984. 13.95 (*0-525-18839-8*, DCB) Dutton Child Bks.
Stone, L. Mapaches (Raccoons) 1991. 8.95s.p. (*0-86592-798-7*) Rourke Enter.
Stone, Lynn. Raccoons. (Illus.). 24p. (gr. k-5). 1990. lib. bdg. 11.94 (*0-86593-045-7*); lib. bdg. 8.95s.p. (*0-685-46450-4*) Rourke Corp.
Weaver, Harriett E. Frosty: A Raccoon to Remember. Dewey, Jennifer O., illus. (gr. 5-7). 1986. pap. 2.50 (*0-671-64088-7*, Archway) PB.

RACCOONS–FICTION

Arnosky, Jim. Raccoons & Ripe Corn. Arnosky, Jim, illus. LC 87-4243. 32p. (ps-3). 1987. 16.00 (*0-688-05455-2*); PLB 15.93 (*0-688-05456-0*) Lothrop.
Barrett, John. Zeke Hatfield & a Ghost Named Rocky. Ruth, Red, illus. (gr. k-10). 1978. 1.99 (*0-686-22892-8*) Silver Dollar.
Boyle, Doe & Thomas, Peter, eds. Big Town Trees: From an Original Article which Appeared in Ranger Rick Magazine, Copyright National Wildlife Federation. Beylon, Cathy, illus. LC 92-34778. 20p. (gr. k-3). 1993. 6.95 (*0-924483-83-0*); incl. audio tape 9.95 (*0-924483-84-9*); incl. audio tape & 13 inch plush toy 35.95 (*0-924483-87-3*); incl. 9 inch plush toy 21.95 (*0-924483-89-X*) Soundprints.
—Rick's First Adventure: From an Original Article Which Appeared in Ranger Rick Magazine, Copyright National Wildlife Federation. Langford, Alton, illus. Luter, Sallie, contrib. by. LC 92-11868. (Illus.). 20p. (gr. k-3). 1992. 6.95 (*0-924483-45-8*); incl. audiocass. tape & 13" toy 35.95 (*0-924483-42-3*); incl. 9" toy 21.95 (*0-924483-43-1*); incl. audiocass. tape 9.95 (*0-924483-44-X*); write for info. audiocass. tape (*0-924483-78-4*) Soundprints.
Brown, Margaret W. Wait till the Moon Is Full. Williams, Garth, illus. LC 48-9278. 32p. (ps-1). 1948. 15.00 (*0-06-020800-7*); PLB 14.89 (*0-06-020801-5*) HarpC Child Bks.
Burgess, Thornton. The Adventures of Bobby Coon. 1992. Repr. lib. bdg. 17.95x (*0-89966-992-1*) Buccaneer Bks.
Burgess, Thornton W. Adventures of Bobby Coon. 18.95 (*0-8488-0383-3*) Amereon Ltd.
Carlson, Nolan. Summer & Shiner. Carlson, John, illus. LC 92-71256. 158p. 1992. pap. text ed. 8.95 (*0-9627947-4-0*) Hearth KS.
Clifford, Eth. Harvey's Mystifying Raccoon Mix-Up. LC 93-27471. 1994. 13.95 (*0-395-68714-4*) HM.
Coleman, Janet W. Fast Eddie. Gillman, Alec, illus. LC 92-31243. 128p. (gr. 3-5). 1993. SBE 13.95 (*0-02-722815-0*, Four Winds) Macmillan Child Grp.
Cosgrove, Stephen. Read on Rita. Edelson, Wendy, illus. 32p. 1993. PLB 12.95 (*1-56674-042-8*, HTS Bks) Forest Hse.
Couderc, Agnes. The Amazing Fate of Raoul Raccoon, Vol. 1. Couderc, Agnes, illus. (ps-3). 1993. 12.95 (*0-316-15829-1*) Little.
Cummings, Pat. Petey Moroni's Camp Runamok Diary. Cummings, Pat, illus. LC 91-45774. 32p. (gr. k-5). 1992. SBE 14.95 (*0-02-725513-1*, Bradbury Pr) Macmillan Child Grp.
Deitz, Lawrence. Jimmy Coon Story Book, No. 1. McCoy, Beverly, illus. 34p. (Orig.). 1985. pap. 2.95 (*0-934750-79-3*) Mntn Memories Bks.
—Jimmy Coon Story Book, No. 2. McCoy, Beverly, illus. 37p. 1985. pap. 2.95 (*0-934750-42-4*) Mntn Memories Bks.
—Jimmy Coon Story Book, No. 5. (Illus.). 40p. (Orig.). (ps up). 1986. pap. 2.95 (*0-938985-02-7*) Mntn Memories Bks.
Greegor, Katherine. Trouble - of the Northwest Territory. Cummins, Lisa, illus. LC 92-61031. 100p. (Orig.). (gr. 3-8). 1992. pap. 5.95 (*0-9633091-7-X*) Promise Land Pubs.
Keane, Glen. Adam Raccoon & the Circusmaster. LC 86-26889. (ps-2). 1987. 6.99 (*1-55513-090-9*, Chariot Bks) Chariot Family.
—Adam Raccoon & the Flying Machine. LC 88-17006. (Illus.). 48p. (ps-2). 1989. 6.99 (*1-55513-287-1*, Chariot Bks) Chariot Family.
—Adam Raccoon & the Mighty Giant. Smith, Julie, ed. Keane, Glen, illus. LC 89-31229. 48p. (gr. 1-3). 1991. 7.99 (*1-55513-362-2*, Chariot Bks) Chariot Family.
—Adam Raccoon at Forever Falls. LC 86-24318. (ps-2). 1987. 6.99 (*1-55513-087-9*, Chariot Bks) Chariot Family.
—Adam Raccoon in Lost Woods. LC 86-30951. (ps-2). 1987. 6.99 (*1-55513-088-7*, Chariot Bks) Chariot Family.
Lassik, Grace E. The Raccoon Connection. rev. ed. Carolock, G. M. & Brown, B. Holborrk, eds. (Illus.). 15p. (ps-2). 1992. pap. 9.95 (*1-880926-00-8*) Four Star SC.
Leonard, Marcia & DeRosa. Little Raccoon Goes to the Beach. (ps-7). 1987. pap. 2.50 (*0-553-15326-9*) Bantam.
McCarthy, Eugene J. Mr. Raccoon & His Friends. Anderson-Miller, Julia, illus. 112p. 1992. 16.00 (*0-89733-377-2*); pap. 6.95 (*0-89733-374-8*) Academy Chi Pubs.
McDonnell, Janet. Raccoon's Adventure in Alphabet Town. Endres, Helen, illus. LC 92-1066. 32p. (ps-2). 1992. PLB 11.80 (*0-516-05418-X*) Childrens.
Maeda, Shintaro. Thomas Raccoon's Fantastic Airshow. Thatch, Nancy R., ed. Maeda, Shintaro, illus. Melton, David, intro. by. (Illus.). 29p. (gr. k-3). 1994. PLB 14.95 (*0-933849-51-6*) Landmark Edns.
Poskanzer, Susan C. Little Raccoon Who Could. Hall, Susan, illus. LC 85-14020. 48p. (Orig.). (gr. 1-3). 1986. PLB 10.59 (*0-8167-0624-7*); pap. text ed. 3.50 (*0-8167-0625-5*) Troll Assocs.
Ricky the Raccoon. (Illus.). (ps-1). 2.98 (*0-517-46985-5*) Random Hse Value.
Roddy, Lee. The Legend of the White Raccoon. 144p. (gr. 3-7). 1986. pap. 4.99 (*0-89693-500-0*, Victor Books) SP Pubns.
Sargent, Dave & Sargent, Pat. Roy Raccoon. 48p. (gr. 2-6). 1992. pap. write for info. (*1-56763-005-7*) Ozark Pub.
Saunders, Dave & Saunders, Julie. Brave Jack. Saunders, Dave, illus. LC 92-23238. 32p. (ps-1). 1993. SBE 14.95 (*0-02-781073-9*, Bradbury Pr) Macmillan Child Grp.
Sharmat, Marjorie W. The Three Hundred Twenty-Ninth Friend. 2nd ed. Szekeres, Cyndy, illus. LC 78-21770. 48p. (gr. k-3). 1992. RSBE 14.95 (*0-02-782259-1*, Four Winds) Macmillan Child Grp.
Stamper, Jamie. Kitty the Raccoon. 2nd ed. Heinonen, Susan, illus. 50p. (gr. k-10). 1989. pap. 8.95 (*0-9623072-0-3*) S Ink WA.
Swan-Brown, Peter, illus. Stories from Toadstool Village. LC 94-13815. (gr. 1 up). 1994. 3.99 (*0-517-11866-1*) Random Bks Yng Read.

RACE

Adams, Pam. All Kinds: Race & Colour. LC 90-45703. (gr. 4 up). 1990. 7.95 (*0-85953-363-8*); pap. 3.95 (*0-85953-353-0*) Childs Play.
Delany, Martin R. Origin of Races & Color: With an Archeological Compendium of Ethiopian & Egyptian Civilization. LC 90-82685. 100p. 1991. 19.95 (*0-933121-51-2*); pap. 8.95 (*0-933121-50-4*) Black Classic.

RACE DISCRIMINATION

see Race Problems

RACE PROBLEMS

see also Discrimination; Immigration and Emigration; Intercultural Education;
also names of countries, cities, etc. with the subdivision Race Relations, e.g. U. S.–Race Relations

Bullard, Sara. Free At Last: A History of the Civil Rights Movement & Those Who Died in the Struggle. Bond, Julian, intro. by. LC 92-38174. (Illus.). 112p. 1993. PLB 20.00 (*0-19-508381-4*) OUP.
Cozic, Charles P., ed. Nationalism & Ethnic Conflict. LC 93-19854. 1994. lib. bdg. 16.95 (*1-56510-080-8*); pap. 9.95 (*1-56510-079-4*) Greenhaven.
Dudley, William & Cozic, Charles. Racism in America: Opposing Viewpoints. LC 91-14293. (Illus.). 240p. (gr. 10 up). 1991. lib. bdg. 17.95 (*0-89908-182-7*); pap. 9.95 (*0-89908-157-6*) Greenhaven.
Hays, Scott. Racism. LC 93-40422. 1994. 14.95 (*1-85435-615-1*) Marshall Cavendish.
Katz, William L. Minorities Today. LC 92-47438. (Illus.). 96p. (gr. 7-8). 1992. PLB 22.80 (*0-8114-6281-1*) Raintree Steck-V.
Kronenwetter, Michael. United They Hate: White Supremacists in America. 133p. 1992. 14.95 (*0-8027-8162-4*); lib. bdg. 15.85 (*0-8027-8163-2*) Walker & Co.
Landau, Elaine. The White Power Movement: America's Racist Hate Groups. LC 92-40920. (Illus.). 96p. (gr. 7 up). 1993. PLB 15.40 (*1-56294-327-8*) Millbrook Pr.
Langone, John J. Spreading Poison: A Book about Racism & Prejudice. LC 92-17847. 1993. 15.95 (*0-316-51410-1*) Little.
Levine, Ellen. Freedom's Children: Young Civil Rights Activists Tell Their Own Stories. 224p. 1993. 16.95 (*0-399-21893-9*) Putnam Pub Group.
McKissack, Patricia & McKissack, Frederick. Taking a Stand Against Racism & Racial Discrimination. LC 89-28627. 1990. PLB 14.40 (*0-531-10924-0*) Watts.
Milios, Ray. Working Together Against Racism. LC 94-1023. 1994. 14.95 (*0-8239-1840-8*) Rosen Group.
Mizell, Linda. Racism. 160p. (gr. 7 up). 1992. PLB 15.85 (*0-8027-8113-6*); pap. 9.95 (*0-8027-7365-6*) Walker & Co.

RACE PROBLEMS–FICTION

Armstrong, William H. Sour Land. LC 70-135783. 128p. (gr. 6 up). 1971. PLB 13.89 (*0-06-020142-8*) HarpC Child Bks.
—Sour Land. LC 70-135783. 128p. (gr. 7 up). 1976. pap. 3.95 (*0-06-440074-3*, Trophy) HarpC Child Bks.
Blume, Judy. Iggie's House. LC 70-104340. 128p. (gr. 4-6). 1982. SBE 13.95 (*0-02-711040-0*, Bradbury Pr) Macmillan Child Grp.
Collier, James L. & Collier, Christopher. Promises to Keep. LC 93-37655. 1994. 15.95 (*0-385-32028-0*) Delacorte.
Gordon, Sheila. Waiting for the Rain. LC 87-7638. 224p. (gr. 7 up). 1987. 12.95 (*0-531-05726-7*); PLB 12.99 (*0-531-08326-8*) Orchard Bks Watts.
Greene, Patricia B. The Sabbath Garden. (Illus.). 192p. (gr. 7 up). 1993. 15.99 (*0-525-67430-6*, Lodestar Bks) Dutton Child Bks.
Hammond, Pearle L. The Prize in the Packard. La Mont, Violet, illus. 100p. (Orig.). (gr. 5-8). 1990. pap. 8.95 (*0-9615161-6-X*) Incline Pr.
Holland, Isabelle. Behind the Lines. LC 93-2576. (Illus.). 240p. (gr. 7 up). 1994. 13.95 (*0-590-45113-8*, Scholastic Hardcover) Scholastic Inc.
Hughes, Dean. End of the Race. LC 92-37747. 160p. (gr. 5 up). 1993. SBE 13.95 (*0-689-31779-4*, Atheneum Child Bk) Macmillan Child Grp.
Hurmence, Belinda. Dixie in the Big Pasture. LC 93-9983. (gr. 4 up). 1994. write for info. (*0-395-52002-9*, Clarion) HM.
Krisher, Trudy. Spite Fences. LC 94-8665. 1994. 14.95 (*0-385-32088-4*) Delacorte.

Martin, Ann M. Hello Mallory. 1993. pap. 3.25 (*0-590-43385-7*) Scholastic Inc.
—Hello, Mallory. large type ed. 176p. (gr. 4 up). 1993. PLB 15.93 (*0-8368-1018-X*) Gareth Stevens Inc.
—Little Miss Stoneybrook-- & Dawn. large type ed. LC 93-8100. 176p. (gr. 4 up). 1993. PLB 15.93 (*0-8368-1019-8*) Gareth Stevens Inc.
Meyer, Carolyn. White Lilacs. LC 92-30503. 1993. write for info. (*0-15-200641-9*) HarBrace.
—White Lilacs. (gr. 4-7). 1993. pap. 3.95 (*0-15-295876-2*, HB Juv Bks) HarBrace.
Miles, Betty. All It Takes Is Practice. LC 76-13057. 128p. (gr. 3-7). 1989. pap. 3.99 (*0-394-82053-3*) Knopf Bks Yng Read.
Nelson, Vaunda M. Mayfield Crossing. Jenkins, Leonard, illus. LC 92-10564. 96p. (gr. 3-7). 1993. 14.95 (*0-399-22331-2*, Putnam) Putnam Pub Group.
Prather, Ray. Fish & Bones. LC 91-44227. 272p. (gr. 5-9). 1992. 14.00 (*0-06-025121-2*); PLB 14.89 (*0-06-025122-0*) HarpC Child Bks.
Sebestyen, Ouida. Words by Heart. 144p. (gr. 4-8). 1983. pap. 3.99 (*0-553-27179-2*, Starfire) Bantam.
Sims, Claudette E. The Rainbow People. Williams, Mauri, illus. (Orig.). (ps-5). 1992. pap. 6.95x (*0-9616121-1-8*) Impressions TX.
Smothers, Ethel F. Moriah's Pond. Ransome, James, illus. LC 94-6490. 128p. (gr. 3-8). 1995. 14.00 (*0-679-84504-6*); lib. bdg. write for info. (*0-679-94504-0*) Knopf Bks Yng Read.
Taylor, Mildred D. The Road to Memphis. 304p. (gr. 5-9). 1992. pap. 3.99 (*0-14-036077-8*, Puffin) Puffin Bks.
Viglucci, Pat C. Cassandra Robbins, Esq. 176p. (Orig.). (gr. 8-12). 1987. pap. 4.95 (*0-938961-01-2*, Stamp Out Sheep Pr) Sq One Pubs.
Woodson, Jacqueline. I Hadn't Meant to Tell You This. LC 93-8733. 1994. 14.95 (*0-385-32031-0*) Delacorte.
Young, Ronder Y. Learning by Heart. LC 92-46887. 1993. 13.95 (*0-395-65369-X*) HM.

RACES OF MAN
see Ethnology

RACIAL BALANCE IN SCHOOLS
see Segregation in Education

RADAR
see also Radar; Sound–Recording and Reproducing
Hitzeroth, Deborah. Radar: The Silent Detector. LC 90-35500. (Illus.). 96p. (gr. 5-8). 1990. PLB 15.95 (*1-56006-201-0*) Lucent Bks.

RADIATION
see also Light; Radioactivity; Sound; X Rays

RADIATION, SOLAR
see Solar Radiation

RADICALS AND RADICALISM
see Reformers; Revolutions

RADIO
Aero Products Research, Inc., Industries Division Staff. Official CB Crossword Puzzles for Big Dummy's. (Illus.). (gr. 8 up). 1977. pap. 1.98 (*0-912682-18-3*) Aero Products.
Balcziak, B. Radio. (Illus.). 48p. (gr. 4-8). 1989. lib. bdg. 17.27 (*0-86592-057-5*); 12.95s.p. (*0-685-58625-1*) Rourke Corp.
Carter, Alden R. Radio: From Marconi to the Space Age. LC 86-23335. (Illus.). 96p. (gr. 4-9). 1987. PLB 10.90 (*0-531-10310-2*) Watts.
Piersel. Photophonics I. (Illus.). (gr. 1-5). 1968. pap. 1.99x (*0-87783-073-8*); tchr's guide 0.29x (*0-685-03702-9*) Oddo.
—Photophonics II. (Illus.). (gr. 1-5). 1968. pap. 2.39x (*0-87783-074-6*); tchr's guide 0.29x (*0-685-03703-7*) Oddo.
Radio. (Illus.). 72p. (gr. 6-12). 1989. pap. 1.85 (*0-8395-3333-0*, 33333) BSA.
Sabin, Louis. Television & Radio. Veno, Joseph, illus. LC 84-8446. 32p. (gr. 3-6). 1985. PLB 9.49 (*0-8167-0310-8*); pap. text ed. 2.95 (*0-8167-0311-6*) Troll Assocs.
Stwertka, Eve & Stwertka, Albert. Tuning in the Sounds of the Radio: The Sounds of the Radio. Dolobowsky, Mena, illus. LC 91-16058. 40p. (gr. 2-5). 1993. lib. bdg. 10.98 (*0-671-69460-X*, J Messner); pap. 5.95 (*0-671-69466-9*, J Messner) S&S Trade.

RADIO–APPARATUS AND SUPPLIES
Becker, Jim & Mayer, Andy. Build Your Own Radio. (Illus.). 64p. (Orig.). (gr. 3 up). 1992. incls. radio kit 19.95 (*1-56138-071-7*) Running Pr.

RADIO–BROADCASTING
see Radio Broadcasting

RADIO–VOCATIONAL GUIDANCE
Chrisfield, Debbie. Radio. LC 93-26393. 1994. text ed. 14.95 (*0-89686-794-3*, Crestwood Hse) Macmillan Child Grp.

RADIO ASTRONOMY
see also names of celestial radio sources, e.g. Quasars

RADIO BROADCASTING
see also Television Broadcasting
Chrisfield, Debbie. Radio. LC 93-26393. 1994. text ed. 14.95 (*0-89686-794-3*, Crestwood Hse) Macmillan Child Grp.
Finkelstein, Norman H. Sounds in the Air: The Golden Age of Radio. LC 92-25354. 144p. (gr. 7 up). 1993. SBE 14.95 (*0-684-19271-3*, Scribners Young Read) Macmillan Child Grp.
Hautzig, David. DJs, Ratings, & Hook Tapes: Pop Music Broadcasting. Hautzig, David, illus. LC 91-33588. 48p. (gr. 3-7). 1993. SBE 15.95 (*0-02-743471-0*, Macmillan Child Bk) Macmillan Child Grp.
Russell, William. Broadcasters. LC 93-44982. 1994. write for info. (*1-57103-054-9*) Rourke Pr.
Wong, Michael A. A Day in the Life of a Disc Jockey. Jann, Gayle, illus. LC 87-10943. 32p. (gr. 4-8). 1988. PLB 11.79 (*0-8167-1125-9*); pap. text ed. 2.95 (*0-8167-1126-7*) Troll Assocs.

RADIO JOURNALISM
see Journalism; Radio Broadcasting

RADIO SCRIPTS
Adorjan, Carol & Rasovsky, Yuri. WKID: Easy Radio Plays. LC 88-132. (Illus.). 80p. (gr. 3-8). 1988. 9.95 (*0-8075-9155-6*) A Whitman.

RADIO SHACK COMPUTERS
see Trs-80 Computers

RADIOACTIVE SUBSTANCE
see Radioactivity

RADIOACTIVE WASTES
Nuclear Waste: The Biggest Clean-up in History. McCuen, Gary, ed. (Illus.). 150p. 1990. lib. bdg. 12.95 (*0-86596-076-3*) G E M.

RADIOACTIVITY
see also Nuclear Physics; X Rays
Dolan, Edward F. & Scariano, Margaret M. Nuclear Waste: The Ten Thousand-Year Challenge. LC 90-34586. (Illus.). 128p. (gr. 9-12). 1990. PLB 14.40 (*0-531-10943-7*) Watts.
Gardiner, Brian. Nuclear Waste. LC 91-30536. (Illus.). 32p. (gr. 2-4). 1992. PLB 11.90 (*0-531-17351-8*, Gloucester Pr) Watts.
Hare, Tony. Nuclear Waste Disposal. (Illus.). (gr. 4-8). 1991. PLB 12.40 (*0-531-17291-0*) Watts.
Milne, Lorus J. & Milne, Margery. Understanding Radioactivity. Hiscock, Bruce, illus. LC 88-7382. 80p. (gr. 4 up). 1989. SBE 14.95 (*0-689-31362-4*, Atheneum Child Bk) Macmillan Child Grp.

RADIOCARBON DATING
Liptak, Karen. Dating Dinosaurs & Other Old Things. LC 91-23072. (Illus.). 72p. (gr. 7 up). 1992. PLB 14.40 (*1-56294-134-8*) Millbrook Pr.

RADIOGRAPHY
see X Rays

RADIUM
see also Radioactivity

RAILROADS
see also Subways
Ammon, Richard. Trains at Work. Ammon, Richard, illus. Peterson, Darrell, photos by. LC 92-33913. (Illus.). 32p. (gr. 1-5). 1993. SBE 14.95 (*0-689-31740-9*, Atheneum Child Bk) Macmillan Child Grp.
Barkan, Joanne. Caboose. Walz, Richard, illus. 12p. (ps-k). 1992. pap. 3.50 POB (*0-689-71574-9*, Aladdin) Macmillan Child Grp.
—Passenger Car. Walz, Richard, illus. 12p. (ps-k). 1992. pap. 3.50 (*0-689-71575-7*, Aladdin) Macmillan Child Grp.
Barton, Byron. Trains. Barton, Byron, illus. LC 85-47898. 32p. (ps-k). 1986. 6.95 (*0-694-00061-2*, Crowell Jr Bks); PLB 13.89 (*0-690-04534-4*) HarpC Child Bks.
Bentley, Judith. Railroad Workers & Loggers. (Illus.). 96p. (gr. 5-8). 1995. bds. 16.95 (*0-8050-2997-4*) TFC Bks NY.
Bowler, Mike. Trains. Herridge, Steve & Higgens, Paul, illus. LC 94-9029. 1994. write for info. (*0-8114-6192-0*) Raintree Steck-V.
Broekel, Ray. Trains. (Illus.). 48p. (gr. k-4). 1981. PLB 12.85 (*0-516-01652-0*); pap. 4.95 (*0-516-41652-9*) Childrens.
Chlad, Dorothy. Stop, Look, & Listen for Trains. LC 83-7213. (Illus.). 32p. (ps-2). 1983. pap. 3.95 (*0-516-41988-9*) Childrens.
Coiley, John. Train. Dunning, Mike, photos by. LC 92-4711. (Illus.). 64p. (gr. 5 up). 1992. 16.00 (*0-679-81684-4*); PLB 16.99 (*0-679-91684-9*) Knopf Bks Yng Read.
Cooper, J. Trains. 1991. 8.95s.p. (*0-86592-490-2*) Rourke Enter.
—Trenes (Trains) 1991. 8.95s.p. (*0-86592-515-1*) Rourke Enter.
Crews, Donald. Freight Train. LC 78-2303. (Illus.). 32p. (gr. k-3). 1978. 16.00 (*0-688-80165-X*); PLB 14.88 (*0-688-84165-1*) Greenwillow.
Dale, Rodney. Early Railways. (Illus.). 64p. 1994. PLB 16.00 (*0-19-521003-4*) OUP.
Dreher, Jean. Iron Horses-Iron Men. (Illus.). 130p. (gr. 10 up). 1984. 12.95 (*0-912113-20-0*); pap. 5.95 (*0-912113-21-9*) Railhead Pubns.
Fisher, Bill. Thirty Years over Donner. LC 90-22185. (Illus.). 198p. (Orig.). (gr. 11). 1991. (Pub. by Trans-Anglo); pap. 19.95 (*0-87046-102-8*, Pub. by Trans-Anglo) Interurban.
Gibbons, Gail. Trains. LC 86-19595. (Illus.). 32p. (ps-3). 1987. reinforced bdg. 15.95 (*0-8234-0640-7*); pap. 5.95 (*0-8234-0699-7*) Holiday.
Griffiths, Rose. Railways. Millard, Peter, photos by. (Illus.). 32p. (gr. 1 up). 1995. PLB 17.27 (*0-8368-1182-8*) Gareth Stevens Inc.
Harvey, T. Railroads. LC 79-5062. (Illus.). 36p. (gr. 3-6). 1980. PLB 13.50 (*0-8225-1184-3*, First Ave Edns); pap. 4.95 (*0-8225-9539-7*, First Ave Edns) Lerner Pubns.
Kanetzke, Howard W. Trains & Railroads. rev. ed. LC 87-20813. (Illus.). 48p. (gr. 2-6). 1987. PLB 10.95 (*0-8172-3263-X*); pap. 4.95 (*0-8114-8222-7*) Raintree Steck-V.
Matthews, L. Railroaders. (Illus.). 32p. (gr. 3-8). 1989. PLB 18.00 (*0-86625-366-1*); 13.50s.p. (*0-685-67677-3*) Rourke Corp.
Prunier, James. Livre des Trains. (FRE.). 93p. (gr. 4-9). 1986. 15.95 (*2-07-039527-8*) Schoenhof.
Railroading. (Illus.). 48p. (gr. 6-12). 1978. pap. 1.85 (*0-8395-3292-X*, 33292) BSA.
Repp, T. O. Main Streets of the Northwest. LC 89-15467. (Illus.). 160p. (gr. 11). 1989. 19.95 (*0-87046-085-4*, Pub. by Trans-Anglo) Interurban.
Richardson, Joy. Trains. LC 93-49731. (Illus.). 1994. write for info. (*0-531-14327-9*) Watts.
Rockwell, Anne. Trains. 1994. pap. 4.50 (*0-14-054979-X*, Puff Unicorn) Puffin Bks.
San Souci, Robert D. & Ginsburg, Max. Kate Shelley: Bound for Legend. LC 93-20438. (gr. 4-7). 1994. write for info. (*0-8037-1289-8*); write for info. (*0-8037-1290-1*) Dial Bks Young.
Scarry, Richard. Richard Scarry's Trains. (Illus.). 24p. (ps-k). 1992. pap. write for info. (*0-307-11536-4*, 11536, Golden Pr) Western Pub.
Warburton, Lois. Railroads: Bridging the Continents. LC 91-23857. (Illus.). 96p. (gr. 5-8). 1991. PLB 15.95 (*1-56006-216-9*) Lucent Bks.
Wood, Sydney. Trains & Railroads. LC 91-58201. (Illus.). 64p. (gr. 3 up). 1992. 11.95 (*1-56458-001-6*); PLB 12.99 (*1-56458-002-4*) Dorling Kindersley.
Young, C. Railways & Trains. (Illus.). 48p. (gr. 2 up). 1992. lib. bdg. 13.96 (*0-88110-441-8*, Usborne); pap. 7.95 (*0-7460-0467-2*, Usborne) EDC.

RAILROADS–FICTION
Ada, Alma F., tr. La Pequena Locomotora Que Si Pudo: The Little Engine That Could. Hauman, George & Hauman, Doris, illus. (SPA.). 48p. (ps-6). 1992. 5.95 (*0-448-41096-6*, Platt & Munk Pubs) Putnam Pub Group.
Ahlberg, Allan. The Ghost Train. Amstutz, Andre, illus. LC 91-39838. 32p. (ps-6). 1992. 14.00 (*0-688-11435-0*) Greenwillow.
Awdry, Rev W. The Midnight Ride of Thomas the Tank Engine. Bell, Owain, illus. LC 93-26587. 16p. (ps-1). 1994. pap. 5.99 (*0-679-85643-9*) Random Bks Yng Read.
Awdry, W. Breakfast-Time for Thomas: Based on the Railway Series. Bell, Owain, illus. LC 89-62527. 32p. (Orig.). (ps-3). 1990. pap. 1.50 (*0-679-80409-9*) Random Bks Yng Read.
—A Cow on the Line & Other Thomas the Tank Engine Stories. Mitton, David & Permane, Terry, photos by. LC 91-21706. (Illus.). 32p. (Orig.). (ps-3). 1992. PLB 5.99 (*0-679-91977-5*); pap. 2.50 (*0-679-81977-0*) Random Bks Yng Read.
—A Cow on the Line & Other Thomas the Tank Engine Stories. Starr, Ringo, narrated by. Mitton, David & Permane, Terry, photos by. (Illus.). 32p. (ps-3). 1992. pap. 5.95 incl. cass. (*0-679-83476-1*) Random Bks Yng Read.
—Diesel's Devious Deed & Other Thomas the Tank Engine Stories. Mitton, David & Permane, Terry, photos by. LC 91-21133. (Illus.). 32p. (Orig.). (ps-3). 1992. PLB 5.99 (*0-679-91976-7*); pap. 2.50 (*0-679-81976-2*) Random Bks Yng Read.
—Diesel's Devious Deed & Other Thomas the Tank Engine Stories. Starr, Ringo, narrated by. Mitton, David & Permane, Terry, photos by. (Illus.). 32p. (ps-3). 1992. pap. 6.95 incl. cass. (*0-679-83474-5*) Random Bks Yng Read.
—Duck Takes Charge. Mitton, David & Permane, Terry, photos by. LC 92-45564. (Illus.). 32p. (ps-2). 1993. 3.50 (*0-679-84763-4*) Random Bks Yng Read.
—Edward, Trevor, & the Really Useful Party. Mitton, David & Permane, Terry, photos by. LC 93-86346. (Illus.). 16p. (ps-k). 1994. bds. 3.99 (*0-679-86186-6*) Random Bks Yng Read.
—Gordon and the Famous Visitor. Mitton, David & Permane, Terry, photos by. LC 92-45569. (Illus.). 32p. (ps-2). 1993. 3.50 (*0-679-84764-2*) Random Bks Yng Read.
—Gordon's Trouble with Mud. Mitton, David & Permane, Terry, photos by. (Illus.). 16p. (ps-k). 1994. bds. 3.99 (*0-679-86185-8*) Random Bks Yng Read.
—Henry the Green Engine & the Tunnel. Spong, Clive, illus. LC 91-67968. 12p. (ps-1). 1992. 3.99 (*0-679-83451-6*) Random Bks Yng Read.
—Henry's Forest. Mitton, David & Permane, Terry, photos by. (Illus.). 16p. (ps-k). 1994. bds. 3.99 (*0-679-86184-X*) Random Bks Yng Read.
—James & the Foolish Freight Cars. LC 91-8035. (Illus.). 32p. (ps-2). 1991. 3.50 (*0-679-82086-8*) Random Bks Yng Read.
—James the Red Engine. Bell, Owain, illus. 7p. (ps-k). 1991. bds. 7.00 with plastic wheels (*0-679-81590-2*) Random Bks Yng Read.
—Meet Thomas the Tank Engine & His Friends. McArthur, Kenny, et al, illus. LC 89-32299. 32p. (ps-1). 1989. 6.95 (*0-679-80102-2*) Random Bks Yng Read.
—Percy Runs Away. LC 91-8707. (Illus.). 32p. (ps-2). 1991. 3.50 (*0-679-82087-6*) Random Bks Yng Read.
—Percy the Small Engine Takes the Plunge. Spong, Clive, illus. LC 91-67970. 12p. (ps-1). 1992. 3.99 (*0-679-83453-2*) Random Bks Yng Read.
—Percy's Promise. Mitton, David & Permane, Terry, photos by. LC 92-43773. (Illus.). 32p. (ps-2). 1993. 3.50 (*0-679-84765-0*) Random Bks Yng Read.
—Los Problemas de Tomas y Otros Cuentos. Saunders, Paola B., tr. LC 93-35947. (Illus.). 32p. (ps-3). 1994. pap. 2.50 (*0-679-85392-8*) Random Bks Yng Read.
—Surprise, Thomas! A Thomas the Tank Engine Book. Bell, Dwain, illus. 22p. (ps-k). 1994. 3.50 (*0-679-85446-0*) Random Bks Yng Read.

—Thomas & the Freight Train. Bell, Owain, illus. LC 90-62371. 22p. (ps). 1991. bds. 3.25 (*0-679-81599-6*) Random Bks Yng Read.

—Thomas & the Hide-&-Seek Animals: A Thomas the Tank Engine Flap Book. Bell, Owain, illus. LC 90-62114. 24p. (ps-1). 1991. 7.95 (*0-679-81316-0*) Random Bks Yng Read.

—Thomas & Trevor. Mitton, David & Permane, Terry, photos by. LC 92-43774. (Illus.). 32p. (ps-2). 1993. 3.50 (*0-679-84766-9*) Random Bks Yng Read.

—Thomas Gets Bumped. LC 93-23326. (Illus.). 32p. 1994. 3.50 (*0-679-86045-2*) Random Bks Yng Read.

—Thomas Gets Tricked & Other Stories: Based on the Railway Series. McArthur, Kenny, photos by. LC 89-8502. (Illus.). 32p. (ps-3). 1989. PLB 5.99 (*0-679-90100-0*); pap. 2.50 (*0-679-80100-6*) Random Bks Yng Read.

—Thomas Gets Tricked & Other Stories. McArthur, Kenny, et al, photos by. Starr, Ringo, contrib. by. (Illus.). 32p. (Orig.). (ps-2). 1991. pap. 6.95 incl. 20-min. cassette (*0-679-80108-1*) Random Bks Yng Read.

—Thomas, Percy, & the Dragon. Mitton, David & Permane, Terry, photos by. (Illus.). 16p. (ps-k). 1994. bds. 3.99 (*0-679-86183-1*) Random Bks Yng Read.

—Thomas the Tank Engine ABC: (Just Right for 2's & 3's) McArthur, Kenny, photos by. LC 89-10605. (Illus.). 24p. (ps). 1990. 5.99 (*0-679-80362-9*) Random Bks Yng Read.

—Thomas the Tank Engine & the Great Race. Bell, Owain, illus. 7p. (ps-k). 1989. bds. 7.00 with plastic wheels (*0-679-80000-X*) Random Bks Yng Read.

—Thomas the Tank Engine & the School Trip. Bell, Owain, illus. LC 92-33711. 32p. (ps-1). 1993. PLB 7.99 (*0-679-94365-X*); pap. 3.50 (*0-679-84365-5*) Random Bks Yng Read.

—Thomas the Tank Engine & the Tractor. Spong, Clive, illus. LC 91-67969. 12p. (ps-1). 1992. 3.99 (*0-679-83452-4*) Random Bks Yng Read.

—Thomas the Tank Engine Goes Fishing. Spong, Clive, illus. LC 91-67967. 12p. (ps-1). 1992. 3.99 (*0-679-83450-8*) Random Bks Yng Read.

—Thomas the Tank Engine Take-along Library, 5 bks. McArthur, Kenny, et al, photos by. (Illus.). (ps-3). 1992. Boxed set incls. A Cow on the Line & Other Stories, Thomas Gets Tricked & Other Stories, Diesel's Devious Deed & Other Stories, Trouble for Thomas & Other Stories, & Catch Me! Catch Me!, 32p. ea. 11.50 (*0-679-83840-6*) Random Bks Yng Read.

—Thomas the Tank Engine Visits a Farm. Bell, Owain, illus. 10p. (ps). 1991. vinyl 3.95 (*0-679-81580-5*) Random Bks Yng Read.

—Thomas the Tank Engine's Noisy Trip. Bell, Owain, illus. LC 89-60089. 28p. 1989. bds. 2.95 (*0-679-80083-2*) Random Bks Yng Read.

—Thomas's Big Railway Pop-up Book. Bell, Owain, illus. 14p. (ps up). 1992. 13.00 (*0-679-83465-6*) Random Bks Yng Read.

—Thomas's Carousel Book. Bell, Owain, illus. 5p. (ps-3). 1993. 8.00 (*0-679-84819-3*) Random Bks Yng Read.

—Toby the Tram Engine. LC 91-7770. (Illus.). 32p. (ps-2). 1991. 3.50 (*0-679-82095-7*) Random Bks Yng Read.

—Toby's Tightrope. LC 93-6292. (Illus.). (ps-2). 1994. 3.50 (*0-679-86047-9*) Random Bks Yng Read.

—Tracking Thomas the Tank Engine & His Friends: A Book with Finger Tabs. Stott, Ken, illus. LC 91-67876. 16p. (ps-1). 1992. bds. 7.99 (*0-679-83458-3*) Random Bks Yng Read.

—Trouble for Thomas & Other Stories. reissue ed. McArthur, Kenny, et al, photos by. Starr, Ringo, contrib. by. (Illus.). 32p. (ps-2). 1991. incl. 20-min. cassette 6.95 (*0-679-80106-5*) Random Bks Yng Read.

—Trouble for Thomas & Other Stories: Based on the Railway Series. McArthur, Kenny, photos by. LC 89-8503. (Illus.). 32p. (ps-3). 1989. pap. 2.50 (*0-679-80101-4*) Random Bks Yng Read.

Awdry, W., created by. Thomas the Tank Engine Storybook. Mitton, David & Permane, Terry, photos by. LC 92-35915. (Illus.). 1993. 8.00 (*0-679-84465-1*) Random Bks Yng Read.

Awdry, W. J. Las Travesuras de Tomas y Otros Cuentos (Thomas Gets Tricked) Saunders, Paola B., tr. LC 93-35948. (Illus.). (ps-3). 1994. pap. 2.50 (*0-679-85391-X*) Random Bks Yng Read.

Aylesworth, Jim. Country Crossing. Rand, Ted, illus. LC 89-78184. 32p. (ps-2). 1991. SBE 13.95 (*0-689-31580-5*, Atheneum Child Bk) Macmillan Child Grp.

Bell, Owain. Stop, Train, Stop! A Thomas the Tank Engine Story. LC 94-15129. (gr. 1 up). 1995. 6.95 (*0-679-85806-7*); 7.99 (*0-679-95806-1*) Beginner.

Bell, Owain, illus. Wave Hello to Thomas! A Thomas the Tank Engine Lift-&-Peek-a-Board Book. Awdry, W., contrib. by. LC 92-80747. (Illus.). 14p. (ps-k). 1993. bds. 4.50 (*0-679-83877-5*) Random Bks Yng Read.

Bibliotheca Press Staff. Posie the Positive Train: Story Edition. (gr. 4-9). 1990. 12.95 (*0-939476-27-4*, Pub. by Biblio Pr GA); pap. 9.95 (*0-939476-28-2*, Pub. by Biblio Pr GA) Prosperity & Profits.

Billout, Guy. The Journey. Billout, Guy, illus. LC 93-17094. 1993. PLB 16.95 (*0-88682-626-8*) Creative Ed.

Brown. Trick Train Ride. (gr. 4-8). 1989. PLB 8.49 (*0-685-70384-3*); pap. 1.95 (*0-87386-065-9*) Jan Prods.

Brown, Margaret W. Two Little Trains. LC 84-43138. 40p. 1986. PLB 12.89 (*0-06-020768-X*) HarpC Child Bks.

Burningham, John. Hey! Get off Our Train. Burningham, John, illus. LC 89-15802. 48p. (ps-4). 1990. 16.00 (*0-517-57638-4*) Crown Bks Yng Read.

Burton, Virginia L. Choo Choo: The Story of a Little Engine Who Ran Away. Burton, Virginia L., illus. LC 37-19461. 56p. (Orig.). (gr. k-8). 1988. pap. 4.80 (*0-395-47942-8*) HM.

Cohen, Daniel. Railway Ghosts & Highway Horrors. Marchesi, Stephen, illus. LC 91-11161. 112p. (gr. 4 up). 1991. 13.95 (*0-525-65071-7*, Cobblehill Bks) Dutton Child Bks.

—Railway Ghosts & Railway Horrors. 112p. (gr. 3-7). 1993. pap. 2.95 (*0-590-45423-4*, Apple Paperbacks) Scholastic Inc.

Crews, Donald. Freight Train. LC 78-2303. (Illus.). 24p. (ps up). 1992. pap. 3.95 (*0-688-11701-5*, Mulberry) Morrow.

—Freight Train: Big Book Edition. (ps up). 1993. pap. 18.95 (*0-688-12940-4*, Mulberry) Morrow.

—Shortcut. LC 91-36312. (Illus.). 32p. (ps-6). 1992. 14.00 (*0-688-06436-1*); PLB 13.93 (*0-688-06437-X*) Greenwillow.

Cross, Genevieve. The Engine That Lost Its Whistle. 10th ed. Cross, Genevieve, illus. 32p. (gr. 1-3). 1988. pap. 12.50 (*0-9621162-0-3*) Van Buren Cty Hist Soc.

Cross, Gilbert B. Terror Train! LC 93-25735. 128p. (gr. 3-7). 1994. pap. 3.95 (*0-689-71765-2*, Aladdin) Macmillan Child Grp.

Damashek, Sandy. Teeny-Tiny Train & Planes, 6 bks. Filippo, Margaret S., illus. (ps-k). 1992. bds. 14.95 (*1-56293-241-1*, Set, mini-board bks. in a tray) McClanahan Bk.

French, Susan M. The Magic Train. Lynn, Patty, illus. 24p. (Orig.). (gr. k-1). 1990. pap. 0.99 (*1-878624-33-4*) McClanahan Bk.

Gauch, Patricia L. Christina Katerina & the Great Bear Train. Primavera, Elise, illus. 32p. 1990. 14.95 (*0-399-21623-5*, Putnam) Putnam Pub Group.

Goble, Paul. Death of the Iron Horse. Goble, Paul, illus. LC 85-28011. 32p. (gr. k-3). 1987. SBE 14.95 (*0-02-737830-6*, Bradbury Pr) Macmillan Child Grp.

—Death of the Iron Horse. Goble, Paul, illus. LC 92-1723. 32p. (ps-3). 1993. pap. 4.95 (*0-689-71686-9*, Aladdin) Macmillan Child Grp.

Green, Suzanne. The Little Choo-Choo: Sounds, Sights & Opposites. Fujita, Miho, illus. 14p. (ps-k). 1988. pap. 8.95 incl. pull toy (*0-385-24426-6*) Doubleday.

Gunning, Thomas G. Dream Trains. LC 92-9802. (Illus.). 72p. (gr. 3 up). 1992. text ed. 14.95 RSBE (*0-87518-558-4*, Dillon) Macmillan Child Grp.

Hamilton, Dorothy. The Blue Caboose. Needler, Jerry, illus. LC 72-5474. 135p. (gr. 3-6). 1973. pap. 3.95 (*0-8361-1696-8*) Herald Pr.

Heller, Nicholas. Peas. LC 92-29740. 24p. 1993. 14.00 (*0-688-12406-2*); PLB 13.93 (*0-688-12407-0*) Greenwillow.

Hillert, Margaret. Little Puff. (Illus.). (ps-2). 1973. PLB 6.95 (*0-8136-5014-3*, TK2328); pap. 3.50 (*0-8136-5514-5*, TK2329) Modern Curr.

Hines, Gary. A Ride in the Crummy. Hines, Anna G., illus. LC 90-30848. 24p. (ps up). 1991. 13.95 (*0-688-09691-3*); PLB 13.88 (*0-688-09692-1*) Greenwillow.

Hooks, William H. The Mighty Santa Fe. Thomas, Angela T., illus. LC 92-17026. 32p. (gr. k-3). 1993. RSBE 14.95 (*0-02-744432-5*, Macmillan Child Bk) Macmillan Child Grp.

Howard, Elizabeth F. Mac & Marie & the Train Toss Surprise. Carter, Gail G., illus. LC 92-17918. 32p. (ps-2). 1993. RSBE 14.95 (*0-02-744640-9*, Four Winds) Macmillan Child Grp.

—The Train to Lulu's. Casilla, Robert, illus. LC 86-33429. 32p. (ps-2). 1988. RSBE 14.95 (*0-02-744620-4*, Bradbury Pr) Macmillan Child Grp.

—The Train to Lulu's. Castille, Robert, illus. LC 93-25565. 32p. (gr. k-2). 1994. pap. 4.95 (*0-689-71797-0*, Aladdin) Macmillan Child Grp.

Johnson, John E., illus. Here Comes the Train. 14p. (gr. 2-5). 1985. 4.99 (*0-394-87551-6*) Random Bks Yng Read.

Keats, Ezra J. John Henry: An American Legend. Schwartz, Anne, ed. LC 65-11444. (Illus.). 32p. (ps-3). 1987. lib. bdg. 12.99 (*0-394-99052-8*); pap. 5.00 (*0-394-89052-3*) Knopf Bks Yng Read.

Ketchum, Mary. The Clapper Rail. 1994. write for info. (*0-8050-2359-3*) H Holt & Co.

Knobbe, Jeff C. The Train. 16p. (gr. 4 up). 1993. pap. 3.95 (*0-9630328-0-1*); 7.95 (*0-9630328-5-2*) SDPI.

Kontoyiannaki, Kosta. Ralph Takes a Train Ride. Kontoyiannaki, Kosta, illus. 18p. (gr. k-3). 1992. pap. 13.95 (*1-895583-24-1*) MAYA Pubs.

Kreeger, Charlene. The Loop Train. Cartwright, Shannon, illus. 48p. 1991. pap. 11.95 (*0-933914-02-4*) Lone Raven.

Kreloff, Elliot, illus. Trains. (ps-k). 1993. Set, lg. bk. 12p., small bk. 6p. bds. 4.95 (*1-56293-357-4*) McClanahan Bk.

Krensky, Stephen. The Iron Dragon Never Sleeps. Fulweiler, Frank, illus. LC 93-31167. 1994. 13.95 (*0-385-31171-0*) Delacorte.

Lewis, Kim. The Last Train. LC 93-32370. (Illus.). 32p. (ps up). 1994. 14.95 (*1-56402-343-5*) Candlewick Pr.

Lippman, Peter. Busy Trains. Lippman, Peter, illus. LC 77-86145. 32p. (ps-3). 1981. lib. bdg. 5.99 (*0-394-93748-1*); pap. 2.25 (*0-394-83748-7*) Random Bks Yng Read.

The Little Engine That Could. 48p. (gr. 1-7). 1978. deluxe ed. 8.95 (*0-448-47373-9*, G&D) Putnam Pub Group.

Little Red Caboose. 1986. 1.30 (*0-307-02152-1*) Western Pub.

London, Jonathan. The Owl Who Became the Moon. Rand, Ted, illus. LC 92-14699. (ps-2). 1993. 13.99 (*0-525-45054-8*, DCB) Dutton Child Bks.

Lyon, George E. A Regular Rolling Noah. Gammell, Stephen, illus. LC 90-39984. 32p. (gr. k-3). 1991. pap. 4.95 (*0-689-71449-1*, Aladdin) Macmillan Child Grp.

McPhail, David. Moony B. Finch, Fastest Draw in the West. LC 93-37408. 1994. lib. bdg. 12.95 (*0-307-17554-5*, Artsts Writrs) Western Pub.

—The Train. (gr. 3-6). 1977. lib. bdg. 15.95 (*0-316-56316-1*, Joy St Bks) Little.

Martin, Lillian. Nosey Rides the Train. Martin, J. V., illus. 22p. (ps-4). 1992. pap. 3.95 (*1-881079-04-X*) Antex Corp.

Mavis. LC 93-23328. 32p. (ps-2). 1994. 3.50 (*0-679-86044-4*) Random Bks Yng Read.

Merriam, Eve. Train Leaves the Station. Gottlieb, Dale, illus. LC 91-28009. 32p. (ps-k). 1992. 14.95 (*0-8050-1934-0*, B Martin BYR) H Holt & Co.

Nesbit, Edith. The Railway Children. Butts, Dennis, intro. by. 224p. 1991. pap. 3.95 (*0-19-282659-X*, 11912) OUP.

—Railway Children. (gr. 4-7). 1992. pap. 3.50 (*0-440-40602-1*) Dell.

—The Railway Children. 1993. 12.95 (*0-679-42534-9*, Everymans Lib) Knopf.

—Railway Children. (gr. 4 up). 1993. pap. 3.25 (*0-553-21415-2*, Bantam Classics) Bantam.

Ong, Cristina, illus. The Little Engine That Could: Little Library, 3 bks. (Set incls. Colors, ABC & Numbers, 20 pgs. ea. bk.). (ps). 1992. Set. bds. 7.95 slipcased (*0-448-40261-0*, Platt & Munk Pubs) Putnam Pub Group.

Pano the Train. (ps-3). 1989. Incl. cass. write for info. (*0-307-13680-9*, 13680, Pub. by Golden Bks) Western Pub.

Parkes, Brenda. One Foggy Night. Cullo, Ned, illus. LC 92-32514. 1993. 4.25 (*0-383-03588-0*) SRA Schl Grp.

Peet, Bill. Caboose Who Got Loose. Peet, Bill, illus. LC 79-155554. 48p. (gr. k-3). 1980. 13.95 (*0-395-14805-7*); pap. 4.80 (*0-395-28715-4*) HM.

—The Caboose Who Got Loose. (gr. 3 up). 1993. pap. 7.95 incl. cassette (*0-395-45740-8*) HM.

Pickney, Gloria J. The Sunday Outing. Pickney, Jerry, illus. LC 93-25383. (gr. k-4). 1994. 14.99 (*0-8037-1198-0*); PLB 14.89 (*0-8037-1199-9*) Dial Bks Young.

Piper, Watty. The Easy-to-Read-Little Engine That Could. Retan, Walter, adapted by. Mateus, illus. 32p. (ps-2). 1986. pap. 2.25 (*0-448-19078-8*, G&D); incl. cassette 5.95 (*0-448-19088-5*) Putnam Pub Group.

—The Little Engine That Could. 40p. 1981. Repr. PLB 15.95x (*0-89966-366-4*) Buccaneer Bks.

—The Little Engine That Could. 69p. 1981. Repr. PLB 10.95x (*0-89967-040-7*) Harmony Raine.

—The Little Engine That Could Board Book. (Illus.). 12p. (ps). 1991. bds. 4.95 (*0-448-40101-0*, G&D) Putnam Pub Group.

—The Little Engine That Could: Miniature Edition. Hauman, George & Hauman, Doris, illus. 48p. 1990. pap. 2.95 (*0-448-40071-5*, Platt & Munk Pubs) Putnam Pub Group.

—The Little Engine That Could: Sixtieth Anniversary Edition. Hauman, George & Hauman, Doris, illus. 48p. 1990. 12.95 (*0-448-40041-3*, Platt & Munk Pubs) Putnam Pub Group.

Piper, Watty, retold by. The Little Engine That Could. 16p. (ps-2). 1993. write for info. (*1-883366-15-1*) YES Ent.

Reynolds, Malvina. Morningtown Ride. Leeman, Michael, illus. 20p. (ps-4). 1984. 10.95 (*0-931793-00-9*) Turn The Page.

Siebert, Diane. Train Song. Wimmer, Mike, illus. LC 88-389. 32p. (ps-3). 1990. 15.00 (*0-690-04726-6*, Crowell Jr Bks); PLB 14.89 (*0-690-04728-2*, Crowell Jr Bks) HarpC Child Bks.

—Train Song. Wimmer, Mike, illus. LC 88-389. 32p. (gr. k-3). 1993. pap. 5.95 (*0-06-443340-4*, Trophy) HarpC Child Bks.

Stevenson, James. All Aboard! LC 94-5825. (Illus.). 32p. 1995. write for info. (*0-688-12438-0*); PLB write for info. (*0-688-12439-9*) Greenwillow.

Stuart, Jesse. A Ride with Huey the Engineer. 3rd ed. Zornes, Rocky, illus. Gifford, James M., intro. by. (Illus.). 112p. (gr. 3 up). 1988. 12.00 (*0-945084-11-0*); pap. 6.00 (*0-945084-10-2*) J Stuart Found.

Terhune, Albert P. Caleb Conover: Railroader. 111p. 1981. Repr. PLB 12.95x (*0-89966-349-4*) Buccaneer Bks.

—Caleb Conover, Railroader. 189p. 1981. Repr. PLB 12.95x (*0-89967-023-7*) Harmony Raine.

Thompson, Richard. Jesse on the Night Train. Fernandes, Eugenie, illus. 32p. (ps-2). 1990. 12.95 (*1-55037-093-6*, Pub. by Annick CN); pap. 4.95 (*1-55037-094-4*, Pub. by Annick CN) Firefly Bks Ltd.

Toot the Train. 1994. 3.99 (*0-517-10279-X*) Random Hse Value.

Tucker, Sian. The Little Train. (Illus.). 10p. (ps-k). 1993. pap. 2.95 (*0-671-79738-7*, Little Simon) S&S Trade.

Warner, Gertrude C. Caboose Mystery. LC 66-10791. (Illus.). 128p. (gr. 2-7). 1966. PLB 10.95 (*0-8075-1008-4*); pap. 3.50 (*0-8075-1009-2*) A Whitman.

Wicentowski, Deborah. The New York Express. Scheinberg, Shepsil, illus. 127p. (gr. 3-5). 1988. 8.95 (*0-935063-46-3*); pap. 6.95 (*0-935063-47-1*) CIS Comm.

Yep, Laurence. Dragon's Gate. LC 92-43649. 288p. (gr. 7 up). 1993. 15.00 (*0-06-022971-3*); PLB 14.89 (*0-06-022972-1*) HarpC Child Bks.

RAILROADS–HISTORY

Campbell, George V. North Shore Line Memories. LC 80-51353. (Illus.). 288p. (gr. 11). 1990. Repr. of 1980 ed. 45.95 (*0-916374-96-3*) Interurban.

Carriker, S. David. North Carolina Railroads: The Common Carrier Railroads of North Carolina. 66p. 1989. pap. 15.00 (*0-936013-08-7*) Herit Pub NC.

Cooper, Alan. Rail Travel. LC 93-16804. 32p. (gr. 5-9). 1993. 14.95 (*1-56847-039-8*) Thomson Lrning.

Donaldson, Stephen E. & Myers, William A. Rails Through the Orange Groves, Vol. 2. LC 89-7619. (Illus.). 144p. (gr. 11). 1990. 34.95 (*0-87046-094-3*, Pub. by Trans-Anglo) Interurban.

Dubin, Arthur D. More Classic Trains. LC 73-92249. (Illus.). 512p. (gr. 11). 1991. Repr. of 1974 ed. 85.95 (*0-916374-85-8*) Interurban.

Edmisten, Donald D. Every Wheel That Turns: Spinning True Tales of California Rails. Rockefeller, Ruth, frwd. by. (Illus.). 53p. (Orig.). 1989. pap. write for info. (*0-9626263-0-9*) DonSyl Pubns.

Elish, Dan. The Transcontinental Railroad: Triumph of a Dream. LC 92-39995. (Illus.). 64p. (gr. 4-6). 1993. PLB 15.40 (*1-56294-337-5*); pap. 5.95 (*1-56294-746-X*) Millbrook Pr.

Fisher, Leonard E. Tracks Across America: The Story of the American Railroad, 1825-1900. LC 91-28244. (Illus.). 192p. (gr. 5 up). 1992. 17.95 (*0-8234-0945-7*) Holiday.

Fraser, Mary A. Ten Mile Day: The Building of the Transcontinental Railroad. Fraser, Mary A., illus. LC 92-3007. 40p. (gr. 3-7). 1993. 15.95 (*0-8050-1902-2*, Bks Young Read) H Holt & Co.

Hanft, Robert M. Pine Across the Mountain. LC 71-164462. (Illus.). 224p. (gr. 11). 1990. Repr. of 1971 ed. 44.95 (*0-87046-099-4*, Pub. by Trans-Anglo) Interurban.

Jones, Robert W. Boston & Maine: Three Colorful Decades of New England Railroading. Drury, George, frwd. by. LC 91-2112. (Illus.). 208p. (gr. 11). 1991. 79.95 (*0-87046-101-X*, Pub. by Trans-Anglo) Interurban.

MacDonald, Fiona. A Nineteenth Century Railway Station: Inside Story. James, John, illus. 48p. (gr. 5 up). 1990. 17.95 (*0-87226-341-X*) P Bedrick Bks.

McKissack, Patricia & McKissack, Frederick. A Long Hard Journey. 144p. (gr. 7-9). 1990. 17.95 (*0-8027-6884-9*); PLB 18.85 (*0-8027-6885-7*) Walker & Co.

McNeese, Tim. America's First Railroads. LC 91-738. (Illus.). 48p. (gr. 5). 1993. text ed. 11.95 RSBE (*0-89686-729-3*, Crestwood Hse) Macmillan Child Grp.

Miller, Marilyn. The Trans-Continental Railroad. LC 85-40167. (Illus.). 64p. (gr. 5 up). 1985. PLB 12.95 (*0-382-06824-6*); pap. 7.95 (*0-382-09912-5*) Silver Burdett Pr.

Murphy, Jim. Across America on an Emigrant Train. LC 92-38650. 160p. 1993. 16.95 (*0-395-63390-7*, Clarion Bks) HM.

Nicholson, Loren. Rails Across the Ranchos: The Pacific Coastline of Southern Pacific Railroad. (Illus.). 197p. (gr. 10-12). 1980. text ed. 18.95 (*0-913548-72-3*) CA HPA.

Scribbins, Jim. The Four Hundred Story. (Illus.). 232p. (gr. 11). 1990. Repr. 49.95 (*0-937658-07-3*) Interurban.

Serpico, Phil. Santa Fe Route to the Pacific. Serpico, Phil, illus. LC 87-46360. 150p. (gr. 6 up). 1988. 25.00 (*0-88418-000-X*) Omni Hawthorne.

Sinnott, Susan. Chinese Railroad Workers. LC 94-50. 1994. write for info. (*0-531-20169-4*) Watts.

Spangenburg, Ray & Moser, Diane. The Story of America's Railroads. (Illus.). 96p. (gr. 6-9). 1991. lib. bdg. 18.95x (*0-8160-2257-7*) Facts on File.

Williams, G. Walton & Kollock, John. The Best Friend. 1991. 10.95 (*0-87844-098-4*); pap. 6.95 (*0-87844-103-4*) Sandlapper Pub Co.

Wormser, Richard. The Iron Horse: How Railroads Changed America. LC 93-12128. (Illus.). 192p. (gr. 4-7). 1993. 18.95 (*0-8027-8221-3*); PLB 19.85 (*0-8027-8222-1*) Walker & Co.

RAILROADS–MODELS

Ferguson, Jane & Ferguson, Gary. Narrow Gauge Fun. Kirkeeide, Deborah, illus. 24p. (ps-6). 1987. pap. 1.98 (*0-9624846-1-X*) J & G Ferguson.

—Sawtooth Mountain Fun. Jenney, David, illus. 24p. (ps-6). 1982. pap. 1.98 (*0-9624846-0-1*) J & G Ferguson.

Goodman, Michael E. Model Railroading. LC 91-15853. (Illus.). 48p. (gr. 5-6). 1993. text ed. 12.95 RSBE (*0-89686-620-3*, Crestwood Hse) Macmillan Child Grp.

LaVoie, Roland. Greenberg's Model Railroading with Lionel Trains, Vol. I. 144p. (Orig.). (gr. 9-12). 1989. pap. 19.95 (*0-89778-054-X*, 10-6745); pap. text ed. 28.95 (*0-685-67522-X*, 10-6745LE) Greenberg Bks.

National TCA Book Committee Staff, et al. Lionel Trains: Standard of the World, 1900-1943. 2nd ed. Witalis-Burke Agency Staff, illus. (Illus.). 256p. 1989. Repr. of 1976 ed. 34.95 (*0-917896-02-5*) TCA PA.

RAILROADS–ROLLING STOCK

see Locomotives

RAILROADS–TRAINS

Brown, James E. Old Freight Train Coloring Book. (SPA & ENG.). 24p. (Orig.). 1992. pap. 0.50 (*0-9632358-0-X*) J E Brown.

Gabriele. Trains. 1986. pap. 1.95 (*0-911211-63-2*) Penny Lane Pubns.

Kanetzke, Howard W. Trains & Railroads. rev. ed. LC 87-20813. (Illus.). 48p. (gr. 2-6). 1987. PLB 10.95 (*0-8172-3263-X*); pap. 4.95 (*0-8114-8222-7*) Raintree Steck-V.

Kindersley, Dorling. Trains. LC 92-12351. (Illus.). 24p. (ps-k). 1992. pap. 7.95 POB (*0-689-71647-8*, Aladdin) Macmillan Child Grp.

McHenry, Ellen J. Inside a Freight Train. McHenry, Ellen J., illus. LC 92-23225. (ps-3). 1993. 9.99 (*0-525-65099-7*, Cobblehill Bks) Dutton Child Bks.

McPhail, David. Train. (ps-3). 1990. write for info.;(Joy St Bks); pap. 5.95 (*0-316-56331-5*, Joy St Bks) Little.

Marshall, Ray. The Train: Watch It Work. Bradley, John F. & Marshall, Ray, illus. 1986. pap. 13.95 (*0-670-81134-3*) Viking Child Bks.

Mott, Evelyn C. Steam Train Ride. (Illus.). 32p. (gr. 4-8). 1991. 13.95 (*0-8027-6995-0*); lib. bdg. 14.85 (*0-8027-6996-9*) Walker & Co.

Piper, Watty. The Fast Rolling Little Engine That Could. Super, Terri, illus. LC 85-70661. 12p. (ps). 1985. 6.95 (*0-448-09878-4*, G&D) Putnam Pub Group.

Steele, Philip. Trains. LC 90-41179. (Illus.). 32p. (gr. 5-6). 1991. text ed. 3.95 RSBE (*0-89686-523-1*, Crestwood Hse) Macmillan Child Grp.

RAILROADS, UNDERGROUND

see Subways

RAILROADS–VOCATIONAL GUIDANCE

Matthews, Morgan. What's It Like to Be a Railroad Worker. Sweat, Lynn, illus. LC 89-34389. 32p. (gr. k-3). 1989. lib. bdg. 10.89 (*0-8167-1815-6*); pap. text ed. 2.95 (*0-8167-1816-4*) Troll Assocs.

RAILWAYS

see Railroads

RAIN AND RAINFALL

see also Floods; Meteorology; Snow; Storms

Brandt, Keith. What Makes It Rain? Miyake, Yoshi, illus. LC 81-7495. 32p. (gr. 2-4). 1982. PLB 11.59 (*0-89375-582-6*); pap. text ed. 2.95 (*0-89375-583-4*) Troll Assocs.

Bright, Michael. Tropical Rainforest. LC 90-44680. (Illus.). 32p. (gr. 2-4). 1991. PLB 11.90 (*0-531-17301-1*, Gloucester Pr) Watts.

Green, Ivah. Splash & Trickle. Connor, Bil, illus. (gr. 2-3). 1978. pap. 1.25 (*0-89508-062-1*) Rainbow Bks.

Greene, Carol. Rain! Rain! LC 82-9509. (Illus.). (ps-2). 1982. PLB 10.25 (*0-516-02034-X*); pap. 2.95 (*0-516-42034-8*) Childrens.

Kahl, Jonathan. Wet Weather: Rain Showers & Snowfall. (Illus.). 64p. (gr. 4-12). 1992. PLB 19.95 (*0-8225-2526-7*) Lerner Pubns.

Kelly, Andrew. Rain. Campbell, Caroline, illus. LC 93-9287. 1994. pap. write for info. (*0-383-03711-5*) SRA Schl Grp.

Kirkpatrick, Rena K. Look at Rainbow Colors. rev. ed. Barnard, Anna, illus. LC 84-26250. 32p. (gr. 2-4). 1985. PLB 10.95 (*0-8172-2356-8*); pap. 4.95 (*0-8114-6902-6*) Raintree Steck-V.

Markle, Sandra. A Rainy Day. Johnson, Cathy, illus. LC 91-17059. 32p. (ps-2). 1993. 14.95 (*0-531-05976-6*); PLB 14.99 (*0-531-08576-7*) Orchard Bks Watts.

Mayes, S. What Makes It Rain? (Illus.). 24p. (gr. 1-4). 1989. lib. bdg. 11.96 (*0-88110-379-9*, Usborne); pap. 3.95 (*0-7460-0274-2*, Usborne) EDC.

Merk, Ann & Merk, Jim. Rain, Snow, & Ice. LC 94-13325. (gr. 3 up). 1994. write for info. (*0-86593-390-1*) Rourke Corp.

Moncure, Jane B. Rain: A Great Day for Ducks. Friedman, Joy, illus. LC 89-24010. 32p. (ps-2). 1990. PLB 13.95 (*0-89565-553-5*) Childs World.

Palmer, Joy. Rain. LC 92-38554. (Illus.). 32p. (gr. 2-3). 1992. PLB 18.99 (*0-8114-3413-3*) Raintree Steck-V.

Robson, Pat, illus. Rain. 32p. (gr. 3-5). 1985. 7.95x (*0-86685-451-7*) Intl Bk Ctr.

Shulevitz, Uri. Rain Rain Rivers. Shulevitz, Uri, illus. LC 73-85370. 32p. (ps-3). 1969. 16.00 (*0-374-36171-1*) FS&G.

Stanish, Bob. Connecting Rainbows. 96p. (gr. 3-12). 1982. 10.95 (*0-86653-081-9*, GA 426) Good Apple.

Steele, Philip. Rain: Causes & Effects. LC 90-41429. (Illus.). 32p. (gr. 5-8). 1991. PLB 12.40 (*0-531-10989-5*) Watts.

Wyler, Rose. Raindrops & Rainbows. Steltenpohl, Jane, ed. Petruccio, Steven, illus. 32p. (gr. k-2). 1989. (J Messner); pap. 4.95 (*0-671-66350-X*) S&S Trade.

RAIN AND RAINFALL–FICTION

Aardema, Verna. Bringing the Rain to Kapiti Plain. Vidal, Beatriz, illus. LC 80-25886. 32p. (ps). 1981. 14.95 (*0-8037-0809-2*); PLB 13.89 (*0-8037-0807-6*) Dial Bks Young.

—Bringing the Rain to Kapiti Plain. Vidal, Beatriz, illus. 32p. (ps-2). 1983. pap. 3.95 (*0-8037-0904-8*, Puff Pied Piper) Puffin Bks.

Alexander, Martha. We Never Get to Do Anything. Alexander, Martha, illus. (ps-3). 1985. Dial Bks Young.

Bauer, Caroline F., ed. Rainy Day: Stories & Poems. Chessare, Michele, illus. LC 85-45170. 96p. (gr. 2-5). 1986. (Lipp Jr Bks); PLB 14.89 (*0-397-32105-8*, Lipp Jr Bks) HarpC Child Bks.

Branley, Franklyn M. Rain & Hail. Barton, Harriett, illus. LC 83-45058. 40p. (gr. k-3). 1983. PLB 14.89 (*0-690-04353-8*, Crowell Jr Bks) HarpC Child Bks.

Brittain, Bill. Dr. Dredd's Wagon of Wonders. Glass, Andrew, illus. LC 86-45775. 208p. (gr. 3-7). 1987. PLB 13.89 (*0-06-020714-0*) HarpC Child Bks.

Carlstrom, Nancy W. What Does the Rain Play? Sorensen, Henry, illus. LC 91-47712. 32p. (ps-2). 1993. RSBE 14.95 (*0-02-717273-2*, Macmillan Child Bk) Macmillan Child Grp.

Charley, Aunt, pseud. The Raindrop Children, Vol. 1. Bruno, Clara E., illus. 24p. (gr. 1-2). 1991. pap. 5.95 (*1-880945-00-2*) Animated Elements.

Chesworth, Michael. Rainy Day Dream. (ps-3). 1992. 14.00 (*0-374-36177-0*) FS&G.

Cole, Sheila. When the Rain Stops. Sorensen, Henri, illus. LC 90-19124. 32p. (ps up). 1991. 13.95 (*0-688-07654-8*) Lothrop.

Conover, Chris. Sam Panda & Thunder Dragon. (ps-3). 1992. 16.00 (*0-374-36393-5*) FS&G.

Corrin, Ruth. It Always Rains for Jackie. Pye, Trevor, illus. 32p. (ps-2). 1990. bds. 8.95 (*0-19-558205-5*) OUP.

Un Dia Lluvioso. (ps-3). 1993. pap. 2.25 (*0-307-50064-0*, Golden Pr) Western Pub.

Ehlert, Lois. Planting a Rainbow. 32p. (ps-3). 1988. 14.95 (*0-15-262609-3*) HarBrace.

Feagan, Mary. Questions to Ask a Cat When It Comes Home from a Trip. (Illus.). 24p. (gr. k-3). 1988. 3.95 (*0-929986-63-6*) Rainbow Cat Pubs.

—The Rainbow Child. (Illus.). 20p. (gr. 1-4). 1988. 8.95 (*0-929986-06-7*) Rainbow Cat Pubs.

Fleming, Candace. Professor Fergus Fahrenheit & His Wonderful Weather Machine. Weller, Don, illus. LC 93-4432. (ps-3). 1994. pap. 14.00 (*0-671-87047-5*, S&S BFYR) S&S Trade.

Gordon, Sheila. Waiting for the Rain. (gr. 7 up). 1989. pap. 3.99 (*0-553-27911-4*, Starfire) Bantam.

Haynes, Max. Sparky's Rainbow Repair. LC 91-1687. (Illus.). (ps-3). 1992. 15.00 (*0-688-11193-9*); PLB 14.93 (*0-688-11194-7*) Lothrop.

Hoban, Julia. Amy Loves the Rain. Hoban, Lillian, illus. LC 87-45851. 24p. (ps). 1993. pap. 3.95 (*0-06-443293-9*, Trophy) HarpC Child Bks.

Hooks, William H. Rainbow Ribbon. 1991. 11.95 (*0-670-82866-1*) Viking Child Bks.

Hooper, Patricia. The Sky's Housekeeper and Her Scarves. Roth, Susan L., illus. LC 93-40106. 1995. 14.95 (*0-316-37255-2*) Little.

James, Betsy. The Mud Family. Morin, Paul, illus. LC 92-43537. 32p. (ps-3). 1994. PLB 15.95 (*0-399-22549-8*, Putnam) Putnam Pub Group.

James, Robin. Napoleon's Rainbow. James, Robin, illus. 32p. (Orig.). (gr. 1-4). 1994. pap. 3.95 (*0-8431-3610-3*) Price Stern.

Johnson, Angela. Rain Feet. Mitchell, Rhonda, illus. LC 93-49391. 12p. (ps). 1994. 4.95 (*0-531-06849-8*) Orchard Bks Watts.

Kalan, Robert. Rain. Crews, Donald, illus. LC 77-25312. 24p. (gr. k-3). 1978. PLB 13.93 (*0-688-84139-2*) Greenwillow.

—Rain. LC 77-25312. (Illus.). 24p. (ps up). 1991. pap. 3.95 (*0-688-10479-7*, Mulberry) Morrow.

Kuskin, Karla. James & the Rain. Cartwright, Reg, illus. LC 93-49345. 1995. 15.00 (*0-671-88808-0*, S&S BFYR) S&S Trade.

L'Engle, Madeleine. Small Rain: A Novel. LC 84-47839. 371p. (gr. 7 up). 1985. pap. 10.00 (*0-374-51912-9*) FS&G.

Maas, Virginia. Niddy Noddy the Noodlemaker. McIntosh, Carolyn, illus. 12p. (ps-2). 1981. pap. 2.75 (*0-933992-15-7*) Coffee Break.

McCaughren, Tom. Rainbows of the Moon. 160p. (gr. 9-12). 1989. 13.95 (*0-947962-45-X*, Pub. by Childrens Pr) Irish Bks Media.

McCoy, James C. Darby's Rainbow. Walker, Timothy, illus. Davenport, May, intro. by. LC 88-70551. (Illus.). 32p. (gr. k-3). 1990. pap. 3.50x (*0-943864-52-6*) Davenport.

Millicer, Jan. When It Rains. Swearingen, Karen M., illus. LC 92-31136. 1993. 2.50 (*0-383-03667-4*) SRA Schl Grp.

Munsch, Robert. Mud Puddle. Suomalaimen, Sami, illus. 32p. (gr. k-3). 1982. pap. 4.95 (*0-920236-28-6*, Pub. by Annick CN) Firefly Bks Ltd.

Nimmo, Jenny. Rainbow & Mr. Zed. 144p. 1994. 14.99 (*0-525-45150-1*) Dutton Child Bks.

Nister, Ernest. Rainbow Round-a-Bout. 10p. 1993. 7.95 (*1-56397-088-0*) Boyds Mills Pr.

Palazzo, Janet. Rainy Day Fun. Ulrich, George, illus. LC 87-10842. 32p. (gr. k-2). 1988. PLB 11.59 (*0-8167-1095-3*); pap. text ed. 2.95 (*0-8167-1096-1*) Troll Assocs.

Pegram, Laura. Rainbow Is Our Face. (ps). 1994. 5.95 (*0-86316-217-7*) Writers & Readers.

Rupprecht, Siegfried P. The Tale of the Vanishing Rainbow. Wilkon, Jozef, illus. Lewis, Naomi, tr. from GER. LC 88-43120. (Illus.). 32p. (gr. k-3). 1989. 14.95 (*1-55858-001-8*) North-South Bks NYC.

Serfozo, Mary. Rain Talk. Narahashi, Keiko, illus. LC 89-12178. 32p. (ps-3). 1990. SBE 13.95 (*0-689-50496-9*, M K McElderry) Macmillan Child Grp.

—Rain Talk. Narahashi, Keiko, illus. LC 92-29562. 32p. (gr. k-3). 1993. pap. 4.95 (*0-689-71699-0*, Aladdin) Macmillan Child Grp.

Short, Sondra J. Unicorns & Rainbows. LC 92-60808. 223p. (gr. 3 up). 1993. 9.95 (*1-55523-537-9*) Winston-Derek.

Spier, Peter. Peter Spier's Rain. LC 81-43506. (Illus.). (gr. k-3). 1987. pap. 7.00 (*0-385-24105-4*, Pub. by Zephyr-BFYR) Doubleday.

Sweeney, Joyce. Right Behind the Rain. LC 86-19953. 192p. (gr. 7 up). 1987. pap. 14.95 (*0-385-29551-0*) Delacorte.
—Right Behind the Rain. 1991. pap. 3.25 (*0-440-20678-2*) Dell.
Taylor, Theodore. Walking up a Rainbow. (gr. k-12). 1988. pap. 2.95 (*0-440-99326-1*, LFL); pap. 2.95 (*0-440-20039-3*) Dell.

RAIN AND RAINFALL–POETRY

Evans, Lezlie. Rain Song. Jabar, Cynthia, illus. LC 94-17368. Date not set. write for info. (*0-395-69865-0*) HM.
Palmer, Michele, ed. Rainy Day Rhymes: A Collection of Chants, Forecasts & Tales. Guerin, Penny, illus. LC 84-60412. 24p. (Orig.). (gr. k up). 1984. pap. 2.95 (*0-932306-02-0*) Rocking Horse.
Radley, Gail, selected by. Rainy Day Rhymes. Kandoian, Ellen, illus. 48p. (gr. 2-5). 1992. 13.45 (*0-395-59967-9*) HM.

RAINFALL

see Rain and Rainfall

RAMS–FICTION

Kalashnikoff, Nicholas. The Defender. Louden, Claire & Louden, George, Jr., illus. LC 92-33560. 144p. (gr. 3-7). 1993. pap. 6.95 (*0-8027-7397-4*) Walker & Co.

RANCH LIFE

see also Cowboys

Bentley, Judith. Farmers & Ranchers. (Illus.). 96p. (gr. 5-8). 1994. bds. 16.95 (*0-8050-2999-0*) TFC Bks NY.
Braly, David. Cattle Barons of Early Oregon. LC 78-105220. (Illus.). 44p. (gr. 7-12). 1982. pap. 4.50 (*0-942206-00-2*) Mediaor Co.
Brown, William F. True Texas Tales. Mazzu, Kenneth, illus. LC 92-93887. 64p. (Orig.). (gr. 7 up). 1992. pap. 8.75 perfect bdg. (*1-881936-14-7*) WFB Ent.
Brusca, Maria C. My Mama's Little Ranch on the Pampas. LC 93-28113. 1994. 15.95 (*0-8050-2782-3*) H Holt & Co.
—On the Pampas. Brusca, Maria C., illus. LC 90-40938. 40p. (ps-2). 1991. 15.95 (*0-8050-1548-5*, Bks Young Read) H Holt & Co.
Henderson, Kathy. I Can Be a Rancher. LC 90-37678. (Illus.). 32p. (gr. k-3). 1990. PLB 11.80 (*0-516-01962-7*); pap. 3.95 (*0-516-41962-5*) Childrens.
Holman, Patsy S. At the Ranch with Taylor. (Illus.). 16p. (ps-3). 1992. PLB 12.99 (*0-9630729-8-6*); pap. 6.99 (*0-9630729-9-4*) KAP Pubns.
Johnson, Neil. Jack Creek Cowboy. Johnson, Neil, photos by. LC 92-921. (Illus.). 32p. (gr. 2-5). 1993. 14.99 (*0-8037-1228-6*); PLB 14.89 (*0-8037-1229-4*) Dial Bks Young.
McGregor, Merideth. Cowgirl. 32p. 1992. 14.95 (*0-8027-8170-5*); PLB 15.85 (*0-8027-8171-3*) Walker & Co.
Morgenroth, Barbara. Get Inside a Ranch. LC 93-41626. (Illus.). 64p. (gr. 4-6). 1994. PLB 12.95 (*1-881889-56-4*) Silver Moon.
—Get Inside a Ranch. Salvini, Donna, illus. 64p. (gr. 4-6). 1994. pap. 6.95 (*1-881889-59-9*) Silver Moon.
Reeve, Agnesa, compiled by. & intro. by. My Dear Mollie: Love Letters of a Texas Sheep Rancher. LC 90-41891. (Illus.). 192p. (gr. 5 up). 1990. 17.95 (*0-937460-62-1*) Hendrick-Long.
Sizemore, Deborah L. The LH7 Ranch in Houston's Shadow: From Longhorns to the Salt Grass Trail. LC 91-20920. (Illus.). 249p. 1991. 22.50 (*0-929398-28-9*) UNTX Pr.

RANCH LIFE–FICTION

Baber, Carolyn S. Little Billy. Fleischman, Luke T., illus. 175p. (gr. 5-9). Date not set. PLB 14.95 (*0-944727-29-8*) Jason & Nordic Pubs.
Biggar, Joan R. High Desert Secrets. 160p. (Orig.). (gr. 5-8). 1992. pap. 3.99 (*0-570-04711-0*) Concordia.
Carey, Karla. Julie & Jackie on the Ranch: The Narration & Music Book. Nolan, Dennis, illus. 91p. 1990. pap. 18.95 complete pkg. (*0-685-35757-0*); pap. 9.95 (*1-55768-204-6*); cassette 9.95 (*0-685-35758-9*) LC Pub.
Cleaver, Vera & Cleaver, Bill. The Kissimmee Kid. LC 80-29262. 160p. (gr. 5 up). 1981. PLB 14.93 (*0-688-51992-X*) Lothrop.
Dominick, Bayard. Sam, a Goat. (Illus.). (gr. 3-5). 1968. 9.95 (*0-8392-3062-1*) Astor-Honor.
Erickson, John. The Case of the Missing Cat: Discover the Land of Enchantment. (Illus.). 144p. 1990. 11.95 (*0-87719-186-7*); pap. 6.95 (*0-87719-185-9*); 2 cass. 15.95 (*0-87719-187-5*) Gulf Pub.
Erickson, John R. Hank the Cowdog: The Case of the Hooking Bull, No. 18. 118p. 1992. 11.95 (*0-87719-213-8*); pap. 6.95 (*0-87719-212-X*); 2 cassettes 15.95 (*0-87719-214-6*) Gulf Pub.
—Hank the Cowdog, Vol. 19: The Case of the Midnight Rustler. Holmes, Gerald, illus. 116p. (Orig.). (gr. 4-6). 1992. 11.95 (*0-87719-219-7*); pap. 6.95 (*0-87719-218-9*); tape 15.95 (*0-87719-220-0*) Gulf Pub.
Field, Rachel. Calico Bush. 1990. pap. 3.99 (*0-440-40368-5*, Pub. by Yearling Classics) Dell.
Gardella, Tricia. Just Like My Dad. Apple, Margot, illus. LC 90-4403. 32p. (ps-3). 1993. 15.00 (*0-06-021937-8*); PLB 14.89 (*0-06-021938-6*) HarpC Child Bks.
Hermes, Patricia. Someone to Count On. LC 93-13502. (ps-6). 1993. 14.95 (*0-316-35925-4*) Little.
Kehret, Peg. Nightmare Mountain. Mckeating, Eileen, illus. LC 89-1535. 176p. (gr. 5 up). 1989. 13.95 (*0-525-65008-3*, Cobblehill Bks) Dutton Child Bks.
Kuchn, Nora A. Thunder, the Maverick Mustang. 96p. 1991. pap. 6.95 (*0-8163-0932-9*) Pacific Pr Pub Assn.

Loder, Ann. The Wet Hat: And Other Stories from Beyond the Black Stump. Peters, Terry, illus. 102p. (Orig.). (gr. 4 up). 1993. pap. write for info. (*0-9636643-0-1*) A L Loder.
THE WET HAT, & OTHER STORIES FROM BEYOND THE BLACK STUMP is a collection of Australian short stories taken from the author's childhood & family album growing up on an Australian sheep ranch. The stories concern family pets; a gutsy pony, two heroic dogs; a kookaburra, (a native Australian bird), a chicken, & a tale about a tiny silkworm. There is a mystery story about a lost ring. Lastly, there is a humorous one. Each story is based on fact & is suitable for children from fourth to eighth grade, up. A dog is featured on the full color cover & there is a black & white illustration with each story. Order from: American Business Communications, 251 Michelle Ct., South San Francisco, CA 94080. FAX: (415) 952-3716 (att: Noel Loder). 415-952-8700.
Publisher Provided Annotation.

Metzler, Rosemary M. Snooty the Fox. 23p. 1993. 5.95 (*0-9637381-0-0*) Snooty Prods.
Rosemary Mezler's irresistible read-aloud children's adventure story, SNOOTY THE FOX, the snootiest, snootiest fox of the Foxville Clan will cast a spell over its readers. This exciting story is for the millions of boys & girls who fall asleep dreaming of being in the saddle during a cattle drive. In this first SNOOTY THE FOX adventure series, Snooty the Fox, the snootiest, snootiest fox, Foxville, England, is invited to his Auntie Margaret Foxville's Colorado cattle ranch to help with the big cattle drive. On the morning of the cattle drive Snooty the Fox dressed in his elegant plaid riding jacket, white breeches & black top hat wants to prove himself to be worthwhile--a true Foxville! Rosemary Metzler has written a page turning story filled with breathtaking escapades.
Publisher Provided Annotation.

Murphy, Barbara B. Annie At the Ranch. (gr. 4-7). 1991. pap. 2.99 (*0-553-15960-7*) Bantam.
Nelson, A. A Long Hard Day on the Ranch. (Illus.). 24p. (ps-8). 1989. pap. 4.95 (*0-88753-184-9*, Pub. by Black Moss Pr CN) Firefly Bks Ltd.
Noble, Trinka H. Meanwhile Back at the Ranch. Ross, Tony, illus. LC 86-11651. 32p. (ps-3). 1987. 13.95 (*0-8037-0353-8*); PLB 13.89 (*0-8037-0354-6*) Dial Bks Young.
O'Brien, Elaine F. Anita of Rancho del Mar. Cunningham, Richard W., illus. LC 90-19711. 176p. (Orig.). (gr. 4-8). 1991. pap. 8.95 (*0-931832-79-9*) Fithian Pr.
Paulsen, Gary. The Haymeadow. (gr. 4-7). 1992. 15.95 (*0-385-30621-0*) Doubleday.
Rodriguez, Gina M. Green Corn Tamales - Tamales de Elote. (SPA & ENG., Illus.). 40p. 1994. 14.95 (*0-938243-00-4*) Hispanic Bk Dist.
Saban, Vera. Johnny Egan of the Paintrock. Saban, Sonja, illus. LC 85-30958. 130p. (Orig.). (gr. 4-8). 1986. pap. 6.95 (*0-914565-13-3*, Timbertrails) Capstan Pubns.
Schaefer, Jack. Shane. McCormick, J., illus. (gr. 7 up). 1954. 15.95 (*0-395-07090-2*) HM.
Schenker, Dona. Fearsome's Hero. LC 93-8601. 144p. (gr. 4-8). 1994. 15.00 (*0-679-85424-X*) Knopf Bks Yng Read.
Scott, Ann H. A Brand is Forever. Himler, Ronald, illus. 48p. (gr. k-3). 1993. 12.95 (*0-395-60118-5*, Clarion Bks) HM.
Steinbeck, John. Of Mice & Men. (gr. 9-12). 1970. pap. 2.75 (*0-553-26675-6*) Bantam.
Storybook Heirlooms Staff. A Visit to Storybook Ranch. (Illus.). 10p. (Orig.). 1993. 9.00 (*0-9638614-0-9*) Strybook Heirlooms.
Von Tempski, Armine. Bright Spurs. Brown, Paul, illus. LC 92-24540. x, 284p. 1992. pap. 14.95 (*0-918024-95-1*) Ox Bow.
—Pam's Paradise Ranch: A Story of Hawaii. Brown, Paul, illus. LC 92-24538. viii, 334p. 1992. pap. 14.95 (*0-918024-96-X*) Ox Bow.

RANDOLPH, ASA PHILIP, 1889-

Cwiklik, Robert. A. Philip Randolph & the Labor Movement. LC 92-32167. (Illus.). 32p. (gr. 2-4). 1993. PLB 12.90 (*1-56294-326-X*); pap. 4.95 (*1-56294-788-5*) Millbrook Pr.
Hanley, Sally. A. Philip Randolph. King, Coretta Scott, intro. by. (Illus.). 112p. (gr. 5 up). 1989. 17.95 (*1-55546-607-9*); pap. 9.95 (*0-7910-0222-5*) Chelsea Hse.

RAPE

Bandon, Alexandra. Date Rape. LC 93-24063. (gr. 10 up). 1994. text ed. 13.95 (*0-89686-806-0*, Crestwood Hse) Macmillan Child Grp.
Bode, Janet. The Voices of Rape. 144p. (gr. 9-12). 1990. 13.95 (*0-531-15184-0*); PLB 13.90 (*0-531-10959-3*) Watts.
Booher, Dianna D. Rape: What Would You Do If...? LC 81-914. 128p. (gr. 7 up). 1983. PLB 12.98 (*0-671-42201-4*, J Messner); pap. 4.95 (*0-671-49485-6*) S&S Trade.
—Rape: What Would You Do If? rev. ed. 160p. (gr. 7 up). 1991. lib. bdg. 13.98 (*0-671-74538-7*, J Messner); pap. 6.95 (*0-671-74546-8*) S&S Trade.
Dizeno, Patricia. Why Me? The Story of Jenny. (gr. 7 up). 1976. pap. 3.50 (*0-380-00563-8*, Flare) Avon.
Guernsey, JoAnn B. Rape. LC 90-33666. (Illus.). 48p. (gr. 5-6). 1990. text ed. 12.95 RSBE (*0-89686-533-9*, Crestwood Hse) Macmillan Child Grp.
McGuire, Leslie. Victims. LC 91-11041. 64p. (gr. 5-7). 1991. 12.95s.p. (*0-86593-120-8*) Rourke Corp.
Mufson, Susan & Kranz, Rachel. Straight Talk about Date Rape. Ryan, Elizabeth A., ed. 128p. (gr. 9-12). 1993. 16.95x (*0-8160-2863-X*) Facts on File.
Shuker-Haines, Frances. Everything You Need to Know about Date Rape. rev. ed. Rosen, Ruth, ed. (gr. 7-12). 1992. PLB 14.95 (*0-8239-1509-3*) Rosen Group.

RAPE–FICTION

Geras, Adele. Watching the Roses. LC 92-8160. 1992. write for info. (*0-15-294816-3*, HB Juv Bks) HarBrace.
Miklowitz, Gloria D. Did You Hear What Happened to Andrea? LC 78-72972. 1979. 7.95 (*0-440-01923-0*) Delacorte.
—Did You Hear What Happened to Andrea? 176p. (gr. 7 up). 1986. pap. 1.75 (*0-440-91853-7*, LE) Dell.
Peck, Richard. Are You in the House Alone? (gr. 10 up). 1976. pap. 15.00 (*0-670-13241-1*) Viking Child Bks.
Rodowsky, Colby. Lucy Peale. 208p. 1992. 15.00 (*0-374-36381-1*) FS&G.
Tamar, Erika. Fair Game. 1993. pap. 3.95 (*0-685-65843-0*, HB Juv Bks) HarBrace.
—No Defense. LC 93-3248. (gr. 9-12). 1993. write for info. (*0-15-278537-X*) HarBrace.
White, Ruth. Weeping Willow. 256p. (gr. 7 up). 1992. 16.00 (*0-374-38255-7*) FS&G.

RAPHAEL SANZIO, 1483-1520

Muhlberger, Richard, text by. What Makes a Raphael a Raphael? (Illus.). 48p. (gr. 5 up). 1993. 9.95 (*0-670-85204-X*) Viking Child Bks.

RATS

Powell, E. Sandy. Rats. Boucher, Jerry, photos by. LC 93-40925. 48p. (gr. 2-3). 1994. PLB 18.95 (*0-8225-3003-1*) Lerner Pubns.
Zinsser, Hans. Rats, Lice & History. (gr. 9 up). 1984. (Pub. by Atlantic Monthly Pr); pap. 12.95 (*0-316-98896-0*) Little.

RATS–FICTION

Allen, Jeffery. Nosey Mrs. Rat. Marshall, James, illus. LC 84-19618. 32p. (ps-3). 1985. pap. 11.95 (*0-670-80880-6*) Viking Child Bks.
Bernardson, Derek. Emma's Rat-Tastic Adventure. Wilcox, Cathy, illus. 96p. (Orig.). (gr. k-4). 1993. pap. 6.95 (*0-04-442345-4*, Pub. by Allen & Unwin Aust Pty AT) IPG Chicago.
Browning, Robert. The Pied Piper of Hamelin: A Classic Tale. Jose, Eduard, adapted by. Suire, Diane D., tr. Rovira, Francesc, illus. LC 88-35313. 32p. (gr. k-2). 1988. PLB 19.95 (*0-89565-471-7*); PLB 13.95s.p. (*0-685-56031-7*) Childs World.
Campbell, Martha S. Patarick Packrat & His Very Old House. Light-Waller, Sara, illus. 32p. (Orig.). (gr. 1-5). 1993. pap. 6.95 (*0-918080-68-1*) Treasure Chest.
The Cat & the Rat EV, Unit 6. (gr. 2). 1991. 5-pack 21.25 (*0-88106-750-4*) Charlesbridge Pub.
Chenoweth, Russ. Shadow Walkers. LC 92-18798. 176p. (gr. 5 up). 1993. SBE 13.95 (*0-684-19447-3*, Scribner Young Read) Macmillan Child Grp.
Conly, Jane L. R-T, Margaret, & the Rats of NIMH. Lubin, Leonard, illus. LC 89-19968. 288p. (gr. 4-7). 1990. 14.00 (*0-06-021363-9*); PLB 13.89 (*0-06-021364-7*) HarpC Child Bks.
—R-T, Margaret, & the Rats of NIMH. 1990. PLB 15.89 (*0-06-023647-7*) HarpC Child Bks.
—R-T, Margaret, & the Rats of NIMH. Lubin, Leonard, illus. LC 89-19968. 272p. (gr. 4-7). 1991. pap. 3.95 (*0-06-440387-4*, Trophy) HarpC Child Bks.
—Rasco & the Rats of NIMH. Lubin, Leonard, illus. LC 85-42634. 288p. (gr. 4-7). 1986. 15.00 (*0-06-021361-2*); PLB 14.89 (*0-06-021362-0*) HarpC Child Bks.

Couture, Susan A. Alfonso's Dream. LC 93-5784. 1996. 14.95 (*0-02-724827-5*, Macmillan Child Bk) Macmillan Child Grp.
Firmin, Peter. Happy Miss Rat. 1990. pap. 2.95 (*0-440-40382-0*, YB) Dell.
Giff, Patricia R. Rat Teeth. (gr. k-6). 1990. pap. 3.25 (*0-440-47457-4*, YB) Dell.
Hamilton, Carol. The Dawn Seekers. Levine, Abby, ed. LC 86-15820. (Illus.). 144p. (gr. 3-7). 1987. PLB 11.95 (*0-8075-1480-2*) A Whitman.
Kasza, Keiko. The Rat & the Tiger. (Illus.). 32p. (ps-3). 1993. PLB 14.95 (*0-399-22404-1*, Putnam) Putnam Pub Group.
La Fontaine. The Lion & the Rat. Wildsmith, Brian, illus. 32p. 1987. 16.00 (*0-19-279607-0*); pap. 7.50 (*0-19-272167-4*) OUP.
McCutcheon, Elsie. The Rat War. LC 85-4593. 111p. (gr. 4 up). 1986. 13.00 (*0-374-36182-7*) FS&G.
Mrs. Frisby & the Rats of NIMH: L-I-T Guide. 8.95 (*0-685-69341-4*) Educ Impress.
O'Donovan, Dermot. Silas Rat & the Nuclear Tail. Booth, Tim, illus. 125p. 1988. pap. 7.95 (*0-947962-22-0*, Pub. by Children's Pr) Irish Bks Media.
Porte, Barbara A. Harry in Trouble. 1990. pap. 2.95 (*0-440-40370-7*, YB) Dell.
Potter, Beatrix. The Roly-Poly Pudding. LC 93-34679. (Illus.). 1994. 6.95 (*0-681-45606-X*) Longmeadow Pr.
Spicer, Venetia. The Adventures of Chatrat. (Illus.). 48p. 1981. 9.95 (*0-7043-2269-2*, Pub. by Quartet England) Charles River Bks.
Storr, Catherine, retold by. The Pied Piper of Hamelin. LC 84-26971. (Illus.). 32p. (gr. k-5). 1984. PLB 19.97 (*0-8172-2107-7*); PLB 29.28 incl. cassette (*0-8172-2238-3*) Raintree Steck-V.
Trezise, Percy. Black Duck & Water Rat. (ps-3). 1994. pap. 7.00 (*0-207-18349-X*, Pub. by Angus & Robertson AT) HarpC.
Velthuijs, Max. Frog & the Stranger. Velthuijs, Max, illus. LC 93-26401. 32p. 1994. 14.00 (*0-688-13267-7*, Tambourine Bks); PLB 13.93 (*0-688-13268-5*, Tambourine Bks) Morrow.
Verne, Jules. The Adventures of the Rat Family. Copeland, Evelyn, tr. Taves, Brian, afterword by. LC 92-36983. 72p. 1993. 14.95 (*0-19-508114-5*) OUP.
Vlakos, Jon, illus. Ladle Rat Rotten Hut. 6th ed. 12p. 1988. pap. 2.00 (*0-934714-05-3*) Swamp Pr.
Ward, Helen. The Moonrat & the White Turtle. 40p. (ps-4). 1992. pap. 4.95 (*0-8249-8580-X*, Ideals Child) Hambleton-Hill.
Westcott, Alvin. Billy Lump's Adventure. LC 68-56817. (Illus.). 32p. (gr. 2-4). 1968. PLB 9.95 (*0-87783-002-9*) Oddo.

RAVENS–FICTION

Peck, Sylvia. Kelsey's Raven. 240p. (gr. 5 up). 1992. 14.00 (*0-688-09583-6*) Morrow Jr Bks.
Sopko, Eugen. The White Raven & the Black Sheep. Sopko, Eugen, illus. Graves, Helen, tr. from GER. LC 91-7254. (Illus.). 32p. (gr. k-3). 1991. 14.95 (*1-55858-118-9*) North-South Bks NYC.

RAYBURN, SAM TALIAFERRO, 1882-1961

Liles, Maurine W. Sam & the Speaker's Chair. LC 93-42374. 1994. 14.95 (*0-89015-946-7*) Sunbelt Media.

RAYS, ROENTGEN

see X Rays

REACTORS (NUCLEAR PHYSICS)

see Nuclear Reactors

READERS

Here are entered school readers in english. For readers in other languages, use the name of the language with the subdivision Readers, e.g. French Language–Readers.

see also Primers

Adventure at the Castle. (Illus.). (ps-5). 3.50 (*0-7214-0022-1*) Ladybird Bks.
Adventure on the Island. (Illus.). (ps-5). 3.50 (*0-7214-0010-8*); o.p. (*0-317-03996-2*) Ladybird Bks.
Armstrong, Vicki. A Dragon Drinks Just One Drop. Armstrong, Bruce, illus. 32p. (gr. 1-6). 1990. wkbk. 5.99 (*0-933367-01-5*) See the Sounds.
—Pigs Pet People. Armstrong, Bruce, illus. (ps-4). 1985. wkbk. 5.99 (*0-933367-00-7*) See the Sounds.
Averill, Esther. Fire Cat. Averill, Esther, illus. LC 60-10234. 64p. (gr. k-3). 1960. PLB 13.89 (*0-06-020196-7*) HarpC Child Bks.
Baker, Betty. Little Runner of the Longhouse. Lobel, Arnold, illus. LC 62-8040. 64p. (gr. k-3). 1962. PLB 13.89 (*0-06-020341-2*) HarpC Child Bks.
Balcomb, Philip E. The Clock Repair First Reader: Second Steps for the Beginner. Balcomb, Philip E., illus. 160p. (Orig.). (gr. 9 up). 1989. pap. 14.95 (*0-9620456-1-6*) Tempus Pr.
Begin, S., et al. Suspicious Minds: A Radio Play Developing Listening Strategies & Lifeskills. 1990. pap. text ed. 13.50 (*0-8013-0287-0*, 75937); cass. 37.95 (*0-8013-0288-9*, 75938) Longman.
Benchley, Nathaniel. Red Fox & His Canoe. Lobel, Arnold, illus. LC 64-16650. 64p. (gr. k-3). 1964. PLB 13.89 (*0-06-020476-1*) HarpC Child Bks.
The Big House. (Illus.). (ps-5). 3.50 (*0-7214-0544-4*) Ladybird Bks.
The Big Secret. (Illus.). (ps-2). 1990. 3.50 (*0-7214-1324-2*); parent/tchr's. guide 3.95 (*0-7214-4203-X*) Ladybird Bks.
Bolinske, Janet L., ed. Big Bug Softcover Package. (Illus., Orig.). (gr. k-1). 1989. Set of 6 bks., 24 pgs. ea. bk. pap. 27.00 (*0-88335-539-6*) Milliken Pub Co.
Bonsall, Crosby N. Case of the Cat's Meow. Bonsall, Crosby N., illus. LC 65-11451. 64p. (gr. k-3). 1965. PLB 13.89 (*0-06-020561-X*) HarpC Child Bks.
—Case of the Dumb Bells. Bonsall, Crosby N., illus. LC 66-8267. 64p. (gr. k-3). 1966. PLB 13.89 (*0-06-020624-1*) HarpC Child Bks.
—Case of the Hungry Stranger. Bonsall, Crosby N., illus. LC 91-13345. 64p. (gr. k-3). 1963. 13.00 (*0-06-020570-9*); PLB 12.89 (*0-06-020571-7*) HarpC Child Bks.
—Tell Me Some More. Siebel, Fritz, illus. LC 61-5773. 64p. (gr. k-3). 1961. PLB 13.89 (*0-06-020601-2*) HarpC Child Bks.
—What Spot? Bonsall, Crosby N., illus. LC 63-8005. 64p. (gr. k-3). 1963. PLB 13.89 (*0-06-020611-X*) HarpC Child Bks.
—Who's a Pest? Bonsall, Crosby N., illus. LC 62-13310. 64p. (gr. k-3). 1962. PLB 13.89 (*0-06-020621-7*) HarpC Child Bks.
Books Are Exciting. (Illus.). (ps-5). 3.50 (*0-7214-0646-7*) Ladybird Bks.
Boyd, Frances & Quinn, David. Stories from Lake Wobegon: Advanced Listening & Conversation Skills. 1990. pap. text ed. 18.95 (*0-8013-0312-5*, 78017); cass. 37.95 (*0-8013-0492-X*, 78344) Longman.
Boys & Girls. (Illus.). (ps-5). 3.50 (*0-7214-0015-9*); Series No. S705. wkbk. 3 1.95 (*0-317-04007-3*); o.p. (*0-317-04009-X*) Ladybird Bks.
Bradshaw, Georgene & Wrighton, Charlene A. Zoo-Phonics Level B Reader: (a-b-c) (Illus.). 48p. (gr. 1). 1987. pap. text ed. 4.50 (*0-9617342-2-1*) Zoo-phonics.
Bradshaw, Georgene E. & Wrighton, Charlene A. A Zoo-Phonics Reader: Level A. Clark, Irene, illus. 32p. (ps-1). 1986. pap. text ed. 3.50 (*0-9617342-1-3*) Zoo-Phonics.
—Zoo-Phonics Reader: Level B (d-e-f) (Illus.). 48p. (gr. 1). 1987. pap. text ed. 4.50 (*0-9617342-3-X*) Zoo-phonics.
—Zoo-Phonics Reader: Level C (g-h-i) (Illus.). 48p. (gr. 1). 1988. pap. text ed. 5.50 (*0-9617342-4-8*) Zoo-phonics.
Brandenberg, Franz. It's Not My Fault. Aliki, illus. LC 79-24157. 64p. (gr. 1-3). 1980. 14.00 (*0-688-80235-4*) Greenwillow.
Brannon, Tom & Cooke, Tom, illus. Open Sesame Multilevel Book. Baigelman, Simon, photos by. pap. 7.95 (*0-19-434261-1*) OUP.
Brooks, Robert F. Nwandu's Child of Life Reader. (Illus.). 20p. (Orig.). (gr. k-4). pap. 2.00 (*0-936868-00-7*) Freeland Pubns.
Buckman, Mary. Leap Frog. LC 89-63379. (Illus., Orig.). (gr. k-2). 1989. pap. text ed. 12.95 (*1-879414-05-8*) Mary Bee Creat.
A Busy Night. (Illus.). (ps-2). 1990. 3.50 (*0-7214-1329-3*); parent/tchr's. guide 3.95 (*0-317-04039-1*) Ladybird Bks.
Carlile, Candy. Book Report Big Top. 48p. (gr. 1-4). 1980. 5.95 (*0-88160-009-1*, LW 111) Learning Wks.
Chapman, Mary W. Why? McKissack, Patricia & McKissack, Fredrick, eds. LC 88-60387. (Illus.). 32p. (Orig.). (gr. 1-3). 1988. text ed. 8.95 (*0-88335-781-X*); pap. text ed. 4.95 (*0-88335-793-3*) Milliken Pub Co.
Children's Classics, Reading Well, Big Bug Books, & Sherlock Street Detectives Series, 64 bks. (Illus., Orig.). (gr. k-3). 1989. Set. pap. 285.00 (*0-88335-716-X*) Milliken Pub Co.
Childs, Phyllis. The Language Ladder, Bk. I. Sterling, Suzanne, illus. 76p. (ps-k). 1985. wkbk. 6.50 (*0-931749-01-8*) PJC Lrng Mtrls.
Chodkowski, Dick. Snakes Alive! It's Reptile Clive! McKissack, Patricia & McKissack, Fredrick, eds. Chodkowski, Dick, illus. LC 88-60391. 32p. (Orig.). (gr. 1-3). 1990. text ed. 8.95 (*0-88335-787-9*); pap. text ed. 4.95 (*0-88335-799-2*) Milliken Pub Co.
Clark, Raymond C. & Jerald, Michael. Summer Olympic Games: Exploring International Athletic Competition. (Illus.). 96p. (gr. 5 up). 1987. 10.50x (*0-86647-021-2*) Pro Lingua.
Cole, Joanna. Ready Set Read. 1990. pap. 17.95 (*0-385-41416-1*) Doubleday.
Collins, David R. Grandfather Woo Goes to School. McKissack, Patricia & McKissack, Fredrick, eds. Wilson, Deborah, illus. LC 88-60389. 32p. (Orig.). (gr. 1-3). 1990. text ed. 8.95 (*0-88335-784-4*); pap. text ed. 4.95 (*0-88335-796-8*) Milliken Pub Co.
Crane, Barbara J. The Baby Jay. (Illus.). (gr. k-2). 1977. pap. 4.85 (*0-89075-095-5*) Bilingual Ed Serv.
Cresswall, Helen. The Weather Cat. rev. ed. Walker, Barbara, illus. 32p. (gr. k-2). 1990. Repr. of 1989 ed. PLB 10.95 (*1-878363-06-9*) Forest Hse.
Davies, Gillian. Why Worms? rev. ed. Kramer, Robin, illus. 32p. (gr. k-2). 1990. Repr. of 1989 ed. PLB 10.95 (*1-878363-07-7*) Forest Hse.
The Day Trip. (Illus.). (ps-2). 1990. 3.50 (*0-7214-1320-X*); parent/tchr's. guide 3.95 (*0-317-04635-7*) Ladybird Bks.
Dee, Abbie & Scott, Annie. Betsy's Riddles. 11p. (ps-1). 1991. pap. text ed. 21.00 big bk. (*1-56843-035-3*); pap. text ed. 4.25 (*1-56843-083-3*) BGR Pub.
—Brittany the Brontosaurus. 8p. (ps-1). 1991. pap. text ed. 21.00 big bk. (*1-56843-032-9*); pap. text ed. 4.25 (*1-56843-080-9*) BGR Pub.
—Four Seasons. 9p. (ps-1). 1991. pap. text ed. 21.00 big bk. (*1-56843-026-4*); pap. text ed. 4.25 (*1-56843-074-4*) BGR Pub.
—Nature Hike. 18p. (ps-1). 1991. pap. text ed. 21.00 big bk. (*1-56843-028-0*); pap. text ed. 4.25 (*1-56843-076-0*) BGR Pub.
—Opposites at the Zoo. 12p. (ps-1). 1991. pap. text ed. 21.00 big bk. (*1-56843-029-9*); pap. text ed. 4.25 (*1-56843-077-9*) BGR Pub.
—Pets on Parade. 14p. (ps-1). 1991. pap. text ed. 21.00 big bk. (*1-56843-027-2*); pap. text ed. 4.25 (*1-56843-075-2*) BGR Pub.
—Sea Horse, Sea Horse. 10p. (ps-1). 1991. pap. text ed. 21.00 big bk. (*1-56843-031-0*); pap. text ed. 4.25 (*1-56843-079-5*) BGR Pub.
Delton, Judy. My Mom Hates Me in January. Faulkner, John, illus. LC 77-5749. (gr. 1-3). 1977. PLB 11.95 (*0-8075-5356-5*) A Whitman.
DeWitt, Lisa F. Nobel Prize Winners: Biographical Sketches for Listening & Reading. (Illus.). 142p. (gr. 8 up). 1991. 12.50x (*0-86647-047-6*); three cassette tapes 27.00x (*0-86647-049-2*) Pro Lingua.
Dodd, Lynley. Dragon in a Wagon. Sherwood, Rhoda, ed. Dodd, Lynley, illus. LC 88-42925. 32p. (gr. 1-2). 1988. PLB 17.27 (*1-55532-911-X*) Gareth Stevens Inc.
Dodd, Lynley & Croser, Nigel. Gold Star First Readers, 14 vols. Aldridge, George, illus. 360p. (gr. 1-2). 1989. Set. PLB 241.73 (*0-8368-0775-8*) Gareth Stevens Inc.
Dodds, Siobhan. Words & Pictures: Reading with Picture Clues. LC 91-71817. (Illus.). 32p. (ps up). 1994. pap. 4.99 (*1-56402-285-4*) Candlewick Pr.
The Dolphin Chase. (Illus.). (ps-2). 1990. 3.50 (*0-7214-1327-7*); parent/tchr's. guide 3.95 (*0-317-04037-5*) Ladybird Bks.
Donatelli, Betty. A Good Book to Toot About. Donatelli, Betty, illus. 11p. (Orig.). (gr. 1-2). 1984. pap. 2.00 (*0-912981-10-5*) Hse BonGiovanni.
The Dream. (Illus.). (ps-2). 1990. 3.50 (*0-7214-1319-6*); parent/tchr's. guide 3.95 (*0-317-04759-0*); Series 9011-6, No. 6. activity bk. 2.95 (*0-7214-3225-5*) Ladybird Bks.
Duyff, Roberta L. Smiles for Smiles. McKissack, Patricia & McKissack, Fredrick, eds. Dorenkamp, Michelle, illus. LC 88-60386. 32p. (Orig.). (gr. 1-3). 1988. text ed. 8.95 (*0-88335-780-1*); pap. text ed. 4.95 (*0-88335-792-5*) Milliken Pub Co.
Easy to Sound. (Illus.). (ps-5). 3.50 (*0-7214-0031-0*) Ladybird Bks.
Enjoying Reading. (Illus.). (ps-5). 3.50 (*0-7214-0552-5*) Ladybird Bks.
Fehiner, Paul. Dog & Cat. LC 90-30164. (Illus.). 28p. (ps-2). 1990. PLB 10.50 (*0-516-05353-1*); pap. 3.95 (*0-516-45353-X*) Childrens.
The Fierce Giant. (Illus.). (ps-2). 1990. 3.50 (*0-7214-1325-0*); parent/tchr's. guide 3.95 (*0-317-04035-9*) Ladybird Bks.
First Word Book. (Illus.). (ps-k). 3.50 (*0-7214-8104-3*) Ladybird Bks.
First Words. (Illus.). (ps-2). 1990. 3.50 (*0-7214-1338-2*); parent/tchr's. guide 3.95 (*0-7214-3219-0*) Ladybird Bks.
Forte, Imogene. Read about It: Middle Grades. LC 82-80502. (Illus.). 80p. (gr. 4-6). 1982. pap. text ed. 7.95 (*0-86530-007-0*, IP 070) Incentive Pubns.
Frankel, Julie. Hare & Bear Go Shopping. McKissack, Patricia & McKissack, Fredrick, eds. Smith, Ted, illus. LC 88-60394. 32p. (Orig.). (gr. 1-3). 1990. text ed. 8.95 (*0-88335-778-X*); pap. text ed. 4.95 (*0-88335-790-9*) Milliken Pub Co.
Friskey, Margaret. Pollito Pequenito Cuenta hasta Diez - Chicken Little Count-to-Ten. Kratky, Lada, tr. from ENG. Evans, K., illus. (SPA.). 32p. (gr. k-3). 1984. pap. 3.95 (*0-516-53431-9*) Childrens.
Fun with Sounds. (Illus.). (ps-5). 3.50 (*0-7214-0551-7*) Ladybird Bks.
Goldstein, Nettie & Warner, Norma. How Hip Are You, Bk 1. (Illus.). (gr. 5-12). 1977. wkbk. 5.95 (*0-87594-160-5*) Book-Lab.
Goley. Respect, Reading Level 2. (Illus.). 32p. (gr. 1-4). 1989. PLB 14.60 (*0-86592-387-6*); 11.95 (*0-685-58788-6*) Rourke Corp.
Gordon, Sharon. Christmas Surprise. Magine, John, illus. 32p. (gr. k-2). 1980. PLB 7.89 (*0-89375-373-4*); pap. 1.95 (*0-89375-273-8*) Troll Assocs.
—Dinosaur in Trouble. Harvey, Paul, illus. 32p. (gr. k-2). 1980. PLB 7.89 (*0-89375-374-2*); pap. 1.95 (*0-89375-274-6*) Troll Assocs.
—Easter Bunny's Lost Egg. Magine, Sharon, illus. 32p. (gr. k-2). 1980. PLB 7.89 (*0-89375-375-0*); pap. 1.95 (*0-89375-275-4*) Troll Assocs.
—Friendly Snowman. Magine, John, illus. 32p. (gr. k-2). 1980. PLB 7.89 (*0-89375-377-7*); pap. 1.95 (*0-89375-277-0*) Troll Assocs.
—Pete the Parakeet. Harvey, Paul, illus. 32p. (gr. k-2). 1980. PLB 7.89 (*0-89375-384-X*); pap. 1.95 (*0-89375-284-3*) Troll Assocs.
—Sam the Scarecrow. Silverstein, Don, illus. 32p. (gr. k-2). 1980. PLB 7.89 (*0-89375-387-4*); pap. 1.95 (*0-89375-287-8*) Troll Assocs.
—Three Little Witches. Sims, Deborah, illus. 32p. (gr. k-2). 1980. PLB 7.89 (*0-89375-390-4*); pap. 1.95 (*0-89375-290-8*) Troll Assocs.
—What a Dog. Sims, Deborah, illus. 32p. (gr. k-2). 1980. PLB 7.89 (*0-89375-393-9*); pap. 1.95 (*0-89375-293-2*) Troll Assocs.
Graham, Carolyn. The Electric Elephant & Other Stories. (Illus., Orig.). (gr. 7-12). 1982. pap. text ed. 7.95x (*0-19-503229-2*) OUP.
Greene, Carol. Miss Apple's Hats. McKissack, Patricia & McKissack, Fredrick, eds. Martin, Clovis, illus. LC 88-60395. 32p. (Orig.). (gr. 1-3). 1988. text ed. 8.95 (*0-88335-779-8*); pap. text ed. 4.95 (*0-88335-791-7*) Milliken Pub Co.
Greene, Jane F. & Woods, Judy F. J & J Language Readers: Level I. Ranson, Peggy, illus. (ps-2). 1992. Set of 18 units, 45p. ea. pap. text ed. 49.00 (*0-944584-86-1*) Sopris.

—J & J Language Readers: Level II. Ranson, Peggy, illus. (gr. 2-4). 1992. Set of 18 units, 45p. ea. pap. text ed. 49.00 (*0-944584-87-X*) Sopris.
—J & J Language Readers: Level III. Ranson, Peggy, illus. (gr. 3-5). 1992. Set of 18 units, 45p. ea. pap. text ed. 49.00 (*0-944584-88-8*) Sopris.
Gregorich, Barbara. The Comprehension Adventure. 48p. (gr. 7-12). 1984. 5.95 (*0-88160-109-8*, LW 1004) Learning Wks.
—The Fox, the Goose & the Corn: Reading Workbook. Hoffman, Joan, ed. Laurent, Richard & Pape, Richard, illus. 32p. (Orig.). (gr. k-2). 1988. 1.99 (*0-88743-107-0*) Sch Zone Pub Co.
—It's Magic. Hoffman, Joan, ed. Pape, Richard, illus. 32p. (gr. k-2). 1987. 1.99 (*0-88743-104-6*, 02604) Sch Zone Pub Co.
—Nicole Digs a Hole. Hoffman, Joan, ed. Brooks, Nan, illus. 32p. (gr. k-2). 1987. wkbk. 1.99 (*0-88743-101-1*, 02601) Sch Zone Pub Co.
—Reading Railroad. Hofman, Joan, ed. Alexander, Barbara, et al, illus. 32p. (ps-1). 1986. wkbk. 1.99 (*0-88743-130-5*, 02506) Sch Zone Pub Co.
—Trouble Again: Reading Workbook. Hoffman, Joan, ed. Murdocca, Sal & Pape, Richard, illus. 32p. (Orig.). (gr. k-2). 1988. 1.99 (*0-88743-110-0*) Sch Zone Pub Co.
Greydanus, Rose. Animals at the Zoo. Hall, Susan T., illus. 32p. (gr. k-2). 1980. PLB 7.89 (*0-89375-371-8*); pap. 1.95 (*0-89375-271-1*) Troll Assocs.
—Big Red Fire Engine. Harvey, Paul, illus. 32p. (gr. k-2). 1980. PLB 7.89 (*0-89375-372-6*); pap. 1.95 (*0-89375-272-X*) Troll Assocs.
—Climb Aboard. Ulrich, George, illus. LC 87-19150. 32p. (gr. k-2). 1988. PLB 11.59 (*0-8167-1099-6*); pap. text ed. 2.95 (*0-8167-1100-3*) Troll Assocs.
—Freddie the Frog. (Illus.). 32p. (gr. k-2). 1980. PLB 7.89 (*0-89375-376-9*); pap. 1.95 (*0-89375-276-2*) Troll Assocs.
—Mike's New Bike. Sims, Deborah, illus. 32p. (gr. k-2). 1980. PLB 7.89 (*0-89375-382-3*); pap. 1.95 (*0-89375-282-7*) Troll Assocs.
—My Secret Hiding Place. Harvey, Paul, illus. 32p. (gr. k-2). 1980. PLB 7.89 (*0-89375-383-1*); pap. 1.95 (*0-89375-283-5*) Troll Assocs.
—Susie Goes Shopping. Apple, Margot, illus. 32p. (gr. k-2). 1980. PLB 7.89 (*0-89375-389-0*); pap. 1.95 (*0-89375-289-4*) Troll Assocs.
—Tree House Fun. Demarest, Chris, illus. 32p. (gr. k-2). 1980. PLB 7.89 (*0-89375-391-2*); pap. 1.95 (*0-89375-291-6*) Troll Assocs.
—Willie the Slowpoke. Eberbach, Andrea, illus. 32p. (gr. k-2). 1980. PLB 7.89 (*0-89375-394-7*); pap. 1.95 (*0-89375-294-0*); cassette 8.95 (*0-685-04954-X*) Troll Assocs.
Halloran, Phyllis. Oh, Brother! Oh, Sister! McKissack, Patricia & McKissack, Fredrick, eds. Shoemaker, Katheryn, illus. LC 88-60392. 32p. (Orig.). (gr. 1-3). 1988. text ed. 8.95 (*0-88335-788-7*); pap. text ed. 4.95 (*0-88335-767-4*) Milliken Pub Co.
Harris, Raymond. Best Short Stories: Advanced Level. Burgoyne, Mari-Ann S., illus. 560p. (Orig.). (gr. 9 up). 1990. text ed. 18.00 (*0-89061-705-8*, 620H); pap. text ed. 14.25 (*0-89061-701-5*, 620) Jamestown Pubs.
Have a Go. (Illus.). (ps-5). 3.50 (*0-7214-0474-X*); Ser. S705, No. 2. wkbk. 1.95 (*0-317-04004-9*); o.p. (*0-317-04006-5*) Ladybird Bks.
Heilbroner, Joan. This Is the House Where Jack Lives. Aliki, illus. LC 62-7311. 64p. (gr. k-3). 1962. PLB 13.89 (*0-06-022286-7*) HarpC Child Bks.
Heyer, Sandra. More True Stories in the News: A Beginning Reader. (Illus.). 1989. pap. text ed. 12.95 (*0-8013-0223-4*, 75881) Longman.

Hill, Charlotte M. Wee Folks Readers: A Phonetic Approach to Beginning Reading, 5 vols. Shortridge, Cleona, ed. Fields, Theodore, et al, illus. LC 90-832256. 70p. (Orig.). (gr. k-5). 1992. Set. pap. write for info. (*0-9620182-9-5*) Charill Pubs.
This five volume reading series is an eclectic approach to beginning reading. Phonics is introduced in story form, lending itself to building comprehension, skills & simultaneously, sight words to build vocabulary as well. Each sound is introduced with illustrations that represent that sound. Books One through Four teach the vowel sounds & this teaching of sounds in context allows for the immediate application of phonetic skills learned. This approach follows the principle of use & reinforcement. Book Five, "Wee Folks on Top" (Adventures in Reading), contains stories, fables & poetry with follow-up questions to improve comprehension. A bookstore owner & mother of a six year old daughter who lives in San Antonio, Texas, wrote, "My daughter was reading the first hour after I started her in Book I. I called relatives all over the country to tell them that she was reading." A director of a Prep School in Seattle, Washington, writes, "Your reading series is excellent. I am an experienced teacher & have always believed that a phonics based reading program is the best way to teach reading."
Publisher Provided Annotation.

Hillert, Margaret. Purple Pussycat. (Illus.). (ps-k). 1981. PLB 6.95 (*0-8136-5072-0*, TK2357); pap. 3.50 (*0-8136-5572-2*, TK2358) Modern Curr.
—The Snow Baby. (Illus.). (ps-k). 1969. PLB 6.95 (*0-8136-5055-0*, TK2363); pap. 3.50 (*0-8136-5555-2*, TK2364) Modern Curr.
—Who Goes to School? (Illus.). (ps-k). 1981. pap. 3.50 (*0-685-38662-7*, TK2383) Modern Curr.
—The Witch Who Went... (Illus.). (ps-k). 1981. PLB 6.95 (*0-8136-5105-0*, TK2386); pap. 3.50 (*0-8136-5605-2*, TK2387) Modern Curr.
Hoban, Russell. Bargain for Frances. Hoban, Lillian, illus. LC 91-12265. 64p. (gr. k-3). 1970. 14.00 (*0-06-022329-4*); PLB 13.89 (*0-06-022330-8*) HarpC Child Bks.
—Tom & the Two Handles. Hoban, Lillian, illus. LC 65-11459. 64p. (gr. k-3). 1965. PLB 13.89 (*0-06-022431-2*) HarpC Child Bks.
Hoff, Syd. Chester. Hoff, Syd, illus. LC 61-5768. 64p. (gr. k-3). 1961. PLB 13.89 (*0-06-022456-8*) HarpC Child Bks.
—Danny & the Dinosaur. Hoff, Syd, illus. LC 92-13609. 64p. (gr. k-3). 1958. 14.00 (*0-06-022465-7*); PLB 13.89 (*0-06-022466-5*) HarpC Child Bks.
—Grizzwold. Hoff, Syd, illus. LC 64-14366. 64p. (gr. k-3). 1963. PLB 13.89 (*0-06-022481-9*) HarpC Child Bks.
—Julius. Hoff, Syd, illus. LC 59-8971. 64p. (gr. k-3). 1959. PLB 13.89 (*0-06-022491-6*) HarpC Child Bks.
—Little Chief. Hoff, Syd, illus. LC 61-12098. 64p. (gr. k-3). 1961. PLB 13.89 (*0-06-022501-7*) HarpC Child Bks.
—Oliver. Hoff, Syd, illus. LC 60-5779. 64p. (gr. k-3). 1960. PLB 13.89 (*0-06-022516-5*) HarpC Child Bks.
—Sammy the Seal. Hoff, Syd, illus. LC 59-5316. 64p. (gr. k-3). 1959. PLB 13.89 (*0-06-022526-2*) HarpC Child Bks.
—Who Will Be My Friends? Hoff, Syd, illus. 32p. (gr. k-2). 1960. PLB 13.89 (*0-06-022556-4*) HarpC Child Bks.
Hoffman, Joan. Mouse & Owl. Gregorich, Barbara, ed. Sanford, John, illus. 32p. (gr. k-2). 1987. wkbk. 1.99 (*0-88743-102-X*, 02602) Sch Zone Pub Co.
How Can I, Dainty Dinosaur? (Illus.). (ps-k). 1990. lib. bdg. 6.95 (*0-8136-5226-X*, TK7291); pap. 3.50 (*0-685-38661-9*, TK7294) Modern Curr.
Hsiung, S. I. Lady Precious Stream. Taylor, C. W., retold by. (Illus.). (gr. k-6). 1971. pap. text ed. 3.95x (*0-19-638235-1*) OUP.
Hurd, Edith T. Last One Home Is a Green Pig. Hurd, Clement, illus. LC 59-8972. 64p. (gr. k-3). 1959. PLB 11.89 (*0-06-022716-8*) HarpC Child Bks.
I Like to Write. (Illus.). (ps-5). 3.50 (*0-7214-0479-0*); Ser. S705, No. 2. wkbk. 1.95 (*0-317-04018-9*) Ladybird Bks.
I Wish. (Illus.). (ps-5). 3.50 (*0-7214-8004-7*); Ser. S50. wkbk. C 1.95 (*0-7214-8009-8*) Ladybird Bks.
I'm Reading...All By Myself! rev. ed. 34p. (gr. k-2). 1982. incl. cass. 12.95 (*0-88679-249-5*) Educ Insights.
Isaak, Betty. Garbage Games. 112p. (gr. 1-4). 1980. 9.95 (*0-88160-012-1*, LW 115) Learning Wks.
It Will Be Fun, Dainty Dinosaur. (Illus.). (ps-2). 1991. PLB 6.95 (*0-8136-5215-4*, TK7297); pap. 3.50 (*0-8136-5715-6*, TK7298) Modern Curr.
Jaspersohn, William. How the Forest Grew. Eckart, Chuck, illus. LC 79-16286. 56p. (gr. 1 up). 1989. Repr. of 1980 ed. 13.95 (*0-688-80232-X*) Greenwillow.
Javernick, Ellen. Gifted & Talented Beginning Readers: Double the Trouble. 32p. 1994. 6.95 (*0-685-72656-8*) Lowell Hse Juvenile.
—Gifted & Talented Beginning Readers: Time for Bed! 32p. (gr. 3 up). 1994. 6.95 (*1-56565-163-4*) Lowell Hse Juvenile.
Johnson, Crockett. Picture for Harold's Room. Johnson, Crockett, illus. LC 60-6372. 64p. (gr. k-3). 1960. PLB 13.89 (*0-06-023006-1*) HarpC Child Bks.
Johnson, John E., illus. My First Book of Things. LC 78-64609. (ps). 1979. 3.95 (*0-394-84128-X*) Random Bks Yng Read.
Jump from the Sky. (Illus.). (ps-5). 3.50 (*0-7214-0545-2*) Ladybird Bks.
Kamm, Karlyn & Chastain, Gerald, Jr. Central Thought. (gr. 5). Date not set. incl. software 95.00 (*0-912899-14-X*) Lrning Multi-Systs.
—Central Thought. (gr. 3). Date not set. incl. software 70.00 (*0-912899-10-7*) Lrning Multi-Systs.
—Paraphrase. (gr. 5). Date not set. incl. software 95.00 (*0-912899-16-6*) Lrning Multi-Systs.
—Paraphrase. (gr. 3). Date not set. incl. software 70.00 (*0-912899-12-3*) Lrning Multi-Systs.
—Relationships - Conclusions. (gr. 3). Date not set. incl. software 70.00 (*0-912899-13-1*) Lrning Multi-Systs.
—Sequence. (gr. 5). Date not set. incl. software 95.00 (*0-912899-15-8*) Lrning Multi-Systs.
—Sequence. (gr. 3). Date not set. incl. software 70.00 (*0-912899-11-5*) Lrning Multi-Systs.
—SolarTrack. (gr. 5). Date not set. incl. software 95.00 (*0-912899-17-4*) Lrning Multi-Systs.
Kapelman, Helen H. Nini's Way, Bk. 1. Kapelman, Helen H., illus. (gr. k-2). 1988. 4.95 (*0-9621807-0-X*) H H Kapelman.
Kate & the Crocodile. (Illus.). (ps-2). 1990. 3.50 (*0-7214-1318-8*); parent/tchr's. guide 3.95 (*0-317-04029-4*); Series 9011-5, No. 5. activity bk. 1.95 (*0-7214-3224-7*) Ladybird Bks.
Kessler, Leonard. Here Comes the Strikeout. newly illus. ed. Kessler, Leonard, illus. LC 91-14717. 64p. (gr. k-3). 1965. 14.00 (*0-06-023155-6*); PLB 13.89 (*0-06-023156-4*) HarpC Child Bks.
Laird, Elizabeth. American Homes. (Illus.). 31p. 1989. pap. text ed. 5.25 (*0-582-01716-5*, 78664) Longman.
—Americans on the Move. (Illus.). 31p. (Orig.). 1989. pap. text ed. 5.25 (*0-582-01715-7*, 78663) Longman.
Learning Is Fun. (Illus.). (ps-5). 3.50 (*0-7214-0628-9*) Ladybird Bks.
Lecourt, Nancy. Rainbow. 32p. (gr. 2). 1980. pap. 1.95 (*0-8127-0290-5*) Review & Herald.
Let Me Write. (Illus.). (ps-5). 3.50 (*0-7214-0027-2*); Ser. S705. wkbk. No. 3 1.95 (*0-317-04758-2*) Ladybird Bks.
Let's Play. (Illus.). (ps-2). 1990. 3.50 (*0-7214-1314-5*); parent/tchr's. guide 3.95 (*0-317-04025-1*); Series 9011-1, No. 1. activity bk. 1.95 (*0-7214-3220-4*) Ladybird Bks.
Lewison, Wendy C., et al. But Why? Reading Workbook. Murdocca, Sal, illus. Pape, Richard, designed by. (Illus.). 32p. (Orig.). (gr. k-2). 1988. wkbk. 1.99 (*0-88743-109-7*) Sch Zone Pub Co.
Lexau, Joan M. Rooftop Mystery. Hoff, Syd, illus. LC 68-16821. 64p. (gr. k-3). 1968. PLB 13.89 (*0-06-023865-8*) HarpC Child Bks.
Litchfield, Ada B. A Cane in Her Hand. Rubin, Caroline, ed. Mill, Eleanor, illus. LC 77-14255. (gr. 1-3). 1977. PLB 13.95 (*0-8075-1056-4*) A Whitman.
Lovelady, Janet. Aladdin Literature Mini-Unit. (Illus.). 32p. (gr. 3-5). 1990. wkbk. 4.95 (*1-56096-016-7*) Mari.
—Annie & the Old One Literature Mini-Unit. (Illus.). 32p. (gr. 3-5). 1990. wkbk. 4.95 (*1-56096-018-3*) Mari.
—Big Bad Bruce Literature Mini-Unit. (Illus.). 32p. (gr. 2-4). 1989. wkbk. 4.95 (*1-56096-001-9*) Mari.
—Bread & Jam for Frances Literature Mini-Unit. (Illus.). 32p. (gr. 2-4). 1989. wkbk. 4.95 (*1-56096-002-7*) Mari.
—Bremen-Town Musicians Literature Mini-Unit. (Illus.). 32p. (gr. 2-4). 1989. wkbk. 4.95 (*1-56096-004-3*) Mari.
—The Drinking Gourd Literature Mini-Unit. (Illus.). 32p. (gr. 3-5). 1990. wkbk. 4.95 (*1-56096-019-1*) Mari.
—Hill of Fire Literature Mini Unit. (Illus.). 32p. (gr. 2-4). 1989. wkbk. 4.95 (*1-56096-005-1*) Mari.
—The Hundred Dresses Literature Mini-Unit. (Illus.). 32p. (gr. 3-5). 1990. wkbk. 4.95 (*1-56096-014-0*) Mari.
—The Little House Literature Mini-Unit. (Illus.). 32p. (gr. 2-4). 1989. wkbk. 4.95 (*1-56096-000-0*) Mari.
—Long Way to a New Land Literature Mini-Unit. (Illus.). 32p. (gr. 3-5). 1990. wkbk. 4.95 (*1-56096-013-2*) Mari.
—Make Way for Ducklings Literature Mini-Unit. (Illus.). 32p. (gr. 2-4). 1989. wkbk. 4.95 (*1-56096-006-X*) Mari.
—Miss Rumphius Literature Mini-Unit. (Illus.). 32p. (gr. 2-4). 1989. wkbk. 4.95 (*1-56096-003-5*) Mari.
—Sam, Bangs & Moonshine Literature Mini-Unit. (Illus.). 32p. (gr. 3-5). 1990. wkbk. 4.95 (*1-56096-012-4*) Mari.
—Shoeshine Girl Literature Mini-Unit. (Illus.). 32p. (gr. 3-5). 1990. wkbk. 4.95 (*1-56096-017-5*) Mari.
—Song of the Swallows Literature Mini-Unit. (Illus.). 32p. (gr. 2-4). 1989. wkbk. 4.95 (*1-56096-007-8*) Mari.
—Stone Soup Literature Mini-Unit. (Illus.). 32p. (gr. 2-4). 1989. wkbk. 4.95 (*1-56096-008-6*) Mari.
—Strega Nona Literature Mini-Unit. (Illus.). 32p. (gr. 2-4). 1989. wkbk. 4.95 (*1-56096-009-4*) Mari.
—The Ugly Duckling Literature Mini-Unit. (Illus.). 32p. (gr. 3-5). 1990. wkbk. 4.95 (*1-56096-015-9*) Mari.
—Velveteen Rabbit Literature Mini-Unit. (Illus.). 32p. (gr. 3-5). 1990. wkbk. 4.95 (*1-56096-011-6*) Mari.
—Wagon Wheels Literature Mini-Unit. (Illus.). 32p. (gr. 3-5). 1990. wkbk. 4.95 (*1-56096-010-8*) Mari.
Lucky Dip. (Illus.). (ps-5). 3.50 (*0-7214-8000-4*); Ser. S50. wkbk. A 1.95 (*0-7214-8007-1*) Ladybird Bks.
Lukasevich, Ann. Food & Fantasy, Vol. 2: Literature-Based Thematic Units for Early Primary. (ps-3). 1993. pap. 18.95 (*0-201-49037-4*) Addison-Wesley.
McFarland, Philip J., et al. Focus on People. (Illus.). (gr. 8). 1981. HM.
McGuffey, William H. The Original McGuffey's Eclectic Series, 7 Vols. (gr. k-12). 1982. Repr. of 1837 ed. 89.95 (*0-88062-014-5*) Mott Media.
McKissack, Patricia & McKissack, Fredrick. No Need for Alarm. Smith, Phil, illus. LC 88-60388. 32p. (Orig.). (gr. 1-3). 1990. text ed. 8.95 (*0-88335-783-6*); pap. text ed. 4.95 (*0-88335-795-X*) Milliken Pub Co.
McKissack, Patricia & McKissack, Fredrick. Reading Well Softcover Package, 24 bks. (Illus., Orig.). (gr. 1-3). 1989. Set, 32p. ea. pap. 107.00 (*0-88335-739-9*) Milliken Pub Co.
McKissack, Patricia & McKissack, Fredrick. A Troll in a Hole. Bartholomew, illus. LC 88-60384. 32p. (Orig.). (gr. 1-3). 1988. text ed. 8.95 (*0-88335-782-8*); pap. text ed. 4.95 (*0-88335-794-1*) Milliken Pub Co.

McKissack, Patricia & McKissack, Frederick, eds. Reading Well Hardcover Package, 24 bks. (Illus.). (gr. 1-3). 1989. Set, 32p. ea. 190.00 (*0-88335-717-8*) Milliken Pub Co.

Magic Music. (Illus.). (ps-2). 1990. 3.50 (*0-7214-1323-4*); parent/tchr's. guide 3.95 (*0-317-04034-0*) Ladybird Bks.

Mayberry, Claude. Discovering Seeds of Change. (ps-3). 1993. pap. 4.95 (*0-201-49001-3*) Addison-Wesley.

—Discovering Seeds of Change. (ps-3). 1993. pap. 4.95 (*0-201-49002-1*) Addison-Wesley.

—Discovering Seeds of Change. 1993. pap. 4.95 (*0-201-49003-X*) Addison-Wesley.

Miles, Betty. How to Read: A Book for Beginners. LC 93-25884. Date not set. write for info. (*0-679-85644-7*) Knopf.

Minarik, Else H. Father Bear Comes Home. Sendak, Maurice, illus. LC 59-5794. 64p. (gr. k-3). 1959. 14.00 (*0-06-024230-2*); PLB 13.89 (*0-06-024231-0*) HarpC Child Bks.

—Little Bear. Sendak, Maurice, illus. 64p. (gr. k-3). 1957. 14.00i (*0-06-024240-X*); PLB 13.89 (*0-06-024241-8*) HarpC Child Bks.

—Little Bear's Friend. Sendak, Maurice, illus. LC 60-6370. 64p. (gr. k-3). 1960. 14.00i (*0-06-024255-8*); PLB 13.89 (*0-06-024256-6*) HarpC Child Bks.

—Little Bear's Visit. Sendak, Maurice, illus. LC 61-11451. 64p. (ps-3). 1961. 14.00 (*0-06-024265-5*); PLB 13.89 (*0-06-024266-3*) HarpC Child Bks.

—No Fighting, No Biting! Sendak, Maurice, illus. LC 58-5293. 64p. (gr. k-3). 1958. 13.00 (*0-06-024290-6*); PLB 13.89 (*0-06-024291-4*) HarpC Child Bks.

Moncure, Jane B. My "c" Sound Box. Sommers, Linda, illus. LC 78-23638. (ps-2). 1979. PLB 14.95 (*0-89565-052-5*) Childs World.

—My "g" Sound Box. Sommers, Linda, illus. LC 78-22037. (ps-2). 1979. PLB 14.95 (*0-89565-053-3*) Childs World.

—My "j" Sound Box. Sommers, Linda, illus. LC 78-23178. (ps-2). 1979. PLB 14.95 (*0-89565-049-5*) Childs World.

—My "k" Sound Box. Sommers, Linda, illus. LC 78-22034. (ps-2). 1979. PLB 14.95 (*0-89565-050-9*) Childs World.

—My "m" Sound Box. Sommers, Linda, illus. LC 78-24458. (ps-2). 1979. PLB 14.95 (*0-89565-051-7*) Childs World.

—My "n" Sound Box. Sommers, Linda, illus. LC 78-22053. (ps-2). 1979. PLB 14.95 (*0-89565-054-1*) Childs World.

—My "q" Sound Box. Sommers, Linda, illus. LC 79-13085. (ps-2). 1979. PLB 14.95 (*0-89565-100-9*) Childs World.

—My Sound Parade. Sommers, Linda, illus. LC 79-15930. (ps-2). 1979. PLB 14.95 (*0-89565-103-3*) Childs World.

—My "v" Sound Box. Sommers, Linda, illus. LC 79-13084. (ps-2). 1979. PLB 14.95 (*0-89565-101-7*) Childs World.

—My "x, y, z" Sound Box. Sommers, Linda, illus. LC 79-13086. (ps-2). 1979. PLB 14.95 (*0-89565-102-5*) Childs World.

—Play with A & T. McCallum, Jodi, illus. LC 89-774. 32p. (gr. k-2). 1989. PLB 14.95 (*0-89565-505-5*) Childs World.

—Play with E & D. (Illus.). 32p. (gr. k-2). 1989. PLB 14.95 (*0-89565-508-X*) Childs World.

—Play with I & G. (Illus.). 32p. (gr. k-2). 1989. PLB 14.95 (*0-89565-507-1*) Childs World.

—Play with O & G. (Illus.). 32p. (gr. k-2). 1989. PLB 14.95 (*0-89565-506-3*) Childs World.

—Play with U & G. (Illus.). 32p. (gr. k-2). 1989. PLB 14.95 (*0-89565-509-8*) Childs World.

—Short A & Long A Play a Game. Endres, Helen, illus. LC 79-10300. (gr. k-2). 1979. PLB 14.95 (*0-89565-089-4*) Childs World.

—Short E & Long E Play a Game. Endres, Helen, illus. LC 79-10305. (gr. k-2). 1979. PLB 14.95 (*0-89565-090-8*) Childs World.

—Short I & Long I Play a Game. Endres, Helen, illus. LC 79-10303. (gr. k-2). 1979. PLB 14.95 (*0-89565-091-6*) Childs World.

—Short O & Long O Play a Game. Endres, Helen, illus. LC 79-10304. (gr. k-2). 1979. PLB 14.95 (*0-89565-092-4*) Childs World.

—Short U & Long U Play a Game. Endres, Helen, illus. LC 79-10306. (gr. k-2). 1979. PLB 14.95 (*0-89565-093-2*) Childs World.

Moore, Elaine. Mixed-Up Sam. McKissack, Patricia & McKissack, Fredrick, eds. Boddy, Joe, illus. LC 88-60390. 32p. (Orig.). (gr. 1-3). 1988. text ed. 8.95 (*0-88335-786-0*); pap. text ed. 4.95 (*0-88335-798-4*) Milliken Pub Co.

More Sounds to Say. (Illus.). (ps-5). 3.50 (*0-7214-0029-9*); Ser. S705, No. 5. wkbk. 1.95 (*0-317-04020-0*) Ladybird Bks.

Morse, Joyce. Peter Sinks in the Water. 32p. (Orig.). (gr. 2). 1980. pap. 1.95 (*0-8127-0281-6*) Review & Herald.

Mountain, Lee, et al. Jamestown Heritage Reader, Bk. A. (Illus.). 160p. (gr. 1). 1991. 12.10 (*0-89061-710-4*); pap. 9.10 (*0-89061-951-4*); tchr's. ed. 22.10 (*0-89061-961-1*) Jamestown Pubs.

—Jamestown Heritage Reader, Bk. C. 256p. (gr. 3). 1991. 14.95 (*0-89061-712-0*); pap. 11.95 (*0-89061-953-0*); tchr's. ed. 24.95 (*0-89061-963-8*) Jamestown Pubs.

—Jamestown Heritage Reader, Bk. E. 256p. (gr. 5). 1991. 16.50 (*0-89061-714-7*); pap. 13.50 (*0-89061-955-7*); tchr's. ed. 26.50 (*0-89061-965-4*) Jamestown Pubs.

—Jamestown Heritage Reader, Bk. F. 246p. (gr. 6). 1991. 17.20 (*0-89061-715-5*); pap. 14.20 (*0-89061-956-5*); tchr's. ed. 27.20 (*0-89061-966-2*) Jamestown Pubs.

Mylet, Trish. Children, Today's Joy & Tomorrow's Hope, 8 bks, Set 2. Sheffield, Antoinette, illus. 224p. (ps-3). 1991. Set. pap. text ed. 16.00 (*0-945590-62-8*) Pals 1, Pals 2, Pals 3, Pals 4, Pals 5, Pals 6, Pals 7, Pals 8. Sizzy Bks.

—Fun with Phonics, 19 bks. Sheffield, Antoinette, illus. 448p. (ps-3). 1991. Set 1 & 2. pap. text ed. 39.95 (*1-881754-70-7*) Set 1: Jan & Pam, The Van, Rex & Tex, The Bed, Siz & Liz, The Pit, Dod & Bob, The Box, Hun & Sun, The Hut, Pals. Set 2: Pals 1, Pals 2, Pals, 3, Pals 4, Pals 5, Pals, 6, Pals 7, Pals 8. Dolphin Lrning.

FUN WITH PHONICS: Set 1 & Set 2, 19 books. This SERIES consists of two Sets of books. Set 1 contains 11 beginning reader & activity books. Set 2 contains 8 books of short stories & activity books. The CHILDREN SERIES consists of positive global readers incorporating geography (the fifty United States & the District of Columbia), phonics (short & long vowels, blends, diagraphs), number recognition & self expression & explores the areas of zoology, botany, history & global unity. Each pair of books in Set 1 & each story in Set 2 contain a state reference page with a dot-to-dot exercise in the shape of that state's outline. The first sixteen books include sentence completion exercises & that story's word list. In Set 2 at least one story in each book has an O. Henry-type ending in which the child decides how the story ends. The SERIES includes a Reference Guide. Building on Set 1's themes of fun & fantasy, Set 2 expands & concludes with joy, fact & hope. This warmly written & illustrated series has been well received worldwide by Early Education, Special Education & English as a Second Language teachers, parents & most importantly, children. $39.95. Trish Mylet, author. Antoinette Sheffield, illustrator. Dolphin Publishing Group, Box 2570, Fair Oaks, CA 95628. ISBN 1-881754-70-7 Write for brochure.

Publisher Provided Annotation.

Myrick, Mildred. Secret Three. Lobel, Arnold, illus. LC 63-13323. 64p. (gr. k-3). 1963. PLB 13.89 (*0-06-024356-2*) HarpC Child Bks.

North, A. C. & Attwood, Teresa K. Protein Structure. 3rd ed. Head, J. J., ed. (Illus.). 32p. (gr. 10 up). 1991. pap. 3.00 (*0-89278-434-2*, 45-9634) Carolina Biological.

Open Door to Reading. (Illus.). (ps-5). 3.50 (*0-7214-0036-1*) Ladybird Bks.

Our Friends. (Illus.). (ps-5). 3.50 (*0-7214-0508-8*); Ser. S705, No. 6. wkbk. 1.95 (*0-7214-3067-8*); Series S05, Set 1. flash cards 4.75 (*0-317-03987-3*) Ladybird Bks.

Out in the Sun. (Illus.). (ps-5). 3.50 (*0-7214-0541-X*); Ser. S705, No. 5. wkbk. 1.95 (*0-317-04013-8*) Ladybird Bks.

Paltrowitz, Stuart & Paltrowitz, Donna. Content Area Reading Skills-Competency Canada: Main Idea. (Illus.). (gr. 4). 1987. pap. text ed. 3.25 (*0-89525-853-6*) Ed Activities.

—Content Area Reading Skills-Competency Mexico: Locating Details. (Illus.). (gr. 4). 1987. pap. text ed. 3.25 (*0-89525-854-4*) Ed Activities.

—Content Area Reading Skills-Competency U. S. History: Detecting Sequence. (Illus.). (gr. 4). 1987. pap. text ed. 3.25 (*0-89525-856-0*) Ed Activities.

—Content Area Reading Skills U. S. Geography: Cause & Effect. (Illus.). (gr. 4). 1987. pap. text ed. 3.25 (*0-89525-855-2*) Ed Activities.

Pape, et al. Oddo Sound Series: 1968, 1974, 1978, 10 vols. (Illus.). (gr. 2-5). 1978. Set. PLB 109.50 (*0-87783-165-3*) Oddo.

Parish, Peggy. Amelia Bedelia & the Surprise Shower. Siebel, Fritz, illus. LC 66-18655. 64p. (gr. k-3). 1966. 14.00 (*0-06-024642-1*); PLB 13.89 (*0-06-024643-X*) HarpC Child Bks.

—Come Back, Amelia Bedelia. Tripp, Wallace, illus. LC 73-121799. 64p. (ps-3). 1971. 14.00 (*0-06-024667-7*); PLB 13.89 (*0-06-024668-5*) HarpC Child Bks.

Peters, Sharon. Fun at Camp. Trivas, Irene, illus. 32p. (gr. k-2). 1980. PLB 7.89 (*0-89375-378-5*); pap. 1.95 (*0-89375-278-9*) Troll Assocs.

—Happy Birthday. Harvey, Paul, illus. 32p. (gr. k-2). 1980. PLB 7.89 (*0-89375-379-3*); pap. 1.95 (*0-89375-279-7*) Troll Assocs.

—Happy Jack. Harvey, Paul, illus. 32p. (gr. k-2). 1980. PLB 7.89 (*0-89375-380-7*); pap. 1.95 (*0-89375-280-0*) Troll Assocs.

—Messy Mark. Trivas, Irene, illus. 32p. (gr. k-2). 1980. PLB 7.89 (*0-89375-381-5*); pap. 1.95 (*0-89375-281-9*) Troll Assocs.

—Puppet Show. Lee, Alan, illus. 32p. (gr. k-2). 1980. PLB 7.89 (*0-89375-385-8*); pap. 1.95 (*0-89375-286-X*) Troll Assocs.

—Ready, Get Set, Go! Trivas, Irene, illus. 32p. (gr. k-2). 1980. PLB 7.89 (*0-89375-386-6*); pap. 1.95 (*0-89375-285-1*) Troll Assocs.

—Stop That Rabbit. Silverstein, Don, illus. 32p. (gr. k-2). 1980. PLB 7.89 (*0-89375-388-2*); pap. 1.95 (*0-89375-288-6*) Troll Assocs.

—Trick or Treat Halloween. Hall, Susan T., illus. 32p. (gr. k-2). 1980. PLB 7.89 (*0-89375-392-0*); pap. 1.95 (*0-89375-292-4*) Troll Assocs.

Phleger, Frederick B. Red Tag Comes Back. Lobel, Arnold, illus. LC 61-11452. 64p. (gr. k-3). 1961. PLB 13.89 (*0-06-024706-1*) HarpC Child Bks.

Play with Us. (Illus.). (ps-5). 3.50 (*0-7214-0001-9*); Ser. S705, No. 1. wkbk. 1.95 (*0-7214-3062-7*) Ladybird Bks.

Polette, Keith. The Winter Duckling. McKissack, Patricia & McKissack, Fredrick, eds. Martin, Clovis, illus. LC 88-60393. 32p. (Orig.). (gr. 1-3). 1990. text ed. 8.95 (*0-88335-777-1*); pap. text ed. 4.95 (*0-88335-789-5*) Milliken Pub Co.

Polette, Nancy. Amelia Bedelia Thinking Book. expanded ed. (Illus.). 48p. (gr. k-3). 1994. pap. 5.95 (*1-879287-10-2*) Bk Lures.

—Frog & Toad Thinking Book. expanded ed. (Illus.). 48p. (gr. k-3). 1992. pap. 5.95 (*1-879287-09-9*) Bk Lures.

Polette, Nancy & O'Neal, Kathleen. Easy Reader Thinking Book. expanded ed. (Illus.). 48p. (gr. k-3). 1994. pap. 5.95 (*1-879287-08-0*) Bk Lures.

Pollack, Cecelia. How Hip Are You, Bk. 2. (Illus.). (gr. 5-12). 1978. wkbk. 5.95 (*0-87594-162-1*) Book Lab.

—How Hip Are You, Bk. 4. (Illus.). (gr. 5-12). 1978. wkbk. 5.95 (*0-87594-163-X*) Book Lab.

Pomeroy, Johanna P. Content Area Reading Skills Electricity & Magnetism. (Illus.). (gr. 4). 1987. pap. text ed. 3.25 (*0-89525-859-5*) Ed Activities.

—Content Area Reading Skills Geology: Detecting Sequence. (Illus.). (gr. 4). 1987. pap. text ed. 3.25 (*1-55737-085-0*) Ed Activities.

—Content Area Reading Skills Light: Main Idea. (Illus.). (gr. 3). 1989. pap. text ed. 3.25 (*1-55737-687-5*) Ed Activities.

—Content Area Reading Skills Machines: Detecting Sequence. (Illus.). (gr. 3). 1989. pap. text ed. 3.25 (*1-55737-690-5*) Ed Activities.

—Content Area Reading Skills Matter: Locating Details. (Illus.). (gr. 4). 1988. pap. text ed. 3.25 (*1-55737-086-9*) Ed Activities.

—Content Area Reading Skills Mechanics: Cause & Effect. (Illus.). (gr. 4). 1988. pap. text ed. 3.25 (*1-55737-088-5*) Ed Activities.

—Content Area Reading Skills Oceans: Main Idea. (Illus.). (gr. 4). 1987. pap. text ed. 3.25 (*0-89525-857-9*) Ed Activities.

—Content Area Reading Skills Our Earth: Locating Details. (Illus.). (gr. 3). 1989. pap. text ed. 3.25 (*1-55737-688-3*) Ed Activities.

—Content Area Reading skills Reproduction & Heredity: Main Idea. (Illus.). (gr. 4). 1988. pap. text ed. 3.25 (*1-55737-087-7*) Ed Activities.

—Content Area Reading Skills Solar System: Locating Details. (Illus.). (gr. 4). 1987. pap. text ed. 3.25 (*0-89525-858-7*) Ed Activities.

—Content Area Reading Skills Sound & Hearing: Detecting Sequence. (Illus.). (gr. 4). 1987. pap. text ed. 3.25 (*0-89525-860-9*) Ed Activities.

—Content Area Reading Skills Weather: Cause & Effect. (Illus.). (gr. 3). 1989. pap. text ed. 3.25 (*1-55737-689-1*) Ed Activities.

Radlauer, Ed. Bears, Bears & More Bears. Radlauer Productions Staff, illus. 32p. (ps-4). 1991. PLB 10.95 (*1-878363-34-4*) Forest Hse.

Rap, Le. The Secret of the Sheep. 15p. (gr. k-2). 1991. pap. text ed. 23.00 big bk. (*1-56843-037-X*); pap. text ed. 4.50 (*1-56843-084-1*) BGR Pub.

Read & Write. (Illus.). (ps-5). 3.50 (*0-7214-0025-6*); Ser. S705, No. 1. wkbk. 1.95 (*0-317-04017-0*) Ladybird Bks.

Reading with Sounds. (Illus.). (ps-5). 3.50 (*0-7214-0549-5*); Ser. S705, No. 6. wkbk. 1.95 (*0-317-04021-9*) Ladybird Bks.

Ready Set Read Nonfiction, 12 titles. 1992. Set. write for info. (*0-8172-3587-6*) Raintree Steck-V.

Reese, Bob. Ten Word Book Series, 10 bks. Wasserman, Dan, ed. Reese, Bob, illus. (gr. k-1). 1979. Set. write for info. (*0-89868-077-8*) ARO Pub.

Reid, E., et al. Complete Set of Readers & Workbooks: Short Vowels, Long Vowels, & Digraphs, 30 vols. 440p. (ps-3). 1986. Set. pap. text ed. 49.95 (*1-56422-045-1*) Start Reading.

—Digraph Readers, 5 vols. 40p. (ps-3). 1986. Set. pap. text ed. 9.95 (*1-56422-038-9*) Start Reading.
—Digraph Readers & Workbooks, 10 vols. 144p. (ps-3). 1986. Set. pap. text ed. 18.95 (*1-56422-044-3*) Start Reading.
—Digraph Readers & Workbooks, 150 vols. 2160p. (ps-3). 1986. Set. pap. text ed. 269.95 (*1-56422-048-6*) Start Reading.
—Digraph Workbooks, 5 vols. 104p. (ps-3). 1986. Set. pap. text ed. 9.95 (*1-56422-041-9*) Start Reading.
—Long Vowel Readers, 5 vols. 40p. (ps-3). 1986. Set. pap. text ed. 9.95 (*1-56422-037-0*) Start Reading.
—Long Vowel Readers & Workbooks, 10 vols. 164p. (ps-3). 1986. Set. pap. text ed. 18.95 (*1-56422-043-5*) Start Reading.
—Long Vowel Readers & Workbooks, 150 vols. 2460p. (ps-3). 1986. Set. pap. text ed. 269.95 (*1-56422-047-8*) Start Reading.
—Long Vowel Workbooks, 5 vols. 124p. (ps-3). 1986. Set. pap. text ed. 9.95 (*1-56422-040-0*) Start Reading.
—Mastery Workbook for Ann: Short "a" Sound. 12p. (ps-3). 1986. pap. 1.99 wkbk. (*1-56422-015-X*) Start Reading.
—Mastery Workbook for the Blue Boat: Long "o" Sound. 28p. (ps-3). 1986. pap. 1.99 wkbk. (*1-56422-023-0*) Start Reading.
—Mastery Workbook for the Brown Mule: Long "u" Sound. 16p. (ps-3). 1986. pap. 1.99 wkbk. (*1-56422-024-9*) Start Reading.
—Mastery Workbook for the Chimp: Ch Sound. 20p. (ps-3). 1986. pap. 1.99 wkbk. (*1-56422-027-3*) Start Reading.
—Mastery Workbook for the Green Jeep: Long "e" Sound. 28p. (ps-3). 1986. pap. 1.99 wkbk. (*1-56422-021-4*) Start Reading.
—Mastery Workbook for the Queen: Qu Sound. 20p. (ps-3). 1986. pap. 1.99 wkbk. (*1-56422-028-1*) Start Reading.
—Mastery Workbook for the Red Plane: Long "a" Sound. 32p. (ps-3). 1986. pap. 1.99 wkbk. (*1-56422-020-6*) Start Reading.
—Mastery Workbook for the Shark: SH Sound. 20p. (ps-3). 1986. pap. 1.99 wkbk. (*1-56422-026-5*) Start Reading.
—Mastery Workbook for the Thing: Th Sound. 20p. (ps-3). 1986. pap. 1.99 wkbk. (*1-56422-029-X*) Start Reading.
—Mastery Workbook for the Whale: Wh Sound. 24p. (ps-3). 1986. pap. 1.99 wkbk. (*1-56422-025-7*) Start Reading.
—Mastery Workbook for the White Bike: Long "i" Sound. 20p. (ps-3). 1986. pap. 1.99 wkbk. (*1-56422-022-2*) Start Reading.
—Mastery Workbook for Top Dog: Short "o" Sound. 24p. (ps-3). 1986. pap. 1.99 wkbk. (*1-56422-016-8*) Start Reading.
—Mastery Workbook for up & Up: Short "u" Sound. 20p. (ps-3). 1986. pap. 1.99 wkbk. (*1-56422-018-4*) Start Reading.
—Mastery Worksheets. 72p. (ps-3). 1989. reproducible masters 39.95 (*1-56422-032-X*) Start Reading.
—Mastery Worksheets. 86p. (ps-3). 1989. reproducible masters 39.95 (*1-56422-033-8*) Start Reading.
—Mastery Worksheets. 73p. (ps-3). 1989. reproducible masters 39.95 (*1-56422-034-6*) Start Reading.
—Short Vowel, Long Vowel, Digraph Readers & Workbooks, 450 vols. 6600p. (ps-3). 1986. Set. pap. text ed. 649.95 (*1-56422-049-4*) Start Reading.
—Short Vowel Readers, 5 vols. 40p. (ps-3). 1986. Set. pap. text ed. 9.95 (*1-56422-036-2*) Start Reading.
—Short Vowel Readers & Workbooks, 10 vols. 132p. (ps-3). 1986. Set. pap. text ed. 18.95 (*1-56422-042-7*) Start Reading.
—Short Vowel Workbooks, 5 vols. 92p. (ps-3). 1986. Set. pap. text ed. 9.95 (*1-56422-039-7*) Start Reading.
—Start Reading with Ann: Short "A" Sound. 8p. (ps-3). 1986. pap. text ed. 1.99 (*1-56422-000-1*) Start Reading.
—Start Reading with Get Set: Short "e" Sound. 8p. (ps-3). 1986. pap. text ed. 1.99 (*1-56422-004-4*) Start Reading.
—Start Reading with Red Plane: Long "a" Sound. 8p. (ps-3). 1986. pap. text ed. 1.99 (*1-56422-005-2*) Start Reading.
—Start Reading with the Blue Boat: Long "o" Sound. 8p. (ps-3). 1986. pap. text ed. 1.99 (*1-56422-006-0*) Start Reading.
—Start Reading with the Brown Mule: Long "u" Sound. 8p. (ps-3). 1986. pap. text ed. 1.99 (*1-56422-009-5*) Start Reading.
—Start Reading with the Chimp: Ch Sound. 8p. (ps-3). 1986. pap. text ed. 1.99 (*1-56422-012-5*) Start Reading.
—Start Reading with the Green Jeep: Long "e" Sound. 8p. (ps-3). 1986. pap. text ed. 1.99 (*1-56422-007-9*) Start Reading.
—Start Reading with the Queen: Qu Sound. 8p. (ps-3). 1986. pap. text ed. 1.99 (*1-56422-013-3*) Start Reading.
—Start Reading with the Thing: Th Sound. 8p. (ps-3). 1986. pap. text ed. 1.99 (*1-56422-010-9*) Start Reading.
—Start Reading with the Whale: Wh Sound. 8p. (ps-3). 1986. pap. text ed. 1.99 (*1-56422-014-1*) Start Reading.
—Start Reading with the White Bike: Long "i" Sound. 8p. (ps-3). 1986. pap. text ed. 1.99 (*1-56422-008-7*) Start Reading.
—Start Reading with Tip: Short "i" Sound. 8p. (ps-3). 1986. pap. text ed. 1.99 (*1-56422-001-X*) Start Reading.
—Start Reading with Top Dog: Short "o" Sound. 8p. (ps-3). 1986. pap. text ed. 1.99 (*1-56422-002-8*) Start Reading.
—Start Reading with up & Up: Short "u" Sound. 8p. (ps-3). 1986. pap. text ed. 1.99 (*1-56422-003-6*) Start Reading.
Reiss, Elayne & Freidman, Rita. A-Choo. (Illus.). (gr. k-1). 1990. 12.50 (*0-89796-864-6*) New Dimens Educ.
Reiss, Elayne & Friedman, Rita. A Buttonmat for Beautiful Buttons. (gr. k-1). 1978. 12.50 (*0-89796-865-4*) New Dimens Educ.
Richard-Amato, Patricia A. Reading in the Content Areas: An Interactive Approach for Advanced Students. 1990. pap. text ed. 20.50 (*0-8013-0247-1*, 75902) Longman.
Richecky, Janet. Excuse Me. Connelly, Gwen, illus. 32p. (ps-2). 1989. PLB 12.95 (*0-89565-539-X*) Childs World.
Riehecky, Janet. After You. Connelly, Gwen, illus. 32p. (ps-2). 1989. PLB 12.95 (*0-89565-538-1*) Childs World.
The Robbery. (Illus.). (ps-2). 1990. 3.50 (*0-7214-1328-5*); parent/tchr's. guide 3.95 (*0-317-04038-3*) Ladybird Bks.
Roop, Peter & Roop, Connie. Snips the Tinker. McKissack, Patricia & McKissack, Fredrick, eds. Brown, Craig M., illus. LC 88-60385. 32p. (Orig.). (gr. 1-3). 1990. text ed. 8.95 (*0-88335-785-2*); pap. text ed. 4.95 (*0-88335-797-6*) Milliken Pub Co.
Salaz, Ruben D. Cosmic Reader of the Southwest for Young People. Aragon, Loretta, illus. (gr. 4 up). 1976. pap. 6.95 (*0-932492-00-2*) Cosmic Hse NM.
—La Lectura Cosmica del Suroeste-para los Jovenes. Minkin, Rita, tr. from ENG. Aragon, Loretta, illus. (SPA.). (gr. 7 up). 1978. pap. 6.95 (*0-932492-01-0*) Cosmic Hse NM.
Say the Sound. (Illus.). (ps-5). 3.50 (*0-7214-0028-0*); Ser. S705, No. 4. wkbk. 1.95 (*0-317-04019-7*) Ladybird Bks.
Scarry, Richard. Best Word Book. (FRE.). (gr. 3-8). 14.95 (*0-685-28441-7*) Fr & Eur.
Seashell Magic. (Illus.). (ps-2). 1991. PLB 6.95 (*0-8136-5191-3*, TK7255); pap. 3.50 (*0-8136-5691-5*, TK7256) Modern Curr.
Selsam, Millicent E. Greg's Microscope. Lobel, Arnold, illus. LC 63-8002. 64p. (gr. k-3). 1963. PLB 13.89 (*0-06-025296-0*) HarpC Child Bks.
Smith, Mary M. Orla's Upside Down Day. rev. ed. Lewis, Jan, illus. 32p. (gr. k-2). 1990. Repr. of 1989 ed. PLB 10.95 (*1-878363-05-0*) Forest Hse.
Snow, Pegeen. Eat Your Peas, Louise! Venezia, Mike, illus. LC 84-27445. 32p. (ps-2). 1985. PLB 10.25 (*0-516-02067-6*); pap. 2.95 (*0-516-42067-4*); pap. 22. 95 big bk. (*0-516-49452-X*) Childrens.
Speedsters Series. (Illus.). (gr. 2-5). write for info. (*0-525-44950-7*) Dutton Child Bks.
Stewart, Jeffrey E. Food! A Reading Program. (Illus.). 116p. (Orig.). (gr. 4 up). 1987. pap. 32.50 (*1-877866-00-8*) J E Stewart.
—More Food! A Reading Program. (Illus.). 116p. (Orig.). (gr. 4 up). 1988. pap. 32.50 (*1-877866-01-6*) J E Stewart.
Stolz, Mary. Emmett's Pig. Williams, Garth, illus. LC 58-7763. 64p. (gr. k-3). 1959. PLB 13.89 (*0-06-025856-X*) HarpC Child Bks.
Stuart, Jesse. A Jesse Stuart Reader. 4th ed. Bogart, Max & DeMers, Ellafrwd. by. 344p. (gr. 8 up). 1988. Repr. of 1963 ed. text ed. 20.00 (*0-945084-05-6*) J Stuart Found.
Things We Do. (Illus.). (ps-5). 3.50 (*0-7214-0540-1*); Ser. S705, No. 4. wkbk. 1.95 (*0-7214-3065-1*) Ladybird Bks.
Things We Like. (Illus.). (ps-5). 3.50 (*0-7214-0003-5*); Ser. S705, No. 3. wkbk. 1.95 (*0-7214-3064-3*) Ladybird Bks.
Thompson, Timothy J. Figs & Nuts. Thompson, Timothy J., illus. LC 80-83134. 15p. (Orig.). (ps-1). 1980. pap. text ed. 3.50 (*0-915676-03-6*) Ed Sys Pub.
—Ten Red Rods. Thompson, Timothy J., illus. LC 80-83135. 16p. (Orig.). (ps-1). 1980. pap. text ed. 3.50 (*0-915676-02-8*) Ed Sys Pub.
Tom's Storybook. (Illus.). (ps-2). 1990. 3.50 (*0-7214-1321-8*); parent/tchr's. guide 3.95 (*0-317-04636-5*) Ladybird Bks.
Waugh, Charles & Greenberg, Martin, eds. The Newbery Award Reader. Hamilton, Virginia, intro. by. 252p. (gr. 7 up). 1984. 14.95 (*0-15-257034-9*, HB Juv Bks) HarBrace.
We Have Fun. (Illus.). (ps-5). 3.50 (*0-7214-0002-7*); Ser. S705, No. 2. wkbk. 1.95 (*0-7214-3063-5*) Ladybird Bks.
We Like to Help. (Illus.). (ps-5). 3.50 (*0-7214-0542-8*); Ser. S705, No. 6. wkbk. 1.95 (*0-317-04015-4*) Ladybird Bks.
Westcott, Alvin. Billy Lump's Adventure. LC 68-56817. (Illus.). 32p. (gr. 2-4). 1968. PLB 9.95 (*0-87783-002-9*) Oddo.
Where We Go. (Illus.). (ps-5). 3.50 (*0-7214-0005-1*); Ser. S705, No. 5. wkbk. 1.95 (*0-7214-3066-X*) Ladybird Bks.
Wise, Francis H. Ann. Wise, Joyce M., ed. & illus. 21p. (ps-1). 1983. pap. 1.50 (*0-915766-60-4*) Wise Pub.
—The Beach. Wise, Joyce M., ed. & illus. 21p. (ps-1). 1983. pap. 1.50 (*0-915766-63-9*) Wise Pub.
—Ed, 20 bks. 3rd ed. Wise, Joyce M., ed. (Illus.). 21p. (ps-1). 1983. pap. 1.50 (*0-915766-59-0*) Wise Pub.
Wise, Francis H. & Wise, Joyce M. Bernie, the Saint. new ed. (Illus.). 21p. (Orig.). (gr. 1). 1980. pap. 1.50 (*0-915766-41-8*) Wise Pub.
—Park the Car. Wise, Joyce M., illus. (ps-1). 1975. pap. text ed. 1.50 (*0-915766-32-9*) Wise Pub.
—Play Ball. Wise, Joyce M., illus. (ps-1). 1975. pap. text ed. 1.50 (*0-915766-31-0*) Wise Pub.
—Sit By Me. Wise, Joyce M., illus. (ps-1). 1975. pap. text ed. 1.50 (*0-915766-33-7*) Wise Pub.
Wiseman, Bernard. Morris Goes to School. Wiseman, Bernard, illus. LC 75-77944. 64p. (gr. k-3). 1970. PLB 13.89 (*0-06-026548-5*) HarpC Child Bks.
Wittwer, Sylvan H. The Greenhouse Effect. Head, J. J., ed. Steffen, Ann T., illus. LC 84-45833. 16p. (Orig.). (gr. 10 up). 1988. pap. text ed. 2.75 (*0-89278-363-X*, 45-9763) Carolina Biological.
Witty, Bruce. A Different Tune. Hoffman, Joan, ed. Laurent, Richard, illus. 32p. (gr. k-2). 1987. wkbk. 1.99 (*0-88743-103-8*, 02603) Sch Zone Pub Co.
Witty, Bruce & Gregorich, Barbara. Noise in the Night: Reading Workbook. Hoffman, Joan, ed. Nerlove, Miriam & Pape, Richard, illus. 32p. (Orig.). (gr. k-2). 1988. 1.99 (*0-88743-106-2*) Sch Zone Pub Co.
—The Raccoon on the Moon: Reading Workbook. Hoffman, Joan, ed. Sandford, John & Pape, Richard, illus. 32p. (Orig.). (gr. k-2). 1988. 1.99 (*0-88743-108-9*) Sch Zone Pub Co.
Young, Karen E. A Day at the Beach. 16p. (ps-1). 1991. pap. text ed. 21.00 big bk. (*1-56843-034-5*); pap. text ed. 4.25 (*1-56843-082-5*) BGR Pub.
—The Great Space Race. 7p. (ps-1). 1991. pap. text ed. 21.00 big bk. (*1-56843-033-7*); pap. text ed. 4.25 (*1-56843-081-7*) BGR Pub.
—Somewhere in Africa. 14p. (ps-1). 1991. pap. text ed. 21.00 big bk. (*1-56843-030-2*); pap. text ed. 4.25 (*1-56843-078-7*) BGR Pub.
Zak & Ben. (Illus.). (ps-2). 1991. PLB 6.95 (*0-8136-5161-1*, TK3833); pap. 3.50 (*0-8136-5661-3*, TK3834) Modern Curr.
Zion, Gene. Harry & the Lady Next Door. Graham, Margaret B., illus. LC 60-9452. 64p. (gr. k-3). 1978. pap. 3.50 (*0-06-444008-7*, Trophy) HarpC Child Bks.

READING

Here are entered books on methods of teaching reading and general books on the art of reading. Works on teaching retarded readers are entered under Reading–Remedial Teaching. books on the cultural aspects of reading and general discussions of books to read are entered under Books and Reading.
see also Books and Reading

Allington, Richard L. & Krull, Kathleen. Reading. Naprstek, Joel, illus. LC 80-16547. 32p. (ps-2). 1985. pap. 3.95 (*0-8114-8235-9*) Raintree Steck-V
Amerikaner, Susan. Gifted & Talented Reading Workbook. Whitten, Leesa, illus. 96p. (ps-3). 1992. pap. 3.95 (*0-929923-83-9*) Lowell Hse.
—The Gifted & Talented Reading Workbook. Whitten, Leesa, illus. 96p. (gr. 1-3). 1993. pap. 3.95 (*1-56565-040-9*) Lowell Hse.
Appell, Clara & Appell, Morey. Glenn Learns to Read. 2nd ed. Szasz, Suzanne, photos by. Appell, Clara T., intro. by. LC 87-62285. (Illus.). 64p. (ps-2). 1987. pap. 6.25 (*0-943501-00-8*) M L Appell.
Artman, John. Good Apple & Reading Fun. 144p. (gr. 3-7). 1981. 12.95 (*0-86653-046-0*, GA 278) Good Apple.
Baggiani, J. M. & Tewell, V. M. Phonics; a Tool for Better Reading & Spelling, Bk. I. Birt, Jane L., illus. (gr. 1-2). 1982. pap. 9.50 student's copy (*0-934329-00-1*); tchr's. manual 10.75 (*0-934329-01-X*) Baggiani-Tewell.
—Phonics: A Tool for Better Reading & Spelling, Bk. II. Jacobson, Mary M., illus. (gr. 3-6). 1967. pap. 3.50 (*0-934329-02-8*); wkbk. 2.00 (*0-934329-03-6*) Baggiani-Tewell.
—Phonics: A Tool for Better Reading & Spelling, Bk. III. Jacobson, Mary M. & Davis, Mary I., illus. (gr. 5-12). 1984. pap. 5.75 (*0-934329-04-4*); wkbk. 4.00 (*0-934329-05-2*) Baggiani-Tewell.
Bernholz, Jean F. & Sumner, Patricia H. Success in Reading & Writing. 2nd ed. (Illus.). 288p. (gr. 3). 1991. 27.95 (*0-673-36005-9*) GdYrBks.
Berry, Marilyn. Help Is on the Way for Reading Skills. (Illus.). 48p. (gr. 4-6). 1987. pap. 4.95 (*0-516-43232-X*) Childrens.
Beyond Basics: A Developmental Reading Program. 216p. (Orig.). (gr. 4). 1987. pap. text ed. 11.95 (*0-89061-429-6*); tchr's. ed. 17.00 (*0-89061-438-5*) Jamestown Pubs.
Beyond Basics: A Developmental Reading Program. (Illus.). 216p. (gr. 5). 1987. pap. text ed. 11.95 (*0-89061-430-X*); tchr's. ed. 17.00 (*0-89061-439-3*) Jamestown Pubs.
Beyond Basics: A Developmental Reading Program. (Illus.). 216p. (gr. 6). 1987. pap. text ed. 11.95 (*0-89061-431-8*); tchr's. ed. 17.00 (*0-89061-440-7*) Jamestown Pubs.
Beyond Basics: A Developmental Reading Program. (Illus.). 216p. (gr. 7). 1987. pap. text ed. 11.95 (*0-89061-432-6*); tchr's. ed. 17.00 (*0-89061-441-5*) Jamestown Pubs.
Beyond Basics: A Developmental Reading Program. (Illus.). 216p. (gr. 8). 1987. 11.95 (*0-89061-433-4*); tchr's. ed. 17.00 (*0-89061-442-3*) Jamestown Pubs.

Beyond Basics: A Developmental Reading Program. (Illus.). 216p. (gr. 9). 1987. pap. text ed. 11.95 (*0-89061-434-2*); tchr's. ed. 17.00 (*0-89061-443-1*) Jamestown Pubs.
Beyond Basics: A Developmental Reading Program. (Illus.). 216p. (gr. 10). 1987. pap. text ed. 11.95 (*0-89061-435-0*); tchr's. ed. 17.00 (*0-89061-444-X*) Jamestown Pubs.
Beyond Basics: A Developmental Reading Program. (Illus.). 216p. (gr. 11). 1987. 11.95 (*0-89061-436-9*); tchr's. ed. 17.00 (*0-89061-445-8*) Jamestown Pubs.
Beyond Basics: A Developmental Reading Program. (Illus.). 216p. (gr. 12). 1987. pap. text ed. 11.95 (*0-89061-437-7*); tchr's. ed. 17.00 (*0-89061-446-6*) Jamestown Pubs.
Billings, Henry & Billings, Melissa. Heroes. (Illus.). 160p. (gr. 6 up). 1985. pap. text ed. 8.75x (*0-89061-450-4*) Jamestown Pubs.
Blue, Rose. Me & Einstein: Breaking Through the Reading Barrier. Luks, Peggy, illus. (gr. 3 up). 1984. 14.95 (*0-87705-388-X*); pap. 9.95 (*0-89885-185-8*) Human Sci Pr.
Borba, Michele & Ungaro, Dan. Bookends. 128p. (gr. 1-4). 1982. 11.95 (*0-86653-065-7*, GA 432) Good Apple.
Brooks, Bearl. Jumbo Reading Yearbook: Kindergarten. 96p. (gr. k). 1980. 18.00 (*0-8209-0011-7*, JRY R) ESP.
Brown, Frances. My First Book of Words. LC 78-58344. 144p. (gr. k-6). 1979. Walker Educ.
Butrick, Lyn M. If This... & That.. Then What. Cooper, William R., ed. Butrick, Lyn M., illus. LC 83-50783. 27p. (gr. 1-3). 1983. Set. pap. 15.80 (*0-914127-13-6*); Vol. 1. 3.93 (*0-914127-04-7*) Univ Class.
Carter, Mary. Reading for Comprehension Skills. (Illus.). (gr. 2-7). 1982. wkbk. 4.50 (*0-89525-177-9*) Ed Activities.
Christman, Ernest. Dr. Christman's Learn to Read Book. Christman, Catherine, illus. 256p. (Orig.). 1990. pap. 15.95 (*0-933025-17-3*) Blue Bird Pub.
Clay, Marie. Stones: Concepts About Print Test. (Orig.). (ps-2). 1980. pap. text ed. 3.00x (*0-435-00556-1*, 00556) Heinemann.
Crane, Barbara J. BS 1 Skillbooklet, No. I. (Illus.). (gr. k-2). 1982. pap. text ed. 2.49 (*0-89075-031-9*) Bilingual Ed Serv.
Crisfield, Deborah. Literacy. LC 91-39567. (Illus.). 48p. (gr. 5-6). 1992. text ed. 12.95 RSBE (*0-89686-750-1*, Crestwood Hse) Macmillan Child Grp.
Daniel, Becky. Reading Brainstorms. 80p. (gr. 1-4). 1990. 9.95 (*0-86653-560-8*, GA1171) Good Apple.
—Reading Thinker Sheets. 64p. (gr. 4-8). 1989. 8.95 (*0-86653-501-2*, GA1097) Good Apple.
Davis, Beatrice G. On the Road to Reading: One Hundred One Creative Activities for Prereaders & New Readers. (Illus.). 96p. 1994. 6.95 (*0-685-71599-X*, 490) W Gladden Found.
Donatelli, Betty. Growing in Reading. Donatelli, Betty, illus. 11p. (Orig.). (gr. 1-2). 1984. pap. 2.00 (*0-912981-07-5*) Hse BonGiovanni.
—Merry Words for You. Donatelli, Betty, illus. 11p. (Orig.). (gr. 1-2). 1984. pap. 2.00 (*0-912981-09-1*) Hse BonGiovanni.
Dramer, Dan. Monsters. (Illus.). 160p. (gr. 6 up). 1985. pap. text ed. 8.75x (*0-89061-451-2*) Jamestown Pubs.
Duncan, Leonard C. Learn to Read with Phonetic & Non-Phonetic Words. Incl. Bk. 1. 97p; Bk. 2. 85p (*0-941414-12-4*); Bk. 3. 99p (*0-941414-13-2*); Bk. 4. 110p (*0-941414-14-0*); Bk. 5. Nursery Rhymes. 109p. (Illus., Orig.). (gr. 1-3). pap. 10.00 (*0-317-11632-0*) LCD.
Evans, A. J. & Palmer, Marilyn. More Writing about Pictures: Using Pictures to Develop Language & Writing Skills. (gr. 1-3). 1982. Bk. 1: Familiar Places. pap. 3.95x (*0-8077-6037-4*); Bk. 2: Action & Activity. pap. 3.95x (*0-8077-6038-2*); Bk. 3: Supplement-Fables. pap. 3.95x (*0-8077-6039-0*); tchr's. manual 2.95x (*0-8077-6040-4*) Tchrs Coll.
Fearn, Leif. Reading in the Mind. 41p. (gr. 1-7). 1984. 25.00 (*0-940444-22-4*) Kabyn.

Fields, Harriette. Phonics for the New Reader: Step-by-Step. Cox, Anne, illus. LC 90-70334. 128p. (Orig.). (ps-2). 1991. 17.95x (*0-9625802-0-1*); pap. 8.95 (*0-9625802-1-X*) Words Pub CO. "The author provides a ready-to-use blueprint for helping young children understand phonics & provides the necessary tools for that understanding," says former President of the National Association of State Boards of Education, Roseann Bentley. "This book provides clear, well-organized directions, & I think this would be an excellent book for people striving to learn English as a second language." TABLE OF CONTENTS: Lesson 1- Letter Names, Shapes & Sounds; Lesson 2- Short Vowels; Lesson 3- Long Vowels; Lesson 4- Special Words & Letters; Lesson 5- Reading Consonant Combinations; Lesson 6- Reading Vowel Combinations; Lesson 7- Special Vowel Combinations; Lesson 8- Reading Vowel-Consonant Combinations.
Publisher Provided Annotation.

Forte, Imogene. Read about It: Beginning Readers. LC 82-81720. (Illus.). 80p. (gr. k-1). 1982. pap. text ed. 7.95 (*0-86530-005-4*, IP 05-4) Incentive Pubns.
—Read about It: Primary. LC 82-80499. (Illus.). 80p. (gr. 2-4). 1982. pap. text ed. 7.95 (*0-86530-006-2*, IP-062) Incentive Pubns.
Foust, Sylvia J. Reading Comprehension. (Illus.). 48p. (gr. 2-6). 1986. wkbk. 6.95 (*1-55734-340-3*) Tchr Create Mat.
Gerber, Carole. Master Comprehension Workbook Grade One. (ps-3). 1990. pap. 4.95 (*1-56189-041-3*) Amer Educ Pub.
—Master Comprehension Workbook Grade Three. (ps-3). 1990. pap. 4.95 (*1-56189-043-X*) Amer Educ Pub.
—Master Comprehension Workbook Grade Two. (ps-3). 1990. pap. 4.95 (*1-56189-042-1*) Amer Educ Pub.
—Master Reading Workbook Grade Five. (gr. 4-7). 1990. pap. 4.95 (*1-56189-005-7*) Amer Educ Pub.
—Master Reading Workbook Grade Four. (gr. 4-7). 1990. pap. 4.95 (*1-56189-004-9*) Amer Educ Pub.
—Master Reading Workbook Grade K. (ps-3). 1990. pap. 4.95 (*1-56189-000-6*) Amer Educ Pub.
—Master Reading Workbook Grade One. (ps-3). 1990. pap. 4.95 (*1-56189-001-4*) Amer Educ Pub.
—Master Reading Workbook Grade Six. (gr. 4-7). 1990. pap. 4.95 (*1-56189-006-5*) Amer Educ Pub.
—Master Reading Workbook Grade Three. (ps-3). 1990. pap. 4.95 (*1-56189-003-0*) Amer Educ Pub.
—Master Reading Workbook Grade Two. (ps-3). 1990. pap. 4.95 (*1-56189-002-2*) Amer Educ Pub.
Getting Ready to Read. 1986. pap. 9.95 (*0-394-88317-9*) Random Bks Yng Read.
Gibson, R. Reading Games. (Illus.). 32p. (ps-9). 1993. lib. bdg. 13.96 (*0-88110-645-3*, Usborne); pap. 5.95 (*0-7460-1292-6*, Usborne) EDC.
Gibson, Ray. Learning Games. (Illus.). 64p. (ps-1). 1993. pap. 8.95 (*0-7460-1296-9*, Usborne) EDC.
Gould, Toni S. & Warnke, Marie. Learn to Read Program. (gr. 1-3). 1985. 59.95x (*0-8027-9244-8*) Walker & Co.
Grades K-One Early Learner Workbook. 192p. (ps-1). 1990. pap. 4.95 wkbk. (*0-87449-999-2*) Modern Pub NYC.
Gregorich, Barbara. Context Clues. Pape, Richard, illus. 24p. (gr. 3-4). 1980. wkbk. 2.95 (*0-89403-602-5*) EDC.
—Reading: First Grade. Hoffman, Joan, ed. Koontz, Robin M., illus. 32p. (gr. 1). 1990. wkbk. 2.29 (*0-88743-183-6*) Sch Zone Pub Co.
—Reading: Second Grade. Hoffman, Joan, ed. Koontz, Robin M., illus. 32p. (gr. 2). 1990. wkbk. 2.29 (*0-88743-189-5*) Sch Zone Pub Co.
—Reading Survival Skills. (Illus.). 72p. (gr. 7-12). 1982. 7.95 (*0-88160-084-9*, LW 1002) Learning Wks.
Gruber, Barbara. Building Literacy. (Illus.). 64p. (gr. k-6). 1992. 7.95 (*0-86734-139-4*, FS-8323) Schaffer Pubns.
Gutkoska, Joseph P. Developing Comprehension Skills Through the Use of Analogies. (Orig.). (gr. 5-12). 1985. pap. 6.95 (*0-930723-00-7*) Nutshell Enterprises.
Harnois, Veronica. The Harnois Program: Decoding Skills for Dyslexic Readers. 80p. 1994. GBC 9.95 (*0-8059-3539-8*) Dorrance.
Henry, Marcia K. Words. (gr. 3-9). 1990. write for info. (*1-878653-00-8*) Lex Pr.
Herr, Selma E. Read for Understanding, Bk. I. new ed. Anyone Can Read Press Staff, ed. Herr, Selma E., illus. 225p. (Orig.). (gr. 6-12). 1987. pap. 6.95 (*0-914275-04-6*) Anyone Can Read Bks.
Hill, Charlotte M. & Hill, Fred D. Wee Folks on Top: Adventures in Reading. Shortridge, Cleona, ed. Fields, Theodore, illus. LC 92-90056. 66p. (Orig.). (gr. 3-5). 1992. pap. 8.95 (*0-9620182-7-9*) Charill Pubs.
Home Run Reading. (gr. k-2). 1992. Boxed Set. wkbks., incl. tapes 129.00 (*0-8449-4250-2*) Good Morn Tchr.
Insel, Eunice & Edson, Ann. Ready-Go-Begin-To-Learn. (Illus.). (ps-1). 1980. wkbk. 4.25 (*0-89525-098-5*) Ed Activities.
King-Dickman, Kathy. Dinosaurs: Games That Teach: Children's Literature Through Whole Language - A Board Game. (Illus.). 20p. (gr. 1-6). 1990. pap. text ed. 15.95 tchr's. guide, incl. gameboard (*0-927867-06-0*) SkippingStone Pr.
King-Dickman, Kathy & Kulp, Katherine. Friendship: Games That Teach: Children's Literature Through Whole Language - A Board Game. (Illus.). 34p. (gr. 1-6). 1990. pap. text ed. 15.00 tchr's. guide, incl. gameboard (*0-927867-08-7*) SkippingStone Pr.
—Games That Teach: Humor: Children's Literature Through Whole Language - A Board Game. (Illus.). 20p. (gr. 1-6). 1990. pap. text ed. 10.00 incl. gameboard (*0-927867-07-9*) SkippingStone Pr.
Kramkowski, Bernice C. Syllabic Reading. LC 83-90226. (Illus.). 118p. (Orig.). (gr. 1-5). 1983. comb bdg. 9.95 (*0-912145-00-5*) MMI Pr.
LeGros, Lucy C. Reading Success for School & Home. rev. ed. (Illus.). 230p. (Orig.). 1989. pap. 10.95 (*0-318-41420-1*) Creat Res NC.
Littlefield, Kathy M. & Littlefield, Robert S. Read to Me! Stark, Steve, illus. 28p. (Orig.). (gr. 3-6). 1990. pap. text ed. 8.95 (*1-879340-04-6*, K0105) Kidspeak.
Lloyd, Sue & Wernham, Sara. Finger Phonics, 7 bks. Stephen, Lib, illus. (ps-2). 1994. Set. 39.50 (*1-870946-31-6*, Pub. by Jolly Lrning UK) Am Intl Dist.
—Finger Phonics, Bk. 1: S, A, T, I, P, N. Stephen, Lib, illus. 14p. (ps-2). 1994. 5.95 (*1-870946-24-3*, Pub. by Jolly Lrning UK) Am Intl Dist.
—Finger Phonics, Bk. 2: CK, E, H, R, M, D. Stephen, Lib, illus. 14p. (ps-2). 1994. 5.95 (*1-870946-25-1*, Pub. by Jolly Lrning UK) Am Intl Dist.
—Finger Phonics, Bk. 3: G, O, U, L, F, B. Stephen, Lib, illus. 14p. (ps-2). 1994. 5.95 (*1-870946-26-X*, Pub. by Jolly Lrning UK) Am Intl Dist.
—Finger Phonics, Bk. 4: AI, J, OA, IE, EE, OR. Stephen, Lib, illus. 14p. (ps-2). 1994. 5.95 (*1-870946-27-8*, Pub. by Jolly Lrning UK) Am Intl Dist.
—Finger Phonics, Bk. 5: Z, W, NG, V, OO, OO. Stephen, Lib, illus. 14p. (ps-2). 1994. 5.95 (*1-870946-28-6*, Pub. by Jolly Lrning UK) Am Intl Dist.
—Finger Phonics, Bk. 6: Y, X, CH, SH, TH, TH. Stephen, Lib, illus. 14p. (ps-2). 1994. 5.95 (*1-870946-29-4*, Pub. by Jolly Lrning UK) Am Intl Dist.
—Finger Phonics, Bk. 7: QU, OU, OI, UE, ER, AR. Stephen, Lib, illus. 14p. (ps-2). 1994. 5.95 (*1-870946-30-8*, Pub. by Jolly Lrning UK) Am Intl Dist.
—Phonic Wall Frieze. Stephen, Lib, illus. (ps-2). 1994. 8.95 (*1-870946-32-4*, Pub. by Jolly Lrning UK) Am Intl Dist.
Longanecker, Georgia. Howdy Out There! Phonics Fun. LC 76-62681. (Illus.). (ps-3). 1977. soft cover 6.95 (*0-9601126-1-8*) Longanecker.
Maberly, Norman C. Mastering Speed Reading. 127p. (gr. 9-12). 1989. pap. 3.50 (*0-451-15511-4*, Sig) NAL-Dutton.
—Mastering Speed Reading. 127p. (gr. 7 up). 1966. pap. 4.99 (*0-451-16644-2*, Sig) NAL-Dutton.
Mackall, Dandi D. So I Can Read. (ps-3). 1993. pap. 4.99 (*0-8066-2686-0*, Augsburg) Augsburg Fortress.
Miles, Betty. How to Read: A Book for Beginners. LC 93-25884. Date not set. write for info. (*0-679-85644-7*) Knopf.
Moretti, Stephanie. The At Book. (Illus.). 18p. (ps-1). 1991. large format easle book 18.95 (*1-879567-08-3*, Valeria Bks) Wonder Well.
Murtha, Philly. Creative Reading: You Can Be a Free Reader. Redpath, Ann, ed. 32p. (gr. 6 up). 1984. PLB 11.95 (*0-87191-997-4*) Creative Ed.
—Reading Fast: You Can Be a Reading Athlete. Redpath, Ann, ed. 32p. (gr. 4 up). 1984. PLB 11.95 (*0-87191-996-6*) Creative Ed.
Mylet, Trish. Phonetic Readers for the Short Vowels, 11 bks, Set 1. Sheffield, Antoinette, illus. 224p. (ps-2). 1988. Set includes Jan & Pam, The Van, Rex & Tex, The Bed, Siz & Liz, The Pit, Dod & Bob, The Box, Hun & Sun, The Hut, Pals. pap. text ed. 16.00 (*0-945590-00-8*) Sizzy Bks.
O'Brien-Palmer, Michelle. Read & Write: Fun Literature & Writing Connections for Kids. (gr. 4-7). 1994. pap. 16.95 (*1-879235-04-8*) MicNik Pubns.
Oxendine, Reginald. Our Family Can Read, 2 bks. Scott, Ricky, illus. 76p. (Orig.). (gr. k up). 1992. Set. pap. text ed. 29.95 incl. audio cass. (*0-944049-00-1*); 29.95 (*0-944049-01-X*); 29.95 (*0-944049-02-8*) Arrow Pub NC.
Peterson, Elizabeth J. Beginning Reading at Home. Dewagian, Jeanette, illus. 136p. (ps-1). 1992. Repr. of 1986 ed. write for info. (*0-938911-00-7*) Indiv Educ Syst.
Piequet, Miriam. Fingertip Phonics. Anyone Can Read Staff, ed. Ritchie, Fern, illus. Piequet, M., intro. by. (Illus.). 290p. (Orig.). (gr. 1-12). 1985. 19.95 (*0-914275-05-4*) Anyone Can Read Bks.
Preschool Early Learner Workbook. 192p. (ps-1). 1990. pap. 4.95 wkbk. (*0-87449-989-5*) Modern Pub NYC.
Price, Betty G. & Caujolle, Claude. See Me Read. Ferguson, Elizabeth T., illus. (ps-k). 1985. pap. 19.95 (*0-9614374-0-5*) Prof Reading Serv.
The Private & Personal Reading Journal. 16p. (gr. 3-7). 1989. pap. 3.50 (*0-8352-2842-8*) Bowker.
Read Today! Read Today, Unit 1. (gr. 1). 1991. 29.50 (*0-88106-700-8*) Charlesbridge Pub.
Reading. (Illus.). 32p. (gr. 6-12). 1983. pap. 1.85 (*0-8395-3393-4*, 33378) BSA.
Reading & Understanding Nonfiction: Level One. 372p. (gr. 9-10). 1990. 15.50 (*0-89061-690-6*); pap. 12.75 (*0-89061-487-3*); tchr's. ed. 3.95 (*0-89061-495-4*) Jamestown Pubs.
Reading & Understanding Nonfiction: Level Two. 388p. (gr. 11-12). 1990. 16.50 (*0-89061-694-9*); pap. 13.75 (*0-89061-491-1*); tchr's. ed. 3.95 (*0-89061-499-7*) Jamestown Pubs.
Reading & Understanding Plays: Level One. 404p. (gr. 9-10). 1990. 18.50 (*0-89061-691-4*); pap. 15.75 (*0-89061-488-1*); tchr's. ed. 3.95 (*0-89061-496-2*) Jamestown Pubs.
Reading & Understanding Plays: Level Two. 356p. (gr. 11-12). 1990. 19.50 (*0-89061-695-7*); pap. 16.75 (*0-89061-492-X*); tchr's. ed. 3.95 (*0-89061-525-X*) Jamestown Pubs.

Reading & Understanding Poems: Level One. 274p. (gr. 9-10). 1990. 12.50 (*0-89061-692-2*); pap. 9.75 (*0-89061-489-X*); tchr's. ed. 3.95 (*0-89061-497-0*) Jamestown Pubs.
Reading & Understanding Poems: Level Two. 242p. (gr. 11-12). 1990. 13.50 (*0-89061-696-5*); pap. 10.75 (*0-89061-493-8*); tchr's. ed. 3.95 (*0-89061-526-8*) Jamestown Pubs.
Reading & Understanding Short Stories: Level One. 356p. (gr. 9-10). 1990. 15.50 (*0-89061-689-2*); pap. 12.75 (*0-89061-486-5*); tchr's. ed. 3.95 (*0-89061-494-6*) Jamestown Pubs.
Reading & Understanding Short Stories: Level Two. 340p. (gr. 11-12). 1990. 16.50 (*0-89061-693-0*); pap. 13.75 (*0-89061-490-3*); tchr's. ed. 3.95 (*0-89061-498-9*) Jamestown Pubs.
Reed, Crafton C., III. Thiu Soo-Pr Pum-Kn: The Super Pumpkin. (Illus.). (gr. 2-5). 1980. pap. text ed. 3.50 (*0-87881-091-9*) Mojave Bks.

Reichenberg, Monte. Sam, Old Kate & I. Brasch, Susan, illus. 32p. (Orig.). (ps-4). 1994. pap. 3.00 (*0-9640260-2-3*) MM & I Ink.
"Learning should be fun," says author Monte Reichenberg, "and that is precisely why I wrote SAM, OLD KATE & I & its companion book CHEATING CHET." SAM, OLD KATE & I is a delightfully illustrated children's story & activity book which uses various rhyming "A" words in a humorous story line. This whole language concept allows beginning readers to actually see the difference between words with long & short "A" sounds & the second rhyming word has blanks with a starter letter to encourage student creativity & develop rhyming skills. The author, who is approved as an Artist-in-the-Schools in Nebraska & Kansas, has successfully used SAM, OLD KATE & I at all grade levels, not only to get students excited about reading & writing poetry & stories, but also to demonstrate the ease with which they can be written. Fast paced & entertaining, SAM, OLD KATE & I will encourage & excite even the most ardent anti-readers. Wholesale discount rates are available to Teachers/schools making volume purchases. Dealer/distributor inquiries welcome. SAM, OLD KATE & I, 32 pages with illustrations. $3.00 each to M M & I Ink, Rt. 1, Box 432, Bayard, NE 69334.
Publisher Provided Annotation.

Robinson, Jacqueline S. I'm Ready for Reading. (ps-k). 1990. 19.95 (*0-9624827-0-6*) A Plus Lrn.
—More Ready for Reading. (gr. k-2). 1990. 19.95 (*0-9624827-1-4*) A Plus Lrn.
Rybak, Bob. I Love a Mystery. (Illus.). 176p. (gr. 3-7). 1992. 13.95 (*0-86653-655-8*, GA1388) Good Apple.
—I Love an Adventure. (Illus.). 176p. (gr. 3-7). 1992. 13.95 (*0-86653-656-6*, GA1389) Good Apple.
Savage, John F. Dyslexia: Understanding Reading Problems. (Illus.). 96p. (gr. 4-8). 1985. lib. bdg. 10.98 (*0-685-28823-4*, J Messner) S&S Trade.
Schaffer, Frank, Publications Staff. Getting Ready for Reading. (Illus.). 24p. (ps-k). 1980. wkbk. 3.98 (*0-86734-019-3*, FS-3032) Schaffer Pubns.
—Reading Comprehension. (Illus.). 24p. (gr. 3-5). 1978. wkbk. 3.98 (*0-86734-011-8*, FS-3012) Schaffer Pubns.
Shangold, Helen. Cloze Stories for Reading Success. (gr. k-3). 1981. 13.95x (*0-8027-9124-7*) Walker & Co.
Shapiro, Mary F. Learn-to-Read. Hinchberger, William D. & Hron, Debi, illus. 52p. (ps-k). 1986. 15.99 (*0-934361-11-8*) Kinder Read.

Shapiro, Mary S. Learn-to-Read Series, 3 bks. Hron, Debi, illus. (ps-k). 1984. Set. 14.95 (*0-934361-00-2*) Kinder Read.
KinderRead's LEARN-TO-READ SERIES contains three boardbooks, RED GREEN YELLOW, STOP START, & PLAY with a CONTROLLED VOCABULARY & one "play book", MY PLAYBOOK I, which reinforces basic vocabulary with a game & a variety of playful activities. Both the boardbooks & one "play book" are colorful with heavy gauge, super-durable coated pages & include a wipe-off crayon color page. Simple vocabulary such as "stop," "on," "start," color words, etc. that are used & seen everyday by young children are introduced SLOWLY & repeated in a variety of interesting ways so that CHILDREN PRACTICALLY TEACH THEMSELVES! This is a relaxing, non-threatening way for parents (& teachers) to introduce simple vocabulary words & GIVE CHILDREN A HAPPY EXPERIENCE & A HEAD START BEFORE ENTERING FORMAL READING INSTRUCTION. Praised by parents, teachers & enthusiastic children who are thrilled with being able to read their first books, the KinderRead LEARN-TO-READ SERIES is a must for all preschoolers & kindergarten children. To order, write KinderRead, P.O. Box 18, Ingomar, PA 15127 or call (412) 366-9761. Add $2.50 s&h. A parent guide & carrying case are included.
Publisher Provided Annotation.

Sirimarco. Illiteracy. 1991. 12.95s.p. (*0-86593-115-1*); PLB 17.26 (*0-685-59206-5*) Rourke Corp.
Spellman, Linda. Book Report Backpack. 48p. (gr. 4-6). 1980. 5.95 (*0-88160-035-0*, LW 220) Learning Wks.
The Sport of Reading: Read Fast, Read Smart, Boost Your Grades. (Illus.). 24p. (gr. 4 up). write for info. (*0-930251-01-6*) Bluechip Pubs.
Stauffer, Russell G. & Berg, Jean H. Super Reading. 295p. (gr. 10-12). 1981. Includes audiocass. pap. text ed. 49.95 (*1-55678-036-2*) Learn Inc.
—Super Reading Junior. 256p. 1981. Includes audiocassettes. pap. text ed. 49.95 (*1-55678-039-7*) Learn Inc.
Steffens, J. & Carr, J. Action & Adventure. (gr. 7-12). 1983. 9.95 (*0-88160-101-2*, LW 1007) Learning Wks.
Szabos, Janice. Reading - A Novel Approach. Filkins, Vanessa, illus. 112p. (gr. 4-8). 1984. wkbk. 11.95 (*0-86653-186-6*, GA 529) Good Apple.
Taylor, Nancy R. The Write to Read Method "Jotter" 27p. (Orig.). (gr. k-2). 1992. pap. 10.00 wkbk. (*0-9634324-2-7*) Progress Educ.
Thompson, Kim M. & Hilderbrand, Karen M. A Little Rhythm, Rhyme & Read: Colors & Shapes. Kozjak, Goran, illus. 28p. (ps-1). 1993. Wkbk., incl. audio cass. 9.98 (*1-882331-16-8*) Twin Sisters.
—A Little Rhythm, Rhyme & Read: Letters & Numbers. Kozjak, Goran, illus. 28p. (ps-1). 1993. Wkbk., incl. audio cass. 9.98 (*1-882331-15-X*) Twin Sisters.
Tilkin, Sheldon L. Establishing Sequence. Conoway, Judith, illus. 24p. (gr. 3-4). 1980. wkbk. 2.95 (*0-89403-570-3*) EDC.
—Finding the Main Idea. Conoway, Judith, illus. 24p. (gr. 3-4). 1980. wkbk. 2.95 (*0-89403-569-X*) EDC.
—Following Directions. Conoway, Judith, illus. 24p. (gr. 3-4). 1980. wkbk. 2.95 (*0-89403-571-1*) EDC.
—Recalling Details. Conoway, Judith, illus. 24p. (gr. 4-5). 1980. wkbk. 2.95 (*0-89403-568-1*) EDC.
—Recognizing Cause & Effect. (Illus.). 24p. (gr. 3-4). 1980. 2.95 (*0-89403-574-6*) EDC.
Tilkin, Sheldon L. & Conoway, Judith. Distinguishing Between Fact & Opinion. (Illus.). 24p. (gr. 4-5). 1980. wkbk. 2.95 (*0-89403-582-7*) EDC.
—Drawing Conclusions. (Illus.). 24p. (gr. 3-4). 1980. wkbk. 2.95 (*0-89403-573-8*) EDC.
—Drawing Conclusions. (Illus.). 24p. (gr. 4-5). 1980. wkbk. 2.95 (*0-89403-583-5*) EDC.
—Establishing Sequence. (Illus.). 24p. (gr. 4-5). 1980. wkbk. 2.95 (*0-89403-580-0*) EDC.
—Finding the Main Idea. (Illus.). 24p. (gr. 4-5). 1980. wkbk. 2.95 (*0-89403-579-7*) EDC.
—Following Directions. (Illus.). 24p. (gr. 4-5). 1980. wkbk. 2.95 (*0-89403-581-9*) EDC.
—Recalling Details. (Illus.). 24p. (gr. 4-5). 1980. wkbk. 2.95 (*0-89403-578-9*) EDC.
—Recognizing Cause & Effect. (Illus.). 24p. (gr. 4-5). 1980. wkbk. 2.95 (*0-89403-584-3*) EDC.
—Recognizing Mood, Character & Plot. (Illus.). 24p. (gr. 4-5). 1980. wkbk. 2.95 (*0-89403-586-X*) EDC.
—Recognizing Mood, Character & Plot. (Illus.). 24p. (gr. 3-4). 1980. wkbk. 2.95 (*0-89403-576-2*) EDC.
Tlkin, Sheldon L. & Conoway, Judith. Distinguishing Between Fact & Opinion. (Illus.). 24p. (gr. 3-4). 1980. wkbk. 2.95 (*0-89403-572-X*) EDC.
Tyler, J. & Round, G. Ready for Reading. (Illus.). 24p. (ps up). 1989. pap. 3.50 (*0-7460-0267-X*, Usborne) EDC.
Wayman, Joe. The Other Side of Reading. 144p. (gr. k-8). 1980. 12.95 (*0-916456-64-1*, GA 183) Good Apple.
Wilson, Barbara A. Study & Writing Skills Manual. 34p. 1992. tchr's. ed. 8.00 (*1-56778-042-3*) Wilson Lang Trning.
Wise, Beth A. Beginning to Read. Nayer, Judith E., ed. Banek, Yvette, illus. 32p. (gr. k-1). 1991. wkbk. 1.95 (*1-878624-62-8*) McClanahan Bk.
Wise, Beth A. & Levin, Amy. I Can Read. Naver, Judith E., ed. Krupinski, Loretta, illus. 32p. (gr. k-1). 1991. wkbk. 1.95 (*1-878624-63-6*) McClanahan Bk.
Womack, Randy L. & Lew, Christina. Read 'n Draw: Following Directions, Bk. 1. (Illus.). 64p. (gr. 3-5). wkbk. 6.95 (*0-685-57592-6*) Gldn Educ.
—Read 'n Draw: Following Directions, Bk. 2. (Illus.). 48p. (gr. 4-6). 1992. wkbk. 6.95 (*1-56500-032-3*) Gldn Educ.
Zakalik, Leslie S. The Comprehension Carnival. 76p. (gr. 2-4). 1977. 7.95 (*0-88160-005-9*, LW 106) Learning Wks.

READING–FICTION

Benson, Rita. Rosa's Diary. Campbell, Caroline, illus. LC 93-28972. 1994. 4.25 (*0-383-03772-7*) SRA Schl Grp.
Birdseye, Tom. Just Call Me Stupid. 128p. (gr. 4-7). 1993. 14.95 (*0-8234-1045-5*) Holiday.
Bloom, Daniel H. The Magic of Johnny Readingseed. Julien, Claudia, illus. 48p. (gr. 5-9). 1990. 9.95 (*0-944007-60-0*) Shapolsky Pubs.
Bowers, Ruth B. Little Thumb. LC 88-51387. (Illus.). 110p. (gr. k-3). 1989. pap. 5.95 (*1-55523-196-9*) Winston-Derek.
Brown, Margaret W. Four Fur Feet. Charlip, Remy, illus. 48p. (gr. 1-3). 1989. Repr. of 1961 ed. 13.95 (*0-929077-03-2*, Hopscotch Bks); PLB 12.95 (*0-317-92548-2*, Hopscotch Bks) Watermark Inc.
Cohen, Miriam. When Will I Read? Hoban, Lillian, illus. LC 76-28320. 32p. (ps-3). 1977. 16.00 (*0-688-80073-4*); PLB 15.93 (*0-688-84073-6*) Greenwillow.
Collins, Pat L. Don't Tease the Guppies. Hafner, Marylin, illus. LC 92-25336. 32p. (ps-1). 1994. 14.95 (*0-399-22530-7*) Putnam Pub Group.
Dr. Seuss. I Can Read with My Eyes Shut! Dr. Seuss, illus. LC 78-7193. (gr. 1-3). 1978. 6.95 (*0-394-83912-9*); lib. bdg. 7.99 (*0-394-93912-3*) Random Bks Yng Read.
Elliott, Dan. Grover Learns to Read. Chartier, Normand, illus. LC 84-27692. 40p. (ps-3). 1993. pap. 2.99 (*0-679-83949-6*) Random Bks Yng Read.
Giff, Patricia R. The Girl Who Knew It All. 128p. (gr. k-6). 1989. pap. 3.25 (*0-440-42855-6*, YB) Dell.
Gilson, Jamie. Do Bananas Chew Gum? LC 80-11414. 160p. (gr. 5-9). 1980. 12.95 (*0-688-41960-7*); PLB 12.88 (*0-688-51960-1*) Lothrop.
Greene, Constance C. Isabelle & Little Orphan Frannie. (gr. 4 up). 1990. pap. 3.95 (*0-14-032916-1*, Puffin) Puffin Bks.
Hallinan, P. K. Just Open a Book. Hallinan, P. K., illus. LC 80-22099. 32p. (ps-3). 1981. pap. 3.95 (*0-516-43521-3*) Childrens.
Herbert, Laurence. Leona Devours Books. (Illus.). 32p. (gr. k-2). 1991. 12.95 (*0-89565-755-4*) Childs World.
Hoban, Lillian. Arthur's Prize Reader. Hoban, Lillian, illus. LC 77-25637. 64p. (ps-3). 1978. PLB 13.89 (*0-06-022380-4*) HarpC Child Bks.
—Arthur's Prize Reader. LC 77-25637. (Illus.). 64p. (ps-3). 1985. incl. cassette 5.98 (*0-694-00016-7*, Trophy); pap. 3.50 (*0-06-444049-4*, Trophy) HarpC Child Bks.
Hubbard, Inez. Danny. Edgell, Kyle, illus. LC 84-62082. 48p. (Orig.). (gr. k-3). 1984. pap. 3.95 (*0-931571-00-6*) Lifetime Pr.
Hutchins, Pat. The Tale of Thomas Mead. LC 79-6398. (Illus.). 1988. pap. 3.95 (*0-688-08422-2*, Mulberry) Morrow.
Lester, Alison. Bibs & Boots. (Illus.). 16p. (ps-k). 1989. 3.50 (*0-670-81988-3*) Viking Child Bks.
—Crashing & Splashing. (Illus.). 16p. (ps-k). 1989. pap. 3.50 (*0-670-81989-1*) Viking Child Bks.
McPhail, David. Santa's Book of Names. LC 92-37279. 1993. 14.95 (*0-316-56335-8*, Joy St Bks) Little.

Mire, Betty. T-Pierre Frog & T-Felix Frog Go to School. Mire, Betty, illus. LC 93-74275. 32p. (Orig.). (gr. 1-3). 1994. PLB 6.95 (*0-9639378-0-4*) Cajun Bay Pr.
T-PIERRE FROG & T-FELIX FROG GO TO SCHOOL focuses on the importance of education & reading. This unique book is incorporated with the CAJUN FRENCH language (approximately one CAJUN FRENCH sentence on every page of text). And for every CAJUN FRENCH sentence there is a cute cartoon picture associated with it. It's a book that parents will enjoy reading to their children. The story begins with the first

day of school on the Louisiana bayous. T-PIERRE FROG likes going to school & he loves to read. He tells his friend T-FELIX FROG that he wants to learn all he can, because he wants to one day become an astronaut. But T-FELIX FROG doesn't like school. And he tells T-PIERRE that he doesn't have to learn, because his only wish is to become a lazy hobo taking it easy in the shade. Sometimes wishes come true. T-FELIX finds that out, but not without woes. Although T-FELIX FROG is soon enlightened on the importance of an education through a dream or rather a nightmare. T-PIERRE FROG & T-FELIX FROG GO TO SCHOOL is simultaneously entertaining & educational. The book is complete with pronunciation guide. *Publisher Provided Annotation.*

Olaf Reads, Unit 4. (gr. 1). 1991. 5-pack 21.25 (*0-88106-734-2*) Charlesbridge Pub.

Paul, Sherry. Blossom Bird Falls in Love. Miller, Bob, illus. 32p. (Orig.). (ps-2). 1981. pap. 14.10 Bks. only (*0-685-01192-5*); pap. 16.20 bks & Skill Masters (*0-685-01193-3*) CPI Pub.

—Blossom Bird Finds a Family. Miller, Bob, illus. 32p. (Orig.). (ps-2). 1981. pap. 14.10 set (*0-686-31343-7*); Bks. & Skill Masters Set 16.20 (*0-685-01194-1*) CPI Pub.

—Blossom Bird Goes South. Miller, Bob, illus. 32p. (Orig.). (ps-2). 1981. pap. 14.10 set (*0-675-01080-2*); Bks. & Skillmasters set 16.20 (*0-685-01195-X*) CPI Pub.

—Finn the Foolish Fish: Trouble with Bubbles. Miller, Bob, illus. 32p. (Orig.). (ps-2). pap. 14.10 set (*0-675-01084-5*); Bks. & Skillmasters set 16.20 (*0-685-01196-8*) CPI Pub.

—Two-B & the Rock 'n' Roll Band. Murphy, Bob, illus. 32p. (Orig.). (ps-2). pap. 14.10 set (*0-675-01082-9*); Bks & Skillmasters set 16.20 (*0-685-01197-6*) CPI Pub.

—Two-B & the Space Visitor. Murphy, Bob, illus. 32p. (Orig.). (ps-2). pap. 14.10 bks. only (*0-685-01198-4*); pap. 16.20 Bks. & Skill Masters (*0-685-01199-2*) CPI Pub.

Paulsen, Gary. Nightjohn. LC 92-1222. 96p. 1993. pap. 14.00 (*0-385-30838-8*) Doubleday.

Pelham, David. Worms Wiggle. Foreman, Michael, illus. (ps-1). 1989. pap. 9.95 (*0-671-67218-5*, Little Simon) S&S Trade.

Roberts, Sarah. Bert & the Missing Mop Mix-Up. Mathieu, Joe, illus. LC 82-22971. 40p. (gr. k-2). 1983. 4.95 (*0-394-85752-6*) Random Bks Yng Read.

Rowe, W. W. Small Tall Tales. LC 88-51388. 78p. 1989. 5.95 (*1-55523-200-0*) Winston-Derek.

Schlieper, Anne. The Best Fight. Mathews, Judith, ed. Schwark, Mary B., illus. 64p. (gr. 3-7). 1994. PLB 10. 95 (*0-8075-0662-1*) A Whitman.

Shearer, Marilyn J. The Adventures of Curious Eric: Learning Concepts. Roberts, Tom, illus. LC 90-60397. 16p. (ps-6). 1990. 19.95 (*0-685-33064-8*); pap. 10.95 (*1-878389-01-7*) L Ashley & Joshua.

Sullivan Associates Staff. I Can Read, 8 bks. (gr. k-1). 1992. Set. pap. 36.00 (*0-8449-2998-0*) Good Morn Tchr.

Thomas, Claire & Thomas, Thornton. Naming Game: Storybook to Color. Jones, S. Max, illus. 22p. (Orig.). (gr. k-3). 1988. pap. 3.95 (*0-317-92517-2*) Sparky Star Pr.

Ziefert, Harriet. Hello Reading. (ps-3). 1990. pap. 42.00 (*0-14-778673-8*) Puffin Bks.

READING–REMEDIAL TEACHING

Dwyer, Kathleen M. What Do You Mean I Have a Learning Disability? (Illus.). 32p. (gr. 5-9). 1991. 14.95 (*0-8027-8102-0*); PLB 15.85 (*0-8027-8103-9*) Walker & Co.

Rue, Nancy N. Coping with An Illiterate Parent. Rosen, Roger, ed. 64p. (gr. 7-12). 1990. PLB 14.95 (*0-8239-1070-9*) Rosen Group.

READING–STUDY AND TEACHING

see Reading

READING CLINICS

see Reading–Remedial Teaching

READING INTERESTS

see Books and Reading

READING INTERESTS OF CHILDREN

see Children–Books and Reading

REAGAN, RONALD WILSON, PRESIDENT U.S., 1911-

Behrens, June. Ronald Reagan: An All-American. LC 81-9993. (Illus.). 32p. (gr. 2 up). 1981. PLB 11.80 (*0-516-03565-7*) Childrens.

De La Mare, Walter. Peacock Pie: A Book of Rhymes. LC 89-1828. (Illus.). (gr. 2-4). 1989. 17.95 (*0-8050-1124-2*, Bks Young Read) H Holt & Co.

Kent, Zachary. Ronald Reagan. LC 89-33746. 100p. (gr. 3 up). 1989. PLB 14.40 (*0-516-01373-4*); pap. 6.95 (*0-516-41373-2*) Childrens.

Robbins, Neal E. Ronald W. Reagan: Fortieth President of the United States. Young, Richard G., ed. LC 89-39955. (Illus.). 128p. (gr. 5-9). 1990. PLB 17.26 (*0-944483-66-6*) Garrett Ed Corp.

Sandak, Cass R. The Reagans. LC 92-37838. (Illus.). 48p. (gr. 5). 1993. text ed. 4.95 RSBE (*0-89686-646-7*, Crestwood Hse) Macmillan Child Grp.

Schwartzberg, Renee. Ronald Reagan. (Illus.). 136p. (gr. 5 up). 1991. 17.95 (*1-55546-849-7*) Chelsea Hse.

Sullivan, George. Ronald Reagan. LC 85-13688. (Illus.). 128p. (gr. 5 up). 1985. lib. bdg. 10.98 (*0-671-60168-7*, J Messner) S&S Trade.

REAL ESTATE

Here are entered general works on real property in the legal sense i.e., ownership of land and buildings (immovable property) as opposed to personal property. Works limited to the buying and selling of real property are entered under Real Estate busimess. general works on land without the ownership aspect are entered under Land.

see also Farms

REASONING

see also Intellect; Logic

Learning Works Staff. Solution Sleuth. (gr. 4-8). 1989. 7.95 (*0-88160-170-5*, LW 278) Learning Wks.

Schwartz, L. Analogy Adventure. (gr. 4-8). 1989. 5.95 (*0-88160-173-X*, LW 280) Learning Wks.

Schwatrz, L. Think on Your Feet. (gr. 4-8). 1989. 7.95 (*0-88160-172-1*, LW 283) Learning Wks.

Tilkin, Sheldon L. & Conoway, Judith. Making Judgments. (Illus.). 24p. (gr. 3-4). 1980. wkbk. 2.95 (*0-89403-577-0*) EDC.

—Making Judgments. (Illus.). 24p. (gr. 4-5). 1980. wkbk. 2.95 (*0-89403-587-8*) EDC.

Wassermann, Selma & Wassermann, Jack. The Book of Imagining. Smith, Dennis, illus. LC 89-77869. 32p. (gr. k-3). 1990. PLB 12.85 (*0-8027-6948-9*); pap. 4.95 (*0-8027-9454-8*) Walker & Co.

REBUSES

see Riddles

RECIPES

see Cookery

RECLAMATION OF LAND

Here are entered general works on reclamation, including drainage and irrigation.

see also Marshes; Sand

RECLAMATION OF LAND–FICTION

Sharpe, Susan. Waterman's Boy. LC 89-39332. 96p. (gr. 3-6). 1990. SBE 14.95 (*0-02-782351-2*, Bradbury Pr) Macmillan Child Grp.

RECONSTRUCTION

Here are entered works dealing with reconstruction in the u. s. following the Civil War.

see also Blacks; Ku Klux Klan

Cooper, Michael L. Slave, Civil War Hero: The Story of Robert Smalls. LC 93-44169. (Illus.). 64p. (gr. 3-6). 1994. 13.99 (*0-525-67489-6*, Lodestar Bks) Dutton Child Bks.

Mettger, Zak. Reconstruction: America after the Civil War. (Illus.). 96p. 1994. 16.99 (*0-525-67490-X*, Lodestar Bks) Dutton Child Bks.

Smith, Carter, ed. One Nation Again: A Sourcebook on the Civil War. LC 92-16661. (Illus.). 96p. (gr. 5-8). 1993. PLB 18.90 (*1-56294-266-2*) Millbrook Pr.

RECORD PLAYERS

see Phonograph

RECREATION

Here are entered works on the psychological and social aspects of recreation and works on organized recreational projects.

see also Amusements; Games; Hobbies; Play; Playgrounds; Sports

Cribbs, Dianna G. A Kid's Guide to Fishing & Fun Things to Do! Cribbs, Dianna G., illus. 113p. (gr. 1-5). 1990. pap. 6.95 (*0-943487-27-7*) Sevgo Pr.

Drake, Jane & Love, Ann. The Kids' Summer Handbook. Collins, Heather, illus. LC 93-2524. 208p. (gr. 3 up). 1994. 15.95 (*0-395-68711-X*); pap. 10.95 (*0-395-68709-8*) Ticknor & Flds Bks Yng Read.

Goffe, Toni. Relax. (ps-3). 1993. 7.95 (*0-85953-789-7*) Childs Play.

Italia, Bob. Bungee Jumping. LC 93-15331. (gr. 6 up). 1993. PLB 9.99 (*1-56239-230-1*) Abdo & Dghtrs.

Kalman, Bobbie. People at Play. (Illus.). 32p. (gr. 2-3). 1986. 15.95 (*0-86505-069-4*); pap. 7.95 (*0-86505-091-0*) Crabtree Pub Co.

Killeen, Leah R. At the Park. Killeen, Leah R., illus. 32p. (ps-2). Date not set. 11.95 (*1-56065-154-7*) Capstone Pr.

Levinson, Nancy S. & Rocklin, Joanne. Feeling Great: Reaching Out to the World, Reaching in to Yourself--Without Drugs. 2nd, rev. ed. LC 92-16217. (Illus.). 112p. (gr. 8-12). 1992. pap. 7.95 (*0-89793-087-8*) Hunter Hse.

Neil, Marilyn. Stars, Wings, & Fun Things: Three Hundred Sixty-Five Activities for Children. (Illus.). 68p. (Orig.). (gr. k-3). 1991. pap. text ed. 8.95 (*0-945301-05-7*) Druid Pr.

West, Rose. Go & Have a Good Time. (gr. 2-8). 1990. pap. 10.95 (*0-8224-3500-4*) Fearon Teach Aids.

Winston, Lynn. Recreation & Sports: An Activity Guide. Garee, Betty, ed. LC 85-72420. 72p. (Orig.). (gr. 9-12). 1985. pap. 4.95 (*0-915708-18-3*, #1770) Cheever Pub.

RECREATIONS, MATHEMATICAL

see Mathematical Recreations

RECREATIONS, SCIENTIFIC

see Scientific Recreations

RECTORS

see Clergy

RED CHINA

see China (People's Republic of China)

RED CLOUD, OGLALA SIOUX CHIEF, 1822-1909

Goble, Paul. Brave Eagle's Account of the Fetterman Fight. LC 91-23198. (Illus.). 64p. 1992. pap. 9.95 (*0-8032-7032-1*, Bison Books) U of Nebr Pr.

Sanford, William R. Red Cloud: Sioux Warrior. LC 93-42256. (Illus.). 48p. (gr. 4-10). 1994. lib. bdg. 14.95 (*0-89490-513-9*) Enslow Pubs.

RED CROSS

Pollard, Michael. The Red Cross & the Red Crescent. LC 93-26383. 1994. text ed. 13.95 (*0-02-774720-4*, New Discovery Bks) Macmillan Child Grp.

RED CROSS, U. S. AMERICAN NATIONAL RED CROSS

Barton, Clara. Story of the Red Cross. Gemme, Francis R., illus. (gr. 4 up). 1968. pap. 1.50 (*0-8049-0170-8*, CL-170) Airmont.

REDUCING (BODY WEIGHT CONTROL)

see Weight Control

REDWOOD

Anderson, Tammy L., ed. California Redwoods Color Book. 26p. (ps-8). 1988. pap. 1.95 (*0-915687-03-8*) FVN Corp.

Guhm, Susan & Guhm, Karl. The Great Sierra Redwood Activity Book. (Illus.). 32p. (gr. 1-6). 1990. write for info. (*0-9627621-0-5*) Froggy Bywater. This is NOT just a coloring book. This activity book contains two WORD SCRAMBLES, two CROSSWORD PUZZLES, two WORD SEARCHES, two DOT-TO-DOTS, one FINISH-THE-PICTURE, one BOARD GAME, one MATH PUZZLE, several COLORING PAGES, plus two answer pages - each & every page about the Sierra Redwood (also called Giant Sequoia, Sequoiadendron giganteum, & Giant Sequoia). Illustrations depict features of the tree in a simple humorous manner - height (as tall as 20 one-story houses or 30 school buses), weight (as heavy as 12 million hamburgers or 120,000 50-pound bags of dog food), their antiquity, their seeds & seedlings, how they grow, tree rings, associated plants & animals in the surrounding forest, etc. THE GREAT SIERRA REDWOOD BOOK is perfect for educators looking for an exciting way to teach their class about redwoods, with a redwood unit or as part of a plants unit in general. Whether visiting a Sierra Redwood forest or not, this activity book is entertaining & educational. For order information call or write: Froggy Bywater Press, P.O. Box 7920, Fresno, CA 93747; 209-251-0243. *Publisher Provided Annotation.*

Vieira, Linda. The Ever-Living Tree: The Life & Times of a Coast Redwood. Canyon, Christopher, illus. LC 93-31688. 32p. (gr. 2-4). 1994. 14.95 (*0-8027-8277-9*); PLB 15.85 (*0-8027-8278-7*) Walker & Co.

REFERENCE BOOKS

see also Books and Reading–Best Books; Encyclopedias and Dictionaries

Anthony, Susan C. Facts Plus: An Almanac of Essential Information. 3rd ed. (Illus.). 256p. (gr. 3-9). 1995. pap. 15.95 (*1-879478-03-X*) Instr Res Co.

Cook, Sybilla. Reference Flipper: A Guide to Reference Material. 49p. (gr. 4 up). 1988. Repr. of 1983 ed. trade edition 5.95 (*1-878383-09-4*) C Lee Pubns.

Everyday Things. 96p. (gr. 2-4). 1981. 12.95 (*0-86020-491-X*) EDC.

Eyewitness Series: Spanish Version. (SPA.). 1989. write for info. (*1-56014-411-4*) Santillana. The Spanish version of the popular Eyewitness Series, BIBLIOTECA VISUAL, is a tremendous informational resource for Spanish speakers of all ages. Twenty-five volumes provide an in-depth presentation of nature, history, science,

& technology through a magnificent collection of photographs & illustrations. Titles include: LOS SECRETOS DE LAS PLANTAS (Secrets of Plants), ROCAS Y MINERALES (Rocks & Minerals), LOS PECES (Fish), EL RIO Y LA LAGUNA (Rivers & Lakes), LA ORILLA DEL MAR (Seashore), EL ARBOL (Trees), LOS MAMIFEROS (Mammals), LOS INSECTOS (Insects), EL PAJARO Y SU NIDO (Birds & their Nests), DE LA ORUGA A LA MARIPOSA (From Moths to Butterflies). Other titles include: LOS FOSILES (Fossils), LOS DINOSAURIOS (Dinosaurs), ESQUELITOS (Skeltons), ARMAS Y ARMADURAS (Arms & Armor), MAQUINAS VOLADORAS (Flying Machines), AUTOMOVILES (Cars), LA MUSICA (Music), HOMBRES PRIMATIVOS (Primitive Man), EL ANTIGUO EGIPTO (Ancient Egypt), LA ANTIGUO ROMA (Ancient Rome). To order: Santillana Publishing Co., 901 W. Walnut, Compton, CA 90220. 1-800-245-8584.
Publisher Provided Annotation.

Goldman, Phyllis B. Monkeyshines on Strange & Wonderful Facts. Grigni, John, illus. 116p. (Orig.). (ps-8). 1991. pap. 8.95 (*0-9620900-2-6*) NC Learn Inst Fitness.
Information Please Staff. Information Please Student Almanac, 1993: Fast Facts for Students. 96p. (gr. 9-12). 1992. pap. 2.80 (*0-395-56006-3*) HM.
Kid's Address & Writing Book. (Illus.). 112p. (Orig.). (ps-8). 1990. pap. 5.95 (*0-943400-45-7*) Marlor Pr.
Levine, Michael. The Kid's Address Book. rev. ed. 244p. 1994. pap. 9.00 (*0-399-51875-4*, Perigee Bks) Berkley Pub.
McCutcheon, Randall. Can You Find It? Twenty-Five Library Scavenger Hunts to Sharpen Your Research Skills. rev. ed. LC 91-30105. (Illus.). 208p. (gr. 9 up). pap. 10.95 (*0-915793-38-5*) Free Spirit Pub.
Martin, Claire & Martin, Steve. My Best Book: A Year-Long Record of "Personal Bests" Martin, Diane, illus. 40p. (Orig.). (gr. 3-5). 1988. pap. 7.95 (*0-929545-00-1*) Black Birch Bks.
Slater, Barbara & Slater, Ron. Tracking Down Trivia. 48p. (gr. 5-12). 1982. 7.95 (*0-86653-078-9*, GA 423) Good Apple.
Webster's Beginning Book of Facts. LC 78-18414. 384p. 1978. 12.95 (*0-87779-074-4*) Merriam-Webster Inc.

REFORM, SOCIAL
see Social Problems

REFORM OF CRIMINALS
see Crime and Criminals

REFORMATION
see also Europe–History–1492-1789; Protestantism
Fehlauer, Adolph. Life & Faith of Martin Luther. (gr. 6-9). 1981. pap. 6.95 (*0-8100-0125-X*, 15N0376) Northwest Pub.
Schwiebert, Ernest G. Luther & His Times: The Reformation from a New Perspective. (Illus.). (gr. 9 up). 1950. 26.95 (*0-570-03246-6*, 15-1164) Concordia.

REFORMERS
Morin, Isobel V. Women Who Reformed Politics. LC 93-46336. 160p. (gr. 5-12). 1994. PLB 14.95 (*1-881508-16-1*) Oliver Pr MN.

REFUGEES
Bergman, Tamar. Along the Tracks. Swirsky, Michael, tr. 256p. (gr. 6-9). 1991. 14.45 (*0-395-55328-8*, Sandpiper) HM.
Donahue, David M. & Flowers, Nancy. The Uprooted: Refugees & the United States - A Resource Curriculum. (Illus.). 224p. (Orig.). (gr. 7-12). 1994. pap. 15.95x (*0-89793-122-X*) Hunter Hse.
Drucker, Olga L. Kindertransport. LC 92-14121. (gr. 5-8). 1992. 14.95 (*0-8050-1711-9*, Bks Young Read) H Holt & Co.
Graff, Nancy P. Where the River Runs: A Portrait of a Refugee Family. Howard, Richard, photos by. LC 92-24184. (Illus.). 80p. 1993. 16.95 (*0-316-32287-3*) Little.
Hitchcox, Linda. Refugees. LC 90-3230. (Illus.). 32p. (gr. 5-8). 1990. PLB 12.40 (*0-531-17242-2*, Gloucester Pr) Watts.
Kent, Zachary. The Story of the Saigon Airlift. LC 91-15847. (Illus.). 32p. (gr. 3-6). 1991. PLB 12.30 (*0-516-04760-4*); pap. 3.95 (*0-516-44760-2*) Childrens.
Seymour-Jones, Carole. Refugees. LC 92-14803. (Illus.). 48p. (gr. 6 up). 1992. text ed. 12.95 RSBE (*0-02-735402-4*, New Discovery) Macmillan Child Grp.
Trier, Jean. United Nations High Commissioner for Refugees. LC 94-5772. 1995. text ed. 13.95 (*0-02-726335-5*, New Discovery Bks) Macmillan Child Grp.

REFUGEES–FICTION
Baylis-White, Mary. Sheltering Rebecca. 112p. (gr. 5-9). 1993. pap. 3.99 (*0-14-036448-X*, Puffin) Puffin Bks.
Crew, Linda. Children of the River. LC 88-20401. (gr. 7 up). 1989. 14.95 (*0-440-50122-9*) Delacorte.
Holm, Anne. North to Freedom. 239p. (gr. 3-7). 1990. pap. 3.95 (*0-15-257553-7*, Odyssey) HarBrace.
Huynh Quang Nhuong. The Land I Lost. (gr. 4-7). 1992. 17.00 (*0-8446-6586-X*) Peter Smith.
Lingard, Joan. Between Two Worlds. 192p. (gr. 7 up). 1991. 14.95 (*0-525-67360-1*, Lodestar Bks) Dutton Child Bks.
—Tug of War. 192p. (gr. 5 up). 1992. pap. 4.50 (*0-14-036072-7*, Puffin) Puffin Bks.
Temple, Frances. Grab Hands & Run. LC 92-34063. 176p. (gr. 5 up). 1993. 14.95 (*0-531-05480-2*); PLB 14.99 (*0-531-08630-5*) Orchard Bks Watts.
Whelan, Gloria. Goodbye, Vietnam. LC 91-3660. 112p. (gr. 3-7). 1992. 13.00 (*0-679-82263-1*); PLB 13.99 (*0-679-92263-6*) Knopf Bks Yng Read.
—Goodbye, Vietnam. LC 91-3660. 144p. (gr. 3-7). 1993. pap. 3.99 (*0-679-82376-X*, Bullseye Bks) Random Bks Yng Read.

REFUSE AND REFUSE DISPOSAL
see also Sewage Disposal; Waste Products; Water–Pollution
Amos, Janine. Waste & Recycling. LC 92-16339. (Illus.). 32p. (gr. 2-3). 1992. PLB 18.99 (*0-8114-3406-0*) Raintree Steck-V.
Anderson, Robert. Garbage: Understanding Words in Context. LC 91-22100. (Illus.). 32p. (gr. 4-7). 1991. PLB 10.95 (*0-89908-609-8*) Greenhaven.
Asimov, Isaac. Where Does Garbage Go? LC 91-50361. (Illus.). 24p. (gr. 2-3). 1992. PLB 15.93 (*0-8368-0742-1*) Gareth Stevens Inc.
—Why Does Litter Cause Problems? LC 92-5349. 1992. PLB 15.93 (*0-8368-0799-5*) Gareth Stevens Inc.
Bailey, Donna. What We Can Do about Litter. LC 90-45006. (Illus.). 32p. (gr. k-4). 1991. PLB 11.40 (*0-531-11016-8*) Watts.
—What We Can Do about Recycling Garbage. (Illus.). 32p. (gr. k-4). 1991. PLB 11.40 (*0-531-11017-6*) Watts.
Becklake, Sue. Waste Disposal & Recycling. LC 91-9702. (Illus.). 40p. (gr. 5-8). 1991. PLB 12.90 (*0-531-17305-4*, Gloucester Pr) Watts.
Berger, Melvin. Where Does All the Garbage Go? (Illus.). 16p. (ps-2). 1992. pap. text ed. 14.95 (*1-56784-002-7*) Newbridge Comms.
Blashfield, Jean F. & Black, Wallace B. Recycling. LC 90-400. (Illus.). 128p. (gr. 4-8). 1991. PLB 20.55 (*0-516-05502-X*) Childrens.
Bonar, Veronica & Daniel, Jamie, eds. Coping with - Food Trash. Kenyon, Tony, illus. LC 93-32478. 1994. 17.27 (*0-8368-1056-2*) Gareth Stevens Inc.
Daniel, Jamie & Bonar, Veronica. Coping with - Glass Trash. Kenyon, Tony, illus. LC 93-32483. 32p. (gr. 2 up). 1994. PLB 17.27 (*0-8368-1057-0*) Gareth Stevens Inc.
—Coping with - Metal Trash. Kenyon, Tony, illus. LC 93-32482. 32p. (gr. 2 up). 1994. PLB 17.27 (*0-8368-1058-9*) Gareth Stevens Inc.
—Coping with - Paper Trash. Kenyon, Tony, illus. LC 93-37688. 32p. (gr. 2 up). 1994. PLB 17.27 (*0-8368-1059-7*) Gareth Stevens Inc.
—Coping with - Plastic Trash. Kenyon, Tony, illus. LC 93-37687. 32p. (gr. 2 up). 1994. PLB 17.27 (*0-8368-1060-0*) Gareth Stevens Inc.
—Coping with - Wood Trash. Kenyon, Tony, illus. LC 93-37686. 32p. (gr. 2 up). 1994. PLB 17.27 (*0-8368-1061-9*) Gareth Stevens Inc.
—Trash Busters Series, 6 vols. Kenyon, Tony, illus. (gr. 2 up). 1994. PLB 103.62 Set (*0-8368-1055-4*) Gareth Stevens Inc.
Davis, Kay & Oldsfield, Wendy. Waste. LC 91-23414. (Illus.). 32p. (gr. 2-5). 1991. PLB 19.97 (*0-8114-3000-6*); pap. 4.95 (*0-8114-1531-7*) Raintree Steck-V.
Foster, Joanna. Cartons, Cans, & Orange Peels: Where Does Our Garbage Go? (Illus.). 64p. (gr. 3-6). 1991. 15.95 (*0-395-56436-0*, Clarion Bks) HM.
Garbage & Recycling. LC 91-50343. (Illus.). 32p. (gr. 3-8). 1993. PLB 17.27 (*0-8368-0700-6*); PLB 17.27 s.p. (*0-685-70865-9*) Gareth Stevens Inc.
Gay, Kathlyn. Garbage & Recycling. LC 91-7130. (Illus.). 128p. (gr. 6 up). 1991. lib. bdg. 17.95 (*0-89490-321-7*) Enslow Pubs.
Gibbons, Gail. Recycle! A Handbook for Kids. Gibbons, Gail, illus. 32p. (ps-3). 1992. 14.95 (*0-316-30971-0*) Little.
Gutnik, Martin J. Recycling: Learning the Four R's: Reduce, Reuse, Recycle, Recover. LC 92-24330. (Illus.). 104p. (gr. 6 up). 1993. lib. bdg. 17.95 (*0-89490-399-3*) Enslow Pubs.
Hadingham, Evan & Hadingham, Janet. Garbage! Where It Comes from, Where It Goes. (Illus.). 48p. (gr. 5 up). 1990. pap. 14.95 jacketed (*0-671-69424-3*, Little Simon); pap. 5.95 (*0-671-69426-X*, Little Simon) S&S Trade.
Hare, Tony. Domestic Waste. LC 91-34099. (Illus.). 32p. (gr. 4-8). 1992. PLB 12.40 (*0-531-17347-X*, Gloucester Pr) Watts.
Heilman, Joan R. Tons of Trash: Why You Should Recycle & What Happens When You Do. 80p. (gr. 2-4). 1992. pap. 3.50 (*0-380-76379-6*, Camelot) Avon.
Leggett, Jeremy. Waste War. LC 90-46573. (Illus.). 48p. (gr. 5-9). 1991. PLB 12.95 (*1-85435-277-6*) Marshall Cavendish.
Leggett, Jeremy & Leggett, Dennis. Operation Earth Series, 6 vols. (Illus.). (gr. 5-9). 1991. PLB 77.70 (*1-85435-273-3*) Marshall Cavendish.
Lepthien, Emilie U. & Kalbacken, Joan. Recycling. LC 90-21275. (Illus.). 48p. (gr. k-4). 1991. PLB 12.85 (*0-516-01118-9*); pap. 4.95 (*0-516-41118-7*) Childrens.
Mandel, Linda & Mandel, Heidi. The Treasure of Trash: A Recycling Story. Codor, Dick, illus. LC 92-41222. 48p. (gr. 4 up). 1993. pap. 12.95 (*0-89529-575-X*) Avery Pub.
Mayes, S. Where Does Rubbish Go? (Illus.). 24p. (gr. 1 up). 1992. PLB 11.96 (*0-88110-551-1*, Usborne); pap. 3.95 (*0-7460-0627-6*, Usborne) EDC.
Nielsen, Shelly. Trash! Trash! Trash! Berg, Julie, ed. LC 93-18952. 1993. PLB 14.96 (*1-56239-192-5*) Abdo & Dghtrs.
O'Connor, Karen. Garbage. LC 89-9382. (Illus.). 96p. (gr. 5-8). 1989. PLB 14.95 (*1-56006-100-6*) Lucent Bks.
Palmer, Joy A. Recycling Plastic. LC 90-32527. (Illus.). 32p. (gr. 5-7). 1991. PLB 12.40 (*0-531-14119-5*) Watts.
Peak, Jan & Hennig, Anna. Trash to Treasure Crafts: From Recyclable Materials. Peak, Jan, illus. 80p. (gr. 3 up). 1992. wkbk. 8.99 (*0-87403-890-1*, 14-02146) Standard Pub.
Showers, Paul. Where Does the Garbage Go? rev. ed. Chewning, Randy, illus. LC 91-46115. 32p. (gr. k-4). 1994. 15.00 (*0-06-021054-0*); PLB 14.89 (*0-06-021057-5*) HarpC Child Bks.
—Where Does the Garbage Go? rev. ed. Chewning, Paul, illus. LC 91-46115. 32p. (gr. k-4). 1994. pap. 4.95 (*0-06-445114-3*, Trophy) HarpC Child Bks.
Silverstein, Alvin, et al. Recycling: Meeting the Challenge of the Trash Crisis. (Illus.). 128p. (gr. 5-9). 1992. 15.95 (*0-399-22190-5*, Putnam) Putnam Pub Group.
Spence, Margaret. Toxic Waste. LC 91-30535. (Illus.). 32p. (gr. 2-4). 1992. PLB 11.90 (*0-531-17297-X*, Gloucester Pr) Watts.
Stefoff, Rebecca. Recycling. (Illus.). 128p. (gr. 5 up). 1991. lib. bdg. 19.95 (*0-7910-1573-4*) Chelsea Hse.
Stenstrup, Allen. Hazardous Waste. LC 91-25864. 128p. (gr. 4-8). 1991. PLB 20.55 (*0-516-05506-2*) Childrens.
Swertka, Eve & Swertka, Albert. Cleaning Up: How Trash Becomes Treasure. Dolobowsky, Mena, illus. LC 91-28777. 40p. (gr. 2-5). 1993. lib. bdg. 10.98 (*0-671-69461-8*, J Messner); pap. 5.95 (*0-671-69467-7*, J Messner) S&S Trade.
Wheeler, Jill C. The Throw-Away Generation. Kallen, Stuart A., ed. LC 91-73071. 202p. 1991. 12.94 (*1-56239-030-9*) Abdo & Dghtrs.
Wilcox, Charlotte. Trash! Bushey, Jerry, illus. 40p. (gr. k-4). 1988. PLB 19.95 (*0-87614-311-7*) Carolrhoda Bks.

REFUSE AND REFUSE DISPOSAL–FICTION
Brownell, Rick. Trixie. Shaw, Peter, illus. LC 93-169. 1994. write for info. (*0-383-03670-4*) SRA Schl Grp.
Delton, Judy. Trash Bash. (ps-3). 1992. pap. 3.25 (*0-440-40592-0*, YB) Dell.
Fuzellier, Michel. Rufus Recycles Paper. LC 93-13933. (Illus.). (gr. 1-5). 1994. 14.95 (*1-56766-105-X*) Childs World.
—Rufus Recycles Trash. LC 93-35706. (Illus.). (gr. 1-5). 1994. 14.95 (*1-56766-106-8*) Childs World.
Hartmann, Wendy. All the Magic in the World. Daly, Niki, illus. LC 92-38289. 32p. (gr. k-3). 1993. 12.99 (*0-525-45092-0*, DCB) Dutton Child Bks.
Korman, Gordon. A Semester in the Life of a Garbage Bag. 1993. pap. 3.25 (*0-590-44429-8*) Scholastic Inc.
Kraus, Robert. How Spider Stopped Litterbugs. (ps-3). 1991. pap. 2.50 (*0-590-44462-X*) Scholastic Inc.
Lord. Garbage! The Trashiest Book. 1993. pap. 2.75 (*0-590-46024-2*) Scholastic Inc.
McEwan, Elaine K. Operation Garbage: A Josh McIntire Book. LC 92-43761. 1993. pap. 4.99 (*0-7814-0121-6*, Chariot Bks) Chariot Family.
Madden, Don. The Wartville Wizard. LC 92-22246. (Illus.). 32p. (gr. k-3). 1993. pap. 4.95 (*0-689-71667-2*, Aladdin) Macmillan Child Grp.
Morris, Martha. Katherine & the Garbage Dump. Cathcart, Yvonne, illus. 24p. (gr. 1-4). 1992. 12.95 (*0-929005-39-2*, Pub. by Second Story Pr CN); pap. 5.95 (*0-929005-38-4*, Second Story Pr CN) InBook.
Spinelli, Jerry. Dump Days. (gr. 4-7). 1991. pap. 3.25 (*0-440-40421-5*) Dell.
Toussaint, Michael E. The Playland Kids, Featuring Marcus Toussaint, the Recycler. Hamburg, Cary, illus. 24p. (Orig.). (gr. k-6). 1992. pap. 2.95 (*0-9630905-0-X*) Michael T Enter.
Van Laan, Nancy. Round & Round Again. Westcott, Nadine B., illus. LC 93-45918. 32p. (ps-3). 1994. 13.95 (*0-7868-0009-7*); PLB 13.89 (*0-7868-2005-5*) Hyprn Child.
Wilcox, Charlotte. Trash! Bushey, Jerry, illus. 40p. (gr. k-4). 1989. pap. 5.95 (*0-87614-511-X*, First Ave Edns) Lerner Pubns.

REGATTAS
see Rowing

REGIONAL PLANNING
see also City Planning

REGISTERS OF PERSONS
see names of countries, cities, etc. and names of colleges, universities, etc. with the subdivision Registers, e.g. U. S. –Registers
REHABILITATION
see classes of people with subdivision Rehabilitation, e.g. Physically Handicapped–Rehabilitation
REIGN OF TERROR
see France–History–Revolution, 1789-1799
REINDEER
Arnold, Caroline. Reindeer. Johnson, Pamela, illus. LC 93-12981. (gr. 4-7). 1993. pap. 3.95 (*0-590-46943-6*) Scholastic Inc.
Bernhard, Emery. Reindeer. Bernhard, Durga, illus. LC 93-45327. 32p. (ps-3). 1994. reinforced bdg. 15.95 (*0-8234-1097-8*) Holiday.
Lepthien, Emilie U. Reindeer. LC 93-33513. (Illus.). 48p. (gr. k-4). 1994. PLB 12.85 (*0-516-01059-X*) Childrens.
Postell, Alice E. Where Did the Reindeer Come From? Alaska Experience the First Fifty Years. York, Susan P., ed. DeArmond, Robert N., frwd. by. LC 90-146. (Illus.). 144p. (gr. 9 up). 1990. write for info. (*0-9626090-0-5*) Amaknak Pr.
REINDEER–FICTION
Haywood, Carolyn. How the Reindeer Saved Santa. Ambrus, Victor G., illus. LC 85-28456. 32p. (ps-3). 1986. 12.95 (*0-688-05903-1*); lib. bdg. 12.88 (*0-688-05904-X*) Morrow Jr Bks.
Lemmons, Cherilynn. Randolph's Wonderful Adventure. (Illus.). 48p. (gr. 1-6). 1992. 6.95 (*0-8059-3289-5*) Dorrance.
Lester, Vivian. Wee-Dolph, the Tiniest Reindeer. (gr. 1-3). 1990. pap. text ed. 4.95 (*1-881079-00-7*) Antex Corp.
Lindman, Maj. Snipp, Snapp, Snurr & the Reindeer. (Illus.). 32p. 1993. Repr. lib. bdg. 14.95x (*1-56849-005-4*) Buccaneer Bks.
May, Robert L. Rudolph the Red-Nosed Reindeer. (ps). 1993. 4.95 (*0-307-12396-0*, Golden Pr) Western Pub.
Olson, Jim. The Reindeer & the Easter Bunny. Van Vleck, Jane & Olson, Sally, eds. (Illus.). 18p. (Orig.). (gr. 1-4). 1981. pap. 4.95 (*0-943806-00-3*) Neahtawanta Pr.
Ritchie, Sheri & Lavranos, Destini. Goodnight Little Reindeer. (Illus.). 2p. (ps-k). 1993. 14.95 (*0-9638393-1-4*) Bedtime Bks.
Rudolph Shines Again. 14.95 (*0-695-81557-1*) Modern Curr.
Rudolph the Red-Nosed Reindeer. 14.95 (*0-8136-6022-X*) Modern Curr.
RELATIVITY (PHYSICS)
Swisher, Clarice. Relativity: Opposing Viewpoints. LC 90-3910. (Illus.). 112p. (gr. 5-8). 1990. PLB 14.95 (*0-89908-076-6*) Greenhaven.
Tauber, Gerald E. Relativity: From Einstein to Black Holes. Kline, Marjory, ed. LC 87-25964. (Illus.). 128p. (gr. 6-12). 1988. PLB 13.40 (*0-531-10482-6*) Watts.
RELAXATION
see Recreation
RELIGION
see also Belief and Doubt; Faith; God; Indians of North America–Religion and Mythology; Mythology; Religions; Spiritual Life; Superstition; Theology; Worship
Barker, Dan. Just Pretend: A Freethought Book for Children. Cuebas, Alma, illus. 72p. (Orig.). (ps-6). 1988. pap. 10.00 (*0-318-42495-9*) Freedom Rel Found.
Bawa, Ujagar S. Bichitra Naatik: A Part of Sikh Scriptures. 172p. (gr. 8-12). 1991. pap. 10.00x (*0-942245-06-7*) Wash Sikh Ctr.
—Sikhism: A Short Expose. 30p. (gr. 8-12). 1988. pap. 2. 00x (*0-942245-02-4*) Wash Sikh Ctr.
—Sri Sukhmani Sahib: A Part of Sikh Scriptures. 304p. (gr. 8-12). 1990. pap. 10.00x (*0-942245-05-9*) Wash Sikh Ctr.
Cook, Bob. Speaking in Tongues: Is That All There Is? Van Someron, Terry, illus. 48p. (gr. 9-12). 1982. pap. text ed. 1.50 (*0-88243-932-4*, 02-0932); leader's guide 3.95 (*0-88243-935-9*, 02-0935) Gospel Pub.
Daughters of St. Paul. God Loves Me. (gr. 1-6). 1982. pap. 1.95 (*0-8198-3032-1*); tchr's. manual 3.95 (*0-8198-3031-3*) St Paul Bks.
Fahs, Sophia L. & Cobb, Alice. Old Tales for a New Day. 2nd ed. Stair, Gobin, illus. 201p. (gr. 4-9). 1992. pap. 15.95 (*0-87975-730-2*) Prometheus Bks.
Hunt, Arnold, et al. Ethics of World Religions. 2nd, rev. ed. LC 91-21259. (Illus.). 180p. (gr. 10 up). 1991. lib. bdg. 16.95 (*0-89908-824-4*); pap. 9.95 (*0-89908-823-6*) Greenhaven.
Huntington, Mairi. The Great Game. 173p. 1987. pap. 6.00 (*1-57043-063-2*) ECKANKAR.
Johnson, Tom. What Religious Science Is. 18p. (gr. 7-12). 1989. Repr. of 1977 ed. 2.00 (*0-941992-19-5*) Los Arboles Pub.
Livre des Religions. (FRE.). 261p. (gr. 4-9). 1989. 29.95 (*2-07-039556-1*) Schoenhof.
McIndoo, Ethel. Discover Girls in Action. (SPA.). 22p. (Orig.). (gr. 4-6). 1988. pap. text ed. 1.50 (*0-936625-74-0*) Womans Mission Union.
—Discover Girls in Action. 22p. (Orig.). (gr. 4-6). 1988. pap. text ed. 1.50 (*0-936625-41-4*) Womans Mission Union.
Makhlouf, Georgia. The Rise of Major Religions. Moeller, Walter O., tr. from FRE. Welply, Michael, illus. 77p. (gr. 7 up). 1988. 12.95 (*0-382-09482-4*) Silver Burdett Pr.
Martin, John D. Living Together on God's Earth. (gr. 3). 1974. 15.00x (*0-87813-915-X*); tchr's. guide 19.65x (*0-87813-910-9*) Christian Light.
Minchin-Comm, Dorothy. Gates of Promise. Wheeler, Gerald, ed. 96p. (gr. 7 up). 1989. pap. 6.95 (*0-8280-0470-6*) Review & Herald.
The New Saint Joseph Baltimore Catechism, 2 bks. (gr. 3-8). No. 1, Gr. 3-5. 1.80 (*0-89942-241-1*, 241/05); No. 2, Gr. 6-8. 1.95 (*0-89942-242-X*, 242/05) Catholic Bk Pub.
Pelton, Jeanette. Natural Morning. Pelton, Dan, ed. Pelton, Fawn, illus. 100p. (Orig.). (gr. 5-7). 1993. pap. 6.00 (*1-879564-06-8*) Long Acre Pub.
St. Augustine. Confessions of Saint Augustine. (gr. 11 up). 1968. pap. 1.95 (*0-8049-0190-2*, CL-190) Airmont.
Stein, Wendy. Shamans: Opposing Viewpoints. LC 91-14498. (Illus.). 112p. (gr. 5-8). 1991. PLB 14.95 (*0-89908-088-X*) Greenhaven.
VanderGriend, Donna. Faith Talk. 132p. (Orig.). (gr. 10-12). 1989. pap. text ed. 24.95 leader's guide (*0-930265-56-4*) CRC Pubns.
RELIGION–PHILOSOPHY
Hamilton, Dorothy. Last One Chosen. Converse, James, illus. LC 82-3150. 112p. (Orig.). (gr. 5-10). 1982. pap. 3.95 (*0-8361-3306-4*) Herald Pr.
RELIGION–STUDY AND TEACHING
see Religious Education
RELIGION AND SCIENCE
see also Creation; Evolution; Man–Origin and Antiquity
Rohr, Janelle. Science & Religion: Opposing Viewpoints. LC 87-38066. (Illus.). (gr. 10 up). 1988. pap. text ed. 9.95 (*0-89908-406-0*) Greenhaven.
RELIGION AND STATE
see Church and State
RELIGIONS
see also Bahaism; Buddha and Buddhism; Christianity; Confucius and Confucianism; Hinduism; Judaism; Mythology; Religion; Sects
Boraks, Lucius. Religions of the West. LC 87-63499. 116p. (Orig.). 1988. pap. 7.95 (*1-55612-141-5*) Sheed & Ward MO.
Counterfeit Religions. 48p. (gr. 9-12). 1990. pap. 8.99 (*1-55945-207-2*) Group Pub.
Hakowski, Maryann. Vine & Branches, Vol. 3. Stamschror, Robert, ed. Price, Carolyn, illus. 168p. (Orig.). (gr. 6-7). 1994. pap. 22.95 (*0-88489-323-5*) St Marys.
Maestro, Betsy. The Story of Religion. Weihs, Erika, illus. LC 92-38980. 1994. write for info (*0-395-62364-2*, Clarion Bks) HM.
Morris, Scott, ed. Religions of the World. De Blij, Harm J., intro. by. LC 92-22282. (Illus.). 1993. 15.95 (*0-7910-1810-5*, Am Art Analog); pap. write for info. (*0-7910-1823-7*, Am Art Analog) Chelsea Hse.
Pollard, Michael. Beliefs & Believers. Stefoff, Rebecca, ed. LC 91-36503. (Illus.). 48p. (gr. 5-9). 1992. PLB 19. 93 (*1-56074-037-X*) Garrett Ed Corp.
Prior, Katherine. Initiation Customs. LC 93-516. 32p. (gr. 4-8). 1993. 13.95 (*1-56847-035-5*) Thomson Lrning.
Singh, Bhagat. The Story of Krishna. (Illus.). 20p. (Orig.). (ps-5). 1976. pap. 2.50 (*0-89744-135-4*, Pub. by Hemkunt India) Auromere.
Singh, Nikkyh-Guninder. Sikhism. (Illus.). 128p. (gr. 7-12). 1992. bds. 17.95x (*0-8160-2446-4*) Facts on File.
Thomas, M. Angele & Ramey, Mary L. Many Children: Religions Around the World. Lucas, Patti L., illus. LC 87-91771. 70p. (Orig.). (gr. 2-6). 1987. pap. text ed. 6.95 (*0-9619293-0-8*) M A Thomas.
Whiting, Roger. Religions for Today. 3rd, rev. & updated ed. (Illus.). 270p. 1991. pap. 21.00x (*0-7487-0586-4*, Pub. by S Thornes UK) Dufour.
Wright, Tom. Bringing the Church to the World. 192p. (Orig.). 1993. pap. 8.99 (*1-55661-318-0*) Bethany Hse.
RELIGIONS–BIOGRAPHY
Here are entered collections of biographies of religious leaders not limited to the Christian religion.
see also Christian Biography
Burch, Joann J. Fine Print: A Story about Johann Gutenberg. Aldrich, Kent A., illus. 64p. (gr. 3-6). 1991. lib. bdg. 14.95 (*0-87614-682-5*) Carolrhoda Bks.
Clarke, Brenda. Fighting for Their Faith. LC 89-71372. (Illus.). 48p. (gr. 4-8). 1990. PLB 11.95 (*0-8114-2753-6*) Raintree Steck-V.
Lappin, Peter. Stories of Don Bosco. 2nd ed. LC 78-72525. (Illus.). 272p. (gr. 5-12). 1979. pap. 2.95 (*0-89944-036-3*) Don Bosco Multimedia.
Majumdar, Lila. Jorasanko House. (Illus.). (gr. 1-9). 1979. pap. 2.50 (*0-89744-176-1*) Auromere.
Treece, Patricia. Soldier of God. Chatton, Ray, illus. 32p. (gr. 1-8). 1982. pap. 1.00 (*0-913382-22-1*, 111-1) Prow Bks-Franciscan.
RELIGIONS–FICTION
Baba Hari Dass. Mystic Monkey. Kelley, Elizabeth A., illus. LC 81-51051. 64p. (Orig.). (gr. 4-8). 1984. pap. 9.95 (*0-918100-05-4*) Sri Rama.
Babbitt, Lucy C. Where the Truth Lies: A Novel. LC 92-34061. 208p. (gr. 7 up). 1993. 15.95 (*0-531-05473-X*); PLB 15.99 (*0-531-08623-2*) Orchard Bks Watts.
Barrie, J. M. The Little Minister. 232p. 1981. Repr. PLB 18.95 (*0-89966-329-X*) Buccaneer Bks.
—The Little Minister. 300p. 1980. Repr. PLB 18.95x (*0-89967-007-5*) Harmony Raine.
Blume, Judy. Are You There God? It's Me, Margaret. LC 90-44484. 156p. (gr. 4-7). 1990. Repr. of 1970 ed. SBE 14.95 (*0-02-710991-7*, Bradbury Pr) Macmillan Child Grp.
Carney, Mary L. How Do You Hug an Angel? A Devotional Novel for Junior Highers. 144p. (gr. 6-9). 1993. pap. 6.99 (*0-310-59411-1*, Pub. by Youth Spec) Zondervan.
Devi-Doolin, Daya. Dormck & the Temple of the Healing Light. LC 89-63461. (Illus.). 50p. (Orig.). (gr. 4-8). 1989. pap. text ed. 6.50 incl. cassette (*1-877945-05-6*) Padaran Pubns.

Griffin, Peggy A. Talking Treasures. Pulliam, Darrell, illus. 82p. 1994. pap. 12.95 (*1-884056-01-6*) Scribes Pubns. TALKING TREASURES is a book of folk stories being retold from the oral tradition of African Americans in Appalachia. Each of the five stories contains moral lessons for juveniles. Animal characters & children of past ages come alive on fully illustrated pages to entertain, entrance & entreat young readers. TO THE FAIR is an animal story of a race between the frog & the turtle. THE MAGNIFICENT BUTTERFLY travels around the world looking for flowers that are beautiful enough for him. He discovers that he left the most wonderful flowers back home. SHILDA is a pretty, witty, but spoiled little girl who manages to have her own way. She meets a tragedy in the woods as a result of her disobedience to her parents & teacher. BILLY'S BIRTHDAY is a heartwarming scene between three generations who discuss the privileges of young people. Billy discovers that he is not grown up as he thought. UPHILL DOWNHILL: Young teenagers go on a mountain trip to search for snipes. They have many adventures & learn a secret. TALKING TREASURES will be enjoyed by the entire family. It is a treasure that will have the whole family talking, even to each other. Order form Scribes Publishing, 1448 E. 52nd St. #418, Chicago, IL 60615. *Publisher Provided Annotation.*

Groner, Judyth & Wikler, Madeine. Let's Build a Sukkah. Kahn, Katherine J., illus. LC 86-81717. 12p. (ps). 1986. bds. 4.95 (*0-930494-58-X*) Kar Ben.
Jones, Rebecca C. The Believers. 144p. (gr. 6 up). 1989. 13.95 (*1-55970-035-1*) Arcade Pub Inc.
Le Guin, Ursula K. Solomon Leviathan's Nine Hundred Thirty-First Trip Around the World. Austin, Alicia, illus. 40p. (gr. 7 up). 1983. 70.00 (*0-941826-03-1*) Cheap St.
Lockman, Vic. Super Bug Leads Tim Burr to the Gospel in the Woods. Lockman, Vic, illus. 24p. (Orig.). (gr. 8 up). 1991. pap. 2.95 (*0-936175-14-1*) V Lockman.
Oberman, Sheldon. The Always Prayer Shawl. Lewin, Ted, illus. 32p. (gr. 2 up). 1994. 14.95 (*1-878093-22-3*) Boyds Mills Pr.
Paterson, Katherine. Rebels of the Heavenly Kingdom. 240p. (gr. 7 up). 1984. pap. 2.95 (*0-380-68304-0*, Flare) Avon.
Pender, Gresilda. God's Little People. 1993. 7.95 (*0-8062-4631-6*) Carlton.
Saypol, Judyth R. & Wikler, Madeline. The Purim Parade. Kahn, Katherine J., illus. LC 86-71816. 12p. (ps). 1986. bds. 4.95 (*0-930494-60-1*) Kar Ben.
Thomsen, Paul. Flight of the Falcon. 80p. (gr. 4 up). 1991. pap. 4.95 (*1-56121-056-0*) Wolgemuth & Hyatt.
RELIGIOUS ART
see Christian Art and Symbolism
RELIGIOUS BELIEF
see Belief and Doubt; Faith
RELIGIOUS BIOGRAPHY
see Christian Biography; Religions–Biography
RELIGIOUS CEREMONIES
see Rites and Ceremonies
RELIGIOUS DENOMINATIONS
see Sects
RELIGIOUS EDUCATION
see also Bible–Study; Character Education
Ahlers, Julia. Special Topics in Justice & Peace: Nine Articles for Student Handouts. Allaire, Barbara, ed. 48p. (Orig.). (gr. 11-12). 1990. pap. text ed. 8.95 stitched (*0-88489-244-1*) St Marys.
Aronoff, Daisy P. ABC Bible & Holiday Stories. Danciger, Leila N., illus. 58p. (ps-7). 1992. pap. 15.95 (*1-878612-28-X*) Sunflower Co.

Beckman, Beverly. Shapes in God's World. LC 56-1462. (ps-k). 1984. 6.99 (*0-570-04094-9*) Concordia.
—Sizes in God's World. (ps-k). 1984. 6.99 (*0-570-04095-7*, 56-1463) Concordia.
Boden, Robert. Teen Talks with God. (gr. 7-12). 1980. pap. 3.99 (*0-570-03812-X*, 12-2921) Concordia.
Branson, Mary. Fun Around the World: Games, Crafts, Food & Dress Ideas You Can Use! Gross, Karen, ed. 64p. (Orig.). (gr. 1-6). 1992. pap. text ed. 4.95 (*1-56309-052-X*, New Hope) Womans Mission Union.
Case, Riley B., et al. We Believe - Discovery. rev. ed. 64p. 1988. wkbk. 4.35 (*0-917851-26-9*) Bristol Hse.
Caswell, Helen R. God's World Makes Me Feel So Little. Caswell, Helen R., illus. LC 84-14545. 32p. (gr. k-3). 1985. 5.95 (*0-687-15510-X*) Abingdon.
Clark, Suzanne. Blackboard Blackmail. La Haye, Beverly. 220p. (Orig.). 1989. pap. 8.95 (*1-877818-02-X*) Footstool Pubns.
Coleman, Bill & Coleman, Patty. My Confirmation Journal. rev. ed. 112p. (gr. 6-9). 1991. pap. 4.95 (*0-89622-483-X*, B67) Twenty-Third.
Cone, Molly. About Belonging. Perl, Susan, illus. 64p. (Orig.). (gr. 1-2). 1972. pap. 6.00 (*0-8074-0234-6*, 101083) UAHC.
Crowther, Jean D. Growing up in the Church: Gospel Principles & Practices for Children. rev. ed. Perry, Lucille R., illus. LC 67-25433. 84p. (gr. 2-6). 1973. Repr. of 1965 ed. 7.98 (*0-88290-024-2*) Horizon Utah.
Cumming, James T. & Moll, Hans G. And, God, What About...? 1980. 5.99 (*0-570-03806-5*, 12-2915) Concordia.
Dean, Bessie. Let's Go to Church. Dean, Bessie, illus. LC 76-3995. 63p. (ps-3). 1993. pap. 3.98 (*0-88290-062-5*) Horizon Utah.
Doolittle, Robert. Be Alive in Christ. Stamschror, Robert P., ed. St. George, Carolyn, illus. 188p. (Orig.). (gr. 9-12). 1991. pap. 16.95 (*0-88489-246-8*) St Marys.
Fehlauer, Adolph. Catechism Lessons: Pupil's Book. Grunze, Richard, ed. May, Lawrence, illus. 336p. (gr. 5-6). 1981. 6.95 (*0-938272-09-8*) WELS Board.
—Catechism Lessons-Teacher's Book. Grunze, R., ed. 392p. (gr. 5-6). 1978. 3-ring binder 9.95 (*0-938272-08-X*) WELS Board.
Foling, Debra & Sherbondy, Sharon. Super Sketches for Youth Ministry: Thirty Creative Topical Dramas from Willow Creek Community Church. 192p. 1991. pap. 12.99 (*0-310-53411-9*, Pub. by Youth Spec) Zondervan.
Fretz, Clarence Y. Story of God's People. (gr. 7). 1978. pap. 5.90x (*0-87813-900-1*); tchr's. guide 8.75x (*0-87813-901-X*) Christian Light.
Garces, David F., compiled by. Ideas Para Actividade Especiales - Ideas for Special Activities. (SPA.). 64p. (Orig.). (gr. 12 up). 1992. pap. 3.50 (*0-311-12251-5*) Casa Bautista.
Griffin, Jeannie. Seven Key Scriptures to Lead Someone to the Lord. 128p. (Orig.). (gr. 12). 1990. pap. 5.00 (*0-9625016-3-8*) Jeannie Griffin.
Groomer, Vera. Quiet Because. (ps). 1979. pap. 2.15 (*0-8127-0253-0*) Review & Herald.
Haas, Lois J. Tell Me about God: 12 Lessons, Vol. 1. (ps). 1966. complete kit 14.95 (*0-86508-011-9*); text only 3.50 (*0-86508-012-7*); color & action book 1.75 (*0-86508-013-5*) BCM Pubn.
—Tell Me about Jesus: 16 Lessons, Vol. 2. (ps). 1967. complete kit 14.95 (*0-86508-014-3*); text only 3.50 (*0-86508-015-1*); color & action book 1.75 (*0-86508-016-X*) BCM Pubn.
Hakowski, Maryann. Vine & Branches, Vol. 1. Stamschror, Robert P., ed. St. George, Carolyn, illus. 158p. (gr. 7-12). 1992. spiral bdg. 22.95 (*0-88489-255-7*) St Marys.
—Vine & Branches, Vol. 2. Stamschror, Robert P., ed. St. George, Carolyn, illus. 166p. (gr. 7-12). 1992. spiral bdg. 22.95 (*0-88489-278-6*) St Marys.
Hand, Phyllis. Celebrate God & Country. Nygaard, Elizabeth, illus. 144p. (gr. k-6). 1987. pap. 11.95 (*0-86653-390-7*, SS 843, Shining Star Pubns) Good Apple.
Harrison House Staff. Confessions for Kids. Titolo, Nancy, illus. 29p. (Orig.). (gr. 1-3). 1984. pap. 0.98 (*0-89274-322-0*) Harrison Hse.
Hillert, Margaret. God's Big Book. Hohag, Linda, illus. 24p. (gr. k-1). 1988. 4.99 (*0-87403-457-4*, 24-03696) Standard Pub.
Hutchens, Paul. Sugar Creek Gang & the Chicago Adventure & One Stormy Day. (gr. 3-7). 1968. pap. 6.99 (*0-8024-1237-8*) Moody.
—The Thousand Dollar Fish. (gr. 2-7). 1966. pap. 4.99 (*0-8024-4815-1*) Moody.
—The Timber Wolf. (gr. 3-7). 1965. pap. 4.99 (*0-8024-4823-2*) Moody.
Johnston, Dorothy G. & Abbas, Kathleen. Church Time for Children. LC 80-67855. 120p. (Orig.). (gr. 1-6). 1981. 10.95 (*0-89636-056-3*, Chariot Bks) Cook.
Lea, Thomas D. & Latham, Bill. Sigueme 3. Martinez, Mario, tr. from ENG. (SPA.). 128p. (Orig.). (gr. 5 up). 1989. pap. 3.75 (*0-311-13847-0*) Casa Bautista.
Lecciones y Actividades Misioneras para Ninos de 3 y 4 anos, No. 1. (SPA.). 96p. (ps). 1988. pap. 3.50 (*0-311-12039-3*) Casa Bautista.
Lecciones y Actividades Misioneras Para Ninos de 3 y 4 Anos - Missionary Lessons & Activities for Children 3 & 4, No. 2. (SPA., Illus.). 96p. (Orig.). (ps). 1989. pap. 3.50 (*0-311-12044-X*) Casa Bautista.
Lee, Sylvia, ed. The Holy Spirit in Christian Education. LC 88-80549. 144p. (Orig.). (gr. k up). 1988. pap. 2.95 tchr's. bk. (*0-88243-854-9*, 02-0854) Gospel Pub.
Leichner, Jeannine T. Making Things Right: The Sacrament of Reconciliation. (Illus.). 62p. (Orig.). (gr. 2-4). 1980. pap. 3.95 (*0-87973-351-9*, 351); Spanish Edition. 3.95 (*0-87973-349-7*, 349) Our Sunday Visitor.
MacKenthun, Carole & Dwyer, Paulinus. Kindness. Filkins, Vanessa, illus. 48p. (gr. 2 up). 1987. pap. 7.95 (*0-86653-379-6*, SS880, Shining Star Pubns) Good Apple.
Murphy, Elspeth C. Sometimes I Get Mad. LC 81-67739. (ps-2). 1981. pap. 3.99 (*0-89191-493-5*, 54932, Chariot Bks) Chariot Family.
—Sometimes I Have to Cry. Nelson, Jane, illus. (ps-2). 1981. pap. 3.99 (*0-89191-494-3*, 54940, Chariot Bks) Chariot Family.
—Sometimes I Need to Be Hugged. LC 81-67740. (Illus.). (ps-2). 1981. pap. 3.99 (*0-89191-492-7*, 54924, Chariot Bks) Chariot Family.
Neighbour, Ralph W., Jr. Sigueme, Edicion para Ninos. Geiger, Mary J. & Ditmore, Shirley, trs. from ENG. (SPA., Illus.). 64p. (Orig.). 1989. pap. 2.65 (*0-311-13848-9*) Casa Bautista.
Nystrom, Carolyn. The Holy Spirit in Me. 32p. (ps-2). 1980. pap. 4.99 (*0-8024-6152-2*) Moody.
Olsen, Warren & Rinden, David, eds. Explanation of Luther's Small Catechism. 2nd ed. 128p. (gr. 7-8). 1992. text ed. 7.95 (*0-943167-20-5*) Faith & Fellowship Pr.
Programas y Actividades para Muchachos y Jovencitos, No. 5. (SPA.). 96p. (gr. 4-10). 1988. pap. 3.50 (*0-311-12041-5*) Casa Bautista.
Programas y Actividades para Muchachos y Jovencitos, No. 6. (SPA., Illus.). 96p. (Orig.). 1989. pap. 2.95 (*0-311-12046-6*) Casa Bautista.
Programas y Actividades para Ninas y Jovencitas, No. 5. (SPA.). 96p. (gr. 4-10). 1988. pap. 3.50 (*0-311-12040-7*) Casa Bautista.
Programas y Actividades para Ninas y Jovencitas, No. 6. (SPA., Illus.). 96p. (Orig.). 1989. pap. 3.50 (*0-311-12045-8*) Casa Bautista.
Prose, Francine. Stories from Our Living Past. new ed. Harlow, Jules, ed. Weihs, Erika, illus. LC 74-8514. 128p. (gr. 3-4). 1974. 7.95 (*0-87441-081-9*); wkbk. 1 2.95 (*0-87441-083-5*); wkbk. 2 2.95 (*0-87441-084-3*); tchr's guide 14.95 (*0-87441-082-7*) Behrman.
Rice, Wayne & Yaconelli, Mike. Creative Activities for Small Youth Groups. Stamschror, Robert P., ed. Youth Specialities Clip Art Staff, illus. 101p. (gr. 7-12). 1991. pap. 12.95 (*0-88489-264-6*) St Marys.
—Creative Communication & Discussion Activities. Stamschror, Robert P., ed. Youth Specialties Clip Art Staff, illus. 96p. (gr. 7-12). 1991. pap. 12.95 (*0-88489-266-2*) St Marys.
Rummel, Mary. God's Love for Happiness: A Return to Family Values. Dirks, Nathan & Brandt, Bill, illus. LC 92-91032. 64p. (Orig.). (gr. k up). 1992. pap. 9.95 (*0-9635091-0-1*) Olive Brnch.
St. John, Patricia M. Rainbow Garden. (gr. 2-5). pap. 4.99 (*0-8024-0028-0*) Moody.
Schneck, Susan & Strohl, Mary. Vacation Bible School Ideas & Summertime Fun. (Illus.). 96p. (ps-2). 1989. 10.95 (*0-86653-477-6*, SS1813, Shining Star Pubns) Good Apple.
Solomon, Marti. StudiAct: Queen. Butler, Cathy, ed. 31p. (Orig.). 1991. pap. text ed. 2.25 (*1-56309-006-6*) Womans Mission Union.
—StudiAct: Queen Regent. Turrentine, Jan, ed. 32p. (Orig.). (gr. 7-12). 1991. pap. text ed. 2.25 (*1-56309-003-1*) Womans Mission Union.
—StudiAct: Queen Regent in Service. Turrentine, Jan, ed. 31p. (Orig.). (gr. 7-12). 1991. pap. text ed. 2.25 (*1-56309-004-X*) Womans Mission Union.
—StudiAct: Queen with Scepter. Turrentine, Jan, ed. 31p. (Orig.). (gr. 7-12). Date not set. pap. text ed. 2.25 (*1-56309-005-8*) Womans Mission Union.
—StudiAct: Service Aide. Turrentine, Jan, ed. 16p. (Orig.). (gr. 7-12). 1991. pap. text ed. 2.25 (*1-56309-002-3*) Womans Mission Union.
Stadler, Bernice & Reese, Nancy. Celebrations of the Word for Children: Cycle C. LC 88-90102. 104p. (Orig.). (gr. 3-8). 1988. pap. text ed. 9.95 (*0-89622-362-0*) Twenty-Third.
Walsh, Chad. Knock & Enter. 208p. (gr. 6-9). 1953. pap. 4.95 (*0-8192-1076-5*) Morehouse Pub.
Ward, Elaine. Using God's World in Christian Education. 12p. (Orig.). (gr. 1-8). 1987. pap. 5.75 (*0-940754-40-1*) Ed Ministries.
Watkins, Dawn L. The Medallion. (Illus.). 223p. (Orig.). (gr. 4). 1985. pap. 6.94 (*0-89084-282-5*) Bob Jones Univ Pr.
You Are an Acolyte: A Manual for Acolytes. (Illus.). 24p. (gr. 6-9). 1977. pap. 4.99 (*0-8066-1552-4*, 10-7409, Augsburg) Augsburg Fortress.

RELIGIOUS FESTIVALS
see Fasts and Feasts
RELIGIOUS FREEDOM
see Religious Liberty
RELIGIOUS HISTORY
see Church History
RELIGIOUS LIBERTY
see also Church and State

Evans, J. Edward. Freedom of Religion. (Illus.). 88p. (gr. 4 up). 1990. PLB 14.95 (*0-8225-1754-X*) Lerner Pubns.
Merlin, Lester. Courage for a Cross, Teacher's Guide To. (gr. 1-6). 1987. pap. 9.95 (*0-377-00169-4*) Friendship Pr.
Nichols, Joan K. A Matter of Conscience: The Trial of Anne Hutchinson. Krovatin, Dan, illus. LC 92-18087. 101p. (gr. 2-5). 1992. PLB 21.34 (*0-8114-7233-7*) Raintree Steck-V.
Sherrow, Victoria. Separation of Church & State. LC 91-39770. (Illus.). 144p. (gr. 7-12). 1992. PLB 13.90 (*0-531-13000-2*) Watts.
Walters, Jean. Freedom or Fear. 32p. (Orig.). 1984. pap. 3.50 (*0-941992-21-7*) Los Arboles Pub.

RELIGIOUS LITERATURE
see also Catholic Literature

Angers, Joann. Meeting the Forgiving Jesus: A Child's First Penance Book. 32p. (gr. 1-3). 1983. pap. 2.95 (*0-89243-201-2*) Liguori Pubns.
Bhaktivedanta, Swami A. C. Prahlad, Picture & Story Book. LC 72-2032. (Illus.). (gr. 2-6). 1973. pap. 4.00 (*0-685-47513-1*) Bhaktivedanta.
Burgess, Beverly C. The Little Red Hen. (Illus.). 32p. (gr. 1-3). 1984. pap. 3.98 (*0-89274-312-3*) Harrison Hse.
—Little Red Riding Hood. (Illus.). 32p. (Orig.). (gr. 1-3). 1983. pap. 3.98 (*0-89274-289-5*) Harrison Hse.
Coleman, William L. Listen to the Animals. LC 79-11312. 128p. (ps-6). 1979. pap. 6.99 (*0-87123-341-X*) Bethany Hse.
—Singing Penguins & Puffed-up Toads. LC 81-1079. 125p. (ps-4). 1981. pap. 6.99 (*0-87123-554-4*) Bethany Hse.
Dueland, Joy. God's Great Adventure. (Illus.). 111p. (ps up). 1980. 8.95 (*0-685-08285-7*) Phunn Pubs.
Geller, Norman. Talk to God... I'll Get the Message: Catholic Version. Tomlinson, Albert, illus. 23p. (gr. 1-4). 1983. pap. 4.95 (*0-915753-03-0*) N Geller Pub.
—Talk to God... I'll Get the Message: Jewish Version. Tomlinson, Albert J., illus. 23p. (gr. 1-4). 1983. pap. 4.95 (*0-915753-02-2*) N Geller Pub.
—Talk to God... I'll Get the Message: Protestant Version. Tomlinson, Albert J., illus. 23p. (gr. 1-4). 1983. pap. 4.95 (*0-915753-04-9*) N Geller Pub.
The Illustrated Pilgrim's Progress. (Illus.). 1989. 12.99 (*0-8423-1605-1*) Tyndale.
Jones, Tim & Butterworth, Jim. Another Way of Putting It: Twenty Short Plays with a Point. 128p. (gr. 7-12). 1991. pap. 7.99 (*0-87403-854-5*, 14-03354) Standard Pub.
Muhaiyaddeen, M. R. Bawa. Come to the Secret Garden: Sufi Tales of Wisdom. LC 83-49210. (Illus.). 450p. 1985. 20.00 (*0-914390-27-9*) Fellowship Pr PA.
The Queen Who Saved Her People. 32p. (gr. 3-6). 1973. pap. 1.99 (*0-570-06075-3*, 59-1194) Concordia.
Richardson, Arleta. In Grandma's Attic. LC 74-75541. 112p. (Orig.). (gr. 3-7). 1984. pap. 3.99 (*0-912692-32-4*, Chariot Bks) Chariot Family.
Richter, Betts & Jacobsen, Alice. Make It So! A Child's Book on Self-Direction Through Affirmations. 3rd ed. LC 79-84946. (Illus.). 55p. (gr. k-4). 1988. pap. 7.95 (*0-87516-599-0*) DeVorss.
Rizzo, Kay D. Gospel in the Grocery Store. Wheeler, Penny E., ed. 96p. (gr. 7 up). 1989. pap. 4.95 (*0-8280-0446-3*) Review & Herald.
Schlink, Basilea. What Made Them So Brave? (Illus.). (gr. 3 up). 1978. gift edition 2.25 (*3-87209-655-9*) Evang Sisterhood Mary.
Wheeler, Penny E., ed. Morning Riser. 384p. (gr. 3-6). 1988. 9.50 (*0-8280-0457-9*) Review & Herald.

RELIGIOUS MUSIC
see Church Music
RELIGIOUS PAINTING
see Christian Art and Symbolism
RELIGIOUS POETRY
see also Carols; Hymns

Alexander, Martha. Poems & Prayers for the Very Young. (Illus.). (ps-1). 1973. pap. 2.25 (*0-394-82705-8*) Random Bks Yng Read.
Fletcher, Cynthia H. My Jesus Pocketbook of Nursery Rhymes. Sherman, Erin, illus. LC 80-52041. 32p. (Orig.). (ps-3). 1980. pap. 0.69 (*0-937420-00-X*) Stirrup Assoc.
Grimes, Nikki. From a Child's Heart. Joysmith, Brenda, illus. LC 93-79000. 32p. (gr. 2-6). 1993. 15.95 (*0-940975-44-0*); pap. 7.95 (*0-940975-43-2*) Just Us Bks.
Pree, Bernice W. Quiet Time. Hyman, Mark, ed. 82p. (Orig.). Date not set. pap. write for info. (*0-915515-03-2*) Way Pub.

RELIGIOUS SYMBOLISM
see Christian Art and Symbolism
REMBRANDT HERMANSZOON VAN RIJN, 1606-1669

Bonafoux, Pascal. A Weekend with Rembrandt. LC 91-40507. (Illus.). 64p. (gr. 1-6). 1992. 19.95 (*0-8478-1441-6*) Rizzoli Intl.
Muhlberger, Richard, text by. What Makes a Rembrandt a Rembrandt? (Illus.). 48p. (gr. 5 up). 1993. 9.95 (*0-670-85199-X*) Viking Child Bks.
Raboff, Ernest. Rembrandt. Rembrandt, illus. LC 87-45148. 32p. (gr. 1 up). 1987. pap. 7.95 (*0-06-446072-X*, Trophy) HarpC Child Bks.
Schwartz, Gary. Rembrandt. (Illus.). 92p. 1992. 19.95 (*0-8109-3760-3*) Abrams.
Sturgis, Alexander. Introducing Rembrandt. LC 93-11418. (gr. 4 up). 1994. 15.95 (*0-316-82022-9*) Little.
Venezia, Mike. Rembrandt. Venezia, Mike, illus. LC 87-33014. 32p. (ps-4). 1988. PLB 12.85 (*0-516-02272-5*); pap. 4.95 (*0-516-42272-3*) Childrens.

REMEDIAL READING
see Reading–Remedial Teaching

REMINGTON, FREDERIC, 1861-1909

Raboff, Ernest. Frederic Remington. Remington, Frederic, illus. LC 87-17698. 32p. (gr. 1 up). 1988. pap. 7.95 (*0-06-446079-7*, Trophy) HarpC Child Bks.

Van Steenwyk, Elizabeth. Frederic Remington. (Illus.). 64p. (gr. 4-6). 1994. PLB 13.51 (*0-531-20172-4*) Watts.

RENAISSANCE

see also Art, Renaissance; Civilization, Medieval; Middle Ages

Howarth, Sarah. Renaissance People. LC 92-4990. (Illus.). 48p. (gr. 4-6). 1992. PLB 14.40 (*1-56294-088-0*) Millbrook Pr.

—Renaissance Places. LC 92-7537. (Illus.). 48p. (gr. 4-6). 1992. PLB 14.40 (*1-56294-089-9*) Millbrook Pr.

Sabin, Francene. Renaissance. Frenck, Hal, illus. LC 84-2695. 32p. (gr. 3-6). 1985. PLB 9.49 (*0-8167-0246-2*); pap. text ed. 2.95 (*0-8167-0247-0*) Troll Assocs.

Ventura, Piero. Fourteen Ninety-Two: The Year of the New World. 96p. 1992. 19.95 (*0-399-22332-0*, Putnam) Putnam Pub Group.

Wood, Tim. The Renaissance. (Illus.). 48p. (gr. 3-7). 1993. 14.99 (*0-670-85149-3*) Viking Child Bks.

RENAISSANCE–FICTION

Caselli, Giovanni. The Everyday Life of a Cathedral Builder. Caselli, Giovanni, illus. LC 87-29787. 32p. (gr. 3-6). 1992. PLB 12.95 (*0-87226-115-8*) P Bedrick Bks.

Juster, Norton. Alberic the Wise. Baskin, Leonard, illus. LC 92-7807. 28p. (gr. 1 up). 1992. 16.95 (*0-88708-243-2*) Picture Bk Studio.

Verges, Gloria & Verges, Oriol. The Renaissance. Rius, Maria & Peris, Carme, illus. 32p. (gr. 2-4). 1988. pap. 6.95 (*0-8120-3396-5*); El Renacimiento. pap. 6.95 (*0-8120-3397-3*) Barron.

REPAIRING

see also Building–Repair and Reconstruction

REPORTERS AND REPORTING

see also Journalism

Fitz-Gerald, Christine M. I Can Be a Reporter. LC 86-9614. (Illus.). 32p. (gr. k-3). 1986. pap. 3.95 (*0-516-41899-8*) Childrens.

Fleming, Thomas. Behind the Headlines. (gr. 5 up). 1989. 14.95 (*0-8027-6890-3*); PLB 15.85 (*0-8027-6891-1*) Walker & Co.

Trainer, David. A Day in the Life of a TV News Reporter. Sanacore, Stephen, photos by. LC 78-68810. (Illus.). 32p. (gr. 4-8). 1980. PLB 11.79 (*0-89375-228-2*); pap. 2.95 (*0-89375-232-0*) Troll Assocs.

REPORTERS AND REPORTING–FICTION

Hiser, Constance. Scoop Snoops. Smith, Cat B., illus. LC 92-25922. 112p. (gr. 3-7). 1993. 13.95 (*0-8234-1011-0*) Holiday.

Pageler, Elaine. The Riddle Street Mystery Series, 5 bks. Kratoville, B L, ed. (Illus.). 48p. (gr. 1 up). 1994. pap. 15.00 Set (*0-87879-983-4*) Acad Therapy.

Set of five books: The Wrong Robber Mystery, The Market Stake-Out Mystery, The Haunted Apartment House Mystery, The Book Party Mystery, The Radio Station Mystery. Fiction written at a first grade reading level, yet appealing to older youngsters with reading difficulties & to those in literary programs is historically hard to come by. It takes a very special talent to depart from the hackneyed "Dick & Jane" approach yet come up with colorful characters, exciting plots & realistic dialogue all bound together skillfully written first grade level prose. The photographer Brad & the reporter Meg have been assigned the Riddle Street beat by their city editor. Of course, they stumble onto mysteries &, of course, they are on hand to solve them. Plots involving a crooked giveaway, haunted elevator, supermarket scam, bank robbery & book autograph party are all well paced & eminently readable.

Publisher Provided Annotation.

Schmidt, Annie M. Minnie. Salway, Lance, tr. from DUT. LC 93-35924. 1994. pap. 6.95 (*0-915943-95-6*) Milkweed Ed.

REPRODUCTION

see also Cells; Embryology; Pregnancy; Sex

Andry, Andrew C. & Schepp, Steven. How Babies Are Made. Hampton, Blake, illus. LC 99-944003. 88p. 1984. pap. 9.95 (*0-316-04227-7*) Little.

Avraham, Regina. The Reproductive System. (Illus.). 128p. (gr. 6-12). 1991. 18.95 (*0-7910-0025-7*) Chelsea Hse.

Back, Christine. Chicken & Egg. LC 86-10019. (Illus.). 25p. (gr. k-4). 1991. 5.95 (*0-382-09292-9*); PLB 7.95 (*0-382-09284-8*); pap. 3.95 (*0-382-09959-1*) Silver Burdett.

Baker, Sue. The Birds & the Bees. LC 91-39758. (gr. 3 up). 1991. 9.95 (*0-85953-400-6*) Childs Play.

Bryan, Jenny. Reproduction. LC 93-2038. (Illus.). 48p. (gr. 5 up). 1993. text ed. 13.95 RSBE (*0-87518-589-4*, Dillon) Macmillan Child Grp.

Cole, Babette. Mommy Laid an Egg. (ps-3). 1992. 13.95 (*0-8118-0350-3*) Chronicle Bks.

Mayes, S. Where Do Babies Come From? (Illus.). 24p. (gr. 1 up). 1992. PLB 11.96 (*0-88110-547-3*, Usborne); pap. 3.95 (*0-7460-0690-X*, Usborne) EDC.

Newman, Matt & Lemay, Nita K. Human Reproductive Systems. Green, James, et al, illus. (gr. 5-8). 1980. pap. text ed. 165.00 4 filmstrips, 4 cass., 24 skill sheets, Guide (*0-89290-101-2*, A794-SATC) Soc for Visual.

Nilsson, Lennart. How Was I Born? Reproduction & Birth for Children. LC 75-24725. (Illus.). 32p. (ps-3). 1975. pap. 14.95 (*0-385-28624-4*, Sey Lawr) Delacorte.

Pomeroy, Johanna P. Content Area Reading skills Reproduction & Heredity: Main Idea. (Illus.). (gr. 4). 1988. pap. text ed. 3.25 (*1-55737-087-7*) Ed Activities.

Selsam, Millicent E. Egg to Chick. rev. ed. Wolff, Barbara, illus. LC 74-85034. 64p. (ps-3). 1970. PLB 13.89 (*0-06-025290-1*) HarpC Child Bks.

Silverstein, Alvin & Silverstein, Virginia. Reproductive System. (Illus.). 96p. (gr. 5-8). 1994. bds. 16.95 (*0-8050-2838-2*) TFC Bks NY.

Stein, Sara B. Making Babies. LC 73-15267. (Illus.). 48p. (gr. 1 up). 1974. 10.95 (*0-8027-6171-2*) Walker & Co.

—Making Babies. LC 73-15267. (Illus.). 48p. (ps-8). 1984. pap. 7.95 (*0-8027-7221-8*) Walker & Co.

Thiry, Joan. Discovering the Whole You. Sititra, illus. 64p. (Orig.). (gr. 5-6). 1991. pap. text ed. 6.00 (*0-935046-05-4*); tchr's. edition 14.00 (*0-935046-06-2*) Chateau Thierry.

Twist, Clint. Reproduction to Birth: Projects with Biology. LC 91-6818. (Illus.). 32p. (gr. 5-8). 1991. PLB 12.40 (*0-531-17294-5*, Gloucester Pr) Watts.

Wood, A. J. Egg! A Dozen Eggs, What Will They Be? Unfold Each Page & You Will See! Stillwell, Stella, illus. LC 92-17930. 1993. 12.95 (*0-316-81616-7*) Little.

REPTILES

see also Crocodiles; Lizards; Snakes; Turtles

Armstrong, B. Reptiles. 32p. (gr. 1-6). 1988. 3.95 (*0-88160-164-0*, LW 269) Learning Wks.

Ballard, Lois. Reptiles. LC 81-38525. (Illus.). 48p. (gr. k-4). 1982. PLB 12.85 (*0-516-01644-X*); pap. 4.95 (*0-516-41644-8*) Childrens.

Bender, Lionel. Fish to Reptiles. Khan, Aziz, illus. LC 89-81607. 40p. (gr. 6-8). 1988. PLB 12.40 (*0-531-17093-4*, Gloucester Pr) Watts.

Berkowitz, Henry. Amphibians & Reptiles. Berkowitz, Henry, illus. 32p. (Orig.). (gr. 1-9). 1985. pap. 2.50 (*0-317-66182-5*) Banyan Bks.

Brennan, Frank. Reptiles. Livingstone, Malcolm, illus. LC 91-26684. 32p. (Orig.). (ps-2). 1992. pap. 5.95 (*0-689-71587-0*, Aladdin) Macmillan Child Grp.

Brenner, Barbara A. & Chardiet, Bernice. Hide & Seek Science: Where's That Reptile? Schwartz, Carol, illus. LC 92-20905. 1993. 10.95 (*0-590-45212-6*) Scholastic Inc.

Caitlin, Stephen. Discovering Reptiles & Amphibians. Johnson, Pamela, illus. LC 89-4972. 32p. (gr. 2-4). 1990. PLB 11.59 (*0-8167-1753-2*); pap. text ed. 2.95 (*0-8167-1754-0*) Troll Assocs.

Chermayeff, Ivan, et al. Scaly Facts. LC 94-2958. 1995. 10.95 (*0-15-200109-3*) HarBrace.

Conant, Roger, et al. Peterson First Guide to Reptiles & Amphibians. Conant, Roger, et al, illus. 128p. (gr. 5 up). 1992. pap. 4.80 (*0-395-62232-8*) HM.

Cutts, David. I Can Read About Reptiles. LC 72-96954. (Illus.). (gr. 2-4). 1973. pap. 2.50 (*0-89375-058-1*) Troll Assocs.

Hornblow, Leonora & Hornblow, Arthur. Reptiles Do the Strangest Things. Frith, Michael K., illus. LC 70-106500. (gr. 2-4). 1970. 6.95 (*0-394-80074-5*); lib. bdg. 8.99 (*0-394-90074-X*, 90074) Random Bks Yng Read.

Howell, Catherine H. Reptiles & Amphibians; Mammals, 2 vols. (gr. 1-3). 1993. Set 24.95 (*0-87044-891-9*); incl. Mammals 24.95 (*0-685-70128-X*) Natl Geog.

Illustrated Encyclopedia of Wildlife, Vol. 9: Reptiles & Amphibians. 304p. (gr. 7 up). 1990. lib. bdg. write for info. (*1-55905-045-4*) Grey Castle.

Johnston, Ginny & Cutchins, Judy. Scaly Babies: Reptiles Growing Up. LC 87-18599. (Illus.). 48p. (gr. 2-5). 1988. 13.95 (*0-688-07305-0*); PLB 13.88 (*0-688-07306-9*, Morrow Jr Bks) Morrow Jr Bks.

—Scaly Babies: Reptiles Growing Up. LC 87-18599. (Illus.). 48p. (gr. 2 up). 1990. pap. 4.95 (*0-688-09998-X*, Pub. by Beech Tree Bks) Morrow.

Kuchalla, Susan. What Is a Reptile? Harvey, Paul, illus. LC 81-11364. 32p. (gr. k-2). 1982. PLB 11.59 (*0-89375-672-5*); pap. 2.95 (*0-89375-673-3*) Troll Assocs.

Lindblom, Steven. Golden Book of Snakes & Other Reptiles. 1990. write for info. (*0-307-15852-7*, Pub. by Golden Bks) Western Pub.

Ling, Mary. Amazing Crocodiles & Other Reptiles. Young, Jerry, photos by. LC 90-19239. (Illus.). 32p. (Orig.). (gr. 1-5). 1991. PLB 9.99 (*0-679-90689-4*); pap. 7.99 (*0-679-80689-X*) Knopf Bks Yng Read.

Losito, Linda, et al. Reptiles & Amphibians. (Illus.). 96p. 1989. 17.95x (*0-8160-1965-7*) Facts on File.

McCarthy, Colin & Arnold, Nick. Reptile. Keates, Colin & Arnold, Nick, photos by. LC 90-4890. (Illus.). 64p. (gr. 5 up). 1991. 16.00 (*0-679-80783-7*); PLB 16.99 (*0-679-90783-1*) Knopf Bks Yng Read.

McConnell, Keith. The ReptAlphabet Encyclopedia. McConnell, Keith, illus. 48p. (Orig.). (gr. 4 up). 1984. pap. 5.95 (*0-88045-045-2*) Stemmer Hse.

Markert, Jenny. Reptiles. (gr. 1-8). 1992. PLB 15.95 (*0-89565-850-X*) Childs World.

Martin, Louise. Reptile Discovery Library, 6 bks, Reading Level 2. (Illus.). 144p. (gr. k-5). 1989. Set. PLB 71.60 (*0-86592-573-9*) Rourke Corp.

Matero, Robert. Eyes on Nature: Reptiles. (Illus.). 32p. 1992. pap. 4.95 (*1-56156-151-7*) Kidsbks.

Mattern, Joanne. Reptiles & Amphibians. Stone, Lynn M., illus. LC 92-20189. 24p. (gr. 4-7). 1992. pap. 1.95 (*0-8167-2954-9*, Pub. by Watermill Pr) Troll Assocs.

Nayer, Judy. Reptiles. Goldberg, Grace, illus. 10p. (ps-2). 1992. bds. 6.95 (*1-56293-220-9*) McClanahan Bk.

Parker, Nancy W. Frogs, Toads, Lizards & Salamanders. Wright, Joan R., illus. (gr. 1 up). 1990. 15.00 (*0-688-08680-2*); PLB 14.93 (*0-688-08681-0*) Greenwillow.

Parker, Steve. Revolting Reptiles. Savage, Ann, illus. LC 92-43725. 38p. (gr. 3-6). 1992. PLB 19.97 (*0-8114-0692-X*) Raintree Steck-V.

Peissel, Michel & Allen, Missy. Dangerous Reptilian Creatures. (Illus.). 112p. (gr. 5 up). 1993. PLB 19.95 (*0-7910-1789-3*, Am Art Analog) Chelsea Hse.

Phillips, Gina. First Facts about Snakes & Reptiles. Persico, F. S., illus. 24p. (Orig.). 1991. pap. 2.50 (*1-56156-037-5*) Kidsbks.

—First Facts about Snakes & Reptiles. Persico, F. S., illus. 24p. 1991. write for info. (*1-56156-060-X*) Kidsbks.

Pope, Joyce. Reptiles. (Illus.). 32p. (gr. 4-6). 1991. 13.95 (*0-237-60166-4*, Pub. by Evans Bros Ltd) Trafalgar.

Quinn, Kaye. Reptiles! Quinn, Kaye, illus. 40p. (Orig.). (gr. k-4). 1987. pap. 2.95 (*0-8431-1892-X*) Price Stern.

Reptile & Amphibian Study. (Illus.). 64p. (gr. 6-12). 1972. pap. 1.85 (*0-8395-3342-X*, 33288) BSA.

Reptiles. (gr. 4-6). pap. 2.95 (*0-8431-4273-1*, Wonder-Treas) Price Stern.

Reptiles. 20p. (gr. k up). 1990. laminated, wipe clean surface 3.95 (*0-88679-823-X*) Educ Insights.

Ricciuti, Edward. Reptiles. (Illus.). 64p. (gr. 4-8). 1993. PLB 16.95 (*1-56711-047-9*) Blackbirch.

—Reptiles. (Illus.). 64p. (gr. 3-7). 1993. 14.95 (*1-56711-063-0*) Blackbirch.

Richardson, Joy. Reptiles. LC 92-32912. (Illus.). 32p. (gr. 2-4). 1993. PLB 11.40 (*0-531-14254-X*) Watts.

Roberts, M. L. World's Weirdest Reptiles. LC 93-8493. (Illus.). 32p. (gr. 2-9). 1993. PLB 11.89 (*0-8167-3229-9*, Pub. by Watermill Pr); pap. 2.95 (*0-8167-3221-3*, Pub. by Watermill Pr) Troll Assocs.

Sabin, Louis. Reptiles & Amphibians. Zink-White, Nancy, illus. LC 84-8445. 32p. (gr. 3-6). 1985. PLB 9.49 (*0-8167-0294-2*); pap. text ed. 2.95 (*0-8167-0295-0*) Troll Assocs.

Scott, Mary. A Picture Book of Reptiles & Amphibians. Kinnelay, Janice, illus. LC 92-19054. 24p. (gr. 1-4). 1992. lib. bdg. 9.59 (*0-8167-2838-0*); pap. text ed. 2.50 (*0-8167-2839-9*) Troll Assocs.

Selsam, Millicent E. & Hunt, Joyce. A First Look at Snakes, Lizards & Other Reptiles. Springer, Harriet, illus. LC 74-26315. 32p. (gr. 1-4). 1975. PLB 12.85 (*0-8027-6211-5*) Walker & Co.

Snakes & Reptiles. (Illus.). 32p. (gr. 2-6). 1989. pap. 3.50 (*0-88625-240-7*) Durkin Hayes Pub.

Snedden, Robert. What Is a Reptile? Lascom, Adrian, illus. LC 94-14422. (gr. 1 up). 1995. write for info. (*0-87156-493-9*) Sierra.

Spellerberg, Ian & McKerchar, Marit. Reptile World. Quinn, David, illus. 32p. (gr. 4-7). 1985. PLB 13.96 (*0-88110-174-5*, Pub. by Usborne); pap. 5.95 (*0-86020-845-1*) EDC.

Spinelli, Eileen. Reptiles. (Illus.). 64p. (gr. k-4). 1992. PLB 13.75 (*1-878363-88-3*, HTS Bks) Forest Hse.

Spizzirri, Peter M. Reptiles Dot to Dot: Educational Activity-Coloring Book. Spizzirri, Linda, ed. (Illus.). 32p. (gr. k-3). 1992. pap. 1.00 (*0-86545-207-5*) Spizzirri.

Spizzirri Publishing Co. Staff. Reptiles: An Educational Coloring Book. Spizzirri, Linda, ed. Fuller, Glenn, et al, illus. 32p. (gr. 1-8). 1981. pap. 1.75 (*0-86545-031-5*) Spizzirri.

Steele, Philip. Reptiles. LC 90-42017. (Illus.). 32p. (gr. 5-6). 1991. text ed. 3.95 RSBE (*0-89686-582-7*, Crestwood Hse) Macmillan Child Grp.

—Reptiles & Amphibians. (gr. 4-7). 1991. lib. bdg. 4.95 (*0-671-72238-7*, J Messner) S&S Trade.

—Reptiles & Amphibians. (gr. 4-7). 1991. lib. bdg. 9.98 (*0-671-72237-9*, J Messner) S&S Trade.

REPTILES, FOSSIL

see also Dinosaurs

Eldridge, David. Sea Monsters, Ancient Reptiles That Ruled the Sea. Nodel, Norman, illus. LC 79-87964. 32p. (gr. 3-6). 1980. PLB 10.79 (*0-89375-240-1*); pap. 2.95 (*0-89375-244-4*) Troll Assocs.

Gabriele, Joseph. Prehistoric Reptiles of the Sea & Air: Text Editions. Hurst, Margaret, illus. 32p. (gr. 1-3). 1985. pap. 1.95 (*0-911211-58-6*, Pub. by Know & Show Bks) Penny Lane Pubns.
Massare, Judy A. Prehistoric Marine Reptiles: Sea Monsters During the Age of Dinosaurs. LC 91-17057. (Illus.). 64p. (gr. 5-8). 1991. PLB 14.90 (*0-531-11022-2*) Watts.
Steele, Philip. Extinct Reptiles: And Those in Danger of Extinction. Kline, Marjory, ed. (Illus.). 32p. (gr. 5-8). 1991. PLB 11.90 (*0-531-11030-3*) Watts.
Wexo, John B. Reptiles. 24p. (gr. 3 up). 1991. PLB 14.95 (*0-88682-392-7*) Creative Ed.

RESCUE WORK
see also First Aid
Barrett, Norman S. Picture World of Air Rescue. LC 90-31222. (Illus.). 32p. (gr. k-4). 1991. PLB 12.40 (*0-531-14089-X*) Watts.
—Picture World of Sea Rescue. LC 90-31019. (Illus.). 32p. (gr. k-4). 1991. PLB 12.40 (*0-531-14093-8*) Watts.
Marston, Hope I. To the Rescue. LC 90-2575. (Illus.). 48p. (gr. 2-5). 1991. 14.95 (*0-525-65059-8*, Cobblehill Bks) Dutton Child Bks.
Patent, Dorothy H. Hugger to the Rescue. Munoz, William, photos by. LC 93-32031. 1994. write for info. (*0-525-65161-6*, Cobblehill Bks) Dutton Child Bks.
Shea, George. Amazing Rescues. Peck, Marshall H., III, illus. LC 90-53221. 48p. (gr. 2-3). 1992. PLB 7.99 (*0-679-91107-3*); pap. 3.50 (*0-679-81107-9*) Random Bks Yng Read.
Stewart, Janet & Pelowich, Nadia, eds. Amazing Rescues. (Illus.). 48p. (gr. 4). 1987. PLB 14.65 (*0-88625-172-9*); pap. 5.95 (*0-88625-151-6*) Durkin Hayes Pub.

RESCUE WORK–FICTION
Cowan, James. Emergency Rescue! Nightmare at Norton's Mills. (gr. 4-7). 1993. pap. 2.95 (*0-590-46019-6*) Scholastic Inc.
—Emergency Rescue: Trouble at Moosehead Lake. (gr. 4-7). 1993. pap. 2.95 (*0-590-46018-8*) Scholastic Inc.
Dicks, Terrance. Sally Ann & the Mystery Picnic. Sims, Blanche, illus. LC 92-22074. (gr. 1-3). 1993. pap. 14.00 JRT (*0-671-79427-2*, S&S BFYR) S&S Trade.
Halak, Glenn. A Grandmother's Story. LC 91-18058. (Illus.). 48p. (ps). 1992. 14.00 (*0-671-74953-6*, Green Tiger) S&S Trade.
Hendrie, Alison. Kid Heroes. (gr. 4 up). 1993. pap. 3.50 (*0-440-84816-4*) Dell.
Mikaelsen, Ben. Rescue Josh McGuire. LC 91-71386. 272p. (gr. 5-9). 1993. pap. 4.50 (*1-56282-523-2*) Hyprn Ppbks.
Pepper Bird Staff. Pea Island Rescue. Rose, Ann C., illus. 48p. (Orig.). (gr. 4-7). 1993. pap. 4.95 (*1-56817-002-5*) Pepper Bird.
Proysen, Alf. Mrs. Pepperpot to the Rescue. (gr. k-6). 1987. pap. 16.25 (*0-440-45597-9*, YB) Dell.
Rescue Nine-One-One: Amazing. 1993. pap. 3.50 (*0-440-40909-8*) Dell.
Roddy, Lee. The Legend of Fire. 148p. (gr. 3-6). 1989. pap. 4.99 (*0-929608-17-8*) Focus Family.
Sharp, Margery. Rescuers. (gr. 4-7). 1994. 4.95 (*0-316-78355-2*) Little.
Spier, Peter. Father, May I Come? LC 92-31328. 1993. 13.95 (*0-385-30935-X*) Doubleday.

RESEARCH
see also Learning and Scholarship; Psychical Research; also subjects with the subdivision Research, e.g. Agriculture–Research; Medicine–Research
Blustein, Lotte & Geary, Rosemary J. Writing the Research Paper. 70p. (gr. 9 up). 1992. pap. text ed. 7.50 (*0-9605248-3-5*) Blustein-Geary.
Direct, R. F. Doing Basic Research for Pay. 130p. (gr. 10). 1988. pap. text ed. 39.95x (*0-945661-01-0*) PASE Pubns.
Donovan, Melissa. Research Challanges. Schneider, Al, illus. 168p. (gr. 4-8). 1985. wkbk. 13.95 (*0-86653-271-4*, GA 660) Good Apple.
McCutcheon, Randall. Can You Find It? Twenty-Five Library Scavenger Hunts to Sharpen Your Research Skills. rev. ed. LC 91-30105. (Illus.). 208p. (gr. 9 up). pap. 10.95 (*0-915793-38-5*) Free Spirit Pub.
Martin, Susan & Green, Harriet. Research Workout. Melton, Gerald, illus. 144p. (gr. 4-9). 1984. wkbk. 12.95 (*0-86653-194-7*, GA 551) Good Apple.
Petreshene, Susan S. Research Pleasers. Sussman, Ellen, ed. Rundell, Wendi S., illus. (Orig.). (gr. 3-6). 1982. pap. text ed. 5.95 (*0-933606-19-2*, MS-618) E Sussman Educ.
Schrecengost, Maity. Research to Write. LC 94-2639. 56p. 1994. pap. 9.50 (*0-917846-37-0*, 33897, Alleyside) Highsmith Pr.
Schwartz, Linda. Search & Research. 48p. (gr. 4-6). 1984. 5.95 (*0-88160-116-0*, LW 248) Learning Wks.
Suid, Murray. For the Love of Research. (Illus.). 64p. (gr. 4-6). 1986. pap. 6.95 (*0-912107-50-2*) Monday Morning Bks.
Weitzman, David. My Backyard History Book. Robertson, James, illus. 128p. (gr. 4 up). 1975. 15.95 (*0-316-92901-8*); pap. 10.95 (*0-316-92902-6*) Little.

RESIDENCES
see Architecture, Domestic; Houses

RESOURCES
see Marine Resources

RESPIRATION
Adler, David A. You Breathe In, You Breathe Out: All about Your Lungs. Roxas, Reni, ed. Paterson, Diane, illus. 32p. (gr. 1-4). 1991. PLB 12.90 (*0-531-10700-0*) Watts.
Bailey, Donna. All about Your Lungs. LC 90-41009. (Illus.). 48p. (gr. 2-6). 1990. PLB 20.70 (*0-8114-2782-X*) Raintree Steck-V.
Bryan, Jenny. Breathing: The Respiratory System. LC 92-36353. (Illus.). 48p. (gr. 5 up). 1993. text ed. 13.95 RSBE (*0-87518-563-0*, Dillon) Macmillan Child Grp.
Ganeri, Anita. Breathing. (Illus.). 32p. (gr. 2-4). 1994. PLB 18.99 (*0-8114-5520-3*) Raintree Steck-V.
Kerby, Mona. Asthma. LC 89-8905. (Illus.). 128p. (gr. 7-12). 1989. PLB 12.90 (*0-531-10697-7*) Watts.
Kittredge, Mary. The Respiratory System. Koop, C. Everett, intro. by. (Illus.). 112p. (gr. 6-12). 1989. 18.95 (*0-7910-0026-5*) Chelsea Hse.
Lungs & Breathing. 48p. (gr. 5-8). 1988. PLB 10.95 (*0-382-09701-7*) Silver Burdett Pr.
Ostrow, William & Ostrow, Vivian. All about Asthma. Levine, Abby, ed. Sims, Blanche, illus. LC 89-5254. 32p. (gr. 2-6). 1989. PLB 11.95 (*0-8075-0276-6*); pap. 4.95 (*0-8075-0275-8*) A Whitman.
Parker, Steve. The Lungs & Breathing. rev. ed. Mayron-Parker, Alan, contrib. by. LC 88-51609. (Illus.). 48p. (gr. 5-6). 1989. PLB 12.90 (*0-531-10710-8*) Watts.
—The Lungs & Breathing. rev. ed. (Illus.). 48p. (gr. 5 up). 1991. pap. 6.95 (*0-531-24605-1*) Watts.
Savage, Eileen. Winning over Asthma. (Illus.). 40p. (Orig.). (ps-3). pap. write for info. (*0-9622868-0-X*) Dolan Pr.
Silverstein, Alvin & Silverstein, Virginia. Respiratory System. (Illus.). 96p. (gr. 5-8). 1994. bds. 16.95 (*0-8050-2831-5*) TFC Bks NY.
Ward, Brian. Breathing: And Your Health. LC 90-31226. (Illus.). 32p. (gr. 5-8). 1991. PLB 12.40 (*0-531-14094-6*) Watts.

RESTAURANTS, BARS, ETC.
Franck, Irene M. & Brownstone, David M. Restaurateurs & Innkeepers. (Illus.). 176p. 1988. 17.95x (*0-8160-1451-5*) Facts on File.
Gibbons, Gail. Marge's Diner. Gibbons, Gail, illus. LC 88-26789. 32p. (gr. 1-4). 1989. (Crowell Jr Bks); PLB 12.89 (*0-690-04606-5*, Crowell Jr Bks) HarpC Child Bks.
Lee, Mary P. & Lee, Richard. Careers in the Restaurant Industry. rev. ed. Rosen, R., ed. (Illus.). 160p. (gr. 7-12). 1990. 14.95 (*0-8239-1142-X*) Rosen Group.
Waters, Alice L. Fanny at Chez Panisse: A Child's Restaurant Adventure with Forty-Two Recipes. LC 92-52586. (Illus.). 1992. 23.00 (*0-06-016896-X*, HarpT) HarpC.

RESTAURANTS, BARS, ETC.–FICTION
Calmenson, Stephanie. Dinner at the Panda Palace. Westcott, Nadine B., illus. LC 90-33720. 32p. (ps-3). 1991. 15.00 (*0-06-021010-9*); PLB 14.89 (*0-06-021011-7*) HarpC Child Bks.
Cummings, Priscilla. Sid & Sal's Famous Channel Marker Diner. Cohen, A. R., illus. LC 91-65255. 30p. (gr. k-5). 1992. 8.95 (*0-87033-423-9*) Tidewater.
Davis, Jenny. Checking on the Moon. LC 91-8284. 224p. (gr. 6 up). 1991. 14.95 (*0-531-05960-X*); RLB 14.99 (*0-531-08560-0*) Orchard Bks Watts.
Egan, Tim. Friday Night at Hodges' Cafe. LC 93-11290. 1994. 14.95 (*0-395-68076-X*) HM.
The Ghost in Dobbs Diner. 42p. (ps-3). 1992. PLB 13.27 (*0-8368-0884-3*); PLB 13.26 s.p. (*0-685-61518-9*) Gareth Stevens Inc.
Greenberg, Melanie H. My Father's Luncheonette. Greenberg, Melanie H., illus. LC 90-45586. 32p. (ps-2). 1991. 12.95 (*0-525-44725-3*, DCB) Dutton Child Bks.
Hemingway, Ernest. A Clean, Well-Lighted Place. (gr. 4-9). 1989. 13.95 (*0-88682-345-5*, 97212-098) Creative Ed.
Kerr, M. E. Linger. LC 92-30988. 224p. (gr. 7 up). 1993. 15.00 (*0-06-022879-2*); PLB 14.89 (*0-06-022882-2*) HarpC Child Bks.
Korman, Gordon. Losing Joe's Place. 240p. 1991. pap. 3.25 (*0-590-42769-5*, Point) Scholastic Inc.
Kovalski, Maryann. Pizza for Breakfast. Kovalski, Maryann, illus. LC 90-46078. 32p. (gr. k up). 1991. Repr. of 1990 ed. 13.95 (*0-688-10409-6*); PLB 13.88 (*0-688-10410-X*, Morrow Jr Bks) Morrow Jr Bks.
Levy, Elizabeth. Something Queer in the Cafeteria. Gerstein, Mordicai, illus. LC 93-31343. 48p. (gr. 2-5). 1994. 13.95 (*0-7868-0001-1*); pap. 4.95 (*0-7868-1000-9*) Hyprn Child.
Moss, Marissa. Mel's Diner. Moss, Marissa, illus. LC 93-38683. 32p. (gr. k-3). 1994. PLB 13.95 (*0-8167-3460-7*); pap. text ed. 3.95 (*0-8167-3461-5*) BrdgeWater.
Peters, Sharon. Contento Juan. Harvey, Paul, illus. (SPA.). 32p. (gr. k-2). 1981. PLB 7.89 (*0-89375-552-4*); pap. 1.95 (*0-685-04945-0*) Troll Assocs.
Pinkwater, Daniel. The Phantom of the Lunch Wagon. LC 92-3051. (Illus.). 32p. (gr. k up). 1992. RSBE 13.95 (*0-02-774641-0*, Macmillan Child Bk) Macmillan Child Grp.
—Spaceburger: A Kevin Spoon & Mason Mintz Story. Pinkwater, Daniel, illus. LC 93-6658. 32p. (gr. k-3). 1993. RSBE 13.95 (*0-02-774643-7*, Macmillan Child Bk) Macmillan Child Grp.
Rylant, Cynthia. An Angel for Solomon Singer. Catalanotto, Peter, illus. LC 91-15957. 32p. 1992. 14.95 (*0-531-05978-2*); lib. bdg. 14.99 (*0-531-08578-3*) Orchard Bks Watts.
Smith, D. The Waitress. 144p. 1992. pap. 2.95 (*0-590-45063-8*, Point) Scholastic Inc.
Tchudi, Stephen N. The Burg-O-Rama Man. LC 82-14075. 192p. (gr. 7 up). 1983. pap. 13.95 (*0-385-29239-2*) Delacorte.
Warner, Gertrude C., created by. The Pizza Mystery. Tang, Charles, illus. LC 92-32263. 128p. (gr. 2-7). 1993. PLB 10.95 (*0-8075-6534-2*); pap. 3.50 (*0-8075-6535-0*) A Whitman.

RETAIL TRADE
see also Advertising; Salesmen and Salesmanship; Supermarkets
Bentley, Judith. Miners, Merchants, & Maids. (Illus.). 96p. (gr. 5-8). 1995. bds. 16.95 (*0-8050-2998-2*) TFC Bks NY.
Greenberg, Keith. Sam Walton. LC 92-45123. 1993. 15.93 (*0-86592-047-8*); 11.95s.p. (*0-685-66419-8*) Rourke Enter.

REVERE, PAUL, 1735-1818
Brandt, Keith. Paul Revere: Son of Liberty. LC 81-23147. (Illus.). 48p. (gr. 4-6). 1982. PLB 10.79 (*0-89375-766-7*); pap. text ed. 3.50 (*0-89375-767-5*) Troll Assocs.
Forbes, Esther. America's Paul Revere. Ward, Lynd, illus. 48p. (gr. 3-5). 1990. pap. 5.70 (*0-395-24907-4*) HM.
—America's Paul Revere. LC 90-48984. (Illus.). 88p. (gr. 6-10). 1991. PLB 13.95 (*1-55905-093-4*) Marshall Cavendish.
—Paul Revere & the World He Lived In. (Illus.). 528p. (gr. 4-8). 1972. pap. 10.70 (*0-395-08370-2*) HM.
Fritz, Jean. And Then What Happened, Paul Revere? Tomes, Margot, illus. 48p. (gr. 2-6). 1973. 13.95 (*0-698-20274-0*, Coward); pap. 6.95 (*0-698-20541-3*) Putnam Pub Group.
Gleiter, Jan & Thompson, Kathleen. Paul Revere. Balistreri, Francis, illus. 32p. (gr. 2-5). 1986. PLB 19.97 (*0-8172-2644-3*) Raintree Steck-V.
Grant, Matthew G. Paul Revere. LC 73-18076. 1988. PLB 14.95 (*0-88682-186-X*) Creative Ed.
Graves, Charles P. Paul Revere: Rider for Liberty. (Illus.). 80p. (gr. 2-6). 1991. Repr. of 1964 ed. lib. bdg. 12.95 (*0-7910-1419-3*) Chelsea Hse.
Paul Revere. (Illus.). (gr. 2-5). 1989. 29.28 (*0-8172-2957-4*) Raintree Steck-V.
Stein, R. Conrad. The Story of Lexington & Concord. LC 82-23518. (Illus.). 32p. (gr. 3-6). 1983. pap. 3.95 (*0-516-44661-4*) Childrens.
Stevenson, Augusta. Paul Revere: Boston Patriot. Nicholas, Frank, illus. LC 86-10743. 192p. (gr. 2-6). 1986. pap. 3.95 (*0-02-042090-0*, Aladdin) Macmillan Child Grp.
The Story of Paul Revere. (gr. k-6). 1990. pap. 2.95 (*0-440-40361-8*, YB) Dell.
Weinberg, Lawrence. Paul Revere. De John, Marie, illus. 48p. (gr. 2-4). 1988. pap. 2.50 (*0-681-40688-7*) Longmeadow Pr.

REVERE, PAUL, 1735-1818–FICTION
Lawson, Robert. Mr. Revere & I. (gr. 3-6). 1973. pap. 2.95 (*0-440-45897-8*, YB) Dell.
—Mr. Revere & I. Lawson, Robert, illus. (gr. 7-10). 1953. 16.95 (*0-316-51739-9*) Little.
—Mr. Revere & I. Lawson, Robert, illus. 152p. (gr. 3-6). 1988. pap. 5.95 (*0-316-51729-1*) Little.

REVIVAL OF LETTERS
see Renaissance

REVOLUTION, AMERICAN
see U. S.–History–Revolution

REVOLUTION, FRENCH
see France–History–Revolution, 1789-1799

REVOLUTIONS
see also France–History–Revolution, 1789-1799; Hungary–History–Revolution, 1956; Social Conflict; U. S. –History–Revolution
Millard. The Age of Revolutions. (Illus.). (gr. 4-9). 1979. (Usborne-Hayes); PLB 13.96 (*0-88110-112-5*); pap. 6.95 (*0-86020-263-1*) EDC.
Pollard, Michael. Revolutionary Power. Stefoff, Rebecca, ed. LC 91-36504. (Illus.). 48p. (gr. 5-8). 1992. PLB 19.93 (*1-56074-039-6*) Garrett Ed Corp.

RHETORIC
see also Criticism; Debates and Debating; Letter Writing; Punctuation; Satire
Alward, Edgar C. Research Paper, Step-by-Step. rev. ed. (gr. 9 up). 1991. pap. 22.00 (*0-9620092-7-X*) Pine Isl Pr.
Ehrenhaft, George. Write Your Way into College. 2nd, rev. ed. LC 93-13380. 120p. (gr. 9 up). 1993. pap. 8.95 (*0-8120-1415-4*) Barron.
Fearn, Leif. First I Think: Then I Write My Think. 160p. (gr. 3-12). 1981. 6.95 (*0-940444-13-5*) Kabyn.
Fearn, Leif & Goldman, Elizabeth. Writing Kabyn: Assessment & Editing. 96p. (gr. 2-9). 1981. classroom kit 27.50 (*0-940444-11-9*) Kabyn.
—Writing Kabyn: Products. 148p. (gr. 2-9). 1982. classroom kit 48.00 (*0-940444-09-7*) Kabyn.
—Writing Kabyn: Sentences-Paragraphs. 125p. (gr. 2-9). 1982. classroom kit 69.00 (*0-940444-08-9*) Kabyn.
—Writing Kabyn: Technology. 76p. (gr. 2-9). 1981. classroom Kit 49.00 (*0-940444-10-0*) Kabyn.
Hunter, Mollie. Talent Is Not Enough: Mollie Hunter on Writing for Children. LC 76-3841. 144p. 1990. pap. 9.95 (*0-06-446105-X*, Trophy) HarpC Child Bks.
Kadesch, M., et al. Insights into Academic Writing: Strategies for Advanced Students. 176p. (gr. 9 up). 1991. pap. text ed. 19.95 (*0-8013-0364-8*, 78139) Longman.
Kane, Andrea L. & Martorana, Barbara. Writing Competency Practice. (gr. 7-12). 1980. wkbk. 5.75 (*0-89525-134-5*) Ed Activities.

Littlefield, Kathy M. & Littlefield, Robert S. What's Your Point? Stark, Steve, illus. 32p. (Orig.). (gr. 3-6). 1990. pap. text ed. 8.95 (*1-879340-05-4*, K0106) Kidspeak.

McCabe, Ann C. & Fairbanks, Eugene B. English Writing: Fifteen-Day Competency Review Text. Gamsey, Wayne H., ed. Fairbanks, Eugene B., illus. 160p. (Orig.). (gr. 7-12). 1992. pap. text ed. 4.95 (*0-935487-56-5*) N & N Pub Co.

Mason, Michael. How to Write a Winning College-Application Essay. 250p. (Orig.). (gr. 10 up). 1991. pap. 8.95 (*1-55958-083-6*) Prima Pub.

Sebranek, et al. Write Source Two Thousand: A Guide to Writing, Thinking, & Learning. Krenzke, Chris, illus. 400p. (Orig.). (gr. 4-9). 1990. text ed. 11.95 (*0-939045-34-6*); pap. text ed. 9.95 (*0-939045-33-8*); tchr's. ed., 116p. 9.95 (*0-939045-52-4*) Write Source.

—Writers Inc: A Guide to Writing, Thinking, & Learning. 2nd ed. Krenzke, Chris, illus. 360p. (gr. 9 up). 1990. text ed. 10.95 (*0-939045-49-4*); pap. text ed. 8.95 (*0-939045-48-6*); Inc Sights, 94p. tchr's. ed. 7.95 (*0-939045-32-X*) Write Source.

Sebranek, Patrick. Revising & Editing Two: A Program of Revising & Editing Activities & Strategies to Accompany Writers Inc. Krenzke, Christian R., illus. 92p. (Orig.). (gr. 11-12). 1991. wkbk. 9.95 (*0-939045-51-6*); tchr's. ed. 7.95 (*0-939045-56-7*); reproducible set 39.95 (*0-939045-59-1*) Write Source.

Sebranek, patrick, et al. Revising & Editing One: A Program of Revising & Editing & Strategies to Accompany Writers Inc. (Illus.). 92p. (Orig.). (gr. 9-10). 1991. pap. 6.95 wkbk. (*0-939045-50-8*); tchr's. ed. 7.95 (*0-939045-55-9*); reproducible set 39.95 (*0-939045-58-3*) Write Source.

Stevens, Jared & Michaels, Judy. How to Write for Everyday Living. (Illus.). (gr. 7 up). 1981. wkbk. 4.95 (*0-89525-132-9*) Ed Activities.

Weisberg, Valerie H. Students' Discourse: Comprehensive Examples & Explanations of All Expository Modes & Argument, Precis, Narrative, Examination Writing & MLA Reccomendations for Research Paper Documentation Writing Exposition. 2nd ed. 126p. 1990. pap. 9.95 (*0-685-49571-X*) V H Pub.

RHINOCEROSES–FICTION

Alexander, Scott. Rhinoceros Success. 25th ed. Smallwood, Laurie, illus. LC 80-51648. 123p. (Orig.). (gr. 1 up). 1985. pap. 5.95 (*0-937382-00-0*) Rhinos Pr.

Beutler, Eve R. & Beutler, Bryce D. Whinosaurus Rex. (Illus.). 36p. (ps-3). 1993. pap. 6.95 (*0-9637262-0-X*) Evening Pearl.

Damjan, Mischa. The Big Squirrel & the Little Rhinoceros. De Beer, Hans, illus. Hort, Lenny, tr. from GER. LC 91-17865. (Illus.). 32p. (gr. k-3). 1991. 14.95 (*1-55858-117-0*) North-South Bks NYC.

De Brunhoff, Laurent. Babar's Battle. De Brunhoff, Laurent, illus. LC 91-53169. 36p. (ps-3). 1992. 10.00 (*0-679-81068-4*); PLB 10.99 (*0-679-91068-9*) Random Bks Yng Read.

—Isabelle's New Friend: A Babar Book. De Brunhoff, Laurent, illus. LC 89-3727. 32p. (ps-1). 1990. PLB 5.99 (*0-394-92880-6*); pap. 2.25 (*0-394-82880-1*) Random Bks Yng Read.

Green, Carl R. & Sanford, William R. The African Rhinos. (Illus.). 48p. (gr. 5). 1987. text ed. 12.95 RSBE (*0-89686-327-1*, Crestwood Hse) Macmillan Child Grp.

Noble, Kate. Oh Look, It's a Nosserus. Bass, Rachel, illus. 32p. (ps-4). 1993. 14.95 (*0-9631798-2-9*) Silver Seahorse. Robbi is a young rhino who lives in a game park in Africa. He can't wait to have a horn as beautiful as his Mama's; he gets teased for being clumsy, & he sets out to save his friends from terrible danger. Children who loved & laughed with Kimbi in BUBBLE GUM will be delighted to meet Robbi & his zebra & giraffe friends. Once again, Rachel Bass creates the beauty of Africa & the charm of its animals in her vivid paintings. BUBBLE GUM. Kate Noble (Africa Stories Ser.) (Illus. by Rachel Bass). 32p. 1992. pre K-4th gr. 14.95 (0-9631798-0-2) Kimbi is a young baboon who lives in a park in Africa. He wishes tourists didn't pay so much attention to the lions. He loves sweets, & he stumbles into an amazing adventure. The illustrations for this delightful story capture the magic of the African landscape. There's also a learning plus: the details of animal behavior are correct, & the pictures show both black & white children & adults. Silver Seahorse Press, 2568 N. Clark St., Suite 320, Chicago, IL 60614; 312-871-1772; FAX: 312-327-8978. Distributed by Lifetime Books, Inc., 2131 Hollywood Blvd., Hollywood, FL 33020-6750; 1-800-771-3355; FAX: 1-800-931-7411. *Publisher Provided Annotation.*

Palmer, Todd S. Rhino & Mouse. Lanfredi, Judy, illus. LC 93-33299. 40p. (ps-3). 1994. 12.99 (*0-8037-1322-3*); PLB 12.89 (*0-8037-1323-1*) Dial Bks Young.

Rogers, Alan. Red Rhino. Rogers, Alan, illus. LC 90-9830. 16p. (ps-1). 1990. PLB 13.27 (*0-8368-0403-1*) Gareth Stevens Inc.

Samton, Sheila W. Tilly & the Rhinoceros. (Illus.). 32p. (ps-3). 1993. PLB 14.95 (*0-399-21973-0*, Philomel Bks) Putnam Pub Group.

Silverstein, Shel. Who Wants a Cheap Rhinoceros? rev. ed. LC 82-23945. (Illus.). 56p. (ps-3). 1983. RSBE 12.95 (*0-02-782690-2*, Macmillan Child Bk) Macmillan Child Grp.

Sis, Peter. Rainbow Rhino. reissued ed. Sis, Peter, illus. LC 87-2679. 40p. (ps-2). 1993. pap. 4.99 (*0-679-85005-8*) Knopf Bks Yng Read.

Storms, John. Ralph the Rhino. Ooka, Dianne & Squellati, Liz, eds. Storms, Bob, illus. 24p. (Orig.). (gr. k-3). 1994. pap. 4.95 (*0-89346-793-6*) Heian Intl.

RHODE ISLAND

Carole Marsh Rhode Island Books, 44 bks. 1994. PLB 1027.80 set (*0-7933-1314-7*); pap. 587.80 set (*0-7933-5200-2*) Gallopade Pub Group.

Carpenter, Allan. Rhode Island. LC 78-16446. (Illus.). 96p. (gr. 4 up). 1979. PLB 16.95 (*0-516-04139-8*) Childrens.

Fradin, Dennis. Rhode Island: In Words & Pictures. Wahl, Len, illus. LC 80-22497. 48p. (gr. 2-5). 1981. PLB 12.95 (*0-516-03939-3*) Childrens.

Fradin, Dennis B. The Rhode Island Colony. LC 89-744. (Illus.). 160p. (gr. 4 up). 1989. PLB 17.95 (*0-516-00391-7*) Childrens.

Gavan, Terrence. Complete Guide to Newport. (Illus.). 64p. (Orig.). 1988. pap. 5.95 (*0-929249-00-3*) Pineapple Pubns.

Grosvenor, Richard. An Airplane Ride over Newport. 8p. (gr. k-2). 1993. pap. write for info. (*1-882563-02-6*) Lamont Bks.

Heinrichs, Ann. Rhode Island. LC 89-25284. (Illus.). 144p. (gr. 4 up). 1990. PLB 20.55 (*0-516-00485-9*) Childrens.

—Rhode Island. 195p. 1993. text ed. 15.40 (*1-56956-165-6*) W A T Braille.

MacDonald, Sandra. Ben of Colonial Newport. 8p. (gr. k-2). 1993. pap. write for info. (*1-882563-08-5*) Lamont Bks.

Marsh, Carole. Avast, Ye Slobs! Rhode Island Pirate Trivia. (Illus.). 1994. PLB 24.95 (*0-7933-1004-0*); pap. 14.95 (*0-7933-1003-2*); computer disk 29.95 (*0-7933-1005-9*) Gallopade Pub Group.

—The Beast of the Rhode Island Bed & Breakfast. (Illus.). 1994. PLB 24.95 (*0-7933-1965-X*); pap. 14.95 (*0-7933-1966-8*); computer disk 29.95 (*0-7933-1967-6*) Gallopade Pub Group.

—Bow Wow! Rhode Island Dogs in History, Mystery, Legend, Lore, Humor & More! (Illus.). (gr. 3-12). 1994. PLB 24.95 (*0-7933-3584-1*); pap. 14.95 (*0-7933-3585-X*); computer disk 29.95 (*0-7933-3586-8*) Gallopade Pub Group.

—Christopher Columbus Comes to Rhode Island! Includes Reproducible Activities for Kids! (Illus.). (gr. 3-12). 1994. PLB 24.95 (*0-7933-3737-2*); pap. 14.95 (*0-7933-3738-0*); computer disk 29.95 (*0-7933-3739-9*) Gallopade Pub Group.

—The Hard-to-Believe-But-True! Book of Rhode Island History, Mystery, Trivia, Legend, Lore, Humor & More. (Illus.). 1994. PLB 24.95 (*0-7933-1001-6*); pap. 14.95 (*0-7933-1000-8*); computer disk 29.95 (*0-7933-1002-4*) Gallopade Pub Group.

—If My Rhode Island Mama Ran the World! (Illus.). 1994. lib. bdg. 24.95 (*0-7933-1974-9*); pap. 14.95 (*0-7933-1975-7*); computer disk 29.95 (*0-7933-1976-5*) Gallopade Pub Group.

—Jurassic Ark! Rhode Island Dinosaurs & Other Prehistoric Creatures. (gr. k-12). 1994. PLB 24.95 (*0-7933-7545-2*); pap. 14.95 (*0-7933-7546-0*); computer disk 29.95 (*0-7933-7547-9*) Gallopade Pub Group.

—Let's Quilt Our Rhode Island County. 1994. lib. bdg. 24.95 (*0-7933-7230-5*); pap. text ed. 14.95 (*0-7933-7231-3*); disk 29.95 (*0-7933-7232-1*) Gallopade Pub Group.

—Let's Quilt Our Rhode Island Town. 1994. lib. bdg. 24.95 (*0-7933-7080-9*); pap. text ed. 14.95 (*0-7933-7081-7*); disk 29.95 (*0-7933-7082-5*) Gallopade Pub Group.

—Let's Quilt Rhode Island & Stuff it Topographically! (Illus.). 1994. PLB 24.95 (*0-7933-1957-9*); pap. 14.95 (*1-55609-065-X*); computer disk 29.95 (*0-7933-1958-7*) Gallopade Pub Group.

—Meow! Rhode Island Cats in History, Mystery, Legend, Lore, Humor & More! (Illus.). (gr. 3-12). 1994. PLB 24.95 (*0-7933-3431-4*); pap. 14.95 (*0-7933-3432-2*); computer disk 29.95 (*0-7933-3433-0*) Gallopade Pub Group.

—My First Book about Rhode Island. (gr. k-4). 1994. PLB 24.95 (*0-7933-5686-5*); pap. 14.95 (*0-7933-5687-3*); computer disk 29.95 (*0-7933-5688-1*) Gallopade Pub Group.

—Patch, the Pirate Dog: A Rhode Island Pet Story. (ps-4). 1994. PLB 24.95 (*0-7933-5533-8*); pap. 14.95 (*0-7933-5534-6*); computer disk 29.95 (*0-7933-5535-4*) Gallopade Pub Group.

—Rhode Island & Other State Greats (Biographies) (Illus.). 1994. PLB 24.95 (*0-7933-1977-3*); pap. 14.95 (*0-7933-1978-1*); computer disk 29.95 (*0-7933-1979-X*) Gallopade Pub Group.

—Rhode Island Bandits, Bushwackers, Outlaws, Crooks, Devils, Ghosts, Desperadoes & Other Assorted & Sundry Characters! (Illus.). 1994. PLB 24.95 (*0-7933-0986-7*); pap. 14.95 (*0-7933-0985-9*); computer disk 29.95 (*0-7933-0987-5*) Gallopade Pub Group.

—Rhode Island Classic Christmas Trivia: Stories, Recipes, Activities, Legends, Lore & More! (Illus.). 1994. PLB 24.95 (*0-7933-0989-1*); pap. 14.95 (*0-7933-0988-3*); computer disk 29.95 (*0-7933-0990-5*) Gallopade Pub Group.

—Rhode Island Coastales. (Illus.). 1994. PLB 24.95 (*0-7933-1971-4*); pap. 14.95 (*0-7933-1972-2*); computer disk 29.95 (*0-7933-1973-0*) Gallopade Pub Group.

—Rhode Island Coastales! 1994. lib. bdg. 24.95 (*0-7933-7304-2*) Gallopade Pub Group.

—Rhode Island Dingbats! Bk. 1: A Fun Book of Games, Stories, Activities & More about Our State That's All in Code! for You to Decipher. (Illus.). (gr. 3-12). 1994. PLB 24.95 (*0-7933-3890-5*); pap. 14.95 (*0-7933-3891-3*); computer disk 29.95 (*0-7933-3892-1*) Gallopade Pub Group.

—Rhode Island Festival Fun for Kids! (Illus.). (gr. 3-12). 1994. lib. bdg. 24.95 (*0-7933-4043-8*); pap. 14.95 (*0-7933-4044-6*); disk 29.95 (*0-7933-4045-4*) Gallopade Pub Group.

—The Rhode Island Hot Air Balloon Mystery. (Illus.). (gr. 2-9). 1994. 24.95 (*0-7933-2669-9*); pap. 14.95 (*0-7933-2670-2*); computer disk 29.95 (*0-7933-2671-0*) Gallopade Pub Group.

—Rhode Island Jeopardy! Answers & Questions about Our State! (Illus.). (gr. 3-12). 1994. PLB 24.95 (*0-7933-4196-5*); pap. 14.95 (*0-7933-4197-3*); computer disk 29.95 (*0-7933-4198-1*) Gallopade Pub Group.

—Rhode Island "Jography" A Fun Run Thru Our State! (Illus.). 1994. PLB 24.95 (*0-7933-1954-4*); pap. 14.95 (*0-7933-1955-2*); computer disk 29.95 (*0-7933-1956-0*) Gallopade Pub Group.

—Rhode Island Kid's Cookbook: Recipes, How-to, History Lore & More! (Illus.). 1994. PLB 24.95 (*0-7933-0998-0*); pap. 14.95 (*0-7933-0997-2*); computer disk 29.95 (*0-7933-0999-9*) Gallopade Pub Group.

—Rhode Island Quiz Bowl Crash Course! (Illus.). 1994. PLB 24.95 (*0-7933-1968-4*); pap. 14.95 (*0-7933-1969-2*); computer disk 29.95 (*0-7933-1970-6*) Gallopade Pub Group.

—Rhode Island Rollercoasters! (Illus.). (gr. 3-12). 1994. PLB 24.95 (*0-7933-5341-6*); pap. 14.95 (*0-7933-5342-4*); computer disk 29.95 (*0-7933-5343-2*) Gallopade Pub Group.

—Rhode Island School Trivia: An Amazing & Fascinating Look at Our State's Teachers, Schools & Students! (Illus.). 1994. PLB 24.95 (*0-7933-0995-6*); pap. 14.95 (*0-7933-0994-8*); computer disk 29.95 (*0-7933-0996-4*) Gallopade Pub Group.

—Rhode Island Silly Basketball Sportsmysteries, Vol. 1. (Illus.). 1994. PLB 24.95 (*0-7933-0992-1*); pap. 14.95 (*0-7933-0991-3*); computer disk 29.95 (*0-685-45968-3*) Gallopade Pub Group.

—Rhode Island Silly Basketball Sportsmysteries, Vol. 2. (Illus.). 1994. PLB 24.95 (*0-7933-1980-3*); pap. 14.95 (*0-7933-1981-1*); computer disk 29.95 (*0-7933-1982-X*) Gallopade Pub Group.

—Rhode Island Silly Football Sportsmysteries, Vol. 1. (Illus.). 1994. PLB 24.95 (*0-7933-1959-5*); pap. 14.95 (*0-7933-1960-9*); computer disk 29.95 (*0-7933-1961-7*) Gallopade Pub Group.

—Rhode Island Silly Football Sportsmysteries, Vol. 2. (Illus.). 1994. PLB 24.95 (*0-7933-1962-5*); pap. 14.95 (*0-7933-1963-3*); computer disk 29.95 (*0-7933-1964-1*) Gallopade Pub Group.

—Rhode Island Silly Trivia! (Illus.). 1994. PLB 24.95 (*0-7933-1951-X*); pap. 14.95 (*0-7933-1952-8*); computer disk 29.95 (*0-7933-1953-6*) Gallopade Pub Group.

—Rhode Island's (Most Devastating!) Disasters & (Most Calamitous!) Catastrophies! (Illus.). 1994. PLB 24.95 (*0-7933-0983-2*); pap. 14.95 (*0-7933-0982-4*); computer disk 29.95 (*0-685-45966-7*) Gallopade Pub Group.

Thompson, Kathleen. Rhode Island. 48p. (gr. 3 up). 1986. PLB 19.97 (*0-86514-457-5*) Raintree Steck-V.

Warner, J. F. Rhode Island: Hello U. S. A. (gr. 4-7). 1993. 17.50 (*0-8225-2731-6*) Lerner Pubns.

RHODE ISLAND–FICTION

Flood, E. L. Secret in the Moonlight: Welcome Inn. LC 93-50936. (Illus.). 144p. (gr. 3-6). 1994. pap. 2.95 (*0-8167-3427-5*) Troll Assocs.

Nicholson, Peggy & Warner, John F. The Case of the Squeaky Thief. 120p. (gr. 4-7). 1994. RTB 14.95 (*0-8225-0711-0*) Lerner Pubns.

RHODE ISLAND–HISTORY

Carbotti, Richard. Newport Houses. 8p. (gr. k-2). 1993. pap. write for info. (*1-882563-01-8*) Lamont Bks.

Gavan, Terrence. The Barons of Newport: A Guide to the Gilded Age. (Illus.). 88p. (Orig.). 1988. pap. 7.50 (*0-929249-01-1*) Pineapple Pubns.

Marsh, Carole. Chill Out: Scary Rhode Island Tales Based on Frightening Rhode Island Truths. (Illus.). 1994. lib. bdg. 24.95 (*0-7933-4771-8*); pap. 14.95 (*0-7933-4772-6*); disk 29.95 (*0-7933-4773-4*) Gallopade Pub Group.

—Rhode Island "Crinkum-Crankum" A Funny Word Book about Our State. (Illus.). (gr. 3-12). 1994. 24.95 (*0-7933-4925-7*); pap. 14.95 (*0-7933-4926-5*); computer disk 29.95 (*0-7933-4927-3*) Gallopade Pub Group.

—The Rhode Island Mystery Van Takes Off! Book 1: Handicapped Rhode Island Kids Sneak Off on a Big Adventure. (Illus.). (gr. 3-12). 1994. 24.95 (*0-7933-5078-6*); pap. 14.95 (*0-7933-5079-4*); computer disk 29.95 (*0-7933-5080-8*) Gallopade Pub Group.

—Rhode Island Timeline: A Chronology of Rhode Island History, Mystery, Trivia, Legend, Lore & More. (Illus.). (gr. 3-12). 1994. PLB 24.95 (*0-7933-5992-9*); pap. 14.95 (*0-7933-5993-7*); computer disk 29.95 (*0-7933-5994-5*) Gallopade Pub Group.

—Rhode Island's Unsolved Mysteries (& Their "Solutions") Includes Scientific Information & Other Activities for Students. (Illus.). (gr. 3-12). 1994. PLB 24.95 (*0-7933-5839-6*); pap. 14.95 (*0-7933-5840-X*); computer disk 29.95 (*0-7933-5841-8*) Gallopade Pub Group.

—Uncle Rebus: Rhode Island Picture Stories for Computer Kids. (Illus.). (gr. k-3). 1994. PLB 24.95 (*0-7933-4618-5*); pap. 14.95 (*0-7933-4619-3*); disk 29. 95 (*0-7933-4620-7*) Gallopade Pub Group.

RHODESIA

Laure, Jason. Zimbabwe. LC 87-35426. (Illus.). 127p. (gr. 4-8). 1988. PLB 20.55 (*0-516-02704-2*) Childrens.

RHYMES

see Limericks; Nonsense Verses; Nursery Rhymes; Poetry–Collections

RHYTHM

Hayes, Sarah. Stamp Your Feet. Ormerod, Jan, illus. LC 87-29779. 32p. (ps-1). 1988. 13.00 (*0-688-07694-7*); PLB 12.88 (*0-688-07695-5*) Lothrop.

Lobel, Arnold. Whiskers & Rhymes. Lobel, Arnold, illus. LC 83-25424. 48p. (gr. k-3). 1985. 13.00 (*0-688-03835-2*); lib. bdg. 12.88 (*0-688-03836-0*) Greenwillow.

—Whiskers & Rhymes. LC 83-25424. (Illus.). 48p. 1988. pap. 4.95 (*0-688-08291-2*, Mulberry) Morrow.

Morrison, Lillian. Rhythm Road: Poems to Move To. LC 87-4071. (gr. 4 up). 1988. PLB 14.00 (*0-688-07098-1*) Lothrop.

RICE

Brice, Raphaelle. Rice: The Little Grain That Feeds the World. Bogard, Vicki, tr. from FRE. Riquier, Aline, illus. LC 90-50775. 38p. (gr. k-5). 1991. 5.95 (*0-944589-30-8*, 308) Young Discovery Lib.

Johnson, Sylvia A. Rice. Moriya, Noboru, illus. 48p. (gr. 4 up). 1985. PLB 19.95 (*0-8225-1466-4*) Lerner Pubns.

Merrison, Lynne. Rice. Yeats, John, illus. 32p. (gr. 1-4). 1990. PLB 13.50 (*0-87614-417-2*) Carolrhoda Bks.

Thomson, Ruth. Rice. Stefoff, Rebecca, ed. Das, Prodeepta, photos by. LC 90-40367. (Illus.). 32p. (gr. 3-5). 1990. PLB 15.93 (*0-944483-71-2*) Garrett Ed Corp.

RICE–FICTION

Barry, David. The Rajah's Rice. 32p. 1994. text ed. write for info. (*0-7167-6568-3*) W H Freeman.

Pittman, Helena C. A Grain of Rice. LC 84-4670. (Illus.). (gr. k-4). 1986. lib. bdg. 12.95 (*0-8038-9289-6*) Hastings.

RICHARD 3RD, KING OF ENGLAND, 1452-1485–FICTION

Stevenson, Robert Louis. Black Arrow. (gr. 6 up). 1964. pap. 2.95 (*0-8049-0020-5*, CL-20) Airmont.

RICHELIEU, ARMAND JEAN DU PLESSIS, CARDINAL, DUC DE, 1585-1642

Glossop, Pat. Cardinal Richelieu. (Illus.). 112p. (gr. 5 up). 1990. 17.95 (*1-55546-822-5*) Chelsea Hse.

RIDDLES

see also Puzzles

Adler, David A. Bunny Rabbit Rebus. Linden, Madelaine G., illus. LC 82-45574. 40p. (gr. 1-4). 1983. (Crowell Jr Bks); (Crowell Jr Bks) HarpC Child Bks.

—The Carsick Zebra & Other Animal Riddles. De Paola, Tomie, illus. LC 82-48750. 64p. (gr. 1-4). 1983. reinforced bdg. 12.95 (*0-8234-0479-X*) Holiday.

—The Carsick Zebra & Other Animal Riddles. De Paola, Tomie, illus. 64p. (Orig.). (gr. 1). 1985. pap. 2.25 (*0-553-15487-7*) Bantam.

—The Dinosaur Princess & Other Prehistoric Riddles. Leedy, Loreen, illus. LC 87-25121. 64p. (gr. 1-4). 1988. reinforced bdg. 12.95 (*0-8234-0686-5*) Holiday.

—The Dinosaur Princess & Other Prehistoric Riddles. (gr. k-3). 1992. pap. 2.99 (*0-553-15793-0*, Skylark) Bantam.

—The Purple Turkey & Other Thanksgiving Riddles. Hafner, Marylin, illus. LC 86-310. 64p. (gr. 1-4). 1986. reinforced bdg. 12.95 (*0-8234-0613-X*) Holiday.

—Remember Betsy Floss & Other Colonial American Riddles. Wallner, John, illus. LC 87-45333. 64p. (gr. 1-4). 1987. reinforced bdg. 12.95 (*0-8234-0664-4*) Holiday.

—A Teacher on Roller Skates & Other School Riddles. Wallner, John, illus. LC 89-1929. 64p. (gr. 1-4). 1989. reinforced bdg. 12.95 (*0-8234-0775-6*) Holiday.

—The Twisted Witch & Other Spooky Riddles. Chess, Victoria, illus. LC 85-909. 64p. (gr. 1-4). 1985. reinforced bdg. 12.95 (*0-8234-0571-0*) Holiday.

—The Twisted Witch & Other Spooky Riddles. 64p. 1986. pap. 2.25 (*0-553-15447-8*) Bantam.

Adler, Larry. Help Wanted: Riddles about Jobs. Burke, Susan S., illus. 32p. (gr. 1-4). 1989. PLB 11.95 (*0-8225-2325-6*) Lerner Pubns.

Ainsworth, Catherine H. Black & White & Said All over: Riddles. LC 72-5461. 36p. (ps-12). 1976. 5.00 (*0-933190-02-6*) Clyde Pr.

Artell, Mike. The Wackiest Ecology Riddles on Earth. LC 91-45773. (Illus.). 96p. (gr. 3-8). 1992. 12.95 (*0-8069-1250-2*) Sterling.

Ask a Riddle, Unit 4. (gr. 1). 1991. 29.50 (*0-88106-727-X*) Charlesbridge Pub.

Barry, Sheila A., ed. Kids' Funniest Jokes. Sinclair, Jeff, illus. LC 93-23045. 96p. (gr. 2-10). 1994. 12.95 (*0-8069-0449-6*); pap. 3.95 (*0-8069-0448-8*) Sterling.

Beisner, Monika. Monika Beisner's Book of Riddles. LC 83-81529. (Illus.). 32p. (ps up). 1983. 15.00 (*0-374-30866-7*) FS&G.

Benjamin, Alan. Halloween Riddles Chubby Board Book. (ps-6). 1993. pap. 3.95 (*0-671-87067-X*, Little Simon) S&S Trade.

Benny, Mike. The World's Punniest Joke Book. Hoffman, Sanford, illus. LC 92-42578. 96p. 1993. 12.95 (*0-8069-8544-5*) Sterling.

Bernstein, Joanne & Cohen, Paul. Creepy, Crawly, Critter Riddles. Tucker, Kathleen, ed. Hoffman, Rosekrans, illus. LC 86-15911. 32p. (gr. 1-5). 1986. PLB 8.95 (*0-8075-1345-8*) A Whitman.

—Unidentified Flying Riddles. Fay, Ann, ed. Seltzer, Meyer, illus. LC 83-17097. 32p. (gr. 1-5). 1983. PLB 8.95 (*0-8075-8329-4*) A Whitman.

Bernstein, Joanne E. & Cohen, Paul. Happy Holiday Riddles to You. Fay, Ann, ed. Seltzer, Meyer, illus. LC 85-717. 32p. (gr. 1-5). 1985. PLB 8.95 (*0-8075-3154-5*) A Whitman.

—Riddles to Take on Vacation. Fay, Ann, ed. LC 87-2071. (Illus.). (gr. 1-5). 1987. PLB 8.95 (*0-8075-6999-2*) A Whitman.

—Sporty Riddles. Mathews, Judith, ed. Harvey, Paul, illus. LC 89-5294. 32p. (gr. 1-5). 1989. PLB 8.95 (*0-8075-7590-9*) A Whitman.

—What Was the Wicked Witch's Real Name? & Other Character Riddles. Iosa, Ann, illus. LC 86-1648. 32p. (gr. 1-5). 1986. 8.95 (*0-8075-8854-7*) A Whitman.

Bierhorst, John, ed. & tr. Lightning Inside You: And Other Native American Riddles. Brierley, Louise, illus. LC 91-21744. 112p. (gr. 2 up). 1992. 14.00 (*0-688-09582-8*) Morrow Jr Bks.

Birney, Betty. Who Am I? Berret, Lisa, illus. 16p. (ps). 1992. pap. 5.95 pop-up bk. (*0-671-76914-6*, Little Simon) S&S Trade.

Bishop, Ann. Riddle Ages! Rubin, Caroline, ed. Warshaw, Jerry, illus. LC 77-12828. (gr. 1-4). 1977. PLB 8.95 (*0-8075-6965-8*) A Whitman.

Bolton, Martha. TV Jokes & Riddles. Sinclair, Jeff, illus. LC 91-25297. 96p. 1992. pap. 3.95 (*0-8069-7246-7*) Sterling.

Brandreth, Gyles. Super Silly Riddles. 1991. 3.99 (*0-517-07352-8*) Random Hse Value.

Bridwell, Norman. Clifford's Riddles. Bridwell, Norman, illus. 32p. (gr. k-3). 1984. pap. 2.25 (*0-590-44282-1*) Scholastic Inc.

Brittain, Bill. The Mystery of the Several Sevens. Warhola, James, illus. LC 93-47076. 96p. (gr. 2-5). 1994. 11.95 (*0-06-024459-3*); PLB 11.89 (*0-06-024462-3*) HarpC Child Bks.

Brown, Kenneth. Barn House Book: Rhymes, Riddles, & Jokes. Brown, Kenneth, illus. Date not set. 12.95 (*1-56743-046-5*) Amistad Pr.

Buggy Riddles. 1992. pap. 4.99 (*0-14-036178-2*) Puffin Bks.

Burns, Diane & Burns, Andy. Home on the Range: Ranch-Style Riddles. Burke, Susan S., photos by. LC 93-19158. (Illus.). 32p. (ps-3). 1994. PLB 13.50 (*0-8225-2341-8*); pap. 3.95 (*0-8225-9657-1*) Lerner Pubns.

Burns, Diane L. & Scholten, Dan. Here's to Ewe: Riddles about Sheep. Burke, Susan S., illus. 32p. (gr. 1-4). 1989. PLB 11.95 (*0-8225-2326-4*) Lerner Pubns.

Burns, Marilyn. The One Dollar Word Riddle Book. Weston, Martha, illus. 48p. (Orig.). (gr. 3-8). 1990. pap. 6.95 (*0-938587-29-3*) Cuisenaire.

—One Dollar Word Riddle Book. (gr. 4-7). 1990. pap. 6.95 (*0-201-48025-5*) Addison-Wesley.

Calmenson, Stephanie. What Am I? Very First Riddles. Gundersheimer, Karen, illus. LC 87-22959. 32p. (ps-2). 1989. 11.95 (*0-06-020997-6*); PLB 11.89 (*0-06-020998-4*) HarpC Child Bks.

Cerf, Bennett A. Bennett Cerf's Book of Animal Riddles. LC 64-11246. (gr. 2-3). 1964. lib. bdg. 7.99 (*0-394-90034-0*) Beginner.

—Bennett Cerf's Book of Riddles. LC 60-13492. (Illus.). 72p. (gr. 1-2). 1960. 6.95 (*0-394-80015-X*); lib. bdg. 7.99 (*0-394-90015-4*) Beginner.

—More Riddles. LC 61-11727. (Illus.). 72p. (gr. k-3). 1961. 6.95 (*0-394-80024-9*); lib. bdg. 7.99 (*0-394-90024-3*) Beginner.

Chemielewski, Gary. Riddles. Clark, Ron G., illus. LC 86-17720. (gr. 2-3). 1986. PLB 13.27 (*0-86592-686-7*); 9.95 (*0-685-58363-5*) Rourke Corp.

Chmielewski, Gary. Teacher Jokes. Clark, Ron G., illus. LC 86-17773. (gr. 2-3). 1986. 13.27 (*0-86592-688-3*); 9.95s.p. (*0-685-58365-1*) Rourke Corp.

Coco, Eugene. Jokes & Riddles. Jarka, Jeff, illus. 24p. (ps-2). 1993. pap. text ed. 0.99 (*1-56293-350-7*) McClanahan Bk.

Cole, Joanna. Six Sick Sheep. LC 92-5715. 1993. pap. 6.95 (*0-688-11068-1*, Pub. by Beech Tree Bks) Morrow.

Cole, Joanna & Calmenson, Stephanie. Why Did the Chicken Cross the Road? And Other Riddles, Old & New. LC 94-2582. (gr. 3 up). 1994. write for info. (*0-688-12202-7*); PLB write for info. (*0-688-12203-5*) Morrow Jr Bks.

Ertner, James D. Super Silly Animal Riddles. Sinclair, Jeff, illus. LC 92-41919. 96p. 1993. 12.95 (*0-8069-0333-3*) Sterling.

Fischer, Richard, et al. Little Biddle Riddle Book. 32p. 1991. 3.95 (*0-935284-89-3*) Patrice Pr.

Fox, Lori M. The Craziest Riddle Book in the World. Hoffman, Sanford, illus. LC 91-13209. 96p. (gr. 3-9). 1992. 12.95 (*0-8069-8406-6*); pap. 3.95 (*0-8069-8407-4*) Sterling.

—Oodles of Riddles. LC 89-4549. (Illus.). 96p. (gr. 2-8). 1989. 12.95 (*0-8069-6880-X*); PLB 15.69 (*0-8069-6881-8*) Sterling.

—Riddlemania. Hoffman, Sanford, illus. LC 90-43230. 96p. (gr. 2-7). 1991. 12.95 (*0-8069-7352-8*) Sterling.

—Riddlemania. Hoffman, Sanford, illus. LC 90-43230. 96p. (gr. 1-7). 1992. pap. 3.95 (*0-8069-7353-6*) Sterling.

Gallant, Morrie. The Nuttiest Riddle Book in the World. Hoffman, Sanford, illus. LC 93-7871. 96p. (gr. 2-10). 1993. 12.95 (*0-8069-0420-8*) Sterling.

Gerberg, Mort. Geographunny: A Book of Global Riddles. Gerberg, Mort, illus. 64p. (gr. 3 up). 1991. 14.45 (*0-395-52449-0*, Clarion Bks); pap. 7.70 (*0-395-60312-9*, Clarion Bks) HM.

Gordon, Jeffie R. Hide & Shriek: Riddles about Ghosts & Goblins. (Illus.). 32p. (gr. 1-4). 1991. PLB 11.95 (*0-8225-2336-1*); pap. 3.95 (*0-8225-9594-X*) Lerner Pubns.

Hafner, Everett. Sports Riddles. Hafner, Marylin, illus. 48p. (gr. 1-4). 1991. pap. 3.95 (*0-14-032497-6*, Puffin) Puffin Bks.

Hall, Katy. Snakey Riddles. 1990. 9.95 (*0-8037-0669-3*); PLB 9.89 (*0-8037-0670-7*) Dial Bks Young.

Hall, Katy & Eisenberg, Lisa. Batty Riddles. Rubel, Nicole, illus. LC 91-20777. 48p. (ps-3). 1993. 11.99 (*0-8037-1217-0*); lib. bdg. 11.89 (*0-8037-1218-9*) Dial Bks Young.

—Buggy Riddles. Taback, Simms, illus. LC 85-1450. 48p. (ps-3). 1986. 9.95 (*0-8037-0139-X*); PLB 9.89 (*0-8037-0140-3*) Dial Bks Young.

—Buggy Riddles. Taback, Simms, illus. LC 85-1450. 48p. (ps-3). 1988. pap. 4.95 (*0-8037-0554-9*) Dial Bks Young.

—Buggy Riddles. Taback, Simms, illus. LC 93-6556. (gr. 1-4). 1993. pap. 3.25 (*0-14-036543-5*) Puffin Bks.

—Bunny Riddles. Rubel, Nicole, illus. LC 93-13241. (ps-4). 1995. write for info. (*0-8037-1519-6*); PLB write for info. (*0-8037-1521-8*) Dial Bks Young.

—Fishy Riddles. LC 82-22135. (Illus.). 48p. (ps-3). 1983. pap. 4.99 (*0-8037-2419-5*) Dial Bks Young.

—Fishy Riddles. Taback, Simms, illus. (gr. 3-5). 1985. bk. & cassette 19.95 (*0-941078-72-8*); pap. 12.95 bk. & cassette (*0-941078-70-1*); cassette, 4 paperbacks & guide 27.95 (*0-941078-71-X*) Live Oak Media.

—Fishy Riddles. Taback, Simms, illus. LC 93-6551. (gr. 1-4). 1993. pap. 3.25 (*0-14-036546-X*, Puffin) Puffin Bks.

—Grizzly Riddles. Rubel, Nicole, illus. LC 86-29275. 48p. (ps-3). 1992. pap. 3.99 (*0-14-036116-2*, Dial Easy to Read) Puffin Bks.

—Sheepish Riddles. Alley, Robert, illus. LC 93-32212. 1995. write for info. (*0-8037-1535-8*); lib. bdg. write for info. (*0-8037-1536-6*) Dial Bks Young.

—Snakey Riddles. Taback, Simms, illus. 48p. (ps-3). 1993. pap. 3.99 (*0-14-054588-3*) Puffin Bks.

—Spacey Riddles. LC 90-42508. (Illus.). 48p. (ps-3). 1992. 11.00 (*0-8037-0814-9*); PLB 10.89 (*0-8037-0815-7*) Dial Bks Young.

Hartman, Victoria. The Silliest Joke Book Ever. Alley, R. W., photos by. LC 92-22161. (Illus.). 1993. 14.00 (*0-688-10109-7*); lib. bdg. 13.93 (*0-688-10110-0*) Lothrop.

Hartman, Victoria G. Westward Ho, Ho, Ho. Karas, G. Brian, illus. 48p. (gr. 2-6). 1994. pap. 3.99 (*0-14-036851-5*) Puffin Bks.

Heck, Joseph. Dinosaur Riddles. Barish, Wendy, ed. Hoffman, Sandy, illus. 128p. (gr. 3-7). 1982. 9.29 (*0-685-05613-9*, Little Simon) S&S Trade.

Highlights for Children Editors. Rebus Treasury 2: Forty-Four Stories Kids Can Read by Following the Pictures. (Illus.). 48p. (Orig.). (ps-2). 1993. pap. 4.95 (*1-56397-063-5*) Boyds Mills Pr.

Hillert, Margaret. What Am I? (Illus.). (ps-k). 1981. PLB 6.95 (*0-8136-5066-6*, TK2376); pap. 3.50 (*0-8136-5566-8*, TK2377) Modern Curr.

—What Is It? (Illus.). (ps-2). 1978. PLB 6.95 (*0-8136-5056-9*, TK2378); pap. 3.50 (*0-8136-5556-0*, TK2379) Modern Curr.

Hindman, Darwin A. Eighteen Hundred Riddles, Enigmas & Conundrums. 159p. (Orig.). (gr. 4 up). 1963. pap. 3.50 (*0-486-21059-6*) Dover.

Johnson, Harriet. Honolulu Zoo Riddles. Thompson, Judi, illus. (ps-5). 1974. pap. 1.25 (*0-914916-07-6*) Topgallant.

Jones, Evelyn. World's Wackiest Riddle Book. 1991. 3.99 (*0-517-07353-6*) Random Hse Value.

Kallen, Stuart A. Brain Teasers. LC 92-14774. 1992. 12. 94 (*1-56239-130-5*) Abdo & Dghtrs.

—Only the Funniest Joke Book. LC 92-14778. 1992. 12. 94 (*1-56239-133-X*) Abdo & Dghtrs.

—Ridiculous Riddles. LC 92-14772. 1992. 12.94 (*1-56239-126-7*) Abdo & Dghtrs.
Keller, Charles. Astronauts: Space Jokes & Riddles. (gr. 4-7). 1991. pap. 2.95 (*0-671-73984-0*, Little Simon) S&S Trade.
—Colossal Fossils: Dinosaur Riddles. 64p. (gr. 4-7). 1991. pap. 2.95 (*0-671-73985-9*, Little Simon) S&S Trade.
—Count Draculations: Monster Riddles. 64p. (gr. 4-7). 1991. pap. 2.95 (*0-671-73983-2*, Little Simon) S&S Trade.
—Planet of the Grapes: Show Biz Jokes & Riddles. Richter, Mischa, illus. 40p. (gr. 3-7). 1992. 13.95 (*0-945912-17-X*) Pippin Pr.
—Take Me to Your Liter: Science & Math Jokes. Filling, Gregory, illus. 40p. (gr. 2-5). 1991. PLB 13.95 (*0-945912-13-7*) Pippin Pr.
Keller, Charles, et al, eds. Star-Spangled Banana: And Other Revolutionary Riddles. (Illus.). 62p. (gr. 2 up). 1978. 3.95 (*0-13-842971-5*, Pub. by Treehouse) P-H.
Kessler, Leonard. Old Turtle's Ninety Knock-Knocks, Jokes, & Riddles. LC 89-77505. (Illus.). 48p. (gr. k up). 1991. 13.95 (*0-688-09585-2*); PLB 13.88 (*0-688-09586-0*) Greenwillow.
—Old Turtle's Ninety Knock-Knocks, Jokes, & Riddles. (Illus.). 48p. (gr. 1 up). 1993. pap. 4.95 (*0-688-04586-3*, Mulberry) Morrow.
—Old Turtle's Riddle & Joke Book. Kessler, Leonard, illus. LC 85-12565. 48p. (gr. 1-4). 1986. 14.00 (*0-688-05953-8*); PLB 13.93 (*0-688-05954-6*) Greenwillow.
—Old Turtle's Riddle & Joke Book. (gr. k-6). 1990. pap. 2.95 (*0-440-40268-9*, YB) Dell.
Koontz, Robin M. I See Something You Don't See: A Riddle-Me Picture Book. Koontz, Robin M., illus. LC 91-8025. 32p. (ps-3). 1992. 13.00 (*0-525-65077-6*, Cobblehill Bks) Dutton Child Bks.
Lang, Margaret A. Gramma's Stories & Rhymes for Little Christians. Smith, Linda G., illus. 104p. (ps-5). 1982. 9.95 (*0-685-42235-6*) Lang Pubns.
Lee, Greg. Money. LC 92-44074. 1993. 12.67 (*0-86593-268-9*); 9.50s.p. (*0-685-66360-4*) Rourke Corp.
—School. LC 92-44073. (gr. 3 up). 1993. 12.67 (*0-86593-269-7*); 9.50s.p. (*0-685-66359-0*) Rourke Corp.
—Vacation. LC 92-45692. 1993. 12.67 (*0-86593-270-0*); 9.50s.p. (*0-685-66420-1*) Rourke Corp.
Lee, Greg, compiled by. Food: Wacky Words. LC 92-41730. (gr. 3 up). 1993. 12.67 (*0-86593-265-4*); 9.50s.p. (*0-685-66289-6*) Rourke Corp.
—Outer Space: Wacky Words. LC 92-43965. (gr. 3 up). 1993. 12.67 (*0-86593-267-0*); 9.50s.p. (*0-685-66292-6*) Rourke Corp.
—Pets: Wacky Words. LC 92-43964. (gr. 3 up). 1993. 12.67 (*0-86593-266-2*); 9.50s.p. (*0-685-66291-8*) Rourke Corp.
Levine, Caroline. Riddles to Tell Your Cat. Grant, Christy, ed. Seltzer, Meyer, illus. 32p. (gr. 1-4). 1992. PLB 8.95 (*0-8075-7006-0*) A Whitman.
—Silly School Riddles & Other Classroom Crack-Ups. Levine, Abby, ed. Munsinger, Lynn, illus. LC 84-17300. 32p. (gr. 1-5). 1984. 8.95 (*0-8075-7359-0*) A Whitman.
Levine, Caroline A. The Silly Kid Joke Book. Maestro, Giulio, illus. LC 82-17727. 64p. (gr. 1-3). 1983. 10.95 (*0-525-44039-9*, DCB) Dutton Child Bks.
Lewis, J. Patrick. Riddle-Icious. Roberts, Victoria, illus. LC 93-43759. 1995. 15.00 (*0-679-84011-7*); PLB write for info. (*0-679-94011-1*) Knopf.
Livingston, Myra C. My Head Is Red & Other Riddle Rhymes. LoPrete, Tere, illus. LC 89-24528. 32p. (ps-3). 1990. reinforced bdg. 12.95 (*0-8234-0806-X*) Holiday.
Livingston, Myra C., selected by. Riddle-Me Rhymes. Perry, Rebecca, illus. LC 93-25179. 96p. (gr. 3-7). 1994. SBE 13.95 (*0-689-50602-3*, M K McElderry) Macmillan Child Grp.
Longo, Linda. Troll Jokes & Riddles. LC 92-22571. (Illus.). 48p. (gr. 1-7). 1992. pap. 1.95 (*0-8167-2940-9*) Troll Assocs.
Lord. One Hundred One Thanksgiving Knock-Knocks, Jokes, & Riddles. 1993. pap. 1.95 (*0-590-47163-5*) Scholastic Inc.
Low, Joseph. A Mad Wet Hen & Other Riddles. LC 76-44329. (Illus.). 56p. (gr. 3 up). 1992. pap. 3.95 (*0-688-11511-X*, Mulberry) Morrow.

Macias, Benjamin. One Hundred One Bible Riddles for All Ages. Macias, Daniel, illus. 112p. (Orig.). (gr. 1 up). 1993. pap. 7.95 (*0-9638277-1-5*) Fam of God.
This Bible riddle book is the most complete collection of fully illustrated Bible riddles for children, adolescents & adults. Each humorous Bible riddle has its own unique, creative & vivid illustration that perfectly describes the riddle. These Bible riddles have been shared with young & old & all agree that it is a treasure of wit & humor for ages to come. You will certainly find this Bible riddle book worthy of sharing with those who also have an appreciation for wholesome & clean riddles. In addition, this witty book can be used in children's activities & programs & young people can also incorporate it in their social activities. Parents can also share it as a gift to their children, knowing satisfactorily that the riddles are children oriented. This Bible riddle indeed is for all ages & ages to come. Family of God Publishing House, P.O. Box 758, Vista, CA 92083-0758. (619) 598-3629, FAX (619) 966-0312.
Publisher Provided Annotation.

McKie, Roy. The Riddle Book. LC 77-85237. (ps-2). 1978. lib. bdg. 5.99 (*0-394-93732-5*); pap. 2.25 (*0-394-83732-0*) Random Bks Yng Read.
Maestro, Giulio. Halloween Howls: Riddles That Are a Scream. LC 83-1419. (Illus.). 64p. (gr. 2-7). 1992. pap. 4.99 (*0-14-036115-4*, Puff Unicorn) Puffin Bks.
—Macho Nacho & Other Rhyming Riddles. LC 93-47137. (Illus.). 48p. (gr. 2-7). 1994. 12.99 (*0-525-45261-3*) Dutton Child Bks.
—More Halloween Howls: Riddles That Come Back to Haunt You. LC 91-23505. (Illus.). 64p. (gr. 2-7). 1992. 12.00 (*0-525-44899-3*, DCB) Dutton Child Bks.
—Razzle-Dazzle Riddles. Maestro, Giulio, illus. LC 85-3785. 64p. (Orig.). (gr. 2-5). 1985. 11.95 (*0-89919-382-X*, Clarion Bks); pap. 5.95 (*0-89919-405-2*, Clarion Bks) HM.
—Riddle Romp. LC 83-2067. (Illus.). 64p. (gr. k-3). 1983. (Clarion Bks); pap. 4.95 (*0-89919-207-6*, Clarion Bks) HM.
—Riddle Roundup: A Wild Bunch to Beef up Your Word Power. Maestro, Giulio, illus. LC 86-33404. 64p. (gr. 2-5). 1989. (Clarion Bks); pap. 5.70 (*0-89919-537-7*, Clarion Bks) HM.
—What's a Frank Frank? Tasty Homograph Riddles. Maestro, Giulio, illus. LC 84-5021. 64p. (gr. 2-5). 1984. 13.95 (*0-89919-297-1*, Clarion Bks); pap. 5.95 (*0-89919-317-X*, Clarion Bks) HM.
—What's Mite Might? Homophone Riddles to Boost Your Word Power! Maestro, Giulio, illus. LC 86-2665. 64p. (gr. 2-5). 1986. 11.95 (*0-89919-434-6*, Clarion Bks); pap. 4.95 (*0-89919-435-4*, Clarion Bks) HM.
Maestro, Marco & Maestro, Giulio. Riddle City USA: A Book of Geography Riddles. Maestro, Giulio, illus. LC 93-16665. 64p. (gr. 2-5). 1994. 15.00 (*0-06-023368-0*); PLB 14.89 (*0-06-023369-9*) HarpC Child Bks.
Marks, Burton. Animals. Harvey, Paul, illus. LC 91-3656. 24p. (gr. k-2). 1992. PLB 9.89 (*0-8167-2415-6*); pap. text ed. 2.50 (*0-8167-2416-4*) Troll Assocs.
Marzollo, Jean. I Spy, Mystery: A Book of Picture Riddles. Wick, Walter, photos by. LC 92-40863. (Illus.). 1993. 12.95 (*0-590-46294-6*) Scholastic Inc.
Marzollo, Jean, compiled by. The Rebus Treasury. Carson, Carol D., illus. LC 85-16133. 64p. (ps up). 1989. pap. 5.95 (*0-8037-0644-8*) Dial Bks Young.
Mase, Thomas. What's Gnu? Riddles from the Zoo. Burke, Susan S., illus. 32p. (gr. 1-4). 1989. PLB 11.95 (*0-8225-2330-2*) Lerner Pubns.
Mathews, Judith. Knock-Knock Knees & Funny Bones: Riddles for Every Body. (ps-3). 1993. 8.95 (*0-8075-4203-2*) A Whitman.
Mathews, Judith & Robinson, Fay. Oh, How Waffle! Riddles You Can Eat. Levine, Abby, ed. Whiting, Carl, illus. LC 92-13478. 32p. (gr. 1-4). 1992. 8.95g (*0-8075-5907-5*) A Whitman.
Matthews, Morgan. One Hundred Two Out of This World Jokes. Matthews, Morgan, illus. LC 91-45021. 64p. (gr. 2-6). 1992. pap. text ed. 2.95 (*0-8167-2789-9*) Troll Assocs.
—One Hundred Two School Cafeteria Jokes. LC 91-30055. (Illus.). 64p. (gr. 2-6). 1991. pap. text ed. 2.95 (*0-8167-2611-6*) Troll Assocs.
Michaels, Ski. One Hundred Two Animal Jokes. LC 91-30061. (Illus.). 64p. (gr. 2-6). 1991. pap. text ed. 2.95 (*0-8167-2613-2*) Troll Assocs.
Milne, A. A. Winnie the Pooh & Some Bees Storybooks. 128p. (ps-2). 1993. (DCB); pap. 4.99 (*0-525-45033-5*, DCB) Dutton Child Bks.
Most, Bernard. Zoodles. 1992. write for info. (*0-15-299969-8*, HB Juv Bks) HarBrace.
Neitzel, Shirley. The Bag I'm Taking to Grandma's. Parker, Nancy W., illus. LC 94-4115. 32p. Date not set. write for info. (*0-688-12960-9*); PLB write for info. (*0-688-12961-7*) Greenwillow.
—The Dress I'll Wear to the Party. Parker, Nancy W., illus. LC 91-30906. 32p. (ps-4). 1992. 14.00 (*0-688-09959-9*); PLB 13.93 (*0-688-09960-2*) Greenwillow.
—The Jacket I Wear in the Snow. Cohr, Amy, ed. Parker, Nancy W., illus. LC 92-43789. 32p. (ps up). 1994. pap. 4.95 (*0-688-04587-1*, Mulberry) Morrow.
Nelson, Jeffrey. Spooky Jokes & Riddles Books. (Illus.). 24p. (gr. 3 up). 1988. pap. 1.95 (*1-56288-344-5*) Checkerboard.
Nelson, Jeffrey S. Animal Jokes & Riddles. Nelson, Jeffrey S., illus. LC 90-27676. 24p. (gr. 3 up). 1991. pap. 1.95 (*1-56288-016-0*) Checkerboard.
—Family Jokes & Riddles. Nelson, Jeffrey S., illus. 24p. (gr. 3 up). 1991. pap. 1.95 (*1-56288-015-2*) Checkerboard.
—Jungle Jokes & Riddles. Nelson, Jeffrey S., illus. 24p. (gr. 3 up). 1991. pap. 1.95 (*1-56288-017-9*) Checkerboard.
—Yucky Jokes & Riddles. Nelson, Jeffrey S., illus. 24p. (gr. 3 up). 1991. pap. 1.95 (*1-56288-014-4*) Checkerboard.
Nims, Bonnie L. Just Beyond Reach. Anema, George, illus. 48p. 1992. 13.95 (*0-590-44077-2*, Scholastic Hardcover) Scholastic Inc.
Owl Magazine Editors. Jokes & Riddles. (Illus.). 96p. (gr. 3 up). 1992. pap. 3.95 (*0-919872-85-9*, Pub. by Greey dePencier CN) Firefly Bks Ltd.
Parenteau. One Hundred Plus Super Pig Jokes, Puns, & Riddles. 1993. pap. 1.95 (*0-590-41656-1*) Scholastic Inc.
Pellowski, Michael. One Hundred Two Cat & Dog Jokes. LC 91-42769. (Illus.). 64p. (gr. 2-6). 1992. pap. text ed. 2.95 (*0-8167-2790-2*) Troll Assocs.
—One Hundred Two Wacky Monster Jokes. LC 91-44702. (Illus.). 64p. (gr. 2-6). 1992. pap. text ed. 2.95 (*0-8167-2746-5*) Troll Assocs.
—One Hundred Two Wild & Wacky Jokes. LC 91-30783. (Illus.). 64p. (gr. 2-6). 1991. pap. text ed. 2.95 (*0-8167-2612-4*) Troll Assocs.
Pellowski, Michael J. Wackiest Jokes in The World. Hoffman, Sanford, illus. LC 93-38242. 96p. 1994. 12.95 (*0-8069-0493-3*) Sterling.
Perkins, Gary. Silly Goofy Jokes. Nevins, Dan, illus. LC 92-20779. 64p. (gr. 2-6). 1992. pap. text ed. 1.95 (*0-8167-2965-4*, Pub. by Watermill Pr) Troll Assocs.
—Silly Haunted Jokes. Nevins, Dan, illus. LC 92-20760. 64p. (gr. 2-6). 1992. pap. text ed. 1.95 (*0-8167-2963-8*, Pub. by Watermill Pr) Troll Assocs.
—Silly School Jokes. Nevins, Dan, illus. LC 92-20437. 64p. (gr. 2-6). 1992. pap. text ed. 1.95 (*0-8167-2964-6*, Pub. by Watermill Pr) Troll Assocs.
Peterson, Scott K. Out on a Limb: Riddles about Trees & Plants. Burke, Susan S., illus. 32p. (gr. 1-4). 1989. PLB 11.95 (*0-8225-2328-0*) Lerner Pubns.
—Wing It! Riddles about Birds. (Illus.). 32p. (gr. 1-4). 1991. PLB 11.95 (*0-8225-2333-7*) Lerner Pubns.
—Wing It: Riddles about Birds. (ps-3). 1991. pap. 3.95 (*0-8225-9591-5*) Lerner Pubns.
Phillips, Bob. Ultimate Good Clean Jokes for Kids. 1993. pap. 3.99 (*1-56507-085-2*) Harvest Hse.
Phillips, Louis. Going Ape: Jokes from the Jungle. Shein, Bob, illus. 64p. (gr. 2 up). 1990. pap. 3.95 (*0-14-032263-9*, Puffin) Puffin Bks.
—Invisible Oink: Pig Jokes. Dubanevich, Arlene, illus. LC 92-24803. 64p. 1993. 11.99 (*0-670-84387-3*) Viking Child Bks.
—Riddlegrams. (Illus.). 48p. (Orig.). (gr. 2 up). 1989. pap. 2.95 incl. chipboard (*0-8431-2404-0*) Price Stern.
—School Daze: Jokes Your Teacher Will Hate! Natti, Susanna, illus. LC 93-41484. 64p. (gr. 2-6). 1994. 11.99 (*0-670-84929-4*) Viking Child Bks.
—The Upside down Riddle Book. Gardner, Beau, illus. LC 82-73. 32p. (gr. k up). 1982. 16.00 (*0-688-00931-X*); PLB 15.93 (*0-688-00932-8*) Lothrop.
Pirotta, Saviour. Hey Riddle Riddle! Hellen, Nancy, illus. LC 88-34356. 32p. (gr. 2 up). 1989. PLB 9.95 (*0-87226-408-4*, Bedrick Blackie) P Bedrick Bks.
Riddles & Jokes. (Illus.). (ps-2). 1991. pap. 3.50 (*0-8136-5961-2*, TK2360) Modern Curr.
Rosenbloom, Joseph. Biggest Riddle Book in the World. Behr, Joyce, illus. LC 76-1165. (gr. 5 up). 1979. pap. 5.95 (*0-8069-8884-3*) Sterling.
—The Funniest Riddle Book Ever! Wilhelm, Hans, illus. LC 84-16192. 24p. (ps up). 1985. 12.95 (*0-8069-4698-9*) Sterling.
—Monster Madness. 1991. 3.99 (*0-517-07354-4*) Random Hse Value.
—Six Hundred Ninety-Six Silly School Jokes & Riddles. Kendrick, Dennis, illus. 128p. (gr. 2 up). 1987. pap. 3.95 (*0-8069-6392-1*) Sterling.
—The Zaniest Riddle Book in the World. Hoffman, Sanford, illus. LC 83-18102. 128p. (gr. 3 up). 1985. pap. 3.95 (*0-8069-6252-6*) Sterling.
Rothaus, Jim. Bug Riddles. Woodworth, Viki, illus. (gr. 1-4). 1992. PLB 13.95 (*0-89565-864-X*) Childs World.
—Fairy Tale Jokes. Woodworth, Viki, illus. (gr. 1-4). 1992. PLB 13.95 (*0-89565-862-3*) Childs World.
—Monster Riddles. Woodworth, Viki, illus. (gr. 1-4). 1992. PLB 13.95 (*0-89565-863-1*) Childs World.
Rox, Lori M. Oodles of Riddles. Hoffman, Sanford, illus. LC 89-4549. 96p. (gr. 3-8). 1990. pap. 3.95 (*0-8069-7202-5*) Sterling.
Salinas, Roger. Silly Ghost Riddles. Rodriguez, Carlos, illus. 32p. (Orig.). (gr. 3-5). 1987. pap. 2.95 (*0-942673-00-X*) Salinas Salinas & Matthews.
Schaff, Joanne. What Am I? Schaff, Joanne, illus. 38p. (Orig.). (ps-3). 1987. pap. 2.00 (*0-9619365-0-9*) Tree City Pr.
Schecter, Ellen. The Boy Who Cried Wolf. (ps-3). 1994. pap. 3.99 (*0-553-37232-7*) Bantam.
Schecter, Ellen, retold by. The Boy Who Cried Wolf! Chalk, Gary, illus. (gr. 4 up). 1994. 10.95 (*0-553-09043-7*) Bantam.
Schenk De Regniers, Beatrice. It Does Not Say Meow & Other Animal Riddle Rhymes. LC 72-75704. 40p. (gr. k-3). 1983. pap. 4.95 (*0-89919-043-X*, Clarion Bks) HM.
Schwartz, Alvin. Unriddling. Truesdell, Sue, illus. LC 82-48778. 128p. (gr. 4 up). 1983. PLB 13.89 (*0-397-32030-2*, Lipp Jr Bks) HarpC Child Bks.

—Unriddling: All Sorts of Riddles to Puzzle Your Guessary. Truesdell, Sue, illus. LC 82-48778. 128p. (gr. 4 up). 1987. pap. 4.95 (*0-06-446057-6*, Trophy) HarpC Child Bks.

Seltzer, Meyer. Petcetera: The Pet Riddle Book. Fay, Ann, ed. LC 88-21. (Illus.). 32p. (gr. 1-5). 1988. PLB 8.95 (*0-8075-6515-6*) A Whitman.

Sesame Street Staff. Sesame Street Pop-up Riddle Book. Sutherland, David, illus. LC 77-70852. (ps-3). 1977. bds. 8.99 (*0-394-83546-8*) Random Bks Yng Read.

Shannon, J. Michael. Riddles & More Riddles. Magnuson, Diana, illus. LC 82-19765. 48p. (gr. 1-5). 1983. pap. 3.95 (*0-516-41873-4*) Childrens.

—Still More Riddles. Magnuson, Diana, illus. LC 85-29065. 48p. (gr. 1-5). 1986. pap. 3.95 (*0-516-41869-6*) Childrens.

Shofner, Myra. Second Ark Book of Riddles. Walles, Dwight, illus. (gr. 3-7). 1981. pap. 3.99 (*0-89191-531-1*, 55319, Chariot Bks) Chariot Family.

Sloat, Teri & Sloat, Robert. Rib Ticklers: A Book of Punny Animals. LC 93-48619. (Illus.). 1994. 15.00 (*0-688-12519-0*); PLB 14.93 (*0-688-12520-4*) Lothrop.

Smith, William J. & Ra, Carol, eds. Behind the King's Kitchen Door. Hnizdovsky, Jacques, illus. LC 91-66056. 56p. (gr. 5 up). 1992. 18.95 (*1-56397-024-4*, Wordsong) Boyds Mills Pr.

Spires, Elizabeth, ed. One White Wing: Puzzles in Poems & Pictures. Blegvad, Erik, illus. LC 94-12927. 1995. 16.00 (*0-689-50622-8*, M K McElderry) Macmillan Child Grp.

Sterne, Noelle. Tyrannosaurus Wrecks: A Book of Dinosaur Riddles. Chess, Victoria, illus. LC 78-22499. 32p. (gr. 1-4). 1979. PLB 15.89 (*0-690-03960-3*, Crowell Jr Bks) HarpC Child Bks.

Swann, Brian. A Basket Full of White Eggs: Riddle-Poems. Goembel, Ponder, illus. LC 87-11220. 32p. (gr. k-3). 1988. 14.95 (*0-531-05734-8*); PLB 14.99 (*0-531-08334-9*) Orchard Bks Watts.

Swanson, June. Summit Up: Riddles about Mountains. Burke, Susan S., illus. LC 93-19157. 32p. (gr. 1-4). 1994. PLB 13.50 (*0-8225-2342-6*); pap. 3.95 (*0-8225-9842-6*) Lerner Pubns.

—Summit Up: Riddles about Mountains. (ps-3). 1994. pap. 3.95 (*0-8225-9658-X*) Lerner Pubns.

—That's for Shore: Riddles from the Beach. Burke, Susan S., illus. 32p. (gr. 1-4). 1991. PLB 11.95 (*0-8225-2332-9*) Lerner Pubns.

—That's for Shore: Riddles from the Beach. (ps-3). 1991. pap. 3.95 (*0-8225-9592-3*) Lerner Pubns.

Teitelbaum, Michael. Ghastly Giggles & Ghoulish Guffaws. Billin-Frye, Paige, illus. LC 91-60998. 96p. (Orig.). (gr. 1-6). 1992. pap. 2.99 (*0-679-81787-5*) Random Bks Yng Read.

—Why Did the Vampire Cross the Road? And Other Horrific Howlers. Billin-Frye, Paige, illus. LC 91-61001. 96p. (Orig.). (gr. 1-6). 1992. pap. 2.99 (*0-679-81788-3*) Random Bks Yng Read.

Terban, Marvin. The Dove Dove: Funny Homograph Riddles. Huffman, Tom, illus. LC 88-2611. 64p. (gr. 4-7). 1988. 12.95 (*0-89919-723-X*, Clarion Bks); pap. 6.95 (*0-89919-810-4*, Clarion Bks) HM.

—Eight Ate: A Feast of Homonym Riddles. Maestro, Giulio, illus. LC 81-12203. 64p. (gr. 1-3). 1982. 13.45 (*0-89919-067-7*, Clarion Bks); pap. 6.95 (*0-89919-086-3*, Clarion Bks) HM.

—Funny You Should Ask: How to Make up Jokes & Riddles with Wordplay. O'Brien, John, illus. 64p. (gr. 4-7). 1992. 13.95 (*0-395-60556-3*, Clarion Bks); pap. 5.95 (*0-395-58113-3*, Clarion Bks) HM.

—Hey, Hay! A Wagonful of Funny Homonym Riddles. Stevenson, Dinah, ed. Hawkes, Kevin, illus. 64p. (gr. 3-7). 1991. 14.95 (*0-395-54431-9*, Clarion Bks); pap. 5.70 (*0-395-56183-3*, Clarion Bks) HM.

—Too Hot to Hoot: Funny Palindrome Riddles. Maestro, Giulio, illus. LC 84-14942. 64p. (gr. 2-5). 1985. 13.95 (*0-89919-319-6*, Clarion Bks); pap. 6.95 (*0-89919-320-X*, Clarion Bks) HM.

Thaler, Mike. Earth Mirth: The Ecology Riddle Book. Brown, Rick, illus. LC 93-37818. 1994. text ed. write for info. (*0-7167-6521-7*); pap. text ed. write for info. (*0-7167-6529-2*) W H Freeman.

—Oinkers Away! Pig Riddles, Cartoons & Jokes. (gr. 3-6). 1989. pap. 2.50 (*0-671-67456-0*, Minstrel Bks) PB.

—The Riddle King's Camp Riddles. Harvey, Paul, illus. LC 88-63193. 32p. (gr. 1-5). 1989. pap. 1.25 (*0-394-83995-1*) Random Bks Yng Read.

—The Riddle King's Food Riddles. Harvey, Paul, illus. LC 88-63190. 32p. (gr. 1-5). 1989. pap. 1.25 (*0-394-84041-0*) Random Bks Yng Read.

—The Riddle King's Pet Riddles. Harvey, Paul, illus. LC 88-63191. 32p. (gr. 1-5). 1989. pap. 1.25 (*0-394-83977-3*) Random Bks Yng Read.

—The Riddle King's School Riddles. Harvey, Paul, illus. LC 88-63192. 32p. (gr. 1-5). 1989. pap. 1.25 (*0-394-84004-6*) Random Bks Yng Read.

Time Life Inc., Staff. Purple Parrots Eating Carrots: A Rebus Reader. Kagan, Neil, ed. 64p. (ps-2). 1991. write for info. (*0-8094-9262-8*); lib. bdg. write for info. (*0-8094-9263-6*) Time-Life.

Vaughn, Marcia. Riddle by the River. Ruffins, Reynold, illus. LC 93-46890. (gr. 1 up). 1994. write for info. (*0-382-24603-9*); pap. write for info. (*0-382-24451-6*); PLB write for info. (*0-382-24602-0*) Silver Burdett Pr.

Wallner, Alexandra. Ghoulish Giggles & Monster Riddles. Tucker, Kathy, ed. Wallner, Alexandra, illus. LC 82-10969. 32p. (gr. 1-5). 1983. PLB 8.95 (*0-8075-2863-3*) A Whitman.

Walton, Ann & Walton, Rick. Alphabatty: Riddles from A to Z. Burke, Susan S., illus. 32p. (gr. 1-4). 1991. PLB 11.95 (*0-685-49141-2*) Lerner Pubns.

Walton, Rick. Alphabatty: Riddles from A to Z. (ps-3). 1991. pap. 3.95 (*0-8225-9593-1*) Lerner Pubns.

—Hoop-la: Riddles about Basketball. (gr. 4-7). 1993. pap. 3.95 (*0-8225-9639-3*) Lerner Pubns.

—Off Base: Riddles about Baseball. (gr. 4-7). 1993. pap. 3.95 (*0-8225-9638-5*) Lerner Pubns.

—Take a Hike: Riddles about Football. (gr. 4-7). 1993. pap. 3.95 (*0-8225-9640-7*) Lerner Pubns.

Walton, Rick & Walton, Ann. Ho Ho Ho! Riddles about Santa Claus. (Illus.). 32p. (gr. 1-4). 1991. PLB 11.95 (*0-8225-2337-X*); pap. 3.95 (*0-8225-9595-8*) Lerner Pubns.

—Hoop-La: Riddles about Basketball. Burke, Susan S., illus. LC 92-25771. 1993. 11.95 (*0-8225-2339-6*) Lerner Pubns.

—I Toad You So: Riddles about Frogs & Toads. Burke, Susan S., illus. 32p. (gr. 1-4). 1991. PLB 11.95 (*0-8225-2331-0*); pap. 3.95 (*0-8225-9590-7*) Lerner Pubns.

—Off Base: Riddles about Baseball. Burke, Susan S., illus. LC 92-19857. 1993. 11.95 (*0-8225-2338-8*) Lerner Pubns.

—On with the Show: Show Me Riddles. Burke, Susan S., illus. 32p. (gr. 1-4). 1989. PLB 11.95 (*0-8225-2327-2*) Lerner Pubns.

—Take a Hike: Riddles about Football. Burke, Susan S., illus. LC 92-27011. 1993. 11.95 (*0-8225-2340-X*) Lerner Pubns.

—Weather or Not: Riddles for Rain & Shine. Burke, Susan S., illus. 32p. (gr. 1-4). 1989. PLB 8.95 (*0-8225-2329-9*) Lerner Pubns.

Wattenberg, Jane. Mrs. Mustard's Name Games. LC 92-16128. (Illus.). 48p. 1993. 7.95 (*0-8118-0259-0*) Chronicle Bks.

Williams, Linda. Big Golden Book of Riddles, Jokes, Giggles, & Rhymes. (gr. 4-7). 1993. 10.95 (*0-307-17877-3*, Golden Pr) Western Pub.

Young, Frederica. Super-Duper Jokes. (gr. 4-7). 1993. 13.00 (*0-374-37301-9*); pap. 4.95 (*0-374-47353-6*) FS&G.

Zimmerman, Andrea G. Riddle Zoo. 64p. (gr. 3-7). 1981. (Dutton) NAL-Dutton.

RIDING

see Horsemanship

RIGHT TO WORK

see Discrimination in Employment

RIGHTS, CIVIL

see Civil Rights

RINGLING BROTHERS

Glendinning, Richard & Glendinning, Sally. The Ringling Brothers: Circus Family. Hutchinson, William, illus. 80p. (gr. 2-6). 1991. Repr. of 1972 ed. lib. bdg. 12.95 (*0-7910-1468-1*) Chelsea Hse.

RINGLING BROTHERS AND BARNUM AND BAILEY CIRCUS

Duncan, Lois. The Circus Comes Home. Steinmetz, Joseph J., photos by. LC 92-7481. (Illus.). 1993. 16.95 (*0-385-30689-X*) Doubleday.

RIO GRANDE RIVER

Bragg, Bea. The Very First Thanksgiving: Pioneers on the Rio Grande. LC 89-15562. (Illus.). 64p. (Orig.). (gr. 3-5). 1989. pap. 7.95 (*0-943173-22-1*) Harbinger AZ.

RIOTS–FICTION

Bunting, Eve. Smoky Night. Diaz, David, illus. LC 93-14885. (gr. 4 up). 1994. 14.95 (*0-15-269954-6*) Harbrace.

RIOTS

Archer, Jules. Rage in the Streets: Mob Violence in America. LC 93-5710. 1994. write for info. (*0-15-277691-5*, Browndeer Pr) HarBrace.

Steele, Philip. Riots. LC 92-24195. (Illus.). 48p. (gr. 6 up). 1993. text ed. 12.95 RSBE (*0-02-786883-4*, New Discovery) Macmillan Child Grp.

RITES AND CEREMONIES

see also Baptism; Fasts and Feasts; Funeral Rites and Ceremonies; Manners and Customs; Marriage Customs and Rites;

also classes of people and ethnic groups with the subdivision Rites and Ceremonies, e.g. Jews–Rites and Ceremonies

Guentert, Kenneth. The Young Server's Book of the Mass. LC 86-60894. 88p. (gr. 6-8). 1987. pap. 4.95 (*0-89390-078-8*) Resource Pubns.

Halliburton, Warren J. Celebrations of African Heritage. LC 92-7989. (Illus.). 48p. (gr. 6). 1992. text ed. 13.95 RSBE (*0-89686-676-9*, Crestwood Hse) Macmillan Child Grp.

Liptak, Karen. Coming-of-Age: Traditions & Rituals Around the World. LC 93-1414. (Illus.). 128p. (gr. 7 up). 1994. PLB 15.90 (*1-56294-243-3*) Millbrook Pr.

Lovasik, Lawrence G. The Seven Sacraments. (Illus.). (gr. 1-6). 1978. flexible bdg 0.95 (*0-89942-278-0*, 278) Catholic Bk Pub.

RITUAL

see Rites and Ceremonies

RIVERA, DIEGO, 1886-1957

Braun, Barbara. A Weekend with Diego Rivera. LC 93-38905. 64p. 1994. 19.95 (*0-8478-1749-0*) Rizzoli Intl.

Cockcroft, James D. Diego Rivera. (Illus.). 112p. (gr. 5 up). 1991. lib. bdg. 17.95 (*0-7910-1252-2*) Chelsea Hse.

Hargrove, Jim. Diego Rivera: Mexican Muralist. LC 89-25453. (Illus.). 128p. (gr. 4 up). 1990. PLB 14.40 (*0-516-03268-2*); pap. 5.95 (*0-516-43268-0*) Childrens.

Venezia, Mike. Diego Rivera. LC 94-11650. (Illus.). 48p. (gr. 4 up). 1994. PLB 17.20 (*0-516-02299-7*); pap. 4.95 (*0-516-42299-5*) Childrens.

Winter, Jonah. Diego. Prince, Amy, tr. Winter, Jeanette, illus. LC 90-25923. (ENG & SPA.). 40p. (gr. k-4). 1991. 15.00 (*0-679-81987-8*); PLB 15.99 (*0-679-91987-2*) Knopf Bks Yng Read.

RIVERS

see also Dams; Floods; Water–Pollution; Water Power

also names of rivers

Arvetis, Chris & Palmer, Carole. Lakes & Rivers. LC 93-499. (Illus.). 1993. write for info. (*0-528-83572-6*) Rand McNally.

Ayer, Eleanor. Our Great Rivers & Waterways. (Illus.). 48p. (gr. 2-4). 1994. 13.40 (*1-56294-441-X*) Millbrook Pr.

Bains, Rae. Wonders of Rivers. Miyake, Yoshi, illus. LC 81-7423. 32p. (gr. 2-4). 1982. PLB 11.59 (*0-89375-570-2*); pap. text ed. 2.95 (*0-89375-571-0*) Troll Assocs.

Baker, Susan. First Look at Rivers. LC 91-9419. (Illus.). 32p. (gr. 1-2). 1991. PLB 17.27 (*0-8368-0679-4*) Gareth Stevens Inc.

Bender, Lionel. River. FS Staff, ed. LC 87-51706. (Illus.). 32p. (gr. 1-6). 1988. PLB 11.90 (*0-531-10554-7*) Watts.

Bentley, John & Charlton, Bill. Finding Out about Streams. (Illus.). 64p. (gr. 7-12). 1985. 19.95 (*0-7134-4425-8*, Pub. by Batsford UK) Trafalgar.

Bramwell, Martyn. Rivers & Lakes. (Illus.). 32p. (gr. 5-8). 1994. PLB write for info. (*0-531-14305-8*) Watts.

Carlisle, Norman & Carlisle, Madelyn. Rivers. LC 81-38448. (Illus.). 48p. (gr. k-4). 1982. PLB 12.85 (*0-516-01645-8*) Childrens.

Cherry, Lynne. A River Ran Wild. 1992. 14.95 (*0-15-200542-0*, HB Juv Bks) HarBrace.

Corke, Philip, illus. Rivers. 32p. (gr. 3-5). 1985. 7.95x (*0-86685-452-5*) Intl Bk Ctr.

Craighead, Charles. The Eagle & the River. Mangelsen, Tom, photos by. LC 92-23240. (Illus.). (gr. 1-5). 1994. RSBE 14.95 (*0-02-762265-7*, Macmillan Child Bk) Macmillan Child Grp.

Crump, Donald J., ed. Let's Explore a River. (Illus.). (gr. k-4). 1988. Set. 13.95 (*0-87044-741-6*); Set. PLB 16.95 (*0-87044-746-7*) Natl Geog.

Deming, Susan. The River: A Nature Panorama. Deming, Susan, illus. 7p. (ps-3). 1991. bds. 5.95 (*0-87701-812-X*) Chronicle Bks.

Emil, Jane. All about Rivers. LC 83-4868. (Illus.). 32p. (gr. 3-6). 1984. lib. bdg. 10.59 (*0-89375-979-1*); pap. text ed. 2.95 (*0-89375-980-5*) Troll Assocs.

Fowler, Allan. All along the River. LC 93-39646. (Illus.). 32p. (ps-2). 1994. PLB 10.75 (*0-516-06019-8*) Childrens.

Frahm, Randy. Rivers. LC 93-46804. 40p. 1994. 18.95 (*0-88682-708-6*) Creative Ed.

Hester, Nigel. The Living River. LC 90-32526. (Illus.). 32p. (gr. 3-5). 1991. PLB 12.40 (*0-531-14121-7*) Watts.

Jeunesse, Gallimard & Bour, Laura, eds. The River. Bour, Laura, illus. LC 92-41415. 1993. 11.95 (*0-590-47128-7*) Scholastic Inc.

Mariner, Tom. Rivers. LC 89-9824. (Illus.). 32p. (gr. 3-8). 1990. PLB 9.95 (*1-85435-191-5*) Marshall Cavendish.

Morgan, Patricia G. A River Adventure. Plunkett, Micheal, illus. LC 87-3485. 32p. (gr. 3-6). 1988. PLB 10.79 (*0-8167-1171-2*); pap. text ed. 2.95 (*0-8167-1172-0*) Troll Assocs.

Parker, Steve. Pond & River. Dowell, Philip, photos by. LC 88-1575. (Illus.). 64p. (gr. 5 up). 1988. 16.00 (*0-394-89615-7*); lib. bdg. 16.99 (*0-394-99615-1*) Knopf Bks Yng Read.

Rowland-Entwistle, Theodore. Rivers & Lakes. (Illus.). 48p. (gr. 5-8). 1987. PLB 12.95 (*0-382-09499-9*) Silver Burdett Pr.

Russell, Naomi. The Stream. Russell, Naomi, illus. LC 90-47497. 32p. (ps-1). 1991. 9.95 (*0-525-44729-6*, DCB) Dutton Child Bks.

Santrey, Laurence. Rivers. Sweat, Lynn, illus. LC 84-8818. 32p. (gr. 3-6). 1985. lib. bdg. 9.49 (*0-8167-0210-1*); pap. text ed. 2.95 (*0-8167-0211-X*) Troll Assocs.

Smalley, Mark. The Rhine. Cumming, David, illus. LC 92-24041. 48p. (gr. 5-6). 1993. PLB 22.80 (*0-8114-3102-9*) Raintree Steck-V.

Steele, Philip. River Through the Ages. Ingpen, Robert, illus. LC 91-33279. 32p. (gr. 3-6). 1993. PLB 11.89 (*0-8167-2735-X*); pap. text ed. 3.95 (*0-8167-2736-8*) Troll Assocs.

Stewart, G. On the Water. (Illus.). 32p. (gr. 3-8). 1989. lib. bdg. 15.94 (*0-86592-109-1*); 11.95s.p. (*0-685-58597-2*) Rourke Corp.

Swenson, Peter J. Secrets of Rivers & Streams. Jack, Susan, ed. Sabaka, Donna, illus. 90p. (gr. 4-10). 1982. pap. 3.95 (*0-930096-31-2*) G Gannett.

Taylor, Barbara. Rivers & Oceans: Geography Facts & Experiments. LC 92-28421. (Illus.). 32p. (gr. 1-4). 1993. 10.95 (*1-85697-876-1*, Kingfisher LKC); pap. 5.95 (*1-85697-939-3*) LKC.

Valiappa, Al. Story of Our Rivers: Book II. Chakravarty, Pranab, illus. (gr. 1-9). 1979. pap. 2.50 (*0-89744-184-2*) Auromere.

Wood, Jenny. Waterfalls: Nature's Thundering Splendor. (Illus.). 32p. (gr. 3-4). 1991. PLB 17.27 (*0-8368-0633-6*) Gareth Stevens Inc.

RIVERS–FICTION

Baer, Judy. Silent Tears No More. LC 89-82689. 144p. (Orig.). (gr. 7-10). 1990. 3.99 (*1-55661-119-6*) Bethany Hse.

Beveridge, Barbara. The Stream. Crossett, Warren, illus. LC 92-33738. 1993. 3.75 (*0-383-03657-7*) SRA Schl Grp.

Clark, Billy C. Song of the River. rev. ed. Gifford, James M., et al, eds. LC 92-31483. (Illus.). 176p. (gr. 7 up). 1993. Repr. of 1957 ed. 15.00 (*0-945084-35-8*) J Stuart Found.

Coran, Pierre. River at Risk. (Illus.). 32p. (gr. k-2). 1991. 12.95 (*0-89565-747-3*) Childs World.

Garden, Nancy. Peace, O River. 245p. (gr. 7 up). 1986. 15.00 (*0-374-35763-3*) FS&G.

Gilliland, Judith H. River. (ps-3). 1993. 14.95 (*0-395-55963-4*, Clarion Bks) HM.

Grahame, Kenneth. The Wind in the Willows. Shepard, Ernest H., illus. LC 88-8046. 272p. (ps up). 1989. pap. 4.95 (*0-689-71310-X*, Aladdin) Macmillan Child Grp.

Halpern, Shari. My River. Halpern, Shari, illus. LC 91-33582. 32p. (ps-2). 1992. RSBE 13.95 (*0-02-741980-0*, Macmillan Child Bk) Macmillan Child Grp.

Kovacs, Deborah. Moonlight on the River. Shattuck, William, illus. LC 92-28377. (ps-3). 1993. 13.99 (*0-670-84463-2*) Viking Child Bks.

Lillegard, Dee. The Hee Haw River. 1995. write for info. (*0-8050-2375-5*) H Holt & Co.

Locker, Thomas. Where the River Begins. (Illus.). 32p. 1993. pap. 4.99 (*0-14-054595-6*) Puffin Bks.

Meigs, Cornelia. Swift Rivers. Orr, Forrest W., illus. 288p. (Orig.). (gr. 4-7). 1994. pap. 6.95 (*0-8027-7419-9*) Walker & Co.

Paulsen, Gary. River. 1993. pap. 4.50 (*0-440-40753-2*) Dell.

Roddy, Lee. The Hermit of Mad River. 132p. (gr. 3-7). 1988. pap. 4.99 (*0-89693-475-6*, Victor Books) SP Pubns.

Sanders, Scott R. The Floating House. Cogancherry, Helen, illus. LC 94-15277. 1995. 15.00 (*0-02-778137-2*, BRadbury Pr) Macmillan Child Grp.

Say, Allen. A River Dream. Say, Allen, illus. 32p. (gr. k-3). 1993. pap. 4.95 (*0-395-65749-0*) HM.

Stevenson, James. The Pattaconk Brook. LC 92-29404. 32p. (ps up). 1993. 14.00 (*0-688-11954-9*); lib. bdg. 13.93 (*0-688-11955-7*) Greenwillow.

RIVERS–POLLUTION

see Water–Pollution

ROAD CONSTRUCTION

see Roads

ROAD RUNNER (BIRD)

Reese, Bob. Rapid Robert Roadrunner. LC 81-6090. (Illus.). 24p. (ps-2). 1981. pap. 2.95 (*0-516-42305-3*) Childrens.

ROAD SIGNS

see Signs and Signboards

ROADS

Gibbons, Gail. From Path to Highway: The Story of the Boston Post Road. Gibbons, Gail, illus. LC 85-47897. 32p. (gr. 1-4). 1986. (Crowell Jr Bks); PLB 14.89 (*0-690-04514-X*) HarpC Child Bks.

—New Road! LC 82-45917. (Illus.). 32p. (gr. k-4). 1983. (Crowell Jr Bks); PLB 14.89 (*0-690-04343-0*) HarpC Child Bks.

—New Road! Gibbons, Gail, illus. LC 82-45917. 32p. (gr. k-4). 1987. pap. 4.95 (*0-06-446059-2*, Trophy) HarpC Child Bks.

Hennessy, B. G. Road Builders. Taback, Simms, illus. 32p. (ps-2). 1994. 14.99 (*0-670-83390-8*) Viking Child Bks.

Royston, Angela & Thompson, Graham. Monster Road Builders. (Illus.). 24p. (ps-2). 1989. 9.95 (*0-8120-6126-8*) Barron.

Sauvain, Philip. Roads. Stefoff, Rebecca, ed. LC 90-40359. (Illus.). 48p. (gr. 4-7). 1990. PLB 17.26 (*0-944483-77-1*) Garrett Ed Corp.

Spangenburg, Ray & Moser, Diane. The Story of America's Roads. (Illus.). 96p. (gr. 6-9). 1991. lib. bdg. 18.95x (*0-8160-2255-0*) Facts on File.

Steele, Philip. Road Through the Ages. Howett, Andrew & Davidson, Gordon, illus. LC 91-35878. 32p. (gr. 3-6). 1993. PLB 11.89 (*0-8167-2737-6*); pap. text ed. 3.95 (*0-8167-2738-4*) Troll Assocs.

Unstead, R. J. Travel by Road Through the Ages. (Illus.). (gr. 7-10). 1983. 14.95 (*0-7136-1812-4*) Dufour.

Williams, Owen. How Roads Are Made. (Illus.). 32p. 1989. 12.95x (*0-8160-2041-8*) Facts on File.

ROADS–FICTION

Cohen, Daniel. Railway Ghosts & Highway Horrors. Marchesi, Stephen, illus. LC 91-11161. 112p. (gr. 4 up). 1991. 13.95 (*0-525-65071-7*, Cobblehill Bks) Dutton Child Bks.

Goodall, John S. The Story of a Main Street. Goodall, John S., illus. LC 87-60644. 60p. 1987. SBE 14.95 (*0-689-50436-5*, M K McElderry) Macmillan Child Grp.

Lyon, George-Ella. Who Came Down That Road? Catalanotto, Peter, illus. LC 91-20742. 32p. (ps-2). 1992. 15.95 (*0-531-05987-1*); PLB 15.99 (*0-531-08587-2*) Orchard Bks Watts.

ROANOKE ISLAND–HISTORY

Bosco, Peter I. Roanoke: The Story of the Lost Colony. LC 91-19887. (Illus.). 64p. (gr. 4-6). 1992. PLB 14.90 (*1-56294-111-9*) Millbrook Pr.

Larsen, Anita. The Roanoke Missing Persons Case. Watling, James, illus. LC 91-19524. 48p. (gr. 5-6). 1992. text ed. 11.95 RSBE (*0-89686-619-X*, Crestwood Hse) Macmillan Child Grp.

ROBBERS AND OUTLAWS

Collins, William & Levene, Bruce. Black Bart: The True Story of California's Most Famous Stagecoach Robber. LC 91-67893. (Illus.). 224p. (Orig.). (gr. 4-7). 1992. pap. 15.95 (*0-933391-10-2*) Pac Transcript.

Gintzler, A. S. Rough & Ready Outlaws & Lawmen. (Illus.). 48p. (gr. 4-7). 1994. 12.95 (*1-56261-163-1*) John Muir.

Green, Carl R. & Sanford, William R. Outlaws & Lawmen of the Wild West Series, 6 bks. (Illus.). (gr. 4-10). Set. lib. bdg. 89.70 (*0-89490-391-8*) Enslow Pubs.

Lindgren, Astrid. Ronia, the Robber's Daughter. (Illus.). 176p. (gr. 4-7). 1985. pap. 3.99 (*0-14-031720-1*, Puffin) Puffin Bks.

Stewart, Gail B. Where Lies Butch Cassidy? LC 91-25368. (Illus.). 48p. (gr. 5-6). 1992. text ed. 11.95 RSBE (*0-89686-618-1*, Crestwood Hse) Macmillan Child Grp.

ROBBERS AND OUTLAWS–FICTION

Ahlberg, Allan. Burglar Bill. Ahlberg, Janet, illus. 1992. pap. 3.99 (*0-14-050301-3*) Viking Child Bks.

Alcock, Vivien. Kind of Thief. (gr. 4-7). 1994. pap. 3.50 (*0-440-40916-0*) Dell.

Alexander, Martha. We're in Big Trouble, Blackboard Bear. Alexander, Martha, illus. LC 79-20631. (ps-2). 1980. Dial Bks Young.

Avi. Emily Upham's Revenge. ALC Staff, ed. Zelinsky, Paul, illus. LC 92-9572. 192p. (gr. 5 up). 1992. pap. 3.95 (*0-688-11899-2*, Pub. by Beech Tree Bks) Morrow.

—Man from the Sky. ALC Staff, ed. LC 92-1496. 96p. (gr. 5 up). 1992. pap. 3.95 (*0-688-11897-6*, Pub. by Beech Tree Bks) Morrow.

Bains, Rae. Case of the Great Train Robbery. Harvey, Paul, illus. LC 81-7525. 48p. (gr. 2-4). 1982. PLB 10.89 (*0-89375-588-5*); pap. text ed. 3.50 (*0-89375-589-3*) Troll Assocs.

Berry, James. A Thief in the Village & Other Stories. LC 87-24695. 160p. (gr. 6 up). 1988. PLB 12.95 (*0-531-05745-3*); PLB 12.99 (*0-531-08345-4*) Orchard Bks Watts.

Best, Elizabeth. Mr. McGillicuddy's Clocks. Culic, Ned, illus. LC 93-26928. 1994. 4.25 (*0-383-03765-4*) SRA Schl Grp.

Blackmore, Richard D. Lorna Doone. 272p. (gr. 4-6). 1984. pap. 2.95 (*0-14-035021-7*, Puffin) Puffin Bks.

Cohen, Caron L. Bronco Dogs. Shepherd, Roni, illus. LC 90-47952. 32p. (ps-3). 1991. 12.95 (*0-525-44721-0*, DCB) Dutton Child Bks.

Collier, James L. My Crooked Family. LC 90-27747. 288p. (gr. 5-9). 1991. pap. 15.00 jacketed, 3-pc. bdg. (*0-671-74224-8*, S&S BFYR) S&S Trade.

Dickens, Charles. Oliver Twist. Martin, Les, adapted by. Zallinger, Jean, illus. LC 89-24279. 96p. (gr. 2-6). 1990. PLB 5.99 (*0-679-90391-7*); pap. 2.99 (*0-679-80391-2*) Random Bks Yng Read.

Enderle, Judith R., et al. Nell Nugget & the Cow Caper. Yalowitz, Paul, photos by. LC 94-10189. 1995. 15.95 (*0-02-733385-X*, Four Winds) Macmillan Child Grp.

Fleischman, Sid. The Whipping Boy. Sis, Peter, illus. LC 85-17555. 96p. (gr. 2-6). 1986. PLB 15.00 (*0-688-06216-4*) Greenwillow.

Galbraith, Kathryn O. Something Suspicious. 128p. (gr. 3 up). 1987. pap. 2.50 (*0-380-70253-3*, Camelot) Avon.

Galt, Hugh. Horse Thief. 208p. (gr. 5-10). 1993. pap. 9.95 (*0-86278-278-3*, Pub. by OBrien Pr IE) Dufour.

Gezi, Kal & Bradford, Ann. The Mystery in the Secret Club House. McLean, Mina G., illus. LC 78-6418. (gr. k-3). 1978. PLB 12.95 (*0-89565-027-4*) Childs World.

Haseley, Dennis. The Thieves' Market. Desimini, Lisa, illus. LC 90-38440. 32p. (gr. 1-5). 1991. HarpC Child Bks.

Hogrogian, Nonny. The Contest. LC 75-40389. (Illus.). 32p. (gr. k-3). 1976. 16.00 (*0-688-80042-4*); PLB 15.93 (*0-688-84042-6*) Greenwillow.

Johnson, Paul B. Frank Fister's Hidden Talent: Story & Pictures. LC 93-4883. 1994. write for info. (*0-531-06813-7*); lib. bdg. write for info. (*0-531-08663-1*) Orchard Bks Watts.

Kahrimanis, Leola. Blue Hills Robbery. Roberts, M., ed. (Illus.). 128p. (gr. 6-8). 1991. 10.95 (*0-89015-753-7*) Sunbelt Media.

McPhail, David. Moony B. Finch, Fastest Draw in the West. LC 93-37408. 1994. lib. bdg. 12.95 (*0-307-17554-5*, Artsts Writrs) Western Pub.

Mahy, Margaret. Great Piratical Rumbustification the Librarian & the Robbers. Blake, Quentin, illus. LC 85-45966. 64p. 1986. 11.95 (*0-87923-629-9*) Godine.

Martin, Ann M. Jessi and the Jewel Thieves: Baby-sitters Club Mystery Ser. (gr. 4-7). 1993. pap. 3.50 (*0-590-44959-1*) Scholastic Inc.

Novak, Matt. Elmer Blunt's Open House. LC 91-38424. (Illus.). 24p. (ps-1). 1992. 14.95 (*0-531-05998-7*); PLB 14.99 (*0-531-08598-8*) Orchard Bks Watts.

Noyes, Alfred. The Highwayman. Keeping, Charles, illus. 32p. 1987. pap. 7.50 (*0-19-272133-X*) OUP.

Oana. Timmy Tiger & the Masked Bandit. LC 80-82955. (Illus.). 32p. (ps-4). 1981. PLB 9.95x (*0-87783-161-0*) Oddo.

Palazzo-Craig, Janet. The Upside-Down Boy. Burns, Ray, illus. LC 85-14067. 48p. (Orig.). (gr. 1-3). 1986. PLB 10.59 (*0-8167-0604-2*); pap. text ed. 3.50 (*0-8167-0605-0*) Troll Assocs.

Parish, Peggy. The Cats' Burglar. Sweat, Lynn, illus. LC 82-11751. 64p. (gr. 1-3). 1983. 12.95 (*0-688-01825-4*); PLB 13.93 (*0-688-01826-2*) Greenwillow.

Roberts, Willo D. Jo & the Bandit. LC 91-4100. 192p. (gr. 4-7). 1992. SBE 15.00 (*0-689-31745-X*, Atheneum Child Bk) Macmillan Child Grp.

Rosenbloom, Joseph. Deputy Dan & the Bank Robbers. Raglin, Tim, illus. LC 84-159969. 48p. (gr. 2-3). 1985. lib. bdg. 7.99 (*0-394-97045-4*); 3.50 (*0-394-87045-X*) Random Bks Yng Read.

Saller, Carol. Pug, Slug, & Doug the Thug. Redenbaugh, Vicki J., illus. LC 92-44340. 1993. 13.95 (*0-87614-803-8*) Carolrhoda Bks.

Soto, Gary. Crazy Weekend. LC 93-13967. 144p. (gr. 3-7). 1994. 13.95 (*0-590-47814-1*) Scholastic Inc.

Steig, William. El Verdadero Ladron: The Real Thief. (ps-3). 1993. 15.00 (*0-374-30458-0*, Mirasol) FS&G.

Stevens, Kathleen. Aunt Skilly & the Stranger. Parker, Robert A., illus. LC 93-38235. 32p. (ps-2). 1994. 14.95 (*0-395-68712-8*, Ticknor & Flds Yng Read) Ticknor & Fields.

Stine, Megan & Stine, H. William. Young Indiana Jones & the Lost Gold of Durango. 132p. (Orig.). (gr. 3-7). 1993. pap. 3.50 (*0-679-84926-2*, Bullseye Bks) Random Bks Yng Read.

Swan, Walter. Stick 'em up! I've Got You Covered! Swan, Deloris, ed. Asch, Connie, illus. 16p. (Orig.). (ps-8). 1989. pap. 1.50 (*0-927176-03-3*) Swan Enterp.

Ungerer, Tomi. The Three Robbers. 2nd ed. Ungerer, Tomi, illus. LC 91-246. 40p. (gr. k-3). 1991. pap. 4.95 (*0-689-71511-0*, Aladdin) Macmillan Child Grp.

—Los Tres Bandidos - The Three Robbers. Azaola, Miguel, tr. Ungerer, Tomi, illus. (SPA.). 36p. (gr. 2-4). 1990. pap. write for info. (*84-204-5084-7*) Santillana.

Wettasinghe, Sybil. The Umbrella Thief. (Illus.). 32p. (ps-3). 1987. 11.95 (*0-916291-12-X*) Kane-Miller Bk.

Wood, Audrey. Twenty-Four Robbers. Wood, Audrey, illus. LC 90-46182. 32p. (ps-2). 1989. 7.95 (*0-85953-100-7*); pap. 3.95 (*0-85953-324-7*) Childs Play.

Wright, Bob. Gold Coin Robbery. Bourne, Phyllis & Tusquets, Eugenia, trs. (SPA & ENG., Illus.). 96p. (gr. 1-5). 1989. pap. text ed. 4.95 (*0-87879-667-3*) High Noon Bks.

Yates, Elizabeth. Hue & Cry. 182p. (gr. 7-12). 1991. pap. 4.95 (*0-89084-536-0*) Bob Jones Univ Pr.

ROBESON, PAUL

Greenfield, Eloise. Paul Robeson. Ford, George, illus. LC 74-13663. 40p. (gr. 1-5). 1975. PLB 15.89 (*0-690-00660-8*, Crowell Jr Bks) HarpC Child Bks.

Hamilton, Virginia. Paul Robeson: The Life & Times of a Free Black Man. LC 72-82892. (Illus.). 240p. (gr. 7 up). 1974. 14.89 (*0-06-022189-5*) HarpC Child Bks.

Holmes, Burnham. Paul Robeson: A Voice of Struggle. Shenton, James., intro. by. LC 94-12665. (gr. 5 up). 1994. write for info. (*0-8114-2381-6*) Raintree Steck-V.

McKissack, Patricia & McKissack, Fredrick. Paul Robeson: A Voice to Remember. LC 92-2582. (Illus.). 32p. (gr. 1-4). 1992. lib. bdg. 12.95 (*0-89490-310-1*) Enslow Pubs.

Paul Robeson: Mini Play. (gr. 5 up). 1977. 6.50 (*0-89550-371-9*) Stevens & Shea.

Plumpp, Sterling. Paul Robeson. Burrowes, Adjoa J., illus. 1992. pap. 5.95 (*0-88378-065-8*) Third World.

Samuels, Steven. Paul Robeson. King, Coretta Scott, intro. by. (Illus.). 112p. (Orig.). (gr. 5 up). 1988. 17.95 (*1-55546-608-7*); pap. 9.95 (*0-7910-0206-3*) Chelsea Hse.

ROBIN HOOD

Creswick, Paul. Robin Hood. Wyeth, N. C., illus. LC 92-50796. 376p. (gr. 6 up). 1993. 16.95 (*1-56138-265-5*) Running Pr.

Green, Roger L. Adventures of Robin Hood. (Orig.). (gr. 2-5). 1984. pap. 2.99 (*0-14-035034-9*, Puffin) Puffin Bks.

Green, Roger L., retold by. The Adventures of Robin Hood. LC 94-5862. 1994. 13.95 (*0-679-43636-7*, Evrymans Lib Childs) Knopf.

Haynes, Sarah, retold by. Robin Hood. Benson, Patrick, illus. LC 89-33419. 80p. (gr. 4-6). 1989. 12.95 (*0-8050-1206-0*, Bks Young Read) H Holt & Co.

Heyer, Carol, retold by. & illus. Robin Hood. LC 93-18591. 32p. (ps-3). 1993. 14.95 (*0-8249-8634-2*, Ideals Child); PLB 15.00 (*0-8249-8648-2*) Hambleton-Hill.

Ingle, Annie, adapted by. Robin Hood. reissued ed. D'Andrea, Domenick, illus. LC 90-23078. 96p. (Orig.). (gr. 2-6). 1993. pap. 2.99 (*0-679-81045-5*) Random Bks Yng Read.

Leeson, Robert, retold by. The Story of Robin Hood. Lofthouse, Barbara, illus. LC 94-651. 96p. (gr. 5 up). 1994. 16.95 (*1-85697-988-1*, Kingfisher LKC) LKC.

McGovern, Ann. Robin Hood of Sherwood Forest. 128p. (gr. 3-7). 1991. pap. 2.95 (*0-590-45441-2*) Scholastic Inc.

Miles, Bernard. Robin Hood: His Life & Legend. Ambrus, Victor G., illus. LC 79-64615. 128p. (gr. 4 up). 12.95 (*1-56288-412-3*) Checkerboard.

Pawczuk, Eugene. Robin Hood. Pronk, Mary, ed. Pawczuk, Eugene, illus. 32p. (Orig.). (gr. 1-6). 1992. PLB 15.55 (*0-88625-266-0*); pap. 5.95 (*0-88625-264-4*) Durkin Hayes Pub.

Pyle, Howard. The Merry Adventures of Robin Hood. Pyle, Howard, illus. LC 68-55820. xxii, 296p. (gr. 3-6). 1968. pap. 6.95 (*0-486-22043-5*) Dover.

—The Merry Adventures of Robin Hood. Mattern, Joanne, ed. Sauber, Robert, illus. LC 92-12702. 48p. (gr. 3-6). 1992. PLB 12.89 (*0-8167-2858-5*); pap. text ed. 3.95 (*0-8167-2859-3*) Troll Assocs.

—Robin Hood. abr. ed. Arneson, D. J., retold by. Clift, Eva, illus. 128p. 1991. pap. 2.95 (*1-56156-028-6*) Kidsbks.

Robin Hood. 1988. 2.98 (*0-671-09223-5*) S&S Trade.

Storr, Catherine, retold by. Robin Hood. LC 83-24417. (Illus.). 32p. (gr. k-5). 1984. PLB 19.97 (*0-8172-2109-3*); PLB 29.28 incl. cassette (*0-8172-2235-9*) Raintree Steck-V.

Vivian, E. Charles. Adventures of Robin Hood. Vivian, E. Charles, illus. (gr. 5 up). 1965. pap. 1.75 (*0-8049-0067-1*, CL-67) Airmont.

Wu, William F. Time Tours No. 1: Robin Hood Ambush. 1990. pap. 3.50 (*0-06-106003-8*, Harp PBks) HarpC.

ROBINS

Robin Bird House. 1993. 9.95 (*1-56828-049-1*) Red Jacket Pr.

ROBINS–FICTION

Kent, Jack. Round Robin. Kent, Jack, illus. 32p. (ps-3). 1984. P-H.

Wise Robin. (ARA., Illus.). (gr. 1-4). 1987. 3.95x (*0-86685-243-3*) Intl Bk Ctr.

Yost, Carolyn K. The Robins Knew. Gardner, Katherine W., illus. 32p. (gr. k-2). 1991. pasted 2.50 (*0-87403-817-0*, 24-03917) Standard Pub.

ROBINSON, BROOKS CALBERT, 1937-

Wolff, Rick. Brooks Robinson. Murray, Jim, intro. by. (Illus.). 64p. (gr. 3 up). 1991. lib. bdg. 14.95 (*0-7910-1186-0*) Chelsea Hse.

ROBINSON, FRANK, 1935-

Macht, Norm. Frank Robinson. Murray, Jim, intro. by. (Illus.). 64p. (gr. 3 up). 1991. lib. bdg. 14.95 (*0-7910-1187-9*) Chelsea Hse.

ROBINSON, JOHN ROOSEVELT, 1919-1972

Adler, David A. Jackie Robinson, He Was the First. LC 88-32394. (Illus.). 48p. (gr. 2-5). 1989. reinforced bdg. 14.95 (*0-8234-0734-9*) Holiday.

—Jackie Robinson: He Was the First. Casilla, Robert, illus. LC 88-32394. 48p. (gr. 2-5). 1990. pap. 5.95 (*0-8234-0799-3*) Holiday.

—A Picture Book of Jackie Robinson. Casilla, Robert, illus. LC 93-27224. (ps-3). 1994. reinforced bdg. 15.95 (*0-8234-1122-2*) Holiday.

Brandt, Keith. Jackie Robinson: A Life of Courage. Ramsey, Marcy, illus. LC 91-17852. 48p. (gr. 4-6). 1992. PLB 10.79 (*0-8167-2505-5*); pap. text ed. 3.50 (*0-8167-2506-3*) Troll Assocs.

Cohen, Barbara. Thank You, Jackie Robinson. Cuffari, Richard, illus. LC 87-29341. (gr. 3-6). 1988. PLB 15.00 (*0-688-07909-1*) Lothrop.

—Thank You, Jackie Robinson. 1989. pap. 2.95 (*0-590-42378-9*) Scholastic Inc.

Davidson, Margaret. The Story of Jackie Robinson: Bravest Man in Baseball. (Orig.). (gr. k-6). 1988. pap. 3.50 (*0-440-40019-8*, YB) Dell.

Diamond, Arthur. Jackie Robinson. LC 92-19871. (Illus.). 112p. (gr. 5-8). 1992. PLB 14.95 (*1-56006-029-8*) Lucent Bks.

Farr, Naunerle C. Babe Ruth-Jackie Robinson. Caravana, Tony & Cruz, Nardo, illus. (gr. 4-12). 1979. pap. text ed. 2.95 (*0-88301-359-2*); wkbk 1.25 (*0-88301-383-5*) Pendulum Pr.

Farrell, Edward. Young Jackie Robinson, Baseball Hero. Stuart, Dennis, illus. LC 91-26480. 32p. (gr. k-2). 1992. text ed. 11.59 (*0-8167-2536-5*); pap. text ed. 2.95 (*0-8167-2537-3*) Troll Assocs.

Golenbock, Peter. Teammates. Bacon, Paul, illus. (gr. 1-4). 1990. 15.95 (*0-15-200603-6*) HarBrace.

Grabowski, John. Jackie Robinson. Murray, Jim, intro. by. (Illus.). 64p. (gr. 3 up). 1991. lib. bdg. 14.95 (*0-7910-1188-7*) Chelsea Hse.

Green, Carl R. & Sanford, William R. Jackie Robinson. LC 91-23921. (Illus.). 48p. (gr. 5). 1992. text ed. 11.95 RSBE (*0-89686-743-9*, Crestwood Hse) Macmillan Child Grp.

Greene, Carol. Jackie Robinson: Baseball's First Black Major Leaguer. Dobson, Steven, illus. LC 89-28816. 48p. (gr. k-3). 1990. PLB 12.85 (*0-516-04211-4*); pap. 4.95 (*0-516-44211-2*) Childrens.

Keyla Activity Book: Jackie Robinson. 24p. (gr. 4-6). 1992. pap. text ed. 4.95 (*1-882962-03-6*) Keyla.

O'Connor, Jim. Jackie Robinson & the Story of All-Black Baseball. Butcher, Jim, illus. LC 88-18466. 48p. (Orig.). (gr. 2-4). 1989. PLB 7.99 (*0-394-92456-8*); pap. 3.50 (*0-394-82456-3*) Random Bks Yng Read.

Reiser, Howard. Jackie Robinson: Baseball Pioneer. Rich, Mary P., ed. LC 91-28617. (Illus.). 64p. (gr. 3-5). 1992. PLB 12.90 (*0-531-20095-7*) Watts.

Robinson, Jackie & Duckett, Alfred. Breakthrough to the Big League: The Story of Jackie Robinson. LC 90-48588. (Illus.). 160p. (gr. 6-10). 1991. PLB 13.95 (*1-55905-094-2*) Marshall Cavendish.

Sabin, Francene. Jackie Robinson. Sheean, Michael, illus. LC 84-2603. 32p. (gr. 3-6). 1985. PLB 9.49 (*0-8167-0164-4*); pap. text ed. 2.95 (*0-8167-0165-2*) Troll Assocs.

Scott, Richard. Jackie Robinson. King, Coretta Scott, intro. by. (Illus.). 112p. (Orig.). (gr. 5 up). 1987. 17.95 (*1-55546-609-5*); pap. 9.95 (*0-7910-0200-4*) Chelsea Hse.

Shorto, Russell. Jackie Robinson & the Breaking of the Color Barrier. (Illus.). 32p. (gr. 2-4). 1991. PLB 12.90 (*1-878841-15-7*); pap. 4.95 (*1-878841-35-1*) Millbrook Pr.

Weber, Bruce. Jackie Robinson: Classic Sports Shots. 1993. pap. 1.25 (*0-590-47021-3*) Scholastic Inc.

Weidhorn, Manfred. Jackie Robinson. LC 92-15248. (Illus.). 160p. (gr. 5-9). 1993. SBE 15.95 (*0-689-31644-5*, Atheneum Child Bk) Macmillan Child Grp.

Weinberg, Lawrence. Jackie Robinson. Ford, George, illus. 48p. (gr. 2-4). 1988. pap. 2.50 (*0-681-40690-9*) Longmeadow Pr.

ROBOTS

Berger, Fredericka. Robots - What They Are, What They Do. Huffman, Tom, illus. LC 91-14128. 48p. (gr. 1 up). 1992. 14.00 (*0-688-09863-0*); PLB 13.93 (*0-688-09864-9*) Greenwillow.

Cummings, Richard. Make Your Own Robots. 1985. 8.95 (*0-679-20686-8*) McKay.

Greene, Carol. Robots. LC 82-17872. (Illus.). 48p. (gr. k-4). 1983. PLB 12.85 (*0-516-01684-9*); pap. 4.95 (*0-516-41684-7*) Childrens.

Gutmann, John W. Robot Hobby: The Complete Manual for Individuals & Clubs. (Illus.). 320p. (Orig.). (gr. 5-12). 1992. text ed. 36.95 (*0-9634272-5-3*); pap. 29.95 (*0-9634272-4-5*) Machine Pr.

Harrar, George. Radical Robots: Can You Be Replaced? (Illus.). 48p. (gr. 5 up). 1990. (S&S BFYR); (S&S BFYR) S&S Trade.

Hitzeroth, Deborah. Robots: Mechanical Laborers. (Illus.). (gr. 5-8). Date not set. 15.95 (*1-56006-254-1*) Lucent Bks.

Lauber, Patricia. Get Ready for Robots. Kelley, True, illus. LC 85-48255. 32p. (ps-3). 1987. PLB 13.89i (*0-690-04578-6*, Crowell Jr Bks) HarpC Child Bks.

Pouts-Lajus, Serge. Robots y Ordenadores (Robots & Computers) Villanueva, Marciano, tr. Davot, Francois, illus. (SPA.). 96p. (gr. 4 up). 1992. PLB 15.90 (*1-56294-178-X*) Millbrook Pr.

Riehecky, Janet. Robots: Here They Come! Hohag, Linda, illus. LC 90-30634. 32p. (ps-2). 1990. PLB 13.95 (*0-89565-577-2*) Childs World.

Salant, Michael A. Our Industrious Robots: A Guide to What Robots Can Do & How They Work. LC 84-90027. (Illus.). 128p. (gr. 6 up). Date not set. 17.95 (*0-9609288-3-9*); pap. 12.95 (*0-9609288-2-0*) M A Salant.

Silverstein, Alvin & Silverstein, Virginia B. The Robots Are Here. LC 83-9555. (Illus.). 128p. (gr. 5-9). 1986. P-H.

Skurzynski, Gloria. Robots: Your High-Tech World. LC 89-70805. (Illus.). 64p. (gr. 4 up). 1990. SBE 16.95 (*0-02-782917-0*, Bradbury Pr) Macmillan Child Grp.

Sylvester, Diane. Inventions, Robots, Future. 112p. (gr. 4-6). 1984. 9.95 (*0-88160-108-X*, LW 905) Learning Wks.

Thro, Ellen. Robotics. (Illus.). 128p. (gr. 7 up). 1993. PLB 17.95x (*0-8160-2628-9*) Facts on File.

Vowles, Andrew. Robotics. Bastien, Charles, illus. 32p. (gr. 5-9). 1985. pap. 5.95 (*0-88625-113-3*) Durkin Hayes Pub.

ROBOTS–FICTION

Altman, Adelaide. Professor Pishposh & the Robots. Altman, Adelaide, illus. 48p. (ps-2). 1988. 12.95 (*0-933905-05-X*); pap. 9.95 (*0-933905-16-5*) Claycomb Pr.

Asimov, Janet & Asimov, Isaac. Norby & the Court Jester. 128p. (gr. 3-7). 1991. 14.95 (*0-8027-8131-4*); PLB 15.85 (*0-8027-8132-2*) Walker & Co.

—Norby & the Queen's Necklace. LC 86-11120. 144p. (gr. 4-9). 1986. 11.95 (*0-8027-6659-5*); PLB 12.85 (*0-8027-6660-9*) Walker & Co.

—Norby & Yobo's Great Adventure. 224p. (gr. 4-9). 1989. 12.95 (*0-8027-6893-8*); PLB 13.85 (*0-8027-6894-6*) Walker & Co.

—Norby, the Mixed up Robot. LC 82-25173. 96p. (gr. 5-7). 1983. PLB 10.85 (*0-8027-6496-7*) Walker & Co.

Black, Christopher. The Android Invasion. (Orig.). (gr. 4-8). 1984. pap. 2.50 (*0-440-40081-3*, YB) Dell.

Cone, Molly. Mishmash. MacDonald, Patricia, ed. Shortall, Leonard, illus. 128p. 1991. pap. 2.95 (*0-671-70937-2*, Minstrel Bks) PB.

—Mishmash. (gr. 4-7). 1962. 13.95 (*0-395-06711-1*) HM.

Fettig, Art. The Three Robots Find a Grandpa. Carpenter, Joe, illus. LC 84-80378. 96p. (Orig.). (gr. k-7). 1984. pap. 3.95 (*0-9601334-8-8*); cassette incl. Growth Unltd.

Gallo, Donald R. Short Circuits. 1993. pap. 4.99 (*0-440-21889-6*) Dell.

Hautzig, Deborah. Night of Sentinels. 1994. 7.99 (*0-679-96029-5*); pap. 3.50 (*0-679-86029-0*) Random.

Herge. Adventures of Tintin, Vol. 1. (gr. 4-7). 1994. 15.95 (*0-316-35940-8*) Little.

—Adventures of Tintin, Vol. 2. (gr. 4-7). 1994. 15.95 (*0-316-35942-4*) Little.

—Adventures of Tintin, Vol. 3. (gr. 4-7). 1994. 15.95 (*0-316-35944-0*) Little.

Hoban, Lillian & Hoban, Phoebe. The Laziest Robot in Zone One. Hoban, Lillian, illus. LC 82-48613. 64p. (gr. k-3). 1983. HarpC Child Bks.

Hoover, H. M. Orvis. 192p. (gr. 4 up). 1990. pap. 3.95 (*0-14-032113-6*, Puffin) Puffin Bks.

Kroll, Steven. Otto. Delaney, Ned, illus. LC 82-19024. 48p. (ps-3). 1983. 5.95 (*0-8193-1105-7*); PLB 5.95 (*0-8193-1106-5*) Parents.

Lorkowski, Tommy. Dr. Nim & the Nombex. LC 94-60703. (Illus.). 30p. (gr. 4 up). 1994. pap. 9.95 (*0-914127-20-9*) Univ Class. You liked stories by Dr. Seuss, you will love DR. NIM & THE NOMBEX. This exciting book in full color is 8" X 11" with 80# coated quality paper. Dr. Nim became concerned about the hard work the people of Nime had to perform. Working in his lab he invented a robot & named it Nombex. Nombex soon was able to relieve the people of their many tasks such as laying bricks, & all the other tasks they had to perform. He even fed them so they soon lost control of their hands, arms & legs since they no longer used them. You will find out what happened to the Nimians as you read the story. It will cause you to wonder if there are any Nimians in your community. These beautiful full-page illustrations are classics in themselves. Book II, DR. NIM & THE STRANGE QUEST will be available soon.
Publisher Provided Annotation.

Mahy, Margaret. Raging Robots & Unruly Uncles. Stevenson, Peter, illus. 94p. (gr. 3-7). 1993. 13.95 (*0-87951-469-8*) Overlook Pr.

Maris, Ron. Rescuing Robot. (Illus.). 32p. (ps-k). 1992. 16.95 (*1-85681-260-X*, Pub. by J MacRae UK) Trafalgar.

Pienkowski, Jan. Robot. Pienkowski, Jan, illus. 12p. (gr. 1 up). 1981. 9.95 (*0-440-07459-2*) Delacorte.

—Robot. 1992. 15.00 (*0-440-40539-4*, YB) Dell.

Robert's Robot. (Illus.). (ps-2). 1991. PLB 6.95 (*0-8136-5145-X*, TK3397); pap. 3.50 (*0-8136-5645-1*, TK3398) Modern Curr.

Robin Drake, a Robot. (Illus.). (ps-2). 1991. PLB 6.95 (*0-8136-5165-4*, TK3835); pap. 3.50 (*0-8136-5665-6*, TK3836) Modern Curr.

Teitelbaum, Michael. Sonic the Hedgehog. Teitelbaum, Michael, illus. LC 93-14029. (gr. 2-4). 1993. pap. 2.50 (*0-8167-3199-3*) Troll Assocs.

—Sonic the Hedgehog: Robotnik's Revenge. Hanson, Glen, illus. LC 93-48920. 64p. (gr. 2-4). 1994. pap. 2.50 (*0-8167-3438-0*) Troll Assocs.

Waddell, Martin. Harriet & the Robot. Burgess, Mark, illus. LC 86-17435. (gr. 3-7). 1987. 12.95 (*0-316-91624-2*, Joy St Bks) Little.

Wyatt, Pam. I Can Go! Buell-Bakke, Karen, illus. (ps-1). 1988. lib. bdg. 9.95 (*0-945286-00-7*) Red Bus Pub.

ROCK CLIMBING

see Mountaineering

ROCK MUSIC

Adams, Barbara. Rock Video Strikes Again. (Orig.). (gr. 2-6). 1986. pap. 2.50 (*0-440-47170-2*, YB) Dell.

Amelar, Chris. Stand Alone Rock. 32p. pap. 9.95 (*0-88284-544-6*, 4430) Alfred Pub.

Bad Boyz of Rap. 32p. (gr. 5 up). 1993. pap. 3.95 (*0-307-20102-3*, 20102, Golden Pr) Western Pub.

Barnard, Stephen. The Illustrated History of Rock. (Illus.). 256p. (gr. 7 up). 1987. text ed. 70.00 (*0-02-870251-4*) Schirmer Bks.

Busnar, Gene. It's Rock 'n' Roll. LC 79-10927. (Illus.). 256p. (gr. 7 up). 1979. (J Messner); pap. 4.95 (*0-685-03343-0*) S&S Trade.

Clinton, Susan. Live Aid. LC 92-33423. (Illus.). 32p. (gr. 3-6). 1993. PLB 12.30 (*0-516-06665-X*); pap. 3.95 (*0-516-46665-8*) Childrens.

Conord, Bruce W. John Lennon. LC 92-39113. (Illus.). 1994. 18.95 (*0-7910-1739-7*, Am Art Analog); pap. 7.95 (*0-7910-1740-0*, Am Art Analog) Chelsea Hse.

Crocker, Chris. Cyndi Lauper. Arico, Diane, ed. (Illus.). 64p. (gr. 3-7). 1985. 9.29 (*0-685-09958-X*) S&S Trade.

—Wham! Arico, Diane, ed. (Illus.). 64p. (gr. 3-7). 1985. lib. bdg. 8.79 (*0-685-10386-2*); pap. 3.50 (*0-685-10387-0*) S&S Trade.

—Wham. LC 85-10572. (Illus.). 64p. (gr. 3-7). 1985. (J Messner) S&S Trade.

Frankl, Ron. Bruce Springsteen. LC 93-1850. (gr. 7 up). 1994. 18.95 (*0-7910-2327-3*, Am Art Analog); pap. write for info. (*0-7910-2352-4*, Am Art Analog) Chelsea Hse.

Godwin, Jeff. What's Wrong with Christian Rock? LC 90-85347. (Illus.). (gr. 7-12). 1990. pap. 8.95 (*0-937958-36-0*) Chick Pubns.

Hair, Johnny. Who's Hot -- Red Hot Chili Peppers. (gr. 4-7). 1993. pap. 1.49 (*0-440-21595-1*) Dell.

Hopkins, Del & Hopkins, Margaret. Careers As a Rock Musician. Rosen, Ruth, ed. (gr. 7-12). 1993. PLB 14.95 (*0-8239-1518-2*); pap. 9.95 (*0-8239-1725-8*) Rosen Group.

Jones, Davy & Green, Alan. Monkees, Memories & Media Madness. Kirshner, Don, frwd. by. (Illus.). 176p. (gr. 9 up). 1992. 39.95 (*0-9631235-1-3*); pap. 29.95 (*0-9631235-0-5*) Click Pub.

Kallen, Stuart. Renaissance of Rock: British Invasion - The Sixties. Italia, Bob, ed. LC 89-84917. (Illus.). 48p. (gr. 4). 1989. PLB 12.94 (*0-939179-75-X*) Abdo & Dghtrs.

—Renaissance of Rock: Sounds of America - The Sixties. Italia, Bob, ed. LC 89-84916. (Illus.). 48p. (gr. 4). 1989. PLB 12.94 (*0-939179-74-1*) Abdo & Dghtrs.
—Retrospect of Rock: The Eighties. Italia, Bob, ed. LC 89-84919. (Illus.). 48p. (gr. 4). 1989. PLB 12.94 (*0-939179-77-6*) Abdo & Dghtrs.
—Revolution of Rock: The Seventies. Italia, Bob, ed. LC 89-84918. (Illus.). 48p. (gr. 4). 1989. PLB 12.94 (*0-939179-76-8*) Abdo & Dghtrs.
—Roots of Rock, Vol. 2: The Fifties. Italia, Bob, ed. LC 89-84914. (Illus.). 48p. (gr. 4). 1989. PLB 12.94 (*0-939179-73-3*) Abdo & Dghtrs.
Korman, Justine. Yellow Dog - MTV. (gr. 4-7). 1994. pap. 3.50 (*0-8167-3342-2*) Troll Assocs.
Krohn, Katherine E. Elvis Presley: The King. LC 93-23905. (gr. 4 up). 1993. 29.95 (*0-8225-2877-0*) Lerner Pubns.
Lantz, Frances. Rock, Rap, & Rad: How to Be a Rock Or Rap Star. 224p. (Orig.). 1992. pap. 3.99 (*0-380-76793-7*, Flare) Avon.
Martin, Susan. Duran Duran. 1984. 8.29 (*0-685-09673-4*) S&S Trade.
Matthews, Gordon. Madonna. (Illus.). 64p. (gr. 3-7). 1985. PLB 8.79 (*0-685-11123-7*, J Messner) S&S Trade.
—Prince. Arico, Diane, ed. (Illus.). 64p. (gr. 3 up). 1985. pap. 3.50 (*0-685-09758-7*) S&S Trade.
Paige, David. A Day in the Life of a Rock Musician. Ruhlin, Roger, photos by. LC 78-68808. (Illus.). 32p. (gr. 4-8). 1980. PLB 11.79 (*0-89375-225-8*); pap. 2.95 (*0-89375-229-0*) Troll Assocs.
Rowley, Kay. Rock Concerts. LC 91-21367. (Illus.). 32p. (gr. 5). 1992. text ed. 13.95 RSBE (*0-89686-715-3*, Crestwood Hse) Macmillan Child Grp.
—Rock Music. LC 91-22085. (Illus.). 32p. (gr. 5). 1992. text ed. 13.95 RSBE (*0-89686-714-5*, Crestwood Hse) Macmillan Child Grp.
—Rock Stars. LC 91-15077. (Illus.). 32p. (gr. 5). 1992. text ed. 13.95 RSBE (*0-89686-713-7*, Crestwood Hse) Macmillan Child Grp.
—Rock Videos. LC 91-15073. (Illus.). 32p. (gr. 5). 1992. text ed. 13.95 RSBE (*0-89686-712-9*, Crestwood Hse) Macmillan Child Grp.
Strasser, Todd. Rock It to the Top. 1987. write for info. Delacorte.
—Rock 'n Roll Nights. LC 81-12618. 224p. (gr. 7 up). 1982. pap. 10.95 (*0-385-28855-7*) Delacorte.

ROCKEFELLER, JOHN DAVISON, 1839-1937

Shuker, Nancy. John D. Rockefeller. Furstinger, Nancy, ed. (Illus.). 140p. (gr. 7-10). 1989. PLB 7.95 (*0-382-09583-9*) Silver Burdett Pr.

ROCKET FLIGHT

see Space Flight

ROCKETRY

see also Guided Missiles; Rockets (Aeronautics); Space Vehicles

Baird, Anne. The U. S. Space Camp Book of Rockets. Graham, David, photos by. Aldrin, Edwin E. & Buckbee, Edward O.frwd. by. LC 93-26148. (Illus.). (gr. 3 up). 1994. 15.00 (*0-688-12228-0*); PLB 14.93 (*0-688-12229-9*) Morrow Jr Bks.
Branley, Franklyn M. Rockets & Satellites. rev. ed. Maestro, Giulio, illus. LC 86-47748. 32p. (ps-3). 1987. (Crowell Jr Bks) HarpC Child Bks.
Lampton, Christopher. Rocketry: From Goddard to Space Travel. Kline, Marjory, ed. LC 87-21558. (Illus.). 96p. (gr. 7-9). 1988. PLB 10.90 (*0-531-10483-4*) Watts.

ROCKETS (AERONAUTICS)

see also Guided Missiles

Arno, Roger. The Story of Space & Rockets. (Illus.). (gr. 5). 1978. pap. 3.95 (*0-88388-063-6*) Bellerophon Bks.
Asimov, Isaac. Rockets, Probes & Satellites. 1990. pap. 4.95 (*0-440-40351-0*, YB) Dell.
Baird, Anne. The U. S. Space Camp Book of Rockets. Graham, David, photos by. Aldrin, Edwin E. & Buckbee, Edward O.frwd. by. LC 93-26148. (Illus.). (gr. 3 up). 1994. 15.00 (*0-688-12228-0*); PLB 14.93 (*0-688-12229-9*) Morrow Jr Bks.
Dudley, Mark. An Eye to the Sky. LC 91-33880. (Illus.). 48p. (gr. 5-6). 1992. text ed. 12.95 RSBE (*0-89686-691-2*, Crestwood Hse) Macmillan Child Grp.
How It Works: The Motor Car. (ARA., Illus.). (gr. 5-12). 1987. 3.95x (*0-86685-256-5*) Intl Bk Ctr.
Myring. Rockets & Spaceflight. (gr. 2-5). 1982. (Usborne-Hayes); pap. 3.95 (*0-86020-584-3*) EDC.
Sabin, Francene. Rockets & Satellites. Maccabe, Richard, illus. LC 84-2738. 32p. (gr. 3-6). 1985. PLB 9.49 (*0-8167-0288-8*); pap. text ed. 2.95 (*0-8167-0289-6*) Troll Assocs.
Spizzirri Publishing Co. Staff. Rockets: An Educational Coloring Book. Spizzirri, Linda, ed. (Illus.). 32p. (gr. 1-8). 1986. pap. 1.75 (*0-86545-072-2*) Spizzirri.

ROCKETS (AERONAUTICS)–FICTION

Newell, Peter. The Rocket Book. Newell, Peter, illus. LC 69-12080. 52p. (gr. k-4). 1969. Repr. of 1912 ed. 14.95 (*0-8048-0505-9*) C E Tuttle.
—The Rocket Book. (Illus.). 48p. (gr. 4-7). 1992. pap. 3.95t (*0-685-52838-3*) Dover.
—Rocket Book. LC 91-3120. (gr. 4-7). 1992. pap. 3.95 (*0-486-26961-2*) Dover.

ROCKETS (AERONAUTICS)–MODELS

Humphreys, B. J. A Hundred Ways to Save Money on Model Rocket Building. (Illus.). 1977. pap. text ed. 1.50 (*0-912468-19-X*) CA Rocketry.

ROCKNE, KNUTE KENNETH, 1888-1931

Riper, Guernsey V., Jr. Knute Rockne: Young Athlete. Doremus, Robert, illus. LC 86-10791. 192p. (gr. 2-6). 1986. pap. 3.95 (*0-02-042110-9*, Aladdin) Macmillan Child Grp.

ROCKS

see also Crystallography; Geology; Mineralogy

Arem, Joel. Rocks & Minerals. Boltin, Lee & Arem, Joel, photos by. LC 91-74106. (Illus.). 160p. (gr. 7-12). 1991. pap. 8.95 (*0-945005-06-7*) Geoscience Pr.
Arem, Joel E. Descubre Rocas y Minerales. University of Mexico City Staff, tr. from SPA. O'Neill, Pablo M. & Robare, Lorie, illus. 48p. (gr. 3-8). 1993. PLB 16.95 (*1-56674-051-7*, HTS Bks) Forest Hse.
Arneson, D. J. Rocks & Minerals. Friedman, Howard, illus. 32p. (Orig.). 1990. pap. 2.50 (*0-942025-90-3*) Kidsbks.
Bains, Rae. Rocks & Minerals. Maccabe, Richard, illus. LC 84-8644. 32p. (gr. 3-6). 1985. PLB 9.49 (*0-8167-0186-5*); pap. text ed. 2.95 (*0-8167-0187-3*) Troll Assocs.
Barnes-Svarney, Patricia L. Born of Heat & Pressure: Mountains & Metamorphic Rocks. LC 89-25856. (Illus.). 64p. (gr. 6 up). 1991. lib. bdg. 15.95 (*0-89490-276-8*) Enslow Pubs.
Baylor, Byrd. Everybody Needs a Rock. Parnall, Peter, illus. LC 74-9163. 32p. (ps-3). 1974. RSBE 15.00 (*0-684-13899-9*, Scribners Young Read) Macmillan Child Grp.
—Everybody Needs a Rock. Parnall, Peter, illus. LC 74-9163. 32p. (gr. k-3). 1985. pap. 4.95 (*0-689-71051-8*, Aladdin) Macmillan Child Grp.
Beattie, Laura C. Discover Rocks & Minerals: Activity Book. Creative Company Staff, illus. 24p. (gr. 3-8). 1991. wkbk. 2.95 (*0-911239-36-7*) Carnegie Mus.
Benanti, Carol. Rocks & Minerals. (Illus.). 32p. (gr. 3 up). 1994. pap. 10.00 (*0-679-85072-4*) Random Bks Yng Read.
Brown, Vinson, et al. Rocks & Minerals of California. 3rd. rev. ed. LC 72-13423. (Illus.). 200p. (gr. 4 up). 1972. 17.95 (*0-911010-59-9*); pap. 9.95 (*0-911010-58-0*) Naturegraph.
Cork, B. & Bramwell, M. Rocks & Fossils. Jackson, I. & Suttie, A., illus. 32p. (gr. 5-8). 1983. PLB 13.96 (*0-88110-159-1*); pap. 6.95 (*0-86020-765-X*) EDC.
Cunningham, Timothy. The Geode Kit. (Illus.). 64p. 1992. 17.95 (*1-56138-144-6*) Running Pr.
Evans, David & Williams, Claudette. Rocks & Soil. LC 92-53478. (Illus.). 24p. (gr. k-3). 1993. 9.95 (*1-56458-209-4*) Dorling Kindersley.
Fowler, Allan. It Could Still Be a Rock. LC 92-39260. (Illus.). 32p. (ps-2). 1993. big bk. 22.95 (*0-516-49641-7*); PLB 10.75 (*0-516-06010-4*); pap. 3.95 (*0-516-46010-2*) Childrens.
Gans, Roma. Rock Collecting. 2nd ed. Keller, Holly, illus. LC 83-46170. 32p. (gr. k-3). 1984. PLB 14.89 (*0-690-04266-3*, Crowell Jr Bks) HarpC Child Bks.
—Rock Collecting. Keller, Holly, illus. LC 83-46170. 32p. (ps-3). 1987. pap. 4.50 (*0-06-445063-5*, Trophy) HarpC Child Bks.
Gattis, L. S., III. Rocks & Minerals for Pathfinders: A Basic Youth Enrichment Skill Honor Packet. (Illus.). 22p. (Orig.). (gr. 5 up). 1987. pap. 5.00 tchr's. ed. (*0-936241-29-2*) Cheetah Pub.
Horenstein, Sidney. Rocks Tell Stories. LC 92-16562. (Illus.). 72p. (gr. 4-6). 1993. PLB 15.40 (*1-56294-238-7*); pap. 6.95 (*1-56294-766-4*) Millbrook Pr.
Hyler, Nelson W. Rocks & Minerals. Shannon, Kenyon, illus. (gr. 4-6). pap. 2.95 (*0-8431-4274-X*, Wonder-Treas) Price Stern.
Jennings, Terry. Rocks & Soil. LC 88-22889. (Illus.). 32p. (gr. 3-6). 1989. pap. 4.95 (*0-516-48407-9*) Childrens.
Jennings, Terry J. Rocks. Stefoff, Rebecca, ed. Barber, Ed, photos by. LC 91-18190. (Illus.). 32p. (gr. 3-5). 1991. PLB 15.93 (*1-56074-000-0*) Garrett Ed Corp.
Lye, Keith. Rocks & Minerals. LC 92-31817. (Illus.). 32p. (gr. 2-3). 1992. PLB 18.99 (*0-8114-3411-7*) Raintree Steck-V.
—Rocks, Minerals & Fossils. (Illus.). 48p. (gr. 5-8). 1991. PLB 12.95 (*0-382-24226-2*) Silver Burdett Pr.
Mariner, Tom. Rocks. LC 89-17321. (Illus.). 32p. (gr. 3-8). 1990. PLB 9.95 (*1-85435-194-X*) Marshall Cavendish.
Metcalf, Doris & Marson, Ron. Rocks & Minerals. Marson, Peg, illus. 88p. (gr. 7-12). 1989. tchr's. ed. 15.70 (*0-941008-23-1*) Tops Learning.
Morris, Scott, ed. Rocks & Minerals of the World. De Blij, Harm J., intro. by. LC 92-22910. (Illus.). 1993. 15.95 (*0-7910-1803-2*, Am Art Analog); pap. write for info. (*0-7910-1816-4*, Am Art Analog) Chelsea Hse.
Oliver, Ray. Rocks & Fossils. LC 92-44791. (Illus.). 80p. (gr. 5 up). 1993. 13.00 (*0-679-82661-0*); PLB 13.99 (*0-679-92661-5*) Random Bks Yng Read.
Parker, Steve. Rock & Minerals. LC 93-12643. (Illus.). 64p. (gr. 3-6). 1993. 9.95 (*1-56458-394-5*) Dorling Kindersley.
Podendorf, Illa. Rocks & Minerals. LC 81-38494. (Illus.). 48p. (gr. k-4). 1982. PLB 12.85 (*0-516-01648-2*); pap. 4.95 (*0-516-41648-0*) Childrens.
Rocks. (gr. k-5). 1991. write for info. (*0-307-12852-0*, Golden Pr) Western Pub.
Russell, William. Rocks & Minerals. LC 94-507. (gr. 3 up). 1994. write for info. (*0-86593-362-6*) Rourke Corp.
Selsam, Millicent E. & Hunt, Joyce. A First Look at Rocks. LC 83-40394. 32p. (gr. 1-4). 1984. PLB 12.85 (*0-8027-6531-9*) Walker & Co.
Shedenhelm, W. R. Discover Rocks & Minerals. (Illus.). 48p. (gr. 3-6). 1992. PLB 14.95 (*1-878363-70-0*, HTS Bks) Forest Hse.
Tilling, Robert I. Born of Fire: Volcanoes & Igneous Rocks. LC 89-25781. (Illus.). 64p. (gr. 6 up). 1991. lib. bdg. 15.95 (*0-89490-151-6*) Enslow Pubs.
Walker, Sally M. Born Near the Earth's Surface: Sedimentary Rocks. LC 90-42436. (Illus.). 64p. (gr. 6 up). 1991. lib. bdg. 15.95 (*0-89490-293-8*) Enslow Pubs.
Woolley, Alan. Rocks & Minerals. (Illus.). 64p. (gr. 7 up). 1992. pap. 4.95 (*0-86020-112-0*) EDC.
Zim, Herbert S. & Shaffer, Paul R. Rocks & Minerals. Perlman, Raymond, illus. (gr. 6 up). 1957. pap. write for info. (*0-307-24499-7*, Golden Pr) Western Pub.

ROCKS–AGE

see Geology, Stratigraphic

ROCKY MOUNTAINS

Bullock, Robert. The Rocky Mountains: A Young Reader's Journal. Bullock, Robert, illus. LC 93-77117. 64p. (Orig.). (gr. k-5). 1993. pap. 8.95 (*0-943972-18-3*) Homestead WY.
Burns, Diane. Rocky Mountain Seasons: From Valley to Mountaintop. Dannen, Kent & Dannen, Donna, photos by. LC 92-22833. (Illus.). 32p. (gr. 1-5). 1993. RSBE 14.95 (*0-02-716142-0*, Macmillan Child Bk) Macmillan Child Grp.
Petersen, David. Rocky Mountain National Park. LC 93-798. (Illus.). 48p. (gr. k-4). 1993. PLB 12.85 (*0-516-01196-0*); pap. 4.95 (*0-516-41196-9*) Childrens.

ROCKY MOUNTAINS–FICTION

MacDougall, Mary-Katherine. Black Jupiter. Gruver, Kate E., ed. Moyers, William, illus. 181p. (gr. 5 up). 1983. 8.95 (*0-940175-01-0*) Now Comns.
"It was late for the horses to be so high in the mountains. By this time in other years they had already found winter quarters in a lower area. But this fall they were waiting for a colt." That colt was Black Jupiter. Snow came. The horses had to leave through the rock gateway the black mare could not yet get through. The stallion stayed with her. The next dawn the colt came but did not move or make a sound. The horses left the newborn colt alone in the snow. Jim Peters, a prospector, living alone in his cabin, was sensitive to wildlife. He felt something was wrong when he heard two horses leaving a day after the herd. He found Black Jupiter alive but not strong. He took him to his cabin. There are Gregg & Jenine Jordan, children of a mining engineer, a threat to Jim & his mining plans. In turn, Jim is suspected of stealing from the surveying crew. Black Jupiter, set in the Rocky Mountains with a factual copper mining background, is a mystery story of distrust & misunderstanding, healed by love & a colt. There is a happy Christmas chapter. Black & white illustrations.
Publisher Provided Annotation.

Woods, Becky. A Rocky Mountain Rabbit. LC 90-70093. (Illus.). 86p. (gr. 4-8). 1991. 12.95 (*0-932433-65-0*) Windswept Hse.

RODEOS

Acton, Avis. Behind the Chutes at Cheyenne Frontier Days: Your Pocket Guide to Rodeo. Garretson-Weibel, Cindy, ed. Wagner, Randy, photos by. (Illus.). 112p. (Orig.). (gr. 6 up). 1991. pap. 7.95 (*0-9627412-0-5*) ABC Pub.
Bellville, Cheryl W. Rodeo. LC 84-14981. (Illus.). 32p. (gr. k-4). 1985. PLB 19.95 (*0-87614-272-2*) Carolrhoda Bks.
—Rodeo. (Illus.). 32p. (gr. k-4). 1985. pap. 5.95 (*0-87614-492-X*, First Ave Edns) Lerner Pubns.
Bryant, Thomas A. Rodeo, America's Number One Sport. 2nd ed. Wagner, E. Vernel, illus. 64p. (gr. 3-5). 1986. pap. 3.00 (*0-941875-00-8*) Wolverine Gallery.
Fain, James W. Rodeos. LC 82-23460. (SPA.). 48p. (gr. k-4). 1987. PLB 12.85 (*0-516-31685-0*); pap. 4.95 (*0-516-51685-X*) Childrens.
Rice, James. Cowboy Rodeo. Rice, James, illus. LC 91-34924. 32p. 1992. 14.95 (*0-88289-903-1*) Pelican.

RODEOS–FICTION

Bryant, Bonnie. Rodeo Rider. (gr. 4 up). 1990. pap. 3.50 (*0-553-15821-X*) Bantam.
Toriseva, Jonelle. Rodeo Day. Casilla, Robert, illus. LC 92-39475. 32p. (ps-2). 1994. RSBE 14.95 (*0-02-789405-3*, Bradbury Pr) Macmillan Child Grp.

ROENTGEN, WILHELM CONRAD, 1845-1923

Gherman, Beverly. The Mysterious Rays of Dr. Roentgen. Marchesi, Stephen, illus. LC 92-38966. 32p. (gr. 2-5). 1994. SBE 14.95 (*0-689-31839-1*, Atheneum Child Bk) Macmillan Child Grp.

ROENTGEN RAYS

see X Rays

ROGERS, WILL, 1879-1935

Anderson, Peter. Will Rogers: American Humorist. LC 91-35057. (Illus.). 32p. (gr. 2-5). 1992. PLB 11.80 (*0-516-04183-5*); pap. 3.95 (*0-516-44183-3*) Childrens.

Keith, Harold. Will Rogers, a Boy's Life: An Indian Territory Childhood. rev. ed. LC 91-62354. 271p. (gr. 3 up). 1992. 17.00 (*0-927562-08-1*); pap. 11.00 (*0-927562-09-X*) Levite Apache.

Sonneborn, Elizabeth. Will Rogers: Cherokee Entertainer. (Illus.). 112p. (gr. 5 up). 1994. PLB 18.95 (*0-7910-1719-2*, Am Art Analog); pap. write for info. (*0-7910-1988-8*, Am Art Analog) Chelsea Hse.

ROGUES AND VAGABONDS–FICTION

Fitzgerald, John D. The Great Brain Reforms. LC 72-7601. (Illus.). 176p. (gr. 4-7). 1973. PLB 11.89 (*0-8037-3068-3*) Dial Bks Young.

ROLLER-SKATING–FICTION

Calmenson, Stephanie. Roller Skates! 1992. 2.95 (*0-590-45716-0*, Cartwheel) Scholastic Inc.

Diestel-Feddersen, Mary. Try Again, Sally Jane. Ashley, Yvonne, illus. LC 86-42810. 30p. (gr. 2-3). 1987. PLB 18.60 (*1-55532-150-X*) Gareth Stevens Inc.

Fraser, Sheila. I Can Roller Skate. Kopper, Lisa, illus. 24p. (ps-3). 1991. 5.95 (*0-8120-6228-0*) Barron.

ROLLING STOCK

see Locomotives

ROMAN ANTIQUITIES

see Rome–Antiquities

ROMAN CATHOLIC CHURCH

see Catholic Church

ROMAN LITERATURE

see Latin Literature

ROMAN MYTHOLOGY

see Mythology, Classical

ROME

Here are entered works about the Roman Empire. works only on the modern city of Rome are entered under Rome (City).

Amery & Vanage. Rome & Romans. (gr. 4-9). 1976. (Usborne-Hayes); PLB 13.96 (*0-88110-101-X*); pap. 6.95 (*0-86020-070-1*) EDC.

Bombarde, Odile & Moatti, Claude. Living in Ancient Rome. Matthews, Sarah, tr. from FRE. Place, Francois, illus. LC 87-37113. 38p. (gr. k-5). 1988. 5.95 (*0-944589-08-1*, 081) Young Discovery Lib.

Chrisp, Peter. The Romans. LC 93-29441. 1994. write for info. (*0-7910-2707-4*); write for info. (*0-7910-2731-7*) Chelsea Hse.

Church, Alfred J. Roman Life in the Days of Cicero. LC 61-24994. (gr. 7-11). 1968. 22.00 (*0-8196-0105-5*) Biblo.

Corbishley, Mike. Growing up in Ancient Rome. Molan, Chris, illus. LC 91-14851. 32p. (gr. 3-5). 1993. PLB 11.89 (*0-8167-2721-X*); pap. text ed. 3.95 (*0-8167-2722-8*) Troll Assocs.

—What Do We Know about the Romans? LC 91-28763. (Illus.). 40p. (gr. 3-7). 1992. PLB 16.95 (*0-87226-352-5*) P Bedrick Bks.

Davis, William S. Day in Old Rome. LC 61-24993. (Illus.). (gr. 7 up). 1963. 20.00 (*0-8196-1206-5*) Biblo.

Jackson, Ralph, et al. The Romans. (Illus.). (gr. 2-6). pap. 3.95 (*0-7141-1282-8*, Pub. by Brit Mus UK) Parkwest Pubns.

Lamprey, Louise. Children of Ancient Rome. LC 61-12876. (Illus.). (gr. 7-11). 1967. 18.00 (*0-8196-0114-4*) Biblo.

Macdonald, Fiona. A Roman Fort. Wood, Gerald, illus. LC 93-16397. 48p. (gr. 5 up). 1993. 17.95 (*0-87226-370-3*); pap. 8.95 sewn (*0-87226-259-6*) P Bedrick Bks.

Morley, Jacqueline & James, John. A Roman Villa: Inside Story. LC 92-15279. (Illus.). 48p. (gr. 5 up). 1992. 17.95 (*0-87226-360-6*) P Bedrick Bks.

Mulvihill, Margaret. Roman Forts. LC 89-28778. 1990. PLB 12.40 (*0-531-17201-5*, Gloucester Pr) Watts.

Steele, Philip. In Ancient Rome. LC 93-28384. (Illus.). 32p. (gr. 6 up). 1995. text ed. 14.95 RSBE (*0-02-726321-5*, New Discovery Bks) Macmillan Child Grp.

Tingay, Graham I. & Badcock, John. These Were the Romans. 1985. pap. 25.00 (*0-7175-0591-X*) Dufour.

ROME–ANTIQUITIES

Hicks, Peter. The Romans. LC 93-11653. (Illus.). 32p. (gr. 4-6). 1994. 14.95 (*1-56847-063-0*) Thomson Lrning.

ROME–BIOGRAPHY

Coolidge, Olivia. Lives of Famous Romans. Johnson, Milton, illus. LC 91-40360. 248p. (gr. 8-12). 1992. Repr. of 1965 ed. lib. bdg. 19.50 (*0-208-02333-X*, Pub. by Linnet) Shoe String.

Place, Robin. The Romans: Fact & Fiction. (Illus.). 32p. 1989. 12.95 (*0-521-33267-2*); pap. 7.50 (*0-521-33787-9*) Cambridge U Pr.

ROME–FICTION

Bretecher, Claire. Agrippina. 50p. 1992. pap. 9.95 (*0-7493-0812-5*, Pub. by Mandarin UK) Heinemann.

Goodman, Joan E. Songs from Home. LC 93-46248. (gr. 5 up). 1994. 10.95 (*0-15-203590-7*); pap. 4.95 (*0-15-203591-5*) HarBrace.

Hawthorne, Nathaniel. Marble Faun. Fisher, N. H., intro. by. (gr. 11 up). 1966. pap. 1.95 (*0-8049-0104-X*, CL-104) Airmont.

Hull, Robert. Roman Stories. Smith, Tony, illus. LC 93-29996. 48p. (gr. 5-9). 1993. 15.95 (*1-56847-105-X*) Thomson Lrning.

ROME–HISTORY

Abbott, Frank F. The Common People of Ancient Rome: Studies of Roman Life & Literature. LC 65-23487. (gr. 7 up). 1965. Repr. of 1911 ed. 25.00 (*0-8196-0157-8*) Biblo.

—A History & Description of Roman Political Institutions. 3rd ed. LC 63-10766. 451p. (gr. 7 up). 1910. 24.00 (*0-8196-0117-9*) Biblo.

—Society & Politics in Ancient Rome: Essays & Sketches. LC 63-10767. 267p. (gr. 7 up). 1909. 24.00 (*0-8196-0118-7*) Biblo.

Ancient Greece & Rome. (Illus.). 20p. 1994. 6.95 (*1-56458-716-9*) Dorling Kindersley.

Artman, John. Ancient Rome. 64p. (gr. 4-8). 1991. 8.95 (*0-86653-638-8*, GA1343) Good Apple.

Badcock, John & Tingay, Graham I. The Romans & Their Empire. (Illus.). 75p. (Orig.). (gr. 6-8). 1992. pap. 14.95x (*0-7487-1186-4*, Pub. by S Thornes UK) Dufour.

Bombarde, Odile & Moatti, Claude. Living in Ancient Rome. Place, Francois, illus. 40p. (gr. k-5). 1993. PLB 9.95 (*1-56674-060-6*, HTS Bks) Forest Hse.

Brandt, Keith. Ancient Rome. Frenck, Hal, illus. LC 84-2684. 32p. (gr. 3-6). 1985. PLB 9.49 (*0-8167-0298-5*); pap. text ed. 2.95 (*0-8167-0299-3*) Troll Assocs.

Burland, Cottie A. Ancient Rome. (Illus.). (gr. 4-8). 1974. Repr. of 1958 ed. 10.95 (*0-7175-0015-2*) Dufour.

Burrell, Roy. The Romans. Connolly, Peter, illus. 112p. (gr. 5-9). 1991. bds. 19.95 (*0-19-917162-9*, 5084) OUP.

Chisholm, Jan. Roman Times. McCaig, Rob, illus. 24p. (gr. 3-6). 1982. PLB 11.96 (*0-88110-105-2*); pap. 4.50 (*0-86020-619-X*) EDC.

Clare, John D., ed. Classical Rome. LC 92-30502. 1993. write for info. (*0-15-200513-7*, Gullivar Bks) HarBrace.

Corbishley, Mike. Everyday Life in Roman Times. LC 93-21191. 1994. write for info. (*0-531-14288-4*) Watts.

—Rome & the Ancient World. (Illus.). 80p. (gr. 2-6). 1993. 17.95x (*0-8160-2786-2*) Facts on File.

Cortes, Jose L. The Roman Empire. LC 92-34595. (Illus.). 36p. (gr. 3 up). 1993. PLB 14.95 (*0-516-08382-1*); pap. 6.95 (*0-516-48382-X*) Childrens.

Dineen, Jacqueline. The Romans. LC 91-511. (Illus.). 64p. (gr. 6 up). 1992. text ed. 14.95 RSBE (*0-02-730651-8*, New Discovery) Macmillan Child Grp.

Grant, Neil. Roman Conquests. (Illus.). 32p. (gr. 3-9). 1991. PLB 10.95 (*1-85435-262-8*) Marshall Cavendish.

Hall, Andy & Hall, Maggie. The Romans Pop-Up. (Illus.). 32p. (Orig.). (gr. 3 up). 1985. pap. 7.95 (*0-906212-29-4*, Pub. by Tarquin UK) Parkwest Pubns.

Hicks, Peter. The Romans. LC 93-11653. (Illus.). 32p. (gr. 4-6). 1994. 14.95 (*1-56847-063-0*) Thomson Lrning.

Hodge, Peter. Roman House. (Illus.). 64p. (Orig.). (gr. 7-12). 1971. pap. text ed. 9.00 (*0-582-20300-7*, 70709) Longman.

Jackson, Ralph, et al. The Roman's Activity Book. (Illus.). 16p. 1994. pap. 5.95 (*0-500-27765-6*) Thames Hudson.

Lamprey, Louise. Children of Ancient Gaul. LC 60-16708. (Illus.). (gr. 7-11). 1968. 20.00 (*0-8196-0109-8*) Biblo.

Moore, Frank G. The Roman's World. LC 65-23486. (Illus.). 502p. (gr. 7 up). 1936. 25.00 (*0-8196-0155-1*) Biblo.

Odijk, Pamela. The Romans. (Illus.). 48p. (gr. 5-8). 1989. PLB 12.95 (*0-382-09885-4*); 7.95 (*0-382-24260-2*); tchr's. guide 4.50 (*0-382-24275-0*) Silver Burdett Pr.

The Romans. (Illus.). (gr. 5 up). 1990. pap. 3.95 (*1-85543-006-1*) Ladybird Bks.

Steele, Philip. The Romans & Pompeii. (Illus.). 32p. (gr. 6 up). 1994. text ed. 13.95 RSBE (*0-87518-538-X*, Dillon) Macmillan Child Grp.

Steffens, Bradley. The Fall of the Roman Empire: Opposing Viewpoints. LC 93-11025. 1994. 14.95 (*1-56510-098-0*) Greenhaven.

Tingay, G. & Marks, A. The Romans. (Illus.). 96p. 1990. PLB 16.96 (*0-88110-439-6*); pap. 10.95 (*0-7460-0340-4*) EDC.

Whitehead, Albert C. The Standard Bearer: A Story of Army Life in the Time of Caesar. (Illus.). (gr. 7-11). 1943. 20.00 (*0-8196-0116-0*) Biblo.

ROME–HISTORY–FICTION

Anderson, Paul L. Pugnax the Gladiator. LC 61-1111. (Illus.). (gr. 7-11). 1939. 16.00 (*0-8196-0104-7*) Biblo.

—With the Eagles. LC 57-9447. (Illus.). (gr. 7-11). 1929. 20.00 (*0-8196-0100-4*) Biblo.

Church, Alfred J. Lucius, Adventures of a Roman Boy. LC 60-16706. (gr. 7-11). 1969. 20.00 (*0-8196-0108-X*) Biblo.

Dillon, Eilis. Living in Imperial Rome. (Illus.). 176p. (gr. 4-8). 1991. pap. 10.95 (*0-86278-264-3*, Pub. by OBrien Pr IE) Dufour.

Morris, Neil & Morris, Ting. Battle of the Gladiators. (Illus.). 24p. (gr. 3-5). 1991. 13.95 (*0-237-51021-9*, Pub. by Evans Bros Ltd) Trafalgar.

—In the Slave Market. (Illus.). 24p. (gr. 3-5). 1991. 13.95 (*0-237-51019-7*, Pub. by Evans Bros Ltd) Trafalgar.

Wallace, Lewis. Ben Hur. 450p. 1981. Repr. lib. bdg. 27.95x (*0-89966-289-7*) Buccaneer Bks.

Wells, Reuben F. With Caesar's Legions. LC 60-16709. (Illus.). (gr. 7-11). 1951. 18.00 (*0-8196-0110-1*) Biblo.

ROME–HISTORY–REPUBLIC, 510-30 B.C.

James, Simon. Ancient Rome. (Illus.). 48p. (gr. 3-7). 1992. 15.00 (*0-670-84493-4*) Viking Child Bks.

Judson, Harry P. Caesar's Army: A Study of the Military Art of the Romans in the Last Days of the Republic. LC 61-12877. (Illus.). 127p. (gr. 7 up). 1888. 24.00 (*0-8196-0113-6*) Biblo.

Poulton, Michael. Augustus & the Ancient Romans. Molan, Christine, illus. LC 92-5824. 63p. (gr. 6-7). 1992. PLB 24.26 (*0-8114-3350-1*) Raintree Steck-V.

ROME–HISTORY–EMPIRE, 30 B.C.-476 A.D.

Guittard, Charles. The Romans: Life in the Empire. LaRose, Mary K., tr. from FRE. Martin, Annie-Claude, illus. LC 92-9467. 64p. (gr. 4-6). 1992. PLB 15.40 (*1-56294-200-X*) Millbrook Pr.

Hughes, Jill. Imperial Rome. (Illus.). 32p. (gr. 4-6). 1991. 13.95 (*0-237-60167-2*, Pub. by Evans Bros Ltd) Trafalgar.

Poulton, Michael. Augustus & the Ancient Romans. Molan, Christine, illus. LC 92-5824. 63p. (gr. 6-7). 1992. PLB 24.26 (*0-8114-3350-1*) Raintree Steck-V.

Sauvain, Philip. Over Sixteen Hundred Years Ago in the Roman Empire. LC 91-43328. (Illus.). 32p. (gr. 6 up). 1992. text ed. 13.95 RSBE (*0-02-781083-6*, New Discovery) Macmillan Child Grp.

ROMMEL, ERWIN, 1891-1944

Blanco, Richard L. Rommel the Desert Warrior: The Afrika Korps in World War II. LC 82-2293. 192p. (gr. 7 up). 1982. (J Messner); pap. write for info. (*0-671-49582-8*) S&S Trade.

ROOSEVELT, ELEANOR (ROOSEVELT) 1884-1962

Adler, David A. A Picture Book of Eleanor Roosevelt. Casilla, Robert, illus. LC 90-39212. 32p. (ps-3). 1991. reinforced 14.95 (*0-8234-0856-6*) Holiday.

Faber, Doris. Eleanor Roosevelt: First Lady of the World. Ruff, Donna, photos by. LC 84-20861. (Illus.). 64p. (gr. 2-6). 1985. pap. 10.95 (*0-670-80551-3*) Viking Child Bks.

—Eleanor Roosevelt: First Lady of the World. Ruff, Doris, illus. 64p. (gr. 2-6). 1986. pap. 4.50 (*0-14-032103-9*, Puffin) Puffin Bks.

Jacobs, William J. Eleanor Roosevelt: A Life of Happiness & Tears. LC 90-48974. (Illus.). 128p. (gr. 6-10). 1991. PLB 13.95 (*1-55905-095-0*) Marshall Cavendish.

Lazo, Caroline. Eleanor Roosevelt. LC 93-6610. (Illus.). 64p. (gr. 4 up). 1993. text ed. 13.95 RSBE (*0-87518-594-0*, Dillon) Macmillan Child Grp.

Sabin, Francene. Young Eleanor Roosevelt. Ramsey, Marcy D., illus. LC 89-33939. 48p. (gr. 4-6). 1990. PLB 10.79 (*0-8167-1779-6*); pap. text ed. 3.50 (*0-8167-1780-X*) Troll Assocs.

Sandak, Cass R. The Franklin Roosevelts. LC 91-30256. (Illus.). 48p. (gr. 5). 1992. text ed. 4.95 RSBE (*0-89686-639-4*, Crestwood Hse) Macmillan Child Grp.

Toor, Rachel. Eleanor Roosevelt. Horner, Matina S., intro. by. (Illus.). 112p. (gr. 5 up). 1989. 17.95 (*1-55546-674-5*) Chelsea Hse.

Vercelli, Jane A. Eleanor Roosevelt. LC 94-5132. 1994. write for info. (*0-7910-1772-9*); pap. write for info. (*0-7910-2136-X*) Chelsea Hse.

Weidt, Maryann N. Stateswoman to the World: A Story about Eleanor Roosevelt. Anderson, Lydia M., illus. LC 90-23216. 64p. (gr. 3-6). 1991. PLB 9.95 (*0-87614-663-9*) Carolrhoda Bks.

—Stateswoman to the World: A Story about Eleanor Roosevelt. (gr. 4-7). 1992. pap. 5.95 (*0-87614-562-4*) Carolrhoda Bks.

Weil, Ann. Eleanor Roosevelt. LC 89-37781. (Illus.). 192p. (gr. 2-6). 1989. pap. 3.95 (*0-689-71348-7*, Aladdin) Macmillan Child Grp.

Winner, David. Eleanor Roosevelt: Defender of Human Rights & Democracy. LC 91-291. (Illus.). 68p. (gr. 5-6). 1992. PLB 19.93 (*0-8368-0218-7*) Gareth Stevens Inc.

ROOSEVELT, FRANKLIN DELANO, PRESIDENT U. S. 1882-1945

Cross, Robin. Roosevelt: And the Americans at War. LC 90-31227. (Illus.). 64p. (gr. 5-8). 1990. PLB 12.90 (*0-531-17254-6*, Gloucester Pr) Watts.

Devaney, John. Franklin Delano Roosevelt, President. LC 86-46254. (Illus.). 76p. (gr. 5-9). 1987. 12.95 (*0-8027-6713-3*); PLB 13.85 (*0-8027-6714-1*) Walker & Co.

Farr, Naunerle C. Abraham Lincoln - Franklin D. Roosevelt. Redondo, Nestor & LoFamia, Jun, illus. (gr. 4-12). 1979. pap. text ed. 2.95 (*0-88301-354-1*); wkbk. 1.25 (*0-88301-378-9*) Pendulum Pr.

Freedman, Russell. Franklin Delano Roosevelt. (Illus.). 208p. (gr. 4 up). 1990. 16.95 (*0-89919-379-X*, Clarion Bks) HM.

Greenblatt, Miriam. Franklin D. Roosevelt: Thirty-Second President of the United States. Young, Richard G., ed. LC 87-36121. (Illus.). (gr. 5-9). 1989. PLB 17.26 (*0-944483-06-2*) Garrett Ed Corp.

Hacker, Jeffrey. Franklin D. Roosevelt. LC 90-48973. (Illus.). 176p. (gr. 6-10). 1991. PLB 13.95 (*1-55905-096-9*) Marshall Cavendish.

Israel, Fred L. Franklin D. Roosevelt. (Illus.). 112p. (gr. 5 up). 1985. lib. bdg. 17.95x (*0-87754-573-1*); pap. 9.95 (*0-7910-0599-2*) Chelsea Hse.

Italia, Bob. Franklin D. Roosevelt. Walner, Rosemary, ed. LC 90-82619. (Illus.). 32p. (gr. 4). 1990. PLB 11.96 (*0-939179-82-2*) Abdo & Dghtrs.

Larsen, Rebecca. Franklin D. Roosevelt: Man of Destiny. (Illus.). 224p. (gr. 9-12). 1991. PLB 15.40 (*0-531-11068-0*) Watts.

Osinski, Alice. Franklin D. Roosevelt. (Illus.). 100p. (gr. 3 up). 1987. PLB 14.40 (*0-516-01395-5*); pap. 6.95 (*0-516-41395-3*) Childrens.

Sandak, Cass R. The Franklin Roosevelts. LC 91-30256. (Illus.). 48p. (gr. 5). 1992. text ed. 4.95 RSBE (*0-89686-639-4*, Crestwood Hse) Macmillan Child Grp.

Schlesinger, Arthur, Jr., intro. by. Franklin Roosevelt. (Illus.). 128p. (gr. 7-12). PLB 16.95 (*0-685-21876-7*, 087250) Know Unltd.

Shebar, Sharon. Franklin D. Roosevelt & the New Deal. (Illus.). 144p. (gr. 3-6). 1987. pap. 4.95 (*0-8120-3916-5*) Barron.

ROOSEVELT, FRANKLIN DELANO, PRESIDENT U. S. 1882-1945–DRAMA

Franklin D. Roosevelt Mini-Play: Mini-Play, 2 pts. (gr. 8 up). 1978. Pt. 1. 6.50 (*0-89550-314-X*) Pt. 2. 6.50 (*0-89550-319-0*) Stevens & Shea.

ROOSEVELT, THEODORE, PRESIDENT U. S. 1858-1919

Beach, James C. Theodore Roosevelt: Man of Action. (Illus.). 80p. (gr. 2-6). 1991. Repr. of 1960 ed. lib. bdg. 12.95 (*0-7910-1450-9*) Chelsea Hse.

DeStefano, Susan. Theodore Roosevelt: Conservation President. Castro, Antonio, illus. 80p. (gr. 4-7). 1993. PLB 14.95 (*0-8050-2122-1*) TFC Bks NY.

Fritz, Jean. Bully for You, Teddy Roosevelt! (Illus.). 128p. 1991. 15.95 (*0-399-21769-X*, Putnam) Putnam Pub Group.

Kent, Zachary. The Story of the Rough Riders. LC 90-22444. (Illus.). 32p. (gr. 3-6). 1991. PLB 12.30 (*0-516-04756-6*); pap. 3.95 (*0-516-44756-4*) Childrens.

—Theodore Roosevelt. LC 87-35184. (Illus.). 100p. (gr. 3 up). 1988. PLB 14.40 (*0-516-01354-8*); pap. 6.95 (*0-516-41354-6*) Childrens.

Luthor. Theodore Roosevelt. Date not set. PLB write for info. (*0-8050-2274-0*) H Holt & Co.

McCafferty, Jim. Holt & the Teddy Bear. Davis, Florence S., illus. LC 90-44060. 40p. (gr. 4-8). 1991. 12.95 (*0-88289-823-X*) Pelican.

Markham, Lois. Theodore Roosevelt. LC 90-48981. (Illus.). 96p. (gr. 6-10). 1991. PLB 13.95 (*1-55905-098-5*) Marshall Cavendish.

Parks, Edd W. Teddy Roosevelt: Young Rough Rider. Morrow, Gray, illus. LC 89-37819. 192p. (gr. 2-6). 1989. pap. 3.95 (*0-689-71349-5*, Aladdin) Macmillan Child Grp.

Quackenbush, Robert. Don't You Dare Shoot That Bear. LC 84-4693. 1990. pap. 11.95 (*0-671-66295-3*) S&S Trade.

Sabin, Lou. Teddy Roosevelt, Rough Rider. Baxter, Robert, illus. LC 85-1090. 48p. (gr. 4-6). 1986. lib. bdg. 10.79 (*0-8167-0555-0*); pap. text ed. 3.50 (*0-8167-0556-9*) Troll Assocs.

Sandak, Cass R. The Theodore Roosevelts. LC 91-7377. (Illus.). 48p. (gr. 5). 1991. text ed. 12.95 RSBE (*0-89686-634-3*, Crestwood Hse) Macmillan Child Grp.

Stefoff, Rebecca. Theodore Roosevelt: 26th President of the United States. Young, Richard G., ed. LC 87-35953. (Illus.). (gr. 5-9). 1988. PLB 17.26 (*0-944483-09-7*) Garrett Ed Corp.

Theodore Roosevelt: Mini-Play. (gr. 5 up). 1979. 6.50 (*0-89550-316-6*) Stevens & Shea.

Weitzman, David. The Mountain Man & the President. Shaw, Charles, illus. LC 92-23040. 40p. (gr. 2-5). 1992. PLB 19.97 (*0-8114-7224-8*) Raintree Steck-V.

Whitelaw, Nancy. Theodore Roosevelt Takes Charge. Levine, Abby, ed. LC 90-29181. 192p. (gr. 4-8). 1992. 11.95 (*0-8075-7849-5*) A Whitman.

ROOSEVELT, THEODORE, PRESIDENT U. S. 1858-1919–FICTION

Kay, Helen. The First Teddy Bear. Detwiler, Susan, illus. LC 85-2706. 40p. (gr. 1 up). 1985. 12.95 (*0-88045-042-8*) Stemmer Hse.

Monjo, F. N. The One Bad Thing about Father. Negri, Rocco, illus. LC 71-85036. 64p. (gr. k-3). 1987. pap. 3.50 (*0-06-444110-5*, Trophy) HarpC Child Bks.

ROOSEVELT FAMILY

Sandak, Cass R. The Theodore Roosevelts. LC 91-7377. (Illus.). 48p. (gr. 5). 1991. text ed. 12.95 RSBE (*0-89686-634-3*, Crestwood Hse) Macmillan Child Grp.

ROOSTERS–FICTION

Berrill, Margaret. Chanticleer. Bottomley, Jane, illus. LC 86-6746. 32p. (gr. 2-5). PLB 19.97 (*0-8172-2626-5*) Raintree Steck-V.

Cole, Sheila. The Hen That Crowed. LC 92-4907. (ps-3). 1993. 14.00 (*0-688-10112-7*); PLB 13.93 (*0-688-10113-5*) Lothrop.

Conrad, Pam. The Rooster's Gift. Beddows, Eric, illus. LC 93-14490. 1995. 15.00 (*0-06-023603-5*); PLB 14.89 (*0-06-023604-3*) HarpC Child Bks.

Crawford, Thomas. Rooster Who Refused to Crow. (Illus.). (gr. 3-4). 1972. pap. 1.95 (*0-89375-050-6*) Troll Assocs.

Denslow, Sharon P. Hazel's Circle. McGinley-Nally, Sharon, illus. LC 91-18182. 32p. (ps-2). 1992. RSBE 14.95 (*0-02-728683-5*, Four Winds) Macmillan Child Grp.

Fox, Robin. Poulet: A Rooster Who Laid Eggs. (FRE., Illus.). 3.50 (*0-685-11509-7*) Fr & Eur.

Froehlich, Margaret W. That Kookoory! Frazee, Marla, illus. LC 93-41833. 1995. write for info. (*0-15-277650-8*, Browndeer Pr) HarBrace.

Harper-Deiters, Cyndi. Jonathan Michael & the Perilous Flight. Ruggles, Robert & Ruggles, Grace, eds. Bowers, Helen M., illus. 34p. (gr. 2-4). Date not set. pap. 4.95 (*0-9632513-3-3*) Cntry Home.

—The Jonathan Michael Series. Ruggles, Robert & Ruggles, Grace, eds. Bowers, Helen M., illus. (Orig.). (gr. 2-5). 1993. pap. text ed. write for info. (*0-9632513-4-1*) Cntry Home.

—Jonathan Michael: The Resident Rooster. LC 92-70663. 40p. (gr. 3). 1992. pap. 4.95 (*0-9632513-0-9*) Cntry Home.

Kimmel, Eric A. Valiant Red Rooster. 1995. write for info. (*0-8050-2781-5*) H Holt & Co.

Lewison, Wendy C. The Rooster Who Lost His Crow. Wickstrom, Thor, illus. LC 93-28059. 1994. write for info. (*0-8037-1545-5*); PLB write for info. (*0-8037-1546-3*) Dial Bks Young.

McLean, Janet. Hector & Maggie. McLean, Andrew, illus. 32p. (Orig.). (gr. k-2). 1993. 16.95 (*0-04-442162-1*, Pub. by Allen & Unwin Aust Pty AT); pap. 6.95 (*0-04-442245-8*, Pub. by Allen & Unwin Aust Pty AT) IPG Chicago.

Peet, Bill. Cock-a-Doodle Dudley. Peet, Bill, illus. 48p. (gr. k-3). 1990. 14.45 (*0-395-55331-8*) HM.

—Cock-A-Doodle Dudley. Peet, Bill, illus. 48p. (gr. k-3). 1993. pap. 4.80 (*0-395-65745-8*) HM.

Peters, Sharon. The Rooster & the Weather Vane. Harvey, Paul, illus. LC 86-30838. 32p. (gr. k-2). 1988. PLB 7.89 (*0-8167-0980-7*); pap. text ed. 1.95 (*0-8167-0981-5*) Troll Assocs.

Scamell, Ragnhild. Rooster Crows. Riches, Judith, illus. LC 93-31348. 1994. 15.00 (*0-688-13290-1*, Tambourine Bks); PLB 14.93 (*0-688-13291-X*, Tambourine Bks) Morrow.

Threadgall, Colin. Proud Rooster & the Fox. LC 91-15004. (Illus.). 32p. (ps-3). 1992. 14.00 (*0-688-11123-8*, Tambourine Bks); PLB 13.93 (*0-688-11124-6*, Tambourine Bks) Morrow.

Toepperwein, Emilie & Toepperwein, Fritz. Chinto, The Chaparral Cock. (gr. 4-7). 2.95 (*0-910722-04-8*) Highland Pr.

Uchida, Yoshiko. The Rooster Who Understood Japanese. 8.95 (*0-684-14672-X*) JACP Inc.

ROPE

Hindley, Judy. A Piece of String Is a Wonderful Thing. Chamberlain, Margaret, illus. LC 92-53137. 32p. (ps up). 1993. 14.95 (*1-56402-147-5*) Candlewick Pr.

Severn, Bill. Bill Severn's Magic with Rope, Ribbon, & String. LC 93-17893. (Illus.). 224p. 1994. pap. 12.95 (*0-8117-2533-2*) Stackpole.

—Magic with Rope, Ribbon, & String. 224p. (gr. 6 up). 1981. 9.95 (*0-679-20813-5*) McKay.

ROSES–FICTION

Brisson, Pat. Wanda's Roses. Cocca-Leffler, Maryann, illus. 32p. (ps-3). 1994. 14.95 (*1-56397-136-4*) Boyds Mills Pr.

Helldorfer, M. C. Cabbage Rose. Downing, Julie, illus. LC 91-9833. 32p. (ps-3). 1993. RSBE 14.95 (*0-02-743513-X*, Bradbury Pr) Macmillan Child Grp.

Ichikawa, Satomi. Nora's Roses. (Illus.). 32p. (ps up). 1993. PLB 14.95 (*0-399-21968-4*, Philomel Bks) Putnam Pub Group.

Johnson, Janice. Rosamund. Haeffele, Deborah, illus. LC 92-44115. (gr. k-3). 1994. pap. 15.00 (*0-671-79329-2*, S&S BFYR) S&S Trade.

Lobel, Arnold. The Rose in My Garden. Lobel, Anita, illus. LC 92-24588. 40p. (ps up). 1993. pap. 4.95 (*0-688-12265-5*, Mulberry) Morrow.

ROSH HASHONAH

Bin-Nun, Judy & Einhorn, Franne. Rosh Hashanah: A Holiday Funtext. Steinberger, Heidi, illus. (gr. 1-3). 1978. pap. 5.00 (*0-8074-0230-3*, 101300) UAHC.

Chaikin, Miriam. Sound the Shofar: The Story & Meaning of Rosh HaShanah & Yom Kippur. Weihs, Erika, illus. LC 86-2651. 96p. (gr. 3-7). 1986. (Clarion Bks); pap. 4.95 (*0-89919-427-3*, Clarion Bks) HM.

Eisenberg, Ann. I Can Celebrate. Schanzer, Roz, illus. LC 88-83567. 12p. (ps). 1989. bds. 4.95 (*0-930494-93-8*) Kar Ben.

Epstein, Sylvia. How the Rosh Hashanah Challah Became Round. Migron, Hagit, illus. 28p. 1993. 8.95 (*0-317-05847-9*, Pub. by Gefen Pub Hse IS) Gefen Bks.

Friedman, Audrey M. & Zwerin, Raymond. High Holy Day Do It Yourself Dictionary. Ruten, Marlene L., illus. 32p. (gr. k-3). 1983. pap. 5.00 (*0-8074-0162-5*, 101100) UAHC.

Gellman, Ellie. It's Rosh-Hashanah. Kahn, Katherine J., illus. LC 85-80783. 12p. (ps). 1985. bds. 4.95 (*0-930494-50-4*) Kar Ben.

Goldin, Barbara D. World's Birthday. LC 89-29208. 28p. (ps-3). 1990. 13.95 (*0-15-299648-6*) HarBrace.

Kahn, Katherine, illus. The Shofar Calls to Us. LC 91-60592. 12p. (ps). 1991. bds. 4.95 (*0-929371-61-5*) Kar Ben.

Levin, Carol. A Rosh Hashanah Walk. Kahn, Katherine J., illus. LC 87-3106. (ps-3). 1987. 4.95 (*0-930494-70-9*) Kar Ben.

Simon, Norma. Rosh Hashanah. Gordon, Ayala, illus. (ps-k). 1961. plastic cover 4.50 (*0-8381-0700-1*) United Syn Bk.

ROSS, BETSY (GRISCOM) 1752-1836

Spencer, Eve. A Flag for Our Country. Eagle, Mike, illus. LC 92-14414. 32p. (gr. 2-5). 1992. PLB 18.51 (*0-8114-7211-6*) Raintree Steck-V.

Wallner, Alexandra. Betsy Ross. Wallner, Alexandra, illus. LC 93-3559. 32p. (ps-3). 1994. reinforced bdg. 15.95 (*0-8234-1071-4*) Holiday.

Weil, Ann. Betsy Ross: Designer of Our Flag. Fiorentino, Al, illus. LC 86-10775. 192p. (gr. 2 up). 1986. pap. 3.95 (*0-02-042120-6*, Aladdin) Macmillan Child Grp.

ROUND TABLE

see Arthur, King

ROUSSEAU, HENRI JULIEN FELIX, 1844-1910

Plazy, Gilles. A Weekend with Rousseau. LC 93-12187. (Illus.). 64p. 1993. 19.95 (*0-8478-1717-2*) Rizzoli Intl.

ROUTES OF TRADE

see Trade Routes

ROWING

Rowing. (Illus.). 48p. (gr. 6-12). 1981. pap. 1.85 (*0-8395-3392-6*, 33290) BSA.

ROWING–FICTION

Kingman, Lee. The Luck of the Miss L. LC 92-24600. 160p. (gr. 5 up). 1993. pap. 4.95 (*0-688-11779-1*, Pub. by Beech Tree Bks) Morrow.

ROYALTY

see Kings and Rulers; Queens

RUBBER

Curtis, Neil & Greenland, Peter. How Tires Are Made. (Illus.). 24p. (gr. 1-3). 1992. PLB 13.50 (*0-8225-2377-9*) Lerner Pubns.

Lewington, Anna. Antonio's Rain Forest. Parker, Edward, photos by. (Illus.). 48p. (gr. 2-5). 1993. 21.50 (*0-87614-749-X*) Carolrhoda Bks.

Mitgutsch, Ali. From Rubber Tree to Tire. Lerner, Mark, tr. from GER. Mitgutsch, Ali, illus. 24p. (ps-3). 1986. lib. bdg. 10.95 (*0-87614-297-8*) Carolrhoda Bks.

RUBBER TIRES

see Tires

RUDOLPH, WILMA, 1940-

Coffey, Wayne. Wilma Rudolph. (Illus.). 64p. (gr. 3-7). 1993. PLB 14.95 (*1-56711-004-5*) Blackbirch.

RUINS

see Cities and Towns, Ruined, Extinct, Etc.

RULERS

see Kings and Rulers; Queens

RULES OF ORDER

see Parliamentary Practice

RUMANIA

Carran, Betty B. Romania. LC 87-35423. (Illus.). 124p. (gr. 5-9). 1988. PLB 20.55 (*0-516-02703-4*) Childrens.

Gligor, Adrian & Strauss, Karen. Romanian Traditions & Customs. Strauss, Karen, illus. 32p. (Orig.). (ps-4). 1993. pap. 11.95 (*0-9634797-1-7*) K Strauss & A Gligor.

Lerner Publications Company, Geography Department Staff. Romania: In Pictures. LC 92-32861. 1993. PLB 17.50 (*0-8225-1894-5*) Lerner Pubns.

Stewart, Gail B. Romania. LC 90-24946. (Illus.). 48p. (gr. 6-7). 1991. text ed. 12.95 RSBE (*0-89686-600-9*, Crestwood Hse) Macmillan Child Grp.

RUMANIA–FICTION

Orlev, Uri. Lydia: Queen of Palestine. Halkin, Hillel, tr. from HEB. LC 93-12488. 1993. 13.95 (*0-395-65660-5*) HM.

Pullein-Thompson, Christine. The Long Search. LC 92-40349. 160p. (gr. 5-9). 1993. SBE 13.95 (*0-02-775445-6*, Bradbury Pr) Macmillan Child Grp.

RUNAWAYS

Redpath, Ann. What Happens If You Run Away from Home? (Illus.). 48p. (gr. 3-6). Date not set. PLB 12.95 (*1-56065-133-4*) Capstone Pr.

Switzer, Ellen. Anyplace but Here: Young, Alone & Homeless: What to Do. LC 92-15. 176p. (gr. 5 up). 1992. SBE 14.95 (*0-689-31694-1*, Atheneum Child Bk) Macmillan Child Grp.

Walsh, Joy & Fuda, Siri, eds. Life Junkies: On Our Own. (Illus.). 200p. (Orig.). (gr. 9-12). 1990. pap. 8.00 (*0-938838-51-2*) Textile Bridge.

RUNAWAYS–FICTION

Avi. Encounter at Easton. Cohn, Amy, ed. LC 94-81. 144p. (gr. 5 up). 1994. pap. 4.95 (*0-688-05296-7*, Pub. by Beech Tree Bks) Morrow.

Blacker, Terence. Homebird. LC 92-23536. 144p. (gr. 7 up). 1993. SBE 13.95 (*0-02-710685-3*, Bradbury Pr) Macmillan Child Grp.

Bunting, Eve. The Hideout. D'Andrade, Diane, ed. 133p. (gr. 3-7). 1991. 14.95 (*0-15-233990-6*) HarBrace.

Cleary, Beverly. Runaway Ralph. 176p. (gr. k-6). 1981. pap. 3.25 (*0-440-47519-8*, YB) Dell.

Corcoran, Barbara. The Hideaway. LC 86-28849. 128p. (gr. 5-9). 1987. SBE 13.95 (*0-689-31353-5*, Atheneum Child Bk) Macmillan Child Grp.

Cresswell, Helen. The Watchers: A Mystery at Alton Towers. LC 93-41683. (gr. 3-7). 1994. 14.95 (*0-02-725371-6*, Macmillan Child Bk) Macmillan Child Grp.

Doherty, Berlie. Street Child. large type ed. (Illus.). (gr. 1-8). 1994. 15.95 (*0-7451-2225-6*, Galaxy etc.) Chivers N Amer.

Garden, Nancy. Lark in the Morning. 288p. (gr. 9-12). 1991. 14.95 (*0-374-34338-1*) FS&G.

Gleitzman, Morris. Worry Warts. LC 92-22631. 1993. 12.95 (*0-15-299666-4*) HarBrace.

Gorman, Carol. The Taming of Roberta Parsley. Koehler, Ed, illus. LC 93-38312. 96p. (Orig.). (gr. 4-7). 1994. pap. 3.99 (*0-570-04628-9*) Concordia.

Grater, Lindsay. Runaway Row. Grater, Lindsay, illus. 24p. (ps-3). 1992. PLB 15.95 (*1-55037-213-0*, Pub. by Annick CN); pap. 5.95 (*1-55037-210-6*, Pub. by Annick CN) Firefly Bks Ltd.

Gregory, Kristiana. Legend of Jimmy Spoon. 165p. (gr. 3-7). 1990. 15.95 (*0-15-200506-4*) HarBrace.

Griffin, Peni R. Hobkin. LC 91-24079. 208p. (gr. 4-7). 1992. SBE 14.95 (*0-689-50539-6*, M K McElderry) Macmillan Child Grp.

—Hobkin. LC 93-7758. 208p. (gr. 3-7). 1993. pap. 3.99 (*0-14-036356-4*, Puffin) Puffin Bks.
Hamilton, Morse. Effie's House. LC 89-11918. 224p. (gr. 7 up). 1990. 13.95 (*0-688-09307-8*) Greenwillow.
Haugen, Tormod. Zeppelin. Diamond, Donna, illus. Jacobs, David R., tr. from NOR. LC 92-8319. (Illus.). 128p. (gr. 4-7). 1994. 15.00 (*0-06-020881-3*); PLB 14.89 (*0-06-020882-1*) HarpC Child Bks.
Hooks, William H. & Boegehold, Betty D. The Rainbow Ribbon. Munsinger, Lynn, illus. LC 93-27706. 32p. 1995. pap. 3.99 (*0-14-054092-X*) Puffin Bks.
Killingsworth, Monte. Circle Within a Circle. LC 93-17244. 176p. (gr. 7 up). 1994. SBE 14.95 (*0-689-50598-1*, M K McElderry) Macmillan Child Grp.
Kiser, SuAnn. The Catspring Somersault Flying One-Handed Flip-Flop. Catalanotto, Peter, illus. LC 92-44519. 32p. (ps-2). 1993. 14.95 (*0-531-05493-4*); PLB 14.99 (*0-531-08643-7*) Orchard Bks Watts.
Konigsburg, E. L. From the Mixed-Up Files of Mrs. Basil E. Frankweiler. LC 86-25903. (Illus.). 176p. (gr. 4-7). 1987. pap. 3.95 (*0-689-71181-6*, Aladdin) Macmillan Child Grp.
Lexau, Joan M. Emily & the Klunky Baby & the Next-Door Dog. Alexander, Martha, illus. LC 77-181789. 40p. (ps-3). 1972. 5.95 (*0-8037-2309-1*) Dial Bks Young.
McCully, Emily A. My Real Family. LC 92-46290. 1994. 13.95 (*0-15-277698-2*, Browndeer Pr) HarBrace.
Macken, Walter. Flight of the Doves. LC 91-3922. 1992. pap. 14.00 (*0-671-73801-1*, S&S BFYR) S&S Trade.
Nelson, Theresa. The Beggars' Ride. LC 90-52515. 256p. (gr. 6-12). 1992. 15.95 (*0-531-05896-4*); PLB 15.99 (*0-531-08496-5*) Orchard Bks Watts.
Pascal, Francine. Todd Runs Away. 1994. pap. 3.50 (*0-553-48100-2*) Bantam.
Paulsen, Gary. Tiltawhirl John. 1990. pap. 3.95 (*0-14-034312-1*, Puffin) Puffin Bks.
Percy Runs Away. (gr. 2 up). Date not set. write for info. (*0-679-86208-0*) Random Bks Yng Read.
Radley, Gail. The Golden Days. LC 92-19526. 160p. (gr. 5 up). 1992. pap. 3.99 (*0-14-036002-6*) Puffin Bks.
Robins, Joan. Addie Runs Away. Truesdell, Sue, illus. LC 88-24350. 32p. (ps-2). 1991. pap. 3.50 (*0-06-444147-4*, Trophy) HarpC Child Bks.
Schories, Pat. He's Your Dog. (ps-3). 1993. 15.00 (*0-374-32906-0*) FS&G.
Schur, Maxine R. The Circlemaker. LC 93-17983. 1994. 13.99 (*0-8037-1354-1*) Dial Bks Young.
Smucker, Barbara. Runaway to Freedom. (gr. 4-8). 1992. 17.00 (*0-8446-6585-1*) Peter Smith.
Uspenski, Eduard. Uncle Fedya, His Dog, & His Cat. Shpitalnik, Vladimir, illus. Heim, Michael, tr. from RUS. LC 92-44491. (Illus.). 144p. (gr. 1-5). 1993. 14.00 (*0-679-82064-7*) Knopf Bks Yng Read.
Van Raven, Pieter. Pickle & Price. LC 89-10846. 224p. (gr. 7 up). 1990. SBE 14.95 (*0-684-19162-8*, Scribners Young Read) Macmillan Child Grp.
Wright, Richard. Rite of Passage. Rampersad, Arnold, afterword by. LC 93-2473. 128p. (gr. 7 up). 1994. 12.95 (*0-06-023419-9*); PLB 12.89 (*0-06-023420-2*) HarpC Child Bks.

RUNNING
see Track Athletics

RURAL ARCHITECTURE
see Architecture, Domestic

RURAL LIFE
see Country Life; Outdoor Life

RURAL LIFE–FICTION
Carlstrom, Nancy W. Baby-O. Stevenson, Sucie, illus. 32p. (ps-3). 1992. 14.95 (*0-316-12851-1*) Little.
Casad, Mary B. Bluebonnet of the Hill Country. Binder, Pat, illus. (gr. k-4). 1983. 11.95 (*0-89015-395-7*, Pub. by Panda Bks) Sunbelt Media.
Chambers, Vickie. In the Silence of the Hills. Taylor, LaVonne, ed. (Illus.). (gr. 9-12). 1994. write for info. (*0-9627735-1-4*) Excllnc Entrps.
Johnson, Allen, Jr. The Christmas Tree Express. Keetle, Lisbeth, illus. (gr. 4-8). Date not set. 12.95 (*1-878561-21-9*) Seacoast AL.

RUSSELL, BILL, 1934-
Shapiro, Miles. Bill Russell. King, Coretta Scott, intro. by. (Illus.). 112p. (gr. 5 up). 1991. lib. bdg. 17.95 (*0-7910-1136-4*) Chelsea Hse.

RUSSIAN LANGUAGE
Amery, Heather & Kirilenko, Katrina. The First Thousand Words in Russian. Cartwright, Stephen, illus. 64p. (gr. k-7). 1983. 11.95 (*0-86020-769-2*) EDC.
Anpilogova, B. G., et al. Foundation Dictionary of Russian: Three Thousand High Semantic Frequency Words. (RUS & ENG.). 178p. (gr. 9-12). 1967. pap. 4.95 (*0-486-21860-0*) Dover.
Mahoney, Judy. Teach Me Russian. Gybin, Sasha, tr. 20p. (Orig.). (ps-6). 1991. pap. 11.95 incl. audiocassette (*0-934633-51-7*); tchr's. ed. 5.95 (*0-934633-31-2*) Teach Me.

RUSSIAN LITERATURE
Volkov, Alexander. The Wizard of Emerald City & Urfin Jus & His Wooden Soldiers. Blystone, Peter L., tr. from RUS. LC 90-62416. (gr. 4 up). 1991. pap. 11.95 (*1-878941-16-X*) Red Branch Pr.
Volkov, Alexander M. The Seven Underground Kings; & The Fiery God of the Marrans. Blystone, Peter L., tr. from RUS. & afterword by. LC 90-83409. 384p. (Orig.). (gr. 4 up). 1993. pap. 13.95 (*1-878941-18-6*) Red Branch Pr.

RUSSIAN SATELLITE COUNTRIES
see Communist Countries

RUSSIANS IN THE U. S.
Brown, Tricia. L' Chaim: The Story of a Russian Emigre Boy. LC 93-44853. (gr. 2-5). 1994. 15.95 (*0-8050-2354-2*) H Holt & Co.
Magosci, Paul R. The Russian Americans. Moynihan, Daniel P., intro. by. (Illus.). 112p. (gr. 5 up). 1989. 17.95x (*0-87754-899-4*) Chelsea Hse.
Rosenblum, Richard. Journey to the Golden Land. Rosenblum, Richard, illus. LC 91-44941. 32p. (gr. k-4). 1992. 14.95 (*0-8276-0405-X*) JPS Phila.

RUSSWURM, JOHN BROWN, 1799-1851
Borzendowski, Janice. John Russwurm. (Illus.). 112p. (gr. 5 up). 1989. 17.95 (*1-55546-610-9*) Chelsea Hse.

RUTH (BIBLICAL CHARACTER)
Alexander, Matilda. Ruth. Butcher, Sam, illus. 48p. (gr. k-6). 1972. pap. text ed. 9.45 (*1-55976-017-6*) CEF Press.
Berg, Jean H., adapted by. The Story of Ruth. Palm, Felix & Crouch, Ellen, illus. 32p. pap. 9.95 (*0-87510-273-5*, G81244) Christian Sci.
Frank, Penny. Ruth's New Family. Morris, Tony, et al, illus. 24p. (ps-3). 3.99 (*0-85648-740-6*) Lion USA.
Miller, R. Edward. Romance of Redemption. 213p. (Orig.). (gr. 10). 1990. pap. 7.95 (*0-945818-09-2*) Peniel Pubns.
Ruth. (gr. 3 up). pap. 2.50 perfect bdg. (*1-55748-173-3*) Barbour & Co.

RUTH, GEORGE HERMAN, 1895-1948
Bains, Rae. Babe Ruth. Smolinski, Dick, illus. LC 84-2595. 32p. (gr. 3-6). 1985. PLB 9.49 (*0-8167-0144-X*); pap. text ed. 2.95 (*0-8167-0145-8*) Troll Assocs.
Berke, Art. Babe Ruth: The Best There Ever Was. Rakos, Jennie, ed. LC 87-27366. (Illus.). 128p. (gr. 7-12). 1988. PLB 14.40 (*0-531-10472-9*) Watts.
Brandt, Keith. Babe Ruth, Home Run Hero. Frenck, Hal, illus. LC 85-1091. 48p. (gr. 4-6). 1986. lib. bdg. 10.79 (*0-8167-0553-4*); pap. text ed. 3.50 (*0-8167-0554-2*) Troll Assocs.
Eisenberg, Lisa. The Story of Babe Ruth. (gr. k-6). 1990. pap. 2.95 (*0-440-40274-3*, YB) Dell.
Farr, Naunerle C. Babe Ruth-Jackie Robinson. Caravana, Tony & Cruz, Nardo, illus. (gr. 4-12). 1979. pap. text ed. 2.95 (*0-88301-359-2*); wkbk 1.25 (*0-88301-383-5*) Pendulum Pr.
Green, Carl R. & Sanford, William R. Babe Ruth. LC 91-21639. (Illus.). 48p. (gr. 5). 1992. text ed. 11.95 RSBE (*0-89686-741-2*, Crestwood Hse) Macmillan Child Grp.
Jacobs, William J. They Shaped the Game. LC 94-14007. (gr. 4-6). 1994. 15.95 (*0-684-19734-0*, Scribner) Macmillan.
Macht, Norm. Babe Ruth. Murray, Jim, intro. by. (Illus.). 64p. (gr. 3 up). 1991. lib. bdg. 14.95 (*0-7910-1189-5*) Chelsea Hse.
Rothaus, Jim. Babe Ruth. (ENG & SPA.). (gr. 2-6). 1992. PLB 14.95 (*0-89565-962-X*) Childs World.
Van Riper, Guernsey, Jr. Babe Ruth: One of Baseball's Greatest. Fleishman, Seymour, illus. LC 86-10957. 192p. (gr. 2-6). 1986. pap. 3.95 (*0-02-042130-3*, Aladdin) Macmillan Child Grp.
Weber, Bruce. Babe Ruth: Classic Sports Shots. 1993. pap. 1.25 (*0-590-47018-3*) Scholastic Inc.

S

SABBATH
Abrams, Judith Z. Shabbat: A Family Service. Kahn, Katherine J., illus. LC 91-31640. 24p. (Orig.). (gr. k-3). 1992. pap. text ed. 3.95 (*0-929371-29-1*) Kar Ben.
Groner, Judye & Wikler, Madeline. Shabbat Shalom. Yaffa, illus. LC 88-83568. 12p. (ps). 1989. bds. 4.95 (*0-930494-91-1*) Kar Ben.
Kobre, Faige. A Sense of Shabbat. LC 89-40361. (Illus.). 32p. 1990. 11.95 (*0-933873-44-1*) Torah Aura.
Robinson, Glen. Fifty-Two Things to Do on Sabbath. Wheeler, Gerald, ed. Kinzer, Kaaren, illus. (Orig.). 1983. pap. 2.95 (*0-8280-0199-5*) Review & Herald.
Saypol, Judyth R. & Wikler, Madeline. Come Let Us Welcome Shabbat. LC 83-25638. (Illus.). 32p. (ps up). 1978. pap. 2.95 (*0-930494-04-0*) Kar Ben.
Schwartz, Howard & Rush, Barbara, eds. Sabbath Lion: A Jewish Folktale from Algeria. LC 91-35766. (Illus.). 32p. (gr. k-4). 1992. 14.00 (*0-06-020853-8*); PLB 13.89 (*0-06-020854-6*) HarpC Child Bks.
Simon, Norma. Every Friday Night. Weiss, Harvey, illus. (ps-k). plastic cover 4.50 (*0-8381-0708-7*) United Syn Bk.

SABBATH–FICTION
Schur, Maxine R. Day of Delight: A Jewish Sabbath in Ethiopia. Pinkney, Brian, illus. LC 93-31451. (gr. 3 up). 1994. 15.99 (*0-8037-1413-0*); PLB 15.89 (*0-8037-1414-9*) Dial Bks Young.
Snyder, Carol. God Must Like Cookies, Too. Glick, Beth, illus. LC 92-26886. 32p. (ps-3). 1993. 16.95 (*0-8276-0423-8*) JPS Phila.

SABIN, FLORENCE, 1871-1953
Kronstadt, Janet. Florence Sabin. Horner, Matina S., intro. by. (Illus.). 112p. (gr. 5 up). 1990. 17.95 (*1-55546-676-1*) Chelsea Hse.

SACAJAWEA, 1786-1884
Bryant, Martha F. Sacajawea: A Native American Heroine. Gilliland, Hap, ed. Sargent, Heather & Gilliland, Hap, illus. 256p. (Orig.). 1989. 21.95 (*0-89992-420-4*); pap. 15.95 (*0-89992-120-5*) Coun India Ed.
Gleiter, Jan & Thompson, Kathleen. Sacagawea. Miyake, Yoshi, illus. 32p. (gr. 2-5). 1987. PLB 19.97 (*0-8172-2651-6*) Raintree Steck-V.
Jassem, Kate. Sacajawea, Wilderness Guide. new ed. LC 78-60118. (Illus.). 48p. (gr. 4-6). 1979. PLB 10.59 (*0-89375-160-X*); pap. 3.50 (*0-89375-150-2*) Troll Assocs.
O'Dell, Scott. Streams to the River, River to the Sea: A Novel of Sacagawea. 1986. 14.45 (*0-395-40430-4*) HM.
Raphael, Elaine & Bolognese, Don. Sacajawea: The Journey West. LC 93-49002. (gr. 1-3). 1994. 12.95 (*0-590-47898-2*) Scholastic Inc.
Seymour, Flora W. Sacagawea: American Pathfinder. Doremus, Robert, illus. LC 90-23267. 192p. (gr. 3-7). 1991. pap. 3.95 (*0-689-71482-3*, Aladdin) Macmillan Child Grp.

SACCO-VANZETTI CASE
Rappaport, Doreen. The Sacco-Vanzetti Trial. LC 91-47509. (Illus.). 176p. (gr. 5 up). 1992. 14.00 (*0-06-025115-8*); PLB 13.89 (*0-06-025116-6*) HarpC Child Bks.
—The Sacco-Vanzetti Trial. LC 91-47509. (Illus.). 176p. (gr. 5 up). 1994. pap. 4.95 (*0-06-446113-0*, Trophy) HarpC Child Bks.

SACRED ART
see Christian Art and Symbolism

SACRED MUSIC
see Church Music

SAFETY EDUCATION
see also Accidents–Prevention
Ahbe, Dottie & Pluta, Terry. Safety Always Matters. Saba Designs, Inc. Staff & Ahbe, S., illus. 16p. (gr. 1-3). 1992. wkbk. 0.59 (*0-9620584-1-6*) Safety Always Matters.
—Safety Always Matters. Saba Designs, Inc. Staff & Ahbe, S., illus. 16p. (ps-k). 1992. wkbk. 0.59 (*0-9620584-0-8*) Safety Always Matters.
—Safety Always Matters. Saba Designs, Inc. Staff & Ahbe, S., illus. 16p. (gr. 4-6). 1992. wkbk. 0.59 (*0-9620584-2-4*) Safety Always Matters.
—Safety Always Matters. Saba Designs, Inc. Staff & Ahbe, S., illus. 32p. (ps-k). 1991. wkbk. 2.00 (*0-9620584-3-2*) Safety Always Matters.
—Safety Always Matters. Saba Designs, Inc. Staff & Ahbe, S., illus. 32p. (gr. 1-3). 1988. wkbk. 2.00 (*0-9620584-4-0*) Safety Always Matters.
—Safety Always Matters. Saba Designs, Inc. Staff & Ahbe, S., illus. 32p. (gr. 4-6). 1988. wkbk. 2.00 (*0-9620584-5-9*) Safety Always Matters.
Arnosky, Jim. Crinkleroot's Guide to Walking in Wild Places. Arnosky, Jim, illus. LC 92-45775. 32p. (gr. k-5). 1993. pap. 4.95 (*0-689-71753-9*, Aladdin) Macmillan Child Grp.
Boyer. Let's Walk Safely. LC 80-82953. (Illus.). 32p. (gr. 1-6). 1981. PLB 9.95 (*0-87783-159-9*) Oddo.
—Oddo Safety Series. (Illus.). (ps-6). Set of 4 vols. PLB 44.60 (*0-87783-170-X*); three cassettes o.s.i. 23.82x (*0-87783-235-8*) Oddo.
Brady, Janeen. Safety Kids Personal Safety, Vol. 1. Underwood, Oscar, tr. (SPA., Orig.). (gr. k-6). 1984. dialogue bk. 1.50 (*0-944803-18-0*); Trans. by Oscar Underwood, in Spanish, 1984, 6pgs. pap. text ed. 1.50 dialogue bk. (*0-944803-19-9*); songbk. 6.95 (*0-944803-15-6*); act. bk. 2.50 (*0-944803-16-4*); cassette & bk. 10.95 (*0-944803-17-2*) Brite Music.
—Safety Kids Personal Safety, Vol. 1. Twede, Evan, illus. 14p. (gr. k-6). 1983. Set of 20. wkbk. 12.00 (*0-944803-20-2*) Brite Music.
—Safety Kids Play it Smart: Stay Safe from Drugs, Vol. 2. Twede, Evan, illus. 14p. (gr. k-6). 1985. Set of 20. wkbk. 12.00 (*0-944803-25-3*) Brite Music.
—Safety Kids, Vol. 3: Protect Their Minds. 24p. (Orig.). (gr. k-6). Date not set. pap. text ed. 1.50 dialogue script (*0-944803-82-2*) Brite Music.
Buschman, Janis & Hunley, Debbie. Strangers Don't Look Like the Big Bad Wolf! Lyons, Carole & Meyer, Linda D., eds. Megale, Marina, illus. McMorris, Sharon, intro. by. LC 85-80513. (Illus.). 38p. (Orig.). (gr. 2-4). 1985. lib. bdg. 9.00 (*0-932091-04-0*); pap. 3.95 (*0-932091-05-9*) Franklin Pr WA.
Carratello, Patricia. Let's Investigate Health & Safety. (Illus.). 48p. (gr. 1-4). 1984. wkbk. 6.95 (*1-55734-214-8*) Tchr Create Mat.
Chlad, Dorothy. Los Animales Pueden Ser Amigos Especiales - Animals Can Be Special Friends. LC 84-23300. (SPA., Illus.). 32p. (ps-2). 1987. pap. 3.95 (*0-516-51978-6*) Childrens.
—Los Cerillos, los Encendedores y los Triquitraques No Son Juguetes (Matches, Lighters & Firecrackers Are Not Toys) Halverson, Lydia, illus. LC 81-18125. (SPA.). 32p. (ps-2). 1987. pap. 3.95 (*0-516-51982-4*) Childrens.
—Cuando Cruzo la Calle (When I Cross the Street) Kratky, Lada, tr. Halverson, Lydia, illus. LC 85-31397. (SPA.). 32p. (ps-2). 1986. pap. 3.95 (*0-516-51985-9*) Childrens.
—Cuando viajo en auto (When I Ride in a Car) Halverson, Lydia, illus. LC 83-7382. (ENG & SPA.). 32p. (ps-2). 1989. pap. 3.95 (*0-516-51987-5*) Childrens.

—Matches, Lighters, & Firecrackers Are not Toys. LC 81-18125. (Illus.). (gr. k-3). 1982. pap. 3.95 (*0-516-41982-X*) Childrens.

—Playing on the Playground. Halverson, Lydia, illus. LC 87-5197. 32p. (ps-2). 1987. pap. 3.95 (*0-516-41989-7*) Childrens.

—Strangers. LC 81-18109. (Illus.). (gr. k-3). 1982. pap. 3.95 (*0-516-41984-6*) Childrens.

—Viajando en Autobus (Riding on a Bus) Halverson, Lydia, illus. LC 85-12570. (SPA.). 32p. (ps-2). 1988. pap. 3.95 (*0-516-51979-4*) Childrens.

—When I Cross the Street. LC 81-18108. (Illus.). (gr. k-3). 1982. pap. 3.95 (*0-516-41985-4*) Childrens.

—When I Ride in a Car. LC 83-7382. (Illus.). 32p. (ps-2). 1983. pap. 3.95 (*0-516-41987-0*) Childrens.

Courson, Diana. Let's Learn about Safety. Foster, Tom, illus. 64p. (ps-2). 1987. pap. 7.95 (*0-86653-382-6*, GA1011) Good Apple.

Crary, Elizabeth. I'm Lost. Megale, Marina, illus. LC 84-62128. 32p. (Orig.). (ps-2). 1985. PLB 15.95 (*0-943990-08-4*); pap. 4.95 (*0-943990-09-2*) Parenting Pr.

Elbek, Gail. What Every Child Must Know about Grownups. Jaworski, Jo, ed. Taylor, Neil, illus. LC 86-40333. 65p. (gr. k-4). 1990. 5.95 (*1-55523-015-6*) Winston-Derek.

Forte, Imogene. I'm Ready to Learn about Safety. (Illus.). (gr. k-1). 1986. pap. text ed. 1.95 (*0-86530-120-4*, IP 110-8) Incentive Pubns.

Glaser, Nily. Be Street Smart - Be Safe: Raising Safety Minded Children. Kids Against Crime Organization Staff, et al, illus. LC 93-80451. 96p. (Orig.). (gr. k-6). 1994. pap. 9.95 (*0-9632663-2-2*) Gan Pub.
THE MOST COMPREHENSIVE & ENJOYABLE GUIDE TO ONE OF TODAY'S MOST CONCERNING ISSUES: CHILD SAFETY!--WRITTEN BY A VETERAN EDUCATOR. Using rhyme & delightful illustrations, Careful Lee the hound teaches children grades K-6 to: *Differentiate between safe & unsafe situations, without making them fearful *Say an unequivocal NO! when faced by a potentially dangerous situation *Refuse to cooperate with those trying to tempt them. *Distance themselves from unsafe places & people *Use common sense & trust their intuition. "...(This) work is truly important in the fight against crime."--Office of Pete Wilson, Governor of California. "This safety book is long over due!...It is very comprehensive, well thought-out, creative & POSITIVE...It provides a sound foundation that is a must for every home that has children."--Susan Rifkin, School Principal. "This book must be in the hands of every parent & child...A great help in teaching children to minimize potential danger... Important Work!"--Huguette Salti, M.D., Pediatrician. "...a great tool... offers a delightful way to teach children, parents & teachers how to be safety smart...I highly recommend this book to every child, parent & teacher." --Police Sgt. Walter Snyder. May be ordered from publisher 909-381-8844, or Baker & Taylor.
Publisher Provided Annotation.

—Be Street Smart - Be Safe: Raising Safety Minded Children. Kids Against Crime Organization Kids & Cardoza, Julian, illus. LC 93-80451. 72p. (gr. k-6). 1994. pap. 9.95 (*0-9632663-3-0*) Gan Pub.

Hall, Judy A. Don't Just Say No! Safety Workbook for Children. 2nd ed. Edwards, Juanita, ed. Hall, Judy A., illus. 40p. (Orig.). (gr. k-5). 1991. pap. text ed. write for info. saddlestitch (*0-9629597-1-5*) Personal Prods.

—What Every Child Should Know & Do...for Surviving in the 90's: A Small Picture Book. Edwards, Juanita, ed. Hall, Judy A., illus. 24p. (Orig.). (gr. k-5). 1992. saddlestitched 9.95 (*0-9629597-0-7*) Personal Prods.

Hubbard, Kate & Berlin, Evelyn. Help Yourself to Safety: A Guide to Avoiding Dangerous Situations with Strangers & Friends. Meyer, Linda D., ed. Megale, Marina, illus. Walsh, John & Walsh, Whiteintro. by. Lyons, Carole, ed. LC 84-82541. (Illus.). 48p. (Orig.). (gr. 4-6). 1985. lib. bdg. 9.00 (*0-932091-00-8*); pap. 3.95 (*0-932091-01-6*) Franklin Pr WA.

Jance, Judy. Dial Zero for Help: A Story of Parental Kidnapping. Meyer, Linda D. & Lyons, Carole, eds. Megale, Marina, illus. 30p. (Orig.). (gr. k-4). 1985. lib. bdg. 9.00 (*0-932091-06-7*); pap. 3.95 (*0-932091-07-5*) Franklin Pr WA.

—It's Not Your Fault. Meyer, Linda D. & Lyons, Carole R., eds. Megale, Mauna, illus. LC 85-70434. 32p. (gr. k-4). 1985. lib. bdg. 9.00 (*0-932091-03-2*) Franklin Pr Wa.

KIDZ Safety Rap Car Rap Book & Audio Cassette. (Illus.). 64p. (Orig.). (gr. 1). 1993. incl. audiocassette 9.95 (*1-56138-278-7*) Running Pr.

Klingel, Cynthia. Safety First: Fire. LC 86-72672. (ps up). 1986. PLB 12.95 (*0-88682-080-4*) Creative Ed.

Klingel, Cynthia F. Safety First - School. LC 86-72593. (ps up). 1986. PLB 12.95 (*0-88682-084-7*) Creative Ed.

—Safety First - Water. LC 86-72673. (ps up). 1986. PLB 12.95 (*0-88682-083-9*) Creative Ed.

Lehman, Yvette K. Know & Tell: A Work Book for Parents & Children. Myles, Glenn, ed. 50p. (ps-3). 1991. pap. write for info. Artmans Pr.

McGee, Eddie. The Emergency Handbook. Arico, Diane, ed. Barnes-Murphy, Rowan, illus. 176p. (gr. 8-12). 1985. lib. bdg. 9.79 (*0-671-60484-8*); pap. 4.95 (*0-671-60483-X*) S&S Trade.

MacHovec, et al. The Aware Bears. Downey, John & Cohen, Lois, eds. (Illus., Orig.). (gr. k-2). 1991. Set. pap. 39.50 (*0-89976-236-0*) Oceana Educ Comm.

Olah, Suzann M. My Phone Book. 18p. (ps-2). 1991. pap. 6.95 (*0-9630985-0-0*) RJB Enter.

Peissel, Michel & Allen, Missy. The Encyclopedia of Danger, 10 vols. (Illus.). (gr. 5 up). 1993. Set. PLB 199.50 (*0-7910-1784-2*, Am Art Analog) Chelsea Hse.

Poulet, Virginia. Blue Bug's Safety Book. Charles, Donald, illus. LC 72-8348. 32p. (gr. k-3). 1973. PLB 11.80 (*0-516-03419-7*) Childrens.

Reihecky, Janet. Carefulness. Hutton, Kathryn, illus. LC 89-71195. (ENG & SPA.). 32p. (ps-2). 1990. PLB 13.95 (*0-89565-564-0*) Childs World.

Rogers, Quint. The Guardian Coloring Book, Safety Tips for Children. (Illus.). 20p. (gr. k-4). 1993. pap. 1.50 (*0-9637930-0-4*) Creat Wrld.

Safety. (Illus.). 48p. (gr. 6-12). 1986. pap. 1.85 (*0-8395-3347-0*, 33347) BSA.

Santrey, Laurence. Safety. Gold, Ethel, illus. LC 84-2700. 32p. (gr. 3-6). 1985. PLB 9.49 (*0-8167-0230-6*); pap. text ed. 2.95 (*0-8167-0231-4*) Troll Assocs.

Say No to Strangers. 16p. 1994. 0.95 (*0-685-71924-3*, 731) W Gladden Found.

Scott, Kay & Shouse, Lucille. Help Me Bear Shows You How to Call 911. Semingson, Roberta, tr. Scott, Kay & Shouse, Lucille, illus. (ENG & SPA.). 16p. (Orig.). (gr. k-4). 1988. write for info. tchr's. ed. (*0-9620819-1-4*); write for info. color bk. (*0-9620819-0-6*) L Shouse.

Starbuck, Marnie. The Gladimals Fire Safety Book. (Illus.). 16p. 1990. 0.75 (*1-56456-206-9*, 476) W Gladden Found.

—The Gladimals Practice Home Safety. (Illus.). 16p. 1990. 0.75 (*1-56456-205-0*, 475) W Gladden Found.

Student Lifeline, Inc., Staff. Police Officer Friendly's Safety Tips Activity & Coloring Book. rev. ed. Milisello, Clif, illus. 32p. (gr. k-3). 1993. pap. text ed. 1.79x (*1-884888-00-3*) Student Lifeline.
POLICE OFFICER FRIENDLY is a 36 page coloring/activity book which illustrates the primary causes of injury sustained by young children here in the U.S.A. Each "color-in" page is a lesson in safety with an "I promise..." text, for which the child is instructed to print its name. These books are great for teaching safety lessons & prove to be significant regarding the "retention value" of each lesson among tots since the child is actively coloring-in & promising. FREE SUPPLIES ARE MADE AVAILABLE VIA AD SPONSORS FOR LIBRARIES, SCHOOL DISTRICTS & YOUTH POLICE OFFICERS. CALL (516) 327-0800 FOR MORE INFORMATION. EXAMPLE PAPERS: Strangers, 911, electric appliances & water, crossing the street, bike safety, touching, opening the door, windows, ropes, plastic bags, cords, choking, medicine, playing with bad children, roaming away from home, etc.
Publisher Provided Annotation.

Thomas J. Safe at Home, Safe Alone. (Illus.). 64p. (Orig.). (gr. 3-5). 1985. pap. 4.95 (*0-917917-01-4*) Miles River.

World Book, Inc. Staff, ed. Play It Safe! With the Alphabet Pals: Hide- & -Seek Safety. (Illus.). 20p. (ps). 1989. lib. bdg. write for info. (*0-7166-1901-6*) World Bk.

SAFETY EDUCATION–FICTION

Berenstain, Stan & Berenstain, Janice. The Berenstain Bears Learn about Strangers. (Illus.). 32p. (ps-1). 1986. pap. 5.95 (*0-394-88346-2*) Random Bks Yng Read.

Berg, Eric. Bernie's Safe Ideas. LC 93-8905. 1993. write for info. (*1-56071-324-0*) ETR Assocs.

Bissett, Isabel. That's Dangerous. Tulloch, Coral, illus. LC 92-31947. 1993. 3.75 (*0-383-03596-1*) SRA Schl Grp.

Boyer. Accident Kids. LC 73-93019. (Illus.). 32p. (gr. 2-5). 1974. PLB 9.95 (*0-87783-119-X*); pap. 3.94 deluxe ed. (*0-87783-120-3*) cassettes o.s.i. 7.94x (*0-87783-175-0*) Oddo.

—Lucky Bus. LC 73-87801. (Illus.). 32p. (gr. k-2). 1974. PLB 12.35 prebound (*0-87783-131-9*); cassette o.s.i. 7.94x (*0-87783-193-9*) Oddo.

—Safety on Wheels. LC 73-87802. (Illus.). 32p. (gr. k-5). 1974. PLB 12.35 prebound (*0-87783-133-5*); pap. 3.94 deluxe ed. (*0-87783-134-3*); cassette 7.94x (*0-87783-199-8*) Oddo.

Brady, Janeen J. Safety Kids, Vol. 3: Protect Their Minds. Twede, Evan, illus. 32p. (Orig.). (gr. k-6). 1992. pap. 2.50 (*0-944803-78-4*); pap. 10.95 incl. cassette (*0-944803-77-6*) Brite Music.

Chlad, Dorothy. Los Desconocidos (Strangers) Kratky, Lada, tr. from ENG. Halverson, Lydia, illus. LC 81-18109. (SPA.). 32p. (ps-2). 1984. PLB 15.27 (*0-516-31984-1*); pap. 3.95 (*0-516-51984-0*) Childrens.

—Playing Outdoors in the Winter. Halverson, Lydia, illus. LC 90-22258. 32p. (ps-2). 1991. pap. 3.95 (*0-516-41972-2*) Childrens.

—Los Venenos Te Hacen Dano (Poisons Make You Sick) Kratky, Lada, tr. Halverson, Lydia, illus. LC 85-30738. (SPA.). 32p. (ps-2). 1986. PLB 15.27 (*0-516-31976-0*); pap. 3.95 (*0-516-51976-X*) Childrens.

ETR Associates Staff. A Helmet for Harry. Paley, Nina, illus. LC 92-8357. 1992. write for info. (*1-56071-102-7*) ETR Assocs.

Franklin, Herb. Fireman Fred's, Fire Safety Coloring Book. Miller, Jackie, illus. 8p. (gr. 1-5). 1990. pap. 0.50 (*0-945145-02-0*) Miller Family Pubns.

Jagen, Edward J. A Good Knight Story: The Quest for the Missing Children. Gregory, G., et al, eds. Blank, Diane, et al, illus. McCarthy, Dennis, intro. by. 64p. (Orig.). (gr. k-7). 1990. pap. 14.95x (*0-9625641-0-9*); wkbk. 4.95 (*0-9625641-2-5*) White Feather & Co.

—The Quest of the Junior Blue Knights. Blank, Diane, illus. Jagen, E. J., intro. by. (Illus.). 32p. (gr. k-7). 1990. wkbk. 4.95 (*0-9625641-1-7*) White Feather & Co.

Matthews, Cecily. Why Not? Culic, Ned, illus. LC 93-9280. 1994. write for info. (*0-383-03727-1*) SRA Schl Grp.

Moore-Slater, Carole. Dana Doesn't Like Guns Anymore. (Illus., Orig.). 1991. 10.95 (*0-377-00246-1*) Friendship Pr.

Petty, Kate. Mr. Toad to the Rescue. Baker, Alan, illus. 24p. (ps-2). 1992. 8.95 (*0-8120-6273-6*) Barron.

—Mr. Toad's Narrow Escape. (ps-3). 1992. pap. 4.95 (*0-8120-1475-8*) Barron.

—Mr. Toad's Narrow Escapes. (ps-3). 1992. 8.95 (*0-8120-6289-2*) Barron.

Poulet, Virginia. El Libro de Seguridad de Azulin: Blue Bug's Safety Book. LC 72-8348. (SPA., Illus.). 32p. (ps-3). 1992. PLB 11.80 (*0-516-33419-0*); pap. 3.95 (*0-516-53419-X*) Childrens.

Rathmann, Peggy. Officer Buckle & Gloria. LC 93-43887. 1995. write for info. (*0-399-22616-8*, Putnam) Putnam Pub Group.

Shaver, Beth. In Friggleland...Safety Is No Accident! 1993. text ed. 12.95 personalized (*1-883842-07-7*); text ed. 7.95 (*1-883842-06-9*) Kids at Heart.

Steel, Danielle. Martha & Hillary & the Stranger. (ps-3). 1991. 9.95 (*0-385-30212-6*) Delacorte.

Tester, Sylvia R. Magic Monsters Learn about Safety. Magine, John, illus. LC 78-24365. (ps-3). 1979. PLB 14.95 (*0-89565-060-6*) Childs World.

Waters, Sarah. Keeping Safe. LC 92-62550. (Illus.). (ps-2). 1993. 9.95 (*0-89577-475-5*, Dist. by Random) RD Assn.

Ziefert, Harriet. Oh No, Nicky! Brown, Richard, illus. 20p. (ps-1). 1992. pap. 5.99 (*0-14-054521-2*) Puffin Bks.

SAFETY EDUCATION–POETRY

Glaser, Nily. Be Street Smart - Be Safe: Raising Safety Minded Children. Kids Against Crime Organization Staff, et al, illus. LC 93-80451. 96p. (Orig.). (gr. k-6). 1994. pap. 9.95 (*0-9632663-2-2*) Gan Pub.
THE MOST COMPREHENSIVE & ENJOYABLE GUIDE TO ONE OF TODAY'S MOST CONCERNING

SAFETY MEASURES
see Accidents–Prevention;
also subjects with the subdivision Safety Measures, e.g. Aeronautics–Safety Measures

SAHARA DESERT
Halliburton, Warren J. Nomads of the Sahara. LC 91-47153. (Illus.). 48p. (gr. 6). 1992. text ed. 13.95 RSBE (*0-89686-678-5*, Crestwood Hse) Macmillan Child Grp.
Murray, Peter. The Sahara. LC 93-25782. (ENG & SPA.). (gr. 2-6). 1993. 15.95 (*1-56766-023-1*) Childs World.
Reynolds, Jan. Sahara Vanishing Cultures. 30p. (gr. 2 up). 1991. 16.95 (*0-15-269959-7*); pap. 8.95 (*0-15-269958-9*) HarBrace.
Scoones, Simon. The Sahara & Its People. LC 93-16803. 48p. (gr. 5-8). 1993. 15.95 (*1-56847-088-6*) Thomson Lrning.

SAHARA DESERT–FICTION
De Saint-Exupery, Antoine. Little Prince. Woods, Katherine, tr. De Saint-Exupery, Antoine, illus. LC 67-1144. 91p. (gr. 3-7). 1943. 13.95 (*0-15-246503-0*, HB Juv Bks) HarBrace.
—The Little Prince. Woods, Katherine, tr. LC 92-37907. (gr. 4 up). 1993. 50.00 (*0-15-243820-3*) HarBrace.
Kaufmann, Herbert. Adventure in the Desert. Karlin, Eugene, illus. (gr. 7 up). 1961. 10.95 (*0-8392-3000-1*) Astor-Honor.
—Lost Sahara Trail. (gr. 7 up). 1962. 10.95 (*0-8392-3022-2*) Astor-Honor.
Kessler, Cristina. Al Hamdillilai! Schoenherr, Ian, illus. LC 94-6734. 1995. 15.95 (*0-399-22726-1*, Philomel Bks) Putnam Pub Group.

SAILING
see also Boats and Boating; Navigation
Bailey, Donna. Sailing. LC 90-36489. (Illus.). 32p. (gr. 1-4). 1990. PLB 18.99 (*0-8114-2853-2*); pap. 3.95 (*0-8114-4709-X*) Raintree Steck-V.
Barrett, Norman S. Sailing. Franklin Watts Ltd., ed. (Illus.). 32p. (ps-6). 1988. 11.90 (*0-531-10351-X*) Watts.
Crews, Donald. Sail Away. LC 94-6004. (Illus.). 32p. 1995. write for info. (*0-688-11053-3*); lib. bdg. write for info. (*0-688-11054-1*) Greenwillow.
Evans, Jeremy. Sailing. LC 91-12321. (Illus.). 48p. (gr. 5-6). 1992. text ed. 13.95 RSBE (*0-89686-682-3*, Crestwood Hse) Macmillan Child Grp.
Roth, Julee. Get Ready Get Set Go! An Advanced Sailing Manual. (Illus.). 208p. (Orig.). (gr. 7-12). 1993. pap. text ed. 15.95 (*0-9637423-0-2*) JRC Pubns.
Rudder Editors. Good Sailing: An Illustrated Course on Sailing. (Illus.). (gr. 7 up). 1976. pap. 5.95 (*0-679-50630-6*) McKay.
Ships & Sailing. LC 91-60900. (Illus.). 64p. (gr. 6 up). 1991. 14.95 (*1-879431-20-3*); PLB 15.99 (*1-879431-35-1*) Dorling Kindersley.

SAILING–FICTION
Alvord, Douglas. Sarah's Boat: A Young Girl Learns the Art of Sailing. Alvord, Douglas, illus. LC 93-37971. 48p. (gr. 3-8). 1994. 16.95 (*0-88448-117-4*) Tilbury Hse.
Bjorke, Drew. The Magic Sail. Bjorke, Drew, illus. 12p. (ps). 1993. 4.95 (*1-56828-036-X*) Red Jacket Pr.
Calhoun, Mary. Henry the Sailor Cat. Ingraham, Erick, illus. LC 92-29794. 40p. (gr. k up). 1994. 15.00g (*0-688-10840-7*); PLB 14.93 (*0-688-10841-5*) Morrow Jr Bks.
Clements, Bruce. Coming About. 1993. pap. 3.95 (*0-374-41339-8*) FS&G.
Cooper, Marva. Livingston's Vision. (Illus.). (gr. 1-7). 3.95 (*1-882185-08-0*) Crnrstone Pub.
Fry, Ed. Paseo en Barco de Vela - Sailboat Ride. (ENG & SPA., Illus.). 24p. (gr. k-1). 1992. pap. 23.75 (*0-89061-721-X*) Jamestown Pubs.
Haskell, Bess C. Sailing to Pint Pot. Poole, Ann M., illus. 72p. (Orig.). (gr. 4 up). 1993. pap. 10.95 (*0-9626857-4-7*) Coastwise Pr.
Helldorfer, Mary C. Sailing to the Sea. Krupinski, Loretta, illus. 32p. (ps-3). 1993. pap. 4.99 (*0-14-054317-1*, Puffin) Puffin Bks.
Kovacs, Deborah. Moonlight on the River. Shattuck, William, illus. LC 92-28377. (ps-3). 1993. 13.99 (*0-670-84463-2*) Viking Child Bks.
Locke, Eleanor G., ed. Sail Away. Goodfellow, Robin, illus. 164p. (Orig.). 1987. pap. 17.00 (*0-913932-24-8*) Boosey & Hawkes.
Locker, Thomas. Sailing with the Wind. Locker, Thomas, illus. LC 85-23381. 32p. (ps up). 1986. 15.00 (*0-8037-0311-2*); PLB 14.89 (*0-8037-0312-0*) Dial Bks Young.
MacGill-Callahan, Sheila. How the Boats Got Their Sails. LC 93-45966. 1995. write for info. (*0-8037-1541-2*); lib. bdg. write for info. (*0-8037-1542-0*) Dial Bks Young.
One White Sail. (gr. 3 up). 1993. 4.95 (*0-671-87894-8*, Little Simon) S&S Trade.

Smith, E. Boyd. The Seashore Book. Smith, E. Boyd, illus. LC 84-22483. 56p. (gr. k-12). 1985. Repr. of 1912 ed. 13.45 (*0-395-38015-4*) HM.
Swolgaard, Carole. Sailboat Coloring Guide: A Great Five Star Super Deluxe Coloring Book. Seablom, Victoria, ed. Seablom, Seth H., illus. 32p. (Orig.). (gr. 1-6). 1979. pap. 2.50 saddle stitched (*0-918800-07-2*) Seablom.
Weil, Ann. Red Sails to Capri. (gr. 5-9). 16.50 (*0-8446-6413-8*) Peter Smith.

SAILORS
see Seamen

SAILORS' LIFE
see Seafaring Life

ST. LAWRENCE RIVER
Willis, Terri. St. Lawrence River & Seaway. LC 94-3023. (Illus.). 64p. (gr. 5-8). 1994. PLB write for info. (*0-8114-6370-2*) Raintree Steck-V.

ST. LAWRENCE RIVER–FICTION
Holling, Holling C. Paddle-to-the-Sea. (Illus.). (gr. 4-6). 1980. 17.45 (*0-395-15082-5*); pap. 7.95 (*0-395-29203-4*) HM.

ST. LAWRENCE SEAWAY
Gibbons, Gail. The Great St. Lawrence Seaway. Gibbons, Gail, illus. LC 91-9851. 40p. (gr. 1 up). 1992. 15.00 (*0-688-06984-3*); PLB 14.93 (*0-688-06985-1*) Morrow Jr Bks.
Willis, Terri. St. Lawrence River & Seaway. LC 94-3023. (Illus.). 64p. (gr. 5-8). 1994. PLB write for info. (*0-8114-6370-2*) Raintree Steck-V.

ST. LOUIS
Ford, Barbara. St. Louis. LC 88-35912. (Illus.). 60p. (gr. 3 up). 1989. text ed. 13.95 RSBE (*0-87518-402-2*, Dillon) Macmillan Child Grp.

ST. LOUIS–FICTION
Betancourt, Jeanne. Sweet Sixteen & Never... 144p. (Orig.). (gr. 7-12). 1991. pap. 3.50 (*0-553-25534-7*, Starfire) Bantam.

ST. LOUIS CARDINALS (BASEBALL TEAM)
Goodman, Michael. St. Louis Cardinals. 48p. (gr. 4-10). 1992. PLB 14.95 (*0-88682-461-3*) Creative Ed.
Saint Louis Cardinals. (gr. 4-7). 1993. pap. 1.49 (*0-553-56427-7*) Bantam.

ST. PATRICK'S DAY
Barth, Edna. Shamrocks, Harps, & Shillelaghs: The Story of the St. Patrick's Day Symbols. Arndt, Ursula, illus. LC 77-369. 96p. (gr. 3-6). 1982. 15.45 (*0-395-28845-2*, Clarion Bks); pap. 5.95 (*0-89919-038-3*, Clarion) HM.
Davis, Nancy M., et al. St. Patrick's. Davis, Nancy M., illus. 29p. (Orig.). (ps-4). 1986. pap. 4.95 (*0-937103-08-X*) DaNa Pubns.
Freeman, Dorothy R. St. Patrick's Day. LC 91-43098. (Illus.). 48p. (gr. 1-4). 1992. lib. bdg. 14.95 (*0-89490-383-7*) Enslow Pubs.
Gibbons, Gail. St. Patrick's Day. Gibbons, Gail, illus. LC 93-29570. 32p. (ps-3). 1994. reinforced bdg. 15.95 (*0-8234-1119-2*) Holiday.
Johnson, Pamela. Let's Celebrate St. Patricks's Day: A Book of Drawing Fun. LC 87-61374. (Illus.). (gr. 2-6). 1988. PLB 10.65 (*0-8167-1135-6*); pap. 1.95 (*0-8167-1136-4*) Troll Assocs.
Kessel, Joyce K. St. Patrick's Day. Gilchrist, Cathy, illus. LC 82-1254. 48p. (gr. k-4). 1982. lib. bdg. 14.95 (*0-87614-193-9*); pap. 3.95 (*0-87614-482-2*) Carolrhoda Bks.
Riehecky, Janet. St. Patrick's Day. Endres, Helen, illus. LC 93-47640. 32p. (ps-2). 1994. PLB 16.40 (*0-516-00696-7*); pap. 3.95 (*0-516-40696-5*) Childrens.
Ziegler, Sandra. Our St. Patrick's Day Book. Connelly, Gwen, illus. LC 86-31726. 32p. (ps-3). 1987. PLB 13.95 (*0-89565-344-3*) Childs World.

ST. VALENTINE'S DAY
see Valentine's Day

SAINTS
see also Legends
Beebe, Catherine. Saint John Bosco & the Children's Saint Dominic Savio. 2nd ed. LC 92-71930. 157p. 1992. pap. 9.95 (*0-89870-416-2*) Ignatius Pr.
Bisignano, Judith & Sanders, Corine. Saints Alive! Mirocha, Kay, illus. LC 86-63988. 64p. (gr. 5-7). 1987. wkbk. 7.95 (*1-55612-038-9*) Sheed & Ward MO.
Bunson, Margaret & Bunson, Matthew. Kateri Tekakwitha. Bunson, Margaret, illus. LC 92-61548. 56p. (Orig.). 1993. 9.95 (*0-87973-786-7*, 786); pap. 7.95 (*0-87973-560-0*, 560) Our Sunday Visitor.
—St. Patrick. Bunson, Margaret, illus. LC 92-61547. 56p. (Orig.). 1993. 9.95 (*0-87973-785-9*, 785); pap. 7.95 (*0-87973-559-7*, 559) Our Sunday Visitor.
The Children's Book of Saints. (gr. 1-4). 1989. 5.95 (*0-88271-130-X*) Regina Pr.
Daughters of St. Paul. Bells of Conquest. LC 68-28105. (gr. 3-7). 1987. 3.00 (*0-8198-0228-X*); pap. 2.00 (*0-8198-1109-2*) St Paul Bks.
—The Country Road Home. (gr. 3-7). 1987. 3.00 (*0-8198-0232-8*) St Paul Bks.
—Fifty-Seven Saints for Boys & Girls. (Illus.). (gr. 5-8). 1963. 16.95 (*0-8198-0044-9*) St Paul Bks.
—Saints for Young People for Every Day, Vol. 1: January-June. (Illus.). 302p. (gr. 4-8). 1984. pap. 4.50 (*0-8198-0144-5*) St Paul Bks.
DePaola, Tomie. Christopher: The Holy Giant. DePaola, Tomie, illus. 32p. (ps-3). 1994. PLB 15.95 reinforced bdg. (*0-8234-0862-0*) Holiday.
Donze, Mary T. I Can Pray with the Saints. (SPA & ENG., Illus.). 64p. (gr. 2-4). 1993. pap. text ed. 2.95 (*0-89243-514-3*) Liguori Pubns.
Egan, Patricia. St. Brigid: The Girl Who Loved to Give. (Illus.). 24p. (Orig.). (gr. 4-7). 1994. pap. 4.50 (*1-853902-22-5*, Pub. by Veritas Pubns ER) Irish Bks Media.
Greene, Carol. Beggars, Beasts & Easter Fire: Stories of Early Saints. Klausmeier, Robert, ed. Root, Kimberly B., illus. LC 92-31408. 128p. (gr. 3-6). 1993. 15.95 (*0-7459-2221-X*) Lion USA.
Heffernan, Anne E. Fifty-Seven Saints. rev. ed. Myers, Theresa F., ed. Rizzo, Jerry, illus. LC 94-1866. 288p. (gr. 5-8). 1994. 16.95 (*0-8198-2657-X*); pap. 10.95 (*0-8198-2656-1*) St Paul Bks.
Lappin, Peter. Dominic Savio Teenage Saint. rev. ed. LC 81-67928. 145p. (gr. 4-10). 1981. pap. 2.95 (*0-89944-055-X*, Patron) Don Bosco Multimedia.
Panunzi, Paul. Love As Strong As Death. LC 66-30822. (gr. 3-7). 1966. 3.00 (*0-8198-0239-5*) St Paul Bks.
Patterson, Yvonne. Doubting Thomas. (gr. k-4). 1981. pap. 1.99 (*0-570-06144-X*, 59-1261) Concordia.
Scott, Lesbia, text by. I Sing a Song of the Saints of God. LC 91-10393. (Illus.). 32p. (ps-5). 1994. pap. 6.95 (*0-8192-1618-6*) Morehouse Pub.

Scotti, Juliet & Linksman, Ricki. Kirpal Singh: The Story of a Saint. 2nd ed. Tarrant, Valerie, illus. Zaffina, Bruno, intro. by. LC 77-79840. (Illus.). 96p. (gr. 1-7). 1982. pap. 13.00 (*0-918224-05-5*) S K Pubns.

Seco, Nina. The Life of St. Nina. Duckworth, Ruth, illus. (Orig.). (ps-1). 1991. pap. 6.00 (*0-913026-28-X*) St Nectarios.

Seco, Nina & Pilutik, Anastasia D. Saints Adrian & Natalie. Duckworth, Ruth, illus. (Orig.). (ps-1). 1991. pap. write for info. (*0-913026-29-8*) St Nectarios.

Seco, Nina, et al. A Cloud of Witnesses Series. Duckworth, Ruth, illus. (Orig.). (ps-1). 1991. pap. write for info. (*0-913026-27-1*) St Nectarios.

Stone, Elaine M. Elizabeth Bayley Seton: An American Saint. Mitchell, Mark, illus. LC 92-42020. 96p. 1993. pap. 4.95 (*0-8091-6609-7*) Paulist Pr.

Windeatt, Mary F. The Cure of Ars: The Story of Saint John Vianney, Patron Saint of Parish Priests. Harmon, Gedge, illus. LC 90-71827. 211p. (gr. 5-9). 1991. pap. 9.00 (*0-89555-418-6*) TAN Bks Pubs.

—The Little Flower: The Story of Saint Therese of the Child Jesus. Harmon, Gedge, illus. LC 90-71829. 167p. (gr. 5-9). 1991. pap. 7.00 (*0-89555-413-5*) TAN Bks Pubs.

—Patron Saint of First Communicants: The Story of Blessed Imelda Lambertini. Harmon, Gedge, illus. LC 90-71824. 85p. (gr. 5-9). 1991. pap. 4.00 (*0-89555-416-X*) TAN Bks Pubs.

—Saint Catherine of Siena: The Story of the Girl Who Saw Saints in the Sky. Beccard, Helen L., illus. LC 93-60320. 64p. 1993. pap. 4.00 (*0-89555-421-6*) TAN Bks Pubs.

—St. Christopher. Harmon, Gedge, illus. 32p. (gr. 1-5). 1989. Repr. of 1954 ed. wkbk. 3.00 (*0-89555-376-7*) TAN Bks Pubs.

—St. Hyacinth of Poland: The Story of the Apostle of the North. Mary Jean, illus. LC 93-83094. 189p. 1993. pap. 8.00 (*0-89555-422-4*) TAN Bks Pubs.

—St. Louis de Montfort: The Story of Our Lady's Slave. Grout, Paul A., illus. LC 90-71826. 211p. (gr. 5-9). 1991. pap. 9.00 (*0-89555-414-3*) TAN Bks Pubs.

—St. Maria Goretti. Harmon, Gedge, illus. 32p. (gr. 1-5). 1989. Repr. of 1954 ed. wkbk. 3.00 (*0-89555-374-0*) TAN Bks Pubs.

—St. Martin de Porres: The Story of the Little Doctor of Lima, Peru. Mary Jean, illus. LC 93-83095. 122p. 1993. pap. 6.00 (*0-685-70391-6*) TAN Bks Pubs.

—St. Meinrad. Harmon, Gedge, illus. 32p. (gr. 1-5). 1989. Repr. of 1954 ed. wkbk. 3.00 (*0-89555-377-5*) TAN Bks Pubs.

—St. Philomena. Harmon, Gedge, illus. 32p. (gr. 1-5). 1989. Repr. of 1954 ed. wkbk. 3.00 (*0-89555-373-2*) TAN Bks Pubs.

—St. Rose of Lima: The Story of the First Canonized Saint of the Americas. Mary Jean, illus. LC 93-83096. 132p. 1993. pap. 7.00 (*0-89555-424-0*) TAN Bks Pubs.

Windham, Joan. Sixty Saints for Boys. 416p. (gr. 1-6). 1988. pap. 13.95 (*0-87061-149-6*) Chr Classics.

—Sixty Saints for Girls. 384p. (gr. 1-6). 1988. pap. 13.95 (*0-87061-150-X*) Chr Classics.

Young, John. Heroes of Faith: Stories of Saints for Young & Old. 1989. pap. 6.95 (*0-937032-61-1*) Light&Life Pub Co MN.

SAINTS–DICTIONARIES

Daughters of St Paul. Saints for Young People for Every Day of the Year, Vol. 2: July to December. (Illus.). 338p. (gr. 4 up). 1984. pap. 4.50 (*0-8198-0648-X*) St Paul Bks.

SAINTS–FICTION

Christopher, Matt. Beloved St. Anne. LC 92-56932. (Illus.). 69p. (gr. 6-11). 1993. pap. 6.95 (*1-55523-569-7*) Winston-Derek.

De Paola, Tomie. Nuestra Senora de Guadalupe. LC 79-19609. (SPA., Illus.). 48p. (gr. k-4). 1980. reinforced bdg. 16.95 (*0-8234-0374-2*); pap. 6.95 (*0-8234-0404-8*) Holiday.

Hunger, Bill. When Two Saints Meet. Ripley, Jill, ed. Martin, Alice, et al, illus. 100p. (Orig.). (gr. 6-12). pap. 9.95 (*0-9625782-0-7*) Two Saints Pub.

Mohan, Claire J. Kaze's True Home: The Young Life of a Modern Day Saint, Mother Maria Kaupas. Thomer, Susannah, illus. Xuzmickus, Marilyn, intro. by. LC 91-66722. (Illus.). 64p. (gr. 4-9). 1992. 8.95 (*0-9621500-5-3*) Young Sparrow Pr.

Talwalker, Gopinath. Some Indian Saints. Jomra, J., illus. 64p. (Orig.). (gr. 5 up). 1980. pap. 2.50 (*0-89744-208-3*, Pub. by Natl Bk Trust IA) Auromere.

Windeatt, Mary F. St. Teresa of Avila. Harmon, Gedge, illus. 32p. (gr. 1-5). 1989. Repr. of 1954 ed. wkbk. 3.00 (*0-89555-372-4*) TAN Bks Pubs.

SAINTS–LEGENDS

Egan, Patricia. Saint Patrick & the Snakes. (Illus.). 28p. (gr. 1-8). 1990. 9.95 (*1-85390-059-1*, Pub. by Veritas Pubns ER) Irish Bks Media.

Sabuda, Robert. Saint Valentine. Sabuda, Robert, illus. LC 91-25012. 32p. (gr. 1-4). 1992. SBE 14.95 (*0-689-31762-X*, Atheneum Child Bk) Macmillan Child Grp.

Simms, George O. Brendan the Navigator: Exploring the Ancient World. LC 89-82004. (Illus.). 96p. (gr. 7-12). 1989. 13.95 (*0-86278-202-3*, Pub. by OBrien Pr IE) Dufour.

SALADS

Drew, David. Make a Salad Face. Robertson, Ian, illus. LC 92-34335. 1993. 2.50 (*0-383-03640-2*) SRA Schl Grp.

SALAMANDERS

George, Jean C. The Moon of the Salamanders. new ed. Werner, Marlene H., illus. LC 90-25591. 48p. (gr. 3-7). 1992. 15.00 (*0-06-022609-9*); PLB 14.89 (*0-06-022694-3*) HarpC Child Bks.

Selsam, Millicent E. & Hunt, Joyce. A First Look at Frogs, Toads & Salamanders. Spunger, Harriett, illus. 32p. (gr. 2-4). 1976. PLB 12.85 (*0-8027-6244-1*) Walker & Co.

Souza, D. M. Shy Salamanders. LC 94-9108. 1994. write for info. (*0-87614-826-7*) Carolrhoda Bks.

SALEM, MASSACHUSETTS–HISTORY

Kent, Zachary. The Story of the Salem Witch Trials. Canaday, Ralph, illus. LC 86-9632. 32p. (gr. 3-6). 1986. pap. 3.95 (*0-516-44704-1*) Childrens.

Van der Linde, Laurel. The Devil in Salem Village: The Story of the Salem Witchcraft Trials. LC 91-24403. (Illus.). 64p. (gr. 4-6). 1992. PLB 15.40 (*1-56294-144-5*) Millbrook Pr.

SALESMEN AND SALESMANSHIP

see also Advertising; Business

Boy Scouts of America. Salesmanship. LC 19-600. (Illus.). 40p. (gr. 6-12). 1987. pap. 1.85 (*0-8395-3351-9*, 33351) BSA.

Estes, Sherrill Y. Sell Like a Pro! The Secrets of Consultative Selling. (Illus.). 192p. (gr. 7 up). 1988. 18.95 (*0-87491-917-7*) Acropolis.

Mandino, Og. Greatest Salesman in the World. LC 68-10798. (gr. 9 up). 1987. 12.95 (*0-8119-0067-3*) Lifetime.

SALESMEN AND SALESMANSHIP–FICTION

Brittain, Bill. Professor Popkin's Prodigious Polish. Glass, Andrew, illus. LC 89-78221. 160p. (gr. 3-7). 1991. pap. 3.95 (*0-06-440386-6*, Trophy) HarpC Child Bks.

Field, Rachel. General Store. Laroche, Giles, illus. LC 87-37218. (ps-3). 1988. 15.95 (*0-316-28163-8*) Little.

Hautzig, Deborah. It's Not Fair! Leigh, Tom, illus. LC 85-30154. 40p. (ps-3). 1993. pap. 2.99 (*0-679-83951-8*) Random Bks Yng Read.

McOmber, Rachel B., ed. McOmber Phonics Storybooks: The Lemonade Sale. rev. ed. (Illus.). write for info. (*0-944991-41-6*) Swift Lrn Res.

Merrill, Jean. The Pushcart War. Solbert, Ronni, illus. LC 84-43131. 224p. (gr. 5-8). 1992. PLB 14.89 (*0-06-020822-8*) HarpC Child Bks.

Williams-Garcia, Rita. Fast Talk on a Slow Track. 176p. (gr. 7 up). 1991. 15.00 (*0-525-67334-2*, Lodestar Bks) Dutton Child Bks.

SALESMEN AND SALESMANSHIP–VOCATIONAL GUIDANCE

Epstein, Lawrence. Exploring Careers in Computer Sales. Rosen, Roger, ed. 64p. (gr. 7-12). 1990. PLB 14.95 (*0-8239-0667-1*) Rosen Group.

SALK, JONAS, 1914-

Bredeson, Carmen. Jonas Salk: Discoverer of the Polio Vaccine. LC 93-12097. (Illus.). 112p. (gr. 6 up). 1993. lib. bdg. 17.95 (*0-89490-415-9*) Enslow Pubs.

Curson, Marjorie. Jonas Salk. Gallin, Richard, ed. (Illus.). 144p. (gr. 5-9). 1990. PLB 10.95 (*0-382-09966-4*); pap. 6.95 (*0-382-09971-0*) Silver Burdett Pr.

Hargrove, Jim. The Story of Jonas Salk & the Discovery of the Polio Vaccine. LC 89-25361. (Illus.). 32p. (gr. 3-6). 1990. PLB 12.30 (*0-516-04747-7*); pap. 3.95 (*0-516-44747-5*) Childrens.

Sherrow, Victoria. Jonas Salk: Research for a Healthier World. LC 92-32302. (Illus.). 128p. (gr. 6-9). 1993. 16. 95x (*0-8160-2805-2*) Facts on File.

Tomlinson, Michael. Jonas Salk. LC 92-46284. 1993. 19. 93 (*0-86625-495-1*); 14.95s.p. (*0-685-66537-2*) Rourke Pubns.

SALMON

Field, Nancy & Machlis, Sally. Discovering Salmon. Machlis, Sally, illus. 32p. (Orig.). (gr. k-6). 1984. pap. 3.95 (*0-941042-05-7*) Dog Eared Pubns.

Guiberson, Brenda Z. Salmon Story. Guiberson, Brenda, illus. LC 93-1360. 64p. (gr. 2-4). 1993. 14.95 (*0-8050-2754-8*, Bks Young Read) H Holt & Co.

Hogan, Paula Z. The Salmon. Hockerman, Dennis, illus. LC 78-21178. 32p. (gr. 1-4). 1979. PLB 19.97 (*0-8172-1255-8*); pap. 4.95 (*0-8114-8178-6*); pap. 9.95 incl. cassette (*0-8114-8186-7*) Raintree Steck-V.

—The Salmon. LC 78-21178. (Illus.). 32p. (gr. 1-4). 1984. PLB 29.28 incl. cassette (*0-8172-2232-4*) Raintree Steck-V.

Lavies, Bianca. The Atlantic Salmon. Lavies, Bianca, photos by. LC 91-27990. (Illus.). 32p. (gr. 2-5). 1992. 14.50 (*0-525-44860-8*, DCB) Dutton Child Bks.

Phleger, Frederick B. Red Tag Comes Back. Lobel, Arnold, illus. LC 61-11452. 64p. (gr. k-3). 1961. PLB 13.89 (*0-06-024706-1*) HarpC Child Bks.

SALOMON, HAYM, 1740?-1785

Milgrim, Shirley. Haym Salomon: Liberty's Son. Fish, Richard, illus. LC 75-17349. 120p. (gr. 5-8). 1975. 7.95 (*0-8276-0073-9*) JPS Phila.

SALOONS

see Restaurants, Bars, Etc.

SALT

Bracy, Norma M. Salt. (Illus.). 32p. (gr. k-12). 1986. pap. text ed. 2.00 (*0-915783-03-7*) Book Binder.

Joly, Dominique. Grains of Salt. Perols, Sylvaine, illus. LC 87-34534. 38p. (gr. k-5). 1988. 4.95 (*0-944589-20-0*, 200) Young Discovery Lib.

Langton, Jane, retold by. Salt. LC 91-74007. (Illus.). 40p. (ps-4). 1994. 5.95 (*1-56282-681-6*) Hyprn Ppbks.

Mebane, Robert & Rybolt, Thomas. Salts & Solids. (Illus.). 64p. (gr. 5-8). 1994. bds. 15.95 (*0-8050-2841-2*) TFC Bks NY.

Mitgutsch, Ali. From Sea to Salt. Mitgutsch, Ali, illus. LC 84-17466. 24p. (ps-3). 1985. PLB 10.95 (*0-87614-232-3*) Carolrhoda Bks.

SALUTATIONS

see Etiquette; Letter Writing

SALVADOR

Adams, Faith. El Salvador: Beauty among the Ashes. LC 85-6945. (Illus.). 136p. (gr. 5 up). 1986. text ed. 14.95 RSBE (*0-87518-309-3*, Dillon) Macmillan Child Grp.

Bachelis, Faren M. El Salvador. LC 89-25419. (Illus.). 128p. (gr. 5-9). 1990. PLB 20.55 (*0-516-02718-2*) Childrens.

Cheney, Glenn A. El Salvador: Country in Crisis. LC 89-38708. (gr. 4-7). 1990. PLB 13.40 (*0-531-10916-X*) Watts.

Cummins, Ronnie & Welch, Rose. Children of the World: El Salvador. Welch, Rose, photos by. LC 89-43137. (Illus.). 64p. (gr. 5-6). 1990. PLB 21.26 (*0-8368-0220-9*) Gareth Stevens Inc.

Haverstock, Nathan A. El Salavador in Pictures. (Illus.). 64p. (gr. 5 up). 1987. PLB 17.50 (*0-8225-1806-6*) Lerner Pubns.

Sanders, Renfield. El Salvador. (Illus.). 104p. (gr. 5 up). 1988. lib. bdg. 14.95 (*1-55546-781-4*) Chelsea Hse.

Stewart, Gail B. El Salvador. LC 90-47691. (Illus.). 48p. (gr. 6-7). 1991. text ed. 4.95 RSBE (*0-89686-602-5*, Crestwood Hse) Macmillan Child Grp.

SALVAGE

see also Skin Diving; Shipwrecks

Graham, Ian. Salvage at Sea. (Illus.). 32p. (gr. 5-8). 1990. PLB 12.40 (*0-531-17177-9*) Watts.

SAMSON, JUDGE OF ISRAEL–FICTION

Kolbrek, Loyal & Larsen, Chris. Samson's Secret. (Orig.). (ps-4). 1970. pap. 1.99 (*0-570-06052-4*, 59-1168) Concordia.

SAN ANTONIO–FICTION

Bruni, Mary A. Rosita's Christmas Wish. Ricks, Thom, illus. LC 85-52040. 48p. (gr. k-8). 1985. 13.95 (*0-935857-00-1*); ltd. ed. 125.00 (*0-935857-03-6*); write for info. (*0-935857-09-5*); pap. write for info. (*0-935857-01-X*); pap. write for info. (*0-935857-10-9*) Texart.

Griffin, Peni R. A Dig in Time. LC 92-18958. 160p. (gr. 3-7). 1992. pap. 3.99 (*0-14-036001-8*) Puffin Bks.

—Switching Well. 224p. (gr. 5 up). 1994. pap. 3.99 (*0-14-036910-4*) Puffin Bks.

SAN ANTONIO–HISTORY

Lee, Sally. San Antonio. LC 91-34303. (Illus.). 60p. (gr. 4 up). 1992. text ed. 13.95 RSBE (*0-87518-510-X*, Dillon) Macmillan Child Grp.

SAN DIEGO PADRES (BASEBALL TEAM)

Goodman, Michael. San Diego Padres. 48p. (gr. 4-10). 1992. PLB 14.95 (*0-88682-463-X*) Creative Ed.

San Diego Padres. (gr. 4-7). 1993. pap. 1.49 (*0-553-56433-1*) Bantam.

SAN FRANCISCO

Climo, Shirley. City! San Francisco. LC 89-32912. (Illus.). 64p. (gr. 3-7). 1990. RSBE 16.95 (*0-02-719030-7*, Macmillan Child Bk) Macmillan Child Grp.

Grout, Harry & Grout, Susan. Fun & Easy Guide to San Francisco. Grout, Harry, illus. 32p. (Orig.). (gr. 2). 1991. pap. 5.95 (*0-9626868-4-0*) Locations Plus.

Haddock, Patricia. San Francisco. LC 88-20200. (Illus.). 60p. (gr. 3 up). 1988. text ed. 13.95 RSBE (*0-87518-383-2*, Dillon) Macmillan Child Grp.

Junior League of San Francisco Staff & Brown, Tricia. The City by the Bay: A Magical Journey Around San Francisco. Kleven, Elisa, illus. LC 92-32104. 1993. 12. 95 (*0-8118-0233-7*) Chronicle Bks.

Wilder, Laura I. West from Home: Letters of Laura Ingalls Wilder, San Francisco 1915. MacBride, Roger L., ed. LC 73-14342. 176p. (gr. 7 up). 1974. 15.00 (*0-06-024110-1*); PLB 14.89 (*0-06-024111-X*) HarpC Child Bks.

Zibart, Rosemary. Kidding Around San Francisco: A Young Person's Guide to the City. St. Marie, Janice, illus. 64p. (Orig.). (gr. 3 up). 1989. pap. 9.95 (*0-945465-23-8*) John Muir.

SAN FRANCISCO–EARTHQUAKE AND FIRE, 1906

Hamilton, Sue. San Francisco Earthquake. Hamilton, John, ed. LC 88-71723. (Illus.). 32p. (gr. 4). 1989. PLB 11.96 (*0-939179-43-1*) Abdo & Dghtrs.

House, James & Steffens, Bradley. The San Francisco Earthquake. LC 89-33558. (Illus.). 64p. (gr. 5-8). 1989. PLB 11.95 (*1-56006-003-4*) Lucent Bks.

Stein, R. Conrad. The Story of the San Francisco Earthquake. LC 83-10135. (Illus.). 32p. (gr. 3-6). 1983. pap. 3.95 (*0-516-44664-9*) Childrens.

SAN FRANCISCO–FICTION

Caen, Herb. The Cable Car & the Dragon. Byfield, Barbara N., illus. LC 85-32004. 40p. 1986. 9.95 (*0-87701-390-X*) Chronicle Bks.

Cruise, Beth. Saved by the Bell: California Scheming. LC 92-2739. 144p. (Orig.). (gr. 5 up). 1992. pap. 2.95 (*0-02-042776-X*, Collier Young Ad) Macmillan Child Grp.

Elmore, Patricia. Susannah & the Purple Mongoose Mystery. LC 91-43643. (Illus.). 120p. (gr. 3-7). 1992. 15.00 (*0-525-44907-8*, DCB) Dutton Child Bks.

Kudlinski, Kathleen V. Earthquake! A Story of Old San Francisco. Himler, Ronald, illus. 64p. (gr. 2-6). 1993. RB 12.99 (*0-670-84874-3*) Viking Child Bks.

Levine, Ellen. If You Lived at the Time of the Great San Francisco Earthquake. Williams, Richard, illus. 64p. 1992. pap. 4.95 (*0-590-45157-X*) Scholastic Inc.

Nasaw, Jonathan. Shakedown Street. LC 92-43046. 1993. 14.95 (*0-385-31071-4*) Delacorte.

Salat, Cristina. Living in Secret. LC 92-20889. 1993. 15. 00 (*0-553-08670-7*, Skylark) Bantam.
—Living in Secret. (gr. 4-7). 1994. pap. 3.99 (*0-440-40950-0*) Dell.
Schulte, Elaine L. Daniel Colton Kidnapped: Daniel Strikes a Bad Bargain - Now He Must Outsmart His Captors. (Illus.). 144p. (gr. 3-7). 1993. pap. 5.99 (*0-310-57261-4*, Pub. by Youth Spec) Zondervan.
Yep, Laurence. Child of the Owl. LC 76-24314. 224p. (gr. 7 up). 1977. PLB 12.89 (*0-06-026743-7*) HarpC Child Bks.

SAN FRANCISCO–HISTORY

Climo, Shirley. City! San Francisco. LC 89-32912. (Illus.). 64p. (gr. 3-7). 1990. RSBE 16.95 (*0-02-719030-7*, Macmillan Child Bk) Macmillan Child Grp.
Wilder, Laura I. West from Home: Letters of Laura Ingalls Wilder, San Francisco 1915. MacBride, Roger L., ed. LC 73-14342. (Illus.). 176p. (gr. 7 up). 1976. pap. 3.95 (*0-06-440081-6*, Trophy) HarpC Child Bks.
Wilson, Kate. Earthquake! San Francisco, Nineteen Hundred Six. Courtney, Richard, illus. LC 92-18081. 62p. (gr. 2-5). 1992. PLB 19.97 (*0-8114-7216-7*) Raintree Steck-V.

SAN FRANCISCO GIANTS (BASEBALL TEAM)

Goodman, Michael. San Francisco Giants. 48p. (gr. 4-10). 1992. PLB 14.94 (*0-88682-453-2*) Creative Ed.
The San Francisco Giants. 1991. 2.99 (*0-517-05789-1*) Random Hse Value.
San Francisco Giants. (gr. 4-7). 1993. pap. 1.49 (*0-553-56434-X*) Bantam.

SANATORIUMS

see Hospitals

SAND

Carlisle, Madelyn W. Let's Investigate Soft, Shimmering Sand. Banek, Yvette S., illus. 32p. (gr. 3-7). 1993. pap. 4.95 (*0-8120-4972-1*) Barron.
De Paola, Tomie. The Quicksand Book. LC 76-28762. (Illus.). 32p. (ps-3). 1977. reinforced bdg. 15.95 (*0-8234-0291-6*); pap. 5.95 (*0-8234-0532-X*) Holiday.

SAND DUNES

Bannan, Jan G. Sand Dunes. (Illus.). 48p. (gr. 3-6). 1989. lib. bdg. 19.95 (*0-87614-321-4*); pap. 6.95 (*0-87614-513-6*) Carolrhoda Bks.

SAND DUNES–FICTION

Petrie, Catherine. Sandbox Betty. Elzaurdia, Sharon, illus. LC 81-15547. 32p. (ps-2). 1982. PLB 10.25 (*0-516-03578-9*); pap. 2.95 (*0-516-43578-7*) Childrens.

SANDBURG, CARL, 1878-1967

Mitchell, Barbara. Good Morning Mr. President: A Story about Carl Sandburg. Collins, Dane, illus. LC 88-7265. 56p. (gr. 3-6). 1988. PLB 14.95 (*0-87614-329-X*) Carolrhoda Bks.
Sandburg, Carl. Prairie-Town Boy. Hague, Michael & Krush, Joe, illus. 228p. (gr. 3-7). 1990. pap. 4.95 (*0-15-263332-4*, Odyssey) HarBrace.

SANGER, MARGARET HIGGINS, 1883-1966

Whitelaw, Nancy. Margaret Sanger: Every Child a Wanted Child. LC 93-13635. (Illus.). 160p. (gr. 4 up). 1994. text ed. 13.95 RSBE (*0-87518-581-9*, Dillon) Macmillan Child Grp.

SANITARY AFFAIRS

see Sanitation

SANITATION

see also Cemeteries; Hygiene; Public Health; Refuse and Refuse Disposal; Water Supply

Colman, Penny, photos by. Toilets, Bathtubs, Sinks, & Sewers: A History of the Bathroom. LC 93-48413. (Illus.). (gr. 5-9). 1994. 14.95 (*0-689-31894-4*, Atheneum Child Bks) Macmillan Child Grp.
Johnson, Jean. Sanitation Workers: A to Z. (Illus.). (gr. k-3). 1988. 11.95 (*0-8027-6772-9*); PLB 12.85 (*0-8027-6773-7*) Walker & Co.
Nardo, Don. Hygiene. Koop, C. Everett, intro. by. LC 92-32086. 1993. pap. write for info. (*0-7910-0460-0*) Chelsea Hse.
Poskanzer, Susan C. Sanitation Worker. Eitzen, Allan, illus. LC 88-10044. 32p. (gr. k-3). 1989. PLB 10.89 (*0-8167-1436-3*); pap. text ed. 2.95 (*0-8167-1437-1*) Troll Assocs.

SANTA CLAUS

Adler, Bill, compiled by. Children's Letters to Santa Claus. LC 93-25377. (Illus.). (ps-3). 1993. 9.95 (*1-55972-196-0*, Birch Ln Pr) Carol Pub Group.
Barkan, Joanne. A Very Merry Santa Story. 1992. 3.95 (*0-590-46020-X*, Cartwheel) Scholastic Inc.
Baum, L. Frank. The Life & Adventures of Santa Claus. (gr. 2-6). 1985. 4.98 (*0-517-42062-7*) Random Hse Value.
—The Life & Adventures of Santa Claus. Apple, Max, afterword by. 160p. 1994. pap. 2.95 (*0-451-52064-5*, Sig Classics) NAL-Dutton.
—The Life & Adventures of Santa Claus. 16.95 (*0-8488-0428-7*) Amereon Ltd.
Benjamin, Alan. Dear Santa Chubby Board Book. (ps-6). 1993. pap. 3.95 (*0-671-87068-8*, Little Simon) S&S Trade.
Birenbaum, Barbara. The Cupdeer. Birenbaum, Barbara, illus. LC 92-33093. 1993. PLB write for info. (*0-935343-04-0*); pap. write for info. (*0-935343-02-4*) Peartree.
Briggs, Raymond. Father Christmas. (Illus.). 32p. (gr. k-3). 1981. pap. 3.95 (*0-14-050125-8*, Puffin) Puffin Bks.
Brooke, Roger. Santa's Christmas Journey. LC 84-9796. (Illus.). 32p. (gr. k-5). 1984. PLB 19.97 (*0-8172-2116-6*); PLB 29.28 incl. cassette (*0-8172-2244-8*) Raintree Steck-V.
Brown, Marc T. Arthur's Christmas. Brown, Marc T., illus. LC 84-4373. (ps-3). 1985. 14.95 (*0-316-11180-5*, Joy St Bks); pap. 4.95 (*0-316-10993-2*) Little.
Bryant, Gary. The First Ride: The Real Story of Santa Claus. 40p. 1992. pap. 4.95 (*1-881442-00-4*) New Legends Pub.
Bushell, Isobel, illus. Santa Claus Is Coming to Town: Musical Board Book. 12p. (ps). 1993. 5.95 (*0-694-00563-0*, Festival) HarpC Child Bks.
Campbell, Louisa. Gargoyles' Christmas. Taylor, Bridget S., illus. LC 94-4035. 32p. (gr. k-2). 1994. 15.95 (*0-87905-587-1*) Gibbs Smith Pub.
CCC of America Staff. Nicholas: The Boy Who Became Santa. CCC of America Staff, illus. 35p. (Orig.). (ps-4). 1989. incl. video 21.95 (*1-56814-003-7*); pap. text ed. 2.95 book (*0-685-62400-5*) CCC of America.
Church, Francis P. Yes, Virginia, There Is a Santa Claus. Allison, Christine, intro. by. LC 92-12268. 1992. 10.00 (*0-385-30854-X*) Delacorte.
Civardi, Annie. The Secrets of Santa. Scruton, Clive, illus. LC 91-130. 32p. (ps-1). 1991. pap. 13.95 jacketed (*0-671-74270-1*, S&S BFYR) S&S Trade.
Clements, Andrew. Santa's Secret Helper. Santini, Debrah, illus. LC 90-8601. 32p. (gr. k up). 1991. pap. 14.95 (*0-88708-136-3*) Picture Bk Studio.
Compton, Kenn. Happy Christmas to All! Compton, Kenn, illus. LC 90-29078. 32p. (ps-3). 1991. reinforced 14.95 (*0-8234-0890-6*) Holiday.
Craig, Janet A. A Letter to Santa. Rader, Laura, illus. LC 93-2214. 32p. (gr. k-2). 1993. PLB 11.59 (*0-8167-3252-3*); pap. text ed. 2.95 (*0-8167-3253-1*) Troll Assocs.
Cuyler, Margery. Fat Santa. LC 86-31962. 32p. (ps-2). 1989. 14.95 (*0-8050-0423-8*, Bks Young Read); pap. 4.95 (*0-8050-1167-6*, Bks Young Read) H Holt & Co.
Dadey, Debbie & Jones, Marcia. Santa Claus Doesn't Mop Floors. 80p. 1991. pap. 2.75 (*0-590-44477-8*) Scholastic Inc.
Dear Santa. (Illus.). 5p. (gr. k-3). 1991. 9.95 (*0-8167-2455-5*) Troll Assocs.
Egan, Louise B. Santa's Christmas Ride: A Storybook with Real Presents. Officer, Robyn, illus. 52p. 1993. incl. gifts 16.95 (*0-8362-4505-9*) Andrews & McMeel.
Ellison, Harold. Santa's Gone Away. LC 88-51034. 44p. (gr. k-3). 1988. 6.95 (*1-55523-180-2*) Winston-Derek.
Elves. The Story of Santa Claus. 96p. (ps-3). 1993. 19.95 (*1-878685-45-7*) Turner Pub GA.
Ewing, Juliana H. Old Father Christmas: Based on a Story by Juliana Horatia Ewing. Doherty, Berlie, retold by. Meloni, Maria T., illus. LC 92-43820. 42p. (ps-3). 1993. 12.95 (*0-8120-6354-6*) Barron.
Fass, Bernie & Wolfson, Mack. United Santas of America. 48p. (gr. 3-12). 1987. pap. 16.95 (*0-86704-038-6*); student bk. 2.95 (*0-86704-039-4*) Clarus Music.
Geyer, Waldon M. Santa & Friends. 32p. 1991. 14.95 (*1-880695-01-4*); incl. cassette 23.95 (*1-880695-03-0*); pap. 8.95 (*1-880695-02-2*); pap. 15.95 incl. cassette (*1-880695-04-9*); cassette 7.95 (*1-880695-00-6*) Santa & Friends.
Giblin, James C. The Truth about Santa Claus. LC 85-47541. (Illus.). 96p. (gr. 3-7). 1985. (Crowell Jr Bks); PLB 15.89 (*0-690-04484-4*, Crowell Jr Bks) HarpC Child Bks.
Gimbel, Cheryl & Maners, Wendelin. Why Does Santa Celebrate Christmas? Lovelady, J., ed. (Illus.). 36p. (gr. k up). 1990. 12.95 (*0-915190-67-2*, JP9067-2) Jalmar Pr.
Great Aunt Adeline, pseud. The Legend of Sinter Klaas. (Illus.). 32p. (Orig.). (gr. k-4). 1992. pap. text ed. 5.95 (*0-9632863-0-7*) Ebner & Steffes.
Greenburg, Dan. Young Santa. Miller, Warren, illus. LC 93-7482. 80p. 1993. pap. 4.99 (*0-14-034773-9*, Puffin) Puffin Bks.
Greene, George W. Santa's Hat. Hatter, Laurie, illus. (ps). 1993. 4.95 (*1-56828-021-1*) Red Jacket Pr.
Hausman, Suzanne, illus. Yes, Virginia. 6.95 (*0-685-86235-6*) Pubns Devl Co TX.
Haywood, Carolyn. How the Reindeer Saved Santa. Ambrus, Victor G., illus. LC 85-28456. 32p. (ps up). 1991. pap. 4.95 (*0-688-11073-8*, Mulberry) Morrow.
—Santa Claus Forever! Ambrus, Victor G., illus. LC 83-1017. 32p. (gr. k-3). 1983. 11.95 (*0-688-10998-5*); lib. bdg. 11.88 (*0-688-02345-2*) Morrow Jr Bks.
Hazen, Barbara S. The Story of Santa Claus. (Illus.). 32p. (ps up). 1989. write for info. (*0-307-12097-X*, Pub. by Golden Bks) Western Pub.
Hover, M. Here Comes Santa Claus. Santoro, Christopher, illus. 14p. (ps). 1982. write for info. (*0-307-12267-0*, Golden Bks.) Western Pub.
Huang, Benrei, illus. Pop-up Santa's Workshop. 14p. (ps-1). 1992. 3.95 (*0-448-40252-1*, G&D) Putnam Pub Group.
Ives, Penny. Santa's Christmas Journey: A Scrolling Picture Book. (Illus.). (ps-3). 1994. 14.95 (*0-7868-0023-2*) Hyprn Child.
James, Emily. Santa's Surprise. (ps). 1992. 3.99 (*0-553-37117-7*) Bantam.
Kahn, Peggy. The Care Bears Help Santa. Fleming, Denise, illus. LC 84-3385. 40p. (ps-3). 1984. lib. bdg. 4.99 (*0-394-96807-7*, BYR) Random Bks Yng Read.

Kapraun, Francis. Santa's Red Toy Bag: (How It All Began) Archer, Jolynn, illus. 14p. 1994. write for info. (*0-9643313-0-6*) Inspired Ink.

Many years ago, Santa used boxes to deliver toys around the world. SANTA'S RED TOY BAG (How it all began) tells us WHY he is now seen with his famous huge toy bag & WHO sparked the idea for its use. A delightful story children will enjoy & remember. This is a twenty-four page activity book with story pages to color & pages to draw. To order, contact: Inspired Ink Productions by Kapraun, 36745 Hill St., Lower Salem, OH 45745; 614-585-2706.
Publisher Provided Annotation.

Kessler, Leonard. That's Not Santa! LC 93-39653. (ps-4). 1994. 2.95 (*0-590-48140-1*) Scholastic Inc.
Kroll, Steven. Santa's Crash-Bang Christmas. De Paola, Tomie, illus. LC 77-3025. 32p. (ps-3). 1977. reinforced bdg. 14.95 (*0-8234-0302-5*); pap. 5.95 (*0-8234-0621-0*) Holiday.
Lane, Julie. The Life & Adventures of Santa Claus. (Illus.). 144p. 1987. 12.95 (*0-685-19459-0*) Equity Pub NH.
—The Life & Legends of Santa Claus. Hokie, illus. Zinnott, Nicholas H., intro. by. LC 84-2741. (Illus.). 160p. (gr. 3-6). 1983. 10.95 (*0-917057-00-7*) Tonnis.
Lippman, Peter. Mini House Books: Santa's Workshop. (Illus.). 20p. (ps-1). 1993. bds. 9.95 (*1-56305-499-X*, 3499) Workman Pub.
Lockhart, Barbara. Santa. Lockhart, Lynne, illus. 12p. 1993. 4.95 (*1-56828-026-2*) Red Jacket Pr.
Mayo, Virginia. Dont' Forget Me Santa Claus. (ps). 1993. 12.95 (*0-8120-6391-0*) Barron.
Mercurio, Helen C. The Miracle Santa's Beard. Mercurio, Mary M., ed. Adjoian, Eva M., illus. 29p. 1985. 12.00 (*0-9616079-0-4*) Tiffany Pub.
Merriam, Robert L. Santa Claus' Snack. Roberts, William, illus. 14p. (ps-6). 1970. pap. 2.00x (*0-686-32491-9*) R L Merriam.
Miller, Sherry. Santa's Helper. Martinez, Jesse, illus. LC 83-72493. 32p. (Orig.). (gr. k-5). 1983. pap. 1.95 saddle-stitched (*0-913379-00-X*) Double M Pub.
Mora, Emma. Mortimer Visits Santa Claus. Kennedy, illus. (ps-1). 1987. 3.95 (*0-8120-5808-9*) Barron.
Night Santa Got Stuck. 13p. (gr. k-3). 1991. pap. 2.95 (*0-8167-2193-9*) Troll Assocs.
Novak, Matt. The Last Christmas Present. Novak, Matt, illus. LC 92-44513. 32p. (ps-1). 1993. 14.95 (*0-531-05495-0*); PLB 14.99 (*0-531-08645-3*) Orchard Bks Watts.
Packard, Mary. Christmas Kitten. (Illus.). 28p. (ps-2). 1994. PLB 14.00 (*0-516-05364-7*) Childrens.
Paulsen, Gary. A Christmas Sonata. Bowman, Leslie W., illus. LC 90-46891. 80p. (gr. 3-7). 1992. 14.95 (*0-385-30441-2*) Delacorte.
Pellegrini, Nina. Charlie Claus: Santa's Best Friend. LC 93-1495. (Illus.). (ps-6). 1993. 4.99 (*0-517-09309-X*, Pub. by Derrydale Bks) Random Hse Value.
Peters, Sharon. Santa's New Sled. Dole, Bob, illus. LC 81-5028. 32p. (gr. k-2). 1981. PLB 11.59 (*0-89375-523-0*); pap. text ed. 2.95 (*0-89375-524-9*) Troll Assocs.

Pickett, Margaret E. What's Keeping You, Santa? A Christmas Story Book. Brown, Blanche M., illus. LC 83-50122. 64p. 1983. Autographed. PLB 24.95 (*0-913939-00-5*) TP Assocs. Classified a "Rare Book" by Carnegie Mellon University Library & is in the Rare Book Room of the Library of Congress. WHAT'S KEEPING YOU, SANTA? is a story about a Santa who runs his toyland by computer which breaks down...& what happens in the little town of Zwingely, Maine...the town Santa forgot! Oscar Dystel, Publisher's Consultant & FORMER PUBLISHER OF BANTAM BOOKS says, "This delightful story has an innocence & lack of sophistication about it that makes it so appealing I believe it might well take its place along with THE NIGHT BEFORE CHRISTMAS & Dickens' A CHRISTMAS CAROL as part of the Christmas legend." Also available is the CHRISTMAS MUSICAL PRODUCTION PACKAGE of WHAT'S KEEPING YOU, SANTA? ($60.00) (for performance as a Christmas play) containing a 74-page

song book & a cassette tape of the songs on one side: What's Keeping You, Santa?, Bells Are Ringing, Snowflake Song & Dance, & Santa's Helpers with piano accompaniment ONLY on the second side for use in rehearsal. A refreshing new approach on the Christmas theme which will delight children as well as grownups for generations to come. To order, contact Margaret Pickett, TP Associates, 21462 Pacific Coast Highway, #210, Huntington Beach, CA 92648.
Publisher Provided Annotation.

Pierce, Anne M. So Many Gifts. Campbell, Donna P., illus. 30p. (ps up). 1989. 14.95 (*0-685-44721-9*); 7.50x (*0-685-27188-9*) Forword MN.

—So Many Gifts. Campbell, Donna P., illus. 32p. (gr. k-6). 1989. Repr. of 1990 ed. 14.95g (*0-9623937-0-3*) Forword MN.

Porter-Chase, Mary. The Return of Sinta Claus: A Family Winter Solstice Tale. Walsh, Lloyd, illus. (Orig.). (gr. 3-12). 1991. pap. 6.00 (*0-9630798-0-8*) Samary Pr.

Richter, Konrad. Wipe Your Feet, Santa Claus. Wilkon, Jozef, illus. LC 85-7246. 24p. (gr. k-2). 1985. 14.95 (*1-55858-016-6*) North-South Bks NYC.

Rojany, Lisa. Santa's New Suit! Lester, Mike, illus. 24p. (ps-2). 1993. 7.95 (*0-8431-3587-5*) Price Stern.

Ross, Pat. M & M & the Santa Secrets. Hafner, Marylin, illus. (gr. 1-4). pap. 2.95 (*0-317-62234-X*, Puffin) Puffin Bks.

—M & M & the Santa Secrets. (Illus.). 1987. pap. 3.99 (*0-14-032222-1*, Puffin) Puffin Bks.

Santa Claus Has a Busy Night. 3.95 (*0-7214-5077-6*) Ladybird Bks.

Santa Claus Is Coming to Town: Timeless Tales. 1992. 4.99 (*0-517-06970-9*) Random Hse Value.

Santa's New Suit Storybook. (ps-6). 1972. 3.00 (*0-686-00005-6*) B A Scott.

Scheidl, Gerda M. Can We Help You, Saint Nicholas? Corderoc'h, Jean-Pierre, illus. Lanning, Rosemary, tr. from GER. LC 92-5231. (Illus.). 32p. (gr. k-3). 1992. 14.95 (*1-55858-154-5*); PLB 14.88 (*1-55858-155-3*) North-South Bks NYC.

Schmid, Eleonore. Wake up, Dormouse, Santa Claus Is Here. Schmid, Eleonore, illus. LC 89-42610. 32p. (gr. k-3). 1989. 14.95 (*1-55858-020-4*) North-South Bks NYC.

Sharmat, Marjorie W. I'm Santa Claus & I'm Famous. Hafner, Marylin, illus. LC 90-55106. 32p. (ps-4). 1990. reinforced 14.95 (*0-8234-0826-4*) Holiday.

Sheppard, Dorothy M. & Sheppard, Jack G. Jo Jo the Elf Meets Santa's Enemy. Roxbury, David, et al, illus. 65p. (gr. 1-6). Date not set. PLB 12.95 (*0-9634300-1-7*); pap. 7.95 (*0-9634300-0-9*) D & J Arts Pubs.
JO JO THE ELF MEETS SANTA'S ENEMY, a children's fantasy, opens a new frontier for Santa & a loveable elf named Jo Jo. Jo Jo is a woods elf from the Black Forest of Germany who sails with Santa on Christmas Eve to protect him from an evil wizard named Natanzo. Natanzo is determined to steal Santa's bag, which has special magical powers that any wizard would crave to possess. Jo Jo battles giant birds, monsters, dragons, & Natanzo, Master of Evil in order to save Santa's bag, so toys can be delivered to all the children of the world. It's an adventure from start to finish, as Jo Jo fights to defeat evil. He not only wins his battles, but is guaranteed to win the hearts of all ages & emerge to become a new Christmas hero for all time. This exciting book, with 27 beautiful full-color illustrations, will encourage children to read. How to order info: Baker & Taylor Books.
Publisher Provided Annotation.

Siegenthaler, Kathrin. Santa Claus & the Woodcutter. Crawford, Elizabeth, tr. from GER. Pfister, Marcus, illus. 32p. (gr. k-3). 1989. pap. 2.95 (*1-55858-032-8*) North-South Bks NYC.

Smith, George S. The Christmas Eve Cattle Drive. Bacon, Eliza, illus. 32p. (gr. 1-4). 1991. pap. 3.95 (*0-89015-820-7*) Sunbelt Media.

Stevenson, James. The Oldest Elf. LC 94-25355. 1995. write for info. (*0-688-13755-5*); write for info. (*0-688-13756-3*) Greenwillow.

Stickland, Henrietta. The Christmas Bear. Stickland, Paul, illus. LC 93-10157. 32p. (ps-3). 1993. 15.99 (*0-525-45062-9*, DCB) Dutton Child Bks.

Stone, Bev. Santa Plus Martha. Stone, Gary, illus. 62p. (gr. k-6). 1992. pap. 12.95 (*0-9619791-1-9*) Stone Studios.

—The Secret of Santa Claus: Flower Blue & Snowie Elves Help Santa Meet His Brothers. rev. ed. Stone, Gary, illus. 64p. (ps-6). 1990. pap. 12.95 (*0-9619791-0-0*) Stone Studios.
AT LAST! THE SECRET OF SANTA CLAUS REVEALED! * How can Santa Claus be in so many stores at once? * How does he enter homes with no chimneys? * Why does Santa live at the North Pole? * How do the reindeer fly? * How does Santa know if children have been good? Meet new characters. * Ice Family * Flower Blue & Snowie Elves * Claus Brothers. This charming story of Nicholas Claus, a "guide" to the fabled Santa Claus, will help children to give, to share, to deal with problems like adoption, living with two families, etc. Children are encouraged to meet Santa Claus as a friend almost from the day they are born. When Santa says everyone needs at least four hugs everyday, use your manners & be polite, children will respond, as proven by thousands of children captivated by this story in school assemblies presented by the author Bev Stone & husband Gary Stone who illustrates as she speaks. Newspapers, parents & teachers call it a new Christmas classic. The first of a series is ideal for adults to read to children who eagerly look for hidden pictures in illustrations.
Publisher Provided Annotation.

Stout, Robert T. Children's Favorite Story of Santa Claus. Stout, Robert T., illus. 32p. (ps-6). 1982. 5.95 (*0-911049-08-8*); pap. 3.95 (*0-911049-04-5*) Yuletide Intl.

—The Original Story of Santa Claus. Stout, Robert T., illus. 56p. (ps-8). 1981. 6.95 (*0-911049-00-2*) Yuletide Intl.

Upton, Richard & Fair, Sharon. The Search for the Smell of Christmas. Buerkle, Bonnie K., illus. 32p. 1992. 14. 95x (*0-9633348-0-8*) Aromatique.

Warren, Jean. Huff & Puff's Foggy Christmas: A Totline Teaching Tale. Cubley, Kathleen, ed. Piper, Molly & Ekberg, Jean, illus. LC 93-38780. 32p. (Orig.). (ps-2). 1994. 12.95 (*0-911019-97-9*); pap. text ed. 5.95 (*0-911019-96-0*) Warren Pub Hse.

Watson, Fay. Milford the Moose Helped Santa One Year. Watson, Fay, illus. 1994. pap. 6.95 (*0-9642893-6-9*) Milford Prod.
Old Santa had a bit of a problem one particular year. The reindeer had the flu & were unable to pull Santa's sleigh. Milford was a friendly moose that hung around Santa's neighborhood. Since Milford was big & strong, Santa recruited him to make the trip that night. Milford was a bit clumsy & uncoordinated. The job did get done. There were a few mishaps along the way, & Santa was a bit unnerved, Milford did save that night. Order from: Milford Production Enterprise, P.O. Box 131, Lewistown, MT 59457.
Publisher Provided Annotation.

Weil, Lisl. Santa Claus Around the World. Weil, Lisl, illus. LC 87-45334. 32p. (ps-3). 1987. reinforced 13.95 (*0-8234-0665-2*) Holiday.

Wild, Margaret. Thank You, Santa. (Illus.). 1992. 12.95 (*0-590-45805-1*, Scholastic Hardcover) Scholastic Inc.

Ziefert, Harriet. When Will Santa Come? Schumacher, Claire, illus. 16p. (ps-3). 1991. pap. 5.95 (*0-06-107440-3*) HarpC Child Bks.

SANTA CLAUS–POETRY

Kearney, Jill. A Fishmas Carol. LC 94-6198. 1994. write for info. (*0-681-00582-3*) Longmeadow Pr.

Moore, Clement C. The Night Before Christmas. De Paola, Tomie, illus. LC 80-11758. 32p. (ps up). 1980. reinforced bdg. 15.95 (*0-8234-0414-5*); pap. 6.95 (*0-8234-0417-X*) Holiday.

—The Night Before Christmas. Amoss, Berthe, illus. 10p. (ps-7). 1989. pap. 3.95 (*0-922589-06-2*) More Than Card.

—The Night Before Christmas. Ferris, Lynn B., illus. 24p. 1991. 6.95 (*0-8362-4917-8*) Andrews & McMeel.

—The Night Before Christmas. Hirashima, Jean, illus. LC 92-27138. 32p. (ps-3). 1993. pap. 2.25 (*0-448-40482-6*, G&D) Putnam Pub Group.

—Twas the Night Before Christmas. Downing, Julie, illus. LC 93-40243. (ps up). 1994. 14.95 (*0-02-767646-3*, Bradbury Pr) Macmillan Child Grp.

—A Visit from St. Nicholas. Hader, Berta & Hader, Elmer, illus. LC 93-33703. (gr. 2 up). 1994. pap. write for info. (*0-486-27978-2*) Dover.

Trosclair. Cajun Night Before Christmas: Full-Color Edition. Jacobs, Howard, ed. Rice, James, illus. LC 92-8375. 48p. (gr. k-3). 1992. 14.95 (*0-88289-940-6*); boxed ed. 25.00 (*0-88289-947-3*); audio 9.95 (*0-88289-914-7*) Pelican.

SANTA FE, NEW MEXICO

Hillerman, Anne. Children's Guide to Santa Fe. LC 84-8782. (Illus.). 48p. (Orig.). (gr. 3 up). 1984. pap. 4.95 (*0-86534-030-7*) Sunstone Pr.

Patterson, Don. A Child's Trip to Christmas in Santa Fe: A Photographic Documentary. LC 91-62868. (Illus.). 120p. (gr. k-3). 1991. 29.95 (*0-9629093-2-7*) MyndSeye.

York, Susan. Kidding Around Santa Fe: A Young Person's Guide to the City. Blakemore, Sally, illus. 64p. (Orig.). (gr. 3 up). 1991. pap. 9.95 (*0-945465-99-8*) John Muir.

SANTA FE TRAIL

Hill, William E. & Hill, Jan C. Heading Southwest: Along the Santa Fe Trail. (Illus.). 32p. (Orig.). (gr. k-4). 1993. pap. 3.95 (*0-9636071-1-1*) HillHouse Pub.

Lavender, David S. The Santa Fe Trail. LC 94-16638. 1995. write for info. (*0-8234-1153-2*) Holiday.

Yoder, Walter D. Santa Fe Trail Activity Book: Pioneer Settlers in the Southwest. Smith, James C., Jr., ed. (Illus.). 48p. (Orig.). (gr. 3-9). 1994. pap. 7.95 (*0-86534-217-2*) Sunstone Pr.

SANTA FE TRAIL–FICTION

Holling, Holling C. Tree in the Trail. (Illus.). (gr. 4-6). 16. 45 (*0-395-18228-X*) HM.

SASQUATCH

Carmichael, Carrie. Bigfoot: Man, Monster, or Myth? LC 77-21317. (Illus.). 48p. (gr. 4 up). 1977. PLB 20.70 (*0-8172-1052-0*) Raintree Steck-V.

Gaffron, Norma. Bigfoot: Opposing Viewpoints. LC 88-24376. (Illus.). 112p. (gr. 5-8). 1989. PLB 14.95 (*0-89908-058-8*) Greenhaven.

Odor, Ruth S. Bigfoot. Magnuson, Diana, illus. LC 88-7882. 100p. (gr. 3-7). 1989. PLB 14.95 (*0-89565-455-5*) Childs World.

Sonberg, Lynn. The Bigfoot Mystery. (gr. 4-9). 1983. pap. 2.25 (*0-553-15436-2*) Bantam.

SATAN

see Devil

SATELLITES, ARTIFICIAL

see Artificial Satellites

SATIRE

Swift, Jonathan. Gulliver's Travels. LC 92-53687. 220p. 1992. 5.98 (*1-56138-169-1*) Courage Bks.

SAUDI ARABIA

Foster, Leila M. Saudi Arabia. LC 92-8890. (Illus.). 128p. (gr. 5-9). 1993. PLB 20.55 (*0-516-02611-9*) Childrens.

Honeyman, Susannah. Saudi Arabia. LC 94-17104. (gr. 4 up). 1995. write for info. (*0-8114-2786-2*) Raintree Steck-V.

Janin, Hunt. Saudi Arabia. LC 92-13448. 1992. 21.95 (*1-85435-532-5*) Marshall Cavendish.

McCarthy, Kevin. Saudi Arabia: A Desert Kingdom. LC 85-6941. (Illus.). 128p. (gr. 5 up). 1986. text ed. 14.95 RSBE (*0-87518-295-X*, Dillon) Macmillan Child Grp.

SAUL, KING OF ISRAEL

Segal, Lore. The Story of King Saul & King David. LC 90-52544. (Illus.). 144p. 1991. 19.50 (*0-8052-4088-8*) Pantheon.

Wengrov, Charles. Tales of King Saul. (Illus.). (gr. 5-10). 1969. 3.00 (*0-914080-21-0*) Shulsinger Sales.

SAXONS

see Anglo-Saxons

SAYINGS

see Epigrams; Proverbs; Quotations

SCANDINAVIA

Garrett, Dan. Scandinavia. LC 91-6422. (Illus.). 96p. (gr. 6-11). 1991. PLB 22.80 (*0-8114-2444-8*) Raintree Steck-V.

SCANDINAVIANS IN THE U. S.

Brownstone & Franck, eds. The Scandinavian-American Heritage. LC 88-45086. 128p. (gr. 5-9). 1988. 16.95x (*0-8160-1626-7*) Facts On File.

SCARECROWS–FICTION

Amery, H. Scarecrow's Secret. (Illus.). 16p. (ps-3). 1992. pap. 3.95 (*0-7460-0584-9*) EDC.

Cazet, Denys. Nothing at All. LC 93-25204. (Illus.). 32p. (ps-1). 1994. 14.95 (*0-531-06822-6*); lib. bdg. 14.99 RLB (*0-531-08672-0*) Orchard Bks Watts.

Dillon, Jana. Jeb Scarecrow's Pumpkin Patch. Dillon, Jana, illus. LC 91-16423. 32p. (ps-3). 1992. 14.45 (*0-395-57578-8*) HM.

Fleischman, Sid. The Scarebird. Sis, Peter, illus. LC 87-4099. 32p. (gr. k-3). 1988. 15.00 (*0-688-07317-4*); lib. bdg. 14.93 (*0-688-07318-2*) Greenwillow.

—The Scarebird. Sis, Peter, illus. LC 93-11726. 32p. (ps up). 1994. pap. 4.95 (*0-688-13105-0*, Mulberry) Morrow.

Gordon, Sharon. Samuel el Espantapajaros. Silverstein, Don, illus. (SPA.). 32p. (gr. k-2). 1981. PLB 7.89 (*0-89375-556-7*); pap. 1.95 (*0-89375-958-9*) Troll Assocs.

Levin, Betty. Starshine & Sunglow. Smith, Joseph A., illus. LC 93-26672. 96p. (gr. 4-7). 1994. PLB 14.00 (*0-688-12806-8*) Greenwillow.

Lifton, Betty J. Joji & the Dragon. Mitsui, Eiichi, illus. LC 88-8434. 64p. (gr. 1-3). 1989. Repr. of 1957 ed. lib. bdg. 16.00 (*0-208-02245-7*, Pub. by Linnet) Shoe String.

Littlewood, Valerie. Scarecrow. (Illus.). 32p. (gr. 2-6). 1992. 15.00 (*0-525-44948-5*, DCB) Dutton Child Bks.

Oana, Katy D. Robbie & the Raggedy Scarecrow. LC 77-18349. (Illus.). 32p. (gr. 2-4). 1978. PLB 9.95 (*0-87783-154-8*) Oddo.

—Robbie & the Raggedy Scarecrow. Stephens, Jacquelyn S., illus. LC 77-18349. (gr. k-2). 1978. PLB 5.95 (*0-89508-065-6*) Rainbow Bks.

San Souci, Robert D. Feathertop: Based on the Tale by Nathaniel Hawthorne. San Souci, Daniel, illus. LC 91-10104. 32p. (gr. 1-5). 1992. pap. 16.00 (*0-385-42044-7*) Doubleday.

Stolz, Mary. The Scarecrows & Their Child. Schwartz, Amy, illus. LC 87-115. 80p. (gr. 3-6). 1987. HarpC Child Bks.

Vainio, Pirkko. Don't Be Scared, Scarecrow. LC 93-42052. (Illus.). 32p. (gr. k-3). 1994. 14.95 (*1-55858-275-4*); PLB 14.88 (*1-55858-276-2*) North-South Bks NYC.

SCENERY

see Views

SCENERY (STAGE)

see Theaters–Stage Setting and Scenery

SCHOLARSHIP

see Learning and Scholarship

SCHOLARSHIPS, FELLOWSHIPS, ETC.

Carr, Roberta, ed. Art & Music Scholarships. 75p. (Orig.). (gr. 9-12). 1992. pap. text ed. 12.50x (*1-880468-06-9*) Col Connect.

—Scholarships for Catholic Colleges & Universities. 75p. (Orig.). (gr. 9-12). 1992. pap. text ed. 12.50x (*1-880468-07-7*) Col Connect.

Fossey, Keith R. The Football Scholarship Guide: How to Maximize Scholarship Potential. Thomas, Roger, frwd. by. LC 92-90842. (Illus.). 309p. (Orig.). (gr. 9-12). 1992. pap. 24.95 (*0-9633495-0-3*) Pigskin Pr.

Herb, James A. & Herb, Marcy E. In Search of the Athletic Scholarship: A Manual for Student Athletes & Parents. rev. ed. 94p. (gr. 9-12). 1994. pap. 24.50 (*0-9641479-0-4*) J A Herb. Collegiate athletic scholarships are not just given away. It takes hard work to accomplish what many high school athletes dream of. The secret of securing an athletic scholarship is exposure & starting early. Increase your chances in being offered an athletic scholarship. IN SEARCH OF THE ATHLETIC SCHOLARSHIP was designed for the high school student athlete & his/her parents. This book takes a unique "do it yourself" approach & has helped several athletes being placed at Division I & Division II colleges across the country. IN SEARCH OF THE ATHLETIC SCHOLARSHIP provides a step-by-step approach to this process. It is in use by several high school counselors & is rapidly becoming a very valuable reference for high school athletes, parents, counselors, & coaches. Topics included in this manual are: How to Start This Process, Preparing Your Athletic Resume, How & When to Contact Coaches, Questions to Ask of a College Coach, Face-to-Face Meetings with College Coaches, Academic Eligibility, The National Letter of Intent, & also includes sample forms, letters, & much more. Book is spiral bound 8 1/2" x 11" - 94 pages (ISBN 0-9641479-0-4). Cost: California Residents - $24.50 (includes tax, priority mail); Non-CA Residents - $23.00 (includes priority mail). To order, contact: J. A. Herb, P.O. Box 3656, La Habra, CA 90632-3656; 714-870-4998.

Publisher Provided Annotation.

Lahey, David. Athletic Scholarships: Making Your Sports Pay. 200p. 1992. pap. 12.95 (*1-895629-06-3*, Pub. by Warwick Pub CN) Firefly Bks Ltd.

SCHOOL ADMINISTRATION AND ORGANIZATION

see also Teaching

Cobb, Vicki. The Secret Life of School Supplies. Morrison, Bill, illus. LC 81-47108. 96p. (gr. 5 up). 1981. PLB 13.89 (*0-397-31925-8*, Lipp Jr Bks) HarpC Child Bks.

Greeley, Sheila. S.T.A.R. Patrol. 30p. (Orig.). 1993. pap. text ed. 7.95 (*0-9622812-1-2*) FAFCTPC.

Rogers, Donald J. Banned! Censorship in the Schools. LC 87-7736. 128p. (gr. 5 up). 1987. lib. bdg. 12.98 (*0-671-63708-8*, J Messner) S&S Trade.

SCHOOL AND HOME

see Home and School

SCHOOL ATTENDANCE

see also Child Labor; Dropouts

Gross, Alan. I Don't Want to Go to School Book. LC 81-17034. (Illus.). (ps-3). 1982. pap. 3.95 (*0-516-43496-9*) Childrens.

Paschos, Jacqueline & Destang, Francoise. Come to School. (ps). 1986. pap. 0.35 (*0-8091-6505-8*) Paulist Pr.

Ready for School. 32p. (ps). 1985. pap. write for info. (*0-307-03585-9*, Pub. by Golden Bks) Western Pub.

Shles, Larry. Do I have to Go to School Today? Squib Measures Up. Winch, Bradley L., ed. Shles, Larry, illus. 64p. (Orig.). (gr. k up). 1989. pap. 7.95 (*0-915190-62-1*, JP9062-1) Jalmar Pr.

SCHOOL ATTENDANCE–FICTION

Cartwright, Stephen, illus. Going to School. 16p. (ps up). 1986. pap. 3.95 (*0-7460-1269-1*) EDC.

Eyles, Heather. Well, I Never! Ross, Tony, illus. 32p. (ps-3). 1990. 11.95 (*0-87951-383-7*) Overlook Pr.

Hogan, Paula Z. Sometimes I Don't Like School. Ford, Pam, illus. Smith, David L., intro. by. LC 79-24055. (Illus.). 32p. (gr. k-6). 1980. PLB 19.97 (*0-8172-1357-0*) Raintree Steck-V.

L'Engle, Madeleine. And Both Were Young. (Orig.). (gr. 7 up). 1983. pap. 3.99 (*0-440-90229-0*, LFL) Dell.

Tester, Sylvia R. We Laughed a Lot, My First Day of School. Hook, Frances, illus. LC 78-10900. (ps-3). 1979. PLB 14.95 (*0-89565-020-7*) Childs World.

SCHOOL INTEGRATION

see Segregation in Education

SCHOOL LIBRARIES

see also Children's Literature; Libraries

SCHOOL DROPOUTS

see Dropouts

SCHOOL LIFE

see Students

SCHOOL ENROLLMENT

see School Attendance

SCHOOL MANAGEMENT

see School Administration and Organization

SCHOOL INSPECTION

see School Administration and Organization

SCHOOL MUSIC

see Music–Study and Teaching

SCHOOL ORGANIZATION

see School Administration and Organization

SCHOOL PLAYGROUNDS

see Playgrounds

SCHOOL SPORTS

see also Coaching (Athletics)

Belfiglio, Val. Pride of the Southwest: Outstanding Athletes of the Southwest Conference. Carter, Bo, intro. by. (Illus.). 144p. (gr. 4-7). 1992. 14.95 (*0-89015-822-3*) Sunbelt Media.

Carlson, Nancy. Making the Team. Carlson, Nancy, illus. LC 85-3775. 32p. (ps-3). 1985. PLB 13.50 (*0-87614-281-1*) Carolrhoda Bks.

Gould, Marilyn. Playground Sports: A Book of Ball Games. (Illus.). 62p. (gr. 2 up). 1991. 10.95 (*0-9632305-2-2*) Allied Crafts.

Matovcik, Gerard. Academic Sportfolio: Excuse Notes Are No Excuse. Pranzo, Donard, ed. (Illus.). (gr. 9-12). 1989. portfolio ser. 50.00 (*0-924086-11-4*) Acad Sportfolio.

Norberg, Jon. Academic Sportfolio. Gallup, Beth, ed. Norberg, Jon, illus. 1200p. (gr. 3-6). 1987. 495.00 (*0-685-24265-X*) Acad Sportfolio.

—Academic Sportfolio: Excuse Notes Are No Excuse. Pranzo, Donard, ed. Norberg, Jon, illus. (gr. 3-6). 1987. portfolio ser. 50.00 (*0-924086-00-9*) Acad Sportfolio.

Pranzo, Donard. Academic Sportfolio: Excuse Notes Are No Excuse. rev. ed. Gallup, Beth, ed. (Illus.). 1985. group of 40 lessons 249.00 (*0-924086-28-9*); Group 1, 400 photo masters incl. write for info. (*0-924086-29-7*); Group 2, 400 photo masters incl. write for info (*0-924086-30-0*) Acad Sportfolio.

SCHOOL TEACHING

see Teaching

SCHOOL WITHDRAWALS

see Dropouts

SCHOOLS

see also Colleges and Universities; Education; Kindergarten; Public Schools

Alvarez Del Real, Maria E., ed. El Dato Escolar. 3rd ed. LC 81-72099. (SPA., Illus.). 352p. (gr. 2). 1985. pap. 6.00x (*0-944499-11-2*) Editorial Amer.

—Diccionario Escolar. 2nd ed. LC 83-80787. (SPA., Illus.). 228p. (gr. 2). 1986. pap. 3.75x (*0-944499-13-9*) Editorial Amer.

Berry, Joy W. Teach Me about School. Dickey, Kate, ed. LC 85-45093. (Illus.). 36p. (ps). 1986. 4.98 (*0-685-10732-9*) Grolier Inc.

Blackburn, Lynn B. The Class in Room Forty-Four: When a Classmate Dies. Johnson, Joy, ed. Borum, Shari, illus. 24p. (Orig.). (gr. 1-6). 1990. pap. 3.60 (*1-56123-025-1*) Centering Corp.

College Admissions Planner & Organizer. (gr. 9-12). 1990. pap. write for info. (*1-87851-401-6*, CE 4891); pap. write for info.; write for info. inserts (*1-87851-403-2*, CE 9892) Cole Enter.

Dentemaro, Christine & Kranz, Rachel. Straight Talk about Student Life. LC 92-31488. 1993. write for info. (*0-8160-2735-8*) Facts on File.

Gatch, Jean. School Makes Sense...Sometimes. Turnbull, Jean, illus. LC 80-10281. 32p. (gr. k-5). 1980. 16.95 (*0-87705-494-0*) Human Sci Pr.

Glaser, Nily. Be Street Smart - Be Safe: Raising Safety Minded Children. Kids Against Crime Organization Staff, et al, illus. LC 93-80451. 96p. (Orig.). (gr. k-6). 1994. pap. 9.95 (*0-9632663-2-2*) Gan Pub. THE MOST COMPREHENSIVE & ENJOYABLE GUIDE TO ONE OF TODAY'S MOST CONCERNING ISSUES: CHILD SAFETY!--WRITTEN BY A VETERAN EDUCATOR. Using rhyme & delightful illustrations, Careful Lee the hound teaches children grades K-6 to: *Differentiate between safe & unsafe situations, without making them fearful *Say an unequivocal NO! when faced by a potentially dangerous situation *Refuse to cooperate with those trying to tempt them. *Distance themselves from unsafe places & people *Use common sense & trust their intuition. "...(This) work is truly important in the fight against crime."--Office of Pete Wilson, Governor of California. "This safety book is long over due!...It is very comprehensive, well thought-out, creative & POSITIVE...It provides a sound foundation that is a must for every home that has children."--Susan Rifkin, School Principal. "This book must be in the hands of every parent & child...A great help in teaching children to minimize potential danger... Important Work!"--Huguette Salti, M.D., Pediatrician. "...a great tool... offers a delightful way to teach children, parents & teachers how to be safety smart...I highly recommend this book to every child, parent & teacher." --Police Sgt. Walter Snyder. May be ordered from publisher 909-381-8844, or Baker & Taylor.

Publisher Provided Annotation.

Goldentyer, Debra. Dropping Out of School. LC 93-14251. (Illus.). 80p. (gr. 6-9). 1993. PLB 21.34 (*0-8114-3526-1*) Raintree Steck-V.

Hains, Harriet. My New School. LC 92-52812. (Illus.). 24p. (ps-1). 1993. 9.95 (*1-56458-116-0*) Dorling Kindersley.

Hough, Judith M. My School Days Memories: Grades K-6. Hough, Judith, illus. 40p. (gr. k-6). 1992. pap. 7.95 (*0-9633769-0-X*) Touch The Sky.

Howlett, Bud. I'm New Here. LC 92-7478. 1993. 14.95 (*0-395-64049-0*) HM.

Hunter, Latoya. Diary of Latoya Hunter. LC 92-8384. 1992. 16.00 (*0-517-58511-1*, Crown) Crown Pub Group.

Kalman, Bobbie. Early Schools. (Illus.). 64p. (gr. 4-5). 1982. 15.95 (*0-86505-015-5*); pap. 7.95 (*0-86505-014-7*) Crabtree Pub Co.

—A One Room School. (Illus.). 32p. (Orig.). (gr. k-9). 1994. PLB 15.95 (*0-86505-497-5*); pap. 7.95 (*0-86505-517-3*) Crabtree Pub Co.

Kaufman, Tanya & Wishny, Judith. School Events. Piltch, Benjamin, ed. Bartick, Robert, illus. 64p. (gr. 2-5). 1983. 4.00 (*0-934618-04-6*) Learning Well.

Kuklin, Susan. Going to My Nursery School. Kuklin, Susan, illus. LC 89-37077. 40p. (ps-k). 1990. RSBE 13.95 (*0-02-751237-1*, Bradbury Pr) Macmillan Child Grp.

Lewis, Lois F. Carlin School, A History Book: The Story of a School in Ravenna, Ohio, U. S. A. Lewis, William B., illus. 28p. (Orig.). (gr. 5). 1989. pap. text ed. write for info. (*0-9620136-3-3*) L F Lewis.

—West Main School, a History Book: The Story of a School in Ravenna, Ohio, U. S. A. Lewis, William B., illus. (Orig.). (gr. 5). 1988. pap. text ed. 2.00 (*0-9620136-0-9*) L F Lewis.

Loeper, John J. Going to School in 1876. LC 83-15669. (Illus.). 96p. (gr. 4-7). 1984. SBE 15.00 (*0-689-31015-3*, Atheneum) Macmillan Child Grp.

McCune, Dianne, et al. The Welcome Back to School Book. Hierstein, Judy, illus. 112p. (gr. k-4). 1987. pap. 10.95 (*0-86653-383-4*, GA1001) Good Apple.

Mernit, Susan. Everything You Need to Know about Changing Schools. (gr. 7-12). 1992. PLB 14.95 (*0-8239-1326-0*) Rosen Group.

Osborne, Judy. My Teacher Said Goodbye Today: Planning for the End of the School Year. 2nd ed. Osborne, John, photos by. (Illus.). 39p. (ps-6). 1987. pap. text ed. 9.95 (*0-9618303-8-7*) Emijo Pubns.

Petersen, Suni & Straub, Ron L. School Crisis Survival Guide. 195p. (gr. k-12). 1994. 34.95 (*0-685-71634-1*, 785) W Gladden Found.

Riddell, Edwina. My First Day at Preschool. (Illus.). 32p. (ps). 1992. 9.95 (*0-8120-6261-2*) Barron.

Roby, Cynthia. Feeling Different, Feeling Fine: Kids Talk about Their Learning Problems. LC 93-6532. 1993. write for info. (*0-8075-2334-8*) A Whitman.

Sayler, Mary H. First Days in High School: Devotions to Cheer You On. 208p. 1994. 8.99 (*0-8054-5372-5*, 4253-72) Broadman.

Schneider, Meg. Help! My Teacher Hates Me: A School Survival Guide for Kids 10-14 Years Old. (gr. 4-9). 1994. pap. 5.95 (*1-56305-492-2*) Workman Pub.

Winitz, Harris. School: All about Language Ser. Baker, Syd, illus. 50p. (Orig.). (gr. 7 up). 1987. pap. text ed. 31.00 incl. 2 cass. (*0-939990-49-0*) Intl Linguistics.

Wirths, Claudine G. & Bowman-Kruhm, Mary. I Hate School! How to Hang In & When to Drop Out. Stren, Patti, illus. LC 85-48248. 128p. (gr. 7 up). 1986. pap. 7.95 (*0-06-446054-1*, Trophy) HarpC Child Bks.

—Your New School. Stren, Patti, illus. LC 93-8513. 64p. (gr. 5-8). 1993. PLB 14.95 (*0-8050-2074-8*, TFC Bks NY) H Holt & Co.

Woodworth, Viki. School Jokes. (Illus.). 32p. (gr. 1-4). 1991. 13.95 (*0-89565-726-0*) Childs World.

SCHOOLS–ADMINISTRATION

see School Administration and Organization

SCHOOLS–FICTION

see also Universities and Colleges–Fiction

Adams, Barbara. The Not-Quite-Ready-for-Prime-Time Bandits. (Orig.). (gr. 3-6). 1986. pap. 2.50 (*0-440-49551-2*, YB) Dell.

Adams, Nicholas. Final Curtain. 1991. pap. 3.50 (*0-06-106079-8*, Harp PBks) HarpC.

—Heartbreaker. (gr. 9-12). 1991. pap. 3.50 (*0-06-106037-2*, PL) HarpC.

—I. O. U. 1991. pap. 3.50 (*0-06-106106-9*, Harp PBks) HarpC.

—Mr. Popularity. (gr. 9-12). 1990. pap. 3.50 (*0-06-106018-6*, PL) HarpC.

—New Kid on the Block. (gr. 9-12). 1991. pap. 3.50 (*0-06-106061-5*, PL) HarpC.

—Santa Claws. 1991. pap. 3.50 (*0-06-106108-5*, Harp PBks) HarpC.

Adams, Pam. Dolly Dolphin's Play School. 1981. 6.95 (*0-85953-266-6*) Childs Play.

Adler, David A. Eaton Stanley & the Mind Control Experiment. Drescher, Joan, illus. LC 84-21135. 96p. (gr. 2-6). 1985. 11.95 (*0-525-44117-4*, DCB) Dutton Child Bks.

—Wacky Jacks: A Houdini Club Magic Mystery. Malone, Heather H., illus. LC 93-51259. 80p. (Orig.). (gr. 1-4). 1994. PLB 2.99 (*0-679-84696-4*); pap. 9.99 (*0-679-94696-9*) Random.

Adler, Susan S. Samantha Learns a Lesson: A School Story. Thieme, Jeanne, ed. Niles, Nancy & Lusk, Nancy N, illus. 72p. (gr. 2-5). 1986. PLB 12.95 (*0-937295-83-3*); pap. 5.95 (*0-937295-13-2*) Pleasant Co.

Ahlberg, Allan. The Cinderella Show. Ahlberg, Janet, illus. (ps-3). 1987. pap. 4.95 (*0-670-81037-1*) Viking Child Bks.

—Starting School. Ahlberg, Janet, illus. LC 88-50053. (ps-1). 1988. pap. 11.95 (*0-670-82175-6*) Viking Child Bks.

Ahlberg, Janet. Starting School. 1990. pap. 4.95 (*0-14-050843-0*, Puffin) Puffin Bks.

Albright, Molly. The Mascot Mess. Connor, Eulala, illus. LC 88-15879. 96p. (gr. 3-6). 1989. PLB 9.89 (*0-8167-1484-3*); pap. text ed. 2.95 (*0-8167-1485-1*) Troll Assocs.

Alcott, Louisa May. Little Men. 1991. 12.99 (*0-517-03088-8*) Random Hse Value.

Alexander, Martha. Move over, Twerp. Alexander, Martha, illus. 32p. (ps-2). 1989. pap. 3.95 (*0-8037-5814-6*) Dial Bks Young.

Arnold, Tedd. Green Wilma. Arnold, Tedd, illus. LC 91-31501. 32p. (ps-3). 1993. 13.99 (*0-8037-1313-4*); PLB 13.89 (*0-8037-1314-2*) Dial Bks Young.

Asher, Sandy. Missing Pieces. LC 83-14381. 144p. (gr. 7 up). 1984. 12.95 (*0-385-29318-6*) Delacorte.

—Out of Here: A Senior Class Yearbook. LC 92-35188. 160p. (gr. 7 up). 1993. 14.99 (*0-525-67418-7*, Lodestar Bks) Dutton Child Bks.

Ashley, Bernard. Cleversticks. Brazell, Derek, illus. LC 91-34669. 32p. (ps-2). 1992. 10.00 (*0-517-58878-1*); PLB 10.99 (*0-517-58879-X*) Crown Bks Yng Read.

Avi. Nothing but the Truth: A Documentary Novel. LC 91-9200. 192p. (gr. 6 up). 1991. 14.95 (*0-531-05959-6*); RLB 14.99 (*0-531-08559-7*) Orchard Bks Watts.

—Nothing But the Truth: A Documentary Novel. large type ed. LC 93-42497. 1994. 15.95 (*0-7862-0131-2*) Thorndike Pr.

Baehr, Patricia. School Isn't Fair. Alley, R. W., illus. LC 91-38485. 32p. (ps-k). 1992. pap. 4.95 (*0-689-71544-7*, Aladdin) Macmillan Child Grp.

Baer, Edith. This Is the Way We Go to School. Bjorkman, Steve, illus. 32p. (ps-1). 1992. pap. 3.95 (*0-590-43162-5*, Blue Ribbon Bks) Scholastic Inc.

Baer, Judy. Price of Silence. 1994. pap. 3.99 (*1-55661-387-3*) Bethany Hse.

—Risky Assignment. 1994. pap. 3.99 (*1-55661-386-5*) Bethany Hse.

Baker, Barbara. Third Grade Is Terrible. Shepherd, Roni, illus. LC 88-3631. 80p. (gr. 2-5). 1989. 11.95 (*0-525-44425-4*, DCB) Dutton Child Bks.

—Third Grade Is Terrible. MacDonald, Patricia, ed. Shepard, Roni, illus. 112p. 1991. pap. 2.99 (*0-671-70379-X*, Minstrel Bks) PB.

—The William Problem. Iosa, Ann, illus. LC 93-32598. 1994. write for info. (*0-525-45235-4*, DCB) Dutton Child Bks.

Ball, Jacqueline A. Battle of the Class Clowns. 1990. pap. 2.95 (*0-06-106007-0*, PL) HarpC.

Banks, Jacqueline T. New One. (gr. 4-7). 1994. 13.95 (*0-395-66610-4*) HM.

Barrie, Barbara. Adam Zigzag. LC 93-8735. 1994. 14.95 (*0-385-31172-9*) Delacorte.

Bates, A. Final Exam. 1990. pap. 3.25 (*0-590-43291-5*, Point) Scholastic Inc.

Bates, Betty. Everybody Say Cheese. (gr. 3-6). 1986. pap. 2.50 (*0-440-42446-1*, YB) Dell.

Bechard, Margaret. My Sister, My Science Report. 96p. (gr. 3-7). 1992. pap. 4.99 (*0-14-034408-X*, Puffin) Puffin Bks.

—Really No Big Deal. LC 93-31065. 144p. (gr. 3-7). 1994. 13.99 (*0-670-85444-1*) Viking Child Bks.

Beck, Amanda. The Pegasus Club & Me. Yoshi Miyake, illus. LC 91-38330. 32p. (gr. 2-6). 1992. PLB 19.97 (*0-8114-3577-6*) Raintree Steck-V.

Beere, Peter. School for Terror: Going to School Can Be Murder. 1994. pap. 3.50 (*0-590-48319-6*) Scholastic Inc.

Bemelmans, Ludwig. Mad about Madeline. Quindlen, Anna, intro. by. (Illus.). 352p. 1993. 35.00 (*0-670-85187-6*) Viking Child Bks.

Benjamin, Saragail K. My Dog Ate It. LC 93-25218. 128p. (gr. 3-7). 1994. 14.95 (*0-8234-1047-1*) Holiday.

Berenstain, Stan & Berenstain, Jan. The Berenstain Bears Accept No Substitutes. Berenstain, Stan & Berenstain, Jan, illus. 112p. (Orig.). (gr. 2-6). 1993. PLB 7.99 (*0-679-94035-9*); pap. 3.50 (*0-679-84035-4*) Random Bks Yng Read.

—The Berenstain Bears & the Nerdy Nephew. Berenstain, Stan & Berenstain, Jan, illus. LC 92-32564. 112p. (Orig.). (gr. 2-6). 1993. PLB 7.99 (*0-679-93610-6*); pap. 3.50 (*0-679-83610-1*) Random Bks Yng Read.

Berenstain, Stan & Berenstain, Janice. The Berenstain Bears Go to School. LC 77-79853. (Illus.). (ps-2). 1978. lib. bdg. 5.99 (*0-394-93736-8*); pap. 2.25 (*0-394-83736-3*) Random Bks Yng Read.

Berg, Eric. Bernie's Safe Ideas. LC 93-8905. 1993. write for info. (*1-56071-324-0*) ETR Assocs.

—Five Special Senses. LC 93-8906. 1993. write for info. (*1-56071-328-3*) ETR Assocs.

Bergen, J. P. Media Madness. LC 94-10859. (gr. 5 up). 1994. pap. 2.95 (*0-02-045472-4*, Collier) Macmillan.

—Middlefield Mayhem. LC 94-14228. (gr. 5 up). 1994. pap. 2.95 (*0-02-045473-2*, Collier) Macmillan Child Grp.

—New Kids on Campus. LC 94-14482. (gr. 5 up). 1994. pap. 2.95 (*0-02-045471-6*, Collier) Macmillan.

Bernthal, Mark. Baby Bop Goes to School. Dowdy, Linda C., ed. Full, Dennis, illus. LC 93-74290. 24p. (ps-k). 1994. 4.95 (*1-57064-020-3*) Barney Pub.

Betancourt, Jeanne. My Name Is Brain Brian. LC 92-16513. 176p. (gr. 3-7). 1993. 13.95 (*0-590-44921-4*) Scholastic Inc.

Bianchi, John. Spring Break at Pokeweed Public School. (Illus.). 24p. (gr. 1-4). 1994. PLB 14.95 (*0-921285-33-7*, Pub. by Bungalo Bks CN); pap. 4.95 (*0-685-72193-0*, Pub. by Bungalo Bks CN) Firefly Bks Ltd.

Bird, Malcolm. The School in Murky Wood. (Illus.). 40p. (ps-3). 1993. 10.95 (*0-8118-0544-1*) Chronicle Bks.

Birdseye, Tom. Just Call Me Stupid. 128p. (gr. 4-7). 1993. 14.95 (*0-8234-1045-5*) Holiday.

Birnbaum, Bette. My School, Your School. (Illus.). 24p. 1990. PLB 17.10 (*0-8172-3583-3*); pap. 10.95 pkg. of 3 (*0-8114-2931-8*) Raintree Steck-V.

Blanchette, Rick. Choice Adventure: Class Project Showdown. LC 92-30501. 1993. 4.99 (*0-8423-5047-0*) Tyndale.

Bliss, Corinne D. The Shortest Kid in the World. LC 93-45421. 1994. write for info. (*0-679-85809-1*) Random Bks Yng Read.

Bloom, Hanya. Vic the Vampire, No. 1: School Ghoul. (gr. 4-7). 1990. pap. 2.95 (*0-06-106004-6*, Harp PBks) HarpC.

Blume, Judy. Tales of a Fourth Grade Nothing. (gr. k-6). 1976. pap. 3.99 (*0-440-48474-X*, YB) Dell.

—Tales of a Fourth Grade Nothing. Doty, Roy, illus. LC 70-179050. 128p. (gr. 2-5). 1972. 11.95 (*0-525-40720-0*, DCB) Dutton Child Bks.

Boegehold, Betty D. Fight. (ps-3). 1991. 9.99 (*0-553-07086-X*) Bantam.

—Fight. (ps-3). 1991. pap. 3.99 (*0-553-35206-7*) Bantam.

Boston, Lucy M. The Children of Green Knowe. Deeter, Catherine & Boston, Peter, illus. 183p. (gr. 3-7). 1989. pap. 3.95 (*0-15-217151-7*, Odyssey) HarBrace.

—An Enemy at Green Knowe. Deeter, Catherine & Boston, Peter, illus. 176p. (gr. 4-7). 1989. pap. 3.95 (*0-15-225973-2*, Odyssey) HarBrace.

—A Stranger at Green Knowe. Deeter, Catherine & Boston, Peter, illus. 199p. (gr. 3-7). 1989. pap. 3.95 (*0-15-281755-7*, Odyssey) HarBrace.

Bourgeois, Paulette. Too Many Chickens! (ps-3). 1991. 12.95 (*0-316-10358-6*) Little.

Bradford, Jan. Caroline Zucker Gets Her Wish. Ramsey, Marcy D., illus. LC 90-31549. 96p. (gr. 2-5). 1991. PLB 9.89 (*0-8167-2019-3*); pap. text ed. 2.95 (*0-8167-2020-7*) Troll Assocs.

Brennan, Melissa. Sneaking Around. 1992. pap. 3.50 (*0-06-106069-0*, Harp PBks) HarpC.

Breslin, Theresa. New School Blues. (gr. 3-5). 1994. pap. 6.95 (*0-685-71177-3*, Pub. by Cnngt UK) Trafalgar.

Bridgers, Sue E. Keeping Christina. LC 92-22061. 288p. (gr. 7 up). 1993. 15.00 (*0-06-021504-6*); PLB 14.89 (*0-06-021505-4*) HarpC Child Bks.

Bridwell, Norman. The Witch Goes to School. LC 92-12091. (ps-3). 1992. pap. 2.95 (*0-590-45831-0*) Scholastic Inc.

Brooks, Chelsea. A California Night's Dream. LC 94-17924. (gr. 5 up). 1994. pap. 2.95 (*0-02-041652-0*, Collier) Macmillan.

Brooks, Jerome. Knee Holes. LC 91-25398. 144p. (gr. 7 up). 1992. 14.95 (*0-531-05994-4*); lib. bdg. 14.99 (*0-531-08594-5*) Orchard Bks Watts.

Brown, Marc T. Arthur's Teacher Trouble. Brown, Marc T., illus. 32p. (ps-3). 1989. 15.95 (*0-316-11244-5*, Joy St Bks); pap. 4.95 (*0-316-11186-4*, Joy St Bks) Little.

—The True Francine. Brown, Marc T., illus. 32p. (ps-3). 1981. 15.95 (*0-316-11212-7*, Joy St Bks) Little.

Buchanan, Heather S. George & Matilda Mouse & the Floating School. LC 89-22036. (Illus.). 40p. (ps-3). 1990. pap. 13.95 (*0-671-70613-6*) S&S Trade.

Bunt, Sandra K. The Other Side of the Desk. DeVito, Pam, illus. LC 90-71374. 135p. (Orig.). (gr. 3-6). 1992. pap. 9.95 (*0-932433-80-4*) Windswept Hse.

Bunting, Eve. The Girl in the Painting. (Illus.). 64p. (gr. 3-8). 1992. 8.95 (*0-89565-770-8*) Childs World.

—Our Sixth-Grade Sugar Babies. LC 90-5487. 160p. (gr. 4-6). 1990. 13.00 (*0-397-32451-0*, Lipp Jr Bks); PLB 12.89 (*0-397-32452-9*, Lipp Jr Bks) HarpC Child Bks.

—Our Teacher's Having a Baby. De Groat, Diane, illus. 32p. (ps-3). 1992. 13.45 (*0-395-60470-2*, Clarion Bks) HM.

—Spying on Miss Muller. LC 94-15003. (gr. 1-8). 1995. write for info. (*0-395-69172-9*, Clarion Bks) HM.

Burch, Robert. Queenie Peavy. 160p. (gr. 3-7). 1987. pap. 3.99 (*0-14-032305-8*, Puffin) Puffin Bks.

Burnett, Frances H. Little Princess. Tudor, Tasha, illus. LC 63-15435. (gr. 4-6). 1963. 16.00 (*0-397-30693-8*, Lipp Jr Bks); PLB 15.89 (*0-397-31339-X*, Lipp Jr Bks) HarpC Child Bks.

—Little Princess. (gr. 3 up). 1993. pap. 4.99 (*0-88070-527-2*, Gold & Honey) Questar Pubs.

—A Little Princess. Dubowski, Cathy E., ed. LC 93-14000. 1994. 2.99 (*0-679-85090-2*) Random.

—A Little Princess. Dubowski, Cathy E., adapted by. 108p. (Orig.). (gr. 2-6). 1994. pap. 2.99 (*0-685-71036-X*) Random Bks Yng Read.

—Little Princess. 14.95 (*0-8488-1253-0*) Amereon Ltd.

Butcher, Samuel J. & Butcher, Jon. Precious Moments Learning Can Be Fun. LC 93-11671. (Illus.). 176p. (ps). 1993. 14.99 (*0-8010-1059-4*) Baker Bk.

Butterworth, Nick. Field Day. (gr. 1-3). 1993. pap. 2.99 (*0-553-37250-5*) Bantam.

—School Trip. (gr. 1-3). 1993. pap. 2.99 (*0-553-37249-1*) Bantam.

Calder, Lyn. Gold-Star Homework. LC 90-85434. (Illus.). 32p. (gr. k-3). 1991. 5.95 (*1-56282-035-4*) Disney Pr.

Calmenson, Stephanie. The Principal's New Clothes. Brunkus, Denise, illus. (ps-3). 1989. pap. 12.95 (*0-590-41822-X*) Scholastic Inc.

—The Principal's New Clothes. Brunkus, Denise, illus. 40p. (ps-2). 1991. pap. 3.95 (*0-590-44778-5*, Blue Ribbon Bks) Scholastic Inc.

Calvert, Patricia. Writing to Richie. LC 94-14458. (gr. 4-6). 1994. 14.95 (*0-684-19764-2*, Scribner) Macmillan.

Caple, Kathy. The Wimp. LC 94-7121. 1994. 14.95 (*0-395-63115-7*) HM.

Carlson, Nancy. Arnie & the New Kid. (Illus.). 32p. (ps-3). 1992. pap. 3.99 (*0-14-050945-3*, Puffin) Puffin Bks.

—Loudmouth George & the Sixth Grade Bully. Carlson, Nancy, illus. (gr. k-3). 1986. pap. 12.95 incl. cassette (*0-87499-014-9*); incl. cassette 19.95 (*0-87499-016-5*); incl. cassette, 4 paperbacks guide 27.95 (*0-317-40166-1*) Live Oak Media.

Carroll, Jeri, et al. Back to School in January. Smith, Bron, illus. 144p. (gr. k-5). 1989. wkbk. 12.95 (*0-86653-470-9*, GA1067) Good Apple.

Case, Mary & Shaffer, Dianna. Katie Koala Bear in What Will Katie Wear to School? (Illus.). 20p. (Orig.). 1989. pap. 4.95 (*1-877995-06-1*) Koala Pub Co.

Caseley, Judith. Mr. Green Peas. LC 93-24183. 1994. write for info. (*0-688-12859-9*); PLB write for info. (*0-688-12860-2*) Greenwillow.

Caudill, Rebecca. Schoolhouse in the Woods. (gr. k-6). 1989. pap. 2.75 (*0-440-40170-4*, YB) Dell.

—Schoolroom in the Parlor. (gr. k-6). 1989. pap. 2.75 (*0-440-40200-X*, YB) Dell.

Cazet, Denys. Are There Any Questions? LC 91-42977. (Illus.). 32p. (ps-2). 1992. 14.95 (*0-531-05451-9*); PLB 14.99 (*0-531-08601-1*) Orchard Bks Watts.

—Never Spit on Your Shoes. LC 89-35164. (Illus.). 32p. (ps-1). 1990. 14.95 (*0-531-05847-6*); PLB 14.99 (*0-531-08447-7*) Orchard Bks Watts.

Chardiet, Bernice & Maccarone, Grace. Merry Christmas, What's Your Name School Friends. Karas, G. Brian, illus. 32p. (ps-2). 1991. 2.50 (*0-590-43306-7*) Scholastic Inc.

—We Scream for Ice Cream. Karas, G. Brian, illus. 48p. (ps-3). 1992. pap. 2.50 (*0-590-44934-6*) Scholastic Inc.

Christian, Mary B. But Everybody Does It: Peer Pressure. Brubaker, Lee W., illus. LC 85-17112. 72p. (Orig.). (gr. 4-7). 1986. pap. 3.99 (*0-570-03636-4*, 39-1098) Concordia.

—Swamp Monsters. Brown, Marc T., illus. LC 93-25616. (gr. 1-4). 1994. pap. 3.25 (*0-14-036841-8*, Puffin) Puffin Bks.

Clark, Catherine. What's So Funny about Ninth Grade? LC 91-2494. 128p. (gr. 6-9). 1992. lib. bdg. 9.89 (*0-8167-2396-6*); pap. text ed. 2.95 (*0-8167-2397-4*) Troll Assocs.

Clarkson, Margaret. Susie's Babies: A Clear & Simple Explanation of the Everyday Miracle of Birth. 72p. 1992. pap. 7.99 (*0-8028-4053-1*) Eerdmans.

Clayton, Elaine. Pup in School. Clayton, Elaine, illus. LC 92-18457. 24p. (ps-1). 1993. 12.00 (*0-517-59085-9*); PLB 12.99 (*0-517-59086-7*) Crown Bks Yng Read.

Cleary, Beverly. Beverly Cleary, 4 vols. (gr. 4-7). 1991. Set. pap. 14.00 boxed (*0-380-71719-0*, Camelot) Avon.

—Dear Mr. Henshaw. large type ed. Zelinsky, Paul O., illus. 141p. (gr. 2-6). 1987. Repr. of 1983 ed. lib. bdg. 14.95 (*1-55736-001-4*, Crnrstn Bks) BDD LT Grp.

—Ellen Tebbits. Darling, Louis, illus. LC 51-11430. 160p. (gr. 3-7). 1951. 12.95 (*0-688-21264-6*); PLB 12.88 (*0-688-31264-0*, Morrow Jr Bks) Morrow Jr Bks.

—Henry & Beezus. 1923. pap. 1.75 (*0-440-73295-6*) Dell.

—Jean & Johnny. Krush, Beth & Krush, Joe, illus. LC 59-7806. 288p. (gr. 6-9). 1959. 12.95 (*0-688-21740-0*); PLB 12.88 (*0-688-31740-5*, Morrow Jr Bks) Morrow Jr Bks.

—Muggie Maggie. Life, Kay, illus. LC 89-38959. 80p. (gr. 7 up). 1990. 11.95 (*0-688-08553-9*); PLB 11.88 (*0-688-08554-7*) Morrow Jr Bks.

—Otis Spofford. Darling, Louis, illus. LC 53-6660. 192p. (gr. 3-7). 1953. 12.95 (*0-688-21720-6*); PLB 12.88 (*0-688-31720-0*) Morrow Jr Bks.

—Ramona Quimby, Age 8. large type ed. Tiegreen, Alan, illus. 142p. (gr. 2-6). 1987. Repr. of 1981 ed. lib. bdg. 14.95 (*1-55736-000-6*, Crnrstn Bks) BDD LT Grp.

—Ramona the Brave. Tiegreen, Alan, illus. LC 74-16494. 192p. (gr. 3-7). 1975. 13.95 (*0-688-22015-0*); PLB 13.88 (*0-688-32015-5*) Morrow Jr Bks.

—Ramona the Pest. Darling, Louis, illus. LC 68-12981. (gr. 3-7). 1968. 13.95 (*0-688-21721-4*); PLB 13.88 (*0-688-31721-9*) Morrow Jr Bks.

—Strider. Zelinsky, Paul O., illus. LC 90-6608. 192p. (gr. 3 up). 1991. 13.95 (*0-688-09900-9*); PLB 13.88 (*0-688-09901-7*) Morrow Jr Bks.

Cohen, Barbara. Two Hundred Thirteen Valentines. Clay, Wil, illus. LC 91-7151. 64p. (gr. 2-4). 1991. 13.95 (*0-8050-1536-1*, Redfeather BYR) H Holt & Co.

Cohen, Miriam. Best Friends. Hoban, Lillian, illus. LC 70-146620. 32p. (ps-1). 1971. RSBE 13.95 (*0-02-722800-2*, Macmillan Child Bk) Macmillan Child Grp.

—Don't Eat Too Much Turkey! Hoban, Lillian, illus. LC 86-25660. 32p. (gr. k-3). 1987. 15.00 (*0-688-07141-4*); lib. bdg. 14.93 (*0-688-07142-2*) Greenwillow.

—First Grade Takes a Test. Hoban, Lillian, illus. (gr. k-3). 1983. pap. 2.95 (*0-440-42500-X*, YB) Dell.

—Jim's Dog Muffins. Hoban, Lillian, illus. LC 83-14090. 32p. (gr. k-3). 1984. 13.95 (*0-688-02564-1*); PLB 13.88 (*0-688-02565-X*) Greenwillow.

—No Good in Art. Hoban, Lillian, illus. LC 79-16566. 32p. (gr. k-3). 1980. PLB 14.93 (*0-688-84234-8*) Greenwillow.

—Second Grade Friends. 1993. pap. 2.75 (*0-590-47463-4*) Scholastic Inc.

—Second Grade-Friends Again! (ps-3). 1994. pap. 2.95 (*0-590-45906-6*) Scholastic Inc.

—See You in Second Grade! Hoban, Lillian, illus. LC 87-14869. 32p. (ps up). 1989. 13.95 (*0-688-07138-4*); PLB 13.88 (*0-688-07139-2*) Greenwillow.

—When Will I Read? Hoban, Lillian, illus. LC 76-28320. 32p. (ps-3). 1977. 16.00 (*0-688-80073-4*); PLB 15.93 (*0-688-84073-6*) Greenwillow.

—Will I Have a Friend? Hoban, Lillian, illus. LC 67-10127. 32p. (ps-1). 1967. RSBE 13.95 (*0-02-722790-1*, Macmillan Child Bk) Macmillan Child Grp.

Cole, Joanna. The Magic School Bus at the Waterworks. Degen, Bruce, illus. 40p. (gr. 1-4). 1988. pap. 3.95 (*0-590-40360-5*, Scholastic Hardcover) Scholastic Inc.

Coleman, Clay. Resolved: Your Dead. 1990. pap. 3.50 (*0-06-106019-4*, PL) HarpC.

Conford, Ellen. The Alfred G. Graebner Memorial High School Handbook of Rules & Regulations. (gr. 7-12). 1976. 14.95 (*0-316-15293-5*) Little.

—Dear Lovey Hart: I Am Desperate. 224p. (gr. 4-6). 1975. 14.95 (*0-316-15306-0*) Little.

—Dear Mom, Get Me Out of Here! LC 92-438. 1992. 14.95 (*0-316-15370-2*) Little.

Coombs, Patricia. Dorrie & the Haunted Schoolhouse. Coombs, Patricia, illus. 32p. (ps-3). 1992. 13.45 (*0-395-60116-9*, Clarion Bks) HM.

Cooney, Barbara. Miss Rumphius. Cooney, Barbara, illus. (ps-3). 1994. pap. 6.99 incl. cassette (*0-14-095026-5*, Puffin) Puffin Bks.

Cooney, Caroline B. Driver's Ed. LC 94-445. 1994. 15.95 (*0-385-32087-6*) Delacorte.

Cooney, Linda A. Freshman Affair. 1992. pap. 3.50 (*0-06-106711-3*, Harp PBks) HarpC.

—Freshman Christmas. 1992. pap. 4.50 (*0-06-106723-7*, Harp PBks) HarpC.

—Freshman Dreams. (gr. 9-12). 1991. pap. 3.50 (*0-06-106040-2*, PL) HarpC.

—Freshman Games. (gr. 9-12). 1991. pap. 3.50 (*0-06-106035-6*, PL) HarpC.

—Freshman Guys. (gr. 9-12). 1990. pap. 3.50 (*0-06-106011-9*, PL) HarpC.

—Freshman Lies. 1990. pap. 3.50 (*0-06-106005-4*, Harp PBks) HarpC.

—Freshman Nights. (gr. 9-12). 1990. pap. 3.50 (*0-06-106012-7*, PL) HarpC.

—Freshman Roommate. 1993. pap. 3.99 (*0-06-106730-X*, Harp PBks) HarpC.

Cooper, Ilene. Choosing Sides. (Illus.). 218p. (gr. 3-7). 1992. pap. 3.99 (*0-14-036097-2*, Puffin) Puffin Bks.

—The New, Improved Gretchen Hubbard. LC 92-6197. 208p. (gr. 4 up). 1992. 14.00 (*0-688-08432-X*) Morrow Jr Bks.

—Queen of the Sixth Grade. 160p. (gr. 3 up). 1992. pap. 3.99 (*0-14-036098-0*, Puffin) Puffin Bks.

—Trick or Trouble. (gr. 4 up). 1994. write for info. Viking Penguin.

Cormier, Robert. Little Raw on Monday Mornings. 1992. pap. 3.99 (*0-440-21134-4*) Dell.

Corrin, Ruth. Charlie Best. Moyes, Lesley, illus. LC 93-9229. 1994. write for info. (*0-383-03681-X*) SRA Schl Grp.

Coryell, Susan. Eaglebait. 187p. (gr. 7 up). 1989. 14.95 (*0-15-200442-4*, Gulliver Bks) HarBrace.

Coville, Bruce. My Teacher Fried My Brains. MacDonald, Patricia, ed. 128p. (Orig.). 1991. pap. 3.99 (*0-671-72710-9*, Minstrel Bks) PB.

Craig, Lynn. New Friends in New Places. LC 94-1929. 1994. pap. 4.99 (*0-8407-9239-5*) Nelson.

Crew, Linda. Nekomah Creek Christmas. Robinson, Charles, illus. LC 94-478. 1994. 14.95 (*0-385-32047-7*) Delacorte.

Crews, Donald. School Bus. LC 85-576. (Illus.). 32p. (ps-1). 1985. pap. 3.99 (*0-14-050549-0*, Puffin) Puffin Bks.

Cross, Gillian. The Demon Headmaster. large type ed. 208p. (gr. 3 up). 1990. lib. bdg. 16.95x (*0-7451-1150-5*, Lythway Large Print) Hall.

Cruise, Beth. Best Friend's Girl. LC 94-11670. (gr. 5 up). 1994. pap. 2.95 (*0-02-042786-7*) Macmillan.

—Computer Confusion. 144p. (Orig.). (gr. 5 up). 1994. pap. 2.95 (*0-02-042784-0*, Collier Young Ad) Macmillan Child Grp.

—Going, Going, Gone! LC 94-14475. (gr. 3-7). 1994. pap. 3.95 (*0-689-71852-7*, Aladdin Bks) Macmillan Child Grp.

—Saved by the Bell: Bayside Madness. LC 91-46070. 144p. (Orig.). (gr. 5 up). 1992. pap. 2.95 (*0-02-042775-1*, Collier Young Ad) Macmillan Child Grp.

—Saved by the Bell: Zack Strikes Back. LC 92-5182. 144p. (Orig.). (gr. 5 up). 1992. pap. 2.95 (*0-02-042777-8*, Collier Young Ad) Macmillan Child Grp.

—Saved By the Bell: Zack's Last Scam. LC 92-31733. 144p. (gr. 5 up). 1992. pap. 2.95 (*0-02-042767-0*, Collier Young Ad) Macmillan Child Grp.

Crutcher, Chris. Staying Fat for Sarah Byrnes. large type ed. (gr. 9-12). 1993. 15.95 (*0-7862-0062-6*) Thorndike Pr.

—Stotan! LC 85-12712. 192p. (gr. 7 up). 1986. reinforced trade ed. 12.00 (*0-688-05715-2*) Greenwillow.

Cullen, Lynn. The Backyard Ghost. LC 92-24580. 160p. (gr. 4-7). 1993. 13.95 (*0-395-64527-1*, Clarion Bks) HM.

—Meeting the Make-Out King. LC 93-38850. 1994. 13.95 (*0-395-67889-7*, Clarion Bks) HM.

Dahl, Roald. Matilda. LC 94-5864. 1994. 12.95 (*0-679-43651-0*, Evrymans Lib Childs) Knopf.

Danziger, Paula. Amber Brown Is Not a Crayon. Ross, Tony, illus. LC 92-34678. 80p. (gr. 1-4). 1994. 11.95 (*0-399-22509-9*, Putnam) Putnam Pub Group.

—The Cat Ate My Gymsuit. LC 74-5501. 128p. (gr. 7 up). 1974. 14.95 (*0-385-28183-8*); PLB 14.95 (*0-385-28194-3*) Delacorte.

—This Place Has No Atmosphere. (gr. k-6). 1989. pap. 3.50 (*0-440-40205-0*, YB) Dell.

Davis, M. J. Beverly Hills, 90210: Exposed. 1991. pap. 4.50 (*0-06-106137-9*, Harp PBks) HarpC.

DeClements, Barthe. How Do You Lose Ninth Grade Blues? 144p. (gr. 5 up). 1993. pap. 3.99 (*0-14-036333-5*, Puffin) Puffin Bks.

—Nothing's Fair in Fifth Grade. 144p. (gr. 8-12). 1995. pap. 3.99 (*0-14-034443-8*, Puffin) Puffin Bks.

—Seventeen & In-Between. 180p. (gr. 7-9). 1984. pap. 13.95 (*0-670-63615-0*) Viking Child Bks.

—Seventeen & In-Between: A Novel. LC 92-37596. 176p. (gr. 7 up). 1993. pap. 3.99 (*0-14-036475-7*, Puffin) Puffin Bks.

—Sixth Grade Can Really Kill You. LC 85-40382. 146p. (gr. 5-8). 1985. pap. 12.95 (*0-670-80656-0*) Viking Child Bks.

Degroat, Diane. Annie Pitts, Artichoke. LC 91-759108. (gr. 4-7). 1992. pap. 12.00 (*0-671-75910-8*, S&S BFYR) S&S Trade.

Delton, Judy. My Mom Made Me Go to School. (gr. 1-3). 1993. pap. 2.99 (*0-553-37252-1*) Bantam.

—The New Girl at School. Hoban, Lillian, illus. LC 79-11409. (gr. k-3). 1979. 12.95 (*0-525-35780-7*, DCB) Dutton Child Bks.

Denton, Terry. The School for Laughter. Denton, Terry, illus. 32p. (gr. k-3). 1990. 13.45 (*0-395-53353-8*) HM.

Deru, Myriam & Alen, Paule. My First Day at School. (SPA & ENG., Illus.). 32p. (ps-1). 1991. 5.99 (*0-517-65557-8*) Random Hse Value.

De Saint Mars, Dominique. Max Doesn't Like School. Bloch, Serge, illus. LC 93-23773. (gr. 2-4). Date not set. 8.95 (*1-56766-103-3*) Childs World.

Dicks, Terrance. Teacher's Pet. Littlewood, Valerie, illus. 52p. (gr. 2-5). 1992. pap. 3.50 (*0-8120-4820-2*) Barron.

Domke, Todd. Grounded. LC 81-14267. 192p. (gr. 4-7). 1982. pap. 9.95 (*0-394-85163-3*) Knopf Bks Yng Read.

Draper, Sharon. Tears of a Tiger. LC 94-10278. (gr. 7 up). 1994. 14.95 (*0-689-31878-2*, Atheneum) Macmillan.

Duey, Kathleen. The Third Grade's Skinny Pig. 80p. (Orig.). (gr. 1). 1993. pap. 3.50 (*0-380-76730-9*, Camelot Young) Avon.

Duncan, Lois. Wonder Kid Meets the Evil Lunch Snatcher. Sanfilippo, Margaret, illus. LC 87-26490. 76p. (gr. 7-10). 1988. 12.95 (*0-316-19558-8*) Little.

Dunn, Ben. Ninja High School, Vol. 1: Graphic Album. 2nd ed. Castro, Carlos & Dunn, Ben, illus. 126p. (gr. 10). 1990. pap. 9.95 (*0-944735-13-4*) Malibu Graphics.

Dygard, Thomas J. Backfield Package. LC 93-7721. 208p. (gr. 5 up). 1993. pap. 3.99 (*0-14-036348-3*, Puffin) Puffin Bks.

—Forward Pass. LC 89-33427. (Illus.). 192p. (gr. 7 up). 1989. 11.95 (*0-688-07961-X*) Morrow Jr Bks.

—Game Plan. LC 92-47252. 224p. (gr. 7 up). 1993. 14.00 (*0-688-12007-5*) Morrow Jr Bks.

—The Rebounder. LC 94-51257. 1994. write for info. (*0-688-12821-1*) Morrow Jr Bks.

Ehrlich, Fred. A Class Play with Ms. Vanilla. Gradisher, Martha, illus. 32p. (ps-3). 1992. 9.00 (*0-670-84651-1*) Viking Child Bks.

—Lunch Boxes. Gradisher, Martha, illus. LC 93-2724. (gr. k-3). 1993. pap. 3.25 (*0-14-036555-9*, Puffin) Puffin Bks.

Elias, Miriam L. Thanks to You! LC 94-44850. 1994. write for info. (*0-87306-663-4*); pap. write for info. (*0-87306-664-2*) Feldheim.

Ellis, Jana. Better Than the Truth. LC 88-15881. 160p. (gr. 7 up). 1988. pap. text ed. 2.50 (*0-8167-1362-6*) Troll Assocs.

—Never Stop Smiling. LC 88-12390. 160p. (gr. 7 up). 1988. pap. text ed. 2.50 (*0-8167-1360-X*) Troll Assocs.

—Playing Games. LC 88-12389. 160p. (gr. 7 up). 1988. pap. text ed. 2.50 (*0-8167-1358-8*) Troll Assocs.

Ewers, Joe, illus. Little Yellow School Bus. 14p. (ps-k). 1992. bds. 4.99 (*0-679-83243-2*) Random Bks Yng Read.

Faber, Adele & Mazlish, Elaine. Bobby & the Brockles Go to School. Morehouse, Hank, illus. LC 93-42884. 64p. (Orig.). 1994. pap. 15.00 (*0-380-77068-7*) Avon.

Feder, Paula K. Where Does the Teacher Live? Hoban, Lillian, illus. LC 78-13157. 48p. (gr. 1-3). 1979. 12.95 (*0-525-42586-1*, DCB) Dutton Child Bks.

—Where Does the Teacher Live? Hoban, Lillian, illus. LC 78-13157. 48p. (gr. 1-3). 1992. pap. 3.99 (*0-525-44889-6*, Unicorn Pbks) Dutton Child Bks.

Fine, Anne. Flour Babies & the Boys of Room 8. LC 93-35698. 1994. Repr. of 1992 ed. 14.95 (*0-316-28319-3*) Little.

Fitzgerald, John D. The Great Brain at the Academy. 164p. (gr. k-6). 1982. pap. 3.99 (*0-440-43113-1*, YB) Dell.

—The Great Brain at the Academy. Mayer, Mercer, illus. LC 72-712. 176p. (gr. 4-7). 1985. 12.95 (*0-8037-3039-X*); PLB 11.89 (*0-8037-3040-3*) Dial Bks Young.

Fitzhugh, Louise. Harriet the Spy. large type ed. Fitzhugh, Louise, illus. 282p. (gr. 2-6). 1987. Repr. of 1964 ed. lib. bdg. 13.95 (*1-55736-012-X*, Crnrstn Bks) BDD LT Grp.

Fleetwood, Jennie. Happy Birthday: Nine Birthday Stories. Willow, illus. 96p. (gr. 2-4). 1993. 16.95 (*0-460-88050-0*, Pub. by J M Dent & Sons) Trafalgar.

Fleischman, Paul. Time Train. Ewart, Claire, illus. LC 90-27357. 32p. (gr. k-4). 1991. 15.00 (*0-06-021709-X*); PLB 14.89 (*0-06-021710-3*) HarpC Child Bks.

Fleisher, Gila M. Dan Goes to First Grade. Kriss, David, tr. from HEB. Eagle, Mike, illus. 24p. (Orig.). (ps). 1992. pap. text ed. 3.00x (*1-56134-166-5*) Dushkin Pub.

—Daniel Entra Al Primer Grado. Writer, C. C. & Nielsen, Lisa C., trs. Eagle, Mike, illus. (SPA.). 24p. (Orig.). (ps). 1992. pap. text ed. 3.00x (*1-56134-176-2*) Dushkin Pub.
Frandsen, Karen G. I Started School Today. LC 83-23169. (Illus.). 32p. (ps-2). 1984. pap. 3.95 (*0-516-43495-0*) Childrens.
—Michael's New Haircut. Frandsen, Karen G., illus. LC 86-11696. 32p. (ps-3). 1986. pap. 3.95 (*0-516-43545-0*) Childrens.
Frederick, Ruth. Where's Tommy? O'Connell, Ruth A., illus. 32p. (gr. 1-2). 1991. pap. 3.99 saddle stitch (*0-87403-806-5*, 24-03896) Standard Pub.
Gabler, Mirko. Brackus, Krakus. Gabler, Mirko, illus. LC 92-25819. 32p. (ps-3). 1993. 14.95 (*0-8050-1963-4*, Bks Young Read) H Holt & Co.
Gantos, Jack. Heads or Tails: Stories from the Sixth Grade. LC 93-43117. 1994. 16.00 (*0-374-32909-5*) FS&G.
Garland, Sarah. Billy & Belle. Garland, Sarah, illus. 32p. (ps-3). 1992. 13.00 (*0-670-84396-2*) Viking Child Bks.
Gehman, Mary W. Abdi & the Elephants. 104p. (Orig.). (gr. 6-8). 1995. pap. 5.95 (*0-8361-3699-3*) Herald Pr.
Geller, Mark. My Life in the Seventh Grade. LC 85-45265. 160p. (gr. 5-7). 1986. PLB 11.89 (*0-06-021982-3*) HarpC Child Bks.
Geras, Adele. Pictures of the Night. LC 92-27425. 1993. write for info. (*0-15-261588-1*) HarBrace.
—The Tower Room. 1992. 15.95 (*0-15-289627-9*, HB Juv Bks) HarBrace.
Gifaldi, David. Toby Scudder, Ultimate Warrior. LC 92-39532. 1993. 13.95 (*0-395-66400-4*, Clarion Bks) HM.
Giff, Patricia R. The Case of the Cool-Itch Kid. (gr. k-6). 1989. pap. 3.50 (*0-440-40199-2*) Dell.
—Count Your Money with the Polk Street School. (ps-3). 1994. pap. 3.99 (*0-440-40929-2*) Dell.
—The Fourth Grade Celebrity. 128p. (gr. k-6). 1989. pap. 3.50 (*0-440-42676-6*, YB) Dell.
—Fourth Grade Celebrity. Morrill, Leslie, illus. 128p. (gr. 4-6). 1984. 8.95 (*0-385-28308-3*) Delacorte.
—Fourth Grade Celebrity. Morrill, Leslie, illus. LC 79-50678. (gr. 4-6). 1979. 8.95 (*0-440-02725-X*); PLB 8.89 (*0-440-02726-8*) Delacorte.
—Garbage Juice for Breakfast. (gr. 1-4). 1989. pap. 3.25 (*0-440-40207-7*, YB) Dell.
—The Great Shamrock Disaster. (ps-3). 1993. pap. 3.25 (*0-440-40778-8*) Dell.
—New Kids of the Polk Street School, 6 vols. (gr. 4-7). 1990. pap. 16.50 boxed set (*0-440-36029-3*) Dell.
—Next Year I'll Be Special. Hafner, Marylin, photos by. LC 92-20749. 1993. 13.95 (*0-385-30903-1*, Zephyr-BFYR) Doubleday.
—Pickle Puss. (Orig.). (gr. k-3). 1986. pap. 3.50 (*0-440-46844-2*, YB) Dell.
—Pickle Puss. Sims, Blanche, illus. (ps-3). 1986. pap. 8.95 (*0-385-29477-8*) Delacorte.
—Postcard Pest: Polk Street Special, No. 3. (ps-3). 1994. pap. 3.99 (*0-440-40973-X*) Dell.
—Purple Climbing Days. Sims, Blanche, illus. (ps-3). 1986. pap. 8.95 (*0-385-29500-6*) Delacorte.
—Say "Cheese" Sims, Blanche, illus. (ps-3). 1986. pap. 8.95 (*0-385-29501-4*) Delacorte.
—Say "Cheese, No. 10. Sims, Blanche, illus. (gr. 6-9). 1985. pap. 3.50 (*0-440-47639-9*, YB) Dell.
—Stacy Says Good-Bye. Sims, Blanche, illus. 80p. (gr. k-3). 1989. pap. 3.50 (*0-440-40135-6*, YB) Dell.
—Sunny Side Up. (Orig.). (gr. k-3). 1986. pap. 3.50 (*0-440-48406-5*, YB) Dell.
—Today Was a Terrible Day. Natti, Susanna, illus. 1993. pap. 6.99 incl. cassette (*0-14-095119-9*, Puffin) Puffin Bks.
—War Began at Supper: Letters to Miss Loria. (gr. 4-7). 1991. pap. 2.95 (*0-440-40572-6*) Dell.
—Watch Out! Man-Eating Snake. 80p. (Orig.). (gr. k-6). 1988. pap. 3.50 (*0-440-40085-6*, YB) Dell.
Gilden, Mel. Beverly Hills, 90210. 1991. pap. 3.99 (*0-06-100417-0*, Harp PBks) HarpC.
—Fifth Grade Monsters, No. 12: Werewolf Come Home. 1990. pap. 2.75 (*0-380-75908-X*, Camelot) Avon.
—Fifth Grade Monsters, No. 15: The Secret of Dinosaur Bog. 96p. (Orig.). (gr. 5). 1991. pap. 2.99 (*0-380-76308-7*, Camelot) Avon.
—How to Be a Vampire in One Easy Lesson. 1990. pap. 2.75 (*0-380-75906-3*, Camelot) Avon.
—Island of the Weird. 96p. 1990. pap. 2.95 (*0-380-75907-1*, Camelot) Avon.
Gilligan, Shannon. The Locker Thief. (gr. 4-7). 1991. pap. 2.99 (*0-553-15895-3*) Bantam.
Gilson, Jamie. Itchy Richard. De Groat, Diane, illus. 64p. (gr. 1-5). 1991. 13.45 (*0-395-59282-8*, Clarion Bks) HM.
—Sticks & Stones & Skeleton Bones. DeRosa, Dee, illus. (gr. 3-6). 1991. 14.00 (*0-688-10098-8*) Lothrop.
—You Don't Know Beans about Bats. De Groat, Diane, illus. LC 93-559. 1994. write for info. (*0-395-67063-2*, Clarion Bks) HM.
Gordon, Sharon. Show & Tell. Kolding, Richard M., illus. LC 86-30855. 32p. (gr. k-2). 1988. PLB 7.89 (*0-8167-0994-7*); pap. text ed. 1.95 (*0-8167-0995-5*) Troll Assocs.
Gorman, Carol. Biggest Bully in Brookdale. (Illus.). 80p. (gr. 2-4). 1992. pap. 3.99 (*0-570-04713-7*) Concordia.
—Million Dollar Winner. Koehler, Ed, illus. LC 93-36935. 96p. (Orig.). (gr. 4-7). 1994. pap. 3.99 (*0-570-04630-0*) Concordia.
—The Taming of Roberta Parsley. Koehler, Ed, illus. LC 93-38312. 96p. (Orig.). (gr. 4-7). 1994. pap. 3.99 (*0-570-04628-9*) Concordia.
Gormley, Beatrice. Fifth Grade Magic. McCully, Emily A., illus. 128p. (gr. 3-7). 1984. pap. 3.50 (*0-380-67439-4*, Camelot) Avon.
—More Fifth Grade Magic. 112p. 1990. pap. 3.50 (*0-380-70883-3*, Camelot) Avon.
Goudge, Eileen. Winner All the Way. 160p. (Orig.). (gr. 7-12). 1984. pap. 2.25 (*0-440-99480-2*, LFL) Dell.
Greenaway, Elizabeth. Bitty Goes to School. (Illus.). 24p. (Orig.). (ps-2). 1994. pap. 2.50 (*0-679-86182-3*) Random Bks Yng Read.
Greene, Constance C. A Girl Called Al. 128p. (gr. 5-9). 1977. pap. 2.95 (*0-440-42810-6*, YB) Dell.
Greenwald, Sheila. Move Over, Columbus, Rosy Cole Discovers America! LC 92-12480. 1992. 13.95 (*0-316-32721-2*, Joy St Bks) Little.
Haas, Dorothy. Trouble at Alcott School. 1989. pap. 2.50 (*0-590-41509-3*) Scholastic Inc.
Haas, Jessie. Skipping School. LC 91-37642. (gr. 6-12). 1992. 14.00 (*0-688-10179-8*) Greenwillow.
Hackett, Christine. Little House in the Classroom. Filkins, Vanessa, illus. 112p. (gr. 3-5). 1989. wkbk. 10.95 (*0-86653-444-X*, GA1052) Good Apple.
Hallinan, P. K. My First Day of School. Hallinan, P. K., illus. 24p. (ps-2). 1987. perfect bdg. 4.95 (*0-8249-8533-8*, Ideals Child) Hambleton-Hill.
Hamilton, Dorothy. Rosalie. Unada, illus. LC 76-39961. 128p. (gr. 3-10). 1977. pap. text ed. 3.95 (*0-8361-1807-3*) Herald Pr.
Harding, William H. Alvin's Famous No-Horse. Chesworth, Michael, illus. LC 92-13834. 64p. (gr. 2-4). 1992. alk. paper 14.95 (*0-8050-2227-9*, Redfeather BYR) H Holt & Co.
Harrell, Janice. Tiffany, the Disaster. Ashby, Ruth, ed. 112p. (Orig.). (gr. 3-6). 1992. pap. 2.99 (*0-671-72860-1*, Minstrel Bks) PB.
Harrison, David. Somebody Catch My Homework. 32p. (gr. 4-7). 1993. 13.95 (*1-878093-87-8*, Wordsong) Boyds Mills Pr.
Hart, Avery & Mantell, Paul. Ninth Grade Outcast. LC 91-2492. 128p. (gr. 6-9). 1992. lib. bdg. 9.89 (*0-8167-2392-3*); pap. text ed. 2.95 (*0-8167-2393-1*) Troll Assocs.
Hart, Jan S. The Many Adventures of Minnie. Wilson, Kay, illus. LC 92-17740. 96p. (gr. 4-7). 1992. 12.95 (*0-89015-859-2*) Sunbelt Media.
Harvey, Jayne. Great-Uncle Dracula. Carter, Abby, illus. LC 91-31460. 80p. (Orig.). (gr. 2-4). 1992. PLB 6.99 (*0-679-92448-5*); pap. 2.50 (*0-679-82448-0*) Random Bks Yng Read.
Hawkins, Laura. The Cat That Could Spell Mississippi. LC 92-8025. 160p. (gr. 3-5). 1992. 13.95 (*0-395-61627-1*) HM.
—Valentine to a Flying Mouse. (ps-7). 1993. 13.95 (*0-395-61628-X*) HM.
Hayashi, Nancy. The Fantastic Stay-Home-from-School Day. Hayashi, Nancy, illus. LC 91-21095. 105p. (gr. 2-5). 1992. 12.00 (*0-525-44864-0*, DCB) Dutton Child Bks.
Haynes, Betsy. Grade Me. (gr. 7). 1989. pap. 2.75 (*0-685-33584-4*) Bantam.
—Seventh-Grade Menace. (gr. 4 up). 1989. pap. 2.75 (*0-553-15763-9*) Bantam.
Haywood, Carolyn. B Is for Betsy. Haywood, Carolyn, illus. LC 85-16381. 159p. (gr. 1-5). 1939. 12.95 (*0-15-204975-4*, HB Juv Bks) HarBrace.
—B Is for Betsy. Yakovetic, Joe, contrib. by. 120p. (gr. 2-5). 1990. pap. 3.95 (*0-15-204977-0*, Odyssey) HarBrace.
—Back to School with Betsy. Haywood, Carolyn, illus. LC 85-16380. 176p. (gr. 1-5). 1943. 12.95 (*0-15-205512-6*, HB Juv Bks) HarBrace.
—Back to School with Betsy. Yakovetic, Joe, contrib. by. 135p. (gr. 2-5). 1990. pap. 3.95 (*0-15-205515-0*, Odyssey) HarBrace.
—Betsy & Billy. Haywood, Carolyn, illus. LC 41-51926. 119p. (gr. 1-5). 1941. 12.95 (*0-15-206765-5*, HB Juv Bks) HarBrace.
—Betsy & Billy. Yakovetic, Joe, contrib. by. 119p. (gr. 2-5). 1990. pap. 3.95 (*0-15-206768-X*) HarBrace.
—Betsy & the Boys. Yakovetic, Joe, contrib. by. 140p. (gr. 2-5). 1990. pap. 3.95 (*0-15-206947-X*) HarBrace.
Henkes, Kevin. Chrysanthemum. LC 90-39803. (Illus.). 32p. (ps up). 1991. 13.95 (*0-688-09699-9*); PLB 13.88 (*0-688-09700-6*) Greenwillow.
Hennessy, B. G. School Days. Pearson, Tracey C., illus. LC 92-12008. (gr. 4 up). 1992. pap. 3.99 (*0-14-054179-9*, Puffin) Puffin Bks.
Hentoff, Nat. Does This School Have Capital Punishment? 160p. (gr. 7-11). 1983. pap. 3.50 (*0-440-92070-1*, LFL) Dell.
Herman, Charlotte. Millie Cooper, 3B. Cogancherry, Helen, illus. 80p. (gr. 3-7). 1986. pap. 3.95 (*0-14-032072-5*, Puffin) Puffin Bks.
Herman, Debbie. The Incredible Brocho Machine. (Illus.). 190p. (gr. 3-5). 1994. 8.95 (*1-56871-045-3*) Targum Pr.
Herman, Emmi S. My First Day at School. Flanigan, Ruth J., illus. 24p. (ps-2). 1992. pap. 0.99 (*1-56293-106-7*) McClanahan Bk.
Herman, Gail. Time for School, Little Dinosaur. Gorbaty, Norman, illus. LC 89-70331. 24p. (Orig.). (ps-2). 1990. pap. 2.25 (*0-679-80789-6*) Random Bks Yng Read.
Hermes, Patricia. Friends Are Like That. LC 83-18407. 128p. (gr. 3-7). 1984. 14.95 (*0-15-229722-7*, HB Juv Bks) HarBrace.
—I Hate Being Gifted. 144p. 1990. 14.95 (*0-399-21687-1*, Putnam) Putnam Pub Group.
—A Place for Jeremy. LC 86-31793. (Illus.). 160p. (gr. 3-7). 1987. 13.95 (*0-15-262350-7*) HarBrace.
Hess, Debra. Wilson Sat Alone. Greenseid, Diane, illus. LC 93-17616. (ps-2). 1994. pap. 14.00 (*0-671-87046-7*, S&S BFYR) S&S Trade.
Hiller, B. B. Rent a Third Grader. 192p. (gr. 2-4). 1988. pap. 2.75 (*0-590-40966-2*) Scholastic Inc.
Hilton, James. Good-Bye, Mr. Chips. (Illus.). (gr. 7 up). 1962. 17.95 (*0-316-36420-7*, Pub. by Atlantic Monthly Pr) Little.
—Goodbye, Mr. Chips. (gr. 7 up). 1969. pap. 2.95 (*0-553-25613-0*) Bantam.
Hirsch, Karen. Ellen Ånders on Her Own. LC 93-13350. 96p. (gr. 3-7). 1994. SBE 13.95 (*0-02-743975-5*, Macmillan Child Bk) Macmillan Child Grp.
Hodge, Merle. For the Life of Laetitia. 1993. 15.00 (*0-374-32447-6*) FS&G.
Hoestlandt, Jo. Back to School with Mom. (Illus.). 48p. (gr. 3-8). 1990. 8.95 (*0-89565-815-1*) Childs World.
Hogan, Paula Z. Sometimes I Don't Like School. (ps-3). 1993. pap. 3.95 (*0-8114-7155-1*) Raintree Steck-V.
Holt. Holt Little Class Special. (gr. 3 up). 1993. write for info. (*0-8050-3107-3*) H Holt & Co.
Hopper, Nancy J. Hang on, Harvey! 96p. (gr. 5-9). 1984. pap. 2.25 (*0-440-43371-1*, YB) Dell.
—I Was a Fifth-Grade Zebra. LC 92-30731. (gr. 3-6). 1993. 13.99 (*0-8037-1420-3*); PLB 13.89 (*0-8037-1595-1*) Dial Bks Young.
—The Interrupted Education of Huey B. 192p. (gr. 7 up). 1991. 14.95 (*0-525-67336-9*, Lodestar Bks) Dutton Child Bks.
—The Queen of Put-Down. LC 92-19559. 112p. (gr. 4-6). 1993. pap. 3.95 (*0-689-71670-2*, Aladdin) Macmillan Child Grp.
Hughes, Dean. Lucky's Cool Club. LC 93-28534. 141p. (gr. 3-7). 1993. pap. 4.95 (*0-87579-786-5*) Deseret Bk.
—One-Man Team. LC 93-44676. (Orig.). (gr. 4-9). 1994. PLB write for info. (*0-679-95441-4*, Bullseye Bks); pap. 3.99 (*0-679-85441-X*) Random Bks Yng Read.
—Re-elect Nutty. LC 94-12776. 1995. 14.00 (*0-689-31862-6*, Atheneum) Macmillan.
Hughes, Thomas. Tom Brown's School Days. 1987. Repr. lib. bdg. 21.95x (*0-89966-554-3*) Buccaneer Bks.
Hughes, Thomas P. Tom Brown's Schooldays. Sanders, Andrew, ed. (Illus.). 456p. 1989. pap. 4.95 (*0-19-282198-9*) OUP.
Hurwitz, Johanna. Class Clown. Hamanaka, Sheila, illus. LC 86-23624. 112p. (gr. 1-4). 1987. 12.95 (*0-688-06723-9*) Morrow Jr Bks.
—Class President. Hamanaka, Sheila, illus. LC 89-28600. 96p. (gr. 2 up). 1990. 12.95 (*0-688-09114-8*) Morrow Jr Bks.
—Teacher's Pet. Hamamaka, Sheila, illus. LC 87-24003. 128p. (gr. 2-5). 1988. 12.95 (*0-688-07506-1*) Morrow Jr Bks.
—Teacher's Pet. (gr. 2-5). 1989. pap. 2.75 (*0-590-42031-3*, Apple Paperbacks) Scholastic Inc.
Hutchins, Pat. Three-Star Billy. LC 93-26517. 32p. 1994. 15.00 (*0-688-13078-X*); lib. bdg. 14.93 (*0-688-13079-8*) Greenwillow.
Jackson, Alison. Blowing Bubbles with the Enemy. LC 93-2888. 120p. (gr. 3-7). 1993. 13.99 (*0-525-45056-4*, DCB) Dutton Child Bks.
Jackson, Kim. First Day of School. Goodman, John, illus. LC 84-8631. 32p. (gr. k-2). 1985. PLB 11.59 (*0-8167-0359-0*); pap. text ed. 2.95 (*0-8167-0439-2*) Troll Assocs.
Jackson, Shirley. Charles. 1991. PLB 13.95s.p. (*0-88682-470-2*) Creative Ed.
James. Shoebag. 1992. pap. 2.95 (*0-590-43030-0*, Apple Paperbacks) Scholastic Inc.
James, Mary. Frankenlouse. LC 93-39651. (gr. 6 up). 1994. 13.95 (*0-590-46528-7*) Scholastic Inc.
James, Sara. Boots Goes to School. Barcita, Pamela, illus. 24p. 1993. 3.98 (*1-56156-132-0*) Kidsbks.
—Bootsflat: Boots Goes to School. (Illus.). 24p. (ps). 1993. 3.98 (*0-8317-0606-6*) Smithmark.
Johnston, Annie F. The Little Colonel at Boarding School. (gr. 5 up). 13.95 (*0-89201-032-0*) Zenger Pub.
Johnston, Janet. Ellie Brader Hates Mr. G. 144p. (gr. 3-6). 1991. 13.45 (*0-395-58195-8*, Clarion Bks) HM.
Johnston, Norma. The Image Game. LC 93-39764. (Illus.). 160p. (gr. 5-8). 1994. PLB 13.95 (*0-8167-3472-0*); pap. text ed. 2.95 (*0-8167-3473-9*) BrdgeWater.
Jones, William E. & Goldberg, Minerva J. Going to School. LC 68-56811. (Illus.). 32p. (ps-1). 1968. PLB 9.95 (*0-87783-015-0*) Oddo.
Kahaner, Ellen. Fourth Grade Loser. Henderson, David F., illus. LC 90-26791. 96p. (gr. 3-5). 1992. lib. bdg. 9.89 (*0-8167-2384-2*); pap. text ed. 2.95 (*0-8167-2385-0*) Troll Assocs.
—What's So Great about Fourth Grade? Henry, Paul, illus. LC 89-20602. 96p. (gr. 3-5). 1990. PLB 9.89 (*0-8167-1702-8*); pap. text ed. 2.95 (*0-8167-1703-6*) Troll Assocs.
Kassem, Lou. Middle School Blues. 192p. (gr. 3-7). 1987. pap. 3.50 (*0-380-70363-7*, Camelot) Avon.
Kaye, Marilyn. The Atonement of Mindy Wise. Van Doren, Liz, ed. 160p. (gr. 7 up). 1991. 15.95 (*0-15-200402-5*, Gulliver Bks) HarBrace.
—Camp Sunnyside Back to School Special: School Daze. 128p. (Orig.). 1992. pap. 3.50 (*0-380-76920-4*, Camelot) Avon.
—A Friend Like Phoebe, No. 5. 132p. (gr. 3-7). 1989. 13.95 (*0-15-200450-5*, Gulliver Bks) HarBrace.

Keene, Carolyn. Junior Class Trip. Greenberg, Ann, ed. 224p. (Orig.). 1991. pap. 2.95 (*0-671-73124-6*, Archway) PB.

Keller, Holly. The New Boy. LC 90-41757. (Illus.). 24p. (ps up). 1991. 13.95 (*0-688-09827-4*); PLB 13.88 (*0-688-09828-2*) Greenwillow.

Kerby, Mona. Thirty-Eight Weeks Till Summer Vacation. Rosales, Melodye, illus. 128p. (gr. 3-7). 1989. pap. 12. 00 (*0-670-82887-4*) Viking Child Bks.

Kerr, M. E. Fell Back. LC 88-35762. 192p. (gr. 7 up). 1989. 12.00 (*0-06-023292-7*); PLB 11.89 (*0-06-023293-5*) HarpC Child Bks.

Khdir, Kate & Nash, Sue. Little Ghost. Church, Caroline, illus. 32p. (ps-2). 1991. incl. dust jacket 12.95 (*0-8120-6203-5*); pap. 5.95 (*0-8120-4779-6*) Barron.

Kiesel, Stanley. The War Between the Pitiful Teachers & the Splendid Kids. 208p. (gr. 7 up). 1982. pap. 3.50 (*0-380-57802-6*, Flare) Avon.

Kingman, Lee. Break a Leg, Betsy, Maybe. 192p. (gr. 7 up). 1979. pap. 1.50 (*0-440-90794-2*, LFL) Dell.

—Break a Leg, Betsy Maybe. LC 92-26975. 256p. (gr. 7 up). 1993. pap. 4.95 (*0-688-11789-9*, Pub. by Beech Tree Bks) Morrow.

Kirkland, Dianna C. Last Year I Failed...but. Orlowski, Dennis, illus. 32p. (Orig.). (ps-5). 1981. pap. 6.50 (*0-940370-04-2*); counseling activity guide-failure 6.50 (*0-940370-07-7*) Aid-U Pub.

Klein, Leah. Flying High. 200p. (gr. 6-9). 1993. pap. 9.95 (*1-56871-019-4*) Targum Pr.

Kline, Suzy. Herbie Jones & the Class Gift. Williams, Richard, illus. 96p. (gr. 3-7). 1989. pap. 3.99 (*0-14-032723-1*, Puffin) Puffin Bks.

—Horrible Harry & the Christmas Surprise. Remkiewicz, Frank, illus. LC 93-15137. 64p. (gr. 2-5). 1993. pap. 2.99 (*0-14-034452-7*, Puffin) Puffin Bks.

—Horrible Harry & the Kickball Wedding. Remkiewicz, Frank, illus. LC 92-5827. 64p. (gr. 2-5). 1992. 11.00 (*0-670-83358-4*) Viking Child Bks.

—Horrible Harry in Room 2B. Remkiewicz, Frank, illus. 64p. (gr. 2-5). 1990. pap. 2.99 (*0-14-032825-4*, Puffin) Puffin Bks.

—Horrible Harry's Secret. Remkiewicz, Frank, illus. 64p. (gr. 2-5). 1992. pap. 2.99 (*0-14-032915-3*) Puffin Bks.

—Mary Marony, Mummy Girl. Sims, Blanche, illus. LC 93-14348. 80p. (gr. 1-4). 1994. 13.95 (*0-399-22609-5*, Putnam) Putnam Pub Group.

—Song Lee & the Hamster Hunt. Remkiewicz, Frank, illus. 64p. (gr. 2-6). 1994. 11.99 (*0-670-84773-9*) Viking Child Bks.

—Song Lee in Room Two B. Remkiewicz, Frank, illus. 64p. (gr. 2-5). 1993. RB 10.99 (*0-670-84772-0*) Viking Child Bks.

—Who's Orp's Girlfriend? 112p. (gr. 3-6). 1993. 13.95 (*0-399-22431-9*, Putnam) Putnam Pub Group.

Koosak, Tara. School Biz Is.., Bk. 1. rev. ed. LC 90-70016. (Illus.). 52p. (gr. 1-8). 1991. pap. 3.50 (*0-934426-33-3*) NAPSAC Reprods.

Korman, Gordon. Beware the Fish. (Illus., Orig.). (gr. 4-7). 1991. pap. 2.95 (*0-590-44205-8*, Apple Paperbacks) Scholastic Inc.

—Macdonald Hall Goes Hollywood. 176p. (gr. 3-7). 1991. 12.95 (*0-590-43940-5*, Scholastic Hardcover) Scholastic Inc.

—The Twinkie Squad. 1992. 13.95 (*0-590-45249-5*, Scholastic Hardcover) Scholastic Inc.

Korman, Justine H. The Monster in Room 202. Chesworth, Michael D., illus. LC 93-2215. 32p. (gr. 2-4). 1993. pap. text ed. 9.59 (*0-8167-3182-9*); pap. 2.95 (*0-8167-3183-7*) Troll Assocs.

Kraus, Robert. Miss Gator's School House, 6 bks. Kraus, Robert, illus. (gr. k-3). 1989. Set, 48p. ea. lib. bdg. 53. 88 (*0-671-94105-4*, J Messner); Set, 48p. ea. pap. 21. 00 (*0-671-94106-2*) S&S Trade.

Kroll, Steven. I'm George Washington & You're Not! LC 93-7536. (Illus.). 64p. (gr. 2-5). 1994. 11.95 (*1-56282-579-8*); PLB 11.89 (*1-56282-580-1*) Hyprn Child.

—Otto. Delaney, Ned, illus. LC 82-19024. 48p. (ps-3). 1983. 5.95 (*0-8193-1105-7*); PLB 5.95 (*0-8193-1106-5*) Parents.

—Will You Be My Valentine? Hoban, Lillian, illus. 32p. (ps-3). 1993. reinforced bdg. 14.95 (*0-8234-0925-2*) Holiday.

Krulik, Nancy E. Ring Out the Old, Ring in the New Scrapbook. (gr. 4-7). 1994. pap. 4.95 (*0-590-48086-3*) Scholastic Inc.

Kubler, Annie. Annie's Body Paint Academy. (ps-3). 1993. pap. 13.95 (*0-85953-527-4*) Childs Play.

Kunhardt, Edith. Red Day, Green Day. Hafner, Marylin, illus. LC 90-38490. 32p. (ps up). 1992. 14.00 (*0-688-09399-X*); PLB 13.93 (*0-688-09400-7*) Greenwillow.

Kurtz, Jane. Fire on the Mountain. Lewis, Earl B., illus. LC 93-11477. (gr. k-2). 1994. 15.00 (*0-671-88268-6*, S&S BFYR) S&S Trade.

Lakin, Patricia. Get Ready to Read! Cushman, Doug, illus. LC 93-49842. 1994. write for info. (*0-8114-3866-X*) Raintree Steck-V.

—The Mystery Illness. Cushman, Doug, illus. LC 93-49843. 1994. write for info. (*0-8114-3867-8*) Raintree Steck-V.

—Trash & Treasure. Cushman, Doug, illus. LC 93-49844. 1994. write for info. (*0-8114-3865-1*) Raintree Steck-V.

—A True Partnership. Cushman, Doug, illus. LC 94-660. (gr. 5 up). 1994. write for info. (*0-8114-3869-4*) Raintree Steck-V.

—Up a Tree. Cushman, Doug, illus. LC 93-49847. 1994. write for info. (*0-8114-3868-6*) Raintree Steck-V.

Lamb, Nancy & Singer, Muff. The World's Greatest Toe Show. Sims, Blanche, illus. LC 93-28440. 64p. (gr. 2-5). 1993. PLB 13.95 (*0-8167-3322-8*); pap. 3.95 (*0-8167-3323-6*) BrdgeWater.

Landin, Les & Gardner, Mary. Homework Sweet Homework. 1990. pap. 6.95 (*0-8224-3603-5*) Fearon Teach Aids.

Lantz, Frances. Dear Celeste, My Life Is a Mess. (gr. 4-7). 1992. pap. 3.25 (*0-553-15961-5*) Bantam.

Lantz, Francess. Marissa's Dance. LC 93-43225. (Illus.). 128p. (gr. 3-7). 1994. pap. text ed. 2.95 (*0-8167-3475-5*) Troll Assocs.

—Randy's Raiders. LC 93-44345. (Illus.). 176p. (gr. 3-6). 1994. pap. 2.95 (*0-8167-3474-7*) Troll Assocs.

Larson, Kirby. Second Grade Pig Pals. Poydar, Nancy, illus. LC 93-16061. 96p. (gr. 1-5). 1994. 14.95 (*0-8234-1107-9*) Holiday.

Lasky, Kathryn. Lunch Bunnies. Hafner, Marylin, illus. LC 92-31554. 1993. 13.95 (*0-316-51525-6*, Joy St Bks) Little.

—Pageant. LC 86-12087. 240p. (gr. 7 up). 1986. SBE 14. 95 (*0-02-751720-9*, Four Winds) Macmillan Child Grp.

Lawlor, Laurie. How To Survive Third Grade. Levine, Abby, ed. LC 87-25430. (Illus.). 72p. (gr. 2-5). 1988. PLB 9.95 (*0-8075-3433-1*) A Whitman.

—How to Survive Third Grade. Zarins, Joyce A., illus. (gr. 2-4). 1991. pap. 2.99 (*0-671-67713-6*, Minstrel Bks) PB.

Lebowitz, Clara. Tuvia & the Tiny Teacher. (Illus.). 100p. (gr. 3-4). 1991. 8.95 (*1-56062-105-2*) CIS Comm.

Lee, Marie G. Finding My Voice. LC 92-2947. 176p. (gr. 6 up). 1992. 13.95 (*0-395-62134-8*) HM.

L'Engle, Madeleine. And Both Were Young. (Orig.). (gr. 7 up). 1983. pap. 3.99 (*0-440-90229-0*, LFL) Dell.

Leonard, Marcia. Hannah the Hamster Hunter. Brook, Bonnie, ed. Chambliss, Maxie & Iosa, Ann W., illus. 24p. (ps-1). 1990. 4.95 (*0-671-70404-4*); lib. bdg. 6.95 (*0-671-70399-4*) Silver Pr.

Lerangis, Peter. Yearbook. 1994. pap. 3.50 (*0-590-46678-X*) Scholastic Inc.

Leroe, Ellen. Heebie Jeebies at H.O.W.L. High. MacDonald, Patricia, ed. 144p. (gr. 3-6). 1992. pap. 2.99 (*0-671-75415-7*, Minstrel Bks) PB.

—H.O.W.L. High, No. 1. MacDonald, Patricia, ed. 144p. (gr. 4-7). 1991. pap. 2.95 (*0-671-68568-6*, Minstrel Bks) PB.

—Meet Your Match, Cupid Delaney. 160p. (gr. 7 up). 1990. 13.95 (*0-525-67309-1*, Lodestar Bks) Dutton Child Bks.

Levene, Nancy S. Crocodile Meatloaf. LC 92-32615. (ps-6). 1993. pap. 4.99 (*0-7814-0000-7*, Chariot Bks) Chariot Family.

—Master of Disaster. LC 94-17356. Date not set. write for info. (*0-7814-0089-9*, Chariot Bks) Chariot Family.

Leverich, Kathleen. Best Enemies. Lamb, Susan C., illus. LC 88-19150. (gr. 1 up). 1989. 10.95 (*0-688-08316-1*) Greenwillow.

Levy, Elizabeth. Cheater, Cheater. LC 92-33455. 1993. 13.95 (*0-590-45865-5*) Scholastic Inc.

—Keep Ms. Sugarman in the Fourth Grade. Henderson, Dave, illus. LC 91-22576. 96p. (gr. 3-6). 1992. 13.00 (*0-06-020426-5*); PLB 12.89 (*0-06-020427-3*) HarpC Child Bks.

—Nice Little Girls. Gerstein, Mordicai, illus. LC 73-15394. (gr. k-3). 1978. pap. 2.75 (*0-440-06360-4*) Delacorte.

—School Spirit Sabotage: A Brian & Pea Brain Mystery. Ulrich, George, illus. LC 93-23029. 96p. 1994. 14.00 (*0-06-023407-5*); PLB 13.89 (*0-06-023408-3*) HarpC Child Bks.

—Something Queer at the Haunted School. Gerstein, Mordicai, illus. 48p. (gr. 1-4). 1983. pap. 3.25 (*0-440-48461-8*, YB) Dell.

—Something Queer in the Cafeteria. Gerstein, Mordicai, illus. LC 93-31343. 48p. (gr. 2-5). 1994. 13.95 (*0-7868-0001-1*); pap. 4.95 (*0-7868-1000-9*) Hyprn Child.

Lewis, Beverley. The Six-Hour Mystery. Johnson, Meredith, illus. LC 93-35020. (gr. 4 up). 1993. 3.99 (*0-8066-2666-6*) Augsburg Fortress.

Lewis, Beverly. Holly's First Love. LC 92-47055. 1993. pap. 2.99 (*0-310-38051-0*) Zondervan.

Lindberg, Becky T. Chelsea Martin Turns Green. Tucker, Kathy, ed. Poydar, Nancy, illus. LC 92-31613. 144p. (gr. 2-4). 1993. PLB 11.95 (*0-8075-1134-X*) A Whitman.

Lindbergh, Anne. Nick of Time. LC 93-20777. 1994. 14. 95 (*0-316-52629-0*) Little.

Lindgren, Astrid. I Want to Go to School, Too! Lucas, Barbara, tr. from SWE. Wikland, Llon, illus. 32p. (ps up). 1987. 10.95 (*91-29-58328-4*, Pub. by R & S Bks) FS&G.

Lipniacka, Ewa. School Trip. Bogdanowicz, Basia, illus. LC 92-33325. 1993. 6.95 (*1-56656-121-3*, Crocodile Bks) Interlink Pub.

Little, Jean. Listen for the Singing. LC 90-40250. 272p. (gr. 4-7). 1991. pap. 3.95 (*0-06-440394-7*, Trophy) HarpC Child Bks.

—Listen for the Singing. LC 90-40019. 272p. (gr. 4-7). 1991. PLB 14.89 (*0-06-023910-7*) HarpC Child Bks.

Littledale, Freya. The Snow Child. Lavallee, Barbara & Shtainmets, Leon, illus. 32p. (gr. 2-5). 1989. pap. 2.50 (*0-590-42141-7*) Scholastic Inc.

Lovelace, Maud H. Betsy & Joe. Neville, Vera, illus. LC 48-8096. 256p. (gr. 5 up). 1948. 14.95 (*0-690-13378-2*, Crowell Jr Bks) HarpC Child Bks.

—Betsy Was a Junior. Neville, Vera, illus. LC 46-11995. 248p. (gr. 5 up). 1947. 14.95 (*0-690-13946-2*, Crowell Jr Bks) HarpC Child Bks.

McCants, William D. Anything Can Happen in High School: And It Usually Does. LC 92-32982. 1993. write for info. (*0-15-276604-9*); pap. write for info. (*0-15-276605-7*) HarBrace.

McDonald, Megan. Insects Are My Life. Johnson, Paul B., illus. LC 94-21960. (gr. 1-8). 1995. write for info. (*0-531-06874-9*); pap. write for info. (*0-531-08724-7*) Orchard Bks Watts.

McDonnell, Janet. Celebrating Earth Day. LC 93-37714. (Illus.). 32p. (ps-2). 1994. PLB 12.30 (*0-516-00689-4*) Childrens.

McEwan, Elaine K. Murphy's Mansion. Norton, LoraBeth, ed. 96p. (gr. 3-6). Date not set. pap. 4.99 (*0-7814-0160-7*, Chariot Bks) Chariot Family.

—Operation Garbage: A Josh McIntire Book. LC 92-43761. 1993. pap. 4.99 (*0-7814-0121-6*, Chariot Bks) Chariot Family.

McGugan, Jim. Josepha. Kimber, Murray, illus. LC 94-6603. 1994. 13.95 (*0-8118-0802-5*) Chronicle Bks.

McGuire, Leslie. Is There Life after Sixth Grade? Henry, Paul, illus. LC 89-20615. 96p. (gr. 4-6). 1990. PLB 9.89 (*0-8167-1706-0*); pap. text ed. 2.95 (*0-8167-1707-9*) Troll Assocs.

—The Terrible Truth about Third Grade. Henderson, David F., illus. LC 90-26788. 96p. (gr. 2-4). 1992. lib. bdg. 9.89 (*0-8167-2382-6*); pap. text ed. 2.95 (*0-8167-2383-4*) Troll Assocs.

McKee, David. The School Bus Comes at Eight O'Clock. LC 93-79583. (Illus.). 32p. (ps-3). 1994. 14.95 (*1-56282-662-X*); PLB 14.89 (*1-56282-663-8*) Hyprn Child.

McKenna, Colleen O. Fourth Grade Is a Jinx. LC 88-23897. 176p. (gr. 4-6). 1989. pap. 10.95 (*0-590-41735-5*) Scholastic Inc.

—Fourth Grade Is a Jinx. (ps-3). 1990. pap. 2.95 (*0-590-41736-3*, Apple Paperbacks) Scholastic Inc.

—Good Grief, Third Grade. LC 92-33457. 1993. 13.95 (*0-590-45123-5*) Scholastic Inc.

—Roger Friday: Live from the Fifth Grade. LC 93-13706. (gr. 3-7). 1994. 13.95 (*0-590-46684-4*) Scholastic Inc.

—The Truth about Sixth Grade. 1991. pap. 12.95 (*0-590-44388-7*) Scholastic Inc.

McKenzie, Ellen K. Stargone John. Low, William, illus. LC 90-34119. 80p. (gr. 2-4). 1990. 13.95 (*0-8050-1451-9*, Redfeather BYR) H Holt & Co.

MacLachlan, Patricia. Three Names. Pertzoff, Alexander, illus. LC 90-4444. 32p. (gr. k-4). 1991. 14.95 (*0-06-024035-0*); PLB 14.89 (*0-06-024036-9*) HarpC Child Bks.

McMillan, Bruce. Mouse Views: What the Class Pet Saw. LC 92-25921. (Illus.). 32p. (ps-3). 1993. reinforced bdg. 15.95 (*0-8234-1008-0*); pap. 5.95 (*0-8234-1132-X*) Holiday.

McMullan, Kate. The Great Eggspectations of Lila Fenwick. De Groat, Diane, illus. 148p. (gr. 3-7). 1991. bds. 13.95 jacketed (*0-374-32774-2*) FS&G.

McOmber, Rachel B., ed. McOmber Phonics Storybooks: The Wizz Kid. rev. ed. (Illus.). write for info. (*0-944991-23-8*) Swift Lrn Res.

Maguire, Gregory. Seven Spiders Spinning. LC 93-30478. 1994. 13.95 (*0-395-68965-1*, Clarion Bks) HM.

Maguire, Jesse. Breaking the Rules, No. 6: Nowhere High. (Orig.). 1992. pap. 3.99 (*0-8041-0849-8*) Ivy Books.

—Nowhere High No. 4: On the Edge. 192p. 1991. pap. 3.50 (*0-8041-0447-6*) Ivy Books.

Mahy, Margaret. The Birthday Burglar & a Very Wicked Headmistress. Chamberlain, Margaret, illus. LC 92-46599. 144p. (gr. 5 up). 1993. pap. 4.95 (*0-688-12470-4*, Pub. by Beech Tree Bks) Morrow.

Maiboroda, Tanya. School. (Illus.). 48p. (gr. 4-7). 1987. Price Stern.

Mallett, Jerry & Bartch, Marian. First-Last Gravelsburg Elementary School Spelling Bee. Smith, Mark D., illus. 55p. (gr. 2-5). 1986. PLB 7.50 (*0-8479-9928-9*, 101440) Perma-Bound.

Malmgren, Dallin. The Ninth Issue. LC 88-22881. (gr. 7 up). 1989. pap. 14.95 (*0-440-50124-5*) Delacorte.

Manes, Stephen. Comedy High. 176p. (gr. 7 up). 1992. 13.95 (*0-590-44436-0*, Scholastic Hardcover) Scholastic Inc.

Mango, Karin N. Portrait of Miranda. LC 92-8191. 240p. (gr. 7 up). 1993. 16.00 (*0-06-021777-4*); PLB 15.89 (*0-06-021778-2*) HarpC Child Bks.

Marshall, Edward. Fox at School. Marshall, James, illus. LC 93-2721. (gr. 1-4). 1993. pap. 3.25 (*0-14-036544-3*, Puffin) Puffin Bks.

Martin, Ann M. Claudia & Middle School. (gr. 4-7). 1991. pap. 3.25 (*0-590-44082-9*) Scholastic Inc.

—Karen's School. (gr. 4-7). 1993. pap. 2.95 (*0-590-47041-8*) Scholastic Inc.

Marzollo, Jean. Slam Dunk Saturday. Sins, Blanche, illus. 64p. (Orig.). (gr. 2-4). 1994. PLB 7.99 (*0-679-92366-7*); pap. 2.99 (*0-679-82366-2*) Random Bks Yng Read.

Maurer, Donna. Annie, Bea, & Chi Chi Dolores: A School Day Alphabet. Cazet, Denys, illus. LC 92-25104. 32p. (ps-k). 1993. 14.95 (*0-531-05467-5*); PLB 14.99 (*0-531-08617-8*) Orchard Bks Watts.

Merry Christmas, What's Your Name. (ps-3). 1990. 11.95 (*0-590-44334-8*, Scholastic Hardcover) Scholastic Inc.

Meyer, Kathleen. Little Bear Finds a Friend. Boerke, Carole, illus. 32p. (gr. k-2). 1991. pasted 2.50 (*0-87403-815-4*, 24-03915) Standard Pub.
Meyers, Marsha A. A Child's Fear: Vision of Hope. 1993. pap. 12.95 (*0-9637083-9-2*) Myi-Way Prod.
Miklowitz, Gloria D. The Emerson High Vigilantes. LC 87-25657. 160p. (gr. 7 up). 1988. 14.95 (*0-385-29637-1*) Delacorte.
Mills, Claudia. Dinah for President. LC 91-34839. 128p. (gr. 3-7). 1992. SBE 13.95 (*0-02-766999-8*, Macmillan Child Bk) Macmillan Child Grp.
—Dinah for President. LC 93-44668. (gr. 3-7). 1994. pap. 3.95 (*0-689-71854-3*, Aladdin) Macmillan Child Grp.
Mitchell, Debbie. Diary of a First Class Jerk. LC 87-50267. 96p. (gr. 6-8). 1987. 8.95 (*1-55523-079-2*) Winston-Derek.
Moncure, Jane B. What's So Special about This Fall? I'm Going to School: I'm Going to School. Williams, Jenny, illus. LC 88-2868. 32p. (ps-2). 1988. PLB 14.95 (*0-89565-420-2*) Childs World.
—Word Bird's New Friend. Hohag, Linda, illus. LC 90-37002. 32p. (ps-2). 1990. PLB 14.95 (*0-89565-616-7*) Childs World.
Moore, Elaine. The Substitute Teacher from Mars. LC 93-37527. (Illus.). 96p. (gr. 2-6). 1993. pap. text ed. 2.95 (*0-8167-3283-3*) Troll Assocs.
Mooser, Stephen. Babe Ruth & the Home Run Derby. Ulrich, George, illus. 80p. (Orig.). (gr. 2-5). 1992. pap. 3.25 (*0-440-40486-X*, YB) Dell.
—Disaster in Room 101. MacDougall, Rob, illus. LC 93-24055. 80p. (gr. 2-4). 1993. PLB 2.95 (*0-8167-3278-7*); pap. text ed. 2.95 (*0-8167-3279-5*) Troll Assocs.
—It's a Weird, Weird School. 1989. 13.95 (*0-385-29812-9*) Doubleday.
Morgan, Trudy. Where's Alex Best? LC 93-35925. 1994. write for info. (*0-8280-0736-5*) Review & Herald.
Morpugo, Michael. The War of Jenkins' Ear. LC 94-7602. 1995. 15.95 (*0-399-22735-0*, Philomel Bks) Putnam Pub Group.
Morris, Judy K. The Kid Who Ran for Principal. LC 89-2729. 224p. (gr. 3-7). 1989. (Lipp Jr Bks); PLB 12.89 (*0-397-32360-3*, Lipp Jr Bks) HarpC Child Bks.
Morrow, Catherine. The Jellybean Principal. Wummer, Amy, illus. LC 93-26537. 48p. (gr. 1-3). 1994. 7.99 (*0-679-94743-4*); pap. 3.50 (*0-679-84743-X*) Random Bks Yng Read.
Moss, Marissa. But Not Kate. Donovan, Melanie, ed. Moss, Marissa, illus. LC 90-25751. 32p. (ps-3). 1992. 14.00 (*0-688-10600-5*); PLB 13.93 (*0-688-10601-3*) Lothrop.
—Regina's Big Mistake. Moss, Marissa, illus. 32p. (gr. k-3). 1990. 13.45 (*0-395-55330-X*) HM.
Mozelle, Shirley. Zack's Alligator Goes to School. Watts, James, illus. LC 92-29871. 64p. (gr. k-3). 1994. 14.00 (*0-06-022887-3*); PLB 13.89 (*0-06-022888-1*) HarpC Child Bks.
Mulford, Philippa G. The World Is My Eggshell. LC 85-16198. (gr. 7 up). 1986. pap. 14.95 (*0-385-29432-8*) Delacorte.
Myers, Bill & West, Robert. The Blunder Years. LC 93-964. (Illus.). 1993. 3.99 (*0-8423-4117-X*) Tyndale.
Myers, Laurie. Earthquake in the Third Grade. LC 92-26609. 1993. 13.95 (*0-395-65360-6*, Clarion Bks) HM.
—Guinea Pigs Don't Talk. Taylor, Cheryl, illus. LC 93-39642. 1994. 13.95 (*0-395-68967-8*, Clarion Bks) HM.
Myers, Walter D. Darnell Rock Reporting. LC 94-8666. 1994. 14.95 (*0-385-32096-5*) Delacorte.
—The Test. 1993. pap. 3.50 (*0-553-29722-8*) Bantam.
Nabb, Magdalen. Josie Smith at School. Vainio, Pirkko, illus. LC 91-10970. 112p. (gr. 1-5). 1991. SBE 12.95 (*0-689-50533-7*, M K McElderry) Macmillan Child Grp.
Naylor, Phyllis R. Alice in April. LC 92-17016. 176p. (gr. 4-8). 1993. SBE 14.95 (*0-689-31805-7*, Atheneum Child Bk) Macmillan Child Grp.
—Reluctantly Alice. LC 90-37956. 192p. (gr. 3-7). 1991. SBE 13.95 (*0-689-31681-X*, Atheneum Child Bk) Macmillan Child Grp.
Nelson, Vaunda M. Mayfield Crossing. Jenkins, Leonard, illus. LC 92-10564. 96p. (gr. 3-7). 1993. 14.95 (*0-399-22331-2*, Putnam) Putnam Pub Group.
Nesbit, Jeffrey A. The Great Nothing Strikes Back. 256p. (Orig.). (gr. 9-12). 1991. pap. 6.99 (*0-87788-323-8*) Shaw Pubs.
—A War of Words. LC 92-27663. (Illus.). 1992. pap. 4.99 (*0-89693-076-9*, Victor Books) SP Pubns.
Noble, Trinka H. The Day Jimmy's Boa Ate the Wash. Kellogg, Steven, illus. 32p. (ps-3). 1993. pap. 4.99 (*0-14-054623-5*, Puff Pied Piper) Puffin Bks.
Nordstrom, Ursula. Secret Language. Chalmers, Mary, illus. LC 60-7701. 192p. (gr. 3-5). 1960. PLB 12.89 (*0-06-024576-X*) HarpC Child Bks.
Odgers, Sally F. Mrs. Honey's List. Cooper-Brown, Jean, illus. LC 93-6572. 1994. write for info. (*0-383-03703-4*) SRA Schl Grp.
Okimoto, Jean D. Talent Night. LC 93-34591. 1995. 13.95 (*0-590-47809-5*) Scholastic Inc.
Palmer, Martha. Fractions. Hoffman, Joan, ed. Cook, Chris, illus. 32p. (gr. 5-6). 1981. wkbk. 1.99 (*0-938256-43-2*) Sch Zone Pub Co.
Palumbo, Nancy. J.J. Goes to School: J.J. Va a L E'cole. Weaver, Judith, illus. 32p. (gr. k-6). 1989. wkbk. 5.95 (*0-927024-13-6*) Crayons Pubns.
—J.J. Goes to School: J.J. Va a la Escuela. Weaver, Judith, illus. 32p. (gr. k-6). 1989. wkbk. 5.95 (*0-927024-12-8*) Crayons Pubns.
Park, Barbara. Maxie, Rosie, & Earl...Partners in Grime. Strogart, Alexander, illus. LC 89-28027. 128p. (gr. 3-7). 1990. 13.00 (*0-679-80212-6*); PLB 13.99 (*0-679-90212-0*) Random Bks Yng Read.
—Rosie Swanson: Fourth-Grade Geek for President. LC 91-8616. 114p. (gr. 3-6). 1991. 14.00 (*0-679-82094-9*) Knopf Bks Yng Read.
Parker, Roberta N. & Parker, Harvey C. Making the Grade: An Adolescent's Struggle with ADD. DiMatteo, Richard, tr. (Illus.). 48p. (Orig.). (gr. 5-10). 1992. pap. 12.00 (*0-9621629-1-4*) Spec Pr FL.
Pascal, Francine. Jealous Lies. 144p. (Orig.). (gr. 7-12). 1986. pap. 2.75 (*0-553-25816-8*) Bantam.
—Lovestruck. 160p. (Orig.). (gr. 7-12). 1986. pap. 2.75 (*0-553-26750-7*) Bantam.
—The Middle School Gets Married. (gr. 4-7). 1993. pap. 3.25 (*0-553-48055-3*) Bantam.
—Spring Fever: Spring Super Edition, No. 2. 240p. (Orig.). (gr. 7-12). 1987. pap. 3.50 (*0-553-26420-6*) Bantam.
—Steven's Bride. large type ed. LC 93-1350. 1993. 15.95 (*1-56054-756-1*) Thorndike Pr.
—Sweet Valley Twins. 96p. (Orig.). (gr. 7-12). 1987. pap. 2.50 (*0-553-15474-5*) Bantam.
—Winter Carnival. (Orig.). (gr. 7-12). 1986. pap. 3.50 (*0-553-26159-2*) Bantam.
Pascal, Francine, created by. Against the Rules. 96p. (Orig.). (gr. 7-12). 1987. pap. 2.50 (*0-553-15518-0*) Bantam.
—Alone in the Crowd. 160p. (Orig.). (gr. 7-12). 1986. pap. 2.75 (*0-553-26825-2*) Bantam.
—Choosing Sides. 96p. (Orig.). (gr. 7-12). 1986. pap. 2.50 (*0-553-15459-1*) Bantam.
—Leaving Home High. (Illus.). 144p. (gr. 7-12). 1987. pap. 3.50 (*0-553-27631-X*) Bantam.
—The New Jessica. 160p. (Orig.). (gr. 7-12). 1986. pap. 2.75 (*0-553-26113-4*) Bantam.
—Taking Sides. 160p. (Orig.). (gr. 7-12). 1986. pap. 2.75 (*0-553-25886-9*) Bantam.
Paterson, Diane. Someday. Paterson, Diane, illus. LC 92-11401. 40p. (gr. 1-3). 1993. SBE 12.95 (*0-02-770565-X*, Bradbury Pr) Macmillan Child Grp.
Paulsen, Gary. The Boy Who Owned the School. LC 89-23048. 112p. (gr. 6-9). 1990. 12.95 (*0-531-05865-4*); PLB 12.99 (*0-531-08465-5*) Orchard Bks Watts.
—The Boy Who Owned the School. 1991. pap. 3.50 (*0-440-70694-7*) Dell.
Pearce, J. C. Tug of War. LC 93-15037. 144p. (gr. 3-7). 1993. pap. 2.99 (*0-14-036663-6*, Puffin) Puffin Bks.
Pearson, Sue. The Haunted School. Pearson, Sue, illus. (gr. 3-6). 1992. pap. 7.95 (*1-56680-509-0*) Mad Hatter Pub.
Pearson, Susan. The Green Magician Puzzle. Fiammenghi, Gioia, illus. LC 90-22436. 1991. pap. 11.95 (*0-671-74054-7*, S&S BFYR); pap. 2.95 (*0-671-74053-9*, S&S BFYR) S&S Trade.
Peck, Richard. Bel-Air Bambi & the Mall Rats. LC 92-29377. 1993. 15.95 (*0-385-30823-X*) Delacorte.
Peck, Robert N. Soup for President. (gr. 3-6). 1986. pap. 3.50 (*0-440-48188-0*, YB) Dell.
—Soup on Wheels. Robinson, illus. LC 80-17661. 128p. (gr. 3 up). 1981. PLB 11.99 (*0-394-94581-6*) Knopf Bks Yng Read.
Pellowski, Michael J. Class Clown, No. 7. LC 91-74005. (Illus.). 128p. (Orig.). (gr. 4-8). 1992. pap. 2.99 (*1-56282-113-X*) Hyprn Child.
Perkins, Thornton. Junior High Champs. Chappick, Joseph, illus. 49p. (Orig.). (gr. 6-9). 1989. pap. 3.00 (*0-9623407-0-7*) NVEM.
Petersen, P. J. Going for the Big One. (gr. k-12). 1987. pap. 2.95 (*0-440-93158-4*, LFL) Dell.
—Here's to the Sophomores. LC 83-14362. 192p. (gr. 7 up). 1984. pap. 13.95 (*0-385-29319-4*) Delacorte.
—Here's to the Sophomores. 192p. (gr. 6 up). 1986. pap. 2.50 (*0-440-93394-3*, LFL) Dell.
—The Sub. Johnson, Meredith, illus. LC 92-22269. (gr. 2-5). 1993. 12.99 (*0-525-45059-9*, DCB) Dutton Child Bks.
Peterson, P. J. Some Days, Other Days. LC 93-3871. (gr. k-2). 1994. 14.95 (*0-684-19595-X*, Scribner) Macmillan.
Petty, Kate. Being Bullied. Firmin, Charlotte, illus. 24p. (ps-2). 1991. pap. 4.95 (*0-8120-4661-7*) Barron.
Pevsner, Stella. The Night the Whole Class Slept Over. McDonald, Patricia, ed. 176p. (gr. 3-6). 1992. pap. 3.50 (*0-671-78157-X*, Minstrel Bks) PB.
Piercy, Patricia A. The Great Encounter: A Special Meeting Before Columbus. Wilkerson, Napoleon, illus. 47p. (gr. 1-7). 1991. pap. 5.95 (*0-913543-26-8*) African Am Imag.
Pinkwater, Daniel. Author's Day. Pinkwater, Daniel, illus. LC 92-18154. 32p. (gr. k-3). 1993. RSBE 13.95 (*0-02-774642-9*, Macmillan Child Bk) Macmillan Child Grp.
Pinkwater, Jill. Mister Fred. 160p. (gr. 5-8). 1994. 15.99 (*0-525-44778-4*) Dutton Child Bks.
Porter, Penny. The Keymaker: Born to Steal. (Illus.). 144p. (Orig.). (gr. 7-12). 1994. pap. 10.95 (*0-943173-99-X*) Harbinger AZ.
Poulet, Virginia. Blue Bug Goes to School. Anderson, Peggy P., illus. LC 84-23161. 32p. (ps-3). 1985. PLB 11.80 (*0-516-03416-2*); pap. 3.95 (*0-516-43416-0*) Childrens.
Powell, E. Sandy. Chance to Grow. (ps-3). 1992. 13.50 (*0-87614-741-4*) Carolrhoda Bks.
Pryor, Bonnie. Horses in the Garage. LC 92-7287. 160p. (gr. 4 up). 1992. 14.00 (*0-688-10567-X*) Morrow Jr Bks.
—Poison Ivy & Eyebrow Wigs. Owens, Gail, illus. LC 92-38881. 176p. (gr. 3 up). 1993. 14.00 (*0-688-11200-5*) Morrow Jr Bks.
Pulver, Robin. Mrs. Toggle & the Dinosaur. Alley, R. W., illus. LC 90-35771. 32p. (ps-2). 1991. RSBE 13.95 (*0-02-775452-9*, Four Winds) Macmillan Child Grp.
—Mrs. Toggle's Beautiful Blue Shoe. Alley, R. W., illus. LC 92-40824. 32p. (ps-2). 1994. RSBE 13.95 (*0-02-775456-1*, Four Winds) Macmillan Child Grp.
—Mrs. Toggle's Zipper. LC 88-37251. (Illus.). 32p. (ps-2). 1990. RSBE 13.95 (*0-02-775451-0*, Four Winds Press) Macmillan Child Grp.
—Mrs. Toggle's Zipper. Alley, Robert W., illus. LC 92-39355. 32p. (ps-2). 1993. pap. 3.95 (*0-689-71689-3*, Aladdin) Macmillan Child Grp.
—Nobody's Mother Is in Second Grade. Karas, G. Brian, illus. LC 91-16395. 32p. (gr. k-3). 1992. 13.50 (*0-8037-1210-3*); PLB 13.89 (*0-8037-1211-1*) Dial Bks Young.
Quackenbush, Robert. First Grade Jitters. Quackenbush, Robert, illus. LC 81-47757. 32p. (gr. k-2). 1982. PLB 11.89 (*0-397-31981-9*, Lipp Jr Bks) HarpC Child Bks.
Quin-Harkin, Janet. Roni's Dream Boy, No. 2. LC 93-50680. (Illus.). 176p. (gr. 3-6). 1994. pap. 2.95 (*0-8167-3415-1*) Troll Assocs.
Rabe, Berniece. The Balancing Girl. Hoban, Lillian, illus. LC 80-22100. (ps-2). 1981. 12.95 (*0-525-26160-5*, 0995-300, DCB) Dutton Child Bks.
Randle, Kristen D. The Only Alien on the Planet. LC 93-34594. 1994. 13.95 (*0-590-46309-8*) Scholastic Inc.
Ransom, Candice F. Third Grade Stars: Tales from Third Grade. LC 93-7868. (Illus.). 128p. (gr. 2-4). 1993. PLB 9.89 (*0-8167-2994-8*); pap. 2.95 (*0-8167-2995-6*) Troll Assocs.
—Who Needs Third Grade? LC 92-30754. 128p. (gr. 2-4). 1992. PLB 9.89 (*0-8167-2988-3*); pap. text ed. 2.95 (*0-8167-2989-1*) Troll Assocs.
—Why Are Boys So Weird? LC 93-6222. (Illus.). 128p. (gr. 2-6). 1994. PLB 9.89 (*0-8167-2990-5*); pap. text ed. 2.95 (*0-8167-2991-3*) Troll Assocs.
Rapp, Adam. Missing the Piano: A Novel. LC 93-44110. 1994. 14.99 (*0-670-85340-2*, Viking) Viking Penguin.
Rathmann, Peggy. Officer Buckle & Gloria. LC 93-43887. 1995. write for info. (*0-399-22616-8*, Putnam) Putnam Pub Group.
—Ruby the Copycat. 32p. 1991. 13.95 (*0-590-43747-X*, Scholastic Hardcover) Scholastic Inc.
Reese, Bernnie, et al. Tahquitz Exchange. (Orig.). (gr. 12). 1993. pap. write for info. (*0-9628802-3-X*) DeChamp CA.
Reese, Bob. ABCs. Reese, Bob, illus. LC 92-12188. 24p. (ps-2). 1992. PLB 9.75 (*0-516-05577-1*) Childrens.
—Art. Reese, Bob, illus. LC 92-12187. 24p. (ps-2). 1992. PLB 9.75 (*0-516-05578-X*) Childrens.
—Field Trip. Reese, Bob, illus. LC 92-12186. 24p. (ps-2). 1992. PLB 9.75 (*0-516-05579-8*) Childrens.
—Glasses. Reese, Bob, illus. LC 92-12185. 24p. (ps-2). 1992. PLB 9.75 (*0-516-05580-1*) Childrens.
—Recess. Reese, Bob, illus. LC 92-12184. 24p. (ps-2). 1992. PLB 9.75 (*0-516-05581-X*) Childrens.
—Sack Lunch. Reese, Bob, illus. LC 92-12183. 24p. (ps-2). 1992. PLB 9.75 (*0-516-05582-8*) Childrens.
Regan, Dana. At My School: Paint Box Fun. (ps-3). 1993. pap. 1.95 (*0-590-46291-1*) Scholastic Inc.
Regan, Dian C. The Class with the Summer Birthdays. Guevara, Susan, illus. 80p. (gr. 2-4). 1991. 13.95 (*0-8050-1657-0*, Redfeather BYR) H Holt & Co.
—The Curse of the Trouble Dolls. Chesworth, Michael, illus. LC 91-28572. 64p. (gr. 2-4). 1992. 14.95 (*0-8050-1944-8*, Bks Young Read) H Holt & Co.
—The Peppermint Race. Dewdney, Anna, illus. (gr. 2-4). 1994. 14.95 (*0-8050-2753-X*) H Holt & Co.
Reuter, Bjarne. Buster, the Sheikh of Hope Street. Bell, Anthea, illus. LC 91-19397. 144p. (gr. 4 up). 1991. 13.95 (*0-525-44772-5*, DCB) Dutton Child Bks.
Rice, Bebe F. Class Trip. 1993. pap. 3.50 (*0-06-106731-8*, Harp PBks) HarpC.
Rider, Joanne. First Grade Valentines. Lewin, Betsy, illus. LC 92-35388. 32p. (gr. k-2). 1992. PLB 9.79 (*0-8167-3004-0*); pap. text ed. 2.95 (*0-8167-3005-9*) Troll Assocs.
Robinson, Barbara. The Worst Best School Year Ever. LC 93-50891. 96p. (gr. 3 up). 1994. 12.95 (*0-06-023039-8*); PLB 12.89 (*0-06-023043-6*) HarpC Child Bks.
Robinson, Nancy K. Wendy on the Warpath. LC 93-32739. (gr. 3 up). 1994. 13.95 (*0-590-45571-0*) Scholastic Inc.
Rocard, Ann. Hobee Scrogneenee at Joey's School. Degano, Marino, illus. 28p. (ps-4). 1991. smythe sewn reinforced bdg. 9.95 (*1-56182-001-6*) Atomium Bks.
Rockwell, Anne. When Hugo Went to School. LC 89-13211. (Illus.). 32p. (ps-1). 1991. RSBE 13.95 (*0-02-777305-1*, Macmillan Child Bk) Macmillan Child Grp.
Rodgers, Elizabeth. Ollie Goes to School. (Illus.). 32p. (ps-2). 1992. pap. 2.50 (*0-590-44785-8*, Cartwheel) Scholastic Inc.
Roos, Stephen. My Horrible Secret. Newsom, Carol, illus. LC 82-14954. 128p. (gr. 4-6). 1983. pap. 10.95 (*0-385-29246-5*) Delacorte.
—The Terrible Truth: Secrets of a Sixth-Grader. Newsom, Carol, illus. 128p. (gr. 4-7). 1991. pap. 3.25 (*0-440-48578-9*, YB) Dell.
Rosen, Michael J. A School for Pompey Walker. Robinson, Aminah B., illus. LC 94-6240. 1995. write for info. (*0-15-200114-X*, HB Juv Bks) Harbrace.

Ross, Pat. M & M & the Superchild Afternoon. Hafner, Marylin, illus. LC 86-28128. (gr. 1-4). 1987. pap. 9.95 (*0-670-81208-0*) Viking Child Bks.
Ross, Sandra J. The Nicelies Go to School: A Lil'l Charmers Book. (Illus.). 74p. (gr. 3-7). 1994. pap. 5.95 (*1-881235-02-5*) Creat Opport.
Ruckman, Ivy. What's an Average Kid Like Me Doing Way up Here? LC 82-72820. 144p. (gr. 4-6). 1983. PLB 11.89 (*0-440-08893-3*); pap. 11.95 (*0-385-29251-1*) Delacorte.
Russo, Marisabina. I Don't Want to Go Back to School. LC 93-5479. 32p. 1994. 15.00 (*0-688-04601-0*); PLB 14.93 (*0-688-04602-9*) Greenwillow.
Ryder, Joanne. First Grade Elves. Lewin, Betsy, illus. LC 93-25543. 32p. (ps-2). 1993. PLB 9.79 (*0-8167-3010-5*); pap. text ed. 2.95 (*0-8167-3011-3*) Troll Assocs.
—First Grade Ladybugs. Lewin, Betsy, illus. LC 92-43528. 32p. (ps-2). 1993. PLB 9.79 (*0-8167-3006-7*); pap. text ed. 2.95 (*0-8167-3007-5*) Troll Assocs.
—Hello, First Grade. Lewin, Betsy, illus. LC 93-9041. 32p. (ps-2). 1993. PLB 9.79 (*0-8167-3008-3*); pap. text ed. 2.95 (*0-8167-3009-1*) Troll Assocs.
—One Small Fish. Schwartz, Carol, illus. LC 92-21563. 32p. (gr. k up). 1993. 15.00 (*0-688-07059-0*); PLB 14.93 (*0-688-07060-4*) Morrow Jr Bks.
Sachan, Louis. Wayside School Is Falling Down. Schick, Joel, illus. LC 88-674. 192p. (gr. 3-7). 1989. 13.00 (*0-688-07868-0*) Lothrop.
Sachar, Louis. Dogs Don't Tell Jokes. LC 91-2042. 176p. (gr. 5-9). 1991. lib. bdg. 14.99 (*0-679-92017-X*) Knopf Bks Yng Read.
—Marvin Redpost: Is He a Girl? Sullivan, Barbara, illus. LC 92-40784. 80p. (Orig.). (gr. 1-4). 1993. PLB 9.99 (*0-679-91948-1*); pap. 2.99 (*0-685-71893-X*) Random Bks Yng Read.
—Sixth Grade Secrets. LC 86-4298. 208p. (gr. 4-6). 1987. pap. 12.95 (*0-590-40709-0*, Scholastic Hardcover) Scholastic Inc.
—Sixth Grade Secrets. 208p. (gr. 3-7). 1992. pap. 2.95 (*0-590-46075-7*, Apple Paperbacks) Scholastic Inc.
—Someday Angeline. Samuels, Barbara, illus. 160p. (Orig.). (gr. 3-7). 1983. pap. 3.99 (*0-380-83444-8*, Camelot) Avon.
—Wayside School Is Falling Down. 192p. 1990. pap. 3.99 (*0-380-75484-3*, Camelot) Avon.
Sachs, Betsy. The Trouble with Santa. Apple, Margot, illus. LC 89-24257. 64p. (Orig.). (gr. 2-4). 1990. pap. 2.50 (*0-679-80410-2*) Random Bks Yng Read.
Sachs, Marilyn. Circles. LC 90-37516. 144p. (gr. 5-9). 1991. 14.95 (*0-525-44683-4*, DCB) Dutton Child Bks.
—Circles. LC 92-20287. 144p. (gr. 5 up). 1992. pap. 3.99 (*0-14-034931-6*) Puffin Bks.
Salem, Lynn & Stewart, Josie. What a School. Hartman, David, illus. 16p. (gr. 1). 1992. pap. 3.50 (*1-880612-10-0*) Seedling Pubns.
Saltzburg, Barney. Show & Tell. LC 93-47365. (Illus.). 32p. (gr. k-3). 1994. 14.95 (*0-7868-0020-8*); PLB 14.89 (*0-7868-2016-0*) Hyprn Child.
Saunders, Susan. Starring Stephanie. (Illus.). 96p. (Orig.). (gr. 4-6). 1987. pap. 2.50 (*0-590-40642-6*) Scholastic Inc.
—Tyrone Goes to School. (Illus.). 64p. (gr. 2-5). 1992. 11.99 (*0-525-44981-7*, DCB) Dutton Child Bks.
Scarry, Richard. Richard Scarry's Great Big Schoolhouse. Scarry, Richard, illus. (ps-2). 1969. 12.00 (*0-394-80874-6*) Random Bks Yng Read.
Schanback, Mindy. Does Third Grade Last Forever? Henry, Paul, illus. LC 89-20603. 96p. (gr. 2-4). 1990. PLB 9.89 (*0-8167-1700-1*); pap. text ed. 2.95 (*0-8167-1701-X*) Troll Assocs.
—What's New in Sixth Grade? LC 90-26792. 96p. (gr. 4-6). 1992. lib. bdg. 9.89 (*0-8167-2388-5*); pap. text ed. 2.95 (*0-8167-2389-3*) Troll Assocs.
Schenker, Dona. Fearsome's Hero. LC 93-8601. 144p. (gr. 4-8). 1994. 15.00 (*0-679-85424-X*) Knopf Bks Yng Read.
Schlieper, Anne. The Best Fight. Mathews, Judith, ed. Schwark, Mary B., illus. 64p. (gr. 3-7). 1994. PLB 10.95 (*0-8075-0662-1*) A Whitman.
Schreiber, Perel. B.Y. High, No. 2: Making Her Mark. 160p. (gr. 7-10). 1994. 9.95 (*1-56871-040-2*) Targum Pr.
Schwartz, Amy. Bea & Mr. Jones. Schwartz, Amy, illus. LC 93-20572. 32p. (gr. k-2). 1994. pap. 3.95 (*0-689-71796-2*, Aladdin) Macmillan Child Grp.
Schwartz, Linda. All about My School. LC 93-86209. 32p. (gr. 1-6). 1994. 4.95 (*0-88160-236-1*, LW331) Learning Wks.
Scribner, Virginia. Gopher Takes Heart. Wilson, Janet, illus. LC 92-25939. 128p. (gr. 3-7). 1993. 13.99 (*0-670-84839-5*) Viking Child Bks.
Sells, Carole G. Rainbow Dragon: Lessons in Basic Values. Zellers, Toby, illus. Guese, Raymond F., intro. by. (Illus.). 34p. (Orig.). (ps-6). 1988. pap. 3.95 (*0-926739-00-X*) Sells Pub.
Selway, Martina. I Hate Roland Roberts. Selway, Martina, illus. LC 93-30916. 32p. (ps-2). 1994. 12.95 (*0-8249-8660-1*, Ideals Child) Hambleton-Hill.
—I Hate Roland Roberts. LC 93-30916. (Illus.). 32p. (ps-2). 1995. pap. 4.95 (*0-8249-8675-X*) Hambleton-Hill.
Sempe, Jean-Jacques. Chronicles of Little Nicholas. 1993. 15.00 (*0-374-31275-3*) FS&G.
Shahan, Sherry. Fifth Grade Crush. (Illus.). 128p. (gr. 3-5). 1993. 2.50 (*0-87406-139-3*) Willowisp Pr.
Shalant, Phyllis. The Rock Star, the Rooster, & Me, the Reporter. Robinson, Charles, illus. 169p. (gr. 3-7). 1991. pap. 3.95 (*0-14-034596-5*, Puffin) Puffin Bks.
—The Transformation of Faith Futterman. 144p. (gr. 3-7). 1992. pap. 3.99 (*0-14-036026-3*) Puffin Bks.
Shannon, Jacqueline. I Hate My Hero. LC 92-890. (gr. 4-7). 1992. pap. 13.00 (*0-671-75442-4*, S&S BFYR) S&S Trade.
Sharmat, Marjorie W. The Cooking Class. (gr. 4-7). 1991. pap. 2.99 (*0-06-106026-7*, PL) HarpC.
—The Great Genghis Khan Look-Alike Contest. Rigie, Mitch, illus. 80p. (Orig.). (gr. 1-4). 1993. PLB 9.99 (*0-679-95002-8*); pap. 2.99 (*0-679-85002-3*) Random Bks Yng Read.
—Kids on the Bus, No. 3: Bully on the Bus. (gr. 4-7). 1991. pap. 2.95 (*0-06-106027-5*, Harp PBks) HarpC.
—Kids on the Bus, No. 4: The Secret Notebook. (gr. 4-7). 1991. pap. 2.95 (*0-06-106028-3*, Harp PBks) HarpC.
—Maggie Marmelstein for President. Shecter, Ben, illus. LC 75-6300. 128p. (gr. 4-6). 1975. PLB 13.89 (*0-06-025555-2*) HarpC Child Bks.
—Maggie Marmelstein for President. LC 75-6300. (Illus.). 128p. (gr. 3-7). 1976. pap. 3.95 (*0-06-440079-4*, Trophy) HarpC Child Bks.
Sharmat, Marjorie W. & Sharmat, Andrew. The Haunted Bus. (gr. 1-6). 1991. pap. 2.99 (*0-06-106030-5*, Harp PBks) HarpC.
Sharmat, Marjorie W. & Sharmat, Mitchell. The Princess of the Fillmore Street School. Brunkus, Denise, illus. LC 89-1106. (gr. 2-4). 1989. 12.95 (*0-385-29811-0*) Delacorte.
Shaw, Janet. Kirsten Learns a Lesson: A School Story. Thieme, Jeanne, ed. Graef, Renee, illus. 72p. (gr. 2-5). 1986. PLB 12.95 (*0-937295-82-5*); pap. 5.95 (*0-937295-10-8*) Pleasant Co.
Shles, Larry. Do I have to Go to School Today? Squib Measures Up. Winch, Bradley L., ed. Shles, Larry, illus. 64p. (Orig.). (gr. k up). 1989. pap. 7.95 (*0-915190-62-1*, JP9062-1) Jalmar Pr.
Shreve, Susan. The Flunking of Joshua T. Bates. De Groat, Diane, illus. LC 83-19636. 96p. (gr. 2-6). 1984. PLB 13.99 (*0-394-96380-6*) Knopf Bks Yng Read.
—The Gift of the Girl Who Couldn't Hear. LC 91-2247. 80p. (gr. 3 up). 1991. 12.95 (*0-688-10318-9*, Tambourine Bks) Morrow.
—The Gift of the Girl Who Couldn't Hear. LC 92-43763. 80p. (gr. 5 up). 1993. pap. 3.95 (*0-688-11694-9*, Pub. by Beech Tree Bks) Morrow.
—Joshua T. Bates Takes Charge. Andreasen, Dan, illus. LC 92-19708. 112p. (gr. 3-5). 1993. 15.00 (*0-394-84362-2*) Knopf Bks Yng Read.
Shreve, Susan R. The Bad Dreams of a Good Girl. DeGroat, Diane, illus. LC 92-24593. 96p. (gr. 4 up). 1993. pap. 3.95 (*0-688-12113-6*, Pub. by Beech Tree Bks) Morrow.
Sidney, Margaret. Five Little Peppers at School. 1987. Repr. lib. bdg. 25.95x (*0-89966-552-7*) Buccaneer Bks.
—Five Little Peppers at School. (Orig.). (gr. k-6). 1988. pap. 4.95 (*0-440-40035-X*, YB) Dell.
Siegal, Barbara & Siegel, Scott. Final Frenzy. MacDonald, Pat, ed. 160p. (Orig.). 1993. pap. 3.50 (*0-671-75948-5*, Archway) PB.
Silly Schoolhouse Look & Look Again. 1991. pap. 3.99 (*0-517-06140-6*) Random Hse Value.
Simmons, Alex. Grounded for Life? Tiegreen, Alan, illus. DeMasco, Steve, created by. LC 93-22061. (Illus.). 64p. (gr. 1-4). 1993. PLB 9.59 (*0-8167-3102-0*); pap. 2.50 (*0-8167-3103-9*) Troll Assocs.
Singer, Marilyn. The Case of the Sabotaged School Play: A Sam & Dave Mystery. Glasser, Judy, illus. LC 83-48437. 64p. (gr. 3-7). 1987. pap. 3.95 (*0-06-440207-X*, Trophy) HarpC Child Bks.
Skinner, David. The Wrecker. LC 93-46895. 1995. PLB 14.00 (*0-671-79771-9*, S&S BFYR) S&S Trade.
Slepian, Jan. Broccoli Tapes. (gr. 4-7). 1990. pap. 2.95 (*0-590-44263-5*) Scholastic Inc.
Smath, Jerry. Elephant Goes to School. LC 93-7769. 1993. PLB 13.27 (*0-8368-0967-X*) Gareth Stevens Inc.
Smith, David B. Bucky Gets Busted. LC 93-37921. 1993. write for info. (*0-8280-0807-8*) Review & Herald.
Smith, Janice L. The Baby Blues: An Adam Joshua Story. Gackenbach, Dick, illus. LC 93-14492. 96p. (gr. 1-4). 1994. 12.00 (*0-06-023642-6*, HarpT); PLB 11.89 (*0-06-023643-4*, HarpT) HarpC.
—It's Not Easy Being George: Stories about Adam Joshua (& His Dog) Gackenbach, Dick, illus. LC 88-33075. 128p. (gr. 1-4). 1989. PLB 10.89 (*0-06-025853-5*) HarpC Child Bks.
—Serious Science: An Adam Joshua Story. Gackenbach, Dick, illus. LC 91-30824. 80p. (gr. 1-4). 1993. 12.00 (*0-06-020779-5*); PLB 11.89 (*0-06-020782-5*) HarpC Child Bks.
Smith, Joanne. Show & Tell. (Illus.). 32p. (ps-2). 1994. PLB 13.80 (*0-516-02026-9*); pap. 2.95 (*0-516-42026-7*) Childrens.
Sommer, Karen. Satch & the Motormouth. LC 86-24031. (gr. 3-7). 1987. pap. 4.99 (*1-55513-063-1*, Chariot Bks) Chariot Family.
Sonnenmark, Laura A. Something's Rotten in the State of Maryland. 1990. pap. 12.95 (*0-590-42876-4*) Scholastic Inc.
Soto, Gary. The Mustache. Hinojosa, Celina, illus. LC 93-42395. 1995. 14.95 (*0-399-22617-6*, Putnam) Putnam Pub Group.
Spinelli, Eileen. Somebody Loves You, Mr. Hatch. Yalowitz, Paul, photos by. LC 94-794. (gr. 3 up). 1995. pap. 5.95 (*0-689-71872-1*, Aladdin) Macmillan Child Grp.
Spinelli, Jerry. Fourth Grade Rats. (ps-3). 1991. 13.95 (*0-590-44243-0*, Scholastic Hardcover) Scholastic Inc.
—Fourth Grade Rats. (gr. 4-7). 1993. pap. 2.95 (*0-590-44244-9*, Apple Classics) Scholastic Inc.
—Report to the Principal's Office! 1992. 2.95 (*0-590-46277-6*, Apple Paperbacks) Scholastic Inc.
—There's a Girl in My Hammerlock. LC 91-8765. 208p. (gr. 5-9). 1991. pap. 13.00 jacketed, 3-pc. bdg. (*0-671-74684-7*, S&S BFYR) S&S Trade.
Stadler, John. The Adventures of Snail at School. Stadler, John, illus. LC 91-45403. 64p. (gr. k-3). 1993. 14.00 (*0-06-021041-9*); PLB 13.89 (*0-06-021042-7*) HarpC Child Bks.
Stafford, Jean. The Scarlet Letter. LC 92-44056. 1994. 13.95 (*0-88682-588-1*) Creative Ed.
Stahl, Hilda. Daisy Punkin: Meet Daisy Punkin. 128p. (gr. 2-5). 1991. pap. 4.99 (*0-89107-617-4*) Crossway Bks.
—Sendi Lee Mason & the Big Mistake. 128p. (Orig.). (gr. 1-4). 1991. pap. 4.95 (*0-89107-613-1*) Crossway Bks.
Standish, Burt L. Frank Merriwell's Chums. Rudman, Jack, ed. (gr. 9 up). 1970. 9.95 (*0-8373-9302-7*); pap. 3.95 (*0-8373-9002-8*) F Merriwell.
Steel, Danielle. Martha's New School. Rogers, Jacqueline, illus. (ps-2). 1989. 8.95 (*0-385-29800-5*) Delacorte.
Steffy, Jan. The School Picnic. Bond, Denny, illus. LC 87-14867. 32p. (ps-3). 1987. 12.95 (*0-934672-52-0*) Good Bks PA.
Steiber, Ellen. Eighth Grade Changes Everything. LC 91-2495. 128p. (gr. 6-9). 1992. lib. bdg. 9.89 (*0-8167-2390-7*); pap. text ed. 2.95 (*0-8167-2391-5*) Troll Assocs.
Steiner, Barbara. Oliver Dibbs & the Dinosaur Cause. Christelow, Eileen, illus. LC 86-9941. 128p. (gr. 3-7). 1986. SBE 13.95 (*0-02-787880-5*, Four Winds) Macmillan Child Grp.
Stevenson, James. That Dreadful Day. Stevenson, James, illus. LC 84-4164. 32p. (gr. k-3). 1985. 15.00 (*0-688-04035-7*); lib. bdg. 14.93 (*0-688-04036-5*) Greenwillow.
Stewart, Dianne. Paper Chase. (ps-3). 1992. pap. 2.95 (*0-7910-2904-2*) Chelsea Hse.
Stine, Megan & Stine, H. William. How I Survived Fifth Grade. LC 90-26790. 96p. (gr. 4-6). 1992. lib. bdg. 9.89 (*0-8167-2386-9*); pap. text ed. 2.95 (*0-8167-2387-7*) Troll Assocs.
Stolz, Mary. Bully of Barkham Street. Shortall, Leonard, illus. LC 68-2661. 224p. (gr. 3-6). 1963. PLB 14.89 (*0-06-025821-7*) HarpC Child Bks.
Stowe, Cynthia M. Dear Mom, in Ohio for a Year. 1992. 13.95 (*0-590-45060-3*, 024, Scholastic Hardcover) Scholastic Inc.
Surat, Michele M. Angel Child, Dragon Child. Vo-Dinh Mai, illus. LC 83-8606. 32p. (gr. 3-6). 1983. PLB 12.96 (*0-940742-12-8*) Raintree Steck-V.
Sutherland, Colleen. Jason Goes to Show & Tell. Weller, Linda, illus. 32p. (ps-k). 1992. bds. 9.95 (*1-878093-89-4*) Boyds Mills Pr.
Tada, Joni E. & Jensen, Steve. Darcy & the Meanest Teacher in the World. LC 92-33075. (gr. 3-7). 1993. pap. 4.99 (*0-7814-0885-7*, Chariot Bks) Chariot Family.
Tamar, Erika. Fair Game. 1993. pap. 3.95 (*0-685-65843-0*, HB Juv Bks) HarBrace.
—No Defense. LC 93-3248. (gr. 9-12). 1993. write for info. (*0-15-278537-X*) HarBrace.
Tankersley-Cusick, Richie. The Locker. 1994. pap. 3.99 (*0-671-79404-3*, Archway) PB.
Taylor, Theodore. The Weirdo. 240p. 1993. pap. 3.50 (*0-380-72017-5*, Flare) Avon.
Taylor, William. Knitwits. 1992. 13.95 (*0-590-45778-0*, 022, Scholastic Hardcover) Scholastic Inc.
Thaler, Mike. The Schmo Must Go On. Lee, Jared, illus. LC 93-4317. 32p. (gr. k-3). 1994. lib. bdg. 9.89 (*0-8167-3519-0*); pap. 2.95 (*0-8167-3520-4*) Troll Assocs.
Thompson, Julian F. Goofbang Value Daze. (gr. 7 up). 1989. pap. 12.95 (*0-590-41946-3*) Scholastic Inc.
—Goofbang Value Daze. 1990. pap. 2.95 (*0-590-41945-5*) Scholastic Inc.
Thureen, Faythe D. Jenna's Big Jump. Sandeen, Eileen, illus. 112p. (gr. 2-5). 1993. SBE 12.95 (*0-689-31834-0*, Atheneum Child Bk) Macmillan Child Grp.
Today Was a Terrible Day. (ps-3). 1988. pap. 6.95 (*0-14-095073-7*, Puffin) Puffin Bks.
Tolan, Stephanie S. Plague Year. LC 89-13605. (Illus.). 208p. (gr. 7 up). 1990. 12.95 (*0-688-08801-5*) Morrow Jr Bks.
Topek, Susan R. A Turn for Noah: A Hanukkah Story. Springer, Sally, illus. LC 92-22958. 1992. 12.95 (*0-929371-37-2*); pap. 4.95 (*0-929371-38-0*) Kar Ben.
Tripp, Valerie. Molly Learns a Lesson: A School Story. Thieme, Jeanne, ed. Payne, C. F., illus. 72p. (gr. 2-5). 1986. PLB 12.95 (*0-937295-84-1*); pap. 5.95 (*0-937295-16-7*) Pleasant Co.
—Samantha Saves the Day: A Summer Story. Thieme, Jeanne, ed. Grace, Robert & Niles, Nancy, illus. 72p. (gr. 2-5). 1988. PLB 12.95 (*0-937295-92-2*); pap. 5.95 (*0-937295-41-8*) Pleasant Co.
Tryon, Leslie. Albert's Field Trip. Tryon, Leslie, illus. LC 92-43686. 32p. (gr. k-3). 1993. SBE 14.95 (*0-689-31821-9*, Atheneum Child Bk) Macmillan Child Grp.
Udry, Janice M. What Mary Jo Shared. Sayles, Elizabeth, illus. 32p. (ps-3). 1991. pap. 3.95 (*0-590-43757-7*) Scholastic Inc.

Vail, Rachel. Wonder. LC 91-10576. 128p. (gr. 6 up). 1991. 13.95 (0-531-05964-2); RLB 13.99 (0-531-08564-3) Orchard Bks Watts.
—Wonder. 128p. (gr. 5 up). 1993. pap. 3.99 (0-14-036167-7, Puffin) Puffin Bks.
Vallet, Muriel. When We Ride the School Bus. Vallet, Muriel, illus. 17p. (gr. k-3). 1994. pap. 8.95 (1-895583-68-3) MAYA Pubs.
Van der Beek, Deborah. Melinda & the Class Photograph. 28p. (gr. k-4). 1991. PLB 18.95 (0-87614-694-9) Carolrhoda Bks.
Villanueva, Marie. Nene & the Horrible Math Monster. Unson, Ria, illus. LC 92-35425. 36p. (gr. 2-4). 1993. 12.95 (1-879965-02-X) Polychrome Pub.
Voigt, Cynthia. Building Blocks. 1994. pap. 3.95 (0-590-47732-3) Scholastic Inc.
Waber, Bernard. Nobody Is Perfick. (ps-3). 1991. pap. 4.80 (0-395-31669-3) HM.
Wallace, Art. Toby & the Phantoms of the Fourth Grade. LC 93-760. (Illus.). (gr. 4-7). 1994. Repr. of 1971 ed. 11.95 (0-89015-917-3) Sunbelt Media.
Wallace, Bill. True Friends. LC 94-6449. 160p. (gr. 4-6). 1994. 14.95 (0-8234-1141-9) Holiday.
Wardlaw, Lee. The Eye & I. Stouffer, Deborah, illus. LC 88-15664. 75p. (Orig.). (gr. 3-6). 1988. pap. 3.50 (0-931093-10-4) Red Hen Pr.
—Operation Rhinoceros. Stouffer, Deborah, illus. LC 92-15933. 120p. (Orig.). (gr. 3-6). 1992. pap. 3.50 (0-931093-14-7) Red Hen Pr.
Warren, Jean. Huff & Puff Go to School: A Totline Teaching Tale. Cubley, Kathleen, ed. Piper, Molly & Ekberg, Marion, illus. LC 93-34859. 32p. (Orig.). (ps-2). 1994. 12.95 (0-911019-95-2); pap. 5.95 (0-911019-94-4) Warren Pub Hse.
Weil, Judith. School for One. (gr. 4 up). 1992. 11.95 (0-87306-620-0); pap. 9.95 (0-87306-621-9) Feldheim.
Weiss, Leatie. My Teacher Sleeps in School. Weiss, Ellen, illus. LC 85-40449. 32p. (ps-3). 1985. pap. 4.50 (0-14-050559-8, Puffin) Puffin Bks.
Weiss, Nicki. An Egg Is an Egg. (Illus.). 32p. (ps-1). 1990. 14.95 (0-399-22182-4, Putnam) Putnam Pub Group.
Wells, Rosemary. First Tomato. Wells, Rosemary, illus. LC 91-41599. 32p. (ps-3). 1992. PLB 12.89 (0-8037-1175-1) Dial Bks Young.
Weyn, Suzanne. All Alone in the Eighth Grade. LC 91-10162. 128p. (gr. 6-9). 1992. lib. bdg. 9.89 (0-8167-2394-X); pap. text ed. 2.95 (0-8167-2395-8) Troll Assocs.
White, Ruth. Weeping Willow. 256p. (gr. 7 up). 1992. 16.00 (0-374-38255-7) FS&G.
Wiggins, VeraLee. Shelby's Best Friend. LC 93-27279. 1994. 8.95 (0-8163-1189-7) Pacific Pr Pub Assn.
Wild, Margaret. Beast. LC 93-34596. 1994. 13.95 (0-590-47158-9) Scholastic Inc.
Wilkinson, Brenda. Ludell & Willie. LC 76-18402. (gr. 7 up). 1977. PLB 13.89 (0-06-026488-8) HarpC Child Bks.
Williams, Karen S. Best Friends Are for Keeps. LC 92-10988. 1992. write for info. (0-8280-0660-1) Review & Herald.
Willis, Val. The Mystery in the Bottle. Shelley, John, illus. 32p. (gr. k-3). 1991. bds. 14.95 (0-374-35194-5) FS&G.
—Surprise in the Wardrobe. (gr. 4-8). 1990. 15.00 (0-374-37309-4) FS&G.
Willner-Pardo, Gina. Jason & the Losers. LC 93-44156. 1996. write for info. (0-395-70160-0, Clarion Bks) HM.
—Natalie Spitzer's Turtles. Levine, Abby, ed. Delaney, Molly, illus. LC 92-3342. 32p. (gr. k-3). 1992. 13.95g (0-8075-5515-0) A Whitman.
Winthrop, Elizabeth. Luke's Bully. Porter, Pat G., illus. 64p. (gr. 2-5). 1990. pap. 11.95 (0-670-83103-4) Viking Child Bks.
Wiseman, Bernard. Morris Goes to School. Wiseman, Bernard, illus. LC 75-77944. 64p. (gr. k-3). 1970. PLB 13.89 (0-06-026548-5) HarpC Child Bks.
—Morris Goes to School. LC 75-77944. (Illus.). 64p. (gr. k-3). 1983. pap. 3.50 (0-06-444045-1, Trophy) HarpC Child Bks.
Wolfe, Elle. Palm Beach Prep, No. 3: The Girls Against the Boys. (gr. 4-7). 1990. pap. 2.95 (0-8125-1063-1) Tor Bks.
—Palm Beach Prep, No. 5: Troublemaker. (gr. 4-7). 1990. pap. 2.95 (0-8125-1065-8) Tor Bks.
—Upstaged, No. 6. (gr. 4-7). 1990. pap. 2.95 (0-8125-1077-1) Tor Bks.
Wolff, Patricia R. & Root, Kimberly B. The Toll-Bridge Troll. LC 93-32298. (gr. 3 up). 1995. write for info. (0-15-277665-6) Harbrace.
Woo, Dianne. The Computer Munched My Homework. 128p. (Orig.). 1992. pap. 3.99 (0-8125-2050-5) Tor Bks.
Woodruff, Elvira. Awfully Short for the Fourth Grade. 1990. pap. 3.50 (0-440-40366-9, Pub. by Yearling Classics) Dell.
—The Magnificent Mummy Maker. LC 93-7870. 160p. (gr. 4-7). 1994. 13.95 (0-590-45742-X) Scholastic Inc.
—Show-&-Tell. Brunkus, Denise, illus. LC 90-23588. 32p. (ps-3). 1991. reinforced 14.95 (0-8234-0883-3) Holiday.
Wyeth, Sharon D. Lisa, We Miss You. 1990. pap. 2.95 (0-440-40393-6) Dell.
—Super Pen Pals, No. 1. (Orig.). (gr. 4-7). 1990. pap. 3.50 (0-440-40395-2, Pub. by Yearling Classics) Dell.
Wyman, Andrea. Faith, Hope & Chicken Feathers. LC 93-26293. 1994. 15.95 (0-8234-1117-6) Holiday.
Yashima, Taro. Crow Boy. Yashima, T., illus. (gr. k-3). 1955. pap. 14.99 (0-670-24931-9) Viking Child Bks.
Yates, Madeleine. It's School Picture Day. (ps-3). 1993. pap. 2.99 (0-440-40781-8) Dell.
Yepsen, Roger. Smarten Up. (gr. 4-7). 1990. 13.95 (0-316-96864-1) Little.
Yolen, Jane & Greenberg, Martin H., eds. Things That Go Bump in the Night: A Collection of Original Stories. LC 88-39338. 288p. (gr. 5 up). 1989. 15.00 (0-06-026802-6); PLB 14.89 (0-06-026803-4) HarpC Child Bks.
Yorke, Malcolm. Ritchie F. Dweebly Thunders On. Chamberlain, Margaret, illus. LC 93-5003. 32p. (gr. 1-4). 1994. 10.95 (1-56458-199-3) Dorling Kindersley.
Young, Selina. Ned. LC 92-33518. 26p. (ps-1). 1993. 14.95 (1-56566-033-1) Thomasson-Grant.
Zach, Cheryl. Benny & the No-Good Teacher. Wilson, Janet, illus. LC 91-30588. 80p. (gr. 2-6). 1992. SBE 12.95 (0-02-793706-2, Bradbury Pr) Macmillan Child Grp.
Zeier, Joan T. Stick Boy. LC 92-23326. 144p. (gr. 2-6). 1993. SBE 13.95 (0-689-31835-9, Atheneum Child Bk) Macmillan Child Grp.
Ziefert, Harriet. Harry Gets Ready for School. Smith, Mavis, illus. (ps-2). 1993. pap. 3.25 (0-14-036539-7, Puffin) Puffin Bks.
—Today Is Monday. (Illus.). 12p. (ps-3). 1992. 9.95 (0-694-00407-3) HarpC Child Bks.
—Trip Day (Mr. Rose's Class) Brown, Richard, illus. 64p. 1988. pap. 2.50 (0-553-15618-7, Skylark) Bantam.
—Worm Day (Mr. Rose's Class) Brown, Richard, illus. 64p. 1988. pap. 2.50 (0-553-15619-5, Skylark) Bantam.
Zimelman, Nathan. How the Second Grade Got 8,205.50 to Visit the Statue of Liberty. Mathews, Judith, ed. Slavin, Bill, illus. LC 92-996. 32p. (gr. k-3). 1992. 13.95g (0-8075-3431-5) A Whitman.
—Please Excuse Jaspar. (ps-3). 1993. pap. 2.99 (0-440-40783-4) Dell.
Zindel, Paul. Harry & Hortense at Hormone High. 160p. (gr. 7-12). 1985. pap. 3.99 (0-553-25175-9, Starfire) Bantam.

SCHOOLS–MANAGEMENT AND ORGANIZATION
see School Administration and Organization

SCHOOLS, COMMERCIAL
see Business Education

SCHOOLS, MILITARY
see Military Education

SCHUMANN, ROBERT ALEXANDER, 1810-1856

Rachlin, Ann. Schumann. Hellard, Susan, illus. LC 92-26965. 24p. (gr. k-3). 1993. pap. 5.95 (0-8120-1544-4) Barron.

SCHWEITZER, ALBERT, 1875-1965

Bentley, James. Albert Schweitzer: The Doctor Who Devoted His Life to Africa's Sick. Lantier, Patricia, adapted by. LC 90-9974. (Illus.). 64p. (gr. 3-4). 1991. PLB 19.93 (0-8368-0457-0) Gareth Stevens Inc.
—Albert Schweitzer: The Doctor Who Gave up a Brilliant Career to Serve the People of Africa. LC 88-17731. (Illus.). 68p. (gr. 5-6). 1989. PLB 19.93 (1-55532-823-7) Gareth Stevens Inc.
Crawford, Gail & Renna, Giani. Albert Schweitzer. (Illus.). 104p. (gr. 5-8). 1990. 9.95 (0-382-09976-1); pap. 5.95 (0-382-24003-0) Silver Burdett Pr.
Greene, Carol. Albert Schweitzer: Friend of All Life. LC 93-12975. (Illus.). 48p. (gr. k-3). 1993. PLB 12.85 (0-516-04258-0); pap. 4.95 (0-516-44258-9) Childrens.
Robles, Harold. Albert Schweitzer: An Adventurer for Humanity. Miller, Rhena S., pref. by. (Illus.). 64p. (gr. 4-6). 1994. 15.40 (1-56294-352-9) Millbrook Pr.
Schweitzer, Albert. Albert Schweitzer. Repath, Ann, ed. Winston, Richard & Winston, Clara, trs. Delessert, Etienne, illus. 32p. (gr. 9 up). 1986. PLB 12.95 (0-88682-013-8) Creative Ed.

SCIENCE
see also Astronomy; Bacteriology; Biology; Botany; Chemistry; Crystallography; Ethnology; Fossils; Geology; Mathematics; Meteorology; Mineralogy; Natural History; Physics; Physiology; Space Sciences; Zoology; also headings beginning with the word Scientific

Aaseng, Nathan. Science vs. Pseudoscience? LC 93-30014. (Illus.). 144p. (gr. 9-12). 1994. PLB 13.40 (0-531-11182-2) Watts.
Adair, R., et al. Brinca de Alegria Hacia la Primavera con las Matematicas y Ciencias. (SPA & ENG.). 94p. (gr. k-1). 1988. pap. text ed. 16.95 (1-881431-21-5) AIMS Educ Fnd.
—Caete de Gusto Hacid el Otono con las Matematicas y Ciencias. (SPA & ENG.). 116p. (gr. k-1). 1988. pap. text ed. 16.95 (1-881431-19-3) AIMS Educ Fnd.
—Patine al Invierno con Matematicas y Ciencias. (SPA & ENG.). 105p. (gr. k-1). 1988. pap. text ed. 16.95 (1-881431-20-7) AIMS Educ Fnd.
Alberti, Delbert & Mason, George. Laboratory Laughter. Firmhand, Zelda, illus. (Orig.). (gr. 2-9). 1974. pap. 7.95 (0-918932-25-4) Activity Resources.
Aronson, Billy. Scientific Goofs. LC 94-4492. 1994. text ed. write for info. (0-7167-6537-3, Sci Am Yng Rdrs); pap. text ed. write for info. (0-7167-6553-5) W H Freeman.
—Scientific Goofs. LC 94-4492. 1994. text ed. write for info. (0-7167-6537-3, Sci Am Yng Rdrs); pap. text ed. write for info. (0-7167-6553-5) W H Freeman.
Asimov, Isaac. Is There Life on Other Planets? 1991. pap. 4.95 (0-440-40348-0, YB) Dell.
Barr, George. Science Projects for Young People. 153p. (gr. 5 up). 1986. pap. 3.50 (0-486-25235-3) Dover.
—Sports Science for Young People. 1990. pap. 3.95 (0-486-26527-7) Dover.
Berenstain, Stan & Berenstain, Janice. The Berenstain Bears' Science Fair. Berenstain, Stan & Berenstain, Janice, illus. LC 76-8121. (gr. 1-4). 1977. PLB 11.99 (0-394-93294-3) Random Bks Yng Read.
Berger, Melvin. Bubbles, Bubbles Everywhere. (Illus.). 16p. (ps-2). 1994. pap. text ed. 14.95 (1-56784-017-5) Newbridge Comms.
—Kids for the Earth. (Illus.). 16p. (ps-2). 1994. pap. text ed. 14.95 (1-56784-020-5) Newbridge Comms.
—The Native Americans Told Us So. 16p. (gr. 2-4). 1994. pap. 14.95 (1-56784-211-9) Newbridge Comms.
—The Web of Life. 16p. (gr. 2-4). 1994. pap. 14.95 (1-56784-206-2) Newbridge Comms.
Bochinski, Julianne B. The Complete Handbook of Science Fair Projects. 1991. text ed. 29.95 (0-471-52729-7) Wiley.
Bombaugh, Ruth. Science Fair Success. LC 89-7798. (Illus.). 96p. (gr. 6 up). 1990. lib. bdg. 16.95 (0-89490-197-4) Enslow Pubs.
Bourne, Phyllis M. Things Change. (Illus.). 24p. (Orig.). (gr. 1-3). 1992. pap. text ed. 29.95 big bk. (1-56334-067-4); pap. text ed. 6.00 small bk. (1-56334-073-9) Hampton-Brown.
Bousquet, Catherine. Incredibly Hidden. LC 93-9459. (Illus.). 48p. (gr. 6 up). 1993. text ed. 14.95 RSBE (0-02-711737-5, New Discovery Bks) Macmillan Child Grp.
Boy Scouts of America Staff. Cub Scout Academics: Science. (Illus.). 44p. 1991. pap. 1.35 (0-8395-3030-7, 33030) BSA.
Bramwell, Martyn. How Things Work. Mostyn, David, illus. 38p. (ps-3). 1985. PLB 7.95 (0-7460-0415-X, Pub. by Usborne) EDC.
Bremmer, T., et al. Book of Knowledge. (Illus.). 243p. (gr. 3 up). 24.95 (0-7460-0360-9) EDC.
Bridge, Michael. Starseed: An Introduction (for children) to the World. Haughey, Karen, illus. 32p. 1992. 22.95 (0-944963-34-X); PLB 20.95 (0-944963-15-3); pap. 16.95 (0-685-60191-9) Glastonbury Pr.
BSCS Staff. Science for Life & Living: Integrating Science, Technology & Health. 368p. (gr. 5). 1991. case-sewn 26.90 (0-8403-5998-5) Kendall-Hunt.
Calder, Nigel & Newell, John. On the Frontiers of Science: How Scientists See Our Future. (Illus.). 256p. 1989. 35.00x (0-8160-2205-4) Facts on File.
Carratello, John & Carratello, Patty. All about Science Fairs. Chellton, Anna, illus. 96p. (gr. 1-8). 1989. wkbk. 10.95 (1-55734-228-8) Tchr Create Mat.
—Problem Solving Science Investigations. Chellton, Anna, illus. 96p. (gr. 1-8). 1989. wkbk. 10.95 (1-55734-229-6) Tchr Create Mat.
Chisholm, J. Book of Science. Beeson, D., illus. 48p. (gr. 3-6). 1984. 14.95 (0-86020-721-8); pap. 3.95 (0-7460-0830-9) EDC.
Collins, Nancy. Places to Sleep. Neaville, Michelle, illus. LC 92-14392. 32p. (ps-2). Date not set. 11.95 (1-56065-165-2) Capstone Pr.
Conaway, Judith. More Science Secrets. LC 86-16084. (Illus.). 48p. (gr. 1-5). 1987. PLB 11.89 (0-8167-0866-5); pap. text ed. 3.50 (0-8167-0867-3) Troll Assocs.
Cooper, Chris & Insley, Jane. How Does It Work? 64p. (gr. 4-7). 15.95x (0-8160-1066-8) Facts on File.
Crump, Donald J., ed. On the Brink of Tomorrow: Frontiers of Science. LC 81-48075. 200p. (gr. 7 up). 1982. 12.95 (0-87044-414-X) Natl Geog.
—You Won't Believe Your Eyes. LC 86-7637. (Illus.). 104p. (gr. 3-8). 1987. 8.95 (0-87044-611-8); PLB 12.50 (0-87044-616-9) Natl Geog.
Daab, Marcia J. Science Fair Workshop. (gr. 4-8). 1990. pap. 6.95 (0-8224-6374-1) Fearon Teach Aids.
Daitz, Myrna. Crafty Ideas from Science. Montgomery, Margaret, ed. Chapman, Gillian, illus. 48p. 1993. pap. 4.99 (1-85015-392-2) Exley Giftbooks.
Darneille, Diane D. Season Science 1: Seasonal Mystery of Animal Coat Change. Porter, Robin A., illus. 32p. (Orig.). (gr. k-5). 1992. pap. 13.95 (0-9634246-1-0) Sci Passport.
Dashefsky, H. Steven. Microbiology: Forty-Nine Science Fair Projects. (gr. 3 up). 1994. text ed. 19.95 (0-07-015659-X) McGraw.
Davies, Kay & Oldfield, Wendy. My Apple. Pragoff, Fiona, photos by. LC 94-7107. (Illus.). 32p. (gr. 1 up). 1994. PLB 17.27 (0-8368-1114-3) Gareth Stevens Inc.
Davies, Kay, et al. First Step Science, 4 vols. Pragoff, Fiona, photos by. (Illus.). (gr. 1 up). 1994. PLB 69.08 Set (0-8368-1113-5) Gareth Stevens Inc.
—First Step Science, 4 vols. Pragoff, Fiona, photos by. (Illus.). (gr. 1 up). 1995. PLB 69.08 (0-8368-1184-4) Gareth Stevens Inc.
—First Step Science, 8 vols. Pragoff, Fiona, photos by. (Illus.). (gr. 1 up). Date not set. PLB 138.18 (0-8368-1189-5) Gareth Stevens Inc.
—My Jumper. Pragoff, Fiona, photos by. (Illus.). 32p. (gr. 1 up). 1995. PLB 17.27 (0-8368-1187-9) Gareth Stevens Inc.
DeBruin, Jerry. Creative Hands-on Science Cards & Activities. 336p. (gr. 3-9). 1990. 19.95 (0-86653-538-1, GA1150) Good Apple.
—School Yard-Backyard, Cycles of Science. 160p. (gr. 3-9). 1989. 12.95 (0-86653-489-X, GA1084) Good Apple.
DeCloux, Tina. Tina's Science Adventures. Werges, Rosanne, ed. Sullivan, Tara, illus. 80p. (ps-3). 1992. pap. 12.95 spiral bdg. (0-9615903-3-5) Symbiosis Bks.

Dempsey, Michael, ed. Growing up with Science: The Illustrated Encyclopedia of Invention. (Illus.). 2496p. (gr. 3-10). 1990. 239.95 (*0-87475-839-4*) Marshall Cavendish.
Diagram Group Staff. Junior Science on File Collection. 288p. (gr. 4-6). 1991. 155.00 (*0-8160-2706-4*) Facts on File.
Diebert, Linda. Science for Me. 112p. (ps-2). 1991. 11.95 (*0-86653-597-7*, GA1318) Good Apple.
Disney, Walt, Productions Staff. Simple Science. 1986. 5.95 (*0-553-05415-5*) Bantam.
Dolan, Edward F. Science. 1995. PLB write for info. (*0-8050-2863-3*) H Holt & Co.
Dreher, Barbara S. Sounds of Science. LC 89-52116. (Illus.). 44p. (gr. k-3). 1990. 5.95 (*1-55523-310-4*) Winston-Derek.
Durant. Prize-Winning Science Fair Projects. 1992. pap. 2.95 (*0-590-44019-5*) Scholastic Inc.
Emberley, Ed. Ed Emberley's Three Science Flip Books. (ps-3). 1994. 10.95 (*0-316-23456-7*) Little.
Embry, Lynn. Scientific Encounters of the Curious Kind. McClure, Nancee, illus. 64p. (gr. 4-7). 1984. wkbk. 8.95 (*0-86653-176-9*, GA 550) Good Apple.
—Scientific Encounters of the Endangered Kind. McClure, Nancee, illus. 64p. (gr. 4-7). 1986. wkbk. 8.95 (*0-86653-353-2*, GA 694) Good Apple.
English, Timothy M. & English, Gayla I. Science Fun Centers. (Illus.). 48p. (Orig.). (gr. 3-5). 1990. pap. text ed. 4.69 (*1-878931-00-8*, 3B90-001) English Enterprises.
Everix, Nancy. Windows to the World. Everix, Nancy, illus. 128p. (gr. 2-8). 1984. wkbk. 11.95 (*0-86653-173-4*, GA 527) Good Apple.
Field, Nancy, et al. Nature Discovery Library. Machlis, Sally & Torvik, Sharon, illus. (gr. 3-6). 1990. Set. pap. text ed. 42.50 (*0-941042-15-4*) Dog Eared Pubns.
Filson, Brent. Superconductors & Other New Breakthroughs in Science. (Illus.). 128p. (gr. 5-9). 1989. lib. bdg. 13.98 (*0-671-65857-3*, J Messner); PLB 9.74s.p. (*0-685-24680-9*) S&S Trade.
Fleisher, Paul. Secrets of the Universe: Discovering the Universal Laws of Science. Keeler, Patricia, illus. LC 86-14001. 224p. (gr. 5-9). 1987. SBE 17.95 (*0-689-31266-0*, Atheneum Child Bk) Macmillan Child Grp.
Ford, B. G. Do You Know? One Hundred Fascinating Facts. McNaught, Harry, illus. LC 78-62132. (ps-1). 1979. pap. 2.25 (*0-394-84070-4*) Random Bks Yng Read.
Forte, Imogene. Science Fun. LC 84-62935. (Illus.). 80p. (gr. k-6). 1985. pap. text ed. 3.95 (*0-86530-100-X*, IP 91-4) Incentive Pubns.
Fowler, Allan. Hearing Things Big Book. (Illus.). 32p. (ps-2). 1991. PLB 22.95 (*0-516-49469-4*) Childrens.
—Seeing Things Big Book. (Illus.). 32p. (ps-2). 1991. PLB 22.95 (*0-516-49470-8*) Childrens.
—Smelling Things Big Book. (Illus.). 32p. (ps-2). 1991. PLB 22.95 (*0-516-49472-4*) Childrens.
—Tasting Things Big Book. (Illus.). 32p. (ps-2). 1991. PLB 22.95 (*0-516-49471-6*) Childrens.
Friedhoffer, Robert. Magic Tricks, Science Facts. 1990. pap. 6.95 (*0-531-15186-7*) Watts.
—More Magic Tricks, Science Facts. 1993. pap. 6.95 (*0-531-15669-9*) Watts.
Gabb, Michael. Everyday Science. LC 79-64387. (Illus.). 36p. (gr. 3-6). 1980. PLB 13.50 (*0-8225-1179-7*, First Ave Edns); pap. 4.95 (*0-8225-9508-7*, First Ave Edns) Lerner Pubns.
Gabet, Marcia. Fun with Science. Gabet, Marcia, illus. 48p. (gr. k-3). 1985. wkbk. 6.95 (*1-55734-036-6*) Tchr Create Mat.
Gallant, Roy A. A Young Person's Guide to Science: Ideas That Change the World. LC 92-12332. (Illus.). 256p. (gr. 5 up). 1993. SBE 16.95 (*0-02-735775-9*, Macmillan Child Bk) Macmillan Child Grp.
Ganeri, Anita. Earth Science. LC 93-16753. (Illus.). 48p. (gr. 5 up). 1993. text ed. 13.95 RSBE (*0-87518-577-0*, Dillon) Macmillan Child Grp.
—Indoor Science. LC 93-72569. (Illus.). 48p. (gr. 5 up). 1993. text ed. 13.95 RSBE (*0-87518-578-9*, Dillon) Macmillan Child Grp.
Gardner, Robert. Robert Gardner's Science Activity Books, 4 vols. (Illus.). 544p. (gr. 4-8). 1989. Set. PLB 47.92 (*0-671-94217-4*, J Messner); Set. PLB 35.94s.p. (*0-685-47080-6*); Set. pap. 19.80 (*0-671-94218-2*); Set. pap. 14.84s.p. (*0-685-47081-4*) S&S Trade.
Ginns, Russell. Midnight Science. LC 94-4142. 1994. pap. text ed. write for info. (*0-7167-6569-1*) W H Freeman.
Glass, Don, ed. Why You Can Never Get to the End of the Rainbow & Other Moments of Science. Singh, Paul, contrib. by. LC 92-34770. 1993. 29.95 (*0-253-32591-9*); pap. 10.95 (*0-253-20780-0*) Ind U Pr.
Godlewski, Lorraine, et al. Preparing for the Science RCT. (Illus., Orig.). 1987. wkbk. 3.45 (*0-937323-08-X*) United Pub Co.
Haught, James A. Science in a Nanosecond: Illustrated Answers to 100 Basic Science Questions. (Illus.). 110p. (Orig.). (gr. 4 up). 1991. pap. 14.95 (*0-87975-637-3*) Prometheus Bks.
Heddle, Rebecca & Shipton, Paul. Science Activities, Vol. III. (Illus.). 72p. (gr. k-5). 1993. pap. 9.95 (*0-7460-1427-9*, Usborne) EDC.
Henry, Lucia K. Science & Ourselves. (gr. 1-3). 1989. pap. 6.95 (*0-8224-6456-X*) Fearon Teach Aids.
—Science in Special Places. (gr. 1-3). 1989. pap. 6.95 (*0-8224-6457-8*) Fearon Teach Aids.
—Science Through the Seasons. (gr. 1-3). 1989. pap. 6.95 (*0-8224-6304-0*) Fearon Teach Aids.
Hessler, Edward W. & Stubbs, Harriett. Acid Rain Science Projects. 20p. (Orig.). (gr. 5-12). 1987. pap. 9.95 (*0-935577-09-2*) Acid Rain Found.
Hillen, Judith A. Piezas y Disenos, un Mosaico de Matematicas y Ciencias. (SPA & ENG.). 160p. (gr. 5-9). 1992. pap. text ed. 16.95 (*1-881431-31-2*) AIMS Educ Fnd.
Hiscock, Bruce. The Big Rock. Hiscock, Bruce, illus. LC 87-31834. 32p. (gr. 1-5). 1988. RSBE 14.95 (*0-689-31402-7*, Atheneum Child Bk) Macmillan Child Grp.
Hurt, Roger. Exploring Science: Practice at Home Science Activity. Trotter, Stuart, illus. 24p. (Orig.). (gr. 2-5). 1992. pap. 2.95 wkbk. (*0-7214-3246-8*) Ladybird Bks.
Hy Kim. Showy Science: Exciting Hands-on Activities That Explore the World Around Us. (Illus.). 320p. (Orig.). (gr. 3-6). 1994. pap. 19.95 (*0-673-36091-1*) GdYrBks.
Iozzi, Louis A. & Bastardo, Peter J. Decisions for Today & Tomorrow. (gr. 9-12). 1990. tchr's. ed. 60.00 (*0-944584-22-5*) Sopris.
Jennings, Terry. Balancing. Anstey, David, illus. LC 88-83615. 28p. (gr. k-4). 1989. PLB 10.90 (*0-531-17175-2*, Gloucester Pr) Watts.
—Structures. LC 88-22879. (Illus.). 32p. (gr. 3-6). 1989. pap. 4.95 (*0-516-48409-5*) Childrens.
Johnston, Tom. Light! Color! Action! Pooley, Sarah, illus. LC 87-42754. 32p. (gr. 4-6). 1988. PLB 17.27 (*1-55532-409-6*) Gareth Stevens Inc.
—Science in Action, 6 vols. Pooley, Sarah, illus. 32p. (gr. 4-6). 1987. Set. PLB 103.60 (*1-55532-412-6*) Gareth Stevens Inc.
Kanetzke, Howard W. Airplanes & Balloons. rev. ed. LC 87-23230. (Illus.). 48p. (gr. 2-6). 1987. PLB 10.95 (*0-8172-3251-6*) Raintree Steck-V.
Kerrod, Robin. Air in Action. LC 89-997. (Illus.). 32p. (gr. 3-8). 1990. PLB 9.95 (*1-85435-152-4*) Marshall Cavendish.
—Fire & Water. LC 89-917. (Illus.). 32p. (gr. 3-8). 1990. PLB 9.95 (*1-85435-153-2*) Marshall Cavendish.
—How Things Work. LC 89-918. (Illus.). 32p. (gr. 3-8). 1990. PLB 9.95 (*1-85435-154-0*) Marshall Cavendish.
—Is It Magic. LC 89-919. (Illus.). 32p. (gr. 3-8). 1990. PLB 9.95 (*1-85435-155-9*) Marshall Cavendish.
—Let's Investigate Science. (Illus.). (gr. 5 up). 1994. Group 1, The Solar System, Animal Life, Force & Motion, Communications, The Environment. PLB write for info.; Group 2, Electricity & Magnetism, Plant Life, Natural Resources, Transportation, Weather. PLB write for info. (*1-85435-688-7*) Marshall Cavendish.
—Light Fantastic. LC 89-998. (Illus.). 32p. (gr. 3-8). 1990. PLB 9.95 (*1-85435-156-7*) Marshall Cavendish.
—Plants in Action. LC 89-996. (Illus.). 32p. (gr. 3-8). 1990. PLB 9.95 (*1-85435-157-5*) Marshall Cavendish.
—S&S Young Reader's Book of Science. 1991. pap. 12.95 (*0-671-73128-9*, S&S BFYR); pap. 7.95 (*0-671-73240-4*, S&S BFYR) S&S Trade.
—Secrets of Science Series, 6 vols. (Illus.). (gr. 3-8). 1990. PLB 65.70 (*1-85435-151-6*) Marshall Cavendish.
—Secrets of Science Series: Group Two, 4 vols. (Illus.). (gr. 3-8). 1991. Set. PLB 39.80 (*1-85435-268-7*) Marshall Cavendish.
Kids' Smithsonian Experience. 32p. (ps-8). pap. 29.50 (*0-87474-585-3*) Smithsonian.
Klitzner, Carol. Reading Books for Science: A Study Guide. Friedland, Joyce & Kessler, Rikki, eds. (gr. 1-3). 1991. pap. text ed. 19.95 (*0-88122-691-2*) LRN Links.
Koenig, Herbert G., et al. RCT Science Review. 6th ed. Gamsey, Wayne H., ed. Fairbanks, Eugene B., illus. 288p. (gr. 7-12). 1992. pap. text ed. 5.17 (*0-935487-09-3*) N & N Pub Co.
Kohl, MaryAnn & Potter, Jean. ScienceArts: Discovering Science Through Art Experiences. Macleod, Andi, illus. 144p. (Orig.). (ps-4). 1993. pap. text ed. 15.95 (*0-935607-04-8*) Bright Ring.
Kuebler, Sharon. Noon to Night. Kirkeeide, Deborah, illus. 32p. (ps-2). Date not set. 11.95 (*1-56065-161-X*) Capstone Pr.
Kuntz, Margy, et al. Big Fearon Book of Doing Science. (gr. 1-6). 1989. pap. 25.95 (*0-8224-2737-0*) Fearon Teach Aids.
Library of Science, 6 vols. (gr. 4-9). 1989. Set. 113.70 (*1-85435-069-2*) Marshall Cavendish.
Luine, Jerome. Science Mysteries. 80p. 1994. pap. 4.95 (*1-56565-173-1*) Lowell Hse Juvenile.
McKelway, Margaret. A World of Things to Do. Crump, Donald J., ed. (Illus.). 104p. 1987. 8.95 (*0-87044-610-X*); PLB 12.50 (*0-87044-615-0*) Natl Geog.
McMillan, Dana & Martin, Shirley. Science Boosters. 64p. (gr. 2-6). 1988. 6.95 (*0-912107-82-0*, MM998) Monday Morning Bks.
Macmillan Educational Company Staff. Macmillan Encyclopedia of Science, 12 vols. (Illus.). 1991. Set. text ed. 360.00 (*0-02-941346-X*) Macmillan.
Maine, Diana, ed. Science. LC 92-54482. (Illus.). 1993. write for info. (*1-56458-248-5*) Dorling Kindersley.
Markham, Lois. Discoveries That Changed Science. (Illus.). 48p. (gr. 4-8). 1994. PLB write for info. (*0-8114-4936-X*) Raintree Steck-V.
Markle, Sandra. Primary Science Sampler. 112p. (gr. 1-3). 1980. 9.95 (*0-88160-008-3*, LW 110) Learning Wks.
—Science Mini-Mysteries. LC 87-17420. (Illus.). 72p. (gr. 3-7). 1988. SBE 14.95 (*0-689-31291-1*, Atheneum Child Bk) Macmillan Child Grp.
—Science Sampler. 112p. (gr. 4-8). 1980. 9.95 (*0-88160-031-8*, LW 216) Learning Wks.
—Science to the Rescue. LC 92-41096. (Illus.). 48p. (gr. 3-7). 1994. SBE 15.95 (*0-689-31783-2*, Atheneum Child Bk) Macmillan Child Grp.
Markle, Sandras. Science: Just Add Salt. (gr. 4-7). 1994. pap. 2.95 (*0-590-46537-6*) Scholastic Inc.
Marsh, Carole. Gee! Ology: Trivia for Kids. (Illus.). (gr. 3-12). 1994. PLB 24.95 (*1-55609-305-5*); pap. 14.95 (*1-55609-306-3*); computer disk 29.95 (*1-55609-307-1*) Gallopade Pub Group.
Martin, Paul D. Science: It's Changing Your World. Crump, Donald J., ed. LC 85-2936. (Illus.). 104p. (gr. 3-8). 1985. 8.95 (*0-87044-516-2*); PLB 12.50 (*0-87044-521-9*) Natl Geog.
Mayes, S., et al. Starting Point Science, Vol. 2. (gr. 4-7). 1992. 11.95 (*0-7460-0655-1*, Usborne) EDC.
Meredith, S. & Tahta, S. Starting Point Science, Vol. 3. (Illus.). 96p. (gr. 2-7). 1992. 11.95 (*0-7460-0970-4*, Usborne) EDC.
Moore, Jo E. & Tryon, Leslie. The Big Book of Science Stories. (Illus.). 64p. (gr. k-2). 1991. pap. 11.95 (*1-55799-210-X*) Evan-Moor Corp.
Moutron, Julia S. Collecting Bugs & Things: A Science Activity Storybook. (Illus.). 48p. (gr. k up). 1988. pap. 2.95 (*0-8431-2226-9*) Price Stern.
Myers, Jack. What Makes Popcorn Pop? And Other Questions about the World Around Us. (Illus.). 64p. (gr. 1-7). 1994. 7.95 (*1-56397-402-9*) Boyds Mills Pr.
Nelson, Bonnie E. Science & Computer Activities for Children 3 to 9 Years Old. 2nd, rev. ed. (Illus.). 146p. (gr. k-3). 1988. 28.00x (*0-931642-21-3*) Lintel.
Norden, Carroll R. The Jungle. rev. ed. LC 87-20820. (Illus.). 48p. (gr. 2-6). 1987. PLB 10.95 (*0-8172-3256-7*) Raintree Steck-V.
Ollerenshaw, Chris & Triggs, Pat. Toy Box Science, 4 vols, Set. Millard, Peter J., photos by. (Illus.). (gr. 3 up). Date not set. PLB 69.08 (*0-8368-1118-6*) Gareth Stevens Inc.
Oppenheim, Carol. Science Is Fun Activity Package: For Families & Classroom Groups - Sing a Song of Science with Carol & the Kids. 1993. incl. song tape 23.90 (*0-9633555-6-2*) Cracom.
—Science Is Fun! For Families & Classroom Groups. Schmitt, Judy & Cooney, Cynthia D., illus. LC 92-35717. 198p. (Orig.). (ps up). 1993. pap. 14.95 (*0-9633555-1-1*) Cracom.
Parker, Steve. How It Works. Pleasance, Geoff, illus. 48p. (gr. 3-6). 1992. pap. 2.95 (*1-56680-010-2*) Mad Hatter Pub.
Pearce, Q. L. Amazing Science Series, 8 bks. (Illus.). 256p. (gr. 4-6). 1989. Set. PLB 77.88 (*0-671-94111-9*, J Messner); Set. pap. 35.70 (*0-671-94112-7*) S&S Trade.

Directions encourage children to explore, invent, & learn the value of risk-taking in science & art processes. *Author/Artist Carolyn Petty is an internationally recognized education consultant. *Extensively Classroom Tested--Child Approved! Their testimony says it all, "Do we have to go to recess now?"
Publisher Provided Annotation.

Platt, Richard. Del Interior de las Cosas - Incredible Cross-Sections. Puncel, Maria & Vasquez, Juan J., eds. Bermejo, Ana & Aixela, Javier F., trs. Bietsy, Stephen, illus. (SPA.). 48p. (gr. 5-12). 1992. write for info. (*84-372-4524-9*) Santillana.

Pollard, Michael. The House That Science Built. (Illus.). 48p. (gr. 1-4). 1987. 12.95x (*0-8160-1780-8*) Facts on File.

Pringle, Laurence. Rain of Troubles: The Science & Politics of Acid Rain. LC 87-34950. (Illus.). 128p. (gr. 7 up). 1988. SBE 14.95 (*0-02-775370-0*, Macmillan Child Bk) Macmillan Child Grp.

Puncel, Maria, ed. Las Cosas de Cada Dia - Everyday Things. Aixela, Javier F., tr. (SPA., Illus.). 64p. (gr. 5-12). 1992. write for info. (*84-372-4527-3*) Santillana.

Pyke, Magnus. Weird & Wonderful Science Facts. Burton, Terry, illus. LC 83-24288. 128p. (gr. 5 up). 1985. pap. 3.95 (*0-8069-6254-2*) Sterling.

Roberts, Allene. The Curiosity Club: Kids' Nature Activity Book. 192p. 1992. text ed. cancelled (*0-471-55590-8*); pap. text ed. 14.95 (*0-471-55589-4*) Wiley.

Salem Press Editors, ed. The Twentieth Century: Great Scientific Achievements, 10 vols. (Illus.). 1800p. (gr. 6 up). 1994. Set. lib. bdg. 250.00 (*0-89356-860-0*) Salem Pr.

Schaffer, Frank, Publications Staff. Getting Ready for Science. (Illus.). 24p. (ps-k). 1980. wkbk. 3.98 (*0-86734-021-5*, FS-3034) Schaffer Pubns.

Schwartz, L. Trivia Trackdown - Animals & Science. (gr. 4-6). 1985. 3.95 (*0-88160-119-5*, LW 252) Learning Wks.

The Science Almanac for Kids. 128p. (gr. 3-7). 1993. pap. 7.95 (*1-56293-356-6*) McClanahan Bk.

Science & Technology. 160p. 1993. 30.00 (*0-19-910143-4*) OUP.

Science Magic. 1987. write for info. P-H.

Science Starter. 88p. (ps-3). 1990. 15.93 (*0-8094-4881-5*); lib. bdg. 21.27 (*0-8094-4882-3*) Time-Life.

Science Surprises. (Illus.). 32p. (gr. 2-5). 1986. pap. 4.95 (*0-86020-914-8*) EDC.

Science Tricks & Magic. (Illus.). 32p. (gr. 2-5). 1986. pap. 4.95 (*0-86020-916-4*) EDC.

Science Yellow Pages for Students & Teachers. LC 87-82070. 64p. (gr. k-8). 1988. pap. text ed. 6.95 (*0-318-32626-4*, IP 89-2) Incentive Pubns.

Selsam, Millicent E. Is This a Baby Dinosaur? & Other Science Picture Puzzles. LC 72-76508. (Illus.). 32p. (ps-3). 1972. PLB 13.89 (*0-06-025303-7*) HarpC Child Bks.

Sheely, Robert. Entertainment Lab. 64p. (gr. 4-6). 1994. PLB 12.95 (*1-881889-63-7*) Silver Moon.

Short, Edward P. Checkpoint: A Science Project Survival Guide...for Kids & Adults. (Illus.). 48p. (Orig.). (gr. 3-8). 1992. pap. 9.95 (*0-9636375-1-7*) Quest Dists.
Students groan, their parents shudder, the media specialist threatens to resign. ..It's science fair time again! Science projects have been notorious stress inducers for students, teachers, & parents ever since the first blue ribbon was pinned on a backboard. But they don't need to be. There's a way to survive & even have fun while learning how to develop a quality scientific presentation. Developed & proven in the classroom, CHECKPOINT is designed to be used by students in grades 3-8 with their parents' or teachers' help. In its workbook format, it is concise & practical as it separates a complex task into 14 small, easy-to-follow segments. It also provides motivation & strategies that instill confidence in students while keeping them on a painless track toward a successful science project. Teachers, parents, students & librarians say: "In high demand by our students." "Very useful tool." "Most appropriate project resource." "Got us started & guided us to the end." Call or write for ordering information & discounts: Edward Short - Publisher, 215 Beachwood Blvd., Melbourne Beach, Fl 32951; 407-676-5903.
Publisher Provided Annotation.

Simon, Seymour. Einstein Anderson Sees Through the Invisible Man. Winkowski, Fred, illus. (gr. 3-7). 1987. pap. 3.95 (*0-14-032306-6*, Puffin) Puffin Bks.

Stacy, Tom. Earth, Sea & Sky. Forsey, Chris, illus. LC 90-42976. 40p. (Orig.). (gr. 2-5). 1991. pap. 4.99 (*0-679-80861-2*) Random Bks Yng Read.

Stangl, Jean. Science Toolbox: Making & Using the Tools of Science. LC 93-29389. (ps-3). 1993. 17.95 (*0-8306-4605-1*); pap. 9.95 (*0-8306-4352-4*) TAB Bks.

—The Tools of Science: Ideas & Activities for Guiding Young Scientists. rev. ed. (Illus.). 160p. 1989. 16.95 (*0-8306-9216-9*); pap. 8.95 (*0-8306-3216-6*) TAB Bks.

Stein, Sara. The Science Book. LC 79-64786. (Illus.). 288p. (gr. 4-7). 1980. pap. 9.95 (*0-89480-120-1*, 291) Workman Pub.

Stine, Megan, et al. Smithsonian Science Activity Book. Solimini, Cheryl, ed. (Illus.). 100p. (gr. 2-6). 1987. pap. text ed. 8.95 (*0-939456-51-6*) Galison.

Story of Science, Bk. 1. (ARA., Illus.). (gr. 5-12). 1987. 3.95x (*0-86685-229-8*) Intl Bk Ctr.

Sullivan, Dianna J. Big & Easy Science. Adkins, Lynda, illus. 48p. (ps-2). 1988. wkbk. 6.95 (*1-55734-105-2*) Tchr Create Mat.

Supraner, Robyn. Science Secrets. Barto, Renzo, illus. LC 80-23794. 48p. (gr. 1-5). 1981. PLB 11.89 (*0-89375-426-9*); pap. 3.50 (*0-89375-427-7*) Troll Assocs.

Things Around Us. 88p. (ps-3). 1989. 15.93 (*0-8094-4845-9*); lib. bdg. 21.27 (*0-8094-4846-7*) Time-Life.

Unwin, M. Science Activities, Vol. II. (Illus.). 24p. (gr. 1-4). 1993. 9.95 (*0-7460-1081-8*) EDC.

Vaughan, Jenny. The World of Science. (Illus.). 36p. (gr. 2-6). 1990. 3.99 (*0-517-69907-9*) Random Hse Value.

Victor Raintree Publishers Inc. Staff. The Poles. LC 87-28697. (Illus.). 64p. (Orig.). (gr. 5-9). 1988. PLB 11.95 (*0-8172-3078-5*) Raintree Steck-V.

Weiss, Ann E. Seers & Scientists: Can the Future Be Predicted? (Illus.). 80p. (gr. 7 up). 1986. 13.95 (*0-15-272850-3*, HB Juv Bks) HarBrace.

Wexo, John B. Life Begins. 24p. (gr. 3 up). 1991. PLB 14.95 (*0-88682-387-0*) Creative Ed.

Weyland, Jack. Megapowers: Can Science Fact Defeat Science Fiction. Steacy, Ken, illus. LC 92-5441. 1992. pap. 8.61 (*0-201-58115-9*) Addison-Wesley.

White, Laurence B. Shazam! Simple Science Magic. (ps-3). 1994. pap. 4.95 (*0-8075-7333-7*) A Whitman.

White, Laurence B., Jr. Science Games & Puzzles. Brown, Marc T., illus. LC 84-40786. 1979. pap. 4.95 (*0-201-08606-9*, Lipp Jr Bks) HarpC Child Bks.

—Science Toys & Tricks. Brown, Marc T., illus. LC 84-40787. 1980. pap. 4.95 (*0-201-08659-X*, Lipp Jr Bks) HarpC Child Bks.

Why on Earth? LC 88-25486. (Illus.). 96p. (gr. 3-6). 1988. 8.95 (*0-87044-701-7*); PLB 12.50 (*0-87044-706-8*) Natl Geog.

Wicks, Keith. Science Can Be Fun. Kostal, Pavel, illus. 32p. (gr. 4-7). 1988. PLB 14.95 (*0-8225-0896-6*, First Ave Edns); pap. 4.95 (*0-8225-9559-1*, First Ave Edns) Lerner Pubns.

Wilkes. Simple Science. (Illus.). 38p. (gr. 2-5). 1983. 10.95 (*0-86020-761-7*) EDC.

Wilkins, Mary-Jane. Air, Light & Water. Forsey, Chris, illus. LC 90-12975. 40p. (gr. 4-5). 1991. PLB 12.40 (*0-531-19104-4*, Warwick) Watts.

Williams, Brenda & Williams, Brian. The Random House Book of One Thousand-One Wonders of Science. Kerrod, Robin, et al, illus. LC 89-3954. 160p. 1990. PLB 11.99 (*0-679-90080-2*); pap. 13.00 (*0-679-80080-8*) Random Bks Yng Read.

Wolfe, Connie. Search: A Research Guide for Science Fairs & Independent Study. 96p. (Orig.). (gr. 4-8). 1988. pap. text ed. 12.95 (*0-913705-30-6*) Zephyr Pr AZ.

Wong, Herbert H. The Backyard Detective: A Guide for Beginning Naturalists. Greer, Deborah, illus. LC 92-63342. 64p. (Orig.). (gr. k-5). 1993. pap. 7.95 (*1-882489-00-4*) NatureVision.
THE BACKYARD DETECTIVE provides children with a headstart in science while they have fun exploring their own environment. This book & nature kit invite children to study nature by direct observation in easily accessible environments. With this fully-illustrated guide as an outdoor companion, they use simple science tools & basic comparison charts to investigate nature's clues & uncover their own areas of interest. Young Backyard Detectives will have the opportunity to examine, identify, measure, grow, feed, & collect organisms. They will learn how to keep their own nature journal. This book encourages children to enjoy & respect their natural environment. Dr. Herbert H. Wong, the author, is a zoologist & science educator whose children's science books have become standard favorites among children & their teachers. The ecological concepts he uses to form the framework for THE BACKYARD DETECTIVE are diversity, interrelationships, adaptations & change. THE BACKYARD DETECTIVE is available in book form only, & also with the complete exploration kit (carrying case, magnifier, observation jar, pencil & measuring tape). AVAILABLE THROUGH BOOKPEOPLE & QUALITY BOOKS.
Publisher Provided Annotation.

Wood, Barbara S. Messages Without Words. rev. ed. LC 87-23315. (Illus.). 48p. (gr. 2-6). 1987. PLB 10.95 (*0-8172-3258-3*) Raintree Steck-V.

Woods, Geraldine. Science in Ancient Egypt. LC 87-23746. (Illus.). 96p. (gr. 5-8). 1988. PLB 10.90 (*0-531-10486-9*) Watts.

World Book Editors. World Book's Science Desk Reference. LC 91-65996. (Illus.). 415p. (gr. 4-6). 1991. lib. bdg. write for info. (*0-7166-3242-X*) World Bk.

World Book Editors, ed. World Book's Young Scientist, 10 vols. rev. ed. LC 93-60294. (Illus.). 1270p. (gr. 3-6). 1993. Set. PLB write for info. (*0-7166-2794-9*) World Bk.

World Book Editors & Verlagsgruppe Bertelsmann International Staff, eds. The World Book Encyclopedia of Science, 8 vols. rev. ed. LC 90-70521. (Illus.). 1200p. 1994. Set. PLB write for info. (*0-7166-3393-0*) World Bk.

Wroble, Lisa. Natural Science. Nolte, Larry, illus. 48p. (gr. 3-6). Date not set. PLB 12.95 (*1-56065-112-1*) Capstone Pr.

Wyler, Rose. Science Fun Series, 6 vols. Stewart, Pat, illus. 288p. (gr. 2-4). 1988. (J Messner); Set. PLB 51.24s.p. (*0-685-47066-0*); Set. pap. 29.70 (*0-671-93018-4*); Set. pap. 22.26s.p. (*0-685-47067-9*) S&S Trade.

SCIENCE–DICTIONARIES

Ardley, Neil. Dictionary of Science. LC 93-29811. 1994. write for info. (*1-56458-349-X*) Dorling Kindersley.

Clarke, Donald & Dartford, Mark, eds. The New Illustrated Science & Invention Encyclopedia: How It Works. LC 93-3331. (Illus.). 1994. Set. 349.95 (*0-86307-491-X*) Marshall Cavendish.

Craig, A. & Rosney, C. Science Encyclopedia. (Illus.). 128p. 1989. lib. bdg. 16.96 (*0-88110-390-X*); pap. 14.95 (*0-7460-0419-2*) EDC.

Dempsey, Michael W. Children's First Science Encyclopedia. 1987. 6.98 (*0-671-07745-7*) S&S Trade.

Ford, Brian J. First Encyclopedia of Science. LC 92-44792. (Illus.). 192p. (gr. 2-6). 1993. 19.00 (*0-679-83698-5*); PLB 21.99 (*0-679-93698-X*) Random Bks Yng Read.

Headlam, Catherine, ed. The Kingfisher Science Encyclopedia. 808p. (gr. 3 up). 1993. 39.95 (*1-85697-842-7*, Kingfisher LKC) LKC.

Heese. Jugendhandbuch Naturwissen: Saeugetiere, Vol. 3. (GER.). 144p. 1976. pap. 5.95 (*0-7859-0933-8*, M-7488, Pub. by Rowohlt) Fr & Eur.

—Jugendhandbuch Naturwissen, Vol. 4: Erde und Weltall. (GER.). 128p. 1976. pap. 5.95 (*0-7859-0412-3*, M7489) Fr & Eur.

—Jugendhandbuch Naturwissen, Vol. 5: Energie. (GER.). 128p. 1976. pap. 5.95 (*0-7859-0413-1*, M7490) Fr & Eur.

—Jugendhandbuch Naturwissen, Vol. 6: Elektrizitaet und Elektronic. (GER.). 144p. 1976. pap. 5.95 (*0-7859-0414-X*, M7491) Fr & Eur.

Jugendhandbuch Naturwissen: Bausteine des Lebens, 6 vols, Vol. 1. (GER.). 144p. pap. 750.00 (*3-499-16203-2*, M-7486, Pub. by Rowohlt) Fr & Eur.

Let's Discover, 16 vols. (Illus.). (gr. k-6). 1981. Set. PLB 199.00 per set (*0-8172-1782-7*) Raintree Steck-V.

Pearce, Q. L. The Checkerboard Press Kids' Science Dictionary. LC 88-71150. (Illus.). 124p. (gr. 4-6). 1991. Repr. of 1989 ed. 12.95 (*1-56288-003-9*) Checkerboard.

Pitt, Valeria. Enciclopedia Juvenil de la Ciencia. (SPA.). 260p. 1975. 95.00 (*0-8288-5870-5*, S26475) Fr & Eur.

Rabkin, Sarah. My First Science Dictionary. Burke, Dianne O., illus. 64p. (gr. k-3). 1992. 10.95 (*1-56288-215-5*) Checkerboard.

Rabkin, Ssarah. My First Science Dictionary. Burke, Dianne O., illus. 64p. 1994. pap. 5.95 (*1-56565-177-4*) Lowell Hse Juvenile.

The Raintree Illustrated Science Encyclopedia, 18 vols. LC 78-12093. (Illus.). (gr. 3 up). 1991. Repr. of 1984 ed. PLB 470.00 (*0-8172-3800-X*) Raintree Steck-V.

Shaw, Jean M. & Dyches, Richard W. First Science Dictionary. Sornat, Czeslaw, illus. LC 91-7528. 104p. (gr. k-4). 1991. PLB 15.90 (*0-531-11110-5*) Watts.

Simon, Seymour. The Science Dictionary. (Illus.). 256p. (gr. 4 up). 1994. 29.95 (*0-06-025629-X*); PLB 29.89 (*0-06-025630-3*) HarpC Child Bks.

Stone, Jeanne. The Julian Messner Illustrated Dictionary of Science. (Illus.). 192p. (gr. 5 up). 1985. lib. bdg. 9.79 (*0-671-54548-5*, J Messner) S&S Trade.

Wertheim, J. & Oxlade, C. Dictionary of Science: Physics, Chemistry & Biology Facts. (Illus.). 128p. (gr. 6 up). 1988. pap. 23.95 (*0-86020-989-X*) EDC.

World Book Editors & Verlagsgruppe Bertelsmann International Staff, eds. The World Book Encyclopedia of Science, 8 vols. rev. ed. LC 90-70521. (Illus.). 1200p. 1994. Set. PLB write for info. (*0-7166-3393-0*) World Bk.

World Book Staff, ed. Science Year - 1993: The World Book Annual Science Supplement. LC 65-21776. (Illus.). 400p. (gr. 6 up). 1992. PLB write for info. (*0-7166-0593-7*) World Bk.

World of Science Series, 18 vols. (gr. 4-7). 1985. Set. bds. 225.00x (*0-8160-1563-5*) Facts on File.

SCIENCE–EXPERIMENTS

see also particular branches of science with the subdivision Experiments, e.g. Chemistry–Experiments, etc.

Adventures with Science Series, 5 bks. (Illus.). (gr. 4-9). Set. lib. bdg. 84.75 (*0-89490-375-6*) Enslow Pubs.

Aldridge, Bill G. The Ultimate Science Quiz Book. LC 94-15518. (gr. 5 up). 1994. lib. bdg. 14.98 (*0-531-11198-9*) Watts.

Allison, Linda & Katz, David. Gee Wiz! How to Mix Art & Science or the Art of Thinking Scientifically. Allison, Linda, illus. LC 83-9834. 128p. (gr. 4 up). 1983. pap. 10.95 (*0-316-03445-2*) Little.

Amato, Carol. Super Science Fair Projects. (Illus.). 64p. (gr. 6 up). 1994. pap. 3.95 (*1-56565-141-3*) Lowell Hse Juvenile.

Amato, Carol & Ladizinsky, Eric. Fifty Nifty Science Fair Projects. Manwaring, Kerry, illus. 64p. (Orig.). (gr. 3-7). 1993. pap. 4.95 (*1-56565-053-0*) Lowell Hse.

Amery. Experiments. (gr. 4-6). 1977. pap. 6.95 (*0-86020-135-X*, Usborne-Hayes) EDC.

Ardley, Neil. Science Book of Color. 29p. (gr. 2-5). 1991. 9.95 (*0-15-200576-5*) HarBrace.

—The Science Book of Gravity. 1992. 9.95 (*0-15-200621-4*, Gulliver Bks) HarBrace.

—The Science Book of Motion. 1992. 9.95 (*0-15-200622-2*, Gulliver Bks) HarBrace.

—Science Book of Water. 29p. (gr. 2-5). 1991. 9.95 (*0-15-200575-7*) HarBrace.

—The Science Book of Weather. 1992. 9.95 (*0-15-200624-9*, Gulliver Bks) HarBrace.

Baker, Wendy & Haslam, Andrew. Earth: A Creative Hands-on Approach to Science. LC 92-27573. (Illus.). 48p. (gr. 2-5). 1993. pap. 12.95 POB (*0-689-71662-1*, Aladdin) Macmillan Child Grp.

—Plants: A Creative Hands-on Approach to Science. LC 92-24559. (Illus.). 48p. (gr. 2-5). 1993. pap. 12.95 POB (*0-689-71664-8*, Aladdin) Macmillan Child Grp.

—Sound: A Creative Hands-on Approach to Science. LC 92-30104. (Illus.). 48p. (gr. 2-5). 1993. pap. 12.95 POB (*0-689-71665-6*, Aladdin) Macmillan Child Grp.

Barber, Jacqueline. Bubble-ology. Bergman, Lincoln & Fairwell, Kay, eds. Baker, Lisa H., et al, illus. Barber, Jacqueline & Sneider, Cary I., photos by. 53p. (gr. 5-9). 1987. pap. 8.50 (*0-912511-11-7*) Lawrence Science.

Barr, George. Fascinating Science Experiments for Young People. LC 93-8111. (Illus.). 160p. (gr. 7-8). 1993. pap. text ed. 3.95t (*0-486-27670-8*) Dover.

Bell, J. L. Soap Science: A Science Book Bubbling with 36 Experiments. (gr. 4-7). 1993. pap. 9.57 (*0-201-62451-6*) Addison-Wesley.

Bingham, J. Science Experiments. (Illus.). 64p. (gr. 5 up). 1992. PLB 13.96 (*0-88110-515-5*, Usborne); pap. 7.95 (*0-7460-0806-6*, Usborne) EDC.

Bochinski, Julianne B. Complete Handbook of Science Fair Projects. 1991. pap. text ed. 12.95 (*0-471-52728-9*) Wiley.

Bonnet, Robert L. & Keen, G. Daniel. Botany: Forty-Nine More Science Fair Projects. (Illus.). 170p. (gr. 4-7). 1990. 16.95 (*0-8306-7416-0*, 3416); pap. 9.95 (*0-8306-3416-9*) TAB Bks.

—Space & Astronomy: Forty-Nine Science Fair Projects. 144p. 1991. 16.95 (*0-8306-3939-X*); pap. 9.95 (*0-8306-3938-1*) TAB Bks.

Bower, Miranda. Experiment with Weather. LC 92-41126. 1993. 17.50 (*0-8225-2458-9*) Lerner Pubns.

Broekel, Ray. Experiments with Air. LC 87-34146. (Illus.). 48p. (gr. k-4). 1988. PLB 12.85 (*0-516-01213-4*); pap. 4.95 (*0-516-41213-2*) Childrens.

—Experiments with Straws & Paper. LC 90-2173. (Illus.). 48p. (gr. k-4). 1990. PLB 12.85 (*0-516-01104-9*); pap. 4.95 (*0-516-41104-7*) Childrens.

—Experiments with Water. LC 87-34147. (Illus.). 48p. (gr. k-4). 1988. PLB 12.85 (*0-516-01215-0*); pap. 4.95 (*0-516-41215-9*) Childrens.

Brown, Bob. More Science for You: One Hundred Twelve Illustrated Experiments. (Illus.). 128p. (ps-8). 1988. 12.95 (*0-8306-9125-1*, 3125); pap. 7.95 (*0-8306-3125-9*, 3125) TAB Bks.

Brown, Sam E. Bubbles, Rainbows & Worms: Science Experiments for Pre-School Children. Stamper, Silas, illus. LC 80-84598. 105p. (ps-1). 1981. pap. 8.95 (*0-87659-100-4*) Gryphon Hse.

Byles, Monica. Experiment with Senses. LC 92-41110. 1993. 17.50 (*0-8225-2455-4*) Lerner Pubns.

—Experiments with Plants. Anderson, Nancy, illus. LC 92-43117. 1993. 17.50 (*0-8225-2456-2*) Lerner Pubns.

Cain, Nancy W. Animal Behavior Science Projects. Date not set. pap. text ed. 12.95 (*0-471-02636-0*) Wiley.

Carson, Mary S. The Scientific Kid: Projects, Experiments, Adventures. LC 88-45551. 80p. (Orig.). 1989. pap. 14.00 (*0-06-096316-6*, PL 6316, PL) HarpC.

Cash, Terry & Taylor, Barbara. One Hundred Seventy-Five More Science Experiments to Amuse & Amaze Your Friends. Kuo Kang Chen & Bull, Peter, illus. LC 90-39250. 176p. (Orig.). (gr. 4-7). 1991. pap. 12.00 (*0-679-80390-4*) Random Bks Yng Read.

Catherall, Ed. Exploring Plants. LC 91-40544. (Illus.). 48p. (gr. 4-8). 1992. PLB 22.80 (*0-8114-2601-7*) Raintree Steck-V.

CES Industries, Inc. Staff. Ed-Lab Eight Hundred Experiment Manual: Thermal Probe Sensor. (Illus., Orig.). (gr. 9-12). 1983. pap. write for info. (*0-86711-073-2*) CES Industries.

Challand, Helen. Activities in the Earth Sciences. LC 82-9444. (Illus.). (gr. 5 up). 1982. PLB 13.95 (*0-516-00506-5*) Childrens.

—Activities in the Life Sciences. LC 82-9442. (Illus.). (gr. 5 up). 1982. PLB 13.95 (*0-516-00507-3*) Childrens.

Challand, Helen J. Science Projects & Activities. Kimball, Linda H., illus. LC 84-23252. 93p. (gr. 5-8). 1985. PLB 13.95 (*0-516-00569-3*) Childrens.

Charman, Andrew. Energy. LC 92-6079. (Illus.). 32p. (gr. 5-8). 1993. PLB 12.40 (*0-531-14233-7*) Watts.

—Materials. LC 92-6078. (Illus.). 32p. (gr. 5-8). 1993. PLB 12.40 (*0-531-14232-9*) Watts.

Churchill, E. Richard. Amazing Science Experiments with Everyday Materials. Zweifel, Frances, illus. LC 90-20641. 128p. (gr. 4-12). 1992. 12.95 (*0-8069-7372-2*); pap. 4.95 (*0-8069-7371-4*) Sterling.

Cobb, Vicki. Bet You Can: Science Possibilities to Fool You. (Illus.). 112p. 1990. 12.95 (*0-688-09865-7*) Lothrop.

—More Science Experiments You Can Eat. Maestro, Giulio, illus. LC 78-12732. (gr. 5 up). 1979. 13.00 (*0-397-31828-6*, Lipp Jr Bks); PLB 14.89 (*0-397-31878-2*, Lipp Jr Bks) HarpC Child Bks.

—More Science Experiments You Can Eat. LC 78-12732. (Illus.). 128p. (gr. 5-8). 1984. pap. 4.95 (*0-06-446003-7*, Trophy) HarpC Child Bks.

—Science Experiments You Can Eat. LC 71-151474. (Illus.). 128p. (gr. 5-8). 1972. pap. 4.95 (*0-685-31398-0*, Trophy) HarpC Child Bks.

—Science Experiments You Can Eat. (ps-3). 1984. pap. 4.95 (*0-06-446002-9*, PL) HarpC.

—Science Experiments You Can Eat. rev. ed. Cain, David, illus. LC 93-13679. 160p. (gr. 5-9). 1994. 15.00 (*0-06-023534-9*); PLB 14.89 (*0-06-023551-9*) HarpC Child Bks.

Cobb, Vicki & Darling, Kathy. Bet You Can! Science Possibilities to Fool You. Ormai, Stella, illus. 112p. (gr. 3-7). 1983. pap. 3.50 (*0-380-82180-X*, Camelot) Avon.

—Bet You Can't! Science Impossibilities to Fool You. Weston, Martha, illus. LC 79-9254. 128p. (gr. 5 up). 1980. 13.00 (*0-688-41905-4*); PLB 12.93 (*0-688-51905-9*) Lothrop.

—Bet You Can't: Science Impossibilities to Fool You. Weston, Martha, illus. 128p. (gr. 3-7). 1983. pap. 3.50 (*0-380-54502-0*, Camelot) Avon.

Conaway, Judith. More Science Secrets. LC 86-16084. (Illus.). 48p. (gr. 1-5). 1987. PLB 11.89 (*0-8167-0866-5*); pap. text ed. 3.50 (*0-8167-0867-3*) Troll Assocs.

D'Amico, J. & Drummond, Karen E. The Science Chef: One Hundred Fun Food Experiments & Recipes for Kids. Cash-Walsh, Tina, illus. LC 94-9045. 1994. pap. text ed. 12.95 (*0-471-31045-X*) Wiley.

Darling, David. Between Fire & Ice: The Science of Heat. LC 91-40966. (Illus.). 60p. (gr. 5 up). 1992. text ed. 13.95 RSBE (*0-87518-501-0*, Dillon) Macmillan Child Grp.

—From Glasses to Gases: The Science of Matter. LC 91-38233. (Illus.). 60p. (gr. 5 up). 1992. text ed. 13.95 RSBE (*0-87518-500-2*, Dillon) Macmillan Child Grp.

Davies, Kay & Oldfield, Wendy. Sound & Music. LC 91-23475. (Illus.). 32p. (gr. 2-5). 1991. PLB 19.97 (*0-8114-3003-0*); pap. 4.95 (*0-8114-1534-1*) Raintree Steck-V.

Davis, Kay & Oldsfield, Wendy. Electricity & Magnetism. LC 91-30069. (Illus.). 32p. (gr. 2-5). 1991. PLB 19.97 (*0-8114-3004-9*); pap. 4.95 (*0-8114-1532-5*) Raintree Steck-V.

—Floating & Sinking. LC 91-25756. (Illus.). 32p. (gr. 2-5). 1991. PLB 19.97 (*0-8114-3001-4*); pap. 4.95 (*0-8114-1529-5*) Raintree Steck-V.

—Light. LC 91-30067. (Illus.). 32p. (gr. 2-5). 1991. PLB 19.97 (*0-8114-3006-5*); pap. 4.95 (*0-8114-1530-9*) Raintree Steck-V.

—Weather. LC 91-30066. (Illus.). 32p. (gr. 2-5). 1991. PLB 19.97 (*0-8114-3007-3*); pap. 4.95 (*0-8114-1535-X*) Raintree Steck-V.

DeBruin, Jerry. Creative, Hands-on Science Experiences. 256p. (gr. k-6). 1980. 15.95 (*0-916456-87-0*, GA 165) Good Apple.

—Science Fairs with Style. 336p. (gr. 5-12). 1991. 19.95 (*0-86653-606-X*, GA1325) Good Apple.

Devonshire, Hilary. Flight. LC 92-6077. (Illus.). 32p. (gr. 5-8). 1993. PLB 12.40 (*0-531-14234-5*) Watts.

—Light. LC 91-8401. (Illus.). 32p. (gr. 5-7). 1992. PLB 12.40 (*0-531-14126-8*) Watts.

—Movement. LC 92-7837. (Illus.). 32p. (gr. 5-8). 1993. PLB 12.40 (*0-531-14229-9*) Watts.

—Water. LC 91-8378. (Illus.). 32p. (gr. 5-7). 1992. PLB 12.40 (*0-531-14125-X*) Watts.

Diehn, Gwen & Krautwurst, Terry. Science Crafts for Kids: 50 Fantastic Things to Invent & Create. LC 93-39112. 144p. 1993. 19.95 (*0-8069-0283-3*, Pub. by Lark Bks) Sterling.

Durant, Penny R. Bubblemania. LC 93-38274. 96p. (gr. 3 up). 1994. pap. 3.99 (*0-380-77373-2*, Camelot) Avon.

Dwyer, Derek & Corby, Jill. More Fun with Science: Practice at Home. Lobban, John, illus. 24p. (Orig.). (gr. 3-5). 1992. pap. 2.95 wkbk. (*0-7214-3240-9*, S9115-3) Ladybird Bks.

Echols, Jean C. Buzzing a Hive. Bergman, Lincoln & Fairwell, Kay, eds. Baker, Lisa H., illus. Curtis, Elizabeth, et al, photos by. (Illus.). 97p. (Orig.). (gr. 1-3). 1987. pap. 12.50 (*0-912511-12-5*) Lawrence Science.

Edom, H. Science with Magnets. (Illus.). 24p. (gr. 1-4). 1991. PLB 12.96 (*0-88110-629-1*, Usborne); pap. 4.95 (*0-7460-1259-4*, Usborne) EDC.

Farndon, John. How the Earth Works: One Hundred Ways Parents & Kids Can Share the Secrets of the Earth. LC 91-45004. (Illus.). 192p. (gr. 3 up). 1992. 24.00 (*0-89577-411-9*, Dist. by Random) RD Assn.

Filson, Brent. Famous Experiments & How to Repeat Them. Fuhrmann, Brigita, illus. LC 85-22259. 64p. (gr. 4 up). 1986. lib. bdg. 12.98 (*0-671-55687-8*, J Messner) S&S Trade.

Flint, David. Weather & Climate: Projects with Geography. LC 91-6806. (Illus.). 32p. (gr. 5-8). 1991. PLB 12.40 (*0-531-17321-6*, Gloucester Pr) Watts.

Gardner, Robert. Electricity. LC 92-34075. (gr. 4 up). 1993. lib. bdg. 14.98 (*0-671-69039-6*, J Messner); pap. 9.95 (*0-671-69044-2*, J Messner) S&S Trade.

—Experimenting with Science in Sports. (Illus.). 128p. (gr. 7-12). 1993. PLB 13.40 (*0-531-12543-2*); pap. 6.95 (*0-531-15682-6*) Watts.

—Experimenting with Sound. LC 91-4012. (Illus.). 128p. (gr. 9-12). 1991. PLB 13.40 (*0-531-12503-3*) Watts.

—Experimenting with Water. LC 93-15586. (Illus.). 144p. (gr. 7-12). 1993. PLB 13.40 (*0-531-12549-1*) Watts.

—Ideas for Science Projects. LC 86-9238. (Illus.). 144p. (gr. 7-12). 1989. PLB 13.90 (*0-531-10246-7*); pap. 6.95 (*0-531-15125-5*) Watts.

—Robert Gardner's Challenging Science Experiments. LC 92-21116. (Illus.). 176p. (gr. 9-12). 1993. PLB 13.90 (*0-531-11090-7*); pap. 6.95 (*0-531-15671-0*) Watts.

—Science Around the House. (Illus.). 136p. (gr. 4-8). 1989. lib. bdg. 11.98 (*0-671-54663-5*, J Messner); pap. 4.95 (*0-671-68139-7*); 8.99s.p. (*0-685-47084-9*) S&S Trade.

—Science Projects about Chemistry. LC 94-959. (Illus.). 128p. (gr. 6 up). 1994. lib. bdg. 17.95 (*0-89490-531-7*) Enslow Pubs.

—Science Projects about Electricity & Magnets. LC 93-45252. (Illus.). 128p. (gr. 6 up). 1994. lib. bdg. 17.95 (*0-89490-530-9*) Enslow Pubs.

—Science Projects about Light. LC 93-23719. (Illus.). 128p. (gr. 6 up). 1994. lib. bdg. 17.95 (*0-89490-529-5*) Enslow Pubs.

—Science Projects about the Human Body. LC 92-43802. (Illus.). 104p. (gr. 6 up). 1993. lib. bdg. 17.95 (*0-89490-443-4*) Enslow Pubs.

Gardner, Robert & Kemer, Eric. Making & Using Scientific Models. LC 92-21124. (Illus.). 144p. (gr. 9-12). 1993. PLB 13.90 (*0-531-10986-0*); pap. 6.95 (*0-531-15662-1*) Watts.

—Science Projects about Temperature & Heat. (Illus.). 128p. (gr. 6 up). 1994. lib. bdg. 17.95 (*0-89490-534-1*) Enslow Pubs.

—Temperature & Heat. LC 92-32367. (gr. 3-7). 1993. lib. bdg. 14.98 (*0-671-69040-X*, J Messner); pap. 9.95 (*0-671-69045-0*, J Messner) S&S Trade.

Gardner, Robert & Webster, David. Science in Your Backyard. (Illus.). 136p. (gr. 4-8). 1987. lib. bdg. 11.98 (*0-671-55565-0*, J Messner); lib. bdg. 4.95 (*0-671-63835-1*); PLB 8.99s.p. (*0-685-47087-3*); pap. 3.71s.p. (*0-685-47088-1*) S&S Trade.

—Science Projects about Weather. LC 93-48720. (Illus.). 128p. (gr. 6 up). 1994. lib. bdg. 17.95 (*0-89490-533-3*) Enslow Pubs.

Ginns. Scientific American Activity Book. 128p. 1994. text ed. write for info. (*0-7167-6558-6*) W H Freeman.

Glover, David. Batteries, Bulbs & Wires. LC 92-40215. 32p. (gr. 1-4). 1993. 10.95 (*1-85697-837-0*, Kingfisher LKC); pap. 5.95 (*1-85697-933-4*) LKC.

—Flying & Floating. LC 92-40212. 32p. (gr. 1-4). 1993. 10.95 (*1-85697-843-5*, Kingfisher LKC); pap. 5.95 (*1-85697-937-7*) LKC.

—Solids & Liquids. LC 92-40214. 32p. (gr. 1-4). 1993. 10.95 (*1-85697-845-1*, Kingfisher LKC); pap. 5.95 (*1-85697-934-2*) LKC.

—Sound & Light. LC 92-40213. 32p. (gr. 1-4). 1993. 10.95 (*1-85697-839-7*, Kingfisher LKC); pap. 5.95 (*1-85697-935-0*) LKC.

Green, Carl R. & Sanford, William R. Exploring the Unknown Series, 6 bks. (Illus.). (gr. 4-10). Set. lib. bdg. 89.70 (*0-89490-475-2*) Enslow Pubs.

Gurley, Heather & Larson, Bob. Sunlight Works: Solar Science: Educational Activities. Word, Reagan, illus. 31p. (gr. 1-6). 1993. wkbk. 10.00 (*0-9634694-2-8*) Sun Light Wks.

Gutnik, Martin J. Experiments That Explore Acid Rain. LC 91-19958. (Illus.). 72p. (gr. 5-8). 1992. PLB 14.40 (*1-56294-115-1*) Millbrook Pr.

—Experiments That Explore the Greenhouse Effect. (Illus.). 72p. (gr. 5-8). 1991. PLB 14.40 (*1-56294-012-0*) Millbrook Pr.

Hall, Godfrey. Mind Twisters. Oxford Illustrators Staff, et al, illus. LC 91-27688. 96p. (Orig.). (gr. 3-7). 1992. pap. 10.00 (*0-679-82038-8*) Random Bks Yng Read.

Harker, Jillian. First Science: Practice at Home Science Activity. James, Claire, illus. 24p. (gr. k-2). 1992. pap. 2.95 wkbk. (*0-7214-3244-1*) Ladybird Bks.

—Fun with Science: Practice at Home. Sliwinska, Sara, illus. 24p. (Orig.). 1992. pap. 2.95 wkbk. (*0-7214-3239-5*, S9115-2) Ladybird Bks.

Harlow, Rosie & Morgan, Gareth. Cycles & Seasons. Peperell, Liz, illus. LC 91-2567. 40p. (gr. 5-8). 1991. PLB 12.90 (*0-531-19123-0*, Warwick) Watts.

—Energy & Growth. Kuo Kang Chen & Fitzsimmons, Cecilia, illus. 40p. (gr. 5-8). 1991. PLB 12.90 (*0-531-19124-9*, Warwick) Watts.

—Observing Minibeasts. Kuo Kang Chen, illus. 40p. (gr. 5-8). 1991. PLB 12.90 (*0-531-19125-7*, Warwick) Watts.

—Trees & Leaves. Peperell, Liz, illus. LC 91-7461. 40p. (gr. 5-8). 1991. PLB 12.90 (*0-531-19126-5*, Warwick) Watts.

Heddle, R. Science & Your Body. (Illus.). 24p. (gr. 1-4). 1993. PLB 12.96 (*0-88110-632-1*); pap. 4.95 (*0-7460-1425-2*) EDC.

Heddle, Rebecca & Shipton, Paul. Science Activities, Vol. III. (Illus.). 72p. (gr. k-5). 1993. pap. 9.95 (*0-7460-1427-9*, Usborne) EDC.

Herbert, Don. Mr. Wizard's Experiments for Young Scientists. 1990. pap. 10.95 (*0-385-26585-9*) Doubleday.

—Mr. Wizard's Supermarket Science. McKie, Roy, illus. LC 79-27217. 96p. (gr. 4-7). 1980. pap. 9.00 (*0-394-83800-9*) Random Bks Yng Read.

Hershey, David R. Plant Biology Science Projects. LC 94-12934. 1995. write for info. (*0-471-04983-2*) Wiley.

Hessler, Edward W. & Stubbs, Harriett. Acid Rain Science Projects. 20p. (Orig.). (gr. 5-12). 1987. pap. 9.95 (*0-935577-09-2*) Acid Rain Found.

Hewitt, Sally. Puff & Blow. LC 94-16910. (Illus.). 24p. (ps-3). 1994. PLB 14.40 (*0-516-07993-X*); pap. 4.95 (*0-516-47993-8*) Childrens.

—Squeak & Roar. LC 94-12309. (Illus.). 24p. (ps-3). 1994. PLB 14.40 (*0-516-07995-6*); pap. 4.95 (*0-516-47995-4*) Childrens.

Hickman, Pamela M. Habitats. English, Sarah J., illus. LC 93-12683. 1993. write for info. (*0-201-62651-9*); pap. 9.57 (*0-201-62618-7*) Addison-Wesley.

Hoffman, Jane. Backyard Scientist, Series Four. Ostroff, Lanny, illus. 54p. (ps-7). 1992. pap. text ed. 8.50 (*0-9618663-4-9*) Backyard Scientist.

—Backyard Scientist, Exploring Earthworms with Me: Simple & Fun Experiments to Do with Earthworms. Ostroff, Lanny, illus. 56p. (gr. k-6). 1994. pap. text ed. 8.95 (*0-9618663-5-7*) Backyard Scientist.
The Backyard Scientist Series, Hoffman, Jane. THE ORIGINAL BACKYARD SCIENTIST, $8.50, ISBN 0-9618663-1-4; BACKYARD SCIENTIST, SERIES ONE, $8.50, ISBN 0-9618663-0-6; BACKYARD SCIENTIST, SERIES TWO, $8.50, ISBN 0-9618663-2-2; BACKYARD SCIENTIST, SERIES THREE, $8.50, ISBN 0-9618663-3-0; BACKYARD SCIENTIST, SERIES FOUR, $8.50, ISBN 0-9618663-4-9; BACKYARD SCIENTIST, EXPLORING EARTHWORMS WITH ME, $8.95, ISBN 0-9618663-5-7. These sprightly illustrated books contain simple-to-perform, hands-on science experiments in chemistry, physics & solid sciences (except as noted below) for budding scientists 4 to 14 years old. Using commonly available materials (most are found in the average home), the experiments will allow the student to explore & understand complex scientific concepts. SERIES THREE's focus is on the life sciences. EXPLORING EARTHWORMS WITH ME allows the young scientist to learn the physiology & environmental needs of this beneficial animal. The books are excellent for use in the home & classroom. The author, Jane Hoffman, is a sought-after provider of teacher in-service workshops & workshop leader at educational conferences. Backyard Scientist, Inc., P.O. Box 16966, Irvine, CA 92713; 714-551-2392; FAX 714-552-5351.
Publisher Provided Annotation.

—Backyard Scientist: Series One. Ostroff, Lanny, illus. 52p. (Orig.). (gr. k-6). 1987. pap. text ed. 8.50 (*0-9618663-0-6*) Backyard Scientist.

—Backyard Scientist: Series Two. (Illus.). (gr. 4-9). 1989. pap. 8.50 (*0-9618663-2-2*) Backyard Scientist.

—Backyard Scientist, Series 3: Experiments in the Life Sciences. (Illus.). 52p. (gr. k-7). 1990. text ed. 8.50 (*0-9618663-3-0*) Backyard Scientist.

—The Original Backyard Scientist. Ostroff, Lanny, illus. 58p. (Orig.). (gr. k-6). 1987. text ed. 8.50 (*0-9618663-1-4*) Backyard Scientist.

Hurt, Roger. Exploring Science: Practice at Home Science Activity. Trotter, Stuart, illus. 24p. (Orig.). (gr. 2-5). 1992. pap. 2.95 wkbk. (*0-7214-3246-8*) Ladybird Bks.

Ingram, Jay. Real Live Science: Top Scientists Present Amazing Activities Any Kid Can Do. Ingram, Jay, illus. 48p. (gr. 4 up). 1992. text ed. 16.95 (*1-895688-00-0*, Pub. by Greey de Pencier CN); pap. 8.95 (*0-920775-87-X*, Pub. by Greey de Pencier CN) Firefly Bks Ltd.

Johnson, M., et al. Science Fun. (Illus.). 192p. (gr. 4 up). 1993. pap. 9.95 (*0-7460-0361-7*) EDC.

Junior Science Experiments on File. LC 93-33381. 1993. write for info. (*0-8160-2921-0*) Facts on File.

Kallen, Stuart A. Mad Science Experiments. LC 92-14776. 1992. 12.94 (*1-56239-128-3*) Abdo & Dghtrs.

Katz, Phyllis & Frekko, Janet. Great Science Fair Projects. (Illus.). 80p. (gr. 3-6). 1992. PLB 12.40 (*0-531-11015-X*) Watts.

—Great Science Fair Projects. (Illus.). 80p. (gr. 5-8). 1992. pap. 6.95 (*0-531-15628-1*) Watts.

Kelley, Colleen. Kids' Stuff: Simple Science & Nature Projects for Children. Kelley, Colleen, illus. 96p. (gr. k-6). 1989. pap. text ed. 4.95 (*0-9618052-2-6*) Daily Hampshire.

Kerrod, Robin. Sounds & Music. LC 90-25543. (Illus.). 32p. (gr. 3-8). 1991. PLB 9.95 (*1-85435-270-9*) Marshall Cavendish.

King, Virginia. Vibrating Things Make Sound. Mancini, Rob, illus. LC 93-114. 1994. pap. write for info. (*0-383-03724-7*) SRA Schl Grp.

Kneidel, Sally S. Creepy Crawlies & the Scientific Method: Over 100 Hands-on Science Experiments for Children. LC 92-53033. (Illus.). 224p. (Orig.). 1993. pap. 15.95 (*1-55591-118-8*) Fulcrum Pub.

Kramer, Alan. How to Make a Chemical Volcano & Other Mysterious Experiments. Harvey, Paul, illus. 112p. (gr. 5 up). 1991. pap. 6.95 (*0-531-15610-9*) Watts.

Krieger, Melanie J. How to Excel in Science Competitions. LC 91-17790. (Illus.). 144p. (gr. 9-12). 1991. PLB 13.90 (*0-531-11004-4*) Watts.

Ladizinsky, Eric. More Magical Science: Magic Tricks for Young Scientists. Burke, Dianne O., illus. 64p. (gr. 3-7). 1994. pap. 4.95 (*1-56565-110-3*) Lowell Hse.

Levine, Shar & Grafton, Allison. Projects for a Healthy Planet: Simple Environmental Experiments for Kids. 1992. pap. text ed. 10.95 (*0-471-55484-7*) Wiley.

Lewis, James. Hocus Pocus Stir & Cook, The Kitchen Science Magic Book. LC 91-30403. (Illus.). 79p. 1991. pap. 7.00 (*0-88166-183-X*) Meadowbrook.

Lynn, Sara & James, Diane. Rain & Shine. Wright, Joe, illus. LC 93-36420. 32p. (gr. k-2). 1994. 14.95 (*1-56847-142-4*) Thomson Lrning.

McCarthy, Donald. More Fun with Science Magic. LC 91-75095. (Illus.). 80p. (Orig.). 1991. pap. 6.33 (*0-914127-12-8*) Univ Class.

McCarthy, Donald W. Fun with Science Magic. Cooper, William H., ed. LC 84-50893. (Illus.) 80p. (gr. 4-9). 1984. pap. 5.27 (*0-914127-15-2*) Univ Class.

McGowan, Christopher. Discover Dinosaurs: Become a Dinosaur Detective. Holdcroft, Tina, illus. LC 92-42627. 96p. (gr. 4-7). 1993. pap. 9.57 (*0-201-62267-X*) Addison-Wesley.

McGregor, Diana, et al. Fizzle, Bubble, Pop & WOW! Simple Science Experiments for Young Children. 63p. (ps-4). 1992. pap. 12.00 (*0-9638539-0-2*) Exper First Pr.

Mandell, Muriel. Simple Science Experiments with Everyday Materials. Zweifel, Frances W., illus. LC 88-31201. 128p. (gr. 4-10). 1989. 12.95 (*0-8069-6794-3*) Sterling.

—Simple Science Experiments with Everyday Materials. LC 88-31201. (Illus.). 128p. (gr. 4-10). 1990. pap. 4.95 (*0-8069-5764-6*) Sterling.

—Simple Weather Experiments with Everyday Materials. LC 90-37915. (Illus.). 128p. (gr. 4-10). 1990. 12.95 (*0-8069-7296-3*) Sterling.

—Two Hundred & Twenty Easy-to-Do Science Experiments for Young People: Three Complete Books. 287p. (gr. 3 up). 1985. pap. 10.50 (*0-486-24874-7*) Dover.

Markle, Sandra. Earth Alive! (Illus.). 48p. (gr. 4-7). 1991. 14.95 (*0-688-09360-4*); PLB 14.88 (*0-688-09361-2*) Lothrop.

—Exploring Summer: A Season of Science Activities, Puzzlers, & Games. Markle, Sandra, illus. LC 86-17322. 176p. (gr. 3-7). 1987. SBE 14.95 (*0-689-31212-1*, Atheneum Child Bk) Macmillan Child Grp.

—Measuring Up: Experiments, Puzzles & Games Exploring Measurement. LC 94-19240. 1995. 16.00 (*0-689-31904-5*, Atheneum) Macmillan.

—Power Up: Experiments, Puzzles & Games Exploring Electricity. LC 88-7772. (Illus.). 48p. (gr. 3-7). 1989. SBE 14.95 (*0-689-31442-6*, Atheneum Child Bk) Macmillan Child Grp.

—Science to the Rescue. LC 92-41096. (Illus.). 48p. (gr. 3-7). 1994. SBE 15.95 (*0-689-31783-2*, Atheneum Child Bk) Macmillan Child Grp.

—The Young Scientist's Guide to Successful Science Projects. Byrd, Bob, photos by. LC 89-45290. (Illus.). 128p. (gr. 3-7). lib. bdg. 12.93 (*0-688-07217-8*) Lothrop.

Melton, Lisa & Ladizinsky, Eric. Fifty Nifty Science Experiments. Yamamoto, Neal, illus. 64p. (ps-3). 1992. pap. 3.95 (*0-929923-92-8*) Lowell Hse.

Mind & Perception: The Marshall Cavendish Guide to Projects & Experiments, 6 vols. (Illus.). (gr. 4-9). 1990. Set. PLB 89.95 (*1-85435-307-1*) Marshall Cavendish.

Molleson, Diane. Easy Science Experiments. (ps-3). 1993. pap. 3.95 (*0-590-45304-1*) Scholastic Inc.

Morris, Neil. What Is My Shadow Made Of? Questions Kids Ask about Everyday Science. Brown, Mik, illus. LC 94-14120. 1994. write for info. (*0-89577-609-X*, Readers Digest Kids) RD Assn.

Morris, Ting & Morris, Neil. Growing Things. (Illus.). 32p. (gr. 2-4). 1994. PLB 12.40 (*0-531-14284-1*) Watts.

Munson, Howard R. Science Activities with Simple Things. (gr. 4-8). 1972. pap. 7.95 (*0-8224-6320-2*) Fearon Teach Aids.

Murphy, Bryan. Experiment with Air. 32p. (gr. 2-5). 1991. PLB 17.50 (*0-8225-2452-X*) Lerner Pubns.

—Experiment with Movement. 32p. (gr. 2-5). 1991. PLB 17.50 (*0-8225-2451-1*) Lerner Pubns.

—Experiment with Water. 32p. (gr. 2-5). 1991. PLB 17.50 (*0-8225-2453-8*) Lerner Pubns.

Murray, Peter. Professor Solomon Snickerdoodle Looks at Water. Mitchell, Anastasia, illus. LC 93-1322. (gr. 2-6). 1995. 14.95 (*1-56766-081-9*) Childs World.

—Silly Science Tricks. LC 92-18903. (gr. 2-6). 1992. PLB 14.95 (*0-89565-976-X*) Childs World.

Newton, David E. Science - Technology - Society Projects for Young Scientists. LC 91-17825. (Illus.). 144p. (gr. 9-12). 1991. PLB 13.90 (*0-531-11047-8*) Watts.

Nye, Bill. Bill Nye the Science Guy's Big Blast of Science. (Illus.). 176p. 1993. pap. 12.45 (*0-201-60864-2*) Addison-Wesley.

Olsav Lautenschlaeger, Susan J. Blooming Discoveries: Fun Language Activities to Explore Everyday Wonders Based on Bloom's Taxonomy. 80p. (gr. k-5). 1991. pap. 15.95 (*1-55999-206-9*) LinguiSystems.

O'Neil, Karen E. Health & Medicine Projects for Young Scientists. LC 92-42745. (Illus.). 128p. (gr. 8-9). 1993. PLB 13.90 (*0-531-11050-8*); pap. 6.95 (*0-531-15668-0*) Watts.

Ontario Science Center Staff. Scienceworks: Sixty-Five Experiments That Introduce the Fun & Wonder of Science. Holdcroft, Tina, illus. (gr. 2-7). 1986. pap. 9.57 (*0-201-16780-8*) Addison-Wesley.

Parker, Steve. Nerves to Senses: Projects with Biology. LC 91-8737. (Illus.). 32p. (gr. 5-8). 1991. PLB 12.40 (*0-531-17295-3*, Gloucester Pr) Watts.

Penrose, Gordon. Dr. Zed's Science Surprises. 1990. pap. 6.95 (*0-671-70541-5*) PB.

—Magic Mud & Other Great Experiments. Holdcroft, Tina, illus. 48p. 1994. pap. 9.95 (*0-920775-18-7*, Pub. by Greey dePencier CN) Firefly Bks Ltd.

—More Science Surprises from Dr. Zed. LC 91-38935. (Illus.). 32p. (gr. k-3). 1992. pap. 12.00 (*0-671-77810-2*, S&S BFYR); pap. 6.00 (*0-671-77811-0*, S&S BFYR) S&S Trade.

—Sensational Science Activities with Dr. Zed. LC 90-9724. (Illus.). 48p. (gr. 3-7). 1990. (S&S BFYR); pap. 5.95 (*0-671-72553-X*, S&S BFYR) S&S Trade.

Pressling, Robert. My Magnet. Pragoff, Fiona, photos by. LC 94-7110. (Illus.). 32p. (gr. 1 up). 1994. PLB 17.27 (*0-8368-1117-8*) Gareth Stevens Inc.

Prochnow, Dave & Prochnow, Kathy. How? More Experiments for the Young Scientist. (Illus.). 160p. 1992. 16.95 (*0-8306-4024-X*, 4177); pap. 9.95 (*0-8306-4025-8*, 4177) TAB Bks.

—Why? Experiments for the Young Scientist. (Illus.). 160p. (gr. 4-7). 1992. 16.95 (*0-8306-4015-0*, 4176); pap. 9.95 (*0-8306-4023-1*, 4176) TAB Bks.

Rainis, Kenneth G. Exploring with a Magnifying Glass. LC 91-18329. (Illus.). 144p. (gr. 9-12). 1991. PLB 13.90 (*0-531-12508-4*) Watts.

Reuben, Gabriel. Electricity Experiments for Children. (Illus.). 88p. (gr. 5-9). pap. 2.95 (*0-486-22030-3*) Dover.

Richards, Roy. One Hundred-One Science Tricks: Fun Experiments with Everyday Materials. LC 91-13263. (Illus.). 104p. (gr. 3-10). 1991. 14.95 (*0-8069-8388-4*) Sterling.

Robson, Pam. Clocks, Scales & Measurements. (Illus.). 32p. (gr. 5-7). 1993. PLB 12.40 (*0-531-17419-0*, Gloucester Pr) Watts.

—Electricity. LC 92-37099. (Illus.). 32p. (gr. 5-8). 1993. PLB 12.40 (*0-531-17398-4*, Gloucester Pr) Watts.

—Magnetism. LC 92-37098. (Illus.). 32p. (gr. 5-8). 1993. PLB 12.40 (*0-531-17399-2*, Gloucester Pr) Watts.

—Water, Paddles, & Boats. LC 92-375. 1992. 12.40 (*0-531-17376-3*, Gloucester Pr) Watts.

Rodecker, Stephen B. & Quon-Warner, Maryanna. Las Ciencias Fisicas: Metodos, Investigaciones, Retos y Actividades - M.I.R.A. Appel, Sergio, tr. 342p. (gr. 7 up). 1993. lab manual 39.95 (*0-9638008-1-7*) Spectrum CA.

—Laboratory Experiments & Activities in Physical Science: L.E.A.P.S. 342p. (gr. 7 up). 1993. lab manual 39.95 (*0-9638008-0-9*) Spectrum CA.

Rowe, Julian & Perham, Molly. Amazing Magnets. LC 94-16942. (Illus.). 32p. (gr. 1-4). 1994. PLB 18.60 (*0-516-08137-3*); pap. 4.95 (*0-516-48137-1*) Childrens.

—Build It Strong! LC 94-16941. (Illus.). 32p. (gr. 1-4). 1994. PLB 18.60 (*0-516-08138-1*); pap. 4.95 (*0-516-48138-X*) Childrens.

—Colorful Light. LC 93-8217. (Illus.). 32p. (gr. 1-4). 1993. PLB 13.95 (*0-516-08131-4*) Childrens.

—Make It Move! LC 93-13737. (Illus.). 32p. (gr. 1-4). 1993. PLB 13.95 (*0-516-08135-7*) Childrens.

—Making Sounds. LC 92-13738. (Illus.). 32p. (gr. 1-4). 1993. PLB 13.95 (*0-516-08136-5*) Childrens.

—Using Energy. LC 94-13911. (Illus.). 32p. (gr. 1-4). 1994. PLB 18.60 (*0-516-08140-3*); pap. 4.95 (*0-516-48140-1*) Childrens.

—Watch It Grow! LC 94-12258. (Illus.). 32p. (gr. 1-4). 1994. PLB 18.60 (*0-516-08141-1*); pap. 4.95 (*0-516-48141-X*) Childrens.

Rowe, Julina & Perham, Molly. Keep it Afloat! LC 93-8213. (Illus.). 32p. (gr. 1-4). 1993. PLB 13.95 (*0-516-08134-9*) Childrens.

Rybolt, Thomas R. & Mebane, Robert C. Environmental Experiments about Air. LC 92-26297. (Illus.). 96p. (gr. 4-9). 1993. lib. bdg. 16.95 (*0-89490-409-4*) Enslow Pubs.

—Environmental Experiments about Energy. LC 93-48543. (Illus.). 96p. (gr. 4-9). 1994. lib. bdg. 16.95 (*0-89490-579-1*) Enslow Pubs.

—Environmental Experiments about Land. LC 93-15581. (Illus.). 96p. (gr. 4-9). 1993. lib. bdg. 16.95 (*0-89490-411-6*) Enslow Pubs.

—Environmental Experiments about Life. LC 93-15582. (Illus.). 96p. (gr. 4-9). 1993. lib. bdg. 16.95 (*0-89490-412-4*) Enslow Pubs.

—Environmental Experiments about Water. LC 92-41235. (Illus.). 96p. (gr. 4-9). 1993. lib. bdg. 16.95 (*0-89490-410-8*) Enslow Pubs.

—Science Experiments for Young People Series, 5 bks. (Illus.). (gr. 4-9). Set. lib. bdg. 84.75 (*0-89490-448-5*) Enslow Pubs.

Savan, Beth. Earthwatch: Earthcycles & Ecosystems. Cupples, Pat, illus. 96p. 1992. pap. 9.57 (*0-201-58148-5*) Addison-Wesley.

Science Crafts for Kids Book & Kit. 1994. 40.00 (*0-8069-0900-5*, Pub. by Lark Bks) Sterling.

Searle-Barnes, Bonita. Air. (Illus.). 32p. (gr. k-3). 1993. 6.99 (*0-7459-2694-0*) Lion USA.

—Light. (Illus.). 32p. (gr. k-3). 1993. 6.99 (*0-7459-2695-9*) Lion USA.

—Sound. (Illus.). 32p. (gr. k-3). 1993. 6.99 (*0-7459-2692-4*) Lion USA.

—Water. (Illus.). 32p. (gr. k-3). 1993. 6.99 (*0-7459-2693-2*) Lion USA.

—The Wonder of God's World: Air. Smithson, Colin, illus. LC 92-44575. 1993. 6.99 (*0-7459-2021-7*) Lion USA.

—The Wonder of God's World: Light. Smithson, Colin, illus. LC 92-44275. 1993. 6.99 (*0-7459-2022-5*) Lion USA.

—The Wonder of God's World: Water. Smithson, Colin, illus. LC 92-44274. 1993. 6.99 (*0-7459-2024-1*) Lion USA.

Seller, Mick. Air, Wind, & Flight. LC 92-374. 1992. 12.40 (*0-531-17375-5*, Gloucester Pr) Watts.

—Wheels, Pulleys & Levers. (Illus.). 32p. (gr. 5-7). 1993. PLB 12.40 (*0-531-17420-4*, Gloucester Pr) Watts.

Shipton, P. Science with Batteries. (Illus.). 24p. (gr. 1-4). 1993. PLB 12.96 (*0-88110-633-X*); pap. 4.95 (*0-7460-1423-6*) EDC.

Shubkagel, Judy F. Show Me How to Write an Experimental Science Fair Paper: A Fill-in-the-Blank Handbook. 44p. (gr. 4-8). 1993. wkbk. 9.95 (*1-883484-00-6*) Show Me How.
It is the "Writing of the Experimental Science Fair Paper that Drives Everybody Nuts!" This book was written by a science teacher to help 4th through 8th grade students, their parents & teachers know exactly what is expected on each page of the science fair paper. Included in this book is a complete science fair paper on a paper airplane project from the title page to the bibliography. Each section includes "a" & "b" pages. The "a" pages have three sections: the SAMPLE project, a REMINDER section, & an EXPLANATION of how to write each page. The REMINDER section includes helpful hints such as "You will need two copies of this page, one for the backboard & one for the notebook." The SAMPLE & EXPLANATION pages also emphasize & identify independent, dependent & constant variables. These variables are identified throughout the book with single, double, or dashed lines. Opposite the "a" pages are the "b" reproducible fill in the blank pages. Also included are sections on Variables, Selecting Topics, Using a Timeline, Backboard & Display & alternative charts & graphs. This book is very precise & complete... A MUST HAVE FOR FIRST TIME EXPERIMENTERS! Show Me How Publications. 15606 E. 44th St., Independence, MO 64055. Shubkagel (816) 373-7819.
Publisher Provided Annotation.

Silvani, Harold. Kitchen, Garage & Garbage Can Science, Bks. A-C. Garcia, Joe, illus. 35p. (gr. 1-8). 1992. Bk. A. wkbk. 6.95 (*1-878669-47-8*) Bk. B. wkbk. 6.95 (*1-878669-45-1*); Bk. C. wkbk. 6.95 (*1-878669-46-X*) Crea Tea Assocs.

Simple Science Projects, 8 vols. (Illus.). 256p. (gr. 2-4). 1992. Set. PLB 138.16 (*0-8368-0773-1*) Gareth Stevens Inc.

Smith, Norman F. How to Do Successful Science Projects. rev. ed. Steltenpohl, Jane, ed. (Illus.). 128p. (gr. 6-9). 1990. lib. bdg. 11.98 (*0-671-70685-3*, J Messner); pap. 5.95 (*0-671-70686-1*) S&S Trade.

Sneider, Cary I. Oobleck: What Do Scientists Do? rev. ed. Bergman, Lincoln & Fairwell, Kay, eds. Baker, Lisa H. & Peterson, Adria, illus. Sneider, Cary I., photos by. 28p. (gr. 4-8). 1988. pap. 8.50 (*0-912511-64-8*) Lawrence Science.

Sneider, Cary I. & Gould, Alan. The Wizard's Lab. Bergman, Lincoln & Fairwell, Kay, eds. Bevilacqua, Carol & Klofkorn, Lisa, illus. Hoyt, Richard, photos by. 72p. 1989. pap. 20.00 (*0-912511-71-0*) Lawrence Science.

Spurgeon, R. Energy & Power. (Illus.). 48p. 1990. PLB 13.96 (*0-88110-418-3*); pap. 7.95 (*0-7460-0422-2*) EDC.

Stacy, Dennis. Nifty (& Thrifty) Science Activities. (gr. 2-6). 1988. pap. 6.95 (*0-8224-4777-0*) Fearon Teach Aids.

Stangl, Jean. The Tools of Science: Ideas & Activities for Guiding Young Scientists. rev. ed. (Illus.). 160p. 1989. 16.95 (*0-8306-9216-9*); pap. 8.95 (*0-8306-3216-6*) TAB Bks.

Stine, Megan, et al. Hands-On Science: Color & Light. Taback, Simms, illus. LC 92-56889. 1993. PLB 18.60 (*0-8368-0954-8*) Gareth Stevens Inc.

—Hands-On Science: Food & the Kitchen. Taback, Simms, illus. LC 92-56890. 1993. PLB 18.60 (*0-8368-0955-6*) Gareth Stevens Inc.

—Hands-On Science: Fun Machines. Taback, Simms, illus. LC 92-56891. 1993. PLB 18.60 (*0-8368-0956-4*) Gareth Stevens Inc.

—Hands-On Science: Games, Puzzles, & Toys. Taback, Simms, illus. LC 92-56892. 1993. PLB 18.60 (*0-8368-0957-2*) Gareth Stevens Inc.

—Hands-On Science: Mystery & Magic. Taback, Simms, illus. LC 92-56893. 1993. PLB 18.60 (*0-8368-0958-0*) Gareth Stevens Inc.

—Hands-On Science: Things That Grow. Taback, Simms, illus. LC 92-56894. 1993. PLB 18.60 (*0-8368-0959-9*) Gareth Stevens Inc.

—More Science Activities. Solimini, Cheryl, ed. (Illus.). 100p. (gr. 2-6). 1988. pap. text ed. 8.95 (*0-939456-16-8*) Galison.

—Still More Science Activities. 3rd ed. Taback, Simms, illus. Falk, John, intro. by. (Illus.). 100p. (gr. 2-6). 1989. pap. text ed. 8.95 (*0-929648-01-3*) Galison.

Stone, George K. Science Projects You Can Do. Peck, Stephen R., illus. 101p. (gr. 7-9). 1973. (Pub. by Treehouse) P-H.

Stover, Susan G. & Macdonald, R. Heather. On the Rocks: Earth Science Activities. (Illus.). 204p. (gr. 1-8). 1993. pap. text ed. 9.00 (*1-56576-005-0*) SEPM.

Sundquist, Nancy & Brin, Susannah. Fifty Science Experiments I Can Do. (Illus.). 48p. (Orig.). (gr. 1-5). 1988. pap. 2.95 (*0-8431-1867-9*) Price Stern.

Suzuki, David. Looking at Insects. (Illus.). 96p. 1992. text ed. 22.95 (*0-471-54747-6*); pap. text ed. 9.95 (*0-471-54050-1*) Wiley.

—Looking at Plants. (Illus.). 96p. 1992. text ed. 22.95 (*0-471-54748-4*); pap. text ed. 9.95 (*0-471-54049-8*) Wiley.

Tant, Carl. Science Fair Spelled W-I-N. Crask, Tammy & Setzer, Debra, illus. 112p. (Orig.). (gr. 7-12). 1992. pap. 14.95 (*1-880319-02-0*) Biotech.

Taylor, Barbara. Air & Flight. (Illus.). 40p. (gr. k-4). 1991. PLB 12.90 (*0-531-19129-X*, Warwick) Watts.

—Batteries & Magnets. LC 91-2558. (Illus.). 40p. (gr. k-4). 1991. PLB 12.90 (*0-531-19130-3*, Warwick) Watts.

—Color & Light. LC 91-9571. (Illus.). 40p. (gr. k-4). 1991. PLB 12.90 (*0-531-19127-3*, Warwick) Watts.

—Green Thumbs Up! The Science of Growing Plants. Bull, Peter, et al, illus. LC 91-4290. 40p. (Orig.). (gr. 2-5). 1992. pap. 4.95 (*0-679-82042-6*) Random Bks Yng Read.

—Growing Plants. LC 91-2568. (Illus.). 40p. (gr. k-4). 1991. PLB 12.90 (*0-531-19128-1*, Warwick) Watts.

—I Wonder Why Soap Makes Bubbles & Other Questions about Science. LC 94-2313. 32p. (gr. k-3). 1994. 8.95 (*1-85697-995-4*, Kingfisher LKC) LKC.

—More Power to You! The Science of Batteries & Magnets. Bull, Peter, et al, illus. LC 91-4293. 40p. (Orig.). (gr. 2-5). 1992. pap. 4.95 (*0-679-82040-X*) Random Bks Yng Read.

—Over the Rainbow! The Science of Color & Light. Bull, Peter, et al, illus. LC 91-4291. 40p. (Orig.). (gr. 2-5). 1992. pap. 4.95 (*0-679-82041-8*) Random Bks Yng Read.

—Sound & Music. LC 91-8740. (Illus.). 32p. (gr. 5-8). 1991. PLB 12.40 (*0-531-14185-3*) Watts.

—Up, Up & Away! The Science of Flight. Bull, Peter, et al, illus. LC 91-4292. 40p. (Orig.). (gr. 2-5). 1992. pap. 4.95 (*0-679-82039-6*) Random Bks Yng Read.

Taylor, Ron. Projects. (Illus.). 64p. (gr. 4-7). 1985. 15.95x (*0-8160-1076-5*) Facts on File.

Thomas, David A. Math Projects for Young Scientists. LC 87-21064. (Illus.). 128p. (gr. 7-12). 1988. PLB 13.90 (*0-531-10523-7*) Watts.

Time-Life Inc. Editors. Simple Experiments. Kinney, Karin, ed. (Illus.). 88p. (gr. k-3). 1994. write for info. (*0-8094-9470-1*); PLB write for info. (*0-8094-9471-X*) Time-Life.

Tocci, Salvatore. How to Do a Science Fair Project. (Illus.). 128p. (gr. 7-12). 1989. PLB 13.90 (*0-531-10245-9*); pap. 6.95 (*0-531-15123-9*) Watts.

Twist, Clint. Jungles & Forests: Projects with Geography. LC 92-33916. 1993. 12.40 (*0-531-17397-6*, Gloucester Pr) Watts.

—Reproduction to Birth: Projects with Biology. LC 91-6818. (Illus.). 32p. (gr. 5-8). 1991. PLB 12.40 (*0-531-17294-5*, Gloucester Pr) Watts.

UNESCO Staff. Seven Hundred Science Experiments for Everyone. rev. ed. LC 64-10638. (Illus.). 252p. (gr. 5-9). 1964. pap. 16.95 (*0-385-05275-8*) Doubleday.

VanCleave, Janice. A-Plus Projects in Biology: Winning Science Fair Ideas. 240p. 1993. text ed. 22.95 (*0-471-58629-3*); pap. text ed. 12.95 (*0-471-58628-5*) Wiley.

—A-Plus Projects in Chemistry: Winning Science Fair Ideas. 240p. (gr. 7 up). 1993. text ed. 22.95 (*0-471-58631-5*); pap. text ed. 12.95 (*0-471-58630-7*) Wiley.

—Janice VanCleave's Earthquakes. 88p. (Orig.). 1993. pap. text ed. 9.95 (*0-471-57107-5*) Wiley.

—Janice VanCleave's Electricity: Mind-Boggling Experiments You Can Turn into Science Fair Projects. LC 93-40913. 1994. pap. text ed. 9.95 (*0-471-31010-7*) Wiley.

—Janice VanCleave's Machines. 87p. (Orig.). (gr. 4 up). 1993. pap. text ed. 9.95 (*0-471-57108-3*) Wiley.

—Janice VanCleave's Magnets. 87p. (Orig.). 1993. pap. text ed. 9.95 (*0-471-57106-7*) Wiley.

—Janice VanCleave's Microscopes & Magnifying Lenses: Mind-Boggling Chemistry & Biology Experiments You Can Turn into Science Fair Projects. 112p. (gr. 3 up). 1993. pap. text ed. 9.95 (*0-471-58956-X*) Wiley.

—Janice VanCleave's Two Hundred Gooey, Slippery, Slimy, Weird, & Fun Experiments. (Illus.). 128p. (gr. 3-7). 1992. pap. text ed. 12.95 (*0-471-57921-1*) Wiley.

—Janice VanCleave's Volcanoes: Mind-Boggling Experiments You Can Turn into Science Fair Projects. (Orig.). 1994. pap. text ed. 9.95 (*0-471-30811-0*) Wiley.
New in The Spectacular Science Projects series: Mount Vesuvius. Mauna Loa. Mount St. Helens. Your kitchen. All of these locations may have one thing in common. An active volcano. From what we hear, smoke & lava are spewing from erupting volcanoes in homes & schools everywhere! Now Janice VanCleave offers practical tips for this classic experiment along with lots of other volcanic phenomena. Activities

transport children to the edge of a volcanic crater to explore & learn exactly how & why volcanoes occur. Their discoveries will be the launch pad for the best science fair projects ever! 20 easy-to-do activities, plus dozens of tips & tricks for developing original science fair projects. Kids can make the classic erupting volcano, create their own molten lava rock, or build their own spud launcher. Explains where most volcanoes are found, how scientists predict volcanic eruptions, & how liquid rock moves through the earth.
Publisher Provided Annotation.

—Janice VanCleave's Weather: Mind-Boggling Experiments You Can Turn into Science Fair Projects. LC 94-25646. 1995. write for info. (*0-471-03231-X*) Wiley.

—Two Hundred One Awesome, Magical, Bizarre, & Incredible Experiments. LC 93-29807. 1994. pap. text ed. 12.95 (*0-471-31011-5*) Wiley.
Unlocking the secrets of the universe...& having a blast! Why does a cat have a rough tongue? Why is the sky blue? Why does a person snore? How does a submarine rise & submerge? Following on the heels of the best-selling, 200 GOOEY, SLIPPERY, SLIMY, WEIRD, & FUN EXPERIMENTS, everyone's favorite science teacher is back with more fantastic ways for children to discover the science in the world around them through fun & easy experiments in biology, chemistry, physics, earth science, & astronomy. With plenty of complete experiments to choose from, kids can find just the right project for their science fair, discover which science subjects most capture their interests, or just have fun messing around. 201 wacky experiments in five different science areas. Simple step-by-step instructions. Easy-to-find materials from around the house. Greatest hits from previous books plus 40 all-new experiments.
Publisher Provided Annotation.

Vancleave, Janice P. Janice Vancleave's Astronomy for Every Kid: 101 Easy Experiments That Really Work. 1991. text ed. 24.95 (*0-471-54285-7*); pap. text ed. 10. 95 (*0-471-53573-7*) Wiley.

—Janice VanCleave's Human Body Book for Every Kid: Easy Activities that Make Learning Science Fun. LC 94-20862. (gr. k up). 1995. write for info. (*0-471-02413-9*); pap. write for info. (*0-471-02408-2*) Wiley.

—Physics for Every Kid: One Hundred One Easy Experiments in Motion, Heat, Light, Machines & Sound. 1991. pap. text ed. 10.95 (*0-471-52505-7*) Wiley.

Vecchione, Glen. One Hundred Amazing Make-It-Yourself Science Fair Projects. LC 93-41681. (Illus.). 224p. 1994. 17.95 (*0-8069-0366-X*) Sterling.

Vessel, M. F. & Wong, H. H. Science Bulletin Boards. (gr. 1-8). 1962. pap. 6.95 (*0-8224-6290-7*) Fearon Teach Aids.

Vowles, A. Amazing Experiments. (Illus.). 32p. (gr. 2-6). 1985. pap. 5.95 (*0-88625-073-0*) Durkin Hayes Pub.

Walpole, Brenda. One Hundred Seventy-Five Science Experiments to Amuse & Amaze Your Friends. Kuo Kang Chen & Bull, Peter, illus. LC 88-4526. 176p. (Orig.). (gr. 4-7). 1988. pap. 12.00 (*0-394-89991-1*) Random Bks Yng Read.

Webster, Vera. Experimentos Cientificos (Science Experiments) Kratky, Lada, tr. LC 85-31403. (SPA., Illus.). 48p. (gr. k-4). 1986. PLB 12.85 (*0-516-31646-X*); pap. 4.95 (*0-516-51646-9*) Childrens.

—Science Experiments. LC 82-4429. 48p. (gr. k-4). 1982. PLB 12.85 (*0-516-01646-6*); pap. 4.95 (*0-516-41646-4*) Childrens.

Wellnitz, William R. Be a Kid Physicist. LC 92-40506. 1993. 17.95 (*0-8306-4091-6*); pap. 9.95 (*0-8306-4092-4*) TAB Bks.

—Homemade Slime & Rubber Bones! Awesome Science Experiments. LC 92-41238. (gr. 3 up). 1993. 17.95 (*0-8306-4093-2*); pap. 9.95 (*0-8306-4094-0*) TAB Bks.

—Science Magic for Kids: Simple & Safe Experiments. (Illus.). 128p. 1990. 17.95 (*0-8306-8423-9*, 3423); pap. 9.95 (*0-8306-3423-1*) TAB Bks.

Whalley, Margaret. Experiment with Magnets & Electricity. LC 92-41109. 1993. 17.50 (*0-8225-2457-0*) Lerner Pubns.

White, Laurence B., Jr. Science Toys & Tricks. Brown, Marc T., illus. LC 85-43036. 96p. (gr. 1-4). 1985. pap. 6.95 (*0-06-446014-2*, Trophy) HarpC Child Bks.

White, Laurence B., Jr. & Broekel, Ray. Shazam! Simple Science Magic. Mathews, Judith, ed. Seltzer, Meyer, illus. LC 90-42441. 48p. (gr. 3-7). 1991. 11.95 (*0-8075-7332-9*) A Whitman.

Wiebe, Ann. Soap Films & Bubbles. (gr. 4-9). 1990. pap. text ed. 14.95 (*1-881431-25-8*) AIMS Educ Fnd.

Wiese, Jim. Roller Coaster Science: 50 Wet, Wacky, Wild, Dizzy Experiments about Things Kids Like Best. 1994. pap. text ed. 12.95 (*0-471-59404-0*) Wiley.

Wilkes, Angela. My First Science Book. (Illus.). 48p. (gr. 1-5). 1990. 13.00 (*0-679-80583-4*); PLB 13.99 (*0-679-90583-9*) Knopf Bks Yng Read.

Williams, John. Simple Science Projects with Air. LC 91-50543. (Illus.). 32p. (gr. 2-4). 1992. PLB 17.27 (*0-8368-0765-0*) Gareth Stevens Inc.

—Simple Science Projects with Color & Light. LC 91-50544. (Illus.). 32p. (gr. 2-4). 1992. PLB 17.27 (*0-8368-0766-9*) Gareth Stevens Inc.

—Simple Science Projects with Electricity. LC 91-50545. (Illus.). 32p. (gr. 2-4). 1992. PLB 17.27 (*0-8368-0767-7*) Gareth Stevens Inc.

—Simple Science Projects with Flight. LC 91-50546. (Illus.). 32p. (gr. 2-4). 1992. PLB 17.27 (*0-8368-0768-5*) Gareth Stevens Inc.

—Simple Science Projects with Machines. LC 91-50547. (Illus.). 32p. (gr. 2-4). 1992. PLB 17.27 (*0-8368-0769-3*) Gareth Stevens Inc.

—Simple Science Projects with Time. LC 91-50548. (Illus.). 32p. (gr. 2-4). 1992. PLB 17.27 (*0-8368-0770-7*) Gareth Stevens Inc.

—Simple Science Projects with Water. LC 91-50549. (Illus.). 32p. (gr. 2-4). 1992. PLB 17.27 (*0-8368-0771-5*) Gareth Stevens Inc.

—Simple Science Projects with Wheels. LC 91-50550. (Illus.). 32p. (gr. 2-4). 1992. PLB 17.27 (*0-8368-0772-3*) Gareth Stevens Inc.

Wong, Ovid. Experiments with Animal Behavior. LC 87-33779. (Illus.). 48p. (gr. k-4). 1988. PLB 12.85 (*0-516-01214-2*); pap. 4.95 (*0-516-41214-0*) Childrens.

—Hands-On Ecology. LC 91-12751. (Illus.). 128p. (gr. 5 up). 1991. PLB 13.95 (*0-516-00539-1*) Childrens.

Wong, Ovid K. Experimenting with Electricity & Magnetism. LC 92-37672. (gr. 7-12). 1993. 13.40 (*0-531-12547-5*) Watts.

—Experimenting with Electricity & Magnetism. (Illus.). 128p. (gr. 7-12). 1993. pap. 6.95 (*0-531-15681-8*) Watts.

—Is Science Magic? LC 88-36961. (Illus.). 128p. (gr. 5 up). 1989. PLB 13.95 (*0-516-00570-7*) Childrens.

Wood, Robert W. Science for Kids: Thirty-nine Easy Engineering Experiments. (gr. 3-8). 1991. 16.95 (*0-8306-1946-1*); pap. 9.95 (*0-8306-1943-7*) TAB Bks.

—Thirty-Nine Easy Astronomy Experiments. (Illus.). 160p. 1991. 16.95 (*0-8306-7597-3*, 3597); pap. 9.95 (*0-8306-3597-1*) TAB Bks.

—Thirty-Nine Easy Plant Biology Experiments. 160p. 1991. 16.95 (*0-8306-1941-0*, 5003); pap. 9.95 (*0-8306-1935-6*) TAB Bks.

—What? Experiments for the Young Scientists. (gr. 4-7). 1994. pap. text ed. 10.95 (*0-07-051636-7*) McGraw.

—When? Experiments for the Young Scientists. (gr. 4-7). 1994. pap. 10.95 (*0-07-051640-5*) McGraw.

Woodward, K. Science in the Kitchen. (Illus.). 24p. (gr. 1-4). 1992. PLB 12.96 (*0-88110-284-9*); pap. 4.95 (*0-7460-0974-7*) EDC.

Wroble, Lisa. Astronomy. Nolte, Larry, illus. 48p. (gr. 3-6). Date not set. PLB 12.95 (*1-56065-110-5*) Capstone Pr.

Wyler, Rose. Science Fun with Drums, Bells, & Whistles. Stewart, Pat, illus. LC 87-7838. 48p. (gr. 2-4). 1987. lib. bdg. 11.38 (*0-671-63783-5*, J Messner); lib. bdg. 4.95 (*0-671-64760-1*); PLB 8.54s.p. (*0-685-47070-9*); pap. 3.71s.p. (*0-685-47071-7*) S&S Trade.

—Science Fun With Mud & Dirt. Stewart, Pat, illus. 48p. (gr. 3). 1987. pap. 4.95 (*0-317-56794-2*) S&S Trade.

—Science Fun with Mud & Dirt. Stewart, Pat, illus. LC 86-8388. 48p. (gr. 2-4). 1986. lib. bdg. 11.38 (*0-671-55569-3*, J Messner); lib. bdg. 4.95 (*0-671-62904-2*); PLB 8.54s.p. (*0-685-47076-8*); pap. 3.71s.p. (*0-685-47077-6*) S&S Trade.

—Science Fun with Peanuts & Popcorn. Stewart, Pat, illus. 48p. (gr. 2-4). 1986. lib. bdg. 11.38 (*0-671-55572-3*, J Messner); lib. bdg. 4.95 (*0-671-62452-0*); PLB 8.54s.p. (*0-685-54164-9*); pap. 3.71s.p. (*0-685-54165-7*) S&S Trade.

—Science Fun with Toy Boats & Planes. Stewart, Pat, illus. 48p. (gr. 3). 1987. pap. 4.95 (*0-317-56816-7*) S&S Trade.

—Science Fun with Toy Cars & Trucks. Stewart, Pat, illus. LC 87-20326. 48p. (gr. 2-4). 1988. lib. bdg. 11.38 (*0-671-63784-3*, J Messner); lib. bdg. 4.95 (*0-671-65854-9*); PLB 8.54s.p. (*0-685-47068-7*); pap. 3.71s.p. (*0-685-47069-5*) S&S Trade.

Zubrowski, Bernie. Making Waves: Finding Out about Rhythmic Motion. Doty, Roy, illus. LC 93-35455. 96p. (gr. 5 up). 1994. pap. 6.95 (*0-688-11788-0*) Morrow Jr Bks.

—Making Waves: Finding Out about Rhythmic Motion. Doty, Roy, illus. 96p. (gr. 3 up). 1994. PLB 13.93 (*0-688-11787-2*) Morrow Jr Bks.

—Mirrors. Doty, Roy, illus. LC 91-29142. 96p. (gr. 5 up). 1992. pap. 6.95 (*0-688-10591-2*, Pub. by Beech Tree Bks) Morrow.

—Mirrors: Finding Out about the Properties of Light. Doty, Roy, illus. LC 91-29142. 96p. (gr. 3 up). 1992. PLB 13.93 (*0-688-10592-0*) Morrow Jr Bks.

—Mobiles: Building & Experimenting with Balancing Toys. Doty, Roy, illus. LC 92-28408. 104p. (gr. 3 up). 1993. Repr. PLB 13.93 (*0-688-10590-4*) Morrow Jr Bks.

SCIENCE–FICTION

see Science Fiction

SCIENCE–HISTORY

Beshore, George. Science in Ancient China. LC 87-23748. (Illus.). 96p. (gr. 5-8). 1988. PLB 10.90 (*0-531-10485-0*) Watts.

—Science in Early Islamic Culture. LC 88-2660. (Illus.). 72p. (gr. 5-8). 1988. PLB 10.90 (*0-531-10596-2*) Watts.

Duvall, Jill. The Penobscot. (Illus.). 48p. (gr. k-4). 1993. PLB 12.85 (*0-516-01194-4*); pap. 4.95 (*0-516-41194-2*) Childrens.

Gay, Kathlyn. Science in Ancient Greece. LC 87-23747. (Illus.). 96p. (gr. 5-8). 1988. PLB 10.90 (*0-531-10487-7*) Watts.

Harris, Jacqueline L. Science in Ancient Rome. LC 88-2649. (Illus.). 72p. (gr. 5-8). 1988. PLB 10.90 (*0-531-10595-4*) Watts.

Moss, Carol. Science in Ancient Mesopotamia. LC 88-2649. (Illus.). 72p. (gr. 5-8). 1988. PLB 10.90 (*0-531-10594-6*) Watts.

Ross, Frank, Jr. Oracles Bones, Stars & the Wheelbarrows: Ancient Chinese Science & Technology. 1990. pap. 4.80 (*0-395-54967-1*) HM.

Spangenburg, Ray & Moser, Diane K. The History of Science from the Ancient Greeks to the Scientific Revolution. LC 92-33180. (Illus.). 192p. (gr. 6-9). 1993. 17.95x (*0-8160-2739-0*) Facts on File.

—The History of Science from 1946 to the 1990s. (Illus.). 192p. (gr. 7-12). 1994. 18.95x (*0-8160-2743-9*) Facts on File.

—The History of Science in the 19th Century. LC 93-10576. 1993. 18.95x (*0-8160-2741-2*) Facts on File.

SCIENCE–METHODOLOGY

see also Logic

Aronson, Billy. Scientific Goofs. LC 94-4492. 1994. text ed. write for info. (*0-7167-6537-3*, Sci Am Yng Rdrs); pap. text ed. write for info. (*0-7167-6553-5*) W H Freeman.

Kramer, Stephen P. How to Think Like a Scientist: Answering Questions by the Scientific Method. Bond, Felicia, illus. LC 85-43604. 48p. (gr. 3-7). 1987. (Crowell Jr Bks); PLB 13.89 (*0-690-04565-4*, Crowell Jr Bks) HarpC Child Bks.

Nye, Bill. Bill Nye the Science Guy's Big Blast of Science. (Illus.). 176p. 1993. pap. 12.45 (*0-201-60864-2*) Addison-Wesley.

Ruchlis, Hy. How Do You Know It's True? Discovering the Difference Between Science & Superstition. (Illus.). 112p. (Orig.). 1991. pap. 13.95 (*0-87975-657-8*) Prometheus Bks.

VanCleave, Janice. Janice VanCleave's Weather: Mind-Boggling Experiments You Can Turn into Science Fair Projects. LC 94-25646. 1995. write for info. (*0-471-03231-X*) Wiley.

SCIENCE–POETRY

Min, Kellet I. Modern Informative Nursery Rhymes: General Science, Book I. Hansen, Heidi, illus. LC 89-91719. 64p. (Orig.). (gr. 2-5). 1993. pap. 10.95 (*0-9623411-4-2*) Rhyme & Reason.

Moore, Jo E. & Tryon, Leslie. The Big Book of Science Rhymes & Chants. (Illus.). 64p. (gr. k-2). 1991. pap. 11.95 (*1-55799-211-8*, EMC306) Evan-Moor Corp.

SCIENCE–SOCIAL ASPECTS

see Science and Civilization

SCIENCE–STUDY AND TEACHING

see also Nature Study

American Institute for Research. Science Success for Students with Disabilities. 1993. pap. text ed. 18.50 (*0-201-81939-2*) Addison-Wesley.

Berman, Sally. Catch Them Thinking in Science: A Handbook of Classroom Strategies. LC 93-78421. (Illus.). 112p. (Orig.). (gr. 6-12). 1993. pap. 15.95 (*0-932935-55-9*) IRI-Skylght.

Geoffrion, Sondra. Power Study to up Your Grades in Science. LC 88-61275. 60p. (gr. 11 up). 1989. pap. text ed. 3.95 (*0-88247-785-4*) R & E Pubs.

Kumbaraci, Turkan & Gardenier, George H. Branching Trees: Statistical Methods: Games & Songs. Gardenier, Turhan K., illus. LC 89-90944. 27p. (gr. 1-8). 1989. 30.00x (*0-685-29039-5*, 0003) Teka Trends.

Tchudi, Stephen. Probing the Unknown: From Myth to Science. LC 89-35938. (Illus.). 160p. (gr. 7 up). 1990. SBE 14.95 (*0-684-19086-9*, Scribners Young Read) Macmillan Child Grp.

Zeman, Anne & Kelly, Kate. Everything You Need to Know about Science Homework. LC 93-49352. 1994. 19.95 (*0-590-49356-6*); pap. 8.95 (*0-590-49357-4*) Scholastic Inc.

SCIENCE–VOCATIONAL GUIDANCE

Shapiro, Stanley J. Exploring Careers in Science. rev. ed. Rosen, Ruth, ed. (gr. 7-12). 1989. PLB 14.95 (*0-8239-0969-7*) Rosen Group.

SCIENCE–YEARBOOKS

World Book Editors, ed. Science Year, 1994: The World Book Annual Science Supplement. LC 65-21776. (Illus.). 368p. (gr. 6 up). 1993. PLB write for info. (*0-7166-0594-5*) World Bk.

World Book Staff, ed. Science Year, 1992: The World Book Annual Science Supplement. LC 65-21776. (Illus.). 400p. (gr. 7-12). 1991. lib. bdg. write for info. (*0-7166-0592-9*) World Bk.

SCIENCE AND CIVILIZATION

Asimov, Isaac. Ask Isaac Asimov, 41 vols. (Illus.). 24p. (gr. 1-8). PLB 570.01 subscription set (*0-8368-0789-8*); PLB 14.60 ea., standing order (*0-8368-0788-X*) Gareth Stevens Inc.

Encyclopaedia Britannica Publishers, Inc. Staff. Hombre, Ciencia y Tecnologia. (SPA., Illus.). 3160p. 1992. write for info. (*1-56409-005-1*) EBP Latin Am.

SCIENCE AND RELIGION

see Religion and Science

SCIENCE AND SPACE

see Space Sciences

SCIENCE FICTION

Abbott, Tony. Danger Guys Blast Off. Scribner, Joanne, illus. LC 93-31806. 80p. (gr. 2-5). 1994. pap. 3.95 (*0-06-440520-6*, Trophy) HarpC Child Bks.

Allington, Richard L. & Krull, Kathleen. Science. Teason, James, illus. LC 82-101711. 32p. (gr. k-3). 1985. pap. 8.95 (*0-8172-2486-6*) Raintree Steck-V.

Amthor, Terry K. Rivendell, the House of Elrond. McBride, Angus, illus. 36p. (Orig.). (gr. 10-12). 1987. pap. 7.00 (*0-915795-87-6*, 8080) Iron Crown Ent Inc.

Anderson, Margaret J. In the Circle of Time. LC 78-10156. (gr. 5-9). 1979. lib. bdg. 6.99 (*0-394-94029-6*) Knopf Bks Yng Read.

Angell, Judie. What's Best for You? 192p. (gr. 6-9). 1983. pap. 2.25 (*0-440-98959-0*, LFL) Dell.

Anthony, Piers. Balook. Woodroffe, Patrick, illus. 200p. 1990. 24.95 (*0-88733-069-X*); signed ed. 75.00 (*0-685-53972-5*) Underwood-Miller.

Appleton, Victor. Cyborg Kickboxer. Greenberg, Ann, ed. 160p. (Orig.). 1991. pap. 2.95 (*0-671-67825-6*, Archway) PB.

—The DNA Disaster. Greenberg, Anne, ed. 160p. (Orig.). 1991. pap. 2.95 (*0-671-67826-4*, Archway) PB.

—Fire Biker. Greenberg, Anne, ed. 160p. 1992. pap. 2.99 (*0-671-75652-4*, Archway) PB.

—The Microbots. Greenberg, Anne, ed. 160p. (Orig.). 1992. pap. 2.99 (*0-671-75651-6*) PB.

—Mind Games. Greenberg, Anne, ed. 160p. (Orig.). 1992. pap. 2.99 (*0-671-75654-0*, Archway) PB.

—Monster Machine. Greenberg, Anne, ed. 160p. (Orig.). 1991. pap. 2.99 (*0-671-67827-2*, Archway) PB.

—Mutant Beach. Greenberg, Anne, ed. 160p. (Orig.). (gr. 7 up). 1992. pap. 2.99 (*0-671-75657-5*, Archway) PB.

—The Negative Zone. Greenberg, Anne, ed. 176p. (Orig.). 1991. pap. 2.95 (*0-671-67824-8*, Archway) PB.

—Tom Swift & His Airship. (ps-3). 1992. 12.95 (*1-55709-177-3*) Applewood.

—Tom Swift & His Motor Boat. (ps-3). 1992. 12.95 (*1-55709-176-5*) Applewood.

—Tom Swift & His Motor Cycle. (ps-3). 1992. 12.95 (*1-55709-175-7*) Applewood.

Armintrout, W. G. Death Game 2090. Barrett, Kevin, ed. Aulisio, Janet, et al, illus. 48p. (Orig.). (gr. 12). 1990. pap. 9.00 (*1-55806-132-0*, 5106) Iron Crown Ent Inc.

Asamiya, Kia. Gunhed: Gun Unit - Heavy Elimination Device. Horibuchi, Seiji, ed. Fujii, Satoru, tr. from JPN. (Illus.). 136p. (Orig.). (gr. 10 up). 1991. pap. 14. 95 (*0-929279-14-X*) Viz Commns Inc.

Asimov, Isaac. All the Troubles of World. 40p. (gr. 5). 1989. PLB 13.95s.p. (*0-88682-233-5*) Creative Ed.

—Fantastic Voyage. 192p. (gr. 7 up). 1984. pap. 3.50 (*0-553-27151-2*, Spectra) Bantam.

—Franchise. 40p. (gr. 5). 1989. PLB 13.95 (*0-88682-232-7*) Creative Ed.

—It's Such a Beautiful Day. Redpath, Ann, ed. Delessert, Etienne, illus. 64p. (gr. 4 up). 1985. PLB 13.95 (*0-88682-008-1*) Creative Ed.

—Oceans of Venus & the Big Sun of Mercury. (gr. 4 up). 1993. pap. 4.99 (*0-553-56254-1*, Spectra) Bantam.

—Robbie. 40p. (gr. 5). 1989. 13.95 (*0-88682-231-9*) Creative Ed.

—Sally. 40p. (gr. 5). 1989. PLB 13.95 (*0-88682-230-0*) Creative Ed.

—Visions of Fantasy: Tales from the Masters. 1991. pap. 3.50 (*0-553-29356-7*) Bantam.

Asimov, Janet. The Package in Hyperspace. Gampert, John, illus. (gr. 4-7). 1988. 13.95 (*0-8027-6822-9*); PLB 14.85 (*0-8027-6823-7*) Walker & Co.

Asimov, Janet & Asimov, Isaac. Norby Down to Earth. (Illus.). (gr. 4-9). 1989. 12.95 (*0-8027-6866-0*); PLB 13.85 (*0-8027-6867-9*) Walker & Co.

—Norby Finds a Villain. (gr. 4-9). 1987. 12.95 (*0-8027-6710-9*); PLB 13.85 (*0-8027-6711-7*) Walker & Co.

Askounis, Christina. The Dream of the Stone. 272p. (gr. 7 up). 1992. 17.00 (*0-374-31877-8*) FS&G.

Baker. The Time Machine & The Chef. Abell, ed. & illus. (Orig.). (gr. 8 up). 1992. PLB 25.00 (*1-56611-014-9*); pap. 15.00 (*1-56611-041-6*) Jonas.

Baldry, Cherith. Rite of Brotherhood. Reck, Sue, ed. 160p. (gr. 8-12). Date not set. pap. 4.99 (*0-7814-0094-5*, Chariot Bks) Chariot Family.

Ball, Duncan. Emily Eyefinger. Ulrich, George, illus. LC 91-20751. 96p. (gr. 2-5). 1992. pap. 13.00 jacketed (*0-671-74618-9*, S&S BFYR) S&S Trade.

Baron, Nick. Glory's End. (gr. 9-12). 1990. pap. 3.50 (*0-06-106013-5*, PL) HarpC.

Barrett, Kevin. Black Guard. Charlton, S. Coleman, ed. Jones, J. Wallace, et al, illus. 40p. (Orig.). (gr. 12). 1990. pap. 8.00 (*1-55806-115-0*, 7012) Iron Crown Ent Inc.

Barron, Thomas A. Heartlight. 272p. (gr. 5-9). 1990. 15. 95 (*0-399-22180-8*, Philomel Bks) Putnam Pub Group.

Beattie, Owen & Geiger, John. Buried in Ice. 64p. 1992. 15.95 (*0-590-43848-4*, Scholastic Hardcover) Scholastic Inc.

Bellairs, John. The Eyes of the Killer Robot. LC 86-2148. 176p. (gr. 5 up). 1986. 11.95 (*0-8037-0324-4*) Dial Bks Young.

Benet, Stephen Vincent. By the Waters of Babylon. 32p. (gr. 6). 1990. PLB 13.95s.p. (*0-88682-294-7*) Creative Ed.

Bennie, Scott. Day of the Destroyer. Bell, Rob, ed. Phillips, Joe & Dunn, Ben, illus. 32p. (Orig.). (gr. 12). 1990. pap. 7.00 (*1-55806-101-0*, 408) Iron Crown Ent Inc.

Bianchi, John. Flight of the Space Quester. Bianchi, John, illus. 24p. 1993. lib. bdg. 14.95 (*0-921285-31-0*, Pub. by Bungalo Bks CN); pap. 4.95 (*0-921285-30-2*, Pub. by Bungalo Bks CN) Firefly Bks Ltd.

Birkner, Malthias & Birkner, Karen. Denizens of the Dark Wood. Ney, Jessica, ed. McBride, Angus & Danforth, Liz, illus. 32p. (Orig.). (gr. 12). 1989. pap. 6.00 (*1-55806-081-2*, 8111) Iron Crown Ent Inc.

Black, J. R. Sea Creature, No. 7. (gr. 4 up). 1994. 3.50 (*0-679-86180-7*) Random.

Blackwood, Gary L. The Dying Sun. LC 88-27517. 224p. (gr. 6-9). 1989. SBE 14.95 (*0-689-31482-5*, Atheneum Child Bk) Macmillan Child Grp.

Bohl, Al. Zaanan: Fatal Limit. Bohl, Al, illus. 224p. (gr. 4-8). 1989. pap. text ed. 2.50 (*1-55748-101-6*) Barbour & Co.

Bouton, Steve. Cyber Rogues. Barrett, Kevin, ed. Aulisio, Janet, illus. 32p. (Orig.). (gr. 12). 1990. pap. 10.00 (*1-55806-125-8*, 5103) Iron Crown Ent Inc.

Bradbury, Ray. Dandelion Wine. (gr. 6 up). 1985. pap. 5.50 (*0-553-27753-7*) Bantam.

—The Foghorn. Kelley, Gary, illus. 32p. 1987. PLB 13.95 (*0-88682-107-X*) Creative Ed.

—Illustrated Man. (gr. 6-12). 1969. pap. 3.50 (*0-553-25483-9*) Bantam.

—The Smile. 1991. PLB 13.95 (*0-88682-466-4*) Creative Ed.

—Something Wicked This Way Comes. (gr. 6-12). 1983. pap. 3.50 (*0-553-25774-9*) Bantam.

Brennan, Herbie. The Mystery Machine. Marks, Alan, illus. LC 94-4185. 1995. 14.00 (*0-689-50615-5*, M K McElderry) Macmillan Child Grp.

Brenner, Barbara A. Moon Boy. 1990. 9.99 (*0-553-05858-4*) Bantam.

Bridges, Laurie. Magic Show. (ps-7). 1987. pap. 2.25 (*0-553-25096-5*) Bantam.

Brinkley, Chad & Barrett, Kevin. The Body Bank. Aulisio, Janet, illus. 32p. (Orig.). (gr. 12). 1990. pap. 10.00 (*1-55806-128-2*, 5104) Iron Crown Ent Inc.

Brittain, Bill. Shape-Changer. LC 93-27268. 112p. (gr. 3-7). 1994. 14.00 (*0-06-024238-8*); PLB 13.89 (*0-06-024239-6*) HarpC Child Bks.

Brown, Charles. Demons Rule. Bell, Rob, ed. Boonthanakit, Ted & Chacon, Joe, illus. 32p. (Orig.). (gr. 12). 1990. pap. 7.00 (*1-55806-110-X*, 412) Iron Crown Ent Inc.

Buller, Jon & Schade, Susan. The Video Kids. Buller, Jon & Schade, Susan, illus. LC 93-26923. 48p. (gr. 2-3). 1994. 7.99 (*0-448-40181-9*, G&D); pap. 3.50 (*0-448-40180-0*, G&D) Putnam Pub Group.

—Yo! It's Captain Yo-Yo. Buller, Jon & Schade, Susan, illus. LC 92-44306. 48p. (gr. 2-3). 1993. 7.99 (*0-448-40192-4*, G&D); pap. 3.50 (*0-448-40191-6*, G&D) Putnam Pub Group.

Bullock, Harold B. The Battle for the Worlds. Anderson, Jean, ed. Menefee, Paige & Smith, Patti, illus. 1990. 14.95 (*0-9626219-4-3*) Summit TX.

Bunting, Eve. The Island of One. (Illus.). 64p. 1992. 8.95 (*0-89565-768-6*) Childs World.

—The Mask. (Illus.). 64p. (gr. 3-8). 1992. 8.95 (*0-89565-769-4*) Childs World.

—The Mirror Planet. (Illus.). 64p. 1992. 8.95 (*0-89565-767-8*) Childs World.

—The Space People. (Illus.). 64p. (gr. 3-8). 1992. 8.95 (*0-89565-765-1*) Childs World.

Burke, Terrill M. Dolphin Magic: The Ancient Knowledge. 310p. (Orig.). (gr. 6 up). 1993. pap. 12.25 (*1-880485-51-6*) Alpha-Dolphin.

Cameron, Eleanor. Mr. Bass's Planetoid. Darling, Louis, illus. (gr. 3-7). 1958. 14.95 (*0-316-12525-3*, Joy St Bks) Little.

Carella, C. J. & Siembieda, Kevin. Pantheons of the Megaverse. Marciniszyn, Alex, et al, eds. Zeleznik, John, et al, illus. 208p. (Orig.). (gr. 8 up). 1994. pap. 19.95 (*0-916211-68-1*, 811) Palladium Bks.

Carlson, Dale. The Plant People. 96p. (gr. 5 up). 1979. pap. 1.25 (*0-440-96959-X*, LFL) Dell.

Carlson, Larry G. Molecular Ramjet: And Other Bedtime Stories... Valenzuela, Walter V., illus. 212p. (gr. 7-9). 1989. pap. 4.95 (*0-929301-01-3*) TadAlex Bks.

Carr, Barbara. The Planet of the Dinosaurs. Bear, Alice, illus. LC 92-9287. 32p. (gr. k-3). 1992. 12.95 (*0-89334-161-4*, 161-4) Humanics Ltd.

Cartwright, Pauline. Escape from Zarcay. Campbell, Caroline, illus. LC 90-10075. 32p. (gr. 2-5). 1990. PLB 17.28 (*0-8114-2694-7*) Raintree Steck-V.

Children of the Storm. 192p. (Orig.). (gr. 7-9). 1989. pap. 2.95 (*0-8041-0460-3*) Ivy Books.

Christian, D. & Siembieda, Kevin. Robotech: Zentraedi Breakout. Marciniszyn, Alex, et al, eds. Miller, Tom & Breaux, Wayne, illus. 64p. (Orig.). (gr. 8 up). 1994. pap. 9.95 (*0-916211-67-3*, 561) Palladium Bks.

Christopher, John. The City of Gold & Lead. 2nd ed. LC 88-16118. (Illus.). 224p. (gr. 7 up). 1988. pap. 3.95 (*0-02-042701-8*, Collier Young Ad) Macmillan Child Grp.

—Dragon Dance. LC 85-31149. 160p. (gr. 5-9). 1986. 12. 95 (*0-525-44227-8*, DCB) Dutton Child Bks.

—A Dusk of Demons. LC 92-31730. 176p. (gr. 5-9). 1994. SBE 14.95 (*0-02-718425-0*, Macmillan Child Bk) Macmillan Child Grp.

—The Guardians. 2nd ed. LC 91-44197. 224p. (gr. 7 up). 1992. pap. 4.95 (*0-02-042681-X*, Collier Young Ad) Macmillan Child Grp.

—The Lotus Caves. LC 74-78074. 160p. (gr. 5-9). 1971. pap. 4.95 (*0-02-042690-9*, Collier Young Ad) Macmillan Child Grp.

—The Lotus Caves. 2nd ed. LC 91-27715. 224p. (gr. 7 up). 1992. pap. 4.95 (*0-02-042691-7*, Collier Young Ad) Macmillan Child Grp.

—The Pool of Fire. LC 68-23062. 192p. (gr. 5-9). 1970. SBE 14.95 (*0-02-718350-5*, Macmillan Child Bk); (Collier Young Ad) Macmillan Child Grp.

—The Pool of Fire. 2nd ed. LC 88-16117. 224p. (gr. 7 up). 1988. pap. 3.95 (*0-02-042721-2*, Collier Young Ad) Macmillan Child Grp.

—The Pool of Fire. large type ed. 280p. (gr. 3 up). 1990. 18.95 (*0-7451-1176-9*) G K Hall.

—The Prince in Waiting. (gr. 5-9). 1984. 16.75 (*0-8446-6157-0*) Peter Smith.

—The Prince in Waiting. (Illus.). 224p. (gr. 7 up). 1989. pap. 3.95 (*0-02-042573-2*, Collier Young Ad) Macmillan Child Grp.

—The Sword of the Spirits. 224p. (gr. 7 up). 1989. pap. 3.95 (*0-02-042574-0*, Collier Young Ad) Macmillan Child Grp.

—The Tripods Trilogy. 2nd ed. 224p. (gr. 7 up). 1988. Boxed Set. pap. 11.95 (*0-02-042571-6*, Collier Young Ad) Macmillan Child Grp.

—When the Tripods Came. LC 90-1436. 160p. (gr. 7 up). 1990. pap. 3.95 (*0-02-042575-9*, Collier Young Ad) Macmillan Child Grp.

—The White Mountains. 2nd ed. LC 88-16119. (Illus.). 224p. (gr. 7 up). 1988. pap. 3.95 (*0-02-042711-5*, Collier Young Ad) Macmillan Child Grp.

—The White Mountains. large type ed. 256p. (gr. 3 up). 1990. 16.95 (*0-7451-1043-6*) G K Hall.

—Wild Jack. 2nd ed. 160p. (gr. 7 up). 1991. pap. 3.95 (*0-02-042576-7*, Collier Young Ad) Macmillan Child Grp.

Cooke, Tim. Calenhad: A Beacon of Gondor. Ney, Jessica, ed. Martin, David, et al, illus. 48p. (Orig.). (gr. 12). 1990. pap. 9.00 (*1-55806-097-9*, 8203) Iron Crown Ent Inc.

Cooper, Clare. Ashar of Qarius. 163p. (gr. 3-7). 1990. 14. 95 (*0-15-200409-2*, Gulliver Bks) HarBrace.

Cover, Arthur B. The Rings of Saturn. 144p. (gr. 5 up). 1985. pap. 2.25 (*0-553-25797-8*) Bantam.

Coville, Bruce. My Teacher Flunked the Planet. MacDonald, Pat, ed. Fisher, Steve, illus. 176p. (Orig.). 1992. pap. 3.50 (*0-671-75081-X*, Minstrel Bks) PB.

—Space Brat. MacDonald, Pat, ed. Coville, Katherine, illus. 80p. (Orig.). 1992. pap. 3.50 (*0-671-74567-0*, Minstrel Bks) PB.

—Space Brat. MacDonald, Pat, ed. Coville, Katherine, illus. 1993. 12.00 (*0-671-87059-9*, Minstrel Bks) PB.

—Space Brat Two: Blork's Evil Twin. Coville, Bruce, illus. 80p. (Orig.). (gr. 2-4). 1993. 12.00 (*0-671-87038-6*, Minstrel Bks); pap. 3.50 (*0-671-77713-0*, Minstrel Bks) PB.

—Space Brat 3: The Wrath of Squat. Coville, Katherine, illus. LC 93-50602. 1994. 3.50 (*0-671-86844-6*, Minstrel bks) PB.

Crisfield, Deborah. The Amityville Horror. LC 91-4528. (Illus.). 48p. (gr. 5-6). 1991. text ed. 13.95 RSBE (*0-89686-576-2*, Crestwood Hse) Macmillan Child Grp.

Crist, Harold L. Twice a Hero. 112p. (Orig.). 1990. pap. 5.95 (*0-9621743-1-9*) H L Crist.

Crowdis, John. Disaster on Adonis Three. LaDell, Leo, ed. Ridge, Jeff & Midgette, Darrell, illus. 32p. (Orig.). (gr. 12). 1989. pap. 6.00 (*1-55806-039-1*, 9107) Iron Crown Ent Inc.

—Ghosts of the Southern Arduin. Ney, Jessica & Fenlon, Peter C., Jr., eds. McBride, Angus & Midgette, Darrell, illus. 32p. (Orig.). (gr. 12). 1989. pap. 6.00 (*1-55806-030-8*, 8109) Iron Crown Ent Inc.

—Hazards of the Harod Wood. Ney, Jessica, ed. McBride, Angus & Danforth, Liz, illus. 32p. (Orig.). (gr. 12). 1990. pap. 6.00 (*1-55806-096-0*, 8112) Iron Crown Ent Inc.

—Rogues of the Borderlands. Ney, Jessica, ed. McBride, Angus & Jermy, Paul, illus. 40p. (Orig.). (gr. 12). 1990. pap. 7.00 (*1-55806-083-9*, 8014) Iron Crown Ent Inc.

Crutchfield, Charles. Forest of Tears. Ney, Jessica, ed. McBride, Angus & Danforth, Liz, illus. 40p. (Orig.). (gr. 12). 1989. pap. 7.00 (*1-55806-084-7*, 8015) Iron Crown Ent Inc.

—Warlords of the Desert. Ney, Jessica, ed. McBride, Angus & Robin, Jeremy, illus. 40p. (Orig.). (gr. 12). 1989. pap. 7.00 (*1-55806-058-8*, 8012) Iron Crown Ent Inc.
Cunningham, Lowell. The Men in Black. Ulm, Chris, ed. Carruthers, Sandy, illus. 76p. 1990. pap. 7.95 (*0-944735-60-6*) Malibu Graphics.
Danziger, Paula. This Place Has No Atmosphere. (gr. k-12). 1987. pap. 3.99 (*0-440-98726-1*, LFL) Dell.
—This Place Has No Atmosphere. large type ed. 190p. 1989. Repr. of 1986 ed. lib. bdg. 15.95 (*1-55736-130-4*, Crnrstn Bks) BDD LT Grp.
David, Peter. Starfleet Academy, No. 2: Worf's Mission. 128p. (Orig.). (gr. 3-6). 1993. pap. 3.99 (*0-671-87085-8*, Minstrel Bks) PB.
—Survival. Fry, James, illus. 128p. (Orig.). 1993. pap. 3.99 (*0-671-87086-6*, Minstrel Bks) PB.
Davids, Paul. Mission from Mount Yoda. (gr. 4-7). 1993. pap. 3.99 (*0-553-15890-2*) Bantam.
—Prophets of the Dark Side. (gr. 4-7). 1993. pap. 3.99 (*0-553-15892-9*) Bantam.
—Queen of the Empire. (gr. 4-7). 1993. pap. 3.99 (*0-553-15891-0*) Bantam.
Davids, Paul & Davids, Hollace. Glove of Darth Vader. (gr. 4-7). 1992. pap. 3.99 (*0-553-15887-2*, Starfire) Bantam.
—Jabba the Hutt's Revenge. 1992. pap. 3.99 (*0-553-15889-9*) Bantam.
—Lost City of the Jedi. (gr. 4-7). 1992. pap. 3.99 (*0-553-15888-0*, Starfire) Bantam.
Deem, James M. How to Catch a Flying Saucer. Kelley, True, illus. 192p. 1993. pap. 3.50 (*0-380-71898-7*, Camelot) Avon.
—How to Travel Through Time. 128p. (Orig.). 1993. pap. 3.50 (*0-380-76681-7*, Camelot) Avon.
De Haven, Tom. Joe Gosh. Reese, Ralph, illus. (gr. 7 up). 1988. 15.95 (*0-8027-6824-5*) Walker & Co.
Derman, Karen. The Magic Hole in the Sky. Neel, Jennifer & Williams, Roger, illus. 48p. (Orig.). 1992. pap. 14.95 (*0-9630026-0-0*) Childlight Pr.
Dershem, Kurt. The Olympians. Bell, Rob, ed. Perez, George & Sutherland, Jackie, illus. 48p. (Orig.). (gr. 12). 1990. pap. 9.00 (*1-55806-114-2*, 414) Iron Crown Ent Inc.
De Saint-Exupery, Antoine. Le Petit Prince. De Saint-Exupery, Antoine, illus. LC 43-5812. (FRE.). 91p. (gr. 3-7). 1943. 14.95 (*0-15-243818-1*, HB Juv Bks) HarBrace.
Dever, Joe. Lone Wolf, No. 13: The Plague Lords of Ruel. 1992. pap. 3.50 (*0-425-13245-5*) Berkley Pub.
Dever, Sara. A Nickel for a Gumball Buys an Alien. LC 92-91120. 64p. (gr. 2 up). 1994. pap. 7.00 limited ed. (*1-56002-261-2*, Univ Edtns) Aegina Pr.
Dickinson, Peter. AK. 1994. pap. 3.99 (*0-440-21897-7*) Dell.
Dicks, Terrance. A Cat Called Max: Max's Amazing Summer. Goffe, Toni, illus. 52p. (gr. 3-6). 1992. pap. 3.50 (*0-8120-4819-9*) Barron.
Dillon, Barbara. My Stepfather Shrank! LC 91-23901. (Illus.). 128p. (gr. 3-7). 1992. 13.00 (*0-06-021574-7*); PLB 12.89 (*0-06-021581-X*) HarpC Child Bks.
Dixon, Franklin W. The Alien Factor. Greenberg, Anne, ed. 224p. (Orig.). 1993. pap. 3.99 (*0-671-79532-5*, Archway) PB.
—Endangered Species. Greenberg, Anne, ed. 160p. (Orig.). 1992. pap. 3.99 (*0-671-73100-9*, Archway) PB.
Doyle, Arthur Conan. The Lost World. 256p. 1993. pap. 4.99 (*0-8125-3468-9*) Tor Bks.
Doyle, Debra. Timecrime Inc. (gr. 9-12). 1991. pap. 3.50 (*0-06-106014-3*, PL) HarpC.
Duane, Diane E. So You Want to Be a Wizard. (gr. 5 up). 1992. 3.50 (*0-440-40638-2*, YB) Dell.
Dunn, Ben. Ninja High School, Vol. 2: Beware of Dog. Ulm, Chris, ed. Dunn, Ben, illus. 121p. 1990. pap. 9.95 (*0-944735-59-2*) Malibu Graphics.
Edwards, Roger. Max Science & the Glowing Firefly. Sanchez, Brenda L., ed. Beard, Derrick, illus. 26p. (gr. k-5). 1991. pap. 3.95 (*1-879350-01-7*) Max Sci Pub.
Engdahl, Sylvia. Enchantress from the Stars. Shackell, Rodney, illus. 288p. (gr. 7 up). 1989. pap. 3.95 (*0-02-043031-0*, Collier Young Ad) Macmillan Child Grp.
—Enchantress from the Stars. (gr. 6-10). 1991. 16.75 (*0-8446-6448-0*) Peter Smith.
Eyes of the Tarot. (gr. 7-12). 1983. pap. 2.50 (*0-553-26685-3*) Bantam.
FamilyVision Press Staff. Kidnapped to the Center of the Earth. LC 93-71554. (Illus.). 48p. 1993. 14.95 (*1-56969-125-8*) FamilyVision.
Farmer, Nancy. The Ear, the Eye & the Arm. LC 93-11814. 320p. (gr. 7 up). 1994. 16.95 (*0-531-06829-3*); lib. bdg. 16.99 RLB (*0-531-08679-8*) Orchard Bks Watts.
Farrow, Peter & Lampert, Diane. Twyllyp. (Illus.). (gr. 3-7). 1963. 10.95 (*0-8392-3040-0*) Astor-Honor.
Feild, William B., Jr. & Stassun, Peter G. Perils on the Sea of Rhun. Ney, Jessica, ed. Hook, Richard & Danforth, Liz, illus. 32p. (Orig.). (gr. 12). 1989. pap. 6.00 (*0-685-37962-0*, 8110) Iron Crown Ent Inc.
Fenlon, Peter C., Jr., ed. Lords of Middle-Earth, Vol. 2: The Mannish Races. McBride, Angus, illus. 112p. (Orig.). (gr. 10-12). 1987. pap. 12.00 (*0-915795-32-9*, 8003) Iron Crown Ent Inc.
Ferrone, John M. Ghost Warriors. Ney, Jessica, ed. McBride, Angus & Danforth, Liz, illus. 48p. (Orig.). (gr. 12). 1990. pap. 10.00 (*1-55806-107-X*, 8016) Iron Crown Ent Inc.
Fine, Anne. The True Story of Harrowing Farm. Fisher, Cynthia, illus. LC 92-33935. 1993. 12.95 (*0-316-28316-9*, Joy St Bks) Little.
Fleischman, Paul. Time Train. Ewart, Claire, illus. LC 90-27357. 32p. (gr. k-4). 1994. pap. 4.95 (*0-06-443351-X*, Trophy) HarpC Child Bks.
Flood, E. L. The Fly. LC 91-7376. (Illus.). 48p. (gr. 5-6). 1991. text ed. 13.95 RSBE (*0-89686-574-6*, Crestwood Hse) Macmillan Child Grp.
Foley, Tod. War on a Distant Moon. LaDell, Leo, ed. Velez, Waller & Waltrip, Jason, illus. 32p. (Orig.). (gr. 12). 1988. pap. 6.00 (*1-55806-020-0*, 9104) Iron Crown Ent Inc.
Ford, Noel. An Earful of Aliens. 64p. (gr. 2-4). 1994. 5.95 (*0-340-56914-X*, Pub. by Hodder & Stoughton UK) Trafalgar.
Forman, Vicki, adapted by. Days of Future Past. adpt. ed. Ruiz, Aristides, illus. 108p. (Orig.). (gr. 2 up). 1994. pap. 3.50 (*0-679-86181-5*) Random Bks Yng Read.
Friedman, Michael J. Star Trek: The Next Generation - The Star Lost. Kahan, Bob, ed. (Illus.). 144p. (Orig.). 1993. pap. 14.95 (*1-56389-084-4*) DC Comics.
Fryman, Alice J. Nobody Sees Tomorrow. 1992. 7.95 (*0-533-10017-8*) Vantage.
Garfield, Leon. The Night of the Comet. (gr. k-6). 1988. pap. 3.25 (*0-440-40070-8*, YB) Dell.
Gasperini, Jim. The Mystery of Atlantis. 144p. (Orig.). (gr. 5 up). 1985. pap. 2.25 (*0-553-25073-6*) Bantam.
Gentle, Mary. Golden Witchbreed. (gr. 9-12). 1990. pap. 3.95 (*0-451-13606-3*, Sig) NAL-Dutton.
Gerrold, David. Voyage of Star Wolf. 240p. 1990. pap. 5.99 (*0-553-26466-4*, Spectra) Bantam.
—When Harlie Was One. 288p. 1988. pap. 3.95 (*0-553-26465-6*, Spectra) Bantam.
Gibson, Robert W. Captain Harlock Returns. Ulm, Chris, ed. Duke, Pat, et al, illus. 86p. 1991. pap. 9.95 (*0-944735-75-4*) Malibu Graphics.
Gilden, Mel. Outer Space & All That Junk. LaVigne, Daniel, illus. LC 88-37110. 176p. (gr. 5-9). 1989. (Lipp Jr Bks); PLB 12.89 (*0-397-32307-7*, Lipp Jr Bks) HarpC Child Bks.
—The Planetoid of Amazement. LC 91-7261. 224p. (gr. 5-9). 1991. 14.95 (*0-06-021713-8*) HarpC Child Bks.
—Pumpkins of Time. (gr. 6-9). 1994. pap. write for info. (*0-15-200889-6*) HarBrace.
—The Pumpkins of Time. LC 94-16894. (gr. 6-9). 1994. 10.95 (*0-15-276603-0*) HarBrace.
—The Return of Captain Conquer. (gr. 5-8). 1985. 12.95 (*0-685-11811-8*) HM.
Glugg, Professor. The Blue Skidoo Crew. Glugg, Professor, illus. LC 92-75278. 32p. (Orig.). (ps up). 1993. pap. 3.95 (*1-881905-03-9*) Glue Bks.
—Glugg-A-Lug Bug. Glugg, Professor, illus. LC 92-74768. 32p. (Orig.). (ps up). 1993. pap. 3.95 (*1-881905-02-0*) Glue Bks.
Goldin, Stephen & Mason, Mary. Jade Darcy & the Zen Pirates. (gr. 9-12). pap. 3.95 (*0-451-16157-2*, Sig) NAL-Dutton.
Good, Sharon. Alpha, Beta & Gamma: A Small Story. LC 90-86292. (Illus.). 48p. 1991. pap. 6.95 (*0-9627226-1-8*) Excalibur Publishing.
Gormley, Beatrice. Travelers Through Time: Back to the Titanic. (gr. 4-7). 1994. pap. 3.25 (*0-590-46226-1*) Scholastic Inc.
Greer, Gery & Ruddick, Robert. Jason & the Aliens down the Street. Sims, Blanche L., illus. LC 90-47386. 96p. (gr. 2-5). 1991. 12.95 (*0-06-021761-8*); PLB 12.89 (*0-06-021762-6*) HarpC Child Bks.
—Jason & the Escape from Bat Planet. Sims, Blanche L. illus. LC 92-41169. 96p. (gr. 2-5). 1993. 14.00 (*0-06-021221-7*); PLB 13.89 (*0-06-021222-5*) HarpC Child Bks.
—Jason & the Lizard Pirates. Sims, Blanche L., illus. LC 91-14327. 96p. (gr. 2-5). 1992. PLB 13.89 (*0-06-022722-2*) HarpC Child Bks.
—Let Me off This Spaceship! Sims, Blanche L., illus. LC 90-47386. 80p. (gr. 2-5). 1992. pap. 3.95 (*0-06-440436-6*, Trophy) HarpC Child Bks.
—Max & Me & the Time Machine. LC 87-45284. 128p. (gr. 3-7). 1988. pap. 3.95 (*0-06-440222-3*, Trophy) HarpC Child Bks.
Gross, Edward. The Alien Nation Companion. (Illus.). 112p. (gr. 9-12). 1991. pap. 12.95 (*0-9627508-1-6*) Image NY.
Guymon, Maurine B. The Adventures of Micki Microbe. Zagone, Arlene T., illus. 88p. (gr. 2-5). 1987. 15.00 (*0-9618650-0-8*) MoDel Pubs.
Hamilton, Virginia. Planet of Junior Brown. large type, unabr. ed. 400p. (gr. 5 up). 1988. lib. bdg. 13.95 (*0-8161-4642-X*) G K Hall.
Hammer, Jeff. Field Trip. 160p. (gr. 6). 1991. pap. 2.99 (*0-380-76144-0*, Flare) Avon.
Harris, Mark. The Doctor Who Technical Manual. Nathan-Turner, John, intro. by. LC 83-42868. (Illus.). 64p. (gr. 5 up). 1983. lib. bdg. 6.99 (*0-394-96214-1*) Random Bks Yng Read.
Hautzig, Deborah. Night of Sentinels. 1994. 7.99 (*0-679-96029-5*); pap. 3.50 (*0-679-86029-0*) Random.
Haycock, Kate. Science Fiction Films. LC 91-31672. (Illus.). 32p. (gr. 5). 1992. text ed. 13.95 RSBE (*0-89686-716-1*, Crestwood Hse) Macmillan Child Grp.
Hayes, Bert. Nineteen Seventy-Eight: The Human Race Begins. Courington, D., as told to. (Illus.). 64p. (Orig.). 1989. pap. 4.95 (*0-318-41429-5*) M C Cook.
Heinlein, Robert A. Citizen of the Galaxy. LC 86-26172. 312p. (gr. 7 up). 1987. SBE 15.95 (*0-684-18818-X*, Scribners Young Read) Macmillan Child Grp.
Heintze, Ty. Valley of the Eels: A Science Fiction Mystery. Heintze, Ty, illus. LC 93-2906. 1993. 14.95 (*0-89015-904-1*) Sunbelt Media.
Heisel, Sharon E. Wrapped in a Riddle. LC 92-26954. 1993. 13.95 (*0-395-65026-7*) HM.
Herdling, Glenn. Illuminator Enter Metatron, Bk. 4. (gr. 4-7). 1993. pap. 4.99 (*0-8407-6255-0*) Nelson.
—Illuminator the Channel Master the Fun & the Fury, Bk. 3. (gr. 4-7). 1993. pap. 2.95 (*0-8407-6253-4*) Nelson.
Hess, Debra. Alien Alert! Newsom, Carol, illus. LC 95-528. 128p. (gr. 3-6). 1993. pap. 3.50 (*1-56282-567-4*) Hyprn Ppbks.
—Escape from Earth. Newsom, Carol, illus. 128p. (gr. 3-7). 1994. pap. 3.50 (*1-56282-682-4*) Hyprn Child.
—Spies, Incorporated. Newsom, Carol, illus. LC 93-34116. 128p. (gr. 3-6). 1994. pap. 3.50 (*1-56282-683-2*) Hyprn Ppbks.
Hill, Douglas. The Caves of Klydor. 144p. 1986. pap. 2.75 (*0-553-25929-6*, Spectra) Bantam.
Hillman, Ben. That Pesky Toaster. LC 94-9831. 1995. write for info. (*0-7868-0033-X*); PLB write for info. (*0-7868-2028-4*) Hyprn Child.
Hinton, S. E. Big David, Little David. Daniel, Alan, illus. LC 93-32307. 1995. 14.95 (*0-385-31093-5*) Doubleday.
Hoover, H. M. Only Child. LC 91-33037. 128p. (gr. 4-7). 1992. 13.00 (*0-525-44865-9*, DCB) Dutton Child Bks.
Hudson, Randolph. The Methuselah Factor. 237p. 1992. pap. 5.25 (*0-9632097-0-1*) Rattlesnake.
Hughes, Dean. Nutty Knows All. LC 90-40282. 160p. (gr. 3-7). 1991. pap. 3.95 (*0-689-71470-X*, Aladdin) Macmillan Child Grp.
Hughes, Monica. The Crystal Drop. LC 92-27706. (gr. 5-9). 1993. pap. 14.00 JR3 (*0-671-79195-8*, S&S BFYR) S&S Trade.
—Invitation to the Game. LC 90-22832. (Illus.). 192p. (gr. 5-9). 1991. pap. 14.00 jacketed, 3-pc. bdg. (*0-671-74236-1*, S&S BFYR) S&S Trade.
—Invitation to the Game. LC 90-22832. 208p. (gr. 5-9). 1993. pap. 3.95 (*0-671-86692-3*, Half Moon Bks) S&S Trade.
Hughes, Ted. The Iron Woman. LC 94-25485. 1995. write for info. (*0-8037-1796-2*); write for info. (*0-8037-1797-0*) Dial Bks Young.
Hunt, Dave. The Archon Conspiracy. LC 89-31535. 256p. (Orig.). (gr. 9 up). 1989. pap. 8.99 (*0-89081-766-9*) Harvest Hse.
Huxley, Aldous. Brave New World. abr. ed. 137p. 1973. pap. text ed. 5.95 (*0-582-53033-4*) Longman.
Ingrid, Charles. Lasertown Blues. (gr. 9-12). 1988. pap. 3.50 (*0-88677-260-5*) DAW Bks.
—Solar Kill. (gr. 9-12). 1987. pap. 3.50 (*0-88677-209-5*) DAW Bks.
Jackson, Steve & Livingstone, Ian. Rebel Planet. (Orig.). (gr. 5 up). 1986. pap. 2.50 (*0-440-97360-0*, LFL) Dell.
Jacobs, Paul S. Sleepers, Wake. (ps-3). 1991. 13.95 (*0-590-42397-5*) Scholastic Inc.
Johnson, Larry. Road Kill. Tabb, Doug, ed. (Illus.). 32p. (Orig.). (gr. 12). 1991. pap. 7.00 (*1-55806-117-7*, 415) Iron Crown Ent Inc.
Jones, Diana W. Hexwood. LC 93-18172. 304p. (gr. 6 up). 1994. 16.00 (*0-688-12488-7*) Greenwillow.
Kane, Thomas. Tales of the Loremasters. Amthor, Terry K. & Ruemmler, John D., eds. Roberts, Tony & Jaquays, Paul, illus. 32p. (Orig.). (gr. 12). 1989. pap. 6.00 (*1-55806-073-1*, 6004) Iron Crown Ent Inc.
Kane, Tom. Tales of the Loremasters, Book 2. Ruemmler, John D., ed. Martin, David & Jaquays, Paul, illus. 32p. (Orig.). (gr. 12). 1989. pap. 6.00 (*1-55806-034-0*, 6008) Iron Crown Ent Inc.
Kelly, Karla, et al. The Adventure of the Wandering Wolves in Vulcan's Vent. Crosby, Harriet, ed. Chan, Peter, illus. 40p. (Orig.). (gr. 1-6). 1993. pap. 6.95 (*1-883871-01-8*) Nature Co.
King, Buzz. Silicon Songs. 1992. pap. 3.25 (*0-440-21164-6*) Dell.
Klause, Annette C. Alien Secrets. LC 92-31326. 1993. 15.95 (*0-385-30928-7*) Delacorte.
Koike, Kazuo. Shades of Death, Pt. 1: Crying Freeman Graphic Novel. Horibuchi, Seiji, ed. Fujii, Satoru, tr. from JPN. Ikegami, Ryoichi, illus. 212p. (Orig.). (gr. 12 up). 1991. pap. 14.95 (*0-929279-75-1*) Viz Commns Inc.
—Shades of Death, Pt. 2: Crying Freeman Graphic Novel. Horibuchi, Seiji, ed. Fujii, Satoru, tr. from JPN. Ikegami, Ryoichi, illus. 212p. (Orig.). (gr. 12 up). 1992. pap. 14.95 (*0-929279-76-X*) Viz Commns Inc.
—Shades of Death, Pt. 3: Crying Freeman Graphic Novel. Horibuchi, Seiji, ed. Fujii, Satoru, tr. from JPN. Ikegami, Ryoichi, illus. 212p. (gr. 12 up). 1992. pap. 14.95 (*0-929279-77-8*) Viz Commns Inc.
Krensky, Stephen. The Dragon Circle. 128p. (gr. 7 up). 1990. pap. 3.95 (*0-689-71365-7*, Aladdin) Macmillan Child Grp.
LaDell, Leo. The Durandrium Find. Amthor, Terry K., ed. Velez, Waller & Martin, Ellisa, illus. 32p. (Orig.). (gr. 12). 1989. pap. 6.00 (*1-55806-021-9*, 9105) Iron Crown Ent Inc.
—Legacy of the Ancients. Amthor, Terry K., ed. Ridge, Jeff & Waltrip, Jason, illus. 32p. (Orig.). (gr. 12). 1989. pap. 6.00 (*1-55806-035-9*, 9106) Iron Crown Ent Inc.
Lankford, Robert D. Dream Weaver: Survive until Dawn, Vol. 1, Issue 1. Lankford, Robert D., illus. 24p. (gr. 11 up). 1987. pap. 1.95 (*0-9621811-0-2*) Lankford Comics.

Lapka, Fay S. Dark Is a Color. 264p. (Orig.). (gr. 9-12). 1990. pap. 6.99 (*0-87788-163-4*) Shaw Pubs.
—Hoverlight. (Orig.). 1991. pap. 6.99 (*0-87788-352-1*) Shaw Pubs.
Lawrence, Louise. Andra. LC 90-38595. 240p. (gr. 7 up). 1991. PLB 14.89 (*0-06-023705-8*) HarpC Child Bks.
—Extinction Is Forever & Other Stories. LC 92-35464. 1993. 15.00 (*0-06-022913-6*, HarpT); PLB 14.89 (*0-06-022914-4*, HarpT) HarpC.
—The Patchwork People. LC 93-40830. 1994. 14.95 (*0-395-67892-7*, Clarion Bks) HM.
Lawson, A. Star Baby. Apple, Margot, illus. 1992. 15.95 (*0-15-200905-1*, HB Juv Bks) HarBrace.
Le Guin, Ursula K. Catwing's Return. (ps-3). 1991. pap. 2.95 (*0-590-42832-2*) Scholastic Inc.
L'Engle, Madeleine. An Acceptable Time. (gr. 7 up). 1989. 16.00 (*0-374-30027-5*) FS&G.
—Madeleine L'Engle's Time Quartet, 4 vols. (gr. 4 up). 1987. pap. 14.00 (*0-440-95208-5*) Dell.
—Many Waters. LC 86-14911. 310p. (gr. 4 up). 1986. 17. 00 (*0-374-34796-4*); ltd. ed. o.s.i. 50.00 (*0-374-34797-2*) FS&G.
—A Swiftly Tilting Planet. LC 78-9648. 288p. (gr. 5 up). 1978. 17.00 (*0-374-37362-0*) FS&G.
—Swiftly Tilting Planet. (gr. 4-7). 1981. pap. 4.50 (*0-440-40158-5*) Dell.
—A Wind in the Door. 224p. (gr. 5-9). 1974. pap. 3.99 (*0-440-48761-7*, YB) Dell.
—A Wrinkle in Time. 224p. (gr. 5-9). 1973. pap. 4.50 (*0-440-49805-8*, YB) Dell.
—A Wrinkle in Time. LC 62-7203. 224p. (gr. 7 up). 1962. 17.00 (*0-374-38613-7*) FS&G.
Levin, Betty. Mercy's Mill. LC 91-31483. (gr. 7 up). 1992. 14.00 (*0-688-11122-X*) Greenwillow.
Lewis, C. S. Out of the Silent Planet. Date not set. 18.95 (*0-8488-0563-1*) Yestermorrow.
—Perelandra. 1976. 19.95 (*0-8488-0564-X*) Amereon Ltd.
Lewis, Dallas & Lewis, Lisa. The Planet Yes. Lewis, Dallas, illus. 32p. (Orig.). (gr. 3). 1994. 13.95x (*0-9634087-1-2*); pap. 6.95x (*0-9634087-2-0*) Silly Billys Bks.
Lindbergh, Anne. Nick of Time. LC 93-20777. 1994. 14. 95 (*0-316-52629-0*) Little.
Lively, Penelope. The Voyage of QV66. large type ed. Jones, Harold, illus. 280p. 1992. 16.95 (*0-7451-1548-9*, Galaxy Child Lrg Print) Chivers N Amer.
Loback, Tom. Halls of the Elven-King. Ruemmler, John D., ed. Martin, David, illus. 32p. (Orig.). (gr. 12). 1988. pap. 6.00 (*1-55806-015-4*, 8204) Iron Crown Ent Inc.
Longyear, Barry B. The Homecoming. Clark, Alan M., illus. 224p. 1989. 15.95 (*0-8027-6863-6*) Walker & Co.
Lowry, Lois. The Giver. large type ed. LC 93-21002. (gr. 9-12). 1993. 15.95 (*0-7862-0055-3*) Thorndike Pr.
McCaffrey, Anne. Dragondrums. Marcellino, Fred, illus. LC 78-11318. 256p. (gr. 6 up). 1979. SBE 16.95 (*0-689-30685-7*, Atheneum Child Bk) Macmillan Child Grp.
—Dragonsong. Lydecker, Laura, illus. LC 75-30530. 224p. (gr. 5-9). 1976. 16.95 (*0-689-30507-9*, Atheneum Child Bk) Macmillan Child Grp.
McEvoy, Seth. Planet Hunters. 128p. (Orig.). (gr. 3 up). 1985. pap. 1.95 (*0-553-24532-5*) Bantam.
—The Red Rocket. 120p. (Orig.). (gr. 4). 1985. pap. 2.25 (*0-553-26676-4*) Bantam.
McKeage, Jeffrey. Dark Mage of Rhudaur. Ney, Jessica, ed. McBride, Angus & Danforth, Liz, illus. 40p. (Orig.). (gr. 12). 1989. pap. 7.00 (*1-55806-072-3*, 8013) Iron Crown Ent Inc.
McOmber, Rachel B., ed. McOmber Phonics Storybooks: Tale of the Green Glob. rev. ed. (Illus.). write for info. (*0-944991-65-3*) Swift Lrn Res.
Maguire, Gregory. I Feel Like the Morning Star. LC 88-21544. 288p. (gr. 7 up). 1989. HarpC Child Bks.
Mantell, Paul & Hart, Avery, eds. The Slaves of Genosha. (Illus.). 32p. (Orig.). (ps-3). 1994. pap. 2.50 (*0-679-86202-1*) Random Bks Yng Read.
Marino, Tony. Intergalatic Grudge Match. LC 92-12845. (gr. 2). 1992. 13.99 (*1-56239-154-2*) Abdo & Dghtrs.
Martin, George R. Aces High, No. 2. 288p. (Orig.). 1987. pap. 5.50 (*0-553-26464-8*, Spectra) Bantam.
Marzollo, Jean & Marzollo, Claudio. Ruthie's Rude Friends. Meddaugh, Susan, illus. LC 84-1707. (ps-3). 1984. Dial Bks Young.
Matsumoto, Leiji. Captain Harlock Television Scripts, Vol. 1. Villa, Mickie & Mason, Tom, eds. Dunn, Ben, illus. Gibson, Robert, intro. by. (Illus.). 135p. 1990. pap. 19.95 (*0-944735-63-0*) Malibu Graphics.
Mayakovsky, Stanislaw & Geary, Rick. Cyberantics. (Illus.). 56p. (Orig.). 1992. 14.95 (*1-878574-29-9*) Dark Horse Comics.
Mayhar, Ardath. A Place of Silver Silence. Ortega, Pat, illus. (gr. 7 up). 1988. 15.95 (*0-8027-6825-3*) Walker & Co.
Merwin, Richard. Mega-Slank from Titanium. LC 92-12842. (gr. 2). 1992. 13.99 (*1-56239-151-8*) Abdo & Dghtrs.
Miyazaki, Hayao. Nausicaa of the Valley of the Wind, Vols. 1-2. (Illus.). (gr. 7-12). 1993. Vol. 1. 19.95 (*4-19-086975-9*) Vol. 2. 19.95 (*4-19-086976-7*) Tokuma Pub.
Moore, Silas. Scarlet Arena 30303. Oddo, Genevieve, ed. Luering, Jacqueline M., illus. LC 74-190272. 196p. (gr. 8-12). 1972. PLB 3.95 (*0-87783-063-0*) Oddo.
Mooser, Stephen. Disaster in Room 101. MacDougall, Rob, illus. LC 93-24055. 80p. (gr. 2-4). 1993. PLB 2.95 (*0-8167-3278-7*); pap. text ed. 2.95 (*0-8167-3279-5*) Troll Assocs.
Morin, John B. Sea-Lords of Gondor. McBride, Angus, illus. Fenlon, Peter C., Jr., ed. 64p. (Orig.). (gr. 10-12). 1987. pap. 12.00 (*0-915795-88-4*, 3400) Iron Crown Ent Inc.
Moulton, Deborah. Children of Time. (gr. 7 up). 1989. 14.95 (*0-8037-0607-3*) Dial Bks Young.
Mueller, Kate. Antimatter Universe. (gr. 6 up). 1994. pap. 3.50 (*0-553-56391-2*) Bantam.
Ney, Jessica, ed. The Necromancer's Lieutenant. Danforth, Liz & Martin, David, illus. 32p. (Orig.). (gr. 12). 1990. pap. 7.00 (*1-55806-113-4*, 8113) Iron Crown Ent Inc.
Obergfoll, Michael. Super Santa of All Space & Beyond Assisted by His Galaxy Elves. Jew, Flora, illus. 38p. (gr. 2-12). 1988. 2.95 (*0-929052-00-5*) Super Santa Prodns.
—Super Santa of All Space & Beyond Assisted by His Galaxy Elves: Coloring Activity Book. Obergfoll, Michael, illus. LC 72-847. 34p. (gr. 2-12). 1988. 10.95 (*0-929052-01-3*) Super Santa Prodns.
O'Brien, Jane. Alien. (Illus.). 48p. (gr. 5-6). 1991. text ed. 13.95 RSBE (*0-89686-573-8*, Crestwood Hse) Macmillan Child Grp.
O'Brien, Robert C. Z for Zachariah. LC 74-76736. 256p. (gr. 7 up). 1975. SBE 15.95 (*0-689-30442-0*, Atheneum Child Bk) Macmillan Child Grp.
Oppel, Kenneth. Dead Water Zone. LC 92-37282. 1993. 14.95 (*0-316-65102-8*, Joy St Bks) Little.
Ostrander, John & Wein, Len. Legends. Kahan, Bob, ed. Byrne & Kesel, illus. 160p. 1993. pap. 9.95 collector's ed. (*1-56389-095-X*) DC Comics.
Ouellette, et al. Macross II: Deck Plans, Vol. 1. Siembieda, Kevin, et al, eds. Long, Kevin & Durocher, Dominique, illus. 64p. (Orig.). (gr. 8 up). 1994. pap. 9.95 (*0-916211-66-5*, 592) Palladium Bks.
Oxley, Dorothy. Quest. 144p. (Orig.). (gr. 7-10). 1990. pap. 4.99 (*0-7459-1846-8*) Lion USA.
Pace, Sue. The Last Oasis. LC 92-20223. 1993. 15.00 (*0-385-30881-7*) Delacorte.
Packard, Edward. Comet Crash. (gr. 4-7). 1994. pap. 3.50 (*0-553-56009-3*) Bantam.
—The Comet Masters. (gr. 4-7). 1991. pap. 2.99 (*0-553-28961-6*) Bantam.
—The Fiber People. (gr. 4-7). 1991. pap. 2.99 (*0-553-29355-9*) Bantam.
—Return to the Cave of Time. 128p. (Orig.). (gr. 4). 1985. pap. 2.25 (*0-553-25495-2*) Bantam.
—The Space Fortress. (gr. 4-7). 1991. pap. 2.99 (*0-553-28899-7*) Bantam.
—The Third Planet from Altair. 128p. (Orig.). (gr. 5 up). 1989. pap. 2.50 (*0-553-23185-5*) Bantam.
Pascal, Francine. Date with a Werewolf. 1994. pap. 3.50 (*0-553-56228-2*) Bantam.
Pausacker, Jenny. Fast Forward. Rawlins, Donna, illus. (gr. 4-7). 1991. 12.95 (*0-688-10195-X*) Lothrop.
Peel, John. Uptime Downtime. LC 90-27570. 1992. pap. 14.00 jacketed, 3-pc. bdg. (*0-671-73274-9*, S&S BFYR) S&S Trade.
Petersen, P. J. Would You Settle for Improbable? 160p. (gr. 5-9). 1983. pap. 3.25 (*0-440-99733-X*, LFL) Dell.
Peyton, K. M. The Edge of the Cloud. (gr. 7 up). 1992. 16.50 (*0-8446-6566-5*) Peter Smith.
Pfeffer, Susan B. Future Forward. Glass, Andrew, illus. (gr. 5 up). 1989. 13.95 (*0-385-29740-8*) Delacorte.
Pinkwater, Daniel. Guys from Space. Pinkwater, Daniel, illus. LC 91-20100. 32p. (gr. k-3). 1992. pap. 3.95 (*0-689-71590-0*, Aladdin) Macmillan Child Grp.
—I Was a Second Grade Werewolf. Pinkwater, Daniel, illus. (gr. 1-3). 1986. incl. cassette 19.95 (*0-87499-010-6*); pap. 12.95 incl. cassette (*0-87499-008-4*); incl. cassette, 4 paperbacks guide 27. 95 (*0-87499-009-2*) Live Oak Media.
—Ned Feldman, Space Pirate. Pinkwater, Daniel, illus. LC 93-40893. (gr. k-3). 1994. 14.95 (*0-02-774633-X*, Macmillan Child Bk) Macmillan Child Grp.
Pinkwater, Daniel M. I Was a Second Grade Werewolf. Pinkwater, Daniel M., illus. LC 82-17715. 32p. (ps-2). 1985. pap. 3.95 (*0-525-44194-8*, DCB) Dutton Child Bks.
Plante, Edmund. Alone in the House. 176p. (Orig.). (gr. 5). 1991. pap. 3.50 (*0-380-76424-5*, Flare) Avon.
Platt, Kin. Dracula, Go Home. Mayo, Frank, illus. 96p. (gr. 7 up). 1981. pap. 1.25 (*0-440-92022-1*, LE) Dell.
Poppel, George. Planet of Trash. Moyer, Barry S., illus. 32p. (ps-3). 1987. 9.95 (*0-915765-42-X*, Pub. by Panda Monium Bks.) Natl Pr Bks.
Prowense, Mary J. Pamela & the Revolution. Schatz, Molly, ed. Kear, Suzanne, illus. 130p. (gr. 7 up). 1993. 12.95 (*0-9635107-2-X*) Marc Anthony.
Pyle, Howard. The Garden Behind the Moon: The Real Story of the Moon Angel. (Illus.). 176p. (gr. 6-8). 1991. pap. 10.95 (*0-930407-22-9*) Parabola Bks.
Rebellion, Boxer. The Invisible Man & The Butler. Abell, ed. & illus. (gr. 8 up). 1992. PLB 25.00 (*1-56611-013-0*); pap. 15.00 (*1-56611-149-8*) Jonas.
Roberts, Willo D. The Girl with the Silver Eyes. LC 80-12391. 192p. (gr. 4-7). 1980. SBE 14.95 (*0-689-30786-1*, Atheneum Child Bk) Macmillan Child Grp.
Roos, Stephen. Twelve-Year-Old Vows Revenge: After Being Dumped by Extraterrestrial on First Date. (gr. 4-7). 1991. pap. 3.25 (*0-440-40465-7*) Dell.
Rubenstein, Gillian. Space Demons. MacDonald, Pat, ed. (gr. 6-9). 1989. pap. 2.95 (*0-671-67912-0*, Archway) PB.
Rubinstein. Galax-Arena. Date not set. PLB 13.89 (*0-06-023450-4*) HarpC Child Bks.
Rubinstein, Gillian. Galax-Arena. LC 93-1118. 1994. 14. 00 (*0-06-023449-0*, HarpT) HarpC.
—Skymaze. LC 90-43796. 192p. (gr. 6-9). 1991. 14.95 (*0-531-05929-4*); PLB 14.99 (*0-531-08529-5*) Orchard Bks Watts.
Russo, Joe, et al. Planet of the Apes Revisited. Heston, Charlton, intro. by. (Illus.). 212p. (Orig.). (gr. 9-12). 1991. pap. 12.95 (*0-9627508-2-4*) Image NY.
Ryan, Mary C. Me Two. (gr. 4-7). 1991. 16.95 (*0-316-76376-4*) Little.
Rymer, Alta M. Beep-Bap-Zap-Jack. LC 74-20428. (Illus.). 48p. (gr. 5-7). 1974. 20.00 (*0-9600792-0-3*) Rymer Bks.
—Captain Zomo. Rymer, Alta M. & Rymer, Tracy J., illus. LC 79-67651. 48p. (Orig.). (gr. 5-7). 1993. 20. 00x (*0-9600792-2-X*) Rymer Bks.
—Stars of Obron: Chambo Returns. Rymer, Alta M., illus. 56p. (Orig.). (gr. 5-7). 1987. pap. text ed. 25.00 (*0-9600792-3-8*) Rymer Bks.
Sadler, Marilyn. Alistair & the Alien Invasion. Bollen, Roger, illus. LC 92-22828. 1994. pap. 15.00 (*0-671-75957-4*, S&S BFYR) S&S Trade.
Sampson, Fay. Finnglas & the Stones of Choosing. (Illus.). 128p. (gr. 4-8). 1989. pap. 4.99 (*0-7459-1124-2*) Lion USA.
—Finnglas of the Horses. (Illus.). 178p. (gr. 4-8). 1989. pap. 4.99 (*0-85648-899-2*) Lion USA.
Saunders, Susan. The Green Slime. 64p. (gr. 1-8). 1982. pap. 2.25 (*0-553-15480-X*) Bantam.
Schmid, Eleonore. The Air Around Us. Schmid, Eleonore & James, J. Alison, illus. LC 92-9830. 32p. (gr. k-3). 1992. 14.95 (*1-55858-165-0*); PLB 14.88 (*1-55858-166-9*) North-South Bks NYC.
Scott, Michael. Gemini Game. LC 93-39972. 160p. 1994. 14.95 (*0-8234-1092-7*) Holiday.
Sculfield, Byron. Hello! My Name Is Mr. ImGonChop. Omalade, Kip, illus. 1993. pap. 5.95 (*0-88378-097-6*) Third World.
Senn, Oscar S. Loonie Louie Meets the Space Fungus. 112p. 1991. pap. 2.95 (*0-380-75894-6*, Camelot) Avon.
Service, Pamela F. Stinker's Return. LC 92-21800. 96p. (gr. 4-6). 1993. SBE 12.95 (*0-684-19542-9*, Scribners Young Read) Macmillan Child Grp.
—Under Alien Stars. LC 89-28025. 224p. (gr. 4-8). 1990. SBE 14.95 (*0-689-31621-6*, Atheneum Child Bk) Macmillan Child Grp.
Shusterman, Neil. Dissidents. 192p. 1994. pap. 3.99 (*0-8125-3461-1*) Tor Bks.
Silverberg, Robert. Letters from Atlantis. Gould, Robert, illus. LC 90-562. 144p. (gr. 7 up). 1990. SBE 14.95 (*0-689-31570-8*, Atheneum Child Bk) Macmillan Child Grp.
—Project Pendulum. (gr. 8 up). 1987. 15.95 (*0-8027-6712-5*) Walker & Co.
Simmons, Aaron. Surface Thoughts. Thornton, Don, intro. by. Soto, Zachary & Bostick, Matthew, illus. 48p. (Orig.). (gr. 5-12). 1993. pap. 5.00 (*1-882913-01-9*) Thornton LA.
Simpkins, Mark A. Rames Two. (gr. 4-7). 1986. pap. 5.95 (*0-916095-10-X*) Pubs Pr UT.
Sleator, William. The Boy Who Reversed Himself. LC 86-19700. 176p. (gr. 5-11). 1986. 13.95 (*0-525-44276-6*, DCB) Dutton Child Bks.
—The Duplicate. (gr. 5 up). 1990. pap. 3.99 (*0-553-28634-X*, Starfire) Bantam.
—The Green Futures of Tycho. 144p. (gr. 7 up). 1991. pap. 3.95 (*0-14-034581-7*, Puffin) Puffin Bks.
—House of Stairs. LC 73-17417. 176p. (gr. 7 up). 1985. 14.95 (*0-525-32335-X*, DCB) Dutton Child Bks.
—House of Stairs. (Illus.). 172p. (gr. 7 up). 1991. pap. 3.95 (*0-14-034580-9*, Puffin) Puffin Bks.
—Interstellar Pig. 224p. (gr. 6 up). 1986. pap. 3.50 (*0-553-25564-9*, Starfire) Bantam.
—Strange Attractors. LC 89-33840. 176p. (gr. 5-11). 1990. 13.95 (*0-525-44530-7*, DCB) Dutton Child Bks.
—Strange Attractors. (Illus.). 144p. (gr. 7 up). 1991. pap. 3.99 (*0-14-034582-5*, Puffin) Puffin Bks.
Slobodkin, Louis. The Space Ship Returns to the Apple Tree. Slobodkin, Louis, illus. LC 93-10747. 128p. (gr. 3-7). 1994. pap. 3.95 (*0-689-71768-7*, Aladdin) Macmillan Child Grp.
—The Space Ship under the Apple Tree. 2nd ed. Slobodkin, Louis, illus. LC 92-42712. 128p. (gr. 3-7). 1993. pap. 3.95 (*0-689-71741-5*, Aladdin) Macmillan Child Grp.
Slote, Alfred. My Trip to Alpha I. Berson, Harold, illus. LC 78-6463. 96p. (gr. 2-5). 1992. (Lipp Jr Bks); PLB 13.89 (*0-397-32510-X*, Lipp Jr Bks) HarpC Child Bks.
Snell, Gordon. Tom's Amazing Machine Zaps Back! (Illus.). 144p. (gr. 4-6). 1992. 15.95 (*0-09-173888-1*, Pub. by Hutchinson UK) Trafalgar.
Sparger, Rex. The Doll. (ps-7). 1987. pap. 2.50 (*0-553-26759-0*) Bantam.
Specter, B. J. Camp Fright. MacDonald, Pat, ed. 96p. (Orig.). 1992. pap. 2.99 (*0-671-75559-5*, Minstrel Bks) PB.
—Twisted Tours. Ashby, Ruth, ed. 128p. (Orig.). 1992. pap. 2.99 (*0-671-75558-7*, Minstrel Bks) PB.
Spinner, Stephanie. Aliens for Dinner. Bjorkman, Steve & Sims, Blanche, illus. LC 93-47105. 80p. (Orig.). (gr. 2-4). 1994. PLB 7.99 (*0-679-95858-4*); pap. 2.99 (*0-679-85858-X*) Random.

Staplehurst, Graham. Mouths of the Entwash. Fenlon, Peter C., Jr., ed. Sharp, Shawn & McBride, Angus, illus. 40p. (Orig.). (gr. 12). 1988. pap. 7.00 (*1-55806-010-3*, 8011) Iron Crown Ent Inc.
Stauffer, Brooke. Fruit Blasterz from Outer Space. 96p. (Orig.). 1993. pap. 3.50 (*0-380-76404-0*, Camelot Young) Avon.
Stevenson, Robert Louis. Dr. Jekyll & Mr. Hyde. (gr. 8 up). 1964. pap. 2.25 (*0-8049-0042-6*, CL-42) Airmont.
—Master of Ballantrae. (gr. 8 up). 1964. pap. 1.95 (*0-8049-0047-7*, CL-47) Airmont.
Stevermer, C. River Rats. 1992. 16.95 (*0-15-200895-0*, HB Juv Bks) HarBrace.
Stine, R. L. Bozos on Patrol. 160p. 1992. pap. 2.75 (*0-590-44747-5*, Apple Paperbacks) Scholastic Inc.
Strickland, Brad. Stowaways. (gr. 6 up). 1994. pap. 3.99 (*0-671-88000-4*, Minstrel Bks) PB.
Stuart, W. J. Forbidden Planet. 212p. (gr. 5 up). 1990. pap. 3.95 (*0-374-42445-4*, Sunburst) FS&G.
Tallis, Robyn. Fire in the Sky. (gr. 6 up). 1989. pap. 2.95 (*0-8041-0463-8*) Ivy Books.
Taylor, Tim. Cyclops Vale & Other Tales. Ruemmler, John D., ed. Roberts, Tony & Jaquays, Paul, illus. 32p. (Orig.). (gr. 12). 1989. pap. 6.00 (*1-55806-042-1*, 6009) Iron Crown Ent Inc.
Taylor, Timothy. The Orgillion Horror. Ruemmler, John D., ed. Martin, David & Jaquays, Paul, illus. 32p. (Orig.). (gr. 12). 1989. pap. 6.00 (*1-55806-029-4*, 6006) Iron Crown Ent Inc.
Teague, Mark. Moog-Moog, Space Barber. 32p. 1991. pap. 4.95 (*0-590-43331-8*) Scholastic Inc.
Teitelbaum, Michael. Sonic the Hedgehog. Teitelbaum, Michael, illus. LC 93-14029. (gr. 2-4). 1993. pap. 2.50 (*0-8167-3199-3*) Troll Assocs.
—Sonic the Hedgehog: Robotnik's Revenge. Hanson, Glen, illus. LC 93-48920. 64p. (gr. 2-4). 1994. pap. 2.50 (*0-8167-3438-0*) Troll Assocs.
Thorne, Ian. The Blob. LC 81-19633. (Illus.). 48p. (gr. 4-8). 1982. text ed. 11.95 RSBE (*0-89686-212-7*, Crestwood Hse) Macmillan Child Grp.
—Godzilla. LC 76-51148. (Illus.). 48p. (gr. 3 up). 1977. text ed. 11.95 RSBE (*0-913940-68-2*, Crestwood Hse); cass. 7.95 (*0-89686-486-3*) Macmillan Child Grp.
Time Life Inc. Editors. Voyage of the Micronauts: A Book about the Human Body. Fallow, Allan, ed. Cooke, Tom, illus. 64p. (ps-2). 1992. write for info. (*0-8094-9295-4*); PLB write for info. (*0-8094-9296-2*) Time-Life.
Time Warp: Golden Mini Play Lights. (ps-3). 1993. 14.95 (*0-307-75400-6*, Pub. by Golden Bks) Western Pub.
Timlin, William M. The Ship That Sailed to Mars. (Illus.). 104p. (gr. 4-5). 1992. Repr. of 1923 ed. 25.00 (*0-9633212-6-9*) V Wagner Pubns.
Townsend, Tom. Ghost Flyers. LC 93-19906. 1993. 11.95 (*0-89015-897-5*) Sunbelt Media.
—Trader Wooly & the Ghost in the Colonel's Jeep. (Illus.). 110p. (gr. 6-8). 1991. 10.95 (*0-89015-807-X*) Sunbelt Media.
Transformers Project BR. (Illus.). 1986. pap. 1.25 (*0-440-82136-3*) Dell.
Tzannes, Robin. Professor Puffendorf's Secret Potions. Paul, Korky, illus. 40p. (ps-5). 1992. 16.95 (*1-56288-267-8*) Checkerboard.
Verne, Jules. De la Terre a la Lune. (gr. 7-12). 1970. pap. 6.95 (*0-88436-048-2*, 40275) EMC.
—De la Terre a la Lune. (FRE.). 246p. (gr. 5-10). 1977. pap. 9.95 (*2-07-056625-0*) Schoenhof.
—From the Earth to the Moon. Lowndes, R. A., intro. by. (gr. 8 up). 1967. pap. 1.75 (*0-8049-0142-2*, CL-142) Airmont.
—Journey to the Center of the Earth. Lowndes, R. A., intro. by. (gr. 6 up). 1965. pap. 3.50 (*0-8049-0060-4*, CL-60) Airmont.
—Journey to the Center of the Earth. 253p. (gr. 5 up). 1986. pap. 2.99 (*0-14-035049-7*, Puffin) Puffin Bks.
—A Journey to the Center of the Earth. James, Raymond, adapted by. Geehan, Wayne, illus. LC 89-20560. 48p. (gr. 3-6). 1990. lib. bdg. 12.89 (*0-8167-1867-9*); pap. text ed. 3.95 (*0-8167-1868-7*) Troll Assocs.
—Master of the World. Lowndes, R. A., intro. by. (gr. 7 up). 1965. pap. 1.25 (*0-8049-0073-6*, CL-73) Airmont.
—Michael Strogoff. (gr. 8 up). 1964. pap. 1.50 (*0-8049-0048-5*, CL-48) Airmont.
—Mysterious Island. (gr. 8 up). 1965. pap. 1.95 (*0-8049-0077-9*, CL-77) Airmont.
—Round the Moon. (gr. 7 up). 1968. pap. 1.50 (*0-8049-0182-1*, CL-182) Airmont.
—Twenty Thousand League under the Sea. 285p. 1992. pap. 3.25 (*0-590-45179-0*) Scholastic Inc.
—Twenty Thousand Leagues under the Sea. rev. ed. Grund, Diane F., ed. (Illus.). 128p. 1990. pap. 2.95 (*0-942025-85-7*) Kidsbks.
Waite, Michael P. Emma Wimble, Accidental Astronaut. LC 88-10946. 112p. (gr. 3-7). 1988. pap. 4.99 (*1-55513-639-7*, Chariot Bks) Chariot Family.
Wallis, James & Sienbieda, Kevin. Mutants in Orbit. Marciniszyn, Alex, et al, eds. Gustovich, Mike & Ewell, Newton, illus. 112p. (Orig.). (gr. 8 up). 1992. pap. 11.95 (*0-916211-48-7*, 514) Palladium Bks.
Ward, David. The Misenberg Accelerator. LC 94-10517. 1994. 4.99 (*0-8407-9235-2*) Nelson.
Wells, H. G. First Men in the Moon. Lowndes, R. A., intro. by. (gr. 7 up). 1965. pap. 1.25 (*0-8049-0078-7*, CL-78) Airmont.
—Food of the Gods. (gr. 7 up). 1965. pap. 0.95 (*0-8049-0059-0*, CL-59) Airmont.
—Guerre des Mondes. Bozellac, Anne, illus. (FRE.). 288p. (gr. 5-10). 1990. pap. 9.95 (*2-07-033567-4*) Schoenhof.
—In the Days of the Comet. Lowndes, R. A., intro. by. (gr. 7 up). pap. 1.25 (*0-8049-0111-2*, CL-111) Airmont.
—Invisible Man. (gr. 8 up). 1964. pap. 1.75 (*0-8049-0040-X*, CL-40) Airmont.
—Invisible Man. (gr. 4-7). 1990. pap. 2.95 (*0-590-44016-0*) Scholastic Inc.
—Invisible Man. (gr. 4-7). 1993. pap. 2.95 (*0-89375-415-3*) Troll Assocs.
—Seven Science Fiction Novels. 1015p. (gr. 9 up). 29.95 (*0-486-20264-X*) Dover.
—The Strange Orchid. rev. ed. (gr. 9-12). 1989. Repr. of 1898 ed. multi-media kit 35.00 (*0-685-31127-9*) Balance Pub.
—Time Machine. (gr. 7 up). 1964. pap. 2.50 (*0-8049-0044-2*, CL-44) Airmont.
—The Time Machine. Binder, Otto, ed. Nino, Alex, illus. LC 73-75467. 64p. (Orig.). (gr. 5-10). 1973. pap. 2.95 (*0-88301-102-6*) Pendulum Pr.
—The Time Machine. Martin, Les, adapted by. Edens, John, illus. LC 89-39506. 96p. (gr. 2-6). 1994. pap. 2.99 (*0-679-80371-8*) Random Bks Yng Read.
—The Time Machine. James, Raymond, ed. Deal, Jim, illus. LC 92-5804. 48p. (gr. 3-6). 1992. PLB 12.89 (*0-8167-2872-0*); pap. text ed. 3.95 (*0-8167-2873-9*) Troll Assocs.
—War of the Worlds. (gr. 8 up). 1964. 2.50 (*0-8049-0045-0*, CL-45) Airmont.
—The War of the Worlds. (gr. 3 up). 1960. lib. bdg. 5.39 (*0-394-90471-0*) Random Bks Yng Read.
—The War of the Worlds. 226p. 1993. pap. 2.50 (*0-8125-0515-8*) Tor Bks.
—War of the Worlds. (gr. 4-7). 1993. pap. 2.95 (*0-89375-347-5*) Troll Assocs.
Wells, H. G. & Geary, Rick. The Invisible Man. (Illus.). 52p. Date not set. pap. 4.95 (*1-57209-020-0*) Classics Int Ent.
Wells, H. G., et al. The Island of Dr. Moreau. (Illus.). 52p. Date not set. pap. 4.95 (*1-57209-012-X*) Classics Int Ent.
Welty, Harry R. Visit to the Attic. Lee, Marlene K., illus. LC 92-90838. 250p. (Orig.). (gr. 6-8). 1992. pap. 6.95 (*0-9632953-0-6*) Welty Pr.
Wheeler, Thomas G. Lost Threshold. LC 68-16349. (Illus.). (gr. 7 up). 1968. 21.95 (*0-87599-140-8*) S G Phillips.
White, John. The Tower of Geburah. LC 78-2078. (Illus.). 404p. (gr. 4 up). 1978. pap. 10.99 (*0-87784-560-3*, 560) InterVarsity.
Wiesner, David. June 29, 1999. Wiesner, David, illus. 32p. (ps-3). 1992. 15.95 (*0-395-59762-5*, Clarion Bks) HM.
Wildsmith, Brian & Wildsmith, Rebecca. Jack & the Meanstalk. LC 93-30374. 1994. 15.00 (*0-679-85810-5*); pap. 15.99 (*0-679-95810-X*) Knopf Bks Yng Read.
Williams, Lorraine D., ed. Buck Rogers: The First 60 Years in the 25th Century. LC 88-50400. (Illus.). 368p. 1988. 24.95 (*0-88038-604-5*) TSR Inc.
Williams, Sheila. Loch Moose Monster: More Stories from Isaac Asimov's Science Fiction Magazine. LC 91-36291. 1993. 16.00 (*0-385-30600-8*) Doubleday.
Williams, Sheila & Ardai, Charles, eds. Why I Left Harry's All-Night Hamburgers: And Other Short Stories from Isaac Asimov's Science Fiction Magazine. 288p. (gr. 7 up). 1992. pap. 3.99 (*0-440-21394-0*, LFL) Dell.
Williams, Travis. Changes. Thatch, Nancy R., ed. Williams, Travis, illus. Melton, David, intro. by. LC 93-13420. (Illus.). 29p. (gr. 6-9). 1993. PLB 14.95 (*0-933849-44-3*) Landmark Edns.
Wilson, Robert A. Schrodinger's Cat Trilogy. 1988. pap. 13.95 (*0-440-50070-2*, Dell Trade Pbks) Dell.
Wolff, Robert S. The Caves of Mars. LC 87-34252. 168p. (gr. 7 up). 1988. PLB 15.00 (*0-208-02190-6*, Linnet) Shoe String.
Woodruff, Elvira. The Disappearing Bike Shop. LC 91-29863. 176p. (gr. 3-7). 1992. 13.95 (*0-8234-0933-3*) Holiday.
Wrightson, Bernie. Captain Stern: Running Out of Time, No. 3. Amara, Phil, ed. Wrightson, Bernie, illus. 48p. (gr. 6 up). 1994. pap. 4.95 (*0-87816-230-5*) Kitchen Sink.
—Captain Stern: Running Out of Time, No. 4. Amara, Phil, ed. Wrightson, Bernie, illus. 48p. (gr. 4 up). 1994. pap. 4.95 (*0-87816-231-3*) Kitchen Sink.
Yolen, Jane. Commander Toad & the Planet of the Grapes. Degen, Bruce, illus. 64p. (gr. 1-4). 1982. (Coward); pap. 6.95 (*0-698-20540-5*) Putnam Pub Group.
—Two Thousand Forty-One: Twelve Stories about the Future by Top Science Fiction Writers. 1994. pap. 3.99 (*0-440-21898-5*) Dell.
Zakalik, Leslie S. Super Science Fiction. 48p. (gr. 4-6). 1977. 5.95 (*0-88160-026-1*, LW 211) Learning Wks.
Zelazny, Roger. The Courts of Chaos. 144p. (gr. 9 up). 1979. pap. 4.99 (*0-380-47175-2*) Avon.

SCIENCE FICTION–HISTORY AND CRITICISM

Asimov, Isaac. Science Fiction Science Fact. (gr. 4-7). 1991. pap. 4.95 (*0-440-40352-9*) Dell.
—Space Spotters Guide. (gr. 4-7). 1991. pap. 4.95 (*0-440-40388-X*) Dell.
L'Engle, Madeleine. A Wrinkle in Time: (Una Arruga en el Tiempo) (gr. 1-6). 15.95 (*84-204-4074-4*) Santillana.
Payson, Patricia. Science Fiction: A Zephyr Learning Packet. 79p. (gr. k-8). 1980. pap. 19.95 spiral bdg. (*0-913705-18-7*) Zephyr Pr AZ.

SCIENTIFIC APPARATUS AND INSTRUMENTS

see also names of groups of instruments, e.g. Aeronautical Instruments; Astronomical Instruments; Chemical Apparatus; Electric Apparatus and Appliances; Meteorological Instruments

Newton, David E. Making & Using Scientific Equipment. LC 92-38039. (Illus.). 128p. (gr. 9-12). 1993. PLB 13.90 (*0-531-11176-8*); pap. 6.95 (*0-531-15663-X*) Watts.

SCIENTIFIC EDUCATION

see Science–Study and Teaching

SCIENTIFIC EXPEDITIONS

see also names of regions explored, e.g. Antarctic Regions; Arctic Regions; and names of expeditions

Stefoff, Rebecca. Scientific Explorers. (Illus.). 144p. 1992. PLB 22.00 (*0-19-507689-3*) OUP.

SCIENTIFIC EXPERIMENTS

see Science–Experiments;
also particular branches of science with the subdivision Experiments, e.g. Chemistry–Experiments

SCIENTIFIC INSTRUMENTS

see Scientific Apparatus and Instruments

SCIENTIFIC METHOD

see special subjects with the subdivision Methodology, e.g. Science–Methodology

SCIENTIFIC RECREATIONS

see also Mathematical Recreations

Allison, Linda & Ferguson, Tom. The Get-Well-Quick Kit. Allison, Linda & Wells, William S., illus. LC 92-42626. 1993. 14.38 (*0-201-63213-6*) Addison-Wesley.
Barr, George. Fun with Science: Forty Six Entertaining Demonstrations. LC 93-45547. (Illus.). 160p. pap. 3.95 (*0-486-28000-4*) Dover.
—Outdoor Science Projects for Young People. (Illus.). 160p. pap. 3.95 (*0-486-26855-1*) Dover.
—Science Tricks & Magic for Young People. (Illus.). 126p. (gr. 3-11). 1987. pap. 3.95 (*0-486-25453-4*) Dover.
Bisignano, Judith. Trivial Pursuit - Science (Junior High) (Illus.). 64p. (gr. 7-9). 1992. 12.95 (*0-86653-651-5*, GA1387) Good Apple.
Book, David L. Problems for Puzzlebusters. LC 92-90284. (Illus.). 358p. (gr. 7-12). 1992. 24.95 (*0-9633217-0-6*) Enigmatics.
Charles, Kirk. Magic Tricks. LC 92-9012. (Illus.). (gr. 2-6). 1992. PLB 14.95 (*0-89565-964-6*) Childs World.
Cobb, Vicki & Darling, Kathy. Wanna Bet! Science Challenges Bound to Fool You. LC 92-8962. 1992. 13.00 (*0-688-11213-7*) Lothrop.
Friedhoffer, Robert. Magic Tricks, Science Facts. LC 89-28487. 1990. PLB 12.90 (*0-531-10902-X*) Watts.
Ginns, Russell. Midnight Science. LC 94-4142. 1994. pap. text ed. write for info. (*0-7167-6569-1*) W H Freeman.
Hall, Godfrey. Mind Twisters. Oxford Illustrators Staff, et al, illus. LC 91-27688. 96p. (Orig.). (gr. 3-7). 1992. pap. 10.00 (*0-679-82038-8*) Random Bks Yng Read.
Jacome, Karen & Jacome, Felipe. Trivial Pursuit - Science (Intermediate) (Illus.). 64p. (gr. 4-6). 1992. 12.95 (*0-86653-649-3*, GA1386) Good Apple.
Kallen, Stuart A. Mad Science Experiments. LC 92-14776. 1992. 12.94 (*1-56239-128-3*) Abdo & Dghtrs.
Kerrod, Robin. Sounds & Music. LC 90-25543. (Illus.). 32p. (gr. 3-8). 1991. PLB 9.95 (*1-85435-270-9*) Marshall Cavendish.
McGowan, Christopher. Discover Dinosaurs: Become a Dinosaur Detective. Holdcroft, Tina, illus. LC 92-42627. 96p. (gr. 4-7). 1993. pap. 9.57 (*0-201-62267-X*) Addison-Wesley.
Markle, Sandra. Exploring Summer. 176p. (gr. 7-8). 1991. pap. 2.95 (*0-380-71320-9*, Camelot) Avon.
—Measuring Up: Experiments, Puzzles & Games Exploring Measurement. LC 94-19240. 1995. 16.00 (*0-689-31904-5*, Atheneum) Macmillan.
Murray, Peter. Professor Solomon Snickerdoodle Looks at Water. Mitchell, Anastasia, illus. LC 93-1322. (gr. 2-6). 1995. 14.95 (*1-56766-081-9*) Childs World.
—Silly Science Tricks. LC 92-18903. (gr. 2-6). 1992. PLB 14.95 (*0-89565-976-X*) Childs World.
Oxlade, Chris. Air. Thompson, Ian, illus. LC 94-5547. 30p. (gr. 2-5). 1994. 12.95 (*0-8120-6444-5*); pap. 4.95 (*0-8120-1983-0*) Barron.
—Light. Thompson, Ian, illus. LC 94-5549. 30p. (gr. 2-5). 1994. 12.95 (*0-8120-6445-3*); pap. 4.95 (*0-8120-1984-9*) Barron.
—Science Magic with Sound. Thompson, Ian, illus. LC 94-5550. 30p. (gr. 2-5). 1994. 12.95 (*0-8120-6446-1*); pap. 4.95 (*0-8120-1985-7*) Barron.
—Water. Thompson, Ian, illus. LC 94-5548. 30p. (gr. 2-5). 1994. 12.95 (*0-8120-6448-8*); pap. 4.95 (*0-8120-1986-5*) Barron.
Packard, Ann & Stafford, Shirley. Space. 58p. (ps-3). 1981. write for info. (*0-9607580-2-X*) S Stafford.
Penrose, Gordon. Dr. Zed's Dazzling Book of Science Activities. Bucholtz-Ross, Linda, illus. 48p. 1993. pap. 7.95 (*0-919872-78-6*, Pub. by Greey dePencier CN) Firefly Bks Ltd.
—More Science Surprises from Dr. Zed. LC 91-38935. (Illus.). 32p. (gr. k-3). 1992. pap. 12.00 (*0-671-77810-2*, S&S BFYR); pap. 6.00 (*0-671-77811-0*, S&S BFYR) S&S Trade.

290p. (gr. 4-8). 1994. PLB 28.50g (*0-9642898-0-6*) Larchmere Ltd. WATERDRUM SCIENCE is a beautifully illustrated activity book for children. Parents & teachers will appreciate the useful chapter introductions. Two hundred exciting, hands-on science/art projects help kids explore fifty science concepts from life, earth, space, physics & the environment. These activities from many nations invite all children to discover the science & art of the First Americans, focusing on the people of the Woodlands. WATERDRUM SCIENCE features: *Science-Based Legends from many cultures. Delightful stories stimulate curiosity & concept exploration. *Fascinating Facts connect science concepts with American Indian art & culture. *Science-Art Activities for each concept encourage creative problem-solving. *Sample Activities: Anatomy Puppets; Animal Drawing; Patterns in Plants, Baskets, Beading, Stars, Dance & Music; Painting Fossils, Rocks, Habitats, & Rainbows; Electric Pow Wow Storytelling; Weather Symbols; Eagle & Airplane Design; Volcano/ Earthquake Legends; Circles of Life; Solar Calendars; Waves of water, sound & light... *Clear, Open-Ended Directions encourage children to explore, invent, & learn the value of risk-taking in science & art processes. *Author/Artist Carolyn Petty is an internationally recognized education consultant. *Extensively Classroom Tested--Child Approved! Their testimony says it all, "Do we have to go to recess now?"
Publisher Provided Annotation.

Prohaska, Elizabeth. Trivial Pursuit - Science (Primary) (Illus.). 64p. (gr. 1-3). 1992. 12.95 (*0-86653-647-7*, GA1385) Good Apple.

Richards, Roy. One Hundred One Science Surprises: Exciting Experiments with Everyday Materials. Pang, Alex, illus. LC 92-32491. 104p. 1993. 14.95 (*0-8069-8822-3*) Sterling.

Silverstein, Herma. Scream Machines. 112p. 1991. pap. 2.95 (*0-380-71461-2*, Camelot) Avon.

Stine, Megan, et al. Hands-On Science: Color & Light. Taback, Simms, illus. LC 92-56889. 1993. PLB 18.60 (*0-8368-0954-8*) Gareth Stevens Inc.

—Hands-On Science: Food & the Kitchen. Taback, Simms, illus. LC 92-56890. 1993. PLB 18.60 (*0-8368-0955-6*) Gareth Stevens Inc.

—Hands-On Science: Fun Machines. Taback, Simms, illus. LC 92-56891. 1993. PLB 18.60 (*0-8368-0956-4*) Gareth Stevens Inc.

—Hands-On Science: Games, Puzzles, & Toys. Taback, Simms, illus. LC 92-56892. 1993. PLB 18.60 (*0-8368-0957-2*) Gareth Stevens Inc.

—Hands-On Science: Mystery & Magic. Taback, Simms, illus. LC 92-56893. 1993. PLB 18.60 (*0-8368-0958-0*) Gareth Stevens Inc.

—Hands-On Science: Things That Grow. Taback, Simms, illus. LC 92-56894. 1993. PLB 18.60 (*0-8368-0959-9*) Gareth Stevens Inc.

Thomson, Ruth. Autumn. LC 94-16940. (Illus.). 24p. (ps-3). 1994. PLB 14.40 (*0-516-07986-7*); pap. 4.95 (*0-516-47986-5*) Childrens.

—Spring. LC 94-16916. (Illus.). 24p. (ps-3). 1994. PLB 14.40 (*0-516-07994-8*); pap. 4.95 (*0-516-47994-6*) Childrens.

VanCleave, Janice. Janice VanCleave's Two Hundred Gooey, Slippery, Slimy, Weird, & Fun Experiments. (Illus.). 128p. (gr. 3-7). 1992. pap. text ed. 12.95 (*0-471-57921-1*) Wiley.

—Two Hundred One Awesome, Magical, Bizarre, & Incredible Experiments. LC 93-29807. 1994. pap. text ed. 12.95 (*0-471-31011-5*) Wiley. Unlocking the secrets of the universe...& having a blast! Why does a cat have a rough tongue? Why is the sky blue? Why does a person snore? How does a submarine rise & submerge? Following on the heels of the best-selling, 200 GOOEY, SLIPPERY, SLIMY, WEIRD, & FUN EXPERIMENTS, everyone's favorite science teacher is back with more fantastic ways for children to discover the science in the world around them through fun & easy experiments in biology, chemistry, physics, earth science, & astronomy. With plenty of complete experiments to choose from, kids can find just the right project for their science fair, discover which science subjects most capture their interests, or just have fun messing around. 201 wacky experiments in five different science areas. Simple step-by-step instructions. Easy-to-find materials from around the house. Greatest hits from previous books plus 40 all-new experiments.
Publisher Provided Annotation.

Vivian, Charles. Science Experiments & Amusements for Children. Watts, S. A., photos by. LC 67-28142. (ps-6). 1967. pap. 2.95 (*0-486-21856-2*) Dover.

Wellnitz, William R. Homemade Slime & Rubber Bones! Awesome Science Experiments. LC 92-41238. (gr. 3 up). 1993. 17.95 (*0-8306-4093-2*); pap. 9.95 (*0-8306-4094-0*) TAB Bks.

SCIENTISTS

see also Science–Vocational Guidance; also classes of scientists, e.g. Astronomers; Chemists; Geologists; Mathematicians; Naturalists; Physicists, etc.; and names of scientists

Asimov, Isaac. Isaac Asimov's Pioneers of Science & Exploration, 3 vols. (Illus.). 64p. (gr. 3-4). 1991. Set. PLB 55.80 (*0-8368-0754-5*) Gareth Stevens Inc.

Baldwin, Joyce Y. DNA Pioneer: James Watson & the Double Helix. LC 93-31090. 160p. (gr. 4-6). 1994. 14.95 (*0-8027-8297-3*); PLB 15.85 (*0-8027-8298-1*) Walker & Co.

Balsamo, Kathy. Exploring the Lives of Gifted People-The Sciences. Johnson, Phyllis, illus. 80p. (gr. 4 up). 1987. pap. 8.95 (*0-86653-417-2*, GA 1038) Good Apple.

Burns, Virginia L. Gentle Hunter: Biography of Alice Evans, Bacteriologist. (Illus.). 224p. (gr. 5-12). 1993. PLB 22.00 (*0-9604726-5-7*) Enterprise Pr.

Carwell, Hattie. Blacks in Science: Astrophysicist to Zoologist. Earls, Julian, intro. by. (Illus.). 96p. (gr. 8 up). 1988. pap. 7.00 (*0-682-48911-5*); 10.00 (*0-685-22950-5*) H Carwell.

Coil, Suzanne M. Robert Hutchings Goddard. (Illus.). 128p. (gr. 7-12). 1992. lib. bdg. 16.95x (*0-8160-2591-6*) Facts on File.

DeBruin, Jerry. Scientists Around the World. Junkasem, Rochana, illus. 160p. (gr. 4-12). 1987. pap. 12.95 (*0-86653-416-4*, GA1005) Good Apple.

Deitch, Kenneth M. & Yeamans, Joseph R. J. Robert Oppenheimer & the Birth of the Atomic Age. Weisman, JoAnne B., ed. (Illus.). 128p. 1994. PLB 19.95 (*1-878668-21-8*); pap. 9.95 (*1-878668-29-3*) Disc Enter Ltd.

Gallardo, Evelyn. Among the Orangutans: The Birute Galdikas Story. LC 92-25777. 1993. 12.95 (*0-8118-0031-8*) Chronicle Bks.

Gelman, Rita G. What Are Scientists? What Do They Do? Let's Find Out. (ps-3). 1991. pap. 3.95 (*0-590-43184-6*) Scholastic Inc.

Hayden, Robert. Seven African-American Scientists. rev. ed. (Illus.). 173p. (gr. 5-8). 1992. Repr. of 1970 ed. PLB 14.95 (*0-8050-2134-5*) TFC Bks NY.

Heckart, Barbara H. Edmond Halley: The Man & His Comet. LC 83-24000. (Illus.). 112p. (gr. 4 up). 1984. PLB 14.40 (*0-516-03202-X*) Childrens.

Henderson, Harry. Stephen Hawking. LC 93-49488. (Illus.). 112p. (gr. 5-8). 1994. 14.95 (*1-56006-050-6*) Lucent Bks.

McGovern, Ann. Shark Lady: True Adventures of Eugenie Clark. reissued ed. Chew, Ruth, illus. LC 78-22126. 96p. (gr. 3-7). 1984. 13.95 (*0-02-767060-0*, Four Winds) Macmillan Child Grp.

McKissack, Patricia & McKissack, Fredrick. African-American Scientists. LC 93-11226. (Illus.). 96p. (gr. 4-6). 1994. PLB 17.90 (*1-56294-372-3*) Millbrook Pr.

McPartland, Scott. Edwin Land. LC 93-22077. (gr. 7-8). 1993. 15.93 (*0-86592-150-4*); 11.95s.p. (*0-685-66592-5*) Rourke Enter.

Newton, David E. Linus Pauling: Scientist & Advocate. LC 93-31719. (Illus.). 128p. 1994. 16.95x (*0-8160-2959-8*) Facts on File.

Parker, Steve. Aristotle & Scientific Thought. LC 94-8263. 1994. write for info. (*0-7910-3004-0*) Chelsea Hse.

—Louis Pasteur & Germs. LC 94-8262. 1994. write for info. (*0-7910-3002-4*) Chelsea Hse.

Perry, Susan. Scientists. (Illus.). 128p. (gr. 3-6). Date not set. 19.95 (*1-56065-122-9*) Capstone Pr.

Polacco, Patricia. Meteor! Polacco, Patricia, illus. 32p. (gr. k-3). 1987. 14.95 (*0-399-21699-5*, Putnam) Putnam Pub Group.

Reid, S. & Fara, P. Scientists. (Illus.). 48p. (gr. 4 up). 1993. PLB 14.96 (*0-88110-587-2*); pap. 7.95 (*0-7460-1009-5*) EDC.

Rich, Beverly. Louis Pasteur: The Scientist Who Found the Cause of Infectious Disease & Invented Pasteurization. LC 88-24867. (Illus.). 64p. (gr. 5-6). 1989. PLB 19.93 (*1-55532-839-3*) Gareth Stevens Inc.

Sherrow, Victoria. Great Scientists. (Illus.). 160p. (gr. 7-12). 1992. lib. bdg. 16.95x (*0-8160-2540-1*) Facts on File.

Veglahn, Nancy. Women Scientists. (Illus.). 128p. (gr. 6-10). 1992. lib. bdg. 16.95x (*0-8160-2482-0*) Facts on File.

Verheyden-Hilliard, Mary E. Mathematician & Computer Scientist, Caryn Navy. Rom, Holly M., illus. LC 87-82595. 32p. (Orig.). (gr. 1-4). 1988. pap. 5.00 (*0-932469-12-4*) Equity Inst.

—Scientist & Activist, Phyllis Stearner. Rom, Holly M., illus. LC 87-82597. 32p. (Orig.). (gr. 1-4). 1988. pap. 5.00 (*0-932469-15-9*) Equity Inst.

—Scientist & Physician, Judith Pachciarz. Stanier, Linda, illus. LC 87-82599. 32p. (Orig.). (gr. 1-4). 1988. pap. 5.00 (*0-932469-13-2*) Equity Inst.

—Scientist & Strategist, June Rooks. Rom, Holly M., illus. LC 87-82596. 32p. (Orig.). (gr. 1-4). 1988. pap. 5.00 (*0-932469-14-0*) Equity Inst.

—Scientist & Teacher, Anne Barrett Swanson. Rom, Holly M., illus. LC 87-82598. 32p. (Orig.). (gr. 1-4). 1988. pap. 5.00 (*0-932469-16-7*) Equity Inst.

Yount, Lisa. Black Scientists. (Illus.). (gr. 5-12). 1991. lib. bdg. 16.95x (*0-8160-2549-5*) Facts on File.

—William Harvey: Discoverer of How Blood Circulates. (Illus.). 128p. (gr. 4-10). 1994. lib. bdg. 17.95 (*0-89490-481-7*) Enslow Pubs.

SCOPES, JOHN THOMAS, 1901-

Blake, Arthur. The Scopes Trial: Defending the Right to Teach. LC 93-37018. (Illus.). 64p. (gr. 4-6). 1994. PLB 15.40 (*1-56294-407-X*) Millbrook Pr.

SCORPIONS

Mell, Jan. Scorpion. LC 89-28273. (Illus.). 48p. (gr. 5). 1990. text ed. 12.95 RSBE (*0-89686-520-7*, Crestwood Hse) Macmillan Child Grp.

Myers, Walter D. Scorpions. LC 85-45815. 160p. (gr. 7 up). 1988. 14.00 (*0-06-024364-3*); PLB 13.89 (*0-06-024365-1*) HarpC Child Bks.

—Scorpions. LC 85-45815. 224p. (gr. 7 up). 1990. pap. 3.95 (*0-06-447066-0*, Trophy) HarpC Child Bks.

Pringle, Laurence. Scorpion Man: Exploring the World of Scorpions. Polis, Gary A., photos by. LC 93-34936. (gr. 5 up). 1994. 15.95 (*0-684-19560-7*, Scribner) MacMillan.

Spiders & Scorpions. (ps-3). 1991. pap. 2.50 (*0-89954-548-3*) Antioch Pub Co.

Storad, Conrad J. Scorpions. Jansen, Paula, photos by. LC 94-4634. (Illus.). 48p. (gr. 2-3). 1994. 18.95 (*0-8225-3004-X*) Lerner Pubns.

SCOTCH IN THE U. S.

Aman, Catherine. The Scottish Americans. (Illus.). 112p. (gr. 5 up). 1991. lib. bdg. 17.95 (*1-55546-132-8*) Chelsea Hse.

Brownstein, Robin & Guttmacher, Peter. The Scotch-Irish Americans. (Illus.). 112p. (gr. 5 up). 1988. lib. bdg. 17.95 (*0-87754-875-7*) Chelsea Hse.

Johnson, James E. The Scots & Scotch-Irish in America. LC 66-10151. (Illus.). 88p. (gr. 5 up). 1991. PLB 15.95 (*0-8225-0242-9*) Lerner Pubns.

—Scots & Scotch-Irish in America. 1992. pap. 5.95 (*0-8225-1038-3*) Lerner Pubns.

SCOTLAND

Lerner Publications, Department of Geography Staff, ed. Scotland in Pictures. (Illus.). 64p. (gr. 5 up). 1991. PLB 17.50 (*0-8225-1875-9*) Lerner Pubns.

Meek, James. The Land & People of Scotland. LC 88-27215. (Illus.). 256p. (gr. 6 up). 1990. 18.00 (*0-397-32332-8*, Lipp Jr Bks); PLB 14.89 (*0-397-32333-6*, Lipp Jr Bks) HarpC Child Bks.

Sutherland, Dorothy B. Scotland. LC 84-23227. (Illus.). 128p. (gr. 5-9). 1985. PLB 20.55 (*0-516-02787-5*) Childrens.

Taylor, Doreen. Scotland. LC 90-10028. (Illus.). 96p. (gr. 6-11). 1990. PLB 22.80 (*0-8114-2431-6*) Raintree Steck-V.

SCOTLAND–FICTION

Anderson, Ken. Nessie & the Little Blind Boy of Loch Ness. Fiott, Steve, intro. by. (Illus.). 72p. 1992. collector's ed. 49.95 (*0-941613-27-5*) Stabur Pr.

Barrie, James. Little Minister. (gr. 10 up). 1968. pap. 0.75 (*0-8049-0187-2*, CL-187) Airmont.

Bawden, Nina. The Witch's Daughter. 192p. (gr. 3-7). 1991. 13.45 (*0-395-58635-6*, Clarion Bks) HM.

Cameron, Eleanor. Beyond Silence. LC 80-10350. 208p. (gr. 5-9). 1980. 9.95 (*0-525-26463-9*, DCB) Dutton Child Bks.

Duncan, Jane. Janet Reachfar & the Kelpie. Hedderwick, Mairi, illus. LC 75-44166. 32p. (ps-3). 1976. 7.50 (*0-685-02316-8*, Clarion Bks) HM.

Dunlop, Eileen. Finn's Search. LC 93-44880. 128p. (gr. 5-9). 1994. 14.95 (*0-8234-1099-4*) Holiday.

—Green Willow. LC 92-33402. 160p. (gr. 5-9). 1993. 14.95 (*0-8234-1021-8*) Holiday.

Hendry, Frances M. The Jackdaw: Quest for a Queen. 256p. (gr. 4 up). 1994. pap. 7.95 (*0-86241-437-7*, Pub. by Cnngt UK) Trafalgar.

—Quest for a Maid. 240p. (gr. 5 up). 1992. pap. 4.95 (*0-374-46155-4*, Sunburst) FS&G.

Hunter, Mollie. A Sound of Chariots. LC 72-76523. 256p. (gr. 7 up). 1972. PLB 12.89 (*0-06-022669-2*) HarpC Child Bks.
MacDonald, George. Wee Sir Gibbie of the Highlands. Phillips, Michael R., ed. 240p. (gr. 2-7). 1990. 10.99 (*1-55661-139-0*) Bethany Hse.
Masters, Anthony. Klondyker. LC 92-351. 1992. pap. 15.00 (*0-671-79173-7*, S&S BFYR) S&S Trade.
Ollivant, Alfred. Bob, Son of Battle. (Illus.). (gr. 5 up). 1967. pap. 2.50 (*0-8049-0141-4*, CL-141) Airmont.
Paton Walsh, Jill. Matthew & the Sea Singer. (ps-3). 1993. 13.00 (*0-374-34869-3*) FS&G.
Robertson, Jenny. Fear in the Glen. 128p. (gr. 5-8). 1990. pap. 4.99 (*0-7459-1874-3*) Lion USA.
Stevenson, Robert Louis. Kidnapped. (gr. 8 up). 1964. pap. 1.95 (*0-8049-0010-8*, CL-10) Airmont.
Stewart, A. C. Ossian House. LC 76-9645. (gr. 6 up). 1976. PLB 21.95 (*0-87599-219-6*) S G Phillips.
Wandelmaier, Roy. Mystery at Loch Ness. Mulkey, Kim, illus. LC 85-2532. 112p. (gr. 3-6). 1985. lib. bdg. 9.49 (*0-8167-0529-1*) Troll Assocs.
Weems, David B. Son of an Earl...Sold for a Slave. Magellan, Mauro, illus. LC 92-27917. 112p. (gr. 5 up). 1992. 10.95 (*0-88289-921-X*) Pelican.

SCOTLAND–HISTORY–FICTION

Porter, Jane. The Scottish Chiefs. reissued ed. Wyeth, N. C., illus. LC 91-8521. 528p. 1991. SBE 26.95 (*0-684-19340-X*, Scribners Young Read); limited ed. 75.00 (*0-684-19339-6*, Scribners Young Read) Macmillan Child Grp.
Stevenson, Robert Louis. Kidnapped. Mattern, Joanne, retold by. Parton, Steve, illus. LC 92-5803. 48p. (gr. 3-6). 1992. PLB 12.89 (*0-8167-2862-3*); pap. text ed. 3.95 (*0-8167-2863-1*) Troll Assocs.
—Kidnapped. LC 94-5859. 1994. 13.95 (*0-679-43638-3*, Evrymans Lib Childs) Knopf.

SCOTLAND–KINGS AND RULERS–FICTION

Porter, Jane. The Scottish Chiefs. reissued ed. Wyeth, N. C., illus. LC 91-8521. 528p. 1991. SBE 26.95 (*0-684-19340-X*, Scribners Young Read); limited ed. 75.00 (*0-684-19339-6*, Scribners Young Read) Macmillan Child Grp.

SCOTT, DRED, 1795-1858

Herda, D. J. The Dred Scott Case: Slavery & Citizenship. LC 93-22402. (Illus.). 104p. (gr. 6 up). 1994. lib. bdg. 17.95 (*0-89490-460-4*) Enslow Pubs.

SCOTT, ROBERT FALCON, 1868-1912

Sauvain, Philip. Robert Scott in the Antarctic. LC 93-18209. (Illus.). 32p. (gr. 4-6). 1993. text ed. 13.95 RSBE (*0-87518-532-0*, Dillon) Macmillan Child Grp.
Sipiera, Paul. Roald Amundsen & Robert Scott: Race for the South Pole. LC 90-2178. (Illus.). 128p. (gr. 3 up). 1990. PLB 20.55 (*0-516-03056-6*) Childrens.

SCOTTISH POETRY

Campbell, Aileen, illus. The Wee Scot Book: Scottish Poems & Stories. Greenberg, Linda, ed. LC 93-28728. (Illus.). 1994. 19.95 (*1-56554-018-2*); audio 9.95 (*1-56554-019-0*) Pelican.
Stevenson, Robert Louis. A Child's Garden of Verses. Robinson, Charles, illus. LC 92-53175. 128p. 1992. 12.95 (*0-679-41799-0*, Evrymans Lib Childs Class) Knopf.

SCOUTS AND SCOUTING

see also Boy Scouts; Girl Scouts

Beard, Lina & Beard, Adelia. American Girls Handybook: How to Amuse Yourself & Others. LC 86-46262. 480p. 1987. 11.95 (*0-87923-666-3*) Godine.
Toliusis, Juozas, ed. Ausra, Jubiliejine Stovykla. (LIT., Illus.). 72p. (gr. 1 up). 1983. pap. write for info. (*0-9611488-1-0*) Lith Scouts.

SCOUTS AND SCOUTING–FICTION

Delton, Judy. Peanut Butter Pilgrims. 80p. (Orig.). (gr. k-6). 1988. pap. 3.25 (*0-440-40066-X*, YB) Dell.
—The Pooped Troop. Tiegreen, Alan, illus. 80p. (ps-3). 1989. pap. 3.50 (*0-440-40184-4*, YB) Dell.
Little Critter at Scout Camp. (Illus.). (ps-3). 1991. write for info. (*0-307-12629-3*, Golden Pr) Western Pub.
Nye, Julie. Scout. 177p. (Orig.). 1987. pap. 4.95 (*0-89084-413-5*) Bob Jones Univ Pr.
Thaler, Mike. Pack 109. Chartier, Normand, illus. (gr. k-3). 1993. pap. 3.25 (*0-14-036548-6*, Puffin) Puffin Bks.

SCREEN PRINTING

see Silk Screen Printing

SCRIPTURES, HOLY

see Bible

SCUBA DIVING

see Skin Diving

SCULLING

see Rowing

SCULPTORS

Italia, Robert. Maya Lin: Honoring Our Forgotten Heroes. LC 93-10257. 1993. 12.94 (*1-56239-234-4*) Abdo & Dghtrs.
Reef, Pat. Bernard Langlais, Sculptor. LC 84-81337. (Illus.). 48p. (gr. 3-7). 1985. pap. 9.95 (*0-933858-06-X*) Kennebec River.
Reichel, Cara. A Stone Promise. Thatch, Nancy R., ed. Reichel, Cara, illus. Melton, David, intro. by. LC 91-15059. (Illus.). 26p. (gr. 5 up). 1991. PLB 14.95 (*0-933849-35-4*) Landmark Edns.
Von Rosenberg, Marjorie. Elisabet Ney: Sculptor of American Heroes. Von Roesnberg, Marjorie, illus. 64p. (gr. 4-7). 1990. 10.95 (*0-89015-747-2*) Sunbelt Media.

SCULPTURE

see also Mobiles (Sculpture); Modeling; Monuments

Ancona, George. Stone Cutters, Carvers & the Cathedral. LC 94-10549. 1995. write for info. (*0-688-12056-3*); lib. bdg. write for info. (*0-688-12057-1*) Lothrop.
Brommer, Gerald F. Wire Sculpture & Other Three Dimensional Construction. LC 68-19999. (Illus.). 128p. (gr. 5-12). 1968. 15.95 (*0-87192-025-5*) Davis Mass.
Greenberg, Jan & Jordan, Sandra. The Sculptor's Eye: Looking at Contemporary American Art. LC 92-16323. 1993. 19.95 (*0-385-30902-3*) Delacorte.
Hellman, Nina & Brouwer, Norman. A Mariner's Fancy: The Whaleman's Art of Scrimshaw. Aron, Jack R. & Neill, Peterpref. by. (Illus.). 96p. (Orig.). 1992. pap. 22.50 (*0-917439-14-7*) Balsam Pr.
Johnson, Peter D., intro. by. Clay Modelling for Everyone: Sculpture, Pottery & Jewellery Without a Wheel. De La Bedoyere, Charlotte, tr. (Illus.). 112p. (Orig.). (gr. 7 up). 1988. pap. 16.95 (*0-85532-564-X*, Pub. by Search Pr UK) A Schwartz & Co.
Morgan, Judith. An Art Text-Workbook: Sculpture (Introduction) Wallace, Dorathye, ed. (Illus.). 113p. (gr. 8-10). 1990. 13.27 (*0-914127-34-9*) Univ Class.
Pekarik, Andrew. Sculpture. LC 92-52988. (Illus.). 64p. (gr. 3-7). 1992. 18.95 (*1-56282-294-2*); PLB 18.89 (*1-56282-295-0*) Hyprn Child.
Slade, Richard. Your Book of Modelling. (gr. 4 up). 1968. 7.95 (*0-571-08387-0*) Transatl Arts.

SCULPTURE–FICTION

Fleischman, Paul. Graven Images. LC 81-48649. (Illus.). 96p. (gr. 6 up). 1982. 14.00 (*0-06-021906-8*); PLB 14.89 (*0-06-021907-6*) HarpC Child Bks.
Hwa-I Publishing Co., Staff. Chinese Children's Stories, Vol. 5: Sun Valley, A Stone Carver's Dream. Ching, Emily, et al, eds. Wonder Kids Publications Staff, tr. from CHI. (Illus.). 28p. (gr. 3-6). 1991. Repr. of 1988 ed. 7.95 (*0-685-49019-X*) Wonder Kids.

SCULPTURE–HISTORY

Levine, Bobbie, et al. A Child's Walk Through Twentieth Century American Painting & Sculpture. (Illus.). 29p. (gr. 2-6). 1986. spiral bdg. 1.50 (*0-912303-37-9*) Michigan Mus.

SCULPTURE, RELIGIOUS

see Christian Art and Symbolism

SCULPTURE–TECHNIQUE

see also Modeling

Sculpture. (Illus.). 24p. (gr. 6-12). 1969. pap. 1.85 (*0-8395-3322-5*, 33322) BSA.
Solga, Kim. Make Sculptures! (Illus.). 48p. (gr. 1-6). 1992. 11.95 (*0-89134-420-9*, 30378) North Light Bks.

SEA

see Ocean

SEA ANIMALS

see Marine Animals

SEA FISHERIES

see Fisheries

SEA-HORSE

Fowler, Allan. Podria Ser un Pez - Libro Grande: (It Could Still Be a Fish Big Book) LC 90-2203. (SPA., Illus.). 32p. (ps-2). 1993. 22.95 (*0-516-59462-1*) Childrens.
Schlein, Miriam. The Dangerous Life of the Sea Horse. Cole, Gwen, illus. LC 85-26857. 40p. (gr. 3-6). 1986. SBE 13.95 (*0-689-31180-X*, Atheneum Child Bk) Macmillan Child Grp.

SEA-HORSE–FICTION

Tate, Suzanne. Stevie B. Sea Horse: A Tale of a Proud Papa. Melvin, James, illus. LC 93-86779. 28p. (Orig.). (gr. k-3). 1993. pap. 3.95 (*1-878405-09-8*) Nags Head Art.

SEA LIFE

see Seafaring Life; Seamen;
also names of countries with the subhead Navy, e.g., U. S. Navy

SEA LIONS

see Seals (Animals)

SEA MOSSES

see Algae

SEA POETRY

Daniel, Mark, compiled by. A Child's Treasury of Seaside Verse. LC 90-2819. (Illus.). 144p. (ps up). 1991. 16.95 (*0-8037-0889-0*) Dial Bks Young.

SEA POWER

see also Disarmament; Naval History; Warships;
also names of countries with the subhead Navy or the subdivision History, Naval, e.g. U.S. Navy; U.S.–History, Naval, etc.

Walmer, Max & Rawlinson, Jon. Sea Power Library, 6 bks, Reading Level 5. (Illus.). 288p. (gr. 3-8). 1989. Set. PLB 111.60 (*0-86625-087-5*); 18.60 (*0-685-58760-6*); 13.95 (*0-685-58761-4*) Rourke Corp.

SEA ROUTES

see Trade Routes

SEA SHELLS

see Shells

SEA SHORE

see Seashore

SEA STORIES

Adams, Richard. Watership Down. LC 73-6044. 444p. 1974. text ed. 40.00 (*0-02-700030-3*) Macmillan Child Grp.
Ahlberg, Allan. Skeleton Crew. Amstutz, Andre, illus. LC 91-39161. 32p. (ps-6). 1992. 14.00 (*0-688-11436-9*) Greenwillow.
Avi. Captain Grey. LC 92-37643. 160p. (gr. 5 up). 1993. pap. 3.95 (*0-688-12234-5*, Pub. by Beech Tree Bks) Morrow.
—The True Confessions of Charlotte Doyle. Murray, Ruth E., illus. LC 90-30624. 224p. (gr. 6-8). 1990. 15.95 (*0-531-05893-X*); PLB 15.99 (*0-531-08493-0*) Orchard Bks Watts.
Barber, Antonia. The Mousehole Cat. Bayley, Nicola, illus. LC 90-31533. 40p. (gr. k-3). 1990. SBE 14.95 (*0-02-708331-4*, Macmillan Child Bk) Macmillan Child Grp.
Berleth, Richard. Mary Patten's Voyage. Mathews, Judith, ed. Otero, Ben, illus. LC 93-45919. 40p. (gr. 3-6). 1994. PLB 14.95 (*0-8075-4987-8*) A Whitman.
Bligh, William. Mutiny on Board HMS Bounty. Teitel, N. R., intro. by. (gr. 8 up). 1965. pap. 1.95 (*0-8049-0088-4*, CL-88) Airmont.
Calhoun, Mary. Henry the Sailor Cat. Ingraham, Erick, illus. LC 92-29794. 40p. (gr. k up). 1994. 15.00g (*0-688-10840-7*); PLB 14.93 (*0-688-10841-5*) Morrow Jr Bks.
Carrie, Christopher. Search for the Sea Treasure. (Illus.). 40p. (gr. k up). 1990. 1.59 (*0-86696-246-8*) Binney & Smith.
Chrisman, Arthur B. Shen of the Sea. Hasselriis, Else, illus. (gr. 4-7). 1968. 15.00 (*0-525-39244-0*, DCB) Dutton Child Bks.
Cohen, Daniel. Ghosts of the Deep. LC 92-34669. 112p. (gr. 5-9). 1993. 14.95 (*0-399-22435-1*, Putnam) Putnam Pub Group.
Conrad, Joseph. Lord Jim. Gemme, F. R., intro. by. (gr. 10 up). 1965. pap. 1.95 (*0-8049-0054-X*, CL-54) Airmont.
Conrad, Pam. The Lost Sailor. Egielski, Richard, illus. LC 91-39640. 32p. (gr. k-4). 1992. 15.00 (*0-06-021695-6*); PLB 14.89 (*0-06-021696-4*) HarpC Child Bks.
Cooper, Susan. Seaward. LC 83-7055. 180p. (gr. 5 up). 1983. SBE 14.95 (*0-689-50275-3*, M K McElderry) Macmillan Child Grp.
Dana, Richard H. Two Years Before the Mast. Bennet, C. L., intro. by. (gr. 8 up). 1965. pap. 2.25 (*0-8049-0085-X*, CL-85) Airmont.

Fine, John C. The Tested Man. Whitaker, Kate, ed. 130p. 1994. pap. 12.00 (*1-883650-00-3*) Windswept Hse. Eight soul-searching, rugged tales of men against the elements. John Fine has written fifteen books including award-winning books dealing with the problems of ocean pollution (Oceans in Peril) & world hunger (The Hunger Road). He was elected to the Academy of Underwater Arts & Sciences in honor of his books in the field of education. His children's book, The Boy & the Dolphin (Windswept House, 1990), received the 1991 Herman Melville Literary Award. Fine, a trained biologist with a Doctor of Jurisprudence degree, has received international recognition for his pioneering work investigating toxic waste contamination of our land & water resources. He received the Freedom Award at the World Underwater Congress in recognition of his work in the marine environment. Fine is a trustee of the International Oceanographic Foundation, a recipient of the Marine Environment Award, given by the Foundation for Ocean Research, has three times been named Diver of the Year, & holds the highest professional licenses as an underwater instructor. Fine writes with strength, sincerity & great understanding of the sea & the men who sail on it. These are stories you will never forget.
Publisher Provided Annotation.

Foreman, Michael. Jack's Fantastic Voyage. 1992. write for info. (*0-15-239496-6*, HB Juv Bks) HarBrace.
Forester, C. S. Commodore Hornblower. (gr. 7 up). 1989. pap. 11.95 (*0-316-28938-8*) Little.
—Lieutenant Hornblower. (gr. 7 up). 1984. 17.95 (*0-316-28907-8*); pap. 11.95 (*0-316-28921-3*) Little.
—Lord Hornblower, Vol. 1. (gr. 7 up). 1989. 17.95 (*0-316-28908-6*); pap. 11.95 (*0-316-28943-4*) Little.
—Mr. Midshipman Hornblower. (gr. 7 up). 1950. 17.95 (*0-316-28909-4*) Little.
Ghrist, Julie, illus. Taelly's Counting Adventures: At Sea. 12p. (ps). 1993. 4.95 (*1-56828-027-0*) Red Jacket Pr.
Guiberson, Brenda Z. Lobster Boat. Lloyd, Megan, illus. LC 92-4055. 32p. (ps-3). 1993. 14.95 (*0-8050-1756-9*, Bks Young Read) H Holt & Co.
Holling, Holling C. Seabird. (Illus.). (gr. 4-6). 1973. 17.95 (*0-395-18230-1*) HM.

Hulme, Joy N. Sea Squares. Schwartz, Carol, illus. LC 91-71381. 32p. (ps-3). 1993. pap. 4.95 (*1-56282-520-8*) Hyprn Ppbks.
Jenkin-Pearce, Susie. Seashell Song. LC 91-772960. (Illus.). (ps-3). 1993. 15.00 (*0-688-11725-2*); PLB 14.93 (*0-688-11726-0*) Lothrop.
Kipling, Rudyard. Captains Courageous. (gr. 6 up). 1964. pap. 1.75 (*0-8049-0027-2*, CL-27) Airmont.
Lewis, Thomas P. Clipper Ship. Sandin, Joan, illus. LC 77-11858. 64p. (ps-3). 1978. 11.95 (*0-06-023808-9*); PLB 11.89 (*0-06-023809-7*) HarpC Child Bks.
Lightbourne, K. A. Grandfather Played the Trumpet: Sailors Fantasies. 375p. (Orig.). 1988. pap. 12.50 (*0-9621212-0-7*) Sailors Fantasies Pub.
London, Jack. Martin Eden. (gr. 9 up). 1969. pap. 3.50 (*0-8049-0209-7*, CL-209) Airmont.
—Sea Wolf. Gall, M., intro. by. (gr. 6 up). 1965. pap. 2.50 (*0-8049-0064-7*, CL-64) Airmont.
Major, Kevin. Far from Shore. 224p. (gr. 7 up). 1983. pap. 2.95 (*0-440-92585-1*, LFL) Dell.
Marston, Elsa. Cynthia & the Runaway Gazebo. Henstra, Friso, illus. LC 91-32548. 32p. (gr. k-4). 1992. 14.00 (*0-688-10282-4*, Tambourine Bks); PLB 13.93 (*0-688-10283-2*, Tambourine Bks) Morrow.
Melville, Herman. Billy Budd. Fisher, N. H., intro. by. Bd. with The Encantadas. (gr. 9 up). 1966. pap. 1.75 (*0-8049-0116-3*, CL-116) Airmont.
—Billy Budd. (Illus.). 64p. (gr. 4-12). 1979. pap. text ed. 2.95 (*0-88301-385-1*); student activity bk. 1.25 (*0-88301-409-2*) Pendulum Pr.
—Moby Dick. (gr. 11 up). 1964. pap. 3.95 (*0-8049-0033-7*, CL-33) Airmont.
—Moby Dick. new ed. Shapiro, Irwin, ed. Nino, Alex, illus. LC 73-75458. 64p. (Orig.). (gr. 5-10). 1973. pap. 2.95 (*0-88301-099-2*) Pendulum Pr.
—Typee. Thomas, C., intro. by. (gr. 10 up). 1965. pap. 1.50 (*0-8049-0053-1*, CL-53) Airmont.
Newton, Jill. Cat-Fish. LC 91-42858. (Illus.). 32p. (ps up). 1992. 14.00 (*0-688-11423-7*); PLB 13.93 (*0-688-11424-5*) Lothrop.
Paulsen, Gary. The Voyage of the Frog. LC 88-15261. (Illus.). 160p. (gr. 6-8). 1989. 13.95 (*0-531-05805-0*); PLB 13.99 (*0-531-08405-1*) Orchard Bks Watts.
Rushdie, Salman. Haroun & the Sea of Stories. large type ed. (gr. 1-8). 1991. 16.95 (*0-7451-1428-8*, Galaxy Child Lrg Print) Chivers N Amer.
Sobel, Barbara. The Jewels from the Sea. LC 87-81237. (gr. 3-6). 1987. 7.59 (*0-87386-043-8*); bk. & cassette 16.99 (*0-317-55335-6*); pap. 1.95 (*0-87386-042-X*) Jan Prods.
Sohl, Marcia & Dackerman, Gerald. Moby Dick Student Activity Book. Nino, Alex, illus. (gr. 4-10). 1976. pap. 1.25 (*0-88301-181-6*) Pendulum Pr.
Stevenson, Robert Louis. Master of Ballantrae. (gr. 8 up). 1964. pap. 1.95 (*0-8049-0047-7*, CL-47) Airmont.
Swift, Hildegarde H. & Ward, Lynd. The Little Red Lighthouse & the Great Gray Bridge. LC 73-12861. (Illus.). 52p. (ps-3). 1974. pap. 4.95 (*0-15-652840-1*, Voyager Bks) HarBrace.
Van Allsburg, Chris. The Wretched Stone. Van Allsburg, Chris, illus. 32p. 1991. 17.45 (*0-395-53307-4*, Sandpiper) HM.
Verne, Jules. Twenty Thousand Leagues under the Sea. (gr. 8 up). 1964. pap. 3.25 (*0-8049-0012-4*, CL-12) Airmont.
—Twenty Thousand Leagues under the Sea. new ed. Binder, Otto, ed. Gamboa, Romy & Patricio, Ernie, illus. LC 73-75466. 64p. (Orig.). (gr. 5-10). 1973. pap. 2.95 (*0-88301-104-2*); student activity bk. 1.25 (*0-88301-180-8*) Pendulum Pr.
—Twenty Thousand Leagues under the Sea. Butz, Steve, illus. Nordlicht, Lillian, adapted by. LC 79-23887. 48p. (gr. 4 up). 1983. PLB 20.70 (*0-8172-1652-9*) Raintree Steck-V.
Waters, Tony. Sailor's Bride. (ps-3). 1991. pap. 13.95 (*0-385-41440-4*) Doubleday.
Whelan, Gloria. Goodbye, Vietnam. LC 91-3660. 112p. (gr. 3-7). 1992. 13.00 (*0-679-82263-1*); PLB 13.99 (*0-679-92263-6*) Knopf Bks Yng Read.
—Goodbye, Vietnam. LC 91-3660. 144p. (gr. 3-7). 1993. pap. 3.99 (*0-679-82376-X*, Bullseye Bks) Random Bks Yng Read.
Williams, Vera B. Stringbean's Trip to The Shining Sea. Williams, Jennifer & Williams, Vera B., illus. LC 86-29502. 48p. (gr. k-3). 1988. 13.95 (*0-688-07161-9*); lib. bdg. 13.88 (*0-688-07162-7*) Greenwillow.

SEA WAVES
see Ocean Waves

SEAFARING LIFE
see also Seamen
Hoare, Robert. Travel by Sea. Unstead, R. J., ed. (gr. 7 up). 1975. 14.95 (*0-7136-0119-1*) Dufour.

SEALS (ANIMALS)
Allan, Doug. The Seal on the Rocks. Oxford Scientific Film Staff, illus. LC 87-9950. 32p. (gr. 4-6). 1988. PLB 17.27 (*1-55532-271-9*) Gareth Stevens Inc.
Arnold, Caroline. Sea Lion. Hewett, Richard, photos by. LC 93-27007. (Illus.). 1994. write for info. (*0-688-12027-X*); lib. bdg. write for info. (*0-688-12028-8*) Morrow Jr Bks.
Baker, Lucy. Seals. (Illus.). 32p. (gr. 2-6). 1990. pap. 4.95 (*0-14-034436-5*, Puffin) Puffin Bks.
Bare, Colleen S. Elephants on the Beach. Bare, Colleen S., photos by. LC 89-32267. (Illus.). 32p. (ps-3). 1990. 12.95 (*0-525-65018-0*, Cobblehill Bks) Dutton Child Bks.
Barrett, Norman S. Seals & Walruses. LC 90-32150. (Illus.). 32p. (gr. k-4). 1991. PLB 11.90 (*0-531-14115-2*) Watts.
Cossi, Olga. Harp Seals. (Illus.). 48p. (gr. 2-5). 1991. PLB 19.95 (*0-87614-437-7*) Carolrhoda Bks.
—Harp Seals. (ps-3). 1992. pap. 6.95 (*0-87614-567-5*) Carolrhoda Bks.
Cousteau Society Staff. Seals. LC 91-34459. (Illus.). 24p. (ps-1). 1992. pap. 3.95 (*0-671-77061-6*, Little Simon) S&S Trade.
Cowcher, Helen. Antarctica. Cowcher, Helen, illus. Grammer, Red, contrib. by. (Illus.). 32p. (gr. k-3). 1990. incl. audiocassette 19.95 (*0-924483-24-5*); incl. audio cass. tape & stuffed penguin toy 44.95 (*0-924483-65-2*) Soundprints.
Dalmais. Seal, Reading Level 3-4. (Illus.). 28p. (gr. 2-5). 1983. PLB 16.67 (*0-86592-867-3*); 12.50s.p. (*0-685-58825-4*) Rourke Corp.
Duden, Jane. Harp Seal. LC 89-28274. (Illus.). 48p. (gr. 5). 1990. text ed. 12.95 RSBE (*0-89686-516-9*, Crestwood Hse) Macmillan Child Grp.
Evans, Phyllis R. The Sea World Book of Seals & Sea Lions. LC 85-27100. (Illus.). (gr. 4-7). 1986. (HB Juv Bks); pap. 9.95 (*0-15-271955-5*) HarBrace.
Green, Carl R. & Sanford, William R. The Elephant Seal. LC 87-22349. (Illus.). 48p. (gr. 5). 1987. text ed. 12.95 RSBE (*0-89686-330-1*, Crestwood Hse) Macmillan Child Grp.
Highlights for Children Editors. Seals. (Illus.). 32p. (Orig.). (gr. 2-5). 1993. pap. 3.95 (*1-56397-286-7*) Boyds Mills Pr.
Hoffman, Mary. Seal. LC 86-17806. (Illus.). 24p. (gr. k-5). 1987. PLB 9.95 (*0-8172-2702-4*); pap. 3.95 (*0-8114-6887-9*) Raintree Steck-V.
Johnson, Sylvia A. Elephant Seals. Lanting, Frans, photos by. LC 88-12924. (Illus.). 48p. (gr. 4 up). 1989. PLB 19.95 (*0-8225-1487-7*) Lerner Pubns.
Leon, Vicki. Seals & Sea Lions. (Illus.). 40p. (Orig.). (gr. 5 up). 1988. pap. 7.95 (*0-918303-15-X*) Blake Pub.
Martin, L. Seals. (Illus.). 24p. (gr. k-5). 1988. PLB 11.94 (*0-86592-999-8*) Rourke Corp.
Palmer, S. Leones Marinos (Sea Lions) 1991. 8.95s.p. (*0-86592-674-3*) Rourke Enter.
—Sea Lions. (Illus.). 24p. (gr. k-5). 1989. lib. bdg. 11.94 (*0-86592-362-0*); lib. bdg. 8.95s.p. (*0-685-58622-7*) Rourke Corp.
—Sea Otters. (Illus.). 24p. (gr. k-5). 1989. lib. bdg. 11.94 (*0-86592-361-2*) Rourke Corp.
Papastavrou, Vassili. Seals & Sea Lions. LC 91-9127. (Illus.). 32p. (gr. 2-5). 1992. PLB 12.40 (*0-531-18455-2*, Pub. by Bookwright Pr) Watts.
Patent, Dorothy H. Seals, Sea Lions & Walruses. LC 90-55101. (Illus.). 96p. (gr. 3-7). 1990. reinforced 14.95 (*0-8234-0834-5*) Holiday.
Petty, Kate. Baby Animals: Seals. (Illus.). 24p. (ps-3). 1992. pap. 3.95 (*0-8120-4970-5*) Barron.
—Seals. (Illus.). 24p. (gr. k-3). 1991. PLB 10.90 (*0-531-17285-6*, Gloucester Pr) Watts.
Rotter, Charles. Seals & Sea Lions. 32p. (gr. 2-6). 1991. 15.95 (*0-89565-714-7*) Childs World.
Saintsing, David & Allan, Douglas. The World of Seals. LC 87-6524. (Illus.). 32p. (gr. 2-3). 1987. PLB 17.27 (*1-55532-300-6*) Gareth Stevens Inc.
The Seal. (gr. 2-5). 1988. pap. 3.50 (*0-8167-1575-0*) Troll Assocs.
Sherrow, Victoria. Seals, Sea Lions, & Walruses. updated ed. LC 91-4663. (Illus.). 64p. (gr. 3-4). 1991. PLB 11.90 (*0-685-52512-0*) Denison.
Sobol, Richard & Sobol, Jonah. Seal Journey. Sobol, Richard, photos by. LC 92-25974. (Illus.). 32p. (gr. 1-5). 1993. 14.99 (*0-525-65126-8*, Cobblehill Bks) Dutton Child Bks.
Soller, Joelle. The Seal. (Illus.). 28p. (gr. 3-8). 1992. pap. 6.95 (*0-88106-428-9*) Charlesbridge Pub.
Two Can Publishing Ltd. Staff. Seals. (Illus.). 32p. (gr. 2-7). 1991. pap. 3.50 (*0-87534-218-3*) Highlights.
Wexo, John B. Seals, Sea Lions, Walruses. 24p. (gr. 4). 1989. PLB 14.95 (*0-88682-271-8*) Creative Ed.
Wildlife Education, Ltd. Staff. Seals & Sea Lions. Stuart, Walter, illus. 20p. (Orig.). (gr. 5 up). 1985. pap. 2.75 (*0-937934-33-X*) Wildlife Educ.

SEALS (ANIMALS)–FICTION
Allen, Judy. Seal. Humphries, Tudor, illus. LC 93-3642. 32p. (ps up). 1994. 14.95 (*1-56402-145-9*) Candlewick Pr.
Aschenbrenner, Gerald. Jack, the Seal, & the Sea. Fink, Joanne, adapted by. Aschenbrenner, Gerald, illus. 30p. (gr. 2-5). 1988. PLB 10.95 (*0-382-09985-0*); pap. 4.95 (*0-382-09986-9*) Silver Burdett Pr.
Davis, Deborah. The Secret of the Seal. Davis, Deborah, illus. (gr. 2 up). 1988. 15.00 (*0-517-56725-3*) Crown Bks Yng Read.
Farry, Liane. Frank & Sam's Summer at Aramoana. Wells, Gregory, illus. LC 93-11733. 1994. 4.25 (*0-383-03744-1*) SRA Schl Grp.
Gerstein, Mordicai. The Seal Mother. (ps-3). 1990. pap. 3.95 (*0-8037-0743-6*) Dial Bks Young.
Hoff, Syd. Sammy the Seal. Hoff, Syd, illus. LC 59-5316. 64p. (gr. k-3). 1959. PLB 13.89 (*0-06-022526-2*) HarpC Child Bks.
—Sammy the Seal. Hoff, Syd, illus. LC 59-5316. 64p. (gr. k-3). 1980. pap. 3.50 (*0-06-444028-1*, Trophy) HarpC Child Bks.
Paton Walsh, Jill. Matthew & the Sea Singer. (ps-3). 1993. 13.00 (*0-374-34869-3*) FS&G.
Peck, Sylvia. Seal Child. Parker, Robert A., illus. LC 89-33700. 208p. (gr. 4 up). 1989. 12.95 (*0-688-08682-9*) Morrow Jr Bks.
—Seal Child. (gr. 3-7). 1991. Repr. 3.50 (*0-553-15868-6*, Skylark) Bantam.
Rand, Gloria. Prince William. Rand, Ted, illus. LC 91-25180. 32p. (gr. 1-3). 1992. 14.95 (*0-8050-1841-7*, Bks Young Read) H Holt & Co.
Sammy Seal. (Illus.). (ps). 1.79 (*0-517-46416-0*) Random Hse Value.
Shachtman, Tom. Driftwhistler: A Story of Daniel au Fond. (Illus.). 160p. (gr. 5 up). 1991. 14.95 (*0-8050-1285-0*, Bks Young Read) H Holt & Co.
Tafuri, Nancy. Follow Me! LC 89-23259. (Illus.). 24p. (ps up). 1990. 13.95 (*0-688-08773-6*); lib. bdg. 13.88 (*0-688-08774-4*) Greenwillow.
Yolen, Jane. Greyling. (Illus.). 40p. (ps-3). 1991. 14.95 (*0-399-22262-6*, Philomel Bks) Putnam Pub Group.
Zoehfeld, Kathleen W. Seal Pup Grows Up: The Story of a Harbor Seal. Bonforte, Lisa, illus. Thomas, Peter, Jr., contrib. by. LC 93-27269. (Illus.). 32p. (ps-2). 1994. 14.95 (*1-56899-026-X*); incl. audiocassette 19.95 (*1-56899-039-1*); incl. 14" plush toy 26.95 (*1-56899-038-3*); mini-sized bk. 4.50 (*1-56899-027-8*); mini-sized bk., incl. 7" plush toy 9.95 (*1-56899-040-5*); audiocassette avail. (*1-56899-037-5*) Soundprints.

SEAMANSHIP
see also Navigation
Boy Scouts of America. Sea Exploring Manual. 272p. (gr. 6-12). 1987. pap. 12.85 (*0-8395-3229-6*, 33239) BSA.

SEAMEN
see also Pilots and Pilotage; Seafaring Life
also names of countries with the subhead Navy, e.g. U.S. Navy, etc.
Coote, Roger. The Sailor Through History. Smith, Tony, illus. LC 92-43640. 48p. (gr. 5-8). 1993. 15.95 (*1-56847-012-6*) Thomson Lrning.
Lattimore, Deborah N. The Sailor Who Captured the Sea. Lattimore, Deborah N., illus. LC 89-26937. 40p. (gr. 2-5). 1993. pap. 5.95 (*0-06-443342-0*, Trophy) HarpC Child Bks.
Strom, Kay M. John Newton: The Angry Sailor. (Orig.). (gr. 2-7). 1984. pap. 4.50 (*0-8024-0335-2*) Moody.

SEAMEN–LEGENDS
Edwards, Roberta, retold by. Five Silly Fishermen: A Step One Book. Wickstrom, Sylvie, illus. LC 89-42508. 32p. (Orig.). (ps-1). 1989. PLB 7.99 (*0-679-90092-6*); pap. 3.50 (*0-679-80092-1*) Random Bks Yng Read.
Lobel, Arnold. Uncle Elephant. Lobel, Arnold, illus. LC 80-8944. 64p. (gr. k-3). 1981. 14.00 (*0-06-023979-4*); PLB 13.89 (*0-06-023980-8*) HarpC Child Bks.

SEARCH AND RESCUE OPERATIONS
see Rescue Work

SEASHORE
Arnold, Caroline. A Walk by the Seashore. Brook, Bonnie, ed. Tanz, Freya, illus. 32p. (ps-1). 1990. 4.95 (*0-671-68666-6*); lib. bdg. 6.95 (*0-671-68662-3*) Silver Pr.
Behm, Barbara J. Exploring Seashores. LC 93-37058. 1994. 17.27 (*0-8368-1067-8*) Gareth Stevens Inc.
Brown, Vinson. Exploring Pacific Coast Tide Pools. rev. & enl. ed. Rovetta, Ane, illus. 80p. (gr. 4 up). 1966. pap. 8.95 (*0-87961-217-7*) Naturegraph.
Buehler, Paula. Who's on Second Beach? 8p. (gr. k-2). 1993. pap. write for info. (*1-882563-07-7*) Lamont Bks.
Burgess, Thornton W. Burgess Sea Shore Book for Children. 24.95 (*0-8488-0403-1*) Amereon Ltd.
Corbett, Julia. Sea Life at the Ocean's Edge. Warren, Hank & Moore, Shirley, eds. Kahler, Carole, illus. 24p. (gr. 4-6). 1984. pap. text ed. 3.95 (*0-685-34734-6*) NW Interpretive.
Crump, Donald J., ed. The World's Wild Shores. (Illus.). 1990. 12.95 (*0-87044-716-5*); lib. bdg. 12.95 (*0-87044-721-1*) Natl Geog.
De Hieronymis, Elve F. Beach. LC 92-72119. (ps). 1992. 4.50 (*1-56397-204-2*) Boyds Mills Pr.
Farmer, Wesley M. Seashore Discoveries. Hamann, Jeff, illus. 124p. (Orig.). (gr. 9 up). 1986. pap. text ed. 7.95x (*0-937772-01-1*) W M Farmer.
Fox, Paula. The Village by the Sea. LC 88-60099. 160p. (gr. 5-7). 1988. 13.95 (*0-531-05788-7*); PLB 13.99 (*0-531-08388-8*) Orchard Bks Watts.
Glaser, Michael. The Nature of the Seashore. Glaser, Michael, illus. 16p. (Orig.). (gr. 1-6). 1986. pap. 4.95 (*0-911635-02-5*) Knickerbocker.
Goodall, John S. The Story of the Seashore. LC 89-8328. (Illus.). 54p. 1990. SBE 14.95 (*0-689-50491-8*, M K McElderry) Macmillan Child Grp.
Gregory, Elizabeth. Beach Colors & Beach Creatures. (Illus.). 1981. 6.95 (*0-933184-17-4*); pap. 5.50 (*0-933184-18-2*) Flame Intl.
Hansen, Judith. Seashells in My Pocket: A Child's Nature Guide to Exploring the Atlantic Coast. 2nd ed. Sabaka, Donna, illus. LC 92-24397. 160p. (gr. 6 up). 1992. pap. 10.95 (*1-878239-15-5*) AMC Books.
Hecht, Jeff. Shifting Shores: Rising Seas, Retreating Coastlines. LC 89-37812. (Illus.). 160p. (gr. 7 up). 1990. SBE 14.95 (*0-684-19087-7*, Scribners Young Read) Macmillan Child Grp.
Hedgpeth, Joel. Common Seashore Life of Southern California. Hinton, Sam, illus. 64p. (gr. 4 up). 1961. 14.95 (*0-911010-63-7*); pap. 6.95 (*0-911010-62-9*) Naturegraph.
Heller, Ruth. Designs for Coloring Seashells. (Illus.). 64p. 1992. pap. 3.95 (*0-448-03144-2*, G&D) Putnam Pub Group.

Howard, Jean G. Bound by the Sea: A Summer Diary. LC 86-50255. (Illus.). 96p. (gr. 6-12). 1986. text ed. 15.00 (*0-930954-25-4*); pap. 10.00 (*0-930954-26-2*) Tidal Pr.

Hurd, Edith T. Starfish. Bloch, Lucienne, illus. LC 62-7742. 40p. (gr. k-2). 1962. PLB 13.89 (*0-690-77069-3*, Crowell Jr Bks) HarpC Child Bks.

Jennings, Terry. Sea & Seashore. LC 89-454. (Illus.). 32p. (gr. 3-6). 1989. pap. 4.95 (*0-516-48441-9*) Childrens.

Jeunesse, Gallimard & Cohat, Elisabeth, eds. The Seashore. De Hugo, Pierre, illus. LC 94-25896. 1995. 11.95 (*0-590-20303-7*) Scholastic Inc.

Kandoian, Ellen. Molly's Seasons. Kandoian, Ellen, illus. LC 91-8039. 32p. (ps-3). 1992. 13.00 (*0-525-65076-8*, Cobblehill Bks) Dutton Child Bks.

Kirkpatrick, Rena K. Look at Shore Life. rev. ed. Milne, Annabel & Stebbing, Peter, illus. LC 84-26249. 32p. (gr. 2-4). 1985. PLB 10.95 (*0-8172-2358-4*); pap. 4.95 (*0-8114-6904-2*) Raintree Steck-V.

Kricher, John C. & Morrison, Gordon. Peterson First Guide to Seashores. Kricher, John C. & Morrison, Gordon, illus. 128p. (gr. 5 up). 1992. pap. 4.80 (*0-395-61901-7*) HM.

Lawlor, Elizabeth P. Discover Nature at the Seashore: Things to Know & Things to Do. Archer, Pat, illus. LC 91-17260. 224p. 1992. pap. 12.95 (*0-8117-3079-4*) Stackpole.

Lazier, Christine. Seashore Life. Bogard, Vicki, tr. from FRE. Underhill, Graham, illus. LC 90-50781. 38p. (gr. k-5). 1991. 5.95 (*0-944589-39-1*, 391) Young Discovery Lib.

Lye, Keith. Coasts. Furstinger, Nancy, ed. (Illus.). 48p. (gr. 5-8). 1989. PLB 12.95 (*0-382-09790-4*) Silver Burdett Pr.

Macht, Philip. Circles in the Sand. Rosenthal, Linda, illus. LC 84-90597. 64p. (gr. 7 up). 1985. 12.95 (*0-930339-00-2*) Maxrom Pr.

Maidoff, Ilka. Let's Explore the Shore. (Illus.). (gr. 5 up). 1962. 9.95 (*0-8392-3017-6*) Astor-Honor.

Malnig, Anita. Where the Waves Break: Life at the Edge of the Sea. LC 84-9614. (Illus.). 48p. (gr. 2-5). 1985. PLB 19.95 (*0-87614-226-9*) Carolrhoda Bks.

—Where the Waves Break: Life at the Edge of the Sea. (Illus.). 48p. (gr. 1-5). 1987. pap. 6.95 (*0-87614-477-6*, First Ave Edns) Lerner Pubns.

Manuel, Mark, et al. Our Coast. LC 93-33362. 1994. pap. write for info. Cambridge U Pr.

Mason, Helen. Life at the Seashore. (Illus.). 32p. (gr. 2-5). 1990. PLB 14.25 (*0-88625-270-9*); pap. 3.50 (*0-88625-269-5*) Durkin Hayes Pub.

Miller, Christina G. & Berry, Louise A. Coastal Rescue: Preserving Our Seashores. LC 88-27520. (Illus.). 144p. (gr. 5-9). 1989. SBE 14.95 (*0-689-31288-1*, Atheneum Child Bk) Macmillan Child Grp.

O'Connor, Karen. Let's Take a Walk on the Beach. Axeman, Lois, illus. LC 86-9551. 32p. (ps-2). 1986. PLB 14.95 (*0-89565-354-0*) Childs World.

Oda, Hidetomo. Animals of the Seashore. LC 85-28192. (Illus.). 32p. (gr. 3-7). 1986. PLB 10.95 (*0-8172-2543-9*) Raintree Steck-V.

On the Beach. (Illus.). (ps-5). 3.50 (*0-7214-8001-2*); Ser. S50. wkbk. A 1.95 (*0-317-04022-7*) Ladybird Bks.

Parker, Steve. Seashore. King, Dave, illus. LC 88-27173. 64p. (gr. 5 up). 1989. 16.00 (*0-394-82254-4*); PLB 16. 99 (*0-394-92254-9*) Knopf Bks Yng Read.

—Seashore. (Illus.). 48p. (gr. 7-9). 1992. 13.95 (*0-563-34410-5*, BBC-Parkwest); pap. 6.95 (*0-563-34411-3*, BBC-Parkwest) Parkwest Pubns.

Podendorf, Illa. Animals of Sea & Shore. LC 81-38453. (Illus.). 48p. (gr. k-4). 1982. PLB 12.85 (*0-516-01615-6*); pap. 4.95 (*0-516-41615-4*) Childrens.

Rius, Maria & Parramon, J. M. The Seaside. (ps). 1986. 6.95 (*0-8120-5747-3*); pap. 6.95 (*0-8120-3699-9*) Barron.

Rockwell, Anne. At the Beach. Rockwell, Harlow, illus. LC 86-2943. 24p. (ps-1). 1987. RSBE 13.95 (*0-02-777940-8*, Macmillan Child Bk) Macmillan Child Grp.

Salts, Bobbi. Beaches Are for Kids! An Activity Book for Kids. Parker, Steve, illus. 32p. (gr. 1-6). 1990. pap. 2.95 (*0-929526-09-0*) Double B Pubns.

Silver, Donald M. Seashore. (gr. 7-12). 1993. text ed. write for info. (*0-7167-6511-X*, Sci Am Yng Rdrs) W H Freeman.

Silverstein, Alvin. Life in a Tidal Pool, Vol. 1. (gr. 4-7). 1990. 14.95 (*0-316-79120-2*, Joy St Bks) Little.

Solomon, Joan. A Day by the Sea. (Illus.). 25p. (gr. 2-4). 1991. 12.95 (*0-237-60152-4*, Pub. by Evans Bros Ltd) Trafalgar.

Stevenson, James. July. Stevenson, James, illus. LC 88-37584. (gr. k up). 1990. 12.95 (*0-688-08822-8*); PLB 12.88 (*0-688-08823-6*) Greenwillow.

Stone, L. Seashores. (Illus.). 48p. (gr. 4-8). 1989. lib. bdg. 15.94 (*0-86592-435-X*); 11.95s.p. (*0-685-58575-1*) Rourke Corp.

Swanson, Diane. Squirts & Snails & Skinny Green Tails: Seashore Nature Activities for Kids. (gr. 2 up). 1994. pap. 5.95 (*1-55850-389-7*) Adams Inc MA.

Swenson, Allan. Secrets of a Seashore. (Illus.). 80p. (gr. 4-10). 1981. pap. 3.95 (*0-930096-28-2*) G Gannett.

Talkabout the Beach. (ARA., Illus.). (gr. 1-3). 1987. 3.95x (*0-86685-232-8*) Intl Bk Ctr.

Taylor, Barbara. Shoreline. Greenaway, Frank, photos by. LC 92-53491. (Illus.). 32p. (gr. 2-5). 1993. 9.95 (*1-56458-213-2*) Dorling Kindersley.

Time-Life Inc. Editors. How Big Is the Ocean? First Questions & Answers about the Beach. Fallow, Allan, ed. (Illus.). 48p. (ps-k). 1994. write for info. (*0-7835-0897-2*) Time-Life.

Vasiliu, Mircea. A Day at the Beach. LC 76-24169. (ps-2). 1977. Random Bks Yng Read.

Wyler, Rose. Seashore Surprises. (Illus.). 32p. (gr. k-3). 1991. lib. bdg. 11.98 (*0-671-69165-1*, J Messner); pap. 4.95 (*0-671-69167-8*) S&S Trade.

SEASHORE–FICTION

Agell, Charlotte. I Wear Long Green Hair in Summer. Agell, Charlotte, illus. LC 93-33612. 32p. (ps up). 1994. 7.95 (*0-88448-113-1*) Tilbury Hse.

Akkerman, Dinnie. King on the Beach. (ps). 1994. 12.95 (*0-8120-6430-5*); pap. 4.95 (*0-8120-1957-1*) Barron.

Alden, Laura. Squirrel's Adventure in Alphabet Town. Collins, Judi, illus. LC 92-1314. 32p. (ps-2). 1992. PLB 11.80 (*0-516-05419-8*) Childrens.

Baker, Leslie. Morning Beach. (ps-3). 1990. 14.95 (*0-316-07835-2*) Little.

Bat-Ami, Miriam. Sea, Salt, & Air. Young, Mary O., illus. LC 91-34140. 32p. (gr. 1-5). 1993. RSBE 14.95 (*0-02-708495-7*, Macmillan Child Bk) Macmillan Child Grp.

Beames, Margaret. Juno Loves Barney. Campbell, Caroline, illus. LC 93-20030. 1994. pap. write for info. (*0-383-03698-4*) SRA Schl Grp.

Beveridge, Barbara. Waves. Costeloe, Brenda, illus. LC 92-31948. 1993. 3.75 (*0-383-03603-8*) SRA Schl Grp.

Brown, Margaret W. The Seashore Noisy Book. new ed. Weisgard, Leonard, illus. LC 92-31433. 48p. (ps-1). 1993. 15.00 (*0-06-020840-6*); PLB 15.89 (*0-06-020841-4*) HarpC Child Bks.

Calmenson, Stephanie. Hotter Than a Hot Dog! Savadier, Elivia, illus. LC 93-313. (gr. 1-8). 1994. 14.95 (*0-316-12479-6*) Little.

Carpenter, Mimi G. Of Lucky Pebbles & Mermaid's Tears. Carpenter, Mimi G., illus. 32p. (ps-5). 1994. pap. 9.95 (*0-9614628-2-5*) Beachcomber Pr. Author/Illustrator Mimi Gregoire Carpenter (What The Sea Left Behind, 1981), presents a rhyming fantasy with an environmental theme for children through fifth grade (Includes a shell identification page). "Mimi Gregoire Carpenter conveys a child-like sense of wonder in her artwork & writing. As revealed in her work, her inspiration comes from the sea & its creatures. Mimi's philosophy, spirituality & love... of the environment are embodied in her beautiful illustrations & storylines."-- New England Science Center, Worcester, Mass. Don't miss this unusual bunch of creatures - Sea Uglies & Sandcreatures, Tidal Pool Trolls & Lagoonies. Learn about the environment, mischief, being different, being creative - about things you can change & about things you cannot & while you're at it - learn about why we call beachglass "Mermaid's Tears" & why pebbles with rings around them are called "Lucky." Shorah, a "non-traditional" mermaid & the story's main character, learns to face the consequences of her actions after she conjures a storm that disrupts the sea world. 8 1/2" X 10 1/2" - detailed opaque watercolors & graphite - durable coated paper - stapled binding - paperback 32pp. $9.95. Write or call Beachcomber "Studio" Press, RR3, Box 2220, Oakland, ME 04963; 207-465-7197.

Publisher Provided Annotation.

Cole, Sheila. When the Tide Is Low. Wright-Frierson, Virginia, illus. LC 84-10023. 32p. (ps-1). 1985. 16.00 (*0-688-04066-7*); PLB 15.93 (*0-688-04067-5*) Lothrop.

Condra, Estelle. See the Ocean. Crockett-Blassingame, Linda, illus. LC 94-4234. 1994. reinforced bdg. 14.95 (*1-57102-005-5*, Ideas Child) Hambleton-Hill.

Cooney, Barbara. Hattie & the Wild Waves: A Story from Brooklyn. Cooney, Barbara, illus. LC 92-40723. 40p. 1993. pap. 4.99 (*0-14-054193-4*, Puffin) Puffin Bks.

Craig, Janet. Homer the Beachcomber. Mahan, Ben, illus. LC 87-10913. 32p. (gr. k-2). 1988. PLB 11.59 (*0-8167-1085-6*); pap. text ed. 2.95 (*0-8167-1086-4*) Troll Assocs.

Dawe, Karen. The Beach Book & Beach Bucket. LC 87-40648. (Illus.). (gr. k-5). 1988. pap. 7.95 incl. bucket (*0-89480-590-8*, 1590) Workman Pub.

DeSaix, Frank. The Girl Who Danced with Dolphins. DeSaix, Debbi D., illus. 32p. (gr. k-3). 1991. 14.95 (*0-374-32626-6*) FS&G.

Dexter, Alison. Grandma. Dexter, Alison, illus. LC 92-6473. 32p. (ps-2). 1993. 15.00 (*0-06-021143-1*); PLB 14.89 (*0-06-021144-X*) HarpC Child Bks.

Drescher, Henrick. Down by the Bay. 16p. (ps-2). 1994. text ed. 3.95 (*0-673-36201-9*) GdYrBks.

Farry, Liane. Frank & Sam's Summer at Aramoana. Wells, Gregory, illus. LC 93-11733. 1994. 4.25 (*0-383-03744-1*) SRA Schl Grp.

Florian, Douglas. Beach Day. LC 89-1933. (Illus.). 32p. (ps up). 1990. 12.95 (*0-688-09104-0*); lib. bdg. 12.88 (*0-688-09105-9*) Greenwillow.

Frank, John. Erin's Voyage. Schutzer, Dena, illus. LC 92-31783. (ps-1). 1994. pap. 15.00 (*0-671-79585-6*, S&S BFYR) S&S Trade.

Gauthier, Bertrand. Zachary in Camping Out. Sylvestre, Daniel, illus. LC 93-15457. 1993. 15.93 (*0-8368-1012-0*) Gareth Stevens Inc.

Graham, Bob. Greetings from Sandy Beach. Graham, Bob, illus. 32p. (ps-3). 1992. 12.95 (*0-916291-40-5*) Kane-Miller Bk.

Greaves, Margaret. The Serpent Shell. Nesbitt, Jan, illus. 32p. (ps-3). 1993. 13.95 (*0-8120-6350-3*) Barron.

Greenberg, Melanie H. At the Beach. Greenberg, Melanie H., illus. LC 88-29995. 24p. (ps-2). 1989. 11.95 (*0-525-44474-2*, DCB) Dutton Child Bks.

Guild, Anne V. Mickey Mouse in Let's Go...on a Beach Picnic. Scholefield, Ron, et al, illus. 26p. (ps up). 1987. pap. 14.95 (*1-55578-800-9*) Worlds Wonder.

Harrison, Troon. The Long Weekend. Foreman, Michael, illus. LC 93-307. (gr. k). 1994. 14.95 (*0-15-248842-1*) HarBrace.

Helldorfer, M. C. Harmonica Night. Natchev, Alexi, illus. LC 93-40669. 1995. 16.95 (*0-02-743518-0*, Bradbury Pr) Macmillan Child Grp.

Hines, Anna G. Gramma's Walk. LC 92-30085. 32p. (ps up). 1993. 14.00 (*0-688-11480-6*); PLB 13.93 (*0-688-11481-4*) Greenwillow.

Hosie, Bounar. Life Belts. LC 92-43048. 1993. 14.95 (*0-385-31074-9*) Delacorte.

Hughes, Shirley. Here Comes Charlie Moon. Hughes, Shirley, illus. LC 85-24125. 128p. (gr. 2-5). 1986. Repr. of 1980 ed. 11.95 (*0-688-06401-9*) Lothrop.

—Lucy & Tom at the Seaside. (Illus.). 32p. (ps-k). 1994. 17.95 (*0-575-05227-9*, Pub. by Gollancz UK) Trafalgar.

Jackson, Darcy. Another Fuzz Bugg Adventure. Sheppard, Scott O., illus. 40p. (gr. k-5). 1993. 15.95 (*1-883016-00-2*) Moonglow Pubns.

Jesep, Paul P. A December Gift from the Shoals. Bowdren, John, illus. 16p. (Orig.). (gr. 4). 1993. pap. 5.95 (*0-9634360-1-5*) Seacoast Pubns New Eng.

Johnson, Angela. Joshua by the Sea. Mitchell, Rhonda, illus. LC 93-46411. (ps). 1994. 4.95 (*0-531-06846-3*) Orchard Bks Watts.

Kesselman, Wendy & Himler, Ronald. Sand in my Shoes. LC 94-12038. (Illus.). 1995. write for info. (*0-7868-0057-7*); PLB write for info. (*0-7868-2045-4*) Hyprn Child.

Kimball, Kathleen M. Big Foot, Little Foot. LoBue, Elisa M., illus. LC 78-68822. (ps). 1979. 6.95 (*0-933308-00-0*) West Village.

King, Virginia. Sand. Quinn, Annie, illus. LC 92-31959. 1993. 2.50 (*0-383-03591-0*) SRA Schl Grp.

Lakin, Patricia. Dad & Me in the Morning. Steele, Robert, illus. LC 93-36169. (ps-3). 1994. 14.95 (*0-8075-1419-5*) A Whitman.

Leopold, Nikia C. Sandcastle Seahorses. LC 87-35978. 45p. (Orig.). 1988. pap. 5.95 (*0-913123-17-X*) Galileo.

Lessing, Doris. Through the Tunnel. (gr. 4-12). 1989. 13. 95 (*0-88682-346-3*, 97224-098) Creative Ed.

Lester, Alison. Magic Beach. Lester, Alison, illus. 32p. (ps-3). 1992. 13.95 (*0-316-52177-9*, Joy St Bks) Little.

Levine, Evan. Not the Piano, Mrs. Medley! Schindler, Stephen D., illus. LC 90-29085. 32p. (ps-2). 1991. 14. 95 (*0-531-05956-1*); RLB 14.99 (*0-531-08556-2*) Orchard Bks Watts.

Levy, Elizabeth. Something Queer on Vacation. Gerstein, Mordicai, illus. LC 78-72858. (gr. 1-3). 1980. 10.95 (*0-440-08346-X*); pap. 6.95 (*0-385-28987-1*) Delacorte.

Light, John. Beachcombers. LC 91-38130. (gr. 4 up). 1991. 2.95 (*0-85953-502-9*) Childs Play.

Lionni, Leo. On the Beach There Are Many Pebbles. Cohn, Amy, ed. LC 94-6484. (Illus.). 32p. (ps up). 1994. pap. 4.95 (*0-688-13284-7*, Mulberry) Morrow.

MacDonald, Maryann. Ben at the Beach. McTaggart, David, illus. 32p. (ps-3). 1991. 14.95 (*0-670-83920-5*) Viking Child Bks.

Marshal, Edward. Four on the Shore. (ps-3). 1993. pap. 4.99 (*0-14-036186-3*, Puffin) Puffin Bks.

Marshall, Edward. Four on the Shore. Marshall, James, illus. (gr. 1-4). 1994. pap. 3.25 (*0-14-037006-4*) Puffin Bks.

—La Pandilla en la Orilla - Four on the Shore. Marshall, James, illus. (SPA.). 52p. (gr. 2-4). 1990. pap. write for info. (*84-204-4678-5*) Santillana.

—Three by the Sea. Marshall, James, illus. 48p. (ps-3). 1981. PLB 10.89 (*0-8037-8687-5*) Dial Bks Young.

—Three by the Sea. Marshall, James, illus. (gr. k-3). 1994. pap. 3.25 (*0-14-037004-8*) Puffin Bks.

Martin, Antoinette T. Famous Seaweed Soup. Mathews, Judith, ed. Westcott, Nadine B., illus. LC 92-31612. 32p. (ps-2). 1993. PLB 13.95 (*0-8075-2263-5*) A Whitman.

Nabb, Magdalen. Josie Smith at the Seashore. Vainio, Pirkko, illus. LC 89-8168. 96p. (gr. 1-5). 1990. SBE 12.95 (*0-689-50492-6*, M K McElderry) Macmillan Child Grp.

—Josie Smith at the Seaside. large type ed. Vainio, Pirkko, illus. 1993. 16.95 (*0-7451-1808-9*, Galaxy Child Lrg Print) Chivers N Amer.

Oana. Bobby Bear Goes to the Beach. LC 80-82951. (Illus.). 32p. (ps-1). 1981. PLB 9.95 (*0-87783-153-X*) Oddo.

Oxenbury, Helen. Tom & Pippo on the Beach. Oxenbury, Helen, illus. LC 92-53130. 24p. (ps). 1993. 5.95 (*1-56402-181-5*) Candlewick Pr.

Paraskevas, Betty. Monster Beach. Paraskevas, Michael, illus. LC 93-46927. 1995. write for info. (*0-15-292882-0*) HarBrace.

—On the Edge of the Sea. Paraskevas, Michael, illus. LC 91-31489. 32p. 1992. 14.00 (*0-8037-1130-1*); PLB 13.89 (*0-8037-1263-4*) Dial Bks Young.

—The Strawberry Dog. Paraskevas, Michael, illus. LC 92-18216. (ps-3). 1993. 13.99 (*0-8037-1367-3*); PLB 13.89 (*0-8037-1368-1*) Dial Bks Young.

Pascal, Francine. Malibu Summer. 208p. (Orig.). (gr. 4). 1986. pap. 3.50 (*0-553-26050-2*) Bantam.

Ray, Mary L. Alvah & Arvilla. Root, Barry, illus. LC 93-31874. (gr. k-3). 1994. 14.95 (*0-15-202655-X*) HarBrace.

Reid, Mary C. Come to the Ocean with Me. LC 91-71035. 32p. 1991. pap. 4.99 (*0-8066-2551-1*) Augsburg Fortress.

Rockwell, Anne. At the Beach. Rockwell, Harlow, illus. LC 90-45620. 24p. (ps-1). 1991. pap. 3.95 (*0-689-71494-7*, Aladdin) Macmillan Child Grp.

—The Way to Captain Yankee's. Rockwell, Anne, illus. LC 92-44644. 32p. (ps-2). 1994. RSBE 13.95 (*0-02-777271-3*, Macmillan Child Bk) Macmillan Child Grp.

Ryder, Joanne. A House by the Sea. Sweet, Melissa, illus. LC 93-22149. 32p. (ps up). 1994. 15.00g (*0-688-12675-8*); PLB 14.93 (*0-688-12676-6*) Morrow Jr Bks.

Rylant, Cynthia. Henry & Mudge & the Forever Sea: The Sixth Book of Their Adventures. Stevenson, Sucie, illus. LC 88-6130. 48p. (gr. 1-3). 1989. RSBE 12.95 (*0-02-778007-4*, Bradbury Pr) Macmillan Child Grp.

—Henry & Mudge & the Forever Sea: The Sixth Book of Their Adventures. Stevenson, Sucie, illus. LC 92-28646. 48p. (gr. 1-3). 1993. pap. 3.95 (*0-689-71701-6*, Aladdin) Macmillan Child Grp.

Sharmat, Marjorie W. Nate the Great & the Boring Beach Bag. Simont, Marc, illus. 48p. (gr. 1-4). 1989. pap. 3.25 (*0-440-40168-2*, YB) Dell.

Singleton, Linda J. Spring Break. LC 94-4570. (gr. 7 up). 1994. 3.95 (*1-56565-144-8*) Lowell Hse Juvenile.

Sis, Peter. Beach Ball. Sis, Peter, illus. LC 89-2076. 24p. (ps). 1990. 12.95 (*0-688-09181-4*); PLB 12.88 (*0-688-09182-2*) Greenwillow.

Smith, E. Boyd. The Seashore Book. Smith, E. Boyd, illus. LC 84-22483. 56p. (gr. k-12). 1985. Repr. of 1912 ed. 13.45 (*0-395-38015-4*) HM.

Steele, David H. The Pebble Searcher. 16p. (gr. 7-10). 1986. 22.00x (*0-317-52595-6*, Pub. by A H Stockwell England) St Mut.

Stevens, Kathleen. Bully for the Beast! Bowler, Ray, illus. LC 88-33090. 32p. (gr. 2-3). 1990. PLB 18.60 (*0-8368-0020-6*) Gareth Stevens Inc.

Stevenson, James. Emma at the Beach. LC 88-3491. (Illus.). (gr. k up). 1990. 12.95 (*0-688-08806-6*); lib. bdg. 12.88 (*0-688-08807-4*) Greenwillow.

—The Worst Person in the World at Crab Beach. LC 86-31931. (Illus.). 32p. (gr. k-3). 1988. 13.95 (*0-688-07298-4*); lib. bdg. 13.88 (*0-688-07299-2*) Greenwillow.

Stine, R. L. Beach Party. 1990. pap. 3.50 (*0-590-43278-8*, Point) Scholastic Inc.

Stock, Catherine. Sophie's Bucket. (ps-1). 1994. pap. 4.95 (*0-15-277162-X*) HarBrace.

Streib, Sally. Treasures by the Sea. 159p. (gr. 4 up). 1991. pap. 7.95 (*0-8163-0933-7*) Pacific Pr Pub Assn.

Turkle, Brinton. Do Not Open. Turkle, Brinton, illus. LC 80-10289. 32p. (ps-2). 1981. pap. 13.95 (*0-525-28785-X*, 01258-370, DCB) Dutton Child Bks.

Verrier, Suzy. Titus Tidewater. Verrier, Suzy, illus. LC 70-112636. 48p. (gr. 2-4). 1990. Repr. of 1970 ed. 12.95 (*0-89272-289-4*) Down East.

Waddell, Martin. The Big, Big Sea. Eachus, Jennifer, illus. LC 93-33228. 32p. 1994. 15.95 (*1-56402-066-5*) Candlewick Pr.

Warner, Gertrude C. Mystery in the Sand. Cunningham, David, illus. LC 70-165823. 128p. (gr. 2-7). 1971. PLB 10.95 (*0-8075-5373-5*); pap. 3.50 (*0-8075-5372-7*) A Whitman.

Weir, Bob & Weir, Wendy. Baru Bay. LC 93-23325. (Illus.). 1995. incl. cassette 19.95 (*1-56282-622-0*); PLB 14.95 (*1-56282-623-9*) Hyprn Child.

Welles, Laura & Welles, Ted. Will & Grandmother Change the Seashore. McCloskey, Maris, ed. Welles, Laura, illus. LC 92-62260. 40p. (Orig.). (gr. k-7). 1992. pap. 7.95 (*0-915189-07-0*) Oceanus.

—Will & Grandmother Change the Seashore. McCloskey, Maris, ed. Welles, Laura, illus. LC 92-62260. 40p. (Orig.). (gr. k-7). 1993. text ed. 24.00 (*0-915189-08-9*) Oceanus.

Wild, Margaret. The Queen's Holiday. O'Loughlin, Sue, illus. LC 91-14024. 32p. (ps-1). 1992. 13.95 (*0-531-05973-1*); PLB 13.99 (*0-531-08573-2*) Orchard Bks Watts.

Zamost, Barbara. Handstands in the Sand. Nalerio, Claudio, illus. 48p. (ps-6). 1992. 12.95 (*1-881970-00-0*) Saras Prints.

Zion, Gene. Harry by the Sea. Graham, Margaret B., illus. LC 65-21302. 32p. (ps-3). 1976. pap. 4.95 (*0-06-443010-3*, JP 10, Trophy) HarpC Child Bks.

Zolotow, Charlotte. The Seashore Book. Minor, Wendell, illus. LC 91-22783. 32p. (ps-3). 1992. 15.00 (*0-06-020213-0*); PLB 14.89 (*0-06-020214-9*) HarpC Child Bks.

—Seashore Book. LC 91-22783. (ps). 1994. pap. 5.95 (*0-06-443364-1*) HarpC Child Bks.

SEASONS

see also names of the seasons, e.g. Autumn, etc.

Alexander, Sue. There's More...Much More. Brewster, Patience, illus. LC 86-33632. 32p. (ps-3). 1987. 12.95 (*0-15-200605-2*, Gulliver Bks) HarBrace.

Allison, Linda. The Reasons for Seasons: The Great Cosmic Megagalactic Trip Without Moving from Your Chair. Allison, Linda, illus. 128p. (gr. 4 up). 1975. pap. 9.95 (*0-316-03440-1*) Little.

Asimov, Isaac. Why Do We Have Different Seasons? LC 90-26061. (Illus.). 24p. (gr. 2-3). 1991. PLB 15.93 (*0-8368-0439-2*) Gareth Stevens Inc.

Bank Street College of Education Editors. Let's Explore the Seasons. (gr. 1-2). 1986. pap. 2.95 (*0-8120-3625-5*) Barron.

Baxter, Roberta. Turn of the Seasons. Sagati, Miriam, illus. 32p. (ps-2). Date not set. 11.95 (*1-56065-146-6*) Capstone Pr.

Bennett, David. Seasons. Kightley, Rosalinda, illus. 32p. (ps up). 1988. pap. 3.95 (*0-553-05480-5*) Bantam.

Bilyeu, Linda M. Celebrate Spring. Grossmann, Dan, illus. 144p. (gr. k-3). 1984. wkbk. 11.95 (*0-86653-209-9*, SS 836, Shining Star Pubns) Good Apple.

Borden, Louise. Caps, Hats, Socks, & Mittens: A Book about the Four Seasons. Hoban, Lillian, illus. 1992. pap. 3.95 (*0-590-44872-2*, Blue Ribbon Bks) Scholastic Inc.

Brandt, Keith. Wonders of the Seasons. Watling, James, illus. LC 81-7411. 32p. (gr. 2-4). 1982. PLB 11.59 (*0-89375-580-X*); pap. text ed. 2.95 (*0-89375-581-8*) Troll Assocs.

Branley, Franklyn M. Sunshine Makes the Seasons. rev. ed. Maestro, Giulio, illus. LC 85-47540. 32p. (ps-3). 1985. PLB 14.89 (*0-690-04482-8*, Crowell Jr Bks) HarpC Child Bks.

Burns, Diane. Rocky Mountain Seasons: From Valley to Mountaintop. Dannen, Kent & Dannen, Donna, photos by. LC 92-22833. (Illus.). 32p. (gr. 1-5). 1993. RSBE 14.95 (*0-02-716142-0*, Macmillan Child Bk) Macmillan Child Grp.

Busch, Phyllis S. Science Safaris to the Nearest Wilderness: Your Own Back Yard. LC 93-48410. (Illus.). 1995. 16.00 (*0-02-715655-9*) Macmillan Child Grp.

Butler, Daphne. First Look at the Changing Seasons. LC 90-10246. (Illus.). 32p. (gr. 1-2). 1991. PLB 17.27 (*0-8368-0504-6*) Gareth Stevens Inc.

Butterfield, Sherri. Seasons. (Illus.). 48p. (gr. 2-5). 1990. 5.95 (*0-88160-190-X*, LW 149) Learning Wks.

Cohen, Lynn. Weather & Seasons. 64p. (ps-2). 1988. 6.95 (*0-912107-79-0*, MM983) Monday Morning Bks.

Darneille, Diane D. Season Science 1: Seasonal Mystery of Animal Coat Change. Porter, Robin A., illus. 32p. (Orig.). (gr. k-5). 1992. pap. 13.95 (*0-9634246-1-0*) Sci Passport.

De Bourgoing, Pascale. Weather. Kniffke, Sophie, illus. 24p. 1991. pap. 10.95 (*0-590-45234-7*, Cartwheel) Scholastic Inc.

Doyle, Tara. All about the Seasons Activity Book. (ps-3). 1993. pap. 1.95 (*0-590-46296-2*) Scholastic Inc.

Dvorak, David, Jr. A Sea of Grass: The Tallgrass Prairie. Dvorak, David, Jr., illus. LC 93-19507. 32p. (gr. 1-4). 1994. RSBE 14.95 (*0-02-733245-4*, Macmillan Child Bk) Macmillan Child Grp.

Fass, Bernie & Caggiano, Rosemary. The Four Seasons. 48p. (gr. k-6). 1976. pap. 14.95 (*0-86704-001-7*) Clarus Music.

The Four Seasons. (Illus.). (ps). 1985. bds. 3.98 (*0-517-47339-9*) Random Hse Value.

Graube, Ireta S. Seasons - A Thematic Unit. Apodaca, Blanqui, illus. 80p. (ps-1). 1990. wkbk. 8.95 (*1-55734-251-2*) Tchr Create Mat.

Greydanus, Rose. Changing Seasons. Hall, Susan, illus. LC 82-19959. 32p. (gr. k-2). 1983. PLB 11.59 (*0-89375-902-3*); pap. 2.95 (*0-8167-1478-9*) Troll Assocs.

Hand, Phyllis. Seasonal Bulletin Boards That Teach. Henson, Grace, illus. 48p. (gr. 1-5). 1984. wkbk. 7.95 (*0-86653-203-X*, SS 820, Shining Star Pubns) Good Apple.

Harlow, Rosie & Morgan, Gareth. Cycles & Seasons. Peperell, Liz, illus. LC 91-2567. 40p. (gr. 5-8). 1991. PLB 12.90 (*0-531-19123-0*, Warwick) Watts.

Kalman, Bobbie. Time & the Seasons. (Illus.). 32p. (gr. 2-3). 1986. 15.95 (*0-86505-072-4*); pap. 7.95 (*0-86505-094-5*) Crabtree Pub Co.

Kurtz, John & Kurtz, John, illus. Disney's Pop-up Book of Seasons. LC 92-56161. 12p. (ps-k). 1994. 7.95 (*1-56282-508-9*) Disney Pr.

Linker, Corinne. Circle of Seasons. Kirkeeide, Debi, illus. 32p. (ps-2). Date not set. 11.95 (*1-56065-157-1*) Capstone Pr.

Little People Big Book About Seasons. 64p. (ps-1). 1989. write for info. (*0-8094-7470-0*); PLB write for info. (*0-8094-7471-9*) Time-Life.

Lynn, Sara & James, Diane. Rain & Shine. Wright, Joe, illus. LC 93-36420. 32p. (gr. k-2). 1994. 14.95 (*1-56847-142-4*) Thomson Lrning.

Magoldi, Mary. Daily Close-Ups for Spring. McClure, Nancee, illus. Russell, Bruce, ed. 96p. (gr. k-6). 1984. wkbk. 9.95 (*0-86653-255-2*, GA 563) Good Apple.

—Daily Close-Ups for Winter. Hall, Robyn, illus. Russell, Bruce, ed. 96p. (gr. k-6). 1984. wkbk. 9.95 (*0-86653-256-0*, GA 562) Good Apple.

Magoldi, Mary & Russell, Bruce. Daily Close-Ups for Fall. 96p. (gr. k-6). 1984. wkbk. 9.95 (*0-86653-254-4*, GA 561) Good Apple.

Marcus, Elizabeth. Our Wonderful Seasons. Boyd, Patti, illus. LC 82-17372. 32p. (gr. 3-6). 1983. PLB 10.59 (*0-89375-896-5*); pap. text ed. 2.95 (*0-89375-897-3*) Troll Assocs.

Milburn, Constance. Let's Look at the Seasons. Caulkins, Janet, ed. LC 87-71740. (Illus.). 32p. (gr. k-6). 1988. PLB 11.40 (*0-531-18179-0*, Pub. by Bookwright Pr) Watts.

Palmer, Glenda. Blue Galoshes in Spring: God's Wonderful World of Seasons. LC 92-34716. (Illus.). 1993. pap. 4.99 (*0-7814-0710-9*, Chariot Bks) Chariot Family.

Plattner, Sandra S. Connecting with the Seasons. (ps-k). 1991. pap. 10.95 (*0-86653-977-8*) Fearon Teach Aids.

Podendorf, Illa. Seasons. LC 81-7751. (Illus.). 48p. (gr. k-4). 1981. PLB 12.85 (*0-516-01647-4*); pap. 4.95 (*0-516-41647-2*) Childrens.

Provensen, Alice & Provensen, Martin. A Book of Seasons. Provensen, Alice & Provensen, Martin, illus. LC 75-36470. 32p. (ps-1). 1976. pap. 2.25 (*0-394-83242-6*) Random Bks Yng Read.

Russo, Monica. The Tree Almanac: A Year-Round Activity Guide. Byron, Kevin, photos by. LC 92-41347. (Illus.). (gr. 3 up). 1993. 14.95 (*0-8069-1252-9*) Sterling.

Sabin, Francene. Seasons. Burns, Raymond, illus. LC 84-2713. 32p. (gr. 3-6). 1985. PLB 9.49 (*0-8167-0308-6*); pap. text ed. 2.95 (*0-8167-0309-4*) Troll Assocs.

Spizman, Robyn. Bulletin Boards: Seasonal Ideas & Activities. Pesiri, Evelyn, illus. 64p. (gr. k-6). 1984. wkbk. 7.95 (*0-86653-218-8*, GA 568) Good Apple.

—Bulletin Boards to Promote Good Study Skills & Positive Self-Concept. Pesiri, Evelyn, illus. 48p. (gr. k-6). 1984. wkbk. 6.95 (*0-86653-261-7*, GA 575) Good Apple.

Supraner, Robyn. I Can Read About Seasons. LC 74-24990. (Illus.). (gr. 2-4). 1975. pap. 2.50 (*0-89375-068-9*) Troll Assocs.

Updike, John. A Child's Calendar. Burkert, Nancy E., illus. LC 61-21555. 32p. (gr. k-3). 1965. 11.95 (*0-394-81059-7*) Knopf Bks Yng Read.

Wallace, Jeffery S. Discovering the Four Seasons. Bittner, Bob, ed. LC 92-43796. (Illus.). 128p. (gr. 3-6). 1993. pap. 7.99 (*0-7459-2617-7*) Lion USA.

Walsh, Abigail. Exploring the Seasons. Dowling, Marilyn, illus. 24p. (ps-2). Date not set. PLB 11.95 (*1-56065-109-1*) Capstone Pr.

Whitfield, Philip & Pope, Joyce. Why Do the Seasons Change? Questions on Nature's Rhythms & Cycles Answered by the Natural History Museum. LC 87-40133. 96p. (ps up). 1987. pap. 16.95 (*0-670-81860-7*) Viking Child Bks.

Wildsmith, Brian. Seasons. (Illus.). 32p. (ps up). 1991. pap. 5.95 (*0-19-272175-5*, 12409) OUP.

SEASONS–FICTION

Ackerman, Karen. Leaves in October. 1993. pap. 3.50 (*0-440-40868-7*) Dell.

Agell, Charlotte. Wind Spins Me Around in the Fall. Agell, Charlotte, illus. 40p. (ps up). 1994. 7.95 (*0-88448-114-X*) Tilbury Hse.

Anderson, Janet. The Key into Winter. Soman, David, illus. LC 93-13017. 1993. write for info. (*0-8075-4170-2*) A Whitman.

Annable, Toni & Kaspar, Maria H. The Four Seasons: Las Cuatro Estaciones. Viola, Amy, tr. Lumetta, Lawrence, illus. 40p. (Orig.). (gr. 5 up). 1992. pap. 4.95 (*1-882828-02-X*); pap. 10.95 incl. audio (*1-882828-14-3*) Kasan Imprints.

—The Four Seasons: Les Quatre Saisons. Lumetta, Lawrence, illus. 40p. (Orig.). (gr. 5 up). 1992. pap. 4.95 (*1-882828-03-8*); pap. 10.95 incl. audio (*1-882828-15-1*) Kasan Imprints.

Aver, Kate. Joey's Way. Himler, Ronald, illus. LC 92-7830. 48p. (gr. 1-4). 1992. SBE 13.95 (*0-689-50552-3*, M K McElderry) Macmillan Child Grp.

Beers, V. Gilbert, text by. Precious Moments Through-the-Year Stories. Butcher, Samuel J., illus. LC 89-17848. 288p. (gr. 2-6). 1989. 14.99 (*0-8010-0973-1*) Baker Bk.

Bissett, Isabel. Molly's Bracelet. Strahan, Heather, illus. LC 92-34337. 1993. 3.75 (*0-383-03641-0*) SRA Schl Grp.

Blades, Ann. Fall. Blades, Ann, illus. (ps-k). 1990. bds. 4.95 (*0-688-09232-2*) Lothrop.

Boyd, Candy D. Seasons. 144p. (gr. 3-7). 1994. pap. 3.99 (*0-14-036583-4*) Puffin Bks.

Carlstrom, Nancy W. How Do You Say It Today, Jesse Bear? Degen, Bruce, illus. LC 91-21939. 32p. (ps-1). 1992. RSBE 13.95 (*0-02-717276-7*, Macmillan Child Bk) Macmillan Child Grp.

Chanin, Michael. Grandfather Four Winds & Rising Moon. Smith, Sally J., illus. LC 93-2689. 32p. 1994. 14.95 (*0-915811-47-2*) H J Kramer Inc.
Christiansen, C. B. Sycamore Street. Sweet, Melissa, illus. LC 92-33685. 48p. (gr. 1-3). 1993. SBE 13.95 (*0-689-31784-0*, Atheneum Child Bk) Macmillan Child Grp.
Clifton, Lucille. Everett Anderson's Year. rev. ed. Grifalconi, Ann, illus. LC 92-4683. 32p. (ps-2). 1992. 14.95 (*0-8050-2247-3*, Bks Young Read) H Holt & Co.
Coats, Laura J. The Almond Orchard. LC 90-38009. (Illus.). 32p. (gr. 1-4). 1991. RSBE 14.95 (*0-02-719041-2*, Macmillan Child Bk) Macmillan Child Grp.
Cushman, Doug. Mouse & Mole & the Year - Round Garden. LC 93-37202. (gr. 4 up). 1993. text ed. write for info. (*0-7167-6524-1*, Sci Am Yng Rdrs) W H Freeman.
Davis, Rhonda K. Sons & Daughters of Autumn, Vol. I. Davis, Rhonda K. & Beck, Arthello, illus. 32p. (Orig.). (ps-4). 1992. pap. 3.00 (*1-881967-14-X*) Express In Writing.
De Paola, Tomie. Four Stories for Four Seasons. LC 76-8837. (Illus.). (ps-3). 1980. (Pub. by Treehouse); PLB 9.95 o. p. (*0-13-330175-3*) P-H.
—Four Stories for Four Seasons. LC 76-8837. (Illus.). 48p. (ps-2). 1987. pap. 15.00 jacketed (*0-671-66686-X*, Little Simon) S&S Trade.
—Four Stories for Four Seasons. (ps-3). 1994. pap. 5.95 (*0-671-88633-9*, Half Moon Bks) S&S Trade.
Dupasquier, Philippe. Our House on the Hill. (Illus.). 32p. (ps-3). 1990. pap. 3.95 (*0-14-054227-2*, Puffin) Puffin Bks.
Ferguson, Virginia & Durkin, Peter. Autumn Leaves. Swan, Susan, illus. LC 92-34253. 1993. 3.75 (*0-383-03615-1*) SRA Schl Grp.
Fowler, Susi G. When Summer Ends. Russo, Marisabina, illus. 32p. (ps-3). 1992. pap. 4.50 (*0-14-054472-0*, Puffin) Puffin Bks.
George, Jean C. Dear Rebecca, Winter Is Here. Krupinski, Loretta, illus. LC 92-9515. 32p. (ps-3). 1993. 15.00 (*0-06-021139-3*); PLB 14.89 (*0-06-021140-7*) HarpC Child Bks.
Gerstein, Mordicai. The Story of May. Gerstein, Mordicai, illus. LC 90-22410. 48p. (ps-3). 1993. 16.00 (*0-06-022288-3*); PLB 15.89 (*0-06-022289-1*) HarpC Child Bks.
Gibbons, Gail. The Seasons of Arnold's Apple Tree. LC 84-4484. (Illus.). 32p. (ps-3). 1984. 14.95 (*0-15-271246-1*, HB Juv Bks) HarBrace.
Ginsburg, Mirra, adapted by. The Old Man & His Birds. Ruff, Donna, illus. LC 93-26705. 24p. 1994. 15.00 (*0-688-04603-7*); PLB 14.93 (*0-688-04604-5*) Greenwillow.
Good, Elaine W. Fall Is Here! I Love It! Wenger, Susie S., illus. LC 90-71115. 32p. (ps-1). 1990. text ed. 12. 95 (*1-56148-007-X*) Good Bks PA.
Hawkes, Kevin. His Royal Buckliness. LC 91-40347. (Illus.). 32p. (ps up). 1992. 15.00 (*0-688-11062-2*); PLB 14.93 (*0-688-11063-0*); poster avail. Lothrop.
Hopkins, Lee B., ed. The Sky Is Full of Song. Zimmer, Dirk, illus. LC 82-48263. 48p. (gr. 3-7). 1983. PLB 13. 89 (*0-06-022583-1*) HarpC Child Bks.
Horton, Barbara S. What Comes in Spring? Young, Ed, illus. LC 89-39695. 40p. (ps-1). 1992. 14.00 (*0-679-80268-1*); PLB 14.99 (*0-679-90268-6*) Knopf Bks Yng Read.
Iwamura, Kazuo. The Fourteen Forest Mice & the Harvest Moon Watch. Knowlton, Mary L., tr. from JPN. Iwamura, Kazuo, illus. LC 90-50706. 32p. (gr. k-3). 1991. PLB 17.27 (*0-8368-0497-X*) Gareth Stevens Inc.
Kroll, Virginia. The Seasons & Someone. Kiuchi, Tatsuro, illus. LC 93-11123. (ps-3). 1994. write for info. (*0-15-271233-X*) HarBrace.
Maass, Robert. When Autumn Comes. LC 90-32069. (Illus.). 32p. (ps-2). 1992. pap. 5.95 (*0-8050-2349-6*, Bks Young Read) H Holt & Co.
Mayorga, Dolores. David Plays Hide-&-Seek in Celebrations: David Juega Al Escondite y Celebra. Mayorga, Dolores, illus. (ENG & SPA.). 24p. (gr. 2-5). 1992. PLB 18.95 (*0-8225-2001-X*) Lerner Pubns.
Muller, Gerda. Around the Oak. LC 93-32310. (gr. 3 up). 1994. write for info. (*0-525-45239-7*, DCB) Dutton Child Bks.
Owen, Roy. The Ibis & the Egret. Sabuda, Robert, illus. LC 92-26220. 32p. (ps-3). 1993. 14.95 (*0-399-22504-8*, Philomel Bks) Putnam Pub Group.
Patience, John. The Seasons in Fern Hollow. (Illus.). 64p. (ps-1). 2.98 (*0-517-45857-8*) Random Hse Value.
Peters. October Smiled Back. 1993. 14.95 (*0-8050-1776-3*) H Holt & Co.
Rockwell, Anne. Ducklings & Polliwogs. Rockwell, Lizzy, illus. LC 93-16600. (ps-2). 1994. 14.95 (*0-02-777452-X*) Macmillan Child Grp.
Rogers, Alan. Green Bear. Rogers, Alan, illus. LC 90-9831. (ps). 1990. PLB 13.27 (*0-8368-0406-6*) Gareth Stevens Inc.
Rylant, Cynthia. Henry & Mudge in the Green Time: The Third Book of Their Adventures. Stevenson, Sucie, illus. LC 91-24942. 48p. (gr. 1-3). 1992. pap. 3.95 (*0-689-71582-X*, Aladdin) Macmillan Child Grp.
—Henry & Mudge under the Yellow Moon: The Fourth Book of Their Adventures. Stevenson, Sucie, illus. LC 91-23135. 48p. (gr. 1-3). 1992. pap. 3.95 (*0-689-71580-3*, Aladdin) Macmillan Child Grp.
—This Year's Garden. Szilagyi, Mary, illus. LC 86-22224. 32p. (ps-3). 1987. pap. 4.95 (*0-689-71122-0*, Aladdin) Macmillan Child Grp.
Sesame Street October. 1923. pap. 0.50 (*0-440-85998-0*) Dell.
Sesame Street September. 1923. pap. 0.50 (*0-440-86041-5*) Dell.
Sesame Street September. 1973. pap. 0.40 (*0-440-88258-3*) Dell.
Shecter, Ben. When Will the Snow Trees Grow? Shecter, Ben, illus. LC 92-32557. 32p. (gr. k-3). 1993. 14.00 (*0-06-022897-0*); PLB 13.89 (*0-06-022898-9*) HarpC Child Bks.
Stewart, Sarah. The Money Tree. Small, David, illus. 32p. (gr. k up). 1991. 14.95 (*0-374-35014-0*) FS&G.
Weiss, Nicki. On a Hot, Hot Day. Weiss, Nicki, illus. 32p. (ps-1). 1992. PLB 13.95 (*0-399-22119-0*, Putnam) Putnam Pub Group.
Wells, Rosemary. Night Sounds. McPhail, David, illus. LC 93-31815. (gr. k up). 1994. 14.99 (*0-8037-1301-0*); PLB 14.89 (*0-8037-1302-9*) Dial Bks Young.
Whittington, Mary K. Winter's Child. Brown, Sue E., illus. LC 91-25011. 32p. (ps-3). 1992. SBE 14.95 (*0-689-31685-2*, Atheneum Child Bk) Macmillan Child Grp.
Wildsmith, Brian. Seasons. Wildsmith, Brian, illus. (ps-3). 1980. 9.95 (*0-19-279730-1*) OUP.

SEASONS–LEGENDS

Witters, Judith. When the Earth Was Bare. Cammarata, Kathleen, illus. LC 93-26930. 1994. 4.25 (*0-383-03785-9*) SRA Schl Grp.

SEASONS–POETRY

Annable, Toni & Kaspar, Maria H. The Four Seasons. Viola, Amy, tr. Lumetta, Lawrence, illus. 80p. (Orig.). (gr. 5 up). 1992. Set. pap. text ed. 8.95 (*1-882828-09-7*) Vol. 1: English-Spanish, Las Cuatro Estaciones. Vol. 2: English-French, Les Quatre Saisons. Kasan Imprints.
Bruchac, Joseph & London, Jonathan, eds. Thirteen Moons on Turtle's Back: A Native American Year of Moons. Locker, Thomas, illus. 32p. (ps-8). 1992. PLB 15.95 (*0-399-22141-7*, Philomel Bks) Putnam Pub Group.
Demi, selected by. & illus. In the Eyes of the Cat. Tze-Si Huang, tr. from JPN. LC 91-27729. 80p. (gr. 1-3). 1992. 15.95 (*0-8050-1955-3*, Bks Young Read) H Holt & Co.
Jacobs. Just Around the Corner. 1993. write for info. (*0-8050-3024-7*) H Holt & Co.
Jacobs, Leland B. Just Around the Corner: Poems about the Seasons. Kaufman, Jeff, illus. LC 93-18342. 32p. (gr. k-3). 1993. 14.95 (*0-8050-2676-2*, Bks Young Read) H Holt & Co.
Schmidt, Gary D., ed. Robert Frost: Poetry for Young People. Sorenson, Henri, illus. LC 94-11161. 48p. 1994. 14.95 (*0-8069-0633-2*) Sterling.
Singer, Marilyn. Turtle in July. Pinkey, Jerry, illus. LC 93-14430. 32p. (gr. 3-7). 1994. pap. 4.95 (*0-689-71805-5*, Aladdin) Macmillan Child Grp.
Turner, Ann. A Moon for Seasons. Noricka, Robert, illus. LC 92-36857. 40p. (gr. 1-5). 1994. RSBE 14.95 (*0-02-789513-0*, Macmillan Child Bk) Macmillan Child Grp.
Yolen, Jane. Ring of Earth: A Child's Book of Seasons. Wallner, John, illus. LC 86-4800. 32p. (ps up). 1986. 14.95 (*0-15-267140-4*, HB Juv Bks) HarBrace.

SEATTLE

Bass, Sophie F. Pig-Tail Days in Old Seattle. Clark, Florenz, illus. LC 72-77591. 190p. (gr. 4-6). 1973. 12. 50 (*0-8323-0206-6*) Binford Mort.
Loewen, N. Seattle. (Illus.). (gr. 5 up). 1989. lib. bdg. 15. 94 (*0-86592-545-3*); 11.95 (*0-685-58592-1*) Rourke Corp.
Snelson, Karin. Seattle. LC 91-38232. (Illus.). 64p. (gr. 4 up). 1992. text ed. 13.95 RSBE (*0-87518-509-6*, Dillon) Macmillan Child Grp.
Steves, Rick. Kidding Around Seattle: A Young Person's Guide to the City. Meier, Melissa, illus. 64p. (Orig.). (gr. 3 up). 1991. pap. 9.95 (*0-945465-84-X*) John Muir.

SEAWEEDS

see Algae

SEX CRIMES

Benedict, Helen. Safe, Strong & Streetwise: The Teenager's Guide to Preventing Sexual Assault. (Illus.). 192p. (gr. 7 up). 1987. pap. 6.95 (*0-87113-100-5*) Little.

SECONDARY EDUCATION

see Education, Secondary

SECONDARY SCHOOLS

see Education, Secondary; High Schools; Public Schools

SECRET SERVICE

see also Detectives; Spies;
also names of wars with the subdivision Secret Service, e.g. World War, 1939-1945–Secret Service, etc.

SECRET WRITING

see Cryptography

SECRETARIES–FICTION

Pearson, Susan. Lenore's Big Break. Carlson, Nancy, illus. 32p. (gr. k up). 1992. PLB 14.00 (*0-670-83474-2*) Viking Child Bks.

SECTS

see also names of churches and sects, e.g. Methodist Church, etc.

Beit-Hallahmi, Benjamin. The Illustrated Encyclopedia of Active New Religions, Sects, & Cults. Rosen, Roger, ed. 1993. 49.95 (*0-8239-1505-0*) Rosen Group.
Cohen, Daniel. Cults. LC 94-966. (Illus.). 128p. (gr. 7 up). 1994. PLB 15.90 (*1-56294-324-3*) Millbrook Pr.
Evenhouse, Bill. Reasons One, Sects & Cults with Non-Christian Roots. rev. ed. 120p. 1991. 5.75 (*0-930265-97-1*); tchr's. manual, 60p. 5.75 (*1-56212-007-7*) CRC Pubns.
Hamilton, Sue. The Death of a Cult Family: Jim Jones. Hamilton, John, ed. LC 89-84906. (Illus.). 32p. (gr. 4). 1989. PLB 11.96 (*0-939179-58-X*) Abdo & Dghtrs.
Israel, Fred L. The Amish. Moynihan, Daniel P., intro. by. (Illus.). 112p. 1986. lib. bdg. 17.95 (*0-87754-853-6*) Chelsea Hse.
Nardo, Don & Belgum, Erik. Voodoo: Opposing Viewpoints. LC 91-14497. (Illus.). 112p. (gr. 5-8). 1991. PLB 14.95 (*0-89908-089-8*) Greenhaven.
Ross, Terry. Cults. (Illus.). 64p. (gr. 7 up). 1990. lib. bdg. 17.27 (*0-86593-070-8*); lib. bdg. 12.95s.p. (*0-685-36323-6*) Rourke Corp.
Smith, Richard. Waco Cult Inferno. LC 93-5154. 1993. 11.96 (*1-56239-260-3*) Abdo & Dghtrs.
Stevens, Sarah. Cults. LC 91-17774. (Illus.). 48p. (gr. 5-6). 1992. text ed. 12.95 RSBE (*0-89686-723-4*, Crestwood Hse) Macmillan Child Grp.
Tolan, Stephanie S. A Good Courage. LC 87-31306. 240p. (gr. 7 up). 1988. 12.95 (*0-688-07446-4*) Morrow Jr Bks.
What Is Scientology? The Comprehensive Reference on the World's Fastest Growing Religion. 834p. 1992. 85. 00 (*0-88404-633-8*) Bridge Pubns Inc.

SECURITIES

see also Investments; Stocks

SECURITIES EXCHANGE

see Stock Exchange

SECURITY, INTERNATIONAL

see also Disarmament; International Organization

SEDITION

see Political Crimes and Offenses; Revolutions

SEEDS

Andersen, Honey. Which Comes First? Berry, Ruth, illus. LC 93-18113. 1994. write for info. (*0-383-03726-3*) SRA Schl Grp.
Berger, Melvin. All about Seeds: A Hands-On Science Book. 32p. 1992. pap. 2.95 (*0-590-44909-5*) Scholastic Inc.
—Seeds Get Around. (Illus.). 16p. (ps-2). 1993. pap. text ed. 14.95 (*1-56784-006-X*) Newbridge Comms.
Dietl, Ulla. The Plant-&-Grow Project Book. LC 93-24788. (Illus.). 48p. (gr. 2-10). 1993. 12.95 (*0-8069-0456-9*) Sterling.
Jennings, Terry. Seeds & Seedlings. LC 88-22890. (Illus.). 32p. (gr. 3-6). 1989. pap. 4.95 (*0-516-48408-7*) Childrens.
Jordan, Helene J. How a Seed Grows. rev. ed. Krupinski, Loretta, illus. LC 91-10166. 32p. (ps-1). 1992. 14.00 (*0-06-020104-5*); PLB 14.89 (*0-06-020185-1*) HarpC Child Bks.
—How a Seed Grows. rev. ed. Krupinski, Loretta, illus. LC 91-10165. 32p. (ps-1). 1992. pap. 4.95 (*0-06-445107-0*, Trophy) HarpC Child Bks.
Kuchalla, Susan. All about Seeds. McBee, Jane, illus. LC 81-11480. 32p. (gr. k-2). 1982. lib. bdg. 11.59 (*0-89375-658-X*); pap. 2.95 (*0-89375-659-8*) Troll Assocs.
Lauber, Patricia. Seeds: Pop Stick Glide. Wexler, Jerome, photos by. LC 80-14553. (Illus.). 64p. (gr. 2-4). 1991. lib. bdg. 14.99 (*0-517-58554-5*) Crown Bks Yng Read.
Moncure, Jane B. How Seeds Travel: Popguns & Parachutes. Endres, Helen, illus. LC 89-71171. 32p. (ps-2). 1990. PLB 14.95 (*0-89565-569-1*) Childs World.
Overbeck, Cynthia. How Seeds Travel. LC 81-17217. (Illus.). 48p. (gr. 4 up). 1982. PLB 19.95 (*0-8225-1474-5*) Lerner Pubns.
—How Seeds Travel. Hani, Shabo, photos by. (Illus.). 48p. (gr. 4 up). Repr. of 1982 ed. 5.95g (*0-8225-9569-9*) Lerner Pubns.
Sabin, Louis. Plants, Seeds & Flowers. Moylan, Holly, illus. LC 84-2720. 32p. (gr. 3-6). 1985. PLB 9.49 (*0-8167-0226-8*); pap. text ed. 2.95 (*0-8167-0227-6*) Troll Assocs.
Stagg, Mildred A. & Lamb, Cecile. Song of the Seed. Faltico, Mary L., illus. 28p. (ps). 1992. 2.50 (*0-87403-956-8*, 24-03596) Standard Pub.
Swartzentruber. God Makes Seeds That Grow. 1976. 2.50 (*0-686-18182-4*) Rod & Staff.
Tant, Carl. Seeds, etc... Crask, Tammy & Setzer, Debra, illus. LC 91-76151. 160p. (gr. 6-9). 1992. pap. 13.95 (*1-880319-01-2*) Biotech.
White, Nancy. Seeds Get Around: Student Edition. (Illus.). 16p. (ps-2). 1993. pap. text ed. 14.95 (*1-56784-031-0*) Newbridge Comms.

SEEING EYE DOGS

see Guide Dogs

SEGREGATION IN EDUCATION

see also Discrimination in Education

Dudley, Mark E. Brown vs. Board of Education (1954) School Desegregation. LC 93-32712. 1994. text ed. 14.95 (*0-02-736271-X*, New Discovery Bks) Macmillan Child Grp.
Elish, Dan. James Meredith & School Desegregation. LC 93-9383. (Illus.). 32p. (gr. 2-4). 1994. 12.90 (*1-56294-379-0*) Millbrook Pr.
Kelso, Richard. Days of Courage: The Little Rock Story. Williges, Mel, illus. LC 92-12805. 88p. (gr. 2-5). 1992. PLB 21.34 (*0-8114-7230-2*) Raintree Steck-V.

SEISMOGRAPHY

see Earthquakes

SEISMOLOGY
see Earthquakes
SELECTIVE SERVICE
see Military Service, Compulsory
SELF-CONTROL

MacKenthun, Carole & Dwyer, Paulinus. Self-Control. Filkins, Vanessa, illus. 48p. (gr. 2 up). 1987. pap. 7.95 (*0-86653-396-6*, SS878, Shining Star Pubns) Good Apple.

Moser, Adolph J. Don't Pop Your Cork on Mondays! The Children's Anti-Stress Book. Pilkey, Dav, illus. LC 88-13912. 48p. (gr. k up). 1988. PLB 14.95 (*0-933849-18-4*) Landmark Edns.

Ward, Ruth M. Self Esteem: A Gift from God. (gr. 9 up). 1984. pap. 7.99 (*0-8010-9664-2*) Baker Bk.

SELF-CULTURE
see also Books and Reading

Bold, Mary. How to Improve Your Mind over Summer Vacation. Small, Carol B., illus. 65p. (gr. 4-6). 1987. wkbk. 6.95 (*0-938267-05-1*) Bold Prodns.

Christophersen, Susan & Farr, J. Michael. Knowing Yourself: Learning about Your Skills, Values & Planning Your Life. Croy, Greg, ed. Kreffel, Mike, illus. 64p. (gr. 9-12). 1990. pap. 5.95 (*0-942784-58-8*, KY) JIST Works.

Duco, Joyce. Workbook for Self Image Is the Key. LC 89-92547. 26p. (Orig.). (gr. 7-12). 1990. Set. pap. 5.00 (*0-9612896-2-7*) J Duco.

Hooker, Dennis. I Am (Already) Successful: Getting Motivated, Being Me. Holcomb, Ann, ed. Kreffel, Mike, illus. 156p. (gr. 7-12). 1990. pap. 7.95 (*0-942784-41-3*, AM); instr's. manual, 32p. 12.95 (*0-942784-42-1*, AMIG) JIST Works.

Long, Lynellyn D. & Podnecky-Spiegel, Janet. In Print: Beginning Literacy Through Cultural Awareness. (Illus.). 192p. 1988. pap. text ed. 9.95 (*0-201-12023-2*); tchrs., 128 p 7.95 (*0-201-12024-0*) Addison-Wesley.

Sidy, Richard V. Rebellion with Purpose: A Young Adult's Guide to the Improvement of Self & Society. 192p. (gr. 10 up). 1993. pap. text ed. 9.95 (*0-9633744-1-9*) SNS Pr.

Taylor-Gerdes, Elizabeth. Straight Up! A Teenager's Guide to Taking Charge of Your Life. Crouse, Jane, ed. Harris, Cortrell, illus. 110p. (gr. 7-12). 1994. pap. 9.95 (*1-885242-00-X*) Lindsey Pubng.
STRAIGHT UP! is a personal guide that provides teenagers the tools necessary to help them overcome the many barriers they face daily with courage & wisdom. Tools needed to help them expand their potential to be winners in life. Through timeless wisdom & practical tools, STRAIGHT UP! helps youths discover they have the personal power to take control of their lives in these forceful times. This book describes today's world with its great opportunities & pressure. It explains a teenager's role in this world. It also explains the important lessons that are passed on from their ancestors. STRAIGHT UP! discusses the 10 universal laws of mind & spirit that are operating in their lives at this very moment & at their command. It shows teens how to use these laws to enhance their lives regardless of race, gender, education or social status. STRAIGHT UP! is written by Dr. Elizabeth Taylor-Gerdes, a recognized leader in the fields of personal development, motivation & metaphysics. She received her Master's Degree from the University of San Francisco & Doctorate from Union Institute in Cincinnati. She counsels & conducts workshops in self-esteem, personal management & professional development.
Publisher Provided Annotation.

SELF-DEFENSE
see also Boxing; Judo; Karate

Craven, Jerry. Aikido. LC 94-4093. 1994. write for info. (*0-86593-364-2*) Rourke Corp.

—Ninja. LC 94-2528. (Illus.). 1994. write for info. (*0-86593-365-0*) Rourke Corp.

—Taekwondo. LC 94-4086. 1994. write for info. (*0-86593-367-7*) Rourke Corp.

Friedl, Michael. Ah...To Be A Kid: Three Dozen Aikido Games for Children of All Ages. Ransom, Stefan P., illus. 55p. (Orig.). 1994. pap. 9.95 (*0-9638530-1-5*, Castle Capers) Magical Michael.

Jwing-Ming, Yang. How to Defend Yourself: Effective & Practical Martial Arts Techniques. Dougall, Alan, ed. Painter, John, frwd. by. (Illus.). 120p. (Orig.). 1992. pap. text ed. 12.95 (*0-940871-27-0*) Yangs Martial Arts.

Mijares, David P. Modern Samurai Training. Mijares, David P., illus. 100p. (Orig.). 1989. pap. 9.95 (*0-9623400-0-6*) Group M Probelications.

Mitchell, David. The Young Martial Artist. (Illus.). 128p. 1992. 19.95 (*0-87951-422-1*) Overlook Pr.

Neff, Fred. Basic Self-Defense Manual. Reid, James, illus. LC 75-38473. 56p. (gr. 5 up). 1976. PLB 14.95 (*0-8225-1152-5*) Lerner Pubns.

—Hand-Fighting Manual for Self-Defense & Sport Karate. Reid, James, illus. LC 75-38475. 56p. (gr. 5 up). 1977. PLB 11.95 (*0-8225-1154-1*) Lerner Pubns.

—Lessons from the Art of Kempo: Subtle & Effective Self-Defense. Wolfe, Bob & Wolfe, Diane, photos by. (Illus.). 96p. (gr. 5 up). 1987. PLB 14.95 (*0-8225-1160-6*, First Ave Edns); pap. 4.95 (*0-8225-9532-X*, First Ave Edns) Lerner Pubns.

—Lessons from the Samurai: Ancient Self-Defense Strategies & Techniques. Wolfe, Bob & Wolfe, Diane, illus. 96p. (gr. 5 up). 1987. PLB 14.95 (*0-8225-1161-4*, First Ave Edns); pap. 4.95 (*0-8225-9531-1*, First Ave Edns) Lerner Pubns.

—Lessons from the Western Warriors. O'Leary, Patrick, photos by. (Illus.). 112p. (gr. 5 up). 1994. PLB 14.95 (*0-8225-1166-5*) Lerner Pubns.

—Lessons from the Western Warriors: Dynamic Self-Defense Techniques. Wolfe, Bob & Wolfe, Diane, illus. 96p. (gr. 5 up). 1987. PLB 14.95 (*0-8225-1159-2*, First Ave Edns); pap. 4.95 (*0-8225-9533-8*, First Ave Edns) Lerner Pubns.

Pfluger, A. Karate: Basic Principles. Kuttner, Paul & Cunningham, Dale S., trs. LC 67-27760. (Illus.). (gr. 8 up). 1969. Repr. of 1967 ed. 6.95 (*0-8069-4432-3*); PLB 7.49 (*0-8069-4433-1*) Sterling.

Webster-Doyle, Terrence. The Eye of the Hurricane: Tales of the Empty-Handed Masters. Cameron, Rod, illus. 128p. (gr. 4-8). 1992. PLB 17.95 (*0-942941-25-X*); pap. 12.95 (*0-942941-24-1*) Atrium Soc Pubns.

SELF-GOVERNMENT
see Democracy
SELF-INSTRUCTION
see Self-Culture
SELF-RESPECT

AESOP Enterprises, Inc. Staff & Crenshaw, Gwendolyn J. Malcolm X: Developing Self-Esteem, Self-Love, & Self-Dignity. 27p. (gr. 3-12). 1991. pap. write for info. incl. cassette (*1-880771-00-4*) AESOP Enter.

Anderson, Jill. Bright Beginnings Storybook: Building Self-Esteem Skills with Pumsy. Soasey, Beverly, illus. 42p. (gr. k-1). 1990. text ed. 3.95 (*0-9608284-7-8*); leader's guide 80.00 (*0-9608284-6-X*) Timberline Pr.

—Pumsy Storybook. Soasey, Beverly, illus. 40p. (Orig.). (gr. 1-4). 1990. pap. text ed. 3.95 (*0-9608284-2-7*) Timberline Pr.

Anderson, Lisa. Proud to Be Me, Peewee Platypus. Messer, Cathy, illus. 40p. (Orig.). (ps-4). 1990. pap. 12.95 (*0-9628323-0-8*) Ridge Enter.

Banks, Joann. Brandon's First Baseball Game. Robinson, Famous, illus. LC 90-63290. 37p. (Orig.). (ps-6). 1990. pap. text ed. 5.00 (*0-9627951-0-0*) JRBB Pubs.

Bennett, Geraldine M. Opening the Door to Your Inner Self: My Lessons. Bennett, Geraldine M., illus. LC 91-67122. 122p. (Orig.). (gr. 2 up). 1993. pap. 12.98 (*0-9630718-5-8*, 1-87122) New Dawn NY.

Blount, Lucy D. The Story of Lucy What's-Her-Name! And Your Name Too! Long, Woodie, illus. 48p. 1992. Spiral bdg. pap. 12.00 (*0-9630017-2-8*) Light-Bearer.

Brady, Janeen. Someone Special - You! Clarkson & Twede, illus. 26p. (gr. k-9). 1991. activity bk. 2.50 (*0-944803-76-8*); cassette & bklt. 10.95 (*0-944803-74-1*) Brite Music.

Byers, Reggie. The Esteem Team in "The Best I Can Be" Byers, Reggie, illus. 48p. (gr. k-4). 1993. 9.95 (*1-882732-05-7*) Ctr Applied Psy.

Cavanaugh, Joe & Dorn, Katie. Healing Hearts: A Young Person's Guide to Discovering the Goodness Within. Wright, Wendy, ed. (Illus.). 64p. (Orig.). (gr. 6 up). 1994. pap. text ed. 10.99 (*0-9640435-0-5*) Nantucket Pubng.
Joe Cavanaugh is a nationally recognized inspirational speaker specializing in youth issues. He was most recently featured on a PBS special, "Respectfully, Joe Cavanaugh," a program addressing self-esteem, values & goals of today's youth. HEALING HEARTS, his first book in a planned series, grew out of a need for young people to have a tool & ongoing journal to deal with these important issues. The testimonies of parents, teachers & students alike reiterate the power of his message. Tom E. McNellis, a parent, commented, "From a parent's perspective, Joe says so many things that we've wanted to say but are unable to say ourselves. He has a special talent & a very important message that should be heard by all." A junior high student's review says, "I learned a lot about my friends & about myself. I took away ideas & impressions that will last a lifetime." As Joe says on the first page of his book, "If I could sum up this book in a few words, it would be that its purpose is not to give you all the answers. Its purpose is to help you struggle through the questions. Questions about looking inside yourself & others & seeing the goodness more clearly." Call or write for information to order, Nantucket Publications, P.O. Box 1789, Minnetonka, MN 55345; 612-937-5492. This book is distributed by The Bookmen Inc. (800) 328-8411.
Publisher Provided Annotation.

Cavanaugh, Kate. Pete & His Elves Series. Kiner, K. C., illus. 28p. 1992. Set. pap. write for info. (*0-9622353-4-2*) KAC.

Childre, Doc L. The How-to Book of Teen Self Discovery: Helping Teens Find Balance, Security & Esteem. 2nd ed. Cryer, Bruce & Rozman, Deborah, eds. Putman, Brian, illus. (SPA.). 128p. (ps-12). 1992. pap. 8.95 (*1-879052-36-9*) Planetary Pubns.

Churchill, E. Richard & Churchill, Linda R. Who I Am & Who I Want to Be. 110p. (gr. 6-9). 1994. 7.95 (*0-685-71630-9*, 781) W Gladden Found.

Clarissa. (gr. 1-4). 1992. incl. storybk., video & tchr's. guide 79.95 (*1-55942-025-1*, 9369); tchr's. guide, 24p., by Sandy Stryker 16.95 (*1-55942-024-3*, 1032) Marshfilm.

Clinkscale, Lonnie J. Hey Dummy! A Testimony of an Overcomer. LC 94-94507. 112p. (gr. 3 up). 1994. pap. 6.95 (*0-9640311-0-8*) Clinkscale Pubns.
There are few things more devastating to a child's fragile self-esteem than being humiliated before classmates & called a "dummy" by friends, teachers & even family members. But millions of bright, sensitive, yet learning disabled children live this nightmare every day...clinging to the hope that one day, perhaps, they can achieve their life's goals. Everyone has a turning point in their life. For Lonnie Clinkscale, author of HEY DUMMY!, it was a newly discovered faith in God & the help of one special teacher. He'll tell you how he was given the strength to overcome incredible odds: * A paralyzing learning disability that prevented him from spelling his name or adding 2 plus 2 on the blackboard. * Severe stuttering, rendering even simple sentences almost unintelligible. * Insensitive taunting from fellow students, & even a guidance counselor who encouraged him to join the army because he "wasn't college material." * A deprived childhood, marred by family tensions, divorce & poverty. Once encouraged & made to feel like a "somebody," Clinkscale's natural abilities blossomed & he progressed from being unable to read aloud to winning speech tournaments & becoming an honors student. Today, he is an administrative executive at Ohio's 12th largest hospital. The books can be purchased through Clinkscale

Publications & Productions, Inc. by calling 1-800-505-6464 or by writing to Clinkscale Publications & Productions, Inc., P.O. Box 5696, Youngstown, OH 44504 (volume discounts are available). *Publisher Provided Annotation.*

Daniells, Trenna. One to Grow On! Series. James, Henry, tr. (Illus., Orig.). (gr. 1-2). 1992. Per vol., incl. audio cass. pap. 10.95 (*1-56956-000-5*) W A T Braille.
Offered on audio-cassettes for several years, this popular children's series is now available in a format ideal for blind children who are developing their braille reading skills. Each of the 16 titles is produced in grade 1 & grade 2 braille plus print, so reading can be shared by blind & sighted children, parents & educators. The 30-minute audio-cassette, with music & sound effects, is included, allowing children to practice reading skills independently. The ONE TO GROW ON! series promotes self-responsibility & encourages high self-esteem. Children relate to & identify with the characters, which helps develop the determination & courage to approach life with a positive & successful attitude. Each adventure is filled with fun-loving characters, depicted in braille graphics to stimulate the imagination. Available in grade 1 & grade 2 braille. I Don't Want to Be a Lion Anymore!: Be True to Yourself. Gr. 1 ISBN 1-56956-001-3, Gr. 2 ISBN 1-56956-026-9; The Keeper of Dreams: No More Nightmares. Gr. 1, ISBN 1-56956-002-1, Gr. 2 ISBN 1-56956-027-7; When Jokes Aren't Fun: The Hyena Who Teased Too Much. Gr. 1 ISBN 1-56956-003-X, Gr. 2 ISBN 1-56956-028-5; Maylene the Mermaid: All Things Change. Gr. 1 ISBN 1-56956-004-8, Gr. 2 ISBN 1-56956-029-3; Travis & the Dragon: Accepting Others As They Are. Gr. 1 ISBN 1-56956-005-6, Gr. 2 ISBN 1-56956-030-7; Cody Caterpillar Turns Over a New Leaf: Taking the Problem Out of Bedtime. Gr. 1 ISBN 1-56956-006-4, Gr. 2 ISBN 1-56956-031-5; Timothy Chicken Learns to Lead: Don't Blame Others. Gr. 1 ISBN 1-56956-007-2, Gr. 2 ISBN 1-56956-016-1; Oliver's Adventures on Monkey Island: It's Okay to Be Different. Gr. 1 ISBN 1-56956-008-0, Gr. 2 ISBN 1-56956-017-X. To Order, contact Jeri Brubaker, Braille International, Inc., 3290 S.E. Slater St., Stuart, FL 34997; 1-800-336-3142.
Publisher Provided Annotation.

Educational Assessment Publishing Company Staff. Parent - Child Learning Library: Self-Esteem. (Illus.). 40p. 1991. text ed. 9.95 (*0-942277-53-8*) Am Guidance.

—Parent - Child Learning Library: Self-Esteem English Big Book. (Illus.). 40p. (gr. k-3). 1991. text ed. 16.95 (*0-942277-46-5*) Am Guidance.

—Parent - Child Learning Library: Self-Esteem Spanish Big Book. (SPA., Illus.). 40p. (gr. k-3). 1991. text ed. 16.95 (*0-942277-47-3*) Am Guidance.

—Parent - Child Learning Library: Self-Esteem Spanish Edition. (SPA.). 40p. (ps). 1991. text ed. 9.95 (*0-942277-89-9*) Am Guidance.

—Parent - Child Learning Library: Your Uniqueness. (Illus.). 32p. (ps-k). 1991. text ed. 9.95 (*0-942277-63-5*) Am Guidance.

—Parent - Child Learning Library: Your Uniqueness English Big Book. (Illus.). 32p. (gr. k-3). 1991. text ed. 16.95 (*0-942277-79-1*) Am Guidance.

—Parent - Child Learning Library: Your Uniqueness Spanish Big Book. (SPA., Illus.). 32p. (gr. k-3). 1991. text ed. 16.95 (*0-942277-80-5*) Am Guidance.

—Parent - Child Learning Library: Your Uniqueness Spanish Edition. (SPA.). 32p. (ps). 1991. text ed. 9.95 (*0-942277-95-3*) Am Guidance.

Espeland, Pamela & Wallner, Rosemary. Making the Most of Today: Daily Readings for Young People on Self-Awareness, Creativity & Self-Esteem. LC 91-14494. 392p. (Orig.). (gr. 5 up). 1991. pap. 8.95 (*0-915793-33-4*) Free Spirit Pub.

Finch, Carolyn B. Socks Says! Barrows, Jack, illus. 40p. (Orig.). 1993. pap. 8.95 (*1-882956-00-1*) Bogart Comm.

Fleming, Beverly A. Scott the Dot: A Self-Esteem Tale for Children. Fleming, Beverly A., illus. LC 91-44898. 32p. (Orig.). (ps-3). 1992. pap. 3.95 (*0-915166-73-9*) Impact Pubs Cal.

Goffe, Toni, illus. How to Be Rich. LC 93-9575. 1993. 5.95 (*0-85953-405-7*) Childs Play.

Gray, Barbara J. Problem Solving for Teens: An Interactive Approach to Real-Life Problem Solving. (Illus.). (gr. 7-12). 1990. spiral bdg. 29.95 (*1-55999-113-5*) LinguiSystems.

Gray, Mattie E. Images: A Workbook for Enhancing Self-Esteem & Promoting Career Preparation, Especially for Young Black Girls. (Illus.). 184p. (gr. 6-12). 1988. pap. 8.00 (*0-8011-0782-2*) Calif Education.

Greene, Ida. How to Improve Self-Esteem in the African American Child: Self-Esteem - the Essence of You. Edwards, Eddie, illus. 60p. (Orig.). (gr. k-8). 1995. pap. text ed. 4.95 (*1-881165-15-9*) People Skills.
Self-esteem is not a privilege. It is a right. However, every African-American child struggles on a daily basis to keep & maintain their cultural identity or sense of self. Children are open & loving. They lack the skills to nurture, to protect, or to maintain their sense of self against: subtle bias, exclusivity & rejection. Children must first like, respect & appreciate themselves before they can do this for another human being. To order contact: People Skills International, 2910 Bailey Ave., San Diego, CA 92105; (619) 262-9951.
Publisher Provided Annotation.

Greene, Leia A. Mommy! Why Is Everyone Staring at Me? Greene, Leia A., illus. (gr. k-12). 1992. wkbk. 4.95 (*1-880737-11-6*) Crystal Jrns.

Harmon, Ed & Jarmin, Marge. Haciendome Cargo de Mi Vida: Opciones, Cambios y Yo. Lerma, Olivia, tr. Feign, Larry, illus. (SPA.). (gr. 5-12). 1993. pap. 9.95 (*0-918588-26-X*) Barksdale Foun.

Hollis, Dave & Hollis, Dotty. Traditions of Honor. Woodburn, Mary S., ed. 297p. (Orig.). (gr. 8-12). 1994. pap. 12. 95 (*0-9640894-1-6*) BPCOA.
TRADITIONS OF HONOR is the first book to rewrite the "THREE R'S" of education to include RESPONSIBILITY, RESPECT & REPUTATION. It identifies, illustrates & examples the specific behaviors, beliefs & methods to easily instill & maintain the virtues of Honesty & Integrity, Self-discipline, Compassion, Life Long Learning, Friendship, Courage & Loyalty within our children. It deals directly with the realities of life & sets forth the rules of conduct to preserve our honor, dignity & fine reputation. It offers a soft but direct approach to resolving key issues & concerns between people, parents & peers. TRADITIONS OF HONOR sets forth the fundamental principles to building & maintaining a fine character in a highly changing & challenging world. A world that often places little or no value on the fine qualities of individuals. It helps our parents & children read through the many mixed messages of our world. TRADITIONS OF HONOR helps our children gain the kind of recognition & respect we all need & deserve for ourselves & our families. It is not a book of religious or political views & is strong in its convictions about basic rights & wrongs. It offers the fundamentals for responsible behavior.
Publisher Provided Annotation.

Hutson, Joan. I'm Glad I Am: Christian Affirmations for Children. Hutson, Joan, illus. LC 92-10627. 48p. (Orig.). (gr. 1-4). 1992. pap. 3.95 (*0-8198-3623-0*) St Paul Bks.

Jacobs, Marjorie, et al. Building a Positive Self-Concept. Shanafelt, Noreen, illus. 126p. 1994. 16.95 (*0-685-71632-5*, 783) W Gladden Found.

Johnson, Julie T. Celebrate You: Building Your Self-Esteem. 72p. (gr. 5 up). 1990. PLB 15.95 (*0-8225-0046-9*) Lerner Pubns.

Key Concepts in Personal Development Series. (gr. 1-4). 1992. 16.95 (*1-55942-050-2*) Marshfilm.

Kramer, Patricia. Discovering Self-Confidence. (gr. 7-12). 1991. PLB 14.95 (*0-8239-1275-2*) Rosen Group.

Loomans, Diane. Today I Am Lovable, Three Hundred Sixty-Five Self-Esteem Activities for Kids: And for the Kid in All of Us. (Illus.). 1994. calendar 10.95 (*1-56838-012-7*) Hazelden.

Loomans, Diane. Lovables in the Kingdom of Self-Esteem. Carleton, Nancy, ed. Howard, Kim, illus. LC 90-52633. 32p. (ps-5). 1991. 14.95 (*0-915811-25-1*) H J Kramer Inc.

Loomans, Diane & Loomans, Julia. Full Esteem Ahead: One Hundred Ways to Build Self-Esteem in Children & Adults. Carleton, Nancy, ed. Canfield, Jack & Schultz, Skyfrwd. by. (Orig.). (ps up). 1994. pap. 12.95 (*0-915811-57-X*) H J Kramer Inc.
As a nationally recognized speaker, trainer & consultant on the topics of creativity, self-esteem & the power of laughter & play, Diane Loomans was determined to raise her daughter with a high level of self-esteem. She realized she needed to consciously do things differently & to treat herself & her daughter with consistent respect & kindness. When she was able to act in alignment with her values, her personal self-esteem was enhanced & she was able to model creative methods of conflict resolution & playful interaction. She began to write down her most successful methods. Over sixteen years, the two have originated many fun-filled techniques, games, & processes & collected others from friends. They assembled one hundred of their favorites to present in FULL ESTEEM AHEAD. These techniques are designed to make day-to-day family interactions easier & more joyful. The simple methods are presented in a bite-sized format so a busy parent can quickly find some inspiration. Diane Loomans is co-author of The Laughing Classroom: Everyone's Guide to Teaching With Humor & Play, author of The Loveables in the Kingdom of Self-Esteem, & with daughter Julia, co-author of Positively Mother Goose. "This is the best book on self-esteem & parenting that I've seen." - Jack Canfield, Author, CHICKEN SOUP FOR THE SOUL.
Publisher Provided Annotation.

McAllister, Dawson. Self Esteem & Loneliness. Lamb, Jim, illus. (gr. 5-12). 1989. pap. 3.95 (*0-923417-02-8*) Shepherd Minst.

—Student Conference Follow-Up Manual. Lamb, Jim, illus. (gr. 5-12). 1989. pap. 2.95 (*0-923417-10-9*) Shepherd Minst.

McFarland, Rhoda. Coping Through Self-Esteem. rev. ed. Rosen, Ruth, ed. (gr. 7 up). 1993. PLB 14.95 (*0-8239-1654-5*) Rosen Group.

—Coping with Stigma. Rosen, Ruth, ed. (gr. 7-12). 1989. PLB 14.95 (*0-8239-0998-0*) Rosen Group.
Manber, David. Zachary of the Wings. 88p. (gr. 9-12). 1993. PLB 10.95 (*1-879567-27-X*) Wonder Well.
Marton, Jirina. I'll Do It Myself. Marton, Jirina, illus. 1990. 14.95 (*1-550370-63-4*, Pub. by Annick CN); pap. 5.95 (*1-550370-62-6*, Pub. by Annick CN) Firefly Bks Ltd.

Mawe, Sheelagh M. Dandelion: The Triumphant Life of a Misfit, a Story for All Ages. 165p. (Orig.). (gr. 4). 1994. pap. 6.95 (*0-9642168-0-9*) Totally Unique.
Dandelion is a lowly, mis-bred Irish farm horse. As is true of all creatures, she begins her life with a sense of her own worth. But little by little, the "circumstances" of her life erode that belief. Dandelion becomes dispirited & eventually gives up her dreams. Nevertheless, given a chance at freedom, she has wits enough to pursue it, only to find that "freedom" was not quite what she was looking for! Dandelion's subsequent journey leads her to her true destination. It leads her to herself. In this enchanting book, readers of all ages will find in Dandelion an inspirational symbol of all those who have overcome poverty, prejudice, background & self-doubt to make a resounding success of their lives. To order contact: TOTALLY UNIQUE THOUGHTS, A Division of TUT Enterprises, 1713 Acme St., Orlando, FL 32805-3603. 407-246-7040.
Publisher Provided Annotation.

Moser, Adolph. Don't Feed the Monster on Tuesdays! The Children's Self-Esteem Book. Thatch, Nancy R., ed. Melton, David, illus. Moser, Adolph, intro. by. LC 91-12941. (Illus.). 55p. (gr. k-12). 1991. PLB 14.95 (*0-933849-38-9*) Landmark Edns.
Nielsen, Shelly. Self Esteem. Wallner, Rosemary, ed. LC 91-73047. 1992. 13.99 (*1-56239-061-9*) Abdo & Dghtrs.
Papa Piccolo. 32p. (gr. 1-4). 1992. incl. storybk., video & tchr's. guide 79.95 (*1-55942-031-6*, 9370); tchr's. guide, 24p., by Sandy Stryker 16.95 (*1-55942-030-8*, 1033) Marshfilm.
Parkison, Jami. Pequena the Burro. Maeno, Itoko, illus. LC 93-30377. 32p. (gr. 1-4). 1994. 16.95 (*1-55942-055-3*, 7657); video, tchr's. guide & storybook 79.95 (*1-55942-058-8*, 9376) Marshfilm.
Path Works Staff. Feeling Good about Me. Nelson, Colleen, illus. 20p. (gr. 3-5). 1993. incl. tchr's. guide 1.95 (*0-685-71609-0*, 741) W Gladden Found.
Perinchief, Robert. Hamel the Camel: A Different Mammal. Nordensten, Ellen H., illus. 21p. (ps-5). 1993. 12.95 (*1-882809-00-9*) Perry Pubns.
Potash, Dorothy. The Tale of Ned & His Nose. Sperling, Thomas, illus. 24p. (gr. k-4). 1993. PLB 13.95 (*1-879567-23-7*, Valeria Bks) Wonder Well.
Rogers, George L. Mac & Zach from Hackensack. Eskander, Stefanie C., illus. 32p. (gr. k-6). 1992. PLB 12.95 (*0-938399-07-1*); pap. 4.95 (*0-938399-06-3*) Acorn Pub MN.
Rose, John R. Keys to Success. 128p. 1992. pap. write for info. (*1-881170-00-4*) Rose Pub OR.

Roth-Nelson, Stephanie. S. E. E. K. Self-Esteem Enhancement Kit. Zilis, Tom, illus. LC 93-29345. 176p. (Orig.). (gr. 6-12). 1993. pap. 14.95 (*0-942097-49-1*) BPPbks.
S.E.E.K. belongs in school & resource agency libraries. S.E.E.K. sparks discussion about emotions, helps teens practice self-respect & respect for others, deal with anger, examine their beliefs & values. Teens like its "short attention-span" concept, examples & illustrations. "With a refreshing & straightforward style, Roth-Nelson speaks to teens in a language they can understand. No issue is too sensitive or too weird: AIDS, sex, pregnancy, gangs, depression, school. This workbook will stimulate teens to look at themselves & their world in a new & empowering way. Educators, therapists & parents will also find much value here." (NAPRA). Middle, high school, health & special education teachers, counselors & dropout prevention & drug-free schools coordinators use S.E.E.K. U.S. & Canadian juvenile detention facilities & residential treatment centers use it, too. The 123-page Facilitator's Guide (ISBN 0-9642097-48-3, $29.95) makes S.E.E.K. perfect for groups. Session plans for each section offer 38 group activities using role playing, art, discussions, movies, field trips, planning, visualization activities & 42 reproducible masters for handouts. Guide & 10 non-consumable workbooks: $120. Training available, too. For information or to order, contact Roth-Nelson Consulting, Box 104, Louisville, CO 80027, 1-800-200-0367, or Bookpeople, Moving Books or DeVorss.
Publisher Provided Annotation.

Rubly-Burggraff, Roberta. Magnum Opus: An Affirmation Journal. Robbins-Ptak, Elizabeth, illus. 72p. (Orig.). (gr. 7-12). 1989. pap. 5.95 (*0-937997-14-5*) Hi-Time Pub.
Rudner, Barry. The Bumblebee & the Ram. Fahsbender, Thomas, illus. LC 89-81585. 32p. (Orig.). 1989. pap. 5.95 (*0-925928-03-8*) Tiny Thought.
Rutman, Shereen G. All about Me. Jordan, Polly, illus. 32p. (ps). 1992. wkbk. 1.95 (*1-56293-174-1*) McClanahan Bk.
Sanders, Bill. Stand Tall: Learning to Really Love Yourself. LC 92-13985. 160p. (Orig.). 1992. pap. 7.99 (*0-8007-5452-2*) Revell.
Schenkerman, Rona D. Growing up with Self-Esteem. 16p. (gr. 3-8). 1993. 1.95 (*1-56688-119-6*) Bur For At-Risk.
Schwartz, Linda. Monkey See, Monkey Do. LC 90-62597. (ps-3). 1991. pap. 4.95 (*0-88160-187-X*, LW1201) Learning Wks.
—Responsible Rascal. LC 90-62595. (ps-3). 1991. pap. 4.95 (*0-88160-188-8*, LW1202) Learning Wks.
Sciacca, Fran & Sciacca, Jill. So What's Wrong with a Big Nose? Building Self-Esteem. 64p. 1992. pap. 3.99 saddle stitch bdg. (*0-310-48051-5*) Zondervan.
Self-Esteem. (Illus.). 32p. (gr. 5 up). 1989. lib. bdg. 15.94 (*0-86625-288-6*); 11.95s.p. (*0-685-58600-6*) Rourke Corp.
Self Esteem - Be a Winner. 16p. 1994. 0.95 (*0-685-71603-1*, 728) W Gladden Found.
Shapiro, Lawrence E. Sometimes I Drive My Mom Crazy, but I Know She's Crazy about Me: A Self-Esteem Book for Overactive & Impulsive Children. Shore, Hennie M., ed. Parrotte, Timothy, illus. 80p. (gr. k-6). 1993. 9.95 (*1-882732-03-0*) Ctr Applied Psy.
Simmons, Cassandra W. Becoming Myself: True Stories about Learning from Life. Espeland, Pamela, ed. 136p. (Orig.). (gr. 5 up). 1994. pap. 4.95 (*0-915793-69-5*) Free Spirit Pub.
Starbuck, Marnie. The Gladimals Talk about Self Esteem. (Illus.). 16p. 1990. 0.75 (*1-56456-201-8*, 471) W Gladden Found.
Talley, Carol. Clarissa. Maeno, Itoko, illus. LC 91-29958. 32p. (gr. 1-4). 1992. 16.95 (*1-55942-014-6*, 7650) Marshfilm.
Teen Esteem. 366p. (Orig.). (gr. 6-12). 1992. spiral bdg. 7.00 (*1-882835-09-3*) STA-Kris.
Thomas, Alicia. Self-Esteem. (gr. 7-12). 1991. PLB 14.95 (*0-8239-1225-6*) Rosen Group.
Trahey, Jerome. Building Self-Esteem: A Workbook for Teens. Guelzow, Diane, illus. 176p. (Orig.). (gr. 7-12). 1992. pap. 16.95 (*0-89390-231-4*) Resource Pubns.
Walk Thru the Bible Staff. Youthwalk Again. 272p. 1993. pap. 9.99 (*0-310-54601-X*, Pub. by Daybreak Bks) Zondervan.
Walters-Lucy, Jean. Look Ma, I'm Flying. Tabesh, Delight, ed. & illus. LC 92-13953. 48p. (Orig.). (ps-5). 1992. pap. 6.95 perfect bdg. (*0-941992-28-4*) Los Arboles Pub.
Wood, Bill. Marty the Marathon Bear. Kaluza, Mary K. & Carreiro, Bob, illus. Kauffman, Helen, photos by. 136p. (Orig.). (gr. 3-7). 1988. pap. text ed. 6.95 (*0-317-93376-0*) Rallysport Video Prodns.
Youngs, Bettie B. You & Self-Esteem: It's the Key to Happiness & Success. 160p. (gr. 5-12). 1992. pap. 16.95 (*0-915190-83-4*, JP-9083-4) Jalmar Pr.

SELLING
see Salesmen and Salesmanship

SEMANTICS
see also Words, New

Tavzel, Carolyn. Blooming Holidays. (ps-5). 1989. pap. 15.95 (*1-55999-025-2*) LinguiSystems.

SENATORS–U. S.
see U. S. Congress

SENEGAL

Barboza, Steven. Door of No Return: The Legend of Goree Island. LC 93-21163. (Illus.). 48p. (gr. 5 up). 1994. 14.99 (*0-525-65188-8*, Cobblehill Bks) Dutton Child Bks.
Department of Geography, Lerner Publications. Senegal in Pictures. (Illus.). 64p. (gr. 5 up). 1988. 17.50 (*0-8225-1827-9*) Lerner Pubns.

SENSES AND SENSATION
see also Color Sense; Hearing; Smell; Touch; Vision

Aliki. My Five Senses. rev. ed. LC 88-35350. (Illus.). 32p. (gr. 1-3). 1989. pap. 4.95 (*0-06-445083-X*, Trophy) HarpC Child Bks.
—My Five Senses. rev. ed. Aliki, illus. LC 88-35350. 32p. (ps-1). 1991. 19.95 (*0-06-020050-2*) HarpC Child Bks.
—My Five Senses. rev. ed. Aliki, illus. LC 88-853500. 228p. (ps-3). 1989. 15.00 (*0-690-04792-4*, Crowell Jr Bks); PLB 13.89 (*0-685-58944-7*) HarpC Child Bks.
Ardley, Neil. Science Book of the Senses. (gr. 4-7). 1992. 9.95 (*0-15-200614-1*, HB Juv Bks) HarBrace.
Bailey, Donna. All about Your Senses. LC 90-10051. (Illus.). 48p. (gr. 2-6). 1990. PLB 20.70 (*0-8114-2776-5*) Raintree Steck-V.
Berg, Eric. Five Special Senses. LC 93-8906. 1993. write for info. (*1-56071-328-3*) ETR Assocs.
Berger, Melvin. See, Hear, Touch, Taste, Smell. (Illus.). 16p. (ps-2). 1993. pap. text ed. 14.95 (*1-56784-009-4*) Newbridge Comms.
—See, Hear, Touch, Taste, Smell: Student Edition. (Illus.). 16p. (ps-2). 1994. pap. text ed. 14.95 (*1-56784-034-5*) Newbridge Comms.
Berry, Joy W. Teach Me about Tasting. Dickey, Kate, ed. LC 85-45088. (Illus.). 36p. (ps). 1986. 4.98 (*0-685-10727-2*) Grolier Inc.
Bertrand, Cecile. Noni Tastes. (ps). 1993. 4.95 (*0-307-15687-7*, Artsts Writrs) Western Pub.
Brandt, Keith. Five Senses. Green, Gloria, illus. LC 84-2633. 32p. (gr. 3-6). 1985. PLB 9.49 (*0-8167-0168-7*); pap. text ed. 2.95 (*0-8167-0169-5*) Troll Assocs.
Broekel, Ray. Tus Cinco Sentidos (Your Five Senses) LC 84-7603. (SPA.). 48p. (gr. k-4). 1987. PLB 12.85 (*0-516-31932-9*); pap. 4.95 (*0-516-51932-8*) Childrens.
—Your Five Senses. LC 84-7603. (Illus.). 48p. (gr. k-4). 1984. PLB 12.85 (*0-516-01932-5*); pap. 4.95 (*0-516-41932-3*) Childrens.
Brooks, Bruce. Making Sense: Animal Perception & Communication. LC 93-10474. 1993. 17.00 (*0-374-34742-5*) FS&G.
Bryan, Jenny. Smell, Taste & Touch. (Illus.). 48p. (gr. 5). 1994. text ed. 13.95 RSBE (*0-87518-590-8*, Dillon) Macmillan Child Grp.
—Sound & Vision. LC 93-37306. (Illus.). 48p. (gr. 5). 1994. text ed. 13.95 RSBE (*0-87518-591-6*, Dillon) Macmillan Child Grp.
Byles, Monica. Experiment with Senses. LC 92-41110. 1993. 17.50 (*0-8225-2455-4*) Lerner Pubns.
Carratello, Patricia & Carratello, John. Let's Investigate the Senses. Chacon, Rick, illus. 48p. (gr. 1-4). 1984. wkbk. 6.95 (*1-55734-213-X*) Tchr Create Mat.
Clasing, Elisabeth. Sesame Street: Come to the Playground. Cooke, Tom, illus. 12p. (ps). 1992. write for info. (*0-307-12003-1*, 12003, Golden Pr) Western Pub.
Cole, Joanna. You Can't Smell a Flower with Your Ear! All about Your 5 Senses. Smith, Mavis, illus. LC 93-27264. 48p. (gr. 1-3). 1994. 7.99 (*0-448-40470-2*, G&D); pap. 3.50 (*0-448-40469-9*, G&D) Putnam Pub Group.
Crowdy, Deborah. Let's Take a Walk in the Park. Axeman, Lois, illus. LC 86-17598. 32p. (ps-2). 1986. PLB 14.95 (*0-89565-357-5*) Childs World.
The Five Senses. 48p. (gr. 5-8). 1988. PLB 10.95 (*0-382-09707-6*) Silver Burdett Pr.
Fowler, Allan. Feeling Things. LC 90-22526. (Illus.). 32p. (ps-2). 1991. PLB 10.75 (*0-516-04908-9*); pap. 3.95 (*0-516-44908-7*) Childrens.
—El Gusto de las Cosas: Tasting Things. LC 90-21647. (SPA., Illus.). 32p. (ps-2). PLB 10.75, Apr. 1992 (*0-516-34911-2*); pap. 3.95, Jul. 1992 (*0-516-54911-1*) Childrens.
—Hearing Things. LC 90-22524. (Illus.). 32p. (ps-2). 1991. PLB 10.75 (*0-516-04909-7*); pap. 3.95 (*0-516-44909-5*) Childrens.
—Lo Que Escuchas: Hearing Things. LC 90-22524. (SPA., Illus.). 32p. (ps-2). PLB 10.75, Apr. 1992 (*0-516-34909-0*); pap. 3.95, Jul. 1992 (*0-516-54909-X*) Childrens.
—Lo Que Sientes Al Tocar: Feeling Things. LC 90-22526. (SPA., Illus.). 32p. (ps-2). PLB 10.75, Apr. 1992 (*0-516-34908-2*); pap. 3.95, Jul. 1992 (*0-516-54908-1*) Childrens.
—Lo Que Ves: Seeing Things. LC 91-22527. (SPA., Illus.). 32p. (ps-2). PLB 10.75, Apr. 1992 (*0-516-34910-4*); pap. 3.95, Jul. 1992 (*0-516-54910-3*) Childrens.
—El Olor De las Cosas: Smelling Things. LC 90-22123. (SPA., Illus.). 32p. (ps-2). PLB 10.75, Apr. 1992 (*0-516-34912-0*); pap. 3.95, Jul. 1992 (*0-516-54912-X*) Childrens.
—Seeing Things. LC 90-22527. (Illus.). 32p. (ps-2). 1991. PLB 10.75 (*0-516-04910-0*); pap. 3.95 (*0-516-44910-9*) Childrens.
—Smelling Things. LC 90-22123. (Illus.). 32p. (ps-2). 1991. PLB 10.75 (*0-516-04912-7*); pap. 3.95 (*0-516-44912-5*) Childrens.

—Tasting Things. LC 90-21647. (Illus.). 32p. (ps-2). 1991. PLB 10.75 (*0-516-04911-9*); pap. 3.95 (*0-516-44911-7*) Childrens.

Gardner, Karen A. My Life As an Ear. rev. ed. (Illus.). 37p. (ps-2). 1984. Set of 1-4. PLB 1.70 (*0-931421-01-2*) Psychol Educ Pubns.

Hoover, Rosalie & Murphy, Barbara. Learning about Our Five Senses. 64p. (gr. k-3). 1981. 7.95 (*0-86653-013-4*, GA 241) Good Apple.

Kohl, Judith & Kohl, Herbert. The View from the Oak. Bayless, Roger, illus. 112p. (gr. 5 up). 1988. 15.95 (*0-316-50137-9*) Little.

Koomar, Jane & Friedman, Barbara. Your Balance Sense. Wolf, Elizabeth, illus. 20p. (ps-3). 1992. pap. text ed. 11.00 (*0-910317-88-7*) Am Occup Therapy.

Littler, Angela. What Can You See. Galvani, Maureen & Littler, Angela, illus. 20p. (ps-1). 1988. (J Messner) S&S Trade.

McMillan, Bruce. Sense Suspense. McMillan, Bruce, photos by. LC 93-30272. (Illus.). (ps-2). 1994. 14.95 (*0-590-47904-0*) Scholastic Inc.

Martin, Paul D. Messengers to the Brain: Your Fantastic Five Senses. Crump, Donald J., ed. LC 82-45636. 104p. (gr. 3-8). 1984. 8.95 (*0-87044-499-9*); PLB 12.50 (*0-87044-504-9*) Natl Geog.

Micallef, Mary. Listening: The Basic Connection. Micallef, Mary, illus. 96p. (gr. 3-8). 1984. wkbk. 9.95 (*0-86653-188-2*, GA 555) Good Apple.

Miller, Margaret. My Five Senses. LC 93-1956. 1994. 15.00 (*0-671-79168-0*, S&S BFYR) S&S Trade.

Moncure, Jane B. The Five Senses: Treasures Outside. Axeman, Lois, illus. LC 90-30635. 32p. (ps-2). 1990. PLB 13.95 (*0-89565-575-6*) Childs World.

—A Tasting Party. Axeman, Lois, illus. LC 82-4411. 32p. (ps-3). 1982. pap. 3.95 (*0-516-43253-2*) Childrens.

O'Connor, Karen. Let's Take a Walk on the Beach. Axeman, Lois, illus. LC 86-9551. 32p. (ps-2). 1986. PLB 14.95 (*0-89565-354-0*) Childs World.

O'Connor, Karen & Crowdy, Deborah. Let's Take a Walk in the City. Axeman, Lois, illus. LC 86-20746. 32p. (ps-2). 1986. PLB 14.95 (*0-89565-355-9*) Childs World.

Otto, Carolyn B. I Can Tell by Touching. Westcott, Nadine B., illus. LC 93-18630. 32p. (ps-1). 1994. 15.00 (*0-06-023324-9*); PLB 14.89 (*0-06-023325-7*) HarpC Child Bks.

—I Can Tell by Touching. Westcott, Nadine B., illus. LC 93-18630. 32p. (ps-1). 1994. pap. 4.95 (*0-06-445125-9*, Trophy) HarpC Child Bks.

Parker, Steve. Animals Can Think? LC 94-19405. (gr. k up). 1995. write for info. (*0-8114-3882-1*) Raintree Steck V.

—Learning a Lesson: How You See, Think & Remember. LC 89-77860. (Illus.). 32p. (gr. k-4). 1991. PLB 11.40 (*0-531-14087-3*) Watts.

—Nerves to Senses: Projects with Biology. LC 91-8737. (Illus.). 32p. (gr. 5-8). 1991. PLB 12.40 (*0-531-17295-3*, Gloucester Pr) Watts.

—Touch, Taste & Smell. rev. ed. Mayron-Parker, Alan, contrib. by. LC 88-51607. (Illus.). 48p. (gr. 5-6). 1989. PLB 12.90 (*0-531-10655-1*) Watts.

—Touch, Taste & Smell. rev. ed. (Illus.). 48p. (gr. 5 up). 1991. pap. 6.95 (*0-531-24607-8*) Watts.

Parramon Editorial Team Staff. The Senses. (Illus.). 96p. (ps-1). 1994. 16.95 (*0-8120-6442-9*) Barron.

—Los Sentidos. (Illus.). 96p. (ps-1). 1994. 16.95 (*0-8120-6443-7*) Barron.

Parramon, J. M. & Puig, J. J. Taste. Rius, Maria, illus. 32p. (ps). 1985. pap. 6.95 (*0-8120-3566-6*); Span. ed. pap. 6.95 (*0-8120-3608-5*) Barron.

Parramon, J. M., et al. Five Senses, 5 bks. (ps). 1985. pap. 32.95 boxed set (*0-8120-7365-7*) Barron.

Ripoll, Jamie. How Our Senses Work. (Illus.). 1994. 13.95 (*0-7910-2128-9*, Am Art Analog) Chelsea Hse.

Rowe, Julian & Perham, Molly. Feel & Touch! LC 93-8214. (Illus.). 32p. (gr. 1-4). 1993. PLB 13.95 (*0-516-08132-2*) Childrens.

—Keeping Your Balance. LC 93-8215. (Illus.). 32p. (gr. 1-4). 1993. PLB 13.95 (*0-516-08133-0*) Childrens.

Royston, Angela. The Senses. Riddell, Edwina, illus. LC 92-25715. 24p. (ps-3). 1993. 13.95 (*0-8120-6272-8*) Barron.

Senses. (Illus.). 32p. (gr. 3-8). 1991. PLB 9.95 (*1-85435-271-7*) Marshall Cavendish.

Showers, Paul. Listening Walk. Aliki, illus. LC 61-10495. 40p. (gr. k-3). 1961. PLB 13.89 (*0-690-49663-X*, Crowell Jr Bks) HarpC Child Bks.

—Look at Your Eyes. rev. ed. Kelley, True, illus. LC 91-10167. 32p. (ps-1). 1992. 14.00 (*0-06-020188-6*); PLB 13.89 (*0-06-020189-4*) HarpC Child Bks.

Silverstein, Alvin, et al. Smell, the Subtle Sense. Neumann, Ann, illus. LC 91-21745. 96p. (gr. 3 up). 1992. 14.00 (*0-688-09396-5*); PLB 13.93 (*0-688-09397-3*) Morrow Jr Bks.

Simon, Seymour. Professor I. Q. Explores the Senses. (Illus.). 48p. (gr. 4-7). 1993. 13.95 (*1-878093-28-2*) Boyds Mills Pr.

Smith, Kathie B. & Crenson, Victoria. Tasting. LC 87-5884. (Illus.). 24p. (gr. k-3). 1988. PLB 10.59 (*0-8167-1014-7*); pap. text ed. 2.50 (*0-8167-1015-5*) Troll Assocs.

Snell, Nigel. Tasting & Smelling. (Illus.). 32p. (gr. k-2). 1991. 10.95 (*0-237-60258-X*, Pub. by Evans Bros Ltd) Trafalgar.

Suhr, Mandy. Sight. Gordon, Mike, illus. LC 93-44193. 1993. 13.50 (*0-87614-834-8*) Carolrhoda Bks.

—Smell. Gordon, Mike, illus. LC 93-44189. 1993. 13.50 (*0-87614-835-6*) Carolrhoda Bks.

—Taste. Gordon, Mike, illus. LC 93-44191. 1993. 13.50 (*0-87614-836-4*) Carolrhoda Bks.

—Touch. Gordon, Mike, illus. LC 93-44192. 1993. 13.50 (*0-87614-837-2*) Carolrhoda Bks.

Talbot, Mary. The Senses. (Illus.). 112p. (gr. 6-12). 1990. 18.95 (*0-7910-0027-3*) Chelsea Hse.

Van Der Meer, Ron & Van Der Meer, Atie. Your Amazing Senses: Thirty-Six Games, Puzzles & Tricks to Show How Your Senses Work. Van Der Meer, Ron & Van Der Meer, Atie, illus. 12p. (gr. 4-7). 1987. pap. 9.95 (*0-689-71184-0*, Aladdin) Macmillan Child Grp.

West, Cindy. Disney's That Tickles! The Disney Book of Senses. Moore, Larry, illus. LC 92-53444. 32p. (ps-k). 1993. 9.95 (*1-56282-383-3*) Disney Pr.

Wood, Nicholas. Touch...What Do You Feel? Willey, Lynne, illus. LC 90-10925. 32p. (gr. k-3). 1991. PLB 11.59 (*0-8167-2126-2*); pap. text ed. 3.95 (*0-8167-2127-0*) Troll Assocs.

Wright, Lillian. Hearing: First Starts Ser. LC 94-10719. (Illus.). 32p. (gr. 2-4). 1994. PLB 18.99 (*0-8114-5516-5*) Raintree Steck-V.

—Seeing. LC 94-10720. (Illus.). 32p. (gr. 2-4). 1994. PLB 18.99 (*0-8114-5515-7*) Raintree Steck-V.

Ziefert, Harriet. What Do I Hear? 1988. pap. 3.95 (*0-553-05452-X*) Bantam.

—What Do I Taste? 1988. 3.95 (*0-553-05453-8*) Bantam.

—What Do I Taste: The Five Senses. Smith, Mavis, illus. (ps-1). 1988. pap. 3.95 (*0-317-69282-8*) Bantam.

SEPARATION (LAW)

see Divorce

SEQUOIA

George, Michael. Sequoias. 40p. (gr. 4-7). 1993. 15.95 (*1-56846-055-4*) Creat Editions.

SEQUOIA NATIONAL PARK

McCormick, Maxine. Sequoia & Kings Canyon. LC 88-20214. (Illus.). 48p. (gr. 4-5). 1988. text ed. 13.95 RSBE (*0-89686-409-X*, Crestwood Hse) Macmillan Child Grp.

Salts, Bobbi. Sequoia & Kings Canyon Discovery. Parker, Steve, illus. 36p. (Orig.). (gr. 1-6). 1992. pap. 3.95 (*1-878441-05-1*) Sequoia Nat Hist Assn.

SEQUOYA, CHEROKEE INDIAN, 1700?-1843

Cwiklik, Robert. Sequoyah. Furstinger, Nancy, ed. (Illus.). 142p. (gr. 5-7). 1989. PLB 10.95 (*0-382-09570-7*); pap. 7.95 (*0-382-09759-9*) Silver Burdett Pr.

Oppenheim, Joanne. Sequoyah, Cherokee Hero. new ed. LC 78-60117. (Illus.). 48p. (gr. 4-6). 1979. PLB 10.59 (*0-89375-159-6*); pap. 3.50 (*0-89375-149-9*) Troll Assocs.

Petersen, David. Sequoyah: Father of the Cherokee Alphabet. LC 91-13313. 32p. (gr. 2-4). 1991. PLB 11.80 (*0-516-04180-0*); pap. 3.95 (*0-516-44180-9*) Childrens.

Shumate, Jane A. Sequoyah: Inventor of the Cherokee Alphabet. LC 93-18107. (Illus.). (gr. 5 up). 1994. PLB 18.95 (*0-7910-1720-6*, Am Art Analog); pap. write for info. (*0-7910-1990-X*, Am Art Analog) Chelsea Hse.

Wheeler, Jill. The Story of Sequoyah. Deegan, Paul, ed. Dodson, Liz, illus. LC 89-84909. 32p. (gr. 4). 1989. PLB 11.96 (*0-939179-70-9*) Abdo & Dghtrs.

SERIALS

see Periodicals

SERIGRAPHY

see Silk Screen Printing

SERMON ON THE MOUNT

Gonsalves, Carol. Sermon on the Mountain. (gr. k-4). 1981. pap. 1.89 (*0-570-06149-0*, 59-1304) Concordia.

Parolini, Stephen. Sermon on the Mount. (Illus.). 48p. (gr. 6-8). 1992. pap. 8.99 (*1-55945-129-7*) Group Pub.

SERMONS

Benjamin, Don-Paul & Miner, Ron. Come Sit with Me Again: Sermons for Children. LC 86-30588. (Illus.). 128p. (Orig.). 1987. pap. 8.95 (*0-8298-0748-9*) Pilgrim OH.

Cross, Luther. Object Lessons for Children. (Illus.). 99p. (Orig.). (gr. 2-5). 1967. pap. 4.99 (*0-8010-2315-7*) Baker Bk.

Metcalf, Calvin S. Voices from the Bible: Dramatic Monologs in Worship. LC 90-53277. (Illus.). 144p. (Orig.). 1990. pap. 9.95 (*0-916260-70-4*, B173) Meriwether Pub.

O'Connor, Francine M. The ABCs Lessons of Love: Sermon on the Mount for Children. Boswell, Kathryn, illus. 48p. (gr. 6-8). 1991. pap. text ed. 4.95 (*0-89243-345-0*) Liguori Pubns.

Steindam, Harold. Growing Together: Sermons for Children. Heck, J. Parker, illus. LC 88-28718. 136p. (Orig.). 1989. pap. 9.95 (*0-8298-0800-0*) Pilgrim OH.

Timmer, John. Once upon a Time: Story Sermons for Children. 144p. 1992. pap. 8.99 (*0-310-58621-6*, Pub. by Minister Res Lib) Zondervan.

Weisheit, E. Sixty-One Worship Talks for Children. rev. ed. LC 68-20728. (gr. 3-6). 1975. pap. 7.99 (*0-570-03714-X*, 12-2616) Concordia.

SERPENTS

see Snakes

SERRA, JUNIPERO, 1713-1784

Dolan, Sean. Junipero Serra. (Illus.). 112p. (gr. 5 up). 1991. lib. bdg. 17.95 (*0-7910-1255-7*) Chelsea Hse.

—Junipero Serra: Hispanics of Achievement. (gr. 4-7). 1992. pap. 7.95 (*0-7910-1282-4*) Chelsea Hse.

Duque, Sarah. Sally & Fr. Serra. (Illus.). 104p. (gr. 4-8). 1987. 9.95 (*0-89505-504-X*, 21105) Tabor Pub.

Helen, Mary. Wait for Me: The Life of Junipero Serra. Thien, Denis, illus. LC 88-13103. 100p. (gr. 4-8). 1988. 3.00 (*0-8198-8232-1*) St Paul Bks.

Junipero Serra. (Illus.). 32p. (gr. 3-6). 1988. PLB 19.97 (*0-8172-2909-4*); pap. 4.95 (*0-8114-6765-1*) Raintree Steck-V.

Martin, Teri. Junipero Serra: God's Pioneer. Novack, Kevin, illus. 64p. (gr. 7-9). 1990. pap. 4.95 (*0-8091-6589-9*) Paulist Pr.

Meyer, Kathleen A. Father Serra: Traveler on the Golden Chain. LC 89-63335. (Illus.). 72p. (Orig.). 1990. 9.95 (*0-87973-139-7*); pap. 6.50 (*0-87973-141-9*) Our Sunday Visitor.

Rawls, James J. Never Turn Back: Father Serra's Mission. Guzzi, George, illus. LC 92-12814. 52p. (gr. 2-5). 1992. PLB 19.97 (*0-8114-7221-3*) Raintree Steck-V.

White, Florence. Father Junipero Serra & the American. (Orig.). (gr. k-6). 1987. pap. 3.50 (*0-440-42495-X*, YB) Dell.

SERVICE, COMPULSORY MILITARY

see Military Service, Compulsory

SET THEORY

see also Arithmetic; Numbers Theory

Oliver, Stephen, photos by. Sorting. LC 90-8575. (Illus.). 24p. (ps-k). 1991. 6.95 (*0-679-81162-1*) Random Bks Yng Read.

SETS (MATHEMATICS)

see Set Theory

SEVEN WONDERS OF THE WORLD

McLeish, Kenneth. The Seven Wonders of the World. 32p. (gr. 4-7). 1986. 17.95 (*0-521-26538-X*) Cambridge U Pr.

SEWAGE DISPOSAL

see also Refuse and Refuse Disposal; Water-Pollution

Asimov, Isaac. What Happens When I Flush the Toilet? (Illus.). 24p. (gr. 1-8). 1992. PLB 15.93 (*0-8368-0801-0*); PLB 11.95 s.p. (*0-685-61487-5*) Gareth Stevens Inc.

SEWING

see also Embroidery; Needlework

Arrants, Cheryl & Arrants, Dennis. Thimbelina & the Notion Parade. Arrants, Cheryl & Arrants, Dennis, illus. 32p. (Orig.). (gr. k-4). 1983. pap. text ed. 2.50 (*0-943704-03-0*) Arrants & Assoc.

Cherry, Winky. My First Machine Sewing Book. Cherry, Winky, illus. 40p. (Orig.). (gr. 2 up). 1989. pap. 12.00 (*0-317-93839-8*) ITS Pub.

—My First Sewing Book. Cherry, Winky, illus. 40p. (Orig.). (ps-6). 1984. pap. 10.00 (*0-317-93840-1*) ITS Pub.

Coleman, Anne. Fabrics & Yarns. (Illus.). 32p. (gr. 2-6). 1990. lib. bdg. 15.94 (*0-86592-483-X*); lib. bdg. 11.95s.p. (*0-685-46441-5*) Rourke Corp.

Hoffman, Christine. Sewing by Hand. Barton, Harriett, illus. LC 92-9516. 32p. (ps-3). 1994. 14.00 (*0-06-021146-6*); PLB 13.89 (*0-06-021147-4*) HarpC Child Bks.

Mainwaring, S. Learning Through Sewing & Pattern Design. 35p. (gr. k-3). 1976. pap. 8.00 (*0-931114-86-1*) High-Scope.

Pyman, Kit, ed. Every Kind of Smocking. Messent, Jan, et al, illus. 126p. (Orig.). 1989. pap. 17.95 (*0-85532-632-8*, Pub. by Search Pr UK) A Schwartz & Co.

Siegel, Beatrice. The Sewing Machine. LC 83-40397. 64p. (gr. 5 up). 1984. PLB 10.85 (*0-8027-6532-7*) Walker & Co.

Smith, Nancy & Milligan, Lynda. Sewing Machine Fun. Holmes, Sharon, ed. Robinson, Marilyn, illus. 72p. (gr. 1-12). 1993. pap. 15.95 GBC bdg. (*1-880972-04-2*, DreamSpinners) Pssblts Denver.

—Sewing Machine Fun: Activity Kit. Holmes, Sharon, ed. Robinson, Marilyn, illus. 72p. (gr. 1-12). 1993. pap. 29.95 (*1-880972-10-7*, DreamSpinners) Pssblts Denver.

—Step into Patchwork. Holmes, Sharon, ed. Robinson, Marilyn, illus. 72p. (gr. 1-12). 1994. pap. 15.95 plastic comb bdg. (*1-880972-09-3*, DreamSpinners) Pssblts Denver.

Smith, Nancy J. & Milligan, Lynda. More Sewing Machine Fun. Holmes, Sharon, ed. Robinson, Marilyn, illus. 72p. (gr. 2-8). 1993. pap. 15.95 plastic comb. (*1-880972-05-0*) Pssblts Denver.

Wood, Marina. Crayon Creations. Wood, Marina, illus. 40p. (Orig.). (gr. 4-8). 1984. pap. 6.00 (*0-932946-12-7*) Burdett CA.

SEX

see also Reproduction;

also headings beginning with the word Sexual

Bode, Janet & Mack, Stan. Heartbreak & Roses: Real-Life Stories of Troubled Love. LC 93-39012. 1994. 15.95 (*0-385-32068-X*) Delacorte.

Bosworth, et al. Human Sexuality. (gr. 7-12). Date not set. incl. software 120.00 (*0-912899-55-7*) Lrning Multi-Systs.

Chetin, Helen. My Father Raped Me: Frances Ann Speaks Out. 2nd ed. Olsen, Karen, illus. 20p. (gr. 5 up). 1977. pap. 4.95 (*0-938678-05-1*) New Seed.

Cohen, Richard A. Alfie's Home. Sherman, Elizabeth, illus. LC 93-78368. 30p. (gr. 3-12). 1993. 14.95 (*0-9637058-0-6*) Intl Healing.

Eager, George B. Save Sex. 2nd ed. Philbrook, Diana, illus. 29p. (gr. 6-12). 1993. pap. 3.00x (*1-879224-07-0*) Mailbox.

—Understanding Your Sex Drive. rev. ed. Philbrook, Diana, illus. LC 93-80758. 96p. (gr. 6-12). 1994. 12.95 (*1-879224-19-4*); pap. 7.95 (*1-879224-12-7*) Mailbox.

Fox, F. Earle. Biblical Sexuality & the Battle for Science. LC 88-80409. 208p. (Orig.). (gr. 9-12). 1988. pap. 5.45 (*0-945778-00-7*) Emmaus Ministries.

Gittelsohn, Roland B. Love in Your Life: A Jewish View of Teenage Sexuality. (gr. 7-9). 1991. pap. 9.95 (*0-8074-0460-8*, 142685) UAHC.

Harvey & McGuire. So, There Are Laws about Sex! Answers on Legal Sex for Canadian Children & Youth. 48p. 1989. pap. 10.00 (*0-409-88936-9*) Butterworth Legal Pubs.

Hyde, Margaret O. Teen Sex. LC 88-101. 120p. (gr. 7-12). 1988. 10.00 (*0-664-32726-5*, Westminster) Westminster John Knox.

Jennings, Donna A. Baby Brendon's Busy Day: A Sexuality Primer. Hall, Bruce, illus. Wilson, Pamela M., intro. by. LC 93-79755. (Illus.). 32p. (ps-k). 1994. 15.95 (*0-9638079-0-0*) Goose Pond.

Johnson, Kathryn T. & Balczon, Mary-Lynne J. The Sexual Dictionary: Terms & Expressions for Teens & Parents. St. John, Charlotte, ed. (Illus.). 176p. 1993. pap. 12.95 (*0-89896-400-8*) Larksdale.

Lawson, Michael & Skipp, David. Sexo y Mas: Guia Para la Juventud. (SPA., Illus.). 110p. (Orig.). (gr. 10-12). 1988. pap. 2.95 (*0-945792-02-6*) Editorial Unilit.

Mast, Coleen K. Sex Respect: The Option of True Sexual Freedom: A Public Health Manual for Teachers. Evans, Wendy M. & Evans, Dolly B., illus. 61p. (Orig.). (gr. 7-9). 1986. pap. 12.95 (*0-945745-00-1*) Respect Inc.

—Sex Respect: The Option of True Sexual Freedom: A Public Health Guide for Parents. Evans, Wendy M. & Evans, Dolly B., illus. 61p. (Orig.). (gr. 7-9). 1986. pap. text ed. 8.95 (*0-945745-01-X*) Respect Inc.

—Sex Respect: The Option of True Sexual Freedom: A Public Health Workbook for Students. Evans, Wendy M. & Evans, Dolly B., illus. 61p. (Orig.). (gr. 7-9). 1986. pap. text ed. 7.95 (*0-945745-02-8*) Respect Inc.

Miller, Deborah. Coping with Incest. rev. ed. (gr. 4-7). 1994. 14.95 (*0-8239-1949-8*) Rosen Group.

Nourse, Alan E. Teen Guide to Safe Sex. 1990. pap. 4.95 (*0-531-15211-1*) Watts.

Phiffer, Cynthia L. My Body, My Choice. Coy, Stanley C., ed. 40p. (Orig.). (gr. 7-12). 1994. pap. 2.00 (*1-881459-17-9*) Eagle Pr SC.

Polish, Daniel F., et al. Drugs, Sex, & Integrity: What Does Judaism Say? Diaz, Jose, illus. LC 90-28763. (gr. 7-9). 1991. pap. 10.00 (*0-8074-0459-4*, 168505) UAHC.

Rench, Janice. Understanding Sexual Identity. 1992. pap. 4.95 (*0-8225-9602-4*) Lerner Pubns.

St. Clair, Barry & Jones, Bill. Sex: Desiring the Best. 140p. (Orig.). 1993. pap. 5.99 (*1-56476-190-8*, Victor Books) SP Pubns.

Sciacca, Fran & Sciacca, Jill. Sex: When to Say Yes. 1987. pap. 3.95 (*0-89066-099-9*) World Wide Pubs.

Speck, Greg. Sex: It's Worth Waiting For. Hillam, Corbin A., illus. (Orig.). 1989. pap. 6.99 (*0-8024-7692-9*) Moody.

Spies, Karen. Everything You Need to Know about Incest. (gr. 7-12). 1992. PLB 14.95 (*0-8239-1325-2*) Rosen Group.

SEX INSTRUCTION

Ameiss, Bill & Graver, Jane. Love, Sex & God. 128p. (gr. 9 up). 1988. pap. 7.99 (*0-570-08485-7*, 14-1625) Concordia.

Baker, Sue. The Birds & the Bees. LC 91-39758. (gr. 3 up). 1991. 9.95 (*0-85953-400-6*) Childs Play.

Bausch, William J. Becoming a Man: Basic Information, Guidance, & Attitudes on Sex for Boys. LC 87-51569. 324p. (Orig.). (gr. 5-12). 1988. pap. 9.95 (*0-89622-357-4*) Twenty-Third.

Bell, Alison & Rooney, Lisa. Your Body, Yourself: A Guide to Your Changing Body. (Illus.). 144p. 1993. pap. 6.95 (*1-56565-045-X*) Lowell Hse.

Bimler, Rich, illus. Sex & the New You. 64p. (gr. 6-9). 1988. pap. 7.99 (*0-570-08484-9*, 14-1624) Concordia.

Blank, Joani. Playbook for Kids About Sex. Costanzo, Lana, illus. 56p. (gr. 2-6). 1980. pap. 5.00 (*0-9602324-6-X*, Yes Pr) Down There Pr.

Bleich, Alan R. Coping with Health Risks & Risky Behavior. Rosen, Roger, ed. (gr. 7-12). 1990. PLB 14.95 (*0-8239-1072-5*) Rosen Group.

Bourgeois & Wolfish. Changes in You & Me: A Book about Puberty, Mostly for Boys. LC 94-1162. (gr. 7-12). 1994. 14.95 (*0-8362-2814-6*) Andrews & McMeel.

Bourgeois, Paulette & Wolfish, Martin. Changes in You & Me: A Book about Puberty, Mostly for Girls. Phillips, Louise & Yu, Kam, illus. LC 94-1161. (gr. 7-12). 1994. 14.95 (*0-8362-2815-4*) Andrews & McMeel.

Butterworth, Nick & Inkpen, Mick, illus. Who Made Me? Doney, Malcolm, text by. LC 92-20748. 1992. write for info. (*0-551-01476-8*) Zondervan.

Canterbury, Joyce C. Time We Talk: The Pre-Teen Years. Canterbury, Joyce C., illus. LC 92-73621. 24p. (Orig.). (gr. 4-7). 1993. pap. 4.25 (*0-9634737-0-0*) Hoffman Spec.

Center for Learning Network. Chastity: the Only Choice: Looking at Life. 12p. (gr. 7-12). 1992. pap. text ed. 0.80 (*1-56077-221-2*) Ctr Learning.

Cole, Babette. Mommy Laid an Egg. (ps-3). 1992. 13.95 (*0-8118-0350-3*) Chronicle Bks.

Cole, Joanna. How You Were Born. LC 83-17314. (Illus.). 48p. (ps-3). 1984. 12.95 (*0-688-01710-X*); lib. bdg. 12.88 (*0-688-01709-6*, Morrow Jr Bks); pap. 4.95 (*0-685-08263-6*, Mulberry Bks) Morrow Jr Bks.

Cush, Cathie. Pregnancy. LC 93-25155. (Illus.). (gr. 6-9). 1993. PLB 21.34 (*0-8114-3530-X*) Raintree Steck-V.

Diggs, Richard N. Let's Talk about Sex: Facts, Statistics & Information Which May Help You Avoid...Screwin up Your Life! Clancey, Eleanor, ed. (Illus.). 60p. (Orig.). (gr. 8-10). 1992. pap. 5.95 (*0-937157-11-2*) Progressive Pubns.

—The Sex Education Handbook. (Illus.). 216p. (gr. 6-12). 1994. pap. text ed. 17.95 (*0-937157-13-9*) Progressive Pubns.

Eager, George B. Love, Dating & Sex: What Teens Want to Know. Philbrook, Diana, illus. 208p. (gr. 7-12). 1989. PLB 14.95 (*0-9603752-9-5*); pap. text ed. 9.95 (*0-9603752-8-7*) Mailbox.

—Understanding Your Sex Drive. Philbrook, Diana, illus. 29p. (Orig.). (gr. 6-12). 1993. pap. 3.00x (*1-879224-05-4*) Mailbox.

Elgin, Kathleen & Osterritter, John F. Twenty-Eight Days. LC 73-77779. (Illus.). 64p. (gr. 5 up). 1973. pap. 5.95 (*0-679-51382-5*) McKay.

Family Life Education: Understanding Human Sexuality. (gr. 5-7). 1989. 29.00 (*1-877844-14-4*, 2058) Meridian Educ.

Fenwick, Elizabeth & Walker, Richard. How Sex Works: A Clear, Comprehensive Guide for Teenagers to Emotional, Physical & Sexual Maturity. LC 93-37638. (Illus.). 96p. 1994. 14.95 (*1-56458-505-0*) Dorling Kindersley.

Fiedler, Jean & Fiedler, Hal. Be Smart about Sex: Facts for Young People. LC 89-7919. (Illus.). 128p. (gr. 6 up). 1990. lib. bdg. 17.95 (*0-89490-168-0*) Enslow Pubs.

Fox, Robert J. The Gift of Sexuality: A Guide for Young People. LC 88-63528. (Orig.). (gr. 9 up). 1989. pap. 7.95 (*0-87973-425-6*, 425) Our Sunday Visitor.

Gardner-Loulan, JoAnn, et al. Period. updated ed. Quackenbush, Marcia, illus. & LC 90-46065. 95p. (gr. 4-8). 1991. pap. 9.95 incl. removable parents' guide (*0-912078-88-X*) Volcano Pr.

Gee, R. & Meredith, S. Facts of Life (B - U) (Illus.). 96p. (gr. 5-9). pap. 12.95 (*0-86020-851-6*) EDC.

Gitchel, Sam & Foster, Lorri. Let's Talk about...S-E-X: A Read & Discuss Guide for People 9 to 12 & Their Parents. Cooper, Andrea, illus. 59p. (gr. 4-8). 1983. pap. 4.95 (*0-9610122-0-X*) Plan Par Ctrl CA.

Gordon, Sol. Girls Are Girls & Boys Are Boys: So What's the Difference? Cohen, Vivien, illus. 48p. (Orig.). (gr. 3-7). 1991. pap. 9.95 (*0-87975-686-1*) Prometheus Bks.

—Protect Yourself from Becoming an Unwanted Parent. (Illus., Orig.). (gr. 9-12). 1983. pap. 1.95 (*0-934978-08-5*) Ed-U-Pr.

Gordon, Sol & Cohen, Judith. Did the Sun Shine Before You Were Born: A Sex Education Primer. LC 74-82733. (ps-2). 1974. 12.00 (*0-89388-179-1*) Okpaku Communications.

Gordon, Sol & Gordon, Judith. Did the Sun Shine Before You Were Born? A Sex Education Primer. (ps-3). 1982. pap. 7.95 (*0-934978-03-4*) Ed-U Pr.

—Did the Sun Shine Before Your Were Born? Cohen, Vivien, illus. 48p. (Orig.). (gr. k-5). 1992. pap. 8.95 (*0-87975-723-X*) Prometheus Bks.

Graver, Jane. How You Are Changing. 64p. (gr. 3-6). 1988. 7.99 (*0-570-08483-0*, 14-1623) Concordia.

Greene, Carol. Why Boys & Girls Are Different. 32p. (ps up). 1988. 7.99 (*0-570-08481-4*, 14-1621) Concordia.

Harris, Robie H. It's Perfectly Normal: Changing Bodies, Sex, & Sexual Health. Emberley, Michael, illus. LC 93-48365. 96p. (gr. 3-8). 1994. 19.95 (*1-56402-199-8*) Candlewick Pr.

Hoch, Dean & Hoch, Nancy. The Sex Education Dictionary for Today's Teens & Preteens. Severe, Camille H., illus. LC 89-63577. 128p. (Orig.). (gr. 5-12). 1990. pap. 12.95 (*0-9624209-0-5*) Landmark ID.

Hummel, Ruth. Where Do Babies Come From? 32p. (gr. 1-3). 1988. 7.99 (*0-570-08482-2*, 14-1622) Concordia.

Jakobson, Cathryn. Teenage Pregnancy. rev. ed. 160p. (gr. 7 up). 1992. PLB 15.85 (*0-8027-8128-4*); pap. 9.95 (*0-8027-7372-9*) Walker & Co.

Johnson, Eric W. People, Love, Sex & Families. Wool, David, illus. 144p. (gr. 4 up). 1985. PLB 14.85 (*0-8027-6605-6*) Walker & Co.

Johnson, Greg & Shellenberger, Susie. Getting Ready for the Guy-Girl Thing: Two Ex-Teenagers Reveal the Shocking Truth about God's Plan for Success with the Opposite Sex! Duncan, Kyle, ed. Fisher, Barbara L., illus. LC 91-14818. 200p. (gr. 5-9). 1991. pap. 8.99 (*0-8307-1485-5*, 5422705) Regal.

Kelly, Gary F. Sex & Sense: A Contemporary Guide for Teenagers. 240p. 1993. pap. 7.95 (*0-8120-1446-4*) Barron.

Koch, Janice. Our Baby: A Birth & Adoption Story. Goldberg, Pat, illus. LC 85-6392. 27p. (ps-2). 1985. 10.95 (*0-9609504-3-5*) Perspect Indiana.

LaBarre, Alice, et al. Sexual Abuse! What Is It? An Informational Book for the Hearing Impaired. Nelson, Mary F., illus. LC 92-80161. 80p. (gr. 1-6). 1992. pap. 9.00 (*0-9629302-1-0*) Liberty.

Lee, Michele. Teenage Sexuality. LC 93-47225. 1994. 14.95 (*1-85435-616-X*) Marshall Cavendish.

Lena, Dan & Howard, Marie. Sexual Assault: How to Defend Yourself. (gr. 10 up). 1990. pap. 6.95 (*0-8119-0677-9*) Lifetime.

Lena, Daniel S. & Howard, Marie. Hands off... I'm Special! How to Tell Your Boyfriend No. Bartimole, John, ed. (Illus.). 96p. (Orig.). (gr. 7 up). 1988. pap. 6.95 (*0-936320-30-3*) Compact Books.

McCoy, Kathy & Wibbelsman, Charles. The New Teenage Body Book. rev. ed. (Illus.). 288p. (Orig.). (gr. 9-12). 1992. pap. 15.00 (*0-399-51725-1*, Body Pr-Perigee) Berkley Pub.

McIlhaney, Joe S., Jr. Sexuality & Sexually Transmitted Diseases: A Doctor Confronts the Myth of "Safe" Sex. LC 90-649. 176p. (Orig.). 1990. pap. 8.99 (*0-8010-6274-8*) Baker Bk.

Mahoney, Ellen V. Coping with Safer Sex. Rosen, Ruth, ed. (gr. 7-12). 1989. PLB 14.95 (*0-8239-0999-9*) Rosen Group.

Mayle, Peter. What's Happening to Me? Walter, Paul & Robins, Arthur, illus. LC 75-14410. 56p. (gr. 3 up). 1975. 12.00 (*0-8184-0221-0*); pap. 6.95 (*0-8184-0312-8*) Carol Pub Group.

Morgan, Marcia K. My Feelings. 2nd ed. Hilty, Christi S., illus. (ps-5). 1984. pap. text ed. 3.95 (*0-930413-00-8*, TX-1-361-947) Equal Just Con.

Morrison, Jan. A Safe Place: Beyond Sexual Abuse. 180p. (Orig.). 1990. pap. 7.99 (*0-87788-747-0*) Shaw Pubs.

Neutens, James J. Healthy Sexual Development, Course I. (Illus.). 144p. (gr. 6-8). 1993. text ed. 7.50 wkbk. (*1-56269-056-6*); tchr's. manual, 152p. 17.50 (*1-56269-057-4*) Am Guidance.

—Healthy Sexual Development, Course II. (Illus.). 144p. (gr. 9-12). 1993. text ed. 7.50 wkbk. (*1-56269-058-2*); tchr's. manual, 152p. 17.50 (*1-56269-059-0*) Am Guidance.

Noble, Elizabeth & Sorger, Leo. The Joy of Being a Boy. 115p. 1994. pap. 4.95 (*0-9641183-0-0*) New Life Images. The first book to reassure the young boy & his family that for his penis to remain intact as nature intended is the BEST way. Circumcision is the only surgical procedure where the decision to operate is made solely by parents who know little about the structure & function of the penis & foreskin. In simple words & photographs, THE JOY OF BEING A BOY explains these facts. It is an essential reading for: families with young boys, doctor's offices, libraries, day care centers & schools. This book will educate those who blindly follow tradition or believe in such medical fallacies that surgery is necessary for cleanliness & disease prevention. Even physicians often do not know that the foreskin should be left alone until it naturally retracts in childhood. The United States is the only country that circumcises most male infants for non-ritualistic reasons. According to the Universal Declaration of Human Rights & the United Nations Convention on the Rights of the Child "no-one shall be subjected to torture or to cruel, inhuman or degrading treatment or punishment." As well as psychological harm, for the adult male an average of twelve square inches of erogenous tissue is lost by this medically-unnecessary genital mutilation.
Publisher Provided Annotation.

Nourse, Alan E. Sexually Transmitted Diseases. LC 91-21707. (Illus.). 128p. (gr. 9-12). 1992. PLB 14.40 (*0-531-11065-6*) Watts.

—Teen Guide to Safe Sex. Kline, Marjory, ed. (Illus.). 64p. (gr. 6-12). 1988. PLB 13.40 (*0-531-10592-X*) Watts.

—Teen Guide to Survival. LC 90-12267. (Illus.). 64p. (gr. 9-12). 1990. PLB 13.40 (*0-531-10968-2*) Watts.

Orlandi, Mario, et al. Human Sexuality. (Illus.). 128p. 1989. 18.95x (*0-8160-1666-6*) Facts on File.

Poe, Elizabeth A. Focus on Sexuality. 225p. 1990. lib. bdg. 39.50 (*0-87436-116-8*) ABC-CLIO.

Pomeroy, Wardell B. Boys & Sex. rev. ed. 176p. (Orig.). (gr. 7 up). 1981. pap. 3.25 (*0-440-90753-5*, LE) Dell.

—Boys & Sex. 3rd ed. 1991. pap. 3.95 (*0-440-20811-4*) Dell.

—Girls & Sex. rev. ed. 176p. (Orig.). (gr. 7 up). 1981. pap. 3.25 (*0-440-92904-0*, LE) Dell.

Rachner, Mary J. Kerry's Thirteenth Birthday: Everything Your Parents & Their Friends Know about Sex but Are Too Polite to Talk About. rev. ed. LC 93-84599. 80p. (gr. 8 up). 1993. pap. text ed. 9.95 (*0-9623133-4-3*) Oxner Inst.

Rench, Janice E. Teen Sexuality: Decisions & Choices. (Illus.). 72p. (gr. 6 up). 1988. lib. bdg. 15.95 (*0-8225-0041-8*) Lerner Pubns.

Stone, Bob & Palmer, Bob. The Dating Dilemma: Handling Sexual Pressures. 160p. (Orig.). 1990. pap. 9.99 (*0-8010-8314-1*) Baker Bk.

Swisher, Karin L., et al, eds. Teenage Sexuality: Opposing Viewpoints. LC 93-30962. (Illus.). 264p. (gr. 10 up). 1994. PLB 17.95 (*1-56510-103-0*); pap. text ed. 9.95 (*1-56510-102-2*) Greenhaven.

Tengbom, Mildred. Talking Together about Love & Sexuality. LC 85-22837. 160p. (gr. 4-8). 1985. pap. 7.99 (*0-87123-804-7*) Bethany Hse.

Watkins, James N. Sex Is Not a Four-Letter Word. 1991. pap. 7.95 (*0-8423-7001-3*) Tyndale.

Westheimer, Ruth. Dr. Ruth Talks to Kids: Where You Came from, How Your Body Changes, & What Sex Is All About. DeGroat, Diane, illus. LC 92-11397. 96p. (gr. 4-9). 1993. SBE 13.95 (*0-02-792532-3*, Macmillan Child Bk) Macmillan Child Grp.

Wingerd, William N. Understanding & Enjoying Adolescence. 1988. pap. text ed. 13.05 (*0-8013-0215-3*, 75873) Longman.

Wingfield, Jack & Wingfield, Angela. Growing up Now. (Illus.). 48p. (gr. 4-8). 1992. 14.95 (*0-7459-1537-X*) Lion USA.

Zimet, Susan & Goodman, Victor. The Great Cover-Up: A Condom Compendium. Silbur, Stephanie, illus. LC 88-92769. 136p. (Orig.). (gr. 10 up). 1989. pap. text ed. 7.95 (*0-9621700-0-3*) Civan Inc.

SEX ROLE–FICTION

Berenstain, Stan & Berenstain, Jan. The Berenstain Bears & the Female Fullback. Berenstain, Stan & Berenstain, Jan, illus. 112p. (Orig.). (gr. 2-6). 1993. PLB 7.99 (*0-679-93611-4*); pap. 3.50 (*0-679-83611-X*) Random Bks Yng Read.

—Los Osos Berenstain, No Se Permiten Ninas. LC 93-29904. (SPA.). 32p. (ps-3). 1994. pap. 2.50 (*0-679-85431-2*) Random Bks Yng Read.

Cristaldi, Kathryn. Baseball Ballerina. Carter, Abby, illus. LC 90-20234. 48p. (Orig.). (gr. 1-3). 1992. PLB 7.99 (*0-679-91734-9*); pap. 3.50 (*0-679-81734-4*) Random Bks Yng Read.

Davis, Jenny. Sex Education. LC 87-30441. 160p. (gr. 7 up). 1988. 13.95 (*0-531-05756-9*); PLB 13.99 (*0-531-08356-X*) Orchard Bks Watts.

Dygard, Thomas J. Forward Pass. LC 89-33427. (Illus.). 192p. (gr. 7 up). 1989. 11.95 (*0-688-07961-X*) Morrow Jr Bks.

Emerson, Mark. The Mean Lean Weightlifting Queen. 120p. (gr. 9-12). 1992. 17.95 (*0-936389-26-5*) Tudor Pubs.

Hague, Kathleen & Hague, Michael. The Man Who Kept House. Hague, Michael, illus. LC 80-26258. 32p. (ps-3). 1981. 12.95 (*0-15-251698-0*, HB Juv Bks) HarBrace.

Houston, Gloria. Mountain Valor. Allen, Thomas B., illus. LC 92-26218. 240p. (gr. 8 up). 1994. 14.95 (*0-399-22519-6*, Philomel Bks) Putnam Pub Group.

Hyatt, Pat R. Coast to Coast with Alice. LC 94-25750. (gr. 1-8). 1995. write for info. (*0-87614-789-9*) Carolrhoda Bks.

Jackson, Alison. Blowing Bubbles with the Enemy. LC 93-2888. 120p. (gr. 3-7). 1993. 13.99 (*0-525-45056-4*, DCB) Dutton Child Bks.

Kroll, Virginia L. A Carp for Kimiko. Roundtree, Katherine, illus. LC 93-6940. 32p. 1993. 14.95 (*0-88106-412-2*); PLB 15.88 (*0-88106-413-0*) Charlesbridge Pub.

Lantz, Francess. Randy's Raiders. LC 93-44345. (Illus.). 176p. (gr. 3-6). 1994. pap. 2.95 (*0-8167-3474-7*) Troll Assocs.

Lattimore, Deborah N. Frida Maria: A Story of the Old Southwest. LC 93-17250. 1994. 14.95 (*0-15-276636-7*, Browndeer Pr) HarBrace.

Leggat, Bonnie-Alise. Punt, Pass & Point! Thatch, Nancy R., ed. Leggat, Bonnie-Alise, illus. Melton, David, intro. by. LC 92-17598. (Illus.). 26p. (gr. 3-5). 1992. PLB 14.95 (*0-933849-39-7*) Landmark Edns.

Le Guin, Ursula K. Fish Soup. Wynne, Patrick, illus. LC 91-29740. 40p. (gr. 2-4). 1992. SBE 13.95 (*0-689-31733-6*, Atheneum Child Bk) Macmillan Child Grp.

Mulford, Philippa G. If It's Not Funny, Why Am I Laughing? LC 82-70321. 144p. (gr. 7 up). 1982. 9.95 (*0-440-03961-4*) Delacorte.

Neuberger, Anne E. The Girl-Son. LC 94-6725. 1994. write for info. (*0-87614-846-1*) Carolrhoda Bks.

Nixon, Joan L. Land of Dreams. LC 93-8734. 1994. 14.95 (*0-385-31170-2*) Delacorte.

Pamplin, Laurel J. Masquerade on the Western Trail. Roberts, M., ed. (Illus.). 112p. (gr. 4-8). 1991. 9.95 (*0-89015-755-3*) Sunbelt Media.

Sachar, Louis. Marvin Redpost: Is He a Girl? Sullivan, Barbara, illus. LC 92-40784. 80p. (Orig.). (gr. 1-4). 1993. PLB 9.99 (*0-679-91948-1*); pap. 2.99 (*0-685-71893-X*) Random Bks Yng Read.

Sadler, Marilyn. P. J. Funnybunny Camps Out: A Step One Book. Bollen, Roger, illus. LC 92-6156. 32p. (Orig.). (ps-3). 1994. PLB 7.99 (*0-679-93269-0*); pap. 3.50 (*0-679-83269-6*) Random Bks Yng Read.

Savage, Deborah. To Race a Dream. 1994. 15.95 (*0-395-69252-0*) HM.

Staples, Suzanne F. Haveli. LC 92-29054. 1993. write for info. (*0-06-798443-6*) Knopf.

Stops, Sue. Dulcie Dando, Soccer Star. Gliori, Debi, illus. LC 92-2259. (ps-2). 1992. 14.95 (*0-8050-2413-1*, Bks Young Read) H Holt & Co.

Sullivan, Ann. Molly Maguire: Wide Receiver. 112p. (Orig.). 1992. pap. 2.99 (*0-380-76114-9*, Camelot) Avon.

Turin, Adela & Saccaro, Margherita. The Breadtime Story. (Illus.). 32p. (gr. 3-6). 1980. 6.95 (*0-904613-61-5*) Writers & Readers.

Ure, Jean. What If They Saw Me Now? LC 83-14981. 160p. (gr. 7 up). 1984. 13.95 (*0-385-29317-8*) Delacorte.

SEXUAL EDUCATION

see Sex Instruction

SEXUAL ETHICS

see also Birth Control

Black, Beryl. Coping with Sexual Harassment. rev. ed. Rosen, Ruth, ed. 149p. (gr. 7 up). 1992. PLB 14.95 (*0-8239-1174-8*); pap. 8.95 (*0-8239-0764-3*) Rosen Group.

Bouchard, Elizabeth. Everything You Need to Know about Sexual Harassment. rev. ed. (gr. 4-7). 1994. 14.95 (*0-8239-2037-2*) Rosen Group.

Center for Learning Network. Chastity: the Only Choice: Looking at Life. 12p. (gr. 7-12). 1992. pap. text ed. 0.80 (*1-56077-221-2*) Ctr Learning.

Cozic, Charles P., ed. Sexual Values: Opposing Viewpoints. LC 94-4978. (Illus.). 264p. (gr. 10 up). 1995. PLB 17.95 (*1-56510-211-8*); pap. text ed. 9.95 (*1-56510-210-X*) Greenhaven.

Doolittle, Robert. Searching Young Hearts: Adolescent Sexuality & Spirituality. Stamschror, Robert, ed. (Illus.). 72p. (gr. 7-12). 1993. stitched 8.95 (*0-88489-292-1*) St Marys.

Family of the America's Staff & Sincro Communications Staff. If You Love Me...Show Me! CCC of America Staff, illus. 41p. (Orig.). (gr. 5-7). 1992. incl. video 21.95 (*1-56814-400-8*); pap. text ed. 6.95 book (*0-685-62406-4*) CCC of America.

Fox, Robert J. The Gift of Sexuality: A Guide for Young People. LC 88-63528. (Orig.). (gr. 9 up). 1989. pap. 7.95 (*0-87973-425-6*, 425) Our Sunday Visitor.

Gage, Rodney. Let's Talk about AIDS & Sex. LC 92-30853. 1992. 5.99 (*0-8054-6073-X*) Broadman.

Hadland, Beverly J. Hang on to Your Hormones: Straight Talk on Sex, Love & Dating. Paterson, Jim, illus. 192p. (Orig.). 1992. pap. 4.95x (*0-919225-38-1*) Life Cycle Bks.

It's Not Fun, It's Illegal: A Curriculum for the Identification & Prevention of Sexual Harassment in the Schools. (Illus.). 70p. (Orig.). (gr. 7-12). 1991. pap. text ed. 25.00x (*0-941375-43-9*) Diane Pub.

Knot, Madonna. Sex for Straights: A Call for Critical Thinking by Teenagers Who Oppose Sexual Perversion. Rachner, Mary J., intro. by. Turner, William, illus. 34p. (gr. 7-12). 1993. PLB 49.95 (*0-9623133-5-1*) Oxner Inst.

McAllister, Dawson. How to Know If You're Really in Love. LC 93-40906. 1994. 8.99 (*0-8499-3312-9*) Word Pub.

McCauslin, Mark. Sexually Transmitted Diseases. LC 91-18445. (Illus.). 48p. (gr. 5-6). 1992. text ed. 12.95 RSBE (*0-89686-720-X*, Crestwood Hse) Macmillan Child Grp.

Mast, Coleen K. Sex Respect: The Option of True Sexual Freedom: A Public Health Workbook for Students. rev. ed. Forrestal, Julienne, ed. Greiner, William, illus. 118p. (gr. 7-9). 1990. pap. text ed. 8.95 (*0-945745-05-2*) Respect Inc.

Nystrom, Carolyn & Floding, Matthew. Sexuality: God's Good Idea. (Illus.). 64p. (Orig.). (gr. 9-12). 1988. saddle-stitched student ed. 3.99 (*0-87788-764-0*); saddle-stitched tchr's. ed. 4.99 (*0-87788-765-9*) Shaw Pubs.

Ozer, Elizabeth M. & Toure, Nkenge. Staying Safe: How to Protect Yourself Against Sexual Assault. Hamilton, Linda, illus. 23p. (Orig.). (gr. 2-6). 1984. pap. text ed. 3.00 (*0-318-04650-4*) Rape Crisis Ctr.

Pomeroy, Wardell B. Girls & Sex. rev. ed. 176p. (Orig.). (gr. 7 up). 1981. pap. 3.25 (*0-440-92904-0*, LE) Dell.

Sex: A Christian Perspective. 48p. (gr. 9-12). 1990. pap. 8.99 (*1-55945-206-4*) Group Pub.

Stafford, Tim. Love, Sex & the Whole Person: Everything You Want to Know. 280p. 1991. pap. 9.99 (*0-310-71181-9*, Campus Life) Zondervan.

Strauss, Susan & Espeland, Pamela. Sexual Harassment & Teens, a Program for Positive Change. 160p. 1994. 17.95 (*0-685-71633-3*, 784) W Gladden Found.

Wekesser, Carol, et al, eds. Sexual Harassment. LC 92-23593. 200p. (gr. 10 up). 1992. PLB 16.95 (*1-56510-021-2*); pap. text ed. 9.95 (*1-56510-020-4*) Greenhaven.

Why Say No When the World Says Yes. iii, 204p. (gr. 8-12). 1993. 12.95 (*0-87579-736-9*) Deseret Bk.

SHADES AND SHADOWS

Bulla, Clyde R. What Makes a Shadow? rev. ed. Otani, June, illus. LC 92-36350. 32p. (ps-1). 1994. 15.00 (*0-06-022915-2*); PLB 14.89 (*0-06-022916-0*) HarpC Child Bks.

—What Makes a Shadow? rev. ed. Otani, June, illus. LC 92-36350. 32p. (ps-1). 1994. pap. 4.95 (*0-06-445118-6*, Trophy) HarpC Child Bks.

Cosgrove, Stephen E. Shadow Chaser. Edelson, Wendy, illus. 32p. (ps-3). 1990. PLB 14.95 (*0-89565-663-9*) Childs World.

Dorros, Arthur. Me & My Shadow. (ps-3). 1990. pap. 12.95 (*0-590-42772-5*) Scholastic Inc.

Goor, Ron & Goor, Nancy. Shadows: Here, There, & Everywhere. Goor, Ron, photos by. LC 81-43036. (Illus.). 48p. (gr. k-3). 1981. PLB 13.89 (*0-690-04133-0*, Crowell Jr Bks) HarpC Child Bks.

Hoban, Tana. Shadows & Reflections. LC 89-30461. (Illus.). 32p. (ps up). 1990. 12.95 (*0-688-07089-2*); lib. bdg. 12.88 (*0-688-07090-6*) Greenwillow.

Michaels, William. Clare & Her Shadow. Michaels, William, illus. LC 90-8487. 32p. (ps-k). 1991. lib. bdg. 15.00 (*0-208-02301-1*, Linnet) Shoe String.

Montgomery, Rutherford G. Pekan the Shadow. Nenninger, Jerome D., illus. LC 78-84779. (gr. 8-12). 1970. 3.95 (*0-87004-132-0*) Caxton.

Simon, Seymour. Shadow Magic. Ormai, Stella, illus. LC 84-4433. 48p. (ps-3). 1985. PLB 14.93 (*0-688-02682-6*) Lothrop.

Ward, Nick. Shadowland. (Illus.). 32p. (ps-1). 1994. 19.95 (*0-09-176211-1*, Pub. by Hutchinson UK) Trafalgar.

Webb, Phila H. & Corby, Jose. Shadowgraphs: Anyone Can Make. LC 90-50896. (Illus.). 32p. (gr. 1-4). 1991. Repr. of 1927 ed. 8.95 (*1-56138-014-8*) Running Pr.

SHADOW PANTOMIMES AND PLAYS

Bursill, Henry. Hand Shadows to Be Thrown upon a Wall. 42p. (gr. 1-6). pap. 1.95 (*0-486-21779-5*) Dover.

—More Hand Shadows to Be Thrown Upon a Wall. (Illus.). 39p. (gr. 1-6). 1971. pap. 1.95 (*0-486-21384-6*) Dover.

SHAKERS

Bial, Raymond. Shaker Home. LC 93-17917. 1994. 15.95 (*0-395-64047-4*) HM.

Bolick, Nancy O. & Randolph, Sallie G. Shaker Villages. LoTurco, Laura, illus. LC 92-34587. 96p. (gr. 5 up). 1993. 12.95 (*0-8027-8209-4*); PLB 13.85 (*0-8027-8210-8*) Walker & Co.

Campion, Nardi R. Mother Ann Lee, Morning Star of the Shakers. Sprigg, June, frwd. by. LC 90-50305. (Illus.). 205p. (gr. 9-10). 1990. pap. 12.95 (*0-87451-527-0*) U Pr of New Eng.

Ray, Mary L. Angel Baskets: A Little Story about the Shakers. Colquhoun, Jean, illus. LC 87-50789. 32p. (Orig.). 1987. pap. write for info. (*0-9609384-3-5*) M Wetherbee.

—Shaker Boy. Winter, Jeanette, illus. LC 93-1333. (gr. k-3). 1994. 15.95 (*0-15-276921-8*) HarBrace.

Shaver, Elizabeth, ed. Fifteen Years a Shakeress. Shaker Almanac, 1886, NYS Library Staff & Lee, Elizabeth, illus. 105p. 1990. Repr. of 1872 ed. perfect bdg. 5.95 (*0-318-49991-6*) Shaker Her Soc.

Sherburne, Trudy R. As I Remember It: A Detailed Description of the North Family of the Watervliet, N. Y. Shaker Community. (Illus., Orig.). (gr. 5-10). 1987. pap. 4.95 (*0-944178-00-6*) World Shaker.

SHAKESPEARE, WILLIAM, 1564-1616

Birch, Beverley. Shakespeare's Stories: Histories. Green, Robina, illus. LC 88-15693. 126p. (gr. 7-12). 1990. pap. 6.95 (*0-87226-226-X*) P Bedrick Bks.

—Shakespeare's Stories: Tragedies. Kerins, Tony, illus. LC 88-18112. 126p. (gr. 7-12). 1990. pap. 6.95 (*0-87226-227-8*) P Bedrick Bks.

Birch, Beverley, retold by. Shakespeare's Stories: Comedies. Tarrant, Carol, illus. LC 88-16947. 126p. 1990. pap. 6.95 (*0-87226-225-1*) P Bedrick Bks.

Garfield, Leon. Shakespeare Stories. Foreman, Michael, illus. LC 85-1971. 288p. (gr. 5 up). 1991. 24.95 (*0-395-56397-6*) HM.

Marsh, Carole. Bill S: Shakespeare for Kids. (Illus.). (gr. 4-12). 1994. PLB 24.95 (*1-55609-156-7*); pap. 14.95 (*0-935326-10-3*) Gallopade Pub Group.

Martin, C. Shakespeare. (Illus.). 112p. (gr. 7 up). 1989. lib. bdg. 19.94 (*0-86592-296-9*); 14.95s.p. (*0-685-58633-2*) Rourke Corp.

Marydass, C. A Compendium of Shakespeare. 180p. (gr. 7 up). 1988. text ed. 25.00x (*81-207-0713-3*, Pub. by Sterling Pubs IA) Apt Bks.

Mulherin, Jennifer. As You Like It: Shakespeare for Everyone. Thompson, George, illus. LC 90-478. 32p. (gr. 3-7). 1990. PLB 12.95 (*0-87226-339-8*) P Bedrick Bks.

SHAKESPEARE, WILLIAM, 1564-1616–ADAPTATIONS

Coville, Bruce. William Shakespeare's the Tempest. (ps-3). 1994. pap. text ed. 16.95 (*0-385-32056-6*) Doubleday.

Foster, Cass. Shakespeare for Children: The Story of Romeo & Juliet. Molyneux, Lisa, illus. LC 89-80371. 105p. (gr. 2 up). 1989. pap. 9.95 (*0-9619853-3-X*) Five Star AZ.

—The Sixty-Minute Shakespeare: Romeo & Juliet. Hawkins, Mary E., ed. LC 89-82072. 136p. 1990. pap. 3.95 (*0-9619853-8-0*); 5.00 (*1-877749-00-1*) Five Star AZ.

Garfield, Leon. Shakespeare Stories II. Foreman, Michael, illus. LC 94-10515. 1995. write for info. (*0-395-70893-1*) HM.

Guida, Frank J. Romeo & Juliet - with a Happy Ending, Vol. 1. rev. ed. Guida, Frank J., illus. 20p. 1991. lib. bdg. write for info. (*1-878476-00-9*) Rockmasters Intl.
This children's adaptation of William Shakespeare's classic ROMEO & JULIET is intended to cultivate at an early age some of the most dramatic writing in literature. Wait till you hear your youngster reading, understanding & quoting The Bard! "What a wonderful treasure you have added to the shelves of children's literature in your adaptation of Romeo & Juliet. I

thank & applaud you as future generations are certain to do likewise."--Constance F. Zimmerman, Chairperson, Norfolk Reading Council. "The presentation is superb; the art work attractive; & the text very interesting."--James Cullinan, Finnbar Books, Kent, England. "I like your story Mr. Guida because it's with a happy ending. If they're sad, I start to cry & I have bad dreams. But I wonder where you got that name wink milch?"--Crystal (Drew School, 8 years old, Washington, D.C.). "My favorite part is when the two families become friends again & nobody gets killed!"--Brett (Drew School, 9 years old). "In a unique adaptation, Frank Guida has forged a new method of bringing great literary works to young minds."--(Julie Cimino, Educator, Wash., D.C.). "Guida's adaptation incorporates portions of the original in all capital letters, such as Juliet's famous balcony scene."--Philip Walzer (Virginian-Pilot, Norfolk, Va.).
Publisher Provided Annotation.

Lamb, Charles & Lamb, Mary. Tales from Shakespeare. (gr. k-6). 1986. 8.98 (*0-685-16860-3*, 621568) Random Hse Value.

Lester, Julius. Othello: A Retelling. LC 94-12833. 1995. write for info. (*0-590-41967-6*) Scholastic Inc.

Miles, Bernard. Favorite Tales from Shakespeare. Ambrus, Victor G., illus. 128p. (gr. 4-7). 1993. Repr. of 1976 ed. 14.95 (*1-56288-257-0*) Checkerboard.

Shakespeare, William. Hamlet. Davidson, Diane, ed. LC 83-12310. (Illus.). 154p. (gr. 8-12). 1983. pap. 5.95 (*0-934048-12-6*) Swan Books.

—Hamlet. Gill, Roma, ed. (Illus.). 160p. 1992. PLB 7.50 (*0-19-831960-6*) OUP.

—Hamlet for Young People. Davidson, Diane, ed. & illus. 64p. (gr. 5-8). 1993. pap. text ed. 4.95 (*0-934048-24-X*) Swan Books.

—Macbeth: A Facing-Page Edition--The Original Text & a Translation into Modern English. Zuesse, Eric, tr. 192p. (Orig.). 1990. pap. 3.95 (*0-9628103-0-4*) Shakespere VT.

—Merchant of Venice. Davidson, Diane, ed. LC 83-12308. (Illus.). 112p. (gr. 8-12). 1983. pap. 5.95 (*0-934048-08-8*) Swan Books.

—Midsummer Night's Dream. Davidson, Diane, ed. LC 83-12311. (Illus.). 99p. (gr. 8-12). 1983. pap. 5.95 (*0-934048-10-X*) Swan Books.

—Much Ado about Nothing for Young People. Davidson, Diane, ed. (Illus.). 64p. (gr. 5-8). 1994. pap. 4.95 (*0-934048-25-8*) Swan Books.

—Romeo & Juliet. Davidson, Diane, ed. LC 83-12309. (Illus.). 129p. (gr. 8-12). 1983. pap. 5.95 (*0-934048-06-1*) Swan Books.

SHAKESPEARE, WILLIAM, 1564-1616–CRITICISM, INTERPRETATION, ETC.

Eidenier, Betty. Warp Zone Shakespeare! Active Learning Lessons for the Gifted. (gr. 6-12). 1990. 12.00 (*0-910609-23-3*) Gifted Educ Pr.

Kerr, Jessica. Shakespeare's Flowers. Dowden, Anne O., illus. LC 68-13585. 96p. (gr. 7 up). 1982. (Crowell Jr Bks); (Crowell Jr Bks) HarpC Child Bks.

Kester, Ellen S. Word Magic: Shakespeare's Rhetoric for Gifted Students: Elementary & Secondary Shakespearian Excerpts. 2nd ed. Turner, Joseph R., III, illus. 194p. 1989. pap. text ed. 35.00 (*0-685-26279-0*) Pickwick Pubs.

Lipson, Greta & Solomon, Susan. Romeo & Juliet: Plainspoken. Kropa, Susan, illus. 256p. (gr. 7-12). 1985. 15.95 (*0-86653-283-8*, GA 659) Good Apple.

Norris, Crystal. Julius Caesar - Study Guide. Friedland, Joyce & Kessler, Rikki, eds. (gr. 9-12). 1993. pap. text ed. 14.95 (*0-88122-102-3*) Lrn Links.

Peitz, Mary. Romeo & Juliet - Study Guide. Friedland, Joyce & Kessler, Rikki, eds. (gr. 9-12). 1993. pap. text ed. 14.95 (*0-88122-127-9*) Lrn Links.

Shakespeare, William. Hamlet. Mack, Maynard & Boynton, Robert W., eds. 180p. (gr. 9-12). 1990. pap. 4.50 (*0-86709-019-7*, 0019) Boynton Cook Pubs.

—Midsummer Night's Dream. Adams, Richard, ed. 1990. pap. text ed. 4.29 (*0-582-01345-3*, 78421) Longman.

—Romeo & Juliet. Mack, Maynard & Boynton, Robert W., eds. 159p. (gr. 9-12). 1990. pap. text ed. 4.50 (*0-86709-035-9*, 0035) Boynton Cook Pubs.

—Romeo & Juliet. Gibson, Rex, ed. (Illus.). 224p. 1992. pap. 5.95 (*0-521-39574-7*) Cambridge U Pr.

—Twelfth Night. Adams, Richard, ed. 1989. pap. text ed. 4.29 (*0-582-01346-1*, 78433) Longman.

Stockdale, Marina. William's Window: An Introduction to Shakespeare's Plays for Young People. 36p. (gr. 3-8). 1983. pap. 3.00 (*0-88680-209-1*); royalty on application 35.00 (*0-685-57865-8*) I E Clark.

Walters, Michael E. Teaching Shakespeare to Gifted Students: An Examination of the Sensibility of Genius. (gr. 6-12). 1990. 12.00 (*0-910609-22-5*) Gifted Educ Pr.

SHAKESPEARE, WILLIAM, 1564-1616–FICTION

Dhondy, Farrukh. Black Swan. LC 92-30425. 208p. (gr. 6 up). 1993. 14.95 (*0-395-66076-9*) HM.

Lepscky, Ibi. William Shakespeare. Cardoni, Paolo, illus. 28p. (gr. k-3). 1989. 7.95 (*0-8120-6106-3*) Barron.

SHAKESPEARE, WILLIAM, 1564-1616, JULIUS CAESAR

Mulherin, Jennifer. Julius Caesar: Shakespeare for Everyone. Payne, Roger, illus. LC 90-476. 32p. (gr. 3-7). 1990. 12.95 (*0-87226-338-X*) P Bedrick Bks.

Shakespeare, William. Julius Caesar. Davidson, Diane, ed. LC 83-12307. (Illus.). 121p. (gr. 8-12). 1983. pap. 5.95 (*0-934048-04-5*) Swan Books.

—Julius Caesar. Mack, Maynard & Boynton, Robert W., eds. 148p. (gr. 9-12). 1990. pap. text ed. 4.50 (*0-86709-023-5*, 0023) Boynton Cook Pubs.

—Julius Caesar for Young People. Davidson, Diane, ed. LC 90-43038. (Illus.). 64p. (gr. 5-8). 1990. pap. text ed. 4.95 (*0-934048-22-3*) Swan Books.

SHAKESPEARE, WILLIAM, 1564-1616, MACBETH

Shakespeare, William. Macbeth. Davidson, Diane, ed. LC 83-12312. (Illus.). 111p. (gr. 8-12). 1983. pap. 5.95 (*0-934048-02-9*) Swan Books.

—Macbeth. Mack, Maynard & Boynton, Robert W., eds. 141p. (gr. 9-12). 1990. pap. text ed. 4.50 (*0-86709-021-9*, 0021) Boynton Cook Pubs.

—Macbeth: A Facing-Page Edition--The Original Text & a Translation into Modern English. Zuesse, Eric, tr. 192p. (Orig.). 1990. pap. 3.95 (*0-9628103-0-4*) Shakespere VT.

SHAKESPEARE, WILLIAM, 1564-1616–STAGE HISTORY

Brown, John R. Shakespeare & His Theatre. Gentleman, David, illus. LC 81-8441. 64p. (gr. 6 up). 1982. 15.00 (*0-688-00850-X*) Lothrop.

SHAPE

see Size and Shape

SHARES OF STOCK

see Stocks

SHARKS

Arnold, Caroline. Watch out for Sharks! Hewett, Richard, photos by. (Illus.). 48p. (gr. 3-6). 1991. 15.45 (*0-395-57560-5*, Clarion Bks) HM.

Bailey, Donna. Sharks. LC 90-22114. (Illus.). 32p. (gr. 1-4). 1992. PLB 18.99 (*0-8114-2649-1*); pap. 3.95 (*0-8114-4618-2*) Raintree Steck-V.

Barrett, Norman S. Tiburones. LC 90-70892. (SPA., Illus.). 32p. (gr. k-4). 1990. PLB 11.90 (*0-531-07910-4*) Watts.

Behrens, June. Sharks! LC 89-25375. (Illus.). 48p. (gr. 1-4). 1990. PLB 12.30 (*0-516-00571-5*); pap. 5.95 (*0-516-40571-3*) Childrens.

Berkowitz, Henry. Sharks: An Educational Coloring Book. (Illus.). 32p. (Orig.). (gr. 1-9). 1988. pap. 2.50 (*0-938059-01-7*) Henart Bks.

Berman, Ruth. Sharks. Rotman, Jeffrey L., photos by. LC 94-21468. 1995. write for info. (*0-87614-870-4*) Carolrhoda Bks.

Carrick, Carol. Sand Tiger Shark. Carrick, Donald, illus. 32p. (ps-3). 1991. pap. 5.70 (*0-395-59701-3*, Clarion Bks) HM.

Cerullo, Mary M. Sharks: Challengers of the Deep. Rotman, Jeffrey L., photos by. LC 92-14206. 64p. (gr. 4 up). 1993. 15.00 (*0-525-65100-4*, Cobblehill Bks) Dutton Child Bks.

Chinery, Michael. Shark. Doubilet, David, et al, illus. LC 90-33361. 32p. (gr. 4-6). 1991. lib. bdg. 11.59 (*0-8167-2104-1*); pap. text ed. 3.95 (*0-8167-2105-X*) Troll Assocs.

Coupe, Sheena. Sharks. 72p. (gr. 5-12). 1990. 17.95 (*0-8160-2270-4*) Facts on File.

Dingerkus, Guido. The Shark Watcher's Guide. Burkel, Dietrich, illus. 176p. (gr. 7 up). 1989. PLB 10.98 (*0-671-50234-4*, J Messner); pap. 5.95 (*0-671-68815-4*) S&S Trade.

Doudt, Kenny. Surfing with the Great White Shark. LC 92-90967. (Orig.). Date not set. pap. 8.95 (*0-9633342-7-1*) Shark-Bite.

Freedman, Russell. Sharks. Freedman, Russell, illus. LC 85-42881. 40p. (gr. 1-4). 1985. reinforced bdg. 13.95 (*0-8234-0582-6*) Holiday.

Gay, Tanner O. Sharks in Action. Cassels, Jean, illus. 16p. (ps-4). 1990. pap. 8.95 POB (*0-689-71435-1*, Aladdin) Macmillan Child Grp.

Gibbons, Gail. Sharks. LC 91-31524. (Illus.). 32p. (ps-3). 1992. reinforced bdg. 15.95 (*0-8234-0960-0*) Holiday.

Green, Carl R. & Sanford, William R. The Great White Shark. LC 85-14936. (Illus.). 48p. (gr. 5). 1986. text ed. 12.95 RSBE (*0-89686-281-X*, Crestwood Hse) Macmillan Child Grp.

Hall, Howard. Sharks: The Perfect Predators. rev. ed. Leon, Vicki, ed. LC 93-27061. (Illus.). 48p. (gr. 5 up). 1993. pap. 9.95 (*0-918303-36-2*) Blake Pub.

Herge. The Red Sea Sharks. (gr. k up). 1976. pap. 7.95 (*0-316-35848-7*, Joy St Bks) Little.

Lopez, Gary. Sharks. 32p. (gr. 2-6). 1991. 15.95 (*0-89565-705-8*) Childs World.

McGovern, Ann. Sharks. Tinkelman, Murray, illus. 48p. (gr. k-3). 1987. pap. 2.50 (*0-590-41360-0*) Scholastic Inc.

MacQuitty, Miranda. Shark. Greenaway, Frank & King, Dave, photos by. LC 92-4712. (Illus.). 64p. 1992. 16.00 (*0-679-81683-6*); PLB 16.99 (*0-679-91683-0*) Knopf Bks Yng Read.

Maestro, Betsy. Sea Full of Sharks. (ps-3). 1990. 12.95 (*0-590-43100-5*) Scholastic Inc.

Naden, C. J. I Can Read About Sharks. LC 78-73736. (Illus.). (gr. 2-6). 1979. pap. 2.50 (*0-89375-218-5*) Troll Assocs.

Palmer, S. Great White Sharks. (Illus.). 24p. (gr. k-5). 1988. PLB 11.94 (*0-86592-462-7*); 8.95s.p. (*0-685-58314-7*) Rourke Corp.

—Hammerhead Sharks. (Illus.). 24p. (gr. k-5). 1988. PLB 11.94 (*0-86592-461-9*); 8.95s.p. (*0-685-67680-3*) Rourke Corp.

—Mako Sharks. (Illus.). 24p. (gr. k-5). 1989. PLB 11.94 (*0-86592-458-9*); 8.95s.p. (*0-685-58310-4*) Rourke Corp.

—Nurse Sharks. (Illus.). 24p. (gr. k-5). 1988. PLB 11.94 (*0-86592-459-7*); 8.95s.p. (*0-685-58311-2*) Rourke Corp.

—Thresher Sharks. (Illus.). 24p. (gr. k-5). 1988. PLB 11.94 (*0-86592-460-0*); PLB 8.95s.p. (*0-685-58313-9*) Rourke Corp.

—Whale Sharks. (Illus.). 24p. (gr. k-5). 1988. PLB 11.94 (*0-86592-463-5*); PLB 8.95s.p. (*0-685-58309-0*) Rourke Corp.

Palmer, Sarah. World of Sharks, 6 vols. 1990. 7.99 (*0-517-02747-X*) Random Hse Value.

Penny, Malcolm. Let's Look At Sharks. LC 89-31200. (ps-3). 1990. PLB 11.40 (*0-531-18308-4*, Pub. by Bookwright Pr) Watts.

Penzler, Otto. Hunting the Killer Shark. LC 75-23409. (Illus.). 32p. (gr. 5-10). 1976. PLB 10.79 (*0-89375-009-3*); pap. 2.95 (*0-89375-025-5*) Troll Assocs.

Radlauer, Edward. Shark Mania. 1986. pap. 3.95 (*0-516-47410-3*) Childrens.

Resnick, Jane. All about Sharks. (Illus.). 32p. (Orig.). (gr. 1-8). 1994. pap. 3.95 (*1-884506-10-0*) Third Story.

Robson, Denny A. Sharks. LC 91-34966. (Illus.). 32p. (gr. 1-4). 1992. PLB 11.90 (*0-531-17354-2*, Gloucester Pr) Watts.

Sattler, Helen R. Sharks, the Super Fish. Zallinger, Jean D., illus. LC 84-4381. 96p. (gr. 9 up). 1985. 16.00 (*0-688-03993-6*) Lothrop.

Selsam, Millicent E., et al. A First Look at Sharks. Springer, Harriet, illus. (gr. k-3). 1979. PLB 12.85 (*0-8027-6373-1*) Walker & Co.

Serventy, Vincent. Shark & Ray. LC 84-15097. (Illus.). 24p. (gr. k-5). 1984. PLB 9.95 (*0-8172-2402-5*); pap. 3.95 (*0-8114-6888-7*) Raintree Steck-V.

Server, Lee. Sharks. (Illus.). 128p. 1989. 14.99 (*0-517-69091-8*) Random Hse Value.

Shark & Whale. (Illus.). 20p. 1994. 6.95 (*1-56458-717-7*) Dorling Kindersley.

Sharks. (Illus.). 32p. (gr. 3 up). 1993. 5.95 (*1-56138-229-9*) Running Pr.

Simon. Sharks. 1995. 16.00 (*0-06-023029-0*); PLB 15.89 (*0-685-68958-1*) HarpC Child Bks.

Spinelli, Eileen. Sharks. (Illus.). 64p. (gr. k-4). 1992. PLB 13.75 (*1-878363-89-1*, HTS Bks) Forest Hse.

Spizzirri Publishing Co. Staff. Sharks: An Educational Coloring Book. Spizzirri, Linda, ed. Fuller, Glenn, et al, illus. 32p. (gr. 1-8). 1981. pap. 1.75 (*0-86545-029-3*) Spizzirri.

Stevens, John, ed. Sharks. (Illus.). 240p. 1987. 35.00 (*0-8160-1800-6*) Facts on File.

Stoops, Erik D. & Stoops, Sherrie. Sharks. LC 93-43336. (Illus.). 80p. 1994. 14.95 (*0-8069-0374-0*) Sterling.

Wildlife Education, Ltd. Staff. Sharks. Hoopes, Barbara, illus. 20p. (gr. 5 up). 1983. pap. 2.75 (*0-937934-15-1*) Wildlife Educ.

Wilson, Lynn. Sharks! Courtney Studios, Inc. Staff, illus. 32p. (ps-3). 1992. (Platt & Munk Pubs); pap. 2.25 (*0-448-40300-5*, Platt & Munk Pubs) Putnam Pub Group.

SHARKS–FICTION

Campbell, Eric. The Shark Callers. LC 93-44881. (gr. 7 up). 1994. 10.95 (*0-15-200007-0*); pap. 4.95 (*0-15-200010-0*) HarBrace.

Crisfield, Deborah. Jaws. LC 90-47941. (Illus.). 48p. (gr. 5-6). 1991. text ed. 13.95 RSBE (*0-89686-578-9*, Crestwood Hse) Macmillan Child Grp.

Gibbons, Gail. Sharks. (Illus.). 1993. pap. 5.95 (*0-8234-1068-4*) Holiday.

Laird, Donivee M. Ula Li'i & the Magic Shark. LC 86-3390. (Illus.). 42p. (gr. k-3). 1985. 7.95x (*0-940350-12-2*) Barnaby Bks.

McBarnet, Gill. The Shark Who Learned a Lesson. McBarnet, Gill, illus. 32p. (ps-2). 1990. 7.95 (*0-9615102-5-0*) Ruwanga Trad.

Mahy, Margaret. The Great White Man-Eating Shark: A Cautionary Tale. Allen, Jonathan, illus. (ps-3). 1990. 13.00 (*0-8037-0749-5*) Dial Bks Young.

Mellor, Corinne. Clark the Toothless Shark. (ps-3). 1994. 14.95 (*0-307-17606-1*, Artsts Writrs) Western Pub.

Ossorio, Joseph D. & Salvadeo, Michele B. Misadventures of the Friendly Shark. (Illus.). 60p. (gr. 3-5). 1994. pap. 6.95 (*1-56721-054-6*) Twnty-Fifth Cent Pr.

Thiele, Colin. Shadow Shark. LC 87-45566. 224p. (gr. 5-7). 1988. PLB 14.89 (*0-06-026179-X*) HarpC Child Bks.

SHAVU'OTH (FEAST OF WEEKS)–FICTION

Wengrov, Charles. The Story of Shavuot. (Illus.). (gr. k-7). 1965. pap. 2.50 (*0-914080-55-5*) Shulsinger Sales.

SHEEP

Ahlstrom, Mark. The Sheep. LC 83-25215. (Illus.). 48p. (gr. 5). 1984. text ed. 12.95 RSBE (*0-89686-248-8*, Crestwood Hse) Macmillan Child Grp.

Clayton, Gordon, photos by. Lamb. (Illus.). 24p. (gr. k-3). 1992. 6.95 (*0-525-67359-8*, Lodestar Bks) Dutton Child Bks.
Fowler, Allan. Ovejas Lanudas y Cabras Hambrientas: (Woolly Sheep & Hungry Goats) LC 92-36366. (SPA., Illus.). 32p. (ps-2). 1993. PLB 10.75 (*0-516-36014-0*); pap. 3.95 (*0-516-56014-X*) Childrens.
—Woolly Sheep & Hungry Goats. LC 92-36366. (Illus.). 32p. (ps-2). 1993. big bk. 22.95 (*0-516-49645-X*); PLB 10.75 (*0-516-06014-7*); pap. 3.95 (*0-516-46014-5*) Childrens.
Gambill, Henrietta, ed. Little Lost Lamb. (Illus.). 18p. 1994. 7.99 (*0-7847-0234-9*, 24-03120) Standard Pub.
Hall, Katy & Eisenberg, Lisa. Sheepish Riddles. Alley, Robert, illus. LC 93-32212. 1995. write for info. (*0-8037-1535-8*); lib. bdg. write for info. (*0-8037-1536-6*) Dial Bks Young.
Herriot, James. Smudge, the Little Lost Lamb. Brown, Ruth, illus. 32p. 1991. 12.95 (*0-312-06404-7*) St Martin.
—Smudge, the Little Lost Lamb. Brown, Ruth, illus. 32p. 1994. pap. 6.95 (*0-312-11067-7*) St Martin.
Keller, Holly. Ten Sleepy Sheep. Keller, Holly, illus. LC 83-1477. 32p. (gr. k-3). 1983. 10.25 (*0-688-02306-1*); PLB 13.93 (*0-688-02307-X*) Greenwillow.
Kratky, Lada J. The Shaggy Sheep. Freire, Carlos, illus. 16p. (Orig.). (gr. 1-3). 1992. pap. text ed. 29.95 big bk. (*1-56334-068-2*); pap. text ed. 6.00 small bk. (*1-56334-074-7*) Hampton-Brown.
Paladino, Catherine. Spring Fleece: A Day of Sheepshearing. (ps-3). 1990. 14.95 (*0-316-68890-8*, Joy St Bks) Little.
Royston, Angela. Sheep. LC 89-22531. 1990. PLB 10.90 (*0-531-19082-X*, Warwick) Watts.
Simmons, Paula & Salsbury, Darrell L. Your Sheep: A Kid's Guide to Raising & Showing. Steege, Gwen, ed. LC 91-57947. (Illus.). 128p. 1992. (Garden Way Pub); pap. 12.95 (*0-88266-769-6*, Garden Way Pub) Storey Comm Inc.
Stone, L. Ovejas (Sheep) 1991. 8.95s.p. (*0-86592-915-7*) Rourke Enter.
Stone, Lynn. Sheep. (Illus.). 24p. (gr. k-5). 1990. lib. bdg. 11.94 (*0-86593-038-4*); lib. bdg. 8.95s.p. (*0-685-36313-9*) Rourke Corp.

SHEEP–FICTION

Alda, Arlene. Sheep, Sheep, Sheep: Help Me Fall Asleep. Alda, Arlene, photos by. LC 91-43006. (Illus.). 32p. (ps-2). 1992. pap. 13.50 (*0-385-30791-8*) Doubleday.
Amery, H. The Naughty Sheep. (Illus.). 16p. (ps). 1989. 3.95 (*0-7460-0261-0*, Usborne); lib. bdg. 7.96 (*0-88110-376-4*, Usborne) EDC.
Blanchard, Arlene. The Naughty Lamb. Wells, Tony, illus. LC 88-4098. 32p. (ps-1). 1989. 9.95 (*0-8037-0577-8*) Dial Bks Young.
Bursik, Rose. Zoe's Sheep. 1994. 14.95 (*0-8050-2530-8*) H Holt & Co.
Carrick, Carol. Valentine. Bouma, Paddy, illus. LC 93-35911. 1995. write for info. (*0-395-66554-X*, Clarion Bks) HM.
Demi. Little Baby Lamb. Demi, illus. 12p. (ps). 1993. bds. 3.95 (*0-448-40580-6*, G&D) Putnam Pub Group.
Dunn, Judy. The Little Lamb. Dunn, Phoebe, illus. LC 76-24167. (ps-2). 1978. lib. bdg. 5.99 (*0-394-93455-5*); pap. 2.25 (*0-394-83455-0*) Random Bks Yng Read.
Enderle, Judith R. & Tessler, Stephanie G. Six Creepy Sheep. O'Brien, John, illus. 24p. (ps-1). 1992. PLB 12.95 (*1-56397-092-9*) Boyds Mills Pr.
—Six Creepy Sheep. O'Brien, John, illus. LC 93-7140. 26p. (ps-1). 1993. pap. 4.99 (*0-14-054994-3*, Puffin) Puffin Bks.
—Six Snowy Sheep. O'Brien, John, illus. LC 93-73307. 24p. (ps-1). 1994. 14.95 (*1-56397-138-0*) Boyds Mills Pr.
Ernst, Lisa C. Nattie Parsons' Good-Luck Lamb. (Illus.). 32p. (ps-3). 1990. pap. 3.95 (*0-14-050772-8*, Puffin) Puffin Bks.
Goldthwaite, Howard. The Little Lost Lamb. (Illus.). 6p. 1994. pop-up bk. 3.99 (*1-56476-171-1*, Victor Books) SP Pubns.
Gordon, Jeffie R. Six Sleepy Sheep. O'Brien, John, illus. 24p. (ps-1). 1993. pap. 4.99 (*0-14-054848-3*, Puffin) Puffin Bks.
Hale, Sarah J. Mary Had a Little Lamb. 1992. 3.95 (*0-590-43774-7*, 045, Blue Ribbon Bks) Scholastic Inc.
Hooks, William H. & Brenner, Barbara A. Lion & Lamb, Level 3. Degen, Bruce, illus. (ps-3). 1989. pap. 3.50 (*0-553-34692-X*) Bantam.
—Lion & Lamb: Level 3. Degen, Bruce, illus. (ps-3). 1989. 9.99 (*0-553-05829-0*) Bantam.
Hughes, Francine. A Sheepful of Dollars. Thompson, Dana, illus. LC 93-83722. 32p. (Orig.). (ps-3). 1993. pap. 2.25 (*0-679-85111-9*) Random Bks Yng Read.
Ichikawa, Satomi. Nora's Surprise. Ichikawa, Satomi, illus. LC 92-39308. 32p. (ps-3). 1994. 14.95 (*0-399-22535-8*, Philomel Bks) Putnam Pub Group.
Inkpen, Mick. If I Had a Sheep. Inkpen, Mick, illus. (ps). 1988. 7.95 (*0-316-41888-9*) Little.
—If I Had a Sheep. (ps). 1992. pap. 3.99 (*0-440-40612-9*, Pub. by Yearling Classics) Dell.
Kanno, Wendy. Bags the Lamb. Reese, Bob, illus. (gr. k-2). 1984. 7.95 (*0-89868-165-0*); pap. 2.95 (*0-89868-166-9*) ARO Pub.
Kiser, Kevin. Sherman the Sheep. Barnes-Murphy, Rowan, illus. LC 92-22745. 32p. (gr. k-3). 1994. RSBE 14.95 (*0-02-750825-0*, Macmillan Child Bk) Macmillan Child Grp.
Kitamura, Satoshi. When Sheep Cannot Sleep. LC 86-45000. (Illus.). 32p. (ps up). 1986. 13.00 (*0-374-38311-1*) FS&G.
Krumgold, Joseph. And Now Miguel. Charlot, Jean, illus. LC 53-8415. 245p. (gr. 5 up). 1987. 16.00 (*0-690-09118-4*, Crowell Jr Bks); PLB 15.89 (*0-690-04696-0*, Crowell Jr Bks) HarpC Child Bks.
Laughlin, Charlotte. Where's the Lost Sheep? 1992. 9.99 (*0-8499-0919-8*) Word Inc.
Lenski, Lois. Strawberry Girl. Lenski, Lois, illus. LC 45-7609. 192p. (gr. 4-6). 1945. 16.00 (*0-397-30109-X*, Lipp Jr Bks); PLB 15.89 (*0-397-30110-3*, Lipp Jr Bks) HarpC Child Bks.
Levine, Arthur A. Sheep Dreams. Lanfredi, Judy, illus. LC 91-44929. 32p. (ps-3). 1993. 13.99 (*0-8037-1194-8*); PLB 13.89 (*0-8037-1195-6*) Dial Bks Young.
Lewis, Kim. Emma's Lamb. Lewis, Kim, illus. LC 90-3863. 32p. (ps-1). 1991. SBE 13.95 (*0-02-758821-1*, Four Winds) Macmillan Child Grp.
Little Lost Lamb. LC 92-62559. 20p. (ps). 1993. 4.99 (*0-89577-484-4*, Dist. by Random) RD Assn.
Macaulay, David. BAAA. LC 85-2316. (Illus.). 64p. (gr. 6 up). 1985. 13.45 (*0-395-38948-8*); pap. 4.80 (*0-395-39588-7*) HM.
McGee, Barbara. Counting Sheep. McGee, Barbara, illus. 24p. (gr. k-3). 1991. 12.95 (*1-55037-157-6*, Pub. by Annick CN); pap. 4.95 (*1-55037-160-6*, Pub. by Annick CN) Firefly Bks Ltd.
Mother Goof. The Sheep Who Was Allergic to Wool. Mother Goof, illus. LC 92-60096. 32p. (gr. 3 up). 1992. 8.95 (*0-9623184-1-8*) Sunflower Hill.
Novak, Matt. While the Shepherd Slept. LC 90-7733. (Illus.). 32p. (ps-2). 1991. 13.95 (*0-531-05915-4*); PLB 13.99 (*0-531-08515-5*) Orchard Bks Watts.
O'Brien, Mary. Counting Sheep to Sleep. (ps-3). 1992. 13.95 (*0-316-62206-0*) Little.
Parry, Alan. The Lost Sheep. (Illus.). 24p. (ps-5). 1994. 3.99 (*0-8499-1089-7*) Word Inc.
Paulsen, Gary. The Haymeadow. (gr. 4-7). 1992. 15.95 (*0-385-30621-0*) Doubleday.
Portlock, Rob. Buster the Biker Sheep. Portlock, Rob, illus. LC 93-19201. 32p. (Orig.). (ps-2). 1993. pap. 4.99 (*0-8308-1904-5*, 1904) InterVarsity.
Ray, Sandy. The Lamb. Sytsma, Cheryle, ed. (Illus.). 15p. (Orig.). 1991. pap. write for info. (*1-879068-10-9*) Ray-Ma Natsal.
Roddie, Shen. Mrs. Wolf: A Three-Dimensional Picture Book. Paul, Korky, illus. LC 92-1202. 24p. (gr. k-3). 1993. 13.99 (*0-8037-1300-2*) Dial Bks Young.
Sanders, Scott R. Warm As Wool. LC 91-34987. (Illus.). 32p. (gr. k-5). 1992. RSBE 14.95 (*0-02-778139-9*, Bradbury Pr) Macmillan Child Grp.
Scamell, Ragnhild. Three Bags Full. Hobson, Sally, illus. LC 92-50882. 32p. (ps-1). 1993. 14.95 (*0-531-05486-1*) Orchard Bks Watts.
Shaw, Elizabeth. Little Black Sheep. 1985. 7.95 (*0-86278-102-7*, Pub. by O'Brien Press Ltd Eire) Dufour.
Shaw, Nancy. Sheep in a Jeep. Apple, Margot, illus. LC 86-3101. 32p. (ps-k). 1986. 13.95 (*0-395-41105-X*) HM.
—Sheep in a Shop. Apple, Margot, illus. LC 90-4139. 32p. (ps-k). 1991. 13.45 (*0-395-53681-2*) HM.
—Sheep on a Ship. Apple, Margot, illus. (ps). 1989. 13.45 (*0-395-48160-0*) HM.
—Sheep on a Ship. (ps-3). 1992. pap. 3.80 (*0-395-64376-7*) HM.
—Sheep Out to Eat. Apple, Margot, illus. LC 91-38425. 32p. (ps-1). 1992. 13.45 (*0-395-61128-8*) HM.
—Sheep Take a Hike. Apple, Margot, illus. LC 93-30725. 1994. 13.95 (*0-395-68394-7*) HM.
Sopko, Eugen. The White Raven & the Black Sheep. Sopko, Eugen, illus. Graves, Helen, tr. from GER. LC 91-7254. (Illus.). 32p. (gr. k-3). 1991. 14.95 (*1-55858-118-9*) North-South Bks NYC.
Strete, Craig K. Big Thunder Magic. Brown, Craig, illus. LC 89-34613. 32p. (ps up). 1990. 12.95 (*0-688-08853-8*); PLB 12.88 (*0-688-08854-6*) Greenwillow.
Stubblefield, Fern. Tim & His Lamp. 52p. (gr. k-6). pap. 0.40 (*0-686-29170-0*); pap. 1.00 3 copies (*0-686-29171-9*) Faith Pub Hse.
Sundgaard, Arnold. The Lamb & the Butterfly. Carle, Eric, illus. LC 88-60092. 32p. (ps-2). 1988. 14.95 (*0-531-05779-8*); PLB 14.99 (*0-531-08379-9*) Orchard Bks Watts.
Taylor, William. Agnes the Sheep. 176p. (gr. 5 up). 1991. 13.95 (*0-590-43365-2*, Scholastic Hardcover) Scholastic Inc.
—Agnes the Sheep. (gr. 4-7). 1994. pap. 3.25 (*0-590-43364-4*) Scholastic Inc.
Wallace, Brooks B. Argyle. Sandford, John, illus. LC 91-76021. 32p. (ps-3). 1992. 13.95 (*1-56397-043-0*) Boyds Mills Pr.
Wellington, Monica. The Sheep Follow. Wellington, Monica, illus. LC 91-3420. 32p. (ps-k). 1992. 13.00 (*0-525-44837-3*, DCB) Dutton Child Bks.
Willis, Patricia. Out of the Storm. LC 94-2133. Date not set. write for info. (*0-395-68708-X*, Clarion Bks) HM.
Wood, A. J. Sunny Stories: The Sheep that Liked to Sing. 1989. 1.98 (*0-671-09892-6*) S&S Trade.
Yates, Elizabeth. Mountain Born. Unwin, Nora S., illus. LC 92-40545. 128p. (gr. 3-7). 1993. pap. 6.95 (*0-8027-7402-4*) Walker & Co.

SHELLFISH

see Mollusks

SHELLS

see also Mollusks

Abbott, R. Tucker. Seashells of North America. Zim, Herbert S., ed. Sandstrom, George F., illus. (gr. 9 up). 1969. (Golden Pr); pap. write for info (*0-307-13657-4*) Western Pub.
—Seashells of the World. Rev. ed. Zim, Herbert S., ed. Sandstrom, George F. & Sandstrom, Marita, illus. (gr. 9 up). 1985. pap. write for info. (*0-307-24410-5*, Golden Pr) Western Pub.
Arthur, Alex. Shell. Einsiedel, Andreas, photos by. LC 88-13449. (Illus.). 64p. (gr. 5 up). 1989. 16.00 (*0-394-82256-0*); lib. bdg. 16.99 (*0-394-92256-5*) Knopf Bks Yng Read.
Benanti, Carol. Seashells. (Illus.). 32p. (gr. 3 up). 1994. pap. 10.00 (*0-679-85071-6*) Random Bks Yng Read.
Cate, Jean M. & Raskin, Selma. It's Easy to Say Crepidula! A Phonetic Guide to Pronunciation of the Scientific Names of Sea Shells. Vasquez, Gina, illus. 158p. (Orig.). (gr. 5-7). 1986. pap. 19.95 (*0-938509-00-4*) Pretty Penny Pr.
Coldrey, Jennifer. Shells. LC 92-54310. (Illus.). 64p. (gr. 3 up). 1993. 9.95 (*1-56458-229-9*) Dorling Kindersley.
Davies, Kay, et al. My Shell. Pragoff, Fiona, photos by. (Illus.). 32p. (gr. 1 up). 1995. PLB 17.27 (*0-8368-1188-7*) Gareth Stevens Inc.
Fichter, George S. Starfish, Seashells, & Crabs. Sandstrom, George, illus. 36p. (gr. k-3). 1993. 4.95 (*0-307-11430-9*, 11430, Golden Pr) Western Pub.
Florian, Douglas. Discovering Seashells. Florian, Douglas, illus. LC 86-11903. 32p. (ps-2). 1986. SBE 13.95 (*0-684-18740-X*, Scribners Young Read) Macmillan Child Grp.
Fredlee. Magic of Sea Shells. rev. ed. (Illus.). 36p. (gr. 1-3). 1985. pap. 3.50 (*0-685-47437-2*) Windward Pub.
Gattis, L. S., III. Shells for Pathfinders: A Basic Youth Enrichment Skill Honor Packet. (Illus.). 26p. (Orig.). (gr. 5 up). 1989. pap. 5.00 tchr's. ed. (*0-936241-47-0*) Cheetah Pub.
Saunders, Graham. Shells. (Illus.). 64p. (gr. 8 up). 1993. pap. 4.95 (*0-86020-454-5*, Usborne) EDC.
Seashells. (gr. k-5). 1991. write for info. (*0-307-12854-7*, Golden Pr) Western Pub.
Selsam, Millicent E. & Hunt, Joyce. A First Look at Seashells. Springer, Hariett, illus. LC 83-5876. 32p. (gr. 1-3). 1983. PLB 12.85 (*0-8027-6503-3*) Walker & Co.
Shells. LC 91-60532. (Illus.). 24p. (ps-3). 1991. 8.95 (*1-879431-10-6*) Dorling Kindersley.
Zoehfeld, Kathleen W. What Lives in a Shell? Davie, Helen K., illus. LC 93-12428. 32p. (ps-1). 1994. 15.00 (*0-06-022998-5*); PLB 14.89 (*0-06-022999-3*) HarpC Child Bks.

SHEPHERDS–FICTION

Caudill, Rebecca. A Certain Small Shepherd. (gr. k-6). 1987. pap. 2.99 (*0-440-41194-7*, YB) Dell.
Franklin, Kristine L. The Shepherd Boy (El Nino Pastor) Ada, Alma F., tr. Kastner, Jill, illus. LC 93-34823. 40p. (ps-1). 1994. SBE, English ed. 14.95 (*0-689-31809-X*, Atheneum Child Bk); SBE, Spanish ed. 14.95 (*0-689-31918-5*, Atheneum Child Bk) Macmillan Child Grp.
Haseley, Dennis. The Cave of Snores. Beddows, Eric, illus. LC 85-48845. 40p. (gr. k-4). 1987. HarpC Child Bks.
Hort, Lenny. Goatherd & the Shepherdess. Bloom, Lloyd, illus. LC 93-18178. 1994. 14.99 (*0-8037-1352-5*); PLB 14.89 (*0-8037-1353-3*) Dial Bks Young.
Hunt, Angela E. Singing Shepherd. (Illus.). 32p. (ps-6). 1992. 13.95 (*0-7459-2224-4*) Lion USA.
Laughlin, Charlotte. Where's the Lost Sheep? 1992. 9.99 (*0-8499-0919-8*) Word Inc.
Lewis, Kim. The Shepherd Boy. Lewis, Kim, illus. LC 89-23679. 32p. (ps-1). 1990. SBE 13.95 (*0-02-758581-6*, Four Winds) Macmillan Child Grp.
Mehl, Ron, Jr. & Gundersen, Sandy. The Littlest Shepherd. (Illus.). 40p. (ps-3). 1991. pap. 4.99 (*0-88070-449-7*, Gold & Honey) Questar Pubs.
Rowzee, Janet Z. & Watson, James A. The Song of the Shepherd Boy. 20p. (gr. 4-8). 1993. pap. 6.95 saddle bdg. (*0-9638941-0-2*) Eagles Three.
Tharlet, Eve. Simon & the Holy Night. Clements, Andrew, tr. (Illus.). 28p. (gr. k up). 1991. pap. 14.95 (*0-88708-185-1*) Picture Bk Studio.
—Simon & the Holy Night. Clements, Andrew, adapted by. Tharlet, Eve, illus. LC 93-306. 1993. 4.95 (*0-88708-324-2*) Picture Bk Studio.
Wright, Harold B. Shepherd of the Hills. rev. ed. Phillips, Michael R., ed. LC 88-10311. 256p. 1988. pap. 7.99 (*0-87123-916-7*) Bethany Hse.

SHIPBUILDING

see also Boatbuilding; Ships; Steamboats

SHIPPING–FICTION

Goudge, Elizabeth. I Saw Three Ships. (Orig.). 1990. pap. 2.95 (*0-440-40367-7*, Pub. by Yearling Classics) Dell.
Slater, Teddy. Shopping with Samantha. Hearn, Diane D., illus. 24p. (ps-1). 1991. 4.95 (*0-671-72984-5*); PLB 6.95 (*0-671-72983-7*) Silver Pr.

SHIPS

see also Boats and Boating; Navigation; Sailing; Steamboats; Submarines; Warships

Asimov, Isaac. How Do Big Ships Float? (Illus.). 24p. (gr. 1-8). 1992. PLB 15.93 (*0-8368-0802-9*); PLB 15.93 s.p. (*0-685-61488-3*) Gareth Stevens Inc.
Atkinson, I. The Viking Ships. LC 77-17510. (Illus.). 48p. (gr. 7 up). 1979. pap. 8.95 (*0-521-21951-5*) Cambridge U Pr.

Barton, Byron. Boats. Barton, Byron, illus. LC 85-47900. 32p. (ps-k). 1986. 4.95 (*0-694-00059-0*, Crowell Jr Bks); PLB 13.89 (*0-690-04536-0*) HarpC Child Bks.
Baxter, Leon. Famous Ships. (gr. 2-5). 1993. pap. 7.95 (*0-8249-8612-1*, Ideals Child) Hambleton-Hill.
Biesty, Stephen & Platt, Richard. Cross Sections: Man-of-War. Biesty, Steven, illus. LC 92-21227. 32p. (gr. 3 up). 1993. 16.95 (*1-56458-321-X*) Dorling Kindersley.
Blackman, Steven. Ships & Shipwrecks. (Illus.). 32p. (gr. 5-7). 1993. PLB 11.90 (*0-531-14278-7*) Watts.
Buschini, Henny & Buschini, Luciano. The Ship in the Field. Buschini, Henny & Buschini, Luciano, illus. LC 77-174719. 32p. (gr. k-3). 1973. 6.95 (*0-87592-045-4*) Scroll Pr.
Canright, David. Ships & the River. Cambell, Janet, ed. Canright, David, intro. by. (Illus.). 32p. (gr. 2-6). 1975. pap. 2.00 (*0-913344-22-2*) South St Sea Mus.
Carter, Katherine. Ships & Seaports. LC 82-4463. (Illus.). (gr. k-4). 1982. pap. 4.95 (*0-516-41656-1*) Childrens.
Chant, Chris. Sailing Ships. Batchelor, John, illus. LC 88-28706. 63p. (gr. 3 up). 1990. PLB 16.95 (*1-85435-091-9*) Marshall Cavendish.
Cooper, J. Boats & Ships. 1991. 8.95s.p. (*0-86592-492-9*) Rourke Enter.
—Botes y Barcos (Boats & Ships) 1991. 8.95s.p. (*0-86592-474-0*) Rourke Enter.
Emert, Phyllis R. Mysteries of Ships & Planes. 128p. 1990. pap. 2.50 (*0-8125-9427-4*) Tor Bks.
Gibbons, Gail. Boat Book. Gibbons, Gail, illus. LC 82-15851. 32p. (ps-3). 1983. reinforced bdg. 15.95 (*0-8234-0478-1*); pap. 5.95 (*0-8234-0709-8*) Holiday.
Hoare, Robert. Travel by Sea. Unstead, R. J., ed. (gr. 7 up). 1975. 14.95 (*0-7136-0119-1*) Dufour.
Humble, Richard. Ships. Cornwall, Peter, illus. LC 93-19705. 32p. (gr. 4-6). 1993. PLB 19.97 (*0-8114-6158-0*) Raintree Steck-V.
—Ships: Sailors & the Sea. LC 91-6805. (Illus.). 48p. (gr. 5-8). 1991. 13.95 (*0-531-15234-0*) Watts.
Hutchinson, Gillian. The Story of Boats. James, John, illus. LC 91-39010. 32p. (gr. 1-4). 1993. PLB 11.89 (*0-8167-2705-8*); pap. text ed. 3.95 (*0-8167-2706-6*) Troll Assocs.
Jeunesse, Gallimard, created by. Boats. Broutin, Christian, illus. LC 92-41414. 1993. 11.95 (*0-590-47131-7*) Scholastic Inc.
Kindersley, Dorling. Ships & Boats. LC 91-25687. (Illus.). 24p. (ps-k). 1992. pap. 7.95 POB (*0-689-71566-8*, Aladdin) Macmillan Child Grp.
Let's Discover Ships & Boats. LC 80-22959. (Illus.). 80p. (gr. k-6). 1983. per set 199.00 (*0-8172-1774-6*); 14.95 ea. Raintree Steck-V.
Matthews, Rupert. Let's Look At Ships & Boats. LC 89-9710. (ps-3). 1990. PLB 11.40 (*0-531-18322-X*, Pub. by Bookwright Pr) Watts.
Richardson, Joy. Ships. LC 93-49730. (Illus.). 1994. write for info. (*0-531-14326-0*) Watts.
Riegel, Martin P. The Ships of the Orange Coast. Riegel, Martin P., illus. LC 88-92522. 40p. (Orig.). (gr. 9 up). 1988. PLB 11.00 (*0-944871-08-9*); pap. 4.75 (*0-944871-09-7*) Riegel Pub.
Rutland, Jonathan. Amazing Fact Book of Ships. (Illus.). 32p. (gr. 4-8). 1987. PLB 14.95 (*0-87191-849-8*) Creative Ed.
Ships. (Illus.). 32p. (gr. 1-4). 1994. pap. 5.95 (*1-56458-521-2*) Dorling Kindersley.
Ships & Sailing. LC 91-60900. (Illus.). 64p. (gr. 6 up). 1991. 14.95 (*1-879431-20-3*); PLB 15.99 (*1-879431-35-1*) Dorling Kindersley.
Spizzirri Publishing Co. Staff. Ships: An Educational Coloring Book. Spizzirri, Linda, ed. Fuller, Glenn & Spizzirri, Peter M., illus. 32p. (gr. 1-8). 1981. pap. 1.75 (*0-86545-035-8*) Spizzirri.
Thomas, David A. How Ships Are Made. LC 89-31328. (Illus.). 32p. (gr. 4-8). 1989. 12.95x (*0-8160-2040-X*) Facts on File.
Walmer, M. Frigates. (Illus.). 48p. (gr. 3-8). 1989. lib. bdg. 18.60 (*0-86625-082-4*); 13.95s.p. (*0-685-58643-X*) Rourke Corp.

SHIPS–FICTION

Brett, Bernard. The Fighting Ship. Batchelor, John & Lapper, Ivan, illus. 96p. (gr. 7 up). 1988. 17.95 (*0-19-273155-6*) OUP.
Cabral, Olga. So Proudly She Sailed. (Illus.). (gr. 5-9). 1981. 13.45 (*0-395-31670-7*) HM.
Crawford, F. Marion. Nightmare Ship. Richardson, I. M., adapted by. Toulmin-Rothe, Ann, illus. LC 81-21805. 32p. (gr. 5-10). 1982. PLB 10.79 (*0-89375-632-6*); pap. text ed. 2.95 (*0-89375-633-4*) Troll Assocs.
Defoe, Daniel. Robinson Crusoe. Lindskoog, Kathryn, ed. (gr. 3-7). 1991. pap. 4.99 (*0-88070-438-1*, Gold & Honey) Questar Pubs.
Fredeking, Jean T. My Trip n a Ship. 16p. 1987. pap. 25.00x (*0-317-59267-X*, Pub. by A H Stockwell England) St Mut.
Hawes, Charles B. The Dark Frigate. rev. ed. Chappell, Warren, illus. (gr. 7 up). 1971. 18.95 (*0-316-35096-6*, Joy St Bks) Little.
Lattimore, Deborah N. Lady with the Ship on Her Head. (ps-3). 1992. pap. 4.95 (*0-15-243526-3*) HarBrace.
Lewis, J. Patrick. The Fat-Cats at Sea. Chess, Victoria, illus. 40p. (ps-3). 1994. 15.00 (*0-679-82639-4*, Apple Soup Bks); PLB 15.99 (*0-679-92639-9*, Apple Soup Bks) Knopf Bks Yng Read.
Ryan, John. Pugwash & the Ghost Ship. Ryan, John, illus. LC 68-23218. (gr. k-3). 1968. 21.95 (*0-87599-146-7*) S G Phillips.
Winter, Jeanette. The Christmas Tree Ship. LC 93-36341. (Illus.). 32p. (ps up). 1994. PLB 14.95 (*0-399-22693-1*, Philomel Bks) Putnam Pub Group.

SHIPS–HISTORY

Berenstain, Michael. The Ship Book. (Illus.). (gr. k-3). 1978. 6.95 (*0-679-20449-0*) McKay.
Burns, Phillys B. Iron Lady at Sea: From Shipyard to Voyage: A Story of the Great Iron-Hulled Sailing Ship, Star of India. (Illus.). 108p. (Orig.). 1988. pap. 6.95 (*0-685-20061-2*) Cove Pr CA.
Grady, Sean M. Ships: Crossing the World's Oceans. LC 92-9162. (Illus.). 96p. (gr. 5-8). 1992. 15.95 (*1-56006-220-7*) Lucent Bks.
Humble, Richard. Ships: Sailors & the Sea. LC 91-6805. (Illus.). 48p. (gr. 5-8). 1991. 13.95 (*0-531-15234-0*) Watts.
Kentley, Eric. Boat. Stevenson, Jim, photos by. LC 91-53136. (Illus.). 64p. (gr. 5 up). 1992. 16.00 (*0-679-81678-X*); PLB 16.99 (*0-679-91678-4*) Knopf Bks Yng Read.
Lord, Walter. Night to Remember. (gr. 6-12). 1983. pap. 4.99 (*0-553-27827-4*) Bantam.
Macaulay, David. Ship. (gr. 4-7). 1993. 19.95 (*0-395-52439-3*) HM.
Mitchell, John C. Great Lakes & Great Ships: An Illustrated History for Children. Woodruff, Thomas R., illus. 52p. (gr. 2-7). 1991. 15.95 (*0-9621466-1-7*) Suttons Bay Pubns.
Riegel, Martin P. Historic Ships of Hawaii. LC 88-92776. (Illus.). 44p. (Orig.). 1988. 11.00 (*0-944871-12-7*); pap. 4.95 (*0-944871-13-5*) Riegel Pub.
—Historic Ships of Oregon. LC 88-92771. (Illus.). 48p. (Orig.). 1988. 11.00 (*0-944871-14-3*); pap. 4.95 (*0-944871-15-1*) Riegel Pub.
—Historic Ships of Washington. LC 88-63929. (Illus.). 52p. (Orig.). 1988. 11.00 (*0-944871-16-X*); pap. 4.95 (*0-944871-17-8*) Riegel Pub.
—The Ships of the California Gold Rush. LC 88-92421. (Illus.). 48p. (Orig.). 1988. 11.00 (*0-944871-11-9*); pap. 4.95 (*0-685-24979-4*) Riegel Pub.

SHIPWRECKS

see also Salvage; Survival (After Airplane Accidents, Shipwrecks, etc.);
also names of wrecked ships

Blackman, Steven. Ships & Shipwrecks. (Illus.). 32p. (gr. 5-7). 1993. PLB 11.90 (*0-531-14278-7*) Watts.
Fine, John C. Sunken Ships & Treasures. LC 86-3652. (Illus.). 128p. (gr. 3 up). 1986. SBE 16.95 (*0-689-31280-6*, Atheneum Child Bk) Macmillan Child Grp.
Geography Department Staff. Sunk! Exploring Underwater Archaeology. LC 93-42008. 1994. lib. bdg. write for info. (*0-8225-3205-0*, Runestone Pr) Lerner Pubns.
Hawcock, David. Shipwrecks: A Three-Dimensional Exploration. Walton, Garry, illus. 24p. (gr. 2 up). 1993. 15.95 (*0-694-00452-9*, Festival) HarpC Child Bks.
Humphrey, Kathryn L. Shipwrecks: Terror & Treasure. LC 91-16962. (Illus.). 64p. (gr. 5-8). 1991. PLB 12.90 (*0-531-20031-0*) Watts.
Kent, Deborah. The Titanic. LC 93-12688. (Illus.). 32p. (gr. 3-6). 1993. PLB 12.30 (*0-516-06672-2*); pap. 3.95 (*0-516-46672-0*) Childrens.
Macaulay, David. Ship. (gr. 4-7). 1993. 19.95 (*0-395-52439-3*) HM.
Nottridge, Rhoda. Sea Disasters. LC 93-6830. 48p. (gr. 4-6). 1993. 15.95 (*1-56847-084-3*) Thomson Lrning.
Rathe, Gustave. The Wreck of the Barque Stefano off the North West Cape of Australia in 1875. (Illus.). 160p. 1992. 17.00 (*0-374-38585-8*) FS&G.

SHIPWRECKS–FICTION

Brink, Carol R. Baby Island. Sewell, Helen, illus. LC 92-45577. 160p. (gr. 3-7). 1993. pap. 3.95 (*0-689-71751-2*, Aladdin) Macmillan Child Grp.
Conrad, Pam. The Lost Sailor. Egielski, Richard, illus. LC 91-39640. 32p. (gr. k-4). 1992. 15.00 (*0-06-021695-6*); PLB 14.89 (*0-06-021696-4*) HarpC Child Bks.
Crofford, Emily. Born in the Year of Courage. 184p. (gr. 4-6). 1991. PLB 19.95 (*0-87614-679-5*) Carolrhoda Bks.
Defoe, Daniel. Robinson Crusoe. (gr. 6 up). 1964. pap. 2.25 (*0-8049-0022-1*, CL-22) Airmont.
—Robinson Crusoe. Ward, Lynd, illus. (gr. 4-6). 1963. 13.95 (*0-448-06021-3*, G&D) Putnam Pub Group.
—Robinson Crusoe. 1993. 13.95 (*0-679-42819-4*, Everymans Lib) Knopf.
Grimm, Jacob & Grimm, Wilhelm K. The Elves & the Shoemaker. Watts, Bernadette, illus. LC 85-63306. 32p. (gr. k-2). 1986. 14.95 (*1-55858-035-2*) North-South Bks NYC.
Martin, Les. Young Indiana Jones & the Titanic Adventure. 132p. (Orig.). (gr. 3-7). 1993. pap. 3.50 (*0-679-84925-4*, Bullseye Bks) Random Bks Yng Read.
Marvin, Isabel R. Shipwrecked on Padre Island. Miller, Lyle L., illus. 160p. (gr. 4 up). 1993. 14.95 (*0-937460-83-4*) Hendrick-Long.
Paton Walsh, Jill. Grace. 256p. (gr. 7 up). 1992. 16.00 (*0-374-32758-0*) FS&G.
Spier, Peter. Father, May I Come? LC 92-31328. 1993. 13.95 (*0-385-30935-X*) Doubleday.
Taylor, Theodore. Timothy of the Cay: A Prequel-Sequel. 192p. (gr. 4-7). 1993. 13.95 (*0-15-288358-4*, HB Juv Bks) HarBrace.
Treece, Henry. Further Adventures of Robinson Crusoe. Nickless, Will, illus. LC 58-9623. (gr. 7-11). 1958. 21.95 (*0-87599-116-5*) S G Phillips.
Von Tempski, Armine. Judy of the Islands: A Story of the South Seas. Burger, Carl, illus. LC 92-24539. viii, 280p. 1992. pap. 14.95 (*0-918024-97-8*) Ox Bow.
Wandelmaier, Roy. Shipwrecked on Mystery Island. Pinkney, Brian J. LC 85-2531. (Illus.). 112p. (gr. 3-6). 1985. lib. bdg. 9.49 (*0-8167-0533-X*); pap. text ed. 2.95 (*0-8167-0534-8*) Troll Assocs.
Warner, Gertrude C. The Ghost Ship Mystery. Tang, Charles, illus. LC 93-40889. (gr. 4-7). 1994. 10.95 (*0-8075-2856-0*); pap. 3.95 (*0-8075-2855-2*) A Whitman.
Wyss, Johann. Swiss Family Robinson. Ward, Lynd & Gregori, Lee, illus. (gr. 4-6). 1949. 14.95 (*0-448-06022-1*, G&D) Putnam Pub Group.

SHOES AND SHOE INDUSTRY

Badt, Karin L. On Your Feet! LC 94-11651. (Illus.). 32p. (gr. 3-7). 1994. PLB 17.20 (*0-516-08189-6*); pap. 5.95 (*0-516-48189-4*) Childrens.
Barnes, Lilly. Lace Them Up. Fernandes, Eugenie, illus. 32p. (ps-2). 1992. 8.95 (*1-56282-282-9*) Hyprn Child.
Dorros, Arthur. Alligator Shoes. Dorros, Arthur, illus. LC 82-2409. 24p. (ps-k). 1988. pap. 3.95 (*0-525-44428-9*) Dutton Child Bks.
Havill, Juanita. Jamaica & Brianna. O'Brien, Anne S., illus. LC 92-36508. 1993. 13.95 (*0-395-64489-5*) HM.
Miller, Margaret. Whose Shoe? LC 90-38491. (Illus.). 40p. (ps up). 1991. 13.95 (*0-688-10008-2*); PLB 13.88 (*0-688-10009-0*) Greenwillow.
Nayer, Judy. Who Wears Shoes? Rader, Laura, illus. 16p. (ps-2). 1994. pap. text ed. 14.95 (*1-56784-303-4*) Newbridge Comms.
Petty, Kate. New Shoes. Barber, Ed, photos by. (Illus.). 32p. (gr. 2 up). 1992. bds. 12.95 (*0-7136-3483-9*, Pub. by A&C Black UK) Talman.
Strauss, Lucy. The Story of Shoes. (Illus.). 32p. (gr. 1-4). 1989. PLB 18.99 (*0-8172-3534-5*); pap. 3.95 (*0-8114-6732-5*) Raintree Steck-V.
Tafuri, Nancy. Two New Sneakers. LC 87-8418. (Illus.). 12p. (ps). 1988. bds. 3.95 (*0-688-07462-6*) Greenwillow.
Young, Robert. Sneakers: The Shoes We Choose. LC 90-26473. (Illus.). 64p. (gr. 3 up). 1991. text ed. 14.95 RSBE (*0-87518-460-X*, Dillon) Macmillan Child Grp.

SHOOTING

see also Hunting

Boy Scouts of America Staff. Varsity Shooting Sports. (Illus.). 87p. 1990. pap. 3.15 (*0-8395-3457-4*, 3457) BSA.

SHOOTING STARS

see Meteors

SHOPPER'S GUIDES

see Consumer Education; Shopping

SHOPPING

see also Consumer Education

Milios, Rita. Shopping Savvy. Rosen, Ruth, ed. (gr. 7-12). 1992. 13.95 (*0-8239-1455-0*) Rosen Group.
Oliver, Stephen, photos by. Shopping. LC 90-23567. (Illus.). 24p. (ps-k). 1991. 7.00 (*0-679-81803-0*) Random Bks Yng Read.
Shopping. (Illus.). (ps). 3.50 (*0-7214-1120-7*) Ladybird Bks.
Tucker, Sian. Nursery Board: Shopping. (ps-2). 1994. pap. 2.95 (*0-671-88262-7*, Little Simon) S&S Trade.
Washington, Dolores E. Begin Basic Budget Saving Shopping Spending, Vol. I. 13p. (gr. 11 up). 1989. wkbk. 2.50x (*0-685-26101-8*) Dew Educational.

SHOPPING–FICTION

Aylesworth, Jim. McGraw's Emporium. 1995. write for info. (*0-8050-3192-8*) H Holt & Co.
Barnett, Ada, et al. Eddycat Goes Shopping with Becky Bunny. Hoffmann, Mark, illus. LC 93-56884. 32p. (gr. 1 up). 1993. Repr. of 1991 ed. PLB 17.27 incl. tchr's. guide (*0-8368-0947-5*) Gareth Stevens Inc.
Bates, Artie A. Ragsale. Chapman-Crane, Jeff, illus. LC 94-17366. (gr. 1-8). 1995. write for info. (*0-395-70030-2*) HM.
Day, Alexandra. Carl Goes Shopping. (Illus.). (gr. 3 up). 1989. 12.95 (*0-374-31110-2*) FS&G.
Edwards, Linda S. The Downtown Day. Edwards, Linda S., illus. LC 82-4645. 48p. (gr. k-3). 1983. Pantheon.
French, Vivian. Little Tiger Goes Shopping. Cooke, Andy, illus. LC 92-43771. 24p. (gr. 3 up). 1993. 3.99 (*1-56402-263-3*) Candlewick Pr.
Fyleman, Rose. Fairy Went A-Marketing. LC 86-4468. (Illus.). 24p. (ps-1). 1990. pap. 3.95 (*0-525-44556-0*, DCB) Dutton Child Bks.
Grossman, Bill. Tommy at the Grocery Store. Chess, Victoria, illus. LC 88-35756. 32p. (ps-2). 1989. 13.00 (*0-06-022408-8*) HarpC Child Bks.
Haynes, Betsy. Mall Mania. (gr. 4-7). 1991. pap. 2.95 (*0-553-15852-X*) Bantam.
Hutchins, Pat. Don't Forget the Bacon! LC 75-17935. (Illus.). 32p. (gr. k-3). 1976. 13.95 (*0-688-06787-5*); PLB 14.93 (*0-688-06788-3*) Greenwillow.
Lobel, Arnold. On Market Street. Lobel, Anita, illus. LC 80-21418. 40p. (gr. k-3). 1981. 14.00 (*0-688-80309-1*); PLB 13.93 (*0-688-84309-3*); Greenwillow.
Loomis, Christine. At the Mall. Poydar, Nancy, illus. 1994. 14.95 (*0-590-72832-6*); pap. 4.95 (*0-590-49490-2*) Scholastic Inc.
Matthews, Cecily. Mr. Clutterbus. Hunnam, Lucinda, illus. LC 92-34257. 1993. 4.25 (*0-383-03642-9*) SRA Schl Grp.
Oxenbury, Helen. Shopping Trip. LC 81-69274. 14p. (ps-k). 1982. bds. 3.50 (*0-8037-7939-9*) Dial Bks Young.

Peck, Richard. Secrets of the Shopping Mall. 192p. (gr. k-6). 1989. pap. 3.99 (*0-440-40270-0*, LFL); pap. 3.99 (*0-440-98099-2*) Dell.
Ross, Christine. Lily & the Present. Ross, Christine, illus. LC 91-41134. 28p. (ps-3). 1992. 13.95 (*0-395-61127-X*) HM.
Ross, Pat. M & M & the Big Bag. 48p. (ps-3). 1985. pap. 3.99 (*0-14-031852-6*, Puffin) Puffin Bks.
—M & M & the Big Bag I Am Reading Book. Hafner, Marilyn, illus. LC 80-23299. 48p. (gr. 1-4). 1981. 6.95 (*0-394-84340-1*) Pantheon.
Shapiro, Arnold. Shopping Trip. (ps-3). 1992. pap. 12.95 (*0-8167-2747-3*) Troll Assocs.
Shaw, Nancy. Sheep in a Shop. Apple, Margot, illus. LC 90-4139. 32p. (ps-k). 1991. 13.45 (*0-395-53681-2*) HM.
Weiss, Monica. Shopping Spree: Identifying Shapes. Berlin, Rosemary, illus. LC 91-3986. 24p. (gr. k-2). 1992. PLB 10.59 (*0-8167-2490-3*); pap. text ed. 2.95 (*0-8167-2491-1*) Troll Assocs.
Yee, Patrick. Little Buddy Goes Shopping. LC 92-16432. (ps). 1993. 10.95 (*0-670-84804-2*) Viking Child Bks.

SHORT STORIES

Abeel, Samantha. Reach for the Moon: What Once was White. Murphy, Charles R., illus. LC 93-46417. 48p. 1994. 17.95 (*1-57025-013-8*) Pfeifer-Hamilton.
Accorsi, William. Short Short Short Stories. LC 90-48179. (Illus.). 32p. (ps up). 1991. 13.95 (*0-688-10180-1*); PLB 13.88 (*0-688-10181-X*) Greenwillow.
Ada, Alma F., et al. Choices & Other Stories from the Caribbean. LC 92-43134. 1993. pap. 6.95 (*0-377-00257-7*) Friendship Pr.
Ahlberg, Janet & Ahlberg, Allan. The Clothes Horse & Other Stories. (Illus.). 32p. (ps-3). 1992. pap. 4.99 (*0-14-032907-2*) Puffin Bks.
Aiken, Joan. A Fit of Shivers: Tales for Late at Night. LC 92-6130. 144p. (gr. 6 up). 1992. 15.00 (*0-385-30691-1*) Delacorte.
—The Last Slice of Rainbow: And Other Stories. Berenzy, Alix, illus. LC 87-45271. 160p. (gr. 3-7). 1988. HarpC Child Bks.
Aleichem, Sholom. Holiday Tales of Sholom Aleichem. Shevrin, Aliza, tr. DiGrazia, Thomas, illus. LC 79-753. 145p. (gr. 5 up). 1985. pap. 5.95 (*0-689-71034-8*, Aladdin) Macmillan Child Grp.
Alexander, Liza. When Oscar Was a Little Grouch & Other Good-Night Stories. (Illus.). 24p. (ps-1). 1989. write for info. (Pub. by Golden Bks) Western Pub.
Alexander, Liza, et al. The Sesame Street Treasury: Featuring Jim Henson's Sesame Street Muppets. Chartier, Normand, et al, illus. LC 93-8326. Date not set. write for info. (*0-679-84655-7*); PLB write for info. (*0-679-94655-1*) Random.
Allen, Steve & Meadows, Jayne. Shakin' Loose with Mother Goose. Bullock, Kathleen, illus. 128p. (ps-2). 1987. 4 bks. & 2 forty minute tapes in gift box ed. 19.95 (*0-89411-010-1*) Kids Matter.
Allen, Wynell. Nature Stories for Children. 1993. 6.95 (*0-8062-4454-2*) Carlton.
—Tales for Little Children. (Illus.). 32p. 1992. pap. 3.95 (*0-8059-3316-6*) Dorrance.
Alpha Pyramis Publishing Staff. Story Time Stories That Rhyme, Vol. 1: Fish Convention, Rainbow, Miss Divine Sunshine & Others. 106p. (gr. 4-12). 1992. binder 27.95 (*0-913597-99-6*, Pub. by Alpha Pyramis) Prosperity & Profits.
American Heritage Magazine Editorial Staff. The American Heritage Junior Library, 20 vols. (gr. 5-12). 1989. 14.95 (*0-8167-1536-X*) Troll Assocs.
Amery, H. First Stories. Cartwright, Stephen, illus. 48p. 1988. 8.95 (*0-7460-0191-6*) EDC.
Andersen, Hans Christian. Twelve Tales. Blegvad, Erik, tr. & illus. LC 93-6927. 96p. (gr. 3-7). 1994. SBE 18.95 (*0-689-50584-1*, M K McElderry) Macmillan Child Grp.
Arnold, Arnold. Pictures & Stories from Forgotten Children's Books. (Illus.). 170p. (Orig.). (gr. k-6). 1970. pap. 7.50 (*0-486-22041-9*) Dover.
Asch, Frank. George's Store. Wiseman, Bernard, illus. LC 82-22298. 48p. (ps-3). 1983. 5.95 (*0-8193-1101-4*); PLB 5.95 (*0-8193-1102-2*) Parents.
Babbitt, Natalie. The Devil's Other Storybook. LC 86-32760. (Illus.). 112p. (gr. 3 up). 1987. 13.00 (*0-374-31767-4*) FS&G.
—Devil's Other Storybook. (gr. 4-7). 1989. pap. 3.50 (*0-374-41704-0*) FS&G.
—The Devil's Storybook. Babbitt, Natalie, illus. LC 74-5488. 102p. (gr. 3-7). 1984. pap. 3.95 (*0-374-41708-3*) FS&G.
Baisden, E. Bertram, et al. Anthology of Caribbean Short Stories. 125p. (Orig.). (gr. 7-12). 1989. pap. text ed. write for info. Caribbean Rsch Ctr.

Ball, Douglas H., et al. Stories Worth Reading. Bruns, Stan & Capron, Michael W., illus. 192p. (Orig.). (gr. 8-11). 1990. pap. 7.00 (*0-9621844-0-3*) Printemps Bks.
Companion books, two anthologies of inspired original stories by both highly regarded, established writers & brilliant new authors. These fresh new stories, selected by experienced teachers, respond to a wide range of young reader interests. Action stories of adventure, animals, surprise, nostalgia, fantasy, heroic deeds, & modern stories based on African proverbs "grab" & hold attention. Reading expert's comment: "Your anthologies are truly worth reading. I would like to see them in libraries & personal collections. They offer some high interest, low vocabulary literature for young readers & some captivating read-aloud material for teachers & parents. Through an assortment of exciting escapades involving runaways, rogues & renegades, the authors spin their tales of quiet heroism & bold confrontations. Older students with their own rebellious tendencies should relate to the 15-year-old who befriends a washed-out boxer or an 8th grader who just can't stay out of trouble in a new school. If these stories were indeed collected to 'compel readers to turn the page, eager to find out what happens next,' that goal has been accomplished." (Marietta Castle, Special Interest Council, International Reading Assn.) Order from Printemps Books, 1120 Harbor Drive South, Venice, FL 34285.
Publisher Provided Annotation.

Baltuck, Naomi. Crazy Gibberish & Other Story Hour Stretches from a Storyteller's Bag of Tricks. (Illus.). 1993. PLB 25.00 (*0-208-02336-4*, Pub. by Linnet); pap. text ed. 15.00 (*0-208-02337-2*, Pub. by Linnet) Shoe String.
Bauer, Caroline F., ed. Windy Day: Stories & Poems. Zimmer, Dirk, illus. LC 86-42994. 96p. (gr. 2-5). 1988. (Lipp Jr Bks); PLB 14.89 (*0-397-32208-9*) HarpC Child Bks.
Bauer, Marion D. Am I Blue? Coming Out from the Silence. LC 93-29574. 224p. (gr. 9 up). 1994. 15.00 (*0-06-024253-1*); PLB 14.89 (*0-06-024254-X*) HarpC Child Bks.
Benforado, Sally. Bring Me a Story. rev. ed. (gr. 6-10). 14.95 (*0-915745-08-9*) Floricanto Pr.
Bernard, Robert, ed. All Problems Are Simple & Other Stories: Nineteen Views of the College Years. (gr. 12 up). 1988. 3.50 (*0-318-37398-X*, LF) Dell.
Berry, James. The Future-Telling Lady & Other Stories. LC 92-13759. 144p. (gr. 5 up). 1993. 14.00 (*0-06-021434-1*); PLB 13.89 (*0-06-021435-X*) HarpC Child Bks.
Big Bear's Treasury, Vol. 2: A Children's Anthology. LC 91-71859. 96p. (ps up). 1992. 19.95 (*1-56402-113-0*) Candlewick Pr.
Blishen, Edward, ed. Children's Classics to Read Aloud. LC 92-53097. (Illus.). 256p. (gr. 2 up). 1992. 16.95 (*1-85697-825-7*, Kingfisher LKC) LKC.
Blishen, Edward & Blishen, Nancy, eds. A Treasury of Stories for Five Year Olds. Noakes, Polly, illus. LC 92-53107. 160p. (Orig.). (gr. k-5). 1992. pap. 5.95 (*1-85697-827-3*, Kingfisher LKC) LKC.
—A Treasury of Stories for Seven Year Olds. Ludlow, Patricia, illus. LC 92-53109. 160p. (Orig.). (gr. k-5). 1992. pap. 5.95 (*1-85697-829-X*, Kingfisher LKC) LKC.
—A Treasury of Stories for Six Year Olds. Knowles, Tizzie, illus. LC 92-53108. 160p. (Orig.). (gr. k-5). 1992. pap. 5.95 (*1-85697-828-1*, Kingfisher LKC) LKC.
Blishen, Nancy & Blishen, Edward. Treasury of Stories for Four Year Olds. Dinan, Carolyn, illus. LC 94-2337. 1994. 5.95 (*1-85697-984-9*, Kingfisher LKC) LKC.
Bolden, Tonya, ed. Rites of Passage: Stories about Growing up by Black Writers from Around the World. Johnson, Charles, frwd. by. LC 93-31304. 240p. (gr. 5 up). 1993. 16.95 (*1-56282-688-3*) Hyprn Child.
Bond, Michael. Paddington's Storybook. Fortnum, Peggy, illus. 160p. (gr. 1-5). 1984. 19.95 (*0-395-36667-4*) HM.
Bramos, Helen. My Favorite Bed Time Stories. Bramos, Ann S., tr. & illus. LC 91-76687. 63p. (Orig.). 1992. pap. 7.00 (*1-56002-152-7*) Aegina Pr.
Branfield, John. The Day I Shot My Dad: And Other Stories. 160p. (gr. 6-9). 1990. 18.95 (*0-575-04486-1*, Pub. by Gollancz England) Trafalgar.
British & American Short Stories. 1993. pap. text ed. 6.50 (*0-582-09681-2*, 79816) Longman.
Brooke, William J. Teller of Tales. LC 93-43421. 128p. (gr. 5 up). 1994. 15.00 (*0-06-023399-0*); PLB 14.89 (*0-06-023400-8*) HarpC Child Bks.
—A Telling of the Tales: Five Stories. Egielski, Richard, illus. LC 89-36588. 144p. (gr. 3-7). 1990. 13.00 (*0-06-020688-8*); PLB 12.89 (*0-06-020689-6*) HarpC Child Bks.
Brooks, Martha. Paradise Cafe & Other Stories. (gr. 7 up). 1990. 14.95 (*0-316-10978-9*, Joy St Bks) Little.
—Paradise Cafe: And Other Stories. 1993. pap. 2.95 (*0-590-45562-1*) Scholastic Inc.
—Traveling on into the Light: And Other Stories. LC 94-9136. 144p. (gr. 7 up). 1994. 14.95 (*0-531-06863-3*); PLB 14.99 (*0-531-08713-1*) Orchard Bks Watts.
Brown, Roberta. The Walking Trees & Other Scary Stories. 139p. (gr. 4 up). 1991. 8.95 (*0-87483-143-1*) August Hse.
Buck, Pearl S. The Enemy. LC 85-30005. 64p. (gr. 6 up). 1986. PLB 13.95 (*0-88682-059-6*) Creative Ed.
Burgess, Thornton W. Tales from the Storyteller's House. 19.95 (*0-8488-0930-0*) Amereon Ltd.
Burnett, Frances H. The Troubles of Queen Silver-Bell: As Told by Queen Crosspatch. Cady, Harrison, illus. 56p. (gr. 3-6). 1992. 4.99 (*0-517-07247-5*, Pub. by Derrydale Bks) Random Hse Value.
Cahill, Susan, ed. Women & Fiction: Short Stories by & About Women. (gr. 7 up). 1975. pap. 4.50 (*0-451-62411-4*, ME2263, Ment) NAL-Dutton.
Calderon, Frank, ed. Washington Irving's Pilgrim of Love: From the Tales of the Alhambra. 2nd ed. Pontet, Daniel G., illus. 64p. (gr. 4 up). 1990. text ed. 19.95 (*0-939193-20-5*) Edit Concepts.
Callen, Larry. Who Kidnapped the Sheriff? Gammill, Stephen L., illus. 176p. (gr. 4 up). 1985. 14.95 (*0-316-12499-0*, Joy St Bks) Little.
Cameron, Ann. More Stories Julian Tells. Strugnell, Ann, illus. LC 84-10095. 96p. (gr. k-3). 1989. pap. 2.99 (*0-394-82454-7*) Knopf Bks Yng Read.
Camille, Pamela, intro. by. Children of the Mountains: Short Stories by the Elementary School Children of Pagosa Springs, Colorado. LC 88-81602. (Illus.). 150p. (Orig.). (gr. 4-8). 1988. pap. 7.95 (*0-945985-01-0*) Freedom Lights Pr.
Carlson, Anna L. Stories to Treasure. Wynne, Diana, illus. 24p. (Orig.). (ps-5). 1984. pap. 62.40 (*0-939938-06-5*) Karwyn Ent.
Carusone, Al. Don't Open the Door after the Sun Goes Down: Tales of the Real & Unreal. Glass, Andrew, illus. LC 94-7406. (gr. 4 up). 1994. 13.95 (*0-395-65225-1*, Clarion Bks) HM.
Chadwick, Roxane. Once upon a Felt Board. Skiles, Janet, illus. 128p. (gr. k-4). 1986. wkbk. 11.95 (*0-86653-338-9*, GA 798) Good Apple.
Chaikin, Miriam. Hinkl & Other Schlemiel Stories. (Illus.). 96p. (Orig.). (gr. 3-12). 1987. 10.95 (*0-933503-15-6*) Shapolsky Pubs.
Chekhov, Anton. A Day in the Country. Redpath, Ann, ed. (Illus.). 32p. (gr. 4 up). 1986. PLB 13.95 (*0-88682-004-9*) Creative Ed.
Child Study Association of America Staff. Read-to-Me Storybook. Lenski, Lois L., illus. LC 47-31488. (ps-1). 1947. 16.95i (*0-690-68832-6*, Crowell Jr Bks) HarpC Child Bks.
Chorao, Kay. The Baby's Story Book. Chorao, Kay, illus. LC 84-26005. 64p. (ps-1). 1989. 13.95 (*0-525-44200-6*, DCB); bk. & cassette 17.95 (*0-525-44507-2*) Dutton Child Bks.
—The Child's Story Book. Chorao, Kay, illus. LC 87-8899. 64p. (ps-3). 1987. 12.95 (*0-525-44328-2*, 01258-370, DCB) Dutton Child Bks.
Cole, Joanna & Calmenson, Stephanie, eds. The Read-Aloud Treasury: Favorite Nursery Rhymes, Poems, Stories & More for the Very Young. Schweninger, Ann, illus. 256p. 1988. pap. 18.95 (*0-385-18560-X*) Doubleday.
Colum, Padraic. The Children of Odin: The Book of Northern Myths. Pogany, Willy, illus. LC 83-20368. 280p. (gr. 5up). 1984. SBE 15.95 (*0-02-722890-8*, Macmillan Child Bk); pap. 8.95 (*0-02-042100-1*, Collier Young Ad) Macmillan Child Grp.
Conari Press Editors. Kids' Random Acts of Kindness. (Illus.). 168p. (Orig.). 1994. pap. 8.95 (*0-943233-62-3*) Conari Press.
Conford, Ellen. I Love You, I Hate You, Get Lost. LC 93-8588. 176p. 1994. 13.95 (*0-590-45558-3*) Scholastic Inc.
Copping, Harold. Children's Stories from Dickens. Copping, Harold, illus. LC 92-37666. 1993. 8.99 (*0-517-08485-6*, Pub. by Derrydale Bks) Random Hse Value.
Corrin, Sara. Stories for Five-Year-Olds. (ps-3). 1989. pap. 9.95 (*0-571-12998-6*) Faber & Faber.
Corrin, Sara & Corrin, Stephen, eds. Laugh out Loud: More Funny Stories for Children. Rose, Gerald, illus. 116p. (gr. k-2). 1991. pap. 2.95 (*0-571-14177-3*) Faber & Faber.
—Stories for Nine-Year-Olds. Hughes, Shirley, illus. LC 79-670371. 160p. (gr. 2-5). 1979. pap. 10.95 (*0-571-12931-5*) Faber & Faber.
Courageous Captain. 32p. (Orig.). (gr. 1-5). 1989. 14.95 (*0-89800-194-3*); pap. 7.95 (*0-89800-195-1*) Dharma Pub.
Cranch, Christopher P. Three Children's Novels. Little, Greta D. & Myerson, Joel, eds. LC 92-24894. (Illus.). 200p. (gr. 4 up). 1993. 30.00x (*0-8203-1507-9*) U of Ga Pr.
Crane, Stephen. Maggie & Other Stories. Gemme, F. R., intro. by. (gr. 11 up). 1968. pap. 2.75 (*0-8049-0166-X*, CL-166) Airmont.
Crutcher, Chris. Athletic Shorts. LC 91-4418. (gr. 12 up). 1991. 14.00 (*0-688-10816-4*) Greenwillow.

Dahl, Roald. Roald Dahl: Charlie & the Chocolate Factory, Charlie & the Great Glass Elevator & The BFG, 3 bks. 1989. Set. pap. 11.95 (*0-685-30573-2*) Viking Child Bks.

Davis, Richard H. Ranson's Folly & Other Stories. (gr. 9 up). 1968. pap. 1.95 (*0-8049-0192-9*, CL-192) Airmont.

DeGrote, Barbara. Take the Pizza & Run: And Other Stories for Children about Stewardship. Martens, Ray, illus. 32p. 1992. pap. 5.99 (*0-8066-2599-6*, 10-25996) Augsburg Fortress.

De Maupassant, Guy. Best Short Stories of Guy de Maupassant. Canon, R. R., intro. by. (gr. 9 up). 1968. pap. 2.75 (*0-8049-0161-9*, CL-161) Airmont.

Demi, illus. A Chinese Zoo: Fables & Proverbs. LC 86-33562. 32p. (ps-3). 1987. 14.95 (*0-15-217510-5*, HB Juv Bks) HarBrace.

Dickens, Charles. The Bagman's Story. 48p. (gr. 4 up). 1983. PLB 13.95 (*0-87191-922-2*) Creative Ed.

Dickinson, Karle. Love Notes: Boys on the Brain & Other Junior-High Stories. Dickinson, Karle, illus. LC 93-44343. 128p. (gr. 6-9). 1994. pap. 3.50 (*0-8167-3468-2*) Troll Assocs.

Disney Babies Bedtime Stories. 112p. 1994. 9.98 (*1-57082-141-0*) Mouse Works.

Dittberner-Jax, Norita, ed. The Ragged Heart. Wood, Marce, illus. 164p. (Orig.). 1989. pap. 8.00 (*0-927663-14-7*) COMPAS.

Dobkin, Bonnie. Go-with Words. (Illus.). 32p. (ps-2). 1993. PLB 10.25 (*0-516-02016-1*); pap. 2.95 (*0-516-42016-X*) Childrens.

Donatelli, Betty. Sunny, Funny Stories. Donatelli, Betty, illus. 11p. (Orig.). (gr. 1-2). 1984. pap. 1.00 (*0-912981-08-3*) Hse BonGiovanni.

Doyle, Arthur Conan. Great Stories of Sherlock Holmes. 287p. (gr. 5 up). 1962. pap. 1.75 (*0-440-93190-8*, LFL) Dell.

Dr. Seuss. Six by Seuss: A Treasury of Dr. Seuss Classics. Dr. Seuss, illus. LC 91-6311. 352p. 1991. 25.00 (*0-679-82148-1*) Random Bks Yng Read.

—Yertle the Turtle & Other Stories. Dr. Seuss, illus. (gr. k-3). 1958. 14.00 (*0-394-80087-7*); PLB 13.99 (*0-394-90087-1*) Random Bks Yng Read.

Dyer, Jane, illus. The Random House Book of Bedtime Stories. LC 94-2631. 160p. (gr. 1 up). 1994. 18.00 (*0-679-80832-9*); PLB 18.99 (*0-679-90832-3*) Random.

Eagle, Kin. It's Raining, It's Pouring. Gilbert, Robert, illus. LC 93-40897. (ps-3). 1994. 14.95 (*1-879085-88-7*) Whsprng Coyote Pr.

Eisen, Armand. Treasury of Children's Literature. LC 92-2847. (Illus.). 304p. (gr. 3-7). 1992. 24.45 (*0-395-53349-X*) HM.

Ellis, Joyce K., compiled by. Saved by a Broken Pole & Other Stories. 75p. (Orig.). (gr. 2-6). 1980. pap. 1.25 (*0-89323-007-3*, 096) Bible Memory.

The Emergent Reader. (ps-1). 1991. Big Bks. pap. 21.00 (*1-56843-025-6*); Little Bks. 4.25 (*0-685-62345-9*) BGR Pub.

Erickson, John R. Alkali County Tales. Holmes, Gerald, illus. 100p. (Orig.). (gr. 3up). 1984. 9.95 (*0-916941-06-X*); pap. 5.95 (*0-9608612-8-9*) Maverick Bks.

ETR Associates Staff. Everyday Decisions. Paley, Nina, illus. LC 93-20725. 1993. write for info. (*1-56071-316-X*) ETR Assocs.

Evans, Mary J. & Anderson, Deborah. Tales from Hans Christian Andersen. (gr. k up). 1983. pap. 4.50 (*0-87602-257-3*) Anchorage.

Fager, Charles. Life, Death & Two Chickens. 100p. (gr. 3-6). 1990. pap. 10.95 (*0-945177-04-6*) Kimo Pr.

Field Drake, Christin. The Sleepy Baker: A Collection of Stories & Recipes for Children. Eldridge, Alexandra, illus. LC 92-56509. 56p. (gr. k-5). 1993. 12.95 (*0-87358-551-8*) Northland AZ.

Fifty-Two Stories & Poems for Children. (Illus.). 160p. (gr. 2-5). 1987. casebound 7.99 (*0-570-04158-9*, 56-1616) Concordia.

Fisher, Barbara & Spiegel, Richard, eds. Streams. (Illus.). 138p. (Orig.). (gr. 9-12). 1987. pap. 5.00 (*0-934830-39-8*) Ten Penny.

—Streams, No. 2. (Illus.). 142p. (gr. 9-12). 1988. pap. 5.00 (*0-934830-42-8*) Ten Penny.

—Streams, No. 3. (Illus.). (gr. 9-12). 1989. pap. 5.00 (*0-934830-43-6*) Ten Penny.

Fourie, Corlia. Ganekwane & the Green Dragon: Four Stories from Africa. Grant, Christy, ed. Epanya, Christian A., illus. LC 93-45922. 40p. (gr. 3-6). 1994. PLB 14.95 (*0-8075-2744-0*) A Whitman.

Fremont, Eleanor, adapted by. Tales from the Crypt, Vol. 1: Introduced by the Crypt-Keeper. Davis, Jack, illus. LC 90-23916. 96p. (Orig.). (gr. 4-7). 1991. pap. 2.99 (*0-679-81799-9*) Random Bks Yng Read.

French, Vivian. Under the Moon. Fisher, Chris, illus. LC 93-877. 96p. (gr. 3-6). 1994. 14.95 (*1-56402-330-3*) Candlewick Pr.

Fuentes, Vilma M. Kimod & the Swan Maiden. Inis, Ninabeth R., illus. 36p. (Orig.). (gr. k-3). 1984. pap. 3.50 (*971-10-0135-7*, Pub. by New Day Pub PI) Cellar.

Furman, Abraham L., ed. Everygirls Career Stories. (Illus.). (gr. 6-10). PLB 7.19 (*0-8313-0049-3*) Lantern.

—Everygirls Companion. LC 68-11184. (gr. 5-9). 1968. PLB 7.19 (*0-685-13773-2*) Lantern.

Gale, David. Funny You Should Ask: The Yearling Book of Original Humorous Short Stories. (gr. 4-7). 1994. pap. 3.99 (*0-440-40922-5*) Dell.

Gale, David, ed. Don't Give up the Ghost: The Delacorte Book of Original Ghost Stories. LC 92-47088. 1993. 14.95 (*0-385-31109-5*) Delacorte.

Gallo, Donald R. Within Reach: Ten Stories. LC 92-29378. 192p. (gr. 5 up). 1993. 15.00 (*0-06-021440-6*); PLB 14.89 (*0-06-021441-4*) HarpC Child Bks.

Gallo, Donald R., ed. Join In: Multiethnic Short Stories by Outstanding Writers for Young Adults. LC 92-43169. 1993. 15.95 (*0-385-31080-3*) Delacorte.

—Sixteen: Short Stories by Outstanding Writers for Young Adults. LC 84-3250. 208p. (gr. 7 up). 1984. 16.95 (*0-385-29346-1*) Delacorte.

—Sixteen: Short Stories by Outstanding Young Adult Writers. 192p. (gr. 5-12). 1985. pap. 4.50 (*0-440-97757-6*, LFL) Dell.

—Visions: Nineteen Short Stories by Outstanding Writers for Young Adults. (gr. k-12). 1988. pap. 3.99 (*0-440-20208-6*, LFL) Dell.

—Visions: 19 Short Stories by Outstanding Writers for Young Adults. LC 87-6787. 240p. (gr. 7 up). 1987. pap. 16.95 (*0-385-29588-X*) Delacorte.

Garner, Alan. A Bag of Moonshine. Lynch, Patrick J., illus. LC 86-13362. 160p. (gr. k-5). 1986. pap. 15.95 (*0-385-29517-0*) Delacorte.

George A. Jackson School Students. The Literary Lion, 1993. (Illus.). 164p. (Orig.). 1993. pap. 10.00 (*0-940429-11-X*) M B Glass Assocs.

Geras, Adele. Golden Windows: And Other Stories of Jerusalem. LC 92-39885. 160p. (gr. 3-7). 1993. 14.00 (*0-06-022941-1*); PLB 13.89 (*0-06-022942-X*) HarpC Child Bks.

Gibson, Andrew. The Rollickers & Other Stories. (Illus.). 160p. (gr. 3 up). 1993. 15.95 (*0-571-16687-3*) Faber & Faber.

Gikow, Louise. Bye-Bye, Pacifier. Cooke, Tom, illus. 18p. (ps). 1992. bds. 3.50 (*0-307-12330-8*, 12330, Golden Pr) Western Pub.

Gold, Robert S. Stepping Stones: Seventeen Powerful Stories of Growing Up. 320p. (gr. 7 up). 1981. pap. 3.25 (*0-440-98269-3*, LFL) Dell.

Goodman, Burton. More Conflicts. 160p. (gr. 8). 1993. pap. 9.50 (*0-89061-718-X*) Jamestown Pubs.

Goodman, Burton, et al. Conflicts. 160p. (gr. 8). 1993. pap. 9.50 (*0-89061-717-1*) Jamestown Pubs.

Gorog, Judith. On Meeting Witches at Wells. (gr. 3 up). 1991. 14.95 (*0-399-21803-3*, Philomel) Putnam Pub Group.

Greenberg, Martin H. & Waugh, Charles G., eds. A Newbery Halloween: Thirteen Scary Stories by Newbery Award-Winning Authors. LC 92-43877. 1993. pap. 16.95 (*0-385-31028-5*) Doubleday.

Hague, Michael, illus. The Fairy Tales of Oscar Wilde. LC 92-14305. 192p. 1993. 19.95 (*0-8050-1009-2*, Bks Young Read) H Holt & Co.

Hale, Edward E. Man Without a Country & Other Stories. (gr. 5 up). 1968. pap. 1.95 (*0-8049-0185-6*, CL-185) Airmont.

Hamel, Jean-Marie. Heart Tales: A Collection of Stories from a Child's Heart. Hamel, Jean-Marie, illus. 40p. (ps-3). 1990. 12.95g (*0-929684-50-8*) Silver Forest Pub.

The Hands of Pablo Santos. 96p. (gr. 6-9). 1985. pap. 6.50 (*0-521-31706-1*) Cambridge U Pr.

Handy, Bob. The Kids in Us. (Illus.). 1994. saddlestitched 14.95 (*0-8059-3543-6*) Dorrance.

Hardegrove, Nelle A. Ten Stories for Children. Miller, Dennis, illus. 10p. (Orig.). (gr. 1-5). 1987. pap. text ed. 7.95 (*0-9619227-3-7*) N A Hardegrove.

Harris, Raymond. Best Short Stories: Advanced Level. Burgoyne, Mari-Ann S., illus. 560p. (Orig.). (gr. 9 up). 1990. text ed. 18.00 (*0-89061-705-8*, 620H); pap. text ed. 14.25 (*0-89061-701-5*, 620) Jamestown Pubs.

Harris, Raymond, ed. Best-Selling Chapters: Middle Level. 2nd ed. 460p. (gr. 6-8). 1994. pap. 13.95 (*0-89061-755-4*) Jamestown Pubs.

—Best-Selling Chapters: Middle Level. 2nd ed. 460p. (gr. 6-8). 1994. 17.00 (*0-89061-756-2*) Jamestown Pubs.

—Best Short Stories Hardcover: Middle Level. 2nd ed. 460p. (gr. 6-8). 1994. pap. 17.00 (*0-89061-754-6*) Jamestown Pubs.

—Best Short Stories: Middle Level. 2nd ed. 460p. (gr. 6-8). 1994. pap. 13.95 (*0-89061-753-8*) Jamestown Pubs.

Harris, Rosemary. The Lotus & the Grail: Legends from East to East. Le Cain, Erro, illus. 272p. (gr. 7 up). 1985. pap. 7.95 (*0-571-13536-6*) Faber & Faber.

Hawthorn, Philip. Bedtime Stories. Cartwright, Stephen, illus. (ps-4). 1992. 10.95 (*0-7460-0538-5*, Usborne) EDC.

Heart of Gold. 32p. (Orig.). (gr. 1-5). 1989. 14.95 (*0-89800-192-7*); pap. 7.95 (*0-89800-193-5*) Dharma Pub.

Heins, Ethel L., retold by. The Cat & the Cook & Other Fables of Krylov. Lobel, Anita, illus. 32p. (gr. 1 up). Date not set. write for info. (*0-688-12310-4*); PLB write for info. (*0-688-12311-2*) Greenwillow.

Highlights for Children Staff. In the Shadow of an Eagle: And Other Adventure Stories. LC 91-77001. (Illus.). 96p. (gr. 3-7). 1992. pap. 2.95 (*1-56397-078-3*) Boyds Mills Pr.

—Marvin Composes a Tea: And Other Humorous Stories. LC 90-85916. (Illus.). 96p. (gr. 3-7). 1992. pap. 2.95 (*1-878093-40-1*) Boyds Mills Pr.

—No Pets Allowed! And Other Animal Stories. LC 91-77000. (Illus.). 96p. (gr. 3-7). 1992. pap. 2.95 (*1-56397-102-X*) Boyds Mills Pr.

—Storm's Fury: And Other Horse Stories. LC 90-85910. (Illus.). 96p. (gr. 3-7). 1992. pap. 2.95 (*1-878093-31-2*) Boyds Mills Pr.

Hill, Mary, ed. Creepy Classics. Langeneckert, Mark, illus. LC 94-5079. 128p. (gr. 4-8). 1994. pap. 4.99 (*0-679-86692-2*) Random Bks Yng Read.

Hindley, Judy. Zoom on a Broom: Six Fun-Filled Stories. Goffe, Toni, illus. LC 92-53100. 72p. (gr. k-3). 1992. 10.95 (*1-85697-826-5*, Kingfisher LKC) LKC.

Hitchcock, Alfred. Alfred Hitchcock's Spellbinders in Suspense. Isen, Harold, illus. (gr. 7-11). 1982. 4.99 (*0-394-84900-0*) Random Bks Yng Read.

Hollander, Cass. Teddy Bear Bedtime Stories. Bates, Louise, illus. 24p. (ps-2). 1992. pap. 0.99 (*1-56293-115-6*) McClanahan Bk.

Howe, Irving & Greenberg, Eliezer, eds. Favorite Yiddish Stories. 128p. 1992. Repr. 5.99 (*0-517-06656-4*, Pub. by Wings Bks) Random Hse Value.

Hughes, Shirley. The Shirley Hughes Nursery Collection. LC 93-47395. (Illus.). 1994. 17.00 (*0-688-13583-8*) Lothrop.

—Stories by Firelight. LC 92-38207. (Illus.). 64p. 1993. 16.00 (*0-688-04568-5*) Lothrop.

Hurwood, Bernhardt J. Eerie Tales of Terror & Dread. 1992. 2.95 (*0-590-44650-9*, Point) Scholastic Inc.

Hwa-I Publishing Co., Staff. Chinese Children's Stories, Vol. 10: The Money Tree, The Coxcomb. Ching, Emily, et al, eds. Wonder Kids Publications Staff, tr. from CHI. Hwa-I Publishing Co., Staff, illus. LC 90-60792. 28p. (gr. 3-6). 1991. Repr. of 1988 ed. 7.95x (*1-56162-010-6*) Wonder Kids.

—Chinese Children's Stories, Vol. 100: From Rice into Flowers, The Shy Rainbow. Ching, Emily, et al, eds. Wonder Kids Publications Staff, tr. from CHI. Hwa-I Publishing Co., Staff, illus. LC 90-60811. 28p. (gr. 3-6). 1991. Repr. of 1988 ed. 7.95x (*1-56162-100-5*) Wonder Kids.

—Chinese Children's Stories, Vol. 12: The Snail & the Ox, Sparrows Can't Walk. Ching, Emily, et al, eds. Wonder Kids Publications Staff, tr. from CHI. Hwa-I Publishing Co., Staff, illus. LC 90-60793. 28p. (gr. 3-6). 1991. Repr. of 1988 ed. 7.95x (*1-56162-012-2*) Wonder Kids.

—Chinese Children's Stories, Vol. 13: Rooster Summons the Sun, The White-Haired Bird. Ching, Emily, et al, eds. Wonder Kids Publications Staff, tr. from CHI. Hwa-I Publishing Co., Staff, illus. LC 90-60793. 28p. (gr. 3-6). 1991. Repr. of 1988 ed. 7.95x (*1-56162-013-0*) Wonder Kids.

—Chinese Children's Stories, Vol. 14: Weasel Steals the Chickens, Why is the Crow Black? Ching, Emily, et al, eds. Wonder Kids Publications Staff, tr. from CHI. Hwa-I Publishing Co., Staff, illus. LC 90-60793. 28p. (gr. 3-6). 1991. Repr. of 1988 ed. 7.95x (*1-56162-014-9*) Wonder Kids.

—Chinese Children's Stories, Vol. 15: Jiggle in the Wind, The Bat Can't See the Sun. Ching, Emily, et al, eds. Wonder Kids Publications Staff, tr. from CHI. Hwa-I Publishing Co., Staff, illus. LC 90-60793. 28p. (gr. 3-6). 1991. Repr. of 1988 ed. 7.95x (*1-56162-015-7*) Wonder Kids.

—Chinese Children's Stories, Vol. 17: The Monkey & the Fire, Lazy Wife & the Bread Ring. Ching, Emily, et al, eds. Wonder Kids Publications Staff, tr. from CHI. Hwa-I Publishing Co., Staff, illus. LC 90-60794. 28p. (gr. 3-6). 1991. Repr. of 1988 ed. 7.95x (*1-56162-017-3*) Wonder Kids.

—Chinese Children's Stories, Vol. 18: The Little Bamboo Pole, The Wise Old Man. Ching, Emily, et al, eds. Wonder Kids Publications Staff, tr. from CHI. Hwa-I Publishing Co., Staff, illus. LC 90-60794. 28p. (gr. 3-6). 1991. Repr. of 1988 ed. 7.95x (*1-56162-018-1*) Wonder Kids.

—Chinese Children's Stories, Vol. 19: Crow Moves Away, Baby Lion & Baby Rhino. Ching, Emily, et al, eds. Wonder Kids Publications Staff, tr. from CHI. Hwa-I Publishing Co., Staff, illus. LC 90-60794. 28p. (gr. 3-6). 1991. Repr. of 1988 ed. 7.95x (*1-56162-019-X*) Wonder Kids.

—Chinese Children's Stories, Vol. 2: The Blind Man & the Cripple, Orchard Village. Ching, Emily, et al, eds. Wonder Kids Publications Staff, tr. (Illus.). 28p. (gr. 3-6). 1991. Repr. of 1988 ed. 7.95 (*1-56162-002-5*) Wonder Kids.

—Chinese Children's Stories, Vol. 20: Ah-Liu Picks Corn, Cuckoo's Winter. Ching, Emily, et al, eds. Wonder Kids Publications Staff, tr. from CHI. Hwa-I Publishing Co., Staff, illus. LC 90-60794. 28p. (gr. 3-6). 1991. Repr. of 1988 ed. 7.95x (*1-56162-020-3*) Wonder Kids.

—Chinese Children's Stories, Vol. 21: Seamless Clothing, The Big Clam & the Snipe. Ching, Emily, et al, eds. Wonder Kids Publications Staff, tr. from CHI. (Illus.). 28p. (gr. 3-6). 1991. Repr. of 1988 ed. 7.95 (*1-56162-021-1*) Wonder Kids.

—Chinese Children's Stories, Vol. 22: The Steal a Bell, The Dropout. Ching, Emily, et al, eds. Wonder Kids Publications Staff, tr. from CHI. Hwa-I Publishing Co., Staff, illus. LC 90-60796. 28p. (gr. 3-6). 1991. Repr. of 1988 ed. 7.95x (*1-56162-022-X*) Wonder Kids.

—Chinese Children's Stories, Vol. 23: Dummy Afa, The Fox in a Tiger's Suit. Ching, Emily, et al, eds. Wonder Kids Publications Staff, tr. from CHI. Hwa-I Publishing Co., Staff, illus. LC 90-60796. 28p. (gr. 3-6). 1991. Repr. of 1988 ed. 7.95x (*1-56162-023-8*) Wonder Kids.

—Chinese Children's Stories, Vol. 24: Running Fifty vs. One-Hundred Strides, Atu Yanks the Rice Seedlings. Ching, Emily, et al, eds. Wonder Kids Publications Staff, tr. from CHI. Hwa-I Publishing Co., Staff, illus. LC 90-60796. 28p. (gr. 3-6). 1991. Repr. of 1988 ed. 7.95x (*1-56162-024-6*) Wonder Kids.

—Chinese Children's Stories, Vol. 25: The Blindmen & the Elephant, Little Frog in the Well. Ching, Emily, et al, eds. Wonder Kids Publications Staff, tr. from CHI. Hwa-I Publishing Co., Staff, illus. LC 90-60796. 28p. (gr. 3-6). 1991. Repr. of 1988 ed. 7.95x (*1-56162-025-4*) Wonder Kids.

—Chinese Children's Stories, Vol. 26: Celebrating New York, Miss Yuan-Tsau. Ching, Emily, et al, eds. Wonder Kids Publications Staff, tr. from CHI. (Illus.). 28p. (gr. 3-6). 1991. Repr. of 1988 ed. 7.95 (*1-56162-026-2*) Wonder Kids.

—Chinese Children's Stories, Vol. 27: Sky-Mending Festival, Decorative Paper for Graves. Ching, Emily, et al, eds. Wonder Kids Publications Staff, tr. from CHI. Hwa-I Publishing Co., Staff, illus. LC 90-60797. 28p. (gr. 3-6). 1991. Repr. of 1988 ed. 7.95x (*1-56162-027-0*) Wonder Kids.

—Chinese Children's Stories, Vol. 28: Mih-Ro River, The Herder & the Seamstress. Ching, Emily, et al, eds. Wonder Kids Publications Staff, tr. from CHI. Hwa-I Publishing Co., Staff, illus. LC 90-60797. 28p. (gr. 3-6). 1991. Repr. of 1988 ed. 7.95x (*1-56162-028-9*) Wonder Kids.

—Chinese Children's Stories, Vol. 29: Moon Cake, Fei's Adventure. Ching, Emily, et al, eds. Wonder Kids Publications Staff, tr. from CHI. Hwa-I Publishing Co., Staff, illus. LC 90-60797. 28p. (gr. 3-6). 1991. Repr. of 1988 ed. 7.95x (*1-56162-029-7*) Wonder Kids.

—Chinese Children's Stories, Vol. 30: La-Ba Porridge, The Stove God. Ching, Emily, et al, eds. Wonder Kids Publications Staff, tr. from CHI. Hwa-I Publishing Co., Staff, illus. LC 90-60797. 28p. (gr. 3-6). 1991. Repr. of 1988 ed. 7.95x (*1-56162-030-0*) Wonder Kids.

—Chinese Children's Stories, Vol. 32: Dumplings, Ham. Ching, Emily, et al, eds. Wonder Kids Publications Staff, tr. from CHI. Hwa-I Publishing Co., Staff, illus. LC 90-60798. 28p. (gr. 3-6). 1991. Repr. of 1988 ed. 7.95x (*1-56162-032-7*) Wonder Kids.

—Chinese Children's Stories, Vol. 33: Noodles over the Bridge, Steamed Bread. Ching, Emily, et al, eds. Wonder Kids Publications Staff, tr. from CHI. Hwa-I Publishing Co., Staff, illus. LC 90-60798. 28p. (gr. 3-6). 1991. Repr. of 1988 ed. 7.95x (*1-56162-033-5*) Wonder Kids.

—Chinese Children's Stories, Vol. 34: The Stuffed Steamed Bao, Miss Freckle's Tofu. Ching, Emily, et al, eds. Wonder Kids Publications Staff, tr. from CHI. Hwa-I Publishing Co., Staff, illus. LC 90-60798. 28p. (gr. 3-6). 1991. Repr. of 1988 ed. 7.95x (*1-56162-034-3*) Wonder Kids.

—Chinese Children's Stories, Vol. 35: Monks' Beef Stew, Yue's Tofu Store. Ching, Emily, et al, eds. Wonder Kids Publications Staff, tr. from CHI. Hwa-I Publishing Co., Staff, illus. LC 90-60798. 28p. (gr. 3-6). 1991. Repr. of 1988 ed. 7.95x (*1-56162-035-1*) Wonder Kids.

—Chinese Children's Stories, Vol. 37: Confucius' Bookkeeping, The Scissors Shop. Ching, Emily, et al, eds. Wonder Kids Publications Staff, tr. from CHI. Hwa-I Publishing Co., Staff, illus. LC 90-60799. 28p. (gr. 3-6). 1991. Repr. of 1988 ed. 7.95x (*1-56162-037-8*) Wonder Kids.

—Chinese Children's Stories, Vol. 38: The Peace Drum, Comb. Ching, Emily, et al, eds. Wonder Kids Publications Staff, tr. from CHI. Hwa-I Publishing Co., Staff, illus. LC 90-60799. 28p. (gr. 3-6). 1991. Repr. of 1988 ed. 7.95x (*1-56162-038-6*) Wonder Kids.

—Chinese Children's Stories, Vol. 39: Brush Pen, Duan's Ink-Slab. Ching, Emily, et al, eds. Wonder Kids Publications Staff, tr. from CHI. Hwa-I Publishing Co., Staff, illus. LC 90-6079. 28p. (gr. 3-6). 1991. Repr. of 1988 ed. 7.95x (*1-56162-039-4*) Wonder Kids.

—Chinese Children's Stories, Vol. 40: The Ink-Stick, Shiuan Paper. Ching, Emily, et al, eds. Wonder Kids Publications Staff, tr. from CHI. Hwa-I Publishing Co., Staff, illus. LC 90-60799. 28p. (gr. 3-6). 1991. Repr. of 1988 ed. 7.95x (*1-56162-040-8*) Wonder Kids.

—Chinese Children's Stories, Vol. 42: Tiger Seeks a Master, Why Are Cats Afraid of Dogs? Ching, Emily, et al, eds. Wonder Kids Publications Staff, tr. from CHI. Hwa-I Publishing Co., Staff, illus. LC 90-60800. 28p. (gr. 3-6). 1991. Repr. of 1988 ed. 7.95x (*1-56162-042-4*) Wonder Kids.

—Chinese Children's Stories, Vol. 43: The Bunny's Tail, Fox, Monkey, Rabbit & Horse. Ching, Emily, et al, eds. Wonder Kids Publications Staff, tr. from CHI. Hwa-I Publishing Co., Staff, illus. LC 90-60800. 28p. (gr. 3-6). 1991. Repr. of 1988 ed. 7.95x (*1-56162-043-2*) Wonder Kids.

—Chinese Children's Stories, Vol. 44: Snake's Lost Drum, Ox & Buffalo Change Clothes. Ching, Emily, et al, eds. Wonder Kids Publications Staff, tr. from CHI. Hwa-I Publishing Co., Staff, illus. LC 90-60800. 28p. (gr. 3-6). 1991. Repr. of 1988 ed. 7.95x (*1-56162-044-0*) Wonder Kids.

—Chinese Children's Stories, Vol. 45: The Goat & the Camel, The Wolf & the Pig. Ching, Emily, et al, eds. Wonder Kids Publications Staff, tr. from CHI. Hwa-I Publishing Co., Staff, illus. LC 90-60800. 28p. (gr. 3-6). 1991. Repr. of 1988 ed. 7.95x (*1-56162-045-9*) Wonder Kids.

—Chinese Children's Stories, Vol. 47: The Crane-Riding Immortal, Lyu Dungbin & Guanyin. Ching, Emily, et al, eds. Wonder Kids Publications Staff, tr. from CHI. Hwa-I Publishing Co., Staff, illus. LC 90-60801. 28p. (gr. 3-6). 1991. Repr. of 1988 ed. 7.95x (*1-56162-047-5*) Wonder Kids.

—Chinese Children's Stories, Vol. 48: Sir Thunder & Lady Lightning, The Door Guards. Ching, Emily, et al, eds. Wonder Kids Publications Staff, tr. from CHI. Hwa-I Publishing Co., Staff, illus. LC 90-60801. 28p. (gr. 3-6). 1991. Repr. of 1988 ed. 7.95x (*1-56162-048-3*) Wonder Kids.

—Chinese Children's Stories, Vol. 49: The Slippery Nose Deity, Under the Moonlight. Ching, Emily, et al, eds. Wonder Kids Publications Staff, tr. from CHI. Hwa-I Publishing Co., Staff, illus. LC 90-60801. 28p. (gr. 3-6). 1991. Repr. of 1988 ed. 7.95x (*1-56162-049-1*) Wonder Kids.

—Chinese Children's Stories, Vol. 50: Zung Kuei & the Little Ghost, Earth God & Earth Goddess. Ching, Emily, et al, eds. Wonder Kids Publications Staff, tr. from CHI. Hwa-I Publishing Co., Staff, illus. LC 90-60801. 28p. (gr. 3-6). 1991. Repr. of 1988 ed. 7.95x (*1-56162-050-5*) Wonder Kids.

—Chinese Children's Stories, Vol. 52: Joining the Army, Beating up the Tiger. Ching, Emily, et al, eds. Wonder Kids Publications Staff, tr. from CHI. Hwa-I Publishing Co., Staff, illus. LC 90-60802. 28p. (gr. 3-6). 1991. Repr. of 1988 ed. 7.95x (*1-56162-052-1*) Wonder Kids.

—Chinese Children's Stories, Vol. 53: Meeting an Angel, The Child in the Deer Skin. Ching, Emily, et al, eds. Wonder Kids Publications Staff, tr. from CHI. Hwa-I Publishing Co., Staff, illus. LC 90-60802. 28p. (gr. 3-6). 1991. Repr. of 1988 ed. 7.95x (*1-56162-053-X*) Wonder Kids.

—Chinese Children's Stories, Vol. 54: The Story of Shun, Village of Filial Piety. Ching, Emily, et al, eds. Wonder Kids Publications Staff, tr. from CHI. Hwa-I Publishing Co., Staff, illus. LC 90-60802. 28p. (gr. 3-6). 1991. Repr. of 1988 ed. 7.95x (*1-56162-054-8*) Wonder Kids.

—Chinese Children's Stories, Vol. 55: Two Baskets of Mulberries, Trun's Little Daughter. Ching, Emily, et al, eds. Wonder Kids Publications Staff, tr. from CHI. Hwa-I Publishing Co., Staff, illus. LC 90-60802. 28p. (gr. 3-6). 1991. Repr. of 1988 ed. 7.95x (*1-56162-055-6*) Wonder Kids.

—Chinese Children's Stories, Vol. 56: Catching a Thief, The Plum Tree by the Road. Ching, Emily, et al, eds. Wonder Kids Publications Staff, tr. from CHI. (Illus.). 28p. (gr. 3-6). 1991. Repr. of 1988 ed. 7.95 (*1-56162-056-4*) Wonder Kids.

—Chinese Children's Stories, Vol. 57: The Little-Boy God, A Rooster's Egg. Ching, Emily, et al, eds. Wonder Kids Publications Staff, tr. from CHI. Hwa-I Publishing Co., Staff, illus. LC 90-60803. 28p. (gr. 3-6). 1991. Repr. of 1988 ed. 7.95x (*1-56162-057-2*) Wonder Kids.

—Chinese Children's Stories, Vol. 58: Three Princes & the Firewood, Wang's Memory. Ching, Emily, et al, eds. Wonder Kids Publications Staff, tr. from CHI. Hwa-I Publishing Co., Staff, illus. LC 90-60803. 28p. (gr. 3-6). 1991. Repr. of 1988 ed. 7.95x (*1-56162-058-0*) Wonder Kids.

—Chinese Children's Stories, Vol. 59: A Tankful of Water, The Little Hero. Ching, Emily, et al, eds. Wonder Kids Publications Staff, tr. from CHI. Hwa-I Publishing Co., Staff, illus. LC 90-60803. 28p. (gr. 3-6). 1991. Repr. of 1988 ed. 7.95x (*1-56162-059-9*) Wonder Kids.

—Chinese Children's Stories, Vol. 60: Weighing an Elephant, The Distant Homeland. Ching, Emily, et al, eds. Wonder Kids Publications Staff, tr. from CHI. Hwa-I Publishing Co., Staff, illus. LC 90-60803. 28p. (gr. 3-6). 1991. Repr. of 1988 ed. 7.95x (*1-56162-060-2*) Wonder Kids.

—Chinese Children's Stories, Vol. 62: To Catch the Suns, Two Quarrelsome Brothers. Ching, Emily, et al, eds. Wonder Kids Publications Staff, tr. from CHI. Hwa-I Publishing Co., Staff, illus. LC 90-60804. 28p. (gr. 3-6). 1991. Repr. of 1988 ed. 7.95x (*1-56162-062-9*) Wonder Kids.

—Chinese Children's Stories, Vol. 63: To Speak or Not, The Dark Village. Ching, Emily, et al, eds. Wonder Kids Publications Staff, tr. from CHI. Hwa-I Publishing Co., Staff, illus. LC 90-60804. 28p. (gr. 3-6). 1991. Repr. of 1988 ed. 7.95x (*1-56162-063-7*) Wonder Kids.

—Chinese Children's Stories, Vol. 64: Why Is the Sky So High?, Turning into Stone. Ching, Emily, et al, eds. Wonder Kids Publications Staff, tr. from CHI. Hwa-I Publishing Co., Staff, illus. LC 90-60804. 28p. (gr. 3-6). 1991. Repr. of 1988 ed. 7.95x (*1-56162-064-5*) Wonder Kids.

—Chinese Children's Stories, Vol. 65: Lugging Mountains, What's a Life Span? Ching, Emily, et al, eds. Wonder Kids Publications Staff, tr. from CHI. Hwa-I Publishing Co., Staff, illus. LC 90-60804. 28p. (gr. 3-6). 1991. Repr. of 1988 ed. 7.95x (*1-56162-065-3*) Wonder Kids.

—Chinese Children's Stories, Vol. 66: The Chiao Sisters, Zhou under the Bed. Ching, Emily, et al, eds. Wonder Kids Publications Staff, tr. from CHI. (Illus.). 28p. (gr. 3-6). 1991. Repr. of 1988 ed. 7.95 (*1-56162-066-1*) Wonder Kids.

—Chinese Children's Stories, Vol. 67: The After-Meal Bell, Passing the Three Gorges. Ching, Emily, et al, eds. Wonder Kids Publications Staff, tr. from CHI. Hwa-I Publishing Co., Staff, illus. LC 90-60805. 28p. (gr. 3-6). 1991. Repr. of 1988 ed. 7.95x (*1-56162-067-X*) Wonder Kids.

—Chinese Children's Stories, Vol. 68: The Donkey-Riding Poet, The Backyard Song. Ching, Emily, et al, eds. Wonder Kids Publications Staff, tr. from CHI. Hwa-I Publishing Co., Staff, illus. LC 90-60805. 28p. (gr. 3-6). 1991. Repr. of 1988 ed. 7.95x (*1-56162-068-8*) Wonder Kids.

—Chinese Children's Stories, Vol. 69: The Young Family, Tsuei's Beautiful Bride. Ching, Emily, et al, eds. Wonder Kids Publications Staff, tr. from CHI. Hwa-I Publishing Co., Staff, illus. LC 90-60805. 28p. (gr. 3-6). 1991. Repr. of 1988 ed. 7.95x (*1-56162-069-6*) Wonder Kids.

—Chinese Children's Stories, Vol. 7: Dragon Eye & Cassia Circle, The Conceited Barber. Ching, Emily, et al, eds. Wonder Kids Publications Staff, tr. from CHI. Hwa-I Publishing Co., Staff, illus. LC 90-60792. 28p. (gr. 3-6). 1991. Repr. of 1988 ed. 7.95x (*1-56162-007-6*) Wonder Kids.

—Chinese Children's Stories, Vol. 70: Ji's Jokes, The Scrooge. Ching, Emily, et al, eds. Wonder Kids Publications Staff, tr. from CHI. Hwa-I Publishing Co., Staff, illus. LC 90-60805. 28p. (gr. 3-6). 1991. Repr. of 1988 ed. 7.95x (*1-56162-070-X*) Wonder Kids.

—Chinese Children's Stories, Vol. 71: The Magic Glass Jar, The Pear Tree. Ching, Emily, et al, eds. Wonder Kids Publications Staff, tr. from CHI. (Illus.). 28p. (gr. 3-6). 1991. Repr. of 1988 ed. 7.95 (*1-56162-071-8*) Wonder Kids.

—Chinese Children's Stories, Vol. 72: The Lotus Child, The Ghost in the Basin. Ching, Emily, et al, eds. Wonder Kids Publications Staff, tr. from CHI. Hwa-I Publishing Co., Staff, illus. LC 90-60806. 28p. (gr. 3-6). 1991. Repr. of 1988 ed. 7.95x (*1-56162-072-6*) Wonder Kids.

—Chinese Children's Stories, Vol. 73: Walking through Walls, Who Is the Real Lord Ji? Ching, Emily, et al, eds. Wonder Kids Publications Staff, tr. from CHI. Hwa-I Publishing Co., Staff, illus. LC 90-60806. 28p. (gr. 3-6). 1991. Repr. of 1988 ed. 7.95x (*1-56162-073-4*) Wonder Kids.

—Chinese Children's Stories, Vol. 74: Chaos in the Heavenly Palace, Eating the Ginseng Fruit. Ching, Emily, et al, eds. Wonder Kids Publications Staff, tr. from CHI. Hwa-I Publishing Co., Staff, illus. LC 90-60806. 28p. (gr. 3-6). 1991. Repr. of 1988 ed. 7.95x (*1-56162-074-2*) Wonder Kids.

—Chinese Children's Stories, Vol. 75: Tang's Strange Journey, Dwarfs & Giants. Ching, Emily, et al, eds. Wonder Kids Publications Staff, tr. from CHI. Hwa-I Publishing Co., Staff, illus. LC 90-60806. 28p. (gr. 3-6). 1991. Repr. of 1988 ed. 7.95x (*1-56162-075-0*) Wonder Kids.

—Chinese Children's Stories, Vol. 77: Sir Guan's Big Red Face, Turning Cranes into Words. Ching, Emily, et al, eds. Wonder Kids Publications Staff, tr. from CHI. Hwa-I Publishing Co., Staff, illus. LC 90-60807. 28p. (gr. 3-6). 1991. Repr. of 1988 ed. 7.95x (*1-56162-077-7*) Wonder Kids.

—Chinese Children's Stories, Vol. 78: Tang Buohu's Drawings, The General & the Water Tank. Ching, Emily, et al, eds. Wonder Kids Publications Staff, tr. from CHI. Hwa-I Publishing Co., Staff, illus. LC 90-60807. 28p. (gr. 3-6). 1991. Repr. of 1988 ed. 7.95x (*1-56162-078-5*) Wonder Kids.

—Chinese Children's Stories, Vol. 79: Black-Faced Sir Bao, Doctor Hwa-Tuo. Ching, Emily, et al, eds. Wonder Kids Publications Staff, tr. from CHI. Hwa-I Publishing Co., Staff, illus. LC 90-60807. 28p. (gr. 3-6). 1991. Repr. of 1988 ed. 7.95x (*1-56162-079-3*) Wonder Kids.

—Chinese Children's Stories, Vol. 8: The Millets Won't Go Home, The Immortal Palm. Ching, Emily, et al, eds. Wonder Kids Publications Staff, tr. from CHI. Hwa-I Publishing Co., Staff, illus. LC 90-60792. 28p. (gr. 3-6). 1991. Repr. of 1988 ed. 7.95x (*1-56162-008-4*) Wonder Kids.

—Chinese Children's Stories, Vol. 80: The Dwarf Minister, The Fabulous Chimera's Gift. Ching, Emily, et al, eds. Wonder Kids Publications Staff, tr. from CHI. Hwa-I Publishing Co., Staff, illus. LC 90-60807. 28p. (gr. 3-6). 1991. Repr. of 1988 ed. 7.95x (*1-56162-080-7*) Wonder Kids.

—Chinese Children's Stories, Vol. 82: The Fish Minister, The Hidden Sword. Ching, Emily, et al, eds. Wonder Kids Publications Staff, tr. from CHI. Hwa-I Publishing Co., Staff, illus. LC 90-60808. 28p. (gr. 3-6). 1991. Repr. of 1988 ed. 7.95x (*1-56162-082-3*) Wonder Kids.

—Chinese Children's Stories, Vol. 83: The Revenge of Chao's Orphan, Tien's Wonderful Strategies. Ching, Emily, et al, eds. Wonder Kids Publications Staff, tr. from CHI. Hwa-I Publishing Co., Staff, illus. LC 90-60808. 28p. (gr. 3-6). 1991. Repr. of 1988 ed. 7.95x (*1-56162-083-1*) Wonder Kids.

—Chinese Children's Stories, Vol. 84: Who Is the Real Liu Bong?, Kong Borrows the East Wind. Ching, Emily, et al, eds. Wonder Kids Publications Staff, tr. from CHI. Hwa-I Publishing Co., Staff, illus. LC 90-60808. 28p. (gr. 3-6). 1991. Repr. of 1988 ed. 7.95x (*1-56162-084-X*) Wonder Kids.

—Chinese Children's Stories, Vol. 85: The Battle of the Fei River, The Princess' Engagement. Ching, Emily, et al, eds. Wonder Kids Publications Staff, tr. from CHI. Hwa-I Publishing Co., Staff, illus. LC 90-60808. 28p. (gr. 3-6). 1991. Repr. of 1988 ed. 7.95x (*1-56162-085-8*) Wonder Kids.

—Chinese Children's Stories, Vol. 86: From Crows into Bricks, Two Treasured Swords. Ching, Emily, et al, eds. Wonder Kids Publications Staff, tr. from CHI. (Illus.). 28p. (gr. 3-6). 1991. Repr. of 1988 ed. 7.95 (*1-56162-086-6*) Wonder Kids.

—Chinese Children's Stories, Vol. 87: Fan Bridge & Escape Alley, The Stream of Flowers. Ching, Emily, et al, eds. Wonder Kids Publications Staff, tr. from CHI. Hwa-I Publishing Co., Staff, illus. LC 90-60809. 28p. (gr. 3-6). 1991. Repr. of 1988 ed. 7.95x (*1-56162-087-4*) Wonder Kids.

—Chinese Children's Stories, Vol. 88: Five Stone Goats, Six-Foot Street. Ching, Emily, et al, eds. Wonder Kids Publications Staff, tr. from CHI. Hwa-I Publishing Co., Staff, illus. LC 90-60809. 28p. (gr. 3-6). 1991. Repr. of 1988 ed. 7.95x (*1-56162-088-2*) Wonder Kids.

—Chinese Children's Stories, Vol. 89: Peach Blossom Cave, Mt. Lee. Ching, Emily, et al, eds. Wonder Kids Publications Staff, tr. from CHI. Hwa-I Publishing Co., Staff, illus. LC 90-60809. 28p. (gr. 3-6). 1991. Repr. of 1988 ed. 7.95x (*1-56162-089-0*) Wonder Kids.

—Chinese Children's Stories, Vol. 9: The Story of Rice, The Cows & the Trumpet. Ching, Emily, et al, eds. Wonder Kids Publications Staff, tr. from CHI. Hwa-I Publishing Co., Staff, illus. LC 90-60792. 28p. (gr. 3-6). 1991. Repr. of 1988 ed. 7.95x (*1-56162-009-2*) Wonder Kids.

—Chinese Children's Stories, Vol. 90: The Dragon Who Puts out Fires, The Golden Hairpin Well. Ching, Emily, et al, eds. Wonder Kids Publications Staff, tr. from CHI. Hwa-I Publishing Co., Staff, illus. LC 90-60809. 28p. (gr. 3-6). 1991. Repr. of 1988 ed. 7.95x (*1-56162-090-4*) Wonder Kids.

—Chinese Children's Stories, Vol. 91: A Little City, Beating the Devil. Ching, Emily, et al, eds. Wonder Kids Publications Staff, tr. from CHI. (Illus.). 28p. (gr. 3-6). 1991. Repr. of 1988 ed. 7.95 (*1-56162-091-2*) Wonder Kids.

—Chinese Children's Stories, Vol. 92: White-Rice Magic Cave, Sun-Moon Lake. Ching, Emily, et al, eds. Wonder Kids Publications Staff, tr. from CHI. Hwa-I Publishing Co., Staff, illus. LC 90-60810. 28p. (gr. 3-6). 1991. Repr. of 1988 ed. 7.95x (*1-56162-092-0*) Wonder Kids.

—Chinese Children's Stories, Vol. 93: Mt. Anvil & the Sword Well, Two Waters. Ching, Emily, et al, eds. Wonder Kids Publications Staff, tr. from CHI. Hwa-I Publishing Co., Staff, illus. LC 90-60810. 28p. (gr. 3-6). 1991. Repr. of 1988 ed. 7.95x (*1-56162-093-9*) Wonder Kids.

—Chinese Children's Stories, Vol. 94: Muddy Water Stream, Sister Lakes & Brother Trees. Ching, Emily, et al, eds. Wonder Kids Publications Staff, tr. from CHI. Hwa-I Publishing Co., Staff, illus. LC 90-60810. 28p. (gr. 3-6). 1991. Repr. of 1988 ed. 7.95x (*1-56162-094-7*) Wonder Kids.

—Chinese Children's Stories, Vol. 95: Half-Shield Mountain, The Adopted Daughter Lake. Ching, Emily, et al, eds. Wonder Kids Publications Staff, tr. from CHI. Hwa-I Publishing Co., Staff, illus. LC 90-60810. 28p. (gr. 3-6). 1991. Repr. of 1988 ed. 7.95x (*1-56162-095-5*) Wonder Kids.

—Chinese Children's Stories, Vol. 97: Tiger Aunty, Ah-Long & Ah-Hwa. Ching, Emily, et al, eds. Wonder Kids Publications Staff, tr. from CHI. Hwa-I Publishing Co., Staff, illus. LC 90-60811. 28p. (gr. 3-6). 1991. Repr. of 1988 ed. 7.95x (*1-56162-097-1*) Wonder Kids.

—Chinese Children's Stories, Vol. 98: Ai-Yu Jello, Granny & the Fox. Ching, Emily, et al, eds. Wonder Kids Publications Staff, tr. from CHI. Hwa-I Publishing Co., Staff, illus. LC 90-60811. 28p. (gr. 3-6). 1991. Repr. of 1988 ed. 7.95x (*1-56162-098-X*) Wonder Kids.

—Chinese Children's Stories, Vol. 99: The Underground People, Half-Street Lai. Ching, Emily, et al, eds. Wonder Kids Publications Staff, tr. from CHI. Hwa-I Publishing Co., Staff, illus. LC 90-60811. 28p. (gr. 3-6). 1991. Repr. of 1988 ed. 7.95x (*1-56162-099-8*) Wonder Kids.

Irving, Washington. The Legend of Sleepy Hollow. Van Nutt, Robert, adapted by. & illus. LC 88-33375. 32p. (ps up). 1991. pap. 14.95 (*0-88708-088-X*, Rabbit Ears); incl. cassette 19.95 (*0-88708-089-8*, Rabbit Ears) Picture Bk Studio.

—Legend of Sleepy Hollow & Other Stories. (gr. 6 up). 1964. pap. 2.95 (*0-8049-0050-7*, CL-50) Airmont.

—Washington Irving's Tales of the Supernatural. Wagenknecht, Edward, ed. Alley, R. W., illus. LC 80-29313. 288p. (gr. 6 up). 1982. 17.95 (*0-916144-64-X*) Stemmer Hse.

Is Seeing Believing? Selected from Highlights for Children. LC 92-73627. (Illus.). 96p. (gr. 2-5). 1993. pap. 2.95 (*1-56397-192-5*) Boyds Mills Pr.

Jacob, Max. The Story of King Kabul the First & Gawain the Kitchen-Boy: Histoire du Roi Kaboul Ier et du Marmiton Gauwain; Followed by Vulcan's Crown, la Couronne de Vulcan. Black, Moishe & Green, Maria, trs. Blachon, Roger, illus. LC 93-5362. viii, 79p. 1994. 20.00 (*0-8032-2577-6*) U of Nebr Pr.

Jacques, Brian. Seven Strange & Ghostly Tales. (gr. 3 up). 1991. 14.95 (*0-399-22103-4*, Philomel Bks) Putnam Pub Group.

James, Henry. Daisy Miller & Other Stories. LC 84-29480. (gr. 9 up). 1968. pap. 1.75 (*0-8049-0178-3*, CL-178) Airmont.

Janger, Kathie, ed. Rainbow Collection, 1987: Stories & Poetry by Young People. Ishikawa, Yoko, illus. Johnson, Rafer, intro. by. (Illus.). 160p. (gr. 1-8). 1987. pap. text ed. 6.00 (*0-929889-02-9*) Young Writers Contest Found.

—Rainbow Collection, 1988: Stories & Poetry by Young People. Turtiainen, Tuomas, illus. Valenti, Jack, intro. by. (Illus.). 160p. (gr. 1-8). 1988. pap. 6.00 (*0-929889-03-7*) Young Writers Contest Found.

Janger, Kathie & Korenblit, Joan, eds. Rainbow Collection, 1985: Stories & Poetry by Young People. Allen, Steve, frwd. by. 160p. (gr. 1-8). 1985. pap. 6.00 (*0-929889-00-2*) Young Writers Contest Found.

—Rainbow Collection, 1986: Stories & Poetry by Young People. Scott, Willard, frwd. by. 160p. (gr. 1-8). 1986. pap. 6.00 (*0-929889-01-0*) Young Writers Contest Found.

Janssen, Lawrence H. Green Lake Tales & Trails. Janssen, Beverly B., illus. LC 84-71073. 96p. (ps-6). 1984. pap. 4.95 (*0-917575-00-8*) Cedars WI.

Jennings, Paul. Uncanny! Even More Surprising Stories. 144p. (gr. 5 up). 1993. pap. 3.99 (*0-14-034909-X*, Puffin) Puffin Bks.

—Unmentionable! More Amazing Stories. LC 92-25930. 112p. (gr. 5 up). 1993. 14.99 (*0-670-84734-8*) Viking Child Bks.

—Unreal! Eight Surprising Stories. 112p. (gr. 5 up). 1993. pap. 3.99 (*0-14-034910-3*, Puffin) Puffin Bks.

Johnson, Liliane & Dufton, Jo S. Children's Chillers & Thrillers. Bruhn, Joan, illus. 136p. (Orig.). Date not set. pap. 10.00 (*0-930069-04-8*) Jasmine Pr.

Johnson, Ralph E. Children's Stories Two: Coloring Nature's Harmony. Johnson, Paul T., ed. Clark, Melissa & Johnson, Gloria, illus. Johnson, Paul. 100p. (Orig.). (gr. k-12). 1989. pap. write for info. (*0-9621929-0-2*) J-p Press.

Jones, Michael P. Works in Progress, Vol. 1. (Illus.). 16p. 1984. pap. text ed. 1.60 (*0-89904-075-6*) Crumb Elbow Pub.

Jones, Michael P., ed. Writing Works Catalogue: Wholesale Edition Vol. 1. (Illus.). 202p. 1984. pap. 5.00 (*0-89904-059-4*); composition 6.00 (*0-89904-058-6*) Crumb Elbow Pub.

Jones, Terry. Fantastic Stories. large type ed. Foreman, Michael, illus. 1993. 16.95 (*0-7451-1908-5*, Galaxy Child Lrg Print) Chivers N Amer.

Jordan, Cathleen, ed. Fun & Games at the Whacks Museum & Other Horror Stories: From Alfred Hitchcock Mystery Magazine & Ellery Queen's Mystery Magazine. LC 93-34862. (gr. 5-9). 1994. 15. 00 (*0-671-89005-0*, S&S BFYR) S&S Trade.

Kallen, Stuart A. Vampires, Werewolves, & Zombies. LC 91-73062. 1991. 12.94 (*1-56239-039-2*) Abdo & Dghtrs.

Kennedy, Richard. Richard Kennedy: Collected Stories. Sewall, Marcia, illus. LC 86-45495. 416p. (gr. 2-6). 1987. HarpC Child Bks.

King, Clive, ed. Adventure Stories. Walker, Brian, illus. LC 92-26452. 1993. pap. 6.95 (*1-85697-882-6*, Kingfisher LKC) LKC.

Kipling, Rudyard. The Elephant's Child & Other Just So Stories. (Illus.). 96p. 1993. pap. text ed. 1.00t (*0-486-27821-2*) Dover.

—Just So Stories. (Illus.). 224p. (gr. 2-9). 1979. 5.99 (*0-517-26655-5*) Random Hse Value.

—Just So Stories. Kipling, Rudyard, illus. LC 92-53177. 192p. 1992. 12.95 (*0-679-41797-4*, Evrymans Lib Childs Class) Knopf.

—New Illustrated Just So Stories. Nicholas, illus. (gr. 1-7). 1952. PLB o.p. (*0-385-02180-1*) Doubleday.

Kittelson, Pat & Connor, Brooke. Cedar Breaks for Kids. (Illus.). (gr. k-4). 1979. pap. 1.00 (*0-915630-14-1*) Zion.

Koftan, Jenelle & Koftan, Kenneth. Long-Distance Grandparenting Series. Mar, Carl, illus. (Orig.). 1988. Set. pap. 37.95 (*0-945184-06-9*) Spring Creek Pubns.

Helpful, informative series. Three activity books to provide grandparents or parents with personalized adventures to read to their special child. Helps build self-esteem, family values, attitudes toward caring & sharing. Lighthearted verse & songs make each adventure a delight. The adult inserts the child's name into the stories, then reads the adventure into a tape recorder & mails the tape recording with tear-out activity pages to the child. "...next best thing to being there might be a tape recorder & an activity book grandparents can use to communicate with grandchildren who live far away." - MATURE OUTLOOK. "...enough material in each volume to last for about two years, provided the grandparents stick to a leisurely schedule. Each story's built around some activity the child & grandparent are to imagine they are sharing." - SINGLE PARENT. Each book has complete instructions & many suggestions for increasing inter-generational communication. Great for parents on business trips & for divorced parents. Books sold separately at $12.95 each. ISBN 0-945184-00-x, ages 3-5 years. ISBN 0-945184-01-8, ages 5-7 years. ISBN 0-945184-02-6, ages 8-10 years. Spring Creek Publications, P.O. Box 243, Rose Hill, KS 67133; 316-788-2182.

Publisher Provided Annotation.

Konigsburg, E. L. Altogether, One at a Time. Haley, Gail E., et al, illus. LC 70-134814. 88p. (gr. 4-7). 1971. SBE 13.95 (*0-689-20638-0*, Atheneum Child Bk) Macmillan Child Grp.

Kornbluth, Adina F. Kaleidoscope. Nodel, Norman, illus. 160p. (gr. 6-10). 1992. 10.95 (*0-922613-31-1*); pap. 8.95 (*0-922613-32-X*) Hachai Pubns.

Kraus, Robert. Fables Aesop Never Wrote. Kraus, Robert, illus. 32p. (gr. k up). 1994. PLB 14.99 (*0-670-85630-4*) Viking Child Bks.

Krayer, Christina, ed. Crossroads, 84 titles. (Illus.). (gr. 9-12). Date not set. Set. pap. 299.00 (*1-882869-00-1*) Read Advent.

—It's a Hit, 86 titles. (Illus.). (gr. 3-8). Date not set. Set. pap. 299.00 (*1-882869-06-0*) Read Advent.

—Laugh Track, 96 titles. (Illus.). (gr. 3-8). Date not set. Set. pap. 299.00 (*1-882869-04-4*) Read Advent.

—Simply Romance, 95 titles. (Illus.). (gr. 6-10). Date not set. Set. pap. 329.00 (*1-882869-02-8*) Read Advent.

—Spine Tinglers, 96 titles. (Illus.). (gr. 3-8). Date not set. Set. pap. 299.00 (*1-882869-03-6*) Read Advent.

Kudalis, Eric. Dracula & Other Vampire Stories. 48p. (gr. 3-10). 1994. PLB 17.27 (*1-56065-212-8*) Capstone Pr.

—Frankenstein & Other Stories of Man-Made Monsters. 48p. (gr. 3-10). 1994. PLB 17.27 (*1-56065-213-6*) Capstone Pr.

—Stories of Mummies & the Living Dead. 48p. (gr. 3-10). 1994. PLB 17.27 (*1-56065-214-4*) Capstone Pr.

Lawrence, Louise. Extinction Is Forever & Other Stories. LC 92-35464. 1993. 15.00 (*0-06-022913-6*, HarpT); PLB 14.89 (*0-06-022914-4*, HarpT) HarpC.

Lenski, Lois. Lois Lenski's Big Big Book of Mr. Small. (Illus.). 300p. (ps-1). 1985. 5.98 (*0-517-46307-5*) Random Hse Value.

Leroe, Ellen. H. O. W. L. High Goes Bats. MacDonald, Patricia, ed. 144p. (Orig.). 1993. pap. 2.99 (*0-671-79838-3*, Minstrel Bks) PB.

Lester, Julius. The Knee-High Man & Other Tales. Pinto, Ralph, illus. LC 72-181785. 32p. (ps-3). 1985. pap. 3.95 (*0-8037-0234-5*, 0383-120, Puff Pied Piper) Puffin Bks.

Lewis, Shari & O'Kun, Lan. One-Minute Teddy Bear Stories. Lisi, Victoria, illus. LC 92-23033. 1993. pap. 12.95 (*0-385-30909-0*) Doubleday.

Lillington, Kenneth. The Real Live Dinosaur & Other Stories. Floyd, Gareth, illus. 144p. (gr. 3-7). 1992. pap. 4.95 (*0-571-16318-1*) Faber & Faber.

Lines, Kathleen, ed. The Faber Book of Magical Tales. Howard, Alan, illus. LC 85-4437. 176p. (Orig.). (gr. 5-9). 1985. pap. 7.95 (*0-571-13648-6*) Faber & Faber.

London, Jack. Jack London in the High School Aegis. Sisson, James E., ed. Lttell, Katherine, pref. by. (Illus.). 125p. (Orig.). (gr. 7-12). 1980. pap. 5.95 (*0-932458-01-7*) Star Rover.

—Short Stories. (gr. 9 up). 1969. pap. 2.50 (*0-8049-0198-8*, CL-198) Airmont.

Love, Glen A., ed. The World Begins Here: An Anthology of Oregon Short Fiction. LC 92-43642. (Illus.). 320p. (Orig.). 1993. text ed. 35.95x (*0-87071-369-8*); pap. 21.95t (*0-87071-370-1*) Oreg St U Pr.

Lucille Clifton Library. 1993. PLB write for info. (*0-8050-3074-3*) H Holt & Co.

MacDonald, Caroline. Hostilities: Nine Bizarre Stories. LC 93-19019. 112p. (gr. 7 up). 1994. 13.95 (*0-590-46063-3*) Scholastic Inc.

McDonald, Collin. The Chilling Hour: Tales of the Real & Unreal. (Illus.). 128p. (gr. 4 up). 1992. 14.00 (*0-525-65101-2*, Cobblehill Bks) Dutton Child Bks.

—Nightwaves: Scary Tales for after Dark. 112p. (gr. 3-7). 1992. pap. 3.95 (*0-06-440447-1*, Trophy) HarpC Child Bks.

—Shadows & Whispers: Tales from the Other Side. LC 94-2143. 160p. (gr. 4 up). 1994. 13.99 (*0-525-65184-5*, Cobblehill Bks) Dutton Child Bks.

McKinley, Robin. A Knot in the Grain & Other Stories. LC 93-17557. 208p. (gr. 6 up). 1994. 14.00 (*0-688-09201-2*) Greenwillow.

McKissack, Patricia. The Dark-Thirty: Southern Tales of the Supernatural. Pinkney, Brian, illus. LC 92-3021. 128p. (gr. 3-7). 1992. 15.00 (*0-679-81863-4*); PLB 15.99 (*0-679-91863-9*) Knopf Bks Yng Read.
McQueen, Priscilla L. We Can Read: Story Pack-54 Little Stories. 1973. pap. 18.66 (*0-685-47089-X*) McQueen.
Magic Flute & Other Children's Stories. (gr. 5 up). 1981. pap. 4.95 (*0-8351-0850-3*) China Bks.
Magorian, James. Plucked Chickens. LC 80-68263. (Illus.). 32p. (gr. 4-6). 1981. 5.00 (*0-930674-04-9*) Black Oak.
Mahy, Margaret. The Birthday Burglar & a Very Wicked Headmistress. Chamberlain, Margaret, illus. LC 92-46599. 144p. (gr. 5 up). 1993. pap. 4.95 (*0-688-12470-4*, Pub. by Beech Tree Bks) Morrow.
—The Chewing-Gum Rescue & Other Stories. Ormerod, Jan, illus. 142p. (gr. 3-7). 1991. 12.95 (*0-87951-424-8*) Overlook Pr.
—The Chewing Gum Rescue & Other Stories. LC 93-35963. 192p. (gr. 5 up). 1994. pap. 4.95 (*0-688-12798-3*, Pub. by Beech Tree Bks) Morrow.
—The Girl with the Green Ear: Stories about Magic in Nature. Hughes, Shirley, illus. LC 91-14992. 112p. (gr. 3-7). 1992. 15.00 (*0-679-82231-3*); PLB 15.99 (*0-679-92231-8*) Knopf Bks Yng Read.
—The Great Piratical Rumbustification & The Librarian & The Robbers. Blake, Quentin, illus. LC 92-43777. 64p. (gr. 5 up). 1993. pap. 3.95 (*0-688-12469-0*, Pub. by Beech Tree Bks) Morrow.
—A Tall Story & Other Tales. Nesbitt, Jan, illus. LC 91-62222. 96p. (gr. 3-7). 1992. SBE 15.95 (*0-689-50547-7*, M K McElderry) Macmillan Child Grp.
—Tick Tock Tales. Smith, Wendy, illus. 96p. (gr. k-4). 1994. SBE 16.95 (*0-689-50604-X*, M K McElderry) Macmillan Child Grp.
Mark, Jan. In Black & White & Other Stories. large type ed. 216p. (gr. 3-7). 1992. 16.95 (*0-7451-1584-5*, Galaxy Child Lrg Print) Chivers N Amer.
Mark, Jan, ed. The Oxford Book of Children's Stories. 480p. 1995. 25.00 (*0-19-214228-3*); pap. 14.95 (*0-19-282397-3*) OUP.
Marsh, Carole. The Drawers of Ocracoke. (Illus., Orig.). (ps-7). 1994. 24.95 (*1-55609-163-X*); pap. 14.95 (*1-55609-236-9*) Gallopade Pub Group.
—Island of the Calamari. (Illus., Orig.). (ps-7). 1994. 24.95 (*1-55609-172-9*); pap. 14.95 (*0-317-66069-1*) Gallopade Pub Group.
—Palm Fever. (Illus.). (gr. 4-12). 1994. 24.95 (*1-55609-185-0*); pap. 14.95 (*1-55609-237-7*) Gallopade Pub Group.
—Saturnalia. (Illus., Orig.). (gr. 4-12). 1994. 24.95 (*1-55609-187-7*); pap. 14.95 (*1-55609-238-5*) Gallopade Pub Group.
Marshall, James. Rats on the Range & Other Stories. LC 92-28918. (gr. 1-5). 1993. 12.99 (*0-8037-1384-3*); PLB 12.89 (*0-8037-1385-1*) Dial Bks Young.
—Rats on the Roof: And Other Stories. Marshall, James, illus. LC 90-44084. 80p. (gr. 1-5). 1991. 13.00 (*0-8037-0834-3*); lib. bdg. 12.89 (*0-8037-0835-1*) Dial Bks Young.
Marten, Phyllis. Why Papa Went Away & Other Stories. 112p. (gr. 8 up). 1987. pap. 4.95 (*0-919797-45-8*) Kindred Pr.
Maruya, Saiichi. Rain in the Wind: Four Stories. Keene, Dennis, tr. from JPN. 190p. 1990. 18.95 (*0-87011-940-0*) Kodansha.
Mathias, Beverley. A Treasury of Christmas Stories. Aldous, Kate, illus. LC 93-50708. 160p. (ps-3). 1994. write for info. (*1-85697-985-7*, Kingfisher LKC) LKC.
Matthews, Andrew, retold by. Stories from Hans Christian Andersen. Snow, Alan, illus. LC 92-45627. 96p. (gr. 2-5). 1993. 18.95 (*0-531-05463-2*) Orchard Bks Watts.
Matthews, Penny, compiled by. Amazing & Bizarre: Ten Wonderfully Weird Stories. 80p. (Orig.). (gr. 4-7). 1992. pap. 3.50 (*0-440-40705-2*, YB) Dell.
Mazer, Anne, intro. by. America Street: A Multicultural Anthology of Stories. 1993. 14.95 (*0-89255-190-9*); pap. 4.95 (*0-89255-191-7*) Persea Bks.
Medlicott, Mary, ed. Tales for Telling: From Around the World. Williams, Sue, illus. LC 92-53095. 96p. (gr. k-5). 1992. 16.95 (*1-85697-824-9*, Kingfisher LKC) LKC.
Menez, Annie R. Why the Kalaw Wears a Casque & Other Stories for Children. (Illus.). 34p. (Orig.). (gr. 1-3). 1993. pap. 3.00 (*971-10-0494-1*, Pub. by New Day Pub PI) Cellar.
Menzies, Edna. Storytime. (Illus.). 128p. (gr. 6-8). 1993. pap. 4.95 (*1-879224-15-1*) Mailbox.
Milam, June M. I've Got an Idea. Gilmer, Chris, ed. McIntosh, Chuck, illus. 20p. (ps-k). 1994. pap. text ed. 24.95 (*1-884307-07-8*); student's ed. 4.95 (*1-884307-08-6*) Dev Res Educ.
Miller, Teresa & Pellowski, Anne. Joining In: An Anthology of Audience Participation Stories & How to Tell Them. Livo, Norma J., ed. Simms, Laura, intro. by. 125p. (Orig.). 1988. pap. text ed. 11.95 (*0-938756-21-4*) Yellow Moon.
Minor, Lee. Table in the Sky. LC 88-51386. 53p. (gr. k-3). 1989. 5.95 (*1-55523-197-7*) Winston-Derek.
Miranda, Lydia. Redheads: Stories & Narrations for School Students. 1993. 9.95 (*0-8062-4521-2*) Carlton.
Monrad, Jean. How Many Kisses Goodnight: Just Right for 2's & 3's. Wilkin, Eloise, illus. LC 88-6453. 24p. (ps). 1986. 6.00 (*0-394-88253-9*) Random Bks Yng Read.
Moore, Lilian & Lobel, Arnold. The Magic Spectacles & Other Easy to Read Stories. 80p. (Orig.). (gr. 6). 1985. pap. 2.25 (*0-553-15329-3*) Bantam.
The Moth & Other Stories. (Illus.). 128p. (Orig.). 1962. pap. text ed. 5.95 (*0-582-53018-0*) Longman.
Mowry, Jess. Rats in the Trees: Stories. LC 89-27909. 160p. (Orig.). 1990. pap. 8.95 (*0-936784-81-4*) J Daniel.
Mugo, Phoebe, ed. Lodu's Escape: And Other Stories from Africa. (Illus.). 64p. (Orig.). (gr. 3-5). 1994. pap. 6.95 (*0-377-00269-0*) Friendship Pr.
Muntean, Michaela. Bert & the Magic Lamp & Other Good-Night Stories. (Illus.). 24p. (ps-1). 1989. write for info. (*0-307-12073-2*, Pub. by Golden Bks) Western Pub.
—Sesame Street: Ernie & His Merry Monsters & Other Good-Night Stories. Leigh, Tom, illus. 24p. (ps-3). 1992. write for info. (*0-307-12336-7*, 12336, Golden Pr) Western Pub.
—What's in Oscar's Trash Can? And Other Good-Night Stories. Cooke, Tom, illus. (ps-1). 1991. 3.25 (*0-307-12342-1*, Golden Pr) Western Pub.
Myers, Ruth S. & Banfield, Beryle, eds. Embers: Stories for a Changing World. LC 82-73499. (Illus.). 175p. (gr. 3-6). 1983. pap. 8.95 (*0-930040-47-3*); tchr's manual 18.95 (*0-930040-46-5*) CIBC.
Nehemias, Paulette. A Tree in Sprocket's Pocket: Stories about God's Green Earth. Harris, Jim, illus. LC 92-26033. 128p. (Orig.). (gr. 3-5). 1993. pap. 4.99 (*0-570-04730-7*) Concordia.
—Wiggler's Worms: Stories about God's Green Earth. Harris, Jim, illus. LC 92-28486. 128p. (Orig.). (gr. 3-5). 1993. pap. 4.99 (*0-570-04731-5*) Concordia.
Nesbit, Edith. Whereyouwantogoto: And Other Unlikely Tales. Millar, H. R. & Shepperson, Claude, illus. LC 93-18685. 224p. 1993. 6.00 (*1-56957-904-0*) Shambhala Pubns.
Offen, Hilda, illus. A Treasury of Bedtime Stories. Yeatman, Linda, compiled by. (Illus.). 160p. (ps-3). 1981. pap. 13.00 (*0-671-44463-8*, S&S BFYR) S&S Trade.
O. Henry. Four Million & Other Stories. (gr. 8 up). 1964. pap. 1.25 (*0-8049-0025-6*, CL-25) Airmont.
O. Henry & Gianni, Gary. The Gift of the Magi & Other Stories. (Illus.). 52p. Date not set. pap. 4.95 (*1-57209-013-8*) Classics Int Ent.
Outlet Staff. More Five Minute Bunny Tales for Bedtime. 1993. 7.99 (*0-517-08769-3*) Random Hse Value.
Outstanding Short Stories. 1993. pap. text ed. 6.50 (*0-582-09678-2*, 79822) Longman.
Oxenbury, Helen. First Day of School. (Illus.). 24p. (ps-1). 1993. pap. 3.99 (*0-14-054977-3*, Puff Pied Piper) Puffin Bks.
—Helen Oxenbury's First Nursery Stories. Oxenbury, Helen, illus. 32p. (ps-k). 1994. pap. 3.95 (*0-689-71825-X*, Aladdin) Macmillan Child Grp.
Paley, Nina, illus. Inside-Out Feelings. LC 93-8953. 1993. write for info. (*1-56071-315-1*) ETR Assocs.
Pascal, Francine. Left Back. 1992. pap. 2.99 (*0-553-48005-7*) Bantam.
Paton Walsh, Jill. Green Book. LC 81-12620. (Illus.). 80p. (gr. 5 up). 1986. pap. 3.95 (*0 374-42802-6*) FS&G.
Paulsen, Gary. Madonna Stories. (gr. 4-7). 1993. pap. 8.95 (*0-15-655116-0*, HB Juv Bks) HarBrace.
Pearce, Philippa. Who's Afraid? & Other Strange Stories. LC 86-14299. 160p. (gr. 5-9). 1987. 10.25 (*0-688-06895-2*) Greenwillow.
Pearce, Q. L. Still More Scary Stories for Sleepovers. LC 93-12822. (Illus.). 128p. (Orig.). (gr. 3-6). 1993. pap. 4.95 (*0-8431-3588-3*) Price Stern.
Pellowski, Anne, ed. A World of Children's Stories. Ortiz, Gloria, illus. LC 93-13509. 192p. (Orig.). (gr. 3-6). 1993. pap. 19.95 (*0-377-00259-3*) Friendship Pr.
Pepper, Dennis, ed. The Oxford Book of Scary Tales. (Illus.). 160p. 1992. 20.00 (*0-19-278131-6*) OUP.
Perez, Rachel L. Ms. Pea's Pet Store & Other Children's Tales. 1994. 7.95 (*0-533-10836-5*) Vantage.
Philadelphia Schools Students. From the Young at Heart: A Student Anthology. Goodman, Sharon L., ed. Saahaddin, Anwar, et al, illus. 20p. (Orig.). (gr. 1-8). 1989. pap. write for info. (*0-935369-19-8*) In Tradition Pub.
Phillips, Gina, ed. Three Minute Bedtime Stories. Persico, F. S., illus. 24p. 1991. 2.98 (*1-56156-087-1*) Kidsbks.
Pickering, H. G. The Pickering Collection: Neighbors Have My Ducks, Merry Xmas, Mr. Williams Dog Days on Trout Waters & Angling of the Test. Timmins, Harry L. & Gardner, Donald, illus. 189p. (gr. 10 up). 1993. Repr. of 1933 ed. 40.00 (*1-56416-047-5*) Derrydale Pr.
The Play of the Week: Selected from Highlights for Children. LC 92-73626. (Illus.). 96p. (gr. 2-5). 1993. pap. 2.95 (*1-56397-193-3*) Boyds Mills Pr.
Poe, Edgar Allan. Edgar Allan Poe, Stories & Poems. (gr. 9 up). 1962. pap. 3.25 (*0-8049-0008-6*, CL-8) Airmont.
—Ghostly Tales & Eerie Poems of Edgar Allan Poe. Schwinger, Larry, illus. LC 92-30884. 256p. 1993. 13.95 (*0-448-40533-4*, G&D) Putnam Pub Group.
Porte, Barbara A. Jesse's Ghost & Other Stories. LC 83-1451. 128p. (gr. 7 up). 1983. reinforced 10.25 (*0-688-02301-0*) Greenwillow.
Potter, Beatrix. Peter Rabbit & Eleven Other Favorite Tales. Stewart, Pat, adapted by. Potter, Beatrix, illus. LC 93-14417. 96p. 1994. pap. 1.00t (*0-486-27845-X*) Dover.
The Power of a Promise. 32p. (Orig.). (gr. 1-5). 1989. 14.95 (*0-89800-196-X*); pap. 7.95 (*0-89800-197-8*) Dharma Pub.
Powling, Chris, compiled by. Faces in the Dark: A Book of Scary Stories. Bailey, Peter, illus. LC 93-46911. 80p. (gr. 2-6). 1994. 16.95 (*1-85697-986-5*, Kingfisher LKC) LKC.
Prenzlau, Sheryl, ed. Everything under the Sun: An Anthology for Young Teens. 448p. (gr. 5 up). 1993. 17.95 (*1-56871-020-8*); pap. 14.95 (*1-56871-021-6*) Targum Pr.
Prevert, Jacques. Contes pour Enfants pas Sages. Henriquez, Elsa, illus. (FRE.). 88p. (gr. 1-5). 1990. pap. 12.95 (*2-07-031181-3*) Schoenhof.
Proysen, Alf. Little Old Mrs. Pepperpot. (gr. 1-4). 1960. 12.95 (*0-8392-3021-4*) Astor-Honor.
—Mrs. Pepperpot Again. Berg, Bjorn, illus. (gr. 1-4). 1961. 12.95 (*0-8392-3023-0*) Astor-Honor.
Pyle, Howard. Tales of Pirates & Buccaneers. Pyle, Howard, illus. LC 93-44689. 1994. write for info. (*0-517-10162-9*) Random Hse Value.
—The Wonder Clock or, Four & Twenty Marvelous Tales, Being One for Each Hour of the Day. (Illus.). xiv, 319p. (gr. 3-6). pap. 7.95 (*0-486-21446-X*) Dover.
The Rabbit in the Moon. 32p. (Orig.). (gr. 1-5). 1989. 14.95 (*0-89800-190-0*); pap. 7.95 (*0-89800-191-9*) Dharma Pub.
Ramos, Lindsey. Four Chinese Children's Stories. Troupe, Connie, illus. 1991. 14.95 (*0-9628563-0-4*) Lttle Peop Pr.
The Random House Book of Easy-to-Read Stories. LC 92-40179. 256p. (ps-3). 1993. 18.00 (*0-679-83438-9*); PLB 18.99 (*0-679-93438-3*) Random Bks Yng Read.

Razzi, Jim. Terror in the Mirror. LC 89-5230. 96p. (gr. 7 up). 1990. PLB 9.89 (*0-8167-1684-6*); pap. text ed. 2.95 (*0-8167-1685-4*) Troll Assocs.
Relf, Pat. Hurry! Hurry! 24p. (ps up). 1992. write for info. (*0-307-74802-2*, 64802) Western Pub.
Richardson, Arleta. More Stories from Grandma's Attic. LC 78-73125. (Illus.). (gr. 3-7). 1979. pap. 3.99 (*0-89191-131-6*, Chariot Bks) Chariot Family.
Robbins, Bonnie N. Nap-Time Tales. 1992. 7.95 (*0-533-10232-4*) Vantage.
Roberts, Ann, ed. The Children's Treasury of Animal Stories. Machalek, Jan, illus. 192p. (ps-5). 1993. 18.95 (*1-55013-504-X*, Pub. by Key Porter Bks CN) Natl Bk Netwk.
Rochman, Hazel. Who Do You Think You Are? Stories of Friends & Enemies. 1993. 15.95 (*0-316-75355-6*) Little.
Rosen, Michael, compiled by. Funny Stories. Blundell, Tony, illus. LC 92-26447. 256p. (gr. 4-9). 1993. 6.95 (*1-85697-883-4*, Kingfisher LKC) LKC.
Rosen, Michael, ed. South & North, East & West: The Oxfam Book of Children's Stories. Goldberg, Whoopi, intro. by. LC 91-58749. (Illus.). 96p. (ps up). 1992. 19.95 (*1-56402-117-3*) Candlewick Pr.
Rosentheil, Agnes. Mimi Makes a Splash. Stryker, Sandra & Paine, Penelope, eds. Paine, Penelope, tr. LC 91-11286. (Illus.). 48p. (Orig.). (ps-4). 1991. pap. 6.95 (*0-911655-51-4*) Advocacy Pr.

—Mimi Takes Charge. Stryker, Sandra & Paine, Penelope, eds. Paine, Penelope, tr. LC 91-11285. (Illus.). 48p. (Orig.). (ps-4). 1991. pap. 6.95 (0-911655-50-6) Advocacy Pr.

Rosman, Steven M. The Twenty-Two Gates to the Garden. LC 93-35944. 224p. 1994. pap. 24.95 (1-56821-124-4) Aronson.

Rossner, Richard. The Whole Story: Short Stories for Pleasure & Language Improvement. (gr. 9-12). 1988. pap. text ed. 14.95 (0-582-79109-X, 78326); cass. 22. 95 (0-582-01887-0, 78325) Longman.

Roy, Cal. Bubble, the Birds, & the Noise. Roy, Cal, illus. (gr. k-4). 1968. 8.95 (0-8392-3069-9) Astor-Honor.

Sakade, Florence. Kintaro's Adventures & Other Japanese Children's Stories. Hayashi, Yoshio, illus. 60p. (gr. 1-5). 1958. pap. 8.95 (0-8048-0343-9) C E Tuttle.

—Little One-Inch & Other Japanese Children's Favorite Stories. (Illus.). 60p. (gr. 1-5). 1958. pap. 8.95 (0-8048-0384-6) C E Tuttle.

—Peach Boy & Other Japanese Children's Favorite Stories. Kurosaki, Yoshisuke, illus. 58p. (gr. 1-5). 1958. pap. 8.95 (0-8048-0469-9) C E Tuttle.

Sakade, Florence, ed. Urashima Taro & Other Japanese Children's Stories. (Illus.). 58p. (gr. 1-6). 1958. pap. 8.95 (0-8048-0609-8) C E Tuttle.

Salerno, Tony, et al. Tony Salerno's Good News Express. Thompson, Del, et al, illus. 64p. (Orig.). (gr. k-6). Date not set. pap. write for info. (1-881597-00-8) Magination CA.

Salkey, Andrew. Brother Anancy & Other Stories. LC 93-24266. 1993. write for info. (0-582-22581-7, Pub. by Longman UK) Longman.

Sandburg, Carl. Rootabaga Stories. Cott, Jonathan, ed. Petersham, Maud & Petersham, Miska, illus. LC 93-41102. (ps). 1994. pap. 7.50 (1-56957-925-3) Barefoot Bks.

—Rootabaga Stories, Pt. 2. Hague, Michael, illus. 179p. (gr. 3-7). 1989. 19.95 (0-15-269062-X) HarBrace.

—Rootabaga Stories, Pt. 2. Hague, Michael, contrib. by. 158p. (gr. 3-7). 1990. pap. 4.95 (0-15-269063-8, Odyssey) HarBrace.

Saro-Wiwa, Ken. A Forest of Flowers: Short Stories. 151p. (Orig.). (gr. 10 up). pap. 10.00 (9-78246-004-4) Three Continents.

Sauerwein, Leigh. The Way Home. LC 93-10097. 1993. 15.00 (0-374-38247-6) FS&G.

Scarry, Richard. Richard Scarry's Best Story Book Ever. Scarry, Richard, illus. (gr. 1-5). 1968. write for info. (0-307-16548-5, Golden Bks) Western Pub.

Schrader, Richard A. Fungi: More Crucian Stories. Emanuel, Charles A., intro. by. LC 92-96921. (Illus.). 114p. 1993. pap. text ed. write for info. (0-9622987-3-5) R A Schrader.

Schultz, Dave. Little Ditties. Ferrante, Len, intro. by. 64p. (Orig.). pap. 3.00 (0-937393-08-8) Fred Pr.

Schwartz. Wonder Child & Other Jewish Fairytales. Date not set. 16.00 (0-06-023517-9); PLB 15.89 (0-06-023518-7) HarpC Child Bks.

Schwartz, Alvin. All of Our Noses Are Here & Other Noodle Tales. Weinhaus, Karen A., illus. LC 84-48330. 64p. (gr. k-3). 1987. pap. 3.50 (0-06-444108-3, Trophy) HarpC Child Bks.

—Gold & Silver, Silver & Gold: Tales of Hidden Treasure. 1993. pap. 8.95 (0-374-42583-3, Sunburst) FS&G.

—More Scary Stories to Tell in the Dark. Gammell, Stephen, illus. LC 83-49494. 112p. (gr. 4 up). 1986. pap. 3.95 (0-06-440177-4, Trophy) HarpC Child Bks.

—Whoppers: Tall Tales & Other Lies. LC 74-32024. (Illus.). 128p. (gr. 4 up). 1975. 14.00 (0-397-31575-9, Lipp Jr Bks) HarpC Child Bks.

Scieszka, Jon. The Stinky Cheese Man: And Other Fairly Stupid Tales. Smith, Lane, illus. 56p. (gr. 1). 1992. 16. 00 (0-670-84487-X) Viking Child Bks.

Segal, Lore. Tell Me a Mitzi. LC 69-14980. (Illus.). 40p. (ps-3). 1991. pap. 5.95 (0-374-47502-4) FS&G.

—Tell Me a Trudy. Wells, Rosemary, illus. (ps up). 1989. pap. 4.95 (0-374-47504-0) FS&G.

Segel, Elizabeth. Short Takes. (gr. 4-7). 1992. pap. 3.99 (0-440-40581-5) Dell.

—Short Takes: A Collection of Short Stories. Smith, Joseph A., illus. 160p. (gr. 9 up). 1986. 12.95 (0-688-06092-7) Lothrop.

Selleck, Richelle R. Take-Home Stories. 96p. (ps-2). 1990. 10.95 (0-86653-567-5, GA1169) Good Apple.

Sendak, Maurice. Nutshell Library. Incl. Alligators All Around; Chicken Soup with Rice; One Was Johnny; Pierre. LC 62-13315. (ps-3). 1962. Set. 15.00i (0-06-025500-5) HarpC Child Bks.

Shannon, George. Stories to Solve: Folktales from Around the World. Sis, Peter, illus. LC 84-18656. 56p. (gr. 3-5). 1985. 14.00 (0-688-04303-8); PLB 13.93 (0-688-04304-6) Greenwillow.

Sharmat, Marjorie W. Get Rich Mitch! Lustig, Loretta, illus. LC 85-8799. 160p. (gr. 3-7). 1985. 13.95 (0-688-05790-X) Morrow Jr Bks.

Shealy, Daniel, ed. Louisa May Alcott's Fairy Tales & Fantasy Stories. LC 91-43144. (Illus.). 432p. (Orig.). 1992. text ed. 37.95x (0-87049-752-9); pap. 24.95 (0-87049-758-8) U of Tenn Pr.

Sierra, Judy. The Flannel Board Storytelling Book. LC 87-6260. 216p. (ps-4). 1987. 40.00 (0-8242-0747-5) Wilson.

Sieruta, Peter D. Heartbeats: And Other Stories. LC 88-21351. 224p. (gr. 7 up). 1989. HarpC Child Bks.

—Heartbeats: And Other Stories. LC 88-21351. 224p. (gr. 7 up). 1991. pap. 3.50 (0-06-447064-4, Trophy) HarpC Child Bks.

The Silly Tail Book. 1994. 13.27 (0-8368-0986-6) Gareth Stevens Inc.

Silverman, Maida. The Glass Menorah & Other Stories for Jewish Holidays. Levine, Marge, illus. LC 91-13890. 64p. (gr. 1-4). 1992. RSBE 14.95 (0-02-782682-1, Four Winds) Macmillan Child Grp.

Simms, Donna A. The Hillsborough Tales. (Illus.). 76p. (gr. 4-7). write for info. (0-942078-22-5) R Tanner Assocs Inc.

Singer, Isaac Bashevis. Shrewd Todie & Lyzer the Miser: And Other Children's Stories. (gr. 2 up). 1994. 6.00 (1-56957-927-X) Barefoot Bks.

—Stories for Children. LC 84-13612. 338p. (gr. k up). 1984. 22.95 (0-374-37266-7); ltd. ed. o.s.i. 30.00 (0-374-37267-5) FS&G.

—Stories for Children. LC 84-13612. 338p. (gr. k up). 1985. pap. 12.95 (0-374-46489-8, Sunburst) FS&G.

—Zlateh the Goat & Other Stories. Sendak, Maurice, illus. LC 66-8114. (gr. 1-6). 1966. 16.00 (0-06-025698-2) HarpC Child Bks.

—Zlateh the Goat & Other Stories. Shub, Elizabeth, tr. Sendak, Maurice, illus. LC 66-8114. 96p. (gr. 3-7). 1984. pap. 4.95 (0-06-440147-2, Trophy) HarpC Child Bks.

Skaggs, Calvin, ed. The American Short Story, Vol. I. 400p. (gr. 7 up). 1979. pap. 5.99 (0-440-30294-3, LE) Dell.

Skinner, Ada M. & Skinner, Eleanor L. A Child's Book of Country Stories. Smith, Jessie W., illus. 224p. (gr. 1-7). 1992. 12.99 (0-517-69333-X, Child Classics) Random Hse Value.

Smith, Bruce. The Silver Locket: A Charleston Christmas Storybook. Smith, Bruce, illus. LC 94-78135. 110p. (Orig.). (ps up). 1994. pap. 11.95 (0-9642620-0-2) Marsh Wind Pr. Children's tales of the joy of the Christmas season set against a backdrop of America's most charming city. Share the wonder of a small boy who greets one of Claus' reindeer beneath the foggy, moss-shrouded oaks of Charleston's historic Battery; Meet Butter the golden retriever, who nurses an injured teal back to health in the marshes along the Ashley River; Ride cobbled streets with Magnolia, the carriage horse who refuses to pull without a carriage filled with children; Discover the magic of The Silver Locket, in which two young girls share a wondrous Charleston snowfall & learn the true meaning of the season. Ten stories by award-winning journalist, poet, & writer Bruce Smith - the Charleston correspondent for the Associated Press whose stories about Charleston & the South Carolina coast have been published throughout the South, across the nation & around the world. 110 page, perfect bound trade paperback. Illustrated with black & white renderings of Charleston scenes. Cover illuminated in silver, red & black. $11.95 retail. To order: Marsh Wind Press, Box 1596, Mount Pleasant, SC 29465. 803-884-5957. ***Publisher Provided Annotation.***

Smith, Janice L. The Kid Next Door & Other Headaches: More Stories about Adam Joshua. Gackenbach, Dick, illus. LC 83-47689. 160p. (gr. 1-4). 1986. pap. 3.95 (0-06-440182-0, Trophy) HarpC Child Bks.

—The Show-&-Tell War: And Other Stories about Adam Joshua. Gackenbach, Dick, illus. LC 85-45842. 176p. (gr. 1-4). 1988. PLB 12.89 (0-06-025815-2) HarpC Child Bks.

Sohn, David A., ed. Ten Top Stories. Bd. with Flowers for Algernon. Keyes; So Much Unfairness of Things. Bryan; Backward Boy. Coghlan; Denton's Daughter. Lowenberg; Hoods I Have Known. Spatt; Planet of the Condemned. Murphy; Test. Thomas; See How They Run. Coxe; Polar Night. Burke; The Turtle. Vukelich. (Orig.). (gr. 6-12). 1985. pap. 3.95 (0-553-25326-3) Bantam.

Sonnenfeld, Shlomo Z. Jerusalem Gems: Great Tales about Everyday People In Old Jerusalem. Dershowitz, Y., illus. 160p. 1987. 12.95 (0-89906-839-1); pap. 9.95 (0-89906-840-5) Mesorah Pubns.

Sorenson, Stephen. Growing up Is an Adventure, Lord. LC 92-27056. 112p. (gr. 3-7). 1992. pap. 5.99 (0-8066-2647-X, 9-2647) Augsburg Fortress.

Soto, Gary. Local News. LC 92-37905. 1993. 13.95 (0-15-248117-6) HarBrace.

Stamper, Judith B. Even More Tales for the Midnight Hour. 112p. (gr. 4 up). 1992. pap. 2.75 (0-590-44143-4, Point) Scholastic Inc.

—Five Funny Frights. Raglin, Tim, illus. LC 92-44538. (gr. 4 up). 1993. pap. 2.95 (0-590-46416-7) Scholastic Inc.

—Night Frights: Thirteen Scary Stories. (gr. 4-7). 1993. pap. 2.95 (0-590-46046-3) Scholastic Inc.

—Still More Tales for the Midnight Hour. 1992. pap. 2.95 (0-685-53518-5, Point) Scholastic Inc.

Stangl, Jean. Paper Stories. LC 84-60238. (ps-3). 1984. pap. 10.95 (0-8224-5402-5) Fearon Teach Aids.

Starr, Aloa. I Want to Know. Tyree, Michael, illus. (Orig.). (ps-6). 1990. pap. 7.00 (0-929686-02-0, Dist. by Aloa Starr) Temple Golden Pubns.

Stevens, Margaret M. Stepping Stones Three. Stevens, David, illus. 32p. (gr. 1-8). 1983. pap. 4.50 (0-87516-518-4) DeVorss.

Stockton, Frank. Lady or the Tiger & Other Stories. Gennie, F. R., intro. by. (gr. 5 up). 1968. pap. 1.95 (0-8049-0163-5, CL-163) Airmont.

Stop the Balloon! Selected from Highlights for Children. LC 92-73625. (Illus.). 96p. (gr. 2-5). 1993. pap. 2.95 (1-56397-194-1) Boyds Mills Pr.

Stories of Detection & Mystery. 1993. pap. text ed. 6.50 (0-582-08465-2, 79828) Longman.

Story Time Stories That Rhyme Staff. Holiday Storytelling: Christmas, Easter, Halloween. (Illus.). 1992. binder 21.95 (1-56820-002-1) Story Time.

—Stories with Activities That Educate & Inform: Sea Shell Edition. (Illus., Orig.). 1992. GBC bdg. 19.95 (1-56820-006-4) Story Time.

—Story Menus for Schools & Educational Locations to Duplicate & Use. (Illus.). 1992. binder 29.95 (1-56820-000-5) Story Time.

Strasser, Todd & Duke, Richard. Disney's It's Magic: Stories from the Films. DiCicco, Gil, illus. 80p. 1994. 14.95 (0-7868-3001-8); PLB 14.89 (0-7868-5000-0) Disney Pr.

Talkington, Bruce. Walt Disney's Tales from the Cottage: Stories by the Seven Dwarfs. Williams, Don, illus. 96p. (ps-3). 1994. 14.95 (0-7868-3008-5); PLB 14.89 (0-7868-5003-5) Disney Pr.

Tate, Eleanor E. Front Porch Stories: At the One-Room School. (gr. 4-7). 1994. pap. 3.50 (0-440-40901-2) Dell.

Taylor, B., ed. American Short Stories. (Illus.). 119p. 1964. pap. text ed. 5.95 (0-582-53026-1) Longman.

Terhune, Albert P. Great Dog Stories. 1993. 12.99 (0-517-09337-5) Random Hse Value.

Thomas, Piri. Stories from el Barrio. LC 78-328. (gr. 5-9). 1992. 15.00 (0-394-83568-9) Knopf Bks Yng Read.

Thomas, Vernon. More Stories from the Arabian Nights. Bose, R. K., illus. 135p. (gr. 1 up). 1981. 7.50 (0-89744-232-6, Pub. by Hemkunt India) Auromere.

Thompson, Richard. Tell Me One Good Thing: Bedtime Stories. Fernandes, Eugenie, illus. 48p. (ps-3). 1992. PLB 15.95 (1-55037-215-7, Pub. by Annick CN); pap. 7.95 (1-55037-212-2, Pub. by Annick CN) Firefly Bks Ltd.

Thornley, G. C., ed. Stories from Many Lands. (Illus.). 133p. (Orig.). 1964. pap. text ed. 5.95 (0-582-53025-3) Longman.

Toure, Masee. Mariamah's Good Fortune & Other Stories. (Illus.). (gr. 6-9). 1993. 10.95 (0-533-10292-8) Vantage.

Tournier, Michel. Sept Contes. Hezard, Pierre, illus. (FRE.). 161p. (gr. 5-10). 1990. pap. 9.95 (2-07-033497-X) Schoenhof.

Troudet, Farideh. Trudy's Short Stories. 1993. pap. 8.95 (0-533-10451-3) Vantage.

Trussell, Margaret E. Sierra Summers: Fireside Tales to Share with Young & Old. Van Kleeck, Cynthia, illus. Trussell, Margaret E., et al, photos by. Bechtol, Bruce, intro. by. LC 89-51208. (Illus.). 200p. (Orig.). (gr. 8-9). 1989. pap. 10.95 (0-9624235-1-3) Talking Mntn.

Twain, Mark. The Celebrated Jumping Frog of Calaveras County. (CHI.). 32p. (gr. 6). 1990. PLB 13.95 (0-88682-296-3) Creative Ed.

—Mark Twain: Short Stories & Tall Tales. LC 93-70552. 320p. (gr. 4 up). 1993. 5.98 (1-56138-323-6) Courage Bks.

—Short Stories of Mark Twain. Franklin, B., intro. by. (gr. 8 up). 1968. pap. 3.95 (0-8049-0171-6, CL-171) Airmont.

—The Signet Classic Book of Mark Twain's Short Stories. 688p. (gr. 5 up). 1989. pap. 4.50 (0-451-52220-6, Sig Classics) NAL-Dutton.

Two in One Books, Bk. 1. 1991. pap. 1.97 (1-56297-078-X) Lee Pubns KY.

Two in One Books, Bk. 2. 1991. pap. 1.97 (1-56297-079-8) Lee Pubns KY.

Umansky, Kaye. Phantasmagoria. Smedley, Chris, illus. 64p. (gr. 2-6). 14.95 (0-7136-3072-8, Pub. by A&C Black UK) Talman.

Upgren, H. Ted, Jr. Across the Wheatgrass: A Collection of Hearthside Stories about Uncommon People, Wildlife, Days Afield, & Things, Times & Places of Some Centennial Years. Calkins, Burdette & Bruner, Mike, illus. LC 88-50045. 211p. (Orig.). (gr. 8-12). 1988. 18.95 (0-9620122-0-3); pap. 12.95 (0-9620122-1-1) Windfeather Pr.

Uttley, Alison. Ten Candelight Tales. Hawkins, Irene, illus. 112p. (gr. k-2). 1991. pap. 3.95 (0-571-14289-3) Faber & Faber.

—The Weather Cock & Other Tales. Innes, Nancy, illus. 111p. (gr. k-3). 1991. pap. 2.95 (0-571-14174-9) Faber & Faber.

Vincenzi, Harry. Changes. LC 94-94044. (gr. 6-9). 1994. pap. text ed. 9.95 (*0-9640402-1-2*) Future Press.

Vollaro, Joseph. Skeletons in the Closet: A Collection of Short Stories. Paretta, Joseph, ed. Van Brunt, John, illus. 208p. (Orig.). (gr. 9-12). 1993. pap. 13.95 (*0-9633309-3-4*) Rightway Educ.

Von Konigslow, A. Wayne. Toilet Tales. (Illus.). 24p. (ps-8). 1985. PLB 14.95 (*0-920303-14-5*, Pub. by Annick CN); pap. 4.95 (*0-920303-13-7*, Pub. by Annick CN) Firefly Bks Ltd.

—Toilet Tales. Von Konigslow, Andrea W., illus. 24p. (ps-2). 1989. pap. 0.99 (*0-920303-81-1*, Pub. by Annick CN) Firefly Bks Ltd.

Von Munchhausen, Angelita. The Real Munchhausen: Baron of Bodenwerder. Carter, Harry, illus. 224p. (gr. 6 up). 1960. 10.00 (*0-8159-6701-2*) Devin.

Vonsild, Fred. Tales from the "Ile" of Mulberry. 1989. 7.95 (*0-533-08213-7*) Vantage.

Wagner, Paul. Thirteen, Vol. 1: Short Stories. 228p. (Orig.). (gr. 9-12). 1991. pap. text ed. 3.95 (*0-9628653-0-3*) USA Entrps.

Walker, Warren S., ed. Twentieth Century Short Story Explication New Series, 1989-1990, Vol. 1. LC 92-22790. vi, 366p. 1993. lib. bdg. 49.50 (*0-208-02340-2*) Shoe String.

Wallace, Latressia & Wilson, Annette. Black Wallstreet Children's Storybook: A Black City Made of Gold! Wilson, Jay J. & Wallace, Ron, eds. Wilson, Mike, illus. 32p. (Orig.). (ps-5). 1993. pap. text ed. 8.95 (*1-884265-02-2*) Black Wallst.

Walt Disney Story Land. 1987. write for info. (*0-317-66556-1*, Golden Bks) Western Pub.

Watson, Wendy. Tales for a Winter's Eve. LC 87-13467. (Illus.). 32p. (ps up). 1988. 13.00 (*0-374-37373-6*) FS&G.

—Tales for a Winter's Eve. (Illus.). 32p. (ps up). 1991. pap. 4.95 (*0-374-47419-2*) FS&G.

Weinberg, Larry. Shivers & Shakes. Tavonatti, Mia, illus. LC 93-24445. 1993. pap. 2.95 (*0-8167-3281-7*) Troll Assocs.

Welch, R. C. Twisted Tales: The Dripping Head & Other Gruesome Stories. Fike, Scott, illus. 128p. (Orig.). (gr. 3-7). 1992. pap. 4.95 (*1-56288-314-3*) Checkerboard.

—Twisted Tales: The Slithering Corpse & Other Sinister Stories. Fike, Scott, illus. 128p. (Orig.). (gr. 3-7). 1992. pap. 4.95 (*1-56288-315-1*) Checkerboard.

Welch, Sheila K. A Horse for All Seasons: Collected Stories. LC 93-94237. 160p. (gr. 4-8). 1994. 16.95 (*0-9638819-0-6*); pap. 9.95 (*0-9638819-1-4*) ShadowPlay Pr.

Wells, H. G. This Misery of Boots. 48p. (ps-12). 1987. pap. text ed. 2.50 (*0-930997-01-8*, W-01) East Bay Bks.

West, Mark I., ed. A Wondrous Menagerie: Animal Fantasy Stories from American Children's Literature. xvi, 139p. 1994. lib. bdg. 25.00 (*0-208-02383-6*, Pub. by Archon Bks) Shoe String.

Westall, Robert. Christmas Spirit: Two Stories. Lawrence, John, illus. LC 94-9847. (gr. 3 up). 1994. 14.00 (*0-374-31260-5*) FS&G.

—Echoes of War. 96p. (gr. 7 up). 1991. 13.95 (*0-374-31964-2*) FS&G.

—In Camera: And Other Stories. LC 92-13815. 176p. (gr. 7 up). 1993. 13.95 (*0-590-45920-1*) Scholastic Inc.

—Shades of Darkness: More of the Ghostly Best Stories of Robert Westall. LC 93-42229. 1994. 17.00 (*0-374-36758-2*) FS&G.

Westall, Robert, selected by. Ghost Stories. Eckett, Sean, illus. LC 92-26451. 256p. (gr. 4-9). 1993. 6.95 (*1-85697-884-2*, Kingfisher LKC) LKC.

What You See Is What... (Illus.). (ps-2). 1991. PLB 6.95 (*0-8136-5084-4*, TK2380); pap. 3.50 (*0-8136-5584-6*, TK2381) Modern Curr.

What's for Dinner? And Other Stories. 140p. (ps-1). 1994. 17.95 (*0-340-58988-4*, Pub. by Hodder & Stoughton UK); pap. 6.95 (*0-340-58996-5*, Pub. by Hodder & Stoughton UK) Trafalgar.

Whitcher, Susan. Real Mummies Don't Bleed: Friendly Tales for October Nights. (gr. 4-7). 1993. 15.00 (*0-374-36213-0*) FS&G.

White, Stephen. BJ's Silly Story. Daste, Larry, illus. LC 94-71998. 16p. (ps-k). 1994. bds. 4.95 (*1-57064-018-1*) Barney Pub.

Wilde, Oscar. Stories for Children. Lynch, P. J., illus. LC 90-38854. 96p. (gr. 3 up). 1991. 14.95 (*0-02-792765-2*, Macmillan Child Bk) Macmillan Child Grp.

Willard, Nancy. Telling Time: Angels, Ancestors, & Stories. LC 93-16390. (gr. 4-7). 1993. pap. 10.95 (*0-15-693130-3*, HB Juv Bks) HarBrace.

Willcox Smith, Jessie. A Child's Book of Stories. (gr. k-6). 1986. 8.98 (*0-685-16856-5*, 618869) Random Hse Value.

Williams, Sheila. Loch Moose Monster: More Stories from Isaac Asimov's Science Fiction Magazine. LC 91-36291. 1993. 16.00 (*0-385-30600-8*) Doubleday.

Williams, Sheila & Ardai, Charles, eds. Why I Left Harry's All-Night Hamburgers: And Other Short Stories from Isaac Asimov's Science Fiction Magazine. 288p. (gr. 7 up). 1992. pap. 3.99 (*0-440-21394-0*, LFL) Dell.

Wilson, Budge. The Leaving. 208p. (gr. 6 up). 1992. 14. 95 (*0-399-21878-5*, Philomel Bks) Putnam Pub Group.

Wilson, Jack. Glacier Wings & Tales. 2nd ed. Clark, Marvin, ed. Benson, Carl, intro. by. (Illus.). 220p. (gr. 9 up). 1990. pap. 19.95 (*0-937708-18-6*) Great Northwest.

Wise, Francis H. & Wise, Joyce M. Storybooks. (Illus.). 105p. (gr. k-1). 1979. pap. 7.50 (*0-685-05433-0*) Wise Pub.

Wonder Kids Publications Group Staff (USA) & Hwa-I Publishing Co., Staff. Animal Tales: Chinese Children's Stories, Vols. 11-15. Ching, Emily, et al, eds. Wonder Kids Publication Staff, tr. from CHI. Hwa-I Publishing Co., Staff, illus. LC 90-60793. 28p. (gr. 3-6). 1991. Repr. of 1988 ed. Five vol. set, 28p. ea. bk. 39.75 (*0-685-58702-9*) Wonder Kids.

—Chinese Sites: Chinese Children's Stories, Vols. 86-90. Ching, Emily, et al, eds. Wonder Kids Publications Staff, tr. from CHI. Hwa-I Publishing Co., Staff, illus. LC 90-60809. (gr. 3-6). 1991. Repr. of 1988 ed. Five vol. set, 28p. ea. bk. 39.75 (*0-685-58717-7*) Wonder Kids.

—Festivals: Chinese Children's Stories, Vols. 26-30. Ching, Emily, et al, eds. Wonder Kids Publications Staff, tr. from CHI. Hwa-I Publishing Co., Staff, illus. LC 90-60797. (gr. 3-6). 1991. Repr. of 1988 ed. Five vol. set, 28p. ea. bk. 39.75 (*0-685-58705-3*) Wonder Kids.

—Filial Piety: Chinese Children's Stories, Vols. 51-55. Ching, Emily, et al, eds. Wonder Kids Publications Staff, tr. from CHI. Hwa-I Publishing Co., Staff, illus. LC 90-60802. (gr. 3-6). 1991. Repr. of 1988 ed. Five vol. set, 28p. ea. bk. 39.75 (*0-685-58710-X*) Wonder Kids.

—Folklore: Chinese Children's Stories, Vols. 1-5. Ching, Emily, et al, eds. Wonder Kids Publications Staff, tr. from CHI. Hwa-I Publishing Co., Staff, illus. LC 90-60791. 28p. (gr. 3-6). 1991. Repr. of 1988 ed. Five vol. set, 28p. ea. bk. 39.75 (*0-685-58701-0*); Set (100 vols.) 795.00 (*1-56162-120-X*) Wonder Kids.

—Heroes: Chinese Children's Stories, Vols. 76-80. Ching, Emily, et al, eds. Wonder Kids Publications Staff, tr. from CHI. Hwa-I Publishing Co., Staff, illus. LC 90-60807. (gr. 3-6). 1991. Repr. of 1988 ed. Five vol. set, 28p. ea. bk. 39.75 (*0-685-58715-0*) Wonder Kids.

—Historical Accounts: Chinese Children's Stories, Vols. 81-85. Ching, Emily, et al, eds. Wonder Kids Publications Staff, tr. from CHI. Hwa-I Publishing Co., Staff, illus. LC 90-60808. (gr. 3-6). 1991. Repr. of 1988 ed. Five vol. set, 28p. ea. bk. 39.75 (*0-685-58716-9*) Wonder Kids.

—Idioms: Chinese Children's Stories, Vols. 21-25. Ching, Emily, et al, eds. Wonder Kids Publications Staff, tr. from CHI. Hwa-I Publishing Co., Staff, illus. LC 90-60796. (gr. 3-6). 1991. Repr. of 1988 ed. Five vol. set, 28p. ea. bk. 39.75 (*0-685-58704-5*) Wonder Kids.

—Inventions: Chinese Children's Stories, Vols. 36-40. Ching, Emily, et al, eds. Wonder Kids Publications Staff, tr. from CHI. Hwa-I Publishing Co., Staff, illus. LC 90-60799. (gr. 3-6). 1991. Repr. of 1988 ed. Five vol. set, 28p. ea. bk. 39.75 (*0-685-58707-X*) Wonder Kids.

—Literature: Chinese Children's Stories, Vols. 66-70. Ching, Emily, et al, eds. Wonder Kids Publications Staff, tr. from CHI. Hwa-I Publishing Co., Staff, illus. LC 90-60805. (gr. 3-6). 1991. Repr. of 1988 ed. Five vol. set, 28p. ea. bk. 39.75 (*0-685-58713-4*) Wonder Kids.

—Popular Narratives: Chinese Children's Stories, Vols. 71-75. Ching, Emily, et al, eds. Wonder Kids Publications Staff, tr. from CHI. Hwa-I Publishing Co., Staff, illus. LC 90-60806. (gr. 3-6). 1991. Repr. of 1988 ed. Five vol. set, 28p. ea. bk. 39.75 (*0-685-58714-2*) Wonder Kids.

—Taiwanese Sites: Chinese Children's Stories, Vols. 91-95. Ching, Emily, et al, eds. Wonder Kids Publications Staff, tr. from CHI. Hwa-I Publishing Co., Staff, illus. LC 90-60810. (gr. 3-6). 1991. Repr. of 1988 ed. Five vol. set, 28p. ea. bk. 39.75 (*0-685-58718-5*) Wonder Kids.

—Tales about Food: Chinese Children's Stories, Vols. 31-35. Ching, Emily, et al, eds. Wonder Kids Publications Staff, tr. from CHI. Hwa-I Publishing Co., Staff, illus. LC 90-60798. (gr. 3-6). 1991. Repr. of 1988 ed. Five vol. set, 28p. ea. bk. 39.75 (*0-685-58706-1*) Wonder Kids.

—Twelve Beasts & the Years: Chinese Children's Stories, Vols. 41-45. Ching, Emily, et al, eds. Wonder Kids Publications Staff, tr. from CHI. Hwa-I Publishing Co., Staff, illus. LC 90-60800. (gr. 3-6). 1991. Repr. of 1988 ed. Five vol. set, 28p. ea. bk. 39.75 (*0-685-58708-8*) Wonder Kids.

—Wonder Kids: Chinese Children's Stories, Vols. 56-60. Ching, Emily, et al, eds. Wonder Kids Publications Staff, tr. from CHI. Hwa-I Publishing Co., Staff, illus. LC 90-60803. (gr. 3-6). 1991. Repr. of 1988 ed. Five vol. set, 28p. ea. bk. 39.75 (*0-685-58711-8*) Wonder Kids.

World's Best Christmas Stories. LC 93-27249. (Illus.). 80p. (gr. 4-6). 1993. pap. 1.95 (*0-8167-3142-X*, Pub. by Watermill Pr) Troll Assocs.

Worth, Bonnie. Bye-Bye, Blankie. Cooke, Tom, illus. 18p. (ps). 1992. bds. 3.50 (*0-307-12329-4*, 12329, Golden Pr) Western Pub.

Wulffson, Don L. Time Fix: And Other Tales of Terror. 96p. 1994. 13.99 (*0-525-65140-3*, Cobblehill Bks) Dutton Child Bks.

Yashinsky, Dan, ed. Next Teller: A Book of Canadian Storytelling. (Illus.). 224p. (gr. 7 up). 1994. pap. 12.95 (*0-921556-46-2*, Pub. by Gynergy-Ragweed CN) InBook.

Yolen, Jane. Here There Be Unicorns. Wilgus, David, illus. LC 94-1790. (gr. 5 up). 1994. write for info. (*0-15-209902-6*) HarBrace.

—Two Thousand Forty-One: Twelve Stories about the Future by Top Science Fiction Writers. 1994. pap. 3.99 (*0-440-21898-5*) Dell.

Yolen, Jane, ed. Camelot. LC 92-39322. 1994. 21.95 (*0-399-22540-4*, Philomel Bks) Putnam Pub Group.

Yolen, Jane & Greenberg, Martin H., eds. Vampires. LC 90-27888. 240p. (gr. 5 up). 1991. 15.00 (*0-06-026800-X*); PLB 14.89 (*0-06-026801-8*) HarpC Child Bks.

Young, Judy D. & Young, Richard, eds. Stories from the Days of Columbus: A Multicultural Collection for Young Readers. 160p. 1992. 17.95 (*0-87483-199-7*); pap. 8.95 (*0-87483-198-9*) August Hse.

Zolotow, Charlotte, ed. Early Sorrow: Ten Stories of Youth. LC 79-2669. 224p. (gr. 7 up). 1986. PLB 14.89 (*0-06-026937-5*) HarpC Child Bks.

Zorn, Steven, as told by. Mostly Ghostly: Eight Spooky Tales to Chill Your Bones. Brodley, John, illus. LC 91-71087. 56p. (gr. 2 up). 1991. 9.98 (*1-56138-033-4*) Courage Bks.

SHRIMPS

Russell, Ching Y. A Day on a Shrimp Boat. Littlejohn, Beth, ed. Russell, Phillip K., illus. 57p. (gr. 3-6). 1993. 13.95 (*0-87844-120-4*) Sandlapper Pub Co.

SHRUBS

Gattis, L. S., III. Shrubs for Pathfinders: A Basic Youth Enrichment Skill Honor Packet. (Illus.). 20p. (Orig.). (gr. 5 up). 1989. pap. 5.00 tchr's. ed. (*0-936241-41-1*) Cheetah Pub.

SHULA, DON, 1930-

Stein, R. Conrad. Don Shula: Football's Winningest Coach. LC 94-9915. (Illus.). 48p. (gr. 2-8). 1994. PLB 15.80 (*0-516-04385-4*); pap. 3.95 (*0-516-44385-2*) Childrens.

SIAMESE TWINS

Collins, David R. Eng & Chang: The Original Siamese Twins. LC 93-26295. (Illus.). 112p. (gr. 4-7). 1994. text ed. 13.95 RSBE (*0-87518-602-5*, Dillon Pr) Macmillan Child Grp.

SIBERIA

Hautzig, Esther. Endless Steppe: Growing up in Siberia. LC 68-13582. 256p. (gr. 7 up). 1992. 15.00 (*0-690-26371-6*, Crowell Jr Bks); PLB 14.89 (*0-690-04919-6*, Crowell Jr Bks) HarpC Child Bks.

SIBERIA–FICTION

Kalashnikoff, Nicholas. The Defender. Louden, Claire & Louden, George, Jr., illus. LC 92-33560. 144p. (gr. 3-7). 1993. pap. 6.95 (*0-8027-7397-4*) Walker & Co.

SICILY–FICTION

Valens, Amy. Danilo the Fruit Man. Valens, Amy, illus. LC 91-46893. 32p. (ps-3). 1993. 12.99 (*0-8037-1151-4*); PLB 12.89 (*0-8037-1152-2*) Dial Bks Young.

SIDEREAL SYSTEM

see Stars

SIERRA LEONE

Milsome, John. Sierra Leone. (Illus.). 96p. (gr. 5 up). 1988. 14.95 (*0-7910-0106-7*) Chelsea Hse.

SIERRA NEVADA MOUNTAINS

Williams, George, III. Hot Springs of the Eastern Sierra. 2nd, rev. ed. Dalton, Bill, ed. LC 87-16230. (Illus.). 80p. (gr. 8-12). 1993. text ed. 14.95 (*0-935174-35-4*); pap. 9.95 (*0-935174-34-6*) Tree by River.

SIERRA NEVADA MOUNTAINS–FICTION

Nesbit, Jeff. Cougar Chase. LC 93-40145. 1994. pap. 4.99 (*0-8407-9255-7*) Nelson.

—Mountaintop Rescue. LC 93-49796. (gr. 4 up). 1994. pap. 4.99 (*0-8407-9257-3*) Nelson.

—Setting the Trap. LC 93-41025. 1994. pap. 4.99 (*0-8407-9256-5*) Nelson.

Nesbit, Jeffrey A. The Legend of the Great Grizzly. LC 93-39765. 1994. pap. 4.99 (*0-8407-9254-9*) Nelson.

SIGHT

see Vision

SIGN BOARDS

see Signs and Signboards

SIGN LANGUAGE

see Indians of North America–Sign Language

SIGNALS AND SIGNALING

see also Flags; Radio

Greene, Laura & Dicker, Eva B. Sign Language Talk. Solomon, Maury, ed. Caraway, Caren, illus. 96p. (gr. 5 up). 1989. PLB 11.90 o.s. (*0-531-10597-0*) Watts.

SIGNERS OF THE DECLARATION OF INDEPENDENCE

see U. S. Declaration of Independence

SIGNS (ADVERTISING)

see Signs and Signboards

SIGNS AND SIGNBOARDS

see also Posters

Finton, Esther. Bulletin Boards Should Be More Than Something to Look At. 64p. (gr. k-6). 1979. 7.95 (*0-916456-32-3*, GA97) Good Apple.

Hoban, Tana. I Walk & Read. Hoban, Tana, illus. LC 83-14215. 32p. (ps-1). 1984. 17.00 (*0-688-02575-7*); PLB 16.93 (*0-688-02576-5*) Greenwillow.

SIGNS AND SIGNBOARDS–FICTION

Arnold, Tedd. The Signmaker's Assistant. Arnold, Tedd, illus. LC 90-19537. 32p. (ps-3). 1992. 14.00 (*0-8037-1010-0*); PLB 13.89 (*0-8037-1011-9*) Dial Bks Young.

SIGNS AND SYMBOLS

see also Ciphers; Cryptography; Heraldry; Signals and Signaling; Symbolism

Bartusch, Nancy. Sign Numbers. (Illus.). 54p. (Orig.). (ps-3). 1988. pap. 5.00 (*0-916708-17-9*) Modern Signs.

Hausman, Gerald. Turtle Island ABC: A Gathering of Native American Symbols. Moser, Barry & Moser, Cara, illus. LC 92-14982. 32p. (gr. 1 up). 1994. 15.00 (*0-06-021307-8*); PLB 14.89 (*0-06-021308-6*) HarpC Child Bks.
Hefter, Richard. Watch Out! Hefter, Richard, illus. LC 83-2190. 32p. (ps-1). 1983. 5.95 (*0-911787-03-8*) Optimum Res Inc.
Hovanec, Helene. Doubletalk: Codes, Signs & Symbols. Wimmer, Chuck, illus. (gr. 7-10). 1993. pap. 1.25 (*0-553-37218-1*) Bantam.
Nelson, Nigel. Signs & Symbols. De Saulles, Tony, illus. LC 93-27779. 32p. (gr. k-2). 1993. 12.95 (*1-56847-100-9*) Thomson Lrning.
Schneider, D. Douglas. Symbolically Speaking. Holbrook, Clifford & LaMothe, Becky, illus. Michael, ed. 85p. (ps up). 1987. pap. 5.95 (*0-939169-01-0*) World Peace Univ.

SIKORSKY, IGOR IVANOVICH, 1889-

Otfinski, Steven. Igor Sikorsky. LC 93-2822. 1993. 15.93 (*0-86592-100-8*); 11.95s.p. (*0-685-66610-7*) Rourke Enter.

SILK

see also Silkworms

Strathern, Paul. Exploration by Land. LC 93-7147. (Illus.). 48p. (gr. 6 up). 1994. text ed. 15.95 RSBE (*0-02-788375-2*, New Discovery Bks) Macmillan Child Grp.

SILK SCREEN PRINTING

O'Reilly, Susie. Stencils & Screens. LC 93-28349. (Illus.). 32p. (gr. 4-6). 1994. 14.95 (*1-56847-068-1*) Thomson Lrning.

SILKWORMS

Johnson, Sylvia A. Silkworms. Kishida, Isao, illus. LC 82-250. 48p. (gr. 4 up). 1982. PLB 19.95 (*0-8225-1478-8*, First Ave Edns); pap. 5.95 (*0-8225-9557-5*, First Ave Edns) Lerner Pubns.
Miller, Billie M. Soo Ling: The Story of the Silkworm. Guerra, Mauricio, illus. Luna, Rose Mary, tr. (SPA & ENG., Illus.). 12p. 1991. 12.00 (*1-878742-01-9*); pap. 6.00 (*1-878742-02-7*) Kidship Assoc.

SILVER

see also Money

Cobb, Vicki. Feeding Yourself. Hafner, Marylin, illus. LC 88-14192. 32p. (gr. k-3). 1989. (Lipp Jr Bks); PLB 11.89 (*0-397-32325-5*, Lipp Jr Bks) HarpC Child Bks.
Rickard, G. Silver. (Illus.). 48p. (gr. 5 up). 1985. PLB 17.27 (*0-86592-273-X*); 12.95 (*0-685-58323-6*) Rourke Corp.
Russell, William. Gold & Silver. LC 94-504. (gr. 3 up). 1994. write for info. (*0-86593-359-6*) Rourke Corp.

SILVERSMITHING

see also Metalwork

SIMHAT TORAH

Simon, Norma. Simhat Torah. Gordon, Ayala, illus. (ps-k). 1960. bds. 4.50 lam. (*0-8381-0704-4*) United Syn Bk.

SINGAPORE

Brown, Marion M. Singapore. LC 89-34280. 128p. (gr. 5-9). 1989. PLB 20.55 (*0-516-02715-8*) Childrens.
Layton, Lesley. Singapore. LC 89-25465. (Illus.). 128p. (gr. 5-9). 1991. PLB 21.95 (*1-85435-295-4*) Marshall Cavendish.
Wee, Jessie. Singapore. (Illus.). 96p. (gr. 5 up). 1988. 14.95 (*0-222-00988-8*) Chelsea Hse.
Wright, David K. Singapore. LC 89-43196. (Illus.). 64p. (gr. 5-6). 1991. PLB 21.26 (*0-8368-0255-1*) Gareth Stevens Inc.

SINGERS

Algarin, Miguel, ed. Aloud! Voices. (gr. 6 up). 1994. write for info. (*0-8050-3275-4*) H Holt & Co.
Amdur, Richard. Linda Ronstadt: Mexican-American Singer. (Illus.). 112p. (gr. 6-12). 1994. PLB 18.95 (*0-7910-1781-8*, Am Art Analog); pap. write for info. (*0-7910-2025-8*, Am Art Analog) Chelsea Hse.
Anderson, Tom. Sing Choral Music at Sight. Blakeslee, Michael, ed. (Illus.). 128p. (Orig.). (gr. 1-12). 1992. pap. 36.00 tchr's. ed. (*1-56545-007-8*) Music Ed Natl.
Burke, Bronwen. Garth Brooks. (Illus.). 48p. 1992. 1.49 (*0-440-21433-5*) Dell.
Byars, Betsy C. The Glory Girl. (ps-3). 1985. pap. 3.95 (*0-14-031785-6*, Puffin) Puffin Bks.
De Veaux, Alexis. Don't Explain (A Song of Billie Holiday) LC 78-19471. (Illus.). 160p. (gr. 7 up). 1980. PLB 12.89 (*0-06-021630-1*) HarpC Child Bks.
Dinero, G. Who's Hot! Vanessa Williams. (gr. 4-7). 1993. pap. 1.49 (*0-440-21479-3*) Dell.
Ford, M. Thomas. Paula Abdul: Straight Up. LC 91-40231. (Illus.). 72p. (gr. 3 up). 1992. text ed. 13.95 RSBE (*0-87518-508-8*, Dillon) Macmillan Child Grp.
—Who's Hot -- Clint Black. (gr. 4-7). 1993. pap. 1.49 (*0-440-21598-6*) Dell.
Garza, Hedda. Joan Baez. (Illus.). 120p. (gr. 5 up). 1991. lib. bdg. 17.95 (*0-7910-1233-6*) Chelsea Hse.
Gillianti, Simone. Rick Springfield. 1984. lib. bdg. write for info. (*0-671-53104-2*) S&S Trade.
Gonzalez, Fernando. Gloria Estefan, Cuban-American Singing Star. LC 92-39798. (Illus.). 32p. (gr. 2-4). 1993. PLB 12.90 (*1-56294-371-5*); pap. 4.95 (*1-56294-809-1*) Millbrook Pr.
Haskins, James S. Diana Ross: Star Supreme. Spence, Jim, photos by. LC 84-21897. (Illus.). 64p. (gr. 2-6). 1985. pap. 10.95 (*0-670-80549-1*) Viking Child Bks.
—Diana Ross: Star Supreme. Spence, Jim, illus. 64p. (gr. 2-6). 1986. pap. 3.95 (*0-14-032096-2*, Puffin) Puffin Bks.
—I'm Gonna Make You Love Me: The Story of Diana Ross. 176p. (gr. 7 up). 1982. pap. 2.25 (*0-440-94172-5*, LFL) Dell.
Haskins, James S. & Stifle, J. M. Donna Summer: An Unauthorized Biography. (Illus.). 144p. (gr. 7 up). 1983. 14.95 (*0-316-35003-6*, Joy St Bks) Little.
Heller, Jeffrey. Joan Baez: Singer with a Cause. LC 90-21046. (Illus.). 152p. (gr. 4 up). 1991. PLB 14.40 (*0-516-03271-2*); pap. 5.95 (*0-516-43271-0*) Childrens.
Italia, Bob. Amy Grant. Wallner, Rosemary, ed. LC 92-16692. 1992. PLB 12.94 (*1-56239-145-3*) Abdo & Dghtrs.
Keith, Evan. Amy Grant: Who's Hot! 48p. (gr. 4-7). 1992. pap. 1.49 (*0-440-21377-0*) Dell.
Marx, Fonda. Who's Hot! Nirvana. (gr. 4-7). 1993. pap. 1.49 (*0-440-21478-5*) Dell.
Nazel, Joseph. B. B. King: Jazz Musician. (Illus.). 192p. 1994. pap. 3.95 (*0-87067-792-6*, Melrose Sq) Holloway.
Parker, Steve. Singing a Song: How You Sing, Speak & Make Sounds. Kline, Marjory, ed. LC 91-17018. (Illus.). 32p. (gr. k-4). 1992. PLB 11.40 (*0-531-14212-4*) Watts.
Peeples, Freda. C & C Music Factory. (Illus.). 48p. 1992. 1.49 (*0-440-21435-1*) Dell.
—D. J. Jazzy Jeff & the Fresh Prince. (Illus.). 48p. 1992. 1.49 (*0-440-21429-7*) Dell.
—Queen Latifah. (Illus.). 48p. 1992. 1.49 (*0-440-21428-9*) Dell.
Press, Skip. Natalie & Nat King Cole. LC 94-22429. 1995. text ed. 13.95 (*0-89686-879-6*, Crestwood Hse) Macmillan Child Grp.
Rooth, Marianne. Sarah Vaughn: Jazz Singer. (Illus.). 208p. (Orig.). 1994. pap. 3.95 (*0-87067-592-3*, Melrose Sq) Holloway.
Rowley, Kay. Rock Stars. LC 91-15077. (Illus.). 32p. (gr. 5). 1992. text ed. 13.95 RSBE (*0-89686-713-7*, Crestwood Hse) Macmillan Child Grp.
Shirley, David. Gloria Estefan. LC 93-48090. (gr. 5-8). 1994. pap. write for info. (*0-7910-2117-3*) Chelsea Hse.
Steins, Richard. Leontyne Price: Opera Star. (Illus.). 64p. (gr. 3-7). 1993. PLB 14.95 (*1-56711-009-6*) Blackbirch.
Tager, Miriam. Paula Abdul. (Illus.). 48p. 1992. 1.49 (*0-440-21434-3*) Dell.
Wallner, Rosemary. Garth Brooks. LC 93-4175. 1993. 12.94 (*1-56239-229-8*) Abdo & Dghtrs.
Wyman, Carolyn. Ella Fitzgerald: Jazz Singer Supreme. (Illus.). 144p. (gr. 9-12). 1993. PLB 14.40 (*0-531-13031-2*) Watts.
—Ella Fitzgerald: Jazz Singer Supreme. (Illus.). 144p. (gr. 7-12). 1993. pap. 6.95 (*0-531-15679-6*) Watts.

SINGING–FICTION

Andersen, Torsten. Debbie Dare. 1992. 7.95 (*0-533-10279-0*) Vantage.
Angelou, Maya. Now Sheba Sings the Song. Feelings, Tom, illus. LC 86-19876. 56p. 1988. pap. 9.95 (*0-525-48374-8*, DCB) Dutton Child Bks.
Beall, Pamela C. & Nipp, Susan H. Wee Sing Children's Songs & Fingerplays. (Illus.). 64p. (ps-2). 1982. bk. & cass. 9.95 (*0-8431-3793-2*); pap. 2.95 (*0-8431-3807-6*) Price Stern.
Birdseye, Tom & Birdseye, Debbie. She'll Be Comin' Round the Mountain. Glass, Andrew, illus. LC 92-37641. 32p. (ps-3). 1994. reinforced bdg. 15.95 (*0-8234-1032-3*) Holiday.
Butler, Dale. Blossom. Caffin, Liz, illus. LC 92-34265. 1993. 14.00 (*0-383-03620-8*) SRA Schl Grp.
Christian, Mary B. Singin' Somebody Else's Song. LC 88-12000. 192p. (gr. 7 up). 1988. SBE 14.95 (*0-02-718500-1*, Macmillan Child Bk) Macmillan Child Grp.
Cutler, Ivor. Doris. Munoz, Claudio, illus. LC 92-5923. 32p. (gr. k-3). 1992. PLB 14.00 (*0-688-11939-5*, Tambourine Bks) Morrow.
De Gasztold, Carmen B. Creature's Choir. (FRE., Illus.). (gr. 3-8). 29.95 (*0-8288-9331-4*, F140841) Fr & Eur.
Geras, Adele. Pictures of the Night. LC 92-27425. 1993. write for info. (*0-15-261588-1*) HarBrace.
Grimm, Jacob & Grimm, Wilhelm K. Grimm's Fairy Tales. (SPA & FRE.). Span. ed. 8.95 (*0-685-23350-2*); fr. ed 5.50 (*0-685-23351-0*) Fr & Eur.
Higginsen, Vy & Bolden, Tonya. Mama, I Want to Sing. 1992. 13.95 (*0-590-44201-5*, Scholastic Hardcover) Scholastic Inc.
Hunt, Angela E. The Chance of a Lifetime. LC 92-20635. 1993. pap. 4.99 (*0-8423-1118-1*) Tyndale.
—Singing Shepherd. (Illus.). 32p. (ps-6). 1992. 13.95 (*0-7459-2224-4*) Lion USA.
Johnston, Tony. Grandpa's Song. Sneed, Brad, illus. LC 90-43836. 32p. (ps-3). 1991. 12.95 (*0-8037-0801-7*); lib. bdg. 12.89 (*0-8037-0802-5*) Dial Bks Young.
Martin, Marla. A Sweet Singer. (gr. 2-4). 1976. 2.55 (*0-686-15487-8*) Rod & Staff.
Paterson, Katherine. Come Sing, Jimmy Jo. LC 84-21123. 208p. (gr. 5 up). 1985. 12.95 (*0-525-67167-6*, Lodestar Bks) Dutton Child Bks.
Peterson, Jeanne W. My Mama Sings. Speidel, Sandra, illus. LC 91-72. 32p. (ps-3). 1994. 15.00 (*0-06-023854-2*); PLB 14.89 (*0-06-023859-3*) HarpC Child Bks.
Rice, Eve. What Sadie Sang. (ps). 1983. 11.95 (*0-688-02179-4*) Greenwillow.
Robinson, Fay. Old MacDonald Had a Farm. Iosa, Ann W., illus. LC 92-10757. 32p. (ps-2). 1993. PLB 11.60 (*0-516-02372-1*); pap. 3.95 (*0-516-42372-X*) Childrens.
Sherlock, Patti. Some Fine Dog. LC 91-856. 160p. (gr. 3-7). 1992. 14.95 (*0-8234-0947-3*) Holiday.
Thomas, Joyce C. When the Nightingale Sings. LC 92-6045. 160p. (gr. 7 up). 1992. 14.00 (*0-06-020294-7*); PLB 13.89 (*0-06-020295-5*) HarpC Child Bks.
Wharton, Thomas. Hildegard Sings. (Illus.). 32p. (gr. k-3). 1991. 10.95 (*0-374-33242-8*) FS&G.
—Hildegard Sings. (ps-3). 1993. pap. 4.95 (*0-374-43070-5*, Sunburst) FS&G.

SINGING GAMES

Chase, Richard. Singing Games & Playparty Games. Tolford, Joshua, illus. 63p. (gr. 1-4). 1949. pap. 2.50 (*0-486-21785-X*) Dover.
Corbett, Pie. Playtime Treasury. 1990. 16.95 (*0-385-26448-8*) Doubleday.
Rae, Mary M., illus. The Farmer in the Dell: A Singing Game. 32p. (ps-1). 1990. pap. 3.95 (*0-14-050788-4*, Puffin) Puffin Bks.

SISTERHOODS

see Monasticism and Religious Orders for Women

SISTERS–FICTION

Adler, C. S. The Lump in the Middle. 160p. 1991. pap. 3.50 (*0-380-71176-1*, Camelot) Avon.
—Split Sisters. LC 89-18308. 176p. (gr. 4-7). 1990. pap. 3.95 (*0-689-71369-X*, Aladdin) Macmillan Child Grp.
Adorjan, Carol. I Can! Can You? rev. ed. Levine, Abby, ed. Nerlove, Miriam, illus. LC 90-37665. 24p. (ps). 1990. 11.95 (*0-8075-3491-9*) A Whitman.
Alcott, Louisa May. Little Women. (Illus.). (gr. 6 up). 1966. pap. 2.95 (*0-8049-0106-6*, CL-106) Airmont.
—Little Women. Magagna, Anna M. & Jambor, Louis, illus. (gr. 4-6). 1981. (G&D); deluxe ed. 15.95 (*0-448-06019-1*) Putnam Pub Group.
—Little Women. (gr. 6 up). 1974. 250.00 (*0-8490-0547-7*) Gordon Pr.
—Little Women. Smith, Jessie W., illus. (gr. 7 up). 1968. 19.95 (*0-316-03095-3*) Little.
—Little Women. 320p. (gr. 3-7). 1983. pap. 2.25 (*0-14-035008-X*, Puffin) Puffin Bks.
—Little Women. (gr. 5 up). 1963. 37.50 (*0-685-20188-0*, 144-7) Saphrograph.
—Little Women. (gr. 6 up). 1983. Repr. lib. bdg. 18.95x (*0-89966-408-3*) Buccaneer Bks.
—Little Women. Douglas, Ann, intro. by. 480p. (gr. 3 up). 1983. pap. 3.95 (*0-451-52341-5*, Sig Classic) NAL-Dutton.
—Little Women. Edwards, Gunvor, illus. Gliberry, Lysbeth, retold by. (Illus.). 48p. (gr. 7-12). 1975. pap. text ed. 3.25x (*0-19-421804-X*) OUP.
—Little Women. LC 62-20197. (gr. 4 up). 1986. pap. 5.00 (*0-02-041240-1*, Collier Young Ad) Macmillan Child Grp.
—Little Women. Smith, Jessie W. & Merrill, Frank, illus. 400p. (gr. 2 up). 1988. 12.99 (*0-517-63489-9*) Random Hse Value.
—Little Women. (Orig.). (gr. k-6). 1987. pap. 6.95 (*0-440-44768-2*, Pub. by Yearling Classics) Dell.
—Little Women. Showalter, Elaine, intro. by. 608p. 1989. pap. 5.95 (*0-14-039069-3*, Penguin Classics) Viking Penguin.
—Little Women. 1989. Repr. of 1867 ed. lib. bdg. 79.00 (*0-7812-1627-3*) Rprt Serv.
—Little Women. Auerbach, Nina, afterword by. 480p. 1983. pap. 3.95 (*0-553-21275-3*, Bantam Classics Spectra) Bantam.
—Little Women. large type ed. 336p. 1987. 15.95 (*0-7089-8384-7*, Charnwood) Ulverscroft.
—Little Women. 1986. pap. 3.25 (*0-590-43797-6*, Apple Paperbacks) Scholastic Inc.
—Little Women. 1988. 2.98 (*0-671-09222-7*) S&S Trade.
—Little Women. Kulling, Monica, adapted by. LC 93-38237. 108p. (gr. 2-6). 1994. pap. 3.50 (*0-679-86175-0*, Bullseye Bks) Random Bks Yng Read.
—Little Women. LC 94-5865. 1994. 15.95 (*0-679-43642-1*, Evrymans Lib Childs) Knopf.
—Little Women, or, Meg, Jo, Beth, & Amy. Hague, Michael, illus. LC 93-18943. 308p. (gr. 4-8). 1993. 15.95 (*0-8050-2767-X*, Bks Young Read) H Holt & Co.
—Little Women, Vol. 1: Four Funny Sisters. Lindskoog, Kathryn, ed. (Illus.). (gr. 3-7). 1991. pap. 4.99 (*0-88070-437-3*, Gold & Honey) Questar Pubs.
—Reader's Digest Best Loved Books for Young Readers: Little Women. Ogburn, Jackie, ed. English, Mark, illus. 176p. (gr. 4-12). 1989. 3.99 (*0-945260-25-3*) Choice Pub NY.
Alexander, Martha. Nobody Asked Me If I Wanted a Baby Sister. Alexander, Martha, illus. (gr. k-2). 1977. pap. 3.95 (*0-8037-6410-3*) Dial Bks Young.
Angel, Ann. Real for Sure Sister. LC 87-29217. (Illus.). 72p. (gr. 3-6). 1988. 10.95 (*0-9609504-7-8*) Perspect Indiana.
Athkins, D. E. Mirror, Mirror. 144p. 1992. pap. 3.25 (*0-590-45246-0*, Point) Scholastic Inc.
Bauer, Marion D. A Taste of Smoke. LC 92-32585. (gr. 5 up). 1993. 13.95 (*0-395-64341-4*, Clarion Bks) HM.
Benson, Elizabeth. My Sister, My Sorrow. (gr. 9-12). 1993. pap. 3.50 (*0-06-106760-1*, Harp PBks) HarpC.
Bradford, Jan. Caroline Zucker & the Birthday Disaster. Ramsey, Marcy, illus. LC 90-11159. 96p. (gr. 2-5). 1991. lib. bdg. 9.89 (*0-8167-2021-5*); pap. text ed. 2.95 (*0-8167-2022-3*) Troll Assocs.
—Caroline Zucker Helps Out. Ramsey, Marcy, illus. LC 90-11156. 96p. (gr. 2-5). 1991. PLB 9.89 (*0-8167-2025-8*); pap. text ed. 2.95 (*0-8167-2026-6*) Troll Assocs.

Brink, Carol R. Baby Island. Sewell, Helen, illus. LC 92-45577. 160p. (gr. 3-7). 1993. pap. 3.95 (*0-689-71751-2*, Aladdin) Macmillan Child Grp.

Byars, Betsy C. Golly Sisters Go West. LC 84-48474. (Illus.). 64p. (gr. k-3). 1989. pap. 3.50 (*0-06-444132-6*, Trophy) HarpC Child Bks.

—Hooray for the Golly Sisters! Truesdell, Sue, illus. LC 89-48147. 64p. (gr. k-3). 1990. 14.00 (*0-06-020898-8*); PLB 13.89 (*0-06-020899-6*) HarpC Child Bks.

—Hooray for the Golly Sisters! Truesdell, Sue, contrib. by. LC 89-48147. (Illus.). 64p. (gr. k-3). 1992. pap. 3.50 (*0-06-444156-3*, Trophy) HarpC Child Bks.

Calmenson, Stephanie. The Little Witch Sisters. Alley, R. W., illus. LC 93-15454. 1993. 13.27 (*0-8368-0970-X*) Gareth Stevens Inc.

Carlstrom, Nancy W. Kiss Your Sister, Rose Marie! Wickstrom, Thor, illus. LC 90-48671. 32p. (ps-1). 1992. RSBE 13.95 (*0-02-717271-6*, Macmillan Child Bk) Macmillan Child Grp.

Cleary, Beverly. Beezus & Ramona. 130p. 1992. text ed. 10.40 (*1-56956-108-7*) W A T Braille.

—Sister of the Bride. 240p. (Orig.). (gr. 6). 1992. pap. 3.99 (*0-380-70928-7*, Flare) Avon.

Clifford, Eth. Will Somebody Please Marry My Sister? Eagle, Ellen, illus. 128p. (gr. 3-6). 1992. 13.45 (*0-395-58037-4*) HM.

Cocca-Leffler, Maryann. What a Pest! Cocca-Leffler, Maryann, illus. 32p. (ps-1). 1994. 7.99 (*0-448-40399-4*, G&D); pap. 3.50 (*0-448-40393-5*, G&D) Putnam Pub Group.

Colli, Monica. Twins. LC 91-36606. 1992. 5.95 (*0-85953-394-8*) Childs Play.

Corcoran, Barbara. Wolf at the Door. LC 92-45108. 192p. (gr. 3-7). 1993. SBE 14.95 (*0-689-31870-7*, Atheneum Child Bk) Macmillan Child Grp.

Dahlback, Helena. My Sister Lotta & Me. Ramel, Charlotte, illus. Lesser, Rika, tr. from SWE. (Illus.). 32p. (gr. k-3). 1993. 15.95 (*0-8050-2558-8*, Bks Young Read) H Holt & Co.

Dunrea, Olivier. Eppie M. Says... Dunrea, Olivier, illus. LC 89-8134. 32p. (ps-2). 1990. RSBE 14.95 (*0-02-733205-5*, Macmillan Child Bk) Macmillan Child Grp.

Eversole, Robyn H. The Magic House. Palagonia, Peter, illus. LC 91-17824. 32p. (ps-2). 1992. 13.95 (*0-531-05924-3*); lib. bdg. 13.99 (*0-531-08524-4*) Orchard Bks Watts.

Flood, E. L. Secret in the Moonlight: Welcome Inn. LC 93-50936. (Illus.). 144p. (gr. 3-6). 1994. pap. 2.95 (*0-8167-3427-5*) Troll Assocs.

Galbraith, Kathryn O. Roommates. LC 89-33434. (Illus.). 48p. (gr. 1-4). 1990. SBE 12.95 (*0-689-50487-X*, M K McElderry) Macmillan Child Grp.

—Roommates. 48p. (gr. 1-4). 1991. pap. 2.99 (*0-380-71357-8*, Camelot) Avon.

—Roommates Again. Graham, Mark, illus. LC 93-8709. 48p. (ps-2). 1994. SBE 14.95 (*0-689-50592-2*, M K McElderry) Macmillan Child Grp.

—Roommates Again. Graham, Mark, illus. LC 93-8709. 48p. (gr. 1-4). 1994. SBE 12.95 (*0-689-50597-3*, M K McElderry) Macmillan Child Grp.

—Roommates & Rachel. 48p. (gr. 1). 1993. pap. 3.50 (*0-380-71762-X*, Camelot Young) Avon.

Gerber, Merrill J. Handsome As Anything. 1990. 13.95 (*0-590-43019-X*) Scholastic Inc.

Griffin, Peni R. Hobkin. LC 91-24079. 208p. (gr. 4-7). 1992. SBE 14.95 (*0-689-50539-6*, M K McElderry) Macmillan Child Grp.

—Hobkin. LC 93-7758. 208p. (gr. 3-7). 1993. pap. 3.99 (*0-14-036356-4*, Puffin) Puffin Bks.

Grove, Vicki. Rimwalkers. LC 92-36091. 224p. (gr. 5 up). 1993. 14.95 (*0-399-22430-0*, Putnam) Putnam Pub Group.

Hallinan, P. K. We're Very Good Friends, My Sister & I. Hallinan, P. K., illus. 24p. (ps-2). 1990. 4.95 (*0-8249-8470-6*, Ideals Child) Hambleton-Hill.

Hamilton, Morse. Little Sister for Sale. Fiammenghi, Gioia, illus. LC 91-8139. 32p. (ps-3). 1992. 13.00 (*0-525-65078-4*, Cobblehill Bks) Dutton Child Bks.

Hendry, Diana. Double Vision. LC 92-52996. 272p. (gr. 7-11). 1993. 14.95 (*1-56402-125-4*) Candlewick Pr.

Hesse, Karen. Wish on a Unicorn. LC 92-26792. 112p. (gr. 3-7). 1993. pap. 3.99 (*0-14-034935-9*) Puffin Bks.

Hines, Anna G. Jackie's Lunch Box. LC 90-39715. (Illus.). 24p. (ps up). 1991. 13.95 (*0-688-09693-X*); PLB 13.88 (*0-688-09694-8*) Greenwillow.

Hiser, Constance. Sixth-Grade Star. LC 92-52856. 96p. (gr. 3-7). 1992. 13.95 (*0-8234-0967-8*) Holiday.

Holland, Isabelle. Journey Home. (gr. 4-7). 1990. 13.95 (*0-590-43110-2*) Scholastic Inc.

Hooks, William H. & Boegehold, Betty D. The Rainbow Ribbon. Munsinger, Lynn, illus. LC 93-27706. 32p. 1995. pap. 3.99 (*0-14-054092-X*) Puffin Bks.

Howard, Elizabeth F. The Train to Lulu's. Castille, Robert, illus. LC 93-25565. 32p. (gr. k-2). 1994. pap. 4.95 (*0-689-71797-0*, Aladdin) Macmillan Child Grp.

—What's in Aunt Mary's Room? Lucas, Cedric, illus. LC 94-4985. Date not set. write for info. (*0-395-69845-6*, Clarion Bks) HM.

Kaye, Marilyn. Camp Sunnyside Friends, No. 13: Big Sister Blues. 128p. (Orig.). 1991. pap. 2.95 (*0-380-76551-9*, Camelot) Avon.

Kehret, Peg. Sisters, Long Ago. Kelly, Kathleen M., illus. LC 89-38677. 160p. (gr. 5 up). 1990. 14.95 (*0-525-65021-0*, Cobblehill Bks) Dutton Child Bks.

Lattimore, Deborah N. Punga: The Goddess of Ugly. LC 92-23191. 32p. 1993. 14.95 (*0-15-292862-6*) HarBrace.

Lerner, Harriet G. & Goldhor, Susan H. What's So Terrible about Swallowing an Appleseed. O'Neill, Catharine, illus. LC 94-2769. Date not set. 15.00 (*0-06-024523-9*); PLB 14.89 (*0-06-024524-7*) HarpC.

Lillie, Patricia. Floppy Teddy Bear. Baker, Karen L., illus. LC 93-26516. 32p. 1995. write for info. (*0-688-12570-0*); PLB write for info. (*0-688-12571-9*) Greenwillow.

Little Women. Centennial ed. (Illus.). (gr. 3-7). 1968. 19.95 (*0-685-47121-7*) Little.

McKay, Hilary. The Exiles at Home. LC 94-14225. (gr. 4-7). 1994. 15.95 (*0-689-50610-4*, M K McElderry) Macmillan Child Grp.

Martin, Ann M. Dawn's Wicked Stepsister. (gr. 4-7). 1990. pap. 3.25 (*0-590-42497-1*) Scholastic Inc.

Martin, JeanRead & Marx, Patricia. Now I Will Never Leave the Dinner Table. Chast, Roz, illus. LC 94-3209. (gr. 4 up). Date not set. 15.00 (*0-06-024794-0*); PLB 14.89 (*0-06-024795-9*) HarpC.

Naylor, Phyllis R. Boys Start the War. LC 92-249. (gr. 4-7). 1993. 14.95 (*0-385-30814-0*) Doubleday.

Noll, Sally. That Bothered Kate. LC 90-38488. (Illus.). 32p. (ps up). 1991. 13.95 (*0-688-10095-3*); PLB 13.88 (*0-688-10096-1*) Greenwillow.

—That Bothered Kate. LC 92-40167. (Illus.). 32p. (ps-3). 1993. pap. 4.99 (*0-14-054885-8*, Puffin) Puffin Bks.

Pascal, Francine. Psychic Sisters. (gr. 4-6). 1993. pap. 3.25 (*0-553-48057-X*) Bantam.

—Stepsisters. 1993. pap. 3.25 (*0-553-29850-X*) Bantam.

Paterson, Katherine. Jacob Have I Loved. LC 80-668. 256p. (gr. 5 up). 1990. pap. 3.95 (*0-06-440368-8*, Trophy) HarpC Child Bks.

Patron, Susan. Maybe Yes, Maybe No, Maybe Maybe. Donahue, Dorothy, illus. LC 92-34067. 96p. (gr. 3-5). 1993. 14.95 (*0-531-05482-9*); PLB 14.99 (*0-531-08632-1*) Orchard Bks Watts.

Pearson, Gayle. The Fog Doggies & Me. LC 92-41069. 128p. (gr. 4-8). 1993. SBE 13.95 (*0-689-31845-6*, Atheneum Child Bk) Macmillan Child Grp.

Peters, Lisa W. The Hayloft. Plum, K. D., illus. LC 93-18718. Date not set. write for info. (*0-8037-1490-4*); lib. bdg. write for info. (*0-8037-1491-2*) Dial Bks Young.

Pfeffer, Susan B. Twin Surprises. Carter, Abby, illus. 64p. (gr. 2-4). 1991. 13.95 (*0-8050-1850-6*, Redfeather BYR) H Holt & Co.

—Twin Troubles. Carter, Abby, illus. LC 92-5773. 1992. 14.95 (*0-8050-2146-9*, Redfeather BYR) H Holt & Co.

Porte, Barbara A. When Aunt Lucy Rode A Mule & Other Stories. Chambliss, Maxie, illus. LC 93-4874. 32p. (gr. k-2). 1994. 15.95 (*0-531-06816-1*); PLB 15.99 (*0-531-08666-6*) Orchard Bks Watts.

Powell, Pamela. The Turtle Watchers. LC 92-5822. 160p. (gr. 3-7). 1992. 13.00 (*0-670-84294-X*) Viking Child Bks.

Rice, Bebe F. My Sister, My Sorrow. 1992. pap. 3.50 (*0-440-21296-0*) Dell.

Richardson, Jean. Out of Step: The Twins Were So Alike. ..but So Different. Holmes, Dawn, illus. LC 92-39666. 28p. (ps-3). 1993. 12.95 (*0-8120-5790-2*); pap. 5.95 (*0-8120-1553-3*) Barron.

Rinaldi, Ann. In My Father's House. LC 91-46839. 304p. (gr. 7 up). 1993. 13.95 (*0-590-44730-0*) Scholastic Inc.

Roos, Stephen. Never Trust a Sister over Twelve. De Groat, Diane, illus. LC 92-34406. 1993. 13.95 (*0-385-31048-X*) Delacorte.

Ross, Pat. Hannah's Fancy Notions: A Story of Industrial New England. Dodson, Bert, illus. LC 92-20286. 64p. (gr. 2-6). 1992. pap. 3.99 (*0-14-032389-9*) Puffin Bks.

Sachs, Marilyn. What My Sister Remembered. 128p. (gr. 5 up). 1994. pap. 3.99 (*0-14-036944-9*) Puffin Bks.

Samuels, Barbara. What's So Great about Cindy Snappleby? LC 91-17809. (Illus.). 32p. (ps-1). 1992. 13.95 (*0-531-05979-0*); lib. bdg. 13.99 (*0-531-08579-1*) Orchard Bks Watts.

Smith, Jane D. Mary by Myself. LC 93-47457. 128p. (gr. 3 up). 1994. 14.00 (*0-06-024517-4*); PLB 13.89 (*0-06-024518-2*) HarpC Child Bks.

Smothers, Ethel F. Moriah's Pond. Ransome, James, illus. LC 94-6490. 128p. (gr. 3-8). 1995. 14.00 (*0-679-84504-6*); lib. bdg. write for info. (*0-679-94504-0*) Knopf Bks Yng Read.

Springer, Nancy. The Great Pony Hassle. Duffy, Daniel M., illus. LC 92-34781. (gr. 3-7). 1993. 12.99 (*0-8037-1306-1*); PLB 13.89 (*0-8037-1308-8*) Dial Bks Young.

Tolles, Martha. Secret Sister. (gr. 4-7). 1992. pap. 2.95 (*0-590-45245-2*) Scholastic Inc.

Tsutsui, Yoriko. Anna in Charge. Hayashi, Akiki, illus. 32p. (ps-3). 1991. pap. 3.95 (*0-14-050733-7*, Puffin) Puffin Bks.

Van Leeuwen, Jean. Two Girls in Sister Dresses. Benson, Linda, illus. LC 91-23633. 56p. (gr. 1-5). 1994. 12.99 (*0-8037-1230-8*); PLB 12.89 (*0-8037-1231-6*) Dial Bks Young.

Widerberg, Siv. The Big Sister. Sjogren, Birgitta, tr. from SWE. Torudd, Cecilia, illus. 1989. 9.95 (*91-29-59186-4*, Pub. by R&S Bks) FS&G.

Williams, Carol L. Kelly & Me. LC 92-20492. 1993. 13.95 (*0-385-30897-3*) Delacorte.

Winer, Yvonne. Ssh, Don't Wake the Baby! Power, Margaret, illus. LC 92-34160. 1993. 3.75 (*0-383-03655-0*) SRA Schl Grp.

Wood, Audrey. Three Sisters. Hoffman, Rosekrans, illus. LC 85-29392. 48p. (ps-3). 1989. 4.95 (*0-8037-0597-2*) Dial Bks Young.

Wood, Marcia. Always, Julia. LC 91-40460. 128p. (gr. 5-9). 1993. SBE 13.95 (*0-689-31728-X*, Atheneum Child Bk) Macmillan Child Grp.

Wright, Betty R. My Sister Is Different. (ps-3). 1993. pap. 3.95 (*0-8114-7158-6*) Raintree Steck-V.

SITTING BULL, DAKOTA CHIEF, ca. 1831-1890

Adler, David A. A Picture Book of Sitting Bull. Byrd, Samuel, illus. LC 92-47119. 32p. (ps-3). 1993. reinforced bdg. 15.95 (*0-8234-1044-7*) Holiday.

Bernatas, Bob. Sitting Bull. (gr. 4-7). 1993. pap. 7.95 (*0-7910-1968-3*) Chelsea Hse.

Bernotas, Bob. Sitting Bull. (Illus.). 112p. (gr. 5 up). 1992. lib. bdg. 17.95 (*0-7910-1703-6*) Chelsea Hse.

Black, Sheila. Sitting Bull. Furstinger, Nancy, ed. (Illus.). 144p. (gr. 5-7). 1989. PLB 10.95 (*0-382-09572-3*); pap. 7.95 (*0-382-09761-0*) Silver Burdett Pr.

Bodow, Steven. Sitting Bull. LC 92-16518. (Illus.). 128p. (gr. 7-10). 1992. PLB 22.80 (*0-8114-2328-X*) Raintree Steck-V.

Bruchac, Joseph. A Boy Called Slow. Baviera, Rocco, illus. LC 93-21233. 1994. write for info. (*0-399-22692-3*, Philomel Bks) Putnam Pub Group.

Fleischer, Jane. Sitting Bull, Warrior of the Sioux. new ed. LC 78-18047. (Illus.). 48p. (gr. 4-6). 1979. PLB 10.59 (*0-89375-154-5*); pap. 3.50 (*0-89375-144-8*) Troll Assocs.

Grey, Alan. Chief Sitting Bull. Hagar, Ashley, illus. 64p. 1993. pap. 5.00 (*1-56883-031-9*) Colonial Pr AL.

Sanford, William R. Sitting Bull: Sioux Warrior. LC 93-42255. (Illus.). 48p. (gr. 4-10). 1994. lib. bdg. 14.95 (*0-89490-514-7*) Enslow Pubs.

Smith, Kathie B. Sitting Bull. (Illus.). 32p. (gr. k-5). 1987. pap. 2.25 (*0-671-64027-5*, Little Simon) S&S Trade.

—Sitting Bull. Seward, James, illus. LC 86-33888. 24p. (gr. 4-6). 1987. lib. bdg. 7.98 (*0-671-64603-6*, J Messner); PLB 5.99s.p. (*0-685-47297-3*) S&S Trade.

Stein, R. Conrad. The Story of Little Bighorn. LC 83-6594. (Illus.). 32p. (gr. 3-6). 1983. pap. 3.95 (*0-516-44663-0*) Childrens.

Wheeler, Jill. The Story of Sitting Bull. Deegan, Paul, ed. Dodson, Liz, illus. LC 89-94912. 32p. (gr. 4). 1989. PLB 11.96 (*0-939179-67-9*) Abdo & Dghtrs.

SIX DAY WAR

see Israel-Arab War, 1967-

SIZE AND SHAPE

see also Mensuration

All about Shapes. (Illus.). 32p. (Orig.). 1994. pap. 8.95 incl. cass. (*0-7935-2381-8*, 00330504) H Leonard.

Allen, Jonathan. Big Owl, Little Towel. Allen, Jonathan, illus. LC 91-39349. 12p. (ps). 1992. 3.95 (*0-688-11783-X*, Tambourine Bks) Morrow.

Allington, Richard L. Shapes. Ehlert, Lois, illus. LC 79-19852. 32p. (gr. k-3). 1985. pap. 3.95 (*0-8114-8238-3*) Raintree Steck-V.

Barnes-Murphy, Rowan. Shapes. Barnes-Murphy, Rowan, illus. 16p. (ps). 1993. bds. 3.95 (*0-8249-8606-7*, Ideals Child) Hambleton-Hill.

Barrett, Peter & Barrett, Susan. The Circle Sarah Drew. Barrett, Peter & Barrett, Susan, illus. Incl. The Line Sophie Drew. LC 76-174716. 8.95 (*0-87592-029-2*); The Square Ben Drew. 8.95 (*0-87592-049-7*). LC 72-89449. (Illus.). 32p. (ps-2). 1973. (*0-87592-012-8*) Scroll Pr.

Bishop, Roma. Shapes. (Illus.). 14p. (ps-k). 1991. pap. 2.95 (*0-671-74830-0*, Little Simon) S&S Trade.

Borgo, Deborah C., illus. Thomas the Tank Engine - Shapes & Sizes. Awdry, W., contrib. by. (Illus.). 14p. (ps). 1993. bds. 2.29 (*0-679-81643-7*) Random Bks Yng Read.

Boyle, Alison. Playdays Colours & Shapes. Johnson, Paul, illus. 32p. (ps-2). 1992. pap. 2.95 (*0-563-20887-2*, BBC-Parkwest) Parkwest Pubns.

Bradbury, Lynne. Shapes & Colors. Grundy, Lynn N., illus. 28p. (ps). 1992. Series 921. 3.50 (*0-7214-1510-5*) Ladybird Bks.

Brown, Margery W. Afro-Bets: Book of Colors. Blair, Culverson, illus. LC 91-76334. 24p. (Orig.). (ps-1). 1991. pap. 3.95 (*0-940975-28-9*) Just Us Bks.

Bryant-Mole, K. Shapes. (Illus.). 24p. (ps up). 1991. pap. 3.50 (*0-7460-0593-8*, Usborne) EDC.

Buddle, Jacqueline. Fun with Sizes & Shapes. Davis, Annelies, illus. 32p. (gr. k). 1988. PLB 14.97 (*0-88625-162-1*); pap. 2.95 (*0-88625-143-5*) Durkin Hayes Pub.

Carle, Eric. My Very First Book of Shapes. reissued ed. Carle, Eric, illus. LC 72-83778. 10p. (ps-1). 1985. 4.95 (*0-694-00013-2*, Crowell Jr Bks) HarpC Child Bks.

Chermayeff, Ivan & Chermayeff, Jane C. First Shapes. (Illus.). 32p. 1991. 16.95 (*0-8109-3819-7*) Abrams.

Clement, Rod. Counting on Frank. LC 90-27558. (Illus.). 32p. (gr. 1-3). 1991. PLB 18.60 (*0-8368-0358-2*) Gareth Stevens Inc.

Colors & Shapes. (Illus.). (ps). pap. 1.25 (*0-7214-9555-9*) Ladybird Bks.

Cony, Sue, illus. Shapes. 8p. (ps-k). 1991. bds. 4.95 (*1-56293-149-0*) McClanahan Bk.

Dillion, Leo & Dillion, Diane. What Am I? LC 93-48835. (gr. 1 up). 1994. 13.95 (*0-590-47885-0*, Blue Sky Press) Scholastic Inc.

Disney's Pop-up Book of Shapes. LC 90-85430. (Illus.). 12p. (ps-k). 1991. 6.95 (*1-56282-019-2*) Disney Pr.

Dodds, Dayle A. The Shape of Things. Lacome, Julie, illus. LC 93-47255. 1994. write for info. (*1-56402-224-2*) Candlewick Pr.

Dr. Seuss. Shape of Me & Other Stuff. Dr. Seuss, illus. (ps-1). 1973. 6.95 (*0-394-82687-6*); lib. bdg. 7.99 (*0-394-92687-0*) Random Bks Yng Read.

Ehrlich, Robert. The Cosmological Milkshake: A Semi-Serious Look at the Size of Things. Ehrlich, Gary, illus. LC 93-28135. 1994. 24.00 (0-8135-2045-2) Rutgers U Pr.

Ferarro, Bonita. Colors & Shapes. Robison, Don, illus. 32p. (Orig.). (ps). 1993. wkbk. 1.99 (1-56189-058-8) Amer Educ Pub.

Les Formes. (FRE., Illus.). 3.50 (0-7214-1429-X) Ladybird Bks.

Fun Forms, Set 7. (gr. 3 up). 1991. pap. 1.97 (1-56297-147-6, FF-74) Lee Pubns KY.

Gabriele. Shapes. 1985. pap. 1.95 (0-911211-67-5) Penny Lane Pubns.

Gave, Marc. Walt Disney's Pinocchio: Fun with Shapes & Sizes. Kurtz, John, illus. 14p. (ps-k). 1992. bds. write for info. (0-307-12332-4, 12332, Golden Pr) Western Pub.

Gorbaty, Norman, illus. Puppy Round & Square. 12p. (ps). 1991. pap. 3.95 (0-671-74436-4, Little Simon) S&S Trade.

Greenway, Shirley. How Big Am I? Oxford Scientific Films, photos by. LC 93-18593. (Illus.). 32p. (ps-1). 1993. PLB 11.00 (0-8249-8625-3, Ideals Child); pap. 3.95 (0-8249-8601-6) Hambleton-Hill.

Gregorich, Barbara. Alike-Not Alike & Go-Togethers: Kindergarten. Hoffman, Joan, ed. Koontz, Robin M., illus. 32p. (gr. k). 1990. wkbk. 2.29 (0-88743-176-3) Sch Zone Pub Co.

—Igual O Diferente: Same or Different. Hoffman, Joan, ed. Shepherd-Bartram, tr. from ENG. Pape, Richard, illus. (SPA.). 32p. (Orig.). (ps). 1987. wkbk. 1.99 (0-938256-80-7) Sch Zone Pub Co.

Griffiths, Rose. Circles. Millard, Peter, photos by. LC 94-9592. (Illus.). 32p. (gr. 1 up). 1994. PLB 17.27 (0-8368-1109-7) Gareth Stevens Inc.

Groening, Matt & Groening, Maggie. Maggie Simpson's Book of Colors & Shapes. LC 91-2864. (Illus.). 32p. (ps-1). 1991. HarpC Child Bks.

Helwig, Barbara & Stewart, Susan. Shape Alert. (Illus.). 90p. (gr. 2-6). 1992. spiral bdg. 4.95 (1-881285-04-9) Arbus Pub.

Hill, Eric. Book of Shapes. (ps). 6.95 (0-317-13666-6) Determined Prods.

Hoban, Tana. Blanco en Negro. LC 93-42643. (SPA., Illus.). (ps up). 1994. bds. 4.95 (0-688-13653-2) Greenwillow.

—Is It Larger? Is It Smaller? LC 84-13719. (Illus.). 32p. (ps-1). 1985. 14.95 (0-688-04027-6); PLB 14.88 (0-688-04028-4) Greenwillow.

—Negro en Blanco. LC 93-42644. (SPA., Illus.). 12p. (ps up). 1994. bds. 4.95 (0-688-13652-4) Greenwillow.

—Spirals, Curves, Fanshapes, & Lines. LC 91-30159. (Illus.). 32p. (ps-4). 1992. 14.00 (0-688-11228-5); PLB 13.93 (0-688-11229-3) Greenwillow.

—Who Are They? LC 93-33644. (Illus.). 12p. (ps up). 1994. bds. 4.95 (0-688-12921-8) Greenwillow.

In the Play Room: A Book about Shapes. (gr. 3 up). 1992. pap. 2.99 (0-517-03588-X) Random Hse Value.

Karlin, Bernie. Shapes: Circle - Square - Triangle, 3 bks. (Illus., 12 pgs. ea. bk.). (ps). 1992. Set. pap. 6.95 (0-671-74625-1, Little Simon) S&S Trade.

Lambert, Jonathan, illus. Shapes. 18p. (ps-1). 1992. bds. 1.95 (0-681-41564-9) Longmeadow Pr.

Learn with Jemima Puddle Duck: Shapes. 1993. 2.99 (0-517-07699-3) Random Hse Value.

Levin, Ina M. & Sterling, Mary E. Readiness Manipulatives: Shapes. Vasconcelles, Keith, illus. 28p. (Orig.). (ps-1). 1992. wkbk. 7.95 (1-55734-180-X) Tchr Create Mat.

Loveland Comm. Staff. Discover Sizes & Shapes. 1992. 4.49 (1-55513-909-4, Chariot Bks) Chariot Family.

MacKinnon, Debbie. What Shape? Sieveking, Anthea, photos by. LC 91-34700. (Illus.). 24p. (ps-k). 1992. 10. 99 (0-8037-1244-8) Dial Bks Young.

—What Size. Sieveking, Anthea, photos by. LC 93-40103. 1995. write for info. (0-8037-1745-8) Dial Bks Young.

McMillan, Bruce. Fire Engine Shapes. McMillan, Bruce, photos by. LC 87-38145. (Illus.). 32p. (ps-2). 1988. 12. 95 (0-688-07842-7); PLB 12.88 (0-688-07843-5) Lothrop.

Moncure, Jane B. Hide-&-Seek Word Bird. Hohag, Linda S., illus. LC 81-18068. (ps-2). 1982. PLB 14.95 (0-89565-218-8) Childs World.

Morgan, Sally. Circles & Spheres. (Illus.). 32p. (gr. 1-3). 1994. 14.95 (1-56847-235-8) Thomson Lrning.

—Squares & Cubes. (Illus.). 32p. (gr. 1-3). 1994. 14.95 (1-56847-234-X) Thomson Lrning.

Morris, Neil. Holly & Harry: A Fun Book of Sizes. Stevenson, Peter, illus. 32p. (ps-2). 1991. PLB 13.50 (0-87614-673-6) Carolrhoda Bks.

—Rummage Sale: A Fun Book of Shapes & Colors. Stevenson, Peter, illus. 32p. (ps-2). 1991. PLB 13.50 (0-87614-676-0) Carolrhoda Bks.

Murphy, Chuck. My First Book of Shapes. (Illus.). 12p. 1993. 6.95 (0-590-46303-9) Scholastic Inc.

My Book of Shapes & Colors. (ps-2). 3.95 (0-7214-5148-9) Ladybird Bks.

My Very First Colors, Shapes, Sizes, & Opposites Book. 1993. write for info. (1-56458-377-5) Dorling Kindersley.

Myller, Rolf. How Big Is a Foot? 1991. pap. 3.50 (0-440-40495-9) Dell.

Oliver, Stephen, photos by. My First Look at Shapes. LC 89-63087. (Illus.). 24p. (ps-k). 1990. 7.00 (0-679-80534-6) Random Bks Yng Read.

—My First Look at Sizes. LC 89-63086. (Illus.). 24p. (ps-k). 1990. 7.00 (0-679-80532-X) Random Bks Yng Read.

One, Two, Three Board Shape Book. (Illus.). (ps). 1985. bds. 1.69 (0-517-46320-2) Random Hse Value.

Palmer, Glenda. Sidewalk Squares & Triangle Birds: God's Wonderful World of Shapes. LC 92-34717. (Illus.). 1993. pap. 4.99 (0-7814-0711-7, Chariot Bks) Chariot Family.

Parramon, J. M. My First Shapes. (Illus.). 32p. (ps). 1991. pap. 5.95 (0-8120-4724-9) Barron.

Pienkowski, Jan. Shapes. Pienkowski, Jan, illus. (ps). 1989. 2.95 (0-671-68135-4, Little Simon) S&S Trade.

—Sizes. Pienkowski, Jan, illus. 24p. (ps-k). 1991. pap. 2.95 (0-671-72844-X, Little Simon) S&S Trade.

Push 'n' Pull Book of Opposites. 12p. 1992. pap. 8.95 (0-590-45088-3) Scholastic Inc.

Radlauer, Ed. Bears, Bears & More Bears. Radlauer Productions Staff, illus. 32p. (ps-4). 1991. PLB 10.95 (1-878363-34-4) Forest Hse.

Rikys, Bodel. Red Bear's Fun with Shapes. LC 91-46997. (Illus.). 32p. (ps-k). 1993. 10.99 (0-8037-1317-7) Dial Bks Young.

Ross, Anna. Little Grover's Book of Shapes. Gorbaty, Norman, illus. LC 91-4920. 24p. (ps). 1992. 3.99 (0-679-82237-2) Random Bks Yng Read.

Rutman, Shereen G. Shapes. Heck, Ed, illus. 16p. (ps). 1992. wkbk. 2.25 (1-56293-188-1) McClanahan Bk.

Schwager, Istar. Matching. Siede, George & Preis, Donna, photos by. (Illus.). 24p. (ps-3). 1993. PLB 12.95 (1-56674-068-1, HTS Bks) Forest Hse.

—Sorting. Siede, George & Preis, Donna, photos by. (Illus.). 24p. (ps-3). 1993. PLB 12.95 (1-56674-069-X, HTS Bks) Forest Hse.

Shapes & Sizes. (Illus.). 24p. (ps). 1994. bds. 2.95 (1-56458-536-0) Dorling Kindersley.

Shapes of Christmas. (gr. k-2). 1991. pap. 3.95 (0-8167-2188-2) Troll Assocs.

Shaping Up. (Illus.). (gr. 2 up). 1991. 5.95 (0-87449-579-2) Modern Pub NYC.

Siede, George & Preis, Donna, photos by. Shapes: Active Minds. Schwager, Istar, contrib. by. (Illus.). 24p. (ps-3). 1992. PLB 9.95 (1-56674-005-3) Forest Hse.

Simon, Seymour. Little Giants. Carroll, Pamela, illus. LC 82-14139. 48p. (gr. k-5). 1983. PLB 14.88 (0-688-01731-2) Morrow Jr Bks.

Smalley, Guy, illus. My Very Own Book of Sizes. 24p. (ps-2). 1989. 9.95 (0-929793-04-8) Camex Bks Inc.

Smith, Matthew V. Shapes & Colours. Smith, Matthew V., illus. 12p. 1992. pap. 4.95 (1-895583-03-9) MAYA Pubs.

Smith, Mavis. Circles. (ps-8). 1991. 3.95 (1-55782-366-9, Pub. by Warner Juvenile Bks) Little.

—Squares. (ps-8). 1991. 3.95 (1-55782-364-2, Pub. by Warner Juvenile Bks) Little.

—Triangles. (ps-8). 1991. 3.95 (1-55782-365-0, Pub. by Warner Juvenile Bks) Little.

Smoothey, Marion. Shape Patterns. Evans, Ted, illus. LC 92-36223. 1993. 15.95 (1-85435-465-5) Marshall Cavendish.

—Shapes. Evans, Ted, illus. LC 92-36224. 1993. 15.95 (1-85435-464-7) Marshall Cavendish.

—Solids. Evans, Ted, illus. LC 92-36220. 1993. 15.95 (1-85435-469-8) Marshall Cavendish.

Taulbee, Annette. Shapes & Colors. (Illus.). 24p. (ps-k). 1986. 3.98 (0-86734-068-1, FS-3061) Schaffer Pubns.

Taylor, Barbara. Hear! Hear! The Science of Sound. Bull, Peter, et al, illus. LC 90-42617. 40p. (Orig.). (gr. 2-5). 1991. pap. 4.95 (0-679-80813-2) Random Bks Yng Read.

Things That Go Board Shape Book. (Illus.). (ps). 1985. bds. 1.69 (0-517-46322-9) Random Hse Value.

Thompson, Kim M. & Hilderbrand, Karen M. A Little Rhythm, Rhyme & Read: Colors & Shapes. Kozjak, Goran, illus. 28p. (ps-1). 1993. Wkbk., incl. audio cass. 9.98 (1-882331-16-8) Twin Sisters.

Tucker, Sian. Sizes. (Illus.). 24p. (ps-k). 1992. pap. 2.95 (0-671-76909-X, Little Simon) S&S Trade.

Tyler, J. & Round, G. Sizes. (Illus.). 24p. (ps up). 1989. pap. 3.50 (0-7460-0269-6, Usborne) EDC.

University of Mexico City Staff, tr. Formas: Mentes Activas. Siede, George & Preis, Donna, photos by. Schwager, Istar, contrib. by. (SPA., Illus.). 24p. (ps-8). 1992. PLB 11.95 (1-56674-041-X) Forest Hse.

Weissman, Bari. Dial Playshapes: Circle. LC 91-73549. (Illus.). 10p. (ps). 1992. 3.95 (0-8037-1144-1) Dial Bks Young.

—Dial Playshapes: Square. LC 91-73550. (Illus.). 10p. (ps). 1992. 3.95 (0-8037-1146-8) Dial Bks Young.

—Dial Playshapes: Triangle. LC 91-73551. (Illus.). 10p. (Orig.). (ps). 1992. 3.95 (0-8037-1147-6) Dial Bks Young.

Wells, Robert E. Is a Blue Whale the Biggest Thing There Is? LC 93-2703. (Illus.). (gr. 1-6). 1993. 13.95 (0-8075-3655-5); pap. 6.95 (0-8075-3656-3) A Whitman.

Wise, Beth A. Colors, Shapes, & Sizes. Morgado, Richard, illus. 32p. (ps). 1992. wkbk. 1.95 (1-56293-168-7) McClanahan Bk.

—Sizes. Loh, Carolyn, illus. 16p. (ps). 1992. wkbk. 2.25 (1-56293-187-3) McClanahan Bk.

Yenawine, Philip. Shapes. (Illus.). (gr. 2-5). 1991. 14.95 (0-385-30255-X); PLB 14.99 (0-385-30315-7) Delacorte.

SIZE AND SHAPE–FICTION

Allen, Constance. Grover's Book of Cute Things to Touch. (ps). 1990. write for info. (0-307-12320-0, Golden Pr) Western Pub.

Ashwill, Beverley. Too Little, Too Big, Just Right. Ashwill, Betty J., illus. LC 90-83314. 18p. (ps-3). 1990. pap. 3.98 (0-941381-04-8) BJO Enterprises.

Bliss, Corinne D. The Shortest Kid in the World. LC 93-45421. 1994. write for info. (0-679-85809-1) Random Bks Yng Read.

Brenner, Barbara. Mr. Tall & Mr. Small. Shenon, Mike, illus. LC 93-8256. (gr. k-3). 1994. 14.95 (0-8050-2757-2) H Holt & Co.

Bridwell, Norman. Clifford's Puppy Days. LC 93-1802. (Illus.). 32p. (ps-6). 1994. 12.95 (0-590-43339-3, Cartwheel) Scholastic Inc.

Brown, Marc T. D. W. Just Big Enough. LC 92-19947. 1993. 11.95 (0-316-11305-0, Joy St Bks) Little.

Brown, Margaret W. The Little Fireman. new ed. Slobodkina, Esphyr, illus. LC 92-17571. 40p. (ps-3). 1993. 12.00 (0-06-021476-7); PLB 11.89 (0-06-021477-5) HarpC Child Bks.

Burns, Marilyn. The Greedy Triangle. Silveria, Gordon, illus. LC 94-11308. 1994. write for info. (0-590-48991-7) Scholastic Inc.

Cebulash, Mel. Batboy. Krych, Duane, illus. (gr. 3-8). 1992. PLB 8.95 (0-89565-882-8) Childs World.

Clement, Claude. Be Patient, Little Chick. Jensen, Patricia, adapted by. Erost, illus. LC 93-2951. 22p. (ps-3). 1993. 5.98 (0-89577-503-4, Readers Digest Kids) RD Assn.

Cooke, Trish. When I Grow Bigger. Brunello, John B., illus. LC 93-42601. 32p. (ps up). 1994. 13.95 (1-56402-430-X) Candlewick Pr.

Las Cosas Grandes y Chicas. (SPA.). (ps-3). 1993. pap. 2.25 (0-307-50073-X, Golden Pr) Western Pub.

Las Cosas que Conejito Ve. (SPA.). (ps-3). 1993. pap. 5.95 (0-307-91591-3, Golden Pr) Western Pub.

Cuneo, Mary L. What Can a Giant Do? Huang, Benrei, illus. LC 92-8307. 32p. (ps-1). 1994. 15.00 (0-06-021214-4); PLB 14.89 (0-06-021217-9) HarpC Child Bks.

Dahl, Roald. Esio Trot. Blake, Quentin, illus. LC 92-16931. 64p. (gr. 3-7). 1992. pap. 3.99 (0-14-036099-9) Puffin Bks.

Dillon, Barbara. My Stepfather Shrank! LC 91-23901. (Illus.). 128p. (gr. 3-7). 1992. 13.00 (0-06-021574-7); PLB 12.89 (0-06-021581-X) HarpC Child Bks.

DuQuette, Keith. Hotel Animal. DuQuette, Keith, illus. LC 93-14531. 32p. (ps-3). 1994. PLB 13.99 (0-670-85056-X) Viking Child Bks.

Eitan, Ora. Sometimes Big, Sometimes Small. Kriss, David, tr. from HEB. Elcanan, illus. 24p. (Orig.). (ps). 1992. pap. text ed. 3.00x (1-56134-139-8) Dushkin Pub.

Esh, Olivia. The Fence Was Too High. Childress, Rhonda, illus. LC 93-34499. 1994. PLB 19.97 (0-8114-4460-0) Raintree Steck-V.

Falwell, Cathryn. Clowning Around. LC 90-29064. (Illus.). 32p. (ps-1). 1991. 13.95 (0-531-05952-9); RLB 13.99 (0-531-08552-X) Orchard Bks Watts.

Farmer, Tony. How Small Is an Ant? (ps-3). pap. 3.95 (0-85953-518-5) Childs Play.

Farmer, Tony & Farmer, Lynne. How BIG Is an Elephant? LC 91-285. (gr. 3 up). 1991. 3.95 (0-85953-516-9) Childs Play.

Friedman, Frieda. Dot for Short. 168p. 1981. Repr. PLB 10.95x (0-89967-038-5) Harmony Raine.

Gackenbach, Dick. Tiny for a Day. Gackenbach, Dick, illus. LC 92-37580. 1993. 14.45 (0-395-65616-8, Clarion Bks) HM.

Gerstein, Mordicai. The Gigantic Baby. Levin, Arnie, illus. LC 90-35537. 32p. (gr. k-3). 1991. PLB 14.89 (0-06-022106-2) HarpC Child Bks.

Gleeson, Libby. Uncle David. Greder, Armin, illus. & photos by LC 92-18155. 32p. (ps up). 1993. 15.00 (0-688-12417-8, Tambourine Bks); PLB 14.93 (0-688-12418-6, Tambourine Bks) Morrow.

Gliori, Debi. When I'm Big. LC 92-43346. (Illus.). 32p. (ps up). 1994. 3.99 (1-56402-241-2) Candlewick Pr.

Gordon, Sharon. Playground Fun. Karas, G. Brian, illus. LC 86-30854. 32p. (gr. k-2). 1988. lib. bdg. 7.89 (0-8167-0990-4); pap. text ed. 1.95 (0-8167-0991-2) Troll Assocs.

Hellings, Colette. Too Little, Too Big: Trop Petite, Trop Grande. Maes, Dominique, illus. 40p. (ps-3). 1993. 10. 95 (0-8118-0530-1) Chronicle Bks.

Henkes, Kevin. The Biggest Boy. Tafuri, Nancy, illus. LC 94-4574. 32p. 1995. write for info. (0-688-12829-7); PLB write for info. (0-688-12830-0) Greenwillow.

Hoban, Lillian. Joe & Betsy the Dinosaur. Hoban, Lillian, photos by. LC 93-44725. (Illus.). (gr. k up). 1995. 14. 00 (0-06-024473-9) HarpC.

Hodges, Margaret, retold by. Gulliver in Lilliput. Root, Kimberly B., illus. LC 94-15037. (gr. 4 up). 1995. write for info. (0-8234-1147-8) Holiday.

Hutchins, Pat. Titch. Hutchins, Pat, illus. LC 92-1642. 40p. (ps-1). 1993. pap. 4.95 (0-689-71688-5, Aladdin) Macmillan Child Grp.

Jonas, Ann. Holes & Peeks. Jonas, Ann, illus. LC 83-14128. 24p. (ps-1). 1984. 16.00 (0-688-02537-4); PLB 15.93 (0-688-02538-2) Greenwillow.

Joyce, William. George Shrinks. Joyce, William, illus. LC 90-46285. 32p. (ps-2). 1991. 3.95 (0-06-023299-4) HarpC Child Bks.

Kellogg, Steven. Much Bigger Than Martin. Kellogg, Steven, illus. LC 75-27599. (ps-3). 1976. pap. 3.95 (0-8037-5811-1) Dial Bks Young.

Krasilovsky, Phyllis. The Very Little Boy. (Illus.). (ps). 1992. pap. 4.95 (0-590-44762-9, 030, Cartwheel) Scholastic Inc.

—The Very Little Girl. (Illus.). (ps). 1992. pap. 4.95 (0-590-44761-0, 029, Cartwheel) Scholastic Inc.

Leditschke, Anna. Tiny Timothy Turtle. McLean-Carr, Carol, illus. 32p. (ps-2). 1991. PLB 18.60 (*0-8368-0667-0*) Gareth Stevens Inc.
Levy, Elizabeth. The Runt. (Orig.). (gr. k-6). 1986. pap. 2.95 (*0-440-47538-4*, YB) Dell.
McDaniel, Becky B. Katie Couldn't. Axeman, Lois, illus. LC 85-11666. 30p. (gr. 1-2). 1985. PLB 10.25 (*0-516-02069-2*); pap. 2.95 (*0-516-42069-0*) Childrens.
Mayer, Marianna & McDermott, Gerald. The Brambleberrys Animal Book of Shapes. LC 91-70421. (Illus.). 32p. (ps up). 1991. 3.95 (*1-878093-77-0*) Boyds Mills Pr.
Miss Lori. Shapeless & the Magic Box, Bk. 1. White, Lori G., ed. Miss Lori, illus. 18p. (Orig.). (ps-1). 1990. pap. 11.99 (*0-9623368-3-1*) Shapeless Enterprises.
Mitchell, Rita P. Hue Boy. Binch, Caroline, illus. LC 92-18560. 32p. (ps-3). 1993. 13.99 (*0-8037-1448-3*) Dial Bks Young.
Mogensen, Jan. The Land of the Big. Mogensen, Jan, illus. LC 92-18302. 32p. (ps-3). 1993. 14.95 (*1-56656-111-6*, Crocodile Bks) Interlink Pub.
Mollel, Tololwa M. Big Boy. Lewis, E. B., illus. LC 93-21176. 1995. write for info (Clarion Bks) HM.
Moncure, Jane B. Magic Monsters Look for Shapes. Magnuson, Diana, illus. LC 78-21529. (ps-3). 1979. PLB 14.95 (*0-89565-057-6*) Childs World.
Moses, Amy. If I Were an Ant. Dunnington, Tom, illus. LC 92-12947. 32p. (ps-2). 1992. PLB 10.25 (*0-516-02011-0*) Childrens.
—If I Were an Ant. Dunnington, Tom, illus. LC 92-12947. 32p. (ps-2). 1993. pap. 2.95 (*0-516-42011-9*) Childrens.
Myers, Walter D. Hoops. 192p. (gr. 7 up). 1983. pap. 3.99 (*0-440-93884-8*, LFL) Dell.
O'Connor, Jane. Splat! Mets, Marilyn, illus. LC 93-34127. 32p. (ps-1). 1994. 7.99 (*0-448-40220-3*, G&D); pap. 3.50 (*0-448-40219-X*, G&D) Putnam Pub Group.
Patron, Susan. Five Bad Boys, Billy Que, & the Dustdobbin. Shenon, Mike, illus. LC 91-736. 32p. (ps-1). 1992. 13.95 (*0-531-05989-8*); PLB 13.99 (*0-531-08589-9*) Orchard Bks Watts.
Paul, Ann W. Shadows are About. Graham, Mark, illus. 32p. 1992. 13.95 (*0-590-44842-0*, Scholastic Hardcover) Scholastic Inc.
Petersen, P. J. The Fireplug Is First Base. James, Betsy, illus. LC 92-18956. 64p. (gr. 2-5). 1992. pap. 3.99 (*0-14-036165-0*) Puffin Bks.
Pienkowski, Jan. Small Talk. (Illus.). 10p. (ps up). 1991. 4.95 (*0-8431-2966-2*) Price Stern.
Potts, Jim. The House That Makes Shapes. LC 92-5847. (Illus.). 32p. (gr. k-3). 1992. 14.95 (*0-943173-74-4*) Harbinger AZ.
Rogers, Mary. Too Little. 30p. (ps-k). 1992. pap. text ed. 23.00 big bk. (*1-56843-002-7*); pap. text ed. 4.50 (*1-56843-052-3*) BGR Pub.
Shaw, Charles G. It Looked Like Spilt Milk Board Book. Shaw, Charles G., illus. LC 47-30767. 24p. (ps-1). 1993. 4.95 (*0-694-00491-X*, Festival) HarpC Child Bks.
Skofield, James. Round & Round. Hale, James G., illus. LC 90-32831. 32p. (ps-2). 1993. 15.00 (*0-06-025746-6*); PLB 14.89 (*0-06-025747-4*) HarpC Child Bks.
Stinson, Kathy. Big or Little. Lewis, Robin B., illus. 24p. (ps-1). 1987. pap. 0.99 (*0-920303-19-6*, Pub. by Annick CN) Firefly Bks Ltd.
Sweat, Lynn & Phillips, Louis. The Smallest Stegosaurus. Sweat, Lynn, illus. 32p. (ps-k). 1993. PLB 13.99 (*0-670-83865-9*) Viking Child Bks.
Tomioka, Chiyoko. Rise & Shine, Mariko-Chan! Tsuchida, Yoshiharu, illus. 32p. (ps-1). 1992. pap. 3.95 (*0-590-45507-9*) Scholastic Inc.
Weiss, Ellen. Oh Beans! Starring String Bean. Hall, Susan, illus. LC 88-4907. 32p. (gr. k-3). 1989. PLB 8.79 (*0-8167-1396-0*); pap. text ed. 1.95 (*0-8167-1397-9*) Troll Assocs.
Weiss, Monica. Shopping Spree: Identifying Shapes. Berlin, Rosemary, illus. LC 91-3986. 24p. (gr. k-2). 1992. PLB 10.59 (*0-8167-2490-3*); pap. text ed. 2.95 (*0-8167-2491-1*) Troll Assocs.
White, Stephen. Baby Bop Discovers Shapes. Hartley, Linda, ed. Daste, Larry, illus. LC 93-77867. 14p. (ps-k). 1993. bds. 4.95 chunky board die-cut (*1-57064-010-6*) Barney Pub.
Wisler, G. Clifton. Jericho's Journey. LC 92-36701. 144p. (gr. 5-9). 1993. 13.99 (*0-525-67428-4*, Lodestar Bks) Dutton Child Bks.
Yeager, Nancy & Yeager, Doug. A Tiny Little Story. 32p. (ps-k). 1993. pap. write for info. (*1-879911-01-9*) Rams Horn Bks.

SKATEBOARDS

Andrejtschitsch, Jan, et al. Action Skateboarding. LC 91-40328. (Illus.). 128p. (gr. 10-12). 1992. 16.95 (*0-8069-8500-3*) Sterling.
—Action Skateboarding. (Illus.). 128p. (gr. 10-12). 1993. pap. 10.95 (*0-8069-8501-1*) Sterling.
Caitlin, Stephen. Skateboard Fun. LC 87-19179. (ps-1). 1988. PLB 7.89 (*0-8167-1233-6*); pap. 1.95 (*0-8167-1234-4*) Troll Assocs.
Evans, Jeremy. Skateboarding. LC 93-18165. (Illus.). 48p. (gr. 5-6). 1994. text ed. 13.95 RSBE (*0-89686-822-2*, Crestwood Hse) Macmillan Child Grp.
Gould, Marilyn. Skateboarding. 48p. (gr. 3-4). 1991. PLB 11.95 (*1-56065-048-6*) Capstone Pr.
Hills, Gavin. Skate Boarding. LC 92-8433. (gr. 4 up). 1993. 17.50 (*0-8225-2483-X*) Lerner Pubns.
Italia, Bob. Skateboarding. 2nd ed. Wallner, Rosemary, ed. LC 91-73020. 32p. 1992. PLB 9.99 (*1-56239-077-5*) Abdo & Dghtrs.
King, Ron. Rad Boards: Skateboarding, Snowboarding, Bodyboarding. (gr. 4-7). 1991. pap. 9.95 (*0-316-49355-4*, Spts Illus Kids) Little.
Leder, Jane M. Learning How: Skateboarding. James, Jody, ed. Concept of Design Staff, illus. 48p. (gr. 4-7). 1992. lib. bdg. 14.95 (*0-944280-33-1*); pap. 5.95 (*0-944280-42-0*) Bancroft-Sage.
Thatcher, Kevin & Brannon, Brian. Thrasher: The Radical Skateboard Book. LC 91-52544. (Illus.). 72p. (Orig.). (gr. 3 up). 1992. PLB 11.99 (*0-679-92207-5*); pap. 7.99 (*0-679-82207-0*) Random Bks Yng Read.
Wilkins, Kevin. Skateboarding. LC 93-85515. (Illus.). 96p. (Orig.). 1994. pap. 12.95 (*1-56138-377-5*) Running Pr.

SKATING

Bailey, Donna. Skating. LC 90-36525. (Illus.). 32p. (gr. 1-4). 1990. PLB 18.99 (*0-8114-2854-0*); pap. 3.95 (*0-8114-4715-4*) Raintree Steck-V.
Boy Scouts of America. Cub Scout Sports: Skating. (Illus.). 64p. (Orig.). (gr. 2-5). 1986. pap. 1.35 (*0-8395-4083-3*, 34083) BSA.
Breitenbucher, Cathy. Bonnie Blair: Speediest Skater. LC 94-5744. 1994. 17.50 (*0-8225-2883-5*); pap. 13.13 (*0-8225-9665-2*) Lerner Pubns.
Brimner, Larry D. Rolling - In-Line! LC 93-51255. (gr. 3 up). 1994. write for info. (*0-531-20171-6*) Watts.
Donohue, Shiobhan. Kristi Yamaguchi: Artist on Ice. LC 92-38272. 1993. 13.50 (*0-8225-0522-3*) Lerner Pubns.
—Kristi Yamaguchi: Artist on Ice. (gr. 4-7). 1993. pap. 4.95 (*0-8225-9649-0*) Lerner Pubns.
Hilgers, Laura. Great Skates. (Illus.). (gr. 3-7). 1991. pap. 14.95 (*0-316-36240-9*, Spts Illus Kids) Little.
Italia, Robert. In-Line Skating. Wallner, Rosemary, ed. LC 91-73021. 32p. 1991. PLB 9.95 (*1-56239-076-7*) Abdo & Dghtrs.
Martin, John. In-Line Skating: Extreme Blading. 48p. (gr. 3-10). 1994. PLB 17.27 (*1-56065-202-0*) Capstone Pr.
Penner, Fred. Rollerskating. Hicks, Barbara, illus. 32p. (Orig.). (gr. 2-6). 1990. pap. 5.95 (*0-920534-64-3*, Pub. by Hyperion Pr Ltd CN) Sterling.
Quinn, Robert J. & Quinn, Nancy D. Figure Skating Pins. LC 87-60429. (Illus.). 152p. (Orig.). (gr. 7-12). 1987. pap. 15.00 (*0-9618349-1-9*) Quin Tel Prodns.
Sanford, William R. & Green, Carl R. Dorothy Hamill. LC 92-21356. (Illus.). 48p. (gr. 5). 1993. text ed. 11.95 RSBE (*0-89686-779-X*, Crestwood Hse) Macmillan Child Grp.
Savage, Jeff. Kristi Yamaguchi: Pure Gold. LC 92-42190. (Illus.). 64p. (gr. 3 up). 1993. text ed. 13.95 RSBE (*0-87518-583-5*, Dillon) Macmillan Child Grp.
Skating. (Illus.). 64p. (gr. 6-12). 1983. pap. 1.85 (*0-8395-3250-4*, 33250) BSA.
Sullivan, George. In-Line Skating: A Complete Guide for Beginners. LC 92-25896. (Illus.). 48p. (gr. 4 up). 1993. 13.99 (*0-525-65124-1*, Cobblehill Bks) Dutton Child Bks.
—In-Line Skating: A Complete Guide for Beginners. 48p. (gr. 4 up). 1993. pap. 4.99 (*0-14-054987-0*, Puff Unicorn) Puffin Bks.
Trenary, Jill. The Day I Skated for the Gold. 1989. pap. 14.95 (*0-671-68315-2*, S&S BFYR) S&S Trade.
Winter, Ginny L. Skating Book. Winter, Ginny L., illus. (gr. k-3). 1963. 8.95 (*0-8392-3035-4*) Astor-Honor.
Wood, Tim. Ice Skating. Fairclough, Chris, photos by. LC 89-49272. (Illus.). 32p. (gr. k-4). 1990. PLB 11.40 (*0-531-14051-2*) Watts.

SKATING–FICTION

Christopher, Matt. Skateboard Tough. (gr. 4-7). 1991. 15.95 (*0-316-14247-6*) Little.
Dodge, Mary M. Hans Brinker. (gr. k-6). 1985. pap. 4.95 (*0-440-43446-7*, Pub. by Yearling Classics) Dell.
—Hans Brinker. Betts, Louise, adapted by. Elwell, Peter, illus. LC 87-15472. 48p. (gr. 3-6). 1988. PLB 12.89 (*0-8167-1205-0*); pap. text ed. 3.95 (*0-8167-1206-9*) Troll Assocs.
—Hans Brinker or The Silver Skates. 1993. pap. 2.50 (*0-8125-3342-9*) Tor Bks.
—Hans Brinker: Or The Silver Skates. (gr. 4 up). 1993. pap. 4.99 (*0-88070-528-0*, Gold & Honey) Questar Pubs.
—Hans Brinker: The Silver Skates. LC 54-14472. (gr. 5 up). 1966. pap. 1.50 (*0-8049-0099-X*, CL-99) Airmont.
Fenner, Carol. The Skates of Uncle Richard. Forberg, Ati, illus. LC 78-55910. (gr. 2-5). 1978. PLB 9.99 (*0-394-93553-5*) Random Bks Yng Read.
Gutman, Bill. Skateboarding. 128p. 1992. pap. 6.99 cancelled (*0-8125-1938-8*) Tor Bks.
Holabird, Katharine. Angelina Ice Skates. Craig, Helen, illus. 32p. (ps-2). 1993. 15.00 (*0-517-59619-9*, Clarkson Potter) Crown Bks Yng Read.
Johnson, Mildred. Wait, Skates! Dunnington, Tom, illus. LC 82-22228. 32p. (ps-2). 1983. PLB 10.25 (*0-516-02039-0*); pap. 2.95 (*0-516-42039-9*) Childrens.
Kirk, Daniel. Skateboard Monsters. (Illus.). 32p. (ps-1). 1993. 12.95 (*0-685-66619-0*) Universe.
Koda-Callan, Elizabeth. Shiny Skates. LC 92-50293. (ps-3). 1992. 12.95 (*1-56305-309-8*, 3309) Workman Pub.
Laird, Elizabeth. The Day the Ducks Went Skating. Reeder, Colin, illus. LC 90-25899. 32p. (gr. k up). 1991. 11.95 (*0-688-10246-8*, Tambourine Bks); PLB 11.88 (*0-688-10247-6*, Tambourine Bks) Morrow.
Levy, Elizabeth. Cold As Ice. LC 88-12898. 176p. (gr. 7 up). 1988. 12.95 (*0-688-06579-1*) Morrow Jr Bks.
Lowell, Melissa. Breaking the Ice. 1993. pap. 3.50 (*0-553-48134-7*) Bantam.
—Competition. (gr. 4-7). 1994. pap. 3.50 (*0-553-48136-3*, Skylark) Bantam.
—Going for the Gold. (gr. 4-7). 1994. pap. 3.50 (*0-553-48137-1*, Skylark) Bantam.
—In the Spotlight. 1993. pap. 3.50 (*0-553-48135-5*) Bantam.
Marshall, Edward. Fox on Wheels. Marshall, James, illus. (gr. 1-4). 1993. pap. 3.25 (*0-14-036541-9*, Puffin) Puffin Bks.
Mooser, Stephen. Scary Scraped-up Skaters. Ulrich, George, illus. 80p. (Orig.). (gr. 2-5). 1992. pap. 3.25 (*0-440-40488-6*, YB) Dell.
Mumma, Barbara J. Two to Tango. (gr. 6 up). 1989. pap. 2.95 (*0-449-13466-0*) Fawcett.
Peters, Sharon. Champ on Ice. Paterson, Diane, illus. LC 87-10908. 32p. (gr. k-2). 1988. PLB 11.59 (*0-8167-1093-7*); pap. text ed. 2.95 (*0-8167-1094-5*) Troll Assocs.
Radin, Ruth Y. A Winter Place. O'Kelley, Mattie L., illus. LC 82-15349. 32p. (gr. 3 up). 1982. 15.95 (*0-316-73218-4*, Joy St Bks) Little.
Sawyer, Ruth. Roller Skates. Angelo, Valenti, illus. 192p. (gr. 4-7). 1969. pap. 1.50 (*0-440-47499-X*, YB) Dell.
Smith, Kaitlin M. Skating with Katie. Smith, Kaitlin M., illus. 15p. (gr. k-3). 1992. pap. 17.95 (*1-895583-19-5*) MAYA Pubs.
Streatfeild, Noel. Skating Shoes. (Orig.). (gr. 5 up). 1982. pap. 2.75 (*0-440-47731-X*, YB) Dell.
Warner, Gertrude C. The Mystery on the Ice. (gr. 4-7). 1993. 10.95 (*0-8075-5414-6*); pap. 3.50 (*0-8075-5413-8*) A Whitman.
Wojciechowska, Maia. Dreams of Ice Dancing. Karsky, A. K., illus. 52p. 1994. 14.50 (*1-883740-08-8*) Pebble Bch Pr Ltd.

SKELETON

Bailey, Donna. All about Your Skeleton. LC 90-10114. (Illus.). 48p. (gr. 2-6). 1990. PLB 20.70 (*0-8114-2780-3*) Raintree Steck-V.
Balestrino, Philip. The Skeleton Inside You. rev. ed. Kelley, True, illus. LC 88-23672. 32p. (gr. k-3). 1989. 14.00 (*0-690-04731-2*, Crowell Jr Bks); PLB 13.89 (*0-690-04733-9*) HarpC Child Bks.
—The Skeleton Inside You. rev. ed. Kelley, True, illus. LC 88-24600. 32p. (gr. k-3). 1989. pap. 4.95 (*0-06-445087-2*, Trophy) HarpC Child Bks.
Bones & Skeletons. 8.95 (*1-56458-041-5*) Dorling Kindersley.
Broekel, Ray. Your Skeleton & Skin. LC 84-7746. (Illus.). 48p. (gr. k-4). 1984. PLB 12.85 (*0-516-01934-1*) Childrens.
Cumbaa, Stephen. The Bones Book & Skeleton. LC 90-50368. (Illus.). 64p. (Orig.). (gr. 1-7). 1991. pap. 14.95 (*0-89480-860-5*, 1860) Workman Pub.
Feinberg, Brian. The Musculoskeletal System. Garell, Dale C. & Snyder, Solomon H., eds. (Illus.). 112p. (gr. 7-12). 1994. 19.95 (*0-7910-0028-1*, Am Art Analog) Chelsea Hse.
—The Musculoskeletal System. Koop, C. Everett, intro. by. LC 92-21956. 1993. pap. write for info. (*0-7910-0463-5*) Chelsea Hse.
Ganeri, Anita. Moving. (Illus.). 32p. (gr. 2-4). 1994. PLB 18.99 (*0-8114-5521-1*) Raintree Steck-V.
Gross, Ruth B. A Book about Your Skeleton. Bjorkman, Steve, illus. LC 93-49824. (ps-4). 1994. 2.95 (*0-590-48312-9*, Cartwheel) Scholastic Inc.
Incredible Skeleton Secrets. 32p. (ps-k). 1994. 4.95 (*1-56458-727-4*) Dorling Kindersley.
Johnson, Jinny. Skeletons: An Inside Look at Animals. Gray, Elizabeth, illus. LC 94-62. (gr. 3 up). 1994. 16.95 (*0-89577-604-9*) RD Assn.
Kahney, Regina. The Glow-in-the Dark Book of Animal Skeletons. Santoro, Christopher, illus. LC 91-3810. 24p. (gr. 2-5). 1992. 14.00 (*0-679-81080-3*) Random Bks Yng Read.
Morrison, Rob. X-Rays. Black, Don, illus. LC 93-28983. 1994. 4.25 (*0-383-03789-1*) SRA Schl Grp.
Murray, Peter. Your Bones: An Inside Look at Skeletons. LC 92-7460. (Illus.). (gr. 1-8). 1992. PLB 14.95 (*0-89565-968-9*) Childs World.
Nelson, JoAnne. Nose to Toes. Keith, Doug, illus. LC 91-34706. 24p. (Orig.). (gr. k-2). 1993. pap. 5.95 (*0-935529-16-0*) Comprehen Health Educ.
Parker, Steve. Skeleton. Dowell, Philip, photos by. LC 87-26314. (Illus.). 64p. (gr. 5 up). 1988. 16.00 (*0-394-89620-3*); lib. bdg. 16.99 (*0-394-99620-8*) Knopf Bks Yng Read.
—The Skeleton & Movement. rev. ed. (Illus.). 48p. (gr. 5 up). 1991. pap. 6.95 (*0-531-24606-X*) Watts.
Silverstein, Alvin & Silverstein, Virginia. Skeletal System. (Illus.). 96p. (gr. 5-8). 1995. bds. 15.95 (*0-8050-2837-4*) TFC Bks NY.
Skeleton & Movement. 48p. (gr. 5-8). 1988. PLB 10.95 (*0-382-09702-5*) Silver Burdett Pr.
Thompson, Brenda & Giesen, Rosemary. Bones & Skeletons. Viner, Carole & Giesen, Rosemary, illus. LC 76-22420. (gr. k-3). 1977. PLB 7.95 (*0-8225-1352-8*) Lerner Pubns.

SKETCHING

see Drawing

SKIING

see Skis and Skiing

SKIING, WATER

see Water Skiing

SKIN

Asimov, Isaac & Dierks, Carrie. Why Do People Come in Different Colors? LC 93-20157. 1993. PLB 15.93 (*0-8368-0808-8*) Gareth Stevens Inc.

Bailey, Donna. All about Your Skin, Hair & Teeth. LC 90-10050. (Illus.). 48p. (gr. 2-6). 1990. PLB 20.70 (*0-8114-2783-8*) Raintree Steck-V.

Broekel, Ray. Your Skeleton & Skin. LC 84-7746. (Illus.). 48p. (gr. k-4). 1984. PLB 12.85 (*0-516-01934-1*) Childrens.

Hammerslough, Jane. Everything You Need to Know about Skin Care. LC 93-45386. 1994. 14.95 (*0-8239-1686-3*) Rosen Group.

Machotka, Hana. Outstanding Outsides. LC 92-19517. (Illus.). 32p. (gr. k up). 1993. 15.00 (*0-688-11752-X*); PLB 14.96 (*0-688-11753-8*) Morrow Jr Bks.

Montagna, William. Human Skin. Head, J. J., ed. Ito, Joel, illus. LC 84-45831. 16p. (Orig.). (gr. 10 up). 1986. pap. text ed. 2.75 (*0-89278-159-9*, 45-9759) Carolina Biological.

Nelson, JoAnne. Nose to Toes. Keith, Doug, illus. LC 91-34706. 24p. (Orig.). (gr. k-2). 1993. pap. 5.95 (*0-935529-16-0*) Comprehen Health Educ.

Rauzon, Mark. Skin, Scales, Feathers, & Fur. LC 90-409858. (ps-3). 1993. 13.00 (*0-688-10232-8*); PLB 12.93 (*0-688-10233-6*) Lothrop.

Riedman, Sarah R. & Barish, Wendy. The Good Looks Skin Book. (Illus.). 144p. (gr. 10 up). 1983. 9.29 (*0-685-06727-0*) S&S Trade.

Showers, Paul. Your Skin & Mine. rev. ed. Kuchera, Kathleen, illus. LC 90-37430. 32p. (gr. k-4). 1991. PLB 13.89 (*0-06-022523-8*) HarpC Child Bks.

—Your Skin & Mine. rev. ed. Kuchera, Kathleen, illus. LC 90-37429. 32p. (gr. k-4). 1991. pap. 4.50 (*0-06-445102-X*, Trophy) HarpC Child Bks.

Skin. (Illus.). (gr. 5 up). 1987. lib. bdg. 15.94 (*0-86625-276-2*); 11.95 (*0-685-73924-4*) Rourke Corp.

SKIN, COLOR OF

see Color of Man

SKIN–DISEASES

Lamberg, Lynn. Skin Disorders. (Illus.). 112p. (gr. 6-12). 1990. 18.95 (*0-7910-0076-1*) Chelsea Hse.

Robins, Perry. Play It Safe in the Sun. Podwal, Michael, illus. 40p. 1994. pap. 9.95 (*0-9627688-1-2*) Skin Cancer Fndtn.

PLAY IT SAFE IN THE SUN is the first book on sun safety written especially for children. This practical guide tells children everything they need to know about year-round sun protection & early detection of skin cancer. With 40 pages of reading fun, 18 clever full-color illustrations & entertaining puzzles, the book has an interactive learning format that challenges children & stimulates group participation. Reproduction masters are included for a "sunword" puzzle, a sun-sense test & a coloring page. With warmth & humor, Dr. Robins discusses skin cancer, ozone depletion, the danger of tanning machines, use of sunscreens, as well as a range of other objects related to sun protection & skin health. Written by the president & founder of the Foundation & illustrated by 10-year-old artist Michael Podwal, this book is ideal for reading at home with the entire family & for use in classrooms, camps & clubs, doctor's offices & child care facilities. To order, send $9.95 plus $2.50, shipping & handling, (check, money order, MasterCard or VISA). Special discount: 25 copies/$174.

Publisher Provided Annotation.

Silverstein, Alvin, et al. Overcoming Acne: The How & Why of Healthy Skin Care. Papa, Christopher M., pref. by. LC 89-13748. (Illus.). 112p. (gr. 7 up). 1990. 12.95 (*0-688-08344-7*) Morrow Jr Bks.

SKIN DIVING

see also Underwater Exploration

Barrett, Norman S. Scuba Diving. LC 88-50372. (Illus.). 32p. (gr. k-6). 1990. 11.90 (*0-531-10631-4*) Watts.

Holbrook, Mike. Snorkeling. LC 92-45219. (Illus.). 48p. (gr. 5-6). 1994. text ed. 13.95 RSBE (*0-89686-823-0*, Crestwood Hse) Macmillan Child Grp.

Jennet, Judith. Snorkeling for Kids. 2nd ed. Nakanishi, Nadine, illus. 56p. (ps-9). 1992. pap. text ed. 5.95 (*0-916974-50-2*, 212) NAUI.

SKIS AND SKIING

see also Water Skiing

Bailey, Donna. Skiing. LC 90-36125. (Illus.). 32p. (gr. 1-4). 1990. PLB 18.99 (*0-8114-2856-7*); pap. 3.95 (*0-8114-4710-3*) Raintree Steck-V.

Claridge, M. Skiing. (Illus.). 64p. (gr. 6 up). 1987. pap. 7.95 (*0-7460-0096-0*) EDC.

Dieterich, Michele. Skiing. (Illus.). 48p. (gr. 4-12). 1992. PLB 17.50 (*0-8225-2478-3*) Lerner Pubns.

Evans, Jeremy. Skiing. LC 91-32025. (Illus.). 48p. (gr. 5-6). 1992. text ed. 13.95 RSBE (*0-89686-681-5*, Crestwood Hse) Macmillan Child Grp.

Godlington, Douglas. Skiing. (Illus.). 80p. (gr. 7 up). 1991. pap. 6.95 (*0-7063-6823-1*, Pub. by Ward Lock UK) Sterling.

Haycock, Kate. Skiing. LC 91-670. (Illus.). 48p. (gr. 6). 1991. text ed. 13.95 RSBE (*0-89686-669-6*, Crestwood Hse) Macmillan Child Grp.

Hulbert, Elizabeth M. I Love to Ski. Hulbert, Elizabeth M., illus. LC 87-51331. 64p. (Orig.). (gr. 1-3). 1986. pap. 4.95 (*0-932433-25-1*) Windswept Hse.

Italia, Bob. Skiing on the Edge. LC 93-19134. 66p. 1993. 9.95 (*1-56239-231-X*) Abdo & Dghtrs.

Italia, Robert. Jet Skiing. Wallner, Rosemary, ed. LC 91-73022. 32p. 1992. PLB 9.99 (*1-56239-075-9*) Abdo & Dghtrs.

Marozzi, Alfred. Skiing Basics. Gow, Bill, illus. 48p. (gr. 3-7). 1984. 4.95 (*0-13-812264-4*) P-H.

Sanchez, Isidro & Peris, Carme. Winter Sports. (Illus.). 32p. (ps-1). 1992. pap. 5.95 (*0-8120-4868-7*) Barron.

Skiing. (Illus.). 56p. (gr. 6-12). 1980. pap. 1.85 (*0-8395-3364-0*, 33365) BSA.

Smith, Alias & Pelkowski, Robert. Skiing: Speedy Slopes & Fluffy Snow in Ski School. 32p. (ps-3). 1989. pap. 3.95 (*0-8120-4244-1*) Barron.

Symons & Westcott, Alvin. Dips 'n' Doodles. LC 74-108726. (Illus.). 48p. (gr. 3-5). 1970. PLB 10.95 (*0-87783-011-8*); pap. 3.94 deluxe ed. (*0-87783-090-8*) Oddo.

SKIS AND SKIING–FICTION

Beskow, Elsa. Ollie's Ski Trip. Ernest Benn Ltd. Staff, tr. from SWE. Beskow, Elsa, illus. (ps-2). Repr. of 1960 ed. 14.95 (*0-86315-091-8*, Pub. by Floris Bks UK) Gryphon Hse.

Cavanna, Betty. Angel on Skis. (gr. 4-7). 1992. pap. 2.50 (*0-8167-1268-9*) Troll Assocs.

De Brunhoff, Laurent. Babar Fait Du Ski. (FRE.). (gr. 2-3). 14.95 (*0-685-11029-X*) Fr & Eur.

Delton, Judy. Pee Wee's on Skis. 1993. pap. 3.25 (*0-440-40885-7*) Dell.

Kaye, Marilyn. Camp Sunnyside Friends, No. 15: Christmas Break. 128p. (Orig.). 1991. pap. 2.99 (*0-380-76553-5*, Camelot) Avon.

Krementz, Jill. A Very Young Skier. LC 89-28760. (Illus.). 48p. (gr. k up). 1992. pap. 5.99 (*0-8037-1141-7*, Puff Pied Piper) Puffin Bks.

MacLean, John. When the Mountain Sings. LC 91-26720. 212p. (gr. 5-9). 1992. 14.95 (*0-395-59917-2*) HM.

Patterson, Don. Ski Vacation. Patterson, Don, photos by. (Illus.). 40p. (gr. k-6). 1991. 13.95 (*0-9629093-3-5*) MyndSeye.

Stine, R. L. Ski Weekend. large type ed. (gr. 6 up). Date not set. PLB 14.60 (*0-8368-1159-3*) Gareth Stevens Inc.

SKULL

see Brain

SKUNKS

Green, Carl R. & Sanford, William R. The Striped Skunk. LC 87-6652. (Illus.). 48p. (gr. 5). 1987. text ed. 12.95 RSBE (*0-89686-338-7*, Crestwood Hse) Macmillan Child Grp.

Lepthien, Emilie U. Skunks. LC 93-3410. (Illus.). 48p. (gr. k-4). 1993. PLB 12.85 (*0-516-01197-9*); pap. 4.95 (*0-516-41197-7*) Childrens.

Stone, L. Zorrillos (Skunks) 1991. 8.95s.p. (*0-86592-799-5*) Rourke Enter.

Stone, Lynn. Skunks. (Illus.). 24p. (gr. k-5). 1990. lib. bdg. 11.94 (*0-86593-046-5*); lib. bdg. 8.95s.p. (*0-685-36341-4*) Rourke Corp.

SKUNKS–FICTION

Burgess, Thornton. The Adventures of Jimmy Skunk. 1992. Repr. lib. bdg. 17.95x (*0-89966-993-X*) Buccaneer Bks.

Burgess, Thornton W. Adventures of Jimmy Skunk. 18.95 (*0-8488-0384-1*) Amereon Ltd.

—The Adventures of Jimmy Skunk. (Illus.). 96p. 1994. pap. 1.00 (*0-486-28023-3*) Dover.

Fontenot, Mary A. Clovis Crawfish & Batiste Bete Puante. Blazek, Scott R., illus. LC 93-1249. 32p. (gr. k-3). 1993. 14.95 (*0-88289-952-X*) Pelican.

Hanson, Fred E. Norman. Hanson, Ann R., ed. & illus. LC 89-90961. 63p. (Orig.). (gr. 4-6). 1989. pap. 7.95 (*0-685-28895-1*) Black Willow Pr.

—Norman. 2nd ed. Hanson, Ann R., illus. 64p. (gr. 3-5). 1989. pap. 7.95 (*0-9624292-0-1*) Black Willow Pr.

Levine, Evan. What's Black & White & Came to Visit? Lewin, Betsy, illus. LC 93-46418. 32p. (ps-2). 1994. 14.95 (*0-531-06852-8*); lib. bdg. 14.99 (*0-531-08702-6*) Orchard Bks Watts.

McMullen, Shawn A. It's What's Inside That Counts. Haley, Amanda, illus. 32p. (ps-2). 1991. pap. text ed. 3.99 (*0-87403-808-1*, 24-03898) Standard Pub.

Sargent, Dave & Sargent, Pat. Sammy the Skunk. 64p. (gr. 2-6). 1992. pap. write for info. (*1-56763-011-1*) Ozark Pub.

Service, Pamela F. Stinker's Return. LC 92-21800. 96p. (gr. 4-6). 1993. SBE 12.95 (*0-684-19542-9*, Scribners Young Read) Macmillan Child Grp.

Sherrow, Victoria. Skunk at Hemlock Circle. Davis, Allen, illus. Komisar, Alexi, contrib. by. LC 93-35511. (Illus.). 32p. (ps-2). 1994. 14.95 (*1-56899-031-6*); incl. audiocassette 19.95 (*1-56899-047-2*); incl. 12" plush toy 29.95 (*1-56899-046-4*); mini-sized bk. 4.50 (*1-56899-032-4*); mini-sized bk., incl. 6" plush toy 12.95 (*1-56899-048-0*); audiocassette avail. (*1-56899-045-6*) Soundprints.

Spohn, David. Nate's Treasure. (Illus.). (ps-3). 1991. 9.95 (*0-688-10092-9*) Lothrop.

Zwahlen, Diana. Pee-U I Think There Is a Skunk in Our School. LC 93-60230. (Illus.). 44p. (ps-3). 1994. 7.95 (*1-55523-607-3*) Winston-Derek.

SKYDIVING–FICTION

Rodriguez, Agatha A. Paracaidas, Paracaidas. Medina, Mary L., illus. (SPA.). 20p. (Orig.). 1992. pap. 5.00 (*0-933196-05-9*) Bilingue Pubns.

SKYSCRAPERS

Cooper, J. Rascacielos (Skyscrapers) (SPA.). 1991. 8.95s.p. (*0-86592-935-1*) Rourke Enter.

—Skyscrapers. 1991. 8.95s.p. (*0-86592-637-9*) Rourke Enter.

Dunn, Andrew. Skyscrapers. LC 92-43944. (Illus.). 32p. (gr. 5-8). 1993. PLB 13.95 (*1-56847-027-4*) Thomson Lrning.

Gibbons, Gail. Up Goes the Skyscraper! Gibbons, Gail, illus. LC 85-16245. 32p. (gr. k-3). 1986. RSBE 14.95 (*0-02-736780-0*, Four Winds) Macmillan Child Grp.

—Up Goes the Skyscraper! Gibbons, Gail, illus. LC 90-31777. 32p. (gr. k-3). 1990. pap. 4.95 (*0-689-71411-4*, Aladdin) Macmillan Child Grp.

Giblin, James C. The Skyscraper Book. Kramer, Anthony, illus. Anderson, David, photos by. LC 81-43038. (Illus.). 96p. (gr. 3-6). 1981. (Crowell Jr Bks); PLB 14.89 (*0-690-04155-1*, Crowell Jr Bks) HarpC Child Bks.

Michael, Duncan. How Skyscrapers Are Made. (Illus.). 32p. (gr. 5-12). 1987. 12.95x (*0-8160-1692-5*) Facts on File.

Richardson, Joy. Skyscrapers. (Illus.). 32p. (gr. 2-4). 1994. PLB 11.40 (*0-531-14291-4*) Watts.

Sauvain, Philip. Skyscrapers. Stefoff, Rebecca, ed. LC 90-40358. (Illus.). 48p. (gr. 4-7). 1990. PLB 17.26 (*0-944483-78-X*) Garrett Ed Corp.

Wilcox, Charlotte. A Skyscraper Story. Boucher, Jerry, photos by. (Illus.). 48p. (ps-4). 1990. PLB 19.95 (*0-87614-392-3*) Carolrhoda Bks.

SLATER, SAMUEL, 1768-1835

Simonds, Christopher. Samuel Slater's Mill & the Industrial Revolution. (Illus.). 64p. (gr. 5 up). 1990. PLB 12.95 (*0-382-09951-6*); pap. 7.95 (*0-382-09947-8*) Silver Burdett Pr.

SLAVE TRADE

Barboza, Steven. Door of No Return: The Legend of Goree Island. LC 93-21163. (Illus.). 48p. (gr. 5 up). 1994. 14.99 (*0-525-65188-8*, Cobblehill Bks) Dutton Child Bks.

Dudley, William, ed. Slavery: Opposing Viewpoints. LC 92-21796. 288p. 1992. lib. bdg. 17.95 (*1-56510-013-1*); pap. 9.95 (*1-56510-012-3*) Greenhaven.

Fox, Paula. The Slave Dancer. Eros, Keith, illus. LC 73-80642. 192p. (gr. 5-8). 1982. SBE 14.95 (*0-02-735560-8*, Bradbury Pr) Macmillan Child Grp.

Leas, Allan. Abolition of the Slave Trade. (Illus.). 72p. (gr. 7-10). 1989. 19.95 (*0-7134-5668-X*, Pub. by Batsford UK) Trafalgar.

Meltzer, Milton. All Times, All Peoples: A World History of Slavery. Fisher, Leonard E., illus. LC 79-2810. 80p. (gr. 5-9). 1980. PLB 15.89 (*0-06-024187-X*) HarpC Child Bks.

Nardo, Don. Braving the New World, 1619-1784: From the Arrival of the Enslaved Africans to the End of the American Revolution. LC 94-2963. (gr. 7 up). 1994. write for info. (*0-7910-2259-5*); pap. write for info. (*0-7910-2685-X*) Chelsea Hse.

Ofosu-Appiah, L. H. People in Bondage: African Slavery in the Modern Era. (Illus.). 132p. (gr. 5-12). 1993. PLB 19.95 (*0-8225-1437-0*) Lerner Pubns.

Sullivan, George. Slave Ship: The Story of the Henrietta Marie. LC 93-47653. (Illus.). 80p. (gr. 5 up). 1994. 14.99 (*0-525-65174-8*, Cobblehill Bks) Dutton Child Bks.

SLAVERY–FICTION

Anderson, Paul L. Slave of Catiline. LC 57-9446. 255p. (gr. 7-11). 1930. 18.00 (*0-8196-0101-2*) Biblo.

Armstrong, Jennifer. Steal Away. LC 91-18504. 224p. (gr. 6 up). 1992. 15.95 (*0-531-05983-9*); lib. bdg. 15.99 (*0-531-08583-X*) Orchard Bks Watts.

Berry, James. Ajeemah & His Son. LC 92-6615. 96p. (gr. 7 up). 1992. 13.00 (*0-06-021043-5*); PLB 12.89 (*0-06-021044-3*) HarpC Child Bks.

Clark, Margaret G. Freedom Crossing. 160p. (gr. 3-7). 1991. 2.95 (*0-590-44569-3*) Scholastic Inc.

Coleman, Evelyn. The Footwarmer & the Black Crow. Minter, Daniel, illus. LC 92-38352. (gr. 1 up). 1994. 14.95 (*0-02-722816-9*, Macmillan Child Bk) Macmillan Child Grp.

Collier, James L. & Collier, Christopher. Jump Ship to Freedom. LC 81-65492. 192p. (gr. 4-6). 1981. pap. 13.95 (*0-385-28484-5*) Delacorte.

—Who Is Carrie? LC 83-23947. 192p. (gr. 4-6). 1984. 14.95 (*0-385-29295-3*) Delacorte.

Connelly, Bernardine. Follow the Drinking Gourd. Buchanan, Yvonne, illus. LC 93-19247. 1993. 14.95 (*0-88708-336-6*, Rabbit Ears); incl. cass. 19.95 (*0-88708-335-8*, Rabbit Ears) Picture Bk Studio.

Cromer, Mary L. Stories for Jason. LC 93-37765. 110p. 1993. pap. 8.95 (*0-944350-28-3*) Friends United.

Endore, Guy. Babouk. rev. ed. Kincaid, Jamaica & Trouillot, Michel-Rolphintro. by. 352p. (gr. 9-12). 28. 00 (*0-85345-759-X*); pap. 9.00 (*0-85345-745-X*) Monthly Rev.

Gaeddert, LouAnn. Breaking Free. LC 93-22600. 144p. (gr. 3-7). 1994. SBE 14.95 (*0-689-31883-9*, Atheneum Child Bk) Macmillan Child Grp.

Goldin, Barbara D. Red Means Good Fortune: A Story of San Francisco's Chinatown. Ma, Wenhai, illus. 64p. (gr. 2-6). 1994. PLB 12.99 (*0-670-85352-6*) Viking Child Bks.

Harris, Deborah. Sweet Clara & the Freedom Quilt. Ransome, James, illus. LC 91-11601. 40p. (gr. k-5). 1993. 15.00 (*0-679-82311-5*); PLB 15.99 (*0-679-92311-X*) Knopf Bks Yng Read.

Hoobler, Dorothy & Hoobler, Thomas. Next Stop, Freedom: The Story of a Slave Girl. Hanna, Cheryl, illus. 64p. (gr. 4-6). 1991. 5.95 (*0-382-24152-5*); PLB 7.95 (*0-382-24145-2*); pap. 3.95 (*0-382-24347-1*) Silver Burdett Pr.

Hooks, William H. Freedom's Fruit. Ransome, James E., illus. LC 93-235. 1995. write for info. (*0-679-82438-3*); lib. bdg. write for info. (*0-679-92438-8*) Knopf.

Hurmence, Belinda. A Girl Called Boy. 180p. (gr. 3-6). 1982. 14.45 (*0-395-31022-9*, Clarion Bks) HM.

Johnson, Dolores. Now Let Me Fly: The Story of a Slave Family. Johnson, Dolores, illus. LC 92-33683. 32p. (gr. k-5). 1993. RSBE 14.95 (*0-02-747699-5*, Macmillan Child Bk) Macmillan Child Grp.

Marie, D. Tears for Ashan. Childers, Norman, illus. LC 88-63766. 32p. (ps-3). 1989. 11.95 (*0-9621681-0-6*) Creative Pr Works.

Meltzer, Milton. Underground Man. 261p. (gr. 3-7). 1990. pap. 4.95 (*0-15-292846-4*, Odyssey) HarBrace.

Monjo, F. N. The Drinking Gourd. Brenner, Fred, illus. LC 92-10823. 64p. (gr. k-3). 1983. pap. 3.50 (*0-06-444042-7*, Trophy) HarpC Child Bks.

Paulsen, Gary. Nightjohn. LC 92-1222. 96p. 1993. pap. 14.00 (*0-385-30838-8*) Doubleday.

Rinaldi, Ann. Wolf by the Ears. 1991. 13.95 (*0-590-43413-6*, Scholastic Hardcover) Scholastic Inc.

Rosen, Michael J. A School for Pompey Walker. Robinson, Aminah B., illus. LC 94-6240. 1995. write for info. (*0-15-200114-X*, HB Juv Bks) Harbrace.

Rowe, William. Viu's Night Book. (Illus.). 55p. (gr. 3-6). 1995. pap. 7.95 (*0-9641330-0-8*) Portunus Pubng.

Smalls-Hector, Irene. Irene Jennie & the Christmas Masquerade: The Johnkankus. Goodnight, Paul, illus. LC 93-7037. 1994. 15.95 (*0-316-79878-9*) Little.

Smucker, Barbara. Runaway to Freedom. Lilly, Charles, illus. LC 77-11834. 160p. (gr. 4-8). 1979. pap. 3.95 (*0-06-440106-5*, Trophy) HarpC Child Bks.

Sterne, Emma G. The Slave Ship. 1988. 2.95 (*0-590-44360-7*) Scholastic Inc.

Stolz, Mary. Cezanne Pinto. LC 92-46765. 256p. (gr. 7 up). 1994. 15.00 (*0-679-84917-3*) Knopf Bks Yng Read.

Stowe, Harriet Beecher. Uncle Tom's Cabin. Corrigan, R. A., intro. by. (gr. 9 up). 1967. pap. 3.50 (*0-8049-0143-0*, CL-143) Airmont.

Turner, Glennette T. Running for Our Lives. Byrd, Samuel, illus. LC 93-28430. 208p. (gr. 3-7). 1994. 15. 95 (*0-8234-1121-4*) Holiday.

Twain, Mark. Pudd'nhead Wilson. Gemme, F. R., intro. by. (Illus.). (gr. 8 up). 1966. pap. 2.50 (*0-8049-0124-4*, CL-124) Airmont.

Weinberg, Larry. Ghost Hotel. LC 94-2970. (Illus.). 160p. (gr. 3-6). 1994. pap. 2.95 (*0-8167-3420-8*) Troll Assocs.

Wright, Courtni C. Jumping the Broom. Griffith, Gershom, illus. LC 92-45575. 32p. (ps-3). 1994. reinforced bdg. 15.95 (*0-8234-1042-0*) Holiday.

SLAVERY IN THE U. S.

see also Abolitionists; Slave Trade; Southern States–History; Underground Railroad

Adler, David A. A Picture Book of Harriet Tubman. Byrd, Samuel, illus. LC 91-19628. 32p. (ps-3). 1992. reinforced bdg. 15.95 (*0-8234-0926-0*) Holiday.

Bial, Raymond. The Underground Railroad. LC 94-19614. 1995. write for info. (*0-395-69937-1*) HM.

Brill, Marlene T. Allen Jay & the Underground Railroad. Porter, Janice L., illus. LC 92-25279. 1993. 14.95 (*0-87614-776-7*); pap. write for info. (*0-87614-605-1*) Carolrhoda Bks.

Coil, Suzanne M. Slavery & Abolitionists. (Illus.). 64p. (gr. 5-8). 1995. bds. 15.95 (*0-8050-2984-2*) TFC Bks NY.

Connell, Kate. Tales from the Underground Railroad. Heller, Debbe, illus. LC 92-14415. 68p. (gr. 2-5). 1992. PLB 19.97 (*0-8114-7223-X*) Raintree Steck-V.

Davidson, Margaret. Frederick Douglass Fights for Freedom. 80p. (gr. 2-5). 1989. pap. 2.50 (*0-590-42218-9*, Apple Paperbacks) Scholastic Inc.

Davis, Ossie. Escape to Freedom: A Play about Young Frederick Douglass. (gr. 4-7). 1990. pap. 3.99 (*0-14-034355-5*, Puffin) Puffin Bks.

Dupre, Rick. Agassu: Legend of the Leopard King. Dupre, Rick, illus. 40p. (gr. 1-4). 1993. 18.95 (*0-87614-764-3*) Carolrhoda Bks.

Ferris, Jeri. Go Free or Die: A Story about Harriet Tubman. Ritz, Karen, illus. 64p. (gr. 3-6). 1989. pap. 5.95 (*0-87614-504-7*, First Ave Edns) Lerner Pubns.

Gaines, Edith M. Freedom Light: Underground Railroad Stories from Ripley, Ohio. Clay, Cliff, illus. (Orig.). (gr. 5-8). 1991. pap. 6.95 (*0-913678-20-1*) New Day Pr.

Goldman, Martin S. Nat Turner: And the Southampton Revolt of 1831. LC 91-36618. (Illus.). 160p. (gr. 9-12). 1992. PLB 14.40 (*0-531-13011-8*) Watts.

Hamilton, Virginia. Anthony Burns: The Defeat & Triumph of a Fugitive Slave. LC 87-38063. 192p. (gr. 5 up). 1988. lib. bdg. 12.99 (*0-394-98185-5*); pap. 3.99 (*0-679-83997-6*) Knopf Bks Yng Read.

—Many Thousand Gone: African-Americans from Slavery to Freedom. Dillon, Leo & Dillon, Diane, illus. LC 89-19988. 160p. (gr. 4-9). 1992. 16.00 (*0-394-82873-9*); PLB 16.99 (*0-394-92873-3*) Knopf Bks Yng Read.

Haskins, Jim. Get On Board: The Story of the Underground Railroad. LC 92-13247. 160p. (gr. 4-7). 1993. 13.95 (*0-590-45418-8*) Scholastic Inc.

Herda, D. J. The Dred Scott Case: Slavery & Citizenship. LC 93-22402. (Illus.). 104p. (gr. 6 up). 1994. lib. bdg. 17.95 (*0-89490-460-4*) Enslow Pubs.

Johnson, LaVerne C. Harriet Tubman: Writer. Perry, Craig R., illus. LC 92-35251. 1992. 3.95 (*0-922162-92-1*) Empak Pub.

Katz, William L. The Westward Movement & Abolitionism, 1815-1850. LC 92-14965. (Illus.). 96p. (gr. 7-8). 1992. PLB 22.80 (*0-8114-6276-5*) Raintree Steck-V.

Lester, Julius. This Strange New Feeling. 164p. (gr. 7 up). 1985. pap. 2.75 (*0-590-44047-0*) Scholastic Inc.

—To Be a Slave. Feelings, Tom, illus. LC 68-28738. (gr. 7-12). 1968. 14.95 (*0-8037-8955-6*) Dial Bks Young.

—To Be a Slave. 1986. pap. 3.25 (*0-590-42460-2*) Scholastic Inc.

McKissack, Patricia C. & McKissack, Frederick. Christmas in the Big House, Christmas in the Quarters. Thompson, John, illus. LC 92-33831. (gr. 3-8). 1994. 15.95 (*0-590-43027-0*) Scholastic Inc.

Marsh, Carole. Out of the Mouths of Slaves. (gr. 3-12). 1994. PLB 24.95 (*1-55609-312-8*); pap. 14.95 (*1-55609-311-X*); computer disk 29.95 (*1-55609-313-6*) Gallopade Pub Group.

Northup, Soloman. Twelve Years a Slave, Eighteen Forty-One to Eighteen Fifty-Three. Eakin, Sue, retold by. Dean, W. A., illus. LC 89-82295. 205p. (gr. 6-12). 1990. lib. bdg. 16.50 (*0-944419-27-5*); pap. text ed. 9. 95x (*0-944419-17-8*) Everett Cos Pub.

Northup, Solomon. Twelve Years a Slave: Excerpts from the Narrative of Solomon Northup. abr. ed. Lucas, Alice, ed. (Illus.). 48p. (Orig.). (gr. 5-12). Date not set. pap. text ed. 25.00 incl. 3 audio tapes (*0-936434-39-2*, Pub. by Zellerbach Fam Fund); pap. text ed. 5.00 tchr's. guide (*0-936434-59-7*) SF Study Ctr.

Excerpts in print & on audiotape from the true story of Solomon Northup, a free African American from New York who was kidnapped & sold into slavery in Louisiana. He lived as a slave for 12 years before regaining his freedom in 1853. Northup told of his harrowing experiences in a full-length book which Frederick Douglass called truth that is "stranger than fiction." African American actor/singer Wendell Brooks dramatically retells this moving story, enhancing the text by singing work songs & spirituals from the period. Actor Ossie Davis calls it "a powerful work. I recommend it without reservation." Reviewed in SLJ, 5/93, p. 71. BOOKLIST, 5/15/93, p. 1716, calls this 48-page illustrated excerpt: "excellent primary source material for the study of slavery in the United States." Also recorded on three 30-minute audiocassettes, TWELVE YEARS A SLAVE is excellent for schools, fifth grade through junior college. Also for church groups, other adult settings. Make checks payable to Many Cultures Publishing, P.O. Box 425646, San Francisco, CA 94142-5646. Toll Free 1-800-484-4173, ext. 1073, FAX 415-626-7276. California purchasers add sales tax.
Publisher Provided Annotation.

Perseverance. (Illus.). 256p. (gr. 9 up). 1993. write for info. (*0-7835-2250-9*); PLB write for info. (*0-7835-2251-7*) Time-Life.

Petry, Ann. Tituba of Salem Village. LC 64-20691. 254p. (gr. 7 up). 1988. PLB 14.89 (*0-690-04766-5*, Crowell Jr Bks) HarpC Child Bks.

Rappaport, Doreen. Escape from Slavery: Five Journeys to Freedom. Lilly, Charles, illus. LC 90-38170. 128p. (gr. 4-7). 1991. 13.00 (*0-06-021631-X*); PLB 12.89 (*0-06-021632-8*) HarpC Child Bks.

Rivers, Larry. Some American History: Slavery: The Black Man & the Man. Childs, Charles, intro. by. LC 72-153088. 50p. (Orig.). 1971. pap. text ed. 8.95 (*0-318-42723-0*, Dist. by U of TX Pr) Inst for the arts.

Rogers, James T. The Antislavery Movement. LC 93-40960. 1994. write for info. (*0-8160-2907-5*) Facts on File.

Shuter, Jane. Ball Charles: Charles Ball & American Slavery. LC 94-25546. 1995. write for info. (*0-8114-8281-2*) Raintree Steck-V.

Steins, Richard. The Nation Divides: The Civil War (1820-1880) LC 93-24993. (Illus.). 64p. (gr. 5-8). 1993. PLB 15.95 (*0-8050-2583-9*) TFC Bks NY.

Warner, Lucille S. From Slave to Abolitionist: The Life of William Wells Brown. Feelings, Tom, illus. LC 76-2288. 144p. (gr. 6 up). 1993. 13.99 (*0-8037-2743-7*) Dial Bks Young.

Yates, Elizabeth. Amos Fortune, Free Man. Unwin, Nora S., illus. (gr. 7 up). 1967. 15.00 (*0-525-25570-2*, DCB) Dutton Child Bks.

SLEEP

see also Dreams

Asimov, Isaac & Dierks, Carrie. Why Do We Need Sleep? LC 92-20154. 1993. PLB 15.93 (*0-8368-0806-1*) Gareth Stevens Inc.

Coad, Penelope. Goodnight. Falla, Dominique, illus. LC 92-31960. 1993. 4.25 (*0-383-03569-4*) SRA Schl Grp.

Edelson, Edward. Sleep. (Illus.). 112p. (gr. 6-12). 1992. lib. bdg. 18.95 (*0-7910-0092-3*) Chelsea Hse.

Feldman, Eve B. Animals Don't Wear Pajamas: A Book about Sleeping. Owens, Mary B., illus. LC 91-25192. 32p. (ps-3). 1992. 14.95 (*0-8050-1710-0*, Bks Young Read) H Holt & Co.

Hirschi, Ron. A Time for Sleeping. Mangelsen, Thomas D., photos by. LC 92-21408. (Illus.). 32p. (ps-3). 1993. 13.99 (*0-525-65128-4*, Cobblehill Bks) Dutton Child Bks.

Hobson, J. Allan. Sleep & Dreams. Head, J. J., ed. Whittingtor Julianne S., illus. 16p. (Orig.). (gr. 10 up). 1992. pap. text ed. 2.75 (*0-89278-117-3*, 45-9617) Carolina Biological.

Lanton, Sandy. Bedtime. Sagasti, Miriam, illus. 32p. (ps-2). Date not set. 11.95 (*1-56065-141-5*) Capstone Pr.

Little People Big Book About Bedtime. 64p. (ps-1). 1989. write for info. (*0-8094-7454-9*); PLB write for info. (*0-8094-7455-7*) Time-Life.

Myers, Jack. How Do We Dream? And Other Questions about Your Body. (Illus.). 64p. (gr. 1-5). 1992. bds. 12. 95 (*1-56397-091-0*) Boyds Mills Pr.

Parker, Steve. Dreaming in the Night: How You Rest, Sleep & Dream. (Illus.). 32p. (gr. k-4). 1991. PLB 11. 40 (*0-531-14099-7*) Watts.

Showers, Paul. Sleep Is for Everyone. Watson, Wendy, illus. LC 72-83785. 40p. (ps-3). 1974. PLB 14.89 (*0-690-01118-0*, Crowell Jr Bks) HarpC Child Bks.

Time Life Inc. Editors. Where Does the Sun Sleep? First Questions & Answers about Bedtime. Kagan, Neil, ed. (Illus.). 48p. (ps). 1993. write for info. (*0-7835-0866-2*); lib. bdg. write for info. (*0-7835-0867-0*) Time-Life.

Ziefert, Harriet. My Getting-Ready-for-Bed Book. Smith, Mavis, illus. LC 89-62012. 12p. (ps-1). 1990. 13.95 (*0-694-00299-2*) HarpC Child Bks.

SLEEP–FICTION

Adams, Pam, illus. There Were Ten in the Bed. LC 90-45580. 24p. (ps-2). 1979. 9.95 (*0-85953-095-7*, Pub. by Child's Play England) Childs Play.

Alda, Arlene. Sheep, Sheep, Sheep: Help Me Fall Asleep. Alda, Arlene, photos by. LC 91-43006. (Illus.). 32p. (ps-2). 1992. pap. 13.50 (*0-385-30791-8*) Doubleday.

Appelt, Kathi. A Colorful Goodnight Poem to a "Bayou Gal" Waldman, Neil, illus. LC 94-16639. (gr. 4-7). Date not set. write for info. (*0-688-12856-4*); PLB write for info. (*0-688-12857-2*) Morrow Jr Bks.

Asher, Sandy. Princess Bee & the Royal Good-Night Story. Mathews, Judith, ed. Smith, Cat B., illus. LC 89-35790. 32p. (ps-1). 1990. 13.95 (*0-8075-6624-1*) A Whitman.

Ashforth, Camilla. Horatio's Bed. Ashforth, Camilla, illus. LC 91-58737. 32p. (ps up). 1992. 15.95 (*1-56402-057-6*) Candlewick Pr.

—Horatio's Bed. LC 91-58737. (Illus.). 32p. (ps up). 1994. pap. 4.99 (*1-56402-277-3*) Candlewick Pr.

Beckman, Kaj. Lisa Can't Sleep. Beckman, Per, illus. 28p. (ps). 1990. 7.95 (*91-29-59768-4*, Pub. by R & S Bks) FS&G.

Benson, Rita. What Angela Needs. McClelland, Linda, illus. LC 92-34266. 1993. 14.00 (*0-383-03666-6*) SRA Schl Grp.

Boelts, Maribeth. Dry Days, Wet Nights. Parkinson, Kathy, illus. LC 93-28674. 1994. write for info. (*0-8075-1723-2*) A Whitman.

Brown, Hayden & Dickins, Roberts. The Sombrero. Dickins, Robert, illus. LC 93-6633. 1994. write for info. (*0-383-03714-X*) SRA Schl Grp.

Brown, Margeret W. Little Donkey Close Your Eyes. Wolff, Ashley, illus. LC 94-16523. (gr. 2-5). 1995. 15. 00 (*0-06-024482-8*); PLB 14.89 (*0-06-024483-6*) HarpC.

Calhoun, Mary. While I Sleep. Young, Ed, illus. LC 90-25488. 32p. (ps up). 1992. 14.00 (*0-688-08200-9*); PLB 13.93 (*0-688-08201-7*) Morrow Jr Bks.
Campbell, Alison & Barton, Julia. Are You Asleep, Rabbit? Scriven, Gill, illus. 32p. (ps-3). 1992. pap. 3.99 (*0-14-054495-X*) Puffin Bks.
Carlstrom, Nancy W. No Nap for Benjamin Badger. Nolan, Dennis, illus. LC 90-42564. 32p. (ps-1). 1991. RSBE 13.95 (*0-02-717285-6*, Macmillan Child Bk) Macmillan Child Grp.
Caseley, Judith. Sophie & Sammy's Library Sleepover. LC 91-48160. (Illus.). 32p. (ps up). 1993. 14.00 (*0-688-10615-3*); PLB 13.93 (*0-688-10616-1*) Greenwillow.
Cazet, Denys. I'm Not Sleepy. Cazet, Denys, illus. LC 91-15958. 32p. (ps-1). 1992. 14.95 (*0-531-05898-0*); lib. bdg. 14.99 (*0-531-08498-1*) Orchard Bks Watts.
—Mother Night. LC 88-36439. (Illus.). 32p. (ps-1). 1989. 14.95 (*0-531-05830-1*); PLB 14.99 (*0-531-08430-2*) Orchard Bks Watts.
Dale, Penny. Wake Up, Mr. B.! LC 91-58763. (Illus.). 32p. (ps up). 1994. pap. 4.99 (*1-56402-382-6*) Candlewick Pr.
DeClements, Barthe. Wake Me at Midnight. 160p. (gr. 3-7). 1993. pap. 3.99 (*0-14-036486-2*, Puffin) Puffin Bks.
Dormir. (SPA.). (ps-3). 1993. pap. 2.95 (*0-307-96084-6*, Golden Pr) Western Pub.
Dragonwagon, Crescent. Half a Moon & One Whole Star. Pinkney, Jerry, illus. LC 89-18643. 32p. (gr. k-3). 1990. pap. 3.95 (*0-689-71415-7*, Aladdin) Macmillan Child Grp.
Dr. Seuss. Dr. Seuss's Sleep Book. Dr. Seuss, illus. (gr. 3-7). 1962. 13.00 (*0-394-80091-5*); lib. bdg. 13.99 (*0-394-90091-X*) Random Bks Yng Read.
Fox, Mem. Night Noises. 30p. (ps-2). 1989. 13.95 (*0-15-200543-9*) HarBrace.
Ginsburg, Mirra. Asleep, Asleep. Tafuri, Nancy, illus. LC 91-14393. 24p. (ps up). 1992. 14.00 (*0-688-09153-9*); PLB 13.93 (*0-688-09154-7*) Greenwillow.
Gregorich, Barbara. Say Good Night. Hoffman, Joan, ed. Stasiak, Krystyna, illus. 16p. (Orig.). (gr. k-2). 1984. pap. 2.25 (*0-88743-010-4*, 06010) Sch Zone Pub Co.
—Say Good Night. Hoffman, Joan, ed. (Illus.). 32p. (gr. k-2). 1992. pap. 3.95 (*0-88743-408-8*, 06060) Sch Zone Pub Co.
Hamm, Diane J. Rockabye Farm. Brown, Richard, illus. LC 91-19127. 40p. (ps-1). 1992. pap. 14.00 jacketed (*0-671-74773-8*, S&S BFYR) S&S Trade.
Hamm, Diane Johnston. Rockabye Farm. LC 91-109127. (ps-3). 1994. pap. 4.95 (*0-671-88630-4*, Half Moon Bks) S&S Trade.
Hennessy, B. G. Sleep Tight. Carnabuci, Anthony, illus. 32p. (ps-1). 1992. RB 14.00 (*0-670-83567-6*) Viking Child Bks.
Hest, Amy. Pajama Party. Trivas, Irene, illus. LC 91-13676. 48p. (gr. 2 up). 1992. 14.00 (*0-688-07866-4*); PLB 13.93 (*0-688-07870-2*) Morrow Jr Bks.
Hiccups for Elephant. LC 94-15585. 2.95 (*0-590-48588-1*) Scholastic Inc.
Hindley, Judy. The Sleepy Book: A Lullaby. Aggs, Patrice, illus. LC 91-15787. 32p. (ps-1). 1992. 12.95 (*0-531-05971-5*); lib. bdg. 12.99 (*0-531-08571-6*) Orchard Bks Watts.
Hood, Thomas. Before I Go to Sleep. Begin-Callanan, Maryjane, illus. 32p. (ps-1). 1992. pap. 4.95 (*0-399-22440-8*, Putnam) Putnam Pub Group.
Howard, Jane R. When I'm Sleepy. Cherry, Lynne, illus. LC 84-25895. 24p. (ps-3). 1985. 12.95 (*0-525-44204-9*, DCB) Dutton Child Bks.
Irving, Washington. Rip Van Winkle. Rackham, Arthur, illus. LC 92-9843. 128p. (gr. 1). 1992. 19.00 (*0-8037-1264-2*) Dial Bks Young.
James, Mary. Shuteyes. (gr. 4-7). 1994. pap. 3.25 (*0-590-45070-0*) Scholastic Inc.
James, Sara. Boots Sleeps Over. Barcita, Pamela, illus. 24p. 1993. 3.98 (*1-56156-135-5*) Kidsbks.
—Boots Sleeps Over. Barcita, Pamela, illus. 24p. (ps-k). 1993. 3.98 (*0-8317-0604-X*) Smithmark.
Jensen, Patricia & Clement, Claude. Go to Sleep, Little Groundhog. Nouvelle, Catherine, illus. LC 91-46234. 24p. (ps-3). 1993. 6.99 (*0-89577-487-9*, Dist. by Random) RD Assn.
Leman, Jill. Sleepy Kittens. Leman, Martin, illus. LC 93-24232. 32p. 1994. 14.00 (*0-688-13288-X*, Tambourine Bks); PLB 13.93 (*0-688-13289-8*, Tambourine Bks) Morrow.
Lewison, Wendy C. Going to Sleep on the Farm. Wijngaard, Juan, illus. LC 91-3737. 32p. (ps-2). 1992. 13.00 (*0-8037-1096-8*); PLB 12.89 (*0-8037-1097-6*) Dial Bks Young.
Lipniacka, Ewa. Asleep at Last. Bogdanowicz, Basia, illus. LC 92-33326. 1993. 6.95 (*1-56656-118-3*, Crocodile Bks) Interlink Pub.
—To Bed...or Else! Bogdanowicz, Basia, illus. LC 91-22118. 32p. (ps-3). 1992. 13.95 (*0-940793-85-7*, Crocodile Bks) Interlink Pub.
Locker, Thomas, adapted by. & illus. Rip Van Winkle. LC 87-24448. 32p. (ps up). 1988. 15.95 (*0-8037-0520-4*); PLB 15.89 (*0-8037-0521-2*) Dial Bks Young.
McDaniel, Lurlene. Now I Lay Me Down to Sleep. 1991. pap. 3.50 (*0-553-28897-0*) Bantam.
McGuire, Leslie. Time for Bed? (ps-3). 1994. 11.95 (*0-89577-572-7*, Readers Digest Kids) RD Assn.
McLerran, Alice. Dreamsong. Vasiliev, Valery, illus. LC 91-32622. 32p. (gr. k up). 1992. 14.00 (*0-688-10105-4*, Tambourine Bks); PLB 13.93 (*0-688-10106-2*, Tambourine Bks) Morrow.
McMullan, Kate. Goodnight, Stella. Clark, Emma C., illus. LC 93-876. 32p. (ps up). 1994. 14.95 (*1-56402-065-7*) Candlewick Pr.
McOmber, Rachel B., ed. McOmber Phonics Storybooks: Snores & More. rev. ed. (Illus.). write for info. (*0-944991-59-9*) Swift Lrn Res.
Masurel, Claire. Good Night! Henry, Marie H., illus. LC 93-30198. 1994. 12.95 (*0-8118-0644-8*) Chronicle Bks.
Matthews, Morgan. Whoo's Too Tired? Kolding, Richard M., illus. LC 88-1285. 48p. (Orig.). (gr. 1-4). 1988. PLB 10.59 (*0-8167-1331-6*); pap. text ed. 3.50 (*0-8167-1332-4*) Troll Assocs.
Michaels, Ski. Wake up, Sam! Garry-McCord, Kathi, illus. LC 85-14115. 48p. (Orig.). (gr. 1-3). 1986. PLB 10.59 (*0-8167-0580-1*); pap. text ed. 3.50 (*0-8167-0581-X*) Troll Assocs.
Moerbeek, Kees. Can't Sleep. Moerbeek, Kees, illus. 12p. (ps-3). 1994. 9.95 (*0-8431-3689-8*) Price Stern.
Muir, Jim. Little Girls Have to Sleep. Barwick, Mary, illus. Moore, Robert, contrib. by. LC 92-37456. (Illus.). 1994. 16.00 (*1-881320-03-0*) Black Belt Pr.
Ormerod, Jan. Midnight Pillow Fight. Ormerod, Jan, illus. LC 92-53011. 32p. (ps up). 1993. 14.95 (*1-56402-169-6*) Candlewick Pr.
Packard, Mary. Sleep-over Mouse. (Illus.). 28p. (ps-2). 1994. PLB 14.00 (*0-516-05367-1*); pap. 3.95 (*0-516-45367-X*) Childrens.
Paschkis. Wide Awake So Sleepy. (ps-1). 1994. 12.95 (*0-8050-3174-X*) H Holt & Co.
Que Duermas Bien. (SPA.). (ps-3). 1993. pap. 2.25 (*0-307-50026-8*, Golden Pr) Western Pub.
Reiser, Lynn. Night Thunder & the Queen of the Wild Horses. LC 93-25734. 1994. write for info. (*0-688-11791-0*); PLB write for info. (*0-688-11792-9*) Greenwillow.
Rodgers, Frank. I Can't Get to Sleep. LC 90-19607. (Illus.). 32p. (ps-1). 1993. pap. 7.95 (*0-671-79848-0*, S&S BYR) S&S Trade.
Rogers, Jacqueline. Best Friends Sleep Over. LC 92-56895. 1993. write for info. (*0-590-44793-9*) Scholastic Inc.
Ross, Anna. Naptime. Gorbaty, Norman, illus. LC 89-34545. 24p. (ps). 1990. 3.95 (*0-394-85828-X*) Random Bks Yng Read.
Ross, Tony. Happy Blanket. (Illus.). 32p. (ps-2). 1990. 12.95 (*0-374-32843-9*) FS&G.
Sage, James. To Sleep. Hutton, Warwick, illus. LC 89-36931. 32p. (ps-3). 1990. SBE 13.95 (*0-689-50497-7*, M K McElderry) Macmillan Child Grp.
Schmidt, Bridget. Bayla & the SleepStone. (ps-3). 1992. pap. 14.99 (*0-9634525-0-9*) Bayla Prods.
Schuchman, Joan. Two Places to Sleep. LaMarche, Jim, illus. LC 79-88201. 32p. (gr. 1-4). 1979. PLB 13.50 (*0-87614-108-4*) Carolrhoda Bks.
Shepperson, Bob. The Sandman. Shepperson, Bob, illus. 32p. (ps-3). 1991. pap. 4.95 (*0-374-46450-2*) FS&G.
Singer, Marilyn. Nine O'Clock Lullaby. Lessac, Frane, illus. LC 90-32116. 32p. (ps-3). 1993. pap. 4.95 (*0-06-443319-6*, Trophy) HarpC Child Bks.
Splendor, Meg. Dream Catcher: A Starlight Journey with Meg Splendor. LC 93-1015. 77p. (Orig.). (ps up). 1993. pap. 12.95 incl. 17 min. audio tape (*1-882979-17-6*) What the Heck.
Stevenson, James. We Can't Sleep. LC 81-20307. (Illus.). 32p. (gr. k-3). 1982. 13.95 (*0-688-01213-2*); PLB 13.88 (*0-688-01214-0*) Greenwillow.
Stinson, Kathy. Who Is Sleeping in Aunty's Bed? (ps-3). 1994. pap. 6.95 (*0-19-540852-7*) OUP.
Storr, Catherine, retold by. Rip Van Winkle. LC 83-26996. (Illus.). 32p. (gr. k-5). 1984. PLB 19.97 (*0-8172-2108-5*); PLB 29.28 incl. cassette (*0-8172-2236-7*) Raintree Steck-V.
Szekeres, Cyndy. Cyndy Szekeres' Teeny Mouse Counts Herself. Szekeres, Cyndy, illus. 12p. (ps). 1992. bds. write for info. (*0-307-06118-3*, 6118, Golden Pr) Western Pub.
Tiller, Ruth. Cinnamon, Mint, & Mothballs: A Visit to Grandmother's House. Sogabe, Aki, illus. LC 92-32981. 1993. write for info. (*0-15-276617-0*) HarBrace.
Trent, John T. There's a Duck in My Closet. Love, Judy, illus. LC 93-15707. (gr. k-5). 1993. 12.99 (*0-8499-1037-4*) Word Pub.
Twining, Edith. Sandman. (ps-4). 1991. pap. 12.95 (*0-385-41258-4*) Doubleday.
Waber, Bernard. Ira Sleeps over. (gr. k-5). 1984. incl. cassette 19.95 (*0-941078-36-1*); pap. 12.95 incl. cassette (*0-941078-34-5*); incl. 4 bks., cassette, & guide 27.95 (*0-941078-35-3*); filmstrip 22.95 (*0-941078-43-4*) Live Oak Media.
Wahl, Jan. The Sleepytime Book. Johnson, Arden, illus. LC 91-10176. 32p. (ps-3). 1992. 15.00 (*0-688-10275-1*, Tambourine Bks); PLB 14.93 (*0-688-10276-X*, Tambourine Bks) Morrow.
Wallace, Karen. Why Count Sheep? a Bedtime Book. Aggs, Patrice, illus. LC 92-56140. 32p. (ps-1). 1993. 13.95 (*1-56282-528-3*); PLB 13.89 (*1-56282-529-1*) Hyprn Child.
Warburton, Nick. Mr. Tite's Belongings. Warburton, Nick, illus. 32p. (ps-3). 1992. 13.95 (*0-670-84155-2*) Viking Child Bks.
Wells, Rosemary. Good Night, Fred. Wells, Rosemary, illus. LC 81-65849. 32p. (ps-3). 1981. Dial Bks Young.
Wilkin, Eloise, illus. My Goodnight Book. 14p. (ps-k). 1981. write for info. (*0-307-12258-1*, Golden Bks.) Western Pub.
Wood, Audrey. Into the Napping House. Wood, Don, illus. Shaylen, Carl, contrib. by. (Illus.). (ps-2). 1990. Incl. cassette. 19.95 (*0-15-256709-7*) HarBrace.
—The Napping House. Wood, Don, illus. LC 83-13035. 32p. (ps-3). 1984. 13.95 (*0-15-256708-9*, HB Juv Bks) HarBrace.
Worth, Bonnie. I Can Take a Nap. (ps). 1994. 3.95 (*0-307-12426-6*, Golden Pr) Western Pub.
Zolotow, Charlotte. The Summer Night. Shecter, Ben, illus. LC 88-44522. 32p. (ps-3). 1991. PLB 13.89 (*0-06-026917-0*) HarpC Child Bks.

SLEIGHT OF HAND
see Magic

SLOTHS
Fowler, Allan. The Upside-Down Sloth. LC 93-18981. (Illus.). 32p. (ps-2). 1993. PLB 10.75 (*0-516-06018-X*); pap. 3.95 (*0-516-46018-8*) Childrens.

SLOTHS–FICTION
Bond, Felicia. Poinsettia & Her Family. Bond, Felicia, illus. LC 81-43035. 32p. (ps-3). 1981. PLB 13.89 (*0-690-04145-4*, Crowell Jr Bks) HarpC Child Bks.
Turnbull, Ann. Too Tired. Clark, Emma C., illus. LC 93-10825. 1994. write for info. (*0-15-200549-8*) HarBrace.

SLOW LEARNING CHILDREN–FICTION
Byars, Betsy C. Summer of the Swans. CoConis, Ted, illus. (gr. 7 up). 1970. pap. 14.00 (*0-670-68190-3*) Viking Child Bks.

SLUMBER SONGS
see Lullabies

SLUMS
see Housing

SMALL ARMS
see Firearms

SMALL BUSINESS
Ashmore, M. Catherine, et al. Risks & Rewards of Entrepreneurship. LC 87-21787. 128p. (Orig.). 1987. pap. text ed. 7.95 (*0-8219-0323-3*, 25658); tchr's. resource guide 19.00 (*0-8219-0324-1*, TRG-25803) EMC.
Bernstein, Daryl. Better Than a Lemonade Stand: Business Ideas for Kids. (Illus.). (gr. 2-10). 1992. pap. 7.95 (*0-941831-75-2*) Beyond Words Pub.
Ratcliffe, Dolores. Women Entrepreneurs, Networking & Sweet Patato Pie: Business Survival Guide. (gr. 10-12). 1987. pap. 14.95 (*0-933016-03-4*) Corita Comm.
Riehm, Sarah. Teenage Entrepreneur's Guide: 50 Money-Making Business Ideas. 2nd ed. LC 87-1904. (Illus., Orig.). (gr. 7-12). 1990. pap. 10.95 (*0-940625-17-2*) Surrey Bks.
Thompson, Terri. Biz Kids Guide to Success: Money-Making Ideas for Young Entrepreneurs. (Illus.). 96p. (gr. 3 up). 1992. pap. 4.95 (*0-8120-4831-8*) Barron.

SMALLS, ROBERT, 1839-1915
Cooper, Michael L. Slave, Civil War Hero: The Story of Robert Smalls. LC 93-44169. (Illus.). 64p. (gr. 3-6). 1994. 13.99 (*0-525-67489-6*, Lodestar Bks) Dutton Child Bks.

SMELL
Allington, Richard L. & Krull, Kathleen. Smelling. Gatzke, Lee, illus. LC 79-27147. 32p. (gr. k-3). 1985. PLB 9.95 (*0-8172-1293-0*); pap. 9.27 (*0-8172-2488-2*) Raintree Steck-V.
Fowler, Allan. Smelling Things. LC 90-22123. (Illus.). 32p. (ps-2). 1991. PLB 10.75 (*0-516-04912-7*); pap. 3.95 (*0-516-44912-5*) Childrens.
Moncure, Jane B. What Your Nose Knows! Axeman, Lois, illus. LC 82-9464. 32p. (ps-3). 1982. pap. 3.95 (*0-516-43255-9*) Childrens.
Parramon, J. M. & Puig, J. J. Smell. Rius, Maria, illus. 32p. (ps). 1985. pap. 6.95 (*0-8120-3565-8*); pap. 6.95 (*0-8120-3607-7*) Span. ed. Barron.
Silverstein, Alvin, et al. Smell, the Subtle Sense. Neumann, Ann, illus. LC 91-21745. 96p. (gr. 3 up). 1992. 14.00 (*0-688-09396-5*); PLB 13.93 (*0-688-09397-3*) Morrow Jr Bks.
Smith, Kathie B. & Crenson, Victoria. Smelling. Storms, Robert S., illus. LC 87-5887. 24p. (gr. k-3). 1988. PLB 10.59 (*0-8167-1010-4*); pap. text ed. 2.50 (*0-8167-1011-2*) Troll Assocs.
Snell, Nigel. Tasting & Smelling. (Illus.). 32p. (gr. k-2). 1991. 10.95 (*0-237-60258-X*, Pub. by Evans Bros Ltd) Trafalgar.
Stuchbury, Dianne. Taste & Smell! Stuchbury, Dianne, illus. 24p. (ps-1). 1991. 4.99 (*0-7459-2003-9*) Lion USA.
Suhr, Mandy. Smell. Gordon, Mike, illus. LC 93-44189. 1993. 13.50 (*0-87614-835-6*) Carolrhoda Bks.
Ziefert, Harriet. What Do I Smell? 1988. pap. 3.95 (*0-553-05457-0*) Bantam.

SMELL–FICTION
Ernie Usa su Nariz. (SPA.). (ps-3). 1993. pap. 4.95 (*0-307-52321-7*, Golden Pr) Western Pub.

SMITH, JEDEDIAH STRONG, 1799-1831
Allen, John L. Jedediah Smith & the Mountain Men of the American West. Goetzmann, William H., ed. Collins, Michael, intro. by. (Illus.). 112p. (gr. 5 up). 1991. lib. bdg. 18.95 (*0-7910-1319-7*) Chelsea Hse.
Vogt, Esther L. God's Mountain Man: The Story of Jedediah Strong Smith. LC 90-25278. (Illus.). 160p. (gr. 6-8). 1991. pap. 5.95 (*0-88243-563-9*, 02-0563) Gospel Pub.

SMITH, JOHN, 1580-1631
Graves, Charles P. John Smith. (Illus.). 96p. (gr. 3-5). 1991. Repr. of 1965 ed. PLB 12.95 (*0-7910-1499-1*) Chelsea Hse.

SMITHSONIAN INSTITUTION

Lucas, Daryl. Choice Adventures, No. 2: The Smithsonian Connection. (gr. 3-7). 1991. PLB 4.99 (*0-8423-5026-8*) Tyndale.

Thomson, Peggy. Auks, Rocks & the Odd Dinosaur: Inside Stories from the Smithsonian's Museum of Natural History. LC 85-47744. (Illus.). 128p. (gr. 3-7). 1985. PLB 14.89 (*0-690-04492-5*, Crowell Jr Bks) HarpC Child Bks.

SMOKING

see also Tobacco Habit

Bosworth, et al. Smoking. (gr. 7-12). Date not set. incl. software 120.00 (*0-912899-56-5*) Lrning Multi-Systs.

Cohen, Philip. Tobacco. LC 91-32583. (Illus.). 64p. (gr. 6-12). 1991. PLB 22.80 (*0-8114-3202-5*) Raintree Steck-V.

Gano, Lila. Smoking. LC 89-12650. (Illus.). 96p. (gr. 5-8). 1989. PLB 14.95 (*1-56006-103-0*) Lucent Bks.

Keyishian, Elizabeth. Everything You Need to Know about Smoking. rev. ed. Rosen, Ruth, ed. (gr. 7-12). 1993. PLB 14.95 (*0-8239-1615-4*) Rosen Group.

Lee, Richard S. & Lee, Mary P. Caffeine & Nicotine. LC 94-2279. (gr. 7 up). 1994. write for info. (*0-8239-1701-0*) Rosen Group.

Marr, John S. A Breath of Air & a Breath of Smoke. Sweat, Lynn, illus. LC 70-161362. 48p. (gr. 3 up). 1970. 4.95 (*0-87131-038-4*) M Evans.

Sanders, Peter A., Jr. Why Do People Smoke? (Illus.). 32p. (gr. 2-5). 1989. PLB 11.40 (*0-531-17192-2*) Watts.

Say No to Smoking! 16p. 1994. 0.95 (*0-685-71923-5*, 730) W Gladden Found.

Stronck, David. Tobacco - The Real Story. Nelson, Mary & Clark, Kay, eds. Ransom, Robert D., illus. 30p. (gr. 5-8). 1987. pap. text ed. 2.95 (*0-941816-34-6*) ETR Assocs.

Szumski, Bonnie. Smoking: Distinguishing Between Fact & Opinion. LC 89-2153. (Illus.). 32p. (gr. 3-6). 1990. PLB 10.95 (*0-89908-642-X*) Greenhaven.

Traynor, Pete. Cigarettes, Cigarettes. Traynor, Pete, illus. Reynolds, Patrick, frwd. by. LC 92-31033. (Illus.). 24p. 1994. 14.95 (*0-9629978-7-0*) Sights Prods.

SMUGGLING

Steele, Philip. Smuggling. LC 92-13611. (Illus.). 48p. (gr. 6 up). 1993. text ed. 12.95 RSBE (*0-02-786884-2*, New Discovery) Macmillan Child Grp.

SMUGGLING–FICTION

Avi. Smuggler's Island. LC 93-35964, 192p. (gr. 5 up). 1994. 14.00g (*0-688-12796-7*); pap. 3.95 (*0-688-12797-5*, Pub. by Beech Tree Bks) Morrow Jr Bks.

Westcott, Alvin. Rockets & Crackers. LC 75-108729. (Illus.). 80p. (gr. 4 up). 1970. PLB 10.95 (*0-87783-033-9*); pap. 3.94 deluxe ed. (*0-87783-105-X*) Oddo.

SNAILS

Buholzer, Theres. Life of the Snail. Simon, Noel, tr. from GER. (Illus.). 48p. (gr. 2-5). 1987. PLB 19.95 (*0-87614-246-3*) Carolrhoda Bks.

Johnson, Sylvia A. Snails. Masuda, Modoki, illus. LC 82-10086. 48p. (gr. 4 up). 1982. PLB 19.95 (*0-8225-1475-3*, First Ave Edns); pap. 5.95 (*0-8225-9544-3*, First Ave Edns) Lerner Pubns.

Olesen, Jens. Snail. LC 86-10084. (Illus.). 25p. (gr. k-4). 1986. 5.95 (*0-382-09304-6*); PLB 7.95 (*0-382-09289-9*) pap. 3.95 (*0-382-24019-7*) Silver Burdett Pr.

Watts, Barrie. Slugs & Snails. 32p. (gr. k-4). 1991. pap. 4.95 (*0-531-15623-0*) Watts.

SNAILS–FICTION

Chottin, Ariane. A Home for Little Turtle. Wirth, Pascale, illus. LC 91-40650. 24p. (ps-3). 1992. 6.99 (*0-89577-420-8*, Dist. by Random) RD Assn.

Fontenot, Mary A. Clovis Crawfish & Etienne Escargot. Blazek, Scott R., illus. LC 91-26896. 32p. (ps-3). 1992. 12.95 (*0-88289-826-4*) Pelican.

Giganti, Paul, Jr. How Many Snails? LC 87-26281. (Illus.). 24p. (ps-1). 1988. 15.00 (*0-688-06369-1*); lib. bdg. 14.93 (*0-688-06370-5*) Greenwillow.

Greenberg, David. Slugs. Chase, Victoria, illus. LC 82-10017. 32p. (gr. k-5). 1983. 13.95 (*0-316-32658-5*, Joy St Bks); pap. 4.95i (*0-316-32659-3*, Joy St Bks) Little.

Himmelman, John. Simpson Snail Sings. (Illus.). 48p. (gr. k-2). 1992. 11.00 (*0-525-44978-7*, DCB) Dutton Child Bks.

—The Ups & Downs of Simpson Snail. Himmelman, John, illus. LC 89-30547. 48p. (ps-3). 1989. 9.95 (*0-525-44542-0*, DCB) Dutton Child Bks.

Lowesdale School Children. Sarah Snail. Shaw, Peter, illus. LC 92-27084. 1993. 3.75 (*0-383-03592-9*) SRA Schl Grp.

Napoli, Donna J. Prince of the Pond. LC 91-40340. (Illus.). 112p. (gr. 2-5). 1992. 13.00 (*0-525-44976-0*, DCB) Dutton Child Bks.

Ryder, Joan. The Snail's Spell. Cherry, Lynne, illus. (gr. 3-8). 1988. pap. 4.99 (*0-14-050891-0*, Puffin) Puffin Bks.

Ryder, Joanne. The Snail's Spell. Cherry, Lynne, illus. 32p. (ps-3). 1992. PLB 14.00 (*0-670-84385-7*) Viking Child Bks.

Stadler, John. The Adventures of Snail at School. Stadler, John, illus. LC 91-45403. 64p. (gr. k-3). 1993. 14.00 (*0-06-021041-9*); PLB 13.89 (*0-06-021042-7*) HarpC Child Bks.

—Hooray for Snail! LC 83-46164. (Illus.). 32p. (ps-2). 1984. PLB 14.89 (*0-690-04413-5*, Crowell Jr Bks) HarpC Child Bks.

Stevenson, James. The Pattaconk Brook. LC 92-29404. 32p. (ps up). 1993. 14.00 (*0-688-11954-9*); lib. bdg. 13.93 (*0-688-11955-7*) Greenwillow.

SNAKES

Arnold, Caroline. Snake. Hewett, Richard, photos by. LC 90-22591. (Illus.). 48p. (gr. 2 up). 1991. 13.95 (*0-688-09409-0*); PLB 13.88 (*0-688-09410-4*) Morrow Jr Bks.

Bailey, Donna. Las Serpientes. LC 91-23778. (SPA., Illus.). 32p. (gr. 1-4). 1992. PLB 18.99 (*0-8114-2657-2*) Raintree Steck-V.

Baker, Lucy. Snakes. (Illus.). 32p. (gr. 2-6). 1990. pap. 4.95 (*0-14-034434-9*, Puffin) Puffin Bks.

Bargar & Johnson. Anacondas. (Illus.). 24p. (gr. 1-4). 1987. PLB 11.94 (*0-86592-249-7*) Rourke Corp.

—Coral Snakes. (Illus.). 24p. (gr. 1-4). 1987. PLB 11.94 (*0-86592-246-2*) Rourke Corp.

—King Snakes. (Illus.). 24p. (gr. 1-4). 1987. PLB 11.94 (*0-86592-248-9*); 8.95s.p. (*0-685-67603-X*) Rourke Corp.

—Pythons. (Illus.). 24p. (gr. 1-4). 1987. PLB 11.94 (*0-86592-244-6*) Rourke Corp.

—Rat Snakes. (Illus.). 24p. (gr. 1-4). 1987. PLB 11.94 (*0-86592-247-0*) Rourke Corp.

—Tree Vipers. (Illus.). 24p. (gr. 1-4). 1987. PLB 11.94 (*0-86592-245-4*); PLB 8.95s.p. (*0-685-67604-8*) Rourke Corp.

Bargar, Sherie & Johnson, Linda. Boas Constrictoras. Palacios, Argentina, tr. from ENG. Van Horn, George, photos by. LC 93-8391. (SPA., Illus.). 1993. write for info. (*0-86593-333-2*) Rourke Corp.

Barger & Johnson. Boa Constrictors, Reading Level 2. (Illus.). 24p. (gr. k-5). 1986. PLB 11.94 (*0-86592-959-9*) Rourke Corp.

—Cobras, Reading Level 2. (Illus.). 24p. (gr. k-5). 1986. PLB 11.94 (*0-86592-955-6*) Rourke Corp.

—Copperheads, Reading Level 2. (Illus.). 24p. (gr. k-5). 1986. PLB 11.94 (*0-86592-957-2*) Rourke Corp.

—Cottonmouths, Reading Level 2. (Illus.). 24p. (gr. k-5). 1986. PLB 11.94 (*0-86592-958-0*) Rourke Corp.

—Mambas, Reading Level 2. (Illus.). 24p. (gr. k-5). 1986. PLB 11.94 (*0-86592-960-2*); 8.95s.p. (*0-685-58805-X*) Rourke Corp.

—Rattlesnake, Reading Level 2. (Illus.). 24p. (gr. k-5). 1986. PLB 11.94 (*0-86592-956-4*) Rourke Corp.

—Snake Discovery Library, 6 bks, Set I, Reading Level 2. (Illus.). 144p. (gr. k-5). 1986. Set. PLB 71.60 (*0-86592-954-8*); PLB 53.70s.p. (*0-685-58804-1*) Rourke Corp.

Barrett, Norman S. Serpientes. LC 90-70891. (SPA., Illus.). 32p. (gr. k-4). 1990. PLB 11.90 (*0-531-07909-0*) Watts.

Brenner, Barbara A. A Snake-Lover's Diary. Brenner, Barbara A., illus. LC 84-43136. 96p. (gr. 4-6). 1990. PLB 15.89 (*0-06-020697-7*) HarpC Child Bks.

Broekel, Ray. Snakes. LC 81-38487. (Illus.). 48p. (gr. k-4). 1982. PLB 12.85 (*0-516-01649-0*); pap. 4.95 (*0-516-41649-9*) Childrens.

Byars, Betsy C. The Moon & I. (Illus.). 112p. (gr. 7 up). 1992. 12.95 (*0-671-74166-7*, J Messner); lib. bdg. 14.98 (*0-671-74165-9*, J Messner) S&S Trade.

Cole, Joanna. A Snake's Body. Wexler, Jerome, photos by. LC 81-9443. (Illus.). 48p. (gr. k-3). 1981. 12.95 (*0-688-00702-3*); 12.88 (*0-688-00703-1*, Morrow Jr Bks) Morrow Jr Bks.

Collard, Sneed B. Sea Snakes. 32p. (gr. 4-7). 1993. 12.95 (*1-56397-004-X*) Boyds Mills Pr.

Fichter, George S. Snakes & Lizards: A Golden Junior Guide. (ps-3). 1993. 4.95 (*0-307-11432-5*, Golden Pr) Western Pub.

Fine, Edith H. The Python & Anaconda. LC 88-5421. (Illus.). 48p. (gr. 5). 1988. text ed. 12.95 RSBE (*0-89686-391-3*, Crestwood Hse) Macmillan Child Grp.

Fowler, Allan. It's Best to Leave a Snake Alone. LC 91-39245. (Illus.). 32p. (ps-2). 1992. PLB 10.75 (*0-516-04926-7*); PLB 22.95 big bk. (*0-516-49627-1*); pap. 3.95 (*0-516-44926-5*) Childrens.

Gerholdt, James E. Snakes. LC 94-7795. 1994. write for info. (*1-56239-307-3*) Abdo & Dghtrs.

Gove, Doris. A Water Snake's Year. Duncan, Beverly, illus. LC 90-673. 40p. (gr. 2-6). 1991. SBE 13.95 (*0-689-31597-X*, Atheneum Child Bk) Macmillan Child Grp.

Green, Carl R. & Sanford, William R. The Cobra. LC 85-14969. (Illus.). 48p. (gr. 5). 1986. text ed. 12.95 RSBE (*0-89686-266-6*, Crestwood Hse) Macmillan Child Grp.

Gross, Ruth B. Snakes. reissued ed. LC 89-38254. (Illus.). 64p. (ps-3). 1990. Repr. of 1973 ed. RSBE 14.95 (*0-02-737022-4*, Four Winds Press) Macmillan Child Grp.

—Snakes. 64p. (gr. 1-4). 1989. pap. 2.50 (*0-590-44090-X*) Scholastic Inc.

Harrison, Virginia. The World of Snakes. Oxford Scientific Films Staff, photos by. LC 89-4634. (Illus.). 32p. (gr. 2-3). 1989. PLB 17.27 (*0-8368-0143-1*) Gareth Stevens Inc.

Hess, Lilo. That Snake in the Grass. Hess, Lilo, photos by. LC 86-24826. (Illus.). 48p. (gr. 3-6). 1987. SBE 13.95 (*0-684-18591-1*, Scribners Young Read) Macmillan Child Grp.

Hoffman, Mary. Snake. LC 86-6774. (Illus.). 24p. (gr. k-5). 1986. PLB 9.95 (*0-8172-2398-3*); pap. 3.95 (*0-8114-6889-5*) Raintree Steck-V.

Hunziker, Ray. Your First Snake. (Illus.). 34p. (Orig.). (gr. 1-6). 1991. pap. 1.95 (*0-86622-072-0*, YF-115) TFH Pubns.

Johnson, Sylvia A. Snakes. Masuda, Modoki, photos by. LC 87-7162. (Illus.). 48p. (gr. 4 up). 1986. PLB 19.95 (*0-8225-1484-2*, First Ave Edns); pap. 5.95 (*0-8225-9503-6*, First Ave Edns) Lerner Pubns.

Julivert, Maria A. El Fascinante Mundo: Las Serpientes, The Fascinating World of Snakes. Marcel Socias Studio Staff, ed. Arridondo, F., illus. 32p. (gr. 3-7). 1993. pap. 7.95 (*0-8120-1799-4*) Barron.

—The Fascinating World of Snakes. Marcel Socias Studio Staff & Arridondo, F., illus. 32p. (gr. 3-7). 1993. 11.95 (*0-8120-6346-5*); pap. 7.95 (*0-8120-1564-9*) Barron.

Lauber, Patricia. Snakes Are Hunters. Keller, Holly, illus. LC 87-47695. 32p. (ps-3). 1988. (Crowell Jr Bks); PLB 13.89 (*0-690-04630-8*, Crowell Jr Bks) HarpC Child Bks.

Lavies, Bianca. A Gathering of Garter Snakes. Lavies, Bianca, photos by. (Illus.). 32p. (gr. 3 up). 1993. reinforced bdg. 14.99 (*0-525-45099-8*, DCB) Dutton Child Bks.

—Secretive Timber Rattlesnake. LC 90-31964. (Illus.). 32p. (gr. 3-6). 1990. 13.95 (*0-525-44572-2*, DCB) Dutton Child Bks.

Lee, Sandra. Rattlesnakes. (gr. 2-6). 1992. PLB 15.95 (*0-89565-842-9*) Childs World.

Lindblom, Steven. Golden Book of Snakes & Other Reptiles. 1990. write for info. (*0-307-15852-7*, Pub. by Golden Bks) Western Pub.

Linley, Mike. The Snake in the Grass. Oxford Scientific Films Staff, photos by. LC 89-4621. (Illus.). 32p. (gr. 4-6). 1989. PLB 17.27 (*0-8368-0118-0*) Gareth Stevens Inc.

—The Snake: Smooth Scaly & Successful. Stefoff, Rebecca, ed. LC 92-10248. (Illus.). 32p. (gr. 3-6). 1992. PLB 17.26 (*1-56074-053-1*) Garrett Ed Corp.

—Snakes. LC 91-8558. 32p. (gr. 2-5). 1993. 14.95 (*1-56847-006-1*) Thomson Lrning.

McClung. Snakes. 1991. 14.95 (*0-8050-1917-0*) H Holt & Co.

McClung, Robert. Snakes: Their Place in the Sun. Dennis, David M., illus. 64p. (gr. 2-4). 1991. 14.95 (*0-8050-1718-6*, Bks Young Read) H Holt & Co.

Maestro, Betsy. Take a Look at Snakes. (Illus.). 1992. 14.95 (*0-590-44935-4*, Scholastic Hardcover) Scholastic Inc.

Morris, Dean. Snakes & Lizards. rev. ed. LC 87-16697. (Illus.). 48p. (gr. 2-6). 1987. PLB 10.95 (*0-8172-3212-5*) Raintree Steck-V.

Murray, Peter. Snakes. (gr. 2-6). 1992. PLB 15.95 (*0-89565-849-6*) Childs World.

National Wildlife Federation Staff. Let's Hear It for Herps. (gr. k-8). 1991. pap. 7.95 (*0-945051-42-5*, 75034) Natl Wildlife.

Palmer, William M. Poisonous Snakes of North Carolina. (Illus.). 22p. (gr. 6-12). 1974. pap. 2.00 (*0-917134-00-1*) NC Natl Sci.

Parsons, Alexandra. Amazing Snakes. Young, Jerry, photos by. LC 89-38944. (Illus.). 32p. (gr. 1-5). 1990. 7.99 (*0-679-80225-8*); PLB 9.99 (*0-679-90225-2*) Knopf Bks Yng Read.

Penner, Lucille R. S-s-s-snakes! LC 93-46799. (Illus.). 48p. (gr. k-2). 1994. PLB 7.99 (*0-679-94777-9*); pap. 3.50 (*0-679-84777-4*) Random Bks Yng Read.

Phillips, Gina. First Facts about Snakes & Reptiles. Persico, F. S., illus. 24p. (Orig.). 1991. pap. 2.50 (*1-56156-037-5*) Kidsbks.

—First Facts about Snakes & Reptiles. Persico, F. S., illus. 24p. 1991. write for info. (*1-56156-060-X*) Kidsbks.

Rattlesnakes. 1991. PLB 14.95 (*0-88682-426-5*) Creative Ed.

Ray, Stephen & Murdoch, Kathleen. Some Snakes. Ruth, Trevor, illus. LC 93-113. 1994. pap. write for info. (*0-383-03715-8*) SRA Schl Grp.

—Tall Stories about Snakes. Forss, Ian, illus. LC 93-6630. 1994. pap. write for info. (*0-383-03716-6*) SRA Schl Grp.

Robson, Denny A. Snakes. (Illus.). 32p. (gr. 1-4). 1992. PLB 11.90 (*0-531-17355-0*, Gloucester Pr) Watts.

Roever, Joan M. Snake Secrets. Roever, Joan M., illus. LC 78-4318. (gr. 5 up). 1979. PLB 11.85 (*0-8027-6333-2*) Walker & Co.

Sanford, William R. & Green, Carl R. The Boa Constrictor. LC 86-32868. (Illus.). 48p. (gr. 5). 1987. text ed. 12.95 RSBE (*0-89686-320-4*, Crestwood Hse) Macmillan Child Grp.

Selsam, Millicent E. A First Look at Poisonous Snakes. 32p. (gr. 1-4). 1987. 11.95 (*0-8027-6681-1*); PLB 12.85 (*0-8027-6683-8*) Walker & Co.

Simon, Seymour. Poisonous Snakes. Downey, William R., illus. LC 85-24202. 80p. (gr. 3-7). 1984. SBE 14.95 (*0-02-782850-6*, Four Winds) Macmillan Child Grp.

—Snakes. Simon, Seymour, illus. LC 91-15948. 32p. (gr. k-3). 1992. 16.00 (*0-06-022529-7*); PLB 15.89 (*0-06-022530-0*) HarpC Child Bks.

—Snakes. Simon, Seymour, illus. LC 91-15948. 32p. (gr. k-3). 1994. pap. 5.95 (*0-06-446165-3*, Trophy) HarpC Child Bks.

Smith, Mavis. A Snake Mistake. Smith, Mavis, illus. LC 90-43152. 32p. (gr. k-3). 1991. PLB 11.89 (*0-06-026909-X*); pap. 3.95 (*0-06-107426-8*) HarpC Child Bks.

Smith, Patricia. Snakes! Moffatt, Judith, illus. LC 92-24466. 48p. (gr. 1-3). 1993. lib. bdg. 7.99 (*0-448-40514-8*, G&D); pap. 3.50 (*0-448-40513-X*, G&D) Putnam Pub Group.

Smith, Roland. Snakes in the Zoo. Munoz, William, illus. LC 91-45588. 64p. (gr. 3-6). 1992. PLB 14.40 (*1-56294-211-5*) Millbrook Pr.

Snake Discovery Library, 6 bks, Set II, Reading Level 2. (Illus.). 144p. (gr. k-5). 1987. Set. PLB 71.60 (*0-86592-243-8*); PLB 53.70s.p. (*0-685-58806-8*) Rourke Corp.
Snakes. (gr. 4-6). 1975. pap. 2.95 (*0-685-09281-X*, Wonder-Treas) Price Stern.
Snakes. 1991. PLB 14.95 (*0-88682-331-5*) Creative Ed.
Snakes. (Illus.). 64p. (gr. 3-6). 1994. 15.95 (*0-87156-490-4*) Sierra.
Snakes of Arizona. (Illus.). 32p. (gr. 3 up). 1984. pap. 1.00 (*0-935810-17-X*) Primer Pubs.
Spizzirri Publishing Co. Staff. Poisonous Snakes: Educational Coloring Book. Spizzirri, Linda, ed. (Illus.). 32p. (gr. 1-8). 1984. pap. 1.75 (*0-86545-054-4*) Spizzirri.
Stoops, Erik D. & Wright, Annette T. Snakes. LC 92-18995. (Illus.). 80p. (gr. 10-12). 1992. 14.95 (*0-8069-8482-1*) Sterling.
Tropea, S. Snakes, A Photo Fact Book. (Illus.). 24p. (Orig.). 1988. pap. 1.95 (*0-942025-15-6*) Kidsbks.
Vrbova, Zuza. Snakes. McAulay, Robert, illus. 48p. 1990. PLB 9.95 (*0-86622-557-9*, J-007) TFH Pubns.
Wildlife Education, Ltd. Staff. Snakes. Hoopes, Barbara & Oden, Dick, illus. 20p. (Orig.). (gr. 5 up). 1981. pap. 2.75 (*0-937934-05-4*) Wildlife Educ.
Wimberly, Christine A. Poisonous Snakes of Alabama. DeJarnette, Tom, illus. 46p. (Orig.). (gr. 4-12). 1970. pap. 3.35 (*0-9605938-0-2*) Explorer Bks.
World of Snakes, 12 vols. in 1. 1990. 9.99 (*0-517-03756-4*) Random Hse Value.
Zim, Herbert S. Snakes. Irving, James G., illus. LC 49-10266. 64p. (gr. 3-7). 1949. PLB 12.88 (*0-688-31549-6*) Morrow Jr Bks.

SNAKES–FICTION

Ata, Te & Moroney, Lynn, eds. Baby Rattlesnake. LC 89-9892. (Illus.). 32p. (ps-5). 1989. 13.95 (*0-89239-049-2*) Childrens Book Pr.
—Baby Rattlesnake. (Illus.). 32p. (gr. 1-7). 1993. pap. 5.95 (*0-89239-111-1*) Childrens Book Pr.
Barrett, Judi. A Snake Is Totally Tail. Johnson, Lonni S., illus. LC 83-2657. 32p. (ps-1). 1983. SBE 13.95 (*0-689-30979-1*, Atheneum Child Bk) Macmillan Child Grp.
Buckley, Richard. The Greedy Python. Carle, Eric, illus. LC 92-6633. 28p. (ps). 1993. Repr. Mini-bk. 4.95 (*0-88708-268-8*) Picture Bk Studio.
Cebulash, Mel. Rattler. (gr. 3-8). 1992. PLB 8.95 (*0-89565-880-1*) Childs World.
Charbonnet, Gabrielle. Snakes Are Nothing to Sneeze At. Carter, Abby, illus. 80p. (gr. 2-4). 1990. 13.95 (*0-8050-1373-3*, Bks Young Read) H Holt & Co.
Clifford, E. Harvey's Horrible Snake Disaster. 1990. pap. 2.95 (*0-671-72957-8*, Minstrel Bks) PB.
Clifford, Eth. Harvey's Horrible Snake Disaster. LC 83-27299. 128p. (gr. 3-6). 1984. 13.45 (*0-395-35378-5*, 5-83913) HM.
Cosgrove, Stephen. Kartusch. James, Robin, illus. 32p. (Orig.). (gr. 1-9). 1978. pap. 3.95 (*0-8431-0568-2*) Price Stern.
Coxe, Molly. Maxie & Mirabel. LC 92-26528. (Illus.). 64p. (gr. k-3). 1994. 14.00 (*0-06-022868-7*); PLB 13.89 (*0-06-022869-5*) HarpC Child Bks.
Czernecki, Stefan & Rhodes, Timothy. The Singing Snake. Czernecki, Stefan, illus. LC 92-85515. 40p. (ps-2). 1993. 14.95 (*1-56282-399-X*); PLB 14.89 (*1-56282-400-7*) Hyprn Child.
Edler, Timothy J. Maurice the Snake & Gaston the Near-Sighted Turtle: Tim Edler's Tales from the Atchafalaya. (Illus.). 36p. (gr. k-8). 1977. pap. 6.00 (*0-931108-00-4*) Little Cajun Bks.
Eisemann, Henry. His-Her, The Shy Serpent. O'Grady-Steinberg, Chrissy, illus. 32p. (Orig.). (gr. k-6). 1992. pap. 6.95 (*0-938129-05-8*) Emprise Pubns.
Gray, Libba M. Small Green Snake. Meade, Holly, illus. LC 93-49396. 32p. (ps-1). 1994. 14.95 (*0-531-06844-7*); PLB 14.99 (*0-531-08694-1*) Orchard Bks Watts.
Johnson, Angela. The Girl Who Wore Snakes. Ransome, James E., illus. LC 92-44521. 32p. (ps-2). 1993. 14.95 (*0-531-05491-8*); PLB 14.99 (*0-531-08641-0*) Orchard Bks Watts.
Johnson, Terry C. Slither McCreep & His Brother, Joe. Chess, Victoria, illus. 1992. 13.95 (*0-15-276100-4*, HB Juv Bks) HarBrace.
Kahn, Jonathan. Patulous: The Prairie Rattlesnake. Thatch, Nancy R., ed. Kahn, Jonathan, illus. Melton, David, intro. by. LC 91-13652. (Illus.). 26p. (gr. k-4). 1991. PLB 14.95 (*0-933849-36-2*) Landmark Edns.
Kastner, Jill. Snake Hunt. Kastner, Jill, illus. LC 92-32601. 32p. (ps-2). 1993. RSBE 14.95 (*0-02-749395-4*, Four Winds) Macmillan Child Grp.
Kipling, Rudyard. Rikki-Tikki-Tavi. 1992. 16.95 (*0-15-267015-7*, HB Juv Bks) HarBrace.
Kudrna, C. Imbior. To Bathe a Boa. Kudrna, C. Imbiore., illus. 32p. (ps-4). 1986. PLB 18.50 (*0-87614-306-0*); pap. 5.95 (*0-87614-490-3*) Carolrhoda Bks.
Lauber, Patricia. Snakes Are Hunters. LC 87-47695. (Illus.). 32p. (ps-4). 1989. pap. 4.95 (*0-06-445091-0*, Trophy) HarpC Child Bks.
Lester, Alison. Tessa Snaps Snakes. Lester, Alison, illus. LC 91-2665. 32p. (ps-k). 1991. pap. 13.95 (*0-685-52551-1*, Sandpiper) HM.
Noble, Trinka H. Day Jimmy's Boa Ate the Wash. enl. ed. (ps-3). 1991. pap. 17.95 (*0-8037-1073-9*, Puff Pied Piper) Puffin Bks.
—The Day Jimmy's Boa Ate the Wash. Kellogg, Steven, illus. 32p. (ps-3). 1993. pap. 4.99 (*0-14-054623-5*, Puff Pied Piper) Puffin Bks.
—The Day Jimmy's Boa Ate the Wash: Giant Edition. (ps-3). 1991. pap. 18.99 (*0-14-054622-7*) Viking Penguin.
—Jimmy's Boa & the Big Splash Birthday Bash. Kellog, Steven, illus. LC 88-10933. 32p. (ps-3). 1989. 13.95 (*0-8037-0539-5*); PLB 13.89 (*0-8037-0540-9*) Dial Bks Young.
—Jimmy's Boa & the Big Splash Birthday Bash. Kellogg, Steven, illus. 32p. (ps-3). 1993. pap. 4.99 (*0-14-054921-8*, Puff Pied Piper) Puffin Bks.
—Jimmy's Boa Bounces Back. Kellog, Steven, illus. LC 83-14289. 32p. (ps-3). 1984. 13.95 (*0-8037-0049-0*); PLB 13.89 (*0-8037-0050-4*) Dial Bks Young.
—Jimmy's Boa Bounces Back. Kellogg, Steven, illus. 32p. (ps-3). 1993. pap. 4.99 (*0-14-054654-5*, Puff Pied Piper) Puffin Bks.
Ray, Stephen & Murdoch, Kathleen. Snake. Campbell, Carolinee, illus. LC 92-21453. 1993. 4.25 (*0-383-03653-4*) SRA Schl Grp.
Reed, Lynn R. Rattlesnake Stew. LC 90-55163. (Illus.). 32p. (gr. k-3). 1990. 13.95 (*0-374-36190-8*) FS&G.
Reese, Bob. Slitherfoot Snake. Reese, Bob, illus. (gr. k-6). 1987. 7.95 (*0-89868-191-X*); pap. 2.95 (*0-89868-192-8*) ARO Pub.
Rodieck, Jorma. The Little Bitty Snake. Burnett, Yumiko M. & Contreras, Moyra, trs. LC 82-60393. (Illus.). 24p. (ps up). 1983. English-Japanese. pap. 4.95 (*0-940880-07-5*); English-Spanish. pap. 4.95 (*0-940880-03-2*); English-French. pap. 4.95 (*0-940880-05-9*) Open Hand.
Roughsey, Dick. Rainbow Serpent. (ps-3). 1994. pap. 7.00 (*0-207-17433-4*, Pub. by Angus & Robertson AT) HarpC.
Schleifer, Jay. Cobra. LC 92-14530. (Illus.). 48p. (gr. 5). 1993. text ed. 13.95 RSBE (*0-89686-701-3*, Crestwood Hse) Macmillan Child Grp.
Shannon, George. April Showers. Aruego, Jose & Dewey, Ariane, illus. LC 94-6266. 24p. 1995. write for info. (*0-688-13121-2*); PLB write for info. (*0-688-13122-0*) Greenwillow.
Stuart, Jesse. Old Ben. rev. ed. Gifford, James M. & Charles, Chuck D., eds. Cuffari, Richard, illus. LC 91-35578. 64p. (gr. 3-6). 1992. 10.00 (*0-945084-22-6*); pap. 3.00 (*0-945084-23-4*) J Stuart Found.
Tate, Lindsey. Claire & the Friendly Snakes. (ps-3). 1993. 15.00 (*0-374-31337-7*) FS&G.
Tea, K. Snake in the Grass. Abell, J., ed. & illus. 50p. (ps-1). 1994. 25.00 (*1-56611-501-9*); pap. 15.00 (*1-56611-502-7*) Jonas.
Turpin, Lorna. The Sultan's Snakes. (gr. 4 up). 1991. 7.95 (*0-85953-511-8*); pap. 3.95 (*0-85953-512-6*) Childs Play.
Waber, Bernard. The Snake: A Very Long Love Story. Waber, Bernard, illus. (ps-1). 1978. PLB 7.95 (*0-685-02310-9*) HM.
Wildsmith, Brian. Python's Party. (Illus.). 32p. (ps up). 1991. pap. 7.50 (*0-19-272229-8*, 12355) OUP.
Woodruff, Elvira. Secret Funeral of Slim Jim the Snake. (gr. 4-7). 1994. pap. 3.50 (*0-440-40945-4*) Dell.

SNORKELLING

see Skin Diving

SNOW

Bauer, Caroline F., ed. Snowy Day: Stories & Poems. Tomes, Margot, illus. LC 85-45858. 80p. (gr. 2-5). 1992. pap. 5.95 (*0-06-446123-8*, Trophy) HarpC Child Bks.
Bentley, W. A. & Humphreys, W. J. Snow Crystals. (Illus.). (gr. 5 up). 24.75 (*0-8446-1660-5*) Peter Smith.
Bianchi, John & Edwards, Frank B. Snow: Learning for the Fun of It. Binachi, John, illus. 48p. (gr. 5 up). 1992. PLB 17.95 (*0-921285-15-9*, Pub. by Bungalo Bks CN); pap. 7.95 (*0-921285-09-4*, Pub. by Bungalo Bks CN) Firefly Bks Ltd.
Branley, Franklyn M. Snow Is Falling. rev. ed. Keller, Holly, illus. LC 85-48256. 32p. (ps-3). 1986. (Crowell Jr Bks); PLB 14.89 (*0-690-04548-4*, Crowell Jr Bks) HarpC Child Bks.
Cech, John. First Snow, Magic Snow. McGinley-Nally, Sharon, illus. LC 91-42988. 40p. (gr. k-2). 1992. RSBE 14.95 (*0-02-717971-0*, Four Winds) Macmillan Child Grp.
Kahl, Jonathan. Wet Weather: Rain Showers & Snowfall. (Illus.). 64p. (gr. 4-12). 1992. PLB 19.95 (*0-8225-2526-7*) Lerner Pubns.
Lampton, Christopher. Blizzard. (Illus.). 64p. (gr. 4-6). 1991. PLB 13.90 (*1-56294-029-5*); pap. 5.95 (*1-56294-775-3*) Millbrook Pr.
—Blizzard: A Disaster Book. (gr. 4-7). 1992. pap. 5.95 (*0-395-63641-8*) HM.
McKie, Roy & Eastman, Philip D. Snow. LC 62-15114. (Illus.). 72p. (gr. 1-2). 1962. 6.95 (*0-394-80027-3*); lib. bdg. 7.99 (*0-394-90027-8*) Beginner.
Merk, Ann & Merk, Jim. Rain, Snow, & Ice. LC 94-13325. (gr. 3 up). 1994. write for info. (*0-86593-390-1*) Rourke Corp.
Otfinoski, Steven. Blizzards. (Illus.). 64p. (gr. 5-8). 1994. bds. 15.95 (*0-8050-3093-X*) TFC Bks NY.
Palmer, Joy. Snow & Ice. LC 92-38438. (Illus.). 32p. (gr. 2-3). 1992. PLB 18.99 (*0-8114-3414-1*) Raintree Steck-V.
Phillips, Louise S. The First Snowflake of Winter. LC 87-62210. (Illus.). 40p. (gr. k-4). 1987. pap. 6.95 (*0-932433-36-7*) Windswept Hse.
Riehecky, Janet. Snow: When Will It Fall? Friedman, Joy, illus. LC 89-28084. 32p. (ps-2). 1990. PLB 13.95 (*0-89565-560-8*) Childs World.
Rockwell, Anne & Rockwell, Harlow. The First Snowfall. Rockwell, Harlow, illus. LC 91-41247. 24p. (ps-1). 1992. pap. 3.95 (*0-689-71614-1*, Aladdin) Macmillan Child Grp.
Steele, Philip. Snow: Causes & Effects. LC 90-45020. (Illus.). 32p. (gr. 4-6). 1991. PLB 12.40 (*0-531-10990-9*) Watts.
Stonehouse, Bernard. Snow, Ice, & Cold. LC 92-26298. (Illus.). 48p. (gr. 6 up). 1993. text ed. 13.95 RSBE (*0-02-788530-5*, New Discovery) Macmillan Child Grp.
Tresselt, Alvin. White Snow Bright Snow. Duvoisin, Roger, illus. LC 88-10018. 32p. (ps up). 1988. pap. 3.95 (*0-688-08294-7*, Mulberry) Morrow.
Williams, Terence T. & Major, Ted. The Secret Language of Snow. Dewey, Jennifer, illus. LC 83-19410. 144p. (gr. 3-7). 1984. 10.95 (*0-394-86574-X*, Pant Bks Young) Pantheon.

SNOW–FICTION

Ahlberg, Allan. The Black Cat. Amstutz, Andre, illus. LC 92-45621. 32p. (gr. k up). 1993. pap. text ed. 4.95 (*0-688-12679-0*, Mulberry) Morrow.
Barkan, Joanne. A Very Merry Snowman Story. 1992. 3.95 (*0-590-46021-8*, Cartwheel) Scholastic Inc.
Bauer, Caroline F., ed. Snowy Day: Stories & Poems. Tomes, Margot, illus. LC 85-45858. 80p. (gr. 2-5). 1986. (Lipp Jr Bks); PLB 14.89 (*0-397-32177-5*) HarpC Child Bks.
Beveridge, Barbara. Hooray for Snow. Greenhatch, Betty, illus. LC 92-27098. 1993. 3.75 (*0-383-03573-2*) SRA Schl Grp.
Braby, Marie. The Longest Wait. Ward, John, illus. LC 94-24875. 1995. write for info. (*0-531-06871-4*); PLB write for info. (*0-531-08721-2*) Orchard Bks Watts.
Briggs, Raymond. The Snowman. Briggs, Raymond, illus. LC 78-55904. 32p. (ps-3). 1978. 16.00 (*0-394-83973-0*) Random Bks Yng Read.
—The Snowman. miniature ed. LC 90-60078. (Illus.). 32p. (ps-8). 1990. 4.95 (*0-679-80906-6*) Random Bks Yng Read.
—The Snowman Board Books. Briggs, Raymond, illus. Incl. Building the Snowman (*0-316-10813-8*); Dressing up. 1985. pap. 3.95 (*0-316-10814-6*); Walking in the Air. 1985. pap. 3.95 (*0-316-10815-4*); The Party. (Illus.). (ps-k). 1985. pap. 3.95 (*0-685-73726-8*) Little.
—The Snowman Clock Book. Briggs, Raymond, illus. LC 91-67874. 16p. (ps-3). 1992. pap. 7.99 (*0-679-83261-0*) Random Bks Yng Read.
—The Snowman Cuddle Cloth Book. Briggs, Raymond, illus. 12p. (ps). 4.99 (*0-679-82696-3*) Random Bks Yng Read.
—The Snowman Storybook. Briggs, Raymond, illus. LC 90-8029. 24p. (ps). 1990. 6.00 (*0-679-80840-X*) Random Bks Yng Read.
Brown, Margaret W. Animals in the Snow. Schwartz, Carol, illus. LC 94-8470. 1995. write for info. (*0-7868-0039-9*); pap. write for info. (*0-7868-2032-2*) Hyprn Child.
Burton, Virginia L. Katy & the Big Snow. (Illus.). (gr. k-3). 1973. reinforced bdg. 13.45 (*0-395-18155-0*) HM.
Butterworth, Nick. One Snowy Night. (ps-3). 1990. 13.95 (*0-316-11918-0*) Little.
Carlson, Nancy. Take Time to Relax. (ps-3). 1991. 14.00 (*0-670-83287-1*) Viking Child Bks.
—Take Time to Relax! LC 92-26584. 1993. pap. 4.99 (*0-14-054242-6*, Puffin) Puffin Bks.
Carlstrom, Nancy W. The Snow Speaks. Dyer, Jane, illus. (ps-3). 1992. 15.95 (*0-316-12861-9*) Little.
Chapman, Cheryl. Snow on Snow on Snow. St. James, Synthia, illus. 1994. write for info. (*0-8037-1456-4*); PLB write for info. (*0-8037-1457-2*) Dial Bks Young.
Chardiet, Bernice & Maccarone, Grace. The Snowball War. 1992. 2.50 (*0-590-44933-8*) Scholastic Inc.
Coleridge, Sara. January Brings the Snow. Chartier, Normand, illus. (ps-3). 1990. (Little Simon); pap. 2.25 (*0-671-72338-3*) S&S Trade.
Damon, Laura. Fun in the Snow. Paterson, Diane, illus. LC 87-10843. 32p. (gr. k-2). 1988. PLB 11.59 (*0-8167-1081-3*); pap. text ed. 2.95 (*0-8167-1082-1*) Troll Assocs.
Edwards, Amelia B. The Phantom Coach. Richardson, I. M., adapted by. Ashmead, Hal, illus. LC 81-19862. 32p. (gr. 5-10). 1982. PLB 10.79 (*0-89375-634-2*); pap. text ed. 2.95 (*0-89375-635-0*) Troll Assocs.
Estvanik, Nicole B. Snowman Who Wanted to See July. (ps-3). 1993. pap. 4.95 (*0-8114-5210-7*) Raintree Steck-V.
Ewart, Claire. One Cold Night. (Illus.). 32p. (ps-1). 1992. 14.95 (*0-399-22341-X*, Putnam) Putnam Pub Group.
Frosty the Snowman & the Magic Day. (Illus.). (ps-3). 1991. write for info. (*0-307-12339-1*, Golden Pr) Western Pub.
Grandpa Bill. Let It Snow: Three Snow Stories for Children. 1992. 7.95 (*0-533-10159-X*) Vantage.
Greene, Carol. Snow Joe. LC 82-9403. (Illus.). (ps-2). 1982. PLB 10.25 (*0-516-02035-8*); pap. 2.95 (*0-516-42035-6*) Childrens.
Greene, George W. Me & My Snowman. Hatter, Laurie, illus. (ps). 1993. 4.95 (*1-56828-020-3*) Red Jacket Pr.
Hader, Elmer & Hader, Berta. The Big Snow. LC 48-10240. (Illus.). 48p. (gr. 1-3). 1972. RSBE 14.95 (*0-02-737910-8*, Macmillan Child Bk) Macmillan Child Grp.
Harshman, Marc. Snow Company. LC 89-23941. (Illus.). (ps-3). 1990. 12.95 (*0-525-65029-6*, Cobblehill Bks) Dutton Child Bks.

Heo, Yumi. Father's Rubber Shoes. LC 94-21961. (gr. 1-8). 1995. write for info. (*0-531-06873-0*); PLB write for info. (*0-531-08723-9*) Orchard Bks Watts.

Hiscock, Bruce. When Will It Snow? LC 94-9385. (Illus.). 1996. 15.95 (*0-689-31937-1*, Atheneum) Macmillan.

Hoban, Julia. Amy Loves the Snow. Hoban, Lillian, illus. LC 87-45852. 24p. (ps). 1993. pap. 3.95 (*0-06-443294-7*, Trophy) HarpC Child Bks.

Hoff, Syd. When Will It Snow? Chalmers, Mary, illus. LC 64-16657. 32p. (gr. k-3). 1971. HarpC Child Bks.

Horneck, Heribert. Tracks in the Snow. Young, Richard G., ed. Mangold, Paul, illus. LC 89-11890. 24p. (gr. 1-3). 1989. PLB 14.60 (*0-944483-53-4*) Garrett Ed Corp.

Huddy, Delia. Snowman's Christmas. 1990. 13.95 (*0-385-30173-1*) Delacorte.

Hudson, Jan. Sweetgrass. 1991. pap. 2.95 (*0-590-43486-1*) Scholastic Inc.

Hutchins, H. Ben's Snow Song. (Illus.). 24p. (ps-8). 1987. 12.95 (*0-920303-91-9*, Pub. by Annick CN); pap. 4.95 (*0-920303-90-0*, Pub. by Annick CN) Firefly Bks Ltd.

—Norman's Snowball. (Illus.). 24p. (ps-8). 1989. 12.95 (*1-55037-053-7*, Pub. by Annick CN); pap. 4.95 (*1-55037-050-2*, Pub. by Annick CN) Firefly Bks Ltd.

Inkpen, Mick. Penguin Small. (ps-3). 1993. pap. 14.95 (*0-15-200567-6*) HarBrace.

Joosse, Barbara M. Snow Day! Plecas, Jennifer, illus. LC 94-17012. (gr. 1-8). Date not set. write for info. (*0-395-66588-4*, Clarion Bks) HM.

Keats, Ezra J. Un Dia de Nieve. (SPA.). (ps). 1991. 12.95 (*0-670-83747-4*) Viking Child Bks.

—Un Dia de Nieve. (SPA., Illus.). 32p. (ps-1). 1991. pap. 4.50 (*0-14-054363-5*, Puffin) Puffin Bks.

—The Snowy Day. Keats, Ezra J., illus. LC 62-15441. 40p. (ps-1). 1962. pap. 13.00 (*0-670-65400-0*) Viking Child Bks.

—Snowy Day. (SPA.). (ps-3). 1993. pap. 19.95 (*0-590-72632-3*) Scholastic Inc.

—Snowy Day. (ps-3). 1993. pap. 19.95 (*0-590-73323-0*) Scholastic Inc.

Keown, Elizabeth. Emily's Snowball: The World's Biggest. Trivas, Irene, illus. LC 90-1181. 32p. (ps-3). 1992. SBE 13.95 (*0-689-31518-X*, Atheneum Child Bk) Macmillan Child Grp.

Kessler, Ethel & Kessler, Leonard. Stan the Hot Dog Man. Kessler, Leonard, illus. LC 89-34474. 64p. (gr. k-3). 1990. PLB 13.89 (*0-06-023280-3*) HarpC Child Bks.

Khalsa, Dayal K. The Snow Cat. Khalsa, Dayal K., illus. LC 92-8988. 32p. (ps-2). 1992. 14.00 (*0-517-59183-9*, Clarkson Potter) Crown Bks Yng Read.

Leavitt, Melvin J. A Snow Story. McAllister Stammen, JoEllen, illus. LC 94-21532. 1995. 14.00 (*0-02-754633-0*, S&S BFYR) S&S Trade.

Lewis, Kim. First Snow. Lewis, Kim, illus. LC 92-54413. 32p. (ps up). 1993. 14.95 (*1-56402-194-7*) Candlewick Pr.

Lobe, Mira. The Snowman Who Went for a Walk. Opgenoorth, Winifried, illus. LC 83-27298. 32p. (ps-2). 1984. 11.95 (*0-688-03865-4*); PLB 11.88 (*0-688-03866-2*) Morrow Jr Bks.

Lockhart, Barbara. The Snowman. Lockhart, Lynne, illus. 12p. (ps). 1993. 4.95 (*1-56828-024-6*) Red Jacket Pr.

London, Jonathan. Froggy Gets Dressed. Remkiewicz, Frank, illus. 32p. (ps-1). 1992. 13.00 (*0-670-84249-4*) Viking Child Bks.

The Lonely Snowman: Timeless Tales. 1992. 4.99 (*0-517-06969-5*) Random Hse Value.

Loretan, Sylvia. Bob the Snowman. (ps-3). 1991. 13.95 (*0-670-83677-X*) Viking Child Bks.

Lucas, Barbara M. Snowed In. Stock, Catherine, illus. LC 92-39081. 32p. (ps-3). 1993. RSBE 14.95 (*0-02-761465-4*, Bradbury Pr) Macmillan Child Grp.

McAllister, Angela. The Snow Angel. Fletcher, Claire, illus. LC 92-44155. 1993. 14.00 (*0-688-04569-3*) Lothrop.

McArthur, Dalton R. The First Snowflake. Minson, Grant L., illus. 32p. (Orig.). (ps-4). 1991. pap. 4.95x (*0-9626111-0-7*) McArthur UT.

McCraw, Louise H. As the Snow on the High Hills. 198p. (Orig.). 1979. pap. 1.00 (*0-89323-001-4*, 771) Bible Memory.

McKie, Roy & Eastman, Philip D. Snow. LC 62-15114. (Illus.). 72p. (gr. 1-2). 1962. 6.95 (*0-394-80027-3*); lib. bdg. 7.99 (*0-394-90027-8*) Beginner.

Mayper, Monica. Oh Snow. Otani, June, illus. LC 90-42088. 32p. (ps-1). 1991. PLB 14.89 (*0-06-024204-3*) HarpC Child Bks.

Mazer, Harry. Snow Bound. 144p. (gr. 5 up). 1975. pap. 3.99 (*0-440-96134-3*, LFL) Dell.

Mendez, Phil. The Black Snowman. Byard, Carole, illus. 48p. 1991. pap. 4.95 (*0-590-44873-0*, Blue Ribbon Bks) Scholastic Inc.

Miller, Ned. Emmett's Snowball. Guevara, Susan, illus. LC 89-77787. 40p. (ps-2). 1990. 14.95 (*0-8050-1394-6*, Bks Young Read) H Holt & Co.

Moncure, Jane B. Biggest Snowball of All. Friedman, Joy, illus. LC 88-25600. (ENG & SPA.). 32p. (ps-2). 1989. PLB 14.95 (*0-89565-391-5*) Childs World.

Neitzel, Shirley. The Jacket I Wear in the Snow. Cohr, Amy, ed. Parker, Nancy W., illus. LC 92-43789. 32p. (ps up). 1994. pap. 4.95 (*0-688-04587-1*, Mulberry) Morrow.

Nelson, Steve & Rollins, Jack. Frosty the Snowman: Book & Cookie Cutter Set. Zimmerman, Jerry, illus. 17p. (ps-2). 1993. Incl. 2 cookie cutters. pap. 3.95 (*0-590-69016-7*, Cartwheel) Scholastic Inc.

Outlet Staff. Missing Snowman: Look & Look Again. 1991. 3.99 (*0-517-06142-2*) Random Hse Value.

Prelutsky, Jack. It's Snowing! It's Snowing! Titherington, Jeanne, illus. LC 83-16583. 48p. (gr. 1-3). 1984. 12.95 (*0-688-01512-3*); PLB 14.93 (*0-688-01513-1*) Greenwillow.

Pryor, Bonnie. Birthday Blizzard. Delaney, Molly, illus. LC 92-1713. 32p. (gr. k up). 1993. 15.00 (*0-688-09423-6*); PLB 14.93 (*0-688-09424-4*) Morrow Jr Bks.

Ripley, Dorothy. Winter Barn. Schories, Pat, illus. LC 93-32420. 32p. (ps-1). 1995. pap. 2.50 (*0-679-84472-4*) Random Bks Yng Read.

Sachs, Marilyn. A Secret Friend. 128p. (gr. 3-7). 1987. pap. 2.95 (*0-590-40403-2*, Apple Paperback) Scholastic Inc.

Sanfield, Steve. Snow. Winter, Jeanette, illus. LC 94-8754. 1995. 15.95 (*0-399-22751-2*, Philomel Bks) Putnam Pub Group.

Silk, Silvia. Gramma Jasmine Musical Stories. (Illus.). 53p. (Orig.). (gr. 1 up). pap. write for info. (*0-938861-04-2*); cassette avail. (*0-938861-05-0*) Jasmine Texts.

The Snow Lion. 42p. (ps-3). 1992. PLB 13.27 (*0-8368-0888-6*) Gareth Stevens Inc.

Spinelli. Deep Snow. Date not set. 15.00 (*0-06-023370-2*); PLB 14.89 (*0-06-023371-0*) HarpC Child Bks.

Spooner, Michael. Legend of Snowshoes. 1995. write for info. (*0-8050-3137-5*) H Holt & Co.

Stine, R. L. Snowman. 1991. pap. 3.50 (*0-590-43280-X*) Scholastic Inc.

Tallarico, Tony, illus. Snowboy & Snowgirl. 12p. (ps-1). 1990. bds. 3.95 (*0-448-40336-6*, Tuffy) Putnam Pub Group.

Tresselt, Alvin. White Snow, Bright Snow. Duvoisin, Roger, illus. (ps-3). 1989. 16.00 (*0-688-41161-4*); PLB 15.93 (*0-688-51161-9*) Lothrop.

Van Leeuwen, Jean. Oliver & Amanda & the Big Snow. Schweninger, Ann, illus. LC 93-48598. 1995. write for info. (*0-8037-1762-8*); lib. bdg. write for info. (*0-8037-1763-6*) Dial Bks Young.

Wahl, Jan. Emily Rosebush's Snowflake: A Christmas Story. Wahl, Jan, illus. LC 94-22713. 32p. (gr. k-3). 1995. pap. 2.25 (*0-8167-3573-5*, Whistlestop) Troll Assocs.

Wise, Francis H. & Wise, Joyce M. Snowman. Wise, Joyce M., illus. (gr. 1). 1976. pap. 1.50 (*0-915766-37-X*) Wise Pub.

Zolotow, Charlotte. Something Is Going to Happen. Stock, Catherine, illus. LC 87-26661. 32p. (ps-3). 1988. PLB 13.89 (*0-06-027029-2*) HarpC Child Bks.

SOAP

Simon, Seymour. Soap Bubble Magic. Ormai, Stella, illus. LC 84-4432. 48p. (ps-3). 1985. PLB 13.93 (*0-688-02685-0*) Lothrop.

SOARING FLIGHT

see Gliding and Soaring

SOCCER

Abangma, Julius. Soccer for Beginners: How to Understand & Play the Game of Soccer. (Illus.). 128p. (gr. 7-12). 1994. pap. 10.95 (*1-885392-07-9*) Allied Publishers.
This book may easily be THE MOST COMPLETE SOCCER MANUAL EVER PRINTED. It may be used by players of all ages & levels. The basic skills of stopping, passing, kicking & heading the ball have been given special attention. A total of 54 illustrations have been used to facilitate comprehension. The book has 11 chapters & a glossary of soccer terms, including a chapter on the history of the game, one on goalkeeping & one on soccer injuries & drugs--the author strongly believes no sports manual will be complete without a discussion on drugs & the athlete. Also, there are several drills to help develop basic skills, & "practice sessions" to explain the use of basic skills in actual game situations. It is a book for soccer players of all ages. The author, a native of Cameroon (the great soccer nation), has played soccer all his life. Contact Allied Publishers, Box 1172, Silver Spring, MD 20910, Attention (SB); 301-754-1242.
Publisher Provided Annotation.

Arnold, Caroline. Soccer: From Neighborhood Play to the World Cup. LC 91-12830. (Illus.). 64p. (gr. 5-8). 1991. PLB 12.90 (*0-531-20037-X*) Watts.

Bauer, Gerhard. Soccer Techniques, Tactics & Teamwork. Beckenbauer, Franz, intro. by. (Illus.). 160p. (gr. 10-12). 1993. pap. 14.95 (*0-8069-8730-8*) Sterling.

Brown, Michael. Soccer Techniques in Pictures. (Illus.). 80p. (Orig.). 1991. pap. 8.95 (*0-399-51701-4*, Perigee Bks) Berkley Pub.

Bryce, James, et al. Power Basics of Soccer. LC 84-22839. 112p. 1984. 5.95 (*0-13-688326-5*, Busn) P-H.

Coleman, Lori. Fundamental Soccer. King, Andy, contrib. by. LC 94-11907. 1994. 21.50 (*0-8225-3451-7*) Lerner Pubns.

Dewazien, Karl. Fundamental Soccer Goalkeeping. Lavery, Vincent J., ed. (Illus.). 128p. (Orig.). (gr. 6). 1986. pap. 7.95 (*0-9619139-1-6*) Fun Soccer Ent.

—Fundamental Soccer Practice. Lavery, Vincent J., ed. Garcia, Joseph G., illus. 128p. (Orig.). (gr. 6). 1985. pap. 7.95 (*0-9619139-0-8*) Fun Soccer Ent.

—FUNdamental Soccer Series. Maher, Alan, ed. Garcia, Joe, illus. 128p. (gr. 1 up). 1991. pap. 4.95 (*0-9619139-4-0*) Fun Soccer Ent.

—Fundamental Soccer Tactics. Lavery, Vincent J., ed. (Illus.). 128p. (Orig.). (gr. 6). 1987. pap. 7.97 (*0-9619139-2-4*) Fun Soccer Ent.

Gemme, Leila B. El Futbol es Nuestro Juego: Soccer Is Our Game. LC 79-13245. 32p. (gr. k-3). 1990. PLB 12.30 (*0-516-33615-0*); pap. 3.95 (*0-516-53615-X*) Childrens.

—Soccer Is Our Game. Caliger, Roberta, illus. LC 79-13245. 32p. (gr. k-3). 1979. PLB 12.30 (*0-516-03615-7*); pap. 3.95 (*0-516-43615-5*) Childrens.

Goodman, Michael. The World Cup (Soccer) 32p. (gr. 4). 1990. PLB 14.95 (*0-88682-320-X*) Creative Ed.

Grosshandler, Janet. Winning Ways in Soccer. Grosshandler, Janet, photos by. LC 90-48620. (Illus.). 32p. (gr. k-3). 1991. 13.95 (*0-525-65064-4*, Cobblehill Bks) Dutton Child Bks.

Gutman, Bill. Soccer. LC 89-7379. (Illus.). 64p. (gr. 3-8). 1990. PLB 14.95 (*0-942545-90-7*) Marshall Cavendish.

—World Cup Action! LC 93-41721. (Illus.). 32p. (gr. 2-6). 1994. pap. text ed. 3.95 (*0-8167-3376-7*) Troll Assocs.

Harris, Paul & Walsh, Adrian. You Can Control the Soccer Ball: World Champion Adrian Walsh's Little Book of Secrets. (Illus.). (gr. 2-6). 1977. pap. 3.95 (*0-916802-05-1*) Soccer for Am.

Howard, Dale E. Soccer Around the World. (Illus.). 48p. 1994. PLB 13.45 (*0-516-08046-6*) Childrens.

—Soccer Stars. (Illus.). 48p. 1994. PLB 13.45 (*0-516-08047-4*) Childrens.

Humber, Bill. Kids' Soccer. (gr. 4-7). 1994. pap. 9.95 (*0-8362-4511-3*) Andrews & McMeel.

Jackson, C. Paul. How to Play Better Soccer. Madden, Don, illus. LC 76-51450. (gr. 3-7). 1978. (Crowell Jr Bks); (Crowell Jr Bks) HarpC Child Bks.

Laitin, Ken & Laitin, Steve. Playing Soccer. Laitin, Lindy, illus. LC 79-63980. (gr. 2-7). 1979. pap. 9.95 (*0-916802-22-1*) Soccer for Am.

Leder, Jane M. Learning How: Soccer. James, Jody, ed. Concept of Design Staff, illus. 48p. (gr. 4-7). 1992. lib. bdg. 14.95 (*0-944280-32-3*); pap. 5.95 (*0-944280-38-2*) Bancroft-Sage.

Lineker, Gary. The Young Soccer Player. LC 93-41145. (Illus.). 32p. (gr. 2-6). 1994. 7.95 (*1-56458-592-1*) Dorling Kindersley.

Pollock, Bruce. Soccer for Juniors. 1980. 9.95 (*0-684-16487-6*, Scribner) Macmillan.

Rosenthal, Bert. Soccer. LC 82-19753. (Illus.). 48p. (gr. k-4). 1983. PLB 12.85 (*0-516-01658-X*); pap. 4.95 (*0-516-41658-8*) Childrens.

Rosenthal, Gary. Soccer: The Game & How to Play It. rev. ed. Bolle, Frank, illus. LC 72-129116. 256p. (gr. 3-9). 1978. PLB 14.95 (*0-87460-258-0*) Lion Bks.

Russell, Robin. Soccer. LC 91-9556. (Illus.). 32p. (gr. 2-5). 1992. PLB 11.90 (*0-531-18462-5*, Pub. by Bookwright Pr) Watts.

Wilner, Barry. Soccer. Seiden, Art, illus. Photo Shoppe Staff, photos by. Charlton, Bobby, intro. by. LC 93-1525. 1993. PLB 21.34 (*0-8114-5777-X*) Raintree Steck-V.

Woods, P. Soccer Skills. (Illus.). 48p. (gr. 6-10). 1987. pap. 5.95 (*0-7460-0167-3*) EDC.

SOCCER–FICTION

Auch, Mary J. Angel & Me. 1989. 9.95 (*0-316-05914-5*) Little.

Avi. S.O.R. Losers. LC 84-11022. 112p. (gr. 5-7). 1984. 14.00 (*0-02-793410-1*, Bradbury Pr) Macmillan Child Grp.

Barnett, Ada & Wurfer, Nicole. Eddycat Brings Soccer to Mannersville. Hoffmann, Mark, illus. LC 92-56879. Date not set. PLB 17.27 (*0-8368-0941-6*) Gareth Stevens Inc.

Berenstain, Stan & Berenstain, Janice. The Berenstain Bears' Soccer Star. LC 83-60055. (Illus.). 32p. (ps-2). 1983. pap. 1.50 (*0-394-85922-7*) Random Bks Yng Read.

Bughes, Dean. Back-Up Star. LC 94-15128. (gr. 1 up). 1995. pap. 3.99 (*0-679-85442-8*, Bullseye Bks); 4.99 (*0-679-95442-2*) Random Bks Yng Read.

Chapin, Kim. The Road to Wembley. LC 93-50815. (gr. 4-7). 1994. 15.00 (*0-374-34849-9*) FS&G.

Christopher, Matt. Soccer Halfback. Johnson, Larry, illus. (gr. 4-6). 1985. 15.95 (*0-316-13946-7*); pap. 3.95 (*0-316-13981-5*) Little.

—Top Wing. (Illus.). (gr. 8-12). 1994. 14.95 (*0-316-14099-6*) Little.

Dygard, Thomas J. Soccer Duel. 224p. (gr. 4 up). 1990. pap. 3.99 (*0-14-034116-1*, Puffin) Puffin Bks.

Eller, Scott. That Soccer Season. (gr. 4-7). 1993. pap. 2.95 (*0-590-42829-2*) Scholastic Inc.
Ettinger, Tom & Jaspersohn, William. My Soccer Book. (Illus.). 48p. (gr. 3-7). 1993. 10.95 (*0-694-00478-2*, Festival) HarpC Child Bks.
Fraser, Sheila. I Can Play Soccer. Kopper, Lisa, illus. 24p. (ps-3). 1991. 5.95 (*0-8120-6225-6*) Barron.
Gilson, Jamie. Soccer Circus. LC 92-9716. 1993. 12.00 (*0-688-12021-0*) Lothrop.
Hallowell, Tommy. Shot from Midfield. 112p. (gr. 3 up). 1990. pap. 3.50 (*0-14-032912-9*, Puffin) Puffin Bks.
—Shot from Midfield. (gr. 4-7). 1991. 12.95 (*0-670-83730-X*) Viking Child Bks.
Hughes, Dean. Psyched! Lyall, Dennis, illus. LC 91-24715. 112p. (Orig.). (gr. 2-6). 1992. pap. 2.99 (*0-679-82636-X*) Knopf Bks Yng Read.
—Quick Moves. Lyall, Dennis, illus. LC 92-44933. 112p. (Orig.). (gr. 2-6). 1993. pap. 3.50 (*0-679-84358-2*, Bullseye Bks) Random Bks Yng Read.
—Shake-Up. Lyall, Dennis, illus. LC 92-44932. 112p. (Orig.). (gr. 2-6). 1993. pap. 3.50 (*0-679-84357-4*) Random Bks Yng Read.
—Victory Goal. Lyall, Dennis, illus. LC 91-23321. 112p. (Orig.). (gr. 2-6). 1992. pap. 2.99 (*0-679-82637-8*, Bullseye Bks) Knopf Bks Yng Read.
Jenkins, Jerry. The Weird Soccer Match. (Orig.). (gr. 7-12). 1986. pap. text ed. 4.99 (*0-8024-8237-6*) Moody.
Joosse, Barbara M. The Losers Fight Back. Truesdell, Sue, illus. LC 92-40783. 1994. 13.95 (*0-395-62335-9*, Clarion Bks) HM.
Kessler, Leonard. Old Turtle's Soccer Team. LC 87-14870. (Illus.). 48p. (gr. k-3). 1988. 12.95 (*0-688-07157-0*); lib. bdg. 12.88 (*0-688-07158-9*) Greenwillow.
—Old Turtle's Soccer Team. 1990. pap. 2.95 (*0-440-40285-9*) Dell.
Kira, Gene S. Understanding Soccer: Rules & Procedures for Players, Parents & Coaches. (Illus.). 84p. (Orig.). (gr. 5 up). 1994. pap. 9.95 (*0-929637-02-X*) Apples & Oranges Inc.
Lakin, Patricia. A Good Sport! Cushman, Doug, illus. LC 93-49845. 1994. write for info. (*0-8114-3870-8*) Raintree Steck-V.
Levene, Nancy S. Hero for a Season. Reck, Sue, ed. LC 93-21126. 96p. (gr. 3-6). 1994. pap. 4.99 (*0-7814-0702-8*, Chariot Bks) Cook.
Maccarone, Grace. Soccer Game! Johnson, Meredith, illus. LC 93-43742. (ps-4). 1994. 2.95 (*0-590-48369-2*) Scholastic Inc.
Marzollo, Claudio. Kenny & the Little Kickers. Rogers, Jacqueline, illus. 32p. 1992. pap. 2.95 (*0-590-45417-X*) Scholastic Inc.
Marzollo, Jean. Soccer Sam. Sims, Blanche, illus. LC 86-47533. 48p. (gr. 1-3). 1987. lib. bdg. 7.99 (*0-394-98406-4*); pap. 3.50 (*0-394-88406-X*) Random Bks Yng Read.
Murrow, Liza K. Twelve Days in August: A Novel. LC 92-54489. 160p. (gr. 7 up). 1993. 14.95 (*0-8234-1012-9*) Holiday.
Napoli, Donna J. Soccer Shock. Johnson, Meredith, illus. LC 91-20706. 192p. (gr. 4-7). 1991. 13.95 (*0-525-44827-6*, DCB) Dutton Child Bks.
—Soccer Shock. Johnson, Meredith, illus. LC 93-7483. 192p. (gr. 3-7). 1993. pap. 3.99 (*0-14-036482-X*, Puffin) Puffin Bks.
Packard, Edward. Soccer Star. 1994. pap. 3.50 (*0-553-56011-5*) Bantam.
Park, Margaret & Iosa, Ann. Harvey & Rosie...& Ralph. LC 91-43306. (Illus.). 64p. (gr. 2-5). 1992. 11.00 (*0-525-44836-5*, DCB) Dutton Child Bks.
Roper, Gail. Seventh Grade Soccer Star. LC 88-9496. 132p. (gr. 3-7). 1988. pap. 4.99 (*1-55513-507-2*, Chariot Bks) Chariot Family.
Russman, Penny & Wright, Sheila. Changing Bodies, Changing Goals & Other Youth Soccer Stories. Woog, Dan, ed. Wright, Curt, photos by. LC 84-71345. (Illus.). 96p. (Orig.). (gr. 5-9). 1984. pap. 5.95 (*0-9613538-0-5*) Ascot Pr.
Seabrooke, Brenda. Jerry on the Line. LC 90-1745. 128p. (gr. 3-5). 1990. SBE 13.95 (*0-02-781432-7*, Bradbury Pr) Macmillan Child Grp.
—Jerry on the Line. 128p. (gr. 3-7). 1992. pap. 3.99 (*0-14-034868-9*) Puffin Bks.
Stops, Sue. Dulcie Dando, Soccer Star. Gliori, Debi, illus. LC 92-2259. (ps-2). 1992. 14.95 (*0-8050-2413-1*, Bks Young Read) H Holt & Co.
Tamar, Erika. Soccer Mania! 64p. (Orig.). (gr. 2-4). 1993. PLB 6.99 (*0-679-93396-4*); pap. 2.50 (*0-679-83396-X*) Random Bks Yng Read.
Wallace, Bill. Never Say Quit. LC 92-54420. 160p. (gr. 3-7). 1993. 14.95 (*0-8234-1013-7*) Holiday.
Wojciechowska, Maia. Dreams of Soccer. Karsky, A. K., illus. 70p. 1994. pap. 6.50 (*1-883740-06-1*) Pebble Bch Pr Ltd.

SOCIAL ADJUSTMENT

Parkison, Ralph F. The Pea in the Pod, Bk. 3. Withrow, Marion O., ed. Bush, William, illus. 10p. (Orig.). (gr. 2-6). 1988. pap. text ed. 3.00 (*0-929949-02-1*) Little Wood Bks.

SOCIAL CHANGE

Greene, Laura. Change: Getting to Know about Ebb & Flow. Mayo, Gretchen, illus. LC 80-81081. 32p. (gr. k-3). 1981. 16.95 (*0-87705-401-0*) Human Sci Pr.
Middleton, Nick. Atlas of Social Issues. (Illus.). 64p. 1990. 16.95x (*0-8160-2024-8*) Facts on File.

SOCIAL CONDITIONS

see also Economic Conditions; Labor and Laboring Classes; Social Problems

Middleton, Nick. Atlas of Social Issues. (Illus.). 64p. 1990. 16.95x (*0-8160-2024-8*) Facts on File.

SOCIAL CONFLICT

Schmidt, Fran & Friedman, Alice. Creative Conflict Solving for Kids: Grades 5-9. 2nd., rev. ed. Cranford, Kay K., et al, illus. 80p. (gr. 4-9). 1985. Incl. poster. pap. text ed. 21.95 (*1-878227-00-9*) Peace Educ.
—Creative Conflict Solving for Kids: Grades 3-4. 90p. (Orig.). (gr. 3-4). 1991. Incl. poster. 21.95 (*1-878227-10-6*); Set of 5, 24p. 11.95 (*1-878227-11-4*) Peace Educ.
—Peacemaking Skills for Little Kids. Le Shane, Phyllis, contrib. by. (Illus.). 76p. (Orig.). (gr. k-2). 1988. pap. text ed. 54.95 incl. poster, puppet, cassette (*1-878227-03-3*) Peace Educ.
Schmidt, Fran, et al. Mediation for Kids. 2nd ed. (Illus.). 68p. (gr. 4-12). 1992. Incl. poster. 21.95 (*1-878227-13-0*); Set of 5, 28p. 11.95 (*1-878227-14-9*) Peace Educ.

SOCIAL CUSTOMS

see Manners and Customs

SOCIAL HISTORY

see Social Conditions

SOCIAL HYGIENE

see Hygiene; Public Health

SOCIAL LIFE AND CUSTOMS

see Manners and Customs

SOCIAL PROBLEMS

see also Child Labor; Crime and Criminals; Discrimination; Divorce; Housing; Immigration and Emigration; Juvenile Delinquency; Migrant Labor; Public Health; Race Problems

Barden, Renardo. Gangs. (Illus.). 64p. (gr. 7 up). 1990. lib. bdg. 17.27 (*0-86593-073-2*); 12.95s.p. (*0-685-36324-4*) Rourke Corp.
—Gun Control. (Illus.). 64p. (gr. 7 up). 1990. lib. bdg. 17.27 (*0-86593-072-4*); lib. bdg. 12.95s.p. (*0-685-36325-2*) Rourke Corp.
Crary, Elizabeth. I Can't Wait. Horosko, Marina M., illus. LC 82-6277. 32p. (Orig.). (ps-2). 1982. PLB 15.95 (*0-9602862-6-8*); pap. 4.95 (*0-9602862-3-3*) Parenting Pr.
—I Want It. Horosko, Marina M., illus. LC 82-2129. 32p. (Orig.). (ps-2). 1982. PLB 15.95 (*0-9602862-5-X*); pap. 4.95 (*0-9602862-2-5*) Parenting Pr.
—I Want to Play. Horosko, Marina M., illus. LC 82-3610. 32p. (Orig.). (ps-2). 1982. PLB 15.95 (*0-9602862-7-6*); pap. 4.95 (*0-9602862-4-1*) Parenting Pr.
Fagan, Margaret. The Fight Against Homelessness. LC 90-3214. (Illus.). 64p. (gr. 5-8). 1990. PLB 12.40 (*0-531-17251-1*) Watts.
Greenberg, Keith E. Erik Is Homeless. Halebian, Carol, photos by. (Illus.). 40p. (gr. 4-8). 1992. PLB 17.50 (*0-8225-2551-8*) Lerner Pubns.
Hurwitz, Eugene & Hurwitz, Sue. Working Together Against Homelessness. LC 94-1022. 1994. 14.95 (*0-8239-1772-X*) Rosen Group.
Hyde, Margaret O. The Homeless: Profiling the Problem. LC 88-21195. (Illus.). 96p. (gr. 6 up). 1989. lib. bdg. 16.95 (*0-89490-159-1*) Enslow Pubs.

Issues of Our Time Series. (Illus.). 64p. (gr. 5-8). 1994. lib. bdg. 175.45 (*0-8050-3662-8*) TFC Bks NY. ISSUES OF OUR TIME is an ongoing series that introduces young readers to some of the complex social issues facing society today. These issues, the causes of which are often debatable & the solutions elusive, directly affect the world around us. Each title looks at a particular topic by integrating history with current positions & solutions. The well-rounded, unbiased discussions are presented in a clear, readable style, enhanced & reinforced with full-color photographs, charts & graphs. Although these books cannot attempt to offer any clear-cut answers, they encourage readers to form their own conclusions, or to pursue the subject further. The eleven issues now covered are: ADOLESCENT RIGHTS; CENSORSHIP; HOMELESSNESS; THE AMERICAN FAMILY; THE DEATH PENALTY; DRUGS IN SOCIETY; FAMILY ABUSE; GUN CONTROL; IMMIGRATION; TEEN PREGNANCY, & TEEN SUICIDE. For more information, or to order, call or write to: Marketing Director, Twenty-First Century Books, 115 West 18th Street,New York, NY 10011. (800-628-9658, ext. 9387).
Publisher Provided Annotation.

Johnson, Joan J. Kids Without Homes. (Illus.). 192p. (gr. 9-12). 1991. PLB 14.40 (*0-531-11064-8*) Watts.
Jones, Norma, et al, eds. Social Welfare: A Helping Hand? 44p. 1992. pap. text ed. 11.95 (*1-878623-34-6*) Info Plus TX.
McCauslin, Mark. The Homeless. LC 93-24106. 1994. text ed. 13.95 (*0-89686-805-2*, Crestwood Hse) Macmillan Child Grp.
Marx, Doug. Homeless. (Illus.). 64p. (gr. 7 up). 1990. lib. bdg. 17.27 (*0-86593-071-6*); lib. bdg. 12.95s.p. (*0-685-36326-0*) Rourke Corp.
Metlzer, Milton. Who Cares? Millions Do-- LC 94-4082. 1994. write for info. (*0-8027-8324-4*); Reinforced. write for info. (*0-8027-8325-2*) Walker & Co.
Miller, Maryann. Working Together Against Gun Violence. LC 94-1021. 1994. 14.95 (*0-8239-1779-7*) Rosen Group.
Redpath, Ann. What Happens If You Become Homeless. (Illus.). 48p. (gr. 3-6). Date not set. PLB 12.95 (*1-56065-132-6*) Capstone Pr.
Shelby, Anne. What to Do about Pollution. Trivas, Irene, illus. LC 92-24173. 32p. (ps-1). 1993. 14.95 (*0-531-05471-3*); PLB 14.99 (*0-531-08621-6*) Orchard Bks Watts.
Vorspan, Albert & Saperstein, David. Tough Choices: Jewish Perspectives on Social Justice. LC 92-31747. 1992. pap. 11.00 (*0-8074-0482-9*, 167275) UAHC.

SOCIAL PROBLEMS–FICTION

Baker, C. G. Taking Charge. LC 93-15038. 144p. (gr. 3-7). 1993. pap. 3.50 (*0-14-036568-0*, Puffin) Puffin Bks.
Bonham, Frank. Mystery of the Fat Cat. Smith, Alvin, illus. 160p. (gr. 5-9). 1971. pap. 1.25 (*0-440-46226-6*, YB) Dell.
Herzig, Alison C. & Mali, Jane L. Sam & the Moon Queen. 176p. (gr. 3-7). 1992. pap. 3.99 (*0-14-034979-0*, Puffin) Puffin Bks.
Hinton, Susie E. That Was Then, This Is Now. Siegel, Hal, illus. (gr. 7 up). 1971. 13.95 (*0-670-69798-2*) Viking Child Bks.
Mandrell, Louise. Kimi's American Dream: A Story about the Meaning of Martin Luther King Day. (gr. 4-7). 1993. 12.95 (*1-56530-045-9*) Summit TX.
Staples, Suzanne F. Shabanu: Daughter of the Wind. LC 89-2714. (Illus.). 256p. (gr. 7 up). 1989. 18.00 (*0-394-84815-2*); lib. bdg. 18.99 (*0-394-94815-7*) Knopf Bks Yng Read.
Tolan, Stephanie S. Sophie & the Sidewalk Man. Avishai, Susan, illus. LC 91-17317. 80p. (gr. 2-4). 1992. SBE 13.95 (*0-02-789365-0*, Four Winds) Macmillan Child Grp.
Wagner, Jane. J. T. Parks, Gordon, photos by. (Illus.). 128p. (gr. 3-8). 1972. pap. 3.99 (*0-440-44275-3*, YB) Dell.
Wild, Margaret. Space Travelers. Rogers, Gregory, illus. LC 91-30252. 40p. (gr. 1-4). 1993. 14.95 (*0-590-45598-2*) Scholastic Inc.

SOCIAL PSYCHOLOGY

see also Attitude (Psychology); Human Relations; Psychology, Applied; Social Adjustment

SOCIAL REFORM

see Social Problems

SOCIAL SCIENCES

see also Economics; Political Science; Social Change; Sociology

Chan, Barbara J. Kid Pix Around the World: A Computer & Activities Book. Chan, Barbara J., illus. LC 92-46141. 1993. pap. 12.95 (*0-201-62226-2*) Addison-Wesley.
Cobb, Vicki. This Place Is Cold. Lavallee, Barbara, illus. (gr. 2-4). 1989. 14.95 (*0-8027-6852-0*); PLB 13.85 (*0-8027-6853-9*) Walker & Co.
—This Place Is Dry. Lavallee, Barbara, illus. (gr. 2-4). 1989. 12.95 (*0-8027-6854-7*); PLB 13.85 (*0-8027-6855-5*) Walker & Co.
Coleccion Mi Mundo, 29 bks. rev. ed. (SPA., Illus., Orig.). (ps-2). 1991. Set of 29 bks. 32 pgs. ea. pap. 232.00 (*1-56334-017-8*) Hampton-Brown.
Cumpiano, Ina. Que Semana, Luchito! Halverson, Lydia, illus. (SPA.). 24p. (Orig.). (gr. 1-3). 1991. pap. text ed. 29.95 big bk. (*1-56334-023-2*); pap. text ed. 6.00 small bk. (*1-56334-037-2*) Hampton-Brown.
Frinks, Donna. All about Me. (gr. k). 1989. text incl. activity program 160.00 (*0-318-41077-X*) Southwinds Pr.
Gabet, Marcia. Fun with Social Studies. Gabet, Marcia, illus. 48p. (gr. k-3). 1985. wkbk. 6.95 (*1-55734-037-4*) Tchr Create Mat.
Gakken Co. Ltd. Editors, ed. World We Live In. Time-Life Books Inc Editors, tr. 90p. (gr. k-3). 1989. write for info. (*0-8094-4885-8*); PLB write for info. (*0-8094-4886-6*) Time-Life.
Grunsell, Angela. Hablemos del Rascismo. Mlawer, Teresa, tr. from ENG. (SPA., Illus.). 32p. (gr. 4-6). 1993. 12.95 (*1-880507-09-9*) Lectorum Pubns.
Hargreaves, Margaret & Davis, Pat. At Home & School. (Illus.). (gr. 1). 1988. text incl. activity program 259.00 (*0-318-41078-8*) Southwinds Pr.
—Extending My World. (gr. 3). 1988. text incl. activity program 259.00 (*0-318-41080-X*) Southwinds Pr.
—My Neighborhood & Me. (gr. 2). 1988. text incl. activity program 259.00 (*0-318-41081-8*) Southwinds Pr.

I Love the World. (Illus.). 36p. (Orig.). (gr. 1-6). 1993. pap. 7.00 (*1-56334-327-4*) Hampton-Brown.
Issues for the Nineteen Nineties Series, 6 bks. (Illus.). (gr. 7-10). 1989. Set. PLB 77.88 (*0-671-94194-1*, J Messner) S&S Trade.
Kratky, Lada J. Meet the Villarreals. Lovell, Craig, photos by. (Illus.). 24p. (Orig.). (gr. 1-3). 1991. pap. text ed. 29.95 big bk. (*1-56334-050-X*); pap. text ed. 6.00 small bk. (*1-56334-056-9*) Hampton-Brown.
Laird, Elizabeth. American Homes. (Illus.). 31p. 1989. pap. text ed. 5.25 (*0-582-01716-5*, 78664) Longman.
—Americans on the Move. (Illus.). 31p. (Orig.). 1989. pap. text ed. 5.25 (*0-582-01715-7*, 78663) Longman.
Maestro, Betsy & Maestro, Giulio. El Descubrimiento de las Americas. Arturo, Juan G., tr. (Illus.). 48p. (gr. 5-8). 1992. 13.95 (*0-9625162-9-5*) Lectorum Pubns.
—Una Union Mas Perfecta: La Historia de Nuestra Constitucion. Marcuse, Aida, tr. (Illus.). 48p. (gr. 5). 1992. 13.95 (*0-9625162-8-7*) Lectorum Pubns.
Newton, David E. Science - Technology - Society Projects for Young Scientists. LC 91-17825. (Illus.). 144p. (gr. 9-12). 1991. PLB 13.90 (*0-531-11047-8*) Watts.
Pilar, Arlene. Reading Books for Social Studies: A Study Guide. Friedland, Joyce & Kessler, Rikki, eds. (gr. 1-3). 1991. pap. text ed. 19.95 (*0-88122-692-0*) LRN Links.
Porter, Mark. Wow, What a Week! Halverson, Lydia, illus. 24p. (Orig.). (gr. 1-3). 1991. pap. text ed. 29.95 big bk. (*1-56334-051-8*); pap. text ed. 6.00 small bk. (*1-56334-057-7*) Hampton-Brown.
Rothlein, Liz & Wild, Terri C. Read It Again! Multicultural Books for the Intermediate Grades. (Illus.). 144p. (Orig.). (gr. 3-5). 1994. pap. 9.95 (*0-673-36081-4*) GdYrBks.
San Souci, Robert. Los Peregrinos de N. C. Wyeth. Romo, Alberto, tr. (Illus.). 34p. (gr. 4-6). 1992. 14.95 (*1-880507-03-X*) Lectorum Pubns.
Schwartz, L. Trivia Trackdown - Social Studies & Famous People. (gr. 4-6). 1985. 3.95 (*0-88160-120-9*, LW 253) Learning Wks.

SOCIAL SCIENCES–STUDY AND TEACHING

Cherryholmes, C. & Manson, G. Investigating Societies. (Illus.). (gr. 6). 1979. text ed. 28.04 (*0-07-011986-4*) McGraw.
Clarke, Joy A. Multicultural Social Studies Unit: Who Am I? Blocker, Kearn, illus. 150p. (gr. 3-8). 1991. 3-ring binder 79.95 (*0-9626984-1-5*); pap. 69.95 (*0-685-62443-9*) Clarke Enterprise.
Geoffrion, Sondra. Power Study to up Your Grades in Social Studies. LC 88-61277. 60p. (gr. 11 up). 1989. pap. text ed. 3.95 (*0-88247-786-2*) R & E Pubs.
Hegeman, Kathryn T. Our Community. Hegeman, Mark, et al, illus. (Orig.). (gr. k-3). 1982. tchr's manual 10.00 (*0-89824-034-4*); wkbk. 4.99 (*0-89824-035-2*) Trillium Pr.
Moore, Jo E. Who Discovered America? (Illus.). 48p. 1991. pap. 5.95 (*1-55799-218-5*) Evan-Moor Corp.

SOCIAL SERVICE
see Social Work

SOCIAL SETTLEMENTS
see also Playgrounds;
also names of settlements, e.g. Hull House, Chicago; etc.

SOCIAL STUDIES
see Geography; Social Sciences

SOCIAL WELFARE
see Social Problems; Social Work

SOCIAL WORK

Campolo, Anthony. Ideas for Social Action. 160p. (gr. 9-12). 1985. pap. 9.99 (*0-310-45251-1*, 11375P, Pub. by Youth Specialities) Zondervan.
Cytron, Phyllis. Myriam Mendilow: The Mother of Jerusalem. LC 93-15119. 1993. write for info. (*0-8225-4919-0*) Lerner Pubns.
McPherson, Stephanie S. Peace & Bread: The Story of Jane Addams. LC 93-6736. 1993. 17.50 (*0-87614-792-9*) Carolrhoda Bks.
Seymour-Jones, Carole. Homelessness. LC 92-39445. (Illus.). 48p. (gr. 6 up). 1993. text ed. 12.95 RSBE (*0-02-786882-6*, New Discovery) Macmillan Child Grp.
Weiss, Ann E. Welfare: Helping Hand or Trap? LC 89-16843. 128p. (gr. 6 up). 1990. lib. bdg. 17.95 (*0-89490-169-9*) Enslow Pubs.

SOCIAL WORK–FICTION

Peterseil, Tehila. Secret Files of Lisa Weiss. 1990. 11.95 (*0-87306-549-2*); pap. 9.95 (*0-87306-550-6*) Feldheim.

SOCIALISM
see also Communism; Individualism; Labor and Laboring Classes; Labor Unions; National Socialism

SOCIETY, PRIMITIVE
see also Art, Primitive; Indians of North America–Social Life and Customs; Man, Prehistoric

SOCIETY OF FRIENDS
see Friends, Society of

SOCIOLOGY
see also Cities and Towns; Civilization; Communism; Immigration and Emigration; Individualism; Labor and Laboring Classes; Population; Race Problems; Social Change; Social Conditions; Social Problems; Psychology

Beckelman, Laurie. The Homeless. LC 89-1432. (Illus.). 48p. (gr. 5-6). 1989. text ed. 12.95 RSBE (*0-89686-439-1*, Crestwood Hse) Macmillan Child Grp.
McSharry, Patra & Rosen, Roger, eds. The People of This Place: Natural & Unnatural Habitats. (gr. 7-12). 1993. 16.95 (*0-8239-1381-3*); pap. 8.95 (*0-8239-1382-1*) Rosen Group.
Petrikin, Jonathan S., ed. Male - Female Roles: Opposing Viewpoints. LC 94-4975. (Illus.). 264p. (gr. 10 up). 1995. PLB 17.95 (*1-56510-174-X*); pap. text ed. 9.95 (*1-56510-175-8*) Greenhaven.
Stull, Donald D., ed. On the Banks of the Grasshopper: Oral Traditions of the Kansas Kickapoo. Thomas, Fred, frwd. by. (Illus.). 82p. (Orig.). (gr. 7-12). 1984. pap. text ed. 7.95 (*0-317-13553-8*) Kickapoo Tribal.
Troubled Society Series, 6 bks, Set II. 1991. 77.70s.p. (*0-86593-109-7*) Rourke Corp.
Trundle. People of the World. (gr. 4-9). 1978. (Usborne-Hayes); PLB 13.96 (*0-88110-116-8*); pap. 6.95 (*0-86020-189-9*) EDC.

SOCIOLOGY, RURAL
see also Country Life

SOCIOLOGY, URBAN
see also Cities and Towns

SOFTBALL

Berst, Barbara J. I Love Softball. LC 84-62470. (Illus.). 72p. (Orig.). (gr. 3-6). 1985. pap. 4.25 (*0-9614126-0-7*) Natl Lilac Pub.
Gregory, Paul. Baseball & Softball. (Illus.). 80p. (gr. 10-12). 1992. pap. 6.95 (*0-7063-6667-0*, Pub. by Ward Lock UK) Sterling.
Gutman, Bill. Softball. LC 89-7608. (Illus.). 64p. (gr. 3-8). 1990. PLB 14.95 (*0-942545-91-5*) Marshall Cavendish.
McCrory, G. Jacobs. Softball Rules in Pictures. rev. ed. (Illus.). 80p. (Orig.). 1992. pap. 7.95 (*0-399-51728-6*, Perigee Bks) Berkley Pub.

SOFTBALL–FICTION

Killien, Christi. The Daffodils. 144p. 1992. 13.95 (*0-590-44241-4*, Scholastic Hardcover) Scholastic Inc.
Martin, Ann M. Kristy & the Walking Disaster. large type ed. 176p. (gr. 4 up). 1993. PLB 15.93 (*0-8368-1024-4*) Gareth Stevens Inc.
Ripslinger, Jon. Triangle. (gr. 7 up). 1994. write for info. (*0-15-200048-8*); pap. write for info. (*0-15-200049-6*) HarBrace.

SOIL CONSERVATION
see also Erosion

Soil & Water Conservation. (Illus.). 96p. (gr. 6-12). 1983. pap. 1.85 (*0-8395-3291-1*, 33291) BSA.

SOIL EROSION
see Erosion

SOIL FERTILITY
see Soils

SOILS
see also Clay
also headings beginning with the word Soil

Bourgeois, Paulette. Amazing Dirt Book. 1990. pap. 7.64 (*0-201-55096-2*) Addison-Wesley.
Catherall, Ed. Exploring Soil & Rocks. LC 90-10024. (Illus.). 48p. (gr. 4-8). 1990. PLB 22.80 (*0-8114-2595-9*) Raintree Steck-V.
Evans, David & Williams, Claudette. Rocks & Soil. LC 92-53478. (Illus.). 24p. (gr. k-3). 1993. 9.95 (*1-56458-209-4*) Dorling Kindersley.
Jennings, Terry. Rocks & Soil. LC 88-22889. (Illus.). 32p. (gr. 3-6). 1989. pap. 4.95 (*0-516-48407-9*) Childrens.
Lavies, Bianca. Compost Critters. Lavies, Bianca, illus. LC 92-35651. 32p. (gr. 2-6). 1993. 14.99 (*0-525-44763-6*, DCB) Dutton Child Bks.
Murray, Peter. Dirt, Wonderful Dirt! Dann, Penny, illus. LC 92-42741. (gr. 2-6). 1995. 14.95 (*1-56766-079-7*) Childs World.
Nielsen, Shelly. I Love Dirt. Berg, Julie, ed. LC 93-18956. (gr. 3 up). 1993. 14.96 (*1-56239-188-7*) Abdo & Dghtrs.
Petty, Kate. Earth. LC 90-31022. (Illus.). 32p. (gr. k-4). 1991. PLB 11.90 (*0-531-14098-9*) Watts.
Pluckrose, Henry. Under the Ground. LC 93-45659. 1994. PLB 11.95 (*0-516-08122-5*) Childrens.
Stille, Darlene. Soil Erosion & Pollution. LC 89-25360. (Illus.). 48p. (gr. k-4). 1990. 12.85 (*0-516-01188-X*); pap. 4.95 (*0-516-41188-8*) Childrens.
Winckler, Suzanne & Rodgers, Mary M. Our Engandered Planet: Soil. LC 92-39902. 1993. PLB 21.50 (*0-8225-2508-9*) Lerner Pubns.
Wyler, Rose. Science Fun with Mud & Dirt. Stewart, Pat, illus. LC 86-8388. 48p. (gr. 2-4). 1986. lib. bdg. 11.38 (*0-671-55569-3*, J Messner); lib. bdg. 4.95 (*0-671-62904-2*); PLB 8.54s.p. (*0-685-47076-8*); pap. 3.71s.p. (*0-685-47077-6*) S&S Trade.

SOLAR ENERGY

Asimov, Isaac. How Did We Find Out about Solar Power? Wool, David, illus. 64p. (gr. 4-7). 1983. PLB 12.85 (*0-8027-6423-1*) Walker & Co.
Brooke, Bob. Solar Energy. (Illus.). (gr. 5 up). 1992. lib. bdg. 19.95 (*0-7910-1590-4*) Chelsea Hse.
Crump, Donald J., ed. Exploring Your Solar System. (gr. 3-8). 1989. 8.95 (*0-87044-703-3*) Natl Geog.
Gould, Alan. Hot Water & Warm Homes from Sunlight. Bergman, Lincoln & Fairwell, Kay, eds. Baker, Lisa H. & Byal, Chris, illus. Sneider, Cary I., photos by. 40p. (Orig.). (gr. 4-8). 1986. pap. 10.00 (*0-912511-24-9*) Lawrence Science.
Hillerman, Anne. Done in the Sun: Solar Projects for Children. Yamashita, Mina, illus. LC 83-638. 48p. (Orig.). (gr. 3-5). 1983. pap. 6.95 (*0-86534-018-8*) Sunstone Pr.
Kaufman, Allan. Exploring Solar Energy: Principles & Projects. LC 86-60262. (Illus.). 98p. (gr. 7-12). 1989. pap. 8.95 (*0-911168-60-5*) Prakken.
Petersen, David. Solar Energy at Work. LC 84-23208. (Illus.). 48p. (gr. k-4). 1985. PLB 12.85 (*0-516-01942-2*) Childrens.
Rickard, Graham. Solar Energy. (Illus.). 32p. (gr. 4-6). 1991. PLB 17.27 (*0-8368-0709-X*) Gareth Stevens Inc.
Spence, Margaret. Solar Power. LC 92-33920. (Illus.). 32p. (gr. k-4). 1993. PLB 11.90 (*0-531-17378-X*, Gloucester Pr) Watts.

SOLAR HEAT
see Solar Energy; Sun

SOLAR PHYSICS
see Sun

SOLAR POWER
see Solar Energy

SOLAR RADIATION
see also Solar Energy

Robins, Perry. Play It Safe in the Sun. Podwal, Michael, illus. 40p. 1994. pap. 9.95 (*0-9627688-1-2*) Skin Cancer Fndtn.
PLAY IT SAFE IN THE SUN is the first book on sun safety written especially for children. This practical guide tells children everything they need to know about year-round sun protection & early detection of skin cancer. With 40 pages of reading fun, 18 clever full-color illustrations & entertaining puzzles, the book has an interactive learning format that challenges children & stimulates group participation. Reproduction masters are included for a "sunword" puzzle, a sun-sense test & a coloring page. With warmth & humor, Dr. Robins discusses skin cancer, ozone depletion, the danger of tanning machines, use of sunscreens, as well as a range of other objects related to sun protection & skin health. Written by the president & founder of the Foundation & illustrated by 10-year-old artist Michael Podwal, this book is ideal for reading at home with the entire family & for use in classrooms, camps & clubs, doctor's offices & child care facilities. To order, send $9.95 plus $2.50, shipping & handling, (check, money order, MasterCard or VISA). Special discount: 25 copies/$174.
Publisher Provided Annotation.

SOLAR SYSTEM

Adams, Richard. Our Wonderful Solar System. Burns, Raymond, illus. LC 82-17413. 32p. (gr. 3-6). 1983. PLB 10.59 (*0-89375-872-8*); pap. text ed. 2.95 (*0-89375-873-6*) Troll Assocs.
Asimov, Isaac. What Is an Eclipse? LC 90-26062. (Illus.). 24p. (gr. 2-3). 1991. PLB 15.93 (*0-8368-0440-6*) Gareth Stevens Inc.
Asimov, Isaac, et al. Cosmic Debris: The Asteroids. rev. & updated ed. (Illus.). (gr. 3 up). 1994. PLB 17.27 (*0-8368-1130-5*) Gareth Stevens Inc.
—Our Planetary System. rev. & updated ed. (Illus.). (gr. 3 up). 1994. PLB 17.27 (*0-8368-1134-8*) Gareth Stevens Inc.
Berger, Melvin & Berger, Gilda. Where Are the Stars During the Day? A Book about Stars. Sims, Blanche, illus. LC 92-18200. (gr. k-3). 1993. 12.00 (*0-8249-8644-X*, Ideals Child); pap. 4.50 (*0-8249-8607-5*) Hambleton-Hill.
Brandt, Keith. Planets & the Solar System. Veno, Joseph, illus. LC 84-2714. 32p. (gr. 3-6). 1985. PLB 9.49 (*0-8167-0300-0*); pap. text ed. 2.95 (*0-8167-0301-9*) Troll Assocs.
Branley, Franklyn M. Eclipse: Darkness in Daytime. rev. ed. Crews, Donald, illus. LC 87-47692. 32p. (ps-3). 1988. (Crowell Jr Bks); PLB 14.89 (*0-690-04619-7*, Crowell Jr Bks) HarpC Child Bks.
—Eclipse: Darkness in Daytime. rev. ed. Crews, Donald, illus. LC 87-45276. 32p. (ps-3). 1988. pap. 4.50 (*0-06-445081-3*, Trophy) HarpC Child Bks.
—The Planets in Our Solar System. rev. ed. Madden, Don, illus. LC 86-45171. 32p. (ps-3). 1987. pap. 4.95 (*0-06-445064-3*, Trophy) HarpC Child Bks.
Brown, Peter L. Astronomy. LC 84-1654. (Illus.). 64p. (gr. 7 up). 15.95x (*0-87196-985-8*) Facts on File.
Burack, Jonathan. A Trip to the Planets. (Illus.). 12p. (ps-3). incl. filmstrip, cass. 25.00 (*0-915291-90-8*, 5154) Know Unltd.
Cirou, Alain. Incredibly Far. LC 93-20078. (Illus.). 48p. (gr. 6 up). 1993. text ed. 14.95 RSBE (*0-02-718650-4*, New Discovery) Macmillan Child Grp.
Cole, Joanna. The Magic School Bus Lost in the Solar System. Degen, Bruce, illus. 40p. 1992. pap. 3.95 (*0-590-41429-1*, Scholastic Hardcover) Scholastic Inc.
Cole, Norma. Blast Off! A Space Counting Book. Peck, Marshall, III, illus. LC 93-28794. 32p. (ps-4). 1994. 14.95 (*0-88106-499-8*); PLB 15.88 (*0-88106-493-9*); pap. 6.95 (*0-88106-498-X*) Charlesbridge Pub.

Couper, H. & Henbest, Nigel. The Space Atlas: A Pictorial Guide to our Universe. 1992. 16.95 (*0-15-200598-6*, HB Juv Bks) HarBrace.
Fowler, Allan. The Sun's Family of Planets. LC 92-7405. (Illus.). 32p. (ps-2). 1992. PLB 10.75 (*0-516-06004-X*); big bk. 22.95 (*0-516-49631-X*) Childrens.
George, Michael. Galaxies. (gr. 4-7). 1993. 15.95 (*1-56846-053-8*) Creat Editions.
Gouck, Maura M. The Solar System. LC 93-17027. (SPA & ENG.). (gr. 2-6). 1993. 15.95 (*1-56766-061-4*) Childs World.
Ingle, Annie. The Glow-in-the-Dark Planetarium Book. Enik, Ted, illus. LC 92-29932. 16p. (Orig.). (ps-1). 1993. pap. 4.99 (*0-679-84367-1*) Random Bks Yng Read.
Kerrod, Robin. The Solar System. Evans, Ted, illus. LC 93-4339. 64p. (gr. 5 up). 1993. Set. write for info. (*1-85435-620-8*); PLB 15.95 (*1-85435-621-6*) Marshall Cavendish.
Leedy, Loreen. Postcards from Pluto: A Tour of the Solar System. LC 92-32658. (Illus.). 32p. (ps-3). 1993. reinforced bdg. 15.95 (*0-8234-1000-5*) Holiday.
Lewellen, John. La Luna, el Sol, y las Estrellas (Moon, Sun, & Stars) Kratky, Lada, tr. from ENG. LC 81-7749. (SPA., Illus.). 48p. (gr. k-4). 1984. PLB 12.85 (*0-516-31637-0*); pap. 4.95 (*0-516-51637-X*) Childrens.
Lhommedieu, Arthur J. Children of the Sun. (ps-3). 1993. 7.95 (*0-85953-931-8*) Childs Play.
Maynard, Christopher & Verdet, Jean-Pierre. The Universe. LC 94-9085. (Illus.). 128p. (gr. k-4). 1994. pap. 5.95 (*1-85697-527-4*, Kingfisher LKC) LKC.
Notre Planete dans l'Univers. (FRE.). 77p. 1990. 24.95 (*2-07-035901-8*) Schoenhof.
Pomeroy, Johanna P. Content Area Reading Skills Solar System: Locating Details. (Illus.). (gr. 4). 1987. pap. text ed. 3.25 (*0-89525-858-7*) Ed Activities.
Simon, Seymour. The Long View into Space. LC 78-11388. (Illus.). (gr. 2-4). 1987. 13.95 (*0-517-53659-5*) Crown Bks Yng Read.
—Neptune. LC 90-13213. (Illus.). 32p. (gr. k up). 1991. 13.95 (*0-688-09631-X*); PLB 13.88 (*0-688-09632-8*, Morrow Jr Bks) Morrow Jr Bks.
Sorensen, Lynda. Planets. LC 93-14874. (ps-6). 1993. 12.67 (*0-86593-274-3*); 9.50s.p. (*0-685-66588-7*) Rourke Corp.
Spangenburg, Ray & Moser, Diane. Exploring the Reaches of the Solar System. 1990. 22.95x (*0-8160-1850-2*) Facts on File.
Stacy, Tom. Sun, Stars & Planets. Bull, Peter, illus. LC 90-42979. 40p. (Orig.). (gr. 2-5). 1991. pap. 4.99 (*0-679-80862-0*) Random Bks Yng Read.
Teitelbaum, Michael. First Facts about the Solar System. Friedman, Jon, illus. 24p. 1991. 2.98 (*1-56156-085-5*) Kidsbks.
Verba, Joan M. Voyager: Exploring the Outer Planets. 64p. (gr. 5 up). 1991. PLB 19.95 (*0-8225-1597-0*) Lerner Pubns.
Verdet, Jean-Pierre. The Earth & Sky. (Illus.). 1992. bds. 10.95 (*0-590-45268-1*, 040, Cartwheel) Scholastic Inc.

SOLDIERS

Here are entered works dealing with members of the armed forces in general, including the Navy, Marine Corps, etc. as well as the Army.
see also Generals; Military Art and Science; Military Service–Vocational Guidance; Scouts and Scouting also names of countries with the subdivision Army–Military Life, e.g. U. S. Army–Military life; etc.

Chrisp, Peter. The Soldier Through History. Smith, Tony, illus. LC 92-40639. 48p. (gr. 5-8). 1993. 15.95 (*1-56847-010-X*) Thomson Lrning.
Murphy, Jim. A Young Patriot: The American Revolution As Experienced by One Boy. LC 93-38789. 1995. write for info. (*0-395-60523-7*, Clarion Bks) HM.

SOLDIERS, DISABLED

see Physically Handicapped

SOLDIERS–FICTION

Adams, Pam. Oh, Soldier! Soldier! LC 90-48946. (ps-3). 1990. pap. 5.95 (*0-85953-092-2*, Pub. by Child's Play England) Childs Play.
Adams, Pam, illus. Oh, Soldier! Soldier! LC 90-48946. 16p. (ps-2). 1978. 11.95 (*0-85953-093-0*, Pub. by Child's Play England) Childs Play.
Brown, Marcia. Sopa de Piedras. Mlawer, Teresa, tr. from ENG. Brown, Marcia, illus. (gr. 5-7). 1991. PLB 12.95 (*0-9625162-1-X*) Lectorum Pubns.
—Stone Soup. reissued ed. Brown, Marcia, illus. LC 86-10964. 48p. (ps-2). 1986. pap. 3.95 (*0-689-71103-4*, Aladdin) Macmillan Child Grp.
Collington, Peter. The Angel & the Soldier Boy. Schulman, Janet, ed. Collington, Peter, illus. LC 86-20169. 32p. (ps-3). 1994. 13.00 (*0-394-88626-7*); lib. bdg. 10.99 (*0-394-98626-1*) Knopf Bks Yng Read.
Garland, Hamlin. The Return of a Private. LC 92-44051. 1994. 13.95 (*0-88682-583-0*) Creative Ed.
Greene, Bette. Summer of My German Soldier. 208p. (gr. 7-12). 1984. pap. 3.50 (*0-553-27247-0*) Bantam.
—Summer of My German Soldier. 224p. (gr. 7 up). 1973. 14.95 (*0-8037-8321-3*) Dial Bks Young.
—The Summer of My German Soldier. large type ed. 272p. 1989. Repr. of 1973 ed. lib. bdg. 15.95 (*1-55736-134-7*, Crnrstn Bks) BDD LT Grp.
Greeson, Janet. An American Army of Two. Mulvihill, Patricia, illus. 48p. (gr. k-4). 1991. PLB 14.95 (*0-87614-664-7*) Carolrhoda Bks.
Johnston, Annie F. The Little Colonel: Maid of Honor. (gr. 5 up). 13.95 (*0-89201-034-7*) Zenger Pub.
—The Little Colonel Stories: First Series. (gr. 5 up). 13.95 (*0-89201-070-3*) Zenger Pub.
—The Little Colonel Stories: Second Series. (gr. 5 up). 15.95 (*0-89201-071-1*) Zenger Pub.
—The Little Colonel's Chum: Mary Ware. (gr. 5 up). 13.95 (*0-89201-036-3*) Zenger Pub.
—The Little Colonel's Hero. (gr. 5 up). 13.95 (*0-89201-037-1*) Zenger Pub.
—The Little Colonel's Knight Comes Riding. (gr. 5 up). 13.95 (*0-89201-072-X*) Zenger Pub.
Lerangis, Peter. The Sultan's Secret. (gr. 8 up). 1988. pap. 2.95 (*0-345-35099-5*) Ballantine.
Mandrell, Louise. All American Hero: A Story about the Meaning of Veterans Day. (gr. 4-7). 1993. 12.95 (*1-56530-010-6*) Summit TX.
Nimmo, Jenny. The Chestnut Soldier. LC 90-21532. 164p. (gr. 6 up). 1991. 14.95 (*0-525-44656-7*, DCB) Dutton Child Bks.
Strasser, Todd, adapted by. Disney's the Three Musketeers. LC 93-71247. (gr. 4-7). 1993. pap. 3.50 (*1-56282-590-9*) Disney Pr.
Windrow, Martin & Hook, Richard. The Footsoldier. (Illus.). 80p. (ps-5). 1988. bds. 17.95 (*0-19-273147-5*) OUP.

SOLDIERS–U. S.

Matthews, L. Soldiers. (Illus.). 32p. (gr. 3-8). 1989. PLB 18.00 (*0-86625-365-3*); 13.50 (*0-685-67678-1*) Rourke Corp.
The World War II Soldier at Monte Cassino. 48p. (gr. 5-6). 1991. lib. bdg. 11.95 (*1-56065-005-2*) Capstone Pr.

SOLDIERS' LIFE

see Soldiers

SOLID GEOMETRY

see Geometry

SOLOMON, KING OF ISRAEL

Frank, Penny. Solomon's Golden Temple. (Illus.). 24p. (ps-4). 1987. 3.99 (*0-85648-745-7*) Lion USA.
MacGill-Callahan, Sheila. When Solomon Was King. Johnson, Stephen T., illus. LC 93-28058. 1995. write for info. (*0-8037-1589-7*); PLB write for info. (*0-8037-1590-0*) Dial Bks Young.
Orgel, Doris & Schecter, Ellen. The Flower of Sheba. Kelly, Laura, illus. LC 92-33477. 1994. pap. 3.50 (*0-553-37235-1*, Little Rooster, Little Rooster) Bantam.
Renberg, Dalia H. King Solomon & the Bee. Heller, Ruth, illus. LC 92-30411. 32p. (ps-3). 1994. 15.00 (*0-06-022899-7*); PLB 14.89 (*0-06-022902-0*) HarpC Child Bks.
Tangvald, Christine H. Yea, Hooray! The Son Came Home Today, & Other Bible Stories about Wisdom. Sasaki, Ellen J., illus. LC 93-9244. 1993. 7.99 (*0-7814-0927-6*, Chariot Bks) Chariot Family.
Wise King Solomon. 1989. text ed. 3.95 cased (*0-7214-5261-2*) Ladybird Bks.

SOLOMON, KING OF ISRAEL–FICTION

Las Minas Del Rey Salomon. (SPA.). 1990. casebound 3.50 (*0-7214-1402-8*) Ladybird Bks.

SOMME, 2ND BATTLE OF THE, 1918

Tames, Richard. The First Day of the Somme. (Illus.). 64p. (gr. 7-11). 1990. 19.95 (*0-85219-829-9*, Pub. by Batsford UK) Trafalgar.

SONG BOOKS

see Songbooks

SONGBOOKS

Andrews, Janice. Tunes for Tots. (ps). 1987. write for info. incl. tape & tchr's. guide (*1-878079-04-2*) Arts Pubns.
Baron, Phil. The Do-Along Songbook. Forse, Ken, ed. High, David, et al, illus. 26p. (ps). 1986. 9.95 (*0-934323-34-8*); pre-programmed audio cass. tape incl. Alchemy Comms.
Barratt, C. Mother Goose Songbook. (gr. k up). 1986. 4.98 (*0-685-16882-4*, 615754) Random Hse Value.
Beal, K. Big Book Package, 4 vols. (Illus.). 16p. (gr. 1-3). 1990. Set. pap. text ed. 80.25 (*0-201-52205-5*) Addison-Wesley.
—Here It's Winter Big Book. (Illus.). 16p. (gr. 1-3). 1990. pap. text ed. 22.95 (*0-201-52203-9*) Addison-Wesley.
—I Like You Big Book. (Illus.). 16p. (gr. 1-3). 1990. pap. text ed. 22.95 (*0-201-52204-7*) Addison-Wesley.
—I Like You Little Book. (Illus.). 16p. (gr. 1-3). 1990. pap. text ed. 4.50 (*0-201-52209-8*) Addison-Wesley.
—I Like You Little Books Four-Pack. (Illus.). 16p. (gr. 1-3). 1990. Set. pap. text ed. 12.95 (*0-201-52213-6*) Addison-Wesley.
—I Love My Family Big Book. (Illus.). 16p. (gr. 1-3). 1990. pap. text ed. 22.95 (*0-201-52202-0*) Addison-Wesley.
—I Love My Family Little Book. (Illus.). 16p. (gr. 1-3). 1990. pap. text ed. 4.50 (*0-201-52207-1*) Addison-Wesley.
—I Love My Family Little Books Four-Pack. (Illus.). 16p. (gr. 1-3). 1990. Set. pap. text ed. 12.95 (*0-201-52211-X*) Addison-Wesley.
—It's Pink I Think Big Book. (Illus.). 16p. (gr. 1-3). 1990. pap. text ed. 22.95 (*0-201-52201-2*) Addison-Wesley.
—It's Pink I Think Little Book. (Illus.). 16p. (gr. 1-3). 1990. pap. text ed. 4.50 (*0-201-52206-3*) Addison-Wesley.
—It's Pink I Think Little Books Four-Pack. (Illus.). 16p. (gr. 1-3). 1990. Set. pap. text ed. 12.95 (*0-201-52210-1*) Addison-Wesley.
—It's Winter Little Book. (Illus.). 16p. (gr. 1-3). 1990. pap. text ed. 4.50 (*0-201-52208-X*) Addison-Wesley.
—It's Winter Little Books Four-Pack. (Illus.). 16p. (gr. 1-3). 1990. Set. pap. text ed. 12.95 (*0-201-52212-8*) Addison-Wesley.
Beall, Pamela C. & Nipp, Susan H. Wee Sing Dinosaurs. (Illus.). 64p. (ps-2). 1991. pap. 2.95 (*0-8431-3809-2*); pap. 9.95 bk. & cass. (*0-8431-3801-7*) Price Stern.
—Wee Sing for Christmas. (Illus.). 64p. (Orig.). (ps-2). 1984. pap. 2.95 (*0-8431-3808-4*); pap. 9.95 bk. & cass. (*0-8431-3800-9*) Price Stern.
Belling, Andrew. Let's Sing about America. O'Malley, Kevin, illus. LC 92-763081. 32p. (gr. k-2). 1992. PLB 12.89 (*0-8167-2982-4*); pap. text ed. 3.95 (*0-8167-2983-2*) Troll Assocs.
Biene, Susanna & Moneli, illus. Sing Through the Seasons: Ninety-Nine Songs for Children. Society of Brothers Staff, ed. LC 70-164916. 144p. (gr. k-6). 1972. 17.00 (*0-87486-006-7*); cassette 7.00 (*0-87486-048-2*) Plough.
Bock, Fred. Charlie Brown's Favorite Sunday School Songs. Schulz, Charles, illus. 24p. (Orig.). (gr. 1-6). 1992. pap. 7.95 (*1-56516-012-6*) Houston IN.
Boy Scouts of America. Boy Scout Songbook. 128p. (gr. 6-12). 1970. pap. 1.55 (*0-8395-3224-5*, 33224) BSA.
Brady, Janeen. Standin' Tall Songbook, Vol. 2. 71p. (ps-6). 1988. pap. text ed. 7.95 (*0-944803-63-6*) Brite Music.
—Standin' Tall Songbook, Vol. 3. 72p. (ps-6). 1989. pap. text ed. 7.95 (*0-944803-64-4*) Brite Music.
Bryer, James. Reading Skills Songbook, Vol. 1: Read, Rapp, & Rock to the Skills of Reading. Evangelist, Gary, illus. 48p. (Orig.). (gr. 2-6). 1989. pap. 14.95 incl. audiocassette (*0-9622499-0-4*) Soundbox Pubns.
Caggiano, Rosemary & Martinez, Larry. The Circus. 48p. (gr. k-6). 1978. pap. 14.95 (*0-86704-000-9*) Clarus Music.
Cassidy, John & Cassidy, Nancy. Kids Songs Two: Another Holler-Along Handbook. M'Guinness, Jim, illus. 70p. (Orig.). 1989. pap. 10.95 incl. 48-min. stereo cassette (*0-932592-20-1*) Klutz Pr.
Cassidy, Nancy. Kids Songs: Sleepyheads. 50p. 1991. Incl. cassette tape. wiro-bound 10.95 (*1-878257-11-0*) Klutz Pr.
Charney, Steve. Let's Sing about Silly People. Barnes-Murphy, Rowan, illus. LC 92-24713. 32p. (gr. k-2). 1992. PLB 12.89 (*0-8167-2978-6*); pap. text ed. 3.95 (*0-8167-2979-4*) Troll Assocs.
Cinderella - Night Songs. (Illus.). 72p. (gr. 9-12). 1988. saddle-stitch 18.95 (*0-88188-766-8*, HL00692375) H Leonard.
Cooper, Don. Dino-Songs. Boyd, Patti, illus. 32p. (ps-3). 1988. bk. & cassette pkg. 6.95 (*0-394-89810-9*) Random Bks Yng Read.
Cooper, Don, read by. Songs of America. Fritz, Ron, illus. 32p. (ps-3). 1990. Includes audio cassette. 6.95 (*0-394-85225-7*) Random Bks Yng Read.
Coopersmith, Harry, ed. More of the Songs We Sing. Oechsli, K., illus. (ENG & HEB.). 288p. (gr. 4-10). 1970. 9.50x (*0-8381-0217-4*) United Syn Bk.
Darin, Bobby & Murray, Jean. Splish Splash. Peterson, Bryan, illus. 24p. 1993. 9.95 (*0-7935-1841-5*, 00183010) H Leonard.
Dr. Seuss. Cat in the Hat Songbook. LC 67-21921. (Illus.). 72p. (gr. k up). 1993. 12.00 (*0-394-81695-1*) Random Bks Yng Read.
Ellis, Cathy. Holiday Guitar: Songs for Christmas & Hanukah. rev. ed. 48p. 1992. Repr. of 1985 ed. lab manual 18.95 (*1-879542-11-0*); audiotape 14.95 (*1-879542-12-9*) Ellis Family Mus.
Emerson, Sally. Nursery Rhyme Songbook: With Easy Music to Play for Piano & Guitar. Maclean, Colin & Maclean, Moira, illus. LC 92-53106. 72p. (ps-k). 1992. 16.95 (*1-85697-823-0*, Kingfisher LKC) LKC.
Fass, Bernie & Caggiano, Rosemary. Children Are People. 48p. (gr. 2-10). 1977. pap. 14.95 (*0-86704-003-3*) Clarus Music.
—The Four Seasons. 48p. (gr. k-6). 1976. pap. 14.95 (*0-86704-001-7*) Clarus Music.
—Happy Birthday Party Time. 48p. (gr. k-6). 1976. pap. 14.95 (*0-86704-002-5*) Clarus Music.
—The Power Is You. 48p. (gr. 2-12). 1979. pap. 14.95 (*0-86704-005-X*) Clarus Music.
—The Weather Company. 48p. (gr. k-8). 1978. pap. 14.95 (*0-86704-004-1*) Clarus Music.
Fass, Bernie, et al. Old MacDonald Had a Farm. 32p. (gr. k-4). 1981. pap. 14.95 (*0-86704-007-6*) Clarus Music.
Favorite Children's Songs. 48p. (ps-8). 1986. pap. 5.95 (*0-88188-495-2*, 00240251) H Leonard.
Gallina, Michael & Gallina, Jill. Movin' Right along with Me. (gr. k-6). 1989. 14.95 (*0-931205-51-4*) Jenson Pubns.
Garson, Eugenia, ed. The Laura Ingalls Wilder Songbook: Favorite Songs from the "Little House" Books. reissued ed. Williams, Garth, illus. LC 68-24327. 160p. (gr. 4 up). 1968. 19.00 (*0-06-021933-5*); PLB 18.89 (*0-06-021934-3*) HarpC Child Bks.
Gerson, Trina. Holiday Songs. Gerson, Ivan, illus. 84p. (ps-7). 1984. pap. text ed. write for info. (*0-9605878-2-9*) Anirt Pr.
Girl Scouts of the U. S. A. Staff. Brownies' Own Songbook. Roos, Ann, et al. 48p. (gr. 1-3). 1968. pap. 4.00 (*0-88441-351-9*, 23-130) Girl Scouts USA.
—Girl Scout Pocket Songbook: For Juniors, Cadettes, Seniors, & Leaders. 56p. (gr. 3 up). 1973. pap. 1.00 (*0-88441-306-3*, 20-192) Girl Scouts USA.
Glazer, Tom. Tom Glazer's Christmas Songbook. Corrigan, Barbara, illus. 1989. 16.00 (*0-685-29548-6*) Doubleday.
Goldstein, Rose B. Songs to Share. Schloss, E., illus. (HEB & ENG.). 64p. (ps-5). 2.95x (*0-8381-0720-6*, 10-720) United Syn Bk.

Gutmann, Bessie P. Nursery Songs & Lullabies. (Illus.). 32p. 1990. 9.95x (*0-448-23457-2*, G&D) Putnam Pub Group.

Harper, Jo. Pals, Potions, & Pixies: Family Songbook. George, R. Jefferson, photos by. Boustany, Robert, illus. (SPA & ENG.). 20p. (Orig.). (gr. 1-5). 1988. pap. 8.95 incl. cassette (*0-929932-01-3*) JCH Pr.

Hart, Jane, ed. Singing Bee! A Collection of Favorite Children's Songs. Lobel, Anita, illus. LC 82-15296. 160p. 1989. Repr. of 1982 ed. 22.95 (*0-688-41975-5*) Lothrop.

Holland, Alex N. Time to Sing Songs. Holland, Alex N., illus. 13p. (gr. k-3). 1992. pap. 12.95 (*1-895583-10-1*) MAYA Pubs.

Holland, Margaret. Willowisp Christmas Songbook. (Illus.). 24p. (gr. k-8). 1987. incl. cassette 3.50 (*0-87406-253-5*) Willowisp Pr.

James, George. Let's Sing about Animals. Hoggan, Pat, illus. LC 91-763080. 32p. (gr. k-2). 1992. lib. bdg. 12.89 (*0-8167-2980-8*); pap. text ed. 2.95 (*0-8167-2981-6*) Troll Assocs.

Johnson, Mark. Sing-Along Fun: Cowboy Classics, Fun-to-Sing, Campfire Favorites & Good 'n Gross, 4 vols. (Illus.). 24p. (Orig.). (gr. k-12). 1993. Set, incl. 4 audio cass. pap. 31.99 (*1-883988-05-5*) RSV Prods.

Lansky, Vicki. Vicki Lansky's Sing Along as You Ride Along Travel Songs. (ps-1). 1988. pap. 5.95 (*0-590-63233-7*) Scholastic Inc.

Lennon, John & McCartney, Paul. Yellow Submarine. Chojnacki, Cathy, illus. 24p. 1993. 9.95 (*0-7935-1859-8*, 00183013) H Leonard.

Masters, Brien, ed. The Waldorf Song Book. 1988. pap. 8.50 (*0-86315-059-4*, 20243) Gryphon Hse.

Mattox, Cheryl W., ed. Shake It to the One That You Love the Best: Play Songs & Lullabies from Black Musical Traditions. Honeywood, Varnette P. & Joysmith, Brenda, illus. (Orig.). (ps-6). 1990. pap. 7.95 (*0-9623381-0-9*) Warren-Mattox.

Metropolitan Museum of Art Staff. Go in & out the Window: An Illustrated Songbook for Children. Marks, Claude, commentary by. LC 87-752208. (Illus.). 144p. (gr. k up). 1987. 24.95 (*0-8050-0628-1*, Bks Young Read) H Holt & Co.

Mochnick, Beth R. New Holiday Songs for Children: A Creative Approach. Davis, Barbara, ed. (Illus.). iv, 44p. 1988. pap. text ed. 14.95 (*0-916656-25-X*) Mark Foster Mus.

Music for Very Little People. 9.95 (*0-685-62474-9*, XH1001) Astor Bks.

Mussiett, Salomon R., ed. Cancionero para Preescolares. (SPA.). 54p. (ps). 1989. pap. 3.50 (*0-311-32226-3*) Casa Bautista.

My Play a Tune Book: The Berenstain Bears' Family Favorites. (gr. k-5). 1990. 15.95 (*0-938971-08-5*) JTG Nashville.

Okun, Milton & Sosin, Donald, eds. Magic of Music - Children's Song: Piano - Vocal. Payor, Terry, illus. 80p. (Orig.). 1988. pap. text ed. 9.95 (*0-89524-372-5*) Cherry Lane.

Olshansky, Joanne. The Pizza Boogie Songbook. Colucci, Kristina & Boughton, Narda, illus. 33p. (Orig.). (gr. k-6). 1990. pap. 9.95 (*0-9626239-0-3*) JHO Music.

Oram, Hiawyn. Creepy Crawly Song Book. (ps-3). 1993. 17.00 (*0-374-31639-2*) FS&G.

Paris, Pat. This Old Man. (Illus.). 12p. (ps-1). 1989. text ed. 9.95 (*0-8120-6109-8*) Barron.

Peraza, Michael, illus. Disney's the Little Mermaid: An Under the Sea Christmas: A Holiday Songbook. LC 93-70939. 48p. 1993. 9.95 (*1-56282-504-6*) Disney Pr.

Phillips, Mark, et al, eds. America Takes Note: Official Menc Songbook: Piano - Vocal. (Illus.). 112p. (Orig.). 1988. pap. text ed. 14.95 (*0-89524-369-5*) Cherry Lane.

Polisar, Barry L. Noises from under the Rug: The Barry Louis Polisar Songbook. Stewart, Michael, illus. 208p. (gr. k-6). 1985. 18.98 (*0-9615696-0-3*); pap. 13.95 (*0-9615696-1-1*) Rainbow Morn.

Raffi. The Raffi Everything Grows Songbook. (Illus.). 48p. (ps up). 1989. 16.00 (*0-517-57110-2*) Crown Bks Yng Read.

Raposo, Joe. Bein' Green. Macari, Mario, illus. 24p. 1993. 9.95 (*0-7935-1680-3*, 00183008) H Leonard.

—C Is for Cookie & Other Kids' Favorites. (Illus.). 1993. plastic clam shell 6.95 (*0-7935-1954-3*, 00823016) H Leonard.

—Sing. Backhaus, Kenn, illus. 24p. 1993. 9.95 (*0-7935-1860-1*, 00183012) H Leonard.

—Sing & Other Kids' Favorites. (Illus.). 1993. plastic clam shell 6.95 (*0-7935-1955-1*, 00823020) H Leonard.

Running Press Staff, ed. KIDZ Family Car Songbook & Audiocassette. (Illus.). 128p. (Orig.). (gr. 1 up). 1991. incl. audiocassette 9.95 (*0-89471-996-3*) Running Pr.

—KIDZ Kids' Car Songbook & Audiocassette. (Illus.). 112p. (gr. 1 up). 1991. incl. audiocassette 9.95 (*1-56138-074-1*) Running Pr.

—KIDZ Merry Christmas Car Songbook & Audiocassette. (Illus.). 80p. (gr. 1 up). 1991. incl. audiocassette 9.95 (*1-56138-051-2*) Running Pr.

—KIDZ Sing along Car Songbook. (Illus.). 128p. 1992. incl. audiocass. 9.95 (*1-56138-177-2*) Running Pr.

Russell, Hannah. Songs about the Sky. rev. ed. Hendrickson, June, illus. 18p. 1988. pap. 4.50 (*0-9614089-2-8*) Avitar Bks.

Shipman, Gary, illus. Tinga Layo. 16p. (ps-2). 1992. pap. 14.95 (*1-55799-228-2*) Evan-Moor Corp.

Sing-Along Songbook: A Songbook for Younger Girl Scouts. 80p. 1990. 9.50 (*0-88441-367-5*, 23-102) Girl Scouts USA.

Smollin, Michael, illus. Laugh-Along Songs. 32p. (Orig.). (ps-2). 1990. pap. 6.95 incl. cass. (*0-679-80305-X*) Random Bks Yng Read.

Songs for Well Behaved Children. (gr. k-6). 1979. incls. cassette 9.95 (*0-9615696-6-2*) Rainbow Morn.

Stevens, Ray. Everything Is Beautiful. Karpinski, John E., illus. 24p. 1993. 9.95 (*0-7935-1856-3*, 00183011) H Leonard.

Supancich, Jo, illus. Second Story Window. 16p. (ps-2). 1992. pap. 14.95 (*1-55799-227-4*) Evan-Moor Corp.

—Skip to My Lou. 16p. (ps-2). 1992. pap. 14.95 (*1-55799-229-0*) Evan-Moor Corp.

Walt Disney's Peter Pan. (Illus.). 32p. (gr. 4-12). 1985. 7.95 (*0-88188-414-6*, HL 00360819) H Leonard.

Warren, Jean & Shroyer, Susan. Piggyback Songs to Sign. Kimmel, Joan, illus. LC 85-50433. 96p. 1992. 8.95 (*0-911019-53-7*, WPH 0209) Warren Pub Hse.

Weiss, George D. & Thiele, Bob. What a Wonderful World. Graef, Renee, illus. 24p. 1993. 9.95 (*0-7935-1840-7*, 00183009) H Leonard.

Young, Roger & Caggiano, Rosemary. The Safari. 48p. (gr. k-8). 1979. pap. 14.95 (*0-86704-006-8*) Clarus Music.

SONGS

see also Ballads; Carols; Folk Songs; Hymns; Lullabies; Music, Popular (Songs, Etc.); National Songs; Songbooks

All about Dinosaurs. (Illus.). 32p. (Orig.). 1994. pap. 8.95 incl. cass. (*0-7935-2379-6*, 00330502) H Leonard.

All about Me. (Illus.). 32p. (Orig.). 1994. pap. 8.95 incl. cass. (*0-7935-2380-X*, 00330503) H Leonard.

All about Shapes. (Illus.). 32p. (Orig.). 1994. pap. 8.95 incl. cass. (*0-7935-2381-8*, 00330504) H Leonard.

Allen, Linda & Snider, Chrystle L., eds. Washington Songs & Lore. Green, Donald A., illus. 200p. (gr. 1-12). 1988. pap. 15.95 (*0-9616441-3-3*); Abridged ed., 72 pg. comb bdg. 8.95 (*0-9616441-4-1*) Melior Dist.

Allert, Kathy, illus. The Golden Nursery Song Book: Favorite Songs & Singing Games for Children. 48p. (ps-k). 1993. 7.95 (*0-307-15863-2*, 15863, Golden Pr) Western Pub.

Argent, Philip, illus. Sing Nowell! 64p. (gr. 1-6). 1991. pap. 14.95 (*0-7136-5695-6*, Pub. by A&C Black UK) Talman.

Arnsteen, Katy K. Children's Songs: Hide 'n' Seek. 1990. 3.99 (*0-517-02569-8*) Random Hse Value.

Bacon, M. Songs That Every Child Should Know. (ps-6). 1972. 59.95 (*0-8490-1086-1*) Gordon Pr.

Baltuck, Naomi. Crazy Gibberish & Other Story Hour Stretches from a Storyteller's Bag of Tricks. (Illus.). 1993. PLB 25.00 (*0-208-02336-4*, Pub. by Linnet); pap. text ed. 15.00 (*0-208-02337-2*, Pub. by Linnet) Shoe String.

Barchas, Sarah. Get Ready, Get Set, Sing! Songs for Early Childhood & ESL. Hoffman, David & Gething, Elizabeth, illus. 40p. (Orig.). (ps-k). 1994. Incl. audio cass. pap. 12.95 (*0-9632621-1-4*); Incl. CD. pap. 15.98 (*0-9632621-2-2*) High Haven Mus. This zestful, dynamic 52-minute sound recording & illustrated lyrics book of child-tested original & traditional songs will bring joy & sing-along fun to young children in preschool through the primary grades. The 31 songs in GET READY, GET SET, SING! invite sharing, participation, learning & delight. Children can sing their way to ESL & through early childhood, exploring the world around them in songs of alphabet, people, family, feelings, colors, clothes, days of the week, numbers from 1 to 20, farm & pet animals, body, shapes, foods, months of the year, riddle rhymes, school & transportation. The charming, illustrated lyrics book will entice children to read-along as they sing-along. From the inviting "ABC Train" to the exuberant "Going for A Ride," these songs are ideal for ESL, & are for ALL young children exploring language & life with vitality & spark. Ordering information: High Haven Music, P.O. Box 246, Sonoita, AZ 85637-0246.
Publisher Provided Annotation.

—Pinata! Bilingual Songs for Children. 24p. (gr. k-6). 1991. Incl. audio cass. pap. 12.95 (*0-9632621-0-6*) High Haven Mus.
Hispanic culture & language are celebrated in 17 original songs in this 40 minute cassette with illustrated lyrics book. The songs evoke pride in traditions, holidays & contributions of Hispanic culture & people; explore basic concepts & joy in reading; share delight & value in knowing two languages & paving the way for three. These bilingual songs have Spanish & English interwoven, or in alternating verses, or in separate language versions making them accessible to speakers of either or both languages. Young people can lean on the language they know best & stretch to the language they seek to acquire. PINATA! can be used for any context inviting second language acquisition (ESL, SSL, bilingual) & any context inviting multicultural awareness & valuing of Hispanic culture. It can be used to integrate with the curriculum in social studies, language arts & music, including history & biography. It can enhance acceptance & understanding of self & others. "Fun for sing-alongs in schools with Spanish-speaking students, where Spanish is taught, or as an enrichment for multicultural studies." (ESLC, Brodart, 1994). Ordering information: High Haven Music, P.O. Box 246, Sonoita, AZ 85637-0246.
Publisher Provided Annotation.

Bates, Katharine L. America the Beautiful. Waldman, Neil, illus. LC 92-46199. 32p. 1993. SBE 14.95 (*0-689-31861-8*, Atheneum Child Bk) Macmillan Child Grp.

—O Beautiful for Spacious Skies. Thiebaud, Wayne, illus. Boyers, Sara J., ed. LC 94-6599. 1994. 13.95 (*0-8118-0832-7*) Chronicle Bks.

Beall, Pamela C. & Nipp, Susan H. Wee Sing Activity Book. Klein, Nancy, illus. 48p. (ps-2). 1992. pap. 2.95 (*0-8431-1423-1*) Price Stern.

—Wee Sing & Play. (Illus.). 64p. (Orig.). (ps-2). 1983. pap. 2.95 (*0-8431-3812-2*); pap. 9.95 incl. cassette (*0-8431-3796-7*) Price Stern.

—Wee Sing Around the World. Klein, Nancy S., illus. 65p. (ps-6). 1994. pap. 2.95 (*0-8431-3740-1*); incl. cass. 9.95 (*0-8431-3729-0*) Price Stern.

—Wee Sing Silly Songs. (Illus.). 64p. (ps-2). 1983. pap. 2.95 (*0-8431-3813-0*); pap. 9.95 bkl & cass. (*0-8431-3803-3*) Price Stern.

—Wee Sing Sing-Alongs. (Illus.). 64p. (ps-2). 1983. pap. 2.95 (*0-8431-3814-9*); pap. 9.95 bk. & cass. (*0-8431-3804-1*) Price Stern.

Beers, V. Gilbert. The Toddler's First Songbook. 168p. 1994. incl. cass. 15.99 (*1-56476-300-5*, Victor Books) SP Pubns.

The Best Easy Listening Songs Ever. 336p. (gr. 5 up). 1986. 15.95 (*0-7935-0972-6*, 00101542) H Leonard.

Bleiler, E. F. Mother Goose Melodies. 128p. (ps up). 1985. pap. 2.95 (*0-486-22577-1*) Dover.

Brady, Janeen. I Have a Song for You, Vol. 1: About People & Nature. rev. ed. (Illus.). (ps-4). Illus. by Linda Howard, 1986, 50pgs. pap. text ed. 7.95 activity bk. (*0-944803-02-4*); Ed. by Ted Brady, Illus. by Phyllis & Warren Luch, 1979, 39pgs. songbook 7.95 (*0-944803-00-8*); cassette 8.95 (*0-944803-01-6*) Brite Music.

—I Have a Song for You, Vol. 2: About Seasons & Holidays. (Illus., Orig.). (ps-4). Illus. by Linda Howard, 1987, 50pgs. pap. text ed. 7.95 activity bk. (*0-944803-05-9*); Ed. by Ted Brady, Illus. by Phyllis & Warren Luch, 1979, 45 pgs. songbook 7.95 (*0-944803-03-2*); cassette 8.95 (*0-944803-04-0*) Brite Music.

—I Have a Song for You, Vol. 3: About Animals. Howard, Linda, illus. 50p. (ps-4). 1988. pap. text ed. 7.95 activity bk. (*0-944803-08-3*); Ed. by Ted Brady, Illus. by Phyllis & Warren Luch, 1979, 42pgs. songbook 7.95 (*0-944803-06-7*); cassette 8.95 (*0-944803-07-5*) Brite Music.

—Standin' Tall Songbook, Vol. 1. 52p. (ps-6). 1987. pap. text ed. 7.95 (*0-944803-62-8*) Brite Music.

—Watch Me Sing, Vol. 1. Noyce, Robert, illus. 31p. (ps-2). 1977. pap. text ed. 6.95 songbk. (*0-944803-09-1*); cassette 8.95 (*0-944803-10-5*) Brite Music.

—Watch Me Sing, Vol. 2. Twede, Evan & Nelson, Eloise, illus. 30p. (ps-2). 1986. pap. text ed. 6.95 songbk. (*0-944803-11-3*); cassette 8.95 (*0-944803-12-1*) Brite Music.

Brahms' Lullaby. (Illus.). 6p. (gr. k-2). 1993. bds. 14.95 (*1-56144-348-4*, Honey Bear Bks) Modern Pub NYC.
Briggs, Raymond. Snowman: Songbook. 1993. pap. 7.95 (*0-7935-1831-8*, 50489170) H Leonard.
Brimhall, John. Children's Songs for Piano. 96p. (Orig.). (gr. 1-6). 1985. pap. text ed. 7.95 (*0-8494-2264-7*, 0496) Hansen Ed Mus.
—My Favorite Classics Level One. 120p. (Orig.). (gr. 3-6). pap. text ed. 10.95 (*0-8494-2180-2*, 0114) Hansen Ed Mus.
Burgie, Irving. Caribbean Carnival: Songs of the West Indies. Lessac, Frane, illus. Guy, Rosa, intro. by. LC 91-760838. (Illus.). 32p. (gr. 1 up). 1992. 15.00 (*0-688-10779-6*, Tambourine Bks); PLB 14.93 (*0-688-10780-X*, Tambourine Bks) Morrow.
Carey, Karla. Julie & Jackie at Christmas-Time: The Play & Musical Play (with Music Book, Story-&-Song Cassette & Piano Cassette) Nolan, Dennis, illus. LC 88-12909. 39p. 1990. pap. 35.00 complete pkg. (*1-55768-151-1*); pap. 25.00 book only (*1-55768-026-4*); story-&-song or piano cass. 8.00 (*0-685-19710-7*) LC Pub.
—Julie & Jackie at the Circus: The Play & Musical Play (with Music Book, Story-&-Song Cassette & Piano Cassette) Nolan, Dennis, illus. LC 88-12910. 44p. 1990. pap. 35.00 complete pkg. (*1-55768-152-X*); pap. 25.00 book only (*1-55768-177-5*); story-&-song or piano cass. 8.00 (*1-55768-027-2*) LC Pub.
—Julie & Jackie Go a'Journeying: The Play & Musical Play (with Music Book, Story-&-Song Cassette & Piano Cassette) Nolan, Dennis, illus. LC 88-9171. 73p. 1990. pap. 35.00 complete pkg. (*1-55768-153-8*); pap. 25.00 book only (*1-55768-028-0*); story-&-song or piano cass. 8.00 (*0-685-19711-5*) LC Pub.
—Julie & Jackie on the Ranch: The Play & Musical Play (with Music Book, Story-&-Song Cassette & Piano Cassette) Nolan, Dennis, illus. LC 88-12911. 46p. 1990. pap. 35.00 complete pkg. (*1-55768-154-6*); pap. 25.00 book only (*1-55768-029-9*); story-&-song or piano cass. 8.00 (*0-685-19712-3*) LC Pub.
Carle, Eric. Today Is Monday. Carle, Eric, illus. 32p. (ps-3). 1993. 14.95 (*0-399-21966-8*, Philomel Bks) Putnam Pub Group.
Cassidy, Nancy & Cassidy, John. Kid's Songs: A Holler-Along Handbook. M'Guinness, Jim, illus. 86p. (Orig.). 1986. pap. 10.95 incl. 48 min. stereo cassette (*0-932592-13-9*) Klutz Pr.
Chapin, Tom & Forster, John. Sing a Whale Song. Smath, Jerry, illus. 32p. 1993. incl. cass. 14.00 (*0-679-83478-8*) Random Bks Yng Read.
Cheech Marin: Me Llamo Cheech, el Chofer Del Autobus De la Escuela. (SPA.). 16p. (Orig.). 1992. pap. 9.98 incl. cass. (*1-56668-200-2*); pap. 13.98 incl. compact disc (*1-56668-202-9*) BMG Kidz.
Child, Lydia M. Over the River & Through the Wood. Westcott, Nadine B., illus. LC 92-14979. 32p. (gr. 1-5). 1993. 14.00 (*0-06-021303-5*); PLB 13.89 (*0-06-021304-3*) HarpC Child Bks.
Children at Sunrise Ranch, illus. Songs for the Joy of Living. 50p. (gr. 1-10). 1985. ring-bound 11.95 (*0-932869-01-7*) Emissaries.
Christmas Reindeer. (Illus.). 6p. (gr. k-3). 1993. bds. 12.95 (*1-56144-382-4*, Honey Bear Bks) Modern Pub NYC.
Christmas Santa. (Illus.). 6p. (gr. k-3). 1993. bds. 12.95 (*1-56144-381-6*, Honey Bear Bks) Modern Pub NYC.
Christmas Snowman. (Illus.). 6p. (gr. k-3). 1993. bds. 12.95 (*1-56144-380-8*, Honey Bear Bks) Modern Pub NYC.
Christmas Tree. (Illus.). 6p. (gr. k-3). 1993. bds. 12.95 (*1-56144-383-2*, Honey Bear Bks) Modern Pub NYC.
Clark, Kenneth B., ed. Traditional Black Music Series, 15 vols. (Illus.). (gr. 5 up). 1993. Set. PLB 224.25 (*0-7910-1826-1*, Am Art Analog) Chelsea Hse.
Clarkson, Ginger. Stop, Look & Listen: Songs of Awareness for Young Children. (ps). 1986. pap. text ed. 4.95 (*0-8497-5924-2*, WE8) KJOS.
Collier Books Staff. Sesame Street Songbook: Sixty-Four Favorite Songs. 1994. pap. 20.00 (*0-02-019201-0*) Macmillan Child Grp.
Collier, Roberta, illus. Sing with Me Lullabies. (ps-1). 1987. Incl cassette. 5.95 (*0-394-88811-1*) Random Bks Yng Read.
Cooper, Don. Recycled Songs. Alley, R. W., illus. 32p. (ps-3). 1992. incl. cassette 7.99 (*0-679-82643-2*) Random Bks Yng Read.
—Spooky Tunes. Daniel, Frank, illus. 32p. (Orig.). (ps-3). 1990. pap. 6.95 incl. cassette (*0-679-80303-3*) Random Bks Yng Read.
Cooper, Don, read by. Star Tunes. Fritz, Ronald, illus. 32p. (Orig.). (ps-3). 1991. pap. 6.95 incls. cassette (*0-679-81243-1*) Random Bks Yng Read.
Coplon, Emily, et al. She'll Be Coming Round the Mountain. LC 93-20627. (Illus.). (gr. 4 up). 1994. 10.95 (*0-553-09044-5*); pap. 3.99 (*0-553-37340-4*) Bantam.
Cross, David & Morse, Sarah. Easy As One Two Three: Fifty Dulcimer Tunes for Beginners. (Illus.). 32p. (Orig.). (gr. 1-6). 1985. pap. text ed. 2.25 (*0-9614939-4-1*); tchr's. ed. 5.95 (*0-9614939-5-X*) Backyard Music.
Davisge, Bud. The Mummer's Song. Wallace, Ian, illus. Major, Kevin, afterword by. LC 93-5773. (Illus.). 32p. (gr. k-3). 1994. 14.95 (*0-531-06825-0*); lib. bdg. 14.99 (*0-531-08675-5*) Orchard Bks Watts.
Delacre, Lulu. Arroz Con Leche: Popular Songs & Rhymes from Latin America. (Illus.). (ps-3). 1989. pap. 13.95 (*0-590-41887-4*) Scholastic Inc.
Delacre, Lulu, illus. Sing with Me Mother Goose. (ps-1). 1987. incl. cassette 5.95 (*0-394-88812-X*) Random Bks Yng Read.
De La Mare, Walter. Songs of Childhood. 106p. (gr. 3 up). pap. 4.50 (*0-486-21972-0*) Dover.
DiSilvestro, Frank. Sing Along with Me. Likht, Marina, illus. 52p. (gr. 8-10). 1985. pap. 7.95 (*0-934591-00-8*) Songs & Stories.
Disney Children's Favorites Songbook. 112p. 1992. 17.95 (*0-7935-1155-0*, 00311545) H Leonard.
Disney Favorites. 16p. (gr. 3 up). 1992. Incl. xylotone. 14.95 (*0-7935-1391-X*, 00824002) H Leonard.
Disney Songs from Animated Film Classics. 16p. (gr. 3 up). 1992. Incl. xylotone. 14.95 (*0-7935-1393-6*, 00824004) H Leonard.
Disney Songs from Animated Film Classics. 24p. (gr. 3 up). 1992. Incl. harmonica. 9.95 (*0-7935-1644-7*, 00850123) H Leonard.
Disney, Walt. Disney's Silly Songs. (ps-3). 1993. pap. 9.95 (*0-7935-1829-6*, 0290187) H Leonard.
Duke, Kate, illus. Tingalayo. (ps-2). 1988. 9.95 (*0-517-56926-4*) Crown Bks Yng Read.
Edge, Nellie, adapted by. La Cancion De Opuestos. Zamora-Pearson, Marissa, tr. from ENG. Nichols, Barry & Nicholas, Barry, illus. (SPA.). (ps-2). 1993. pap. text ed. 15.00 (*0-922053-25-1*) N Edge Res.
—Opposite Song Big Book. Nichols, Barry, illus. (ps-2). 1988. pap. text ed. 14.00 (*0-922053-06-5*) N Edge Res.
Edge, Nellie, compiled by. Songs & Rhymes for a Rainy Day Big Book. Saylor, Melissa, illus. (ps-2). 1988. pap. text ed. 15.00 (*0-922053-07-3*) N Edge Res.
Elkins, Stephen. Stories That End with a Song. Menck, Kevin, illus. 32p. (gr. k-8). Date not set. 12.98 (*0-685-68095-9*) Wonder Wkshop.
Ellis, John S., ed. My Play a Tune Book: All Time Disney Classics. (Illus.). 26p. 1988. 15.95 (*0-938971-07-7*) JTG Nashville.
Ellis, John S. & Leary, Mary B., eds. My Play a Tune Book: Children's Songs. Trebing, Tom, illus. 26p. (ps up). 1985. 14.95 (*0-938971-00-X*) JTG Nashville.
Ellis, Toni. My Play a Tune Book: Nintendo. Nintendo, illus. 26p. 1989. 15.95 (*0-938971-21-2*) JTG Nashville.
Ellis, Toni, ed. My Play a Tune Book: American Songs. (Illus.). 26p. 1988. PLB 15.95 (*0-938971-12-3*) JTG Nashville.
Engvick, William, ed. Lullabies & Night Songs. Sendak, Maurice, illus. LC 65-22880. (ps-3). 1965. 26.00 (*0-06-021820-7*) HarpC Child Bks.
Everybody Once Was A Kid: Gemini-Fun Songs & Activites for Kids. (Illus.). 32p. 1993. Book & cassette pkg. pap. 9.95 (*0-7935-2875-5*); Book & CD pkg. pap. 9.95 (*0-7935-2874-7*) H Leonard.
Fass, Bernie & Caggiano, Rosemary. Children Are People. 48p. (gr. 2-10). 1977. pap. 14.95 (*0-86704-003-3*) Clarus Music.
Ferguson, Virginia & Durkin, Peter. I Went to Visit a Friend One Day. Fleming, Leanne, illus. LC 92-31926. 1993. 4.25 (*0-383-03575-9*) SRA Schl Grp.
Fiarotta, Noel & Fiarotta, Phyllis. Music Crafts for Kids: The How-to Book of Music Dicovery. LC 93-24114. (Illus.). 160p. (gr. 3 up). 1993. 17.95 (*0-8069-0406-2*) Sterling.
Finckel, Edwin A. Now We'll Make the Rafters Ring: Classic & Contemporary Rounds for Everyone. Morice, David, illus. LC 92-43866. 144p. (Orig.). (gr. k-12). 1993. pap. 11.95 (*1-55652-186-3*) A cappella Bks.

Finger Fun-ics: A Collection of Finger Plays, Action Verses & Songs. (Illus.). 1995. pap. text ed. 9.95 (*0-9635535-1-8*) Kinder Kollege.
FINGER FUN-ICS is a delightful series of fingerplays, action verses, & songs designed to encourage participatory learning & to develop language skills. FINGER FUN-ICS is an invaluable teaching tool for teachers & parents of preschoolers. The daily use of FINGER FUN-ICS strengthens a child's memory & attention span. Through happy play, children learn to follow directions cheerfully while having fun. FINGER FUN-ICS opens up exciting worlds to young children in simple language & catchy rhythms. *Publisher Provided Annotation.*

Flanders, Michael & Swann, Donald. The Hippopotamus Song: A Muddy Love Story. Westcott, Nadine B., illus. (ps-3). 1991. 14.95 (*0-316-28557-9*) Little.
Fritz, Ron. Let's Have a Party! Scott, Dennis, illus. LC 92-28560. 32p. (gr. k-2). 1992. PLB 12.89 (*0-8167-2984-0*); pap. text ed. 3.95 (*0-8167-2985-9*) Troll Assocs.
Fullen, Dave. The Mountain Song. Farley, Brendon, illus. Oremus, Earl, contrib. by. (Illus.). 20p. (Orig.). (gr. 1-6). 1992. pap. 14.95 incl. cass. (*1-881650-00-6*) Mntn Bks.
Galdone, Paul. Cat Goes Fiddle-I-Fee. LC 85-2686. (Illus.). (ps-1). 1988. pap. 5.95 (*0-89919-705-1*, Clarion Bks) HM.
Gilbert, Yvonne. Baby's Book of Lullabies & Cradle Songs. LC 89-25898. (Illus.). 48p. (ps). 1990. 12.95 (*0-8037-0794-0*); PLB 12.89 (*0-8037-0795-9*) Dial Bks Young.
Gill, Madelaine & Pliska, Greg. Praise for the Singing: Song for Children. (Illus.). 1993. 18.95 (*0-316-52627-4*) Little.
Glazer, Tom, ed. Tom Glazer's Treasury of Songs for Children. (Illus.). (gr. 1-6). 1988. 12.95 (*0-686-74302-4*) J R Pubns.
Goode, Diane. Diane Goode's Book of Silly Stories & Songs. LC 91-38192. (Illus.). 64p. (ps-6). 1992. 15.00 (*0-525-44967-1*, DCB) Dutton Child Bks.
Goodman, Ailene S. Abe Lincoln in Song & Story. LC 88-753827. (gr. 4-12). 1989. incl. audio cass. & guidebook 11.98 (*0-9620704-0-8*) A S Goodman.
Greene, Carol. Columbus & Frankie the Cat. Dunnington, Tom, illus. LC 88-33067. 32p. (ps-2). 1989. pap. 3.95 (*0-516-43462-4*) Childrens.
—My Bible Stories: The Hop-Aboard Handbook & Sing-along Cassette. (Illus.). 64p. (Orig.). (ps). 1993. pap. 13.99 (*0-570-04752-8*) Concordia.
—The Pilgrims Are Marching. Dunnington, Tom, illus. LC 88-20219. 32p. (ps-2). 1988. PLB 11.80 (*0-516-08234-5*); pap. 3.95 (*0-516-48234-3*) Childrens.
Hale, Beverly M. A Rainbow Book of Song: Key of "C" 2nd ed. Hale, Beverly M., illus. 57p. (ps up). 1993. Blue spine bdg. pap. text ed. 13.95 (*0-9634305-1-3*) E-Z Keys Method.
Hamilton, Arthur. Sing a Rainbow Big Book. Izaguirre, Oscar, illus. (ps-2). 1988. pap. text ed. 14.00 (*0-922053-21-9*) N Edge Res.
Hammerstein, Oscar, II & Rodgers, Richard. Rodgers & Hammerstein's My Favorite Things. Warhola, James, illus. LC 93-26116. (ps-1). 1994. 15.00 (*0-671-79457-4*, S&S BFYR) S&S Trade.
Happy Songs for Kids. 32p. (gr. 3 up). 1992. Incl. cass., songbk., crayons. 6.95 (*0-7935-1082-1*, 00850113) H Leonard.
Harrop, Beatrice, compiled by. Sing Hey Diddle Diddle. Harris, Frank & Cheese, Bernard, illus. 96p. (ps-3). 1991. pap. 14.95 (*0-317-04680-2*, Pub. by A&C Black UK) Talman.
Haskins, Jim. Amazing Grace: The Story Behind the Song. LC 91-20999. (Illus.). 48p. (gr. 3-5). 1992. PLB 14.40 (*1-56294-117-8*) Millbrook Pr.
Hawthorn, P. & Roberts, S. Easy Recorder Tunes. (Illus.). 64p. (gr. 2-6). 1990. PLB 14.96 (*0-88110-414-0*, Usborne); pap. 8.95 (*0-7460-0457-5*, Usborne) EDC.
Hoban, Russell. Egg Thoughts & Other Frances Songs. newly illustrated ed. Hoban, Lillian, illus. LC 92-44004. 32p. (ps-3). 1972. 15.00 (*0-06-022331-6*); PLB 14.89 (*0-06-022332-4*) HarpC Child Bks.
Hunt, Brian, compiled by. Count Me In. Axworthy, Anni, illus. 64p. (ps-3). 12.95 (*0-7136-2622-4*, Pub. by A&C Black UK) Talman.
Johnson, James Weldon. Lift Every Voice & Sing. Catlett, Elizabeth, illus. 36p. 1993. 14.95 (*0-8027-8250-7*); PLB 15.85 (*0-8027-8251-5*) Walker & Co.
—Lift Ev'ry Voice & Sing. Gilchrist, Jan S., illus. LC 92-32283. (ps up). 1995. 14.95 (*0-590-46982-7*) Scholastic Inc.
Johnson, Mark. Campfire Favorites: A Songbook for Balance-Control Karaoke. Johnson, Mark, illus. 24p. (Orig.). (gr. k-12). 1993. pap. 2.49 (*1-883988-08-X*); pap. 8.99 incl. cassette (*1-883988-02-0*) RSV Prods.
—Cowboy Classics: A Songbook for Balance-Control Karaoke. Johnson, Mark, illus. 24p. (Orig.). (gr. k-12). 1993. pap. 2.49 (*1-883988-06-3*); pap. 8.99 incl. cassette (*1-883988-00-4*) RSV Prods.
—Fun-to-Sing: A Songbook for Balance-Control Karaoke. Johnson, Mark, illus. 24p. (Orig.). (gr. k-12). 1993. pap. 2.49 (*1-883988-07-1*); pap. 8.99 incl. cassette (*1-883988-01-2*) RSV Prods.
—Good 'n Gross: A Songbook for Balance-Control Karaoke. Johnson, Mark, illus. 24p. (Orig.). (gr. k-12). 1993. pap. 2.49 (*1-883988-09-8*); pap. 8.99 incl. cassette (*1-883988-03-9*) RSV Prods.
Juengst, Sara C. Silver Ships-Green Fields. Pace, Anne, illus. 52p. (Orig.). (gr. 1-6). 1986. pap. 5.95 (*0-377-00161-9*) Friendship Pr.
Kahn, Elithe A. Lani Goose Sings...for Hawaii's Children. Ruble, Allison, illus. (Orig.). (ps up). 1988. pap. 14.95 incl. audio cassette (*0-944264-03-4*) Lani Goose Pubns.
Kerr, Sandra, compiled by. Sing for Your Life. Samapatti, illus. 80p. (gr. 3 up). 12.95 (*0-7136-5546-1*, Pub. by A&C Black UK) Talman.
Kid Songs with Krazy Sounds. (Illus.). 20p. (ps up). 1992. write for info. (*0-307-74302-0*, 64302, Golden Pr) Western Pub.
Kids in Motion. (Illus.). 104p. (Orig.). 1994. pap. 14.95 (*0-7935-2797-X*, 00815016) H Leonard.
King, Bob. Sitting on the Farm. Slavin, Bill, illus. LC 91-17253. 32p. (ps-1). 1992. 13.95 (*0-531-05985-5*); lib. bdg. 13.99 (*0-531-08585-6*) Orchard Bks Watts.
Kolosick, Timothy & Kolosick, Helga. The Canons Austrian Children Sing. (Illus.). 32p. (Orig.). (gr. k-8). 1987. pap. text ed. 15.00 (*0-943121-00-0*) AZU Music Pr.
Kovalski, Maryann. Jingle Bells. (Illus.). (ps-3). 1991. pap. 4.95 (*0-316-50261-8*) Little.

Krull, Kathleen, selected by. Gonna Sing My Head Off! Garns, Allen, illus. Guthrie, Arlo, intro. by. LC 89-49562. (Illus.). 160p. 1992. 20.00 (*0-394-81991-8*) Knopf Bks Yng Read.

Lancaster, Francine. Favorite Animal Songs. (gr. k up). 1985. Boxed Set incl. cassette. 16.95 (*0-930647-01-7*) Lancaster Prodns.

Landes, William-Alan & Rizzo, Jeff. Rumpelstiltskin: Music & Lyrics. rev. ed. (gr. 3-12). 1985. pap. text ed. 15.00 (*0-88734-004-0*) Players Pr.

Langstaff, John. Oh, A-Hunting We Will Go. Parker, Nancy W., illus. LC 74-76274. 32p. (ps-3). 1974. SBE 14.95 (*0-689-50007-6*, M K McElderry) Macmillan Child Grp.

Langstaff, Nancy & Langstaff, John. Sally Go Round the Moon & Other Revels Songs & Singing Games for Young Children. Pienkowski, Jan, illus. LC 86-90535. 127p. (ps-1). 1986. pap. 12.95 (*0-9618334-0-8*) Revels Pubns.

Lavender, Cheryl. Moans, Groans & Skeleton Boans: Fun Songs & Activities for Kids. (Illus.). 32p. (Orig.). 1993. pap. text ed. 12.95 incl. CD (*0-7935-2371-0*, HL00330604) H Leonard.

—Moans, Groans & Skeleton Bones: Fun Songs & Activities for Kids. (Illus.). 32p. (Orig.). 1993. pap. text ed. 9.95 incl. cass. (*0-7935-2372-9*, HL00330605) H Leonard.

Lee, Kristina, et al. Songs of the Season. (Illus.). 80p. (Orig.). 1991. pap. 7.95 (*0-89084-555-7*) Bob Jones Univ Pr.

Lemberg, Stephen H. Alphabet Town. Baker, Darrell C., illus. (ps-k). 1993. Incl. cass. 7.95 (*1-882500-02-4*) SmartSong.

—Learning Land. Baker, Darrell C., illus. (ps-k). 1993. Incl. cass. 7.95 (*1-882500-00-8*) SmartSong.

—Numberville. Baker, Darrell C., illus. (ps-k). 1993. Incl. cass. 7.95 (*1-882500-03-2*) SmartSong.

—Rainbow Village. Baker, Darrell C., illus. (ps-k). 1993. Incl. cass. 7.95 (*1-882500-01-6*) SmartSong.

Let's Sing about America. (ps-3). 1993. pap. 7.95 incl. cassette (*0-8167-3107-1*) Troll Assocs.

Let's Sing about Silly People. (ps-3). 1993. pap. 7.95 incl. cassette (*0-8167-3105-5*) Troll Assocs.

Lewis, O. G. Good News. (Illus.). (gr. k-6). 1978. visualized song 2.99 (*3-90117-005-7*) CEF Press.

Leyerle, Anne L. & Leyerle, William D. Song Anthology One. 3rd, rev. ed. LC 79-90829. 159p. (gr. 9 up). 1985. pap. 12.95 plastic comb (*0-9602296-3-9*) Leyerle Pubns.

Leyerle, Anne L. & Leyerle, William D., eds. Song Anthology Two. 159p. (gr. 9 up). 1984. pap. 12.95 plastic comb. (*0-9602296-4-7*) Leyerle Pubns.

The Linda Arnold Songbook. (Illus.). 64p. (Orig.). 1994. pap. 9.95 (*0-7935-2377-X*, 00815002) H Leonard.

Lippman, Sidney, et al. A You're Adorable. Alexander, Martha, illus. LC 93-931. 32p. (ps up). 1994. 9.95 (*1-56402-237-4*) Candlewick Pr.

Little Peter's Christmas Secret. (Illus.). 16p. (gr. k-2). 1993. 14.95 (*1-56144-312-3*, Honey Bear Bks) Modern Pub NYC.

Livingston, Myra C. Space Songs. Fisher, Leonard E., illus. LC 87-19628. 32p. (ps-3). 1988. reinforced bdg. 15.95 (*0-8234-0675-X*) Holiday.

Lowry, Robert. Nothing but the Blood. (Illus.). (gr. k-6). illustrated song 2.99 (*3-90117-009-X*) CEF Press.

MacArthur, Barbara. Sing, Dance, Laugh, & Eat Quiche 3. Jensen, Robert, illus. (FRE.). 35p. (Orig.). (ps-12). 1992. pap. 17.95 (*1-881120-07-4*) Frog Pr WI.

—Sing, Dance, Laugh & Learn German. Jensen, Robert, illus. (ENG & GER.). 18p. (Orig.). (ps-8). 1993. pap. 12.95 incl. cass. (*1-881120-11-2*) Frog Pr WI.

McKernan, Llewellyn. More Songs of Gladness (Suppl.) (Illus.). 24p. (gr. k-4). 1987. pap. 1.99 (*0-570-09004-0*, 59-1432) Concordia.

McKinney, Roberta, ed. Songs for Children of the World. 16p. (Orig.). (gr. 1-8). 1984. pap. 12.95 set of 10 (*0-87487-740-7*, Suzuki Method) Summy-Birchard.

McMaster, Clara W. Sing a Happy Song: Beloved Children's Favorites. 1992. 8.98 (*0-88290-451-5*, 2929) Horizon Utah.

Magers, Pat, illus. Sing with Me Animal Songs. (ps-1). 1987. incl. cassette 5.95 (*0-394-88809-X*) Random Bks Yng Read.

Manson, Christopher, adapted by. & illus. The Tree in the Wood: An Old Nursery Song. LC 92-23524. 32p. (gr. k-3). 1993. 14.95 (*1-55858-192-8*); PLB 14.88 (*1-55858-193-6*) North-South Bks NYC.

Mary Had a Little Lamb. (Illus.). 6p. (gr. k-2). 1993. bds. 14.95 (*1-56144-351-4*, Honey Bear Bks) Modern Pub NYC.

Mayfield, Larry. Jesus Is Caring for You. Behl, Deborah, illus. 20p. (gr. k-6). 1982. visualized song 5.99 (*3-90117-026-X*) CEF Press.

Milne, A. A. The Songs of Winnie-the-Pooh. Shepard, Ernest H., illus. 10p. (gr. 4-7). 1994. pap. 5.99 (*0-525-45206-0*, DCB) Dutton Child Bks.

Miranda, Anne. Night Songs. Miranda, Anne, illus. LC 92-251. 32p. (ps-1). 1993. RSBE 13.95 (*0-02-767250-6*, Bradbury Pr) Macmillan Child Grp.

Mister Rogers - Won't You Be My Neighbor. (Illus.). 32p. (Orig.). 1994. pap. 9.95 incl. cass. (*0-7935-2927-1*, 00815023) H Leonard.

Mister Rogers - Won't You Be My Neighbor. (Illus.). 32p. (Orig.). 1994. pap. 12.95 incl. CD (*0-7935-2926-3*, 00815024) H Leonard.

Mister Rogers - You Are Special. (Illus.). 32p. (Orig.). 1994. pap. 9.95 incl. cass. (*0-7935-2925-5*, 00815025) H Leonard.

Mister Rogers - You Are Special. (Illus.). 32p. (Orig.). 1994. pap. 12.95 incl. CD (*0-7935-2924-7*, 00815026) H Leonard.

The Mister Roger's Songbook. (Illus.). 80p. (Orig.). 1994. pap. 10.95 (*0-7935-2928-X*, 00815027) H Leonard.

Mitchell, Joni. Both Sides Now. (Illus.). 1992. 14.95 (*0-590-45668-7*, Scholastic Hardcover) Scholastic Inc.

My Wonderful Lord Kit. (gr. k-6). 1973. 19.99 (*1-55976-107-5*) CEF Press.

Nelson, Esther L., ed. The Fun-to-Sing Songbook. LC 86-752869. (Illus.). 96p. (Orig.). (gr. k-6). 1986. 14.95 (*0-8069-4760-8*); pap. 10.95 (*0-8069-4762-4*) Sterling.

Nikola-Lisa, W. No Babies Asleep. Palagonia, Peter, illus. LC 93-20589. 32p. (ps-1). 1995. SBE 15.00 (*0-689-31841-3*, Atheneum) Macmillan Child Grp.

Norworth, Jack. Take Me Out to the Ballgame. LC 91-18555. (Illus.). 40p. (ps up). 1992. RSBE 14.95 (*0-02-735991-3*, Four Winds) Macmillan Child Grp.

Okun, Milton, ed. All My Life - Karla Bonoff (Piano - Vocal) (Illus.). 64p. (Orig.). Date not set. pap. 14.95 (*0-89524-707-0*) Cherry Lane.

—Eric Andersen Selected Songs (Piano - Vocal) (Illus.). 96p. (Orig.). 1993. pap. text ed. 17.95 (*0-89524-733-X*) Cherry Lane.

—The Leslie Bricusse Children's Songbook (Piano - Vocal) (Illus.). 282p. (Orig.). Date not set. pap. text ed. 24.95 (*0-89524-693-7*) Cherry Lane.

Old MacDonald's Farm. (Illus.). 6p. (gr. k-2). 1993. bds. 14.95 (*1-56144-349-2*, Honey Bear Bks) Modern Pub NYC.

Omodt, Jimm. The Chronicles of Caroltune: Scherzo Finds a Home. Omodt, Mary, ed. & illus. 40p. (Orig.). (gr. 3-8). 1993. pap. text ed. 10.00 (*1-881026-05-1*) Scherzo Pub.

Omodt, Jimm A. The Huge Hairy Horse Comes Back with Twenty-Six More. Omodt, Mary, ed. & illus. 40p. (Orig.). (ps-5). 1993. pap. text ed. 10.00 (*1-881026-03-5*); pap. text ed. 20.00 incl. cassette (*1-881026-02-7*) Scherzo Pub.

One Thousand Two the Complete Children's Song Book: The Complete Children's Song Book. 1990. incl. cass. 24.95 (*0-685-32067-7*, Z019) Hansen Ed Mus.

Oppenheim, Joanne. Row, Row, Row Your Boat. O'Malley, Kevin, illus. LC 92-29015. 1993. 9.99 (*0-553-09498-X*) Bantam.

Page, Parker. Getting Along: A Set of Fun-Filled Stories, Songs, & Activities to Help Children Work & Play Together. Rose, Mitchell, illus. LC 88-71899. 64p. (Orig.). (ps-5). 1989. 12.95 (*0-929831-00-4*) Childrens TV Resource.

Paton, Sandy & Paton, Caroline. I've Got a Song! A Collection of Songs for Youngsters. 2nd ed. Paton, Sandy & Paton, David, illus. 40p. (Orig.). (gr. k-4). 1989. pap. 10.98 (*0-938702-05-X*) Folk-Legacy.

—When the Spirit Says Sing: A Read-along, Sing-along, Coloring Book. Richardson, Joyce, illus. Wood, Chip, intro. by. (Illus.). 40p. (Orig.). (gr. k-8). 1989. pap. 13. 98 (*0-938702-06-8*) Folk-Legacy.

Paxton, Tom & Scharrett, Darcy. A Car Full of Songs. Fairbend, Kerstin, illus. 84p. (Orig.). (ps-6). 1991. 14. 95 (*0-89524-632-5*) Cherry Lane.

—Tom Paxton's Children's Songbook. Fairbend, Kerstin, illus. 68p. (Orig.). (ps-5). 1990. 12.95 (*0-89524-563-9*) Cherry Lane.

Pearce, Elvina T. Four O'Clock Tunes. Clark, Frances & Goss, Louise, eds. (gr. 2 up). 1986. pap. text ed. 3.50 (*0-913277-19-3*) New Schl Mus Study.

Peek, Merle. Roll Over! A Counting Song. Peek, Merle, illus. 32p. (ps-2). 1981. 14.95 (*0-395-29438-X*, Clarion Bks) HM.

—Roll Over! A Counting Song. Peek, Merle, illus. 32p. (ps). 1993. pap. 4.80 (*0-395-58105-2*, Clarion Bks); pap. 7.95 incl. cassette (*0-395-60117-7*, Clarion Bks) HM.

Penner, Fred. Fred Penner's Sing along - Play Along. Hicks, Barbara, illus. 112p. (Orig.). (ps-4). 1991. 14.95 (*0-89524-625-2*) Cherry Lane.

Pennie. Love Songs for Our Children. Szasz, Suzanne, photos by. Siegel, Bernie S., intro. by. (Illus.). 40p. (Orig.). (ps up). 1989. pap. 13.95 incl. cassette (*0-9624135-1-8*) Songs & Co.

Perinchief, Robert. Drug-Free Word Spree. 58p. (ps-12). 1993. 19.95 (*1-882809-01-7*) Perry Pubns.

Perry, Frances B., ed. Let's Sing Together: Favorite Primary Songs of Members of the Church of Jesus Christ of Latter-day Saints. Heaston, Claudia, illus. 96p. (ps-6). 1981. 10.98 (*0-941518-00-0*) Perry Enterprises.

—Let's Sing Together: Favorite Primary Songs. Heaston, Claudia, illus. 96p. (ps-6). 1984. hard cover music 12. 98 (*0-941518-02-7*) Perry Enterprises.

Pfister, Marcus, selected by. & illus. I See the Moon: Good-Night Poems & Lullabies. LC 91-10841. 32p. (ps-k). 1991. 14.95 (*1-55858-119-7*) North-South Bks NYC.

Pinkston, Joan & Tipton, Nancy. Songs of Our Heritage. (Illus.). 80p. (Orig.). 1991. pap. 7.95 (*0-89084-608-1*) Bob Jones Univ Pr.

Play & Sing with Ernie. 20p. (ps-4). 1993. 24.00 (*0-307-74305-5*, 64305, Golden Pr) Western Pub.

Plotz, Helen. A Week of Lullabies. Russo, Marisabina, illus. LC 86-18458. 32p. (ps-3). 1988. 11.95 (*0-688-06652-6*); lib. bdg. 11.88 (*0-688-06653-4*) Greenwillow.

Poffenberger, Nancy. Instant Fun With Sacred Songs. 24p. (gr. k up). pap. 5.95 (*0-938293-27-3*) Fun Pub OH.

Pooley, Sarah. A Night of Lullabies. (Illus.). 64p. (ps-1). 1992. 16.95 (*0-370-31491-3*, Pub. by Bodley Head UK) Trafalgar.

Powell, Harriet, compiled by. Game-Songs with Prof Dogg's Troupe. (Illus.). 64p. (ps-3). 1991. pap. 13.95 (*0-7136-2306-3*, Pub. by A&C Black UK) Talman.

Race, Donna. Favorite Mother Goose Songs: A Musical Pop-up Book with Five Different Melodies. (Illus.). 12p. (ps-1). 1993. pap. 12.95 POB (*0-689-71684-2*, Aladdin) Macmillan Child Grp.

Rae, Mary M., illus. The Farmer in the Dell: A Singing Game. 32p. (ps-1). 1990. pap. 3.95 (*0-14-050788-4*, Puffin) Puffin Bks.

Raffi. Baby Beluga. Wolff, Ashley, illus. LC 89-49367. 32p. (ps-2). 1992. pap. 3.99 (*0-517-58362-3*) Crown Bks Yng Read.

—Everything Grows. McMillan, Bruce, illus. LC 88-37162. 32p. (ps-2). 1993. pap. 3.99 (*0-517-88098-9*) Crown Bks Yng Read.

—Like Me & You. Hoban, Lillian, illus. LC 93-9840. (ps-2). 1994. 13.00 (*0-517-59587-7*); PLB 13.99 (*0-517-59588-5*) Crown Bks Yng Read.

—The Spider on the Floor. Kelley, True, illus. LC 92-33442. 32p. (ps-3). 1993. 13.00 (*0-517-59381-5*); PLB 13.99 (*0-517-59464-1*) Crown Bks Yng Read.

—Tingalayo. Duke, Kate, illus. LC 88-3562. 32p. (ps-2). 1993. pap. 3.99 (*0-517-88099-7*) Crown Bks Yng Read.

Reader's Digest Editors, ed. The Reader's Digest Children's Songbook. (Illus.). 252p. (ps up). 1985. lie-flat spiral bdg. 29.95 (*0-89577-214-0*, Dist. by Random) RD Assn.

Reichmeier, Betty, illus. Sing with Me Play-along & Counting Songs. (ps-1). 1987. incl. cassette 5.95 (*0-394-88810-3*) Random Bks Yng Read.

Reynolds, Malvina. Tweedles & Foodles for Young Noodles. Robbin, Jodi, illus. LC 73-80670. 42p. (gr. k-4). 1961. pap. 5.75 (*0-915620-08-1*) Schroder Music.

Rivera, Edgard & Rodriguez, Pilar, eds. Canciones Bajo El Arbol De Titeres - Songs under the Puppet Tree, Vol. 1: Canciones Infantiles Latinoamericanas - Latin American Children Songs. Rivera, Edgard & Rodriguez, Pilar, trs. from SPA. Murguia, Veronica, illus. 24p. (Orig.). (ps-5). 1993. 16.00 (*0-9629025-2-7*) Anarca Prodns.

Roberts, Sheena, compiled by. Birds & Beasts. Price, David, illus. 80p. (gr. 1-6). 12.95 (*0-7136-5653-0*, Pub. by A&C Black UK) Talman.

Robson, Tom. Musical Wisdom: Songs & Drawings for the Child in Us All. James, Nancy V., illus. 88p. (Orig.). (gr. k-6). 1992. pap. 16.95 (*0-9633332-0-8*) Laughing Cat.

Rohmer, Harriet, adapted by. Uncle Nacho's Hat (El Sombrero de Tio Nacho) Flor Ada, Alma & Zubizarreta, Rosalma, trs. Reisberg, Veg, illus. LC 88-37090. (ENG & SPA.). 32p. (ps-5). 1989. 13.95 (*0-89239-043-3*) Childrens Book Pr.

Ronnholm, Ursula O. Two Way Bilingual Songs for Elementary School. Archo, Mayra, illus. 41p. (gr. k-12). 1987. Incl. cass. pap. text ed. 8.00 (*0-941911-06-3*) Two Way Bilingual.

Rosen, Gary & Shontz, Bill. Sing a Happy Song. Petach, Heidi, illus. 24p. (ps-1). 1990. pap. 9.95 incl. cassette (*0-679-80805-1*) Random Bks Yng Read.

Rosen, Michael J. The Lullaby & Goodnight Sleepkit: The Gift of Sweet Dreams & Family Memories. Hague, Scott, illus. 32p. (ps-3). 1992. Boxed gift set incl. cass. & parents' guide. deluxe ed. 29.95 (*1-880444-00-3*); Mini ed. mini ed. cass & parents' guide, Aug. 1992 14.95 (*1-880444-02-X*) Times to Treas.

Ross, Brad. Kidz Sing-Along Poems Car Songbook & Audiocassette. (Illus.). 128p. (Orig.). 1994. 9.95 (*1-56138-414-3*) Running Pr.

Roth, Kevin. Songs for a Merry Christmas. Bollinger, Kristine, illus. 24p. (Orig.). (ps-1). 1992. pap. 9.95 incl. cass. (*0-679-83253-X*) Random Bks Yng Read.

Roth, Kevin, read by. Dinosaurs & Dragons. Byrd, Robert, illus. 24p. (ps-1). 1991. pap. 9.95 incls. cassette (*0-679-81744-1*) Random Bks Yng Read.

—Unbearable Bears. Hearn, Diane D., illus. 24p. (Orig.). (ps-1). 1991. pap. 9.95 incls. cassette (*0-679-81742-5*) Random Bks Yng Read.

Row Your Boat. 1993. pap. 3.50 (*0-553-37193-2*) Bantam.

Royer, Katherine, ed. Nursery Songbook. (Illus.). 48p. (ps). 1957. pap. 3.95x (*0-8361-1278-4*) Herald Pr.

Rubenstein, Judith S. & Rubenstein, Howard S., eds. Songs of the Seder: A Music Book to Accompany the Passover Haggadah - Twenty-Three Songs, Prayers, & Chants - Traditional & Contemporary - Transliteration & English - Keys That Are Easy to Sing & Play - Chords for Piano & Guitar. 70p. (Orig.). 1994. pap. 9.95 (*0-9638886-1-7*) Granite Hills Pr.

Sabatier, C. & Sabatier, R. Livre des Chansons de France: Deuxieme Livre. (FRE.). 163p. (gr. 4-9). 1990. 18.95 (*2-07-039529-4*) Schoenhof.

—Livre des Chansons de France: Troisieme Livre. (FRE.). 165p. (gr. 4-9). 1990. 18.95 (*2-07-039535-9*) Schoenhof.

Sabatier, Roland. Livre des Chansons de France. (FRE.). 157p. (gr. 4-9). 1991. 18.95 (*2-07-039516-2*) Schoenhof.

Scelsa, Greg & Millang, Steve. Dancin' Machine. Fritz, Ron, illus. 24p. (ps-1). 1992. incl. cassette 9.95 (*0-679-82378-6*) Random Bks Yng Read.

—Everybody Has Music Inside: Fun Songs & Activities for Kids. (Illus.). 32p. (Orig.). 1993. pap. text ed. 9.95 incl. cass. (*0-7935-2374-5*, HL00330607) H Leonard.

—Everybody Has Music Inside: Fun Songs & Activities for Kids. (Illus.). 32p. (Orig.). 1993. pap. text ed. 12. 95 incl. CD (*0-7935-2373-7*, HL00330606) H Leonard.
—The World Is a Rainbow. Holub, Joan, illus. 24p. (ps-1). 1992. incl. cassette 9.95 (*0-679-81979-7*) Random Bks Yng Read.
Schackburg, Richard. Yankee Doodle. Emberley, Ed, contrib. by. LC 93-28633. 1994. 14.00 (*0-671-88559-6*, S&S BFYR) S&S Trade.
—Yankee Doodle. Emberley, Ed. LC 93-28633. 1994. pap. 5.95 (*0-671-88645-2*, Half Moon Bks) S&S Trade.
Sesame Street Songbook: Sixty Favorite Songs. (ps-3). 1992. text ed. 25.00 (*0-02-525141-4*, Macmillan Child Bk) Macmillan Child Grp.
Sharon & Lois. Sharon, Lois & Bram Sing A to Z. LaFave, Kim, illus. LC 91-18990. 64p. (Orig.). (ps-4). 1992. 9.99 (*0-517-58723-8*) Crown Bks Yng Read.
Siebert, Diane. Truck Song. Barton, Byron, illus. LC 83-46173. 32p. (ps-3). 1984. (Crowell Jr Bks); PLB 14.89 (*0-690-04411-9*) HarpC Child Bks.
Silverman, Jerry. African Roots. Clark, Kenneth B., intro. by. (Illus.). 64p. (gr. 5 up). 1994. PLB 15.95 (*0-7910-1828-8*, Am Art Analog); pap. 7.95 (*0-7910-1844-X*, Am Art Analog) Chelsea Hse.
—Childrens' Songs. (Illus.). (gr. 5 up). 1992. PLB 15.95 (*0-7910-1831-8*, Am Art Analog); pap. 7.95 (*0-7910-1847-4*, Am Art Analog) Chelsea Hse.
—Slave Songs. Clark, Kenneth B., intro. by. (Illus.). 64p. (gr. 5 up). 1994. PLB 15.95 (*0-7910-1837-7*, Am Art Analog); pap. 7.95 (*0-7910-1853-9*, Am Art Analog) Chelsea Hse.
—Songs of Protest & Civil Rights. Clark, Kenneth B., intro. by. (Illus.). 64p. (gr. 5 up). 1992. 15.95 (*0-7910-1827-X*, Am Art Analog); pap. 7.95 (*0-7910-1843-1*, Am Art Analog) Chelsea Hse.
Simon, Paul. At the Zoo. (ps up). 1991. 15.00 (*0-385-41771-3*); PLB 15.99 (*0-385-41906-6*) Doubleday.
Sing-a-Long. 16p. 1991. write for info. incl. cassette (*1-880459-01-9*) Arrow Trad.
Sing-a-Long. 16p. 1991. write for info. incl. cassette (*1-880459-05-1*) Arrow Trad.
Songs & Prayers for Children. 32p. (ps-k). 1993. 3.98 (*0-8317-5184-3*) Smithmark.
Songs of Sesame Street. (Illus.). 64p. 1993. pap. 4.95 (*0-7935-0186-5*, 00001408) H Leonard.
Songs We Sing Around the Clock. 1990. 3.50 (*0-685-31996-2*, H480) Hansen Ed Mus.
Songs We Sing on the Bus. 1990. 3.50 (*0-685-31995-4*, G011) Hansen Ed Mus.
Staines, Bill. All God's Critters Got a Place in the Choir. Zemach, Margot, illus. LC 88-31696. 32p. (ps-2). 1989. 13.95 (*0-525-44469-6*, DCB) Dutton Child Bks.
—All God's Critters Got a Place in the Choir. Zemach, Margot, illus. 32p. (ps-2). 1993. pap. 4.99 (*0-14-054838-6*) Puffin Bks.
—River. Spohn, Kate, illus. LC 93-27864. 1994. 13.99 (*0-670-85353-4*) Viking Child Bks.
Steele, Mary Q. Anna's Summer Songs. Anderson, Lena, illus. LC 86-27109. (SWE.). 32p. (gr. k-3). 1988. 11.95 (*0-688-07180-5*); lib. bdg. 11.88 (*0-688-07181-3*) Greenwillow.
Stewart, Margaret A. The Best Book a Mother Ever Had. Imholte, Max, illus. 146p. (ps-3). 1985. pap. 12.95 spiral bdg. (*0-931047-00-5*) KinderPr.
Super Songs with Silly Sounds. (Illus.). 20p. (ps up). 1992. write for info. (*0-307-74301-2*, 64301, Golden Pr) Western Pub.
Swinger, Marlys. Sing Through the Day: Ninety Songs for Younger Children. 3rd ed. Society of Brothers Staff, ed. Jeanie And Joanie And Judy, photos by. LC 68-9673. (Illus.). 144p. (gr. 5 up). 1968. 17.00 (*0-87486-005-9*); cassette 7.00 (*0-87486-047-4*) Plough.
Teach Me Now 2. 80p. (ps). 1982. 4.95 (*1-55976-402-3*); 6.99 (*0-685-30468-X*) CEF Press.
Theo Carus Harter, Kaboblin. Turnabout Songs Program Complete Set: A Shortcut to Knowledge. Smith, Betty N. & Anderson, Catherine, eds. Gunder Heimer, Jocelyn C., illus. 262p. 1993. 2 in. 3-hole ring binder, incl. 9 cass. & cass. locator guide 150.00 (*0-944528-41-4*) Child Mus Wkshop.

Thornton, Suzi. Sometimes Childhood Stinks. Thornton, Don, intro. by. Lassalle, Cindy & Logan, Anne, illus. 64p. (Orig.). (gr. k-6). 1994. pap. 15.00 (*1-882913-06-X*) Thornton LA. SOMETIMES CHILDHOOD STINKS is a compilation of poems & songs about childhood. Characters in the poems/songs are reminiscent of the author as child & as teacher. Many of the poems/songs reflect painful experiences of childhood such as parent unemployment, divorce, or loneliness. Other poem/songs invest in the more humorous side of childhood with selections like Loose Tooth, Lost & Found, & Fried Liver. The poems are records of climatic moments in the lives of children. Songs have been written for fifteen of the thirty-four poems. The music score is included in the book. The spiral binding allows the book to open flat for use on a music stand or piano. The cassette includes all fifteen songs sung by the author. The work is especially appropriate for the elementary level for elocution & for musical presentations. The songs were written about childhood to be sung to children or performed by children. Those who do not read music or are uncomfortable singing alone can use the tape as a sing-along. *Publisher Provided Annotation.*

Todd, Cynthia & Ziemann, Debbie. David David. Woessner, Circe, illus. 23p. (gr. k-6). 1990. PLB 7.95 (*1-879056-01-1*) Alpenhorn Pr.
—Heidelberg Castle. Woessner, Circe, illus. 28p. (gr. k-6). 1990. PLB 9.95 (*1-879056-00-3*) Alpenhorn Pr.
—Mother Earth. Woessner, Circe, illus. 24p. Date not set. pap. 9.95 (*1-879056-03-8*) Alpenhorn Pr.
—Nessie. 2nd ed. Woessner, Circe, illus. 9p. (gr. k-6). 1990. PLB 9.95 (*1-879056-02-X*) Alpenhorn Pr.
—People from Outer Space. Woessner, Circe, illus. 9p. 1991. PLB 9.95 (*0-685-51627-X*) Alpenhorn Pr.
—Take One Hand. Woessner, Circe, illus. 25p. (gr. k-6). 1990. PLB 9.95 (*1-879056-05-4*) Alpenhorn Pr.
Traugh, Steven. All about Colors. (Illus.). 32p. (Orig.). 1993. pap. text ed. 8.95 (*0-7935-2384-2*, HL00330501) H Leonard.
Twinkle, Twinkle Little Star. (Illus.). 6p. (gr. k-2). 1993. bds. 14.95 (*1-56144-350-6*, Honey Bear Bks) Modern Pub NYC.
Veriat, I. Russian Songs: Text in Romanized Russian, English, & Music. 32p. (gr. 6-8). 1994. pap. 7.95 (*1-882427-23-8*) Aspasia Pubns.
Warhola, James, illus. Rodgers & Hammerstein's "The Surrey with the Fringe on Top" Hammerstein, Oscar, II, contrib. by. LC 92-2462. (Illus.). 1993. pap. 14.00 (*0-671-79456-6*, S&S BFYR) S&S Trade.
Watch. (gr. k-6). 1969. illustrated song 4.50 (*3-90117-008-1*) CEF Press.
Watson, Clyde. Father Fox's Feast of Songs. Watson, Wendy, illus. 32p. 1992. PLB 14.95 (*1-878093-84-3*) Boyds Mills Pr.
Watson, Wendy. Frog Went A-Courting. Watson, Wendy, illus. LC 89-63022. 32p. (ps-2). 1990. 13.95 (*0-688-06539-2*) Lothrop.
We All Live Together Plus. (Illus.). 160p. (Orig.). 1994. pap. 19.95 (*0-7935-2378-8*, 00815003) H Leonard.
Weimer, Tonja E. Space Songs for Children: Fun Songs & Activities about Outer Space. Kozlina, Yvonne, illus. 100p. (Orig.). (ps-3). 1993. 13.98 (*0-936823-11-9*); cassette 9.95 (*0-936823-12-7*) Pearce Evetts.
Weissman, Jackie. Sniggles, Squirrels & Chicken Pox: Forty Original Songs with Activities for Early Childhood. 64p. (ps-5). 1984. pap. 9.95 (*0-939514-06-0*); Vol. I. album 9.95 (*0-685-09111-2*); cassette 9.95 (*0-685-09112-0*); Vol. II. album 9.95 (*0-685-09113-9*); cassette 9.95 (*0-685-09114-7*) Miss Jackie.
Wilkon, Jozef & Moers, Hermann. Lullaby for a Newborn King. Wilkon, Jozef, illus. Lanning, Rosemary, tr. from GER. LC 91-11684. (Illus.). 32p. (gr. k-3). 1991. 14. 95 (*1-55858-123-5*) North-South Bks NYC.
Williams, Sue, compiled by. Strawberry Fair. Rothero, Chris, illus. 96p. (gr. 1-6). 14.95 (*0-7136-2676-3*, Pub. by A&C Black UK) Talman.
Wilson, Etta, ed. My Play a Tune Book: Christmas Songs. Harrison, Susan, illus. 26p. (gr. k up). 1987. 15.95 (*0-938971-05-0*) JTG Nashville.
—My Play a Tune Book: Twelve Favorite Bible Songs. Mahan, Benton, illus. 26p. (ps up). 1988. 12.95 (*0-687-27554-7*) JTG Nashville.
Wilson, Valerie & Hull, Shirley, eds. Preschoolers Sing & Say. (ps). 1976. wire spiral bdg. 3.50 (*0-87227-045-9*) Reg Baptist.
The World Is a Rainbow. (Illus.). 80p. (Orig.). 1994. pap. 10.95 (*0-7935-2934-4*, 00815028) H Leonard.
Yolen, Jane. Jane Yolen's Old MacDonald Songbook. Hoffman, Rosekrans, illus. LC 93-73303. 96p. (ps-1). 1994. 16.95 (*1-56397-281-6*) Boyds Mills Pr.
—The Lullaby Songbook. Mikolaycak, Charles, illus. LC 85-752885. 32p. (ps up). 1986. 13.95 (*0-15-249903-2*, HB Juv Bks) HarBrace.
Yolen, Jane, ed. Jane Yolen's Mother Goose Songbook. Hoffman, Rosekrans, illus. Stemple, Adam, contrib. by. (Illus.). 96p. (ps-7). 1992. PLB 16.95 (*1-878093-52-5*) Boyds Mills Pr.
—Jane Yolen's Songs of Summer. Moore, Cyd, illus. Stemple, Adam, designed by. LC 92-85034. (Illus.). 32p. 1993. 12.95 (*1-56397-110-0*, Wordsong) Boyds Mills Pr.

SONGS, NATIONAL
see National Songs
SONGS, POPULAR
see Music, Popular (Songs, etc.)
SOOTHSAYING
see Divination
SOPORIFICS
see Narcotics
SORCERY
see Occult Sciences; Witchcraft
SOTO, HERNANDO DE, 1500?-1542

Carson, Robert. Hernando de Soto: Expedition to the Mississippi River. LC 91-12665. 128p. (gr. 3 up). 1991. PLB 20.55 (*0-516-03065-5*) Childrens.
Whitman, Sylvia. Hernando de Soto & the Explorers of the American South. Goetzmann, William H., ed. Collins, Michael, intro. by. (Illus.). 112p. (gr. 5 up). 1991. lib. bdg. 18.95 (*0-7910-1301-4*) Chelsea Hse.

SOUND

Ardley, Neil. Science Book of Sound. 29p. (gr. 2-5). 1991. 9.95 (*0-15-200579-X*, HB Juv Bks) HarBrace.
—Sound Waves to Music: Projects with Sound. LC 90-3249. (Illus.). 32p. (gr. 5-8). 1990. PLB 12.40 (*0-531-17236-8*, Gloucester Pr) Watts.
Barrett, Sally. The Sound of the Week. 144p. (gr. k-4). 1980. 12.95 (*0-916456-63-3*, GA 184) Good Apple.
Berger, Melvin. All about Sound. (ps-3). 1994. pap. 3.95 (*0-590-46760-3*) Scholastic Inc.
Brandt, Keith. Sound. Sweat, Lynn, illus. LC 84-2632. 32p. (gr. 3-6). 1985. PLB 9.49 (*0-8167-0128-8*); pap. text ed. 2.95 (*0-8167-0129-6*) Troll Assocs.
Brown, Craig. City Sounds. LC 90-25632. (Illus.). 24p. (ps-4). 1992. 14.00 (*0-688-10028-7*); PLB 13.93 (*0-688-10029-5*) Greenwillow.
Cash, Terry. Sound. Chen, Kuo K. & Bull, Peter, illus. LC 89-50001. 40p. (gr. 5-6). 1989. PLB 12.90 (*0-531-19064-1*, Warwick) Watts.
Cooper, Jason. Sound. LC 92-8809. 1992. 12.67 (*0-86593-167-4*); 9.50s.p. (*0-685-59296-0*) Rourke Corp.
Darling, David. Sounds Interesting: The Science of Acoustics. LC 91-4002. (Illus.). 60p. (gr. 4-6). 1991. text ed. 13.95 RSBE (*0-87518-477-4*, Dillon) Macmillan Child Grp.
Davies, Kay & Oldfield, Wendy. Sound & Music. LC 91-23475. (Illus.). 32p. (gr. 2-5). 1991. PLB 19.97 (*0-8114-3003-0*); pap. 4.95 (*0-8114-1534-1*) Raintree Steck-V.
Evans, David & Williams, Claudette. Sound & Music. LC 92-53481. (Illus.). 24p. (gr. k-3). 1993. 9.95 (*1-56458-206-X*) Dorling Kindersley.
Kettelkamp, Larry. The Magic of Sound. Rev. ed. Kramer, Anthony, illus. LC 82-6510. 96p. (gr. 4-6). 1982. lib. bdg. 12.88 (*0-688-01493-3*) Morrow Jr Bks.
Knight, David C. All about Sound. Johnson, Lewis, illus. LC 82-17387. 32p. (gr. 3-6). 1983. PLB 10.59 (*0-89375-878-7*); pap. text ed. 2.95 (*0-89375-879-5*) Troll Assocs.
Lampton, Christopher F. Sound: More Than What You Hear. LC 91-22331. (Illus.). 96p. (gr. 6 up). 1992. lib. bdg. 16.95 (*0-89490-327-6*) Enslow Pubs.
Morgan, Sally & Morgan, Adrian. Using Sound. LC 93-31720. (Illus.). 48p. (gr. 5-9). 1994. 14.95x (*0-8160-2981-4*) Facts on File.
Oxlade, Chris. Science Magic with Sound. Thompson, Ian, illus. LC 94-5550. 30p. (gr. 2-5). 1994. 12.95 (*0-8120-6446-1*); pap. 4.95 (*0-8120-1985-7*) Barron.
Peacock, Graham. Sound. LC 93-7521. (Illus.). (gr. 2-5). 1993. 14.95 (*1-56847-074-6*) Thomson Lrning.
Pomeroy, Johanna P. Content Area Reading Skills Sound & Hearing: Detecting Sequence. (Illus.). (gr. 4). 1987. pap. text ed. 3.25 (*0-89525-860-9*) Ed Activities.
Preschool Color & Learn: Sounds All Around. (ps). 1992. pap. 1.95 (*0-590-45037-9*) Scholastic Inc.
Robinson, Fay. Sound All Around. LC 93-38592. (Illus.). 32p. (ps-2). 1994. PLB 10.75 (*0-516-06024-4*) Childrens.
Searle-Barnes, Bonita. Sound. (Illus.). 32p. (gr. k-3). 1993. 6.99 (*0-7459-2692-4*) Lion USA.
—The Wonder of God's World: Sound. Smithson, Colin, illus. LC 92-44284. 1993. 6.99 (*0-7459-2023-3*) Lion USA.
Sound. (Illus.). 56p. (gr. 7-12). 1990. 8.80 (*0-941008-88-6*) Tops Learning.
Thompson, Bob. How to Whistle. Regan, Dan, illus. LC 93-40396. 24p. (gr. 3-6). 1994. pap. 1.95 (*0-8167-3443-7*, Pub. by Watermill Pr) Troll Assocs.
Wittner, Seth H. Sounds Around Us. Nusbaum, Linda, illus. 32p. (Orig.). (ps). 1988. Incl. audio-cassette. pap. 9.95 (*0-9619269-8-8*) Sound World Record.
Wood, Robert W. Forty-Nine Easy Experiments with Acoustics. (Illus.). 224p. 1990. 16.95 (*0-8306-7392-X*, 3392); pap. 9.95 (*0-8306-3392-8*) TAB Bks.

SOUND–EXPERIMENTS

Baker, Wendy & Haslam, Andrew. Sound: A Creative Hands-on Approach to Science. LC 92-30104. (Illus.). 48p. (gr. 2-5). 1993. pap. 12.95 POB (*0-689-71665-6*, Aladdin) Macmillan Child Grp.
Davies, Kay & Oldfield, Wendy. Sound & Music. LC 91-23475. (Illus.). 32p. (gr. 2-5). 1991. PLB 19.97 (*0-8114-3003-0*); pap. 4.95 (*0-8114-1534-1*) Raintree Steck-V.
Gardner, Robert. Experimenting with Sound. LC 91-4012. (Illus.). 128p. (gr. 9-12). 1991. PLB 13.40 (*0-531-12503-3*) Watts.
Glover, David. Sound & Light. LC 92-40213. 32p. (gr. 1-4). 1993. 10.95 (*1-85697-839-7*, Kingfisher LKC); pap. 5.95 (*1-85697-935-0*) LKC.
Hewitt, Sally. Puff & Blow. LC 94-16910. (Illus.). 24p. (ps-3). 1994. PLB 14.40 (*0-516-07993-X*); pap. 4.95 (*0-516-47993-8*) Childrens.
—Squeak & Roar. LC 94-12309. (Illus.). 24p. (ps-3). 1994. PLB 14.40 (*0-516-07995-6*); pap. 4.95 (*0-516-47995-4*) Childrens.

Kerrod, Robin. Sounds & Music. LC 90-25543. (Illus.). 32p. (gr. 3-8). 1991. PLB 9.95 (*1-85435-270-9*) Marshall Cavendish.

King, Virginia. Vibrating Things Make Sound. Mancini, Rob, illus. LC 93-114. 1994. pap. write for info. (*0-383-03724-7*) SRA Schl Grp.

Rowe, Julian & Perham, Molly. Making Sounds. LC 92-13738. (Illus.). 32p. (gr. 1-4). 1993. PLB 13.95 (*0-516-08136-5*) Childrens.

Searle-Barnes, Bonita. Sound. (Illus.). 32p. (gr. k-3). 1993. 6.99 (*0-7459-2692-4*) Lion USA.

Seller, Mick. Sound, Noise & Music. LC 92-33923. (Illus.). 32p. (gr. 5-8). 1993. PLB 12.40 (*0-531-17408-5*, Gloucester Pr) Watts.

Taylor, Barbara. Sound. LC 92-348. 1992. 12.40 (*0-531-17382-8*, Gloucester Pr) Watts.

—Sound & Music. LC 91-8740. (Illus.). 32p. (gr. 5-8). 1991. PLB 12.40 (*0-531-14185-3*) Watts.

Ward, Alan. Experimenting with Sound. (Illus.). 48p. (gr. 2-7). 1991. lib. bdg. 12.95 (*0-7910-1511-4*) Chelsea Hse.

—Sound & Music. LC 92-370. 1993. 11.40 (*0-531-14237-X*) Watts.

SOUND-RECORDING AND REPRODUCING

Shipton, Alyn. Singing. LC 93-20006. (Illus.). 32p. (gr. 1-8). 1993. PLB 19.97 (*0-8114-2315-8*) Raintree Steck-V.

SOUND EFFECTS

see Sounds

SOUND WAVES

Wood, Nicholas & Rye, Jennifer. Listen...What Do You Hear? Douglas, Julie, illus. LC 90-40136. 32p. (gr. k-3). 1991. lib. bdg. 11.59 (*0-8167-2120-3*); pap. text ed. 3.95 (*0-8167-2121-1*) Troll Assocs.

SOUNDS

Arnold, Tedd, illus. Sounds. 16p. (ps). 1992. pap. 3.95 (*0-671-77826-9*, Little Simon) S&S Trade.

Conrad, Pam. Animal Lingo. Falk, Barbara B., illus. LC 93-22163. 1995. 15.00 (*0-06-023401-6*); PLB 14.89 (*0-06-023402-4*) HarpC Child Bks.

De Zutter, Hank. Who Says a Dog Goes Bow-Wow? LC 92-4232. (ps-3). 1993. pap. 15.00 (*0-385-30659-8*) Doubleday.

Dodds, Dayle A. Do Bunnies Talk? Dubanevich, Arlene, illus. LC 91-13434. 32p. (ps-1). 1992. 15.00 (*0-06-020248-3*); PLB 14.89 (*0-06-020249-1*) HarpC Child Bks.

Ferarro, Bonita. Letters & Sounds. Robison, Don, illus. 32p. (Orig.). (ps). 1993. wkbk. 1.99 (*1-56189-059-6*) Amer Educ Pub.

Gelbart, Ofra. Sounds I Hear. Kriss, David, tr. from HEB. Eagle, Mike, illus. 24p. (Orig.). (ps). 1992. pap. text ed. 3.00x (*1-56134-138-X*) Dushkin Pub.

Gregorich, Barbara. Los Sonidos para Empezar: Beginning Sounds. Hoffman, Joan, ed. Shepherd-Bartram, tr. from ENG. Pape, Richard, illus. (SPA.). 32p. (Orig.). (ps). 1987. wkbk. 1.99 (*0-938256-77-7*, 02077) Sch Zone Pub Co.

Hughes, Joleen. Sounds! LC 93-46323. 1994. PLB 4.99 (*0-517-10152-1*, Derrydale Bks) Random Hse Value.

Jennings, Terry. Making Sounds. LC 90-3227. (Illus.). 24p. (gr. k-4). 1990. PLB 10.90 (*0-531-17212-0*, Gloucester Pr) Watts.

—Sounds. LC 88-36213. (Illus.). 32p. (gr. 3-6). 1989. pap. 4.95 (*0-516-48443-5*) Childrens.

Kratky, Lada J. Los Animales y Sus Crias. (SPA., Illus.). 24p. (Orig.). (gr. 1-3). 1991. pap. text ed. 29.95 big bk. (*1-56334-020-8*); pap. text ed. 6.00 small bk. (*1-56334-034-8*) Hampton-Brown.

Lieberman, Lillian. ABC Sounds. 64p. (gr. k-2). 1984. 6.95 (*0-912107-11-1*) Monday Morning Bks.

McConnell, Em. Strange Sounds. Moser, Jeanie W., illus. (gr. k-3). Bk. & cassette 4.95 (*0-932715-09-5*) Evans FL.

MacKinnon, Debbie. What Noise? Sieveking, Anthea, photos by. LC 92-43651. (Illus.). (gr. 4 up). 1994. 10. 99 (*0-8037-1510-2*) Dial Bks Young.

Mangelsen, Thomas D. A Time for Singing. LC 93-36772. (Illus.). 32p. (ps-3). 1994. 13.99 (*0-525-65096-2*, Cobblehill Bks) Dutton Child Bks.

Morris, Neil. What a Noise: A Fun Book of Sounds. Stevenson, Peter, illus. 32p. (ps-2). 1991. PLB 13.50 (*0-87614-670-1*) Carolrhoda Bks.

Oliver, Stephen, photos by. Noises. LC 90-8587. (Illus.). 24p. (ps-k). 1991. 6.95 (*0-679-81161-3*) Random Bks Yng Read.

Robinson, Marc. Cock-a-Doodle Doo! What Does It Sound Like to You? Jenkins, Steve, illus. LC 92-30961. 32p. 1993. 12.95 (*1-55670-267-1*) Stewart Tabori & Chang.

Ross, Katharine. The Little Quiet Book. Hirashima, Jean, illus. LC 88-62101. 28p. (ps). 1989. bds. 2.95 (*0-394-82899-2*) Random Bks Yng Read.

Silvers, Vicki. Sing a Song of Sound. Ehlert, Lois, illus. LC 72-90695. 32p. (ps-2). 1973. 7.95 (*0-87592-046-2*) Scroll Pr.

Snow, Alan. The Monster Book of ABC Sounds. Snow, Alan, illus. LC 90-39384. 32p. (ps-2). 1991. 12.95 (*0-8037-0935-8*) Dial Bks Young.

Spier, Peter. Crash! Bang! Boom! (ps-1). 1990. 5.95 (*0-385-26569-7*) Doubleday.

Tallarico, Tony. Sounds. (Illus.). 28p. (ps). 1992. 2.95 (*0-448-40428-1*, G&D) Putnam Pub Group.

World's Best Scary, Spooky Sounds, 2 bks. (gr. 4 up). 1992. pap. 10.99 incl. cassette (*0-8069-5690-9*) Sterling.

SOUNDS-FICTION

Alda, Arlene. Pig, Horse, or Cow, Don't Wake Me Now. Alda, Arlene, photos by. LC 93-44695. (Illus.). 1994. 13.95 (*0-385-32032-9*) Doubleday.

Artell, Mike. Who Said "Moo"? Artell, Mike, illus. 12p. (ps-k). 1994. pap. 7.95 (*0-689-71811-X*, Aladdin) Macmillan Child Grp.

Baylor, Byrd. The Other Way to Listen. Parnall, Peter, illus. LC 78-23430. 32p. (ps-3). 1978. SBE 14.95 (*0-684-16017-X*, Scribners Young Read) Macmillan Child Grp.

Bridwell, Norman. Clifford's Noisy Day. (Illus.). 1992. bds. 3.95 (*0-590-45737-3*, 036, Cartwheel) Scholastic Inc.

Brown, Margaret W. The Country Noisy Book. Weisgard, Leonard, photos by. LC 93-4755. 48p. (ps-1). 1988. 15.00 (*0-06-020810-4*); PLB 14.89 (*0-06-020811-2*) HarpC Child Bks.

—The Indoor Noisy Book. new ed. Weisgard, Leonard, illus. LC 92-46879. 48p. (ps-1). 1986. 15.00 (*0-06-020820-1*); PLB 15.89 (*0-06-020821-X*) HarpC Child Bks.

—The Noisy Book. new ed. Weisgard, Leonard, illus. LC 92-8322. 48p. (ps-1). 1939. 15.00 (*0-06-020830-9*); PLB 14.89 (*0-06-020831-7*) HarpC Child Bks.

—The Noisy Book. new ed. Weisgard, Leonard, illus. LC 92-8322. 48p. (ps-1). 1939. pap. 4.95 (*0-06-443001-4*, Trophy) HarpC Child Bks.

—The Quiet Noisy Book. new ed. Weisgard, Leonard, illus. LC 92-8320. 40p. (ps-1). 1993. pap. 4.95 (*0-06-443215-7*, Trophy) HarpC Child Bks.

—The Seashore Noisy Book. new ed. Weisgard, Leonard, illus. LC 92-31433. 48p. (ps-1). 1993. 15.00 (*0-06-020840-6*); PLB 15.89 (*0-06-020841-4*) HarpC Child Bks.

—The Summer Noisy Book. new ed. Weisgard, Leonard, illus. LC 92-31435. 40p. (ps-1). 1993. 15.00 (*0-06-020855-4*); PLB 15.89 (*0-06-020856-2*) HarpC Child Bks.

—The Winter Noisy Book. new ed. Shaw, Charles G., illus. LC 92-46880. 48p. (ps-1). 1986. 15.00 (*0-06-020865-1*); PLB 15.89 (*0-06-020866-X*) HarpC Child Bks.

Burton, Marilee R. One Little Chickadee. Street, Janet, illus. LC 93-27271. (gr. 2 up). 1993. 15.00 (*0-688-12651-0*, Tambourine Bks); PLB 14.93 (*0-688-12652-9*) Morrow.

Carroll, Kathleen S. One Red Rooster. Barbier, Suzette, illus. 32p. (ps). 1992. 13.45 (*0-395-60195-9*) HM.

Christiansen, C. B. Mara in the Morning. Stock, Catherine, illus. LC 90-25049. 32p. (gr. k-3). 1991. RSBE 13.95 (*0-689-31616-X*, Atheneum Child Bk) Macmillan Child Grp.

Cohen, Caron L. Whiffle Squeek. Rand, Ted, illus. 32p. (ps-3). 1994. pap. 4.99 (*0-14-050448-6*) Puffin Bks.

Cosgrove, Stephen. Tinkling. (ps-3). 1992. pap. 3.95 (*0-307-13451-2*) Western Pub.

Dijs, Carla & Moerbeek, Kees. Bee Says Buzz. (gr. 3 up). 1990. 9.95 (*0-85953-222-4*) Childs Play.

Dr. Seuss. Mr. Brown Can Moo! Can You? - The Foot Book, 2 bks. reissue ed. Dr. Seuss, illus. (ps-1). 1991. Set, 32p. ea. incl. 2 20-min. cassette 8.95 (*0-679-82036-1*) Random Bks Yng Read.

Grindley, Sally. Shhh! A Lift the Flap Book. Utton, Peter, illus. 32p. (ps-3). 1992. 13.95 (*0-316-32899-5*, Joy St Bks) Little.

Heam, Emily. Woosh! I Heard a Sound. Cooper, Heather, illus. 24p. (ps-1). 1987. pap. 0.99 (*0-920303-21-8*, Pub. by Annick CN) Firefly Bks Ltd.

Hindley, Judy. Soft & Noisy. Aggs, Patrice, illus. LC 91-39110. 32p. (ps). 1992. 13.95 (*1-56282-224-1*); PLB 13.89 (*1-56282-225-X*) Hyprn Child.

Johnson, Angela. Joshua's Night Whispers. Mitchell, Rhonda, illus. LC 93-46412. 12p. (ps). 1994. 4.95 (*0-531-06847-1*) Orchard Bks Watts.

Kline, Suzy W. SHHHH! Fay, Ann, ed. LC 83-26032. (Illus.). (ps-1). 1984. PLB 11.95 (*0-8075-7321-3*) A Whitman.

Koch, Michelle. Hoot, Howl, Hiss. LC 90-38484. (Illus.). 24p. (ps up). 1991. 13.95 (*0-688-09651-4*); PLB 13.88 (*0-688-09652-2*) Greenwillow.

Lotz, Karen E. Snowsong Whistling. Kleven, Elisa, illus. LC 92-47117. 32p. (ps-2). 1993. 14.99 (*0-525-45145-5*, DCB) Dutton Child Bks.

Lunn, Carolyn. Un Murmullo Es Silencioso: A Whisper Is Quiet. Martin, Clovis, illus. LC 88-11968. (SPA.). 32p. (ps-2). 1991. PLB 10.25 (*0-516-32087-4*); pap. 2.95 (*0-516-52087-3*) Childrens.

Maccarone, Grace. Oink! Moo! How Do You Do? Wilhelm, Hans, illus. LC 93-45962. (ps). 1994. 6.95 (*0-590-48161-4*) Scholastic Inc.

McDonald, Megan. Whoo-oo Is It? Schindler, Stephen D., illus. LC 91-18494. 32p. (ps-1). 1992. 14.95 (*0-531-05974-X*); lib. bdg. 14.99 (*0-531-08574-0*) Orchard Bks Watts.

Manushkin, Fran. Peeping & Sleeping. Plecas, Jennifer, illus. LC 93-26297. (ps-3). 1994. 14.95 (*0-395-64339-2*, Clarion Bks) HM.

Martin, Bill, Jr. Polar Bear, Polar Bear, What Do You Hear? Big Book. Carle, Eric, illus. LC 91-13322. 32p. (ps-2). 1992. pap. 18.95 (*0-8050-2346-1*, Bks Young Read) H Holt & Co.

Munsch, Robert. Agu, Agu, Agu: Murmel, Murmel, Murmel. Martchenko, Michael, illus. (SPA.). 32p. (ps-2). 1991. pap. 5.95 (*1-55037-095-2*, Pub. by Annick CN) Firefly Bks Ltd.

Myers, Bernice. Ding-a-Ling-a-Ling. 16p. (ps-2). 1992. pap. 14.95 (*1-56784-055-8*) Newbridge Comms.

Ogburn, Jacqueline K. Noise Lullaby. Sandford, John, illus. LC 93-37417. (gr. 2 up). 1994. 14.00 (*0-688-10452-5*); 13.93 (*0-688-10453-3*) Lothrop.

Potter, Beatrix. Farmyard Noises. 12p. 1991. bds. 3.50 (*0-7232-3784-0*) Warne.

Roennfeldt, Mary. What's That Noise? Roennfeldt, Robert, illus. LC 91-16215. 32p. (ps-1). 1992. 13.95 (*0-531-05972-3*); lib. bdg. 13.99 (*0-531-08572-4*) Orchard Bks Watts.

Scamell, Ragnhild. Buster's Echo. Webster, Genevieve, illus. LC 92-29868. 32p. (ps-2). 1993. 14.00 (*0-06-022883-0*); PLB 13.89 (*0-06-022884-9*) HarpC Child Bks.

Schoberle, Cecile & Stevenson, Harvey. Morning Sounds, Evening Sounds. LC 93-16786. (gr. 4 up). 1994. pap. 14.00 (*0-671-87437-3*, S&S BFYR) S&S Trade.

Serfozo, Mary. Joe Joe. Montezinos, Nina, illus. LC 92-30133. 32p. (ps-k). 1993. SBE 15.95 (*0-689-50578-7*, M K McElderry) Macmillan Child Grp.

Shebar, Sharon. Nightmonsters. Wasserman, Dan, ed. Reese, Bob, illus. (gr. k-1). 1979. 7.95 (*0-89868-068-9*); pap. 2.95 (*0-89868-079-4*) ARO Pub.

Showers, Paul. The Listening Walk. Aliki, illus. LC 90-30526. 32p. (ps-2). 1993. pap. 4.95 (*0-06-443322-6*, Trophy) HarpC Child Bks.

Simon, Francesca. But What Does the Hippopotamus Say? Floate, Helen, illus. LC 93-32297. (ps-1). 1994. 11.95 (*0-15-200029-1*, Gulliver Bks) HarBrace.

Sloat, Teri & Westcott, Nadine B. The Thing That Bothered Farmer Brown. LC 94-24873. (gr. 1-8). 1995. write for info. (*0-531-06883-8*); PLB write for info. (*0-531-08733-6*) Orchard Bks Watts.

Thompson, R. Gurgle Bubble Splash. (Illus.). 24p. (ps-8). 1989. 12.95 (*1-55037-029-4*, Pub. by Annick CN); pap. 4.95 (*1-55037-028-6*, Pub. by Annick CN) Firefly Bks Ltd.

Time-Life Books Editors. Barnyard Babies: Oink, Baa, Moo, Meow, Neigh, Peep. Marshall, Blaine, ed. Time-Life Books Staff, illus. 6p. (ps). 1993. 16.95 (*0-8094-6692-9*) Time-Life.

Wise Brown, Margaret. Seashore Noisy Book. Weisgard, Leonard, illus. LC 92-31433. 48p. (ps-1). 1993. pap. 4.95 (*0-06-443329-3*, Trophy) HarpC Child Bks.

Ziefert, Harriet. Oh What a Noisy Farm. Bolum, Emily, illus. LC 94-15171. 1994. write for info. (*0-688-13260-X*, Tambourine Bks); PLB write for info. (*0-688-13261-8*, Tambourine Bks) Morrow.

Zimmerman, Andrea G. & Clemesha, David. The Cow Buzzed. Meisel, Paul, illus. LC 91-31905. 32p. (ps-1). 1993. 15.00 (*0-06-020808-2*); PLB 14.89 (*0-06-020809-0*) HarpC Child Bks.

SOUNDS-POETRY

Kuskin, Karla. City Noise. Flower, Renee, illus. LC 91-44213. 32p. (ps-3). 1994. 15.00 (*0-06-021076-1*); PLB 14.89 (*0-06-021077-X*) HarpC Child Bks.

SOUPS

Palmer, Michele. Zoup Soup. Gugler, Janine, illus. LC 78-66342. (ps-1). 1978. pap. 1.95 (*0-932306-00-4*) Rocking Horse.

SOUSA, JOHN PHILIP, 1854-1932

Greene, Carol. John Philip Sousa: The March King. LC 91-37891. (Illus.). 48p. (gr. k-3). PLB 12.85 (*0-516-04226-2*); pap. 4.95, Jul. 1992 (*0-516-44226-0*) Childrens.

SOUTH, THE

see Southern States

SOUTH AFRICA

see Africa, South

SOUTH AFRICA, REPUBLIC OF

Angelou, Maya. My Painted House, My Friendly Chicken, & Me. Courtney-Clarke, Margaret, photos by. LC 93-45735. (Illus.). 48p. (ps-5). 1994. 16.00 (*0-517-59667-9*, Clarkson Potter) Crown Pub Group.

Griffiths, I. Crisis in South Africa. (Illus.). 80p. (gr. 7 up). 1988. PLB 18.60 (*0-86592-035-4*) Rourke Corp.

Harris, Sarah. Sharpeville. (gr. 7 up). 1989. 19.95 (*0-85219-767-5*, Pub. by Batsford UK) Trafalgar.

Hoobler, Dorothy & Hoobler, Thomas. Mandela: The Man, the Struggle, the Triumph. (Illus.). 144p. (gr. 9-12). 1992. PLB 14.40 (*0-531-11141-5*) Watts.

Jacobsen, Karen. South Africa. LC 89-10044. 48p. (gr. k-4). 1989. PLB 12.85 (*0-516-01176-6*); pap. 4.95 (*0-516-41176-4*) Childrens.

Leas, Allan. South Africa. (Illus.). 72p. (gr. 7-12). 1992. 22.95 (*0-7134-6499-2*, Pub. by Batsford UK) Trafalgar.

Paton, Jonathan. The Land & People of South Africa. LC 89-2477. (Illus.). 304p. (gr. 6 up). 1990. 19.00 (*0-397-32361-1*, Lipp Jr Bks); PLB 18.89 (*0-397-32362-X*, Lipp Jr Bks) HarpC Child Bks.

Pogrund, Benjamin. Nelson Mandela. LC 91-50541. (Illus.). 68p. (gr. 3-4). 1992. PLB 19.93 (*0-8368-0621-2*) Gareth Stevens Inc.

Rosmarin, Ike. South Africa. LC 92-38755. 1993. 21.95 (*1-85435-575-9*) Marshall Cavendish.

SOUTH AFRICA, REPUBLIC OF-FICTION

Case, Dianne. Love, David. Andreasen, Dan, illus. 144p. (gr. 3-7). 1991. 14.95 (*0-525-67350-4*, Lodestar Bks) Dutton Child Bks.

Gordon, Sheila. Middle of Somewhere: A Story of South Africa. (gr. 4-7). 1992. pap. 3.50 (*0-553-15991-7*) Bantam.

Isadora, Rachel. At the Crossroads. Isadora, Rachel, illus. 32p. (ps up). 1994. pap. 4.95 (*0-688-13103-4*, Mulberry) Morrow.

—Over the Green Hills. LC 91-12761. 32p. (ps up). 1992. 14.00 (*0-688-10509-2*); PLB 13.93 (*0-688-10510-6*) Greenwillow.

Lewin, Hugh. Jafta. Kopper, Lisa, illus. 24p. (ps-3). 1989. pap. 4.95 (*0-87614-494-6*, First Ave Edns) Lerner Pubns.
—Jafta & the Wedding. Kopper, Lisa, illus. LC 82-12836. 24p. (ps-3). 1983. pap. 4.95 (*0-87614-497-0*) Carolrhoda Bks.
—Jafta: The Homecoming. Kopper, Lisa, illus. LC 93-12945. 32p. (ps-2). 1994. 8.99 (*0-679-84722-7*); PLB 9.99 (*0-679-94722-1*) Knopf Bks Yng Read.
—Jafta's Father. Kopper, Lisa, illus. 24p. (ps-3). 1989. pap. 4.95 (*0-87614-496-2*, First Ave Edns) Lerner Pubns.
—Jafta's Mother. Kopper, Lisa, illus. 24p. (ps-3). 1989. pap. 4.95 (*0-87614-495-4*, First Ave Edns) Lerner Pubns.
Maartens, Maretha. Paper Bird: A Novel of South Africa. 144p. (gr. 4-9). 1991. 13.45 (*0-395-56490-5*, Clarion Bks) HM.
Mennen, Ingrid & Daly, Niki. Somewhere in Africa. Maritz, Nicolaas, illus. LC 91-19379. 32p. (ps-3). 1992. 13.00 (*0-525-44848-9*, DCB) Dutton Child Bks.
Naidoo, Beverley. Chain of Fire. Velasquez, Eric, illus. LC 89-27551. 256p. (gr. 6 up). 1990. (Lipp Jr Bks); PLB 13.89 (*0-397-32427-8*, Lipp Jr Bks) HarpC Child Bks.
—Chain of Fire. LC 89-27551. 256p. (gr. 6 up). 1993. pap. 3.95 (*0-06-440468-4*, Trophy) HarpC Child Bks.
—Journey to Jo'burg: A South African Story. reissued ed. Velasquez, Eric, illus. LC 85-45508. 96p. (gr. 4-7). 1986. 14.00 (*0-397-32168-6*, Lipp Jr Bks); PLB 13.89 (*0-397-32169-4*) HarpC Child Bks.
Rochman, Hazel, ed. Somehow Tenderness Survives: Stories of Southern Africa. LC 88-916. 160p. (gr. 7 up). 1988. PLB 12.89 (*0-06-025023-2*) HarpC Child Bks.
Sacks, Margaret. Beyond Safe Boundaries. LC 88-27311. 160p. (gr. 7 up). 1989. 13.95 (*0-525-67281-8*, Lodestar Bks) Dutton Child Bks.
—Themba. Clay, Wil, illus. LC 92-9754. 48p. (gr. 2-5). 1992. 12.00 (*0-525-67414-4*, Lodestar Bks) Dutton Child Bks.
Silver, Norman. Python Dance. 192p. (gr. 8 up). 1993. 14.99 (*0-525-45161-7*, DCB) Dutton Child Bks.
Williams, Michael. Crocodile Burning. 192p. (gr. 7 up). 1992. 15.00 (*0-525-67401-2*, Lodestar Bks) Dutton Child Bks.
—The Genuine Half-Moon Kid. 192p. (gr. 7 up). 1994. 15.99 (*0-525-67470-5*, Lodestar Bks) Dutton Child Bks.
—Into the Valley. LC 92-25116. 176p. (gr. 5-9). 1993. 14.95 (*0-399-22516-1*, Philomel Bks) Putnam Pub Group.

SOUTH AMERICA

Byrnes, Ron. Exploring the Developing World: Life in Africa & Latin America. (Illus.). (gr. 7-12). 1993. pap. 26.95 (*0-943804-78-7*) U of Denver Teach.
Georges, D. V. South America. LC 86-9584. (Illus.). 48p. (gr. k-4). 1986. PLB 12.85 (*0-516-01296-7*); pap. 4.95 (*0-516-41296-5*) Childrens.
Greene, Carol. Simon Bolivar: South American Liberator. LC 89-34663. (gr. 4 up). 1989. PLB 14.40 (*0-516-03267-4*) Childrens.
Henry-Biabaud, Chantal. Living in South America. Bogard, Vicki, tr. from FRE. Dagan, Bernard, illus. LC 90-50773. 38p. (gr. k-5). 1991. 5.95 (*0-944589-28-6*, 286) Young Discovery Lib.
Morrison, Marion. Ecuador, Peru, Bolivia. (Illus.). 96p. (gr. 6-12). 1992. PLB 22.80 (*0-8114-2453-7*) Raintree Steck-V.
Sabin, Francene. South America. Eitzen, Allan, illus. LC 84-8586. 32p. (gr. 3-6). 1985. PLB 9.49 (*0-8167-0292-6*); pap. text ed. 2.95 (*0-8167-0293-4*) Troll Assocs.

SOUTH AMERICA–DISCOVERY AND EXPLORATION

see America–Discovery and Exploration

SOUTH AMERICA–FICTION

Lester, Alison. Isabella's Bed. Lester, Alison, illus. LC 92-22935. 32p. (gr. k-3). 1993. Repr. of 1991 ed. 14.95 (*0-395-65565-X*) HM.
Schaefer, Jackie. Miranda's Day to Dance. Schaefer, Jackie, illus. LC 94-9372. (ps-k). 1994. 14.95 (*0-02-781111-5*) Macmillan.
Windle, Jeanette. Parker Twins: Adventures in South America. 412p. 1994. pap. 8.99 (*0-88070-647-3*, Multnomah Bks) Questar Pubs.

SOUTH AMERICA–HISTORY

Adler, David A. A Picture Book of Simon Bolivar. Casilla, Robert, illus. LC 91-19419. 32p. (ps-3). 1992. reinforced bdg. 14.95 (*0-8234-0927-9*) Holiday.
Hobbler, Dorothy & Hobbler, Thomas. South American Portraits. LC 93-38361. 1994. PLB 22.80 (*0-8114-6383-4*) Raintree Steck-V.
Simon Bolivar. (Illus.). 32p. (gr. 3-5). 1988. PLB 19.97 (*0-8172-2902-7*) Raintree Steck-V.

SOUTH ATLANTIC STATES

see Atlantic States

SOUTH CAROLINA

Aylesworth, Thomas G. & Aylesworth, Virginia L. Lower Atlantic (North Carolina, South Carolina) (Illus.). 64p. (gr. 3 up). 1991. lib. bdg. 16.95 (*0-7910-1042-2*) Chelsea Hse.
Carole Marsh South Carolina Books, 45 bks. 1994. PLB 1052.75 set (*0-7933-1315-5*); pap. 602.75 set (*0-7933-5202-9*) Gallopade Pub Group.
Carpenter, Allan. South Carolina. LC 79-11453. (Illus.). 96p. (gr. 4 up). 1979. PLB 16.95 (*0-516-04140-1*) Childrens.
Coy, Stanley C. Beaufort County: "Queen of the Carolina Sea Islands" Activity Book. 21p. (gr. 3-5). 1992. pap. 3.95 (*1-881459-00-4*) Eagle Pr SC.
Fradin, Dennis B. South Carolina. LC 91-32921. 64p. (gr. 3-5). 1992. PLB 16.45 (*0-516-03840-0*); pap. 5.95 (*0-516-43840-9*) Childrens.
Fredeen, Charles. South Carolina. 72p. (gr. 3-6). 1991. PLB 17.50 (*0-8225-2712-X*) Lerner Pubns.
Gasque, Pratt. Rum Gully Tales from Tuck'em Inn. (Illus.). 148p. 1990. 14.95 (*0-87844-094-1*); pap. 8.95 (*0-87844-095-X*) Sandlapper Pub Co.
Hembree, Mike, et al. Journey Home. Todd, Sharon, ed. (Illus.). 208p. (gr. 8 up). 1988. text ed. 22.95 (*0-685-22594-1*) GNP Pub.
Jones, Lewis P. South Carolina: One of the Fifty States. LC 85-1882. (Illus.). 720p. (gr. 8). 1985. text ed. 30.95 (*0-87844-062-3*); tchr's. manual avail. (*0-87844-063-1*) Sandlapper Pub Co.
Kent, Deborah. South Carolina. LC 89-858. 144p. (gr. 4 up). 1989. PLB 20.55 (*0-516-00486-7*) Childrens.
—South Carolina. 188p. 1993. text ed. 15.40 (*1-56956-172-9*) W A T Braille.
McDaniel, Thomas. At Home in South Carolina. (gr. 3). 1991. 29.95 (*0-87844-099-2*) Sandlapper Pub Co.
Marsh, Carole. Avast, Ye Slobs! South Carolina Pirate Trivia. (Illus.). 1994. PLB 24.95 (*0-7933-1028-8*); pap. 14.95 (*0-7933-1027-X*); computer disk 29.95 (*0-7933-1029-6*) Gallopade Pub Group.
—The Beast of the South Carolina Bed & Breakfast. (Illus.). 1994. PLB 24.95 (*0-7933-1995-1*); pap. 14.95 (*0-7933-1996-X*); computer disk 29.95 (*0-7933-1997-8*) Gallopade Pub Group.
—Bow Wow! South Carolina Dogs in History, Mystery, Legend, Lore, Humor & More! (Illus.). (gr. 3-12). 1994. PLB 24.95 (*0-7933-3587-6*); pap. 14.95 (*0-7933-3588-4*); computer disk 29.95 (*0-7933-3589-2*) Gallopade Pub Group.
—Christopher Columbus Comes to South Carolina! Includes Reproducible Activities for Kids! (Illus.). (gr. 3-12). 1994. PLB 24.95 (*0-7933-3740-2*); pap. 14.95 (*0-7933-3741-0*); computer disk 29.95 (*0-7933-3742-9*) Gallopade Pub Group.
—The Hard-to-Believe-But-True! Book of South Carolina History, Mystery, Trivia, Legend, Lore, Humor & More. (Illus.). 1994. PLB 24.95 (*0-7933-1025-3*); pap. 14.95 (*0-7933-1024-5*); computer disk 29.95 (*0-7933-1026-1*) Gallopade Pub Group.
—If My South Carolina Mama Ran the World! (Illus.). 1994. lib. bdg. 24.95 (*0-7933-2003-8*); pap. 14.95 (*0-7933-2004-6*); computer disk 29.95 (*0-7933-2005-4*) Gallopade Pub Group.
—Jurassic Ark! South Carolina Dinosaurs & Other Prehistoric Creatures. (gr. k-12). 1994. PLB 24.95 (*0-7933-7548-7*); pap. 14.95 (*0-7933-7549-5*); computer disk 29.95 (*0-7933-7550-9*) Gallopade Pub Group.
—Let's Quilt Our South Carolina County. 1994. lib. bdg. 24.95 (*0-7933-7233-X*); pap. text ed. 14.95 (*0-7933-7234-8*); disk 29.95 (*0-7933-7235-6*) Gallopade Pub Group.
—Let's Quilt Our South Carolina Town. 1994. lib. bdg. 24.95 (*0-7933-7083-3*); pap. text ed. 14.95 (*0-7933-7084-1*); disk 29.95 (*0-7933-7085-X*) Gallopade Pub Group.
—Let's Quilt South Carolina & Stuff It Topographically! (Illus.). 1994. PLB 24.95 (*0-7933-1987-0*); pap. 14.95 (*1-55609-053-6*); computer disk 29.95 (*0-7933-1988-9*) Gallopade Pub Group.
—Meow! South Carolina Cats in History, Mystery, Legend, Lore, Humor & More! (Illus.). (gr. 3-12). 1994. PLB 24.95 (*0-7933-3434-9*); pap. 14.95 (*0-7933-3435-7*); computer disk 29.95 (*0-7933-3436-5*) Gallopade Pub Group.
—My First Book about South Carolina. (gr. k-4). 1994. PLB 24.95 (*0-7933-5689-X*); pap. 14.95 (*0-7933-5690-3*); computer disk 29.95 (*0-7933-5691-1*) Gallopade Pub Group.
—Patch, the Pirate Dog: A South Carolina Pet Story. (ps-4). 1994. PLB 24.95 (*0-7933-5536-2*); pap. 14.95 (*0-7933-5537-0*); computer disk 29.95 (*0-7933-5538-9*) Gallopade Pub Group.
—South Carolina & Other State Greats (Biographies) (Illus.). 1994. PLB 24.95 (*0-7933-2006-2*); pap. 14.95 (*0-7933-2007-0*); computer disk 29.95 (*0-7933-2008-9*) Gallopade Pub Group.
—South Carolina Bandits, Bushwackers, Outlaws, Crooks, Devils, Ghosts, Desperadoes & Other Assorted & Sundry Characters! (Illus.). 1994. PLB 24.95 (*0-7933-1010-5*); pap. 14.95 (*0-7933-1009-1*); computer disk 29.95 (*0-7933-1011-3*) Gallopade Pub Group.
—South Carolina Classic Christmas Trivia: Stories, Recipes, Activities, Legends, Lore & More! (Illus.). 1994. PLB 24.95 (*0-7933-1013-X*); pap. 14.95 (*0-7933-1012-1*); computer disk 29.95 (*0-7933-1014-8*) Gallopade Pub Group.
—South Carolina Coastales. (Illus.). 1994. PLB 24.95 (*0-7933-2001-1*); pap. 14.95 (*1-55609-115-X*); computer disk 29.95 (*0-7933-2002-X*) Gallopade Pub Group.
—South Carolina Coastales! 1994. lib. bdg. 24.95 (*0-7933-7305-0*) Gallopade Pub Group.
—South Carolina Dingbats! Bk. 1: A Fun Book of Games, Stories, Activities & More about Our State That's All in Code! for You to Decipher. (Illus.). (gr. 3-12). 1994. PLB 19.95 (*0-7933-3893-X*); pap. 14.95 (*0-7933-3894-8*); computer disk 29.95 (*0-7933-3895-6*) Gallopade Pub Group.
—South Carolina Festival Fun for Kids! (Illus.). (gr. 3-12). 1994. lib. bdg. 24.95 (*0-7933-4046-2*); pap. 14.95 (*0-7933-4047-0*); disk 29.95 (*0-7933-4048-9*) Gallopade Pub Group.
—The South Carolina Hot Air Balloon Mystery. (Illus.). (gr. 2-9). 1994. 24.95 (*0-7933-2678-8*); pap. 14.95 (*0-7933-2679-6*); computer disk 29.95 (*0-7933-2680-X*) Gallopade Pub Group.
—South Carolina Jeopardy! Answers & Questions about Our State! (Illus.). (gr. 3-12). 1994. PLB 24.95 (*0-7933-4199-X*); pap. 14.95 (*0-7933-4200-7*); computer disk 29.95 (*0-7933-4201-5*) Gallopade Pub Group.
—South Carolina "Jography" A Fun Run Thru Our State! (Illus.). 1994. PLB 24.95 (*0-7933-1985-4*); pap. 14.95 (*1-55609-049-8*); computer disk 29.95 (*0-7933-1986-2*) Gallopade Pub Group.
—South Carolina Jography: A Fun Run Through the Palmetto State. (Illus.). 50p. (Orig.). (gr. 3-9). 1994. pap. 14.95 (*0-935326-96-0*) Gallopade Pub Group.
—South Carolina Kid's Cookbook: Recipes, How-to, History, Lore & More! (Illus.). 1994. PLB 24.95 (*0-7933-1022-9*); pap. 14.95 (*0-7933-1021-0*); computer disk 29.95 (*0-7933-1023-7*) Gallopade Pub Group.
—South Carolina Quiz Bowl Crash Course! (Illus.). 1994. PLB 24.95 (*0-7933-1998-6*); pap. 14.95 (*0-7933-1999-4*); computer disk 29.95 (*0-7933-2000-3*) Gallopade Pub Group.
—South Carolina Rollercoasters! (Illus.). (gr. 3-12). 1994. PLB 24.95 (*0-7933-5344-0*); pap. 14.95 (*0-7933-5345-9*); computer disk 29.95 (*0-7933-5346-7*) Gallopade Pub Group.
—South Carolina School Trivia: An Amazing & Fascinating Look at Our State's Teachers, Schools & Students! (Illus.). 1994. PLB 24.95 (*0-7933-1019-9*); pap. 14.95 (*0-7933-1018-0*); computer disk 29.95 (*0-7933-1020-2*) Gallopade Pub Group.
—South Carolina Silly Basketball Sportsmysteries, Vol. 1. (Illus.). 1994. PLB 24.95 (*0-7933-1016-4*); pap. 14.95 (*0-7933-1015-6*); computer disk 29.95 (*0-7933-1017-2*) Gallopade Pub Group.
—South Carolina Silly Basketball Sportsmysteries, Vol. 2. (Illus.). 1994. PLB 24.95 (*0-7933-2009-7*); pap. 14.95 (*0-7933-2010-0*); computer disk 29.95 (*0-7933-2011-9*) Gallopade Pub Group.
—South Carolina Silly Football Sportsmysteries, Vol. 1. (Illus.). 1994. PLB 24.95 (*0-7933-1989-7*); pap. 14.95 (*0-7933-1990-0*); computer disk 29.95 (*0-7933-1991-9*) Gallopade Pub Group.
—South Carolina Silly Football Sportsmysteries, Vol. 2. (Illus.). 1994. PLB 24.95 (*0-7933-1992-7*); pap. 14.95 (*0-7933-1993-5*); computer disk 29.95 (*0-7933-1994-3*) Gallopade Pub Group.
—South Carolina Silly Trivia! (Illus.). 1994. PLB 24.95 (*0-7933-1983-8*); pap. 14.95 (*0-685-54060-X*); computer disk 29.95 (*0-7933-1984-6*) Gallopade Pub Group.
—South Carolina's (Most Devastating!) Disasters & (Most Calamitous!) Catastrophies! (Illus.). 1994. PLB 24.95 (*0-7933-1007-5*); pap. 14.95 (*0-7933-1006-7*); computer disk 29.95 (*0-7933-1008-3*) Gallopade Pub Group.
Russell, Ching Y. A Day on a Shrimp Boat. Littlejohn, Beth, ed. Russell, Phillip K., illus. 57p. (gr. 3-6). 1993. 13.95 (*0-87844-120-4*) Sandlapper Pub Co.
Thompson, Kathleen. South Carolina. 48p. (gr. 3 up). 1986. PLB 19.97 (*0-86514-475-3*) Raintree Steck-V.

SOUTH CAROLINA–FICTION

Bodie, Idella. Ghost in the Capitol. Kovach, Gay H., illus. 116p. (gr. 4-6). 1986. pap. 6.95 (*0-87844-072-0*) Sandlapper Pub Co.
Hogan, Stephen. Johnny Lynch. Nivens, Chuck, illus. 165p. (gr. 5-6). 1991. PLB 13.00x (*0-945253-07-9*) Thornsbury Bailey Brown.
Houston, Gloria. Young Will: A Sunny Land with a Sunny Brook. Sabuda, Robert, illus. LC 94-15220. 1995. write for info. (*0-399-22740-7*, Philomel Bks) Putnam Pub Group.
Schroeder, Alan. Carolina Shout! Fuchs, Bernie, illus. LC 94-17125. (gr. 1-8). 1995. PLB write for info. (*0-8037-1678-8*); write for info. (*0-8037-1676-1*) Dial Bks Young.
Seabrooke, Brenda. The Bridges of Summer. LC 92-11642. 160p. (gr. 5 up). 1992. 14.00 (*0-525-65094-6*, Cobblehill Bks) Dutton Child Bks.
Smothers, Thelma W. Sweet Savannah. Pitt, Jo J. & Lumpkins, Debbie B., eds. 219p. (gr. 8 up). 1994. PLB 20.00 (*1-882188-06-3*) Magnolia Mktg.

SOUTH CAROLINA–HISTORY

Bagwell, Joyce B. Low Country Quake Tales. 88p. 1986. pap. 7.50 (*0-89308-593-6*, SC 84) Southern Hist Pr.
Bahlinger, Nanette M. The Jekyll Island Historic District Coloring Book. Bahlinger, Nanette M., illus. 32p. (Orig.). (gr. 5). 1993. wkbk. 4.00 (*0-9638256-1-5*) N M Bahlinger.
Fradin, Dennis B. The South Carolina Colony. LC 91-32330. (Illus.). 190p. (gr. 4 up). 1992. PLB 17.95 (*0-516-00397-6*) Childrens.
Harris, Hazel. The History of South Carolina in the Building of the Nation. (Illus.). 330p. (gr. 8). 1991. tchr's ed. 15.00 (*0-9628232-1-X*) A G Furman.
Huff, Archie V., Jr. The History of South Carolina in the Building of the Nation. (Illus.). 528p. (gr. 8). 1991. text ed. 20.99 (*0-9628232-0-1*) A G Furman.

Marsh, Carole. Chill Out: Scary South Carolina Tales Based on Frightening South Carolina Truths. (Illus.). 1994. lib. bdg. 24.95 (*0-7933-4774-2*); pap. 14.95 (*0-7933-4775-0*); disk 29.95 (*0-7933-4776-9*) Gallopade Pub Group.

—South Carolina "Crinkum-Crankum" A Funny Word Book about Our State. (Illus.). (gr. 3-12). 1994. 24.95 (*0-7933-4928-1*); pap. 14.95 (*0-7933-4929-X*); computer disk 29.95 (*0-7933-4930-3*) Gallopade Pub Group.

—The South Carolina Mystery Van Takes Off! Book 1: Handicapped South Carolina Kids Sneak Off on a Big Adventure. (Illus.). (gr. 3-12). 1994. 24.95 (*0-7933-5081-6*); pap. 14.95 (*0-7933-5082-4*); computer disk 29.95 (*0-7933-5083-2*) Gallopade Pub Group.

—South Carolina Timeline: A Chronology of South Carolina History, Mystery, Trivia, Legend, Lore & More. (Illus.). (gr. 3-12). 1994. PLB 24.95 (*0-7933-5995-3*); pap. 14.95 (*0-7933-5996-1*); computer disk 29.95 (*0-7933-5997-X*) Gallopade Pub Group.

—South Carolina's Unsolved Mysteries (& Their "Solutions") Includes Scientific Information & Other Activities for Students. (Illus.). (gr. 3-12). 1994. PLB 24.95 (*0-7933-5842-6*); pap. 14.95 (*0-7933-5843-4*); computer disk 29.95 (*0-7933-5844-2*) Gallopade Pub Group.

—Uncle Rebus: South Carolina Picture Stories for Computer Kids. (Illus.). (gr. k-3). 1994. PLB 24.95 (*0-7933-4621-5*); pap. 14.95 (*0-7933-4622-3*); disk 29.95 (*0-7933-4623-1*) Gallopade Pub Group.

SOUTH DAKOTA

Ames, Mary. Memories of the Pasque & Prairie. Wong, Vera M., illus. Thornley, Phyllis, intro. by. (Illus.). 79p. (gr. 9-12). 1987. 13.95 (*0-9619407-0-0*) Country Messenger Inc.

Burdick, Gerry & Schuett, Julie. Puzzling about South Dakota. Gleich, Shannon & Long, Lori, illus. 61p. (Orig.). (gr. 8 up). 1992. pap. 4.95 (*0-9632844-0-1*, 050111557) Dakota Desktop.

Carole Marsh South Dakota Books, 44 bks. 1994. PLB 1027.80 set (*0-7933-1316-3*); pap. 587.80 set (*0-7933-5204-5*) Gallopade Pub Group.

Fradin, Dennis. South Dakota: In Words & Pictures. Wahl, Richard, illus. LC 80-25349. 48p. (gr. 2-5). 1981. PLB 12.95 (*0-516-03941-5*) Childrens.

Jensen, Delwin A. Fort Pierre-Deadwood Trail: Route to the Gold Fields of the Black Hills. (Illus.). 60p. (Orig.). (gr. 8-12). 1989. pap. text ed. 4.00 (*0-9624413-0-9*) D A Jensen.

Lepthien, Emilie U. South Dakota. LC 90-21137. 144p. (gr. 4 up). 1991. PLB 20.55 (*0-516-00487-5*) Childrens.

—South Dakota. 195p. 1993. text ed. 15.40 (*1-56956-143-5*) W A T Braille.

Marsh, Carole. Avast, Ye Slobs! South Dakota Pirate Trivia. (Illus.). 1994. PLB 24.95 (*0-7933-1052-0*); pap. 14.95 (*0-7933-1051-2*); computer disk 29.95 (*0-7933-1053-9*) Gallopade Pub Group.

—The Beast of the South Dakota Bed & Breakfast. (Illus.). 1994. PLB 24.95 (*0-7933-2026-7*); pap. 14.95 (*0-7933-2027-5*); computer disk 29.95 (*0-7933-2028-3*) Gallopade Pub Group.

—Bow Wow! South Dakota Dogs in History, Mystery, Legend, Lore, Humor & More! (Illus.). (gr. 3-12). 1994. PLB 24.95 (*0-7933-3590-6*); pap. 14.95 (*0-7933-3591-4*); computer disk 29.95 (*0-7933-3592-2*) Gallopade Pub Group.

—Chill Out: Scary South Dakota Tales Based on Frightening South Dakota Truths. (Illus.). 1994. lib. bdg. 24.95 (*0-7933-4777-7*); pap. 14.95 (*0-7933-4778-5*); disk 29.95 (*0-7933-4779-3*) Gallopade Pub Group.

—Christopher Columbus Comes to South Dakota! Includes Reproducible Activities for Kids! (Illus.). (gr. 3-12). 1994. PLB 24.95 (*0-7933-3743-7*); pap. 14.95 (*0-7933-3744-5*); computer disk 29.95 (*0-7933-3745-3*) Gallopade Pub Group.

—The Hard-to-Believe-But True! Book of South Dakota History, Mystery, Trivia, Legend, Lore, Humor & More. (Illus.). 1994. PLB 24.95 (*0-7933-1049-0*); pap. 14.95 (*0-7933-1048-2*); computer disk 29.95 (*0-7933-1050-4*) Gallopade Pub Group.

—If My South Dakota Mama Ran the World! (Illus.). 1994. lib. bdg. 24.95 (*0-7933-2035-6*); pap. 14.95 (*0-7933-2036-4*); computer disk 29.95 (*0-7933-2037-2*) Gallopade Pub Group.

—Jurassic Ark! South Dakota Dinosaurs & Other Prehistoric Creatures. (gr. k-12). 1994. PLB 24.95 (*0-7933-7551-7*); pap. 14.95 (*0-7933-7552-5*); computer disk 29.95 (*0-7933-7553-3*) Gallopade Pub Group.

—Let's Quilt Our South Dakota County. 1994. lib. bdg. 24.95 (*0-7933-7236-4*); pap. text ed. 14.95 (*0-7933-7237-2*); disk 29.95 (*0-7933-7238-0*) Gallopade Pub Group.

—Let's Quilt Our South Dakota Town. 1994. lib. bdg. 24.95 (*0-7933-7086-8*); pap. text ed. 14.95 (*0-7933-7087-6*); disk 29.95 (*0-7933-7088-4*) Gallopade Pub Group.

—Let's Quilt South Dakota & Stuff It Topographically! (Illus.). 1994. lib. bdg. 24.95 (*0-7933-2018-6*); pap. 14.95 (*1-55609-136-2*); computer disk 29.95 (*0-7933-2019-4*) Gallopade Pub Group.

—Meow! South Dakota Cats in History, Mystery, Legend, Lore, Humor & More! (Illus.). (gr. 3-12). 1994. PLB 24.95 (*0-7933-3437-3*); pap. 14.95 (*0-7933-3438-1*); computer disk 29.95 (*0-7933-3439-X*) Gallopade Pub Group.

—My First Book about South Dakota. (gr. k-4). 1994. PLB 24.95 (*0-7933-5692-X*); pap. 14.95 (*0-7933-5693-8*); computer disk 29.95 (*0-7933-5694-6*) Gallopade Pub Group.

—Patch, the Pirate Dog: A South Dakota Pet Story. (ps-4). 1994. PLB 24.95 (*0-7933-5539-7*); pap. 14.95 (*0-7933-5540-0*); computer disk 29.95 (*0-7933-5541-9*) Gallopade Pub Group.

—South Dakota & Other State Greats (Biographies) (Illus.). 1994. PLB 24.95 (*0-7933-2038-0*); pap. 14.95 (*0-7933-2039-9*); computer disk 29.95 (*0-7933-2040-2*) Gallopade Pub Group.

—South Dakota Bandits, Bushwackers, Outlaws, Crooks, Devils, Ghosts, Desperadoes & Other Assorted & Sundry Characters! (Illus.). 1994. PLB 24.95 (*0-7933-1034-2*); pap. 14.95 (*0-7933-1033-4*); computer disk 29.95 (*0-7933-1035-0*) Gallopade Pub Group.

—South Dakota Classic Christmas Trivia: Stories, Recipes, Activities, Legends, Lore & More! (Illus.). 1994. PLB 24.95 (*0-7933-1037-7*); pap. 14.95 (*0-7933-1036-9*); computer disk 29.95 (*0-7933-1038-5*) Gallopade Pub Group.

—South Dakota Coastales. (Illus.). 1994. PLB 24.95 (*0-7933-2032-1*); pap. 14.95 (*0-7933-2033-X*); computer disk 29.95 (*0-7933-2034-8*) Gallopade Pub Group.

—South Dakota Coastales! 1994. lib. bdg. 24.95 (*0-7933-7306-9*) Gallopade Pub Group.

—South Dakota "Crinkum-Crankum" A Funny Word Book about Our State. (Illus.). (gr. 3-12). 1994. 24.95 (*0-7933-4931-1*); pap. 14.95 (*0-7933-4932-X*); computer disk 29.95 (*0-7933-4933-8*) Gallopade Pub Group.

—South Dakota Dingbats! Bk. 1: A Fun Book of Games, Stories, Activities & More about Our State That's All in Code! for You to Decipher. (Illus.). (gr. 3-12). 1994. PLB 19.95 (*0-7933-3896-4*); pap. 14.95 (*0-7933-3897-2*); computer disk 29.95 (*0-7933-3898-0*) Gallopade Pub Group.

—South Dakota Festival Fun for Kids! (Illus.). (gr. 3-12). 1994. lib. bdg. 19.95 (*0-7933-4049-7*); pap. 14.95 (*0-7933-4050-0*); disk 29.95 (*0-7933-4051-9*) Gallopade Pub Group.

—The South Dakota Hot Air Balloon Mystery. (Illus.). (gr. 2-9). 1994. 24.95 (*0-7933-2687-7*); pap. 14.95 (*0-7933-2688-5*); computer disk 29.95 (*0-7933-2689-3*) Gallopade Pub Group.

—South Dakota Jeopardy! Answers & Questions about Our State! (Illus.). (gr. 3-12). 1994. PLB 24.95 (*0-7933-4202-3*); pap. 14.95 (*0-7933-4203-1*); computer disk 29.95 (*0-7933-4204-X*) Gallopade Pub Group.

—South Dakota "Jography" A Fun Run Thru Our State! (Illus.). 1994. PLB 24.95 (*0-7933-2015-1*); pap. 14.95 (*0-7933-2016-X*); computer disk 29.95 (*0-7933-2017-8*) Gallopade Pub Group.

—South Dakota Kid's Cookbook: Recipes, How-to, History, Lore & More! (Illus.). 1994. PLB 24.95 (*0-7933-1046-6*); pap. 14.95 (*0-7933-1045-8*); computer disk 29.95 (*0-7933-1047-4*) Gallopade Pub Group.

—The South Dakota Mystery Van Takes Off! Book 1: Handicapped South Dakota Kids Sneak Off on a Big Adventure. (Illus.). (gr. 3-12). 1994. 24.95 (*0-7933-5084-0*); pap. 14.95 (*0-7933-5085-9*); computer disk 29.95 (*0-7933-5086-7*) Gallopade Pub Group.

—South Dakota Quiz Bowl Crash Course! (Illus.). 1994. PLB 24.95 (*0-7933-2029-1*); pap. 14.95 (*0-7933-2030-5*); computer disk 29.95 (*0-7933-2031-3*) Gallopade Pub Group.

—South Dakota Rollercoasters! (Illus.). (gr. 3-12). 1994. PLB 24.95 (*0-7933-5347-5*); pap. 14.95 (*0-7933-5348-3*); computer disk 29.95 (*0-7933-5349-1*) Gallopade Pub Group.

—South Dakota School Trivia: An Amazing & Fascinating Look at Our State's Teachers, Schools & Students! (Illus.). 1994. PLB 24.95 (*0-7933-1043-1*); pap. 14.95 (*0-7933-1042-3*); computer disk 29.95 (*0-7933-1044-X*) Gallopade Pub Group.

—South Dakota Silly Basketball Sportsmysteries, Vol. 1. (Illus.). 1994. PLB 24.95 (*0-7933-1040-7*); pap. 14.95 (*0-7933-1039-3*); computer disk 29.95 (*0-7933-1041-5*) Gallopade Pub Group.

—South Dakota Silly Basketball Sportsmysteries, Vol. 2. (Illus.). 1994. PLB 24.95 (*0-7933-2041-0*); pap. 14.95 (*0-7933-2042-9*); computer disk 29.95 (*0-7933-2043-7*) Gallopade Pub Group.

—South Dakota Silly Football Sportsmysteries, Vol. 1. (Illus.). 1994. PLB 24.95 (*0-7933-2020-8*); pap. 14.95 (*0-7933-2021-6*); computer disk 29.95 (*0-7933-2022-4*) Gallopade Pub Group.

—South Dakota Silly Football Sportsmysteries, Vol. 2. (Illus.). 1994. PLB 24.95 (*0-7933-2023-2*); pap. 14.95 (*0-685-45970-5*); computer disk 29.95 (*0-7933-2025-9*) Gallopade Pub Group.

—South Dakota Silly Trvia! (Illus.). 1994. PLB 24.95 (*0-7933-2012-7*); pap. 14.95 (*0-7933-2013-5*); computer disk 29.95 (*0-7933-2014-3*) Gallopade Pub Group.

—South Dakota Timeline: A Chronology of South Dakota History, Mystery, Trivia, Legend, Lore & More. (Illus.). (gr. 3-12). 1994. PLB 24.95 (*0-7933-5998-8*); pap. 14.95 (*0-7933-5999-6*); computer disk 29.95 (*0-7933-6000-5*) Gallopade Pub Group.

—South Dakota's (Most Devastating!) Disasters & (Most Calamitous!) Catastrophies! (Illus.). 1994. PLB 24.95 (*0-7933-1031-8*); pap. 14.95 (*0-7933-1030-X*); computer disk 29.95 (*0-7933-1032-6*) Gallopade Pub Group.

—South Dakota's Unsolved Mysteries (& Their "Solutions") Includes Scientific Information & Other Activities for Students. (Illus.). (gr. 3-12). 1994. PLB 24.95 (*0-7933-5845-0*); pap. 14.95 (*0-7933-5846-9*); computer disk 29.95 (*0-7933-5847-7*) Gallopade Pub Group.

—Uncle Rebus: South Dakota Picture Stories for Computer Kids. (Illus.). (gr. k-3). 1994. PLB 24.95 (*0-7933-4624-X*); pap. 14.95 (*0-7933-4625-8*); disk 29.95 (*0-7933-4626-6*) Gallopade Pub Group.

Sirvaitis, Karen. South Dakota. LC 94-5451. 1994. lib. bdg. write for info. (*0-8225-2747-2*) Lerner Pubns.

Thompson, Kathleen. South Dakota. 48p. (gr. 3 up). 1986. PLB 19.97 (*0-86514-458-3*) Raintree Steck-V.

SOUTH DAKOTA–FICTION

Kinyon, Jeannette. Over Home. LC 92-71059. 244p. (gr. 4-8). 1992. PLB 24.95 (*1-880531-01-1*); pap. 13.95 (*1-880531-02-X*) East Eagle.
Set in the 1920s in Huron, South Dakota, OVER HOME captures the essence of small-town rural America through the eyes of an 11-year old girl. It is a story of family relationships & rituals brought to life by a richly detailed cast of characters caught up in a real-life murder mystery. The estranged wife of one of Grandpa & Grandma Weise's boarders has been murdered & Scharmann can't keep her nose out of it. The inquisitive Scharmann is both horrified & fascinated. An active imagination leads Scharmann through a series of colorful adventures which sometimes are nothing but trouble. Mamma & Daddy say it's none of her business, but, for Scharmann, secrets are to be discovered & mysteries are to be solved. Like Laura Ingalls Wilder, Jeannette Kinyon writes with a depth of vivid description. OVER HOME reverberates with the customs & fashions of days gone by, yet the lessons of family & adolescence are strikingly familiar for all time. Hardback (ISBN 1-880531-01-1) & paperback (ISBN 1-880531-02-X). Call or write for information to order, East Eagle Company, P.O. Box 812, Huron, SD 57350, 605-352-5875.
Publisher Provided Annotation.

Wilder, Laura Ingalls. Little Town on the Prairie. rev. ed. Williams, Garth, illus. LC 52-7531. 308p. (gr. 3-7). 1961. 15.95 (*0-06-026450-0*); PLB 15.89 (*0-06-026451-9*) HarpC Child Bks.

—The Long Winter. rev. ed. Williams, Garth, illus. LC 52-7530. 334p. (gr. 3-7). 1961. 15.95 (*0-06-026460-8*); PLB 15.89 (*0-06-026461-6*) HarpC Child Bks.

—These Happy Golden Years. rev. ed. Williams, Garth, illus. LC 52-7532. 304p. (gr. 3-7). 1961. 15.95 (*0-06-026480-2*); PLB 15.89 (*0-06-026481-0*) HarpC Child Bks.

SOUTH POLE

Flaherty, Leo & Goetzmann, William H. Roald Amundsen & the Quest for the South Pole. Collins, Michael, intro. by. (Illus.). 112p. (gr. 6-12). 1993. PLB 18.95 (*0-7910-1308-1*) Chelsea Hse.

SOUTH SEA ISLANDS

see Islands of the Pacific

SOUTHEAST ASIA

see Asia, Southeastern

SOUTHERN STATES

Aylesworth, Thomas G. & Aylesworth, Virginia L. South Central (Louisiana, Arkansas, Missouri, Kansas, Oklahoma) (Illus.). 64p. (Orig.). (gr. 3 up). 1988. lib. bdg. 16.95 (*1-55546-561-7*); pap. 6.95 (*0-7910-0542-9*) Chelsea Hse.

—The South (Mississippi, Alabama, Florida) (Illus.). 64p. (gr. 3 up). 1991. lib. bdg. 16.95 (*0-7910-1044-9*) Chelsea Hse.

—The Southeast (Kentucky, Tennessee, Georgia) (Illus.). 64p. (gr. 3 up). 1991. lib. bdg. 16.95 (*0-7910-1043-0*) Chelsea Hse.

Brown, Anne H. The Colonial South. LC 93-49008. 1994. write for info. (*0-86625-509-5*) Rourke Pubns.

Greenfield, Eloise & Little, Lessie J. Childtimes: A Three-Generation Memoir. Pinkney, Jerry, illus. LC 77-26581. 160p. (gr. 5 up). 1979. (Crowell Jr Bks); PLB 13.89 (*0-690-03875-5*, Crowell Jr Bks) HarpC Child Bks.

Herda, D. J. Environmental America: The South Central States. (Illus.). 64p. (gr. 5-8). 1991. PLB 15.40 (*1-878841-09-2*) Millbrook Pr.

—Environmental America: The Southeastern States. (Illus.). 64p. (gr. 5-8). 1991. PLB 15.40 (*1-878841-07-6*) Millbrook Pr.

—Historical America: The Southeastern States. LC 92-16315. (Illus.). 64p. (gr. 5-8). 1993. PLB 15.40 (*1-56294-119-4*) Millbrook Pr.

Nickens, Bessie. Walking the Log: Memories of a Southern Childhood. LC 94-10803. (Illus.). 32p. (gr. 2 up). 1994. 14.95 (*0-8478-1794-6*) Rizzoli Intl.

Touchstone, Samuel J. Jessie Jackson Touchstone Clan & Parallel Touchstones. LC 90-81215. (Illus.). 80p. (Orig.). (gr. 6-12). 1990. pap. text ed. 9.95 (*0-914917-06-4*) Folk-Life.

SOUTHERN STATES–FICTION

Bernardini, Robert. Southern Love for Christmas. Rice, James, illus. 32p. (gr. k-3). 1993. 14.95 (*0-88289-974-0*) Pelican.

—A Southern Time Christmas. Rice, James, illus. LC 91-12467. 32p. 1991. 14.95 (*0-88289-828-0*) Pelican.

Duke, Mary A. Victoria Scarlett Jones. LC 93-70815. (Illus.). 55p. (Orig.). (gr. 3-5). 1993. Incls. Victoria Scarlett & the Big Black Bear; Victoria Scarlett & Clara at Christmas; Victoria Scarlett Says, "Recess Was a Mess!" pap. 5.95 (*1-883241-05-7*) Cognitive Pr.

Harris, Joel C. Uncle Remus Stories. (gr. 5-6). 22.95 (*0-89190-311-9*, Pub. by Am Repr) Amereon Ltd.

McKissack, Patricia C. Mirandy & Brother Wind. Tyson, Cicely, narrated by. Pinkney, Jerry, illus. LC 87-349. 32p. (ps up). 1992. incl. cassette 17.00 (*0-679-82668-8*) Knopf Bks Yng Read.

Peck, Kay. Folsom Boy. LC 88-51030. 174p. 1989. pap. 6.95 (*1-55523-173-X*) Winston-Derek.

Pyrnelle, Louise-Clarke. Diddie, Dumps & Tot. (Illus.). 117p. (gr. 4-8). 1963. 14.95 (*0-911116-17-6*) Pelican.

Reaver, Chap. Bill. 1994. 14.95 (*0-385-31175-3*) Delacorte.

Standish, Burt L. Frank Merriwell Down South. Rudman, Jack, ed. (gr. 9 up). Date not set. 9.95 (*0-8373-9305-1*); pap. 3.95 (*0-8373-9005-2*) F Merriwell.

Young, Ronder Y. Learning by Heart. LC 92-46887. 1993. 13.95 (*0-395-65369-X*) HM.

SOUTHERN STATES–HISTORY

Jameson, W. C. Buried Treasures of the American South. (Illus.). 224p. (gr. 6 up). 1992. pap. 9.95 (*0-87483-286-1*) August Hse.

Stone, Lynn. Plantations. LC 93-771. (ps-6). 1993. 15.93 (*0-86625-446-3*); 11.95s.p. (*0-685-66594-1*) Rourke Pubns.

SOUTHERN STATES–RACE RELATIONS

Kent, Deborah. The Freedom Riders. LC 92-33424. (Illus.). 32p. (gr. 3-6). 1993. PLB 12.30 (*0-516-06662-5*); pap. 3.95 (*0-516-46662-3*) Childrens.

SOUTHWEST, NEW

Here are entered works on that part of the United States which corresponds roughly with the old Spanish province of New Mexico, including the present Arizona, New Mexico, southern Colorado, Utah, Nevada and California.

Alpers, Jody. T Is for Tortilla: A Southwestern Alphabet Book. Johnson, Celeste, illus. 30p. (gr. k-6). 1993. pap. 5.95 (*0-9640533-0-6*) Libros de Ninos.

Anderson, Joan. Spanish Pioneers of the Southwest. Ancona, George, photos by. LC 88-16121. (Illus.). 64p. (gr. 3-6). 1989. 14.95 (*0-525-67264-8*, Lodestar Bks) Dutton Child Bks.

Aylesworth, Thomas G. & Aylesworth, Virginia L. The Southwest (Texas, New Mexico, Colorado) (Illus.). 64p. 1988. lib. bdg. 16.95x (*1-55546-562-5*); pap. 6.95 (*0-7910-0545-3*) Chelsea Hse.

Herda, D. J. Environmental America: The Southwestern States. LC 91-29901. (Illus.). 64p. (gr. 5-8). 1991. PLB 15.40 (*1-878841-11-4*) Millbrook Pr.

—Historical America: The Southwestern States. LC 92-28206. (Illus.). 64p. (gr. 5-8). 1993. PLB 15.40 (*1-56294-123-2*) Millbrook Pr.

Hill, William E. & Hill, Jan C. Heading Southwest: Along the Santa Fe Trail. (Illus.). 32p. (Orig.). (gr. k-4). 1993. pap. 3.95 (*0-9636071-1-1*) HillHouse Pub.

McCarty, John L. Maverick Town: The Story of Old Tascosa. Bugbee, Harold D., illus. Sonnichsen, C. L., frwd. by. LC 87-5946. (Illus.). 320p. (gr. 6-12). 1968. pap. 13.95 (*0-8061-2089-4*) U of Okla Pr.

Petersen, David. The Anasazi. LC 91-3036. 48p. (gr. k-4). 1991. PLB 12.85 (*0-516-01121-9*); pap. 4.95 (*0-516-41121-7*) Childrens.

Weisberg, Barbara. Coronado's Golden Quest. Eagle, Mike, illus. LC 92-18078. 79p. (gr. 2-5). 1992. PLB 21.34 (*0-8114-7232-9*); pap. 4.95 (*0-8114-8072-0*) Raintree Steck-V.

SOUTHWEST, NEW–FICTION

Geis, Jacqueline. Where the Buffalo Roam. Geis, Jacqueline, illus. LC 92-7733. 32p. (gr. 1-3). 1994. pap. 4.95 (*0-8249-8661-X*, Ideals Child) Hambleton-Hill.

Hobbs, Will. The Big Wander. LC 92-825. 192p. (gr. 5-9). 1992. SBE 14.95 (*0-689-31767-0*, Atheneum Child Bk) Macmillan Child Grp.

Johnston, Tony. Alice Nizzy Nazzy, the Witch of Santa Fe. DePaola, Tomie, illus. LC 93-44375. 1995. write for info. (*0-399-22788-1*, Putnam) Putnam Pub Group.

Lattimore, Deborah N. Frida Maria: A Story of the Old Southwest. LC 93-17250. 1994. 14.95 (*0-15-276636-7*, Browndeer Pr) HarBrace.

Lowell, Susan. The Three Little Javelinas. Harris, Jim, illus. LC 92-14232. 32p. (ps-2). 1992. 14.95 (*0-87358-542-9*) Northland AZ.

Oberman, Sheldon. The White Stone of Casa Loma. Tait, Les, illus. LC 93-61791. 24p. (gr. 1-6). 1994. 16.95 (*0-88776-333-2*) Tundra Bks.

SOVEREIGNS

see Kings and Rulers; Queens

SOVIET UNION

Baker. Soviet Air Force. LC 88-12121. (Illus.). 48p. (gr. 3-8). 1987. PLB 18.60 (*0-86625-331-9*); PLB 13.95s.p. (*0-685-58301-5*) Rourke Corp.

—Soviet Forces in Space. LC 88-14050. (Illus.). 48p. (gr. 3-8). 1987. PLB 18.60 (*0-86625-335-1*); PLB 13.95s.p. (*0-685-58299-X*) Rourke Corp.

Boyette, William. Soviet Georgia. (Illus.). 104p. (gr. 5 up). 1988. lib. bdg. 14.95 (*1-55546-779-2*) Chelsea Hse.

Bradley, Catherine. Kazakhstan. Channon, John, contrib. by. LC 92-2243. (Illus.). 32p. (gr. 4-6). 1992. PLB 14.40 (*1-56294-308-1*) Millbrook Pr.

Buettner, Dan, photos by. Sovietrek: A Journey by Bicycle across Southern Russia. LC 94-5449. (Illus.). 104p. (gr. 5 up). 1994. 22.95 (*0-8225-2950-5*) Lerner Pubns.

Carrion, Esther. The Empire of the Czars. (Illus.). 36p. (gr. 3 up). 1994. PLB 20.00 (*0-516-08391-0*); pap. 6.95 (*0-516-48391-9*) Childrens.

Clark, Mary J. The Commonwealth of Independent States. LC 92-20745. (Illus.). 64p. (gr. 5-8). 1992. PLB 15.90 (*1-56294-081-3*) Millbrook Pr.

Dolphin, Laurie. Georgia to Georgia: Making Friends in the U. S. S. R. McGee, E. Alan, illus. LC 90-47494. 40p. (gr. 2 up). 1991. 13.95 (*0-688-09896-7*, Tambourine Bks); PLB 13.88 (*0-688-09897-5*, Tambourine Bks) Morrow.

Fannon, Cecilia. Soviet Union. (Illus.). 64p. (gr. 7 up). 1990. lib. bdg. 17.27 (*0-86593-092-9*); lib. bdg. 12.95s.p. (*0-685-36367-8*) Rourke Corp.

Finney, Susan. The Revised Soviet Union. 64p. (gr. 4-8). 1991. 7.95 (*0-86653-580-2*, GA1453) Good Apple.

Flint, David. Russia. LC 92-43190. (Illus.). 32p. (gr. 3-4). 1992. PLB 19.24 (*0-8114-2941-5*) Raintree Steck-V.

Franco, Betsy. Around the World, Vol. 3: Russia. (Illus.). 48p. (gr. 1-3). 1993. pap. text ed. 7.95 (*1-55799-258-4*) Evan-Moor Corp.

Gillies, John. The New Russia. LC 93-25380. (Illus.). 128p. (gr. 5 up). 1994. text ed. 14.95 RSBE (*0-87518-481-2*, Dillon) Macmillan Child Grp.

Gosnell, Kelvin. Belarus, Ukraine, & Moldavia. Channon, John, contrib. by. LC 92-2241. (Illus.). 32p. (gr. 4-6). 1992. PLB 14.40 (*1-56294-306-5*) Millbrook Pr.

Hyde, Margaret O. Peace & Friendship: Russian & American Teens Meet. (Illus.). 96p. (gr. 6 up). 1992. 14.00 (*0-525-65107-1*, Cobblehill Bks) Dutton Child Bks.

Jackson, W. A., ed. Soviet Union. rev. ed. LC 87-83270. (Illus.). 160p. (gr. 6 up). 1988. text ed. 16.95 (*0-934291-34-9*); tchr's. guide 9.95 (*0-934291-35-7*); mastery test packet 5.95 (*0-934291-40-3*) Gateway Pr MI.

Jacobsen, Karen. The Commonwealth of Independent States. LC 92-12946. (Illus.). 48p. (gr. k-4). 1992. PLB 12.85 (*0-516-02194-X*) Childrens.

—The Russian Federation. LC 93-36996. (Illus.). 48p. (gr. k-4). 1994. PLB 12.85 (*0-516-01060-3*) Childrens.

—The Soviet Union. LC 90-2177. (Illus.). 48p. (gr. k-4). 1990. PLB 12.85 (*0-516-01109-X*); pap. 4.95 (*0-516-41109-8*) Childrens.

Kendall, Russ. Russian Girl: Life in an Old Russian Town. LC 93-13198. (Illus.). 40p. (ps-4). 1994. 14.95 (*0-590-45789-6*) Scholastic Inc.

Kort, Michael G. The Cold War. LC 93-1934. (Illus.). 160p. (gr. 7 up). 1994. PLB 16.90 (*1-56294-353-7*) Millbrook Pr.

Kotlyarskaya, Elena. Women in Society: Russia. LC 93-49762. 1994. 22.95 (*1-85435-561-9*) Marshall Cavendish.

Lerner Geography Department Staff, ed. Armenia. (Illus.). 64p. (gr. 5-12). 1993. PLB 19.95 (*0-8225-2806-1*) Lerner Pubns.

—Azerbaijan. (Illus.). 64p. (gr. 5-12). 1993. PLB 19.95 (*0-8225-2810-X*) Lerner Pubns.

—Belarus. (Illus.). 64p. (gr. 5-12). 1993. PLB 19.95 (*0-8225-2811-8*) Lerner Pubns.

—Georgia. (Illus.). 64p. (gr. 5-12). 1993. PLB 19.95 (*0-8225-2807-X*) Lerner Pubns.

—Kazakhstan. (Illus.). 64p. (gr. 5-12). 1993. PLB 19.95 (*0-8225-2815-0*) Lerner Pubns.

—Kirghyzstan. (Illus.). 64p. (gr. 5-12). 1993. PLB 19.95 (*0-8225-2814-2*) Lerner Pubns.

—Moldova. (Illus.). 64p. (gr. 5-12). 1993. PLB 19.95 (*0-8225-2809-6*) Lerner Pubns.

—Russia. (Illus.). 64p. (gr. 5-12). 1992. PLB 19.95 (*0-8225-2805-3*) Lerner Pubns.

—Tadzhikistan. (Illus.). 64p. (gr. 5-12). 1993. PLB 19.95 (*0-8225-2816-9*) Lerner Pubns.

—Turkmenistan. (Illus.). 64p. (gr. 5-12). 1993. PLB 19.95 (*0-8225-2813-4*) Lerner Pubns.

—Uzbekistan. (Illus.). 64p. (gr. 5-12). 1993. PLB 19.95 (*0-8225-2812-6*) Lerner Pubns.

Lerner Publications, Department of Geography Staff, ed. Soviet Union in Pictures. (Illus.). 64p. (gr. 5 up). 1989. PLB 17.50 (*0-8225-1864-3*) Lerner Pubns.

Miller. Soviet Navy. LC 88-11327. (Illus.). 48p. (gr. 3-8). 1988. PLB 18.60 (*0-86625-336-X*); PLB 13.95s.p. (*0-685-58300-7*) Rourke Corp.

—Soviet Rocket Forces. LC 88-11367. (Illus.). 48p. (gr. 3-8). 1988. PLB 18.60 (*0-86625-333-5*); PLB 13.95s.p. (*0-685-58297-3*) Rourke Corp.

—Soviet Submarines. (Illus.). 48p. (gr. 3-8). 1987. PLB 18.60 (*0-86625-332-7*); PLB 13.95s.p. (*0-685-58296-5*) Rourke Corp.

Murphy, Claire R. Friendship Across Arctic Waters: Alaskan Cub Scouts Visit Their Soviet Neighbors. Mason, Charles, photos by. (Illus.). 48p. (gr. 3-8). 1991. 15.95 (*0-525-67348-2*, Lodestar Bks) Dutton Child Bks.

Perrin, Penelope. Russia. LC 93-30422. (Illus.). 32p. (gr. 4 up). 1994. text ed. 13.95 RSBE (*0-89686-775-7*, Crestwood Hse) Macmillan Child Grp.

Resnick, Abraham. The Commonwealth of Independent States. (Illus.). 128p. (gr. 5-9). 1993. PLB 20.55 (*0-516-02613-5*) Childrens.

—The Union of Soviet Socialist Republics. LC 84-7602. (Illus.). 128p. (gr. 5-9). 1985. PLB 20.55 (*0-516-02789-1*) Childrens.

Riordan, James. Russia & the Commonwealth of Independent States. (Illus.). 48p. (gr. 5 up). 1992. PLB 12.95 (*0-382-24378-1*) Silver Burdett Pr.

Roberts, Elizabeth. Georgia, Armenia, & Azerbaijan. Akiner, Sharon, contrib. by. LC 92-2242. (Illus.). 32p. (gr. 4-6). 1992. PLB 14.40 (*1-56294-309-X*) Millbrook Pr.

Stewart, Gail B. The Baltic States. LC 92-40. (Illus.). 48p. (gr. 6-7). 1992. text ed. 12.95 RSBE (*0-89686-747-1*, Crestwood Hse) Macmillan Child Grp.

—The Soviet Union. LC 90-38408. (Illus.). 48p. (gr. 6-7). 1990. text ed. 12.95 RSBE (*0-89686-537-1*, Crestwood Hse) Macmillan Child Grp.

Tolhurst, Marilyn. U. S. S. R. (Illus.). 48p. (gr. 4-8). 1987. PLB 14.95 (*0-382-09507-3*) Silver Burdett Pr.

Wood. Soviet Army. (Illus.). 48p. (gr. 3-8). 1987. PLB 18.60 (*0-86625-334-3*); PLB 13.95s.p. (*0-685-58298-1*) Rourke Corp.

SOVIET UNION–BIOGRAPHY

AESOP Enterprises, Inc. Staff & Crenshaw, Gwendolyn J. Aleksandr Sergeyevich Pushkin: Poetic Freedom Fighter for the People. 16p. (gr. 3-12). 1991. pap. write for info. incl. cassette (*1-880771-15-2*) AESOP Enter.

Ausbrook, Michael. Raisa Gorbachev. (Illus.). 112p. (gr. 5 up). 1992. lib. bdg. 17.95 (*0-7910-1625-0*) Chelsea Hse.

Ayer, Eleanor H. Boris Yeltsin: Man of the People. LC 92-16607. (Illus.). 144p. (gr. 5 up). 1992. text ed. 13.95 RSBE (*0-87518-543-6*, Dillon) Macmillan Child Grp.

Hoobler, Dorothy & Hoobler, Thomas. Russian Portraits. LC 93-38362. 1994. PLB 22.80 (*0-8114-6380-X*) Raintree Steck-V.

Kossman, Nina. Behind the Border. LC 93-48617. 1994. 14.00 (*0-688-13494-7*) Lothrop.

McGuire, Leslie. Anastasia: Czarina or Fake? Opposing Viewpoints. LC 89-35584. (Illus.). 112p. (gr. 5-8). 1989. 14.95 (*0-89908-074-X*) Greenhaven.

Moga, Jerome. Mikhail Gorbachev. (gr. 4-7). 1991. pap. 3.50 (*0-553-15898-8*) Bantam.

Mokrinskaia, Nina. Moia Zhizn' (My Life) Detstvo v Sibiri, junost' v Shankkhaie 1914-1392 gody. Valk, Gabriel, ed. LC 90-85815. (RUS., Illus.). 224p. (Orig.). 1991. pap. 16.00 (*0-911971-61-0*) Effect Pub.

Oleksy, Walter. Mikhail Gorbachev: A Leader for Soviet Change. LC 88-36960. (Illus.). 152p. (gr. 4 up). 1989. PLB 14.40 (*0-516-03265-8*) Childrens.

Schecter, Kate S. Boris Yeltsin. LC 92-37474. (Illus.). 1993. 18.95 (*0-7910-1749-4*, Am Art Analog); pap. write for info. (*0-7910-1795-8*, Am Art Analog) Chelsea Hse.

Selfridge, John W. Mikhail Gorbachev. (Illus.). 72p. (gr. 3-5). 1991. lib. bdg. 12.95 (*0-7910-1567-X*) Chelsea Hse.

Sproule, Anna. Mikhail Gorbachev. LC 91-50542. 68p. (gr. 3-4). 1992. PLB 19.93 (*0-8368-0619-0*) Gareth Stevens Inc.

Sproyle, Anna. Mikhail Gorbachev: Revolutionary for Democracy. LC 90-10010. (Illus.). 64p. (gr. 5-6). 1991. PLB 19.93 (*0-8368-0401-5*) Gareth Stevens Inc.

Streissguth, Thomas. Soviet Leaders from Lenin to Gorbachev. LC 92-19903. (Illus.). 160p. (gr. 5-12). 1992. PLB 14.95 (*1-881508-02-1*) Oliver Pr MN.

Sullivan, George. Mikhail Gorbachev. rev. ed. (Illus.). 128p. (gr. 7 up). 1990. lib. bdg. 13.98 (*0-671-72913-6*, J Messner); lib. bdg. 7.95 (*0-671-72914-4*) S&S Trade.

Wheeler, Jill. Raisa Gorbachev. LC 92-16678. 1992. 12.94 (*1-56239-118-6*) Abdo & Dghtrs.

SOVIET UNION–FICTION

Bunn, T. Davis. Winter Palace. 400p. (Orig.). 1993. pap. 9.99 (*1-55661-324-5*) Bethany Hse.

Cole, Joanna. Bony-Legs. Zimmer, Dirk, illus. LC 85-5070. 48p. (ps-3). 1984. RSBE 13.95 (*0-02-722970-X*, Four Winds) Macmillan Child Grp.

Dostoyevsky, Fyodor. Brothers Karamazov. Rudzik, O. H., intro. by. (gr. 11 up). 1966. pap. 3.95 (*0-8049-0128-7*, CL-128) Airmont.

—Crime & Punishment. Canon, R. R., intro. by. (Illus.). (gr. 11 up). 1967. pap. 3.95 (*0-8049-0145-7*, CL-145) Airmont.

Franklin, Kristine L. The Wolfhound. LC 94-14595. 1995. write for info. (*0-688-13674-5*); PLB write for info. (*0-688-13675-3*) Lothrop.

Gogol, Nikolai V. Dead Souls. Girling, Z., intro. by. (gr. 11 up). 1966. pap. 1.75 (*0-8049-0122-8*, CL-122) Airmont.

Gross, Sukey S. Passport to Russia. Backman, Aidel, illus. 158p. (gr. 5-8). 1989. 10.95 (*0-935063-59-5*); pap. 7.95 (*0-935063-60-9*) CIS Comm.

Holman, Felice. The Wild Children. LC 85-3541. 152p. (gr. 5-9). 1985. pap. 4.99 (*0-14-031930-1*, Puffin) Puffin Bks.

Kasakov. Goluboe i Zelenoe. (gr. 7-12). 1972. pap. 6.95 (*0-88436-053-9*, 65253) EMC.

Laskin. Spasibo za Vnimanie. (gr. 7-12). pap. 6.95 (*0-88436-052-0*, 65251) EMC.

Matas, Carol. Sworn Enemies. LC 92-6188. 148p. 1993. 16.00 (*0-553-08326-0*) Bantam.

Pargment, Lila, adapted by. How the Moolah Was Taught a Lesson & Other Tales from Russia. Titiev, Estelle, adapted by. LC 75-9200. (Illus.). 56p. 1985. (Dial); PLB 5.47 (*0-8037-5746-8*, Dial) Doubleday.

Phillips, Michael & Pella, Judith. A House Divided. 400p. (Orig.). 1992. pap. 9.99 (*1-55661-173-0*) Bethany Hse.

Polacco, Patricia & Polacco, Patricia. Babushka Baba Yaga. LC 92-30361. (Illus.). 32p. 1993. 14.95 (*0-399-22531-5*, Philomel Bks) Putnam Pub Group.

Posell, Elsa. Homecoming. 230p. (gr. 7 up). 1987. 14.95 (*0-15-235160-4*, HB Juv Bks) HarBrace.

Price, Susan. Ghost Song. 1992. 15.00 (*0-374-32544-8*) FS&G.

Samstag, Nicholas. Kay Kay Comes Home. Shahn, Ben, illus. (gr. 5-7). 1962. 10.95 (*0-8392-3015-X*) Astor-Honor.

Schloneger, Florence E. Sara's Trek. Quinn, Sidney, illus. 100p. (gr. 7 up). 1982. pap. 4.95 (*0-87303-071-0*) Faith & Life.

Schur, Maxine R. The Circlemaker. LC 93-17983. 1994. 13.99 (*0-8037-1354-1*) Dial Bks Young.

Segal, Jerry. The Place Where Nobody Stopped. Cohn, Amy, ed. Pilkey, Dar, illus. LC 94-86. 160p. (gr. 5 up). 1994. pap. 4.95 (*0-688-12567-0*, Pub. by Beech Tree Bks) Morrow.

Shulevitz, Uri. Soldier & Tsar in the Forest: A Russian Tale. Lourie, Richard, tr. from RUS. Shulevitz, Uri, illus. LC 72-188254. 32p. (ps-3). 1972. 16.00 (*0-374-37126-1*) FS&G.

Trivas, Irene. Annie... Anya: A Month in Moscow. LC 91-46433. (Illus.). 32p. (gr. k-2). 1992. 14.95 (*0-531-05452-7*); PLB 14.99 (*0-531-08602-X*) Orchard Bks Watts.

Turgenev, Ivan S. Fathers & Sons. Garnett, Constance, tr. Canon, R. R., intro. by. (gr. 11 up). 1967. pap. 1.95 (*0-8049-0129-5*, CL-129) Airmont.

Ushinsky, Konstantin. How a Shirt Grew in the Field. Rudolph, Marguerita, adapted by. Weihs, Erika, illus. 32p. (ps-3). 1992. 13.45 (*0-395-59761-7*, Clarion Bks) HM.

SOVIET UNION–HISTORY

Andrews, William G. The Land & People of the Soviet Union. LC 90-5746. (Illus.). 320p. (gr. 6 up). 1991. PLB 17.89 (*0-06-020035-9*) HarpC Child Bks.

Barbour, William, ed. The Breakup of the Soviet Union: Opposing Viewpoints. LC 93-1809. 1994. lib. bdg. 17.95 (*1-56510-068-9*); pap. 9.95 (*1-56510-067-0*) Greenhaven.

Geza von, Habsburg. Carl Faberge. LC 93-26856. 1994. 19.95 (*0-8109-3324-1*) Abrams.

Jacobsen, Karen. Commonwealth of Independent States. LC 92-12946. (Illus.). 48p. (gr. k-4). 1993. pap. 4.95 (*0-516-42194-8*) Childrens.

Jones, Dianne. Old Russia 1400-1917. 60p. (gr. k-8). 1989. 19.95 (*0-913705-46-2*) Zephyr Pr AZ.

Kallen, Stuart A. Before the Communist Revolution. Wallner, Rosemary, ed. LC 92-13472. 1992. PLB 13.99 (*1-56239-100-3*) Abdo & Dghtrs.

—The Brezhnev Era. Wallner, Rosemary, ed. LC 92-13475. 1992. PLB 13.99 (*1-56239-104-6*) Abdo & Dghtrs.

—Gorbachev-Yeltsin: The Fall of Communism. Wallner, Rosemary, ed. LC 92-13477. 1992. PLB 13.99 (*1-56239-105-4*) Abdo & Dghtrs.

—The Khrushchev Era. Wallner, Rosemary, ed. LC 92-13476. 1992. PLB 13.99 (*1-56239-103-8*) Abdo & Dghtrs.

Kort, Michael. The Rise & Fall of the Soviet Union. (Illus.). 128p. (gr. 9-12). 1992. PLB 13.90 (*0-531-11040-0*) Watts.

Nadel, Laurie. The Kremlin Coup. LC 91-36892. (Illus.). 64p. (gr. 5-8). 1992. PLB 15.90 (*1-56294-170-4*) Millbrook Pr.

—Kremlin Coup. 1992. pap. 4.95 (*0-395-62468-1*) HM.

Resnick, Abraham. Russia: A History to 1917. LC 83-7369. (Illus.). 128p. (gr. 5-9). 1983. PLB 20.55 (*0-516-02785-9*) Childrens.

Roberson, John R. Transforming Russia, 1682-1991. LC 92-1377. (Illus.). 192p. (gr. 5 up). 1992. SBE 15.95 (*0-689-31495-7*, Atheneum Child Bk) Macmillan Child Grp.

SOVIET UNION–HISTORY–FICTION

Asmar, Ramsey. The Birth of a New Tradition. Yerkes, Lane, illus. LC 92-35284. 32p. (gr. 4-6). 1992. PLB 19.97 (*0-8114-3583-0*) Raintree Steck-V.

Krichevsky, David J. What Price Revolution. LC 76-18448. 175p. (gr. 9-12). 1976. 8.95 (*0-87881-052-8*) Mojave Bks.

Phillips, Michael & Pella, Judith. The Russians 1-3 Giftset. 1992. 29.99 (*1-55661-770-4*) Bethany Hse.

SOVIET UNION–HISTORY–1689-1800

Stanley, Diane. Peter the Great. Stanley, Diane, illus. LC 85-13060. 32p. (gr. k-3). 1986. RSBE 15.95 (*0-02-786790-0*, Four Winds) Macmillan Child Grp.

SOVIET UNION–HISTORY–1917-

Campling, Elizabeth. U. S. S. R. Since Nineteen Forty-Five. (Illus.). 64p. (gr. 7-11). 1990. 19.95 (*0-7134-6063-6*, Pub. by Batsford UK) Trafalgar.

Kallen, Stuart A. The Lenin Era. Wallner, Rosemary, ed. LC 92-13473. 1992. PLB 13.99 (*1-56239-101-1*) Abdo & Dghtrs.

Smith, Brenda. Collapse of the Soviet Union. LC 93-17097. (gr. 6-9). 1994. 14.95 (*1-56006-142-1*) Lucent Bks.

SOVIET UNION–HISTORY–REVOLUTION, 1917-1921

Clark, Philip. Russian Revolution. (Illus.). 32p. (gr. 3-9). 1988. PLB 10.95 (*0-86307-935-0*) Marshall Cavendish.

Dunn, John M. The Russian Revolution. LC 93-22869. (gr. 6-9). 1994. 14.95 (*1-56006-234-7*) Lucent Bks.

Kindle, Pat & Finney, Susan. Russia to the Revolution. McKay, Ardis, illus. 64p. (gr. 4-8). 1987. pap. 8.95 (*0-86653-398-2*, GA 1020) Good Apple.

Ross, Stewart. The Russian Revolution, Nineteen Fourteen to Nineteen Twenty-Four. LC 87-73500. (Illus.). 64p. (gr. 7-12). 1989. PLB 13.40 (*0-531-18221-5*, Pub. by Bookwright Pr) Watts.

SOVIET UNION–HISTORY–1925-1953

Kallen, Stuart A. The Stalin Era. Wallner, Rosemary, ed. LC 92-13474. 1992. PLB 13.99 (*1-56239-102-X*) Abdo & Dghtrs.

SOVIET UNION–POLITICS AND GOVERNMENT

Ayer, Eleanor H. Boris Yeltsin: Man of the People. LC 92-16607. (Illus.). 144p. (gr. 5 up). 1992. text ed. 13.95 RSBE (*0-87518-543-6*, Dillon) Macmillan Child Grp.

Harbor, Bernard. Conflicts: The Breakup of the Soviet Union. LC 92-19917. (Illus.). 48p. (gr. 6 up). 1993. text ed. 13.95 RSBE (*0-02-742625-4*, New Discovery) Macmillan Child Grp.

Hawkes, Nigel. Glasnost & Perestroika. (Illus.). 48p. (gr. 5 up). 1990. lib. bdg. 18.60 (*0-86592-149-0*); lib. bdg. 13.95s.p. (*0-685-36378-3*) Rourke Corp.

Lambroza, Shlomo. World Leaders - Boris Yeltsin. LC 92-46479. 1993. 19.93 (*0-86625-482-X*); 14.95s.p. (*0-685-66417-1*) Rourke Pubns.

Perkovich, George. Thinking about the Soviet Union. (Illus.). 256p. (Orig.). 1989. pap. text ed. 25.00 (*0-942349-00-8*) Eductrs Soc Respons.

Roberts, Elizabeth. Glasnost: The Gorbachev Revolution. (Illus.). 64p. (gr. 9-12). 1991. 16.95 (*0-237-60042-0*, Pub. by Evans Bros Ltd) Trafalgar.

Ross, Stewart. The U. S. S. R. under Stalin. LC 90-24373. (Illus.). 64p. (gr. 9-12). 1991. 13.40 (*0-531-18409-9*, Pub. by Bookwright Pr) Watts.

Sproule, Anna. Mikhail Gorbachev. LC 91-50542. 68p. (gr. 3-4). 1992. PLB 19.93 (*0-8368-0619-0*) Gareth Stevens Inc.

Sproyle, Anna. Mikhail Gorbachev: Revolutionary for Democracy. LC 90-10010. (Illus.). 64p. (gr. 5-6). 1991. PLB 19.93 (*0-8368-0401-5*) Gareth Stevens Inc.

Sullivan, George. Mikhail Gorbachev. LC 87-20273. (Illus.). 128p. (gr. 7 up). 1988. PLB 10.98 (*0-671-63263-9*, J Messner); pap. 5.95 (*0-671-66937-0*) S&S Trade.

Trager, Oliver, ed. Gorbachev's Glasnost: Red Star Rising. 224p. (gr. 7-12). 1989. 29.95x (*0-8160-2220-8*) Facts on File.

Yost, Graham. The KGB. (Illus.). 160p. (gr. 8-12). 1989. 16.95x (*0-8160-1940-1*) Facts on File.

SPACE, OUTER

see Outer Space

SPACE AND TIME

see also Relativity (Physics)

Ferguson, Kitty. Black Holes in Space-Time. LC 91-2111. (Illus.). 128p. (gr. 7-9). 1991. PLB 13.40 (*0-531-12524-6*) Watts.

Gribbin, John & Gribbin, Mary. Time & Space. LC 93-44285. (Illus.). 64p. 1994. 15.95 (*1-56458-619-7*) Dorling Kindersley.

Gribbin, John R. & Gribbin, Mary. Time & Space. LC 93-44285. (Illus.). 64p. (gr. 7 up). 1994. 15.95 (*1-56458-478-X*) Dorling Kindersley.

SPACE AND TIME–FICTION

Ambrus, Victor G. What Time Is It, Dracula? Ambrus, Victor G., illus. LC 91-41260. 24p. (ps-1). 1992. 3.99 (*0-517-58970-2*) Crown Bks Yng Read.

Banks, Lynne R. The Secret of the Indian. (gr. 5 up). 1989. pap. 15.95 (*0-385-26292-2*) Doubleday.

Bellairs, John. The Trolley to Yesterday. LC 88-7113. (Illus.). 192p. (gr. 5 up). 1989. 13.95 (*0-8037-0581-6*); PLB 13.89 (*0-8037-0582-4*) Dial Bks Young.

Boston, Lucy M. Treasure of Green Knowe. Deeter, Catherine & Boston, Peter, illus. 214p. (gr. 3-7). 1989. pap. 3.95 (*0-15-289982-0*, Odyssey) HarBrace.

Cameron, Eleanor. Beyond Silence. LC 80-10350. 208p. (gr. 5-9). 1980. 9.95 (*0-525-26463-9*, DCB) Dutton Child Bks.

—The Court of the Stone Children. 192p. (gr. 4 up). 1990. pap. 4.99 (*0-14-034289-3*, Puffin) Puffin Bks.

Captives of Time. 1987. pap. 14.95 (*0-440-50227-6*) Dell.

Chetwin, Grace. Jason's Seven Magical Night Rides. Chetwin, Grace, illus. LC 93-21125. 128p. (gr. 2-6). 1994. SBE 14.95 (*0-02-718221-5*, Bradbury Pr) Macmillan Child Grp.

Cresswell, Helen. The Watchers: A Mystery at Alton Towers. LC 93-41683. (gr. 3-7). 1994. 14.95 (*0-02-725371-6*, Macmillan Child Bk) Macmillan Child Grp.

Dijs, Carla. What Do I Do at Eight O'Clock? (Illus.). 22p. (ps). 1993. pap. 8.95 casebound (*0-671-79526-0*, S&S BFYR) S&S Trade.

Eager, Edward. The Time Garden. Bodecker, N. M., illus. (gr. 4-6). 17.50 (*0-8446-6233-X*) Peter Smith.

—The Time Garden. Treherne, Katie T. & Bodecker, N. M., illus. 193p. (gr. 3-7). 1990. pap. 4.95 (*0-15-288193-X*, Odyssey) HarBrace.

Essley, Roger. Paul's Fantastic Photos. LC 93-12035. (ps-6). 1994. 16.00 (*0-671-86722-9*, S&S BFYR) S&S Trade.

Foley, Bernice W. Spaceships of the Ancients. Hoffman, Lee, illus. LC 78-59116. (gr. 3-6). 1978. 6.95 (*0-915964-04-X*) Veritie Pr.

Hahn, Mary D. Time for Andrew: A Ghost Story. LC 93-2877. 1994. 13.95 (*0-395-66556-6*, Clarion Bks) HM.

Hoppe, Joanne. Dream Spinner. LC 92-5258. 240p. (gr. 7 up). 1992. 14.00 (*0-688-08559-8*) Morrow Jr Bks.

Jones, Diana W. The Homeward Bounders. LC 81-1905. 224p. (gr. 5 up). 1981. 11.75 (*0-688-00678-7*) Greenwillow.

Jordan, Sherryl. Time of Darkness. (gr. 9-12). 1990. 13.95 (*0-590-43363-6*) Scholastic Inc.

—Time of Darkness. 1992. pap. 3.25 (*0-590-43362-8*, Point) Scholastic Inc.

Kipling, Rudyard. Puck of Pook's Hill: And Rewards & Fairies. Mackenzie, Donald, ed. LC 92-14450. 496p. (gr. 4 up). 1993. pap. 7.95 (*0-19-282575-5*) OUP.

Kurjian, Judi. In My Own Backyard. Wagner, David, illus. LC 93-18472. 32p. (ps-8). 1993. 14.95 (*0-88106-442-4*); PLB 15.88 (*0-88106-443-2*) Charlesbridge Pub.

MacGrory, Yvonne. The Secret of the Ruby Ring. Miller, Terry, illus. LC 93-35950. 189p. 1994. pap. 6.95 (*0-915943-92-1*) Milkweed Ed.

McOmber, Rachel B., ed. McOmber Phonics Storybooks: The Time Box. rev. ed. (Illus.). write for info. (*0-944991-52-1*) Swift Lrn Res.

Peck, Richard. The Dreadful Future of Blossom Culp. 224p. (gr. 7-12). 1984. pap. 2.95 (*0-440-92162-7*, LFL) Dell.

Pinkwater, Daniel. Borgel. LC 89-13421. 160p. (gr. 5 up). 1990. SBE 13.95 (*0-02-774671-2*, Macmillan Child Bk) Macmillan Child Grp.

—Borgel. LC 91-42914. 176p. (gr. 3-7). 1992. pap. 3.95 (*0-689-71620-6*, Aladdin) Macmillan Child Grp.

Pirotta, Saviour. Follow That Cat! Melnyczuk, Peter, illus. LC 92-38287. 32p. (gr. k-3). 1993. 13.99 (*0-525-45125-0*, DCB) Dutton Child Bks.

Reiss, Kathryn. Time Windows. 260p. (gr. 5 up). 1991. 15.95 (*0-15-288205-7*, HB Juv Bks) HarBrace.

Rodda, Emily. Finders Keepers. LC 90-47850. (Illus.). (gr. 5 up). 1991. 13.95 (*0-688-10516-5*) Greenwillow.

—Finders Keepers. Young, Noela, illus. LC 92-43776. 192p. (gr. 5 up). 1993. pap. 3.95 (*0-688-11846-1*, Pub. by Beech Tree Bks) Morrow.

—The Timekeeper. Young, Noela, illus. LC 92-31512. 160p. (gr. 5 up). 1993. 14.00 (*0-688-12448-8*) Greenwillow.

Rowe, W. W. Gully's Travels in Space-Time. LC 90-71370. 61p. (gr. k-3). 1991. pap. 5.95 (*1-55523-385-6*) Winston-Derek.

Russell, Sharman A. The Humpbacked Fluteplayer. LC 92-44492. 1994. 16.00 (*0-679-82408-1*) Knopf Bks Yng Read.

Taber, Anthony. The Boy Who Stopped Time. Taber, Anthony, illus. LC 92-398. 32p. (ps-3). 1993. SBE 13.95 (*0-689-50460-8*, M K McElderry) Macmillan Child Grp.

Wandelmaier, Roy. Secret of the Old Museum. Smolinski, Dick, illus. LC 85-2533. 112p. (gr. 3-6). 1985. lib. bdg. 9.49 (*0-8167-0531-3*); pap. text ed. 2.95 (*0-8167-0532-1*) Troll Assocs.

Wilde, Nicholas. Down Came a Blackbird. LC 92-20209. 208p. (gr. 5 up). 1992. 15.95 (*0-8050-2001-2*, Bks Young Read) H Holt & Co.

Williams, Ruth L. The Silver Tree. LC 91-16399. 224p. (gr. 3-7). 1992. PLB 13.89 (*0-06-020297-1*) HarpC Child Bks.

Winthrop, Elizabeth. The Battle for the Castle. LC 92-54490. 160p. (gr. 3-7). 1993. 14.95 (*0-8234-1010-2*) Holiday.

SPACE EXPLORATION (ASTRONAUTICS)

see Outer Space–Exploration

SPACE FLIGHT

see also Interplanetary Voyages; Outer Space–Exploration

Apfel, Necia H. Voyager to the Planets. Briley, Dorothy, ed. (Illus.). 48p. (gr. 3 up). 1991. 15.45 (*0-395-55209-5*, Clarion Bks) HM.

Baker, D. Danger on Apollo Thirteen. (Illus.). 32p. (gr. 4 up). 1988. PLB 17.27 (*0-86592-871-1*); 12.95 (*0-685-58289-2*) Rourke Corp.

Berliner, Don. Distance Flights. (Illus.). 72p. (gr. 5 up). 1990. 21.50 (*0-8225-1589-X*) Lerner Pubns.

—Living in Space. LC 92-24847. (Illus.). 72p. (gr. 5 up). 1993. 14.95 (*0-8225-1599-7*) Lerner Pubns.

Blackman, Steven. Space Travel. LC 93-13310. (Illus.). 32p. (gr. 5-7). 1993. PLB 11.90 (*0-531-14275-2*) Watts.

Bondar, Barbara & Bondar, Roberta. On the Shuttle: Eight Days in Space. 64p. Date not set. PLB 16.95 (*1-895688-12-4*, Pub. by Greey dePencier CN); pap. 8.95 (*1-895688-10-8*, Pub. by Greey dePencier CN) Firefly Bks Ltd.

Branley, Franklyn M. Is There Life in Outer Space? Maddem, Don, illus. LC 85-45057. 32p. (gr. k-3). 1986. pap. 4.95 (*0-06-445049-X*, Trophy) HarpC Child Bks.

Darling, David. Could You Ever Fly to the Stars? (Illus.). 60p. (gr. 5 up). 1991. text ed. 14.95 RSBE (*0-87518-446-4*, Dillon) Macmillan Child Grp.

DeOld, Alan R. & Judge, Joseph W. Space Travel: A Technological Frontier. (Illus.). 144p. (Orig.). (gr. 7-12). 1990. pap. text ed. 13.81 (*0-87192-206-1*) Delmar.

Embury, Barbara & Crouch, Tom D. The Dream Is Alive: A Flight of Discovery Aboard the Space Shuttle. LC 90-55194. (Illus.). 64p. (gr. 3-7). 1991. 14.95 (*0-06-021813-4*) HarpC Child Bks.

Friskey, Margaret. Space Shuttles. LC 81-16648. (Illus.). 48p. (gr. k-4). 1982. PLB 12.85 (*0-516-01655-5*); pap. 4.95 (*0-516-41655-3*) Childrens.

Gold, Susan D. The Kennedy Space Center: Gateway to Space. LC 91-42566. (Illus.). 48p. (gr. 5-6). 1992. text ed. 12.95 RSBE (*0-89686-690-4*, Crestwood Hse) Macmillan Child Grp.

—To Space & Back: The Story of the Shuttle. LC 91-42565. (Illus.). 48p. (gr. 5-6). 1992. text ed. 12.95 RSBE (*0-89686-688-2*, Crestwood Hse) Macmillan Child Grp.

Hansen, Rosanna & Bell, Robert. My First Book about Space. (ps-3). 1985. pap. 9.95 (*0-671-60262-4*, S&S BFYR) S&S Trade.

Hawkes, Nigel. Space & Aircraft. (Illus.). 32p. (gr. 5-8). 1994. bds. 13.95 (*0-8050-3416-1*) TFC Bks NY.

Kelch, Joseph W. Millions of Miles to Mars. Byrne, Connell, illus. LC 93-33798. (gr. 3 up). 1995. 17.00 (*0-671-88249-X*, J Messner); pap. 10.95 (*0-671-88250-3*, J Messner) S&S Trade.

Kettelkamp, Larry. Living in Space. LC 92-35118. (Illus.). 128p. (gr. 3 up). 1993. 14.00 (*0-688-10018-X*) Morrow Jr Bks.

Lauber, Patricia. Seeing Earth from Space. LC 89-77523. (Illus.). 80p. (gr. 5 up). 1990. 19.95 (*0-531-05902-2*); PLB 19.99 (*0-531-08502-3*) Orchard Bks Watts.

McDonnell, Janet. Space Travel: Blast-Off Day. Collette, Rondi, illus. LC 89-23999. 32p. (ps-2). 1990. PLB 13.95 (*0-89565-556-X*) Childs World.

Maynard, Christopher. The Space Shuttle. LC 93-41941. 1994. 8.95 (*1-85697-512-6*, Kingfisher LKC) LKC.

Nelson, Nigel. Space. LC 93-7257. 32p. (gr. k-2). 1993. 14.95 (*1-56847-109-2*) Thomson Lrning.

Petty, Kate. Into Space. Wood, Jakki, illus. 32p. (gr. 2-4). 1993. pap. 5.95 (*0-8120-1761-7*) Barron.

Schultz, Charles., illus. Land & Space. LC 94-15492. (gr. 2 up). 1994. 9.99 (*0-517-11895-5*, Pub. by Derrydale Bks) Random Hse Value.

Smith, Howard E., Jr. Daring the Unknown: A History of N. A. S. A. LC 86-33617. (Illus.). 128p. (gr. 3-7). 1987. 16.95 (*0-15-200435-1*, Gulliver Bks) HarBrace.

Souza, D. M. Space Sailing. LC 92-45176. 1993. 19.95 (*0-8225-2850-9*) Lerner Pubns.

Space Exploration. (Illus.). 64p. (gr. 6-12). 1983. pap. 1.85 (*0-8395-3354-3*, 33354) BSA.

Steele, Philip. Space Travel. LC 90-20735. (Illus.). 32p. (gr. 5-6). 1991. text ed. 3.95 RSBE (*0-89686-585-1*, Crestwood Hse) Macmillan Child Grp.

Stewart, G. In Space. (Illus.). 32p. (gr. 3-8). 1989. lib. bdg. 11.95s.p. (*0-86592-116-4*); PLB 15.74 (*0-685-58599-9*) Rourke Corp.

Wroble, Lisa. Space Science. Nolte, Larry, illus. 48p. (gr. 3-6). Date not set. PLB 12.95 (*1-56065-114-8*) Capstone Pr.

SPACE FLIGHT–FICTION

Atkinson, Stuart. Journey into Space. Asimov, Isaac, intro. by. 80p. (gr. 5-7). 1988. pap. 14.95 (*0-670-82306-6*) Viking Child Bks.

Blumberg, Rhoda. The First Travel Guide to the Moon: What to Pack, How to Go, & What to See When You Get There. Doty, Roy, illus. LC 84-28757. 96p. (gr. 3-7). 1984. Repr. of 1980 ed. 13.95 (*0-02-711680-8*, Four Winds) Macmillan Child Grp.

Bowles, Charles. The Sometimes Invisible Spaceship. LC 87-71712. 113p. (Orig.). 1987. pap. 6.00 (*0-916383-25-3*) Aegina Pr.

Brooks, Walter R. Freddy & the Men from Mars. Morrill, Leslie & Wiese, Kurt, illus. LC 86-40421. 256p. (gr. 3-7). 1987. pap. 3.95 (*0-394-88887-1*) Knopf Bks Yng Read.

Cameron, Eleanor. Stowaway to the Mushroom Planet. Henneberger, Robert, illus. (gr. 3-7). 1956. 14.95 (*0-316-12534-2*, Joy St Bks) Little.

—Stowaway to the Mushroom Planet. (gr. 3-7). 1988. pap. 6.95 (*0-316-12541-5*); pap. text ed. write for info. Little.

Cohen, Della. Jeff Rides a Spaceship. Van Wright, Cornelius, illus. 24p. (ps-2). 1992. pap. 0.99 (*1-56293-107-5*) McClanahan Bk.

Davids, Paul. Mission from Mount Yoda. (gr. 4-7). 1993. pap. 3.99 (*0-553-15890-2*) Bantam.

—Prophets of the Dark Side. (gr. 4-7). 1993. pap. 3.99 (*0-553-15892-9*) Bantam.

—Queen of the Empire. (gr. 4-7). 1993. pap. 3.99 (*0-553-15891-0*) Bantam.

Greydanus, Rose. Trouble in Space. Page, Don, illus. LC 81-5114. 32p. (gr. k-2). 1981. PLB 11.59 (*0-89375-517-6*); pap. text ed. 2.95 (*0-89375-518-4*) Troll Assocs.

Herge. Explorers on the Moon: The Adventures of Tintin. Herge, illus. 24p. (ps-3). 1992. 16.95 (*0-316-35860-6*, Joy St Bks) Little.

Hill, Douglas. The Moon Monster. Ford, Jeremy, illus. 42p. (gr. 2-4). 1989. 3.95 (*0-8120-6138-1*) Barron.

Hirst, Robin & Hirst, Sally. My Place in Space. Harvey, Roland & Levine, Joe, illus. LC 89-37893. 40p. (ps-2). 1992. pap. 5.95 (*0-531-07030-1*) Orchard Bks Watts.

Hobbs, Clara M. Begin-Again Land. 1993. 10.95 (*0-533-10386-X*) Vantage.

Idore. Space Needle Journey to Mars. Trebor Eugol, illus. 38p. (gr. k-3). 1991. pap. 4.95 (*0-926060-07-4*) Anschell Pub Co.

—Space Needle: Journey to Mars. 2nd ed. Eugol, Trebor, illus. 37p. (Orig.). (ps-3). 1991. pap. 4.95 (*0-926060-08-2*) Anschell Pub Co.

Ionesco, Eugene. Conte..., 3: Contes Numero 3 (Pour Enfants de Moins de Trois Ans) (FRE., Illus.). 32p. 1985. pap. 9.95 (*0-685-73256-8*) Fr & Eur.

Lawhead, Steve. Howard Had a Spaceship. (Illus.). 32p. (gr. k-3). 1986. 7.99 (*0-7459-1101-3*) Lion USA.

Livingston, Cohn. Space Songs. Fisher, Leonard E., illus. (ps-3). 1993. pap. 5.95 (*0-8234-1029-3*) Holiday.

MacDonald, Suse. Space Spinners. (ps-3). 1991. 13.95 (*0-8037-1008-9*); PLB 13.89 (*0-8037-1009-7*) Dial Bks Young.

Marshall, Edward. Space Case. Marshall, James, illus. 40p. (gr. k-3). 1982. pap. 4.99 (*0-8037-8431-7*) Dial Bks Young.

Marshall, James. Merry Christmas, Space Case. Marshall, James, illus. LC 85-1664. 32p. (ps-3). 1986. 11.95 (*0-8037-0215-9*) Dial Bks Young.

Moncure, Jane B. The Magic Moon Machine. Hohag, Linda, illus. LC 87-30959. 32p. (ps-2). 1987. PLB 14.95 (*0-89565-410-5*); pap. 6.96 (*0-89565-438-5*) Childs World.

Murdock, M. S. Armageddon off Vesta. LC 88-51716. (Illus.). 288p. (Orig.). 1989. pap. 3.95 (*0-88038-761-0*) TSR Inc.

—Rebellion 2456. LC 88-51714. 288p. (Orig.). 1989. pap. 3.95 (*0-88038-728-9*) TSR Inc.

Nord, Barry M. The Spaceship Earth. Palmer, Norman D., illus. 64p. (Orig.). (gr. 6 up). pap. 9.95 (*0-935656-09-X*) Nords Studio.

Oana, Katherine. Spacebear Lands on Earth. Baird, Tate, ed. Wallace, Dorathye, illus. LC 86-51210. 16p. (Orig.). (ps up). 1988. pap. 3.72 (*0-914127-26-8*) Univ Class.

Peppe, Rodney. Mice on the Moon. (gr. 4 up). 1993. pap. 13.95 (*0-385-30839-6*) Doubleday.

Phillips, Dave. Space Age Mazes. (gr. 2 up). 1988. pap. 2.95 (*0-486-25659-6*) Dover.

Pinkwater, Daniel M. Fat Men from Space. Pinkwater, Daniel M., illus. 64p. (gr. 4-6). 1980. pap. 3.25 (*0-440-44542-6*, YB) Dell.

Pollotta, Nick & Foglio, Phil. Illegal Aliens. Foglio, Phil, illus. LC 88-51727. 320p. (Orig.). 1989. pap. 3.95 (*0-88038-715-7*) TSR Inc.

Pryor, Bonnie. Mr. Munday & Space Creatures. (gr. k-3). 1991. pap. 4.95 (*0-671-73620-5*, S&S BFYR) S&S Trade.

Raichert, Lane. D.C. Hopper, the First Starbunny. Raichert, Lane, illus. LC 91-23055. 32p. (gr. 2-6). 1992. 15.95 (*1-880009-81-1*, DC-P1) Blue Zero Pub.

Rodgers, G. Kryptic: The Little Space Guy. (Illus.). 32p. (gr. 2-6). 1989. 10.95 (*0-88625-246-6*) Durkin Hayes Pub.

Rubel, Nicole. Pirate Jupiter & the Moondogs. Rubel, Nicole, illus. LC 84-13815. 32p. (ps-3). 1985. Dial Bks Young.

Rubinstein, Gillian. Space Demons. LC 87-27542. 240p. (gr. 5-9). 1988. 13.95 (*0-8037-0534-4*) Dial Bks Young.

Russomanno, Diane. The Journey Begins. 32p. 1991. pap. text ed. write for info. (*1-880501-03-1*) Know Booster.

Rymer, Alta M. Oopletrump's Odyssey, Bk. 4. Rymer, Alta M., illus. LC 85-61861. 48p. (Orig.). (gr. 5-7). 1987. pap. text ed. 20.00 (*0-9600792-5-4*) Rymer Bks.

Saunders, Susan. Runaway Spaceship. 64p. 1985. pap. 2.25 (*0-553-15463-X*) Bantam.

Svaren, Jacqueline. Lojor's Letters: A Space-Age Story about a Boy & a Gnome & Learning Italic Handwriting. Kisvet, Fran, illus. Reynolds, Lloyd J., intro. by. LC 78-60185. (Illus.). 72p. (Orig.). (gr. 1 up). 1981. pap. 10.00 (*0-931474-04-3*) TBW Bks.

Sweeney, Toni. Spacedog's Best Friend. Sweeney, Toni, illus. (Orig.). (gr. 5-12). 1989. pap. 6.95 (*0-933025-13-0*) Blue Bird Pub.

Teague, Mark. Moog-Moog, Space Barber. (gr. 4-7). 1990. 12.95 (*0-590-43332-6*) Scholastic Inc.

Wells, H. G. First Men in the Moon. Lowndes, R. A., intro. by. (gr. 7 up). 1965. pap. 1.25 (*0-8049-0078-7*, CL-78) Airmont.

Wilhelm, Doug. The Mystery of the Forgotten Planet. (gr. 4-7). 1993. pap. 3.50 (*0-553-29303-6*) Bantam.

Yolen, Jane. Commander Toad & the Space Pirates. Degen, Bruce, illus. 64p. (gr. 1-4). 1987. (Coward); pap. 6.95 (*0-698-20633-9*, Coward) Putnam Pub Group.

Zebrowski, George. The Stars Will Speak. LC 85-42638. 224p. (gr. 7 up). 1987. pap. 2.95 (*0-06-447050-4*, Trophy) HarpC Child Bks.

SPACE FLIGHT, MANNED

see Manned Space Flight

SPACE FLIGHT TO THE MOON

see also Apollo Project; Moon–Exploration

Bay, Timothy. First to the Moon. LC 92-75989. 1993. 9.95 (*0-383-03818-9*) SRA Schl Grp.

Charleston, Gordon. Armstrong Lands on the Moon. LC 93-32918. (Illus.). 32p. (gr. 4 up). 1994. text ed. 13.95 RSBE (*0-87518-530-4*, Dillon) Macmillan Child Grp.

Collins, Michael. Flying to the Moon: An Astronaut's Story. 2nd, rev. ed. LC 93-42001. 1994. pap. 4.50 (*0-374-42356-3*, Sunburst) FS&G.

Englehart, Steve. Countdown to the Moon. LC 94-5135. (Illus.). 96p. (Orig.). 1994. pap. 3.99 (*0-380-77538-7*, Camelot) Avon.

Fraser, Mary A. One Giant Leap. Fraser, Mary A., illus. LC 92-41044. 40p. (gr. 3-7). 1993. 15.95 (*0-8050-2295-3*) H Holt & Co.

Gold, Susan D. Countdown to the Moon. LC 91-30360. (Illus.). 48p. (gr. 5-6). 1992. text ed. 12.95 RSBE (*0-89686-689-0*, Crestwood Hse) Macmillan Child Grp.

Sullivan, George. Day We Walked On the Moon: A Photo History of Space Exploration. (Illus.). (gr. 3-9). 1990. 14.95 (*0-590-43632-5*); pap. 4.95 (*0-685-58532-8*) Scholastic Inc.

SPACE MEDICINE

see also Manned Space Flight

Rambaut, Paul. Space Medicine. Head, J. J., ed. LC 84-45837. (Illus.). 16p. (Orig.). (gr. 10 up). 1985. pap. text ed. 2.75 (*0-89278-366-4*, 45-9766) Carolina Biological.

SPACE PROBES

Robinson, Fay. Space Probes to the Planets. Grant, Christy, ed. LC 92-10792. (Illus.). 32p. (gr. k-3). 1993. 14.95g (*0-8075-7548-8*) A Whitman.

SPACE RESEARCH

see Outer Space–Exploration; Space Sciences

SPACE SCIENCES

see also Astronautics; Astronomy; Geophysics; Outer Space; Space Medicine

Cabellero, Jane A. Aerospace Projects for Young Children. rev. ed. LC 79-90481. (Illus.). 112p. (Orig.). (ps-3). 1987. pap. 14.95 (*0-89334-100-2*) Humanics Ltd.

Gaffney, T. Kennedy Space Center. LC 85-11317. 48p. (gr. k-4). 1985. pap. 4.95 (*0-516-41269-8*) Childrens.

Gardner, Robert. Projects in Space Science. (Illus.). 136p. (gr. 4-8). 1988. lib. bdg. 11.98 (*0-671-63639-1*, J Messner); lib. bdg. 5.95 (*0-671-65993-6*); PLB 8.99s.p. (*0-685-47085-7*); pap. 3.71s.p. (*0-685-47086-5*) S&S Trade.

Graham, Ian. Space Science. LC 92-18319. 48p. (gr. 5). 1992. PLB 22.80 (*0-8114-2806-0*) Raintree Steck-V.

McKay, David W. & Smith, Bruce G. Space Science Projects for Young Scientists. LC 86-7745. (Illus.). 128p. (gr. 7-12). 1986. PLB 13.90 (*0-531-10244-0*) Watts.

SPACE SHIPS–PILOTS

see Astronauts

SPACE TELECOMMUNICATION

see Interstellar Communication

SPACE TRAVEL

see Interplanetary Voyages; Manned Space Flight; Space Flight

SPACE VEHICLES

see also Artificial Satellites; Space Probes

Abernathy, Susan. Space Machines. LaPadula, Tom, illus. (gr. 3-6). 1991. 8.50 (*0-307-17872-2*, Golden Pr) Western Pub.

Barrett, Norman. Space Machines. LC 93-33237. (Illus.). 48p. (gr. 5-7). 1994. PLB 13.95 (*0-531-14300-7*) Watts.

Blackman, Steven. Space Travel. LC 93-13310. (Illus.). 32p. (gr. 5-7). 1993. PLB 11.90 (*0-531-14275-2*) Watts.

Branley, Franklyn M. Rockets & Satellites. rev. ed. Maestro, Giulio, illus. LC 86-47748. 32p. (ps-3). 1987. (Crowell Jr Bks) HarpC Child Bks.

Coords, Arthur E. The Space Apple Story: The Children's Tribute to the Seven Challenger Astronauts. (Illus.). 32p. (gr. 2-6). 1992. PLB 7.70 (*0-9631106-0-8*) A E Coords.

Friskey, Margaret. Lanzaderas Espaciales (Space Shuttles) Kratky, Lada, tr. from ENG. LC 81-16648. (SPA., Illus.). 48p. (gr. k-4). 1984. pap. 4.95 (*0-516-51655-8*) Childrens.

Gabriele. Astronauts & Spacecraft. 1985. pap. 1.95 (*0-911211-62-4*) Penny Lane Pubns.

Graham, Ian. Spacecraft. Stewart, Roger, illus. LC 94-2875. 1994. write for info. (*0-8114-6193-9*) Raintree Steck-V.

Hamilton, Sue. Space Shuttle Challenger's Explosion. Hamilton, John, ed. LC 88-71720. (Illus.). 32p. (gr. 4). 1989. PLB 11.96 (*0-939179-40-7*) Abdo & Dghtrs.

Italia, Bob. Voyagers One & Two. Walner, Rosemary, ed. LC 90-82622. (Illus.). 32p. (gr. 4). 1990. PLB 11.96 (*0-939179-96-2*) Abdo & Dghtrs.

Kerrod, Robin. Spacecraft. Full, Roger, et al, illus. LC 88-17655. 24p. (Orig.). (gr. 2-5). 1989. PLB 5.99 (*0-394-99989-4*) Random Bks Yng Read.

Rockwell, Anne & Brion, David. Space Vehicles. LC 93-43594. (Illus.). 24p. (ps-1). 1994. 13.99 (*0-525-45270-2*, DCB) Dutton Child Bks.

Shaw, Dena. Ronald McNair. LC 94-2759. 1994. pap. write for info. (*0-7910-2116-5*, Am Art Analog) Chelsea Hse.

The Space Boat. (Illus.). (ps-2). 1990. 3.50 (*0-7214-1316-1*); parent/tchr's. guide 3.95 (*0-317-04027-8*); Series 9011-3, No. 3. activity bk. 2.95 (*0-7214-3222-0*) Ladybird Bks.

Spacecraft. LC 92-52832. 24p. (ps-3). 1993. 8.95 (*1-56458-136-5*) Dorling Kindersley.

Spizzirri Publishing Co. Staff. Shuttle Craft: An Educational Coloring Book. Spizzirri, Linda, ed. (Illus.). 32p. (gr. 1-8). 1986. pap. 1.75 (*0-86545-077-3*) Spizzirri.

—Space Craft: An Educational Coloring Book. Spizzirri, Linda, ed. Spizzirri, Peter M., illus. 32p. (gr. 1-8). 1981. pap. 1.75 (*0-86545-036-6*) Spizzirri.

Stille, Darlene. Spacecraft. LC 90-19992. (Illus.). 48p. (gr. k-4). 1991. PLB 12.85 (*0-516-01120-0*); pap. 4.95 (*0-516-41120-9*) Childrens.

Vogt, Gregory. The Space Shuttle. (Illus.). 112p. (gr. 4-6). 1991. PLB 15.90 (*1-56294-049-X*) Millbrook Pr.

SPAIN

Bailey, Donna. Spain. LC 91-23716. (Illus.). 32p. (gr. 1-4). 1992. PLB 18.99 (*0-8114-2569-X*); pap. 3.95 (*0-8114-7186-1*) Raintree Steck-V.

Biggs, Betsey. Kidding Around Spain: A Young Person's Guide. D'Agostino, Anthony, illus. 108p. (Orig.). (gr. 3 up). 1991. pap. 12.95 (*0-945465-97-1*) John Muir.

Butler, Daphne. Spain. LC 92-17032. (Illus.). 32p. (gr. 3-4). 1992. PLB 19.24 (*0-8114-3678-0*) Raintree Steck-V.

Chambers, Catherine & Wright, Rachel. Spain. LC 92-27137. 1993. 11.90 (*0-531-14257-4*) Watts.

Cross, Wilbur & Cross, Esther. Spain. LC 85-16588. 128p. (gr. 5-9). 1985. PLB 20.55 (*0-516-02786-7*) Childrens.

Cumming, David. Spain. LC 91-7340. (Illus.). 32p. (gr. 2-4). 1992. PLB 12.40 (*0-531-18443-9*, Pub. by Bookwright Pr) Watts.

Getting to Know Spain. 48p. 1990. 8.95 (*0-8442-7627-8*, Natl Textbk) NTC Pub Grp.

James, Ian. Spain. LC 89-8873. (Illus.). 32p. (gr. k-6). 1989. PLB 11.90 (*0-531-10834-1*) Watts.

Leahy, Philippa. Spain. LC 93-2663. (Illus.). 32p. (gr. 5). 1993. text ed. 13.95 RSBE (*0-89686-772-2*, Crestwood Hse) Macmillan Child Grp.

Loader, Mandy. Guide to Spain. Turpin, Lorna, illus. LC 93-38366. 32p. (gr. 1-4). 1994. 3.95 (*1-85697-961-X*, Kingfisher LKC) LKC.

Loewen, Nancy. Food in Spain. LC 90-43595. 32p. (gr. 3-5). 1991. 11.95s.p. (*0-86625-346-7*) Rourke Pubns.

Lye, Keith. Passport to Spain. rev. ed. LC 93-21186. (Illus.). 48p. (gr. 5-8). 1994. PLB 13.90 (*0-531-14294-9*) Watts.

Miller, Arthur. Spain. (Illus.). 112p. (gr. 5 up). 1989. lib. bdg. 14.95 (*1-55546-795-4*) Chelsea Hse.

Selby, Anna. Spain. LC 93-28438. 1993. PLB 22.80 (*0-8114-1848-0*) Raintree Steck-V.

Shubert, Adrian. The Land & People of Spain. LC 91-9971. (Illus.). 256p. (gr. 6 up). 1992. 18.00 (*0-06-020217-3*); PLB 17.89 (*0-06-020218-1*) HarpC Child Bks.

Tollhurst, Marilyn. Spain. (Illus.). 48p. (gr. 4-8). 1989. lib. bdg. 14.95 (*0-382-09821-8*) Silver Burdett Pr.

Woods, Geraldine. Spain: A Shining New Democracy. (Illus.). (gr. 4 up). 1987. RSBE 14.95 (*0-87518-363-8*, Dillon) Macmillan Child Grp.

Wright, David & Wright, Jill. Spain. (Illus.). 32p. (gr. 4-6). 1991. 17.95 (*0-237-60183-4*, Pub. by Evans Bros Ltd) Trafalgar.

Wright, Nicola. Getting to Know: Spain & Spanish. Wooley, Kim, illus. 32p. (gr. 3-7). 1993. 12.95 (*0-8120-6339-2*); pap. 5.95 (*0-8120-1535-5*) Barron.

SPAIN–FICTION

Baroja. Las Inquietudes de Shanti Andia. (gr. 7-12). 1973. pap. 6.95 (*0-88436-062-8*, 70267) EMC.

Bellerophon Books Staff. Don Quixote. (gr. 4-7). 1992. pap. 3.95 (*0-88388-182-9*) Bellerophon Bks.

Braun, Lutz. Faster Than the Bull. Moore, Stephen, illus. LC 92-37947. 32p. (gr. 4-6). 1992. PLB 19.97 (*0-8114-3580-6*) Raintree Steck-V.

Bunuel. Las Tres de la Madrugada. 1972. pap. 5.95 (*0-88436-061-X*, 70265) EMC.

De Cervantes Saavedra, Miguel. Don Quixote. (gr. 11 up). 1967. pap. 2.75 (*0-8049-0153-8*, CL-153) Airmont.

Hahn, Mary D. The Spanish Kidnapping Disaster. 144p. 1993. pap. 3.50 (*0-380-71712-3*, Camelot) Avon.

Hodges, Margaret, adapted by. Don Quixote & Sancho Panza. Marchesi, Stephen, illus. LC 90-24098. 80p. (gr. 6 up). 1992. SBE 16.95 (*0-684-19235-7*, Scribners Young Read) Macmillan Child Grp.

Johnson, Jane. The Princess & the Painter. LC 93-39987. (ps-3). 1994. 15.00 (*0-374-36118-5*) FS&G.

Kimmel, Eric A. Bernal & Florinda: A Spanish Tale. Rayevsky, Robert, illus. LC 93-37917. 32p. (ps-3). 1994. reinforced bdg. 15.95 (*0-8234-1089-7*) Holiday.

Leaf, Munro. The Story of Ferdinand. Lawson, Robert, illus. LC 36-19452. (gr. k-3). 1936. pap. 13.00 (*0-670-67424-9*) Viking Child Bks.

Levinson, Riki. Mira Como Salen las Estrellas. (SPA., Illus.). 32p. (ps-3). 1992. 15.00 (*0-525-44958-2*, DCB) Dutton Child Bks.

O'Dell, Scott. The Spanish Smile. (gr. 7 up). 1982. 13.95 (*0-395-32867-5*) HM.

Pelgrom, Els. The Acorn Eaters. Prins, Johanna H. & Prins, Johanna W., trs. from DUT. LC 93-34210. (gr. 4 up). 1994. 16.00 (*0-374-30029-1*) FS&G.

Reeves, James, retold by. Exploits of Don Quixote. Ardizzone, Edward, illus. LC 85-11170. (gr. 5 up). 1985. 12.95 (*0-87226-025-9*, Bedrick Blackie); (Bedrick Blackie) P Bedrick Bks.

Sherrow, Victoria. Los Puerquitos Se Escaparon. Writer, C. C. & Nielsen, Lisa C., trs. Eagle, Mike, illus. (SPA.). 24p. (Orig.). (ps). 1992. pap. text ed. 3.00x (*1-56134-171-1*) Dushkin Pub.

Toto in Spain. (ENG & SPA., Illus.). 1992. 12.95 (*0-8442-9170-6*, Natl Textbk) NTC Pub Grp.

Williams, Marcia, adapted by. & illus. Don Quixote. LC 92-52995. 32p. (gr. 2 up). 1993. 13.95 (*1-56402-174-2*) Candlewick Pr.

Wojciechowska, Maia. Shadow of a Bull. LC 91-27716. 160p. (gr. 3-7). 1992. pap. 3.95 (*0-689-71567-6*, Aladdin) Macmillan Child Grp.

SPAIN–HISTORY

Bachrach, Deborah. The Inquisition. (Illus.). 128p. (gr. 6-9). 1994. 14.95 (*1-56006-247-9*) Lucent Bks.

Juan Carlos. (Illus.). 112p. (gr. 6-12). 1993. PLB 17.95 (*0-7910-1555-6*) Chelsea Hse.

SPAIN–HISTORY–FICTION

Cervantes Saavedra, Miguel de. Don Quijote de la Mancha: Primer Parte. (gr. 7-12). pap. 6.95 (*0-88436-056-3*, 70275) EMC.

Lehmann, Marcus. Family y Aguilar. Breuer, Jacob, adapted by. (gr. 7 up). 9.95 (*0-87306-122-5*) Feldheim.

SPAIN–HISTORY–711-1516

Koslow, Philip. El Cid: Spanish Military Leader. LC 92-33377. (Illus.). 1993. PLB 18.95 (*0-7910-1239-5*, Am Art Analog); pap. write for info. (*0-7910-1266-2*, Am Art Analog) Chelsea Hse.

McCaughrean, Geraldine. El Cid. Ambrus, Victor G., illus. 128p. (gr. 5 up). 1989. 19.95 (*0-19-276077-7*) OUP.

SPAIN–HISTORY–CIVIL WAR, 1936-1939

Katz, William L. & Crawford, Marc. The Lincoln Brigade: A Picture History. LC 88-27522. (Illus.). 96p. (gr. 5 up). 1989. SBE 14.95 (*0-689-31406-X*, Atheneum Child Bk) Macmillan Child Grp.

SPANISH AMERICA

see Latin America

SPANISH-AMERICAN WAR, 1898

see U. S.–History–War of 1898

SPANISH LANGUAGE

Ada, Alma F. Caballito Blanco y Otras Poesias Favoritas: Green Small Book Set. (SPA., Illus.). 40p. (Orig.). (gr. 1-3). 1992. Set, 6 copies. pap. 42.00 (*1-56334-118-2*) Hampton-Brown.

—Chart Set: Green Set. (SPA., Illus., Orig.). (gr. 1-3). 1992. Set incl. anthology, tapes, charts. pap. 179.95 (*1-56334-122-0*) Hampton-Brown.

—Cinco Pollitos y Otras Poesias Favoritas: Tan Small Book Set, 6 bks. (SPA., Illus.). 40p. (Orig.). (ps-6). 1991. Set. pap. 420.00 (*1-56334-117-4*) Hampton-Brown.

—Classroom Set: Green Set. (SPA., Illus., Orig.). (gr. 1-3). 1992. pap. 250.00 set, incl. anthology, 4 tapes, tan charts, (12) small bks. (*1-56334-120-4*) Hampton-Brown.

—Sale el Oso. (SPA., Illus.). 16p. (Orig.). (gr. 1-3). 1992. pap. 36.00 set (6 copies) (*1-56334-140-9*) Hampton-Brown.

—Los Seis Deseos de la Jirafa. (SPA., Illus.). 16p. (Orig.). (gr. 1-3). 1992. pap. 36.00 set (6 copies) (*1-56334-139-5*) Hampton-Brown.

Amery, H. Usborne First Thousand Words in Spanish. 1994. Incl. cassette. pap. 19.95 (*0-88110-686-0*) EDC.

Babin, Veronique. Enciclopedia Mega-Chiquitin. (SPA., Illus.). 116p. (ps-2). 1993. Repr. of 1989 ed. 9.95 (*970-607-181-4*, Larousse LKC) LKC.

Berlitz Jr., No. Two: Spanish. LC 93-36122. (SPA & ENG.). 1995. Set, incl. cass. pap. 19.95 (*0-689-71819-5*, Aladdin); pap. 19.95 bk. only (*0-689-71818-7*, Aladdin); write for info. cass. (Aladdin) Macmillan Child Grp.

Bouwman, Constance, et al. Beginning Spanish: A Teacher's Manual: Comprehension Based Activities for the Learnables, Book One. Baker, Syd, illus. 163p. (gr. 7 up). 1989. pap. text ed. 28.00 (*0-939990-78-4*) Intl Linguistics.

Burchard, Elizabeth & Lopez-Solar, Joyce. Spanish: In a Flash. 479p. (gr. 7-12). 1994. pap. 9.95 (*1-881374-10-6*) Flash Blasters.

Colors & Opposites. (Illus.). 32p. (ps-1). 1992. pap. 2.95 (*1-56144-107-4*, Honey Bear Bks) Modern Pub NYC.

Colvin, L. & Irving, N. Essential Spanish. (Illus.). 64p. 1990. lib. bdg. 12.96 (*0-88110-421-3*); pap. 5.95 (*0-7460-0320-X*) EDC.

Criminale, Ulrike & The Language School of the American Cultural Exchange Staff. Springboard to Spanish: Introduction to the Spanish Language. rev. ed. Porter, Mary D., illus. (gr. k-4). 1991. Incl. cassettes. 19. 95 (*1-880770-02-4*) ACE Pub. SPRINGBOARD is a set of easy, encouraging foreign language lessons for young children ages 4-8. This popular series features two 90-minute cassette tapes on which a native speaker of the foreign language leads the child in short, playful sessions through a variety of actions by repeating simple commands in both the foreign language & in English. The child is not required to read or write the language. Instead, the language is absorbed almost effortlessly as the child enjoys a progression of music, games & activities. The program emphasizes well-planned lessons for the adult leader & can be enjoyed by anyone in the home setting as well as in class. Because the cassettes guide the activity, the adult is not required to know the language, but instead simply participates with the child. The accompanying Springboard books provide attractive illustrations & a word-for-word transcript of the cassettes along with a comprehensive Vocabulary Chart for review & an Activities Supplement with suggestions for further learning. The Series is available in French, German & Spanish &, will soon be available in Japanese. For information on placing orders, please call (206) 535-8104.
Publisher Provided Annotation.

Daizovi, Lonnie G. & Saxon, Ed. Spanish Alive, Level I. (SPA., Illus.). 177p. (Orig.). (ps-3). 1990. Repr. of 1986 ed. songbook & cassette 11.95 (*0-935301-50-X*); tchr's. manual 18.95 (*0-935301-59-3*) Vibrante Pr.

De Brunhoff, Laurent. Je Parle Espagnol avec Babar. (FRE., Illus.). (gr. 4-6). 15.95 (*0-685-11273-X*) Fr & Eur.

Dupre, Jean-Paul, et al. Enciclopedia Mega-Junior. (SPA., Illus.). 296p. (gr. 1-4). 1993. Repr. of 1989 ed. 19.95 (*970-607-104-0*, Larousse LKC) LKC.

Emberley, Rebecca. My Day: A Book in Two Languages - Mi Dia: un Libro en Dos Lenguas. LC 92-37277. (ENG & SPA.). 1993. 15.95 (*0-316-23454-0*) Little.

Farris, Katherine, ed. Let's Speak Spanish! A First Book of Words. Hendry, Linda, illus. 48p. (ps-5). 1993. 11. 99 (*0-670-84994-4*) Viking Child Bks.

First Words. (Illus.). 32p. (ps-1). 1992. pap. 2.95 (*1-56144-105-8*, Honey Bear Bks) Modern Pub NYC.

Flora, James. The Fabulous Firework Family. Flora, James, illus. LC 93-11472. 32p. (gr. k-4). 1994. SBE 14.95 (*0-689-50596-5*, M K McElderry) Macmillan Child Grp.

Garcia, Yolanda P. Spanish in a Taco Shell. Garcia, Veronica J., illus. (ENG & SPA., Orig.). (gr. 4-9). 1991. pap. 10.95 (*0-935303-04-9*) Victory Pub.

Garvy, Helen. Bingo Book, No. 4: Spanish. LC 93-87278. 128p. (Orig.). 1994. pap. 6.00 (*0-918828-15-5*) Shire Pr.

Grisewood, John. Fun to Learn Spanish. Sleight, Katy, illus. LC 91-28906. 48p. (gr. 2-5). 1992. 12.95 (*0-531-15242-1*, Warwick); PLB 12.90 (*0-531-19112-5*, Warwick) Watts.

Gross, Ramon G. Pequeno Larousse Ilustrado 1993. (SPA., Illus.). 1736p. 1993. 34.95 (*970-607-156-3*, Larousse LKC) LKC.

Harrison, William F. & Welker, Dorothy W. Spanish Memory Book: A New Approach to Vocabulary Building. Nelson, Anita, illus. LC 93-12717. 96p. (Orig.). (gr. 7-12). 1993. text ed. 22.50x (*0-292-73079-9*); pap. 8.95 (*0-292-73081-0*) U of Tex Pr.

Hazzan, Anne-Francoise. Let's Learn Spanish Coloring Book. (Illus.). 64p. (gr. 4 up). 1988. pap. 3.95 (*0-8442-7549-2*, Natl Textbk) NTC Pub Grp.

La Hora de la Comida. (SPA., Illus.). 12p. (ps). 1992. bds. 4.95 (*0-525-44855-1*, DCB) Dutton Child Bks.

La Hora del Bano. (SPA., Illus.). 12p. (ps). 1992. bds. 4.95 (*0-525-44857-8*, DCB) Dutton Child Bks.

A Jugar! (SPA., Illus.). 12p. (ps). 1992. bds. 4.95 (*0-525-44854-3*, DCB) Dutton Child Bks.

Kidship Associates Staff. Lluvia de Palabras. Kidship Associates Staff, illus. (SPA.). 109p. (gr. 1-3). 1988. pap. text ed. 2.00 (*1-878742-00-0*) Kidship Assoc.

Levin, James. Ayudar. Carter, Jackie, ed. LC 94-729. 1994. write for info. (*0-590-29365-6*) Scholastic Inc.

MacArthur, Barbara. Canten Navidad. Jensen, Robert, illus. (ENG & SPA.). 15p. (Orig.). (ps-12). 1993. pap. 12.95 incl. cass. (*1-881120-09-0*) Frog Pr WI.

—Sing, Dance, Laugh & Eat Cheeseburgers. Jensen, Robert, illus. 35p. (Orig.). (ps-9). 1992. pap. text ed. 17.95 (*1-881120-06-6*) Frog Pr WI.

—Sing, Dance, Laugh & Eat Tacos. Jensen, Robert, illus. (SPA.). 35p. (Orig.). (ps-9). 1990. pap. text ed. 17.95 incl. cass. (*1-881120-04-X*) Frog Pr WI.

—Sing, Dance, Laugh & Eat Tacos 2. Jensen, Robert, illus. (SPA.). 36p. (Orig.). (ps-9). 1991. pap. text ed. 17.95 incl. cass. (*1-881120-05-8*) Frog Pr WI.

—Sing, Dance, Laugh & Learn Spanish. Jensen, Robert, illus. 18p. (Orig.). (ps-4). 1993. pap. 12.95 (*1-881120-08-2*) Frog Pr WI.

Mahoney, Judy. Teach Me More Spanish. (Illus.). 20p. (ps-6). 1989. pap. 13.95 incl. audiocassette (*0-934633-14-2*); tchr's. ed. 6.95 (*0-934633-37-1*) Teach Me.

Martinez, Eliseo R. & Martinez, Irma C. Spanish Readiness Skills, Vol. 1. (Illus.). 78p. (ps-3). 1986. wkbk. 8.75 (*1-878300-01-6*) Childrens Work.

Mirame! (SPA., Illus.). 12p. (ps). 1992. bds. 4.95 (*0-525-44853-5*, DCB) Dutton Child Bks.

Morgan-Williams, Louise. I Can Sing en Espanol! Fun Songs for Learning Spanish. (gr. 4-7). 1994. 8.95 (*0-8442-7168-3*, Natl Textbk) NTC Pub Grp.

Noffs, David & Noffs, Laurie. Harold: Revista. rev. ed. Noffs, Laurie, illus. (SPA.). 24p. 1991. wkbk. 2.50 (*0-929875-11-7*) Noffs Assocs.

Numbers & Shapes. (Illus.). 32p. (ps-1). 1992. pap. 2.95 (*1-56144-106-6*, Honey Bear Bks) Modern Pub NYC.

Pen Notes Staff. Learn to Print Spanish: (Aprendiendo a Escribir las Letras. (ps up). 1989. Bilingual instrns. 10.95 (*0-939564-17-3*) Pen Notes.

Piette, Nadine, illus. Mi Primer ABC. (SPA.). 60p. (ps). 1993. Repr. of 1991 ed. 3.95 (*970-607-186-5*, Larousse LKC) LKC.

—Mis Primeros Conocimentos. (SPA.). 60p. (ps). 1993. Repr. of 1991 ed. 3.95 (*970-607-188-1*, Larousse LKC) LKC.

Reid, Elizabeth. Bilingual ABC: Spanish & English. (SPA & ENG., Illus.). 64p. (gr. k-3). 1995. pap. text ed. 2.50 (*0-9627080-6-2*) In One EAR.

—Moms & Dads - Mamis y Papis: Bilingual Coloring Book. (SPA & ENG., Illus.). 64p. (gr. 1-4). 1992. pap. 1.95 (*0-9627080-5-4*) In One EAR.

Ricklen, Neil, illus. My Clothes: Mi Ropa. LC 93-27162. (ENG & SPA.). 14p. (ps-k). 1994. pap. 3.95 (*0-689-71773-3*, Aladdin) Macmillan Child Grp.

—My Colors: Mis Colores. LC 93-27195. (ENG & SPA.). 14p. (ps-k). 1994. pap. 3.95 (*0-689-71772-5*, Aladdin) Macmillan Child Grp.

—My Numbers: Mis Numeros. LC 93-27165. (ENG & SPA.). 14p. (ps-k). 1994. pap. 3.95 (*0-689-71770-9*, Aladdin) Macmillan Child Grp.

Root, Betty. Three Hundred First Words - Palabras Primeras. Dann, Geoff, photos by. (ENG & SPA.). 156p. (ps). 9.95 (*0-8120-6358-9*) Barron.

Schott, Darlyne F. Bono el Mono En la Escuela, Vol. 6: Pasitos Spanish Language Development Books. 25p. (gr. k-1). 1990. pap. text ed. 11.00 (*1-56537-055-4*) D F Schott Educ.

—Calabazas Opuestas, Vol. 5: Pasitos Spanish Language Development Books. 16p. (gr. k-1). 1990. pap. text ed. 11.00 (*1-56537-054-6*) D F Schott Educ.

—Cuatro Regalos, Vol. 2: Pasitos Spanish Language Development Books. 32p. (gr. k-1). 1990. pap. text ed. 11.00 (*1-56537-051-1*) D F Schott Educ.

—Cuento Del Manzano, Vol. 9: Pasitos Spanish Language Development Books. 16p. (gr. k-1). 1990. pap. text ed. 11.00 (*1-56537-058-9*) D F Schott Educ.

—Esta Nevando!, Vol. 10: Pasitos Spanish Language Development Books. 18p. (gr. k-1). 1990. pap. text ed. 11.00 (*1-56537-059-7*) D F Schott Educ.

—Mi Papalote Rojo, Vol. 8: Pasitos Spanish Language Development Books. 11p. (gr. k-1). 1990. pap. text ed. 11.00 (*1-56537-057-0*) D F Schott Educ.

—Oruga, Oruga, Vol. 3: Pasitos Spanish Language Development Books. 15p. (gr. k-1). 1990. pap. text ed. 11.00 (*1-56537-052-X*) D F Schott Educ.

—Pasitos Reading Readiness Kit, A E I O U. (gr. k-1). 1984. Incl. 5 tchr's. manuals, 100 workbooks, copy masters, alphabet picture cards, 20 student alphabet cards. 330.00 (*1-56537-001-5*) D F Schott Educ.

—Pasitos Spanish Language Development Books. (gr. k-1). 1990. pap. text ed. 105.00 (*1-56537-090-2*) D F Schott Educ.

—Pasitos Student Workbook, Libro 1: Pasitos Reading Readiness Kit, A E I O U. 17p. (gr. k-1). 1984. 1.25 (*1-56537-021-X*) D F Schott Educ.

—Pasitos Student Workbook, Libro 10. Schott, Darlyne F., illus. (SPA.). 8p. (Orig.). (gr. k-1). 1991. pap. text ed. 1.25 (*1-56537-131-3*, 131) D F Schott Educ.

—Pasitos Student Workbook, Libro 2: Pasitos Reading Readiness Kit, A E I O U. 17p. (gr. k-1). 1984. 1.25 (*1-56537-022-8*) D F Schott Educ.

—Pasitos Student Workbook, Libro 3: Pasitos Reading Readiness Kit, A E I O U. 17p. (gr. k-1). 1985. 1.25 (*1-56537-023-6*) D F Schott Educ.

—Pasitos Student Workbook, Libro 4: Pasitos Reading Readiness Kit, A E I O U. 17p. (gr. k-1). 1985. 1.25 (*1-56537-024-4*) D F Schott Educ.

—Pasitos Student Workbook, Libro 5: Pasitos Reading Readiness Kit, A E I O U. 17p. (gr. k-1). 1985. 1.25 (*1-56537-025-2*) D F Schott Educ.

—Pasitos Student Workbook, Libro 6. Schott, Darlyne F., illus. (SPA.). 8p. (Orig.). (gr. k-1). 1991. pap. text ed. 1.25 (*1-56537-126-7*, 126) D F Schott Educ.

—Pasitos Student Workbook, Libro 7. Schott, Darlyne F., illus. (SPA.). 8p. (Orig.). (gr. k-1). 1991. pap. text ed. 1.25 (*1-56537-127-5*, 127) D F Schott Educ.

—Pasitos Student Workbook, Libro 8. Schott, Darlyne F., illus. (SPA.). 8p. (Orig.). (gr. k-1). 1991. pap. text ed. 1.25 (*1-56537-128-3*, 128) D F Schott Educ.

—Pasitos Student Workbook, Libro 9. Schott, Darlyne F., illus. (SPA.). 8p. (Orig.). (gr. k-1). 1991. pap. text ed. 1.25 (*1-56537-129-1*, 129) D F Schott Educ.

—Pasitos Teachers' Manual, Libro 1: Pasitos Reading Readiness Kit, A E I O U. 54p. (gr. k-1). 1985. 20.00 (*1-56537-011-2*) D F Schott Educ.

—Pasitos Teachers' Manual, Libro 2: Pasitos Reading Readiness Kit, A E I O U. 44p. (gr. k-1). 1985. 20.00 (*1-56537-012-0*) D F Schott Educ.

—Pasitos Teachers' Manual, Libro 3: Pasitos Reading Readiness Kit, A E I O U. 56p. (gr. k-1). 1985. 20.00 (*1-56537-013-9*) D F Schott Educ.

—Pasitos Teachers' Manual, Libro 4: Pasitos Reading Readiness Kit, A E I O U. 33p. (gr. k-1). 1985. 20.00 (*1-56537-014-7*) D F Schott Educ.

—Pasitos Teachers' Manual, Libro 5: Pasitos Reading Readiness Kit, A E I O U. 40p. (gr. k-1). 1985. 20.00 (*1-56537-015-5*) D F Schott Educ.

—El Puerco Raro, Vol. 1: Pasitos Spanish Language Development Books. 16p. (gr. k-1). 1990. pap. text ed. 11.00 (*1-56537-050-3*) D F Schott Educ.

—Tres Osos, Tres Tamanos, Vol. 4: Pasitos Spanish Language Development Books. 25p. (gr. k-1). 1990. pap. text ed. 11.00 (*1-56537-053-8*) D F Schott Educ.

—Valentin Bonito, Vol. 7: Pasitos Spanish Language Development Books. 19p. (gr. k-1). 1990. pap. text ed. 11.00 (*1-56537-056-2*) D F Schott Educ.

Shott, Stephen, photos by. El Mundo del Bebe. (SPA., Illus.). 48p. (ps). 1992. 14.95 (*0-525-44846-2*, DCB) Dutton Child Bks.

Stockham, Leslie C. Divirtamonos Con el Abecedario. Stockham, Leslie C., illus. 96p. (gr. k-2). 1993. wkbk. 8.95 (*0-9624096-2-6*) Bilingual Lang Mat.

—Divirtamonos Con Letras y Sonidos. (Illus.). 56p. (Orig.). (gr. k-2). 1993. pap. 5.98 (*0-9624096-1-8*) Bilingual Lang Mat.

Wilkes, Angela. Spanish for Beginners. 48p. (ps-1). 1988. 8.95 (*0-8442-7628-6*, Natl Textbk) NTC Pub Grp.

Winitz, Harris. Basic Structures - Spanish, Bk. 1: A Textbook for the Learnables. Sagarna, Blanca, tr. Baker, Syd, illus. 106p. (gr. 7 up). 1991. pap. text ed. 45.00 incl. 4 cass. tapes (*0-939990-61-X*) Intl Linguistics.

Wolfe, Gerard R. Spanish Study Aid. 1978. pap. 2.75 (*0-87738-033-3*) Youth Ed.

SPANISH LANGUAGE–CONVERSATION AND PHRASE BOOKS

Berlitz. Berlitz Jr. Spanish. (ps-2). 1989. text ed. 19.95 incl. cassette (*0-689-71317-7*, Aladdin) Macmillan Child Grp.

Berlitz Jr., No. Two: Spanish. LC 93-36122. (SPA & ENG.). 1995. Set, incl. cass. pap. 19.95 (*0-689-71819-5*, Aladdin); pap. 19.95 bk. only (*0-689-71818-7*, Aladdin); write for info. cass. (Aladdin) Macmillan Child Grp.

Bishop, Dorothy S., et al. Las Manchos Del Sapo. (SPA & ENG., Illus.). 72p. 1987. pap. 4.95 (*0-8442-7171-3*, Natl Textbk) NTC Pub Grp.

—El Muchacho Que Grito el Lobo! (ENG & SPA., Illus.). 72p. 1991. pap. 4.95 (*0-8442-7295-7*, Natl Textbk) NTC Pub Grp.

—El Pajaro Cu. (SPA & ENG., Illus.). 72p. 1991. pap. 4.95 (*0-8442-7163-2*, Natl Textbk) NTC Pub Grp.

Cosby, Bill, et al. Universal Spanish--Cambios: Descubriendo lo Mejor Que Hay en Ti. Callejas, Juan, et al, eds. Trevant, Pierre, tr. from ENG. Ordonez, Maria A. & Espada, Frank, illus. (SPA.). 181p. (Orig.). (gr. 6-8). 1988. pap. text ed. 6.85 (*0-933419-44-9*) Quest Intl.

Disney's First Words in Spanish: A Pull-the-Tab Word Book. (ENG & SPA.). 12p. (ps-1). 1994. 10.95 (*0-7868-3002-6*) Disney Pr.

Farnes, C. Survive in Five Languages. (Illus.). 64p. (gr. 8 up). 1993. PLB 12.96 (*0-88110-623-2*); pap. 6.95 (*0-7460-1034-6*) EDC.

Finocchiaro, Mary, ed. Children's Living Spanish. (Illus.). 1988. manual, incl. cassette 18.95 (*0-517-56333-9*, Crown); dictionary 5.00 (*0-517-56336-3*); manual 5.00 (*0-517-56335-5*) Crown Pub Group.

Foster, Lorri & Gitchel, Sam. Hablemos Acerca del...S-E-X-O: Un Libro para Toda la Familia Acerca de la Pubertad. (SPA & ENG., Illus.). 90p. (gr. 4-8). 1985. pap. 4.95 (*0-9610122-1-8*) Plan Par Ctrl CA.

Gregorich, Barbara. Los Colores. Hoffman, Joan, ed. Shepherd-Bartram, tr. from ENG. Pape, Richard, illus. (SPA.). 32p. (Orig.). (ps). 1987. wkbk. 1.99 (*0-938256-78-5*) Sch Zone Pub Co.

Irving, N. Learn Spanish. (Illus.). 64p. (gr. 6 up). 1993. PLB 13.96 (*0-88110-598-8*); pap. 7.95 (*0-7460-0536-9*) EDC.

Lyric Language - Spanish, Series 1 & 2. (Illus.). (ps-8). Series 1. 9.95 (*1-56015-226-5*) Series 2. 9.95 (*1-56015-239-7*) Penton Overseas.

Mealer, Tamara. My World in Spanish Coloring Book. (SPA., Illus.). 64p. 1991. pap. 4.95 (*0-8442-7552-2*, Natl Textbk) NTC Pub Grp.

Morgan-Williams, Louise. I Can Sing en Espanol: Fun Songs for Learning Spanish. (gr. 4-7). 1994. pap. 12.95 incl. cassette (*0-8442-7172-1*) NTC Pub Grp.

Palmer, Helen. A Fish Out of Water in English & Spanish. Rivera, Carlos, tr. (Illus.). (gr. k-3). 1967. lib. bdg. 5.99 (*0-394-91598-4*) Random Bks Yng Read.

Ronnholm, Ursula O. Aprende a Leer a Trave's de Musica, Juegos y Ritmos. rev. ed. Rabell, Edda, ed. & tr. Montero, Miguel, illus. (SPA.). 42p. (gr. k-2). 1989. pap. text ed. 20.00 incl. cass. (*0-941911-07-1*) Two Way Bilingual.

Sagarna, Blanca. Medios de Transporte: Transportation - Spanish. Baker, Syd, illus. Winitz, Harris, intro. by. (SPA., Illus.). 50p. (gr. 7 up). 1989. pap. text ed. 22.00 incl. cass. (*0-939990-75-X*) Intl Linguistics.

Saloom, Barbara B. Conversational Spanish: Quick & Easy. Cogger, Virginia & Ricardo-Gil, Jose, eds. Mrvien, Mark, illus. 120p. (Orig.). 1988. pap. text ed. 12.95 (*0-9627755-0-9*) B B Saloom.

Schwartz, Linda. Que Piensas Tu? (SPA.). 184p. (gr. 3-7). 1994. 9.95 (*0-88160-238-8*, LW333) Learning Wks.

Segal, Bertha E. Aprendemos el Espanol por Medio de Accion. (SPA.). 106p. (Orig.). (gr. 3-12). 1987. pap. text ed. 12.99 (*0-938395-12-2*) B Segal.

Smith, Neraida. Let's Sing & Learn in Spanish. (SPA & ENG., Illus.). 64p. 1991. pap. text ed. 9.95 incl. audiocassette (*0-8442-7075-X*, Natl Textbk) NTC Pub Grp.

Utley, Derek. Espana Viva. (SPA.). 224p. 1988. pap. text ed. 12.50 (*0-8219-0335-7*, 70291); tchr's. guide 5.95 (*0-8219-0336-5*, TG-70826); text-wkbk. 19.95 (*0-8219-0337-3*, TXTWK-70662) EMC.

Watson, Carol & De Saulles, Janet. Five Hundred Spanish Words & Phrases for Children. McNicholas, Shelagh, illus. (SPA & ENG.). 32p. (gr. 1-2). 1994. 8.95 (*0-7818-0262-8*) Hippocrene Bks.

Winitz, Harris. Text for the Learnables, Spanish, Bk. 1. Sagarna, Blanca, tr. (SPA.). 36p. (gr. 3 up). 1990. pap. text ed. 6.50 (*0-939990-68-7*) Intl Linguistics.

SPANISH LANGUAGE–DICTIONARIES

Aprendamos Espanol Diccinario Ilustrado. (SPA., Illus.). 80p. (gr. 4-7). 1993. pap. 9.95 (*0-8442-7499-2*, Natl Textbk) NTC Pub Grp.

Bailey, Kenneth. Enciclopedia Juvenil Molino en Color, 5 vols. 2nd ed. (SPA.). 510p. 1985. Set 150.00 (*0-7859-5113-X*, S22861) Fr & Eur.

Corbeil, Jean-Claude. The Facts on File English - Spanish Visual Dictionary. (Illus.). 928p. 1992. 39.95 (*0-8160-1546-5*) Facts on File.

Diccionario Infantil Ilustrado. (SPA.). 190p. 1975. 20.50 (*0-7859-0876-5*, S50006); pap. 17.95 (*0-8288-5827-6*, S50007) Fr & Eur.

Enciclopedia Tematica Juvenil: La Agricultura, los Arboles, la Arqueologia, las Aves, la Caramica, el Cuerpo Humano, la Fisica, los Insectos, los Minerales, los Animales Prehistoricos, el Transporte, la Vivienda, 12 vols. (SPA.). 624p. 1976. Set. leatherette 250.00 (*84-201-0188-5*) Fr & Eur.

Langronet, Michel. Enciclopedia Juvenil Larousse: Childrens Larousse Encyclopedia, 8 vols. 4th ed. (SPA.). 1552p. 1978. Set. 495.00 (*0-8288-5226-X*, S50479) Fr & Eur.

Montousse, Juan L. & Perez, Candi. First Two Hundred Words in Spanish. Sleight, Katy, illus. LC 93-29561. (SPA & ENG.). 32p. (gr. 1-4). 1994. 3.95 (*1-85697-957-1*, Kingfisher LKC) LKC.

My First Spanish & English Dictionary: Elementary. 72p. 1993. 6.95 (*0-8442-0055-7*, Natl Textbk) NTC Pub Grp.

Passport Books Staff, ed. Let's Learn Spanish: Picture Dictionary. Goodman, Marlene, illus. 72p. 1991. 9.95 (*0-8442-7558-1*, Natl Textbk) NTC Pub Grp.

Sheheen, Dennis, illus. A Child's Picture English-Spanish Dictionary. LC 84-71801. (gr. k-2). 1984. 9.95 (*0-915361-11-6*, 09407-3) Modan-Adama Bks.

Wilkes, Angela & Borgia, Rubi. Mi Primer Libro de Palabras de Espanol. LC 92-56498. (SPA., Illus.). 64p. (ps-3). 1993. 12.95 (*1-56458-262-0*) Dorling Kindersley.

SPANISH LANGUAGE–DICTIONARIES–ENGLISH

Berlitz. Berlitz Jr. Spanish Dictionary. LC 91-43927. (Illus.). 144p. (ps-2). 1992. pap. 11.95 POB (*0-689-71538-2*, Aladdin) Macmillan Child Grp.

Cirker, Hayward & Steadman, Barbara. Spanish Picture Word Book: Learn over Five Hundred Commonly Used Spanish Words Through Pictures. (SPA & ENG., Illus.). 32p. (Orig.). 1993. pap. text ed. 2.95t (*0-486-27779-8*) Dover.

Livesey, Rupert & Proctor, Astrid. Barrons: Diccionario Juvenil Illustrado - Ingles para Hispanos. (Illus.). 180p. (gr. 2 up). 1994. 14.95 (*0-8120-6457-7*) Barron.

My First One Hundred Words in Spanish & English. 24p. (ps-3). 1992. pap. 11.00 casebound, pull-tab bk. (*0-671-74965-X*, S&S BFYR) S&S Trade.

Passport Books Editors. Apredamos Ingles Diccionario Ilustrado. (gr. 4-7). 1994. 9.95 (*0-8442-7489-5*, Passport Bks) NTC Pub Grp.

Robinson, Linton H. Mexican Slang: A Guide. 160p. (Orig.). 1994. pap. 6.95 (*0-9627080-7-0*) In One EAR.

Watermill Press Staff. Webster's English-Spanish - Espanol-Ingles Dictionary. 224p. (gr. 4-7). 1992. pap. 2.95 (*0-8167-2918-2*, Pub. by Watermill Pr) Troll Assocs.

SPANISH LANGUAGE–GRAMMAR

Collins, Stephen. VerbMaster: Spanish. (SPA.). 29p. (Orig.). (gr. 9 up). 1990. pap. 4.95 (*0-9626328-1-3*) F One Servs.

Deru, Myriam & Alen, Paule. The Birthday Surprise. (SPA & ENG., Illus.). 32p. (ps-1). 1991. 5.99 (*0-517-65556-X*) Random Hse Value.

—My First Day at School. (SPA & ENG., Illus.). 32p. (ps-1). 1991. 5.99 (*0-517-65557-8*) Random Hse Value.

Faulkner, Keith. My First Phrases in Spanish & English. Johnson, Paul, illus. 14p. (ps-4). 1993. pap. 11.00 casebound (*0-671-86595-1*, S&S BFYR) S&S Trade.

Hendirckson, James M. Spanish Grammar Flipper: A Guide to Correct Spanish Usage, No. 2. 49p. (gr. 7 up). 1988. trade edition 5.95 (*1-878383-11-6*) C Lee Pubns.

Piette, Nadine, illus. Mis Primeras Palabras en Ingles. (ENG & SPA.). 60p. (ps). 1993. Repr. of 1991 ed. 3.95 (*970-607-187-3*, Larousse LKC) LKC.

Rico, Armando B. School Adventures: Aventuras Escolares. 27p. (Orig.). 1989. pap. text ed. 4.95 (*1-879219-04-2*) Veracruz Pubs.

Ronnholm, Ursula O. Mi Libro de Escritura. Montero, Miguel, illus. (SPA.). 74p. (gr. k-3). 1986. 4.00 (*0-941911-05-5*) Two Way Bilingual.

SPANISH LANGUAGE–READERS

Ada, Alma F. Manzano, Manzano! Kalthoff, Sandra C., illus. 24p. (Orig.). (gr. k-3). 1989. Six-Pack Set. pap. text ed. 36.00 (*0-917837-46-0*) Hampton-Brown.

—Manzano, Manzano! (Big Book) Kalthoff, Sandra C., illus. (SPA.). 24p. (Orig.). (gr. k-3). 1989. pap. text ed. 29.95 (*0-917837-09-6*) Hampton-Brown.

—El Oso Mas Elegante. Kalthoff, Sandra C., illus. 24p. (Orig.). (gr. k-3). 1989. Six-Pack Set. pap. text ed. 36. 00 (*0-917837-43-6*) Hampton-Brown.

—El Oso Mas Elegante (Big Book) Kalthoff, Sandra C., illus. (SPA.). 24p. (Orig.). (gr. k-3). 1989. pap. text ed. 29.95 (*0-917837-10-X*) Hampton-Brown.

—Los Seis Deseos de la Jirafa (Big Book) Roy, Doug, illus. (SPA.). 16p. (Orig.). (gr. k-3). 1988. pap. text ed. 29.95 (*0-917837-02-9*) Hampton-Brown.

—Una Semilla Nada Mas (Big Book) Remkiewicz, Frank, illus. (SPA.). 16p. (Orig.). (gr. k-3). 1990. pap. text ed. 29.95 (*0-917837-56-8*) Hampton-Brown.

Amery, Heather. First Thousand Words in Spanish. Cartwrigh, Stephen, illus. 50p. (ps-7). 1979. 11.95 (*0-86020-277-1*) EDC.

Behrens, June. El Libro de los Modales (The Manners Book) LC 79-22377. (SPA., Illus.). 32p. (gr. k-3). 1987. pap. 3.95 (*0-516-58750-1*) Childrens.

Big Book - Tape Set. (ENG & SPA.). 1989. tchr's. ed. 143p., 2 cass. tapes 180.00 (*0-917837-26-6*) Hampton-Brown.

Big Book - Tape Set. (ENG & SPA., Orig.). (gr. k-3). 1990. Set incls. 4 big bks. 16p. ea., 2 cass. tapes & tchr's. ed. pap. text ed. 180.00 (*0-917837-61-4*) Hampton-Brown.

Blocksma, Mary. Chirrinchinchina - Que Hay en la Tina? (Rub-a-Dub-Dub - What's in the Tub?) Martin, Sandra K., illus. LC 84-12139. (SPA.). 24p. (ps-2). 1988. pap. 3.95 (*0-516-51586-1*) Childrens.

—Manzano, Manzano! - Libro Grande: Apple Tree! Apple Tree! - Big Book. (Illus.). 24p. (ps-2). 1990. PLB 22.95 (*0-516-59514-8*) Childrens.

—Manzano, Manzano! Apple Tree! Apple Tree! LC 86-19270. (Illus.). 24p. (ps-2). 1986. PLB 9.45 (*0-516-31584-6*); pap. 3.95 (*0-516-51584-5*) Childrens.

—El Oso Mas Elegante (The Best Dressed Bear) LC 86-19272. (Illus.). 24p. (ps-2). 1986. PLB 9.75 (*0-516-31585-4*); pap. 3.95 (*0-516-51585-3*) Childrens.

Cenicienta: Cinderella. LC 86-21526. 32p. (ps-2). 1986. PLB 10.25 (*0-516-32361-X*); pap. 3.95 (*0-516-52361-9*) Childrens.

Classroom Set. (ENG & SPA.). 1989. incls. 4 big bks. 24p., tchr's. ed. 3-ring binder, 143p., 24 small PB (6 of 4 titles) 24p. ea. & 2 cass. tapes 295.00 set (*0-917837-25-8*) Hampton-Brown.

Classroom Set. (ENG & SPA., Orig.). (gr. k-3). 1990. pap. text ed. 260.00 set incls. 4 big bks. 16p., tchr's. guide, 20 copies consumable bks. & 2 cass. tapes (*0-917837-60-6*) Hampton-Brown.

Cuentitos Mios. (SPA.). 72p. (Orig.). (gr. k-3). 1988. pap. text ed. 7.50 (*0-917837-08-8*) Hampton-Brown.

Cuentitos Mios. (SPA.). 65p. (Orig.). (gr. k-3). 1990. pap. text ed. 7.50 (*0-917837-58-4*) Hampton-Brown.

Cuentitos Mios Twenty-Pack. (SPA., Illus.). 72p. (Orig.). (gr. k-3). 1988. Set. pap. text ed. 130.00 (*0-917837-51-7*) Hampton-Brown.

Cuentitos Mios Twenty-Pack. (SPA.). 65p. (Orig.). (gr. k-3). 1990. Set. pap. text ed. 80.00 (*0-917837-65-7*) Hampton-Brown.

Cumpiano, Ina. Pan, Pan, Gran Pan (Big Book) Murdocca, Sal, illus. (SPA.). 16p. (Orig.). (gr. k-3). 1990. pap. text ed. 29.95 (*0-917837-52-5*) Hampton-Brown.

Dr. Seuss. The Cat in the Hat in English & Spanish. Dr. Seuss, illus. Rivera, Carlos, tr. LC 67-5819. (Illus.). 72p. (gr. 1-2). 1967. 6.95 (*0-394-81626-9*) Beginner.

Eastman, Patricia. A Veces las Cosas Cambian-Libro Grande: Sometimes Things Change-Big Book. (Illus.). 32p. (ps-2). 1988. PLB 22.95 (*0-516-59509-1*) Childrens.

—A Veces las Cosas Cambian (Sometimes Things Change) Fleishman, Seymour, illus. LC 83-10090. (SPA.). 32p. (ps-2). 1988. PLB 10.25 (*0-516-32044-0*); pap. 2.95 (*0-516-52044-X*) Childrens.

Elkin, Benjamin. Seis Pescadores Disparatados - Six Foolish Fisherman. LC 86-21611. (Illus.). 32p. (gr. k-3). 1986. pap. 3.95 (*0-516-53601-X*) Childrens.

Emberley, Rebecca. My House, My Casa: A Book in Two Languages. Emberley, Rebecca, illus. LC 89-12893. (ps-2). 1990. 15.95 (*0-316-23637-3*) Little.

Eyewitness Series: Spanish Version. (SPA.). 1989. write for info. (*1-56014-411-4*) Santillana. The Spanish version of the popular Eyewitness Series, BIBLIOTECA VISUAL, is a tremendous informational resource for Spanish speakers of all ages. Twenty-five volumes provide an in-depth presentation of nature, history, science, & technology through a magnificent collection of photographs & illustrations. Titles include: LOS SECRETOS DE LAS PLANTAS (Secrets of Plants), ROCAS Y MINERALES (Rocks & Minerals), LOS PECES (Fish), EL RIO Y LA LAGUNA (Rivers & Lakes), LA ORILLA DEL MAR (Seashore), EL ARBOL (Trees), LOS MAMIFEROS (Mammals), LOS INSECTOS (Insects), EL PAJARO Y SU NIDO (Birds & their Nests), DE LA ORUGA A LA MARIPOSA (From Moths to Butterflies). Other titles include: LOS FOSILES (Fossils), LOS DINOSAURIOS (Dinosaurs), ESQUELITOS (Skeltons), ARMAS Y ARMADURAS (Arms & Armor), MAQUINAS VOLADORAS (Flying Machines), AUTOMOVILES (Cars), LA MUSICA (Music), HOMBRES PRIMATIVOS (Primitive Man), EL ANTIGUO EGIPTO (Ancient Egypt), LA ANTIGUO ROMA (Ancient Rome). To order: Santillana Publishing Co., 901 W. Walnut, Compton, CA 90220. 1-800-245-8584.
Publisher Provided Annotation.

Foreman, Mary M., tr. from ENG. Encuentralo con Elena. King, Ed, illus. (SPA.). 24p. 1992. pap. 3.95 (*1-56288-238-4*) Checkerboard.

—Investigalo con Ines. King, Ed, illus. (SPA.). 24p. 1992. pap. 3.95 (*1-56288-239-2*) Checkerboard.

Four Paperback Classroom Set. (SPA.). 32p. (Orig.). (gr. k-3). 1990. Set. pap. text ed. 32.00 (*0-917837-74-6*) Hampton-Brown.

Fradin, Dennis. California en Palabras y Fotos: C·lifornia: In Words & Pictures. LC 86-21526. (Illus.). 48p. (gr. 2-6). 1986. pap. 4.95 (*0-516-53905-1*) Childrens.

—Texas en Palabras y Fotos: Texas: In Words & Pictures. 48p. (gr. 2-6). 1986. pap. 4.95 (*0-516-53943-4*) Childrens.

Fradsen, Karen. Hoy Fue Mi Primer Dia de Escuela: I Started School Today. LC 86-21623. (Illus.). 32p. (gr. k-3). 1986. PLB 11.30 (*0-516-33495-6*); pap. 3.95 (*0-516-53495-5*) Childrens.

Garcia, Maria. The Adventures of Connie & Diego (Los aventuras de Connie y Diego) LC 86-17132. (ENG & SPA., Illus.). 32p. (gr. 2-9). 1987. 13.95 (*0-89239-028-X*) Childrens Book Pr.

Jarvis-Sladky, Kay. Un Grabado de Goya: Reader 3. Bakke, Eric, illus. LC 81-7783. (SPA.). 40p. (Orig.). (gr. 7-12). 1982. pap. 3.25 (*0-88436-860-2*, 70261) EMC.

—La Guitarra Misteriosa: Reader 1. Bakke, Eric, illus. LC 81-7785. (SPA.). 40p. (Orig.). (gr. 7-12). 1982. pap. 3.25 (*0-88436-858-0*, 70259) EMC.

—El Penitente Elusivo: Reader 4. Bakke, Eric, illus. LC 81-7842. (SPA., Orig.). (gr. 7-12). 1982. pap. 3.25 (*0-88436-861-0*, 70262) EMC.

—Secretos de Famalia: Reader 2. Bakke, Eric, illus. LC 81-7780. (SPA.). 40p. (Orig.). (gr. 7-12). 1982. pap. 3.25 (*0-88436-859-9*, 70260) EMC.

Kratky, Lada J. Chirrinchinchina Que Hay en la Tina? Kalthoff, Sandra C., illus. (SPA.). 24p. (Orig.). (gr. k-3). 1989. pap. text ed. 29.95 big bk. (*0-917837-11-8*) Hampton-Brown.

—Chirrinchinchina Que Hay en la Tina? Kalthoff, Sandra C., illus. (SPA.). 24p. (Orig.) (gr. k-3). 1989. pap. text ed. 6.00 small bk. (*0-917837-13-4*) Hampton-Brown.

—Chirrinchinchina Que Hay en la Tina? Kalthoff, Sandra C., illus. (SPA.). 24p. (Orig.). (gr. k-3). 1989. Six-Pack Set. pap. text ed. 36.00 (*0-917837-44-4*) Hampton-Brown.

—El Chivo en la Huerta (Big Book) Remkiewicz, Frank, illus. (SPA.). 16p. (Orig.). (gr. k-3). 1988. pap. text ed. 29.95 (*0-917837-04-5*) Hampton-Brown.

—La Gallinita, el Gallo y el Frijol. Yerkes, Lane, illus. (SPA.). 24p. (Orig.). (gr. k-3). 1988. pap. text ed. 29. 95 big bk. (*0-917837-05-3*) Hampton-Brown.

—Pequeno Coala Busca Casa. Kalthoff, Sandra C., illus. (SPA.). 24p. (Orig.). (gr. k-3). 1989. pap. text ed. 6.00 (*0-917837-14-2*) Hampton-Brown.

—Pequeno Coala Busca Casa. Kalthoff, Sandra C., illus. (SPA.). 24p. (Orig.). (gr. k-3). 1989. Six-Pack Set. pap. text ed. 36.00 (*0-917837-45-2*) Hampton-Brown.

—Pequeno Coala Busca Casa (Big Book) Kalthoff, Sandra C., illus. (SPA.). 24p. (Orig.). (gr. k-3). 1989. pap. text ed. 29.95 (*0-917837-12-6*) Hampton-Brown.

—Pinta, Pinta, Gregorita (Big Book) Hockerman, Dennis, illus. (SPA.). 16p. (Orig.). (gr. k-3). 1990. pap. text ed. 29.95 (*0-917837-53-3*) Hampton-Brown.

—Veo, Veo, Que Veo? (Big Book) Yerkes, Lane, illus. (SPA.). 16p. (Orig.). (gr. k-3). 1990. pap. text ed. 29. 95 (*0-917837-57-6*) Hampton-Brown.

Lionni, Leo. Pulgada a Pulgada. (SPA., Illus.). (gr. k-1). 1961. 10.95 (*0-8392-3030-3*) Astor-Honor.

Lopez, N. C. King Pancho & the First Clock. Gutierrez, M., illus. LC 63-16396. 32p. (gr. 2-7). 1967. PLB 9.95 (*0-87783-020-7*); pap. 3.94 deluxe ed. (*0-87783-098-3*); cassette 7.94x (*0-685-03701-0*) Oddo.

Lopez, Norbert. Cuento Del Rey Pancho y el Primer Reloj. LC 70-108730. (Illus.). 32p. (gr. 2-7). 1970. PLB 9.95 (*0-87783-010-X*); pap. 3.94 deluxe ed. (*0-87783-104-1*); cassette 7.94x (*0-685-03700-2*) Oddo.

McKissack, Patricia & McKissack, Fredrick. Ada, la Desordenada - Libro Grande: Messey Bessey-Big Book. 32p. (ps-2). 1988. PLB 22.95 (*0-516-59508-3*) Childrens.

—Ada, la Desordenada (Messy Bessey) Hackney, Richard, illus. LC 87-15079. (SPA.). 32p. (ps-2). 1988. PLB 10.25 (*0-516-32083-1*); pap. 2.95 (*0-516-52083-0*) Childrens.

—La Gallinita Roja: The Little Red Hen. LC 86-20801. (Illus.). 32p. (ps-2). 1986. PLB 10.25 (*0-516-32363-6*); pap. 4.95 (*0-516-52363-5*) Childrens.

—El Ratoncito del Campo y el Ratoncito de la Ciudad: Country Mouse & City Mouse. LC 86-21565. 32p. (ps-2). 1986. pap. 3.95 (*0-516-52362-7*) Childrens.

—Los Tres Chivitos. Dunnington, Tom, illus. LC 86-33450. (SPA.). 32p. (ps-2). 1988. PLB 13.27 (*0-516-32366-0*); pap. 3.95 (*0-516-52366-X*) Childrens.

Matthias, Catherine. Los Gatos Me Gustan Mas (I Love Cats) Dunnington, Tom, illus. LC 83-7215. (SPA.). 32p. (ps-2). 1988. pap. 2.95 (*0-516-52041-5*) Childrens.

Moreno, Leslie B. Companeros: Activity Book in Spanish & English for Children. 144p. (gr. 7-11). 1983. pap. 5.95 (*0-917168-09-7*) Executive Comm.

Neasi, Barbara J. Escuchame (Listen to Me) Sharp, Gene, illus. LC 86-10665. (SPA.). 32p. (ps-2). 1988. PLB 10. 25 (*0-516-32072-6*); PLB 22.95 big bk. (*0-516-59507-5*); pap. 2.95 (*0-516-52072-5*) Childrens.

—Igual Que Yo (Just Like Me) Axeman, Lois, illus. LC 83-23154. (SPA.). 32p. (ps-2). 1988. PLB 10.25 (*0-516-32047-5*); PLB 22.95 big bk. (*0-516-59506-7*); pap. 2.95 (*0-516-52047-4*) Childrens.

Ozaeta, Pablo. Mis Primeros Cuentos. Frank, Marjorie & Lono, Luz P., eds. Sussman, Dee, illus. LC 75-16546. (gr. 4-8). 1985. pap. 6.60 student ed. (*0-8325-9642-6*, Natl Textbk); tchr's ed. 10.60 (*0-8325-9641-8*, Natl Textbk); program pkg. (1 tchr's. ed. & 10 student wkbks.) 76.60 (*0-8325-9640-X*, Natl Textbk) NTC Pub Grp.

Padilla, Jaime & Taylor, Maurie. Easy Spanish Word Games. (SPA., Illus.). 64p. (gr. 4 up). 1985. pap. 4.95 (*0-8442-7242-6*, Natl Textbk) NTC Pub Grp.

El Perro y el Gato (Dog & Cat) (SPA., Illus.). 28p. (ps-2). 1991. PLB 11.55 (*0-516-35353-5*); pap. 3.95 (*0-516-55353-4*) Childrens.

Petrie, Catherine. A Pedro Perez le Gustan los Camiones (Joshua James Likes Trucks) Warshaw, Jerry, illus. LC 81-17076. (SPA.). 32p. (ps-2). 1988. pap. 2.95 (*0-516-53525-0*) Childrens.

Ramboz, Ina W. Christmas Songs in Spanish. (SPA.). 32p. (gr. 6-9). 1985. pap. 7.95 (*0-8442-7097-0*, Passport Bks) NTC Pub Grp.

Rivera, Carlos & Eastman, P. D., trs. Are You My Mother? (SPA & ENG.). (gr. 2-4). 1967. 8.95 (*0-394-81596-3*) Random Bks Yng Read.

Tallon, Robert, illus. ABCDEFGHIJKLMNOPQRSTUVWXYZ. LC 76-86987. (ENG & SPA.). 64p. (gr. k-2). 1969. PLB 15. 95 (*0-87460-131-2*) Lion Bks.

Twenty-Four Paperback Classroom Set. (SPA.). 32p. (Orig.). (gr. k-3). 1990. Set. pap. text ed. 192.00 (*0-917837-73-8*) Hampton-Brown.

Wylie, Joanne & Wylie, David. Little Monster: Learning about Size. LC 85-14988. (Illus.). 32p. (ps-2). 1985. pap. 3.95 (*0-516-44495-6*) Childrens.

SPANISH LITERATURE

Garcia, Yolanda. Espanol Divertido: Spanish Fun. LC 86-90286. (Illus.). (gr. 1-6). 1986. pap. 7.95 (*0-935303-00-6*) Victory Pub.

SPANISH POETRY–COLLECTIONS

El Cuento Del Gato y Otras Poesias Favoritas: Blue Set. (SPA., Illus.). 40p. (Orig.). (ps-2). 1992. pap. text ed. 7.00 small bk. (*1-56334-155-7*) Hampton-Brown.

Cumpiano, Ina. Rosario y el Dinosaurio. Winkowski, Fredric, illus. (SPA.). 24p. (Orig.). (gr. 1-3). 1992. pap. text ed. 29.95 big bk. (*1-56334-168-9*) Hampton-Brown.

—Rosario y el Dinosaurio. Winkowski, Fredric, illus. (SPA.). 24p. (Orig.). (gr. 1-3). 1992. pap. text ed. 6.00 small bk. (*1-56334-170-0*) Hampton-Brown.

Del Rosario Marquez, Nieves. Raices y Alas (Poesias Para Ninos y Jovenes) Montes, Jesus, illus. LC 81-65415. (Orig.). (gr. 6). 1981. pap. 5.00 (*0-89729-289-8*) Ediciones.

Kratky, Lada J. El Aguila del Viento. Johnston, David M., illus. (SPA.). 16p. (Orig.). (gr. 2-4). 1992. pap. text ed. 29.95 big bk. (*1-56334-172-7*) Hampton-Brown.

—El Aguila del Viento. Johnston, David M., illus. (SPA.). 16p. (Orig.). (gr. 2-4). 1992. pap. text ed. 6.00 small bk. (*1-56334-173-5*) Hampton-Brown.

—El Chivo en la Huerta. (SPA., Illus.). 16p. (Orig.). (gr. 1-3). 1992. pap. text ed. 36.00 set (6 copies) (*1-56334-141-7*) Hampton-Brown.

—En el Pais de Dulcehogar. Morse, Deborah, illus. (SPA.). 24p. (Orig.). (gr. 1-3). 1992. pap. text ed. 29. 95 big bk. (*1-56334-169-7*) Hampton-Brown.
—En el Pais de Dulcehogar. Morse, Deborah, illus. (SPA.). 24p. (Orig.). (gr. 1-3). 1992. pap. text ed. 6.00 small bk. (*1-56334-171-9*) Hampton-Brown.
—La Gallinita, El Gallo y El Frijol. (SPA., Illus.). 16p. (Orig.). (gr. 1-3). 1992. pap. 36.00 6 copies (*1-56334-142-5*) Hampton-Brown.
—Veo, Veo, Que Veo? (SPA., Illus.). 16p. (Orig.). (ps-2). 1992. Set of 6 bks. pap. 36.00 (*1-56334-124-7*) Hampton-Brown.
La Vida Set, 4 bks. (SPA., Orig.). (gr. 1-3). 1991. pap. 32. 00 set (*1-56334-113-1*) Hampton-Brown.
La Vida Set, 24 bks. (SPA., Orig.). (gr. 1-3). 1991. pap. 192.00 set (*1-56334-112-3*) Hampton-Brown.

SPARRING
see Boxing

SPARROWS
Arnold, Caroline. House Sparrows Everywhere. Hewett, Richard R., photos by. (Illus.). 48p. (gr. 2-5). 1992. 19. 95 (*0-87614-696-5*) Carolrhoda Bks.
George, Jean C. The Moon of the Winter Bird. Nasta, Vincent, illus. LC 91-15237. 48p. (gr. 3-7). 1992. 15. 00 (*0-06-020267-X*); PLB 14.89 (*0-06-020268-8*) HarpC Child Bks.
Pohl, Kathleen. Sparrows. (Illus.). 32p. (gr. 3-7). 1986. PLB 10.95 (*0-8172-2719-9*) Raintree Steck-V.

SPARROWS–FICTION
Bauer, Fred & Reufenacht, Peter. Chilp. LC 72-89351. (Illus.). 24p. (gr. k-4). 1973. 7.95 (*0-87592-011-X*) Scroll Pr.
Bernardson, Derek. The Sparrows & the Circus. Kelly, Geoff, illus. 96p. (Orig.). (gr. 1-3). 1993. pap. 6.95 (*1-86373-061-3*, Pub. by Allen & Unwin Aust Pty AT) IPG Chicago.
—The Sparrows & the Spies. Kelly, Geoff, illus. 96p. (Orig.). (gr. 1-3). 1993. pap. 6.95 (*1-86373-042-7*, Pub. by Allen & Unwin Aust Pty AT) IPG Chicago.
Doney, Meryl. The Very Worried Sparrow. Geldart, William, illus. 32p. (ps-6). 1991. 11.95 (*0-7459-1919-7*) Lion USA.
Richmond, Gary. The Early Bird. 32p. 1992. 7.99 (*0-8499-0924-4*) Word Inc.

SPASTIC PARALYSIS
see Cerebral Palsy

SPEAKING
see Debates and Debating; Public Speaking; Rhetoric; Voice

SPECIE
see Money

SPECIMENS, PRESERVATION OF
see Zoological Specimens–Collection and Preservation

SPECTACLES
see Eyeglasses

SPECTERS
see Apparitions; Ghosts

SPEECH
see also Language and Languages; Phonetics; Voice
Boudreau, Cathy. Speech Takes Off. (Illus.). 176p. (gr. k-6). 1991. 24.95 (*0-937857-30-0*, 1595) Speech Bin.
Childs, Phyllis. Speak Up. 78p. (ps-k). 1985. wkbk. 6.50 (*0-931749-00-X*) PJC Lrng Mtrls.
Cooper, Gary J. Take a Chance. (gr. 2-8). 1993. 16.95 (*0-937857-46-7*, 1544) Speech Bin.
DeVaney, Janet S. Speech Stations: The One-Stop Speech Book. DeVaney, Janet S., illus. 205p. (ps-5). 1987. 24. 95 (*0-937857-03-3*, 1552) Speech Bin.
Fehling, Roberta H. Thinking Speech: A Blueprint for Carryover. 112p. (gr. 3 up). 1991. 16.95 (*0-937857-28-9*, 1593) Speech Bin.
Grigas, Denise. SAYdee. (Illus.). (ps-12). 1993. 20.00 (*0-937857-47-5*, 1546) Speech Bin.
Littlefield, Kathy M. & Littlefield, Robert S. Speak Up! Stark, Steve, illus. 32p. (Orig.). (gr. 3-6). 1989. pap. text ed. 8.95 (*1-879340-00-3*, K0101) Kidspeak.
—What Did You Say? Stark, Steve, illus. 32p. (Orig.). (gr. 3-6). 1989. pap. text ed. 8.95 (*1-879340-01-1*, K0102) Kidspeak.
Minn, Loretta. Teach Speech. 64p. (gr. 3-7). 1982. 8.95 (*0-86653-058-4*, GA 418) Good Apple.
Moncure, Jane B. My "e" Sound Box. Gohman, Vera, illus. LC 84-17021. 32p. (ps-2). 1984. PLB 14.95 (*0-89565-297-8*) Childs World.
—My "i" Sound Box. Gohman, Vera K., illus. LC 84-17022. 32p. (ps-2). 1984. PLB 14.95 (*0-89565-298-6*) Childs World.
—My "o" Sound Box. Gohman, Vera, illus. LC 84-17023. 32p. (ps-2). 1984. PLB 14.95 (*0-89565-299-4*) Childs World.
Pinkney, Nathaniel, illus. Conversation Games: Vol. I-People Times. 87p. (Orig.). (ps-6). 1978. pap. 15.00 (*0-939632-17-9*) ILM.
—Conversation Games: Vol. II-Experiences. 87p. (Orig.). (ps-6). 1978. pap. 15.00 (*0-939632-20-9*) ILM.
Reville, Julie D. The Many Voices of Paws: A Workbook for Young Stutterers. Metayer, Phil, illus. 64p. (ps-3). 1989. 25.00 (*0-937857-11-4*, 1568) Speech Bin.
Rosenbloom, Joseph. World's Toughest Tongue Twisters. Kendrick, Dennis, illus. LC 86-5983. 128p. (gr. 2-8). 1987. pap. 3.95 (*0-8069-6596-7*) Sterling.
Showers, Paul. How You Talk. rev. ed. Lloyd, Megan, illus. LC 90-1484. 32p. (gr. k-4). 1992. PLB 14.89 (*0-06-022768-0*) HarpC Child Bks.
—How You Talk. rev. ed. Lloyd, Megan, illus. LC 90-4056. 32p. (gr. k-4). 1992. pap. 4.50 (*0-06-445099-6*, Trophy) HarpC Child Bks.
Silverstein, Alvin & Silverstein, Virginia. Wonders of Speech. LC 87-31370. (Illus.). 160p. (gr. 7 up). 1988. 12.95 (*0-688-06534-1*) Morrow Jr Bks.
Waugh, Michelle. Winning In Speech: A Workbook for Fluency. (Illus.). 98p. (gr. k-5). 1991. 16.95 (*0-937857-29-7*, 1594) Speech Bin.

SPEECH, LIBERTY OF
see Free Speech

SPEECH THERAPY
Shaw, Janet M. Speech Sports: Games for Speech & Language Fun. (Illus.). 98p. (gr. k-8). 1991. 23.95 (*0-937857-23-8*, 1590) Speech Bin.
Weber, John C. Coping for Kids Who Stutter. (Illus.). 32p. (gr. k-12). 1993. 14.95 (*0-937857-43-2*, 1543) Speech Bin.

SPEECH THERAPY–FICTION
Hulme, Joy N. The Other Side of the Door. LC 90-41020. 168p. (gr. 3-6). 1990. pap. 4.95 (*0-87579-412-2*) Deseret Bk.
Samuelson, Rita. Super Speech Adventures. Madsen, Kris, illus. 96p. (gr. k-4). 1991. pap. 10.00 (*0-930599-65-9*) Thinking Pubns.

SPELEOLOGY
see Caves

SPELLING
see names of languages with the subdivision Spelling, e.g. English Language–Spelling

SPHERICAL TRIGONOMETRY
see Trigonometry

SPICES
Pallotta, Jerry. The Great Tasting Alphabet Book. LC 94-5178. (gr. k up). 1994. 14.95 (*0-685-72620-7*); PLB 15.00 (*0-685-72621-5*); pap. 6.95 (*0-685-72622-3*) Charlesbridge Pub.
—The Spice Alphabet Book: Herbs, Spices, & Other Natural Flavors. Evans, Leslie, illus. 32p. (Orig.). (ps-4). 1994. 14.95 (*0-88106-898-5*); PLB 15.00 (*0-88106-899-3*); pap. 6.95 (*0-88106-897-7*) Charlesbridge Pub.
Reid, Struan. Exploration by Sea. LC 93-14693. (Illus.). 48p. (gr. 6 up). 1994. text ed. 15.95 RSBE (*0-02-775801-X*, New Discovery Bks) Macmillan Child Grp.

SPIDERS
Back, Christine & Watts, Barrie. Spider's Web. LC 86-10017. (Illus.). 25p. (gr. k-4). 1986. 7.95 (*0-382-09288-0*); pap. 3.95 (*0-382-24020-0*) Silver Burdett Pr.
Bailey, Donna. Spiders. LC 90-22113. (Illus.). 32p. (gr. 1-4). 1992. PLB 18.99 (*0-8114-2648-3*); pap. 3.95 (*0-8114-4623-9*) Raintree Steck-V.
Barrett, Norman S. Aranas. LC 90-70883. (SPA., Illus.). 32p. (gr. k-4). 1990. PLB 11.90 (*0-531-07901-5*) Watts.
Climo, Shirley. Someone Saw a Spider: Spider Facts & Folktales. LC 85-45340. (Illus.). 128p. (gr. 4-7). 1985. (Crowell Jr Bks); PLB 13.89 (*0-690-04436-4*, Crowell Jr Bks) HarpC Child Bks.
Craig, Janet. Amazing World of Spiders. Helmer, Jean, illus. LC 89-5005. 32p. (gr. 2-4). 1990. PLB 11.59 (*0-8167-1751-6*); pap. text ed. 2.95 (*0-8167-1752-4*) Troll Assocs.
Dallinger, Jane. Spiders. LC 80-27548. (Illus.). 48p. (gr. 4 up). 1981. PLB 19.95 (*0-8225-1456-7*, First Ave Edns); pap. 5.95 (*0-8225-9534-6*, First Ave Edns) Lerner Pubns.
Dewey, Jennifer. Spiders near & Far. (Illus.). 48p. (gr. 5 up). 1993. 14.99 (*0-525-44979-5*, DCB) Dutton Child Bks.
Gibbons, Gail. Spiders. LC 92-54414. (Illus.). 32p. (ps-3). 1993. reinforced bdg. 15.95 (*0-8234-1006-4*) Holiday.
—Spiders. Gibbons, Gail, illus. 1994. pap. 5.95 (*0-8234-1081-1*) Holiday.
Green, Carl R. & Sanford, William R. The Tarantulas. LC 87-22342. (Illus.). 48p. (gr. 5). 1987. text ed. 12.95 RSBE (*0-89686-339-5*, Crestwood Hse) Macmillan Child Grp.
Hawcock, David. Spider. Montgomery, Lee, illus. LC 93-85207. 12p. (ps-3). 1994. 5.99 (*0-679-85471-1*) Random Bks Yng Read.
Hillyard, Paul. Insects & Spiders. LC 93-19074. (Illus.). 1993. write for info. (*1-56458-385-6*) Dorling Kindersley.
Hopf, Alice L. Spiders. Moreton, Ann, illus. LC 89-9716. 64p. (gr. 5 up). 1990. 13.95 (*0-525-65017-2*, Cobblehill Bks) Dutton Child Bks.
Horton, et al. Amazing Fact Book of Spiders. (Illus.). 32p. 1987. PLB 14.95 (*0-87191-850-1*) Creative Ed.
Insect World. LC 92-30847. 176p. 1993. 18.60 (*0-8094-9687-9*); lib. bdg. 24.60 (*0-8094-9688-7*) Time-Life.
Jennings, Terry. Spiders. Anstey, David, illus. LC 88-83614. 24p. (gr. 1-3). 1989. PLB 10.40 (*0-531-17176-0*) Denison.
Julivert, Maria A. Fascinating World of Spiders. (gr. 4-7). 1992. pap. 6.95 (*0-8120-1377-8*) Barron.
LaBonte, Gail. The Tarantula. (Illus.). 60p. (gr. 3 up). 1991. text ed. 13.95 RSBE (*0-87518-452-9*, Dillon) Macmillan Child Grp.
Lane, Margaret. The Spider. Firth, Barbara, illus. 32p. (gr. k-4). 1994. pap. 4.99 (*0-14-055277-4*, Puff Pied Piper) Puffin Bks.
Levi, Herbert W. & Levi, Lorna R. Spiders & Their Kin. rev. ed. Zim, Herbert S. & Fichter, George S., eds. Strekalovsky, Nicholas, illus. (gr. 9 up). 1969. pap. write for info. (*0-307-24021-5*, Golden Pr) Western Pub.
Lovett, Sarah, text by. Extremely Weird Spiders. (Illus.). 48p. (gr. 3 up). 1991. 9.95 (*1-56261-007-4*) John Muir.
Markle, Sandra. Outside & Inside Spiders. Markle, Sandra, illus. LC 93-22643. 40p. (gr. k-3). 1994. SBE 15.95 (*0-02-762314-9*, Bradbury Pr) Macmillan Child Grp.
Martin, L. Bird Eating Spiders. (Illus.). 24p. (gr. k-5). 1988. PLB 11.94 (*0-86592-966-1*) Rourke Corp.
—Black Widow Spiders. (Illus.). 24p. (gr. k-5). 1988. PLB 11.94 (*0-86592-965-3*) Rourke Corp.
—Fishing Spiders. (Illus.). 24p. (gr. k-5). 1988. PLB 11.94 (*0-86592-964-5*); 8.95s.p. (*0-685-58305-8*) Rourke Corp.
—Funnel Web Spiders. (Illus.). 24p. (gr. k-5). 1988. PLB 11.94 (*0-86592-962-9*); 8.95s.p. (*0-685-58304-X*) Rourke Corp.
—Tarantulas. (Illus.). 24p. (gr. k-5). 1988. PLB 11.94 (*0-86592-967-X*); PLB 8.95s.p. (*0-685-58302-3*) Rourke Corp.
—Trapdoor Spiders. (Illus.). 24p. (gr. k-5). 1988. PLB 11. 94 (*0-86592-963-7*); PLB 8.95s.p. (*0-685-58303-1*) Rourke Corp.
Merrians, Deborah. I Can Read About Spiders. McKeown, Gloria, illus. LC 76-54576. (gr. 2-5). 1977. pap. 2.50 (*0-89375-043-3*) Troll Assocs.
Morris, Dean. Spiders. rev. ed. LC 87-16695. (Illus.). 48p. (gr. 2-6). 1987. PLB 10.95 (*0-8172-3213-3*) Raintree Steck-V.
Murray, Peter. Black Widows. (gr. 2-6). 1992. PLB 15.95 (*0-89565-845-3*) Childs World.
—Spiders. (gr. 2-6). 1992. PLB 15.95 (*0-89565-847-X*) Childs World.
—Tarantulas. (gr. 2-6). 1993. 15.95 (*1-56766-060-6*) Childs World.
Nielsen, Nancy. Black Widow Spider. LC 89-28271. (Illus.). 48p. (gr. 5). 1990. text ed. 12.95 (*0-89686-513-4*, Crestwood Hse) Macmillan Child Grp.
Parker, Steve. Scary Spiders. Savage, Ann, illus. LC 93-27876. 1993. 19.97 (*0-8114-2345-X*) Raintree Steck-V.
Parsons, Alexandra. Amazing Spiders. Young, Jerry, photos by. LC 89-38833. (Illus.). 32p. (gr. 1-5). 1990. 7.99 (*0-679-80226-6*); PLB 9.99 (*0-679-90226-0*) Knopf Bks Yng Read.
Petersen, Candyce A. Silky the Spider. Stoffregen, Jill A., illus. 24p. (ps-3). Date not set. 11.95 (*1-56065-098-2*) Capstone Pr.
Podendorf, Illa. Spiders. LC 81-38444. (Illus.). 48p. (gr. k-4). 1982. PLB 12.85 (*0-516-01653-9*); pap. 4.95 (*0-516-41653-7*) Childrens.
Sarracino, William L., illus. Mother Spider & Her Little Ones. 16p. (Orig.). (ps-7). 1982. pap. 3.75 (*0-915347-11-3*) Pueblo Acoma Pr.
Schnieper, Claudia. Amazing Spiders. Meier, Max, photos by. (Illus.). 48p. (gr. 2-5). 1989. 19.95 (*0-87614-342-7*); pap. 6.95 (*0-87614-518-7*) Carolrhoda Bks.
Spiders. 1991. PLB 14.95 (*0-88682-410-9*) Creative Ed.
Spiders & Scorpions. (ps-3). 1991. pap. 2.50 (*0-89954-548-3*) Antioch Pub Co.
Steele, Philip. Insects. 32p. (gr. 3-5). 1991. lib. bdg. 9.98 (*0-671-72235-2*, J Messner); pap. 4.95 (*0-671-72236-0*) S&S Trade.
Tesar, Jenny. Spiders. (Illus.). 64p. (gr. 4-8). 1993. PLB 16.95 (*1-56711-043-6*) Blackbirch.
—Spiders. (Illus.). 64p. (gr. 3-7). 1993. 14.95 (*1-56711-062-2*) Blackbirch.
Watts, Barrie. Spiders. 32p. (gr. k-4). 1991. pap. 4.95 (*0-531-15624-9*) Watts.
Wildlife Education, Ltd. Staff. Spiders. Stuart, Walter, et al, illus. 20p. (Orig.). (gr. 5 up). 1985. pap. 2.75 (*0-937934-39-9*) Wildlife Educ.
—Spiders. Stuart, Walter, illus. 24p. 1992. 13.95 (*0-937934-88-7*) Wildlife Educ.
The World in Your Backyard: And Other Stories of Insects & Spiders. (Illus.). 63p. (gr. 3-5). 1989. 10.95 (*0-88309-132-1*) Zaner-Bloser.

SPIDERS–FICTION
Fontenot, Mary A. Clovis Crawfish & the Spinning Spider. LC 86-23778. (Illus.). 32p. (ps-3). 1987. 12.95 (*0-88289-644-X*) Pelican.
Graham, Margaret B. Be Nice to Spiders. Graham, Margaret B., illus. LC 67-17101. 32p. (gr. k-3). 1967. PLB 14.89 (*0-06-022073-2*) HarpC Child Bks.
Kajpust, Melissa. A Dozen Silk Diapers. Tomova, Veselina, illus. LC 92-41937. 32p. (ps-2). 1993. 13.95 (*1-56282-456-2*); PLB 13.89 (*1-56282-457-0*) Hyprn Child.
Kirk, David. Miss Spider's Tea Party. LC 93-15710. (Illus.). 32p. 1994. 15.95 (*0-590-47724-2*) Scholastic Inc.
Kraus, Robert. How Spider Saved Thanksgiving. 32p. 1991. pap. 2.50 (*0-590-44411-5*) Scholastic Inc.
—How Spider Saved the Flea Circus. (ps-3). 1991. pap. 2.50 (*0-590-42459-9*) Scholastic Inc.
Lane, Margaret. The Spider. Firth, Barbara, illus. LC 82-71354. 32p. (ps-4). 1983. 9.95 (*0-8037-8303-5*, 0339-110) Dial Bks Young.
McDermott, Gerald, retold by & illus. Anansi the Spider: A Tale from the Ashanti. LC 76-150028. 48p. (ps-2). 1987. reinforced bdg. 15.95 (*0-8050-0310-X*, Bks Young Read); pap. 5.95 (*0-8050-0311-8*) H Holt & Co.
MacDonald, Suse. Space Spinners. (ps-3). 1991. 13.95 (*0-8037-1008-9*); PLB 13.89 (*0-8037-1009-7*) Dial Bks Young.

McNulty, Faith. The Lady & the Spider. Marstall, Bob, illus. LC 85-5427. 48p. (gr. 1-4). 1986. PLB 14.89 (*0-06-024192-6*) HarpC Child Bks.
Maguire, Gregory. Seven Spiders Spinning. LC 93-30478. 1994. 13.95 (*0-395-68965-1*, Clarion Bks) HM.
Martin, C. L. G. Three Brave Women. Elwell, Peter, illus. LC 89-77770. 32p. (gr. k-3). 1991. RSBE 13.95 (*0-02-762445-5*, Macmillan Child Bk) Macmillan Child Grp.
Morley, Carol. A Spider & a Pig. LC 92-53215. 1993. 14. 95 (*0-316-58405-3*) Little.
Nimmo, Jenny. The Snow Spider. LC 87-5429. 144p. (gr. 5 up). 1987. 11.95 (*0-525-44306-1*, DCB) Dutton Child Bks.
—The Snow Spider. 136p. (gr. 5-9). 1990. pap. 2.95 (*0-8167-2264-1*) Troll Assocs.
Parker. I Love Spiders. 1993. pap. 28.67 (*0-590-50153-4*) Scholastic Inc.
Rouss, Sylvia A. Sammy Spider's First Hanukkah. Kahn, Katherine J., illus. LC 92-39639. 1993. 13.95 (*0-929371-45-3*); pap. 5.95 (*0-929371-46-1*) Kar Ben.
Sardegna, Jill. The Roly Poly Spider. Arnold, Tedd, illus. LC 93-40653. (ps-1). 1994. 13.95 (*0-590-47119-8*) Scholastic Inc.
Simons, Scott & Simons, Jamie. Why Spiders Spin: A Story of Arachne. Winograd, Deborah, illus. 32p. (gr. 2-5). 1992. 8.95 (*0-671-69124-4*); PLB 10.95 (*0-671-69120-1*) Silver Pr.
White, E. B. Charlotte's Web. Williams, Garth, illus. LC 52-9760. (gr. 2-6). 1952. 13.00 (*0-06-026385-7*); PLB 12.89 (*0-06-026386-5*) HarpC Child Bks.
—Charlotte's Web. LC 52-9760. (Illus.). 1974. pap. 3.95 (*0-06-440055-7*, Trophy) HarpC Child Bks.
—Charlotte's Web. (Illus.). 192p. (ps-8). 1990. Repr. lib. bdg. 21.95x (*0-89966-696-5*) Buccaneer Bks.
—E. B. White Boxed Set. Incl. Charlotte's Web; The Trumpet of the Swan; Stuart Little. (Illus.). (gr. 3 up). 1972. 39.00 (*0-06-026399-7*) HarpC Child Bks.
—E. B. White Boxed Set. Incl. Charlotte's Web; The Trumpet of the Swan; Stuart Little. (Illus.). (gr. 3 up). 1974. pap. 11.85 (*0-06-440061-1*, Trophy) HarpC Child Bks.
—Tela Charlottae. Fox, Bernice, tr. Williams, Garth, illus. LC 90-55691. (LAT.). 256p. (gr. 2 up). 1991. 18.95 (*0-06-026401-2*) HarpC Child Bks.
Williams, Ursula M. Spid. large type ed. 192p. (gr. 3-7). 1991. 16.95 (*0-7451-1321-4*, Galaxy Child Lrg Print) Chivers N Amer.

SPIES
see also World War, 1939-1945–Underground Movements
Larsen, Anita. The Rosenbergs. Ramsey, Mercy, illus. LC 91-22311. 48p. (gr. 5-6). 1992. text ed. 11.95 RSBE (*0-89686-612-2*, Crestwood Hse) Macmillan Child Grp.
Levine, Ellen. Secret Missions: Four True Life Stories. (Illus.). 128p. (gr. 3-7). 1988. pap. 2.50 (*0-590-41183-7*) Scholastic Inc.
McCarthy, Rick. Spymaster. (gr. 6-10). 1991. write for info. (*0-9629205-0-9*) Develop Solutions.
Reit, Seymour V. Behind Rebel Lines: The Incredible Story of Emma Edmonds, Civil War Spy. 114p. (gr. 3-7). 1991. pap. 4.95 (*0-15-200424-6*, Odyssey) HarBrace.
Stevens, Bryna. Frank Thompson: Her Civil War Story. LC 91-45382. (Illus.). 144p. (gr. 5-9). 1992. SBE 13.95 (*0-02-788185-7*, Macmillan Child Bk) Macmillan Child Grp.
Travis, F. & Hindley, J. Spycraft. (Illus.). 32p. (gr. 3-6). 1977. pap. 6.95 (*0-86020-005-1*) EDC.

SPIES–FICTION
Arthur, Robert, ed. Spies & More Spies. Lambert, Saul, illus. (gr. 7-11). 1972. lib. bdg. 5.39 (*0-394-91673-5*) Random Bks Yng Read.
Ball, Duncan. Emily Eyefinger, Secret Agent. Ulrich, George, illus. LC 92-30518. 96p. (gr. 2-5). 1993. pap. 13.00 JRT (*0-671-79827-8*, S&S BFYR) S&S Trade.
Carmichael, Jack B. Black Knight. 89p. (Orig.). (gr. 12). 1991. pap. 9.95 (*0-9626948-1-9*) Dynamics MI.
—Tales of the Cousin. 80p. (Orig.). (gr. 12). 1992. pap. 9.95 (*0-9626948-2-7*) Dynamics MI.
Fitzhugh, Louise. Harriet the Spy. Fitzhugh, Louise, illus. LC 64-19711. 224p. (gr. 4-7). 1964. 16.00 (*0-06-021910-6*); PLB 15.89 (*0-06-021911-4*) HarpC Child Bks.
—Harriet the Spy. Fitzhugh, Louise, illus. LC 64-19711. 304p. (gr. 3-7). 1990. pap. 3.95 (*0-06-440331-9*, Trophy) HarpC Child Bks.
Follett, Ken. The Key to Rebecca. 352p. (gr. 9-12). 1981. pap. 4.95 (*0-451-15510-6*, Sig) NAL-Dutton.
Gerson, Corinne. My Grandfather the Spy. 1990. 14.95 (*0-8027-6955-1*) Walker & Co.
Griffin, Judith B. Phoebe the Spy. 48p. (gr. 3-6). 1991. pap. 2.75 (*0-590-42432-7*) Scholastic Inc.
Herndon, Ernest. Double-Crossed in Gator Country. 144p. 1994. pap. 4.99 (*0-310-38261-0*) Zondervan.
—Night of the Jungle Cat. (gr. 5 up). 1994. pap. 4.99 (*0-310-38271-8*) Zondervan.
Hoobler, Dorothy & Hoobler, Thomas. The Sign Painter's Secret: The Story of a Revolutionary Girl. Ayers, Donna, illus. 64p. (gr. 4-6). 1991. 5.95 (*0-382-24150-9*); PLB 7.95 (*0-382-24143-6*); pap. 3.95 (*0-382-24345-5*) Silver Burdett Pr.
Kidd, Ronald. A Legend in His Own Mind. Jones, Bob, illus. 80p. (gr. 3-6). 1992. pap. 2.99 (*0-14-034986-3*, Puffin) Puffin Bks.
Lawson, Don & Barish, Wendy. The French Resistance. 192p. (gr. 3-7). 1984. PLB 8.79 (*0-685-07808-6*) S&S Trade.
Leibold, Jay. Spy for George Washington. 128p. (gr. 4). 1985. pap. 2.25 (*0-553-25497-9*) Bantam.
Leppard, Lois G. Mandie & the Foreign Spies. 160p. (Orig.). (gr. 3-8). 1990. pap. 3.99 (*1-55661-147-1*) Bethany Hse.
—Mandie & the Silent Catacombs. 160p. (gr. 3-8). 1990. 3.99 (*1-55661-148-X*) Bethany Hse.
Lisle, Janet T. Sirens & Spies. LC 84-21518. 192p. (gr. 7 up). 1985. SBE 14.95 (*0-02-759150-6*, Bradbury Pr) Macmillan Child Grp.
Locke, Mary. Summer the Spies Moved In. (gr. 4-7). 1991. pap. 2.75 (*0-590-43723-2*, Apple Paperbacks) Scholastic Inc.
Luttrell, Wanda. Stranger in Williamsburg. LC 94-20574. 1995. write for info. (*0-7814-0902-0*, Chariot Bks) Chariot Family.
McCay, William, adapted by. The Secret Peace. LC 91-58100. (Illus.). 136p. (Orig.). (gr. 4-8). 1992. PLB cancelled (*0-679-92777-8*); pap. 3.50 (*0-679-82777-3*) Random Bks Yng Read.
Martini, Teri. Secret Is Out. (gr. 4-7). 1990. 14.95 (*0-316-54864-2*, Joy St Bks) Little.
Matus, Joel. Leroy & the Caveman. LC 92-24647. 144p. (gr. 3-7). 1993. SBE 13.95 (*0-689-31812-X*, Atheneum Child Bk) Macmillan Child Grp.
Olson, Marjorie T. The Sly Spy & Other Stories. Reusable ed. (Illus.). 64p. (gr. 2-3). 1979. pap. 6.50 (*0-87879-830-7*, Ann Arbor Div) Acad Therapy.
Peel, John. Where in the World Is Carmen San Diego? 48p. (gr. 4-7). 1991. pap. 3.95 (*0-307-22301-9*, 22301) Western Pub.
—Where in Time Is Carmen San Diego? 48p. (gr. 4-7). 1991. pap. 3.95 (*0-307-22302-7*, 22302) Western Pub.
Rinaldi, Ann. Finishing Becca: A Story of Peggy Shippen & Benedict Arnold. (gr. 7 up). 1994. pap. 3.95 (*0-15-200879-9*); 10.95 (*0-15-200880-2*) HarBrace.
Sathre, Vivian. J. B. Wigglebottom & the Parade of Pets. O'Neill, Catherine, illus. LC 92-17375. 96p. (gr. 2-6). 1993. SBE 12.95 (*0-689-31811-1*, Atheneum Child Bk) Macmillan Child Grp.
Schenkman, Richard, ed. The Illustrated James Bond, 007. McLusky, John, illus. 90p. (Orig.). (gr. 5 up). 1981. pap. 6.95 (*0-9605838-0-7*) Bond Double-O Seven.
Sharmat, Marjorie W. Sly Spy: Olivia Sharp, Agent for Secrets. 1990. 12.95 (*0-385-29974-5*) Doubleday.
—Spy in the Neighborhood. 1989. pap. 2.75 (*0-590-42633-8*) Scholastic Inc.
Sobol, Donald J. Encyclopedia Brown's Book of Wacky Spies. Enik, Ted, illus. 112p. (gr. 4-6). 1984. pap. 2.25 (*0-553-15369-2*, Skylark) Bantam.
Vincent, John. High Stakes. (Illus.). 128p. (gr. 3-7). 1992. pap. 2.99 (*0-14-036048-4*, Puffin) Puffin Bks.

SPINAL PARALYSIS, ANTERIOR
see Poliomyelitis

SPIRIT OF ST. LOUIS (AIRPLANE)
Stein, R. Conrad. The Spirit of St. Louis. LC 94-9491. (Illus.). 32p. 1994. PLB 16.40 (*0-516-06682-X*); pap. 3.95 (*0-516-46682-8*) Childrens.
Younkin, Paula. The Spirit of St. Louis. LC 93-3292. (Illus.). 48p. (gr. 5-6). 1994. text ed. 13.95 RSBE (*0-89686-832-X*, Crestwood Hse) Macmillan Child Grp.

SPIRITS
see Apparitions; Ghosts; Witchcraft

SPIRITUAL LIFE
see also Christian Life; Faith
Anderson, Neil T. & Park, Dave. Stomping Out the Darkness: Realizing the Incredible Power of Who You Really Are in Christ. Daly, Jean, ed. LC 93-26385. (Illus.). 180p. (gr. 8-12). 1993. pap. 8.99 (*0-8307-1640-8*, 5422307) Regal.
Auer, Jim. Ten Ways to Meet God: Spirituality for Teens. 64p. (gr. 7-12). 1989. pap. 2.95 (*0-89243-299-3*) Liguori Pubns.
Bennett, Geraldine M. Katrina & Elishia Learn about Ouija Boards. Shell, Audery & Granger, Debby, eds. Poe, Ty, illus. 50p. (Orig.). (gr. 5 up). 1994. 6.98 (*1-882786-13-0*); pap. 7.98 (*1-882786-04-1*) New Dawn NY.
—The Katrina Tells Series. (gr. 3 up). 1994. pap. write for info. (*1-882786-99-8*) New Dawn NY.
Brownlow, Bette H. Tyler's Descent. (Illus.). 32p. (Orig.). 1993. pap. 5.25 (*1-883516-00-5*) Peregrine & Hayes.
Brunton, Paul. Inspiration & the Overself: The Notebooks of Paul Brunton, Vol. 14. Cash, Paul & Smith, Timothy, eds. (Illus.). 256p. (gr. 7 up). 1988. 25.00 (*0-943914-40-X*, Dist. by NBN); pap. 14.95 (*0-943914-41-8*, Dist. by NBN) Larson Pubns.
Burrill, Richard. Somewhere Behind the Eyes: A New Way of Being & Seeing. (Orig.). (gr. 9-12). 1990. 15. 95 (*1-878464-04-3*); pap. 8.95 (*1-878464-05-1*) Anthro Co.
Carrozzi, Craig J. Wedding of the Waters. LC 88-60526. (Illus.). 396p. (Orig.). 1988. pap. 10.95 (*0-9620286-0-6*) Suthrn Trails Pub.
Case, Riley B. & Keysor, Charles W. We Believe - Confirmation Student Guide: Jr. High. rev. ed. Heidinger, James V., II, et al, eds. Myers, Glenn, illus. 60p. (gr. 6-9). 1988. wkbk. 4.35 (*0-917851-20-X*) Bristol Hse.
Conwell, Russell H. Acres of Diamonds: All Good Things Are Possible, Right Where You Are, & Now! Leonardo, Bianca, ed. 160p. (gr. 8-12). 1993. pap. text ed. 10.95 (*0-930852-25-7*) Tree Life Pubns.
Curtis, Donald. New Age Understanding. LC 72-92276. 144p. 1990. pap. 7.95 (*0-941992-23-3*) Los Arboles Pub.
Ekberg, Susan. Pink Stars & Angel Wings. Neavill, Michelle, illus. LC 91-91216. 32p. (ps up). 1992. 16.95 (*0-9630419-0-8*) Spiritseeker.
Hebblethwaite, Margaret. My Secret Life: A Friendship with God. LC 90-21550. 32p. (gr. 3-7). 1991. 11.95 (*0-8192-1538-4*) Morehouse Pub.
Hodgson, Joan. Hullo Sun. Ripper, Peter, illus. (ps-3). 1972. 6.95 (*0-85487-019-9*) DeVorss.
Johnson, Tom. Heaven Is an Action, Not a Place. 32p. (Orig.). 1990. pap. 3.50 (*0-941992-22-5*) Los Arboles Pub.
Jones, James A., III. Conversations with Children. Cook, Debbie, illus. LC 85-40201. 96p. (gr. 4-8). 1985. 8.95 (*0-938232-72-X*) Winston-Derek.
Keith, Gretchen L. The Life to Come: Stories for Children about the Spiritual World. Cook, Richard J., illus. 89p. (Orig.). (gr. 3-7). 1990. pap. 5.00 (*0-945003-03-X*) General Church.
Landon, Linda L. Earth Angel Child: You May Be One. Landon, Linda L., illus. (Orig.). (gr. 3 up). 1992. pap. 8.80 (*0-9633759-0-3*) Harmony Hill.
Lehn, Cornelia. Peace Be with You. Neely, Keith R., illus. Regier, Harold R. & Schwartzentruber, Hubertintro. by. LC 80-70190. (Illus.). 126p. (gr. k-5). 1981. 12.95 (*0-87303-061-3*) Faith & Life.
Lindstrom, Marilyn. The Voice from Inner Space: Answers Who Am I? Why Am I Here? Beckman, Jean, ed. LC 90-35087. 112p. (Orig.). 1990. pap. 7.95 (*0-941992-20-9*) Los Arboles Pub.
MacKenthun, Carole & Dwyer, Paulinus. Gentleness. Filkins, Vanessa, illus. 48p. (gr. 2 up). 1987. pap. 7.95 (*0-86653-395-8*, SS879, Shining Star Pubns) Good Apple.
Murphy, Louise S. A Teenager Who Dared Obey God. 97p. (Orig.). 1985. pap. text ed. 3.95 (*0-937580-44-9*) LeSEA Pub Co.
Narayaneeyam. pap. 5.95 (*0-87481-474-X*, Pub. by Ramakrishna Math India) Vedanta Pr.
Paramananda. Problem of Life & Death. pap. 1.95 (*0-87481-543-6*, Pub. by Ramakrishna Math India) Vedanta Pr.
Ray, Sandy. The Little Seed. Sytsma, Cheryle, ed. LC 90-63623. (Illus.). 30p. (Orig.). (gr. k-5). 1991. pap. write for info. (*1-879068-01-X*) Ray-Ma Natsal.
—Sir Joshua, Himself. Sytsma, Cheryle, ed. LC 90-63622. (Illus.). 30p. (Orig.). (gr. k-5). 1991. pap. write for info. (*1-879068-02-8*) Ray-Ma Natsal.
Roberts, Sharon L. Somebody Lives Inside: The Holy Spirit. (Illus.). 24p. (Orig.). (gr. k-4). 1986. pap. 3.99 saddlestitched (*0-570-08530-6*, 56-1557) Concordia.
Snyder, Linda. School Struggles. 48p. (Orig.). (gr. 9-12). 1990. pap. 8.99 (*1-55945-201-3*) Group Pub.
Stelling, Bill. Simply Spiritual Exercise Workbook. 38p. (Orig.). (gr. 10 up). 1992. pap. 6.00 (*0-940829-08-8*) Eagle Wing Bks.
Sutphen, Dick. The Nasty Dragon Who Became a Nice Puppy: Reincarnation for Young People. (Illus.). 32p. (Orig.). (ps-3). 1992. pap. 10.98 incl. tape (*0-87554-528-9*) Valley Sun.
Taylor, Connie R. Before Birth, Beyond Death. LC 87-82117. 64p. (gr. 4-6). 1987. pap. 6.98 (*0-88290-315-2*) Horizon Utah.
Vissell, Rami. Rami's Book: The Inner Life of a Child. Vissell, Rami, illus. Vissell, Barry, intro. by. LC 88-91345. (Illus.). 56p. 1990. 13.95 (*0-9612720-4-X*, 104) Ramira Pub.
Wenig, Laurin J. The Prophets: Showing Us the Way to Justice & Peace. (Illus.). 80p. (Orig.). (gr. 9-12). 1990. pap. text ed. 4.90 (*0-937997-16-1*); tchr's. ed. 8.90 (*0-937997-17-X*) Hi-Time Pub.
Woody, Sandra. Run So Fast. Sytsma, Cheryle, ed. LC 90-63615. (Illus.). 25p. (Orig.). (gr. k-5). 1991. pap. write for info. (*1-879068-05-2*) Ray-Ma Natsal.

SPIRITUALS
Bryan, Ashley. All Night, All Day: A Child's First Book of African-American Spirituals. Bryan, Ashley, illus. LC 90-753145. 48p. (ps-4). 1991. SBE 14.95 (*0-689-31662-3*, Atheneum Child Bk) Macmillan Child Grp.
Langstaff, John. What a Morning! The Christmas Story in Black Spirituals. Bryan, Ashley, illus. LC 87-750130. 32p. 1987. SBE 14.95 (*0-689-50422-5*, M K McElderry) Macmillan Child Grp.

SPLICING
see Knots and Splices

SPOCK, BENJAMIN MCLANE, 1903-
Kaye, Judith. The Life of Benjamin Spock. (Illus.). 80p. (gr. 4-7). 1993. PLB 13.95 (*0-8050-2301-1*) TFC Bks NY.

SPORTS
see also Amusements; Athletics; Coaching (Athletics); Games; Gymnastics; Olympic Games; Outdoor Life; Physical Education and Training; Rodeos; School Sports; Water Sports; Winter Sports
also names of sports, e.g. baseball; etc.
Aaseng, Nathan. The Locker Room Mirror: How Sports Reflect Society. LC 92-34582. (Illus.). 144p. (gr. 5 up). 1993. 14.95 (*0-8027-8217-5*); PLB 15.85 (*0-8027-8218-3*) Walker & Co.
Adoff, Arnold. Sports Pages. Kuzma, Steve, illus. LC 85-45169. 80p. (gr. 3 up). 1990. pap. 5.95 (*0-06-446098-3*, Trophy) HarpC Child Bks.
Allen, Anne. Sports for the Handicapped. (gr. 6 up). 1981. lib. bdg. 10.85 reinforced (*0-8027-6437-1*) Walker & Co.

Barrett, Norman S. Sport: Players, Games & Spectacle. LC 93-7936. (Illus.). 48p. (gr. 5-8). 1993. 13.95 (0-531-15262-6) Watts.

Beard, Daniel C. American Boys Handy Book: What to Do & How to Do It. facs. ed. LC 66-15858. (Illus.). 392p. (gr. 4 up). 1966. 14.95 (0-8048-0006-5) C E Tuttle.

Bonner, Staci. Sports: Careers in Sports. LC 93-9887. (Illus.). 48p. (gr. 5-6). 1994. text ed. 14.95 RSBE (0-89686-789-7, Crestwood Hse) Macmillan Child Grp.

Boy Scouts of America Staff. Varsity Triathlon. (Illus.). 41p. 1990. pap. 3.15 (0-8395-3456-6, 3456) BSA.

Braden, Vic & Phillips, Louis. Sportsathon Puzzles, Jokes, Facts & Games. Eberbach, Andrea, illus. (ps-k). 1986. pap. 4.95 (0-14-032028-8, Puffin) Puffin Bks.

Clark, Raymond C. & Jerald, Michael. Summer Olympic Games: Exploring International Athletic Competition. (Illus.). 96p. (gr. 5 up). 1987. 10.50x (0-86647-021-2) Pro Lingua.

Constanzo, Christie. Hot Air Ballooning. 48p. (gr. 3-4). 1991. PLB 11.95 (1-56065-049-4) Capstone Pr.

Cook, J. & Way, P. Windsurfing. (Illus.). (gr. 6 up). 1988. pap. 7.95 (0-7460-0195-9) EDC.

Crisfield, Deborah. Sports Injuries. (Illus.). 48p. (gr. 5-6). 1991. text ed. 12.95 RSBE (0-89686-663-7, Crestwood Hse) Macmillan Child Grp.

Dudley, William. Sports in America: Opposing Viewpoints. LC 93-30961. (Illus.). 264p. (gr. 10 up). 1994. PLB 17.95 (1-56510-105-7); pap. text ed. 9.95 (1-56510-104-9) Greenhaven.

Duncanson, Neil. Sports Technology. LC 91-17570. (Illus.). 48p. (gr. 5-7). 1992. PLB 12.90 (0-531-18401-3, Pub. by Bookwright Pr) Watts.

Field, Shelly. Career Opportunities in the Sports Industry. 264p. (gr. 9-12). 1992. pap. 14.95 (0-8160-2672-6) Facts on File.

FS Staff & Mohun, Janet. Drugs Steroids & Sports. LC 88-50494. (Illus.). 64p. (gr. 6-12). 1988. PLB 12.40 (0-531-10626-8) Watts.

Gay, Kathlyn. They Don't Wash Their Socks! 112p. 1991. pap. 3.50 (0-380-71302-0, Camelot) Avon.

Gilbert, Nancy. The Special Olympics. 32p. (gr. 4). 1990. PLB 14.95 (0-88682-311-0) Creative Ed.

Gould, Marilyn. Playground Sports: A Book of Ball Games. (Illus.). 62p. (gr. 2 up). 1991. 10.95 (0-9632305-2-2) Allied Crafts.

Grosshandler, Henry & Grosshandler, Janet. Everyone Wins at Tee Ball. Grosshandler, Henry & Grosshandler, Janet, illus. LC 89-7875. 32p. (gr. k-3). 1990. 12.95 (0-525-65016-4, Cobblehill Bks) Dutton Child Bks.

Guthrie, Robert. Freestyle Skiing & Snowboarding. (Illus.). 48p. (gr. 3-6). 1992. PLB 12.95 (1-56065-052-4) Capstone Pr.

Gutman, Bill. Go for It Sports Library Series, 12 vols. (gr. 3-8). 1990. Set. PLB 179.40 (0-942545-98-2) Marshall Cavendish.

Hamilton, Harley & Jones, Nancy K. Sport Signs. Incl. Signs & Printed Words, General Vocabulary. 64p. pap. 6.00 (0-317-42767-9); Football. 48p. pap. 5.00 (0-317-42768-7); Basketball. 48p. pap. 5.00 (0-317-42769-5); Baseball-Softball. 48p. pap. 5.00 (0-317-42770-9); Track & Field. 40p. pap. 4.00 (0-317-42771-7); Volley Ball. 28p. pap. 3.00 (0-317-42772-5). 1985. pap. 17.00 set (0-317-42766-0) Modern Signs.

Hammond, Tim. Sports. King, Dave, photos by. LC 88-1573. (Illus.). 64p. (gr. 5 up). 1988. 16.00 (0-394-89616-5); lib. bdg. 16.99 (0-394-99616-X) Knopf Bks Yng Read.

Hays, Scott. Landsailing. (Illus.). 48p. (gr. 3-6). 1992. PLB 12.95 (1-56065-057-5) Capstone Pr.

Herzog, Brad. Heads Up! Puzzles for Sports Brains. (gr. 4-7). 1994. pap. 2.99 (0-553-48160-6) Bantam.

Highlights for Children Staff. Action Book of Sports. Highlights for Children Staff, illus. 32p. (gr. 3-8). 1988. pap. 2.95 (0-87534-229-9) Highlights.

—Summer Games. Highlights for Children Staff, illus. 48p. (gr. 3-7). 1990. pap. 2.95 (0-87534-352-X) Highlights.

Hinds, Bill. Buzz Beamer's Radical Sports. (gr. 4-7). 1990. pap. 3.95 (0-316-36448-7, Spts Illus Kids) Little.

Hollander, Phyllis & Hollander, Zander. Amazing but True Sports Stories. (Illus.). 128p. (Orig.). (gr. 3 up). 1986. pap. 2.50 (0-590-43736-4) Scholastic Inc.

Jennings, Jay. Comebacks. (Illus.). 64p. (gr. 5-7). 1991. PLB 10.95 (0-382-24109-6); pap. 5.95 (0-382-24115-0); pap. 6.71s.p. (0-685-47014-8) Silver Burdett Pr.

—Sports Triumphs Series, 4 vols. (Illus.). 256p. (gr. 5-7). 1991. Set. PLB 43.80s.p. (0-685-47011-3); Set. pap. 26.85s.p. (0-685-47012-1) Silver Burdett Pr.

Kallen, Stuart A. Spectacular Sports Records. Wallner, Rosemary, ed. LC 91-73056. 1991. PLB 12.94 (1-56239-045-7) Abdo & Dghtrs.

Kaplan, Andrew. Careers for Sports Fans. (Illus.). 64p. (gr. 7 up). 1991. PLB 14.40 (1-56294-023-6); pap. 4.95 (1-56294-773-7) Millbrook Pr.

—Careers for Sports Fans. 1992. pap. 4.95 (0-395-63562-4) HM.

Kettelkamp, Larry. Modern Sports Science. LC 86-8754. (Illus.). 160p. (gr. 7 up). 1986. 12.95 (0-688-05494-3) Morrow Jr Bks.

Kristy, Davida. Coubertin's Olympics: How the Games Began. LC 94-12889. 1994. 21.50 (0-8225-3327-8) Lerner Pubns.

Langley, Andrew. Sports & Politics. (Illus.). 48p. (gr. 5 up). 1990. lib. bdg. 18.60 (0-86592-117-2); lib. bdg. 13. 95 s.p. (0-685-46458-X) Rourke Corp.

Lerner Publications, Department of Geography Staff, ed. Sri Lanka in Pictures. (Illus.). 64p. (gr. 5 up). 1988. 17.50 (0-8225-1853-8) Lerner Pubns.

Let's Discover Sport & Entertainment. (Illus.). 80p. (gr. k-6). 1981. per set 199.00 (0-8172-1768-1) Raintree Steck-V.

Liss, Howard. The Giant Book of More Strange but True Sports Stories. Mathieu, Joe, illus. LC 82-13236. 160p. (gr. 5-10). 1983. pap. 8.95 (0-394-85633-3) Random Bks Yng Read.

—The Giant Book of Strange but True Sports Stories. Mathieu, Joe, illus. LC 76-8132. (gr. 5-9). 1976. 9.00 (0-394-83287-6) Random Bks Yng Read.

Loeffelbein, Robert L. The Recreation Handbook: Three-Hundred Forty-Two Games & Other Activities for Teams & Individuals. LC 92-50310. (Illus.). 255p. 1992. pap. 24.95x (0-89950-744-1) McFarland & Co.

Masciantonio, Rudolph. Greco Roman Sports & Games. 64p. (gr. 7-12). 1991. spiral bdg. 4.50 (0-939507-28-5, B 314) Amer Classical.

Meer, Jeff. Drugs & Sports. (Illus.). 32p. (gr. 5 up). 1991. pap. 4.49 (1-55546-996-5) Chelsea Hse.

Myers, Gail A. A World of Sports for Girls. LC 81-10440. (Illus.). 160p. (gr. 5-9). 1981. 11.00 (0-664-32683-8, Westminster) Westminster John Knox.

Nardo, Don. Drugs & Sports. LC 90-6686. (Illus.). 112p. (gr. 5-8). 1990. PLB 14.95 (1-56006-112-X) Lucent Bks.

Nash, Bruce & Zullo, Allan. Freebies for Sports Fans. Doty, Roy, illus. 96p. (gr. 1 up). 1990. pap. 4.95 (0-671-70339-0, S&S BFYR) S&S Trade.

—The Greatest Sports Stories Never Told. Ward, Bernie, compiled by. Gampert, John, illus. LC 92-15352. 1993. pap. 8.95 (0-671-75938-8) S&S Trade.

—The Sports Hall of Shame: Young Fans Edition. MacDonald, Patricia, ed. 176p. 1990. pap. 2.95 (0-671-69355-7, Archway) PB.

Nelson, Cordner. Careers in Pro Sports. rev. ed. Rosen, Ruth, ed. LC 89-37641. (Illus.). 143p. (gr. 7-12). 1992. PLB 14.95 (0-8239-1456-9) Rosen Group.

Nuwer, Hank. Sports Scandals. LC 93-26317. (Illus.). 196p. (gr. 9-12). 1994. PLB 13.90 (0-531-11183-0) Watts.

O'Sullivan, Carol. Drugs & Sports: Locating the Author's Main Idea. LC 89-36322. (Illus.). 32p. (gr. 3-6). 1990. PLB 10.95 (0-89908-637-3) Greenhaven.

The Parents' Guide to Kids' Sports. (Illus.). (gr. 3-7). 1990. pap. 8.95 (0-316-77471-5) Little.

Parietti, Jeff. One Hundred & One Wacky Sports Quotes. (gr. 4-7). 1991. pap. 1.95 (0-590-44146-9) Scholastic Inc.

Peissel, Michel & Allen, Missy. Dangerous Sports. (Illus.). 112p. (gr. 5 up). 1993. PLB 19.95 (0-7910-1791-5, Am Art Analog) Chelsea Hse.

—Dangerous Sports. LC 92-23546. 1993. pap. write for info. (0-7910-1942-X) Chelsea Hse.

Richardson, Allen F. Careers Without College: Sports. Colton, Kitty, ed. Schmidt, Peggy, contrib. by. LC 93-4488. 96p. (gr. 10-12). 1993. pap. 7.95 (1-56079-250-7) Petersons Guides.

Rigby, Julie. Career Portraits: Sports. LC 94-15315. 1994. 12.95 (0-8442-4361-2, VGM Career Bks) NTC Pub Grp.

Rolfe, John. Curveballs Strikes Again: More Wacky Facts to Bat Around. Kopecky, Robert, illus. 32p. (gr. 3-7). 1992. pap. 4.95 (0-316-75460-9, Spts Illus Kids) Little.

Rowen, Larry. Beyond Winning: Group Centered Games & Sports. (gr. 2-6). 1990. pap. 9.95 (0-8224-3380-X) Fearon Teach Aids.

Sanchez, Isidro & Peris, Carme. The World of Sports Series, 4 bks. (Illus.). 32p. (ps-1). 1992. Boxed set. pap. 23.95 (0-8120-7862-4) Barron.

Schneider, Tom. Everybody's a Winner: A Kid's Guide to New Sports & Fitness. (Illus.). (gr. 3 up). 1976. 14.95 (0-316-77398-0, Brown Paper School); pap. 10.95 (0-316-77399-9) Little.

Schulman, L. M., ed. The Random House Book of Sports Stories. Allen, Thomas B., illus. LC 89-12834. 256p. (gr. 5 up). 1990. lib. bdg. 16.99 (0-394-92874-1); pap. 16.00 (0-394-82874-7) Random Bks Yng Read.

Schultz, Ron. Looking Inside Sports Aerodynamics. (Illus.). 48p. (Orig.). (gr. 3 up). 1992. pap. 9.95 (1-56261-065-1) John Muir.

Schwartz, Linda. Trivia Trackdown-Sports & Space. (Illus.). 32p. (gr. 4-6). 1986. 3.95 (0-88160-138-1, LW257) Learning Wks.

Seibert, Patricia. Mush! Across Alaska in the World's Longest Sled-dog Race! (gr. 4-7). 1992. pap. 4.95 (0-395-64537-9) HM.

Sheely, Robert. Sports Lab. LC 93-41621. 64p. (gr. 4-6). 1994. PLB 12.95 (1-881889-49-1) Silver Moon.

Sobol, Donald J. Encyclopedia Brown's Book of Wacky Sports. Enik, Ted, illus. 128p. (Orig.). (gr. 3-7). 1984. pap. 2.50 (0-553-15497-4, Skylark) Bantam.

Sports. (Illus.). 72p. (gr. 6-12). 1972. pap. 1.85 (0-8395-3255-5, 33255) BSA.

Sports & Entertainment. (Illus.). 80p. (gr. k-6). 1986. pap. 199.00 per set (0-8172-2590-0); 14.95 ea. Raintree Steck-V.

Sports & Recreation, 11 vols. (Illus.). 96p. (gr. 3 up). 1987. Set. PLB 240.00 (0-317-64441-6); pap. 13.27 (0-8172-3061-0) Raintree Steck-V.

Sports Curriculum, Vols. I-VII. rev. ed. (Illus.). 552p. (gr. 3-8). 1994. pap. text ed. write for info. Set, incl. job cards Spts Curriculum.

The Sports Day. (Illus.). (ps-2). 1990. 3.50 (0-7214-1322-6); parent/tchr's. guide 3.95 (0-317-04760-4) Ladybird Bks.

Sports: Superdoodles. LC 92-74098. (gr. 1-6). 1993. pap. 4.95 (0-88160-221-3, LW305) Learning Wks.

Stevens, Philippa J. Bonk! Goes the Ball. Martin, Clovis, illus. LC 89-48561. 32p. (ps-2). 1990. PLB 10.25 (0-516-02061-7); pap. 2.95 (0-516-42061-5) Childrens.

Stine, Megan, et al. Hands-On Science: Games, Puzzles, & Toys. Taback, Simms, illus. LC 92-56892. 1993. PLB 18.60 (0-8368-0957-2) Gareth Stevens Inc.

Super Giant Sports Question & Answer Book. (Illus.). 278p. 1991. pap. 2.99 (0-517-02239-7) Random Hse Value.

Tallarico, Tony. I Didn't Know That about Sports. (Illus.). 32p. 1992. pap. 2.95 (1-56156-163-0) Kidsbks.

—I Didn't Know That about Sports. (Illus.). 32p. 1992. 9.95 (1-56156-115-0); pap. 2.95 (1-56156-111-8) Kidsbks.

Three Hundred Sixty-Five Amazing Days in Sports. (Illus.). (gr. 3-7). 1990. pap. 12.95 (0-316-78537-7, Spts Illus Kids) Little.

Time-Life Inc. Editors. Play Ball: Sports Math. Mark, Sara, et al, eds. (Illus.). 64p. (gr. k-4). 1993. write for info. (0-8094-9970-3); lib. bdg. write for info. (0-8094-9971-1) Time-Life.

Trager, Oliver, ed. Sports in America: Paradise Lost? 224p. 1990. 29.95x (0-8160-2412-X) Facts on File.

Weber. More Weird Moments in Sports. 1993. pap. 2.50 (0-590-43522-1) Scholastic Inc.

Weiss, Ann E. Money Games: The Business of Sports. LC 92-25002. 240p. (gr. 5-9). 1993. 14.45 (0-395-57444-7) HM.

Winston, Lynn. Recreation & Sports: An Activity Guide. Garee, Betty, ed. LC 85-72420. 72p. (Orig.). (gr. 9-12). 1985. pap. 4.95 (0-915708-18-3, #1770) Cheever Pub.

Woodworth, Viki. Sports Jokes. (Illus.). 32p. (gr. 1-4). 1991. 13.95 (0-89565-727-9) Childs World.

Young, Robert S. Sports Cards. LC 92-33761. (Illus.). 72p. (gr. 5 up). 1993. text ed. 13.95 RSBE (0-87518-519-3, Dillon) Macmillan Child Grp.

Zadra, Dan. The Secrets to Goal-Setting. (Illus.). 32p. (gr. 6 up). 1986. PLB 12.95 (0-88682-017-0) Creative Ed.

Zinsser, Nate. Dear Dr. Psych. (gr. 3-7). 1991. pap. 5.95 (0-316-98898-7, Spts Illus Kids) Little.

SPORTS–BIOGRAPHY

Boga, Steve. On Their Own: Adventure Athletes in Solo Sports, 3 bks. Kratoville, B. L., ed. (Illus.). (gr. 3-9). 1992. Set, 64p. ea. bk. pap. text ed. 11.00 (0-87879-928-1); wkbk. 12.50 (0-87879-929-X) High Noon Bks.

Ellis, Lucy. American Gladiators. (Illus.). 48p. 1993. 1.49 (0-440-21436-X) Dell.

Gutman, Bill. Pro Sports Champions. (Illus.). 144p. (Orig.). (gr. 5 up). 1990. pap. 2.75 (0-671-69334-4, Archway) PB.

The Lincoln Library of Sports Champions, 20 vols. (gr. 6-12). 1989. Set. 419.00 (0-685-44870-3) Ency Brit Ed.

Ogden, Dale. Hoosier Sports Heroes. Day, Richard, illus. LC 90-84308. 192p. 1990. 19.95 (1-878208-01-2) Guild Pr In.

Salem Press Editors. The Twentieth Century: Great Athletes, 20 vols. (Illus.). 2924p. (gr. 6 up). 1992. lib. bdg. 400.00x (0-89356-775-2) Salem Pr.

Smith, Simpson E. Bear Bryant: Football's Winning Coach. LC 83-40404. (Illus.). 128p. (gr. 7 up). 1984. 11.95 (0-8027-6526-2) Walker & Co.

Sports Great Books Series, 24 bks. (Illus.). (gr. 4-10). Set. lib. bdg. 382.80 (0-89490-342-X) Enslow Pubs.

SPORTS–DICTIONARIES

Sullivan, George. Complete Sports Dictionary. (gr. 4-7). 1993. pap. 3.25 (0-590-40411-3) Scholastic Inc.

SPORTS–FICTION

Baker, Carin G. High Pressure. 128p. (gr. 3-7). 1992. pap. 3.50 (0-14-036025-5) Puffin Bks.

—Karate Club, No. 5: Out of Control. LC 92-19941. 144p. (gr. 3-7). 1992. pap. 3.50 (0-14-036264-9) Puffin Bks.

Barnett, Ada & Wurfer, Nicole. Eddycat Brings Soccer to Mannersville. Hoffmann, Mark, illus. LC 92-56879. Date not set. PLB 17.27 (0-8368-0941-6) Gareth Stevens Inc.

Bryant, Bonnie. Team Play. (gr. 4-7). 1991. pap. 3.50 (0-553-15862-7) Bantam.

Carrier, Roch. Un Champion. Cohen, Sheldon, illus. LC 90-70134. (FRE.). 24p. (gr. 3 up). 1991. 14.95 (0-88776-250-6) Tundra Bks.

Christopher, Matt. Long Shot For Paul. (gr. 3-7). 1990. pap. 3.95 (0-316-14244-1) Little.

—Red-Hot Hightops. Mock, Paul D., illus. 128p. (gr. 4-6). 1987. 14.95 (0-316-14056-2) Little.

Cornell, Donald. Ice Told Tales. Rosoff, Barbara, tr. Cornell, Donald, illus. (ENG & FRE.). 58p. (Orig.). (ps-2). 1991. pap. 4.00 (0-9620738-1-4) D Cornell.

Dagavarian, Debra A., ed. A Century of Children's Sports Stories. 200p. (gr. 5-8). 1993. lib. bdg. 16.95 (0-88736-852-2) Mecklermedia.

D'Andrea, Joseph. If I Played Baseball: Or Football, or Soccer, or... Ayers, Michael B., illus. 12p. (ps-k). 1991. 4.99 (1-878338-05-6) Picture Me Bks.

Dixon, Franklin W. Sabotage at Sports City. Winkler, Ellen, ed. 160p. (Orig.). 1992. pap. 3.99 (0-671-73062-2, Minstrel Bks) PB.

Dygard, Thomas J. Point Spread. (gr. 4-7). 1991. pap. 3.95 (0-14-034591-4, Puffin) Puffin Bks.

Ellis, Lucy. Pink Parrots, No. 4: Fielder's Choice. (gr. 4-7). 1991. pap. 3.50 (0-316-12447-8, Spts Illus Kids) Little.

Fleischman, Sid. McBroom & the Great Race. Lorraine, Walter H., illus. 64p. (gr. 3-7). 1980. 13.95 (0-316-28568-4, Joy St Bks) Little.

French, Michael. The Throwing Season. LC 79-53598. (gr. 9-12). 1980. 8.95 (0-440-08600-0) Delacorte.

Friend, David. Baseball, Football, Daddy & Me. Brown, Richard, illus. 32p. (ps-3). 1992. pap. 3.99 (0-14-050914-3) Puffin Bks.

Gilligan, Shannon. The Search for Champ. Kramer, Anthony, illus. 50p. (gr. 4). 1983. pap. 2.25 (0-553-15442-7) Bantam.

Golenbock, Peter. Teammates. LC 89-3816. (ps-3). 1992. pap. 4.95 (0-15-284286-1, HB Juv Bks) HarBrace.

Gorman, S. S. Goal Maker. Clancy, Lisa, ed. 128p. (Orig.). (gr. 4-6). 1993. pap. 2.99 (0-671-78905-8, Minstrel Bks) PB.

Gregorich, Barbara. Jace, Mace, & the Big Race. Hoffman, Joan, ed. (Illus.). 32p. (gr. k-2). 1992. pap. 3.95 (0-88743-416-9, 06068) Sch Zone Pub Co.

Gutman, Bill. Rookie Summer. (gr. 7-12). 1988. PLB 2.95 (0-89872-300-0) Turman Pub.

Hey Coach. (Illus.). 8p. (Orig.). 1993. pap. text ed. write for info. (1-882225-13-9) Tott Pubns.

Highlights for Children Staff. The Bears' Blitz: And Other Sports Stories. LC 90-85908. (Illus.). 96p. (gr. 3-7). 1992. pap. 2.95 (1-878093-29-0) Boyds Mills Pr.

Hiller, B. B. Next Karate Kid. 1994. pap. 3.95 (0-590-48444-3) Scholastic Inc.

—Next Karate Kid. (gr. 4-7). 1994. pap. 3.95 (0-590-48445-1) Scholastic Inc.

Howker, Janni. Isaac Campion. LC 86-9843. 128p. (gr. 5 up). 1987. 10.25 (0-688-06658-5) Greenwillow.

Hughes, Dean. Winning Streak. (Illus.). 96p. (gr. 2-4). 1990. PLB 9.99 (0-679-90428-X); pap. 2.95 (0-679-80428-5) Knopf Bks Yng Read.

Jack B. Quick, Sports Detective: The Case of the Missing Playbook & Other Mysteries. (Illus.). (gr. 3-7). 1990. pap. 3.50 (0-316-72911-6, Spts Illus Kids) Little.

Jenkins, Jerry. The Angry Gymnast. (Orig.). (gr. 7-12). 1986. pap. text ed. 4.99 (0-8024-8235-X) Moody.

Johnson, Annabel & Johnson, Edgar. Gamebuster. Marchesi, Stephen, illus. LC 90-1330. 192p. (gr. 7 up). 1990. 14.95 (0-525-65033-4, Cobblehill Bks) Dutton Child Bks.

Jordan, James L. Ricky's Last Chance. 104p. (gr. 4-6). 1991. pap. 3.95 (0-9630534-0-X) Living Water.

Kehret, Peg. The Winner. (gr. 7-12). 1988. PLB 2.95 (0-89872-302-7) Turman Pub.

Kessler, Leonard. Big Mile Race. (gr. 4-7). 1991. pap. 2.95 (0-440-40413-4) Dell.

—The Worst Team Ever. Kessler, Leonard, illus. LC 84-25883. 47p. (gr. 1-3). 1985. 10.25 (0-688-04234-1); lib. bdg. 10.88 (0-688-04235-X) Greenwillow.

—Worst Team Ever. (ps-3). 1991. pap. 2.95 (0-440-40428-2) Dell.

Klass, David. Wrestling with Honor. 208p. (gr. 8-12). 1990. pap. 2.95 (0-590-43187-0) Scholastic Inc.

Knudson, R. R. Rinehart Lifts. 88p. (gr. 4-7). 1982. pap. 1.95 (0-380-57059-9, 57059-9, Camelot) Avon.

—Rinehart Shouts. LC 86-29540. 115p. (gr. 4 up). 1987. 13.00 (0-374-36296-3) FS&G.

Kubler, Annie. The Champion. LC 90-24246. (gr. 4 up). 1991. 3.95 (0-85953-531-2) Childs Play.

Levy. Go for the Gold. 1992. pap. 2.95 (0-590-45253-3, Apple Paperbacks) Scholastic Inc.

Levy, Elizabeth. The Captain of the Team. 1989. pap. 2.75 (0-590-42820-9) Scholastic Inc.

—Crush on the Coach. 1990. pap. 2.75 (0-590-42821-7) Scholastic Inc.

—The New Coach? 128p. (gr. 3-7). 1991. pap. 2.75 (0-590-44695-9) Scholastic Inc.

—Tough at the Top. (gr. 4-7). 1991. pap. 2.75 (0-590-44694-0) Scholastic Inc.

—Tumbling Ghosts. 1989. pap. 2.75 (0-590-42221-9) Scholastic Inc.

Lipsyte, Robert. The Contender. LC 67-19623. 176p. (gr. 7 up). 1987. pap. 3.95 (0-06-447039-3, Trophy) HarpC Child Bks.

Lurie, Susan. Rally! (gr. 7-10). 1993. pap. 3.50 (0-553-48092-8) Bantam.

McBrier, Page. The Kickball Crisis. 96p. 1989. pap. 2.50 (0-380-75781-8, Camelot) Avon.

McOmber, Rachel B., ed. McOmber Phonics Storybooks: A Game for Champions. rev. ed. (Illus.). write for info. (0-944991-68-8) Swift Lrn Res.

Miklowitz, Gloria D. Standing Tall, Looking Good. 160p. 1992. pap. 3.50 (0-440-21263-4, LFL) Dell.

Miles, Betty. All It Takes Is Practice. LC 76-13057. (gr. 4-8). 1976. lib. bdg. 10.99 (0-394-93325-7) Knopf Bks Yng Read.

Mooser, Stephen. Amazing Stories. (gr. 4-7). 1993. pap. 3.25 (0-440-40646-3) Dell.

—Muscle Mania. (ps-3). 1993. pap. 3.25 (0-440-40564-5) Dell.

Nicklaus, Carol. Silver Sports Series, 4 vols. Nicklaus, Carol, illus. (ps-1). 1991. Set, 32p. ea. lib. bdg. 23.80 (0-671-31271-5); Set, 32p. ea. pap. 11.80 (0-671-31272-3) Silver Pr.

Parachute Press Staff. Over in the Meadow. 1987. pap. 2.95 (0-553-15573-3) Bantam.

Pascal, Francine. The Big Race. (ps-3). 1993. pap. 2.99 (0-553-48011-1) Bantam.

Paulsen, Gary. Coach Amos. (gr. 4-7). 1994. 3.50 (0-440-40930-6) Dell.

Peet, Bill. Merle the High Flying Squirrel. Peet, Bill, illus. 30p. (gr. k-3). 1983. pap. 5.70 (0-395-34923-0) HM.

Perkins, Thornton. Junior High Champs. Chappick, Joseph, illus. 49p. (Orig.). (gr. 6-9). 1989. pap. 3.00 (0-9623407-0-7) NVEM.

Potash, Dorothy. The Tale of Ned & His Nose. Sperling, Thomas, illus. 24p. (gr. k-4). 1993. PLB 13.95 (1-879567-23-7, Valeria Bks) Wonder Well.

Riddell, Ruth. Ice Warrior. LC 91-29506. 144p. (gr. 4-7). 1992. SBE 13.95 (0-689-31710-7, Atheneum Child Bk) Macmillan Child Grp.

Sanchez, Isidro & Peris, Carme. City Sports. 32p. (ps-1). 1992. pap. 5.95 (0-8120-4866-0) Barron.

Sobol, Donald J. Encyclopedia Brown's Book of Wacky Sports. Enik, Ted, illus. LC 82-84250. 128p. (gr. 3-7). 1984. 11.95 (0-688-03884-0) Morrow Jr Bks.

Sports Day. 22p. (ps-1). 1985. 1.98 (0-517-42789-3) Random Hse Value.

Standish, Burt L. Frank Merriwell's Sports Afield. Rudman, Jack, ed. (gr. 9 up). Date not set. 9.95 (0-8373-9310-8); pap. 3.95 (0-8373-9010-9) F Merriwell.

Story Time Collection Staff. Tennis Shoes: A Story Rhyme. (Illus.). 20p. (Orig.). (ps-6). 1992. pap. text ed. 6.95 (0-939476-75-4, Pub. by Biblio Pr) Prosperity & Profits.

Tab, Joan & Jon. The House That Played Ball. rev. ed. Abel, J., illus. 50p. (gr. k-2). 1992. PLB 25.00 (1-56611-424-1); pap. 15.00 (1-56611-006-8) Jonas.

Taylor, Theodore. Tuck Triumphant. (gr. 4-7). 1992. pap. 3.99 (0-380-71323-3, Camelot) Avon.

Tiny Toon Adventures: The Big Race. (gr. k-2). 1991. write for info. (0-307-11698-0, Golden Pr) Western Pub.

Von Moshzisker, Felix. Playoff Champion. (gr. 4-7). 1993. pap. 3.50 (0-553-56000-X) Bantam.

Williams-Garcia, Rita. Fast Talk on a Slow Track. 1992. pap. 3.50 (0-553-29594-2) Bantam.

Winthrop, Elizabeth. Sledding. Wilson, Sarah, illus. LC 89-1761. 32p. (ps-2). 1989. PLB 13.89 (0-06-026566-3) HarpC Child Bks.

Yamate, Sandra S. The Best of Intentions. Lee, Wendy K., illus. LC 93-45794. 1994. 12.95 (1-879965-09-7) Polychrome Pub.

SPORTS–HISTORY

Benson, Michael. Dream Teams: The Best Teams of All Time. (gr. 4-7). 1991. 17.95 (0-316-08993-1, Spts Illus Kids) Little.

Great Sports Performances. 48p. (gr. 5-6). 1991. PLB 11.95 (1-56065-063-X) Capstone Pr.

Sperling, Anita. Sports Tracing Fun Book. (gr. 3-7). 1990. pap. 1.95 (0-590-42492-0) Scholastic Inc.

SPORTS–POETRY

Foster, John, ed. Sports Poems. (Illus.). 16p. (gr. 1 up). 1992. pap. 2.95 (0-19-916428-2) OUP.

SPORTS–YEARBOOKS

Stevens, Tim. North Carolina High School Record Book. 96p. (gr. 9 up). 1991. pap. 3.00 (0-935400-17-6) News & Observer.

SPORTS JOURNALISM

Feinberg, Jeremy R. Reading the Sports Page: A Guide to Understanding Sports Statistics. LC 92-18972. (Illus.). 80p. (gr. 6 up). 1992. text ed. 12.95 RSBE (0-02-734420-7, New Discovery) Macmillan Child Grp.

SPRING

Allington, Richard L. & Krull, Kathleen. Spring. Rahn, Dee, illus. LC 80-25093. 32p. (gr. k-3). 1985. PLB 9.95 (0-8172-1342-2); pap. 3.95 (0-8114-8244-8) Raintree Steck-V.

Anglund, Joan W. Spring Is a New Beginning. Anglund, Joan W., illus. LC 63-7892. 32p. (ps up). 1991. 8.95 (0-15-278161-7, HB Juv Bks) HarBrace.

Barker, Cicely M. Flower Fairies of the Spring. Barker, Cicely M., illus. (ps up). 1991. 5.95 (0-7232-3753-0) Warne.

Beach, Judy & Spencer, Kathleen. Minds-on Fun for Spring. (gr. k-4). 1991. pap. 9.95 (0-86653-946-8) Fearon Teach Aids.

Davis, Nancy M., et al. Spring & May. Davis, Nancy M., illus. 46p. (Orig.). (ps-4). 1986. pap. 5.95 (0-937103-11-X) DaNa Pubns.

Fowler, Allan. How Do You Know It's Spring? LC 91-12760. 32p. (ps-2). 1991. PLB 10.75 (0-516-04914-3); PLB 22.95 big bk. (0-516-49474-0); pap. 3.95 (0-516-44914-1) Childrens.

Glover, Susanne & Grewe, Georgeann. A Splash of Spring. Grewe, Georgeann, illus. 128p. (gr. 2-5). 1987. pap. 11.95 (0-86653-412-1, GA1026) Good Apple.

Hirschi, Ron. Spring. LC 89-49039. (Illus.). (ps-3). 1990. 13.95 (0-525-65037-7, Cobblehill Bks) Dutton Child Bks.

Kalman, Bobbie. We Celebrate Spring. (Illus.). 56p. (gr. 3-4). 1985. 15.95 (0-86505-043-0); pap. 7.95 (0-86505-053-8) Crabtree Pub Co.

Maass, Robert. When Spring Comes. LC 93-29816. 1994. 14.95 (0-8050-2085-3, Bks Young Read) H Holt & Co.

Maniscalco, Joe. Old Barn: Springtime. Wheeler, Penny E., ed. 32p. (gr. 2-4). 1988. pap. 3.95 (0-8280-0423-4) Review & Herald.

Markle, Sandra. Exploring Spring: A Season of Science Activities, Puzzlers & Games. LC 89-394. (Illus.). 128p. (gr. 3-7). 1990. SBE 14.95 (0-689-31341-1, Atheneum Child Bk) Macmillan Child Grp.

Mason, John. Spring Weather. LC 90-14397. (Illus.). 32p. (gr. 1-5). 1991. PLB 11.90 (0-531-18437-4, Pub. by Bookwright Pr) Watts.

Moncure, Jane B. Step into Spring: A New Season. Williams, Jenny, illus. LC 90-30375. 32p. (ps-2). 1990. PLB 13.95 (0-89565-571-3) Childs World.

—Word Bird's Spring Words. Gohman, Vera, illus. LC 85-5902. 32p. (gr. k-2). 1985. PLB 14.95 (0-89565-310-9) Childs World.

Ottenheimer, Laurence. Livre du Printemps. (FRE.). 96p. (gr. 4-9). 1983. 15.95 (2-07-039507-3) Schoenhof.

Parramon, J. M., et al. La Primavera. (SPA.). (ps). 1986. pap. 6.95 (0-8120-3648-4) Barron.

Rosen, Mike. Spring Festivals. LC 90-41064. (Illus.). 32p. (gr. 4-6). 1991. PLB 11.90 (0-531-18384-X, Pub. by Bookwright Pr) Watts.

Santrey, Louis. Spring. Sabin, Francene, illus. LC 82-19381. 32p. (gr. 4-7). 1983. lib. bdg. 10.79 (0-89375-909-0); pap. text ed. 2.95 (0-89375-910-4) Troll Assocs.

Schweninger, Ann. Springtime. LC 92-22204. (Illus.). 32p. 1993. 13.50 (0-670-82757-6) Viking Child Bks.

Sibley, Kenneth E. A Spring Surprise. (Illus.). 19p. (Orig.). (gr. 7 up). 1989. pap. 6.95 (0-9619934-1-3) K E Sibley.

Stone, Lynne M. Spring. LC 93-41104. 1994. write for info. (1-55916-018-7) Rourke Bk Co.

Thomson, Ruth. Spring. 1990. PLB 11.90 (0-531-14018-0) Watts.

—Spring. LC 94-16916. (Illus.). 24p. (ps-3). 1994. PLB 14.40 (0-516-07994-8); pap. 4.95 (0-516-47994-6) Childrens.

SPRING–FICTION

Agell, Charlotte. Mud Makes Me Dance in the Spring. Agell, Charlotte, illus. LC 93-33610. 32p. (ps up). 1994. 7.95 (0-88448-112-3) Tilbury Hse.

Barnes, Jill & Ishinabe, Fusako. Spring Snowman. Rubin, Caroline, ed. Japan Foreign Rights Centre Staff, tr. from JPN. Ishinabe, Fusako, illus. LC 90-37748. 32p. (gr. k-3). 1990. PLB 14.60 (0-944483-83-6) Garrett Ed Corp.

Bronstein, Ruth L. Rabbit's Good News. LC 93-30719. (gr. 4 up). Date not set. write for info. (0-395-68700-4, Clarion Bks) HM.

Brown, Craig. In the Spring. LC 92-17465. (Illus.). 24p. (ps up). 1994. 14.00 (0-688-10983-7); PLB 13.93 (0-688-10984-5) Greenwillow.

Brown, Margaret W. Animals in the Snow. Schwartz, Carol, illus. LC 94-8470. 1995. write for info. (0-7868-0039-9); pap. write for info. (0-7868-2032-2) Hyprn Child.

Clifton, Lucille. The Boy Who Didn't Believe in Spring. Turkle, Brinton, illus. (gr. 3-4). 1973. 13.95 (0-525-27145-7, DCB); pap. 1.95 (0-525-45038-6, DCB) Dutton Child Bks.

—The Boy Who Didn't Believe in Spring. Turkle, Brinton, illus. LC 87-27145. 32p. (ps-3). 1988. pap. 4.95 (0-525-44365-7, 0383-120, DCB) Dutton Child Bks.

—The Boy Who Didn't Believe in Spring. (ps-3). 1992. pap. 4.99 (0-14-054739-8) Viking Child Bks.

Emberley, Michael. Welcome Back, Sun. LC 92-9786. (gr. 4 up). 1993. 14.95 (0-316-23647-0) Little.

Gordon, Sharon. First Day of Spring. Willis, Christine, illus. LC 81-2750. 32p. (gr. k-2). 1981. PLB 11.59 (0-89375-531-1); pap. text ed. 2.95 (0-89375-532-X) Troll Assocs.

Greenleaf, Ann. Max & Molly's Spring. 1993. 4.99 (0-517-09153-4) Random Hse Value.

Hurwitz, Johanna. Up & down Spring. (gr. 4-7). 1994. pap. 3.25 (0-590-47736-6) Scholastic Inc.

Iwamura, Kazuo. The Fourteen Forest Mice & the Spring Meadow Picnic. Knowlton, Mary L., tr. from JPN. Iwamura, Kazuo, illus. LC 90-50704. 32p. (gr. k-3). 1991. PLB 17.27 (0-8368-0498-8) Gareth Stevens Inc.

Johnson, Crockett. Will Spring Be Early or Will Spring Be Late? Johnson, Crockett, illus. LC 59-9424. 48p. (gr. k-3). 1961. PLB 13.89 (0-690-89423-6, Crowell Jr Bks) HarpC Child Bks.

—Will Spring Be Early? or Will Spring Be Late? Johnson, Crockett, illus. LC 59-9424. 48p. (gr. k-3). 1990. pap. 3.95 (0-06-443224-6, Trophy) HarpC Child Bks.

Kinsey-Warnock, Natalie. When Spring Comes. Schuett, Stacey, illus. LC 92-14066. (ps-3). 1993. 14.99 (0-525-45008-4, DCB) Dutton Child Bks.

Krensky, Stephen. Lionel in the Spring. LC 88-30885. 1990. 9.95 (0-8037-0630-8); PLB 9.89 (0-8037-0631-6) Dial Bks Young.

—Lionel in the Spring. Natti, Susanna, illus. LC 88-30885. 48p. (ps-3). 1992. pap. 3.99 (0-14-036117-0, Dial Easy to Read) Puffin Bks.

Kroll, Steven. I Love Spring. Shoemaker, Kathryn E., illus. LC 86-14844. 32p. (ps-3). 1987. reinforced bdg. 12.95 (0-8234-0634-2) Holiday.

Kroll, Virginia L. Naomi Knows It's Springtime. Kastner, Jill, illus. LC 92-71267. 32p. (ps-3). 1993. reinforced 14.95 (1-56397-006-6) Boyds Mills Pr.

Lambert, Matthew. My First Spring Day. Beckes, Shirley, illus. 1994. PLB 19.97 (0-8114-4459-7) Raintree Steck-V.

Lucht, Irmgard. In This Night... Lucht, Irmgard, illus. LC 92-54620. 32p. (ps-3). 1993. 13.95 (1-56282-408-2) Hyprn Child.

McDonnell, Janet. Spring: New Life Everywhere. Hohag, Linda, illus. LC 93-10309. 32p. (gr. 2 up). 1993. PLB 12.30 (0-516-00677-0) Childrens.

Markle, Sandra. Exploring Spring. 128p. (gr. 4-7). 1992. pap. 2.99 (0-380-71319-5, Camelot) Avon.

Minarik, Else H. It's Spring! Graham, Margaret B., illus. LC 87-37202. 24p. (ps up). 1989. 11.95 (*0-688-07619-X*); PLB 11.88 (*0-688-07620-3*) Greenwillow.

Pfister, Marcus. Hopper Hunts for Spring. Pfister, Marcus, illus. Lanning, Rosemary, tr. from GER. LC 91-29671. (Illus.). 32p. (gr. k-3). 1992. 14.95 (*1-55858-139-1*); lib. bdg. 14.88 (*1-55858-147-2*) North-South Bks NYC.

Pragoff, Fiona. Spring. (Illus.). 20p. (ps). 1993. pap. 5.95 (*0-689-71707-5*, Aladdin) Macmillan Child Grp.

Preller, James. Wake Me in Spring. (Illus.). (gr. 2). 1994. pap. 2.95 (*0-590-48189-4*, Cartwheel) Scholastic Inc.

Rockwell, Anne. First Comes Spring. LC 84-45331. (Illus.). 32p. (ps-1). 1985. 14.95 (*0-694-00106-6*, Crowell Jr Bks); PLB 12.89 (*0-690-04455-0*) HarpC Child Bks.

—First Comes Spring. Rockwell, Anne, illus. LC 84-45331. 32p. (ps-1). 1991. pap. 4.95 (*0-06-107412-8*) HarpC Child Bks.

Smith, Viola B. Touch of Spring. Michel, Sandra S., ed. Keane, Marie, illus. (gr. k up). 1976. pap. 4.00 (*0-917178-02-5*) Lenape Pub.

Tibo, Gilles. Simon Celebra la Primavera (Simon Welcomes Spring) Salazar, Arturo, tr. from ENG. Tibo, Gilles, illus. LC 92-85471. (SPA.). 24p. (Orig.). (gr. k-3). 1993. pap. 5.95 (*0-88776-297-2*) Tundra Bks.

—Simon Welcomes Spring. Tibo, Gilles, illus. LC 90-70132. 24p. (ps-4). 1990. 10.95 (*0-88776-247-6*) Tundra Bks.

—Simon Welcomes Spring. (Illus.). 24p. (gr. k-3). 1993. pap. 4.95 (*0-88776-279-4*) Tundra Bks.

Vyner, Sue. Arctic Spring. Vyner, Tim, illus. LC 92-32280. (ps-3). 1993. 13.99 (*0-670-84934-0*) Viking Child Bks.

Whittington, Mary K. Winter's Child. Brown, Sue E., illus. LC 91-25011. 32p. (ps-3). 1992. SBE 14.95 (*0-689-31685-2*, Atheneum Child Bk) Macmillan Child Grp.

Wood, Audrey, retold by. When the Root Children Wake Up. Weatherby, Mark A., illus. LC 93-32737. 1995. Repr. of 1906 ed. 14.95 (*0-590-42517-X*) Scholastic Inc.

SPRING–POETRY

Hull, Robert. Poems for Spring. LC 90-20592. (Illus.). 48p. (gr. 3-7). 1991. PLB 21.34 (*0-8114-7802-5*) Raintree Steck-V.

Katz, Bobbi, ed. Puddle Wonderful: Poems to Welcome Spring. Morgan, Mary, illus. LC 91-8066. 32p. (Orig.). (ps-1). 1992. pap. 2.25 (*0-679-81493-0*) Random Bks Yng Read.

SQUANTO, WAMPANOAG INDIAN, d. 1622

Bulla, Clyde R. Squanto, Friend of the Pilgrims. 112p. 1990. pap. 2.95 (*0-590-44055-1*) Scholastic Inc.

Jassem, Kate. Squanto, the Pilgrim Adventure. new ed. LC 78-18042. (Illus.). 48p. (gr. 4-6). 1979. PLB 10.59 (*0-89375-161-8*); pap. 3.50 (*0-89375-151-0*) Troll Assocs.

The Story of Squanto. 1990. pap. 3.50 (*0-440-40360-X*, YB) Dell.

Zadra, Dan. Indians of America: Squanto. rev. ed. (gr. 2-4). 1987. PLB 14.95 (*0-88682-161-4*) Creative Ed.

Ziner, Feenie. Squanto. LC 88-13982. x, 158p. (gr. 7 up). 1988. 17.50 (*0-208-02218-X*, Linnet); pap. 12.50 (*0-208-02274-0*, Linnet) Shoe String.

SQUANTO, WAMPANOAG INDIAN, d. 1622–FICTION

Fontes, Ron & Korman, Justine. Walt Disney Pictures Presents The Indian Warrior: A Novel. Fontes, Ron & Korman, Justine, illus. LC 93-48122. 32p. (gr. k-3). 1994. pap. 3.50 (*0-8167-2502-0*) Troll Assocs.

SQUIRRELS

Bare, Colleen S. Busy, Busy Squirrels. Bare, Colleen S., photos by. LC 90-44219. (Illus.). 32p. (gr. 1-4). 1991. 12.95 (*0-525-65063-6*, Cobblehill Bks) Dutton Child Bks.

Berger, Melvin. Squirrels All Year Long. (Illus.). 16p. (ps-2). 1992. pap. text ed. 14.95 (*1-56784-003-5*) Newbridge Comms.

—Squirrels All Year Long: Student Edition. (Illus.). 16p. (ps-2). 1993. pap. text ed. 14.95 (*1-56784-028-0*) Newbridge Comms.

Coldrey, Jennifer. The Squirrel in the Trees. LC 85-30292. (Illus.). 32p. (gr. 4-6). 1986. 17.27 (*1-55532-062-7*) Gareth Stevens Inc.

—The World of Squirrels. LC 85-30296. (Illus.). 32p. (gr. 2-3). 1987. PLB 17.27 (*1-55532-065-1*) Gareth Stevens Inc.

Dalmais. Squirrel, Reading Level 3-4. (Illus.). 28p. (gr. 2-5). 1983. PLB 16.67 (*0-86592-857-6*); 12.50 (*0-685-58826-2*) Rourke Corp.

George, Jean C. The Moon of the Chickarees. new ed. Rodell, Don, illus. LC 90-22409. 48p. (gr. 3-7). 1992. 15.00 (*0-06-022507-6*); PLB 14.89 (*0-06-022508-4*) HarpC Child Bks.

Komoto, Sachiko. Chessie, the Long Island Squirrel. Komoto, Sachiko, illus. LC 90-46860. 64p. (gr. 1-3). 1993. PLB 19.93 (*0-8368-0198-9*) Gareth Stevens Inc.

Lane, Margaret. The Squirrel. Lilly, Kenneth, illus. LC 81-1229. 32p. (gr. k-4). 1993. 13.99 (*0-8037-8230-6*) Dial Bks Young.

Lepthien, Emilie U. Squirrels. LC 92-9207. (Illus.). 48p. (gr. k-4). 1993. pap. 4.95 (*0-516-41947-1*) Childrens.

McConoughey, Jana. Squirrels. LC 83-2085. (Illus.). 48p. (gr. 5). 1983. text ed. 12.95 RSBE (*0-89686-223-2*, Crestwood Hse) Macmillan Child Grp.

Ryden, Hope, photos by & text by. The Raggedy Red Squirrel. (Illus.). 48p. (gr. k-3). 1992. 16.00 (*0-525-67400-4*, Lodestar Bks) Dutton Child Bks.

Schlein, Miriam. Squirrel Watching. Pillar, Marjorie, illus. LC 91-6481. 64p. (gr. 2-6). 1992. PLB 14.89 (*0-06-022754-0*) HarpC Child Bks.

Stone, Lynn M. Flying Squirrels. LC 93-4146. 1993. write for info. (*0-86593-298-0*) Rourke Corp.

Wildsmith, Brian. Squirrels. (Illus.). 32p. 1992. bds. 16.00 (*0-19-279699-2*) OUP.

SQUIRRELS–FICTION

Alden, Laura. Squirrel's Adventure in Alphabet Town. Collins, Judi, illus. LC 92-1314. 32p. (ps-2). 1992. PLB 11.80 (*0-516-05419-8*) Childrens.

Beeson, Bob. What Time Is It, Mr. Wolf? Beeson, Bob, illus. 32p. (ps). 1994. 12.95 (*0-8249-8649-0*, Ideals Child) Hambleton-Hill.

Brennan, Gale. Earl the Squirrel. Flint, Russ, illus. 16p. (Orig.). (gr. k-6). 1981. pap. 1.25 (*0-685-02455-5*) Brennan Bks.

Browne, Eileen. Tick-Tock. Parkins, David, illus. LC 93-927. 32p. (ps up). 1994. 14.95 (*1-56402-300-1*) Candlewick Pr.

Burgess, Thornton W. The Adventures of Chatterer the Red Squirrel. unabr. ed. Kliros, Thea, adapted by. Cady, Harrison, illus. LC 92-14627. 96p. 1992. pap. 1.00 (*0-486-27399-7*) Dover.

—Adventures of Chatterer the Red Squirrel. 18.95 (*0-8488-0376-0*) Amereon Ltd.

Carnes, Pauline. A Squirrel's Tale. 1993. 7.75 (*0-8062-4664-2*) Carlton.

Chottin, Ariane. Beaver Gets Lost. Geneste, Marcelle, illus. LC 91-40651. 24p. (ps-3). 1992. 6.99 (*0-89577-419-4*, Dist. by Random) RD Assn.

Clement, Claude. Little Squirrel's Special Nest. Jensen, Patricia, adapted by. LC 93-4243. (Illus.). 22p. (ps-3). 1993. 5.98 (*0-89577-542-5*, Reader's Digest Kids) RD Assn.

Cosgrove, Stephen. Squeakers. James, Robin, illus. 32p. (Orig.). (gr. 1-4). 1985. pap. 3.95 (*0-8431-1442-8*) Price Stern.

Cowley, Stewart. Squirrel's Party. LC 93-77348. (Illus.). 22p. (ps-3). 1993. 6.99 (*0-89577-514-X*, Dist. by Random) RD Assn.

Damjan, Mischa. The Big Squirrel & the Little Rhinoceros. De Beer, Hans, illus. Hort, Lenny, tr. from GER. LC 91-17865. (Illus.). 32p. (gr. k-3). 1991. 14.95 (*1-55858-117-0*) North-South Bks NYC.

Downing, Johnette. A Squirrel Jumped Out of the Tree. Downing, Johnette, illus. (ps). 1990. pap. 2.50 (*0-938991-57-4*) Colonial Pr AL.

Ehlert, Lois. Nuts to You! LC 92-19441. (Illus.). 32p. (ps-3). 1993. 14.95 (*0-15-257647-9*, HB Juv Bks) HarBrace.

Elish, Dan. The Great Squirrel Uprising. Cazet, Denys, illus. LC 91-27145. 128p. (gr. 4 up). 1992. 14.95 (*0-531-05995-2*); lib. bdg. 14.99 (*0-531-08595-3*) Orchard Bks Watts.

Ernst, Lisa C. Squirrel Park. Ernst, Lisa C., illus. LC 92-27920. 40p. (ps-2). 1993. RSBE 15.95 (*0-02-733562-3*, Bradbury Pr) Macmillan Child Grp.

Fowler, Richard. Squirrel's Tale. 24p. (ps-3). 1984. 9.95 (*0-88110-157-5*) EDC.

Gordon, Sharon. Show & Tell. Kolding, Richard M., illus. LC 86-30855. 32p. (gr. k-2). 1988. PLB 7.89 (*0-8167-0994-7*); pap. text ed. 1.95 (*0-8167-0995-5*) Troll Assocs.

Hannah, Valerie. Cyril Squirrel & Sheryl: An Ecological Tale. Herrick, George H., ed. Meek, Barbara, illus. 46p. (Orig.). (gr. k-3). 1991. pap. 6.95 (*0-941281-78-7*) V H Pub.

Henderson, Angela. JoJo Meets Scrappy. (Illus.). (ps-3). 1992. write for info. (*1-882185-07-2*) Crnrstone Pub.

James, Simon. The Wild Woods. James, Simon, illus. LC 92-54582. 32p. (ps up). 1993. 13.95 (*1-56402-219-6*) Candlewick Pr.

Kesey, Ken. Little Tricker the Squirrel Meets Big Double the Bear. Moser, Barry, illus. 1990. 14.95 (*0-670-81136-X*) Viking Child Bks.

—The Little Trickler, The Squirrel. 1988. write for info. Viking Child Bks.

Kroll, Steven. The Squirrels' Thanksgiving. Bassett, Jeni, illus. LC 89-77513. 32p. (ps-3). 1991. reinforced 14.95 (*0-8234-0823-X*) Holiday.

Lane, Margaret. The Squirrel. Lilly, Kenneth, illus. 32p. (gr. k-4). 1993. pap. 4.99 (*0-14-054926-9*, Puff Pied Piper) Puffin Bks.

McCabe, Eugene. Cyril: Quest of an Orphaned Squirrel. 72p. (ps-8). 1987. 13.95 (*0-86278-116-7*, Pub. by O'Brien Press Ltd Eire); pap. 7.95 (*0-86278-131-0*, Pub. by O'Brien Press Ltd Eire) Dufour.

McMullen, Shawn. A New Home. Haley, Amanda, illus. LC 91-43071. 32p. (gr. 4-8). 1992. saddle-stitched 5.99 (*0-87403-976-2*, 24-03866) Standard Pub.

—That's What Friends Are For. Haley, Amanda, illus. LC 91-43656. (gr. 4-8). 1992. saddle-stitched 5.99 (*0-87403-975-4*, 24-03865) Standard Pub.

McMullen, Shawn A. Justin Ordinary Squirrel. Haley, Amanda, illus. 32p. (ps-2). 1991. pap. text ed. 3.99 (*0-87403-807-3*, 24-03897) Standard Pub.

Malone, P. M. Out of the Nest. Lewison, Terry, illus. 198p. (Orig.). (gr. 1-8). 1991. pap. text ed. 11.95 (*0-9631957-0-0*) Raspberry Hill.

Miller, Edna. Scamper: A Gray Tree Squirrel. Miller, Edna, illus. 32p. (gr. k-3). 1991. PLB 14.95 (*0-945912-12-9*) Pippin Pr.

Peet, Bill. Merle the High Flying Squirrel. Peet, Bill, illus. LC 73-18371. 32p. (gr. k-3). 1974. reinforced bdg. 14.95 (*0-395-18452-5*) HM.

Potter, Beatrix. Meet Squirrel Nutkin. (Illus.). 12p. (ps). 1987. bds. 2.95 (*0-7232-3452-3*) Warne.

—Noisette l'Ecureuil. (FRE.). 58p. 1990. 10.95 (*2-07-056075-9*) Schoenhof.

—Noisette l'Ecureuil. (FRE., Illus.). 58p. 1990. 9.95 (*0-7859-3629-7*, 2070560759) Fr & Eur.

—The Tale of Squirrel Nutkin. Atkinson, Allen, illus. 64p. 1984. pap. 2.25 (*0-553-15205-X*) Bantam.

—The Tale of Squirrel Nutkin. 1987. 5.95 (*0-7232-3461-2*); pap. 2.25 (*0-7232-3486-8*) Warne.

—The Tale of Squirrel Nutkin. Bond, Gary, read by. (Illus.). (ps-3). 1989. pap. 6.95 bk. & tape (*0-7232-3671-2*) Warne.

—The Tale of Squirrel Nutkin. (Illus.). 60p. (gr. 1-5). 1972. pap. 1.75 (*0-486-22828-2*) Dover.

—Tale of Squirrel Nutkin. 1992. 3.99 (*0-517-07239-4*) Random Hse Value.

Potter, Beatrix, created by. Squirrel Nutkin. Schoonover, Pat & Nelson, Anita, illus. 24p. (gr. 2-4). 1992. PLB 10.95 (*1-56674-009-6*, HTS Bks) Forest Hse.

Prather, Jo Beecher. Mississippi Beau. Quinn, Kenneth M., illus. LC 93-50614. 1994. 12.95 (*0-89015-961-0*) Sunbelt Media.

Rylant, Cynthia. Gooseberry Park. LC 94-11578. (Illus.). (gr. 1-8). 1995. write for info (*0-15-232242-6*) Harbrace.

Sammy the Squirrel. (Illus.). (ps-1). 2.98 (*0-517-46987-1*) Random Hse Value.

Shannon, George. The Surprise. Aruego, Jose & Dewey, Ariane, illus. LC 83-1434. 32p. (gr. k-3). 1983. 13.95 (*0-688-02313-4*) Greenwillow.

Sir. Squirrel Starts a Business. (Illus.). (ps-1). 1.98 (*0-517-45740-7*) Random Hse Value.

Squirrels on the Move (EV, Unit 8. (gr. 2). 1991. 5-pack 21.25 (*0-88106-765-2*) Charlesbridge Pub.

Wilmer, Diane. Nuts about Nuts. rev. ed. Dowling, Paul, illus. 32p. (gr. k-2). 1990. Repr. of 1989 ed. PLB 10.95 (*1-878363-09-3*) Forest Hse.

Yep, Laurence. The Curse of the Squirrel. Zimmer, Dirk, illus. LC 87-4612. 64p. (gr. 2-4). 1987. lib. bdg. 6.99 (*0-394-98200-2*); pap. 1.95 (*0-394-88200-8*, Random Juv) Random Bks Yng Read.

Young, Miriam. Miss Suzy's Easter Surprise. Lobel, Arnold, illus. LC 80-16966. 48p. (ps-3). 1984. Repr. of 1972 ed. RSBE 13.95 (*0-02-793680-5*, Four Winds) Macmillan Child Grp.

—Miss Suzy's Easter Surprise. LC 89-37842. (Illus.). 48p. (ps-3). 1990. pap. 4.95 (*0-689-71374-6*, Aladdin) Macmillan Child Grp.

SRI LANKA

Asia-Australia, 6 vols. (Illus.). (gr. 5-9). 1991. Set. 131.70 (*1-85435-397-7*) Marshall Cavendish.

Wanasundera, Nanda P. Sri Lanka. LC 91-18399. (Illus.). 128p. (gr. 5-9). 1991. PLB 21.95 (*1-85435-398-5*) Marshall Cavendish.

Zimmermann, Robert. Sri Lanka. LC 91-35252. 128p. (gr. 5-9). 1992. PLB 20.55 (*0-516-02606-2*) Childrens.

STABILIZATION IN INDUSTRY

see Economic Conditions

STAGE

see Acting; Actors and Actresses; Theater

STAGE SCENERY

see Theaters–Stage Setting and Scenery

STAGE SETTING

see Theaters–Stage Setting and Scenery

STAINED GLASS

see Glass Painting and Staining

STALIN, JOSEPH VISSARIONOVICH, 1879-1953

Caulkins, Janet. Joseph Stalin. (Illus.). 160p. (gr. 7-12). 1990. PLB 14.40 (*0-531-10945-3*) Watts.

Italia, Bob. Joseph Stalin. Walner, Rosemary, ed. LC 90-82614. (Illus.). 32p. (gr. 4). 1990. PLB 13.99 (*0-939179-83-0*) Abdo & Dghtrs.

Kallen, Stuart A. The Stalin Era. Wallner, Rosemary, ed. LC 92-13474. 1992. PLB 13.99 (*1-56239-102-X*) Abdo & Dghtrs.

Marrin, Albert. Stalin: Russia's Man of Steel. 256p. (gr. 7 up). 1988. pap. 14.95 (*0-670-82102-0*) Viking Child Bks.

—Stalin: Russia's Man of Steel. LC 93-3798. 256p. (gr. 7 up). 1993. pap. 5.99 (*0-14-032605-7*, Puffin) Puffin Bks.

Otfinoski, Steven. Joseph Stalin: Russia's Last Czar. LC 92-41143. (Illus.). 128p. (gr. 2-4). 1992. 15.90 (*1-56294-240-9*) Millbrook Pr.

Ross, Stewart. The U. S. S. R. under Stalin. LC 90-24373. (Illus.). 64p. (gr. 9-12). 1991. 13.40 (*0-531-18409-9*, Pub. by Bookwright Pr) Watts.

Whitelaw, Nancy. Josef Stalin: From Peasant to Premier. LC 92-5747. (Illus.). 160p. (gr. 5 up). 1992. text ed. 13.95 RSBE (*0-87518-557-6*, Dillon) Macmillan Child Grp.

STAMINA, PHYSICAL

see Physical Fitness

STAMPS, POSTAGE

see Postage Stamps

STANDARD OF VALUE

see Money

STANDARD TIME

see Time

STANLEY, SIR HENRY MORTON, 1841-1904

Clinton, Susan. Henry Stanley & David Livingstone: Explorers of Africa. LC 90-2172. (Illus.). 128p. (gr. 3 up). 1990. PLB 20.55 (*0-516-03055-8*) Childrens.

Graves, Charles P. Henry Morton Stanley. (Illus.). 96p. (gr. 3-5). 1991. Repr. of 1967 ed. lib. bdg. 12.95 (*0-7910-1507-6*) Chelsea Hse.

Twist, Clint. Stanley & Livingstone: Expeditions Through Africa. LC 94-21642. 1995. write for info. (*0-8114-3976-3*) Raintree Steck-V.

STANTON, ELIZABETH CADY, 1815-1902

Connell, Kate. They Shall Be Heard: The Story of Susan B. Anthony & Elizabeth Cady Stanton. Kiwak, Barbara, illus. LC 92-18088. 85p. (gr. 2-5). 1992. PLB 21.34 (*0-8114-7228-0*) Raintree Steck-V.

Cullen-Dupont, Kathryn. Elizabeth Cady Stanton & Women's Liberty. (Illus.). 144p. (gr. 6-12). 1992. lib. bdg. 16.95x (*0-8160-2413-8*) Facts on File.

Gleiter, Jan & Thompson, Kathleen. Elizabeth Cady Stanton. (Illus.). 32p. (Orig.). (gr. 2-5). 1988. PLB 19. 97 (*0-8172-2677-X*) Raintree Steck-V.

Kendall, Martha E. Elizabeth Cady Stanton. Knight, Anne R., illus. LC 88-81556. 72p. (gr. 3-5). 1987. text ed. 10.95 (*0-945783-03-5*); pap. 5.95 (*0-945783-02-7*) Highland Pub Group.

Schlank, Carol H. & Metzger, Barbara. Elizabeth Cady Stanton: A Biography for Young Children. Bond, Janice, illus. 32p. (ps-2). 1991. lib. bdg. 14.95 (*0-87659-177-2*); pap. 6.95 (*0-87659-176-4*) Gryphon Hse.

STARFISHES

Fichter, George S. Starfish, Seashells, & Crabs. Sandstrom, George, illus. 36p. (gr. k-3). 1993. 4.95 (*0-307-11430-9*, 11430, Golden Pr) Western Pub.

Hurd, Edith T. Starfish. Bloch, Lucienne, illus. LC 62-7742. 40p. (gr. k-2). 1962. PLB 13.89 (*0-690-77069-3*, Crowell Jr Bks) HarpC Child Bks.

STARLINGS

Pope, Joyce. The Starling. (Illus.). 24p. (gr. 3-6). 1991. 8.95 (*0-237-60251-2*, Pub. by Evans Bros Ltd) Trafalgar.

STARR, BELLE, 1848-1899

Green, Carl R. & Sanford, William R. Belle Starr. LC 91-22310. (Illus.). 48p. (gr. 4-10). 1992. lib. bdg. 14.95 (*0-89490-363-2*) Enslow Pubs.

STARS

see also Astrology; Astronomy; Astrophysics; Meteors; Planets; Solar System

Asimov, Isaac. Birth & Death of Stars. (gr. 4-7). 1991. pap. 4.99 (*0-440-40446-0*, YB) Dell.

—Colonizing Planets & Stars. (gr. 4-7). 1991. pap. 4.99 (*0-440-40447-9*, YB) Dell.

—Why Do Stars Twinkle? (Illus.). 24p. (gr. 2-3). 1991. PLB 15.93 (*0-8368-0437-6*) Gareth Stevens Inc.

Asimov, Isaac, et al. Mysteries of Deep Space: Black Holes, Pulsars, & Quasars. rev. & updated ed. (Illus.). (gr. 3 up). 1994. PLB 17.27 (*0-8368-1133-X*) Gareth Stevens Inc.

—A Star Gazer's Guide. rev. & updated ed. (Illus.). (gr. 3 up). 1995. PLB 17.27 (*0-8368-1197-6*) Gareth Stevens Inc.

Bailey, Donna. Looking at Stars. LC 90-40076. (Illus.). 48p. (gr. 2-6). 1990. PLB 19.97 (*0-8114-2522-3*); pap. 4.95 (*0-8114-6626-4*) Raintree Steck-V.

Baker, David. Flight to the Stars. (Illus.). 48p. (gr. 3-8). 1989. lib. bdg. 18.60 (*0-86592-373-6*); 13.95s.p. (*0-685-58640-5*) Rourke Corp.

Barrett, Norman S. The Picture World of Sun & Stars. LC 90-11992. (Illus.). 32p. (gr. k-4). 1990. PLB 12.40 (*0-531-14058-X*) Watts.

Branley, Franklyn M. The Big Dipper. rev. ed. Coxe, Molly, illus. LC 90-33198. 32p. (ps-1). 1991. pap. 4.95 (*0-06-445100-3*, Trophy) HarpC Child Bks.

—The Big Dipper. rev. ed. Coxe, Molly, illus. LC 90-31199. 32p. (ps-1). 1991. PLB 13.89 (*0-06-020512-1*) HarpC Child Bks.

—The Sky Is Full of Stars. Bond, Felicia, illus. LC 81-43037. 40p. (gr. k-3). 1981. PLB 13.89 (*0-690-04123-3*, Crowell Jr Bks) HarpC Child Bks.

Dickinson, Terence. Exploring the Night Sky: The Equinox Astronomy Guide for Beginners. Bianchi, John, illus. 72p. (Orig.). (gr. 5 up). 1989. 17.95 (*0-920656-64-1*, Pub. by Camden Hse CN); pap. 9.95 (*0-920656-66-8*, Pub. by Camden Hse CN) Firefly Bks Ltd.

Discovery Atlas of Planets & Stars. LC 93-16805. 1993. write for info. (*0-528-83580-7*) Rand McNally.

Estalella, Robert. The Stars. (Illus.). 32p. (gr. 4-8). 1993. 12.95 (*0-8120-6371-6*); pap. 6.95 (*0-8120-1738-2*) Barron.

Eugene, Toni. Descubre Estrellas y Planetas. University of Mexico City Staff, tr. from SPA. O'Neill, Pablo M. & Robare, Lorie, illus. 48p. (gr. 3-8). 1993. PLB 16.95 (*1-56674-052-5*, HTS Bks) Forest Hse.

—Discover Stars & Planets. (Illus.). 48p. (gr. 3-6). 1992. PLB 14.95 (*1-878363-71-9*, HTS Bks) Forest Hse.

Gallant, Roy A. The Constellations: How They Came to Be. rev. ed. LC 84-28755. (Illus.). 224p. (gr. 7 up). 1991. SBE 15.95 (*0-02-735776-7*, Four Winds) Macmillan Child Grp.

George, Michael. Galaxies. (gr. 5 up). 1993. PLB 18.95 (*0-88682-433-8*) Creative Ed.

—Stars. 1992. PLB 18.95 (*0-88682-400-1*) Creative Ed.

—Stars. 40p. (gr. 4-7). 1993. 15.95 (*1-56846-063-5*) Creat Editions.

Gustafson, John R. Stars, Clusters, & Galaxies. LC 92-11228. (gr. 3-7). 1993. lib. bdg. 12.98 (*0-671-72536-X*, J Messner); pap. 6.95 (*0-671-72537-8*, J Messner) S&S Trade.

Hatchett, Clint. The Glow-in-the-Dark Night Sky Book. Marchesi, Stephen, illus. LC 87-61531. 24p. (gr. 3-7). 1988. 13.00 (*0-394-89113-9*) Random Bks Yng Read.

Herbst, Judith. The Golden Book of Stars & Planets. LaPadula, Tom, illus. 48p. (gr. 3-7). 1988. write for info. (*0-307-15572-2*) Western Pub.

Ingle, Annie. The Glow-in-the-Dark Planetarium Book. Enik, Ted, illus. LC 92-29932. 16p. (Orig.). (ps-1). 1993. pap. 4.99 (*0-679-84367-1*) Random Bks Yng Read.

Jefferies, Lawrence. All about Stars. Veno, Joseph, illus. LC 82-20027. 32p. (gr. 3-6). 1983. PLB 10.59 (*0-89375-888-4*); pap. text ed. 2.95 (*0-89375-889-2*) Troll Assocs.

Maynard. Stars & Planets. (Illus.). 32p. (gr. 4-8). 1976. PLB 13.96 (*0-88110-313-6*); pap. 6.95 (*0-86020-094-9*) EDC.

Maynard, Chris. I Wonder Why Stars Twinkle & Other Questions about Space: And Other Questions about Space. Forsey, Chris & Kenyon, Tony, illus. LC 92-44259. 32p. (gr. k-3). 1993. 8.95 (*1-85697-881-8*, Kingfisher LKC) LKC.

The Night Sky: A Guide to the Stars. LC 93-85525. 240p. (Orig.). 1994. pap. 5.95 (*1-56138-386-4*) Running Pr.

Ottewell, Guy. To Know the Stars. (Illus.). 41p. (gr. 3 up). 1983. pap. 7.00 (*0-934546-12-6*) Astron Wkshp.

Rey, H. A. Find the Constellations. rev. ed. (Illus.). 80p. (gr. 3-7). 1976. 17.95 (*0-395-24509-5*) HM.

—Find the Constellations. rev. ed. Rey, H. A., illus. 72p. (gr. 3-7). 1976. pap. 8.70 (*0-395-24418-8*, Sandpiper) HM.

—The Stars: A New Way to See Them. 3rd ed. (Illus.). (gr. 8 up). 1973. 16.45 (*0-395-08121-1*) HM.

Ridpath, Ian. Atlas of Stars & Planets. LC 92-32463. 80p. (gr. 5-10). 1993. 16.95 (*0-8160-2926-1*) Facts on File.

Rosen, Sidney. Can You Find a Planet? 40p. (gr. k-2). 1991. lib. bdg. 19.95 (*0-87614-683-3*) Carolrhoda Bks.

Sabin, Louis. Stars. Acosta, Andres, illus. LC 84-2605. 32p. (gr. 3-6). 1985. PLB 9.49 (*0-8167-0152-0*); pap. text ed. 2.95 (*0-8167-0153-9*) Troll Assocs.

Santrey, Laurence. Discovering the Stars. Watling, James, illus. LC 81-7489. 32p. (gr. 2-4). 1982. PLB 11.59 (*0-89375-568-0*); pap. text ed. 2.95 (*0-89375-569-9*); cassette 9.95 (*0-685-04946-9*) Troll Assocs.

Seiger, Barbara. Seeing Stars: A Book & Poster about the Constellations. Calsbeek, Craig, illus. LC 92-43199. 24p. (gr. 2-6). 1993. pap. 7.95 (*0-448-40198-3*, G&D) Putnam Pub Group.

Simon, Seymour. Galaxies. LC 87-23967. (Illus.). 32p. (ps-3). 1988. 14.95 (*0-688-08002-2*); PLB 14.88 (*0-688-08004-9*, Morrow Jr Bks) Morrow Jr Bks.

Sneider, Cary I. Earth, Moon, & Stars. Bergman, Lincoln & Fairwell, Kay, eds. Baker, Lisa H. & Bevilacqua, Carol, illus. Sneider, Cary I., photos by. 50p. (Orig.). (gr. 5-9). 1986. pap. 10.00 (*0-912511-18-4*) Lawrence Science.

Sorensen, Lynda. Stars. LC 93-10475. 1993. write for info. (*0-86593-276-X*) Rourke Corp.

The Stars' Trip to Earth. (Illus.). 24p. (gr. k-3). 1993. 5.99 (*0-87406-650-6*) Willowisp Pr.

Wandelmaier, Roy. Stars. Trivas, Irene, illus. LC 84-8642. 32p. (gr. k-2). 1985. PLB 11.59 (*0-8167-0339-6*); pap. text ed. 2.95 (*0-8167-0442-2*) Troll Assocs.

Zim, Herbert S. & Baker, Robert H. Stars. rev. ed. Irving, James G., illus. (gr. 6 up). 1985. pap. write for info. (*0-307-24493-8*, Golden Pr) Western Pub.

STARS, FALLING

see Meteors

STARS–FICTION

Baer, Judy. Vanishing Star. 144p. (Orig.). (gr. 7-9). 1991. pap. 3.99 (*1-55661-197-8*) Bethany Hse.

Booht, David. Til All the Stars Have Fallen. (gr. 4-7). 1990. 14.95 (*0-670-83272-3*) Viking Child Bks.

Clement, Claude. The Man Who Lit the Stars. Howe, John, illus. (ps-3). 1992. 15.95 (*0-316-14741-9*) Little.

Conlon-McKenna, Marita. Little Star. Coady, Christopher, illus. LC 92-22132. 1993. 13.95 (*0-316-15375-3*) Little.

Davis, Karen. Star Light, Star Bright. LC 92-17120. (ps-2). 1993. 15.00 (*0-671-79455-8*, Green Tiger) S&S Trade.

Edens, Cooper. The Starcleaner Reunion. Edens, Cooper, illus. 1991. (Green Tiger) S&S Trade.

Field, Susan. The Sun, the Moon, & the Silver Baboon. Field, Susan, illus. LC 92-44496. 32p. (ps-2). 1993. 14. 00 (*0-06-022990-X*); PLB 13.89 (*0-06-022991-8*) HarpC Child Bks.

Ginolfi, Arthur. Tiny Star. Schories, Pat, illus. 32p. 1989. 6.95 (*1-56288-134-5*) Checkerboard.

Goldsmith, Howard. The Christmas Star. Appleget, Byron, illus. 48p. (ps-5). 1994. write for info. saddlestitch (*0-9642651-8-4*); PLB write for info. (*0-9642651-1-7*); text ed. write for info. (*0-9642651-2-5*); pap. 6.95 (*0-9642651-3-3*); pap. text ed. write for info. (*0-9642651-4-1*); tchr's. ed. avail. (*0-9642651-5-X*); wkbk. avail. (*0-9642651-6-8*); lab manual avail. (*0-9642651-7-6*) Reading Video.

Sad & lonely that no one answered its signal, TWINKLE, THE CHRISTMAS STAR decides to take a trip in the sky to try & find a friend. Exciting & unexpected adventures await him in the vast sky. The adventures of TWINKLE make a heartwarming story with endearing pictures that most certainly will capture the hearts of young readers. Howard Goldsmith was an Arthur Rackham Predoctoral Fellow at the University of Michigan, where he received a M.A. He is the author of about forty-five juvenile books for all ages. In addition, his stories have appeared in Disney Adventures, Scholastic, Child Life, Highlights for Children, Weekly Reader, Ideals, & others. To order contact "The" Reading Video, Inc., P.O. Box 42761, Indianapolis, IN 46241. Retail Price $6.95.

Publisher Provided Annotation.

Harrison, David. The Boy Who Counted Stars. Lewin, Betsy, illus. LC 92-61632. 32p. (gr. 1-5). 1994. 14.95 (*1-56397-125-9*) Boyds Mills Pr.

Hort, Lenny. How Many Stars in the Sky. Ransome, James, illus. LC 90-36044. 32p. (ps-3). 1991. 13.95 (*0-688-10103-8*, Tambourine Bks); PLB 13.88 (*0-688-10104-6*, Tambourine Bks) Morrow.

Ichikawa, Satomi. Nora's Stars. Ichikawa, Satomi, illus. 32p. (ps-3). 1989. 14.95 (*0-399-21616-2*, Philomel Bks) Putnam Pub Group.

—Nora's Stars. (Illus.). 32p. (ps up). 1992. pap. 5.95 (*0-399-21887-4*, Philomel Bks) Putnam Pub Group.

Kormann, Gordon. Twinkle Squad. (gr. 4-7). 1994. pap. 2.95 (*0-590-45250-9*) Scholastic Inc.

Lowry, Lois. Number the Stars. (gr. 4-7). 1992. pap. 1.99 (*0-440-21372-X*) Dell.

Luttrell, Ida. The Star Counters. Pretro, Korinna, illus. LC 93-20342. 32p. 1994. 15.00 (*0-688-12149-7*, Tambourine Bks); PLB 14.93 (*0-688-12150-0*, Tambourine Bks) Morrow.

McMahan, Dean & Rose, Willi. Ajuna's Star. rev. ed. McMahan, Dean, illus. LC 90-80841. 24p. (ps-2). 1990. pap. 4.95 (*0-9626254-1-8*); write for info. audio-cassette (*0-9626254-2-6*) Ajuna Unlimited.

Morey, Walt. Sandy & the Rock Star. LC 78-12375. (gr. 4-7). 1979. 13.95 (*0-525-38785-4*, DCB) Dutton Child Bks.

Newman, Leslea. Too Far Away to Touch, Close Enough to See. Stock, Catherine, illus. LC 93-30327. 1995. write for info. (*0-395-68968-6*, Clarion Bks) HM.

Northrop, Nancy. Mystari. St. James, Jim, illus. 16p. 1991. bds. 5.95 spiral bdg. (*0-9627894-1-0*) LNR Pubns.

Stone, Kazuko. Aligay Saves the Stars. 32p. 1991. 13.95 (*0-590-44382-8*, Scholastic Hardcover) Scholastic Inc.

Taylor, Jane. Twinkle, Twinkle, Little Star. Noonan, Julia, illus. (ps-3). 1993. pap. 4.95 (*0-590-45928-7*, Cartwheel) Scholastic Inc.

Vautier, Ghislaine. The Way of the Stars. McLeish, Kenneth, adapted by. (Illus.). 1989. pap. 9.95 (*0-521-37913-X*) Cambridge U Pr.

Widman, Christine. The Star Grazers. Spowart, Robin, illus. LC 87-29377. 32p. (ps-3). 1989. HarpC Child Bks.

Wright, Kit. Tigerella. Bailey, Peter, illus. LC 93-34218. (ps-2). 1994. 14.95 (*0-590-48171-1*) Scholastic Inc.

STARS–POETRY

Trapani, Iza. Twinkle Twinkle Little Star. LC 93-33635. (gr. 2 up). 1994. 14.95 (*1-879085-87-9*) Whsprng Coyote Pr.

STATE AND CHURCH

see Church and State

STATE CHURCH

see Church and State

STATE FLOWERS

Dowden, Anne O. State Flowers. Reissue. ed. Dowden, Anne O., illus. LC 78-41927. 96p. (gr. 5 up). 1978. PLB 14.89 (*0-690-03884-4*, Crowell Jr Bks) HarpC Child Bks.

Landau, Elaine. State Flowers: Including the Commonwealth of Puerto Rico. LC 92-8950. 1992. 13. 90 (*0-531-20059-0*) Watts.

STATE GOVERNMENTS

see also Governors;

also names of states with the subdivision Politics and Government, e.g. New York (State)–Politics and government; etc.

Black, S. Fabulous Facts about Fifty States. (gr. 4-7). 1991. pap. 2.75 (*0-590-44886-2*) Scholastic Inc.

Feinberg, Barbara S. State Governments. LC 92-27368. 1993. lib. bdg. 12.90 (*0-531-20154-6*) Watts.

Santrey, Laurence. State & Local Government. Dole, Bob, illus. LC 84-8440. 32p. (gr. 3-6). 1985. PLB 9.49 (*0-8167-0270-5*); pap. text ed. 2.95 (*0-8167-0271-3*) Troll Assocs.

Silvani, Harold. States & Capitals, 2 bks. Creative Teaching Assocs. Staff, illus. (gr. 3-6). 1975. Bks. A & B. write for info. set (*1-878669-12-5*, 4348) Bk. A, 28p. 6.95 (*1-878669-13-3*, 4348); Bk. B, 53p. 6.95 (*0-685-74213-X*, 4395) Crea Tea Assocs.

STATE TREES
Brandt, Sue R. State Trees: Including the Commonwealth of Puerto Rico. LC 92-8946. 1992. 13.90 (*0-531-20000-0*) Watts.
STATESMEN
see also Diplomats
Beilenson, John. Sukarno. Schlsinger, Arthur M., intro. by. (Illus.). 112p. (gr. 5 up). 1990. 17.95 (*1-55546-853-5*) Chelsea Hse.
Berry, Lynn. Wojciech Jaruzelski. (Illus.). 112p. (gr. 5 up). 1990. 17.95 (*1-55546-838-1*) Chelsea Hse.
Butson, Thomas. Mikhail Gorbachev. Schlesinger, Arthur M., Jr., intro. by. (Illus.). 112p. (Orig.). (gr. 5 up). 1989. 17.95 (*1-55546-200-6*); pap. 9.95 (*0-7910-0571-2*) Chelsea Hse.
Cockcroft, James D. Mohammed Reza Pahlevi. Schlesinger, Arthur M., intro. by. (Illus.). 112p. (gr. 5 up). 1989. 17.95x (*1-55546-847-0*) Chelsea Hse.
Condit, Erin. Francois & Jean-Claude Duvalier. Schlesinger, Arthur M., Jr., intro. by. (Illus.). 112p. (gr. 5 up). 1989. 17.95 (*1-55546-832-2*) Chelsea Hse.
Eide, Lorraine. Robert Mugabe. Schlesinger, Arthur M., intro. by. (Illus.). 112p. (gr. 5 up). 1989. 17.95 (*1-55546-845-4*) Chelsea Hse.
Fortier, E. H. Judas Maccabeus. Schlesinger, Arthur M., Jr., intro. by. (Illus.). 112p. (gr. 5 up). 1988. lib. bdg. 17.95 (*0-87754-539-1*) Chelsea Hse.
Franklin, Benjamin. Autobiography of Benjamin Franklin. Bigoness, J. W., intro. by. LC 80-26312. (gr. 8 up). 1965. pap. 2.75 (*0-8049-0071-X*, CL-71) Airmont.
Friese, Kai. Tenzin Gyatso. (Illus.). 112p. (gr. 5 up). 1990. 17.95 (*1-55546-836-5*) Chelsea Hse.
Geelan, Agnes. The Dakota Maverick. (Illus.). 186p. (gr. 9-12). 1983. pap. 7.95 (*0-911007-03-2*) Prairie Hse.
Gordon, Matthew. Hafez al-Assad. (Illus.). (gr. 5 up). 1989. 17.95 (*1-55546-827-6*) Chelsea Hse.
Gordon, Matthew S. The Gemayels. Schlesinger, Arthur M., Jr., intro. by. (Illus.). 112p. (gr. 5 up). 1988. 17.95 (*1-55546-834-9*) Chelsea Hse.
Haney, John. Clement Attlee. Schlesinger, Arthur M., Jr., intro. by. (Illus.). 112p. (gr. 5 up). 1988. lib. bdg. 17.95 (*0-87754-508-1*) Chelsea Hse.
Hicks, Nancy. The Honorable Shirley Chisholm: Congresswoman from Brooklyn. (gr. 7 up). PLB 12.95 (*0-87460-259-9*) Lion Bks.
Jacobs, William J. Great Lives: World Government. LC 91-42368. (Illus.). 320p. (gr. 4-6). 1993. SBE 22.95 (*0-684-19285-3*, Scribners Young Read) Macmillan Child Grp.
Kaye, Tony. Lech Walesa. (Illus.). 112p. (gr. 5 up). 1989. 17.95 (*1-55546-856-X*); pap. 9.95 (*0-7910-0689-1*) Chelsea Hse.
Kellner, Douglas. Ernesto "Che" Guevara. Schlesinger, Arthur M., intro. by. (Illus.). 112p. (gr. 5 up). 1989. 17.95 (*1-55546-835-7*) Chelsea Hse.
King, Perry. Pericles. Schlesinger, Arthur M., Jr., intro. by. (Illus.). 112p. (gr. 5 up). 1988. lib. bdg. 17.95 (*0-87754-547-2*) Chelsea Hse.
Kittredge, Mary. Marc Antony. Schlesinger, Arthur M., Jr., intro. by. (Illus.). 112p. (gr. 5 up). 1988. lib. bdg. 17.95 (*0-87754-505-7*) Chelsea Hse.
Kuckreja, Madhari. Prince Norodom Sihanouk. (Illus.). 112p. (gr. 5 up). 1990. 17.95 (*1-55546-851-9*) Chelsea Hse.
Kurkowski, David C., ed. Current Leaders of Nations. LC 89-81456. (Illus.). 180p. (gr. 9-12). 1990. 3-ring binder 95.00 (*0-9624900-0-8*) Current Leaders Pub.
Liles, Maurine W. Sam & the Speaker's Chair. LC 93-42374. 1994. 14.95 (*0-89015-946-7*) Sunbelt Media.
Lubetkin, Wendy. Deng Xiaoping. Schlesinger, Arthur M., Jr., intro. by. (Illus.). 112p. (gr. 5 up). 1988. 17.95 (*1-55546-830-6*) Chelsea Hse.
Matusky, Gregory & Hayes, John P., Jr. Hussein. (Illus.). 112p. (gr. 5 up). 1987. lib. bdg. 17.95 (*0-87754-533-2*) Chelsea Hse.
Mayberry, Jodine. Leaders Who Changed the Twentieth Century. LC 93-19032. (Illus.). 48p. (gr. 5-7). 1993. PLB 22.80 (*0-8114-4926-2*) Raintree Steck-V.
Navazelskis, Ina. Alexander Dubcek. (Illus.). 112p. (gr. 5 up). 1991. 17.95 (*1-55546-831-4*) Chelsea Hse.
Powers, Elizabeth. Nero. Schlesinger, Arthur M., Jr., intro. by. (Illus.). 112p. (gr. 5 up). 1988. lib. bdg. 17.95 (*0-87754-544-8*) Chelsea Hse.
Ragan, John D. Emiliano Zapata. Schlesinger, Arthur M., intro. by. (Illus.). 112p. (gr. 5 up). 1989. 17.95 (*1-55546-823-3*) Chelsea Hse.
Shearman, Deirdre. David Lloyd George. (Illus.). 112p. (gr. 5 up). 1988. lib. bdg. 17.95 (*0-87754-581-2*) Chelsea Hse.
Slack, Gordy. Ferdinand Marcos. Schlesinger, Arthur M. (Illus.). 112p. (gr. 5 up). 1988. 17.95 (*1-55546-842-X*) Chelsea Hse.
Solecki, John. Hosni Mubarak. (Illus.). (gr. 5 up). 1991. 17.95 (*1-55546-844-6*) Chelsea Hse.
Stefoff, Rebecca. Faisal. (Illus.). 112p. (gr. 5 up). 1989. 17.95 (*1-55546-833-0*) Chelsea Hse.
—Pol Pot. (Illus.). 112p. (gr. 5 up). 1990. 17.95 (*1-55546-848-9*) Chelsea Hse.
Stockwell, John. Daniel Ortega. Schlesinger, Arthur M., Jr., intro. by. (Illus.). 112p. (gr. 5 up). 1991. 17.95 (*1-55546-846-2*) Chelsea Hse.
Viola, Tom. Willy Brandt. Schlesinger, Arthur M., Jr., intro. by. (Illus.). 112p. (gr. 5 up). 1988. lib. bdg. 17.95 (*0-87754-512-X*) Chelsea Hse.
Walworth, Nancy Z. Constantine. (Illus.). 112p. (gr. 5 up). 1990. 17.95 (*1-55546-805-5*) Chelsea Hse.
STATISTICS
see also Probabilities;
also general subjects and names of countries, cities, etc. with the subdivision Statistics, e.g. U. S.–Statistics; etc.
Gardenier, George E. Statistical Methods: Games & Songs. Gardenier, T. K., ed. Gardenier, Jason C., illus. 99p. (gr. 3 up). 1989. 89.00 (*0-685-29043-3*) Teka Trends.
Kumbaraci, Turkan & Gardenier, George H. Branching Trees: Statistical Methods: Games & Songs. Gardenier, Turhan K., illus. LC 89-90944. 27p. (gr. 1-8). 1989. 30.00x (*0-685-29039-5*, 0003) Teka Trends.
Smoothey, Marion. Statistics. Evans, Ted, illus. LC 92-35574. 1993. 15.95 (*0-685-62557-5*) Marshall Cavendish.
—Statistics. Evans, Ted, illus. 64p. (gr. 4-8). 1993. text ed. 16.95 (*1-85435-468-X*) Marshall Cavendish.
Srivastava, Jane J. Statistics. Reiss, John, illus. LC 72-7559. (gr. 1-5). 1973. PLB 12.89 (*0-690-77300-5*, Crowell Jr Bks) HarpC Child Bks.
STATUE OF LIBERTY, NEW YORK
Birenbaum, Barbara. Lady Liberty's Light. Birenbaum, Barbara, illus. LC 85-32061. 50p. (gr. 3-5). 1986. 10.95 (*0-935343-12-1*); pap. 5.95 (*0-935343-11-3*) Peartree.
Fisher, Leonard E. The Statue of Liberty. Fisher, Leonard E., illus. LC 85-42878. 64p. (gr. 3-7). 1985. reinforced bdg. 14.95 (*0-8234-0586-9*) Holiday.
Gabriele. Statue of Liberty & Ellis Island. 1986. pap. 1.95 (*0-911211-79-9*) Penny Lane Pubns.
Goodman, Roger B. The Statue of Liberty & Ellis Island. (Illus.). 74p. (Orig.). (gr. 9 up). 1990. pap. 6.50 (*0-9632191-0-3*); pap. text ed. 6.50 (*0-9632191-1-1*); tchr's. ed. 6.50 (*0-9632191-2-X*); wkbk. 3.00 (*0-685-57051-7*) Pulitzer-Goodman.
Haskins, Jim. The Statue of Liberty: America's Proud Lady. LC 85-18061. (Illus.). 48p. (gr. 4-8). 1986. lib. bdg. 14.95 (*0-8225-1706-X*) Lerner Pubns.
Kushner, Ellen. Statue of Liberty Adventure. 1986. pap. 2.75 (*0-553-28176-3*) Bantam.
Maestro, Betsy. The Story of the Statue of Liberty. Maestro, Giulio, illus. LC 85-11324. 40p. (ps-3). 1986. PLB 16.93 (*0-688-05774-8*) Lothrop.
—The Story of the Statue of Liberty. LC 85-11324. (Illus.). 48p. (gr. k up). 1989. pap. 5.95 (*0-688-08746-9*, Mulberry) Morrow.
Marsh, Carole. Will Somebody Hold This Thing a Minute? Statue of Liberty Silly Trivia Book. (Illus.). 60p. (Orig.). (gr. 3-12). 1994. 24.95 (*1-55609-192-3*); pap. 14.95 (*0-935326-75-8*) Gallopade Pub Group.
Miller, Natalie. The Statue of Liberty. LC 91-44647. (Illus.). 32p. (gr. 3-6). 1992. PLB 12.30 (*0-516-06655-2*) Childrens.
—The Statue of Liberty. LC 91-44647. (Illus.). 32p. (gr. 3-6). 1993. pap. 3.95 (*0-516-46655-0*) Childrens.
Our Statue of Liberty. (Illus.). (ps-2). 1991. pap. 3.50 (*0-8136-5960-4*, TK3913) Modern Curr.
Sorensen, Lynda. The Statue of Liberty. LC 94-7052. 1994. write for info. (*1-55916-046-2*) Rourke Bk Co.
Wolf, D. M. A Bird's Eye View of the Statue of Liberty: As Seen by Lorenzo the Parrot. McDaniel, Jerry, illus. 32p. (gr. 3-4). 1988. pap. 4.95 (*0-9617057-2-8*) Storyviews Pub.
STAUFFENBERG, BERTHOLD VON, 1907-1944
Forman, James. Code Name Valkyrie: Count Claus von Stauffenberg & the Plot to Kill Hitler. LC 72-12581. (Illus.). 256p. (gr. 9-12). 1973. PLB 24.95 (*0-87599-188-2*) S G Phillips.
STEAM ENGINES
Siegel, Beatrice. The Steam Engine. LC 86-5616. (Illus.). 64p. (gr. 5 up). 1986. 10.95 (*0-8027-6655-2*); PLB 10.85 (*0-8027-6656-0*) Walker & Co.
STEAM ENGINES–FICTION
Coco, Eugene. Sammy the Steamroller. Samuels, Mark, illus. 24p. (ps-2). 1993. pap. text ed. 0.99 (*1-56293-347-7*) McClanahan Bk.
Tootle. (Illus.). 24p. (ps up). 1992. write for info. incl. long-life batteries (*0-307-74806-5*, 64806, Golden Pr) Western Pub.
STEAM-SHOVELS–FICTION
Burton, Virginia L. Mike Mulligan & His Steam Shovel. (Illus.). (gr. k-3). 1939. PLB 11.95 (*0-395-06681-6*) HM.
STEAMBOATS
Braynard, Frank O. U. S. Steamships: A Picture Postcard History. Cronkite, Walter, intro. by. (Illus.). 144p. (Orig.). 1991. pap. 14.95 (*0-930256-20-4*) Almar.
Chant, Chris. Steamships. Batchelor, John, illus. LC 88-28764. 63p. (gr. 3-9). 1989. PLB 16.95 (*1-85435-086-2*) Marshall Cavendish.
McCall, Edith. Mississippi Steamboatman: The Story of Henry Miller Shreve. LC 85-13795. (Illus.). 115p. (gr. 5-8). 1986. 11.95 (*0-8027-6597-1*) Walker & Co.
McNeese, Tim. West by Steamboat. LC 91-22822. (Illus.). 48p. (gr. 5). 1993. text ed. 11.95 RSBE (*0-89686-728-5*, Crestwood Hse) Macmillan Child Grp.
Stein, R. Conrad. The Story of Mississippi Steamboats. Dunnington, Tom, illus. 32p. (gr. 3-6). 1987. pap. 3.95 (*0-516-44726-2*) Childrens.
STEAMSHIPS
see Steamboats
STEEL
see also Iron;
also headings beginning with the word Steel
Curtis, Neil & Greenland, Peter. How Steel Is Made. (Illus.). 24p. (gr. 1-3). 1992. PLB 13.50 (*0-8225-2378-7*) Lerner Pubns.
Lambert, M. Iron & Steel. (Illus.). 48p. (gr. 5 up). 1985. PLB 17.27 (*0-86592-268-3*); 12.95 (*0-685-58325-2*) Rourke Corp.
Langley, Andrew. Steel. LC 93-6834. 32p. (gr. 3-6). 1993. 13.95 (*1-56847-044-4*) Thomson Lrning.
STEEL INDUSTRY AND TRADE
see also Iron Industry and Trade
STEIN, GERTRUDE, 1874-1946
La Farge, Ann. Gertrude Stein. Horner, Matina, intro. by. (Illus.). 112p. (gr. 5 up). 1988. lib. bdg. 17.95 (*1-55546-678-8*) Chelsea Hse.
STEINBECK, JOHN ERNST, 1902-1968
Ito, Tom. John Steinbeck. LC 93-40923. (gr. 5-8). 1994. 14.95 (*1-56006-049-2*) Lucent Bks.
STENCIL WORK
see also Silk Screen Printing
Bartok, Mira & Ronan, Christine. Indians of the Great Plains: Stencils. (Illus.). 32p. (Orig.). 1993. pap. 9.95 (*0-673-36138-1*) GdYrBks.
—West Africa: Nigeria: Stencils. (Illus.). 32p. (Orig.). 1993. pap. 9.95 (*0-673-36137-3*) GdYrBks.
Buckingham, Sandra. Stencil It! (Illus.). 64p. Date not set. PLB 17.95 (*0-921820-75-5*, Pub. by Camden Hse CN); pap. 9.95 (*0-921820-73-9*, Pub. by Camden Hse CN) Firefly Bks Ltd.
Lynn, Sara & James, Diane. Play with Paint. (Illus.). 24p. (ps-2). 1993. 18.95 (*0-87614-755-4*) Carolrhoda Bks.
O'Reilly, Susie. Stencils & Screens. LC 93-28349. (Illus.). 32p. (gr. 4-6). 1994. 14.95 (*1-56847-068-1*) Thomson Lrning.
Pumpkin Cut-Ups: Super Stencils for Perfect Pumpkins. (ps-3). 1992. pap. 1.95 (*0-590-46204-0*) Scholastic Inc.
Walton, Sally & Walton, Stewart. Stencil It! Over One Hundred Step-by-Step Projects. LC 92-36177. (Illus.). 80p. (gr. 4-10). 1993. 14.95 (*0-8069-0346-5*) Sterling.
STEVENSON, ROBERT LOUIS, 1850-1894
Greene, Carol. Robert Louis Stevenson: Author of A Child's Garden of Verses. (Illus.). 32p. (gr. 2-4). 1994. PLB 17.20 (*0-516-04265-3*); pap. 4.95 (*0-516-44265-1*) Childrens.
Murphy, Jim. Across America on an Emigrant Train. LC 92-38650. 160p. 1993. 16.95 (*0-395-63390-7*, Clarion Bks) HM.
Sabin, Francene. Robert Louis Stevenson: Young Storyteller. Johnson, Pamela, illus. LC 91-3924. 48p. (gr. 4-6). 1992. PLB 10.79 (*0-8167-2507-1*); pap. text ed. 3.50 (*0-8167-2508-X*) Troll Assocs.
Willard, Nancy, et al. The Voyage of the Ludgate Hill: A Journey with Robert Louis Stevenson. Provensen, Martin & Provensen, Alice, illus. LC 86-19502. 32p. (gr. k-3). 1987. 14.95 (*0-15-294464-8*) HarBrace.
STOCK EXCHANGE
see also Investments; Stocks
Fisher, Clayton P. The Stock Market Explained for Young Investors: Young Investors Ser. (Illus.). 175p. (gr. 9 up). 1993. 17.95 (*0-931133-02-5*, Busn Class) Pac Pub Grp.
King, Nadia. Inside Truths about the Stock Brokerage Business. Kriks, Bill, ed. 75p. (Orig.). 1989. pap. text ed. 5.00 (*0-685-29786-1*) Kings Inc.
Young, Robin. The Stock Market. (Illus.). 80p. (gr. 5 up). 1991. PLB 21.50 (*0-8225-1780-9*) Lerner Pubns.
STOCK MARKET
see Stock Exchange
STOCK RAISING
see Livestock
STOCKS
see also Investments; Stock Exchange
Dunnan, Nancy. The Stock Market. (Illus.). 128p. (gr. 7-10). 1990. lib. bdg. 9.95 (*0-382-09914-1*); pap. 5.95 (*0-382-24025-1*) Silver Burdett Pr.
Fisher, Clayton P. The Stock Market Explained for Young Investors: Young Investors Ser. (Illus.). 175p. (gr. 9 up). 1993. 17.95 (*0-931133-02-5*, Busn Class) Pac Pub Grp.
STONE
see also Masonry; Rocks
STONE AGE
see also Man, Prehistoric
Ask about Prehistoric Life. 64p. (gr. 4-5). 1987. PLB 11.95 (*0-8172-2879-9*) Raintree Steck-V.
Carrick, Carol. Patrick's Dinosaurs. Carrick, Donald, illus. LC 83-2049. 32p. (gr. k-3). 1983. 13.95 (*0-89919-189-4*, Clarion Bks) HM.
Craig, A. Prehistoric Facts. (Illus.). 48p. (gr. 3-7). 1986. PLB 12.96 (*0-88110-228-8*); pap. 5.95 (*0-86020-973-3*) EDC.
Dunrea, Olivier. Skara Brae: The Story of a Prehistoric Village. Dunrea, Olivier, illus. LC 85-42882. 40p. (gr. 3-7). 1986. reinforced bdg. 13.95 (*0-8234-0583-4*) Holiday.
Killingray, David. The Neolithic Revolution. Yapp, Malcolm, et al, eds. (Illus.). 32p. (gr. 6-11). 1980. pap. text ed. 3.45 (*0-89908-105-3*) Greenhaven.
Let's Discover the Prehistoric World. LC 80-22949. (Illus.). 80p. (gr. k-9). 1981. 14.95 (*0-8172-1776-2*) Raintree Steck-V.
McCord, A. Prehistoric Life (B - U) (Illus.). 96p. (gr. 2-7). 1993. pap. 12.95 (*0-86020-490-1*) EDC.
Spizzirri Publishing Co. Staff. Prehistoric Birds: An Educational Coloring Book. Spizzirri, Linda, ed. Spizzirri, Peter M., illus. 32p. (gr. 1-8). 1981. pap. 1.75 (*0-86545-023-4*) Spizzirri.
—Prehistoric Sea Life: An Educational Coloring Book. Spizzirri, Linda, ed. Kohn, Arnie, illus. 32p. (gr. 1-8). 1981. pap. 1.75 (*0-86545-020-X*) Spizzirri.

STONE AGE–FICTION

Little Treasury of Flintstones. 1989. 5.95 (0-318-41671-9) Random Hse Value.

STONEHENGE

Abels, Harriette S. Stonehenge. LC 87-13638. (Illus.). 48p. (gr. 5-6). 1987. text ed. 12.95 RSBE (0-89686-346-8, Crestwood Hse) Macmillan Child Grp.

Lyon, Nancy. The Mystery of Stonehenge. LC 77-10044. (Illus.). 48p. (gr. 4 up). 1983. PLB 20.70 (0-8172-1049-0) Raintree Steck-V.

Roop, Peter & Roop, Connie. Stonehenge: Opposing Viewpoints. LC 89-37441. (Illus.). 112p. (gr. 5-8). 1989. PLB 14.95 (0-89908-066-9) Greenhaven.

STONES, PRECIOUS

see Precious Stones

STONEWARE

see Pottery

STORIES

see also Animals–Fiction; Ballet–Fiction; Bible Stories; Birds–Fiction; Christmas–Fiction; Fairy Tales; Horror Stories; Legends; Mystery and Detective Stories; Sea Stories; Short Stories; Storytelling; Trees–Fiction; Vocational Stories

Abrams, Rita. Stepping Out. 1991. bds. 12.95 incl. song tape (0-938971-75-1) JTG Nashville.

Adoff, Arnold. The Cabbages Are Chasing the Rabbits. Stevens, Janet, illus. LC 85-893. 32p. (gr. k-3). 1985. 15.95 (0-15-213875-7, HB Juv Bks) HarBrace.

Aguiar, Elithe. Legends of Hawaii As Told By Lani Goose. Aguiar, Elithe & Sakamoto, Dean, illus. 20p. (gr. k up). 1986. pap. 8.95 incl. audio cassette (0-944264-00-X) Lani Goose Pubns.

Aiken, Joan. A Touch of Chill. (gr. k up). 1989. pap. 3.50 (0-440-20459-3, LFL) Dell.

Albright, Nancy T. Do Tell! Holiday Draw & Tell Stories. rev. & enl. ed. (ps-4). 1989. pap. 5.00 (0-913545-13-9) Moonlight FL.

Alexander, Lloyd. Time Cat. Sokol, Bill, illus. (gr. 4-7). 16.25 (0-8446-6237-2) Peter Smith.

Allard, Harry. Miss Nelson Has a Field Day. Marshall, James, illus. LC 84-27791. 32p. (gr. k-3). 1985. 13.45 (0-395-36690-9) HM.

Amoss, Berthe. Lost Magic. LC 93-10082. 192p. (gr. 5 up). 1993. 14.95 (1-56282-573-9) Hyprn Child.

Ancona, George. Bananas. (gr. 4-7). 1990. pap. 5.70 (0-395-54787-3, Clarion Bks) HM.

Andersen, Hans Christian. It's Perfectly True! LC 87-7567. (Illus.). 32p. (ps-3). 1988. reinforced bdg. 13.95 (0-8234-0672-5) Holiday.

Andrews, Jean F. The Flying Fingers Club. LC 88-19875. 104p. (Orig.). (gr. 3-5). 1988. pap. 4.95 (0-930323-44-0, Kendall Green Pubns) Gallaudet Univ Pr.

Armstrong, Velma. The Banana Horse. Graves, Helen, ed. LC 85-51966. 104p. (gr. 3-6). 1986. pap. 6.95 (0-938232-98-3) Winston-Derek.

Arroyo, Anita. El Grillo Grunon: Cuentos para Chicos y Grandes. Robain, Armando O., illus. LC 84-13199. (SPA.). 122p. (Orig.). (gr. 1-6). 1984. pap. 5.50 (0-8477-3527-3) U of PR Pr.

Atwell, Lucy. Lucy Atwell's Goodnight Stories. (Illus.). (ps-1). 1985. 3.98 (0-517-46903-0) Random Hse Value.

Ayme, Marcel. Probleme. Sabatier, Roland, illus. (FRE.). 71p. (ps-1). 1989. pap. 9.95 (2-07-031198-8) Schoenhof.

Baldner, Jean V. Pebbles in the Wind. Webster, Carroll, illus. 52p. (Orig.). (gr. 7 up). pap. 5.95 (0-9615317-0-3) Baldner J V.

Bang, Molly. Dawn. LC 83-886. (Illus.). 32p. (ps up). 1983. 11.95 (0-688-02400-9); PLB 13.88 (0-688-02404-1) Morrow Jr Bks.

Barrett, Judith. Cloudy with a Chance of Meatballs. LC 87-29643. (Illus.). (ps-3). 1982. pap. 3.95 (0-689-70749-5, Aladdin) Macmillan Child Grp.

Barth, Nancy & Wittenborn, Sally. On Halloween Night. Wittenborn, Sally, illus. 12p. (Orig.). (ps-1). 1987. pap. 4.95 (0-942565-00-2) Country Schl Pubns.

Bashful Bard. Being Part of a Family. Bashful Bard, illus. LC 89-84968. 28p. (Orig.). (ps-1). 1989. Kenney Pubns.

—Cricket Gets the Monster: Fears & Feelings. Bashful Bard, illus. LC 89-84969. 28p. (Orig.). (ps-1). 1989. Kenney Pubns.

—Cricket Loses His Shadow. Bashful Bard, illus. LC 89-84963. 28p. (Orig.). (ps-1). 1989. Kenney Pubns.

—A Dragon in Dew Drop Dell. Bashful Bard, illus. LC 89-84965. 28p. (Orig.). (ps-1). 1989. Kenney Pubns.

—Having Fun Outdoors. Bashful Bard, illus. LC 89-84966. 28p. (Orig.). (ps-1). 1989. Kenney Pubns.

—Things to Wonder About. Bashful Bard, illus. LC 89-84970. 28p. (Orig.). (ps-1). 1989. Kenney Pubns.

—Work & Responsibility. Bashful Bard, illus. LC 89-84967. 24p. (Orig.). (gr. k-1). 1989. Kenney Pubns.

Bauer, Caroline F., ed. Rainy Day: Stories & Poems. Chessare, Michele, illus. LC 85-45170. 96p. (gr. 2-5). 1986. (Lipp Jr Bks); PLB 14.89 (0-397-32105-8, Lipp Jr Bks) HarpC Child Bks.

Baum, L. Frank. The Surprising Adventures of the Magical Monarch of Mo & His People. (gr. 5-6). 20.95 (0-88411-771-5, Pub. by Aeonian Pr) Amereon Ltd.

Bawden, Nina. Squib. (gr. k-6). 1990. pap. 3.50 (0-440-40326-X, YB) Dell.

Beamer, Winona D. Talking Story with Nona Beamer: Stories of a Hawaiian Family. Kahalewai, Marilyn, illus. Hannahs, Neil J., afterword by. LC 83-70357. (Illus.). 80p. (gr. 2-6). 1984. 9.95 (0-935848-20-7) Bess Pr.

Beers, V. Gilbert. My Bedtime Anytime Storybook. O'Connor, Tim, illus. LC 92-8376. 1992. 12.99 (0-8407-9166-6) Nelson.

Belle, Barbara. Pixel Helps Pooper out of a Pickle. (Illus.). 24p. (Orig.). (gr. 1-5). pap. 3.25 (0-935163-02-6) Pixel Prods Pubns.

Bennett, Geraldine M. The Katrina Tells Series. (gr. 3 up). 1994. pap. write for info. (1-882786-99-8) New Dawn NY.

Berleth, Richard. Samuel's Choice. Mathews, Judith, ed. Watling, James, illus. LC 89-77186. 40p. (gr. 3-6). 1990. PLB 14.95 (0-8075-7218-7) A Whitman.

Best-Selling Apples, 4 vols. Incl. Nothing's Fair in Fifth Grade. DeClements, Barthe; Yours Till Niagara Falls, Abby. O'Connor, Jane; Tough-Luck Karen. Hurwitz, Johanna; Amy & Laura. Sachs, Marilyn. (gr. 4-6). 1985. Boxed Set. pap. 9.50 (0-590-63049-0, Apple Paperbacks) Scholastic Inc.

Blacker, Terence. Ms Wiz Spells Trouble. Goffe, Toni, illus. 64p. (gr. 3-6). 1990. pap. 2.95 (0-8120-4420-7) Barron.

Blackwell, B. Believe It or Not Stories. 15p. (gr. 7-10). 1986. 30.00x (0-7223-2003-5, Pub. by A H Stockwell England) St Mut.

Boegehold, Betty D. You Are Much Too Small-Bank Street. (ps-3). 1990. PLB 9.99 (0-553-05895-9, Little Rooster); pap. 3.99 (0-553-34925-2) Bantam.

Boesky, Amy. Planet Was, Vol. 1. (ps-3). 1990. 14.95 (0-316-10084-6, Joy St Bks) Little.

Bond, Felicia. Poinsettia & Her Family. Bond, Felicia, illus. LC 81-43035. 32p. (ps-3). 1985. pap. 4.95i (0-06-443076-6, Trophy) HarpC Child Bks.

Bond, Ruskin. Tales Told at Twilight. 166p. (gr. 4-6). 1970. 1.25 (0-88253-394-0) Ind-US Inc.

Boore, Sara. Bedtime Book. (ps). 1992. pap. 12.95 (1-878257-20-X) Klutz Pr.

Bourque, Nina. The Best Trade of All. Urbanovic, Jackie, illus. LC 83-7352. 32p. (gr. 3-6). 1984. PLB 27.99 incl. cassette (0-8172-2280-4); cassette only 14.00 (0-317-19659-6) Raintree Steck-V.

Bowden, Joan. Pop up Just Ben. 1989. 4.95 (0-671-67555-9) S&S Trade.

Bramos, Helen & Bramos, Ann S. My Little Storybook. Bramos, Ann S., illus. 63p. (Orig.). (gr. 1-6). 1992. pap. 7.00 (0-9635333-0-4) A S Bramos.

Brott, Ardyth. Jeremy's Decision. Martchenko, Michael, illus. 32p. (ps-3). 1990. 12.95 (0-916291-31-6) Kane-Miller Bk.

Brown, Marc T., compiled by. & illus. Scared Silly! A Collection of Stories, Rhymes, & Riddles to Laugh Your Fears Away. LC 93-13501. (ps-4). 1994. 18.95 (0-316-11360-3) Little.

Burnsed, Linda & Chaffin, Garry. A Child's Gift of Bedtime Stories, Vol. 1. Brown, J. Aaron, ed. Ragland, Teresa, illus. 28p. (gr. 1-4). 1993. incl. cass. 12.95 (0-927945-07-X) Someday Baby.

Butler, Dorothy. Higgledy Piggledy Hobbledy Hoy. LC 89-77503. (Illus.). 30p. (ps up). 1991. 13.95 (0-688-08660-8); PLB 13.88 (0-688-08661-6) Greenwillow.

Callenbach, Ernest & Leefeldt, Christine. Humphrey the Wayward Whale. Buell, Carl, illus. 24p. (Orig.). (gr. k-6). 1986. pap. 4.95 (0-930588-23-1) Heyday Bks.

Cameron, Ann. More Stories Julian Tells. Strugnell, Ann, illus. LC 84-10095. 96p. (gr. k-3). 1989. pap. 2.99 (0-394-82454-7) Knopf Bks Yng Read.

—The Stories Julian Tells. Strugnell, Ann, illus. LC 80-18023. 88p. (gr. k-3). 1989. Repr. of 1981 ed. 3.25 (0-394-82892-5) Knopf Bks Yng Read.

Caple, Kathy. The Biggest Nose. Caple, Kathy, illus. LC 84-19745. 32p. (gr. k-3). 1985. 14.45 (0-395-36894-4); pap. 5.70 (0-395-47943-6) HM.

Cardinal, Catherine S. The Button Box. (Illus.). 40p. (Orig.). (gr. 3 up). 1992. write for info. (0-9630655-1-3); pap. write for info. Garden Gate.

Carlson, Lori M. & Ventura, Cynthia L., eds. Where Angels Glide at Dawn: New Stories from Latin America. Ortega, Jose, illus. LC 90-6697. 128p. (gr. 5 up). 1990. 14.00 (0-397-32424-3, Lipp Jr Bks); PLB 13.89 (0-397-32425-1, Lipp Jr Bks) HarpC Child Bks.

Carter, Margaret, retold by. The Three Little Pigs & Other Stories. Offen, Hilda, illus. LC 93-11741. 1994. 3.95 (1-85697-973-3, Kingfisher LKC) LKC.

Castle, Caroline. The Hare & the Tortoise. Weevers, Peter, illus. LC 84-9569. 32p. (ps-3). 1985. 10.95 (0-8037-0138-1) Dial Bks Young.

Chaffin, Gary & Burnsed, Linda. A Child's Gift of Bedtime Stories, Vol. 1. Ragland, Teresa, illus. LC 93-17766. 44p. (ps-6). 1993. 13.95 (1-56566-044-7) Thomasson-Grant.

Chetwin, Grace. Box & Cox. Small, David, illus. LC 88-35337. 32p. (gr. k-3). 1990. SBE 13.95 (0-02-718314-9, Bradbury Pr) Macmillan Child Grp.

Chevalier, Christa. Spence Isn't Spence Anymore. Levine, Abby, ed. Chevalier, Christa, illus. LC 84-29195. 32p. (ps-1). 1985. 11.95 (0-8075-7565-8) A Whitman.

A Child's Treasury of the Worthwhile. (gr. 3-11). 6.95 (0-87741-007-0) Makepeace Colony.

Christian, Mary B. Go West, Swamp Monsters. Brown, Marc T., illus. LC 84-12686. 48p. (ps-3). 1985. 8.95 (0-8037-0091-1) Dial Bks Young.

Christopher, Matt. Supercharged Infield. Downing, Julie, illus. (gr. 4-6). 1985. 15.95 (0-316-13983-1) Little.

Coffin, Carlyn. Noel & His Friends. (Illus.). 130p. (ps up). 1987. pap. 10.95 over boards (0-931474-30-2) TBW Bks.

Cohen, Daniel. The UFOS Third Wave. LC 88-16558. 172p. (gr. 7 up). 1988. 12.95 (0-87131-541-6) M Evans.

Connelly, Tony & Holley, Cindy. Holiday Stories. Champlin, John, ed. (Illus.). 38p. (gr. 3-6). 1982. pap. 8.95 (0-938594-02-8) Spec Lit Pr.

Cooner, Donna D. Twelve Days in Texas. Leland, Bob, illus. 32p. (gr. k-2). 1994. pap. 9.95 (0-937460-85-0) Hendrick-Long.

Coren, Alan. Arthur the Kid. 80p. (gr. 4-6). 1984. pap. text ed. 2.25 (0-553-15169-X, Skylark) Bantam.

Cornell, S. A. Little Eagle Learns to Fly. Jones, John, illus. LC 85-14086. 48p. (Orig.). (gr. 1-3). 1986. lib. bdg. 10.59 (0-8167-0618-2); pap. text ed. 3.50 (0-8167-0619-0) Troll Assocs.

Corrin, Sara & Corrin, Stephen, eds. Stories for Seven-Year-Olds. Hughes, Shirley, illus. 188p. (gr. 1-3). 1982. pap. 9.95 (0-571-12910-2) Faber & Faber.

Cosgrove, Stephen. Crabby Gabby. James, Robin, illus. LC 85-14351. 32p. (Orig.). (gr. 1-4). 1985. pap. 2.95 (0-8431-1441-X) Price Stern.

Craig, Janet. Santa's Cookie Surprise. Loh, Carolyn, illus. LC 88-19997. 32p. (gr. k-2). 1989. lib. bdg. 7.89 (0-8167-1538-6); pap. text ed. 1.95 (0-8167-1539-4) Troll Assocs.

Cresswell, Helen. Time Out. Elwell, Peter, illus. LC 89-36798. 80p. (gr. 2-5). 1990. SBE 13.95 (0-02-725425-9, Macmillan Child Bk) Macmillan Child Grp.

Dahl, Roald. Roald Dahl Boxed Set: Includes; Charlie & the Chocolate Factory; Charlie & the Great Glass Elevator; the Big. (Illus.). (gr. 3-7). 1989. pap. 11.95 (0-14-095040-0) Viking Child Bks.

Dale, Bruce. Collection of Children's Stories. (Illus.). 88p. 1994. pap. 6.95 (0-8059-3515-0) Dorrance.

Daly, Niki. Ben's Gingerbread Man. LC 85-3327. (Illus.). 24p. (ps-1). 1985. 4.95 (0-670-80806-7) Viking Child Bks.

Daniel, Jennifer. Spin-a-Story, Twenty Thousand French Fries under the Sea & Other Crazy Classics. Brown, Jean, illus. 24p. (gr. 4-7). 1990. pap. 2.95 (1-878890-01-8) Palisades Prodns.

Daniel, Kira. Backyard Tent. Burns, Ray, illus. LC 85-14068. 48p. (Orig.). (gr. 1-3). 1986. PLB 10.59 (0-8167-0626-3); pap. text ed. 3.50 (0-8167-0627-1) Troll Assocs.

—The Magic Kite. Getchell, Marianne S., illus. LC 85-14015. 48p. (Orig.). (gr. 1-3). 1986. PLB 10.59 (0-8167-0614-X); pap. text ed. 3.50 (0-8167-0615-8) Troll Assocs.

Danziger, Paula. Make Like a Tree & Leave. (gr. 4-7). 1990. 13.95 (0-385-30151-0) Delacorte.

Davis, Rhonda K. Seven-Series Educational Value Pak. (Illus.). (ps up). 1992. Set. 21.00 (1-881967-07-7) Express In Writing.

Davis, Robert. Kimura. 224p. 1989. 18.95 (0-8027-5736-7) Walker & Co.

Davoll, Barbara. The White Trail. Hockerman, Dennis, illus. 24p. 1988. 6.99 (0-89693-404-7, Victor Books); cassette 9.99 (0-89693-615-5) SP Pubns.

DeFelice, Cynthia. Weasel. LC 89-37794. 128p. (gr. 5 up). 1990. SBE 13.95 (0-02-726457-2, Macmillan Child Bk) Macmillan Child Grp.

Deitz, Lawrence. Jimmy Coon Story Book, No. 3. 37p. 1986. pap. 2.95 (0-934750-85-8) Mntn Memories Bks.

—Jimmy Coon Story Book, No. 4. McCoy, Beverly, illus. 30p. 1986. pap. 2.95 (0-934750-14-9) Mntn Memories Bks.

De Paola, Tomie. Now One Foot, Now the Other. (gr. k-4). 1992. pap. 5.95 (0-399-22400-9, Sandcastle Bks) Putnam Pub Group.

Disney Two-in-One, Set 1. (gr. 3 up). 1991. pap. 1.97 (1-56297-116-6, WD-214) Lee Pubns KY.

Disney Two-in-One, Set 2. (gr. 3 up). 1991. pap. 1.97 (1-56297-117-4, WD-214) Lee Pubns KY.

Disney, Walt. Little Treasury of Walt Disney: Favorite Stories, 6 vols. in 1. 1988. boxed 5.99 (0-517-61630-0) Random Hse Value.

Disney, Walt, Productions Staff. Walt Disney's Story Land. (Illus.). 320p. (gr. 1-5). 1987. write for info. (0-307-16547-7, Golden Bks) Western Pub.

—Words, Riddles, & Stories. LC 85-43074. 80p. 1985. pap. 5.95 (0-553-05535-6) Bantam.

Disney's Box Office: Your Tickets to Reading Adventure, 4 bks. (gr. 2-6). 1993. Boxed Set. pap. 11.80 (1-56282-395-7) Disney Pr.

Disney's Read-It-Yourself Storybook. (gr. k-2). 1991. 10.50 (0-307-16556-6, Golden Pr) Western Pub.

Doyle, Charlotte. Freddie's Spaghetti. Reilly, Nicholas, illus. LC 90-61003. 24p. (Orig.). (ps-2). 1991. pap. 2.25 (0-679-81160-5) Random Bks Yng Read.

Dr. Seuss. And to Think That I Saw It on Mulberry Street. LC 88-38411. (Illus.). 32p. (ps-3). 1989. Repr. of 1937 ed. 13.00 (0-394-84494-7); lib. bdg. 11.99 (0-394-94494-1) Random Bks Yng Read.

East, Helen, compiled by. The Singing Sack. Currie, Mary, illus. 80p. (gr. 2 up). 16.95 (0-7136-3115-5, Pub. by A&C Black UK) Talman.

Edgar, Pamela & Matz, Dale. Adventures of Jason: Mythical Magical Journey into Self-Discovery. LC 85-9695. (Illus.). 64p. (Orig.). (gr. 1-5). 1985. pap. 7.95 (0-941992-05-5) Los Arboles Pub.

Elfman, Eric. The Very Scary Almanac. Suckow, Will, illus. 80p. (Orig.). (gr. 4-7). 1993. pap. 4.99 (0-679-84401-5) Random Bks Yng Read.

Elkins, Stephen. Stories That End with a Hug. Menck, Kevin, illus. 32p. (gr. k-8). 1993. 12.98 (*1-56919-002-X*) Wonder Wkshop.
—Stories That End with a Prayer. Menck, Kevin, illus. 32p. (gr. k-8). Date not set. 12.98 (*1-56919-003-8*) Wonder Wkshop.
—Stories That End with a Song. Menck, Kevin, illus. 32p. (gr. k-8). Date not set. 12.98 (*0-685-68095-9*) Wonder Wkshop.
Ellis, Jana. Junior Weekend. LC 88-19988. 160p. (gr. 7 up). 1988. pap. text ed. 2.50 (*0-8167-1364-2*) Troll Assocs.
Engel, Diana. Josephina, the Great Collector. Engel, Diana, illus. LC 87-20358. 32p. (ps-2). 1988. 12.95 (*0-688-07542-8*); PLB 12.88 (*0-688-07543-6*, Morrow Jr Bks) Morrow Jr Bks.
Ernst, Lisa C. Up to Ten & down Again. LC 84-21852. (Illus.). 40p. (ps). 1986. 14.00 (*0-688-04541-3*); PLB 13.93 (*0-688-04542-1*) Lothrop.
Erskine, Jim. Bedtime Story. Schweninger, Ann, illus. LC 81-3163. 32p. (ps-1). 1981. PLB 8.95 (*0-517-54540-3*) Crown Bks Yng Read.
Evans, Olive. Secrets of the Forest. (gr. 3-12). 1985. pap. 6.00 play script (*0-88734-502-6*) Players Pr.
Fifty Years of Little Golden Books, 1942-1992: A Commemorative Set of the First Twelve Little Golden Books. 504p. (ps-k). 1992. Set. write for info. shrink-wrapped slipcase (*0-307-15543-9*, 15543, Golden Pr) Western Pub.
Fisher, Barbara & Spiegel, Richard, eds. In Search of a Song: Jefferson Market Library, Vol. 3. (Illus.). 64p. (Orig.). (gr. 1-6). 1982. pap. 2.00 (*0-934830-27-4*) Ten Penny.
Five-Minute Bedtime Stories. (Illus.). (ps-1). 1985. 2.98 (*0-517-46988-X*) Random Hse Value.
Fleischman, Paul. Coming-&-Going Men: Four Tales. Gaul, Randy, illus. LC 84-48336. 160p. (gr. 6 up). 1985. PLB 12.89 (*0-06-021884-3*) HarpC Child Bks.
Fleischman, Sid. Jim Ugly. (gr. 4-7). 1993. pap. 3.99 (*0-440-40803-2*) Dell.
Fosburgh, Liza. Cruise Control. 224p. (gr. 7 up). 1988. 13.95 (*0-553-05491-0*, Starfire) Bantam.
Foster, Elizabeth V. Lyrico. 2nd ed. Buba, Joy, illus. 230p. (gr. 6-8). 1991. pap. 10.95 (*0-930407-21-0*) Parabola Bks.
Fox, Mem. With Love, at Christmas. Lippincott, Gary, illus. LC 88-6332. (gr. 2 up). 1988. 12.95 (*0-687-45863-3*) Abingdon.
Fox, Paula. Maurice's Room. reissued ed. Fetz, Ingrid, illus. LC 85-7200. 64p. (gr. 2-6). 1985. SBE 13.95 (*0-02-735490-3*, Macmillan Child Bk) Macmillan Child Grp.
Freeman, Lydia. Corduroy's Party. McCue, Lisa, illus. LC 84-40476. 14p. (ps). 1985. pap. 3.99 (*0-670-80520-3*) Viking Child Bks.
Friend, Janet. To Grow by Storybook Phonics Readers. Capezio, Betsy, illus. (gr. k-3). 1990. Set. pap. text ed. 44.95 (*0-910311-69-2*) Huntington Hse.
Fuentes, Vilma M. Manggob & His Golden Top. Inis, Ninabeth R., illus. 48p. (Orig.). (gr. k-3). 1985. pap. 4.00 (*971-10-0218-3*, Pub. by New Day Pub PI) Cellar.
Galdone, Paul. The Teeny-Tiny Woman. Galdone, Paul, illus. 1993. Incl. cassette. 7.70 (*0-395-52602-7*, Clarion Bks) HM.
Gallico, P. Flowers for Mrs. Harris. abr. ed. (Illus.). 118p. 1964. pap. text ed. 5.95 (*0-582-53024-5*) Longman.
Gars, Lissa, ed. The Lost Child & Other Stories. (Illus.). 80p. (gr. 4-9). 1993. pap. 9.95 (*1-882427-02-5*) Aspasia Pubns.
Gauz, Yaffa. From Head to Toe: A Book About You. (gr. 5-8). 1988. 11.95 (*0-87306-446-1*) Feldheim.
Geiss, Tony, et al. The Sesame Street Bedtime Storybook. Cooke, Tom, et al, illus. LC 77-93774. (ps-2). 1978. 10.00 (*0-394-83843-2*); lib. bdg. 7.99 (*0-394-93843-7*) Random Bks Yng Read.
Gibbons, Gail. Check It Out: The Book about Libraries. Gibbons, Gail, illus. LC 85-5414. 32p. (ps-3). 1985. 12.95 (*0-15-216400-6*, HB Juv Bks) HarBrace.
Gill, Shelley R. Kiana's Iditarod. Cartwright, Shannon, illus. 52p. (Orig.). (gr. 2-6). 1984. pap. 8.95 (*0-934007-00-4*) Paws Four Pub.
Gilson, Jamie. Hello, My Name Is Scrambled Eggs. Wallner, John, illus. LC 84-10075. 160p. (gr. 4-6). 1985. 12.95 (*0-688-04095-0*) Lothrop.
Ginsburg, Mirra. The Sun's Asleep Behind the Hill. Zelinsky, Paul O., illus. LC 81-6615. 32p. (ps-1). 1982. 15.00 (*0-688-00824-0*); PLB 14.93 (*0-688-00825-9*) Greenwillow.
Girst, Jack A. Renfro Would Rather Rest. Girst, Jack A., illus. 32p. (gr. k-2). 1989. pap. 1.99 (*0-87403-633-X*, 3972) Standard Pub.
Goble, Paul. Love Flute. Goble, Paul, illus. (gr. k-4). 1993. 14.95 (*0-685-64813-3*); audiocassette 11.00 (*1-882869-80-X*) Read Advent.
Goffin, Jeffrey. My Gun Is Pink. (Illus.). 32p. (Orig.). (gr. 6 up). 1987. pap. 3.50 (*0-88680-280-6*); royalty on application 35.00 (*0-685-73923-6*) I E Clark.
Good Night, Sammy. (ps-k). 1991. write for info. (*0-307-12238-7*, Golden Pr) Western Pub.
Gottlieb, Jane, photos by. Garden Tales: Classic Stories from Favorite Writers. LC 89-40643. (Illus.). 112p. 1990. 12.95 (*0-670-83173-5*, Viking Studio) Studio Bks.
Goudge, Elizabeth. I Saw Three Ships. (Orig.). 1990. pap. 2.95 (*0-440-40367-7*, Pub. by Yearling Classics) Dell.
Greenwald, Sheila. Mariah Delany's Author-of-the-Month-Club. (gr. 4-7). 1990. 14.95 (*0-316-32713-1*, Joy St Bks) Little.
Grifalconi, Ann. Osa's Pride, Vol. 1. Grifalconi, Ann, illus. (ps-3). 1990. 15.95 (*0-316-32865-0*) Little.
Grohmann, Susan. The Dust under Mrs. Merriweather's Bed. Grohmann, Susan, illus. LC 93-21804. (ps-3). 1993. 14.95 (*1-879085-82-8*) Whsprng Coyote Pr.
Grubbs, Tabitha & McQueen, Tiffany. Different Types of Stories & Poems. (Illus.). 52p. (gr. k-3). 1983. PLB 25. 00 (*1-56611-000-9*); pap. 15.00 (*1-56611-349-0*) Jonas.
Hagman, Harlan L. A Seasonal Present & Other Stories. LC 88-34712. (Illus.). xiv, 341p. (gr. 9 up). 1989. 19. 95 (*0-931600-08-1*) Green Oak Pr.
Haiduck, Robert. Ten Tiny Tales, Bk. 1. 87p. (gr. 1-8). 1990. write for info. (*0-9627661-0-0*) Tiny Tales.
Hall, Leo D. B'tween: Messages from Michael. Warnick, Kelly & Hall, Leo D., illus. 180p. (Orig.). (gr. 6-12). 1992. pap. 8.75 (*0-914107-03-8*) Lion House Pr.
Hands & Feet. (Illus.). (gr. 5 up). 1987. lib. bdg. 15.94 (*0-86625-279-7*); 11.95s.p. (*0-685-67665-X*) Rourke Corp.
Hardinge, Miriam. Long Ago Stories. Wheeler, Gerald, ed. 144p. (Orig.). (ps). 1987. pap. 6.95 (*0-8280-0351-3*) Review & Herald.
Hardt, Elaine. Stories from Beyond the Double Rainbow. (Orig.). (gr. 1-8). 1982. pap. 10.50 (*0-932960-03-0*) Thinking Caps.
Harriot, Ray. Stories for Around the Campfire. 2nd ed. (Illus.). 224p. (gr. 5-10). 1986. pap. 5.95 (*0-317-93072-9*) Campfire Pub.
Hartley, Mary M. Mariposa: A Tough Texan in a Time Capsule. 64p. (gr. 4-7). 1986. 10.95 (*0-89015-544-5*, Pub. by Panda Bks) Sunbelt Media.
Harvey, Brett. Cassie's Journey: Going West in the 1860s. Ray, Deborah K., illus. LC 87-23599. 40p. (gr. 1-4). 1988. reinforced bdg. 13.95 (*0-8234-0684-9*) Holiday.
Hathorn, Elizabeth. The Tram to Bondi Beach. Vivas, Julie, illus. 32p. (gr. 4-8). 1989. 12.95 (*0-916291-20-0*) Kane-Miller Bk.
Havill, Juanita. Jamaica's Find. O'Brien, Anne S., illus. (ps-3). 1986. 13.45 (*0-395-39376-0*) HM.
Heide, Florence P. Tales for the Perfect Child. (gr. 4-7). 1991. pap. 3.99 (*0-440-40463-0*) Dell.
Henkes, Kevin. Shhhh. LC 88-18771. (Illus.). 24p. (ps up). 1989. 11.95 (*0-688-07985-7*); PLB 11.88 (*0-688-07986-5*) Greenwillow.
Herigstad, Joni. I Was So Mad: Storybook for Young Children in Sign Language. Herigstad, Joni, illus. 50p. (Orig.). (ps-4). 1986. pap. 4.95 (*0-916708-16-0*) Modern Signs.
Hezlep, William. Pharaoh's Dagger. LC 92-53871. 70p. (Orig.). (gr. 3-12). 1992. pap. 5.00 play script (*0-88734-404-6*) Players Pr.
Highlights for Children Editors. Gift from the Storm: And Other Stories of Children Around the World. 96p. (Orig.). (gr. 3 up). 1994. pap. 2.95 (*1-56397-268-9*) Boyds Mills Pr.
—Jack's Best Boots: And Other Stories of Long Ago. 96p. 1994. pap. 2.95 (*1-56397-266-2*) Boyds Mills Pr.
—Rupert & the Royal Hiccups: And Other Silly Stories. 96p. (Orig.). 1994. pap. 2.95 (*1-56397-267-0*) Boyds Mills Pr.
Hillert, Margaret. I Like Things. (Illus.). (ps-k). 1982. PLB 6.95 (*0-8136-5102-6*, TK2166); pap. 3.50 (*0-8136-5602-8*, TK2167) Modern Curr.
—Little Runaway. (Illus.). (ps-k). 1966. PLB 6.95 (*0-8136-5052-6*, TK2334); pap. 3.50 (*0-8136-5552-8*, TK2335) Modern Curr.
Hitchcock, Alfred, ed. Alfred Hitchcock's Monster Museum. LC 81-13883. (Illus.). 224p. (gr. 5 up). 1982. pap. 4.99 (*0-394-84899-3*) Random Bks Yng Read.
Holland, Shirley. Grandma Holland's Three Tiny Bedtime Stories. Hansen, Heidi, illus. LC 91-70485. 48p. (ps-5). 1991. 12.95 (*0-89802-574-5*) Beautiful Am.
Hoobler, Thomas. The Revenge of Ho-Tai. 208p. (gr. 7 up). 1989. 15.95 (*0-8027-6870-9*) Walker & Co.
Hopkins, Lila. Talking Turkey. LC 89-31501. 128p. (gr. 7-9). 1990. 13.90 (*0-531-10797-3*) Watts.
Hughes, Ted. Tales of the Early World. (gr. 4-8). 1991. 13.95 (*0-374-37377-9*) FS&G.
Hurst, Ida Olivia. My Kaleidoscope of Poetry & Stories. Meyer, Monty Dale, illus. LC 91-92380. 96p. (Orig.). 1992. pap. 11.95 (*0-9632521-0-0*) Gemstone OR.
Illustrated Classics for Children. 1987. 5.98 (*0-671-08501-8*) S&S Trade.
Jackson, Kathryn. Golden Book of Three Hundred Sixty-Five Stories. Scarry, Richard, illus. 1955. write for info. (*0-307-15557-9*, Golden Bks) Western Pub.
Jackson, Tim. The Case of: The Great Graffiti. Jackson, Tim, illus. 19p. (Orig.). (gr. 5-8). 1987. pap. 1.95 (*0-942675-04-5*) Creative License.
Janger, Kathie, ed. Rainbow Collection, 1990: Stories & Poetry by Young People. Sarecky, Melody, illus. Bush, Barbara, frwd. by. (Illus.). 176p. 1990. pap. 6.00 (*0-929889-06-1*) Young Writers Contest Found.
Johnson, Charles & Chernow, Ron. In Search of a Voice. LC 91-36518. 36p. 1991. pap. 1.00 (*0-685-53462-6*) Lib Congress.
Johnson, Lois W. Secrets of the Best Choice. Peck, Virginia, illus. LC 88-60475. 192p. (Orig.). 1988. pap. 7.00 (*0-89109-232-3*) NavPress.
Johnson, Sue. The Little Green Monsters. Herigstad, Joni, illus. 36p. (ps-6). 1985. pap. 4.75 (*0-916708-15-2*) Modern Signs.
Jonas, Ann. Where Can It Be? Jonas, Ann, illus. LC 86-304. 32p. (ps-1). 1986. 14.95 (*0-688-05169-3*); PLB 14.88 (*0-688-05246-0*) Greenwillow.
Keckeis, M. B. The Black Rose. Steiner, Frank, et al, trs. Cassidy, Christoph, illus. (ENG, SPA, FRE & GER.). 256p. (gr. 3-9). 1991. 23.50 (*1-879870-54-1*) Pro Lingua Pr.
Kerr, Rita. The Immortal Thirty-Two. 64p. (gr. 4-7). 1986. 10.95 (*0-89015-538-0*, Pub. by Panda Bks) Sunbelt Media.
Kingsley, Charles. The Water-Babies. (Illus.). 256p. 1987. Repr. PLB 22.95x (*0-89966-579-9*) Buccaneer Bks.
Kipling, Rudyard. Tales from the Jungle Book. McKinley, Robin, adapted by. Smith, J. A., illus. LC 84-11724. 64p. (gr. k-3). 1985. lib. bdg. 8.99 (*0-394-96940-5*) Random Bks Yng Read.
Klass, Sheila S. Credit-Card Carole. 144p. 1989. pap. 2.95 (*0-553-27355-8*, Starfire) Bantam.
Kohaine, Chayele. Operation C. H. E. S. E. D. & other Stories. Scheinberg, Shepsil, illus. 139p. (gr. 2-5). 1989. 10.95 (*0-935063-81-1*); pap. text ed. 7.95 (*0-935063-82-X*) CIS Comm.
Konigsburg, E. L. The Second Mrs. Giaconda. LC 75-6946. (Illus.). 144p. (gr. 5-9). 1978. pap. 5.95 (*0-689-70450-X*, Aladdin) Macmillan Child Grp.
Korman, Gordon. No Coins, Please. 192p. (Orig.). (gr. 3-7). 1991. pap. 2.95 (*0-590-44208-2*, Apple Paperbacks) Scholastic Inc.
Korman, Justine. Big Bird's New Nest & Other Good-Night Stories. Cooke, Tom, illus. (ps-1). 1989. write for info. (*0-307-12060-0*, 12060) Western Pub.
Koulomzin, Sophie. Sbornik Detskij, Tysacha Let (988-1988) (RUS.). (gr. 2-4). 1985. write for info. RBR.
Krauss, Ruth. Somebody Else's Nut Tree & Other Tales from Children. Sendak, Maurice, illus. LC 89-28056. 43p. (ps-5). 1990. Repr. of 1958 ed. lib. bdg. 14.00 (*0-208-02264-3*, Linnet) Shoe String.
Krensky, Stephen. Lionel at Large. Natti, Susanna, illus. LC 85-15930. 56p. (ps-3). 1988. pap. 4.95 (*0-8037-0556-5*) Dial Bks Young.
—Lionel in the Fall. 1989. pap. 4.95 (*0-8037-0683-9*, Dial) Doubleday.

Krupinsky, Jacquelyn S. Henry, the Hesitant Heron. Cutri, Anne C., illus. (Illus.). 24p. (Orig.). (gr. k-3). 1987. pap. 6.95 (*0-912123-02-8*) Woodbury Pr.
HENRY, THE HESITANT HERON is afraid to fly. In fact, he is afraid to do almost everything until the forces of nature precipitate a crisis. A good friend, Freddy Swallow, comes to his aid. All ends happily with Henry snuggled down in the nest with his parents close by. Good for children who lack self-esteem & are also afraid to try their wings at new skills. Has a bibliography & a foreword from Audubon Canyon Ranch, Inc. (a heron sanctuary). Reviews - "Relates accurate information about Great Blue Heron habitat, but also gives young readers a look into the challenges of growing up." (Downeast Magazine). "A book that's going for classic status." (Courier-Gazette). Available from Woodbury Press, RR1, Box 700, Litchfield, ME 04350. When ordering, add $1.95 for shipping, $.25 for each additional book. Also available from the Maine Writers & Publishers, Brunswick, ME 04011. *Publisher Provided Annotation.*

Ladoux, Cathryn. Yani: Stories for Childhood. (Illus.). 150p. (Orig.). (gr. 4-7). 1993. pap. 19.95 (*0-943861-18-7*) Lone Tree.
Landes, William-Alan. Pyramus & Thisbe. rev. ed. LC 90-53083. (gr. 3 up). 1984. pap. 5.00 play script (*0-88734-103-9*) Players Pr.
Landes, William-Alan & Standish, Marilyn. The Wizard of Oz. rev. ed. LC 89-63872. (gr. 3-12). 1985. pap. 6.00 play script (*0-88734-105-5*); tchr's. ed. 30.00 (*0-88734-011-3*) Players Pr.
—The Wizard of Oz: Music & Lyrics. rev. ed. (gr. 3-12). 1985. pap. text ed. 15.00 (*0-88734-010-5*) Players Pr.
Lawhead, Steve. Howard Had a Shrinking Machine. Lawhead, Steve, illus. 32p. (gr. k-3). 1988. 7.99 (*0-7459-1316-4*) Lion USA.
Lehner, Devony. Tinker's Journey Home. Maloney, P. Dennis, ed. Adamson, Charlotte, illus. 34p. (ps-6). 12. 95 (*0-940305-00-3*) P D Maloney.
Levoy, Myron. Witch of Fourth Street & Other Stories. LC 74-183174. (Illus.). 128p. (gr. 3-7). 1974. pap. 3.95 (*0-06-440059-X*, Trophy) HarpC Child Bks.
Lewis, Shari. One-Minute Scary Stories. (ps-3). 1993. 4.99 (*0-440-40833-4*) Dell.
Lipson, Greta B. Tales with a Twist. 160p. (gr. 5-9). 1991. 12.95 (*0-86653-609-4*, GA1328) Good Apple.

Little Golden Book Story Land. 256p. (ps-2). 1992. write for info. (*0-307-16561-2*, 16561, Golden Pr) Western Pub.

Lobato, Arcadio. The Greatest Treasure. Lobato, Arcadio, illus. LC 89-3612. 28p. (ps up). 1991. pap. 14.95 (*0-88708-093-6*) Picture Bk Studio.

Lolling, Atsuko G. Aki & the Banner of Names: And Other Stories from Japan. (Orig.). (gr. 1-6). pap. 4.95 (*0-377-00218-6*) Friendship Pr.

LoPresti, Joan. Calendar Capers: A Child's School Year in Celebration. Danner, Robert W., illus. LC 90-36812. 32p. (gr. k-3). 1990. PLB 18.60 (*0-8368-0428-7*) Gareth Stevens Inc.

McBrier, Page. Oliver & the Lucky Duck. Sims, Blanche, illus. LC 85-8417. 96p. (gr. 3-6). 1986. PLB 9.89 (*0-8167-0541-0*); pap. text ed. 2.95 (*0-8167-0542-9*) Troll Assocs.

—Oliver's Lucky Day. Sims, Blanche, illus. LC 85-8437. 96p. (gr. 3-6). 1986. lib. bdg. 9.89 (*0-8167-0537-2*); pap. text ed. 2.95 (*0-8167-0538-0*) Troll Assocs.

MacDonald, Amy. Rachel Fister's Blister. Priceman, Marjorie, illus. 32p. (ps-3). 1990. 13.45 (*0-395-52152-1*) HM.

McDowell, Robert E. & Lavitt, Edward, eds. Third World Voices for Children. Isaac, Barbara K., illus. LC 71-169091. 156p. (gr. 5-9). 1981. 7.95 (*0-89388-020-5*, Odarkai) Okpaku Communications.

McKinnon, Elizabeth S. & Warren, Jean, eds. Short-Short Stories: Simple Stories for Young Children Plus Seasonal Activities. Ekberg, Marion, illus. LC 86-51509. 80p. (Orig.). (ps-1). 1987. pap. 7.95 (*0-911019-13-8*) Warren Pub Hse.

McOmber, Rachel B., ed. McOmber Phonics Storybooks: A Trip to China. rev. ed. (Illus.). write for info. (*0-944991-70-X*) Swift Lrn Res.

—McOmber Phonics Storybooks: Choose Which One - 1. rev. ed. (Illus.). write for info. (*0-944991-67-X*) Swift Lrn Res.

—McOmber Phonics Storybooks: Humps & Lumps. rev. ed. (Illus.). write for info. (*0-944991-62-9*) Swift Lrn Res.

—McOmber Phonics Storybooks: Kim. rev. ed. (Illus.). write for info. (*0-944991-07-6*) Swift Lrn Res.

—McOmber Phonics Storybooks: Razz. rev. ed. (Illus.). write for info. (*0-944991-06-8*) Swift Lrn Res.

—McOmber Phonics Storybooks: Ten in the Hut. rev. ed. (Illus.). write for info. (*0-944991-27-0*) Swift Lrn Res.

—McOmber Phonics Storybooks: The Bag. rev. ed. (Illus.). write for info. (*0-944991-03-3*) Swift Lrn Res.

—McOmber Phonics Storybooks: The Big Deal. rev. ed. (Illus.). write for info. (*0-944991-47-5*) Swift Lrn Res.

—McOmber Phonics Storybooks: The Big Hole. rev. ed. (Illus.). write for info. (*0-944991-38-6*) Swift Lrn Res.

—McOmber Phonics Storybooks: The Bon-Bon Box. rev. ed. (Illus.). write for info. (*0-944991-14-9*) Swift Lrn Res.

—McOmber Phonics Storybooks: The Box Mix. rev. ed. (Illus.). write for info. (*0-944991-15-7*) Swift Lrn Res.

—McOmber Phonics Storybooks: The Fumes. rev. ed. (Illus.). write for info. (*0-944991-39-4*) Swift Lrn Res.

—McOmber Phonics Storybooks: The Kit. rev. ed. (Illus.). write for info. (*0-944991-08-4*) Swift Lrn Res.

—McOmber Phonics Storybooks: The Land of Morning. rev. ed. (Illus.). write for info. (*0-944991-82-3*) Swift Lrn Res.

—McOmber Phonics Storybooks: The Map. rev. ed. (Illus.). write for info. (*0-944991-05-X*) Swift Lrn Res.

—McOmber Phonics Storybooks: The Pit Kit. rev. ed. (Illus.). write for info. (*0-944991-09-2*) Swift Lrn Res.

—McOmber Phonics Storybooks: The Prize. rev. ed. (Illus.). write for info. (*0-944991-49-1*) Swift Lrn Res.

—McOmber Phonics Storybooks: The Quiz Is (1) rev. ed. (Illus.). write for info. (*0-944991-34-3*) Swift Lrn Res.

—McOmber Phonics Storybooks: The Quiz Is (2) rev. ed. (Illus.). write for info. (*0-944991-35-1*) Swift Lrn Res.

—McOmber Phonics Storybooks: The Rope. rev. ed. (Illus.). write for info. (*0-944991-45-9*) Swift Lrn Res.

—McOmber Phonics Storybooks: The Tin Lid. rev. ed. (Illus.). write for info. (*0-944991-10-6*) Swift Lrn Res.

—McOmber Phonics Storybooks: Tid Bits. rev. ed. (Illus.). write for info. (*0-944991-36-X*) Swift Lrn Res.

McPhail, David. Emma's Pet. McPhail, David, illus. LC 85-4414. 24p. (ps-k). 1985. 9.95 (*0-525-44210-3*, DCB) Dutton Child Bks.

McQueen, Priscilla L. We Can Read: Story Pack-54 Little Stories. 1973. pap. 18.66 (*0-685-47089-X*) McQueen.

Maglione, Robin S. Alyndoria: Tales of Inner Magic. Wheeling, Darren, illus. 71p. (Orig.). (gr. k-12). 1986. pap. 12.00 (*0-910609-11-X*) Gifted Educ Pr.

Mains, Karen & Mains, David. Tales of the Resistance. Stockman, Jack, illus. 112p. (gr. 4-7). 1986. 16.99 (*0-89191-938-4*) Cook.

Marshall, James. The Cut-ups Cut Loose. (Illus.). 32p. (ps-3). 1987. pap. 12.95 (*0-670-80740-0*) Viking Child Bks.

Matthews, Morgan. Icky, Sticky Gloop. Victor, Ymonne, illus. LC 85-14013. 48p. (Orig.). (gr. 1-3). 1986. lib. bdg. 10.59 (*0-8167-0616-6*); pap. text ed. 3.50 (*0-8167-0617-4*) Troll Assocs.

Mills, Claudia. Dynamite Dinah. LC 89-13300. 128p. (gr. 3-7). 1990. SBE 13.95 (*0-02-767101-1*, Macmillan Child Bk) Macmillan Child Grp.

Mills, Jane L. & Johnson, Larry D. Arnie's Surprise. Hebert, Kim T., illus. LC 86-60363. 14p. (Orig.). (ps). 1986. pap. 4.00 (*0-938155-05-9*); pap. 12.00 set of 3 bks. (*0-685-13523-3*) Read A Bol.

Moncure, Jane B. Butterfly Express. Hohag, Linda, illus. LC 88-22944. (ENG & SPA.). 32p. (ps-2). 1989. PLB 14.95 (*0-89565-392-3*) Childs World.

—My "u" Sound Box. Peltier, Pam, illus. LC 84-17012. 32p. (ps-2). 1984. PLB 14.95 (*0-89565-300-1*) Childs World.

Moore, Lilian. The Magic Spectacles & Other Easy-to-Read Stories. Lobel, Arnold, illus. 1992. pap. 2.99 (*0-553-48026-X*) Bantam.

Mother. Tales of All Times. (Illus.). 138p. (gr. 3-8). 1983. pap. 4.95 (*0-89071-321-9*, Pub. by Sri Aurobindo Ashram IA) Aurobindo Assn.

Mount, Guy. How Steelhead Lost His Stripes: A Children's Story & Coloring Book. (Illus.). (gr. k-6). 1984. pap. 3.00 (*0-9604462-1-4*) Sweetlight.

Munro, Alice. Dance of the Happy Shades & Other Stories. 240p. 1990. pap. 7.95 (*0-14-012408-X*) Viking Child Bks.

Munsch, Robert. Thomas' Snowsuit. Martchenko, Michael, illus. 24p. (gr. k-3). 1985. PLB 14.95 (*0-920303-32-3*, Pub. by Annick CN); pap. 4.95 (*0-920303-33-1*, Pub. by Annick CN) Firefly Bks Ltd.

My Biggest Bedtime Book Ever. 1988. 8.98 (*0-671-07571-3*) S&S Trade.

Myers, Bernice. Sidney Rella & the Glass Sneaker. Myers, Bernice, illus. LC 85-3044. 32p. (gr. k-3). 1985. RSBE 14.95 (*0-02-767790-7*, Macmillan Child Bk) Macmillan Child Grp.

Newman, Robert. The Case of the Baker Street Irregular. LC 77-15463. (gr. 3-7). 1984. pap. 4.95 (*0-689-70766-5*, Aladdin) Macmillan Child Grp.

Norris, Carolyn. Jeans Christmas Stocking. Norris, Carolyn, illus. 24p. (Orig.). (ps-4). 1982. pap. 3.95 (*0-916708-10-1*) Modern Signs.

Noyes, Beppie. Wigglesworth. Noyes, Beppie, illus. LC 85-62022. 74p. (gr. k-4). 1985. pap. 5.95 (*0-932433-08-1*) Windswept Hse.

O. Henry. The Last Leaf. rev. ed. (gr. 9-12). 1989. Repr. of 1906 ed. multi-media kit 35.00 (*0-685-31126-0*) Balance Pub.

One World Readalongs. (gr. k-4). 1993. Set of 8 bks. & cassettes. 199.00 (*1-882869-83-4*) Read Advent.

Orgel, Doris. Whiskers, Once & Always. Newsom, Carol, illus. 96p. (gr. 2-5). 1989. pap. 3.95 (*0-14-032038-5*, Puffin) Puffin Bks.

Oxenbury, Helen. The Helen Oxenbury Nursery Storybook. LC 84-28887. (Illus.). 80p. (ps-1). 1985. 16.00 (*0-394-87519-2*) Knopf Bks Yng Read.

Packard, Mary. Bubble Trouble. Kuckarik, Elena, illus. LC 94-16975. 1995. 3.95 (*0-590-48513-X*) Scholastic Inc.

Pellowski, Michael J. Benny's Bad Day. Cushman, Doug, illus. LC 85-14016. 48p. (Orig.). (gr. 1-3). 1986. PLB 10.59 (*0-8167-0620-4*); pap. text ed. 3.50 (*0-8167-0621-2*) Troll Assocs.

Perrault, Charles & Kipling, Rudyard. Cinderella & How the Elephant Got Its Trunk. (Illus.). 48p. (gr. 1-4). 1985. 5.95 (*0-88110-252-0*) EDC.

Pershall, Mary K. You Take the High Road. 1990. 14.95 (*0-8037-0700-2*) Dial Bks Young.

Peterson, Carolyn S. Story Programs Activities for Older Children. Sterchele, Christina, illus. (Orig.). (gr. 3-6). 1987. 20.00 (*0-913545-11-2*) Moonlight FL.

Pinzon, Scott. Tales of Evermore. 90p. (Orig.). (gr. 7-12). 1991. pap. 4.95 (*0-8474-6621-3*) Back to Bible.

Polacco, Patricia. The Keeping Quilt. Polacco, Patricia, illus. (gr. k-4). 1993. 14.95 (*0-685-64811-7*); audiocassette 11.00 (*1-882869-82-6*) Read Advent.

Polsky, Milton, et al. The King of Escapes. (Orig.). (gr. 3-12). 1985. pap. 6.00 play script (*0-88734-510-7*) Players Pr.

Poppel, Hans & Bodden, Ilona. When the Moon Shines Brightly on the House. 24p. (ps). 1985. 5.95 (*0-8120-5669-8*) Barron.

Poskanzer, Susan C. The Great Soap-Bubble Ride. Fiammenghi, Gioia, illus. LC 85-14022. 48p. (Orig.). (gr. 1-3). 1986. PLB 10.59 (*0-8167-0622-0*); pap. text ed. 3.50 (*0-8167-0623-9*) Troll Assocs.

Potter, Beatrix. Giant Treasury of Beatrix Potter. (Illus.). 52p. (gr. k-6). 1985. 6.99 (*0-517-43121-1*) Random Hse Value.

—The One Hundredth Anniversary 1-12 Presentation Box: The World of Beatrix Potter, 12 bks. (Illus.). 1993. Set. 70.00 (*0-7232-4113-9*) Warne.

—The One Hundredth Anniversary 1-23 Presentation Box: The World of Beatrix Potter, 23 bks. (Illus.). 1993. Set. 135.00 (*0-7232-4112-0*) Warne.

—The One Hundredth Anniversary 13-23 Presentation Box: The World of Beatrix Potter, 11 bks. (Illus.). 1993. Set. 65.00 (*0-7232-4114-7*) Warne.

—The Tale of Peter Rabbit & Benjamin Bunny. (Illus.). 32p. (ps-3). 1993. 4.99 (*0-7232-4124-4*) Warne.

—The Tale of Peter Rabbit & Other Favorite Stories, 7 vols. 447p. (gr. 2 up). Boxed Set. pap. 12.25 (*0-486-23903-9*) Dover.

Pronzini, Bill, ed. More Wild Westerns. 192p. 1989. 19.95 (*0-8027-4097-9*) Walker & Co.

Purdy, Carol. Iva Dunnit & the Big Wind. Kellogg, Steven, illus. LC 84-17441. 32p. (ps-3). 1985. 12.95 (*0-8037-0183-7*) Dial Bks Young.

Quackenbush, Robert. Detective Mole & the Haunted Castle Mystery. LC 84-20141. (Illus.). 32p. (gr. k-3). 1985. 14.93 (*0-688-04640-1*); lib. bdg. 14.93 (*0-688-04641-X*) Lothrop.

Rabe, Berniece. Tall Enough to Own the World. LC 88-39139. 160p. (gr. 5-7). 1989. PLB 13.90 (*0-531-10681-0*) Watts.

Ratnett, Mike. Togg & Leftover. (ps-3). 1993. pap. 7.00 NOP (*0-00-664005-2*) Collins SF.

Read & Discover Library. 1966. pap. 25.00 (*0-7175-0284-8*) Dufour.

Richardson, Frederick, illus. Great Children's Stories: Classic Volland Edition. Hunt, Irene, intro. by. LC 72-83891. (Illus.). 160p. (ps-3). 1938. 12.95 (*1-56288-040-3*) Checkerboard.

Rimas y Risas (Red) Series: Big Book-Tape Set. (ENG & SPA., Illus., Orig.) (gr. k-3). 1991. incls. 4 big bks. (Veo, Veo 180.00 set, Una Semilla Nada Mas, Pinta, Pinta, Gregorita, & Pan, Pan, Gran Pan), tchr's. activity notebk. & 2 cass. tapes (*1-56334-007-0*); classroom set incl. 20 copies of Cuentitos Mios consumable student bk. 305.00 (*1-56334-008-9*); cass. tape set incl. 2 cass. tapes 21.00 (*1-56334-013-5*) Hampton-Brown.

Riskind, Mary. Apple is My Sign. 160p. (gr. 5-9). 1993. pap. 3.80 (*0-395-65747-4*) HM.

Robbins, Sandra. See-More's Stories: A Series of Six Read-Aloud Books & Read-Along - Move-Along Tapes. Oseki, Iku, illus. (ps-4). 1993. Series. pap. 54.95 (*1-882601-22-X*) See-Mores Wrkshop.

See-More books & tapes are based on the musical puppet plays of New York City's award-winning Shadow Box Theatre. These illustrated multicultural tales & holiday stories & companion tapes are designed to stimulate children's creativity. Side I of the tape is a Read-Along format, & Side II outlines the story & contains songs from the show & activities for dancing, singing & acting for pre-K-4th grades. AVAILABLE INDIVIDUALLY OR AS A COMPLETE SERIES consisting of: HOW THE TURTLE GOT ITS SHELL, An African Tale, ISBN 1-882601-04-1; BIG ANNIE, An American Tall Tale, ISBN 1-882601-03-3; TOBIAS TURKEY, An Original Thanksgiving Tale, ISBN 1-882601-06-8; RING AROUND A RAINBOW, A Health Adventure, ISBN 1-882601-05-X; THE GROWING ROCK, A Native American Tale, ISBN 1-882601-15-7; LUMPY BUMPY PUMPKIN, A Halloween Tale, ISBN 1-882601-18-1. Ordering instructions: Contact See-More's Workshop, Inc., 325 West End Ave. #12B, New York, NY 10023-8136; 212-724-0677.
Publisher Provided Annotation.

Rockwell, Anne. The Three Bears & Fifteen Other Stories. LC 74-5381. (Illus.). 128p. (gr. k-5). 1975. (Crowell Jr Bks); PLB 13.89 (*0-690-00598-9*) HarpC Child Bks.

Roland, Donna. Grandfather's Stories from Mexico. (gr. k-3). 1986. pap. 4.95 (*0-941996-09-3*); tchr's. ed. 5.50 (*0-941996-16-6*) Open My World.

—More of Grandfather's Stories from the Philippines. (gr. 1-3). 1985. pap. 4.95x (*0-941996-08-5*); tchr's. ed. 5.50 (*0-941996-17-4*) Open My World.

—More of Grandfather's Stories from Vietnam. (gr. 1-3). 1985. pap. 4.95x (*0-941996-12-3*); tchr's. ed. 5.50 (*0-941996-18-2*) Open My World.

Rosen, Michael. South & North, East & West: The Oxfam Book of Children's Stories. LC 91-58749. (Illus.). 96p. (ps-3). 1994. pap. 12.99 (*1-56402-396-6*) Candlewick Pr.

Ross, Anna. Elmo's Little Playhouse. Cooke, Tom, illus. LC 91-68111. 22p. (ps). 1993. 3.25 (*0-679-83270-X*) Random Bks Yng Read.

Rudolph, Stormy. Many Horses (Sequel to Quest for Courage) (Illus.). (gr. 5-12). 1987. pap. 8.95 (*0-89992-112-4*) Coun India Ed.

Rust, Graham. Secret Garden Notebook. (gr. 4-7). 1991. 12.95 (*0-87923-890-9*) Godine.

Rylant, Cynthia. Every Living Thing. Schindler, Stephen D., illus. LC 85-7701. 96p. (gr. 5-7). 1985. SBE 13.95 (*0-02-777200-4*, Bradbury Pr) Macmillan Child Grp.

—Henry & Mudge in the Sparkle Days: The Fifth Book of Their Adventures. Stevenson, Sucie, illus. LC 86-23432. 40p. (gr. 1-3). 1988. RSBE 12.95 (*0-02-778005-8*, Bradbury Pr) Macmillan Child Grp.

Rymer, Alta M. Hobart & Humbert Gruzzy. Rymer, Alta M., illus. LC 85-61860. 28p. (Orig.). (gr. 4-6). 1988. pap. 12.50 (*0-9600792-6-2*) Rymer Bks.

Santoro, Chris, illus. Open the Box, Find a Prize. LC 91-62573. 22p. (ps-k). 1993. 3.50 (*0-679-80902-3*) Random Bks Yng Read.

Santos, Elsie S. The Frog in the Bog. Santos, Duarte, illus. 44p. (Orig.). (ps-2). 1986. pap. 4.95 (*0-914151-04-5*) E S Santos.

Scarry, Richard. The Funniest Storybook Ever. (Illus.). (ps-2). 1972. 10.00 (*0-394-82432-6*) Random Bks Yng Read.

—Richard Scarry's Bedtime Stories. LC 86-484. (Illus.). 32p. (ps-1). 1990. pap. 5.95 incl. cassette (*0-679-80803-5*) Random Bks Yng Read.

Schwartz, Alvin. All of Our Noses Are Here & Other Noodle Tales. Weinhaus, Karen A., illus. LC 84-48330. 64p. (gr. k-3). 1985. PLB 13.89 (*0-06-025288-X*) HarpC Child Bks.

Schwartz, Betty, ed. The Old-Fashioned Storybook. Howell, Troy, illus. 144p. (gr. k-6). 1985. 12.95 (*0-685-10340-4*) S&S Trade.

Scoppettone, Sandra. Trying Hard to Hear You. LC 91-28058. 264p. (gr. 7-12). 1991. pap. 7.95 (*1-55583-196-6*) Alyson Pubns.

Sesame Street Story Land. LC 86-80134. 192p. (ps-k). 1986. write for info. (*0-307-16530-2*, Pub. by Golden Bks) Western Pub.

Sharmat, Marjorie W. Mitchell Is Moving. Aruego, Jose & Dewey, Ariane, illus. LC 85-47782. 48p. (gr. 1-4). 1985. pap. 3.95 (*0-02-045260-8*, Aladdin) Macmillan Child Grp.

Shearer, Marilyn J. Cinderella & the Glass Slipper: A Retelling. Edwards, Ron, illus. LC 90-60394. 16p. (ps-6). 1990. 19.95 (*0-685-33063-X*); pap. 10.95 (*1-878389-02-5*) L Ashley & Joshua.

Sieruta, Peter D. Heartbeats: And Other Stories. LC 88-21351. 224p. (gr. 7 up). 1991. pap. 3.50 (*0-06-447064-4*, Trophy) HarpC Child Bks.

Sieveking, Anthea. What's Inside? LC 89-11897. 1990. 9.95 (*0-8037-0719-3*) Dial Bks Young.

Signer, Billie T. Cry of the Eagle. Bliss, Bob, illus. 190p. (Orig.). (gr. 5-8). 1990. pap. 4.95 (*0-8198-1455-5*) St Paul Bks.

—Shetland Summer. Bliss, Bob, illus. LC 88-18480. 125p. (Orig.). (gr. 5-8). 1990. pap. 3.95 (*0-8198-6884-1*) St Paul Bks.

Singer, Marilyn. Big Wheel. LC 93-31912. 160p. (gr. 5-9). 1993. 14.95 (*1-56282-583-6*); PLB 14.89 (*1-56282-584-4*) Hyprn Child.

Skinner, Ada M. Little Child's Book of Stories. 1988. 12.99 (*0-517-65959-X*) Random Hse Value.

Skinner, Ada M. & Skinner, Eleanor. Very Little Child's Book of Stories. 1990. 12.99 (*0-517-69332-1*) Random Hse Value.

Slater, Teddy. Is That So? Series, 4 vols. Forest, Sandra & Rankin, Laura, illus. (ps-1). 1991. Set, 24p. ea. 19.80 (*0-671-31251-0*); Set, 24p. ea. lib. bdg. 27.80 (*0-671-31249-9*) Silver Pr.

—What Rhymes? Series. Alley, Robert & Hearn, Diane D., illus. (ps-1). 1991. Set, 24p. ea. 19.80 (*0-671-31245-6*); Set, 24p. ea. lib. bdg. 27.80 (*0-671-31244-8*) Silver Pr.

Small, David. Imogene's Antlers. Small, David, illus. LC 84-12085. 32p. (ps-2). 1988. PLB 12.95 (*0-517-55564-6*); pap. 3.95 (*0-517-56242-1*) Crown Bks Yng Read.

Smith, Elizabeth S. Five First Ladies. (Illus.). 122p. (gr. 10 up). 1986. 12.95 (*0-8027-6640-4*); lib. bdg. 14.85 (*0-8027-6641-2*) Walker & Co.

Smith, Louisa & Smith, Glen, eds. The Not Like Any Other Children's Book, Book. Smith, Glen, illus. 40p. (Orig.). (gr. 2 up). 1982. pap. 8.95 (*0-9609230-0-4*) Smith & Smith Pub.

Smith, M. Sherry & Cendejas, Deena L. Potpourri: Bouquet of Language Activities. (gr. 2-5). 1991. wkbk. 16.95 (*0-937857-25-4*, 1587) Speech Bin.

Smith, Martha. Arabella the Itchy Witch. Graves, Helen, ed. Smith, Martha, illus. LC 85-40893. 86p. (gr. 3 up). 1986. 6.95 (*1-55523-007-5*) Winston-Derek.

Spiegel, Richard & Fisher, Barbara, eds. Streams VI. (Illus.). 152p. (Orig.). (gr. 7-12). 1992. pap. 5.00 (*0-934830-50-9*) Ten Penny.

Squier, Karl. Leapin Lizzie. Love, Judith D., illus. LC 84-27784. 32p. (gr. k-5). 1985. pap. 12.95 incl. cassette (*0-931905-00-1*); pap. 7.95 (*0-931905-01-X*); cassette 7.95 (*0-931905-02-8*) Lady Lake Learn.

Stevenson, Robert Louis. Complete Stories. (gr. 5 up). 1994. 50.00 (*0-8050-3204-5*) H Holt & Co.

—Treasure Island. (gr. 5-6). 20.95 (*0-89190-236-8*, Pub. by Am Repr) Amereon Ltd.

Stimson, Joan. Bedtime: Stories for under Fives. Round, Graham, illus. 44p. (ps-k). 1992. 3.50 (*0-7214-1487-7*) Ladybird Bks.

—Storytime for One Year Olds. Strop, John & Strop, Caroline, illus. 28p. (ps). 1991. 3.50 (*0-7214-1419-2*, 887-7) Ladybird Bks.

Stine, Megan & Stine, H. William. Thriller Diller. 1989. lib. bdg. 6.99 (*0-394-92936-5*) Random Bks Yng Read.

Stolz, Mary. Night of Ghosts & Hermits: Nocturnal Life on the Seashore. Gallagher, Susan, illus. LC 84-15665. 48p. (gr. 3-7). 1985. 12.95 (*0-15-257333-X*, HB Juv Bks) HarBrace.

Story Time Staff. Stories That Educate, Inform, Entertain & Rhyme: Kids Workshop Workbook I. Story Time Staff, illus. 52p. 1992. GBC bdg. 29.95 (*1-56820-040-4*) Story Time.

—Stories That Educate, Inform, Entertain & Rhyme: Kids Workshop Workbook II. Story Time Staff, illus. 52p. 1992. GBC bdg. 29.95 (*1-56820-041-2*) Story Time.

Story Time Stories That Rhyme Staff. Fables, Tales, & Stories That Rhyme. Story Time Stories That Rhyme Staff, illus. 50p. (Orig.). (gr. 4-7). 1992. GBC bdg. 19.95 (*1-56820-016-1*) Story Time.

Storytime for Five Year Olds. (Illus.). (gr. k). 3.50 (*0-7214-1099-5*) Ladybird Bks.

Storytime for Four Year Olds. (Illus.). (ps). 3.50 (*0-7214-1192-4*) Ladybird Bks.

Storytime for Seven Year Olds. (Illus.). (gr. 2). 1990. 3.50 (*0-7214-1347-1*) Ladybird Bks.

Stover, Marjorie. When the Dolls Woke. Levine, Abby, ed. Loccisano, Karen, illus. LC 85-3154. 128p. (gr. 3-6). 1985. PLB 10.95 (*0-8075-8882-2*) A Whitman.

Stovicek, Vratislav. Book of Goodnight Stories. 1983. 5.98 (*0-671-05963-7*) S&S Trade.

Strichartz, Naomi. The Wise Woman. Moore, Ella, illus. 43p. (Orig.). (gr. 2-6). 1986. pap. 3.50 (*0-9618182-0-4*) Cranehill Pr.

Sunanda. Stories & Plays for Children. 91p. (gr. 3-8). 1984. pap. 3.00 (*0-89071-329-4*, Pub. by Sri Aurobindo Ashram IA) Aurobindo Assn.

Swajeski, Donna M. The Revolution Machine. rev. ed. (gr. 3-12). 1985. pap. 6.00 play script (*0-88734-511-5*); music & lyrics 15.00 (*0-88734-031-8*) Players Pr.

Talbott, Hudson. The Lady at Liberty. 32p. (Orig.). 1991. pap. 9.95 (*0-380-76427-X*) Avon.

Taylor, Alice K. My Very Own Stories. Keitz, Roderick, illus. 16p. (gr. 2-8). 1993. PLB 11.95 (*0-9638873-0-0*) J Taylor Ltd.

Teitelbaum, Michael. Slightly Scary Campfire Stories. 1994. 5.98 (*0-8317-1171-X*) Smithmark.

Thomas, Marlo. Free to Be...You & Me. Hart, Carole, ed. 1987. pap. 9.95 (*0-317-62189-0*) McGraw.

Thompson, R. Foo. (Illus.). 24p. (ps-8). 1988. 12.95 (*1-55037-005-7*, Pub. by Annick CN); pap. 4.95 (*1-55037-004-9*, Pub. by Annick CN) Firefly Bks Ltd.

Thornton, Don, ed. & intro. by. Whiffle. (Illus.). 52p. (gr. 4-8). 1986. pap. write for info. (*0-933727-02-X*) Cajun Pubs.

Three Bedtime Stories. (Illus.). (ps-1). 1985. 2.98 (*0-517-46989-8*) Random Hse Value.

Three Hundred Sixty-Five Stories for Bedtime. (ps-1). 1985. 5.98 (*0-517-46715-1*) Random Hse Value.

A Treasury of Disney Little Golden Books: 22 Best-Loved Disney Stories. (ps-1). 1991. write for info. (*0-307-15509-9*, Golden Pr) Western Pub.

Trelease, Jim, ed. Hey! Listen to This: Stories to Read-Aloud. 240p. (Orig.). (gr. k-4). 1992. 22.00 (*0-670-83691-5*, Viking); pap. 11.00 (*0-14-014653-9*) Viking Child Bks.

Tunis, John R. Young Razzle. LC 49-9796. 192p. (gr. 5 up). 1991. pap. 4.95 (*0-688-10153-4*, Pub. by Beech Tree Bks) Morrow.

—Young Razzle. LC 49-9796. 192p. (gr. 5 up). 1991. Repr. of 1949 ed. 11.95 (*0-688-10152-6*) Morrow Jr Bks.

Vail, Virginia. Good Sports. Bode, Daniel, illus. LC 89-31345. 128p. (gr. 4-6). 1990. lib. bdg. 9.89 (*0-8167-1629-3*); pap. text ed. 2.95 (*0-8167-1630-7*) Troll Assocs.

—Horse Play. Bode, Daniel, illus. LC 89-31347. 128p. (gr. 4-6). 1990. lib. bdg. 9.89 (*0-8167-1659-5*); pap. text ed. 2.95 (*0-8167-1660-9*) Troll Assocs.

Valentine, Johnny. The Duke Who Outlawed Jelly Beans & Other Stories. Schmidt, Lynette, illus. 32p. (gr. k-5). 1991. 12.95 (*1-55583-199-0*) Alyson Pubns.

Van Allen, Diane. Always Alvin. Reilly, Veronica, illus. (Orig.). (ps). 1984. pap. 3.95 (*0-939332-11-6*) J Pohl Assocs.

Van Woerkom, Dorothy O. Old Devil Is Waiting: Three Folktales. Brett, Jan, illus. LC 85-919. 64p. (ps-3). 1985. (HB Juv Bks) HarBrace.

Vesper, Joan. Joey Becomes a Boomer. De Faye, Monique, illus. LC 85-70354. 63p. (Orig.). (ps-5). 1985. pap. 5.95 (*0-9615007-0-0*) Green Bough Pr.

Walt Disney's Favorites: Twelve Favorite Little Golden Books - Classics Ser. 288p. (ps-k). 1992. Set. write for info. shrink-wrapped slipcase (*0-307-15491-2*, 15491, Golden Pr) Western Pub.

Walter, Mary W., illus. Story Books for We Can Read. Incl. Eel, Ail, Ole. 5.40 (*0-917186-03-6*); Happenings. 5.40 (*0-917186-04-4*); We Learn at Play. 5.40 (*0-917186-05-2*); Things for All Seasons. 5.40 (*0-917186-06-0*); Tales & Tails. 5.40 (*0-917186-07-9*); Just Like Me. 5.40 (*0-917186-08-7*); All Around Me. 5.40 (*0-917186-09-5*); Bridging the Summer. 5.40 (*0-917186-10-9*). McQueen.

We Read More Stories. pap. 10.62 set (*0-917186-11-7*); tchrs guide 4.72 (*0-917186-12-5*) McQueen.

Weber, Chris, pref. by. Treasures Three: Stories & Art by Students in Japan & Oregon. Lammers, Wayne & Morrison, Clinton D., trs. (Illus.). 258p. (Orig.). (gr. k-12). 1994. pap. 15.95 (*0-9616058-6-3*) OR Students Writing.

Weck, Thomas. Back-Back & the Lima Bear. Graves, Helen, ed. Taylor, Neil, illus. LC 85-51963. 64p. (gr. 1-6). 1986. 6.95 (*0-938232-97-5*) Winston-Derek.

Weinberger, Jane. Kiltie, the Laird of Kiltarnen. 2nd ed. Cap, photos by. (Illus.). 44p. (ps-5). 1987. 5.95 (*0-932433-09-X*) Windswept Hse.

—Lemon Drop. Berber, Richard, illus. LC 85-62023. 64p. (gr. 1-6). 1985. Repr. of 1953 ed. PLB 5.95 (*0-932433-10-3*) Windswept Hse.

Weiss, Ellen. Oh Beans! Starring Bean Sprout. Hall, Susan, illus. LC 88-19980. 32p. (gr. k-3). 1989. lib. bdg. 8.79 (*0-8167-1406-1*); pap. text ed. 1.95 (*0-8167-1407-X*) Troll Assocs.

—Oh Beans! Starring Boston Bean. Hall, Susan, illus. LC 88-19981. 32p. (gr. k-3). 1989. lib. bdg. 8.79 (*0-8167-1414-2*); pap. text ed. 1.95 (*0-8167-1415-0*) Troll Assocs.

—Oh Beans! Starring Green Bean. Hall, Susan, illus. LC 88-19970. 32p. (gr. k-3). 1989. lib. bdg. 8.79 (*0-8167-1398-7*); pap. text ed. 1.95 (*0-8167-1399-5*) Troll Assocs.

—Oh Beans! Starring Lima Bean. Hall, Susan, illus. LC 88-19969. 32p. (gr. k-3). 1989. lib. bdg. 8.79 (*0-8167-1394-4*); pap. text ed. 1.95 (*0-8167-1395-2*) Troll Assocs.

—Oh Beans! Starring Mean Bean. Hall, Susan, illus. LC 88-19982. 32p. (gr. k-3). 1989. lib. bdg. 8.79 (*0-8167-1400-2*); pap. text ed. 1.95 (*0-8167-1401-0*) Troll Assocs.

—Oh Beans! Starring Superbean. Hall, Susan, illus. LC 88-19979. 32p. (gr. k-3). 1989. lib. bdg. 8.79 (*0-8167-1416-9*); pap. text ed. 1.95 (*0-8167-1417-7*) Troll Assocs.

Wells, Christie. A Class Act. LC 88-16940. 128p. (gr. 5-8). 1989. lib. bdg. 9.89 (*0-8167-1500-9*); pap. text ed. 2.95 (*0-8167-1501-7*) Troll Assocs.

—Love Letters. LC 88-16938. 128p. (gr. 5-8). 1989. lib. bdg. 9.89 (*0-8167-1504-1*); pap. text ed. 2.95 (*0-8167-1505-X*) Troll Assocs.

—No More Promises. LC 88-16939. 128p. (gr. 5-8). 1989. lib. bdg. 9.89 (*0-8167-1502-5*); pap. text ed. 2.95 (*0-8167-1503-3*) Troll Assocs.

—Rival Roommates. LC 88-16954. 128p. (gr. 5-8). 1989. lib. bdg. 9.89 (*0-8167-1496-7*); pap. text ed. 2.95 (*0-8167-1497-5*) Troll Assocs.

—Secret Crush. LC 88-16941. 128p. (gr. 5-8). 1989. lib. bdg. 9.89 (*0-8167-1498-3*); pap. text ed. 2.95 (*0-8167-1499-1*) Troll Assocs.

Wells, Rosemary. Hazel's Amazing Mother. Wells, Rosemary, illus. LC 85-1447. 32p. (ps-2). 1985. 13.95 (*0-8037-0209-4*); PLB 13.89 (*0-8037-0210-8*) Dial Bks Young.

Weyland, Jack. Brenda at the Prom. LC 88-14880. viii, 171p. (gr. 7-12). 1988. 9.95 (*0-87579-150-6*) Deseret Bk.

What Belongs? Series, 4 bks. (ps-1). 1992. Set. 23.80x (*0-382-31243-0*); Set. PLB 39.92x (*0-382-31242-2*) Silver.

Wiggin, Kate D. The Birds' Christmas Carol. (Illus.). 66p. 1987. Repr. lib. bdg. 19.95x (*0-89966-580-2*) Buccaneer Bks.

Wilder, Laura Ingalls. Little House Books, 9 vols. Williams, Garth, illus. Incl. Little House in the Big Woods. LC 52-7525. 256p. 1971. pap. 3.95 (*0-06-440001-8*); Little House on the Prairie. 352p. 1971. pap. 3.95 (*0-06-440002-6*); Farmer Boy. 384p. 1971. pap. 3.95 (*0-06-440003-4*); On the Banks of Plum Creek. 352p. 1971. pap. 3.95 (*0-06-440004-2*); By the Shores of Silver Lake. 304p. 1971. pap. 3.95 (*0-06-440005-0*); The Long Winter. 352p. 1971. pap. 3.95 (*0-06-440006-9*); Little Town on the Prairie. 320p. 1971. pap. 3.95 (*0-06-440007-7*); These Happy Golden Years. 304p. 1971. pap. 3.95 (*0-06-440008-5*); The First Four Years. 160p. 1972. pap. 3.95 (*0-06-440031-X*). LC 52-7525. (gr. 3-7). 1973. pap. 35.55 Boxed Set (*0-06-440040-9*, Trophy) HarpC Child Bks.

Willard, Nancy. Sailing to Cythera. McPhail, David, illus. LC 74-5602. 72p. (gr. 5 up). 1985. pap. 5.95 (*0-15-269961-9*, Voyager Bks) HarBrace.

Williams, Karen L. Galimoto. Stock, Catherine, illus. (gr. k-4). 1993. 13.95 (*0-685-64814-1*); audio cass. 11.00 (*1-882869-77-X*) Read Advent.

Williams, Monique M. Peanut Tells His Story. Caroland, Mary, ed. LC 90-71225. (Illus.). 44p. (gr. k-3). 1991. pap. 4.95 (*1-55523-382-1*) Winston-Derek.

Williamson, Tracey. Magic Shadow Show: Four Stories - Four Plays, 2 bks. (Illus.). 24p. (gr. k-4). 1991. 17.95 (*0-525-44765-2*, DCB) Dutton Child Bks.

Wilson, Kay W. Classics Then & Now: Around the World in Eighty Days, the Prince & the Pauper, the Legend of Sleepy Hollow. Kratoville, B. L., ed. (Illus.). 112p. (gr. 3 up). 1991. pap. text ed. 12.00 (*0-87879-919-2*, 919-2); wkbk. 10.00 (*0-87879-920-6*) High Noon Bks.

Wood, Audrey. King Bidgood's in the Bathtub. Wood, Don, illus. LC 85-5472. 32p. (ps-3). 1985. 14.95 (*0-15-242730-9*, HB Juv Bks) HarBrace.

Woodworth, Viki. Would You Wear a Snake? Woodworth, Viki, illus. (gr. 1-8). 1992. PLB 12.95 (*0-89565-821-6*) Childs World.

Worcester, Donald. Lone Hunter & the Cheyennes. Pauley, Paige, illus. LC 85-4746. 78p. (gr. 4 up). 1985. Repr. of 1957 ed. 10.95 (*0-87565-018-X*) Tex Christian.

World's Best Christmas Stories. LC 93-27249. (Illus.). 80p. (gr. 4-6). 1993. pap. 1.95 (*0-8167-3142-X*, Pub. by Watermill Pr) Troll Assocs.

Ziefert, Harriet. Say Good Night! Brown, Richard, illus. 32p. 1987. (Puffin); pap. 3.50 (*0-14-050747-7*, Puffin) Puffin Bks.

—Three Wishes. Jacobson, David, illus. 32p. (ps-3). 1993. 9.00 (*0-670-84569-8*) Viking Child Bks.

Zolotow, Charlotte, ed. An Overpraised Season. LC 73-5499. 204p. (gr. 7 up). 1973. PLB 12.89 (*0-06-026954-5*) HarpC Child Bks.

STORKS–FICTION

Bocheck in Poland. (gr. 2-8). 1980. 9.95 (*0-317-02772-7*) Polanie.

Brown, Margaret W. Wheel on the Chimney. Gergely, Tibor, illus. LC 84-48379. 32p. (ps-3). 1954. 14.00 (*0-397-30288-6*, Lipp Jr Bks); PLB 13.89 (*0-397-30296-7*) HarpC Child Bks.
—Wheel on the Chimney. new ed. Gergely, Tibor, illus. LC 93-29423. 32p. (ps-3). 1995. 15.00 (*0-06-024247-7*); PLB 14.89 (*0-06-024248-5*) HarpC Child Bks.
DeJong, Meindert. Wheel on the School. Sendak, Maurice, illus. LC 54-8945. 256p. (gr. 4-7). 1954. 15.00 (*0-06-021585-7*); PLB 14.89 (*0-06-021586-0*) HarpC Child Bks.
—Wheel on the School. LC 54-8945. (Illus.). (gr. 4-7). 1972. pap. 3.95 (*0-06-440021-2*, Trophy) HarpC Child Bks.
Madsen, Ross M. Stewart Stork. Halsey, Megan, illus. LC 92-30730. 40p. (ps-3). 1993. 11.99 (*0-8037-1325-8*); PLB 11.89 (*0-8037-1326-6*) Dial Bks Young.

STORMS
see also Hurricanes; Meteorology; Rain and Rainfall; Snow; Thunderstorms; Tornadoes; Winds; also other kinds of storms
Borgardt, Marianne. Deadly Storms in Action: An Early Reader Pop-up Book. Harris, Greg, illus. 16p. (Orig.). (ps-3). 1993. pap. 8.95 (*0-689-71719-9*, Aladdin) Macmillan Child Grp.
Broekel, Ray. Storms. LC 81-15455. (Illus.). 48p. (gr. k-4). 1982. PLB 12.85 (*0-516-01654-7*) Childrens.
Deery, Ruth. Tornadoes & Hurricanes. Micallef, Mary, illus. 48p. (gr. 4-8). 1985. wkbk. 7.95 (*0-86653-318-4*, GA 631) Good Apple.
Dineen, Jacqueline. Hurricanes & Typhoons. LC 91-11302. (Illus.). 32p. (gr. 5-8). 1991. PLB 12.40 (*0-531-17339-9*, Gloucester Pr) Watts.
Gross, Virginia T. The Day It Rained Forever: A Story of the Johnstown Flood. Himler, Ronald, illus. 64p. (gr. 2-6). 1991. 11.95 (*0-670-83552-8*) Viking Child Bks.
Knapp, Brian. Storm. LC 89-11536. (Illus.). 48p. (gr. 5-9). 1990. PLB 22.80 (*0-8114-2372-7*) Raintree Steck-V.
Merk, Ann & Merk, Jim. Storms. LC 94-13321. (gr. 3 up). 1994. write for info. (*0-86593-386-3*) Rourke Corp.
Micallef, Mary. Storms & Blizzards. Micallef, Mary, illus. 48p. (gr. 4-8). 1985. wkbk. 7.95 (*0-86653-321-4*, GA 683) Good Apple.
Oana. Bobby Bear & the Blizzard. LC 80-82950. (Illus.). 32p. (ps-1). 1981. PLB 9.95 (*0-87783-151-3*) Oddo.
Simon, Seymour. Storms. LC 88-22045. (Illus.). 32p. (gr. k-3). 1989. 12.95 (*0-688-07413-8*); PLB 12.88 (*0-688-07414-6*, Morrow Jr Bks) Morrow Jr Bks.
—Storms. ALC Staff, ed. LC 88-22045. (Illus.). 32p. (gr. k up). 1992. pap. 4.95 (*0-688-11708-2*, Mulberry) Morrow.
Steele, Philip. Storms: Causes & Effects. LC 90-45021. (Illus.). 32p. (gr. 5-8). 1991. PLB 12.40 (*0-531-11026-5*) Watts.
Twist, Clint. Hurricanes & Storms. LC 91-37269. (Illus.). 48p. (gr. 4-6). 1992. text ed. 13.95 RSBE (*0-02-789685-4*, New Discovery) Macmillan Child Grp.
Wood, Jenny. Storm. LC 92-43947. (Illus.). 32p. (gr. 3-6). 1993. 14.95g (*1-56847-002-9*) Thomson Lrning.
—Storms: Nature's Fury. LC 90-55461. (Illus.). 32p. (gr. 3-4). 1991. PLB 17.27 (*0-8368-0471-6*) Gareth Stevens Inc.

STORMS–FICTION
Crimi, Carolyn. Outside, Inside. Riley, Linnea A., illus. LC 93-46897. 1995. 15.00 (*0-671-88688-6*, S&S BFYR) S&S Trade.
Hest, Amy. Ruby's Storm. Cote, Nancy, illus. LC 92-31242. 32p. (ps-2). 1994. RSBE 14.95 (*0-02-743160-6*, Four Winds) Macmillan Child Grp.
Leavy, Una. Harry's Stormy Night. Utton, Peter, illus. LC 94-12772. (gr. 3 up). 1995. 16.00 (*0-689-50625-2*, M K McElderry) Macmillan Child Grp.
O'Rourke, Frank. Burton & Stanley. Allen, Jonathan, illus. (gr. 4-7). 1993. 15.95 (*0-87923-824-0*) Godine.
Peterson, John. Littles & the Big Storm. (gr. 4-7). 1994. pap. 2.75 (*0-590-42276-6*) Scholastic Inc.
Rockwell, Anne. The Storm. Sauber, Robert, illus. LC 93-40976. 32p. (ps-3). 1994. 15.95 (*0-7868-0017-8*); lib. bdg. 15.89 (*0-7868-2013-6*) Hyprn Child.
Roop, Peter & Roop, Connie. Keep the Lights Burning, Abbie. Hanson, Peter E., illus. (gr. 2-4). 1989. incl. cass. 19.95 (*0-87499-135-8*); pap. 12.95 incl. cass. (*0-87499-134-X*); Set; incl. 4 bks., guide, & cass. pap. 27.95 (*0-87499-136-6*) Live Oak Media.
Sargent, Dave. Tornado & Sweep, Bk. I. Bowen, Jane, ed. Zapata, Miguel, tr. Lenoir, Jane, illus. (SPA.). 48p. (Orig.). (gr. k-6). 1993. PLB 11.95 (*1-56763-106-1*); pap. 4.95 (*1-56763-107-X*) Ozark Pub.
Singer, Marilyn. Storm Rising. 224p. 1992. pap. 3.25 (*0-590-42174-3*, Point) Scholastic Inc.
Stolz, Mary. Storm in the Night. Cummings, Pat, illus. LC 85-45838. 32p. (gr. k-3). 1988. 15.00 (*0-06-025912-4*); PLB 14.89 (*0-06-025913-2*) HarpC Child Bks.
Tregebov, Rhea. The Big Storm. Kovalski, Maryann, illus. LC 92-55040. 32p. (ps-3). 1993. 13.95 (*1-56282-461-9*); PLB 13.89 (*1-56282-462-7*) Hyprn Child.
Zolotow, Charlotte. Hold My Hand. Reissue. ed. Di Grazia, Thomas, illus. LC 72-76506. 32p. (gr. k-3). 1972. PLB 12.89 (*0-06-026952-9*) HarpC Child Bks.
—Storm Book. Graham, Margaret B., illus. LC 52-7880. (gr. k-3). 1952. PLB 13.89 (*0-06-027026-8*) HarpC Child Bks.

STORYTELLING
Bodie, Idella. Ghost Tales for Retelling. Stone, Barbara, ed. (Illus.). 78p. (Orig.). (gr. 6). 1994. pap. 6.95 (*0-87844-125-5*) Sandlapper Pub Co. To encourage young readers in the art - & pleasure - of storytelling, author Idella Bodie has pulled together twenty-seven tall tales she & her friends told around their backyard campfires when she was a girl. Older ghost story lovers will recognize old favorites like THE GOLDEN ARM. Ms. Bodie has organized these scary stories into five categories: flesh-tingling stories, spirits returning, supernatural stories, haunted places, & shapes & shadows. To assist the young storytellers, she has included a list of "Hints for Effective Storytelling." A retired English teacher, Ms. Bodie has previously written nine books for young readers: seven novels & two biographies. Call 1-800-849-7263 to order copies or request additional information.
Publisher Provided Annotation.
Brody, Ed, et al, eds. Spinning Tales, Weaving Hope: Stories, Storytelling & Activities for Peace, Justice, & the Environment. Bond, Lahki, illus. 288p. (Orig.). 1992. lib. bdg. 49.95 (*0-86571-228-X*); pap. 22.95 (*0-86571-229-8*) New Soc Pubs.
Brown, Roberta S. Queen of the Cold-Blooded Tales. 176p. (gr. 7 up). 1993. 19.00 (*0-685-67270-0*) August Hse.
Catron, Carol & Parks, Barbara. Super Story Telling. 239p. (ps). 1986. 15.95 (*0-513-01793-3*) Denison.
Champlin, Connie & DeVasure, John. Storytelling with the Computer. (Illus.). 64p. (gr. k-6). 1986. pap. 29.95 (*0-938594-09-5*); diskette incl. Spec Lit Pr.
Duke, Kate. Aunt Isabel Tells a Good One. Duke, Kate, illus. LC 91-14598. 32p. (ps-2). 1992. 14.00 (*0-525-44835-7*, DCB) Dutton Child Bks.
Littlefield, Kathy M. & Littlefield, Robert S. Tell Me a Story! Stark, Steve, illus. 32p. (Orig.). (gr. 3-6). 1989. pap. text ed. 8.95 (*1-879340-02-X*, K0103) Kidspeak.
Marshall, James. Three up a Tree. Marshall, James, illus. LC 86-2163. 48p. (ps-3). 1986. 9.95 (*0-8037-0328-7*); PLB 9.89 (*0-685-13452-0*) Dial Bks Young.
The Storytelling - Folklore Series. rev. ed. 1992. pap. write for info. (*0-938756-99-0*) Yellow Moon.
Suid, Murray. For the Love of Stories. 64p. (gr. 4-6). 1986. 6.95 (*0-912107-49-9*) Monday Morning Bks.

STORYTELLING–COLLECTIONS
Child Study Association of America Staff. Read-to-Me Storybook. Lenski, Lois L., illus. LC 47-31488. (ps-1). 1947. 16.95i (*0-690-68832-6*, Crowell Jr Bks) HarpC Child Bks.
Robertson, Brian. Brian Robertson's Favorite Texas Tales. Wilson, J. Kay, illus. LC 92-17115. 112p. (gr. 4-7). 1992. 12.95 (*0-89015-862-2*) Sunbelt Media.
Robinson, Matt. Gordon of Sesame Street Storybook. (Illus.). (gr. 7-9). 1972. lib. bdg. 5.99 (*0-394-92406-1*) Random Bks Yng Read.
Young, Richard & Young, Judy D. African-American Folktales. 176p. 1993. 18.95 (*0-87483-308-6*); pap. 9.95 (*0-87483-309-4*) August Hse.

STOWE, HARRIET ELIZABETH (BEECHER), 1811-1896
Ash, Maureen. The Story of Harriet Beecher Stowe. LC 89-25364. (Illus.). 32p. (gr. 3-6). 1990. PLB 12.30 (*0-516-04746-9*); pap. 3.95 (*0-516-44746-7*) Childrens.
Bland, Celia. Harriet Beecher Stowe: Antislavery Author. (Illus.). 80p. (gr. 3-5). 1993. PLB 13.95 (*0-7910-1773-7*, Am Art Analog) Chelsea Hse.
Coil, Suzanne M. Harriet Beecher Stowe. LC 93-13710. (Illus.). 192p. (gr. 7-12). 1993. PLB 14.40 (*0-531-13006-1*) Watts.
Fritz, Jean. Harriet Beecher Stowe & the Beecher Preachers. LC 93-6408. (Illus.). 144p. (gr. 6-9). 1994. 16.95 (*0-399-22666-4*, Putnam) Putnam Pub Group.
Jakoubek, Robert. Harriet Beecher Stowe. Horner, Matina S., intro. by. (Illus.). 112p. (gr. 5 up). 1989. 17.95 (*1-55546-680-X*) Chelsea Hse.
Johnston, Norma. Harriet: The Life & World of Harriet Beecher Stowe. (Illus.). 224p. 1994. SBE 16.95 (*0-02-747714-2*, Four Winds) Macmillan Child Grp.

STRATEGIC MATERIALS
see Materials
STRATIGRAPHIC GEOLOGY
see Geology, Stratigraphic
STRAVINSKII, IGOR FEDOROVICH, 1882-1971
Popov, Nicolai. Stravinsky. Gallaz, Christophe, illus. LC 92-40383. 1993. 14.95 (*0-88682-605-5*) Creative Ed.
STREET TRAFFIC
see Traffic Regulations
STREETS
see also Roads

STRINGED INSTRUMENTS
see also names of stringed instruments, e.g. Guitar; etc.
Dillon, Jacquelyn, et al. Strictly Strings - Piano, Bk. 1: A Comprehensive String Method. (Illus.). 64p. (Orig.). (gr. 4-6). 1992. pap. 11.95 (*0-88284-535-7*, 5298) Alfred Pub.
Flesch, Carl. The Art of Violin Playing, Bk. 1. rev. ed. Martens, Frederick H., tr. (Illus.). 188p. 1924. pap. 24.95 (*0-8258-0135-4*, 01317) Fischer Inc NY.
—The Art of Violin Playing: Artistic Realization & Instruction, Book 2. Martens, Frederick H., tr. 237p. 1930. pap. 24.95 (*0-8258-0136-2*, 0 2046) Fischer Inc NY.
Hunka, Alison & Bunting, Philippa. Violin & Stringed Instruments. (Illus.). 32p. (gr. 4-7). 1993. PLB 12.40 (*0-531-17424-7*, Gloucester Pr) Watts.
Kimura, Hideo M. How to Pick & Strum the Ukulele, Bk. II. rev. ed. Kimura, Hideo M., illus. 44p. (gr. 7 up). 1988. pap. text ed. 9.95 (*0-917822-18-8*) Heedays.
Kreutzer, Rudolph. Forty-Two Studies for Violin. Singer, Edmund, ed. 73p. pap. 8.00 (*0-8258-0025-0*) Fischer Inc NY.
Sevcik, Otakar. School of Technic for Violin, Op. 1, Part 2. (FRE, GER & ENG.). 49p. 1900. pap. 8.00 (*0-8258-0035-8*, L 283) Fischer Inc NY.
—School of Technic for Violin: Op. 1 Part 1. (GER, FRE & ENG.). (gr. 6-12). 1900. pap. 8.95 (*0-8258-0034-X*, L 282) Fischer Inc NY.
Sharma, Elizabeth. Strings. LC 93-7249. (Illus.). 32p. (gr. 4-6). 1993. 14.95 (*1-56847-112-2*) Thomson Lrning.
Wohlfahrt, Franz. Easiest Elementary Method for Violin: Op. 38. 56p. 1894. pap. 7.50 (*0-8258-0053-6*, L1061) Fischer Inc NY.
STRUCTURAL BOTANY
see Botany–Anatomy
STRUCTURAL DRAFTING
see Mechanical Drawing
STUDENT ACTIVITIES
see also School Sports
Reum, Earl. The Spirit of Student Council. Bruce, C., ed. (gr. 7-9). 1981. pap. 7.00 (*0-88210-117-X*) Natl Assn Principals.
STUDENT AID
see Scholarships, Fellowships, Etc.
STUDENT GUIDANCE
see Vocational Guidance
STUDENT LIFE AND CUSTOMS
see Students
STUDENT LOAN FUNDS
see also Scholarships, Fellowships, Etc.
STUDENT MOVEMENT
see Youth Movement
STUDENT PROTESTS
see Youth Movement
STUDENT REVOLT
see Youth Movement
STUDENTS
Balter, Lawrence. Sue Lee Starts School: Adjusting to School. Schanzer, Roz, illus. 40p. (ps-3). 1991. 5.95 (*0-8120-6152-7*) Barron.
Cherry, Charles W., II. Excellence Without Excuse: The Black Student's Guide to Academic Excellence. LC 91-35248. (gr. 7 up). 1993. 24.95 (*1-56385-497-X*); pap. 13.95 (*1-56385-498-8*) Intl Schol Pr.
Dean, Theresa & Lucadamo, Rhonda. Pocket Full of School Memories. Dean, Theresa, illus. 26p. (ps-8). 1992. 18.95 (*1-881511-00-6*) Pockets Pr.
Dentemaro, Christine & Kranz, Rachel. Straight Talk about Student Life. Ryan, Elizabeth A., ed. 128p. (gr. 9-12). Date not set. 16.95x (*0-685-63076-5*) Facts on File.
Doerr, Cathy A. Student Organizational Planbook. 112p. (gr. 3-12). 1992. pap. 5.95 (*0-9632893-0-6*) Skills For Lrn.
Going to School. (Illus.). 32p. (ps). 1990. 2.99 (*0-517-69196-5*) Random Hse Value.
Hough, Judith M. My School Days Memories: Grades K-6. Hough, Judith, illus. 40p. (gr. k-6). 1992. pap. 7.95 (*0-9633769-0-X*) Touch The Sky.
Kalman, Bobbie. I Like School. (Illus.). 32p. (gr. k-2). 1985. 15.95 (*0-86505-064-3*); pap. 7.95 (*0-86505-088-0*) Crabtree Pub Co.
Krell-Oishi, Mary. More Scenes That Happen: Real-Life Snapshots of Teenage Lives. LC 93-40926. 208p. 1994. pap. text ed. 10.95 (*1-56608-000-2*, B112) Meriwether Pub.
Landau, Elaine. Teenagers Talk about School. Steltenpohl, Jane, ed. LC 88-23065. 120p. (gr. 7 up). 1989. PLB 12.98 (*0-671-64568-4*, J Messner); pap. 5.95 (*0-671-68148-6*) S&S Trade.
Loeper, John J. Going to School in 1776. LC 72-86940. (Illus.). 112p. (gr. 4-7). 1973. SBE 14.95 (*0-689-30089-1*, Atheneum) Macmillan Child Grp.
Maher, Robert. Leadership: Self, School, Community. Bruce, C., ed. 96p. (Orig.). (gr. 9-12). 1988. pap. 10.00 (*0-88210-217-6*) Natl Assn Student.
Newlin, Lana S. Surviving Sixth Grade. Morey, Cathy, ed. Newlin, Lana S., illus. 90p. (gr. 5-7). 1990. 16.95 (*0-9625413-0-3*); pap. 9.95 (*0-9625413-1-1*) Christmans.
Nichols, V. Student Planner & Assignment Book. 2nd ed. (Illus.). 120p. (gr. 5-12). 1993. pap. 3.95 (*1-879424-20-7*) Nickel Pr.
Page, Parker, et al. Getting Along Complete Kit. (gr. k-4). 1991. 107.95 (*0-88671-407-9*, 4670) Am Guidance.
—Getting Along Student Activities: Level 1. (Orig.). (gr. k-1). 1991. pap. 2.70 (*0-88671-409-5*, 4672) Am Guidance.

—Getting Along Student Activities: Level 2. (Orig.). (gr. 2-4). 1991. pap. 2.70 (*0-88671-410-9*, 4676) Am Guidance.

Rappaport, Doreen. Tinker vs. Des Moines: Student Rights on Trial. Palencar, John J., illus. LC 92-25019. 160p. (gr. 5 up). 1993. 15.00 (*0-06-025117-4*); PLB 14.89 (*0-06-025118-2*) HarpC Child Bks.

—Tinker vs. Des Moines: Student Rights on Trial. LC 92-25019. (Illus.). 160p. (gr. 5 up). 1994. pap. 4.95 (*0-06-446114-9*, Trophy) HarpC Child Bks.

Rydberg, Denny. How to Survive College. 160p. (Orig.). 1989. pap. 8.99 (*0-310-35351-3*) Zondervan.

Smith, Allan H., ed. How to Make School Fun. Trachsler, Don, illus. LC 84-90227. 200p. (Orig.). (gr. 6-12). 1984. pap. 10.00 (*0-931113-03-2*) Success Publ.

Smith, Margaret D. Mississippi High School Students & the Law, Vol. II. LC 89-3745. 206p. (gr. 8-12). 1990. pap. 9.95 (*0-937552-36-4*) Quail Ridge.

Smith, Sandra L. Coping with Changing Schools. LC 93-20433. 1993. 14.95 (*0-8239-1602-2*) Rosen Group.

Spethman, Martin J. How to Get into & Graduate from College in Four Years with Good Grades, a Useful Major, a Lot of Knowledge, a Little Debt, Great Friends, Happy Parents, Maximum Party Attendance, Minimal Weight Gain, Decent Habits, Fewer Hassles, a Career Goal, & a Super Attitude All While Remaining Extremely Cool. Cabrera, Ralph, illus. 192p. (Orig.). (gr. 11-12). 1993. pap. 10.95 (*0-9633598-0-0*) Westgate Pub & Ent.

Warner, Rachel. Our Class. (Illus.). 25p. (gr. 2-4). 1991. 12.95 (*0-237-60139-7*, Pub. by Evans Bros Ltd) Trafalgar.

Wirths, Claudine G. & Bowman-Kruhm, Mary. Your New School. Stren, Patti, illus. LC 93-8513. 64p. (gr. 5-8). 1993. PLB 14.95 (*0-8050-2074-8*, TFC Bks NY) H Holt & Co.

STUDENTS–EMPLOYMENT

Sullivan, Mick. Spare Time Cash: Every Student's Guide to Making Money on the Side. Moe, Mary, ed. 114p. (Orig.). (gr. 10 up). 1989. pap. 12.95 (*1-878330-00-4*) Sullivan MT.

STUDENTS–FICTION

Anderson, Myra. Big Enough. Reid, Diana S., illus. 32p. (gr. k-3). 1991. 12.95 (*0-9625620-0-9*) DOT Garnet.

Avi. Romeo & Juliet - Together (& Alive) at Last. 128p. 1988. pap. 3.99 (*0-380-70525-7*, Camelot) Avon.

Blair, Alison. Back to School. (gr. 10 up). 1989. pap. 2.95 (*0-8041-0329-1*) Ivy Books.

—Social Studies. (gr. 10 up). 1989. pap. 2.95 (*0-8041-0330-5*) Ivy Books.

—Study Break. (gr. 10 up). 1988. pap. 2.95 (*0-8041-0327-5*) Ivy Books.

Blume, Judy. Tales of a Fourth Grade Nothing. large type ed. Doty, Roy, illus. 174p. (gr. 2-6). 1987. Repr. of 1972 ed. lib. bdg. 14.95 (*1-55736-015-4*, Crnrstn Bks) BDD LT Grp.

Brinmer, Larry D. Cory Coleman Grade 2. 1991. 12.95 (*0-8050-1425-X*) H Holt & Co.

Bunting, Eve. Janet Hamm Needs a Date for the Dance. 112p. 1987. pap. 2.95 (*0-553-15537-7*, Skylark) Bantam.

Catling, Patrick S. John Midas in Dreamtime. 96p. (gr. 3-7). 1987. pap. 2.75 (*0-553-15567-9*, Skylark) Bantam.

Cohen, Barbara. King of the Seventh Grade. LC 82-15247. (gr. 4 up). 1982. 14.00 (*0-688-01302-3*) Lothrop.

Cohen, Daniel. Beverly Hills 90210. 1991. pap. 3.99 (*0-671-77052-7*) S&S Trade.

Cooney, Linda A. Freshman Breakup. 1993. pap. 3.99 (*0-06-106165-4*, Harp PBks) HarpC.

—Freshman Celebrity. 1993. pap. 3.99 (*0-06-106767-9*, Harp PBks) HarpC.

—Freshman Choices. 1991. pap. 3.50 (*0-06-106128-X*, Harp PBks) HarpC.

—Freshman Heartbreak. (gr. 7 up). 1992. pap. 3.50 (*0-06-106140-9*, Harp PBks) HarpC.

—Freshman Holiday. 1993. pap. 4.50 (*0-06-106170-0*, Harp PBks) HarpC.

—Freshman Obsession. 1993. pap. 3.99 (*0-06-106734-2*, Harp PBks) HarpC.

—Freshman Rivals. 1991. pap. 3.50 (*0-06-106122-0*, Harp PBks) HarpC.

—Freshman Scandal. 1992. pap. 3.50 (*0-06-106718-0*, Harp PBks) HarpC.

—Freshman Suspect. 1994. pap. 3.99 (*0-06-106168-9*, Harp PBks) HarpC.

—Freshman Temptation. (gr. 4-7). 1993. pap. 3.99 (*0-06-106166-2*, Harp PBks) HarpC.

—Freshman Truths. 1992. pap. 3.50 (*0-06-106713-X*, Harp PBks) HarpC.

Cooper, Ilene. Mean Streak. LC 90-23103. 208p. (gr. 4 up). 1991. 13.95 (*0-688-08431-1*) Morrow Jr Bks.

—Queen of the Sixth Grade. LC 88-18859. 128p. (gr. 4-7). 1988. 12.95 (*0-688-07933-4*) Morrow Jr Bks.

—Queen of the Sixth Grade. LC 89-36938. (gr. 3 up). 1990. pap. 3.95 (*0-14-034028-9*, Puffin) Puffin Bks.

Coville, Bruce. Aliens Ate My Homework. Coville, Katherine, illus. 160p. (gr. 3-6). 1993. 12.00 (*0-671-87249-4*, Minstrel Bks); pap. 3.50 (*0-671-72712-5*, Minstrel Bks) PB.

Cruise, Beth. Saved by the Bell: Class Trip Chaos. LC 92-35523. 144p. (gr. 5 up). 1992. pap. 2.95 (*0-02-042765-4*, Collier Young Ad) Macmillan Child Grp.

Cruise, Beth & Schleifer, Laura. Impeach Screech. (Illus.). 144p. (Orig.). (gr. 5 up). 1993. pap. 2.95 (*0-02-042762-X*, Collier Young Ad) Macmillan Child Grp.

—One Wild Weekend. LC 93-2905. (Illus.). 144p. (Orig.). (gr. 5 up). 1993. pap. 2.95 (*0-02-042763-8*, Collier Young Ad) Macmillan Child Grp.

—That Old Zack Magic. (Illus.). 144p. (Orig.). (gr. 5 up). 1993. pap. 2.95 (*0-02-042761-1*, Collier Young Ad) Macmillan Child Grp.

DeClements, Barthe. The Fourth Grade Master Wizards. 144p. (gr. 3-7). 1988. pap. 12.95 (*0-670-82290-6*) Viking Child Bks.

—Fourth Grade Wizards. large type ed. 144p. 1989. lib. bdg. 15.95 (*1-55736-111-8*, Crnrstn Bks) BDD LT Grp.

—The Fourth Grade Wizards. 160p. (gr. 8-12). 1995. pap. 3.99 (*0-14-032760-6*, Puffin) Puffin Bks.

—Sixth Grade Can Really Kill You. large type ed. 163p. 1989. lib. bdg. 15.95 (*1-55736-108-8*, Crnrstn Bks) BDD LT Grp.

—Sixth Grade Can Really Kill You. (gr. 3-7). 1986. pap. 2.95 (*0-590-42883-7*, Apple Paperbacks) Scholastic Inc.

Delton, Judy & McCue, Noelle B. Mom Made Me Go to School. 1993. pap. 2.99 (*0-440-40841-5*) Dell.

Duncan, Lois. Killing Mr. Griffin. (gr. 7 up). 1978. 15.95 (*0-316-19549-9*) Little.

Eggleston, Edward. The Hoosier Schoolboy. 1988. Repr. of 1883 ed. lib. bdg. 59.00x (*0-7812-1178-6*) Rprt Serv.

—The Schoolmaster's Stories for Boys & Girls. 1988. Repr. of 1874 ed. lib. bdg. 59.00x (*0-7812-1176-X*) Rprt Serv.

Field Day. 1993. pap. 2.99 (*0-440-40824-5*) Dell.

Fields, Terri. Day the Fifth Grade Disappeared. (gr. 4-7). 1992. pap. 2.95 (*0-590-45403-X*) Scholastic Inc.

Geller, Mark. My Life in the Seventh Grade. LC 85-45265. 128p. (gr. 5 up). 1988. pap. 3.50 (*0-06-440276-2*, Trophy) HarpC Child Bks.

Gilden, Mel. Beverly Hills, 90210: No Secrets. (gr. 7 up). 1992. pap. 3.99 (*0-06-106136-0*, Harp PBks) HarpC.

—Beverly Hills, 90210: Where the Boys Are. (gr. 9-12). 1993. pap. 3.99 (*0-06-106145-X*, Harp PBks) HarpC.

—Beverly Hills, 90210: Which Way to the Beach? 1992. pap. 3.99 (*0-06-106768-7*, Harp PBks) HarpC.

—More Than Words. 1993. pap. 3.99 (*0-06-106146-8*, Harp PBks) HarpC.

—Things That Go Bark in the Park. 96p. 1989. pap. 2.75 (*0-380-75786-9*, Camelot) Avon.

—Two Hearts. 1993. pap. 3.99 (*0-06-106144-1*, Harp PBks) HarpC.

—Yuckers. 96p. 1989. pap. 2.95 (*0-380-75787-7*, Camelot) Avon.

Gilligan, Shannon. Science Lab Sabotage. (gr. 4-7). 1991. pap. 2.99 (*0-553-15913-5*) Bantam.

Godfrey, Martyn N. The Great Science Fair Disaster. 1992. pap. 2.95 (*0-590-44081-0*, Apple Paperbacks) Scholastic Inc.

Gormley, Beatrice. Paul's Volcano. 160p. 1988. pap. 2.50 (*0-380-70562-1*, Camelot) Avon.

Great Homework Chase. 1990. 4.98 (*1-55521-687-0*) Bk Sales Inc.

Greenaway, Elizabeth. Bitty Goes to School. (Illus.). 24p. (Orig.). (ps-2). 1994. pap. 2.50 (*0-679-86182-3*) Random Bks Yng Read.

Gross, Alan. What If the Teacher Calls on Me? Venezia, Mike, illus. LC 79-18560. 32p. (ps-3). 1980. pap. 3.95 (*0-516-43671-6*) Childrens.

Haynes, Betsy. Class Trip Calamity. (gr. 4-7). 1992. pap. 2.99 (*0-553-15969-0*) Bantam.

—The Great Boyfriend Trap. 160p. (gr. 4-7). 1987. pap. 2.75 (*0-553-15530-X*, Skylark) Bantam.

—Seventh-Grade Rumors: The Fabulous Five, No. 1. (gr. 4-7). 1988. pap. 2.95 (*0-553-15625-X*, Skylark) Bantam.

—The Trouble with Flirting. (gr. 4-7). 1988. pap. 2.95 (*0-553-15633-0*, Skylark) Bantam.

—Yearbook Memories. 1992. pap. 3.50 (*0-553-15975-5*) Bantam.

Herman, Emmi S. My First Day at School. Flanigan, Ruth J., illus. 24p. (ps-2). 1992. pap. 0.99 (*1-56293-106-7*) McClanahan Bk.

Hillert, Margaret. Who Goes to School? (Illus.). (ps-k). 1981. PLB 6.95 (*0-8136-5075-5*, TK2382); pap. 3.50 (*0-685-50736-X*, TK2383) Modern Curr.

Hodgman, Ann. Galaxy High School. 96p. (gr. 2-6). 1987. pap. 2.50 (*0-553-15545-8*, Skylark) Bantam.

Hurwitz, Johanna. Class Clown. Hamanaka, Sheila, illus. 112p. (gr. 2-5). 1988. pap. 2.75 (*0-590-41821-1*, Little Apple) Scholastic Inc.

—Class President. Hamanaka, Sheila, illus. LC 89-28600. 96p. (gr. 2 up). 1990. 12.95 (*0-688-09114-8*) Morrow Jr Bks.

—School's Out! Hamanaka, Sheila, illus. 96p. 1992. pap. 2.75 (*0-590-45053-0*, Little Apple) Scholastic Inc.

Janney, Rebecca P. The Exchange Student's Secret. (gr. 4-7). 1994. pap. 4.99 (*0-8499-3536-9*) Word Inc.

Kauffman, M. K. The Right Moves. (gr. 7 up). pap. 2.25 (*0-317-62895-X*) S&S Trade.

Kerr, M. E. Fell. LC 86-45776. 176p. (gr. 7 up). 1988. pap. 3.95 (*0-06-447031-8*, Trophy) HarpC Child Bks.

Klein, Robin. Tearaways: Stories to Make You Think Twice. 144p. (gr. 5-9). 1991. 12.95 (*0-670-83212-X*) Viking Child Bks.

Kline, Suzy. Horrible Harry & the Green Slime. Remkiewicz, Frank, illus. 64p. (gr. 2-5). 1989. pap. 10.95 (*0-670-82468-2*) Viking Child Bks.

Leroe, Ellen. H. O. W. L. High Goes Bats. MacDonald, Patricia, ed. 144p. (Orig.). 1993. pap. 2.99 (*0-671-79838-3*, Minstrel Bks) PB.

Levinson, Marilyn. The Fourth-Grade Four. Bowman, Leslie, illus. LC 89-31109. 64p. (gr. 2-4). 1991. pap. 4.95 (*0-8050-1640-6*, Owlet BYR) H Holt & Co.

Levy, Elizabeth. Something Queer in the Cafeteria. Gerstein, Mordicai, illus. 48p. (gr. 2-5). 1994. pap. 4.95 (*0-685-74694-1*) Hyprn Ppbks.

Locke, Joseph. Kill the Teacher's Pet. 1991. pap. 2.99 (*0-553-29058-4*) Bantam.

Lois, Susan. Reunion Affairs. (Orig.). 1988. pap. 3.95 (*0-440-20213-2*) Dell.

McKenna, Colleen O. Fifth Grade: Here Comes Trouble. 128p. (gr. 3-7). 1991. pap. 2.95 (*0-590-41734-7*, Apple Paperbacks) Scholastic Inc.

—The Truth about Sixth Grade. 192p. (gr. 3-7). 1992. pap. 2.75 (*0-590-44392-5*, Apple Paperbacks) Scholastic Inc.

Maguire, Jesse. Starting Over. (Orig.). 1992. pap. 3.99 (*0-8041-0848-X*) Ivy Books.

—Starting Over. 1992. 3.99 (*0-8041-1016-6*) Ivy Books.

Martin, Thomas. Private High. 25p. (Orig.). (gr. 7 up). 1986. pap. 4.50 playscript (*0-87602-267-0*) Anchorage.

Meastro, Betsy. Snow Day. (ps-3). 1992. pap. 4.95 (*0-590-46083-8*) Scholastic Inc.

Meyers, Marsha A. A Child's Fear: Vision of Hope. 1993. pap. 12.95 (*0-9637083-9-2*) Myi-Way Prod.

Miller, Shirley J. School Days. Casey, Marjorie, illus. 80p. (Orig.). (gr. 2-6). 1993. pap. 6.95 (*1-878580-90-6*) Asylum Arts.

New Seed Press Collective Staff. A Book about Us. (Illus.). (ps-5). 1977. 4.95 (*0-938678-04-3*) New Seed.

O'Sullivan, Anna-Margaret. The Green Bank Year. LC 88-62114. 255p. 1989. pap. 6.95 (*1-55523-183-7*) Winston-Derek.

Oxenbury, Helen. First Day of School. (Illus.). 24p. (ps-1). 1993. pap. 3.99 (*0-14-054977-3*, Puff Pied Piper) Puffin Bks.

Pascal, Francine. Against the Odds. large type ed. 151p. (gr. 5-8). 1989. Repr. of 1988 ed. PLB 10.50 (*1-55905-016-0*, Dist. by Gareth Stevens); 9.50 (*1-55905-006-3*, Dist. by Gareth Stevens) Grey Castle.

—Almost Married. (gr. 7 up). 1994. pap. 3.50 (*0-553-29859-3*) Bantam.

—Beware the Babysitter. 1993. pap. 3.50 (*0-553-29856-9*) Bantam.

—The Boyfriend War. 1994. pap. 3.50 (*0-553-29858-5*) Bantam.

—Cheating to Win. 1991. pap. 2.99 (*0-553-29145-9*) Bantam.

—Ciao, Sweet Valley! (gr. 4-7). 1992. pap. 3.25 (*0-553-15940-2*) Bantam.

—Class Trip. (Orig.). (gr. 7 up). 1988. pap. 3.50 (*0-553-15588-1*) Bantam.

—College Girls. (gr. 6 up). 1993. pap. 3.50 (*0-553-56308-4*) Bantam.

—Decisions. (gr. 6 up). 1988. pap. 2.99 (*0-553-27278-0*) Bantam.

—Double Jeopardy. 214p. (Orig.). (gr. 7-12). 1987. pap. 3.50 (*0-553-26905-4*) Bantam.

—Double Love. large type ed. 186p. (gr. 5-8). 1989. Repr. of 1983 ed. PLB 10.50 (*1-55905-010-1*, Dist. by Gareth Stevens); 9.50 (*1-55905-000-4*) Grey Castle.

—Elizabeth Betrayed. 1992. pap. 3.25 (*0-553-29235-8*) Bantam.

—The Evil Twin. 1993. pap. 3.99 (*0-553-29857-7*) Bantam.

—Family Secrets. 160p. (Orig.). (gr. 7 up). 1988. pap. 2.99 (*0-553-27176-8*) Bantam.

—Jealous Lies. 144p. (Orig.). (gr. 7-12). 1986. pap. 2.75 (*0-553-25816-8*) Bantam.

—Jealous Lies. 1986. pap. 3.25 (*0-553-27558-5*) Bantam.

—Jessica Against Bruce. 1992. pap. 3.50 (*0-553-29232-3*) Bantam.

—Jessica's Unburied Treasure. (ps-3). 1992. pap. 2.99 (*0-553-15926-7*) Bantam.

—Keeping Secrets. 96p. (Orig.). 1987. pap. 3.25 (*0-553-15702-7*, Skylark) Bantam.

—Left Back. 1992. pap. 2.99 (*0-553-48005-7*) Bantam.

—Love Letters for Sale. (gr. 4-7). 1992. pap. 3.25 (*0-553-29234-X*) Bantam.

—Love, Lies & Jessica Wakefield. 1993. pap. 3.50 (*0-553-56306-8*) Bantam.

—The Morning After. 1993. pap. 3.50 (*0-553-29852-6*) Bantam.

—Ms. Quarterback. (gr. 9-12). 1990. pap. 3.25 (*0-553-28767-2*) Bantam.

—My Best Friend's Boyfriend. 1992. pap. 3.50 (*0-553-29233-1*) Bantam.

—New Jessica. 1986. pap. 2.99 (*0-553-27560-7*) Bantam.

—Olivia's Story. 1991. pap. 3.50 (*0-553-29359-1*) Bantam.

—Out of Place. (gr. 7 up). 1988. pap. 3.50 (*0-553-15628-4*) Bantam.

—Out of Reach. large type ed. 151p. (gr. 5-8). 1989. Repr. of 1988 ed. PLB 10.50 (*1-55905-015-2*, Dist. by Gareth Stevens); 9.50 (*1-55905-005-5*) Grey Castle.

—Perfect Shot. 1989. pap. 2.95 (*0-553-27915-7*) Bantam.

—Playing for Keeps. (gr. 7 up). 1988. pap. 3.50 (*0-553-27477-5*) Bantam.

—Playing Hooky. (gr. 6 up). 1988. pap. 3.25 (*0-553-15606-3*) Bantam.

—Playing with Fire. large type ed. 149p. (gr. 5-8). 1989. Repr. of 1983 ed. PLB 10.50 (*1-55905-002-0*); PLB 10.50 (*0-685-26540-4*, Dist. by Gareth Stevens) Grey Castle.

—Power Play. large type ed. 150p. (gr. 5-8). 1989. Repr. of 1983 ed. PLB 10.50 (*1-55905-013-6*, Dist. by Gareth Stevens); 9.50 (*1-55905-003-9*) Grey Castle.
—Promises. 160p. (Orig.). (gr. 7-12). 1985. pap. 2.75 (*0-553-26765-5*) Bantam.
—Rags to Riches. 160p. (Orig.). (gr. 5 up). 1985. pap. 3.25 (*0-553-27431-7*) Bantam.
—Runaway. 1985. pap. 3.25 (*0-553-27566-6*) Bantam.
—Second Chance. (ps-1). 1989. pap. 2.95 (*0-553-27771-5*) Bantam.
—Second Chance. large type ed. 133p. (gr. 5-8). 1989. Repr. of 1989 ed. PLB 10.50 (*1-55905-018-7*, Dist. by Gareth Stevens); 9.50 (*1-55905-008-X*) Grey Castle.
—Secrets. large type ed. 118p. (gr. 5-8). 1989. Repr. of 1983 ed. PLB 10.50 (*1-55905-011-X*, Dist. by Gareth Stevens); 9.50 (*1-55905-001-2*) Grey Castle.
—Slam Book. 1988. pap. 3.95 (*0-553-05496-1*) Bantam.
—Spring Fever: Spring Super Edition, No. 2. 240p. (Orig.). (gr. 7-12). 1987. pap. 3.50 (*0-553-26420-6*) Bantam.
—Starring Jessica. (gr. 9-12). 1991. pap. 3.25 (*0-553-28796-6*) Bantam.
—Sweet Valley: Choosing Sides. 1987. pap. 1.25 (*0-440-82085-5*) Dell.
—Sweet Valley High, No. 68. 1990. pap. 3.25 (*0-553-28618-8*) Bantam.
—Sweet Valley Package. 1987. pap. 3.45 (*0-440-82139-8*) Dell.
—Sweet Valley Sneakin' 1987. pap. 1.25 (*0-440-82144-4*) Dell.
—Sweet Valley: Three's a Crowd. 1987. pap. 1.25 (*0-440-82193-2*) Dell.
—Teamwork. (ps-1). 1989. pap. 3.25 (*0-553-15681-0*, SVT #27) Bantam.
—That Fatal Night. (gr. 7 up). 1989. pap. 3.25 (*0-553-28264-6*) Bantam.
—Todd's Story. 1992. pap. 3.50 (*0-553-29207-2*) Bantam.
—Trouble at Home. 1990. pap. 2.99 (*0-553-28518-1*) Bantam.
—Two-Boy Weekend. 1989. pap. 2.99 (*0-553-27856-8*) Bantam.
—Two-Boy Weekend. large type ed. 150p. (gr. 5-8). 1989. Repr. of 1989 ed. PLB 10.50 (*1-55905-019-5*, Dist. by Gareth Stevens); 9.50 (*1-55905-009-8*) Grey Castle.
—The Verdict. 1993. pap. 3.50 (*0-553-29854-2*) Bantam.
—What Your Parents Don't Know. 1994. pap. 3.50 (*0-553-56307-6*) Bantam.
—White Lies. large type ed. 137p. (gr. 5-8). 1989. Repr. of 1989 ed. PLB 10.50 (*1-55905-017-9*); 9.50 (*1-55905-007-1*, Dist. by Gareth Stevens) Grey Castle.
—Who's to Blame? 1990. pap. 3.25 (*0-553-28555-6*) Bantam.
Pascal, Francine, created by. Against the Odds. 160p. 1989. pap. 2.95 (*0-553-27650-6*) Bantam.
—Alone in the Crowd. 160p. (Orig.). (gr. 7-12). 1986. pap. 2.75 (*0-553-26825-2*) Bantam.
—Buried Treasure. (gr. 3-7). 1987. pap. 2.50 (*0-553-15533-4*, Skylark) Bantam.
—Jumping to Conclusions. 112p. (Orig.). 1988. pap. 3.25 (*0-553-15635-7*) Bantam.
—The New Jessica. 160p. (Orig.). (gr. 7-12). 1986. pap. 2.75 (*0-553-26113-4*) Bantam.
—On the Edge. 160p. (gr. 7 up). 1987. pap. 3.25 (*0-553-27692-1*) Bantam.
—Secret Admirer. 160p. (gr. 7 up). 1987. pap. 2.99 (*0-553-27691-3*) Bantam.
—Standing Out. 112p. 1989. pap. 3.25 (*0-553-15653-5*) Bantam.
—Stretching the Truth. (gr. 3-7). 1987. pap. 3.25 (*0-553-15654-3*, Skylark) Bantam.
—Sweet Valley High. 160p. (Orig.). 1989. pap. 2.95 (*0-553-27720-0*) Bantam.
—Sweet Valley High Super Thriller, No. 3. 240p. (Orig.). 1988. pap. 3.50 (*0-553-27554-2*) Bantam.
—Taking Charge. 112p. (Orig.). 1989. pap. 3.25 (*0-553-15669-1*) Bantam.
—Taking Sides. 160p. (Orig.). (gr. 7-12). 1986. pap. 2.75 (*0-553-25886-9*) Bantam.
Paulsen, Gary. The Boy Who Owned the School. 1991. pap. 3.50 (*0-440-70694-7*) Dell.
—Boy Who Owned the School. (gr. 4-7). 1993. pap. 1.99 (*0-440-21626-5*) Dell.
Pfeffer, Susan B. Twin Surprises. Carter, Abby, illus. LC 91-13968. 64p. (gr. 2-4). 1993. pap. 4.95 (*0-8050-2626-6*, Redfeather BYR) H Holt & Co.
Piasecki, Jerry. They're Torturing Teachers in Room 104. 1992. pap. 3.50 (*0-553-48024-3*) Bantam.
Pike, Christopher. The Graduation. (Orig.). (gr. 9 up). 1991. pap. 3.99 (*0-671-73680-9*, Archway) PB.
Quin-Harkin, Janet. Homecoming Dance. 1991. pap. 3.50 (*0-06-106093-3*, Harp PBks) HarpC.
—New Year's Eve. 1991. pap. 3.50 (*0-06-106094-1*, Harp PBks) HarpC.
—Night of the Prom. (gr. 7 up). 1992. pap. 3.50 (*0-06-106095-X*, Harp PBks) HarpC.
Regan, Dian C. The Class with the Summer Birthdays. Guevara, Susan, illus. LC 90-19670. 80p. (gr. 2-4). 1992. pap. 4.95 (*0-8050-2327-5*, Redfeather BYR) H Holt & Co.
Ronald's Report Card. (Illus.). (ps-2). 1991. PLB 6.95 (*0-8136-5164-6*, TK3831); pap. 3.50 (*0-8136-5664-8*, TK3832) Modern Curr.
Roos, Stephen. Confessions of a Wayward Preppie. (gr. k-12). 1987. pap. 2.75 (*0-440-91586-4*, LFL) Dell.
Sachar, Louis. Sideways Stories from Wayside School. 128p. (gr. 2-6). 1990. Repr. of 1985 ed. PLB 12.99 (*0-679-90413-1*) Random Bks Yng Read.
The School Trip. 1993. pap. 2.99 (*0-440-40823-7*) Dell.
Seniors. 1984. pap. write for info. Dell.
Smith, Josephine A. Being Cool, Going to School: Story-Rhyme & Activity Book. Wilkins, Natiale, ed. Dowley, May, illus. LC 92-74244. 72p. (Orig.). 1994. pap. text ed. 2.99 (*1-881958-02-7*) Hickle Pickle.
Spinelli, Jerry. Fourth Grade Rats. (gr. 4-7). 1993. pap. 2.95 (*0-590-44244-9*, Apple Classics) Scholastic Inc.
—Picklemania. (gr. 8-12). 1993. pap. 2.95 (*0-590-45447-1*) Scholastic Inc.
—Report to the Principal's Office! 1992. 2.95 (*0-590-46277-6*, Apple Paperbacks) Scholastic Inc.
Stine, Megan & Stine, H. William. Fifth Grade Flop. Henry, Paul, illus. LC 89-20624. 96p. (gr. 4-6). 1990. lib. bdg. 9.89 (*0-8167-1704-4*); pap. text ed. 2.95 (*0-8167-1705-2*) Troll Assocs.
Suzanne, Jamie. Teacher's Pet. large type ed. Pascal, Francine, created by. 103p. (gr. 7-12). 1990. Repr. of 1986 ed. 9.95 (*1-55905-065-9*) Grey Castle.
Swanson, Helen M. Angel of Rainbow Gulch. 128p. (Orig.). (gr. 3-6). 1992. pap. 4.95 (*1-880188-08-2*) Bess PR.
Thompson, Julian F. Simon Pure. 336p. (gr. 7 up). 1988. pap. 3.50 (*0-590-41823-8*, Point) Scholastic Inc.
Tunis, John R. Schoolboy Johnson. LC 58-5728. 192p. (gr. 5 up). 1991. pap. 4.95 (*0-688-10150-X*, Pub. by Beech Tree Bks) Morrow.
Vornholt, John. How to Sneak into the Girls' Locker Room. 96p. (Orig.). 1993. pap. 3.50 (*0-380-76859-3*, Camelot) Avon.
Wallace, Bill. The Biggest Klutz in Fifth Grade. MacDonald, Pat, ed. 160p. 1994. pap. 3.50 (*0-671-86970-1*, Minstrel Bks) PB.
Warren, Jean. Huff & Puff Go to School: A Totline Teaching Tale. Cubley, Kathleen, ed. Piper, Molly & Ekberg, Marion, illus. LC 93-34859. 32p. (Orig.). (ps-2). 1994. 12.95 (*0-911019-95-2*); pap. 5.95 (*0-911019-94-4*) Warren Pub Hse.
Wells, Rosemary. Timothy Goes to School. Wells, Rosemary, illus. LC 80-20785. 32p. (ps-2). 1981. 13. 95 (*0-8037-8948-3*); PLB 11.89 (*0-8037-8949-1*) Dial Bks Young.
Wenk, Laurie P. Francine Pascal's Sweet Valley High Slam Book. (gr. 7 up). 1988. pap. 3.95 (*0-318-36514-6*) Bantam.
Young, Ginevra M. I Got My Report Card Today. LC 89-51084. (Illus.). 44p. (gr. k-3). 1990. pap. 5.95 (*1-55523-254-X*) Winston-Derek.
Zindel, Paul. The Fifth-Grade Safari. (gr. 4-7). 1993. pap. 3.50 (*0-553-48085-5*) Bantam.

STUDY, METHOD OF

see also Self-Culture;
also subjects with the subdivision Study and Teaching, e.g. Art–Study and Teaching; etc.

Adams, Kathleen. Family Homework. (ps-1). 1989. pap. 6.95 (*0-8224-3052-5*) Fearon Teach Aids.
American College Testing Program Staff. Study Power Leader's Guide. 99p. (Orig.). (gr. 7 up). 1987. tchr's. ed. 4.00 (*0-937734-63-2*) Am Coll Testing.
—Study Power, Managing Time & Environment. 30p. (Orig.). (gr. 7 up). 1987. wkbk. 1.00 (*0-937734-65-9*) Am Coll Testing.
—Study Power, Preparing for Tests. 14p. (Orig.). (gr. 7 up). 1987. wkbk. 1.00 (*0-937734-69-1*) Am Coll Testing.
—Study Power, Reading Textbooks. 21p. (Orig.). (gr. 7 up). 1987. wkbk. 1.00 (*0-937734-66-7*) Am Coll Testing.
—Study Power, Student Workbook Set. (Orig.). (gr. 7 up). 1987. wkbk. 5.00 (*0-937734-64-0*) Am Coll Testing.
—Study Power, Taking Class Notes. 22p. (Orig.). (gr. 7 up). 1987. wkbk. 1.00 (*0-937734-67-5*) Am Coll Testing.
—Study Power, Taking Tests. 13p. (Orig.). (gr. 7 up). 1987. wkbk. 1.00 (*0-937734-70-5*) Am Coll Testing.
—Study Power, Using Resources. 14p. (Orig.). (gr. 7 up). 1987. wkbk. 1.00 (*0-937734-68-3*) Am Coll Testing.
Bank Street College of Education Staff. Barron's Book of Fun & Learning. 384p. (gr. k). 1987. pap. 19.95 (*0-8120-3822-3*) Barron.
Bergreen, Gary. Coping with Study Strategies. rev. ed. (gr. 7-12). 1990. 14.95 (*0-8239-1140-3*) Rosen Group.
Berry, Marilyn. Help Is on the Way for Reading Skills. (Illus.). 48p. (gr. 4-6). 1987. pap. 4.95 (*0-516-43232-X*) Childrens.
Biener, Laurence, et al. How to Study Study Aid. 1978. pap. 2.50 (*0-317-64276-6*) Youth Ed.
Brown, William F. & Gadzella, Bernadette. Study Skills Test. 28p. (Orig.). 1987. pap. text ed. 3.50 (*1-881936-01-5*) WFB Ent.
Butler, Kathleen A. It's All in Your Mind! A Student's Guide to Learning Style. (Illus.). 96p. (Orig.). (gr. 7-12). 1988. pap. 12.95 (*0-945852-01-0*) Learners Dimension.
Christen, William & Murphy, Thomas. Smart Learning: A Study Skills Guide for Teens. Strother, Deborah B. & Strother, William C., eds. Coverly, Dave, illus. LC 91-48274. 120p. (Orig.). (gr. 6 up). 1992. pap. 10.95 (*0-9628556-5-0*) Grayson Bernard Pubs.
Coil, Carolyn. Becoming an Achiever: A Student Guide. (Illus.). 96p. (gr. 5 up). 1994. pap. 9.95 (*1-880505-07-X*) Pieces of Lrning.
Colman, Penny. One Hundred One Ways to Do Better in School. Bogan, Paulette, illus. LC 93-30872. 1993. pap. 2.95 (*0-8167-3285-X*) Troll Assocs.
Communication & Learning Center Staff. One Hundred Twenty-Five Ways to Be a Better Student: A Program for Study Skills Success. 1987. spiral reproducible wkbk. 27.95 (*1-55999-063-5*) LinguiSystems.
Cummings, Rhoda & Fisher, Gary. The School Survival Guide for Kids with LD (Learning Differences) Ways to Make Learning Easier & More Fun. LC 91-14489. (Illus.). 176p. (gr. 2 up). 1991. pap. 10.95 (*0-915793-32-6*) Free Spirit Pub.
Custer, Susan, et al. Smarts: A Study Skills Resource Guide. rev. ed. Oling, Tom, illus. (gr. 5-7). 1991. tchr's. ed. 11.95 (*0-944584-27-6*) Sopris.
De Ponce, Blanca N. La Aventura de Estudiar: Programa para Desarrollar Destrezas de Estudio e Informacion en el nivel Elemental e Intermedio. Figueroa, Ivelisse, illus. (SPA.). 100p. (Orig.). (gr. 5-9). 1984. write for info. B Ponce.
Dickinson, Lavona & Watts, Ramona. Storytime Learning. (ps). 1989. pap. 15.95 (*0-8224-6277-X*) Fearon Teach Aids.
Falkenberg, P. R. Fifteen Days to Study Power. 2nd ed. (Illus.). 378p. (Orig.). (gr. 7 up). 1985. pap. 12.95 (*0-939800-01-2*) Greencrest.
Feder, Chris W. Brain Quest: Grade 1. (gr. 1). 1992. pap. 9.95 (*1-56305-258-X*, 3258) Workman Pub.
—Brain Quest: Grade 2. (gr. 2). 1992. pap. 9.95 (*1-56305-259-8*, 3259) Workman Pub.
—Brain Quest: Grade 3. (gr. 3). 1992. pap. 9.95 (*1-56305-260-1*, 3260) Workman Pub.
—Brain Quest: Grade 4. (gr. 4). 1992. pap. 9.95 (*1-56305-261-X*, 3261) Workman Pub.
—Brain Quest, Grade 5. (gr. 5). 1992. pap. 9.95 (*1-56305-262-8*, 3262) Workman Pub.
—Brain Quest, Grade 6. (gr. 6). 1992. pap. 9.95 (*1-56305-263-6*, 3263) Workman Pub.
—Brain Quest, Grade 7. (gr. 7). 1992. pap. 9.95 (*1-56305-264-4*, 3264) Workman Pub.
Geoffrion, Sondra. Power Study to up Your Grades & Grade Point Average. LC 88-61283. 60p. (gr. 11 up). 1989. pap. 3.95 (*0-88247-787-0*) R & E Pubs.
Georgiady, Nicholas P. & Romano, Louis G. Focus on Study Habits at School. Dilley, Pamela A., illus. 15p. (Orig.). (gr. 6-8). pap. text ed. 3.00 (*0-918449-05-7*) MI Middle Educ.
Gerber, Carole. Master Study Skills Workbook Grade One. (ps-3) 1990. pap. 4.95 (*1-56189-051-0*) Amer Educ Pub.
—Master Study Skills Workbook Grade Three. (ps-3). 1990. pap. 4.95 (*1-56189-053-7*) Amer Educ Pub.
—Master Study Skills Workbook Grade Two. (ps-3). 1990. pap. 4.95 (*1-56189-052-9*) Amer Educ Pub.
Herr, Ted & Johnson, Ken. Problem Solving Strategies: Crossing the River with Dogs. (gr. 9-12). 1994. 24.95 (*1-55953-068-5*) Key Curr Pr.
—Problem Solving Strategies: Crossing the River with Dogs. (gr. 9-12). 1994. Tchr's. resource bk. & answer key. 19.95 (*1-55953-069-3*) Key Curr Pr.
Heun, Joseph H. Graduate High School - A Formula for Success. LC 91-71723. (Illus.). 150p. (gr. 10). 1991. pap. 19.95 (*0-9629317-0-5*) Ace Pub Prodns.
Hubbard, L. Ron, concept by. Learning How to Learn. 190p. (gr. 3-7). 1992. 34.99 (*0-88404-771-7*) Bridge Pubns Inc.
—Study Skills for Life. 128p. (gr. 7-10). 1992. 34.99 (*0-88404-744-X*) Bridge Pubns Inc.
James, Elizabeth & Barkin, Carol. How to Be School Smart: Secrets of Successful Schoolwork. Doty, Roy, photos by. Greenlaw, M. Jean, intro. by. LC 87-2899. (Illus.). (gr. 4-7). 1988. lib. bdg. 12.93 (*0-688-06799-9*) Lothrop.
—How to Be School Smart: Secrets of Successful Schoolwork. Doty, Roy, illus. LC 87-2899. 96p. (gr. 4 up). 1988. pap. 6.95 (*0-688-06798-0*, Pub. by Beech Tree Bks) Morrow.
Kells, Elizabeth C. Taking Notes in the Classroom: A Guide to Higher Grades, Preparation for Exams, Reduced Study Time, Less Stress. (Orig.). (gr. 10-12). 1993. pap. text ed. 7.95 (*0-9634458-7-1*) Pubs Northeast.
Kesselman-Turkel, Judi & Peterson, Franklynn. Study Smarts: How to Learn More in Less Time. 64p. 1981. pap. 7.93 (*0-8092-5852-8*) Contemp Bks.
Lafferty, Jerry. Learning Power: A Student's Guide to Success. Moore, Melissa, ed. Foss, Debbie, illus. LC 92-72769. 138p. (Orig.). (gr. 7-12). 1993. Incl. six audio cass. pap. 34.95 (*1-881843-29-7*) Alpha Educ Inst.
Learning Forum Staff. Study Skills Set. (gr. 8-12). 1989. 130.00 (*0-945525-13-3*) Supercamp.
McCutcheon, Randall J. Get off My Brain: A Survival Guide for Lazy Students. Wagner, Pete, illus. LC 84-82166. 120p. (gr. 9 up). 1985. pap. 8.95 (*0-915793-02-4*) Free Spirit Pub.
McInerney, Claire. Tracking the Facts: How to Develop Research Skills. Pulver, Harry, illus. 64p. (gr. 4 up). 1990. PLB 14.95 (*0-8225-2426-0*) Lerner Pubns.
Mancuso, Robert A. Question the Direction: A Program for Teaching Careful Listening & the Questioning of Unclear Directions. (gr. 1-7). 1988. manual & reproducible wkbk. 29.95 (*1-55999-065-1*) LinguiSystems.
Mangrum, Charles T., II. Learning to Study, Bks. B-C. 2nd ed. 80p. (gr. 2-3). 1994. pap. 8.00 (*0-89061-725-2*); tchr's. guide 3.95 (*0-89061-732-5*) Jamestown Pubs.
—Learning to Study, Bk. D. 2nd ed. 80p. (gr. 4). 1994. pap. 8.00 (*0-89061-726-0*); tchr's. guide 3.95 (*0-89061-733-3*) Jamestown Pubs.

—Learning to Study, Bk. E. 2nd ed. 96p. (gr. 5). 1994. pap. 8.00 (*0-89061-727-9*); tchr's. guide 3.95 (*0-89061-734-1*) Jamestown Pubs.
—Learning to Study, Bk. F. 2nd ed. 96p. (gr. 6). 1994. pap. 8.00 (*0-89061-728-7*); tchr's. guide 3.95 (*0-89061-735-X*) Jamestown Pubs.
—Learning to Study, Bk. G. 2nd ed. 96p. (gr. 7). 1994. pap. 8.00 (*0-89061-729-5*); tchr's. guide 3.95 (*0-89061-736-8*) Jamestown Pubs.
—Learning to Study, Bk. H. 2nd ed. 96p. (gr. 8). 1994. pap. 8.00 (*0-89061-730-9*); tchr's. guide 3.95 (*0-89061-737-6*) Jamestown Pubs.
—Learning to Study, 6 bks, Bks.B-H. 2nd ed. (gr. 2-8). 1994. Set. pap. 48.00 (*0-89061-724-4*); tchr's. guide 23.70 (*0-89061-731-7*) Jamestown Pubs.
Marsh, Carole. Sorta Silly, Smart-Aleck Study Tips Even Teens Will Like. (gr. 7-12). 1994. PLB 24.95 (*0-7933-7352-2*); pap. 14.95 (*0-7933-7353-0*); computer disk 29.95 (*0-7933-7354-9*) Gallopade Pub Group.
Marshall, Brian. The Secret of Getting Straight A's: Learn More in Less Time with Little Effort. Ferguson, Bill, illus. 182p. (Orig.). (gr. 8 up). 1993. pap. 12.95 (*0-9633357-9-0*) Hathaway Intl.
Martin, Sidney & McMillan, Dana. Learning Ideas Through the Year. 112p. (gr. 2-6). 1989. 9.95 (*0-912107-91-X*, MM1908) Monday Morning Bks.
Mayo, Patty, et al. Study Smart. Madsen, Kris, illus. 59p. (gr. 5-12). 1990. bd. game 39.00 (*0-930599-64-0*) Thinking Pubns.
Mengel, Gail E. The Homework Organizer: Assignment Notebook & Guide. 92p. (gr. 7-12). 1991. 9.95 (*0-9631705-0-3*) Get Organized.
Moran, John, et al. Term Paper Study Aids. 1986. pap. 2.25 (*0-87738-025-2*) Youth Ed.

Murphy, Marsha A. Secrets of Making A's the Easy SpeedLearning Way: Powerful Learning Tools & Study Techniques Revealed. LC 92-75555. (Illus., Orig.). Date not set. Incl. audio tape. pap. 59.95 (*0-9635508-0-2*) DataQuest VA.
The author has coupled a learning resource guide & explanatory audio tape into a "LEARNING KIT" containing richly-informative tips for students of all ages on actually HOW to learn what they are INSTRUCTED to learn. These techniques are useful & adaptable for school, business & all life-long learners. In addition to the multitude of learning & memory techniques graphically explained & simplified here for easy understanding & instant application, there are also chapters included on organization of information, spelling, grammar, writing, reading comprehension, math shortcuts, library usage, study & relaxation tips, test-taking strategies, & speed-reading. Audio, visual, & tactile/kinesthetic techniques are clearly explained, showing students how to learn by circumventing rote memory alone. Mind pictures & mental movies are some of the powerful learning tools described here. These techniques are easy, fun, & will dramatically shorten learning time. Although this three-part guide is divided into sections generally applicable to different age groups, all students will find valuable information in each section. The text is lavishly illustrated & specially formatted for easy readability & understanding. TO ORDER: write DataQuest, P.O. Box 62692, Virginia Beach, VA 23466. ***Publisher Provided Annotation.***

Oudheusden, Susan. Go for It! A Student's Guide to Independent Projects. 75p. (gr. 3-9). pap. 14.95 (*0-936386-51-7*) Creative Learning.
Page, Andrea C. Student Success Tutor Directory: Sarasota & Manatee County Edition, 1991-92. (Illus.). 64p. (gr. k-12). 1991. pap. write for info. Computer Pr.
Paterra, Mary E. Cambridge Stratford Study Skills Course, 20 Hour Edition. (Illus.). 196p. (gr. 6-8). 1986. tchr's. ed. 64.95 (*0-935637-03-6*); wkbk. 12.95 (*0-935637-02-8*); transparency set 60.00 (*0-935637-00-1*); listening tape set 40.00 (*0-935637-01-X*) Cambridge Strat.
—Cambridge Stratford Study Skills Course, 30 Hour Edition. (Illus.). (gr. 9-11). 1986. tchr's. ed. 64.95 (*0-935637-07-9*); wkbk. 12.95 (*0-935637-06-0*); transparency set 120.00 (*0-935637-04-4*); listening tape set 40.00 (*0-935637-05-2*) Cambridge Strat.
Peters, Max & Shostak, Jerome. How to Prepare for Catholic High School Entrance Examinations - COOP & HSPT. 576p. 1992. pap. 11.95 (*0-8120-4955-1*) Barron.
Quackenbush, Ross & Gastineau, Jerrel. Homework? My Locker Ate It! An Effective Method for Parents to Help Their Student Study at Home & Improve in School. Thiesies, Darlene, illus. 143p. (Orig.). (gr. 6-12). 1988. pap. 19.95 (*0-9621701-0-0*) CWP.
Rohrer, Doug. More Thought Provokers. (gr. 9-12). 1994. 9.95 (*1-55953-070-7*) Key Curr Pr.
Rooney, Robert & Lipuma, Anthony. Learn to Be the Master Student: How to Develop Self-Confidence & Effective Study Skills. De Silva, Jessica, illus. LC 92-80281. 248p. (Orig.). (gr. 9-12). 1992. pap. 14.95 (*0-9632530-8-5*) Maydale Pub.
San Fillipo, Patrick R. A Study Workout for Sixth, Seventh, Eighth Graders, Pt. One: A Workout for the Mind. 26p. (gr. 6-8). 1991. wkbk. incls. video 34.95 (*0-9630443-1-1*); wkbk. 11.95 (*0-9630443-0-3*) Educ Excell Via.
Schroeder, Linda M. Becoming Excellent Students Today: Academic Organizer. 102p. (gr. 9-12). Date not set. pap. text ed. 6.95 (*1-883583-01-2*) Gratitude Pub.
—Becoming Excellent Students Today: Assignment Planner. 102p. (gr. 5-8). 1993. pap. text ed. 6.95 (*1-883583-00-4*) Gratitude Pub.
Schumm, Jeanne S. & Radencich, Marguerite. School Power: Strategies for Succeeding in School. Espeland, Pamela, ed. LC 92-10907. (Illus.). 130p. (Orig.). (gr. 5 up). 1992. pap. 11.95 (*0-915793-42-3*) Free Spirit Pub.
Schwartz, Linda. Study Skills Shortcake. 32p. (gr. 4-6). 1979. 3.95 (*0-88160-071-7*, LW 804) Learning Wks.
Sedita, Joan. Landmark Study Skills Guide. LC 89-27870. (Orig.). (gr. 4-12). 1989. pap. text ed. 15.00 (*0-9624119-0-6*) Landmark Found.
Shepherd, C. A., et al. The Sly Fox. (Orig.). (gr. 3-12). 1985. pap. 8.00 play script (*0-88734-503-4*) Players Pr.
Snodgrass, Jameward. Making the Most of School. (Illus.). 48p. (gr. 6-8). 1991. pap. 8.99 (*1-55945-113-0*) Group Pub.
Spainhower, Steven D. School Smart: Behaviors & Skills for Student Success, 93-94. Wilson, Dana & Brown, Steven J., eds. (Illus.). 205p. (Orig.). (gr. 7-12). 1993. pap. text ed. 18.95 (*0-9637573-0-X*) Education Res.
Starbuck, Marnie. The Gladimals Learn to Be Good Students. (Illus.). 16p. 1990. 0.75 (*1-56456-208-5*, 478) W Gladden Found.
Taylor, Mildred G. How to Write a Research Paper. LC 71-180899. (Illus.). 55p. (Orig.). (gr. 7-12). 1974. pap. 1.75 (*0-87015-206-8*) Pacific Bks.
Trent, Linda M. Games That Make Homework Fun! 80p. (Orig.). (gr. 2-8). 1991. pap. 9.95 (*0-9630470-2-7*) For-Kids.
Ulrich, Cindy & Guild, Pat. No Sweat! How to Use Your Learning Style to Be a Better Student. Craig, Dorothy, ed. Hall, Mary A., illus. 52p. (gr. 8-12). 1986. wkbk. 5.95 (*0-317-92552-0*) Teaching Advisory.
Vodraska, Cynthia L. & Vodraska, Kenneth F. Study Skills: Out-Line Format Reference Manual. 175p. (gr. 7-12). 1992. 3-ring binder 36.00 (*0-9632356-0-5*) OLF Pub Co.
Windsor, Laura. Beating the Term Paper Deadline: A Student Guide to Getting Help at the Library - in Record Time. 24p. (Orig.). (ps-12). 1990. 4.95 (*0-918734-34-7*) Reymont.
Wirths, Claudine G. & Bowman-Kruhm, Mary. How to Get up When Schoolwork Gets You Down. LC 93-3050. 1993. pap. 5.99 (*0-7814-0118-6*, Chariot Bks) Chariot Family.
World Book Editors. The World Book Learning Library, 7 vols. rev. ed. LC 89-51413. (Illus.). 896p. (gr. 6-9). 1990. Set. write for info. (*0-7166-3222-5*) World Bk.
World Book Editors, ed. The World Book of Study Power, 2 vols. LC 93-61400. (Illus.). 592p. (gr. 7-12). 1994. Set. PLB write for info. (*0-7166-3594-1*) World Bk.
Young, Ralph C. The Better Grades Handbook. (Illus.). 92p. (Orig.). (gr. 6-11). 1991. pap. text ed. 8.95 (*0-9631476-0-9*) RCY Design.
Zakalik, Leslie S. Study Skills Sorcery. 48p. (gr. 4-6). 1978. 5.95 (*0-88160-028-8*, LW 213) Learning Wks.

STYLE, LITERARY
see also Criticism; Letter Writing; Literature–History and Criticism; Rhetoric

STYLE IN DRESS
see Costume; Fashion

SUBCONSCIOUS
see also Dreams; Hypnotism; Mind and Body; Psychoanalysis; Sleep; Thought Transference

SUBMARINE CABLES
see Cables, Submarine

SUBMARINE DIVING
see Skin Diving

SUBMARINE EXPLORATION
see Underwater Exploration

SUBMARINE GEOLOGY
Arnold, Caroline. A Walk on the Great Barrier Reef. (Illus.). 48p. (gr. 2-5). 1988. PLB 19.95 (*0-87614-285-4*) Carolrhoda Bks.

SUBMARINE TELEGRAPH
see Cables, Submarine

SUBMARINE WARFARE
see also Submarines
Swanson, June. David Bushnell & His Turtle: The Story of America's First Submarine. Eagle, Mike, illus. LC 90-628. 40p. (gr. 2-5). 1991. SBE 13.95 (*0-689-31628-3*, Atheneum Child Bk) Macmillan Child Grp.

SUBMARINES
Baker, David. Anti-Submarine Warfare. 48p. (gr. 3-8). 1989. lib. bdg. 18.60 (*0-86592-532-1*) Rourke Corp.
Gibbons, Tony. Submarines. Gibbons, Tony, et al, illus. 48p. (gr. 5 up). 1987. PLB 14.95 (*0-8225-1383-8*, First Ave Edns); pap. 4.95 (*0-8225-9542-7*, First Ave Edns) Lerner Pubns.
Grady, Sean M. Submarines: Probing the Ocean Depths. LC 93-20628. (gr. 5-8). 1994. 15.95 (*1-56006-227-4*) Lucent Bks.
How Do Submarines Dive? 1991. 3.99 (*0-517-05893-6*) Random Hse Value.
Humble, Richard. A World War Two Submarine. Bergin, Mark, illus. 48p. (gr. 5 up). 1991. 17.95 (*0-87226-351-7*) P Bedrick Bks.
Maynard, Christopher. The Deepsea Sub. LC 93-41691. 1995. 8.95 (*1-85697-510-X*, Kingfisher LKC) LKC.
—Submarines. LC 94-640. 32p. (gr. 2-5). 1994. 3.95 (*1-85697-508-8*, Kingfisher LKC) LKC.
Petersen, David. Submarines. LC 83-26253. (Illus.). 48p. (gr. k-4). 1984. PLB 12.85 (*0-516-01728-4*) Childrens.
Rawlinson, J. Hunter-Killer Submarines. (Illus.). 48p. (gr. 3-8). 1989. lib. bdg. 18.60 (*0-86625-086-7*); 13.95s.p. (*0-685-58644-8*) Rourke Corp.
Submarines. (Illus.). 64p. (gr. 3-9). 1990. PLB 16.95 (*1-85435-116-8*) Marshall Cavendish.
Wagenman, Mark A. Atlantis the Submarine: Coloring & Activity Book. Wagenman, Mark A., illus. 24p. (ps-k). 1990. pap. 2.95 (*0-89610-168-1*) Island Heritage.
Weiss, Harvey. Submarines & Other Underwater Craft. Weiss, Harvey, illus. LC 89-37614. 64p. (gr. 3-7). 1990. (Crowell Jr Bks); PLB 12.89 (*0-690-04761-4*, Crowell Jr Bks) HarpC Child Bks.
White, D. Submarines. (Illus.). 48p. (gr. 3-8). 1989. PLB 18.60 (*0-86592-452-X*) Rourke Corp.

SUBMARINES–FICTION
Anderson, Joan. Sally's Submarine. Ancona, George, contrib. by. LC 94-16644. (gr. 4-7). Date not set. write for info. (*0-688-12690-1*); PLB write for info. (*0-688-12691-X*) Morrow Jr Bks.
Fowler, R. Ted & Dolly's Submarine. (Illus.). 20p. 1991. text ed. 9.95 (*0-88110-569-4*, Usborne) EDC.
Lawhead, Steve. Howard Had a Submarine. (Illus.). 32p. (gr. 1 up). 1987. pap. 7.99 (*0-7459-1179-X*) Lion USA.
McOmber, Rachel B., ed. McOmber Phonics Storybooks: The Sub. rev. ed. (Illus.). write for info. (*0-944991-22-X*) Swift Lrn Res.
Melendez, Francisco. The Mermaid & the Major: or, the True Story of the Invention of the Submarine. Melendez, Francisco, illus. 64p. 1991. 24.95 (*0-8109-3619-4*) Abrams.
Roddy, Lee. Secret of the Sunken Sub. 160p. (Orig.). (gr. 3-6). 1990. pap. 4.99 (*0-929608-63-1*) Focus Family.
Verne, Jules. Reader's Digest Best Loved Books for Young Readers: Twenty Thousand Leagues under the Sea. Ogburn, Jackie, ed. Hildibrand, illus. 176p. (gr. 4-12). 1989. 3.99 (*0-945260-29-6*) Choice Pub NY.
—Twenty Thousand Leagues under the Sea. (gr. 8 up). 1964. pap. 3.25 (*0-8049-0012-4*, CL-12) Airmont.
—Twenty Thousand Leagues under the Sea. new ed. Binder, Otto, ed. Gamboa, Romy & Patricio, Ernie, illus. LC 73-75466. 64p. (Orig.). (gr. 5-10). 1973. pap. 2.95 (*0-88301-104-2*); student activity bk. 1.25 (*0-88301-180-8*) Pendulum Pr.
—Twenty Thousand Leagues under the Sea. Butz, Steve, illus. Nordlicht, Lillian, adapted by. LC 79-23887. 48p. (gr. 4 up). 1983. PLB 20.70 (*0-8172-1652-9*) Raintree Steck-V.
—Twenty Thousand Leagues under the Sea. (gr. 4-7). 1993. pap. 4.95 (*0-8114-6846-1*) Raintree Steck-V.

SUBURBAN HOMES
see Architecture, Domestic

SUBVERSIVE ACTIVITIES
see also Political Crimes and Offenses; Spies

SUBWAYS
Yepsen, Roger. City Trains: Moving Through America's Cities by Rail. Yepsen, Roger, illus. LC 92-2395. 96p. (gr. 3-7). 1993. SBE 14.95 (*0-02-793675-9*, Macmillan Child Bk) Macmillan Child Grp.

SUBWAYS–FICTION
Bahar, Mehrdad. Bastoor. new & rev. ed. Jabbari, Ahmad, ed. Alyeshmreni, Mansoor, tr. from PER. LC 83-60451. (Illus.). 32p. (Orig.). (gr. 1 up). 1983. pap. 4.95 (*0-939214-17-2*) Mazda Pubs.
Crifasi, Kathleen. Woodley Rides the Subway Train. LC 87-62212. 54p. (ps-4). 1987. pap. 6.95 (*0-932433-30-8*) Windswept Hse.
Gabhart, Ann. Wish Come True. 160p. (gr. 7 up). 1988. pap. 2.50 (*0-380-75653-6*, Flare) Avon.
Holman, Felice. Slake's Limbo. LC 74-11675. 126p. (gr. 4-8). 1974. RSBE 14.95 (*0-684-13926-X*, Scribners Young Read) Macmillan Child Grp.
—Slake's Limbo. LC 85-26795. 128p. (gr. 6 up). 1986. pap. 3.95 (*0-689-71066-6*, Aladdin) Macmillan Child Grp.
New York Transit Museum Staff. I've Been Working on the Subway: The Folklore & Oral History of Transit. Webb, William, illus. 54p. (Orig.). (gr. 5-10). 1991. pap. 5.00 incl. curriculum guide (*0-9637492-9-3*) NY Transit Mus.

Rush, Ken. Friday's Journey. LC 93-4871. (Illus.). 1994. write for info. (*0-531-06821-8*); lib. bdg. write for info. (*0-531-08671-2*) Orchard Bks Watts.

Torres, Leyla. Subway Sparrow. LC 92-55104. (ENG, SPA & POL.). 1993. 15.00 (*0-374-37285-3*) FS&G.

SUCCESS

see also Business; Leadership

Aaseng, Nathan. Close Calls: From the Brink of Ruin to Business Success. (Illus.). 80p. (gr. 5 up). 1990. PLB 18.95 (*0-8225-0682-3*) Lerner Pubns.

Alger, Horatio, Jr. Struggling Upward. 1971. Fasc. 6.95 (*0-87874-005-8*, Nautilus) Galloway.

Appleton, C. M. Steve Urkel's Super-Cool Guide to Success! (Illus.). 64p. (gr. 3-8). 1992. pap. 2.95 (*0-590-45744-6*) Scholastic Inc.

Bode, Janet. Beating the Odds: Stories of Unexpected Achievers. LC 91-14215. 144p. (gr. 9-12). 1991. PLB 14.40 (*0-531-10985-2*) Watts.

Brooks, B. David & Paull, Robert C. How to Be Successful in Less Than Ten Minutes a Day. 180p. (gr. 7 up). 1991. tchr's. ed. 65.00 (*0-938308-11-4*); wkbk. 65.00 (*0-685-20975-X*) T Jefferson Ctr.

Brown, H. Jackson, Jr. Life's Little Treasure Book on Success. 96p. (gr. 6 up). 1994. 4.95 (*1-55853-280-3*) Rutledge Hill Pr.

Buhay, Debra. Black & White of Success. 30p. (gr. 12). 1990. pap. 2.00 (*1-878056-01-8*) D Hockenberry.

Cherry, Charles W., II. Excellence Without Excuse: The Black Student's Guide to Academic Excellence. LC 91-35248. (gr. 7 up). 1993. 24.95 (*1-56385-497-X*); pap. 13.95 (*1-56385-498-8*) Intl Schol Pr.

Conway, L. M. Goal Getters. 48p. (gr. 3-7). 1984. 5.95 (*0-88160-105-5*, LW 245) Learning Wks.

Conwell, Russell H. Acres of Diamonds: All Good Things Are Possible, Right Where You Are, & Now! Leonardo, Bianca, ed. 160p. (gr. 8-12). 1993. pap. text ed. 10.95 (*0-930852-25-7*) Tree Life Pubns.

Crystal Clarity Staff. Little Secrets of Success. (gr. 4-7). 1993. 5.95 (*1-56589-603-3*) Crystal Clarity.

David, Ward S. Ask Not for Victory. Grant, Wilda L., ed. Stein, August, illus. 234p. (Orig.). (gr. 8-12). 1991. pap. 9.95 (*0-9630883-3-5*) W S David.

DeVenzio, Richard. Smart Moves: How to Succeed in School, Sports, Career & Life. 293p. (gr. 6-12). 1989. pap. 15.95 (*0-87975-546-6*) Prometheus Bks.

Lena, Dan & Lena, Marie. My Power Book. (Illus.). 60p. 1991. wkbk. 10.00 (*0-9617032-0-2*) D & M Lena.

Longheed, L. Business Small Talk: Five Steps to Success. 1995. pap. text ed. 12.00 (*0-201-54261-7*); write for info cassette (*0-201-54262-5*) Longman.

McDiarmid, T. Making Money. (Illus.). 48p. (gr. 2-6). 1988. pap. 5.95 (*0-88625-152-4*) Durkin Hayes Pub.

Mandino, Og. Og Mandino's Great Trilogy. 1993. 12.98 (*0-8119-0428-8*) Lifetime.

Martin. Reaching Your Goal, 8 bks, Set I, Reading Level 2. (Illus.). 192p. (gr. 1-4). 1987. Set. PLB 116.80 (*0-86592-166-0*); 87.60s.p. (*0-685-58796-7*) Rourke Corp.

Mascola, et al. Reaching Your Goal, 8 bks, Set II, Reading Level 2. (Illus.). 192p. (gr. 1-4). 1989. Set. PLB 116.80 (*0-86592-425-2*); 87.60s.p. (*0-685-58797-5*) Rourke Corp.

Menzies, Linda, et al. A Teen's Guide to Business: The Secrets to a Successful Enterprise. large type ed. LC 93-30254. (gr. 9-12). 1993. 15.95 (*0-7862-0061-8*) Thorndike Pr.

Ormondroyd, Edward. Johnny Castleseed. Thewlis, Diana, illus. LC 85-8189. 32p. (gr. k-3). 1988. 12.95 (*0-395-38355-2*); pap. 4.80 (*0-395-47947-9*) HM.

Peet, Bill. The Luckiest One of All. Peet, Bill, illus. (gr. k-3). 1982. 14.95 (*0-395-31863-7*); pap. 4.80 (*0-395-39593-3*) HM.

Riley, Sue. Success. LC 77-20992. (SPA & ENG., Illus.). (ps-2). 1978. 12.95 (*0-89565-016-9*) Childs World.

Roets, Lois S. Understanding Success & Failure. 36p. (gr. 5 up). 1985. 8.00 (*0-911943-07-2*) Leadership Pubs.

Rolliet, D. G. Your Name & Colors: Secret Keys to Your Beauty, Personality, & Success, the Rolliett Letter-Color Theory. Reanult, Michael & Wolf, Jeannie, eds. Sherwood, Ed, illus. LC 89-91991. 192p. (Orig.). 1990. pap. text ed. 12.95 (*0-9621693-0-7*) Spectra Pubns Hse.

Rutkovsky, Paul. Get. Rutkovsky, Paul, illus. 72p. (Orig.). (gr. 9-12). 1987. pap. 8.95 (*0-89822-048-3*) Visual Studies.

Schlachter, Rita. Good Luck, Bad Luck. Karas, G. Brian, illus. LC 85-14069. 48p. (Orig.). (gr. 1-3). 1986. PLB 10.59 (*0-8167-0572-0*); pap. text ed. 3.50 (*0-8167-0573-9*) Troll Assocs.

Schulman, Janet. The Great Big Dummy. Hoban, Lillian, illus. 32p. (gr. 1-3). 1961. pap. 2.50 (*0-440-43072-0*, YB) Dell.

Seltzer, Joan. Go for It! 62p. (gr. 5-12). 1981. pap. 5.95 (*0-9607732-1-5*); write for info. tchr's ed.; write for info. wkbk. Jory Pubns.

Shea, Richard. The Book of Success. LC 93-30087. 192p. 1993. 12.95 (*1-55853-254-4*) Rutledge Hill Pr.

Symonds, Martha. Think Big. 76p. (gr. 4-6). 1977. 7.95 (*0-88160-024-5*, LW 209) Learning Wks.

Terry, Jim & Terry, Mary. Soaring to the Top: The Success Manual for Young Adults. 300p. 1988. pap. 8.95 (*0-931731-07-0*) Jimar Prodns.

Youngs, Bettie B. & Tracy, Brian S. Achievement, Popularity, & Success: Getting What You Want from Life. 276p. (Orig.). (gr. 6-12). 1988. pap. 12.95 (*0-317-89982-1*) Phoenix Educ Found.

SUFFRAGE

see also classes of people with the subdivision Suffrage, e.g. Women–Suffrage; etc.

SUGAR

Cobb, Vicki. Gobs of Goo. Schatell, Brian, illus. LC 82-48457. 40p. (gr. 1-3). 1983. (Lipp Jr Bks); PLB 13.89 (*0-397-32022-1*) HarpC Child Bks.

Nottridge, Rhoda. Sugar. Yeats, John, illus. 32p. (gr. 1-4). 1990. PLB 14.95 (*0-87614-418-0*) Carolrhoda Bks.

—Sugars. LC 92-21414. 1993. PLB 14.95 (*0-87614-796-1*); pap. 5.95 (*0-87614-611-6*) Carolrhoda Bks.

Wittstock, Laura W. Ininatig's Gift of Sugar: Traditional Native Sugarmaking. Kakkak, Dale, photos by. Dorris, Michael, frwd. by. LC 92-37980. (Illus.). 48p. 1993. 19.95 (*0-8225-2653-0*) Lerner Pubns.

—Ininatig's Gift of Sugar: Traditional Native Sugarmaking. 48p. (gr. 4-7). 1993. pap. 6.95 (*0-8225-9642-3*) Lerner Pubns.

SUGIMOTO, ETSU (INAGAKI) 1874-1950

Sugimoto, Etsu I. Daughter of the Samurai. LC 66-15849. (gr. 9 up). 1966. pap. 14.95 (*0-8048-1655-7*) C E Tuttle.

SUICIDE

Ayer, Eleanor. Teen Suicide: Is It Too Painful to Grow Up? (Illus.). 64p. (gr. 5-8). 1993. PLB 14.95 (*0-8050-2573-1*) TFC Bks NY.

Colman, Warren. Understanding & Preventing Teen Suicide. LC 90-1400. (Illus.). 48p. (gr. k-4). 1990. pap. 6.95 (*0-516-40594-2*) Childrens.

Copeland Lewis, Cynthia. Teen Suicide: Too Young to Die. LC 93-25010. (Illus.). 128p. (gr. 6 up). 1994. lib. bdg. 17.95 (*0-89490-433-7*) Enslow Pubs.

Crook, Marion. Teenagers Talk about Suicide. 128p. (gr. 7-12). 1988. pap. 12.95 (*1-55021-013-0*, Pub. by NC Press CN) U of Toronto Pr.

Dolce, Laura. Suicide. (Illus.). 112p. (gr. 6-12). 1992. 18.95 (*0-7910-0053-2*) Chelsea Hse.

Faulk, Tim. What Causes Our Teens to Take Their Lives? Dying to Live. 80p. (Orig.). (gr. 9 up). 1989. pap. text ed. 5.95 (*0-685-29873-6*) T Faulk Ministries.

Flanders, Stephen A. Suicide. 240p. (gr. 9-12). 1991. 22.95x (*0-8160-1909-6*) Facts on File.

Francis, Dorothy B. Suicide, a Preventable Tragedy. LC 88-26856. 144p. (gr. 7 up). 1989. 13.95 (*0-525-67279-6*, Lodestar Bks) Dutton Child Bks.

Frankel, Bernard & Kranz, Rachel. Straight Talk about Teenage Suicide. Ryan, Elizabeth A., ed. LC 93-38381. 128p. (gr. 7-12). 1994. 16.95x (*0-8160-2987-3*) Facts on File.

Galas, Judith. Teen Suicide. LC 93-11081. 1994. 14.95 (*1-56006-148-0*) Lucent Bks.

Gardner, Sandra & Rosenberg, Gary B. Teenage Suicide. LC 85-14277. 160p. (gr. 7 up). 1986. lib. bdg. 11.98 (*0-671-49975-0*, J Messner); pap. 4.95 (*0-671-63241-8*) S&S Trade.

—Teenage Suicide. rev. ed. (Illus.). 128p. (gr. 7 up). 1990. lib. bdg. 13.98 (*0-671-70200-9*, J Messner); pap. 5.95 (*0-671-70201-7*) S&S Trade.

Hyde, Margaret O. & Forsyth, Elizabeth H. Suicide. 3rd, updated ed. LC 90-46872. (Illus.). 160p. (gr. 9-12). 1991. PLB 14.40 (*0-531-11003-6*) Watts.

Kolehmainen, Janet & Handwerk, Sandra. Teen Suicide: A Book for Friends, Family, & Classmates. 72p. (gr. 7 up). 1986. PLB 15.95 (*0-8225-0037-X*, First Ave Edns); pap. 4.95 (*0-8225-9514-1*, First Ave Edns) Lerner Pubns.

Kuklin, Susan. Surviving Suicide: Young People Speak Up. LC 93-33141. (Illus.). 128p. (gr. 7 up). 1994. 15.95 (*0-399-22605-2*, Putnam); pap. 8.95 (*0-399-22801-2*) Putnam Pub Group.

Langone, John J. Dead End: A Book about Suicide. LC 85-25620. (gr. 6 up). 1986. 14.95 (*0-316-51432-2*) Little.

Leder, Jane M. Dead Serious: A Book for Teenagers about Teenage Suicide. LC 86-25880. 160p. (gr. 7 up). 1987. SBE 14.95 (*0-689-31262-8*, Atheneum Child Bk) Macmillan Child Grp.

—Dead Serious: A Book for Teenagers about Teenage Suicide. 160p. (gr. 7 up). 1989. pap. 3.50 (*0-380-70661-X*, Flare) Avon.

McGuire, Leslie. Suicide. (Illus.). 64p. (gr. 7 up). 1990. lib. bdg. 17.27 (*0-86593-069-4*); lib. bdg. 12.95s.p. (*0-685-46444-X*) Rourke Corp.

Madison, Arnold. Suicide & Young People. LC 77-13240. 144p. (gr. 6 up). 1979. (Clarion Bks); (Clarion) HM.

Miller, Michael. Dare to Live: A Guide to the Prevention & Understanding of Teenage Suicide & Depression. (gr. 7-12). 1989. pap. 9.95 (*0-941831-22-1*) Beyond Words Pub.

Nelson, Richard E. & Galas, Judith. The Power to Prevent Suicide: A Guide for Teens Helping Teens. Espeland, Pamela, ed. Olofsdotter, Marie, illus. LC 94-5594. 160p. (Orig.). (gr. 6 up). 1994. pap. 11.95 (*0-915793-70-9*) Free Spirit Pub.

Norton, Yuri E. Dear Uncle Dave. Waring, Shirley B., photos by. (Illus.). 40p. (Orig.). (gr. 1 up). 1993. PLB 13.95 (*0-9622808-4-4*) S&T Waring.

Powell, Donalyn. A Reason to Live. 160p. (Orig.). (gr. 9 up). 1989. pap. 6.99 (*1-55661-076-9*) Bethany Hse.

Rosenthal, Howard. Not with My Life I Don't: Preventing Your Suicide & That of Others. LC 88-70011. vi, 266p. (gr. 9 up). 1988. pap. text ed. 18.95 (*0-915202-77-8*) Accel Devel.

Schliefer, Jay. Everything You Need to Know about Teen Suicide. rev. ed. (Illus.). 64p. (gr. 7 up). 1993. PLB 14.95 (*0-8239-1612-X*) Rosen Group.

Smith, Judie. Coping with Suicide. rev. ed. LC 86-10076. 128p. (gr. 7-12). 1990. PLB 14.95 (*0-8239-1052-0*) Rosen Group.

Stewart, Gail. Teen Suicide. LC 88-20281. (Illus.). 48p. (gr. 5-6). 1988. text ed. 12.95 RSBE (*0-89686-413-8*, Crestwood Hse) Macmillan Child Grp.

Wilde, Gary. Suicide: The Silent Epidemic. (Illus.). 48p. (gr. 6-8). 1992. pap. 8.99 (*1-55945-145-9*) Group Pub.

SUICIDE–FICTION

Arrick, Fran. Tunnel Vision. 176p. (gr. 7 up). 1981. (LE); tchr's. guide by Lou Stanck 0.50 (*0-685-01410-X*) Dell.

Azaad, Meyer. The Tale of Ringy. Ghanoonparvar, Mohammad R. & Wilcox, Diane L., trs. from PER. Haqiqat, Nahid, illus. 24p. (Orig.). (gr. 3 up). 1983. pap. 4.95 (*0-686-43078-6*) Mazda Pubs.

Bunting, Eve. Face at the Edge of the World. LC 85-2684. 192p. (gr. 7 up). 1985. (Clarion Bks); pap. 6.95 (*0-89919-800-7*) HM.

Cannon, Bettie. A Bellsong for Sarah Raines. LC 87-4299. 192p. (gr. 7 up). 1987. 14.95 (*0-684-18839-2*, Scribners Young Read) Macmillan Child Grp.

Garland, Sherry. I Never Knew Your Name. Greenberg, Sheldon, illus. LC 93-23703. 32p. (gr. k-3). 1994. 14.95 (*0-395-69686-0*) Ticknor & Fields.

Gerson, Corinne. Passing Through. 208p. (gr. 8 up). 1980. pap. 1.50 (*0-440-96958-1*, LFL) Dell.

Grant, Cynthia D. Phoenix Rising: or How to Survive Your Life. LC 88-7370. 160p. 1989. SBE 13.95 (*0-689-31458-2*, Atheneum Child Bk) Macmillan Child Grp.

Hahn, Mary D. The Wind Blows Backwards. large type ed. LC 93-31870. (gr. 9-12). 1993. 15.95 (*0-7862-0064-2*) Thorndike Pr.

Irwin, Hadley. So Long at the Fair. LC 88-12813. 208p. (gr. 9 up). 1988. SBE 14.95 (*0-689-50454-3*, M K McElderry) Macmillan Child Grp.

McDaniel, Lurlene. So Much to Live For. 160p. (gr. 5-8). 1991. pap. 2.99 (*0-685-57448-2*) Willowisp Pr.

Mori, Kyoko. Shizuko's Daughter. LC 92-26956. 256p. (gr. 7 up). 1993. 15.95 (*0-8050-2557-X*, Bks Young Read) H Holt & Co.

Nunes, Lygia B. My Friend the Painter. Pontiero, Giovanni, tr. from POR. 85p. (gr. 3-7). 1991. 13.95 (*0-15-256340-7*) HarBrace.

Tapp, Kathy K. The Sacred Circle of the Hula Hoop. LC 88-27369. 208p. (gr. 6-9). 1989. SBE 14.95 (*0-689-50461-6*, M K McElderry) Macmillan Child Grp.

Thompson, Julian F. The Fling. LC 93-33812. 1994. 15.95 (*0-8050-2881-1*) H Holt & Co.

SUKKOTH

Abrams, Judith. Sukkot: A Family Seder. Kahn, Katherine J., illus. LC 93-7551. 24p. (ps-6). 1993. pap. 3.95 (*0-929371-75-5*) Kar Ben.

Edelman, Lily. Sukkah & the Big Wind. Kessler, Leonard, illus. (gr. k-2). 1956. 5.95 (*0-8381-0716-8*) United Syn Bk.

Simon, Norma. Our First Sukkah. Gordon, Ayala, illus. (ps-k). 1959. plastic cover 4.50 (*0-8381-0703-6*) United Syn Bk.

Springer, Sally, illus. Sukkot & Simchat Torah Fun for Little Hands. 32p. (ps). 1993. wkbk. 3.95 (*0-929371-77-1*) Kar Ben.

SUMER

Florian, Douglas. A Summer Day. LC 87-8484. (Illus.). 24p. (ps-1). 1988. 11.95 (*0-688-07564-9*); lib. bdg. 11.88 (*0-688-07565-7*) Greenwillow.

SUMER–FICTION

Good, Elaine. It's Summertime! LC 89-28895. (Illus.). 32p. (ps-1). 1990. 12.95 (*0-934672-68-7*) Good Bks PA.

Schweninger, Ann. Summertime. (Illus.). 32p. (ps-3). 1994. pap. 4.50 (*0-14-054331-7*) Puffin Bks.

SUMERIANS

Foster, Leila M. The Sumerians. LC 90-12132. (Illus.). 64p. (gr. 5-8). 1990. PLB 12.90 (*0-531-10874-0*) Watts.

Odijk, Pamela. The Sumerians. (Illus.). 48p. (gr. 5-8). 1990. PLB 12.95 (*0-382-09892-7*); 7.95 (*0-382-24268-8*); 4.50 (*0-382-24282-3*) Silver Burdett Pr.

SUMMER

Allington, Richard L. & Krull, Kathleen. Summer. Hockerman, Dennis, illus. LC 80-25097. 32p. (gr. k-3). 1985. PLB 9.95 (*0-8172-1341-4*); pap. 3.95 (*0-8114-8241-3*) Raintree Steck-V.

Allison, Linda. The Sierra Club Summer Book. Allison, Linda, illus. LC 93-41481. 1994. 7.99 (*0-517-10082-7*, Pub. by Wings Bks) Random Hse Value.

Barker, Cicely M. Flower Fairies of the Summer. Barker, Cicely M., illus. (ps up). 1991. 5.95 (*0-7232-3754-9*) Warne.

Beach, Judy & Spencer, Kathleen. Minds-on Fun for Summer. (gr. k-4). 1991. pap. 9.95 (*0-86653-945-X*) Fearon Teach Aids.

Beaton, Clare. Summer Activity Book. (ps-3). 1994. pap. 4.95 (*0-8120-1959-8*) Barron.

Fowler, Allan. Como Sabes Que Es Verano? How Do You Know It's Summer? LC 91-35061. (SPA., Illus.). 32p. (ps-2). 1992. PLB 10.75 (*0-516-34923-6*); pap. 3.95 (*0-516-54923-5*); big bk. 22.95 (*0-516-59624-1*) Childrens.

—How Do You Know It's Summer? LC 91-35061. (Illus.). 32p. (ps-2). 1992. PLB 10.75 (*0-516-04923-2*); PLB 22.95 big bk. (*0-516-49624-7*); pap. 3.95 (*0-516-44923-0*) Childrens.

Hirschi, Ron. Summer. Mangelsen, Thomas D., photos by. LC 90-19596. (Illus.). 32p. (ps-3). 1991. 13.95 (*0-525-65054-7*, Cobblehill Bks) Dutton Child Bks.
Hurwitz, Johanna. Hot & Cold Summer. 1985. pap. 2.95 (*0-590-42858-6*) Scholastic Inc.
Maass, Robert. When Summer Comes. LC 92-26955. (Illus.). 32p. (gr. 1-3). 1993. 14.95 (*0-8050-2087-X*, Bks Young Read) H Holt & Co.
MacKenthun, Carole. Celebrate Summer. Grossman, Dan, illus. 144p. (gr. k-3). 1985. wkbk. 11.95 (*0-86653-265-X*, SS 837, Shining Star Pubns) Good Apple.
Mason, John. Summer Weather. LC 90-41063. (Illus.). 32p. (gr. 1-4). 1991. PLB 11.90 (*0-531-18382-3*, Pub. by Bookwright Pr) Watts.
Moncure, Jane B. Step into Summer: A New Season. McCallum, Jodie, illus. LC 90-30456. 32p. (ps-2). 1990. PLB 13.95 (*0-89565-572-1*) Childs World.
Ottenheimer, Laurence. Livre de l'Ete. Claverie, Jean, illus. (FRE.). 88p. (gr. 4-9). 1983. 15.95 (*2-07-039508-1*) Schoenhof.
Parramon, J. M., et al. El Verano. (SPA.). (ps). 1986. pap. 6.95 (*0-8120-3645-X*) Barron.
Rosen, Mike. Summer Festivals. LC 90-41064. (Illus.). 32p. (gr. 3-7). 1991. PLB 11.90 (*0-531-18383-1*, Pub. by Bookwright Pr) Watts.
Sanchez, Isidro & Peris, Carme. Summer Sports. (Illus.). 32p. (ps-1). 1992. pap. 5.95 (*0-8120-4865-2*) Barron.
Santrey, Louis. Summer. LC 82-19384. (Illus.). 32p. (gr. 4-7). 1983. lib. bdg. 10.79 (*0-89375-911-2*); pap. text ed. 2.95 (*0-89375-912-0*) Troll Assocs.
Schweninger, Ann. Summertime. Schweninger, Ann, illus. 32p. (ps-3). 1992. RB 13.50 (*0-670-83610-9*) Viking Child Bks.
Stone, Lynn M. Summer. LC 93-39058. 1994. write for info. (*1-55916-020-9*) Rourke Bk Co.
Thomson, Ruth. Summer. LC 89-36561. 1990. PLB 11.90 (*0-531-14019-9*) Watts.
Three-D Summertime Fun Book. (Illus.). 1992. pap. 2.95 (*1-56156-107-X*) Kidsbks.
Webber, Helen. Summer Sun. Webber, Helen, illus. (gr. k-6). 1968. 8.95 (*0-8392-3056-7*) Astor-Honor.
Webster, David. Summer. Steadman, Barbara, illus. 48p. (gr. 2-4). 1990. lib. bdg. 10.98 (*0-671-65859-X*, J Messner); pap. 5.95 (*0-671-65984-7*) S&S Trade.

SUMMER–FICTION

Agell, Charlotte. I Wear Long Green Hair in Summer. Agell, Charlotte, illus. LC 93-33612. 32p. (ps up). 1994. 7.95 (*0-88448-113-1*) Tilbury Hse.
Asher. Summer Smith Begins. (gr. 7 up). 1987. pap. 2.50 (*0-553-25883-4*) Bantam.
Ballard, Kimberly M. Light at Summer's End. 160p. (Orig.). (gr. 9-12). 1991. pap. 6.99 (*0-87788-503-6*) Shaw Pubs.
Black, J. R. One Slimy Summer. 132p. (Orig.). (gr. 3-7). 1994. pap. 3.50 (*0-685-71035-1*) Random Bks Yng Read.
Bobo, Carmen P. Sarah's Growing-up Summer. LC 88-62111. 52p. 1989. 6.95 (*1-55523-187-X*) Winston-Derek.
Brown, Margaret W. Summer Noisy Book. new ed. Weisgard, Leonard, illus. LC 92-31435. 40p. (ps-1). 1993. pap. 4.95 (*0-06-443328-5*, Trophy) HarpC Child Bks.
Calmenson, Stephanie. Hotter Than a Hot Dog! Savadier, Elivia, illus. LC 93-313. (gr. 1-8). 1994. 14.95 (*0-316-12479-6*) Little.
Cavanna, Betty. Paintbox Summer. 239p. 1981. Repr. PLB 16.95x (*0-89967-031-8*) Harmony Raine.
Clifford, Eth. The Summer of the Dancing Horse. 1992. pap. 2.95 (*0-590-45400-5*, Apple Paperbacks) Scholastic Inc.
Coville, Bruce. How I Survived My Summer Vacation. Newsom, Tom, illus. 96p. (Orig.). (gr. 3-5). 1988. pap. 3.50 (*0-671-68176-1*, Minstrel Bks) PB.
Crews, Nina. Summer. LC 94-6268. (Illus.). 32p. 1995. write for info. (*0-688-13393-2*); PLB write for info. (*0-688-13394-0*) Greenwillow.
Daly, Maureen. Seventeenth Summer. 288p. 1981. Repr. PLB 19.95x (*0-89967-029-6*) Harmony Raine.
Davidson, Linda. Cool Breezes. (gr. 10 up). 1989. pap. 2.95 (*0-8041-0244-9*) Ivy Books.
—On the Edge. (gr. 10 up). 1988. pap. 2.95 (*0-8041-0243-0*) Ivy Books.
De Angeli, Marguerite. Copper-Toed Boots. LC 88-34417. (Illus.). 96p. (gr. 4 up). 1989. Repr. of 1938 ed. 14.95x (*0-8143-1922-X*) Wayne St U Pr.
De Muth, Jillian. Blue Skies, Green Days. Gamble, Kim, illus. 48p. (gr. 1-6). 1993. 16.95 (*1-86373-062-1*, Pub. by Allen & Unwin Aust Pty AT) IPG Chicago.
Un Dia Caluroso. (SPA.). 1993. pap. 28.67 (*0-590-71798-7*) Scholastic Inc.
Easton, Patricia H. Summer's Chance. LC 87-17728. 150p. (gr. 7 up). 1988. 13.95 (*0-15-200591-9*, Gulliver Bks) HarBrace.
—Summer's Chance. (gr. 4-7). 1992. pap. 4.95 (*0-15-282493-6*) HarBrace.
Effinger, Marta. Bunker & Me: Summer Adventures of Best Friends, Vol. I. Lawrence & Penny, ed. Effinger, Michael, illus. Washington, Pat, intro. by. (Illus.). 30p. (gr. 3-5). 1990. 12.95x (*0-929917-02-2*) Magnolia PA.
Farjam, Farideh & Azaad, Meyer. Uncle Noruz (Uncle New Year) Jabbari, Ahmad, ed. & tr. from PER. Mesqali, Farshid, illus. LC 83-60450. 24p. (Orig.). (gr. k up). 1983. pap. 4.95 (*0-939214-14-8*) Mazda Pubs.
Ferris, Jean. Invincible Summer. 176p. 1994. pap. 3.95 (*0-374-43608-8*) FS&G.
Fowler, Susi G. When Summer Ends. Russo, Marisabina, illus. LC 87-14937. 32p. (ps up). 1989. 11.95 (*0-688-07605-X*); PLB 11.88 (*0-688-07606-8*) Greenwillow.
Fowler, Zinita. The Last Innocent Summer. LC 89-20417. 144p. (gr. 6-9). 1990. pap. 11.95 (*0-87565-045-7*) Tex Christian.
Frame, Janet. Mona Minium & the Smell of the Sun. 96p. (gr. 4-7). 1993. 17.95 (*0-8076-1334-7*) Braziller.
Gilden, Mel. Summer Love. 1993. pap. 3.99 (*0-06-106756-3*, Harp PBks) HarpC.
Girion, Barbara. Indian Summer. (gr. 4-7). 1993. pap. 2.95 (*0-590-42637-0*) Scholastic Inc.
Godden, Rumer. Greengage Summer. 206p. (gr. 7 up). 1986. pap. 3.95 (*0-14-031982-4*, Puffin) Puffin Bks.
Gordon. Pierced by a Ray of Sun. 1995. 16.00 (*0-06-023613-2*); PLB 15.89 (*0-06-023614-0*) HarpC Child Bks.
Greenleaf, Ann. Max & Molly's Summer. 1993. 4.99 (*0-517-09154-2*) Random Hse Value.
Gulley, Judie. Rodeo Summer. LC 84-9129. 192p. (gr. 5-9). 1984. 11.95 (*0-395-36174-5*) HM.
Haith, Betty. Bonnie's Thirteenth Summer. 52p. 1992. pap. 4.95 (*1-882185-01-3*) Crnrstone Pub.
Hakkinen. Summer Legs. 1993. 15.95 (*0-8050-2262-7*) H Holt & Co.
Hawks, Robert. Summer's End. 176p. (Orig.). (gr. 8 up). 1994. pap. 3.99 (*0-380-77440-2*, Flare) Avon.
Hayward, Linda. Ernie & Bert's Summer Project. Nicklaus, Carol, illus. LC 90-60821. 32p. (Orig.). (ps-3). 1991. pap. 1.50 (*0-679-81051-X*) Random Bks Yng Read.
Haywood, Carolyn. Betsy's Busy Summer. Haywood, Carolyn, illus. LC 56-7894. (gr. 3-7). 1956. PLB 13.88 (*0-688-31087-7*) Morrow Jr Bks.
—Summer Fun. Durrell, Julie, illus. LC 85-25864. 128p. (gr. 1-4). 1986. 11.95 (*0-688-04958-3*) Morrow Jr Bks.
—Summer Fun. (gr. 2-4). 1987. pap. 2.95 (*0-8167-1037-6*) Troll Assocs.
Hunter, Mollie. The Mermaid Summer. LC 87-45984. 160p. (gr. 3-7). 1988. PLB 13.89 (*0-06-022628-5*) HarpC Child Bks.
—The Mermaid Summer. LC 87-45984. 128p. (gr. 3-7). 1990. pap. 3.95 (*0-06-440344-0*, Trophy) HarpC Child Bks.
Hurwitz, Johanna. Hot & Cold Summer. Owen, Gail, illus. LC 83-19336. 176p. (gr. 3-5). 1984. 12.95 (*0-688-02746-6*) Morrow Jr Bks.
Iwamura, Kazuo. The Fourteen Forest Mice & the Summer Laundry Day. Knowlton, Mary L., tr. from JPN. Iwamura, Kazuo, illus. LC 90-50705. 32p. (gr. k-3). 1991. PLB 17.27 (*0-8368-0576-3*) Gareth Stevens Inc.
Johnson, Kevin. Why Can't My Life Be a Summer Vacation? 1994. pap. 6.99 (*1-55661-284-2*) Bethany Hse.
Kesselman, Wendy & Himler, Ronald. Sand in my Shoes. LC 94-12038. (Illus.). 1995. write for info. (*0-7868-0057-7*); PLB write for info. (*0-7868-2045-4*) Hyprn Child.
Lasky, Kathryn. My Island Grandma. Schwartz, Amy, illus. LC 91-31000. 32p. (ps up). 1993. 15.00 (*0-688-07946-6*); PLB 14.93 (*0-688-07948-2*) Morrow Jr Bks.
Lee, Robert C. Summer of the Green Star. LC 80-27427. 128p. (gr. 5-9). 1981. 11.00 (*0-664-32681-1*, Westminster) Westminster John Knox.
Leonard, Marcia. Secret Summer. (gr. 3-7). 1990. 12.95 (*0-943021-04-9*) Funchess Jones.
Lipsyte, Robert. Summer Rules. LC 79-2816. 208p. (gr. 7 up). 1992. pap. 3.95 (*0-06-447071-7*, Trophy) HarpC Child Bks.
—The Summerboy. 160p. 1984. pap. 2.25 (*0-553-24130-3*) Bantam.
—The Summerboy. LC 82-47578. 208p. (gr. 7 up). 1992. pap. 3.95 (*0-06-447072-5*, Trophy) HarpC Child Bks.
Lowry, Lois. Summer to Die. 1984. pap. 3.99 (*0-440-21917-5*) Bantam.
McDonnell, Janet. Summer, a Growing Time. Hohag, Linda, illus. LC 93-1182. 32p. (gr. 2 up). 1993. PLB 12.30 (*0-516-00678-9*) Childrens.
McGraw, Eloise J. A Really Weird Summer. LC 90-31542. 224p. (gr. 7 up). 1990. pap. 3.95 (*0-02-044483-4*, Collier Young Ad) Macmillan Child Grp.
Martin, Ann M. Bummer Summer. (gr. 4-7). 1990. pap. 2.95 (*0-590-43622-8*) Scholastic Inc.
—Eleven Kids, One Summer. (gr. 4-7). 1993. pap. 2.95 (*0-590-45917-1*) Scholastic Inc.
Moncure, Jane B. Word Bird's Summer Words. Miracle, Ric, illus. LC 85-5930. 32p. (gr. k-2). 1985. PLB 14.95 (*0-89565-311-7*) Childs World.
Murray, Eleanor B. Cherokee County Summer. Murray, Hubert, photos by. (Illus.). 48p. (Orig.). (gr. 9-12). 1981. pap. 3.98 (*1-879313-01-4*) Murrays Leprechaun Bks.
Nicolai, D. Miles. The Summer the Flowers Had No Scent. 3rd ed. Poyser, Victoria, illus. 28p. (gr. 3-5). 1977. pap. 2.75 (*0-933992-19-X*) Coffee Break.
O'Neal, Zibby. In Summer Light. 160p. (gr. 6 up). 1986. pap. 3.50 (*0-553-25940-7*) Bantam.
Pare, R. Summer Days. (Illus.). 24p. (ps-8). 1988. 12.95 (*1-55037-043-X*, Pub. by Annick CN); pap. 4.95 (*1-55037-044-8*, Pub. by Annick CN) Firefly Bks Ltd.
Parr, Letitia. When Sea & Sky Are Blue. Watts, John, illus. LC 78-151272. 32p. (ps-3). 7.95 (*0-87592-059-4*) Scroll Pr.
Perl, Lila. Telltale Summer of Tina C. 1984. pap. 2.50 (*0-590-41324-4*) Scholastic Inc.
Peters, Lisa W. The Hayloft. Plum, K. D., illus. LC 93-18718. Date not set. write for info. (*0-8037-1490-4*); lib. bdg. write for info. (*0-8037-1491-2*) Dial Bks Young.
Pragoff, Fiona. Summer. (Illus.). 20p. (ps). 1993. pap. 5.95 (*0-689-71706-7*, Aladdin) Macmillan Child Grp.
Prelutsky, Jack. What I Did Last Summer. Abolafia, Yossi, illus. LC 83-11561. 48p. (gr. 1-3). 1984. 13.95 (*0-688-01754-1*) Greenwillow.
Quinn, Patrick. Matthew Pinkowski's Special Summer. Quinn, Patrick, illus. LC 91-10982. 150p. (Orig.). (gr. 5-8). 1991. pap. 5.95 (*0-930323-82-3*, Pub. by K Green Pubns) Gallaudet Univ Pr.
Ransom, Candice F. Shooting Star Summer. Milone, Karen, illus. 32p. (ps-3). 1992. PLB 14.95 (*1-56397-005-8*) Boyds Mills Pr.
Reading, J. P. The Summer of Sassy Jo. LC 88-34130. (gr. 5 up). 1989. 13.45 (*0-395-48950-4*) HM.
—Summer of Sassy Jo. 1993. pap. 4.95 (*0-395-66956-1*) HM.
Rodgers, Mary. Summer Switch. LC 79-2690. 192p. (gr. 5 up). 1982. 14.00 (*0-06-025058-5*); PLB 12.89 (*0-06-025059-3*) HarpC Child Bks.
Ruschak, Lynette. One Hot Day. (ps-3). 1994. 12.95 (*0-307-17607-X*, Artsts Writrs) Western Pub.
Sachs, Marilyn. A Summer's Lease. LC 78-12846. 128p. (gr. 5-9). 1979. 13.95 (*0-525-40480-5*, 0898-270, DCB) Dutton Child Bks.
Scariano, Margaret & Cunningham, Marilyn. Nine to Five Series. (Illus.). (gr. 3-9). 1985. Set. pap. 15.00 (*0-87879-502-2*) High Noon Bks.
Schwartz, Joel L. Upchuck Summer. Degen, Bruce, illus. LC 81-65838. 144p. (gr. 4-6). 1982. 10.95 (*0-385-29099-3*); pap. 10.95 (*0-385-29100-0*) Delacorte.
Scott, Mavis. Birdstone Summer. (ps-3). 1993. pap. 6.95 (*1-86373-231-4*, Pub. by Allen & Unwin Aust Pty AT) IPG Chicago.
Seabrooke, Brenda. The Dragon That Ate Summer. (gr. 4-7). 1993. pap. 2.95 (*0-590-46986-X*) Scholastic Inc.
Shaw, Janet. Kirsten Saves the Day: A Summer Story. Thieme, Jeanne, ed. Graef, Renee, illus. 72p. (gr. 2-5). 1988. PLB 12.95 (*0-937295-91-4*); pap. 5.95 (*0-937295-39-6*) Pleasant Co.
Stanley, Carol. The Last Great Summer. 1992. pap. 3.25 (*0-590-45705-5*, Point) Scholastic Inc.
Staub, Wendy C. Summer Lightning. 1993. pap. 3.50 (*0-06-106778-4*, Harp PBks) HarpC.
Stucky, Naomi R. Sara's Summer. 144p. (Orig.). (gr. 6-12). 1990. pap. 5.95 (*0-8361-3534-2*) Herald Pr.
Summer Job. 1990. 4.98 (*1-55521-688-9*) Bk Sales Inc.
Thacker, Nola. Summer Stories. Low, William, illus. LC 87-45880. 160p. (gr. 3-7). 1988. (Lipp Jr Bks); (Lipp Jr Bks) HarpC Child Bks.
—Summer Stories. Low, William, illus. (gr. 3-7). 1989. pap. 2.75 (*0-590-42191-3*, Apple Paperbacks) Scholastic Inc.
Tibo, Gilles. Simon en Verano. Salazar, Arturo, tr. from ENG. Tibo, Gilles, illus. LC 92-85470. (SPA.). 24p. (Orig.). (gr. k-3). Date not set. pap. 5.95 (*0-88776-298-0*) Tundra Bks.
Tresselt, Alvin. Sun Up. (ps-3). 1991. 14.95 (*0-688-08656-X*); PLB 14.88 (*0-688-08657-8*) Lothrop.
Tripp, Valerie. Molly Saves the Day: A Summer Story. Thieme, Jeanne, ed. Backes, Nick, illus. 72p. (gr. 2-5). 1988. PLB 12.95 (*0-937295-93-0*); pap. 5.95 (*0-937295-43-4*) Pleasant Co.
Vandevenne, Jean. Some Summer! (Illus.). 178p. (Orig.). (gr. 4-6). 1987. pap. 4.95 (*0-89084-380-5*) Bob Jones Univ Pr.
Weiss, Nicki. Sun Sand Sea Sail. LC 88-16391. (Illus.). 32p. (ps up). 1989. 11.95 (*0-688-08270-X*); PLB 11.88 (*0-688-08271-8*) Greenwillow.
Weyn, Suzanne. The Makeover Summer. 128p. (gr. 7 up). 1988. pap. 2.95 (*0-380-75521-1*, Flare) Avon.
Whelan, Gloria. That Wild Berries Should Grow: The Story of a Summer. LC 93-41106. 122p. (gr. 4-6). 1994. 13.99 (*0-8028-3754-9*); pap. 4.99 (*0-8028-5091-X*) Eerdmans.
Woodson, Jacqueline. Last Summer with Maizon. 1990. 13.95 (*0-385-30045-X*) Doubleday.
—Last Summer with Maizon. 1992. pap. 3.50 (*0-440-40555-6*) Dell.
Wyeth, Sharon D. Summer Sizzle. (gr. 4-7). 1991. pap. 3.50 (*0-440-40470-3*) Dell.
Zable, Rona S. An Almost Perfect Summer. (gr. 7 up). 1989. pap. 2.95 (*0-553-27967-X*, Starfire) Bantam.
Ziefert, Harriet. I Love Summer &... Baum, Susan, illus. 16p. (ps-3). 1992. incl. postcards 5.95 (*0-694-00405-7*) HarpC Child Bks.

SUMMER–POETRY

Hull, Robert. Poems for Summer. LC 90-20591. (Illus.). 48p. (gr. 3-7). 1991. PLB 21.34 (*0-8114-7803-3*) Raintree Steck-V.

SUMMER HOMES

see Architecture, Domestic; Houses

SUN

see also Solar Energy; Solar System

Adams, Richard. Our Amazing Sun. Boyd, Patti, illus. LC 82-17419. 32p. (gr. 3-6). 1983. PLB 10.59 (*0-89375-890-6*); pap. text ed. 2.95 (*0-89375-891-4*) Troll Assocs.
Asimov, Isaac. How Did We Find Out about Sunshine. 64p. (gr. 5 up). 1987. 10.95 (*0-8027-6697-8*); PLB 12. 85 (*0-8027-6698-6*) Walker & Co.

Asimov, Isaac, et al. The Sun & Its Secrets. rev. & updated ed. (Illus.). (gr. 3 up). 1994. PLB 17.27 (0-8368-1135-6) Gareth Stevens Inc.

Barrett, Norman S. The Picture World of Sun & Stars. LC 90-11992. (Illus.). 32p. (gr. k-4). 1990. PLB 12.40 (0-531-14058-X) Watts.

Baylor, Byrd. The Way to Start a Day. Parnall, Peter, illus. LC 85-28802. 32p. (gr. 1-4). 1986. pap. 3.95 (0-689-71054-2, Aladdin) Macmillan Child Grp.

Brandt, Keith. Sun. Sweat, Lynn, illus. LC 84-2715. 32p. (gr. 3-6). 1985. PLB 9.49 (0-8167-0190-3); pap. text ed. 2.95 (0-8167-0191-1) Troll Assocs.

Branley, Franklyn M. The Sun: Our Nearest Star. rev. ed. Madden, Don, illus. LC 87-47764. 32p. (ps-3). 1988. (Crowell Jr Bks); PLB 13.89 (0-690-04678-2) HarpC Child Bks.

—Sunshine Makes the Seasons. rev. ed. Maestro, Giulio, illus. LC 85-42750. 32p. (ps-3). 1988. incl. cassette 7.95 (0-694-00203-8, Trophy); pap. 4.95 (0-06-445019-8, Trophy) HarpC Child Bks.

Daily, Bob. The Sun. LC 94-2241. 1994. write for info. (0-531-20105-8) Watts.

Estalella, Robert. Our Star: The Sun. (Illus.). 32p. (gr. 4-8). 1993. 12.95 (0-8120-6370-8); pap. 6.95 (0-8120-1739-0) Barron.

Fowler, Allan. El Sol Siempre Brilla En Alguna Parte: The Sun Is Always Shining Somewhere. LC 90-2176. (SPA., Illus.). 32p. (ps-2). PLB 10.75, Apr. 1992 (0-516-34906-6); pap. 3.95, Jul. 1992 (0-516-54906-5) Childrens.

—The Sun Is Always Shining Somewhere. (Illus.). 32p. (ps-2). 1991. PLB 10.75 (0-516-04906-2); pap. 3.95 (0-516-44906-0) Childrens.

—The Sun Is Always Shining Somewhere Big Book. (Illus.). 32p. (ps-2). 1991. PLB 22.95 (0-516-49466-X) Childrens.

Ganeri, Anita. Outdoor Science. LC 93-13125. (Illus.). 48p. (gr. 5 up). 1993. text ed. 13.95 RSBE (0-87518-579-7, Dillon) Macmillan Child Grp.

Gantschev, Ivan. Good Morning, Good Night. Clements, Andrew, tr. Gantschev, Ivan, illus. LC 91-3603. 28p. (gr. k up). 1991. pap. 14.95 (0-88708-183-5) Picture Bk Studio.

George, Michael. The Sun. 1992. PLB 18.95 (0-88682-402-8) Creative Ed.

—The Sun. LC 92-8413. (SPA & ENG.). (gr. 2-6). 1992. PLB 15.95 (0-89565-855-0) Childs World.

Gibbons, Gail. Sun up, Sun Down. Gibbons, Gail, illus. LC 82-23420. 32p. (gr. 1-5). 1983. 14.95 (0-15-282781-1, HB Juv Bks) HarBrace.

How the Sun Was Born (Como el Sol Nacio) (Illus.). 24p. (gr. k-3). 1993. 5.99 (0-87406-649-2) Willowisp Pr.

Larson, Wendy. Sun. Curti, Anna, illus. 14p. (ps-1). 1994. bds. 4.95 (0-448-40571-7, G&D) Putnam Pub Group.

Moncure, Jane B. The Sun: Our Daytime Star. Endres, Helen, illus. LC 89-24009. 32p. (ps-2). 1990. PLB 13. 95 (0-89565-551-9) Childs World.

Palazzo, Janet. Our Friend the Sun. Hall, Susan, illus. LC 81-11460. 32p. (gr. k-2). 1982. PLB 11.59 (0-89375-650-4); pap. 2.95 (0-89375-651-2) Troll Assocs.

Robson, Denny A. The Sun. LC 91-10316. (Illus.). 32p. (gr. k-4). 1991. PLB 11.90 (0-531-17336-4, Gloucester Pr) Watts.

Shedd, Edith S. & Shedd, Alan. Do It with the Sun. Higginbotham, David, illus. LC 82-81309. 208p. (Orig.). (gr. 6-9). 1982. pap. 12.95 (0-9608358-0-6) Integ Energy.

Sorensen, Lynda. Sun. LC 93-14872. (ps-6). 1993. 12.67 (0-86593-272-7); 9.50s.p. (0-685-66587-9) Rourke Corp.

Ziefert, Harriet. Good Morning Sun. 1988. pap. 3.95 (0-670-81578-0) Viking Child Bks.

SUN–FICTION

Aesop. The Wind & the Sun. Watts, Bernadette, illus. LC 92-2653. 32p. (gr. k-3). 1992. 14.95 (1-55858-162-6); PLB 14.88 (1-55858-163-4) North-South Bks NYC.

Ashley, Bernard. A Break in the Sun. Keeping, Charles, illus. 186p. (gr. 6 up). 1980. 21.95 (0-87599-230-7) S G Phillips.

Baron, Lindamichelle. The Sun Is On. rev. ed. Elam, Keith, illus. Dee, Ruby, intro. by. (Illus.). 48p. (gr. 1-6). 1982. pap. 5.95 (0-940938-02-2) Harlin Jacque.

Berger, Barbara. When the Sun Rose. (Illus.). 32p. (ps-3). 1990. pap. 5.95 (0-399-22175-1, Sandcastle Bks) Putnam Pub Group.

Borrelli, Susan. Freedom in the Sun. LC 91-67500. (Illus.). 44p. (gr. k-3). 1992. pap. 6.95 (1-55523-494-1) Winston-Derek.

Butler, Andrea. Mr. Sun & Mr. Sea. 16p. (ps-2). 1994. text ed. 3.95 (0-673-36198-5) GdYrBks.

Daly, Niki. Why the Sun & Moon Live in the Sky. LC 93-47304. (Illus.). 1994. 15.00 (0-688-13331-2); lib. bdg. 14.93 (0-688-13332-0) Lothrop.

Emberley, Michael. Welcome Back, Sun. LC 92-9786. (gr. 4 up). 1993. 14.95 (0-316-23647-0) Little.

Gerstein, Mordicai. The Sun's Day. LC 88-24738. (Illus.). 32p. (ps-1). 1989. 13.00 (0-06-022404-5); PLB 13.89 (0-06-022405-3) HarpC Child Bks.

Ginsburg, Mirra. Where Does the Sun Go at Night? Aruego, Jose & Dewey, Ariane, illus. LC 79-16151. 32p. (gr. k-3). 1980. 10.95 (0-688-80245-1); PLB 10. 88 (0-688-84245-3) Greenwillow.

Greene, Carol. Shine, Sun! Sharp, Gene, illus. LC 82-19853. 32p. (ps-2). 1983. PLB 10.25 (0-516-02038-2); pap. 2.95 (0-516-42038-0) Childrens.

Hadley, Eric & Hadley, Tessa. Legends of the Sun & Moon. LC 82-17720. (Illus.). 32p. (gr. 3-7). 1989. 14. 95 (0-521-25227-X); pap. 10.95 (0-521-37912-1) Cambridge U Pr.

Harrison, David. Wake up! Sun! Wilhelm, Hans, illus. LC 85-30053. 32p. (ps-1). 1986. 3.50 (0-394-88256-3); lib. bdg. 7.99 (0-394-98256-8) Random Bks Yng Read.

Lagos, Deloris K. The Sun Shall Shine. 1993. 7.95 (0-8062-4786-X) Carlton.

London, Jonathan. Like Butter on Pancakes. Karas, G. Brian, illus. LC 94-9154. 1995. write for info. (0-670-85130-2, Viking) Viking Penguin.

Marzollo, Jean. Sun Song. Date not set. 15.00 (0-06-020787-6, HarpT); PLB 14.89 (0-06-020788-4, HarpT) HarpC.

Matthews, Andrew & Todd, Justin. The Jar of the Sun. (Illus.). 32p. (gr. k-3). 1992. 16.95 (0-09-176400-9, Pub. by Hutchinson UK) Trafalgar.

Pfister, Marcus. Sun & Moon. (gr. 4-7). 1993. pap. 4.95 (0-590-44490-5) Scholastic Inc.

Rahmas, Sigrid. Mother Sun & Her Planet Children. Rahmas, Sigrid, illus. 32p. (Orig.). (ps-3). 1991. 6.25 (0-87157-099-8); pap. 2.95 (0-87157-599-X) Story Hse Corp.

Reid, Barbara. Zoe's Sunny Day. 12p. 1991. pap. 3.95 (0-590-44713-0) Scholastic Inc.

Tomkins, Jasper. My Secret Sunrise. LC 91-22274. (Illus.). 60p. 1991. 11.95 (0-671-74975-7, Green Tiger); pap. 7.95 (0-671-74978-1, Green Tiger) S&S Trade.

Wildsmith, Brian. What the Moon Saw. Wildsmith, Brian, illus. 32p. (ps-3). 1978. 16.00 (0-19-279724-7); pap. 7.50 (0-19-272157-7) OUP.

SUN–RADIATION

see Solar Radiation

SUN-DIALS

see Sundials

SUN GLASSES

see Eyeglasses

SUNDAY

see Sabbath

SUNDIALS

Simon, Seymour. Shadow Magic. Ormai, Stella, illus. LC 84-4433. 48p. (ps-3). 1985. PLB 14.93 (0-688-02682-6) Lothrop.

SUNFLOWERS–FICTION

Hostetler, Jacob. My Backyard Giant. adpt. ed. Sawicki, Mary, adapted by. LC 93-29762. (Illus.). 32p. (ps-2). 1994. 10.95 (0-8120-6399-6); pap. 4.95 (0-8120-1736-6) Barron.

Schwinge, Joan. Sunny Sunflower. (Illus.). 28p. 1992. pap. 6.95 (0-9632902-0-7) Winston Bks.

SUNKEN CITIES

see Cities and Towns, Ruined, Extinct, Etc.

SUNKEN TREASURE

see Buried Treasure

SUPERMARKETS

Hautzig, David. At the Supermarket. LC 93-26976. (Illus.). 32p. (gr. k-3). 1994. 14.95 (0-531-06832-3); lib. bdg. 14.99 RLB (0-531-08682-8) Orchard Bks Watts.

SUPERMARKETS–FICTION

Adler, David A. Onion Sundaes: A Houdini Club Magic Mystery. Malone, Heather H., illus. LC 93-5878. 80p. (Orig.). (gr. 1-4). 1994. PLB 9.99 (0-679-94697-7); pap. 2.99 (0-679-84697-2) Random Bks Yng Read.

Grossman, Bill. Tommy at the Grocery Store. Chess, Victoria, illus. LC 88-35756. 32p. (ps-2). 1991. pap. 4.95 (0-06-443266-1, Trophy) HarpC Child Bks.

Martin, B. Yo, Grocer. (gr. 4 up). 1900. 12.95 (0-8050-0329-0) H Holt & Co.

SUPERNATURAL–FICTION

Bellairs, John. The Drum, the Doll, & the Zombie. Gorey, Edward, illus. Stickland, Brad, contrib. by. LC 93-43964. (gr. 2 up). 1994. 14.99 (0-8037-1462-9); PLB 14.89 (0-8037-1463-7) Dial Bks Young.

—The Ghost in the Mirror. Strickland, Brad, contrib. by. LC 92-18369. 1993. 14.99 (0-8037-1370-3); PLB 14. 89 (0-8037-1371-1) Dial Bks Young.

Briggs, Katherine M. An Encyclopedia of Fairies: Hobgoblins, Brownies, Bogies, & Other Supernatural Creatures. LC 76-12939. (Illus.). (gr. 4 up). 1978. 12. 95 (0-394-40918-3); pap. 19.00 (0-394-73467-X) Pantheon.

Brittain, Bill. Professor Popkin's Prodigious Polish: A Tale of Coven Tree. Glass, Andrew, illus. LC 89-78221. 160p. (gr. 3-7). 1991. PLB 13.89 (0-06-020727-2) HarpC Child Bks.

Brown, Roberta. The Walking Trees & Other Scary Stories. 139p. (gr. 4 up). 1991. 8.95 (0-87483-143-1) August Hse.

Buffie, Margaret. Warnings. 1991. 13.95 (0-590-43665-1, Scholastic Hardcover) Scholastic Inc.

Cannon, A. E. Shadow Brothers. 1992. pap. 3.50 (0-440-21167-0) Dell.

Carmody, Isobelle. The Gathering. LC 93-31844. 1994. write for info. (0-8037-1716-4, Dial) Doubleday.

Chittum, Ida. The Ghost Boy of el Toro. LC 78-1079. (gr. 4 up). 1978. 8.00 (0-8309-0201-5) Ind Pr MO.

Cole, Joanna & Calmenson, Stephanie, eds. The Scary Book. Demarest, Chris, et al, illus. LC 90-26330. 128p. (gr. 2 up). 1991. 12.95 (0-688-10654-4) Morrow Jr Bks.

Connell, David D. Case of the Unnatural. (gr. 4-7). 1993. pap. text ed. write for info. (0-7167-6504-7) W H Freeman.

Crose, Mark. The Terminator. LC 90-28888. (Illus.). 48p. (gr. 5-6). 1991. text ed. 13.95 RSBE (0-89686-580-0, Crestwood Hse) Macmillan Child Grp.

Denan, Corinne. Tales of Magic & Spells. Watling, James, illus. LC 79-66325. 48p. (gr. 3-6). 1980. PLB 9.89 (0-89375-318-1); pap. text ed. 2.95 (0-89375-317-3) Troll Assocs.

Derman, Martha. Tales from Academy Street. (gr. 4-7). 1992. pap. 2.95 (0-590-43704-6) Scholastic Inc.

Garden, Nancy. The Door Between. LC 87-8778. 192p. (gr. 5 up). 1987. 15.00 (0-374-31833-6) FS&G.

—Watersmeet. LC 83-11512. 202p. (gr. 5 up). 1983. 15. 00 (0-374-38244-1) FS&G.

Hawthorne, Nathaniel. Dr. Heidegger's Experiment. 1991. PLB 13.95 (0-88682-465-6) Creative Ed.

Hiser, Constance. Night of the Werepoodle. Fisher, Cynthia, illus. LC 93-25732. 128p. (gr. 2-6). 1994. 14. 95 (0-8234-1116-8) Holiday.

Hitchcock, Alfred, ed. Alfred Hitchcock's Supernatural Tales of Terror & Suspense. (Illus.). (gr. 5 up). 1983. pap. 4.99 (0-394-85622-8) Random Bks Yng Read.

Hite, Sid. Dither Farm. LC 91-31323. 224p. (gr. 7 up). 1992. 15.95 (0-8050-1871-9, Bks Young Read) H Holt & Co.

Hodgman, Ann. Dark Dreams. LC 93-15039. 224p. (gr. 7 up). 1993. pap. 3.50 (0-14-036374-2, Puffin) Puffin Bks.

Honeycutt, Natalie. Invisible Lissa. Rutherford, Jenny, illus. LC 84-20466. 192p. (gr. 4-6). 1985. SBE 14.95 (0-02-744360-4, Bradbury Pr) Macmillan Child Grp.

Jennings, Paul. Uncanny! Even More Surprising Stories. 144p. (gr. 5 up). 1993. pap. 3.99 (0-14-034909-X, Puffin) Puffin Bks.

—Unmentionable! More Amazing Stories. LC 92-25930. 112p. (gr. 5 up). 1993. 14.99 (0-670-84734-8) Viking Child Bks.

Katz, Welwyn W. False Face. LC 88-12847. 176p. (gr. 5-9). 1988. SBE 14.95 (0-689-50456-X, M K McElderry) Macmillan Child Grp.

Keegan, Shannon. Haunted Tacos: Culinary Verse with a Curse. (gr. 4-7). 1992. pap. 2.50 (0-590-45815-9) Scholastic Inc.

Kergueno, Jacqueline & Seignolle, Claude. The Man with Seven Wolves. (Illus.). (gr. 3-8). 1992. PLB 8.95 (0-89565-895-X) Childs World.

Kindl, Patrice. Owl in Love. LC 92-26952. 1993. 13.95 (0-395-66162-5) HM.

—Owl in Love. 208p. (gr. 7 up). 1994. pap. 3.99 (0-14-037129-X) Puffin Bks.

Lisle, Janet T. The Gold Dust Letters. LC 93-11806. 128p. (gr. 3-5). 1994. 14.95 (0-531-06830-7); lib. bdg. 14.99 RLB (0-531-08680-1) Orchard Bks Watts.

—Looking for Juliette. LC 94-6922. 128p. (gr. 3-5). 1994. 14.95 (0-531-06870-6); PLB 14.99 (0-531-08720-4) Orchard Bks Watts.

Littledale, Freya. Stories of Ghosts, Witches, & Demons. (gr. 4-7). 1992. pap. 2.95 (0-590-45556-7) Scholastic Inc.

Lyon, George E. Here & Then. LC 94-6921. 128p. (gr. 5-7). 1994. 14.95 (0-531-06866-8); PLB 14.99 (0-531-08716-6) Orchard Bks Watts.

McDonald, Collin. The Chilling Hour: Tales of the Real & Unreal. (Illus.). 128p. (gr. 4 up). 1992. 14.00 (0-525-65101-2, Cobblehill Bks) Dutton Child Bks.

—Shadows & Whispers: Tales from the Other Side. LC 94-2143. 160p. (gr. 4 up). 1994. 13.99 (0-525-65184-5, Cobblehill Bks) Dutton Child Bks.

McKinley, Robin. A Knot in the Grain & Other Stories. LC 93-17557. 208p. (gr. 6 up). 1994. 14.00 (0-688-09201-2) Greenwillow.

Mahy, Margaret. The Changeover: A Supernatural Romance. LC 83-83446. 224p. (gr. 7 up). 1984. SBE 14.95 (0-689-50303-2, M K McElderry) Macmillan Child Grp.

Martin, Bill, Jr. Old Devil Wind. Root, Barry, illus. LC 92-37908. 1993. 13.95 (0-15-257768-8) HarBrace.

Morgan, Helen. The Witch Doll. (Illus.). 144p. (gr. 3-7). 1992. 14.00 (0-670-84285-0) Viking Child Bks.

Pascal, Francine. Steven & the Zombie. 1994. pap. 3.50 (0-553-48104-5) Bantam.

Peck, Richard. Ghosts I Have Been. LC 77-9469. 224p. (gr. 7 up). 1977. pap. 15.00 (0-670-33813-3) Viking Child Bks.

Peel, John. Tag: You're Dead! LC 92-19939. 128p. (gr. 3-7). 1992. pap. 2.99 (0-14-036053-0) Puffin Bks.

Pike, Christopher. The Immortal. MacDonald, Pat, ed. 256p. (Orig.). 1993. 14.00 (0-671-87039-4, Archway); pap. 3.99 (0-671-74510-7, Archway) PB.

Powling, Chris, compiled by. Faces in the Dark: A Book of Scary Stories. Bailey, Peter, illus. LC 93-46911. 80p. (gr. 2-6). 1994. 16.95 (1-85697-986-5, Kingfisher LKC) LKC.

Reiss, Kathryn. Dreadful Sorry. LC 92-38780. (gr. 5-9). 1993. 16.95 (0-15-224213-9) HarBrace.

—Pale Phoenix. LC 93-32299. (gr. 5 up). 1994. write for info. (0-15-200030-5); pap. write for info. (0-15-200031-3) Harbrace.

Rubel, Nicole. The Ghost Family Meets Its Match. Rubel, Nicole, illus. LC 91-10815. 32p. (ps-3). 1992. 14.00 (0-8037-1093-3); PLB 13.89 (0-8037-1094-1) Dial Bks Young.

Scott, Michael. October Moon. LC 93-8693. 160p. (gr. 7 up). 1994. 14.95 (0-8234-1110-9) Holiday.

Sinykin, Sheri C. Sirens. LC 93-77099. 1993. 13.00 (0-688-12309-0) Lothrop.

Skwarek, Skip. The Horrors of Howling Hall. Compass Productions Staff, illus. LC 91-46526. 10p. (gr. k-4). 1992. 4.95 (0-8037-1185-9) Dial Bks Young.

—In the Deep Dark Dungeon. Compass Productions Staff, illus. LC 91-45515. 10p. (gr. k-4). 1992. 4.95 (*0-8037-1187-5*) Dial Bks Young.
—The Mystery of Maggoty Mill. Compass Productions Staff, illus. LC 91-47021. 10p. (gr. k-4). 1992. 4.95 (*0-8037-1186-7*) Dial Bks Young.
Strange Stories of the Supernatural. (gr. 4-7). 1993. pap. 2.95 (*0-89375-403-X*) Troll Assocs.
Vaughan, Marsha K. Whistling Dixie. Date not set. 15.00 (*0-06-021030-3*, HarpT); 14.89 (*0-06-021029-X*, HarpT) HarpC.
Westall, Robert. The Call & Other Stories. 128p. (gr. 7 up). 1993. 13.00 (*0-670-82484-4*) Viking Child Bks.
—In Camera: And Other Stories. LC 92-13815. 176p. (gr. 7 up). 1993. 13.95 (*0-590-45920-1*) Scholastic Inc.
Wrightson, Patricia. Balyet. 1990. pap. 3.95 (*0-14-034339-3*, Puffin) Puffin Bks.
Wulffson, Don L. Time Fix: And Other Tales of Terror. 96p. 1994. 13.99 (*0-525-65140-3*, Cobblehill Bks) Dutton Child Bks.
Wyllie, Stephen. Ghost Train: A Spooky Hologram Book. Lee, Brian, illus. LC 91-15719. 24p. (gr. k). 1992. 18.00 (*0-8037-1163-8*) Dial Bks Young.
Yolen, Jane. The Faery Flag: Stories & Poems of Fantasy & the Supernatural. LC 88-34866. 128p. (gr. 5 up). 1989. 15.95 (*0-531-05838-7*); PLB 15.99 (*0-531-08438-8*) Orchard Bks Watts.

SUPERSTITION
see also Apparitions; Astrology; Divination; Dreams; Fairies; Folklore; Fortune Telling; Ghosts; Occult Sciences; Witchcraft
Ainsworth, Catherine H. Superstitions from Seven Towns of the United States. LC 43-7320. 64p. (ps-12). 1973. 5.00 (*0-933190-00-X*) Clyde Pr.
Crosby, Nina E. & Marten, Elizabeth H. Don't Teach! Let Me Learn about World War II, Adventure, Dreams & Superstition. Rossi, Richard, illus. 72p. (Orig.). (gr. 3-10). 1984. 8.95 (*0-88047-044-5*, 8411) DOK Pubs.
Jenkins, Steve, text by. & illus. Duck Breath & Mouse Pie: A Collection of Animal Superstitions. LC 94-2499. 32p. (gr. k-3). 1994. 14.95g (*0-395-69688-7*) Ticknor & Flds Bks Yng Read.
Lord, Suzanne. Superstitions. LC 89-70867. (Illus.). 48p. (gr. 5-6). 1990. text ed. 11.95 RSBE (*0-89686-512-6*, Crestwood Hse) Macmillan Child Grp.
Perl, Lila. Don't Sing Before Breakfast, Don't Sleep in the Moonlight: Everyday Superstitions & How They Began. LC 87-24295. (Illus.). 96p. (gr. 3-6). 1988. 13.95 (*0-89919-504-0*, Clarion Bks) HM.
Schwartz, Alvin. Cross Your Fingers, Spit in Your Hat: Superstitions & Other Beliefs. Rounds, Glen, illus. LC 73-21912. 128p. (gr. 4-6). 1990. PLB 13.89 (*0-397-32436-7*, Lipp Jr Bks) HarpC Child Bks.
—Cross Your Fingers, Spit in Your Hat: Superstitions & Other Beliefs. LC 73-21912. (Illus.). 160p. (gr. 3 up). 1993. pap. 4.95 (*0-06-446138-6*, Trophy) HarpC Child Bks.
Vornholt, John. Break a Leg! Famous Curses & Superstitions. LC 94-5119. 96p. (Orig.). 1994. pap. 3.50 (*0-380-76858-5*, Camelot) Avon.

SUPERSTITION–FICTION
Standiford, Natalie, retold by. The Headless Horseman. Cook, Donald, illus. LC 90-53228. 48p. (Orig.). (ps-2). 1992. PLB 7.99 (*0-679-91241-X*); pap. 3.50 (*0-679-81241-5*) Random Bks Yng Read.

SURF
see Ocean Waves

SURFING
Evans, Jeremy. Surfing. LC 92-43227. (Illus.). 48p. (gr. 5-6). 1994. text ed. 13.95 RSBE (*0-89686-824-9*, Crestwood Hse) Macmillan Child Grp.
—Windsurfing. LC 91-7886. (Illus.). 48p. (gr. 5-6). 1992. text ed. 13.95 RSBE (*0-89686-680-7*, Crestwood Hse) Macmillan Child Grp.
Hays, Scott. Surfing. LC 93-32164. 1993. write for info. (*0-86593-349-9*) Rourke Corp.
Holden, Phil. Wind & Surf. (Illus.). 48p. (gr. 4-12). 1992. PLB 17.50 (*0-8225-2477-5*) Lerner Pubns.
Italia, Robert. Sailboarding. Wallner, Rosemary, ed. LC 91-73019. 32p. 1991. PLB 9.95 (*1-56239-078-3*) Abdo & Dghtrs.
King, Ron. Rad Boards: Skateboarding, Snowboarding, Bodyboarding. (gr. 4-7). 1991. pap. 9.95 (*0-316-49355-4*, Spts Illus Kids) Little.
Smith, Don. Surfing, the Big Wave. new ed. LC 75-21847. (Illus.). 32p. (gr. 5-10). 1976. PLB 10.79 (*0-89375-011-5*) Troll Assocs.

SURFING–FICTION
Collington, Peter. The Coming of the Surfman. Collington, Peter, illus. LC 92-41844. 32p. (gr. 3 up). 1994. 16.00 (*0-679-84721-9*) Knopf Bks Yng Read.
Quackenbush, Robert. Surfboard to Peril. LC 85-24430. (gr. 4-7). 1991. pap. 2.95 (*0-671-73344-3*, S&S BFYR) S&S Trade.
Roddy, Lee. Mystery of the Wild Surfer. 160p. (Orig.). (gr. 3-7). 1990. pap. 4.99 (*0-929608-64-X*) Focus Family.
Singer, A. L. Surf Warriors. (gr. 4-7). 1993. pap. 3.50 (*0-440-40799-0*) Dell.
Tomlinson, Theresa. Riding the Waves. LC 92-3942. (Illus.). 144p. (gr. 4-8). 1993. SBE 13.95 (*0-02-789207-7*, Macmillan Child Bk) Macmillan Child Grp.
Winton, Tim. Lockie Leonard, Human Torpedo. (gr. 5 up). 1992. 13.95 (*0-316-94753-9*) Little.

SURGEONS
Crofford, Emily. Frontier Surgeons: A Story about the Mayo Brothers. (ps-3). 1991. pap. 4.95 (*0-87614-553-5*) Carolrhoda Bks.

SURGERY
Facklam, Margery & Facklam, Howard. Spare Parts for People. (Illus.). 143p. (gr. 7 up). 1987. 15.95 (*0-15-277410-6*, HB Juv Bks) HarBrace.
Gay, Kathlyn. Breast Implants: Making Safe Choices. LC 92-35095. (Illus.). 128p. (gr. 6 up). 1993. text ed. 13.95 RSBE (*0-02-737955-8*, New Discovery) Macmillan Child Grp.
Hooper, Tony. Surgery. LC 93-19708. (Illus.). 48p. (gr. 5-8). 1993. PLB 22.80 (*0-8114-2335-2*) Raintree Steck-V.

SURINAM
Beatty, Noelle B. Suriname. (Illus.). 96p. (gr. 5 up). 1988. lib. bdg. 14.95 (*1-55546-196-4*) Chelsea Hse.

SURVEYING
see also Geodesy
Surveying. (Illus.). 64p. (gr. 6-12). 1984. pap. 1.85 (*0-8395-3327-6*, 33327) BSA.

SURVIVAL (AFTER AIRPLANE ACCIDENTS, SHIPWRECKS, ETC.)
see also Wilderness Survival
Donnelly, Judy & Kramer, Sydelle. Survive! Could You? 96p. (Orig.). (gr. 2-7). 1993. PLB 9.99 (*0-679-94363-3*, Bullseye Bks); pap. 2.99 (*0-679-84363-9*, Bullseye Bks) Random Bks Yng Read.
Landsman, Susan. Survival! In the Desert. 112p. (Orig.). 1993. pap. 3.50 (*0-380-76601-9*, Camelot) Avon.
Morris, Deborah. Real Kids, Real Adventures. LC 94-11741. 112p. (gr. 3-10). 1994. 5.99 (*0-8054-4051-8*, 4240-51) Broadman.
Rathe, Gustave. The Wreck of the Barque Stefano off the North West Cape of Australia in 1875. (Illus.). 160p. 1992. 17.00 (*0-374-38585-8*) FS&G.
Smith, L. Survival Skills. (Illus.). 48p. (gr. 6-10). 1987. pap. 5.95 (*0-7460-0169-X*) EDC.

SURVIVAL (AFTER AIRPLANE ACCIDENTS, SHIPWRECKS, ETC.)–FICTION
Baillie, Allan. Adrift. 128p. (gr. 3-7). 1992. 14.00 (*0-670-84474-8*) Viking Child Bks.
—Adrift. 128p. (gr. 3-7). 1994. pap. 3.99 (*0-14-037010-2*) Puffin Bks.
Campbell, Eric. The Shark Callers. LC 93-44881. (gr. 7 up). 1994. 10.95 (*0-15-200007-0*); pap. 4.95 (*0-15-200010-0*) HarBrace.
Defoe, Daniel. Reader's Digest Best Loved Books for Young Readers: The Life & Strange Surprising Adventures of Robinson Crusoe. Ogburn, Jackie, ed. Foster, Robert, illus. 168p. (gr. 4-12). 1989. 3.99 (*0-945260-27-X*) Choice Pub NY.
—Robinson Crusoe. (gr. 6 up). 1964. pap. 2.25 (*0-8049-0022-1*, CL-22) Airmont.
—Robinson Crusoe. Ward, Lynd, illus. (gr. 4-6). 1963. 13.95 (*0-448-06021-3*, G&D) Putnam Pub Group.
—Robinson Crusoe. Dolch, Edward W., et al, eds. (gr. k-3). 1988. pap. 2.95 (*0-590-41841-6*) Scholastic Inc.
—Robinson Crusoe. Lindskoog, Kathryn, ed. (gr. 3-7). 1991. pap. 4.99 (*0-88070-438-1*, Gold & Honey) Questar Pubs.
—Robinson Crusoe. 1993. 13.95 (*0-679-42819-4*, Everymans Lib) Knopf.
Faucher, Elizabeth. Surviving. 1993. pap. 2.95 (*0-590-43731-3*) Scholastic Inc.

Fine, John C. The Tested Man. Whitaker, Kate, ed. 130p. 1994. pap. 12.00 (*1-883650-00-3*) Windswept Hse. Eight soul-searching, rugged tales of men against the elements. John Fine has written fifteen books including award-winning books dealing with the problems of ocean pollution (Oceans in Peril) & world hunger (The Hunger Road). He was elected to the Academy of Underwater Arts & Sciences in honor of his books in the field of education. His children's book, The Boy & the Dolphin (Windswept House, 1990), received the 1991 Herman Melville Literary Award. Fine, a trained biologist with a Doctor of Jurisprudence degree, has received international recognition for his pioneering work investigating toxic waste contamination of our land & water resources. He received the Freedom Award at the World Underwater Congress in recognition of his work in the marine environment. Fine is a trustee of the International Oceanographic Foundation, a recipient of the Marine Environment Award, given by the Foundation for Ocean Research, has three times been named Diver of the Year, & holds the highest professional licenses as an underwater instructor. Fine writes with strength, sincerity & great understanding of the sea & the men who sail on it. These are stories you will never forget.
Publisher Provided Annotation.

Finley, Mary Pearce. Soaring Eagle. LC 92-38263. (gr. 6 up). 1993. pap. 14.00 (*0-671-75598-6*, S&S BFYR) S&S Trade.
Fiore, Carmen A. The Snakeskin. Ferri, Penny J., illus. 112p. (gr. 3-7). 1991. 14.95 (*0-939219-07-7*) Townhouse Pub.
Greene, Laura. Help: Getting to Know about Needing & Giving. Mayo, Gretchen, illus. LC 80-81082. 32p. (ps-3). 1981. 16.95 (*0-87705-402-9*) Human Sci Pr.
Harte, Bret. The Outcasts of Poker Flat. Nuemeier, Marty, illus. 48p. (gr. 6 up). 1980. PLB 13.95 (*0-87191-768-8*) Creative Ed.
Hill, Kirkpatrick. Toughboy & Sister. 128p. (gr. 3-7). 1992. pap. 3.99 (*0-14-034866-2*) Puffin Bks.
Hite, Sid. It's Nothing to a Mountain. LC 93-42048. 1994. 15.95 (*0-8050-2769-6*) H Holt & Co.
Houston, James. Frozen Fire: A Tale of Courage. Houston, James, illus. LC 77-6366. 160p. (gr. 7 up). 1977. SBE 13.95 (*0-689-50083-1*, M K McElderry) Macmillan Child Grp.
—Frozen Fire: A Tale of Courage. 2nd ed. Houston, James, illus. LC 91-46062. 160p. (gr. 3-7). 1992. pap. 4.95 (*0-689-71612-5*, Aladdin) Macmillan Child Grp.
Houston, James R. Long Claws: An Arctic Adventure. (Illus.). 32p. (ps-3). 1992. pap. 4.99 (*0-14-054522-0*, Puffin) Puffin Bks.
Kehret, Peg. Night of Fear. LC 93-24051. 144p. (gr. 5 up). 1994. 13.99 (*0-525-65136-5*, Cobblehill Bks) Dutton Child Bks.
McClung, Robert M. Hugh Glass: Mountain Man. LC 92-43790. 176p. (gr. 7 up). 1993. pap. 3.95 (*0-688-04595-2*, Pub. by Beech Tree Bks) Morrow.
McKinley, Nancy L. Signs of Survival. (Illus.). (gr. 5-12). 1991. 12.00 (*0-930599-69-1*) Thinking Pubns.
Masterton, David S. Get Out of My Face. LC 90-24096. 160p. (gr. 5-9). 1991. SBE 13.95 (*0-689-31675-5*, Atheneum Child Bk) Macmillan Child Grp.
Mayne, William. Low Tide. LC 92-24717. 1993. 14.00 (*0-385-30904-X*) Delacorte.
Mazer, Harry. The Island Keeper: A Tale of Courage & Survival. LC 80-39762. 192p. (gr. 7 up). 1981. pap. 11.95 (*0-385-28446-2*) Delacorte.
—Snow Bound. 144p. (gr. 5 up). 1975. pap. 3.99 (*0-440-96134-3*, LFL) Dell.
Myers, Edward. Climb or Die. LC 93-44861. 192p. (gr. 5-9). 1994. 14.95 (*0-7868-0026-7*); PLB 14.89 (*0-7868-2021-7*) Hyprn Child.
Nesbit, Jeffrey A. The Lost Canoe. 130p. 1991. pap. 4.99 (*0-89693-130-7*) SP Pubns.
Paulsen, Gary. Hatchet. large type ed. 232p. 1989. Repr. of 1987 ed. lib. bdg. 15.95 (*1-55736-117-7*, Crnrstn Bks) BDD LT Grp.
Phleger, Marjorie. Pilot Down, Presumed Dead. LC 63-16244. 224p. (gr. 5-9). 1975. pap. 3.95 (*0-06-440067-0*, Trophy) HarpC Child Bks.
Sis, Peter. A Small, Tall Tale from the Far, Far North. Sis, Peter, illus. LC 92-75906. 40p. (gr. k-5). 1993. 15.00 (*0-679-84345-0*); PLB 15.99 (*0-679-94345-5*) Knopf Bks Yng Read.
Skurzynski, Gloria. Lost in the Devil's Desert. Scrofani, Joseph M., illus. LC 92-45656. 96p. (gr. 5 up). 1993. pap. 3.95 (*0-688-04593-6*, Pub. by Beech Tree Bks) Morrow.

Smith, Duane. Heritage Revealed Series for Younger Readers, 3 Bks. 1994. Set. pap. 13.95 (*1-886218-00-5*); The Legend of the Golden Hawk. pap. 4.95 (*0-9632074-1-5*); Journey to Clay Mountain. pap. 4.95 (*0-9632074-2-3*); Lost on Victoria Lake. pap. 4.95 (*0-9632074-3-1*) Azimuth Ga. Introducing THE HERITAGE REVEALED SERIES FOR YOUNGER READERS! These three stories of cultural understanding & identity from the author of the critically acclaimed novel, THE NUBIAN, are designed for children ages 7 through 14. THE LEGEND OF THE GOLDEN HAWK: A wild hawk becomes trapped in a game preserve. During his capture he loses his memory, & struggles with the despair of his captivity until he is miraculously rescued by the faithfulness of his brother. JOURNEY TO CLAY MOUNTAIN: A small village at the base of a mountain range is dominated

by the shadows from the largest of these, the Clay Mountain. The villagers toil in frustration until a young boy discovers the wonderful secret of the Clay Mountain, a secret which has been hidden for centuries. LOST...ON VICTORIA LAKE: Two children are cast adrift in their father's fishing boat during a storm. They are rescued by the guidance & provision of their royal ancestors, who appear to the children in a series of magnificent visions. For order information, call 1-800-373-5000 or write to the Azimuth Press, 3002 Dayna Dr, College Park, GA 30349. *Publisher Provided Annotation.*

Smith, Roland. Thunder Cave. LC 9-19714. 1995. 14.95 (*0-7868-0068-2*); 14.89 (*0-7868-2055-1*) Hyprn Child.

Sutherland, Robert D. Sticklewort & Feverfew. LC 79-92898. (Illus.). 360p. (gr. 2 up). 1980. 16.00 (*0-936044-00-4*); pap. 9.00 (*0-936044-01-2*) Pikestaff Pr.

Taylor, Theodore. Cay. LC 69-15161. 160p. (gr. 6-9). 1987. pap. 15.95 (*0-385-07906-0*) Doubleday.

—Sweet Friday Island. LC 93-32435. (gr. 7 up). 1994. write for info. (*0-15-200009-7*); pap. write for info. (*0-15-200012-7*) HarBrace.

—Timothy of the Cay: A Prequel-Sequel. 192p. (gr. 4-7). 1993. 13.95 (*0-15-288358-4*, HB Juv Bks) HarBrace.

Thesman, Jean. When the Road Ends. 192p. (gr. 5-9). 1992. 13.45 (*0-395-59507-X*) HM.

Thompson, Julian F. A Question of Survival. 320p. (gr. 8 up). 1984. pap. 2.50 (*0-380-87775-9*, Flare) Avon.

Treece, Henry. Further Adventures of Robinson Crusoe. Nickless, Will, illus. LC 58-9623. (gr. 7-11). 1958. 21.95 (*0-87599-116-5*) S G Phillips.

Ure, Jean. Plague. LC 93-18198. 224p. (gr. 7 up). 1993. pap. 3.99 (*0-14-036283-5*, Puffin) Puffin Bks.

Wyss, Johann. Swiss Family Robinson. (gr. 5 up). 1964. pap. 1.95 (*0-8049-0013-2*, CL-13) Airmont.

—Swiss Family Robinson. Ward, Lynd & Gregori, Lee, illus. (gr. 4-6). 1949. 14.95 (*0-448-06022-1*, G&D) Putnam Pub Group.

—The Swiss Family Robinson. James, Raymond, ed. Beier, Ellen, illus. LC 89-33888. 48p. (gr. 3-6). 1990. lib. bdg. 12.89 (*0-8167-1875-X*); pap. text ed. 3.95 (*0-8167-1876-8*) Troll Assocs.

—Swiss Family Robinson. 1993. 12.99 (*0-517-06022-1*) Random Hse Value.

SUSPENSION BRIDGES

see Bridges

SUTCLIFF, ROSEMARY

Sutcliff, Rosemary. Blue Remembered Hills: A Recollection. (Illus.). 144p. 1992. pap. 8.95 (*0-374-40714-2*, Sunburst) FS&G.

SWALLOWS–FICTION

Politi, Leo. Song of the Swallows. Politi, Leo, illus. 32p. (gr. k-3). 1987. pap. 4.95 (*0-689-71140-9*, Aladdin) Macmillan Child Grp.

—Song of the Swallows. reissue ed. LC 49-8215. (Illus.). 32p. (gr. 1-4). 1987. SBE 14.95 (*0-684-18831-7*, Scribners Young Read) Macmillan Child Grp.

SWAMPS

see Marshes

SWANS

Ayme, Marcel. Cygnes. Sabatier, Roland, illus. (FRE.). 72p. (gr. 1-5). 1990. pap. 9.95 (*2-07-031235-6*) Schoenhof.

Coldrey, Jennifer. The Swan on the Lake. LC 86-5719. (Illus.). 32p. (gr. 4-6). 1987. 17.27 (*1-55532-066-X*) Gareth Stevens Inc.

—The World of Swans. LC 86-5721. (Illus.). 32p. (gr. 2-3). 1987. PLB 17.27 (*1-55532-070-8*) Gareth Stevens Inc.

Curry, Jerri. The Swan: A Storybook for Adults & Other Children. Poppler, Sarah, illus. 21p. (gr. 7 up). 1989. incl. cassette 13.95g (*0-944586-00-7*) WIN Pub.

A Storybook for Adults & Other Children is a series of nine metaphoric family fairytales. The poetic stories have many meanings that allow the audience to explore life's issues. Published: THE SWAN (commitment) with seven-minute audio tape. Crystal learns about love on Puddle Pond as narrated by Thomas the toad. Work in progress: Shy Violet (self esteem) won't bloom because she doesn't think she is pretty. Old Ollie the Octopus (fear) is afraid to leave his rock & the Angel fish succeeds in helping Ollie let go of his rock. Snowflake (control) wants to know where she will land. Klinker the Clown (special needs) learns to accept his multi-striped face when the other clowns have solid color faces. Puffer (friendship) learns how her actions impact those around her. The Musical Miracle Merry-Go-Round (positive thinking) allows David to achieve the ability to believe. Buttercup & the butterflies (competition) want Mother Nature to make a decision about competition. Star (identity) wants to know who she is, so she searches throughout the universe to find out. There are questions & activities at the end of each story. Center for Family Mediation & Counseling, Jerri Curry, Ph.D. MFCC, 1530 Webster St., D, Fairfield, CA 94533; (707) 428-0228. *Publisher Provided Annotation.*

Hogan, Paula Z. The Black Swan. Hockerman, Dennis, illus. LC 78-27416. 32p. (gr. 1-4). 1979. PLB 19.97 (*0-8172-1254-X*) Raintree Steck-V.

—The Black Swan. LC 78-27416. (Illus.). 32p. (gr. 1-4). 1984. PLB 29.28 incl. cassette (*0-8172-2225-1*) Raintree Steck-V.

Horton, Tom. Swanfall: Journey of the Tundra Swans. Harp, Dave, photos by. (Illus.). 48p. (gr. 1-3). 1991. 15.95 (*0-8027-8106-3*); PLB 16.85 (*0-8027-8107-1*) Walker & Co.

Rothaus, Jim. Ducks, Geese, & Swans. 24p. (gr. 3). 1988. PLB 14.95 (*0-88682-224-6*) Creative Ed.

Selsam, Millicent E. & Hunt, Joyce. A First Look at Ducks, Geese & Swans. Springer, Harriet, illus. 32p. (gr. 1-4). 1990. 11.95 (*0-8027-6975-6*); lib. bdg. 12.85 (*0-8027-6976-4*) Walker & Co.

SWANS–FICTION

Andersen, Hans Christian. Ugly Duckling. Ross, Katherine, adapted by. LC 90-61004. (Illus., Orig.). (ps-2). 1991. pap. 2.25 (*0-679-81039-0*) Random Bks Yng Read.

—The Wild Swans. Jeffers, Susan, illus. Ehrlich, Amy, retold by. LC 81-65843. (Illus.). 40p. (gr. k up). 1976. 15.95 (*0-8037-9381-2*) Dial Bks Young.

—Wild Swans. Jeffers, Susan, illus. LC 81-65843. 40p. (gr. k up). 1987. pap. 5.95 (*0-8037-0451-8*) Dial Bks Young.

Dalton, Annie. Swan Sister. large type ed. (gr. 1-8). 1994. sewn 16.95 (*0-7451-2039-3*, Galaxy Child Lrg Print) Chivers N Amer.

Helprin, Mark. Swan Lake. Van Allsburg, Chris, illus. 112p. (gr. 4-7). 1992. pap. 12.95 (*0-395-64647-2*) HM.

Lasky, Kathryn. Sea Swan. Stock, Catherine, illus. LC 88-1444. 32p. (gr. k-3). 1988. RSBE 14.95 (*0-02-751700-4*, Macmillan Child Bk) Macmillan Child Grp.

Mayo, Virginia. The Swan. (Illus.). 32p. (ps-3). 1994. 12.95 (*0-8120-6408-9*); pap. 5.95 (*0-8120-1938-5*) Barron.

Mitchell, Adrian. The Ugly Duckling. Heale, Jonathan, illus. LC 93-39962. 32p. (ps-3). 1994. 14.95 (*1-56458-557-3*) Dorling Kindersley.

El Patito Feo. (SPA.). (gr. 1). 1990. casebound 3.50 (*0-7214-1407-9*) Ladybird Bks.

Salvadeo, Michele B. & Ossorio, Joseph D. The Stuck-up Swan. (Illus.). 48p. (gr. 3-5). 1994. pap. 6.95 (*1-56721-057-0*) Twnty-Fifth Cent Pr.

The Ugly Duckling. (Illus.). 32p. (gr. 3-7). 1993. 10.95 (*1-878685-75-9*, Bedrock Press) Turner Pub GA.

Wellington, Monica. Seasons of Swans. LC 89-28893. (Illus.). 32p. (ps-2). 1990. 12.95 (*0-525-44621-4*, DCB) Dutton Child Bks.

White, E. B. E. B. White Boxed Set. Incl. Charlotte's Web; The Trumpet of the Swan; Stuart Little. (Illus.). (gr. 3 up). 1972. 39.00 (*0-06-026399-7*) HarpC Child Bks.

—E. B. White Boxed Set. Incl. Charlotte's Web; The Trumpet of the Swan; Stuart Little. (Illus.). (gr. 3 up). 1974. pap. 11.85 (*0-06-440061-1*, Trophy) HarpC Child Bks.

—Trumpet of the Swan. Frascino, Edward, illus. LC 72-112484. (gr. 3-6). 1970. 13.00 (*0-06-026397-0*); PLB 12.89 (*0-06-026398-9*) HarpC Child Bks.

—The Trumpet of the Swan. Frascino, Edward, illus. LC 72-112484. 222p. (gr. 3 up). 1973. pap. 3.95 (*0-06-440048-4*, Trophy) HarpC Child Bks.

Willard, Barbara. A Flight of Swans. (gr. k up). 1989. pap. 3.25 (*0-440-20458-5*, LFL) Dell.

SWEDEN

Bailey, Donna. Sweden. LC 91-22052. (Illus.). 32p. (gr. 1-4). 1992. PLB 18.99 (*0-8114-2567-3*) Raintree Steck-V.

Hinz, Martin. Sweden. LC 85-2643. 128p. (gr. 5-9). 1985. PLB 20.55 (*0-516-02788-3*) Childrens.

Zickgraf, Ralph. Sweden. (Illus.). 96p. (gr. 5 up). 1988. lib. bdg. 14.95 (*1-55546-797-0*) Chelsea Hse.

SWEDEN–FICTION

Ayres, Becky H. Per & the Dala Horse. Gilbert, Yvonne, illus. LC 93-38596. 1995. write for info. (*0-385-32075-2*) Doubleday.

Beskow, Elsa. Pelle's New Suit. Beskow, Elsa, illus. 16p. (ps-1). 1929. PLB 13.89 (*0-06-020496-6*) HarpC Child Bks.

Lindgren, Astrid. A Calf for Christmas. Lucas, Barbara, tr. Tornqvist, Marit, illus. 32p. (ps up). 1991. bds. 13.95 (*91-29-59920-2*, Pub. by R & S Bks) FS&G.

—Pippi Goes on Board. Glanzman, Louis S., illus. (gr. 4-6). 1957. pap. 13.00 (*0-670-55677-7*) Viking Child Bks.

—Pippi in the South Seas. Bothmer, Gerry, tr. Glanzman, Louis S., illus. (gr. 4-6). 1959. pap. 13.00 (*0-670-55711-0*) Viking Child Bks.

—Pippi Longstocking. Lamborn, Florence, tr. Glanzman, Louis S., illus. (gr. 4-6). 1950. pap. 12.95 (*0-670-55745-5*) Viking Child Bks.

—The Tomten. Wiberg, Harald, illus. LC 61-10658. (gr. 1-3). 1979. 14.95 (*0-698-20147-7*, Coward); (Coward) Putnam Pub Group.

Nilsson, Ulf. If You Didn't Have Me. Eriksson, Eva, illus. Blecher, Lone T. & Blecher, George, trs. LC 86-21327. (Illus.). 128p. (gr. 2-5). 1987. SBE 13.95 (*0-689-50406-3*, M K McElderry) Macmillan Child Grp.

Schwartz, David. Supergrandpa. (Illus.). (ps-3). 1991. 13.95 (*0-688-09898-3*); 13.88 (*0-688-09899-1*) Lothrop.

SWEDES IN THE U. S.

McGill, Allyson. The Swedish Americans. Moynihan, Daniel P., intro. by. (Illus.). 112p. (gr. 5 up). 1988. lib. bdg. 17.95 (*1-55546-135-2*) Chelsea Hse.

SWEDES IN THE U. S.–FICTION

Munson, Sammye. Goodbye, Sweden, Hello Texas. LC 93-38928. 1994. 14.95 (*0-89015-948-3*) Sunbelt Media.

Nixon, Joan L. Land of Dreams. LC 93-8734. 1994. 14.95 (*0-385-31170-2*) Delacorte.

SWIMMING

see also Diving

American Red Cross Staff. American Red Cross Swimming & Diving. 356p. 1992. pap. 20.00 (*0-8016-6506-X*) Mosby Yr Bk.

Bailey, Donna. Swimming. LC 90-36527. (Illus.). 32p. (gr. 1-4). 1990. PLB 18.99 (*0-8114-2852-4*); pap. 3.95 (*0-8114-4716-2*) Raintree Steck-V.

Carson, Charles. Make the Team: Swimming & Diving. (gr. 4-7). 1991. pap. 5.95 (*0-316-13028-1*, Spts Illus Kids) Little.

Fischel, E. Swimming & Diving Skills. (Illus.). 48p. (gr. 6-12). 1989. (Usborne); pap. 5.95 (*0-7460-0171-1*) EDC.

Gutman, Bill. Swimming. LC 89-7380. (Illus.). 64p. (gr. 3-8). 1990. PLB 14.95 (*0-942545-89-3*) Marshall Cavendish.

Henning, Jean M. Six Days to Swim-Jeff Farrell: A Story of Olympic Courage. Daland, P., intro. by. LC 71-103031. (Illus.). (gr. 6-12). 1970. 3.50 (*0-911822-02-X*) Swimming.

Kolbisen, Irene M. Froggie Kicks & Duck Dives: A Child's Primer for Beginning Swimming. Reiter, John, ed. Zmolek, Sandy D., illus. Graves, Steve, intro. by. (Illus.). (ps). 1990. 12.95 (*1-877863-02-5*); pap. 8.95 (*0-685-26751-2*) I Think I Can.

—Starfish Floats & Motorboats: A Child's Primer for Beginning Swimming. Reiter, John, ed. Zmolek, Sandy D., illus. Graves, Steve, intro. by. (Illus.). 20p. (ps). 1990. 12.95g (*1-877863-01-7*); pap. 8.95g (*0-685-26750-4*) I Think I Can.

—Wiggle-Butts & Up-Faces: A Child's Primer for Beginning Swimming. Reiter, John, ed. Zmolek, Sandy D., illus. Graves, Steve, intro. by. (Illus.). 32p. (ps). 1989. PLB 14.95 (*1-877863-00-9*) I Think I Can.

McSweeney, Sean & Sampson, Rebecca. Swimming. (Illus.). 64p. (gr. 7-10). 1993. 24.95 (*0-7134-7128-X*, Pub. by Batsford UK) Trafalgar.

National Safety Council Staff. Learn to Swim, Journey One. 1993. pap. text ed. 50.00 10 pack (*0-86720-788-4*) Jones & Bartlett.

Noble, Jim. Swimming. LC 91-6314. (Illus.). 32p. (gr. k-4). 1991. 11.90 (*0-531-18466-8*, Pub. by Bookwright Pr) Watts.

Sanborn, Laura & Eberhardt, Lorraine. Swim Free. Jones, Shari, illus. 32p. (gr. 6-12). 1982. pap. 6.95x (*0-910715-00-9*) Search Public.

Sanchez, Isidro & Peris, Carme. Summer Sports. (Illus.). 32p. (ps-1). 1992. pap. 5.95 (*0-8120-4865-2*) Barron.

Sandelson, Robert. Swimming & Diving. LC 91-16117. (Illus.). 48p. (gr. 6). 1991. text ed. 13.95 RSBE (*0-89686-670-X*, Crestwood Hse) Macmillan Child Grp.

Winter, Ginny L. Swimming Book. Winter, Ginny L., illus. (gr. k-3). 1964. 8.95 (*0-8392-3037-0*) Astor-Honor.

YMCA of the U. S. A. Staff. The Minnow Swim Book. 24p. 1990. pap. 2.00 (*0-87322-288-1*, LYMC5089) Human Kinetics.

—The Polliwog Swim Book. 24p. 1990. pap. 2.00 (*0-87322-274-1*, LYMC5087) Human Kinetics.

SWIMMING–FICTION

Borden, Louise. Albie the Lifeguard. Sayles, Elizabeth, illus. LC 91-11327. 32p. (ps-3). 1993. 14.95 (*0-590-44585-5*) Scholastic Inc.

Brown, M. K. Let's Go Swimming with Mr. Sillypants. Brown, M. K., illus. LC 85-29900. 32p. (ps-2). 1992. pap. 4.99 (*0-517-59030-1*) Crown Bks Yng Read.

Byars, Betsy C. The Night Swimmers. Howell, Troy, illus. 144p. (gr. 5-9). 1983. pap. 3.50 (*0-440-45857-9*, YB) Dell.

—Night Swimmers. large type ed. 1990. Repr. PLB 15.95 (*1-55736-177-0*, Crnrstn Bks) BDD LT Grp.

Crutcher, Chris. Stotan! LC 85-12712. 192p. (gr. 7 up). 1986. reinforced trade ed. 12.00 (*0-688-05715-2*) Greenwillow.
Davis, Deborah. My Brother Has AIDS. (gr. 4-8). 1994. 14.95 (*0-689-31922-3*, Atheneum) Macmillan.
Day, Alexandra. River Parade. (Illus.). 32p. (ps-2). 1990. pap. 12.95 (*0-670-82946-3*) Viking Child Bks.
—River Parade. (Illus.). 32p. (gr. 3-7). 1992. pap. 3.99 (*0-14-054158-6*, Puffin) Puffin Bks.
Duder, Tessa. Alex in Rome. LC 91-41275. 166p. (gr. 6 up). 1992. 13.95 (*0-395-62879-2*) HM.
Fraser, Sheila. I Can Swim. Kopper, Lisa, illus. 24p. (ps-3). 1991. 5.95 (*0-8120-6226-4*) Barron.
George, Lindsay B. William & Boomer. George, Lindsay B., illus. LC 86-9789. 24p. (ps-1). 1987. 15.00 (*0-688-06640-2*); PLB 14.93 (*0-688-06641-0*) Greenwillow.
Henley, Claire. Joe's Pool. LC 92-33946. (Illus.). 32p. (ps-1). 1994. 12.95 (*1-56282-431-7*); PLB 12.89 (*1-56282-432-5*) Hyprn Child.
Jenkins, Jerry. The Strange Swimming Coach. (Orig.). (gr. 7-12). 1986. pap. text ed. 4.99 (*0-8024-8238-4*) Moody.
Kessler, Leonard. Last One in Is a Rotten Egg. Kessler, Leonard, illus. LC 69-10209. 64p. (gr. k-3). 1969. PLB 13.89 (*0-06-023158-0*) HarpC Child Bks.
—Last One in Is a Rotten Egg. Kessler, Leonard, illus. LC 69-10209. 64p. (gr. k-3). 1989. pap. 3.50 (*0-06-444118-0*, Trophy) HarpC Child Bks.
Klein, Robin. Boss of the Pool. 96p. (gr. 3-7). 1992. pap. 3.99 (*0-14-036037-9*) Puffin Bks.
Korman, Gordon. Go Jump in the Pool! 192p. (gr. 4-6). 1991. pap. 2.95 (*0-590-44209-0*, Apple Paperbacks) Scholastic Inc.
Lessing, Doris. Through the Tunnel. (gr. 4-12). 1989. 13.95 (*0-88682-346-3*, 97224-098) Creative Ed.
Lindman, Maj. Snipp, Snapp, Snurr Learn to Swim. (Illus.). 32p. 1993. Repr. lib. bdg. 14.95x (*1-56849-006-2*) Buccaneer Bks.
Makris, Kathryn. A Different Way. 192p. 1989. pap. 2.95 (*0-380-75728-1*, Flare) Avon.
Marino, Jan. Like Some Kind of Hero. (gr. 7 up). 1992. 14.95 (*0-316-54626-7*) Little.
Miles, Betty. Sink or Swim. 208p. (gr. 3-7). 1987. pap. 2.95 (*0-380-69913-3*, Camelot) Avon.
Mock, Dorothy. Aqua Kid Saves the Day: The Good News Kids Learn about Peace. (Illus.). 32p. (Orig.). (ps-2). 1992. pap. 3.99 (*0-570-04718-8*) Concordia.
Napoli, Donna J. When the Water Closes over My Head. Poydar, Nancy, illus. LC 93-14486. 60p. (gr. 2-5). 1994. 13.99 (*0-525-45083-1*) Dutton Child Bks.
Percy, Graham. Meg & the Great Race. Percy, Graham, illus. LC 92-44851. (ps-3). 1993. 15.95 (*1-56766-077-0*) Childs World.
Petty, Kate. Mr. Toad to the Rescue. Baker, Alan, illus. 24p. (ps-2). 1992. 8.95 (*0-8120-6273-6*) Barron.
Weston, Martha. Tuck in the Pool. LC 94-7408. 1995. write for info. (*0-395-65479-3*, Clarion Bks) HM.
Williams, Karin. Swimming. Williams, Karin, illus. LC 93-83002. 12p. (ps-1). 1994. 4.99 (*0-679-85000-7*) Random Bks Yng Read.

SWINE
see Hogs

SWING MUSIC
see Jazz Music

SWITZERLAND
Hintz, Martin. Switzerland. LC 86-9581. (Illus.). 128p. (gr. 5-9). 1986. PLB 20.55 (*0-516-02790-5*) Childrens.
Schrepfer, Margaret. Switzerland: The Summit of Europe. LC 88-35913. (Illus.). 144p. (gr. 5 up). 1989. text ed. 14.95 RSBE (*0-87518-405-7*, Dillon) Macmillan Child Grp.

SWITZERLAND–FICTION
Heidi. (Illus.). 24p. (gr. k-3). 1993. pap. 2.50 (*1-56144-296-8*, Honey Bear Bks) Modern Pub NYC.
Obligado, Lilian. The Chocolate Cow. LC 91-27464. (Illus.). 48p. (ps-2). 1993. pap. 14.00 JRT (*0-671-73852-6*, S&S BFYR) S&S Trade.
Pacinelli, Donna, illus. Heidi. 48p. (gr. 2-5). 1991. 6.95 (*0-88101-112-6*) Unicorn Pub.
Spyri, Johanna. Heidi. LC 85-13292. (gr. 5 up). 1964. pap. 1.95 (*0-8049-0018-3*, CL-18) Airmont.
—Heidi. LC 85-13292. (Illus.). (gr. 4-6). 1988. pap. 3.25 (*0-590-42046-1*) Scholastic Inc.
—Heidi. LC 85-13292. 240p. (gr. 3-7). 1983. pap. 2.25 (*0-14-035002-0*, Puffin) Puffin Bks.
—Heidi. Dole, Helen B., tr. Sharp, William, illus. LC 93-50908. 1994. write for info. (*0-448-40563-6*, G&D) Putnam Pub Group.
—Moni, the Goat Boy: And Other Stories. (Illus.). 218p. 1993. pap. 5.95 (*1-883453-00-3*) Deutsche Buchhandlung.

SYMBIOSIS
see Botany–Ecology

SYMBOLISM
see also Christian Art and Symbolism; Heraldry
Barth, Edna. Lilies, Rabbits, & Painted Eggs: The Story of the Easter Symbols. Arndt, Ursula, illus. LC 74-79033. (gr. 3-6). 1979. (Clarion Bks); pap. 5.95 (*0-395-30550-0*, Clarion Bks) HM.
Fisher, Leonard E. Symbol Art: Thirteen Squares, Circles & Triangles from Around the World. Fisher, Leonard E., illus. LC 85-42805. 64p. (gr. 4-6). 1986. SBE 16.95 (*0-02-735270-6*, Four Winds) Macmillan Child Grp.

SYNAGOGUES
Freeman, Grace & Sugarman, Joan. Inside the Synagogue. rev. ed. Mass, Ronald, photos by. (Illus.). 64p. (gr. 1-3). 1984. pap. 6.00 (*0-8074-0268-0*, 301785) UAHC.
Levin, Meyer & Kurzband, Toby. Story of the Synagogue. LC 57-13093. (gr. 4-6). 1957. pap. 6.95x (*0-87441-006-1*); activity bk. 3.50 (*0-87441-007-X*) Behrman.
Rosenblum, Richard. The Old Synagogue. Rosenbloom, Roger, illus. 32p. (gr. k-3). 1989. 12.95 (*0-8276-0322-3*) JPS Phila.
Weisser, M. My Synagogue. Rosenblum, R., illus. 25p. (gr. k-5). 1984. pap. text ed. 4.25 (*0-87441-386-9*) Behrman.

SYNTHETIC PRODUCTS
see also Plastics
also names of snythetic products, e.g. Rubber, Artificial; etc.

SYRIA
Beaton, Margaret. Syria. LC 88-18697. (Illus.). 128p. (gr. 5-9). 1988. PLB 20.55 (*0-516-02708-5*) Childrens.
Lerner Publications, Department of Geography Staff. Syria in Pictures. (Illus.). 64p. (gr. 5 up). 1990. lib. bdg. 17.50 (*0-8225-1867-8*) Lerner Pubns.
Patterson, Charles. Hafez Al-Asad. (Illus.). 128p. (gr. 8 up). 1991. PLB 13.98 (*0-671-69468-5*, J Messner); pap. 7.95 (*0-671-69469-3*) S&S Trade.

SYSTEMS ENGINEERING
see also Bionics

T

T V
see Television

TABLE
Giblin, James C. From Hand to Mouth: Or, How We Invented Knives, Forks, Spoons, & Chopsticks, & the Table Manners To Go with Them. LC 86-29341. (Illus.). 96p. (gr. 3-7). 1987. (Crowell Jr Bks); PLB 13.89 (*0-690-04662-6*, Crowell Jr Bks) HarpC Child Bks.

TABLE TENNIS
see Ping-Pong

TADPOLES
see Frogs

TAFT, WILLIAM HOWARD, PRESIDENT U. S. 1857-1930
Casey, Jane C. William Howard Taft. LC 88-8675. (Illus.). 100p. (gr. 3 up). 1989. PLB 14.40 (*0-516-01366-1*) Childrens.
Falkof, Lucille. William H. Taft: Twenty-Seventh President of the United States. Young, Richard G., ed. LC 89-39947. (Illus.). 128p. (gr. 5-9). 1990. PLB 17.26 (*0-944483-56-9*) Garrett Ed Corp.
Sandak, Cass R. The Tafts. LC 92-37839. (Illus.). 48p. (gr. 5). 1993. text ed. 12.95 RSBE (*0-89686-647-5*, Crestwood Hse) Macmillan Child Grp.

TAHITI–FICTION
Fremantle, Anne. Island of Cats. Sapieha, Christine, illus. (gr. 1-4). 1964. 12.95 (*0-8392-3011-7*) Astor-Honor.

TAILORING
Here are entered works on the cutting and making of men's, or men's and women's clothing. Works limited to the cutting and making of women's clothes are entered under Dressmaking.
see also Uniforms, Military

TAILORS–FICTION
Friedman, Aileen. A Cloak for the Dreamer. Howard, Kim, illus. LC 94-11274. 1994. write for info. (*0-590-48987-9*) Scholastic Inc.
Grimm, Jacob & Grimm, Wilhelm K. The Brave Little Tailor: A Classic Tale. Jose, Eduard, adapted by. Moncure, Jane B., tr. Rovira, Francesc, illus. LC 88-35311. 32p. (gr. 1-4). 1988. PLB 13.95 (*0-89565-460-1*) Childs World.
Littledale, Freya. Brave Little Tailor. 1990. pap. 2.50 (*0-590-42797-0*) Scholastic Inc.
Potter, Beatrix. Tailleur de Gloucester. (FRE.). 58p. 1991. 10.95 (*2-07-056076-7*) Schoenhof.
—Tailleur de Gloucester. (FRE., Illus.). 58p. 1991. 9.95 (*0-7859-3630-0*, 2070560767) Fr & Eur.

TAIWAN
see Formosa

TALES
see Fables; Fairy Tales; Folklore; Legends

TALKING
see Speech

TALL TALES
see American Wit and Humor; Folklore; Legends

TANKS (MILITARY SCIENCE)
Awdry, W. Thomas the Tank Engine Press-out Model Book. (gr. 4-7). 1994. pap. 4.99 (*0-679-84466-X*) Random Bks Yng Read.
Barrett, Norman S. Tanques. (SPA., Illus.). 32p. (gr. k-4). 1991. PLB 11.90 (*0-531-07922-8*) Watts.
Hogg, Ian V. Tanks. Sarson, Peter & Bryan, Tony, illus. LC 84-9650. 48p. (gr. 5 up). 1985. PLB 14.95 (*0-8225-1378-1*, First Ave Edns); pap. 4.95 (*0-8225-9507-9*, First Ave Edns) Lerner Pubns.
Jefferis, David. Battle Kings: The History of Tanks. LC 90-46259. (Illus.). 32p. (gr. 5-8). 1991. PLB 12.40 (*0-531-14193-4*) Watts.
Nicholaus, J. Main Battle Tanks. (Illus.). 48p. (gr. 3-8). 1989. lib. bdg. 18.60 (*0-86592-420-1*); 13.95s.p. (*0-685-58576-X*) Rourke Corp.
Norman, C. J. Tanks. (Illus.). 32p. (gr. 2 up). 1990. pap. 4.95 (*0-531-15145-X*) Watts.

TANZANIA
Aardema, Verna. Bimwili & the Zimwi. Meddaugh, Susan, illus. LC 85-4449. 32p. (ps-3). 1985. 14.99 (*0-8037-0212-4*); PLB 12.89 (*0-8037-0213-2*) Dial Bks Young.
Blauer, Ettagale & Laure, Jason. Tanzania. LC 93-35495. (Illus.). 128p. (gr. 5-8). 1994. PLB 20.55 (*0-516-02622-4*) Childrens.
Department of Geography, Lerner Publications. Tanzania in Pictures. (Illus.). 64p. (gr. 5 up). 1988. PLB 17.50 (*0-8225-1838-4*) Lerner Pubns.
Houston, Dick. Safari Adventure. Houston, Dick, photos by. LC 91-8038. (Illus.). 160p. (gr. 6 up). 1991. 15.95 (*0-525-65051-2*, Cobblehill Bks) Dutton Child Bks.
McCulla, Patricia E. Tanzania. (Illus.). 112p. (gr. 5 up). 1989. lib. bdg. 14.95 (*1-55546-784-9*) Chelsea Hse.

TAOISM
Brown, Stephen F. Taoism. (Illus.). 128p. (gr. 7-12). 1992. bds. 17.95x (*0-8160-2448-0*) Facts on File.
Hoff, Benjamin. The Te of Piglet. (Illus.). 224p. 1992. 16.00 (*0-525-93496-0*, Dutton) NAL-Dutton.

TAVERNS
see Restaurants, Bars, etc.

TAXATION–U. S.
Hirsch, Charles. Taxation. LC 92-5198. (Illus.). 48p. (gr. 5-6). 1992. PLB 21.34 (*0-8114-7356-2*) Raintree Steck-V.

TAXIDERMY
see also Zoological Specimens–Collection and Preservation

TAYLOR, ZACHARY, PRESIDENT U.S. 1784-1850
Collins, David R. Zachary Taylor: Twelfth President of the United States. Young, Richard G., ed. LC 88-24539. (Illus.). (gr. 5-9). 1989. PLB 17.26 (*0-944483-17-8*) Garrett Ed Corp.

TCHAIKOVSKY, PETER ILYICH, 1840-1893
Rachlin, Ann. Tchaikovsky. Hellard, Susan, illus. 24p. (gr. k-3). 1993. pap. 5.95 (*0-8120-1545-2*) Barron.
Tames, Richard. Peter Ilyich Tchaikovsky. (Illus.). 32p. (gr. 5-8). 1991. PLB 12.40 (*0-531-14108-X*) Watts.
Thompson, Wendy. Pyotr Ilyich Tchaikovsky. (Illus.). 48p. (gr. 5 up). 1993. 17.99 (*0-670-84476-4*) Viking Child Bks.
Venezia, Mike. Peter Tchaikovsky. Venezia, Mike, illus. LC 94-9479. 48p. (gr. 4 up). 1994. PLB 17.20 (*0-516-04537-7*); pap. 4.95 (*0-516-44537-5*) Childrens.

TEA ROOMS
see Restaurants, Bars, etc.

TEACHER TRAINING
see Teachers–Training

TEACHERS
see also Educators; Teaching
Beckman, Beatrice. I Can Be a Teacher. LC 84-23236. (Illus.). 32p. (gr. k-3). 1985. PLB 11.80 (*0-516-01843-4*); pap. 3.95 (*0-516-41843-2*) Childrens.
Bentley, Judith. Teachers & Preachers. (Illus.). 96p. (gr. 5-8). 1995. bds. 16.95 (*0-8050-2996-6*) TFC Bks NY.
Braithwaite, E. R. To Sir, with Love. (gr. 9-12). 1992. pap. 3.99 (*0-515-10519-8*) Jove Pubns.
Burchard, Peter. Charlotte Forten: A Black Teacher in the Civil War. LC 94-18305. (Illus.). 96p. (gr. 4-7). 1995. 16.00 (*0-517-59242-8*); PLB write for info. (*0-517-59243-6*) Crown Bks Yng Read.
Daniel, Kira. Teacher. Paterson, Diane, illus. LC 88-10041. 32p. (gr. k-3). 1989. PLB 10.89 (*0-8167-1430-4*); pap. text ed. 2.95 (*0-8167-1431-2*) Troll Assocs.
Eberts, Marjorie & Gisler, Margaret. Career Portraits: Teaching. LC 93-47956. (gr. 9-12). 1995. 13.95 (*0-8442-4362-0*, VGM Career Bks) NTC Pub Grp.
Gilman, Alma B. & Gilman, Clarence R. Revelations in a Schoolroom: And Other Recollections As Remembered in the Year 1984. Custard Paste Art Staff & Loweree, Paul, illus. Kelley, Win, intro. by. 56p. (Orig.). 1984. pap. 3.75 (*0-9613914-0-5*) A B Gilman.
Houston, Gloria M. My Great-Aunt Arizona. Lamb, Susan C., illus. LC 90-44112. 32p. (gr. 1-4). 1992. 15.00 (*0-06-022606-4*); PLB 14.89 (*0-06-022607-2*) HarpC Child Bks.
Johnson, Jean. Teachers: A to Z. (Illus.). (gr. 1-3). 1987. 11.95 (*0-8027-6676-5*); PLB 12.85 (*0-8027-6677-3*) Walker & Co.
Neimark, Anne E. A Deaf Child Listened: Thomas Gallaudet, Pioneer in American Education. LC 82-23942. 160p. (gr. 7up). 1983. 11.95 (*0-688-01719-3*) Morrow Jr Bks.
Page, Andrea C. Student Success Tutor Directory (TM) Manatee & Sarasota County, 1990-91 Edition. (Illus.). 128p. (gr. k-12). 1990. pap. write for info. (*0-9621214-2-8*) Computer Pr.
Unger, Harlow G. Teachers & Educators. LC 94-8628. 1994. write for info. (*0-8160-2990-3*) Facts on File.

TEACHERS–FICTION
Allard, Harry & Marshall, James. Miss Nelson Is Missing! Marshall, James, illus. (gr. k-3). 1985. reinforced bdg. 13.45 (*0-395-25296-2*); pap. 3.80 (*0-395-40146-1*) HM.
Avery, Gillian. Maria Escapes. Snow, Scott, illus. LC 91-36730. 272p. (gr. 4-8). 1992. pap. 15.00 jacketed, 3-pc. bdg. (*0-671-77074-8*, S&S BFYR) S&S Trade.

Avi. Who Was That Masked Man, Anyway? LC 92-7942. 176p. (gr. 4 up). 1992. 14.95 (*0-531-05457-8*); PLB 14.99 (*0-531-08607-0*) Orchard Bks Watts.
Benjamin, Saragail K. My Dog Ate It. LC 93-25218. 128p. (gr. 3-7). 1994. 14.95 (*0-8234-1047-1*) Holiday.
Brooks, Jerome. Knee Holes. LC 91-25398. 144p. (gr. 7 up). 1992. 14.95 (*0-531-05994-4*); lib. bdg. 14.99 (*0-531-08594-5*) Orchard Bks Watts.
Brown, Marc. Arturo y Sus Problemas Con el Professor: Arthur's Teacher Trouble. (ps-3). 1994. 15.95 (*0-316-11379-4*); pap. 5.95 (*0-316-11380-8*) Little.
Brown, Marc T. Arthur's Teacher Trouble. Brown, Marc T., illus. 32p. (ps-3). 1989. 15.95 (*0-316-11244-5*, Joy St Bks); pap. 4.95 (*0-316-11186-4*, Joy St Bks) Little.
Bunt, Sandra K. The Other Side of the Desk. DeVito, Pam, illus. LC 90-71374. 135p. (Orig.). (gr. 3-6). 1992. pap. 9.95 (*0-932433-80-4*) Windswept Hse.
Christian, Mary B. Swamp Monsters. Brown, Marc T., illus. LC 93-25616. (gr. 1-4). 1994. pap. 3.25 (*0-14-036841-8*, Puffin) Puffin Bks.
Cleary, Beverly. Dear Mr. Henshaw. (gr. 4-7). 1992. pap. 1.99 (*0-440-21366-5*) Dell.
Clements, Andrew. Billy & the Bad Teacher. Savadier, Elivia, illus. LC 92-6619. 28p. 1992. pap. 14.95 (*0-88708-244-0*) Picture Bk Studio.
Coville, Bruce. My Teacher Glows in the Dark. MacDonald, Patricia, ed. Pierard, John, illus. 144p. (Orig.). 1991. pap. 3.50 (*0-671-72709-5*, Minstrel Bks) PB.
Cupo, Hortense. No Way Out but Through. LC 93-29519. Date not set. 4.95 (*0-8198-5130-2*) St Paul Bks.
Cusick, Richie T. Teacher's Pet. 224p. (Orig.). (gr. 8-12). 1990. pap. 3.25 (*0-590-43114-5*) Scholastic Inc.
Dicks, Terrance. Teacher's Pet. Littlewood, Valerie, illus. 52p. (gr. 2-5). 1992. pap. 3.50 (*0-8120-4820-2*) Barron.
Ehrlich, Fred. A Class Play with Ms. Vanilla. Gradisher, Martha, illus. 32p. (ps-3). 1992. 9.00 (*0-670-84651-1*) Viking Child Bks.
—A Class Play with Ms. Vanilla. Gradisher, Martha, illus. 32p. (ps-3). 1992. pap. 3.50 (*0-14-054580-8*) Puffin Bks.
Feder, Paula K. Where Does the Teacher Live? Hoban, Lillian, illus. LC 78-13157. 48p. (gr. 1-3). 1979. 12.95 (*0-525-42586-1*, DCB) Dutton Child Bks.
Hallinan, P. K. My Teacher's My Friend. (Illus.). 24p. (ps-3). 1989. pap. 4.95 perfect bdg. (*0-8249-8542-7*, Ideals Child) Hambleton-Hill.
Hilton, James. Goodbye, Mr. Chips. (gr. 7 up). 1969. pap. 2.95 (*0-553-25613-0*) Bantam.
Hoffman, Jim. Fabulous Principal Pie. Hoffman, Joan, ed. (Illus.). 32p. (gr. k-2). 1992. pap. 3.95 (*0-88743-427-4*, 06079) Sch Zone Pub Co.
—Fabulous Principal Pie. Hoffman, Joan, ed. (Illus.). 16p. (gr. k-2). 1992. pap. 2.25 (*0-88743-266-2*, 06033) Sch Zone Pub Co.
Howe, James. The Day the Teacher Went Bananas. Hoban, Lillian, illus. LC 84-1536. 32p. (ps-2). 1984. 12.95 (*0-525-44107-7*, DCB); pap. 3.95 (*0-525-44321-5*, DCB) Dutton Child Bks.
Hurwitz, Johanna. Teacher's Pet. Hamamaka, Sheila, illus. LC 87-24003. 128p. (gr. 2-5). 1988. 12.95 (*0-688-07506-1*) Morrow Jr Bks.
I Want to Be a Teacher. (Illus.). (ps-k). 1991. write for info. (*0-307-12627-7*, Golden Pr) Western Pub.
Irving, Washington. The Legend of Sleepy Hollow. 1991. pap. 7.00 (*0-385-41929-5*) Doubleday.
Kindl, Patrice. Owl in Love. LC 92-26952. 1993. 13.95 (*0-395-66162-5*) HM.
—Owl in Love. 208p. (gr. 7 up). 1994. pap. 3.99 (*0-14-037129-X*) Puffin Bks.
Klass, Sheila S. Kool Ada. (gr. 4-7). 1991. 13.95 (*0-590-43902-2*, Scholastic Hardcover) Scholastic Inc.
Korman, Justine H. The Teacher from Outer Space. Matthews, Bonnie J., illus. LC 93-24846. 32p. (gr. 1-4). 1993. PLB 9.59 (*0-8167-3180-2*); pap. text ed. 2.95 (*0-8167-3181-0*) Troll Assocs.
Levy, Elizabeth. Keep Ms. Sugarman in the Fourth Grade. Henderson, Dave, illus. LC 91-22576. 96p. (gr. 3-6). 1992. 13.00 (*0-06-020426-5*); PLB 12.89 (*0-06-020427-3*) HarpC Child Bks.
—Keep Ms. Sugarman in the Fourth Grade. LC 91-22576. 96p. (gr. 3-6). 1993. pap. 3.95 (*0-06-440487-0*, Trophy) HarpC Child Bks.
McKenna, Colleen O. The Truth about Sixth Grade. 1991. pap. 12.95 (*0-590-44388-7*) Scholastic Inc.
Mallett, Jerry & Bartch, Marian. Close the Curtains. Smith, Mark D., illus. 54p. (gr. 2-5). 1986. PLB 7.50 (*0-8479-9927-0*, 056115) Perma-Bound.
Montgomery, Lucy M. Anne of Avonlea. (gr. 4-7). 1991. pap. 3.25 (*0-590-44556-1*, Apple Classics) Scholastic Inc.
—Anne of Avonlea. 1992. pap. 3.25 (*0-553-15114-2*) Bantam.
Moore, Elaine. The Substitute Teacher from Mars. LC 93-37527. (Illus.). 96p. (gr. 2-6). 1993. pap. text ed. 2.95 (*0-8167-3283-3*) Troll Assocs.
Myers, Laurie. Earthquake in the Third Grade. LC 92-26609. 1993. 13.95 (*0-395-65360-6*, Clarion Bks) HM.
Parish, Peggy. Teach Us, Amelia Bedelia. Sweat, Lynn, illus. 64p. (gr. k-3). 1987. pap. 2.95 (*0-590-43345-8*) Scholastic Inc.
Park, Barbara. Junie B. Jones & Some Sneaky Peeky Spying. Brunkus, Denise, illus. LC 93-5557. 80p. (Orig.). (gr. 1-4). 1994. PLB 9.99 (*0-679-95101-6*); pap. 2.99 (*0-679-85101-1*) Random Bks Yng Read.
Pascal, Francine. Get the Teacher! (ps-3). 1994. pap. 2.99 (*0-553-48106-1*) Bantam.
—The Substitute Teacher. (gr. k-3). 1990. pap. 2.99 (*0-553-15760-4*, Skylark) Bantam.
Petersen, P. J. The Sub. Johnson, Meredith, illus. LC 92-22269. (gr. 2-5). 1993. 12.99 (*0-525-45059-9*, DCB) Dutton Child Bks.
Piasecki, Jerry. They're Torturing Teachers in Room 104. 1992. pap. 3.50 (*0-553-48024-3*) Bantam.
Pinkwater, Jill. Mister Fred. 160p. (gr. 5-8). 1994. 15.99 (*0-525-44778-4*) Dutton Child Bks.
Pulver, Robin. Mrs. Toggle's Beautiful Blue Shoe. Alley, R. W., illus. LC 92-40824. 32p. (ps-2). 1994. RSBE 13.95 (*0-02-775456-1*, Four Winds) Macmillan Child Grp.
Richardson, Arleta. Eighteen & on Her Own. LC 85-29050. 173p. (gr. 3-7). 1986. pap. 3.99 (*0-89191-512-5*, Chariot Bks) Chariot Family.
Sachar, Louis. Marvin Redpost: Alone in His Teacher's House. Sullivan, Barbara, illus. LC 93-19791. 96p. (Orig.). (gr. 1-4). 1994. 2.99 (*0-679-81949-5*); PLB 2.99 (*0-679-91949-X*) Random Bks Yng Read.
Schick, Eleanor. Art Lessons. LC 86-243. (Illus.). 48p. (gr. k-3). 1987. 11.75 (*0-688-05120-0*); lib. bdg. 11.88 (*0-688-05121-9*) Greenwillow.
Shura, Mary F. Our Teacher is Missing. (gr. 4-7). 1993. pap. 2.95 (*0-590-44677-0*) Scholastic Inc.
—Our Teacher is Missing. 1993. pap. 2.95 (*0-590-44597-9*) Scholastic Inc.
Slack, Thomas, ed. The Pleasing Instructor. Graham, Joanne, et al. 368p. 1973. Repr. of 1785 ed. 66.75 (*3-261-01008-8*) P Lang Pubs.
Thaler, Mike. Teacher from the Black Lagoon. (gr. 1-4). 1989. pap. 2.50 (*0-590-41962-5*) Scholastic Inc.
Wolitzer, Meg. Operation: Save the Teacher. 128p. (Orig.). (gr. 4-8). 1993. pap. 3.50 (*0-380-76461-X*, Camelot) Avon.
—Operation: Save the Teacher: Saturday Night Toast. 128p. (Orig.). 1993. pap. 3.50 (*0-380-76462-8*, Camelot) Avon.
—Operation: Save the Teacher: Tuesday Night Pie. 128p. (Orig.). 1993. pap. 3.50 (*0-380-76460-1*, Camelot) Avon.
Yorke, Malcolm. Miss Butterpat Goes Wild. Chamberlain, Margaret, illus. LC 93-20204. 32p. (gr. 1-5). 1993. 10.95 (*1-56458-200-0*) Dorling Kindersley.
—Molly the Mad Basher. Chamberlain, Margaret, illus. LC 93-11407. 32p. (gr. 1-4). 1994. 10.95 (*1-56458-459-3*) Dorling Kindersley.
—Ritchie F. Dweebly Thunders On. Chamberlain, Margaret, illus. LC 93-5003. 32p. (gr. 1-4). 1994. 10.95 (*1-56458-199-3*) Dorling Kindersley.
Zach, Cheryl. Benny & the No-Good Teacher. Wilson, Janet, illus. LC 91-30588. 80p. (gr. 2-6). 1992. SBE 12.95 (*0-02-793706-2*, Bradbury Pr) Macmillan Child Grp.

TEACHERS–TRAINING

Here are entered works dealing with the history and methods of training teachers, including the educational functions of teachers colleges. Works on the study of education as a science are entered under Education–Study and teaching.

Johnston, Janet. Ellie Brader Hates Mr. G. 144p. (gr. 3-6). 1991. 13.45 (*0-395-58195-8*, Clarion Bks) HM.

TEACHERS AND PARENTS

see Home and School

TEACHERS COLLEGES

Here are entered general and historical works about teachers colleges. Works dealing with their educational functions are entered under Teachers–Training.

see also Teachers–Training

TEACHING

see also Child Study; Education; Kindergarten; Study, Method of; Teachers–Training

also subjects with the subdivision Study and Teaching, e.g. Science–Study and Teaching

Bradley, R. C. Teaching for "Self-Directed" Living & Learning in Students - How to Help Students Get in Charge of Their Lives: "Self-Directed" Living & Learning. LC 90-85800. 224p. 1991. text ed. 19.95 (*0-9628624-0-1*) Bassi Bk.
Brisson, Lynn. Three-D Teaching Aids. (Illus.). 64p. (gr. k-6). 1989. pap. text ed. 6.95 (*0-86530-072-0*, IP 166-2) Incentive Pubns.
Dickson, Sue. Complete Classroom Kit. rev. ed. Portadino, Norma, illus. 7968p. (gr. k-3). 1984. pap. 533.00 (*1-55574-000-6*, KC 510) CBN Publishing.
Peterson, Sherrie. Help! for Substitutes. Schmid, Ross, illus. 80p. 1985. tchr's. wkbk. 5.95 (*0-86653-277-3*, GA 642) Good Apple.
Rybak, Sharon. Good Apple Lesson Organizer. 128p. (gr. k-6). 1990. 19.95 (*0-86653-563-2*, GA1149) Good Apple.
—Teach Smarter, Not Harder. 128p. (gr. k-6). 1991. 11.95 (*0-86653-620-5*, GA1339) Good Apple.

TEACHING–VOCATIONAL GUIDANCE

Shockley, Robert & Cutlip, Glen W. Careers in Teaching. rev. ed. 64p. (gr. 7-12). 1990. pap. 9.95 (*0-8239-1718-5*) Rosen Group.

TEACHINGS OF JESUS

see Jesus Christ–Teachings

TEAROOMS

see Restaurants, Bars, etc.

TECHNICAL TERMS

see Technology–Dictionaries

TECHNOLOGY

see also Building; Engineering; Inventions; Machinery; Manufactures

Aaseng, Nathan. Better Mousetraps: Product Improvements That Led to Success. (Illus.). 80p. (gr. 5 up). 1989. PLB 18.95 (*0-8225-0680-7*) Lerner Pubns.
Diamond, Bert. Technology You Can Build. (Illus.). 92p. (Orig.). 1990. pap. text ed. 13.81 (*0-87192-215-0*) Delmar.
Folsom, Michael & Folsom, Marcia. The Macmillan Book of How Things Work. Hammann, Brad, illus. LC 86-23761. 80p. (gr. 3-7). 1987. SBE 16.95 (*0-02-735360-5*, Macmillan Child Bk) Macmillan Child Grp.
Fuller, Melvin L. & Weisberg, Maggie. Student Inventors Lesson Plan. Christensen, Don, illus. 75p. (Orig.). (gr. 4-12). 1989. pap. 14.95x (*0-685-25993-5*) M&M Assocs.
Graham, Ian. How Things Work. LC 94-20013. 1994. write for info. (*0-8160-3218-1*) Facts on File.
Hacker, Michael & Barden, Robert. Living with Technology. 2nd ed. 1991. text ed. 29.95 (*0-8273-4907-6*) Delmar.
Hillman, Susan, et al. Future World. Smith, Guy, et al, illus. LC 89-42981. 48p. (gr. 4-5). 1989. PLB 17.27 (*0-8368-0135-0*) Gareth Stevens Inc.
Iozzi, Louis A. & Bastardo, Peter J. Decisions for Today & Tomorrow. (gr. 9-12). 1990. tchr's. ed. 60.00 (*0-944584-22-5*) Sopris.
McBurney, Jim. Technopoly. Kraven, Mae, ed. Harris, Linda, illus. 96p. (gr. 4-5). 1991. text ed. 19.95 (*0-9629471-0-5*) J McBurney.
Macmillan Educational Company Staff. Macmillan Encyclopedia of Science, 12 vols. (Illus.). 1991. Set. text ed. 360.00 (*0-02-941346-X*) Macmillan.
Marsh, Richard S. Reading & Understanding Technical Information. (Illus.). (gr. 5). 1986. wkbk. 4.95 (*0-89525-758-0*) Ed Activities.
Math, Irwin. Tomorrow's Technology: Experimenting with the Science of the Future. Keith, Hal, illus. LC 91-32341. 80p. (gr. 7 up). 1992. SBE 13.95 (*0-684-19294-2*, Scribners Young Read) Macmillan Child Grp.
Morgan, Sally & Morgan, Adrian. Technology in Action. (Illus.). 48p. (gr. 5-9). 1994. 14.95x (*0-8160-3126-6*) Facts on File.
Newton, David E. Science - Technology - Society Projects for Young Scientists. LC 91-17825. (Illus.). 144p. (gr. 9-12). 1991. PLB 13.90 (*0-531-11047-8*) Watts.
Parker, Steve. The Random House Book of How Things Work. LC 90-9137. (Illus.). 160p. (Orig.). (gr. 3-7). 1991. PLB 19.99 (*0-679-90908-7*); pap. 16.00 (*0-679-80908-2*) Random Bks Yng Read.
Potter, T. & Guild, I. Robotics. Priddy, R., illus. 48p. (gr. 6 up). 1983. PLB 13.96 (*0-88110-661-5*); pap. 6.95 (*0-7460-1466-X*) EDC.
Science & Technology. 160p. 1993. 30.00 (*0-19-910143-4*) OUP.
Simon & Schuster Staff. How Things Work: A Guide to How Human-Made & Living Things Function. (Illus.). 128p. (gr. 3-7). 1988. pap. 9.95 (*0-671-67032-8*, S&S BFYR) S&S Trade.
—Why Things Are: A Guide to Understanding the World Around Us. (Illus.). 128p. (gr. 3-7). 1988. pap. 9.95 (*0-671-67031-X*, S&S BFYR) S&S Trade.
Skurzynski, Gloria. Almost the Real Thing: Simulation in Your High-Tech World. (Illus.). 64p. (gr. 9 up). 1991. SBE 16.95 (*0-02-778072-4*, Bradbury Pr) Macmillan Child Grp.
Technology. 112p. (gr. 4-9). 1989. 18.95 (*1-85435-073-0*) Marshall Cavendish.
Weaver, Rebecca & Dale, Rodney. Machines in the Home. LC 92-21662. (Illus.). 64p. 1993. PLB 16.00 (*0-19-520965-6*) OUP.
Wilkins, Mary-Jane. Everyday Things & How They Work. Bull, Peter, illus. LC 90-12999. 40p. (gr. 4-6). 1991. PLB 12.40 (*0-531-19109-5*, Warwick) Watts.

TECHNOLOGY–DICTIONARIES

Williams, Brian. Science & Technology. LC 92-46589. (Illus.). 96p. (gr. 5 up). 1993. 15.95 (*1-85697-850-8*, Kingfisher LKC); pap. 9.95 (*1-85697-849-4*) LKC.

TECHNOLOGY–FICTION

Discovery with Cap'n Bob & Matey: Voyages of Courage & Adventure. (Illus.). 32p. (gr. 1-4). 1991. 13.95 (*0-931595-08-8*); pap. 7.95 (*0-931595-09-6*) Seascape Enters.
MacGregor, Ellen & Pantell, Dora. Miss Pickerell Meets Mr. H. U. M. new ed. Greer, Charles, illus. 160p. (gr. 2-6). 1974. o.p. (*0-07-044577-X*) McGraw.
Manes, Stephen. It's New!, It's Improved!, It's Terrible! (gr. 2-6). 1989. pap. 3.50 (*0-553-15682-9*, Skylark) Bantam.

TECHNOLOGY–VOCATIONAL GUIDANCE

Southworth, Scott. Exploring High-Tech Careers. rev. ed. Rosen, Roger, ed. 118p. (gr. 7-12). 1993. 14.95 (*0-8239-1502-6*); pap. 9.95 (*0-8239-1717-7*) Rosen Group.

TECHNOLOGY AND CIVILIZATION

see also Machinery in Industry

Encyclopaedia Britannica Publishers, Inc. Staff. Hombre, Ciencia y Tecnologia. (SPA., Illus.). 3160p. 1992. write for info. (*1-56409-005-1*) EBP Latin Am.

TECUMSEH, SHAWNEE CHIEF, 1768-1813

Connell, Kate. These Lands Are Ours: Tecumseh's Fight for the Old Northwest. Jones, Jan N., illus. LC 92-14417. 96p. (gr. 2-5). 1992. PLB 21.34 (*0-8114-7227-2*) Raintree Steck-V.

Fleischer, Jane. Tecumseh, Shawnee War Chief. new ed. LC 78-18046. (Illus.). 48p. (gr. 4-6). 1979. PLB 10.59 (*0-89375-153-7*); pap. 3.50 (*0-89375-143-X*) Troll Assocs.
Ingoglia, Gina. Tecumseh: One Nation for His People. Shaw, Charlie & Bill Smith Studios Staff, illus. LC 92-56162. 80p. (Orig.). (gr. 1-4). 1993. PLB 12.89 (*1-56282-490-2*); pap. 3.50 (*1-56282-489-9*) Disney Pr.
Kent, Zachary. Tecumseh. LC 92-8217. 32p. (gr. 3-6). 1992. PLB 12.30 (*0-516-06660-9*) Childrens.
—Tecumseh. LC 92-8217. (Illus.). 32p. (gr. 3-6). 1993. pap. 3.95 (*0-516-46660-7*) Childrens.
Shorto, Russell. Tecumseh. Furstinger, Nancy, ed. (Illus.). 136p. (gr. 5-7). 1989. PLB 10.95 (*0-382-09569-3*); pap. 7.95 (*0-382-09758-0*) Silver Burdett Pr.

TEEN AGE
see Adolescence; Youth

TEETH
see also Dentistry

All about Our Bodies, Our Teeth. 14p. (gr. k-6). pap. 4.50 (*0-89346-296-9*) Heian Intl.
Asimov, Isaac & Dierks, Carrie. Why Do We Need to Brush Our Teeth. LC 93-20155. 1993. PLB 15.93 (*0-8368-0807-X*) Gareth Stevens Inc.
Bailey, Donna. All about Your Skin, Hair & Teeth. LC 90-10050. (Illus.). 48p. (gr. 2-6). 1990. PLB 20.70 (*0-8114-2783-8*) Raintree Steck-V.
Dievart, Roger. Teeth, Tusks & Fangs. Bogard, Vicki, tr. from FRE. Valat, Pierre-Marie, illus. LC 90-50778. 38p. (gr. k-5). 1991. 5.95 (*0-944589-35-9*, 359) Young Discovery Lib.
Fisher, Barbara. Jolly Molly Molar. Fisher, Barbara, illus. 44p. (Orig.). (gr. 1-3). 1979. pap. 2.00 (*0-934830-10-X*) Ten Penny.
Kleinbard, Gitel. Oh, Zalmy! or, the Tale of the Tooth: Book 2. Kunda, Shmuel, illus. (gr. k-3). 1977. 5.95 (*0-917274-02-4*); pap. 3.95 (*0-917274-03-2*) Mah Tov Pubns.
Lauber, Patricia. What Big Teeth You Have! Weston, Martha, illus. LC 85-47902. 64p. (gr. 2-6). 1986. (Crowell Jr Bks); PLB 13.89 (*0-690-04507-7*, Crowell Jr Bks) HarpC Child Bks.
Le Sieg, Theodore. The Tooth Book. McKie, Roy, illus. LC 80-28320. 48p. (ps-1). 1981. 6.95 (*0-394-84825-X*, XBYR); lib. bdg. 7.99 (*0-394-94825-4*) Random Bks Yng Read.
Nourse, Alan E. The Tooth Book. (gr. 6up). 1977. 6.95 (*0-679-20376-1*) McKay.
Quinlan, Patricia. Brush Them Bright. Fernandes, Eugenie, illus. 32p. (ps-2). 1992. 8.95 (*1-56282-283-7*) Hyprn Child.
Rauzon, Mark. Horns, Antlers, Fangs, & Tusks. LC 90-49726. (ps-3). 1993. 13.00 (*0-688-10230-1*); PLB 12.93 (*0-688-10231-X*) Lothrop.
Showers, Paul. How Many Teeth? Galdone, Paul, illus. 40p. (gr. k-3). 1962. PLB 13.89 (*0-690-40716-5*, Crowell Jr Bks) HarpC Child Bks.
—How Many Teeth? rev. ed. Kelley, True, illus. LC 89-71731. 32p. (ps-1). 1991. pap. 4.95 (*0-06-445098-8*, Trophy) HarpC Child Bks.
—How Many Teeth? rev. ed. Kelley, True, illus. LC 89-13995. 32p. (ps-1). 1991. 15.00 (*0-06-021633-6*); PLB 14.89 (*0-06-021634-4*) HarpC Child Bks.
Ward, Brian. Teeth: And Their Care. (Illus.). 32p. (gr. 5-8). 1991. PLB 12.40 (*0-531-14174-8*) Watts.

TEETH–FICTION

Alberts, Nancy. Teeth Week. (gr. 4-7). 1993. pap. 2.75 (*0-590-45563-X*) Scholastic Inc.
Arthur's Tooth. (ps-3). 1993. pap. 7.95 incl. cass. (*0-316-11339-5*) Little.
Bohonek, Jan B. & Bohonek, Stan B. How Peter Molar Looked for a Smile. Bohonek, Jan & Bohonek, Stan B., illus. Johnsen, David C. LC 83-73507. 32p. (gr. 1-3). 1984. PLB 9.95 (*0-914827-00-6*) Adonis Studio.
Brown, Marc T. Arthur's Tooth, Vol. 1. Brown, Marc T., illus. (ps-3). 1986. pap. 4.95 (*0-316-11246-1*) Little.
Brush Your Teeth Please. (Illus.). 10p. (ps-k). 1993. 9.95 (*0-89577-474-7*, Dist. by Random) RD Assn.
Buller, Jon & Schade, Susan. No Tooth, No Quarter! A Step 3 Book. Buller, Jon, illus. LC 89-30250. 48p. (Orig.). (gr. 2-3). 1989. lib. bdg. 7.99 (*0-394-94956-0*); pap. 3.50 (*0-394-84956-6*, Random Juv) Random Bks Yng Read.
Carrick, Carol. Norman Fools the Tooth Fairy. McCue, Lisa, illus. 32p. 1992. 13.95 (*0-590-42240-5*, Scholastic Hardcover) Scholastic Inc.
Christiana, David. Tooth Fairy's Tale. (ps-3). 1994. 16.00 (*0-374-37677-8*) FS&G.

Dr. Mac: The Tooth Fairy Legend. 50p. (gr. k-3). 1994. 12.95 (*0-9638033-8-7*) Storybk Pub.
Ever wondered or been asked, "What is the story of the Tooth Fairy?" Years ago Dr. Mac, a Dentist & Teacher, was asked this question from children. Not knowing the answer, he decided to find it. He discovered that the origin of the Tooth Fairy was one of the least known & documented stories in our heritage, & that no tale of the Tooth Fairy, based on history & culture, had ever been told. So he wrote THE TOOTH FAIRY LEGEND to give her a place in Western literature. Written to entertain children, the story can enlighten for its basic content is from historical information, folklore, superstitions & customs of the past & present relating to teeth from international sources. His endearing classic, long a favorite of children & adults alike, in this new full-color edition, beautifully illustrated in a classical manner & praised by some of America's leading artists, is still the standard work on this beloved character. For every parent who has ever watched a child place a baby tooth under a pillow, & for every child who has done so in eager anticipation, THE TOOTH FAIRY LEGEND will be an enlightening & fascinating reading. Storybook Publishing, P.O. Box 3218, Manhattan Beach, CA 90266-5133. 310-372-2950.
Publisher Provided Annotation.

Feagles, Anita. The Tooth Fairy. (Illus.). 32p. (gr. k-2). 1993. Repr. of 1962 ed. PLB write for info. (*0-208-02323-2*, Linnet) Shoe String.
Giff, Patricia R. Rat Teeth. Morrill, Leslie, illus. LC 83-16601. 144p. (gr. 4-6). 1984. 12.95 (*0-385-29339-9*); PLB 12.95 (*0-385-29309-7*) Delacorte.
Gillerlain, Gayle. Reverend Thomas's False Teeth. Schutzer, Dena, illus. LC 93-39980. 32p. (gr. k-3). 1995. PLB 14.95 (*0-8167-3303-1*); pap. text ed. 4.95 (*0-8167-3304-X*) BrdgeWater.
Heller, Nicholas. The Tooth Tree. LC 90-39791. (Illus.). 24p. (ps up). 1991. 13.95 (*0-688-09392-2*); PLB 13.88 (*0-688-09393-0*) Greenwillow.
Kroll, Steven. Loose Tooth. (Illus.). 1992. 3.95 (*0-590-45713-6*) Scholastic Inc.
Lipniacka, Ewa. Tooth Fairy. Bogdanowicz, Basia, illus. LC 92-33328. 1993. 6.95 (*1-56656-120-5*, Crocodile Bks) Interlink Pub.
Maccarone, Grace. My Tooth Is about to Fall Out. Lewin, Betsy, illus. LC 94-9772. (gr. 3-7). Date not set. write for info. (*0-590-48376-5*) Scholastic Inc.
Maccarone, Grace & Chardiet, Bernice. Martin & the Tooth Fairy. Karas, G. Brian, illus. 32p. 1991. pap. 2.50 (*0-590-43305-9*) Scholastic Inc.
Macdonald, Maryann. Rosie's Baby Tooth. Sweet, Melissa, illus. LC 90-35923. 32p. (ps-2). 1991. SBE 12.95 (*0-689-31626-7*, Atheneum Child Bk) Macmillan Child Grp.
Marie, Sharon. Granny's Crooked Teeth. 1993. 7.95 (*0-533-10602-8*) Vantage.
Miller, Robert D. Tommy the Toothbrush. Palsa, Soozee, illus. 16p. (gr. 2-4). 1982. write for info Miller OH.
Noll, Sally. I Have a Loose Tooth. LC 91-31456. (Illus.). 32p. (ps-4). 1992. 14.00 (*0-688-11191-2*); PLB 13.93 (*0-688-11192-0*) Greenwillow.
Pohl, Linda. The Wiggly Tooth Book. Kelley, Colleen M., illus. 16p. (ps-2). 1991. 3.95 (*0-9625453-1-7*) L P Pohl.
Showers, Paul. How Many Teeth? LC 68-11004. (Illus.). 40p. (ps-3). 1984. pap. 4.50 (*0-06-445008-2*, Trophy) HarpC Child Bks.
Silverman, Martin. My Tooth Is Loose. Aitken, Amy, illus. 32p. (ps-3). 1992. 8.95 (*0-670-83862-4*) Viking Child Bks.
Taylor, Carol. Toothless Albert. Moroney, Tracey, illus. LC 93-28937. 1994. 4.25 (*0-383-03780-8*) SRA Schl Grp.
Thaler, Mike. The Bully Brothers Trick the Tooth Fairy. Lee, Jared, illus. LC 92-72834. 32p. (ps-3). 1993. pap. 2.25 (*0-448-40519-9*, G&D) Putnam Pub Group.
Tregebov, Rhea. Sasha & the Wiggly Tooth. Desputeaux, Helene, illus. 24p. 1993. 12.95 (*0-317-05541-0*, Pub. by Second Story Pr CN); pap. 5.95 (*0-929005-50-3*, Second Story Pr CN) InBook.
Wilkins, Verna. Dave & the Tooth Fairy. (ps-3). 1993. pap. 3.95 (*0-85953-133-3*) Childs Play.
Williams, Barbara. Albert's Toothache. Chorao, Kay, illus. LC 74-4040. 32p. (ps-1). 1988. pap. 3.95 (*0-525-44363-0*, 0383-120, DCB) Dutton Child Bks.
—Albert's Toothache. Chorao, Kay, illus. (ps-3). pap. 4.99 (*0-14-054733-9*, Puff Unicorn) Puffin Bks.
Zalben, Jane B. Buster Gets Braces. Zalben, Jane B., illus. LC 91-13967. 32p. (ps-2). 1992. 15.95 (*0-8050-1682-1*, Bks Young Read) H Holt & Co.
Ziefert, Harriet. My Tooth is Loose. (Illus.). 32p. (ps-3). 1992. pap. 3.50 (*0-14-054394-5*) Puffin Bks.
—My Tooth Is Loose. (Illus.). (ps-2). 1994. pap. 3.25 (*0-14-037001-3*) Puffin Bks.

TELECOMMUNICATION
see also Cables, Submarine; Interstellar Communication; Radio; Telephone; Television

Graham, Ian. Communications. LC 91-10008. (Illus.). 48p. (gr. 5-8). 1991. PLB 22.80 (*0-8114-2803-6*) Raintree Steck-V.
Kerrod, Robin. Communications. Evans, Ted, illus. LC 93-1913. 64p. (gr. 5 up). 1993. PLB write for info. (*1-85435-624-0*) Marshall Cavendish.
Lampton, Christopher. Telecommunications: From Telegraphs to Modems. LC 90-48230. (Illus.). 96p. (gr. 7-9). 1991. PLB 12.90 (*0-531-12527-0*) Watts.
Mackie, Dan. Communications. (Illus.). 32p. (gr. 4-9). 1987. pap. 5.95 (*0-88625-135-4*) Durkin Hayes Pub.
Skurzynski, Gloria. Get the Message: Telecommunications in Your High-Tech World. LC 92-14892. (Illus.). 64p. (gr. 4 up). 1993. SBE 16.95 (*0-02-778071-6*, Bradbury Pr) Macmillan Child Grp.

TELEGRAPH
see also Cables, Submarine

TELEGRAPH, SUBMARINE
see Cables, Submarine

TELEPATHY
see Thought Transference

TELEPHONE

Adventure Publications. My Very Own Phone Book. (ps-3). 1993. pap. 7.95 (*0-9635490-0-6*) Just Mom & Me.
Becker, Jim & Mayer, Andy. Build Your Own Telephone. LC 93-83372. (Illus.). 64p. (Orig.). (gr. 5 up). 1993. pap. 25.00 (*0-679-83444-3*) Random Bks Yng Read.
Bendick, Jeanne. Eureka! It's a Telephone! Murdocca, Sal, illus. LC 92-5085. 48p. (gr. 2-6). 1993. PLB 15.40 (*1-56294-215-8*) Millbrook Pr.
Melle, Julie. My 911 Book for Help. Collas, Daniel, illus. LC 92-71606. 16p. (ps-6). 1992. pap. text ed. 9.99g (*1-881402-00-2*) CA Storybook.
Skowronski, Deborah. The Non-Reader's Telephone Directory. Jacobson, Julie, illus. LC 82-61510. 36p. 1982. pap. text ed. 2.25 (*0-9609618-0-1*) Sunburst.
Skurzynski, Gloria. Get the Message: Telecommunications in Your High-Tech World. LC 92-14892. (Illus.). 64p. (gr. 4 up). 1993. SBE 16.95 (*0-02-778071-6*, Bradbury Pr) Macmillan Child Grp.
Strazzabosco, Gina & Reynolds, Moira. The Telephone: Uses & Abuses. LC 93-25717. (gr. 5 up). 1993. 13.95 (*0-8239-1608-1*) Rosen Group.
Telephone. (ARA., Illus.). (gr. 5-12). 1987. 3.95x (*0-86685-236-0*) Intl Bk Ctr.
Weiss, Ellen. Telephone Time: A First Book of Telephone Do's & Don'ts. Knight, Hilary, illus. LC 86-42560. 32p. (gr. k-3). 1986. lib. bdg. 5.99 (*0-394-98252-5*) Random Bks Yng Read.
Winitz, Harris. The Telephone. Baker, Syd, illus. 50p. (Orig.). (gr. 7 up). 1987. pap. text ed. 22.00 incl. cass. (*0-939990-50-4*) Intl Linguistics.

TELEPHONE–FICTION

Barnett, Ada, et al. Eddycat Teaches Telephone Skills. Hoffmann, Mark, illus. LC 92-56882. 1993. PLB 17.27 (*0-8368-0944-0*) Gareth Stevens Inc.
Brown, Irene B. Morning Glory Afternoon. Milam, Larry, illus. 224p. (gr. 7 up). 1991. pap. 8.95 (*0-936085-20-7*) Blue Heron OR.
Mazer, Harry. When the Phone Rang. LC 84-6098. (Illus.). 192p. (gr. 7 up). 1985. pap. 11.95 (*0-590-32167-6*, Scholastic Hardcover) Scholastic Inc.
Merriam, Robert L. Abigail Challenges the Telephone Company. Merriam, Robert L., illus. 8p. (Orig.). (ps-6). 1972. pap. 1.50x (*0-686-32483-8*) R L Merriam.
Rodgers, Mary. A Billion for Boris. LC 74-3586. 192p. (gr. 5 up). 1976. pap. 3.95 (*0-06-440075-1*, Trophy) HarpC Child Bks.
Sachs, Marilyn. Hello... Wrong Number. 1993. pap. 2.95 (*0-590-44504-9*) Scholastic Inc.
Stine, R. L. Phone Calls. 160p. (Orig.). (gr. 7 up). 1990. pap. 3.99 (*0-671-69497-9*, Archway) PB.

TELESCOPE

Baker, David. Starwatch. (Illus.). 48p. (gr. 3-8). 1989. lib. bdg. 18.60 (*0-86592-400-7*); lib. bdg. 13.95s.p. (*0-685-58637-5*) Rourke Corp.
Bender, Lionel. Telescopes. LC 91-7802. (Illus.). 32p. (gr. 5-8). 1991. PLB 12.40 (*0-531-17265-1*, Gloucester Pr) Watts.
Hitzeroth, Deborah. Telescopes: Searching the Heavens. LC 91-16711. (Illus.). 96p. (gr. 5-8). 1991. PLB 15.95 (*1-56006-209-6*) Lucent Bks.
Schultz, Ron. Looking Inside Telescopes & the Night Sky. (Illus.). 48p. (Orig.). (gr. 3 up). Date not set. pap. 9.95 (*1-56261-072-4*) John Muir.
Vogt, Gregory. The Hubble Space Telescope. LC 91-25771. (Illus.). 112p. (gr. 4-6). 1992. PLB 15.90 (*1-56294-145-3*) Millbrook Pr.

TELEVISION

Asimov, Isaac. How Does a TV Work? (Illus.). 24p. (gr. 1-8). 1992. PLB 15.93 (*0-8368-0804-5*); PLB 15.93 s.p. (*0-685-61490-5*) Gareth Stevens Inc.
Bendick, Jeanne & Bendick, Robert. Eureka! It's Television! Murdocca, Sal, illus. & designed by. LC 92-15652. 48p. (gr. 2-6). 1993. PLB 15.40 (*1-56294-214-X*); pap. 6.95 (*1-56294-718-4*) Millbrook Pr.
Charren, Peggy & Hulsizer, Carol. The TV-Smart Book for Kids: Puzzles, Games, & Other Good Stuff. Hafner, Marylin, illus. 48p. (gr. 2-7). 1986. Parent's Guide, 16 p. 6.95 (*0-525-44249-9*, DCB) Dutton Child Bks.
Elwell, Sharon. This Is My Homework! Sixty TV Exercises. (Orig.). (gr. 6-12). 1993. wkbk. 10.95 (*0-9626210-7-2*) Rattle OK Pubns.
Gano, Lila. Television: Electronic Pictures. LC 90-6470. (Illus.). 96p. (gr. 5-8). 1990. PLB 15.95 (*1-56006-202-9*) Lucent Bks.

Gee, R. & Inglis, L. Television. (Illus.). 32p. (gr. 3-9). 1992. PLB 13.96 (*0-88110-586-4*); pap. 6.95 (*0-7460-1057-5*) EDC.
Jacobson, Karen. Television. LC 82-4456. (Illus.). (gr. k-4). 1982. pap. 4.95 (*0-516-41659-6*) Childrens.
Lambert, Mark. TV & Video Technology. 1990. PLB 12.90 (*0-531-18327-0*) Watts.
Limousin, Odile & Neumann, Daniele. TV & Films: Behind the Scenes. Vincent, Francois, illus. 40p. (gr. k-5). 1993. PLB 9.95 (*1-56674-073-8*, HTS Bks) Forest Hse.
Potter, Tony. How Television Works. (Illus.). 48p. (gr. 7-9). 1992. 13.95 (*0-563-34579-9*, BBC-Parkwest); pap. 6.95 (*0-563-34578-0*, BBC-Parkwest) Parkwest Pubns.
Sabin, Louis. Television & Radio. Veno, Joseph, illus. LC 84-8446. 32p. (gr. 3-6). 1985. PLB 9.49 (*0-8167-0310-8*); pap. text ed. 2.95 (*0-8167-0311-6*) Troll Assocs.
Teitelbaum, Michael. Family Matters: Behind the Scenes. LC 92-33899. 1992. pap. 2.95 (*0-8167-3038-5*) Troll Assocs.
Television. (ARA., Illus.). (gr. 5-12). 1987. 3.95x (*0-86685-237-9*) Intl Bk Ctr.
Wallner, Rosemary. Beverly Hills 90210. LC 92-16789. 1992. 12.94 (*1-56239-139-9*) Abdo & Dghtrs.
—Family Matters. LC 92-16788. 1992. 12.94 (*1-56239-142-9*) Abdo & Dghtrs.
—Fresh Prince of Bel Air. LC 92-16790. 1992. 12.94 (*1-56239-140-2*) Abdo & Dghtrs.
Ziefert, Harriet. My Television. Rader, Laura, illus. 14p. (ps). 1993. 4.50 (*0-694-00420-0*, Festival) HarpC Child Bks.

TELEVISION–BROADCASTING
see Television Broadcasting

TELEVISION–FICTION
Adams, Barbara. Can This Telethon Be Saved. (gr. k-6). 1987. pap. 2.50 (*0-440-41427-X*, YB) Dell.
—On the Air & off the Wall. (Orig.). (gr. 3-6). 1986. pap. 2.50 (*0-440-46771-3*, YB) Dell.
Barracca, Sal & Barracca, Debra. Maxi, the Star. Ayers, Alan, illus. LC 91-44962. 32p. (ps-3). 1993. 13.99 (*0-8037-1348-7*); PLB 13.89 (*0-8037-1349-5*) Dial Bks Young.
Bower, Tom. Albert Blows a Fuse. Bower, Tom, illus. 32p. (gr. 5-8). 1991. 11.95 (*0-7459-1906-5*) Lion USA.
Byars, Betsy C. The TV Kid. Cuffari, Richard, illus. 128p. (gr. 4-6). 1976. pap. 12.95 (*0-670-73331-8*) Viking Child Bks.
Conford, Ellen. Nibble, Nibble, Jenny Archer. Palmisciano, Diane, illus. LC 92-34306. 1993. 12.95 (*0-316-15371-0*) Little.
Deaver, Julie R. You Bet Your Life. LC 92-28211. 224p. (gr. 7 up). 1993. 15.00 (*0-06-021516-X*); PLB 14.89 (*0-06-021517-8*) HarpC Child Bks.
Denholtz, Roni S. The Day the T. V. Broke. Fontalvo, Nelsy, illus. LC 86-81371. 32p. (gr. k-2). 1986. PLB 7.59 (*0-87386-016-0*); pap. 1.95 (*0-87386-012-8*) Jan Prods.
Everitt, Betsy. TV Dinner. LC 93-19159. (ps-3). 1994. 13.95 (*0-15-283950-X*, HB Juv Bks) HarBrace.
Girion, Barbara. Prime Time Attraction. (Orig.). (gr. k-12). 1987. pap. 2.50 (*0-440-97179-9*, LFL) Dell.
Haynes, Betsy. The Great TV Turnoff. (gr. 4-7). 1991. pap. 2.95 (*0-553-15861-9*) Bantam.
McOmber, Rachel B., ed. McOmber Phonics Storybooks: On TV. rev. ed. (Illus.). write for info. (*0-944991-17-3*) Swift Lrn Res.
—McOmber Phonics Storybooks: The TV Box. rev. ed. (Illus.). write for info. (*0-944991-18-1*) Swift Lrn Res.
—McOmber Phonics Storybooks: The Video Show. rev. ed. (Illus.). write for info. (*0-944991-63-7*) Swift Lrn Res.
McPhail, David. Fix-It. McPhail, David, illus. LC 83-16459. 24p. (ps-k). 1984. 11.00 (*0-525-44093-3*, DCB) Dutton Child Bks.
Manes, Stephen. The Boy Who Turned into a TV Set. Bass, Michael, illus. 32p. (Orig.). (gr. 2-5). 1983. pap. 2.50 (*0-380-62000-6*, Camelot) Avon.
Novak, Matt. Mouse TV. LC 93-49399. (Illus.). 32p. (ps-1). 1994. 14.95 (*0-531-06856-0*); PLB 14.99 (*0-531-08706-9*) Orchard Bks Watts.
O'Connor, Jim & O'Connor, Jane. Slime Time. Porter, Pat, illus. LC 89-77324. 64p. (Orig.). (gr. 2-4). 1990. Random Bks Yng Read.
Sargent, Sarah. Between Two Worlds. LC 93-24533. 1995. 13.95g (*0-395-66425-X*) Ticknor & Flds Bks Yng Read.
Shannon, Jacqueline. I Hate My Hero. LC 92-890. (gr. 4-7). 1992. pap. 13.00 (*0-671-75442-4*, S&S BFYR) S&S Trade.
Swift, Carolyn. Robbers on TV. 160p. (ps-8). 1989. pap. 5.95 (*1-85371-033-4*, Pub. by Poolbeg Press Ltd Eire) Dufour.
West, Dan. The Day the TV Blew Up. Levine, Abby, ed. LC 87-25348. (Illus.). 32p. (gr. 2-5). 1988. PLB 11.95 (*0-8075-1491-8*) A Whitman.
Wright, Betty R. The Day Our TV Broke Down. Bejna, Barbara & Jensen, Shirlee, illus. Holbrook, Thomas, intro. by. LC 80-14434. 32p. (gr. k-6). 1980. PLB 19.97 (*0-8172-1365-1*) Raintree Steck-V.
Ziefert, Harriet. When the TV Broke. Smith, Mavis, illus. LC 92-47097. (ps-2). 1993. pap. 3.25 (*0-14-036540-0*, Puffin) Puffin Bks.

TELEVISION–HISTORY
Balcziak, B. Television. (Illus.). 48p. (gr. 4-8). 1989. lib. bdg. 17.27 (*0-86592-059-1*); lib. bdg. 12.95s.p. (*0-685-58628-6*) Rourke Corp.

TELEVISION–PRODUCTION AND DIRECTION
Geser, Ingrid. TV & Video. Stefoff, Rebecca, ed. LC 90-13868. (Illus.). 32p. (gr. 4-8). 1991. PLB 17.26 (*0-944483-99-2*) Garrett Ed Corp.
Scott, Elaine. Ramona: Behind the Scenes of a Television Show. Miller, Margaret, photos by. LC 87-33313. (Illus.). 96p. (gr. 3-7). 1988. 14.95 (*0-688-06818-9*); PLB 14.88 (*0-688-06819-7*, Morrow Jr Bks) Morrow Jr Bks.
Weiner, Eric & Storey, T. R. Full House: Behind the Scenes. LC 92-34522. (Illus.). 64p. (gr. 2-6). 1993. tchr's. ed. 2.95 (*0-8167-3037-7*) Troll Assocs.

TELEVISION–VOCATIONAL GUIDANCE
Hallenstein, Kathy. I Can Be a TV Camera Operator. LC 84-7665. (Illus.). 32p. (gr. k-3). 1984. pap. 3.95 (*0-516-41842-4*) Childrens.
Vitkus-Weeks, Jessica. Television: Careers in Television. LC 93-446. (Illus.). 48p. (gr. 5-6). 1994. text ed. 14.95 RSBE (*0-89686-783-8*, Crestwood Hse) Macmillan Child Grp.

TELEVISION BROADCASTING
Bridges, Steve. Today's Media. (Illus.). 48p. (gr. 6-8). 1993. pap. 8.99 (*1-55945-144-0*) Group Pub.
Brooks, Chelsea. Behind the Scenes. LC 93-7628. (Illus.). 64p. (gr. 5 up). 1993. pap. 7.95 (*0-02-041650-4*, Collier Young Ad) Macmillan Child Grp.
Calabro, Marian. Zap! A Brief History of Television. LC 91-744. (Illus.). 224p. (gr. 5 up). 1992. SBE 15.95 (*0-02-716242-7*, Four Winds) Macmillan Child Grp.
Freed, Carol. Let's Visit a Television Station. LC 87-3461. (Illus.). 32p. (gr. 2-4). 1988. PLB 10.79 (*0-8167-1165-8*); pap. text ed. 2.95 (*0-8167-1166-6*) Troll Assocs.
Russell, William. Broadcasters. LC 93-44982. 1994. write for info. (*1-57103-054-9*) Rourke Pr.
Trainer, David. A Day in the Life of a TV News Reporter. Sanacore, Stephen, photos by. LC 78-68810. (Illus.). 32p. (gr. 4-8). 1980. PLB 11.79 (*0-89375-228-2*); pap. 2.95 (*0-89375-232-0*) Troll Assocs.

TELEVISION BROADCASTING–BIOGRAPHY
Blue, Rose & Bernstein, Joanne E. Diane Sawyer: Super Newswoman. LC 89-16817. (Illus.). 104p. (gr. 6 up). 1990. lib. bdg. 17.95 (*0-89490-288-1*) Enslow Pubs.
Durrett, Deanne. Jim Henson. LC 93-38681. (gr. 5-8). 1994. 14.95 (*1-56006-048-4*) Lucent Bks.
Fischer, David M. Ted Turner. LC 92-44761. 1993. 19.93 (*0-86625-496-X*); 14.95s.p. (*0-685-66547-X*) Rourke Pubns.
Malone, Mary. Connie Chung: Broadcast Journalist. LC 91-25396. (Illus.). 128p. (gr. 6 up). 1992. lib. bdg. 17.95 (*0-89490-332-2*) Enslow Pubs.
Otfinoski, Steve. Oprah Winfrey: Television Star. (Illus.). 64p. (gr. 3-7). 1993. PLB 14.95 (*1-56711-015-0*) Blackbirch.
Patterson, Lillie & Wright, Cornelia H. Oprah Winfrey: Talk Show Host & Actress. LC 89-17002. (Illus.). 128p. (gr. 6 up). 1990. lib. bdg. 17.95 (*0-89490-289-X*) Enslow Pubs.
St. Pierre, Stephanie. Story of Jim Henson. (gr. 4-7). 1991. pap. 2.95 (*0-440-40453-3*) Dell.

TELL, WILLIAM
Small, Terry. Legend of William Tell. (ps-3). 1991. 14.95 (*0-553-07031-2*) Bantam.

TEMPERATURE
see also Heat; Low Temperatures
Ardley, Neil. The Science Book of Hot & Cold. (gr. 4-7). 1992. 9.95 (*0-15-200612-5*, HB Juv Bks) HarBrace.
Fowler, Allan. Hot & Cold. LC 93-38588. (Illus.). 32p. (ps-2). 1994. PLB 10.14.40 (*0-516-06021-X*); pap. 3.95 (*0-516-46021-8*) Childrens.
Gardner, Robert & Kemer, Eric. Science Projects about Temperature & Heat. (Illus.). 128p. (gr. 6 up). 1994. lib. bdg. 17.95 (*0-89490-534-1*) Enslow Pubs.
—Temperature & Heat. LC 92-32367. (gr. 3-7). 1993. lib. bdg. 14.98 (*0-671-69040-X*, J Messner); pap. 9.95 (*0-671-69045-0*, J Messner) S&S Trade.
Llewellyn, Claire. First Look at Keeping Warm. LC 91-9423. (Illus.). 32p. (gr. 1-2). 1991. PLB 17.27 (*0-8368-0704-9*) Gareth Stevens Inc.
Maury, Jean-Pierre. Heat & Cold. 80p. (gr. 8 up). 1989. pap. 4.95 (*0-8120-4211-5*) Barron.

TEMPERATURES, LOW
see Low Temperatures

TEN COMMANDMENTS
Biffi, Inos. The Ten Commandments. Vignazia, Franco, illus. LC 93-39147. 32p. 1994. pap. 9.99 (*0-8028-3758-1*) Eerdmans.
Cone, Molly. Who Knows Ten? Tales of the Ten Commandments. (Illus., Orig.). (gr. k-3). pap. 6.00 (*0-8074-0080-7*, 102551) UAHC.
De Graaf, Anne. The Two Greatest Commandments. (Illus.). 32p. 1989. 4.95 (*0-310-52760-0*) Zondervan.
Goodman, Roberta L. God's Top Ten: The Meaning of the Ten Commandments. Steinberger, Heidi, illus. 32p. (Orig.). (gr. 4-6). 1992. pap. text ed. 1.85 (*0-933873-73-5*) Torah Aura.
Haffey, Richard. H. R. Cornelius Learns about Love: A Commandments Book for Children. (Illus.). 20p. (Orig.). (gr. 2-5). 1985. pap. 2.95 (*0-89622-235-7*) Twenty-Third.
Lockman, Vic. God's Law for Modern Man. Lockman, Vic, illus. 60p. 1993. stapled 6.00 (*0-936175-25-7*) V Lockman.
Lovasik, Lawrence G. The Ten Commandments. (Illus.). (gr. 1-6). 1978. flexible bdg. 0.95 (*0-89942-287-X*, 287) Catholic Bk Pub.
O'Connor, Francine & Boswell, Kathryn. ABCs of the Ten Commandments. (Illus.). 32p. (Orig.). (gr. 1-4). 1980. pap. 3.95 (*0-89243-125-3*) Liguori Pubns.
Pingry, Patricia. The Story of Moses & the Ten Commandments. Britt, Stephanie, illus. (ps-3). 1990. pap. 3.95 (*0-8249-8418-8*, Ideals Child) Hambleton-Hill.
Roeda, Jack. Decisions. 2nd ed. Stoub, Paul, illus. Smith, Harvey A., intro. by. (Illus.). 80p. (gr. 9-12). 1992. pap. text ed. 6.50 (*0-930265-96-3*, 1240-4920); tchr's. manual 8.50 (*1-56212-000-X*, 1240-4940); session guides 4.95 (*0-685-60757-7*, 1240-4910) CRC Pubns.
Rummel, Mary. God's Love for Happiness: A Return to Family Values. Dirks, Nathan & Brandt, Bill, illus. LC 92-91032. 64p. (Orig.). (gr. k up). 1992. pap. 9.95 (*0-9635091-0-1*) Olive Brnch.
The Ten Commandments. 1989. text ed. 3.95 cased (*0-7214-5262-0*) Ladybird Bks.
Topek, Susan R. Ten Good Rules. Schanzer, Rosalyn, illus. LC 91-32109. 24p. (ps-1). 1992. 12.95 (*0-929371-30-5*); pap. 5.95 (*0-929371-28-3*) Kar Ben.
Truitt, Gloria A. The Ten Commandments: Learning about God's Law. LC 56-1398. (gr. 1 up). 1983. pap. 3.99 (*0-570-08527-6*) Concordia.
Woods, Paul. The Ten Commandments. (Illus.). 48p. (gr. 6-8). 1992. pap. 8.99 (*1-55945-127-0*) Group Pub.

TENNESSEE
Buchart & Associates, Inc. Staff. Knoxville Guide Book for Kids. 28p. (ps-5). 1993. pap. 1.50 (*1-883900-03-4*) Buchart & Assocs.
Cannon, Devereaux D., Jr. Flags of Tennessee. Tullier, Debra L., illus. LC 90-7679. 112p. (gr. 6-8). 1990. 14.95 (*0-88289-794-2*) Pelican.
Carole Marsh Tennessee Books, 44 bks. 1994. PLB 1027.80 set (*0-7933-1317-1*); pap. 587.80 (*0-7933-5206-1*) Gallopade Pub Group.
Carpenter, Allan. Tennessee. LC 78-11522. (Illus.). 96p. (gr. 4 up). 1979. PLB 20.55 (*0-516-04142-8*) Childrens.
Children's Museum of Oak Ridge, Tennessee Staff & Overholt, Jim, eds. Ridges & Valleys: A Mini-Encyclopedia of Anderson County, TN. 3rd ed. (Illus.). 126p. (Orig.). (gr. 5-12). 1990. pap. 5.50 (*0-9606832-5-9*) Chldrns Mus.
Fradin, Dennis. Tennessee: In Words & Pictures. LC 79-19218. (Illus.). 48p. (gr. 2-5). 1980. PLB 12.95 (*0-516-03942-3*); pap. 4.95 (*0-516-43942-1*) Childrens.
Fradin, Dennis B. Tennessee - from Sea to Shining Sea. LC 92-6385. (Illus.). 64p. (gr. 3-5). 1992. PLB 16.45 (*0-516-03842-7*); pap. 5.95 (*0-516-43842-5*) Childrens.
Lynch, Amy. Nashville. LC 90-41611. (Illus.). 60p. (gr. 3 up). 1991. text ed. 13.95 RSBE (*0-87518-453-7*, Dillon) Macmillan Child Grp.
McNair, Sylvia. Tennessee. LC 89-25285. (Illus.). 144p. (gr. 4 up). 1990. PLB 20.55 (*0-516-00488-3*) Childrens.
—Tennessee. 202p. 1993. text ed. 15.40 (*1-56956-162-1*) W A T Braille.
Marsh, Carole. Avast, Ye Slobs! Tennessee Pirate Trivia. (Illus.). 1994. PLB 24.95 (*0-7933-1076-8*); pap. 14.95 (*0-7933-1075-X*); computer disk 29.95 (*0-7933-1077-6*) Gallopade Pub Group.
—The Beast of the Tennessee Bed & Breakfast. (Illus.). 1994. PLB 24.95 (*0-7933-2056-9*); pap. 14.95 (*0-7933-2057-7*); computer disk 29.95 (*0-7933-2058-5*) Gallopade Pub Group.
—Bow Wow! Tennessee Dogs in History, Mystery, Legend, Lore, Humor & More! (Illus.). (gr. 3-12). 1994. PLB 24.95 (*0-7933-3593-0*); pap. 14.95 (*0-7933-3594-9*); computer disk 29.95 (*0-7933-3595-7*) Gallopade Pub Group.
—Christopher Columbus Comes to Tennessee! Includes Reproducible Activities for Kids! (Illus.). (gr. 3-12). 1994. PLB 24.95 (*0-7933-3746-1*); pap. 14.95 (*0-7933-3747-X*); computer disk 29.95 (*0-7933-3748-8*) Gallopade Pub Group.
—The Hard-to-Believe-But-True! Book of Tennessee History, Mystery, Trivia, Legend, Lore, Humor & More. (Illus.). 1994. PLB 24.95 (*0-7933-1073-3*); pap. 14.95 (*0-7933-1072-5*); computer disk 29.95 (*0-7933-1074-1*) Gallopade Pub Group.
—If My Tennessee Mama Ran the World! (Illus.). 1994. lib. bdg. 24.95 (*0-7933-2065-8*); pap. 14.95 (*0-7933-2066-6*); computer disk 29.95 (*0-7933-2067-4*) Gallopade Pub Group.
—Jurassic Ark! Tennessee Dinosaurs & Other Prehistoric Creatures. (gr. k-12). 1994. PLB 24.95 (*0-7933-7554-1*); pap. 14.95 (*0-7933-7555-X*); computer disk 29.95 (*0-7933-7556-8*) Gallopade Pub Group.
—Let's Quilt Our Tennessee County. 1994. lib. bdg. 24.95 (*0-7933-7239-9*); pap. text ed. 14.95 (*0-7933-7240-2*); disk 29.95 (*0-7933-7241-0*) Gallopade Pub Group.
—Let's Quilt Our Tennessee Town. 1994. lib. bdg. 24.95 (*0-7933-7089-2*); pap. text ed. 14.95 (*0-7933-7090-6*); disk 29.95 (*0-7933-7091-4*) Gallopade Pub Group.
—Let's Quilt Tennessee & Stuff It Topographically! (Illus.). 1994. PLB 24.95 (*0-7933-2048-8*); pap. 14.95 (*1-55609-079-X*); computer disk 29.95 (*0-7933-2049-6*) Gallopade Pub Group.
—Meow! Tennessee Cats in History, Mystery, Legend, Lore, Humor & More! (Illus.). (gr. 3-12). 1994. PLB 24.95 (*0-7933-3440-3*); pap. 14.95 (*0-7933-3441-1*); computer disk 29.95 (*0-7933-3442-X*) Gallopade Pub Group.

—My First Book about Tennessee. (gr. k-4). 1994. PLB 24.95 (*0-7933-5695-4*); pap. 14.95 (*0-7933-5696-2*); computer disk 29.95 (*0-7933-5697-0*) Gallopade Pub Group.

—Patch, the Pirate Dog: A Tennessee Pet Story. (ps-4). 1994. PLB 24.95 (*0-7933-5542-7*); pap. 14.95 (*0-7933-5543-5*); computer disk 29.95 (*0-7933-5544-3*) Gallopade Pub Group.

—Tennessee & Other State Greats (Biographies) (Illus.). 1994. PLB 24.95 (*0-7933-1055-5*); pap. 14.95 (*0-7933-1054-7*); computer disk 29.95 (*0-7933-1056-3*) Gallopade Pub Group.

—Tennessee Bandits, Bushwackers, Outlaws, Crooks, Devils, Ghosts, Desperadoes & Other Assorted & Sundry Characters! (Illus.). 1994. PLB 24.95 (*0-7933-1058-X*); pap. 14.95 (*0-7933-1057-1*); computer disk 29.95 (*0-7933-1059-8*) Gallopade Pub Group.

—Tennessee Classic Christmas Trivia: Stories, Recipes, Activities, Legends, Lore & More! (Illus.). 1994. PLB 24.95 (*0-7933-1061-X*); pap. 14.95 (*0-7933-1060-1*); computer disk 29.95 (*0-7933-1062-8*) Gallopade Pub Group.

—Tennessee Coastales. (Illus.). 1994. PLB 24.95 (*0-7933-2062-3*); pap. 14.95 (*0-7933-2063-1*); computer disk 29.95 (*0-7933-2064-X*) Gallopade Pub Group.

—Tennessee Coastales! 1994. lib. bdg. 24.95 (*0-7933-7307-7*) Gallopade Pub Group.

—Tennessee Dingbats! Bk. 1: A Fun Book of Games, Stories, Activities & More about Our State That's All in Code! for You to Decipher. (Illus.). (gr. 3-12). 1994. PLB 24.95 (*0-7933-3899-9*); pap. 14.95 (*0-7933-3900-6*); computer disk 29.95 (*0-7933-3901-4*) Gallopade Pub Group.

—Tennessee Festival Fun for Kids! (Illus.). (gr. 3-12). 1994. lib. bdg. 24.95 (*0-7933-4052-7*); pap. 14.95 (*0-7933-4053-5*); disk 29.95 (*0-7933-4054-3*) Gallopade Pub Group.

—The Tennessee Hot Air Balloon Mystery. (Illus.). (gr. 2-9). 1994. 24.95 (*0-7933-2696-6*); pap. 14.95 (*0-7933-2697-4*); computer disk 29.95 (*0-7933-2698-2*) Gallopade Pub Group.

—Tennessee Jeopardy! Answers & Questions about Our State! (Illus.). (gr. 3-12). 1994. PLB 24.95 (*0-7933-4205-8*); pap. 14.95 (*0-7933-4206-6*); computer disk 29.95 (*0-7933-4207-4*) Gallopade Pub Group.

—Tennessee "Jography" A Fun Run Thru Our State! (Illus.). 1994. PLB 24.95 (*0-7933-2046-1*); pap. 14.95 (*1-55609-089-7*); computer disk 29.95 (*0-7933-2047-X*) Gallopade Pub Group.

—Tennessee Kid's Cookbook: Recipes, How-to, History, Lore & More! (Illus.). 1994. PLB 24.95 (*0-7933-1070-9*); pap. 14.95 (*0-7933-1069-5*); computer disk 29.95 (*0-7933-1071-7*) Gallopade Pub Group.

—Tennessee Quiz Bowl Crash Course! (Illus.). 1994. PLB 24.95 (*0-7933-2059-3*); pap. 14.95 (*0-7933-2060-7*); computer disk 29.95 (*0-7933-2061-5*) Gallopade Pub Group.

—Tennessee Rollercoasters! (Illus.). (gr. 3-12). 1994. PLB 24.95 (*0-7933-5350-5*); pap. 14.95 (*0-7933-5351-3*); computer disk 29.95 (*0-7933-5352-1*) Gallopade Pub Group.

—Tennessee School Trivia: An Amazing & Fascinating Look at Our State's Teachers, Schools & Students! (Illus.). 1994. PLB 24.95 (*0-7933-1067-9*); pap. 14.95 (*0-7933-1066-0*); computer disk 29.95 (*0-7933-1068-7*) Gallopade Pub Group.

—Tennessee Silly Basketball Sportsmysteries, Vol. 1. (Illus.). 1994. PLB 24.95 (*0-7933-1064-4*); pap. 14.95 (*0-7933-1063-6*); computer disk 29.95 (*0-7933-1065-2*) Gallopade Pub Group.

—Tennessee Silly Basketball Sportsmysteries, Vol. 2. (Illus.). 1994. PLB 24.95 (*0-7933-2071-2*); pap. 14.95 (*0-7933-2072-0*); computer disk 29.95 (*0-7933-2073-9*) Gallopade Pub Group.

—Tennessee Silly Football Sportsmysteries, Vol. 1. (Illus.). 1994. PLB 24.95 (*0-7933-2050-X*); pap. 14.95 (*0-7933-2051-8*); computer disk 29.95 (*0-7933-2052-6*) Gallopade Pub Group.

—Tennessee Silly Football Sportsmysteries, Vol. 2. (Illus.). 1994. PLB 24.95 (*0-7933-2053-4*); pap. 14.95 (*0-7933-2054-2*); computer disk 29.95 (*0-7933-2055-0*) Gallopade Pub Group.

—Tennessee Silly Trivia! (Illus.). 1994. PLB 24.95 (*0-7933-2044-5*); pap. 14.95 (*1-55609-036-6*); computer disk 29.95 (*0-7933-2045-3*) Gallopade Pub Group.

—Tennessee Timeline: A Chronology of Tennessee History, Mystery, Trivia, Legend, Lore & More. (Illus.). (gr. 3-12). 1994. PLB 24.95 (*0-7933-6001-3*); pap. 14.95 (*0-7933-6002-1*); computer disk 29.95 (*0-7933-6003-X*) Gallopade Pub Group.

—Tennessee's (Most Devastating!) Disasters & (Most Calamitous!) Catastrophies! (Illus.). 1994. PLB 24.95 (*0-7933-2068-2*); pap. 14.95 (*0-7933-2069-0*); computer disk 29.95 (*0-7933-2070-4*) Gallopade Pub Group.

—Tennessee's Unsolved Mysteries (& Their "Solutions") Includes Scientific Information & Other Activities for Students. (Illus.). (gr. 3-12). 1994. PLB 24.95 (*0-7933-5848-5*); pap. 14.95 (*0-7933-5849-3*); computer disk 29.95 (*0-7933-5850-7*) Gallopade Pub Group.

Sirvaitis, Karen. Tennessee. 72p. (gr. 3-6). 1991. PLB 17.50 (*0-8225-2711-1*) Lerner Pubns.

Thompson, Kathleen. Tennessee. 48p. (gr. 3 up). 1985. PLB 19.97 (*0-86514-444-3*) Raintree Steck-V.

TENNESSEE–FICTION

Galbreath, Bob. Tennessee Red Berry Tales. Garrett, Deborah G., ed. 97p. (Orig.). (gr. 3 up). 1986. pap. 7.95 (*0-9616918-0-8*) Whites Creek Pr.

Isaacs, Anne. Swamp Angel. Zelinsky, Paul O., illus. LC 93-43956. 40p. (ps-4). 1994. 14.99 (*0-525-45271-0*) Dutton Child Bks.

Taylor, Mildred D. The Road to Memphis. Fogelman, Phyllis J., ed. LC 88-33654. (Illus.). 240p. (gr. 7 up). 1990. 14.95 (*0-8037-0340-6*) Dial Bks Young.

TENNESSEE–HISTORY

Hirsch, Virginia R. Heart Country Tennessee: A Tribute to the Tennessee Songmaker. rev. ed. LC 85-82468. 80p. (gr. 5 up). 1986. pap. 5.00 (*0-9616334-0-9*) Heart Ctry Pubns.

Lommel, Cookie. Robert Church: And the Church Family of Memphis. (Illus.). 192p. Date not set. pap. 3.95 (*0-87067-789-6*) Holloway.

McKissack, Patricia & McKissack, Fredrick. Tennessee Trailblazers. 96p. (gr. 4-7). 1993. 13.95 (*0-9634824-0-8*) March Media.

Marsh, Carole. Chill Out: Scary Tennessee Tales Based on Frightening Tennessee Truths. (Illus.). 1994. lib. bdg. 24.95 (*0-7933-4780-7*); pap. 14.95 (*0-7933-4781-5*); disk 29.95 (*0-7933-4782-3*) Gallopade Pub Group.

—Tennessee "Crinkum-Crankum" A Funny Word Book about Our State. (Illus.). (gr. 3-12). 1994. 24.95 (*0-7933-4934-6*); pap. 14.95 (*0-7933-4935-4*); computer disk 29.95 (*0-7933-4936-2*) Gallopade Pub Group.

—The Tennessee Mystery Van Takes Off! Book 1: Handicapped Tennessee Kids Sneak Off on a Big Adventure. (Illus.). (gr. 3-12). 1994. 24.95 (*0-7933-5087-5*); pap. 14.95 (*0-7933-5088-3*); computer disk 29.95 (*0-7933-5089-1*) Gallopade Pub Group.

—Uncle Rebus: Tennessee Picture Stories for Computer Kids. (Illus.). (gr. k-3). 1994. PLB 24.95 (*0-7933-4627-4*); pap. 14.95 (*0-7933-4628-2*); disk 29.95 (*0-7933-4629-0*) Gallopade Pub Group.

Phillips, Margaret I. Governors of Tennessee. LC 77-26845. (Illus.). 193p. (gr. 6-12). 1978. 16.95 (*0-88289-169-3*) Pelican.

TENNIS

Aguon, Jane M. Mr. Munchkin's Tennis. (gr. 4 up). 1993. 10.75 (*0-8062-4719-3*) Carlton.

Bailey, Donna. Tennis. LC 90-23056. (Illus.). 32p. (gr. 1-4). 1991. PLB 18.99 (*0-8114-2904-0*); pap. 3.95 (*0-8114-4711-1*) Raintree Steck-V.

Boy Scouts of America Staff. Varsity Tennis. (Illus.). 42p. 1990. pap. 3.15 (*0-8395-3455-8*, 3455) BSA.

Bradlee, Dick. Instant Tennis. (Illus.). 124p. (gr. 7 up). 1962. 9.95 (*0-8159-5811-0*) Devin.

Ganeri, A. Tennis Skills. (Illus.). 48p. (gr. 6-12). (Usborne); pap. 5.95 (*0-7460-0173-8*) EDC.

Gutman, Bill. Tennis. LC 89-7607. (Illus.). 64p. (gr. 3-8). 1990. PLB 14.95 (*0-942545-88-5*) Marshall Cavendish.

Newcombe, Barry. Tennis: Tactics of Success. (Illus.). 80p. (gr. 10-12). 1992. pap. 8.95 (*0-7063-7098-8*, Pub. by Ward Lock UK) Sterling.

Singleton, Skip. The Junior Tennis Handbook: A Complete Guide to Tennis for Juniors Parents & Coaches. LC 90-21927. (Illus.). 176p. (Orig.). (gr. 5 up). 1991. pap. 12.95 (*1-55870-192-3*, 70065) Shoe Tree Pr.

Sirimarko, Elizabeth. Tennis. LC 93-27152. 1993. write for info. (*0-86593-343-X*) Rourke Corp.

Whitney, Marceil. Teenie Tennis: A Love Game. 72p. (Orig.). (ps up). 1991. pap. write for info. (*0-9629089-0-8*) ATS Pub.

Wimbledon. 32p. (gr. 4). 1990. PLB 14.95 (*0-88682-319-6*) Creative Ed.

TENNIS–BIOGRAPHY

Dell, Pamela. Michael Chang: Tennis Champion. LC 92-6384. (Illus.). 32p. (gr. 2-5). 1992. PLB 11.80 (*0-516-04185-1*); pap. 3.95 (*0-516-44185-X*) Childrens.

Eliot, Chip. Ivan Lendl. LC 88-1829. (Illus.). 48p. (gr. 5-6). 1988. text ed. 11.95 RSBE (*0-89686-380-8*, Crestwood Hse) Macmillan Child Grp.

Goldstein, Margaret J. Jennifer Capriati: Tennis Sensation. LC 92-38867. 1993. 13.50 (*0-8225-0519-3*) Lerner Pubns.

—Jennifer Capriati: Tennis Sensation. (gr. 4-7). 1993. pap. 4.95 (*0-8225-9645-8*) Lerner Pubns.

Green, Carl R. & Ford, Roxanne. Jennifer Capriati. LC 93-39397. 1994. text ed. 13.95 (*0-89686-834-6*, Crestwood Hse) Macmillan Child Grp.

Lakin, Patricia. Jennifer Capriati. LC 93-18131. 1993. 15.93 (*0-86592-090-7*); 11.95s.p. (*0-685-66545-3*) Rourke Enter.

Leder, Jane M. Martina Navratilova. LC 89-99550. (Illus.). 48p. (gr. 5-6). 1985. text ed. 11.95 RSBE (*0-89686-252-6*, Crestwood Hse) Macmillan Child Grp.

Martina Navratilova. (gr. 2-6). 1989. pap. 3.50 (*0-14-033218-9*, Puffin) Puffin Bks.

Monroe, Judy. Steffi Graf. LC 87-30115. (Illus.). 48p. (gr. 5-6). 1988. text ed. 11.95 RSBE (*0-89686-368-9*, Crestwood Hse) Macmillan Child Grp.

Pablo Casals. (Illus.). 112p. (gr. 6-12). 1993. PLB 17.95 (*0-7910-1237-9*); pap. write for info. (*0-7910-1264-6*) Chelsea Hse.

Porter, A. P. Zina Garrison. 56p. (gr. 4-9). 1991. PLB 13.50 (*0-8225-0499-5*) Lerner Pubns.

—Zina Garrison: Ace. (Illus.). 64p. (gr. 4-9). 1992. pap. 3.95 (*0-8225-9596-6*) Lerner Pubns.

Rothaus, James R. Jennifer Capriati. 32p. 1991. 14.95 (*0-89565-738-4*) Childs World.

—Steffi Graf. (SPA & ENG., Illus.). 32p. (gr. 2-6). 1991. 14.95 (*0-89565-734-1*) Childs World.

Sanford, William R. & Green, Carl R. Billie Jean King. LC 92-27458. (Illus.). 48p. (gr. 5). 1993. text ed. 11.95 RSBE (*0-89686-781-1*, Crestwood Hse) Macmillan Child Grp.

Weissberg, Ed. Arthur Ashe. King, Coretta Scott, intro. by. (Illus.). 112p. (gr. 5 up). 1991. lib. bdg. 17.95 (*0-7910-1115-1*) Chelsea Hse.

TENNIS–FICTION

Barbic, Ivo. Playing Tennis with Bouncy & Fuzzy. Blanc, Henry, illus. 96p. 1987. pap. 11.95 (*0-88289-654-7*) Pelican.

Kaye, Marilyn. Camp Sunnyside Friends: The Tennis Trap, No. 12. 128p. (Orig.). (gr. 5). 1991. pap. 2.95 (*0-380-76184-X*, Camelot) Avon.

Lehrman, Robert. Separations. LC 92-26782. 224p. (gr. 5-9). 1993. pap. 3.99 (*0-14-032322-8*) Puffin Bks.

Nesbit, Jeffrey A. Crosscourt Winner. 132p. 1991. pap. 4.99 (*0-89693-129-3*) SP Pubns.

—The Puzzled Prodigy. (Orig.). (gr. 3-6). 1992. pap. 4.99 (*0-89693-075-0*, Victor Books) SP Pubns.

—Struggle with Silence. 129p. 1991. pap. 4.99 (*0-89693-132-3*) SP Pubns.

Schulman, Janet. Jenny & The Tennis Nut. Hafner, Marilyn, illus. 64p. (gr. 1-4). 1981. pap. 2.50 (*0-440-44211-7*, YB) Dell.

Tunis, John R. Champion's Choice. 206p. (gr. 3-7). 1990. pap. 3.95 (*0-15-216074-4*, Odyssey) HarBrace.

Wojciechowska, Maia. Dreams of Wimbledon. Karsky, A. K., illus. 52p. 1994. 14.50 (*1-883740-02-9*) Pebble Bch Pr Ltd.

TERMITES–FICTION

Sickles, William. Herman the Termite. (Illus.). (gr. 3-5). 1968. 10.95 (*0-8392-3066-4*) Astor-Honor.

TERRARIUMS

Broekel, Ray. Aquariums & Terrariums. LC 82-4428. (gr. k-4). 1982. 12.85 (*0-516-01660-1*) Childrens.

TERRESTRIAL PHYSICS

see Geophysics

TERROR, REIGN OF

see France–History–Revolution, 1789-1799

TESLA, NIKOLA, 1856-1943

Dommermuth-Costa, Carol. Nikola Tesla: A Spark of Genius. LC 93-43123. (Illus.). 144p. (gr. 5 up). 1994. 21.50 (*0-8225-4920-4*) Lerner Pubns.

TEST PILOTS

see Air Pilots; Airplanes–Testing

TESTS

see Educational Tests and Measurements

TEXAS

Adams, Carolyn. Stars over Texas. rev. ed. (Illus.). 128p. (gr. 1-6). 1983. 9.95 (*0-89015-411-2*, Pub. by Panda Bks) Sunbelt Media.

Aylesworth, Thomas G. & Aylesworth, Virginia L. The Southwest (Texas, New Mexico, Colorado) (Illus.). 64p. (gr. 3 up). 1992. lib. bdg. 16.95 (*0-7910-1048-1*) Chelsea Hse.

Brown, William F. True Texas Tales. Mazzu, Kenneth, illus. LC 92-93887. 64p. (Orig.). (gr. 7 up). 1992. pap. 8.75 perfect bdg. (*1-881936-14-7*) WFB Ent.

Buhler, June H., et al. Let's Celebrate Texas: Past, Present & Future. LC 86-11961. (Illus.). 171p. (gr. 4-7). 1986. 15.95x (*0-937460-23-0*) Hendrick-Long.

Carole Marsh Texas Books, 44 bks. 1994. PLB 1027.80 set (*0-7933-1318-X*); pap. 587.80 set (*0-7933-5208-8*) Gallopade Pub Group.

Carpenter, Allan. Texas. LC 78-18430. (Illus.). 96p. (gr. 4 up). 1979. PLB 16.95 (*0-516-04143-6*) Childrens.

Elliott, Tony. Texas Outdoors: Read 'n Color Book. Elliott, Tony, illus. (gr. 1-8). 1986. pap. 3.95 (*0-914565-24-9*, 24-9, Timbertrails) Capstan Pubns.

Fradin, Dennis. Texas en Palabras y Fotos: Texas: In Words & Pictures. 48p. (gr. 2-6). 1986. pap. 4.95 (*0-516-53943-4*) Childrens.

—Texas: In Words & Pictures. Wahl, Richard, illus. LC 80-27497. 48p. (gr. 2-5). 1981. PLB 12.95 (*0-516-03943-1*); pap. 4.95 (*0-516-43943-X*) Childrens.

Fradin, Dennis B. Texas. LC 92-9189. (Illus.). 64p. (gr. 3-5). 1992. PLB 16.45 (*0-516-03843-5*); pap. 5.95 (*0-516-43843-3*) Childrens.

—Texas - De Mar a Mar: (Texas - From Sea to Shining Sea) LC 92-9189. (SPA., Illus.). 64p. (gr. 3-5). 1993. PLB 16.45 (*0-516-33843-9*); pap. 5.95 (*0-516-53843-8*) Childrens.

Gipson, Fred. The Trail-Driving Rooster. Lich, Glen, intro. by. (Illus.). 88p. (gr. 4-7). 1987. Repr. of 1955 ed. 9.95 (*0-89015-620-4*, Pub. by Panda Bks) Sunbelt Media.

Hopkins, Jacqueline. Tumbleweed Tom on the Texas Trail. Salem, Kay, illus. 32p. (Orig.). (ps-4). 1994. 14.95 (*0-88106-848-9*); PLB 15.00 (*0-88106-849-7*); pap. 7.95 (*0-88106-847-0*) Charlesbridge Pub.

Jones, Martha T. The Great Texas Scare: A Story of the Runaway Scrape. La Freniere, Annette, ed. LC 88-767. (Illus.). 96p. (gr. 3-7). 1988. lib. bdg. 10.95 (*0-937460-31-1*) Hendrick-Long.

Kerr, Rita. Texas Rebel. Eakin, Edwin M., ed. Kerr, Rita, illus. 80p. (gr. 4-6). 1989. 10.95 (*0-89015-695-6*) Sunbelt Media.

Koch, Susan C. Colormore Travels - Ft. Worth, Texas: The Travel Guide for Kids. Koch, Susan C., illus. (Orig.). (gr. k-4). 1989. pap. 4.50 (*0-945600-02-X*) Colormore Inc.

—Colormore Travels - San Antonio, Texas: The Travel Guide for Kids. Koch, Susan C., illus. 32p. (Orig.). (gr. k-4). 1990. pap. 4.50 (*0-945600-05-4*) Colormore Inc.
McAlister, George A. A Time to Love...a Time to Die. Godfrey, Raymond, illus. 216p. (Orig.). (gr. 10). 1988. pap. 7.95 (*0-924307-01-3*) Docutex Inc.
Magley, Beverly. Texas Wildflowers: A Children's Field Guide to the State's Most Common Flowers. Dowden, D. D., illus. 32p. (Orig.). 1993. pap. 5.95 (*1-56044-183-6*) Falcon Pr MT.
Marsh, Carole. Avast, Ye Slobs! Texas Pirate Trivia. (Illus.). 1990. PLB 24.95 (*0-7933-1100-4*); pap. 14.95 (*0-7933-1099-7*); computer disk 0-7933-1101-2 29.95 (*0-685-45953-5*) Gallopade Pub Group.
—The Beast of the Texas Bed & Breakfast. (Illus.). 1994. PLB 24.95 (*0-7933-2086-0*); pap. 14.95 (*0-7933-2087-9*); computer disk 29.95 (*0-7933-2088-7*) Gallopade Pub Group.
—Bow Wow! Texas Dogs in History, Mystery, Legend, Lore, Humor & More! (Illus.). (gr. 3-12). 1994. PLB 24.95 (*0-7933-3596-5*); pap. 14.95 (*0-7933-3597-3*); computer disk 29.95 (*0-7933-3598-1*) Gallopade Pub Group.
—Christopher Columbus Comes to Texas! Includes Reproducible Activities for Kids! (Illus.). (gr. 3-12). 1994. PLB 24.95 (*0-7933-3749-6*); pap. 14.95 (*0-7933-3750-X*); computer disk 29.95 (*0-7933-3751-8*) Gallopade Pub Group.
—The Hard-to-Believe-But-True! Book of Texas History, Mystery, Trivia, Legend, Lore, Humor & More. (Illus.). 1994. PLB 24.95 (*0-7933-1097-0*); pap. 14.95 (*0-7933-1096-2*); computer disk 29.95 (*0-7933-1098-9*) Gallopade Pub Group.
—If My Texas Mama Ran the World! (Illus.). 1994. PLB 24.95 (*0-7933-2094-1*); pap. 14.95 (*0-7933-2095-X*); computer disk 29.95 (*0-7933-2096-8*) Gallopade Pub Group.
—Jurassic Ark! Texas Dinosaurs & Other Prehistoric Creatures. (gr. k-12). 1994. PLB 24.95 (*0-7933-7557-6*); pap. 14.95 (*0-7933-7558-4*); computer disk 29.95 (*0-7933-7559-2*) Gallopade Pub Group.
—Let's Quilt Our Texas County. 1994. lib. bdg. 24.95 (*0-7933-7242-9*); pap. text ed. 14.95 (*0-7933-7243-7*); disk 29.95 (*0-7933-7244-5*) Gallopade Pub Group.
—Let's Quilt Our Texas Town. 1994. lib. bdg. 24.95 (*0-7933-7092-2*); pap. text ed. 14.95 (*0-7933-7093-0*); disk 29.95 (*0-7933-7094-9*) Gallopade Pub Group.
—Let's Quilt Texas & Stuff It Topographically! (Illus.). 1994. PLB 24.95 (*0-7933-2078-X*); pap. 14.95 (*1-55609-077-3*); computer disk 29.95 (*0-7933-2079-8*) Gallopade Pub Group.
—Meow! Texas Cats in History, Mystery, Legend, Lore, Humor & More! (Illus.). (gr. 3-12). 1994. PLB 24.95 (*0-7933-3443-8*); pap. 14.95 (*0-7933-3444-6*); computer disk 29.95 (*0-7933-3445-4*) Gallopade Pub Group.
—Texas & Other State Greats (Biographies) (Illus.). 1994. PLB 24.95 (*0-7933-2097-6*); pap. 14.95 (*0-7933-2098-4*); computer disk 29.95 (*0-7933-2099-2*) Gallopade Pub Group.
—Texas Bandits, Bushwackers, Outlaws, Crooks, Devils, Ghosts, Desperadoes & Other Assorted & Sundry Characters! (Illus.). 1994. PLB 24.95 (*0-7933-1082-2*); pap. 14.95 (*0-7933-1081-4*); computer disk 29.95 (*0-7933-1083-0*) Gallopade Pub Group.
—Texas Classic Christmas Trivia: Stories, Recipes, Activities, Legends, Lore & More! (Illus.). 1994. PLB 24.95 (*0-7933-1085-7*); pap. 14.95 (*0-7933-1084-9*); computer disk 29.95 (*0-7933-1086-5*) Gallopade Pub Group.
—Texas Coastales. (Illus.). 1994. PLB 24.95 (*0-7933-2092-5*); pap. 14.95 (*1-55609-121-4*); computer disk 29.95 (*0-7933-2093-3*) Gallopade Pub Group.
—Texas Coastales! 1994. lib. bdg. 24.95 (*0-7933-7308-5*) Gallopade Pub Group.
—Texas Dingbats! Bk. 1: A Fun Book of Games, Stories, Activities & More about Our State That's All in Code! for You to Decipher. (Illus.). (gr. 3-12). 1994. PLB 24.95 (*0-7933-3902-2*); pap. 14.95 (*0-7933-3903-0*); computer disk 29.95 (*0-7933-3904-9*) Gallopade Pub Group.
—Texas Festival Fun for Kids! (Illus.). (gr. 3-12). 1994. lib. bdg. 24.95 (*0-7933-4055-1*); pap. 14.95 (*0-7933-4056-X*); disk 29.95 (*0-7933-4057-8*) Gallopade Pub Group.
—The Texas Hot Air Balloon Mystery. (Illus.). (gr. 2-9). 1994. 24.95 (*0-7933-2705-9*); pap. 14.95 (*0-7933-2706-7*); computer disk 29.95 (*0-7933-2707-5*) Gallopade Pub Group.
—Texas Jeopardy! Answers & Questions about Our State! (Illus.). (gr. 3-12). 1994. PLB 24.95 (*0-7933-4208-2*); pap. 14.95 (*0-7933-4209-0*); computer disk 29.95 (*0-7933-4210-4*) Gallopade Pub Group.
—Texas "Jography" A Fun Run Thru Our State! (Illus.). 1994. PLB 24.95 (*0-7933-2076-3*); pap. 14.95 (*1-55609-087-0*); computer disk 29.95 (*0-7933-2077-1*) Gallopade Pub Group.
—Texas Kid's Cookbook: Recipes, How-To, History, Lore & More! (Illus.). 1994. PLB 24.95 (*0-7933-1094-6*); pap. 14.95 (*0-7933-1093-8*); computer disk 29.95 (*0-7933-1095-4*) Gallopade Pub Group.
—Texas Quiz Bowl Crash Course! (Illus.). 1994. PLB 24.95 (*0-7933-2089-5*); pap. 14.95 (*0-7933-2090-9*); computer disk 29.95 (*0-7933-2091-7*) Gallopade Pub Group.
—Texas Rollercoasters! (Illus.). (gr. 3-12). 1994. PLB 24.95 (*0-7933-5353-X*); pap. 14.95 (*0-7933-5354-8*); computer disk 29.95 (*0-7933-5355-6*) Gallopade Pub Group.
—Texas School Trivia: An Amazing & Fascinating Look at Our State's Teachers, Schools & Students! (Illus.). 1994. PLB 24.95 (*0-7933-1091-1*); pap. 14.95 (*0-7933-1090-3*); computer disk 29.95 (*0-7933-1092-X*) Gallopade Pub Group.
—Texas Silly Basketball Sportsmysteries, Vol. 1. (Illus.). 1994. PLB 24.95 (*0-7933-1088-1*); pap. 14.95 (*0-7933-1087-3*); computer disk 29.95 (*0-7933-1089-X*) Gallopade Pub Group.
—Texas Silly Basketball Sportsmysteries, Vol. 2. (Illus.). 1994. PLB 24.95 (*0-7933-2100-X*); pap. 14.95 (*0-7933-2101-8*); computer disk 29.95 (*0-7933-2102-6*) Gallopade Pub Group.
—Texas Silly Football Sportsmysteries, Vol. 1. (Illus.). 1994. PLB 24.95 (*0-7933-2080-1*); pap. 14.95 (*0-7933-2081-X*); computer disk 29.95 (*0-7933-2082-8*) Gallopade Pub Group.
—Texas Silly Football Sportsmysteries, Vol. 2. (Illus.). 1994. PLB 24.95 (*0-7933-2083-6*); pap. 14.95 (*0-7933-2084-4*); computer disk 29.95 (*0-7933-2085-2*) Gallopade Pub Group.
—Texas Silly Trivia! (Illus.). 1994. PLB 24.95 (*0-7933-2074-7*); pap. 14.95 (*1-55609-081-1*); computer disk 29.95 (*0-7933-2075-5*) Gallopade Pub Group.
—Texas's (Most Devastating!) Disasters & (Most Calamitous!) Catastrophies! (Illus.). 1994. PLB 24.95 (*0-7933-1079-2*); pap. 14.95 (*0-7933-1078-4*); computer disk 29.95 (*0-7933-1080-6*) Gallopade Pub Group.
Martinello, Marian & Field, William T., Jr. Who Are the Chinese Texans? Ricks, Thorn, illus. 84p. (Orig.). (gr. 5-8). 8.95 (*0-933164-36-X*); pap. 5.95 (*0-933164-46-7*) U of Tex Inst Tex Culture.
Michael, Linda. Big As Texas: The A to Z Tour of Texas Cities & Places. Lowdermilk, Karen, ed. Lewis, Patrick, illus. LC 87-36793. 64p. (gr. k-3). 1988. pap. 6.95 (*0-937460-34-6*) Hendrick-Long.
O'Rear, Sybil J. Charles Goodnight: Pioneer Cowman. LC 89-48652. (Illus.). 69p. (gr. 5-8). 1990. 10.95 (*0-89015-741-3*) Sunbelt Media.
Peifer, Charles, Jr. Houston. LC 88-20197. (Illus.). 60p. (gr. 3 up). 1988. text ed. 13.95 RSBE (*0-87518-387-5*, Dillon) Macmillan Child Grp.
Petrucelli. Henry Cisneros, Reading Level 2. (Illus.). 24p. (gr. 1-4). 1989. PLB 14.60 (*0-86592-431-7*); 10.95s.p. (*0-685-58799-1*) Rourke Corp.
Reeve, Agnesa, compiled by. & intro. by. My Dear Mollie: Love Letters of a Texas Sheep Rancher. LC 90-41891. (Illus.). 192p. (gr. 5 up). 1990. 17.95 (*0-937460-62-1*) Hendrick-Long.
Sorenson, Richard. Focus on Texas History & Geography. (Illus.). 56p. (gr. 6 up). 1987. pap. 9.95 (*0-937460-29-X*) Hendrick-Long.
Stanush, Barbara E. Texans: A Story of Texan Cultures for Young People. Grades 4-7. write for info. tchr's. guide (*0-86701-045-2*) U of Tex Inst Tex Culture.
Stein, R. Conrad. Texas. LC 88-38400. (Illus.). 144p. (gr. 4 up). 1989. PLB 20.55 (*0-516-00489-1*) Childrens.
—Texas. 193p. 1993. text ed. 15.40 (*1-56956-151-6*) W A T Braille.
Stewart, G. Houston. (Illus.). 48p. (gr. 5 up). 1989. lib. bdg. 15.74 (*0-86592-539-9*); 11.95s.p. (*0-685-58588-3*) Rourke Corp.
Thompson, Kathleen. Texas. LC 85-9980. 48p. (gr. 3 up). 1985. PLB 19.97 (*0-86514-445-1*) Raintree Steck-V.
Veazey, Steve & Porter, John D., Jr. Flags in the History of Texas. McPeek, Ellen, illus. 40p. (gr. 4 up). 1991. pap. 6.95 (*0-937460-73-7*) Hendrick-Long.
Von Rosenberg, Marjorie. Elisabet Ney: Sculptor of American Heroes. Von Roesnberg, Marjorie, illus. 64p. (gr. 4-7). 1990. 10.95 (*0-89015-747-2*) Sunbelt Media.
—Max & Martha: Children from Germany in the Texas Hill Country. (Illus.). 48p. (gr. 4-7). 1986. 8.95 (*0-89015-539-9*, Pub. by Panda Bks) Sunbelt Media.
Wade, Mary D. I Am Houston. (Illus.). 64p. (gr. 3-5). 1993. 10.95 (*1-882539-05-2*); pap. 4.95 (*1-882539-06-0*); tchr's. guide 5.00 (*1-882539-07-9*) Colophon Hse.
Wicks, Kathy. Texas Folklife Festival: A Children's Guide. (Illus.). 30p. 2.25 (*0-86701-035-5*) U of Tex Inst Tex Culture.

TEXAS–FICTION

Abernethy, Francis E. How the Critters Created Texas. Sargent, Ben, illus. LC 82-80440. 40p. (gr. 4-12). 1982. pap. 8.95 (*0-936650-01-X*) E C Temple.
Alter, Judy. After Pa Was Shot. Shaw, Charles, illus. LC 89-12176. 192p. (Orig.). (gr. 4-9). 1991. pap. 5.95 (*0-936650-12-5*) E C Temple.
Anzaldua, Gloria. Friends from the Other Side: Amigos del otro lado. Mendez, Consuelo, illus. LC 92-34384. 32p. (gr. 2-7). 1993. 13.95 (*0-89239-113-8*) Childrens Book Pr.
Baylor, Byrd. The Best Town in the World. Himler, Ronald, illus. LC 86-3381. 32p. (gr. 1-3). 1986. pap. 3.95 (*0-689-71086-0*, Aladdin) Macmillan Child Grp.
Cheadle, J. A. A Donkey's Life: A Story for Children. Thomas, Toni, illus. LC 80-123421. iii, 88p. (Orig.). (gr. 2-6). 1979. pap. 3.50 (*0-9604244-0-7*) Heahstan Pr.
Cherry, Lynne. The Armadillo from Amarillo. LC 93-11185. 1994. 14.95 (*0-15-200359-2*, Gulliver Bks) HarBrace.
Cole, Barbara H. Texas Star. Minton, Barbara, illus. LC 88-25205. 32p. (ps-2). 1990. 14.95 (*0-531-05820-4*); PLB 14.99 (*0-531-08420-5*) Orchard Bks Watts.
Cooner, Donna D. Twelve Days in Texas. Leland, Bob, illus. 32p. (gr. k-2). 1994. pap. 9.95 (*0-937460-85-0*) Hendrick-Long.
Crowder, Dorothy. In the Land of the Wichitas: Stories about Burkburnett, Texas for the Young Reader. (Illus.). 48p. (Orig.). (gr. 3-4). 1986. pap. text ed. 7.50x (*0-317-91365-4*) Dorthenia Pubs.
Dionne, Wanda. The Couturiere of Galvez. LC 92-46147. (Illus.). (gr. 6-9). 1993. 15.95 (*0-89015-860-6*) Sunbelt Media.
Evey, Ethel L. Stowaway to Texas. Darst, Shelia S., ed. 201p. (gr. 4-7). 1986. 9.95 (*0-89896-102-5*, Post Oak Pr); pap. 6.95 (*0-89896-101-7*, Post Oak Pr) Larksdale.
Fowler, Zinita. The Last Innocent Summer. LC 89-20417. 144p. (gr. 6-9). 1990. pap. 11.95 (*0-87565-045-7*) Tex Christian.
Freeman, Peggy P. Swept Back to a Texas Future. Haas, Holly, illus. 40p. (gr. 4-7). 1991. pap. 7.95 (*0-937460-72-9*) Hendrick-Long.
Garland, Sherry. The Silent Storm. LC 92-33690. 1992. write for info. (*0-15-274170-4*) HarBrace.
Giff, Patricia R. Shark in School. LC 93-39016. (gr. 1 up). 1994. 14.95 (*0-385-32029-9*) Delacorte.
Gipson, Fred. Old Yeller. LC 56-8780. (Illus.). (gr. 7-9). 1956. 22.00i (*0-06-011545-9*, HarpT) HarpC.
Griffin, Peni R. The Treasure Bird. Gowing, Toby, illus. LC 91-42773. 144p. (gr. 4-7). 1992. SBE 13.95 (*0-689-50554-X*, M K McElderry) Macmillan Child Grp.
—The Treasure Bird. 144p. (gr. 3-7). 1994. pap. 3.99 (*0-14-036653-9*) Puffin Bks.
Gurasich, Marj. A House Divided. LC 93-14189. 174p. (gr. 5-8). 1994. pap. 9.95 (*0-87565-122-4*) Tex Christian.
Harman, Betty & Meador, Nancy. Paco & the Lion of the North. Roberts, Melissa, ed. 112p. (gr. 4-7). 1987. 10.95 (*0-89015-598-4*, Pub. by Panda Bks) Sunbelt Media.
Harper, Jo. Jalapeno Hal. Haris, Jennifer B., illus. LC 92-16921. 40p. (ps-2). 1993. RSBE 14.95 (*0-02-742645-9*, Four Winds) Macmillan Child Grp.
Hart, Jan S. The Many Adventures of Minnie. Wilson, Kay, illus. LC 92-17740. 96p. (gr. 4-7). 1992. 12.95 (*0-89015-859-2*) Sunbelt Media.
Hicks, Grace R. The Critters of Gazink. Hicks, Bruce & Ashcraft, Karen H., illus. 64p. (gr. 4-7). 1992. 11.95 (*0-89015-816-9*) Sunbelt Media.
Hoff, Carol. Johnny Texas. Myers, Bob, illus. 150p. (gr. 4 up). 1992. lib. bdg. 15.95 (*0-937460-80-X*); pap. 9.95 (*0-937460-81-8*) Hendrick-Long.
—Johnny Texas on the San Antonio Road. (Illus.). 191p. (gr. 4 up). 1984. Repr. of 1953 ed. 13.95 (*0-937460-15-X*) Hendrick-Long.
Jakes, John. Susanna of the Alamo. (Illus.). 32p. (gr. 1-5). 1990. pap. 4.95 (*0-15-200595-1*, Voyager Bks) HarBrace.
Johnston, Tony. The Cowboy & the Blackeyed Pea. Ludwig, Warren, illus. 32p. (ps-3). 1992. 14.95 (*0-399-22330-4*, Putnam) Putnam Pub Group.
Karr, Kathleen. Oh, Those Harper Girls! 176p. (gr. 7 up). 1992. 16.00 (*0-374-35609-2*) FS&G.
Kerr, Rita. Texas Cavalier: The Story of James Butler Bonham. Roberts, Melissa, ed. Kerr, Rita, illus. 64p. (gr. 4-7). 1989. 10.95 (*0-89015-714-6*, Pub. by Panda Bks) Sunbelt Media.
—Texas Footprints. (gr. 3-7). 1988. 10.95 (*0-89015-676-X*, Pub. by Panda Bks) Sunbelt Media.
—The Texas Orphans: A Story of the Orphan Trail Children. Kerr, Rita, illus. LC 94-1995. 1994. 10.95 (*0-89015-962-9*) Sunbelt Media.
—A Wee Bit of Texas. Kerr, Rita, illus. 80p. (gr. 1-4). 1991. 10.95 (*0-89015-809-6*) Sunbelt Media.
Ketner, Mary G. Ganzy Remembers. Sparks, Barbara, illus. LC 89-78261. 32p. (gr. k-3). 1991. SBE 13.95 (*0-689-31610-0*, Atheneum Child Bk) Macmillan Child Grp.
Knapik, Jane A. Sarah's Flag for Texas. Wilson, Jo K., illus. LC 93-16171. (gr. 3-6). 1994. 12.95 (*0-89015-900-9*) Sunbelt Media.
Kudlinski, Kathleen V. Lone Star: A Story of the Texas Rangers. Himler, Ronald, illus. 64p. (gr. 2-6). 1994. PLB 12.99 (*0-670-85179-5*) Viking Child Bks.
Lightfoot, D. J. Trail Fever: The Life of a Texas Cowboy. Bobbish, John, illus. LC 92-5458. 1992. 11.00 (*0-688-11537-3*) Lothrop.
Liles, Maurine W. Rebecca of Blossom Prairie: Grandmother of a Vice President. Roberts, M., ed. (Illus.). 112p. 1990. 10.95 (*0-89015-754-5*) Sunbelt Media.
Mc Donald, Archie. When the Corn Grows Tall in Texas. Peacock, Joe, illus. 96p. (gr. 4-8). 1991. 11.95 (*0-89015-808-8*) Sunbelt Media.
Marvin, Isabel R. Josefina & the Hanging Tree. LC 91-34501. 128p. (gr. 6-9). 1992. pap. 9.95 (*0-87565-103-8*) Tex Christian.
—Shipwrecked on Padre Island. Miller, Lyle L., illus. 160p. (gr. 4 up). 1993. 14.95 (*0-937460-83-4*) Hendrick-Long.
Meyer, Carolyn. White Lilacs. LC 92-30503. 1993. write for info. (*0-15-200641-9*) HarBrace.
—White Lilacs. (gr. 4-7). 1993. pap. 3.95 (*0-15-295876-2*, HB Juv Bks) HarBrace.

Michener, James A. The Eagle & the Raven. Shaw, Charles, illus. LC 90-9684. 228p. 1990. 19.95 (*0-938349-57-0*); ltd. ed. o.p. 100.00 (*0-938349-58-9*) State House Pr.

Munson, Sammye. Goodbye, Sweden, Hello Texas. LC 93-38928. 1994. 14.95 (*0-89015-948-3*) Sunbelt Media.

Nixon, Joan L. Shadowmaker. LC 93-32314. 1994. 14.95 (*0-385-32030-2*) Delacorte.

Paulsen, Gary. Canyons. 1990. 15.95 (*0-385-30153-7*) Delacorte.

Pella, Judith. Frontier Lady. 400p. (Orig.). 1993. pap. 9.99 (*1-55661-293-1*) Bethany Hse.

Penson, Mary. You're an Orphan, Mollie Brown: A Novel. Shaw, Charles, illus. LC 92-23407. 122p. (gr. 5-8). 1993. pap. 9.95 (*0-87565-111-9*) Tex Christian.

Richardson, Jean. Tag-along Timothy Tours Texas. (Illus.). 1992. 10.95 (*0-89015-817-7*) Sunbelt Media.

Roberts, Willo D. Jo & the Bandit. LC 91-4100. 192p. (gr. 4-7). 1992. SBE 15.00 (*0-689-31745-X*, Atheneum Child Bk) Macmillan Child Grp.

Roderus, Frank. Duster. Conoly, Walle, illus. LC 85-14759. 266p. (gr. 4 up). 1987. 14.95 (*0-87565-055-4*); pap. 10.95 (*0-87565-095-3*) Tex Christian.

Schenker, Dona. Fearsome's Hero. LC 93-8601. 144p. (gr. 4-8). 1994. 15.00 (*0-679-85424-X*) Knopf Bks Yng Read.

Searle, Don L. Light in the Harbor. LC 91-17827. viii, 245p. (Orig.). 1991. pap. 8.95 (*0-87579-528-5*) Deseret Bk.

Shefelman, Janice. A Paradise Called Texas. (Illus.). 128p. (gr. 4-7). 1983. 10.95 (*0-89015-409-0*, Pub. by Panda Bks); pap. 5.95 (*0-89015-506-2*) Sunbelt Media.

Sinclair, Dorothy T. Tales of the Texians. Milam, Harris, illus. LC 85-90411. 104p. (Orig.). (gr. 4-7). 1986. 14.95 (*0-9615311-0-X*); pap. 9.95 (*0-9615311-1-8*) Sinclair Ent.

Stem, Jacqueline. The Haunted Tunnel. LC 93-46917. 1994. 11.95 (*0-89015-959-9*) Sunbelt Media.

Stover, Jill. Alamo Across Texas. LC 91-47572. (Illus.). 32p. (ps up). 1993. 13.00 (*0-688-11712-0*); 12.95 (*0-688-11713-9*) Lothrop.

Tilli Comes to Texas. (gr. k up). 1987. incl. cassette & bk. 15.95 (*0-937460-57-5*); cassette tape 6.95 (*0-937460-56-7*) Hendrick-Long.

Tolliver, Ruby C. Boomer's Kids. Miller, Lyle, illus. 128p. (gr. 4 up). 1992. 14.95 (*0-937460-69-9*) Hendrick-Long.

—Have Gun - Need Bullets. Washington, Burl, illus. LC 90-49363. 120p. (gr. 4 up). 1991. 15.95 (*0-87565-085-6*); pap. 10.95 (*0-87565-089-9*) Tex Christian.

—Muddy Banks. LC 85-20851. (Illus.). 154p. (gr. 4up). 1987. 14.95 (*0-87565-062-7*); pap. 6.95 (*0-87565-049-X*) Tex Christian.

Von Rosenberg, Marjorie. Cowboy Bob's Critters Visit Texas Heroes. Von Rosenberg, Marjorie, illus. LC 93-2908. 80p. (gr. 2-5). 1993. 12.95 (*0-89015-905-X*) Sunbelt Media.

Webber, Earlynne. The Secret of the Big Thicket. 1994. 12.95 (*0-89015-958-0*) Sunbelt Media.

Williams, Jeanne. Tame the Wild Stallion. Conoly, Walle, illus. LC 84-16257. 182p. (gr. 4 up). 1985. 14.95 (*0-87565-002-3*); pap. 8.95 (*0-87565-009-0*) Tex Christian.

Wisler, G. Clifton. Piper's Ferry. 144p. (gr. 5-9). 1990. 14.95 (*0-525-67303-2*, Lodestar Bks) Dutton Child Bks.

TEXAS–HISTORY

Baker, Charlotte. Trails North - Stories of Texas Yesterdays. Roberts, Melissa, ed. Gholson, Virginia, illus. 128p. (gr. 4-7). 1991. 10.95 (*0-685-74092-7*) Sunbelt Media.

Barrett, Anna P. Juneteenth. rev. ed. Goodman, Frances B., ed. Costner, Howard, illus. 64p. (gr. k-8). 1993. pap. 9.95 (*0-89896-111-4*) Larksdale.

Cox, Bertha M. True Tales of Texas. Hendrick, Lura A., illus. LC 87-12091. 292p. (gr. 3-8). 1987. PLB 13.95 (*0-937460-28-1*); pap. 9.95 (*0-937460-77-X*) Hendrick-Long.

Cox, Mike. Texas Rangers. (Illus.). 144p. (gr. 6-9). 1992. 14.95 (*0-89015-818-5*) Sunbelt Media.

Crawford, Ann F. New Life, New Land: Women in Early Texas. (Illus.). 48p. 1986. 9.95 (*0-89015-560-7*, Pub. by Panda Bks) Sunbelt Media.

De Boe, David C. Sponsors' Handbook: Junior Historian & Walter Prescott Webb Historical Society. rev. ed. iv, 86p. pap. 5.00 (*0-87611-120-7*) Tex St Hist Assn.

Dennis, Anne T. Marshall Yesterday: An Adventure Back in Time for Children & Adults. 36p. (gr. 4 up). 1991. pap. 5.00 (*1-879703-00-9*) Marshall Regnl Arts.

Durham, Merle. The Lone Star State Divided: Texans & the Civil War. LC 94-1984. 1994. write for info. (*0-937460-97-4*) Hendrick-Long.

Gurasich, Marj. Benito & the White Dove: A Story of Jose Antonio Navarro, Hero of Early Texas. (Illus.). 112p. (gr. 6-8). 1989. 10.95 (*0-89015-693-X*) Sunbelt Media.

—Did You Ever Meet a Texas Hero? LC 91-19544. (Illus.). (gr. 3-5). 1992. 12.95 (*0-89015-819-3*) Sunbelt Media.

Hackney, Ann. The Epic Adventure...Texas. 2nd ed. Hodges, Carol, illus. Johnson, Lady Bird, intro. by. LC 85-24854. (Illus.). 64p. (gr. 4-7). 1985. text ed. 19.95 includes tape (*0-935077-11-1*); pap. 12.95 includes tape (*0-935077-12-X*); paps. 5.95 (*0-935077-07-3*); tchr's guide 16.95 (*0-935077-10-3*); cassette 7.95 (*0-935077-08-1*) Hist Jefferson Found.

Henderson, Shelia & George, Bonnie S. The Littlest Aggie. Darr, S. C., ed. La Rue, Doug, et al, illus. Williams, Clayton, Jr., frwd. by. 56p. 1990. 18.95 (*0-9623171-2-8*); coloring bk. 4.95 (*0-9623171-3-6*) LBCo Pub.

Hennech, Michael C., intro. by. Texas History According to Us. (Illus.). 116p. (Orig.). (gr. 7). 1991. pap. text ed. 7.95 (*1-881301-01-X*) Ale Pub.

Jackson, Sarah & Patterson, Mary Ann. A Child's History of Texas. Jackson, Sarah & Patterson, Mary Ann, illus. (gr. 1-6). 1972. 5.95 (*0-89015-056-7*, Pub. by Panda Bks) Sunbelt Media.

Levine, Ellen. The Tree That Would Not Die. Rand, Ted, illus. LC 94-8394. (ps-3). Date not set. 14.95 (*0-590-43724-0*) Scholastic Inc.

Marsh, Carole. Chill Out: Scary Texas Tales Based on Frightening Texas Truths. (Illus.). 1994. lib. bdg. 24.95 (*0-7933-4783-1*); pap. 14.95 (*0-7933-4784-X*); disk 29.95 (*0-7933-4785-8*) Gallopade Pub Group.

—My First Book about Texas. (gr. k-4). 1994. PLB 24.95 (*0-7933-5698-9*); pap. 14.95 (*0-7933-5699-7*); computer disk 29.95 (*0-7933-5700-4*) Gallopade Pub Group.

—Patch, the Pirate Dog: A Texas Pet Story. (ps-4). 1994. PLB 24.95 (*0-7933-5545-1*); pap. 14.95 (*0-7933-5546-X*); computer disk 29.95 (*0-7933-5547-8*) Gallopade Pub Group.

—Texas "Crinkum-Crankum" A Funny Word Book about Our State. (Illus.). (gr. 3-12). 1994. 24.95 (*0-7933-4937-0*); pap. 14.95 (*0-7933-4938-9*); computer disk 29.95 (*0-7933-4939-7*) Gallopade Pub Group.

—The Texas Mystery Van Takes Off! Book 1: Handicapped Texas Kids Sneak Off on a Big Adventure. (Illus.). (gr. 3-12). 1994. 24.95 (*0-7933-5090-5*); pap. 14.95 (*0-7933-5091-3*); computer disk 29.95 (*0-7933-5092-1*) Gallopade Pub Group.

—Texas Timeline: A Chronology of Texas History, Mystery, Trivia, Legend, Lore & More. (Illus.). (gr. 3-12). 1994. PLB 24.95 (*0-7933-6004-8*); pap. 14.95 (*0-7933-6005-6*); computer disk 29.95 (*0-7933-6006-4*) Gallopade Pub Group.

—Texas's Unsolved Mysteries (& Their "Solutions") Includes Scientific Information & Other Activities for Students. (Illus.). (gr. 3-12). 1994. PLB 24.95 (*0-7933-5851-5*); pap. 14.95 (*0-7933-5852-3*); computer disk 29.95 (*0-7933-5853-1*) Gallopade Pub Group.

—Uncle Rebus: Texas Picture Stories for Computer Kids. (Illus.). (gr. k-3). 1994. PLB 24.95 (*0-7933-4630-4*); pap. 14.95 (*0-7933-4631-2*); disk 29.95 (*0-7933-4632-0*) Gallopade Pub Group.

Martinello, Marian L. Cedar Fever: Story of a German-Texan Girl During World War I. Hudgins, Paul, illus. LC 92-73295. 212p. (gr. 7-9). 1992. 15.95 (*0-931722-90-X*); pap. 7.95 (*0-931722-95-0*) Corona Pub.

Martinello, Marian L. & Nesmith, Samuel P. With Domingo Leal in San Antonio, 1734. Institute of Texan Cultures Staff, ed. Lowther, Marilyn, illus. 78p. (Orig.). (gr. 5-8). 1980. pap. 6.95 (*0-933164-40-8*) U of Tex Inst Tex Culture.

Milligan, Bryce. Comanche Captive: You Are There. Shaw, Charles, illus. 156p. (gr. 5 up). 1989. pap. 3.95 (*0-87719-157-3*, Lone Star Bks) Gulf Pub.

Morgan, Elizabeth D. Jane Long: A Child's Pictorial History. Johnson, Nancy D., photos by. Richards, Ann, intro. by. LC 92-17739. (Illus.). 96p. (gr. 4-7). 1992. 12.95 (*0-89015-861-4*) Sunbelt Media.

—Mirabeau B. Lamar: President of Texas. Johnson, Nancy D., photos by. LC 94-2641. (Illus.). 1994. 11.95 (*0-89015-963-7*) Sunbelt Media.

Munson, Sammye. Our Tejano Heroes: Outstanding Mexican-Americans. Eakin, Edwin M., ed. (Illus.). 96p. (gr. 4-6). 1989. 10.95 (*0-89015-691-3*, Pub. by Panda Bks) Sunbelt Media.

O'Keefe, Candace. Texas Women - A Celebration of History: A Multicultural Guide. Shaw, Charles, illus. 60p. (gr. 4 up). 1991. pap. 8.95 (*0-9606256-2-3*) Hendrick-Long.

Pate, J'Nell L. Ranald Slidell Mackenzie: Brave Cavalry Colonel. LC 93-21952. (gr. 4-8). 1994. 14.95 (*0-89015-901-7*) Sunbelt Media.

Reynolds, Patrick M. Texas Lore, Vols. 1, 2, 3, & 4. Reynolds, Patrick M., illus. 228p. (Orig.). (gr. 8-12). 1992. pap. 12.95 (*0-932514-27-8*) Red Rose Studio.

Rogers, Mary B. & Smith, Sherry A. We Can Fly: Stories of Katherine Stinson & Other Gutsy Texas Women. LC 82-80441. (Illus.). 184p. (Orig.). (gr. 7up). 1983. 14.95 (*0-936650-02-8*) E C Temple.

Seale, Jan. Deaf Smith: The Eyes & Ears of the Texas Army. Seale, Carl, illus. 30p. (gr. k-3). 1987. pap. 2.95 (*0-936927-20-8*) Knowing Pr.

—Dilue Rose: The Girl Who Saw Texas Independence. Seale, Carl, illus. 30p. (gr. k-3). 1986. pap. 2.95 (*0-936927-21-6*) Knowing Pr.

—Juan Seguin: The Tejano Who Wouldn't Give Up. Seale, Carl, illus. 28p. (gr. k-3). 1987. pap. 2.95 (*0-936927-19-4*) Knowing Pr.

—Kian Long: The Slave Girl Who Helped Start Texas. Seale, Carl, illus. 30p. (gr. k-3). 1987. pap. 2.95 (*0-936927-18-6*) Knowing Pr.

—Madam Candelaria: The Nurse at the Alamo. Seale, Carl, illus. 27p. (gr. k-3). 1987. pap. 2.95 (*0-936927-16-X*) Knowing Pr.

—William Goyens: The Texan Who Said No to Failure. Seale, Carl, illus. 29p. (gr. k-3). 1987. pap. 2.95 (*0-936927-17-8*) Knowing Pr.

Smyri, Frank H. Poley Morgan, Son of a Texas Scalawag: (A Historical Novel) Van Horn, Donald, illus. vi, 63p. 1990. 2.00 (*0-910779-00-7*) Tex St Hist Assn.

Sorenson, Richard. Focus on Texas History & Geography. (Illus.). 56p. (gr. 6 up). 1987. pap. 9.95 (*0-937460-29-X*) Hendrick-Long.

Stanush, Barbara E. Texans: The Story of Texan Cultures for Young People. Cosgrove, Jim, illus. LC 88-50983. 122p. (gr. 4-7). 1988. write for info. (*0-86701-040-1*) U of Tex Inst Tex Culture.

Stein, R. Conrad. The Story of the Lone Star Republic. LC 87-35467. (Illus.). 32p. (gr. 3-6). 1988. pap. 3.95 (*0-516-44735-1*) Childrens.

Stewart, Gail. Texans. (Illus.). 32p. (gr. 3-8). 1990. PLB 18.00 (*0-86625-408-0*); PLB 13.50s.p. (*0-685-58650-2*) Rourke Corp.

Teague, Wells. Theo, the Indian Fighter. Eakin, Edwin M., ed. (Illus.). 112p. (gr. 4-7). 1987. 8.95 (*0-89015-614-X*, Pub. by Panda Bks) Sunbelt Media.

Wade, L. Alamo: Battle of Honor & Freedom. 1991. 11.95s.p. (*0-86592-470-8*) Rourke Enter.

Wade, Mary D. Austin: The Son Becomes Father. Finney, Pat, illus. 64p. (gr. 3-5). 1993. 10.95 (*1-882539-08-7*); pap. 4.95 (*1-882539-09-5*); tchr's. guide 5.00 (*1-882539-10-9*) Colophon Hse.

Warren, Betsy. Explorers in Early Texas. Long, Joann M., ed. (Illus.). 128p. (gr. 4 up). 1992. 14.95 (*0-937460-74-5*) Hendrick-Long.

—Let's Remember...Texas, the Twenty-Eighth State. (Illus.). 36p. (gr. 3-7). 1984. pap. 5.95 (*0-937460-13-3*) Hendrick-Long.

—Let's Remember...When Texas Belonged to Spain. Warren, Betsy, illus. 32p. (gr. 3-7). 1982. pap. 5.95 (*0-937460-04-4*) Hendrick-Long.

—Let's Remember...When Texas Was a Republic. Warren, Betsy, illus. 32p. (gr. 3-7). 1983. pap. 5.95 (*0-937460-09-5*) Hendrick-Long.

—The Story of Texas: A History Picture Book. Warren, Betsy, illus. 46p. (gr. 3 up). 1988. pap. 3.50 (*0-9618660-1-2*) Ranch Gate Bks.

—Texas in Historic Sites & Symbols. Warren, Betsy, illus. 28p. (gr. k-3). 1982. pap. 5.50 (*0-937460-05-2*) Hendrick-Long.

—Twenty Texans, Historic Lives for Young Readers. LC 85-13926. (Illus.). 114p. (gr. 3-7). 1985. lib. bdg. 13.95 (*0-937460-17-6*) Hendrick-Long.

Weems, John E. The Story of Texas. 2nd ed. (Illus., Orig.). (gr. 2-6). 1992. pap. 8.95 (*0-940672-35-9*) Shearer Pub.

TEXAS INSTRUMENTS COMPUTERS

Kemnitz, Thomas M. & Mass, Lynne. Kids Working with Computers: The Texas Instruments BASIC Manual. Schlendorf, Lori, illus. 48p. (gr. 4-7). 1983. pap. 4.99 (*0-89824-059-X*) Trillium Pr.

TEXAS RANGERS

Cox, Mike. Texas Rangers. (Illus.). 144p. (gr. 6-9). 1992. 14.95 (*0-89015-818-5*) Sunbelt Media.

Rambeck, Richard. Texas Rangers. 48p. (gr. 4-10). 1992. PLB 14.95 (*0-88682-443-5*) Creative Ed.

TEXTILE FABRICS

see Textile Industry and Fabrics

TEXTILE INDUSTRY AND FABRICS

see also Cotton Manufacture and Trade; Weaving also names of special textile fabrics, (e.g. Silk); and names of articles manufactured, e.g. Carpets

Blood, Charles L. & Link, Martin. The Goat in the Rug. Parker, Nancy W., illus. LC 80-17315. 40p. (ps-3). 1984. Repr. of 1976 ed. RSBE 14.95 (*0-02-710920-8*, Four Winds) Macmillan Child Grp.

Boy Scouts of America. Textile. 64p. (gr. 6-12). 1972. pap. 1.85 (*0-8395-3344-6*, 33344) BSA.

Keeler, Patricia A. & McCall, Francis X., Jr. Unraveling Fibers. LC 93-13906. 1995. 16.00 (*0-689-31777-8*, Atheneum) Macmillan.

Lancaster, John. Fabric Art. LC 90-12281. (Illus.). 48p. (gr. 5-8). 1991. PLB 12.40 (*0-531-14102-0*) Watts.

O'Reilly, Susie. Textiles. LC 91-4472. (Illus.). 48p. (gr. 5-8). 1991. 12.90 (*0-531-18441-2*, Pub. by Bookwright Pr) Watts.

Smith, Elizabeth S. Cloth: Inventions That Changed Our Lives. LC 84-25768. (Illus.). 60p. (gr. 4-7). 1985. PLB 10.85 (*0-8027-6577-7*) Walker & Co.

THAILAND

Bailey, Donna. Thailand. LC 91-22044. (Illus.). 32p. (gr. 1-4). 1992. PLB 18.99 (*0-8114-2570-3*) Raintree Steck-V.

Goldfarb, Mace. Fighters, Refugees, Immigrants: A Story of the Hmong. LC 82-4370. (Illus.). 48p. (gr. 4 up). 1982. lib. bdg. 13.50 (*0-87614-197-1*) Carolrhoda Bks.

Goodman, Jim. Thailand. LC 91-17719. (Illus.). 128p. (gr. 5-9). 1991. PLB 21.95 (*1-85435-402-7*) Marshall Cavendish.

Jacobsen, Karen. Thailand. LC 89-34413. 48p. (gr. k-4). 1989. PLB 12.85 (*0-516-01179-0*); pap. 4.95 (*0-516-41179-9*) Childrens.

Landon, Margaret. Anna & the King of Siam. Ayer, M., illus. 1944. 16.95 (*0-381-98135-5*, A05201); 16.45 (*0-685-02093-2*) HarpC Child Bks.

Lerner Publications, Department of Geography Staff, ed. Thailand in Pictures. (Illus.). 64p. (gr. 5 up). 1989. PLB 17.50 (*0-8225-1866-X*) Lerner Pubns.

McNair, Sylvia. Thailand. LC 86-29933. (Illus.). 128p. (gr. 5-9). 1987. PLB 20.55 (*0-516-02792-1*) Childrens.

Orihara, Kei. Children of the World: Thailand. LC 88-21050. (Illus.). 64p. (gr. 5-6). 1988. PLB 21.26 (*1-55532-223-9*) Gareth Stevens Inc.

THAILAND–BIOGRAPHY

Thomson, Ruth & Thomson, Neil. A Family in Thailand. (Illus.). 32p. (gr. 2-5). 1988. lib. bdg. 13.50 (*0-8225-1684-5*) Lerner Pubns.

THAILAND–FICTION

Ho, Minfong. Rice without Rain. LC 86-33745. 236p. (gr. 7 up). 1990. 12.95 (*0-688-06355-1*) Lothrop.

THAMES RIVER

Rogers, Daniel. The Thames. Lilly, Isabel, illus. LC 92-44702. 48p. (gr. 5-6). 1993. PLB 22.80 (*0-8114-3104-5*) Raintree Steck-V.

THANKSGIVING DAY

Anderson, J. I. I Can Read About the First Thanksgiving. McKeown, Gloria, illus. LC 76-54400. (gr. 2-5). 1977. pap. 2.50 (*0-89375-034-4*) Troll Assocs.

Anderson, Joan. The First Thanksgiving Feast. Ancona, George, photos by. LC 84-58040. (Illus.). (gr. 3-6). 1989. pap. 5.70 (*0-395-51886-5*, Clarion Bks) HM.

Bains, Rae. Pilgrims & Thanksgiving. Wenzel, David, illus. LC 84-2686. 32p. (gr. 3-6). 1985. PLB 9.49 (*0-8167-0222-5*); pap. text ed. 2.95 (*0-8167-0223-3*) Troll Assocs.

Baker, James W. Thanksgiving Magic. Overlie, George, illus. 48p. (gr. 2-5). 1989. 11.95 (*0-8225-2233-0*) Lerner Pubns.

Barkin, Carol & James, Elizabeth. Happy Thanksgiving! Carmi, Giora, illus. LC 86-33734. 96p. (gr. 4-7). 1987. 12.95 (*0-688-06800-6*); PLB 12.88 (*0-688-06801-4*) Lothrop.

Barth, Edna. Turkeys, Pilgrims, & Indian Corn: The Story of the Thanksgiving Symbols. Arndt, Ursula, illus. LC 75-4703. 96p. (gr. 3-6). 1981. pap. 4.95 (*0-89919-039-1*, Clarion Bks) HM.

Boynton, Alice B. Priscilla Alden & the Story of the First Thanksgiving. Brook, Bonnie, ed. Kiefer, Christa, illus. 32p. (gr. k-2). 1990. 4.95 (*0-671-69111-2*); PLB 6.95 (*0-671-69105-8*) Silver Pr.

Bunting, Eve. How Many Days to America? A Thanksgiving Story. Peck, Beth, illus. LC 88-2590. 32p. (gr. k-4). 1988. 15.45 (*0-89919-521-0*, Clarion Bks) HM.

Butler, Elvie. Celebrate Thanksgiving with Stickers. 1989. pap. 3.95 (*0-590-42505-6*) Scholastic Inc.

Celsi, Teresa N. Squanto & the First Thanksgiving. (Illus.). 32p. (gr. 1-4). 1989. PLB 18.99 (*0-8172-3511-6*); pap. 4.95 (*0-8114-6710-4*) Raintree Steck-V.

Child, Lydia M. Over the River & Through the Wood. Westcott, Nadine B., illus. LC 92-14979. 32p. (gr. 1-5). 1993. 14.00 (*0-06-021303-5*); PLB 13.89 (*0-06-021304-3*) HarpC Child Bks.

Conaway, Judith. Happy Thanksgiving: Things to Make & Do. Barto, Renzo, illus. LC 85-16463. 48p. (gr. 1-5). 1986. PLB 11.89 (*0-8167-0668-9*); pap. text ed. 3.50 (*0-8167-0669-7*) Troll Assocs.

Corwin, Judith H. Thanksgiving Crafts. LC 93-6369. (Illus.). (gr. k-4). Date not set. PLB write for info. (*0-531-11147-4*) Watts.

—Thanksgiving Fun. Corwin, Judith H., illus. 64p. (gr. 3 up). 1984. lib. bdg. 10.98 (*0-671-49422-8*, J Messner); lib. bdg. 5.95 (*0-671-50849-0*); PLB 7.71s.p. (*0-685-47062-8*); pap. 4.46s.p. (*0-685-47063-6*) S&S Trade.

Daniel, Frank, illus. Thanksgiving. 20p. (ps). 1993. pap. 3.95 (*0-689-71735-0*, Aladdin) Macmillan Child Grp.

Davis, Nancy M., et al. November & Thanksgiving. Davis, Nancy M., illus. 31p. (Orig.). (ps-2). 1986. pap. 4.95 (*0-937103-02-0*) DaNa Pubns.

Duden, Jane. Thanksgiving. LC 89-25397. (Illus.). 48p. (gr. 5-6). 1990. text ed. 12.95 RSBE (*0-89686-503-7*, Crestwood Hse) Macmillan Child Grp.

Feller, Caroline. Thanksgiving: Stories & Poems. Westcott, Nadine B., illus. LC 93-18631. 96p. (gr. 2-5). 1994. 14.00 (*0-06-023326-5*); PLB 13.89 (*0-06-023327-3*) HarpC Child Bks.

Fradin, Dennis B. Thanksgiving Day. LC 89-7680. (Illus.). 48p. (gr. 1-4). 1990. lib. bdg. 14.95 (*0-89490-236-9*) Enslow Pubs.

George, Jean C. First Thanksgiving. Locker, Thomas, illus. LC 91-46643. 32p. (ps up). 1993. PLB 15.95 (*0-399-21991-9*, Philomel Bks) Putnam Pub Group.

Gibbons, Gail. Thanksgiving Day. Gibbons, Gail, illus. LC 83-175. 32p. (ps-3). 1983. reinforced bdg. 15.95 (*0-8234-0489-7*); pap. 5.95 (*0-8234-0576-1*) Holiday.

Graham-Barber, Lynda. Gobble! The Complete Book of Thanksgiving Words. Lewin, Betsy, illus. LC 90-22770. 128p. (gr. 4-10). 1991. SBE 14.95 (*0-02-708332-2*, Bradbury Pr) Macmillan Child Grp.

Hallinan, P. K. Today Is Thanksgiving. Hallinan, P. K., illus. 24p. (ps-3). 1993. PLB 11.45 (*1-878363-96-4*) Forest Hse.

Hayes, Dan, illus. The Thanksgiving Activity Book. 24p. (ps-3). 1992. pap. 4.95 (*0-8249-8550-8*, Ideals Child) Hambleton-Hill.

Hayward, Linda. The First Thanksgiving. reissue ed. Watling, James, illus. 48p. (gr. k-4). 1992. pap. 6.99 incl. cass. (*0-679-83058-8*) Random Bks Yng Read.

—The First Thanksgiving: A Step 2 Book - Grades 1-3. Watling, James, illus. LC 90-52517. 48p. (Orig.). (gr. k-3). 1990. lib. bdg. 7.99 (*0-679-90218-X*); pap. 3.50 (*0-679-80218-5*) Random Bks Yng Read.

Kessel, Joyce K. Squanto & the First Thanksgiving. Donze, Lisa, illus. LC 82-10313. 48p. (gr. k-4). 1983. PLB 14.95 (*0-87614-199-8*); pap. 5.95 (*0-87614-452-0*) Carolrhoda Bks.

Kinnealy, Janice. Let's Celebrate Thanksgiving: A Book of Drawing Fun. Kinnealy, Janice, illus. LC 87-61373. 32p. (gr. 2-6). 1988. PLB 10.65 (*0-8167-1131-3*); pap. text ed. 1.95 (*0-8167-1132-1*) Troll Assocs.

Lord. One Hundred One Thanksgiving Knock-Knocks, Jokes, & Riddles. 1993. pap. 1.95 (*0-590-47163-5*) Scholastic Inc.

Mock, Dorothy K. The Thanksgiving Parade: The Good News Kids Learn about Faithfulness. Mitter, Kathy, illus. LC 93-2988. 32p. (Orig.). (ps-2). 1993. pap. 3.99 (*0-570-04743-9*) Concordia.

Moncure, Jane B. My First Thanksgiving Book. Connelly, Gwen, illus. LC 84-9433. 32p. (ps-2). 1984. PLB 11.45 (*0-516-02903-7*); pap. 3.95 (*0-516-42903-5*) Childrens.

—Our Thanksgiving Book. rev. ed. Gohman, Vera, illus. LC 85-29077. 32p. (ps-3). 1986. PLB 13.95 (*0-89565-340-0*) Childs World.

Murray, Beth. Thanksgiving Fun: A Bountiful Harvest of Crafts, Recipes, & Games. Matsick, Anni, illus. 32p. (Orig.). (gr. 2-7). 1993. pap. 3.95 (*1-56397-280-8*) Boyds Mills Pr.

Nielsen, Shelly. Thanksgiving. Wallner, Rosemary, ed. LC 91-73033. 1992. 13.99 (*1-56239-068-6*) Abdo & Dghtrs.

Palmer, Glenda. My Thanksgiving Book of Senses. (ps). 1993. 3.99 (*0-8423-3983-3*) Tyndale.

Parker, Margot. What Is Thanksgiving Day? Bates, Matt, illus. LC 88-11112. 48p. (ps-3). 1988. pap. 4.95 (*0-516-43783-6*) Childrens.

Penner, Lucille R. The Thanksgiving Book. Donnelly, Judy, ed. LC 84-518. (Illus.). (gr. 4 up). 1985. 14.95 (*0-8038-7228-3*) Hastings.

Randall, Ronne. Thanksgiving Fun: Great Things to Make & Do. Spenceley, Annabel, illus. LC 93-48615. 32p. (gr. 3-7). 1994. pap. 4.95 (*1-85697-500-2*, Kingfisher LKC) LKC.

Stamper, Judith. Thanksgiving Holiday Grab Bag. Iosa, Ann, illus. LC 92-13420. 48p. (gr. 2-5). 1992. PLB 11.89 (*0-8167-2906-9*); pap. text ed. 3.95 (*0-8167-2907-7*) Troll Assocs.

Stamper, Judith B. New Friends in a New Land: A Thanksgiving Story. Jezierski, Chet, illus. LC 92-18072. 32p. (gr. 2-5). 1992. PLB 18.51 (*0-8114-7213-2*) Raintree Steck-V.

Stevenson, James. Fried Feathers for Thanksgiving. Stevenson, James, illus. LC 86-3100. 32p. (gr. k-3). 1986. 13.95 (*0-688-06675-5*); PLB 13.88 (*0-688-06676-3*) Greenwillow.

Wade, L. Plymouth: Pilgrims' Story of Survival. 1991. 11.95s.p. (*0-86592-469-4*) Rourke Enter.

Williams, Dianna. The Pilgrims' Thanksgiving: With Thanksgiving Journal & Activities. Ross, Connie, illus. 32p. (gr. 2-6). 1991. pap. text ed. 1.95 (*1-878893-16-5*, Telecraft) Telcraft Bks.

Ziefert, Harriet. What Is Thanksgiving? Schumacher, Claire, illus. 16p. (ps). 1992. 5.95 (*0-694-00408-1*, Festival) HarpC Child Bks.

THANKSGIVING DAY–FICTION

Alcott, Louisa May. An Old-Fashioned Thanksgiving. McCurdy, Michael, illus. LC 89-1908. 32p. (gr. 3-7). 1989. reinforced 14.95 (*0-8234-0772-1*) Holiday.

—An Old Fashioned Thanksgiving. Wheeler, Jody, illus. LC 93-20352. 40p. (ps-3). 1993. 13.95 (*0-8249-8620-2*, Ideals Child); PLB 14.00 (*0-8249-8630-X*) Hambleton-Hill.

Alden, Laura & Lexa-Senning, Susan. Thanksgiving. LC 93-13019. (Illus.). 32p. (ps-2). 1993. PLB 12.30 (*0-516-00688-6*); pap. 3.95 (*0-516-40688-4*) Childrens.

Bacon, Joy. Oliver Bean's Thanksgiving. Weinberger, Jane, ed. LC 93-61630. (Illus.). 40p. (Orig.). (ps-3). 1994. pap. 9.95 (*1-883650-13-5*) Windswept Hse.

Barth, Jeff. A Thanksgiving Story in Vermont - 1852. Mitchinson, Shelia, illus. 60p. (Orig.). (gr. 3-8). 1989. pap. write for info. (*0-9624067-0-8*) Parable Pub.

Berenstain, Stan & Berenstain, Janice. The Berenstain Bears & the Prize Pumpkin. Berenstain, Stan & Berenstain, Janice, illus. LC 90-32865. 32p. (Orig.). (ps-1). 1990. lib. bdg. 5.99 (*0-679-90847-1*); pap. 2.25 (*0-679-80847-7*) Random Bks Yng Read.

Bridwell, Norman & Bridwell, Norman. Clifford's Thanksgiving Visit. (Illus.). 32p. (ps-3). 1993. pap. 2.25 (*0-590-46987-8*, Cartwheel) Scholastic Inc.

Brown, Janet M. Thanksgiving at Obaachan's. Brown, Janet M., illus. LC 93-43933. 1994. 12.95 (*1-879965-07-0*) Polychrome Pub.

Brown, Marc T. Arthur's Thanksgiving. Brown, Marc T., illus. LC 83-798. 32p. (gr. 1-3). 1984. 14.95 (*0-316-11060-4*, Joy St Bks); pap. 4.95 (*0-316-11232-1*) Little.

Bunting, Eve. How Many Days to America: A Thanksgiving Story. Bunting, Eve, illus. 32p. (ps-3). 1990. pap. 5.70 (*0-395-54777-6*, Clarion Bks) HM.

—A Turkey for Thanksgiving. De Groat, Diane, illus. 32p. (ps-1). 1991. 13.95 (*0-89919-793-0*, Clarion Bks) HM.

Carlson, Nancy. A Visit to Grandma's. LC 93-18607. (Illus.). 32p. (ps-3). 1993. pap. 4.99 (*0-14-054243-4*, Puffin) Puffin Bks.

Cauper, Eunice. The Story of the Pilgrims & Their Indian Friends: A Thanksgiving Story for Children. 5th ed. Cauper, David, illus. 15p. (gr. k). 1990. pap. 4.95 (*0-9617551-1-3*) E Cauper.

Child, Lydia M. Over the River & Through the Wood. Turkle, Brinton, illus. 32p. (gr. k-3). 1987. pap. 3.95 (*0-590-41190-X*, Blue Ribbons Bks) Scholastic Inc.

—Over the River & Through the Wood. ALC Staff, ed. Van Rynbach, Iris, illus. LC 88-4712. 32p. (ps up). 1992. pap. 3.95 (*0-688-11839-9*, Mulberry) Morrow.

Cohen, Miriam. Don't Eat Too Much Turkey! Hoban, Lillian, illus. LC 86-25660. 32p. (gr. k-3). 1987. 15.00 (*0-688-07141-4*); lib. bdg. 14.93 (*0-688-07142-2*) Greenwillow.

Cuyler, Margery. Daisy's Crazy Thanksgiving. Kramer, Robin, illus. LC 90-4323. 32p. (ps-2). 1990. 14.95 (*0-8050-0559-5*, Owlet BYR) H Holt & Co.

—Daisy's Crazy Thanksgiving. Kramer, Robin, illus. LC 90-4323. 32p. (ps-2). 1992. pap. 4.95 (*0-8050-2348-8*, Owlet BYR) H Holt & Co.

Dalgliesh, Alice. The Thanksgiving Story. Sewell, Helen, illus. LC 87-11471. 32p. (gr. k-3). 1985. pap. 4.95 (*0-689-71053-4*, Aladdin) Macmillan Child Grp.

—The Thanksgiving Story. Sewell, Helen, illus. LC 88-4448. 32p. (gr. k-3). 1988. Repr. of 1954 ed. RSBE 13.95 (*0-684-18999-2*, Scribners Young Read) Macmillan Child Grp.

De Paola, Tomie. My First Thanksgiving. (Illus.). 12p. (ps). 1992. 5.95 (*0-399-22327-4*, Putnam) Putnam Pub Group.

Devlin, Wende & Devlin, Harry. Cranberry Thanksgiving. Devlin, Harry, illus. LC 80-17070. 48p. (ps-3). 1984. Repr. of 1971 ed. RSBE 13.95 (*0-02-729930-9*, Four Winds) Macmillan Child Grp.

—Cranberry Thanksgiving. Devlin, Wende & Devlin, Harry, illus. LC 89-18642. 40p. (gr. k-3). 1990. pap. 4.95 (*0-689-71429-7*, Aladdin) Macmillan Child Grp.

Dragonwagon, Crescent. Alligator Arrived with Apples: A Potluck Alphabet Feast. Aruego, Jose & Dewey, Ariane, illus. LC 91-38490. 40p. (gr. k-3). 1992. pap. 4.95 (*0-689-71613-3*, Aladdin) Macmillan Child Grp.

First Thanksgiving. (Illus.). (ps-2). 1991. pap. 3.50 (*0-8136-5964-7*) Modern Curr.

Gantz, David. The Biggest Thanksgiving Turkey Ever. 32p. 1991. pap. 2.50 (*0-590-45132-4*) Scholastic Inc.

Gibbons, Gail. Thanksgiving Day. Gibbons, Gail, illus. (gr. k-3). 1984. incl. cassette 19.95 (*0-941078-63-9*); pap. 12.95 incl. cassette (*0-941078-61-2*); pap. 27.95 4 bks., cassette & guide (*0-941078-62-0*); sound filmstrip 22.95 (*0-941078-60-4*) Live Oak Media.

Hillert, Margaret. Why We Have Thanksgiving. (Illus.). (ps-k). 1962. PLB 6.95 (*0-8136-5104-2*, TK2384); pap. 3.50 (*0-8136-5604-4*, TK2385) Modern Curr.

Hoban, Lillian. Silly Tilly's Thanksgiving Dinner. Hoban, Lillian, illus. LC 89-29287. 64p. (gr. k-3). 1990. 14.00 (*0-06-022422-3*); PLB 13.89 (*0-06-022423-1*) HarpC Child Bks.

Janice. Little Bear's Thanksgiving. Mariana, illus. LC 67-22593. 32p. (gr. k-3). 1967. PLB 12.93 (*0-688-51078-7*) Lothrop.

Kessel, Joyce K. Squanto & the First Thanksgiving. Donze, Lisa, illus. LC 82-10313. 48p. (gr. k-4). 1983. PLB 14.95 (*0-87614-199-8*); pap. 5.95 (*0-87614-452-0*) Carolrhoda Bks.

Kraus, Robert. How Spider Saved Thanksgiving. 32p. 1991. pap. 2.50 (*0-590-44411-5*) Scholastic Inc.

Kroll, Steven. Oh, What a Thanksgiving! Schindler, Stephen D., illus. LC 88-1973. (gr. k-3). 1988. pap. 12.95 (*0-590-40613-2*, Scholastic Hardcover) Scholastic Inc.

—Oh, What a Thanksgiving! (Illus.). 32p. 1991. pap. 3.95 (*0-590-44874-9*, Blue Ribbon Bks) Scholastic Inc.

—The Squirrels' Thanksgiving. Bassett, Jeni, illus. LC 89-77513. 32p. (ps-3). 1991. reinforced 14.95 (*0-8234-0823-X*) Holiday.

Leedy, Loreen. The Dragon Thanksgiving Feast: Things to Make & Do. Leedy, Loreen, illus. LC 90-55110. 32p. (ps-3). 1990. reinforced 14.95 (*0-8234-0828-0*) Holiday.

Lewis, Beverly. Double Dabble Thanksgiving Surprise. (ps-3). 1993. pap. 3.95 (*1-56233-175-2*, Squeaky Sneaker) Star Song TN.

McGovern, Ann. Pilgrims' First Thanksgiving. 1993. pap. 3.95 (*0-590-46188-5*) Scholastic Inc.

Mandrell, Louise & Collins, Ace. Runaway Thanksgiving: A Story About the Meaning of Thanksgiving. 32p. 1992. 12.95 (*1-56530-011-4*) Summit TX.

Marilue. Bobby Bear's Thanksgiving. LC 77-83623. (Illus.). 32p. (ps-1). 1978. PLB 9.95 (*0-87783-143-2*); cassette o.s.i. 7.94x (*0-87783-187-4*) Oddo.

Markham, Marion M. The Thanksgiving Day Parade Mystery. Cassidy, Dianne, illus. 64p. 1990. pap. 2.95 (*0-380-70967-8*, Camelot) Avon.

Nerlove, Miriam. Thanksgiving. Mathews, Judith, ed. Nerlove, Meriam, illus. LC 89-49363. 24p. (ps-1). 1990. PLB 11.95 (*0-8075-7818-5*) A Whitman.

—Thanksgiving: An Albert Whitman Prairie Book. (ps-3). 1993. pap. 4.95 (*0-8075-7817-7*) A Whitman.

Nixon, Joan L. The Thanksgiving Mystery. Fay, Ann, ed. Cummins, Jim, illus. LC 79-27346. 32p. (gr. 1-3). 1979. PLB 8.95 (*0-8075-7820-7*) A Whitman.

Pascal, Francine. The Best Thanksgiving Ever. (ps-3). 1992. pap. 2.99 (*0-553-48007-3*) Bantam.

Peck, Robert N. Little Soup's Turkey. Robinson, Charles, illus. 80p. (Orig.). (gr. 1-4). 1992. pap. 2.99 (*0-440-40724-9*, YB) Dell.

Pilkey, Dav. Twas the Night Before Thanksgiving. Pilkey, Dav, illus. LC 89-48941. 32p. (ps-2). 1990. 14.95 (*0-531-05905-7*); PLB 14.99 (*0-531-08505-8*) Orchard Bks Watts.

Prelutsky, Jack. It's Thanksgiving. Hafner, Marilyn, illus. 48p. (gr. k-3). 1989. Bk.-Cassette prepack. pap. 5.95 (*0-590-63169-1*); pap. 2.50 (*0-590-41571-9*) Scholastic Inc.

Spinelli, Eileen. Thanksgiving at the Tappletons' Cocca-Leffler, Maryann, illus. LC 84-40793. 32p. (gr. k-3). 1984. 11.95 (*0-201-15892-2*, Lipp Jr Bks) HarpC Child Bks.

—Thanksgiving at the Tappletons' newly illustrated ed. Cocca-Leffler, Maryann, illus. LC 91-33250. 32p. (gr. k-3). 1989. pap. 4.95 (*0-06-443204-1*, Trophy) HarpC Child Bks.
—Thanksgiving at the Tappletons' newly illus. ed. Cocca-Leffler, Maryann, illus. LC 91-33250. 32p. (ps-3). 1992. 15.00 (*0-06-020871-6*); PLB 14.89 (*0-06-020872-4*) HarpC Child Bks.
Stock, Catherine. Thanksgiving Treat. Stock, Catherine, illus. LC 89-49528. 32p. (ps-1). 1990. SBE 11.95 (*0-02-788402-3*, Bradbury Pr) Macmillan Child Grp.
—Thanksgiving Treat. LC 92-43690. (Illus.). 32p. (ps-1). 1993. pap. 3.95 (*0-689-71726-1*, Aladdin) Macmillan Child Grp.
Tripp, Valerie. Squirrel's Thanksgiving Surprise. Martin, Sandra K., illus. LC 87-35518. 24p. (gr. k-2). 1988. pap. 3.95 (*0-516-41568-9*) Childrens.
Tryon, Leslie. Albert's Thanksgiving. LC 94-8025. (gr. k-3). 1994. 14.95 (*0-689-31865-0*, Atheneum) Macmillan Child Grp.
Warren, Jean. Huff & Puff on Thanksgiving: A Totline Teaching Tale. Cubley, Kathleen, ed. Piper, Molly & Ekberg, Marion, illus. LC 93-13545. 32p. (Orig.). (ps-2). 1993. 12.95 (*0-911019-70-7*); pap. 5.95 (*0-911019-71-5*) Warren Pub Hse.
Watson, Wendy. Thanksgiving at Our House. Watson, Wendy, illus. 32p. (ps-1). 1991. 14.45 (*0-395-53626-X*, Clarion Bks) HM.
Weisgard, Leonard. The Plymouth Thanksgiving. (gr. k-3). 1990. pap. 10.00 (*0-385-26754-1*) Doubleday.
Willey. Thanksgiving Uncles. 1995. 15.00 (*0-06-026469-1*); PLB 14.89 (*0-06-026474-8*) HarpC Child Bks.
Williams, Barbara. Chester Chipmunk's Thanksgiving. Chorao, Kay, illus. LC 77-20812. 32p. (gr. k-3). 1988. (DCB); (DCB) Dutton Child Bks.

THEATER

see also Acting; Actors and Actresses; Ballet; Mysteries and Miracle Plays; Opera; Pantomimes; Puppets and Puppet Plays; Shadow Pantomimes and Plays; Theaters

Bishop, Conrad & Fuller, Elizabeth. Get Happy. 36p. (Orig.). (gr. 9-12). 1990. pap. 4.00 acting ed. (*0-9624511-0-X*) WordWorkers.
Boy Scouts of America. Theater. 64p. (gr. 6-12). 1968. pap. 1.85 (*0-8395-3328-4*, 33328) BSA.
Evans, C. Acting & Theater. (Illus.). 64p. (gr. 6 up). 1992. lib. bdg. 13.96 (*0-88110-505-8*, Usborne); pap. 7.95 (*0-7460-0699-3*) EDC.
Franck, Irene M. & Brownstone, David M. Performers & Players. (Illus.). 208p. (gr. 7 up). 1988. 17.95x (*0-8160-1448-5*) Facts on File.
Harris, Aurand. Monkey Magic: Chinese Story Theatre. 58p. (Orig.). (ps-8). 1990. pap. 4.50 playscript (*0-87602-290-5*) Anchorage.
Haycock, Kate. Plays. Stefoff, Rebecca, ed. LC 90-13937. (Illus.). 32p. (gr. 4-8). 1991. PLB 17.26 (*0-944483-98-4*) Garrett Ed Corp.
James, Robert. Twenty Names in Theater. LC 89-23949. (Illus.). 48p. (gr. 3-8). 1990. PLB 12.95 (*1-85435-257-1*) Marshall Cavendish.
Love, Douglas. So You Want to Be a Star. Zimmerman, Robert, illus. 32p. (gr. 5 up). 1993. 18.95 (*0-694-00428-6*, Festival) HarpC Child Bks.
May, Robin. Looking at Theater. LC 89-7155. 48p. (gr. 4-8). 1990. 13.95 (*1-85435-103-6*) Marshall Cavendish.
Morin, Alice. Newspaper Theatre. (gr. 1-8). 1989. pap. 8.95 (*0-8224-6349-0*) Fearon Teach Aids.
Morley, Jacqueline. Entertainment: Screen, Stage & Stars. (Illus.). 48p. (gr. 5-8). 1994. pap. 7.95 (*0-531-15710-5*) Watts.
Novelly, Maria C. Theatre Games for Young Performers. Pijanowski, Kathy & Zapel, Arthur L., eds. LC 85-60572. (Illus.). 160p. (Orig.). (gr. 6-10). 1985. pap. text ed. 10.95 (*0-916260-31-3*, B-188) Meriwether Pub.
Pryor, Nick. Putting on a Play. LC 93-50765. (Illus.). 48p. (gr. 2-5). 1994. 15.95 (*1-56847-104-1*) Thomson Lrning.
Ratliff, Gerald L. & Troth, Susan. Onstage, Producing Musical Theatre. (Illus.). 109p. (gr. 7-12). 1988. PLB 14.95 (*0-8239-0697-3*) Rosen Group.
Tanner, Fran A. Readers Theatre Fundamentals. 2nd ed. (Illus.). 280p. (gr. 10-12). 1993. pap. text ed. 19.33 (*0-931054-30-3*) Clark Pub.

THEATER–FICTION

Auch, Mary J. Glass Slippers Give You Blisters. LC 88-45865. 176p. (gr. 3-7). 1989. 14.95 (*0-8234-0752-7*) Holiday.
Brooks, Chelsea. A California Night's Dream. LC 94-17924. (gr. 5 up). 1994. pap. 2.95 (*0-02-041652-0*, Collier) Macmillan.
Ende, Michael. Ophelia's Shadow Theater. Hechelmann, Friedrich, illus. 32p. (gr. 1 up). 1989. 14.95 (*0-87951-371-3*) Overlook Pr.
Geras, Adele. Happy Endings. Grove, Karen, ed. 173p. (gr. 7 up). 1991. 14.95 (*0-15-233375-4*) HarBrace.
Giff, Patricia R. The Almost Awful Play. Natti, Susanna, illus. LC 84-17922. 32p. (ps-3). 1985. pap. 3.95 (*0-14-050530-X*, Puffin) Puffin Bks.
Gilmore, Kate. Jason & the Bard. LC 92-2680. 240p. (gr. 7 up). 1993. 14.45 (*0-395-62472-X*) HM.
Gorman, Carol. The Great Director. Nappi, Rudi, illus. LC 93-20228. 60p. (Orig.). (gr. 2-4). 1993. pap. 3.99 (*0-570-04746-3*) Concordia.
Hall, Roger. Putting on a Concert: The Television News. Mancini, Rob, illus. LC 93-24527. (gr. 4 up). 1994. 4.25 (*0-383-03770-0*) SRA Schl Grp.
Hill, Elizabeth S. Broadway Chances. 160p. (gr. 3-7). 1992. RB 14.00 (*0-670-84197-8*) Viking Child Bks.
Hillert, Margaret. Let's Have a Play. (Illus.). (ps-k). 1981. PLB 6.95 (*0-8136-5094-1*, TK2168); pap. 3.50 (*0-8136-5594-3*, TK2169) Modern Curr.
Hoffman, Mary. Amazing Grace. (ps-3). 1991. 14.00 (*0-8037-1040-2*) Dial Bks Young.
Johnson, Dolores. The Best Bug to Be. Johnson, Dolores, illus. LC 90-22231. 32p. (gr. k-3). 1992. RSBE 13.95 (*0-02-747842-4*, Macmillan Child Bk) Macmillan Child Grp.
Kingman, Lee. Break a Leg, Betsy, Maybe. 192p. (gr. 7 up). 1979. pap. 1.50 (*0-440-90794-2*, LFL) Dell.
—Break a Leg, Betsy Maybe. LC 92-26975. 256p. (gr. 7 up). 1993. pap. 4.95 (*0-688-11789-9*, Pub. by Beech Tree Bks) Morrow.
Kukkonen, Walter J. Off Broadway. 32p. (Orig.). 1990. pap. text ed. 1.00 (*0-685-49153-6*) Polaris AZ.
Lukas, Cynthia K. Center Stage Summer. 157p. (Orig.). (gr. 8-12). 1988. pap. 4.95 (*0-938961-02-0*, Stamp Out Sheep Press) Sq One Pubs.
Pacovska, Kveta. The Midnight Play. Clements, Andrew, adapted by. LC 93-16258. (Illus.). (ps-8). 1993. 15.95 (*0-88708-317-X*) Picture Bk Studio.
Sachs, Marilyn. Circles. LC 90-37516. 144p. (gr. 5-9). 1991. 14.95 (*0-525-44683-4*, DCB) Dutton Child Bks.
—Circles. LC 92-20287. 144p. (gr. 5 up). 1992. pap. 3.99 (*0-14-034931-6*) Puffin Bks.
Streatfeild, Noel. Theater Shoes. 208p. (gr. k-6). 1983. pap. 2.95 (*0-440-48791-9*, YB) Dell.
Williams, Michael. Crocodile Burning. 192p. (gr. 7 up). 1992. 15.00 (*0-525-67401-2*, Lodestar Bks) Dutton Child Bks.
Wyeth, Sharon D. Annie K's Theater Book: The Mighty Dolphin. (gr. 4-7). 1991. pap. 2.75 (*0-553-15853-8*) Bantam.
—The Chicken Pox Party. 1990. pap. 2.75 (*0-553-15839-2*) Bantam.

THEATER–HISTORY

Haskins, James S. Black Theater in America. LC 81-43874. (Illus.). 160p. (gr. 7 up). 1991. PLB 14.89 (*0-690-04129-2*, Crowell Jr Bks) HarpC Child Bks.
Morley, Jacqueline. Entertainment. LC 93-4826. 1993. write for info. (*0-531-15264-2*) Watts.
Sitarz, Paula G. The Curtain Rises, Vol. II: A History of European Theater from the Eighteenth Century to the Present. (Illus.). 144p. (Orig.). (gr. 7 up). 1993. pap. 12.95 (*1-55870-293-8*, 70205) Betterway Bks.
Sitarz, Paula Gaj. The Curtain Rises, Vol. 1: Early Origins & Eastern Theater. LC 90-21953. (Illus.). 144p. (gr. 5-9). 1991. 14.95 (*1-55870-198-2*, 70036) Shoe Tree Pr.

THEATER–PRODUCTION AND DIRECTION

Baylor, Byrd. Moon Song. Himler, Ronald, illus. LC 81-18427. 24p. (gr. 3-6). 1982. SBE 13.95 (*0-684-17463-4*, Scribners Young Read) Macmillan Child Grp.
Custer, Jim, et al. The Best of the Jeremiah People: Humorous Sketches & Performance Tips by America's Leading Christian Repertory Group. LC 91-34195. 192p. (Orig.). (gr. 9 up). 1991. pap. 14.95 (*0-916260-81-X*, B117) Meriwether Pub.
Garrett, Dan, ed. Masks & Faces. (Illus.). 96p. (Orig.). 1990. pap. 15.00 (*0-333-36056-7*, McMillan Ed UK) Players Pr.
—Scapegoats. (Illus.). 96p. (Orig.). 1990. pap. 15.00 (*0-333-36055-9*, McMillan Ed UK) Players Pr.
Kezer, Claude D. Principles of Stage Combat. (Illus.). 62p. 1983. pap. 12.50 (*0-88680-156-7*) I E Clark.
Poulsson, Emilie. Finger Plays for Nursery & Kindergarten. Bridgman, L. T., illus. LC 74-165397. (ps-k). 1971. pap. 2.25 (*0-486-22588-7*) Dover.
Thompson, Gregory. Step by Step Theatre. (gr. 1-4). 1989. pap. 10.95 (*0-8224-6348-2*) Fearon Teach Aids.

THEATERS

Wright, Lyndie. Toy Theaters. LC 90-31636. (Illus.). 48p. (gr. 5-8). 1991. PLB 12.40 (*0-531-14196-9*) Watts.

THEATERS–STAGE SETTING AND SCENERY

Hodgman, Ann. A Day in the Life of a Theater Set Designer. Jann, Gayle, illus. LC 87-10951. 32p. (gr. 4-8). 1988. PLB 11.79 (*0-8167-1127-5*); pap. text ed. 2.95 (*0-8167-1128-3*) Troll Assocs.
Molyneux, Lynn & Gordner, Brad. Act It Out: Original Plays Plus Crafts for Costumes & Scenery. Marasco, Pam, illus. 192p. (gr. 2-6). 1986. spiral bdg. 12.95 (*0-685-29139-1*) Trellis Bks Inc.

THEATRICAL COSTUME

see Costume

THEATRICAL MAKE-UP

see Make-Up, Theatrical

THEATRICAL SCENERY

see Theaters–Stage Setting and Scenery

THEOLOGY

see also Baptism; Christianity; Church; Ethics; Faith; God; Jesus Christ; Religion; Religion and Science; Spiritual Life; Worship

Fawcett, Cheryl & Newman, Robert C. I Have a Question about God... Doctrine for Children...& Their Parents! Mazellan, Ron, illus. LC 94-3054. (gr. k-7). 1994. 24.95 (*0-87227-180-3*) Reg Baptist.
"Who is God" "Why is night dark?" "How can I be perfect?" "What happens to people when they die?" If you've heard these questions, you know that answering them isn't always easy. I HAVE A QUESTION ABOUT GOD...: DOCTRINE FOR CHILDREN...& THEIR PARENTS! answers those questions & 53 more in a delightful format. Three children - 10-year-old Megan, 8-year-old Toph, & 4-year-old Bobbie - get into all kinds of situations & ask all kinds of questions. You'll start preschool with Bobbie, who can't wait to go to kindergarten & who never stops asking questions. You'll fly to Grandpa & Grandma's with Toph, who has never traveled by himself before. And you'll sympathize with Megan as she deals with a neighbor's injustice & with problems at school. As the kids discover the answers to their questions, usually with the help of their mom or dad, your kids will learn too. The questions fall into eight areas of Biblical teaching or doctrine: God, creation, the Bible, Jesus Christ, sin, salvation, church & the future. Each story includes a beautiful illustration by Ron Mazellan & a few questions to stimulate further thought & discussion. To order: 1-800-727-4440.
Publisher Provided Annotation.

Reynolds, Ralph V. The Cry of the Unborn: Understanding the Spiritual Birth Process. Jones, Jerry, frwd. by. 125p. (Orig.). Date not set. pap. 5.95 (*1-877917-09-5*) Alpha Bible Pubns.
—Dividing the Word of Truth. Sirstad, Raymond, frwd. by. 193p. (gr. 9). Date not set. pap. 14.95 (*1-877917-08-7*) Alpha Bible Pubns.
—Usando Bien la Palabra De Verdad. Geissler, Darry & Geissler, Kimberly, eds. Crossley, Darry, tr. Sirstad, Raymond, frwd. by. (SPA.). 220p. (Orig.). Date not set. pap. 14.95 (*1-877917-12-5*) Alpha Bible Pubns.
The Shorter Catechism: A Baptist Version. 50p. (Orig.). (gr. 5 up). 1991. pap. 7.95 (*0-9622508-4-8*) Simpson NJ.
Tanyi, Enoch N. The Covenant for Young People. (Illus.). 40p. (Orig.). (gr. k-4). 1991. pap. 7.95 (*0-85398-337-2*) G Ronald Pub.

THEOLOGY, DEVOTIONAL

see Prayers

THEORY OF NUMBERS

see Numbers Theory

THEORY OF SETS

see Set Theory

THERMODYNAMICS

see also Heat

Jacobs, Linda. Letting off Steam: The Story of Geothermal Energy. (Illus.). 48p. (gr. 3-6). 1989. lib. bdg. 19.95 (*0-87614-300-1*); pap. 6.95 (*0-87614-510-1*) Carolrhoda Bks.
Rickard, Graham. Geothermal Energy. (Illus.). 32p. (gr. 4-6). 1991. PLB 17.27 (*0-8368-0708-1*) Gareth Stevens Inc.

THERMOMETERS AND THERMOMETRY

see also Temperature

THIEVES

see Robbers and Outlaws

THINKING

see Thought and Thinking

THOMAS AQUINAS, SAINT, 1225?-1274

Maritain, Raissa. St. Thomas Aquinas, the Angel of the Schools: A Book for Children & the Child-Like. (Illus.). 127p. (Orig.). (gr. 3-7). 1993. pap. 5.50 (*0-935952-95-0*) Angelus Pr.
Windeatt, Mary F. St. Thomas Aquinas: The Story of the Dumb Ox. Dorcy, Mary J., illus. LC 92-82033. 81p. 1993. pap. 5.00 (*0-89555-420-8*) TAN Bks Pubs.

THOREAU, HENRY DAVID, 1817-1862

Burleigh, Robert. A Man Named Thoreau. Bloom, Lloyd, illus. LC 85-7947. 48p. (gr. 3 up). 1985. SBE 13.95 (*0-689-31122-2*, Atheneum Child Bk) Macmillan Child Grp.
Miller, Douglas. Henry David Thoreau. Scott, John A., ed. (Illus.). 144p. (gr. 6-10). 1991. lib. bdg. 16.95x (*0-8160-2478-2*) Facts on File.
Montague, William A. Little Mouse: The Mouse Who Lived with Henry David Thoreau at Walden Pond. Roof, Christopher, ed. Payne, Maxine & Montague, William A., illus. LC 93-73231. 56p. (Orig.). (gr. 2-4). 1993. pap. text ed. 7.95 (*0-9638644-0-8*) Concord MouseTrap.
Reef, Catherine. Henry David Thoreau: A Neighbor to Nature. Raymond, Larry, illus. 72p. (gr. 4-7). 1992. PLB 14.95 (*0-941477-39-8*) TFC Bks NY.

Ring, Elizabeth. Henry David Thoreau: In Step with Nature. LC 92-11559. (Illus.). 48p. (gr. 2-4). 1993. PLB 12.90 (*1-56294-258-1*); pap. 5.95 (*1-56294-795-8*) Millbrook Pr.

THOREAU, HENRY DAVID, 1817-1862–DRAMA

Lawrence, Jerome & Lee, Robert E. The Night Thoreau Spent in Jail. 128p. (gr. 8-12). 1983. pap. 4.99 (*0-553-27838-X*) Bantam.

THOROUGHFARES

see Roads

THORPE, JAMES, 1888-1953

Bernotas, Bob. Jim Thorpe. (Illus.). (gr. 5 up). 1993. PLB 17.95 (*0-7910-1722-2*) Chelsea Hse.

Coffey, Wayne. Jim Thorpe. (Illus.). 64p. (gr. 3-7). 1993. PLB 14.95 (*1-56711-005-3*) Blackbirch.

Fago, John N. & Farr, Naunerle C. Jim Thorpe - Althea Gibson. Redondo, Frank & Carrillo, Fred, illus. (gr. 4-12). 1979. pap. text ed. 2.95 (*0-88301-360-6*); wkbk. 1.25 (*0-88301-384-3*) Pendulum Pr.

Green, Carl R. & Sanford, William R. Jim Thorpe. LC 91-32900. (Illus.). 48p. (gr. 5). 1992. text ed. 11.95 RSBE (*0-89686-740-4*, Crestwood Hse) Macmillan Child Grp.

Lipsyte, Robert. Jim Thorpe: Twentieth-Century Jock. LC 92-44069. (Illus.). 112p. (gr. 5-9). 1993. 14.00 (*0-06-022988-8*); PLB 13.89 (*0-06-022989-6*) HarpC Child Bks.

Nardo, Don. Jim Thorpe. LC 93-41138. (gr. 5-8). 1994. 14.95 (*1-56006-045-X*) Lucent Bks.

Richards, Gregory. Jim Thorpe: World's Greatest Athlete. LC 84-14240. (Illus.). 112p. (gr. 4 up). 1984. PLB 14.40 (*0-516-03207-0*) Childrens.

Rivinus, Edward F. Jim Thorpe. Viola, Herman, intro. by. (Illus.). 32p. (gr. 3-6). 1990. PLB 19.97 (*0-8172-3403-9*); pap. 4.95 (*0-8114-4094-X*) Raintree Steck-V.

Santrey, Laurence. Jim Thorpe: Young Athlete. Ulrich, George, illus. LC 82-15982. 48p. (gr. 4-6). 1983. PLB 10.79 (*0-89375-845-0*); pap. text ed. 3.50 (*0-89375-846-9*) Troll Assocs.

Van Riper, Guernsey, Jr. Jim Thorpe: Olympic Champion. Morrow, Gray, illus. LC 86-3478. 192p. (gr. 2-6). 1986. pap. 3.95 (*0-02-042140-0*, Aladdin) Macmillan Child Grp.

THOUGHT AND THINKING

see also Intellect; Logic; Perception; Reasoning

Aten, Jerry. Prime Time Thinking Skills. Filkins, Vanessa, illus. 64p. (gr. 2-5). 1985. wkbk. 8.95 (*0-86653-276-5*, GA 628) Good Apple.

Brody, Norma. Thoughts on Thinking. (SPA., Orig.). (gr. 11 up). 1991. pap. 7.95 (*0-925360-09-0*) Geste Pub.

Carratello, Patty. Literature & Critical Thinking. Apodaca, Blanqui & Vasconcelles, Keith, illus. 96p. (gr. 5-8). 1990. wkbk. 9.95 (*1-55734-316-0*) Tchr Create Mat.

Forte, Imogene. I'm Ready to Learn about Thinking Skills. (Illus.). 64p. (ps-1). 1986. pap. text ed. write for info. (*0-86530-117-4*, IP 111-1) Incentive Pubns.

Johnson, Nancy L. Thinking Is the Key: Questioning Makes the Difference. (Illus.). 96p. (gr. k-12). 1992. pap. 9.95 (*1-880505-01-0*) Pieces of Lrning.

Juntune, Joyce E. Developing Creative Thinking. Dougherty, Edie, illus. 30p. (gr. k-4). 1984. pap. 5.00 (*0-912773-09-X*) One Hund Twenty Creat.

—Developing Creative Thinking: Fun Book, No. 3. Dougherty, Edie, illus. (ps-5). 1985. pap. 6.00 (*0-912773-10-3*) One Hund Twenty Creat.

Katz, Marjorie P. & Arbeiter, Jean S., eds. Pegs to Hang Ideas on: A Book of Quotations. LC 76-187739. 320p. (gr. 6 up). 1976. 12.95 (*0-87131-085-6*) M Evans.

Metos, Thomas H. The Human Mind: How We Think & Learn. (Illus.). 128p. (gr. 9-12). 1990. PLB 13.40 (*0-531-10885-6*) Watts.

Obrien, Thomas C. Woolygoggles & Other Creatures: Problems for Developing Thinking Skills. (gr. 4-7). 1992. pap. 8.50 (*0-201-48018-2*) Addison-Wesley.

Perkins, David N. Thinking Connections: Learning to Think & Thinking to Learn. (gr. 4-7). 1993. pap. 24.95 (*0-201-81998-8*) Addison-Wesley.

Stevens, Lawrence A. Thinking Tools. Radrigan, Roberto, illus. 73p. (Orig.). (gr. 5-10). 1984. pap. text ed. 6.50 (*0-89550-223-2*) Stevens & Shea.

Symonds, M. Think Bigger. 112p. (gr. 4-6). 1993. 8.95 (*0-88160-260-4*, LW255) Learning Wks.

Taulbee, Annette. Kindergarten Thinking Skills. (Illus.). 24p. (ps-k). 1986. 3.98 (*0-86734-067-3*, FS-3060) Schaffer Pubns.

Vallet, Roxanne. Thinking. Vallet, Roxanne, illus. 14p. 1992. pap. 10.95 (*1-895583-39-X*) MAYA Pubs.

Wassermann, Selma & Wassermann, Jack. The Book of Imagining. Smith, Dennis, illus. LC 89-77869. 32p. (gr. k-3). 1990. PLB 12.85 (*0-8027-6948-9*); pap. 4.95 (*0-8027-9454-8*) Walker & Co.

—The Book of Solving Problems. Smith, Dennis, illus. 32p. (gr. k-3). 1990. lib. bdg. 12.85 (*0-8027-6954-3*); pap. 4.95 (*0-8027-9457-2*) Walker & Co.

Westcott, Alvin. Word Bending with Aunt Sarah. LC 68-56821. (Illus.). 48p. (gr. 2-3). 1968. PLB 9.95 (*0-87783-052-5*); pap. 3.94 deluxe ed (*0-87783-118-1*) Oddo.

Wise, Beth A. Thinking. Loh, Carolyn, illus. 16p. (ps). 1992. wkbk. 2.25 (*1-56293-190-3*) McClanahan Bk.

THOUGHT TRANSFERENCE

see also Clairvoyance; Extrasensory Perception; Hypnotism

Insel, Eunice & Edson, Ann. Developing Critical Thinking, Bk. 2. (gr. 5-6). 1983. wkbk. 4.25 (*1-55737-652-2*) Ed Activities.

THUNDERSTORMS

see also Lightning

Branley, Franklyn M. Flash, Crash, Rumble, & Roll. rev. ed. Emberley, Ed E. & Emberley, Barbara, illus. LC 84-45333. 32p. (ps-3). 1985. PLB 13.89 (*0-690-04425-9*, Crowell Jr Bks) HarpC Child Bks.

Cutts, David. I Can Read About Thunder & Lightning. LC 78-66273. (Illus.). (gr. 2-6). 1979. pap. 2.50 (*0-89375-217-7*) Troll Assocs.

Drew, David. The Storm. Costeloe, Brenda, illus. LC 92-30671. 1993. write for info. (*0-383-03656-9*) SRA Schl Grp.

Kahl, Jonathan D. Thunderbolt: Learning about Lightning. LC 92-45177. 1993. 19.95 (*0-8225-2528-3*) Lerner Pubns.

Sanchez, Brenda L. Max Science & the Thunderstorm. Sanchez, J. A., ed. Beard, Derrick, illus. 26p. (gr. k-5). 1991. pap. 3.95 (*1-879350-02-5*) Max Sci Pub.

THUNDERSTORMS–FICTION

Hines, Anna G. Rumble Thumble Boom! LC 91-31808. (Illus.). 24p. (ps-4). 1992. 14.00 (*0-688-10911-X*); PLB 13.93 (*0-688-10912-8*) Greenwillow.

Mayer, Gina & Mayer, Mercer. Just a Thunderstorm. (Illus.). 24p. (ps-k). 1993. pap. 1.45 (*0-307-11540-2*, 11540, Golden Pr) Western Pub.

Nikola-Lisa, W. Storm. Hays, Michael, illus. LC 92-22775. 32p. (ps-2). 1993. SBE 14.95 (*0-689-31704-2*, Atheneum Child Bk) Macmillan Child Grp.

Polacco, Patricia. Thunder Cake. (Illus.). 32p. (ps-3). 1990. 14.95 (*0-399-22231-6*, Philomel Bks) Putnam Pub Group.

Tresselt, Alvin. Sun Up. (ps-3). 1991. 14.95 (*0-688-08656-X*); PLB 14.88 (*0-688-08657-8*) Lothrop.

Tripp, Nathaniel. Thunderstorm! Wijngaard, Juan, illus. LC 93-4612. Date not set. write for info. (*0-8037-1365-7*); PLB write for info. (*0-8037-1366-5*) Dial Bks Young.

Turner, Ann. Rainflowers. Blake, Robert J., illus. LC 90-39629. 32p. (gr. k-3). 1992. 14.00 (*0-06-026041-6*); PLB 13.89 (*0-06-026042-4*) HarpC Child Bks.

TIBET

Gerstein, Mordicai. The Mountains of Tibet. LC 85-45684. (Illus.). 32p. (gr. 2 up). 1989. pap. 5.95 (*0-06-443211-4*, Trophy) HarpC Child Bks.

Halpern, Gina. Where Is Tibet? Jorden, Ngawang, tr. Halpern, Gina, illus. 48p. (gr. k-4). 1991. pap. 12.95 (*0-937938-93-9*) Snow Lion.

Kalman, Bobbie. Tibet. (Illus.). 32p. (gr. 4-5). 1990. PLB 15.95 (*0-86505-213-1*); pap. 7.95 (*0-86505-293-X*) Crabtree Pub Co.

Kendra, Judith. Tibetans. LC 93-36356. (Illus.). 48p. (gr. 6-10). 1994. 16.95 (*1-56847-152-1*) Thomson Lrning.

Perez, Louis G. The Dalai Lama. LC 92-38325. 1993. 19.93 (*0-86625-480-3*); 14.95s.p. (*0-685-67761-3*) Rourke Pubns.

Raimondo, Lois. The Little Lama of Tibet. LC 93-13627. (Illus.). 40p. (ps-4). 1994. 14.95 (*0-590-46167-2*) Scholastic Inc.

TIBET–FICTION

Gerstein, Mordicai. The Mountains of Tibet. LC 85-45684. (Illus.). 32p. (gr. 2 up). 1989. pap. 5.95 (*0-06-443211-4*, Trophy) HarpC Child Bks.

Morpurgo, Michael. King of the Cloud Forest. (Illus.). 160p. (gr. 5-9). 1991. pap. 3.95 (*0-14-032586-7*, Puffin) Puffin Bks.

Rankin, Louise. Daughter of the Mountains. Wiese, Kurt, illus. LC 92-26793. 192p. (gr. 5 up). 1993. pap. 4.99 (*0-14-036335-1*) Puffin Bks.

TIDAL WAVES

see Ocean Waves

TIDES

Bowden, Joan. Why the Tides Ebb & Flow. Brown, Marc T., illus. 48p. (gr. k-3). 1990. pap. 5.95 (*0-395-54952-3*) HM.

Rood, Ronald. Tide Pools. Classen, Martin, illus. LC 92-2581. 48p. (gr. 2-5). 1993. pap. 7.95 (*0-06-446151-3*, Trophy) HarpC Child Bks.

TIDES–FICTION

Arnold, Marsha D. Heart of a Tiger. Henterly, Jamichael, illus. LC 94-17126. (gr. 1-8). 1995. write for info. (*0-8037-1695-8*); PLB write for info. (*0-8037-1696-6*) Dial Bks Young.

Cole, Sheila. When the Tide Is Low. Wright-Frierson, Virginia, illus. LC 84-10023. 32p. (ps-1). 1985. 16.00 (*0-688-04066-7*); PLB 15.93 (*0-688-04067-5*) Lothrop.

Sainz, Frances. La Luna y las Olas. 24p. (ps-1). 1992. pap. text ed. 23.00 big bk. (*1-56843-049-3*); pap. text ed. 4.50 (*1-56843-096-5*) BGR Pub.

TIGERS

Bailey, Jill. Save the Tiger. LC 89-48770. (Illus.). 48p. (gr. 3-7). 1990. PLB 21.34 (*0-8114-2703-X*); pap. 4.95 (*0-8114-6551-9*) Raintree Steck-V.

Bowden, Joan. A World Without Tigers. Cremins, Bob, illus. Moseley, Keith, contrib. by. LC 92-18890. (Illus.). (ps-3). 1993. 7.99 (*0-8037-1381-9*) Dial Bks Young.

Bright, Michael. Tiger. LC 88-83105. (Illus.). 32p. (gr. 5-6). 1989. PLB 12.40 (*0-531-17141-8*, Gloucester Pr) Watts.

Cajacob, Thomas & Burton, Teresa. Close to the Wild: Siberian Tigers in a Zoo. Cajacob, Thomas, photos by. (Illus.). 48p. (gr. 2-5). 1986. PLB 19.95 (*0-87614-227-7*); pap. 6.95 (*0-87614-451-2*) Carolrhoda Bks.

Georgeanne, Irvine. Wild & Wonderful Big Cats at the San Diego Zoo. LC 93-47529. (gr. 3 up). 1995. 16.00 (*0-671-87191-9*, S&S BFYR) S&S Trade.

Goodall, Jane. Jane Goodall's Animal World: Tigers. LC 89-78130. (Illus.). 32p. (gr. 3-7). 1990. pap. 3.95 (*0-689-71393-2*, Aladdin) Macmillan Child Grp.

Hewett, Joan. Tiger, Tiger, Growing Up. Hewett, Richard, photos by. LC 92-9741. (Illus.). 32p. (ps-2). 1993. 13.95 (*0-395-61583-6*, Clarion Bks) HM.

Highlights for Children Editors. Tigers. (Illus.). 32p. (Orig.). (gr. 2-5). 1993. pap. 3.95 (*1-56397-287-5*) Boyds Mills Pr.

Hippo. 1989. 3.50 (*1-87865-732-1*) Blue Q.

Hoffman, Mary. Tiger. LC 84-15120. (Illus.). 24p. (gr. k-5). 1984. PLB 9.95 (*0-8172-2405-X*); pap. 3.95 (*0-8114-6890-9*) Raintree Steck-V.

Hogan, Paula Z. The Tiger. Nachreiner, Tom, illus. LC 79-13604. (gr. 1-4). 1979. PLB 19.97 (*0-8172-1506-9*) Raintree Steck-V.

—The Tiger. LC 79-13604. (Illus.). 32p. (gr. 1-4). 1981. PLB 29.28 incl. cassette (*0-8172-1841-6*) Raintree Steck-V.

Hughes, Jill. Lions & Tigers. (Illus.). 32p. (gr. 4-6). 1991. 13.95 (*0-237-60164-8*, Pub. by Evans Bros Ltd) Trafalgar.

Lewin, Ted. Tiger Trek. Lewin, Ted, illus. LC 89-12710. 40p. (gr. 1-5). 1990. RSBE 14.95 (*0-02-757381-8*, Macmillan Child Bk) Macmillan Child Grp.

Markert, Jenny. Tigers. 32p. (gr. 2-6). 1991. 15.95 (*0-89565-722-8*) Childs World.

Martin, L. Tigers. (Illus.). 24p. (gr. k-5). 1988. PLB 11.94 (*0-86592-995-5*); PLB 8.95s.p. (*0-685-58307-4*) Rourke Corp.

Mattern, Joanne. Lions & Tigers. Stone, Lynn M., illus. LC 92-19053. 24p. (gr. 4-7). 1992. (Pub. by Watermill Pr); pap. 1.95 (*0-8167-2956-5*, Pub. by Watermill Pr) Troll Assocs.

Petty, Kate. Baby Animals: Tigers. (Illus.). 24p. (ps-3). 1992. pap. 3.95 (*0-8120-4971-3*) Barron.

—Tigers. Kline, Marjory, ed. LC 90-18361. (Illus.). 24p. (gr. k-3). 1991. PLB 10.90 (*0-531-17284-8*, Gloucester Pr) Watts.

Royston, Angela. The Tiger. JV-Warwick Press Staff, ed. LC 87-51626. (Illus.). 24p. (gr. 1-3). 1988. 10.40 (*0-531-19043-9*, Warwick) Watts.

Saunier. Tiger, Reading Level 3-4. (Illus.). 28p. (gr. 2-5). 1983. PLB 16.67 (*0-86592-866-5*); lib. bdg. 12.50 (*0-685-58827-0*) Rourke Corp.

Stone, L. Tigers. (Illus.). 24p. (gr. k-5). 1989. lib. bdg. 11.94 (*0-86592-504-6*); lib. bdg. 8.95s.p. (*0-685-58632-4*) Rourke Corp.

Tibbitts, Alison & Roocroft, Alan. Sumatran Tiger. (Illus.). 24p. (ps-2). 1992. PLB 12.95 (*1-56065-105-9*) Capstone Pr.

The Tiger. 28p. (gr. 2-5). 1988. pap. 3.50 (*0-8167-1571-8*) Troll Assocs.

Tiger. 1989. 3.50 (*1-87865-731-3*) Blue Q.

Two Can Publishing Ltd. Staff. Tigers. (Illus.). 32p. (gr. 2-7). 1991. pap. 3.50 (*0-87534-212-4*) Highlights.

Urquhart, Jennifer C. Lions & Tigers & Leopards: The Big Cats. (Illus.). (gr. k-4). 1990. Set. 13.95 (*0-87044-820-X*); Set. PLB 16.95 (*0-87044-825-0*) Natl Geog.

Wexo, John B. Tigers. 24p. (gr. 4). 1989. PLB 14.95 (*0-88682-266-1*) Creative Ed.

Why Are Tigers Striped? 1991. 3.99 (*0-517-05894-4*) Random Hse Value.

Wildlife Education, Ltd. Staff. Tigers. Orr, Richard, et al, illus. 20p. (Orig.). (gr. k-12). 1985. pap. 2.75 (*0-937934-35-6*) Wildlife Educ.

TIGERS–FICTION

Allen, Judy. Tiger. Humphries, Tudor & Humphries, Tudor, illus. LC 91-58760. 32p. (ps up). 1992. 14.95 (*1-56402-083-5*) Candlewick Pr.

—Tiger. LC 91-58760. 32p. (ps-3). 1994. pap. 4.99 (*1-56402-284-6*) Candlewick Pr.

Baker, Keith. Who Is the Beast? Baker, Keith, illus. 28p. (ps-3). 1991. pap. 19.95 (*0-15-296059-7*) HarBrace.

—Who Is the Beast? Baker, Keith, illus. LC 89-29365. 28p. (ps-2). 1990. 12.95 (*0-15-296057-0*) HarBrace.

Bannerman, Helen. Story of Little Black Sambo. (Illus.). (gr. k-3). 1923. 12.00 (*0-397-30006-9*, HarpT) HarpC.

Blaustein, Muriel. Play Ball, Zachary! Blaustein, Muriel, illus. LC 87-45274. 32p. (ps-2). 1988. HarpC Child Bks.

Brooks, Gwendolyn. The Tiger Who Wore White Gloves: Or What You Are You Are. LC 74-75589. 1974. pap. 6.95 (*0-88378-031-3*) Third World.

Cowcher, Helen. La Tigresa. Marcuse, Aida, tr. (SPA.). 32p. (gr. 4-8). 1993. pap. 5.95 (*0-374-47779-5*) FS&G.

—La Tigresa: Tigress. (ps-3). 1993. 16.00 (*0-374-37565-8*, Mirasol) FS&G.

—Tigress. (Illus.). 32p. (ps up). 1991. bds. 14.95 (*0-374-37567-4*) FS&G.

—Tigress. Thomas, Peter, narrated by. Cowcher, Helen, illus. 32p. (gr. k-3). incls. cassette 19.95 (*0-924483-33-4*) Soundprints.

—Tigress. (ps-3). 1993. pap. 5.95 (*0-374-47781-7*) FS&G.

Edmiston, Jim. Mizzy & the Tigers. (ps-3). 1992. pap. 5.95 (*0-8120-4828-8*) Barron.

Edwards, Roland. Tigers. Riches, Judith, illus. LC 91-40098. 32p. (ps-2). 1992. 15.00 (*0-688-11685-X*, Tambourine Bks); PLB 14.93 (*0-688-11686-8*, Tambourine Bks) Morrow.

Egan, Tim. Friday Night at Hodges' Cafe. LC 93-11290. 1994. 14.95 (*0-395-68076-X*) HM.

Hall, Roger. The Tiger & the Millionaire. Newman, Jack, illus. LC 93-28932. 1994. 4.25 (*0-383-03786-7*) SRA Schl Grp.

Harley, Rex. Mary's Tiger. Porter, Sue, illus. LC 89-49009. 23p. (ps-2). 1990. 13.95 (*0-15-200524-2*, Gulliver Bks) HarBrace.

Hawkins, Colin & Hawkins, Jacqui. Terrible, Terrible Tiger. Hawkins, Colin & Hawkins, Jacqui, illus. LC 87-40675. 32p. (ps-3). 1988. bds. 5.95 (*1-55782-043-0*, Pub. by Warner Juvenile Bks) Little.

Jacobs, James & Amiri, Fahimeh, eds. Babri. LC 94-11762. (Illus.). 32p. (ps-2). 1994. 15.95 (*0-87905-622-3*) Gibbs Smith Pub.

Jones, Terry. The Sea Tiger. Foreman, Michael, illus. LC 94-7546. 32p. (gr. k up). 1994. 9.95 (*0-87226-378-9*) P Bedrick Bks.

Kasza, Keiko. The Rat & the Tiger. (Illus.). 32p. (ps-3). 1993. PLB 14.95 (*0-399-22404-1*, Putnam) Putnam Pub Group.

Kerr, Judith. Tiger Who Came to Tea. (ps-3). 1993. NOP 5.95 (*0-00-193798-7*) Collins SF.

Koertge, Ron. Tiger, Tiger, Burning Bright. 160p. (gr. 5 up). 1994. 14.95 (*0-531-06840-4*); lib. bdg. 14.99 RLB (*0-531-08690-9*) Orchard Bks Watts.

Kuntz, J. L. Tennessee Tiger. LC 93-60259. (Illus.). 57p. (ps-3). 1994. 7.95 (*1-55523-611-1*) Winston-Derek.

Kurkul, Edward. Tiger in the Lake. Petie, Haris, illus. LC 68-11183. (gr. 1-3). 1968. write for info. (*0-8313-0076-0*); PLB 7.19 (*0-685-42237-2*) Lantern.

LaFleur, Tom & Brennan, Gale. Tuffy the Tiger. Murtagh, Betty, illus. 16p. (gr. k-6). 1982. pap. 1.25 (*0-685-05557-4*) Brennan Bks.

Lourie, Peter. Everglades: Buffalo Tiger & the River of Grass. Lourie, Peter, photos by. LC 92-73989. (Illus.). 48p. (gr. 3 up). 1994. 16.95 (*1-878093-91-6*) Boyds Mills Pr.

Oetting, Rae. Timmy Tiger & the Elephant. LC 73-108730. (Illus.). 32p. (ps-2). 1970. PLB 9.95 (*0-87783-041-X*); pap. 3.94 deluxe ed (*0-87783-111-4*); cassette 7.94x (*0-87783-277-3*) Oddo.

—Timmy Tiger to the Rescue. LC 70-108733. (Illus.). 32p. (ps-4). 1970. PLB 9.95x (*0-87783-043-6*); pap. 3. 94x deluxe ed (*0-87783-112-2*); cassette 7.94x (*0-87783-229-3*) Oddo.

—Timmy Tiger's New Coat. LC 74-108734. (Illus.). 32p. (ps-2). 1970. PLB 9.95 (*0-87783-044-4*); pap. 3.94 deluxe ed (*0-87783-113-0*); cassette 7.94x (*0-87783-230-7*) Oddo.

—Timmy Tiger's New Friend. LC 77-108732. (Illus.). (ps-2). 1970. PLB 9.95 (*0-87783-042-8*); pap. 3.94 deluxe ed (*0-87783-114-9*); cassette 7.94x (*0-87783-231-5*) Oddo.

Ossorio, Nelson A., et al. Tiger's New Prey. (Illus.). 48p. (gr. 4-6). 1994. pap. 6.95 (*1-56721-074-0*) Twnty-Fifth Cent Pr.

Root, Phyllis. Moon Tiger. Young, Ed, illus. LC 85-7572. 32p. (ps-2). 1988. pap. 4.95 (*0-8050-0803-9*, Bks Young Read) H Holt & Co.

Silver, Norman. No Tigers in Africa. 144p. (gr. 7 up). 1994. pap. 3.99 (*0-14-036935-X*) Puffin Bks.

Smith, Jean B. The Tartan Tiger. (Illus., Orig.). (gr. 7 up). 1986. pap. 8.00 (*0-935827-00-5*) Tartan Tiger.

Stockton, Frank R. The Lady or the Tiger. Carlson, Claudia & DeNieff, Jacqueline S., illus. Horowitz, Paul J., frwd. by. Bd. with The Discourager of Hesitancy. Repr. of 1885 ed. (Orig.). (gr. 1-8). pap. 4.95 (*0-934254-11-7*) Claymont Comm.

Tiger, Take Off Your Hat. (Illus.). 40p. (gr. k-5). 1994. pap. 4.95 (*0-685-71581-7*, 517) W Gladden Found.

Timmy Tiger Series, 6 vols. (Illus.). (ps-4). 1981. Set. PLB 59.70 (*0-87783-166-1*); Set Of 4 Vols. pap. 15.76 deluxe ed (*0-87783-167-X*); cassettes set (4) 31.76x (*0-87783-228-5*) Oddo.

Van Gulik, Robert H. Monkey & the Tiger. 1980. pap. 2.95 (*0-684-16737-9*, Scribner) Macmillan.

Vargo, Vanessa. Tiger Talk. (ps-3). pap. 5.95 (*0-85953-397-2*) Childs Play.

Vaughn, Marcia K. Tingo Tango Mango Tree. Saint James, Synthia, illus. LC 93-44867. 1994. write for info. (*0-382-24605-5*); pap. write for info. (*0-382-24454-0*) Silver.

Wiltshire, Terri. The Tale of Tiki Tiger. Archer, Rebecca, illus. LC 92-40364. 24p. (ps-k). 1993. 7.95 (*1-85697-859-1*, Kingfisher LKC) LKC.

Wright, Kit. Tigerella. Bailey, Peter, illus. LC 93-34218. (ps-2). 1994. 14.95 (*0-590-48171-1*) Scholastic Inc.

Xiong, Blia & Spagnoli, Cathy, eds. Nine-in-One Grr! Grr! LC 89-9891. (Illus.). 32p. (ps-5). 1989. 13.95 (*0-89239-048-4*) Childrens Book Pr.

Zahradka, Miroslav. The Un-Terrible Tiger. Zahradka, Miroslav, illus. LC 78-155815. 32p. (ps-3). 7.95 (*0-87592-056-X*) Scroll Pr.

Zolotow, Charlotte. A Tiger Called Thomas. rev. ed. Stock, Catherine, illus. LC 86-20878. 40p. (ps-3). 1988. PLB 12.88 (*0-688-06697-6*) Lothrop.

TIMBER

see Forests and Forestry; Lumber and Lumbering; Trees; Wood

TIME

see also Calendars; Clocks and Watches

Anastasio, Dina. It's about Time. Smith, Mavis, illus. 24p. (gr. k-3). 1993. 8.95 (*0-448-40551-2*, G&D) Putnam Pub Group.

Awdry, Christopher. Tell the Time with Thomas. Stott, Ken, illus. LC 91-67877. 32p. (ps-3). 1993. 7.99 (*0-679-83461-3*) Random Bks Yng Read.

Baumann, Hans. What Time Is It Around the World? LC 75-24710. (Illus.). (gr. k-5). 1979. 6.95 (*0-87592-061-6*) Scroll Pr.

Beckmann, Beverly. Time in God's World. Edler, Jules, illus. 24p. (gr. 2-5). 1985. 6.99 (*0-570-04128-7*, 56-1539) Concordia.

Bradbury, Lynne. What Is the Time? Grundy, Lynn N., illus. 28p. (ps). 1992. Series 921. 3.50 (*0-7214-1511-3*) Ladybird Bks.

Branley, Franklyn M. Keeping Time. Van Rynbach, Iris, illus. LC 92-6783. 1993. 13.95 (*0-395-47777-8*) HM.

Breiter, Herta S. Time & Clocks. rev. ed. LC 87-23229. (Illus.). 48p. (gr. 2-6). 1987. PLB 10.95 (*0-8172-3262-1*) Raintree Steck-V.

Buck, Peggy J. Tommy Learns about Time & Eternity. Lautermilch, John, illus. 68p. (Orig.). (gr. 1-3). 1980. pap. 1.25 (*0-89323-006-5*, 023) Bible Memory.

Burns, Marilyn. This Book Is about Time. Weston, Martha, illus. LC 78-6614. (gr. 5 up). 1978. 15.95 (*0-316-11752-8*); pap. 10.95 (*0-316-11750-1*) Little.

Cassidy, John. The Time Book. (ps-8). 1991. wire-o bdg. incl. watch 10.95 (*1-878257-08-0*) Klutz Pr.

Darling, David. Could You Ever Build a Time Machine? (Illus.). 60p. (gr. 5 up). 1991. text ed. 14.95 RSBE (*0-87518-456-1*, Dillon) Macmillan Child Grp.

Davies, Kay & Oldfield, Wendy. The Super Science Book of Time. Lloyd, Frances, illus. LC 92-42131. 32p. (gr. 4-8). 1993. 14.95g (*1-56847-020-7*) Thomson Lrning.

Fakih, Kimberly O. Off the Clock: A Lexicon of Time Words & Expressions. LC 94-2082. (Illus.). 144p. (gr. 5 up). 1994. 15.95g (*0-395-66374-1*) Ticknor & Flds Bks Yng Read.

Firmin, Peter, illus. Day & Night. 16p. (ps-1). 1986. 4.50 (*0-7460-0795-7*) EDC.

—Then & Now. 16p. (ps-1). 1986. 4.50 (*0-7460-0794-9*) EDC.

Fortune, J. J. Revenge in the Silent Tomb. 160p. (Orig.). (gr. 7-12). 1984. pap. 2.25 (*0-440-97707-X*, LFL) Dell.

Grey, Judith. What Time Is It? Hall, Susan, illus. LC 81-5113. 32p. (gr. k-2). 1981. PLB 11.59 (*0-89375-509-5*); pap. text ed. 2.95 (*0-89375-510-9*) Troll Assocs.

Kalman, Bobbie. Time & the Seasons. (Illus.). 32p. (gr. 2-3). 1986. 15.95 (*0-86505-072-4*); pap. 7.95 (*0-86505-094-5*) Crabtree Pub Co.

L'Engle, Madeleine. Madeleine L'Engle's Time Trilogy, 3 bks. Incl. A Wrinkle in Time; A Wind in the Door; A Swiftly Tilting Planet. 1986. pap. 9.30 boxed set (*0-440-95207-7*, LE) Dell.

Llewellyn, Claire. My First Book of Time. LC 91-58194. (Illus.). 32p. (ps-3). 1992. 14.95 (*1-879431-78-5*) Dorling Kindersley.

Morris, Neil. Linda's Late: A Fun Book of Time. Stevenson, Peter, illus. 32p. (ps-2). 1991. PLB 13.50 (*0-87614-675-2*) Carolrhoda Bks.

My First Book of Telling the Time. 1994. 3.99 (*0-517-10149-1*) Random Hse Value.

Ockenga, Earl & Rucker, Walt. Telling Time. Dawson, Dave, illus. 16p. (gr. 1). 1990. pap. text ed. 1.25 (*1-56281-120-7*, M120) Extra Eds.

Oliver, Stephen, photos by. Time. LC 90-8576. (Illus.). 24p. (ps-k). 1991. 6.95 (*0-679-81164-8*) Random Bks Yng Read.

Pellowski, Michael J. Teddy on Time. Epstein, Len, illus. LC 85-14127. 48p. (Orig.). (gr. 1-3). 1986. PLB 10.59 (*0-8167-0582-8*); pap. text ed. 3.50 (*0-8167-0583-6*) Troll Assocs.

Pen Notes Staff. Learn to Tell Time. (gr. 1 up). 1982. 8.95 (*0-939564-02-5*) Pen Notes.

Pienkowski, Jan. Time. Pienkowski, Jan, illus. 24p. (ps-k). 1991. pap. 2.95 (*0-671-72847-4*, Little Simon) S&S Trade.

Rand McNally Staff. Children's Atlas of Earth Through Time. Fagan, Elizabeth, ed. (Illus.). 80p. 1990. 14.95 (*0-528-83415-0*) Rand McNally.

Rothman, Joel. A Moment in Time. Leake, Don, illus. LC 72-90693. 32p. (ps-2). 1973. 7.95 (*0-87592-034-9*) Scroll Pr.

Roy, Cal. Time Is Day. (Illus.). (gr. k-3). 1968. 9.95 (*0-8392-3065-6*) Astor-Honor.

Santamaria, Peggy. Arrivals & Departures: How to Use All Kinds of Schedules. LC 93-29642. 1993. 13.95 (*0-8239-1605-7*) Rosen Group.

Shibles, Warren. Time: A Critical Analysis for Children. LC 77-93811. (gr. 4-12). 1978. pap. 6.50 (*0-912386-17-7*) Language Pr.

Singer, Marilyn. Nine O'Clock Lullaby. Lessac, Frane, illus. LC 90-32116. 32p. (ps-3). 1991. PLB 14.89 (*0-06-025648-6*) HarpC Child Bks.

Skutina, Vladimir. Nobody Has Time for Me. Klein, Zanvel, ed. Herrmann, Dagmar, tr. from CZE. Sacre, Marie-Jose, illus. LC 91-4457. 32p. (gr. k-3). 1991. 14. 95 (*0-922984-07-7*) Wellington IL.

Tankel, Lara. My Very First Book of Time. (Illus.). 24p. (ps-3). 1994. write for info. (*1-56458-726-6*) Dorling Kindersley.

Tell Me the Time. (ps-k). 3.95 (*0-7214-5054-7*) Ladybird Bks.

Tell Time with Thomas. (gr. 2 up). Date not set. 95.88 (*0-679-86107-6*) Random Bks Yng Read.

Telling Time. 1993. 3.99 (*0-517-08764-2*) Random Hse Value.

The Time Wipe-Off Book. 24p. (ps-3). 1992. pap. 1.95 (*0-590-45693-8*) Scholastic Inc.

Warren, Jean. Movement Time. 80p. (gr. k-2). 1984. 7.95 (*0-912107-17-0*) Monday Morning Bks.

Williams, John. Simple Science Projects with Time. LC 91-50548. (Illus.). 32p. (gr. 2-4). 1992. PLB 17.27 (*0-8368-0770-7*) Gareth Stevens Inc.

Wing, Ralph. Just Do It! Time Management. Pangaea Press Staff, ed. 144p. (Orig.). (gr. 10 up). 1990. pap. text ed. 6.95 (*0-9625534-0-9*, P100) Pangaea Pr.

Young, Woody. Clockwise, Vol. Two: Learn to Tell Time. White, Craig, illus. 48p. (Orig.). 1985. pap. text ed. 4.95 (*0-939513-02-1*) Joy Pub SJC.

Ziner, Feenie & Thompson, Elizabeth. Time. LC 81-18080. (Illus.). 48p. (gr. k-4). 1982. PLB 12.85 (*0-516-01651-2*) Childrens.

TIME–POETRY

Gordon, Ruth, ed. Time Is the Longest Distance. LC 90-4947. 96p. (gr. 7 up). 1991. 13.95 (*0-06-022297-2*); PLB 13.89 (*0-06-022424-X*) HarpC Child Bks.

TIMEX-SINCLAIR 1000 (COMPUTER)

Hurley, L. ZX-81 TS-1000: Programming for Young Programmers. (Illus.). 96p. (gr. 9up). 1983. pap. text ed. 9.95 (*0-07-031449-7*, BYTE Bks) McGraw.

TIMEX-SINCLAIR COMPUTERS

see also Timex-Sinclair 1000 (Computer)

Kemnitz, Thomas M. & Mass, Lynne. Kids Working with Computers: The Timex-Sinclair BASIC Manual. Schlendorf, Lori, illus. 48p. (gr. 4-7). 1983. pap. 4.99 (*0-89824-058-1*) Trillium Pr.

TIRES

Curtis, Neil & Greenland, Peter. How Tires Are Made. (Illus.). 24p. (gr. 1-3). 1992. PLB 13.50 (*0-8225-2377-9*) Lerner Pubns.

TITANIC (STEAMSHIP)

Ballard, Robert D. Exploring the Titanic. (gr. 4-7). 1991. 14.95 (*0-590-41953-6*); pap. 6.95 (*0-590-41952-8*) Scholastic Inc.

Blos, Joan W. The Heroine of the Titanic: A Tale Both True & Otherwise of the Life of Molly Brown. Dixon, Tennessee, illus. LC 90-35369. 40p. (gr. 1 up). 1991. 14.95 (*0-688-07546-0*); PLB 14.88 (*0-688-07547-9*) Morrow Jr Bks.

Donnelly, Judy. The Titanic: Lost...& Found. Kohler, Keith, illus. LC 86-20402. 48p. (gr. 1-3). 1987. lib. bdg. 7.99 (*0-394-98669-5*); pap. 3.50 (*0-394-88669-0*) Random Bks Yng Read.

Hamilton, Sue. R. M. S. Titanic's Sinking. Hamilton, John, ed. LC 88-71722. (Illus.). 32p. (gr. 4). 1989. PLB 11.96 (*0-939179-42-3*) Abdo & Dghtrs.

Kent, Deborah. The Titanic. LC 93-12688. (Illus.). 32p. (gr. 3-6). 1993. PLB 12.30 (*0-516-06672-2*); pap. 3.95 (*0-516-46672-0*) Childrens.

Lord, Walter. Night to Remember. (gr. 6-12). 1983. pap. 4.99 (*0-553-27827-4*) Bantam.

Rawlinson, J. Titanic. (Illus.). 32p. (gr. 4 up). 1988. PLB 17.27 (*0-86592-873-8*); PLB 12.95s.p. (*0-685-58290-6*) Rourke Corp.

Sloan, Frank. Titanic. LC 87-6214. (Illus.). 96p. (gr. 4-9). 1987. PLB 10.90 (*0-531-10396-X*) Watts.

Stacey, Tom. The Titanic. LC 89-33553. (Illus.). 64p. (gr. 5-8). 1989. PLB 11.95 (*1-56006-006-9*) Lucent Bks.

TITHES

Clawson, Jan. Let's Learn about Tithing. Pardew, Les, illus. 24p. (gr. k-6). 1988. pap. 3.98 (*0-88290-339-X*) Horizon Utah.

TOADS

see Frogs

TOADSTOOLS

see Mushrooms

TOBACCO HABIT

Cohen, Philip. Tobacco. LC 91-32583. (Illus.). 64p. (gr. 6-12). 1991. PLB 22.80 (*0-8114-3202-5*) Raintree Steck-V.

Focus on Nicotine & Caffeine. (Illus.). 64p. (gr. 3-7). 1990. PLB 15.40 (*0-516-07355-9*) Childrens.

Goffe, Toni, illus. No Smoking: Do You Mind If I Don't Smoke? LC 92-10849. 1992. 7.95 (*0-85953-782-X*, Pub. by Child's Play UK); pap. 3.95 (*0-85953-783-8*, Pub. by Childs Play UK) Childs Play.

Gunn, Jeffrey. Pen Pals, Vol. 10: Facts about Nicotine. Wolfe, Debra, illus. (Orig.). (gr. 3). 1990. pap. write for info. (*1-879146-10-X*) Knowldg Pub.

Lee, Richard S. & Lee, Mary P. Caffeine & Nicotine. LC 94-2279. (gr. 7 up). 1994. write for info. (*0-8239-1701-0*) Rosen Group.

Perry, Robert. Focus on Nicotine & Caffeine. (Illus.). 64p. (gr. 2-4). 1990. PLB 14.95 (*0-8050-2217-1*) TFC Bks NY.

Seixas, Judith. Tobacco: What It Is, What It Does. LC 81-837. 56p. (Orig.). (gr. 3-6). 1981. 13.95 (*0-688-00769-4*) Greenwillow.

Seixas, Judith S. Tobacco: What It Is, What It Does. Huffman, Tom, illus. LC 81-837. 56p. (gr. 1 up). 1981. 12.95 (*0-685-42145-7*, Mulberry); (Mulberry) Morrow.

Starbuck, Marnie. The Gladden Book about Tobacco. (gr. 1-4). 1994. 0.75 (*0-685-71638-4*, 655) W Gladden Found.

Traynor, Pete. Cigarettes, Cigarettes. Traynor, Pete, illus. Reynolds, Patrick, frwd. by. LC 92-31033. (Illus.). 24p. 1994. 14.95 (*0-9629978-7-0*) Sights Prods.

TOES

see Foot

TOILET

see Beauty, Personal

TOILET PREPARATIONS

see Cosmetics

TOKYO

Davis, James E. & Hawke, Sharryl D. Tokyo. (Illus.). 64p. (gr. 4-9). 1990. PLB 11.95 (*0-8172-3032-7*) Raintree Steck-V.

Newton, Robert. Tokyo. LC 92-2498. (Illus.). 96p. (gr. 6 up). 1992. text ed. 14.95 RSBE (*0-02-768235-8*, New Discovery) Macmillan Child Grp.

TOLERATION
see also Discrimination; Religious Liberty
Gay, Kathlyn. Bigotry. LC 88-30428. (Illus.). 144p. (gr. 6 up). 1989. lib. bdg. 18.95 (*0-89490-171-0*) Enslow Pubs.
Osborn, Kevin. Tolerance. rev. ed. (gr. 7-12). 1993. 13.95 (*0-8239-1508-5*) Rosen Group.
TOLERATION–FICTION
Ada, Alma F. Friends - Amigos. Koch, Barry, illus. (SPA & ENG.). 26p. (gr. k-2). 1989. Spanish ed. 5.25 (*0-88272-501-7*); English ed. 5.25 (*0-88272-500-9*) Santillana.

Derby, Janice. Are You My Friend? Keenan, Joy D., illus. 40p. (ps-3). 1993. 12.95 (*0-8361-3609-8*) Herald Pr. The expressive watercolors of Joy Dunn Keenan dance across these pages as a boy & his grandfather spend a day at the park. Throughout the day they meet many people & the boy observes how they are different from him. He also notices that they are like him in the things they enjoy seeing & doing. He asks each one, "Are you my friend?" At the end, all the friends gather at the carousel. This book written by Janice Derby allows children to acknowledge characteristics such as language, skin color, being physically or mentally challenged, or having a different economic status that can separate us. By observing that others enjoy the same kinds of activities, children learn that the differences are minor compared to the many similarities we share. For children ages 4-to-8 & the adults who love them.
Publisher Provided Annotation.

TOLKIEN, JOHN RONALD RUEL, 1892-1973
Collins, David R. J. R. R. Tolkien: Master of Fantasy. Heagy, William, illus. 144p. (gr. 4-7). 1992. 21.50 (*0-8225-4906-9*) Lerner Pubns.
Shorto, Russell. J. R. R. Tolkien: Hobbit Chronicler. Tennyson, G. B., frwd. by. (Illus.). 48p. (gr. 5-8). 1988. Kipling Pr.
TOLSTOI, LEV NIKOLAEVICH, GRAF, 1828-1910
Chapman, Lynne F. Leo Tolstoy. LC 93-10629. (gr. 5 up). 1994. 18.95 (*0-88682-620-9*) Creative Ed.
TONGUE
Greenaway, Theresa. Tongues & Tails. Savage, Ann, et al, illus. LC 94-16739. 1995. write for info. (*0-8114-8271-5*) Raintree Steck-V.
Keller, Charles. Tongue Twisters. Fritz, Ron, illus. LC 88-26448. (ps-4). 1989. pap. 13.95 (*0-671-67123-5*, S&S BFYR); pap. 5.95 (*0-671-67975-9*, S&S BFYR) S&S Trade.
Santa Fe Writer's Group Staff. Bizarre & Beautiful Tongues. Brigman, Chris, illus. 48p. (gr. 4-7). 1993. text ed. 14.95 (*1-56261-123-2*) John Muir.
TOOLS
see also Agricultural Machinery; Machine Tools; Machinery
Bracy, Norma N. The Tool Box. (Illus.). 35p. (gr. k-12). 1987. pap. text ed. 2.00 (*0-915783-04-5*) Book Binder.
Gibbons, Gail. Tool Book. Gibbons, Gail, illus. LC 81-13386. 32p. (ps-3). 1982. reinforced bdg. 15.95 (*0-8234-0444-7*); pap. 5.95 (*0-8234-0694-6*) Holiday.
Kelley, True. Hammers & Mops, Pencils & Pots: A First Book of Tools & Gadgets We Use Around the House. Kelley, True, illus. LC 93-25294. 32p. (ps). 1994. 8.99 (*0-517-59626-1*) Crown Bks Yng Read.
Miller, Margaret. Who Uses This? LC 89-30456. (Illus.). 40p. (ps up). 1990. 12.95 (*0-688-08278-5*); PLB 12.88 (*0-688-08279-3*) Greenwillow.
Rockwell, Anne. Toolbox. LC 89-34818. (Illus.). 24p. (ps-1). 1990. pap. 3.95 (*0-689-71382-7*, Aladdin) Macmillan Child Grp.
Rockwell, Anne & Rockwell, Harlow. Toolbox. LC 72-119836. (Illus.). 24p. (ps-2). 1971. RSBE 13.95 (*0-02-777540-2*, Macmillan Child Bk) Macmillan Child Grp.
Sandow, Lyn. My Hammer. Wheeler, Jody, illus. LC 87-40676. (ps up). 1990. bds. 4.95 (*1-55782-307-3*, Pub. by Warner Juvenile Bks) Little.
Shone, Venice. My Activity Box. Shone, Venice, illus. LC 93-3288. 20p. (ps). 1993. 2.99 (*0-525-67449-7*, Lodestar Bks) Dutton Child Bks.
—Tools. (ps). 1991. 9.95 (*0-590-44472-7*) Scholastic Inc.
Timeline of Discovery & Invention: Tracing the Development of Knowledge from Toolmaking. 1993. 12.98 (*0-88394-973-3*) Promntory Pr.
TOOLS–FICTION
Ingle, Annie. Ernie's Little Toolbox: A Sesame Street Book. Cooke, Tom, illus. LC 90-61312. 22p. (ps). 1991. bds. 2.95 (*0-679-80905-8*) Random Bks Yng Read.
Scarry, Richard. Mr. Fix-It: Richard Scarry's Smallest Pop-up Book Ever! (Illus.). 10p. (ps-3). 1992. write for info. (*0-307-12461-4*, 12461, Golden Pr) Western Pub.
TOOLS–HISTORY
Kalman, Bobbie. Tools & Gadgets. (Illus.). 32p. (gr. k-9). 1992. PLB 15.95 (*0-86505-488-6*); pap. 7.95 (*0-86505-508-4*) Crabtree Pub CO.
TOPOGRAPHICAL DRAWING
see also Map Drawing
TORNADOES
see also Storms
Archer, Jules. Tornado! LC 90-45373. (Illus.). 48p. (gr. 5-6). 1991. text ed. 12.95 RSBE (*0-89686-594-0*, Crestwood Hse) Macmillan Child Grp.
Armbruster, Ann & Taylor, Elizabeth A. Tornadoes. (Illus.). 64p. (gr. 5-8). 1993. pap. 5.95 (*0-531-15666-4*) Watts.
Barrett, Norman S. Huracanes y Tornados. LC 90-70889. (SPA., Illus.). 32p. (gr. k-4). 1990. PLB 11.90 (*0-531-07907-4*) Watts.
Branley, Franklyn M. Tornado Alert. Maestro, Giulio, illus. LC 87-29379. 32p. (ps-3). 1988. (Crowell Jr Bks); PLB 14.89 (*0-690-04688-X*) HarpC Child Bks.
—Tornado Alert. Maestro, Giulio, illus. LC 87-29379. 32p. (gr. k-4). 1990. pap. 4.95 (*0-06-445094-5*, Trophy) HarpC Child Bks.
Erlbach, Arlene. Tornadoes. LC 94-10472. (Illus.). 48p. (gr. k-4). 1994. PLB 17.20 (*0-516-01071-9*); pap. 4.95 (*0-516-41071-7*) Childrens.
Farris, John. The Dust Bowl. LC 89-33557. (Illus.). 64p. (gr. 5-8). 1989. PLB 11.95 (*1-56006-005-0*) Lucent Bks.
Greenberg, Keith. Hurricanes & Tornadoes. (Illus.). 64p. (gr. 5-8). 1994. bds. 15.95 (*0-8050-3095-6*) TFC Bks NY.
Hooker, Merrilee. Tornadoes. LC 92-41101. 1993. 12.67 (*0-86593-248-4*); 9.50s.p. (*0-685-66349-3*) Rourke Corp.
Jenison, Norma J. & Benjamin, Starr J. The Eyes of the Storm: Belmond, Iowa Recalls the 1966 Homecoming Day Tornado. LC 89-84423. (Illus.). 256p. (Orig.). 1989. pap. 8.95 (*0-9623288-0-4*) T Lydia Pr.
Kahl, Jonathan D. Storm Warning: The Power of Tornadoes & Hurricanes. LC 92-13627. 1993. 19.95 (*0-8225-2527-5*) Lerner Pubns.
Lampton, Christopher. Tornado. (Illus.). 64p. (gr. 4-6). 1991. PLB 13.90 (*1-56294-032-5*); pap. 5.95 (*1-56294-785-0*) Millbrook Pr.
—Tornado: A Disaster Book. (gr. 4-7). 1992. pap 5.95 (*0-395-63644-2*) HM.
Rotter, Charles. Tornadoes. LC 93-46803. 40p. 1994. 18. 95 (*0-88682-712-4*) Creative Ed.
TORONTO
MacKay, Claire. The Toronto Story. Wales, Johnny, illus. 112p. (Orig.). (gr. 5 up). 1991. 34.95 (*1-55037-137-1*, Pub. by Annick CN); pap. 24.95 (*1-55037-135-5*, Pub. by Annick CN) Firefly Bks Ltd.
Murphy, Wendy & Murphy, Jack. Toronto. (Illus.). 64p. (gr. 3-7). PLB 14.95 (*1-56711-025-8*) Blackbirch.
TORTOISES
see Turtles
TOTALITARIANISM
see also Communism; Dictators; National Socialism
TOTEMS AND TOTEMISM
Batdorf, Carol. Totem Poles: An Ancient Art. Cheney, Tracy, illus. 24p. (Orig.). (gr. 1-6). 1990. pap. 4.95 (*0-88839-248-6*) Hancock House.
TOUCANS–FICTION
McKee, David. Two Can Toucan. McKee, David, illus. 32p. (gr. k-3). 1987. 15.95 (*0-86264-094-6*, Pub. by Anderson Pr UK) Trafalgar.
TOUCH
Berry, Joy W. Teach Me about Touching. Dickey, Kate, ed. LC 85-45089. (Illus.). 36p. (ps). 1986. 4.98 (*0-685-10728-0*) Grolier Inc.
Bertrand, Cecile. Noni Touches. (ps). 1993. 4.95 (*0-307-15688-5*, Artsts Writrs) Western Pub.
Fowler, Allan. Feeling Things. LC 90-22526. (Illus.). 32p. (ps-2). 1991. PLB 10.75 (*0-516-04908-9*); pap. 3.95 (*0-516-44908-7*) Childrens.
Moncure, Jane B. The Touch Book. Axeman, Lois, illus. LC 82-4154. (ps-3). 1982. pap. 3.95 (*0-516-43254-0*) Childrens.
Morris, Neil. Feel! A Fun Book of Touch. Stevenson, Peter, illus. 32p. (ps-2). 1991. PLB 13.50 (*0-87614-672-8*) Carolrhoda Bks.
Otto, Carolyn B. I Can Tell by Touching. Westcott, Nadine B., illus. LC 93-18630. 32p. (ps-1). 1994. 15. 00 (*0-06-023324-9*); PLB 14.89 (*0-06-023325-7*) HarpC Child Bks.
—I Can Tell by Touching. Westcott, Nadine B., illus. LC 93-18630. 32p. (ps-1). 1994. pap. 4.95 (*0-06-445125-9*, Trophy) HarpC Child Bks.
Parramon, J. M. & Puig, J. J. Touch. Rius, Maria, illus. 32p. (Orig.). (ps). 1985. pap. 6.95 (*0-8120-3567-4*); Span. ed. pap. 6.95 (*0-8120-3609-3*) Barron.
Rowe, Julian & Perham, Molly. Feel & Touch! LC 93-8214. (Illus.). 32p. (gr. 1-4). 1993. PLB 13.95 (*0-516-08132-2*) Childrens.
Smith, Kathie B. & Crenson, Victoria. Touching. Storms, Robert S., illus. LC 87-5885. 24p. (gr. k-3). 1988. PLB 10.59 (*0-8167-1012-0*); pap. text ed. 2.50 (*0-8167-1013-9*) Troll Assocs.
Snell, Nigel. Touching. (Illus.). 32p. (gr. k-2). 1991. 10.95 (*0-237-60259-8*, Pub. by Evans Bros Ltd) Trafalgar.
Stuchbury, Dianne. Touch! Stuchbury, Dianne, illus. 24p. (ps-1). 1991. 4.99 (*0-7459-2002-0*) Lion USA.
Suhr, Mandy. Touch. Gordon, Mike, illus. LC 93-44192. 1993. 13.50 (*0-87614-837-2*) Carolrhoda Bks.
Wood, Nicholas. Touch...What Do You Feel? Willey, Lynne, illus. LC 90-10925. 32p. (gr. k-3). 1991. PLB 11.59 (*0-8167-2126-2*); pap. text ed. 3.95 (*0-8167-2127-0*) Troll Assocs.
Ziefert, Harriet. What Do I Touch? 1988. 3.95 (*0-553-05454-6*) Bantam.
TOUCH–FICTION
Isadora, Rachel. I Touch. LC 90 48260. (Illus.). 24p. (ps up). 1991. bds. 6.95 (*0-688-10524-6*) Greenwillow.
Jamieson, Rita. Felt Fun, Flannel Board Stories. Jamieson, Myles, illus. (ps-8). 1990. pap. text ed. 5.00 (*0-9622329-1-2*) R Jamieson.
Peck, Richard. Close Enough to Touch. 144p. (gr. 7 up). 1982. pap. 3.50 (*0-440-91282-2*, LFL) Dell.
Sclavi, Tiziano. Touch & Read. Michelini, Carlo A., illus. 10p. (ps). 1994. bds. 4.95 (*1-56397-343-X*) Boyds Mills Pr.
TOULOUSE-LAUTREC MONFA, HENRI MARIE RAYMOND DE, 1864-1901
Hart, Tony. Toulouse-Lautrec. Hellard, Susan, illus. LC 93-22146. 24p. (ps-3). 1994. pap. 5.95 (*0-8120-1825-7*) Barron.
Raboff, Ernest. Henri de Toulouse-Lautrec. De Toulouse-Lautrec, Henri, illus. LC 87-17703. 32p. (gr. 1 up). 1988. pap. 7.95 (*0-06-446070-3*, Trophy) HarpC Child Bks.
Spizzirri Publishing Co. Staff. Lautrec Posters: Educational Coloring Book. Spizzirr, Linda, ed. (Illus.). 32p. (gr. 1-8). 1983. pap. 1.75 (*0-86545-052-8*) Spizzirri.
TOURIST TRADE
see also Travel
Childs, Valerie. Walt Disney World & Epcot Center. 1990. 7.99 (*0-517-48085-9*) Random Hse Value.
Crisfield, Deborah. Travel: Careers in Travel. LC 93-15211. (Illus.). 48p. (gr. 5-6). 1994. text ed. 14.95 RSBE (*0-89686-790-0*, Crestwood Hse) Macmillan Child Grp.
Grant, Edgar. Exploring Careers in the Travel Industry. rev. ed. Rosen, Ruth, ed. (gr. 7-12). 1989. PLB 14.95 (*0-8239-0961-1*) Rosen Group.
Kennedy, Don. Exploring Careers on Cruise Ships. LC 93-20293. (gr. 7 up). 1993. 14.95 (*0-8239-1665-0*); 9.95 (*0-8239-1714-2*) Rosen Group.
TOURIST TRADE–FICTION
Martin, Charles E. For Rent. Martin, Charles E., illus. LC 85-864. 32p. (gr. k-3). 1986. 11.75 (*0-688-05716-0*); PLB 11.88 (*0-688-05717-9*) Greenwillow.
TOUSSAINT LOUVERTURE, PIERRE DOMINIQUE, 1746?-1803
Hoobler, Dorothy & Hoobler, Thomas. Toussaint L'Ouverture. (Illus.). 112p. (gr. 5 up). 1990. 17.95 (*1-55546-818-7*) Chelsea Hse.
TOWN OFFICERS
see Local Government
TOWN PLANNING
see City Planning
TOWNS
see Cities and Towns
TOXICOLOGY
see Poisons
TOYS
see also Dollhouses; Dolls
Baby's Things. 12p. (ps). 1978. 3.95 (*0-448-40866-X*, G&D) Putnam Pub Group.
Baby's Toys. (Illus.). 10p. (ps-1). 1984. 4.95 (*0-8431-0995-5*) Price Stern.
Bishop, Roma. Toys. (Illus.). 14p. (ps-k). 1991. pap. 2.95 (*0-671-74831-9*, Little Simon) S&S Trade.
Blocksma, Dewey & Blocksma, Mary. Easy-to-Make Water Toys That Really Work. Seiden, Art, illus. LC 84-24913. 64p. (gr. 2-6). 1988. pap. 5.95 (*0-671-66259-7*, S&S BFYR) S&S Trade.
Blocksma, Mary. Todos Mis Juquetes (All My Toys Are on the Floor) Kalthoff, Sandra C., illus. LC 85-27000. (SPA.). 24p. (ps-2). 1989. pap. 3.95 (*0-516-51579-9*) Childrens.
Bourne, Miriam A. Let's Visit a Toy Factory. Plunkett, Micheal, illus. LC 87-3489. 32p. (gr. 2-4). 1988. PLB 10.79 (*0-8167-1159-3*); pap. text ed. 2.95 (*0-8167-1160-7*) Troll Assocs.
Bridgewater, Alan & Bridgewater, Gill. Making Noah's Ark Toys in Wood. LC 88-21040. (Illus.). 164p. (Orig.). (gr. 10-12). 1988. pap. 10.95 (*0-8069-6726-9*) Sterling.
Burns, Elizabeth. Hanky Panky: Traditional Handkerchief Toys. Burns, Elizabeth, illus. 24p. (ps-6). 1989. pap. 4.50 (*0-9624152-0-0*) E Burns.
—Hanky Panky: Traditional Handkerchief Toys, Benefit Edition. (Illus.). 24p. (ps-6). 1991. pap. 4.50 (*0-9624152-2-7*) E Burns.
Churchill, E. Richard. Fast & Funny Paper Toys You Can Make. LC 89-32411. (Illus.). 128p. (gr. 7-12). 1989. 14.95 (*0-8069-5770-0*) Sterling.
—Instant Paper Toys to Pop, Spin, Whirl & Fly. Kendrick, Dennis, illus. LC 85-26229. 112p. (gr. 1-8). 1987. pap. 7.95 (*0-8069-6278-X*) Sterling.
—Paper Action Toys. Michaels, James, illus. LC 93-23860. 128p. (gr. 6 up). 1993. 14.95 (*0-8069-0368-6*) Sterling.
—Paper Science Toys. LC 90-9891. (Illus.). 128p. (gr. 3-10). 1990. 14.95 (*0-8069-5834-0*) Sterling.
Corwin, Judith H. Asian Crafts. Rosoff, Iris, ed. LC 91-13500. (Illus.). 48p. (gr. 1-4). 1992. PLB 12.90 (*0-531-11013-3*) Watts.

Count Ten Fun & Games. (Illus.). 6p. (gr. k-2). 1988. bds. 6.95 (*0-87449-454-0*) Modern Pub NYC.

Count Ten Playtime Toys. (Illus.). 6p. (gr. k-2). 1988. bds. 6.95 (*0-87449-453-2*) Modern Pub NYC.

Davenport, Zoe. Toys. Davenport, Zoe, illus. 16p. (ps). 1995. 4.95 (*0-685-72230-9*) Ticknor & Flds Bks Yng Read.

—Toys. LC 94-20819. 1995. pap. 4.95 (*0-395-71539-3*) Ticknor & Fields.

DeSimone, James. The Official G. I. Joe Collectors Guide to Completing & Collating Your G. I. Joes & Accessories. 1993. pap. 11.94 (*0-9635956-0-1*) GI Joe Collect.

Eden Toys Staff, ed. Toys & Designs from the World of Beatrix Potter. Menchini, Pat, et al. (Illus.). 128p. 1992. 18.00 (*0-7232-4005-1*) Warne.

Flick, Pauline. Discovering Toys & Toy Museums. 2nd ed. (Illus.). 72p. (Orig.). (gr. 6 up). 1977. pap. 3.00 (*0-913714-38-0*) Legacy Bks.

Gibson, Ronald. Folk, Fantasy & Play. 1992. pap. 19.95 (*0-9608982-5-5*) Child Mus.

Greene, Carol. Margarete Steiff: Toy Maker. LC 93-16855. (Illus.). 48p. (gr. k-3). 1993. PLB 12.85 (*0-516-04257-2*); pap. 4.95 (*0-516-44257-0*) Childrens.

Hutchings, Margaret. Big Book of Stuffed Toy & Doll Making: Instructions & Full-Size Patterns for 45 Playthings. (Illus.). 256p. (gr. 7 up). 1983. pap. 8.95 (*0-486-24266-8*) Dover.

Jaffke, Freya. Toymaking with Children. 1988. pap. 10.95 (*0-86315-069-1*, 20244) Gryphon Hse.

Kurland, Alexandra. Teddies to the Rescue. Kenyon, Mark, illus. 56p. (gr. k-4). 1986. 11.95 (*0-938209-27-2*) Bear Hollow Pr.

Lemke, Stefan & Pricken, Marie-Luise L. Making Toys & Gifts. LC 91-3880. (Illus.). 64p. 1991. PLB 15.40 (*0-516-09259-6*); pap. 8.95 (*0-516-49259-4*) Childrens.

Lohf, Sabine. Building Your Own Toys. LC 89-22276. 64p. (gr. 5 up). 1989. lib. bdg. 15.40 (*0-516-09251-0*); pap. 8.95 (*0-516-49251-9*) Childrens.

Lynn, Tim & Lynn, Tom. Making Toy Trains in Wood. LC 90-9978. (Illus.). 136p. (Orig.). (gr. 10-12). 1990. pap. 10.95 (*0-8069-6989-X*) Sterling.

Mapstone, Bryan. Making Wooden Toys for All Ages. LC 92-44019. (Illus.). 172p. (gr. 10-12). 1993. pap. 17. 95 (*0-7153-9809-1*, Pub. by David & Charles Pub UK) Sterling.

Mitgutsch, Ali. From Idea to Toy. (Illus.). 24p. (ps-3). 1988. PLB 10.95 (*0-87614-352-4*) Carolrhoda Bks.

Morris, Ann. How Teddy Bears Are Made. Heyman, Ken, photos by. LC 93-44617. (Illus.). (ps-2). 1994. 10.95 (*0-590-47152-X*, Cartwheel) Scholastic Inc.

My Toys. (ps-k). 1989. bds. 3.50 (*0-7214-9121-9*) Ladybird Bks.

Pfiffner, George. Earth-Friendly Toys: How to Make Fabulous Toys & Games from Reusable Objects. (Illus.). 128p. (gr. 3-7). 1994. pap. text ed. 12.95 (*0-471-00822-2*) Wiley.
These days earth-savvy kids know the value of recycling. They're using old scraps of paper cardboard & foil to make their own erector sets. Or setting up a miniature space station for their action figures using old plastic bottles. Or maybe they're flying a sea plane made of discarded styrofoam. These are just a few of the imaginative toys you'll find in the first title of the exciting Earth-Friendly Series. Includes step-by-step instructions for creating 30 toys, including costumes, dolls, musical instruments, & much more. Lists interesting facts about recycling & other things kids can do to help clean up the planet. Illustrated with over 200 line drawings. Other Earth-Friendly Books coming soon! Earth-Friendly Fashion (Fall 1994), Earth-Friendly Outdoor Fun (Spring 1995), & Earth-Friendly Holidays (Fall 1995).
Publisher Provided Annotation.

Picture Book of Toys. (Illus.). (ps). 3.50 (*0-7214-0750-1*) Ladybird Bks.

Pierce, Sharon. Making Whirligigs & Other Wind Toys. LC 84-26782. (Illus.). 132p. (Orig.). (gr. 10-12). 1985. pap. 9.95 (*0-8069-7980-1*) Sterling.

Sams, Kenneth. Flying Toys. (Illus.). (gr. 9-12). 1992. pap. 7.95 (*1-86351-038-9*, Pub. by S Milner AT) Sterling.

Schael, Hannelore, et al. Toys Made of Clay. LC 89-22253. 64p. 1989. pap. 8.95 (*0-516-49256-X*) Childrens.

Shone, Venice. My Play Box. Shone, Venice, illus. LC 93-3289. 20p. (ps). 1993. 2.99 (*0-525-67448-9*, Lodestar Bks) Dutton Child Bks.

—My Toy Box. Shone, Venice, illus. LC 93-18682. 20p. (ps). 1993. 2.99 (*0-525-67450-0*, Lodestar Bks) Dutton Child Bks.

Sibbett, Ed., Jr. Easy-to-Make Articulated Wooden Toys: Patterns & Instructions for 18 Playthings That Move. (Illus.). 48p. 1983. pap. 2.95 (*0-486-24411-3*) Dover.

Smalley, Guy, illus. My Very Own Book of Toys. 24p. (ps-2). 1989. 9.95 (*0-929793-03-X*) Camex Bks Inc.

Strombeck, Janet A. & Strombeck, Richard H. Making Timeless Toys in Wood: Quality Strom Toys & Plans. (Illus.). 96p. (Orig.). (gr. 10-12). 1986. pap. 9.95 (*0-912355-05-0*) Sun Designs.

Sullivan, S. Adams. Bats, Butterflies, & Bugs, Vol. 1. (ps-3). 1990. 14.95 (*0-316-82185-3*, Joy St Bks) Little.

Toys. 32p. (ps-8). Set of 10. pap. 29.50 (*0-87474-615-9*) Smithsonian.

Toys. LC 91-60534. (Illus.). 24p. (ps-3). 1991. 8.95 (*1-879431-08-4*); PLB 9.99 (*1-879431-23-8*) Dorling Kindersley.

Toys & Games. (ARA., Illus.). (gr. 4-6). 1987. 3.95x (*0-86685-241-7*) Intl Bk Ctr.

Wakefield, David. How to Make Animated Toys. LC 86-42771. 310p. (gr. 10-12). 1987. pap. 14.95 (*0-943822-94-7*) Sterling.

—Making Dinosaur Toys in Wood. LC 90-9466. (Illus.). 260p. (Orig.). (gr. 10-12). 1990. pap. 12.95 (*0-8069-6956-3*) Sterling.

Wiencek, Henry. The World of Lego Toys. (Illus.). 176p. 1987. pap. 19.95 (*0-8109-2362-9*) Abrams.

Wright, Lyndie. Toy Theaters. LC 90-31636. (Illus.). 48p. (gr. 5-8). 1991. PLB 12.40 (*0-531-14196-9*) Watts.

Young, Robert S. Action Figures. LC 92-7697. (Illus.). 64p. (gr. 5 up). 1992. text ed. 13.95 RSBE (*0-87518-516-9*, Dillon) Macmillan Child Grp.

Zuckert, Ellen R., ed. The KIDSTUFF Survey: Parents Rate Toys, Books, Videotapes, Music & Software for Kids under Six. 2nd, rev. ed. Rosenblatt, Barbara G., illus. 240p. (ps-1). 1993. pap. 9.95 (*0-9634785-1-6*) Cove Pt Pr.
The revised edition of The KIDSTUFF Survey is the only comprehensive guide to toys, books, videotapes, music & software for kids under six based on the views of parents nationwide. It is a unique resource; unlike other product guides, the ratings in The KIDSTUFF Survey are drawn exclusively on parents' & kids' experience with more than 1000 items over the course of months & years. There are concise product descriptions, parents' comments' & price information included to help parents & grandparents choose the best items for kids in the market today. The KIDSTUFF Survey also features the "A Lists" of the best products in each category by age group. In addition, the book contains information on more than 50 mail-order catalogues, toll-free telephone numbers of all major toy manufacturers & extensive indexes to help people choose the products they want. The KIDSTUFF Survey, featured in newspaper articles & radio talk shows around the country, is an indispensable guide that brings together the views of parents on toys, books, videotapes, music & software for kids under six.
Publisher Provided Annotation.

TOYS–FICTION

Alborough, Jez. Donde Esta Mi Osito? Where's My Teddy? (SPA., Illus.). 184p. (gr. k-1). 1994. pap. 11.95 (*1-56014-582-X*) Santillana.
Imagine losing your favorite teddy bear. Imagine encountering a giant-size version of a teddy bear searching the forest for his own lost teddy!! What is going on? Zany fun & nonsense, this book has entertained kids around the world in many different languages. Jez Alborough's rhyming text has been recreated in Spanish with all the humor & charm intact. To order: Santillana, 901 West Walnut, Compton, CA 90220. 1-800-245-8584.
Publisher Provided Annotation.

—Where's My Teddy? Alborough, Jez, illus. LC 91-58765. 32p. (ps up). 1992. 15.95 (*1-56402-048-7*) Candlewick Pr.

—Where's My Teddy? LC 91-58765. (Illus.). 32p. (ps up). 1994. pap. 4.99 (*1-56402-280-3*) Candlewick Pr.

Alexander, Martha. Good Night, Lily. Alexander, Martha, illus. LC 92-53005. 14p. (ps). 1993. 4.95 (*1-56402-164-5*) Candlewick Pr.

—Lily & Willy. Alexander, Martha, illus. LC 92-53004. 14p. (ps). 1993. 4.95 (*1-56402-163-7*) Candlewick Pr.

Andersen, Hans Christian. The Steadfast Tin Soldier. Easton, Samantha, retold by. Montgomery, Michael, illus. 1991. 6.95 (*0-8362-4929-1*) Andrews & McMeel.

—The Steadfast Tin Soldier. Lynch, Patrick J., ed. 1992. write for info. (*0-15-200599-4*, Gulliver Bks) HarBrace.

Ashforth, Camilla. Monkey Tricks. Ashforth, Camilla, illus. LC 92-53013. 32p. (ps up). 1993. 15.95 (*1-56402-170-X*) Candlewick Pr.

Bang, Molly. One Fall Day. LC 93-36490. (Illus.). 24p. 1994. 15.00 (*0-688-07015-9*); PLB 14.93 (*0-688-07016-7*) Greenwillow.

—Yellow Ball. LC 92-40722. (Illus.). 32p. (ps-1). 1993. pap. 4.50 (*0-14-054828-9*, Puffin) Puffin Bks.

Banks, Lynne R. The Mystery of the Cupboard. Newsom, Tom, illus. LC 92-39295. 256p. (gr. 5 up). 1993. 13.95 (*0-688-12138-1*); PLB 13.88 (*0-688-12635-9*) Morrow Jr Bks.

—The Secret of the Indian. (gr. 5 up). 1989. pap. 15.95 (*0-385-26292-2*) Doubleday.

Barkan, Joanne, ed. Anna Marie's Blanket. Maze, Deborah, illus. LC 93-50953. (ps-3). 1994. pap. 4.95 (*0-8120-1972-5*) Barron.

Barrett, John. The Day the Toys Came to Silver Dollar City. Ruth, Rod, illus. (gr. k-10). 1978. 1.99 (*0-686-22891-X*) Silver Dollar.

Bertrand, Lynne. Good Night, Teddy Bear. Street, Janet, illus. LC 92-15141. 24p. (ps). 1992. comb-bound 9.95 (*0-9631591-1-9*) Chapters Pub.

—Let's Go! Teddy Bear. Street, Janet, illus. LC 93-71172. 24p. (ps). 1993. combbound 9.95 (*1-881527-15-8*) Chapters Pub.

Bibee, John. The Toy Campaign. Turnbaugh, Paul, illus. LC 87-3261. 225p. (Orig.). (gr. 4 up). 1987. pap. 6.99 (*0-8308-1201-6*, 1201) InterVarsity.

Billam, Rosemary. Fuzzy Rabbit. Julian-Ottie, Vanessa, illus. LC 83-17637. 32p. (ps-3). 1984. pap. 2.25 (*0-394-86346-1*) Random Bks Yng Read.

Brannon, Tom, illus. Sesame Street: Little Elmo's Toy Box. (ps). 1990. pap. write for info. (*0-307-06038-1*, Golden Pr) Western Pub.

—Sesame Street: Little Ernie Loves Rubber Duckie. 12p. (ps). 1992. write for info. nontoxic, washable (*0-307-06064-0*, 6064, Golden Pr) Western Pub.

Breese, Gillian & Langham, Tony. The Amazing Adventures of Teddy Tum Tum. Lowry, Patrick, illus. 32p. (ps-3). 1992. 11.95 (*1-55970-185-4*) Arcade Pub Inc.

Breeze, Lynn. Baby's Toys. (Illus.). 14p. (ps). 1994. bds. 4.50 fold-outs (*0-8120-6412-7*) Barron.

Brown, Marc T., illus. Teddy Bear, Teddy Bear. 8p. (ps-k). 1989. 5.95 (*0-525-44531-5*, DCB) Dutton Child Bks.

Brown, Margaret W. David's Little Indian. Charlip, Remy, illus. 48p. (gr. 2-5). 1989. Repr. of 1954 ed. 10. 95 (*0-929077-02-4*, Hopscotch Bks); PLB 10.95 (*0-317-92547-4*, Hopscotch Bks) Watermark Inc.

Carle, Eric. Mixed-up Chameleon: Miniature Edition. Carle, Eric, illus. LC 91-2497. 32p. (ps-3). 1991. 4.95 (*0-06-020103-7*) HarpC Child Bks.

Carlstrom, Nancy W. Barney Is Best. Hale, James G., illus. LC 92-30376. 32p. (ps-3). 1994. 15.00 (*0-06-022875-X*); PLB 14.89 (*0-06-022876-8*) HarpC Child Bks.

Cartlidge, Michelle. Good Night, Teddy. Cartlidge, Michelle, illus. LC 91-58732. 24p. (ps). 1992. 5.95 (*1-56402-076-2*) Candlewick Pr.

—Teddy's Friends. Cartlidge, Michelle, illus. LC 91-58758. 24p. (ps). 1992. 5.95 (*1-56402-077-0*) Candlewick Pr.

Chorao, Kay. Carousel Round & Round. LC 93-35520. 1995. write for info. (*0-395-63632-9*, Clarion Bks) HM.

Collier, James L. The Teddy Bear Habit. (gr. 5-9). 15.50 (*0-8446-6191-0*) Peter Smith.

Conrad, Pam. The Tub Grandfather. Egielski, Richard, illus. LC 92-31770. 32p. (ps-3). 1993. 15.00 (*0-06-022895-4*); PLB 14.89 (*0-06-022896-2*) HarpC Child Bks.

Cooper, Helen. The Tale of the Bear. LC 94-21054. 1995. write for info. (*0-688-13990-6*) Lothrop.

Darling, Abigail. Teddy Bear's Picnic Cookbook. (ps-3). 1991. 13.95 (*0-670-82947-1*) Viking Child Bks.

Dedieu, Thierry. The Little Christmas Soldier. Dedieu, Thierry, illus. LC 92-40172. 32p. (ps-2). 1993. 15.95 (*0-8050-2612-6*, Bks Young Read) H Holt & Co.

Delamare, David, illus. Steadfast Tin Soldier. Ingram, John W., ed. Delamare, David, illus. LC 90-10927. 48p. (gr. 1-5). 1990. 9.95 (*0-88101-077-4*) Unicorn Pub.

—Steadfast Tin Soldier. 48p. (ps-3). 1992. 4.95 (*0-88101-245-9*) Unicorn Pub.

—Steadfast Tin Soldier. 48p. (ps-3). 1990. 12.95 (*0-88101-237-8*) Unicorn Pub.

Deschaine, Scott. Popcorn! Donovan, Bob, illus. 68p. 1993. pap. 4.95 (*1-878181-06-8*) Discovery Comics.

Desputeaux, Helene. My Toys. (Illus.). 26p. (ps). 1993. bds. 2.95 (*2-921198-26-6*, Pub. by Les Edits Herit CN) Adams Inc MA.

Dicks, Terrance. Sally Ann & the School Show. LC 91-1541. (ps-3). 1992. pap. 14.00 (*0-671-74513-1*, S&S BFYR) S&S Trade.

—Sally Ann on Her Own. Sims, Blanche, illus. LC 91-15379. 64p. (gr. k-3). 1992. pap. 14.00 jacketed (*0-671-74512-3*, S&S BFYR) S&S Trade.

Eure, Wesley. Red Wings of Christmas. Paolillo, Ronald G., illus. LC 92-5457. 160p. (gr. 3-7). 1992. 19.95 (*0-88289-902-3*); audiocassette 14.95 (*0-88289-998-8*) Pelican.

Faulkner, Keith. Monster in My Toybox. Lambert, Tony, illus. 16p. (ps-3). 1993. 4.95 (*0-8431-3481-X*) Price Stern.

Flynn, Amy, illus. Teddy's Busy Night. 24p. (ps). 1993. bds. 2.95 (*0-448-40557-1*, G&D) Putnam Pub Group.

Freeman, Chester D. & McGuire, John E. Runaway Bear. Kuper, Rachel, illus. LC 93-16893. 32p. (gr. k-3). 1993. 14.95 (*0-88289-956-2*); ltd. boxed signed ed. 29. 95 (*1-56554-016-6*) Pelican.

Freeman, Don. Beady Bear. Freeman, Don, illus. LC 54-12295. 48p. (ps-1). 1954. 13.95 (*0-670-15056-8*) Viking Child Bks.

—Corduroy. Freeman, Don, illus. LC 68-16068. 32p. 1968. 12.99 (*0-670-24133-4*) Viking Child Bks.

Freeman, Lydia. Corduroy's Toys. McCue, Lisa, illus. LC 84-40478. 24p. 1985. pap. 3.50 (*0-670-80522-X*) Viking Child Bks.

Gackenbach, Dick. Poppy the Panda. Gackenbach, Dick, illus. LC 84-4952. 32p. (ps-3). 1984. (Pub. by Clarion); pap. 4.80 (*0-89919-492-3*, Pub. by Clarion) HM.

Galbraith, Kathryn. Laura Charlotte. Cooper, Floyd, illus. 32p. (ps-3). 1990. 14.95 (*0-399-21613-8*, Philomel Bks) Putnam Pub Group.

Gantschev, Ivan. The Christmas Teddy Bear. Clements, Andrew, adapted by. LC 93-20121. (gr. 4 up). 1993. write for info. (*0-88708-333-1*) Picture Bk Studio.

—The Christmas Teddy Bear. Gantschev, Ivan, illus. Clements, Andrew, adapted by. LC 94-10270. (Illus.). (gr. k-3). 1994. 14.95 (*1-55858-349-1*); PLB 14.88 (*1-55858-348-3*) North-South Bks NYC.

Godden, Rumer. The Rocking Horse Secret. Smith, Juliet S., photos by. (gr. 3-7). 1988. pap. 3.95 (*0-317-69650-5*, Puffin) Puffin Bks.

Green, Cecile. Tale of Theodore Bear. LC 68-56812. (Illus.). 32p. (gr. 1-2). 1968. PLB 9.95 (*0-87783-038-X*) Oddo.

Greenway, Jennifer. A Real Little Bunny: A Sequel to The Velveteen Rabbit. Officer, Robyn, illus. LC 92-37149. 40p. 1993. 14.95 (*0-8362-4936-4*) Andrews & McMeel.

Gretz, Susanna. Teddy Bears Stay Indoors. Gretz, Susanna, illus. LC 86-19511. 32p. (gr. k-3). 1987. SBE 13.95 (*0-02-738150-1*, Four Winds) Macmillan Child Grp.

Halpern, C. The Homontash That Ran Away. Halpern, C., illus. (ps-4). 2.95 (*0-87306-995-1*) Feldheim.

Hayes, Sarah. This Is the Bear & the Scary Night. Craig, Helen, illus. (ps-1). 1992. 13.95 (*0-316-35250-0*, Joy St Bks) Little.

Hayward, Linda. The Runaway Christmas Toy. Krapinski, Loretta, illus. 24p. (Orig.). (ps-2). 1994. pap. 2.50 (*0-679-86173-4*) Random Bks Yng Read.

Heller, Nicholas. Peas. LC 92-29740. 24p. 1993. 14.00 (*0-688-12406-2*); PLB 13.93 (*0-688-12407-0*) Greenwillow.

Hillert, Margaret. The Ball Book. (Illus.). (ps-k). 1981. PLB 6.95 (*0-8136-5106-9*, TK2158); pap. 3.50 (*0-8136-5606-0*, TK2159) Modern Curr.

Hissey, Jane. Old Bear. (Illus.). 32p. (ps-2). 1986. 14.95 (*0-399-21401-1*, Philomel) Putnam Pub Group.

—Ruff. LC 93-48613. (Illus.). 32p. (ps-3). 1994. 16.00 (*0-679-86042-8*) Random Bks Yng Read.

Hoban, Lillian. Arthur's Honey Bear. Hoban, Lillian, illus. LC 73-14325. 64p. (gr. k-3). 1974. 14.00 (*0-06-022369-3*); PLB 13.89 (*0-06-022370-7*) HarpC Child Bks.

Hoban, Russell. Mouse & His Child. Hoban, Lillian, illus. LC 67-19624. (gr. 1-5). 1967. PLB 14.89 (*0-06-022378-2*) HarpC Child Bks.

Homer. The Return of Odysseus. Richardson, I. M., adapted by. Frenck, Hal, illus. LC 83-14234. 32p. (gr. 4-8). 1984. lib. bdg. 11.79 (*0-8167-0015-X*); pap. text ed. 2.95 (*0-8167-0016-8*) Troll Assocs.

Howe, Deborah & Howe, James. Teddy Bear's Scrapbook. 2nd ed. Rose, David S., illus. LC 93-20919. 80p. (gr. 3-7). 1994. pap. 3.95 (*0-689-71812-8*, Aladdin) Macmillan Child Grp.

Howe, James. Babes in Toyland. Atkinson, Allen, illus. 79p. (gr. 3-7). 1988. pap. 9.95 (*0-15-200410-6*) HarBrace.

Hughes, Shirley. Dogger. LC 92-24602. (Illus.). 32p. (ps up). 1993. pap. 4.95 (*0-688-11704-X*, Mulberry) Morrow.

Inkpen, Mick. Anything Cuddly Will Do! (Illus.). 12p. (gr. 4-7). 1993. 4.99 (*1-878685-71-6*, Bedrock Press) Turner Pub GA.

—Kipper's Toybox. 1992. write for info. (*0-15-200501-3*, Gulliver Bks) HarBrace.

Ivory, Leslie A. The Birthday Cat. Ivory, Leslie A., illus. LC 93-129. 32p. (ps-3). 1993. 15.00 (*0-8037-1622-2*) Dial Bks Young.

Jacobs, Flora G. The Toy Shop Mystery. (Illus.). 96p. 1960. 5.95 (*0-686-31595-2*) Wash Dolls Hse.

Jonas, Ann. Now We Can Go. Jonas, Ann, illus. LC 85-12614. 24p. (ps-1). 1986. 11.75 (*0-688-04802-1*); PLB 11.88 (*0-688-04803-X*) Greenwillow.

Kearns, Kimberly & O'Brien, Marie. Baby Bop's Toys. Hartley, Linda, ed. 24p. (ps). 1993. bds. 3.95 (*0-7829-0369-X*) Lyons Group.

—Baby Bop's Toys. Hartley, Linda, ed. Full, Dennis, photos by. LC 93-77015. (Illus.). 24p. (ps). 1993. bds. 3.95 chunky board (*1-57064-003-3*) Barney Pub.

Kennedy, Fiona. Time for Bed. Endersby, Frank, illus. 26p. (ps-k). 1992. pap. 5.95 (*0-8120-4976-4*) Barron.

Klein, Robin. Boris & Borsch. Wilcox, Cathy, illus. 32p. (Orig.). (gr. k-4). 1993. 16.95 (*0-04-442266-0*, Pub. by Allen & Unwin Aust Pty AT); pap. 6.95 (*1-86373-048-6*, Pub. by Allen & Unwin Aust Pty AT) IPG Chicago.

Koci, Marta. Sarah's Bear. LC 86-30241. (Illus.). 28p. (ps). 1991. pap. 14.95 (*0-88708-038-3*) Picture Bk Studio.

Kudlovich, David. Why Me? 1992. 7.95 (*0-533-09652-9*) Vantage.

Lardner, Kym. Arnold the Prickly Teddy. Lardner, Kym, illus. LC 92-31919. 1993. 14.00 (*0-383-03552-X*) SRA Schl Grp.

Lawrence, D. H. The Rocking Horse Winner. 40p. (gr. 6 up). 1982. PLB 13.95 (*0-87191-893-5*) Creative Ed.

Lecourt, Nancy H. Teddy the Better-Than-New Bear. 32p. 1993. pap. 5.95 (*0-8163-1116-1*) Pacific Pr Pub Assn.

LeRoque, Ellen E. A Tale of a Teddy Bear. Arcaris, Mary, illus. 28p. (Orig.). (ps-2). 1985. pap. 3.95 (*0-932967-03-5*) Pacific Shoreline.

Levy, Elizabeth. Dracula Is a Pain in the Neck. Gerstein, Mordicai, illus. LC 82-47707. 80p. (gr. 2-6). 1983. PLB 12.89 (*0-06-023823-2*) HarpC Child Bks.

Lewis, Shari & O'Kun, Lan. One-Minute Teddy Bear Stories. Lisi, Victoria, illus. LC 92-23033. 1993. pap. 12.95 (*0-385-30909-0*) Doubleday.

Light, John. Playing at Home. LC 90-34356. (gr. 4 up). 1991. 3.95 (*0-85953-336-0*) Childs Play.

Lillegard, Dee. My Yellow Ball. Chamberlain, Sarah, illus. LC 92-27003. (gr. k-3). 1993. 12.99 (*0-525-45078-5*, DCB) Dutton Child Bks.

Linforth, Veda. Toy Shop Tales. 1993. 7.95 (*0-533-10266-9*) Vantage.

Lionni, Leo. Alexander & the Wind-up Mouse. Lionni, Leo, illus. LC 74-2088. 32p. (ps-3). 1974. pap. 4.99 (*0-394-82911-5*) Pantheon.

Lippert, Donald F. Mister B. Hedden, Randall, illus. 32p. (ps). 1989. write for info. Pastel Pubns.

Lyon, David. The Runaway Duck. LC 84-5677. (Illus.). 32p. (ps-1). 1985. 15.93 (*0-688-04002-0*); PLB 16.00 (*0-688-04003-9*) Lothrop.

McClintock, Barbara. The Battle of Luke & Longnose. LC 93-12815. 1994. 14.95 (*0-395-65751-2*) HM.

McDonald, Mandi. Babes in Toyland. Lisi, Victoria & Lisi, Victoria, illus. 72p. (gr. 3-7). 1990. 11.95 (*0-88101-100-2*) Unicorn Pub.

McOmber, Rachel B., ed. McOmber Phonics Storybooks: Boyer's Toy Store. rev. ed. (Illus.). write for info. (*0-944991-66-1*) Swift Lrn Res.

McPhail, David. Those Terrible Toy-Breakers. McPhail, David, illus. LC 80-10450. 48p. (ps-3). 1980. 5.95 (*0-8193-1019-0*); PLB 5.95 (*0-8193-1020-4*) Parents.

Mansell, Dom. My Old Teddy. Mansell, Dom, illus. LC 91-71830. 32p. (ps). 1994. pap. 3.99 (*1-56402-282-X*) Candlewick Pr.

Manushkin, Fran. The Best Toy of All. LC 91-34589. (Illus.). 24p. (ps-1). 1992. 11.00 (*0-525-44897-7*, DCB) Dutton Child Bks.

Maris, Ron. Are You There, Bear? LC 84-4180. (Illus.). 32p. (ps-1). 1985. 15.00 (*0-688-03997-9*); PLB 14.93 (*0-688-03998-7*) Greenwillow.

Marzollo, Jean. The Teddy Bear Book. Schweninger, Ann, illus. LC 87-24538. 32p. (ps-2). 1992. pap. 3.99 (*0-14-054546-8*, Puff Pied Piper) Puffin Bks.

Mathews, Judith. Tuti, Blue Horse, & the Nipnope Man. Powers, Daniel, illus. LC 93-1. 1993. write for info. (*0-8075-8130-5*) A Whitman.

Merriam, Eve. Train Leaves the Station. Gottlieb, Dale, illus. LC 91-28009. 32p. (ps-k). 1992. 14.95 (*0-8050-1934-0*, B Martin BYR) H Holt & Co.

Miller, Margaret. Where Does It Go? LC 91-30160. (Illus.). 40p. (ps-4). 1992. 14.00 (*0-688-10928-4*); PLB 13.93 (*0-688-10929-2*) Greenwillow.

Milne, A. A. Le Meilleur des Ours. (FRE.). (gr. 3-8). 9.95 (*0-685-23403-7*) Fr & Eur.

—Winnie l'Ourson. (FRE., Illus.). (gr. 3-8). 9.95 (*0-685-23402-9*) Fr & Eur.

—World of Christopher Robin. (gr. 1-4). 1958. Boxed with "World of Pooh" 29.95 (*0-525-43348-1*, Dutton) NAL-Dutton.

Mock, Dorothy. One Big Family: The Good News Kids Learn about Kindness. Mitter, Kathy, illus. LC 92-27012. 32p. (Orig.). (ps-2). 1993. pap. 3.99 (*0-570-04737-4*) Concordia.

Morton, Lone. Goodnight Everyone (Bonne Nuit a Tous) Wood, Jakki, illus. Bougard, Marie-Therese, tr. from FRE. LC 94-2434. (ENG & FRE., Illus.). 28p. (ps up). 1994. 6.95 (*0-8120-6453-4*) Barron.

—Goodnight Everyone (Buenos Noches a Todos) Wood, Jakki, photos by. LC 94-2433. (ENG & SPA., Illus.). 28p. (ps up). 1994. 6.95 (*0-8120-6452-6*) Barron.

Nannini, Roger, illus. Josephine's Toy Shop: A Look-&-Play Book with a Special Fold-Out Toy Shop. (ps-2). 1991. 15.95 (*0-8037-1004-6*) Dial Bks Young.

Nemetz, Rowena. Bo's Search for Love & Understanding. LC 86-10379. (Illus.). 48p. (Orig.). (gr. 1-6). 1986. pap. 5.95 (*0-941992-09-8*) Los Arboles Pub.

Nister, Ernest. Playtime Delights. (Illus.). 26p. (ps up). 1993. pop-up 15.95 (*0-399-21898-X*, Philomel Bks) Putnam Pub Group.

O'Connor, Jane. Splat! Mets, Marilyn, illus. LC 93-34127. 32p. (ps-1). 1994. 7.99 (*0-448-40220-3*, G&D); pap. 3.50 (*0-448-40219-X*, G&D) Putnam Pub Group.

Omar, N. Bradley. My Toy Box. 16p. 1980. pap. 2.95 (*0-671-41343-0*) S&S Trade.

Ormondroyd, Edward. Theodore's Rival. Larrecq, John M., illus. LC 76-156876. 40p. (ps-3). 1971. (Pub. by Parnassus); PLB 4.59 (*0-87466-001-7*) HM.

Oxenbury, Helen. Tom & Pippo & the Washing Machine. Oxenbury, Helen, illus. LC 89-37431. 14p. (ps-k). 1988. pap. 5.95 (*0-689-71255-3*, Aladdin) Macmillan Child Grp.

—Tom & Pippo Go for a Walk. Oxenbury, Helen, illus. LC 87-37432. 14p. (ps-k). 1988. pap. 5.95 (*0-689-71254-5*, Aladdin) Macmillan Child Grp.

—Tom & Pippo Make a Mess. Oxenbury, Helen, illus. LC 87-37437. 14p. (ps-k). 1988. pap. 5.95 (*0-689-71253-7*, Aladdin) Macmillan Child Grp.

—Tom & Pippo on the Beach. Oxenbury, Helen, illus. LC 92-53130. 24p. (ps). 1993. 5.95 (*1-56402-181-5*) Candlewick Pr.

—Tom & Pippo Read a Story. Oxenbury, Helen, illus. LC 87-37438. 14p. (ps-k). 1988. pap. 5.95 (*0-689-71252-9*, Aladdin) Macmillan Child Grp.

Phillips, Joan. Lucky Bear. Miller, J. P., illus. LC 85-14467. 32p. (ps-1). 1986. lib. bdg. 7.99 (*0-394-97987-7*); pap. 3.50 (*0-394-87987-2*) Random Bks Yng Read.

Price, Leo. Hoover Wants to Help. LC 88-19188. (Illus.). 35p. (Orig.). (gr. 2-3). 1988. pap. 1.95 (*0-8198-3313-4*) St Paul Bks.

Randall, Ronne. Gingerbread Man. 1988. text ed. 3.95 cased (*0-7214-5102-0*) Ladybird Bks.

Robinson, Fay. A Ghost in the Toy Box. Iosa, Ann W., illus. LC 92-10758. 32p. (ps-2). 1993. PLB 11.50 (*0-516-02371-3*); pap. 3.95 (*0-516-42371-1*) Childrens.

—Old MacDonald Had a Farm. Iosa, Ann W., illus. LC 92-10757. 32p. (ps-2). 1993. PLB 11.60 (*0-516-02372-1*); pap. 3.95 (*0-516-42372-X*) Childrens.

—Pizza Soup. Iosa, Ann W., illus. LC 92-10756. 32p. (ps-2). 1993. PLB 11.60 (*0-516-02373-X*); pap. 3.95 (*0-516-42373-8*) Childrens.

—When Nicki Went Away. Iosa, Ann W., illus. LC 92-13835. 32p. (ps-2). 1992. PLB 11.80 (*0-516-02376-4*) Childrens.

Seymour, Peter. The Magic Toyshop. Welply, Michael, illus. (gr. 3 up). 1988. pap. 14.95 (*0-671-66907-9*, S&S BFYR) S&S Trade.

Shennan, Christopher. Toymaker's Dream. (gr. 6-8). 1984. pap. 2.95 (*0-87508-767-1*) Chr Lit.

Shope, Kimberly A. A Bear Named Song: The Gift of a Lifetime. (Illus.). 32p. 1992. 11.99 (*0-87403-865-0*, 24-03565) Standard Pub.

Shufflebotham, Anne. Baby Bear Cub's Busy Day. LC 91-12965. (gr. 3 up). 1991. 5.99 (*0-85953-425-1*) Childs Play.

—Round & Round the Garden. LC 91-12964. (gr. 4 up). 1991. 5.99 (*0-85953-426-X*) Childs Play.

Smee, Nicola. The Tusk Fairy. Smee, Nicola, illus. LC 93-28444. 32p. (ps-2). 1993. PLB 14.95 (*0-8167-3311-2*); pap. 3.95 (*0-8167-3312-0*) BrdgeWater.

Stain, Dan. Teddy Bears' Halloween Party. (gr. 1-7). 1989. pap. 2.50 (*0-89954-962-4*) Antioch Pub Co.

Stevenson, James. The Night after Christmas. (Illus.). 32p. (ps up). 1993. pap. 4.95 (*0-688-04590-1*, Mulberry) Morrow.

Su, Lucy. Ten Little Teddies. LC 93-24148. 24p. (ps up). 1994. 3.99 (*1-56402-251-X*) Candlewick Pr.

Those Terrible Toy Breakers. 42p. (ps-3). 1992. PLB 13. 27 (*0-8368-0889-4*) Gareth Stevens Inc.

Transformers Autobots. (Illus.). 1986. pap. 1.25 (*0-440-82076-6*) Dell.

Van Leeuwen, Jean. Emma Bean. Wijngaard, Juan, illus. LC 92-29035. 40p. (ps-3). 1993. 13.99 (*0-8037-1392-4*); PLB 13.89 (*0-8037-1393-2*) Dial Bks Young.

Vernon, Tannis. Adriana & the Magic Clockwork Train. LC 89-49368. (Illus.). 32p. 1990. PLB 13.99 (*0-517-57824-7*) Crown Bks Yng Read.

Vulliamy, Clara. Ellen & Penguin. Vulliamy, Clara, illus. LC 92-54590. 32p. (ps up). 1993. 13.95 (*1-56402-193-9*) Candlewick Pr.

Waber, Bernard. Ira Sleeps Over. Waber, Bernard, illus. 48p. (gr. k-3). 1975. pap. 4.80 (*0-395-20503-4*, Sandpiper) HM.

Waddell, Martin. The Toymaker. Milne, Terry A. & Milne, Terry A., illus. LC 91-58762. 32p. (ps up). 1992. 13.95 (*1-56402-103-3*) Candlewick Pr.

Wahl, Jan. The Toy Circus. Bowers, Tim, illus. LC 85-30186. 32p. (ps-3). 1986. 13.95 (*0-15-200609-5*, Gulliver Bks) HarBrace.

Walsh, Ellen S. Brunus & the New Bear. LC 92-29060. 1993. pap. 4.95 (*0-15-212675-9*) HarBrace.

Weatherford, Carole. My Favorite Toy. (ps). 1994. 5.95 (*0-86316-215-0*) Writers & Readers.

Weinbach, Shaindel. Shimmee & the Taste-Me Tree. Backman, Aidel, illus. (ps-2). 2.95 (*0-87306-991-9*) Feldheim.

Weston, Martha. Bea's Four Bears. Weston, Martha, illus. 32p. (ps-k). 1992. 9.70 (*0-395-57791-8*, Clarion Bks) HM.

Williams, Karen L. Galimoto. Stock, Catherine, illus. LC 89-2258. 32p. (gr. k-3). 1990. 13.95 (*0-688-08789-2*); lib. bdg. 13.88 (*0-688-08790-6*) Lothrop.
Williams, Margery. Velveteen Rabbit. (ps-3). 1988. 2.95 (*0-8249-8175-8*, Ideals Child) Hambleton-Hill.
—The Velveteen Rabbit. Officer, Robyn, illus. 40p. 1991. 6.95 (*0-8362-4910-0*) Andrews & McMeel.
—The Velveteen Rabbit. Chandler, Jean, illus. 1991. Incl. book, cass. & toy rabbit. 14.99 (*0-517-66810-6*) Random Hse Value.
—The Velveteen Rabbit. 1991. PLB 13.95 (*0-88682-474-5*) Creative Ed.
—Velveteen Rabbit. LC 82-42887. (ps-3). 1994. pap. 4.95 (*0-671-88248-1*, Halfmoon) S&S Trade.
—The Velveteen Rabbit. Felix, Monique, illus. LC 94-5683. 40p. 1994. 16.95 (*0-88682-732-9*) Creative Ed.
—The Velveteen Rabbit: Or How Toys Become Real. Plume, Ilse, illus. LC 86-33544. 32p. (ps-3). 1987. 10.95 (*0-15-293500-2*) HarBrace.
Wolf, Jill & Moore, Clement C. Teddy Bears Night Before Christmas. Rudegeair, Jean, illus. 24p. (gr. 3-6). 1985. pap. 2.50 (*0-89954-330-8*) Antioch Pub Co.
Wood, A. J. The Tale of the Napkin Rabbit. Downer, Maggie, illus. LC 93-9864. (gr. 3 up). 1993. 14.95 (*0-307-17603-7*, Artsts Writrs) Western Pub.
Young, Selina. Ned. LC 92-33518. 26p. (ps-1). 1993. 14.95 (*1-56566-033-1*) Thomasson-Grant.
Ziefert, Harriet. Come out, Jessie! Smith, Mavis, illus. LC 90-41880. 32p. (ps-1). 1991. pap. 4.95 (*0-06-107414-4*) HarpC Child Bks.

TRACK ATHLETICS
see also Walking
Bailey, Donna. Track & Field. LC 90-23053. (Illus.). 32p. (gr. 1-4). 1991. PLB 18.99 (*0-8114-2901-6*); pap. 3.95 (*0-8114-4747-2*) Raintree Steck-V.
Connolly, Pat. Coaching Evelyn: Fast, Faster, Fastest Woman in the World. LC 90-4835. (Illus.). 224p. (gr. 7 up). 1991. PLB 15.89 (*0-06-021283-7*) HarpC Child Bks.
Durkin, John F. & Newton, Joe. Running to the Top of the Mountain. Cudworth, Chris, illus. 350p. (Orig.). (gr. 9-12). 1988. pap. text ed. 24.95 (*0-9621313-0-X*) J & J Win Edge.
Emmence, Lew. Running. LC 91-15143. (Illus.). 32p. (gr. 2-5). 1992. PLB 11.90 (*0-531-18464-1*, Pub. by Bookwright Pr) Watts.
Gutman, Bill. Track & Field. LC 89-7378. (Illus.). 64p. (gr. 3-8). 1990. PLB 14.95 (*0-942545-87-7*) Marshall Cavendish.
Marx, Doug. Track & Field. LC 93-27154. 1993. write for info. (*0-86593-345-6*) Rourke Corp.
Merrison, Tim. Field Athletics. LC 90-27451. (Illus.). 48p. (gr. 6). 1991. text ed. 13.95 RSBE (*0-89686-665-3*, Crestwood Hse) Macmillan Child Grp.
Parker, Steve. Running a Race: How You Walk, Run & Jump. LC 90-31110. (Illus.). 32p. (gr. k-4). 1991. PLB 11.40 (*0-531-14096-2*) Watts.
Peach, S. Running Skills. (Illus.). 48p. (gr. 6-10). 1988. pap. 5.95 (*0-7460-0165-7*) EDC.
Rosenthal, Burt. Track & Field. LC 93-23281. 1993. PLB 21.34 (*0-8114-5778-8*) Raintree Steck-V.
Sandelson, Robert. Track Athletics. LC 90-27449. (Illus.). 48p. (gr. 6). 1991. text ed. 13.95 RSBE (*0-89686-671-8*, Crestwood Hse) Macmillan Child Grp.
Stanley, Jerry W. The Track & Field Training Diary: Your Personal Workout Record. (gr. 7-12). 1988. plastic bdg. 7.95 (*0-685-44186-5*) Sports Diary Pub.

TRACK ATHLETICS–BIOGRAPHY
Coffey, Wayne. Carl Lewis. Taylor, Dave, illus. 64p. (gr. 3-7). 1993. pap. 7.95 (*1-56711-052-5*) Blackbirch.
Cohen, Neil. Jackie Joyner-Kersee. (Illus.). 144p. (gr. 3-7). 1992. pap. 4.95 (*0-316-15047-9*, Spts Illus Kids) Little.
Fuchs, Carol. Jackie Joyner-Kersee: Track-&-Field Star. LC 92-45244. 1993. 14.60 (*0-86593-261-1*); 10.95s.p. (*0-685-66421-X*) Rourke Corp.
Goldstein, Margaret J. & Larson, Jennifer. Jackie Joyner-Kersee: Super Woman. LC 93-2976. 1993. 13.50 (*0-8225-0524-X*) Lerner Pubns.
Green, Carl R. Jackie Joyner-Kersee. LC 93-456. (Illus.). 48p. (gr. 5-6). 1994. text ed. 13.95 RSBE (*0-89686-838-9*, Crestwood Hse) Macmillan Child Grp.
Koral, April. Florence Griffith Joyner: Track & Field Star. LC 91-32827. (Illus.). 64p. (gr. 3-6). 1992. PLB 12.90 (*0-531-20061-2*) Watts.
Rosenthal, Bert. Carl Lewis: The Second Jesse Owens. LC 83-23984. (Illus.). 48p. (gr. 2-8). 1984. pap. 3.95 (*0-516-44336-4*) Childrens.

TRACK ATHLETICS–FICTION
Bambara, Toni C. Raymond's Run. (gr. 4-9). 1989. 13.95 (*0-88682-351-X*, 97222-098) Creative Ed.
Grubbs, J., et al. Running for Ribbons. 32p. (gr. 1-5). 1984. PLB 25.00 (*1-56611-001-7*); pap. 15.00 (*1-56611-224-9*) Jonas.
Halecroft, David. Setting the Pace. (Illus.). 128p. (gr. 3-7). 1991. pap. 2.95 (*0-14-034547-7*, Puffin) Puffin Bks.
Hoffius, Stephen. Winners & Losers. LC 92-42394. 123p. (gr. 6 up). 1993. pap. 15.00 (*0-671-79194-X*, S&S BFYR) S&S Trade.
Hughes, Dean. End of the Race. LC 92-37747. 160p. (gr. 5 up). 1993. SBE 13.95 (*0-689-31779-4*, Atheneum Child Bk) Macmillan Child Grp.
Hunt, Angela E. The Case of the Terrified Track Star. (Orig.). (gr. 4-7). 1992. pap. 4.99 (*0-8407-4422-6*) Nelson.
Jenkins, Jerry. The Silent Track Star. (Orig.). (gr. 7-12). 1986. pap. text ed. 4.99 (*0-8024-8239-2*) Moody.
Neumann, Peter J. Playing a Virginia Moon. LC 93-25563. 1994. write for info. (*0-395-66562-0*) HM.
Peters, Sharon. Listos, En Sus Marcas, Adelante! Trivas, Irene, illus. (SPA.). 32p. (gr. k-2). 1981. PLB 7.89 (*0-89375-550-8*); pap. 1.95 (*0-89375-957-0*) Troll Assocs.
Platt, Kin. Run for Your Life. 96p. (gr. 7 up). 1979. pap. 1.95 (*0-440-97557-3*, LFL) Dell.
Tunis, John R. Duke Decides. 260p. (gr. 3-7). 1990. pap. 3.95 (*0-15-224308-9*, Odyssey) HarBrace.
—Iron Duke. 262p. (gr. 3-7). 1990. pap. 3.95 (*0-15-238987-3*, Odyssey) HarBrace.
Voigt, Cynthia. The Runner. 224p. (gr. 5 up). 1987. pap. 3.95 (*0-449-70294-4*, Juniper) Fawcett.

TRACKING AND TRAILING
Selsam, Millicent. How to Be a Nature Detective. Donnelly, Marlene H., illus. LC 93-28523. 1995. 15.00 (*0-06-023447-4*); PLB 14.89 (*0-06-023448-2*) HarpC Child Bks.

TRACTION ENGINES
see Tractors

TRACTORS
Young, C. Tractors. (Illus.). 32p. (ps-2). 1992. PLB 13.96 (*0-88110-553-8*, Usborne); pap. 5.95 (*0-7460-0671-3*, Usborne) EDC.
—Tractors. (Illus.). 12p. (ps). 1993. bds. 4.50 (*0-7460-1097-4*) EDC.

TRACTORS–FICTION
Amery, H. The Runaway Tractor. (Illus.). 16p. (ps). 1989. 3.95 (*0-7460-0262-9*, Usborne); lib. bdg. 7.96 (*0-88110-377-2*, Usborne) EDC.
—Tractor in Trouble. (Illus.). 16p. (ps-3). 1992. pap. 3.95 (*0-7460-0588-1*) EDC.
Burton, Virginia L. Katy & the Big Snow. Burton, Virginia L., illus. 40p. (gr. k-3). 1974. pap. 4.80 (*0-395-18562-9*, Sandpiper) HM.
McCormick, Maxine. Pretty As You Please. LC 92-39310. 1994. 15.95 (*0-399-22536-6*, Philomel Bks) Putnam Pub Group.
Pearce, Molly. Big Cat the Proud. Pearce, Molly, illus. LC 91-65488. 32p. (gr. k-2). 1991. pap. 4.95 (*0-9628129-7-8*) Sagebrush Bks.
—Tale of Three Tractors. Pearce, Molly, illus. LC 91-65489. 32p. (gr. k-2). 1991. pap. 4.95 (*0-9628129-8-6*) Sagebrush Bks.
Rucker, Mike. Terry the Tractor. Burchett, Bob, illus. LC 93-94079. 64p. (gr. k up). 1994. pap. 3.95 (*1-56002-382-1*, Univ Edtns) Aegina Pr.
Swan, Walter. The Little Green Tractor. Swan, Deloris, ed. Asch, Connie, illus. 16p. (Orig.). (gr. 2-4). 1989. pap. 1.50 (*0-927176-04-1*) Swan Enterp.

TRADE FAIRS
see Fairs

TRADE ROUTES
Around Africa & Asia by Sea. 128p. 1990. 17.95x (*0-8160-1875-8*) Facts on File.
The European Overland Routes. (Illus.). 160p. 1990. 17.95x (*0-8160-1877-4*) Facts on File.
From Gibraltar to the Ganges. 128p. 1990. 17.95x (*0-8160-1876-6*) Facts on File.
Major, John S. The Silk Route. Fieser, Stephen, illus. LC 92-38169. 1994. 15.00 (*0-06-022924-1*); PLB 14.89 (*0-06-022926-8*) HarpC.
The Northern World. (Illus.). 128p. 1990. 17.95x (*0-8160-1879-0*) Facts on File.
Reid, Struan. Exploration by Sea. LC 93-14693. (Illus.). 48p. (gr. 6 up). 1994. text ed. 15.95 RSBE (*0-02-775801-X*, New Discovery Bks) Macmillan Child Grp.
Strathern, Paul. Exploration by Land. LC 93-7147. (Illus.). 48p. (gr. 6 up). 1994. text ed. 15.95 RSBE (*0-02-788375-2*, New Discovery Bks) Macmillan Child Grp.

TRADE UNIONS
see Labor Unions

TRADE WASTE
see Waste Products

TRADITIONS
see Folklore; Legends; Superstition

TRAFALGAR (CAPE), BATTLE OF, 1805
Balkwill, Richard. Trafalgar. LC 93-2650. (Illus.). 32p. (gr. 6 up). 1993. text ed. 13.95 RSBE (*0-02-726326-6*, New Discovery Bks) Macmillan Child Grp.

TRAFFIC ACCIDENTS
Hjelmeland, Andy. Drinking & Driving. LC 89-25406. (Illus.). 48p. (gr. 5-6). 1990. text ed. 12.95 RSBE (*0-89686-496-0*, Crestwood Hse) Macmillan Child Grp.
Park, Jae S. Now What? Auto Accident Claims Guide. 100p. (Orig.). 1989. pap. text ed. 3.95 (*0-685-28055-1*) Park Pub Co.
Traffic Safety. (Illus.). 64p. (gr. 6-12). 1975. pap. 1.85 (*0-8395-3391-8*, 33391) BSA.

TRAFFIC ACCIDENTS–FICTION
Brown, Margaret W. Red Light, Green Light. Weisgard, Leonard, illus. 40p. 1992. 14.95 (*0-590-44558-8*, Scholastic Hardcover) Scholastic Inc.
Byars, Betsy C. The Glory Girl. (ps-3). 1985. pap. 3.95 (*0-14-031785-6*, Puffin) Puffin Bks.
Colman, Hila. Suddenly. LC 86-28460. 160p. (gr. 7 up). 1987. 12.95 (*0-688-05865-5*) Morrow Jr Bks.
Jordan, Hope D. Haunted Summer. LC 67-15713. (gr. 5 up). 1967. 11.95 (*0-688-41638-1*) Lothrop.
Richmond, Sandra. Wheels for Walking. (Illus.). 176p. (gr. 9-12). 1988. pap. 2.50 (*0-451-15235-2*, Sig) NAL-Dutton.

TRAFFIC REGULATIONS
see also Traffic Accidents
Hoban, Tana. I Read Signs. Hoban, Tana, illus. LC 83-1482. 32p. (ps-1). 1983. 15.00 (*0-688-02317-7*); PLB 14.93 (*0-688-02318-5*) Greenwillow.
—I Read Symbols. Hoban, Tana, illus. LC 83-1481. 32p. (ps-1). 1983. 14.95 (*0-688-02331-2*); PLB 14.88 (*0-688-02332-0*) Greenwillow.

TRAILING
see Tracking and Trailing

TRAINED NURSES
see Nurses and Nursing

TRAINING OF ANIMALS
see Animals–Training

TRAINING OF CHILDREN
see Children–Management

TRAINS, RAILROAD
see Railroads

TRAMPS–FICTION
Buchanan, Paul. The Return of the Eagle. Parker, Liz, ed. Taylor, Marjorie, illus. 45p. (Orig.). (gr. 6-12). 1992. pap. text ed. 2.95 (*1-56254-052-1*) Saddleback Pubns.
Gottlieb, Dale. Seeing Eye Willie. Gottlieb, Dale, illus. LC 91-18606. 40p. (gr. 1-4). 1992. 15.00 (*0-679-82449-9*); PLB 15.99 (*0-679-92449-3*) Knopf Bks Yng Read.
Hamilton, Dorothy. Winter Caboose. Converse, James, illus. LC 83-10816. 104p. (Orig.). (gr. 4-8). 1983. pap. 3.95 (*0-8361-3341-2*) Herald Pr.
North, Jane Y., et al. Old Vagabond in the Railroad Yard. (Illus.). 72p. (gr. 4-6). 1994. pap. 6.95 (*1-56721-077-5*) Twnty-Fifth Cent Pr.
Thompson, Colin. The Paper Bag Prince. Thompson, Colin, illus. LC 91-27453. 32p. (gr. 2-7). 1992. 15.00 (*0-679-83048-0*); PLB 15.99 (*0-679-93048-5*) Knopf Bks Yng Read.

TRANSATLANTIC FLIGHTS
see Aeronautics–Flights

TRANSCONTINENTAL JOURNEYS
see Overland Journeys to the Pacific

TRANSISTORS
Aten, Jerry. Prime Time Reading Skills. Filkins, Vanessa, illus. 64p. (gr. 2-5). 1984. wkbk. 7.95 (*0-86653-185-8*, GA 525) Good Apple.

TRANSPLANTATION OF ORGANS, TISSUES, ETC.
Beckelman, Laurie. Transplants. LC 90-33665. (Illus.). 48p. (gr. 5-6). 1990. text ed. 12.95 RSBE (*0-89686-572-X*, Crestwood Hse) Macmillan Child Grp.
Durrett, Deanne. Organ Transplants. LC 92-42990. (Illus.). 112p. (gr. 5-8). 1993. PLB 14.95 (*1-56006-137-5*) Lucent Bks.
Kittredge, Mary. Organ Transplants. (Illus.). 112p. (gr. 6-12). 1989. lib. bdg. 18.95 (*0-7910-0071-0*) Chelsea Hse.

TRANSPORTATION
see also Aeronautics, Commercial; Automobiles; Bridges; Buses; Canals; Commerce; Harbors; Postal Service; Railroads; Roads; Steamboats; Subways; Trade Routes; Traffic Regulations; Trucks; Waterways
Aunt Peggy. How Did You Come to School Today. Beeching, Mark, illus. LC 93-90173. 42p. 1993. pap. 6.95 (*0-9636185-1-2*) Aunt Peggys Pub.
Baer, Edith. This Is the Way We Go to School. 40p. (ps-2). 1990. 14.95 (*0-590-43161-7*) Scholastic Inc.
The Big Book of Things That Go. LC 94-643. (Illus.). 32p. (ps). 1994. 12.95 (*1-56458-462-3*) Dorling Kindersley.
Bishop, Roma. Things That Go. 1992. pap. 2.95 (*0-671-79129-X*, Little Simon) S&S Trade.
Blackman, Steven. Land Transportation. LC 93-1473. (Illus.). 32p. (gr. 5-7). 1993. PLB 11.90 (*0-531-14276-0*) Watts.
Brandt, Keith. Transportation. Schneider, Rex, illus. LC 84-2584. 32p. (gr. 3-6). 1985. PLB 9.49 (*0-8167-0172-5*); pap. text ed. 2.95 (*0-8167-0173-3*) Troll Assocs.
Brown, Richard. One Hundred Words about Transportation. Brown, Richard, illus. LC 86-22781. 27p. (ps-k). 1987. 5.95 (*0-15-200551-X*, Gulliver Bks) HarBrace.
Brown, Richard, illus. One Hundred Words about Transportation. (ps-1). 1989. pap. 3.95 (*0-15-200555-2*, Voy B) HarBrace.
Cain, Wilma W., ed. Story of Transportation. rev. ed. LC 87-81355. (Illus.). 128p. (gr. 4 up). 1988. 14.95 (*0-934291-24-1*); 11.95 (*0-317-91142-2*) Gateway Pr MI.
Calmenson, Stephanie. Zip, Whiz, Zoom! Stott, Dorothy, illus. (ps-1). 1992. 13.95 (*0-316-12478-8*, Joy St Bks) Little.
Cooper, J. Spanish Language Books, Set 5: Maquinas de Viaje (Traveling Machines, 6 bks. 1991. 53.70s.p. (*0-86592-473-2*) Rourke Enter.
—Traveling Machines Series, 6 bks. 1991. Set. 53.70s.p. (*0-86592-489-9*) Rourke Enter.
Davies, Eryl. Transport: On Land, Road & Rail. (Illus.). 48p. (gr. 4-9). 1992. 13.95 (*0-531-15244-8*) Watts.
Dolan, Edward F. Transportation. 1995. PLB write for info. (*0-8050-2860-9*) H Holt & Co.
Edom, H. Travel & Transport. (Illus.). 24p. (gr. 2-4). 1990. lib. bdg. 11.96 (*0-88110-401-9*); pap. 3.95 (*0-7460-0446-X*) EDC.

Gakken Co. Ltd. Editors, ed. Wheels & Wings. Time-Life Books Inc. Editors, tr. (Illus.). 90p. (gr. k-3). 1988. 15. 93 (*0-8094-4861-0*); PLB 21.27 (*0-8094-4862-9*) Time-Life.

Gardner, Robert. Transportation. (Illus.). 96p. (gr. 5-8). 1994. bds. 16.95 (*0-8050-2853-6*) TFC Bks NY.

Graham, Ian. Transportation. LC 92-20740. 48p. (gr. 5 up). 1992. lib. bdg. 22.80 (*0-8114-2807-9*) Raintree Steck-V.

Harris, Jack C. Personal Watercraft. LC 88-18930. (Illus.). 48p. (gr. 5-6). 1988. text ed. 11.95 RSBE (*0-89686-377-8*, Crestwood Hse) Macmillan Child Grp.

Hawkes, Nigel. Transportation on Land & Sea. (Illus.). 32p. (gr. 5-8). PLB 13.95 (*0-8050-3415-3*) TFC Bks NY.

Jones, Teri C. Little Book of Questions & Answers: Things That Go. Marsh, T. F., illus. 32p. (gr. k-3). 1992. PLB 10.95 (*1-56674-015-0*, HTS Bks) Forest Hse.

Keaton, Phyllis H. Buggies. LC 88-5951. (Illus.). 48p. (gr. 5-6). 1988. text ed. 11.95 RSBE (*0-89686-375-1*, Crestwood Hse) Macmillan Child Grp.

Lambert, Mark. Transportation. LC 93-24990. (Illus.). 32p. (gr. 4-6). 1993. 14.95 (*1-56847-118-1*) Thomson Lrning.

Land Travel. (Illus.). 80p. (gr. k-6). 1986. per set 199.00 (*0-8172-2592-7*); 14.95 ea. Raintree Steck-V.

Little, Karen E. Things on Wheels. (Illus.). 24p. (gr. 2-4). 1987. pap. 3.95 (*0-7460-0090-1*) EDC.

Little, Karen E. & Thomas, A. Wings, Wheels & Water. (Illus.). 72p. (gr. 2-4). 1988. 12.95 (*0-7460-0106-1*) EDC.

Little People Big Book about Things We Ride. 64p. (ps-1). 1989. write for info. (*0-8094-7462-X*); PLB write for info. (*0-8094-7463-8*) Time-Life.

Machines, Cars, Boats, & Airplanes. 224p. (ps-1). 1989. 5.99 (*0-517-68232-X*) Random Hse Value.

Maynard, Chris. I Wonder Why Planes Have Wings & Other Questions about Transport. Quigley, Sebastian, illus. LC 92-42373. 32p. (gr. k-3). 1993. 8.95 (*1-85697-877-X*, Kingfisher LKC) LKC.

Mellet, Peter, et al. Transportation. Smith, Guy & Bull, Peter, illus. LC 89-11358. 48p. (gr. 4-5). 1989. PLB 17.27 (*0-8368-0134-2*) Gareth Stevens Inc.

Moerbeek, Kees. Let's Go. LC 91-38117. 1992. 9.95 (*0-85953-542-8*) Childs Play.

Norris, Ann. On the Go. (Illus.). 32p. 1990. 16.00 (*0-688-06336-5*); PLB 15.93 (*0-688-06337-3*) Lothrop.

Radford, Derek. Let's Look Inside a Bus, Train, Ferry, & Plane. Radford, Derek, illus. LC 92-41487. 20p. (ps). 1993. 9.99 (*0-525-67459-4*, Lodestar Bks) Dutton Child Bks.

Reit, Seymour V. Things That Go: A Traveling Alphabet. 1990. 9.99 (*0-553-05856-8*) Bantam.

Schwartz, Linda. Trivia Trackdown-Communication & Transportation. (Illus.). 32p. (gr. 4-6). 1986. 3.95 (*0-88160-139-X*, LW258) Learning Wks.

Spizzirri Publishing Co. Staff. Transportation: Educational Coloring Book. Spizzirri, Linda, ed. Spizzirri, Peter M., illus. 32p. (gr. 1-8). 1981. pap. 1.75 (*0-86545-038-2*) Spizzirri.

Stacy, Tom. Wings, Wheels & Sails. Bull, Peter, illus. LC 90-42977. 40p. (Orig.). (gr. 2-5). 1991. pap. 3.95 (*0-679-80863-9*) Random Bks Yng Read.

Stein, Barbara. Kids' World Almanac of Transportation: Rockets, Planes, Trains, Cars, Boars & Other Ways to Travel. 1991. 14.95 (*0-88687-491-2*); pap. 6.95 (*0-88687-490-4*) Wrld Almnc.

Steins, Richard. Transportation Milestones & Breakthroughs. (Illus.). 48p. (gr. 4-8). 1994. PLB write for info. (*0-8114-4935-1*) Raintree Steck-V.

Time-Life Editors. Why Are Wagons Red? First Questions & Answers about Transportation. Lesk, Sara M., ed. (Illus.). 48p. (ps-k). 1994. write for info. (*0-7835-0878-6*); PLB write for info. (*0-7835-0879-4*) Time-Life.

Transportation. LC 92-24929. 176p. 1993. 18.60 (*0-8094-9700-X*); lib. bdg. 24.60 (*0-8094-9701-8*) Time-Life.

Transportation. (Illus.). 20p. 1994. 6.95 (*1-56458-479-8*) Dorling Kindersley.

Wheeler, Jill C. Earth Moves: Get There with Energy to Spare. LC 91-73066. 202p. 1991. 12.94 (*1-56239-035-X*) Abdo & Dghtrs.

Williams, Brian. On the Move. LC 92-21678. (Illus.). 128p. (ps-3). 1993. 7.00 (*0-679-83694-2*); PLB 11.99 (*0-679-93694-7*) Random Bks Yng Read.

Yepsen, Roger. City Trains: Moving Through America's Cities by Rail. Yepsen, Roger, illus. LC 92-2395. 96p. (gr. 3-7). 1993. SBE 14.95 (*0-02-793675-9*, Macmillan Child Bk) Macmillan Child Grp.

TRANSPORTATION–FICTION

Ada, Alma F., ed. Olmo y la Mariposa Azul. Escriba, Vivi, illus. 24p. (gr. k-3). 1992. PLB 7.50x (*1-56492-095-X*) Laredo.

Awdry, W. Bertie the Bus Wheel Book. Bell, Owain, illus. 14p. (ps-k). 1993. 4.99 (*0-679-84469-4*) Random Bks Yng Read.

Feldman, B. Going, Going. (Illus.). 24p. (ps-8). 1989. 12. 95 (*1-55037-045-6*, Pub. by Annick CN); pap. 4.95 (*1-55037-046-4*, Pub. by Annick CN) Firefly Bks Ltd.

Hickle, Victoria. Out & about with Brum. Mones, Isidre, illus. 14p. (ps-k). 1993. 4.99 (*0-679-84470-8*) Random Bks Yng Read.

Hillert, Margaret. Funny Ride. (Illus.). (ps-k). 1982. PLB 6.95 (*0-8136-5101-8*, TK2164); pap. 3.50 (*0-8136-5601-X*, TK2165) Modern Curr.

Kingman, Lee. Head over Wheels. 224p. (gr. 7 up). 1981. pap. 1.75 (*0-440-93129-0*, LE) Dell.

McOmber, Rachel B., ed. McOmber Phonics Storybooks: The Tan Cab. rev. ed. (Illus.). write for info. (*0-944991-04-1*) Swift Lrn Res.

Marks, Burton. Let's Go. Harvey, Paul, illus. LC 91-9986. 24p. (gr. k-2). 1992. lib. bdg. 9.89 (*0-8167-2413-X*); pap. text ed. 2.50 (*0-8167-2414-8*) Troll Assocs.

Mitchell, Lucy S., et al. The Taxi That Hurried. reissued ed. Gergely, Tibor, illus. 24p. (ps-k). 1992. write for info. (*0-307-00144-X*, 312-09, Golden Pr) Western Pub.

Nikola-Lisa, W. Wheels Go Round. Conteh-Morgan, Jane, illus. LC 93-38595. 1994. 12.95 (*0-385-32069-8*) Doubleday.

Pootler & Pillion. Take a Ride. LC 93-86728. (Illus.). 32p. (ps-1). 1994. pap. 8.95 (*0-9638479-3-7*) Magnolia MA.

Stuart, Doris. All Aboard! Bracken, Carolyn, illus. LC 87-81766. 22p. (ps). 1988. write for info. (*0-307-12117-8*, Pub. by Golden Bks) Western Pub.

Vail. Number Six All the Way Home. 1993. pap. 2.75 (*0-590-43430-6*) Scholastic Inc.

Ziefert, Harriet. Things That Go. Baum, Susan, illus. 8p. (ps). 1993. 4.95 (*0-694-00507-X*, Festival) HarpC Child Bks.

TRANSPORTATION, HIGHWAY

see also Automobiles; Buses; Trucks

McNeese, Tim. From Trails to Turnpikes. LC 91-41352. (Illus.). 48p. (gr. 5). 1993. text ed. 11.95 RSBE (*0-89686-731-5*, Crestwood Hse) Macmillan Child Grp.

TRANSPORTATION–HISTORY

Leuzzi, Linda. Transportation. LC 94-17183. (gr. 10 up). 1995. write for info. (*0-7910-2840-2*) Chelsea Hse.

McNeese, Tim. Early River Travel. LC 91-42302. (Illus.). 48p. (gr. 5). 1993. text ed. 11.95 RSBE (*0-89686-733-1*, Crestwood Hse) Macmillan Child Grp.

—Western Wagon Trains. LC 91-42076. (Illus.). 48p. (gr. 5). 1993. text ed. 11.95 RSBE (*0-89686-734-X*, Crestwood Hse) Macmillan Child Grp.

Pollard, Michael. From Cycle to Spaceship: The Story of Transport. (Illus.). 48p. (gr. 1-4). 1987. 12.95x (*0-8160-1779-4*) Facts on File.

Unstead, R. J. Travel by Road Through the Ages. (Illus.). (gr. 7-10). 1983. 14.95 (*0-7136-1812-4*) Dufour.

TRANSPORTATION–POETRY

Cassedy, Sylvia. Zoomrimes: Poems About Things That Go. Chessare, Michele, illus. LC 90-1463. 64p. (gr. 3-7). 1993. 14.00 (*0-06-022632-3*); PLB 13.89 (*0-06-022633-1*) HarpC Child Bks.

Livingston, Myra C., ed. Roll Along: Poems on Wheels. LC 92-32714. 80p. (gr. 4 up). 1993. SBE 11.95 (*0-689-50585-X*, M K McElderry) Macmillan Child Grp.

TRAPPING

see also Fur Trade; Hunting

Gilsvik, Bob. The Complete Book of Trapping. Gilsvik, David, illus. 172p. (gr. 7). Repr. of 1976 ed. 14.95 (*0-936622-29-6*) A R Harding Pub.

TRAPPING–FICTION

Morris, Neil. On the Trapping Trail. LC 89-989. (Illus.). 32p. (gr. 3-8). 1989. PLB 9.95 (*1-85435-164-8*) Marshall Cavendish.

Nesbit, Jeff. Setting the Trap. LC 93-41025. 1994. pap. 4.99 (*0-8407-9256-5*) Nelson.

Price, Susan. Ghost Song. 1992. 15.00 (*0-374-32544-8*) FS&G.

Thomas, Jane R. Fox in a Trap. Howell, Troy, illus. LC 86-17412. 96p. (gr. 3-6). 1987. 13.95 (*0-89919-473-7*, Clarion Bks) HM.

TRAVEL

see also Automobiles–Touring; Tourist Trade; Voyages and Travels; Voyages around the World; also names of countries, states, etc. with the subdivision Description and Travel, e.g. U. S.–Description and travel

Birnbaum, Steve, ed. Birnbaum's Walt Disney World for Kids by Kids, 1994. (Illus.). 128p. 1993. pap. 9.95 (*1-56282-750-2*) Hyperion.

Brown, Laurene K. & Brown, Marc T. Dinosaurs Travel: A Guide for Families on the Go. Brown, Marc T., illus. 32p. (ps-3). 1988. 13.95 (*0-316-11076-0*) Little.

Cothran, Betty. Destinations, Detours & Diversions: A Guide to Family Outings & Good Times. (Illus.). 75p. (Orig.). 1989. pap. 4.99 (*0-9625229-0-2*) Seaworthy Pubns.

Helwig, Barbara & Stewart, Susan. Travel Treats: Fun for Kids on the Move, 3 bks. (Illus.). 90p. (gr. 2-6). 1993. Set. spiral bdg. 19.95 (*1-881285-07-3*) Arbus Pub.

Hest, Amy. Travel Tips from Harry: A Guide to Family Vacations in the Sun. Truesdell, Sue, illus. LC 88-39887. 64p. (gr. 2 up). 1989. 11.95 (*0-688-07972-5*); PLB 11.88 (*0-688-09291-8*, Morrow Jr Bks) Morrow Jr Bks.

Kalman, Bobbie. How We Travel. (Illus.). 32p. (gr. 2-3). 1986. 15.95 (*0-86505-076-7*) Crabtree Pub Co.

Kennedy, Don. Exploring Careers on Cruise Ships. LC 93-20293. (gr. 7 up). 1993. 14.95 (*0-8239-1665-0*); 9.95 (*0-8239-1714-2*) Rosen Group.

Klutz Press Staff. Kids Travel: A Backseat Survival Kit. (Illus.). 48p. 1994. wire-o-bound, incl. activity pad, felt pens, colored thread, dice, string, & playing pieces 18. 95 (*1-878257-71-4*) Klutz Pr.

Koken, Tom, et al. AAA Travel Activity Book: The Official AAA Fun Book for Kids. Koken, Tom, et al, illus. 144p. 1990. pap. 4.95 (*1-56288-071-3*) Checkerboard.

Krupp, Robin R. Let's Go Traveling. Krupp, Robin R., illus. LC 91-21845. 40p. (gr. 2 up). 1992. 15.00 (*0-688-08989-5*); PLB 14.93 (*0-688-08990-9*) Morrow Jr Bks.

LaPlaca, Annette. Are We Almost There? The Kids' Book of Travel Fun. Bryer, Debbie, illus. 45p. (Orig.). (gr. 1-5). 1992. pap. 4.99 wkbk. (*0-87788-051-4*) Shaw Pubs.

McKissack, Patricia & McKissack, Fredrick. Big Bug Book of Places to Go. Bartholomew, illus. LC 87-61652. 24p. (Orig.). (gr. k-1). 1987. spiral bdg. 14.95 (*0-88335-765-8*); pap. text ed. 4.95 (*0-88335-775-5*) Milliken Pub Co.

Moore, Kathryn C. My First Flight. rev. ed. Hutson, Ronald, ed. Grant, Leslie, illus. (ps-4). 1991. PLB 3.95 (*0-9633295-0-2*) K Cs Bks N Stuff.

Tucker, Sian. Nursery Board: Let's Go. (ps). 1994. pap. 2.95 (*0-671-88263-5*, Little Simon) S&S Trade.

Wade, Theodore E., Jr. Fun on the Road: Travel Activities. Baptist, Michael, et al, illus. 40p. (Orig.). (gr. k-6). 1990. pap. 2.95 (*0-930192-23-0*) Gazelle Pubns.

Ward, Elaine. Roots & Wings. (Orig.). (gr. 1-6). 1983. pap. 3.95 (*0-377-00130-9*) Friendship Pr.

Windsor, Natalie. How to Fly - for Kids! Your Fun-in-the-Sky Airplane Companion. Azar, Joe, illus. 144p. (gr. 3-7). 1994. pap. 8.95 (*0-944042-33-3*) Globe Pequot.

TRAVEL–FICTION

Barry, Sebastian. Elsewhere. (gr. 1-12). 1985. 15.95 (*0-85105-903-1*, Pub. by Colin Smythe Ltd Britain) Dufour.

Bate, Lucy. How Georgina Drove the Car Very Carefully from Boston to New York. Taylor, Tamar, illus. LC 88-22861. 32p. (ps-1). 1993. pap. 4.99 (*0-517-59324-6*) Crown Bks Yng Read.

Bauer, Caroline F. My Mom Travels a Lot. 48p. (ps-3). 1985. pap. 3.95 (*0-14-050545-8*, Puffin) Puffin Bks.

Beatty, Patricia. Be Ever Hopeful, Hannalee. LC 88-21581. 208p. (gr. 5-9). 1988. 13.00 (*0-688-07502-9*) Morrow Jr Bks.

Bridwell, Norman. Clifford Takes a Trip. 1991. pap. 5.95 incl. cassette (*0-590-63823-8*) Scholastic Inc.

Brisson, Pat. Kate on the Coast. Brown, Rick, illus. LC 91-17046. 40p. (gr. 2-5). 1992. RSBE 13.95 (*0-02-714341-4*, Bradbury Pr) Macmillan Child Grp.

—Your Best Friend, Kate. Brown, Rick, illus. LC 91-15245. 40p. (gr. 1-7). 1992. pap. 4.50 (*0-689-71545-5*, Aladdin) Macmillan Child Grp.

Brown, Margaret W. Four Fur Feet. Charlip, Remy, illus. 48p. (gr. 1-3). 1989. Repr. of 1961 ed. 13.95 (*0-929077-03-2*, Hopscotch Bks); PLB 12.95 (*0-317-92548-2*, Hopscotch Bks) Watermark Inc.

Charlip, Remy. Fortunately. Charlip, Remy, illus. LC 92-22794. 48p. (ps-3). 1993. pap. 4.95 (*0-689-71660-5*, Aladdin) Macmillan Child Grp.

Cheadle, J. A. A Donkey's Life: A Story for Children. Thomas, Toni, illus. LC 80-123421. iii, 88p. (Orig.). (gr. 2-6). 1979. pap. 3.50 (*0-9604244-0-7*) Heahstan Pr.

Desaix, Deborah D. In the Back Seat. (ps-3). 1993. 14.00 (*0-374-33639-3*) FS&G.

Dr. Seuss. Oh, the Places You'll Go! Dr. Seuss, illus. LC 89-36892. 48p. (gr. k up). 1993. 20.00 (*0-679-84736-7*) Random Bks Yng Read.

Eisemann, Henry. Hump-Free Visits Vancouver Expo. Campbell, Jay, illus. (Orig.). (gr. k-6). 1986. pap. 6.95 (*0-938129-01-5*) Emprise Pubns.

Filion, Pierre. Pikolo's Night Voyage. Tibo, Gilles, illus. 32p. (ps-3). 1994. PLB 15.95 (*1-55037-365-X*, Pub. by Annick CN); pap. 5.95 (*1-55037-364-1*, Pub. by Annick CN) Firefly Bks Ltd.

Foreman, Mary M., tr. from ENG. Viaja con Victor. King, Ed, illus. (SPA.). 24p. 1992. pap. 3.95 (*1-56288-237-6*) Checkerboard.

Gilson, Jamie. Four-B Goes Wild. Edwards, Linda S., illus. LC 83-948. 160p. (gr. 4-6). 1983. 12.95 (*0-688-02236-7*) Lothrop.

Gomi, Taro. Coco Can't Wait. Gomi, Taro, illus. (ps-1). 1985. pap. 3.95 (*0-14-050522-9*, Puffin) Puffin Bks.

Halpern-Gold, Julia & Adler, Robin W. Travel Tales: A Mobility Storybook. Binns, Brenda S., illus. LC 88-62588. 107p. (Orig.). (ps-3). 1988. pap. text ed. 20.00 (*0-922637-00-8*) Most Mobil.

Jonas, Ann. Round Trip. Jonas, Ann, illus. LC 82-12026. 32p. (gr. k-3). 1983. 16.00 (*0-688-01772-X*); PLB 15. 93 (*0-688-01781-9*) Greenwillow.

—Round Trip. LC 82-12026. (Illus.). 32p. (ps up). 1990. pap. 3.95 (*0-688-09986-6*, Mulberry) Morrow.

Jones, Sally L. Three Special Journeys, 3 bks. Weissman, Bari, illus. (ps). 1993. Set. 9.99 (*0-7847-0075-3*, 24-03645) Standard Pub.

Juster, Norton. The Phantom Tollbooth. (gr. 5 up). 1972. 16.95 (*0-394-81500-9*) Knopf Bks Yng Read.

Kratky, Lada J. Veo, Veo. Que Veo? (Small Book) Yerkes, Lane, illus. (SPA.). 16p. (Orig.). (gr. k-3). 1992. pap. text ed. 6.00 (*1-56334-082-8*) Hampton-Brown.

L'Engle, Madeleine. The Moon by Night. LC 63-9072. 224p. (gr. 7 up). 1963. 16.00 (*0-374-35049-3*) FS&G.

Lobel, Anita. Away from Home. LC 93-36521. (Illus.). 32p. 1994. 16.00 (*0-688-10354-5*); PLB 15.93 (*0-688-10355-3*) Greenwillow.

Loomie, Christine. We're Going on a Trip. Chambliss, Maxie, illus. LC 93-17592. 48p. (ps up). 1994. PLB 14.93 (*0-688-10173-9*); 15.00 (*0-688-10172-0*) Morrow Jr Bks.

McDonnell, Janet. Turtle's Adventure in Alphabet Town. McDonnell, Janet, illus. LC 92-2984. 32p. (ps-2). 1992. PLB 11.80 (*0-516-05420-1*) Childrens.

Moncure, Jane B. Stop! Go! Word Bird. Hohag, Linda S., illus. LC 80-16273. 32p. (ps-2). 1981. PLB 14.95 (*0-89565-160-2*) Childs World.

Mullin, Penn. Postcards from America Series: The White House Mystery, High Time in New York, Windy City Whirl, Trouble in the Black Hills, San Francisco Adventure. Kratoville, B. L., ed. Rarey, Damon, illus. (Orig.). (gr. 4-12). 1992. pap. 15.00 (*0-87879-957-5*, 957-5) High Noon Bks.

—Postcards from Europe Series, 5 bks. Kratoville, B. L., ed. Rarey, D., illus. 48p. (gr. 6-10). 1994. pap. text ed. 15. 00 (*0-87879-976-1*) High Noon Bks. Four multi-cultural junior high students & their teacher are treated to a trip to Europe by an anonymous benefactor. The four young travelers never stop learning as facts about the historical & cultural treasures of each country are woven into these fast-paced, exciting stories. THE LONDON CONNECTION: The kids climb on board a double-decker bus to see the sights: Buckingham Palace, Westminster Abbey, the Tower of London, & more. PASSPORT TO PARIS: The history of the Arc de Triomphe & the Eiffel Tower, fine art at the Louvre, & folklore & facts about Notre Dame are all part of this whirlwind tour. RIDDLES IN ROME: The kids roam through the ruins at the Forum & the Coliseum, marvel at Michelangelo's Pieta & Sistine Chapel at Vatican City, & enjoy gelato. THE CLUES TO MADRID: In Madrid, the kids are dazzled by the Prado Museum, Picasso's Guernica, & the Plaza Mayor, & end up at the bullfights. SECRETS OF THE MATTERHORN: A fondue dinner & a hike to a Swiss hut on the slopes of the Matterhorn are only a part of this entertaining excursion.
Publisher Provided Annotation.

Neitzel, Shirley. The Bag I'm Taking to Grandma's. Parker, Nancy W., illus. LC 94-4115. 32p. Date not set. write for info. (*0-688-12960-9*); PLB write for info. (*0-688-12961-7*) Greenwillow.

Oxford, Mariesa. Going to Grandma's. (Illus.). (gr. 2-6). 1992. PLB 19.97 (*0-8114-3575-X*) Raintree Steck-V.

Paulsen, Gary. The Car. LC 93-41834. 1994. 13.95 (*0-15-292878-2*) HarBrace.

Peterson, John. Littles Take a Trip. (gr. 4-7). 1993. pap. 2.75 (*0-590-46222-9*) Scholastic Inc.

Raphael, Morris. How Do You Know When You're in Acadiana. Hebert, Carrie, illus. 32p. (Orig.). (gr. 5 up). 1984. pap. 3.95 (*0-9608866-3-X*) M Raphael.

Roberts, Willo D. What Could Go Wrong? LC 92-26177. 176p. (gr. 3-6). 1993. pap. 3.95 (*0-689-71690-7*, Aladdin) Macmillan Child Grp.

Rogers, Paul T. Forget-Me-Not. Berridge, Celia, illus. 32p. (ps-k). 1986. pap. 3.50 (*0-685-43615-2*, Puffin) Puffin Bks.

Sternburg, Sharon. Suzie Q. Mouse Adventures. Coyne, John P., illus. 39p. (Orig.). (ps-1). 1993. pap. 5.99 (*0-9633513-1-1*) S M Resar Pub.

Taylor, Mildred D. The Road to Memphis. Fogelman, Phyllis J., ed. LC 88-33654. (Illus.). 240p. (gr. 7 up). 1990. 14.95 (*0-8037-0340-6*) Dial Bks Young.

Trevor, William. Juliet's Story. LC 93-21790. 1994. pap. 15.00 (*0-671-87442-X*) S&S Trade.

Vallet, Roxanne. Vacation to Marsailles. Vallet, Roxanne, illus. 15p. (gr. k-3). 1992. pap. 13.95 (*1-895583-38-1*) MAYA Pubs.

Viajando. (SPA.). (ps-3). 1993. pap. 2.25 (*0-307-50057-8*, Golden Pr) Western Pub.

Walsh, Jeff. An Open Road & a Full Tank of Gas, Pt. 1. Bonner, Darlene, ed. (Illus.). 108p. (Orig.). 1993. pap. 8.95 (*0-9636883-0-8*) Walsh Assocs.

Walsh, Vivian & Seibold, J. Otto. Mr. Lunch Takes a Plane Ride. Seibold, J. Otto, illus. 40p. (ps-3). 1993. RB 13.99 (*0-670-84775-5*) Viking Child Bks.

Williamson, Duncan. Don't Look Back Jack! Scottish Traveller Tales. 162p. (gr. 5 up). 1994. 13.95 (*0-86241-309-5*, Pub. by Cnngt UK) Trafalgar.

Willis, Jeanne. Earth Mobiles, As Explained by Professor Xargle. Ross, Tony, illus. LC 91-23500. 32p. (ps-2). 1992. 14.00 (*0-525-44892-6*, DCB) Dutton Child Bks.

TRAVELERS
see also Explorers

TRAVELERS–FICTION

Alcock, Vivien. Travelers by Night. (gr. k-6). 1990. pap. 2.95 (*0-440-40292-1*, YB) Dell.

Swann, Carinda. Bootnanny's Trip to Town. LC 62-63255. (Illus.). 44p. (gr. 2-5). 1993. PLB 12.95 (*1-55523-589-1*); pap. 7.95 (*1-55523-657-X*) Winston-Derek.

TRAVELS
see Overland Journeys to the Pacific; Scientific Expeditions; Voyages and Travels; Voyages around the World

TREASURE-TROVE
see Buried Treasure

TREE PLANTING
see also Trees

TREES
see also Forests and Forestry; Fruit Culture; Leaves; Lumber and Lumbering; Nuts; Shrubs; Wood

American Forestry Association Staff. Trees Every Boy & Girl Should Know. 4th ed. (Illus.). 89p. 1977. pap. text ed. 4.50 (*0-685-46347-8*) Am Forests.

Anatta, Ivan M. Trees. LC 92-32286. (gr. 2-6). 1993. 15. 95 (*1-56766-002-9*) Childs World.

Arnosky, Jim. Crinkleroot's Guide to Knowing the Trees. Arnosky, Jim, illus. LC 91-18651. 40p. (ps-5). 1992. RSBE 14.95 (*0-02-705855-7*, Bradbury Pr) Macmillan Child Grp.

Barker, Cicely M. Flower Fairies of the Trees. Barker, Cicely M., illus. (ps up). 1991. 5.95 (*0-7232-3760-3*) Warne.

Bash, Barbara. Tree of Life: The World of the African Baobab. (gr. 1-5). 1989. 15.95 (*0-316-08305-4*, Sierra Club) Little.

—Tree of Life: The World of the African Baobab. (ps-3). 1994. 5.95 (*0-316-08322-4*) Little.

Bianchi, J. The Last of the Tree Ranchers. (Illus.). 24p. (ps-8). 1986. 12.95 (*0-921285-02-7*, Pub. by Bungalo Bks CN); pap. 4.95 (*0-921285-00-0*, Pub. by Bungalo Bks CN) Firefly Bks Ltd.

Binato, Leonardo. What's in the Tree? 12p. (ps-3). 1993. 4.95 (*1-56566-030-7*) Thomasson-Grant.

Brandt, Keith. Discovering Trees. Nigoghossian, Christine W., illus. LC 81-7522. 32p. (gr. 2-4). 1982. PLB 11.59 (*0-89375-566-4*); pap. text ed. 2.95 (*0-89375-567-2*) Troll Assocs.

Brenner, Barbara & Garelick, May. The Tremendous Tree Book. Brenner, Fred, illus. LC 91-73753. 40p. (ps-3). 1992. 14.95 (*1-878093-56-8*) Boyds Mills Pr.

Brockman, C. Frank. Trees of North America. Zim, Herbert S. & Fichter, George S., eds. Merrilees, Rebecca, illus. (gr. 9 up). 1968. pap. write for info (*0-307-13658-2*, Golden Pr) Western Pub.

Broutin, Christian, illus. Arbre. (FRE.). (ps-1). 1989. 12. 95 (*2-07-035712-0*) Schoenhof.

Burnie, David. Tree. Chadwick, Peter, photos by. LC 88-1572. (Illus.). 64p. (gr. 5 up). 1988. 16.00 (*0-394-89617-3*); lib. bdg. 16.99 (*0-394-99617-8*) Knopf Bks Yng Read.

Charman, Andrew. Trees. (Illus.). 48p. (Orig.). (gr. 2 up). 1992. pap. 6.95 (*0-563-35017-2*, BBC-Parkwest) Parkwest Pubns.

Cochrane, Jennifer. Trees of the Tropics. LC 90-10023. (Illus.). 48p. (gr. 5-9). 1990. PLB 21.34 (*0-8114-2731-5*) Raintree Steck-V.

Collard, Sneed. Green Giants. LC 93-15936. (gr. 1-5). 1994. 9.95 (*1-55971-222-8*) NorthWord.

Cooper, J. Arboles (Trees) 1991. 8.95s.p. (*0-86592-498-8*) Rourke Enter.

—Trees. 1991. 8.95s.p. (*0-86592-621-2*) Rourke Enter.

Cowcher, Helen. Whistling Thorns. LC 92-39533. (gr. 6 up). 1993. 14.95 (*0-590-47299-2*) Scholastic Inc.

De Bourgoing, Pascale. Tree. Valat, P. M. & Perols, Sylvie, illus. 24p. 1992. pap. 10.95 (*0-590-45265-7*, Cartwheel) Scholastic Inc.

Dickinson, Jane. All about Trees. D'Adamo, Anthony, illus. LC 82-17382. 32p. (gr. 3-6). 1983. PLB 10.59 (*0-89375-892-2*); pap. text ed. 2.95 (*0-89375-893-0*) Troll Assocs.

Dowden, Anne O., text by. & illus. The Blossom on the Bough: A Book of Trees. LC 93-22726. 80p. (gr. 3 up). 1994. 16.95 (*0-395-68375-0*); pap. 9.95 (*0-395-68943-0*) Ticknor & Flds Bks Yng Read.

Florian, Douglas. Discovering Trees. LC 89-37817. 32p. (ps-2). 1990. pap. 3.95 (*0-689-71377-0*, Aladdin) Macmillan Child Grp.

Flowers & Trees. 88p. (ps-3). 1989. 15.93 (*0-8094-4857-2*); lib. bdg. 21.27 (*0-8094-4858-0*) Time-Life.

Fowler, Allan. It Could Still Be a Tree. LC 90-2207. (Illus.). 32p. (ps-2). 1990. PLB 10.75 (*0-516-04904-6*); pap. 22.95 big bk. (*0-516-49464-3*); pap. 3.95 (*0-516-44904-4*) Childrens.

—Podria Ser un Arbol - Libro Grande: (It Could Still Be a Tree Big Book) LC 90-2207. (SPA., Illus.). 32p. (ps-2). 1993. 22.95 (*0-516-59464-8*) Childrens.

—Podria Ser un Arbol: It Could Still Be a Tree. LC 90-2207. (SPA.). 32p. (ps-2). 1991. PLB 10.75 (*0-516-34904-X*); pap. 3.95 (*0-516-54904-9*) Childrens.

Gackenbach, Dick. Mighty Tree. 1992. 13.95 (*0-15-200519-6*, HB Juv Bks) HarBrace.

Gamlin, Linda. Trees. LC 92-54310. (Illus.). 64p. (gr. 3 up). 1993. 9.95 (*1-56458-230-2*) Dorling Kindersley.

Ganeri, Anita. Trees. Kline, Marjory, ed. (Illus.). 32p. (gr. 4-7). 1993. PLB 12.40 (*0-531-17317-8*, Gloucester Pr) Watts.

Greenaway, Theresa. Woodland Trees. LC 90-37227. (Illus.). 48p. (gr. 5-9). 1990. PLB 21.34 (*0-8114-2732-3*) Raintree Steck-V.

Harlow, Rosie & Morgan, Gareth. Trees & Leaves. Peperell, Liz, illus. LC 91-7461. 40p. (gr. 5-8). 1991. PLB 12.90 (*0-531-19126-5*, Warwick) Watts.

Harris, E. Trees. (Illus.). 64p. (gr. 10 up). 1993. pap. 4.95 (*0-7460-1627-1*) EDC.

Helwig, Barbara & Stewart, Susan. Tree Spree. (Illus.). 56p. (gr. 2-5). 1991. spiral bound 4.95 (*1-881285-01-4*) Arbus Pub.

—Tree Spree. rev. ed. (Illus.). 90p. (gr. 2-6). 1992. spiral bdg. 4.95 (*1-881285-05-7*) Arbus Pub.

Hester, Nigel. The Living Tree. (Illus.). 32p. (gr. 5-8). 1990. PLB 12.40 (*0-531-14007-5*) Watts.

Hindley, Judy. The Tree. Wisenfeld, Alison, illus. LC 89-16105. 32p. (gr. k-3). 1990. (Crown) Crown Pub Group.

Hiscock, Bruce. The Big Tree. Hiscock, Bruce, illus. LC 89-18286. 32p. (gr. 1-5). 1991. RSBE 14.95 (*0-689-31598-8*, Atheneum Child Bk) Macmillan Child Grp.

—The Big Tree. Hiscock, Bruce, illus. LC 93-25564. 32p. (gr. 1-5). 1994. pap. 4.95 (*0-689-71803-9*, Aladdin) Macmillan Child Grp.

Hora, Bayard, ed. Trees & Forests of the World, 2 vols. LC 90-36009. (Illus.). 290p. 1990. PLB 79.95 (*1-85435-330-6*) Marshall Cavendish.

Jennings, Terry. Trees. LC 88-37552. (Illus.). 32p. (gr. 3-6). 1989. pap. 4.95 (*0-516-48444-3*) Childrens.

Jordan, Sandra. Christmas Tree Farm. LC 93-20142. (Illus.). 32p. (ps-2). 1993. 14.95 (*0-531-05499-3*); PLB 14.99 (*0-531-08649-6*) Orchard Bks Watts.

Jorgenson, Lisa. Grand Trees of America: Champion Trees of the Fifty States. (Illus.). 96p. (gr. 2-8). 1992. pap. 8.95 (*1-879373-15-7*) R Rinehart.

Kallen, Stuart A. If the Trees Could Talk. LC 93-18991. (gr. 4 up). 1993. 14.96 (*1-56239-184-4*) Abdo & Dghtrs.

Kalman, Bobbie & Schaub, Janine. How Trees Help Me. (Illus.). 32p. (gr. k-8). 1992. PLB 15.95 (*0-86505-554-8*); pap. 7.95 (*0-86505-580-7*) Crabtree Pub Co.

Keirns, Johanna L. The Cone Connection: A Guide to Cone-Bearing Trees in California's Mountains. 30p. (gr. 3-7). 1992. pap. 5.95 (*1-882346-00-9*) Virgilio Integrat.

—The Cone Connection: The Young Traveler's Guide to Cone-Bearing Trees in California's Mountains. 30p. (gr. 3-7). 1992. pap. 5.95 (*1-882346-01-7*) Virgilio Integrat.

Killion, Bette. The Apartment House Tree. Szilagyi, Mary, illus. LC 88-35700. 32p. (ps-2). 1989. PLB 14. 89 (*0-06-023274-9*) HarpC Child Bks.

Kirkpatrick, Rena K. Look at Trees. rev. ed. Worth, Jo & Knight, Ann, illus. LC 84-26225. 32p. (gr. 2-4). 1985. PLB 10.95 (*0-8172-2359-2*); pap. 4.95 (*0-8114-6905-0*) Raintree Steck-V.

Kirschen, Ya'akov. Trees: The Green Testament. 192p. 1993. pap. text ed. 14.95 (*0-9641252-1-8*) Vital Media.

Lauber, Patricia. Be a Friend to Trees. Keller, Holly, illus. LC 92-24082. 32p. (gr. k-4). 1994. 15.00 (*0-06-021528-3*); PLB 14.89 (*0-06-021529-1*) HarpC Child Bks.

—Be a Friend to Trees. Keller, Holly, illus. LC 92-24082. 32p. (gr. k-4). 1994. pap. 4.95 (*0-06-445120-8*, Trophy) HarpC Child Bks.

Lavies, Bianca. Tree Trunk Traffic. Lavies, Bianca, photos by. LC 88-30001. (Illus.). 32p. (ps-2). 1989. 14.95 (*0-525-44495-5*, DCB) Dutton Child Bks.

Lyon, George-Ella. A B Cedar: An Alphabet of Trees. Parker, Tom, illus. LC 88-22797. 32p. (ps-1). 1989. 14.95 (*0-531-05795-X*); PLB 14.99 (*0-531-08395-0*) Orchard Bks Watts.

Markle, Sandra. Outside & Inside Trees. LC 92-5145. (Illus.). 40p. (ps-3). 1993. RSBE 15.95 (*0-02-762313-0*, Bradbury Pr) Macmillan Child Grp.

Morel, Gaud. Nature's Timekeeper - The Tree. Bogard, Vicki, tr. from FRE. Perols, Sylvaine, illus. LC 92-2710. 38p. (gr. k-5). 1992. 5.95 (*0-944589-43-X*) Young Discovery Lib.

—Nature's Timekeeper: The Tree. Perols, Sylvaine, illus. 40p. (gr. k-5). 1993. PLB 9.95 (*1-56674-072-X*, HTS Bks) Forest Hse.

Nardi, James B. Once upon a Tree: Life from Treetop to Root Tips. Nardi, James B., illus. LC 92-36444. 104p. (gr. 5-10). 1993. 16.95x (*0-8138-0917-7*) Iowa St U Pr.

National Wildlife Federation Staff. Trees Are Terrific. (gr. k-8). 1991. pap. 7.95 (*0-945051-43-3*, 75021) Natl Wildlife.

Petrides, George A. Peterson First Guide to Trees. Petrides, Olivia & Wehr, Janet, illus. Peterson, Roger T., frwd. by. LC 92-36586. 128p. 1993. pap. 4.80 (*0-395-65972-8*) HM.

Pine, Jonathan. Trees. Joudrey, Ken, illus. LC 93-3136. 1994. 15.00 (*0-06-021468-6*); PLB 14.89 (*0-06-021469-4*) HarpC Child Bks.

Pluckrose, Henry. Trees. LC 93-44699. 1994. PLB 11.95 (*0-516-08121-7*) Childrens.

Podendorf, Illa. Trees. LC 81-12313. (Illus.). 48p. (gr. k-4). 1982. PLB 12.85 (*0-516-01657-1*) Childrens.

Quinn, Greg H. Gift of a Tree: Book & Starter Kit. (ps-3). 1994. pap. 6.95 (*0-590-48092-8*) Scholastic Inc.

Richardson, Joy. Trees. LC 93-18652. (Illus.). (gr. 4 up). 1993. 11.40 (*0-531-14273-6*) Watts.

Russo, Monica. The Tree Almanac: A Year-Round Activity Guide. Byron, Kevin, photos by. LC 92-41347. (Illus.). (gr. 3 up). 1993. 14.95 (*0-8069-1252-9*) Sterling.

Ryder, Joanne. Hello, Tree! Hays, Michael, illus. 32p. (gr. k-3). 1991. 13.95 (*0-525-67310-5*, Lodestar Bks) Dutton Child Bks.

Schnieder, Bill. The Tree Giants. Dowden, D. D., illus. LC 88-80225. 32p. 1988. pap. 4.95 (*0-937959-40-5*) Falcon Pr MT.

Seifert, Patty. Exploring Tree Habitats. Doherty, Peg, illus. 24p. (Orig.). (gr. 1-5). 1994. big bk. 21.95 (*1-879531-36-4*); PLB 9.95 (*1-879531-47-X*); pap. 4.95 (*1-879531-35-6*) Mondo Pubng.

Selsam, Millicent E. Tree Flowers. Lerner, Carol, illus. LC 83-17353. 32p. (gr. 4 up). 1984. PLB 12.88 (*0-688-02769-5*) Morrow Jr Bks.

Smith, Kathy B. Trees - It's Our Planet Activity Book. M. J. Studios Staff, illus. 32p. (Orig.). (gr. k-6). 1992. pap. 2.95 (*1-879424-38-X*) Nickel Pr.

Thompson. Trees. (gr. 2-5). 1980. (Usborne-Hayes); PLB 11.96 (*0-88110-071-4*); pap. 3.95 (*0-86020-473-1*) EDC.

Thornhill, Jan. A Tree in a Forest. LC 91-25857. (Illus.). 40p. (ps-3). 1992. pap. 15.00 (*0-671-75901-9*, S&S BFYR) S&S Trade.

Trees of Arizona. (Illus.). 32p. (gr. 1 up). 1994. pap. 1.00 (*0-935810-18-8*) Primer Pubs.

Udry, Janice M. Tree Is Nice. Simont, Marc, illus. LC 56-5153. 32p. (ps-1). 1957. 14.00 (*0-06-026155-2*); PLB 13.89 (*0-06-026156-0*) HarpC Child Bks.

Warren, Elizabeth. I Can Read About Trees & Plants. LC 74-24991. (Illus.). (gr. 2-4). 1975. pap. 2.50 (*0-89375-069-7*) Troll Assocs.

Wiggers, Raymond. Picture Guide to Tree Leaves. (Illus.). 64p. (gr. 5-8). 1992. pap. 5.95 (*0-531-15646-X*) Watts.

Zim, Herbert S. & Martin, Alexander C. Trees. Barlowe, Dorothea & Barlowe, Sy, illus. (gr. 6 up). 1952. pap. write for info. (*0-307-24056-8*, Golden Pr) Western Pub.

TREES–FICTION

Almagor. Plum Tree Is Taken. Date not set. 15.00 (*0-06-023378-8*); PLB 14.89 (*0-06-023379-6*) HarpC Child Bks.

Andersen, Hans Christian. The Fir Tree. Burkert, Nancy E., illus. LC 73-121800. 48p. (ps up). 1986. pap. 6.95 (*0-06-443109-6*, Trophy) HarpC Child Bks.

—The Fir Tree. Goode, Diane, adapted by. & illus. LC 82-62172. 32p. (ps up). 1988. pap. 1.50 (*0-394-81941-1*) Random Bks Yng Read.

—Fir Tree. Britt, Stephanie, illus. 24p. (ps-3). 1989. pap. 2.95 (*0-8249-8389-0*, Ideals Child) Hambleton-Hill.

Anderson, Honey & Reinholdt, Bill. Don't Cut down This Tree. Ruth, Trevor, illus. LC 92-21446. 1993. 3.75 (*0-383-03621-6*) SRA Schl Grp.

Anderson, John W. The Tale of the Great Fruit Tree. Stout, John W., illus. 40p. 1992. 15.00 (*0-9633296-0-X*) Koinonia TX.

Annable, Toni & Kaspar, Maria H. The Silver Tree. Viola, Amy, tr. (Illus.). 80p. (Orig.). (gr. 6 up). 1992. Set. pap. 8.95 (*1-882828-11-9*) Vol. 1 English-Spanish, El Arbol de Plata. Vol. 2 English-French, L'Arbre Argente. Kasan Imprints.

—The Silver Tree: El Arbol de Plata. Viola, Amy, tr. Lumetta, Lawrence, illus. 40p. (Orig.). (gr. 6 up). 1992. pap. 4.95 (*1-882828-06-2*); pap. 10.95 incl. audio (*1-882828-16-X*) Kasan Imprints.

Annble, Toni & Kaspar, Maria H. The Silver Tree: L'Arbre Argente. Lumetta, Lawrence, illus. 40p. (Orig.). (gr. 6 up). 1992. pap. 4.95 (*1-882828-07-0*); pap. 10.95 incl. audio (*1-882828-17-8*) Kasan Imprints.

Barnes, Jill & Sato, Wakiko. Granny, Let Me In. Rubin, Caroline, ed. Japan Foreign Rights Centre Staff, tr. from JPN. Sato, Wakiko, illus. LC 90-37752. 40p. (gr. k-3). 1990. PLB 15.93 (*0-944483-82-8*) Garrett Ed Corp.

Barnes, Jill & Tsurmi, Masao. Giant Tree & the Boy. Rubin, Caroline, ed. Japan Foreign Rights Centre Staff, tr. from JPN. Suzuki, Mamoru, illus. LC 90-37751. 40p. (gr. k-4). 1990. PLB 15.93 (*0-944483-80-1*) Garrett Ed Corp.

Berry. First Palm Trees. Date not set. 15.00 (*0-06-023504-7*); PLB 14.89 (*0-06-023508-X*) HarpC Child Bks.

Blocksma, Mary. Apple Tree! Apple Tree! Kalthoff, Sandra C., illus. LC 82-19852. 24p. (ps-2). 1983. PLB 9.75 (*0-516-01584-2*); pap. 3.95 (*0-516-41584-0*) Childrens.

Bond, Ruskin. Cherry Tree. Eitzen, Allan, illus. LC 90-85731. 32p. (ps-3). 1991. 14.95 (*1-878093-21-5*) Boyds Mills Pr.

Boyle, Doe & Thomas, Peter, eds. Big Town Trees: From an Original Article which Appeared in Ranger Rick Magazine, Copyright National Wildlife Federation. Beylon, Cathy, illus. LC 92-34778. 20p. (gr. k-3). 1993. 6.95 (*0-924483-83-0*); incl. audio tape 9.95 (*0-924483-84-9*); incl. audio tape & 13 inch plush toy 35.95 (*0-924483-87-3*); incl. 9 inch plush toy 21.95 (*0-924483-89-X*) Soundprints.

Brown, Margaret W. The Little Fir Tree. Cooney, Barbara, illus. LC 54-5534. 24p. (gr. k-3). 1979. PLB 13.89 (*0-690-04016-4*, Crowell Jr Bks) HarpC Child Bks.

Bunting, Eve. Someday a Tree. Himler, Ronald, illus. LC 92-24074. 32p. (gr. k-3). 1993. 14.45 (*0-395-61309-4*, Clarion Bks) HM.

Carrier, Lark. A Christmas Promise. LC 91-14556. (Illus.). 28p. (gr. k up). 1991. pap. 4.95 (*0-88708-180-0*) Picture Bk Studio.

Cates, Joe W. The Crooked Tree. Cates, Joe W., illus. 48p. (Orig.). (gr. k-6). 1986. PLB 9.95 (*0-942403-02-9*); pap. 6.00 (*0-942403-00-2*) J Barnaby Dist.

Chanin, Michael. Grandfather Four Winds & Rising Moon. Smith, Sally J., illus. LC 93-2689. 32p. 1994. 14.95 (*0-915811-47-2*) H J Kramer Inc.

Cherry, Lynne. El Gran Capoquero: The Great Kapok Tree. LC 93-36401. (ps-3). 1994. pap. 4.95 (*0-15-232320-1*, HB Juv Bks) HarBrace.

Coran, Pierre. The Tree Poachers. (Illus.). 32p. (gr. k-2). 1991. 12.95 (*0-89565-746-5*) Childs World.

Deedy, Carmen A. Treeman. Ponte, Douglas J., illus. LC 93-1667. 1993. 16.95 (*1-56145-077-4*) Peachtree Pubs.

Dodd, Lynley. The Apple Tree. Dodd, Lynley, illus. LC 85-9774. 26p. (gr. 1-2). 1985. PLB 17.27 (*0-918831-08-3*) Gareth Stevens Inc.

Donahue, Michael & Strawn, Susan. The Grandpa Tree. 24p. (gr. 1-3). 1988. pap. 5.95 (*0-911797-42-4*) R Rinehart.

Ehlert, Lois. Red Leaf, Yellow Leaf. 32p. (ps-3). 1991. 14.95 (*0-15-266197-2*, HB Juv Bks) HarBrace.

Fleischman, Paul. The Birthday Tree. Sewall, Marcia, illus. LC 78-22155. (gr. k-3). 1979. PLB 13.89 (*0-06-021916-5*) HarpC Child Bks.

—The Birthday Tree. Sewall, Marcia, illus. LC 78-22155. 32p. (gr. k-3). 1991. pap. 4.50 (*0-06-443246-7*, Trophy) HarpC Child Bks.

Forbes, Chris. The Tree Stump. 8p. (ps-k). 1994. text ed. 3.95 (*0-673-36191-8*) GdYrBks.

Franklin, Kristine L. Cuando Regresaron los Monos. Roth, Robert, illus. Zubizarreta, Rosa, tr. from ENG. LC 93-46783. (SPA., Illus.). (gr. k-3). 1994. 14.95 (*0-689-31950-9*, Atheneum) Macmillan.

—When the Monkeys Came Back. Roth, Robert, illus. LC 92-33684. 1994. 14.95 (*0-689-31807-3*, Atheneum) Macmillan.

Gardner, Sally. The Little Nut Tree. Gardner, Sally, illus. LC 93-26714. 32p. 1994. 14.00 (*0-688-13297-9*, Tambourine Bks) Morrow.

Glaser, Linda. Tanya's Big Green Dream. McGinnis, Susan, illus. LC 93-9968. 48p. (gr. 1-4). 1994. RSBE 13.95 (*0-02-735994-8*, Macmillan Child Bk) MacMillan Child Grp.

Haynes, Richard T. The Thong Tree. Haynes, Richard T., illus. LC 90-70508. 64p. (gr. 3-7). 1990. 11.95 (*0-929146-02-6*) Voyageur Pub.

Heller, Nicholas. The Tooth Tree. LC 90-39791. (Illus.). 24p. (ps up). 1991. 13.95 (*0-688-09392-2*); PLB 13.88 (*0-688-09393-0*) Greenwillow.

Henwood, Simon. The Hidden Jungle. (Illus.). 32p. (ps-3). 1992. 15.00 (*0-374-33070-0*) FS&G.

Hirokazu Miyazaki. Croc & the Baby Tree. Clements, Andrew, adapted by. & Hirokazu Miyazaki, illus. LC 91-41719. 28p. (gr. k up). 1993. Repr. of 1990 ed. 14.95 (*0-88708-224-6*) Picture Bk Studio.

Holling, Holling C. Tree in the Trail. (Illus.). (gr. 4-6). 16.45 (*0-395-18228-X*) HM.

Howe, James. How the Ewoks Saved the Trees: An Old Ewok Legend. Velez, Walter, illus. LC 83-13708. 48p. (gr. k-3). 1984. lib. bdg. 6.99 (*0-394-96129-3*) Random Bks Yng Read.

Hurwitz, Johanna. Once I Was a Plum Tree. ALC Staff, ed. Fetz, Ingrid, illus. LC 79-23518. 160p. (gr. 5 up). 1992. pap. 3.95 (*0-688-11848-8*, Pub. by Beech Tree Bks) Morrow.

Ikeda, Daisaku. The Cherry Tree. McCaughrean, Geraldine, tr. Wildsmith, Brian, illus. LC 91-22148. 32p. (ps-3). 1992. 15.00 (*0-679-82669-6*); PLB 15.99 (*0-679-92669-0*) Knopf Bks Yng Read.

James, Christopher. Bump & the Trees. (Illus.). 24p. (ps-3). 1990. 6.95 (*0-88625-276-8*) Durkin Hayes Pub.

Johnson, Emily R. A House Full of Strangers. 160p. (gr. 5 up). 1992. 14.00 (*0-525-65091-1*, Cobblehill Bks) Dutton Child Bks.

Jones, Jo. Amanda's Tree. Vansant, Jo, illus. (gr. 3-6). 1977. pap. 3.50 (*0-9602266-0-5*) Jo-Jo Pubns.

Karpin, Florence B. Tree Spirits: The Story of a Boy Who Loved Trees. Karpin, Florence B., illus. 32p. (Orig.). (ps-3). 1992. PLB 14.00 (*0-88150-248-0*) Countryman.

Knutson, Kimberly. Ska-Tat! Knutson, Kimberley, illus. LC 92-38072. 32p. (ps-1). 1993. RSBE 14.95 (*0-02-750846-3*, Macmillan Child Bk) Macmillan Child Grp.

Lavranos, Destini & Ritchie, Sheri. The Magical Tree. Elston, Dino, illus. 2p. (ps-k). 1993. 14.95 (*0-9638393-0-6*) Bedtime Bks.

Levine, Arthur A. Pearl Moscowitz's Last Stand. Roth, Rob, illus. LC 91-10652. 32p. (ps up). 1993. 14.00 (*0-688-10753-2*, Tambourine Bks); PLB 13.93 (*0-688-10754-0*, Tambourine Bks) Morrow.

Lionni, Leo. A Busy Year. LC 91-29149. (Illus.). 36p. (ps-2). 1992. 7.99 (*0-679-82464-2*); PLB 10.99 (*0-679-92464-7*) Knopf Bks Yng Read.

Lisle, Janet T. The Great Dimpole Oak. Gammell, Stephen, illus. LC 87-11092. 144p. (gr. 4-6). 1987. 11.95 (*0-531-05716-X*); PLB 11.99 (*0-531-08316-0*) Orchard Bks Watts.

Luger, Harriet. The Elephant Tree. 112p. (gr. 7-11). 1986. pap. 2.25 (*0-440-92394-8*, LFL) Dell.

Maestro, Betsy. Why Do Leaves Change Color? Krupinski, Loretta, illus. LC 93-9611. 32p. (gr. k-3). 1994. pap. 4.95 (*0-06-445126-7*, Trophy) HarpC Child Bks.

Marshak, Suzanna. The Wizard's Promise. Rand, Ted, illus. LC 92-36507. (ps-2). 1994. pap. 15.00 (*0-671-78431-5*, S&S BFYR) S&S Trade.

Marshall, James. Tres en un Arbol - Three up a Tree. Baro, Ana B., tr. Marshall, James, illus. (SPA.). 48p. (gr. 2-4). 1990. pap. write for info. (*84-204-4637-8*) Santillana.

Mattingley, Christobel. The Miracle Tree. Yamaguchi, Marianne, illus. LC 86-4541. 28p. (gr. 3 up). 1986. 11.95 (*0-15-200530-7*, Gulliver Bks) HarBrace.

Mills, Joyce C. Gentle Willow: A Story for Children about Dying. Chesworth, Michael, illus. LC 93-22770. 32p. (ps-3). 1993. 16.95 (*0-945354-54-1*); pap. 8.95 (*0-945354-53-3*) Magination Pr.

—Gentle Willow: A Story For Children about Dying. Chesworth, Michael, illus. LC 93-38212. (gr. 2 up). 1994. 17.27 (*0-8368-1070-8*) Gareth Stevens Inc.

Oppenheimer, Evelyn. Tilli Comes to Texas. Haverfield, Mary, illus. LC 86-3089. 40p. (gr. k-3). 1986. PLB 9.95 (*0-937460-21-4*) Hendrick-Long.

Pascal, Francine. Jessica Saves the Trees. (gr. 4-7). 1993. pap. 3.25 (*0-553-15946-1*) Bantam.

Patrick, Johnstone G. The Wishing Tree of Honey Hill Wood. 1993. 12.95 (*0-533-10617-6*) Vantage.

Pike, Norman. The Peach Tree. DeWitt, Robin & DeWitt, Patricia, illus. 36p. (ps up). 1984. 10.95 (*0-88045-014-2*) Stemmer Hse.

Pochocki, Ethel. The Gypsies' Tale. Kelly, Laura, illus. LC 93-3320. (gr. 4 up). 1994. pap. 15.00 (*0-671-79934-7*, S&S BFYR) S&S Trade.

Polacco, Patricia. Uncle Vova's Tree. Polacco, Patricia, illus. 32p. (ps-3). 1989. 14.95 (*0-399-21617-0*, Philomel Bks) Putnam Pub Group.

Potok, Chaim. The Tree of Here. Auth, Tony, illus. LC 92-28412. (gr. k-4). 1993. 13.00 (*0-679-84010-9*); PLB 13.99 (*0-679-94010-3*) Knopf Bks Yng Read.

Pryor, Bonnie. The Plum Tree War. Leder, Dora, illus. (gr. 4-7). 1992. pap. 3.25 (*0-440-40619-6*, Pub. by Yearling Classics) Dell.

Roche, Luane. The Proud Tree. 64p. (gr. 2-6). 1981. pap. 2.95 (*0-89243-146-6*) Liguori Pubns.

Romanova, Natalia. Once There Was a Tree. Spirin, Gennady, illus. LC 85-6730. (ps up). 1989. pap. 4.99 (*0-8037-0705-3*) Dial Bks Young.

Ryan, Mary C. The Voice from the Mendelsohns' Maple. 144p. (gr. 5). 1992. pap. 3.50 (*0-380-71140-0*, Camelot) Avon.

Ryder, Donald G. The Inside Story: Living & Learning Through Life's Storms. Mullen, Don, illus. LC 85-27780. 56p. (gr. 7 up). 1985. 14.95 (*0-935973-38-9*) Ryder Pub Co.

Sarai. The Apple Tree That Would Not Let Go of Its Apples. Kozjak, Goran, illus. McNulty, Linda, intro. by. (Illus.). 28p. (Orig.). 1993. pap. 11.50 (*0-938837-13-3*) Behav Sci Ctr Pubs.

Sato, Satoru. I Wish I Had a Big, Big Tree. Murakami, Tsutomu, illus. LC 88-8080. 40p. (ps-2). 1989. 10.95 (*0-688-07303-4*); PLB 10.88 (*0-688-07304-2*) Lothrop.

Seredy, Kate. The Singing Tree. (gr. 4 up). 1992. 17.75 (*0-8446-6588-6*) Peter Smith.

Shaw, Kiki & Shaw, Kathryn. Maya & the Town that Loved a Tree. (Illus.). 32p. (ps-1). 1993. 14.95 (*0-87663-796-9*) Universe.

Smith, Agnes. The Bluegreen Tree. Sharkey, J. Thomas, illus. LC 76-50105. 180p. (Orig.). 1977. 9.00 (*0-87012-271-1*) Westwind Pr.

Spurr, Elizabeth. The Gumdrop Tree. Gorton, Julia, illus. LC 93-38234. 32p. (ps-1). 1994. 13.95 (*0-7868-0008-9*); PLB 13.89 (*0-7868-2004-7*) Hyprn Child.

Stewart, Sarah. The Money Tree. Small, David, illus. 32p. (gr. k up). 1991. 14.95 (*0-374-35014-0*) FS&G.

Stone, Marti. The Singing Fir Tree. Root, Barry, illus. 32p. (ps-3). 1992. 14.95 (*0-399-22207-3*, Putnam) Putnam Pub Group.

Stryker, Sandy. Tonia the Tree. LC 88-16769. (Illus.). 32p. (gr. k-8). 1988. 14.95 (*0-911655-16-6*) Advocacy Pr.

Stuart, Jesse. Split Cherry Tree. rev. ed. Gifford, James M., et al, eds. Wise, Pamela, designed by. LC 90-62198. 56p. (gr. 7 up). 1990. pap. 3.00 (*0-945084-20-X*) J Stuart Found.

Turin, Adela & Selig, Syvie. Of Cannons & Caterpillars. (Illus.). 32p. (gr. 3-6). 1980. 4.95 (*0-904613-62-3*) Writers & Readers.

Van Denend, G. & Vreeman, J. Christopher & the Sycamore Tree. (Illus.). 16p. (Orig.). 1985. pap. 3.95 (*0-918789-00-1*) FreeMan Prods.

Van de Wetering, Janwillem. Hugh Pine & Something Else. Munsinger, Lynn, illus. 96p. (gr. 3 up). 1989. 13.45 (*0-395-49216-5*) HM.

Warren, Jean. Ellie the Evergreen: A Totline Teaching Tale. Cubley, Kathleen, ed. Connelly, Gwen & Tourillotte, Barb, illus. LC 92-62825. 32p. (Orig.). (ps-2). 1993. 12.95 (*0-911019-66-9*); pap. text ed. 5.95 (*0-911019-67-7*) Warren Pub Hse.

—The Wishing Fish: A Totline Teaching Tale. Cubley, Kathleen, ed. Tourtillotte, Barbara, illus. LC 93-12523. 32p. (Orig.). (ps-2). 1994. 12.95 (*0-911019-73-1*); pap. 5.95 (*0-911019-74-X*) Warren Pub Hse.

Watkins, Willie L. Danny Pine & Patty Plum Tree. LC 88-51763. (Illus.). 40p. (Orig.). (gr. k-7). 1989. pap. 8.95 (*0-87516-595-8*) DeVorss.

Wilkins, Vera. Kim's Magic Tree. (ps-2). 1993. pap. 7.95 (*1-870516-05-2*, Pub. by Childs Play UK) Childs Play.

Winter, Ginny L. What's in My Tree. Winter, Ginny L., illus. (gr. k-1). 1962. 8.95 (*0-8392-3044-3*) Astor-Honor.

TREES–POETRY
Behn, Harry. Trees. Endicott, James, illus. LC 91-25179. 32p. (ps-2). 1992. 14.95 (*0-8050-1926-X*, B Martin BYR) H Holt & Co.
Jerris, Tony. The Littlest Spruce. Weinberger, Tanya, illus. 20p. (Orig.). (ps up). 1991. pap. 9.95 (*0-9630107-1-9*) Little Spruce.

TRIAL BY JURY
see Jury

TRIALS
see also Crime and Criminals
Herda, D. J. Roe v. Wade: The Abortion Question. LC 93-22403. (Illus.). 104p. (gr. 6 up). 1994. lib. bdg. 17.95 (*0-89490-459-0*) Enslow Pubs.
Larsen, Anita. The Rosenbergs. Ramsey, Mercy, illus. LC 91-22311. 48p. (gr. 5-6). 1992. text ed. 11.95 RSBE (*0-89686-612-2*, Crestwood Hse) Macmillan Child Grp.
Ogawa, Brian K., et al. To Tell the Truth. Wagstaff, Bob, illus. LC 88-51256. 40p. (gr. 4-6). 1988. text ed. write for info. (*0-9621260-0-4*) VWAP.
Rappaport, Doreen. The Alger Hiss Trial. LC 92-46155. (Illus.). 192p. (gr. 5 up). 1993. 15.00 (*0-06-025119-0*); PLB 14.89 (*0-06-025120-4*) HarpC Child Bks.
—The Alger Hiss Trial. LC 92-46155. (Illus.). 192p. (gr. 5 up). 1993. pap. 4.95 (*0-06-446115-7*, Trophy) HarpC Child Bks.
—The Lizzie Borden Trial. LC 91-23232. (Illus.). 176p. (gr. 5 up). 1992. 14.00 (*0-06-025113-1*); PLB 13.89 (*0-06-025114-X*) HarpC Child Bks.
—The Lizzie Borden Trial. LC 91-23232. (Illus.). 176p. (gr. 5 up). 1993. pap. 4.95 (*0-06-446112-2*, Trophy) HarpC Child Bks.
—The Sacco-Vanzetti Trial. LC 91-47509. (Illus.). 176p. (gr. 5 up). 1992. 14.00 (*0-06-025115-8*); PLB 13.89 (*0-06-025116-6*) HarpC Child Bks.
—Tinker vs. Des Moines: Student Rights on Trial. LC 92-25019. (Illus.). 160p. (gr. 5 up). 1994. pap. 4.95 (*0-06-446114-9*, Trophy) HarpC Child Bks.

TRIALS–FICTION
Alcock, Vivien. Trial of Anna Cotman. (gr. 4-7). 1992. pap. 3.25 (*0-440-40616-1*) Dell.
Lasky, Kathryn. Beyond the Burning Time. 176p. (gr. 7 up). 1994. 13.95 (*0-590-47331-X*, Blue Sky Press) Scholastic Inc.
Rinaldi, Ann. A Break with Charity: A Story about the Salem Witch Trials. LC 92-8858. 1992. 16.95 (*0-15-200353-3*, Gulliver Bks) HarBrace.

TRICKS
see also Card Tricks; Magic
Ames, Gerald & Wyler, Rose. Magic Secrets. Stubis, Talivaldis, illus. LC 67-4229. 64p. (gr. k-3). 1967. PLB 10.89 (*0-06-020069-3*) HarpC Child Bks.
Boy Scouts of America. Cub Scout Magic. (Illus.). 146p. (gr. 3-5). 1960. pap. 7.00x (*0-8395-3219-9*, 33219) BSA.
Disney, Walt, Productions Staff. The Mickey Mouse Magic Book. LC 74-16420. (Illus.). 48p. (gr. 1-2). 1975. 6.95 (*0-394-82567-5*) Random Bks Yng Read.
Eldin, Peter. Trickster's Handbook. LC 89-32073. (Illus.). 96p. (gr. 10-12). 1989. 12.95 (*0-8069-5740-9*) Sterling.
King, Colin. Amazing Book of Puzzles & Tricks. 32p. 1990. 3.50 (*0-517-69194-9*) Random Hse Value.
Knoles, David. Spooky Magic Tricks. (Illus.). 128p. 1994. pap. 4.95 (*0-8069-0419-4*) Sterling.
Longe, Bob. Easy Magic Tricks. LC 94-11207. (Illus.). 128p. 1994. 12.95 (*0-8069-1264-2*) Sterling.
—World's Best Coin Tricks. LC 92-11370. (Illus.). 128p. (gr. 5-10). 1993. pap. 4.95 (*0-8069-8661-1*) Sterling.
Rigney, Francis J. A Beginner's Book of Magic. (Illus.). (gr. 6 up). 1963. 9.95 (*0-8159-5103-5*) Devin.
Severn, Bill. Bill Severn's Magic with Rope, Ribbon, & String. LC 93-17893. (Illus.). 224p. 1994. pap. 12.95 (*0-8117-2533-2*) Stackpole.
Tricks & Puzzles: Superfacts. 1992. 4.99 (*0-517-07327-7*) Random Hse Value.
Van Rensselaer, Alexander. Your Book of Magic. (gr. 9 up). 1968. 7.95 (*0-571-06939-8*) Transatl Arts.
Visual Magic. 64p. 1991. 14.95 (*0-8037-1118-2*) Dial Bks Young.

TRICYCLES
see Bicycles and Bicycling

TRIGONOMETRY
Burchard, Elizabeth & Soroka, Matthew. Algebra Two - Trigonometry: In a Flash. 450p. (gr. 7-12). 1994. pap. 9.95 (*1-881374-14-9*) Flash Blasters.

TRINIDAD–FICTION
Binch, Caroline. Gregory Cool. LC 93-11845. (gr. 3 up). 1994. 14.99 (*0-8037-1577-3*) Dial Bks Young.
Joseph, Lynn. An Island Christmas. Stock, Catherine, illus. 32p. (ps-3). 1992. 14.45 (*0-395-58761-1*, Clarion Bks) HM.

TRIPLETS–FICTION
Pirani, Felix. Rosalie, Sylvia & Melanie. (Illus.). (gr. 3-8). 1992. PLB 8.95 (*0-89565-888-7*) Childs World.

TROJAN WAR
Coolidge, Olivia E. Trojan War. Sandoz, E., illus. (gr. 7-12). 1952. 16.95 (*0-395-06731-6*) HM.
—Trojan War. 1990. pap. 4.80 (*0-395-56151-5*) HM.
Edmondson, Elizabeth. The Trojan War. LC 91-31860. (Illus.). 32p. (gr. 6 up). 1992. text ed. 13.95 RSBE (*0-02-733273-X*, New Discovery) Macmillan Child Grp.
Evslin, Bernard. The Trojan War. 160p. (gr. 5 up). 1988. pap. 2.95 (*0-590-41626-X*) Scholastic Inc.
Homer. Iliad. Lang, Andrew, tr. Budgey, N. F., intro. by. (gr. 9 up). 1966. pap. 2.95 (*0-8049-0115-5*, CL-115) Airmont.
Storr, Catherine. The Trojan Horse. Codd, Mike, illus. LC 84-18292. 32p. (gr. 2-5). 1985. PLB 19.97 (*0-8172-2114-X*) Raintree Steck-V.
Sutcliff, Rosemary. Black Ships Before Troy. Lee, Alan, illus. LC 92-38782. (gr. 4 up). 1993. 19.95 (*0-385-31069-2*) Delacorte.

TROLLS
see Fairies

TROPICAL FISH
Broekel, Ray. Tropical Fish. LC 82-19738. (Illus.). 48p. (gr. k-4). 1983. PLB 12.85 (*0-516-01687-3*) Childrens.
Emmens, Cliff W. A Step-by-Step Book about Tropical Fish. (Illus.). 64p. (gr. 9-12). 1988. pap. 3.95 (*0-86622-471-8*, SK-018) TFH Pubns.
Jameson, P. Tropical Fish. (Illus.). 32p. (gr. 2-5). 1989. lib. bdg. 15.94 (*0-86625-185-5*); lib. bdg. 11.95s.p. (*0-685-58612-X*) Rourke Corp.

TROPICS
Catchpole, Clive. Jungles. Finney, Denise, illus. LC 83-7796. 32p. (ps-4). 1985. pap. 4.95 (*0-8037-0036-9*, 0481-140) Dial Bks Young.
Landau, Elaine. Tropical Rain Forests Around the World. LC 89-24810. (gr. 3-5). 1990. PLB 12.90 (*0-531-10896-1*) Watts.
Marsh, Carole. Jungle Gym! A Monkey's Eye View of the World's Jungles Yesterday, Today & Tomorrow? 36p. (gr. 3-5). 1994. PLB 24.95 (*0-7933-7346-8*); pap. 14.95 (*0-7933-7347-6*); disk 29.95 (*0-7933-7348-4*) Gallopade Pub Group.
Planche, Bernard. Living on a Tropical Island. Matthews, Sarah, tr. from FRE. Broutin, Christian, illus. LC 87-34592. 38p. (gr. k-5). 1988. 5.95 (*0-944589-13-8*, 138) Young Discovery Lib.

TROPICS–DISEASES AND HYGIENE
see also names of tropical diseases, e.g. Yellow Fever

TROUT
Cole, Joanna. A Fish Hatches. LC 78-13445. (Illus.). 40p. (gr. k-3). 1978. PLB 12.88 (*0-688-32153-4*, Morrow Jr Bks) Morrow Jr Bks.
Sargeant, Frank. The Trout Book: A Complete Angler's Guide. LC 92-71318. (Illus.). 160p. (Orig.). 1992. pap. 9.95 (*0-936513-21-7*) Larsens Outdoor.

TROY
Edmondson, Elizabeth. The Trojan War. LC 91-31860. (Illus.). 32p. (gr. 6 up). 1992. text ed. 13.95 RSBE (*0-02-733273-X*, New Discovery) Macmillan Child Grp.

TROY–FICTION
Curtis, Dorris. Skammy: Prince of Troy. Curtis, Dorris, illus. 231p. (gr. 5-9). 1988. lib. bdg. 18.50 (*0-944436-04-8*) Univ Central AR Pr.
Green, Roger L. Tale of Troy. (Illus., Orig.). (gr. 5-7). 1974. pap. 3.95 (*0-14-030120-8*, Puffin) Puffin Bks.

TRS-80 COMPUTERS
Kemnitz, Thomas M. & Mass, Lynne. Kids Working with Computers: TRS-80 BASIC Manual. Schlendorf, Lori, illus. 44p. (gr. 4-7). 1983. pap. 4.99 (*0-89824-055-7*) Trillium Pr.

TRUANCY (SCHOOLS)
see School Attendance

TRUCK DRIVERS
Behrens, June. I Can Be a Truck Driver. LC 84-23246. (Illus.). 32p. (gr. k-3). 1985. PLB 11.80 (*0-516-01848-5*) Childrens.
—Puedo Ser Conductor de Camion (I Can Be a Truck Driver) Kratky, Lada, tr. LC 85-31402. (SPA., Illus.). 32p. (gr. k-3). 1986. PLB 11.80 (*0-516-31848-9*); pap. 3.95 (*0-516-51848-8*) Childrens.
Bourne, Miriam A. A Day in the Life of a Cross-Country Trucker. Jann, Gayle, illus. LC 87-13582. 32p. (gr. 4-8). 1988. PLB 11.79 (*0-8167-1117-8*); pap. text ed. 2.95 (*0-8167-1118-6*) Troll Assocs.
Russell, William. Truckers. LC 93-42484. 1994. write for info. (*1-57103-058-1*) Rourke Pr.

TRUCK DRIVERS–FICTION
Day, Alexandra. Frank & Ernest on the Road. (Illus.). 48p. (ps-3). 1994. 14.95 (*0-590-45048-4*, Scholastic Hardcover) Scholastic Inc.

TRUCK FARMING
see Vegetable Gardening

TRUCKS
Bartle, Brian. Here Comes Tow Truck. Bartle, Brian, illus. 12p. (ps-1). 1992. 4.95 (*0-448-40593-8*, G&D) Putnam Pub Group.
Barton, Byron. Trucks. Barton, Byron, illus. LC 85-47901. 32p. (ps-k). 1986. 6.95 (*0-694-00062-0*, Crowell Jr Bks); PLB 12.89 (*0-690-04530-1*) HarpC Child Bks.
Becker, Jim. You Can Name 100 Trucks! Chewning, Randy, illus. 14p. (ps). 1994. bds. 8.95 (*0-590-46302-0*, Cartwheel) Scholastic Inc.
Boucher, Jerry. Fire Truck Nuts & Bolts. (ps-3). 1993. pap. 5.95 (*0-87614-619-1*) Carolrhoda Bks.
Breverton, David. Here Comes Dump Truck. Bartle, Brian, illus. 12p. (ps-1). 1992. 4.95 (*0-448-40591-1*, G&D) Putnam Pub Group.
—Here Comes Fire Truck. Bartle, Brian, illus. 12p. (ps-1). 1992. 4.95 (*0-448-40592-X*, G&D) Putnam Pub Group.
Broekel, Ray. Trucks. LC 82-17907. (Illus.). 48p. (gr. k-4). 1983. PLB 12.85 (*0-516-01688-1*) Childrens.
Bushey, Jerry. Monster Trucks & Other Giant Machines on Wheels. LC 84-23160. (Illus.). 32p. (gr. k-4). 1985. PLB 19.95 (*0-87614-271-4*); pap. 4.95 (*0-87614-491-1*) Carolrhoda Bks.
Castor, Harriet. Trucks. (Illus.). 12p. (ps). 1993. bds. 4.50 (*0-7460-1098-2*, Usborne) EDC.
Cooper, J. Camiones (Trucks) 1991. 8.95s.p. (*0-86592-509-7*) Rourke Enter.
—Trucks. 1991. 8.95s.p. (*0-86592-491-0*) Rourke Enter.
Crews, Donald. Truck. LC 84-18137. (Illus.). 32p. (ps). 1985. pap. 3.95 (*0-14-050506-7*, Puffin) Puffin Bks.
Donahue, A. K. Four by Fours & Pickups. 48p. (gr. 3-4). 1991. PLB 11.95 (*1-56065-075-3*) Capstone Pr.
Gibbons, Gail. Trucks. Gibbons, Gail, illus. LC 81-43039. 32p. (ps-2). 1981. (Crowell Jr Bks); PLB 14.89 (*0-690-04119-5*) HarpC Child Bks.
Grimm, Rosemary. Truck & Tractor Pullers. LC 87-30592. (Illus.). 48p. (gr. 5-6). 1988. text ed. 11.95 RSBE (*0-89686-358-1*, Crestwood Hse) Macmillan Child Grp.
Hawksley, Gerald. Trucks. Hawksley, Gerald, illus. 10p. (ps). 1990. bds. 4.95 (*1-878624-17-2*) McClanahan Bk.
Johnston, Scott. Monster Truck Racing. 48p. (gr. 3-10). 1994. PLB 17.27 (*1-56065-204-7*) Capstone Pr.
—The Original Monster Truck: Bigfoot. 48p. (gr. 3-10). 1994. PLB 17.27 (*1-56065-200-4*) Capstone Pr.
Kindersley, Dorling. Trucks. LC 90-49260. (Illus.). 24p. (ps-k). 1991. pap. 7.95 POB (*0-689-71405-X*, Aladdin) Macmillan Child Grp.
McNaught, Harry. The Truck Book. LC 77-79851. (ps-2). 1978. pap. 2.25 (*0-394-83703-7*) Random Bks Yng Read.
—Trucks. McNaught, Harry, illus. LC 75-36463. 14p. (ps-1). 1976. Repr. of 1976 ed. bds. 3.95 (*0-394-83240-X*) Random Bks Yng Read.
Marston, Hope I. Big Rigs. rev. & updated ed. LC 92-39881. (Illus.). 48p. (gr. 2-5). 1993. 14.99 (*0-525-65123-3*, Cobblehill Bks) Dutton Child Bks.
Mathieu, Joseph. Big Joe's Trailer Truck. Mathieu, Joseph, illus. LC 74-2538. 32p. (Orig.). (ps-1). 1993. pap. 2.25 (*0-394-82925-5*) Random Bks Yng Read.
Nichols, V. Cars & Trucks Sticker Pad. M. J. Studios Staff, illus. 32p. (gr. k-6). 1993. pap. 2.95 (*1-879424-16-9*) Nickel Pr.
Olson, Norman. I Can Read About Trucks & Cars. LC 72-96957. (Illus.). (gr. 2-4). 1973. pap. 2.50 (*0-89375-055-7*) Troll Assocs.
Rockwell, Anne. Trucks. Rockwell, Anne, illus. LC 84-1556. 24p. (ps-1). 1984. 11.95 (*0-525-44147-6*, DCB) Dutton Child Bks.
—Trucks. Rockwell, Anne, illus. LC 84-1556. 24p. (ps-1). 1988. pap. 3.95 (*0-525-44432-7*, DCB) Dutton Child Bks.
Salter, Andrew. Trucks. Moores, Ian, et al, illus. LC 93-49568. 1994. write for info. (*0-8114-6189-0*) Raintree Steck-V.
Scarry, Richard. Richard Scarry's Cars & Trucks & Things That Go. (Illus.). (ps-2). 1974. write for info. (*0-307-15785-7*, Golden Bks) Western Pub.
Seymour, Peter. The Pop-up Book of Big Trucks. Murphy, Chuck, illus. (ps-3). 1989. 14.95 (*0-316-78197-5*) Little.
Stamper, Judith B. Truck Driver. Ulrich, George, illus. LC 88-10039. 32p. (gr. k-3). 1989. PLB 10.89 (*0-8167-1424-X*); pap. text ed. 2.95 (*0-8167-1425-8*) Troll Assocs.
Steele, Philip. Cars & Trucks. LC 90-41180. (Illus.). 32p. (gr. 5-6). 1991. text ed. 3.95 RSBE (*0-89686-521-5*, Crestwood Hse) Macmillan Child Grp.
Stephen, R. J. The Picture World of Trucks. (Illus.). 32p. (gr. k-4). 1989. PLB 12.40 (*0-531-10729-9*) Watts.
Sullivan, George. Here Come the Monster Trucks. (Illus.). 64p. (gr. 2-6). 1992. pap. 4.99 (*0-525-65085-7*, Dutton Unicorn) Puffin Bks.
Truck Transportation. (Illus.). 32p. (gr. 6-12). 1973. pap. 1.85 (*0-8395-3371-3*, 33371) BSA.
Trucks. LC 92-52833. 24p. (ps-3). 1993. 8.95 (*1-56458-137-3*) Dorling Kindersley.
Young, C. Trucks. (Illus.). 32p. (ps-2). PLB 13.96 (*0-88110-556-2*, Usborne); pap. 5.95 (*0-7460-0722-1*, Usborne) EDC.

TRUCKS–FICTION
Andersen, Honey & Reinholtd, Bill. Pop's Truck. Posey, Pam, illus. LC 93-18050. 1994. write for info. (*0-383-03709-3*) SRA Schl Grp.
Borden, Louise. Neighborhood Trucker. 1990. pap. 12.95 (*0-590-42584-6*) Scholastic Inc.
Bushey, Jerry. Monster Trucks & Other Giant Machines on Wheels. LC 84-23160. (Illus.). 32p. (gr. k-4). 1985. PLB 19.95 (*0-87614-271-4*); pap. 4.95 (*0-87614-491-1*) Carolrhoda Bks.
Cars & Trucks. (Illus.). 24p. (gr. k-2). 1988. 3.95 (*0-87449-501-6*) Modern Pub NYC.
Crews, Donald. Truck: Big Book Edition. Crews, Donald, illus. 32p. (ps up). 1993. pap. 18.95 (*0-688-12611-1*, Mulberry) Morrow.
Dobkin, Bonnie. Truck Stop. (Illus.). 32p. (ps-2). 1994. PLB 13.80 (*0-516-02027-7*); pap. 2.95 (*0-516-42027-5*) Childrens.
Hawksley, Gerald. Trucks Window. (Illus.). 10p. (ps). 1988. 3.95 (*0-681-40469-8*) Longmeadow Pr.
Hoban, Tana. Dig, Drill, Dump, Fill. LC 75-11987. (Illus.). 32p. (ps up). 1992. pap. 3.95 (*0-688-11703-1*, Mulberry) Morrow.
Holm, Astrid. Brum. Mones, Isidre, illus. LC 92-61952. 22p. (ps). 1993. 3.25 (*0-679-84493-7*) Random Bks Yng Read.
Horenstein, Henry. Sam Goes Trucking. (ps-3). 1990. pap. 5.70 (*0-395-54950-7*) HM.
—Sams Goes Trucking. (Illus.). 32p. (gr. k-3). 1990. pap. 4.95 (*0-685-45556-4*) HM.
Korman, Justine. Working Hard with the Mighty Dump Truck. (ps-3). 1993. pap. 2.50 (*0-590-46481-7*) Scholastic Inc.

Kreloff, Elliot, illus. Trucks. (ps-k). 1993. Set, lg. bk. 12p., small bk. 6p. bds. 4.95 (*1-56293-358-2*) McClanahan Bk.

McNaught, Harry. Los Camiones. McNaught, Harry, illus. (SPA.). 32p. (ps-3). 1993. 2.25 (*0-394-85220-6*) Random Bks Yng Read.

Nadler, Ellis. Tiny Tippy Truck. (ps). 1994. 14.95 (*0-316-59688-4*) Little.

Nasta, Cynthia V. Peter & His Pick-up Truck: A Southwestern Children's Tale. Zilka, Pat, illus. LC 89-80351. 24p. (ps-8). 1989. pap. 6.95 (*0-9622064-0-7*) Little Buckaroo.

Parkes, Brenda. Farmer Schnuck. Webb, Philip, illus. LC 92-31078. 1993. 4.25 (*0-383-03568-6*) SRA Schl Grp.

Pearce, Molly. Jimmy the Beet Truck. Pearce, Molly, illus. LC 91-65464. 32p. (gr. k-2). 1991. pap. 4.95 (*0-9628129-9-4*) Sagebrush Bks.

Peck, Marshall H., III, illus. Heavy-Duty Trucks. 14p. (ps-k). 1992. bds. 4.99 (*0-679-83244-0*) Random Bks Yng Read.

Petrie, Catherine. Joshua James Likes Trucks. Warshaw, Jerry, illus. LC 81-17076. 32p. (ps-2). 1982. PLB 10.25 (*0-516-03525-8*); pap. text ed. 2.95 (*0-516-43525-6*) Childrens.

Rockwell, Anne. Trucks. (ps-3). 1992. pap. 4.50 (*0-14-054790-8*) Viking Child Bks.

Smax, Willy. Benny the Breakdown Truck. Ludlow, Karen, illus. LC 93-50048. 64p. (gr. k-4). 1994. 16.00 (*0-517-59921-X*) Crown Bks Yng Read.

Spears-Stewart, Reta. Toby's Big Truck Adventure. LC 92-35750. 1993. 7.95 (*0-8163-1141-2*) Pacific Pr Pub Assn.

Walker, Sloan & Vasey, Andrew. Supertrucks. LC 85-5379. (Illus.). 48p. (gr. 1-4). 1985. 12.95 (*0-8027-6586-6*); PLB 12.85 (*0-8027-6606-4*) Walker & Co.

Williams, Karen L. Tap-Tap. Stock, Catherine, illus. LC 93-13006. (gr. 1-4). 1994. 14.95 (*0-395-65617-6*, Clarion Bks) HM.

Wilmer, Diane. Zap Zero - The Delivery Man. rev. ed. Dowling, Paul, illus. 32p. (gr. k-2). 1990. Repr. of 1989 ed. PLB 10.95 (*1-878363-11-5*) Forest Hse.

Wolf, Sallie. Peter's Trucks. Levine, Abby, ed. Smith, Cat B., illus. LC 91-19251. 24p. (ps-1). 1992. PLB 13.95 (*0-8075-6519-9*) A Whitman.

Ziefert, Harriet. Here Comes a Truck. Brown, Richard, illus. 20p. (ps-1). 1992. pap. 5.99 (*0-14-054520-4*) Puffin Bks.

TRUMAN, HARRY S., PRESIDENT U. S. 1884-1972

Collins, David R. Harry S. Truman: People's President. Frame, Paul, illus. 80p. (gr. 2-6). 1991. Repr. of 1985 ed. lib. bdg. 12.95 (*0-7910-1421-5*) Chelsea Hse.

—Harry S. Truman: 33rd President of the United States. Young, Richard G., ed. LC 87-32750. (Illus.). (gr. 5-9). 1988. PLB 17.26 (*0-944483-00-3*) Garrett Ed Corp.

Farley, Karin C. Harry Truman: The Man from Independence. Steltenpohl, Jane, ed. (Illus.). 160p. (gr. 5-9). 1989. lib. bdg. 11.98 (*0-671-65853-0*, J Messner) S&S Trade.

Feinberg, Barbara S. Harry S. Truman. LC 93-30895. 1994. 14.40 (*0-531-13036-3*) Watts.

Fleming, Thomas. Harry S Truman. LC 93-153. 144p. (gr. 5 up). 1993. 14.95 (*0-8027-8267-1*); lib. bdg. 15.85 (*0-8027-8269-8*) Walker & Co.

Greenberg, Morrie. Harry Truman: The Buck Stops Here. LC 88-20264. (Illus.). 128p. (gr. 5 up). 1991. text ed. 13.95 RSBE (*0-87518-394-8*, Dillon) Macmillan Child Grp.

Hargrove, Jim. Harry S. Truman. (Illus.). 100p. (gr. 3 up). 1987. PLB 14.40 (*0-516-01388-2*) Childrens.

Harry S. Truman: Mini Play. (gr. 8 up). 1977. 6.50 (*0-89550-373-5*) Stevens & Shea.

Hudson, Wilma J. Harry S. Truman: Missouri Farm Boy. Doremus, Robert, illus. LC 92-7513. 192p. (gr. 3-7). 1992. pap. 3.95 (*0-689-71658-3*, Aladdin) Macmillan Child Grp.

Leavell, Perry. Harry S. Truman. (Illus.). 112p. (gr. 5 up). 1988. lib. bdg. 17.95 (*0-87754-558-8*) Chelsea Hse.

Morris, Jeffrey. The Truman Way. (Illus.). 128p. (gr. 5 up). 1994. 22.95 (*0-8225-2927-0*) Lerner Pubns.

O'Neal, Michael. President Truman & the Atomic Bomb: Opposing Viewpoints. LC 90-35611. (Illus.). 112p. (gr. 5-8). 1990. PLB 14.95 (*0-89908-079-0*) Greenhaven.

Sandak, Cass R. The Trumans. LC 92-6879. (Illus.). 48p. (gr. 5). 1992. text ed. 4.95 RSBE (*0-89686-643-2*, Crestwood Hse) Macmillan Child Grp.

TRUST IN GOD

see Faith

TRUTH, SOJOURNER, 1797?-1883

Adler, David A. A Picture Book of Sojourner Truth. Griffith, Gershom, illus. LC 93-7478. 32p. (ps-3). 1994. reinforced bdg. 15.95 (*0-8234-1072-2*) Holiday.

Claflin, Edward B. Sojourner Truth & the Struggle for Freedom. LC 87-19325. (Illus.). 144p. (gr. 3-6). 1987. pap. 5.95 (*0-8120-3919-X*) Barron.

Ferris, Jeri. Walking the Road to Freedom: A Story about Sojourner Truth. Hanson, Peter E., illus. 64p. (gr. 3-6). 1988. lib. bdg. 14.95 (*0-87614-318-4*) Carolrhoda Bks.

—Walking the Road to Freedom: A Story about Sojourner Truth. Hanson, Peter E., illus. 64p. (gr. 3-6). 1989. pap. 5.95 (*0-87614-505-5*, First Ave Edns) Lerner Pubns.

Krass, Peter. Sojourner Truth. King, Coretta Scott, intro. by. (Illus.). 112p. (Orig.). (gr. 5 up). 1988. 17.95 (*1-55546-611-7*); pap. 9.95 (*0-7910-0215-2*) Chelsea Hse.

McKissack, Fredrick, Jr. & McKissack, Patricia C. Sojourner Truth: Ain't I a Woman? (gr. 8-12). 1994. pap. 3.50 (*0-590-44691-6*) Scholastic Inc.

McKissack, Patricia & McKissack, Fredrick. Sojourner Truth: A Voice for Freedom. LC 92-6190. (Illus.). 32p. (gr. 1-4). 1992. lib. bdg. 12.95 (*0-89490-313-6*) Enslow Pubs.

McKissack, Patricia C. & McKissack, Fredrick, Jr. Sojourner Truth: Ain't I a Woman. 1992. 13.95 (*0-590-44690-8*, Scholastic Hardcover) Scholastic Inc.

Obaba, Al-Imam. Sojourner Truth Great Nubian Quiz. (Illus.). 43p. (Orig.). 1989. pap. 3.95 (*0-916157-08-3*) African Islam Miss Pubns.

Ortiz, Victoria. Sojourner Truth: A Self-Made Woman. LC 73-22290. (Illus.). 160p. (gr. 7 up). 1986. PLB 12.89 (*0-397-32134-1*, Lipp Jr Bks) HarpC Child Bks.

Shumate, Jane. Sojourner Truth & the Voice of Freedom. (Illus.). 32p. (gr. 2-4). 1991. PLB 12.90 (*1-56294-041-4*); pap. 4.95 (*1-878841-71-8*) Millbrook Pr.

Taylor-Boyd, Susan. Sojourner Truth: The Courageous Former Slave Whose Eloquence Helped Promote Human Equality. LC 89-4345. (Illus.). 68p. (gr. 5-6). 1990. PLB 19.93 (*0-8368-0101-6*) Gareth Stevens Inc.

—Sojourner Truth: The Courageous Former Slave Who Led Others to Freedom. Tolan, Mary, adapted by. LC 90-37992. (Illus.). 64p. (gr. 3-4). 1991. PLB 19.93 (*0-8368-0458-9*) Gareth Stevens Inc.

TRUTHFULNESS AND FALSEHOOD

Finkelstien, Aurohom. Tzvi Tells the Truth. Friedman, Aaron, illus. 64p. 1991. 10.95 (*1-56062-094-3*) CIS Comm.

Frost, Lesley. Really, Not Really. Remington, Barbara, illus. 64p. (ps-3). 1966. 10.00 (*0-8159-6702-0*) Devin.

Hopper, Nancy J. The Truth or Dare Trap. (gr. 7 up). 1988. pap. 2.50 (*0-380-70269-X*, Flare) Avon.

Johnson, Kevin. Who Should I Listen To: Readings for Early Teens on Identifying Truth from Lies. 1993. pap. 6.99 (*1-55661-283-4*) Bethany Hse.

Kincher, Jonni. The First Honest Book about Lies. Espeland, Pamela, ed. LC 92-13403. (Illus.). 176p. (Orig.). (gr. 7 up). 1992. pap. 12.95 (*0-915793-43-1*) Free Spirit Pub.

Price, Joan. Truth Is a Bright Star. LC 82-1345. 1982. pap. 8.95 (*0-89087-333-X*) Celestial Arts.

Seidler, Tor. Terpin. LC 82-11734. 96p. (gr. 7 up). 1982. 12.00 (*0-374-37413-9*) FS&G.

Sharmat, Marjorie W. A Big Fat Enormous Lie. McPhail, David, illus. LC 77-15645. 32p. (ps-2). 1986. pap. 3.99 (*0-525-44242-1*, DCB) Dutton Child Bks.

Starbuck, Marnie. The Gladimals Learn about Honesty. (Illus.). 16p. 1990. 0.75 (*1-56456-207-7*, 477) W Gladden Found.

Weiss, Ann E. Lies, Deception, & Truth. 160p. (gr. 6 up). 1993. pap. 4.80 (*0-395-65750-4*) HM.

TUAREGS–FICTION

Kaufmann, Herbert. Adventure in the Desert. Karlin, Eugene, illus. (gr. 7 up). 1961. 10.95 (*0-8392-3000-1*) Astor-Honor.

—Lost Sahara Trail. (gr. 7 up). 1962. 10.95 (*0-8392-3022-2*) Astor-Honor.

TUBA–FICTION

Martin, Ann M. Karen's Tuba. (gr. 4-7). 1993. pap. 2.95 (*0-590-45653-9*) Scholastic Inc.

TUBMAN, HARRIET, 1820-1913

Adler, David A. A Picture Book of Harriet Tubman. Byrd, Samuel, illus. LC 91-19628. 32p. (ps-3). 1992. reinforced bdg. 15.95 (*0-8234-0926-0*) Holiday.

AESOP Enterprises, Inc. Staff & Crenshaw, Gwendolyn J. Harriet Tubman: Stand & Deliver. 20p. (gr. 3-12). 1991. pap. write for info. incl. cassette (*1-880771-02-0*) AESOP Enter.

Bains, Rae. Harriet Tubman: The Road to Freedom. LC 81-23145. (Illus.). 48p. (gr. 4-6). 1982. PLB 10.79 (*0-89375-760-8*); pap. text ed. 3.50 (*0-89375-761-6*) Troll Assocs.

Benjamin, Anne. Young Harriet Tubman: Freedom Fighter. Beier, Ellen, illus. LC 91-26404. 32p. (gr. k-2). 1992. PLB 11.59 (*0-8167-2538-1*); pap. text ed. 2.95 (*0-8167-2539-X*) Troll Assocs.

Bentley, Judith. Harriet Tubman. LC 90-12319. (Illus.). 144p. (gr. 9-12). 1990. PLB 14.40 (*0-531-10948-8*) Watts.

Bisson, Terry. Harriet Tubman. King, Coretta Scott, intro. by. (Illus.). 112p. (Orig.). (gr. 5 up). 1991. pap. 9.95 (*0-7910-0249-7*) Chelsea Hse.

Bradford, Sarah. Harriet Tubman, the Moses of Her People. LC 93-34223. 160p. 1993. pap. 8.95 (*1-55709-217-6*) Applewood.

Carter, Polly. Harriet Tubman. Brook, Bonnie, ed. Pinkney, Brian, illus. 32p. (gr. k-2). 1990. 4.95 (*0-671-69115-5*); PLB 6.95 (*0-671-69109-0*) Silver Pr.

Conrad, Earl. Harriet Tubman. 1990. 21.95 (*0-87498-036-4*); pap. 15.95 (*0-685-55179-2*) Assoc Pubs DC.

Ferris, Jeri. Go Free or Die: A Story about Harriet Tubman. Ritz, Karen, illus. 64p. (gr. 3-6). 1988. lib. bdg. 14.95 (*0-87614-317-6*) Carolrhoda Bks.

—Go Free or Die: A Story about Harriet Tubman. Ritz, Karen, illus. 64p. (gr. 3-6). 1989. pap. 5.95 (*0-87614-504-7*, First Ave Edns) Lerner Pubns.

Fitzgerald, Sharon. Harriet Tubman, Patriot. 1992. pap. 3.95 (*0-685-59550-1*, Melrose Sq) Holloway.

Harriet Tubman: Mini Play. (gr. 5 up). 1977. 6.50 (*0-89550-359-X*) Stevens & Shea.

Harriet Tubman, No. 19: Yearling Biography. (Orig.). (gr. k-6). 1991. pap. 3.50 (*0-440-40400-2*, Pub. by Yearling Classics) Dell.

Johnson, LaVerne C. Harriet Tubman: Writer. Perry, Craig R., illus. LC 92-35251. 1992. 3.95 (*0-922162-92-1*) Empak Pub.

Klingel, Cindy. Women of America: Harriet Tubman. (gr. 2-4). 1987. PLB 14.95 (*0-88682-166-5*) Creative Ed.

McClard, Megan. Harriet Tubman: Slavery & the Underground Railroad. (Illus.). 160p. (gr. 5 up). 1990. lib. bdg. 12.95 (*0-382-09938-9*); pap. 7.95 (*0-382-24047-2*) Silver Burdett Pr.

McGovern, Ann. Wanted Dead Or Alive: The True Story of Harriet Tubman. 64p. (gr. 2-4). 1991. 3.95 (*0-590-44212-0*) Scholastic Inc.

Meyer, Linda D. Harriet Tubman: They Called Me Moses. Kerstetter, J., illus. LC 87-43308. 32p. (Orig.). (ps-4). 1988. lib. bdg. 16.95 (*0-943990-33-5*); pap. 5.95 (*0-943990-32-7*) Parenting Pr.

Obaba, Al-Imam. Harriet Tubman Great Nubian Quiz. (Illus.). 43p. (Orig.). 1989. pap. 3.95 (*0-916157-09-1*) African Islam Miss Pubns.

Petry, Ann. Harriet Tubman: Conductor on the Underground Railway. LC 55-9215. 247p. (gr. 7-11). 1955. 16.95 (*0-690-37236-1*, Crowell Jr Bks) HarpC Child Bks.

—Harriet Tubman: Conductor on the Underground Railroad. LC 90-48980. (Illus.). 176p. (gr. 6-10). 1991. PLB 13.95 (*1-55905-097-7*) Marshall Cavendish.

Polcovar, Jane. Harriet Tubman. Bloch, Alex, illus. 48p. (gr. 2-4). 1988. pap. 2.50 (*0-681-40357-8*) Longmeadow Pr.

Sabin, Francene. Harriet Tubman. Frenck, Hal, illus. LC 84-2667. 32p. (gr. 3-6). 1985. PLB 9.49 (*0-8167-0158-X*); pap. text ed. 2.95 (*0-8167-0159-8*) Troll Assocs.

Smith, Kathie B. Harriet Tubman. Steltenpohl, Jane, ed. Seward, James, illus. 24p. (gr. 4-6). 1989. lib. bdg. 7.98 (*0-671-67513-3*, J Messner); PLB 5.99s.p. (*0-685-25427-5*) S&S Trade.

Smith, Kathie B. & Bradbury, Pamela Z. Harriet Tubman. (Illus.). 24p. (ps up). 1989. pap. 2.50 (*0-671-64026-7*, Little Simon) S&S Trade.

Sterling, Dorothy. Freedom Train: The Story of Harriet Tubman. 192p. (gr. 4-6). 1987. pap. 2.95 (*0-590-43628-7*); tchr's. guide o.p. 1.25 (*0-590-40988-3*) Scholastic Inc.

Thompson-Peters, Flossie E. Harriet Tubman: Freedom Fighter. Wilson, Lillian M., illus. 32p. (Orig.). (gr. 3-9). 1988. pap. 4.70 (*1-880784-04-1*) Atlas Pr.

TUBMAN, HARRIET, 1820-1913–POETRY

Lawrence, Jacob. Harriet & the Promised Land. LC 92-33740. 1993. pap. 15.00 (*0-671-86673-7*, S&S BFYR) S&S Trade.

TUGBOATS

Burke, Timothy. Tugboats in Action. LC 93-9131. 1993. write for info. (*0-8075-8112-7*) A Whitman.

Maass, Robert. Tugboat Life. 1994. write for info. (*0-8050-3116-2*) H Holt & Co.

TUGBOATS–FICTION

Crampton, Gertrude. Scuffy the Tugboat. Olson, Gordon, illus. 24p. (ps-k). 1993. 9.00 (*0-307-74813-8*, 64813, Golden Pr) Western Pub.

Gramatky, Hardie. Little Toot. (ps-3). 1992. 14.95 (*0-399-22419-X*) Putnam Pub Group.

O'Hearn, Michael. Hercules the Harbor Tug. (Illus.). 32p. (ps-4). 1994. 15.95 (*0-88106-889-6*); PLB 16.00 (*0-88106-890-X*); pap. 7.95 (*0-88106-888-8*) Charlesbridge Pub.

TUNISIA

Fox, Mary V. Tunisia. LC 90-2199. (Illus.). 128p. (gr. 5-9). 1990. PLB 20.55 (*0-516-02724-7*) Childrens.

Lerner Publications, Department of Geography Staff, ed. Tunisia in Pictures. (Illus.). 64p. (gr. 5 up). 1989. 17.50 (*0-8225-1844-9*) Lerner Pubns.

TUNISIA–FICTION

Wilkins, Verna & McLean, Gill, eds. Five Things to Find: A Story from Tunisia. Wilkinson, Barry, illus. LC 93-12121. 1993. 3.95 (*1-870516-07-9*) Childs Play.

TUNNELS

see also Subways

Dunn, Andrew. Tunnels. LC 92-43945. (Illus.). 32p. (gr. 5-8). 1993. 13.95 (*1-56847-026-6*) Thomson Lrning.

Epstein, Samuel D. & Epstein, Beryl. Tunnels. (Illus.). 128p. (gr. 5 up). 1985. 14.95 (*0-316-24573-9*) Little.

Gaff, Jackie. Buildings, Bridges & Tunnels. Fisher, Michael, et al, illus. LC 91-212. 40p. (Orig.). (gr. 2-5). 1991. pap. 3.99 (*0-679-80865-5*) Random Bks Yng Read.

Gibbons, Gail. Tunnels. Gibbons, Gail, illus. LC 83-18589. 32p. (ps-3). 1984. reinforced bdg. 15.95 (*0-8234-0507-9*); pap. 5.95 (*0-8234-0670-9*) Holiday.

Pluckrose, Henry. Under the Ground. LC 93-45659. 1994. PLB 11.95 (*0-516-08122-5*) Childrens.

Richardson, Joy. Tunnels. LC 93-30057. (Illus.). 32p. (gr. 2-4). 1994. PLB 11.40 (*0-531-14290-6*) Watts.

Sauvain, Philip. Tunnels. Stefoff, Rebecca, ed. LC 90-40248. (Illus.). 48p. (gr. 4-7). 1990. PLB 17.26 (*0-944483-79-8*) Garrett Ed Corp.

Spangenburg, Ray & Moser, Diane K. The Story of America's Tunnels. 96p. (gr. 5 up). 1990. PLB 19.00 (*0-8160-2258-5*) Facts on File.

TURKEY

Bennett, Olivia. Turkish Afternoon. (Illus.). 25p. (gr. 2-4). 1991. 12.95 (*0-237-60119-2*, Pub. by Evans Bros Ltd) Trafalgar.

Department of Geography, Lerner Publications. Turkey in Pictures. (Illus.). 64p. (gr. 5 up). 1988. PLB 17.50 (*0-8225-1831-7*) Lerner Pubns.

Kherdian, David. Road from Home: The Story of an Armenian Girl. LC 78-72511. 256p. (gr. 7 up). 1979. 13.95 (*0-688-80205-2*); PLB 13.93 (*0-688-84205-4*) Greenwillow.

Sheehan, Sean. Turkey. LC 92-35930. 1993. Set. write for info.; 1 vol. 21.95 (*1-85435-576-7*) Marshall Cavendish.

Spencer, William. The Land & People of Turkey. LC 89-2421. (Illus.). 224p. (gr. 6 up). 1990. (Lipp Jr Bks); PLB 14.89 (*0-397-32364-6*, Lipp Jr Bks) HarpC Child Bks.

TURKEY–FICTION

Bruni, Mary-Ann S. Elif: Child of Turkey. (Illus.). 48p. (gr. k-8). 1988. 12.95 (*0-935857-13-3*); pap. text ed. write for info. (*0-935857-14-1*) Texart.

Chetin, Helen. Perihan's Promise: An American Teen Visits Turkey. LC 91-67696. (Illus.). 140p. (gr. 4-9). 1992. pap. 10.95 (*0-938678-13-2*) New Seed. Keeping a promise to her father when she travels to visit her grandmother in Turkey, 14-year-old Perihan keeps a journal for the summer. It's not a stuffy diary, but a reflective, upbeat dialogue with herself about feelings & experiences in a home away from home. Customs, ceremonies, games, clothes, foods & lots of real conversations paint a picture of growing up in another world. Perihan's journey not only takes her to the other side of the world but to a space away from everyday matters where distance equals perspective. Among other things, she attends a village wedding, witnesses an elopement, experiences an earthquake & learns a lot about familial love & tolerance. Both the author & illustrator are American women who have lived in Turkey & raised Turkish-American children. New Seed Press publishes children's books that support people of ethnic diversity, children of different cultures working & playing together & people who take responsibility for their families. Some books are bilingual Spanish - English & one is Chinese - English. Write for a brochure. P. O. Box 9488, Berkeley, CA 94709.
Publisher Provided Annotation.

Hicyilmaz, Gaye. Against the Storm. 176p. (gr. 7 up). 1992. 14.95 (*0-316-36078-3*, Joy St Bks) Little.

St. Pierre, Stephanie. Where's That Turkey Lurking? Book & Cookie Cutter Pack. 16p. (Orig.). (gr. k-3). 1990. pap. 3.95 (*0-590-68984-3*) Scholastic Inc.

TURKEYS

Fowler, Allan. Turkeys That Fly & Turkeys That Don't. LC 94-14765. (Illus.). 32p. (ps-2). 1994. PLB 14.40 (*0-516-06029-5*); pap. 3.95 (*0-516-46029-3*) Childrens.

Patent, Dorothy H. Wild Turkey, Tame Turkey. Munoz, William, illus. LC 89-613. 64p. (gr. 3-6). 1989. 14.45 (*0-89919-704-3*, Clarion Bks) HM.

TURKEYS–FICTION

Balian, Lorna. Sometimes It's Turkey, Sometimes It's Feathers. Balian, Lorna, illus. 32p. (ps-3). 1987. Repr. of 1973 ed. 7.50 (*0-687-37106-6*) Humbug Bks.

Cohen, Miriam. Don't Eat Too Much Turkey. (gr. k-6). 1988. pap. 3.25 (*0-440-40106-2*, YB) Dell.

Patent, Dorothy H. Wild Turkey, Tame Turkey. (gr. 4-7). 1992. pap. 5.70 (*0-395-55275-3*, Clarion Bks) HM.

Smith, Janice L. The Turkeys' Side of It. Gackenbach, Dick, illus. LC 89-78419. 64p. (gr. 1-4). 1992. pap. 3.95 (*0-06-440452-8*, Trophy) HarpC Child Bks.

Turkey in the Straw. (ps-1). Date not set. pap. 7.50 (*0-932970-93-1*) Prinit Pr.

Walters-Lucy, Jean. Look Ma, I'm Flying. Tabesh, Delight, ed. & illus. LC 92-13953. 48p. (Orig.). (ps-5). 1992. pap. 6.95 perfect bdg. (*0-941992-28-4*) Los Arboles Pub.

TURNER, NAT, 1800-1831

Bisson, Terry. Nat Turner. King, Coretta Scott, intro. by. (Illus.). 112p. (Orig.). (gr. 5 up). 1988. 17.95 (*1-55546-613-3*); pap. 9.95 (*0-7910-0214-4*) Chelsea Hse.

Goldman, Martin S. Nat Turner: And the Southampton Revolt of 1831. LC 91-36618. (Illus.). 160p. (gr. 9-12). 1992. PLB 14.40 (*0-531-13011-8*) Watts.

TURTLES

Addison-Wesley Staff. El Conejo la Tortuga - Big Book. (SPA., Illus.). 16p. (gr. k-3). 1989. pap. text ed. 31.75 (*0-201-19937-8*) Addison-Wesley.

—El Conejo la Tortuga - Little Book. (SPA., Illus.). 16p. (gr. k-3). 1989. pap. text ed. 4.50 (*0-201-19709-X*) Addison-Wesley.

—The Hare & the Tortoise Little Book. (Illus.). 16p. (gr. k-3). 1989. pap. text ed. 4.50 (*0-201-19365-5*) Addison-Wesley.

Ancona, George. Turtle Watch. Ancona, George, photos by. LC 87-9316. (Illus.). 48p. (gr. 1-5). 1987. RSBE 14.95 (*0-02-700910-6*, Macmillan Child Bk) Macmillan Child Grp.

Arnold, Caroline. Sea Turtles. Peck, Marshall, illus. LC 93-6353. 1994. 3.95 (*0-590-46945-2*) Scholastic Inc.

Berger, Melvin. Look Out for Turtles! Lloyd, Megan, illus. LC 90-36894. 32p. (gr. k-4). 1992. 15.00 (*0-06-022539-4*); PLB 14.89 (*0-06-022540-8*) HarpC Child Bks.

Cherrill, Paul. Ten Tiny Turtles. Cherrill, Paul, illus. 32p. (ps-2). 1995. 13.95 (*0-395-71250-5*) Ticknor & Flds Bks Yng Read.

Cousteau Society Staff. Turtles. LC 91-32184. (Illus.). 24p. (ps-1). 1992. pap. 3.95 (*0-671-77059-4*, Little Simon) S&S Trade.

Craig, Janet. Turtles. Kelleher, Kathie, illus. LC 81-11448. 32p. (gr. k-2). 1982. PLB 11.59 (*0-89375-664-4*); pap. 2.95 (*0-89375-665-2*) Troll Assocs.

Fichter, George S. Turtles, Toads, & Frogs. Ambler, Barbara H., illus. 36p. (gr. k-3). 1993. 4.95 (*0-307-11433-3*, 11433, Golden Pr) Western Pub.

Fowler, Allan. Las Tortugas So Se Apuran - Turtles Take Their Time. LC 92-7403. (SPA., Illus.). 32p. (ps-2). 1993. big bk. 30.60 (*0-516-59632-2*); PLB 13.93 (*0-516-36005-1*); pap. 3.95 (*0-516-56005-0*) Childrens.

—Turtles Take Their Time. LC 92-7403. (Illus.). 32p. (ps-2). 1992. PLB 10.75 (*0-516-06005-8*); big bk. 22. 95 (*0-516-49632-8*) Childrens.

—Turtles Take Their Time. LC 92-7403. (Illus.). 32p. (ps-2). 1993. pap. 3.95 (*0-516-46005-6*) Childrens.

Frisch. Turtles. 1991. 11.95s.p. (*0-86625-194-4*) Rourke Pubns.

Funston, Sylvia. Leatherback Turtle. Kassian, Olena, illus. 32p. (gr. 1-5). 1992. 4.95 (*0-920775-97-7*, Pub. by Greey de Pencier CN) Firefly Bks Ltd.

Gerholdt, James E. Turtles & Tortoises. LC 94-10696. 1994. write for info. (*1-56239-308-1*) Abdo & Dghtrs.

Hawcock, David. Turtle. (ps). 1994. 3.95 (*0-307-17305-4*, Artsts Writrs) Western Pub.

Holling, Holling C. Minn of the Mississippi. (Illus.). (gr. 4-6). 1992. 16.95 (*0-395-17578-X*) HM.

Kuhn, Dwight R., photos by. Turtle's Day. Hirschi, Ron, text by. LC 93-9006. 1994. write for info. (*0-525-65172-1*, Cobblehill Bks) Nal-Dutton.

Martin, L. Turtles. (Illus.). 24p. (gr. k-5). 1989. lib. bdg. 11.94 (*0-86592-578-X*); lib. bdg. 8.95s.p. (*0-685-58607-3*) Rourke Corp.

Oda, Hidetomo. The Turtle. Pohl, Kathy, ed. LC 85-28234. (Illus.). 32p. (gr. 3-7). 1986. PLB 10.95 (*0-8172-2547-1*) Raintree Steck-V.

Papastavrou, Vassili. Turtles & Tortoises. LC 91-20098. (Illus.). 32p. (gr. 2-5). 1992. PLB 12.40 (*0-531-18453-6*, Pub. by Bookwright Pr) Watts.

Propper. Turtle, Reading Level 3-4. (Illus.). 28p. (gr. 2-5). 1983. PLB 16.67 (*0-86592-856-8*); PLB 12.50s.p. (*0-685-58828-9*) Rourke Corp.

Schafer, Susan. The Galapagos Tortoise. LC 92-7396. (Illus.). 64p. (gr. 4 up). 1992. text ed. 13.95 RSBE (*0-87518-544-4*, Dillon) Macmillan Child Grp.

Serventy, Vincent. Turtle & Tortoise. LC 84-15881. (Illus.). 24p. (gr. k-5). 1985. PLB 9.95 (*0-8172-2403-3*); pap. 3.95 (*0-8114-6891-7*) Raintree Steck-V.

Souza, D. M. What's under that Shell? (Illus.). 40p. (gr. 1-4). 1992. 17.50 (*0-87614-712-0*) Carolrhoda Bks.

Staub, Frank. Sea Turtles. LC 94-4630. (Illus.). 48p. (gr. 2-3). 1994. PLB 18.95 (*0-8225-3005-8*) Lerner Pubns.

Stone, Lynn M. Sea Turtles. LC 93-15691. 1993. write for info. (*0-86593-296-4*) Rourke Corp.

Tortoise. 1989. 3.50 (*1-87865-734-8*) Blue Q.

Turtles. 1991. PLB 14.95 (*0-88682-411-7*) Creative Ed.

White, William, Jr. All about the Turtle. LC 91-41301. (Illus.). 72p. (gr. 7-12). 1992. 14.95 (*0-8069-8276-4*) Sterling.

Wildlife Education, Ltd. Staff. Turtles. Bliss, Rebecca & Stuart, Walter, illus. 24p. (gr. 5 up). 1992. 13.95 (*0-937934-89-5*) Wildlife Educ.

TURTLES–FICTION

Bailey, Jill. Operation Turtle. Green, John, illus. LC 91-19874. 48p. (gr. 3-7). 1992. PLB 21.34 (*0-8114-2713-7*); pap. 4.95 (*0-8114-6546-2*) Raintree Steck-V.

Brown, Ryan & Clarrian, Dean. The Collected Teenage Mutant Ninja Turtles Adventures, Vol. 1. Gaydos, Michael, et al, illus. 96p. 1991. pap. 5.95 (*1-879450-03-8*) Tundra MA.

—The Collected Teenage Mutant Ninja Turtles Adventures, Vol. 2. Mitchroney, Ken, et al, illus. 88p. 1991. pap. 5.95 (*1-879450-04-6*) Tundra MA.

Brown, Ryan, et al. Teenage Mutant Ninja Turtles, Vol. 1. Berger, Dan, et al, illus. 150p. 1990. pap. 9.95 (*1-879450-00-3*) Tundra MA.

Buckley, Richard. The Foolish Tortoise. Carle, Eric, illus. LC 93-20123. (gr. 1-8). 1993. pap. 4.95 (*0-88708-323-4*) Picture Bk Studio.

Castle, Caroline, retold by. Hare & the Tortoise. Weevers, Peter, illus. LC 84-9569. 32p. (ps-3). 1987. pap. 4.95 (*0-8037-0147-0*) Dial Bks Young.

Chottin, Ariane. A Home for Little Turtle. Wirth, Pascale, illus. LC 91-40650. 24p. (ps-3). 1992. 6.99 (*0-89577-420-8*, Dist. by Random) RD Assn.

Clarrain, Dean & Brown, Ryan. Collected Teenage Mutant Ninja Turtles Adventures, Vol. 3. Mutchroney, Ken, et al, illus. 88p. 1991. pap. 5.95 (*1-879450-05-4*) Tundra MA.

—The Collected Teenage Mutant Ninja Turtles Adventures, Vol. 4. Mitchroney, Ken, et al, illus. 88p. 1991. pap. 5.95 (*1-879450-06-2*) Tundra MA.

Dahl, Roald. Esio Trot. Blake, Quentin, illus. 1990. 14.95 (*0-670-83451-3*) Viking Child Bks.

—Esio Trot. Blake, Quentin, illus. LC 92-16931. 64p. (gr. 3-7). 1992. pap. 3.99 (*0-14-036099-9*) Puffin Bks.

De Brunhoff, Laurent. Gregory & the Turtle. 1971. 3.95 (*0-394-82321-4*) Pantheon.

Dodd, Lynley. Smallest Turtle. Dodd, Lynley, illus. LC 85-9771. 29p. (gr. 1-2). 1985. PLB 17.27 (*0-918831-07-5*) Gareth Stevens Inc.

Dr. Seuss. Yertle the Turtle & Other Stories. Dr. Seuss, illus. (gr. k-3). 1958. 14.00 (*0-394-80087-7*); PLB 13. 99 (*0-394-90087-1*) Random Bks Yng Read.

—Yertle the Turtle & Other Stories. reissue ed. Lithgow, John, narrated by. Dr. Seuss, illus. 80p. (ps). 1992. pap. 14.00 incl. cass. (*0-679-83229-7*) Random Bks Yng Read.

Eastman, Kevin & Laird, Peter. Teenage Mutant Ninja Turtles in Intergalactic Wrestling & Other Adventures. Eastman, Kevin & Laird, Peter, illus. 96p. (Orig.). (gr. 2-8). 1991. pap. 6.95 incls. cassette (*0-679-81747-6*) Random Bks Yng Read.

Edler, Timothy J. Maurice the Snake & Gaston the Near-Sighted Turtle: Tim Edler's Tales from the Atchafalaya. (Illus.). 36p. (gr. k-8). 1977. pap. 6.00 (*0-931108-00-4*) Little Cajun Bks.

Florian, Douglas. Turtle Day. Florian, Douglas, illus. LC 88-30321. 32p. (ps-2). 1989. (Crowell Jr Bks); PLB 13. 89 (*0-690-04745-2*, Crowell Jr Bks) HarpC Child Bks.

Fontenot, Mary A. Clovis Crawfish & Bidon Box Turtle. Blazek, Scott R., illus. LC 93-44340. 1996. write for info. (*1-56554-057-3*) Pelican.

Galdone, Paul. The Turtle & the Monkey. Galdone, Paul, illus. 32p. (ps-3). 1990. pap. 6.95 (*0-395-54425-4*, Clarion Bks) HM.

George, William T. Box Turtle at Long Pond. George, Lindsay B., illus. LC 88-18787. 24p. (ps-1). 1989. 15. 00 (*0-688-08184-3*); PLB 14.93 (*0-688-08185-1*) Greenwillow.

Gilbert, Frances. Turtle on a Summer Day. Gilbert, Sara, illus. LC 94-75988. 32p. (ps-2). 1994. 14.95 (*1-880851-15-6*) Greene Bark Pr.

Goldsmith, Howard. Toto the Timid Turtle. LC 80-15096. (Illus.). 32p. (ps-3). 1980. 16.95 (*0-87705-525-4*) Human Sci Pr.

Greene, Elizabeth. Turtle Soup. LC 91-67766. (Illus.). 64p. 1993. pap. 7.00 (*1-56002-166-7*, Univ Edtns) Aegina Pr.

Greene, Shelley. Teenage Mutant Ninja Turtles Totally Awesome Activity Book. Lawson, Jim & Burger, Dan, illus. 96p. (gr. 1-5). 1990. pap. 3.95 (*0-679-81108-7*) Random Bks Yng Read.

Haas, Dorothy. Two Friends Too Many. (gr. 4-7). 1990. pap. 2.50 (*0-590-43557-4*) Scholastic Inc.

Hadithi, Mwenye. Tricky Tortoise. Kennaway, Adrienne, illus. (ps-3). 1988. 15.95 (*0-316-33724-2*) Little.

Hiller, B. B. M-TV. (gr. 4-7). 1991. pap. 3.50 (*0-440-40451-7*) Dell.

—The Sacred Scroll of Death. (gr. 4-7). 1993. pap. 3.99 (*0-440-40800-8*) Dell.

—Teenage Mutant Ninja Turtles. 1990. pap. 2.95 (*0-440-40322-7*) Dell.

—Teenage Mutant Ninja Turtles. 94p. 1991. text ed. 7.52 (*1-56956-320-9*) W A T Braille.

Hoban, Lillian. Stick-in-the-Mud-Turtle. (ps-3). 1992. pap. 2.99 (*0-440-40622-6*) Dell.

—Turtle Spring. (ps-3). 1992. pap. 2.99 (*0-440-40606-4*) Dell.

Holm, Astrid. Teenage Mutant Ninja Turtles: School Daze. Mateu, Franc, illus. LC 90-61185. 32p. (Orig.). (ps-3). 1991. pap. 1.50 (*0-679-81169-9*) Random Bks Yng Read.

Holm, Astrid, adapted by. Teenage Mutant Ninja Turtles: A Visit to Stump Asteroid. Herbert, S. I., illus. LC 90-61217. 48p. (Orig.). (ps-3). 1991. pap. 1.50 (*0-679-81170-2*) Random Bks Yng Read.

Hudson, Eleanor. Teenage Mutant Ninja Turtles Pizza Party: A Step 1 Book - Preschool-Grade 1. Herbert, S. I., illus. LC 90-53243. 32p. (Orig.). (ps-1). 1991. PLB 7.99 (*0-679-91452-8*); pap. 3.50 (*0-679-81452-3*) Random Bks Yng Read.

Katz, Avner. Tortoise Solves a Problem. Katz, Avner, illus. LC 91-32503. 40p. (gr. k-3). 1993. 13.00 (*0-06-020798-1*); PLB 12.89 (*0-06-020799-X*) HarpC Child Bks.

Kessler, Leonard. Old Turtle's Winter Games. (gr. k-6). 1990. pap. 2.95 (*0-440-40261-1*, YB) Dell.

Kraus, Robert, ed. & illus. Wise Old Owl's Canoe Trip Adventure. LC 91-39014. 32p. (ps-3). 1993. text ed. 10.89 (*0-8167-2947-6*); 2.95 (*0-8167-2948-4*) Troll Assocs.

Leditschke, Anna. Tiny Timothy Turtle. McLean-Carr, Carol, illus. 32p. (ps-2). 1991. PLB 18.60 (*0-8368-0667-0*) Gareth Stevens Inc.

Leedy, Loreen. Tracks in the Sand. LC 92-3405. (ps-3). 1993. 15.95 (*0-385-30658-X*) Doubleday.

Lewis, Rob. Tidy up, Trevor. LC 92-30327. (ps-3). 1993. 13.95 (*0-15-200626-5*) HarBrace.

McDonnell, Janet. Turtle's Adventure in Alphabet Town. McDonnell, Janet, illus. LC 92-2984. 32p. (ps-2). 1992. PLB 11.80 (*0-516-05420-1*) Childrens.

MacGill-Callahan, Sheila. And Still the Turtle Watched. (ps-3). 1991. 14.95 (*0-8037-0931-5*); PLB 14.89 (*0-8037-0932-3*) Dial Bks Young.

McGuire-Turcotte, Casey A. How Honu the Turtle Got His Shell. Sakahara, Dick, illus. 30p. (gr. k up). 1991. PLB 19.97 (*0-8172-2783-0*); pap. 3.95 (*0-8114-4304-3*) Raintree Steck-V.

Maury, Jean-Pierre. The Turtleons Are Coming. (Illus.). 48p. (gr. 3-8). 1990. 8.95 (*0-89565-810-0*) Childs World.

Monsell, Mary E. Toohy & Wood. Tryon, Leslie, illus. LC 91-38217. 64p. (gr. 2-5). 1992. SBE 12.95 (*0-689-31721-2*, Atheneum Child Bk) Macmillan Child Grp.

Morris, Dave. Dinosaur Farm. (gr. 4-7). 1991. pap. 3.50 (*0-440-40491-6*) Dell.

—Splinter to the Fore. (gr. 4-7). 1991. pap. 3.50 (*0-440-40492-4*) Dell.

Murphy, Stephen. Monsters among Us: Teenage Mutant Ninja Turtles. 16p. (ps-2). 1993. write for info. (*1-883366-09-7*) YES Ent.

—The Mystery of the Missing Pizza: Teenage Mutant Ninja Turtles. 16p. (ps-2). 1993. write for info. (*1-883366-08-9*) YES Ent.

O'Donnell, Elizabeth L. I Can't Get My Turtle to Move. Chambliss, Maxie, illus. LC 88-22046. 32p. (ps-1). 1989. 11.95 (*0-688-07323-9*); PLB 11.88 (*0-688-07324-7*, Morrow Jr Bks) Morrow Jr Bks.

Oke, Janette. The Impatient Turtle. Peterson, Pete, ed. Mann, Brenda, illus. 110p. (Orig.). (gr. 3-6). 1986. pap. 4.99 (*0-934998-24-8*) Bethel Pub.

Perkins, Anne T. Turtles. Lomax, James, illus. 8p. (ps-k). 1993. 12.00 (*1-884204-00-7*) Teach Nxt Door.

Peters, Tim, ed. Toby Turtle Takes a Tumble. (Illus.). (ps-2). pap. 4.95 (*1-879874-29-6*) T Peters & Co.

Powell, Pamela. The Turtle Watchers. LC 92-5822. 160p. (gr. 3-7). 1992. 13.00 (*0-670-84294-X*) Viking Child Bks.

Robie, Joan H. Teenage Mutant Ninja Turtles Exposed. (gr. 2 up). 1991. pap. 5.95 (*0-914984-31-4*) Starburst.

Roger, Alan. Blue Tortoise. Roger, Alan, illus. LC 90-9833. 16p. (ps-1). 1990. PLB 13.27 (*0-8368-0404-X*) Gareth Stevens Inc.

Ross, Andrea. All about Turtles. LC 89-92455. 24p. (ps-3). 1990. incl. cass. 5.95x (*0-943864-59-3*) Davenport.

Sanfield, Steve. The Great Turtle Drive. Zimmer, Dirk, illus. LC 93-43753. 1994. write for info. (*0-679-85834-2*); lib. bdg. write for info. (*0-679-95834-7*) Knopf.

Schindel, John. I'll Meet You Halfway. Watts, James, illus. LC 91-44019. 32p. (ps-2). 1993. SBE 14.95 (*0-689-50564-7*, M K McElderry) Macmillan Child Grp.

Schlachter, Rita. Winter Fun. Swan, Susan, illus. LC 85-14008. 48p. (Orig.). (gr. 1-3). 1986. PLB 10.59 (*0-8167-0584-4*); pap. text ed. 3.50 (*0-8167-0585-2*) Troll Assocs.

Scotti, Linda. Mr. Peek-a-Boo. 1993. 7.95 (*0-533-10353-3*) Vantage.

Serventy, Vincent. Turtle & Tortoise. (Illus.). 24p. (gr. 1-4). 1987. pap. 2.50 (*0-590-42133-6*) Scholastic Inc.

The Shy Little Turtle. (Illus.). (ps-2). 1991. PLB 6.95 (*0-8136-5171-9*, TK3873); pap. 3.50 (*0-8136-5671-0*, TK3874) Modern Curr.

Stoddard, Sando. Turtle Time. Munsinger, Lynn, illus. LC 93-39192. (gr. 3 up). 1994. write for info. (*0-395-56754-8*) HM.

Tate, Suzanne. Tammy Turtle: A Tale of Saving Sea Turtles. Melvin, James, illus. LC 91-67275. 28p. (Orig.). (gr. k-3). 1991. PLB 3.95 (*1-878405-05-5*) Nags Head Art.

Teenage Mutant Ninja Turtles, 5 vols. (gr. 4-7). 1990. pap. 14.75 boxed set (*0-440-36030-7*) Dell.

Troughton, Joanna, retold by. Tortoise's Dream: An African Folk Tale. Troughton, Joanna, illus. LC 85-15065. 28p. (ps-2). 1986. PLB 14.95 (*0-87226-039-9*, Bedrick Blackie) P Bedrick Bks.

Turner, Charles. The Turtle & the Moon. Mathis, Melissa B., illus. LC 90-43841. 32p. (ps-2). 1991. 14.00 (*0-525-44659-1*, DCB) Dutton Child Bks.

Turtle & Rabbit. (Illus.). (ps-2). 1991. PLB 6.95 (*0-8136-5086-0*, TK2374); pap. 3.50 (*0-8136-5586-2*, TK2375) Modern Curr.

Ward, Helen. The Moonrat & the White Turtle. 40p. (ps-4). 1992. pap. 4.95 (*0-8249-8580-X*, Ideals Child) Hambleton-Hill.

Williams, Barbara. Albert's Toothache. Chorao, Kay, illus. LC 74-4040. 32p. (ps-1). 1974. (Dutton); pap. 3.95 (*0-525-45037-8*) NAL-Dutton.

Willner-Pardo, Gina. Natalie Spitzer's Turtles. Levine, Abby, ed. Delaney, Molly, illus. LC 92-3342. 32p. (gr. k-3). 1992. 13.95g (*0-8075-5515-0*) A Whitman.

Wood, Douglas. Old Turtle. Cheng-Khee Chee, illus. LC 91-73527. 48p. (ps-2). 1991. 17.95 (*0-938586-48-3*) Pfeifer-Hamilton.

TUSKEGEE NORMAL AND INDUSTRIAL INSTITUTE

Washington, Booker T. Up from Slavery. Andrews, C. A., intro. by. (gr. 5 up). 1967. pap. 2.50 (*0-8049-0157-0*, CL-157) Airmont.

TUTANKHAMON, KING OF EGYPT, 1360 B.C.?

Aldred, Cyril. Tut-Ankh-Amun-& His Friends. (gr. 8). 1977. pap. 3.95 (*0-88388-043-1*) Bellerophon Bk.

—Tutankhmun. (Illus.). (gr. 5). 1978. pap. 2.95 (*0-88388-059-8*) Bellerophon Bks.

Donnelly, Judy. Tut's Mummy: Lost & Found. Watling, James, illus. LC 87-20790. (Orig.). (gr. 2-3). 1988. lib. bdg. 7.99 (*0-394-99189-3*); pap. 3.50 (*0-394-89189-9*) Random Bks Yng Read.

Reeves, Nicholas. Into the Mummy's Tomb: The Real-Life Discovery of Tutankhamun's Treasures. 1992. 16.95 (*0-590-45752-7*, Scholastic Hardcover) Scholastic Inc.

Into the Mummy's Tomb: The Real-Life Discovery of Tutankhamun's Treasures. (gr. 4-7). 1993. pap. 6.95 (*0-590-45753-5*) Scholastic Inc.

Reiff, Stephanie A. Secrets of Tut's Tomb & the Pyramids. LC 77-22770. (Illus.). (gr. 4 up). 1983. PLB 20.70 (*0-8172-1051-2*) Raintree Steck-V.

Sabuda, Robert. Tutankhamen's Gift. Sabuda, Robert, illus. LC 93-5401. 32p. (gr. 1-4). 1994. SBE 15.95 (*0-689-31818-9*, Atheneum Child Bk) Macmillan Child Grp.

Smith, Tony, illus. The Treasures of Tutankhamen. 48p. (gr. 3-5). 1987. 7.95x (*0-86685-453-3*) Intl Bk Ctr.

TWAIN, MARK

see Clemens, Samuel Langhorne, 1835-1910

TWENTIETH CENTURY

Campling, Elizabeth. Portrait of a Decade: 1900-1909. (Illus.). 72p. (gr. 7-11). 1990. 19.95 (*0-7134-5989-1*, Pub. by Batsford UK) Trafalgar.

Duden, Jane & Stewart, Gail B. Nineteen Eighties. LC 90-46827. (Illus.). 48p. (gr. 6). 1991. text ed. 11.95 RSBE (*0-89686-599-1*, Crestwood Hse) Macmillan Child Grp.

Fyson, Nance L. Portrait of a Decade: The 1950s. (Illus.). 72p. (gr. 7-11). 1990. 19.95 (*0-7134-6070-9*, Pub. by Batsford UK) Trafalgar.

TWINS

Anderson, Joan. Twins on Toes: A Ballet Debut. Ancona, George, photos by. LC 92-35104. (Illus.). 32p. (gr. 3-7). 1993. 14.99 (*0-525-67415-2*, Lodestar Bks) Dutton Child Bks.

Brennan, Jan. Born Two-Gether. (Illus.). 40p. (Orig.). (ps-2). Date not set. pap. 5.95 (*0-9613536-1-9*) J & L Bks.

Ingram, Jay. Amazing Investigations: Twins. Chan, Harvey, illus. (gr. 3 up). 1989. pap. 12.95 (*0-671-66263-5*) S&S Trade.

Rosenberg, Maxine B. Being a Twin, Having a Twin. Ancona, George, illus. LC 84-17159. 48p. (gr. 1-4). 1985. 11.95 (*0-688-04328-3*); lib. bdg. 11.88 (*0-688-04329-1*) Lothrop.

TWINS–FICTION

Adler, David A. The Fourth Floor Twins & the Fish Snitch Mystery. Trivas, Irene, illus. 64p. (gr. 1-4). 1986. pap. 3.99 (*0-14-032082-2*, Puffin) Puffin Bks.

—The Fourth Floor Twins & the Fortune Cookie Chase. Trivas, Irene, illus. 64p. (gr. 1-4). 1986. pap. 3.95 (*0-14-032083-0*, Puffin) Puffin Bks.

—The Fourth Floor Twins & the Sand Castle Contest. Trivas, Irene, illus. (gr. 2-5). 1988. 9.95 (*0-318-37432-3*) Viking Child Bks.

Anholt, Catherine. Twins, Two by Two. LC 91-71820. 32p. (ps-3). 1994. pap. 4.99 (*1-56402-397-4*) Candlewick Pr.

Banks, Jacqueline T. New One. (gr. 4-7). 1994. 13.95 (*0-395-66610-4*) HM.

Blackman, Malorie. Girl Wonder & the Terrific Twins. Toft, Lis, illus. LC 92-27667. (gr. 2-5). 1993. 12.99 (*0-525-45065-3*, DCB) Dutton Child Bks.

Bryant, Bonnie. Star Rider. (gr. 4-7). 1991. pap. 3.50 (*0-553-15938-0*) Bantam.

Burgess, Barbara H. Oren Bell. 1991. 15.00 (*0-385-30325-4*) Delacorte.

Burgess, Thornton. Buster Bear's Twins. 1992. Repr. lib. bdg. 17.95x (*0-89966-981-6*) Buccaneer Bks.

Cleary, Beverly. Mitch & Amy. Porter, George, illus. LC 67-10041. 224p. (gr. 3-7). 1967. 15.95 (*0-688-21688-9*); PLB 15.88 (*0-688-31688-3*, Morrow Jr Bks) Morrow Jr Bks.

Cohen, Barbara. The Long Way Home. 176p. 1990. 12.95 (*0-688-09674-3*) Lothrop.

Colli, Monica. Twins. LC 91-36606. 1992. 5.95 (*0-85953-394-8*) Childs Play.

—Twins' Party. (ps-3). 1993. 5.95 (*0-85953-404-9*) Childs Play.

Curry, Jane L. What the Dickens! LC 90-26864. 160p. (gr. 4-7). 1991. SBE 13.95 (*0-689-50524-8*, M K McElderry) Macmillan Child Grp.

—What the Dickens! 160p. (gr. 5 up). 1993. pap. 3.99 (*0-14-036284-3*, Puffin) Puffin Bks.

Davis, Natalie L. The Space Twin. Taylor, Neil, illus. 112p. (gr. 4-8). 1987. 7.95 (*1-55523-037-7*) Winston-Derek.

DeVries, Douglas. Matilda & the Twins. (Illus.). 32p. (Orig.). (ps-3). 1990. pap. text ed. 8.00 (*1-877721-02-6*) Jade Ram Pub.

Djolete, Amu. Twins in Trouble. (ps-3). 1992. pap. 2.95 (*0-7910-2905-0*) Chelsea Hse.

Estern, Anne G. Letters from Philippa. (gr. 4-7). 1991. pap. 3.50 (*0-553-15941-0*) Bantam.

Fakih, Kimberly O. Grandpa Putter & Granny Hoe. Pearson, Tracy C., illus. 128p. (gr. 2-5). 1992. 13.00 (*0-374-32762-9*) FS&G.

Follett, Ken. Power Twins. (gr. 4-7). 1991. pap. 2.75 (*0-590-42507-2*) Scholastic Inc.

Fromm, Pete. Monkey Tag. LC 93-34593. (gr. 4-7). 1994. 14.95 (*0-590-46525-2*) Scholastic Inc.

Givens, Terryl. Dragon Scales & Willow Leaves. Portwood, Andrew, illus. LC 93-665. Date not set. write for info. (*0-399-22619-2*, Putnam) Putnam Pub Group.

Greydanus, Rose. Double Trouble. Rodegast, Roland, illus. LC 81-2358. 32p. (gr. k-2). 1981. PLB 11.59 (*0-89375-529-X*); pap. 2.95 (*0-89375-530-3*) Troll Assocs.

Hope, Laura L. Bobbsey Twins, 4 vols. (gr. 4-7). 1990. pap. 11.80 boxed (*0-671-96364-3*) S&S Trade.

The Bobbsey Twins of Lakeport. Gonzalez, Pepe, illus. 120p. (gr. 2-5). 1989. 4.50 (*0-448-09071-6*, G&D) Putnam Pub Group.

—The Case of the Tricky Trickster. Greenberg, Anne, ed. Henderson, David F., illus. 96p. (Orig.). 1992. pap. 2.99 (*0-671-73041-X*) PB.

—The Case of the Vanishing Video. Greenberg, Ann, ed. Henderson, David F., illus. 96p. (Orig.). 1992. pap. 2.99 (*0-671-73040-1*) PB.

—The Clue at Casper Creek. Greenberg, Anne, ed. Henderson, David F., illus. 96p. (Orig.). 1991. pap. 2.99 (*0-671-73038-X*, Minstrel Bks) PB.

—The Monster Mouse Mystery. Greenberg, Ann, ed. Barrett, Randy, illus. 96p. (Orig.). 1991. pap. 2.95 (*0-671-69295-X*, Minstrel Bks) PB.

—Mystery at School. Gonzalez, Pepe, illus. 120p. (gr. 2-5). 1989. 5.95 (*0-448-09074-0*, G&D) Putnam Pub Group.

—The Secret at the Seashore. Gonzalez, Pepe, illus. 120p. (gr. 2-5). 1989. 5.95 (*0-448-09073-2*, G&D) Putnam Pub Group.

Johnson, Lindsay L. & Kowitt, Holly. A Week with Zeke & Zach. (Illus.). 64p. (gr. 2-5). 1993. 11.99 (*0-525-45097-1*, DCB) Dutton Child Bks.

Lasky, Kathryn. Shadows in the Water: A Starbuck Family Adventure. LC 92-8139. 1992. 16.95 (*0-15-273533-X*, HB Juv Bks); pap. write for info. (*0-15-273534-8*) HarBrace.

—Voice in the Wind: A Starbuck Family Adventure. (gr. 4-7). 1993. 16.95 (*0-15-294102-9*, HB Juv Bks); pap. 6.95 (*0-15-294103-7*) HarBrace.

Lattimore, Deborah N. Punga: The Goddess of Ugly. LC 92-23191. 32p. 1993. 14.95 (*0-15-292862-6*) HarBrace.

Leaf, Munro. The Story of Simpson & Sampson. Lawson, Robert, illus. LC 88-39014. 64p. (gr. 1-3). 1989. Repr. of 1941 ed. lib. bdg. 16.50 (*0-208-02244-9*, Pub. by Linnet) Shoe String.

Lindbergh, Anne M. Three Lives to Live. 192p. (gr. 3-7). 1992. 14.95 (*0-316-52628-2*) Little.

McIntire, Jamie. Santa's Christmas Surprise. Henry, Steve, illus. LC 93-24843. (gr. k-3). 1993. pap. text ed. 2.95 (*0-8167-3257-4*) Troll Assocs.

McKissack, Patricia. Who Is Who? LC 83-7361. (Illus.). 32p. (ps-2). 1983. PLB 10.25 (*0-516-02042-0*); pap. 2.95 (*0-516-42042-9*) Childrens.

Maguire, Gregory. Missing Sisters. LC 93-8300. 160p. (gr. 5-9). 1994. SBE 14.95 (*0-689-50590-6*, M K McElderry) Macmillan Child Grp.

Martin, Ann M. Mallory & the Trouble with Twins. 1993. pap. 3.25 (*0-590-43507-8*) Scholastic Inc.

Me & the Terrible Twins. 1986. pap. 1.25 (*0-440-82080-4*) Dell.

Mills, Adam. Cold Chills. (gr. 4 up). 1989. pap. 2.95 (*0-345-35929-1*) Ballantine.

Mulford, Philippa G. The World Is My Eggshell. LC 85-16198. (gr. 7 up). 1986. pap. 14.95 (*0-385-29432-8*) Delacorte.

Neasi, Barbara. Just Like Me. Axeman, Lois, illus. LC 83-23154. 32p. (ps-2). 1984. lib. bdg. 10.25 (*0-516-02047-1*); pap. 2.95 (*0-516-42047-X*) Childrens.

Pascal, Francine. Against the Rules. 1987. pap. 3.25 (*0-553-15676-4*) Bantam.

—Amy Moves In. (gr. 4-7). 1991. pap. 3.25 (*0-553-15837-6*) Bantam.

—April Fool! 1989. pap. 3.50 (*0-553-15688-8*) Bantam.

—The Big Party Weekend. (gr. 4-7). 1991. pap. 3.25 (*0-553-15952-6*) Bantam.

—Boys Against Girls. 1988. pap. 3.25 (*0-553-15666-7*) Bantam.

—Brooke & Her Rock Star Mom. 1992. pap. 3.25 (*0-553-15965-8*) Bantam.

—Buried Treasure. 1987. pap. 3.25 (*0-553-15692-6*) Bantam.

—Center of Attention. 1988. pap. 2.50 (*0-553-15581-4*, Skylark) Bantam.

—Choosing Sides. 1986. pap. 3.25 (*0-553-15658-6*) Bantam.

—Elizabeth's First Kiss. (gr. 4-7). 1990. pap. 3.25 (*0-553-15835-X*) Bantam.

—The Evil Twin. 1993. pap. 3.99 (*0-553-29857-7*) Bantam.

—Haunted House. 1986. pap. 3.25 (*0-553-15657-8*) Bantam.

—Holiday Mischief. 144p. 1988. pap. 3.75 (*0-553-15641-1*, Skylark) Bantam.

—Jessica & the Brat Attack. 1989. pap. 3.50 (*0-553-15695-0*) Bantam.

—Jessica's Secret. (gr. 4-7). 1990. pap. 3.25 (*0-553-15824-4*) Bantam.

—Left Behind. 112p. (Orig.). 1988. pap. 3.25 (*0-553-15609-8*, Skylark) Bantam.

—Lila's Music Video. (gr. 4-7). 1993. pap. 3.25 (*0-553-48059-6*) Bantam.

—Lucky Takes the Reins. (gr. 4-7). 1991. pap. 3.50 (*0-553-15843-0*) Bantam.

—The New Girl. 96p. (Orig.). (gr. 7-12). 1987. pap. 2.50 (*0-553-15475-3*, Skylark) Bantam.

—One of the Gang. 1987. pap. 3.25 (*0-553-15677-2*) Bantam.
—Poor Lila! (gr. 4-7). 1992. pap. 3.50 (*0-553-15962-3*) Bantam.
—Sneaking Out. 1987. pap. 3.50 (*0-553-15659-4*) Bantam.
—Sweet Valley Twins. 1987. pap. 1.25 (*0-440-82187-8*) Dell.
—Sweet Valley Twins First. 1987. pap. 1.25 (*0-440-82138-X*) Dell.
—The Twins & the Wild West. (gr. 3-6). 1990. pap. 2.99 (*0-553-15811-2*) Bantam.
—The Twin's Big Pow-Wow. (ps-3). 1993. pap. 2.99 (*0-553-48098-7*) Bantam.
—The Twins Get Caught. (gr. 4 up). 1990. pap. 3.25 (*0-553-15810-4*) Bantam.
—The Twins Go to the Hospital. (gr. 4-7). 1991. pap. 2.99 (*0-553-15912-7*) Bantam.
—War Between the Twins. (gr. 4-7). 1990. pap. 3.25 (*0-553-15779-5*) Bantam.
—Yours for a Day. (gr. 4-7). 1994. pap. 3.50 (*0-553-48096-0*) Bantam.
Pascal, Francine, created by. Tug of War. 112p. (Orig.). (gr. 7-12). 1987. pap. 3.50 (*0-553-15663-2*, Skylark) Bantam.
Paterson, Katherine. Jacob Have I Loved. LC 80-668. 228p. (gr. 7 up). 1980. 14.00 (*0-690-04078-4*, Crowell Jr Bks); PLB 13.89 (*0-690-04079-2*, Crowell Jr Bks) HarpC Child Bks.
Pfeffer. Twin Troubles. 1994. pap. 4.95 (*0-8050-3272-X*) H Holt & Co.
Pfeffer, Susan B. Twin Surprises. Carter, Abby, illus. 64p. (gr. 2-4). 1991. 13.95 (*0-8050-1850-6*, Redfeather BYR) H Holt & Co.
—Twin Surprises. Carter, Abby, illus. LC 91-13968. 64p. (gr. 2-4). 1993. pap. 4.95 (*0-8050-2626-6*, Redfeather BYR) H Holt & Co.
Radley, Gail. Oakley Duster Day. LC 94-10858. 1995. 14.00 (*0-02-775792-7*) Macmillan Child Grp.
Richardson, Jean. Out of Step: The Twins Were So Alike. ..but So Different. Holmes, Dawn, illus. LC 92-39666. 28p. (ps-3). 1993. 12.95 (*0-8120-5790-2*); pap. 5.95 (*0-8120-1553-3*) Barron.
Rogers, George L. Mac & Zach from Hackensack. Eskander, Stefanie C., illus. 32p. (gr. k-6). 1992. PLB 12.95 (*0-938399-07-1*); pap. 4.95 (*0-938399-06-3*) Acorn Pub MN.
Rogers, Mary. The Twins' First Bike. 34p. (gr. 1). 1992. pap. text ed. 23.00 big bk. (*1-56843-019-1*); pap. text ed. 4.50 (*1-56843-069-8*) BGR Pub.
Roy, J. Soul Daddy. 1992. 16.95 (*0-15-277193-X*, HB Juv Bks) HarBrace.
Ryan, Mary E. Me, My Sister, & I. LC 92-368. 1992. pap. 15.00 (*0-671-73851-8*, S&S BFYR) S&S Trade.
—My Sister Is Driving Me Crazy. LC 90-41263. 224p. (gr. 5-9). 1991. pap. 15.00 jacketed, 3-pc. bdg. (*0-671-73203-X*, S&S BFYR) S&S Trade.
Scott, Michael. Gemini Game. LC 93-39972. 160p. 1994. 14.95 (*0-8234-1092-7*) Holiday.
Silverberg, Robert. Project Pendulum. (gr. 8 up). 1987. 15.95 (*0-8027-6712-5*) Walker & Co.
Snyder, Carol. One Up, One Down. Chambliss, Maxie, illus. LC 93-36282. 1995. 16.00 (*0-689-31828-6*, Atheneum) Macmillan.
Springer, Nancy. The Great Pony Hassle. Duffy, Daniel M., illus. LC 92-34781. (gr. 3-7). 1993. 12.99 (*0-8037-1306-1*); PLB 13.89 (*0-8037-1308-8*) Dial Bks Young.
Stahl, Hilda. The Tyler Twins, No. 3: Pet Show Panic. 144p. (gr. 4-7). 1990. pap. 4.99 (*0-8423-7633-X*) Tyndale.
—The Tyler Twins, No. 5: Tree House Hideaway. 128p. (gr. 4-7). 1990. pap. 4.99 (*0-8423-7635-6*) Tyndale.
Steiber, Ellen. Eighth Grade Changes Everything. LC 91-2495. 128p. (gr. 6-9). 1992. lib. bdg. 9.89 (*0-8167-2390-7*); pap. text ed. 2.95 (*0-8167-2391-5*) Troll Assocs.
Suzanne, Jamie. Against the Rules. large type ed. Pascal, Francine, created by. 104p. (gr. 7-12). 1991. Repr. of 1987 ed. 9.95 (*1-55905-072-1*) Grey Castle.
—Choosing Sides. large type ed. Pascal, Francine, created by. 104p. (gr. 7-12). 1990. Repr. of 1986 ed. 9.95 (*1-55905-067-5*) Grey Castle.
—First Place. large type ed. Pascal, Francine, created by. 106p. (gr. 7-12). 1991. Repr. of 1987 ed. 9.95 (*1-55905-071-3*) Grey Castle.
—One of the Gang. large type ed. Pascal, Francine, created by. 104p. (gr. 7-12). 1991. Repr. of 1987 ed. 9.95 (*1-55905-073-X*) Grey Castle.
—Sneaking Out. large type ed. Pascal, Francine, created by. 106p. (gr. 7-12). 1990. Repr. of 1987 ed. 9.95 (*1-55905-068-3*) Grey Castle.
—Sweet Valley Twins, 10 bks. large type ed. Pascal, Francine, created by. (gr. 7-12). 1990. Repr. Set. 99.50 (*1-55905-074-8*) Grey Castle.
—Three's a Crowd. large type ed. Pascal, Francine, created by. 105p. (gr. 7-12). 1990. Repr. of 1987 ed. 9.95 (*1-55905-070-5*) Grey Castle.
Wallace, Barbara B. The Twin in the Tavern. LC 92-36429. 192p. (gr. 3-7). 1993. SBE 14.95 (*0-689-31846-4*, Atheneum Child Bk) Macmillan Child Grp.
Werlin, Nancy. Are You Alone on Purpose? 1994. 14.95 (*0-395-67350-X*) HM.
Westwood, Chris. Brother of Mine. LC 92-32020. (gr. 5 up). 1993. write for info. (*0-395-66137-4*, Clarion Bks) HM.

TYLER, JOHN, PRESIDENT U.S. 1790-1862
Falkof, Lucille. John Tyler: Tenth President of the United States. Young, Richard G., ed. LC 89-39951. (Illus.). 128p. (gr. 5-9). 1990. PLB 17.26 (*0-944483-60-7*) Garrett Ed Corp.
Lillegard, Dee. John Tyler. LC 87-18202. (Illus.). 100p. (gr. 3 up). 1987. PLB 14.40 (*0-516-01393-9*) Childrens.
TYPESETTING
see also Printing
TYPEWRITING
Andujar, Maria D. & Iglesias, Jose L. Mecanografia Al Dia. rev. ed. (gr. 10 up). 1977. pap. text ed. 3.50 (*0-88345-306-1*, 18482) Prentice ESL.
Marsh, Carole. Typing in Ten Minutes: On Any Keyboard - At Any Age. (Illus.). (gr. k-12). 1994. 24.95 (*1-55609-194-X*); pap. 14.95 (*0-935326-12-X*) Gallopade Pub Group.
Marshall, Grace L. & Haggblade, Berle. Keyboarding & Computer Applications. LC 92-35186. 1994. text ed. 30.95 (*0-538-61877-9*) S-W Pub.
Mountford, Christine. Kids Can Type Too! 32p. (gr. 3-7). 1987. pap. 6.95 (*0-8120-3780-4*) Barron.
Robinson, Jerry W., et al. Applied Keyboarding. LC 93-7454. 1994. text ed. 21.95 (*0-538-62297-0*); text ed. 26.95 (*0-538-62298-9*) S-W Pub.
TYPOGRAPHY
see Printing

U

U BOATS
see Submarines
U. F. O.
see Flying Saucers
U. N.
see United Nations
UGANDA
African Triumph. LC 67-29693. (gr. 3-7). 1978. 3.00 (*0-8198-0225-5*); pap. 2.00 (*0-8198-0226-3*) St Paul Bks.
Lisicky, Paul. Uganda. (Illus.). 96p. (gr. 5 up). 1988. lib. bdg. 14.95 (*1-55546-189-1*) Chelsea Hse.
Sobol, Richard. One More Elephant: The Fight to Save Wildlife in Uganda. Sobol, Richard, photos by. LC 93-45663. 1995. PLB write for info. (*0-525-65179-9*, Cobblehill Bks) Dutton Child Bks.
UKRAINE–FICTION
Larysa & Andrijko Series. (UKR & ENG., Illus.). (gr. 3 up). 1991. Set. 11.75 (*1-882406-04-4*) M A K Pubns.
Maxwell, Cassandre. Yosef's Gift of Many Colors: An Easter Story. Maxwell, Cassandre, illus. LC 92-44189. 32p. (ps-3). 1993. 14.99 (*0-8066-2627-5*, 9-2627) Augsburg Fortress.
ULYSSES
Evslin, Bernard. The Adventures of Ulysses. 1989. pap. 3.25 (*0-590-42599-4*) Scholastic Inc.
Homer. Odyssey. Rouse, William H., tr. (gr. 7 up). 1946. pap. 3.99 (*0-451-62805-5*, Sig Classics) NAL-Dutton.
Uribe, Fernando & Engler, Dan. The Odyssey: A Journey Back Home. CCC of America Staff, illus. 36p. (Orig.). 1992. pap. text ed. write for info. (*1-56814-007-X*) CCC of America.
UMBRELLAS AND PARASOLS–FICTION
Carroll, Jane. The Fly-Away Umbrella. Young, Karen, illus. LC 93-131. 1994. write for info. (*0-383-03687-9*) SRA Schl Grp.
Dundon, Caitlin. Yellow Umbrella. (gr. 2 up). 1994. PLB 15.00 (*0-671-77743-2*, S&S BFYR) S&S Trade.
Mandy's Umbrella. 1989. 2.99 (*0-517-69121-3*) Random Hse Value.
Pinkwater, Daniel M. Roger's Umbrella. Marshall, James, illus. LC 81-2294. 32p. (gr. 1-3). 1982. 11.95 (*0-525-38555-X*, DCB) Dutton Child Bks.
—Roger's Umbrella. Marshall, James, illus. LC 81-2294. 32p. (gr. 1-3). 1985. pap. 3.95 (*0-525-44223-5*, DCB) Dutton Child Bks.
Prelutsky, Jack. Beneath a Blue Umbrella. Williams, Garth, illus. LC 86-19406. 64p. (ps up). 1990. 15.95 (*0-688-06429-9*) Greenwillow.
UNDER WATER EXPLORATION
see Underwater Exploration
UNDERGROUND MOVEMENTS (WORLD WAR, 1939-1945)
see World War, 1939-1945–Underground Movements
UNDERGROUND RAILROAD
see also Slavery in the U. S.
Adler, David A. A Picture Book of Harriet Tubman. Byrd, Samuel, illus. LC 91-19628. 32p. (ps-3). 1992. reinforced bdg. 15.95 (*0-8234-0926-0*) Holiday.
Bial, Raymond. The Underground Railroad. LC 94-19614. 1995. write for info. (*0-395-69937-1*) HM.
Brill, Marlene T. Allen Jay & the Underground Railroad. Porter, Janice L., illus. LC 92-25279. 1993. 14.95 (*0-87614-776-7*); pap. write for info. (*0-87614-605-1*) Carolrhoda Bks.
Connell, Kate. Tales from the Underground Railroad. Heller, Debbe, illus. LC 92-14415. 68p. (gr. 2-5). 1992. PLB 19.97 (*0-8114-7223-X*) Raintree Steck-V.
Cosner, Shaaron. The Underground Railroad. LC 91-18514. (Illus.). 128p. (gr. 9-12). 1991. PLB 13.40 (*0-531-12505-X*) Watts.
Ferris, Jeri. Go Free or Die: A Story about Harriet Tubman. Ritz, Karen, illus. 64p. (gr. 3-6). 1989. pap. 5.95 (*0-87614-504-7*, First Ave Edns) Lerner Pubns.
Hamilton, Virginia. Many Thousand Gone: African-Americans from Slavery to Freedom. Dillon, Leo & Dillon, Diane, illus. LC 89-19988. 160p. (gr. 4-9). 1992. 16.00 (*0-394-82873-9*); PLB 16.99 (*0-394-92873-3*) Knopf Bks Yng Read.
Hansen, Ellen, intro. by. The Underground Railroad: Life on the Road to Freedom. LC 93-72239. (Illus.). 64p. (Orig.). (gr. 5-12). 1993. pap. 4.95 (*1-878668-27-7*) Disc Enter Ltd.
Haskins, Jim. Get On Board: The Story of the Underground Railroad. LC 92-13247. 160p. (gr. 4-7). 1993. 13.95 (*0-590-45418-8*) Scholastic Inc.
Johnson, LaVerne C. Harriet Tubman: Writer. Perry, Craig R., illus. LC 92-35251. 1992. 3.95 (*0-922162-92-1*) Empak Pub.
Marcey, Sally. Choice Adventures, No. 3: The Underground Railroad. (gr. 3-7). 1991. PLB 4.99 (*0-8423-5027-6*) Tyndale.
Petry, Ann. Harriet Tubman: Conductor on the Underground Railway. LC 55-9215. 247p. (gr. 7-11). 1955. 16.95 (*0-690-37236-1*, Crowell Jr Bks) HarpC Child Bks.
Rappaport, Doreen. Escape from Slavery: Five Journeys to Freedom. Lilly, Charles, illus. LC 90-38170. 128p. (gr. 4-7). 1991. 13.00 (*0-06-021631-X*); PLB 12.89 (*0-06-021632-8*) HarpC Child Bks.
Stein, R. Conrad. The Story of the Underground Railroad. LC 82-3801. (Illus.). 32p. (gr. 3-6). 1981. PLB 12.30 (*0-516-04643-8*); pap. 3.95 (*0-516-44643-6*) Childrens.
UNDERGROUND RAILROAD–FICTION
Armstrong, Jennifer. Steal Away. LC 91-18504. 224p. (gr. 6 up). 1992. 15.95 (*0-531-05983-9*); lib. bdg. 15.99 (*0-531-08583-X*) Orchard Bks Watts.
Beatty, Patricia. Who Comes with Cannons? LC 92-6317. 192p. (gr. 5 up). 1992. 14.00 (*0-688-11028-2*) Morrow Jr Bks.
Cromer, Mary L. Stories for Jason. LC 93-37765. 110p. 1993. pap. 8.95 (*0-944350-28-3*) Friends United.
Levine, Ellen. If You Traveled on the Underground Railroad. (gr. 4-7). 1993. pap. 4.95 (*0-590-45156-1*) Scholastic Inc.
Meltzer, Milton. Underground Man. 261p. (gr. 3-7). 1990. 14.95 (*0-15-200617-6*, Gulliver Bks) HarBrace.
—Underground Man. 261p. (gr. 3-7). 1990. pap. 4.95 (*0-15-292846-4*, Odyssey) HarBrace.
Monjo, F. N. The Drinking Gourd. Brenner, Fred, photos by. LC 92-10823. (Illus.). 64p. (gr. k-3). 1970. 14.00 (*0-06-024329-5*); PLB 13.89 (*0-06-024330-9*) HarpC Child Bks.
Ringgold, Faith. Aunt Harriet's Underground in the Sky. Ringgold, Faith, illus. LC 92-20072. 32p. (ps-4). 1993. 16.00 (*0-517-58767-X*); lib. bdg. 17.99 (*0-517-58768-8*) Crown Bks Yng Read.
Rosen, Michael J. A School for Pompey Walker. Robinson, Aminah B., illus. LC 94-6240. 1995. write for info. (*0-15-200114-X*, HB Juv Bks) Harbrace.
Stolz, Mary. Cezanne Pinto. LC 92-46765. 256p. (gr. 7 up). 1994. 15.00 (*0-679-84917-3*) Knopf Bks Yng Read.
Turner, Glennette T. Running for Our Lives. Byrd, Samuel, illus. LC 93-28430. 208p. (gr. 3-7). 1994. 15.95 (*0-8234-1121-4*) Holiday.
Weinberg, Larry. Ghost Hotel. LC 94-2970. (Illus.). 160p. (gr. 3-6). 1994. pap. 2.95 (*0-8167-3420-8*) Troll Assocs.
UNDERGROUND RAILROADS
see Subways
UNDERSEA EXPLORATION
see Underwater Exploration
UNDERSEA TECHNOLOGY
see Oceanography
UNDERSTANDING
see Intellect; Knowledge, Theory of
UNDERWATER EXPLORATION
see also Marine Biology; Skin Diving
Conley, Andrea. Window on the Deep: The Adventures of Underwater Explorer Sylvia Earle. LC 91-17792. (Illus.). 40p. (gr. 5-8). 1991. 14.95 (*0-531-15232-4*); PLB 14.90 (*0-531-11119-9*) Watts.
Crump, Donald J., ed. Hidden Treasures of the Sea. 104p. (gr. 3-8). 1988. PLB 12.50 (*0-87044-663-0*) Natl Geog.
Ferrier, Lucy. Diving the Great Barrier Reef. new ed. LC 75-23411. (Illus.). 32p. (gr. 5-10). 1976. PLB 10.79 (*0-89375-005-0*) Troll Assocs.
Geography Department Staff. Sunk! Exploring Underwater Archaeology. LC 93-42008. 1994. lib. bdg. write for info. (*0-8225-3205-0*, Runestone Pr) Lerner Pubns.
Greenberg, Judith E. & Carey, Helen H. Under the Sea. Tachiera, Andrea, illus. 32p. (gr. 2-4). 1990. 10.95 (*0-8172-3755-0*) Raintree Steck-V.
Hackwell, W. John. Diving to the Past: Recovering Ancient Wrecks. Hackwell, W. John, illus. LC 87-233529. 64p. (gr. 3-7). 1988. RSBE 14.95 (*0-684-18918-6*, Scribners Young Read) Macmillan Child Grp.
Humphrey, Kathryn L. Shipwrecks: Terror & Treasure. LC 91-16962. (Illus.). 64p. (gr. 5-8). 1991. PLB 12.90 (*0-531-20031-0*) Watts.
Johnson, Rebecca L. Diving into Darkness: A Submersible Explores the Sea. (Illus.). 64p. (gr. 5 up). 1989. 22.95 (*0-8225-1587-3*) Lerner Pubns.

McGovern, Ann. Down Under, Down Under: Diving Adventures on the Great Barrier Reef. McGovern, Ann, et al, illus. LC 88-30530. 48p. (gr. 2-6). 1989. SBE 14.95 (*0-02-765770-1*, Macmillan Child Bk) Macmillan Child Grp.

Mackie, D. Undersea. (Illus.). 32p. (gr. 4-9). 1987. pap. 5.95 (*0-88625-156-7*) Durkin Hayes Pub.

Markle, Sandra. Pioneering Ocean Depths. LC 93-33555. 1995. 15.95 (*0-689-31823-5*, Antheneum) Macmillan.

Maynard, Christopher. Submarines. LC 94-640. 32p. (gr. 2-5). 1994. 3.95 (*1-85697-508-8*, Kingfisher LKC) LKC.

Rogers, Daniel. Exploring the Sea. (Illus.). 32p. (gr. 5-8). 1991. 12.40 (*0-531-18389-0*, Pub. by Bookwright Pr) Watts.

Rothman, Cynthia. Under the Sea. 16p. (ps-2). 1994. pap. 14.95 (*1-56784-302-6*) Newbridge Comms.

Starry, Paul & Cleave, Andrew. Underwater. Holmes, David R., et al, illus. LC 92-60795. 32p. (gr. 4-7). 1992. 14.00 (*0-89577-449-6*, Dist. by Random) RD Assn.

Wood, Jenny. Under the Sea. Livingstone, Malcolm, illus. LC 91-7484. 32p. (gr. k-3). 1991. pap. 5.95 (*0-689-71488-2*, Aladdin) Macmillan Child Grp.

UNDERWATER GEOLOGY

see Submarine Geology

UNDERWATER SWIMMING

see Skin Diving

UNICORNS–FICTION

Ada, Alma F. The Unicorn of the West: El Unicornio del Oeste. Zubizarreta, Rosa, tr. Pizer, Abigail, illus. LC 92-7425. (ENG & SPA.). 40p. (gr. 1-3). 1994. English ed. SBE 14.95 (*0-689-31778-6*, Atheneum Child Bk); Spanish ed. SBE 14.95 (*0-689-31916-9*, Atheneum Child Bk) Macmillan Child Grp.

Alden, Laura. Learning about Unicorns. Stasiak, Krystyna, illus. LC 85-9926. 48p. (gr. 2-6). 1985. pap. 4.95 (*0-516-46539-2*) Childrens.

Anderson, J. K. Unicorns-Coloring Book. 1985. pap. 3.95 (*0-88388-086-5*) Bellerophon Bks.

Cherry, Lynne. The Dragon & the Unicorn. LC 92-30321. 1994. write for info. (*0-15-224193-0*) HarBrace.

Cosgrove, Stephen. Morgan & Me. (Illus.). 32p. (Orig.). (gr. 1-4). 1975. pap. 2.95 (*0-8431-0560-7*) Price Stern.

Coville, Bruce. Into the Land of the Unicorns. LC 94-16892. (gr. 3-7). 1994. 12.95 (*0-590-45955-4*) Scholastic Inc.

—Unicorn Treasury: Stories, Poems and Unicorn Lore. (gr. 4-7). 1991. pap. 9.00 (*0-385-41930-9*) Doubleday.

Coville, Bruce & Coville, Katherine. Sarah's Unicorn. LC 79-2408. (Illus.). 48p. (ps-2). 1979. (Lipp Jr Bks); PLB 12.89 (*0-397-31873-1*) HarpC Child Bks.

Coville, Bruce, compiled by. The Unicorn Treasury: Stories, Poems & Unicorn Lore. Hildebrandt, Tim, illus. LC 86-32919. 176p. (gr. 3 up). 1988. pap. 14.95 (*0-385-24000-7*) Doubleday.

Edler, Timothy J. Rhombus: The Cajun Unicorn. (Illus.). 40p. (gr. k up). 1984. pap. 10.00 (*0-931108-10-1*) Little Cajun Bks.

Gibbs, Greg. Willowby's World of Unicorns "Activity Book" 14p. (Orig.). (gr. 2-6). 1984. pap. 4.00x (*0-910349-03-7*) Cloud Ten.

Giblin, James C. The Truth about Unicorns. McDermott, Michael, illus. LC 90-47233. 128p. (gr. 3-7). 1991. 15. 00 (*0-06-022478-9*); PLB 14.89 (*0-06-022479-7*) HarpC Child Bks.

Goodman, Deborah L. The Magic of the Unicorn. 128p. (Orig.). (gr. 4). 1985. pap. 2.25 (*0-553-25242-9*) Bantam.

Greaves, Margaret. The Naming. Baynes, Pauline, illus. 32p. (ps-3). 1993. 14.95 (*0-15-200534-X*) HarBrace.

Hunter, Mollie. Day of the Unicorn. Diamond, Donna, illus. LC 91-44763. 96p. (gr. 2-5). 1994. 14.00 (*0-06-021062-1*, HarpT); PLB 13.89 (*0-06-021063-X*, HarpT) HarpC.

Jones, Shelagh. Save the Unicorns. Myler, Terry, illus. 140p. (gr. 4-7). 1989. 11.95 (*0-947962-48-4*, Pub. by Childrens Pr) Irish Bks Media.

Karim, Sharon L. The Unicorn Without a Name. LC 93-73171. (Illus.). 32p. (ps-3). 1994. 12.95 (*1-883703-00-X*) Big Heart Pub.

Lee, Tanith. Black Unicorn. Cooper, Heather, illus. LC 91-15646. 144p. (gr. 7 up). 1991. SBE 14.95 (*0-689-31575-9*, Atheneum Child Bk) Macmillan Child Grp.

L'Engle, Madeleine. The Young Unicorns. 224p. (gr. 8 up). 1989. pap. 3.99 (*0-440-99919-7*, LFL) Dell.

Luenn, Nancy. Unicorn Crossing. 64p. (gr. 2-9). 1988. pap. 2.50 (*0-8167-1321-9*) Troll Assocs.

Mayer, Marianna. The Unicorn & the Lake. Hague, Michael, illus. LC 82-71356. 32p. (gr. k up). 1982. PLB 13.89 (*0-8037-9338-3*) Dial Bks Young.

—Unicorn & the Lake. giant ed. (ps-3). 1990. 17.99 (*0-8037-0844-0*) Dial Bks Young.

—Unicorn & the Lake. LC 81-5469. (Illus.). 32p. (gr. k up). 1987. pap. 4.95 (*0-8037-0436-4*) Dial Bks Young.

Pierce, Meredith A. Dark Moon. 256p. (gr. 7 up). 1992. 15.95 (*0-685-59346-0*, Joy St Bks) Little.

—Dark Moon, Vol. II: Firebringer Trilogy. (Illus.). (gr. 7 up). 1992. 16.95 (*0-316-70744-9*, Joy St Bks) Little.

Preussler, Otfried. The Tale of the Unicorn. Spirin, Gennady, illus. LC 88-7141. 32p. (ps up). 1989. 12.95 (*0-8037-0583-2*) Dial Bks Young.

—The Tale of the Unicorn. Spirin, Gennady, illus. 32p. (ps up). 1992. pap. 4.99 (*0-14-054568-9*, Puff Pied Piper) Puffin Bks.

Razzi, Jim. Fun with Unicorns. 48p. (gr. 1-3). 1987. pap. 1.95 (*0-590-40787-2*) Scholastic Inc.

Salsitz, Rhondi V. The Twilight Gate. Clark, Alan M., illus. LC 92-22040. 192p. (gr. 7 up). 1993. 16.95 (*0-8027-8213-2*) Walker & Co.

Seitz, Eileen. The Message of the White Unicorn. Seitz, Eileen, illus. LC 87-50260. 35p. (Orig.). (gr. 3-5). 1987. pap. 8.95 (*1-55523-057-1*) Winston-Derek.

Short, Sondra J. Unicorns & Rainbows. LC 92-60808. 223p. (gr. 3 up). 1993. 9.95 (*1-55523-537-9*) Winston-Derek.

Smith, Kathie B. Enchanted Unicorn. 1987. pap. 2.95 incl. stickers (*0-671-63239-6*, Little Simon) S&S Trade.

Stroschin, Jane. A Unicorn Named Beulah Mae. 32p. (gr. k-6). 1993. PLB 15.00 (*1-883960-04-5*) Henry Quill.

Vrooman, Christine W. Willowby's World of Unicorns. Kane, Sandy & Ogden, Peggy, eds. Sidaras, Nanci, illus. 56p. (gr. 2-6). 1982. pap. 8.95 with stickers incl. (*0-685-06580-4*) Cloud Ten.

Walsh, Larry & Walsh, Suella. The Unicorn & Other Children's Stories. 52p. 1993. pap. 4.99 (*1-884754-05-8*) Potpourri Pubns.

UNIDENTIFIED FLYING OBJECTS

see Flying Saucers

UNDERWRITING

see Insurance

UNIFORMS, MILITARY

Military Uniforms. LC 91-58206. (Illus.). 64p. (gr. 6 up). 1992. 14.95 (*1-56458-010-5*); PLB 15.99 (*1-56458-011-3*) Dorling Kindersley.

UNIFORMS, NAVAL

see Uniforms, Military

UNION OF SOUTH AFRICA

see Africa, South

UNION PACIFIC RAILROAD

Sims, Donald. Union Pacific's West. LC 91-2894. (Illus.). (gr. 11). 1991. 42.95 (*0-87046-098-6*) Interurban.

UNIONS, LABOR

see Labor Unions

UNITARIANISM

Evans-Tiller, Jan. Around the Church, Around the Year: Unitarian Universalism for Children. Lewis, Kathryn, et al, eds. Conteh-Morgan, Jane, illus. 144p. (Orig.). (gr. k-3). 1990. pap. text ed. 29.95 (*1-55896-174-7*) Unitarian Univ.

UNITED KINGDOM

see Great Britain

UNITED NATIONS

Brenner, Barbara. The United Nations Fiftieth Anniversary Book. LC 94-12784. 1995. 17.00 (*0-689-31912-6*, Atheneum) Macmillan.

Gikow, Louise & Weiss, Ellen. For Every Child, a Better World. McNally, Bruce, illus. (Illus.). 48p. (gr. k-4). 1993. 9.95 (*0-307-15628-1*, 15628, Golden Pr) Western Pub.

Greene, Carol. The United Nations. LC 83-10068. (Illus.). 48p. (gr. k-4). 1983. PLB 12.85 (*0-516-01710-1*); pap. 4.95 (*0-516-41710-X*) Childrens.

Jacobs, William J. Search for Peace: The Story of the United Nations. LC 93-27149. (Illus.). 144p. (gr. 5-8). 1994. SBE 14.95 (*0-684-19652-2*, Scribners Young Read) Macmillan Child Grp.

Pollard, Michael. United Nations. LC 93-24544. (Illus.). 64p. (gr. 7-9). 1994. text ed. 13.95 RSBE (*0-02-726333-9*, New Discovery Bks) Macmillan Child Grp.

Stein, R. Conrad. The Story of the United Nations. Canaday, Ralph, illus. LC 85-31356. 32p. (gr. 3-6). 1986. pap. 3.95 (*0-516-44698-3*) Childrens.

—The United Nations. LC 93-37030. (Illus.). 32p. (gr. 3-6). 1994. PLB 12.30 (*0-516-06677-3*) Childrens.

Woog, Adam. United Nations. LC 93-3767. (gr. 5-8). 1994. 14.95 (*1-56006-145-6*) Lucent Bks.

UNITED NATIONS–FICTION

Small, David. Ruby Mae Has Something to Say. Small, David, illus. LC 91-33785. 40p. (ps-4). 1992. 12.00 (*0-517-58248-1*); PLB 12.99 (*0-517-58249-X*) Crown Bks Yng Read.

UNITED STATES

see also names of regions of the U. S. and groups of states e.g. Atlantic States; Middle West; Mississippi valley; Northwest, Old; Northwest, Pacific; Southern States; Southwest, New; Southwest, Old; The West

America the Beautiful. 1993. text ed. 15.40 (*1-56956-125-7*) W A T Braille.

American Cavalcade, 25 vols. (gr. 6 up). 1991. Set. lib. bdg. 348.75 (*1-55905-100-0*) Marshall Cavendish.

The American Dream, 6 bks. (Illus.). (gr. 7-10). 1989. Set, 144p. ea. lib. bdg. 47.70 (*0-382-09933-8*) Silver Burdett Pr.

Aten, Jerry. America: From Sea to Shining Sea. 160p. (gr. 4 up). 1988. wkbk. 12.95 (*0-86653-434-2*, GA1044) Good Apple.

—Challenge Across America. 96p. (gr. 4-8). 1990. 12.95 (*0-86653-556-X*, GA1157) Good Apple.

—Fifty Nifty States. (Illus.). 320p. (gr. 4 up). 1990. 20.95 (*0-86653-532-2*, GA1138) Good Apple.

Atkinson, David, illus. The Big Book of America. 56p. 1994. 9.98 (*0-685-71553-1*) Running Pr.

Aylesworth, Thomas G. Kids' World Almanac of the United States. 288p. (gr. 3-7). 1990. 14.95 (*0-88687-479-3*); pap. 7.95 (*0-88687-478-5*) Wrld Almnc.

Baines, John D. The U. S. A. LC 93-26533. 1993. PLB 22.80 (*0-8114-1857-X*) Raintree Steck-V.

Beck, Michael & Scott, Judy. Geography: United States: Geography - History - Maps - Flags (Through Research Activities) Beck, Michael, illus. 240p. (Orig.). (gr. 4-6). 1990. pap. text ed. 20.00 (*0-927867-00-1*) Skippingstone Pr.

Brandt, Sue R. Facts about the Fifty States. 2nd, rev. ed. Greenberg, Lorna, ed. LC 87-25437. (Illus.). 72p. (gr. 4-9). 1988. PLB 10.90 (*0-531-10476-1*) Watts.

Butler, Daphne. U. S. A. LC 92-13647. (Illus.). 32p. (gr. 3-4). 1992. PLB 19.24 (*0-8114-3676-4*) Raintree Steck-V.

Caney, Steven. Steven Caney's Kids' America. LC 77-27465. (Illus.). 416p. (ps-9). 1978. pap. 13.95 (*0-911104-80-1*, 114) Workman Pub.

Cohn, Amy, selected by. From Sea to Shining Sea. Bang, Molly, et al, illus. LC 92-30598. 416p. 1993. 29.95 (*0-590-42868-3*) Scholastic Inc.

Deegan, Paul. A Revolutionary Idea. Abbott, Phyllis, et al, eds. Wadsworth, Elaine, illus. LC 87-71092. 48p. (gr. 4). 1987. lib. bdg. 10.95 (*0-939179-20-2*) Abdo & Dghtrs.

Duffy, Robert. The American Quiz Book. 134p. (gr. 7 up). 1993. pap. 6.95 (*1-85371-187-X*, Pub. by Poolbeg Pr ER) Dufour.

Garrison, Edward T., Jr. Short Stories about States & Capitals. (Illus.). (gr. 5 up). write for info. (*0-9634033-0-3*) E G Photoprint.

Getting to Know United States. (Illus.). 48p. 1990. 7.95 (*0-8442-0682-2*, Natl Textbk) NTC Pub Grp.

Gibson, Roxie C. Hey, God! What Is America? Gibson, James, illus. Harvey, Paul, intro. by. LC 81-71025. (Illus.). 52p. (gr. 3-5). 1982. 4.95 (*0-938232-05-3*, 32795) Winston-Derek.

Glazer, Tom. America the Beautiful. 1987. pap. 12.95 (*0-385-24074-0*) Doubleday.

Harris, Jonathan. This Drinking Nation. (Illus.). 208p. (gr. 5 up). 1994. SBE 15.95 (*0-02-742744-7*, Four Winds) Macmillan Child Grp.

Hartley, Nancy. Quick Facts about the U. S. A. (gr. 4-7). 1994. pap. 2.95 (*0-590-47403-0*) Scholastic Inc.

Johnson, Linda C. Our National Symbols. LC 91-38893. (Illus.). 48p. (gr. 2-4). 1992. PLB 13.40 (*1-56294-108-9*); pap. 5.95 (*1-878841-87-4*) Millbrook Pr.

Johnson, Mabel. One Land - One Nation. (Illus.). 64p. (gr. 7 up). 1987. pap. 3.95 (*0-9600838-6-3*) M Johnson.

Krulik, Nancy E. All about the Fifty States: A Picture Puzzle Book. 1992. pap. 1.95 (*0-590-45223-1*) Scholastic Inc.

Lancaster, Derek. Picture America: States & Capitals. Lancaster, Derek, illus. Anderson, Stevens, ed. (Illus.). 136p. (gr. 5). 1991. pap. 4.95 (*1-880184-02-8*) Compact Classics.

Latta, Rich. State the Facts. 48p. (Orig.). (gr. 2 up). 1990. pap. 2.96 incl. chipboard (*0-8431-2821-6*) Price Stern.

Ronan, Margaret. All about Our Fifty States. rev. ed. Meyerriecks, William & Ronan, Frank, illus. LC 78-16658. (gr. 5-9). 1978. 12.00 (*0-394-80244-6*) Random Bks Yng Read.

Schloredt, Valerie. United States of America. rev. ed. LC 86-15565. (Illus.). 48p. (gr. 5 up). 1986. PLB 12.95 (*0-382-09257-0*) Silver Burdett Pr.

Shapiro, William E., ed. The Kingfisher Young People's Encyclopedia of the United States. LC 93-42501. 808p. (gr. 4-10). 1994. 39.95 (*1-85697-521-5*, Kingfisher LKC) LKC.

—The Young People's Encyclopedia of the United States, 10 vols. LC 91-4141. (Illus.). 800p. (gr. 4-8). 1992. Set. PLB 199.50 (*1-56294-151-8*) Millbrook Pr.

Somerville, L. First Book of America. (Illus.). 32p. 1990. PLB 13.96 (*0-88110-440-X*); pap. 6.95 (*0-7460-0338-2*) EDC.

Stein, R. Conrad. The United States of America. LC 93-35492. (Illus.). 128p. (gr. 5-8). 1994. PLB 20.55 (*0-516-02623-2*) Childrens.

Thompson, Kim M. & Hilderbrand, Karen M. Rhythm, Rhyme & Read: States & Capitals. Kocjak, Gordon, illus. 48p. (gr. 3-6). 1992. 6.99 (*0-9632249-5-6*) Twin Sisters.

—Rhythm, Rhyme & Read Twinset: States & Capitals. Kuzjak, Goran, illus. 48p. (gr. 2-6). 1993. pap. 14.99 wkbk. incl. audiocassette & poster (*1-882331-08-7*, TWIN 306) Twin Sisters.

—States & Capitals. Kuzjak, Goran, illus. (gr. 2-6). 1993. wkbk. incl. audiocassette 9.98 (*1-882331-24-9*, TWIN 406) Twin Sisters.

Zenfell, Martha E. U. S. A. LC 88-18561. (Illus.). 48p. (gr. 4-8). 1988. PLB 14.95 (*0-382-09515-4*) Silver Burdett Pr.

U. S. AIR FORCE

Blue, Rose & Naden, Corinne J. The U. S. Air Force. LC 92-13431. (Illus.). 64p. (gr. 3-6). 1993. PLB 15.40 (*1-56294-217-4*); pap. 5.95 (*1-56294-754-0*) Millbrook Pr.

Hole, Dorothy. The Air Force & You. LC 92-9774. (Illus.). 48p. (gr. 5-6). 1993. text ed. 12.95 RSBE (*0-89686-764-1*, Crestwood Hse) Macmillan Child Grp.

Rhea, John. The Department of the Air Force. (Illus.). 104p. (gr. 5 up). 1990. 14.95 (*0-87754-834-X*) Chelsea Hse.

U. S. AIR FORCE ACADEMY

Smallwood, William L. The Air Force Academy Candidate Book. (Illus.). 200p. (Orig.). (gr. 10-12). 1988. pap. write for info. Beacon Bks.

U. S.–ANTIQUITIES

see also Indians of North America–Antiquities

Wimberly, Christine A. Exploring Prehistoric Alabama Through Archaeology. Anderson, John & Meredith, Marianne, illus. LC 80-70833. 96p. (Orig.). (gr. 5-12). 1981. pap. 8.95 (*0-9605938-3-7*); pap. text ed. 6.18 (*0-9605938-1-0*); tchr's ed. 9.49 (*0-9605938-2-9*) Explorer Bks.

U. S.-ARMED FORCES

see also official names of branches of the Armed Forces, e.g. U. S. Army; U. S. Navy

Cox, Clinton. Undying Glory: The Story of the Massachusetts Fifty-Fourth Regiment. (gr. 4-7). 1993. pap. 3.25 (*0-590-44171-X*) Scholastic Inc.

Italia, Robert. Armed Forces. Wallner, Rosemary, ed. LC 91-73075. 202p. (gr. 4 up). 1991. 13.99 (*1-56239-026-0*) Abdo & Dghtrs.

Nicholaus, John. The Army Library, 6 bks, Reading Level 5. (Illus.). 288p. (gr. 3-8). 1989. Set. PLB 111.60 (*0-86592-417-1*) Rourke Corp.

Oleksy, Walter. Military Leaders of World War II. LC 93-33641. (Illus.). 128p. (gr. 4-11). 1994. 16.95x (*0-8160-3008-1*) Facts on File.

Paananen, Eloise. The Military. LC 92-29008. (Illus.). 48p. (gr. 5-6). 1992. PLB 21.34 (*0-8114-7353-8*) Raintree Steck-V.

White, Carl P. Citizen Soldier: Opportunities in the Reserves. Rosen, Ruth, ed. (gr. 7-12). 1990. PLB 14. 95 (*0-8239-1023-7*) Rosen Group.

U. S.-ARMED FORCES-FICTION

Alphin, Elaine M. The Proving Ground. LC 92-11356. 192p. (gr. 4-7). 1992. 14.95 (*0-8050-2140-X*, Bks Young Read) H Holt & Co.

Emerson, Zack. Hill Five Hundred Sixty-Eight. 1991. pap. 2.95 (*0-590-44592-8*) Scholastic Inc.

—Stand Down. 128p. 1992. pap. 2.95 (*0-590-44594-4*, Point) Scholastic Inc.

—Tis the Season. 256p. 1991. pap. 2.95 (*0-590-44593-6*) Scholastic Inc.

—Welcome to Vietnam. 1991. pap. 2.95 (*0-590-44591-X*) Scholastic Inc.

Hoff, Syd. Captain Cat. Hoff, Syd, illus. LC 91-27518. 48p. (ps-2). 1993. 14.00 (*0-06-020527-X*); PLB 13.89 (*0-06-020528-8*) HarpC Child Bks.

Paananen, Eloise. The Military. LC 92-29008. (Illus.). 48p. (gr. 5-6). 1992. PLB 21.34 (*0-8114-7353-8*) Raintree Steck-V.

Taylor, Norra. My Mom, the Sailor. Laur, Calvin, illus. 1992. 12.95 (*0-533-10302-9*) Vantage.

Wilson, Neil S. Choice Adventures, No. 9: The Tall Ship Shakedown. LC 92-30500. 1993. 4.99 (*0-8423-5046-2*) Tyndale.

U. S.-ARMED FORCES-WOMEN

Stanley, Sandra C. Women in the Military. LC 93-22312. 1993. lib. bdg. 14.98 (*0-671-75549-8*, Messner); pap. 8.95 (*0-671-75550-1*, Messner) S&S Trade.

Wekesser, Carol & Polesetsky, Matt, eds. Women in the Military. LC 91-25056. 200p. (gr. 10 up). 1991. PLB 16.95 (*0-89908-579-2*); pap. text ed. 9.95 (*0-89908-585-7*) Greenhaven.

U. S. ARMY

Cox, Clinton. The Forgotten Heroes: The Story of the Buffalo Soldiers. LC 92-36622. 176p. 1993. 14.95 (*0-590-45121-9*) Scholastic Inc.

Hole, Dorothy. The Army & You. LC 92-2214. (Illus.). 48p. (gr. 5-6). 1993. text ed. 12.95 RSBE (*0-89686-765-X*, Crestwood Hse) Macmillan Child Grp.

Pate, J'Nell L. Ranald Slidell Mackenzie: Brave Cavalry Colonel. LC 93-21952. (gr. 4-8). 1994. 14.95 (*0-89015-901-7*) Sunbelt Media.

U. S. ARMY-ORDNANCE AND ORDNANCE STORES

Italia, Robert. Weapons of War. LC 91-73074. (gr. 4 up). 1991. 13.99 (*1-56239-027-9*) Abdo & Dghtrs.

U. S.-ARTISTS

see Artists, American

U. S.-AUTHORS

see Authors, American

U. S.-BIOGRAPHY

Ashabranner, Brent. People Who Make a Difference. LC 89-34593. (Illus.). (gr. 5 up). 1989. 15.95 (*0-525-65009-1*, Cobblehill Bks) Dutton Child Bks.

Bales, Carol A. Tales of the Elders: A Memory Book of Men & Women Who Came to America as Immigrants, 1900-1930. Bales, Carol A., photos by. LC 92-46729. (Illus.). 160p. (gr. 5 up). 1993. Repr. of 1977 ed. 5.45 (*0-8136-7215-5*); PLB 10.95 (*0-382-24364-1*) Silver Burdett Pr.

Barnes, Jeremy. Samuel Goldwyn. Furstinger, Nancy, ed. (Illus.). 128p. (gr. 7-10). 1989. PLB 7.95 (*0-382-09586-3*) Silver Burdett Pr.

Blos, Joan W. The Heroine of the Titanic: A Tale Both True & Otherwise of the Life of Molly Brown. Dixon, Tennessee, illus. LC 90-35369. 40p. (gr. 1 up). 1991. 14.95 (*0-688-07546-0*); PLB 14.88 (*0-688-07547-9*) Morrow Jr Bks.

Blue, Rose & Naden, Corinne J. Colin Powell: Straight to the Top. LC 91-19121. (Illus.). 48p. (gr. 2-4). 1991. PLB 12.90 (*1-56294-052-X*) Millbrook Pr.

Boyd, Aaron & Causey, Michael. Ross Perot: Businessman Politician. (Illus.). 144p. (gr. 6 up). 1994. PLB 17.95 (*1-883846-04-8*) M Reynolds.

Boynton, LaVerne L. The Enchantment of Beaver Creek. Richards, Linda, illus. 248p. 1988. 12.95 (*0-685-44325-6*) Starlite Pub.

Collins, David. Johnny Appleseed. LC 84-60315. (gr. 3-6). 1985. pap. 6.95 (*0-88062-134-6*) Mott Media.

Davidson, Margaret. The Story of Benjamin Franklin: Amazing American. (Orig.). (gr. k-6). 1988. pap. 3.50 (*0-440-40021-X*, YB) Dell.

Eisenhower, Julie N. Special People. (Illus.). 208p. 1990. pap. text ed. 6.95 (*0-939631-24-5*) Thomas Publications.

Faber, Doris. Calamity Jane: Her Life & Her Legend. LC 91-40050. (Illus.). 80p. (gr. 5-9). 1992. 14.45 (*0-395-56396-8*) HM.

Favors, John & Favors, Kathryne. White Americans Who Cared Kit. 26p. (gr. 4 up). 1990. Repr. of 1978 ed. 299.95 (*1-878794-01-9*) Jonka Enter.

Fowler, Mary J. & Fisher, Margaret, eds. Great Americans. rev. ed. LC 87-81352. (Illus.). 160p. (gr. 4 up). 1988. 14.95 (*0-934291-25-X*); 11.95 (*0-317-91143-0*) Gateway Pr MI.

Frazier, Neta L. Stout-Hearted Seven. 174p. (gr. 4-6). 1984. pap. text ed. 4.95 (*0-914019-22-8*) NW Interpretive.

Gavin, Peggy, compiled by. Meet the Real Me. Kinnealy, Janice, illus. LC 92-21644. 32p. (gr. 2-8). 1992. pap. text ed. 2.50 (*0-8167-2939-5*) Troll Assocs.

Gikow, Louise. Meet Jim Henson. LC 92-30225. 80p. (Orig.). (gr. 2-6). 1993. pap. 2.99 (*0-679-84642-5*, Bullseye Bks) Random Bks Yng Read.

Glassman, Bruce. J. Paul Getty. Furstinger, Nancy, ed. (Illus.). 112p. (gr. 7-10). 1989. PLB 7.95 (*0-382-09584-7*) Silver Burdett Pr.

Green, Carl R. & Sanford, William R. Doc Holliday. LC 94-24845. (gr. 4-10). 1995. write for info. (*0-89490-589-9*) Enslow Pubs.

Griffith, Reva. This Song's for You. LC 92-74144. (Illus.). 240p. (Orig.). (gr. 9-12). 1993. pap. 14.95 (*0-923687-23-8*) Celo Valley Bks.

Hale, Janet. The Conners of Conner Prairie. Baxter, Nancy N., ed. Day, Richard, illus. LC 89-80212. 120p. (gr. 4-6). 1989. 13.95 (*0-9617367-5-5*) Guild Pr IN.

Hammer, Roger A. Hidden America: A Collection of Multi-Cultural Stories, 4 bks. rev. ed. Schlosser, Cy, et al, illus. (gr. 6 up). Set. pap. 29.95 (*0-932991-00-9*) Place in the Woods.

Henry, Carol A. George Mason, Father of the Bill of Rights. Henry, Crystal A., illus. 44p. (Orig.). (gr. k-5). 1991. pap. 9.95 (*0-9633634-3-3*) C A Henry.

Henry, Sondra & Taitz, Emily. Levi Strauss: Everyone Wears His Name. LC 87-32455. (Illus.). 112p. (gr. 5 up). 1990. text ed. 13.95 RSBE (*0-87518-375-1*, Dillon) Macmillan Child Grp.

Hodges, Margaret. Making a Difference: The Story of an American Family. ALC Staff, ed. LC 88-31131. (Illus.). 208p. (gr. 8 up). 1992. pap. 4.95 (*0-688-11780-5*, Pub. by Beech Tree Bks) Morrow.

Italia, Bob. General H. Norman Schwarzkopf. Wallner, Rosemary, ed. LC 92-17393. (gr. 4 up). 1992. PLB 13. 99 (*1-56239-148-8*) Abdo & Dghtrs.

Jacobs, William J. Great Lives: Human Rights. LC 89-37211. (Illus.). 288p. (gr. 4-6). 1990. SBE 23.00 (*0-684-19036-2*, Scribners Young Read) Macmillan Child Grp.

Johnson, Hilda S. A Child's Diary - the 1930's. Johnson, Hilda S., illus. LC 88-51304. 64p. (Orig.). (gr. 3-8). 1988. pap. 3.95 (*0-931563-02-X*) Wishing Rm.

Kurland, Gerald. George Wallace: Southern Governor & Presidential Candidate. Rahmas, D. Steve, ed. 32p. (Orig.). (gr. 7-12). 1972. lib. bdg. 4.95 incl. catalog cards (*0-87157-529-9*) SamHar Pr.

—John D. Rockefeller: Nineteenth Century Industrialist & Oil Baron. Rahmas, D. Steve, ed. 32p. (gr. 7-12). 1972. lib. bdg. 4.95 incl. catalog cards (*0-87157-535-3*) SamHar Pr.

—Lyndon Baines Johnson: President Caught in an Ordeal of Power. Rahmas, D. Steve, ed. LC 76-190243. 32p. (Orig.). (gr. 7-12). 1972. lib. bdg. 4.95 incl. catalog cards (*0-87157-525-6*) SamHar Pr.

—Spiro Agnew: Controversial Vice-President of the Nixon Administration. Rahmas, D. Steve, ed. LC 72-190234. 32p. (Orig.). (gr. 7-12). 1972. PLB 4.95 incl. catalog cards (*0-87157-516-7*) SamHar Pr.

Lessem. John Horner Biography. 48p. 1994. text ed. write for info. (*0-7167-6546-2*); pap. text ed. write for info. (*0-7167-6549-7*) W H Freeman.

Lowe, Jimmy. Jesse Stuart: the Boy from the Dark Hills: A Boyography. Gifford, James M., et al, eds. Wise, Pamela, designed by. LC 90-62199. (Illus.). 79p. (gr. 4-12). 1990. pap. text ed. 15.00 (*0-945084-19-6*) J Stuart Found.

Ludwig, Charles. Susanna Wesley. LC 84-60314. 195p. (gr. 3-6). 1984. pap. 6.95 (*0-88062-110-9*) Mott Media.

Martin, Patricia S. Samantha Smith: Little Ambassador. (Illus.). 24p. (gr. 1-4). 1987. PLB 14.60 (*0-86592-173-3*); 10.95 (*0-685-58131-4*) Rourke Corp.

Mashburn, William H. A Mountain Summer. Gayheart, Willard, illus. LC 88-11782. 140p. (Orig.). (gr. 9-12). 1990. pap. 8.95 (*0-936015-14-4*) Pocahontas Pr.

Mather, Melissa. Rough Road Home. LC 58-9537. 256p. 1988. pap. 9.95 (*0-8397-7237-8*) Eriksson.

Moses, Elbert R. Beating the Odds: A Mini Autobiography. Peters, Claude D., intro. by. (Illus.). 50p. (Orig.). 1992. pap. text ed. 3.95 (*0-922484-03-1*) Poligion Pub.

O'Brien, P. M. The Promoter: His Life & Times. (Illus.). 118p. (gr. 10-12). 1988. pap. 5.65 (*0-9620540-0-3*) P M O'Brien.

Olson, Kenfield & Houghton, Cleo, eds. Collected Memoirs of Central School: Kirkland, Washington, 1890-1980. 67p. (Orig.). (gr. 9-12). 1982. pap. 5.00 (*0-685-28866-8*) Marymoor Mus.

Otfinoski, Steven. Bill Gaines. LC 93-16177. 1993. write for info. (*0-86592-080-X*) Rourke Enter.

Patterson, Lillie. A. Philip Randolph. Scott, John A., ed. (Illus.). 128p. (gr. 7-12). 1994. 16.95x (*0-8160-2827-3*) Facts on File.

People to Know Series, 13 bks. (Illus.). (gr. 6 up). Set. lib. bdg. 233.35 (*0-89490-450-7*) Enslow Pubs.

Raphael, Morris. Weeks Hall: The Master of the Shadows. LC 81-90439. (Illus.). 207p. (gr. 5-12). 1981. 14.95 (*0-9608866-1-3*) M Raphael.

Roberts, Naurice. Andrew Young: Freedom Fighter. rev. ed. LC 83-7633. (Illus.). 32p. (gr. 2-5). 1990. PLB 11. 80 (*0-516-03450-2*); pap. 3.95 (*0-516-43450-0*) Childrens.

Signer, Billie T., pseud. Sonny. Christian, Raleta, illus. Ervis, K. Leroy, intro. by. LC 90-82038. (Illus.). 134p. (gr. 5-8). 1990. lib. bdg. 17.95 (*0-944419-28-3*) Everett Cos Pub.

Smith, Kathie B. The Great Americans Series, 9 vols. Seward, James, illus. 216p. (gr. 4-6). 1989. Set. PLB 71.82 (*0-671-93118-0*, J Messner); Set. PLB 53.91s.p. (*0-685-54168-1*) S&S Trade.

Smith, Kathie B. & Bradbury, Pamela Z. Men of the Constitution. Seward, James, illus. 24p. (gr. 4-6). 1987. (J Messner); PLB 5.99s.p. (*0-685-54169-X*) S&S Trade.

Spies, Karen. Our Folk Heroes. (Illus.). 48p. (gr. 2-4). 1994. 13.40 (*1-56294-440-1*) Millbrook Pr.

Stuart, Jesse. To Teach, To Love. LeMaster, J. R., intro. by. LC 92-808. 317p. (gr. 10 up). 1987. Repr. of 1970 ed. 20.00 (*0-945084-02-1*) J Stuart Found.

Thompson-Peters, Flossie E. The Story of Benjamin Banneker. Clo, Kathy, illus. 32p. (Orig.). (gr. 1-6). 1986. pap. text ed. 4.70 (*1-880784-02-5*) Atlas Pr.

Turk, Ruth. They Reached for the Stars. Tripp, Ned, illus. (gr. 5-9). 1990. pap. 11.95 (*0-933025-20-3*) Blue Bird Pub.

Verheyden-Hilliard, Mary E. American Women in Science & Engineering, 15 bks. Biro, Scarlet & Rom, Holly M., illus. (gr. 1-4). 1988. Set. 75.00 (*0-932469-19-1*) Equity Inst.
This illustrated, 15-book series presents contemporary African-American, American Indian, Asian-American, Hispanic, & Caucasian women who, in girlhood, overcame barriers of gender, race, language, & poverty to become scientists. Five of the books are about girls with physical disabilities who also went on to become scientists. "Inspiring group of biographies of women in science...Children in the lower grades will enjoy these biographies, & those in the upper grades with reading problems can use them for...biographical information."-- SCHOOL LIBRARY JOURNAL. "...useful to teachers who want to help girls become more positive towards mathematics & science... recommended."-- CURRICULUM REVIEW. "...smoothly written texts..."-- BOOKLIST. "...help children...see the connection...between determination to persevere in the face of disabilities & later 'payoff'...in a variety of very exciting careers."-- NEWSLETTER, ASSOCIATION OF BLACK WOMEN IN HIGHER EDUCATION. "...warm, lively & true stories of young girls who went on to become successful scientists..."-- GIFTED CHILDREN MONTHLY. ". ..these books are so attractively produced that I can't imagine elementary classroom teaching without them."-- PERSPECTIVES, National Women Studies Association. Also available are tie-in Teaching Guide $10.00 (ISBN 0-932469-19-3), & video: "You Can Be a Scientist Too!" $46.00 (ISBN 0-932469-11-6). "Shows how exciting & fascinating science can be."-- BOOKLIST.
Publisher Provided Annotation.

Whitfield, Vallie J. Heritage History. 2nd ed. Whitfield, Joanne, ed. LC 87-50112. (Illus.). 265p. (gr. 10 up). 1988. 25.00 (*0-930920-19-8*) Whitfield Bks.

U. S. CENTRAL INTELLIGENCE AGENCY

Archer, Jules. Superspies: The Secret Side of Government. LC 77-72640. (gr. 7up). 1977. pap. 7.95 (*0-440-08136-X*) Delacorte.

U. S.–CHURCH HISTORY

Morrison, Ellen E. The Church That Keeps Memories Alive: The Story of Christ Church, Alexandria, Virginia. 2nd, rev. ed. LC 79-114253. (Illus.). 12p. (gr. 6). 1979. saddle-stitched 1.75 (*0-9622537-0-7*) Morielle Pr.

U. S.–CIVILIZATION

American Cultures. (Illus.). 32p. (gr. 6-12). 1980. pap. 1.85 (*0-8395-3388-8*, 33388) BSA.

Dudley, William & Szumski, Bonnie, eds. America's Future: Opposing Viewpoints. LC 89-25885. (Illus.). 312p. (gr. 10 up). 1990. lib. bdg. 17.95 (*0-89908-448-6*); pap. text ed. 9.95 (*0-89908-423-0*) Greenhaven.

Mayers, Florence C. ABC: National Museum of American History. (Illus.). 32p. 1989. 12.95 (*0-8109-1875-7*) Abrams.

Sinnott, Susan. Extraordinary Hispanic Americans. LC 91-13909. 260p. (gr. 4 up). 1991. PLB 24.65 (*0-516-00582-0*) Childrens.

Thomas, Joyce C. A Gathering of Flowers. LC 90-4043. 256p. (gr. 7 up). 1992. pap. 3.95 (*0-06-447082-2*, Trophy) HarpC Child Bks.

U. S. COAST GUARD

Bishop, Eleanor. Prints in the Sand: The U. S. Coast Guard Beach Patrol During WWII. LC 89-62184. (Illus.). 92p. (Orig.). (gr. 8-12). 1989. pap. 9.95 (*0-929521-22-6*) Pictorial Hist.

Ferrell, Nancy W. The U. S. Coast Guard. (Illus.). 72p. (gr. 5 up). 1989. 22.95 (*0-8225-1431-1*) Lerner Pubns.

Hole, Dorothy. The Coast Guard & You. LC 92-9775. (Illus.). 48p. (gr. 5-6). 1993. text ed. 12.95 RSBE (*0-89686-766-8*, Crestwood Hse) Macmillan Child Grp.

Naden, Corinne J. & Blue, Rose. The U. S. Coast Guard. LC 92-31042. (Illus.). 64p. (gr. 3-6). 1993. PLB 15.40 (*1-56294-321-9*) Millbrook Pr.

Noble, Dennis L. & O'Brien, Mike. U. S. Life-Saving Service 1889-1915, U. S. Coast Guard Service 1915-1989. (Illus.). 24p. (Orig.). (gr. 8 up). 1989. pap. text ed. 2.00 (*0-935549-12-9*) MI City Hist.

U. S.–COLONIES

see U. S.–Territories and Possessions

U. S. CONGRESS

Barba, Harry & Barba, Marian, eds. What's Cooking in Congress? LC 79-83777. (Illus.). 144p. (gr. 5 up). 1979. pap. 9.95 (*0-911906-15-0*) Harian Creative Bks.

Bernstein, Richard & Agel, Jerome. The Congress. LC 88-21025. (gr. 7 up). 1989. 12.95 (*0-8027-6832-6*); PLB 13.85 (*0-8027-6833-4*) Walker & Co.

Blue, Rose & Naden, Corinne J. Barbara Jordan. (Illus.). 112p. (gr. 5 up). 1992. lib. bdg. 17.95 (*0-7910-1131-3*) Chelsea Hse.

Davidson, Sue. A Heart in Politics: Jeannette Rankin & Patsy T. Mink. LC 94-11066. (Illus.). 160p. (Orig.). (gr. 6-12). 1994. pap. 8.95 (*1-878067-53-2*) Seal Pr Feminist.

Fireside, Bryna J. Is There a Woman in the House - or Senate? Levine, Abby, ed. LC 92-28286. (Illus.). 144p. (gr. 4-9). 1993. PLB 14.95 (*0-8075-3662-8*) A Whitman.

Gourse, Leslie. The Congress. LC 94-962. (gr. 3 up). 1994. write for info. (*0-531-20178-3*) Watts.

Green, Carl & Sanford, William. Congress. (Illus.). 96p. (gr. 7 up). 1990. lib. bdg. 18.60 (*0-86593-083-X*); lib. bdg. 13.95s.p. (*0-685-46455-5*) Rourke Corp.

Greene, Carol. Congress. LC 84-23243. (Illus.). 48p. (gr. k-4). 1985. PLB 12.85 (*0-516-01939-2*); pap. 4.95 (*0-516-41939-0*) Childrens.

Jakoubek, Robert. Adam Clayton Powell, Jr. King, Coretta Scott, intro. by. (Illus.). 112p. 1988. lib. bdg. 17.95x (*1-55546-606-0*); pap. 9.95 (*0-7910-0213-6*) Chelsea Hse.

Johnson, Linda C. Barbara Jordan: Congresswoman. (Illus.). 64p. (gr. 3-7). PLB 14.95 (*1-56711-031-2*) Blackbirch.

Nardo, Don. The U. S. Congress. LC 93-41137. (gr. 5-8). 1994. 14.95 (*1-56006-155-3*) Lucent Bks.

Ragsdale, Bruce A. The House of Representatives. Schlesinger, Arthur, Jr., intro. by. (Illus.). 96p. (gr. 5 up). 1989. lib. bdg. 14.95 (*1-55546-112-3*) Chelsea Hse.

Richie, Donald A. The Young Oxford Companion to the Congress of the United States. LC 93-6466. (gr. 5 up). 1993. 35.00 (*0-19-507777-6*) OUP.

Sabin, Louis. Congressperson. Dole, Bob, illus. LC 84-2651. 32p. (gr. 3-6). 1985. PLB 9.49 (*0-8167-0266-7*); pap. text ed. 2.95 (*0-8167-0267-5*) Troll Assocs.

Scheader, Catherine. Shirley Chisholm: Teacher & Congresswoman. LC 89-34451. (Illus.). 128p. (gr. 6 up). 1990. lib. bdg. 17.95 (*0-89490-285-7*) Enslow Pubs.

Stein, R. Conrad. The Story of the Powers of Congress. Neely, Keith, illus. LC 85-10943. 32p. (gr. 3-6). 1985. pap. 3.95 (*0-516-44695-9*) Childrens.

Stern, Gary M. The Congress: America's Lawmakers. LC 92-27030. (Illus.). 48p. (gr. 5-6). 1992. PLB 21.34 (*0-8114-7351-1*); pap. write for info. (*0-8114-5579-3*) Raintree Steck-V.

U. S. CONGRESS. SENATE

Ritchie, Donald A. The Senate. Schlesinger, Arthur M., Jr., intro. by. (Illus.). 96p. (gr. 5 up). 1988. lib. bdg. 14.95 (*1-55546-121-2*) Chelsea Hse.

U. S. CONGRESS. SENATE–BIOGRAPHY

Carrigan, Mellonee. Carol Moseley-Braun: Breaking Barriers. (Illus.). 32p. (gr. 2-4). 1994. PLB 11.80 (*0-516-04190-8*) Childrens.

Gould, Alberta. First Lady of the Senate: A Life of Margaret Chase Smith, U. S. Senator. Weinberger, Jane, ed. LC 89-51315. (Illus.). 150p. (gr. 5-10). 1990. 15.95 (*0-932433-64-2*) Windswept Hse.

Jaspersohn, William. Senator: A Profile of Bill Bradley in the U. S. Senate. 1992. 19.95 (*0-15-272880-5*) HarBrace.

Johnson, Linda C. Barbara Jordan: Congresswomen. (Illus.). 64p. (gr. 3-7). 1993. pap. 7.95 (*1-56711-050-9*) Blackbirch.

Shulman, Jeffrey & Rogers, Teresa. Gaylord Nelson: A Day for the Earth. Raymond, Larry, illus. 68p. (gr. 4-7). 1992. PLB 14.95 (*0-941477-40-1*) TFC Bks NY.

U. S. CONSTITUTION

Abromowitz, Jack & Uva, Kenneth. The Constitution & the Government of the U. S. (gr. 7-12). 1987. pap. text ed. 3.50 (*0-89525-747-5*) Ed Activities.

Colman, Warren. The Bill of Rights. LC 86-33437. (Illus.). 48p. (gr. k-4). 1987. PLB 12.85 (*0-516-01232-0*); pap. 4.95 (*0-516-41232-9*) Childrens.

—La Carta de Derechos: (The Bill of Rights) LC 86-33437. (SPA.). 48p. (gr. k-4). 1989. PLB 12.85 (*0-516-31232-4*); pap. 4.95 (*0-516-51232-3*) Childrens.

—La Constitucion: (The Constitution) LC 86-30968. (SPA.). 48p. (gr. k-4). 1989. PLB 12.85 (*0-516-31231-6*); pap. 4.95 (*0-516-51231-5*) Childrens.

—The Constitution. LC 86-30968. (Illus.). 48p. (gr. k-4). 1987. PLB 12.85 (*0-516-01231-2*); pap. 4.95 (*0-516-41231-0*) Childrens.

Dudley, William. The U. S. Constitution: Locating the Author's Main Idea. LC 90-42328. (Illus.). 32p. (gr. 3-6). 1990. PLB 10.95 (*0-89908-601-2*) Greenhaven.

Fisher, Dorothy C. Our Independence & the Constitution. LC 87-4656. 192p. (gr. 5-9). 1964. pap. 3.95 (*0-394-89175-9*, Random Juv) Random Bks Yng Read.

Glisan, Ellen M. U. S. Constitution Text. rev. ed. (Illus.). 41p. (gr. 7-12). 1989. pap. text ed. write for info. (*0-944791-92-1*, SS505) Peekan Pubns.

Haener, Donald R. & Fry, Janice K. The Era & Our Constitution. rev. ed. Baruffa, Joanne & Tunis, Edwin, illus. (gr. 6 up). 1987. pap. text ed. 5.00 (*0-942661-02-8*) Discovry Enterp.

Howes, Janice. A Classroom Presents the Constitution of the United States: A Story for Elementary School Children. Howes, Janice, illus. LC 87-50078. 35p. (Orig.). (gr. k-5). 1987. pap. 7.00 (*0-942431-00-6*) Teachers Pub Hse.

Jenkins, George. Constitution. (Illus.). 96p. (gr. 7 up). 1990. lib. bdg. 18.60 (*0-86593-085-6*); lib. bdg. 13.95s.p. (*0-685-46456-3*) Rourke Corp.

Johnson, Linda C. Our Constitution. LC 91-43232. (Illus.). 48p. (gr. 2-4). 1992. PLB 13.40 (*1-56294-090-2*); pap. 5.95 (*1-56294-813-X*) Millbrook Pr.

League of Women Voters of Cleveland Educational Fund, Inc. Staff. From Ordinance to Constitution: Government of & by the People. 73p. (gr. 9-12). 1987. pap. text ed. 10.00 (*1-880746-05-0*) LOWV Cleve Educ.

Lindop, Edmund. Birth of the Constitution. LC 86-13380. (Illus.). 160p. (gr. 6 up). 1987. lib. bdg. 18.95 (*0-89490-135-4*) Enslow Pubs.

Maestro, Betsy & Maestro, Giulio. A More Perfect Union: The Story of Our Constitution. LC 87-4083. (Illus.). 48p. (gr. k up). 1990. pap. 5.95 (*0-688-10192-5*, Mulberry) Morrow.

Morris, Richard B. The Constitution. rev. ed. Fisher, Leonard E., illus. 72p. (gr. 5-10). 1985. PLB 13.50 (*0-8225-1702-7*) Lerner Pubns.

Post, Libby, ed. Through the Eyes of Children: Liberty & Justice for All. Wachtter, Sol, intros. by. (Illus.). 48p. (Orig.). 1989. pap. write for info. NY State Alliance.

Prolman, Marilyn. The Story of the Constitution. Glaubke, Robert, illus. LC 69-14680. 32p. (gr. 3-6). 1969. PLB 12.30 (*0-516-04605-5*); pap. 3.95 (*0-516-44605-3*) Childrens.

Richie, Donald A. U. S. Constitution. Schlesinger, Arthur M., Jr., intro. by. (Illus.). 120p. (gr. 5 up). 1989. 14.95 (*0-87754-894-3*) Chelsea Hse.

Scesney, Gladys. It's Your Constitution! rev. ed. Enrees, Michael B., illus. 32p. (gr. 1-6). 1987. pap. 1.50 (*0-9618667-1-3*) Scesney Pubns.

Schmidt, Alex J. Our Federal & State Constitutions. rev. ed. 65p. (gr. 7-11). 1992. pap. text ed. 3.85 (*0-931298-00-8*) A J S Pubns.

Slappey, Mary M. The Constitution of the United States. 17p. (gr. 1 up). 1987. pap. 5.00 (*0-930061-20-9*) Interspace Bks.

Spier, Peter. We the People: The Constitution of the United States of America. (ps). 1991. pap. 8.00 (*0-385-41903-1*) Doubleday.

—We the People: The Story of the U. S. Constitution. Spier, Peter, illus. LC 86-24205. 48p. (gr. k-3). 1987. PLB 16.00 (*0-385-23589-5*) Doubleday.

Wolf, D. M. We the People: Bits, Bytes & Highlights of the U. S. Constitution & Bill of Rights from Honey Bees Tye & Sy. McDaniel, Jerry, illus. 32p. (Orig.). (gr. 3-5). 1987. pap. 4.95 (*0-9617057-1-X*) Storyviews Pub.

U. S. CONSTITUTION–AMENDMENTS

Stein, R. Conrad. The Bill of Rights. LC 91-41541. (Illus.). 32p. (gr. 3-6). PLB 12.30, Apr. 1992 (*0-516-04853-8*); pap. 3.95, Jul. 1992 (*0-516-44853-6*) Childrens.

—The Story of the Nineteenth Amendment. LC 82-4419. (Illus.). 32p. (gr. 3-6). 1982. PLB 12.30 (*0-516-04639-X*); pap. 3.95 (*0-516-44639-8*) Childrens.

U. S. CONSTITUTIONAL CONVENTION, 1787

Hauptly, Denis J. A Convention of Delegates: The Creation of the Constitution. LC 86-17260. (Illus.). 160p. (gr. 3-7). 1987. SBE 14.95 (*0-689-31148-6*, Atheneum Child Bk) Macmillan Child Grp.

McPhillips, Martin. The Constitutional Convention. LC 85-40169. (Illus.). 64p. (gr. 5 up). 1985. PLB 12.95 (*0-382-06827-0*); pap. 7.95 (*0-382-09435-2*) Silver Burdett Pr.

Prolman, Marilyn. The Story of the Constitution. Glaubke, Robert, illus. LC 69-14680. 32p. (gr. 3-6). 1969. PLB 12.30 (*0-516-04605-5*); pap. 3.95 (*0-516-44605-3*) Childrens.

U. S.–CONSTITUTIONAL HISTORY

Faber, Harold & Faber, Doris. We the People: The Story of the United States Constitution since 1787. LC 86-31404. 256p. (gr. 7 up). 1987. SBE 15.95 (*0-684-18753-1*, Scribners Young Read) Macmillan Child Grp.

Henry, Carol A. George Mason, Father of the Bill of Rights. Henry, Crystal A., illus. 44p. (Orig.). (gr. k-5). 1991. pap. 9.95 (*0-9633634-3-3*) C A Henry.

Maestro, Betsy. A More Perfect Union: The Story of Our Constitution. Maestro, Giulio, illus. LC 87-4083. 48p. (gr. 1-5). 1987. 16.00 (*0-688-06839-1*); PLB 15.93 (*0-688-06840-5*) Lothrop.

Smith, Kathie B. Men of the Constitution. (Illus.). 32p. (gr. k-5). 1987. pap. 2.25 (*0-671-64028-3*, Little Simon) S&S Trade.

U. S.–CONSTITUTIONAL LAW

Leinwand, Gerald. Do We Need a New Constitution? LC 93-31847. (Illus.). 136p. (gr. 9-12). 1994. PLB 13.40 (*0-531-11127-X*) Watts.

Meltzer, Milton. The Bill of Rights: How We Got It & What It Means. LC 90-1537. 180p. (gr. 7 up). 1990. (Crowell Jr Bks); PLB 14.89 (*0-690-04807-6*, Crowell Jr Bks) HarpC Child Bks.

Shaver, James R. Understanding the U. S. Constitution. 1986. pap. ɔ.25 (*0-87738-023-6*) Youth Ed.

U. S. DECLARATION OF INDEPENDENCE

Dalgliesh, Alice. Fourth of July Story. Nonnast, Marie, illus. LC 56-6138. 32p. (ps-3). 1972. RSBE 13.95 (*0-684-13164-1*, Scribners Young Read); (Scribner) Macmillan Child Grp.

La Declaracion de Independencia: (The Declaration of Independence) LC 88-11870. (ENG & SPA.). 48p. (gr. k-4). 1989. PLB 12.85 (*0-516-31153-0*); pap. 4.95 (*0-516-51153-X*) Childrens.

Fradin, Dennis B. The Declaration of Independence. LC 88-11870. (Illus.). 48p. (gr. k-4). 1988. PLB 12.85 (*0-516-01153-7*); pap. 4.95 (*0-516-41153-5*) Childrens.

Richards, Norman. The Story of the Declaration of Independence. LC 68-24379. (Illus.). 32p. (gr. 3-6). 1968. pap. 3.95 (*0-516-44606-1*) Childrens.

Sandak, Cass R. The Jeffersons. LC 91-33061. (Illus.). 48p. (gr. 5). 1992. text ed. 12.95 RSBE (*0-89686-637-8*, Crestwood Hse) Macmillan Child Grp.

Schleifer, Jay. Our Declaration of Independence. LC 91-43229. (Illus.). 48p. (gr. 2-4). 1992. PLB 13.40 (*1-56294-205-0*); pap. 5.95 (*1-56294-814-8*) Millbrook Pr.

U. S. DEPARTMENT OF AGRICULTURE

Hurt, R. Douglas. The Department of Agriculture. Schlesinger, Arthur M., Jr., intro. by. (Illus.). 112p. (gr. 5 up). 1989. lib. bdg. 14.95 (*0-87754-833-1*) Chelsea Hse.

U. S. DEPARTMENT OF COMMERCE

Griffin, Robert J., Jr. The Department of Commerce. (Illus.). 104p. (gr. 5 up). 1991. 14.95 (*0-87754-836-6*) Chelsea Hse.

U. S. DEPARTMENT OF DEFENSE

Heinsohn, Beth & Cohen, Andrew. The Department of Defense. (Illus.). 120p. (gr. 5 up). 1990. 14.95 (*0-87754-837-4*) Chelsea Hse.

U. S. DEPARTMENT OF HEALTH, EDUCATION, AND WELFARE

Broberg, Merle. Department of Health & Human Services. (Illus.). 128p. (gr. 5 up). 1989. lib. bdg. 14.95 (*0-87754-840-4*) Chelsea Hse.

Sneigoski, Stephen J. Department of Education. Schlesinger, Arthur M., Jr., intro. by. (Illus.). 96p. (gr. 5 up). 1988. lib. bdg. 14.95 (*0-87754-838-2*) Chelsea Hse.

U. S. DEPARTMENT OF JUSTICE

Dunn, Lynne. The Department of Justice. (Illus.). 112p. (gr. 5 up). 1990. 14.95 (*0-87754-843-9*) Chelsea Hse.

U. S. DEPARTMENT OF STATE

Bartz, Carl. The Department of State. Schlesinger, Arthur M., Jr., intro. by. (Illus.). 120p. (gr. 5 up). 1989. lib. bdg. 14.95 (*0-87754-846-3*) Chelsea Hse.

U. S. DEPARTMENT OF THE INTERIOR

Clement, Fred. Department of the Interior. Schlesinger, Arthur M., Jr., intro. by. (Illus.). 112p. (gr. 5 up). 1989. lib. bdg. 14.95 (*0-87754-842-0*) Chelsea Hse.

U. S.–DESCRIPTION AND TRAVEL

Anderson, Joan. Joshua's Westward Journal. Ancona, George, illus. LC 87-5509. 48p. (gr. 2-5). 1987. 13.00 (*0-688-06680-1*); lib. bdg. 12.88 (*0-688-06681-X*, Morrow Junior Books) Morrow Jr Bks.

Anno, Mitsumasa. Anno's U. S. A. 48p. (ps-8). 1992. 16.95 (*0-399-20974-3*, Philomel Bks); pap. 7.95 (*0-399-21595-6*, Philomel Bks) Putnam Pub Group.

Babbitt, James E., ed. Rainbow Trails: Adventures in Rainbow Bridge Country. Lancaster, John, intro. by. 120p. (Orig.). 1989. pap. 5.95 (*0-317-93359-0*) Glen Canyon Nat Hist Assn.

Bloch, C. America the Beautiful Activity Book. M. J. Studios Staff, illus. 48p. (gr. k-6). 1993. pap. 2.95 (*1-879424-81-9*) Nickel Pr.

Carpenter, Allan. Far-Flung America. new ed. LC 79-12505. (Illus.). 96p. (gr. 4 up). 1979. PLB 16.95 (*0-516-04152-5*) Childrens.

Carratello, John & Carratello, Patty. United States Geography. Chellton, Anna, et al, illus. 48p. (gr. 3-6). 1989. wkbk. 6.95 (*1-55734-160-5*) Tchr Create Mat.

Cool Places U. S. A. Backseat Books. (ps-3). 1994. pap. 3.95 (*0-528-81409-5*) Rand McNally.

Crump, Donald J., ed. Great American Journeys. (Illus.). 1989. 12.95 (*0-87044-669-X*); lib. bdg. 12.95 (*0-87044-674-6*) Natl Geog.

Deltenre, Chantal & Noblet, Martine. The United States. (Illus.). 76p. (gr. 5 up). 1994. 13.95 (*0-8120-6428-3*); pap. 7.95 (*0-8120-1867-2*) Barron.

Duncan, Patsy G. Know America Activity & Coloring Book. 72p. (gr. 2-6). 1989. 2.95 (*0-925449-00-8*) D&M Pubns.

—Know America Coloring & Activity Book. (Illus.). 64p. (Orig.). (gr. 1-6). 1988. pap. text ed. 2.95 (*0-685-25274-4*) D&M Pubns.

Herda, D. J. Environmental America: The Northeastern States. LC 91-29899. (Illus.). 64p. (gr. 5-8). 1991. PLB 15.40 (*1-878841-06-8*) Millbrook Pr.

Koch, Susan C. Colormore Travels - San Antonio, Texas: The Travel Guide for Kids. Koch, Susan C., illus. 32p. (Orig.). (gr. k-4). 1990. pap. 4.50 (*0-945600-05-4*) Colormore Inc.

Lutyk, Carol B., ed. Discover America. (Illus.). 336p. 1989. 26.95 (*0-87044-804-8*); deluxe ed. 36.95 (*0-87044-805-6*); lib. bdg. 39.95 incl. flag (*0-87044-806-4*) Natl Geog.

Marsh, Carole. U. S. A. Jography: A Fun Run Thru the United States, Vol. II. (Illus.). 60p. (gr. k-12). 1994. PLB 24.95 (*1-55609-301-2*); pap. 14.95 (*1-55609-300-4*); computer disk 29.95 (*1-55609-302-0*) Gallopade Pub Group.

Murphy, Jim. Across America on an Emigrant Train. LC 92-38650. 160p. 1993. 16.95 (*0-395-63390-7*, Clarion Bks) HM.

Paltrowitz, Stuart & Paltrowitz, Donna. Content Area Reading Skills U. S. Geography: Cause & Effect. (Illus.). (gr. 4). 1987. pap. text ed. 3.25 (*0-89525-855-2*) Ed Activities.

The Promise of America. (gr. 5-11). 6.95 (*0-87741-008-9*) Makepeace Colony.

Stone, Lynn. Battlefields. LC 93-6781. 1993. write for info. (*0-86625-444-7*) Rourke Pubns.

—Villages. LC 93-16152. 1993. write for info. (*0-86625-448-X*) Rourke Pubns.

Wright, Sarah B. Islands of the Northeastern United States & Eastern Canada. (Illus.). 224p. (Orig.). 1990. pap. text ed. 9.95 (*0-934601-99-2*) Peachtree Pubs.

U. S.–DESCRIPTION AND TRAVEL–MAPS

see U. S.–Maps

U. S.–DISCOVERY AND EXPLORATION

see America–Discovery and Exploration; U. S.–Exploring Expeditions

U. S.–ECONOMIC CONDITIONS

Davies, Nancy M. The Stock Market Crash of Nineteen Twenty-Nine. LC 92-23310. (Illus.). 96p. (gr. 6 up). 1994. text ed. 14.95 RSBE (*0-02-726221-9*, New Discovery Bks) Macmillan Child Grp.

Davis, Bertha. Crisis in Industry. LC 88-38584. (Illus.). 128p. (gr. 10-12). 1990. 12.90 (*0-531-10659-4*) Watts.

O'Toole, Thomas. Economic History of the United States. (Illus.). 88p. (gr. 5 up). 1990. 21.50 (*0-8225-1776-0*) Lerner Pubns.

Woods, Daniel W. Poverty in the U. S. Problems & Policies. LC 87-25246. 1992. PLB 14.85 (*0-8027-6764-8*); pap. 5.95 (*0-8027-6765-6*) Walker & Co.

Wormser, Richard L. Growing up in the Great Depression. LC 93-20686. (Illus.). 112p. (gr. 5-9). 1994. SBE 15.95 (*0-689-31711-5*, Atheneum Child Bk) Macmillan Child Grp.

U. S.–EXPLORING EXPEDITIONS

Here are entered works on exploration within the U. S. and for explorations in other countries which are sponsored by the U. S. Works on early exploration in territory which became a part of the U. S. are entered under America–Discovery and Exploration.

see also names of expeditions, e.g. Lewis and Clark expedition

Halliburton, Warren J. The East-Indian Experience. LC 93-19233. (Illus.). 64p. (gr. 4-6). 1994. PLB 15.40 (*1-56294-340-5*) Millbrook Pr.

U. S. FEDERAL BUREAU OF INVESTIGATION

Archer, Jules. Superspies: The Secret Side of Government. LC 77-72640. (gr. 7up). 1977. pap. 7.95 (*0-440-08136-X*) Delacorte.

Hargrove, Jim. The Story of the FBI. LC 87-36815. (Illus.). 32p. (gr. 3-6). 1988. pap. 3.95 (*0-516-44733-5*) Childrens.

Israel, Fred L. The Federal Bureau of Investigation. Schlesinger, Arthur M., Jr., intro. by. (Illus.). 96p. (gr. 5 up). 1986. lib. bdg. 14.95 (*0-87754-821-8*) Chelsea Hse.

Smith, Carter. A Day in the Life of an FBI Agent-in-Training. Jantzen, Franz, illus. LC 90-11150. 32p. (gr. 4-8). 1991. PLB 11.79 (*0-8167-2210-2*); pap. text ed. 2.95 (*0-8167-2211-0*) Troll Assocs.

U. S.–FICTION

Barracca, Sal & Barracca, Debra. Maxi, the Star. Ayers, Alan, illus. LC 91-44962. 32p. (ps-3). 1993. 13.99 (*0-8037-1348-7*); PLB 13.89 (*0-8037-1349-5*) Dial Bks Young.

Higgins, Bob. Roast Beef in April: An Autobiographical Sketch of the '30's & '40's. Flaming, Doug, ed. 165p. (Orig.). (gr. 7-10). 1993. pap. 9.99 (*0-9637936-2-4*) Deerlick Ent.

Mullin, Penn. Postcards from America Series: The White House Mystery, High Time in New York, Windy City Whirl, Trouble in the Black Hills, San Francisco Adventure. Kratoville, B. L., ed. Rarey, Damon, illus. (Orig.). (gr. 4-12). 1992. pap. 15.00 (*0-87879-957-5*, 957-5) High Noon Bks.

Sonnenmark, Laura A. Something's Rotten in the State of Maryland. 1993. pap. 2.95 (*0-590-42877-2*) Scholastic Inc.

Stuck on the U. S. A. 64p. (gr. 1-7). 1994. pap. 7.95 (*0-448-40179-7*, G&D) Putnam Pub Group.

Swanson, June. I Pledge Allegiance. LC 89-35414. (ps-3). 1991. pap. 5.95 (*0-87614-526-8*) Carolrhoda Bks.

U. S.–FOLKLORE

see Folklore–U. S.

U. S. FOOD AND DRUG ADMINISTRATION

Patrick, Bill. The Food & Drug Administration. Schlesinger, Arthur M., Jr., intro. by. (Illus.). 96p. (gr. 5 up). 1989. lib. bdg. 14.95 (*0-87754-822-6*) Chelsea Hse.

U. S.–FOREIGN POLICY

see U. S.–Foreign Relations

U. S.–FOREIGN POPULATION

see also U. S.–Immigration and Emigration; Minorities; U. S.–Immigration and Emigration;

also Italians in the U. S.; and similar headings

Ashabranner, Brent. An Ancient Heritage: The Arab-American Minority. Conklin, Paul, illus. LC 90-30641. 160p. (gr. 3-7). 1991. PLB 14.89 (*0-06-020049-9*) HarpC Child Bks.

Cantor, David. The Baltic Americans. Moynihan, Daniel P., intro. by. (Illus.). 112p. (gr. 5 up). 1991. 17.95 (*0-87754-890-0*) Chelsea Hse.

Diamond, Arthur. The Romanian Americans. Moynihan, Daniel P., intro. by. (Illus.). 112p. (gr. 5 up). 1988. lib. bdg. 17.95 (*0-87754-898-6*) Chelsea Hse.

Dwyer, Christopher. The Dominican Americans. Moynihan, Daniel P., intro. by. (Illus.). 112p. (gr. 5 up). 1991. lib. bdg. 17.95 (*0-87754-872-2*) Chelsea Hse.

Gernand, Renee. The Cuban Americans. Moynihan, Daniel P., intro. by. (Illus.). 112p. (gr. 5 up). 1989. lib. bdg. 17.95 (*0-87754-869-2*) Chelsea Hse.

Lehrer, Brian. The Korean Americans. Moynihan, Daniel P., intro. by. (Illus.). 112p. (gr. 5 up). 1988. lib. bdg. 17.95 (*0-87754-888-9*) Chelsea Hse.

Lick, Sue. The Iberian Americans. Moynihan, Daniel P., intro. by. (Illus.). 112p. (gr. 5 up). 1990. 17.95 (*0-87754-896-X*) Chelsea Hse.

MacMillan, Dianne & Freeman, Dorothy. My Best Friend Mee-Yung Kim: Meeting a Korean-American Family. Steltenpohl, Jane, ed. Marstall, Bob, illus. 48p. (gr. 3-5). 1989. lib. bdg. 9.98 (*0-671-65691-0*, J Messner) S&S Trade.

Mussari, Mark. The Danish Americans. Moynihan, Daniel P., intro. by. (Illus.). 112p. (gr. 5 up). 1988. lib. bdg. 17.95 (*0-87754-871-4*) Chelsea Hse.

Osborn, Kevin. The Ukrainian Americans. Moynihan, Daniel P., intro. by. (Illus.). 112p. (gr. 5 up). 1989. PLB 17.95 (*1-55546-138-7*) Chelsea Hse.

Shapiro, Ellen. The Croatian Americans. Moynihan, Daniel P. 112p. (gr. 5 up). 1989. 17.95x (*0-87754-891-9*) Chelsea Hse.

Stern, Jennifer. The Filipino Americans. Moynihan, Daniel P., intro. by. (Illus.). 112p. (gr. 5 up). 1990. lib. bdg. 17.95 (*0-87754-877-3*) Chelsea Hse.

Stolarik, Mark. The Slovak Americans. Moynihan, Daniel P., intro. by. (Illus.). 112p. (gr. 5 up). 1988. lib. bdg. 17.95 (*1-55546-134-4*) Chelsea Hse.

Vehiller, Nina. The Haitian Americans. Moynihan, Daniel P., intro. by. (Illus.). 112p. (gr. 5 up). 1991. lib. bdg. 17.95 (*0-87754-882-X*) Chelsea Hse.

U. S.–FOREIGN RELATIONS

Arnoldt, Robert P. Insights: A Guide to the American Experience in Vietnam, 1940 to Present. rev. ed. Marx, Jacqueline A. & Carpenter, Robert S., eds. 100p. (Orig.). (gr. 9 up). 1989. pap. text ed. write for info. Visions Unlimited.

Arnoldt, Robert P. & Marx, Jacqueline A. Vietnam Insights: A Guide to the American Experience in Vietnam 1940 to Present. rev. ed. Carpenter, Robert S., ed. Arnoldt, Robert P., intro. by. LC 89-50664. 232p. (Orig.). (gr. 8 up). 1992. pap. 21.95 (*0-9622776-0-6*) Visions Unlimited.

Cooney, James A. Foreign Policy. rev. ed. 160p. (gr. 7 up). 1992. PLB 15.85 (*0-8027-8116-0*); pap. 9.95 (*0-8027-7368-0*) Walker & Co.

Fincher, Ernest B. Mexico & the United States: Their Linked Destinies. LC 82-45581. (Illus.). 224p. (gr. 7 up). 1983. (Crowell Jr Bks); (Crowell Jr Bks) HarpC Child Bks.

Freeman, Charles. U. S. A. - U. S. S. R. The Superpowers. (Illus.). 72p. (gr. 7-10). 1990. 19.95 (*0-7134-6077-6*, Pub. by Batsford UK) Trafalgar.

Hyde, Margaret O. Peace & Friendship: Russian & American Teens Meet. (Illus.). 96p. (gr. 6 up). 1992. 14.00 (*0-525-65107-1*, Cobblehill Bks) Dutton Child Bks.

Kort, Michael G. The Cold War. LC 93-1934. (Illus.). 160p. (gr. 7 up). 1994. PLB 16.90 (*1-56294-353-7*) Millbrook Pr.

Kuhn, Ferdinand. Commodore Perry & the Opening of Japan. (Illus.). (gr. 4-6). 1955. 2.95 (*0-394-80356-6*) Random Bks Yng Read.

Lawson, Don. The Eagle & the Dragon: The History of U.S.-China Relations. LC 85-47531. (Illus.). 192p. (gr. 7 up). 1985. (Crowell Jr Bks); (Crowell Jr Bks) HarpC Child Bks.

Pascoe, Elaine. Neighbors At Odds: U. S. Policy in Latin America. LC 89-36006. 1990. PLB 14.40 (*0-531-10903-8*) Watts.

Polesetsky, Matthew & Dudley, William, eds. The New World Order: Opposing Viewpoints. LC 91-12374. (Illus.). 240p. (gr. 10 up). 1991. lib. bdg. 17.95 (*0-89908-183-5*); pap. 9.95 (*0-89908-158-4*) Greenhaven.

Wekesser, Carol, ed. American Foreign Policy: Opposing Viewpoints. LC 92-40707. (Illus.). 264p. (gr. 10 up). 1993. PLB 17.95 (*0-89908-199-1*); pap. text ed. 9.95 (*0-89908-174-6*) Greenhaven.

U. S.–GOVERNMENT

see U. S.–Politics and Government

U. S.–HISTORY

Abramowitz, Jack. Readings in American History, Bk. 2. (gr. 4-5). 1987. pap. text ed. 5.25 (*0-89525-862-5*) Ed Activities.

American Heritage Illustrated History of the United States, Vol. 1: The New World. LC 87-73399. (Illus.). 128p. (gr. 7-12). 1988. Repr. of 1963 ed. 3.49 (*0-945260-01-6*) Choice Pub NY.

American Heritage Illustrated History of the United States, 18 vols. LC 87-73397. (gr. 7-12). 1988. Repr. of 1963 ed. Set. 63.00 (*0-945260-00-8*) Choice Pub NY.

The American Way West. (Illus.). 128p. 1990. 17.95x (*0-8160-1880-4*) Facts on File.

Aten, Jerry. Challenge Through American History. (Illus.). 96p. (gr. 4-8). 1992. 12.95 (*0-86653-659-0*, GA1391) Good Apple.

Atkinson, David, illus. Big Book of America. LC 93-85538. 56p. (gr. 3 up). 1994. 9.98 (*1-56138-390-2*) Courage Bks.

Batherman, Muriel. Before Columbus. Batherman, Muriel, illus. 32p. (gr. k-3). 1990. pap. 4.80 (*0-395-54954-X*) HM.

Bouvier, Leon F. Immigration. 160p. (gr. 7 up). 1992. PLB 14.85 (*0-8027-6755-9*); pap. 5.95 (*0-8027-6756-7*) Walker & Co.

Brownstone, David & Franck, Irene. Historic Places of Early America. LC 88-27521. (Illus.). 64p. (gr. 3-7). 1989. pap. 7.95 (*0-689-71234-0*, Aladdin) Macmillan Child Grp.

Burchard, Elizabeth & Allen, Paula. American History: In a Flash. 468p. (gr. 7-12). 1994. pap. 9.95 (*1-881374-12-2*) Flash Blasters.

Burda, Margaret. Amazing States. Sodac, David, illus. 160p. (gr. 4-8). 1984. wkbk. 13.95 (*0-86653-205-6*, GA 546) Good Apple.

Campling, Elizabeth. The Postwar World: The USA since 1945. (Illus.). 64p. (gr. 7-9). 1988. 19.95 (*0-7134-5756-2*, Pub. by Batsford UK) Trafalgar.

Cobblestone Publishing, Inc. Staff. U. S. History Cartoons: For Young People 8-14. (Illus.). 36p. (gr. 4-8). 1987. pap. text ed. 4.95 (*0-942389-02-6*) Cobblestone Pub.

—U. S. History Word Finds: For Young People 8-14. (Illus.). 36p. (gr. 4-8). 1987. pap. 4.95 (*0-9607638-9-9*) Cobblestone Pub.

Etkin, Linda & Willoughby, Bebe, eds. America's Children: Stories, Poems, & Real-Life Adventures of Children Through Our Nation's History. (Illus.). 96p. (gr. 2-7). 1992. write for info. (*0-307-15876-4*, 15876, Golden Pr) Western Pub.

Faber, Doris & Faber, Harold. The Birth of a Nation: The Early Years of the United States. LC 88-30805. (Illus.). 208p. (gr. 7 up). 1989. SBE 14.95 (*0-684-19007-9*, Scribners Young Read) Macmillan Child Grp.

Fast, Suellen M. America's Daughters. Fast, Suellen M., photos by. 100p. (Orig.). (gr. k up). pap. 19.00 (*0-935281-13-4*) Daughter Cult.

Fischer, Max W. American History Simulations. Apodaca, Blanca, illus. 96p. (gr. 5-8). 1993. wkbk. 10.95 (*1-55734-480-9*) Tchr Create Mat.

Fisher, Trevor. Portrait of a Decade: The Nineteen Sixties. (Illus.). 72p. (gr. 7-9). 1988. 19.95 (*0-7134-5603-5*, Pub. by Batsford UK) Trafalgar.

Fry, Annette R. The Orphan Trains. LC 93-29723. (Illus.). 96p. (gr. 6 up). 1994. text ed. 14.95 RSBE (*0-02-735721-X*, New Discovery Bks) Macmillan Child Grp.

Galt, Margot F. The Story in History: Writing Your Way into the American Experience. (Illus.). 280p. (Orig.). 1992. 24.95 (*0-915924-38-2*); pap. 15.95 (*0-915924-39-0*) Tchrs & Writers Coll.

Glassman, Bruce. The Crash of Twenty-Nine & the New Deal. (Illus.). 64p. (gr. 5 up). 1985. PLB 12.95 (*0-382-06831-9*); pap. 7.95 (*0-382-06978-1*) Silver Burdett.

Goldman, Phyllis B., ed. Monkeyshines on How the Fifty States Were Named. Grigni, John, illus. 118p. (Orig.). 1993. pap. 11.95 (*0-9620900-4-2*) NC Learn Inst Fitness.

Goodrich, Charles A. A Child's History of the United States. 1992. Repr. of 1846 ed. lib. bdg. 75.00 (*0-7812-2935-9*) Rprt Serv.

Greenberg, Morrie. American Adventures: True Stories from America's Past, 1770-1870. Long, Laurel, illus. LC 90-2652. 96p. (Orig.). (gr. 4-9). 1991. pap. text ed. 9.95 (*0-9622652-1-7*) Brooke-Richards.

Greene, A. C. The Last Captive. (Illus.). 185p. (gr. 6-9). 1972. 25.00 (*0-88426-004-6*) Encino Pr.

Greene, Jacqueline D. Out of Many Waters. (gr. 5 up). 1988. 16.95 (*0-8027-6811-3*) Walker & Co.

Hakim, Joy. A History of the United States: An Age of Extremes, Vol. 8. (Illus.). 160p. 1994. PLB 19.95 (*0-19-507759-8*); pap. 9.95 (*0-19-507760-1*) OUP.

—A History of the United States: Liberty for All, Vol. 5. (Illus.). 160p. 1994. PLB 19.95 (*0-19-507753-9*); pap. 9.95 (*0-19-507754-7*) OUP.

—A History of the United States: War, Terrible War, Vol. 6. (Illus.). 160p. 1994. PLB 19.95 (*0-19-507755-5*); pap. 9.95 (*0-19-507756-3*) OUP.

—A History of U.S, 10 vols. (Illus.). 1600p. 1995. PLB 199.50 (*0-19-507765-2*); pap. 99.50 (*0-19-507766-0*) OUP.

Higginson, Thomas W. Young Folks' History of the United States. 1992. Repr. of 1875 ed. lib. bdg. 75.00 (*0-7812-3113-2*) Rprt Serv.

Kallen, Stuart. A Modern Nation. Walner, Rosemary, ed. LC 90-82629. (Illus.). 32p. (gr. 4). 1990. PLB 12.94 (*0-939179-91-1*) Abdo & Dghtrs.

—A Nation Divided Eighteen Fifty to Nineteen Hundred. Walner, Rosemary, ed. LC 90-82612. (Illus.). 64p. (gr. 4). 1990. PLB 12.95 (*0-939179-90-3*) Abdo & Dghtrs.

—A Nation United 1780-1850. Walner, Rosemary, ed. LC 90-82610. (Illus.). 64p. (gr. 4). 1990. lib. bdg. 12. 95 (*0-939179-89-X*) Abdo & Dghtrs.

—New Comers to America, Fourteen Hundred to Sixteen Fifty. Walner, Rosemary, ed. LC 90-82616. (Illus.). 64p. (gr. 4). 1990. PLB 12.95 (*0-939179-86-5*) Abdo & Dghtrs.

—Road to Freedom, Seventeen Fifty to Seventeen Eighty-Three. Walner, Rosemary, ed. LC 90-82611. (Illus.). 64p. (gr. 4). 1990. PLB 12.94 (*0-939179-88-1*) Abdo & Dghtrs.

Karl, Jean. America Alive: A History. Schoenherr, Ian, illus. LC 92-40539. 128p. 1994. PLB 22.95 (*0-399-22013-5*, Philomel Bks) Putnam Pub Group.

Killingray, David. The American Frontier. Yapp, Malcolm, et al, eds. (Illus.). 32p. (gr. 6-11). 1980. pap. text ed. 3.45 (*0-89908-206-8*) Greenhaven.

Kranich, Roger E. & Corcoran, Eileen L. Our United States. (Illus.). 256p. (gr. 4-5). 1989. Incl. tchr's. key, 314. pap. text ed. 7.95 (*0-88323-247-2*, 311) Pendergrass Pub.

Kruger, Herbert O., et al. American History Study Aid. 1975. pap. 1.95 (*0-87738-043-0*) Youth Ed.

Kyle, Louisa V. The Witch of Pungo. Dool, Jan, illus. 87p. (gr. 3). 1973. 12.95 (*0-927044-00-5*) Four Oclock Farms.

McNeese, Tim. Conestogas & Stagecoaches. LC 91-24064. (Illus.). 48p. (gr. 5). 1993. text ed. 11.95 RSBE (*0-89686-732-3*, Crestwood Hse) Macmillan Child Grp.

Millard, Catherine. A Children's Companion Guide to America's History. LC 93-78892. (Illus.). 96p. (Orig.). 1993. wkbk. 10.99 (*0-88965-102-7*, Pub. by Horizon Books CN) Chr Pubns.

Munro, Roxie, illus. The Great American Landmarks Adventure. Weeks, Kay, created by. LC 92-31806. (Illus.). 1992. 3.25 (*0-16-038003-0*) USGPO.

Napp, John L. United States History, Bk. I: To 1877. (Illus.). 344p. (gr. 7-12). 1988. text ed. 18.49 (*0-86601-692-9*); tchr's. ed. 12.99 (*0-86601-693-7*); wkbk. 4.99 (*0-86601-694-5*) Media Materials.

Paltrowitz, Stuart & Paltrowitz, Donna. Content Area Reading Skills-Competency U. S. History: Detecting Sequence. (Illus.). (gr. 4). 1987. pap. text ed. 3.25 (*0-89525-856-0*) Ed Activities.

Peel, John. Where in America's Past Is Carmen Sandiego? Nez, John, illus. Vaccarello, Paul, contrib. by. (Illus.). 96p. (gr. 3-7). 1992. pap. 2.95 (*0-307-22205-5*, 22205, Golden Pr) Western Pub.

Roberts, Paul M. Review Text in United States History. 2nd ed. (gr. 7-9). 1989. pap. text ed. 13.33 (*0-87720-857-3*) AMSCO Sch.

Sandak, Cass R. The United States. LC 93-40251. (Illus.). 32p. (gr. 4 up). 1994. text ed. 13.95 RSBE (*0-89686-776-5*, Crestwood Hse) Macmillan Child Grp.

Shifflett, Crandall A. Victorian America. Balkin, Rick, ed. (Illus.). 300p. (gr. 5-10). 1994. 35.00 (*0-8160-2531-2*) Facts on File.

Smock, Raymond W., et al. The American History Slide Collection. 265p. (Orig.). (gr. 7 up). 1977. incl. 2100 slides 895.00 (*0-923805-06-0*) Instruc Resc MD.

—Master Guide to the American History Slide Collection. 265p. (gr. 7 up). 1977. pap. text ed. 25.00 (*0-923805-00-1*) Instruc Resc MD.

Stein, R. Conrad. Ellis Island. 2nd ed. LC 91-33222. (Illus.). 32p. (gr. 3-6). PLB 12.30, Apr. 1992 (*0-516-06653-6*); pap. 3.95, Jul. 1992 (*0-516-46653-4*) Childrens.

Stich, Paul, et al. United States History & Government: A Competency Review Text. 2nd ed. Gamsey, Wayne, ed. Fairbanks, Eugene B., illus. 384p. (gr. 7-12). 1992. pap. text ed. 8.33 (*0-935487-20-4*) N & N Pub Co.

—United States History & Government: A Regents Review Text. 6th ed. Gamsey, Wayne, ed. Fairbanks, Eugene B., illus. 416p. (gr. 7-12). 1992. pap. text ed. 6.22 (*0-935487-21-2*) N & N Pub Co.

—United States History & Government: Ten Day Competency. rev. ed. Gamsey, Wayne, ed. Fairbanks, Eugene B., illus. 128p. (gr. 7-12). 1992. pap. text ed. 4.95 (*0-935487-54-9*) N & N Pub Co.

—United States History & Government: Ten Day Regents Review. rev. ed. Gamsey, Wayne, ed. Fairbanks, Eugene B., illus. 128p. (gr. 7-12). 1992. pap. text ed. 4.95 (*0-935487-49-2*) N & N Pub Co.

Wade, L. Doors to America's Past Series, 8 bks. 1991. Set. 95.60s.p. (*0-86592-464-3*) Rourke Enter.

Wakin, Edward & Wakin, Daniel. Photos That Made U. S. History: From the Cold War to the Space Age, Vol. II. (Illus.). 59p. (gr. 4-7). 1993. 12.95 (*0-8027-8270-1*); PLB 13.85 (*0-8027-8272-8*) Walker & Co.

Weitzman, David. My Backyard History Book. Robertson, James, illus. 128p. (gr. 4 up). 1975. 15.95 (*0-316-92901-8*); pap. 10.95 (*0-316-92902-6*) Little.

Zeman, Anne & Kelly, Kate. Everything You Need to Know about American History Homework. LC 93-46359. (gr. 6 up). 1994. 19.95 (*0-590-49362-0*); pap. 8.95 (*0-590-49363-9*) Scholastic Inc.

U. S.–HISTORY–CHRONOLOGY

see Chronology, Historical

U. S.–HISTORY–DICTIONARIES

Rubel, David. The Scholastic Encyclopedia of the Presidents & Their Times. LC 93-11810. (Illus.). 224p. (gr. 4 up). 1994. 16.95 (*0-590-49366-3*, Scholastic Ref) Scholastic Inc.

U. S.–HISTORY–DRAMA

The Big Four: Mini-Play. (gr. 5 up). 1978. 6.50 (*0-89550-324-7*) Stevens & Shea.

The Flint Sit-Down Strike: Mini-Play. (gr. 5 up). 1978. 6.50 (*0-89550-320-4*) Stevens & Shea.

The Haymarket Affair: Mini-Play. (gr. 5 up). 1978. 6.50 (*0-89550-323-9*) Stevens & Shea.

U. S.–HISTORY, ECONOMIC

see U. S.–Economic Conditions

U. S.–HISTORY–FICTION

Arntson, Herbert E. Caravan to Oregon. LC 57-13207. (Illus.). (gr. 7-11). 1957. 8.95 (*0-8323-0164-7*) Binford Mort.

Aylesworth, Jim. Mr. McGill Goes to Town. Graham, Thomas, illus. LC 89-31111. 32p. (gr. k-2). 1992. pap. 4.95 (*0-8050-2096-9*, Owlet BYR) H Holt & Co.

Carter, Russell G. A Patriot Lad of Old Cape Cod. Pitz, Henry & Sousa, Joseph, illus. LC 75-5092. 224p. (gr. 6-8). 1975. 4.95 (*0-88492-007-0*); pap. 1.95 (*0-88492-008-9*) W S Sullwold.

Collier, James L. & Collier, Christopher. Who Is Carrie? LC 83-23947. 192p. (gr. 4-6). 1984. 14.95 (*0-385-29295-3*) Delacorte.

Curtis, Alice T. A Little Maid of New England. 1991. 7.99 (*0-517-06494-4*) Random Hse Value.

Davidson, Sol M. Wild Jake Hiccup: The History of America's First Frontiersman. Davidson, Penny, illus. LC 91-19499. 160p. (Orig.). (gr. 2-9). 1992. 16.95 (*1-56412-003-1*); pap. 9.95 (*1-56412-004-X*); audio cassette 6.95 (*1-56412-001-5*) Hse Nine Muses. "The story of our tallest unknown folk hero, from his early days in colonial western "Pennsylvanny" to his epic battle with the young Paul Bunyan. Jacob grew up to play no small role in history: he is credited with single-handedly driving the French from Fort Duquesne; suggesting a design for the U.S. flag based on George Washington's pajamas; making Mike Fink the victim of the first April Fool's joke; urging Audubon to add a few birds to his paintings; & inspiring John Chapman, later known as Johnny Peachfuzz - no, Johnny Peanutshell... Johnny Apricotpit something like that. The tale is told in "countrified" prose, illustrated with small, simple line drawings. Readers can absorb a fair dose of history while enjoying the droll adventures of this animal-loving, generally peaceable giant."--KIRKUS REVIEWS, Aug. 1, 1992. "DELICIOUS!"--Mrs. M. Cunningham, 3rd grade teacher, Wash., D.C. "DELIGHTFUL!"--R. Messineo, Administrator, Passaic, N.J. Schools. "CHARMING!"--Mr. J. Wodden, Curriculum Dir., Des Moines, IA, Public Schools. "This book is funny & full of historical information. Overall, this book is very good & on a scale of one to ten, I would give it an eight & a half."--Megan Melamed, Age 12, The Gifted Child Today Magazine (GCT). Also ENJOYING AMERICAN HISTORY: Teacher's Guide to the Mining the Rich Vein of Ideas in Wild Jake Hiccup. Over 200 stimulating projects to make learning American History FUN! 80 pages. Illustrated. ISBN 1-56412-002-3. (softcover.) $5.95. For librarians, parents, grandparents to use with youngsters. Also THE BALLAD OF WILD JAKE HICCUP, audio cassette. Approx. 40 mins. Original words & music composed by John Deltenre & his Pioneer Band. $6. 95. ISBN 1-56412-001-5.
Publisher Provided Annotation.

Davis, Ossie. Just Like Martin. LC 91-4672. 1992. pap. 14.00 (*0-671-73202-1*, S&S BFYR) S&S Trade.

Johnson, Mabel. Escape from Scrooby. (gr. 7 up). 1975. pap. 4.50 (*0-9600838-2-0*) M Johnson.

Langton, Jane & Blegvad, Erik. The Fragile Flag. LC 83-49471. (Illus.). 224p. (gr. 3-7). 1984. PLB 14.89 (*0-06-023699-X*) HarpC Child Bks.

Levy. If You Were There When They Signed the Constitution. 1992. 4.95 (*0-590-45159-6*) Scholastic Inc.

Longmeyer, Carole M. The Lost Colony Storybook. Rhodes, Priscilla, illus. (gr. 4 up). 1994. pap. 14.95 (*0-935326-38-3*) Gallopade Pub Group.

Ormondroyd, Edward. Castaways on Long Ago. 1983. pap. 2.25 (*0-553-15457-5*) Bantam.

O'Sullivan, Anna-Margaret. The Green Bank Year. LC 88-62114. 255p. 1989. pap. 6.95 (*1-55523-183-7*) Winston-Derek.

Pagnucci, Franco & Pagnucci, Susan. Paul Revere & Other Story Hours. (Illus.). 72p. (Orig.). (gr. k-6). 1988. pap. 7.95 (*0-929326-00-8*) Bur Oak Pr Inc.

Stories of the States Series. (gr. 4-6). 1993. PLB 75.00 (*1-881889-45-9*) Silver Moon.

Tripp, Valerie. Molly, 6 bks. (Illus.). 432p. (gr. 2-5). 1991. Boxed Set. lib. bdg. 74.95 (*1-56247-051-5*); Boxed Set. pap. 34.95 (*0-937295-78-7*) Pleasant Co.

U. S.–HISTORY, MILITARY

Chant, Christopher. Military History of the United States, 16 vols. (Illus.). 2000p. 1992. PLB 459.95 (*1-85435-351-9*) Marshall Cavendish.

Foster, Leila M. The Story of the Persian Gulf War. LC 91-4037. (Illus.). 32p. (gr. 3-6). 1991. PLB 12.30 (*0-516-04762-0*); pap. 3.95 (*0-516-44762-9*) Childrens.

Italia, Bob. After the Storm. Wallner, Rosemary, ed. LC 92-17392. (gr. 4 up). 1992. PLB 13.99 (*1-56239-147-X*) Abdo & Dghtrs.

Paton-Walsh, Jill P. Fireweed. (gr. 6 up). 1988. pap. 3.50 (*0-374-42316-4*, Sunburst) FS&G.

Steig, William. Dominic. LC 70-188272. (Illus.). 160p. (gr. 2 up). 1984. pap. 3.95 (*0-374-41826-8*, Sunburst) FS&G.

Stone, Lynn. Battlefields. LC 93-6781. 1993. write for info. (*0-86625-444-7*) Rourke Pubns.

—Forts. LC 93-142. 1993. write for info. (*0-86625-447-1*) Rourke Pubns.

Toussant, Eliza. Soddy Bear: The Persian Gulf War. Rasher, Steven, illus. 76p. (Orig.). (gr. 4 up). 1991. pap. 17.95 (*0-9630583-0-4*) E Toussant.

U. S.–HISTORY, NAVAL

David Farragut. (Illus.). 32p. (gr. 3-6). 1988. PLB 19.97 (*0-8172-2904-3*) Raintree Steck-V.

Foster, Leila M. David Glasgow Farragut: Courageous Naval Officer. LC 91-8031. (Illus.). 152p. (gr. 4 up). 1991. PLB 14.40 (*0-516-03273-9*); pap. 5.95 (*0-516-43273-7*) Childrens.

Sweetman, Jack. American Naval History: An Illustrated Chronology of the U. S. Navy & Marine Corps, 1775-Prese t. 2nd ed. LC 90-29872. (Illus.). 384p. (gr. 7-12). 1991. 42.95 (*1-55750-785-6*) Naval Inst Pr.

U. S.–HISTORY–POETRY

Longfellow, Henry Wadsworth. Paul Revere's Ride. Parker, Nancy W., illus. LC 92-23319. 48p. (gr. 1 up). 1993. pap. 4.95 (*0-688-12387-2*, Mulberry) Morrow.

Min, Kellet I. Modern Informative Nursery Rhymes: American History, Book I. Hansen, Heidi, illus. LC 89-91719. 64p. (Orig.). (gr. 2-5). 1992. pap. 10.95 (*0-9623411-2-6*) Rhyme & Reason.

U. S.–HISTORY, POLITICAL

see U. S.–Politics and Government

U. S.–HISTORY–SOURCES

Smith, Carter, ed. Behind the Lines: A Sourcebook on the Civil War. LC 92-16662. (Illus.). 96p. (gr. 5-8). 1993. PLB 18.90 (*1-56294-265-4*) Millbrook Pr.

—Bridging the Continent: A Sourcebook on the American West. LC 91-31129. (Illus.). 96p. (gr. 5-8). 1992. PLB 18.90 (*1-56294-130-5*) Millbrook Pr.

—The Conquest of the West: A Sourcebook on the American West. LC 91-31130. (Illus.). 96p. (gr. 5-8). 1992. PLB 18.90 (*1-56294-129-1*) Millbrook Pr.
—Eighteen Sixty-Three: The Crucial Year: A Sourcebook on the Civil War. LC 92-16547. (Illus.). 96p. (gr. 5-8). 1993. PLB 18.90 (*1-56294-263-8*) Millbrook Pr.
—Exploring the Frontier: A Sourcebook on the American West. LC 91-31131. (Illus.). 96p. (gr. 5-8). 1992. PLB 18.90 (*1-56294-128-3*) Millbrook Pr.
—The First Battles: A Sourcebook on the Civil War. LC 92-16544. (Illus.). 96p. (gr. 5-8). 1993. PLB 18.90 (*1-56294-262-X*) Millbrook Pr.
—The Legendary Wild West: A Sourcebook on the American West. LC 91-31126. (Illus.). 96p. (gr. 5-8). 1992. PLB 18.90 (*1-56294-133-X*) Millbrook Pr.
—Prelude to War: A Sourcebook on the Civil War. LC 92-16545. (Illus.). 96p. (gr. 5-8). 1993. PLB 18.90 (*1-56294-261-1*) Millbrook Pr.
—The Riches of the West: A Sourcebook on the American West. LC 91-31127. (Illus.). 96p. (gr. 5-8). 1992. PLB 18.90 (*1-56294-132-1*) Millbrook Pr.
—The Road to Appomattox: A Sourcebook on the Civil War. LC 92-16546. (Illus.). 96p. (gr. 5-8). 1993. PLB 18.90 (*1-56294-264-6*) Millbrook Pr.
Steck-Vaughn Company Staff. Voices from America's Past. LC 90-44955. (Illus.). 128p. (gr. 5-9). 1990. PLB 22.80 (*0-8114-2770-6*) Raintree Steck-V.

U. S.–HISTORY–COLONIAL PERIOD

see also Pilgrim Fathers; U. S.–History–French and Indian War, 1755-1763

Alderman, Clifford L. Story of the Thirteen Colonies. Fisher, L. E., illus. (gr. 5-9). 1966. lib. bdg. 9.99 (*0-394-90415-X*) Random Bks Yng Read.
Aliki. The Story of William Penn. Aliki, illus. LC 93-26289. (Orig.). 1994. pap. 14.00 (*0-671-88558-8*, S&S BFYR) S&S Trade.
—Story of William Penn. LC 93-26289. 1994. pap. 5.95 (*0-671-88646-0*, Half Moon Bks) S&S Trade.
American Heritage Illustrated History of the United States, Vol. 2: Colonial America. LC 87-73399. (Illus.). 128p. (gr. 7-12). 1988. Repr. of 1963 ed. 3.49 (*0-945260-02-4*) Choice Pub NY.
Brown, Gene. Discovery & Settlement: Europe Meets the New World (1490-1700) LC 93-8537. (Illus.). 64p. (gr. 5-8). 1993. PLB 15.95 (*0-8050-2574-X*) TFC Bks NY.
Carter, Alden R. The Colonial Wars: Clashes in the Wilderness. (Illus.). 64p. (gr. 5-8). 1993. pap. 5.95 (*0-531-15654-0*) Watts.
Fisher, Margaret & Fowler, Mary J., eds. Colonial America: English Colonies. rev. ed. LC 87-81353. (Illus.). 128p. (gr. 4 up). 1988. 14.95 (*0-934291-23-3*); 11.95 (*0-317-91141-4*) Gateway Pr MI.
Fradin, Dennis B. Colonial Profiles Series, 5 bks. (Illus.). (gr. 3-6). Set. lib. bdg. 74.75 (*0-89490-341-1*) Enslow Pubs.
—The Thirteen Colonies. LC 88-11827. (Illus.). 48p. (gr. k-4). 1988. PLB 12.85 (*0-516-01157-X*); pap. 4.95 (*0-516-41157-8*) Childrens.
Friedenberg, Daniel M. Life, Liberty & the Pursuit of Land: The Plunder of Early America. (Illus.). 423p. 1992. 28.95 (*0-87975-722-1*) Prometheus Bks.
Hakim, Joy. A History of the United States: From Colonies to Country, Vol. 3. (Illus.). 160p. 1993. PLB 19.95 (*0-19-507749-0*); pap. 9.95 (*0-19-507750-4*) OUP.
—A History of the United States: Making Thirteen Colonies, Vol. 2. (Illus.). 160p. 1993. PLB 19.95 (*0-19-507747-4*); pap. 9.95 (*0-19-507748-2*) OUP.
Johnston, Lucile. Celebrations of a Nation: Early American Holidays. 3rd ed. (Illus.). 174p. (gr. 8-12). 1989. 10.95 (*0-9620343-0-4*); pap. 6.95 (*0-9620343-1-2*) Johnston Bicent Found.
Kallen, Stuart. Life in the Thirteen Colonies 1650-1750. Walner, Rosemary, ed. LC 90-82617. (Illus.). 64p. (gr. 4). 1990. PLB 12.94 (*0-939179-87-3*) Abdo & Dghtrs.
Kalman, Bobbie. Colonial Life. (Illus.). 32p. (gr. k-9). 1992. PLB 15.95 (*0-86505-491-6*); pap. 7.95 (*0-86505-511-4*) Crabtree Pub Co.
—A Colonial Town: Williamsburg. (Illus.). 32p. (gr. k-9). 1992. PLB 15.95 (*0-86505-489-4*); pap. 7.95 (*0-86505-509-2*) Crabtree Pub Co.
Katz, William L. From Exploration to the War of 1812, 1492-1814. LC 92-17363. (Illus.). 96p. (gr. 7-8). 1992. PLB 22.80 (*0-8114-6275-7*) Raintree Steck-V.
Longmeyer, Carole M. The Lost Colony Activity Book. Rhodes, Priscilla, illus. (Orig.). (gr. 3 up). 1994. pap. 14.95 (*0-935326-41-3*) Gallopade Pub Group.
Madison, Arnold. How the Colonists Lived. (gr. 7 up). 1980. 8.95 (*0-679-20685-X*) McKay.
Marshall, Peter, et al. The Light & the Glory for Children. LC 92-11727. (Illus.). 160p. (Orig.). (gr. 4-7). 1992. pap. 9.99 (*0-8007-5448-4*) Revell.
Perl, Lila. Slumps, Grunts, & Snickerdoodles: What Colonial America Ate & Why. Cuffari, Richard, illus. LC 75-4894. 128p. (gr. 6 up). 1979. 14.95 (*0-395-28923-8*, Clarion Bks) HM.
Richards, Norman. The Story of the Mayflower Compact. Wiskur, Darrell, illus. LC 67-22901. 32p. (gr. 3-6). 1967. pap. 3.95 (*0-516-44625-8*) Childrens.
Riley, Edward M. Starting America: The Story of Independence Hall. rev. ed. (Illus.). 64p. 1990. pap. text ed. 4.95 (*0-939631-23-7*) Thomas Publications.
St. George, Judith. Mason & Dixon's Line of Fire. LC 90-21625. 128p. (gr. 3-7). 1991. 15.95 (*0-399-22240-5*, Putnam) Putnam Pub Group.
Scott, John A. Settlers on the Eastern Shore 1607-1750. (Illus.). 144p. 1990. 16.95x (*0-8160-2327-1*) Facts on File.
Smith, Carter, ed. Arts & Sciences: A Sourcebook on Colonial America. (Illus.). 96p. (gr. 5-8). 1991. PLB 18.90 (*1-56294-037-6*); pap. 5.95 (*1-878841-67-X*) Millbrook Pr.
—Battles in a New Land: A Sourcebook on Colonial America. LC 91-13940. (Illus.). 96p. (gr. 5-8). 1991. PLB 18.90 (*1-56294-034-1*); pap. 5.95 (*1-878841-65-3*) Millbrook Pr.
—Daily Life: A Sourcebook on Colonial America. LC 91-13941. (Illus.). 96p. (gr. 5-8). 1991. PLB 18.90 (*1-56294-038-4*); pap. 5.95 (*1-878841-68-8*) Millbrook Pr.
—Governing & Teaching: A Sourcebook on Colonial America. (Illus.). 96p. (gr. 5-8). 1991. PLB 18.90 (*1-56294-036-8*); pap. 5.95 (*1-878841-66-1*) Millbrook Pr.
Speare, Elizabeth G. The Witch of Blackbird Pond. 256p. (gr. k-6). 1972. pap. 4.50 (*0-440-49596-2*, YB) Dell.
Stevens, Bernardine S. Colonial American Craftspeople. (Illus.). 112p. (gr. 5-8). 1993. PLB 12.90 (*0-531-12536-X*) Watts.
Tames, Richard. Planters, Pilgrims & Puritans. 64p. (gr. 6-8). 1987. 19.95 (*0-7134-5477-6*, Pub. by Batsford UK) Trafalgar.
Tottle, Edward L. War in the Woods: The Day the United States Began July 9, 1755. (Illus.). (gr. 8). 1992. text ed. 29.00 (*0-937117-05-6*) Educ Materials.
Warner, John F. Colonial American Home Life. (Illus.). 112p. (gr. 5-8). 1993. PLB 12.90 (*0-531-12541-6*) Watts.
Warren, Betsy & Ingerson, Martha. The Thirteen Colonies: A History Picture Book. (Illus.). 32p. (Orig.). (gr. 3 up). 1992. pap. 3.50 (*0-9618660-3-9*) Ranch Gate Bks.
Washburne, Carolyn K. A Multicultural Portrait of Colonial Life. LC 93-10320. (gr. 7 up). 1993. 18.95 (*1-85435-657-7*) Marshall Cavendish.
Zonderman, Jon. A Colonial Printer. LC 94-4015. (gr. 4 up). 1994. write for info. (*1-55916-042-X*) Rourke Bk Co.

U. S.–HISTORY–COLONIAL PERIOD–FICTION

Blackburn, Joyce. The Bloody Summer of Seventeen Forty-Two: A Colonial Boy's Journal. Graham, Critt, illus. 64p. (gr. 5-8). 1985. pap. 4.25 (*0-930803-00-0*) Fort Frederica.
Bulla, Clyde R. Charlie's House. Flavin, Teresa, illus. LC 92-23998. 96p. (gr. 3-6). 1993. 14.00 (*0-679-83841-4*) Knopf Bks Yng Read.
Butters, Dorothy G. The Bells of Freedom. Wilde, Carol, illus. (gr. 4-8). 1984. 15.50 (*0-8446-6162-7*) Peter Smith.
Knight, James E. Blue Feather's Vision, the Dawn of Colonial America. Guzzi, George, illus. LC 81-23082. 32p. (gr. 5-9). 1982. PLB 11.59 (*0-89375-722-5*); pap. text ed. 2.95 (*0-89375-723-3*) Troll Assocs.
—Journey to Monticello, Traveling in Colonial Times. Guzzi, George, illus. LC 81-23156. 32p. (gr. 5-9). 1982. PLB 11.59 (*0-89375-736-5*); pap. text ed. 2.95 (*0-89375-737-3*) Troll Assocs.
—Sailing to America, Colonists at Sea. Guzzi, George, illus. LC 81-23161. 32p. (gr. 5-9). 1982. PLB 11.59 (*0-89375-726-8*); pap. text ed. 2.95 (*0-89375-727-6*) Troll Assocs.
—Salem Days, Life in a Colonial Seaport. Wenzel, David, illus. LC 81-23076. 32p. (gr. 5-9). 1982. PLB 11.59 (*0-89375-732-2*); pap. text ed. 2.95 (*0-89375-733-0*) Troll Assocs.
—The Village, Life in Colonial Times. Palmer, Jan, illus. LC 81-23084. 32p. (gr. 5-9). 1982. PLB 11.59 (*0-89375-728-4*); pap. text ed. 2.95 (*0-89375-729-2*) Troll Assocs.
—The Winter at Valley Forge, Survival & Victory. Guzzi, George, illus. LC 81-23151. 32p. (gr. 5-9). 1982. PLB 11.59 (*0-89375-738-1*); pap. text ed. 2.95 (*0-89375-739-X*) Troll Assocs.
Richter, Conrad. Light in the Forest. (gr. 5-12). 1990. pap. 3.99 (*0-553-26878-3*) Bantam.
Rinaldi, Ann. Fifth of March: A Story of the Boston Massacre. 1993. 10.95 (*0-15-200343-6*) HarBrace.
Speare, Elizabeth G. The Witch of Blackbird Pond. large type ed. 280p. 1989. Repr. of 1958 ed. PLB 15.95 (*1-55736-138-X*, Crnrstn Bks) BDD LT Grp.
Turkle, Brinton, illus. If You Lived in Colonial Times. 1992. pap. 4.95 (*0-590-45160-X*) Scholastic Inc.

U. S.–HISTORY–FRENCH AND INDIAN WAR, 1755-1763

Marrin, Albert. Struggle for a Continent: The French & Indian Wars: 1690-1760. LC 86-26508. (Illus.). 232p. (gr. 5 up). 1987. SBE 15.95 (*0-689-31313-6*, Atheneum Child Bk) Macmillan Child Grp.
Meltzer, Milton. The American Revolutionaries: A History in Their Own Words. LC 86-47846. (Illus.). 256p. (gr. 7 up). 1987. (Crowell Jr Bks); PLB 13.89 (*0-690-04643-X*, Crowell Jr Bks) HarpC Child Bks.
Nardo, Don. The Indian Wars. LC 91-23068. (Illus.). 112p. (gr. 5-8). 1991. PLB 17.95 (*1-56006-403-X*) Lucent Bks.

U. S.–HISTORY–FRENCH AND INDIAN WAR, 1755-1763–FICTION

Cooper, James Fenimore. Last of the Mohicans. (gr. 6 up). 1964. pap. 2.95 (*0-8049-0005-1*, CL-5) Airmont.
—The Last of the Mohicans. Martin, Les, adapted by. Stirnweis, Shannon, illus. 96p. (Orig.). (gr. 2-7). 1993. cancelled (*0-679-94706-X*); pap. 3.50 (*0-679-84706-5*) Random Bks Yng Read.
Keehn, Sally. I Am Regina. 192p. 1991. 15.95 (*0-399-21797-5*, Philomel Bks) Putnam Pub Group.
Mott, Michael. Master Entrick. (gr. 3-6). 1986. pap. 2.95 (*0-440-45818-8*, YB) Dell.
Speare, Elizabeth G. Calico Captive. Mars, Witold T., illus. 288p. (gr. 7-9). 1957. 15.95 (*0-395-07112-7*) HM.

U. S.–HISTORY–REVOLUTION

American Heritage Illustrated History of the United States, Vol. 3: The Revolution. LC 87-73399. (Illus.). 128p. (gr. 7-12). 1988. Repr. of 1963 ed. 3.49 (*0-945260-03-2*) Choice Pub NY.
Bjorkman, Steven. In 1776. Bjorkman, Steven, illus. LC 92-29508. 32p. (ps-3). 1994. 14.95 (*0-590-46973-8*) Scholastic Inc.
Blackburn, Joyce K. Phoebe's Secret Diary: Daily Life & First Romance of a Colonial Girl, 1742. Graham, Critt, illus. 56p. (Orig.). (gr. 3-8). 1993. pap. 6.00 (*0-930803-02-7*) Fort Frederica.
Bliven, Bruce, Jr. American Revolution. (Illus.). (gr. 4-6). 1963. lib. bdg. 9.99 (*0-394-90383-8*) Random Bks Yng Read.
Bovert, Howard E., et al. Book of the American Revolution. Sanchez, Bill, illus. LC 93-21769. (gr. 9-12). 1994. 19.95 (*0-316-96922-2*) Little.
Brenner, Barbara. If You Were There in Seventeen Seventy-Six. (Illus.). 144p. (gr. 3-7). 1994. SBE 15.95 (*0-02-712322-7*, Bradbury Pr) Macmillan Child Grp.
Carter, Alden R. The American Revolution: War for Independence. (Illus.). 64p. (gr. 5-8). 1993. pap. 5.95 (*0-531-15652-4*) Watts.
Clark, Philip. American Revolution. (Illus.). 32p. (gr. 3-9). 1988. PLB 10.95 (*0-86307-930-X*) Marshall Cavendish.
Davis, Burke. Black Heroes of the American Revolution. (gr. 5 up). 1992. pap. 4.95 (*0-15-208561-0*, HB Juv Bks) HarBrace.
De Pauw, Linda G. Founding Mothers: Women of America in the Revolutionary Era. (Illus.). 228p. (gr. 7 up). 1975. 16.95 (*0-395-21896-9*) HM.
Dudley, William, ed. The American Revolution: Opposing Viewpoints. LC 92-21795. 288p. 1992. lib. bdg. 17.95 (*1-56510-011-5*); pap. 9.95 (*1-56510-010-7*) Greenhaven.
Egger-Bovet, Howard. UsKids History: Book of the American Revolution. (gr. 4-7). 1994. 10.95 (*0-316-22204-6*) Little.
Evans, R. E. The War of American Independence. (Illus.). 48p. (gr. 7 up). 1976. pap. 7.95 (*0-521-20903-X*) Cambridge U Pr.
Friedenberg, Daniel M. Life, Liberty & the Pursuit of Land: The Plunder of Early America. (Illus.). 423p. 1992. 28.95 (*0-87975-722-1*) Prometheus Bks.
Fritz, Jean. Can't You Make Them Behave, King George? De Paola, Tomie, illus. 48p. (gr. 3-6). 1982. 13.95 (*0-698-20315-1*, Coward); pap. 6.95 (*0-698-20542-1*) Putnam Pub Group.
—What's the Big Idea, Ben Franklin? (Illus.). 48p. (gr. 2-6). 1982. 13.95 (*0-698-20365-8*, Coward); pap. 6.95 (*0-698-20543-X*, Coward) Putnam Pub Group.
Garrison, Webb. Great Stories of the American Revolution. LC 90-33127. (Illus.). 288p. 1993. pap. 12.95 (*1-55853-270-6*) Rutledge Hill Pr.
Gay, Kathlyn. Revolutionary War. 1995. PLB write for info. (*0-8050-2844-7*) H Holt & Co.
Hakim, Joy. A History of the United States: From Colonies to Country, Vol. 3. (Illus.). 160p. 1993. PLB 19.95 (*0-19-507749-0*); pap. 9.95 (*0-19-507750-4*) OUP.
Harness, Cheryl. Young John Quincy. Harness, Cheryl, illus. LC 92-37266. 48p. (gr. k-5). 1994. RSBE 15.95 (*0-02-742644-0*, Bradbury Pr) Macmillan Child Grp.
Hughes, Libby. Valley Forge. LC 92-23391. (Illus.). 72p. (gr. 4 up). 1993. text ed. 14.95 RSBE (*0-87518-547-9*, Dillon) Macmillan Child Grp.
Jensen, Ann D. The World Turned Upside Down: Children of 1776. Travis-Keene, Gayle, illus. 32p. (Orig.). (gr. 4-5). 1993. pap. 5.95 (*0-9638113-0-4*) Sands Hse.
Johnson, Neil. The Battle of Lexington & Concord. Johnson, Neil, photos by. LC 91-22790. (Illus.). 40p. (gr. 4 up). 1992. RSBE 15.95 (*0-02-747841-6*, Four Winds) Macmillan Child Grp.
Katz, William L. From Exploration to the War of 1812, 1492-1814. LC 92-17363. (Illus.). 96p. (gr. 7-8). 1992. PLB 22.80 (*0-8114-6275-7*) Raintree Steck-V.
Kent, Deborah. The American Revolution: Give Me Liberty, or Give Me Death! LC 93-39046. (Illus.). 128p. (gr. 5 up). 1994. lib. bdg. 17.95 (*0-89490-521-X*) Enslow Pubs.
Marrin, Albert. The War for Independence: The Story of the American Revolution. LC 87-13711. (Illus.). 288p. (gr. 5 up). 1988. SBE 15.95 (*0-689-31390-X*, Atheneum Child Bk) Macmillan Child Grp.
Marshall, Peter, et al. The Light & the Glory for Children. LC 92-11727. (Illus.). 160p. (Orig.). (gr. 4-7). 1992. pap. 9.99 (*0-8007-5448-4*) Revell.
Meltzer, Milton. The American Revolutionaries: A History in Their Own Words. LC 86-47846. (Illus.). 256p. (gr. 7 up). 1987. (Crowell Jr Bks); PLB 13.89 (*0-690-04643-X*, Crowell Jr Bks) HarpC Child Bks.
—American Revolutionaries: A History in Their Own Words 1750-1800. LC 86-47846. (Illus.). 224p. (gr. 7 up). 1993. pap. 6.95 (*0-06-446145-9*, Trophy) HarpC Child Bks.
Merrill, Arthur A. Revolutionary War: An Outline & Calendar. (Illus.). (gr. 7 up). 1976. pap. 2.00 (*0-911894-35-7*) Analysis.

Minks, Louise & Minks, Benton. The Revolutionary War. (Illus.). 128p. (gr. 7 up). 1992. PLB 16.95x (*0-8160-2508-8*) Facts on File.

Morris, Richard B. The American Revolution. rev. ed. Fisher, Leonard E., illus. LC 85-12878. 72p. (gr. 5-10). 1985. PLB 13.50 (*0-8225-1701-9*) Lerner Pubns.

Olesky, Walter. Boston Tea Party. LC 92-26247. (Illus.). 64p. (gr. 4-6). 1993. PLB 12.90 (*0-531-20147-3*) Watts.

Reit, Seymour V. Guns for General Washington: A Story of the American Revolution. (gr. 4-7). 1992. pap. 4.95 (*0-15-232695-2*) HarBrace.

Richards, Dorothy F. George Washington, a Talk with His Grandchildren. Nelson, John, illus. LC 78-8564. (gr. 1-5). 1978. PLB 13.95 (*0-89565-034-7*) Childs World.

Sabin, Francene. American Revolution. Baxter, Robert, illus. LC 84-2582. 32p. (gr. 3-6). 1985. PLB 9.49 (*0-8167-0136-9*); pap. text ed. 2.95 (*0-8167-0137-7*) Troll Assocs.

Schackburg, Richard. Yankee Doodle. Emberley, Ed, contrib. by. LC 93-28633. 1994. 14.00 (*0-671-88559-6*, S&S BFYR) S&S Trade.

Slappey, Mary M. The Constitution of the United States. 17p. (gr. 1 up). 1987. pap. 5.00 (*0-930061-20-9*) Interspace Bks.

Smith, Carter, ed. The Revolutionary War: A Sourcebook on Colonial America. LC 91-13938. (Illus.). 96p. (gr. 5-8). 1991. PLB 18.90 (*1-56294-039-2*); pap. 5.95 (*1-878841-69-6*) Millbrook Pr.

Steen, Sandra & Steen, Susan. Independence Hall. LC 93-5365. (Illus.). 72p. (gr. 4 up). 1994. text ed. 14.95 RSBE (*0-87518-603-3*, Dillon) Macmillan Child Grp.

Steins, Richard. A Nation Is Born: Rebellion & Independence in America (1700-1820) LC 93-24994. (Illus.). 64p. (gr. 5-8). 1993. PLB 15.95 (*0-8050-2582-0*) TFC Bks NY.

Stewart, Gail. The Revolutionary War. LC 91-29889. (Illus.). 112p. (gr. 5-8). 1991. PLB 17.95 (*1-56006-400-5*) Lucent Bks.

Watson, Amy Z. A Colonial Williamsburg ABC. (Illus.). 28p. (ps-k). 1994. 9.95 (*0-87935-127-6*) Williamsburg.

Zall, Paul M. Becoming American: Young People in the American Revolution. LC 92-40199. (Illus.). 208p. (gr. 6-12). 1993. PLB 22.50 (*0-208-02355-0*, Pub. by Linnet) Shoe String.

U. S.–HISTORY–REVOLUTION–BIOGRAPHY

Davis, Burke. Black Heroes of the American Revolution. LC 75-42218. (Illus.). 80p. (gr. 5 up). 1976. 14.95 (*0-15-208560-2*, HB Juv Bks) HarBrace.

Gleiter, Jan & Thompson, Kathleen. Molly Pitcher. Shaw, Charles, illus. 32p. (gr. 2-5). 1987. PLB 19.97 (*0-8172-2652-4*) Raintree Steck-V.

McGovern, Ann. The Secret Soldier: The Story of Deborah Sampson. 64p. (Orig.). (gr. 3-7). 1990. pap. 2.75 (*0-590-43052-1*) Scholastic Inc.

Shelley, Mary V. Dr. Ed: The Story of General Edward Hand. Weatherlow, Regina, illus. LC 78-10331. 36p. (gr. 4-7). 1978. 5.75 (*0-915010-24-0*) Sutter House.

Sherburne, Andrew. Memoirs of Andrew Sherburne: A Pensioneer of the Navy of the Revolution, Written by Himself. Zeinert, Karen, ed. LC 92-20542. (Illus.). 96p. (gr. 7-12). 1993. PLB 15.95 (*0-208-02354-2*, Pub. by Linnet) Shoe String.

Stevenson, Augusta. Molly Pitcher: Young Patriot. Garriott, Gene, illus. LC 86-10744. 192p. (gr. 2-6). 1986. pap. 3.95 (*0-02-042040-4*, Aladdin) Macmillan Child Grp.

Wade, Mary D. Benedict Arnold. LC 94-2574. 1994. write for info. (*0-531-20156-2*) Watts.

U. S.–HISTORY–REVOLUTION–CAMPAIGNS AND BATTLES

Kirby, Philippa. Glorious Days, Dreadful Days: The Battle of Bunker Hill. Edens, John, illus. LC 92-18084. 88p. (gr. 2-5). 1992. PLB 21.34 (*0-8114-7226-4*) Raintree Steck-V.

McPhillips, Martin. The Battle of Trenton. LC 84-40382. (Illus.). 64p. (gr. 5 up). 1984. PLB 12.95 (*0-382-06823-8*); pap. 7.95 (*0-382-09900-1*) Silver Burdett Pr.

Merrill, Arthur A. Battle of White Plains. (Illus.). (gr. 7 up). 1976. pap. 3.00 (*0-911894-27-6*) Analysis.

Murphy, Jim. A Young Patriot: The American Revolution As Experienced by One Boy. LC 93-38789. 1995. write for info. (*0-395-60523-7*, Clarion Bks) HM.

Nordstrom, Judy. Concord & Lexington. LC 92-23392. (Illus.). 72p. (gr. 4 up). 1993. text ed. 14.95 RSBE (*0-87518-567-3*, Dillon) Macmillan Child Grp.

The Revolutionary War Soldier at Saratoga. 48p. (gr. 5-6). 1991. PLB 11.95 (*1-56065-000-1*) Capstone Pr.

Stein, R. Conrad. The Story of Lexington & Concord. LC 82-23518. (Illus.). 32p. (gr. 3-6). 1983. pap. 3.95 (*0-516-44661-4*) Childrens.

—The Story of Valley Forge. Eads, Nancy, illus. LC 84-23203. 32p. (gr. 3-6). 1985. PLB 12.30 (*0-516-04681-0*) Childrens.

—Valley Forge. LC 94-9490. (Illus.). 32p. (gr. 3-6). 1994. PLB 16.40 (*0-516-06683-8*); pap. 3.95 (*0-516-46683-6*) Childrens.

U. S.–HISTORY–REVOLUTION–DRAMA

Hogan, Stephen. Johnny Lynch. Nivens, Chuck, illus. 165p. (gr. 5-6). 1991. PLB 13.00x (*0-945253-07-9*) Thornsbury Bailey Brown.

Lonergan, Carroll V. Brave Boys of Old Fort Ticonderoga. LC 87-22144. (gr. 6 up). 1987. write for info., 192 p. (*0-932334-57-1*, Empire State Bks); pap. 7.95, 144 p. (*1-55787-018-7*, NY16028, Empire State Bks) Heart of the Lakes.

McCaslin, Nellie. Brave New Banner. 20p. 1993. pap. 5.00 (*0-88734-436-4*) Players Pr.

U. S.–HISTORY–REVOLUTION–FICTION

Benchley, Nathaniel. George the Drummer Boy. Bolognese, Don, illus. LC 76-18398. 64p. (gr. k-3). 1977. PLB 13.89 (*0-06-020501-6*) HarpC Child Bks.

—Sam the Minuteman. Lobel, Arnold, illus. LC 68-10211. 64p. (gr. k-3). 1969. PLB 13.89 (*0-06-020480-X*) HarpC Child Bks.

Brown, Drollene. Sybil Rides for Independence. Levine, Abby, ed. Apple, Margot, illus. LC 84-17219. 48p. (gr. 2-5). 1985. 11.95 (*0-8075-7684-0*) A Whitman.

Chalk, Gary. Yankee Doodle. Chalk, Gary, illus. LC 92-53482. 48p. (gr. k-3). 1993. 14.95 (*1-56458-202-7*) Dorling Kindersley.

Clyne, Patricia E. The Corduroy Road. Cary, illus. (gr. 5-9). 1984. 15.25 (*0-8446-6163-5*) Peter Smith.

Collier, James L. & Collier, Christopher. The Bloody Country. 180p. (gr. 9 up). 1985. pap. 3.25 (*0-590-43126-9*) Scholastic Inc.

—My Brother Sam Is Dead. LC 84-28787. 224p. (gr. 7 up). 1984. SBE 15.95 (*0-02-722980-7*, Four Winds) Macmillan Child Grp.

—My Brother Sam Is Dead. 182p. (gr. 9 up). 1985. pap. 2.95 (*0-590-42792-X*) Scholastic Inc.

Cover, Arthur B. American Revolutionary. Martishuis, Walter & Nino, Alex, illus. 144p. (gr. 7-12). 1985. pap. 2.50 (*0-553-26773-6*) Bantam.

Forbes, Esther. Johnny Tremain. Ward, Lynd, illus. 272p. (gr. k-6). 1969. pap. 4.50 (*0-440-94250-0*, YB) Dell.

—Johnny Tremain. Ward, Lynd, illus. (gr. 7-9). 1943. 13.45 (*0-395-06766-9*) HM.

—Johnny Tremain. (gr. 4-8). 1992. 19.25 (*0-8446-6600-9*) Peter Smith.

Ford, Paul L. Janice Meredith. Teitel, N. R., intro. by. (gr. 11 up). 1967. pap. 0.95 (*0-8049-0148-1*, CL-148) Airmont.

Gauch, Patricia L. This Time, Tempe Wick? Tomes, Margot, illus. 48p. (gr. 1-4). 1992. 12.95 (*0-399-21880-7*, Putnam) Putnam Pub Group.

Gerrard, Roy. Sir Cedric Rides Again. (Illus.). 32p. (ps up). 1988. pap. 4.95 (*0-374-46662-9*, Sunburst) FS&G.

Hawthorne, Nathaniel. The Scarlet Letter. Thomson, Hugh, illus. 312p. 1991. 9.99 (*0-517-64302-2*) Random Hse Value.

Hoobler, Dorothy & Hoobler, Thomas. The Sign Painter's Secret: The Story of a Revolutionary Girl. Ayers, Donna, illus. 64p. (gr. 4-6). 1991. 5.95 (*0-382-24150-9*); PLB 7.95 (*0-382-24143-6*); pap. 3.95 (*0-382-24345-5*) Silver Burdett Pr.

Jensen, Dorothea. Riddle of Penncroft Farm. (gr. 3-7). 1989. 14.95 (*0-15-200574-9*) HarBrace.

—Riddle of Penncroft Farm. 242p. (gr. 3-7). 1991. pap. 4.95 (*0-15-266908-6*, Odyssey) HarBrace.

Johnston, Mary. To Have & to Hold. Gemme, F. R., intro. by. (gr. 8 up). 1968. pap. 1.95 (*0-8049-0160-0*, CL-160) Airmont.

Lawson, Robert. Mr. Revere & I. Lawson, Robert, illus. 152p. (gr. 3-6). 1988. pap. 5.95 (*0-316-51729-1*) Little.

Luttrell, Wanda. Stranger in Williamsburg. LC 94-20574. 1995. write for info. (*0-7814-0902-0*, Chariot Bks) Chariot Family.

Marko, Katherine M. Away to Fundy Bay. LC 84-25680. (Illus.). 128p. (gr. 4 up). 1985. 11.95 (*0-8027-6576-9*); PLB 12.85 (*0-8027-6594-7*) Walker & Co.

Moore, Ruth N. Distant Thunder: A Sequel to the Christmas Surprise. LC 91-10845. 160p. (Orig.). (gr. 4-8). 1991. pap. 5.95 (*0-8361-3557-1*) Herald Pr.

Reit, Seymour V. Guns for General Washington: The Impossible Journey. Ross, Richard, illus. 98p. (gr. 3-7). 1990. 15.95 (*0-15-200466-1*, Gulliver Bks) HarBrace.

Rinaldi, Ann. The Fifth of March. 1993. pap. 3.95 (*0-15-227517-7*, HB Juv Bks) HarBrace.

—Finishing Becca: A Story of Peggy Shippen & Benedict Arnold. (gr. 7 up). 1994. pap. 3.95 (*0-15-200879-9*); 10.95 (*0-15-200880-2*) HarBrace.

—A Ride into Morning: The Story of Tempe Wick. Grove, Karen, ed. 289p. (gr. 7 up). 1991. 15.95 (*0-15-200573-0*, Gulliver Bks) HarBrace.

Russomanno, Diane. The Story of the American Flag. 32p. 1991. pap. text ed. write for info. (*1-880501-01-5*) Know Booster.

Smith, Mary P. Boys & Girls of Seventy-Seven. 2nd ed. Silvester, Susan B., ed. Grunwald, C., illus. LC 86-30607. 333p. (gr. 5 up). 1987. Repr. of 1909 ed. 17.00 (*0-913993-08-5*) Paideia MA.

Tharp, Louise H. Tory Hole. (Illus.). (gr. 4up). 1976. pap. 7.50 (*0-686-16261-7*) DCA.

Turner, Ann. Katie's Trunk. Himler, Ronald, illus. LC 91-20409. 32p. (gr. k-3). 1992. RSBE 13.95 (*0-02-789512-2*, Macmillan Child Bk) Macmillan Child Grp.

Walkington, Ethlyn. Betsy Ross, Little Rebel. LC 89-25774. 140p. (Orig.). (gr. 4-6). 1990. pap. 8.95 (*0-944350-13-5*) Friends United.

Wibberley, Leonard. John Treegate's Musket. LC 59-10188. 224p. (gr. 5 up). 1986. pap. 3.95 (*0-374-43788-2*, Sunburst) FS&G.

U. S.–HISTORY–REVOLUTION–NAVAL OPERATIONS

Swanson, June. David Bushnell & His Turtle: The Story of America's First Submarine. Eagle, Mike, illus. LC 90-628. 40p. (gr. 2-5). 1991. SBE 13.95 (*0-689-31628-3*, Atheneum Child Bk) Macmillan Child Grp.

U. S.–HISTORY–REVOLUTION–POETRY

Charles, Carole. The Boston Tea Party. Seible, Bob, illus. LC 75-33156. (gr. 2-6). 1992. PLB 14.95 (*0-913778-18-4*) Childs World.

—John Paul Jones, Victory at Sea. Seible, Bob, illus. LC 75-33157. 32p. (gr. 2-6). 1975. PLB 14.95 (*0-913778-21-4*) Childs World.

U. S.–HISTORY–1783-1809

see also Lewis and Clark Expedition; U. S.–Constitutional History

American Heritage Illustrated History of the United States, Vol. 4: A New Nation. LC 87-73399. (Illus.). 128p. (gr. 7-12). 1988. Repr. of 1963 ed. 3.49 (*0-945260-04-0*) Choice Pub NY.

Friedenberg, Daniel M. Life, Liberty & the Pursuit of Land: The Plunder of Early America. (Illus.). 423p. 1992. 28.95 (*0-87975-722-1*) Prometheus Bks.

Tames, Richard. The American West. (Illus.). 64p. (gr. 7-9). 1988. 19.95 (*0-7134-5731-7*, Pub. by Batsford UK) Trafalgar.

U. S.–HISTORY–1783-1809–FICTION

Connor, Anna T. & Zajdel, Laura C. Seventeen Ninety-Four: Janie Miller's Whiskey Rebellion Saga. (Illus., Orig.). 1994. pap. 11.95 (*0-9640994-0-3*) L C Zajdel.

The government of the fledgling United States imposed an excise tax on whiskey in 1791 to repay its debts from the Revolutionary War. Renewed enforcement of the tax in 1794 created turmoil & hardship in the trade-&-barter economy of western Pennsylvania. Family farmers/distillers sharply debated whether to pay the tax. By mid-1794, the debates turned, in quick succession, to violence, bloodshed, & open rebellion. The United States faced the first test of its domestic strength. President Washington responded by sending federal troops. Ten-year-old Janie Miller was a frontier girl whose family played a key role in the incident of July 15, 1794 which sparked the bloodshed. During the year, Janie's uncle, William Miller, agonized over registering his whiskey still & facing retribution from neighbor "Tom the Tinker," or ignoring the law & facing the consequences in a far-off Philadelphia courtroom. Increasingly pressured to take a stand, he finds himself--& his family--overtaken by events. This dramatic story is seen through Janie's eyes. Pioneer crafts & activities are woven into the story. "1794" is suitable for older children & young adults but can be enjoyed by all ages. L. C. Zajdel, 203 Old Oak Rd., McMurray, PA 15317 (412) 941-2160. ***Publisher Provided Annotation.***

Opie, William. Shenandoah Spector. 120p. (Orig.). 1989. pap. write for info. Opie Pub.

U. S.–HISTORY–1783-1865

Egger-Bovet, Howard, et al. Book of the New American Nation. 1st ed. Rawls, James J., ed. Bruce, Taylor T., illus. LC 94-13075. 1995. 19.95 (*0-316-96923-0*); pap. 10.95 (*0-316-22206-2*) Little.

Hakim, Joy. A History of the United States: The New Nation, Vol. 4. (Illus.). 160p. 1994. PLB 19.95 (*0-19-507751-2*); pap. 9.95 (*0-19-507752-0*) OUP.

Hilton, Suzanne. A Capital Capital City, 1790-1814. LC 91-31340. (Illus.). 160p. (gr. 4 up). 1992. SBE 14.95 (*0-689-31641-0*, Atheneum Child Bk) Macmillan Child Grp.

Steins, Richard. The Nation Divides: The Civil War (1820-1880) LC 93-24993. (Illus.). 64p. (gr. 5-8). 1993. PLB 15.95 (*0-8050-2583-9*) TFC Bks NY.

—A Nation Is Born: Rebellion & Independence in America (1700-1820) LC 93-24994. (Illus.). 64p. (gr. 5-8). 1993. PLB 15.95 (*0-8050-2582-0*) TFC Bks NY.

U. S.–HISTORY–1783-1865–FICTION

Brown, Jane Clark, illus. George Washington's Ghost. LC 93-39194. 1994. 13.95 (*0-395-69452-3*, HM) HM.

Fradin, Dennis B. The Connecticut Colony. LC 89-29205. (Illus.). 160p. (gr. 4 up). 1990. PLB 17.95 (*0-516-00393-3*) Childrens.

U. S.–HISTORY–WAR OF 1812

Berton, Pierre. The Capture of Detroit. (Illus.). 84p. (gr. 5 up). 1992. pap. 5.95 (*0-7710-1425-2*, Pub. by McClelland & Stewart CN) Firefly Bks Ltd.

Bosco, Peter I. War of 1812. (Illus.). 128p. (gr. 7 up). 1991. PLB 16.90 (*1-56294-004-X*) Millbrook Pr.
Carter, Alden R. The War of 1812: Second Fight for Independence. (Illus.). 64p. (gr. 5-8). 1993. pap. 5.95 (*0-531-15659-1*) Watts.
Gay, Kathlyn. War of 1812. 1995. PLB write for info. (*0-8050-2846-3*) H Holt & Co.
Kroll, Steven. By the Dawn's Early Light: The Story of the Star Spangled Banner. Andreasen, Dan, illus. LC 92-27101. 40p. (ps-5). 1994. 14.95 (*0-590-45054-9*) Scholastic Inc.
Marrin, Albert. Eighteen Twelve: The War Nobody Won. LC 84-21623. (Illus.). 190p. (gr. 5 up). 1985. SBE 15.95 (*0-689-31075-7*, Atheneum Child Bk) Macmillan Child Grp.
Morris, Richard B. The War of Eighteen Twelve. rev. ed. Fisher, Leonard E., illus. 72p. (gr. 5-10). 1985. PLB 13.50 (*0-8225-1705-1*) Lerner Pubns.
Nardo, Don. The War of 1812. LC 91-29501. (Illus.). 112p. (gr. 5-8). 1991. PLB 17.95 (*1-56006-401-3*) Lucent Bks.
Whitcraft, Melissa. Francis Scott Key: A Gentleman of Maryland. LC 94-2571. 1994. write for info. (*0-531-20163-5*) Watts.

U. S.–HISTORY–WAR OF 1812–CAMPAIGNS AND BATTLES

The War of Eighteen Twelve Soldier at New Orleans. 48p. (gr. 5-6). 1991. PLB 11.95 (*1-56065-001-X*) Capstone Pr.

U. S.–HISTORY–WAR OF 1812–FICTION

Greeson, Janet. An American Army of Two. (ps-3). 1991. pap. 5.95 (*0-87614-547-0*) Carolrhoda Bks.

U. S.–HISTORY–WAR OF 1812–NAVAL OPERATIONS

Richards, Norman. Story of Old Ironsides. Dunnington, Tom, illus. LC 67-20099. 32p. (gr. 3-6). 1967. pap. 3.95 (*0-516-44628-2*) Childrens.

U. S.–HISTORY–1815-1861

American Heritage Illustrated History of the United States, Vol. 5: Young America. LC 87-73399. 128p. (gr. 7-12). 1988. Repr. of 1963 ed. 3.49 (*0-945260-05-9*) Choice Pub NY.
American Heritage Illustrated History of the United States, Vol. 6: The Frontier. LC 87-73399. 128p. (gr. 7-12). 1988. Repr. of 1963 ed. 3.49 (*0-945260-06-7*) Choice Pub NY.
American Heritage Illustrated History of the United States, Vol. 9: Winning the West. LC 87-73399. 128p. (gr. 7-12). 1988. Repr. of 1963 ed. 3.49 (*0-945260-09-1*) Choice Pub NY.
Berton, Pierre. Revenge of the Tribes. (Illus.). 88p. 1992. pap. 5.99 (*0-7710-1429-5*, Pub. by McClelland & Stewart CN) Firefly Bks Ltd.
Eades, Jo A. A New Salem Primer. (Illus.). 80p. (Orig.). (gr. 5-8). 1989. pap. text ed. 5.95 (*0-685-26274-X*) J A Eades.

U. S.–HISTORY–WAR WITH MEXICO, 1845-1848

American Heritage Illustrated History of the United States, Vol. 7: The War with Mexico. LC 87-73399. 128p. (gr. 7-12). 1988. Repr. of 1963 ed. 3.49 (*0-945260-07-5*) Choice Pub NY.
Jacobs, William J. War with Mexico. LC 92-46115. (Illus.). 64p. (gr. 4-6). 1993. PLB 15.40 (*1-56294-366-9*); pap. 5.95 (*1-56294-776-1*) Millbrook Pr.
Mills, Bronwyn. The Mexican War. Bowman, John, ed. (Illus.). 128p. (gr. 6-12). 1992. lib. bdg. 17.95x (*0-8160-2393-X*) Facts on File.
Nardo, Don. The Mexican-American War. LC 91-16728. (Illus.). 112p. (gr. 5-8). 1991. PLB 17.95 (*1-56006-402-1*) Lucent Bks.

U. S.–HISTORY–CIVIL WAR

see also Slavery in the U. S.

American Heritage Illustrated History of the United States, Vol. 8: The Civil War. LC 87-73399. 128p. (gr. 7-12). 1988. Repr. of 1963 ed. 3.49 (*0-945260-08-3*) Choice Pub NY.
Beller, Susan P. Medical Practices in the Civil War. LC 92-14960. (Illus.). 96p. (Orig.). (gr. 3-7). 1992. pap. 6.95 (*1-55870-264-4*, 70153) Shoe Tree Pr.
Beyer, W. F. & Keydel, D. F., eds. Deeds of Valor: How America's Civil War Heroes Won the Congressional Medal of Honor. (Illus.). 544p. (gr. 3-7). 1992. 9.98 (*0-681-41567-3*) Longmeadow Pr.
Biel, Timothy. The Civil War. LC 91-29500. (Illus.). 112p. (gr. 5-8). 1991. PLB 17.95 (*1-56006-404-8*) Lucent Bks.
Burchard, Peter. Charlotte Forten: A Black Teacher in the Civil War. LC 94-18305. (Illus.). 96p. (gr. 4-7). 1995. 16.00 (*0-517-59242-8*); PLB write for info. (*0-517-59243-6*) Crown Bks Yng Read.
Cannon, Marian G. Robert E. Lee: Defender of the South. LC 93-415. (Illus.). 64p. (gr. 4-6). 1993. PLB 12.90 (*0-531-20120-1*) Watts.
Canon, Jill. Civil War Heroines. Archambault, Alan, illus. (Orig.). (gr. 7 up). 1989. pap. 3.95 (*0-88388-147-0*) Bellerophon Bks.
Carter, Alden R. The Civil War: American Tragedy. (Illus.). 64p. (gr. 5-8). 1993. pap. 5.95 (*0-531-15653-2*) Watts.
Chang, Ina. A Separate Battle: Women & the Civil War. (Illus.). 112p. (gr. 5-9). 1991. 16.00 (*0-525-67365-2*, Lodestar Bks) Dutton Child Bks.
The Civil War Soldier at Atlanta. 48p. (gr. 5-6). 1991. PLB 11.95 (*1-56065-002-8*) Capstone Pr.
Clark, Philip. American Civil War. (Illus.). 32p. (gr. 3-9). 1988. PLB 10.95 (*0-86307-933-4*) Marshall Cavendish.
Coates, Earl J. & Thomas, Dean S. An Introduction to Civil War Small Arms. (Illus.). 96p. 1990. pap. text ed. 7.95 (*0-939631-25-3*) Thomas Publications.
Colman, Penny. Spies! Women in the Civil War. LC 92-18097. (Illus.). 96p. (Orig.). (gr. 3-7). 1992. pap. 6.95 (*1-55870-267-9*, 70158) Shoe Tree Pr.
Cox, Clinton. The Undying Glory. 176p. 1991. 14.95 (*0-590-44170-1*, Scholastic Hardcover) Scholastic Inc.
Currie, Stephen. Music in the Civil War. LC 92-18102. (Illus.). 112p. (Orig.). (gr. 3-7). 1992. pap. 8.95 (*1-55870-263-6*, 70155) Shoe Tree Pr.
Durwood, Thomas A., et al. The History of the Civil War Series, 10 vols. (Illus.). 1600p. (gr. 5 up). 1990. Set. PLB 129.50 (*0-382-09935-4*); Set. pap. 79.50 (*0-382-24044-8*) Silver Burdett Pr.
Gay, Kathlyn. Civil War. (gr. 6 up). 1995. PLB write for info. (*0-8050-2845-5*) H Holt & Co.
Golay, Michael. The Civil War. Bowman, John, ed. (Illus.). 192p. (gr. 6-12). 1992. lib. bdg. 17.95x (*0-8160-2514-2*) Facts on File.
Goodman, Ailene S. Abe Lincoln in Song & Story. LC 88-753827. (gr. 4-12). 1989. incl. audio cass. & guidebook 11.98 (*0-9620704-0-8*) A S Goodman.
Hansen, Joyce. Between Two Fires: Black Soldiers in the Civil War. LC 92-37381. (Illus.). 160p. (gr. 9-12). 1993. PLB 13.90 (*0-531-11151-2*) Watts.
Katz, William L. Breaking the Chains: African-American Slave Resistance. LC 89-36355. (Illus.). 208p. (gr. 5 up). 1990. SBE 15.95 (*0-689-31493-0*, Atheneum Child Bk) Macmillan Child Grp.
Kent, Zachary. The Battle of Antietam. LC 92-12097. (Illus.). 32p. (gr. 3-6). 1993. pap. 3.95 (*0-516-46657-7*) Childrens.
—The Story of the Surrender at Appomattox Court House. LC 87-22468. (Illus.). 32p. (gr. 3-6). 1987. pap. 3.95 (*0-516-44732-7*) Childrens.
McPherson, James M. Marching Toward Freedom: Blacks in the Civil War, 1861-1865. (Illus.). 128p. (gr. 7-12). 1990. 16.95x (*0-8160-2337-9*) Facts on File.
Meltzer, Milton. Voices from the Civil War: A Documentary History of the Great American Conflict. LC 88-34067. (Illus.). 224p. (gr. 7 up). 1989. 15.00 (*0-690-04800-9*, Crowell Jr Bks); PLB 14.89 (*0-690-04802-5*, Crowell Jr Bks) HarpC Child Bks.
—Voices from the Civil War: A Documentary of the Great American Conflict. LC 88-34067. (Illus.). 224p. (gr. 6 up). 1992. pap. 6.95 (*0-06-446124-6*, Trophy) HarpC Child Bks.
Melzer, Milton, ed. Lincoln, in His Own Words. Alcorn, Stephen, illus. LC 92-17431. 240p. 1993. 22.95 (*0-15-245437-3*); ltd. ed. 150.00 (*0-15-245438-1*) HarBrace.
Mettger, Zak. Till Victory Is Won: Black Soldiers in the Civil War. (Illus.). 96p. (gr. 5-9). 1994. 16.99 (*0-525-67412-8*, Lodestar Bks) Dutton Child Bks.
Miller, Howard. Abraham Lincoln's Flag: We Won't Give up a Star. Heiser, John, illus. 26p. (gr. 4-6). 1990. pap. text ed. 4.95 (*0-939631-19-9*) Thomas Publications.
Murphy, Jim. The Boys' War: Confederate & Union Soldiers Talk about the Civil War. (Illus.). 128p. (gr. 4-9). 1990. 15.95 (*0-89919-893-7*, Clarion Bks) HM.
—The Boys' War: Confederate & Union Soldiers Talk about the Civil War. (Illus.). 128p. (gr. 4-7). 1993. pap. 7.70 (*0-395-66412-8*, Clarion Bks) HM.
Piggins, Carol A. A Multicultural Portrait of the Civil War. LC 93-10319. 1993. 18.95 (*1-85435-660-7*, Pub. by M Cavendish Bks UK) Marshall Cavendish.
Powell, Robert M. Recollections of a Texas Colonel at Gettysburg. Coco, Gregory A., ed. (Illus.). 62p. 1990. pap. text ed. 4.95 (*0-939631-26-1*) Thomas Publications.
Ray, Delia. Behind the Blue & Gray: The Soldier's Life in the Civil War. (Illus.). 112p. (gr. 5-9). 1991. 16.00 (*0-525-67333-4*, Lodestar Bks) Dutton Child Bks.
—A Nation Torn: The Story of How the Civil War Began. (Illus.). 128p. (gr. 5-9). 1990. 15.95 (*0-525-67308-3*, Lodestar Bks) Dutton Child Bks.
Reef, Catherine. The Buffalo Soldiers. (Illus.). 80p. (gr. 4-7). 1993. PLB 14.95 (*0-8050-2372-0*) TFC Bks NY.
Reeves, Barbara. The Civil War: A Study Guide. (gr. 5-8). 1991. pap. text ed. 19.95 (*0-88122-688-2*) LRN Links.
Robertson, James I., Jr. Civil War! America Becomes One Nation. LC 91-19177. (Illus.). 192p. (gr. 5-9). 1992. 14.00 (*0-394-82996-4*); PLB 16.99 (*0-394-92996-9*) Knopf Bks Yng Read.
Shorto, Russell. David Farragut & the Great Naval Blockade. (Illus.). 160p. (gr. 5 up). 1990. lib. bdg. 12.95 (*0-382-09941-9*); pap. 7.95 (*0-382-24050-2*) Silver Burdett Pr.
Smith, Carter, ed. Behind the Lines: A Sourcebook on the Civil War. LC 92-16662. (Illus.). 96p. (gr. 5-8). 1993. PLB 18.90 (*1-56294-265-4*) Millbrook Pr.
—Eighteen Sixty-Three: The Crucial Year: A Sourcebook on the Civil War. LC 92-16547. (Illus.). 96p. (gr. 5-8). 1993. PLB 18.90 (*1-56294-263-8*) Millbrook Pr.
—One Nation Again: A Sourcebook on the Civil War. LC 92-16661. (Illus.). 96p. (gr. 5-8). 1993. PLB 18.90 (*1-56294-266-2*) Millbrook Pr.
—Prelude to War: A Sourcebook on the Civil War. LC 92-16545. (Illus.). 96p. (gr. 5-8). 1993. PLB 18.90 (*1-56294-261-1*) Millbrook Pr.
Smith, Gene. Lee & Grant. 448p. (gr. 9-12). 1985. pap. 12.95 (*0-452-01000-4*, Mer) NAL-Dutton.
Steins, Richard. The Nation Divides: The Civil War (1820-1880) LC 93-24993. (Illus.). 64p. (gr. 5-8). 1993. PLB 15.95 (*0-8050-2583-9*) TFC Bks NY.
Stevens, Bryna. Frank Thompson: Her Civil War Story. LC 91-45382. (Illus.). 144p. (gr. 5-9). 1992. SBE 13.95 (*0-02-788185-7*, Macmillan Child Bk) Macmillan Child Grp.
Stewart, Gail B. Why Buy Quantrill's Bones? LC 91-23120. (Illus.). 48p. (gr. 5-6). 1992. text ed. 11.95 RSBE (*0-89686-614-9*, Crestwood Hse) Macmillan Child Grp.
Sullivan, George. Mathew Brady: His Life & Photographs. LC 93-28354. (Illus.). 1994. write for info. (*0-525-65186-1*, Cobblehill Bks) Dutton Child Bks.
Wade, Linda R. Andersonville: A Civil War Tragedy. LC 90-46576. 48p. (gr. 4-7). 1991. 11.95s.p. (*0-86592-472-4*) Rourke Enter.
Weiner, Eric. The Civil War. LC 92-9461. (Illus.). 64p. (gr. 2-6). 1993. 7.98 (*0-8317-2312-2*) Smithmark.

U. S.–HISTORY–CIVIL WAR–BIOGRAPHY

Baxter, Nancy N. Gallant Fourteenth: The Story of an Indiana Civil War Regiment. Niblack, John L., pref. by. 205p. 1986. 16.95 (*0-9617367-8-X*); pap. 12.00 (*0-9617367-0-4*) Guild Pr IN.
Cooper, Michael L. Slave, Civil War Hero: The Story of Robert Smalls. LC 93-44169. (Illus.). 64p. (gr. 3-6). 1994. 13.99 (*0-525-67489-6*, Lodestar Bks) Dutton Child Bks.
De Grummond, Lena & Delaune, Lynn. Jeb Stuart. LC 62-16298. (Illus.). 160p. (gr. 4-6). 1979. pap. 6.95 (*0-88289-247-9*) Pelican.
Johnson, Patricia G. Confederate Woman of New River Border Country. (Illus.). 80p. (Orig.). 1993. pap. 12.00 (*1-878188-03-8*) Walpa Pub.
Reit, Seymour V. Behind Rebel Lines: The Incredible Story of Emma Edmonds, Civil War Spy. 114p. (gr. 3-7). 1991. pap. 4.95 (*0-15-200424-6*, Odyssey) HarBrace.
Shura, Mary F. Gentle Annie: The True Story of a Civil War Nurse. (gr. 4-7). 1994. pap. 2.95 (*0-590-43500-0*) Scholastic Inc.
Tracey, Patrick. Military Leaders of the Civil War. LC 92-34346. (Illus.). 128p. (gr. 6-9). 1993. 16.95x (*0-8160-2671-8*) Facts on File.

U. S.–HISTORY–CIVIL WAR–CAMPAIGNS AND BATTLES

see also names of battles, e.g. Gettysburg, Battle of, 1863

Anderson, Lance. Fort Sumter: The Illustrated Story. (Illus.). 24p. (gr. 2 up). 1993. pap. 3.95 (*0-9640446-0-9*) Typesetters.
Beller, Susan P. Cadets at War: The True Story of Teenage Heroism at the Battle of New Market. LC 90-21952. (Illus.). 96p. (gr. 3-7). 1991. 9.95 (*1-55870-196-6*, 70014) Shoe Tree Pr.
Fritz, Jean. Stonewall. (Illus.). (gr. 3-7). 1979. 15.95 (*0-399-20698-1*, Putnam) Putnam Pub Group.
Kent, Zachary. The Battle of Antietam. LC 92-12097. (Illus.). 32p. (gr. 3-6). 1992. PLB 12.30 (*0-516-06657-9*) Childrens.
—The Battle of Chancellorsville. LC 94-9486. (Illus.). 1994. PLB 16.40 (*0-516-06679-X*); pap. 3.95 (*0-516-46679-8*) Childrens.
—The Story of John Brown's Raid on Harpers Ferry. LC 87-35714. (Illus.). 32p. (gr. 3-6). 1988. PLB 12.30 (*0-516-04734-5*); pap. 3.95 (*0-516-44734-3*) Childrens.
—The Story of the Battle of Bull Run. Catrow, David J., III, illus. LC 86-9642. 32p. (gr. 3-6). 1986. pap. 3.95 (*0-516-44703-3*) Childrens.
—The Story of the Battle of Shiloh. LC 90-21646. (Illus.). 32p. (gr. 3-6). 1991. PLB 12.30 (*0-516-04754-X*); pap. 3.95 (*0-516-44754-8*) Childrens.
Marin, Albert. Unconditional Surrender: U. S. Grant & the Civil War. LC 93-20041. (Illus.). 208p. (gr. 5-9). 1994. SBE 19.95 (*0-689-31837-5*, Atheneum Child Bk) Macmillan Child Grp.
Marrin, Albert. Virginia's General: Robert E. Lee & the Civil War. LC 94-13353. (gr. 5-9). 1994. 19.95 (*0-689-31838-3*, Atheneum) Macmillan.
Murphy, Jim. The Long Road to Gettysburg. (Illus.). 128p. (gr. 4-7). 1992. 15.45 (*0-395-55965-0*, Clarion Bks) HM.
Smith, Carter, ed. The First Battles: A Sourcebook on the Civil War. LC 92-16544. (Illus.). 96p. (gr. 5-8). 1993. PLB 18.90 (*1-56294-262-X*) Millbrook Pr.
—The Road to Appomattox: A Sourcebook on the Civil War. LC 92-16546. (Illus.). 96p. (gr. 5-8). 1993. PLB 18.90 (*1-56294-264-6*) Millbrook Pr.

U. S.–HISTORY–CIVIL WAR–COMMUNICATIONS

Page, Dave. Ship Versus Shore: Civil War Engagements Between Land & Sea. (Illus.). 320p. 1994. 22.95 (*1-55853-267-6*) Rutledge Hill Pr.

U. S.–HISTORY–CIVIL WAR–FICTION

Alphin, Elaine M. The Ghost Cadet. 192p. (gr. 4-6). 1991. 14.95 (*0-8050-1614-7*, Bks Young Read) H Holt & Co.
Banim, Lisa. A Thief on Morgan's Plantation. Yuditskaya, Tatyana, illus. 80p. (gr. 4-6). 1994. PLB 12.95 (*1-881889-62-9*) Silver Moon.
Beachy, J. Wayne. A Bird of Peace Is Born in Petersburg. Hawkins, Beverly, illus. (Orig.). (gr. 5). 1981. pap. 2.50 (*0-9608084-0-X*) B Hawkins Studio.
Beatty, Patricia. Be Ever Hopeful, Hannalee. LC 88-21581. 208p. (gr. 5-9). 1988. 13.00 (*0-688-07502-9*) Morrow Jr Bks.
—Jayhawker. LC 91-17890. 224p. (gr. 5 up). 1991. 13.95 (*0-688-09850-9*) Morrow Jr Bks.
—Who Comes with Cannons? LC 92-6317. 192p. (gr. 5 up). 1992. 14.00 (*0-688-11028-2*) Morrow Jr Bks.
Bellerophon Books Staff. Johnny Reb. (gr. 1-9). 1993. pap. 3.95 (*0-88388-180-2*) Bellerophon Bks.

Biros, Florence K. Dog Jack. Libb, Melva, ed. (Illus.). 192p. (Orig.). 1988. pap. 6.95 (*0-936369-22-1*) Son-Rise Pubns.
Biros, Florence W. Dog Jack. 2nd ed. (Illus.). (gr. 5 up). 1990. 7.95 (*0-936369-47-7*) Son-Rise Pubns.
Charlier, J. M. The Blue Coats. Starwatcher Graphics Staff, tr. from FRE. Giraud, Jean M., illus. 56p. (gr. 12 up). 1990. pap. 7.95 (*0-87416-093-6*, Comcat Comics) Catalan Communs.
Clapp, Patricia C. The Tamarack Tree. 256p. (Orig.). (gr. 5-9). 1988. pap. 3.95 (*0-14-032406-2*, Puffin) Puffin Bks.
Climo, Shirley. A Month of Seven Days. LC 87-5259. 192p. (gr. 5 up). 1987. (Crowell Jr Bks); PLB 12.89 (*0-690-04656-1*, Crowell Jr Bks) HarpC Child Bks.
Collier, James L. & Collier, Christopher. Promises to Keep. LC 93-37655. 1994. 15.95 (*0-385-32028-0*) Delacorte.
Crane, George. Red Badge of Courage. (gr. 4-7). 1993. pap. 4.95 (*0-8114-6837-2*) Raintree Steck-V.
Crane, Stephen. Reader's Digest Best Loved Books for Young Readers: The Red Badge of Courage. Ogburn, Jackie, ed. Barnett, Isa, illus. 120p. (gr. 4-12). 1989. 3.99 (*0-945260-34-2*) Choice Pub NY.
—Red Badge of Courage. (gr. 7 up). 1964. pap. 2.25 (*0-8049-0003-5*, CL-3) Airmont.
—The Red Badge of Courage. Shapiro, Irwin, ed. Cruz, E. R., illus. LC 73-75464. 64p. (Orig.). (gr. 5-10). 1973. pap. 2.95 (*0-88301-101-8*) Pendulum Pr.
—The Red Badge of Courage. Wright, Betty R., adapted by. Shaw, Charles, illus. LC 81-2611. 48p. (gr. 4 up). 1983. PLB 20.70 (*0-8172-1670-7*) Raintree Steck-V.
—The Red Badge of Courage. 1990. pap. 2.50 (*0-8125-0479-8*) Tor Bks.
—The Red Badge of Courage. (Illus.). 224p. 1991. 9.99 (*0-517-66844-0*) Random Hse Value.
—Red Badge of Courage & Other Writings. Chase, Richard, ed. (gr. 9 up). 1972. pap. 9.96 (*0-395-05143-6*, RivEd) HM.
Fleischman, Paul. Bull Run. Frampton, David, illus. LC 92-14745. 112p. (gr. 5 up). 1993. 14.00 (*0-06-021446-5*); PLB 13.89 (*0-06-021447-3*) HarpC Child Bks.
Forman, James D. Becca's Story. LC 92-1375. 192p. (gr. 7 up). 1992. SBE 14.95 (*0-684-19332-9*, Scribners Young Read) Macmillan Child Grp.
Garland, Hamlin. The Return of a Private. LC 92-44051. 1994. 13.95 (*0-88682-583-0*) Creative Ed.
Gauch, Patricia L. Thunder at Gettysburg. Gammell, Stephen, illus. 48p. (gr. 3-6). 1990. 14.95 (*0-399-22201-4*, Putnam) Putnam Pub Group.
Gurasich, Marj. A House Divided. LC 93-14189. 174p. (gr. 5-8). 1994. pap. 9.95 (*0-87565-122-4*) Tex Christian.
Hansen, Joyce. Out from This Place. 144p. 1992. pap. 3.50 (*0-380-71409-4*, Camelot) Avon.
—Which Way Freedom? 128p. 1992. pap. 3.99 (*0-380-71408-6*, Camelot) Avon.
Houston, Gloria. Mountain Valor. Allen, Thomas B., illus. LC 92-26218. 240p. (gr. 8 up). 1994. 14.95 (*0-399-22519-6*, Philomel Bks) Putnam Pub Group.
Hunt, Irene. Across Five Aprils. LC 92-46736. 212p. (gr. 4 up). 1993. PLB 10.95 (*0-382-24358-7*); 8.95 (*0-382-24367-6*) Silver Burdett Pr.
Kassem, Lou. Listen for Rachel. 176p. (gr. 5). 1992. pap. 3.50 (*0-380-71231-8*, Flare) Avon.
Keith, Harold. Rifles for Watie. LC 57-10280. 352p. (gr. 7 up). 1987. pap. 3.95 (*0-06-447030-X*, Trophy) HarpC Child Bks.
—Rifles for Watie. reissued ed. LC 57-10280. 332p. (gr. 7 up). 1991. PLB 14.89 (*0-690-04907-2*, Crowell Jr Bks) HarpC Child Bks.
Lyon, George E. Here & Then. LC 94-6921. 128p. (gr. 5-7). 1994. 14.95 (*0-531-06866-8*); PLB 14.99 (*0-531-08716-6*) Orchard Bks Watts.
Marius, Richard. After the War. LC 94-2927. 640p. pap. 14.95 (*1-55853-273-0*) Rutledge Hill Pr.
Masi, Doris H. Pride O' the Hilltop. 180p. 1992. pap. 12.00 (*0-9628208-6-5*) Canal Side Pubs.
Nixon, Joan L. A Dangerous Promise. LC 94-464. 1994. 15.95 (*0-385-32073-6*) Delacorte.
O'Dell, Scott. Sarah Bishop. (gr. 7 up). 1980. 14.45 (*0-395-29185-2*) HM.
—The Two Hundred Ninety. (gr. 5-9). 1976. 15.45 (*0-395-24737-3*) HM.
Phillips, Michael. Land of the Brave & the Free. 304p. (Orig.). 1993. pap. 8.99 (*1-55661-308-3*) Bethany Hse.
Polacco, Patricia. Pink & Say. LC 93-36340. (Illus.). 48p. (ps-3). 1994. PLB 15.95 (*0-399-22671-0*, Philomel Bks) Putnam Pub Group.
Reeder, Carolyn. Shades of Gray. LC 89-31976. 176p. (gr. 3-7). 1989. SBE 13.95 (*0-02-775810-9*, Macmillan Child Bk) Macmillan Child Grp.
—Shades of Gray. 160p. 1991. pap. 3.99 (*0-380-71232-6*, Camelot) Avon.
Richards, R. W. A Southern Yarn. Bogart, Jeffrey, ed. Willard-Chang, Nancy, illus. LC 89-92811. (Orig.). 1990. pap. write for info. (*0-9625502-0-5*) Rokarn Pubns.
Rinaldi, Ann. In My Father's House. LC 91-46839. 304p. (gr. 7 up). 1993. 13.95 (*0-590-44730-0*) Scholastic Inc.

Rosholt, Malcolm & Rosholt, Margaret. The Story of Old Abe: Wisconsin's Civil War Hero. Mullen, Don, illus. 99p. (gr. 4 up). 1987. PLB 12.95 (*0-910417-09-1*) Rosholt Hse. THE STORY OF OLD ABE, WISCONSIN'S CIVIL WAR HERO, captured as an eaglet in forests of Chippewa County, became a mascot for the Eighth Wisconsin Regiment. He was inducted into the army at Camp Randall in Madison, Wisconsin. He took part in many battles in Mississippi, Missouri, & Illinois. A soldier was assigned to carry the eagle on a roost atop a pole in front of the marching army. The men said he gave them courage. Before the war was over, the Regiment voted to give Old Abe to the Wisconsin Governor, & Abe was given two rooms in the basement of the capitol. Here children came to visit & veterans brought their families. Abe was taken to fairs & veterans' reunions & thousands of his pictures were sold. The money was donated to build a hospital for wounded veterans. Abe's greatest exhibit came in Philadelphia for the Centennial Celebration of the Declaration of Independence in 1876. On May 22, 1911, a delegation of Wisconsin veterans, led by the Governor, were in Vicksburg to dedicate a monument to the men who lost their lives. On top of a tall obelisk in the Wisconsin section of Vicksburg National Cemetery stands a six-foot bronze statue of Old Abe. THE STORY OF OLD ABE won the Award of Merit for literature from The State Historical Society of Wisconsin in 1988. One librarian wrote, "Thank you for making history come alive for children."
Publisher Provided Annotation.

Sohl, Marcia & Dackerman, Gerald. The Red Badge of Courage: Student Activity Book. Cruz, E. R., illus. 16p. (gr. 4-10). 1976. pap. 1.25 (*0-88301-184-0*) Pendulum Pr.
Spier, Peter. Star-Spangled Banner. (ps-3). 1992. pap. 3.99 (*0-440-40697-8*, YB) Dell.
Steele, William O. Perilous Road. 156p. (gr. 3-7). 1990. pap. 3.95 (*0-15-260647-5*, Odyssey) HarBrace.
Tolliver, Ruby C. Muddy Banks. LC 85-20851. (Illus.). 154p. (gr. 4up). 1987. 14.95 (*0-87565-062-7*); pap. 6.95 (*0-87565-049-X*) Tex Christian.
Townsend, Tom. The Battle of Galveston. Eakin, Edwin M., ed. Little, Debbie, illus. 80p. (gr. 9-11). 1989. 10.95 (*0-89015-685-9*, Pub. by Panda Bks); pap. 5.95 (*0-89015-713-8*) Sunbelt Media.
Webber, Earlynne. The Secret of the Big Thicket. 1994. 12.95 (*0-89015-958-0*) Sunbelt Media.
Williams, George F. Bullet & Shell: The Civil War As the Soldier Saw It. (Illus.). 480p. 1992. 9.98 (*0-681-41497-9*) Longmeadow Pr.
Wisler, G. Clifton. Mr. Lincoln's Drummer. 144p. (gr. 7 up). 1994. 14.99 (*0-525-67463-2*, Lodestar Bks) Dutton Child Bks.
—Red Cap. 160p. (gr. 5-9). 1991. 15.00 (*0-525-67337-7*, Lodestar Bks) Dutton Child Bks.

U. S.–HISTORY–CIVIL WAR–NAVAL OPERATIONS

Carter, Alden R. Battle of the Ironclads: The Monitor & the Merrimack. LC 93-417. (Illus.). 64p. (gr. 4-6). 1993. PLB 12.90 (*0-531-20091-4*) Watts.

U. S.–HISTORY–CIVIL WAR–POETRY

Whittier, John Greenleaf. Barbara Frietchie. Parker, Nancy W., illus. LC 90-41755. 32p. (gr. 1 up). 1992. 14.00 (*0-688-09829-0*); PLB 13.93 (*0-688-09830-4*) Greenwillow.

U. S.–HISTORY–1865-1898

American Heritage Illustrated History of the United States, Vol. 11: The Gilded Age. LC 87-73399. (Illus.). 128p. (gr. 7-12). 1988. Repr. of 1963 ed. 3.49 (*0-945260-11-3*) Choice Pub NY.
Brown, Gene. The Struggle to Grow: Expansionism & Industrialization (1880-1913) LC 93-24992. (Illus.). 64p. (gr. 5-8). 1993. PLB 15.95 (*0-8050-2584-7*) TFC Bks NY.
DeMattos, Jack. Masterson & Roosevelt. Earle, James H., illus. DeArment, Robert K., photos by. LC 84-17591. (Illus.). 151p. (gr. 9 up). 1984. 18.95 (*0-932702-31-7*) Creative Texas.
Hakim, Joy. A History of the United States: Reconstruction & Reform, Vol. 7. (Illus.). 160p. 1994. PLB 19.95 (*0-19-507757-1*); pap. 9.95 (*0-19-507758-X*) OUP.
Levinson, Nancy S. Turn of the Century: Our Nation One Hundred Years Ago. LC 93-4604. (Illus.). 144p. (gr. 5-9). 1994. 16.99 (*0-525-67433-0*, Lodestar Bks) Dutton Child Bks.
Mettger, Zak. Reconstruction: America after the Civil War. (Illus.). 96p. 1994. 16.99 (*0-525-67490-X*, Lodestar Bks) Dutton Child Bks.
Wakin, Edward & Wakin, Daniel. Photos That Made U. S. History: From the Civil War to the Atomic Age, Vol. I. (Illus.). 64p. (gr. 4-7). 1993. 12.95 (*0-8027-8230-2*); PLB 13.85 (*0-8027-8231-0*) Walker & Co.

U. S.–HISTORY–1865-1898–FICTION

Morris, Gilbert. The Crossed Sabres. 304p. (Orig.). 1993. pap. 8.99 (*1-55661-309-1*) Bethany Hse.

U. S.–HISTORY–1898-

Wakin, Edward & Wakin, Daniel. Photos That Made U. S. History: From the Civil War to the Atomic Age, Vol. I. (Illus.). 64p. (gr. 4-7). 1993. 12.95 (*0-8027-8230-2*); PLB 13.85 (*0-8027-8231-0*) Walker & Co.

U. S.–HISTORY–1898-1919

American Heritage Illustrated History of the United States, Vol. 12: A World Power. LC 87-73399. (Illus.). 128p. (gr. 7-12). 1988. Repr. of 1963 ed. 3.49 (*0-945260-12-1*) Choice Pub NY.
Brown, Gene. The Struggle to Grow: Expansionism & Industrialization (1880-1913) LC 93-24992. (Illus.). 64p. (gr. 5-8). 1993. PLB 15.95 (*0-8050-2584-7*) TFC Bks NY.
DeMattos, Jack. Masterson & Roosevelt. Earle, James H., illus. DeArment, Robert K., photos by. LC 84-17591. (Illus.). 151p. (gr. 9 up). 1984. 18.95 (*0-932702-31-7*) Creative Texas.

U. S.–HISTORY–WAR OF 1898

Bachrach, Deborah. The Spanish-American War. LC 91-16730. (Illus.). 112p. (gr. 5-8). 1991. PLB 17.95 (*1-56006-405-6*) Lucent Bks.
Carter, Alden R. The Spanish-American War: Imperial Ambitions. LC 91-14753. (Illus.). 64p. (gr. 5-8). 1992. PLB 12.90 (*0-531-20078-7*) Watts.
—The Spanish-American War: Imperial Ambitions. (Illus.). 64p. (gr. 5-8). 1993. pap. 5.95 (*0-531-15657-5*) Watts.
Gay, Kathlyn. Spanish American War. 1995. PLB write for info. (*0-8050-2847-1*) H Holt & Co.
Kent, Zachary. The Story of the Rough Riders. LC 90-22444. (Illus.). 32p. (gr. 3-6). 1991. PLB 12.30 (*0-516-04756-6*); pap. 3.95 (*0-516-44756-4*) Childrens.
—The Story of the Sinking of the Battleship Maine. LC 87-35465. (Illus.). 30p. (gr. 3-6). 1988. pap. 3.95 (*0-516-44736-X*) Childrens.
Marrin, Albert. The Spanish-American War. LC 90-935. (Illus.). 192p. (gr. 5 up). 1991. SBE 15.95 (*0-689-31663-1*, Atheneum Child Bk) Macmillan Child Grp.
The Spanish-American War Soldier at San Juan Hill. 48p. (gr. 5-6). 1991. PLB 11.95 (*1-56065-003-6*) Capstone Pr.

U. S.–HISTORY–WAR OF 1898–FICTION

Howard, Elizabeth F. Papa Tells Chita a Story. Cooper, Floyd, illus. LC 93-1252. 40p. (ps-2). 1995. RSBE 15.00 (*0-02-744623-9*, Four Winds) Macmillan Child Grp.

U. S.–HISTORY–20TH CENTURY

American Heritage Illustrated History of the United States, Vol. 16: Decades of Cold War 1946-1963. LC 87-73399. 128p. (gr. 7-12). 1988. Repr. of 1963 ed. 3.49 (*0-945260-16-4*) Choice Pub NY.
Brown, Gene. Conflict in Europe & the Great Depression: World War I (1914-1940) LC 93-24998. (Illus.). 64p. (gr. 5-8). 1993. PLB 15.95 (*0-8050-2585-5*) TFC Bks Ny.
Gregory, Ross. America 1914 to 1945. Balkin, Rick, ed. (Illus.). 300p. (gr. 5-10). 1994. 35.00 (*0-8160-2532-0*) Facts on File.
Hakim, Joy. All the People. LC 93-28564. 1995. lib. bdg. 19.95 (*0-19-507763-6*); pap. 9.95 (*0-19-507764-4*) OUP.
—War, Peace, & All That Jazz. LC 93-28768. (Illus.). 160p. 1994. PLB 19.95 (*0-19-507761-X*); pap. 9.95 (*0-19-507762-8*) OUP.
Katz, William L. From World War Two to the New Frontier, 1940-1963. LC 92-42801. (Illus.). 96p. (gr. 7-8). 1993. PLB 22.80 (*0-8114-6280-3*) Raintree Steck-V.
—The New Freedom to the New Deal, 1913-1939. LC 92-39948. (Illus.). 96p. (gr. 7-8). 1993. PLB 22.80 (*0-8114-6279-X*) Raintree Steck-V.
Medearis, Angela S. Picking Peas for a Penny. Shaw, Charles, illus. LC 89-49754. 36p. (gr. 1-4). 1990. 11.95 (*0-938349-54-6*) State House Pr.
Meltzer, Milton. Ain't Gonna Study War No More: The Story of America's Peace Seekers. LC 84-48337. (Illus.). 288p. (gr. 7 up). 1985. PLB 14.89 (*0-06-024200-0*) HarpC Child Bks.
—The American Promise: Voices of a Changing Nation, 1945-Present. (Illus.). (gr. 7 up). 1990. 15.95 (*0-553-07020-7*, Starfire) Bantam.
Steins, Richard. Postwar Years: The Cold War & the Atomic Age (1950-1959) (Illus.). 64p. (gr. 5-8). 1993. PLB 15.95 (*0-8050-2587-1*) TFC Bks NY.

Westwood, Phoebe L. & Rohrbacher, Richard W. Yesteryear's Child: Golden Days & Summer Nights. LC 93-77688. 176p. (gr. 3-5). 1993. pap. 11.95

(*0-9623048-7-5*) Heritage West. Learn the answers in Richard Rohrbacher's captivating memoir of life in the first years of the twentieth century. Travel back to a time before television & space travel, before radio, women's suffrage, & penicillin. Discover a familiar world of family work & play. YESTERYEAR'S CHILD: Golden Days & Summer Nights tells of everyday life from town to farm & brings alive a time & place in our collective American past. Outdoor privies were replaced by indoor plumbing; horse-drawn carriages shared the dusty roads with the first automobiles; & the earliest telephone numbers were single digits. This delightful tale will evoke memories in the old & wonder in the young. A must for all school libraries & highly recommended for classrooms. "I now teach third grade, & we teach Valley Days...it helps me explain the 'olden days'," said Norma Brown, teacher, Stockton. "...the ordinary domestic work week is an eye-opener," writes Dan Barnett, The Chico Enterprise. Call or write for information to order, Heritage West Books, 306 Regent Ct., Stockton, CA 95204. 209-464-8818. *Publisher Provided Annotation.*

U. S.–HISTORY–1919-1933

American Heritage Illustrated History of the United States, Vol. 13: World War I. LC 87-73399. (Illus.). 128p. (gr. 7-12). 1988. Repr. of 1963 ed. 3.49 (*0-945260-13-X*) Choice Pub NY.

Blocksma, Mary. Ticket to the Twenties: A Time Traveler's Guide. Dennen, Susan, illus. LC 92-24303. 1993. 15.95 (*0-316-09974-0*) Little.

Johnson, Hilda S. A Child's Diary - the 1930's. Johnson, Hilda S., illus. LC 88-51304. 64p. (Orig.). (gr. 3-8). 1988. pap. 3.95 (*0-931563-02-X*) Wishing Rm.

Meltzer, Milton. Brother, Can You Spare a Dime: The Great Depression 1929-1933. (Illus.). 144p. 1990. 16. 95x (*0-8160-2372-7*) Facts on File.

Schraff, Anne E. The Great Depression & the New Deal: America's Economic Collapse & Recovery. (Illus.). 128p. (gr. 9-12). 1990. PLB 13.90 (*0-531-10964-X*) Watts.

Stein, R. Conrad. The Roaring Twenties. LC 93-37029. (Illus.). 32p. (gr. 3-6). 1994. PLB 12.30 (*0-516-06675-7*) Childrens.

U. S.–HISTORY–1933-1945

American Heritage Illustrated History of the United States, Vol. 14: The Roosevelt Era. LC 87-73399. 128p. (gr. 7-12). 1988. Repr. of 1963 ed. 3.49 (*0-945260-14-8*) Choice Pub NY.

Devaney, John. America Goes to War, 1941. 192p. (gr. 12 up). 1991. 16.95 (*0-8027-6979-9*); lib. bdg. 17.85 (*0-8027-6980-2*) Walker & Co.

—America Storms the Beaches, 1944. LC 92-47057. (Illus.). 176p. (gr. 7 up). 1993. 17.95 (*0-8027-8244-2*); PLB 18.85 (*0-8027-8245-0*) Walker & Co.

Johnson, Hilda S. A Child's Diary - the 1930's. Johnson, Hilda S., illus. LC 88-51304. 64p. (Orig.). (gr. 3-8). 1988. pap. 3.95 (*0-931563-02-X*) Wishing Rm.

Lawson, Don. The Abraham Lincoln Brigade: Americans Fighting Fascism in the Spanish Civil War. LC 88-20263. (Illus.). 176p. (gr. 7 up). 1989. (Crowell Jr Bks); (Crowell Jr Bks) HarpC Child Bks.

Schraff, Anne E. The Great Depression & the New Deal: America's Economic Collapse & Recovery. (Illus.). 128p. (gr. 9-12). 1990. PLB 13.90 (*0-531-10964-X*) Watts.

Stein, Richard C. The Great Depression. LC 93-752. (Illus.). 32p. (gr. 3-6). 1993. PLB 12.30 (*0-516-06668-4*); pap. 3.95 (*0-516-46668-2*) Childrens.

Stewart, Gail B. The New Deal. LC 92-41264. (Illus.). 112p. (gr. 6 up). 1993. text ed. 14.95 RSBE (*0-02-788369-8*, New Discovery Bks) Macmillan Child Grp.

U. S.–HISTORY–WORLD WAR, 1939-1945

see World War, 1939-1945–U. S.

U. S.–HISTORY–1961-

American Heritage Illustrated History of the United States, Vol. 17: Vietnam Era. LC 87-73399. 128p. (gr. 7-12). 1988. Repr. of 1963 ed. 3.49 (*0-945260-17-2*) Choice Pub NY.

American Heritage Illustrated History of the United States, Vol. 18: America Today 1976-1988. LC 87-73399. 128p. (gr. 7-12). 1988. Repr. of 1963 ed. 3.49 (*0-945260-18-0*) Choice Pub NY.

Archer, Jules. The Incredible Sixties: The Stormy Years That Changed America. LC 85-16421. (Illus.). 223p. (gr. 7 up). 1986. 17.95 (*0-15-238298-4*, HB Juv Bks) HarBrace.

Brown, Gene. The Nation in Turmoil: Civil Rights & the Vietnam War (1960-1973) LC 93-24995. (Illus.). 64p. (gr. 5-8). 1993. PLB 15.95 (*0-8050-2588-X*) TFC Bks NY.

Finkelstein, Norman H. Thirteen Days - Ninety Miles: The Cuban Missile Crisis. LC 93-29425. 1994. 15.00 (*0-671-86622-2*, J Messner); pap. write for info. (*0-671-86623-0*, J Messner) S&S Trade.

Garrett, Michael. The Seventies. LC 89-27177. (Illus.). 48p. (gr. 5-9). 1990. PLB 21.99 (*0-8114-4214-4*) Raintree Steck-V.

Goldstein, Toby. Waking from the Dream: America in the Sixties. LC 87-14016. (Illus.). 160p. (gr. 7-12). 1988. (J Messner); pap. 5.95 (*0-671-66051-9*) S&S Trade.

Grey, Edward. The Eighties. LC 89-27178. (Illus.). 48p. (gr. 5-9). 1990. PLB 21.99 (*0-8114-4215-2*) Raintree Steck-V.

—The Sixties. LC 89-21618. (Illus.). 48p. (gr. 5-9). 1990. PLB 21.99 (*0-8114-4213-6*) Raintree Steck-V.

Haskins, James S. & Benson, Kathleen. The Sixties Reader. LC 85-40886. (Illus.). 256p. (gr. 7 up). 1988. pap. 13.95 (*0-670-80674-9*) Viking Child Bks.

Lawson, Don. The United States in the Vietnam War. LC 80-2460. (Illus.). 160p. (gr. 7 up). 1981. (Crowell Jr Bks) HarpC Child Bks.

Martinet, Jeanne. The Year You Were Born, 1983. Lanfredi, Judy, illus. LC 91-31605. 56p. 1992. PLB 13.93 (*0-688-11078-9*, Tambourine Bks); pap. 7.95 (*0-688-11077-0*, Tambourine Bks) Morrow.

Smith, Carter, III. One Giant Leap for Mankind. rev. ed. (Illus.). 64p. (gr. 5 up). 1989. PLB 12.95 (*0-382-09909-5*); pap. 7.95 (*0-382-09910-9*) Silver Burdett Pr.

U. S.–IMMIGRATION AND EMIGRATION

see also U. S.–Foreign Population; also Italians in the U. S.; and similar headings

American Voices Series, 6 bks. 1991. Set. 83.70s.p. (*0-86593-134-8*) Rourke Corp.

Ashabranner, Brent. Still a Nation of Immigrants. Ashabranner, Jennifer, photos by. LC 92-44335. (Illus.). 144p. (gr. 5 up). 1993. 15.99 (*0-525-65130-6*, Cobblehill Bks) Dutton Child Bks.

Bales, Carol A. Tales of the Elders: A Memory Book of Men & Women Who Came to America as Immigrants, 1900-1930. Bales, Carol A., photos by. LC 92-46729. (Illus.). 160p. (gr. 5 up). 1993. Repr. of 1977 ed. 5.45 (*0-8136-7215-5*); PLB 10.95 (*0-382-24364-1*) Silver Burdett Pr.

Bandon, Alexandra. Filipino Americans. LC 92-42205. (Illus.). 112p. (gr. 6 up). 1993. text ed. 14.95 RSBE (*0-02-768143-2*, New Discovery Bks) Macmillan Child Grp.

Berger, Melvin & Berger, Gilda. Where Did Your Family Come From? A Book about Immigrants. Quackenbush, Robert, illus. LC 92-28626. (gr. k-3). 1993. 12.00 (*0-8249-8647-4*, Ideals Child); pap. 4.50 (*0-8249-8610-5*) Hambleton-Hill.

Bratman, Fred. Becoming a Citizen: Adopting a New Home. LC 92-24061. (Illus.). 48p. (gr. 5-6). 1992. PLB 21.34 (*0-8114-7354-6*) Raintree Steck-V.

Fassler, David & Danforth, Kimberly. Coming to America: The Kids' Book about Immigration. (Illus.). 160p. (Orig.). (ps-6). 1992. pap. text ed. 12.95 (*0-914525-23-9*); tchr's. ed. plastic comb spiral bdg. 16.95 (*0-914525-24-7*) Waterfront Bks.

Gordon, Ginger. My Two Worlds. Cooper, Martha, photos by. LC 92-39271. 32p. (gr. 5 up). 1993. 14.95 (*0-395-58704-2*, Clarion Bks) HM.

Herda, D. J. Ethnic America: The North Central States. (Illus.). 64p. (gr. 5-8). 1991. PLB 15.40 (*1-56294-016-3*) Millbrook Pr.

—Ethnic America: The Northeastern States. (Illus.). 64p. (gr. 5-8). 1991. PLB 15.40 (*1-56294-014-7*) Millbrook Pr.

—Ethnic America: The Northwestern States. (Illus.). 64p. (gr. 5-8). 1991. PLB 15.40 (*1-56294-018-X*) Millbrook Pr.

—Ethnic America: The South Central States. (Illus.). 64p. (gr. 5-8). 1991. PLB 15.40 (*1-56294-017-1*) Millbrook Pr.

—Ethnic America: The Southeastern States. (Illus.). 64p. (gr. 5-8). 1991. PLB 15.40 (*1-56294-015-5*) Millbrook Pr.

—Ethnic America: The Southwestern States. (Illus.). 64p. (gr. 5-8). 1991. PLB 15.40 (*1-56294-019-8*) Millbrook Pr.

Hoyt-Goldsmith, Diane. Hoang Anh: A Vietnamese-American Boy. Migdale, Lawrence, photos by. LC 91-28880. (Illus.). 32p. (gr. 3-7). 1992. reinforced bdg. 14. 95 (*0-8234-0948-1*) Holiday.

Jones, Jayne C. The Greeks in America. rev. ed. LC 68-31504. (Illus.). 80p. (gr. 5 up). 1990. PLB 15.95 (*0-8225-0215-1*); pap. 5.95 (*0-8225-1010-3*) Lerner Pubns.

Katz, William L. The Westward Movement & Abolitionism, 1815-1850. LC 92-14965. (Illus.). 96p. (gr. 7-8). 1992. PLB 22.80 (*0-8114-6276-5*) Raintree Steck-V.

Lee, Kathleen. American Origins: Tracing Our Chinese Roots. LC 93-35616. (Illus.). 48p. (gr. 4-7). 1994. 12. 95 (*1-56261-159-3*) John Muir.

Mayberry, Jodine. Eastern Europeans. Cullerton, P., ed. LC 90-12995. (Illus.). 64p. (gr. 5-8). 1991. PLB 13.40 (*0-531-11109-1*) Watts.

Osborn, Kevin. The Peoples of the Arctic. Moynihan, Daniel P., intro. by. (Illus.). 112p. (gr. 5 up). 1990. 17. 95 (*0-685-18912-0*) Chelsea Hse.

Perrin, Linda. Coming to America: Immigrants from the Far East. LC 80-65840. 192p. (gr. 9-12). 1980. 9.95 (*0-440-01072-1*) Delacorte.

Reynolds, Moira. Coping with An Immigrant Parent. Rosen, Ruth, ed. (gr. 7-12). 1992. 14.95 (*0-8239-1462-3*) Rosen Group.

Sandler, Martin W. Immigrants. Billington, James, intro. by. LC 93-44126. 1995. 19.95 (*0-06-024507-7*); PLB 20.89 (*0-06-024508-5*) HarpC Child Bks.

Steltzer, Ulli. The New Americans. Marin, Peter, intro. by. (Illus.). 176p. (gr. 6 up). 1988. pap. 24.95x (*0-939165-07-4*) NewSage Press.

Takai, Ronald T. Journey to Gold Mountain: The Chinese in Nineteenth-Century America. LC 93-4649. (Illus.). 1994. 18.95 (*0-7910-2177-7*, Am Art Analog); pap. write for info. (*0-7910-2277-3*, Am Art Analog) Chelsea Hse.

Takaki, Ronald. Spacious Dreams: The First Wave of Asian Immigration. (Illus.). 1994. 18.95 (*0-7910-2176-9*, Am Art Analog) Chelsea Hse.

U. S.–INDUSTRIES

Clare, John D., ed. Industrial Revolution. LC 93-2554. 1994. 16.95 (*0-15-200514-5*) HarBrace.

U. S.–INSULAR POSSESSIONS

see U. S.–Territories and Possessions

U. S.–LABOR AND LABORING CLASSES

see Labor and Laboring Classes–U. S.

U. S.–LAW

see Law–U. S.

U. S.–LEGENDS

see Legends–U. S.

U. S.–MAIL

see Postal Service

U. S.–MANNERS AND CUSTOMS

see U. S.–Social Life and Customs

U. S.–MANUFACTURES

see U. S.–Industries

U. S.–MAPS

Clouse, Nancy L. Puzzle Maps U. S. A. Clouse, Nancy L., illus. LC 89-24604. 32p. (ps-2). 1990. 15.95 (*0-8050-1143-9*, Bks Young Read) H Holt & Co.

Discovery Atlas of the United States. LC 93-18713. 1993. write for info. (*0-528-83578-5*) Rand McNally.

Harrison, James. The Young People's Atlas of the United States. LC 92-53116. (Illus.). (gr. 3 up). 1992. 17.95 (*1-85697-804-4*, Kingfisher LKC) LKC.

Nichols, V. Notebook World Atlas. (Illus.). 16p. (gr. 5-12). 1993. pap. 1.95 (*1-879424-25-8*) Nickel Pr.

—U. S. Map & Sticker Book. M. J. Studios Staff, illus. 32p. (gr. k-6). 1993. pap. 3.95 (*1-879424-10-X*) Nickel Pr.

Rand McNally & Company Staff. Rand McNally Children's Atlas of the United States. (Illus.). 112p. (gr. 3-6). 1991. Repr. of 1989 ed. PLB 18.95 (*1-878363-37-9*) Forest Hse.

Schwartz, L. U. S. Geography Adventure Kit. (gr. 4-8). 1989. 24.95 (*0-88160-174-8*, LW 284) Learning Wks.

Sticker Atlas of the United States. 5.99 (*1-55748-194-6*) Barbour & Co.

U. S. MARINE CORPS

Guadalcanal Diary. LC 78-50958. (gr. 4-12). 1978. pap. text ed. 2.25 (*0-88301-303-7*) Pendulum Pr.

Hole, Dorothy. The Marines & You. LC 92-9771. (Illus.). 48p. (gr. 5-6). 1993. text ed. 12.95 RSBE (*0-89686-768-4*, Crestwood Hse) Macmillan Child Grp.

Rowan, N. R. Women in the Marines: The Book Camp Challenge. Rowan, N. R., photos by. LC 93-9706. (Illus.). 1993. deluxe ed. 22.95 (*0-8225-1430-3*) Lerner Pubns.

Rummel, Jack. The U. S. Marine Corps. (Illus.). 128p. (gr. 5 up). 1990. 14.95 (*1-55546-110-7*) Chelsea Hse.

U. S. MARINE CORPS–BIOGRAPHY

Davis, Burke. Marine! The Life of Chesty Puller. 1991. pap. 5.99 (*0-553-27182-2*) Bantam.

U. S. MILITARY ACADEMY, WEST POINT

Hughes, Libby. West Point. LC 92-20641. (Illus.). 72p. (gr. 4 up). 1993. text ed. 14.95 RSBE (*0-87518-529-0*, Dillon) Macmillan Child Grp.

U. S. MILITARY ACADEMY, WEST POINT–FICTION

Fleming, Thomas. Band of Brothers. (gr. 8 up). 1988. 13. 95 (*0-8027-6740-0*); PLB 14.85 (*0-8027-6741-9*) Walker & Co.

U. S.–MILITARY HISTORY

see U. S.–History, Military

U. S.–MUSIC

see Music, American

U. S.–MUSICIANS

see Musicians, American

U. S. NATIONAL AERONAUTICS AND SPACE ADMINISTRATION

Dewaard, John. History of NASA: America's Voyage to the Stars. 1984. 12.98 (*0-671-06983-7*) S&S Trade.

U. S.–NATIONAL GUARD

Collins, Robert F. America at Its Best: Opportunities in the National Guard. Rosen, Ruth, ed. (gr. 7-12). 1989. PLB 14.95 (*0-8239-1024-5*) Rosen Group.

U. S. NATIONAL PARK SERVICE
Hallett, Bill & Hallett, Jane. National Park Service: Activities & Adventures for Kids. Paltrow, Robert, illus. 32p. (Orig.). (gr. 3-8). 1991. activity bk. 3.95 (*1-877827-07-X*) Look & See.
Mackintosh, Barry. The National Park Service. Schlesinger, Arthur M., Jr., intro. by. (Illus.). 96p. (gr. 5 up). 1988. lib. bdg. 14.95 (*1-55546-116-6*) Chelsea Hse.
U. S.–NATIONAL PARKS AND RESERVES
see National Parks and Reserves–U. S.
U. S.–NATURAL HISTORY
see Natural History–U. S.
U. S.–NATURAL MONUMENTS
see Natural Monuments
U. S.–NATURAL RESOURCES
see U. S.–Economic Conditions
U. S.–NAVAL HISTORY
see U. S.–History, Naval
U. S. NAVY
Hole, Dorothy. The Navy & You. LC 92-9055. (Illus.). 48p. (gr. 5-6). 1993. text ed. 12.95 RSBE (*0-89686-767-6*, Crestwood Hse) Macmillan Child Grp.
Kraus, Theresa. The Department of the Navy. (Illus.). 112p. (gr. 5 up). 1990. 14.95 (*0-87754-845-5*) Chelsea Hse.
U. S. NAVY–BIOGRAPHY
Dausereau, Raymond J. Tomorrow's Mission: World War II Diary of a Combat Aircrewman Aboard the U. S. S. Yorktown (CV-10), the Fighting Lady, During the Pacific War 1943-1945. LC 92-74143. (Illus.). 396p. (Orig.). (gr. 11-12). 1993. pap. 18.95 (*0-923687-24-6*) Celo Valley Bks.
Worcester, Donald E. John Paul Jones. (gr. 4-6). 1961. 4.36 (*0-395-01755-6*, Piper) HM.
U. S.–PAINTERS
see Painters, American
U. S. PEACE CORPS
Ashabranner, Brent. The Times of My Life: A Memoir. LC 90-40920. (gr. 4-7). 1990. 14.95 (*0-525-65047-4*, Cobblehill Bks) Dutton Child Bks.
Kent, Zachary. The Story of the Peace Corps. LC 90-2113. (Illus.). 32p. (gr. 3-6). 1990. pap. 3.95 (*0-516-44752-1*) Childrens.
Weitsman, Madeline. The Peace Corps. Schlesinger, Arthur M., Jr., intro. by. (Illus.). 128p. (gr. 5 up). 1989. 14.95 (*0-87754-832-3*) Chelsea Hse.
U. S.–POETRY
Bates, Katharine L. O Beautiful for Spacious Skies. Thiebaud, Wayne, illus. Boyers, Sara J., ed. LC 94-6599. 1994. 13.95 (*0-8118-0832-7*) Chronicle Bks.
Panzer, Nora, ed. Celebrate America: In Poetry & Art. LC 93-32336. (Illus.). 96p. (gr. 3 up). 1994. 18.95 (*1-56282-664-6*); PLB 18.89 (*1-56282-665-4*) Hyprn Child.
U. S.–POLITICS AND GOVERNMENT
Arrington, Karen. The Commission on Civil Rights. (Illus.). (gr. 5 up). 1992. 14.95 (*1-55546-127-1*) Chelsea Hse.
Barnes-Svarney, Patricia. The National Science Foundation. Schlesinger, Arthur M., Jr., intro. by. (Illus.). 112p. (gr. 5 up). 1989. lib. bdg. 14.95 (*1-55546-117-4*) Chelsea Hse.
Bernotas, Bob. Department of Housing & Urban Development. Schlesinger, Arthur M., Jr., intro. by. (Illus.). 104p. (gr. 5 up). 1991. lib. bdg. 14.95 (*0-87754-841-2*) Chelsea Hse.
Bernotas, Bob, Jr. The Federal Government: How it Works. (Illus.). 144p. (gr. 5 up). 1990. 14.95 (*0-87754-859-5*) Chelsea Hse.
Bernstein, Richard & Agel, Jerome. The Presidency. LC 88-21026. (gr. 7 up). 1989. 12.95 (*0-8027-6829-6*); PLB 13.85 (*0-8027-6831-8*) Walker & Co.
Burkhardt, Robert. The Federal Aviation Administration. Schlesinger, Arthur M., Jr., intro. by. (Illus.). 112p. (gr. 5 up). 1989. lib. bdg. 14.95 (*1-55546-107-7*) Chelsea Hse.
Clement, Fred. The Nuclear Regulatory Commission. (Illus.). 104p. (gr. 5 up). 1988. 14.95 (*1-55546-129-8*) Chelsea Hse.
Coffey, William E. & Riddel, Frank S. American Government: The U. S. A. & West Virginia. Buckalew, Marshall, ed. Harvey, Eve S. & Harvey, Cliff, illus. 304p. (gr. 8). 1990. 25.00 (*0-914498-08-8*) WV Hist Ed Found.
Crouch, Tom D. The National Aeronautics & Space Administration. (Illus.). 144p. (gr. 5 up). 1990. 14.95 (*1-55546-120-4*) Chelsea Hse.
Davis, Ray J. American Government: Law in Action. 464p. (Orig.). (gr. 11-12). 1991. pap. text ed. 18.67 (*0-931054-23-0*) Clark Pub.
Dickson, Edward & Galan, Mark. The Immigration & Naturalization Service. (Illus.). 112p. (gr. 5 up). 1990. 14.95 (*1-55546-113-1*) Chelsea Hse.
Doggett, Clinton L. Equal Employment Opportunities Commission. (Illus.). 112p. (gr. 5 up). 1990. lib. bdg. 14.95 (*1-55546-106-9*) Chelsea Hse.
Dwyer, Christopher, Jr. The Small Business Administration. (Illus.). 112p. (gr. 5 up). 1991. 14.95 (*1-55546-122-0*) Chelsea Hse.
Faber, Doris & Faber, Harold. Great Lives: American Government. LC 88-4968. (Illus.). 288p. (gr. 4-6). 1988. SBE 22.95 (*0-684-18521-0*, Scribners Young Read) Macmillan Child Grp.
Feinberg, Barbara S. The National Government. LC 92-25915. 1993. lib. bdg. 12.90 (*0-531-20155-4*) Watts.
Fireside, Bryna J. Is There a Woman in the House - or Senate? Levine, Abby, ed. LC 92-28286. (Illus.). 144p. (gr. 4-9). 1993. PLB 14.95 (*0-8075-3662-8*) A Whitman.
Fleming, Thomas. Harry S Truman. LC 93-153. 144p. (gr. 5 up). 1993. 14.95 (*0-8027-8267-1*); lib. bdg. 15.85 (*0-8027-8269-8*) Walker & Co.
Foster, Leila M. The Story of the Great Society. LC 90-22445. (Illus.). 32p. (gr. 3-6). 1991. PLB 12.30 (*0-516-04755-8*); pap. 3.95 (*0-516-44755-6*) Childrens.
Green, Carl, et al. American Government, 4 bks. (Illus.). 384p. (gr. 7 up). 1990. Set. lib. bdg. 74.40 (*0-86593-082-1*); Set. lib. bdg. 55.80s.p. (*0-685-46454-7*) Rourke Corp.
Highland, Jean. The Federal Communications Commission. (Illus.). 112p. (gr. 5 up). 1992. 14.95 (*1-55546-108-5*) Chelsea Hse.
Hopson, Glover E. The Veteran's Administration. Schlesinger, Arthur M., Jr., intro. by. (Illus.). 96p. (gr. 5 up). 1988. lib. bdg. 14.95 (*1-55546-131-X*) Chelsea Hse.
Koslow, Philip. The Securities & Exchange Commission. (Illus.). 112p. (gr. 5 up). 1990. 14.95 (*1-55546-119-0*) Chelsea Hse.
Kownslar, Allan O. & Smart, Terry L. Civics: Citizens & Society. 2nd ed. (Illus.). 576p. (gr. 7-8). 1983. text ed. 31.88 (*0-07-035433-2*) McGraw.
Law, Kevin J. The Environmental Protection Agency. Schlesinger, Arthur M., Jr., intro. by. (Illus.). 96p. (gr. 5 up). 1988. lib. bdg. 14.95 (*1-55546-105-0*) Chelsea Hse.
McKay, David. American Politics & Society. 3rd ed. LC 93-7211. (Illus.). 340p. (gr. 10 up). 1993. pap. text ed. 19.95 (*0-631-18814-2*) Blackwell Pubs.
Matusky, Gregory & Hayes, John P. The U. S. Secret Service. Schlesinger, Arthur M., Jr., intro. by. (Illus.). 96p. (gr. 5 up). 1988. lib. bdg. 14.95 (*1-55546-130-1*) Chelsea Hse.
Meltzer, Milton. American Politics: How It Really Works. LC 88-26635. (Illus.). 192p. (gr. 7 up). 1989. 12.95 (*0-688-07494-4*) Morrow Jr Bks.
Morris, Jeffrey. The Jefferson Way. LC 94-923. (Illus.). 112p. (gr. 5 up). 1994. 22.95 (*0-8225-2926-2*) Lerner Pubns.
—The Washington Way. (Illus.). 128p. (gr. 5 up). 1994. RLB 22.95 (*0-8225-2928-9*) Lerner Pubns.
Parker, Nancy W. The President's Cabinet & How It Grew. Parker, Nancy W., illus. LC 89-70851. 40p. (gr. 3-5). 1991. PLB 14.89 (*0-06-021618-2*) HarpC Child Bks.
Pollack, Jill S. Shirley Chisholm. LC 93-31175. (Illus.). 64p. (gr. 5-8). 1994. PLB 12.90 (*0-531-20168-6*) Watts.
Raber, Thomas R. Election Night. (Illus.). 88p. (gr. 4 up). 1988. lib. bdg. 14.95 (*0-8225-1751-5*) Lerner Pubns.
Rudysmith, Christina. National Archives & Record Administration. Schlesinger, Arthur M., Jr., intro. by. (Illus.). 112p. (gr. 5 up). 1989. 14.95 (*1-55546-073-9*) Chelsea Hse.
Sawyer, Kem K. National Foundation on the Arts & Humanities. (Illus.). 112p. (gr. 5 up). 1989. lib. bdg. 14.95 (*1-55546-115-8*) Chelsea Hse.
Simpson, Andrew L. The Library of Congress. (Illus.). 112p. (gr. 5 up). 1989. 14.95 (*1-55546-109-3*) Chelsea Hse.
Stacy, Darryl. United States: Government & Citizenship. (Illus.). 176p. (gr. 7-9). 1992. text ed. 19.45 (*0-911981-67-5*) Cloud Pub.
—United States: Government & Citizenship. 48p. (gr. 7-9). 1992. wkbk. 5.75 (*0-911981-71-3*) Cloud Pub.
—United States: Government & Citizenship. 48p. (gr. 7-9). 1994. tchr's. ed. 10.45 (*0-911981-70-5*) Cloud Pub.
Stefoff, Rebecca. The Drug Enforcement Administration. (Illus.). 104p. (gr. 5 up). 1990. 14.95 (*0-87754-849-8*) Chelsea Hse.
Stich, Paul, et al. United States History & Government: A Competency Review Text. 2nd ed. Gamsey, Wayne, ed. Fairbanks, Eugene B., illus. 384p. (gr. 7-12). 1992. pap. text ed. 8.33 (*0-935487-20-4*) N & N Pub Co.
—United States History & Government: A Regents Review Text. 6th ed. Gamsey, Wayne, ed. Fairbanks, Eugene B., illus. 416p. (gr. 7-12). 1992. pap. text ed. 6.22 (*0-935487-21-2*) N & N Pub Co.
—United States History & Government: Ten Day Competency. rev. ed. Gamsey, Wayne, ed. Fairbanks, Eugene B., illus. 128p. (gr. 7-12). 1992. pap. text ed. 4.95 (*0-935487-54-9*) N & N Pub Co.
—United States History & Government: Ten Day Regents Review. rev. ed. Gamsey, Wayne, ed. Fairbanks, Eugene B., illus. 128p. (gr. 7-12). 1992. pap. text ed. 4.95 (*0-935487-49-2*) N & N Pub Co.
Stuart, Pamela B. The Federal Trade Commission. (Illus.). 112p. (gr. 5 up). 1991. 14.95 (*1-55546-114-X*) Chelsea Hse.
Suid, Murray. How to Be President of the U. S. A. Barr, Marilynn G., illus. 80p. (Orig.). (gr. 3-8). 1992. pap. text ed. 9.95 (*1-878279-47-5*, MM1963) Monday Morning Bks.
Sullivan, George. How the White House Really Works. 1990. pap. 3.95 (*0-590-43403-9*) Scholastic Inc.
Taylor, Gary. The Federal Reserve System. (Illus.). 104p. (gr. 5 up). 1989. 14.95 (*1-55546-136-0*) Chelsea Hse.
Tuggle, Catherine & Weir, Gary. The Department of Energy. (Illus.). 112p. (gr. 5 up). 1990. 14.95 (*0-87754-839-0*) Chelsea Hse.
U. S.–POLITICS AND GOVERNMENT–DICTIONARIES
Silberdick, Barbara F. Words in the News: A Student's Dictionary of American Government & Politics. Huehnergarth, John, illus. LC 93-19373. 144p. 1993. PLB 13.40 (*0-531-11164-4*) Watts.
U. S.–POLITICS AND GOVERNMENT–FICTION
Liles, Maurine W. The Boy of Blossom Prairie, Who Became Vice-President. 1993. 14.95 (*0-89015-913-0*) Sunbelt Media.
U. S.–POSTAL SERVICE
see Postal Service
U. S.–RACE RELATIONS
Cavan, Seamus. W. E. B. Du Bois & Racial Relations. LC 92-33015. (Illus.). 32p. (gr. 2-4). 1993. PLB 12.90 (*1-56294-288-3*); pap. 4.95 (*1-56294-794-X*) Millbrook Pr.
Dudley, William & Cozic, Charles. Racism in America: Opposing Viewpoints. LC 91-14293. (Illus.). 240p. (gr. 10 up). 1991. lib. bdg. 17.95 (*0-89908-182-7*); pap. 9.95 (*0-89908-157-6*) Greenhaven.
Landau, Elaine. The White Power Movement: America's Racist Hate Groups. LC 92-40920. (Illus.). 96p. (gr. 7 up). 1993. PLB 15.40 (*1-56294-327-8*) Millbrook Pr.
Powledge, Fred. We Shall Overcome: Heroes of the Civil Rights Movement. LC 92-25184. (Illus.). 224p. (gr. 7 up). 1993. SBE 16.95 (*0-684-19362-0*, Scribners Young Read) Macmillan Child Grp.
Walter, Mildred P. Mississippi Challenge. LC 92-6718. (Illus.). 224p. (gr. 6 up). 1992. SBE 18.95 (*0-02-792301-0*, Bradbury Pr) Macmillan Child Grp.
Wright, David K. A Multicultural Portrait of Life in the Cities. LC 93-10318. 1993. 18.95 (*1-85435-659-3*) Marshall Cavendish.
U. S.–RELIGION
Bach, Julie & Modl, Tom, eds. Religion in America: Opposing Viewpoints. LC 88-24359. (Illus.). 250p. (gr. 10 up). 1988. pap. text ed. 9.95 (*0-89908-412-5*) Greenhaven.
Lowry, James W. North America Is the Lord's. (gr. 5). 1980. 18.75x (*0-87813-916-8*) Christian Light.
U. S.–RELIGIOUS HISTORY
see U. S.–Church History
U. S.–SOCIAL CONDITIONS
Archer, Jules. Rage in the Streets: Mob Violence in America. LC 93-5710. 1994. write for info. (*0-15-277691-5*, Browndeer Pr) HarBrace.
Bender, David L., ed. American Values: Opposing Viewpoints. LC 89-36526. (Illus.). 312p. (gr. 10 up). 1989. lib. bdg. 17.95 (*0-89908-436-2*); pap. text ed. 9.95 (*0-89908-411-7*) Greenhaven.
Brown, Gene. The Nation in Turmoil: Civil Rights & the Vietnam War (1960-1973) LC 93-24995. (Illus.). 64p. (gr. 5-8). 1993. PLB 15.95 (*0-8050-2588-X*) TFC Bks NY.
—Violence on America's Streets. LC 91-28929. (Illus.). 64p. (gr. 5-8). 1992. PLB 15.90 (*1-56294-155-0*) Millbrook Pr.
Deutsch, Sarah J. From Ballots to Breadlines: American Women, 1920-1940. LC 93-30664. 1994. 20.00 (*0-19-508063-7*) OUP.
Gardner, Robert & Shortelle, Dennis. The Future & the Past. Steltenpohl, Jane, ed. (Illus.). 176p. (gr. 6-10). 1989. lib. bdg. 14.98 (*0-671-65742-9*, J Messner) S&S Trade.
Goldberg, Michael. Breaking New Ground: American Women, 1800-1848. (Illus.). 144p. 1994. PLB 20.00 (*0-19-508202-8*) OUP.
Haskins, James S. & Benson, Kathleen. The Sixties Reader. LC 85-40886. (Illus.). 256p. (gr. 7 up). 1988. pap. 13.95 (*0-670-80674-9*) Viking Child Bks.
Hays, Scott, et al. Troubled Society, 6 bks. (Illus.). 384p. (gr. 7 up). 1990. Set. lib. bdg. 103.62 (*0-86593-068-6*); Set. lib. bdg. 77.70s.p. (*0-685-36321-X*) Rourke Corp.

DEATH PENALTY; DRUGS IN SOCIETY; FAMILY ABUSE; GUN CONTROL; IMMIGRATION; TEEN PREGNANCY, & TEEN SUICIDE. For more information, or to order, call or write to: Marketing Director, Twenty-First Century Books, 115 West 18th Street,New York, NY 10011. (800-628-9658, ext. 9387). ***Publisher Provided Annotation.***

Johnson, Hilda S. A Child's Diary - the 1930's. Johnson, Hilda S., illus. LC 88-51304. 64p. (Orig.). (gr. 3-8). 1988. pap. 3.95 (*0-931563-02-X*) Wishing Rm.

LaMorte, Kathy & Lewis, Sharen. U. S. Social Studies Yellow Pages for Students & Teachers. Keeling, Jan, ed. LaMorte, Kathy, illus. 64p. (Orig.). 1993. pap. text ed. 7.95 (*0-86530-267-7*) Incentive Pubns.

Landau, Elaine. Terrorism: America's Growing Threat. 128p. (gr. 5-9). 1992. 15.00 (*0-525-67382-2*, Lodestar Bks) Dutton Child Bks.

May, Elaine T. Young Oxford History of Women in the United States, Vol. 9: Pushing the Limits: American Women 1940-1961. (Illus.). 144p. 1993. PLB 20.00 (*0-19-508084-X*) OUP.

The Poor in America. (Illus.). 128p. (gr. 7-10). 1989. 11. 96 (*0-382-09578-2*, J Messner) S&S Trade.

Salmon, Marylynn. The Limits of Independence: American Women, 1760-1800. LC 93-30330. (Illus.). 144p. 1994. PLB 20.00 (*0-19-508125-0*) OUP.

Sigerman, Harriet. An Unfinished Battle: American Women 1848-1865. (Illus.). 144p. 1994. PLB 20.00 (*0-19-508110-2*) OUP.

Wekesser, Carol, ed. America's Children: Opposing Viewpoints. LC 90-24085. (Illus.). 240p. (gr. 10 up). 1991. PLB 17.95 (*0-89908-486-9*); pap. 9.95 (*0-89908-461-3*) Greenhaven.

U. S.–SOCIAL LIFE AND CUSTOMS

Ainsworth, Catherine H. American Calendar Customs, Vol. I. LC 79-52827. 112p. (Orig.). (ps-12). 1979. pap. 12.00 (*0-933190-06-9*) Clyde Pr.

Blocksma, Mary. Ticket to the Twenties: A Time Traveler's Guide. Dennen, Susan, illus. LC 92-24303. 1993. 15.95 (*0-316-09974-0*) Little.

Clark, Raymond C., ed. Max in America, Pt. 1: Communcating in the Culture. (Illus.). 128p. (gr. 8 up). 1987. 5.00x (*0-86647-024-7*) Pro Lingua.

—Max in America, Pt. 2: Communcating in the Culture. (Illus.). 128p. (gr. 8 up). 1987. 5.00x (*0-86647-025-5*) Pro Lingua.

Everyday Life. 88p. (ps-3). 1990. write for info. (*0-8094-4865-3*); lib. bdg. write for info. (*0-8094-4866-1*) Time-Life.

Fix, Philippe. Not So Very Long Ago: Life in a Small Country Village. Fix, Philippe, illus. LC 93-8428. 40p. (gr. 2 up). 1994. 16.99 (*0-525-44594-3*, DCB) Dutton Child Bks.

Garbarino, James. Let's Talk about Living in a World with Violence: An Activity Book for School-Age Children. Csaszar, Sonia, tr. Green, Phillip M., illus. (SPA.). 48p. (gr. k-8). 1993. Wkbk. 10.00 (*0-9639159-0-8*) Erikson Inst. The new activity workbook for school-age children represents the latest step in a violence intervention program developed over the past seven years by Erikson Institute for Advanced Study in Child Development. Written by James Garbarino, Ph.D., the workbook combines reading, writing, drawing & discussion to help children clarify their thoughts, feelings & knowledge about violence. It seeks to help children discover the meaning of violence, that fear is normal & that there are things children can do to feel better & safer with help from caring adults. The workbook encourages a strengthening of the relationships with community resources that can create a positive change for children & families. Two guides--one for parents & one for teachers, counselors & other professionals--accompany the text to assist adults as they use the workbook with children. ***Publisher Provided Annotation.***

Gordon, Alma D. Don't Pig Out on Junk Food: The MK's Guide to Survival in the U. S. LC 93-34545. (Illus.). 160p. (Orig.). (gr. 5-12). 1993. pap. 9.95 (*0-9617751-1-4*) Evangel Missions.

Herda, D. J. Ethnic America: The North Central States. (Illus.). 64p. (gr. 5-8). 1991. PLB 15.40 (*1-56294-016-3*) Millbrook Pr.

—Ethnic America: The Northeastern States. (Illus.). 64p. (gr. 5-8). 1991. PLB 15.40 (*1-56294-014-7*) Millbrook Pr.

—Ethnic America: The Northwestern States. (Illus.). 64p. (gr. 5-8). 1991. PLB 15.40 (*1-56294-018-X*) Millbrook Pr.

—Ethnic America: The South Central States. (Illus.). 64p. (gr. 5-8). 1991. PLB 15.40 (*1-56294-017-1*) Millbrook Pr.

—Ethnic America: The Southeastern States. (Illus.). 64p. (gr. 5-8). 1991. PLB 15.40 (*1-56294-015-5*) Millbrook Pr.

—Ethnic America: The Southwestern States. (Illus.). 64p. (gr. 5-8). 1991. PLB 15.40 (*1-56294-019-8*) Millbrook Pr.

Kalman, Bobbie & Everts, Tammy. A Child's Day. (Illus.). 32p. (Orig.). (gr. k-9). 1994. PLB 15.95 (*0-86505-494-0*); pap. 7.95 (*0-86505-514-9*) Crabtree Pub Co.

Kiebanow, Barbara & Fischer, Sara. American Holidays: Exploring Traditions, Customs, & Backgrounds. (Illus.). 128p. (gr. 5 up). 1986. 10.50x (*0-86647-018-2*) Pro Lingua.

Loeper, John J. Going to School in 1876. LC 83-15669. (Illus.). 96p. (gr. 4-7). 1984. SBE 15.00 (*0-689-31015-3*, Atheneum) Macmillan Child Grp.

Mitchell, Barbara. Hush, Puppies. Wyman, Cherie R., illus. LC 82-4465. 48p. (gr. k-4). 1983. PLB 14.95 (*0-87614-201-3*) Carolrhoda Bks.

Shifflett, Crandall A. Victorian America. Balkin, Rick, ed. (Illus.). 300p. (gr. 5-10). 1994. 35.00 (*0-8160-2531-2*) Facts on File.

Tomscha, Terry. American Customs & Traditions. (Illus.). 31p. (Orig.). 1990. pap. text ed. 5.25 (*0-582-03641-0*, 78662) Longman.

Westwood, Phoebe L. & Rohrbacher, Richard W. Yesteryear's Child: Golden Days & Summer Nights. LC 93-77688. 176p. (gr. 3-5). 1993. pap. 11.95 (*0-9623048-7-5*) Heritage West. Learn the answers in Richard Rohrbacher's captivating memoir of life in the first years of the twentieth century. Travel back to a time before television & space travel, before radio, women's suffrage, & penicillin. Discover a familiar world of family work & play. YESTERYEAR'S CHILD: Golden Days & Summer Nights tells of everyday life from town to farm & brings alive a time & place in our collective American past. Outdoor privies were replaced by indoor plumbing; horse-drawn carriages shared the dusty roads with the first automobiles; & the earliest telephone numbers were single digits. This delightful tale will evoke memories in the old & wonder in the young. A must for all school libraries & highly recommended for classrooms. "I now teach third grade, & we teach Valley Days...it helps me explain the 'olden days'," said Norma Brown, teacher, Stockton. "...the ordinary domestic work week is an eye-opener," writes Dan Barnett, The Chico Enterprise. Call or write for information to order, Heritage West Books, 306 Regent Ct., Stockton, CA 95204. 209-464-8818. ***Publisher Provided Annotation.***

Wormser, Richard L. Growing up in the Great Depression. LC 93-20686. (Illus.). 112p. (gr. 5-9). 1994. SBE 15.95 (*0-689-31711-5*, Atheneum Child Bk) Macmillan Child Grp.

U. S.–SOCIAL LIFE AND CUSTOMS–COLONIAL PERIOD

Coon, Alma S. Amy, Ben, & Catalpa the Cat: A Fanciful Story of This & That. Owens, Gail, illus. 40p. (ps-2). 1990. 8.95 (*0-87935-079-2*) Williamsburg.

Kalman, Bobbie. Colonial Crafts. (Illus.). 32p. (gr. k-9). 1992. PLB 15.95 (*0-86505-490-8*); pap. 7.95 (*0-86505-510-6*) Crabtree Pub CO.

—A Colonial Town: Williamsburg. (Illus.). 32p. (gr. k-9). 1992. PLB 15.95 (*0-86505-489-4*); pap. 7.95 (*0-86505-509-2*) Crabtree Pub Co.

—The Gristmill. (Illus.). 32p. (gr. 3-4). 1991. PLB 15.95 (*0-86505-486-X*); pap. 7.95 (*0-86505-506-8*) Crabtree Pub Co.

—Home Crafts. (Illus.). 32p. (gr. 3-4). 1990. PLB 15.95 (*0-86505-485-1*); pap. 7.95 (*0-86505-505-X*) Crabtree Pub Co.

—The Kitchen. (Illus.). 32p. (gr. 3-4). 1990. PLB 15.95 (*0-86505-484-3*); pap. 7.95 (*0-86505-504-1*) Crabtree Pub Co.

—Tools & Gadgets. (Illus.). 32p. (gr. k-9). 1992. PLB 15. 95 (*0-86505-488-6*); pap. 7.95 (*0-86505-508-4*) Crabtree Pub CO.

Lizon, Karen H. Colonial American Holidays & Entertainment. LC 92-40262. 1993. 12.90 (*0-531-12546-7*) Watts.

Quincannon, Alan, ed. Lifestyles of Colonial America. Lanawn-Shee Studios Staff, illus. 24p. (Orig.). (gr. k-6). 1992. pap. 3.95 (*1-878452-10-X*) Tory Corner Editions.

—More Soldiers of Colonial America. Lanawn-Shee Studios Staff, illus. 24p. (Orig.). (gr. k-6). 1992. pap. 3.95 (*1-878452-12-6*) Tory Corner Editions.

—People of Colonial America. Lanawn-Shee Studios Staff, illus. 20p. (Orig.). (gr. k-6). 1992. pap. 3.95 (*1-878452-09-6*) Tory Corner Editions.

—Soldiers of Colonial America. Lanawn-Shee Studios Staff, illus. 24p. (Orig.). (gr. k-6). 1992. pap. 3.95 (*1-878452-11-8*) Tory Corner Editions.

Sabin, Louis. Colonial Life in America. Frenck, Hal, illus. LC 84-2669. 32p. (gr. 3-6). 1985. PLB 9.49 (*0-8167-0138-5*); pap. text ed. 2.95 (*0-8167-0139-3*) Troll Assocs.

Sherrow, Victoria. Huskings, Quiltings, & Barn Raisings: Work-Play Parties in Early America. Loturco, Laura, illus. LC 92-8725. 78p. 1992. 13.95 (*0-8027-8186-1*); PLB 14.85 (*0-8027-8188-8*) Walker & Co.

Stone, Lynn. Villages. LC 93-16152. 1993. write for info. (*0-86625-448-X*) Rourke Pubns.

Washburne, Carolyn K. A Multicultural Portrait of Colonial Life. LC 93-10320. (gr. 7 up). 1993. 18.95 (*1-85435-657-7*) Marshall Cavendish.

U. S.–SOLDIERS

see Soldiers–U. S.

U. S.–STATE GOVERNMENTS

see State Governments

U. S. SUPREME COURT

Aaseng, Nathan. Great Justices of the Supreme Court. LC 92-18443. (Illus.). 160p. (gr. 5-12). 1992. PLB 14. 95 (*1-881508-01-3*) Oliver Pr MN.

—You Are the Supreme Court Justice. LC 93-46307. (Illus.). 160p. (gr. 5-12). 1994. PLB 14.95 (*1-881508-14-5*) Oliver Pr MN.

Aria, Barbara. The Supreme Court. LC 94-9797. (gr. 4 up). 1994. write for info. (*0-531-20180-5*) Watts.

Bains, Rae. Supreme Court. Dole, Bob, illus. LC 84-2736. 32p. (gr. 3-6). 1985. PLB 9.49 (*0-8167-0272-1*); pap. text ed. 2.95 (*0-8167-0273-X*) Troll Assocs.

Deegan, Paul. Clarence Thomas. Italia, Bob, ed. LC 92-13717. 1992. PLB 13.99 (*1-56239-088-0*) Abdo & Dghtrs.

—Sandra Day O'Connor. Italia, Bob, ed. LC 92-13716. 1992. PLB 13.99 (*1-56239-089-9*) Abdo & Dghtrs.

Fireside, Harvey & Fuller, Sarah B. Brown vs. Board of Education: Equal Schooling for All. LC 93-5897. (Illus.). 104p. (gr. 6 up). 1994. lib. bdg. 17.95 (*0-89490-469-8*) Enslow Pubs.

Gherman, Beverly. Sandra Day O'Connor. (gr. 4-7). 1991. 10.95 (*0-670-82756-8*) Viking Child Bks.

Greene, Carol. The Supreme Court. LC 84-23230. (Illus.). 48p. (gr. k-4). 1985. PLB 12.85 (*0-516-01943-0*) Childrens.

Halliburton, Warren J. Clarence Thomas: Supreme Court Justice. LC 92-30951. (Illus.). 104p. (gr. 6 up). 1993. lib. bdg. 17.95 (*0-89490-414-0*) Enslow Pubs.

Harrison, Maureen & Gilbert, Steve. Landmark Decisions of the United States Supreme Court, No. II. LC 90-84578. 237p. 1991. 15.95 (*0-685-57136-X*) Excellent Bks.

Henry, Christopher E. Ruth Bader Ginsburg: Associate Justice of the United States Supreme Court. LC 94-978. (gr. 4 up). 1994. write for info. (*0-531-20174-0*) Watts.

—Sandra Day O'Connor. LC 94-11287. 1994. lib. bdg. write for info. (*0-531-20175-9*) Watts.

Herda, D. J. Furman vs. Georgia: The Death Penalty Case. LC 93-37512. (Illus.). 104p. (gr. 6 up). 1994. lib. bdg. 17.95 (*0-89490-489-2*) Enslow Pubs.

Italia, Bob. Anthony Kennedy. Deegan, Paul, ed. LC 92-13710. 40p. 1992. PLB 13.99 (*1-56239-094-5*) Abdo & Dghtrs.

—Antonin Scalia. Deegan, Paul, ed. LC 92-13712. 40p. 1992. PLB 13.99 (*1-56239-093-7*) Abdo & Dghtrs.

—Chief Justice William Rehnquist. Deegan, Paul, ed. LC 92-13709. 1992. PLB 13.95 (*1-56239-096-1*) Abdo & Dghtrs.

—Harry Blackmun. Deegan, Paul, ed. LC 92-13711. 1992. PLB 13.99 (*1-56239-090-2*) Abdo & Dghtrs.

—Ruth Bader Ginsburg. LC 93-42168. 1994. write for info. (*1-56239-098-8*) Abdo & Dghtrs.

Italia, Bob & Deegan, Paul. John Paul Stevens. LC 92-13713. 1992. PLB 13.99 (*1-56239-091-0*) Abdo & Dghtrs.

Macht, Norman L. Sandra Day O'Connor. (Illus.). 80p. (gr. 3-5). 1992. lib. bdg. 12.95 (*0-7910-1756-7*) Chelsea Hse.

Patrick, John J. The Young Oxford Companion to the Supreme Court of the United States. LC 93-6467. (gr. 5 up). 1994. 35.00 (*0-19-507877-2*) OUP.

Reef, Catherine. The Supreme Court. LC 93-21506. (Illus.). 72p. (gr. 4-7). 1994. text ed. 14.95 RSBE (*0-87518-626-2*, Dillon) Macmillan Child Grp.
Rierden, Anne B. Reshaping the Supreme Court: New Justices, New Directions. Ribaroff, Margaret, ed. LC 87-25958. (Illus.). 128p. (gr. 7-12). 1988. PLB 13.40 (*0-531-10512-1*) Watts.
Roberts, Jack L. Ruth Bader Ginsburg: Supreme Court Justice. LC 93-39015. (Illus.). 48p. (gr. 2-4). 1994. PLB 12.90 (*1-56294-497-5*); pap. 6.95 (*1-56294-744-3*) Millbrook Pr.
Sherrow, Victoria. Gideon v. Wainwright: Free Legal Counsel. LC 93-45981. (Illus.). 104p. (gr. 6 up). 1995. lib. bdg. 17.95 (*0-89490-507-4*) Enslow Pubs.
Weiss, Ann E. The Supreme Court. LC 86-8929. 96p. (gr. 6 up). 1987. lib. bdg. 16.95 (*0-89490-131-1*) Enslow Pubs.

U. S.–TAXATION
see Taxation–U. S.

U. S.–TERRITORIAL EXPANSION
Ayer, Eleanor H. Ruth Bader Ginsburg. LC 94-17854. 1994. text ed. 13.95 (*0-87518-651-3*, Dillon Pr) Macmillan Child Grp.
Faber, Harold. From Sea to Sea: The Growth of the United States. LC 91-43728. (Illus.). 256p. (gr. 7 up). 1992. SBE 15.95 (*0-684-19442-2*, Scribners Young Read) Macmillan Child Grp.
Petra Press Staff. A Multicultural Portrait of the Move West. LC 93-10317. 1993. 18.95 (*1-85435-658-5*) Marshall Cavendish.

U. S.–TERRITORIES AND POSSESSIONS
Dunnahoo, Terry. U. S. Territories Freely Associated States. Rakos, Jennie, ed. LC 88-16982. (Illus.). 96p. 1988. PLB 13.40 (*0-531-10605-5*) Watts.

U. S. TREASURY DEPARTMENT
Hamilton, John. The Secretary of the Treasury. LC 93-11214. 1993. 13.99 (*1-56239-254-9*) Abdo & Dghtrs.
Walston, Mark. The Department of the Treasury. (Illus.). 128p. (gr. 5 up). 1989. 14.95 (*0-87754-848-X*) Chelsea Hse.

U. S.–VICE-PRESIDENTS
see Vice-Presidents–U. S.

U. S.–WOMEN
see Women in the U. S.

U. S.–WORLD WAR, 1939-1945
see World War, 1939-1945–U. S.

UNITED STATES OF EUROPE (PROPOSED)
see European Federation

UNIVERSAL HISTORY
see World History

UNIVERSE
Asimov, Isaac. How Did We Find Out about the Universe? Wool, David, illus. LC 82-42531. 64p. (gr. 5-8). 1983. PLB 12.85 (*0-8027-6477-0*) Walker & Co.
—Mythology & the Universe. (gr. 4-7). 1991. pap. 4.99 (*0-440-40449-5*, YB) Dell.
Asimov, Isaac, et al. The Birth of Our Universe. rev. & updated ed. (Illus.). (gr. 3 up). 1995. PLB 17.27 (*0-8368-1192-5*) Gareth Stevens Inc.
—Mysteries of Deep Space: Black Holes, Pulsars, & Quasars. rev. & updated ed. (Illus.). (gr. 3 up). 1994. PLB 17.27 (*0-8368-1133-X*) Gareth Stevens Inc.
Blueford, J. R., et al. Universe Cycle - Search for Our Beginning. (gr. k-6). 1992. 20.95 (*1-56638-055-3*) Math Sci Nucleus.
Ciupik, Larry. The Universe. rev. ed. LC 87-20805. (Illus.). 48p. (gr. 2-6). 1987. PLB 10.95 (*0-8172-3264-8*); pap. 4.49 (*0-8114-8221-9*) Raintree Steck-V.
Estalella, Robert. Galaxies. Ferron, Miquel, illus. LC 93-24596. (gr. 4-8). 1994. 12.95 (*0-8120-6367-8*); pap. 6.95 (*0-8120-1742-0*) Barron.
Gallant, Roy A. National Geographic Picture Atlas of Our Universe. Sedeen, Margaret, ed. Collins, Michael, frwd. by. (Illus.). 276p. (gr. 6 up). 1980. 23.95 (*0-87044-356-9*); lib. bdg. 18.95 (*0-87044-357-7*) Natl Geog.
—One Hundred & One Questions & Answers about the Universe. LC 84-7875. (Illus.). 96p. (gr. 1-5). 1984. SBE 13.95 (*0-02-736750-9*, Macmillan Child Bk) Macmillan Child Grp.
Heese. Jugendhandbuch Naturwissen: Saeugetiere, Vol. 3. (GER.). 144p. 1976. pap. 5.95 (*0-7859-0933-8*, M-7488, Pub. by Rowohlt) Fr & Eur.
—Jugendhandbuch Naturwissen, Vol. 4: Erde und Weltall. (GER.). 128p. 1976. pap. 5.95 (*0-7859-0412-3*, M7489) Fr & Eur.
Herbst, Judith. Star Crossing: How to Get Around in the Universe. LC 92-8475. (Illus.). 224p. (gr. 5-9). 1993. SBE 16.95 (*0-689-31523-6*, Atheneum Child Bk) Macmillan Child Grp.
Jacobs, Francine. Cosmic Countdown: What Astronomers Have Learned about the Life of the Universe. Jastrow, Robert, frwd. by. LC 83-5535. (Illus.). 160p. (gr. 7 up). 1983. 9.95 (*0-87131-404-5*) M Evans.
Jespersen, James & Fitz-Randolph, Jane. Looking at the Invisible Universe. Hiscock, Bruce, illus. LC 89-14998. 160p. (gr. 7 up). 1990. SBE 14.95 (*0-689-31457-4*, Atheneum Child Bk) Macmillan Child Grp.
Maynard, Christopher & Verdet, Jean-Pierre. The Universe. LC 94-9085. (Illus.). 128p. (gr. k-4). 1994. pap. 5.95 (*1-85697-527-4*, Kingfisher LKC) LKC.
Miotto, Enrico. The Universe: Origin & Evolution. LC 94-3839. 1994. write for info. (*0-8114-3334-X*) Raintree Steck-V.
Myring. First Guide to the Universe. (gr. 2-5). 1982. 11. 95 (*0-86020-611-4*, Usborne-Hayes) EDC.
Nicolson, Iain. Explore the World of Space & the Universe. Quigley, Sebastian, illus. 48p. (gr. 3-7). 1992. write for info. (*0-307-15608-7*, 15608, Golden Pr) Western Pub.
Paul, Richard. A Handbook to the Universe: Explorations of Matter, Energy, Space, & Time for Beginning Scientific Thinkers. LC 92-39670. (Illus.). 320p. (Orig.). (gr. 6 up). 1993. pap. 14.95 (*1-55652-172-3*) Chicago Review.
Rand McNally Staff. Children's Atlas of the Universe. (Illus.). (gr. 3-7). 1990. 14.95 (*0-528-83408-8*) Rand McNally.
Rothman, Tony. Long Ago Is Far Away: Figuring Out How the Universe Began. LC 92-29745. 1993. write for info. (*0-7167-9000-9*) W H Freeman.
Scrunch the Universe. 48p. (gr. 4-5). 1991. PLB 11.95 (*1-56065-010-9*) Capstone Pr.

UNIVERSITIES AND COLLEGES–FICTION
see also Schools–Fiction
Cooney, Linda A. Freshman Changes. 1991. pap. 3.50 (*0-06-106078-X*, Harp PBks) HarpC.
Grey, Zane. The Young Pitcher. Thorn, John, frwd. by. LC 91-23670. 256p. (gr. 7 up). 1992. Repr. of 1911 ed. 13.00 (*0-688-11090-8*) Morrow Jr Bks.
Holman, Dianne K. Plenty to Do at MSU. (Illus.). 32p. (Orig.). 1989. pap. 5.95 (*0-9626188-0-2*) Cupery Pr.
Lee, Marie G. Finding My Voice. LC 92-2947. 176p. (gr. 6 up). 1992. 13.95 (*0-395-62134-8*) HM.
—Saying Goodbye. LC 93-26092. 1994. write for info. (*0-395-67066-7*) HM.
Montgomery, L. M. Anne of the Island. large type ed. LC 94-1765. 377p. 1994. lib. bdg. 17.95 (*0-7862-0205-X*) Thorndike Pr.
Montgomery, Lucy M. Anne of the Island. 1983. pap. 2.95 (*0-553-21317-2*, Bantam Classics) Bantam.
—Anne of the Island. (gr. 3-7). 1992. pap. 3.50 (*0-553-48066-9*) Bantam.
—Anne of the Island. Graham, Mark, illus. 288p. (gr. 4 up). 1992. 14.95 (*0-448-40311-0*, G&D) Putnam Pub Group.
Quin-Harkin, Janet. Campus Cousins. LC 88-91245. 186p. 1989. pap. 2.95 (*0-8041-0335-6*) Ivy Books.
Schneider, Meg F. I Wonder What College Is Like? Steltenpohl, Jane, ed. (Illus.). 160p. (gr. 7-9). 1989. PLB 13.98 (*0-671-65847-6*, J Messner); pap. 5.95 (*0-671-67815-9*) S&S Trade.
Scholz, Jackson V. The Football Rebels. LC 92-43376. 224p. (gr. 6 up). 1993. pap. 4.95 (*0-688-12643-X*, Pub. by Beech Tree Bks) Morrow.
Standish, Burt L. Frank Merriwell's Schooldays. Rudman, Jack, ed. (gr. 9 up). 1970. 9.95 (*0-8373-9309-4*); pap. 3.95 (*0-8373-9009-5*) F Merriwell.
Tunis, John R. Iron Duke. 262p. (gr. 3-7). 1990. pap. 3.95 (*0-15-238987-3*, Odyssey) HarBrace.

UNIVERSITY OF NOTRE DAME
Deegan, Paul. University of Notre Dame. LC 88-71724. (Illus.). 48p. (gr. 4 up). 1988. lib. bdg. 10.95 (*0-939179-51-2*) Abdo & Dghtrs.
Kaczorek, Keith. The Spirit & Vision of Notre Dame: The First 150 Years. Harrow, Harriett, ed. Griffin, David, et al, illus. Hesburgh, Theodore & Roberson, Kennethfrwd. by. 96p. 1992. 28.00 (*0-9623171-4-4*); pap. 18.50 (*0-9623171-5-2*); pap. text ed. 8.50 black & white ed. (*0-9623171-6-0*); write for info. coloring bk. (*0-9623171-7-9*) LBCo Pub.
Strode, William, photos by. Notre Dame: A Sense of Place. LC 92-80737. (Illus.). (gr. 9 up). 1992. pap. text ed. 21.95 (*0-268-01475-2*) U of Notre Dame Pr.

UNMARRIED MOTHERS
Beauchamp, Andre. Teenage Mothers: Their Experience, Strength, & Hope. Fisher, Rosemarie, tr. from FRE. LC 90-38476. (Illus.). 96p. (Orig.). (gr. 7-12). 1990. pap. 8.95 (*0-89390-180-6*) Resource Pubns.
McGuire, Paula. It Won't Happen to Me: Teenagers Talk about Pregnancy. LC 82-72754. 224p. (gr. 7 up). 1983. 14.95 (*0-385-29244-9*); pap. 6.95 (*0-685-06445-X*) Delacorte.
—It Won't Happen to Me: Teenagers Talk about Pregnancy. Ryan, George M., frwd. by. 1923. pap. 6.95 (*0-385-29201-5*, Delta) Dell.

UNMARRIED MOTHERS–FICTION
Doherty, Berlie. Dear Nobody. 192p. (gr. 6-12). 1992. 14. 95 (*0-531-05461-6*); PLB 14.99 (*0-531-08611-9*) Orchard Bks Watts.
—Dear Nobody. LC 93-9626. 192p. (gr. 8 up). 1994. pap. 4.95 (*0-688-12764-9*, Pub. by Beech Tree Bks) Morrow.
Minshull, Evelyn W. But I Thought You Really Loved Me. LC 76-14992. 150p. (gr. 7 up). 1976. 8.00 (*0-664-32600-5*, Westminster) Westminster John Knox.
Wood, June R. A Share of Freedom. LC 94-6578. 256p. 1994. 15.95 (*0-399-22767-9*, Putnam) Putnam Pub Group.

UPPER ATMOSPHERE
see Atmosphere, Upper

UPPER CLASSES–FICTION
The Great Gatsby. 1993. pap. text ed. 6.50 (*0-582-08485-7*, 79818) Longman.

URBAN RENEWAL
see also City Planning

URUGUAY
Haverstock, Nathan A. Uruguay in Pictures. (Illus.). 64p. (gr. 5 up). 1987. PLB 17.50 (*0-8225-1823-6*) Lerner Pubns.
Morrison, Marion. Uruguay. LC 91-35144. 128p. (gr. 5-9). 1992. PLB 20.55 (*0-516-02607-0*) Childrens.

USEFUL ARTS
see Technology

UTAH
Aylesworth, Thomas G. & Aylesworth, Virginia L. The West (Arizona, Nevada, Utah) (Illus.). 64p. (gr. 3 up). 1992. PLB 16.95 (*0-7910-1049-X*) Chelsea Hse.
Ayres, Becky. Salt Lake City. LC 90-2968. (Illus.). 60p. (gr. 3 up). 1990. text ed. 13.95 RSBE (*0-87518-436-7*, Dillon) Macmillan Child Grp.
Carole Marsh Utah Books, 44 bks. 1994. PLB 1027.80 set (*0-7933-1319-8*); pap. 587.80 set (*0-7933-5210-X*) Gallopade Pub Group.
Carpenter, Allan. Utah. new ed. LC 79-12433. (Illus.). 96p. (gr. 4 up). 1979. PLB 16.95 (*0-516-04144-4*) Childrens.
Fradin, Dennis B. Utah. LC 92-36370. (Illus.). 64p. (gr. 3-5). 1993. PLB 16.45 (*0-516-03844-3*) Childrens.
Hinton, Wayne K. Utah: Unusual Beginning to Unique Present. (Illus.). 192p. (gr. 7 up). 1988. 29.95 (*0-89781-247-6*) Preferred Mktg.
McCarthy, Betty. Utah. LC 89-35083. 144p. (gr. 4 up). 1989. PLB 20.55 (*0-516-00490-5*) Childrens.
—Utah. 199p. 1993. text ed. 15.40 (*1-56956-176-1*) W A T Braille.
Marsh, Carole. Avast, Ye Slobs! Utah Pirate Trivia. (Illus.). 1994. PLB 24.95 (*0-7933-1124-1*); pap. 14.95 (*0-7933-1123-3*); computer disk 29.95 (*0-7933-1125-X*) Gallopade Pub Group.
—The Beast of the Utah Bed & Breakfast. (Illus.). 1994. PLB 24.95 (*0-7933-2117-4*); pap. 14.95 (*0-7933-2118-2*); computer disk 29.95 (*0-7933-2119-0*) Gallopade Pub Group.
—Bow Wow! Utah Dogs in History, Mystery, Legend, Lore, Humor & More! (Illus.). (gr. 3-12). 1994. PLB 24.95 (*0-7933-3599-X*); pap. 14.95 (*0-7933-3600-7*); computer disk 29.95 (*0-7933-3601-5*) Gallopade Pub Group.
—Chill Out: Scary Utah Tales Based on Frightening Utah Truths. (Illus.). 1994. lib. bdg. 24.95 (*0-7933-4786-6*); pap. 14.95 (*0-7933-4787-4*); disk 29.95 (*0-7933-4788-2*) Gallopade Pub Group.
—Christopher Columbus Comes to Utah! Includes Reproducible Activities for Kids! (Illus.). (gr. 3-12). 1994. PLB 24.95 (*0-7933-3752-6*); pap. 14.95 (*0-7933-3753-4*); computer disk 29.95 (*0-7933-3754-2*) Gallopade Pub Group.
—The Hard-to-Believe-But-True! Book of Utah History, Mystery, Trivia, Legend, Lore, Humor & More. (Illus.). 1994. PLB 24.95 (*0-7933-1121-7*); pap. 14.95 (*0-7933-1120-9*); computer disk 29.95 (*0-7933-1122-5*) Gallopade Pub Group.
—If My Utah Mama Ran the World! (Illus.). 1994. PLB 24.95 (*0-7933-2126-3*); pap. 14.95 (*0-7933-2127-1*); computer disk 29.95 (*0-7933-2128-X*) Gallopade Pub Group.
—Jurassic Ark! Utah Dinosaurs & Other Prehistoric Creatures. (gr. k-12). 1994. PLB 24.95 (*0-7933-7560-6*); pap. 14.95 (*0-7933-7561-4*); computer disk 29.95 (*0-7933-7562-2*) Gallopade Pub Group.
—Let's Quilt Our Utah County. 1994. lib. bdg. 24.95 (*0-7933-7245-3*); pap. text ed. 14.95 (*0-7933-7246-1*); disk 29.95 (*0-7933-7247-X*) Gallopade Pub Group.
—Let's Quilt Our Utah Town. 1994. lib. bdg. 24.95 (*0-7933-7095-7*); pap. text ed. 14.95 (*0-7933-7096-5*); disk 29.95 (*0-7933-7097-3*) Gallopade Pub Group.
—Let's Quilt Utah & Stuff It Topographically! (Illus.). 1994. PLB 24.95 (*0-7933-2109-3*); pap. 14.95 (*1-55609-129-X*); computer disk 29.95 (*0-7933-2110-7*) Gallopade Pub Group.
—Meow! Utah Cats in History, Mystery, Legend, Lore, Humor & More! (Illus.). (gr. 3-12). 1994. PLB 24.95 (*0-7933-3446-2*); pap. 14.95 (*0-7933-3447-0*); computer disk 29.95 (*0-7933-3448-9*) Gallopade Pub Group.
—My First Book about Utah. (gr. k-4). 1994. PLB 24.95 (*0-7933-5701-2*); pap. 14.95 (*0-7933-5702-0*); computer disk 29.95 (*0-7933-5703-9*) Gallopade Pub Group.
—Patch, the Pirate Dog: A Utah Pet Story. (ps-4). 1994. PLB 24.95 (*0-7933-5548-6*); pap. 14.95 (*0-7933-5549-4*); computer disk 29.95 (*0-7933-5550-8*) Gallopade Pub Group.
—Uncle Rebus: Utah Picture Stories for Computer Kids. (Illus.). (gr. k-3). 1994. PLB 24.95 (*0-7933-4633-9*); pap. 14.95 (*0-7933-4634-7*); disk 29.95 (*0-7933-4635-5*) Gallopade Pub Group.
—Utah & Other State Greats (Biographies) (Illus.). 1994. PLB 24.95 (*0-7933-2129-8*); pap. 14.95 (*0-7933-2130-1*); computer disk 29.95 (*0-7933-2131-X*) Gallopade Pub Group.
—Utah Bandits, Bushwackers, Outlaws, Crooks, Devils, Ghosts, Desperadoes & Other Assorted & Sundry Characters! (Illus.). 1994. PLB 24.95 (*0-7933-1106-3*); pap. 14.95 (*0-685-45955-1*); computer disk 29.95 (*0-7933-1107-1*) Gallopade Pub Group.
—Utah Classic Christmas Trivia: Stories, Recipes, Activities, Legends, Lore & More! (Illus.). 1994. PLB 24.95 (*0-7933-1109-8*); pap. 14.95 (*0-7933-1108-X*); computer disk 29.95 (*0-7933-1110-1*) Gallopade Pub Group.
—Utah Coastales. (Illus.). 1994. PLB 24.95 (*0-7933-2123-9*); pap. 14.95 (*0-7933-2124-7*); computer disk 29.95 (*0-685-45954-3*) Gallopade Pub Group.
—Utah Coastales! 1994. lib. bdg. 24.95 (*0-7933-7309-3*) Gallopade Pub Group.

—Utah "Crinkum-Crankum" A Funny Word Book about Our State. (Illus.). (gr. 3-12). 1994. 24.95 (*0-7933-4940-0*); pap. 14.95 (*0-7933-4941-9*); computer disk 29.95 (*0-7933-4942-7*) Gallopade Pub Group.

—Utah Dingbats! Bk. 1: A Fun Book of Games, Stories, Activities & More about Our State That's All in Code! for You to Decipher. (Illus.). (gr. 3-12). 1994. PLB 24.95 (*0-7933-3905-7*); pap. 14.95 (*0-7933-3906-5*); computer disk 29.95 (*0-7933-3907-3*) Gallopade Pub Group.

—Utah Festival Fun for Kids! (Illus.). (gr. 3-12). 1994. PLB 24.95 (*0-7933-4058-6*); pap. 14.95 (*0-7933-4059-4*); disk 29.95 (*0-7933-4060-8*) Gallopade Pub Group.

—The Utah Hot Air Balloon Mystery. (Illus.). (gr. 2-9). 1994. 24.95 (*0-7933-2714-8*); pap. 14.95 (*0-7933-2715-6*); computer disk 29.95 (*0-7933-2716-4*) Gallopade Pub Group.

—Utah Jeopardy! Answers & Questions about Our State! (Illus.). (gr. 3-12). 1994. PLB 24.95 (*0-7933-4211-2*); pap. 14.95 (*0-7933-4212-0*); computer disk 29.95 (*0-7933-4213-9*) Gallopade Pub Group.

—Utah "Jography" A Fun Run Thru Our State! (Illus.). 1994. PLB 24.95 (*0-7933-2106-9*); pap. 14.95 (*0-7933-2107-7*); computer disk 29.95 (*0-7933-2108-5*) Gallopade Pub Group.

—Utah Kid's Cookbook: Recipes, How-to, History, Lore & More! (Illus.). 1994. PLB 24.95 (*0-7933-1118-7*); pap. 14.95 (*0-7933-1117-9*); computer disk 29.95 (*0-7933-1119-5*) Gallopade Pub Group.

—The Utah Mystery Van Takes Off! Book 1: Handicapped Utah Kids Sneak Off on a Big Adventure. (Illus.). (gr. 3-12). 1994. 24.95 (*0-7933-5093-X*); pap. 14.95 (*0-7933-5094-8*); computer disk 29.95 (*0-7933-5095-6*) Gallopade Pub Group.

—Utah Quiz Bowl Crash Course! (Illus.). 1994. PLB 24.95 (*0-7933-2120-4*); pap. 14.95 (*0-7933-2121-2*); computer disk 29.95 (*0-7933-2122-0*) Gallopade Pub Group.

—Utah Rollercoasters! (Illus.). (gr. 3-12). 1994. PLB 24.95 (*0-7933-5356-4*); pap. 14.95 (*0-7933-5357-2*); computer disk 29.95 (*0-7933-5358-0*) Gallopade Pub Group.

—Utah School Trivia: An Amazing & Fascinating Look at Our State's Teachers, Schools & Students! (Illus.). 1994. PLB 24.95 (*0-7933-1115-2*); pap. 14.95 (*0-7933-1114-4*); computer disk 29.95 (*0-7933-1116-0*) Gallopade Pub Group.

—Utah Silly Basketball Sportsmysteries, Vol. 1. (Illus.). 1994. PLB 24.95 (*0-7933-1112-8*); pap. 14.95 (*0-7933-1111-X*); computer disk 29.95 (*0-7933-1113-6*) Gallopade Pub Group.

—Utah Silly Basketball Sportsmysteries, Vol. 2. (Illus.). 1994. PLB 24.95 (*0-7933-2132-8*); pap. 14.95 (*0-7933-2133-6*); computer disk 29.95 (*0-7933-2134-4*) Gallopade Pub Group.

—Utah Silly Football Sportsmysteries, Vol. 1. (Illus.). 1994. PLB 24.95 (*0-7933-2111-5*); pap. 14.95 (*0-7933-2112-3*); computer disk 29.95 (*0-7933-2113-1*) Gallopade Pub Group.

—Utah Silly Football Sportsmysteries, Vol. 2. (Illus.). 1994. PLB 24.95 (*0-7933-2114-X*); pap. 14.95 (*0-7933-2115-8*); computer disk 29.95 (*0-7933-2116-6*) Gallopade Pub Group.

—Utah Silly Trivia! (Illus.). 1994. PLB 24.95 (*0-7933-2103-4*); pap. 14.95 (*0-7933-2104-2*); computer disk 29.95 (*0-7933-2105-0*) Gallopade Pub Group.

—Utah Timeline: A Chronology of Utah History, Mystery, Trivia, Legend, Lore & More. (Illus.). (gr. 3-12). 1994. PLB 24.95 (*0-7933-6007-2*); pap. 14.95 (*0-7933-6008-0*); computer disk 29.95 (*0-7933-6009-9*) Gallopade Pub Group.

—Utah's (Most Devastating!) Disasters & (Most Calamitous!) Catastrophies! (Illus.). 1994. PLB 24.95 (*0-7933-1103-9*); pap. 14.95 (*0-7933-1102-0*) (*0-7933-1104-7*) Gallopade Pub Group.

—Utah's Unsolved Mysteries (& Their "Solutions") Includes Scientific Information & Other Activities for Students. (Illus.). (gr. 3-12). 1994. PLB 24.95 (*0-7933-5854-X*); pap. 14.95 (*0-7933-5855-8*); computer disk 29.95 (*0-7933-5856-6*) Gallopade Pub Group.

Page, Jean R. From Hoof to Wheel. Page, Jean R., illus. 75p. (Orig.). (gr. 7-12). 1992. pap. 7.95 (*0-9632755-0-X*) Jean Page.

Salts, Bobbi. Color Sedona. Parker, Steve, illus. 32p. (Orig.). (ps-6). 1991. pap. 2.95 (*0-929526-10-4*) Double B Pubns.

—Utah Is for Kids! Parker, Steve, illus. 32p. (Orig.). (gr. 1-6). 1991. pap. 3.95 (*0-929526-06-6*) Double B Pubns.

Thompson, Kathleen. Utah. 48p. (gr. 3 up). 1985. PLB 19.97 (*0-86514-446-X*) Raintree Steck-V.

Westwood, Dick. Champin' at the Bit: An Autobiography. (Illus.). 161p. (Orig.). (gr. 6-12). 1986. pap. 10.00x (*0-9617118-1-7*) Westwood Ent.

UTAH–FICTION

Fitzgerald, John D. The Great Brain. Mayer, Mercer, illus. LC 67-22252. (gr. 4-8). 1985. 12.95 (*0-8037-3074-8*); PLB 11.89 (*0-8037-3076-4*) Dial Bks Young.

—Me & My Little Brain. 144p. (gr. 4-7). 1972. 3.99 (*0-440-45533-2*, YB) Dell.

—More Adventures of the Great Brain. Mayer, Mercer, illus. LC 73-85547. (gr. 4-8). 1985. 12.95 (*0-8037-5819-7*, 01160-350) Dial Bks Young.

Wunderli, Stephen. The Blue Between the Clouds. LC 91-28010. 80p. (gr. 5 up). 1992. 13.95 (*0-8050-1772-0*, Bks Young Read) H Holt & Co.

UTENSILS, KITCHEN

see Household Equipment and Supplies

V

VACATIONS–FICTION

Ahlberg, Allan. Skeleton Crew. Amstutz, Andre, illus. LC 91-39161. 32p. (ps-6). 1992. 14.00 (*0-688-11436-9*) Greenwillow.

Brandenburg, Franz. A Fun Weekend. Brandenburg, Alexa, illus. LC 89-77502. 24p. (ps up). 1991. 13.95 (*0-688-09720-0*); PLB 13.88 (*0-688-09721-9*) Greenwillow.

Brown, Marc T. Arthur's Family Vacation. LC 92-26650. 1993. 15.95 (*0-316-11312-3*) Little.

Chorao, Kay. The Cherry Pie Baby. (Illus.). 32p. (ps-3). 1994. pap. 4.99 (*0-14-055286-3*, Puff Unicorn) Puffin Bks.

Clarke, J. Al Capsella Takes a Vacation. 160p. (gr. 7 up). 1993. 14.95 (*0-8050-2685-1*, Bks Young Read) H Holt & Co.

Cole, Joanna. The Clown-Arounds Go on Vacation. Smath, Jerry, illus. LC 93-15471. 1993. 13.27 (*0-8368-0966-1*) Gareth Stevens Inc.

Edens, Cooper. Santa Cow Island Vacation. Lane, Daniel, illus. LC 93-30899. (gr. 2 up). 1994. 14.00 (*0-671-88319-4*, Green Tiger) S&S Trade.

Enright, Elizabeth. Gone-Away Lake. Dyer, Jane & Krush, Beth, illus. 256p. (gr. 3-7). 1990. pap. 4.95 (*0-15-231649-3*, Odyssey) HarBrace.

—Return to Gone-Away. Dyer, Jane & Krush, Beth, illus. 212p. (gr. 3-7). 1990. pap. 4.95 (*0-15-266377-0*, Odyssey) HarBrace.

Erickson, Gina & Foster, Kelli C. What a Trip! Gifford, Kerri, illus. 24p. (gr. k-3). 1994. pap. 3.50 (*0-8120-1923-7*) Barron.

Graham, Bob. Greetings from Sandy Beach. Graham, Bob, illus. 32p. (ps-3). 1992. 12.95 (*0-916291-40-5*) Kane-Miller Bk.

Ireland, Shep. Wesley & Wendell: Vacation. Ireland, Shep, illus. 40p. (gr. 1). 1991. lib. bdg. 4.75 (*0-8378-0332-2*) Gibson.

Kerby, Mona. Thirty Eight Weeks Till Summer Vacation. 1991. pap. 3.95 (*0-14-034205-2*, Puffin) Puffin Bks.

Khalsa, Dayal K. My Family Vacation. Khalsa, Dayal K., illus. 24p. (gr. k-8). 1988. 14.95 (*0-88776-226-3*) Tundra Bks.

Kleitsch, Christel & Kelley, True. It Happened at Pickle Lake. (Illus.). 64p. (gr. 2-5). 1993. 11.99 (*0-525-45058-0*, DCB) Dutton Child Bks.

Lessing, Doris. Through the Tunnel. (gr. 4-12). 1989. 13.95 (*0-88682-346-3*, 97224-098) Creative Ed.

Loomie, Christine. We're Going on a Trip. Chambliss, Maxie, illus. LC 93-17592. 48p. (ps up). 1994. PLB 14.93 (*0-688-10173-9*); 15.00 (*0-688-10172-0*) Morrow Jr Bks.

McPhail, David. Emma's Vacation. McPhail, David, illus. LC 86-24066. 24p. (ps-k). 1987. 7.95 (*0-525-44315-0*, DCB) Dutton Child Bks.

Malkin, Michele. Blanche & Smitty, No. 2. 1988. 3.50 (*0-553-05478-3*) Bantam.

Martin, Ann M. Eleven Kids, One Summer. LC 91-55025. 160p. (gr. 3-7). 1991. 14.95 (*0-8234-0912-0*) Holiday.

—Eleven Kids, One Summer. (gr. 4-7). 1993. pap. 2.95 (*0-590-45917-1*) Scholastic Inc.

Mayorga, Dolores. David Plays Hide-&-Seek on Vacation: David Juega Al Escondite En Vacaciones. Mayorga, Dolores, illus. (ENG & SPA.). 24p. (gr. 2-5). 1992. PLB 18.95 (*0-8225-2004-4*) Lerner Pubns.

Nelson, Jackie & Halpern-Segal, Janice. My Trip. Schoonover, Annette, illus. 24p. (Orig.). (ps-3). 1989. pap. 6.95 (*0-685-29177-4*) Take Along Pubns.

Nethery, Mary. Hannah & Jack. Morgan, Mary, illus. LC 93-4651. 1995. 15.95 (*0-02-768125-4*, Bradbury Pr) Macmillan Child Grp.

Nielsen, Shelly. Only Kidding, Victoria. LC 86-8817. 130p. (gr. 3-7). 1986. pap. 4.99 (*0-89191-474-9*, Chariot Bks) Chariot Family.

Noll, Sally. Lucky Morning. LC 93-18188. (Illus.). 32p. (ps up). 1994. 14.00 (*0-688-12474-7*); PLB 13.93 (*0-688-12475-5*) Greenwillow.

Oh, So Silly. 1994. 13.27 (*0-8368-0974-2*) Gareth Stevens Inc.

Pascal, Francine. Ciao, Sweet Valley! (gr. 4-7). 1992. pap. 3.25 (*0-553-15940-2*) Bantam.

—The Unicorns Go Hawaiian. (gr. 4-7). 1991. pap. 3.99 (*0-553-15948-8*) Bantam.

Perl, Lila. Telltale Summer of Tina C. 1984. pap. 2.50 (*0-590-41324-4*) Scholastic Inc.

Porte, Barbara A. When Grandma Almost Fell off the Mountain & Other Stories. Chambliss, Maxie, illus. LC 91-41174. 32p. (ps-2). 1993. 14.95 (*0-531-05965-0*); PLB 14.99 (*0-531-08565-1*) Orchard Bks Watts.

Remkiewicz, Frank. There's Only One Harris. LC 92-44163. (Illus.). (gr. 3-6). 1993. 14.00 (*0-688-11827-5*); PLB 13.93 (*0-688-11828-3*) Lothrop.

Roberts, Willo D. Nightmare. LC 89-7038. 192p. (gr. 5-9). 1989. SBE 14.95 (*0-689-31551-1*, Atheneum Child Bk) Macmillan Child Grp.

Rockwell, Anne. On Our Vacation. Rockwell, Anne, illus. LC 88-29996. 32p. (ps-1). 1989. 12.95 (*0-525-44487-4*, DCB) Dutton Child Bks.

—On Our Vacation. (Illus.). 32p. (ps-1). 1994. pap. 4.50 (*0-14-055287-1*, Puff Unicorn) Puffin Bks.

Sheldon, Dyan. Harry on Vacation. Heap, Sue, illus. LC 92-52999. 144p. (gr. 3-6). 1993. 13.95 (*1-56402-127-0*) Candlewick Pr.

Sieveking, Anthea. What's Inside? (Illus.). 24p. (ps-k). 1994. pap. 4.50 (*0-14-050353-6*, Puff Pied Piper) Puffin Bks.

Singleton, Linda J. Spring Break. LC 94-4570. (gr. 7 up). 1994. 3.95 (*1-56565-144-8*) Lowell Hse Juvenile.

Skurzynski, Gloria. Dangerous Ground. LC 88-31394. 128p. (gr. 3-7). 1989. SBE 14.95 (*0-02-782731-3*, Bradbury Pr) Macmillan Child Grp.

Stack, Richard L. The Doggonest Vacation. Mowrer, Sheri L., illus. 1991. write for info. (*0-9628262-0-0*) Windmill MD.

Stanley, Diane. Moe the Dog in Tropical Paradise. Primavera, Elise, illus. 32p. (ps-3). 1992. 14.95 (*0-399-22127-1*, Putnam) Putnam Pub Group.

Stevenson, James. The Sea View Hotel. LC 78-2749. (Illus.). 48p. 1994. Repr. of 1974 ed. 15.00 (*0-688-13469-6*); PLB 14.93 (*0-688-13470-X*) Greenwillow.

—When I Was Nine. Stevenson, James, illus. LC 85-9777. 32p. (gr. k-3). 1986. 14.00 (*0-688-05942-2*); PLB 13.93 (*0-688-05943-0*) Greenwillow.

Wells, Carolyn. Marjorie's Vacation. 232p. 1981. Repr. PLB 16.95x (*0-89966-337-0*) Buccaneer Bks.

—Marjorie's Vacation. 315p. 1980. Repr. PLB 12.95x (*0-89967-012-1*) Harmony Raine.

Ziefert, Harriet. What's a Vacation: A Lift-the Flap Bk. Schumacher, Claire, illus. 16p. (ps-k). 1993. 5.95 (*0-694-00449-9*, Festival) HarpC Child Bks.

—Where's Bobo? Rader, Laura, illus. LC 92-24495. 24p. (ps up). 1993. 10.95 (*0-688-12327-9*, Tambourine Bks) Morrow.

VACCINATION

see also Immunity

Burge, Michael C. Vaccines: Preventing Disease. LC 92-27851. (Illus.). 96p. (gr. 5-8). 1992. PLB 15.95 (*1-56006-223-1*) Lucent Bks.

VACUUM TUBES

see also Electronics

VALENTINE'S DAY

Barkin, Carol & James, Elizabeth. Happy Valentines Day. LC 87-35812. (Illus.). 96p. (gr. 4-7). 1988. 14.00 (*0-688-06796-4*) Lothrop.

Barth, Edna. Hearts, Cupids, & Red Roses: The Story of the Valentine Symbols. Arndt, Ursula, illus. LC 73-7128. 64p. (gr. 3-6). 1982. pap. 5.95 (*0-89919-036-7*, Clarion Bks) HM.

Bauer, Caroline F., ed. Valentine's Day: Stories & Poems. Sims, Blanche L., illus. LC 91-37641. 96p. (gr. 2-5). 1993. 15.00 (*0-06-020823-6*); PLB 14.89 (*0-06-020824-4*) HarpC Child Bks.

Bennet, Marian. My First Valentine's Day Book. LC 84-21511. (Illus.). 32p. (ps-2). 1985. PLB 11.45 (*0-516-02906-1*); pap. 3.95 (*0-516-42906-X*) Childrens.

Corwin, Judith H. Valentine Crafts. LC 93-11970. 1994. 12.90 (*0-531-11146-6*) Watts.

—Valentine Fun. Corwin, Judith H., illus. LC 82-6047. 64p. (gr. 3 up). 1983. (J Messner); lib. bdg. 5.95 (*0-671-49755-3*); PLB 7.71s.p. (*0-685-47064-4*); pap. 4.46s.p. (*0-685-47065-2*) S&S Trade.

Davis, Nancy M., et al. February & Valentines. Davis, Nancy M., illus. 29p. (Orig.). (ps-2). 1986. pap. 4.95 (*0-937103-07-1*) DaNa Pubns.

Folmer, A. P. Valentine Pop-up Cards to Make. (ps-3). 1991. pap. 3.95 (*0-590-44033-0*) Scholastic Inc.

Fradin, Dennis B. Valentine's Day. LC 89-7682. (Illus.). 48p. (gr. 1-4). 1990. lib. bdg. 14.95 (*0-89490-237-7*) Enslow Pubs.

Graham-Barber, Lynda. Mushy! The Complete Book of Valentine Words. Lewin, Betsy, illus. LC 90-33047. 128p. (gr. 4-10). 1991. 13.95 (*0-02-736941-2*, Bradbury Pr) Macmillan Child Grp.

Kalman, Bobbie. We Celebrate Valentine's Day. (Illus.). 56p. (gr. 3-4). 1986. 15.95 (*0-86505-047-3*); pap. 7.95 (*0-86505-057-0*) Crabtree Pub Co.

Kent, Jack. Jack Kent's Valentine Sticker Book. 40p. (ps-3). 1987. pap. 2.50 (*0-590-32400-4*) Scholastic Inc.

Kessel, Joyce K. Valentine's Day. Ritz, Karen, illus. 48p. (gr. k-4). 1988. pap. 5.95 (*0-87614-502-0*, First Ave Edns) Lerner Pubns.

Make Your Own Valentine Cards. (ps-3). 1992. pap. 2.95 (*0-8167-1613-7*) Troll Assocs.

Moncure, Jane B. Our Valentine's Day Book. Rev. ed. McLean, Mina G., illus. LC 86-28387. 32p. (ps-3). 1987. PLB 13.95 (*0-89565-343-5*) Childs World.

Prelutsky, Jack. It's Valentine's Day. Abolafia, Yossi, illus. 48p. (gr. k-3). 1985. pap. 2.50 (*0-590-40979-4*) Scholastic Inc.

—It's Valentine's Day. Abolafia, Yossi, illus. 48p. (gr. k-3). 1988. pap. 5.95 bk & cassette (*0-590-63172-1*) Scholastic Inc.

Sandak, Cass. Valentine's Day. (Illus.). 48p. (gr. 5-6). 1990. text ed. 12.95 RSBE (*0-89686-504-5*, Crestwood Hse) Macmillan Child Grp.

Spivak, Darlene & Sterling, Mary E. Valentine's Day Activities. Wright, Theresa & Spence, Paula, illus. 48p. (gr. 1-4). 1989. wkbk. 5.95 (*1-55734-009-9*) Tchr Create Mat.

Stamper, Judith. Valentine Holiday Grab Bag. Weissman, Bari & Garcia, T. R., illus. LC 92-13225. 48p. (gr. 2-5). 1992. PLB 11.89 (*0-8167-2910-7*); pap. text ed. 3.95 (*0-8167-2911-5*) Troll Assocs.
Supraner, Robyn. Valentine's Day: Things to Make & Do. Barto, Renzo, illus. LC 80-23780. 48p. (gr. 1-5). 1981. PLB 11.89 (*0-89375-424-2*); pap. 3.50 (*0-89375-425-0*) Troll Assocs.
Tudor, Tasha. The Jenny Wren Book of Valentines. Tudor, Tasha, illus. Wren, Jenny, intro. by. LC 88-51832. (Illus.). 16p. (Orig.). (gr. k up). 1989. pap. 6.95 (*0-9621753-1-5*) Jenny Wren Pr.
Valentine Decorations: Make & Color Your Own. (ps-3). 1989. pap. 1.95 (*0-89375-646-6*) Troll Assocs.
Valentine's Day Search & Find. 24p. (gr. k-4). 1992. pap. 2.50 (*0-8167-1852-0*) Troll Assocs.
Watson, Wendy. A Valentine for You. Briley, Dorothy, ed. Watson, Wendy, illus. 32p. (ps-1). 1991. 14.45 (*0-395-53625-1*, Clarion Bks) HM.
Ziefert, Harriet. My Valentines. Baum, Susan, illus. 8p. (ps-2). 1993. incl. postcards 6.95 (*0-694-00447-2*, Festival) HarpC Child Bks.
—What Is Valentine's Day? Schumacher, Claire, illus. 16p. (ps-k). 1993. 5.95 (*0-694-00413-8*, Festival) HarpC Child Bks.

VALENTINE'S DAY–FICTION

Adams, Adrienne. The Great Valentine's Day Balloon Race. 2nd ed. LC 93-46114. 1995. pap. 4.95 (*0-689-71847-0*, Aladdin) Macmillan Child Grp.
Allen, Helen S. A Valentine Letter to Lynn: Mandy's Adventure in the Snow. 16p. (ps). 1992. pap. text ed. 5.00 (*1-881907-02-3*) Two Bytes Pub.
Balian, Lorna. A Sweetheart for Valentine. Balian, Lorna, illus. 32p. (ps-3). 1988. Repr. of 1980 ed. 7.50 (*0-687-37109-0*) Humbug Bks.
Barth, Nancy & Wittenborn, Sally. But Will You Be My Valentine? (Illus., Orig.). (ps-k). 1987. pap. 4.95 (*0-942565-01-0*) Country Schl Pubns.
Blos, Joan W. One Very Best Valentine's Day. 1990. pap. 8.95 (*0-671-64639-7*) S&S Trade.
—One Very Best Valentine's Day. McCully, Emily A., illus. 32p. (ps-2). 1992. pap. 2.50 (*0-671-75297-9*, Little Simon) S&S Trade.
Brown, Marc T. Arthur's Valentine. Brown, Marc T., illus. (ps-3). 1980. 14.95 (*0-316-11062-0*, Joy St Bks) Little.
Carlson, Nancy. Louanne Pig in the Mysterious Valentine. (ps-3). 1987. pap. 3.95 (*0-14-050604-7*, Puffin) Puffin Bks.
Carrick, Carol. Valentine. Bouma, Paddy, illus. LC 93-35911. 1995. write for info. (*0-395-66554-X*, Clarion Bks) HM.
Cohen, Barbara. Two Hundred Thirteen Valentines. Clay, Wil, illus. LC 91-7151. 64p. (gr. 2-4). 1993. pap. 4.95 (*0-8050-2627-4*, Redfeather BYR) H Holt & Co.
Cohen, Miriam. Bee My Valentine. Hoban, Lillian, illus. LC 77-21950. 32p. (gr. k-3). 1978. PLB 11.88 (*0-688-84129-5*) Greenwillow.
—Bee My Valentine! Hoban, Lillian, illus. (gr. k-3). 1983. pap. 3.25 (*0-440-40507-6*, YB) Dell.
Craig, Janet A. Valentine's Day Mess. Morse, Debby, illus. LC 93-2211. 32p. (gr. k-2). 1993. PLB 11.59 (*0-8167-3254-X*); pap. text ed. 2.95 (*0-8167-3255-8*) Troll Assocs.
Cuyler, Margery. Freckles & Willie: A Valentine's Day Story. Winborn, Marsha, illus. LC 85-8646. 32p. (ps-2). 1986. 12.95 (*0-03-003772-7*, Bks Young Read) H Holt & Co.
Devlin, Wende & Devlin, Harry. Cranberry Valentine. Devlin, Wende & Devlin, Harry, illus. LC 85-24047. 32p. (gr. k-3). 1986. SBE 14.95 (*0-02-729200-2*, Four Winds) Macmillan Child Grp.
—Cranberry Valentine. Devlin, Wende & Devlin, Harry, illus. LC 91-6915. 40p. (gr. k-3). 1992. pap. 3.95 (*0-689-71509-9*, Aladdin) Macmillan Child Grp.
DeWolf, Carol. The Candy Heart. LC 92-82937. (Illus.). 56p. (ps-3). 1993. pap. 3.50 (*0-943864-67-4*) Davenport.
Ehrlich, Fred. A Valentine for Ms. Vanilla. Gradisher, Martha, illus. 32p. (ps-3). 1992. 8.95 (*0-670-84274-5*) Viking Child Bks.
Erickson, Gina C. & Foster, Kelli C. A Valentine That Shines. Gifford, Kerri, illus. 24p. (ps-3). 1994. pap. 3.50 (*0-8120-1838-9*) Barron.
Gantz, David. Biggest Valentine. 1990. pap. 2.50 (*0-590-43329-6*) Scholastic Inc.
Giff, Patricia R. The Red, White, & Blue Valentine. (ps-3). 1993. pap. 3.25 (*0-440-40768-0*) Dell.
—The Valentine Star. Sims, Blanche, illus. 80p. (Orig.). (gr. k-6). 1985. pap. 3.50 (*0-440-49204-1*, YB) Dell.
Greydanus, Rose. Valentine's Day Grump. Page, Don, illus. LC 81-4712. 32p. (gr. k-2). 1981. PLB 11.59 (*0-89375-515-X*); pap. text ed. 2.95 (*0-89375-516-8*) Troll Assocs.
Happy Valentine Bear Read & Color. (ps-3). 1989. pap. 1.25 (*0-8167-0837-1*) Troll Assocs.
Hawkins, Laura. Valentine to a Flying Mouse. (ps-7). 1993. 13.95 (*0-395-61628-X*) HM.
Haynes, Betsy. Melanie's Valentine. (gr. 4-7). 1991. pap. 2.95 (*0-553-15845-7*) Bantam.
Haywood, Carolyn. A Valentine Fantasy. Ambrus, Victor G. & Ambrus, Victor G., illus. LC 75-23083. 32p. (gr. k-3). 1976. PLB 14.88 (*0-688-32055-4*) Morrow Jr Bks.
Hoban, Lillian. Arthur's Great Big Valentine. Hoban, Lillian, illus. LC 88-21202. 64p. (gr. k-3). 1989. PLB 13.89 (*0-06-022407-X*) HarpC Child Bks.
—Arthur's Great Big Valentine. Hoban, Lillian, illus. LC 88-21202. 64p. (gr. k-3). 1991. pap. 3.50 (*0-06-444149-0*, Trophy) HarpC Child Bks.
Hoien, Ruth S. Ruthie's Four Hearts. pap. 2.99 (*0-88019-105-8*) Schmul Pub Co.
Hopkins, Lee B. Good Morning to You, Valentine. 32p. (ps-3). 1991. 9.95 (*1-878093-59-2*) Boyds Mills Pr.
Jeanie's Valentine. (Illus.). (ps-2). 1991. PLB 6.95 (*0-8136-5126-3*, TK2614); pap. 3.50 (*0-8136-5626-5*, TK2613) Modern Curr.
Kelley, True. A Valentine for Fuzzboom. Kelley, True, illus. LC 80-24284. 24p. (gr. k-3). 1982. HM.
Kessel, Joyce K. Valentine's Day. Ritz, Karen, illus. LC 81-3842. 48p. (gr. k-4). 1981. PLB 14.95 (*0-87614-166-1*) Carolrhoda Bks.
Kline, Suzy. Horrible Harry & the Kickball Wedding. Remkiewicz, Frank, illus. LC 92-5827. 64p. (gr. 2-5). 1992. 11.00 (*0-670-83358-4*) Viking Child Bks.
Kraus, Robert. How Spider Saved Valentine's Day. Kraus, Robert, illus. 32p. (Orig.). (ps-1). 1986. pap. 2.50 (*0-590-42514-5*) Scholastic Inc.
Kroll, Steven. Will You Be My Valentine? Hoban, Lillian, illus. 32p. (ps-3). 1993. reinforced bdg. 14.95 (*0-8234-0925-2*) Holiday.
Kunhardt, Edith. Danny's Mystery Valentine. (Illus.). 24p. (ps-1). 1987. 11.75 (*0-688-06853-7*); PLB 11.88 (*0-688-06854-5*) Greenwillow.
Lexau, Joan M. Don't Be My Valentine. Hoff, Syd, illus. (gr. 1-4). 1990. incl. cass. 19.95 (*0-87499-150-1*); pap. 12.95 incl. cass. (*0-87499-149-8*); Set; incl. 4 bks., cass., & guide. pap. 27.95 (*0-685-38539-6*) Live Oak Media.
Lundell, Margo. My Book of Funny Valentines. Evans, Nate, illus. 32p. (ps-3). 1993. pap. 2.50 (*0-590-44187-6*) Scholastic Inc.
McDonnell, Janet. Two Special Valentines. McCallum, Jodie, illus. LC 93-37097. 32p. (ps-2). 1994. PLB 12. 30 (*0-516-00692-4*) Childrens.
Mandrell, Louise. Candy's Frog Prince: A Story about the Meaning of Valentines Day. (gr. 4-7). 1993. 12.95 (*1-56530-046-7*) Summit TX.
Modell, Frank. One Zillion Valentines. LC 81-2215. (Illus.). 32p. (gr. k-3). 1981. 12.93 (*0-688-00565-9*); PLB 11.88 (*0-688-00569-1*) Greenwillow.
Nerlove, Miriam. Valentine's Day. Mathews, Judith, ed. Nerlove, Miriam, illus. LC 91-19289. 24p. (ps-1). 1992. PLB 11.95 (*0-8075-8454-1*) A Whitman.
Peck, Robert N. Soup in Love. (gr. 4-7). 1992. 14.00 (*0-385-30563-X*) Delacorte.
Prelutsky, Jack. It's Valentine's Day. Abolafia, Yossi, illus. LC 83-1449. 48p. (gr. 1-3). 1983. 15.00 (*0-688-02311-8*); PLB 14.93 (*0-688-02312-6*) Greenwillow.
Regan, Dian C. My Zombie Valentine. (gr. 4-7). 1993. pap. 2.95 (*0-590-46038-2*) Scholastic Inc.
Rider, Joanne. First Grade Valentines. Lewin, Betsy, illus. LC 92-35388. 32p. (gr. k-2). 1992. PLB 9.79 (*0-8167-3004-0*); pap. text ed. 2.95 (*0-8167-3005-9*) Troll Assocs.
Roos, Stephen. My Secret Admirer. Newsom, Carol, illus. LC 84-5010. 112p. (gr. 4-6). 1984. 14.95 (*0-385-29342-9*); PLB 13.95 (*0-385-29343-7*) Delacorte.
St. Pierre, Stephanie. Valentine Kittens. 1990. pap. 3.95 (*0-590-63481-X*) Scholastic Inc.
Saunders, Susan. A Valentine for Patti. (gr. 4-7). 1991. pap. 2.75 (*0-590-43927-8*) Scholastic Inc.
Schweninger, Ann. Valentine Friends. (Illus.). 32p. (ps-1). 1990. pap. 4.99 (*0-14-050662-4*, Puffin) Puffin Bks.
Scribner, Virginia. Gopher Takes Heart. Wilson, Janet, illus. LC 92-25939. 128p. (gr. 3-7). 1993. 13.99 (*0-670-84839-5*) Viking Child Bks.
Sharmat, Marjorie W. Best Valentine in the World. LC 81-13345. (Illus.). 32p. (ps-3). 1982. reinforced bdg. 14.95 (*0-8234-0440-4*) Holiday.
—Nate the Great & the Mushy Valentine. Simont, Marc, illus. LC 93-15488. 1994. 12.95 (*0-385-31166-4*) Delacorte.
Smith, Janice L. Nelson in Love: An Adam Joshua Valentine's Day Story. Gackenbach, Dick, illus. LC 91-14667. 80p. (gr. 1-4). 1992. 13.00 (*0-06-020292-0*); PLB 12.89 (*0-06-020293-9*) HarpC Child Bks.
Stahl, Hilda. Daisy Punkin: The Bratty Brother. 128p. (gr. 2-5). 1992. pap. 4.99 (*0-89107-662-X*) Crossway Bks.
Stevenson, James. Happy Valentine's Day, Emma! LC 87-13. (Illus.). 32p. (gr. k-3). 1987. 11.75 (*0-688-07357-3*); lib. bdg. 12.88 (*0-688-07358-1*) Greenwillow.
Stock, Catherine. Secret Valentine. Stock, Catherine, illus. LC 90-1916. 32p. (ps-1). 1991. SBE 11.95 (*0-02-788372-8*, Bradbury Pr) Macmillan Child Grp.
Trumbauer, Lisa. Runaway Valentines. Cote, Pamela, illus. LC 93-14181. (gr. k-2). 1993. pap. 2.95 (*0-8167-3264-7*) Troll Assocs.
Watson, Clyde. Valentine Foxes. Watson, Wendy, illus. LC 88-22392. 32p. (ps-3). 1992. pap. 5.95 (*0-531-07033-6*) Orchard Bks Watts.
Watson, Wendy. A Valentine for You. Watson, Wendy, illus. 32p. (gr. k-3). 1993. pap. 5.95 (*0-395-66411-X*, Clarion Bks) HM.
York, Jami. How Valentine's Day Began, 5 vols, Vol. I. 35p. (gr. 1-6). 1991. Repr. of 1979 ed. 12.95 (*1-880108-04-6*) Apple Valley.
Ziefert, Harriet. A Valentine for Ms. Vanilla. (Illus.). 32p. (ps-3). 1992. pap. 3.50 (*0-14-054460-7*) Puffin Bks.
Ziefert, Harriet & Gradisher, Martha. A Valentine for Ms. Vanilla. (Illus.). (gr. k-3). 1994. pap. 3.25 (*0-14-036871-X*) Puffin Bks.

VALLEY FORGE

Hughes, Libby. Valley Forge. LC 92-23391. (Illus.). 72p. (gr. 4 up). 1993. text ed. 14.95 RSBE (*0-87518-547-9*, Dillon) Macmillan Child Grp.
Stein, R. Conrad. The Story of Valley Forge. Eads, Nancy, illus. LC 84-23203. 32p. (gr. 3-6). 1985. PLB 12.30 (*0-516-04681-0*) Childrens.
—Valley Forge. LC 94-9490. (Illus.). 32p. (gr. 3-6). 1994. PLB 16.40 (*0-516-06683-8*); pap. 3.95 (*0-516-46683-6*) Childrens.

VAN BUREN, MARTIN, PRESIDENT U. S. 1782-1862

Ellis, Rafaela. Martin Van Buren: Eighth President of the United States. Young, Richard G., ed. LC 88-24535. (Illus.). (gr. 5-9). 1989. PLB 17.26 (*0-944483-12-7*) Garrett Ed Corp.
Hargrove, James. Martin Van Buren. LC 87-16023. (Illus.). 100p. (gr. 3 up). 1987. PLB 14.40 (*0-516-01391-2*) Childrens.
Welles, Ted. Van Buren, Wizard of O.K. & 8th U. S. A. President. Johnson, Mercy, ed. LC 87-60750. (Illus.). 96p. (Orig.). (gr. 6 up). 1987. July 30, 1987. lib. bdg. 12.00 (*0-915189-04-6*); June 30, 1987. pap. 5.95 (*0-915189-05-4*) Oceanus.

VANDALISM

see Crime and Criminals

VANILLA

Busenberg, Bonnie. Vanilla, Chocolate, & Strawberry: The Story of Your Favorite Flavors. LC 93-15101. 1993. 23.95 (*0-8225-1573-3*) Lerner Pubns.

VASQUEZ DE CORONADO, FRANCISCO, 1510-1549

Stein, R. Conrad. Francisco de Coronado: Explorer of the American Southwest. LC 91-32207. 128p. (gr. 3 up). 1992. PLB 20.55 (*0-516-03068-X*) Childrens.

VASSALS

see Feudalism

VATICAN (CITY)

Conry, Kieran. The Vatican. (Illus.). 96p. (gr. 5 up). 1988. 14.95 (*0-222-01009-6*) Chelsea Hse.

VAUDEVILLE–FICTION

Slepian, Jan. Pinocchio's Sister. LC 94-1361. 1995. 14.95 (*0-399-22811-X*, Philomel Bks) Putnam Pub Group.

VEGETABLE ANATOMY

see Botany–Anatomy

VEGETABLE GARDENING

see also Vegetables

Berger, Melvin. The Vegetable Garden. (Illus.). 16p. (ps-2). 1995. pap. text ed. 14.95 (*1-56784-024-8*) Newbridge Comms.
Creasy, Rosalind. Blue Potatoes, Orange Tomatoes: How to Grow a Rainbow Garden. Heller, Ruth, illus. LC 92-38800. 48p. (gr. 2-6). 1994. 15.95 (*0-87156-576-5*) Sierra.
Fryer, Lee & Bradford, Leigh. A Child's Organic Garden. Albert, Eddie, frwd. by. 96p. 1989. 9.95 (*0-87491-963-0*); pap. 9.95 (*0-685-28260-0*) Acropolis.
Gardening. (Illus.). 64p. (gr. 6-12). 1982. pap. 1.85 (*0-8395-3240-7*, 33240) BSA.
Handelsman, Judith F. Gardens from Garbage: How to Grow Plants from Recycled Kitchen Scraps. LC 92-9146. (Illus.). 48p. (gr. 4-6). 1993. PLB 13.90 (*1-56294-229-8*) Millbrook Pr.
Walker, Lois. Get Growing! Exciting Plant Projects for Kids. 104p. 1991. pap. text ed. 9.95 (*0-471-54488-4*) Wiley.

VEGETABLE GARDENING–FICTION

Buria, Maria E. Billy the Bean. Siu, Emma, illus. 36p. (Orig.). (ps-k). 1989. pap. 5.95 (*1-878926-04-7*) Colorful Lrngs.
Burningham, John. Avocado Baby. Burningham, John, illus. LC 81-43844. 24p. (ps-3). 1982. 16.00 (*0-690-04243-4*, Crowell Jr Bks); PLB 15.89 (*0-690-04244-2*) HarpC Child Bks.
Coran, Pierre. Old Mr. Bennett's Carrots. (Illus.). 32p. (gr. 3-5). 1991. 12.95 (*0-89565-749-X*) Childs World.
Florian, Douglas. Vegetable Garden. LC 90-20620. (ps-3). 1994. pap. 19.95 (*0-15-200051-8*, HB Juv Bks) HarBrace.
Gaynor, Brigid. The Vegetable Garden. Rollins, Nancy O., illus. 12p. (ps). 1992. 4.95 (*1-56828-016-5*) Red Jacket Pr.
Korman, Gordon. The Zucchini Warriors. 208p. 1991. pap. 3.25 (*0-590-44174-4*, Apple Paperbacks) Scholastic Inc.
Westcott, Nadine B. The Giant Vegetable Garden. (Illus.). 32p. (ps-3). 1981. 14.95i (*0-316-93129-2*, Pub. by Atlantic Monthly Pr); pap. 4.95 (*0-316-93130-6*) Little.

VEGETABLE KINGDOM

see Botany; Plants

VEGETABLES

see also Vegetable Gardening; Vegetarianism

Bergen, Lara R. Pumpkin Heads. Weissman, Bari, illus. 32p. (gr. 1-5). 1994. pap. 5.95 (*0-448-40473-7*, G&D) Putnam Pub Group.
Creasy, Rosalind. Blue Potatoes, Orange Tomatoes: How to Grow a Rainbow Garden. Heller, Ruth, illus. LC 92-38800. 48p. (gr. 2-6). 1994. 15.95 (*0-87156-576-5*) Sierra.
Cross, Gillian. Born of the Sun. LC 84-3740. (Illus.). 240p. (gr. 7 up). 1984. 11.95 (*0-8234-0528-1*) Holiday.
Ford, Beatrice. Royal Eggplant. Duthie, Dorothy B., ed. (Illus.). 1991. pap. write for info. (*1-880172-52-6*) Storyteller.
Green, Harriet & Martin, Sue. Sprouts. 144p. (gr. 3-8). 1981. 12.95 (*0-86653-028-2*, GA256) Good Apple.

Houbre, Gilbert, illus. Carotte. (FRE.). (ps-1). 1989. 13. 95 (*2-07-035711-2*) Schoenhof.
McMillan, Bruce. Growing Colors. McMillan, Bruce, photos by. LC 93-28804. (Illus.). 32p. (ps up). 1994. pap. 4.95 (*0-688-13112-3*, Mulberry) Morrow.
Meltzer, Milton. The Amazing Potato: A Story in Which the Incas, Conquistadors, Marie Antoinette, Thomas Jefferson, Wars, Famines, Immigrants, & French Fries All Play a Part. LC 91-29610. (Illus.). 128p. (gr. 3-7). 1992. 15.00 (*0-06-020806-6*); PLB 14.89 (*0-06-020807-4*) HarpC Child Bks.
Miller, Susanna. Beans & Peas. Yeats, John, illus. 32p. (gr. 1-4). 1990. PLB 14.95 (*0-87614-428-8*) Carolrhoda Bks.
Pohl, Kathleen. Potatoes. (Illus.). 32p. (gr. 3-7). 1986. PLB 10.95 (*0-8172-2723-7*) Raintree Steck-V.
Robinson, Fay. Vegetables, Vegetables. LC 94-14075. (Illus.). 32p. (ps-2). 1994. PLB 14.40 (*0-516-06030-9*); pap. 3.95 (*0-516-46030-7*) Childrens.
Swiader, John M., et al. Producing Vegetable Crops. 4th ed. (Illus.). 626p. (gr. 9-12). 1992. 50.60 (*0-8134-2903-X*); text ed. 35.95 (*0-685-50796-3*); tchr's. manual 9.95 (*0-8134-2904-8*) Interstate.
Turner, Dorothy. Potatoes. Yates, John, illus. 32p. (gr. 1-4). 1989. PLB 14.95 (*0-87614-362-1*) Carolrhoda Bks.
Wake, Susan. Vegetables. (Illus.). 32p. (gr. 1-4). 1990. PLB 14.95 (*0-87614-390-7*) Carolrhoda Bks.
Wasserman, Debra & Stahler, Charles, eds. I Love Animals & Broccoli. Ransom, Ruth, intro. by. 48p. (Orig.). 1985. pap. 5.00 (*0-931411-01-7*) Vegetarian Resc.
Watts, Barrie. Potato. LC 87-16702. (Illus.). 25p. (gr. k-4). 1988. PLB 7.95 (*0-382-09527-8*); pap. 3.95 (*0-382-24018-9*) Silver Burdett Pr.
—Tomato. (Illus.). 25p. (ps-4). 1990. 5.95 (*0-382-24010-3*); PLB 7.95 (*0-382-24008-1*); pap. 3.95 (*0-382-24344-7*) Silver Burdett Pr.
Whitlatch, Issac. Me & My Veggies. Whitlatch, Issac, illus. LC 87-2920. 24p. (gr. 1-7). 1987. PLB 14.95 (*0-933849-16-8*) Landmark Edns.
Wiesbauer, Marciua. The Big Green Bean. Hyman, Trina, illus. LC 94-20372. 1994. pap. 3.95 (*0-382-24661-6*) Silver Burdett Pr.

VEGETABLES–CANNING
see Canning and Preserving

VEGETARIANISM
Bradley, Ann. Cows Are Vegetarians! A Book for Vegetarian Kids. Kramer, Stephen & Huffman, Elise, illus. 24p. (gr. 2-8). 1992. pap. 7.95 (*0-9630893-0-7*) Healthways.
Salter, Charles A. The Vegetarian Teen. (Illus.). 112p. (gr. 7 up). 1991. PLB 15.90 (*1-56294-048-1*) Millbrook Pr.
Singer, Marcia. Eating for a Fresh Start: A P.L.A.Y. Book. Rendal, Camille, illus. LC 90-91969. 64p. (Orig.). (gr. 1-7). 1990. pap. write for info. (*0-9622543-1-2*) PLAY House.
Wolfe, Robert L. Vegetarian Cooking Around the World. (gr. 4-7). 1993. pap. 5.95 (*0-8225-9632-6*) Lerner Pubns.
Wolfe, Robert L. & Wolfe, Diane, photos by. Vegetarian Cooking Around the World. (Illus.). 52p. (gr. 5-12). 1992. PLB 14.95 (*0-8225-0927-X*) Lerner Pubns.

VEHICLES
Barrett, Norman. Sport Machines. LC 93-33236. (Illus.). 48p. (gr. 5-7). 1994. PLB 13.95 (*0-531-14299-X*) Watts.
—Transport Machines. LC 93-33235. (Illus.). 48p. (gr. 5-7). 1994. PLB 13.95 (*0-531-14298-1*) Watts.
Gibbons, Gail. Emergency! LC 94-2109. (Illus.). 32p. (ps-3). 1994. reinforced bdg. 15.95 (*0-8234-1128-1*) Holiday.
Graham, Ian. Cars, Planes, Ships, & Trains. LC 94-16303. 1994. write for info. (*0-8160-3220-3*) Facts on File.
Hawksley, Gerald. Building Wheels. (Illus.). 8p. 1992. bds. 3.95 (*0-681-41557-6*) Longmeadow Pr.
—Farm Wheels. (Illus.). 8p. 1992. bds. 3.95 (*0-681-41556-8*) Longmeadow Pr.
—Racing Wheels. (Illus.). 8p. 1992. bds. 3.95 (*0-681-41558-4*) Longmeadow Pr.
—Rescue Wheels. (Illus.). 8p. 1992. bds. 3.95 (*0-681-41559-2*) Longmeadow Pr.
Lafferty, Peter & Jefferis, David. To the Rescue: The History of Emergency Vehicles. LC 89-21541. (Illus.). 32p. (gr. 5-8). 1990. PLB 12.40 (*0-531-14085-7*) Watts.
Maynard, Chris. I Wonder Why Planes Have Wings & Other Questions about Transport. Quigley, Sebastian, illus. LC 92-42373. 32p. (gr. k-3). 1993. 8.95 (*1-85697-877-X*, Kingfisher LKC) LKC.
Moerbeek, Kees. Let's Go. LC 91-38117. 1992. 9.95 (*0-85953-542-8*) Childs Play.
Radford, Derek. Let's Look Inside a Bus, Train, Ferry, & Plane. Radford, Derek, illus. LC 92-41487. 20p. (ps). 1993. 9.99 (*0-525-67459-4*, Lodestar Bks) Dutton Child Bks.
Rockwell, Anne. Things That Go. LC 86-6199. (Illus.). 24p. (ps-1). 1991. pap. 3.95 (*0-525-44703-2*, Puffin) Puffin Bks.
Royston, Angela. Big Machines. Pastor, Terry, illus. LC 93-16019. (gr. 3 up). 1994. 12.95 (*0-316-76070-6*) Little.
Stacy, Tom. Wings, Wheels & Sails. LC 90-13027. (Illus.). 40p. (gr. 4-6). 1991. PLB 12.40 (*0-531-19105-2*) Watts.
Uggla, Goran, illus. The Car Book. LC 93-4422. 1993. spiral bdg. 17.95 (*0-8118-0514-X*) Chronicle Bks.
Vehicles: Land, Sea, Air. 1991. pap. 3.95 (*0-7214-5322-8*) Ladybird Bks.
Vehicles: Superdoodles. LC 92-74099. (gr. 1-6). 1993. pap. 4.95 (*0-88160-220-5*, LW304) Learning Wks.

VEHICLES, MILITARY
Military Vehicles. (Illus.). 64p. (gr. 3-9). 1990. PLB 16.95 (*1-85435-090-0*) Marshall Cavendish.
Nicholaus, J. Tracked Vehicles. (Illus.). 48p. (gr. 3-8). 1989. lib. bdg. 18.60 (*0-86592-422-8*); lib. bdg. 13. 95s.p. (*0-685-58579-4*) Rourke Corp.

VELAZQUEZ, DIEGO RODRIGUEZ DE SILVA Y, 1599-1660
Beneduce, Ann K., tr. A Weekend with Velazquez. Rodari, Florian, text by. LC 92-33350. (Illus.). 64p. 1993. 19.95 (*0-8478-1647-8*) Rizzoli Intl.
Diego Velazquez. (ps-3). 1993. 18.95 (*0-7910-1779-6*) Chelsea Hse.

VELAZQUEZ, DIEGO RODRIQUEZ DE SILVA Y, 1599-1660–FICTION
De Trevino, Elizabeth B. I, Juan De Pareja. LC 65-19330. 192p. (gr. 7 up). 1965. 16.00 (*0-374-33531-1*); pap. 3.95, 1987 (*0-374-43525-1*, Sunburst) FS&G.
Johnson, Jane. The Princess & the Painter. LC 93-39987. (ps-3). 1994. 15.00 (*0-374-36118-5*) FS&G.

VENEREAL DISEASES
Felman, Yehudi M. Genital Herpes. Head, J. J., ed. Steffen, Ann T. & Whitely, Derek, illus. LC 84-71142. 16p. (Orig.). (gr. 10 up). 1987. pap. text ed. 2.75 (*0-89278-153-X*, 45-9753) Carolina Biological.
Landau, Elaine. Sexually Transmitted Diseases. Heimlich, Hermelie, illus. Armstrong, Donald & Haundsfield, Hunterfrwd. by. LC 85-4349. (Illus.). 96p. (gr. 6 up). 1986. lib. bdg. 16.95 (*0-89490-115-X*) Enslow Pubs.
Little, Marjorie. Sexually Transmitted Diseases. (Illus.). 112p. (gr. 6-12). 1991. 18.95 (*0-7910-0080-X*) Chelsea Hse.
Rico, Armando B. Later with the Latex: AIDS. 44p. (Orig.). 1992. pap. 2.95 (*1-879219-06-9*) Veracruz Pubs.

VENEZUELA
Fox, Geoffrey. The Land & People of Venezuela. LC 90-20431. (Illus.). 208p. (gr. 6 up). 1991. PLB 17.89 (*0-06-022477-0*) HarpC Child Bks.
Lerner Publications, Department of Geography Staff. Venezuela in Pictures. (Illus.). 64p. (gr. 5 up). 1987. PLB 17.50 (*0-8225-1824-4*) Lerner Pubns.
Morrison, Marion. Venezuela. LC 88-30493. (Illus.). 128p. (gr. 5-9). 1989. PLB 20.55 (*0-516-02711-5*) Childrens.
Winter, Jane K. Venezuela. LC 90-22470. (Illus.). 128p. (gr. 5-9). 1991. PLB 21.95 (*1-85435-386-1*) Marshall Cavendish.

VENEZUELA–FICTION
Hudson, William H. Green Mansions. Teitel, N. R., intro. by. (gr. 8 up). 1965. pap. 1.95 (*0-8049-0087-6*, CL-87) Airmont.

VENOM
see Poisons

VENTRILOQUISM
Kraus, Robert. Phil the Ventriloquist. LC 88-11. (Illus.). 32p. (ps up). 1989. 11.95 (*0-688-07987-3*); PLB 11.88 (*0-688-07988-1*) Greenwillow.
McGill, Ormond. Voice Magic: Secrets of Ventriloquism & Voice Conjuring. LC 91-21000. (Illus.). 64p. (gr. 4-6). 1992. PLB 13.40 (*1-56294-137-2*) Millbrook Pr.
Slepian, Jan. Pinocchio's Sister. LC 94-1361. 1995. 14.95 (*0-399-22811-X*, Philomel Bks) Putnam Pub Group.

VENUS (PLANET)
Baker, David. Exploring Venus & Mercury. LC 88-33707. (Illus.). 48p. (gr. 4-6). 1989. PLB 18.60 (*0-86592-371-X*); lib. bdg. 13.95s.p. (*0-685-58638-3*) Rourke Corp.
Branley, Franklyn M. Venus: Magellan Explores Our Twin Planet. LC 92-32990. (Illus.). 64p. (gr. 3-6). 1994. 16.00 (*0-06-020298-X*); PLB 15.89 (*0-06-020384-6*) HarpC Child Bks.
Fradin, Dennis B. Venus. LC 88-39121. (Illus.). 48p. (gr. k-4). 1989. PLB 12.85 (*0-516-01168-5*); pap. 4.95 (*0-516-41168-3*) Childrens.
Schloss, Muriel. Venus. LC 90-13101. (Illus.). 64p. (gr. 3-5). 1991. PLB 12.90 (*0-531-20019-1*) Watts.
Simon, Seymour. Venus. LC 91-12171. (Illus.). 32p. (gr. k up). 1992. 15.00 (*0-688-10542-4*); PLB 14.93 (*0-688-10543-2*) Morrow Jr Bks.
Vogt, Gregory. Magellan & the Radar Mapping of Venus. LC 91-23494. (Illus.). 112p. (gr. 4-6). 1992. PLB 15.90 (*1-56294-146-1*) Millbrook Pr.
Vogt, Gregory L. Venus. LC 93-11217. (Illus.). 32p. (gr. 2-4). 1994. PLB 12.90 (*1-56294-391-X*) Millbrook Pr.

VERDI, GIUSEPPE, 1813-1901
Tames, Richard. Giuseppe Verdi. LC 90-38303. (Illus.). 32p. 1991. PLB 12.40 (*0-531-14109-8*) Watts.

VERMONT
Budbill, David. Snowshoe Trek to Otter River. (Illus.). 96p. (gr. 4-6). 1984. pap. 2.75 (*0-553-15469-9*, Skylark) Bantam.
Carole Marsh Vermont Books, 44 bks. 1994. PLB 1027. 80 set (*0-7933-1320-1*); pap. 587.80 set (*0-7933-5212-6*) Gallopade Pub Group.
Carpenter, Allan. Vermont. new ed. LC 79-829. (Illus.). 96p. (gr. 4 up). 1979. PLB 16.95 (*0-516-04145-2*) Childrens.
Cheney, Cora. Vermont, the State with the Storybook Past. rev. ed. MacLean, Robert, illus. Muller, H. N., III, intro. by. LC 86-60341. (Illus.). 272p. (gr. 5-9). 1986. pap. 18.95 (*0-933050-36-4*) New Eng Pr VT.
Fradin, Dennis. Vermont: In Words & Pictures. LC 79-22069. (Illus.). 48p. (gr. 2-5). 1980. PLB 12.95 (*0-516-03946-6*) Childrens.
Fradin, Dennis B. Vermont. LC 92-36371. (Illus.). 64p. (gr. 3-5). 1993. PLB 16.45 (*0-516-03845-1*) Childrens.
Guyette, Elise. Vermont: A Cultural Patchwork. (Illus.). 144p. (Orig.). (gr. 4-8). 1986. pap. text ed. 9.85 (*0-9607638-5-6*) Cobblestone Pub.
Kelley, Shirley. Little Settlers of Vermont. 1987. 7.95 (*0-685-43894-5*) Equity Pub NH.
Lasky, Kathryn. Sugaring Time. Knight, Christopher G., photos by. LC 86-3468. (Illus.). 64p. (gr. 3-7). 1986. pap. 4.95 (*0-689-71081-X*, Aladdin) Macmillan Child Grp.
McNair, Sylvia. Vermont. LC 90-21117. (Illus.). 144p. (gr. 4 up). 1991. PLB 20.55 (*0-516-00491-3*) Childrens.
—Vermont. 208p. 1993. text ed. 15.40 (*1-56956-160-5*) W A T Braille.
Marsh, Carole. Avast, Ye Slobs! Vermont Pirate Trivia. (Illus.). 1994. PLB 24.95 (*0-7933-1148-9*); pap. 14.95 (*0-685-45958-6*); computer disk 29.95 (*0-7933-1149-7*) Gallopade Pub Group.
—The Beast of the Vermont Bed & Breakfast. (Illus.). 1994. PLB 24.95 (*0-7933-2149-2*); pap. 14.95 (*0-7933-2150-6*); computer disk 29.95 (*0-7933-2151-4*) Gallopade Pub Group.
—Bow Wow! Vermont Dogs in History, Mystery, Legend, Lore, Humor & More! (Illus.). (gr. 3-12). 1994. PLB 24.95 (*0-7933-3602-3*); pap. 14.95 (*0-7933-3603-1*); computer disk 29.95 (*0-7933-3604-X*) Gallopade Pub Group.
—Chill Out: Scary Vermont Tales Based on Frightening Vermont Truths. (Illus.). 1994. lib. bdg. 24.95 (*0-7933-4789-0*); pap. 14.95 (*0-7933-4790-4*); disk 29. 95 (*0-7933-4791-2*) Gallopade Pub Group.
—Christopher Columbus Comes to Vermont! Includes Reproducible Activities for Kids! (Illus.). (gr. 3-12). 1994. PLB 24.95 (*0-7933-3755-0*); pap. 14.95 (*0-7933-3756-9*); computer disk 29.95 (*0-7933-3757-7*) Gallopade Pub Group.
—The Hard-to-Believe-But-True! Book of Vermont History, Mystery, Trivia, Legend, Lore, Humor & More. (Illus.). 1994. PLB 24.95 (*0-7933-1145-4*); pap. 14.95 (*0-7933-1144-6*) (*0-7933-1146-2*) Gallopade Pub Group.
—If My Vermont Mama Ran the World! (Illus.). 1994. PLB 24.95 (*0-7933-2158-1*); pap. 14.95 (*0-7933-2159-X*); computer disk 29.95 (*0-7933-2160-3*) Gallopade Pub Group.
—Jurassic Ark! Vermont Dinosaurs & Other Prehistoric Creatures. (gr. k-12). 1994. PLB 24.95 (*0-7933-7563-0*); pap. 14.95 (*0-7933-7564-9*); computer disk 29.95 (*0-7933-7565-7*) Gallopade Pub Group.
—Let's Quilt Our Vermont County. 1994. lib. bdg. 24.95 (*0-7933-7248-8*); pap. text ed. 14.95 (*0-7933-7249-6*); disk 29.95 (*0-7933-7250-X*) Gallopade Pub Group.
—Let's Quilt Our Vermont Town. 1994. lib. bdg. 24.95 (*0-7933-7098-1*); pap. text ed. 14.95 (*0-7933-7099-X*); disk 29.95 (*0-7933-7100-7*) Gallopade Pub Group.
—Let's Quilt Vermont & Stuff It Topographically! (Illus.). 1994. PLB 24.95 (*0-7933-2141-7*); pap. 14.95 (*1-55609-066-8*); computer disk 29.95 (*0-7933-2142-5*) Gallopade Pub Group.
—Meow! Vermont Cats in History, Mystery, Legend, Lore, Humor & More! (Illus.). (gr. 3-12). 1994. PLB 24.95 (*0-7933-3449-7*); pap. 14.95 (*0-7933-3450-0*); computer disk 29.95 (*0-7933-3451-9*) Gallopade Pub Group.
—My First Book about Vermont. (gr. k-4). 1994. PLB 24. 95 (*0-7933-5704-7*); pap. 14.95 (*0-7933-5705-5*); computer disk 29.95 (*0-7933-5706-3*) Gallopade Pub Group.
—Patch, the Pirate Dog: A Vermont Pet Story. (ps-4). 1994. PLB 24.95 (*0-7933-5551-6*); pap. 14.95 (*0-7933-5552-4*); computer disk 29.95 (*0-7933-5553-2*) Gallopade Pub Group.
—Uncle Rebus: Vermont Picture Stories for Computer Kids. (Illus.). (gr. k-3). 1994. PLB 24.95 (*0-7933-4636-3*); pap. 14.95 (*0-7933-4637-1*); disk 29. 95 (*0-7933-4638-X*) Gallopade Pub Group.
—Vermont & Other State Greats (Biographies) (Illus.). 1994. PLB 24.95 (*0-7933-2161-1*); pap. 14.95 (*0-7933-2162-X*); computer disk 29.95 (*0-7933-2163-8*) Gallopade Pub Group.
—Vermont Bandits, Bushwackers, Outlaws, Crooks, Devils, Ghosts, Desperadoes & Other Assorted & Sundry Characters! (Illus.). 1994. PLB 24.95 (*0-7933-1130-6*); pap. 14.95 (*0-7933-1129-2*) (*0-7933-1131-4*) Gallopade Pub Group.
—Vermont Classic Christmas Trivia: Stories, Recipes, Activities, Legends, Lore & More! (Illus.). 1994. PLB 24.95 (*0-7933-1133-0*); pap. 14.95 (*0-7933-1132-2*); computer disk 29.95 (*0-7933-1134-9*) Gallopade Pub Group.
—Vermont Coastales. (Illus.). 1994. PLB 24.95 (*0-7933-2155-7*); pap. 14.95 (*0-7933-2156-5*); computer disk 29.95 (*0-7933-2157-3*) Gallopade Pub Group.
—Vermont Coastales! 1994. lib. bdg. 24.95 (*0-7933-7310-7*) Gallopade Pub Group.
—Vermont "Crinkum-Crankum" A Funny Word Book about Our State. (Illus.). (gr. 3-12). 1994. 24.95 (*0-7933-4943-5*); pap. 14.95 (*0-7933-4944-3*); computer disk 29.95 (*0-7933-4945-1*) Gallopade Pub Group.

—Vermont Dingbats! Bk. 1: A Fun Book of Games, Stories, Activities & More about Our State That's All in Code! for You to Decipher. (Illus.). (gr. 3-12). 1994. PLB 24.95 (*0-7933-3908-1*); pap. 14.95 (*0-7933-3909-X*); computer disk 29.95 (*0-7933-3910-3*) Gallopade Pub Group.
—Vermont Festival Fun for Kids! (Illus.). (gr. 3-12). 1994. lib. bdg. 24.95 (*0-7933-4061-6*); pap. 14.95 (*0-7933-4062-4*); disk 29.95 (*0-7933-4063-2*) Gallopade Pub Group.
—The Vermont Hot Air Balloon Mystery. (Illus.). (gr. 2-9). 1994. 24.95 (*0-7933-2723-7*); pap. 14.95 (*0-7933-2724-5*); computer disk 29.95 (*0-7933-2725-3*) Gallopade Pub Group.
—Vermont Jeopardy! Answers & Questions about Our State! (Illus.). (gr. 3-12). 1994. PLB 24.95 (*0-7933-4214-7*); pap. 14.95 (*0-7933-4215-5*); computer disk 29.95 (*0-7933-4216-3*) Gallopade Pub Group.
—Vermont "Jography" A Fun Run Thru Our State! (Illus.). 1994. PLB 24.95 (*0-7933-2138-7*); pap. 14.95 (*0-7933-2139-5*); computer disk 29.95 (*0-7933-2140-9*) Gallopade Pub Group.
—Vermont Kids' Cookbook: Recipes, How-to, History, Lore & More! (Illus.). 1994. PLB 24.95 (*0-7933-1142-X*); pap. 14.95 (*0-685-45957-8*); computer disk 29.95 (*0-7933-1143-8*) Gallopade Pub Group.
—The Vermont Mystery Van Takes Off! Book 1: Handicapped Vermont Kids Sneak Off on a Big Adventure. (Illus.). (gr. 3-12). 1994. 24.95 (*0-7933-5096-4*); pap. 14.95 (*0-7933-5097-2*); computer disk 29.95 (*0-7933-5098-0*) Gallopade Pub Group.
—Vermont Quiz Bowl Crash Course! (Illus.). 1994. PLB 24.95 (*0-7933-2152-2*); pap. 14.95 (*0-7933-2153-0*); computer disk 29.95 (*0-7933-2154-9*) Gallopade Pub Group.
—Vermont Rollercoasters! (Illus.). (gr. 3-12). 1994. PLB 24.95 (*0-7933-5359-9*); pap. 14.95 (*0-7933-5360-2*); computer disk 29.95 (*0-7933-5361-0*) Gallopade Pub Group.
—Vermont School Trivia: An Amazing & Fascinating Look at Our State's Teachers, Schools & Students! (Illus.). 1994. PLB 24.95 (*0-7933-1139-X*); pap. 14.95 (*0-7933-1138-1*); computer disk 29.95 (*0-7933-1140-3*) Gallopade Pub Group.
—Vermont Silly Basketball Sportsmysteries, Vol. 1. (Illus.). 1994. PLB 24.95 (*0-7933-1136-5*); pap. 14.95 (*0-7933-1135-7*); computer disk 29.95 (*0-7933-1137-3*) Gallopade Pub Group.
—Vermont Silly Basketball Sportsmysteries, Vol. 2. (Illus.). 1994. PLB 24.95 (*0-7933-2164-6*); pap. 14.95 (*0-7933-2165-4*); 29.95 (*0-7933-2166-2*) Gallopade Pub Group.
—Vermont Silly Football Sportsmysteries, Vol. 1. (Illus.). 1994. PLB 24.95 (*0-7933-2143-3*); pap. 14.95 (*0-7933-2144-1*); computer disk 29.95 (*0-7933-2145-X*) Gallopade Pub Group.
—Vermont Silly Football Sportsmysteries, Vol. 2. (Illus.). 1994. PLB 24.95 (*0-7933-2146-8*); pap. 14.95 (*0-7933-2147-6*); computer disk 29.95 (*0-7933-2148-4*) Gallopade Pub Group.
—Vermont Silly Trivia! (Illus.). 1994. PLB 24.95 (*0-7933-2135-2*); pap. 14.95 (*0-7933-2136-0*); computer disk 29.95 (*0-7933-2137-9*) Gallopade Pub Group.
—Vermont Timeline: A Chronology of Vermont History, Mystery, Trivia, Legend, Lore & More. (Illus.). (gr. 3-12). 1994. PLB 24.95 (*0-7933-6010-2*); pap. 14.95 (*0-7933-6011-0*); computer disk 29.95 (*0-7933-6012-9*) Gallopade Pub Group.
—Vermont's (Most Devastating!) Disasters & (Most Calamitous!) Catastrophies! (Illus.). 1994. PLB 24.95 (*0-7933-1127-6*); pap. 14.95 (*0-7933-1126-8*); computer disk 29.95 (*0-7933-1128-4*) Gallopade Pub Group.
—Vermont's Unsolved Mysteries (& Their "Solutions") Includes Scientific Information & Other Activities for Students. (Illus.). (gr. 3-12). 1994. PLB 24.95 (*0-7933-5857-4*); pap. 14.95 (*0-7933-5858-2*); computer disk 29.95 (*0-7933-5859-0*) Gallopade Pub Group.
Pelta, Kathy. Vermont. LC 93-33389. (Illus.). 72p. (gr. 3-6). 1994. PLB 17.50 (*0-8225-2729-4*) Lerner Pubns.
Peterson, James E. Otter Creek: The Indian Road. LC 90-82089. (Illus.). 176p. (Orig.). (gr. 5 up). 1990. pap. 15.00 (*0-914960-83-0*) Academy Bks.
Thompson, Kathleen. Vermont. 48p. (gr. 3 up). 1986. PLB 19.97 (*0-86514-459-1*) Raintree Steck-V.

VERMONT–FICTION

Carty, Margaret F. Christmas in Vermont: Three Stories. Langley, Marilynn, illus. LC 83-62750. 48p. (Orig.). (gr. 5 up). 1983. pap. 2.95 (*0-933050-21-6*) New Eng Pr VT.
Hurwitz, Johanna. Yellow Blue Jay. Carrick, Donald, illus. LC 92-24597. 128p. (gr. 3 up). 1993. pap. 3.95 (*0-688-12278-7*, Pub. by Beech Tree Bks) Morrow.
Jackson, Edgar N. Green Mountain Hero. 192p. (gr. 6 up). 1988. pap. 9.95 (*0-933050-61-5*) New Eng Pr VT.
Johnson, Allen, Jr. The Christmas Tree Express. Keetle, Lisbeth, illus. (gr. 4-8). Date not set. 12.95 (*1-878561-21-9*) Seacoast AL.
Kinsey-Warnock, Natalie. The Night the Bells Rang. Bowman, Leslie W., illus. LC 91-3053. 80p. (gr. 4 up). 1991. 12.95 (*0-525-65074-1*, Cobblehill Bks) Dutton Child Bks.
Klass, Sheila S. Pork Bellies Are Down. LC 94-20235. 1995. 13.95 (*0-590-46686-0*) Scholastic Inc.
Peck, Robert N. Soup Ahoy. Robinson, Charles, illus. LC 93-14097. 144p. (gr. 2-6). 1994. 15.00 (*0-679-84978-5*); PLB 15.99 (*0-679-94978-X*) Knopf Bks Yng Read.
—Soup in Love. (gr. 4-7). 1992. 14.00 (*0-385-30563-X*) Delacorte.
—Trig. 64p. (gr. 4-6). 1979. pap. 1.25 (*0-440-49098-7*, YB) Dell.
Wells, Rosemary. Waiting for the Evening Star. Jeffers, Susan, illus. LC 92-30492. 40p. (gr. k-3). 1993. 15.00 (*0-8037-1398-3*); PLB 14.89 (*0-8037-1399-1*) Dial Bks Young.

VERNE, JULES, 1828-1905

Teeters, Peggy. Jules Verne: The Man Who Invented Tomorrow. 128p. 1993. 13.95 (*0-8027-8189-6*); PLB 14.85 (*0-8027-8191-8*) Walker & Co.

VERSIFICATION

see also Poetry

VERTEBRATES

see also Amphibians; Birds; Fishes; Mammals; Reptiles

Aaseng, Nathan. Vertebrates. LC 93-13391. (Illus.). 112p. (gr. 7-12). 1993. PLB 13.40 (*0-531-12551-3*) Watts.
Johnson, Jinny. Skeletons: An Inside Look at Animals. Gray, Elizabeth, illus. LC 94-62. (gr. 3 up). 1994. 16.95 (*0-89577-604-9*) RD Assn.
Selsam, Millicent E. & Hunt, Joyce. First Look at...Ser. Springer, Harriet, illus. LC 78-4321. (gr. k-3). 1978. 6.95 (*0-8027-6338-3*); PLB 9.85 (*0-8027-6339-1*) Walker & Co.

VESPUCCI, AMERIGO, 1451-1512

Jaeger, Gerard. Vespucci. 1992. PLB 14.95 (*0-88682-485-0*) Creative Ed.
Nilsen, Frances S. & Salter, James L. Amerigo: The Amerigo Vespucci Story. Salter, Marsha C., illus. LC 92-93878. 253p. (gr. 10-12). 1992. 14.95 (*0-9633937-6-6*) Shamrock TN.

VESSELS (SHIPS)

see Ships

VETERINARIANS

Gibbons, Gail. Say Woof! The Day of a Country Veterinarian. Gibbons, Gail, illus. LC 91-48270. 32p. (gr. k-3). 1992. RSBE 13.95 (*0-02-736781-9*, Macmillan Child Bk) Macmillan Child Grp.
Herriot, James. All Creatures Great & Small. (gr. 6 up). 1985. pap. 6.99 (*0-553-26812-0*) Bantam.
Muntean, Michaela. I Want to Be a Veterinarian. Cooke, Tom, illus. 24p. (ps-k). 1992. pap. write for info. (*0-307-13116-5*, 13116, Golden Pr) Western Pub.
Paige, David. A Day in the Life of a Zoo Veterinarian. Mauney, Michael, illus. LC 84-6538. 32p. (gr. 4-8). 1985. PLB 11.79 (*0-8167-0095-8*); pap. text ed. 2.95 (*0-8167-0096-6*) Troll Assocs.

VETERINARY MEDICINE

Gibbons, Gail. Say Woof! The Day of a Country Veterinarian. Gibbons, Gail, illus. LC 91-48270. 32p. (gr. k-3). 1992. RSBE 13.95 (*0-02-736781-9*, Macmillan Child Bk) Macmillan Child Grp.
Holderness-Roddam, Jane. First Aid. Vincer, Carole, illus. 24p. (Orig.). (gr. 3 up). 1989. pap. 10.00 (*0-901366-98-6*, Pub. by Threshold Bks) Half Halt Pr.
Imershein, Betsy. Animal Doctor. Imershein, Betsy, illus. LC 87-20266. 32p. (gr. 1-5). 1988. (J Messner); lib. bdg. 4.95 (*0-671-65862-X*) S&S Trade.
Lumley, Kay. I Can Be an Animal Doctor. LC 85-12802. 32p. (gr. k-3). 1985. PLB 11.80 (*0-516-01836-1*); pap. 3.95 (*0-516-41836-X*) Childrens.
Veterinary Science. (Illus.). 40p. (gr. 6-12). 1973. pap. 1.85 (*0-8395-3261-X*, 33261) BSA.

VETERINARY MEDICINE–FICTION

Dodd, Lynley. Hairy Maclary's Rumpus at the Vet. Dodd, Lynley, illus. LC 89-43120. 28p. (gr. 1-2). 1989. PLB 17.27 (*0-8368-0126-1*) Gareth Stevens Inc.
Gutkind, Lee. The Veterinarians. 1996. write for info. (*0-8050-3321-1*) H Holt & Co.
Lofting, Hugh. Dr. Dolittle in the Moon. (gr. k-6). 1988. pap. 3.25 (*0-440-40113-5*, YB) Dell.
—Dr. Dolittle's Caravan. (gr. k-6). 1988. pap. 3.50 (*0-440-40071-6*) Dell.
—Dr. Dolittle's Circus. (gr. k-6). 1988. pap. 3.50 (*0-440-40058-9*) Dell.
McDonnell, Janet. Victor's Adventure in Alphabet Town. Peltier, Pam, illus. LC 92-4036. 32p. (ps-2). 1992. PLB 11.80 (*0-516-05422-8*) Childrens.
Thaler, Mike. My Cat Is Going to the Dogs. Lee, Jared, illus. LC 93-18596. 32p. (ps-3). 1993. PLB 9.79 (*0-8167-3022-9*); pap. 2.95 (*0-8167-3023-7*) Troll Assocs.

VETERINARY MEDICINE–VOCATIONAL GUIDANCE

Duncan, Jane C. Careers in Veterinary Medicine. rev. ed. (Illus.). (gr. 7-12). 1994. PLB 13.95 (*0-8239-1678-2*); pap. 9.95 (*0-8239-1719-3*) Rosen Group.
Miller, Louise. Careers for Animal Lovers: And Other Zoological Types. LC 90-50725. 160p. (Orig.). (gr. 7 up). 1991. pap. 9.95 (*0-8442-8125-5*, VGM Career Bks) NTC Pub Grp.
Stamper, Judith. What's It Like to Be a Veterinarian. Ramsey, Marcy D., illus. LC 89-34391. 32p. (gr. k-3). 1990. lib. bdg. 10.89 (*0-8167-1817-2*); pap. text ed. 2.95 (*0-8167-1818-0*) Troll Assocs.
Wolfman, Melvin S. So, You Want to Be a Veterinarian. Steinkraus, Edith, illus. 38p. (Orig.). (gr. 3-12). 1993. pap. 15.00 (*0-9629806-3-3*) Benjamin OH.

VIADUCTS

see Bridges

VIANNEY, JEAN BAPTISTE, MARIE, SAINT, 1786-1859

Daughters of St. Paul. The Country Road Home. (gr. 3-7). 1987. 3.00 (*0-8198-0232-8*) St Paul Bks.

VIBRATION

see also Light; Waves

VICE

see Crime and Criminals

VICE-PRESIDENTS–U. S.

Burford, Betty M. Al Gore: United States Vice President. LC 93-47475. (Illus.). 112p. (gr. 6 up). 1994. lib. bdg. 17.95 (*0-89490-496-5*) Enslow Pubs.
Dell Puzzle Magazine Staff. Story of Bill Clinton & Al Gore. (gr. 4-7). 1993. pap. 3.50 (*0-440-40843-1*) Dell.
Dorman, Michael. Second Man: The Changing Role of the Vice Presidency. LC 67-19765. (gr. 7 up). 1968. pap. 6.95 (*0-440-07703-6*) Delacorte.
Italia, Bob. Al Gore: Vice President of the United States. LC 93-26099. (gr. 5 up). 1993. lib. bdg. 13.99 (*1-56239-253-0*) Abdo & Dghtrs.
Lindop, Edmund. Presidents by Accident. LC 91-17056. (Illus.). 208p. (gr. 9-12). 1991. PLB 15.40 (*0-531-11059-1*) Watts.
Pious, Richard M. The Young Oxford Companion to the Presidency of the United States. LC 93-19908. 1993. Alk. paper. 35.00 (*0-19-507799-7*) OUP.
Stefoff, Rebecca. Al Gore: Vice President. (Illus.). 48p. (gr. 2-4). 1994. 12.90 (*1-56294-433-9*) Millbrook Pr.

VICTORIA, QUEEN OF GREAT BRITAIN, 1819-1901

Young, Lesley. Queen Victoria. (Illus.). 64p. (gr. 5-9). 1991. 11.95 (*0-237-60001-3*, Pub. by Evans Bros Ltd) Trafalgar.

VIDEO GAMES

Arnold, J. Douglas. Awesome Sega Genesis Secrets, No. 1. (Illus.). 256p. (Orig.). 1992. pap. 9.95 (*0-9624676-4-2*, GV1469.3) Sandwich Islands.
DeKeles, Jon C., ed. Video Game Secrets: A Top Secret Guide to One Thousand Tips, Tricks & Codes. (Illus.). 192p. (Orig.). (gr. 6 up). 1990. pap. 9.95 (*0-9625057-3-0*) DMS ID.
DeNure, Dennis. The Age of the Video Athlete. (Illus.). 1984. write for info. (*0-915659-00-X*) Video Athlete.
Game Players Encyclopedia of Game Boy Games, Vol. I. (Illus.). 272p. (ps-12). 1990. pap. 10.95 (*0-929307-13-5*) GP Pubns.
Game Players Encyclopedia of Game Boy Games, Vol. II. (Illus.). 208p. (ps-12). 1991. 10.95 (*0-929307-22-4*) GP Pubns.
Game Players Encyclopedia of Game Boy Games, Vol. III. (Illus.). 208p. (ps-12). 1991. 11.95 (*0-929307-19-4*) GP Pubns.
Game Players Encyclopedia of Nintendo Games, Vol. II. (Illus.). 256p. 1990. pap. 10.95 (*0-929307-12-7*) GP Pubns.
Game Players Encyclopedia of Nintendo Games, Vol. 3. (Illus.). 224p. (ps-12). 1991. 11.95 (*0-929307-16-X*) GP Pubns.
Game Players Encyclopedia of Nintendo Games, Vol. 4. (Illus.). 224p. (ps-12). 1991. 14.95 (*0-929307-17-8*) GP Pubns.
Game Players Encyclopedia of Sega Genesis Games, Vol. 1. (Illus.). 272p. 1990. pap. 10.95 (*0-929307-14-3*) GP Pubns.
Gamepro Magazine Staff. The Official Street Fighter Two Strategy Guide. 164p. (gr. 7-12). 1992. 9.95 (*1-882455-00-2*) Gamepro Pub.
GamePro's Official Mortal Kombat Strategy Guide. 164p. (gr. 7-12). 1993. 9.95 (*1-882455-01-0*) Gamepro Pub.
GP Publications Staff. Game Players Encyclopedia of Nintendo Games, Vol. 1. (Illus.). 272p. (ps-12). 1990. pap. 10.95 (*0-929307-11-9*) GP Pubns.
Lampton, Christopher. Nintendo Action Games. (Illus.). 72p. (gr. 4-6). 1991. PLB 15.40 (*1-878841-26-2*); pap. 2.95 (*1-878841-53-X*) Millbrook Pr.
—Nintendo Role-Playing Games. (Illus.). 72p. (gr. 4-6). 1991. PLB 15.40 (*1-878841-25-4*); pap. 2.95 (*1-878841-52-1*) Millbrook Pr.
Sing 'n' Play with Super Mario Bros. 16p. (gr. 3 up). 1992. Incl. xylotone. 14.95 (*0-7935-1551-3*, 00824010) H Leonard.
Skurzynski, Gloria. Know the Score: Video Games in Your High-Tech World. LC 93-19470. (Illus.). 64p. (gr. 6-9). 1994. RSBE 14.95 (*0-02-782352-0*, Bradbury Pr) Macmillan Child Grp.
—Know the Score: Video Games in Your High-Tech World. Skurzynski, Gloria, illus. LC 93-19470. 64p. (gr. 4 up). 1994. RSBE 16.95 (*0-02-782922-7*, Bradbury Pr) Macmillan Child Grp.
Street Fighter II Turbo Hyper Fighting Strategy Guide. 164p. (gr. 7-12). 1993. 9.95 (*1-882455-02-9*) Gamepro Pub.

VIENNA–FICTION

Henry, Marguerite. The White Stallion of Lipizza. Dennis, Wesley, illus. LC 93-86024. 112p. (gr. 3-7). 1994. Repr. of 1964 ed. SBE 14.95 (*0-02-743628-4*, Macmillan Child Bk) Macmillan Child Grp.
Orgel, Doris. Devil in Vienna. 1988. pap. 4.99 (*0-14-032500-X*, Puffin) Puffin Bks.

VIENNA. SPANISH RIDING SCHOOL

Van der Linde, Laurel. The White Stallions: The Story of the Dancing Horses of Lipizza. LC 93-18919. (Illus.). 72p. (gr. 6 up). 1994. text ed. 14.95 RSBE (*0-02-759055-0*, New Discovery Bks) Macmillan Child Grp.

VIETNAM

Garland, Sherry. Vietnam: Rebuilding a Nation. LC 89-29212. (Illus.). 130p. (gr. 5 up). 1990. text ed. 14.95 RSBE (*0-87518-422-7*, Dillon) Macmillan Child Grp.

Geography Department Staff. Vietnam: In Pictures. LC 93-21343. (Illus.). 64p. (gr. 5 up). 1994. PLB 18.95 (*0-8225-1909-7*) Lerner Pubns.

Jacobsen, Karen. Vietnam. LC 91-35272. (Illus.). 48p. (gr. k-4). 1992. PLB 12.85 (*0-516-01147-2*); pap. 4.95 (*0-516-41147-0*) Childrens.

Nhuong, Nuynh Quang. The Land I Lost: Adventures of a Boy in Vietnam. LC 80-8437. (Illus.). 128p. (gr. 4-7). 1990. (Lipp Jr Bks); PLB 13.89 (*0-397-32448-0*, Lipp Jr Bks) HarpC Child Bks.

Nurland, Patricia. Vietnam. Vu Viet Dung, photos by. LC 89-43178. (Illus.). 64p. (gr. 5-6). 1991. PLB 21.26 (*0-8368-0230-6*) Gareth Stevens Inc.

Parker, Lewis K. Vietnam. LC 94-7558. 1994. write for info. (*1-55916-008-X*) Rourke Bk Co.

Seah, Audrey. Vietnam. LC 93-4380. 1993. 21.95 (*1-85435-584-8*) Marshall Cavendish.

Tran Khan Tuyet. Children of Viet-Nam. (gr. k-2). 1973. 2.50 (*0-686-10278-9*) Asia Resource.

Vietnam Is My Home. 48p. (gr. 2-8). 1992. PLB 18.60 (*0-8368-0905-X*) Gareth Stevens Inc.

Wright, David K. Vietnam. LC 88-30486. (Illus.). 128p. (gr. 5-9). 1989. PLB 20.55 (*0-516-02712-3*) Childrens.

VIETNAM–FICTION

Garland, Sherry. Lotus Seed. LC 92-2913. (gr. 4-7). 1993. 14.95 (*0-15-249465-0*) HarBrace.

—Song of the Buffalo Boy. 1992. 15.95 (*0-15-277107-7*, HB Juv Bks) HarBrace.

—Song of the Buffalo Boy. LC 91-31872. 1994. pap. 3.95 (*0-15-200098-4*, HB Juv Bks) HarBrace.

Gibbons, Alan. The Jaws of the Dragon. LC 94-47126. 156p. (gr. 5 up). 1994. PLB 18.95 (*0-8225-0737-4*) Lerner Pubns.

Huynh Quang Nhuong. The Land I Lost. Vo-Dinh, Mai, illus. LC 80-8437. 128p. (gr. 4-7). 1986. pap. 3.95 (*0-06-440183-9*, Trophy) HarpC Child Bks.

Keller, Holly. Grandfather's Dream. LC 93-18186. (Illus.). 32p. (ps up). 1994. 14.00 (*0-688-12339-2*); PLB 13.93 (*0-688-12340-6*) Greenwillow.

Nhuong. Land I Lost. 1982. 12.95 (*0-06-024592-1*); PLB 12.89 (*0-06-024593-X*) HarpC Child Bks.

Whelan, Gloria. Goodbye, Vietnam. LC 91-3660. 112p. (gr. 3-7). 1992. 13.00 (*0-679-82263-1*); PLB 13.99 (*0-679-92263-6*) Knopf Bks Yng Read.

—Goodbye, Vietnam. LC 91-3660. 144p. (gr. 3-7). 1993. pap. 3.99 (*0-679-82376-X*, Bullseye Bks) Random Bks Yng Read.

VIETNAM–FOREIGN RELATIONS–U. S.

Arnoldt, Robert P. & Marx, Jacqueline A. Vietnam Insights: A Guide to the American Experience in Vietnam 1940 to Present. rev. ed. Carpenter, Robert S., ed. Arnoldt, Robert P., intro. by. LC 89-50664. 232p. (Orig.). (gr. 8 up). 1992. pap. 21.95 (*0-9622776-0-6*) Visions Unlimited.

VIETNAM WAR, 1961-1975

see Vietnamese Conflict, 1961-1975

VIETNAMESE CONFLICT, 1961-1975

Arnoldt, Robert P. Insights: A Guide to the American Experience in Vietnam, 1940 to Present. rev. ed. Marx, Jacqueline A. & Carpenter, Robert S., eds. 100p. (Orig.). (gr. 9 up). 1989. pap. text ed. write for info. Visions Unlimited.

Barr, Roger. The Vietnam War. LC 91-23067. (Illus.). 112p. (gr. 5-8). 1991. PLB 17.95 (*1-56006-410-2*) Lucent Bks.

Becker, Elizabeth. America's Vietnam War: A Narrative History. 160p. (gr. 7 up). 1992. 15.95 (*0-395-59094-9*, Clarion Bks) HM.

Crouse, Joan M., et al. Vietnam. LC 93-14939. 1994. pap. text ed. 19.93 (*0-8013-0865-8*) Longman.

Denenberg, Barry. Voices from Vietnam. LC 93-44886. (gr. 7 up). 1995. 16.95 (*0-590-44267-8*) Scholastic Inc.

Detzer, David. An Asian Tragedy: America & Vietnam. LC 91-37228. (Illus.). 160p. (gr. 7 up). 1992. PLB 16.90 (*1-56294-066-X*) Millbrook Pr.

Devaney, John. The Vietnam War. (Illus.). 64p. (gr. 5-8). 1993. pap. 5.95 (*0-531-15658-3*) Watts.

Donnelly, Judy. A Wall of Names: The Story of the Vietnam Veterans Memorial A Step 4 Book - Grades 2-4. Wenzel, Paul, illus. LC 90-30275. 48p. (Orig.). (gr. 2-4). 1991. PLB 7.99 (*0-679-90169-8*); pap. 3.50 (*0-679-80169-3*) Random Bks Yng Read.

Dudley, William, ed. The Vietnam War: Opposing Viewpoints. rev. ed. LC 90-39794. (Illus.). 240p. (gr. 10 up). 1990. PLB 17.95 (*0-89908-478-8*); pap. text ed. 9.95 (*0-89908-453-2*) Greenhaven.

Edwards, Richard. Vietnam War, Reading Level 8. LC 86-20295. (Illus.). 77p. (gr. 7 up). 1987. PLB 18.60 (*0-86592-031-1*); PLB 13.95s.p. (*0-685-58244-2*) Rourke Corp.

Gibson, Michael. The War in Vietnam. LC 91-9134. (Illus.). 64p. (gr. 7-12). 1992. PLB 13.40 (*0-531-18408-0*, Pub. by Bookwright Pr) Watts.

Griffiths, John. The Last Day in Saigon. 64p. (gr. 6-8). 1987. 19.95 (*0-85219-671-7*, Pub. by Batsford UK) Trafalgar.

Hass, Marv E. Women's Perspectives on the Vietnam War. Starr, Jerold M., ed. (Illus.). 32p. (Orig.). 1991. pap. text ed. 3.00 (*0-945919-14-X*) Ctr Social Studies.

Hoobler, Dorothy & Hoobler, Thomas. Vietnam: An Illustrated History. LC 89-71645. (Illus.). 208p. (gr. 5 up). 1990. 17.95 (*0-394-81943-8*) Knopf Bks Yng Read.

Kent, Deborah. The Vietnam War: "What Are We Fighting For?" LC 93-48471. (Illus.). 128p. (gr. 5 up). 1994. lib. bdg. 17.95 (*0-89490-527-9*) Enslow Pubs.

Kent, Zachary. The Story of the Saigon Airlift. LC 91-15847. (Illus.). 32p. (gr. 3-6). 1991. PLB 12.30 (*0-516-04760-4*); pap. 3.95 (*0-516-44760-2*) Childrens.

Kronenwetter, Michael. The Peace Commandos: Nonviolent Heroes in the Struggle Against War & Injustice. LC 93-31204. (Illus.). 160p. (gr. 4-6). 1994. text ed. 13.95 RSBE (*0-02-751051-4*, New Discovery Bks) Macmillan Child Grp.

Kurland, Gerald. The My Lai Massacre. Rahmas, D. Steve, ed. 32p. (gr. 7-12). 1973. lib. bdg. 4.95 incl. catalog cards (*0-87157-708-9*) SamHar Pr.

Lawson, Don. The United States in the Vietnam War. LC 80-2460. (Illus.). 160p. (gr. 7 up). 1981. (Crowell Jr Bks) HarpC Child Bks.

Lens, Sidney. Vietnam: A War on Two Fronts. (Illus.). 144p. (gr. 7 up). 1990. 15.95 (*0-525-67320-2*, Lodestar Bks) Dutton Child Bks.

Marrin, Albert. America in Vietnam: The Elephant & the Tiger. (Illus.). 256p. (gr. 7 up). 1992. 16.00 (*0-670-84063-7*) Viking Child Bks.

Moss, Nathaniel. Ron Kovic: Antiwar Activist. LC 93-16373. (Illus.). 1994. 18.95 (*0-7910-2076-2*, Am Art Analog); pap. write for info. (*0-7910-2089-4*, Am Art Analog) Chelsea Hse.

Myers, Walter D. A Place Called Heartbreak: A Story of Vietnam. Porter, Frederick, illus. LC 92-14428. 71p. (gr. 2-5). 1992. PLB 21.34 (*0-8114-7237-X*) Raintree Steck-V.

Nickelson, Harry. Vietnam. LC 89-13100. (Illus.). 80p. (gr. 5-8). 1989. PLB 14.95 (*1-56006-110-3*) Lucent Bks.

Rappaport, Doreen. Tinker vs. Des Moines: Student Rights on Trial. Palencar, John J., illus. LC 92-25019. 160p. (gr. 5 up). 1993. 15.00 (*0-06-025117-4*); PLB 14.89 (*0-06-025118-2*) HarpC Child Bks.

Simons, Frank D. You Don't Cry for Heroes. Ferrell, Robert, intro. by. 197p. (Orig.). (gr. 12 up). 1989. pap. 7.95 (*0-685-26939-6*) CFFC POWs MIAs.

Super, Neil. Vietnam War Soldiers. (Illus.). 80p. (gr. 4-7). 1993. PLB 14.95 (*0-8050-2307-0*) TFC Bks NY.

The Vietnam War. LC 87-18224. 768p. (gr. 6 up). 1988. PLB 199.95x (*0-86307-852-4*) Marshall Cavendish.

The Vietnam War Soldier at Con Thien. 48p. (gr. 5-6). 1991. PLB 11.95 (*1-56065-007-9*) Capstone Pr.

Warren, James A. Portrait of a Tragedy: America & the Vietnam War. Summers, Harry G., Jr., frwd. by. LC 88-39560. (Illus.). 208p. (gr. 5 up). 17.95 (*0-688-07454-5*) Lothrop.

Wills, Charles. The Tet Offensive. (Illus.). 64p. (gr. 5 up). 1989. PLB 12.95 (*0-382-09849-8*); pap. 7.95 (*0-382-09855-2*) Silver Burdett Pr.

Wormser, Richard L. Three Faces of Vietnam. LC 93-11099. (Illus.). 160p. (gr. 7-12). 1993. PLB 13.90 (*0-531-11142-3*) Watts.

Wright, David K. The Story of the Vietnam Veterans Memorial. LC 89-713. (Illus.). 32p. (gr. 3-6). 1989. PLB 12.30 (*0-516-04745-0*); pap. 3.95 (*0-516-44745-9*) Childrens.

—War in Vietnam, Bks. I-IV. (Illus.). 144p. (gr. 4 up). 1989. PLB 19.93 (*0-516-02285-7*) Book I, Eve of Battle. Book II, A Wider War. Book III, Vietnamization. Book IV, The Fall of Vietnam. Childrens.

VIETNAMESE CONFLICT, 1961-1975–FICTION

Ashabranner, Brent. Always to Remember: The Story of the Vietnam Veterans Memorial. Ashabranner, Jennifer, photos by. (Illus.). 40p. (gr. 6 up). 1988. 14.95 (*0-399-22031-3*, Putnam) Putnam Pub Group.

Carn, John B. Vietnam Blues. (Orig.). (ps-12). 1988. pap. 3.25 (*0-87067-730-6*) Holloway.

Emerson, Zack. Hill Five Hundred Sixty-Eight. 1991. pap. 2.95 (*0-590-44592-8*) Scholastic Inc.

—Stand Down. 128p. 1992. pap. 2.95 (*0-590-44594-4*, Point) Scholastic Inc.

—Tis the Season. 256p. 1991. pap. 2.95 (*0-590-44593-6*) Scholastic Inc.

—Welcome to Vietnam. 1991. pap. 2.95 (*0-590-44591-X*) Scholastic Inc.

Hahn, Mary D. December Stillness. LC 88-2572. 192p. (gr. 5-9). 1988. 14.95 (*0-89919-758-2*, Clarion Bks) HM.

Jensen, Kathryn. Pocket Change. 192p. (gr. 7 up). 1991. pap. 2.95 (*0-590-43419-5*, Point) Scholastic Inc.

Nelson, Theresa. And One for All. LC 88-22490. 192p. (gr. 6-8). 1989. 12.95 (*0-531-05804-2*); PLB 12.99 (*0-531-08404-3*) Orchard Bks Watts.

Paterson, Katherine. Park's Quest. 160p. (gr. 5 up). 1989. pap. 3.99 (*0-14-034262-1*, Puffin) Puffin Bks.

Paulsen, Gary. The Car. LC 93-41834. 1994. 13.95 (*0-15-292878-2*) HarBrace.

Pettit, Jayne. My Name Is San Ho. 192p. 1992. 13.95 (*0-590-44172-8*, Scholastic Hardcover) Scholastic Inc.

Qualey, Marsha. Come in from the Cold. LC 93-42064. 1994. 14.95 (*0-395-68986-4*) HM.

Rostkowski, Margaret I. The Best of Friends. LC 88-33077. 192p. (gr. 7 up). 1989. HarpC Child Bks.

Talbert, Marc. The Purple Heart. LC 91-23084. 144p. (gr. 4-8). 1992. 14.00 (*0-06-020428-1*); PLB 13.89 (*0-06-020429-X*) HarpC Child Bks.

Wolitzer, Meg. Caribou. 176p. (gr. 7-12). 1986. pap. 2.50 (*0-553-25560-6*) Bantam.

VIETNAMESE LANGUAGE

Nguyen, Kim-Anh. Vietnamese Word Book. My Ly, Ha, illus. LC 93-73560. (VIE & ENG.). 144p. (gr. k-6). 1994. 15.95 (*1-880188-70-8*); pap. 11.95 (*1-880188-51-1*) Bess Pr.

VIEWS

Simon, Seymour. Hidden Worlds: Pictures of the Invisible. LC 83-5407. (Illus.). 48p. (gr. 3up). 1983. 13.95 (*0-688-02464-5*); lib. bdg. 13.88 (*0-688-02465-3*, Morrow Jr Bks) Morrow Jr Bks.

VIKING PROJECT

Vogt, Gregory. Viking & the Mars Landing. (Illus.). 112p. (gr. 4-6). 1991. PLB 15.90 (*1-878841-32-7*); pap. 4.95 (*1-878841-38-6*) Millbrook Pr.

VIKINGS

see Northmen

VILLA, FRANCISCO, 1877-1923

O'Brien, Steven. Pancho Villa: Mexican Revolutionary. LC 93-37890. (Illus.). 112p. (gr. 6-12). 1994. PLB 18.95 (*0-7910-1257-3*, Am Art Analog); PLB write for info. (*0-7910-1284-0*) Chelsea Hse.

VILLAS

see Architecture, Domestic

VIOLINISTS, VIOLONCELLISTS, ETC.

Auh, Yoon-Il. Auh Etudes: Fifth Etude. 35p. (gr. 1-12). 1986. wkbk. 10.00 (*1-882858-26-3*) Yoon-il Auh.

—Auh Etudes: First Etude. 15p. (gr. 5-12). 1992. wkbk. 10.00 (*1-882858-13-1*) Yoon-il Auh.

—Auh Etudes: Fourth Etude. 30p. (gr. 1-12). 1985. wkbk. 10.00 (*1-882858-16-6*) Yoon-il Auh.

—Auh Etudes: Second Etude. 17p. (gr. 5-12). 1992. wkbk. 10.00 (*1-882858-14-X*) Yoon-il Auh.

—Auh Etudes: The Art of Bowing. 20p. (gr. 1-12). 1993. wkbk. 10.00 (*1-882858-07-7*) Yoon-il Auh.

—Auh Etudes: The Art of Double Stop, Bk. I. 20p. (gr. 1-12). 1993. wkbk. 10.00 (*1-882858-08-5*) Yoon-il Auh.

—Auh Etudes: The Art of Double Stop, Bk. II. 20p. (gr. 1-12). 1993. wkbk. 10.00 (*1-882858-09-3*) Yoon-il Auh.

—Auh Etudes: Third Etude. 19p. (gr. 5-12). 1992. wkbk. 10.00 (*1-882858-15-8*) Yoon-il Auh.

—Concert Books for the Young: EZ Duet I. 30p. (gr. 1-12). 1993. wkbk. 10.00 (*1-882858-22-0*) Yoon-il Auh.

—Concert Books for the Young: EZ Duet II. 30p. (gr. 1-12). 1993. wkbk. 10.00 (*1-882858-23-9*) Yoon-il Auh.

—Concert Books for the Young: Moto Perpetuo III. 9p. (gr. 1-8). 1983. wkbk. 10.00 (*1-882858-39-5*) Yoon-il Auh.

—Concert Books for the Young: Moto Perpetuo I. 8p. (gr. 1-8). 1990. wkbk. 10.00 (*1-882858-37-9*) Yoon-il Auh.

—Concert Books for the Young: Moto Perpetuo II. 8p. (gr. 1-8). 1990. wkbk. 10.00 (*1-882858-38-7*) Yoon-il Auh.

—Concert Books for the Young: My First Concert Book. 35p. (gr. k-5). 1988. wkbk. 10.00 (*1-882858-19-0*) Yoon-il Auh.

—Concert Books for the Young: My Second Concert Book. 35p. (gr. k-5). 1988. wkbk. 10.00 (*1-882858-18-2*) Yoon-il Auh.

—Concert Books for the Young: My Third Concert Book. 35p. (gr. k-7). 1988. wkbk. 10.00 (*1-882858-21-2*) Yoon-il Auh.

—Concert Books for the Young: Pizzicato Wonder Land. 22p. (gr. k-8). 1988. wkbk. 10.00 (*1-882858-27-1*) Yoon-il Auh.

—Concert Books for the Young: Theme & Variations I. 12p. (gr. 1-6). 1987. wkbk. 10.00 (*1-882858-24-7*) Yoon-il Auh.

—Concert Books for the Young: Theme & Variations II. 12p. (gr. 1-6). 1987. wkbk. 10.00 (*1-882858-25-5*) Yoon-il Auh.

—Concert Books for the Young: Twenty-Four Contemporary Easy Duets. 25p. 1987. wkbk. 10.00 (*1-882858-41-7*) Yoon-il Auh.

—Concert Books for the Young: Twenty-Four Contemporary Easy Duets. 1987. wkbk. 10.00 (*1-882858-42-5*) Yoon-il Auh.

—Contemporary Rhythm & Dynamics, Bk. I. 20p. (gr. 1-12). 1986. wkbk. 10.00 (*1-882858-43-3*) Yoon-il Auh.

—Contemporary Rhythm & Dynamics: Ten Contemporary EZ Duets. 20p. (gr. 4-12). 1986. wkbk. 10.00 (*1-882858-40-9*) Yoon-il Auh.

—Position Studies: Advance Position Study. 35p. (gr. 1-12). 1985. wkbk. 10.00 (*1-882858-46-8*) Yoon-il Auh.

—Position Studies: Scales & Shifting 1. 30p. (gr. 5-12). 1990. wkbk. 10.00 (*1-882858-11-5*) Yoon-il Auh.

—Position Studies: Scales & Shifting 2. 30p. (gr. 5-12). 1990. wkbk. 10.00 (*1-882858-12-3*) Yoon-il Auh.

—Position Studies: Third Position. 35p. (gr. 5-12). 1986. wkbk. 10.00 (*1-882858-45-X*) Yoon-il Auh.

—Pre-School Virtuoso, Bk. I. 40p. (gr. k-5). 1988. wkbk. 10.00 (*1-882858-03-4*) Yoon-il Auh.

—Pre-School Virtuoso, Bk. II. 40p. (gr. k-5). 1988. wkbk. 10.00 (*1-882858-04-2*) Yoon-il Auh.

—Pre-School Virtuoso, Bk. III. 40p. (gr. k-5). 1988. wkbk. 10.00 (*1-882858-05-0*) Yoon-il Auh.

—Pre-School Virtuoso, Bk. IV. 40p. (gr. k-5). wkbk. 10.00 (*1-882858-06-9*) Yoon-il Auh.

—Preliminary Advance, Bk. 1. 50p. (gr. 1-8). 1983. wkbk. 14.00 (*1-882858-17-4*) Yoon-il Auh.

—Preliminary, Bk. 1. 60p. (gr. 1-8). 1983. wkbk. 14.00 (*1-882858-00-X*) Yoon-il Auh.

—Preliminary, Bk. 2. 60p. (gr. 1-8). 1983. wkbk. 14.00 (*1-882858-01-8*) Yoon-il Auh.

—Preliminary, Bk. 3. 45p. (gr. 1-8). 1983. wkbk. 14.00 (*1-882858-02-6*) Yoon-il Auh.

—Scale System for Young: EZ Scales. 45p. (gr. 1-12). 1993. wkbk. 10.00 (*1-882858-10-7*) Yoon-il Auh.
—Tricks for the Wild Fiddler, Bk. I. 35p. (gr. 1-12). 1985. wkbk. 10.00 (*1-882858-28-X*) Yoon-il Auh.
—Tricks for the Wild Fiddler, Bk. II. 35p. (gr. 1-12). 1985. wkbk. 10.00 (*1-882858-29-8*) Yoon-il Auh.
Chan, Margie. The Eye 'N' Hand, Book One for Violin. (gr. 2). 1988. write for info. GIM-Ho.
—Music Concepts & Vocabulary for Violin, Bk. 1. 41p. (gr. 2 up). 1984. wkbk. 4.95 (*0-9615006-0-3*) Gim-Ho.
—Music Concepts & Vocabulary for Violin, Bk. 2. 48p. (gr. 2 up). 1985. wkbk. 4.95 (*0-9615006-1-1*) Gim-Ho.
Clement, Claude. The Voice of the Wood. Clement, Frederic, photos by. LC 88-22892. (Illus.). 32p. (gr. k up). 1989. 14.95 (*0-8037-0635-9*) Dial Bks Young.
Dillon, Jacquelyn, et al. Strictly Strings: A Comprehensive String Method, Bk. 1: Bass. (Illus.). 40p. (Orig.). (gr. 4-6). 1992. pap. 4.95 (*0-88284-533-0*, 5296) Alfred Pub.
—Strictly Strings: A Comprehensive String Method, Bk. 1: Cello. (Illus.). 40p. (Orig.). (gr. 4-6). 1992. pap. 4.95 (*0-88284-532-2*, 5295) Alfred Pub.
—Strictly Strings: A Comprehensive String Method, Bk. 1: Violin. (Illus.). 40p. (Orig.). (gr. 4-6). 1992. pap. 4.95 (*0-88284-530-6*, 5293) Alfred Pub.
—Strictly Strings: A Comprehensive String Method, Bk. 1: Viola. (Illus.). 40p. (Orig.). (gr. 4-6). 1992. pap. 4.95 (*0-88284-531-4*, 5294) Alfred Pub.
Fleisher, Paul. The Master Violinmaker. Saunders, David, photos by. LC 92-28050. (Illus.). 1993. 14.95 (*0-395-65365-7*) HM.
Moncomble, Gerard. Octave & His Violin. (Illus.). 275p. (Orig.). (gr. 1-5). 1994. pap. 19.95x (*0-572-01967-X*, Pub. by W Foulsham UK) Trans-Atl Phila.
Preucil, Doris. Suzuki Viola School, Viola Part, Vol. 1. Suzuki, Shinichi, ed. 32p. (gr. k-12). 1981. pap. text ed. 6.50 (*0-87487-241-3*) Summy-Birchard.
—Suzuki Viola School, Viola Part, Vol. 2. Suzuki, Shinichi, ed. 32p. (gr. k-12). 1982. pap. text ed. 6.50 (*0-87487-242-1*) Summy-Birchard.
Preucil, Doris & Suzuki, Shinichi, eds. Suzuki Viola School, Vol. A. 64p. (gr. k-12). 1982. pap. text ed. 10.95 (*0-87487-245-6*, Suzuki Method) Summy-Birchard.
Simon, Charnan. Midori: Brilliant Violinist. LC 92-40674. (Illus.). 32p. (gr. 2-4). 1993. PLB 11.80 (*0-516-04187-8*); pap. 3.95 (*0-516-44187-6*) Childrens.
Suzuki, Shinichi. Suzuki Cello School, Cello Part, Vol. 7. 24p. (gr. k-12). 1987. pap. text ed. 6.50 (*0-87487-360-6*, Suzuki Method) Summy-Birchard.
—Suzuki Cello School, Vol. 7: Piano Accompaniments. 32p. (gr. k-12). 1987. pap. text ed. 6.50 (*0-87487-362-2*, Suzuki Method) Summy-Birchard.
—Suzuki Viola School, Piano Accompaniments, Vol. 5. 52p. (gr. k-12). 1986. pap. text ed. 8.95 (*0-87487-250-2*, Suzuki Method) Summy-Birchard.

VIOLONCELLISTS
see Violinists, Violoncellists, etc.

VIPERS
see Snakes

VIRGIN ISLANDS OF THE U. S.

Bailey, Katharine R. & Bourne, Gloria. U. S. Virgin Islands: Jewels of the Caribbean--St. Croix, St. Thomas, St. John. Henle, Fritz, photos by. LC 86-82891. (Illus.). 48p. (Orig.). (gr. 7-12). 1987. pap. 6.95 (*0-88714-012-2*) KC Pubns.
Ellis, Karen S., intro. by. Domino: Traditional Children's Songs, Proverbs & Culture from the American Virgin Islands. Arpino, Alaria, illus. 96p. (Orig.). (gr. 1-6). 1990. Set. pap. 21.50 (*0-9625560-7-6*); pap. text ed. 14.50 (*0-9625560-3-3*); incl. audio tape 10.00 (*0-9625560-0-9*) Guavaberry Bks.
Petersen, Arona. Food & Folklore of the Virgin Islands. 300p. (Orig.). (gr. 9-12). 1990. 20.00 (*0-9626577-0-0*) A Petersen.

VIRGIN MARY
see Mary, Virgin

VIRGINIA

Ashabranner, Brent. A Grateful Nation: The Story of Arlington National Cemetery. (Illus.). 112p. 1990. 15.95 (*0-399-22188-3*, Putnam) Putnam Pub Group.
Aylesworth, Thomas G. & Aylesworth, Virginia L. The Atlantic (Virginia, West Virginia, District of Columbia) (Illus.). 64p. (Orig.). 1990. lib. bdg. 16.95x (*1-55546-555-2*); pap. 6.95 (*0-7910-0533-X*) Chelsea Hse.
Carole Marsh Virginia Books, 46 bks. 1994. PLB 1077.70 set (*0-7933-1321-X*); pap. 617.70 set (*0-7933-5214-2*) Gallopade Pub Group.
Coffey, William E., et al. West Virginia Government. Buckalew, Marshall & Thoenen, Eugenia G., eds. (Illus.). 112p. (Orig.). (gr. 8). 1984. pap. 10.00 (*0-914498-05-3*) WV Hist Ed Found.
Evans, Lynn. Richmond, Virginia: The Travel Guide for Kids. 1991. pap. 5.00 (*0-945600-07-0*) Colormore Inc.
Foster, Sally. The Private World of Smith Island. Foster, Sally, photos by. LC 92-17975. (Illus.). (gr. 3-7). 1993. 14.99 (*0-525-65122-5*, Cobblehill Bks) Dutton Child Bks.
Fradin, Dennis B. Virginia. LC 92-6386. (Illus.). 64p. (gr. 3-5). 1992. PLB 16.45 (*0-516-03846-X*) Childrens.
Goor, Ron & Goor, Nancy. Williamsburg: Cradle of the Revolution. LC 94-9370. (gr. 3-7). 1994. 15.95 (*0-689-31795-6*, Atheneum) Macmillan.
Hamlin, Griffith A. House by the Water: Twelve Generations in Virginia. LC 93-70018. 139p. (gr. 9 up). 1993. 10.95 (*0-9631511-1-8*) G A Hamlin.
Kyle, Louisa V. My Virginia Childhood. (Illus.). 45p. (gr. 3). 1976. write for info. Four Oclock Farms.
McNair, Sylvia. Virginia. LC 88-38203. (Illus.). 144p. (gr. 4 up). 1989. PLB 20.55 (*0-516-00492-1*) Childrens.
—Virginia. 195p. 1993. text ed. 15.40 (*1-56956-170-2*) W A T Braille.
Marsh, Carole. Avast, Ye Slobs! Virginia Pirate Trivia. (Illus.). 1994. PLB 24.95 (*0-7933-1172-1*); pap. 14.95 (*0-7933-1171-3*); computer disk 29.95 (*0-7933-1173-X*) Gallopade Pub Group.
—The Beast of the Virginia Bed & Breakfast. (Illus.). 1994. PLB 24.95 (*0-7933-2179-4*); pap. 14.95 (*0-7933-2180-8*); computer disk 29.95 (*0-7933-2181-6*) Gallopade Pub Group.
—Bow Wow! Virginia Dogs in History, Mystery, Legend, Lore, Humor & More! (Illus.). (gr. 3-12). 1994. PLB 24.95 (*0-7933-3605-8*); pap. 14.95 (*0-7933-3606-6*); computer disk 29.95 (*0-7933-3607-4*) Gallopade Pub Group.
—Chill Out: Scary Virginia Tales Based on Frightening Virginia Truths. (Illus.). 1994. lib. bdg. 24.95 (*0-7933-4792-0*); pap. 14.95 (*0-7933-4793-9*); disk 29.95 (*0-7933-4794-7*) Gallopade Pub Group.
—Christopher Columbus Comes to Virginia! Includes Reproducible Activities for Kids! (Illus.). (gr. 3-12). 1994. PLB 24.95 (*0-7933-3758-5*); pap. 14.95 (*0-7933-3759-3*); computer disk 29.95 (*0-7933-3760-7*) Gallopade Pub Group.
—The Hard-to-Believe-But-True! Book of Virginia History, Mystery, Trivia, Legend, Lore, Humor & More. (Illus.). 1994. PLB 24.95 (*0-7933-1169-1*); pap. 14.95 (*0-7933-1168-3*); computer disk 29.95 (*0-7933-1170-5*) Gallopade Pub Group.
—If My Virginia Mama Ran the World! (Illus.). 1994. PLB 24.95 (*0-7933-2187-5*); pap. 14.95 (*0-7933-2188-3*); computer disk 29.95 (*0-7933-2189-1*) Gallopade Pub Group.
—Jurassic Ark! Virginia Dinosaurs & Other Prehistoric Creatures. (gr. k-12). 1994. PLB 24.95 (*0-7933-7566-5*); pap. 14.95 (*0-7933-7567-3*); computer disk 29.95 (*0-7933-7568-1*) Gallopade Pub Group.
—Let's Quilt Our Virginia County. 1992. lib. bdg. 24.95 (*0-7933-7251-8*); pap. text ed. 14.95 (*0-7933-7252-6*); disk 29.95 (*0-7933-7253-4*) Gallopade Pub Group.
—Let's Quilt Our Virginia Town. 1994. lib. bdg. 24.95 (*0-7933-7101-5*); pap. text ed. 14.95 (*0-7933-7102-3*); disk 29.95 (*0-7933-7103-1*) Gallopade Pub Group.
—Let's Quilt Virginia & Stuff It Topographically! (Illus.). 1994. PLB 24.95 (*0-7933-2171-9*); pap. 14.95 (*1-55609-051-X*); computer disk 29.95 (*0-7933-2172-7*) Gallopade Pub Group.
—Mariner's & More! Virginia People, Places & Things Everyone Should Know. (Illus.). (gr. 9-12). 1994. PLB 24.95 (*0-7933-0000-2*); pap. 14.95 (*0-7933-0001-0*); computer disk 29.95 (*0-7933-0002-9*) Gallopade Pub Group.
—Meow! Virginia Cats in History, Mystery, Legend, Lore, Humor & More! (Illus.). (gr. 3-12). 1994. PLB 24.95 (*0-7933-3452-7*); pap. 14.95 (*0-7933-3453-5*); computer disk 29.95 (*0-7933-3454-3*) Gallopade Pub Group.
—My First Book about Virginia. (gr. k-4). 1994. PLB 24.95 (*0-7933-5707-1*); pap. 14.95 (*0-7933-5708-X*); computer disk 29.95 (*0-7933-5709-8*) Gallopade Pub Group.
—Patch, the Pirate Dog: A Virginia Pet Story. (ps-4). 1994. PLB 24.95 (*0-7933-5554-0*); pap. 14.95 (*0-7933-5555-9*); computer disk 29.95 (*0-7933-5556-7*) Gallopade Pub Group.
—Uncle Rebus: Virginia Picture Stories for Computer Kids. (Illus.). (gr. k-3). 1994. PLB 24.95 (*0-7933-4639-8*); pap. 14.95 (*0-7933-4640-1*); disk 29.95 (*0-7933-4641-X*) Gallopade Pub Group.
—Virginia & Other State Greats (Biographies) (Illus.). 1994. PLB 24.95 (*0-7933-2190-5*); pap. 14.95 (*0-7933-2191-3*); computer disk 29.95 (*0-7933-2192-1*) Gallopade Pub Group.
—Virginia Bandits, Bushwackers, Outlaws, Crooks, Devils, Ghosts, Desperadoes & Other Assorted & Sundry Characters! (Illus.). 1994. PLB 24.95 (*0-7933-1154-3*); pap. 14.95 (*0-7933-1153-5*); computer disk 29.95 (*0-7933-1155-1*) Gallopade Pub Group.
—Virginia Classic Christmas Trivia: Stories, Recipes, Activities, Legends, Lore & More. (Illus.). 1994. PLB 24.95 (*0-7933-1157-8*); pap. 14.95 (*0-7933-1156-X*); computer disk 29.95 (*0-7933-1158-6*) Gallopade Pub Group.
—Virginia Coastales. (Illus.). 1994. PLB 24.95 (*0-685-45962-4*); pap. 14.95 (*1-55609-116-8*); computer disk 29.95 (*0-7933-2186-7*) Gallopade Pub Group.
—Virginia Coastales! 1994. lib. bdg. 24.95 (*0-7933-7311-5*) Gallopade Pub Group.
—Virginia "Crinkum-Crankum" A Funny Word Book about Our State. (Illus.). (gr. 3-12). 1994. 24.95 (*0-7933-4946-X*); pap. 14.95 (*0-7933-4947-8*); computer disk 29.95 (*0-7933-4948-6*) Gallopade Pub Group.
—Virginia Dingbats! Bk. 1: A Fun Book of Games, Stories, Activities & More about Our State That's All in Code! for You to Decipher. (Illus.). (gr. 3-12). 1994. PLB 24.95 (*0-7933-3911-1*); pap. 14.95 (*0-7933-3912-X*); computer disk 29.95 (*0-7933-3913-8*) Gallopade Pub Group.
—Virginia Festival Fun for Kids! (Illus.). (gr. 3-12). 1994. lib. bdg. 24.95 (*0-7933-4064-0*); pap. 14.95 (*0-7933-4065-9*); disk 29.95 (*0-685-41938-X*) Gallopade Pub Group.
—The Virginia Hot Air Balloon Mystery. (Illus.). (gr. 2-9). 1994. 24.95 (*0-7933-2732-6*); pap. 14.95 (*0-7933-2733-4*); computer disk 29.95 (*0-7933-2734-2*) Gallopade Pub Group.
—Virginia Jeopardy! Answers & Questions about Our State! (Illus.). (gr. 3-12). 1994. PLB 24.95 (*0-7933-4217-1*); pap. 14.95 (*0-7933-4218-X*); computer disk 29.95 (*0-7933-4219-8*) Gallopade Pub Group.
—Virginia Jography: A Fun Run Through the Old Dominion State. (Illus.). 50p. (Orig.). (gr. 3-12). 1994. pap. 24.95 (*0-935326-99-5*) Gallopade Pub Group.
—Virginia "Jography" A Fun Run Thru Our State. (Illus.). 1994. PLB 24.95 (*0-685-45960-8*); pap. 14.95 (*1-55609-057-9*); computer disk 29.95 (*0-7933-2170-0*) Gallopade Pub Group.
—Virginia Kid's Cookbook: Recipes, How-to, History, Lore & More! (Illus.). 1994. PLB 24.95 (*0-7933-1166-7*); pap. 14.95 (*0-7933-1165-9*); computer disk 29.95 (*0-7933-1167-5*) Gallopade Pub Group.
—The Virginia Mystery Van Takes Off! Book 1: Handicapped Virginia Kids Sneak Off on a Big Adventure. (Illus.). (gr. 3-12). 1994. 24.95 (*0-7933-5099-9*); pap. 14.95 (*0-7933-5100-6*); computer disk 29.95 (*0-7933-5101-4*) Gallopade Pub Group.
—Virginia Quiz Bowl Crash Courses! (Illus.). 1994. PLB 24.95 (*0-7933-2182-4*); pap. 14.95 (*0-7933-2183-2*); computer disk 29.95 (*0-7933-2184-0*) Gallopade Pub Group.
—Virginia Rollercoasters! (Illus.). (gr. 3-12). 1994. PLB 24.95 (*0-7933-5362-9*); pap. 14.95 (*0-7933-5363-7*); computer disk 29.95 (*0-7933-5364-5*) Gallopade Pub Group.
—Virginia School Trivia: An Amazing & Fascinating Look at Our State's Teachers, Schools & Students! (Illus.). 1994. PLB 24.95 (*0-7933-1163-2*); pap. 14.95 (*0-7933-1162-4*); computer disk 29.95 (*0-7933-1164-0*) Gallopade Pub Group.
—Virginia Silly Basketball Sportsmysteries, Vol. 1. (Illus.). 1994. PLB 24.95 (*0-7933-1160-8*); pap. 14.95 (*0-7933-1159-4*); computer disk 29.95 (*0-7933-1161-6*) Gallopade Pub Group.
—Virginia Silly Basketball Sportsmysteries, Vol. 2. (Illus.). 1994. PLB 24.95 (*0-7933-2195-6*); pap. 14.95 (*0-7933-2196-4*); computer disk 29.95 (*0-7933-2197-2*) Gallopade Pub Group.
—Virginia Silly Football Sportsmysteries, Vol. 1. (Illus.). 1994. PLB 24.95 (*0-685-45961-6*); pap. 14.95 (*0-7933-2174-3*); computer disk 29.95 (*0-7933-2175-1*) Gallopade Pub Group.
—Virginia Silly Football Sportsmysteries, Vol. 2. (Illus.). 1994. PLB 24.95 (*0-7933-2176-X*); pap. 14.95 (*0-7933-2177-8*); computer disk 29.95 (*0-7933-2178-6*) Gallopade Pub Group.
—Virginia Silly Trivia! (Illus.). 60p. (Orig.). (gr. 3-12). 1994. PLB 24.95 (*0-7933-2167-0*); pap. 14.95 (*0-935326-94-4*); computer disk 29.95 (*0-7933-2168-9*) Gallopade Pub Group.
—Virginia Timeline: A Chronology of Virginia History, Mystery, Trivia, Legend, Lore & More. (Illus.). (gr. 3-12). 1994. PLB 24.95 (*0-7933-6013-7*); pap. 14.95 (*0-7933-6014-5*); computer disk 29.95 (*0-7933-6015-3*) Gallopade Pub Group.
—Virginia's (Most Devastating!) Disasters & (Most Calamitous!) Catastrophies! (Illus.). 1994. PLB 24.95 (*0-7933-2193-X*); pap. 14.95 (*0-7933-1150-0*); computer disk 29.95 (*0-7933-2194-8*) Gallopade Pub Group.
—Virginia's Unsolved Mysteries (& Their "Solutions") Includes Scientific Information & Other Activities for Students. (Illus.). (gr. 3-12). 1994. PLB 24.95 (*0-7933-5860-4*); pap. 14.95 (*0-7933-5861-2*); computer disk 29.95 (*0-7933-5862-0*) Gallopade Pub Group.
Sirvaitis, Karen. Virginia. (Illus.). 72p. (gr. 3-6). 1991. PLB 17.50 (*0-8225-2702-2*) Lerner Pubns.

VIRGINIA–FICTION

Flournoy, Valerie. Tanya's Reunion. Pinkey, Jerry, illus. LC 94-13067. 1995. write for info. (*0-8037-1604-4*); PLB write for info. (*0-8037-1605-2*) Dial Bks Young.
Henry, Marguerite. Marguerite Henry's Horseshoe Library: Stormy, Misty's Foal; Sea Star, Orphan of Chincoteague; Misty of Chincoteague, 3 bks. (Illus.). (gr. 3-7). 1992. Set. pap. 11.85 (*0-689-71624-9*, Aladdin) Macmillan Child Grp.
—Misty of Chincoteague. reissued ed. Dennis, Wesley, illus. LC 47-11404. 176p. (gr. 3-7). 1990. SBE 13.95 (*0-02-743622-5*, Macmillan Child Bk) Macmillan Child Grp.
—Stormy: Misty's Foal. Dennis, Wesley, illus. LC 63-13334. 224p. (gr. 2-9). 1987. 8.95 (*0-528-82083-4*, Aladdin Bks); (Aladdin Bks) Macmillan Child Grp.
Hite, Sid. Dither Farm. LC 91-31323. 224p. (gr. 7 up). 1992. 15.95 (*0-8050-1871-9*, Bks Young Read) H Holt & Co.
—It's Nothing to a Mountain. LC 93-42048. 1994. 15.95 (*0-8050-2769-6*) H Holt & Co.
Reeder, Carolyn. Shades of Gray. LC 89-31976. 176p. (gr. 3-7). 1989. SBE 13.95 (*0-02-775810-9*, Macmillan Child Bk) Macmillan Child Grp.
Sharpe, Susan. Waterman's Boy. LC 89-39332. 96p. (gr. 3-6). 1990. SBE 14.95 (*0-02-782351-2*, Bradbury Pr) Macmillan Child Grp.
Turner, Louise. Yesterday to Color at Gunston Hall. Alig, Mary J., illus. 15p. (Orig.). 1990. pap. 3.95 (*1-884085-05-9*) Bd Regents.

VIRGINIA–HISTORY

Beachy, J. Wayne. Richmond Theater Fire, 1862. Hawkins, Beverly, illus. 24p. (Orig.). (gr. 5 up). 1987. pap. 3.00 (*0-9608084-3-4*) B Hawkins Studio.

Byrd, Odell, Jr. Richmond, Virginia: A City of Monuments & Statues. rev. ed. (Illus.). 84p. (gr. 10). 1994. Repr. of 1989 ed. PLB 12.95 (*0-9621739-3-2*) Tambuzi Pubns.

Fradin, Dennis B. The Virginia Colony. LC 86-13639. (Illus.). 160p. (gr. 4 up). 1986. PLB 17.95 (*0-516-00387-9*) Childrens.

Hammond, Gene P. Unmasking a Virginia Myth: Who Visited First the Virgin Valley? What the Schools Did not Teach. Hammond, Rachael W., ed. Johnson, Debbie E., illus. 66p. (gr. 8-12). 1993. write for info. (*1-878014-07-2*); pap. write for info. G P Hammond Pub.

Johnson, Patricia G. The New River Early Settlement. LC 83-81157. (Illus.). 232p. (gr. 6 up). 1991. Repr. of 1983 ed. 20.00 (*0-9614765-3-2*) Walpa Pub.

Kent, Zachary. The Story of the Surrender at Yorktown. LC 89-33784. 32p. (gr. 3-6). 1989. pap. 3.95 (*0-516-44723-8*) Childrens.

Smith, Carter. The Jamestown Colony. (Illus.). 64p. (gr. 5 up). 1991. PLB 12.95 (*0-382-24121-5*); pap. 7.95 (*0-382-24116-9*) Silver Burdett Pr.

Thompson, Kathleen. Virginia. 48p. (gr. 3 up). 1985. PLB 19.97 (*0-86514-447-8*) Raintree Steck-V.

Uchello, Carlo. Virginians All. Barr, Marilyn, illus. LC 92-13634. 144p. (gr. 7-9). 1992. 11.95 (*0-88289-853-1*) Pelican.

VIRUSES

Berger, Melvin. Germs Make Me Sick! Hafner, Marylin, illus. LC 93-27059. 1995. 15.00 (*0-06-024249-3*); PLB 14.89 (*0-06-024250-7*) HarpC Child Bks.

Facklam, Howard & Facklam, Margery. Viruses. (Illus.). 64p. (gr. 5-8). 1994. bds. 15.95 (*0-8050-2856-0*) TFC Bks NY.

Flint, S. Jane. Viruses. Head, J. J., ed. Imrick, Ann T., illus. LC 87-70987. 16p. (Orig.). (gr. 10 up). 1988. pap. text ed. 2.75 (*0-89278-094-0*, 45-9794) Carolina Biological.

LeMaster, Leslie J. Bacteria & Viruses. LC 84-27414. (Illus.). 48p. (gr. k-4). 1985. PLB 12.85 (*0-516-01937-6*) Childrens.

Nourse, Alan E. The Virus Invaders. Mathews, V., ed. LC 91-36650. (Illus.). 96p. (gr. 9-12). 1992. PLB 12.90 (*0-531-12511-4*) Watts.

VISION

see also Blind; Eye; Optical Illusions

Asimov, Isaac & Dierks, Carrie. Why Do Some People Need Glasses? LC 93-20156. 1993. PLB 15.93 (*0-8368-0809-6*) Gareth Stevens Inc.

Bertrand, Cecile. Noni Sees. (ps). 1993. 4.95 (*0-307-15685-0*, Artsts Writrs) Western Pub.

Fleischman, Paul. Finzel the Farsighted. Sewall, Marcia, illus. LC 83-1416. 48p. (gr. 1-5). 1983. 11.95 (*0-525-44057-7*, DCB) Dutton Child Bks.

Forte, Imogene. I'm Ready to Learn about Visual Perception. (gr. k-1). 1986. pap. text ed. 1.95 (*0-86530-114-X*, IP-1112) Incentive Pubns.

Fowler, Allan. Seeing Things. LW 90-22527. (Illus.). 32p. (ps-2). 1991. PLB 10.75 (*0-516-04910-0*); pap. 3.95 (*0-516-44910-9*) Childrens.

Hoban, Tana. Look up, Look Down. LC 91-12613. 32p. (ps up). 1992. 14.00 (*0-688-10577-7*); lib. bdg. 13.93 (*0-688-10578-5*) Greenwillow.

Hobbs, Jack & Salome, Richard. The Visual Experience. (Illus.). 352p. 1990. text ed. 29.96 (*0-87192-226-6*) Davis Mass.

Lauber, Patricia. What Do You See? Wexler, Jerome & Lessin, Leonard, photos by. LC 93-2388. (Illus.). 48p. (gr. 3-7). 1994. 17.00 (*0-517-59390-4*); PLB 17.99 (*0-517-59391-2*) Crown Bks Yng Read.

Legge, Gordon E. & Campbell, Fergus W. Vision of Color & Pattern. Head, J. J., ed. Steffen, Ann T., illus. LC 84-45835. 16p. (Orig.). (gr. 10 up). 1987. pap. text ed. 2.75 (*0-89278-365-6*, 45-9765) Carolina Biological.

Moncure, Jane B. The Look Book. Axeman, Lois, illus. LC 82-4517. 32p. (ps-3). 1982. pap. 3.95 (*0-516-43251-6*) Childrens.

Parker, Steve. Eye & Seeing. LC 88-51606. 1989. PLB 12.90 (*0-531-10654-3*) Watts.

—The Eye & Seeing. rev. ed. (Illus.). 48p. (gr. 5 up). 1991. pap. 6.95 (*0-531-24602-7*) Watts.

Parramon, J. M. & Puig, J. J. Sight. Rius, Maria, illus. 32p. (Orig.). (ps). 1985. pap. 6.95 (*0-8120-3564-X*); pap. 6.95 Spanish ed. (*0-8120-3605-0*) Barron.

Samz, Jane. Vision. (Illus.). 104p. (gr. 6-12). 1990. 18.95 (*0-7910-0031-1*) Chelsea Hse.

Showers, Paul. Look at Your Eyes. rev. ed. Kelley, True, illus. LC 91-10167. 32p. (ps-1). 1992. 14.00 (*0-06-020188-6*); PLB 13.89 (*0-06-020189-4*) HarpC Child Bks.

Sinclair, Sandra. Extraordinary Eyes: How Animals See the World. LC 89-39618. (Illus.). 48p. (gr. 4-7). 1992. 15.00 (*0-8037-0803-3*); PLB 14.89 (*0-8037-0806-8*) Dial Bks Young.

Smith, Kathie B. & Crenson, Victoria. Seeing. Storms, Robert S., illus. LC 87-5862. 24p. (gr. k-3). 1988. PLB 10.59 (*0-8167-1008-2*); pap. text ed. 2.50 (*0-8167-1009-0*) Troll Assocs.

Snell, Nigel. Seeing. (Illus.). 32p. (gr. k-2). 1991. 10.95 (*0-237-60257-1*, Pub. by Evans Bros Ltd) Trafalgar.

Stuchbury, Dianne. Look! Stuchbury, Dianne, illus. 24p. (ps-1). 1991. 4.99 (*0-7459-2000-4*) Lion USA.

Suhr, Mandy. Sight. Gordon, Mike, illus. LC 93-44193. 1993. 13.50 (*0-87614-834-8*) Carolrhoda Bks.

Tytla, Milan & Crystal, Nancy. You Won't Believe Your Eyes. Eldridge, Susan, illus. 88p. (gr. 2-8). 1992. pap. 9.95 (*1-55037-218-1*, Pub. by Annick CN) Firefly Bks Ltd.

Wright, Lillian. Seeing. LC 94-10720. (Illus.). 32p. (gr. 2-4). 1994. PLB 18.99 (*0-8114-5515-7*) Raintree Steck-V.

Ziefert, Harriet. What Do I See? 1988. 3.95 (*0-553-05456-2*) Bantam.

VISUAL INSTRUCTION

see Audio-Visual Education

VITAMINS

Asimov, Isaac. How Did We Find Out About Vitamins? Wool, David, illus. LC 73-92453. 64p. (gr. 5-8). 1974. PLB 11.85 (*0-8027-6184-4*) Walker & Co.

Barber, Jacqueline. Vitamin C Testing. Bergman, Lincoln & Fairwell, Kay, eds. Bevilacqua, Carol, illus. Barber, Jacqueline & Hoyt, Richard, photos by. (Illus.). 48p. (Orig.). (gr. 4-8). 1988. pap. 8.50 (*0-912511-70-2*) Lawrence Science.

Emberley, Rebecca. My Day: A Book in Two Languages - Mi Dia: un Libro en Dos Lenguas. LC 92-37277. (ENG & SPA.). 1993. 15.95 (*0-316-23454-0*) Little.

Muhammad, S. Ifetayo. Vitamin A Through Zinc: An Alphabet of Good Health. 16p. (Orig.). 1985. pap. 1.00 (*0-916157-13-X*) African Islam Miss Pubns.

Nardo, Don. Vitamins & Minerals. (Illus.). (gr. 7-12). 1994. 19.95 (*0-7910-0032-X*, Am Art Analog); pap. write for info. (*0-7910-0472-4*) Chelsea Hse.

Nottridge, Rhoda. Additives. LC 92-33083. 1993. PLB 14.95 (*0-87614-794-5*); pap. 5.95 (*0-87614-609-4*) Carolrhoda Bks.

Seixas, Judith S. Vitamins - What They Are, What They Do. Juffman, Tom, illus. LC 85-17761. 56p. (gr. 1-4). 1986. 12.95 (*0-688-06065-X*); PLB 12.93 (*0-688-06066-8*) Greenwillow.

Silverstein, Alvin, et al. Vitamins & Minerals. Green, Anne C., illus. LC 91-41231. 48p. (gr. 3-6). 1992. PLB 14.40 (*1-56294-206-9*) Millbrook Pr.

VIVARIUMS

see Terrariums

VIVEKANANDA, SWAMI, 1863-1902

Ray, Irene R. & Gupta, Mallika C. Story of Vivekananda. Banerjee, Ramananda, illus. (gr. 4-7). 1971. pap. 1.95 (*0-87481-125-2*, Pub. by Advaita Ashram India) Vedanta Pr.

VOCABULARY

see also Words, New

Ahlberg, Janet & Ahlberg, Allan. The Baby's Catalogue. LC 82-9928. (Illus.). 32p. (gr. k up). 1983. 15.95i (*0-316-02037-0*, Joy St Bks) Little.

Amery, Heather & Cartwright, Stephen. The First Hundred Words. Cartwright, Stephen, illus. 32p. (ps up). 1988. PLB 11.96 (*0-88110-322-5*); pap. 7.95 (*0-7460-0186-X*) EDC.

Anderson, Honey & Reinholtd, Bill. What Are You Called? Bruere, Julian, illus. LC 92-31953. 1993. 3.75 (*0-383-03604-6*) SRA Schl Grp.

Animals, Birds, Bees, & Flowers. 24p. 1989. 5.99 (*0-517-68230-3*) Random Hse Value.

Armstrong, B. Primary Awards Galore. (gr. k-3). 1985. 5.95 (*0-88160-121-7*, LW 132) Learning Wks.

Asher, Sandy. Wild Words & How to Tame Them. Kendrick, Dennis, illus. 96p. (gr. 5 up). 1989. 13.95 (*0-8027-6887-3*); PLB 14.85 (*0-8027-6888-1*) Walker & Co.

Ashton, Christina. Words Can Tell: A Book about Our Language. LC 87-20333. (Illus.). 128p. (gr. 6-9). 1989. lib. bdg. 12.98 (*0-671-65223-0*, J Messner) S&S Trade.

Asimov, Isaac. Words from the Myths. (Illus.). 144p. (gr. 6). 1969. pap. 2.50 (*0-451-14097-4*, Sig) NAL-Dutton.

At Home. (gr. 2-6). 1986. 3.99 (*0-517-05403-5*, 614952) Random Hse Value.

At School. (gr. 2-6). 1986. 3.99 (*0-517-05404-3*, 614960) Random Hse Value.

Awdry, Christopher. Thomas's Big Book of Words. Stott, Ken, illus. LC 91-62681. 32p. (ps-1). 1992. 7.99 (*0-679-82778-1*) Random Bks Yng Read.

Badt, Karin L. Greetings. LC 94-18777. (Illus.). 32p. (gr. 3-7). 1994. PLB 17.20 (*0-516-08188-8*); pap. 5.95 (*0-516-48188-6*) Childrens.

Barrett, Mark, et al. The Word Test--Adolescent - Complete Kit: A Test of Expressive Vocabulary & Semantics. (gr. 7-12). 1989. complete kit 54.95 (*1-55999-096-1*) LinguiSystems.

Bell, Nanci & Lindamood, Phyllis. Vanilla Vocabulary: Visualized-Verbalized Vocabulary Book. Lindamood, Phyllis, illus. 200p. (gr. 4-7). 1992. pap. 19.00 (*0-945856-03-2*) Acad Reading.

Bornstein, Scott. Vocabulary Mastery. Vincent, Ben, illus. 272p. (gr. 9-12). 1982. 22.50 (*0-9602610-1-X*); pap. 14.95 (*0-9602610-2-8*) Bornstein Memory.

Bridwell, Norman. Clifford's Word Book. LC 94-4003. 1994. 10.95 (*0-590-48696-9*) Scholastic Inc.

Bromberg, Murray & Liebb, Julius. Hot Words for the SAT: The Three Hundred Fifty Words You Need to Know. 2nd ed. LC 93-6742. 180p. (gr. 9 up). 1993. pap. 8.95 (*0-8120-1731-5*) Barron.

Brown, Rick. What Rhymes with Snake? A Word & Picture Flap Book. Brown, Rick, illus. LC 92-37870. 24p. 1994. 11.95 (*0-688-12328-7*, Tambourine Bks) Morrow.

Bruce, Lisa. Oliver's Alphabets. Gliori, Debi, illus. LC 92-39471. 24p. (ps-1). 1993. SBE 13.95 (*0-02-735996-4*, Bradbury Pr) Macmillan Child Grp.

Burchard, Elizabeth & Allen, Paula. English Vocabulary: In a Flash. 450p. (gr. 7-12). 1994. pap. 9.95 (*1-881374-08-4*) Flash Blasters.

Cardona, Jose, illus. Disney Pop-up Book of Actions. LC 92-70935. 12p. (ps-k). 1993. 7.95 (*1-56282-506-2*) Disney Pr.

Carle, Eric. My Very First Book of Words. Carle, Eric, illus. LC 72-83779. 10p. (ps-1). 1985. 4.95 (*0-694-00014-0*, Crowell Jr Bks) HarpC Child Bks.

Chirinian, Helene. Camping Out. (Illus.). 48p. (Orig.). (gr. k-3). 1989. pap. 2.95 (*0-8431-2415-6*) Price Stern.

—Future Park. (Illus.). 48p. (Orig.). (gr. k-3). 1989. pap. 2.95 (*0-8431-2416-4*) Price Stern.

—The Great Car Vacation. (Illus.). 48p. (Orig.). (gr. k-3). 1989. pap. 2.95 (*0-8431-2417-2*) Price Stern.

—Scavenger Hunt. (Illus.). 48p. (Orig.). (gr. k-3). 1989. pap. 2.95 (*0-8431-2414-8*) Price Stern.

Clark, Raymond C. Money: Exploring the Ways We Use It. (Illus.). 96p. (gr. 7 up). 1989. 10.50x (*0-86647-029-8*) Pro Lingua.

Clark, Raymond C. & Duncan, Janie L. Getting a Fix on Vocabulary, Using Words in the News: The System of Affixation & Compounding in English. (Illus.). 96p. (gr. 7 up). 1991. 11.00x (*0-86647-038-7*) Pro Lingua.

Daniel, Becky. Word Thinker Sheets. 64p. (gr. 4-8). 1988. wkbk. 8.95 (*0-86653-394-X*, GA1034) Good Apple.

Davenport, Zoe. Animals. LC 94-20821. 1995. 4.95 (*0-395-71537-7*) Ticknor & Flds Bks Yng Read.

—Gardens. LC 94-21456. (gr. 1-8). 1995. 4.95 (*0-395-71538-5*) Ticknor & Flds Bks Yng Read.

—Mealtimes. LC 94-20820. (ps). 1995. 4.95 (*0-395-71536-9*) Ticknor & Flds Bks Yng Read.

—Toys. LC 94-20819. 1995. pap. 4.95 (*0-395-71539-3*) Ticknor & Fields.

De Brunhoff, Laurent. Babar's French & English Word Book. LC 93-27873. (Illus.). 128p. 1994. 16.00 (*0-679-83644-6*) Random Bks Yng Read.

Disney Babies Fun with Words: At Home. 48p. (ps). 1992. 5.98 (*0-8317-2302-5*) Viking Child Bks.

Disney Babies Fun with Words: In the City. 48p. (ps). 1992. 5.98 (*0-8317-2301-7*) Viking Child Bks.

Disney Babies Fun with Words: In the Country. 48p. (ps). 1992. 5.98 (*0-8317-2304-1*) Viking Child Bks.

Disney Babies Fun with Words: On Vacation. 48p. (ps). 1992. 5.98 (*0-8317-2303-3*) Viking Child Bks.

Donatelli, Betty. Sounding Words with Roy & Joy. Donatelli, Betty, illus. 11p. (Orig.). (gr. k-2). 1984. pap. 1.00 (*0-912981-06-7*) Hse BonGiovanni.

Dorling-Kindersley, Ltd. Staff. My Very First Word Book. LC 93-1112. 1993. write for info. (*1-56458-375-9*, D Kindersley) HM.

Duncan, Leonard C. Greek Roots. Bigelow, Holly, illus. 82p. (Orig.). (gr. 6-12). 1982. pap. 10.00 (*0-941414-01-9*) LCD.

Emberley, Rebecca. Let's Go: A Book in Two Languages - Vamos: un Libro en Dos Lenguas. LC 92-37278. (ENG & SPA.). 1993. 15.95 (*0-316-23450-8*) Little.

Feder, Jane. Table, Chair, Bear: A Room in Many Languages. LC 92-40529. (Illus.). 32p. (ps-2). 1995. 13.95g (*0-395-65938-8*) Ticknor & Flds Bks Yng Read.

Gill, Nancy. Vocabulary Boosters I. (gr. 3-6). 1985. pap. 6.95 (*0-8224-7280-5*) Fearon Teach Aids.

—Vocabulary Boosters II. (gr. 3-6). 1985. pap. 6.95 (*0-8224-7281-3*) Fearon Teach Aids.

Gregorich, B. Vocabulary Vampire. (gr. 7-12). 1982. 5.95 (*0-88160-083-0*, LW 1001) Learning Wks.

Gregorich, Barbara. Positional Words & Opposite Words: Kindergarten. Hoffman, Joan, ed. Koontz, Robin M., illus. 32p. (gr. k). 1990. wkbk. 2.29 (*0-88743-180-1*) Sch Zone Pub Co.

—Word Skills: First Grade. Hoffman, Joan, ed. Koontz, Robin M., illus. 32p. (gr. 1). 1990. wkbk. 2.29 (*0-88743-184-4*) Sch Zone Pub Co.

—Word Skills: Second Grade. Hoffman, Joan, ed. Koontz, Robin M., illus. 32p. (gr. 2). 1990. wkbk. 2.29 (*0-88743-190-9*) Sch Zone Pub Co.

—Word Wagon. Hoffman, Joan, ed. Alexander, Barbara, et al, illus. 32p. (Orig.). (ps-1). wkbk. 1.99 (*0-88743-129-1*) Sch Zone Pub Co.

Healey, Tim. My Wonderful Word Box. (ps-3). 1993. 16.00 (*0-89577-528-X*, Readers Digest Kids) RD Assn.

Hill, Charlotte M. Wee Folks Readers: A Phonetic Approach to Beginning Reading, 5 vols. Shortridge, Cleona, ed. Fields, Theodore, et al, illus. LC 90-832256. 70p. (Orig.). (gr. k-5). 1992. Set. pap. write for info. (*0-9620182-9-5*) Charill Pubs.

This five volume reading series is an eclectic approach to beginning reading. Phonics is introduced in story form, lending itself to building comprehension, skills & simultaneously, sight words to build vocabulary as well. Each sound is introduced with illustrations that represent that sound. Books One through Four teach the vowel sounds & this teaching of sounds in context allows for the immediate application of phonetic skills learned. This approach follows the principle of use &

reinforcement. Book Five, "Wee Folks on Top" (Adventures in Reading), contains stories, fables & poetry with follow-up questions to improve comprehension. A bookstore owner & mother of a six year old daughter who lives in San Antonio, Texas, wrote, "My daughter was reading the first hour after I started her in Book I. I called relatives all over the country to tell them that she was reading." A director of a Prep School in Seattle, Washington, writes, "Your reading series is excellent. I am an experienced teacher & have always believed that a phonics based reading program is the best way to teach reading."
Publisher Provided Annotation.

Hill, Eric. Spot's Big Book of Words. (gr. 2 up). 1988. 10.95 (*0-399-21563-8*, Putnam) Putnam Pub Group.

Hoban, Tana. Over, Under & Through. Hoban, Tana, illus. LC 86-20675. 32p. (ps-3). 1987. pap. 3.95 (*0-689-71111-5*, Aladdin) Macmillan Child Grp.

Hollingsworth, Mary. My Very First Book of Bible Words. LC 93-21843. 1993. 4.99 (*0-8407-9226-3*) Nelson.

Honey Bear My First Big Talk about Book. (gr. 2-4). 1991. 6.95 (*0-87449-780-9*) Modern Pub NYC.

Hughes, Joleen. Sounds! LC 93-46323. 1994. PLB 4.99 (*0-517-10152-1*, Derrydale Bks) Random Hse Value.

—Things! LC 93-44877. 1994. 4.99 (*0-517-10151-3*, Pub. by Derrydale Bks) Random Hse Value.

Huisingh, Rosemary, et al. ACHIEV-Blue (Activities for Children Involving Everyday Vocabulary) (ps-5). 1989. complete pkg. 198.70 (*1-55999-002-3*) LinguiSystems.

—ACHIEV-Blue Books (Activities for Children Involving Everyday Vocabulary) (ps-5). 1986. spiral manual 49.95 (*1-55999-004-X*) LinguiSystems.

In the Country. (gr. 2-6). 1986. 2.98 (*0-685-16869-7*, 614987) Random Hse Value.

Johnson, Odette & Johnson, Bruce H. Apples, Alligators, & Also Alphabets. (Illus.). 32p. (ps-1). 1991. 13.95 (*0-19-540757-1*) OUP.

Jones, Carol, illus. The Cat Sat on the Mat. LC 93-14341. 1994. 13.95 (*0-395-68392-0*) HM.

Kelley, True. Hammers & Mops, Pencils & Pots: A First Book of Tools & Gadgets We Use Around the House. Kelley, True, illus. LC 93-25294. 32p. (ps). 1994. 8.99 (*0-517-59626-1*) Crown Bks Yng Read.

Klawitter, P. Wordwise. (gr. 7-12). 1989. 5.95 (*0-88160-193-4*, LW1009) Learning Wks.

Krauss, Ruth. A Hole Is to Dig. Sendak, Maurice, illus. (gr. k-3). 1990. incl. cass. 19.95 (*0-87499-174-9*); pap. 12.95 incl. cass. (*0-87499-173-0*); Set; incl. 4 bks., cass., & guide. pap. 27.95 (*0-87499-175-7*) Live Oak Media.

—Open House for Butterflies. reissued ed. Sendak, Maurice, illus. LC 60-5782. 48p. (ps-3). 1990. 11.00 (*0-06-023445-8*); PLB 10.89 (*0-06-023446-6*) HarpC Child Bks.

Laurita, Raymond E. Building Word Power Through Spelling Mastery: Questions & Answers about Words & Their Origins. 64p. (Orig.). (gr. 6-12). 1991. pap. text ed. 9.50 (*0-914051-25-3*) Leonardo Pr.

Lester, Alison. Tessa Snaps Snakes. Lester, Alison, illus. 32p. (ps-k). 1991. 13.45 (*0-395-59505-3*) HM.

Levey, Judith, ed. The Macmillan Picture Wordbook. rev. ed. LC 90-8274. (Illus.). 64p. (ps-1). 1990. SBE 8.95 (*0-02-754641-1*, Macmillan Child Bk) Macmillan Child Grp.

Levin, James. Ayudar. Carter, Jackie, ed. LC 94-729. 1994. write for info. (*0-590-29365-6*) Scholastic Inc.

Levitt, Paul M., et al. The Weighty Word Book. Stevens, Janet, illus. 99p. (gr. 4-9). 1990. Repr. of 1985 ed. 17.95 (*0-9627979-0-1*) Manuscripts.

Lieberman, Lillian. Vocabulary. 64p. (gr. 2-5). 1987. 6.95 (*0-912107-68-5*) Monday Morning Bks.

—Word Structure. 64p. (gr. k-3). 1987. 6.95 (*0-912107-67-7*) Monday Morning Bks.

LinguiSystems Staff. ACHIEV-Red Sing-a-Longs Manual (Activities for Children Involving Everyday Vocabulary - Home & Family Vocabulary) (ps-3). 1989. 27.95 (*1-55999-006-6*) LinguiSystems.

Longheed, L. Words More Words, & Ways to Use Them. (gr. 7 up). 1993. pap. text ed. 10.95 (*0-201-53961-6*) Longman.

MacCarthy, Patricia. Herds of Words. MacCarthy, Patricia, illus. LC 90-31537. 32p. (ps-3). 1991. 11.95 (*0-8037-0892-0*) Dial Bks Young.

McCulloch, Myrna & Madsen, Sharon, eds. Spelling & Usage Vocabulary Builder. large type ed. (Illus.). 478p. (gr. k-2). 1993. Repr. of 1991 ed. 26.50 (*0-924277-04-1*, Dist. by Riggs Institute Pr) K & M Pub.
This picture/word book's 4832 words have been edited with the mnemonic marketing system for precise speech & correct spelling used in Romalda Spalding's WRITING ROAD TO READING (WRTR), Wm. Morrow, N.Y., also distributed through the Riggs Institute. A truly usable, primary-level reference text; covers word explanations, grammar helps (verb forms including tenses, nouns, formation of plurals, adjectives, adverbs), extensive composition "models" with correct usage & word(s) substitutions (homonyms & antonyms), connected writing models, manuscript printing, syllabication, alphabetization practice & 1200 descriptive pictures. Large (14 point) print, 478 pages (4 to 5 words per page). Editing includes a 7-page Introduction for teachers which describes the WRTR system of teaching, the entire phonetic system for correct spelling, the mnemonic marking system, 28 spelling rules & tips for using multi-sensory, direct instruction. Order from: The Riggs Institute, 4185 SW 102nd Ave., Beaverton, OR 97005; 503-646-9459, FAX 503-644-5191.
Publisher Provided Annotation.

MacKinnon, Debbie. What Color? Sieveking, Anthea, photos by. (Illus.). 24p. (ps-k). 1994. 10.99 (*0-8037-0909-9*) Dial Bks Young.

McNaught, Harry. Five Hundred Words to Grow on. LC 73-2442. (Illus.). (ps-1). 1973. pap. 2.25 (*0-394-82668-X*) Random Bks Yng Read.

Maestro, Betsy. Taxi: A Book of City Words. Maestro, Giulio, illus. LC 88-22867. (ps-3). 1990. pap. 5.70 (*0-395-54811-X*, Clarion Bks) HM.

Marano, Philomena. Word Sandwiches. (gr. 1 up). 1994. pap. 1.95 (*0-590-47588-6*) Scholastic Inc.

Meltzer, Maxine. Pups Speak Up. Schmidt, Karen L., illus. LC 92-33687. 32p. (ps-3). 1994. RSBE 14.95 (*0-02-766710-3*, Bradbury Pr) Macmillan Child Grp.

Middlebrooks-Hutcherson, Gracie. How Many Vehicles Can You Name? I Can Name These Objects! Can You? What Animals Do You See, 3 vols. Clowney, Earle D., tr. Hutcherson, Matthew, III, illus. (SPA & ENG., Orig.). 1992. Set. 25.00 (*1-882485-05-X*); Set. pap. 12.00 (*1-882485-07-6*); write for info. cass. tape (*1-882485-06-8*) Enhance Your Chlds.

Moncure, Jane. The Biggest Snowball of All. Friedman, Joy, illus. 32p. (gr. 1-3). 1993. pap. text ed. 5.95 (*1-56189-348-X*) Amer Educ Pub.

—Butterfly Express. Hohag, Linda, illus. 32p. (gr. 1-3). 1993. pap. text ed. 5.95 (*1-56189-377-3*) Amer Educ Pub.

—Here We Go 'Round the Year. Hohag, Linda & Jacobson, Lori, illus. 32p. (gr. 1-3). 1993. pap. text ed. 5.95 (*1-56189-378-1*) Amer Educ Pub.

—How Many Ways Can You Cut a Pie? Hohag, Linda & Jacobson, Lori, illus. 32p. (gr. 1-3). 1993. pap. text ed. 5.95 (*1-56189-349-8*) Amer Educ Pub.

—Ice-Cream Cows & Mitten Sheep. Friedman, Joy, illus. 32p. (gr. 1-3). 1993. pap. text ed. 5.95 (*1-56189-379-X*) Amer Educ Pub.

—The Magic Moon Machine. Hohag, Linda & Spoden, Dan, illus. 32p. (gr. 1-3). 1993. pap. text ed. 5.95 (*1-56189-375-7*) Amer Educ Pub.

—One Tricky Monkey up on Top. Hohag, Linda & Jacobson, Lori, illus. 32p. (gr. 1-3). 1993. pap. text ed. 5.95 (*1-56189-376-5*) Amer Educ Pub.

—A Pocketful of Pets. Hohag, Linda & Jacobson, Lori, illus. 32p. (gr. 1-3). 1993. pap. text ed. 5.95 (*1-56189-380-3*) Amer Educ Pub.

—Where Is Baby Bear? Friedman, Joy, illus. 32p. (gr. 1-3). 1993. pap. text ed. 5.95 (*1-56189-381-1*) Amer Educ Pub.

Moncure, Jane B. Word Bird Makes Words with Cat. Hohag, Linda, illus. LC 83-23948. 32p. (gr. k-2). 1984. PLB 14.95 (*0-89565-259-5*) Childs World.

—Word Bird Makes Words with Dog. Gohman, Vera, illus. LC 83-23946. 32p. (gr. k-1). 1984. PLB 14.95 (*0-89565-263-3*) Childs World.

—Word Bird Makes Words with Duck. Hohag, Linda, illus. LC 83-23943. 32p. (gr. k-2). 1984. PLB 14.95 (*0-89565-261-7*) Childs World.

—Word Bird Makes Words with Hen. Hohag, Linda, illus. LC 83-23944. 32p. (gr. k-2). 1984. PLB 14.95 (*0-89565-260-9*) Childs World.

—Word Bird's Fall Words. Miracle, Ric, illus. LC 85-5935. 32p. (gr. k-2). 1985. PLB 14.95 (*0-89565-308-7*) Childs World.

—Word Bird's Hats. Gohman, Vera, illus. LC 81-18065. (ps-2). 1982. PLB 14.95 (*0-89565-221-8*) Childs World.

Most, Bernard. There's an Ant in Anthony. Most, Bernard, illus. LC 79-23089. 32p. (gr. k-3). 1980. PLB 12.88 (*0-688-32226-3*) Morrow Jr Bks.

Muldrow, Diane. Disney's Aladdin: Action Words. (ps). 1994. 3.95 (*0-307-12495-9*, Golden Pr) Western Pub.

Murray, William. Picture Word Cards. (ps-2). 1991. flash cards 9.95 (*0-7214-3232-8*, 9113) Ladybird Bks.

Noll, Sally. Jiggle, Wiggle, Prance. LC 92-25332. 1993. pap. 3.99 (*0-14-054883-1*) Puffin Bks.

O'Rourke, Page E., illus. See & Say: A Book of First Words. 12p. (ps). 1993. bds. 4.95 (*0-448-40540-7*, G&D) Putnam Pub Group.

Outlet Staff. At the Farm. 1991. bds. 3.99 (*0-517-05401-9*) Random Hse Value.

Pesiri, Evelyn & Cheney, Martha. Gifted & Talented Word Book: A Reference Workbook for Ages 6-8. 80p. (gr. 1-3). 1994. pap. 3.95 (*1-56565-182-0*) Lowell Hse Juvenile.

Las Primeras Palabras. LC 92-61168. (SPA.). 28p. (ps-3). 1993. 3.25 (*0-679-84170-9*) Random Bks Yng Read.

Rand, Ann & Rand, Paul. Sparkle & Spin. (Illus.). 32p. 1991. Repr. 16.95 (*0-8109-3822-7*) Abrams.

Ricklen, Neil. First Word Books: Opposites. (ps). 1994. pap. 5.95 (*0-671-86728-8*, Little Simon) S&S Trade.

Ricklen, Neil, illus. My Clothes: Mi Ropa. LC 93-27162. (ENG & SPA.). 14p. (ps-k). 1994. pap. 3.95 (*0-689-71773-3*, Aladdin) Macmillan Child Grp.

—My Colors: Mis Colores. LC 93-27195. (ENG & SPA.). 14p. (ps-k). 1994. pap. 3.95 (*0-689-71772-5*, Aladdin) Macmillan Child Grp.

—My Family: Mi Familia. LC 93-30661. (ENG & SPA.). 14p. (ps-k). 1994. pap. 3.95 (*0-689-71771-7*, Aladdin) Macmillan Child Grp.

—My Numbers: Mis Numeros. LC 93-27165. (ENG & SPA.). 14p. (ps-k). 1994. pap. 3.95 (*0-689-71770-9*, Aladdin) Macmillan Child Grp.

Riddell, Edwina. One Hundred First Words. 32p. (ps). 1992. pap. 4.95 (*0-8120-4888-1*) Barron.

Rockwell, Anne. What We Like. Rockwell, Anne, illus. LC 91-4990. 24p. (ps-1). 1992. RSBE 13.95 (*0-02-777274-8*, Macmillan Child Bk) Macmillan Child Grp.

Root, Betty. Three Hundred First Words. Dann, Geoff, photos by. 156p. (ps). 9.95 (*0-8120-6356-2*) Barron.

—Three Hundred First Words - Palabras Primeras. Dann, Geoff, photos by. (ENG & SPA.). 156p. (ps). 9.95 (*0-8120-6358-9*) Barron.

—Three Hundred First Words - Premiers Mots. Dann, Geoff, photos by. (ENG & FRE.). 156p. (ps). 1993. 9.95 (*0-8120-6357-0*) Barron.

Ryan, Elizabeth. How to Build a Better Vocabulary. LC 91-3136. 112p. (gr. 5-9). 1992. lib. bdg. 9.89 (*0-8167-2460-1*); pap. text ed. 3.95 (*0-8167-2461-X*) Troll Assocs.

Salt, Jane. First Words & Pictures. Hawksley, Gerald, illus. LC 92-53115. 96p. (ps-k). 1992. 9.95 (*1-85697-818-4*, Kingfisher LKC) LKC.

—First Words: For Babies & Toddlers. Hawksley, Gerald, illus. LC 90-8037. 192p. (ps-k). 1991. 9.95 (*0-679-80831-0*) Random Bks Yng Read.

—My Giant Word & Number Book. Pooley, Sarah, illus. LC 92-31508. 1993. 9.95 (*1-85697-861-3*, Kingfisher LKC) LKC.

Sarnoff, Jane. Words: A Book about the Origins of Every Day Words & Phrases. Ruffins, Reynold, illus. LC 81-8943. 64p. (gr. 4-8). 1981. SBE 13.95 (*0-684-16958-4*, Scribners Young Read) Macmillan Child Grp.

Sather, Edgar, et al. People at Work: Listening & Communicative Skills, Vocabulary Building. (Illus.). 112p. (gr. 8 up). 1990. student wkbk. only 14.00x (*0-86647-037-9*) Pro Lingua.

—People at Work: Student's Package. (Illus.). 112p. (gr. 8 up). 1990. incl. wkbk. & 3 cassettes 25.00 (*0-86647-033-6*) Pro Lingua.

Scarry, Huck. Things That Go. (ps-1). 1986. 3.98 (*0-685-16834-4*, 616556) Random Hse Value.

—Things That Sail. (ps-1). 1986. 3.98 (*0-685-16828-X*, 616564) Random Hse Value.

Scarry, Richard. Early Words. Scarry, Richard, illus. LC 75-36466. 14p. (ps-1). 1976. 3.95 (*0-394-83238-8*) Random Bks Yng Read.

—Richard Scarry's Best Little Word Book Ever! (Illus.). 24p. (ps-k). 1992. write for info. (*0-307-00136-9*, 312-01, Golden Pr) Western Pub.

—Richard Scarry's Best Word Book Ever. Scarry, Richard, illus. (ps-3). 1963. write for info. (*0-307-15510-2*, Golden Bks) Western Pub.

—Richard Scarry's Biggest Word Book Ever! Scarry, Richard, illus. 12p. (ps-1). 1985. bds. 29.95 (*0-394-87374-2*) Random Bks Yng Read.

—Richard Scarry's First Words. (Illus.). 24p. (ps-k). 1993. pap. 1.45 (*0-307-11543-7*, 11543, Golden Pr) Western Pub.

—Richard Scarry's Lowly Worm Word Book. Scarry, Richard, illus. LC 80-53103. 28p. (ps). 1981. bds. 3.25 (*0-394-84728-8*) Random Bks Yng Read.

—Richard Scarry's Word Book with Huckle Cat & Lowly Worm. (Illus.). 24p. (ps-3). 1993. pap. 1.95 (*0-307-12767-2*, 12767, Golden Pr) Western Pub.

Schaffer, Frank, Publications Staff. My First Words. (Illus.). 24p. (gr. 1-3). 1978. wkbk. 3.98 (*0-86734-005-3*, FS-3006) Schaffer Pubns.

Schuster, E. H. Words Are Important Series. Incl. Level A (Blue) Bk. (gr. 5) (*0-8437-7985-3*); Level B (Red) Bk. (gr. 6) (*0-8437-7991-8*); Level C (Green) Bk. (gr. 7) (*0-8437-7980-2*); Level D (Orange) Bk. (gr. 8) (*0-8437-7950-0*); Level E (Purple) Bk. (gr. 9) (*0-8437-7955-1*); Level F (Brown) Bk. (gr. 10) (*0-8437-7960-8*); Level G (Pink) Bk. (gr. 11) (*0-8437-7965-9*); Level H (Grey) Bk. (gr. 12) (*0-8437-7970-5*). 1985. pap. 3.98 (*0-685-02045-2*) Hammond Inc.

Schwartz, L. I Love Lists! 264p. (gr. 3-7). 1988. 19.95 (*0-88160-157-8*, LW 275) Learning Wks.

—Preschool Teacher's Pet. 192p. (ps). 1989. 14.95 (*0-88160-185-3*, LW 147) Learning Wks.

Schwartz, Linda. The Usage Sleuth. 24p. (gr. 4-6). 1978. 3.95 (*0-88160-055-5*, LW 603) Learning Wks.

Shaw, Marie-Jose. Jumbo Vocabulary Development Yearbook: Grade 3. 96p. (gr. 3). 1980. 18.00 (*0-8209-0052-4*, JVDY 3) ESP.

Shiffman, Lena, illus. My First Book of Words. 64p. 1992. 10.95 (*0-590-45142-1*, Cartwheel) Scholastic Inc.

Shone, Venice. My Activity Box. Shone, Venice, illus. LC 93-3288. 20p. (ps). 1993. 2.99 (*0-525-67449-7*, Lodestar Bks) Dutton Child Bks.

—My Lunch Box. Shone, Venice, illus. LC 93-3287. 20p. (ps). 1993. 2.99 (*0-525-67451-9*, Lodestar Bks) Dutton Child Bks.

—My Play Box. Shone, Venice, illus. LC 93-3289. 20p. (ps). 1993. 2.99 (*0-525-67448-9*, Lodestar Bks) Dutton Child Bks.

—My Toy Box. Shone, Venice, illus. LC 93-18682. 20p. (ps). 1993. 2.99 (*0-525-67450-0*, Lodestar Bks) Dutton Child Bks.

Shott, Stephen, photos by. Baby's World. LC 90-30587. (Illus.). 48p. (ps). 1990. 13.95 (*0-525-44617-6*, DCB) Dutton Child Bks.

Spot's Big Book of Words. (FRE & ENG.). 32p. (ps-k). 1990. 11.95 (*0-399-21826-2*, Putnam) Putnam Pub Group.

Stanford, Gene. McGraw-Hill Vocabulary, Bk. 3. 2nd ed. (Illus.). 128p. 1981. pap. text ed. 6.80 (*0-07-060773-7*) McGraw.

Steffens, J. & Carr, J. Action & Adventure. (gr. 7-12). 1983. 9.95 (*0-88160-101-2*, LW 1007) Learning Wks.

Stern, Leonard & Price, Roger. Spooky Silly Mad Libs. 48p. (Orig.). (gr. 2 up). 1989. pap. 2.95 incl. chipboard (*0-8431-2758-9*) Price Stern.

Stevenson, Peter, illus. Picture Word Book Three. 28p. (ps). 1991. 3.50 (*0-7214-1436-2*, 916-3) Ladybird Bks.

—Picture Word Book Two. 28p. (ps). 1991. 3.50 (*0-7214-1435-4*, 916-2) Ladybird Bks.

Story Time Stories That Rhyme Staff. Water Habitat Convention: Stories & Word Mapping Activity Workbook. Story Time Stories That Rhyme Staff, illus. 50p. (Orig.). (gr. 4-7). 1992. binder 25.95 (*1-56820-018-8*) Story Time.

Supraner, Robyn. I Can Read About Homonyms. Snyder, Joel, illus. LC 76-54442. (gr. 2-5). 1977. pap. 2.50 (*0-89375-036-0*) Troll Assocs.

—I Can Read About Synonyms & Antonyms. McKeown, Gloria, illus. LC 76-54441. (gr. 2-5). 1977. pap. 2.50 (*0-89375-035-2*) Troll Assocs.

Sweet, Melissa, illus. Hippity-Hop. 18p. (ps). 1992. bds. 2.95 (*0-448-40314-5*) Putnam Pub Group.

Terban, Marvin. Superdupers: Really Funny Real Words. Maestro, Giulio, illus. LC 88-38325. 63p. (gr. 4-8). 1989. 13.45 (*0-89919-804-X*, Clarion Bks); pap. 4.80 (*0-395-51123-2*, Clarion Bks) HM.

University of Mexico City Staff, tr. Opuestos: Mentes Activas. Siede, George & Preis, Donna, photos by. Schwager, Istar, contrib. by. (SPA., Illus.). 24p. (ps-8). 1992. PLB 11.95 (*1-56674-040-1*) Forest Hse.

Vacations, Parties, People, & Places. 24p. (ps-1). 1989. 5.98 (*0-517-68229-X*) Random Hse Value.

Vaughn, Jim. Jumbo Vocabulary Development Yearbook: Grade 7. 96p. (gr. 7-9). 1981. 18.00 (*0-8209-0056-7*, JVDY J) ESP.

Weiler, Susan K. Mini-Myths & Maxi-Words. 1986. pap. text ed. 9.99 (*0-88334-191-3*, 76156) Longman.

Welsh, Patricia A. It's My Dictionary. Welsh, Patricia A., illus. 52p. (gr. 1-2). 1978. Repr. of 1978 ed. Wkbk. 4.95 (*1-884620-00-0*) PAW Prods.
In IT'S MY DICTIONARY children ages 5-7 will experience basic dictionary skills while completing a variety of activities. This workbook has been designed to make the dictionary an enjoyable & creative resource for language development. Included in IT'S MY DICTIONARY are one hundred eighty-six words. Activities for each word include one or all of the following: dot-to-dot with letters or numbers, tracing & sentences with missing words. Directions are given for the formation of letters & areas are provided for practice. IT'S MY DICTIONARY has been used successfully in San Francisco & Bay Area schools with individuals, small groups & with entire classrooms. It has been used in regular, bilingual & special education classes. To order IT'S MY DICTIONARY, & other books written & illustrated by the author, please contact Patricia Welsh at PAW Productions, P.O. Box 31603, San Francisco, CA 94131.
Publisher Provided Annotation.

Wilkes, Angela. My First Word Book. LC 91-60897. (Illus.). 64p. (ps-3). 1991. 12.95 (*1-879431-21-1*); PLB 13.99 (*1-879431-36-X*) Dorling Kindersley.

Williams, Joanna, illus. Picture Word Book Four. 28p. (ps). 1991. 3.50 (*0-7214-1437-0*, 916-4) Ladybird Bks.

—Picture Word Book One. 28p. (ps). 1991. 3.50 (*0-7214-1434-6*, 916-1) Ladybird Bks.

Wirths. Your Power with Words. 1993. write for info. (*0-8050-3150-2*) H Holt & Co.

Wise, Beth A. My First Words. McDonough, Chris, illus. 32p. (ps). 1992. wkbk. 1.95 (*1-56293-176-8*) McClanahan Bk.

World Book Editors. The World Book of Word Power, 2 vols. LC 90-72119. (Illus.). 726p. 1991. Set. write for info. (*0-7166-3238-1*) Vol. 1: Language. Vol. 2: Writing & Speaking. World Bk.

World Book Staff, ed. Childcraft Supplement, 5 vols. LC 91-65174. (Illus.). (gr. 2-6). 1991. Set. write for info. (*0-7166-0666-6*) Prehistoric Animals, 304p. About Dogs, 304p. The Magic of Words, 304p. The Indian Book, 304p. The Puzzle Book, 304p. World Bk.

Zachman, Linda, et al. ACHIEV-Red (Activities for Children Involving Everyday Vocabulary) Package. (ps-5). 1989. commplete pkg. 198.70 (*1-55999-001-5*) LinguiSystems.

—ACHIEV-Red Books (Activities for Children Involving Everyday Vocabulary) (ps-5). 1985. spiral manuals 49. 95 (*1-55999-005-8*) LinguiSystems.

Zolotow, Charlotte. Say It! ALC Staff, ed. Stevenson, James, illus. LC 79-25115. 24p. (ps up). 1992. pap. 4.95 (*0-688-11711-2*, Mulberry) Morrow.

VOCAL CULTURE
see Voice

VOCATION, CHOICE OF
see Vocational Guidance

VOCATIONAL GUIDANCE
For general works only. Works on guidance in a specific vocation are entered under such headings as Law–Vocational Guidance.
see also Blind–Education; Counseling; Deaf–Education; Occupations; Professions

Aaseng, Nathan. Midstream Changes: People Who Started over & Made It Work. (Illus.). 80p. (gr. 5 up). 1990. PLB 18.95 (*0-8225-0681-5*) Lerner Pubns.

Abrams, Kathleen S. Guide to Careers Without College. LC 88-5723. (Illus.). 112p. (gr. 7-12). 1988. PLB 13.40 (*0-531-10585-7*) Watts.

Akinsheye, Dexter & Akinsheye, Dayo. I Want to Be... Akiwsheye, Dexter, illus. 56p. (gr. k-4). 1992. pap. 12. 00 (*1-877835-47-1*); pap. text ed. 5.00 (*1-877835-48-X*) TD Pub.

Alexander, Sue. Finding Your First Job. LC 79-26487. (Illus.). (gr. 9 up). 1980. (DCB); (DCB) Dutton Child Bks.

Allman, Paul. Exploring Careers in Video. rev. ed. Rosen, Ruth, ed. (gr. 7-12). 1989. PLB 14.95 (*0-8239-1018-0*) Rosen Group.

Aurich, Charles. How Do I Decide? The Young Adult's Guide to Career Planning. LC 94-92034. (Illus.). 165p. (Orig.). (gr. 7-12). 1994. pap. write for info. (*0-9640083-8-6*) Natl Career.

Barkin, Carol & James, Elizabeth. Jobs for Kids. Doty, Roy, illus. LC 89-45900. 128p. (gr. 5 up). 1991. pap. 6.95 (*0-688-09323-X*, Pub. by Beech Tree Bks) Morrow.

Beckman, Beatrice. Puedo Ser Maestra: (I Can Be a Teacher) LC 84-23236. (SPA.). 32p. (gr. k-3). 1989. PLB 11.80 (*0-516-31843-8*); pap. 3.95 (*0-516-51843-7*) Childrens.

Behrens, June. Puedo Ser Enfermera (I Can Be a Nurse) LC 85-29086. (SPA., Illus.). 32p. (ps-2). 1988. PLB 11.80 (*0-516-31893-4*); pap. 3.95 (*0-516-51893-3*) Childrens.

Bingham, Mindy & Stryker, Sandy. Career Choices: A Guide for Teens & Young Adults: Who Am I? What Do I Want? How Do I Get It? Shafer, Robert, ed. Maeno, Itoko, et al, illus. LC 90-81785. 288p. (Orig.). (gr. 9 up). 1990. pap. 19.95 (*1-878787-02-0*) Acad Innovat.

Bissonnette-Lamendella, Denise. Pathways: A Job Search Curriculum. 275p. (Orig.). 1987. student wkbk. 7.95 (*0-942071-05-0*) M Wright & Assocs.

—Pathways: A Job Search Curriculum. rev. ed. 265p. 1987. Repr. of 1986 ed. tchr's. ed. 87.95 (*0-942071-02-6*) M Wright & Assocs.

Blumenthal, Howard J. You Can Do It! Careers in Baseball. LC 92-9542. 1993. 16.95 (*0-316-10095-1*) Little.

Bonner, Staci. Sports: Careers in Sports. LC 93-9887. (Illus.). 48p. (gr. 5-6). 1994. text ed. 14.95 RSBE (*0-89686-789-7*, Crestwood Hse) Macmillan Child Grp.

Brownley, Margaret. A Youths' Guide to Job Hunting. 28p. (Orig.). (gr. 8-12). 1988. pap. 3.95 (*0-945485-02-6*) Comm Intervention.

Cannastra, Lyn & Raynor, Tom, eds. Career Sourcebook I: A Guide to Career Planning & Job Hunting. 2nd, rev. ed. (Illus.). 184p. (gr. 9-12). 1988. pap. text ed. 10.00 (*0-931032-25-3*) Edison Electric.

Careers: A Beginning. 1988. Repr. of 1981 ed. 3.50 (*1-55646-732-X*, 019972, Career Aids); Set of 10 wkbks. 35.00 (*1-55646-733-8*, 019977, Career Aids) Opportunities Learn.

Christophersen, Susan & Farr, J. Michael. Career Preparation: Getting the Most from Training & Education. Croy, Greg, ed. Kreffel, Mike, illus. 64p. (gr. 9-12). 1990. pap. 6.95 (*0-942784-59-6*, CP) JIST Works.

—Your Career: Thinking about Jobs & Careers. Croy, Greg, ed. Kreffel, Mike, illus. 64p. (gr. 9-12). 1990. pap. 5.95 (*0-942784-60-X*, YC) JIST Works.

Como, Jay. Career Choice & Job Search. 96p. (Orig.). (gr. 9-12). 1986. wkbk. 5.95 (*0-936007-01-X*, 3070); instr's. guide 3.95 (*0-936007-02-8*, 3070) Meridian Educ.

Corbin, William G. & Corbin, Kim. Getting, Keeping, & Growing in a Job in the '90s. 130p. (gr. 10-12). 1994. pap. 9.95 (*0-9634373-1-3*) Beckett-Highland.

Crisfield, Deborah. Travel: Careers in Travel. LC 93-15211. (Illus.). 48p. (gr. 5-6). 1994. text ed. 14.95 RSBE (*0-89686-790-0*, Crestwood Hse) Macmillan Child Grp.

Curless, Maura R. Careers Without College: Kids. Hupping, Carol & Grimaldi, Alicia, eds. LC 93-7078. 96p. (Orig.). 1993. pap. 7.95 (*1-56079-251-5*) Petersons Guides.

Direct, R. F. Art Distribution Manual. (gr. 10). 1989. pap. write for info. (*0-945661-03-7*) PASE Pubns.

—Brochure Distribution Manual. rev. ed. (gr. 12). 1989. pap. text ed. 45.00 (*0-945661-14-2*) PASE Pubns.

—Handwriting Analysis for Pay. rev. ed. (gr. 12). 1989. pap. text ed. 45.00 (*0-945661-13-4*) PASE Pubns.

—Mailing Letters for Pay. rev. ed. (gr. 12). 1989. pap. text ed. 45.00 (*0-945661-12-6*) PASE Pubns.

Dogin, Yvette. Teen-Agers at Work. 64p. (gr. 8 up). 1988. pap. text ed. 3.75 (*0-88323-244-8*, 164); tchr's. key 1.25 (*0-318-33412-7*, 277) Pendergrass Pub.

Dunnan, Nancy. Entrepreneurship. (Illus.). 128p. (gr. 7-10). 1990. lib. bdg. 9.95 (*0-382-09916-8*); pap. 5.95 (*0-382-24027-8*) Silver Burdett Pr.

—Inside Track Library, 4 bks. (Illus.). (gr. 7-10). 1990. Set. lib. bdg. 39.80 (*0-382-09913-3*); pap. 23.80 (*0-382-24024-3*) Silver Burdett Pr.

Edwards, E. W. Exploring Careers Using Foreign Languages. rev. ed. Rosen, Ruth, ed. (gr. 7-12). 1990. PLB 14.95 (*0-8239-0968-9*) Rosen Group.

Farr, J. Michael & Christophersen, Susan. The Skills Advantage: Identify Your Skills for School, Work, & Life. Adams, Sara, ed. (Illus.). 64p. (gr. 6 up). 1993. pap. 5.95 wkbk. (*1-56370-093-X*, SKAD) JIST Works.

Farr, J. Michael & Pavlicko, Marie. The JIST Job Search Course: A Young Person's Guide to Getting & Keeping a Good Job. Croy, Greg, ed. Kreffel, Mike, et al, illus. (gr. 7-12). 1990. pap. 7.95 121p.. (*0-942784-34-0*, YP); data minder, 22p. 1.00 (*0-942784-35-9*, DM) JIST Works.

—The JIST Job Search Course: A Young Person's Guide to Getting & Keeping a Good Job. Croy, Greg, ed. Kreffel, Mike, et al, illus. 138p. (gr. 7-12). 1990. pap. 12.95 instr's. guide (*0-942784-36-7*, YPTM) JIST Works.

Feingold, S. Norman & Feingold, Marilyn N. The Complete Job & Career Handbook: One Hundred One Ways to Get from Here to There. LC 92-39716. (Illus.). 179p. (Orig.). (gr. 9 up). 1993. pap. 15.00 (*1-880774-01-1*) Garrett Pk.

Field, Shelly. Careers As an Animal Rights Activist. Rosen, Ruth, ed. (gr. 7-12). 1993. PLB 14.95 (*0-8239-1465-8*); pap. 9.95 (*0-8239-1722-3*) Rosen Group.

Frydenborg, Kay. They Dreamed of Horses: Careers for Horse Lovers. Wood, Tanya, photos by. LC 93-33023. (Illus.). 128p. (gr. 4-6). 1994. 15.95 (*0-8027-8283-3*); PLB 16.85 (*0-8027-8284-1*) Walker & Co.

Gartner, Bob. Exploring Careers in the National Park Service. Rosen, Ruth, ed. (gr. 7-12). 1993. 14.95 (*0-8239-1414-3*); pap. 9.95 (*0-8239-1726-6*) Rosen Group.

Gilabert, Frank. Business Career Planning Series, 5 bks. (Orig.). (gr. 12). Date not set. Set. pap. 55.00 (*1-884194-05-2*); The Biz Careers Finance Guide: How to Improve Your Business Knowledge about Finance, 100p. pap. 14.95 (*1-884194-02-8*); The Biz Careers Accounting Guide: How to Improve Your Business Knowledge about Accounting, 100p. pap. 14. 95 (*1-884194-01-X*); The Biz Careers Planning Guide: How to Prepare for Your Business Career, 70p. pap. 9.95 (*1-884194-00-1*); The Business Careers Information Systems Guide: How to Improve Your Business Knowledge about Information Systems, 100p. pap. 14.95 (*1-884194-03-6*); The Biz Careers Marketing Guide: How to Improve Your Business Knowledge about Marketing, 100p. pap. 14.95 (*1-884194-04-4*) Biz Careers.

Gourley, Pamela R., ed. Careers to Think About: A Young Person's Guide to Future Job Opportunities. (Illus.). 315p. (Orig.). (gr. 5-9). 1987. PLB 12.95 (*0-943621-21-6*) TechWest Pubns.

Grant, Lesley. Great Careers for People Concerned About the Environment, 6 vols. LC 93-78077. (Illus.). 48p. (gr. 6-9). 1993. 16.95 (*0-8103-9388-3*, 102106, UXL) Gale.

Hamilton, John. ECO-Careers: A Guide to Jobs in the Environental Field. LC 93-7601. 1993. 14.96 (*1-56239-209-3*) Abdo & Dghtrs.

Handville, Elizabeth, ed. OCCU-FACTS: Facts on over 565 Occupations. 624p. (Orig.). (gr. 6 up). 1989. pap. text ed. 38.00 (*0-9623657-0-X*) Careers Inc.

Hechler, Ellen. Simulated Real Life Experiences Using Classified Ads in the Classroom. (Illus.). 54p. (Orig.). (gr. 6-10). 1991. pap. 10.00 (*0-9638483-3-X*) Midmath.

Heron, Jackie. Careers in Health & Fitness. rev. ed. Rosen, Ruth, ed. (Illus.). 160p. (gr. 7 up). 1990. 14.95 (*0-8239-1162-4*) Rosen Group.

Herriott, Joy A. & Herrin, Betty G. Summer Opportunities in Marine & Environmental Science: A Students' Guide to Jobs, Internships & Study, Camp, & Travel Programs. 2nd ed. LC 94-96000. (Illus.). 60p. (gr. 9-12). 1994. pap. 14.95 (*0-9640176-0-1*) White Pond.

Higginson, Mel. Scientists Who Study Fossils. LC 94-6995. 1994. write for info. (*0-86593-375-8*) Rourke Corp.

—Scientists Who Study Ocean Life. LC 94-6999. 1994. write for info. (*0-86593-371-5*) Rourke Corp.

—Scientists Who Study Plants. LC 94-6998. 1994. write for info. (*0-86593-373-1*) Rourke Corp.

—Scientists Who Study the Earth. LC 94-7000. (gr. 4 up). 1994. write for info. (*0-86593-372-3*) Rourke Corp.

—Scientists Who Study Wild Animals. LC 94-6997. 1994. write for info. (*0-86593-374-X*) Rourke Corp.

Hole, Dorothy. The Air Force & You. LC 92-9774. (Illus.). 48p. (gr. 5-6). 1993. text ed. 12.95 RSBE (*0-89686-764-1*, Crestwood Hse) Macmillan Child Grp.

—The Army & You. LC 92-2214. (Illus.). 48p. (gr. 5-6). 1993. text ed. 12.95 RSBE (*0-89686-765-X*, Crestwood Hse) Macmillan Child Grp.

—The Coast Guard & You. LC 92-9775. (Illus.). 48p. (gr. 5-6). 1993. text ed. 12.95 RSBE (*0-89686-766-8*, Crestwood Hse) Macmillan Child Grp.

—The Marines & You. LC 92-9771. (Illus.). 48p. (gr. 5-6). 1993. text ed. 12.95 RSBE (*0-89686-768-4*, Crestwood Hse) Macmillan Child Grp.

Hopkins, Del & Hopkins, Margaret. Careers As a Rock Musician. Rosen, Ruth, ed. (gr. 7-12). 1993. PLB 14.95 (*0-8239-1518-2*); pap. 9.95 (*0-8239-1725-8*) Rosen Group.

How to Get a Job Study Aid. 1975. pap. 1.50 (*0-87738-049-X*) Youth Ed.

How to Write a Book Report Study Aid. 1975. pap. 1.95 (*0-87738-031-7*) Youth Ed.

Jill, Jodi. Childrens Money Making Jobs. 32p. 1993. pap. 6.95 (*1-883438-04-7*) J J Features.

Kaplan, Andrew. Careers for Outdoor Types. (Illus.). 64p. (gr. 7 up). 1991. PLB 14.40 (*1-56294-022-8*); pap. 4.95 (*1-56294-770-2*) Millbrook Pr.

—Careers for Outdoor Types. 1992. pap. 4.95 (*0-395-63561-6*) HM.

—Careers for Sports Fans. (Illus.). 64p. (gr. 7 up). 1991. PLB 14.40 (*1-56294-023-6*); pap. 4.95 (*1-56294-773-7*) Millbrook Pr.

—Careers for Sports Fans. 1992. pap. 4.95 (*0-395-63562-4*) HM.

Kennedy, Don. Exploring Careers on Cruise Ships. LC 93-20293. (gr. 7 up). 1993. 14.95 (*0-8239-1665-0*); 9.95 (*0-8239-1714-2*) Rosen Group.

Lee, Mary P. & Lee, Richard S. Careers in Firefighting. Rosen, Ruth, ed. (gr. 7-12). 1993. PLB 14.95 (*0-8239-1515-8*); pap. 9.95 (*0-8239-1724-X*) Rosen Group.

Lindsay, Norene. Pathfinder - Exploring Career & Educational Paths: Career & Educational Planning for Junior High & High School Students. Adams, Sara, ed. (Illus.). 112p. (gr. 8-12). 1993. pap. 4.95 wkbk. (*1-56370-120-0*, PFP) JIST Works.

Lock, Robert D. Student Activities for Taking Charge of Your Career Direction & Job Search: Career Planning Guide, Bk. 3. 2nd ed. 136p. 1992. pap. 14.95 (*0-534-13659-1*) Brooks-Cole.

Longshoe, Shirley. Careers without College: Office. 96p. (Orig.). 1994. pap. 7.95 (*1-56079-353-8*) Petersons Guides.

Los Angeles Unified School District Staff. Getting a Job. (Illus.). 48p. (Orig.). (gr. 7-12). 1990. Set. 10 wkbks. & tchr's. guide 44.95 (*1-56119-095-0*); wkbk. 4.95 (*1-56119-093-4*); tchr's. guide 1.95 (*1-56119-094-2*) Educ Pr MD.

—Starting Your New Job. (Illus.). 48p. (Orig.). (gr. 7-12). 1990. Set. 10 wkbks. & tchr's. guide 44.95 (*1-56119-098-5*); wkbk. 4.95 (*1-56119-096-9*); tchr's. guide 1.95 (*1-56119-097-7*) Educ Pr MD.

Lytle, Elizabeth S. Careers As an Electrician. LC 93-12776. 1993. 14.95 (*0-8239-1513-1*) Rosen Group.

McCombs, Barbara L. & Brannan, Linda. Help, Please! (Illus.). 32p. (Orig.). (gr. 7-12). 1990. Set. 10 wkbks. & tchr's. guide 44.95 (*1-56119-077-2*); tchr's. guide 1.95 (*1-56119-038-1*); software 39.95 (*1-56119-119-1*) Educ Pr MD.

—How Does It Work? (Illus.). 32p. (Orig.). (gr. 7-12). 1990. Set. 10 wkbks. & tchr's. guide 44.95 (*1-56119-075-6*); tchr's. guide 1.95 (*1-56119-034-9*); software 39.95 (*1-56119-117-5*) Educ Pr MD.

—How Should I Do It? (Illus.). 32p. (Orig.). (gr. 7-12). 1990. Set. 10 wkbks. & tchr's. guide 44.95 (*1-56119-069-1*); tchr's. guide 1.95 (*1-56119-022-5*); software 39.95 (*1-56119-111-6*) Educ Pr MD.

—Keep Calm! (Illus.). 32p. (Orig.). (gr. 7-12). 1990. Set. 10 wkbks. & tchr's. guide 44.95 (*1-56119-070-5*); tchr's. guide 1.95 (*1-56119-024-1*); software 39.95 (*1-56119-112-4*) Educ Pr MD.

—Late Work. (Illus.). 32p. (Orig.). (gr. 7-12). 1990. Set. 10 wkbks. & tchr's. guide 44.95 (*1-56119-065-9*); tchr's. guide 1.95 (*1-56119-014-4*); software 39.95 (*1-56119-107-8*) Educ Pr MD.

—Leaving Early. (Illus.). 32p. (Orig.). (gr. 7-12). 1990. Set. 10 wkbks. & tchr's. guide 44.95 (*1-56119-078-0*); tchr's. guide 1.95 (*1-56119-040-3*); software 39.95 (*1-56119-120-5*) Educ Pr MD.

—May I Try It? (Illus.). 32p. (Orig.). (gr. 7-12). 1990. Set. 10 wkbks. & tchr's. guide 44.95 (*1-56119-085-3*); tchr's. guide 1.95 (*1-56119-054-3*); software 39.95 (*1-56119-127-2*) Educ Pr MD.

McFarland, Rhoda. The World of Work. Rosen, Ruth, ed. (gr. 7-12). 1993. 13.95 (*0-8239-1467-4*) Rosen Group.

Marshall, Mary A. Music: Careers in Music. LC 93-14832. (Illus.). 48p. (gr. 5-6). 1994. text ed. 14.95 RSBE (*0-89686-793-5*, Crestwood Hse) Macmillan Child Grp.

Martin, Phyllis. Job-Hunt Success Plan, High School Edition. rev. & abr. ed. Savage, Kent V., contrib. by. (Illus.). 118p. (gr. 11-12). 1989. pap. text ed. 8.50 (*0-685-31060-4*) Ctr Career Dev.

Menzel-Gerrie, Sharon. Careers in Comedy. LC 93-4962. 1993. 14.95 (*0-8239-1517-4*); pap. 9.95 (*0-8239-1713-4*) Rosen Group.

Menzies, Linda, et al. A Teen's Guide to Business: The Secrets to a Successful Enterprise. large type ed. LC 93-30254. (gr. 9-12). 1993. 15.95 (*0-7862-0061-8*) Thorndike Pr.

Miller, Louise. Career Portraits. LC 93-49056. 1995. 13.95 (*0-8442-4359-0*, VGM Career Bks) NTC Pub Grp.

Miller, Maryann. Your Best Foot Forward: Winning Strategies for the Job Interview. LC 93-44347. 1994. 13.95 (*0-8239-1697-9*) Rosen Group.

Moffett, Carol G. & Strydesky, Rebecca. The Receiving-Checking-Marking-Stocking Clerk. 2nd ed. (Illus.). 160p. (gr. 10-12). 1979. text ed. 13.32 (*0-07-042667-8*) McGraw.

Neufld, Rose. Exploring Nontraditional Jobs for Women. rev. ed. Rosen, Ruth, ed. (gr. 7-12). 1989. PLB 14.95 (*0-8239-0971-9*) Rosen Group.

Ourth, John & Tamarri, Kathie T. Career Caravan. 64p. (gr. 4-8). 1979. 7.95 (*0-916456-52-8*, GA121) Good Apple.

Parker, Julie F. Careers for Women As Clergy. Rosen, Ruth, ed. (gr. 7-12). 1993. PLB 14.95 (*0-8239-1424-0*); pap. 9.95 (*0-8239-1727-4*) Rosen Group.

Parramore, Barbara & Hopke, William E. Career Exploration Activities Booklet: 25 Activities to Help Explore Occupations. 48p. (Orig.). (gr. 6 up). 1989. pap. text ed. 17.75 pkg. of 10 (*0-685-31414-6*) Careers Inc.

Peissel, Michel & Allen, Missy. Dangerous Professions. (Illus.). 112p. (gr. 5 up). 1993. PLB 19.95 (*0-7910-1792-3*, Am Art Analog) Chelsea Hse.

Peterson, Linda. Careers Without College: Emergencies. Hupping, Carol & Grimaldi, Alicia, eds. LC 93-7077. 96p. 1993. pap. 7.95 (*1-56079-252-3*) Petersons Guides.

—Careers without College: Entertainment. (Orig.). 1994. pap. 7.95 (*1-56079-352-X*) Petersons Guides.

Ressler, Ralph. A World of Choice: Careers & You - Student Workbook. LC 77-4182. (Illus.). (gr. 9-12). 1978. pap. 14.95 (*0-88280-050-7*); tchr's. guide 19.95 (*0-88280-051-5*) ETC Pubns.

Rice, Wayne, ed. Ideas Combo Edition 33-36, 4 bks. in 1. (Illus.). 192p. (Orig.). 1988. pap. 19.95 (*0-910125-33-3*) Youth Special.

—One Hundred Ten Tips, Time-Savers & Tricks of the Trade for Youth Workers. Pagaard, Tim, illus. (Illus.). 72p. (Orig.). 1984. pap. 5.95 (*0-910125-04-X*) Youth Special.

Rice, Wayne & McLaughlin, Tim, eds. Ideas Combo Edition 41-44, 4 bks. in 1. Suggs, Robert, illus. 200p. (Orig.). 1988. pap. 19.95 (*0-910125-35-X*) Youth Special.

—Ideas Combo Edition 45-48, 4 bks. in 1. (Illus.). 208p. (Orig.). 1992. pap. 19.95 (*0-910125-36-8*) Youth Special.

—Ideas Combo Edition 49-52, 4 bks. in 1. (Illus.). 192p. (Orig.). 1992. pap. 19.95 (*0-910125-37-6*) Youth Special.

Rice, Wayne & Thigpen, Paul, eds. Ideas Combo Edition 37-40, 4 bks. in 1. Hillam, Corbin, illus. 200p. (Orig.). 1990. pap. 19.95 (*0-910125-34-1*) Youth Special.

Rice, Wayne & Yaconelli, Mike, eds. Ideas Combo Edition 1-4, 4 bks. in 1. (Illus.). 192p. (Orig.). 1979. pap. 19.95 (*0-910125-25-2*) Youth Special.

—Ideas Combo Edition 13-16, 4 bks. in 1. (Illus.). 208p. (Orig.). 1981. pap. 19.95 (*0-910125-28-7*) Youth Special.

—Ideas Combo Edition 17-20, 4 bks. in 1. (Illus.). 206p. (Orig.). 1981. pap. 19.95 (*0-910125-29-5*) Youth Special.

—Ideas Combo Edition 21-24, 4 bks. in 1. (Illus.). 200p. (Orig.). 1984. pap. 19.95 (*0-910125-30-9*) Youth Special.

—Ideas Combo Edition 25-28, 4 bks. in 1. (Illus.). 208p. (Orig.). 1985. pap. 19.95 (*0-910125-31-7*) Youth Special.

—Ideas Combo Edition 29-32, 4 bks. in 1. (Illus.). 200p. (Orig.). 1987. pap. 19.95 (*0-910125-32-5*) Youth Special.

—Ideas Combo Edition 5-8, 4 bks. in 1. (Illus.). 176p. (Orig.). 1984. pap. 19.95 (*0-910125-26-0*) Youth Special.

—Ideas Combo Edition 9-12, 4 bks. in 1. Pegoda, Dan & Wilson, Craig, illus. 180p. (Orig.). 1980. pap. 19.95 (*0-910125-27-9*) Youth Special.

Richardson, Allen F. Careers Without College: Sports. Colton, Kitty, ed. Schmidt, Peggy, contrib. by. LC 93-4488. 96p. (gr. 10-12). 1993. pap. 7.95 (*1-56079-250-7*) Petersons Guides.

Richardson, Peter & Richardson, Bob. Great Careers for People Interested in How Things Work, 6 vols. LC 93-78076. (Illus.). 48p. (gr. 6-9). 1993. 16.95 (*0-8103-9389-1*, 102107, UXL) Gale.

Rigby, Julie. Career Portraits: Sports. LC 94-15315. 1994. 12.95 (*0-8442-4361-2*, VGM Career Bks) NTC Pub Grp.

Rowan, Jim. I Can Be a Zoo Keeper. LC 85-11327. 32p. (gr. k-3). 1985. pap. 3.95 (*0-516-41889-0*) Childrens.

Russell, William. Farmers. LC 93-42481. 1994. write for info. (*1-57103-057-3*) Rourke Pr.

—Fishermen. LC 93-42483. 1994. write for info. Rourke Pr.

—Truckers. LC 93-42484. 1994. write for info. (*1-57103-058-1*) Rourke Pr.

—Zookeepers. LC 93-42482. 1994. write for info. (*1-57103-055-7*) Rourke Pr.

Ryan, Joseph. U. S. Employment Opportunities. 300p. (gr. 12). looseleaf (includes quarterly updates) 184.00 (*0-937801-01-1*) Wash Res Assocs.

Sahlin, Judith. Alphabet Careers: A Career Awareness Program for Grades Two Through Four. 16p. 1994. 10.95 (*1-884063-15-2*) Mar Co Prods.

Schauer, Donald D. Careers in Trucking. rev. ed. Rosen, R., ed. (Illus.). 144p. (gr. 7-12). 1991. PLB 14.95 (*0-8239-1348-1*) Rosen Group.

Serrian, Michael. Now Hiring: Film. LC 93-2018. 1994. text ed. 14.95 (*0-89686-784-6*, Crestwood Hse) Macmillan Child Grp.

Shafe, James C. & Strickland, A. G. Career Direction: Facilitator's Guide. (Illus.). 100p. (gr. 11 up). 1987. tchr's. manual 25.00 (*0-685-26165-4*) Sales & Mgmt Trg.

Shorto, Russell. Careers for Hands-on Types. LC 91-47146. (Illus.). 64p. (gr. 7 up). 1992. PLB 14.40 (*1-56294-065-1*) Millbrook Pr.

—Careers for People Who Like People. LC 91-27662. (Illus.). 64p. (gr. 7 up). 1992. PLB 14.40 (*1-56294-157-7*); pap. 4.95 (*1-56294-771-0*) Millbrook Pr.

—Careers for People Who Like People. 1992. pap. 4.95 (*0-395-63573-X*) HM.

—Careers for the Curious. LC 91-47145. (Illus.). 64p. (gr. 7 up). 1992. PLB 14.40 (*1-56294-064-3*) Millbrook Pr.

Simpson, Carolyn. Careers Inside the World of Offices. LC 94-16189. 1994. write for info. (*0-8239-1897-1*) Rosen Group.

Swanson, Steve. Is There Life after High School? Making Decisions about Your Future. LC 90-15499. 112p. (Orig.). (gr. 9 up). 1991. pap. 5.99 (*0-8066-2500-7*, 9-2500, Augsburg) Augsburg Fortress.

Tomchek, Ann. Puedo Ser Cocinero: (I Can Be a Chef) LC 85-11016. (SPA., Illus.). 32p. (gr. k-3). 1988. PLB 11.80 (*0-516-31886-1*); pap. 3.95 (*0-516-51886-0*) Childrens.

Turner, Peggy & Brewer, Linda S. ABC Career Book for Girls: Introducing the Career Pals. Hollis, Myrlys, ed. Turner, Peggy, illus. Lincoln, Rebecca, intro. by. (Illus.). 32p. (gr. 1-4). 1992. pap. 6.95 (*0-9622514-2-9*) Columbia San Fran.

Unger, Harlow G. But What If I Don't Want to Go to College? A Guide to Successful Careers Through Alternative Education. 176p. 1992. lib. bdg. 19.95x (*0-8160-2534-7*) Facts on File.

U. S. Department of Labor Staff. Exploring Careers: A Young Person's Guide. rev. ed. Farr, J. Michael, ed. LC 89-19881. (Illus.). 462p. (gr. 6-12). 1989. pap. 19.95 (*0-942784-27-8*, EXP) JIST Works.

Wilkes, Donald L. & Hamilton-Wilkes, Viola. Teen Guide Job Search: Ten Easy Steps to Your Future. Carter, Carl, illus. 112p. (gr. 10-12). 1991. pap. 10.95 (*0-9628787-1-5*) Jem Job Educ.

Write into a Job. (gr. 9 up). 1989. 7.95 (*0-936007-28-1*, 3315) Meridian Educ.

Zink, Richard M. Diplomas or Degrees: Fast, Legal, Inexpensive. 5th, rev. ed. (Illus.). 50p. (gr. 9 up). 1994. pap. 14.95x (*0-939469-40-5*) Zinks Career Guide.

VOCATIONAL STORIES

Furman, Abraham L., ed. Everygirls Career Stories. (Illus.). (gr. 6-10). PLB 7.19 (*0-8313-0049-3*) Lantern.

VOCATIONS

see Professions

VOICE

see also Phonetics; Public Speaking; Speech; Ventriloquism

Allington, Richard L. Talking. Thrun, Rick, illus. Krull, Kathleen. LC 80-17021. (Illus.). 32p. (ps-2). 1985. pap. 3.95 (*0-8114-8234-0*) Raintree Steck-V.

Parker, Steve. Singing a Song: How You Sing, Speak & Make Sounds. Kline, Marjory, ed. LC 91-17018. (Illus.). 32p. (gr. k-4). 1992. PLB 11.40 (*0-531-14212-4*) Watts.

Wilbur, Richard. Loudmouse. D'Andrade, Diane, ed. Almquist, Don, illus. 32p. (gr. 1-5). 1991. 12.95 (*0-15-249494-4*) HarBrace.

VOICE CULTURE

see Voice

VOLCANOES

Asimov, Isaac. How Did We Find Out about Volcanoes? Wool, David, illus. 64p. (gr. 4-7). 1981. PLB 12.85 (*0-8027-6412-6*) Walker & Co.

—How did We Find Out about Volcanoes? 64p. (gr. 2-7). 1982. pap. 1.95 (*0-380-59626-1*, 59626-1, Camelot) Avon.

Ask about Volcanoes. 64p. (gr. 4-5). 1987. PLB 11.95 (*0-8172-2878-0*) Raintree Steck-V.

Barrett, Norman S. Volcanes. LC 90-70893. (SPA., Illus.). 32p. (gr. k-4). 1990. PLB 11.90 (*0-531-07911-2*) Watts.

—Volcanoes. (Illus.). 32p. (gr. 2 up). 1991. pap. 4.95 (*0-531-24618-3*) Watts.

Bolt, Bruce A. Discover Volcanoes & Earthquakes. (Illus.). 48p. (gr. 3-6). 1992. PLB 14.95 (*1-56674-031-2*, HTS Bks) Forest Hse.

Booth, Basil. Earthquakes & Volcanoes. LC 91-44878. (Illus.). 48p. (gr. 4-6). 1992. text ed. 13.95 RSBE (*0-02-711735-9*, New Discovery) Macmillan Child Grp.

—Volcanoes & Earthquakes. (Illus.). 48p. (gr. 5-8). 1991. PLB 12.95 (*0-382-24227-0*) Silver Burdett Pr.

Borgardt, Marianne. Volcanoes & Earthquakes in Action: An Early Reader Pop-up Book. Harris, Greg, illus. 16p. (Orig.). (ps-3). 1993. pap. 8.95 (*0-689-71720-2*, Aladdin) Macmillan Child Grp.

Branley, Franklyn M. Volcanoes. Simont, Marc, illus. LC 84-45344. 32p. (ps-3). 1985. (Crowell Jr Bks); PLB 13. 89 (*0-690-04431-3*) HarpC Child Bks.

—Volcanoes. Simont, Marc, illus. LC 84-45344. 32p. (ps-3). 1986. pap. 4.95 (*0-06-445059-7*, Trophy) HarpC Child Bks.

Calderazzo, John. One Hundred One Questions: Volcanoes. Jorgen, Randolph, ed. LC 93-84875. (Illus.). 32p. (Orig.). Date not set. pap. write for info. (*1-877856-33-9*) SW Pks Mnmts.

Carson, Rob. The Living Mountain: Mount St. Helens. Hoffmann, Duane, illus. 84p. (Orig.). (gr. k-8). 1992. pap. 10.95 (*0-9623072-9-7*) S Ink WA.

Challand, Helen J. Volcanoes. LC 82-17888. (Illus.). 48p. (gr. k-4). 1983. PLB 12.85 (*0-516-01690-3*); pap. 4.95 (*0-516-41690-1*) Childrens.

Chiesa, Pierre. Volcanes y Terremotos (Volcanos & Earthquakes) Cobielles, Antonio, tr. Henroit, Jean-Louis, illus. (SPA.). 96p. (gr. 4 up). 1992. PLB 15.90 (*1-56294-176-3*) Millbrook Pr.

Clark, John O. Earthquakes to Volcanoes: Projects with Geography. LC 91-35076. (Illus.). 32p. (gr. 5-9). 1992. PLB 12.40 (*0-531-17316-X*, Gloucester Pr) Watts.

Curran, Eileen. Mountains & Volcanoes. Watling, James, illus. LC 84-8638. 32p. (gr. k-2). 1985. PLB 11.59 (*0-8167-0347-7*); pap. text ed. 2.95 (*0-8167-0348-5*) Troll Assocs.

Damon, Laura. Discovering Earthquakes & Volcanoes. Jones, John R., illus. LC 89-4974. 32p. (gr. 2-4). 1990. PLB 11.59 (*0-8167-1757-5*); pap. text ed. 2.95 (*0-8167-1758-3*) Troll Assocs.

Deery, Ruth. Earthquakes & Volcanoes. Miller-Ray, Sue E., illus. 48p. (gr. 4-8). 1985. wkbk. 7.95 (*0-86653-272-2*, GA 630) Good Apple.

Dineen, Jacqueline. Volcanoes. LC 91-11303. (Illus.). 32p. (gr. 5-8). 1991. PLB 12.40 (*0-531-17338-0*, Gloucester Pr) Watts.

Dudman, John. Volcano. LC 92-41511. 32p. (gr. 3-6). 1993. 14.95 (*1-56847-001-0*) Thomson Lrning.

Elting, Mary. Volcanoes & Earthquakes. Courtney, illus. LC 89-37107. 48p. (gr. 3-7). 1990. pap. 9.95 (*0-671-67217-7*, S&S BFYR) S&S Trade.

Field, Nancy & Machlis, Sally. Discovering Northwest Volcanoes. rev. ed. Machlis, Sally, illus. 32p. (Orig.). (gr. 2-6). 1980. pap. 3.95 (*0-941042-03-0*) Dog Eared Pubns.

Garlie, Gina. Mount St. Helens Is My Home. Elfstrand, Elizabeth, illus. 40p. (gr. k-3). 1993. pap. 5.95 (*0-9637878-0-2*, 574180) Lupine Pr.

George, Michael. Volcanoes. LC 90-22064. (Illus.). 40p. (gr. 3-5). 1992. PLB 18.95 (*0-88682-403-6*) Creative Ed.

—Volcanoes. 40p. (gr. 4-7). 1993. 15.95 (*1-56846-065-1*) Creat Editions.

Greenberg, Judith E. & Carey, Helen H. Volcanoes. Shaw, Charles, illus. 32p. (gr. 2-4). 1990. 10.95 (*0-8172-3756-9*) Raintree Steck-V.

Hamilton, Sue. Mount St. Helens Eruption. Hamilton, John, ed. LC 88-71721. (Illus.). 32p. (gr. 4). 1989. PLB 11.96 (*0-939179-41-5*) Abdo & Dghtrs.

Hoofnagle, Keith L. Hawaii Volcanoes Coloring Book. Hoofnagle, Keith L., illus. 32p. (ps-3). 1979. pap. 1.50 coloring book (*0-940295-07-5*) HI Natural Hist.

Hooker, Merrilee. Volcanoes. LC 92-43121. 1993. 12.67 (*0-86593-244-1*); 9.50s.p. (*0-685-66351-5*) Rourke Corp.

Humphrey, Kathryn L. Pompeii: Nightmare at Midday. LC 89-39711. (Illus.). 1990. PLB 12.90 (*0-531-10895-3*) Watts.

Knapp, Brian. Volcano. LC 89-11584. (Illus.). 48p. (gr. 5-9). 1990. PLB 22.80 (*0-8114-2373-5*) Raintree Steck-V.

Knowledge Unlimited Staff. The Earth Exhales: The Story of Volcanoes. (Illus.). 28p. (gr. 7 up). 1983. incl. filmstrip, cass., guide 25.00 (*0-915291-02-9*) Know Unltd.

Krafft, Maurice. Volcano! Bogard, Vicki, tr. from FRE. Favreau, Luc, illus. LC 92-968. 38p. (gr. k-5). 1992. 5.95 (*0-944589-41-3*) Young Discovery Lib.

—Volcano! Favreau, Luc, illus. 40p. (gr. k-5). 1993. PLB 9.95 (*1-56674-074-6*, HTS Bks) Forest Hse.

Kunhardt, Edith. Pompeii... Buried Alive! Eagle, Michael, illus. LC 87-4512. 48p. (gr. 2-3). 1987. 3.50 (*0-394-88866-9*); lib. bdg. 6.99 (*0-394-98866-3*) Random Bks Yng Read.

Lampton, Christopher. Volcano. (Illus.). 64p. (gr. 4-6). 1991. PLB 13.90 (*1-56294-028-7*); pap. 5.95 (*1-56294-786-9*) Millbrook Pr.

—Volcano: A Disaster Book. (gr. 4-7). 1992. pap. 5.95 (*0-395-63645-0*) HM.

Lasky, Kathryn. Surtsey: The Newest Place on Earth. Knight, Christopher, illus. LC 92-52990. 64p. (gr. 3-7). 1992. 15.95 (*1-56282-300-0*); PLB 15.89 (*1-56282-301-9*) Hyprn Child.

—Surtsey: The Newest Place on Earth. Knight, Christopher G., photos by. (Illus.). 64p. (gr. 3-7). 1994. pap. 6.95 (*0-7868-1004-1*) Hyprn Ppbks.

Lauber, Patricia. Volcano: The Eruption & Healing of Mount St. Helens. LC 85-22442. (Illus.). 64p. (gr. 3-5). 1986. SBE 16.95 (*0-02-754500-8*, Bradbury Pr) Macmillan Child Grp.

—Volcano: The Eruption & Healing of Mount St. Helens. LC 92-23791. (Illus.). 64p. (gr. 2-5). 1993. pap. 6.95 (*0-689-71679-6*, Aladdin) Macmillan Child Grp.

Lye, Keith. Volcanoes. LC 92-32016. (Illus.). 32p. (gr. 2-3). 1992. PLB 18.99 (*0-8114-3412-5*) Raintree Steck-V.

Marcus, Elizabeth. All about Mountains & Volcanoes. Veno, Joseph, illus. LC 83-4834. 32p. (gr. 3-6). 1984. lib. bdg. 10.59 (*0-89375-969-4*); pap. text ed. 2.95 (*0-89375-970-8*) Troll Assocs.

Merrians, Deborah. I Can Read About Earthquakes & Volcanoes. LC 74-24966. (Illus.). (gr. 2-4). 1975. pap. 2.50 (*0-89375-067-0*) Troll Assocs.

O'Meara, Stephen J. & O'Meara, Donna D. Volcanoes: Passion & Fury. LC 93-47387. (Illus.). 1994. 16.95 (*0-933346-70-0*) Sky Pub.

Radlauer, Ruth. Volcanoes. LC 80-24564. (Illus.). 48p. (gr. 3 up). 1981. (Elk Grove Bks); pap. 4.95 (*0-516-47835-4*) Childrens.

Raintree Publishers Inc. Volcanoes. LC 87-27785. (Illus.). 64p. (Orig.). (gr. 5-9). 1988. PLB 11.95 (*0-8172-3081-5*) Raintree Steck-V.

Santrey, Laurence. Earthquakes & Volcanoes. Jones, John, illus. LC 84-2676. 32p. (gr. 3-6). 1985. PLB 9.49 (*0-8167-0212-8*); pap. text ed. 2.95 (*0-8167-0213-6*) Troll Assocs.

Simon, Seymour. Volcanoes. LC 87-33316. (Illus.). 32p. (gr. k-3). 1988. 12.95 (*0-688-07411-1*); PLB 12.88 (*0-688-07412-X*, Morrow Jr Bks) Morrow Jr Bks.

Sotnak, Lewann. Hawaii Volcanoes. LC 89-33550. (Illus.). 48p. (gr. 4-5). 1989. text ed. 13.95 RSBE (*0-89686-432-4*, Crestwood Hse) Macmillan Child Grp.

Stine, Megan. They Survived Mount St. Helens. LC 93-5505. 112p. (gr. 2-5). 1994. PLB 9.99 (*0-679-94362-5*, Bullseye Bks); pap. 2.99 (*0-679-84362-0*, Bullseye Bks) Random Bks Yng Read.

Taylor, Barbara. Mountains & Volcanoes. LC 92-23374. (Illus.). 32p. (gr. 1-4). 1993. 10.95 (*1-85697-874-5*, Kingfisher LKC); pap. 5.95 (*1-85697-938-5*) LKC.

Thomas, Margaret. Volcano! LC 90-45372. (Illus.). 48p. (gr. 5-6). 1991. text ed. 12.95 RSBE (*0-89686-595-9*, Crestwood Hse) Macmillan Child Grp.

Thro, Ellen. Volcanoes of the United States. LC 91-36002. (Illus.). 112p. (gr. 9-12). 1992. PLB 13.90 (*0-531-12522-X*) Watts.

Tilling, Robert I. Born of Fire: Volcanoes & Igneous Rocks. LC 89-25781. (Illus.). 64p. (gr. 6 up). 1991. lib. bdg. 15.95 (*0-89490-151-6*) Enslow Pubs.

VanCleave, Janice. Janice VanCleave's Volcanoes: Mind-Boggling Experiments You Can Turn into Science Fair Projects. (Orig.). 1994. pap. text ed. 9.95 (*0-471-30811-0*) Wiley.

New in The Spectacular Science Projects series: Mount Vesuvius. Mauna Loa. Mount St. Helens. Your kitchen. All of these locations may have one thing in common. An active volcano. From what we hear, smoke & lava are spewing from erupting volcanoes in homes & schools everywhere! Now Janice VanCleave offers practical tips for this classic experiment along with lots of other volcanic phenomena. Activities transport children to the edge of a volcanic crater to explore & learn exactly how & why volcanoes occur. Their discoveries will be the launch pad for the best science fair projects ever! 20 easy-to-do activities, plus dozens of tips & tricks for developing original science fair projects. Kids can make the classic erupting volcano, create their own molten lava rock, or build their own spud launcher. Explains where most volcanoes are found, how scientists predict volcanic eruptions, & how liquid rock moves through the earth.

Publisher Provided Annotation.

Van Rose, Susanna. Volcano & Earthquake. Stevenson, James, photos by. LC 92-4710. (Illus.). 64p. (gr. 5 up). 1992. 15.00 (*0-679-81685-2*); PLB 16.99 (*0-679-91685-7*) Knopf Bks Yng Read.

Vogt, Gregory. Predicting Volcanic Eruptions. (Illus.). 144p. (gr. 7-12). 1989. PLB 13.90 (*0-531-10786-8*) Watts.

—Volcanoes. (Illus.). 64p. (gr. 5-8). 1993. pap. 5.95 (*0-531-15667-2*) Watts.

Walker, Sally M. Volcanoes: Earth's Inner Fire. LC 93-23172. 1994. write for info. (*0-87614-812-7*) Carolrhoda Bks.

Whitfield, Phillip. Why Do Volcanoes Erupt? Questions about Our Unique Planet. 1990. 16.95 (*0-670-83385-1*) Viking Child Bks.

Wood, Jenny. Volcanoes: Fire from Below. LC 90-55460. (Illus.). 32p. (gr. 3-4). 1991. PLB 17.27 (*0-8368-0472-4*) Gareth Stevens Inc.

VOLCANOES–FICTION

Campbell, Eric. The Shark Callers. LC 93-44881. (gr. 7 up). 1994. 10.95 (*0-15-200007-0*); pap. 4.95 (*0-15-200010-0*) HarBrace.

Carpenter, Humphrey. The Solitary Volcano. write for info. HM.

Castaneda, Omar S. Among the Volcanoes. 192p. (gr. 7 up). 1991. 14.95 (*0-525-67332-6*, Lodestar Bks) Dutton Child Bks.

—Among the Volcanoes. (ps-3). 1993. pap. 3.50 (*0-440-40746-X*) Dell.

George. Jean George Volcanoes Book. Date not set. 15. 00 (*0-06-023628-0*); PLB 14.89 (*0-06-023629-9*) HarpC Child Bks.

Gormley, Beatrice. Paul's Volcano. Smith, Catherine B., illus. LC 86-27543. (gr. 4-6). 1987. 13.95 (*0-395-43079-8*) HM.

McBarnet, Gill. Fountain of Fire. McBarnet, Gill, illus. 32p. (gr. k-2). 1987. 7.95 (*0-9615102-3-4*) Ruwanga Trad.

VOLLEYBALL

Costanzo, Christie. Volleyball. LC 93-27153. 1993. write for info. (*0-86593-344-8*) Rourke Corp.

Gutman, Bill. Volleyball. LC 89-7584. (Illus.). 64p. (gr. 3-8). 1990. PLB 14.95 (*0-942545-95-8*) Marshall Cavendish.

Iams, Jim. Competitive Volleyball Drills & Scoring Systems. 63p. (Orig.). (gr. 6-12). 1993. pap. 12.95 (*1-56404-024-0*) Championship Bks & Vid Prodns.

VOLUNTARISM

Adams, Patricia & Marzollo, Jean. The Helping Hands Handbook. Moores, Jeff, illus. LC 91-42947. 96p. (Orig.). (gr. 3 up). 1992. PLB 11.99 (*0-679-92816-2*); pap. 4.99 (*0-679-82816-8*) Random Bks Yng Read.

Gilbert, Sara. Lend a Hand: The How, Where & Why of Volunteering. LC 87-32077. 176p. (gr. 5 up). 1988. 12. 95 (*0-688-07247-X*) Morrow Jr Bks.

Hurwitz, Eugene & Hurwitz, Sue. Working Together Against Homelessness. LC 94-1022. 1994. 14.95 (*0-8239-1772-X*) Rosen Group.

Metlzer, Milton. Who Cares? Millions Do-- LC 94-4082. 1994. write for info. (*0-8027-8324-4*); Reinforced. write for info. (*0-8027-8325-2*) Walker & Co.

Salzman, Marian & Reisgies, Teresa. One Hundred Fifty Ways Teens Can Make a Difference. LC 91-2965. 207p. (Orig.). 1991. pap. 7.95 (*1-56079-093-8*) Petersons Guides.

VOTING

see Elections

VOYAGERS

see Explorers

VOYAGES AND TRAVELS

The AAA Travel Activity Book: The Official AAA Fun Book for Kids. 144p. (gr. k-6). 1990. 4.95 (*0-02-689512-9*, Collier) Macmillan.

Brewer, Annie M. & Brewer, Donald E. Chemicals du Jour: A Traveler's Guide to Tanker Contents. 250p. (Orig.). (gr. 8). 1993. pap. 19.95 (*0-9632341-3-7*) Whitefoord.

Brown, Ann & Bold, Mary. Travel-Ogs: The Do-It-Yourself Survival Kit for Traveling with Parents, Siblings, & Dirty Socks. Small, Carol B., illus. 80p. (Orig.). (gr. 1-6). 1988. wkbk. 6.95 (*0-938267-06-X*) Bold Prodns.

Crump, Donald J., ed. Excursion to Enchantment. (Illus.). 1988. 12.95 (*0-87044-667-3*); lib. bdg. 12.95 (*0-87044-672-X*) Natl Geog.

Davies, Eryl. Water Travel. LC 93-7074. 32p. (gr. 5-9). 1993. 14.95 (*1-56847-038-X*) Thomson Lrning.

Eugene, Toni, ed. Beyond the Horizon: Adventures in Faraway Lands. (Illus.). 1992. 12.95 (*0-87044-831-5*) Natl Geog.

Hogan, Paula. The Compass. LC 82-70439. (Illus.). 64p. (gr. 4-6). 1982. PLB 8.85 (*0-8027-6453-3*) Walker & Co.

Kent, Zachary. Marco Polo: Traveler to Central & Eastern Asia. LC 91-34521. (Illus.). 128p. (gr. 3 up). PLB 20.55 (*0-516-03070-1*); pap. 9.95, Jul. 1992 (*0-516-43070-X*) Childrens.

Kids' U. S. Road Atlas. (gr. 4-7). 1991. pap. 3.95 (*0-528-80547-9*) Rand McNally.

Krupp, Robin R. Let's Go Traveling. Krupp, Robin R., illus. LC 91-21845. 40p. (gr. 2 up). 1992. 15.00 (*0-688-08989-5*); PLB 14.93 (*0-688-08990-9*) Morrow Jr Bks.

Marlor Editors. Kid's Vacation Diary: A Fun Diary & Vacation Book for Use While Traveling! Bree, Marlin, illus. 96p. (Orig.). (gr. 1-7). 1991. pap. 6.95 (*0-943400-56-2*) Marlor Pr.

O'Hare, Jeff. Globe Probe: Exciting Geographical Adventures All Around the World. 32p. (gr. 4-7). 1993. 10.95 (*1-56397-037-6*) Boyds Mills Pr.

Patterson, Jose. A Traveller Child. (Illus.). 25p. (gr. 2-4). 1991. 12.95 (*0-237-60129-X*, Pub. by Evans Bros Ltd) Trafalgar.

Piltch, Benjamin & Smergut, Peter. Class Trips. 64p. (gr. 4-8). 1983. 3.95 (*0-934618-00-3*) Learning Well.

Polo, Marco. Travels of Marco Polo. (gr. 9 up). 1968. pap. 1.50 (*0-8049-0186-4*, CL-186) Airmont.

Prior, Katherine. Pilgrimages & Journeys. LC 93-16318. (Illus.). 32p. (gr. 4-8). 1993. 13.95 (*1-56847-032-0*) Thomson Lrning.

Safari! LC 80-8799. (Illus.). 104p. (gr. 3-8). 1982. 8.95 (*0-87044-385-2*); lib. bdg. 12.50 (*0-87044-390-9*) Natl Geog.

Schwartz, L. The Travel Bug. LC 92-74104. 120p. (gr. 2-9). 1993. 9.95 (*0-88160-256-6*, LW203) Learning Wks.

Stanish, Bob. Lessons from the Hearthstone Traveler. 136p. (gr. 3-12). 1988. wkbk. 12.95 (*0-86653-433-4*, GA1043) Good Apple.

Steele, Philip. Thor Heyerdahl & the Kon-Tiki Voyage. LC 93-9335. (Illus.). 32p. (gr. 4-6). 1993. text ed. 13. 95 RSBE (*0-87518-533-9*, Dillon) Macmillan Child Grp.

Sweetgall, Robert & Peleg, Dorith E. Road Scholars: The Story of Twenty-Eight Kids Who Decided to Take a Hike for Their Health. (Illus.). 64p. (Orig.). 1989. pap. 20.00 (*0-939041-07-3*) Creative Walking.

Twist, Clint. Marco Polo: Overland to Medieval China. LC 93-30744. 1994. PLB 22.80 (*0-8114-7251-5*) Raintree Steck-V.

Vowles, Andrew. My Travel Book. Williams, Harland & O'Halloran, Tim, illus. 32p. (gr. 1-5). 1985. pap. 2.95 (*0-88625-063-3*) Durkin Hayes Pub.

Waterlow, Julia. Journeys. LC 93-6819. (Illus.). 32p. (gr. 4-6). 1993. 14.95 (*1-56847-051-7*) Thomson Lrning.

VOYAGES AND TRAVELS–FICTION

Alexander, Lloyd. Remarkable Journey. 1993. pap. 3.99 (*0-440-40890-3*) Dell.

Ball, Duncan. Jeremy's Tail. Rawlins, Donna, illus. LC 90-28952. 32p. (ps-1). 1991. 14.95 (*0-531-05951-0*); RLB 14.99 (*0-531-08551-1*) Orchard Bks Watts.

Bond, Nancy. Another Shore. LC 87-3907. 320p. (gr. 7 up). 1988. SBE 16.95 (*0-689-50463-2*, M K McElderry) Macmillan Child Grp.

Brisson, Pat. Kate Heads West. Brown, Rick, illus. LC 89-27590. 40p. (gr. k-3). 1990. RSBE 13.95 (*0-02-714345-7*, Bradbury Pr) Macmillan Child Grp.

—Magic Carpet. Schwartz, Amy, illus. LC 89-35993. 32p. (ps-3). 1991. RSBE 14.95 (*0-02-714340-6*, Bradbury Pr) Macmillan Child Grp.

Bursik, Rose. Amelia's Fantastic Flight. Bursik, Rose, illus. LC 91-28809. 32p. (ps-2). 1992. 14.95 (*0-8050-1872-7*, Bks Young Read) H Holt & Co.

Carey, Karla. Julie & Jackie Go a'Journeying: The Narration & Music Book. Nolan, Dennis, illus. 76p. 1990. pap. 18.95 complete pkg. (*0-685-35755-4*); pap. 9.95 (*1-55768-203-8*); cassette 9.95 (*0-685-35756-2*) LC Pub.

Carroll, Lewis. Alice's Adventures in Wonderland. Hitchner, Earle, adapted by. Billin-Frye, Paige, illus. LC 89-33889. 48p. (gr. 3-6). 1990. PLB 12.89 (*0-8167-1861-X*); pap. text ed. 3.95 (*0-8167-1862-8*) Troll Assocs.

Cooney, Barbara. Miss Rumphius. Cooney, Barbara, illus. LC 82-2837. 32p. (gr. k-3). 1982. pap. 14.95 (*0-670-47958-6*) Viking Child Bks.

Dastardly & Muttley's Trip Around the World. (Illus.). 32p. (gr. 6-9). 1993. 12.95 (*1-878685-69-4*, Bedrock Press) Turner Pub GA.

De Brunhoff, Jean. Le Voyage de Babar. (FRE & SPA., Illus.). bds. 15.95 (*0-685-11626-3*) Fr & Eur.

Devi-Doolin, Daya. Dabney, Dormck & Wiggle's Slakadunan Adventure. Devi-Doolin, Daya & Joiner, Eddie, illus. 50p. (Orig.). (gr. 4-8). 1989. pap. text ed. 6.50 (*1-877945-02-1*) Padaran Pubns.

Dickens, Charles. The Baron of Grogzwig. Greenway, Shirley, ed. Barnes-Murphy, Rowan, illus. LC 93-18627. (gr. 2-7). 1993. write for info. (*1-879085-81-X*) Whsprng Coyote Pr.

Farber, Norma. As I Was Crossing Boston Common. Lobel, Arnold, illus. LC 75-6520. 32p. (ps-2). 1991. Repr. 14.95 (*0-525-25960-0*, DCB) Dutton Child Bks.

Faulkner, Matt. The Amazing Voyage of Jackie Grace. Faulkner, Matt, illus. 1991. pap. 3.95 (*0-590-44860-9*) Scholastic Inc.

Garland, Hamlin. Main-Travelled Roads. 1987. Repr. lib. bdg. 18.95x (*0-89966-555-1*) Buccaneer Bks.

Gaskin, Carol. Caravan to China. (gr. 5 up). 1987. pap. 2.50 (*0-317-65091-2*) Bantam.

Gerrard, Roy. Jocasta Carr, Movie Star. LC 92-6751. 1992. 15.00 (*0-374-33654-7*) FS&G.

Goldish, Meish. The Same but Different. (Illus.). 32p. (gr. 1-4). 1989. PLB 18.99 (*0-8172-3528-0*); pap. 3.95 (*0-8114-6729-5*) Raintree Steck-V.

Hopkins, Lee B. Voyages. Mikolaycak, C., ed. 1992. pap. 8.95 (*0-15-294496-6*, HB Juv Bks) HarBrace.

Hunter, Mollie. The Wicked One: A Story of Suspense. LC 76-41515. 136p. (gr. 5-8). 1980. pap. 3.95 (*0-06-440117-0*, Trophy) HarpC Child Bks.

Hyatt, Pat R. Coast to Coast with Alice. LC 94-25750. (gr. 1-8). 1995. write for info. (*0-87614-789-9*) Carolrhoda Bks.

Incredible Journey. 1985. pap. 1.50 (*0-440-82001-4*) Dell.

Jennings, Sharon. Une Journee avec Jeremie et Mme. Ming: When Jeremiah Found Mrs. Ming. Levert, Mireille, illus. (FRE.). 24p. (ps). 1992. PLB 15.95 (*1-55037-247-5*, Pub. by Annick Pr); pap. 6.95 (*1-55037-248-3*, Pub. by Annick Pr) Firefly Bks Ltd.

—When Jeremiah Found Mrs. Ming. Levert, Mireille, illus. 24p. (ps). 1992. PLB 15.95 (*1-55037-237-8*, Pub. by Annick Pr); pap. 5.95 (*1-55037-234-3*, Pub. by Annick Pr) Firefly Bks Ltd.

Joos, Louis, illus. Oregon's Journey. LC 93-11796. 40p. (gr. k-4). 1993. PLB 15.95 (*0-8167-3305-8*); pap. text ed. 3.95 (*0-8167-3306-6*) BrdgeWater.

Joyce, Susan. Post Card Passages. DuBosque, Doug, illus. 1994. 13.95 (*0-939217-27-9*) Peel Prod.

Lasky, Kathryn. Beyond the Divide. LC 82-22867. 264p. (gr. 7 up). 1983. SBE 15.95 (*0-02-751670-9*, Macmillan Child Bk) Macmillan Child Grp.

Lewin, Hugh. Jafta: The Journey. Kopper, Lisa, illus. LC 84-4326. 24p. (ps-3). 1984. PLB 15.95 (*0-87614-265-X*) Carolrhoda Bks.

Lively, Penelope. The Voyage of QV66. large type ed. Jones, Harold, illus. 280p. 1992. 16.95 (*0-7451-1548-9*, Galaxy Child Lrg Print) Chivers N Amer.

Maclachlan, Patricia. Journey. (gr. 4-7). 1993. pap. 3.50 (*0-440-40809-1*) Dell.

Marsh, Carole. Snowshoe & Earmuff Go North. (Illus.). (ps-4). 1994. 24.95 (*1-55609-646-1*); pap. 14.95 (*1-55609-758-1*) Gallopade Pub Group.

Martin, Ann M. Karen's Plane Trip. 144p. (gr. 2-4). 1991. pap. 3.25 (*0-590-44834-X*) Scholastic Inc.

Massi, Jeri. The Myth of the Llama. Thompson, Del & Thompson, Dana, illus. 118p. (Orig.). (gr. 6). 1989. pap. 5.95 (*1-877778-00-1*) Llama Bks.

May, Daryl & Bansemer, Roger. Rachael's Splendifilous Adventure. Little, Carl, ed. Bansemer, Roger, illus. LC 91-66032. 40p. (Orig.). (ps-4). 1992. PLB 10.95 (*0-932433-83-9*) Windswept Hse.

Morpurgo, Michael. Twist of Gold. LC 92-25928. 246p. (gr. 5-9). 1993. 14.99 (*0-670-84851-4*) Viking Child Bks.

Peel, John. Where in the World Is Carmen San Diego? 48p. (gr. 4-7). 1991. pap. 3.95 (*0-307-22301-9*, 22301) Western Pub.

Priceman, Marjorie. How to Make an Apple Pie & See The World. Priceman, Marjorie, illus. LC 93-12341. 40p. (ps-3). 1994. 15.00 (*0-679-83705-1*); lib. bdg. 15. 99 (*0-679-93705-6*) Knopf Bks Yng Read.

Round the World in Eighty Days. 1993. pap. text ed. 6.50 (*0-582-09671-5*, 79826) Longman.

Samton, Sheila W. Jenny's Journey. (Illus.). 32p. (ps-3). 1991. 13.95 (*0-670-83490-4*) Viking Child Bks.

—Jenny's Journey. LC 92-40724. (Illus.). 32p. (ps-3). 1993. pap. 4.99 (*0-14-054308-2*, Puffin) Puffin Bks.

Sandin, Joan. The Long Way Westward. Sandin, Joan, illus. LC 89-2024. 64p. (gr. k-3). 1989. PLB 13.89 (*0-06-025207-3*) HarpC Child Bks.

—The Long Way Westward. Sandin, Joan, illus. LC 89-2024. 64p. (gr. k-3). 1992. pap. 3.50 (*0-06-444198-9*, Trophy) HarpC Child Bks.

Sands, Stella. Odisea. Wolff, Barbara M., illus. (SPA.). 32p. (gr. k-4). 1992. PLB 13.95 (*1-879567-18-0*, Valeria Bks) Wonder Well.

Sansone, Barbara. Holidays in Bloom. (Illus.). 56p. (Orig.). (gr. 3-6). 1990. pap. 6.95 (*0-933606-87-7*, MS-691) E Sussman Educ.

—Special Days in Bloom. (Illus.). 56p. (Orig.). (gr. 3-6). 1990. pap. 6.95 (*0-685-58699-5*, MS-692) E Sussman Educ.

Saul, Carol P. Someplace Else. Root, Barrett, illus. (gr. 4 up). 1995. pap. 14.00 (*0-671-87283-4*, S&S BFYR) S&S Trade.

Say, Allen. Grandfather's Journey. LC 93-18836. 32p. 1993. 16.95 (*0-395-57035-2*) HM.

Sidney, Margaret. Five Little Peppers Abroad. 1987. Repr. lib. bdg. 25.95x (*0-89966-551-9*) Buccaneer Bks.

Smith, Maggie. Counting Our Way to Maine. LC 94-24874. (gr. 2 up). 1995. write for info. (*0-531-06884-6*); pap. write for info. (*0-531-08734-4*) Orchard Bks Watts.

Taylor, Theodore. Walking up a Rainbow: Being the True Version of the Long & Hazardous Journey of Susan D. Carlisle, Mrs. Myrtle Dessery, Drover Bert Pettit & Cowboy Clay Carmer & Others. LC 94-16548. (gr. 7 up). 1994. 14.95 (*0-15-294512-1*) HarBrace.

Time Life Inc. Editors. The Search for the Seven Sisters: A Hidden-Picture Geography Book. (Illus.). 56p. (ps-2). 1991. write for info. (*0-8094-9287-3*); PLB write for info. (*0-8094-9288-1*) Time-Life.

Verne, Jules. Around the World in Eighty Days. (gr. 8 up). 1964. pap. 2.25 (*0-8049-0024-8*, CL-24) Airmont.

—Around the World in Eighty Days. 253p. (gr. 5 up). 1964. pap. 2.95 (*0-440-90285-1*, LFL) Dell.

—Around the World in Eighty Days. Moser, Barry, illus. LC 87-62829. 256p. (gr. 5 up). 1988. 19.95 (*0-688-07508-8*); signed ltd. ed. 175.00 (*0-688-08257-2*, Morrow Jr Bks) Morrow Jr Bks.

—Around the World in Eighty Days. 1990. pap. 3.25 (*0-590-43053-X*) Scholastic Inc.

—Around the World in Eighty Days: Classic Story Books. 1994. 4.98 (*0-8317-1645-2*) Smithmark.

—Master of the World. Lowndes, R. A., intro. by. (gr. 7 up). 1965. pap. 1.25 (*0-8049-0073-6*, CL-73) Airmont.

Warren, Jean. Huff & Puff Around the World: A Totline Teaching Tale. Cubley, Kathleen, ed. Piper, Molly & Ekberg, Marion, illus. LC 93-5490. 32p. (Orig.). (ps-2). 1994. 12.95 (*0-911019-81-2*); pap. 5.95 (*0-911019-80-4*) Warren Pub Hse.

Watson, Harvey. Bob War & Poke. 144p. (gr. 5-9). 1991. 13.45 (*0-395-57038-7*, Sandpiper) HM.

Wild, Margaret. Going Home. Harris, Wayne, illus. LC 93-22975. 32p. (ps-3). 1994. 14.95 (*0-590-47958-X*) Scholastic Inc.

VOYAGES AROUND THE WORLD

see also Adventure and Adventurers; Aeronautics–Flights; Discoveries (In Geography); Explorers; Northwest Passage; Overland Journeys to the Pacific; Scientific Expeditions; Seafaring Life; Seamen; Shipwrecks; Travel; Voyages around the World

also names of countries, continents, etc. with the subdivision Description and Travel (e.g. U. S. –Description and Travel); also names of regions (e.g. Antarctic Regions)

Anno, Mitsumasa. Anno's Journey. 48p. (gr. 4 up). 1981. 15.95 (*0-399-20762-7*, Philomel Bks); (Philomel Bks) Putnam Pub Group.

Coote, Roger. First Voyage Around the World. LC 89-7236. (gr. 4-6). 1990. PLB 11.90 (*0-531-18302-5*, Pub. by Bookwright Pr) Watts.

Jacobs, William J. Magellan: Voyager with a Dream. LC 93-29698. (Illus.). 64p. (gr. 5-8). 1994. PLB 12.90 (*0-531-20139-2*) Watts.

Verne, Jules. Around the World in Eighty Days. new & abr. ed. Calhoun, D'Ann, ed. Redondo, Francisco, illus. (gr. 4-12). 1977. pap. text ed. 2.95 (*0-88301-261-8*) Pendulum Pr.

VOYAGES TO THE MOON

see Space Flight to the Moon

VULTURES–FICTION

Byars, Betsy C. The Blossoms Meet the Vulture Lady. (gr. k-6). 1987. pap. 2.75 (*0-440-40677-3*, YB) Dell.

Victor the Vulture. 7p. (gr. 9 up). 1991. 4.75 (*0-930366-64-6*) Northcountry Pub.

W

WAGNER, RICHARD, 1813-1883

Tames, Richard. Richard Wagner. (Illus.). 32p. (gr. 4-6). 1991. PLB 12.40 (*0-531-14178-0*) Watts.

WALES

Davies, Kath. Wales. LC 90-10192. (Illus.). 96p. (gr. 6-12). 1990. PLB 22.80 (*0-8114-2437-5*) Raintree Steck-V.

Morris, Robert. Bare Ruined Choirs: The Fate of a Welsh Abbey. 52p. (gr. 11 up). 1987. pap. 7.95 (*0-85950-544-8*, Pub. by S Thornes UK) Dufour.

Sutherland, Dorothy B. Wales. LC 86-29954. (Illus.). 128p. (gr. 5-9). 1987. PLB 20.55 (*0-516-02794-8*) Childrens.

WALES–FICTION

Alexander, Lloyd. Castle of Llyr. 192p. (gr. k-6). 1969. pap. 3.99 (*0-440-41125-4*, YB) Dell.

Bawden, Nina. Carrie's War. LC 72-13253. (gr. 4-7). 1973. PLB 14.89 (*0-397-31450-7*, Lipp Jr Bks) HarpC Child Bks.

Bond, Nancy. A String in the Harp. LC 75-28181. 384p. (gr. 4-8). 1976. SBE 16.95 (*0-689-50036-X*, M K McElderry) Macmillan Child Grp.

The Citadel. 1993. pap. text ed. 6.50 (*0-582-09673-1*, 79817) Longman.

Cronin, A. J. The Citadel. 1983. 16.45 (*0-316-16158-6*); pap. 10.95i (*0-316-16183-7*) Little.

Kimmel, Margaret M. Magic in the Mist. Hyman, Trina S., illus. LC 74-18186. 32p. (gr. k-4). 1975. SBE 13.95 (*0-689-50026-2*, M K McElderry) Macmillan Child Grp.

Lawrence, Louise. The Patchwork People. LC 93-40830. 1994. 14.95 (*0-395-67892-7*, Clarion Bks) HM.

Morpurgo, Michael. The Sandman & the Turtles. LC 93-21531. 80p. (gr. 3-7). 1994. 14.95 (*0-399-22672-9*, Philomel Bks) Putnam Pub Group.

Pullman, Philip. The Broken Bridge. LC 91-15893. 256p. (gr. 7 up). 1992. 15.00 (*0-679-81972-X*); PLB 15.99 (*0-679-91972-4*) Knopf Bks Yng Read.

Thomas, Dylan. A Child's Christmas in Wales. Hyman, Trina S., illus. LC 85-766. 48p. (gr. 4-6). 1985. reinforced bdg. 14.95 (*0-8234-0565-6*) Holiday.

—A Conversation about Christmas. 1991. PLB 13.95 (*0-88682-468-0*) Creative Ed.

WALKING

see also Hiking

Arnosky, Jim. Crinkleroot's Guide to Walking in Wild Places. Arnosky, Jim, illus. LC 89-38427. 32p. (gr. k-5). 1990. RSBE 14.95 (*0-02-705842-5*, Bradbury Pr) Macmillan Child Grp.

—Crinkleroot's Guide to Walking in Wild Places. Arnosky, Jim, illus. LC 92-45775. 32p. (gr. k-5). 1993. pap. 4.95 (*0-689-71753-9*, Aladdin) Macmillan Child Grp.

Boy Scouts of America. Hiking. (Illus.). 36p. (gr. 6-12). 1991. pap. 1.85 (*0-8395-3380-2*, 33380) BSA.

Camping & Walking. (Illus.). 128p. (gr. 3 up). 1987. PLB 15.96 (*0-88110-287-3*); pap. 9.95 (*0-7460-0129-0*) EDC.

Erson, Tim. Courageous Pacers: The Complete Guide to Running, Walking & Fitness for Kids (Ages 8-108) Diaz, Michael A., illus. 264p. (Orig.). (gr. 2 up). 1993. Incl. logbook & journal. 18.95 (*0-9636547-0-5*) PRO-ACTIV Pubns.

Hindley, Judy. Funny Walks. Ayliffe, Alex, illus. LC 93-28446. 32p. (ps-2). 1993. PLB 13.95 (*0-8167-3313-9*); pap. 3.95t (*0-8167-3314-7*) BrdgeWater.

Kerber, Karen M. Walking Is Wild, Weird & Wacky. rev. ed. Thatch, Nan, ed. Melton, David, intro. by. LC 89-13547. (Illus.). 32p. (ps-2). 1989. PLB 14.95 (*0-933849-29-X*) Landmark Edns.

Sweetgall, Rob. The Walking Wellness Student Workbook. Neeves, Robert, ed. (Illus.). 80p. (gr. 4-8). 1986. wkbk. 5.00 (*0-939041-00-6*); tchr's. curriculum guidebk. 12.95 (*0-939041-01-4*) Creative Walking.

WALLACE, GEORGE, 1919-

Kurland, Gerald. George Wallace: Southern Governor & Presidential Candidate. Rahmas, D. Steve, ed. 32p. (Orig.). (gr. 7-12). 1972. lib. bdg. 4.95 incl. catalog cards (*0-87157-529-9*) SamHar Pr.

WALRUSES

Darling, Kathy. Walrus: On Location. Darling, Tara, photos by. LC 90-33376. (Illus.). 40p. (gr. 2 up). 1991. 14.95 (*0-688-09032-X*); PLB 14.88 (*0-688-09033-8*) Lothrop.

Green, Carl R. & Sanford, William R. The Walrus. LC 85-17509. (Illus.). 48p. (gr. 5). 1986. text ed. 12.95 RSBE (*0-89686-273-9*, Crestwood Hse) Macmillan Child Grp.

Palmer, S. Morsas (Walruses) 1991. 8.95s.p. (*0-86592-689-1*) Rourke Enter.

—Walruses. (Illus.). 24p. (gr. k-5). 1989. lib. bdg. 11.94 (*0-86592-358-2*); lib. bdg. 8.95s.p. (*0-685-58621-9*) Rourke Corp.

Papastavrou, Vassili. Seals & Sea Lions. LC 91-9127. (Illus.). 32p. (gr. 2-5). 1992. PLB 12.40 (*0-531-18455-2*, Pub. by Bookwright Pr) Watts.

Rotter, Charles. Walruses. LC 92-8410. (gr. 2-6). 1992. PLB 15.95 (*0-89565-841-0*) Childs World.

Schneider, Jeff. My Friend the Walrus: An Ocean Magic Book. Spoon, Wilfred, illus. LC 90-61581. 12p. (ps). 1991. 4.95g (*1-877779-11-3*) Schneider Educational.

Sherrow, Victoria. Seals, Sea Lions, & Walruses. updated ed. LC 91-4663. (Illus.). 64p. (gr. 3-4). 1991. PLB 11. 90 (*0-685-52512-0*) Denison.

WALRUSES–FICTION

Adoff, Arnold. Sports Pages. Kuzma, Steve, illus. LC 85-45169. 80p. (gr. 3-7). 1986. (Lipp Jr Bks); PLB 14.89 (*0-397-32103-1*, Lipp Jr Bks) HarpC Child Bks.

Bantock, Nick. The Walrus & the Carpenter. (Illus.). 12p. 1992. 9.95 (*0-670-84503-5*, Viking) Viking Penguin.

Bonsall, Crosby N. What Spot? Bonsall, Crosby N., illus. LC 63-8005. 64p. (gr. k-3). 1963. PLB 13.89 (*0-06-020611-X*) HarpC Child Bks.

Carroll, Lewis. The Walrus & the Carpenter. Zalben, Jane B., illus. LC 85-7591. 32p. (gr. 2-4). 1986. 13.95 (*0-8050-0071-2*, Bks Young Read) H Holt & Co.

Fleming, Joyce C. The Tale of Lovable, the Baby Walrus. 1993. 6.95 (*0-8062-4703-7*) Carlton.

Hill, Lee. Wally, the Scholarly Walrus. 1990. 6.95 (*0-533-08401-6*) Vantage.

Riddell, Chris. When the Walrus Comes: The Screenplay. Riddell, Chris, illus. LC 89-31718. 1990. 13.95 (*0-385-29858-7*) Doubleday.

Riehecky, Janet. Walrus' Adventure in Alphabet Town. Magnuson, Diana, illus. LC 92-1330. 32p. (ps-2). 1992. PLB 11.80 (*0-516-05423-6*) Childrens.

WAR

see also Aeronautics, Military; Battles; Disarmament; Military Art and Science; Peace; Soldiers; Submarine Warfare

also names of wars, battles, etc., e.g. U. S.–History–Civil War; Gettysburg, Battle of, 1863

Ben-Ner, Yitzhak, et al. Teenage Soldiers-Adult Wars: From the Barracks to the Battlefield. (gr. 7-12). 1991. PLB 16.95 (*0-8239-1304-X*); pap. 8.95 (*0-8239-1305-8*) Rosen Group.

Cipkowski, Peter. Understanding the Crisis in the Persian Gulf. 192p. 1992. text ed. 24.95 (*0-471-54815-4*); pap. text ed. 12.95 (*0-471-54816-2*) Wiley.

Fuller, Bob. Why Is There War? (Illus.). 23p. 1989. pap. 3.99 (*0-89693-989-8*, Victor Bks) SP Pubns.

Goffe, Toni. War & Peace. LC 91-18197. (gr. 4 up). 1991. 7.95 (*0-85953-366-2*); pap. 3.95 (*0-85953-356-5*) Childs Play.

Griscom, Bailey & Griscom, Pam. Why Can't I Be the Leader? (Illus.). 24p. (Orig.). (ps up). 1992. pap. 4.95 (*0-9633705-2-9*) Share Pub CA.

Kennaley, Lucinda H. Only Soldiers Go to War. Curtis, Charmaine, illus. LC 91-65288. 42p. (ps-4). 1991. 14. 95 (*0-9628067-1-4*) Thoth MO.

King, John. The Gulf War. LC 91-25744. (Illus.). 48p. (gr. 4-6). 1991. text ed. 13.95 RSBE (*0-87518-514-2*, Dillon) Macmillan Child Grp.

Kohn, Bernice. One Sad Day. Isaac, Barbara K., illus. LC 78-169153. 48p. 1972. 11.95 (*0-89388-026-4*) Okpaku Communications.

Landau, Elaine. Chemical & Biological Warfare. 128p. (gr. 5-9). 1991. 14.95 (*0-525-67364-4*, Lodestar Bks) Dutton Child Bks.

McCullough, Dennis J., tr. Kids Coping with War: How Young People React to Military Conflict. (Illus.). 112p. 1991. pap. 6.95 (*0-933879-37-7*); audio cassette 9.95 (*0-933879-39-3*) Alegra Hse Pubs.

Parolini, Stephen & Young, Christine. Peace & War. (Illus.). 48p. (gr. 6-8). 1991. pap. 8.99 (*1-55945-123-8*) Group Pub.

Sirimarco, Elizabeth. War & the Environment. LC 93-1194. 1993. 17.27 (*0-8368-1014-7*) Gareth Stevens Inc.

Williams, Brian. War & Weapons. Berry, John, et al, illus. LC 86-26262. 24p. (gr. 2-5). 1987. Random Bks Yng Read.

WAR–FICTION

Anderson, Paul L. Swords in the North. LC 57-9448. 270p. (gr. 7-11). 1935. 20.00 (*0-8196-0103-9*) Biblo.

Bach, Alice. Ragwars. (Orig.). (gr. k-6). 1987. pap. 2.95 (*0-440-47345-4*, YB) Dell.

Baillie, Allan. Rebel. Wu, Di, illus. LC 93-23512. 32p. (ps-2). 1994. reinforced bdg. 13.95 (*0-395-69250-4*) Ticknor & Flds Bks Yng Read.

Beach, Lynn. Invisibility Island. (gr. 8 up). 1988. pap. 2.95 (*0-345-35097-9*) Ballantine.

Carey, Mary. Texas Brat in Alaska: The Cat Train Kid. (Illus.). 96p. (gr. 5-7). 1991. 10.95 (*0-89015-831-2*) Sunbelt Media.

Clapp, Patricia. The Tamarack Tree. LC 86-108. 224p. (gr. 7 up). 1986. 13.00 (*0-688-02852-7*) Lothrop.

Collier, James & Collier, Christopher. War Comes to Willy Freeman. (gr. 4-6). 1992. 17.25 (*0-8446-6596-7*) Peter Smith.

Cooper, Timothy. Sonia. LC 91-73764. 304p. 1991. 19.95 (*0-9619914-1-0*) Americus Pr.

De Brunhoff, Laurent. Babar's Battle. De Brunhoff, Laurent, illus. LC 91-53169. 36p. (ps-3). 1992. 10.00 (*0-679-81068-4*); PLB 10.99 (*0-679-91068-9*) Random Bks Yng Read.

Eco, Umberto. The Bomb & the General. Weaver, William, tr. Carmi, Eugenio, illus. 40p. (ps up). 1989. 12.95 (*0-15-209700-7*) HarBrace.

Falls, Gregory A. The Pushcart War. (Orig.). (gr. 4 up). 1985. pap. 4.50 (*0-87602-248-4*) Anchorage.

Graham, Lorenz. Every Man Heart Lay Down. Browning, Colleen, illus. 48p. (gr. 3 up). 1993. 15.95 (*1-56397-184-4*) Boyds Mills Pr.

Howells, William Dean. Editha. LC 92-44053. 1994. 13. 95 (*0-88682-585-7*) Creative Ed.

Ikeda, Daisaku. The Cherry Tree. McCaughrean, Geraldine, tr. Wildsmith, Brian, illus. LC 91-22148. 32p. (ps-3). 1992. 15.00 (*0-679-82669-6*); PLB 15.99 (*0-679-92669-0*) Knopf Bks Yng Read.

Kisling, Lee. The Fools' War. LC 91-47695. 176p. (gr. 5 up). 1992. 14.00 (*0-06-020836-8*); PLB 13.89 (*0-06-020837-6*) HarpC Child Bks.

Lyon, George-Ella. Cecil's Story. Catalanotto, Peter, illus. LC 90-7775. 32p. (gr. k-2). 1991. 14.95 (*0-531-05912-X*); PLB 14.99 (*0-531-08512-0*) Orchard Bks Watts.

Mazer, Harry. The War on Villa Street. 128p. (gr. 7 up). 1979. pap. 2.95 (*0-440-99062-9*, LFL) Dell.

Moeri, Louise. Forty-Third War. 1993. pap. 4.95 (*0-395-66955-3*) HM.

Perez, N. A. The Slopes of War. (Illus.). 224p. (gr. 7 up). 1990. 14.45 (*0-395-35642-3*, 5-93140); pap. 4.80 (*0-395-54979-5*) HM.

Phillips, Ann. The Peace Child. (Illus.). 160p. (gr. 5 up). 1988. 15.00 (*0-19-271560-7*) OUP.

Pilkey, Dav. World War Won. Pilkey, Dav, illus. LC 87-2711. 32p. (gr. 1 up). 1987. PLB 14.95 (*0-933849-22-2*) Landmark Edns.

Skoglund, Elizabeth R. Alfred MacDuff Is Afraid of War. Johnson, Meredith, illus. 48p. (ps-2). 1991. pap. 3.99 (*0-8423-0032-5*) Tyndale.

Smith, Janice L. The Show-&-Tell War: And Other Stories about Adam Joshua. Gackenbach, Dick, illus. LC 85-45842. 176p. (gr. 1-4). 1990. pap. 3.95 (*0-06-440312-2*, J312, Trophy) HarpC Child Bks.

Steele, William O. Perilous Road. 156p. (gr. 3-7). 1990. pap. 3.95 (*0-15-260647-5*, Odyssey) HarBrace.

Taylor, Theodore. The Battle off Midway Island. 144p. (Orig.). (gr. 7 up). 1981. pap. 3.95 (*0-380-78790-3*, Flare) Avon.

Thompson, Julian F. The Taking of Mariasburg. 288p. (gr. 7 up). 1988. pap. 12.95 (*0-590-41247-7*, Scholastic Hardcover) Scholastic Inc.

Westall, Robert. Echoes of War. 96p. (gr. 7 up). 1991. 13. 95 (*0-374-31964-2*) FS&G.

WAR CORRESPONDENTS

see Reporters and Reporting

WAR CRIPPLES

see Physically Handicapped

WAR OF 1812

see U. S.–History–War of 1812

WAR OF 1939-1945

see World War, 1939-1945

WAR OF SECESSION (U. S.)

see U. S.–History–Civil War

WAR OF THE AMERICAN REVOLUTION

see U. S.–History–Revolution

WAR POETRY

Robb, Laura, compiled by. Music and Drum: Voices of War and Peace, Hope and Dreams. LC 92-39312. 1994. write for info. (*0-399-22024-0*, Philomel Bks) Putnam Pub Group.

WAR SHIPS

see Warships

WARFARE, SUBMARINE

see Submarine Warfare

WARS

see Military History; Naval History

WARSAW–FICTION

Singer, Isaac Bashevis. A Day of Pleasure: Stories of a Boy Growing up in Warsaw. Vishniac, Roman, photos by. LC 70-95461. (Illus.). 160p. (gr. 3 up). 1986. pap. 5.95 (*0-374-41696-6*, Sunburst) FS&G.

WARSHIPS

see also Aircraft Carriers; Submarines;

also names of countries with the subhead Navy (e.g. U. S. Navy)

Drogues, Valerie. Battleship Missouri. LC 93-10423. (Illus.). 48p. (gr. 5-6). 1994. text ed. 13.95 RSBE (*0-89686-825-7*, Crestwood Hse) Macmillan Child Grp.

Norman, C. J. Buques de Guerra. LC 90-71421. (SPA., Illus.). 32p. (gr. k-4). 1991. PLB 11.90 (*0-531-07921-X*) Watts.

Rawlinson, J. Cruisers. (Illus.). 48p. (gr. 3-8). 1989. lib. bdg. 18.60 (*0-86625-085-9*) Rourke Corp.

Stein, R. Conrad. The USS Arizona. LC 91-44646. (Illus.). 32p. (gr. 3-6). 1993. pap. 3.95 (*0-516-46656-9*) Childrens.

Stephen, R. J. Picture World of Warships. LC 89-36499. (Illus.). 1990. PLB 12.40 (*0-531-14013-X*) Watts.

Walmer, M. Battleships. (Illus.). 48p. (gr. 3-8). 1989. lib. bdg. 18.60 (*0-86625-083-2*) Rourke Corp.

—Destroyers. (Illus.). 48p. (gr. 3-8). 1989. lib. bdg. 18.60 (*0-86625-081-6*) Rourke Corp.

WASHINGTON, BOOKER TALIAFERRO, 1859?-1915

Booker T. Washington. (Illus.). (gr. 2-5). 1989. 29.28 (*0-8172-2959-0*) Raintree Steck-V.

Booker T. Washington: Mini Play. (gr. 5 up). 1977. 6.50 (*0-89550-361-1*) Stevens & Shea.

Gleiter, Jan & Thompson, Kathleen. Booker T. Washington. LC 87-26325. (Illus.). 32p. (Orig.). (gr. 2-5). 1987. PLB 19.97 (*0-8172-2663-X*) Raintree Steck-V.

McKissack, Patricia & McKissack, Fredrick. Booker T. Washington: Leader & Educator. LC 92-5356. (Illus.). 32p. (gr. 1-4). 1992. lib. bdg. 12.95 (*0-89490-314-4*) Enslow Pubs.

—The Story of Booker T. Washington. LC 91-15895. (Illus.). 32p. (gr. 3-6). 1991. PLB 12.30 (*0-516-04758-2*); pap. 3.95 (*0-516-44758-0*) Childrens.

Neyland, James. Booker T. Washington, Educator. Locke, Raymond F., ed. (Illus.). 192p. 1993. pap. 3.95 (*0-87067-599-0*, Melrose Sq) Holloway.

Schroeder, Alan. Booker T. Washington. King, Coretta Scott, intro. by. (Illus.). 144p. (gr. 5 up). 1992. 17.95 (*1-55546-616-8*) Chelsea Hse.

—Booker T. Washington: Leader of His People. (Illus.). 80p. (gr. 2-6). 1991. Repr. of 1962 ed. lib. bdg. 12.95 (*0-7910-1427-4*) Chelsea Hse.

Washington, Booker T. Up from Slavery. Andrews, C. A., intro. by. (gr. 5 up). 1967. pap. 2.50 (*0-8049-0157-0*, CL-157) Airmont.

WASHINGTON, GEORGE, PRESIDENT U. S. 1732-1799

Adler, David A. George Washington: Father of Our Country. Garrick, Jacqueline, illus. LC 88-4691. 48p. (gr. 2-5). 1988. reinforced bdg. 14.95 (*0-8234-0717-9*) Holiday.

Alden, Laura. President's Day. Friedman, Joy, illus. LC 93-37095. 32p. (ps-2). 1994. PLB 12.30 (*0-516-00691-6*) Childrens.

Brandt, Keith. George Washington. Frenck, Hal, illus. LC 84-8624. 32p. (gr. 3-6). 1985. PLB 9.49 (*0-8167-0256-X*); pap. text ed. 2.95 (*0-8167-0257-8*) Troll Assocs.

Camp, Norma C. George Washington: Man of Courage & Prayer. Manderfield, Diane, illus. LC 76-3084. (gr. 3-6). 1977. pap. 6.95 (*0-915134-25-X*) Mott Media.

Children of History, 8 vols. (Illus.). 32p. (gr. 3-8). 1989. Set. 87.60 (*0-86307-922-9*) Marshall Cavendish.

D'Aulaire, Ingri & D'Aulaire, Edgar P. George Washington. D'Aulaire, Ingri & D'Aulaire, Edgar P., illus. LC 36-27417. 64p. (gr. 1-4). 1936. pap. 13.95 (*0-385-07306-2*) Doubleday.

Falkof, Lucille. George Washington: First President of the United States. Young, Richard G., ed. LC 88-24564. (Illus.). (gr. 5-9). 1989. PLB 17.26 (*0-944483-19-4*) Garrett Ed Corp.

Farr, Naunerle C. George Washington-Thomas Jefferson. Carrillo, Fred & Cruz, E. R., illus. (gr. 4-12). 1979. pap. text ed. 2.95 (*0-88301-355-X*); wkbk. 1.25 (*0-88301-379-7*) Pendulum Pr.

Fleming, Thomas. First in Their Hearts: A Biography of George Washington. LC 90-48979. (Illus.). 176p. (gr. 6-10). 1991. PLB 13.95 (*1-55905-099-3*) Marshall Cavendish.

Fradin, Dennis B. Washington's Birthday. LC 89-7664. (Illus.). 48p. (gr. 1-4). 1990. lib. bdg. 14.95 (*0-89490-235-0*) Enslow Pubs.

George Washington. (Illus.). 24p. 1987. pap. 2.50 (*0-671-62981-6*, Little Simon) S&S Trade.

George Washington. 1992. 4.99 (*0-517-06997-0*) Random Hse Value.

George Washington Pop-Up. 1991. 8.95 (*0-8167-2567-5*) Troll Assocs.

Giblin, James C. George Washington: A Picture Book Biography. (Illus.). (ps up). 1992. 14.95 (*0-590-42550-1*, 017, Scholastic Hardcover) Scholastic Inc.

Graff, Stewart. George Washington: Father of Freedom. (Illus.). 80p. (gr. 2-6). 1993. Repr. of 1964 ed. lib. bdg. 12.95 (*0-7910-1451-7*) Chelsea Hse.

Greene, Carol. George Washington: First President of the United States. Dobson, Steven, illus. LC 90-22195. 48p. (gr. k-3). 1991. PLB 12.85 (*0-516-04218-1*); pap. 4.95 (*0-516-44218-X*) Childrens.

Hellbroner, Joan. Meet George Washington. Marchesi, Stephen, illus. LC 88-19067. 72p. (gr. 2-4). 1989. pap. 3.50 (*0-394-81965-9*) Random Bks Yng Read.

Heymsfeld, Carla. Where Was George Washington? Koury, Jennifer, illus. LC 92-17341. 1992. 14.95 (*0-931917-20-4*); pap. write for info. (*0-931917-21-2*) Mt Vernon Ladies.

Hilton, Suzanne. The World of Young George Washington. Bock, William S., illus. LC 86-13296. 112p. (gr. 5-9). 1987. 12.95 (*0-8027-6657-9*); PLB 12.85 (*0-8027-6658-7*) Walker & Co.

Hoobler, Dorothy & Hoobler, Thomas. George Washington. Brook, Bonnie, ed. Himler, Ronald, illus. 32p. (gr. k-2). 1990. 4.95 (*0-671-69114-7*); PLB 6.95 (*0-671-69108-2*) Silver Pr.

Hughes, Libby. Valley Forge. LC 92-23391. (Illus.). 72p. (gr. 4 up). 1993. text ed. 14.95 RSBE (*0-87518-547-9*, Dillon) Macmillan Child Grp.

Jacobs, William J. Washington. LC 90-8844. (Illus.). 48p. (gr. 4-6). 1991. SBE 13.95 (*0-684-19275-6*, Scribners Young Read) Macmillan Child Grp.

Kent, Zachary. George Washington. LC 86-12896. (Illus.). 100p. (gr. 3 up). 1986. PLB 14.40 (*0-516-01381-5*); pap. 6.95 (*0-516-41381-3*) Childrens.

Krensky, Stephen. George Washington: The Man Who Would Not Be King. 1991. pap. 2.95 (*0-590-43730-5*) Scholastic Inc.

Meltzer, Milton. George Washington & the Birth of Our Nation. LC 86-9222. 176p. (gr. 9-12). 1986. PLB 14.40 (*0-531-10253-X*) Watts.

Milton, Joyce. George Washington. (Orig.). (gr. k-6). 1988. pap. 2.95 (*0-440-40020-1*, YB) Dell.

Moncure, Jane B. My First Presidents' Day Book. Halverson, Lydia, illus. LC 87-10309. 32p. (ps-2). 1987. pap. 3.95 (*0-516-42910-8*) Childrens.

Morris, Jeffrey. The Washington Way. (Illus.). 128p. (gr. 5 up). 1994. RLB 22.95 (*0-8225-2928-9*) Lerner Pubns.

Osborne, Mary P. George Washington: Leader of a New Nation. LC 90-42601. (Illus.). 96p. (gr. 4-7). 1991. 14.00 (*0-8037-0947-1*); lib. bdg. 13.89 (*0-8037-0949-8*) Dial Bks Young.

Richards, Dorothy F. George Washington, a Talk with His Grandchildren. Nelson, John, illus. LC 78-8564. (gr. 1-5). 1978. PLB 13.95 (*0-89565-034-7*) Childs World.

Roop, Peter & Roop, Connie. Buttons for General Washington. Hanson, Peter E., illus. LC 86-6120. 48p. (gr. k-4). 1986. lib. bdg. 14.95 (*0-87614-294-3*); pap. 4.95 (*0-87614-476-8*) Carolrhoda Bks.

Sandak, Cass R. The Washingtons. (Illus.). 48p. (gr. 5). 1991. text ed. 12.95 RSBE (*0-89686-635-1*, Crestwood Hse) Macmillan Child Grp.

Santrey, Laurence. George Washington: Young Leader. LC 81-23150. (Illus.). 48p. (gr. 4-6). 1982. PLB 10.79 (*0-89375-758-6*); pap. text ed. 3.50 (*0-89375-759-4*) Troll Assocs.

Siegel, Beatrice. George & Martha Washington at Home in New York. Aloise, Frank, illus. LC 88-24534. 80p. (gr. 4-7). 1989. SBE 13.95 (*0-02-782721-6*, Four Winds) Macmillan Child Grp.

Smith, Kathie B. George Washington. Seward, James, illus. 24p. (gr. 4-6). 1987. (J Messner); PLB 5.99s.p. (*0-685-47101-2*) S&S Trade.

Stevenson, Augusta. George Washington: Young Leader. Dreany, E. J., illus. LC 86-10914. 192p. (gr. 2-6). 1986. pap. 3.95 (*0-02-042150-8*, Aladdin) Macmillan Child Grp.

Tunnell, Michael O. The Joke's on George. Osborn, Kathy, illus. LC 92-33312. 32p. (gr. k up). 1993. 14.00 (*0-688-11758-9*, Tambourine Bks); PLB 13.93 (*0-688-11759-7*, Tambourine Bks) Morrow.

Weinberg, Lawrence. George Washington. Bloch, Alex, illus. 48p. (gr. 2-4). 1988. pap. 2.50 (*0-681-40346-2*) Longmeadow Pr.

Williams, Brian. George Washington. (Illus.). 32p. (gr. 3-8). 1988. PLB 10.95 (*0-86307-924-5*) Marshall Cavendish.

Woods, Andrew. Young George Washington: America's First President. Himmelman, John, illus. LC 91-26405. 32p. (gr. k-2). 1992. PLB 11.59 (*0-8167-2540-3*); pap. text ed. 2.95 (*0-8167-2541-1*) Troll Assocs.

WASHINGTON, GEORGE, PRESIDENT U. S. 1732-1799–FICTION

Fritz, Jean. George Washington's Breakfast. Galdone, Paul, illus. (gr. 2-6). 1984. (Coward); pap. 6.95 (*0-698-20616-9*, Coward) Putnam Pub Group.

Gross, Ruth B. If You Grew up with George Washington. (gr. 4-7). 1993. pap. 4.95 (*0-590-45155-3*) Scholastic Inc.

Marshall, James. George & Martha. (gr. 3 up). 1993. pap. 7.95 incl. cass. (*0-395-45739-4*) HM.

Quackenbush, Robert. I Did It with My Hatchet: A Story of George Washington. Quackenbush, Robert, illus. 32p. (gr. 2-6). 1989. 14.95 (*0-945912-04-8*) Pippin Pr.

Small, David. George Washington's Cows. LC 93-39989. 1994. 15.00 (*0-374-32535-9*) FS&G.

Woodruff, Elvira. George Washington's Socks. (gr. 4-7). 1993. pap. 2.95 (*0-590-44036-5*) Scholastic Inc.

WASHINGTON, MARTHA (DANDREGE) CUSTIS, 1731-1802

Anderson, LaVere. Martha Washington: First Lady of the Land. Cary, illus. 80p. (gr. 2-6). 1991. Repr. of 1973 ed. lib. bdg. 12.95 (*0-7910-1452-5*) Chelsea Hse.

Marsh, Joan. Martha Washington. LC 92-24531. (Illus.). 64p. (gr. 5-8). 1993. PLB 12.90 (*0-531-20145-7*) Watts.

Wagoner, Jean B. Martha Washington: America's First First Lady. Goldstein, Leslie, illus. LC 86-10737. 192p. (gr. 2-6). 1986. pap. 3.95 (*0-02-042160-5*, Aladdin) Macmillan Child Grp.

Waldrop, Ruth. Martha Washington. Hendrix, Hurston H., illus. LC 87-61391. 112p. (gr. 3-6). 1987. PLB 10.95 (*0-317-59028-6*); pap. 6.95 (*0-317-59029-4*) RuSk Inc.

WASHINGTON, D. C.

Aylesworth, Thomas G. & Aylesworth, Virginia L. The Atlantic (Virginia, West Virginia, District of Columbia) (Illus.). 64p. (Orig.). 1990. lib. bdg. 16.95x (*1-55546-555-2*); pap. 6.95 (*0-7910-0533-X*) Chelsea Hse.

Bluestone, Carol & Irwin, Susan. Washington, D. C. Guidebook for Kids. rev. ed. LC 87-50322. (Illus.). 64p. (gr. 3-9). 1987. pap. 5.95 (*0-9601022-2-1*) Noodle Pr.

Carlson, Barbara. Our Nation's Capital City. (Illus.). 8p. (ps-3). 1988. incl. filmstrip 19.00 (*1-55933-003-1*, 3187) Know Unltd.

Carole Marsh Washington, D. C. Books, 44 bks. 1994. PLB 1027.80 set (*0-7933-1283-3*); pap. 587.80 set (*0-7933-5138-3*) Gallopade Pub Group.

Carpenter, Allan. District of Columbia. new ed. LC 78-31683. (Illus.). 96p. (gr. 4 up). 1979. PLB 20.55 (*0-516-04151-7*) Childrens.

Climo, Shirley. City! Washington, D. C. Ancona, George, illus. LC 90-1785. 64p. (gr. 3-7). 1991. SBE 16.95 (*0-02-719036-6*, Macmillan Child Bk) Macmillan Child Grp.

Colors of Washington. 16p. (gr. k-6). 1991. 2.50 (*0-9631472-0-X*) Martin Barry Prods.

Davis, James E. & Hawke, Sharryl D. Washington, D. C. (Illus.). 64p. (gr. 4-9). 1990. PLB 11.95 (*0-8172-3026-2*) Raintree Steck-V.

Fradin, Dennis B. Washington, D. C. LC 91-32919. 64p. (gr. 3-5). 1992. PLB 16.45 (*0-516-03851-6*); pap. 5.95 (*0-516-43851-4*) Childrens.

Kennon, Donald R. & Strincer, Richard. Washington Past & Present: A Guide to the Nation's Capital. rev. ed. Schwengel, Fred & Burger, Warren E.frwd. by. (Illus.). 144p. (gr. 7-12). 1993. pap. 5.95t (*0-685-64855-9*) US Capitol Hist.

Kent, Deborah. Washington, D. C. LC 90-35386. (Illus.). 144p. (gr. 4 up). 1990. PLB 20.55 (*0-516-00497-2*) Childrens.

—Washington, D. C. 200p. 1993. text ed. 15.40 (*1-56956-152-4*) W A T Braille.

A Kid's Guide to Washington, D. C. (gr. 1 up). 1989. pap. 8.95 (*0-15-200459-9*, Gulliver Bks) HarBrace.

Loewen, N. Washington, D. C. (Illus.). (gr. 5 up). 1989. lib. bdg. 15.94 (*0-86592-544-5*); lib. bdg. 11.95s.p. (*0-685-58590-5*) Rourke Corp.

Marsh, Carole. Avast, Ye Slobs! Washington, D.C. (Illus.). (gr. 3-12). 1994. PLB 24.95 (*0-7933-0280-3*); pap. 14.95 (*0-7933-0279-X*); computer disk 29.95 (*0-7933-0281-1*) Gallopade Pub Group.

—The Beast of the Washington, D.C. Bed & Breakfast. (Illus.). (gr. 3-12). 1994. PLB 24.95 (*0-7933-1468-2*); pap. 14.95 (*0-7933-1469-0*); computer disk 29.95 (*0-7933-1470-4*) Gallopade Pub Group.

—Bow Wow! Washington D. C. Dogs in History, Mystery, Legend, Lore, Humor & More! (Illus.). (gr. 3-12). 1994. PLB 24.95 (*0-7933-3491-8*); pap. 14.95 (*0-7933-3492-6*); computer disk 29.95 (*0-7933-3493-4*) Gallopade Pub Group.

—Chill Out: Scary Washington D. C. Tales Based on Frightening Washington D. C. Truths. (Illus.). 1994. lib. bdg. 24.95 (*0-7933-4798-X*); pap. 14.95 (*0-7933-4799-8*); disk 29.95 (*0-7933-4800-5*) Gallopade Pub Group.

—Christopher Columbus Comes to Washington D. C.! Includes Reproducible Activities for Kids! (Illus.). (gr. 3-12). 1994. PLB 24.95 (*0-7933-3644-9*); pap. 14.95 (*0-7933-3645-7*); computer disk 29.95 (*0-7933-3646-5*) Gallopade Pub Group.

—The Hard-to-Believe-But-True! Book of Washington, D.C. History, Mystery, Trivia, Legend, Lore, Humor & More. (Illus.). (gr. 3-12). 1994. PLB 24.95 (*0-685-45931-4*); pap. 14.95 (*0-7933-0276-5*); computer disk 29.95 (*0-7933-0278-1*) Gallopade Pub Group.

—If My Washington, D.C. Mama Ran the World! (Illus.). (gr. 3-12). 1994. PLB 24.95 (*0-7933-1477-1*); pap. 14.95 (*0-7933-1478-X*); computer disk 29.95 (*0-7933-1479-8*) Gallopade Pub Group.

—Jurassic Ark! Washington, D. C. Dinosaurs & Other Prehistoric Creatures. (gr. k-12). 1994. PLB 24.95 (*0-7933-7452-9*); pap. 14.95 (*0-7933-7453-7*); computer disk 29.95 (*0-7933-7454-5*) Gallopade Pub Group.

—Let's Quilt Washington, D.C. & Stuff it Topographically! (Illus.). (gr. 3-12). 1994. PLB 24.95 (*1-55609-564-3*); pap. 14.95 (*0-685-45930-6*); computer disk 29.95 (*0-7933-1461-5*) Gallopade Pub Group.

—Meow! Washington DC Cats in History, Mystery, Legend, Lore, Humor & More! (Illus.). (gr. 3-12). 1994. PLB 24.95 (*0-7933-3338-5*); pap. 14.95 (*0-7933-3339-3*); computer disk 29.95 (*0-7933-3340-7*) Gallopade Pub Group.

—Uncle Rebus: Washington, DC Picture Stories for Computer Kids. (Illus.). (gr. k-3). 1994. PLB 24.95 (*0-7933-4645-2*); pap. 14.95 (*0-7933-4646-0*); disk 29.95 (*0-7933-4647-9*) Gallopade Pub Group.

—Washington, D. C. & Other State Greats (Biographies) (Illus.). (gr. 3-12). 1994. PLB 24.95 (*0-7933-1480-1*); pap. 14.95 (*0-7933-1481-X*); computer disk 29.95 (*0-7933-1482-8*) Gallopade Pub Group.

—Washington, D. C. Bandits, Bushwackers, Outlaws, Crooks, Devils, Ghosts, Desperadoes & Other Assorted & Sundry Characters! (Illus.). (gr. 3-12). 1994. PLB 24.95 (*0-7933-0262-5*); pap. 14.95 (*0-7933-0261-7*); computer disk 29.95 (*0-7933-0263-3*) Gallopade Pub Group.

—Washington, D. C. Classic Christmas Trivia: Stories, Recipes, Activities, Legends, Lore & More! (Illus.). (gr. 3-12). 1994. PLB 24.95 (*0-7933-0265-X*); pap. 14.95 (*0-7933-0264-1*); computer disk 29.95 (*0-7933-0266-8*) Gallopade Pub Group.

—Washington, D. C. Coastales. (Illus.). (gr. 3-12). 1994. PLB 24.95 (*0-7933-1474-7*); pap. 14.95 (*0-7933-1475-5*); computer disk 29.95 (*0-7933-1476-3*) Gallopade Pub Group.

—Washington, D. C. Coastales! 1994. lib. bdg. 24.95 (*0-7933-7273-9*) Gallopade Pub Group.

—Washington D. C. "Crinkum-Crankum" A Funny Word Book about Our State. (Illus.). (gr. 3-12). 1994. 24.95 (*0-7933-4952-4*); pap. 14.95 (*0-7933-4953-2*); computer disk 29.95 (*0-7933-4954-0*) Gallopade Pub Group.

—Washington, D. C. Dingbats! Bk. 1: A Fun Book of Games, Stories, Activities & More about Our State That's All in Code! for You to Decipher. (Illus.). (gr. 3-12). 1994. PLB 24.95 (*0-7933-3797-6*); pap. 14.95 (*0-7933-3798-4*); computer disk 29.95 (*0-7933-3799-2*) Gallopade Pub Group.

—Washington, D. C. Festival Fun for Kids! Includes Reproducible Activities for Kids! (Illus.). (gr. 3-12). 1994. PLB 24.95 (*0-7933-3950-2*); pap. 14.95 (*0-7933-3951-0*); computer disk 29.95 (*0-7933-3952-9*) Gallopade Pub Group.

—The Washington D. C. Hot Air Balloon Mystery. (Illus.). (gr. 2-9). 1994. 24.95 (*0-7933-2390-8*); pap. 14.95 (*0-7933-2391-6*); computer disk 29.95 (*0-7933-2392-4*) Gallopade Pub Group.

—Washington, D. C. Jeopardy! Answers & Questions about Our State! (Illus.). (gr. 3-12). 1994. PLB 24.95 (*0-7933-4103-5*); pap. 14.95 (*0-7933-4104-3*); computer disk 29.95 (*0-7933-4105-1*) Gallopade Pub Group.

—Washington, D. C. "Jography" A Fun Run Thru Our State! (Illus.). (gr. 3-12). 1994. PLB 24.95 (*1-55609-562-7*); pap. 14.95 (*1-55609-561-9*); computer disk 29.95 (*0-7933-1460-7*) Gallopade Pub Group.

—Washington, D. C. Kid's Cookbook: Recipes, How-to, History, Lore & More! (Illus.). (gr. 3-12). 1994. PLB 24.95 (*0-7933-0274-9*); pap. 14.95 (*0-7933-0273-0*); computer disk 29.95 (*0-7933-0275-7*) Gallopade Pub Group.

—The Washington D. C. Mystery Van Takes Off! Book 1: Handicapped Washington D. C. Kids Sneak Off on a Big Adventure. (Illus.). (gr. 3-12). 1994. 24.95 (*0-7933-5105-7*); pap. 14.95 (*0-7933-5106-5*); computer disk 29.95 (*0-7933-5107-3*) Gallopade Pub Group.

—Washington, D. C. Quiz Bowl Crash Course! (Illus.). (gr. 3-12). 1994. PLB 24.95 (*0-7933-1471-2*); pap. 14.95 (*0-7933-1472-0*); computer disk 29.95 (*0-7933-1473-9*) Gallopade Pub Group.

—Washington, D. C. Rollercoasters! (Illus.). (gr. 3-12). 1994. PLB 24.95 (*0-7933-5248-7*); pap. 14.95 (*0-7933-5249-5*); computer disk 29.95 (*0-7933-5250-9*) Gallopade Pub Group.

—Washington, D. C. School Trivia: An Amazing & Fascinating Look at Our State's Teachers, Schools & Students! (Illus.). (gr. 3-12). 1994. PLB 24.95 (*0-7933-0271-4*); pap. 14.95 (*0-7933-0270-6*); computer disk 29.95 (*0-7933-0272-2*) Gallopade Pub Group.

—Washington, D. C. Silly Basketball Sportsmysteries, Vol. 1. (Illus.). (gr. 3-12). 1994. PLB 24.95 (*0-7933-0268-4*); pap. 14.95 (*0-7933-0267-6*); computer disk 29.95 (*0-7933-0269-2*) Gallopade Pub Group.

—Washington, D. C. Silly Basketball Sportsmysteries, Vol. 2. (Illus.). (gr. 3-12). 1994. PLB 24.95 (*0-7933-1483-6*); pap. 14.95 (*0-7933-1484-4*); computer disk 29.95 (*0-7933-1485-2*) Gallopade Pub Group.

—Washington, D. C. Silly Football Sportsmysteries, Vol. 1. (Illus.). (gr. 3-12). 1994. PLB 24.95 (*0-7933-1462-3*); pap. 14.95 (*0-7933-1463-1*); computer disk 29.95 (*0-7933-1464-X*) Gallopade Pub Group.

—Washington, D. C. Silly Trivia! (Illus.). (gr. 3-12). 1994. PLB 24.95 (*1-55609-560-0*); pap. 14.95 (*1-55609-559-7*); computer disk 29.95 (*0-7933-1459-3*) Gallopade Pub Group.

—Washington, D. C.'s (Most Devastating!) Disasters & (Most Calamitous!) Catastrophies! (Illus.). (gr. 3-12). 1994. PLB 24.95 (*0-7933-0259-5*); pap. 14.95 (*0-7933-0258-7*); computer disk 29.95 (*0-7933-0260-9*) Gallopade Pub Group.

—Washington, D.C. Silly Football Sportsmysteries, Vol. 2. (Illus.). (gr. 3-12). 1994. PLB 24.95 (*0-7933-1465-8*); pap. 14.95 (*0-7933-1466-6*); computer disk 29.95 (*0-7933-1467-4*) Gallopade Pub Group.

Munro, Roxie. The Inside-Outside Book of Washington, D. C. (Illus.). 48p. 1993. pap. 4.99 (*0-14-054940-4*, Puff Unicorn) Puffin Bks.

—Inside Outside Book of Washington D.C. Munro, Roxie, illus. LC 86-24267. 48p. (ps up). 1987. 13.95 (*0-525-44298-7*, DCB) Dutton Child Bks.

Pedersen, Anne. Kidding Around Washington, D. C., A Young Person's Guide. 2nd ed. Finnell, Jim, illus. 64p. (gr. 3 up). 1993. pap. 9.95 (*1-56261-093-7*) John Muir.

Reef, Catherine. Washington, D. C. LC 89-12025. (Illus.). 60p. (gr. 3 up). 1990. text ed. 13.95 RSBE (*0-87518-411-1*, Dillon) Macmillan Child Grp.

Steins, Richard. Our National Capital. (Illus.). 48p. (gr. 2-4). 1994. 13.40 (*1-56294-439-8*) Millbrook Pr.

Thompson, Kathleen. Washington, D. C. 48p. (gr. 4 up). 1986. PLB 19.97 (*0-86514-472-9*) Raintree Steck-V.

Tippet Shows Off Washington. 32p. (gr. 1-5). 1983. 6.95 (*0-686-47606-9*) Outdoor Bks.

Waters, Kate. The Story of the White House. 1991. 12.95 (*0-590-43335-0*, Scholastic Hardcover) Scholastic Inc.

Westbrook, Charles L. The Talisman of the United States: The Mysterious Street Lines of Washington, D. C. (Illus.). 123p. (Orig.). (gr. 12). 1990. pap. 10.95x (*0-9626554-0-6*) Westcom NC.

Weston, Marti & Decell, Florri. Washington! Adventure for Kids. 2nd ed. LC 90-70168. 64p. (gr. 1-9). 1990. pap. 6.95 (*0-918339-13-8*) Vandamere.

WASHINGTON, D. C. CAPITOL

Prolman, Marilyn. The Story of the Capitol. Wiskur, Darrell, illus. LC 69-14681. 32p. (gr. 3-6). 1969. pap. 3.95 (*0-516-44604-5*) Childrens.

WASHINGTON, D. C.–FICTION

Cook, John M. Inside Four Ninety-Five. Haye, Caroline, ed. (Illus.). 128p. 1989. write for info. J M Cook Pub.

Oestreicher, James. Choice Adventures: Monumental Discovery. 160p. 1992. pap. 4.99 (*0-8423-5030-6*) Tyndale.

Random, Candice F. Jimmy Crack Corn. Haas, Shelly O., illus. LC 93-16657. 1993. 7.00 (*0-87614-786-4*) Carolrhoda Bks.

Service, Pamela F. Stinker's Return. LC 92-21800. 96p. (gr. 4-6). 1993. SBE 12.95 (*0-684-19542-9*, Scribners Young Read) Macmillan Child Grp.

Warner, Gertrude C. The Mystery in Washington, D.C. (gr. 4-7). 1994. 10.95 (*0-8075-5409-X*); pap. 3.75 (*0-8075-5410-3*) A Whitman.

WASHINGTON, D. C.–HISTORY

Hilton, Suzanne. A Capital Capital City, 1790-1814. LC 91-31340. (Illus.). 160p. (gr. 4 up). 1992. SBE 14.95 (*0-689-31641-0*, Atheneum Child Bk) Macmillan Child Grp.

Hoig, Stan. Capital for the Nation. LC 90-2783. (Illus.). (gr. 4-7). 1990. 15.95 (*0-525-65034-2*, Cobblehill Bks) Dutton Child Bks.

Marsh, Carole. My First Book about Washington DC. (gr. k-4). 1994. PLB 24.95 (*0-7933-5593-1*); pap. 14.95 (*0-7933-5594-X*); computer disk 29.95 (*0-7933-5595-8*) Gallopade Pub Group.

—Washington D. C. Timeline: A Chronology of Washington D. C. History, Mystery, Trivia, Legend, Lore & More. (Illus.). (gr. 3-12). 1994. PLB 24.95 (*0-7933-5899-X*); pap. 14.95 (*0-7933-5900-7*); computer disk 29.95 (*0-7933-5901-5*) Gallopade Pub Group.

—Washington D. C.'s Unsolved Mysteries (& Their "Solutions") Includes Scientific Information & Other Activities for Students. (Illus.). (gr. 3-12). 1994. PLB 24.95 (*0-7933-5746-2*); pap. 14.95 (*0-7933-5747-0*); computer disk 29.95 (*0-7933-5748-9*) Gallopade Pub Group.

WASHINGTON, D. C. WHITE HOUSE

Kent, Deborah. The White House. LC 94-9489. (Illus.). 32p. (gr. 3-6). 1994. PLB 16.40 (*0-516-06684-6*); pap. 3.95 (*0-516-46684-4*) Childrens.

Marsh, Carole. Yes, You Have to Wipe Your Feet! White House Trivia. 1994. lib. bdg. 24.95 (*0-7933-6873-1*); pap. text ed. 14.95 (*0-7933-6872-3*); disk 29.95 (*0-7933-6874-X*) Gallopade Pub Group.

St. George, Judith. The White House: Cornerstone of a Nation. (Illus.). 160p. (gr. 6-12). 1990. 16.95 (*0-399-22186-7*, Putnam) Putnam Pub Group.

Sorensen, Lynda. The White House. LC 94-7055. 1994. write for info. (*1-55916-050-0*) Rourke Bk Co.

Waters, Kate. The Story of the White House. 1992. 4.95 (*0-590-43334-2*, Blue Ribbon Bks) Scholastic Inc.

WASHINGTON (STATE)

Carole Marsh Washington, D. C. Books, 44 bks. 1994. PLB 1027.80 set (*0-7933-1322-8*); pap. 587.80 set (*0-7933-5216-9*) Gallopade Pub Group.

Carpenter, Allan. Washington. LC 79-13390. (Illus.). 96p. (gr. 4 up). 1979. PLB 16.95 (*0-516-04147-9*) Childrens.

Cecotti, Loralie. Washington Wildlife. Hamer, Bonnie, illus. 24p. (Orig.). (gr. k-5). 1984. pap. text ed. 2.75 (*0-318-04105-7*) Coffee Break.

Diamond, Lynnell & Mueller, Marge. Let's Discover the San Juan Islands. Diamond, Lynnell & Mueller, Marge, illus. 48p. (Orig.). 1989. pap. 4.95 (*0-89886-220-5*) Mountaineers.

Fradin, Dennis. Washington: In Words & Pictures. Wahl, Richard, illus. LC 80-14745. 48p. (gr. 2-5). 1980. PLB 12.95 (*0-516-03947-4*) Childrens.

Fradin, Dennis B. & Fradin, Judith B. Washington. LC 94-14549. (Illus.). 64p. (gr. 3-5). 1994. PLB 22.00 (*0-516-03847-8*) Childrens.

Johnston, Helen & Elvidge, Vivian, eds. Eastside Historic Coloring Book. Lippie, Joel & Lippie, Jane, illus. McClelland, John M., Jr. 32p. (Orig.). (gr. 1-4). 1985. pap. 2.00 (*0-685-28865-X*) Marymoor Mus.

Johsnton, Helen & Johnston, Richard. Willowmoor: The Story of Marymoor Park. (Illus.). 48p. (Orig.). (gr. 9-12). 1976. pap. 2.50 (*0-685-28867-6*) Marymoor Mus.

League of Women Voters Staff. The State We're In: Washington: A Citizen's Guide to Washington State Government. 3rd ed. Bakke, Jean, ed. Haas, Wanda, intro. by. (Illus.). (gr. 9-12). 1990. pap. 6.95 (*1-878170-00-7*); pap. text ed. 5.50 (*0-685-47519-0*) LWV WA.

Marsh, Carole. Avast, Ye Slobs! Washington Pirate Trivia. (Illus.). 1994. PLB 24.95 (*0-7933-1196-9*); pap. 14.95 (*0-7933-1195-0*); computer disk 29.95 (*0-7933-1197-7*) Gallopade Pub Group.

—The Beast of the Washington Bed & Breakfast. (Illus.). 1994. PLB 24.95 (*0-7933-2212-X*); pap. 14.95 (*0-7933-2213-8*); computer disk 29.95 (*0-7933-2214-6*) Gallopade Pub Group.

—Bow Wow! Washington Dogs in History, Mystery, Legend, Lore, Humor & More! (Illus.). (gr. 3-12). 1994. PLB 24.95 (*0-7933-3608-2*); pap. 14.95 (*0-7933-3609-0*); computer disk 29.95 (*0-7933-3610-4*) Gallopade Pub Group.

—Chill Out: Scary Washington Tales Based on Frightening Washington Truths. (Illus.). 1994. lib. bdg. 24.95 (*0-7933-4795-5*); pap. 14.95 (*0-7933-4796-3*); disk 29.95 (*0-7933-4797-1*) Gallopade Pub Group.

—Christopher Columbus Comes to Washington! Includes Reproducible Activities for Kids! (Illus.). (gr. 3-12). 1994. PLB 24.95 (*0-7933-3761-5*); pap. 14.95 (*0-7933-3762-3*); computer disk 29.95 (*0-7933-3763-1*) Gallopade Pub Group.

—The Hard-to-Believe-But-True! Book of Washington History, Mystery, Trivia, Legend, Lore, Humor & More. (Illus.). 1994. PLB 24.95 (*0-7933-1193-4*); pap. 14.95 (*0-7933-1192-6*); computer disk 29.95 (*0-7933-1194-2*) Gallopade Pub Group.

—If My Washington Mama Ran the World! (Illus.). 1994. PLB 24.95 (*0-7933-2221-9*); pap. 14.95 (*0-7933-2222-7*); computer disk 29.95 (*0-7933-2223-5*) Gallopade Pub Group.

—Jurassic Ark! Washington Dinosaurs & Other Prehistoric Creatures. (gr. k-12). 1994. PLB 24.95 (*0-7933-7569-X*); pap. 14.95 (*0-7933-7570-3*); computer disk 29.95 (*0-7933-7571-1*) Gallopade Pub Group.

—Let's Quilt Our Washington County. 1994. lib. bdg. 24.95 (*0-7933-7254-2*); pap. text ed. 14.95 (*0-7933-7255-0*); disk 29.95 (*0-7933-7256-9*) Gallopade Pub Group.

—Let's Quilt Our Washington Town. 1994. lib. bdg. 24.95 (*0-7933-7104-X*); pap. text ed. 14.95 (*0-7933-7105-8*); disk 29.95 (*0-7933-7106-6*) Gallopade Pub Group.

—Let's Quilt Washington & Stuff It Topographically! (Illus.). 1994. PLB 24.95 (*0-7933-2204-9*); pap. 14.95 (*1-55609-133-8*); computer disk 29.95 (*0-7933-2205-7*) Gallopade Pub Group.

—Meow! Washington Cats in History, Mystery, Legend, Lore, Humor & More! (Illus.). (gr. 3-12). 1994. PLB 24.95 (*0-7933-3455-1*); pap. 14.95 (*0-7933-3456-X*); computer disk 29.95 (*0-7933-3457-8*) Gallopade Pub Group.

—My First Book about Washington. (gr. k-4). 1994. PLB 24.95 (*0-7933-5710-1*); pap. 14.95 (*0-7933-5711-X*); computer disk 29.95 (*0-7933-5712-8*) Gallopade Pub Group.

—Patch, the Pirate Dog: A Washington Pet Story. (ps-4). 1994. PLB 24.95 (*0-7933-5557-5*); pap. 14.95 (*0-7933-5558-3*); computer disk 29.95 (*0-7933-5559-1*) Gallopade Pub Group.

—Uncle Rebus: Washington Picture Stories for Computer Kids. (Illus.). (gr. k-3). 1994. PLB 24.95 (*0-7933-4642-8*); pap. 14.95 (*0-7933-4643-6*); disk 29.95 (*0-7933-4644-4*) Gallopade Pub Group.

—Washington & Other State Greats (Biographies!) (Illus.). 1994. PLB 24.95 (*0-7933-2224-3*); pap. 14.95 (*0-7933-2225-1*); computer disk 29.95 (*0-7933-2226-X*) Gallopade Pub Group.

—Washington Bandits, Bushwackers, Outlaws, Crooks, Devils, Ghosts, Desperadoes & Other Assorted & Sundry Characters! (Illus.). 1994. PLB 24.95 (*0-7933-1178-0*); pap. 14.95 (*0-7933-1177-2*); computer disk 29.95 (*0-7933-1179-9*) Gallopade Pub Group.

—Washington Classic Christmas Trivia: Stories, Recipes, Activities, Legends, Lore & More! (Illus.). 1994. PLB 24.95 (*0-7933-1181-0*); pap. 14.95 (*0-7933-1180-2*); computer dik 29.95 (*0-7933-1182-9*) Gallopade Pub Group.

—Washington Coastales. (Illus.). 1994. PLB 24.95 (*0-7933-2218-9*); pap. 14.95 (*0-7933-2219-7*); computer disk 29.95 (*0-7933-2220-0*) Gallopade Pub Group.

—Washington Coastales! 1994. lib. bdg. 24.95 (*0-7933-7312-3*) Gallopade Pub Group.

—Washington "Crinkum-Crankum" A Funny Word Book about Our State. (Illus.). (gr. 3-12). 1994. 24.95 (*0-7933-4949-4*); pap. 14.95 (*0-7933-4950-8*); computer disk 29.95 (*0-7933-4951-6*) Gallopade Pub Group.

—Washington Dingbats! Bk. 1: A Fun Book of Games, Stories, Activities & More about Our State That's All in Code! for You to Decipher. (Illus.). (gr. 3-12). 1994. PLB 24.95 (*0-7933-3914-6*); pap. 14.95 (*0-7933-3915-4*); computer disk 29.95 (*0-7933-3916-2*) Gallopade Pub Group.

—Washington Festival Fun for Kids! Includes Reproducible Activities for Kids! (Illus.). (gr. 3-12). 1994. PLB 24.95 (*0-7933-4067-5*); pap. 14.95 (*0-7933-4068-3*); computer disk 29.95 (*0-7933-4069-1*) Gallopade Pub Group.

—The Washington Hot Air Balloon Mystery. (Illus.). (gr. 2-9). 1994. 24.95 (*0-7933-2741-5*); pap. 14.95 (*0-7933-2742-3*); computer disk 29.95 (*0-7933-2743-1*) Gallopade Pub Group.

—Washington Jeopardy! Answers & Questions about Our State! (Illus.). (gr. 3-12). 1994. PLB 24.95 (*0-7933-4220-1*); pap. 14.95 (*0-7933-4221-X*); computer disk 29.95 (*0-7933-4222-8*) Gallopade Pub Group.

—Washington "Jography" A Fun Run Thru Our State! (Illus.). 1994. PLB 24.95 (*0-7933-2201-4*); pap. 14.95 (*0-7933-2202-2*); computer disk 29.95 (*0-7933-2203-0*) Gallopade Pub Group.

—Washington Kid's Cookbook: Recipes, How-to, History, Lore & More! (Illus.). 1994. PLB 24.95 (*0-7933-1190-X*); pap. 14.95 (*0-7933-1189-6*); computer disk 29.95 (*0-7933-1191-8*) Gallopade Pub Group.

—The Washington Mystery Van Takes Off! Book 1: Handicapped Washington Kids Sneak Off on a Big Adventure. (Illus.). (gr. 3-12). 1994. 24.95 (*0-7933-5102-2*); pap. 14.95 (*0-7933-5103-0*); computer disk 29.95 (*0-7933-5104-9*) Gallopade Pub Group.

—Washington Quiz Bowl Crash Course! (Illus.). 1994. PLB 24.95 (*0-7933-2215-4*); pap. 14.95 (*0-7933-2216-2*); computer disk 29.95 (*0-7933-2217-0*) Gallopade Pub Group.

—Washington Rollercoasters! (Illus.). (gr. 3-12). 1994. PLB 24.95 (*0-7933-5365-3*); pap. 14.95 (*0-7933-5366-1*); computer disk 29.95 (*0-7933-5367-X*) Gallopade Pub Group.

—Washington School Trivia: An Amazing & Fascinating Look at Our State's Teachers, Schools & Students! (Illus.). 1994. PLB 24.95 (*0-685-45964-0*); pap. 14.95 (*0-7933-1186-1*); computer disk 29.95 (*0-7933-1188-8*) Gallopade Pub Group.

—Washington Silly Basketball Sportsmysteries, Vol. 1. (Illus.). 1994. PLB 24.95 (*0-7933-1184-5*); pap. 14.95 (*0-7933-1183-7*); computer disk 29.95 (*0-7933-1185-3*) Gallopade Pub Group.

—Washington Silly Basketball Sportsmysteries, Vol. 2. (Illus.). 1994. PLB 24.95 (*0-7933-2227-8*); pap. 14.95 (*0-7933-2228-6*); computer disk 29.95 (*0-7933-2229-4*) Gallopade Pub Group.

—Washington Silly Football Sportsmysteries, Vol. 1. (Illus.). 1994. PLB 24.95 (*0-7933-2206-5*); pap. 14.95 (*0-7933-2207-3*); computer disk 29.95 (*0-7933-2208-1*) Gallopade Pub Group.

—Washington Silly Football Sportsmysteries, Vol. 2. (Illus.). 1994. PLB 24.95 (*0-685-45963-2*); pap. 14.95 (*0-7933-2210-3*); computer disk 29.95 (*0-7933-2211-1*) Gallopade Pub Group.

—Washington Silly Trivia! (Illus.). 1994. PLB 24.95 (*0-7933-2198-0*); pap. 14.95 (*0-7933-2199-9*); computer disk 29.95 (*0-7933-2200-6*) Gallopade Pub Group.

—Washington Timeline: A Chronology of Washington History, Mystery, Trivia, Legend, Lore & More. (Illus.). (gr. 3-12). 1994. PLB 24.95 (*0-7933-6016-1*); pap. 14.95 (*0-7933-6017-X*); computer disk 29.95 (*0-7933-6018-8*) Gallopade Pub Group.

—Washington's (Most Devastating!) Disasters & (Most Calamitous!) Catastrophies! (Illus.). 1994. PLB 24.95 (*0-7933-1175-6*); pap. 14.95 (*0-7933-1174-8*); computer disk 29.95 (*0-7933-1176-4*) Gallopade Pub Group.

—Washington's Unsolved Mysteries (& Their "Solutions") Includes Scientific Information & Other Activities for Students. (Illus.). (gr. 3-12). 1994. PLB 24.95 (*0-7933-5863-9*); pap. 14.95 (*0-7933-5864-7*); computer disk 29.95 (*0-7933-5865-5*) Gallopade Pub Group.

Olson, Joan & Olson, Gene. Washington Times & Trails. rev. ed. LC 75-83521. (Illus.). (gr. 7-12). 1983. pap. 8.97x (*0-913366-01-3*) Windyridge.

Powell, E. S. Washington. LC 92-13366. 1993. PLB 17.50 (*0-8225-2726-X*) Lerner Pubns.

Schweizer, William H. Solemn Silence: The Complete Guide to Hood Canal, by Land, & Sea. Amundsen, Richard, illus. 304p. (Orig.). 1992. pap. write for info. (*0-925244-02-3*) EOS Pub.

Seablom, Seth H. Washington State Coloring Guide. (Illus.). 32p. (gr. 1-6). 1978. pap. 2.50 (*0-918800-03-X*) Seablom.

Stein, R. C. Washington. LC 91-13509. 144p. (gr. 4 up). 1991. PLB 20.55 (*0-516-00493-X*) Childrens.

Stein, R. Conrad. Washington. 208p. 1993. text ed. 15.40 (*1-56956-146-X*) W A T Braille.

Thompson, Kathleen. Washington. 48p. (gr. 3 up). 1986. PLB 19.97 (*0-86514-470-2*) Raintree Steck-V.

Way, Nancy. Our Town Redmond. Johnston, Helen, intro. by. (Illus.). (gr. 9-12). 1989. write for info. Marymoor Mus.

Yates, Richard. Our Evergreen State Government: State & Local Government in Washington. Smith-Danell, Paula, illus. 190p. 1989. 13.95 (*0-911927-10-7*) Info Oregon.

WASHINGTON (STATE)–FICTION

Beatty, Patricia. Eight Mules from Monterey. LC 92-24596. 224p. (gr. 6 up). 1993. pap. 4.95 (*0-688-12281-7*, Pub. by Beech Tree Bks) Morrow.

—The Nickel-Plated Beauty. LC 92-23318. 272p. (gr. 5 up). 1993. 14.00 (*0-688-12360-0*); pap. 3.95 (*0-685-61089-6*) Morrow Jr Bks.

Cecotti, Loralie. Seattle Center. Hamer, Bonnie, illus. 24p. (Orig.). (gr. 1-4). 1983. pap. 2.75 (*0-933992-30-0*) Coffee Break.

Dumond, Val. Visiting Olympia. Ballman, Jean, illus. 24p. (Orig.). (gr. 1-4). 1983. pap. 2.75 (*0-933992-39-4*) Coffee Break.

Helstrom, David C. My Tacoma Dome. Hamer, Bonnie, illus. 24p. (Orig.). (gr. 1-4). 1983. pap. 2.75 (*0-933992-29-7*) Coffee Break.

—Visiting Mt. Rainier. Harder, Arvid & Hamer, Bonnie, illus. 28p. (Orig.). (gr. 1-4). 1984. pap. 2.75 (*0-933992-37-8*) Coffee Break.

Luenn, Nancy, ed. A Horse's Tale: Ten Adventures in One Hundred Years. Megale, Marina & Schumacher, Sharon, illus. LC 88-61152. 96p. (Orig.). (gr. 2-6). 1988. lib. bdg. 16.95 (*0-943990-51-3*); pap. 7.95 (*0-943990-50-5*) Parenting Pr.

Parkhurst, Carole. Visiting Tacoma. Hamer, Bonnie, illus. 24p. (Orig.). (gr. 1-4). 1983. pap. 2.75 (*0-933992-38-6*) Coffee Break.

Sharpe, Susan. Spirit Quest. Sharpe, Kate & Sharpe, Alison, illus. LC 91-4417. 128p. (gr. 4-6). 1991. SBE 13.95 (*0-02-782355-5*, Bradbury Pr) Macmillan Child Grp.

—Spirit Quest. 128p. (gr. 3-7). 1993. pap. 3.99 (*0-14-036282-7*) Puffin Bks.

WASPS

Eastman, David. I Can Read About Bees & Wasps. LC 78-73773. (Illus.). (gr. 2-5). 1979. pap. 2.50 (*0-89375-203-7*) Troll Assocs.

Fichter, George S. Bees, Wasps, & Ants. Kest, Kristin, illus. 36p. (gr. k-3). 1993. 4.95 (*0-307-11434-1*, 11434, Golden Pr) Western Pub.

Johnson, Sylvia A. Wasps. Ogawa, Hiroshi, illus. LC 83-23847. 48p. (gr. 4 up). 1984. PLB 19.95 (*0-8225-1460-5*) Lerner Pubns.

Lavies, Bianca. Wasps at Home. Lavies, Bianca, photos by. LC 90-27338. (Illus.). 32p. (gr. 2-5). 1991. 13.95 (*0-525-44704-0*, DCB) Dutton Child Bks.

Ogawa, Hiroshi. The Potter Wasp. Pohl, Kathy, ed. (Illus.). 32p. (gr. 3-7). 1986. PLB 10.95 (*0-8172-2541-2*) Raintree Steck-V.

WASTE DISPOSAL

see Refuse and Refuse Disposal; Sewage Disposal; Waste Products

WASTE PRODUCTS

see also Refuse and Refuse Disposal

Foster, Joanna. Cartons, Cans, & Orange Peels: Where Does Our Garbage Go? (Illus.). 64p. (gr. 3-6). 1991. 15.95 (*0-395-56436-0*, Clarion Bks) HM.

Gutnik, Martin J. Experiments That Explore Recycling. LC 91-26147. (Illus.). 72p. (gr. 5-8). 1992. PLB 14.40 (*1-56294-116-X*) Millbrook Pr.

Hare, Tony. Toxic Waste. LC 91-8666. (Illus.). 32p. (gr. 5-8). 1991. PLB 12.40 (*0-531-17308-9*, Gloucester Pr) Watts.

Klein, Bill. A Kid's Guide to Finding Good Stuff. (Illus.). 64p. (Orig.). (gr. 4-9). 1994. pap. 10.95 (*0-943173-96-5*) Harbinger AZ.

Kouhoupt, Rudy & Marti, Donald B., Jr. How on Earth Do We Recycle Metal? Seiden, Art, illus. LC 91-28953. 64p. (gr. 4-6). 1992. PLB 13.40 (*1-56294-142-9*) Millbrook Pr.

Kronenwetter, Michael. Managing Toxic Wastes. Steltenpohl, Jane, ed. (Illus.). 126p. (gr. 7-10). 1989. lib. bdg. 13.98 (*0-671-69051-5*, J Messner) S&S Trade.

Managing Toxic Wastes. (Illus.). 128p. (gr. 7-10). 1989. 11.96 (*0-382-09577-4*, J Messner) S&S Trade.

Pfiffner, George. Earth-Friendly Wearables: How to Make Fabulous Clothes & Accessories from Reusable Objects. Date not set. pap. text ed. 12.95 (*0-471-00823-0*) Wiley.

Schwartz, Linda. Likeable Recyclables. LC 92-81436. 128p. (gr. 1-6). 1992. 9.95 (*0-88160-210-8*, LW256) Learning Wks.

Snodgrass, M. E. Environmental Awareness: Land Pollution. James, Jody, ed. Vista Three Design Staff, illus. LC 91-8303. 48p. (gr. 4 up). 1991. lib. bdg. 14.95 (*0-944280-29-3*) Bancroft-Sage.

—Environmental Awareness: Solid Waste. James, Jody, ed. Vista Three Design Staff, illus. LC 90-20950. 48p. (gr. 4 up). 1991. PLB 14.95 (*0-944280-28-5*) Bancroft-Sage.

—Environmental Awareness: Toxic Waste. James, Jody, ed. Vista Three Design Staff, illus. LC 91-7427. 48p. (gr. 4 up). 1991. lib. bdg. 14.95 (*0-944280-27-7*) Bancroft-Sage.

Szumski, Bonnie. Toxic Wastes: Examining Cause & Effect Relationships. LC 89-16906. (Illus.). 32p. (gr. 3-6). 1990. PLB 10.95 (*0-89908-643-8*) Greenhaven.

Zipko, Stephen J. Toxic Threat: How Hazardous Substances Poison Our Lives. rev. ed. Steltenpohl, Jane, ed. (Illus.). 208p. (gr. 7 up). 1990. lib. bdg. 14.98 (*0-671-69330-1*, J Messner); pap. 5.95 (*0-671-69331-X*) S&S Trade.

WATCHES

see Clocks and Watches

WATER

see also Floods; Glaciers; Ice; Lakes; Ocean; Rain and Rainfall; Rivers; Snow

Ardley, Neil. Science Book of Water. 29p. (gr. 2-5). 1991. 9.95 (*0-15-200575-7*) HarBrace.

Baines, John. Water. LC 92-45668. (Illus.). 32p. (gr. 3-6). 1993. 13.95 (*1-56847-041-X*) Thomson Lrning.

Bains, Rae. Water. Garcia, T. R., illus. LC 84-2718. 32p. (gr. 3-6). 1985. PLB 9.49 (*0-8167-0194-6*); pap. text ed. 2.95 (*0-8167-0195-4*) Troll Assocs.

Barss, Karen J. Clean Water. (Illus.). (gr. 5 up). 1992. lib. bdg. 19.95 (*0-7910-1583-1*) Chelsea Hse.

Benedict, Kitty. Water: My First Nature Books. Felix, Monique, illus. 32p. (gr. k-2). 1993. pap. 2.95 (*1-56189-169-X*) Amer Educ Pub.

Berger, Melvin. All about Water. (ps-3). 1994. pap. 3.95 (*0-590-46761-1*) Scholastic Inc.

Blueford, J. R., et al. Water Cycle - The Earth's Gift. (gr. k-6). 1992. 19.95 (*1-56638-146-0*) Math Sci Nucleus.

Charman, Andrew. Water. LC 93-20880. 1994. PLB 18.99 (*0-8114-5508-4*) Raintree Steck-V.

Cossi, Olga. Water Wars: The Fight to Control & Conserve Nature's Most Precious Resource. LC 92-43968. (Illus.). 128p. (gr. 6-7). 1993. text ed. 13.95 RSBE (*0-02-724595-0*, New Discovery Bks) Macmillan Child Grp.

Cristini, Ermanno & Puricelli, Luigi. In the Pond. Cristini, Ermanno & Puricelli, Luigi, illus. LC 84-972. 28p. (ps up). 1991. pap. 12.95 (*0-907234-43-7*) Picture Bk Studio.

Devonshire, Hilary. Water. LC 91-8378. (Illus.). 32p. (gr. 5-7). 1992. PLB 12.40 (*0-531-14125-X*) Watts.

Dickinson, Jane. Wonders of Water. Schneider, Rex, illus. LC 82-17388. 32p. (gr. 3-6). 1983. PLB 10.59 (*0-89375-874-4*); pap. text ed. 2.95 (*0-89375-875-2*) Troll Assocs.

Dorros, Arthur. Follow the Water from Brook to Ocean. Dorros, Arthur, illus. LC 90-1438. 32p. (gr. k-4). 1991. PLB 14.89 (*0-06-021599-2*) HarpC Child Bks.

—Follow the Water from Brook to Ocean. LC 90-1438. (Illus.). 32p. (gr. k-4). 1993. pap. 4.95 (*0-06-445115-1*, Trophy) HarpC Child Bks.

Edom, H. Science with Water. (Illus.). 24p. (gr. 1-4). 1991. lib. bdg. 12.96 (*0-88110-630-5*, Usborne); pap. 4.95 (*0-7460-1261-6*, Usborne) EDC.

Ellis, Chris. Water. (Illus.). 48p. (gr. 7-9). 1992. 13.95 (*0-563-34756-2*, BBC-Parkwest); pap. 6.95 (*0-563-34616-7*, BBC-Parkwest) Parkwest Pubns.

Evans, David & Williams, Claudette. Water & Floating. LC 92-53479. (Illus.). 24p. (gr. k-3). 1993. 9.95 (*1-56458-208-6*) Dorling Kindersley.

Fowler, Allan. It Could Still Be Water. LC 92-7402. (Illus.). 32p. (ps-2). 1992. PLB 10.75 (*0-516-06003-1*); big bk. 22.95 (*0-516-49630-1*) Childrens.

—It Could Still Be Water. LC 92-7402. (Illus.). 32p. (ps-2). 1993. pap. 3.95 (*0-516-46003-X*) Childrens.

—Y Aun Podria Ser Agua - It Could Still Be Water. LC 92-7402. (SPA., Illus.). 32p. (ps-2). 1993. big bk. 22.95 (*0-516-59630-6*); PLB 10.75 (*0-516-36003-5*); pap. 3.95 (*0-516-56003-4*) Childrens.

Gable, Kristine & O'Connell, John. Follow Me to the Sea. LC 94-5198. (Illus.). 1994. 7.00 (*0-87842-271-4*) Mountain Pr.

Gans, Roma. Water for Dinosaurs & You. LC 78-158691. (Illus.). (gr. k-3). 1973. PLB 11.89 (*0-690-87027-2*, Crowell Jr Bks); (TYC-J) HarpC Child Bks.

Gardner, Robert. Experimenting with Water. LC 93-15586. (Illus.). 144p. (gr. 7-12). 1993. PLB 13.40 (*0-531-12549-1*) Watts.

Glover, David. Flying & Floating. LC 92-40212. 32p. (gr. 1-4). 1993. 10.95 (*1-85697-843-5*, Kingfisher LKC); pap. 5.95 (*1-85697-937-7*) LKC.

Green, Ivah. Splash & Trickle. Connor, Bil, illus. (gr. 2-3). 1978. pap. 1.25 (*0-89508-062-1*) Rainbow Bks.

Greene, Carol. Caring for Our Water. LC 91-2683. (Illus.). 32p. (gr. k-3). 1991. lib. bdg. 12.95 (*0-89490-356-X*) Enslow Pubs.

Hoff, Mary & Rodgers, Mary M. Our Endangered Planet: Groundwater. (Illus.). 64p. (gr. 4-6). 1991. PLB 21.50 (*0-8225-2500-3*) Lerner Pubns.

—Our Endangered Planet: Rivers & Lakes. (Illus.). 64p. (gr. 4-6). 1991. PLB 21.50 (*0-8225-2501-1*) Lerner Pubns.

Jennings, Terry. Water. LC 88-22871. (Illus.). 32p. (gr. 3-6). 1989. pap. 4.95 (*0-516-48410-9*) Childrens.

Johnston, Tom. Water, Water! Pooley, Sarah, illus. LC 87-42750. 32p. (gr. 4-6). 1988. PLB 17.27 (*1-55532-407-X*) Gareth Stevens Inc.

Kalman, Bobbie & Schaub, Janine. Wonderful Water. (Illus.). 32p. (gr. k-8). 1992. PLB 15.95 (*0-86505-553-X*); pap. 7.95 (*0-86505-579-3*) Crabtree Pub Co.

Larson, Wendy. Water. Curti, Anna, illus. 14p. (ps-1). 1994. bds. 4.95 (*0-448-40572-5*, G&D) Putnam Pub Group.

McClymont, Diane. Water. Young, Richard, ed. LC 91-20536. (Illus.). 32p. (gr. 3-5). 1991. PLB 15.93 (*1-56074-006-X*) Garrett Ed Corp.

Mebane, Robert. Water & Liquids. 1994. PLB write for info. H Holt & Co.

Mebane, Robert & Rybolt, Thomas. Water & Other Liquids. (Illus.). 64p. (gr. 5-8). 1995. bds. 15.95 (*0-8050-2840-4*) TFC Bks NY.

Michel, Francois. Water. Larvor, Yves, illus. LC 92-9715. 1993. 19.95 (*0-688-11427-X*) Lothrop.

Morgan, Sally & Morgan, Adrian. Water. LC 93-31721. (Illus.). 48p. (gr. 5-9). 1994. 14.95x (*0-8160-2982-2*) Facts on File.

Murphy, Bryan. Experiment with Water. 32p. (gr. 2-5). 1991. PLB 17.50 (*0-8225-2453-8*) Lerner Pubns.

Murray, Peter. Professor Solomon Snickerdoodle Looks at Water. Mitchell, Anastasia, illus. LC 93-1322. (gr. 2-6). 1995. 14.95 (*1-56766-081-9*) Childs World.

Nielsen, Shelly & Berg, Julie. I Love Water. LC 93-18957. 1993. PLB 14.96 (*1-56239-190-9*) Abdo & Dghtrs.

Oxlade, Chris. Water. Thompson, Ian, illus. LC 94-5548. 30p. (gr. 2-5). 1994. 12.95 (*0-8120-6448-8*); pap. 4.95 (*0-8120-1986-5*) Barron.

Parramon, J. M., et al. Water. 32p. (ps). 1985. pap. 6.95 (*0-8120-3599-2*) Barron.

Peacock, Graham. Water. LC 93-49799. (Illus.). 32p. (gr. 2-4). 1994. 14.95 (*1-56847-077-0*) Thomson Lrning.

Peters, Lisa W. Water's Way. Rand, Ted, illus. 32p. (ps-2). 1991. 14.95 (*1-55970-062-9*) Arcade Pub Inc.

Reidel, Marlene. From Ice to Rain. Reidel, Marlene, illus. 24p. (ps-3). 1981. PLB 10.95 (*0-87614-157-2*) Carolrhoda Bks.

Richardson, Wendy & Richardson, Jack. Water: Through the Eyes of Artists. LC 90-34280. 48p. (gr. 4 up). 1991. PLB 15.40 (*0-516-09286-3*); pap. 7.95 (*0-516-49286-1*) Childrens.

Robbins. Water. (gr. k-3). 1994. 16.95 (*0-8050-2257-0*) H Holt & Co.

Robson, Pam. Water, Paddles, & Boats. LC 92-375. 1992. 12.40 (*0-531-17376-3*, Gloucester Pr) Watts.

Russell, Naomi. The Stream. Russell, Naomi, illus. LC 90-47497. 32p. (ps-1). 1991. 9.95 (*0-525-44729-6*, DCB) Dutton Child Bks.

Rybolt, Thomas R. & Mebane, Robert C. Environmental Experiments about Water. LC 92-41235. (Illus.). 96p. (gr. 4-9). 1993. lib. bdg. 16.95 (*0-89490-410-8*) Enslow Pubs.

Sauvain, Philip. Water. LC 91-19145. (Illus.). 48p. (gr. 8-9). 1992. text ed. 13.95 RSBE (*0-02-781078-X*, New Discovery) Macmillan Child Grp.

Schmid, Eleonore. The Water's Journey. Schmid, Eleanore, illus. LC 89-42872. 32p. (gr. k-3). 1990. 14.95 (*1-55858-013-1*) North-South Bks NYC.

Searle-Barnes, Bonita. Water. (Illus.). 32p. (gr. k-3). 1993. 6.99 (*0-7459-2693-2*) Lion USA.

—The Wonder of God's World: Water. Smithson, Colin, illus. LC 92-44274. 1993. 6.99 (*0-7459-2024-1*) Lion USA.

Seed, Deborah. Water Science. (Illus.). (gr. 2-7). 1992. pap. 8.61 (*0-201-57778-X*) Addison-Wesley.

Seixas, Judith S. Water- What It Is, What It Does. Huffman, Tom, illus. LC 86-14926. 56p. (gr. 1-4). 1987. 13.00 (*0-688-06607-0*); lib. bdg. 12.93 (*0-688-06608-9*) Greenwillow.

Smith, David. The Water Cycle. LC 93-976. 32p. (gr. 2-5). 1993. 12.95 (*1-56847-092-4*) Thomson Lrning.

Spar, J. Willy, a Story of Water. LC 68-56819. (Illus.). 32p. (gr. 2-3). 1968. PLB 9.95 (*0-87783-051-7*); pap. 3.94 deluxe ed (*0-87783-117-3*) Oddo.

Stangl, Jean. H20 Science. (gr. 3-6). 1990. pap. 9.95 (*0-8224-3604-3*) Fearon Teach Aids.

Stwertka, Eve. Drip Drop Waters Journey. (gr. 4-7). 1990. lib. bdg. 5.95 (*0-671-69462-6*, J Messner) S&S Trade.

Swallow, Su. Water. LC 90-31234. (Illus.). 32p. (gr. k-4). 1990. PLB 11.90 (*0-531-14061-X*) Watts.

Taylor, Barbara. Sink or Swim! The Science of Water. Bull, Peter, et al, illus. LC 90-42618. 40p. (Orig.). (gr. 2-5). 1991. pap. 4.95 (*0-679-80815-9*) Random Bks Yng Read.

—Water & Life. LC 90-32523. (Illus.). 32p. (gr. 5-8). 1991. PLB 12.40 (*0-531-14116-0*) Watts.

—Water at Work. LC 90-32525. (Illus.). 32p. (gr. 4-6). 1991. PLB 12.40 (*0-531-14117-9*) Watts.

Tesar, Jenny. Food & Water: Threats, Shortages & Solutions. (Illus.). 128p. (gr. 7-12). 1992. lib. bdg. 18.95x (*0-8160-2495-2*) Facts on File.

Time-Life Inc. Editors. Do Fish Drink? First Questions & Answers about Water. Kagan, Neil, ed. LC 92-40301. (Illus.). 48p. (ps). 1993. write for info. (*0-7835-0850-6*); PLB write for info. (*0-7835-0851-4*) Time-Life.

Twist, Clint. Rain to Dams: Projects with Water. LC 89-28987. 1990. PLB 12.40 (*0-531-17199-X*, Gloucester Pr) Watts.

Walker, Sally M. Water Up, Water Down: The Hydrolic Cycle. 48p. (gr. 3-6). 1992. PLB 19.95 (*0-87614-695-7*) Carolrhoda Bks.

Walpole, Brenda. Water. Stefoff, Rebecca, ed. Barber, Ed, photos by. LC 90-40381. (Illus.). 32p. (gr. 3-5). 1990. PLB 15.93 (*0-944483-72-0*) Garrett Ed Corp.

Wheeler, Jill. Every Drop Counts: A Book about Water. LC 93-15463. 1993. 12.94 (*1-56239-195-X*) Abdo & Dghtrs.

Wilkins, Mary-Jane. Air, Light & Water. Bull, Peter, illus. LC 90-42620. 40p. (Orig.). (gr. 2-5). 1991. pap. 3.95 (*0-679-80859-0*) Random Bks Yng Read.

WATER–CONSERVATION

see Water Conservation

WATER–POLLUTION

see also Refuse and Refuse Disposal; Sewage Disposal; also Petroleum Pollution of Water and similar headings

Amos, Janine. Pollution. LC 92-16338. (Illus.). 32p. (gr. 2-3). 1992. PLB 18.99 (*0-8114-3405-2*) Raintree Steck-V.
—Pollution. (ps-3). 1993. pap. 4.95 (*0-8114-4917-3*) Raintree Steck-V.
Anderson, Madelyn K. Oil Spills. LC 90-32896. (Illus.). 64p. (gr. 5-8). 1990. PLB 12.90 (*0-531-10872-4*) Watts.
Asimov, Isaac. Why Are Some Beaches Oily? LC 92-5345. 1992. PLB 15.93 (*0-8368-0796-0*) Gareth Stevens Inc.
Berger, Melvin. Oil Spill! Mirocha, Paul, illus. LC 92-34779. 32p. (gr. k-4). 1994. 15.00 (*0-06-022909-8*); PLB 14.89 (*0-06-022912-8*) HarpC Child Bks.
Blashfield, Jean & Black, Wallace. Oil Spills. LC 91-25861. 128p. (gr. 4-8). 1991. PLB 20.55 (*0-516-05508-9*) Childrens.
Breiter, Herta S. Pollution. LC 87-23233. (Illus.). 48p. (Orig.). (gr. 2-6). 1987. PLB 10.95 (*0-8172-3259-1*); pap. 4.95 (*0-8114-8216-2*) Raintree Steck-V.
Bright, Michael. Polluting the Oceans. (Illus.). 32p. (gr. k-4). 1991. PLB 11.90 (*0-531-17353-4*, Gloucester Pr) Watts.
Carr, Terry. Spill! The Story of the Exxon Valdez. LC 90-13104. (Illus.). 64p. (gr. 5-8). 1991. PLB 18.90 (*0-531-10998-4*) Watts.
Conservation of the Sea. LC 93-19872. 1994. write for info. (*0-7910-2102-5*) Chelsea Hse.
Gancri, Anita. Ponds, Rivers, & Lakes. LC 91-5039. (Illus.). 48p. (gr. 5 up). 1992. text ed. 13.95 RSBE (*0-87518-497-9*, Dillon) Macmillan Child Grp.
Gay, Kathlyn. Water Pollution. LC 90-376. (Illus.). 144p. (gr. 7-12). 1990. PLB 13.90 (*0-531-10949-6*) Watts.
Goldman, Linda. Cleaning Up Our Water. LC 94-18025. (Illus.). 96p. (gr. 3-6). 1994. PLB 23.20 (*0-516-05543-7*) Childrens.
Greene, Jack. The Mudgrump. Florman, Lisa, illus. LC 80-68130. 56p. (Orig.). (gr. k-6). 1980. pap. text ed. 3.95 perfect binding (*0-9601258-3-3*) Golden Owl Pub.
Gutnik, Martin J. Experiments That Explore Oil Spills. (Illus.). 72p. (gr. 5-8). 1991. PLB 14.40 (*1-56294-013-9*) Millbrook Pr.
Hamilton, Sue. Exxon Valdez Oil Spill. Hamilton, John, ed. LC 90-82628. (Illus.). 32p. (gr. 4). 1990. PLB 11.96 (*0-939179-84-9*) Abdo & Dghtrs.
Kiefer, Irene. Poisoned Land: The Problems of Hazardous Waste. LC 80-22120. (Illus.). 96p. (gr. 6-9). 1981. SBE 13.95 (*0-689-30837-X*, Atheneum Child Bk) Macmillan Child Grp.
Leggett, Dennis. Troubled Waters. LC 90-46572. (Illus.). 48p. (gr. 5-9). 1991. PLB 12.95 (*1-85435-275-X*) Marshall Cavendish.
Lucas, Eileen. Water: A Resource in Crisis. LC 91-36137. 128p. (gr. 4-8). 1991. PLB 20.55 (*0-516-05509-7*) Childrens.
Nardo, Don. Oil Spills. LC 90-23524. (Illus.). 112p. (gr. 5-8). 1991. PLB 14.95 (*1-56006-151-0*) Lucent Bks.
National Wildlife Federation Staff. Pollution: Problems & Solutions. (gr. k-8). 1991. pap. 7.95 (*0-945051-40-9*, 75045) Natl Wildlife.
O'Neill, Mary. Water Squeeze. Bindon, John, illus. LC 89-77456. 32p. (gr. 3-6). 1989. PLB 12.89 (*0-8167-2080-0*); pap. text ed. 3.95 (*0-8167-2081-9*) Troll Assocs.
Phillips, Anne W. The Ocean. LC 90-36296. (Illus.). 48p. (gr. 6). 1990. text ed. 12.95 RSBE (*0-89686-541-X*, Crestwood Hse) Macmillan Child Grp.
Rothman, Joel. Once There Was a Stream. Roberts, Bruce, photos by. LC 72-90692. (Illus.). 32p. (gr. k-4). 1973. 8.95 (*0-87592-038-1*) Scroll Pr.
Shelby, Anne. What to Do about Pollution. Trivas, Irene, illus. LC 92-24173. 32p. (ps-1). 1993. 14.95 (*0-531-05471-3*); PLB 14.99 (*0-531-08621-6*) Orchard Bks Watts.
Shepherd, John G. The Stream Team on Patrol. LC 93-15386. (gr. 4 up). 1993. 14.96 (*1-56239-207-7*) Abdo & Dghtrs.
Snodgrass, M. E. Environmental Awareness: Water Pollution. James, Jody, ed. Vista Three Design Staff, illus. LC 90-20949. 48p. (gr. 4 up). 1991. PLB 14.95 (*0-944280-26-9*) Bancroft-Sage.
Stille, Darlene. Oil Spills. LC 90-21455. (Illus.). 48p. (gr. k-4). 1991. PLB 12.85 (*0-516-01116-2*); pap. 4.95 (*0-516-41116-0*) Childrens.
—Water Pollution. LC 89-25344. (Illus.). 48p. (gr. k-4). 1990. PLB 12.85 (*0-516-01190-1*); pap. 4.95 (*0-516-41190-X*) Childrens.
Talen, Maria. Ocean Pollution. LC 91-15567. (Illus.). 112p. (gr. 5-8). 1991. PLB 14.95 (*1-56006-104-9*) Lucent Bks.
Turning the Tide on Trash: A Learning Guide on Marine Debris. 78p. (Orig.). (gr. 7-12). 1994. pap. text ed. 40.00x (*0-7881-0392-X*) Diane Pub.

WATER-POLLUTION-FICTION

Asch, Frank. Up River. Levin, Ted & Lehmer, Steve, illus. LC 93-38687. 1995. 16.00 (*0-671-88703-3*, S&S BFYR) S&S Trade.

WATER ANIMALS

see Fresh-Water Animals; Marine Animals

WATER BIRDS

see also names of water birds, e.g. Penguins

Beaty, Dave. Waterfowl. LC 92-32319. (gr. 2-6). 1993. 15.95 (*1-56766-006-1*) Childs World.
Brown, Mary B. Wings along the Waterway. LC 91-18559. (Illus.). 80p. (gr. 3-6). 1992. 17.95 (*0-531-05981-2*); lib. bdg. 17.99 (*0-531-08581-3*) Orchard Bks Watts.
Kerrod, Robin. Birds: Water Birds. Bailey, Jill, contrib. by. (Illus.). 1989. 17.95x (*0-8160-1962-2*) Facts on File.
Mabie, Grace. A Picture Book of Water Birds. Pistolesi, Roseanna, illus. LC 91-34129. 24p. (gr. 1-4). 1992. PLB 9.59 (*0-8167-2436-9*); pap. text ed. 2.50 (*0-8167-2437-7*) Troll Assocs.

WATER COLOR PAINTING

Sanchez, Isidro. Watercolor. Ferron, Miguel, et al, illus. 48p. 1991. pap. 7.95 (*0-8120-4717-6*) Barron.

WATER CONSERVATION

see also Water Supply

Bailey, Donna. What We Can Do about Wasting Water. LC 91-8657. (Illus.). 32p. (gr. k-4). 1992. PLB 11.40 (*0-531-11019-2*) Watts.
Brooks, F. Protecting Rivers & Seas. (Illus.). 24p. (gr. 2-5). 1992. PLB 11.96 (*0-88110-529-5*, Usborne); pap. 4.50 (*0-7460-0687-X*, Usborne) EDC.
Cossi, Olga. Water Wars: The Fight to Control & Conserve Nature's Most Precious Resource. LC 92-43968. (Illus.). 128p. (gr. 6-7). 1993. text ed. 13.95 RSBE (*0-02-724595-0*, New Discovery Bks) Macmillan Child Grp.
Green, Ivah. Splash & Trickle. LC 68-56818. (Illus.). 32p. (gr. 2-3). 1968. PLB 9.95 (*0-87783-037-1*); pap. 3.94 deluxe ed. (*0-87783-109-2*); cassette o.s.i. 7.94x (*0-87783-226-9*) Oddo.
Greene, Carol. Caring for Our Water. LC 91-2683. (Illus.). 32p. (gr. k-3). 1991. lib. bdg. 12.95 (*0-89490-356-X*) Enslow Pubs.
Kohen, Clarita. El Agua y Tu. Barath, Judith, illus. (SPA.). 16p. (gr. k-5). 1993. PLB 7.50x (*1-56492-101-8*) Laredo.
Lucas, Eileen. Water: A Resource in Crisis. LC 91-36137. 128p. (gr. 4-8). 1991. PLB 20.55 (*0-516-05509-7*) Childrens.
Soil & Water Conservation. (Illus.). 96p. (gr. 6-12). 1983. pap. 1.85 (*0-8395-3291-1*, 33291) BSA.

WATER FOWL

see Water Birds

WATER PLANTS

see Marine Plants

WATER POLLUTION

see Water-Pollution

WATER POWER

Bailey, Donna. Energy from Wind & Water. LC 90-39388. (Illus.). 48p. (gr. 2-6). 1990. PLB 19.97 (*0-8114-2519-3*) Raintree Steck-V.
Rickard, Graham. Water Energy. (Illus.). 32p. (gr. 4-6). 1991. PLB 17.27 (*0-8368-0710-3*) Gareth Stevens Inc.
Robson, Pam. Water, Paddles, & Boats. LC 92-375. 1992. 12.40 (*0-531-17376-3*, Gloucester Pr) Watts.
Twist, Clint. Wind & Water Power. LC 92-33921. (Illus.). 32p. (gr. k-4). 1993. PLB 11.90 (*0-531-17377-1*, Gloucester Pr) Watts.

WATER RESOURCES DEVELOPMENT

see also Water Power; Water Supply

WATER SKIING

Benzel, David. Psyching for Slalom: An Illustrated Guide to the Mind & Muscle of the Complete Skier. Robertson, Jo, ed. (Illus.). 127p. (Orig.). 1989. pap. 15.95 (*0-944406-05-X*) World Pub FL.
Finn, Tony. Waterskiboarding - An Illustrated Guide to Learning & Mastering the Sport. Robertson, Jo, ed. LC 88-50675. (Illus.). 113p. (Orig.). 1988. pap. 14.95 (*0-944406-04-1*) World Pub FL.
Italia, Bob. Freestyle Water Skiing. LC 93-19135. 32p. 1992. 9.95 (*1-56239-232-8*) Abdo & Dghtrs.
Kjellander, Mike. Power Slalom - Twenty-Eight Breakthrough Concepts for Mastering the Sport. Robertson, Jo, ed. (Illus.). 100p. (Orig.). 1989. pap. 14.95 (*0-944406-06-8*) World Pub FL.
Klarich, Tony. Hot Dog Slalom Skiing: An Illustrated Guide to over Thirty Amazing Maneuvers. Robertson, Jo, ed. (Illus.). 128p. (Orig.). (gr. 7 up). 1988. pap. 11.95 (*0-944406-02-5*) World Pub FL.
McMillan, Kent. Hydroslide Kneeboarding: An Illustrated Guide to Learning & Mastering the Sport. Robertson, Jo, ed. LC 88-50672. (Illus.). 166p. (Orig.). 1988. pap. 12.95 (*0-944406-03-3*) World Pub FL.
Scarpa, Ron & Dorner, Terrence. Barefoot Water Skiing: An Illustrated Guide to Learning & Mastering the Sport. Robertson, Jo, ed. (Illus.). 176p. (Orig.). (gr. 7 up). 1988. pap. 11.95 (*0-944406-01-7*) World Pub FL.
Walker, Cheryl. Waterskiing & Kneeboarding. (Illus.). 48p. (gr. 3-6). 1992. PLB 12.95 (*1-56065-056-7*) Capstone Pr.
Waterskiing. (Illus.). 48p. (gr. 6-12). 1984. pap. 1.85 (*0-8395-3357-8*, 33245) BSA.

WATER SPORTS

see also Boats and Boating; Canoes and Canoeing; Diving; Fishing; Rowing; Sailing; Skin Diving; Swimming

Barrett, Norman S. Windsurfing. Franklin Watts Ltd., ed. LC 86-51227. (Illus.). 32p. (ps-3). 1988. 11.90 (*0-531-10354-4*) Watts.
Chlad, Dorothy. In the Water...On the Water. Halverson, Lydia, illus. LC 88-12065. 32p. (ps-2). 1988. pap. 3.95 (*0-516-41974-9*) Childrens.
Waterski Magazine Staff. Boating Watersports: The Ultimate Get Started Guide to Towing Fun. Robertson, Jo, ed. LC 89-52016. (Illus.). 100p. 1990. pap. 15.95 (*0-944406-07-6*) World Pub FL.

WATER SPORTS-SAFETY MEASURES

American Red Cross Staff. American Red Cross Child Story Activity Book. (ps-3). 1992. pap. 39.50 pack of 10 (*0-8016-6509-4*) Mosby Yr Bk.
Berenstain, Stan & Berenstain, Janice. Bears' Vacation. Berenstain, Stan & Berenstain, Janice, illus. LC 68-28460. 72p. (gr. k-3). 1968. 6.95 (*0-394-80052-4*) Beginner.
Haskell, Bess C. The Raft. Fetz, Ingrid, illus. (gr. 5 up). 1988. write for info. (*0-933858-26-4*) Kennebec River.

WATER SUPPLY

see also Dams; Water-Pollution; Water Conservation

Cast, C. Vance. Where Does Water Come From? Wilkinson, Sue, illus. 40p. (ps-2). 1992. pap. 5.95 (*0-8120-4642-0*) Barron.
Cole, Joanna. The Magic School Bus at the Waterworks. 1993. pap. 3.95 (*0-590-72488-6*) Scholastic Inc.
Cossi, Olga. Water Wars: The Fight to Control & Conserve Nature's Most Precious Resource. LC 92-43968. (Illus.). 128p. (gr. 6-7). 1993. text ed. 13.95 RSBE (*0-02-724595-0*, New Discovery Bks) Macmillan Child Grp.
Dolan, Edward F. Drought: The Past, Present, & Future Enemy. LC 89-25016. (gr. 9-12). 1990. PLB 13.90 (*0-531-10900-3*) Watts.
Lampton, Christopher. Drought. LC 91-18053. (Illus.). 64p. (gr. 4-6). 1992. PLB 13.90 (*1-56294-125-9*) Millbrook Pr.
—Drought: A Disaster Book. (gr. 4-7). 1992. pap. 5.95 (*0-395-62465-7*) HM.
Splash! Activity Book. 16p. (gr. k-4). 1990. pap. write for info. (*0-89867-517-0*, 70054) Am Water Wks Assn.
Water Magic Water Activities for Students & Teachers. 48p. (gr. k-3). 1991. pap. 4.95 (*0-89867-573-1*, 70060) Am Water Wks Assn.

WATERGATE AFFAIR, 1972-

Feinberg, Barbara S. Watergate: Scandal in the White House. LC 90-34726. (Illus.). 144p. (gr. 9-12). 1990. PLB 13.90 (*0-531-10963-1*) Watts.
Hargrove, Jim. The Story of Watergate. LC 88-11881. (Illus.). 32p. (gr. 3-6). 1988. PLB 12.30 (*0-516-04741-8*); pap. 3.95 (*0-516-44741-6*) Childrens.
Kilian, Pamela. What Was Watergate. 1990. 16.95 (*0-312-04446-1*) St Martin.
Westerfeld, Scott. Watergate. (Illus.). 64p. (gr. 5 up). 1991. PLB 12.95 (*0-382-24126-6*); pap. 7.95 (*0-382-24120-7*) Silver Burdett Pr.

WATERLOO, BATTLE OF, 1815

Sauvain, Philip. Waterloo. LC 92-29564. (Illus.). 32p. (gr. 6 up). 1993. text ed. 13.95 RSBE (*0-02-781096-8*, New Discovery) Macmillan Child Grp.

WATERWAYS

see also Canals; Rivers

Oxlade, Chris. Canals & Waterways. Pyke, Jeremy, illus. Chillmaid, Marty, photos by. LC 93-49749. (Illus.). 1994. write for info. (*0-531-14331-7*) Watts.

WATER WORKS

see Water Supply

WAVES

see also Light; Ocean Waves

Zubrowski, Bernie. Making Waves: Finding Out about Rhythmic Motion. Doty, Roy, illus. LC 93-35455. 96p. (gr. 5 up). 1994. pap. 6.95 (*0-688-11788-0*) Morrow Jr Bks.
—Making Waves: Finding Out about Rhythmic Motion. Doty, Roy, illus. 96p. (gr. 3 up). 1994. PLB 13.93 (*0-688-11787-2*) Morrow Jr Bks.

WEAPONS

see Arms and Armor; Firearms

WEASELS-FICTION

Cosgrove, Stephen E. Gossamer. Edelson, Wendy, illus. 32p. (ps-3). 1990. PLB 14.95 (*0-89565-662-0*) Childs World.
Ernst, Lisa C. Zinnia & Dot. (Illus.). 32p. (ps-3). 1992. 14.00 (*0-670-83091-7*) Viking Child Bks.
Kovacs, Deborah. Brewster's Courage. Mathieu, Joe, illus. LC 91-21481. 112p. (gr. 2-6). 1992. pap. 14.00 jacketed, 3-pc. bdg. (*0-671-74016-4*, S&S BFYR) S&S Trade.
Montgomery, Rutherford G. Pekan the Shadow. Nenninger, Jerome D., illus. LC 78-84779. (gr. 8-12). 1970. 3.95 (*0-87004-132-0*) Caxton.
Potter, Beatrix. Jeremie Peche-a-la-Ligne. (FRE.). 58p. 1990. 10.95 (*2-07-056074-0*) Schoenhof.
Potter, Beatrix, created by. Mr. Jeremy Fisher. Schoonover, Pat & Nelson, Anita, illus. 24p. (gr. 2-4). 1992. PLB 10.95 (*1-56674-019-3*, HTS Bks) Forest Hse.
Seidler, Tor. The Wainscott Weasel. Marcellino, Fred, illus. LC 92-54526. 200p. (gr. 2 up). 1993. 20.00 (*0-06-205032-X*); PLB 19.89 (*0-06-205033-8*) HarpC Child Bks.

WEATHER

see also Climate; Meteorology; Rain and Rainfall; Snow; Storms; Weather Control; Winds

Adler, David. World of Weather. Burns, Raymond, illus. LC 82-17398. 32p. (gr. 3-6). 1983. PLB 10.59 (*0-89375-870-1*); pap. text ed. 2.95 (*0-89375-871-X*) Troll Assocs.
Ardley, Neil. The Science Book of Weather. 1992. 9.95 (*0-15-200624-9*, Gulliver Bks) HarBrace.
Baker, Sue. Child's Play Weather. (ps-3). 1993. 12.95 (*0-85953-929-6*) Childs Play.
Berger, Melvin. Who Cares about the Weather? Student Edition. (Illus.). 16p. (ps-2). 1993. pap. text ed. 14.95 (*1-56784-029-9*) Newbridge Comms.
—Wild Weather. 16p. (gr. 2-4). 1993. pap. 14.95 (*1-56784-203-8*) Newbridge Comms.

Berger, Melvin & Berger, Gilda. How's the Weather? A Look at Weather & How It Changes. Cymerman, John, illus. LC 93-16686. 48p. (gr. k-3). 1993. PLB 12.00 (*0-8249-8641-5*, Ideals Child); pap. 4.50 (*0-8249-8599-0*) Hambleton-Hill.
Bower, Miranda. Experiment with Weather. LC 92-41126. 1993. 17.50 (*0-8225-2458-9*) Lerner Pubns.
Bramwell, Martyn. Weather. (Illus.). 32p. (gr. 5-8). 1994. PLB write for info. (*0-531-14306-6*) Watts.
Branley, Franklyn M. It's Raining Cats & Dogs: All Kinds of Weather & Why We Have It. Kelley, True, illus. LC 86-27546. 128p. (gr. 3-8). 1987. 14.45 (*0-395-33070-X*) HM.
—It's Raining Cats & Dogs: All Kinds of Weather & Why We Have It. 128p. 1993. pap. 3.50 (*0-380-71849-9*, Camelot) Avon.
Breiter, Herta S. Weather. rev. ed. LC 87-23226. (Illus.). 48p. (gr. 2-6). 1987. PLB 10.95 (*0-8172-3265-6*) Raintree Steck-V.
Casey, Denise. Weather Everywhere. Gilmore, Jackie, photos by. LC 92-23239. (Illus.). 40p. (gr. k-4). 1995. RSBE 15.00 (*0-02-717777-7*, Bradbury Pr) Macmillan Child Grp.
Catherall, Ed. Exploring Weather. LC 90-10025. (Illus.). 48p. (gr. 4-8). 1990. PLB 22.80 (*0-8114-2596-7*) Raintree Steck-V.
Cosgrove, Brian. Weather. Shone, Karl & Percival, Keith, photos by. LC 90-4887. (Illus.). 64p. (gr. 5 up). 1991. 16.00 (*0-679-80784-5*); PLB 16.99 (*0-679-90784-X*) Knopf Bks Yng Read.
Cumpiano, Ina. Weather Watch. (Illus.). 24p. (Orig.). (gr. 1-3). 1992. pap. text ed. 29.95 big. bk. (*1-56334-065-8*); pap. text ed. 6.00 small bk. (*1-56334-071-2*) Hampton-Brown.
Davis, Kay & Oldsfield, Wendy. Weather. LC 91-30066. (Illus.). 32p. (gr. 2-5). 1991. PLB 19.97 (*0-8114-3007-3*); pap. 4.95 (*0-8114-1535-X*) Raintree Steck-V.
De Bourgoing, Pascale. Weather. Kniffke, Sophie, illus. 24p. 1991. pap. 10.95 (*0-590-45234-7*, Cartwheel) Scholastic Inc.
DeWitt, Lynda. What Will the Weather Be? Croll, Carolyn, illus. LC 90-1446. 32p. (gr. k-4). 1993. pap. 4.50 (*0-06-445113-5*, Trophy) HarpC Child Bks.
Earth, Sea & Sky. 1989. pap. 1.49 (*0-553-18405-9*) Bantam.
Fass, Bernie & Caggiano, Rosemary. The Weather Company. 48p. (gr. k-8). 1978. pap. 14.95 (*0-86704-004-1*) Clarus Music.
Flint, David. Weather & Climate: Projects with Geography. LC 91-6806. (Illus.). 32p. (gr. 5-8). 1991. PLB 12.40 (*0-531-17321-6*, Gloucester Pr) Watts.
—The World's Weather. LC 93-6827. (Illus.). 32p. (gr. 4-6). 1993. 14.95 (*1-56847-053-3*) Thomson Lrning.
Ford, Adam. Weather Watch. LC 81-637. (Illus.). 48p. (gr. 3-7). 1982. 11.95 (*0-688-00959-X*) Lothrop.
Fowler, Allan. What's the Weather Today? LC 91-3125. 32p. (ps-2). 1991. PLB 10.75 (*0-516-04918-6*); PLB 22.95 big bk. (*0-516-49478-3*); pap. 3.95 (*0-516-44918-4*) Childrens.
Gakken Co. Ltd. Staff, ed. Wind & Weather. Time-Life Books Inc. Editors, tr. (Illus.). 90p. (gr. k-3). 1989. 15.93 (*0-8094-4829-7*); PLB 21.27 (*0-8094-4830-0*) Time-Life.
Ganeri, A. Weather Facts. (Illus.). 48p. (gr. 3-7). 1987. PLB 12.96 (*0-88110-241-5*); pap. 5.95 (*0-86020-975-X*) EDC.
Ganeri, Anita. And Now...the Weather. Wingham, Peter, illus. LC 91-26682. 32p. (ps-2). 1992. pap. 5.95 (*0-689-71583-8*, Aladdin) Macmillan Child Grp.
—The Weather. LC 92-26987. 1993. 11.90 (*0-531-14250-7*) Watts.
Gardner, Robert & Webster, David. Science Projects about Weather. LC 93-48720. (Illus.). 128p. (gr. 6 up). 1994. lib. bdg. 17.95 (*0-89490-533-3*) Enslow Pubs.
Gibbons, Gail. Weather Words & What They Mean. Gibbons, Gail, illus. LC 89-39515. 32p. (ps-3). reinforced bdg. 15.95 (*0-8234-0805-1*); pap. 5.95 (*0-8234-0952-X*) Holiday.
Grumbine, Robert W. Discover Weather. (Illus.). 48p. (gr. 3-6). 1992. PLB 14.95 (*1-56674-032-0*, HTS Bks) Forest Hse.
Heddle, Rebecca & Shipton, Paul. Science with Weather. (Illus.). 24p. (gr. k-5). 1993. PLB 12.96 (*0-88110-654-2*, Usborne); pap. 4.95 (*0-7460-1421-X*, Usborne) EDC.
Hefter, Richard. The Stickybear Book of Weather. Hefter, Richard, illus. LC 83-2191. 32p. (ps-1). 1983. 5.95 (*0-911787-01-1*) Optimum Res Inc.
Hopkins, Lee B., compiled by. Weather. Hall, Melanie, photos by. LC 92-14913. (Illus.). 64p. (gr. k-3). 1994. 14.00 (*0-06-021463-5*); PLB 13.89 (*0-06-021462-7*) HarpC Child Bks.
Jennings, Terry. Weather. Franklin Watts Ltd., ed. Anstey, David, illus. 28p. (gr. k-3). 1990. PLB 10.90 (*0-531-17088-8*, Gloucester Pr) Watts.
Kahl, Jonathan. Weatherwise: Learning about the Weather. (Illus.). 64p. (gr. 4-12). 1992. PLB 19.95 (*0-8225-2525-9*) Lerner Pubns.
—Wet Weather: Rain Showers & Snowfall. (Illus.). 64p. (gr. 4-12). 1992. PLB 19.95 (*0-8225-2526-7*) Lerner Pubns.
Kirkpatrick, Rena K. Look at Weather. rev. ed. Lewin, Janetta, illus. LC 84-26251. 32p. (gr. 2-4). 1985. PLB 10.95 (*0-8172-2360-6*); pap. 4.95 (*0-8114-6906-9*) Raintree Steck-V.
Kohler, Pierre. Weather. (gr. 6 up). 1988. 4.95 (*0-8120-3833-9*) Barron.
Lye, Keith. The Earth. (Illus.). 64p. (gr. 4-6). 1991. PLB 15.40 (*1-56294-025-2*) Millbrook Pr.
McIlveen, J. F. Fundamentals of Weather & Climate. (gr. 5 up). 1991. pap. 39.95 (*0-442-31476-0*) Chapman & Hall.
McMillan, Bruce. The Weather Sky. (Illus.). 40p. (gr. 5 up). 1991. 16.95 (*0-374-38261-1*) FS&G.
McVey, Vicki. Sierra Club Book of Weatherwisdom. (gr. 4-7). 1991. 16.95 (*0-316-56341-2*) Little.
Mandell, Muriel. Simple Weather Experiments with Everyday Materials. LC 90-37915. (Illus.). 128p. (gr. 4-10). 1990. 12.95 (*0-8069-7296-3*) Sterling.
Markle, Sandra. Weather, Electricity, Environmental Investigations. 112p. (gr. 4-6). 1982. 9.95 (*0-88160-082-2*, LW 902) Learning Wks.
Mason, John. Autumn Weather. LC 90-34585. (Illus.). 32p. (gr. 1-5). 1991. PLB 11.90 (*0-531-18357-2*, Pub. by Bookwright Pr) Watts.
—Weather & Climate. (Illus.). 48p. (gr. 5-8). 1991. PLB 12.95 (*0-382-24225-4*) Silver Burdett Pr.
—Winter Weather. LC 90-828. (Illus.). 32p. (gr. 1-5). 1991. PLB 11.90 (*0-531-18358-0*, Pub. by Bookwright Pr) Watts.
Merk, Ann & Merk, Jim. The Weather & Us. LC 94-13322. (gr. 3 up). 1994. write for info. (*0-86593-387-1*) Rourke Corp.
—Weather Signs. LC 94-13323. (gr. 3 up). 1994. write for info. (*0-86593-388-X*) Rourke Corp.
Mogil, H. Michael & Levine, Barbara G. The Amateur Meteorologist: Explorations & Investigations. LC 93-17506. (Illus.). 144p. (gr. 6-9). 1993. PLB 12.90 (*0-531-11045-1*) Watts.
National Wildlife Federation Staff. Wild about Weather. (gr. k-8). 1991. pap. 7.95 (*0-945051-45-X*, 75003) Natl Wildlife.
Parramon, J. M., et al. El Agua. (SPA.). 32p. (ps). 1985. pap. 6.95 (*0-8120-3621-2*) Barron.
—The Four Elements, 4 Bks. (ps). 1985. boxed set 23.95 (*0-8120-7367-3*) Barron.
Petty, Kate. The Sky Above Us. (Illus.). 32p. (gr. 2-4). 1993. pap. 5.95 (*0-8120-1234-8*) Barron.
Pluckrose, Henry A. Weather. LC 93-45660. 1994. PLB 11.95 (*0-516-08123-3*) Childrens.
Pollard, Michael. Air, Water & Weather. (Illus.). 48p. (gr. 1-4). 1987. 12.95x (*0-8160-1781-6*) Facts on File.
Pomeroy, Johanna P. Content Area Reading Skills Weather: Cause & Effect. (Illus.). (gr. 3). 1989. pap. text ed. 3.25 (*1-55737-689-1*) Ed Activities.
Potter, Tony. Weather. (Illus.). 48p. (gr. 7-9). 1992. 13.95 (*0-563-21428-7*, BBC-Parkwest); pap. 6.95 (*0-563-21427-9*, BBC-Parkwest) Parkwest Pubns.
Raintree Publishers Inc. Weather. LC 87-28715. (Illus.). 64p. (Orig.). (gr. 5-9). 1988. lib. bdg. 11.95 (*0-8172-3079-3*) Raintree Steck-V.
Roetger, Doris. Weather Watch. (gr. k-3). 1991. pap. 8.95 (*0-86653-969-7*) Fearon Teach Aids.
Rogers, Paul. What Will the Weather Be Like Today? LC 88-32736. (Illus.). (ps up). 1990. 13.95 (*0-688-08950-X*); lib. bdg. 13.88 (*0-688-08951-8*) Greenwillow.
Rothman, Cynthia. Think about the Weather. 16p. (ps-2). 1994. pap. 14.95 (*1-56784-300-X*) Newbridge Comms.
Rowe, Julian & Perham, Molly. Weather Watch! LC 94-16944. (Illus.). 32p. (gr. 1-4). 1994. PLB 18.60 (*0-516-08142-X*); pap. 4.95 (*0-516-48142-8*) Childrens.
Ruckman, Ivy. Night of the Twisters. LC 83-46168. 160p. (gr. 3-6). 1984. 14.00i (*0-690-04408-9*, Crowell Jr Bks); PLB 13.89 (*0-690-04409-7*, Crowell Jr Bks) HarpC Child Bks.
Sabin, Louis. Weather. Veno, Joseph, illus. LC 84-2706. 32p. (gr. 3-6). 1985. PLB 9.49 (*0-8167-0200-4*); pap. text ed. 2.95 (*0-8167-0201-2*) Troll Assocs.
Seymour, Peter. How the Weather Works. Springer, Sally, illus. 10p. (gr. 2-5). 1985. pap. 8.95 SBE (*0-02-782110-2*, Macmillan Child Bk) Macmillan Child Grp.
Simon, Seymour. Weather. LC 92-31069. (Illus.). 40p. (gr. k up). 1993. 15.00 (*0-688-10546-7*); PLB 14.93 (*0-688-10547-5*) Morrow Jr Bks.
—Weather & Climate. (gr. 4-6). 1969. lib. bdg. 4.99 (*0-394-90804-X*) Random Bks Yng Read.
Summer, Fall, Winter, Spring. 1989. pap. 1.49 (*0-553-18401-6*) Bantam.
Supraner, Robyn. I Can Read About Weather. LC 74-24992. (Illus.). (gr. 2-4). 1975. pap. 2.50 (*0-89375-070-0*) Troll Assocs.
Taylor, Barbara. Weather & Climate: Geography Facts & Experiments. LC 92-28420. 32p. (gr. 1-4). 1993. 10.95 (*1-85697-878-8*, Kingfisher LKC); pap. 5.95 (*1-85697-940-7*) LKC.
—Wind & Weather. LC 90-46260. (Illus.). 32p. (gr. 5-8). 1991. PLB 12.40 (*0-531-14184-5*) Watts.
Tester, Sylvia R. Magic Monsters Learn about Weather. Bowman, Patricia, illus. LC 79-24826. (gr. k-3). 1980. PLB 14.95 (*0-89565-120-3*) Childs World.
Time Life Editors. Why Can't I See the Wind? First Questions & Answers about Weather. Daniels, Pat, ed. (Illus.). 48p. (ps-k). 1994. write for info. (*0-7835-0890-5*); PLB write for info. (*0-7835-0891-3*) Time-Life.
Ward, Alan. Sky & Weather. LC 92-369. 1993. 11.40 (*0-531-14176-4*) Watts.
Watt, F. Weather & Climate. (Illus.). 48p. (gr. 4-11). 1992. PLB 13.96 (*0-88110-511-2*, Usborne); pap. 7.95 (*0-7460-0683-7*, Usborne) EDC.
Weather. 64p. (gr. 6-12). 1963. pap. 1.85 (*0-8395-3274-1*, 33274) BSA.
Weather. LC 93-58990. 32p. (gr. 3 up). 1994. 5.95 (*1-56138-198-5*) Running Pr.
Weather Pack. (gr. 3-6). 1992. pap. 7.95 (*1-56680-502-3*) Mad Hatter Pub.
Webster, Vera. Experimentos Atmosfericos (Weather Experiments) Kratky, Lada, tr. LC 85-31425. (SPA., Illus.). 48p. (gr. k-4). 1986. PLB 12.85 (*0-516-31662-1*); pap. 4.95 (*0-516-51662-0*) Childrens.
—Weather Experiments. LC 81-17062. (Illus.). 48p. (gr. k-4). 1982. PLB 12.85 (*0-516-01662-8*); pap. 4.95 (*0-516-41662-6*) Childrens.
Wilson, Francis. The Weather Pop-Up Book. Jacobs, Philip, illus. Wilgrass, Paul, contrib. by. (Illus.). (gr. 5 up). 1987. pap. 15.00 (*0-671-63699-5*, S&S BFYR) S&S Trade.
Winitz, Harris. Weather. Baker, Syd, illus. 50p. (gr. 7 up). 1986. pap. text ed. 19.00 incl. cass. (*0-939990-47-4*) Intl Linguistics.

WEATHER–FICTION

Arnold, Jeanne G. The Little Cloud That Couldn't: An Environmental Story for Children. Beattie, Linda D., illus. LC 90-62422. 76p. (Orig.). (gr. 3-7). 1990. pap. 4.95 (*0-9620887-1-4*) Media Serv Unltd.
Barrett, Judi. Cloudy with a Chance of Meatballs. Barrett, Ron, illus. LC 78-2945. 32p. (ps-3). 1978. RSBE 14.95 (*0-689-30647-4*, Atheneum Child Bk) Macmillan Child Grp.
Bellairs, John. The Dark Secret of Weatherend. Gorey, Edward, illus. 208p. (gr. 5 up). 1984. 13.95 (*0-8037-0072-5*) Dial Bks Young.
Brittain, Bill. Dr. Dredd's Wagon of Wonders. Glass, Andrew, illus. LC 86-45775. 192p. (gr. 3-7). 1989. pap. 3.50 (*0-06-440289-4*, Trophy) HarpC Child Bks.
Child, A. The Cloud Song. 15p. (gr. 1). 1992. pap. text ed. 23.00 big bk. (*1-56843-023-X*); pap. text ed. 4.50 (*1-56843-073-6*) BGR Pub.
The Day the Dark Clouds Came. (Illus.). (ps-2). 1991. PLB 6.95 (*0-8136-5173-5*, TK3877); pap. 3.50 (*0-8136-5673-7*, TK3878) Modern Curr.
Henley, Claire. Stormy Day. Henley, Claire, illus. LC 92-72025. 32p. (ps). 1993. 11.95 (*1-56282-342-6*); PLB 11.89 (*1-56282-343-4*) Hyprn Child.
—Sunny Day. Henley, Claire, illus. LC 92-72024. 32p. (ps). 1993. 11.95 (*1-56282-340-X*); PLB 11.89 (*1-56282-341-8*) Hyprn Child.
Heuck, Sigrid. The Cloud's Journey. Koch, Sis, illus. 28p. (ps-2). 1991. pap. 9.95 smythe sewn reinforced bdg. (*1-56182-021-0*) Atomium Bks.
Peters, Lisa W. The Sun, the Wind & the Rain. Rand, Ted, illus. LC 87-23808. 48p. (ps-2). 1990. pap. 5.95 (*0-8050-1481-0*, Owlet BYR) H Holt & Co.
Renauld, Christiane. Tomorrow Will Be a Nice Day. (Illus.). 32p. (gr. k-2). 1991. 12.95 (*0-89565-763-5*) Childs World.
Scheffler, Ursel. Sun Jack & Rain Jack. Timm, Jutta, illus. Morice, Dave, contrib. by. LC 93-39229. (Illus.). 32p. (gr. k up). 1994. 18.60 (*0-8368-1089-9*) Gareth Stevens Inc.
Starr, Joyce R. Medal of Drought. 1994. write for info. (*0-8050-3019-0*) H Holt & Co.
Stroschin, Jane. The Cloudy Day. 32p. (gr. k-6). 1989. PLB 15.00 (*1-883960-00-2*) Henry Quill.
Superlove. Sunstar: Sun of Superlove. LC 80-53694. (Illus.). 200p. (Orig.). (gr. 7 up). 1980. pap. 7.00 (*0-9602334-1-5*); 20.00 (*0-685-04821-7*) Superlove.
Vaughan, Marcia. The Stick-Around Cloud. Smith, Craig, illus. LC 93-28962. 1994. 4.25 (*0-383-03777-8*) SRA Schl Grp.
Willis, Jeanne. Earth Weather As Explained by Professor Xargle. Ross, Tony, illus. LC 92-14067. (ps-2). 1993. Repr. of 1991 ed. 14.00 (*0-525-45025-4*, DCB) Dutton Child Bks.
Yolen, Jane. Weather Report. 64p. 1993. 16.95 (*1-56397-101-1*, Wordsong) Boyds Mills Pr.
Ziefert, Harriet. Bear's Weather. Baum, Susan, illus. 12p. (ps). 1993. 4.50 (*0-694-00457-X*, Festival) HarpC Child Bks.

WEATHER CONTROL

DeWitt, Lynda. What Will the Weather Be? Croll, Carolyn, illus. LC 90-1446. 32p. (gr. k-4). 1991. PLB 13.89 (*0-06-021597-6*) HarpC Child Bks.

WEATHER FORECASTING

Gibbons, Gail. Weather Forecasting. Gibbons, Gail, illus. LC 86-7602. 32p. (gr. k-3). 1987. RSBE 13.95 (*0-02-737250-2*, Four Winds) Macmillan Child Grp.
—Weather Forecasting. Gibbons, Gail, illus. LC 92-22264. 32p. (ps-3). 1993. pap. 3.95 (*0-689-71683-4*, Aladdin) Macmillan Child Grp.
Lampton, Christopher. Blizzard. (Illus.). 64p. (gr. 4-6). 1991. PLB 13.90 (*1-56294-029-5*); pap. 5.95 (*1-56294-775-3*) Millbrook Pr.
McVey, Vicki. Sierra Club Book of Weatherwisdom. (gr. 4-7). 1991. 16.95 (*0-316-56341-2*) Little.
Martin, Claire. I Can Be a Weather Forecaster. LC 86-31763. (Illus.). 32p. (gr. k-3). 1987. PLB 11.80 (*0-516-01908-2*); pap. 3.95 (*0-516-41908-0*) Childrens.
Palazzo, Janet. What Makes the Weather. Harvey, Paul, illus. LC 81-11383. 32p. (gr. k-2). 1982. PLB 11.59 (*0-89375-654-7*); pap. 2.95 (*0-89375-655-5*) Troll Assocs.
Ramsey, Dan. Weather Forecasting: A Young Meteorologist's Guide. (Illus.). 144p. 1990. 19.95 (*0-8306-8338-0*, 3338); pap. 10.95 (*0-8306-3338-3*) TAB Bks.
Rowe, Julian & Perham, Molly. Weather Watch! LC 94-16944. (Illus.). 32p. (gr. 1-4). 1994. PLB 18.60 (*0-516-08142-X*); pap. 4.95 (*0-516-48142-8*) Childrens.

Steele, Philip. Frost: Causes & Effects. LC 90-44596. (Illus.). 32p. (gr. 5-8). 1991. PLB 12.40 (*0-531-11025-7*) Watts.
—Heatwave: Causes & Effects. LC 90-46263. (Illus.). 32p. (gr. 5-8). 1991. PLB 12.40 (*0-531-11023-0*) Watts.
—Wind: Causes & Effects. LC 90-46262. (Illus.). 32p. (gr. 5-8). 1991. PLB 12.40 (*0-531-11024-9*) Watts.
Taylor-Cork, Barbara. Weather Forecaster. LC 91-30539. (Illus.). 32p. (gr. 4-7). 1992. PLB 12.40 (*0-531-17267-8*, Gloucester Pr) Watts.

WEAVING
see also Basket Making; Beadwork; Textile Industry and Fabrics;
also names of woven articles, e.g. Carpets
Greenoff, Jane. Crafts for Kids: Cross Stitch Farmyard. (Illus.). 32p. 1994. 9.95 (*0-7153-0248-5*, Pub. by David & Charles Pub UK) Sterling.
—Crafts for Kids: Cross Stitch on the Move: 10 Easy Projects. (Illus.). 32p. 1994. 9.95 (*0-7153-0070-9*, Pub. by David & Charles Pub UK) Sterling.
—Crafts for Kids: Dinosaurs Monsters. (Illus.). 32p. 1994. 9.95 (*0-7153-0249-3*, Pub. by David & Charles Pub UK) Sterling.
—Crafts for Kids: Our World in Cross Stitch: 12 Easy Projects. (Illus.). 32p. 1994. 9.95 (*0-7153-0068-7*, Pub. by David & Charles Pub UK) Sterling.
Harvey, Virginia. Split-Ply Twining. LC 75-4651. (Illus.). 44p. (gr. 7 up). 1976. pap. 7.95 (*0-916658-32-5*) Shuttle Craft.
O'Reilly, Susie. Weaving. Mukhida, Zul, photos by. LC 93-18935. (Illus.). 32p. (gr. 4-6). 1993. 14.95 (*1-56847-067-3*) Thomson Lrning.

WEBSTER, DANIEL, 1782-1852
Allen, Robert. Daniel Webster: Defender of the Union. (Illus.). (gr. 3-6). 1989. pap. 6.95 (*0-88062-156-7*) Mott Media.

WEBSTER, DANIEL, 1782-1852–FICTION
Gibbons, Ted. Daniel Webster & the Blacksmith's Fee. 8p. (Orig.). 1988. pap. 1.95 stiched with dustcover (*0-929985-03-6*) Jackman Pubng.

WEBSTER, NOAH, 1758-1843
Collins, David. Noah Webster: Master of Words. (Illus.). (gr. 3-6). 1989. pap. 6.95 (*0-88062-158-3*) Mott Media.
Ferris, Jeri. What Do You Mean? A Story about Noah Webster. Michaels, Steve, illus. 56p. (gr. 3-6). 1988. PLB 14.95 (*0-87614-330-3*) Carolrhoda Bks.

WEDDINGS
see Etiquette; Marriage; Marriage Customs and Rites

WEEDS
Martin, Alexander C. Weeds. Zallinger, Jean, illus. 160p. (gr. 7 up). 1973. pap. write for info. (*0-307-24353-2*, Golden Pr) Western Pub.
Wexler, Jerome. Queen Anne's Lace. LC 93-29621. 1994. write for info. (*0-8075-6710-8*) A Whitman.

WEIGHT CONTROL
see also Diet; Exercise
Berry, Joy. About Weight Problems & Eating Disorders. (Illus.). 48p. (gr. 3 up). 1990. 12.30 (*0-516-02960-6*); pap. 4.95 (*0-516-42960-4*) Childrens.
Coyle, Neva & Chapian, Marie. Slimming Down & Growing Up. LC 85-15028. 160p. (Orig.). (gr. 4-7). 1985. pap. 5.99 (*0-87123-833-0*) Bethany Hse.
Jones, Lucile. Tony's Tummy. Van Dolson, Bobbie J., ed. 32p. (gr. k up). 1981. pap. 3.95 (*0-8280-0039-5*) Review & Herald.
Kane, June K. Coping with Diet Fads. Rosen, Ruth, ed. (gr. 7-12). 1990. PLB 14.95 (*0-8239-1005-9*) Rosen Group.
Landau, Elaine. Weight: A Teenage Concern. 160p. (gr. 7 up). 1991. 15.00 (*0-525-67335-0*, Lodestar Bks) Dutton Child Bks.
Macmillan, Daniel. Obesity. (Illus.). (gr. 9-12). 1994. lib. bdg. 13.93 (*0-531-11201-2*) Watts.
Ojeda, Linda. Safe Dieting for Teens. LC 92-26432. 116p. (Orig.). (gr. 7-12). 1992. pap. 7.95 (*0-89793-113-0*) Hunter Hse.
Philips, Barbara. Don't Call Me Fatso. Cogancherry, Helen, illus. Okun, Barbara, intro. by. LC 85-24341. (Illus.). 32p. (gr. k-6). 1980. PLB 19.97 (*0-8172-1350-3*) Raintree Steck-V.
Sachs, Marilyn. The Fat Girl. LC 83-11697. 176p. (gr. 6 up). 1984. 13.95 (*0-525-44076-3*, DCB) Dutton Child Bks.
Silverstein, Alvin, et al. So You Think You're Fat? LC 90-40761. 224p. (gr. 7 up). 1991. PLB 13.89 (*0-06-021642-5*) HarpC Child Bks.
Spies, Karen B. Everything You Need to Know about Diet Fads. Rosen, Ruth, ed. (gr. 7-12). 1993. PLB 14. 95 (*0-8239-1533-6*) Rosen Group.

WEIGHT CONTROL–FICTION
Bunting, Eve. Oh, Rick. (Illus.). 64p. (gr. 3-8). 1992. 8.95 (*0-89565-774-0*) Childs World.
Cooper, Ilene. The New, Improved Gretchen Hubbard. LC 92-6197. 208p. (gr. 4 up). 1992. 14.00 (*0-688-08432-X*) Morrow Jr Bks.
DeClements, Barthe. Nothing's Fair in Fifth Grade. 144p. (gr. 8-12). 1995. pap. 3.99 (*0-14-034443-8*, Puffin) Puffin Bks.
Greenberg, Jan. The Pig-Out Blues. LC 82-2552. 121p. (gr. 7 up). 1982. 14.00 (*0-374-35937-7*) FS&G.
Holland, Isabelle. Dinah & the Green Fat Kingdom. 192p. (gr. 5 up). 1986. pap. 1.75 (*0-440-91918-5*, LE) Dell.
Hunt, Angela E. Cassie Perkins: Much Adored Shore. 176p. (gr. 4-8). 1992. pap. 4.99 (*0-8423-1065-7*) Tyndale.
Lipsyte, Robert. One Fat Summer. LC 76-49746. (gr. 7 up). 1977. PLB 14.89 (*0-06-023896-8*) HarpC Child Bks.
—One Fat Summer. LC 76-49746. 240p. (gr. 7 up). 1991. pap. 3.95 (*0-06-447073-3*, Trophy) HarpC Child Bks.
Perl, Lila. Hey, Remember Fat Glenda? 192p. (gr. 3-6). 1981. 14.45 (*0-395-31023-7*, Clarion Bks) HM.
Phillips, Barbara. Don't Call Me Fatso. (ps-3). 1993. pap. 3.95 (*0-8114-5203-4*) Raintree Steck-V.
Ruckman, Ivy. The Hunger Scream. LC 83-6522. 200p. (gr. 6 up). 1983. 14.95 (*0-8027-6514-9*) Walker & Co.

Shaw, G. I. Watermelon in a Cucumber Patch. LC 93-81154. 96p. (Orig.). (gr. 8-11). 1994. pap. 5.00 (*0-9639450-0-9*, Joy Bks) Joy Ent.
On the first day of school, fifteen year-old Stevi is taunted by her classmates because she's overweight. Her best friend offers to help her lose weight, but also gets her involved with a boy that she has a crush on. Stevi overcomes obstacles at home, at work, & in dating as she wades through the confusing world of diets, pills, & exercise. She faces the everyday temptations of teenagers living in the 1990s: shoplifting, sex, & drugs. Finally introduced to a new concept for weight control, she learns how to respect & accept herself, & how to get control of her life. Ms. Shaw lives near Baltimore, Maryland, with her husband, six cats, two dogs & four plus goats. All her life she has struggled to keep her weight under control. "I've always liked doing the opposite of what I'm supposed to do. When I tried to diet I always gained weight. Finding a new idea about successful weight control changed everything. Finally, here was a way of life I could live with." Joy Enterprises, 332 S. Queen Street, Littletown, PA 17340 (717-359-7529).
Publisher Provided Annotation.

WEIGHTS AND MEASURES
see also Mensuration; Metric System
Kerrod, Robin. Weights & Measures. LC 90-25570. (Illus.). 32p. (gr. 3-8). 1991. PLB 9.95 (*1-85435-269-5*) Marshall Cavendish.
Measurements & Conversions: A Complete Guide. 256p. (Orig.). 1994. pap. 5.95 (*1-56138-466-6*) Running Pr.
Robson, Pam. Clocks, Scales & Measurements. (Illus.). 32p. (gr. 5-7). 1993. PLB 12.40 (*0-531-17419-0*, Gloucester Pr) Watts.
Taylor, Barbara. Weight & Balance. LC 89-21504. (Illus.). 32p. (gr. 5-8). 1990. PLB 12.40 (*0-531-14082-2*) Watts.
Weighing. (Illus.). 56p. (gr. 7-12). 1990. 8.80 (*0-941008-75-4*) Tops Learning.

WELFARE STATE
see Economic Policy

WELFARE WORK
see Social Work

WELLS, HERBERT GEORGE, 1866-1946
Martin, C. H. G. Wells. (Illus.). 112p. (gr. 7 up). 1989. lib. bdg. 19.94 (*0-86592-297-7*); 14.95s.p. (*0-685-58636-7*) Rourke Corp.
Nardo, Don. H. G. Wells. LC 92-19870. (Illus.). 112p. (gr. 5-8). 1992. PLB 14.95 (*1-56006-025-5*) Lucent Bks.

WELLS
see also Petroleum; Water Supply

WEST, THE
see also Northwest, Pacific; Pacific States
Aylesworth, Thomas G. & Aylesworth, Virginia L. The West (Arizona, Nevada, Utah) (Illus.). 64p. (Orig.). 1988. lib. bdg. 16.95x (*1-55546-563-3*); pap. 6.95 (*0-7910-0548-8*) Chelsea Hse.
Blanchard, Gerald. The Black West. (gr. 4-6). 1992. print set 75.00 (*1-882205-04-9*) All Media Prods.
Bleeker, Sonia. The Sioux Indians: Hunters & Warriors of the Plains. Sasaki, Kisa N., illus. LC 62-7713. 160p. (gr. 3-6). 1962. PLB 11.88 (*0-688-31457-0*) Morrow Jr Bks.
Courtault, Martine. Going West: Cowboys & Pioneers. Bogard, Vicki, tr. from FRE. Grant, Donald, illus. LC 89-5365. 38p. (gr. k-5). 1989. 5.95 (*0-944589-21-9*, 021) Young Discovery Lib.
D'Apice, R. Gamblers. (Illus.). 32p. (gr. 3-8). 1990. PLB 18.00 (*0-86625-371-8*); 13.50s.p. (*0-685-34711-7*) Rourke Corp.
Emsden, Katharine N. Voices from the West: Life along the Trail. (Illus.). 60p. (Orig.). (gr. 5-12). 1992. pap. 4.95 (*1-878668-18-8*) Disc Enter Ltd.
Erickson, Paul. Daily Life in Covered Wagon. (gr. 4 up). 1994. write for info. (*0-89133-245-6*) Preservation Pr.
Freedman, Russell. Children of the Wild West. (Illus.). (gr. 4-7). 1990. pap. 6.95 (*0-395-54785-7*, Clarion Bks) HM.
Geis, Jacqueline, adapted by. & illus. Where the Buffalo Roam. LC 92-7733. 32p. (gr. k-3). 1992. 13.95 (*0-8249-8570-2*, Ideals Child); PLB 14.00 (*0-8249-8584-2*) Hambleton-Hill.
Green, Carl R. & Sanford, William R. Doc Holliday. LC 94-24845. (gr. 4-10). 1995. write for info. (*0-89490-589-9*) Enslow Pubs.
Kalman, Bobbie & Schimky, Dave. Fort Life. (Illus.). 32p. (Orig.). (gr. k-9). 1994. PLB 15.95 (*0-86505-496-7*); pap. 7.95 (*0-86505-516-5*) Crabtree Pub Co.
Lake, A. L. Women of the West. (Illus.). 32p. (gr. 3-8). 1990. PLB 18.00 (*0-86625-373-4*); PLB 13.50s.p. (*0-685-58656-1*) Rourke Corp.
Medearis, Angela S., compiled by. The Zebra-Riding Cowboy: A Folk Song of the Old West. Brusca, Maria C., illus. LC 91-27941. 32p. (ps-2). 1992. 14.95 (*0-8050-1712-7*, Bks Young Read) H Holt & Co.

Murray, Fred. God Loves Even Cowboys. Murray, Jody L., ed. (Illus.). 177p. (gr. 4 up). 1994. pap. 11.95 (*0-9642685-4-X*) F Murray Pubng.
GOD LOVES EVEN COWBOYS uses true stories of cowboy life to illustrate positive traditional values of daily living. The main theme is to teach children that they are responsible for their actions. Each story contains an illustrated drawing by the author of the action in the story. The book cover features a portrait of the author & his horse by noted equine artist Kim McGuiness entitled COW PONY which will be featured in the January/ February 1995 issue of EQUINE IMAGES. The picture was on exhibit at the 15th annual American Academy of Equine Art National exhibition in Lexington, Kentucky. Over the last 35 years, author Fred Murray, who is known as the cowboy storyteller, has entertained thousands of children & adults with his frontier stories at churches, schools & civic functions. The stories in this book were the most requested by audiences. The stories come from the author's experiences growing up & working on ranches in Western Colorado. He worked with many old-time cowboys & pioneers who shared their experiences with him which he hopes to pass on to future generations. Address your book requests to Murray Publishing, Box 99A, Firth, NE 68358 or call 402-791-5741.
Publisher Provided Annotation.

Sandler, Martin W. Cowboys. Billington, James, illus. LC 93-20386. 96p. (gr. 3 up). 1994. 19.95 (*0-06-023318-4*); PLB 20.89 (*0-06-023319-2*) HarpC Child Bks.
Shapley, R. Boomtowns. (Illus.). 32p. (gr. 3-8). 1990. lib. bdg. 18.00 (*0-86625-370-X*); 13.50s.p. (*0-685-58647-2*) Rourke Corp.
Stein, R. Conrad. The Story of the Lewis & Clark Expedition. Aronson, Lou, illus. LC 78-4648. 32p. (gr. 3-6). 1978. pap. 3.95 (*0-516-44620-7*) Childrens.
Twain, Mark. Roughing It. Girling, Z. N., intro. by. (Illus.). (gr. 8 up). 1967. pap. 2.95 (*0-8049-0134-1*, CL-134) Airmont.
Upton, H. Cattle Ranchers. (Illus.). 32p. (gr. 3-8). 1990. lib. bdg. 18.00 (*0-86625-372-6*) Rourke Corp.
—Trailblazers. (Illus.). 32p. (gr. 3-8). 1990. lib. bdg. 18.00 (*0-86625-369-6*); lib. bdg. 13.50s.p. (*0-685-58653-7*) Rourke Corp.
Williams, Lucy. The American West. LC 90-21738. (Illus.). 24p. (gr. k-4). 1991. 10.90 (*0-531-18387-4*, Pub. by Bookwright Pr) Watts.

WEST, THE–FICTION
Adler, David A. Wild Pill Hickok & Other Old West Riddles. Rounds, Glen, illus. LC 88-6480. 64p. (gr. 1-4). 1988. reinforced bdg. 12.95 (*0-8234-0718-7*) Holiday.

Arntson, Herbert E. Caravan to Oregon. LC 57-13207. (Illus.). (gr. 7-11). 1957. 8.95 (*0-8323-0164-7*) Binford Mort.

Bird, E. J. The Blizzard of Eighteen Ninety-Six. Bird, E. J., illus. 72p. (gr. 2-6). 1990. PLB 14.95 (*0-87614-651-5*) Carolrhoda Bks.

Bly, Stephen. Coyote True. LC 92-8224. 128p. 1992. pap. 4.99 (*0-89107-680-8*) Crossway Bks.

—The Dog Who Would Not Smile. 128p. (gr. 4-7). 1992. pap. 4.99 (*0-89107-656-5*) Crossway Bks.

—Final Justice at Adobe Wells. LC 93-14185. 192p. (Orig.). (gr. 9 up). 1993. pap. 7.99 (*0-89107-744-8*) Crossway Bks.

—You Can Always Trust a Spotted Horse. LC 92-46667. 128p. (Orig.). (gr. 4-7). 1993. pap. 4.99 (*0-89107-716-2*) Crossway Bks.

Bower, B. M. Cabin Fever. 290p. 1981. Repr. of 1918 ed. PLB 16.35x (*0-89966-017-7*) Buccaneer Bks.

—Flying U Ranch. 280p. 1981. Repr. PLB 16.95x (*0-89966-018-5*) Buccaneer Bks.

Brisson, Pat. Kate Heads West. Brown, Rick, illus. LC 89-27590. 40p. (gr. k-3). 1990. RSBE 13.95 (*0-02-714345-7*, Bradbury Pr) Macmillan Child Grp.

Brown, Dee. Cavalry Scout. (gr. 7 up). 1989. pap. 2.95 (*0-440-20227-2*) Dell.

—Yellow Horse. 1989. pap. 2.95 (*0-440-20246-9*) Dell.

Brown, Towana J. Scottie. Brown, Becky E., illus. LC 88-93029. 150p. (Orig.). (gr. 5-6). 1989. pap. 3.50 (*0-9622060-1-6*) T J Brown.

Bulla, Clyde R. Ghost Town Treasure. Freeman, Don, illus. 96p. (gr. 2-5). 1994. pap. 3.99 (*0-14-036732-2*) Puffin Bks.

Byars, Betsy C. The Golly Sisters Ride Again. Truesdell, Sue, illus. & photos by LC 92-23394. 64p. (gr. k-3). 1994. 14.00 (*0-06-021563-1*); PLB 13.89 (*0-06-021564-X*) HarpC Child Bks.

—Hooray for the Golly Sisters! Truesdell, Sue, illus. LC 89-48147. 64p. (gr. k-3). 1990. 14.00 (*0-06-020898-8*); PLB 13.89 (*0-06-020899-6*) HarpC Child Bks.

Cohen, Caron L. Bronco Dogs. Shepherd, Roni, illus. LC 90-47952. 32p. (ps-3). 1991. 12.95 (*0-525-44721-0*, DCB) Dutton Child Bks.

Dutton, June & Schulz, Charles M. Snoopy & the Gang Out West. LC 82-71284. (Illus.). 1983. 6.95 (*0-915696-55-X*); pap. 4.95 (*0-915696-82-7*) Determined Prods.

Ellison, Douglas W. David Lant: The Vanished Outlaw. 232p. (Orig.). 1988. pap. text ed. write for info. (*0-929918-01-0*) Midstates Pub.

Enderle, Judith R., et al. Nell Nugget & the Cow Caper. Yalowitz, Paul, photos by. LC 94-10189. 1995. 15.95 (*0-02-733385-X*, Four Winds) Macmillan Child Grp.

Erickson, John. The Case of the Missing Cat: Discover the Land of Enchantment. (Illus.). 144p. 1990. 11.95 (*0-87719-186-7*); pap. 6.95 (*0-87719-185-9*); 2 cass. 15.95 (*0-87719-187-5*) Gulf Pub.

Erickson, John R. The Case of the Car-Barkaholic Dog. (Illus.). 118p. 1991. 11.95 (*0-87719-198-0*, 9198); pap. 6.95 (*0-87719-199-9*, 9199); incls. 2 cass. 15.95 (*0-87719-200-6*) Gulf Pub.

—Hank the Cowdog: The Case of the Hooking Bull, No. 18. 118p. 1992. 11.95 (*0-87719-213-8*); pap. 6.95 (*0-87719-212-X*); 2 cassettes 15.95 (*0-87719-214-6*) Gulf Pub.

—Moonlight Madness. Holmes, Gerald L., illus. LC 94-14263. 118p. (Orig.). (gr. 3-12). 1994. 11.95 (*0-87719-252-9*); pap. 6.95 (*0-87719-251-0*); Audio cass. 15.95 (*0-87719-253-7*) Gulf Pub. BILLBOARD magazine reports that, "in the past twelve years HANK THE COWDOG has sold more than 90,000 audiobooks & more than a million books, starred in 23 titles, won (1994's) Audie Award for outstanding children's audio...& inspired a fan club with 4,000 members." In his latest adventure, #23 MOONLIGHT MADNESS, Hank meets Eddy the Rac, an orphan raccoon & must guard the crafty masked bandit every moment. Hero, philosopher & head of ranch security, HANK THE COWDOG is a "... marvelous situation comedy."-- SCHOOL LIBRARY JOURNAL. Written by real-life cowboy John Erickson, Hank is available in paperback ($6.95), hardcover ($11.95), & word-for-word cassette tapes ($15.95 two, hour-long, song-filled tapes performed by the author). Teacher's Guides: Grades K-2 & 3-6 embrace the whole-language approach. Now in Spanish. HANK EL PERRO VAQUERO paperbacks #1 through #6 are available in Spanish. For a free catalog all about the adventures of Hank the Cowdog: Head of Ranch Security contact -- Gulf Publishing Company, P.O. Box 2608, Houston, TX 77252-2608. 713-520-4444. FAX: 713-525-4647. Available from your favorite wholesaler.
Publisher Provided Annotation.

Everett, Percival. The One That Got Away. Zimmer, Dirk, illus. 32p. (gr. 1-4). 1992. PLB 14.95 (*0-685-52550-3*, Clarion Bks) HM.

Fleischman, Sid. Jim Ugly. Sewall, Marcia, illus. LC 91-14392. 144p. (gr. 3 up). 1992. 14.00 (*0-688-10886-5*) Greenwillow.

Fontes, Ron & Korman, Justine. Wild Bill Hickok & the Rebel Raiders. Shaw, Charlie & Bill Smith Studios Staff, illus. LC 92-56159. 80p. (Orig.). (gr. 1-4). 1993. PLB 12.89 (*1-56282-494-5*); pap. 3.50 (*1-56282-493-7*) Disney Pr.

Fritz, Jean. Make Way for Sam Houston. Primavera, Elise, illus. LC 85-25601. 109p. (gr. 4-6). 1986. 13.95 (*0-399-21303-1*, Putnam); pap. 6.95 (*0-399-21304-X*) Putnam Pub Group.

Garland, Hamlin. The Long Trail. 1988. Repr. of 1907 ed. lib. bdg. 59.00x (*0-7812-1236-7*) Rprt Serv.

Gerrard, Roy. Rosie & the Rustlers. 32p. (ps up). 1989. 15.00 (*0-374-36345-5*) FS&G.

Gifaldi, David. Gregory, Maw, & the Mean One. Glass, Andrew, illus. 144p. (gr. 7 up). 1992. 13.45 (*0-395-60821-X*, Clarion Bks) HM.

Greer, Gery & Ruddick, Robert. Max & Me & the Wild West. LC 87-12066. 138p. (gr. 4-7). 1988. 12.95 (*0-15-253136-X*) HarBrace.

Guthrie, Alfred B., Jr. The Big Sky. LC 85-4717. 384p. (gr. 6 up). 1984. pap. 5.50 (*0-553-26683-7*) Bantam.

Heisler, Jim. Woody, the Adventurous Tumbleweed. (Illus.). 32p. 1995. pap. 8.00 (*0-8059-3599-1*) Dorrance.

Henry, Marguerite. San Domingo: The Medicine Hat Stallion. Lougheed, Robert, illus. LC 91-46020. 240p. (gr. 3-7). 1992. pap. 3.95 (*0-689-71631-1*, Aladdin) Macmillan Child Grp.

Hudson, Jan. Dawn Rider. 176p. 1992. pap. 3.25 (*0-590-44987-7*, Point) Scholastic Inc.

Hughes, Francine. Westward, Whoa. Thompson, Del, illus. LC 93-83721. 32p. (Orig.). (ps-3). 1993. pap. 2.25 (*0-679-85281-6*) Random Bks Yng Read.

Hughes, Shirley. Charlie Moon & the Big Bonanza Bust-Up. large type ed. 184p. (gr. 3-7). 1990. lib. bdg. 14.95x (*0-7451-1151-3*, Lythway Large Print) Hall.

Jackson, Jack. Comanche Moon. Fehrenbach, T. R., intro. by. 128p. pap. 5.95 (*0-89620-079-5*) Rip Off.

James, Will. Smoky the Cow Horse. 2nd ed. James, Will, illus. LC 92-28753. 324p. (gr. 3-7). 1993. pap. 3.95 (*0-689-71682-6*, Aladdin) Macmillan Child Grp.

Kelley, Shirley. The Good, the Bad & the Two Cookie Kid. Herbst, Eric & Genee, Gloria, eds. Claridy, Jimmy, illus. Cash, Johnny, intro. by. (Illus.). 32p. (ps-4). 1993. Incl. audio cass. 9.95 (*1-882436-02-4*) Better Pl Pub.

Kimmel, Eric A. Charlie Drives the Stage. Rounds, Glen, illus. LC 88-24558. 32p. (ps-3). 1989. reinforced bdg. 13.95 (*0-8234-0738-1*) Holiday.

Lightfoot, D. J. Trail Fever: The Life of a Texas Cowboy. Bobbish, John, illus. LC 92-5458. 1992. 11.00 (*0-688-11537-3*) Lothrop.

Lund, Jillian. Way Out West Lives a Coyote Named Frank. LC 91-46011. (Illus.). 32p. (ps-2). 1993. 13.95 (*0-525-44982-5*, DCB) Dutton Child Bks.

McCall, Edith. Message from the Mountains. Nankin, Fran, ed. LC 85-3142. (Illus.). 122p. (gr. 6-9). 1985. 11.95 (*0-8027-6582-3*) Walker & Co.

McClung, Robert M. Hugh Glass: Mountain Man. LC 92-43790. 176p. (gr. 7 up). 1993. pap. 3.95 (*0-688-04595-2*, Pub. by Beech Tree Bks) Morrow.

McHugh, Elisabet. Wiggie Wins the West. (gr. 4-7). 1991. pap. 3.25 (*0-440-40457-6*) Dell.

MacLachlan, Patricia. Three Names. Pertzoff, Alexander, illus. LC 90-4444. 32p. (gr. k-4). 1991. 14.95 (*0-06-024035-0*); PLB 14.89 (*0-06-024036-9*) HarpC Child Bks.

Morey, Walt. Canyon Winter. 208p. (gr. 5 up). 1994. pap. 3.99 (*0-14-036856-6*) Puffin Bks.

Morris, Neil. Home on the Prairie. LC 89-987. (Illus.). 32p. (gr. 4-8). 1989. PLB 9.95 (*1-85435-165-6*) Marshall Cavendish.

—Longhorn on the Move. LC 89-7153. (Illus.). 32p. (gr. 3-8). 1989. PLB 9.95 (*1-85435-166-4*) Marshall Cavendish.

—On the Trapping Trail. LC 89-989. (Illus.). 32p. (gr. 3-8). 1989. PLB 9.95 (*1-85435-164-8*) Marshall Cavendish.

—Wagon Wheels Roll West. LC 89-988. (Illus.). 32p. (gr. 3-8). 1989. PLB 9.95 (*1-85435-167-2*) Marshall Cavendish.

Morrow, Honore. On to Oregon. Shenton, Edward, illus. LC 90-19554. 240p. (gr. 5 up). 1991. pap. 4.95 (*0-688-10494-0*, Pub. by Beech Tree Bks) Morrow.

Noble, Trinka H. Meanwhile Back at the Ranch. Ross, Tony, illus. 32p. (ps-3). 1992. pap. 3.99 (*0-14-054564-6*, Puff Pied Piper) Puffin Bks.

Pamplin, Laurel J. Masquerade on the Western Trail. Roberts, M., ed. (Illus.). 112p. (gr. 4-8). 1991. 9.95 (*0-89015-755-3*) Sunbelt Media.

Paulsen, Gary. Canyons. (gr. 4-8). 1992. 17.25 (*0-8446-6590-8*) Peter Smith.

—Cowpokes & Desperadoes. (gr. 4-7). 1994. pap. 3.50 (*0-440-40902-0*) Dell.

—Mr. Tucket. LC 93-31180. 1994. 14.95 (*0-385-31169-9*) Delacorte.

Ratz De Tagyos, Paul. Showdown at Lonesome Pellet. LC 93-25733. 1994. 14.95 (*0-395-67645-2*, Clarion Bks) HM.

Reaver, Chap. A Little Bit Dead. LC 92-7185. 192p. (gr. 6 up). 1992. 15.00 (*0-385-30801-9*) Delacorte.

—A Little Bit Dead. large type ed. LC 93-42210. 1994. pap. 15.95 (*0-7862-0139-8*) Thorndike Pr.

Remkiewicz, Frank. The Bone Stranger. LC 93-25214. (Illus.). 1994. 15.00 (*0-688-12041-5*); lib. bdg. 14.93 (*0-688-12042-3*) Lothrop.

Rubel, Nicole. Cyrano the Bear. 1st ed. LC 94-25902. 1995. write for info. (*0-8037-1444-0*); write for info. (*0-8037-1445-9*) Dial Bks Young.

Saban, Vera. Test of the Tenderfoot. Elliott, Tony, illus. LC 89-9729. 147p. (gr. 5-8). 1989. 6.95 (*0-914565-35-4*, Timbertrails) Capstan Pubns.

Saller, Carol. Pug, Slug, & Doug the Thug. Redenbaugh, Vicki J., illus. LC 92-44340. 1993. 13.95 (*0-87614-803-8*) Carolrhoda Bks.

Sauerwein, Leigh. The Way Home. LC 93-10097. 1993. 15.00 (*0-374-38247-6*) FS&G.

Scieszka, Jon. The Good, the Bad, & the Goofy. Smith, Lane, illus. 64p. (gr. 3-7). 1992. 11.00 (*0-670-84380-6*) Viking Child Bks.

—The Good, the Bad, & the Goofy. Smith, Lane, illus. LC 93-15136. 80p. (gr. 2-5). 1993. pap. 2.99 (*0-14-036170-7*, Puffin) Puffin Bks.

Sharmat, Marjorie W. Gila Monsters Meet You at the Airport. Barton, Byron, illus. LC 80-12264. 32p. (gr. k-3). 1980. RSBE 14.95 (*0-02-782450-0*, Macmillan Child Bk) Macmillan Child Grp.

—Gila Monsters Meet You at the Airport. LC 89-38398. (Illus.). 32p. 1990. pap. 4.95 (*0-689-71383-5*, Aladdin) Macmillan Child Grp.

Shub, Elizabeth. The White Stallion. Isadora, Rachel, illus. LC 81-20308. 56p. (gr. 1-3). 1982. 15.95 (*0-688-01210-8*); PLB 15.88 (*0-688-01211-6*) Greenwillow.

Smith, George S. The Christmas Eve Cattle Drive. Bacon, Eliza, illus. 32p. (gr. 1-4). 1991. pap. 3.95 (*0-89015-820-7*) Sunbelt Media.

Sonberg, Lynn. Wild Horse Country. 64p. (gr. 2-4). 1984. pap. 2.25 (*0-553-15489-3*, Skylark) Bantam.

Stahl, Hilda. Sadie Rose & the Outlaw Rustlers. LC 89-50331. 128p. (gr. 4-7). 1989. pap. 4.99 (*0-89107-528-3*) Crossway Bks.

Stine, Megan & Stine, H. William. Young Indiana Jones & the Lost Gold of Durango. 132p. (Orig.). (gr. 3-7). 1993. pap. 3.50 (*0-679-84926-2*, Bullseye Bks) Random Bks Yng Read.

Thomas. Twelve Dark Riders. 1996. 15.00 (*0-06-023477-6*); PLB 14.89 (*0-06-023478-4*) HarpC Child Bks.

Waddell, Martin. Little Obie & the Flood. Lennox, Elsie & Lennox, Elsie, illus. LC 91-58741. 80p. (gr. 3-6). 1992. 13.95 (*1-56402-106-8*) Candlewick Pr.

Wallace, Bill. Buffalo Gal. LC 91-28243. 192p. (gr. 5 up). 1992. 14.95 (*0-8234-0943-0*) Holiday.

Weidt, Maryann. Wild Bill Hickok. Casino, Steve, illus. LC 92-9732. 1992. 11.00 (*0-688-10089-9*) Lothrop.

Weinberg, Larry, adapted by. The Legend of the Lone Ranger Storybook. (Illus.). (gr. 4-7). 1981. lib. bdg. 6.99 (*0-394-94683-9*) Random Bks Yng Read.

West, Colin. The Best of West. (Illus.). 192p. (gr. 5-8). 1992. 22.95 (*0-09-173587-4*, Pub. by Hutchinson UK) Trafalgar.

Williams, Mari. Revolt in the Valley. 1992. pap. 23.00x (*0-86383-778-6*, Pub. by Gomer Pr UK) St Mut.

Wu, William F. Hong on the Range. Hale, Phil & Anderson, Darrel, illus. LC 88-29329. 224p. (gr. 7 up). 1989. 17.95 (*0-8027-6862-8*) Walker & Co.

Yosemite Yarns-Stagecoach Stories. (gr. 7 up). pap. 2.00 (*0-915266-04-0*) Awani Pr.

WEST, THE–HISTORY

Bidwell, John, et al. First Three Wagon Trains. Remington, Frederic, illus. 118p. (gr. 7-9). 1993. pap. 11.95 (*0-8323-0504-9*) Binford Mort.

Brown, Dee. Wounded Knee: An Indian History of the American West. Ehrlick, Emy, adapted by. 192p. (gr. 7 up). 1975. pap. 1.50 (*0-440-95768-0*, LFL) Dell.

Collins, Jim. Settling the American West. LC 92-28301. 1993. PLB 12.90 (*0-531-20070-1*) Watts.

Faber, Doris. Calamity Jane: Her Life & Her Legend. LC 91-40050. (Illus.). 80p. (gr. 5-9). 1992. 14.45 (*0-395-56396-8*) HM.

Fox, Mary V. The Story of Women Who Shaped the West. LC 90-21444. (Illus.). 32p. (gr. 3-6). 1991. PLB 12.85 (*0-516-04757-4*); pap. 3.95 (*0-516-44757-2*) Childrens.

Green, Carl R. & Sanford, William R. Outlaws & Lawmen of the Wild West Series, 6 bks. (Illus.). (gr. 4-10). Set. lib. bdg. 89.70 (*0-89490-391-8*) Enslow Pubs.

Hill, William E. & Hill, Jan C. Heading West: An Activity Book for Children. Hill, William E. & Hill, Jan C., illus. 32p. (Orig.). (gr. k-4). 1992. pap. 3.95 (*0-9636071-0-3*) HillHouse Pub.

McNeese, Tim. West by Steamboat. LC 91-22822. (Illus.). 48p. (gr. 5). 1993. text ed. 11.95 RSBE (*0-89686-728-5*, Crestwood Hse) Macmillan Child Grp.

Miller, Robert. Cowboys. Leonard, Richard, illus. 104p. (gr. 4-7). 1992. PLB 8.95 (*0-382-24079-0*); pap. 4.95 (*0-382-24084-7*) Silver Burdett Pr.

Petra Press Staff. A Multicultural Portrait of the Move West. LC 93-10317. 1993. 18.95 (*1-85435-658-5*) Marshall Cavendish.

Rice, James. Cowboy Rodeo. Rice, James, illus. LC 91-34924. 32p. 1992. 14.95 (*0-88289-903-1*) Pelican.

Salts, Bobbi. Discover Westward Expansion. Parker, Steve, illus. 32p. (Orig.). (gr. 4-6). 1992. pap. text ed. 3.95 (*0-931056-03-9*) Jefferson Natl.

Schlissel. Black Frontiers. 1995. 16.00 (*0-671-73853-4*) S&S Trade.

Shapley, R., et al. Wild West in American History, 14 bks, Set 2. (Illus.). 448p. (gr. 3-8). 1990. Set. lib. bdg. 252.00 (*0-86625-367-X*); Set. lib. bdg. 189.00s.p. (*0-685-36328-7*) Rourke Corp.

Smith, Carter, ed. Bridging the Continent: A Sourcebook on the American West. LC 91-31129. (Illus.). 96p. (gr. 5-8). 1992. PLB 18.90 (*1-56294-130-5*) Millbrook Pr.

—The Conquest of the West: A Sourcebook on the American West. LC 91-31130. (Illus.). 96p. (gr. 5-8). 1992. PLB 18.90 (*1-56294-129-1*) Millbrook Pr.

—Exploring the Frontier: A Sourcebook on the American West. LC 91-31131. (Illus.). 96p. (gr. 5-8). 1992. PLB 18.90 (*1-56294-128-3*) Millbrook Pr.

—The Legendary Wild West: A Sourcebook on the American West. LC 91-31126. (Illus.). 96p. (gr. 5-8). 1992. PLB 18.90 (*1-56294-133-X*) Millbrook Pr.

—The Riches of the West: A Sourcebook on the American West. LC 91-31127. (Illus.). 96p. (gr. 5-8). 1992. PLB 18.90 (*1-56294-132-1*) Millbrook Pr.

Steber, Rick. Grandpa's Stories. Gray, Don, illus. 60p. (Orig.). 1991. pap. 4.95 (*0-945134-10-X*); cassette 9.95 (*0-945134-60-6*) Bonanza Pub.

Stein, R. Conrad. The Oregon Trail. LC 93-36994. (Illus.). 32p. (gr. 3-6). 1994. PLB 12.30 (*0-516-06674-9*) Childrens.

Stewart, Gail. Rivermen. (Illus.). 32p. (gr. 3-8). 1990. PLB 18.00 (*0-86625-409-9*); 13.50 (*0-685-58652-9*) Rourke Corp.

—Scouts. (Illus.). 32p. (gr. 3-8). 1990. PLB 18.00 (*0-86625-404-8*); 13.50 (*0-685-58651-0*) Rourke Corp.

—Trappers & Traders. (Illus.). 32p. (gr. 3-8). 1990. PLB 18.00 (*0-86625-401-3*); PLB 13.50s.p. (*0-685-58655-3*) Rourke Corp.

Stewart, Gail B. Where Lies Butch Cassidy? LC 91-25368. (Illus.). 48p. (gr. 5-6). 1992. text ed. 11.95 RSBE (*0-89686-618-1*, Crestwood Hse) Macmillan Child Grp.

Stiles, T. J. Jesse James. LC 92-45210. (Illus.). 1993. 18.95 (*0-7910-1737-0*, Am Art Analog); pap. write for info. (*0-7910-1738-9*, Am Art Analog) Chelsea Hse.

Tales of the Old West Series, 4 vols. (Illus.). 128p. (gr. 3-8). 1989. Set. PLB 39.80 (*1-85435-163-X*) Marshall Cavendish.

Twist, Clint. Lewis & Clark: Exploring North America. LC 93-33624. 1994. PLB 22.80 (*0-8114-7255-8*) Raintree Steck-V.

Walker, Paul R. Great Figures of the Wild West. (Illus.). 128p. (gr. 7-12). 1992. lib. bdg. 16.95x (*0-8160-2576-2*) Facts on File.

Wilder, Laura I. West from Home: Letters of Laura Ingalls Wilder, San Francisco 1915. MacBride, Roger L., ed. LC 73-14342. (Illus.). 176p. (gr. 7 up). 1976. pap. 3.95 (*0-06-440081-6*, Trophy) HarpC Child Bks.

WEST GERMANY

see Germany (Federal Republic)

WEST INDIES

Brothers, Don. West Indies. (Illus.). 128p. (gr. 5 up). 1989. lib. bdg. 14.95 (*1-55546-793-8*) Chelsea Hse.

Flint, David. West Indies. LC 92-43914. (Illus.). 32p. (gr. 3-4). 1993. PLB 19.24 (*0-8114-2942-3*) Raintree Steck-V.

Ramdin, Ron. West Indies. LC 91-7490. (Illus.). 96p. (gr. 6-12). 1991. PLB 22.80 (*0-8114-2442-1*) Raintree Steck-V.

Russell, William. The West Indies. LC 93-49339. 1994. write for info. (*1-55916-035-7*) Rourke Bk Co.

WEST INDIES–FICTION

Berry, James. The Future-Telling Lady & Other Stories. LC 92-13759. 144p. (gr. 5 up). 1993. 14.00 (*0-06-021434-1*); PLB 13.89 (*0-06-021435-X*) HarpC Child Bks.

Yolen, Jane. Encounter. Shannon, David A., illus. 1992. 14.95 (*0-15-225962-7*, HB Juv Bks) HarBrace.

WEST POINT MILITARY ACADEMY

see U. S. Military Academy, West Point

WEST VIRGINIA

Aylesworth, Thomas G. & Aylesworth, Virginia L. The Atlantic (Virginia, West Virginia, District of Columbia) (Illus.). 64p. (Orig.). 1990. lib. bdg. 16.95x (*1-55546-555-2*); pap. 6.95 (*0-7910-0533-X*) Chelsea Hse.

Carole Marsh West Virginia Books, 44 bks. 1994. PLB 1027.80 set (*0-7933-1323-6*); pap. 587.80 set (*0-7933-5218-5*) Gallopade Pub Group.

Carpenter, Allan. West Virginia. new ed. LC 79-12900. (Illus.). 96p. (gr. 4 up). 1979. PLB 16.95 (*0-516-04148-7*) Childrens.

Di Piazza, Domenica. West Virginia. LC 93-46906. 1994. PLB write for info. (*0-8225-2745-6*) Lerner Pubns.

Doherty, William T. West Virginia: Our Land - Our People. Buckalew, Marshall, ed. Harvey, Eve S. & Harvey, Cliff, illus. 320p. (gr. 8). 1990. 25.00 (*0-914498-07-X*); punched for 3-ring binder tchr's. manual 25.00 (*0-914498-10-X*) WV Hist Ed Found.

Doherty, William T. & Conley, Phil. West Virginia History. (Illus.). 494p. (gr. 8). 1974. 10.25 (*0-914498-00-2*) WV Hist Ed Found.

Fradin, Dennis. West Virginia: In Words & Pictures. Wahl, Richard, illus. LC 80-12133. 48p. (gr. 2-5). 1980. PLB 12.95 (*0-516-03949-0*) Childrens.

Fradin, Dennis B. & Fradin, Judith B. West Virginia. LC 94-17016. (Illus.). 64p. (gr. 3-5). 1994. PLB 22.00 (*0-516-03848-6*) Childrens.

Johnson, Patricia G. The New River Early Settlement. LC 83-81157. (Illus.). 232p. (gr. 6 up). 1991. Repr. of 1983 ed. 20.00 (*0-9614765-3-2*) Walpa Pub.

Marsh, Carole. Avast, Ye Slobs! West Virginia Pirate Trivia. (Illus.). 1994. PLB 24.95 (*0-7933-1220-5*); pap. 14.95 (*0-7933-1219-1*); computer disk 29.95 (*0-7933-1221-3*) Gallopade Pub Group.

—The Beast of the West Virginia Bed & Breakfast. (Illus.). 1994. PLB 24.95 (*0-7933-2244-8*); pap. 14.95 (*0-7933-2245-6*); computer disk 29.95 (*0-7933-2246-4*) Gallopade Pub Group.

—Bow Wow! West Virginia Dogs in History, Mystery, Legend, Lore, Humor & More! (Illus.). (gr. 3-12). 1994. PLB 24.95 (*0-7933-3611-2*); pap. 14.95 (*0-7933-3612-0*); computer disk 29.95 (*0-7933-3613-9*) Gallopade Pub Group.

—Chill Out: Scary West Virginia Tales Based on Frightening West Virginia Truths. (Illus.). 1994. lib. bdg. 24.95 (*0-7933-4801-3*); pap. 14.95 (*0-7933-4802-1*); disk 29.95 (*0-7933-4803-X*) Gallopade Pub Group.

—Christopher Columbus Comes to West Virginia! Includes Reproducible Activities for Kids! (Illus.). (gr. 3-12). 1994. PLB 24.95 (*0-7933-3764-X*); pap. 14.95 (*0-7933-3765-8*); computer disk 29.95 (*0-7933-3766-6*) Gallopade Pub Group.

—The Hard-to-Believe-But-True! Book of West Virginia History, Mystery, Trivia, Legend, Lore, Humor & More. (Illus.). 1994. PLB 24.95 (*0-7933-1217-5*); pap. 14.95 (*0-7933-1216-7*); computer disk 29.95 (*0-7933-1218-3*) Gallopade Pub Group.

—If My West Virginia Mama Ran the World! (Illus.). 1994. PLB 24.95 (*0-7933-2253-7*); pap. 14.95 (*0-7933-2254-5*); computer disk 29.95 (*0-7933-2255-3*) Gallopade Pub Group.

—Jurassic Ark! West Virginia Dinosaurs & Other Prehistoric Creatures. (gr. k-12). 1994. PLB 24.95 (*0-7933-7572-X*); pap. 14.95 (*0-7933-7573-8*); computer disk 29.95 (*0-7933-7574-6*) Gallopade Pub Group.

—Let's Quilt Our West Virginia County. 1994. lib. bdg. 24.95 (*0-7933-7257-7*); pap. text ed. 14.95 (*0-7933-7258-5*); disk 29.95 (*0-7933-7259-3*) Gallopade Pub Group.

—Let's Quilt Our West Virginia Town. 1994. lib. bdg. 24.95 (*0-7933-7107-4*); pap. text ed. 14.95 (*0-7933-7108-2*); disk 29.95 (*0-7933-7109-0*) Gallopade Pub Group.

—Let's Quilt West Virginia & Stuff It Topographically! (Illus.). 1994. PLB 24.95 (*0-7933-2236-7*); pap. 14.95 (*1-55609-052-8*); computer disk 29.95 (*0-7933-2237-5*) Gallopade Pub Group.

—Meow! West Virginia Cats in History, Mystery, Legend, Lore, Humor & More! (Illus.). (gr. 3-12). 1994. PLB 24.95 (*0-7933-3458-6*); pap. 14.95 (*0-7933-3459-4*); computer disk 29.95 (*0-7933-3460-8*) Gallopade Pub Group.

—My First Book about West Virginia. (gr. k-4). 1994. PLB 24.95 (*0-7933-5713-6*); pap. 14.95 (*0-7933-5714-4*); computer disk 29.95 (*0-7933-5715-2*) Gallopade Pub Group.

—Patch, the Pirate Dog: A West Virginia Pet Story. (ps-4). 1994. PLB 24.95 (*0-7933-5560-5*); pap. 14.95 (*0-7933-5561-3*); computer disk 29.95 (*0-7933-5562-1*) Gallopade Pub Group.

—Uncle Rebus: West Virginia Picture Stories for Computer Kids. (Illus.). (gr. k-3). 1994. PLB 24.95 (*0-7933-4648-7*); pap. 14.95 (*0-7933-4649-5*); disk 29.95 (*0-7933-4650-9*) Gallopade Pub Group.

—West Virginia & Other State Greats (Biographies) (Illus.). 1994. PLB 24.95 (*0-7933-2256-1*); pap. 14.95 (*0-7933-2257-X*); computer disk 29.95 (*0-7933-2258-8*) Gallopade Pub Group.

—West Virginia Bandits, Bushwackers, Outlaws, Crooks, Devils, Ghosts, Desperadoes & Other Assorted & Sundry Characters! (Illus.). 1994. PLB 24.95 (*0-7933-1202-7*); pap. 14.95 (*0-7933-1201-9*); computer disk 29.95 (*0-7933-1203-5*) Gallopade Pub Group.

—West Virginia Classic Christmas Trivia: Stories, Recipies, Activities, Legends, Lore & More! (Illus.). 1994. PLB 24.95 (*0-7933-1205-1*); pap. 14.95 (*0-7933-1204-3*); computer disk 29.95 (*0-7933-1206-X*) Gallopade Pub Group.

—West Virginia Coastales. (Illus.). 1994. PLB 24.95 (*0-7933-2250-2*); pap. 14.95 (*0-7933-2251-0*); computer disk 29.95 (*0-7933-2252-9*) Gallopade Pub Group.

—West Virginia Coastales! 1994. lib. bdg. 24.95 (*0-7933-7313-1*) Gallopade Pub Group.

—West Virginia "Crinkum-Crankum" A Funny Word Book about Our State. (Illus.). (gr. 3-12). 1994. 24.95 (*0-7933-4955-9*); pap. 14.95 (*0-7933-4956-7*); computer disk 29.95 (*0-7933-4957-5*) Gallopade Pub Group.

—West Virginia Dingbats! Bk. 1: A Fun Book of Games, Stories, Activities & More about Our State That's All in Code! for You to Decipher. (Illus.). (gr. 3-12). 1994. PLB 24.95 (*0-7933-3917-0*); pap. 14.95 (*0-7933-3918-9*); computer disk 29.95 (*0-7933-3919-7*) Gallopade Pub Group.

—West Virginia Festival Fun for Kids! Includes Reproducible Activities for Kids! (Illus.). (gr. 3-12). 1994. PLB 24.95 (*0-7933-4070-5*); pap. 14.95 (*0-7933-4071-3*); computer disk 29.95 (*0-7933-4072-1*) Gallopade Pub Group.

—The West Virginia Hot Air Balloon Mystery. (Illus.). (gr. 2-9). 1994. 24.95 (*0-7933-2750-4*); pap. 14.95 (*0-7933-2751-2*); computer disk 29.95 (*0-7933-2752-0*) Gallopade Pub Group.

—West Virginia Jeopardy! Answers & Questions about Our State! (Illus.). (gr. 3-12). 1994. PLB 24.95 (*0-7933-4223-6*); pap. 14.95 (*0-7933-4224-4*); computer disk 29.95 (*0-7933-4225-2*) Gallopade Pub Group.

—West Virginia "Jography" A Fun Run Thru Our State! (Illus.). 1994. PLB 24.95 (*0-7933-2233-2*); pap. 14.95 (*0-7933-2234-0*); computer disk 29.95 (*0-7933-2235-9*) Gallopade Pub Group.

—West Virginia Kid's Cookbook: Recipes, How-to, History, Lore & More! (Illus.). 1994. PLB 24.95 (*0-7933-1214-0*); pap. 14.95 (*0-7933-1213-2*); computer disk 29.95 (*0-7933-1215-9*) Gallopade Pub Group.

—The West Virginia Mystery Van Takes Off! Book 1: Handicapped West Virginia Kids Sneak Off on a Big Adventure. (Illus.). (gr. 3-12). 1994. 24.95 (*0-7933-5108-1*); pap. 14.95 (*0-7933-5109-X*); computer disk 29.95 (*0-7933-5110-3*) Gallopade Pub Group.

—West Virginia Quiz Bowl Crash Course! (Illus.). 1994. PLB 24.95 (*0-7933-2247-2*); pap. 14.95 (*0-7933-2248-0*); computer disk 29.95 (*0-7933-2249-9*) Gallopade Pub Group.

—West Virginia Rollercoasters! (Illus.). (gr. 3-12). 1994. PLB 24.95 (*0-7933-5368-8*); pap. 14.95 (*0-7933-5369-6*); computer disk 29.95 (*0-7933-5370-X*) Gallopade Pub Group.

—West Virginia School Trivia: An Amazing & Fascinating Look at Our State's Teachers, Schools & Students! (Illus.). 1994. PLB 24.95 (*0-7933-1211-6*); pap. 14.95 (*0-7933-1210-8*); computer disk 29.95 (*0-7933-1212-4*) Gallopade Pub Group.

—West Virginia Silly Basketball Sportsmysteries, Vol. 1. (Illus.). 1994. PLB 24.95 (*0-7933-1208-6*); pap. 14.95 (*0-7933-1207-8*); computer disk 29.95 (*0-7933-1209-4*) Gallopade Pub Group.

—West Virginia Silly Basketball Sportsmysteries, Vol. 2. (Illus.). 1994. PLB 24.95 (*0-7933-2259-6*); pap. 14.95 (*0-7933-2260-X*); computer disk 29.95 (*0-7933-2261-8*) Gallopade Pub Group.

—West Virginia Silly Football Sportsmysteries, Vol. 1. (Illus.). 1994. PLB 24.95 (*0-7933-2238-3*); pap. 14.95 (*0-7933-2239-1*); computer disk 29.95 (*0-7933-2240-5*) Gallopade Pub Group.

—West Virginia Silly Football Sportsmysteries, Vol. 2. (Illus.). 1994. PLB 24.95 (*0-7933-2241-3*); pap. 14.95 (*0-7933-2242-1*); computer disk 29.95 (*0-685-45965-9*) Gallopade Pub Group.

—West Virginia Silly Trivia! (Illus.). 1994. PLB 24.95 (*0-7933-2230-8*); pap. 14.95 (*0-7933-2231-6*); computer disk 29.95 (*0-7933-2232-4*) Gallopade Pub Group.

—West Virginia Timeline: A Chronology of West Virginia History, Mystery, Trivia, Legend, Lore & More. (Illus.). (gr. 3-12). 1994. PLB 24.95 (*0-7933-6019-6*); pap. 14.95 (*0-7933-6020-X*); computer disk 29.95 (*0-7933-6021-8*) Gallopade Pub Group.

—West Virginia's (Most Devastating!) Disasters & (Most Calamitous!) Catastrophies! (Illus.). 1994. PLB 24.95 (*0-7933-1199-3*); pap. 14.95 (*0-7933-1198-5*); computer disc 29.95 (*0-7933-1200-0*) Gallopade Pub Group.

—West Virginia's Unsolved Mysteries (& Their "Solutions") Includes Scientific Information & Other Activities for Students. (Illus.). (gr. 3-12). 1994. PLB 24.95 (*0-7933-5866-3*); pap. 14.95 (*0-7933-5867-1*); computer disk 29.95 (*0-7933-5868-X*) Gallopade Pub Group.

Stein, R. Conrad. West Virginia. LC 90-33848. (Illus.). 144p. (gr. 4 up). 1990. PLB 20.55 (*0-516-00494-8*) Childrens.

—West Virginia. 195p. 1993. text ed. 15.40 (*1-56956-144-3*) W A T Braille.

Thompson, Kathleen. West Virginia. LC 87-26483. 48p. (gr. 3 up). 1988. 19.97 (*0-86514-476-1*) Raintree Steck-V.

Waura, Grace. The First Families of West Virginia. Waura, Grace M., illus. LC 90-70666. 70p. (Orig.). (gr. 3-6). 1991. pap. 6.00 (*1-56002-007-5*) Aegina Pr.

Williams, Tony L. West Virginia: Our State. Buckalew, Marshall, ed. Harvey, Eve S. & Harvey, Cliff, illus. 288p. (gr. 4). 1990. 20.00 (*0-914498-09-6*); punched for 3-ring binder tchr's. manual 25.00 (*0-685-25544-1*) WV Hist Ed Found.

WEST VIRGINIA–FICTION

McKenna, Colleen O. The Brightest Light. 1992. 13.95 (*0-590-45347-5*, Scholastic Hardcover) Scholastic Inc.

Mills, Patricia. Until the Cows Come Home. Mills, Patricia, illus. LC 92-31049. 32p. (gr. k-3). 1993. 14.95 (*1-55858-190-1*); PLB 14.88 (*1-55858-191-X*) North-South Bks NYC.

Naylor, Phyllis R. Shiloh. LC 90-603. 144p. (gr. 3-7). 1991. SBE 13.95 (*0-689-31614-3*, Atheneum Child Bk) Macmillan Child Grp.
Pool, James M. Among These Hills: A Child's History of Harrison County. Crowder, Beth, illus. 240p. 1985. 12.95 (*0-9615566-0-9*) Clarksburg-Harrison Bicent.
Woodruff, Elvira. Ghosts Don't Get Goosebumps. LC 92-56589. 96p. (gr. 4-7). 1993. 13.95 (*0-8234-1035-8*) Holiday.

WHALES

Allen, Judy. Whale. Humphries, Tudor, illus. LC 92-53019. 32p. (ps up). 1993. 15.95 (*1-56402-160-2*) Candlewick Pr.
Anderson, J. I. I Can Read About Whales & Dolphins. LC 72-96955. (Illus.). (gr. 2-4). 1973. pap. 2.50 (*0-89375-052-2*) Troll Assocs.
Arnold, Caroline. Killer Whale. Hewett, Richard, photos by. LC 93-33668. (gr. 4 up). 1994. write for info. (*0-688-12029-6*); write for info. (*0-688-12030-X*) Morrow Jr Bks.
Asimov, Isaac. Why Are the Whales Vanishing? (Illus.). 24p. (gr. 2-3). 1992. PLB 15.93 (*0-8368-0745-6*) Gareth Stevens Inc.
Barrett, Norman S. Ballenas. LC 90-70885. (SPA., Illus.). 32p. (gr. k-4). 1990. PLB 11.90 (*0-531-07903-1*) Watts.
—Whales. LC 88-51515. (Illus.). 32p. (gr. k-6). 1989. PLB 11.90 (*0-531-10703-5*) Watts.
Barstow, Robbins. Grandiosas Criaturas del Mar: Una Introduccion al Mundo de las Ballenas y Otros Cetaceos. Accent, Inc. Staff, tr. from ENG. Sineti, Donald, illus. (SPA.). 46p. (Orig.). (gr. 7-12). 1988. pap. 5.00 (*0-9618858-2-3*) Cetacean Society.
—Meet the Great Ones: An Introduction to Whales & Other Cetaceans. Sineti, Donald, illus. LC 87-70553. 46p. (Orig.). (gr. 7-12). 1987. pap. 5.95 (*0-9618858-1-5*) Cetacean Society.
Behrens, June. Whales of the World. LC 87-8046. (Illus.). 48p. (gr. 1-4). 1987. PLB 12.30 (*0-516-08877-7*); pap. 4.95 (*0-516-48877-5*) Childrens.
—Whalewatch! Olguin, John, illus. LC 78-7338. 32p. (gr. k-4). 1978. PLB 12.30 (*0-516-08873-4*, Golden Gate); pap. 3.95 (*0-516-48873-2*) Childrens.
Berger, Gilda. Whales. Bonaforte, Lisa, illus. LC 86-16500. 48p. (gr. k-3). 1987. 11.99 (*0-685-18308-4*); PLB 10.95 (*0-685-18309-2*) Doubleday.
Berger, Melvin. As Big As a Whale. 16p. (gr. 2-4). 1993. pap. 14.95 (*1-56784-201-1*) Newbridge Comms.
Bour, Laura. Whales. Bour, Laura, illus. LC 92-41413. 24p. (ps-3). 1993. 11.95 (*0-590-47130-9*, Cartwheel) Scholastic Inc.
Brett, Caroline. The Whale: The Sovereigns of the Sea. Stefoff, Rebecca, ed. LC 92-10242. (Illus.). 31p. (gr. 3-6). 1992. PLB 17.26 (*1-56074-054-X*) Garrett Ed Corp.
Brittain, Mary Ann. A Whale Called Trouble. (Illus.). 24p. (gr. 1-12). 1985. pap. 1.50 (*0-917134-08-7*) NC Natl Sci.
Carrick, Carol. Whaling Days. Frampton, David, illus. 40p. (gr. 4-7). 1993. 15.45 (*0-395-50948-3*, Clarion Bks) HM.
Carwardine, Mark. Whales, Dolphins, & Porpoises. LC 92-7624. (Illus.). 64p. (gr. 3 up). 1992. 11.95 (*1-56458-144-6*) Dorling Kindersley.
Cousteau Society Staff. Whales. LC 92-34176. (Illus.). (ps-1). 1993. pap. 3.95 POB (*0-671-86564-1*, Little Simon) S&S Trade.
Craig, Janet. Discovering Whales & Dolphins. Johnson, Pamela, illus. LC 89-5004. 32p. (gr. 2-4). 1990. PLB 11.59 (*0-8167-1759-1*); pap. text ed. 2.95 (*0-8167-1760-5*) Troll Assocs.
Crump, Donald J., ed. Whales, Bk. 2. (Illus.). (ps-3). 1990. Set. 21.95 (*0-87044-810-2*) Natl Geog.
Dow, Lesley. Whales. 72p. (gr. 5-12). 1990. 17.95 (*0-8160-2271-2*) Facts on File.
D'Vincent, Cynthia. The Whale Family Book. LC 91-41145. (Illus.). 60p. (gr. 5 up). 1992. pap. 15.95 (*0-88708-148-7*) Picture Bk Studio.
Eisemann, Henry. Hump-Free Heads for Hawaii. Campbell, Jay, illus. 24p. (Orig.). (gr. k-6). 1989. pap. 6.95 (*0-938129-02-3*) Emprise Pubns.
Esbensen, Barbara J. Baby Whales Drink Milk. Davis, Lambert, illus. LC 92-30375. 32p. (ps-1). 1994. 15.00 (*0-06-021551-8*); PLB 14.89 (*0-06-021552-6*) HarpC Child Bks.
—Baby Whales Drink Milk. Davis, Lambert, illus. LC 92-30375. 32p. (ps-1). 1994. pap. 4.95 (*0-06-445119-4*, Trophy) HarpC Child Bks.
Fowler, Allan. El Animal Mas Grande del Mundo - The Biggest Animal Ever. LC 92-9410. (SPA., Illus.). 32p. (ps-2). 1993. big bk. 22.95 (*0-516-59628-4*); PLB 10.75 (*0-516-36001-9*); pap. 3.95 (*0-516-56001-8*) Childrens.
—The Biggest Animal Ever. LC 92-9410. (Illus.). 32p. (ps-2). 1992. PLB 10.75 (*0-516-06001-5*); big bk. 22.95 (*0-516-49628-X*) Childrens.
—Podria Ser un Mamifero - Libro Grande: (It Could Still Be a Mammal Big Book) LC 90-2161. (SPA., Illus.). 32p. (ps-2). 1993. 22.95 (*0-516-59463-X*) Childrens.
Fuhr, U. & Sautai, R., illus. Baleine. (FRE.). (ps-1). 1991. 13.95 (*2-07-035729-5*) Schoenhof.
Funston, Sylvia. St. Lawrence Beluga. Kassian, Olena, illus. 32p. (gr. 1-5). 1992. 4.95 (*0-920775-93-4*, Pub. by Greey de Pencier CN) Firefly Bks Ltd.
Gardner, Robert. The Whale Watchers' Guide. Sineti, Don, illus. LC 83-17425. 170p. (gr. 7 up). 1984. lib. bdg. 10.98 (*0-671-45811-6*, J Messner); pap. 5.95 (*0-671-49807-X*) S&S Trade.
Gibbons, Gail. Whales. Gibbons, Gail, illus. LC 91-4507. 32p. (ps-3). 1991. reinforced bdg. 15.95 (*0-8234-0900-7*) Holiday.
—Whales. Gibbons, Gail, illus. (ps-3). 1993. pap. 5.95 (*0-8234-1030-7*) Holiday.
Ginsberg, Daniel. Whales & Dolphins: An Educational Coloring Book. Ginsberg, Daniel, illus. 32p. (Orig.). (gr. 1-4). 1989. pap. 2.95 (*0-9623284-0-5*) R Rinehart.
Gohier, Francois. Humpback Whales. Leon, Vicki, ed. (Illus.). 40p. (Orig.). (gr. 5 up). 1990. pap. 7.95 (*0-918303-26-5*) Blake Pub.
—A Pod of Gray Whales. (Illus.). 40p. (Orig.). (gr. 5 up). 1987. pap. 7.95 (*0-918303-14-1*) Blake Pub.
Gouck, Maura M. Whales. 32p. (gr. 2-6). 1991. 15.95 (*0-89565-717-1*) Childs World.
Graham, Ada & Graham, Frank. Whale Watch. Tyler, D. D., illus. LC 77-20531. (gr. 5 up). 1978. 7.95 (*0-440-09505-0*); pap. 6.46 (*0-440-09506-9*) Delacorte.
Graves, Jack A. What Is a California Gray Whale? Daines, Cameron K., illus. 48p. (gr. 1-4). 1991. pap. 4.95 (*0-929526-13-9*) Double B Pubns.
Green, Carl R. & Sanford, William R. The Humpback Whale. LC 85-9645. (Illus.). 48p. (gr. 5). 1985. text ed. 12.95 RSBE (*0-89686-274-7*, Crestwood Hse) Macmillan Child Grp.
Greenberg, Judith E. & Carey, Helen H. Whales. Fujiwara, Kim, illus. 32p. (gr. 2-4). 1990. PLB 10.95 (*0-8172-3757-7*) Raintree Steck-V.
Greene, Carol. Reading about the Humpback Whale. LC 92-26805. (Illus.). 32p. (gr. k-3). 1993. lib. bdg. 13.95 (*0-89490-426-4*) Enslow Pubs.
Himmelman, John. Ibis: A True Whale Story. 1990. 12.95 (*0-590-42848-9*) Scholastic Inc.
Hogan, Paula Z. The Whale. Ruth, Rod, illus. LC 79-13379. 32p. (gr. 1-4). 1979. PLB 19.97 (*0-8172-1500-X*); pap. 4.95 (*0-8114-8180-8*); pap. 9.95 incl. cassette (*0-8114-8188-3*) Raintree Steck-V.
—The Whale. LC 79-13379. (Illus.). 32p. (gr. 1-4). 1981. PLB 29.28 incl. cassette (*0-8172-1847-5*) Raintree Steck-V.
Hoyt, Eric. Meeting the Whales: The Equinox Guide to Giants of the Deep. Folkens, Pieter, illus. 72p. (gr. 5 up). 1991. lib. bdg. 17.95 (*0-921820-25-9*, Pub. by Camden Hse CN); pap. 9.95 (*0-921820-23-2*, Pub. by Camden Hse CN) Firefly Bks Ltd.
Kalman, Bobbie. Arctic Whales & Whaling. (Illus.). 56p. (gr. 3-4). 1988. 15.95 (*0-86505-146-1*); pap. 7.95 (*0-86505-156-9*) Crabtree Pub Co.
Klobas, John. Life Cycle of the Pacific Gray Whale. Rovetta, Ane, illus. 32p. (gr. 6-9). 1993. 12.95 (*0-89346-532-1*) Heian Intl.
Knapp, Toni, ed. The Six Bridges of Humphrey the Whale. Brown, Craig M., illus. LC 89-8417. 48p. (gr. 8 up). 1989. 15.95 (*1-882092-01-5*) Travis Ilse.
Kovacs, Deborah. All about Whales. (Illus.). 32p. (Orig.). (gr. 1-8). 1994. pap. 3.95 (*1-884506-08-9*) Third Story.
Kraus, Scott & Mallory, Ken. The Search for the Right Whale. LC 92-18091. (Illus.). 36p. (gr. 2-6). 1993. 14.00 (*0-517-57844-1*, Focal); PLB 14.99 (*0-517-57845-X*) Buttrwrth-Heinemann.
Lauber, Patricia. Great Whales: The Gentle Giants. Folkens, Pieter, illus. 64p. (gr. 2-4). 1991. 14.95 (*0-8050-1717-8*, Redfeather BYR) H Holt & Co.
McMillan, Bruce. Going on a Whale Watch. (Illus.). (ps up). 1992. 14.95 (*0-590-45768-3*, 016, Scholastic Hardcover) Scholastic Inc.
Martin, L. Whales. (Illus.). 24p. (gr. k-5). 1988. PLB 11.94 (*0-86592-988-2*); PLB 8.95s.p. (*0-685-67679-X*) Rourke Corp.
Mell, Jan. The Atlantic Gray Whale. LC 89-7868. (Illus.). 48p. (gr. 5-6). 1989. text ed. 12.95 RSBE (*0-89686-458-8*, Crestwood Hse) Macmillan Child Grp.
Miller, Suzanne S. Whales & Sharks. Klimo, Kate, ed. Bonforte, Lisa, illus. 48p. 1982. pap. 9.95 (*0-671-45148-0*, S&S BFYR) S&S Trade.
Milton, Joyce. Whales: The Gentle Giants. Langford, Alton, illus. LC 88-15616. 48p. (Orig.). (gr. k-3). 1989. lib. bdg. 7.99 (*0-394-99809-X*); pap. 3.50 (*0-394-89809-5*) Random Bks Yng Read.
Moore, Jo E., et al. Whales. (Illus.). 48p. (gr. 2-5). 1990. pap. 5.95 (*1-55799-164-2*) Evan-Moor Corp.
Palmer, S. Blue Whales. (Illus.). 24p. (gr. k-5). 1988. PLB 11.94 (*0-86592-480-5*) Rourke Corp.
—Fin Whales. (Illus.). 24p. (gr. k-5). 1988. PLB 11.94 (*0-86592-479-1*); 8.95s.p. (*0-685-58331-7*) Rourke Corp.
—Gray Whales. (Illus.). 24p. (gr. k-5). 1988. PLB 11.94 (*0-86592-477-5*); 8.95s.p. (*0-685-58327-9*) Rourke Corp.
—Humpback Whales. (Illus.). 24p. (gr. k-5). 1988. PLB 11.94 (*0-86592-478-3*); 8.95s.p. (*0-685-58329-5*) Rourke Corp.
—Killer Whales. (Illus.). 24p. (gr. k-5). 1988. PLB 11.94 (*0-86592-481-3*); 8.95s.p. (*0-685-58330-9*) Rourke Corp.
—Narwhals. (Illus.). 24p. (gr. k-5). 1988. PLB 11.94 (*0-86592-476-7*); 8.95s.p. (*0-685-58328-7*) Rourke Corp.
Palmer, Sarah. World of Whales, 6 vols. 1990. 7.99 (*0-517-02746-1*) Random Hse Value.
Papastavrou, Vassili. Whales & Dolphins. LC 90-14400. (Illus.). 32p. (gr. k-4). 1991. 12.40 (*0-531-18394-7*, Pub. by Bookwright Pr) Watts.
Papastavrov, Vasilli. Whale. Greenaway, Frank, illus. 64p. (gr. 5 up). 1993. 16.00 (*0-679-83884-8*); PLB 16.99 (*0-679-93884-2*) Knopf Bks Yng Read.
Parker, Steve. Whales & Dolphins. LC 93-38518. (Illus.). 60p. (gr. 3-6). 1994. 16.95 (*0-87156-465-3*) Sierra.
Patent, Dorothy H. All about Whales. LC 86-27126. (Illus.). 48p. (ps-4). 1987. reinforced bdg. 13.95 (*0-8234-0644-X*) Holiday.
—Humpback Whales. Ferrari, Mark J. & Glockner-Ferrari, Deborah A., illus. LC 89-2026. 32p. (ps-3). 1989. reinforced bdg. 15.95 (*0-8234-0779-9*) Holiday.
—Killer Whales. Ford, John K., photos by. LC 92-23949. (Illus.). 32p. (gr. 3-7). 1993. reinforced bdg. 15.95 (*0-8234-0999-6*) Holiday.
—Whales: Giants of the Deep. Patent, Dorothy H., illus. LC 84-729. 96p. (gr. 3-7). 1984. reinforced bdg. 15.95 (*0-8234-0530-3*) Holiday.
Robinson, Jane. The Whale in Lowell's Cove. Robinson, Jane, illus. LC 91-77670. 48p. (gr. 1-4). 1992. 14.95 (*0-89272-308-4*) Down East.
Sabin, Francene. Whales & Dolphins. Johnson, Pamela, illus. LC 84-2709. 32p. (gr. 3-6). 1985. PLB 9.49 (*0-8167-0286-1*); pap. text ed. 2.95 (*0-8167-0287-X*) Troll Assocs.
Selsam, Millicent E. & Hunt, Joyce. A First Look at Whales. (gr. k-3). 1980. PLB 12.85 (*0-8027-6388-X*) Walker & Co.
Serventy, Vincent. Whale & Dolphin. LC 84-15118. (Illus.). 24p. (gr. k-5). 1985. PLB 9.95 (*0-8172-2401-7*); pap. 3.95 (*0-8114-6892-5*) Raintree Steck-V.
Shark & Whale. (Illus.). 20p. 1994. 6.95 (*1-56458-717-7*) Dorling Kindersley.
Simon, Seymour. Whales. LC 87-45285. (Illus.). 40p. (gr. k-3). 1989. 17.00 (*0-690-04756-8*, Crowell Jr Bks); PLB 16.89 (*0-690-04758-4*, Crowell Jr Bks) HarpC Child Bks.
—Whales. LC 87-45285. (Illus.). 40p. (gr. k-3). 1992. pap. 6.95 (*0-06-446095-9*, Trophy) HarpC Child Bks.
Smith, Roland. Whales, Dolphins, & Porpoises in the Zoo. Munoz, William, photos by. LC 93-35425. (Illus.). 64p. (gr. 3-6). 1994. PLB 14.40 (*1-56294-318-9*) Millbrook Pr.
Smyth, Karen. Crystal: The Story of a Real Baby Whale. LC 85-52440. (Illus.). 96p. (gr. 2 up). 1986. pap. 8.95 (*0-89272-327-0*) Down East.
Spinelli, Eileen. Whales. (Illus.). 64p. (gr. k-4). 1992. PLB 13.75 (*1-878363-90-5*, HTS Bks) Forest Hse.
Spizzirri Publishing Co. Staff. Dot-to-Dot Whales: An Educational Activity-Coloring Book. Spizzirri, Linda, ed. (Illus.). 32p. (gr. 1-8). 1986. pap. 1.00 (*0-86545-079-X*) Spizzirri.
Steele, Philip. The Blue Whale. LC 93-41690. 1994. pap. 8.95 (*1-856975-09-6*, Kingfisher LKC) LKC.
Stone, Lynn M. The Killer Whale. LC 86-32884. (Illus.). 48p. (gr. 5). 1987. text ed. 12.95 RSBE (*0-89686-323-9*, Crestwood Hse) Macmillan Child Grp.
Strachan. Whales & Dolphins. (Illus.). 32p. (gr. 4-6). 1991. 13.95 (*0-237-60168-0*, Pub. by Evans Bros Ltd) Trafalgar.
Tokuda, Wendy & Hall, Richard. Humphrey, the Lost Whale: A True Story. Wakiyama, Hanako, illus. 32p. (gr. k-6). 1992. pap. 5.95 (*0-89346-346-9*) Heian Intl.
Two Can Publishing Ltd. Staff. Whales. (Illus.). 32p. (gr. 2-7). 1991. pap. 3.50 (*0-87534-215-9*) Highlights.
Wade, Larry. Whales in the Classroom, Vol. 1: Oceanography. 2nd ed. Bolles, Stephen, illus. 133p. (gr. 4-8). 1993. pap. 14.95 (*0-9629395-1-X*) Singing Rock.
Waters, John F. Watching Whales. LC 90-28719. (Illus.). 48p. (gr. 4 up). 1991. 14.95 (*0-525-65072-5*, Cobblehill Bks) Dutton Child Bks.
Wexo, John B. Whales. 24p. (gr. 4). 1989. PLB 14.95 (*0-88682-272-6*) Creative Ed.
Whale Museum Staff. Gentle Giants of the Sea. 2nd ed. 214p. (gr. k-6). pap. 15.95 (*0-933331-25-8*) Whale Museum.
Whales & Dolphins. (Illus.). 32p. 1994. incl. chart 5.95 (*1-56138-470-4*) Running Pr.
Whittell, Giles. The Story of the Three Whales. Benson, Patrick, illus. LC 88-35630. 29p. (gr. 2-4). 1988. PLB 17.27 (*0-8368-0092-3*) Gareth Stevens Inc.
Whyte, Malcolm. Dolphins & Whales Model Set. Smith, Daniel, illus. 24p. (gr. 1 up). 1994. pap. 5.95 (*0-8431-2993-X*, Troubador) Price Stern.
Wilson, Lynn. Baby Whale. (Illus.). 32p. (ps-2). 1991. (G&D); pap. 1.95 (*0-448-40072-3*, G&D) Putnam Pub Group.

WHALES–FICTION

Allen, Joseph. Mikey Goes Whale Watching. Trout, M. D., ed. Woodaman, W., illus. 50p. (Orig.). (gr. 1-5). 1986. PLB 13.50 (*0-917071-05-0*); pap. 8.95 (*0-917071-04-2*) Ocean Allen Pub.
Allen, Judy. Whale. Humphries, Tudor, illus. LC 92-53019. 32p. (ps up). 1994. pap. 4.99 (*1-56402-383-4*) Candlewick Pr.
Bailey, Jill. Project Whale. Green, John, illus. LC 90-45159. 48p. (gr. 3-7). 1991. PLB 21.34 (*0-8114-2707-2*); pap. 4.95 (*0-8114-6555-1*) Raintree Steck-V.
Benchley, Nathaniel. Kilroy & the Gull. Schoenherr, John, illus. LC 76-24309. (gr. 4-6). 1978. pap. 3.95 (*0-06-440090-5*, Trophy) HarpC Child Bks.
Boschini, Henny & Boschini, Luciano. Chasing Whales off Norway. LC 72-90690. (Illus.). 32p. (gr. k-4). 1973. 7.95 (*0-87592-010-1*) Scroll Pr.
Chbosky, Stacy. Who Owns the Sun? Chbosky, Stacy, illus. LC 88-12694. 26p. (gr. 3-12). 1988. PLB 14.95 (*0-933849-14-1*) Landmark Edns.

Cosgrove, Stephen. Harmony. Casad, Michael, illus. LC 89-83842. 72p. (gr. 7 up). 1991. 24.95 (*1-55868-008-X*) Gr Arts Ctr Pub.

Craig, Judi. Wally Whale: Wally's Wonderful Wish. Pamiel, illus. 32p. (gr. 1-3). 1994. 14.95 (*0-87604-322-8*) ARE Pr.

Davis, Maggie S. A Garden of Whales. O'Connell, Jennifer B., illus. LC 92-34411. 32p. 1993. 16.95 (*0-944475-36-1*); pap. 6.95 (*0-944475-35-3*) Camden Hse Pub.

Dijs, Carla. Pretend You're a Whale. (Illus.). 14p. (ps). 1992. pap. 6.95 pop-up bk. (*0-671-75980-9*, Little Simon) S&S Trade.

Ellis, Ella T. The Boy Who Loved Whales. 1995. write for info. (*0-8050-3306-8*) H Holt & Co.

Elsemann, Henry. Hump-Free: The Wrong Way Whale. (Illus., Orig.). (gr. k-6). 1985. pap. 6.95 (*0-938129-00-7*) Emprise Pubns.

Evans-Smith, Deborah. The Whale's Tale. Evans, Valeria, illus. LC 85-51791. 25p. (gr. 2-6). 1986. 8.95 (*0-917507-02-9*) Sea Fog Pr.

Faulkner, Keith. Runaway Whale. Lambert, Jonathan, illus. 22p. (gr. 1-3). 1990. 5.95 (*0-681-41014-0*) Longmeadow Pr.

Fisher, R. L. The Prince of Whales. Satter, Denise, illus. 160p. (gr. 3 up). 1987. pap. 2.50 (*0-8125-6635-1*) Tor Bks.

Fuge, Charles & Hayles, Karen. Whale Is Stuck. LC 92-34078. (ps-1). 1993. pap. 14.00 JRT (*0-671-86587-0*, S&S BFYR) S&S Trade.

Heus, John & Robinson, Tom. The Tale of Humphrey the Humpback Whale. Brost, Victoria, illus. 32p. (Orig.). (ps-3). 1985. pap. 6.95 (*0-9616109-0-5*) Brost Heus.

Hillert, Margaret. Mabel the Whale. (Illus.). (ps-2). 1958. PLB 6.95 (*0-8136-5046-1*, TK2336); pap. 3.50 (*0-8136-5546-3*, TK2337) Modern Curr.

Horowitz, Jordan. Free Willy. (gr. 9-12). 1993. pap. 3.25 (*0-590-46755-7*) Scholastic Inc.

Howell, Joyce & Hennessy, B. G. Meet Winslow Whale. Howell, Joyce, illus. 24p. (ps). 1994. 8.99 (*0-670-85632-0*) Viking Child Bks.

Ingoglia, Gina. Walt Disney's Pinocchio & the Whale. Ortiz, Phil & Wakeman, Diana, illus. 40p. (ps-1). 1992. write for info. (*0-307-11583-6*, 11583, Golden Pr) Western Pub.

Johnston, Tony. Whale Song. Young, Ed, illus. 32p. (ps-3). 1987. 14.95 (*0-399-21402-X*, Putnam) Putnam Pub Group.

—Whale Song. Young, Ed, illus. 32p. (ps-3). 1992. pap. 5.95 (*0-399-22408-4*, Putnam) Putnam Pub Group.

Katz, Welwyn W. Whalesinger. 1993. pap. 3.50 (*0-440-21419-X*) Dell.

Kroll, Virginia L. I Saw a Whale! Geehan, Wayne, illus. LC 94-66183. 21p. (Orig.). (gr. 1-4). 1994. pap. 6.95 (*0-9634360-5-8*) Seacoast Pubns New Eng.

Krulik, Nancy E. Free Willy. (ps-3). 1993. pap. 2.95 (*0-590-46757-3*) Scholastic Inc.

Lay, Artie K. & Runnels, Gayle S. Amigo, the Friendly Gray Whale. LC 91-65227. (Illus.). 140p. (gr. 2-6). 1991. incl. audiocassette 24.95 (*0-9628626-0-6*) Blubber Budd.

Lewis, Paul O. Davy's Dream. (Illus.). 64p. (ps-6). 1988. 14.95 (*0-941831-32-9*); pap. 9.95 (*0-941831-28-0*) Beyond Words Pub.

McBarnet, Gill. The Whale Who Wanted to Be Small. McBarnet, Gill, illus. 32p. (gr. k-2). 1985. 7.95 (*0-9615102-0-X*) Ruwanga Trad.

—A Whale's Tale. McBarnet, Gill, illus. 32p. (ps-2). 1988. 6.95 (*0-9615102-4-2*) Ruwanga Trad.

McCloskey, Robert. Burt Dow: Deep-Water Man. McCloskey, Robert, illus. LC 68-364. 64p. (gr. 4-6). 1963. pap. 15.95 (*0-670-19748-3*) Viking Child Bks.

McClung, Robert M. Thor, the Last of the Sperm Whales. Hines, Bob, illus. LC 87-26090. 64p. (gr. 3-7). 1988. Repr. of 1971 ed. PLB 15.00 (*0-208-02186-8*, Linnet) Shoe String.

McFarlane, Sheryl. Waiting for the Whales. Lightburn, Ron, illus. LC 92-25117. 32p. (ps-3). 1993. PLB 14.95 (*0-399-22515-3*, Philomel Bks) Putnam Pub Group.

Melville, Herman. Moby Dick. (gr. 11 up). 1964. pap. 3.95 (*0-8049-0033-7*, CL-33) Airmont.

—Moby Dick. Daniels, Patricia, adapted by. LC 81-15386. (Illus.). 48p. (gr. 4 up). 1983. PLB 20.70 (*0-8172-1679-0*) Raintree Steck-V.

—Moby Dick. Selden, Bernice, adapted by. Gianni, Gary, illus. LC 87-16788. 48p. (gr. 3-6). 1988. PLB 12.89 (*0-8167-1207-7*); pap. text ed. 3.95 (*0-8167-1208-5*) Troll Assocs.

—Moby Dick. Carlson, Donna, ed. (Illus.). 128p. 1992. pap. 2.95 (*1-56156-093-6*) Kidsbks.

—Moby Dick. (gr. 4-7). 1993. pap. 4.95 (*0-8114-6834-8*) Raintree Steck-V.

Melville, Herman, et al. Moby Dick. (Illus.). 52p. Date not set. pap. 4.95 (*1-57209-003-0*) Classics Int Ent.

Morpurgo, Michael. Why the Whales Came. (gr. 5-7). 1990. pap. 10.95 (*0-590-42911-6*) Scholastic Inc.

—Why the Whales Came. 144p. 1992. pap. 2.75 (*0-590-42912-4*, Apple Paperbacks) Scholastic Inc.

Murphy, Catherine F. Songs in the Silence. LC 93-26947. 192p. (gr. 3-7). 1994. SBE 14.95 (*0-02-767730-3*, Macmillan Child Bk) Macmillan Child Grp.

Nobisso, Josephine. Shh! The Whale Is Smiling. Hyde, Maureen, illus. LC 91-21521. 40p. (ps-1). 1992. 14.00 (*0-671-74908-0*, Green Tiger) S&S Trade.

In this rhythmic & poetic book by the creators of GRANDPA LOVED & GRANDMA'S SCRAPBOOK, an older sister comforts a little brother frightened by a wind storm. Knowing his love of whales, she comes to his room to comfort him with a fantastic tale that takes him & the reader right out of the bed & into the undersea world of a loving Humpback who "watches us & guides us through the floating, flying freedom of the deep." Children love joining in on the choruses of "Shh!" & will ask to hear it again & again. One librarian told us, "It's my favorite read-aloud!" Order from Simon & Schuster.
Publisher Provided Annotation.

Raffi. Baby Beluga. Wolff, Ashley, illus. LC 89-49367. 32p. (ps-2). 1990. 13.00 (*0-517-57839-5*); PLB 11.99 (*0-517-57840-9*) Crown Bks Yng Read.

Reese, Bob. Dale the Whale. LC 82-23588. (Illus.). 24p. (ps-2). 1983. pap. 2.95 (*0-516-42313-4*) Childrens.

Rush, Christopher. Venus Peter Saves the Whale. Hedderwick, Mairi, illus. LC 92-7808. 32p. (gr. 4-7). 1992. 14.95 (*0-88289-928-7*) Pelican.

Ryder, Joanne. Winter Whale. Rothman, Michael, illus. LC 90-19174. 32p. (gr. k up). 1991. 13.95 (*0-688-07176-7*); PLB 13.88 (*0-688-07177-5*) Morrow Jr Bks.

Sachs, Elizabeth-Ann. Kiss Me, Janie Tannenbaum. LC 91-28465. 144p. (gr. 5-9). 1992. SBE 13.95 (*0-689-31664-X*, Atheneum Child Bk) Macmillan Child Grp.

Sheldon, Dyan. The Whales' Song. Blythe, Gary, illus. LC 90-46722. 32p. (ps-3). 1991. 15.99 (*0-8037-0972-2*) Dial Bks Young.

Sis, Peter. An Ocean World. LC 91-11692. (Illus.). 24p. (ps-3). 1992. 14.00 (*0-688-09067-2*); PLB 13.93 (*0-688-09068-0*) Greenwillow.

Spinelli, Jerry. Night of the Whale. (gr. k-12). 1988. pap. 3.50 (*0-440-20071-7*, LFL) Dell.

Steele, Philip. The Blue Whale. LC 93-416970. (Illus.). 24p. (gr. 2-5). 1994. 8.95 (*1-85697-514-2*, Kingfisher LKC) LKC.

Steiner, Barbara. Whale Brother. Mayo, Gretchen W., illus. (ps-3). 1988. 12.95 (*0-8027-6804-0*); PLB 13.85 (*0-8027-6805-9*) Walker & Co.

Strange, Florence. Rock-a-Bye Whale. LC 77-83196. (Illus.). (gr. k-4). 1977. 11.95 (*0-931644-00-3*) Manzanita Pr.

Strasser, Todd. Free Willy: Digest Novelization. (gr. 4-7). 1993. pap. 3.25 (*0-590-46756-5*) Scholastic Inc.

Thrush, Robin A., ed. The Gray Whales Are Missing. De Groat, Diane, illus. LC 87-17822. 113p. (gr. 3-7). 1987. 14.95 (*0-15-200455-6*, Gulliver Bks) HarBrace.

Vollmer, Dennis. Joshua Disobeys. Vollmer, Dennis, illus. LC 88-9464. 26p. (gr. k-3). 1988. PLB 14.95 (*0-933849-12-5*) Landmark Edns.

Watanabe, Yuichi. Wally the Whale Who Loved Balloons. Ooka, D. T., tr. from JPN. Watanabe, Yuichi, illus. 32p. (ps-4). 1982. 11.95 (*0-89346-150-4*) Heian Intl.

Ziefert, Harriet. Henry's Wrong Turn, Vol. 1. 1989. 13.95 (*0-316-98778-6*) Little.

WHALING

Carrick, Carol. Whaling Days. Frampton, David, illus. 40p. (gr. 4-7). 1993. 15.45 (*0-395-50948-3*, Clarion Bks) HM.

Graham, Ada & Graham, Frank. Whale Watch. Tyler, D. D., illus. LC 77-20531. (gr. 5 up). 1978. 7.95 (*0-440-09505-0*); pap. 6.46 (*0-440-09506-9*) Delacorte.

Kalman, Bobbie. Arctic Whales & Whaling. (Illus.). 56p. (gr. 3-4). 1988. 15.95 (*0-86505-146-1*); pap. 7.95 (*0-86505-156-9*) Crabtree Pub Co.

WHALING–FICTION

Adams, Pam. Wally Whale & Friends. (gr. 4 up). 1981. pap. 5.95 (*0-85953-268-2*) Childs Play.

Crofford, Emily. Born in the Year of Courage. 184p. (gr. 4-6). 1991. PLB 19.95 (*0-87614-679-5*) Carolrhoda Bks.

Melville, Herman. Moby Dick. new ed. Shapiro, Irwin, ed. Nino, Alex, illus. LC 73-75458. 64p. (Orig.). (gr. 5-10). 1973. pap. 2.95 (*0-88301-099-2*) Pendulum Pr.

—Moby Dick. Kirn, Elaine, adapted by. (Illus.). 62p. (gr. 7 up). 1987. pap. text ed. write for info. (*0-13-586272-8*, 20381) Prentice ESL.

—Moby Dick. Carlson, Donna, ed. (Illus.). 128p. 1992. pap. 2.95 (*1-56156-093-6*) Kidsbks.

Sohl, Marcia & Dackerman, Gerald. Moby Dick Student Activity Book. Nino, Alex, illus. (gr. 4-10). 1976. pap. 1.25 (*0-88301-181-6*) Pendulum Pr.

Tokuda, Wendy & Hall, Richard. Humphrey: The Lost Whale. Wakiyama, Hanako, illus. 32p. (gr. k-4). 1986. 11.95 (*0-89346-270-5*) Heian Intl.

WHARTON, EDITH NEWBOLD (JONES), 1862-1937

Leach, William. Edith Wharton. Horner, Matina, intro. by. (Illus.). 112p. (gr. 5 up). 1987. lib. bdg. 17.95 (*1-55546-682-6*) Chelsea Hse.

Worth, Richard. Edith Wharton. LC 93-23207. 1994. 15.00 (*0-671-86615-X*, J Messner); pap. write for info. (*0-671-86616-8*, J Messner) S&S Trade.

WHEAT

Curtis, Neil & Greenland, Peter. How Bread Is Made. (Illus.). 24p. (gr. 1-3). 1992. PLB 13.50 (*0-8225-2375-2*) Lerner Pubns.

Johnson, Sylvia A. Wheat. Suzuki, Masaharu, illus. 48p. (gr. 4 up). 1990. PLB 19.95 (*0-8225-1490-7*) Lerner Pubns.

Mitgutsch, Ali. From Grain to Bread. Mitgutsch, Ali, illus. LC 80-28592. 24p. (ps-3). 1981. PLB 10.95 (*0-87614-155-6*) Carolrhoda Bks.

WHEATLEY, PHILLIS, 1753?-1784

Jackson, Garnet N. Phillis Wheatley, Poet. Hanna, Cheryl, illus. LC 92-28778. 1992. 56.40 (*0-8136-5233-2*); pap. 28.50 (*0-8136-5706-7*) Modern Curr.

Richmond, Merle. Phyllis Wheatley. Horner, Matina, intro. by. (Illus.). 112p. (Orig.). (gr. 5 up). 1988. 17.95 (*1-55546-683-4*); pap. 9.95 (*0-7910-0218-7*) Chelsea Hse.

Sherrow, Victoria. Phillis Wheatley. (Illus.). 80p. (gr. 3-5). 1992. lib. bdg. 12.95 (*0-7910-1753-2*) Chelsea Hse.

WHEELS

Birchall, Brian. The Magic Wheel. Mancini, Rob, illus. LC 93-18048. 1994. pap. write for info. (*0-383-03701-8*) SRA Schl Grp.

Dunn, Andrew. Wheels at Work. LC 92-41513. 32p. (gr. 3-6). 1993. 13.95 (*1-56847-014-2*) Thomson Lrning.

Fitzpatrick, Julie. Wheels. (Illus.). 30p. (gr. 3-5). 1991. 13.95 (*0-237-60214-8*, Pub. by Evans Bros Ltd) Trafalgar.

Healey, Tim. The Story of the Wheel. Hewetson, Nicholas, illus. LC 91-40417. 32p. (gr. 1-4). 1993. PLB 11.89 (*0-8167-2713-9*); pap. text ed. 3.95 (*0-8167-2714-7*) Troll Assocs.

Hindley, Judy. The Wheeling & Whirling-Around Book. Chamberlain, Margaret, illus. LC 93-28125. 32p. (ps up). 1994. 14.95 (*1-56402-398-2*) Candlewick Pr.

Pienkowski, Jan. Wheels. Pienkowski, Jan, illus. 24p. (ps). 1992. pap. 2.95 (*0-671-74517-4*, Little Simon) S&S Trade.

Seller, Mick. Wheels, Pulleys & Levers. (Illus.). 32p. (gr. 5-7). 1993. PLB 12.40 (*0-531-17420-4*, Gloucester Pr) Watts.

Taylor, Henry T. Know Your Wheels. Bylenok, Marsha, contrib. by. Greenough, Jackie & Taylor, Pamela, illus. 51p. (gr. 4-6). 1981. pap. write for info. (*0-938956-00-0*) H T Taylor.

Williams, John. Simple Science Projects with Wheels. LC 91-50550. (Illus.). 32p. (gr. 2-4). 1992. PLB 17.27 (*0-8368-0772-3*) Gareth Stevens Inc.

WHITMAN, NARCISSA (PRENTISS), 1808-1847

Sabin, Louis. Narcissa Whitman: Brave Pioneer. LC 81-23066. (Illus.). 48p. (gr. 4-6). 1982. PLB 10.79 (*0-89375-762-4*); pap. text ed. 3.50 (*0-89375-763-2*) Troll Assocs.

WHITMAN, WALT, 1819-1892

Loewen, Nancy. Walt Whitman. 48p. (gr. 7 up). 1994. 16.95 (*1-56846-096-1*) Creat Editions.

WHITNEY, ELI, 1765-1825

Latham, Jean L. Eli Whitney: Great Inventor. Cary, illus. 80p. (gr. 2-6). 1991. Repr. of 1963 ed. lib. bdg. 12.95 (*0-7910-1453-3*) Chelsea Hse.

WHITTINGTON, RICHARD, 1358?-1423

Garry-McCord, Kathleen, illus. Dick Whittington. LC 80-28171. 32p. (gr. k-4). 1981. PLB 9.79 (*0-89375-482-X*); pap. text ed. 1.95 (*0-89375-483-8*) Troll Assocs.

WHITTLING

see Wood Carving

WILD ANIMALS

see Animals

WILD BOAR

Nicholson, Darrell. Wild Boars. Blacklock, Craig, photos by. (Illus.). 48p. (gr. 2-5). 1987. PLB 19.95 (*0-87614-308-7*) Carolrhoda Bks.

WILD FLOWERS

Campbell, Carol A. Wildflower Field Guide & Press for Kids. 1993. pap. 13.95 (*1-56305-242-3*, 3242) Workman Pub.

Cooper, J. Flowers. 1991. 8.95s.p. (*0-86592-620-4*) Rourke Enter.

Gales, Donald M. Handbook of Wildflowers, Weeds, Wildlife & Weather of the South Bay & Palos Verdes (California) 3rd, rev. ed. 240p. (gr. 8 up). 1988. pap. 12.00 (*0-317-89904-X*) D M Gales.

Grimmer, Glenna. ABCs of Texas Wildflowers. Roberts, M, ed. Laughlin, Mary J, illus. 64p. (gr. 2-5). 1982. 9.95 (*0-89015-358-2*) Sunbelt Media.

Humphries, C. Wildflowers. (Illus.). 64p. (gr. 10 up). 1993. pap. 4.95 (*0-7460-1628-X*) EDC.

Kelly, M. A. A Child's Book of Wildflowers. Powzyk, Joyce, illus. LC 91-30368. 32p. (gr. k-4). 1992. RSBE 15.95 (*0-02-750142-6*, Four Winds) Macmillan Child Grp.

Landau, Elaine. Wildflowers Around the World. LC 90-13090. (Illus.). 64p. (gr. 3-5). 1991. PLB 12.90 (*0-531-20005-1*) Watts.

—Wildflowers Around the World. 64p. (gr. 5-8). 1992. pap. 5.95 (*0-531-15649-4*) Watts.

McMillan, Bruce. Counting Wildflowers. LC 85-16607. (Illus.). 32p. (ps-1). 1986. 15.00 (*0-688-02859-4*); PLB 14.93 (*0-688-02860-8*) Lothrop.

Magley, Beverly. California Wildflowers. Dowden, D. D., illus. LC 88-83883. 32p. (Orig.). (gr. 3-6). 1989. pap. 4.95 (*0-937959-58-8*) Falcon Pr MT.

—Minnesota Wildflowers: Children's Field Guide. Dowden, D. D., illus. 32p. (Orig.). (gr. 4-7). 1992. pap. 5.95 (*1-56044-117-8*) Falcon Pr MT.
—Montana Wildflowers. Dowden, D. D., illus. 32p. (Orig.). (gr. 4-7). 1992. pap. 5.95 (*1-56044-118-6*) Falcon Pr MT.
—Oregon Wildflowers: Children's Field Guide. Dowden, D. D., illus. 32p. (Orig.). (gr. 4-7). 1992. pap. 5.95 (*1-56044-035-X*) Falcon Pr MT.
—Texas Wildflowers: A Children's Field Guide to the State's Most Common Flowers. Dowden, D. D., illus. 32p. (Orig.). 1993. pap. 5.95 (*1-56044-183-6*) Falcon Pr MT.
Velghe, Anne. Wildflowers: A Garden Primer. 1994. 15. 00 (*0-374-38430-4*) FS&G.

WILD FOWL
see Water Birds

WILD LIFE–CONSERVATION
see Wildlife–Conservation

WILDLIFE–CONSERVATION
see also Birds–Protection; Forests and Forestry; Game Preserves; National Parks and Reserves

Amos, Janine. Animals in Danger. McAllister, David, illus. LC 92-16336. 32p. (gr. 2-3). 1992. PLB 18.99 (*0-8114-3404-4*) Raintree Steck-V.
Ancona, George. The Golden Lion Tamarin Comes Home. LC 93-23705. (gr. 2-6). 1994. 15.95 (*0-02-700905-X*, Macmillan Child Bk) Macmillan Child Grp.
—Man & Mustang. Ancona, George, illus. LC 91-29513. 48p. (gr. 3-7). 1992. RSBE 15.95 (*0-02-700802-9*, Macmillan Child Bk) Macmillan Child Grp.
—Turtle Watch. Ancona, George, photos by. LC 87-9316. (Illus.). 48p. (gr. 1-5). 1987. RSBE 14.95 (*0-02-700910-6*, Macmillan Child Bk) Macmillan Child Grp.
Arnold, Caroline. On the Brink of Extinction: The California Condor. Wallace, Michael, photos by. LC 92-14914. (Illus.). 1993. write for info. (*0-15-257990-7*) HarBrace.
—Sea Lion. Hewett, Richard, photos by. LC 93-27007. (Illus.). 1994. write for info. (*0-688-12027-X*); lib. bdg. write for info. (*0-688-12028-8*) Morrow Jr Bks.
Ashby, Ruth. The Orangutan. LC 93-5754. (Illus.). 60p. (gr. 5 up). 1994. text ed. 13.95 RSBE (*0-87518-600-9*, Dillon) Macmillan Child Grp.
Asimov, Isaac. Why Are Animals Endangered? LC 92-5346. (Illus.). 24p. (gr. 1-8). 1993. PLB 15.93 (*0-8368-0798-7*) Gareth Stevens Inc.
Bailey, Jill. Mission Rhino. LC 90-32529. (Illus.). 48p. (gr. 3-7). 1990. PLB 21.34 (*0-8114-2702-1*); pap. 4.95 (*0-8114-6550-0*) Raintree Steck-V.
—Save the Tiger. LC 89-48770. (Illus.). 48p. (gr. 3-7). 1990. PLB 21.34 (*0-8114-2703-X*); pap. 4.95 (*0-8114-6551-9*) Raintree Steck-V.
Balouet, Jean-Christopher & Behm, Barb. Endangered Animals of the Northern Continents. (Illus.). 32p. (gr. 3 up). Date not set. PLB 18.60 (*0-8368-1079-1*) Gareth Stevens Inc.
—Endangered Animals of the Southern Continents. (Illus.). 32p. (gr. 3 up). Date not set. PLB 18.60 (*0-8368-1080-5*) Gareth Stevens Inc.
—Endangered Wildlife. (Illus.). 32p. (gr. 3 up). Date not set. PLB 18.60 (*0-8368-1077-5*) Gareth Stevens Inc.
Banks, M. Endangered Wildlife. (Illus.). 48p. (gr. 5 up). 1988. PLB 18.60 (*0-86592-284-5*); 13.95 (*0-685-58319-8*) Rourke Corp.
Barton, Miles. Vanishing Species. LC 91-8379. (Illus.). 40p. (gr. 5-8). 1991. PLB 12.90 (*0-531-17306-2*, Gloucester Pr) Watts.
Beattie, Laura C. Discover African Wildlife: Activity Book. Creative Company Staff, illus. 24p. (Orig.). (gr. 3-7). 1993. wkbk. 2.95 (*0-911239-38-3*) Carnegie Mus.
Blashfield, Jean F. Galapagos Islands. LC 94-3030. (Illus.). 64p. (gr. 5-8). 1994. PLB write for info. (*0-8114-6362-1*) Raintree Steck-V.
—Rescuing Endangered Species. LC 94-18009. (Illus.). 96p. (gr. 3-6). 1994. PLB 23.20 (*0-516-05544-5*) Childrens.
Bright, Michael. Killing for Luxury. (Illus.). 32p. (gr. 5-8). 1992. PLB 12.40 (*0-531-17386-0*, Gloucester Pr) Watts.
—Pollution & Wildlife. (Illus.). 32p. (gr. 5-8). 1992. PLB 12.40 (*0-531-17384-4*, Gloucester Pr) Watts.
Brown, Vinson & Lawrence, George. Californian Wildlife Region. 3rd, rev. ed. (Illus.). 224p. (gr. 4 up). Date not set. pap. 8.95 (*0-87961-201-0*) Naturegraph.
Brown, Vinson & Livezey, Robert. The Sierra Nevadan Wildlife Region. 3rd, rev. ed. (Illus.). 192p. (gr. 4 up). 1962. pap. 8.95 (*0-911010-02-5*) Naturegraph.
Brown, Vinson, et al. Wildlife of the Intermountain West. (Illus.). 144p. (gr. 4 up). 1968. 15.95 (*0-911010-15-7*); pap. 7.95 (*0-911010-14-9*) Naturegraph.
Clark, Margaret G. The Vanishing Manatee. LC 89-38676. (Illus.). 64p. (gr. 4 up). 1990. 14.00 (*0-525-65024-5*, Cobblehill Bks) Dutton Child Bks.
Conservation Treaty Support Group Staff. Cites Endangered Species Coloring Book. rev. ed. Dollinger, Peter, ed. Silk, Linda, illus. 72p. 1993. pap. 4.95 (*1-56002-281-7*) Aegina Pr.
Crump, Donald J., ed. Hidden Worlds of Wildlife. (Illus.). 1990. 12.95 (*0-87044-791-2*) Natl Geog.
Cuthbert, Susan. Endangered Creatures. (Illus.). 16p. (gr. 1-6). 1992. pap. 1.99 activity bk. (*0-7459-2144-2*) Lion USA.
DaVolls, Linda. Tano & Binti: Two Chimpanzees Return to the Wild. DaVolls, Andy, illus. LC 93-25403. (gr. k-3). 1994. 14.95 (*0-395-68701-2*, Clarion Bks) HM.
Denton, Peter. The World Wildlife Fund. LC 94-7491. 1995. text ed. 13.95 (*0-02-726334-7*, New Discovery Bks) Macmillan Child Grp.
Dewey, Jennifer. Wildlife Rescue: The Work of Dr. Kathleen Ramsay. MacCarter, Don, photos by. LC 93-71478. (Illus.). 64p. (gr. 3 up). 1994. 16.95 (*1-56397-045-7*) Boyds Mills Pr.
Duden, Jane. Ferret. LC 89-28268. (Illus.). 48p. (gr. 5 up). 1990. text ed. 12.95 RSBE (*0-89686-517-7*, Crestwood Hse) Macmillan Child Grp.
Dunmire, Marj. Wildlife of Cactus & Canyon Country. Dunmire, Marj, illus. 48p. (gr. 2-6). 1988. pap. 3.95 (*0-942559-05-3*) Pegasus Graphics.
Endangered Wildlife of the World. LC 92-14974. 1993. Set. 399.95 (*1-85435-489-2*) Marshall Cavendish.
Few, Roger. Macmillan Children's Guide to Endangered Animals. Pringle, Laurence, frwd. by. LC 92-41433. (Illus.). 96p. (gr. 2 up). 1993. SBE 17.95 (*0-02-734545-9*, Macmillan Child Bk) Macmillan Child Grp.
Field, Nancy & Machlas, Sally. Discovering Endangered Species. (Illus.). 40p. (Orig.). (gr. 3-6). 1990. pap. 4.95 (*0-941042-09-X*) Dog Eared Pubns.
Fishbein, Seymour L. Yellowstone Country: The Enduring Wonder. Crump, Donald J., ed. (Illus.). 1989. 12.95 (*0-87044-713-0*); PLB 12.95 (*0-87044-718-1*) Natl Geog.
Ford, Barbara. Wildlife Rescue. Tucker, Kathleen, ed. Ross, Steve, illus. LC 87-6133. 48p. (gr. 3-7). 1987. PLB 11.95 (*0-8075-9099-1*) A Whitman.
Fraser, Mary Ann. Sanctuary, the Story of Three Arch Rocks. Fraser, Mary A., illus. LC 93-41362. (gr. 3-7). 1994. 15.95 (*0-8050-2920-6*) H Holt & Co.
Gray, Ian. Birds of Prey. LC 90-33768. (Illus.). 32p. (gr. 2-4). 1991. PLB 12.40 (*0-531-18367-X*, Pub. by Bookwright Pr) Watts.
Green, I. Conservation from A to Z. LC 66-11443. (Illus.). 64p. (gr. 4 up). 1968. PLB 10.95 (*0-87783-009-6*); pap. 3.94 deluxe ed. (*0-87783-088-6*) Oddo.
Greene, Carol. Caring for Our Animals. LC 91-9237. (Illus.). 32p. (gr. k-3). 1991. lib. bdg. 12.95 (*0-89490-352-7*) Enslow Pubs.
Greene, Laura O. Wildlife Poaching. (Illus.). 144p. (gr. 9-12). 1994. lib. bdg. 13.95 (*0-531-13007-X*) Watts.
Gutfreund, Geraldine M. Vanishing Animal Neighbors. LC 92-25530. (Illus.). 64p. (gr. 5-8). 1993. PLB 12.90 (*0-531-20060-4*) Watts.
Hare, Tony. Vanishing Habitats. LC 91-11578. (Illus.). 32p. (gr. k-4). 1991. PLB 11.90 (*0-531-17350-X*, Gloucester Pr) Watts.
Head, W. S. The California Chaparral: An Elfin Forest. LC 75-24239. 96p. (gr. 4 up). 1972. 15.95 (*0-87961-003-4*); pap. 7.95 (*0-87961-002-6*) Naturegraph.

Hedren, Tippi & Taylor, Theodore. The Cats of Shambala. rev. ed. Dow, Bill, photos by. (Illus.). 300p. (gr. 6 up). 1992. pap. 14.95 (*0-9631549-0-7*) Tiger Isld Pr.
Here is the riveting, lavishly illustrated saga of how actress Tippi Hedren, in the process of making a feature film as a plea to save wildlife, came to share her home & hearth with its "stars" - some hundred lions, tigers, leopards, cheetahs, & cougars - on a 180 acre preserve in California. Over a hundred photos bring the big cats, & the humans who worked, lived, raised them from cubs & sometimes slept with them, vividly to life. "An exciting read.. ."--Library Journal. "An intriguing tale of obsession..."--Kirkus Review. "This is a rare & captivating book... fascinating, unusual & engrossing"--John Barkham Reviews. "Animal lovers will have difficulty putting Hedren's book down..."--Charleston Evening Post. To order: Tiger Island Press, 6867 Soledad Cyn Rd., Acton, CA 93510.
Publisher Provided Annotation.

Heilman, Joan R. Bluebird Rescue: A Harrowsmith Country Life Nature Guide. rev. ed. LC 91-40618. (Illus.). 48p. (gr. 10 up). 1992. lib. bdg. 16.95 (*0-944475-27-2*); pap. 6.95 (*0-944475-24-8*) Camden Hse Pub.
Irvine, Georgeanne. Protecting Endangered Species at the San Diego Zoo. (Illus.). 48p. (gr. 3-7). 1990. pap. 14. 95 jacketed (*0-671-68776-X*, S&S BFYR) S&S Trade.
Jonas, Ann. Aardvarks, Disembark! (Illus.). 40p. (ps-3). 1994. pap. 4.99 (*0-14-055309-6*) Puffin Bks.
Jones, Norma H., et al. Endangered Animals: Quickly Disappearing. (Illus.). 48p. (Orig.). (gr. 6-9). 1993. pap. text ed. 11.95 (*1-878623-51-6*) Info Plus TX.
Khanduri, K. World Wildlife. (Illus.). 128p. (gr. 2-6). 1994. pap. 17.95 (*0-7460-1982-3*, Usborne) EDC.
Lazo, Caroline E. Endangered Species. LC 90-35494. (Illus.). 48p. (gr. 6). 1990. text ed. 12.95 RSBE (*0-89686-545-2*, Crestwood Hse) Macmillan Child Grp.
Liptak, Karen. Saving Our Wetlands & Their Wildlife. (Illus.). 64p. (gr. 5-8). 1992. pap. 5.95 (*0-531-15648-6*) Watts.
Love, Ann & Drake, Jane. Take Action: An Environmental Book for Kids. Cupples, Pat, illus. LC 92-30412. 96p. (gr. 3 up). 1993. Repr. PLB 13.93 (*0-688-12464-X*, Tambourine Bks) Morrow.
McClung, Robert M. Lost Wild America: The Story of Our Extinct & Vanishing Wildlife. rev., enl. & updated ed. Mines, Bob, illus. LC 93-15657. 312p. (gr. 6-12). 1993. PLB 25.00 (*0-208-02359-3*, Pub. by Linnet) Shoe String.
McNulty, Faith. The Orphan. 48p. 1992. 11.95 (*0-590-43838-7*, Scholastic Hardcover) Scholastic Inc.
Martin, L. Rhinoceros. (Illus.). 24p. (gr. k-5). 1988. PLB 11.94 (*0-86592-997-1*) Rourke Corp.
Matthews, Nancy. Wilderness Preservation. (Illus.). 112p. (gr. 5 up). 1991. PLB 19.95 (*0-7910-1580-7*); pap. write for info. (*0-7910-1605-6*) Chelsea Hse.
Mayfield, Sue. I Carried You on Eagles' Wings. LC 90-28554. 128p. (gr. 6 up). 1991. text ed. 12.95 (*0-688-10597-1*) Lothrop.
Maynard, Thane. Endangered Animal Babies: Saving Species One Birth at a Time. LC 92-33220. (Illus.). 56p. (gr. 5-8). 1993. 15.95 (*0-531-15257-X*); PLB 15. 90 (*0-531-11077-X*) Watts.
—Saving Endangered Birds: Ensuring a Future in the Wild. (Illus.). 56p. (gr. 5-7). 1993. 15.95 (*0-531-15260-X*); PLB 15.90 (*0-531-11094-X*) Watts.
—Saving Endangered Mammals: A Field Guide to Some of the Earth's Rarest Animals. (Illus.). 64p. (gr. 5-8). 1992. PLB 15.90 (*0-531-11076-1*) Watts.
Meyer, Nancy. Endangered Species Coloring-Learning Books Adventure Series. Meyer, George, illus. (ps-3). 1993. write for info. (*1-883408-05-9*) Meyer Pub FL.
Naranjo, Rafael S. Great Animal Refuges. LC 93-3437. (Illus.). 36p. (gr. 3 up). 1993. PLB 14.95 (*0-516-08385-6*); pap. 6.95 (*0-516-48385-4*) Childrens.
Nierman, Lewis G. Lefty's Place. Nierman, Lewis G., illus. 32p. (gr. 1-4). 1994. 18.95g (*0-9636820-0-8*) Kindness Pubns.
Ohanian, Susan. Wolves. Ruth, Trevor, illus. LC 93-28973. 1994. 4.25 (*0-383-03742-5*) SRA Schl Grp.
Our World in Danger. (gr. k-3). 1989. 3.95 (*0-7214-5217-5*) Ladybird Bks.
Papastavrou, Vassili. Seals & Sea Lions. LC 91-9127. (Illus.). 32p. (gr. 2-5). 1992. PLB 12.40 (*0-531-18455-2*, Pub. by Bookwright Pr) Watts.
—Turtles & Tortoises. LC 91-20098. (Illus.). 32p. (gr. 2-5). 1992. PLB 12.40 (*0-531-18453-6*, Pub. by Bookwright Pr) Watts.
Patent, Dorothy H. Places of Refuge: Our National Wildlife Refuge System. Munoz, William, illus. 80p. (gr. 4-9). 1992. 15.95 (*0-89919-846-5*, Clarion Bks) HM.
Penny, Malcolm. Bears. LC 90-35063. (Illus.). 32p. (gr. 2-4). 1991. PLB 12.40 (*0-531-18368-8*, Pub. by Bookwright Pr) Watts.
—Protecting Wildlife. LC 90-9925. (Illus.). 48p. (gr. 4-9). 1990. PLB 21.34 (*0-8114-2389-1*); pap. 5.95 (*0-8114-3455-9*) Raintree Steck-V.
Pollock, Stephen. The Atlas of Endangered Animals. LC 92-20387. (Illus.). 64p. (gr. 6-9). 1993. 17.95 (*0-8160-2856-7*) Facts on File.
Pringle, Laurence. Living Treasure: Saving Earth's Threatened Biodiversity. LC 90-21463. 64p. (gr. 3 up). 1991. 12.95 (*0-688-07709-9*); PLB 12.88 (*0-688-07710-2*, Morrow Jr Bks) Morrow Jr Bks.
Rand McNally Staff. Children's Atlas of World Wildlife. Fagan, Elizabeth, ed. Willis, Jan, illus. 96p. (gr. 3-7). 1990. 14.95 (*0-528-83409-6*) Rand McNally.
Ritchie, Rita. Mountain Gorillas in Danger. Nichols, Michael, photos by. LC 91-10831. (Illus.). 32p. (gr. 2-3). 1991. PLB 17.27 (*0-8368-0447-3*) Gareth Stevens Inc.
Sanger, David. North America's ENDANGERED Species. Lynch, Don, ed. Mathewson, Mel, illus. 97p. (Orig.). (ps-8). 1992. pap. text ed. 4.00 (*0-913205-17-6*); special price 2.40 (*0-685-69239-6*) Grace Dangberg.
Schimmel, Schim. Dear Children of the Earth. Schimmel, Schim, illus. LC 93-47672. 32p. (gr. k-5). 1994. 11.95 (*1-55971-225-2*) NorthWord.
Schlein, Miriam. Project Panda Watch. Shetterly, Robert, illus. LC 84-2914. 96p. (gr. 4 up). 1984. SBE 13.95 (*0-689-31071-4*, Atheneum Child Bk) Macmillan Child Grp.
Sibbald, Jean H. The Manatee. LC 89-26048. (Illus.). 60p. (gr. 3 up). 1990. text ed. 13.95 RSBE (*0-87518-429-4*, Dillon) Macmillan Child Grp.
Sides, Elizabeth. Wildlife at Risk: A Nature & Craft Book, 2 bks. (Illus.). 32p. (Orig.). (gr. 1-5). 1991. Set. pap. 6.95 (*0-685-54745-0*); Bk. 1. pap. 6.95 (*0-86278-252-X*); Bk. 2. pap. 6.95 (*0-86278-253-8*) Dufour.
Silverstein, Alvin, et al. Saving Endangered Animals. LC 92-1765. (Illus.). 128p. (gr. 6 up). 1993. lib. bdg. 17.95 (*0-89490-402-7*) Enslow Pubs.
Smith, Roland. Sea Otter Rescue, the Aftermath of an Oil Spill. LC 89-49446. (Illus.). (gr. 4-7). 1990. 13.95 (*0-525-65041-5*, Cobblehill Bks) Dutton Child Bks.

Sobol, Richard. One More Elephant: The Fight to Save Wildlife in Uganda. Sobol, Richard, photos by. LC 93-45663. 1995. PLB write for info. (*0-525-65179-9*, Cobblehill Bks) Dutton Child Bks.

Spizzirri Publishing, Inc. Staff. Endangered Birds: An Educational Coloring Book. Spizzirri, Linda, ed. (Illus.). 32p. (gr. k-5). 1992. pap. 1.75 (*0-86545-171-0*) Spizzirri.

Steele, Philip. Extinct Land Mammals: And Those in Danger of Extinction. Kline, Marjory, ed. (Illus.). 32p. (gr. 4-7). 1992. PLB 11.90 (*0-531-11028-1*) Watts.

Stone, Lynn M. Back from the Edge: The American Bison. LC 90-38385. (Illus.). 48p. (gr. 4-6). 1991. PLB 16.67 (*0-86593-101-1*); PLB 12.50s.p. (*0-685-59353-3*) Rourke Corp.

—Endangered Animals. LC 83-26323. (Illus.). 48p. (gr. k-4). 1984. PLB 12.85 (*0-516-01724-1*); pap. 4.95 (*0-516-41724-X*) Childrens.

Stuart, Gene S. Wildlife Alert. LC 79-1792. (Illus.). 104p. (gr. 3-8). 1980. 8.95 (*0-87044-318-6*); PLB 12.50 (*0-87044-323-2*) Natl Geog.

Tracqui, Valerie. Polar Bear: Master of the Ice. (Illus.). 28p. (gr. 3-8). 1994. pap. 6.95 (*0-88106-432-7*) Charlesbridge Pub.

Wallin, Carol A. Disappearing Faces: Florida's Animals in Danger. Mydske, Valerie, illus. 64p. (Orig.). (gr. 2 up). 1993. Saddlestitch bdg. pap. 9.95 (*0-9639432-0-0*) Cardinal FL.
DISAPPEARING FACES, recent winner of the NAIP's Interior Design Award for a Softcover Title, is an excellent, creative learning & activity book offering information about many of Florida's animals being threatened or facing extinction. Interesting facts, word & picture puzzles, mini-art projects, & mazes provide areas of fun for children while they discover how & why they should protect Florida's wildlife. Many pages challenge children's imaginations by encouraging them to create their own illustrations or finish activities in their own special way. DISAPPEARING FACES includes lists of conservation groups to whom the children are encouraged to write & learn about the groups' goals as well as ways in which young citizens can help. In the process, children learn how to compose a proper, courteous business letter. All of DISAPPEARING FACES' activities are designed to captivate, stimulate & educate as well as reinforce children's skills in several curriculum areas. And, although the activites have been developed for elementary school-age children, older children & adults may learn something as well. To write or FAX for information on ordering DISAPPEARING FACES, contact: Carol A. Wallin, Publisher, 18721 S. Dixie Hwy. #106, Miami, FL 33157. FAX: 305-253-0110.
Publisher Provided Annotation.

Ward, Lorraine. A Walk in the Wild. 32p. 1993. PLB 16.88 (*0-88106-480-7*); pap. 7.95 (*0-88106-478-5*) Charlesbridge Pub.

Wildlife. (Illus.). 32p. (Orig.). (gr. 1-3). 1994. pap. 4.95 (*1-56458-550-6*) Dorling Kindersley.

Wilkes. Jungles. (gr. 4-6). 1980. (Usborne-Hayes); PLB 11.96 (*0-88110-681-X*); pap. 4.50 (*0-7460-0759-0*) EDC.

—Wild Places. (gr. 4-6). 1980. 10.95 (*0-7460-0798-1*, Usborne-Hayes) EDC.

Wolkomir, Joyce & Wolkomir, Richard. Junkyard Bandicoots & Other Tales of the World's Endangered Species. LC 92-11114. 128p. (gr. 4-7). 1992. pap. text ed. 9.95 (*0-471-57261-6*) Wiley.

Yocom, Charles & Dasmann, Raymond. Pacific Coastal Wildlife Region. rev. ed. (Illus.). 120p. (gr. 4 up). 1965. 15.95 (*0-911010-05-X*); pap. 7.95 (*0-911010-04-1*) Naturegraph.

WILD LIFE–CONSERVATION–FICTION

Bailey, Jill. Operation Elephant. Green, John, illus. LC 90-46056. 48p. (gr. 3-7). 1991. PLB 21.34 (*0-8114-2706-4*); pap. 4.95 (*0-8114-6554-3*) Raintree Steck-V.

Belanger, Mark. Old Slippery. (gr. 4-7). 1993. pap. 4.95 (*0-8114-4305-1*) Raintree Steck-V.

Boyle, Doe & Thomas, Peter, eds. Caribou Country: From an Original Article Which Appeared in Ranger Rick Magazine, Copyright National Wildlife Federation. Langford, Alton, illus. Luther, Sallie, contrib. by. LC 92-7732. (Illus.). 20p. (gr. k-3). 1992. 6.95 (*0-924483-53-9*); incl. audiocass. tape & 13" toy 35.95 (*0-924483-50-4*); incl. 9" toy 21.95 (*0-924483-51-2*); incl. audiocass. tape 9.95 (*0-924483-52-0*); write for info. audiocass. tape (*0-924483-80-6*) Soundprints.

Cowcher, Helen. La Tigresa. Marcuse, Aida, tr. (SPA.). 32p. (gr. 4-8). 1993. pap. 5.95 (*0-374-47779-5*) FS&G.

—La Tigresa: Tigress. (ps-3). 1993. 16.00 (*0-374-37565-8*, Mirasol) FS&G.

—Tigress. Thomas, Peter, narrated by. Cowcher, Helen, illus. 32p. (gr. k-3). incls. cassette 19.95 (*0-924483-33-4*) Soundprints.

Ernst, Lisa C. Squirrel Park. Ernst, Lisa C., illus. LC 92-27920. 40p. (ps-2). 1993. RSBE 15.95 (*0-02-733562-3*, Bradbury Pr) Macmillan Child Grp.

George, Jean C. Who Really Killed Cock Robin? An Ecological Mystery. LC 90-38659. 176p. (gr. 3-7). 1991. 15.00 (*0-06-021980-7*); PLB 14.89 (*0-06-021981-5*) HarpC Child Bks.

Haas, Jessie. Mowing. Smith, Joseph A., photos by. LC 93-12240. 32p. (ps up). 1994. 14.00 (*0-688-11680-9*); lib. bdg. 13.93 (*0-688-11681-7*) Greenwillow.

Henry, Marguerite. Mustang, Wild Spirit of the West. Lougheed, Robert, illus. LC 91-25187. 224p. (gr. 3-7). 1992. pap. 3.95 (*0-689-71601-X*, Aladdin) Macmillan Child Grp.

Herndon, Ernest. The Secret of Lizard Island. LC 93-5011. 144p. 1994. pap. 4.99 (*0-310-38251-3*) Zondervan.

Ichikawa, Satomi. Nora's Duck. Ichikawa, Satomi, illus. 40p. (ps-3). 1991. 14.95 (*0-399-21805-X*, Philomel) Putnam Pub Group.

Kroll, Virginia. Sweet Magnolia. Jacques, Laura, illus. LC 93-11966. 32p. (ps-4). 1994. 14.95 (*0-88106-415-7*); PLB 15.88 (*0-88106-416-5*); pap. 6.95 (*0-88106-414-9*) Charlesbridge Pub.

Lasky, Kathryn. She's Wearing a Dead Bird on Her Head. Catrow, David, illus. LC 94-18204. Date not set. write for info. (*0-7868-0065-8*); pap. write for info. (*0-7868-2052-7*) Hyprn Child.

Loon, Joan & Loon, John. The Lunettes. (Illus.). 16p. (gr. 1-4). 1984. 25.00 (*1-56611-503-5*); pap. 18.00 (*1-56611-504-3*) Jonas.
Our modern society looks to protection of the environment. Two Loons decide to find the best nesting area & begin a trip that takes them over historic London, New York City &, of course, over the sea & through the air. Thinking at last to have found a suitable place to land, an unfortunate accident of the environment happens to them; not spelled out, some creative thinking evolves from today's "select schools" programs. In graded schools best for grades 1-4. Teacher read, explained 1-2. It is done in black & white to cut down on toners throw-off often required by Cannon copiers. Call or write for information. To order: Jonas Publishing, 2603 W. 60th, Indianapolis, IN 46208 (317-255-5220). Prepaid only; checks must accompany. No refunds or returns. Include $2.00 min. for shipping & handling.
Publisher Provided Annotation.

McGee, Charmayne. So Sings the Blue Deer. LC 93-26580. 160p. (gr. 3-7). 1994. SBE 14.95 (*0-689-31888-X*, Atheneum Child Bk) Macmillan Child Grp.

Meeks, Arone R. Enora & the Black Crane. LC 92-32123. 1993. 14.95 (*0-590-46375-6*) Scholastic Inc.

Montgomery, Rutherford G. Pekan the Shadow. Nenninger, Jerome D., illus. LC 78-84779. (gr. 8-12). 1970. 3.95 (*0-87004-132-0*) Caxton.

O'Connor, Karen. The Green Team: The Adventures of Mitch & Molly. Chapin, Patrick O., illus. LC 92-24643. 80p. (Orig.). (gr. 1-4). 1993. pap. 4.99 (*0-570-04726-9*) Concordia.

Powell, Pamela. The Turtle Watchers. LC 92-5822. 160p. (gr. 3-7). 1992. 13.00 (*0-670-84294-X*) Viking Child Bks.

Rush, Christopher. Venus Peter Saves the Whale. Hedderwick, Mairi, illus. LC 92-7808. 32p. (gr. 4-7). 1992. 14.95 (*0-88289-928-7*) Pelican.

Schlein, Miriam. The Year of the Panda. Mak, Kam, illus. LC 89-71307. 96p. (gr. 3-7). 1990. (Crowell Jr Bks); PLB 13.89 (*0-690-04866-1*, Crowell Jr Bks) HarpC Child Bks.

Springstubb, Tricia. Which Way to the Nearest Wilderness? (gr. k-6). 1987. pap. 2.75 (*0-440-49554-7*, YB) Dell.

Vargo, Vanessa. Jaguar Talk. LC 92-4073. 1992. 5.95 (*0-85953-396-4*) Childs Play.

WILDERNESS SURVIVAL

Evans, Jeremy. Camping & Survival. LC 91-39143. (Illus.). 48p. (gr. 5-6). 1992. text ed. 13.95 RSBE (*0-89686-686-6*, Crestwood Hse) Macmillan Child Grp.

Giegling, John. Snowflake Come Home: A Wolf's Story. Oliver, Bryan, illus. 124p. (Orig.). (gr. 7-9). 1992. pap. 4.95 (*0-912661-12-7*) Woodsong Graph.

Goodchild, Peter. The Spark in the Stone: Skills & Projects from the Native American Tradition. LC 90-27324. (Illus.). 144p. (Orig.). (gr. 5 up). 1991. pap. 11.95 (*1-55652-102-2*) Chicago Review.

Landsman, Susan. Survival! In the Jungle. 112p. (Orig.). 1993. pap. 3.50 (*0-380-76605-1*, Camelot) Avon.

McClung, Robert M. The True Adventures of Grizzly Adams. LC 85-8886. (Illus.). 208p. (gr. 5 up). 1985. 11.95 (*0-688-05794-2*) Morrow Jr Bks.

McMurtry, Ken. Survival! in the Mountains. 112p. (Orig.). 1993. pap. 3.50 (*0-380-76602-7*, Camelot) Avon.

Whitefeather, Willy. Willy Whitefeather's Outdoor Survival Handbook for Kids. Whitefeather, Willy, illus. LC 89-26929. 104p. (Orig.). (gr. 3 up). 1990. pap. 9.95 (*0-943173-47-7*) Harbinger AZ.

Wilderness Challenge. LC 79-3241. (Illus.). 104p. (gr. 3-8). 1980. 8.95 (*0-87044-333-X*); PLB 12.50 (*0-87044-338-0*) Natl Geog.

Wilderness Survival. (Illus.). 48p. (gr. 6-12). 1984. pap. 1.85 (*0-8395-3265-2*, 33265) BSA.

WILDERNESS SURVIVAL–FICTION

Dygard, Thomas J. Wilderness Peril. LC 84-25577. 208p. (gr. 7 up). 1985. 12.95 (*0-688-04146-9*) Morrow Jr Bks.

Ferraris, L. E. The Adventures of Kitten & Pachyderm. 1992. 11.95 (*0-533-10132-8*) Vantage.

George, Jean C. My Side of the Mountain. 1991. pap. 4.95 (*0-14-034810-7*) Puffin Bks.

London, Jack. White Fang. LC 85-42971. 272p. (gr. 4-6). 1985. pap. 3.99 (*0-14-035045-4*, Puffin) Puffin Bks.

Paulsen, Gary. The River. 1991. 15.00 (*0-385-30388-2*) Doubleday.

Wyss, Johann D. The Swiss Family Robinson. LC 94-5858. 1994. 13.95 (*0-679-43640-5*, Evrymans Lib Childs) Knopf.

WILKES, CHARLES, 1798-1877

Wolfe, Cheri. Lt. Charles Wilkes & the Great U.S. Exploring Expedition. Goetzmann, William H., ed. Collins, Michael, intro. by. (Illus.). 112p. (gr. 6-12). 1991. PLB 18.95 (*0-7910-1320-0*) Chelsea Hse.

WILLIAMS, DANIEL HALES, 1858-1931

Kaye. Life of Daniel H. Williams. 1993. write for info. (*0-8050-3045-X*) H Holt & Co.

Kaye, Judith. The Life of Daniel Hale Williams. (Illus.). 80p. (gr. 4-7). 1993. PLB 13.95 (*0-8050-2302-X*) TFC Bks NY.

WILLIAMS, THEODORE SAMUEL, 1918-

Weber, Bruce. Ted Williams: Classic Sports Shots. 1993. pap. 1.25 (*0-590-47022-1*) Scholastic Inc.

WILLIAMSBURG, VIRGINIA

Anderson, Joan W. Williamsburg Household. LC 87-33803. (gr. 4-7). 1990. pap. 5.70 (*0-395-54791-1*, Clarion Bks) HM.

Bethell, Jean & Axtell, Susan. A Colonial Williamsburg Activities Book: Fun Things to Do for Children 4 & Up. Wallner, Susan, illus. 40p. (ps). 1984. pap. 4.25 (*0-87935-068-7*) Williamsburg.

Colonial Williamsburg Foundation Staff. Animals at Colonial Williamsburg. (Illus.). 8p. (ps). 1993. bds. 3.95 (*0-87935-092-X*) Williamsburg.

—Colonial Colors. (Illus.). 8p. (ps). 1993. bds. 3.95 (*0-87935-094-6*) Williamsburg.

—Count with the Cooper. (Illus.). 8p. (ps). 1993. bds. 3.95 (*0-87935-093-8*) Williamsburg.

Fortunato, Pat. A Colonial Williamsburg Activities Book: Fun Activities for Young Visitors. Wallner, John, illus. 48p. (Orig.). (gr. 1-4). 1982. pap. 4.25 (*0-87935-062-8*) Williamsburg.

Goor, Ron & Goor, Nancy. Williamsburg: Cradle of the Revolution. LC 94-9370. (gr. 3-7). 1994. 15.95 (*0-689-31795-6*, Atheneum) Macmillan.

Wooten, Vernon. The Colonial Williamsburg Coloring Book. (Illus.). 36p. (Orig.). (gr. 1). 1979. pap. 3.95 (*0-87935-052-0*) Williamsburg.

WILLIAMSBURG, VIRGINIA–FICTION

Coon, Alma S. Amy, Ben, & Catalpa the Cat: A Fanciful Story of This & That. Owens, Gail, illus. 40p. (ps-2). 1990. 8.95 (*0-87935-079-2*) Williamsburg.

Luttrell, Wanda. Stranger in Williamsburg. LC 94-20574. 1995. write for info. (*0-7814-0902-0*, Chariot Bks) Chariot Family.

WILLIAMSBURG, VIRGINIA–HISTORY

Colonial Williamsburg Foundation Staff. The Apprentice. (Illus.). 38p. (Orig.). (gr. 5-7). 1984. pap. 2.95 (*0-87935-103-9*) Williamsburg.

Kent, Zachary. Williamsburg. LC 91-35055. (Illus.). 32p. (gr. 3-6). PLB 12.30, Apr. 1992 (*0-516-04854-6*); pap. 3.95, Jul. 1992 (*0-516-44854-4*) Childrens.

Steen, Sandra & Steen, Susan. Colonial Williamsburg. LC 92-26192. (Illus.). 72p. (gr. 4 up). 1993. text ed. 14.95 RSBE (*0-87518-546-0*, Dillon) Macmillan Child Grp.

WILLS–FICTION

McBurnie, Grant & Polack, Michael. Aunt Wilhelmina's Will. Fleming, Leanne, illus. LC 93-6570. 1994. write for info. (*0-383-03676-3*) SRA Schl Grp.

WILSON, WOODROW, PRESIDENT U. S. 1856-1924

Collins, David R. Woodrow Wilson: Twenty-Eighth President of the United States. Young, Richard G., ed. LC 88-24563. (gr. 5-9). 1989. PLB 17.26 (*0-944483-18-6*) Garrett Ed Corp.

Osinski, Alice. Woodrow Wilson. LC 88-8678. (Illus.). 100p. (gr. 3 up). 1989. PLB 14.40 (*0-516-01367-X*) Childrens.

Randolph, Sallie. Woodrow Wilson. 128p. (gr. 6-9). 1992. 14.95 (*0-8027-8143-8*); PLB 15.85 (*0-8027-8144-6*) Walker & Co.

Sandak, Cass R. The Wilsons. LC 93-3503. (Illus.). 48p. (gr. 5). 1993. text ed. 12.95 RSBE (*0-89686-651-3*, Crestwood Hse) Macmillan Child Grp.

Woodrow Wilson: Mini-Play. (gr. 8 up). 1978. 6.50 (*0-89550-315-8*) Stevens & Shea.

WIND

see Winds

WIND INSTRUMENTS

see also Bands (Music)

Arban, Jean B. Complete Conservatory Method for Trumpet (Cornet) or E-Flat Alto, B-Flat Tenor, Baritone, Euphonium & B-Flat Bass in Treble Clef. Goldman, Edwin F. & Smith, Walter M., eds. 350p. (Orig.). 1936. pap. 25.95 (*0-8258-0010-2*, 021) Fischer Inc NY.

Bunting, Janet. My First Recorder Book. (Illus.). 32p. (gr. 2-6). 1989. Incl. recorder. pap. 14.95 (*0-8120-7618-4*) Barron.

Fun Disney Fav Pack. (Illus., Orig.). 1988. pap. 14.95 (*0-88188-849-4*, HL 00660210) H Leonard.

Klose, Hyacinthe. Celebrated Method for the Clarinet: Complete Edition. Bellison, Simeon, ed. 293p. (Orig.). 1946. pap. 18.95 (*0-8258-0051-X*, 0304) Fischer Inc NY.

Poffenberg, Nancy & Bane, Rosemary. Instant Recorder Package 2. Shaffer, Jim, illus. 32p. (Orig.). (gr. 3-6). 1989. pap. write for info. incl. recorder (*0-938293-17-6*) Fun Pub OH.

Sharma, Elizabeth. Woodwinds. LC 93-709. (Illus.). 32p. (gr. 4-6). 1993. 14.95 (*1-56847-115-7*) Thomson Lrning.

Wagner, Ernst F. Foundation to Flute Playing: An Elementary Method. rev. ed. 120p. (Orig.). 1918. pap. 14.95 (*0-8258-0054-4*, 0223) Fischer Inc NY.

WINDMILLS

Rickard, Graham. Wind Energy. (Illus.). 32p. (gr. 4-6). 1991. PLB 17.27 (*0-8368-0711-1*) Gareth Stevens Inc.

WINDOW GARDENING

see also House Plants

WINDOWS, STAINED GLASS

see Glass Painting and Staining

WINDS

see also Hurricanes; Storms; Tornadoes

Bailey, Donna. Energy from Wind & Water. LC 90-39388. (Illus.). 48p. (gr. 2-6). 1990. PLB 19.97 (*0-8114-2519-3*) Raintree Steck-V.

Cooper, Jason. Wind. LC 92-8811. 1992. 12.67 (*0-86593-171-2*); 9.50s.p. (*0-685-59297-9*) Rourke Corp.

Dorros, Arthur. Feel the Wind. Dorros, Arthur, illus. LC 88-18961. 32p. (ps-3). 1989. (Crowell Jr Bks); PLB 14.89 (*0-690-04741-X*, Crowell Jr Bks) HarpC Child Bks.

—Feel the Wind. Dorros, Arthur, illus. LC 88-18961. 32p. (ps-3). 1990. pap. 4.95 (*0-06-445095-3*, Trophy) HarpC Child Bks.

Felix, Monique. Wind. (ps up). 1993. 7.95 (*1-56846-073-2*) Creat Editions.

Heyes, Eileen. Where the Wind Goes. Christensen, Carrie, illus. 32p. (ps-2). Date not set. 11.95 (*1-56065-148-2*) Capstone Pr.

How Does the Wind Blow? 1991. 3.99 (*0-517-05892-8*) Random Hse Value.

McDonnell, Janet. Wind: What Can It Do? Connelly, Gwen, illus. LC 89-24011. 32p. (ps-2). 1990. PLB 13.95 (*0-89565-555-1*) Childs World.

Michalski, Ute & Michalski, Tilman. Wind Crafts. LC 89-49553. (Illus.). 64p. 1990. 15.40 (*0-516-09258-8*); pap. 8.95 (*0-516-49258-6*) Childrens.

Palmer, Joy. Wind. LC 92-38439. (Illus.). 32p. (gr. 2-3). 1992. PLB 18.99 (*0-8114-3415-X*) Raintree Steck-V.

Santrey, Laurence. What Makes the Wind? Dodson, Bert, illus. LC 81-7486. 32p. (gr. 2-4). 1982. PLB 11.59 (*0-89375-584-2*); pap. text ed. 2.95 (*0-89375-585-0*) Troll Assocs.

Shaw, Alison. Beaufort Wind Scale. 1994. write for info. (*0-8050-2770-X*) H Holt & Co.

Steele, Philip. Wind: Causes & Effects. LC 90-46262. (Illus.). 32p. (gr. 5-8). 1991. PLB 12.40 (*0-531-11024-9*) Watts.

Taylor, Barbara. Wind & Weather. LC 90-46260. (Illus.). 32p. (gr. 5-8). 1991. PLB 12.40 (*0-531-14184-5*) Watts.

Williams, John. Simple Science Projects with Air. LC 91-50543. (Illus.). 32p. (gr. 2-4). 1992. PLB 17.27 (*0-8368-0765-0*) Gareth Stevens Inc.

WINDS–FICTION

Bacon. Wind. 1993. pap. 28.67 (*0-590-72703-6*) Scholastic Inc.

Boyd, Patricia R. The Furry Wind. Spring, Grace J., illus. 28p. (gr. 2-3). 1982. pap. 2.25 (*0-9603840-4-9*) Andrew Mtn Pr.

Corpening, Gene S. I Love to Hear the Cold Wind Howl: (When I'm All Tucked in at Night) 2nd ed. James, Linda, illus. 40p. 1994. Repr. of 1993 ed. PLB 13.95 (*0-9636775-8-6*) Alice Pub.

Downie, Jill. Follow the Wind. (Illus.). 32p. (ps-2). 1992. 15.95 (*0-86264-287-6*, Pub. by Andersen Pr UK) Trafalgar.

Felix, Monique. Wind: Mouse Books. (Illus.). 32p. (ps). 1993. pap. 2.95 (*1-56189-095-2*) Amer Educ Pub.

Fleischman, Sid. McBroom & the Big Wind. Lorraine, Walter H., illus. 48p. (gr. 3 up). 1982. (Pub. by Atlantic Monthly Pr); pap. 3.95 (*0-316-28544-7*) Little.

Fry, Ed. El Viento Fuerte - the Big Wind. (ENG & SPA., Illus.). 24p. (gr. k-1). 1992. pap. 23.75 (*0-89061-722-8*) Jamestown Pubs.

Greene, Carol. Please, Wind? LC 82-4548. (Illus.). (ps-2). 1982. PLB 10.25 (*0-516-02033-1*); pap. 2.95 (*0-516-42033-X*) Childrens.

Guccione, Leslie D. Tell Me How the Wind Sounds. 1992. pap. 3.25 (*0-590-41714-2*, Point) Scholastic Inc.

Hutchins, Pat. The Wind Blew. LC 73-11691. (Illus.). 32p. (ps-2). 1974. RSBE 14.95 (*0-02-745910-1*, Macmillan Child Bk) Macmillan Child Grp.

—The Wind Blew. Hutchins, Pat, illus. 32p. (ps-1). 1986. pap. 3.99 (*0-14-050236-X*, Puffin) Puffin Bks.

—The Wind Blew. Hutchins, Pat, illus. LC 92-44903. 32p. (ps-1). 1993. pap. 4.95 (*0-689-71744-X*, Aladdin) Macmillan Child Grp.

James, Betsy. Blow Away Soon. Vojtech, Anna, illus. LC 93-27135. 1995. 14.95 (*0-399-22648-6*, Putnam) Putnam Pub Group.

Killion, Bette. The Same Wind. LC 92-7786. (Illus.). 32p. (ps-3). 1992. 15.00 (*0-06-021050-8*); PLB 14.89 (*0-06-021051-6*) HarpC Child Bks.

Lasky, Kathryn. The Gates of the Wind. Stevens, Janet, illus. LC 94-8390. 1995. write for info. (*0-15-204264-4*) HarBrace.

Lipson, Michael. How the Wind Plays. (Illus.). 32p. (ps-1). 1994. 14.95 (*1-56282-325-6*); PLB 14.89 (*1-56282-326-4*) Hyprn Child.

McAllister, Angela. The Wind Garden. Fletcher, Claire, illus. LC 93-37435. 1994. 15.00 (*0-688-13280-4*) Lothrop.

MacDonald, Elizabeth. The Very Windy Day. Summers, Lesley, illus. LC 91-690. 40p. (ps-3). 1992. 15.00 (*0-688-11044-4*, Tambourine Bks); PLB 14.93 (*0-688-11045-2*, Tambourine Bks) Morrow.

McKay, Louise & McKay, George. Marny's Ride with the Wind. Smetana, Margaret, illus. (gr. k-3). 1979. 6.95 (*0-934986-00-2*) New Harbinger.

Munsch, Robert. Millicent & the Wind. Duranceau, Suzanne, illus. 24p. (Orig.). (ps-2). 1989. pap. 0.99 (*1-55037-010-3*, Pub. by Annick CN) Firefly Bks Ltd.

Murphy, S. Wind Child. 1995. 15.00 (*0-06-024351-1*); PLB 14.89 (*0-06-024352-X*) HarpC Child Bks.

Murphy, Shirley R. Wind Child. Dillon, Leo & Dillon, Diane, illus. LC 94-13861. 1995. 15.00 (*0-06-024903-X*); PLB 14.89 (*0-06-024904-8*) HarpC.

Pegram, Laura. Windy Day. (ps). 1994. 5.95 (*0-86316-218-5*) Writers & Readers.

Purdy, Carol. Iva Dunnit & the Big Wind. Kellogg, Steven, illus. LC 84-17441. 32p. (ps-3). 1988. pap. 4.99 (*0-8037-0493-3*) Dial Bks Young.

Ross, Christine. The Whirlys & the West Wind. LC 92-39011. 1993. 13.95 (*0-395-65379-7*) HM.

Ryder, Joanne. Catching the Wind. Rothman, Michael, illus. LC 88-23446. 32p. (gr. k up). 1989. 13.95 (*0-688-07170-8*); PLB 13.88 (*0-688-07171-6*, Morrow Jr Bks) Morrow Jr Bks.

—Catching the Wind. (ps-3). 1994. pap. 4.95 (*0-688-13333-9*, Mulberry) Morrow.

Sathre, Vivian. Mouse Chase. Schumaker, Ward, illus. LC 94-17010. Date not set. write for info. (*0-15-200105-0*) HarBrace.

Townsend, Tom. Queen of the Wind. Roberts, Melissa, ed. (Illus.). 144p. (gr. 8-10). 1989. 12.95 (*0-89015-715-4*, Pub. by Panda Bks) Sunbelt Media.

Widman, Christine. Housekeeper of the Wind. Desimini, Lisa, illus. LC 88-10979. 32p. (ps-3). 1990. HarpC Child Bks.

Wildsmith, Brian & Wildsmith, Rebecca. Whose Hat Was That? LC 92-17237. 1993. 6.95 (*0-15-200691-5*); pap. write for info. (*0-15-200690-7*) HarBrace.

WINTER

Allington, Richard L. & Krull, Kathleen. Winter. Wallner, John, illus. LC 80-25115. 32p. (gr. k-3). 1985. PLB 9.95 (*0-8172-1340-6*); pap. 3.95 (*0-8114-8243-X*) Raintree Steck-V.

Bauman, Toni & Zinkgraf, June. Winter Wonders. 240p. (gr. k-6). 1978. 15.95 (*0-916456-29-3*, GA89) Good Apple.

Beach, Judy & Spencer, Kathleen. Minds-on Fun for Winter. (gr. k-4). 1991. pap. 9.95 (*0-86653-947-6*) Fearon Teach Aids.

Craig, Janet. Here Comes Winter. Karas, G. Brian, illus. LC 87-13738. 32p. (gr. k-2). 1988. PLB 7.89 (*0-8167-1225-5*); pap. text ed. 1.95 (*0-8167-1226-3*) Troll Assocs.

Davis, Nancy M., et al. Winter. Davis, Nancy M., illus. 29p. (ps-2). 1986. pap. 4.95 (*0-937103-05-5*) DaNa Pubns.

Dunphy, Madeleine. Here Is the Arctic Winter. Robinson, Alan J., illus. LC 92-72022. 32p. (ps-3). 1993. 14.95 (*1-56282-336-1*) Hyprn Child.

Farber, Norma. Return of the Shadows. Baruffi, Andrea, illus. LC 91-27517. 40p. (gr. k-3). 1992. 15.00 (*0-06-020518-0*); PLB 14.89 (*0-06-020519-9*) HarpC Child Bks.

Fowler, Allan. How Do You Know It's Winter? LC 91-3129. 32p. (ps-2). 1991. PLB 10.75 (*0-516-04915-1*); PLB 22.95 big bk. (*0-516-49475-9*); pap. 3.95 (*0-516-44915-X*) Childrens.

Glover, Susanne & Grewe, Georgeann. A Splash of Winter. Grewe, Georgeann, illus. 128p. (gr. 2-5). 1987. pap. 11.95 (*0-86653-411-3*, GA1025) Good Apple.

Good, Elaine W. White Wonderful Winter. Wenger, Susie S., illus. LC 91-74052. 32p. (ps-1). 1991. pap. 6.95 (*1-56148-018-5*) Good Bks PA.

Grubbs, J., ed. Where Do the Birds Go When It Storms. Abell, J. & Abell, J., illus. (gr. 1-3). 1992. lib. bdg. 25.00 (*1-56611-012-2*); pap. 15.00 (*0-685-66201-2*) Jonas.

Hartwig, Judy. Celebrate Winter. Filkins, Vanessa, illus. 144p. (gr. k-3). 1985. wkbk. 11.95 (*0-86653-266-8*, SS 839, Shining Star Pubns) Good Apple.

Hirschi, Ron. Winter. LC 89-23935. (Illus.). (ps-3). 1990. 14.00 (*0-525-65026-1*, Cobblehill Bks) Dutton Child Bks.

Honda, Tetsuya. Wild Horse Winter. (Illus.). 32p. (ps-3). 1992. 12.95 (*0-8118-0251-5*) Chronicle Bks.

Jackson, Ellen. The Winter Solstice. Ellis, Jan D., illus. LC 92-45065. 32p. (gr. 2-4). 1994. PLB 15.40 (*1-56294-400-2*) Millbrook Pr.

Kalman, Bobbie. We Celebrate Winter. (Illus.). 56p. (gr. 3-4). 1986. 15.95 (*0-86505-046-5*); pap. 7.95 (*0-86505-056-2*) Crabtree Pub Co.

Maass, Robert. When Winter Comes. LC 93-7146. (Illus.). 32p. (gr. 1-3). 1993. 14.95 (*0-8050-2086-1*, Bks Young Read) H Holt & Co.

Markle, Sandra. Exploring Winter. Markle, Sandra, illus. LC 84-3049. 160p. (gr. 3-7). 1984. SBE 14.95 (*0-689-31065-X*, Atheneum Child Bk) Macmillan Child Grp.

Moncure, Jane B. Step into Winter: A New Season. Hohag, Linda, illus. LC 90-30636. 32p. (ps-2). 1990. PLB 13.95 (*0-89565-574-8*) Childs World.

—Word Bird's Winter Words. Gohman, Vera, illus. LC 85-5942. 32p. (gr. k-2). 1985. PLB 14.95 (*0-89565-309-5*) Childs World.

Ottenheimer, Laurence. Livre de L'Hiver. Bour, Daniele, illus. (FRE.). 93p. (gr. 4-9). 1983. 15.95 (*2-07-039505-7*) Schoenhof.

Pragoff, Fiona. Winter. Pragoff, Fiona, illus. 20p. (ps). 1993. pap. 5.95 spiralbound (*0-689-71704-0*, Aladdin) Macmillan Child Grp.

Santrey, Louis. Winter. Sabin, Francene, illus. LC 82-19353. 32p. (gr. 4-7). 1983. lib. bdg. 10.79 (*0-89375-907-4*); pap. text ed. 2.95 (*0-89375-908-2*) Troll Assocs.

Schweninger, Ann. Wintertime. LC 93-16685. 32p. (ps-3). 1993. pap. 4.50 (*0-14-054286-8*, Puffin) Puffin Bks.

Simon, Seymour. Winter Across America. LC 93-45933. (Illus.). 32p. (ps-5). 1994. 14.95 (*0-7868-0019-4*); PLB 14.89 (*0-7868-2015-2*) Hyprn Child.

Stone, Lynn M. Winter. LC 93-39059. 1994. write for info. (*1-55916-021-7*) Rourke Bk Co.

Thomson, Ruth. Winter. LC 89-5830. (Illus.). 32p. (gr. k-4). 1989. PLB 11.90 (*0-531-10733-7*) Watts.

Webster, David. Winter. Steltenpohl, Jane, ed. Steadman, Barbara, illus. 48p. (gr. 2-4). 1989. lib. bdg. 10.98 (*0-671-65861-1*, J Messner); pap. 5.95 (*0-671-65986-3*) S&S Trade.

WINTER–FICTION

Adams, Pam. On a Cold & Frosty Morning. (gr. 4 up). 1990. 5.95 (*0-85953-442-1*) Childs Play.

Agell, Charlotte. I Slide into the White of Winter. Agell, Charlotte, illus. 40p. (ps up). 1994. 7.95 (*0-88448-115-8*) Tilbury Hse.

Andersen, Hans Christian. The Snow Queen. Philip, Neil, tr. from DAN. Holmes, Sally, illus. LC 89-45289. 64p. 1989. 14.95 (*0-688-09047-8*); PLB 14.88 (*0-688-09048-6*) Lothrop.

Barasch, Lynne, text by. & illus. A Winter Walk. LC 92-39804. 32p. (ps-2). 1993. PLB 13.95 (*0-395-65937-X*) Ticknor & Flds Bks Yng Read.

Benjamin, Cynthia. Footprints in the Snow. Rogers, Jacqueline, illus. 48p. (ps-1). 1994. pap. 2.95 (*0-590-46663-1*, Cartwheel) Scholastic Inc.

Briggs, Raymond. The Snowman, No. 8612-4. (Illus.). (ps-4). 1990. 3.50 (*0-7214-1109-6*) Ladybird Bks.

Brown, Margaret W. Animals in the Snow. Schwartz, Carol, illus. LC 94-8470. 1995. write for info. (*0-7868-0039-9*); pap. write for info. (*0-7868-2032-2*) Hyprn Child.

—The Winter Noisy Book. new ed. Shaw, Charles G., illus. LC 92-46880. 48p. (ps-1). 1986. 15.00 (*0-06-020865-1*); PLB 15.89 (*0-06-020866-X*) HarpC Child Bks.

Brutschy, Jennifer. The Winter Fox. Garns, Allen, illus. LC 92-33467. 40p. (ps-3). 1993. 15.00 (*0-679-81524-4*); PLB 15.99 (*0-679-91524-9*) Knopf Bks Yng Read.

Carlstrom, Nancy. Goodbye Geese. Young, Ed, illus. 32p. (ps-3). 1991. 14.95 (*0-399-21832-7*, Philomel) Putnam Pub Group.

Cartwright, Ann. The Winter Hedgehog. Cartwright, Reg, illus. LC 90-5593. 32p. (ps-3). 1990. SBE 13.95 (*0-02-717775-0*, Macmillan Child Bk) Macmillan Child Grp.

Chlad, Dorothy. Playing Outdoors in the Winter. Halverson, Lydia, illus. LC 90-22258. 32p. (ps-2). 1991. pap. 3.95 (*0-516-41972-2*) Childrens.

Christelow, Eileen. The Five-Dog Night. LC 92-36958. 1993. 14.45 (*0-395-62399-5*, Clarion Bks) HM.
Christiansen, Candace. The Ice Horse. LC 92-28964. (Illus.). 32p. (gr. 1-5). 1993. 15.99 (*0-8037-1400-9*); lib. bdg. 15.89 (*0-8037-1401-7*) Dial Bks Young.
Coleridge, Sara. January Brings the Snow. 1989. pap. 4.95 (*0-8037-0704-5*, Dial) Doubleday.
Corey, Deirdre. C U When the Snow Falls. 144p. 1991. pap. 2.75 (*0-590-45109-X*, Apple Paperbacks) Scholastic Inc.
Cunning, Peter. Out on the Ice in the Middle of the Bay. Priestley, Alice, illus. 32p. 1993. lib. bdg. 15.95 (*1-55037-276-9*, Pub. by Annick CN); pap. 5.95 (*1-55037-277-7*, Pub. by Annick CN) Firefly Bks Ltd.
Demi. Demi's Dozen Winter. (ps-2). 1994. 9.95 (*0-8050-2202-3*) H Holt & Co.
Dunphy, Madeleine. Here Is the Arctic Winter. Robinson, Alan J., illus. 32p. (ps-3). 1993. PLB 14.89 (*1-56282-337-X*) Hyprn Child.
Erickson, Gina C. & Foster, Kelli C. The Sled Surprise. Russell, Kerri G., illus. 24p. (ps-2). 1991. pap. 3.50 (*0-8120-4677-3*) Barron.
Ewart, Claire. One Cold Night. (Illus.). 32p. (ps-1). 1992. 14.95 (*0-399-22341-X*, Putnam) Putnam Pub Group.
George, Jean C. Dear Rebecca, Winter Is Here. Krupinski, Loretta, illus. LC 92-9515. 32p. (ps-3). 1993. 15.00 (*0-06-021139-3*); PLB 14.89 (*0-06-021140-7*) HarpC Child Bks.
George, William T. Christmas at Long Pond. George, Lindsay B., illus. LC 91-31475. 32p. (ps-8). 1992. 14. 00 (*0-688-09214-4*); PLB 13.93 (*0-688-09215-2*) Greenwillow.
Greenleaf, Ann. Max & Molly's Winter. 1993. 4.99 (*0-517-09152-6*) Random Hse Value.
Guiberson & Lloyd. Winter Wheat. 1995. 14.95 (*0-8050-1582-5*) H Holt & Co.
Gurney, John S., illus. Over the River & Through the Woods. 1992. pap. 2.50 (*0-590-45258-4*, Cartwheel) Scholastic Inc.
Hader, Berta & Hader, Elmer. The Big Snow. 3rd ed. Hader, Berta & Hader, Elmer, illus. LC 92-46365. 48p. (gr. k-4). 1993. pap. 4.95 (*0-689-71757-1*, Aladdin) Macmillan Child Grp.
Hand, Elizabeth. Winterlong. 1990. pap. 4.95 (*0-553-28772-9*, Spectra) Bantam.
Hartley, Deborah. Up North in Winter. Dabcovich, Lydia, illus. 32p. (ps-3). 1993. pap. 4.99 (*0-14-054943-9*, Puff Unicorn) Puffin Bks.
Hasler, Eveline. Winter Magic. Lemieux, Michele, illus. LC 85-2944. 32p. (ps-3). 1985. lib. bdg. 12.88 (*0-688-05258-4*) Morrow Jr Bks.
Haywood, Carolyn. Betsy's Winterhouse. Haywood, Carolyn, illus. LC 55-8453. 192p. (gr. 3-7). 1958. PLB 13.88 (*0-688-31090-7*) Morrow Jr Bks.
Hiscock, Bruce. When Will It Snow? LC 94-9385. (Illus.). 1996. 15.95 (*0-689-31937-1*, Atheneum) Macmillan.
Hol, Coby. Lisa & the Snowman. Hol, Coby, illus. LC 89-42614. 32p. (gr. k-3). 1989. 13.95 (*1-55858-022-0*) North-South Bks NYC.
Howard, Kim. In Wintertime. LC 93-10979. 1994. 16.00 (*0-688-11378-8*); lib. bdg. 15.93 (*0-688-11379-6*) Lothrop.
Hughes, Shirley. Stories by Firelight. LC 92-38207. (Illus.). 64p. 1993. 16.00 (*0-688-04568-5*) Lothrop.
Hurwitz, Johanna. The Cold & Hot Winter. (gr. 3-7). 1989. pap. 2.95 (*0-590-42619-2*, Apple Paperbacks) Scholastic Inc.
Iwamura, Kazuo. The Fourteen Forest Mice & the Winter Sledding Day. Knowlton, Mary L., tr. from JPN. Iwamura, Kazuo, illus. LC 90-50707. 32p. (gr. k-3). 1991. PLB 17.27 (*0-8368-0499-6*) Gareth Stevens Inc.
Jansson, Tove. Moominland Midwinter. (gr. 4-7). 1992. 14.00 (*0-374-35041-8*) FS&G.
—Moominland Midwinter. (gr. 4-7). 1992. pap. 4.50 (*0-374-45303-9*) FS&G.
Keats, Ezra J. Un Dia de Nieve. (SPA.). (ps). 1991. 12.95 (*0-670-83747-4*) Viking Child Bks.
Krensky, Stephen. Lionel in Winter. Natti, Susanna, illus. LC 92-36121. 1994. write for info. (*0-8037-1333-9*); PLB write for info. (*0-8037-1334-7*) Dial Bks Young.
Landis, Mary M. Ice Slide Winter: Merry Brook Farm Story. (gr. 5 up). 1981. 8.50 (*0-686-30772-0*) Rod & Staff.
Lawson, Robert. The Tough Winter. Lawson, Robert, illus. (gr. 3-7). 1979. pap. 3.95 (*0-14-031215-3*, Puffin) Puffin Bks.
—The Tough Winter. (gr. 2-6). 1992. 16.75 (*0-8446-6565-7*) Peter Smith.
Lewis, Rob. Henrietta's First Winter. (Illus.). 32p. (ps-3). 1990. 11.95 (*0-374-32951-6*) FS&G.
Lotz, Karen E. Snowsong Whistling. Kleven, Elisa, illus. LC 92-47117. 32p. (ps-2). 1993. 14.99 (*0-525-45145-5*, DCB) Dutton Child Bks.
McDonnell, Janet. Winter: Tracks in the Snow. Hohag, Linda, illus. LC 93-20172. 32p. (gr. 2 up). 1993. PLB 12.30 (*0-516-00679-7*) Childrens.
Markle, Sandra. Exploring Winter. 160p. (gr. 7 up). 1992. pap. 2.99 (*0-380-71321-7*, Camelot) Avon.
Martin, Ann M. Snowbound. 240p. 1991. pap. 3.95 (*0-590-44963-X*) Scholastic Inc.
Mason, Margo C. Winter Coats. 1989. pap. 3.50 (*0-553-34726-8*) Bantam.
Mooser, Stephen. The Headless Snowman. Ulrich, George, illus. 80p. (Orig.). (gr. 2-5). 1992. pap. 3.25 (*0-440-40542-4*, YB) Dell.
Munsch, Robert. Thomas' Snowsuit. (CHI., Illus.). 32p. 1993. pap. 5.95 (*1-55037-306-4*, Pub. by Annick CN) Firefly Bks Ltd.
Nelson, Drew. Wild Voices. Schoenherr, John, illus. 96p. (gr. 3 up). 1991. 15.95 (*0-399-21798-3*, Philomel) Putnam Pub Group.
Pare, Roger. Winter Games. Pare, Roger, illus. 24p. 1991. PLB 14.95 (*1-55037-187-8*, Pub. by Annick CN); pap. 4.95 (*1-55037-184-3*, Pub. by Annick CN) Firefly Bks Ltd.
Paulsen, Gary. Winter Room. (gr. 4-7). 1991. pap. 3.50 (*0-440-40454-1*) Dell.
Peters, Sharon. Here Comes Jack Frost. Connor, Eulala, illus. LC 81-4093. 32p. (gr. k-2). 1981. PLB 11.59 (*0-89375-513-3*); pap. text ed. 2.95 (*0-89375-514-1*) Troll Assocs.
Quinlan, Patricia. Anna's Red Sled. Grater, Lindsay, illus. 24p. (ps-2). 1989. 12.95 (*1-55037-073-1*, Pub. by Annick CN); pap. 4.95 (*1-55037-072-3*, Pub. by Annick CN) Firefly Bks Ltd.
Ransome, Arthur. Winter Holiday. LC 87-46246. (gr. 4-6). 1989. pap. 10.95 (*0-87923-661-2*) Godine.
Rice, Eve. Oh, Lewis! Rice, Eve, illus. LC 92-24584. 32p. (ps up). 1993. pap. 4.95 (*0-688-11790-2*, Mulberry) Morrow.

Rundle, Vesta M. Snow Calf. Larison, Arlene, illus. 36p. (Orig.). (gr. 2-8). 1993. pap. 4.50 (*1-882672-01-1*) V M Rundle.
When a fictional family find themselves stranded in their farm home in Western Oklahoma during a record-breaking snow storm it is bad enough; when the calf that Seth is raising to enter in the fair turns up missing it is even worse & a surprise helicopter visit adds to the drama. The magic & the agony of winter are beautifully described as the family survives for nine days without power, telephone service, utilities, or transportation. Readers love the surprise ending about the survival of the calf. A story about pride, disappointment, & hope, the book is arranged in eight very short chapters & could be a first chapter book. There are lovely black & white full-page illustrations & a four-color illustrated cover by California artist Arlene Larison. Response to this book has been enthusiastic from children, teachers, parents, & grandparents. One child: "...my favorite Christmas present." A teacher: "All the fourth grade classes in our school read this story & loved it." A father: "Our family enjoyed this as a bedtime story over several evenings." A junior high reader: "...an animal story I'll always remember." A librarian: "This story could become a classic." Available from: For the Kids Press, 2251 Fourth St., Charleston, IL 61920; Phone (217) 345-2560 or The Distributors, 702 S. Michigan, South Bend, IN 46618.
Publisher Provided Annotation.

Rylant, Cynthia. Henry & Mudge in the Sparkle Days: The Fifth Book of Their Adventures. Stevenson, Sucie, illus. LC 92-42535. 48p. (gr. 1-3). 1993. pap. 3.95 (*0-689-71752-0*, Aladdin) Macmillan Child Grp.
St. John, Patricia. Treasures of the Snow. (gr. 5-8). 1950. pap. 4.50 (*0-8024-0008-6*) Moody.
Schultz, Janice. The First Frost. Caroland, Mary, ed. (Illus.). 44p. 1991. 5.95 (*1-55523-370-8*) Winston-Derek.
Shaw, Janet. Changes for Kirsten: A Winter Story. Thieme, Jeanne, ed. Graef, Renee, illus. 72p. (gr. 2-5). 1988. PLB 12.95 (*0-937295-94-9*) Pleasant Co.
Smith, Dick & Bernard, Felix. Winter Wonderland. Rogers, Jacqueline, illus. 32p. (ps-1). 1993. pap. 2.50 (*0-590-46657-7*, Cartwheel) Scholastic Inc.
Steele, William O. Winter Danger. LC 54-5157. (Illus.). 131p. (gr. 3-7). 1990. pap. 3.95 (*0-685-51103-0*, HB Juv Bks) HarBrace.
Stevenson, James. Brrr! LC 89-34615. (Illus.). 32p. (ps up). 1991. 13.95 (*0-688-09210-1*); PLB 13.88 (*0-688-09211-X*) Greenwillow.
Todhunter, Jean M. Cipher in the Snow. 2nd ed. 6p. (gr. 8-12). 1988. pap. 1.95 stiched with dustcover (*0-929985-07-9*) Jackman Pubng.
Tripp, Valerie. Changes for Samantha: A Winter Story. Thieme, Jeanne, ed. Grace, Robert & Niles, Nancy, illus. 72p. (Orig.). (gr. 2-5). 1988. PLB 12.95 (*0-937295-95-7*); pap. 5.95 (*0-937295-47-7*) Pleasant Co.
Velthuijs, Max. Frog in Winter. Velthuijs, Max, illus. LC 92-20545. 32p. (ps up). 1993. 14.00 (*0-688-12306-6*, Tambourine Bks); PLB 13.93 (*0-688-12307-4*, Tambourine Bks) Morrow.
Weiss, Nicki. Dog Boy Cap Skate. LC 88-16390. (Illus.). 32p. (ps up). 1989. 11.95 (*0-688-08275-0*); PLB 11.88 (*0-688-08276-9*) Greenwillow.
Whittington, Mary K. Winter's Child. Brown, Sue E., illus. LC 91-25011. 32p. (ps-3). 1992. SBE 14.95 (*0-689-31685-2*, Atheneum Child Bk) Macmillan Child Grp.
Willard, Nancy. Starlit Somersault Downhill. (ps-3). 1993. 15.95 (*0-316-94113-1*) Little.
Williams, Amy. The Coasting Kids' Adventures. 1993. 6.95 (*0-533-09631-6*) Vantage.
Yerxa, Leo. Last Leaf First Snowflake to Fall. LC 93-5775. (Illus.). 32p. (gr. k-3). 1994. 14.95 (*0-531-06824-2*); lib. bdg. 14.99 (*0-531-08674-7*) Orchard Bks Watts.
Zolotow, Charlotte. Something Is Going to Happen. Stock, Catherine, illus. LC 87-26661. 32p. (ps-3). 1991. pap. 4.95 (*0-06-443274-2*, Trophy) HarpC Child Bks.

WINTER–POETRY

Hull, Robert. Poems for Winter. LC 90-20589. (Illus.). 48p. (gr. 3-7). 1991. 21.34 (*0-8114-7801-7*) Raintree Steck-V.
Prelutsky, Jack. It's Snowing! It's Snowing! Titherington, Jeanne, illus. LC 83-16583. 48p. (gr. 1-3). 1984. 12.95 (*0-688-01512-3*); PLB 14.93 (*0-688-01513-1*) Greenwillow.
Rogasky, Barbara, selected by. Winter Poems. Hyman, Trina S., illus. 40p. (gr. 2 up). 1994. 15.95 (*0-590-42872-1*, Scholastic Hardcover) Scholastic Inc.

WINTER SPORTS

see also Hockey; Skating; Skis and Skiing

Harris, Jack. The Winter Olympics. 32p. (gr. 4). 1990. PLB 14.95 (*0-88682-317-X*) Creative Ed.
Italia, Robert. Snowboarding. Wallner, Rosemary, ed. LC 91-73024. 32p. 1991. PLB 9.95 (*1-56239-073-2*) Abdo & Dghtrs.
Sanchez, Isidro & Peris, Carme. Winter Sports. (Illus.). 32p. (ps-1). 1992. pap. 5.95 (*0-8120-4868-7*) Barron.
Sandelson, Robert. Ice Sports. LC 91-3881. (Illus.). 48p. (gr. 6). 1991. text ed. 13.95 RSBE (*0-89686-667-X*, Crestwood Hse) Macmillan Child Grp.

WIRELESS

see Radio

WISCONSIN

Aylesworth, Thomas G. & Aylesworth, Virginia L. Western Great Lakes (Illinois, Iowa, Wisconsin, Minnesota) (Illus.). 64p. (Orig.). (gr. 3 up). 1987. lib. bdg. 16.95x (*1-55546-560-9*); pap. 6.95x (*0-7910-0549-6*) Chelsea Hse.
—Western Great Lakes (Illinois, Iowa, Wisconsin, Minnesota) (Illus.). 64p. (gr. 3 up). 1992. lib. bdg. 16. 95 (*0-7910-1046-5*) Chelsea Hse.
Bratvold, Gretchen. Wisconsin. (Illus.). 72p. (gr. 3-6). 1991. PLB 17.50 (*0-8225-2700-6*) Lerner Pubns.
Calhoun, Sharon C. & English, Billy J. The Wisconsin Story. 202p. (gr. 4). 1987. 12.95 (*0-9619484-0-X*, TXU-299476); 49.95 (*0-318-23764-4*) Apple Corps Pubs.
Carole Marsh Wisconsin Books, 44 bks. 1994. PLB 1027. 80 set (*0-7933-1324-4*); pap. 587.80 set (*0-7933-5220-7*) Gallopade Pub Group.
Carpenter, Allan. Wisconsin. new ed. LC 77-13666. (Illus.). 96p. (gr. 4 up). 1978. PLB 20.55 (*0-516-04149-5*) Childrens.
Fradin, Dennis. Wisconsin: In Words & Pictures. Ulm, Robert, illus. LC 77-5330. 48p. (gr. 2-5). 1977. PLB 12.95 (*0-516-03948-2*) Childrens.
Fradin, Dennis B. Wisconsin - From Sea to Shining Sea. LC 92-8135. (Illus.). 64p. (gr. 3-5). 1992. PLB 16.45 (*0-516-03849-4*); pap. 5.95 (*0-516-43849-2*) Childrens.
Goc, Michael J. Stewards of the Wisconsin, the Wisconsin Valley Improvement Company. (Illus.). 152p. 1993. 29.95 (*0-938627-19-8*) New Past Pr.
Hall, Betty L. Wisconsin Survival. rev. ed. 160p. (gr. 10-12). 1986. pap. text ed. 5.84 (*0-936159-01-4*) Westwood Pr.
Marsh, Carole. Avast, Ye Slobs! Wisconsin Pirate Trivia. (Illus.). 1994. PLB 24.95 (*0-7933-1244-2*); pap. 14.95 (*0-7933-1243-4*); computer disk 29.95 (*0-7933-1245-0*) Gallopade Pub Group.
—The Beast of the Wisconsin Bed & Breakfast. (Illus.). 1994. PLB 24.95 (*0-7933-2276-6*); pap. 14.95 (*0-7933-2277-4*); computer disk 29.95 (*0-7933-2278-2*) Gallopade Pub Group.
—Bow Wow! Wisconsin Dogs in History, Mystery, Legend, Lore, Humor & More! (Illus.). (gr. 3-12). 1994. PLB 24.95 (*0-7933-3614-7*); pap. 14.95 (*0-7933-3615-5*); computer disk 29.95 (*0-7933-3616-3*) Gallopade Pub Group.
—Chill Out: Scary Wisconsin Tales Based on Frightening Wisconsin Truths. (Illus.). 1994. lib. bdg. 24.95 (*0-7933-4804-8*); pap. 14.95 (*0-7933-4805-6*); disk 29. 95 (*0-7933-4806-4*) Gallopade Pub Group.
—Christopher Columbus Comes to Wisconsin! Includes Reproducible Activities for Kids! (Illus.). (gr. 3-12). 1994. PLB 24.95 (*0-7933-3767-4*); pap. 14.95 (*0-7933-3768-2*); computer disk 29.95 (*0-7933-3769-0*) Gallopade Pub Group.
—The Hard-to-Believe-But-True! Book of Wisconsin History, Mystery, Trivia, Legend, Lore, Humor & More. (Illus.). 1994. PLB 24.95 (*0-7933-1241-8*); pap. 14.95 (*0-7933-1240-X*); computer disk 29.95 (*0-7933-1242-6*) Gallopade Pub Group.

—If My Wisconsin Mama Ran the World! (Illus.). 1994. PLB 24.95 (*0-7933-2285-5*); pap. 14.95 (*0-7933-2286-3*); computer disk 29.95 (*0-7933-2287-1*) Gallopade Pub Group.

—Jurassic Ark! Wisconsin Dinosaurs & Other Prehistoric Creatures. (gr. k-12). 1994. PLB 24.95 (*0-7933-7575-4*); pap. 14.95 (*0-7933-7576-2*); computer disk 29.95 (*0-7933-7577-0*) Gallopade Pub Group.

—Let's Quilt Our Wisconsin County. 1994. lib. bdg. 24.95 (*0-7933-7260-7*); pap. text ed. 14.95 (*0-7933-7261-5*); disk 29.95 (*0-7933-7262-3*) Gallopade Pub Group.

—Let's Quilt Our Wisconsin Town. 1994. lib. bdg. 24.95 (*0-7933-7110-4*); pap. text ed. 14.95 (*0-7933-7111-2*); disk 29.95 (*0-7933-7112-0*) Gallopade Pub Group.

—Let's Quilt Wisconsin & Stuff It Topographically! (Illus.). 1994. PLB 24.95 (*0-7933-2268-5*); pap. 14.95 (*1-55609-098-6*); computer disk 29.95 (*0-7933-2269-3*) Gallopade Pub Group.

—Meow! Wisconsin Cats in History, Mystery, Legend, Lore, Humor & More! (Illus.). (gr. 3-12). 1994. PLB 24.95 (*0-7933-3461-6*); pap. 14.95 (*0-7933-3462-4*); computer disk 29.95 (*0-7933-3463-2*) Gallopade Pub Group.

—My First Book about Wisconsin. (gr. k-4). 1994. PLB 24.95 (*0-7933-5716-0*); pap. 14.95 (*0-7933-5717-9*); computer disk 29.95 (*0-7933-5718-7*) Gallopade Pub Group.

—Uncle Rebus: Wisconsin Picture Stories for Computer Kids. (Illus.). (gr. k-3). 1994. PLB 24.95 (*0-7933-4651-7*); pap. 14.95 (*0-7933-4652-5*); disk 29.95 (*0-7933-4653-3*) Gallopade Pub Group.

—Wisconsin & Other State Greats (Biographies) (Illus.). 1994. PLB 24.95 (*0-7933-2288-X*); pap. 14.95 (*0-7933-2289-8*); computer Disk 29.95 (*0-7933-2290-1*) Gallopade Pub Group.

—Wisconsin Bandits, Bushwackers, Outlaws, Crooks, Devils, Ghosts, Desperadoes & Other Assorted & Sundry Characters! (Illus.). 1994. PLB 24.95 (*0-7933-1226-4*); pap. 14.95 (*0-7933-1225-6*); computer disk 29.95 (*0-7933-1227-2*) Gallopade Pub Group.

—Wisconsin Classic Christmas Trivia: Stories, Recipes, Activities, Legends, Lore & More. (Illus.). 1994. PLB 24.95 (*0-7933-1229-9*); pap. 14.95 (*0-7933-1228-0*); computer disk 29.95 (*0-7933-1230-2*) Gallopade Pub Group.

—Wisconsin Coastales. (Illus.). 1994. 24.95 (*0-7933-2282-0*); pap. 14.95 (*0-7933-2283-9*); computer disk 29.95 (*0-7933-2284-7*) Gallopade Pub Group.

—Wisconsin Coastales! 1994. lib. bdg. 24.95 (*0-7933-7314-X*) Gallopade Pub Group.

—Wisconsin "Crinkum-Crankum" A Funny Word Book about Our State. (Illus.). (gr. 3-12). 1994. 24.95 (*0-7933-4958-3*); pap. 14.95 (*0-7933-4959-1*); computer disk 29.95 (*0-7933-4960-5*) Gallopade Pub Group.

—Wisconsin Dingbats! Bk. 1: A Fun Book of Games, Stories, Activities & More about Our State That's All in Code! for You to Decipher. (Illus.). (gr. 3-12). 1994. PLB 24.95 (*0-7933-3920-0*); pap. 14.95 (*0-7933-3921-9*); computer disk 29.95 (*0-7933-3922-7*) Gallopade Pub Group.

—Wisconsin Festival Fun for Kids! Includes Reproducible Activities for Kids! (Illus.). (gr. 3-12). 1994. PLB 24.95 (*0-7933-4073-X*); pap. 14.95 (*0-7933-4074-8*); computer disk 29.95 (*0-7933-4075-6*) Gallopade Pub Group.

—The Wisconsin Hot Air Balloon Mystery. (Illus.). (gr. 2-9). 1994. 24.95 (*0-7933-2759-8*); pap. 14.95 (*0-7933-2760-1*); computer disk 29.95 (*0-7933-2761-X*) Gallopade Pub Group.

—Wisconsin Jeopardy! Answers & Questions about Our State! (Illus.). (gr. 3-12). 1994. PLB 24.95 (*0-7933-4226-0*); pap. 14.95 (*0-7933-4227-9*); computer disk 29.95 (*0-7933-4228-7*) Gallopade Pub Group.

—Wisconsin "Jography" A Fun Run Thru Our State! (Illus.). 1994. PLB 24.95 (*0-7933-2265-0*); pap. 14.95 (*0-7933-2266-9*); computer disk 29.95 (*0-7933-2267-7*) Gallopade Pub Group.

—Wisconsin Kid's Cookbook: Recipes, How-To, History, Lore & More! (Illus.). 1994. PLB 24.95 (*0-7933-1238-8*); pap. 14.95 (*0-7933-1237-X*); computer disk 29.95 (*0-7933-1239-6*) Gallopade Pub Group.

—The Wisconsin Mystery Van Takes Off! Book 1: Handicapped Wisconsin Kids Sneak Off on a Big Adventure. (Illus.). (gr. 3-12). 1994. 24.95 (*0-7933-5111-1*); pap. 14.95 (*0-7933-5112-X*); computer disk 29.95 (*0-7933-5113-8*) Gallopade Pub Group.

—Wisconsin Quiz Bowl Crash Course! (Illus.). 1994. PLB 24.95 (*0-7933-2279-0*); pap. 14.95 (*0-7933-2280-4*); computer disk 29.95 (*0-7933-2281-2*) Gallopade Pub Group.

—Wisconsin Rollercoasters! (Illus.). (gr. 3-12). 1994. PLB 24.95 (*0-7933-5371-8*); pap. 14.95 (*0-7933-5372-6*); computer disk 29.95 (*0-7933-5373-4*) Gallopade Pub Group.

—Wisconsin School Trivia: An Amazing & Fascinating Look at Our State's Teachers, Schools & Students! (Illus.). 1994. PLB 24.95 (*0-7933-1235-3*); pap. 14.95 (*0-7933-1234-5*); computer disk 29.95 (*0-7933-1236-1*) Gallopade Pub Group.

—Wisconsin Silly Basketball Sportsmysteries, Vol. 1. (Illus.). 1994. PLB 24.95 (*0-7933-1232-9*); pap. 14.95 (*0-7933-1231-0*); computer disk 29.95 (*0-7933-1233-7*) Gallopade Pub Group.

—Wisconsin Silly Basketball Sportsmysteries, Vol. 2. (Illus.). 1994. PLB 24.95 (*0-7933-2291-X*); pap. 14.95 (*0-7933-2292-8*); computer disk 29.95 (*0-7933-2293-6*) Gallopade Pub Group.

—Wisconsin Silly Football Sportsmysteries, Vol. 1. (Illus.). 1994. PLB 24.95 (*0-7933-2270-7*); pap. 14.95 (*0-7933-2271-5*); computer disk 29.95 (*0-7933-2272-3*) Gallopade Pub Group.

—Wisconsin Silly Football Sportsmysteries, Vol. 2. (Illus.). 1994. PLB 24.95 (*0-7933-2273-1*); pap. 14.95 (*0-7933-2274-X*); computer disk 29.95 (*0-7933-2275-8*) Gallopade Pub Group.

—Wisconsin Silly Trivia! (Illus.). 1994. PLB 24.95 (*0-7933-2262-6*); pap. 14.95 (*0-7933-2263-4*); computer disk 29.95 (*0-7933-2264-2*) Gallopade Pub Group.

—Wisconsin Timeline: A Chronology of Wisconsin History, Mystery, Trivia, Legend, Lore & More. (Illus.). (gr. 3-12). 1994. PLB 24.95 (*0-7933-6022-6*); pap. 14.95 (*0-7933-6023-4*); computer disk 29.95 (*0-7933-6024-2*) Gallopade Pub Group.

—Wisconsin's (Most Devastating!) Disasters & (Most Calamitous!) Catastrophies! (Illus.). 1994. PLB 24.95 (*0-7933-1223-X*); pap. 14.95 (*0-7933-1222-1*); computer disk 29.95 (*0-7933-1224-8*) Gallopade Pub Group.

—Wisconsin's Unsolved Mysteries (& Their "Solutions") Includes Scientific Information & Other Activities for Students. (Illus.). (gr. 3-12). 1994. PLB 24.95 (*0-7933-5869-8*); pap. 14.95 (*0-7933-5870-1*); computer disk 29.95 (*0-7933-5871-X*) Gallopade Pub Group.

Stein, R. Conrad. Wisconsin. LC 87-9376. (Illus.). 144p. (gr. 4 up). 1987. PLB 20.55 (*0-516-00495-6*) Childrens.

—Wisconsin. 210p. 1993. text ed. 15.40 (*1-56956-173-7*) W A T Braille.

Stone, Lynn M. Dairy Country. LC 93-13503. 1993. write for info. (*0-86593-302-2*) Rourke Corp.

Thompson, Kathleen. Wisconsin. 48p. (gr. 3 up). 1985. PLB 19.97 (*0-86514-448-6*) Raintree Steck-V.

WISCONSIN–FICTION

Carter, Alden R. Dogwolf. LC 93-43518. (gr. 7 up). 1994. 14.95 (*0-590-46741-7*) Scholastic Inc.

Chall, Marsha W. Mattie. LC 91-3042. (ps-3). 1992. 11.00 (*0-688-09730-8*) Lothrop.

Clarke, J. Al Capsella Takes a Vacation. 160p. (gr. 7 up). 1993. 14.95 (*0-8050-2685-1*, Bks Young Read) H Holt & Co.

Enright, Elizabeth. Thimble Summer. Enright, Elizabeth, illus. LC 38-27586. 124p. (gr. 6 up). 1938. 16.95 (*0-8050-0306-1*, Bks Young Read) H Holt & Co.

Gelman, Rita G. More Spaghetti, I Say! Gerberg, Mort, illus. 32p. (ps-3). 1993. pap. 2.95 (*0-590-45783-7*) Scholastic Inc.

Qualey, Marsha. Revolutions of the Heart. LC 92-24528. 192p. (gr. 6 up). 1993. 13.45 (*0-395-64168-3*) HM.

Sweeten, Sami. Wolf. LC 93-34493. 1994. write for info. (*0-8075-9160-2*) A Whitman.

Wilder, Laura I. The Deer in the Wood. Graef, Renee, illus. LC 94-18684. 1995. 15.00 (*0-06-024881-5*, Festival); PLB 14.89 (*0-06-024882-3*) HarpC Child Bks.

—Going to Town. Graef, Renee, illus. LC 92-46722. (gr. k-3). Date not set. 15.00 (*0-06-023012-6*); PLB 14.89 (*0-06-023013-4*) HarpC Child Bks.

Wilder, Laura Ingalls. Dance at Grandpa's. Graef, Renee, illus. LC 93-24535. 40p. (ps-3). 1994. 12.00 (*0-06-023878-X*); PLB 11.89 (*0-06-023879-8*) HarpC Child Bks.

—Little House in the Big Woods. rev. ed. Williams, Garth, illus. LC 52-7525. 238p. (gr. 3-7). 1961. 15.95 (*0-06-026430-6*); PLB 15.89 (*0-06-026431-4*) HarpC Child Bks.

—Winter Days in the Big Woods. Graef, Renee, illus. LC 92-45883. 40p. (ps-3). 1994. 12.00 (*0-06-023014-2*); PLB 11.89 (*0-06-023022-3*) HarpC Child Bks.

Wilder, Laura Ingalls, adapted by. Christmas in the Big Woods. Graef, Renee, illus. LC 94-14478. 1995. 12.00 (*0-06-024752-5*, HarpT); PLB 11.89 (*0-06-024753-3*) HarpC Child Bks.

WIT AND HUMOR

see also Epigrams; Humorists; Nonsense Verses; Satire also American Wit and Humor; English Wit and Humor

Ahlberg, Allan. The Black Cat. Amstutz, Andre, illus. LC 92-45621. 32p. (gr. k up). 1993. pap. text ed. 4.95 (*0-688-12679-0*, Mulberry) Morrow.

—Funnybones. Ahlberg, Janet, illus. LC 79-24872. 32p. (gr. k-3). 1981. 15.00 (*0-688-80238-9*); PLB 14.93 (*0-688-84238-0*) Greenwillow.

—Funnybones. Ahlberg, Janet, illus. 32p. (gr. k up). 1993. minibook 4.95 (*0-688-12671-5*, Tupelo Bks) Morrow.

—The Pet Shop. Amstutz, Andre, illus. LC 92-45657. 32p. (gr. k up). 1993. pap. 4.95 (*0-688-12680-4*, Mulberry) Morrow.

Ahlberg, Janet & Ahlberg, Allan. Funnybones. LC 79-24872. (Illus.). 32p. (ps-3). 1990. pap. 3.95 (*0-688-09927-0*, Mulberry) Morrow.

Alden, Laura, compiled by. Dinosaur Jokes. Magnuson, Diana, illus. LC 88-17489. 48p. (gr. 1-5). 1988. pap. 3.95 (*0-516-41865-3*) Childrens.

Allard, Harry. The Stupids Take Off. Marshall, James, illus. 32p. (gr. k-3). 1993. pap. 4.95 (*0-395-65743-1*) HM.

Allard, Harry & Marshall, James. The Stupids Die. (Illus.). (gr. k-3). 1985. 13.45 (*0-395-30347-8*); pap. 4.80 (*0-395-38364-1*) HM.

Allen, Jonathan. Who's at the Door? Allen, Jonathan, illus. LC 92-19618. 32p. (ps up). 1993. 11.95 (*0-688-12257-4*, Tambourine Bks) Morrow.

Alpern, Lynne & Blumenfeld, Esther. In-Laws, Out-Laws & Other Theories of Relativity. Warlick, Cal, illus. 128p. (Orig.). 1990. pap. 6.95 (*0-934601-94-1*) Peachtree Pubs.

Amery & Adair. Jokes & Tricks. (gr. 4-6). 1977. pap. 6.95 (*0-86020-034-5*, Usborne-Hayes) EDC.

Appleton, C. M. Yuk It up with Urkel! (ps-3). 1992. pap. 2.95 (*0-590-45745-4*) Scholastic Inc.

Arnold, Tedd. No More Water in the Tub! LC 93-33741. 1995. write for info. (*0-8037-1581-1*); PLB write for info. (*0-8037-1583-8*) Dial Bks Young.

Artell, Mike. The Wackiest Ecology Riddles on Earth. LC 91-45773. (Illus.). 96p. (gr. 3-8). 1992. 12.95 (*0-8069-1250-2*) Sterling.

Atwater, Richard. Mr. Popper's Penguins. (gr. 4-7). 1992. pap. 1.99 (*0-440-21370-3*) Dell.

Atwater, Richard & Atwater, Florence. Mr. Popper's Penguins: A Pop-Up Book. Williams, Karin, illus. LC 92-53195. 1993. 16.95 (*0-316-05844-0*) Little.

Ball, Duncan. Emily Eyefinger & the Lost Treasure. Ulrich, George, illus. LC 93-39648. (gr. 2-5). 1994. 13.00 (*0-671-86535-8*, S&S BFYR) S&S Trade.

Barry, Sheila A., ed. Kids' Funniest Jokes. Sinclair, Jeff, illus. LC 93-23045. 96p. (gr. 2-10). 1994. 12.95 (*0-8069-0449-6*); pap. 3.95 (*0-8069-0448-8*) Sterling.

Barton, Byron. Buzz, Buzz, Buzz. 1st ed. LC 93-46931. 1995. pap. 4.95 (*0-689-71873-X*, Aladdin) Macmillan Child Grp.

Batchelor, C. Fun, Magic & Jokes. (Illus.). 32p. (gr. 2-6). 1985. pap. 5.95 (*0-88625-072-2*) Durkin Hayes Pub.

Baum, L. Frank. The Woggle-Bug Book. LC 78-6887. (gr. 1-6). 1978. Repr. of 1905 ed. 50.00x (*0-8201-1308-5*) Schol Facsimiles.

Bazaldua, Barbara. Walt Disney's Goofy Joke Book. Baker, Darrell, illus. 24p. (ps-3). 1993. pap. 1.95 (*0-307-12683-8*, 12683, Golden Pr) Western Pub.

Benny, Mike. The World's Punniest Joke Book. Hoffman, Sanford, illus. LC 92-42578. 96p. 1993. 12.95 (*0-8069-8544-5*) Sterling.

Berger, Melvin. Hundred & One Nature Jokes. (gr. 4-7). 1994. pap. 1.95 (*0-590-47763-3*) Scholastic Inc.

—One Hundred & One Spooky Halloween Jokes. (gr. 4-7). 1993. pap. 1.95 (*0-590-47143-0*) Scholastic Inc.

—One Hundred & One Wacky Science Jokes. 1989. pap. 1.95 (*0-590-42388-6*) Scholastic Inc.

—One Hundred & One Wacky State Jokes. 1991. pap. 1.95 (*0-590-44487-5*) Scholastic Inc.

—One Hundred One President Jokes. 1990. pap. 1.95 (*0-590-43166-8*) Scholastic Inc.

Bernstein, Joanne E. & Cohen, Paul. Dizzy Doctor Riddles. Tucker, Kathy, ed. Whiting, Carl, illus. LC 89-35392. 32p. (gr. 1-5). 1989. 8.95 (*0-8075-1648-1*) A Whitman.

—Out to Pasture! Jokes about Cows. Hanson, Joan, illus. 32p. (gr. 1-4). 1988. PLB 11.95 (*0-8225-0998-9*) Lerner Pubns.

—Why Didn't the Dinosaur Cross the Road? And Other Prehistoric Riddles. Tucker, Kathy, ed. Whiting, Carl, illus. LC 90-12726. 32p. (gr. 2-5). 1990. 8.95 (*0-8075-9077-0*) A Whitman.

Bianchi, J. Bushmen Brouhaha. (Illus.). 24p. (ps-8). 1987. 12.95 (*0-921285-10-8*, Pub. by Bungalo Bks CN); pap. 4.95 (*0-921285-08-6*, Pub. by Bungalo Bks CN) Firefly Bks Ltd.

Birchman, David F. A Tale of Tulips, a Tale of Onions. Hunt, Jonathan, illus. LC 92-31240. 40p. (gr. 1-4). 1994. RSBE 15.95 (*0-02-710112-6*, Four Winds) Macmillan Child Grp.

Birdseye, Tom. A Regular Flood of Mishap. Loyd, Megan, illus. LC 93-9888. 32p. (ps-3). 1994. reinforced bdg. 15.95 (*0-8234-1070-6*) Holiday.

Bixenman, Judy. Dinosaur Jokes. (Illus.). 32p. (gr. 1-4). 1991. 13.95 (*0-89565-728-7*) Childs World.

Black, Sonia. Laugh-A-Minute Joke Book. (gr. 4up). 1989. pap. 1.95 (*0-590-42154-9*) Scholastic Inc.

—One Hundred One Outer Space Jokes. 1990. pap. 1.95 (*0-590-42972-8*) Scholastic Inc.

Blume, Judy. Superfudge. 176p. (gr. 2-6). 1981. pap. 3.99 (*0-440-48433-2*, YB) Dell.

Bolton, Martha. T. V. Jokes & Riddles. LC 91-25297. (Illus.). 96p. (gr. 3-10). 1991. 12.95 (*0-8069-7244-0*) Sterling.

—TV Jokes & Riddles. Sinclair, Jeff, illus. LC 91-25297. 96p. 1992. pap. 3.95 (*0-8069-7246-7*) Sterling.

Bonham, Tal D. The Treasury of Clean Jokes for Children. (Orig.). (gr. 1-6). 1987. pap. 3.99 (*0-8054-5721-6*) Broadman.

Border, Rosy, ed. Jokes, Jokes & More Jokes. Green, Barry, illus. 48p. (gr. 3-6). 1992. pap. 2.95 (*1-56680-002-1*) Mad Hatter Pub.

Brandeth, Gyles. The Emergency Excuses Kit, 4 bks. Brown, Judy, illus. (gr. 2-5). 1992. Boxed Set. pap. 4.50 (*0-14-034832-8*) Puffin Bks.

—The Emergency Joke Kit. Brown, Judy, illus. (Orig.). (ps-3). 1988. pap. 3.95 (*0-14-095322-1*, Puffin) Puffin Bks.

Brandreth, Gyles. The Super Joke Book. Barrenger, Nick, illus. LC 83-397. 128p. (gr. 3 up). 1985. 12.95 (*0-8069-4672-5*); pap. 3.95 (*0-8069-6200-3*) Sterling.

Breathed, Berkeley. The Last Basselope: One Ferocious Story. LC 92-14467. (Illus.). 1992. 14.95 (*0-316-10761-1*) Little.

Brill, Michael E. Bamboozled. (Orig.). (gr. 6 up). 1985. pap. 4.50 (*0-87602-240-9*) Anchorage.
Brown, Kenneth. Barn House Book: Rhymes, Riddles, & Jokes. Brown, Kenneth, illus. Date not set. 12.95 (*1-56743-046-5*) Amistad Pr.
Brown, Marc T. Spooky Riddles. LC 83-6051. (Illus.). 48p. (gr. k-3). 1983. 6.95 (*0-394-86093-4*) Beginner.
Brown, Mary K. Let's Go Camping with Mr. Sillypants. LC 94-15991. 1995. write for info. (*0-517-59773-X*); PLB write for info. (*0-517-59774-8*) Crown Pub Group.
Browne, Dik. Hagar the Horrible: Pillage Idiot. 128p. (Orig.). 1986. pap. 1.95 (*0-8125-6788-9*, Dist. by Warner Pub Services & Saint Martin's Press) Tor Bks.
Bunting, Eve. Nasty Stinky Sneakers. LC 93-34641. 128p. (gr. 4-7). 1994. 14.00 (*0-06-024236-1*); PLB 13.89 (*0-06-024237-X*) HarpC Child Bks.
Burgess, Gelett. Goop Tales. (Illus.). (gr. 4-8). 17.75 (*0-8446-4717-9*) Peter Smith.
Burns, Diane & Burns, Clint. Hail to the Chief! Jokes about the Presidents. Hanson, Joan, illus. 32p. (gr. 1-4). 1989. 11.95 (*0-8225-0971-7*, First Ave Edns); pap. 2.95 (*0-8225-9561-3*, First Ave Edns) Lerner Pubns.
Burns, Diane L. Elephants Never Forget! A Book of Elephant Jokes. (Illus.). 32p. (gr. 1-4). 1987. pap. 2.95 (*0-8225-9518-4*, First Ave Edns) Lerner Pubns.
—Snakes Alive! Jokes about Snakes. Hanson, Joan, illus. (gr. 1-4). 1988. PLB 11.95 (*0-8225-0996-2*, First Ave Edns); pap. 2.95 (*0-8225-9543-5*, First Ave Edns) Lerner Pubns.
Calmenson, Stephanie. One Hundred One Silly Summertime Jokes. 1989. pap. 1.95 (*0-590-42556-0*) Scholastic Inc.
Carkeet, David. Quiver River. LC 90-24095. 224p. (gr. 7 up). 1991. HarpC Child Bks.
Carson, Jo. Pulling My Leg. Downing, Julie, illus. LC 89-70978. 32p. (ps-2). 1994. pap. 5.95 (*0-531-07046-8*) Orchard Bks Watts.
Cebulash, Mel. Rattler. (gr. 3-8). 1992. PLB 8.95 (*0-89565-880-1*) Childs World.
Cecil, Laura. Preposterous Pets. Clark, Emma C., photos by. LC 94-6527. (Illus.). 80p. 1995. write for info. RTE (*0-688-13581-1*) Greenwillow.
Cerf, Bennett A. Bennett Cerf's Book of Laughs. LC 59-13387. (Illus.). 72p. (gr. 1-2). 1959. lib. bdg. 7.99 (*0-394-90011-1*) Beginner.
Chmielewski, Gary. Animal Jokes. Clark, Ron G., illus. LC 86-17684. (gr. 2-3). 1986. 13.27 (*0-86592-687-5*); 9.95s.p. (*0-685-58362-7*) Rourke Corp.
—Sports Jokes. Clark, Ron G., illus. (gr. 2-3). 1986. 13.27 (*0-86592-683-2*); lib. bdg. 9.95 (*0-685-58364-3*) Rourke Corp.
—Why Do Bees Hum: And 265 Other Great Jokes for Kids. 1990. 6.99 (*0-517-02536-1*) Random Hse Value.
Clifford, Eth. Flatfoot Fox & the Case of the Missing Whoooo. Lies, Brian, illus. LC 92-21903. 1993. 13.95 (*0-395-65364-9*) HM.
Coco, Eugene. Jokes & Riddles. Jarka, Jeff, illus. 24p. (ps-2). 1993. pap. text ed. 0.99 (*1-56293-350-7*) McClanahan Bk.
Cole, Babette. The Trouble with Uncle. (Illus.). (ps-3). 1992. 14.95 (*0-316-15190-4*) Little.
Cole, Joanna. Get Well, Clown-Arounds. (Illus.). 42p. (ps-3). 1993. PLB 13.27 (*0-8368-0895-9*); PLB 13.26 s.p. (*0-685-61526-X*) Gareth Stevens Inc.
Cole, Joanna & Calmenson, Stephanie. Why Did the Chicken Cross the Road? And Other Riddles, Old & New. LC 94-2582. (gr. 3 up). 1994. write for info. (*0-688-12202-7*); PLB write for info. (*0-688-12203-5*) Morrow Jr Bks.
Cole, Ronny M. Zany Knock Knocks. Garramone, Rich, illus. LC 92-43068. 96p. (gr. 2-7). 1993. pap. 3.95 (*0-8069-8589-5*) Sterling.
Conford, Ellen. Dear Mom, Get Me Out of Here! LC 92-438. 1992. 14.95 (*0-316-15370-2*) Little.
—I Love You, I Hate You, Get Lost. LC 93-8588. 176p. 1994. 13.95 (*0-590-45558-3*) Scholastic Inc.
Cooke, Trish. Mr. Pam Pam & the Hullabazoo. Aggs, Patrice, illus. LC 93-32382. 32p. (ps up). 1994. 14.95 (*1-56402-411-3*) Candlewick Pr.
Corbett, Scott. Jokes to Tell to Your Worst Enemy. Gusman, Annie, illus. LC 83-16564. 80p. (gr. 2-6). 1984. 10.95 (*0-525-44082-8*, DCB) Dutton Child Bks.
Corrin, Sara & Corrin, Sara, eds. A Time to Laugh: Funny Stories for Children. (Illus.). 142p. (ps). 1991. pap. 3.95 (*0-571-15499-9*) Faber & Faber.
Coville, Bruce. Space Brat. MacDonald, Pat, ed. Coville, Katherine, illus. 1993. 12.00 (*0-671-87059-9*, Minstrel Bks) PB.
—Space Brat Two: Blork's Evil Twin. Coville, Bruce, illus. 80p. (Orig.). (gr. 2-4). 1993. 12.00 (*0-671-87038-6*, Minstrel Bks); pap. 3.50 (*0-671-77713-0*, Minstrel Bks) PB.
—Space Brat 3: The Wrath of Squat. Coville, Katherine, illus. LC 93-50602. 1994. 3.50 (*0-671-86844-6*, Minstrel bks) PB.
Crazy Classroom Dictionary. 64p. (Orig.). 1994. pap. 2.99 (*0-8125-9432-0*) Tor Bks.
Crumble, Mortimer. Madison Squid & the Ghost of Slapstick: Hilarious Children's Books for Grown-ups. D'Souza, Edgar, illus. LC 93-79348. 144p. 1994. 19.95 (*0-9636606-1-6*) Streetlight Bks.
Dahl, Roald. Matilda. LC 94-5864. 1994. 12.95 (*0-679-43651-0*, Evrymans Lib Childs) Knopf.
—The Vicar of Nibbleswicke. Blake, Quentin, illus. 24p. 1992. 12.50 (*0-670-84384-9*) Viking Child Bks.
Dahl, Roald & Tannen, Mary. The Twits. Burgoyne, John, illus. LC 80-18410. (ps-5). 1981. 12.00 (*0-394-84599-4*); lib. bdg. 12.99 (*0-394-94599-9*) Knopf Bks Yng Read.
DeGroat, Diane. Annie Pitts, Swamp Monster. LC 93-2474. 1994. pap. 13.00 (*0-671-87004-1*, S&S BFYR) S&S Trade.
Denim, Sue. The Dumb Bunnies. Pilkey, Dav, illus. LC 93-2255. 32p. (ps-3). 1994. 12.95 (*0-590-47708-0*, Blue Sky Press) Scholastic Inc.
Dodds, Dayle A. Wheel Away! Hurd, Thacher, illus. LC 87-27091. 32p. (ps-1). 1989. PLB 14.89 (*0-06-021689-1*) HarpC Child Bks.
Donaldson, Julia. A Squash & a Squeeze. Scheffler, Axel, illus. LC 92-16507. 32p. (ps-3). 1993. SBE 14.95 (*0-689-50571-X*, M K McElderry) Macmillan Child Grp.
Driver, Raymond. Animalimericks. 1994. pap. 5.95 (*0-671-87232-X*, Half Moon Bks) S&S Trade.
Dr. Seuss. Bartholomew & the Oobleck. Dr. Seuss, illus. (gr. k-3). 1949. 12.00 (*0-394-80075-3*); lib. bdg. 12.99 (*0-394-90075-8*) Random Bks Yng Read.
—Daisy-Head Mayzie. Dr. Seuss, illus. LC 94-11349. 1995. 15.00 (*0-679-86712-0*) Random.
—King's Stilts. Dr. Seuss, illus. (gr. k-3). 1939. 9.95 (*0-394-80082-6*); lib. bdg. 9.99 (*0-394-90082-0*) Random Bks Yng Read.
—Mr. Brown Can Moo! Can You? - The Foot Book, 2 bks. reissue ed. Dr. Seuss, illus. (ps-1). 1991. Set, 32p. ea. incl. 2 20-min. cassette 8.95 (*0-679-82036-1*) Random Bks Yng Read.
Dudley, Dick & Kong, Emilie. When Are Pteranodons Sad? (Illus.). 12p. (ps-2). 1992. 5.95 (*1-56288-180-9*) Checkerboard.
—Why Does an Apatosaurus Get Its Way? (Illus.). 12p. 1992. 5.95 (*1-56288-181-7*) Checkerboard.
Eckstein, Joan & Gleit, Joyce. The Best Joke Book for Kids, No. 1. Behr, J., illus. 48p. (gr. 7-12). 1977. pap. 2.99 (*0-380-01734-2*, Camelot) Avon.
—The Best Joke Book for Kids, No. 2. Kohl, Joe, illus. 64p. (gr. 3 up). 1987. pap. 2.99 (*0-380-75209-3*, Camelot) Avon.
—The Best Joke Book for Kids, No. 3. 64p. 1990. pap. 3.50 (*0-380-75872-5*, Camelot) Avon.
—The Best Joke Book for Kids, No. 4. 64p. (Orig.). 1991. pap. 2.95 (*0-380-76263-3*, Camelot) Avon.
Edens, Cooper. If You're Afraid of the Dark, Remember the Night Rainbow. Edens, Cooper, illus. LC 91-15823. 1991. 13.00 (*0-671-74952-8*, Green Tiger) S&S Trade.
Ehrlich, Amy. Parents in the Pigpen, Pigs in the Tub. Kellogg, Steven, illus. LC 91-15601. 40p. (ps-3). 1993. 14.99 (*0-8037-0933-1*); lib. bdg. 14.89 (*0-8037-0928-5*) Dial Bks Young.
Eisenberg, Lisa. Brain Builders...Not! (gr. 4-7). 1993. pap. 1.95 (*0-590-47295-X*) Scholastic Inc.
Eisenberg, Lisa & Hall, Katy. One Hundred One Ghost Jokes. Orehek, Don, illus. (ps up). 1988. pap. 1.95 (*0-590-41811-4*) Scholastic Inc.
Eisneberg, Lisa. More Quickie Comebacks. (gr. 4-7). 1994. pap. 1.95 (*0-590-47296-8*) Scholastic Inc.
Epaminondas. 24p. (ps-3). 1989. 2.25 (*1-56288-163-9*) Checkerboard.
Erickson, John. The Case of the Missing Cat: Discover the Land of Enchantment. (Illus.). 144p. 1990. 11.95 (*0-87719-186-7*); pap. 6.95 (*0-87719-185-9*); 2 cass. 15.95 (*0-87719-187-5*) Gulf Pub.
Erickson, John R. The Case of the Car-Barkaholic Dog. (Illus.). 118p. 1991. 11.95 (*0-87719-198-0*, 9198); pap. 6.95 (*0-87719-199-9*, 9199); incls. 2 cass. 15.95 (*0-87719-200-6*) Gulf Pub.
—Hank the Cowdog: The Case of the Hooking Bull, No. 18. 118p. 1992. 11.95 (*0-87719-213-8*); pap. 6.95 (*0-87719-212-X*); 2 cassettes 15.95 (*0-87719-214-6*) Gulf Pub.
Erkel, Cynthia R. The Farmhouse Mouse. Erkel, Michael, illus. LC 92-27040. 32p. (ps-3). 1994. PLB 14.95 (*0-399-22444-0*, Putnam) Putnam Pub Group.
Ertner, James D. Super Silly Animal Riddles. Sinclair, Jeff, illus. LC 92-41919. 96p. 1993. 12.95 (*0-8069-0333-3*) Sterling.
Euvremer, Teryl. Triple Whammy. Euvremer, Teryl, illus. LC 91-44240. 32p. (gr. k-4). 1993. 15.00 (*0-06-021060-5*); PLB 14.89 (*0-06-021061-3*) HarpC Child Bks.
Feehan, Mary. Book of Children's Jokes. 1990. pap. 5.95 (*0-85342-495-0*) Dufour.
Fidell. More Silly Signs. 1992. pap. 1.95 (*0-590-44837-4*) Scholastic Inc.
Fine, Anne. The True Story of Harrowing Farm. Fisher, Cynthia, illus. LC 92-33935. 1993. 12.95 (*0-316-28316-9*, Joy St Bks) Little.
Fitzgerald, Frank. Where's Kevin? LC 92-33058. (gr. 4-7). 1992. pap. 7.99 (*0-553-37199-1*) Bantam.
Fitzgerald, John D. Me & My Little Brain. Mayer, Mercer, illus. LC 71-153732. (gr. 4-7). 1985. PLB 11.89 (*0-8037-5532-5*) Dial Bks Young.
Fleischman, Sid. Here Comes McBroom. Blake, Quentin, illus. LC 91-32689. 80p. (gr. 1 up). 1992. 14.00 (*0-688-11160-2*) Greenwillow.
—McBroom's Wonderful One-Acre Farm. Blake, Quentin, illus. LC 91-31906. 64p. (gr. 1 up). 1992. 14.00 (*0-688-11159-9*) Greenwillow.
Gackenbach, Dick. Supposes. Gackenbach, Dick, illus. 103p. (ps-3). 1989. 12.95 (*0-15-200594-3*, Gulliver Bks) HarBrace.
Gallant, Morrie. The Nuttiest Riddle Book in the World. Hoffman, Sanford, illus. LC 93-7871. 96p. (gr. 2-10). 1993. 12.95 (*0-8069-0420-8*) Sterling.
Gamiello, Elvira. Silly Jokes & Riddles. (Illus.). 96p. (Orig.). 1988. pap. 1.95 (*0-942025-32-6*) Kidsbks.
Gantos, Jack. Heads or Tails: Stories from the Sixth Grade. LC 93-43117. 1994. 16.00 (*0-374-32909-5*) FS&G.
Garfield, Leon. The Saracen Maid. O'Brien, John, illus. LC 93-6612. (gr. 1-4). 1994. pap. 14.00 (*0-671-86646-X*, S&S BFYR) S&S Trade.
Gedye, Jane. Dinner's Ready! A Pig's Book of Table Manners. 1989. 9.95 (*0-385-26083-0*) Doubleday.
George, Barbara. The Popples' Book of Jokes & Riddles. Henry, Barb, illus. LC 86-62222. 32p. (ps-3). 1987. pap. 1.25 (*0-394-88757-3*) Random Bks Yng Read.
Geronimi, Clyde. Chips Quips. Geronimi, Clyde, illus. LC 83-72694. 55p. (gr. 4 up). 1983. pap. 3.95 (*0-939126-09-5*) Back Bay.
Gibson, Andrew. The Rollickers & Other Stories. (Illus.). 160p. (gr. 3 up). 1993. 15.95 (*0-571-16687-3*) Faber & Faber.
Gleitzman, Morris. Misery Guts. LC 92-22570. 1993. 12.95 (*0-15-254768-1*) HarBrace.
—Worry Warts. LC 92-22631. 1993. 12.95 (*0-15-299666-4*) HarBrace.
Golly Gump Swallowed a Fly. (Illus.). 42p. (ps-3). 1992. PLB 13.27 (*0-8368-0881-9*); PLB 13.26 s.p. (*0-685-61514-6*) Gareth Stevens Inc.
Goodman, Beth. The Norfin Trolls Laugh Out Loud. (Illus.). 1992. 2.50 (*0-590-45925-2*, 046) Scholastic Inc.
Gounaud, Karen J. A Very Mice Joke Book. Munsinger, Lynn, illus. (gr. 2-5). 1981. HM.
Graham, Carolyn. The Electric Elephant & Other Stories. (Illus., Orig.). (gr. 7-12). 1982. pap. text ed. 7.95x (*0-19-503229-2*) OUP.
Greene, Constance C. Odds on Oliver. Schindler, Stephen D., illus. LC 92-25932. 64p. (gr. 2-5). 1993. PLB 12.99 (*0-670-84549-3*) Viking Child Bks.
Grossman, Bill. Cowboy Ed. Wint, Florence, illus. LC 92-23393. 32p. (ps-2). 1993. 15.00 (*0-06-021570-4*); PLB 14.89 (*0-06-021571-2*) HarpC Child Bks.
Hall, Kathy. One Hundred One Cat & Dog Jokes. 1990. pap. 1.95 (*0-590-43336-9*) Scholastic Inc.
Hall, Katy & Eisenberg, Lisa. Bunny Riddles. Rubel, Nicole, illus. LC 93-13241. (ps-4). 1995. write for info. (*0-8037-1519-6*); PLB write for info. (*0-8037-1521-8*) Dial Bks Young.
—One Hundred One School Jokes. Orehek, Don, illus. 96p. (gr. 4-7). 1987. pap. 1.95 (*0-590-41182-9*) Scholastic Inc.
—Sheepish Riddles. Alley, Robert, illus. LC 93-32212. 1995. write for info. (*0-8037-1535-8*); lib. bdg. write for info. (*0-8037-1536-6*) Dial Bks Young.
—Spacey Riddles. LC 90-42508. (Illus.). 48p. (ps-3). 1992. 11.00 (*0-8037-0814-9*); PLB 10.89 (*0-8037-0815-7*) Dial Bks Young.
Hall, Lynn. Dagmar Schultz & the Green-Eyed Monster. LC 90-43524. 80p. (gr. 5-8). 1991. SBE 13.95 (*0-684-19254-3*, Scribners Young Read) Macmillan Child Grp.
Hample, Stoo. Stoo Hample's Silly Joke Book. LC 78-50431. (Illus.). (gr. 1-6). 1978. pap. 5.47 (*0-440-08160-2*); pap. 2.50 (*0-440-08154-8*) Delacorte.
Hartman, Victoria. The Silliest Joke Book Ever. Alley, R. W., photos by. LC 92-22161. (Illus.). 1993. 14.00 (*0-688-10109-7*); lib. bdg. 13.93 (*0-688-10110-0*) Lothrop.
Hartman, Victoria G. The Silly Joke Book. Orehek, Don, illus. 96p. (gr. 4-6). 1987. pap. 1.95 (*0-590-33846-3*) Scholastic Inc.
—Westward Ho, Ho, Ho. Karas, G. Brian, illus. 48p. (gr. 2-6). 1994. pap. 3.99 (*0-14-036851-5*) Puffin Bks.
Hawkins, Colin & Hawkins, Jacqui. Knock! Knock! Hawkins, Colin & Hawkins, Jacqui, illus. LC 91-17313. 28p. 1991. pap. 14.95 POB (*0-689-71475-0*, Aladdin) Macmillan Child Grp.
Hawthorn, P. Jokes. (Illus.). 64p. (gr. 2-5). 1992. pap. 7.95 (*0-7460-0724-8*, Usborne) EDC.
—Silly Jokes. (Illus.). 32p. (gr. 2-5). 1991. PLB 12.96 (*0-88110-532-5*, Usborne); pap. 4.95 (*0-7460-0612-8*, Usborne) EDC.
Hayes, Frederick & Hayes, Jean. The Chile Pot. 1988. 6.95 (*0-925605-00-X*) Pinto Pub.
Hemp, Kevin. Just Hogweed. Hemp, Kevin, illus. 128p. (Orig.). (gr. 9-12). 1988. pap. 4.95 (*0-9622059-0-7*, VA-U-105-990) Wise Guys Pub.
Herman. Max Malone Million. 1992. 13.95 (*0-8050-2332-1*) H Holt & Co.
Herman, Charlotte. Max Malone the Magnificent. Smith, Cat B., illus. LC 92-14123. 64p. (gr. 2-4). 1993. 14.95 (*0-8050-2282-1*, Bks Young Read) H Holt & Co.
Hillman, Ben. That Pesky Toaster. LC 94-9831. 1995. write for info. (*0-7868-0033-X*); PLB write for info. (*0-7868-2028-4*) Hyprn Child.
Himmelman, John. A Guest Is a Guest. Himmelman, John, illus. LC 90-43020. 32p. (ps-2). 1991. 13.95 (*0-525-44720-2*, DCB) Dutton Child Bks.
Hinds, Bill. Buzz Beamer's Radical Olympics. Hinds, Bill, illus. 32p. (gr. 3-7). 1992. pap. 4.95 (*0-316-36452-5*, Spts Illus Kids) Little.
Hirsch, Phil. One Hundred & One Hamburger Jokes. 96p. (gr. 4-7). 1986. pap. 1.95 (*0-590-40374-5*) Scholastic Inc.
Hirsch, Phil & Hirsch, Hope. One Hundred & One Pet Jokes. Eaton, Tom, illus. 96p. (Orig.). (gr. 3-7). 1981. pap. 1.95 (*0-590-30380-5*, Schol Pap) Scholastic Inc.

Hirsh, Phil. One Hundred One Fast Funny Food Jokes. Orehek, Don, illus. 96p. (Orig.). (gr. 4-6). 1987. pap. 1.95 (*0-590-32421-7*) Scholastic Inc.

Hodgman, Ann & Marx, Patty. How to Survive Junior High. Dolobowsky, Mena, illus. LC 93-40968. 160p. (gr. 3-6). 1994. pap. 2.95 (*0-8167-3033-4*) Troll Assocs.

Hoff, Syd. Syd Hoff's Animal Jokes. Hoff, Syd, illus. LC 84-48353. 48p. (gr. k-3). 1986. (Lipp Jr Bks) HarpC Child Bks.

Hughes, Langston. Black Misery. Arouni, illus. Jackson, Jesse & O'Meally, Robert G.intro. by. (Illus.). 64p. 1994. 12.95 (*0-19-509114-0*) OUP.

Hunter, Tammy. Chuckle Mountain. Williams, Harland, illus. 64p. (Orig.). (gr. 3-6). 1992. pap. 2.95 (*0-88625-280-6*) Durkin Hayes Pub.

Jerome, Jerome K. Sense & Nonsense. 208p. (gr. 7-8). 1991. pap. 8.00 (*0-86299-922-7*) A Sutton Pub.

Jillette, Penn & Teller. Penn & Teller's How to Play with Your Food. LC 92-50150. 1992. pap. 20.00 (*0-679-74311-1*, Villard Bks) Random.

Johnson, Crockett. Who's Upside Down? LC 89-28059. (Illus.). 32p. (ps-3). 1990. Repr. of 1952 ed. lib. bdg. 15.00 (*0-208-02276-7*, Pub. by Linnet) Shoe String.

Johnson, Stephanie. Confused Quarterbacks, Jumpy Gymnasts, & Other Sports Jokes. (Orig.). 1994. pap. 3.99 (*0-8125-2052-1*) Tor Bks.

Johnstone, Michael. One Thousand What's What Jokes for Kids. (gr. k up). 1987. pap. 3.95 (*0-345-34654-8*) Ballantine.

Jolly Jester. 8p. (gr. k-3). 1992. pap. 3.95 (*1-56680-602-X*) Mad Hatter Pub.

Juster, Norman. Otter Nonsense. Witte, Michael, illus. LC 93-22041. (gr. 3 up). 1994. write for info. (*0-688-12282-5*); PLB write for info. (*0-688-12283-3*) Morrow Jr Bks.

Kallen, Stuart A. Ridiculous Riddles. LC 92-14772. 1992. 12.94 (*1-56239-126-7*) Abdo & Dghtrs.

—Silly Stories. LC 92-14773. 1992. 12.94 (*1-56239-132-1*) Abdo & Dghtrs.

Keller, Charles. Ballpoint Bananas & Other Jokes for Kids. Barrios, David, illus. LC 72-7338. 96p. (gr. 3-7). 1976. pap. 5.95 (*0-671-66965-6*, S&S BFYR) S&S Trade.

—Belly Laughs! Food Jokes & Riddles. Fritz, Ron, illus. LC 89-28201. 32p. (gr. k-3). 1990. (S&S BFYR); pap. 5.95 (*0-671-70069-3*, S&S BFYR) S&S Trade.

—Driving Me Crazy: Fun on Wheels Jokes. Lorenz, Lee, illus. 40p. (gr. 2-5). 1989. 13.95 (*0-945912-05-6*) Pippin Pr.

—Giggle Puss: Pet Jokes for Kids. Coker, Paul, Jr., illus. LC 76-44837. (gr. 3-7). 1979. (Pub. by Treehouse) P-H.

—It's Raining Cats & Dogs: Cat & Dog Jokes. Quackenbush, Robert, illus. 40p. (gr. 2-6). 1988. 13.95 (*0-945912-01-3*) Pippin Pr.

—Planet of the Grapes: Show Biz Jokes & Riddles. Richter, Mischa, illus. 40p. (gr. 3-7). 1992. 13.95 (*0-945912-17-X*) Pippin Pr.

—Waiter, There's a Fly in My Soup. (gr. 4-7). 1991. pap. 2.95 (*0-671-73982-4*, S&S BFYR) S&S Trade.

Keller, Charles, compiled by. Going Bananas: Jokes for Kids. Wilson, Roger B., illus. (gr. 2-5). 1977. 8.95 (*0-13-357772-4*, Pub. by Treehouse) P-H.

—Lend Me Your Ears: Telephone Jokes. Kessler, Leonard, illus. 40p. (gr. 2-5). 1994. PLB 13.95 (*0-945912-23-4*) Pippin Pr.

—More Ballpoint Bananas. Shortall, Leonard, illus. LC 77-5356. (gr. 1-3). 1980. 7.95 (*0-13-600767-8*, Pub. by Treehouse) P-H.

Kendall, Benjamin. Alien Invasions. Thatch, Nancy R., ed. Kendall, Benjamin, illus. Melton, David, intro. by. LC 93-13423. (Illus.). 29p. (gr. 2-4). 1993. PLB 14.95 (*0-933849-42-7*) Landmark Edns.

Kent, Robert. Gross-Out Jokes: To Make You Heave, Barf, Loose Your Lunch - & Laugh Like a Fool! Weller, Wesla, illus. 96p. (gr. 3-7). 1994. pap. 4.95 (*1-56565-132-4*) Lowell Hse.

Kessler, Leonard. Old Turtle's Ninety Knock-Knocks, Jokes, & Riddles. (Illus.). 48p. (gr. 1 up). 1993. pap. 4.95 (*0-688-04586-3*, Mulberry) Morrow.

—Old Turtle's Riddle & Joke Book. (gr. k-6). 1990. pap. 2.95 (*0-440-40268-9*, YB) Dell.

Kilgarriff, Michael. Oh No! Not Another One Thousand Jokes for Kids. (gr. k up). 1987. pap. 3.95 (*0-345-34035-3*) Ballantine.

—One Thousand Jokes for Kids of All Ages. (gr. k up). 1986. pap. 4.99 (*0-345-33480-9*) Ballantine.

—One Thousand More Jokes for Kids. (gr. k up). 1987. pap. 4.99 (*0-345-34034-5*) Ballantine.

King, Colin. Amazing Book of Jokes. 32p. 1990. 3.50 (*0-517-69192-2*) Random Hse Value.

King Wingnut. 8p. (gr. 1-3). 1992. pap. 3.95 (*1-56680-600-3*) Mad Hatter Pub.

Kline, Rufus. Watch Out for These Weirdos. Carlson, Nancy, illus. 32p. (ps-3). 1990. pap. 12.95 (*0-670-82376-7*) Viking Child Bks.

—Watch Out for These Weirdos! Carlson, Nancy, illus. 32p. (ps-3). 1992. pap. 3.99 (*0-14-050907-0*, Puffin) Puffin Bks.

Komaiko, Leah. Fritzi Fox Flew in from Florida. Hurd, Thacher, illus. LC 93-4754. Date not set. 15.00 (*0-06-021506-2*); PLB 14.89 (*0-06-021507-0*) HarpC Child Bks.

Korman, Gordon. The Toilet Paper Tigers. LC 92-27277. 1993. 13.95 (*0-590-46230-X*) Scholastic Inc.

—The Twinkie Squad. 1992. 13.95 (*0-590-45249-5*, Scholastic Hardcover) Scholastic Inc.

Kowitt, Holly. The Fenderbenders Get Lost in America... Again. (Illus.). 1992. 2.95 (*0-590-45891-4*, 048) Scholastic Inc.

Lando, Miriam. Funny Friday. 176p. 1992. write for info. CIS Comm.

Lattimore, Deborah N. Lady with the Ship on Her Head. 28p. (ps-3). 1990. 14.95 (*0-15-243525-5*) HarBrace.

Lee, Greg. Money. LC 92-44074. 1993. 12.67 (*0-86593-268-9*); 9.50s.p. (*0-685-66360-4*) Rourke Corp.

—School. LC 92-44073. (gr. 3 up). 1993. 12.67 (*0-86593-269-7*); 9.50s.p. (*0-685-66359-0*) Rourke Corp.

—Vacation. LC 92-45692. 1993. 12.67 (*0-86593-270-0*); 9.50s.p. (*0-685-66420-1*) Rourke Corp.

Lee, Greg, compiled by. Food: Wacky Words. LC 92-41730. (gr. 3 up). 1993. 12.67 (*0-86593-265-4*); 9.50s.p. (*0-685-66289-6*) Rourke Corp.

—Outer Space: Wacky Words. LC 92-43965. (gr. 3 up). 1993. 12.67 (*0-86593-267-0*); 9.50s.p. (*0-685-66292-6*) Rourke Corp.

—Pets: Wacky Words. LC 92-43964. (gr. 3 up). 1993. 12.67 (*0-86593-266-2*); 9.50s.p. (*0-685-66291-8*) Rourke Corp.

Leroe, Ellen. Leap Frog Friday. DeRosa, Dee, illus. LC 92-8284. 48p. (gr. 2-5). 1992. 12.00 (*0-525-67370-9*, Lodestar Bks) Dutton Child Bks.

LeSieg, Theo. I Wish That I Had Duck Feet. McKie, Roy, illus. 64p. (ps-1). 1988. bk. & cassette pkg. 6.95 (*0-394-89777-3*) Random Bks Yng Read.

Le Sieg, Theodore. Please Try to Remember the First of Octember. Cumings, Arthur, illus. LC 77-4504. 48p. (gr. 1-4). 1977. lib. bdg. 7.99 (*0-394-93563-2*) Beginner.

Levy, Elizabeth. Dracula Is a Pain in the Neck. Gerstein, Mordicai, illus. LC 82-47707. 80p. (gr. 2-5). 1984. pap. 3.95 (*0-06-440146-4*, Trophy) HarpC Child Bks.

Levy, Elizabeth, adapted by. Fat Albert & the Cosby Kids: Take Two, They're Small. (gr. 2 up). pap. 1.95 (*0-686-74491-8*, YB) Dell.

Lewis, Glenn A. Funny Things. Lewis, Glenn A., illus. 15p. (gr. k-3). 1992. pap. 4.95 (*1-895583-54-3*) MAYA Pubs.

Lewis, J. Patrick. Riddle-Icious. Roberts, Victoria, illus. LC 93-43759. 1995. 15.00 (*0-679-84011-7*); PLB write for info. (*0-679-94011-1*) Knopf.

Light, John. Dig That Hole! LC 91-39036. (gr. 5 up). 1991. 3.95 (*0-85953-503-7*) Childs Play.

—Race Ace Roger. LC 91-33417. (gr. 4 up). 1991. 3.95 (*0-85953-501-0*) Childs Play.

Lincoln, Abraham. Wisdom & Wit. (gr. 8 up). 1965. 6.95 (*0-88088-359-6*) Peter Pauper.

Lindgren, Barbro. Sam's Bath. Eriksson, Eva, illus. LC 83-724. 32p. (ps-k). 1983. 6.95 (*0-688-02362-2*) Morrow Jr Bks.

Little People Big Book about Silly Things. 64p. (ps-1). 1990. write for info. (*0-8094-7520-0*); PLB write for info. (*0-8094-7521-9*) Time-Life.

Lord. One Hundred One Thanksgiving Knock-Knocks, Jokes, & Riddles. 1993. pap. 1.95 (*0-590-47163-5*) Scholastic Inc.

Lots of Laughs Giant Jokes & Riddles. (Illus.). 278p. 1991. pap. 2.99 (*0-517-02235-4*) Random Hse Value.

Lowery, Linda. Twist with a Burger, Jitter with a Bug. Dypold, Pat, illus. LC 93-38236. 32p. 1994. 14.95g (*0-395-67022-5*) Ticknor & Fields.

Lowry, Lois. Anastasia at This Address. LC 90-48308. 112p. (gr. 3-7). 1991. 13.45 (*0-395-56263-5*) HM.

Lyon, George-Ella. The Outside Inn. Rosenberry, Vera, illus. LC 90-14285. 32p. (ps-1). 1991. 13.95 (*0-531-05936-7*); RLB 13.99 (*0-531-08536-8*) Orchard Bks Watts.

McCants, William D. Anything Can Happen in High School: And It Usually Does. LC 92-32982. 1993. write for info. (*0-15-276604-9*); pap. write for info. (*0-15-276605-7*) HarBrace.

McCloskey, Robert. Homer Price. (Illus.). (gr. 3-7). 1976. pap. 3.99 (*0-14-030927-6*, Puffin) Puffin Bks.

MacDonald, Betty. The Mrs. Piggle-Wiggle Treasury. Knight, Hilary, illus. LC 94-15040. 1994. 19.95 (*0-06-024812-2*); PLB 19.89 (*0-06-024813-0*) HarpC Child Bks.

McKay, Hilary. The Exiles. McKeating, Eileen, illus. LC 91-38220. 208p. (gr. 4-7). 1992. SBE 14.95 (*0-689-50555-8*, M K McElderry) Macmillan Child Grp.

—The Exiles at Home. LC 94-14225. (gr. 4-7). 1994. 15.95 (*0-689-50610-4*, M K McElderry) Macmillan Child Grp.

McNamara, Brooks. The Merry Muldoons & the Brighteyes Affair. LC 91-46923. 160p. (gr. 5-12). 1992. 14.95 (*0-531-05454-3*); PLB 14.99 (*0-531-08604-6*) Orchard Bks Watts.

Maguire, Gregory. Seven Spiders Spinning. LC 93-30478. 1994. 13.95 (*0-395-68965-1*, Clarion Bks) HM.

Mahy, Margaret. Bubble Trouble: And Other Poems & Stories. Mahy, Margaret, illus. LC 92-3540. 80p. (gr. 3-7). 1992. SBE 13.95 (*0-689-50557-4*, M K McElderry) Macmillan Child Grp.

—The Great Piratical Rumbustification & The Librarian & The Robbers. Blake, Quentin, illus. LC 92-43777. 64p. (gr. 5 up). 1993. pap. 3.95 (*0-688-12469-0*, Pub. by Beech Tree Bks) Morrow.

Marsh, Carole. How You Know When Your Tush Is Turf. 1994. PLB 24.95 (*0-7933-6924-X*); pap. text ed. 14.95 (*0-7933-6923-1*); disk 29.95 (*0-7933-6925-8*) Gallopade Pub Group.

—Life Isn't Fair: Murphy's Laws for Kids. (Illus.). (gr. 4-12). 1994. 14.95 (*0-935326-08-1*); PLB 24.95 (*0-7933-6916-9*) Gallopade Pub Group.

Marsh, James. From the Heart: Light-Hearted Verse. LC 92-17912. (Illus.). 32p. 1993. 6.99 (*0-8037-1449-1*) Dial Bks Young.

Marshall, James. The Cut-ups Carry On. LC 92-40721. (Illus.). 32p. (ps-3). 1993. pap. 4.99 (*0-14-050726-4*, Puffin) Puffin Bks.

—The Cut-Ups Crack Up. (Illus.). 32p. (ps-3). 1994. pap. 4.99 (*0-14-055318-5*) Puffin Bks.

Martin, Ann M. Ma & Pa Dracula. 128p. 1991. pap. 2.95 (*0-590-43828-X*) Scholastic Inc.

Martin, Prisha. The Poor People of England & Other Works. (Orig.). 1991. pap. write for info. (*1-879019-04-3*) Amer Edit Servs.

Mathews, Judith. Knock-Knock Knees & Funny Bones: Riddles for Every Body. (ps-3). 1993. 8.95 (*0-8075-4203-2*) A Whitman.

Mathews, Judith & Robinson, Fay. Oh, How Waffle! Riddles You Can Eat. Levine, Abby, ed. Whiting, Carl, illus. LC 92-13478. 32p. (gr. 1-4). 1992. 8.95g (*0-8075-5907-5*) A Whitman.

Matthews, Morgan. One Hundred Two Goofy Jokes. LC 91-35176. (Illus.). 64p. (gr. 2-6). 1992. pap. text ed. 2.95 (*0-8167-2697-3*) Troll Assocs.

—One Hundred Two Out of This World Jokes. Matthews, Morgan, illus. LC 91-45021. 64p. (gr. 2-6). 1992. pap. text ed. 2.95 (*0-8167-2789-9*) Troll Assocs.

—One Hundred Two School Cafeteria Jokes. LC 91-30055. (Illus.). 64p. (gr. 2-6). 1991. pap. text ed. 2.95 (*0-8167-2611-6*) Troll Assocs.

Mayer, Mercer. Little Critter's Joke Book. (ps-3). 1993. pap. 2.25 (*0-307-12790-7*, Golden Pr) Western Pub.

Mazer, Norma F. Mrs. Fish, Ape & Me, the Dump Queen. 144p. (Orig.). (gr. 4 up). 1981. pap. 3.50 (*0-380-69153-1*, Flare) Avon.

Merriam, Eve & Ho. The Hole Story. (gr. 3 up). 1995. 16.00 (*0-671-88353-4*, S&S BFYR) S&S Trade.

Messerly, Laura. The Weirdest, Wackiest, Craziest Practical Joke Book in the Universe. Tisserand, Rose-Ann & Huculak, Greg, illus. LC 90-24598. 96p. (gr. 2-10). 1991. pap. 3.95 (*0-8069-8258-6*) Sterling.

Michaels, Ski. One Hundred Two Animal Jokes. LC 91-30061. (Illus.). 64p. (gr. 2-6). 1991. pap. text ed. 2.95 (*0-8167-2613-2*) Troll Assocs.

—One Hundred Two Creepy, Crawly Bug Jokes. Michaels, Ski, illus. LC 91-42737. 64p. (gr. 2-6). 1992. pap. text ed. 2.95 (*0-8167-2745-7*) Troll Assocs.

Miller, Madge. OPQRS, Etc. (Orig.). (gr. 4 up). 1984. pap. 4.50 (*0-87602-246-8*) Anchorage.

Mooser, Stephen. That's So Funny, I Forgot to Laugh. (gr. k-6). 1990. pap. 2.99 (*0-440-40262-X*, YB) Dell.

Most, Bernard. Zoodles. 1992. write for info. (*0-15-299969-8*, HB Juv Bks) HarBrace.

Mulford, Philippa G. If It's Not Funny, Why Am I Laughing. LC 82-70321. 144p. (gr. 7 up). 1982. pap. 10.95 (*0-385-28441-1*) Delacorte.

Murray, Francis. World's Wildest Animal Jokes. LC 91-47701. (Illus.). 96p. (gr. 3-8). 1992. 12.95 (*0-8069-8538-0*) Sterling.

—World's Wildest Animal Jokes. Hoffman, Sanford, illus. 96p. (gr. 2-6). 1993. pap. 3.95 (*0-8069-8539-9*) Sterling.

Myers, Bill. My Life As a Broken Bungee Cord. (gr. 4-7). 1993. pap. 4.99 (*0-8499-3404-4*) Word Inc.

—My Life As a Tornado Test Target. (gr. 4-7). 1994. pap. 4.99 (*0-8499-3538-5*) Word Inc.

—My Life As Alien Monster Bait. (gr. 3-7). 1993. pap. 4.99 (*0-8499-3403-6*) Word Inc.

—My Life As Crocodile Junk Food. (gr. 3-7). 1993. pap. 4.99 (*0-8499-3405-2*) Word Inc.

—My Life As Dinosaur Dental Floss. (gr. 4-7). 1994. pap. 4.99 (*0-8499-3537-7*) Word Inc.

Nelson, Jeffrey. Monster Jokes & Riddles. (Illus.). 24p. (gr. 3 up). 1988. pap. 1.95 (*1-56288-342-9*) Checkerboard.

—Outerspace Jokes & Riddles Book. (Illus.). 24p. (gr. 3 up). 1988. pap. 1.95 (*1-56288-343-7*) Checkerboard.

Nelson, Jeffrey S. Animal Jokes & Riddles. Nelson, Jeffrey S., illus. LC 90-27676. 24p. (gr. 3 up). 1991. pap. 1.95 (*1-56288-016-0*) Checkerboard.

—Family Jokes & Riddles. Nelson, Jeffrey S., illus. 24p. (gr. 3 up). 1991. pap. 1.95 (*1-56288-015-2*) Checkerboard.

—Jungle Jokes & Riddles. Nelson, Jeffrey S., illus. 24p. (gr. 3 up). 1991. pap. 1.95 (*1-56288-017-9*) Checkerboard.

—Yucky Jokes & Riddles. Nelson, Jeffrey S., illus. 24p. (gr. 3 up). 1991. pap. 1.95 (*1-56288-014-4*) Checkerboard.

Nixon, Joan L. That's the Spirit, Claude. Pearson, Tracey C., illus. 32p. (ps-3). 1992. 13.00 (*0-670-83434-3*) Viking Child Bks.

Nordqvist, Sven. Festus & Mercury Go Camping. LC 92-43181. 1993. 18.95 (*0-87614-802-X*) Carolrhoda Bks.

O'Hare, Jeff, ed. Knee Slappers, Side Splitters & Tummy Ticklers: A Book of Riddles & Jokes. LC 91-76204. (Illus.). 48p. (ps-7). 1992. pap. 6.95 (*1-56397-019-8*) Boyds Mills Pr.

Olsen, Alfa-Betty & Efron, Marshall. Gabby the Shrew. Chast, Roz, illus. LC 92-31902. 1994. lib. bdg. write for info. (*0-679-94467-2*) Random.

Otfinoski, Steven. The Truth about Three Billy Goats Gruff. Barnes-Murphy, Rowan, illus. LC 93-42391. 32p. (gr. k-3). 1994. pap. text ed. 2.95 (*0-8167-3013-X*) Troll Assocs.

Owl Magazine Editors. Jokes & Riddles. (Illus.). 96p. (gr. 3 up). 1992. pap. 3.95 (*0-919872-85-9*, Pub. by Greey dePencier CN) Firefly Bks Ltd.
Palacios, Argentina. Peanut Butter, Apple Butter, Cinnamon Toast: Food Riddles for You to Guess. Mahan, Ben, illus. 24p. (ps-2). 1990. PLB 17.10 (*0-8172-3584-1*); PLB 10.95 pkg. of 3 (*0-685-58553-0*) Raintree Steck-V.
Palatini, Margie. Piggie Pie. Fine, Howard, illus. LC 94-19726. 1995. write for info. (*0-395-71691-8*) HM.
Pansini, Anna, ed. Great Riddles, Giggles & Jokes. Loh, Carolyn, illus. LC 89-5200. 48p. (gr. 2-6). 1990. PLB 8.59 (*0-8167-1915-2*); pap. text ed. 2.50 (*0-8167-1916-0*) Troll Assocs.
Parenteau. One Hundred Plus Super Pig Jokes, Puns, & Riddles. 1993. pap. 1.95 (*0-590-41656-1*) Scholastic Inc.
Parish, Peggy. Amelia Bedelia. Siebel, Fritz, illus. LC 91-10163. 64p. (gr. k-3). 1992. 14.00 (*0-06-020186-X*); PLB 13.89 (*0-06-020187-8*) HarpC Child Bks.
—Amelia Bedelia. Siebel, Fritz, illus. LC 91-10164. 64p. (gr. k-3). 1992. pap. 3.50 (*0-06-444155-5*, Trophy) HarpC Child Bks.
—Come Back, Amelia Bedelia. Tripp, Wallace, illus. LC 73-121799. 64p. (ps-3). 1971. 14.00 (*0-06-024667-7*); PLB 13.89 (*0-06-024668-5*) HarpC Child Bks.
—Thank You, Amelia Bedelia. newly illus ed. Thomas, Barbara, illus. LC 92-5746. 64p. (gr. k-3). 1993. 14.00 (*0-06-022979-9*); PLB 13.89 (*0-06-022980-2*) HarpC Child Bks.
Park, Barbara. Junie B. Jones & Some Sneaky Peeky Spying. Brunkus, Denise, illus. LC 93-5557. 80p. (Orig.). (gr. 1-4). 1994. PLB 9.99 (*0-679-95101-6*); pap. 2.99 (*0-679-85101-1*) Random Bks Yng Read.
Paulsen, Gary. Full of Hot Air: Launching, Floating High, & Landing. Heltshe, Mary A., photos by. LC 92-31327. (Illus.). 1993. 14.95 (*0-385-30887-6*) Delacorte.
Peck, Richard. Bel-Air Bambi & the Mall Rats. LC 92-29377. 1993. 15.95 (*0-385-30823-X*) Delacorte.
Pellowski, Michael. One Hundred Two Cat & Dog Jokes. LC 91-42769. (Illus.). 64p. (gr. 2-6). 1992. pap. text ed. 2.95 (*0-8167-2790-2*) Troll Assocs.
—One Hundred Two Wacky Monster Jokes. LC 91-44702. (Illus.). 64p. (gr. 2-6). 1992. pap. text ed. 2.95 (*0-8167-2746-5*) Troll Assocs.
—One Hundred Two Wild & Wacky Jokes. LC 91-30783. (Illus.). 64p. (gr. 2-6). 1991. pap. text ed. 2.95 (*0-8167-2612-4*) Troll Assocs.
Pellowski, Michael J. One Hundred Two School Jokes. Pellowski, Michael, illus. LC 91-20702. 64p. (gr. 2-6). 1991. pap. 2.95 (*0-8167-2579-9*) Troll Assocs.
—Wackiest Jokes in The World. Hoffman, Sanford, illus. LC 93-38242. 96p. 1994. 12.95 (*0-8069-0493-3*) Sterling.
Perkins, Gary. Silly Goofy Jokes. Nevins, Dan, illus. LC 92-20779. 64p. (gr. 2-6). 1992. pap. text ed. 1.95 (*0-8167-2965-4*, Pub. by Watermill Pr) Troll Assocs.
—Silly Haunted Jokes. Nevins, Dan, illus. LC 92-20760. 64p. (gr. 2-6). 1992. pap. text ed. 1.95 (*0-8167-2963-8*, Pub. by Watermill Pr) Troll Assocs.
—Silly School Jokes. Nevins, Dan, illus. LC 92-20437. 64p. (gr. 2-6). 1992. pap. text ed. 1.95 (*0-8167-2964-6*, Pub. by Watermill Pr) Troll Assocs.
Perret, Gene. Funny Comebacks to Rude Remarks. LC 90-37815. (Illus.). 96p. (gr. 3-9). 1990. pap. 3.95 (*0-8069-7240-8*) Sterling.
—Laugh-a-Minute Joke Book. Hoffman, Sanford, illus. LC 90-27674. 96p. (gr. 2-10). 1991. 12.95 (*0-8069-7414-1*) Sterling.
—Laugh-a-Minute Joke Book. Hoffman, Sanford, illus. 96p. (gr. 3-9). 1991. pap. 3.95 (*0-8069-7415-X*) Sterling.
—Super Funny School Jokes. LC 91-22501. (Illus.). 96p. (gr. 2-10). 1991. 12.95 (*0-8069-8294-2*) Sterling.
—Super Funny School Jokes. Hoffman, Sanford, illus. LC 91-22501. 96p. (gr. 1-7). 1992. pap. 3.95 (*0-8069-8295-0*) Sterling.
Peterson, Scott K. Face the Music! Jokes about Music. Hanson, Joan, illus. 32p. (gr. 1-4). 1988. PLB 11.95 (*0-8225-0995-4*) Lerner Pubns.
—What's Your Name? Jokes about Names. Hanson, Joan, illus. 32p. (gr. 1-4). 1987. PLB 11.95 (*0-8225-0994-6*, First Ave Edns); pap. 3.95 (*0-8225-9520-6*, First Ave Edns) Lerner Pubns.
Phillips, Bob. The Best of the Good Clean Jokes. LC 89-32386. 192p. (gr. 5 up). 1989. pap. 4.99 (*0-89081-769-3*) Harvest Hse.
—Good Clean Jokes for Kids. 1991. pap. 3.99 (*0-89081-902-5*) Harvest Hse.
—Loony Good Clean Jokes for Kids. LC 93-23529. 1994. pap. 4.99 (*1-56507-178-6*) Harvest Hse.
—Ultimate Good Clean Jokes for Kids. 1993. pap. 3.99 (*1-56507-085-2*) Harvest Hse.
Phillips, Louis. Alligator Wrestling & You: An Impractical Guide to an Impossible Sport. 96p. (Orig.). (gr. 7-12). 1992. pap. 3.50 (*0-380-76303-6*, Camelot) Avon.
—Going Ape: Jokes from the Jungle. Shein, Bob, illus. 64p. (gr. 2 up). 1990. pap. 3.95 (*0-14-032263-9*, Puffin) Puffin Bks.
—Haunted House Jokes. Marshall, James, illus. 64p. (gr. 2-5). 1988. pap. 3.95 (*0-14-032062-8*, Puffin) Puffin Bks.
—How Do You Get a Horse Out of the Bathtub? Profound Answers to Preposterous Questions. Stevenson, James P., illus. (gr. 4-6). 1983. pap. 4.95 (*0-14-031618-3*, Puffin Bks) Puffin Bks.
—Invisible Oink: Pig Jokes. Dubanevich, Arlene, illus. LC 92-24803. 64p. 1993. 11.99 (*0-670-84387-3*) Viking Child Bks.
—Wackysaurus: Dinosaur Jokes. Barrett, Ron, illus. LC 93-15134. 64p. (gr. 2-5). 1993. pap. 3.99 (*0-14-034687-2*, Puffin) Puffin Bks.
—Way Out! Jokes from Outer Space. Dubanevich, Arlene, illus. LC 89-14700. 58p. (gr. 4-8). 1989. pap. 10.95 (*0-670-82755-X*) Viking Child Bks.
—Way Out! Jokes from Outer Space. (gr. 4-7). 1991. pap. 3.99 (*0-14-034099-8*, Puffin) Puffin Bks.
Pilkey, Dav. Dog Breath! The Horrible Terrible Trouble with Hally Tosis. LC 93-43405. (ps-3). 1994. 14.95 (*0-590-47466-9*, Blue Sky Press) Scholastic Inc.
Pinkwater, Daniel. Borgel. LC 91-42914. 176p. (gr. 3-7). 1992. pap. 3.95 (*0-689-71620-6*, Aladdin) Macmillan Child Grp.
—The Magic Moscow. LC 92-27150. (Illus.). 64p. (gr. 3-7). 1993. pap. 3.95 (*0-689-71710-5*, Aladdin) Macmillan Child Grp.
—Ned Feldman, Space Pirate. Pinkwater, Daniel, illus. LC 93-40893. (gr. k-3). 1994. 14.95 (*0-02-774633-X*, Macmillan Child Bk) Macmillan Child Grp.
Polhamus, Jean B. Dinosaur Funny Bones. Rayburn, Cherie, ed. Claflin, Dale, illus. 27p. (gr. k-6). 1994. pap. text ed. 14.25 (*0-944943-53-5*, 23846-0) Current Inc.
Pollack, Pamela, compiled by. The Random House Book of Humor for Children. Zelinsky, Paul O., illus. LC 86-31478. 320p. (gr. 2-6). 1988. 15.95 (*0-394-88049-8*); lib. bdg. 16.99 (*0-394-98049-2*) Random Bks Yng Read.
Popkin, Arlene. My April Fool Book. (Illus.). (ps-1). 1974. PLB 6.89x (*0-914844-04-0*) J Alden.
Powell, Leroy. Out of My Head: Coon Dogs That Lie to You, Killer Pancakes, & Other Lunacies. Warlick, Cal, illus. LC 89-28418. 240p. 1990. 15.95 (*0-934601-95-X*) Peachtree Pubs.
Price, Roger & Stern, Leonard. Slam Dunk Mad Libs. 48p. (Orig.). (gr. 2 up). 1994. pap. 2.95 incl. chipboard (*0-8431-3722-3*) Price Stern.
Priceman, Marjorie. How to Make an Apple Pie & See The World. Priceman, Marjorie, illus. LC 93-12341. 40p. (ps-3). 1994. 15.00 (*0-679-83705-1*); lib. bdg. 15. 99 (*0-679-93705-6*) Knopf Bks Yng Read.
Protopopescu, Orel O. The Perilous Pit. Chwast, Jacqueline, illus. LC 92-290. 40p. (ps-1). 1993. JRT 14.00 (*0-671-76910-3*, Green Tiger) S&S Trade.
Pulver, Robin. Mrs. Toggle's Beautiful Blue Shoe. Alley, R. W., illus. LC 92-40824. 32p. (ps-2). 1994. RSBE 13.95 (*0-02-775456-1*, Four Winds) Macmillan Child Grp.
—Mrs. Toggle's Zipper. LC 88-37251. (Illus.). 32p. (ps-2). 1990. RSBE 13.95 (*0-02-775451-0*, Four Winds Press) Macmillan Child Grp.
—Mrs. Toggle's Zipper. Alley, Robert W., illus. LC 92-39355. 32p. (ps-2). 1993. pap. 3.95 (*0-689-71689-3*, Aladdin) Macmillan Child Grp.
Quackenbush, Robert M. Henry's Awful Mistake. LC 92-32870. (Illus.). 42p. (ps-3). 1992. PLB 13.27 (*0-8368-0882-7*); PLB 13.26 s.p. (*0-685-61513-8*) Gareth Stevens Inc.
Queen Winnie. 8p. (gr. k-3). 1992. pap. 3.95 (*1-56680-601-1*) Mad Hatter Pub.
Rayner, Shoo. My First Picture Joke Book. (Illus.). 32p. (ps-1). 1993. pap. 3.99 (*0-14-050925-9*) Puffin Bks.
Riddles & Jokes. (Illus.). (ps-2). 1991. pap. 3.50 (*0-8136-5961-2*, TK2360) Modern Curr.
Rissinger, Matt & Yates, Philip. Great Book of Zany Jokes. Corvino, Lucy, illus. LC 93-39189. 1994. 12.95 (*0-8069-0470-4*) Sterling.
Roop, Peter & Roop, Connie. Going Buggy! Jokes about Insects. (Illus.). 32p. (gr. 1-4). 1986. PLB 11.95 (*0-8225-0988-1*, First Ave Edns); pap. 2.95 (*0-8225-9530-3*, First Ave Edns) Lerner Pubns.
—Let's Celebrate! Jokes about Holidays. (Illus.). 32p. (gr. 1-4). 1986. PLB 11.95 (*0-8225-0989-X*, First Ave Edns); pap. 2.95 (*0-8225-9529-X*, First Ave Edns) Lerner Pubns.
—Stick Out Your Tongue! Jokes about Doctors & Patients. (Illus.). 32p. (gr. 1-4). 1986. PLB 11.95 (*0-8225-0990-3*, First Ave Edns); pap. 2.95 (*0-8225-9546-X*, First Ave Edns) Lerner Pubns.
Rose, Anne. The Triumphs of Fuzzy Fogtop. De Paola, Tomie, illus. LC 78-72204. (gr. k-3). 1979. Dial Bks Young.
Rosen, Michael, compiled by. Funny Stories. Blundell, Tony, illus. LC 92-26447. 256p. (gr. 4-9). 1993. 6.95 (*1-85697-883-4*, Kingfisher LKC) LKC.
Rosenbloom, Joseph. Doctor Knock-Knock's Official Knock-Knock Dictionary. Behr, Joyce, illus. LC 76-19796. 128p. (gr. 3 up). 1980. pap. 3.95 (*0-8069-8936-X*) Sterling.
—Funniest Haunted House Book Ever! Wilhelm, Hans, illus. LC 89-38605. 24p. (gr. 1-7). 1989. 12.95 (*0-8069-6818-4*); PLB 15.69 (*0-8069-6819-2*) Sterling.
—Funny Insults & Snappy Put-Downs. Behr, Joyce, illus. LC 82-50547. 128p. (gr. 4 up). 1982. pap. 3.95 (*0-8069-7644-6*) Sterling.
—Gigantic Joke Book. Behr, Joyce, illus. LC 77-93310. 256p. (gr. 4-6). 1981. pap. 5.95 (*0-8069-7514-8*) Sterling.
—Giggles, Gags & Groaners. LC 86-30052. (Illus.). 128p. (gr. 2-8). 1988. pap. 3.95 (*0-8069-6536-3*) Sterling.
—Looniest Limerick Book in the World. 1991. 3.99 (*0-517-07355-2*) Random Hse Value.
—Monster Madness. 1991. 3.99 (*0-517-07354-4*) Random Hse Value.
—Nutty Knock Knocks! Hoffman, Sandy, illus. LC 85-27626. 128p. (Orig.). (gr. 2 up). 1986. pap. 3.95 (*0-8069-6304-2*) Sterling.
—Perfect Put-Downs & Instant Insults. LC 88-11710. (Illus.). 128p. (gr. 2-8). 1989. pap. 3.95 (*0-8069-6940-7*) Sterling.
—Six Hundred Ninety-Six Silly School Jokes & Riddles. Kendrick, Dennis, illus. 128p. (gr. 2 up). 1987. pap. 3.95 (*0-8069-6392-1*) Sterling.
—Spooky Riddles & Jokes. Hoffman, Sanford, illus. LC 87-17972. 128p. (gr. 4 up). 1988. pap. 3.95 (*0-8069-6736-6*) Sterling.
—World's Best Sports Riddles & Jokes. Hoffman, Sanford, illus. LC 87-30434. 128p. (gr. 3-9). 1989. pap. 3.95 (*0-8069-6848-6*) Sterling.
Ross, Dave. How to Prevent Monster Attacks. LC 83-26536. (Illus.). 64p. (gr. 4 up). 1984. 7.00 (*0-688-03790-9*) Morrow Jr Bks.
Rothaus, Jim. Animal Jokes. Woodworth, Viki, illus. (gr. 1-4). 1992. PLB 13.95 (*0-89565-861-5*) Childs World.
—Bug Riddles. Woodworth, Viki, illus. (gr. 1-4). 1992. PLB 13.95 (*0-89565-864-X*) Childs World.
—Fairy Tale Jokes. Woodworth, Viki, illus. (gr. 1-4). 1992. PLB 13.95 (*0-89565-862-3*) Childs World.
Rothman, Joel. The Antcyclopedia. Freshman, Shelley, illus. 4.95 (*0-685-86236-4*) Pubns Devl Co TX.
Rovin, Jeff. Five Hundred Hilarious Jokes for Kids. 144p. (Orig.). 1990. pap. 2.99 (*0-451-16549-7*, Sig) NAL-Dutton.
—Five Hundred More Hilarious Jokes for Kids. 1990. pap. 2.95 (*0-451-16727-9*, Sig) NAL-Dutton.
Rudner, Barry. Nonsense. Fahsbender, Thomas, illus. (gr. k-6). 1991. 5.95 (*0-925928-04-6*) Tiny Thought.
Running Press Staff, ed. KIDZ Laugh-Along Car Jokebook. (Illus.). 64p. (Orig.). 1992. incl. audiocass. 9.95 (*1-56138-178-0*) Running Pr.
Sadler, Marilyn. Bob 'n John's Cat & Mouse Joke Book. (ps-3). 1993. pap. 3.50 (*0-307-11564-X*, Golden Pr) Western Pub.
Saki. The Story-Teller. 1991. PLB 13.95 (*0-88682-476-1*) Creative Ed.
Saller, Carol. Pug, Slug, & Doug the Thug. Redenbaugh, Vicki J., illus. LC 92-44340. 1993. 13.95 (*0-87614-803-8*) Carolrhoda Bks.
Saurus, Alice. One Thousand & One Dinosaur Jokes for Kids. (Orig.). (ps-6). 1993. pap. 3.99 (*0-345-38496-2*) Ballantine.
Schmeltz, Susan A. Oh, So Silly! Cocca, Maryann, illus. LC 83-23754. 48p. (ps-3). 1984. 5.95 (*0-8193-1122-7*) Parents.
Scieszka, Jon. Your Mother Was a Neanderthal. Smith, Lane, illus. 64p. (gr. 2-6). 1993. PLB 10.99 (*0-670-84481-0*) Viking Child Bks.
Sempe, Jean-Jacques. Chronicles of Little Nicholas. 1993. 15.00 (*0-374-31275-3*) FS&G.
Shafner, R. L. & Weisberg, Eric J. Belly's Deli. LC 92-44636. 1993. 13.50 (*0-8225-2101-6*) Lerner Pubns.
—The Hearty Treatment. LC 92-43369. 1993. 13.50 (*0-8225-2103-2*) Lerner Pubns.
—Mrs. Bretsky's Bakery. LC 92-44338. 1993. 13.50 (*0-8225-2102-4*) Lerner Pubns.
Shannon, J. Michael. Still More Jokes. Magnuson, Diana, illus. LC 85-27971. 48p. (gr. 1-5). 1986. pap. 3.95 (*0-516-41867-X*) Childrens.
Shere, Irene & Friedman, Sharon. Cat's out of the Bag: Jokes about Cats. Hanson, Joan, illus. 32p. (gr. 1-4). 1986. 11.95 (*0-8225-0986-5*); pap. 2.95 (*0-8225-9527-3*) Lerner Pubns.
—Grin & Bear It! Jokes about Teddy Bears. (Illus.). 32p. (gr. 1-4). 1986. lib. bdg. 11.95 (*0-8225-0985-7*) Lerner Pubns.
—In the Doghouse! Jokes about Dogs. (Illus.). 32p. (gr. 1-4). 1986. lib. bdg. 11.95 (*0-8225-0987-3*, First Ave Edns); pap. 2.95 (*0-8225-9528-1*, First Ave Edns) Lerner Pubns.
The Silly Tail Book. 1994. 13.27 (*0-8368-0986-6*) Gareth Stevens Inc.
Silverstein, Shel. Giraffe & a Half. Silverstein, Shel, illus. LC 64-19709. 48p. (gr. k-3). 1964. 15.00 (*0-06-025655-9*); PLB 14.89 (*0-06-025656-7*) HarpC Child Bks.
Sir Grumpalot. 8p. (gr. k-3). 1992. pap. 3.95 (*1-56680-605-4*) Mad Hatter Pub.
Sir Laughalot. 8p. (gr. k-3). 1992. pap. 3.95 (*1-56680-604-6*) Mad Hatter Pub.
Sloat, Teri & Sloat, Robert. Rib Ticklers: A Book of Punny Animals. LC 93-48619. (Illus.). 1994. 15.00 (*0-688-12519-0*); PLB 14.93 (*0-688-12520-4*) Lothrop.
Sloat, Teri & Westcott, Nadine B. The Thing That Bothered Farmer Brown. LC 94-24873. (gr. 1-8). 1995. write for info. (*0-531-06883-8*); PLB write for info. (*0-531-08733-6*) Orchard Bks Watts.
Smith, Robert K. Jelly Belly. Jones, Bob, illus. LC 80-23898. 160p. (gr. 4-6). 1981. pap. 13.95 (*0-385-28477-2*) Delacorte.
Smith, William J. Laughing Time: Collected Nonsense. 176p. (gr. 4-8). 1990. 14.00 (*0-374-34366-7*); pap. 3.50 (*0-374-44315-7*, Sunburst) FS&G.
Snow, Alan. How Dogs Really Work! LC 92-54651. 1993. 14.95 (*0-316-80261-1*) Little.
Spirn, Michele. The Know-Nothings. Alley, R. W., illus. LC 93-43533. 1995. 14.00 (*0-06-024499-2*); PLB 13. 89 (*0-06-024500-X*) HarpC Child Bks.
Stamper, Judith B. Five Funny Frights. Raglin, Tim, illus. LC 92-44538. (gr. 4 up). 1993. pap. 2.95 (*0-590-46416-7*) Scholastic Inc.

Steig, William. CDB! LC 80-12376. (Illus.). 48p. (gr. 1-4). 1987. pap. 3.95 (*0-671-66689-4*, S&S BFYR) S&S Trade.

Stine, Bob. One Hundred & One Silly Monster Jokes. Taylor, B. K., illus. 96p. (Orig.). (gr. 4-7). 1986. pap. 1.95 (*0-590-33889-7*) Scholastic Inc.

—One Hundred & One Wacky Kid Jokes. Orehek, Don, illus. 96p. 1988. pap. 1.95 (*0-590-41399-6*) Scholastic Inc.

—One Hundred One More Monster Jokes. 96p. (Orig.). (gr. 4-7). 1990. pap. 1.95 (*0-590-43171-4*) Scholastic Inc.

—One Hundred One School Cafeteria Jokes. 96p. (Orig.). (gr. 3-7). 1990. pap. 1.95 (*0-590-43759-3*) Scholastic Inc.

Stinson, Kathy. Bare Naked Book. Collins, Heather, illus. 32p. (gr. k-2). 1986. PLB 14.95 (*0-920303-52-8*, Pub. by Annick CN); pap. 4.95 (*0-920303-53-6*, Pub. by Annick CN) Firefly Bks Ltd.

—Those Green Things. McLoughlin, Mary, illus. 24p. (gr. k-3). 1985. 12.95 (*0-920303-40-4*, Pub. by Annick CN); pap. 4.95 (*0-920303-41-2*, Pub. by Annick CN) Firefly Bks Ltd.

Stuart, Chad. The Ballymara Flood: A Tale from Old Ireland. Booth, George, illus. LC 94-15162. 1995. write for info. (*0-15-205698-X*) HarBrace.

Stupid Jokes for Kids. 224p. (ps-8). 1991. pap. 3.95 (*0-345-37062-7*) Ballantine.

Suire, Diane, compiled by. Monster Jokes. Hunter, Llyn, illus. LC 88-17487. 48p. (gr. 1-5). 1988. pap. 3.95 (*0-516-41866-1*) Childrens.

Swope, Sam. The Krazees. Rocco, John, photos by. LC 92-24435. (Illus.). 32p. (ps-1). Date not set. 15.00 (*0-06-021541-0*); PLB 14.89 (*0-06-021542-9*) HarpC Child Bks.

Taylor, Theodore. The Trouble with Tuck. 120p. (gr. 5 up). 1993. pap. 3.99 (*0-380-62711-6*, Camelot) Avon.

Terban, Marvin. Guppies in Tuxedos: Funny Eponyms. Maestro, Giulio, illus. LC 87-32630. 64p. (gr. 4-7). 1988. (Clarion Bks); pap. 5.95 (*0-89919-770-1*, Clarion Bks) HM.

Thaler, Mike. Earth Mirth: The Ecology Riddle Book. Brown, Rick, illus. LC 93-37818. 1994. text ed. write for info. (*0-7167-6521-7*); pap. text ed. write for info. (*0-7167-6529-2*) W H Freeman.

—Oinkers Away! Pig Riddles, Cartoons & Jokes. (gr. 3-6). 1989. pap. 2.50 (*0-671-67456-0*, Minstrel Bks) PB.

Time Life Inc. Editors. Mr. Boggle's Peculiar Day: A Visual-Perception Book. Kagan, Neil & Ward, Elizabeth, eds. (Illus.). 56p. (ps-2). 1992. write for info. (*0-8094-9311-X*); lib. bdg. write for info. (*0-8094-9312-8*) Time-Life.

Tompert, Ann. Nothing Sticks Like a Shadow. Munsinger, Lynn, illus. LC 83-18554. 32p. (gr. k-3). 1984. 15.95 (*0-395-35391-2*, 5-97100); pap. 4.80 (*0-395-47950-9*) HM.

Van Laan, Nancy. People, People, Everywhere! Westcott, Nadine B., illus. LC 90-5303. 40p. (ps-2). 1992. 13.00 (*0-679-81063-3*); PLB 13.99 (*0-679-91063-8*) Knopf Bks Yng Read.

Viorst, Judith. Sad Underwear & Other Complications. Hull, Richard, illus. LC 94-3357. 1995. 15.00 (*0-689-31929-0*, Atheneum) Macmillan.

Waldo Wizard. 8p. (gr. k-3). 1992. pap. 3.95 (*1-56680-603-8*) Mad Hatter Pub.

Walker, Barbara K. Laughing Together: Giggles & Grins from Around the Globe. rev. ed. Taback, Simms, illus. LC 91-43784. 128p. (Orig.). (gr. k up). 1992. pap. 12.95 (*0-915793-37-7*) Free Spirit Pub.

Walton, Rick. Off Base: Riddles about Baseball. (gr. 4-7). 1993. pap. 3.95 (*0-8225-9638-5*) Lerner Pubns.

Walton, Rick & Walton, Ann. Can You Match This? Jokes about Unlikely Pairs. Hanson, Joan, illus. 32p. (gr. 1-4). 1989. 11.95 (*0-8225-0973-3*) Lerner Pubns.

—Can You Match This? Jokes about Unlikely Pairs. Hanson, Joan, illus. 36p. pap. 2.95 (*0-8225-9565-6*) Lerner Pubns.

—Dumb Clucks. 12p. 1992. text ed. 0.92 (*1-56956-110-9*) W A T Braille.

—Dumb Clucks! Jokes about Chickens. Hanson, Joan, illus. 32p. (gr. 1-4). 1987. PLB 11.95 (*0-8225-0991-1*) Lerner Pubns.

—Fossil Follies! Jokes about Dinosaurs. Hanson, Joan, illus. 32p. (gr. 1-4). 1989. 11.95 (*0-8225-0974-1*, First Ave Edns); pap. 2.95 (*0-8225-9560-5*, First Ave Edns) Lerner Pubns.

—Hoop-La: Riddles about Basketball. Burke, Susan S., illus. LC 92-25771. 1993. 11.95 (*0-8225-2339-6*) Lerner Pubns.

—Kiss a Frog! Jokes about Fairy Tales, Knights, & Dragons. Hanson, Joan, illus. 32p. (gr. 1-4). 1989. 11.95 (*0-8225-0970-9*) Lerner Pubns.

—Kiss a Frog! Jokes about Fairy Tales, Knights, & Dragons. Hanson, Joan, illus. 40p. (gr. 1-4). pap. 2.95g (*0-8225-9566-4*) Lerner Pubns.

—Off Base: Riddles about Baseball. Burke, Susan S., illus. LC 92-19857. 1993. 11.95 (*0-8225-2338-8*) Lerner Pubns.

—Something's Fishy! Jokes about Sea Creatures. (Illus.). 32p. (gr. 1-4). 1987. PLB 11.95 (*0-8225-0993-8*, First Ave Edns); pap. 2.95 (*0-8225-9519-2*, First Ave Edns) Lerner Pubns.

—Take a Hike: Riddles about Football. Burke, Susan S., illus. LC 92-27011. 1993. 11.95 (*0-8225-2340-X*) Lerner Pubns.

—What a Ham! Jokes about Pigs. Hanson, Joan, illus. 32p. (gr. 1-4). 1989. 11.95 (*0-8225-0972-5*) Lerner Pubns.

—What a Ham! Jokes about Pigs. Hanson, Joan, illus. 40p. (gr. 1-4). pap. 2.95 (*0-8225-9567-2*) Lerner Pubns.

—What's Your Name, Again? More Jokes about Names. Hanson, Joan, illus. 32p. (gr. 1-4). 1988. PLB 11.95 (*0-8225-0997-0*, First Ave Edns); pap. 2.95 (*0-8225-9553-2*, First Ave Edns) Lerner Pubns.

Ward Lock, Ltd. Staff. One Thousand Knock Knock Jokes for Kids. (gr. k up). 1986. pap. 4.99 (*0-345-33481-7*) Ballantine.

Wersba, Barbara. You'll Never Guess the End. LC 91-24771. 144p. (gr. 7 up). 1992. 14.00 (*0-06-020448-6*); PLB 13.89 (*0-06-020449-4*) HarpC Child Bks.

Wilbur, Richard. Runaway Opposites. Drescher, Henrik, illus. LC 94-13188. 1995. write for info. (*0-15-258722-5*) HarBrace.

Williams, Linda. Big Golden Book of Riddles, Jokes, Giggles, & Rhymes. (gr. 4-7). 1993. 10.95 (*0-307-17877-3*, Golden Pr) Western Pub.

Willis, Jeanne. Earth Weather As Explained by Professor Xargle. Ross, Tony, illus. LC 92-14067. (ps-2). 1993. Repr. of 1991 ed. 14.00 (*0-525-45025-4*, DCB) Dutton Child Bks.

—Relativity, As Explained by Professor Xargle. Ross, Tony, illus. LC 93-32606. (gr. 5 up). 1994. write for info. (*0-525-45245-1*, DCB) Dutton Child Bks.

Willis, Val. The Mystery in the Bottle. Shelley, John, illus. 32p. (gr. k-3). 1991. bds. 14.95 (*0-374-35194-5*) FS&G.

Wood, Audrey. Silly Sally. 1992. 13.95 (*0-15-274428-2*, HB Juv Bks) HarBrace.

—The Tickleoctopus. Wood, Don, illus. LC 93-26868. 1994. 14.95 (*0-15-287000-8*) HarBrace.

Wood, Dora. Five Hundred More Wild & Wacky Knock-Knock Jokes for Kids. (gr. 4-7). 1993. pap. 3.99 (*0-345-38161-0*) Ballantine.

Woodworth, Viki. Knock Knock Jokes. (Illus.). 32p. 1991. 13.95 (*0-89565-729-5*) Childs World.

—School Jokes. (Illus.). 32p. (gr. 1-4). 1991. 13.95 (*0-89565-726-0*) Childs World.

—Space Jokes. (Illus.). 32p. (gr. 1-4). 1991. 13.95 (*0-89565-730-9*) Childs World.

—Sports Jokes. (Illus.). 32p. (gr. 1-4). 1991. 13.95 (*0-89565-727-9*) Childs World.

—Teacher Jokes. (Illus.). 32p. (gr. 1-4). 1991. 13.95 (*0-89565-725-2*) Childs World.

Worth, Bonnie. Full House Same to You Duck. (gr. 4-7). 1990. pap. 2.95 (*0-440-40468-1*) Dell.

Yamamoto, Neil. Super Silly School Jokes & Riddles. (gr. 4-7). 1991. pap. 1.95 (*0-8125-9375-8*) Tor Bks.

Yorinks, Arthur. Ugh. Egielski, Richard, illus. 32p. (ps-3). 1990. 13.95 (*0-374-38028-7*) FS&G.

York, Carol B. Pudmuddles. Thiesing, Lisa, illus. LC 91-23596. 48p. (gr. 2-5). 1993. 13.00 (*0-06-020436-2*); PLB 12.89 (*0-06-020437-0*) HarpC Child Bks.

—Pudmuddles. LC 91-23596. (gr. 4-7). 1994. pap. 3.95 (*0-06-440527-3*) HarpC Child Bks.

Yorke, Malcolm. Molly the Mad Basher. Chamberlain, Margaret, illus. LC 93-11407. 32p. (gr. 1-4). 1994. 10.95 (*1-56458-459-3*) Dorling Kindersley.

Young, Frederica. Super-Duper Jokes. (gr. 4-7). 1993. 13.00 (*0-374-37301-9*); pap. 4.95 (*0-374-47353-6*) FS&G.

Young, Frederica & Kohl, Marguerite. Jokes for Children. Patterson, Bob, illus. 128p. (gr. 2 up). 1983. pap. 4.95 (*0-374-43832-3*, Sunburst) FS&G.

—More Jokes for Children. Patterson, Bob, illus. (gr. 2-5). 1984. pap. 4.95 (*0-374-45360-8*, Sunburst) FS&G.

Zadra, Dan. How to Beat the Jitters. (Illus.). 32p. (gr. 6 up). 1986. PLB 12.95 (*0-88682-018-9*) Creative Ed.

Zindel, Paul. One Hundred Percent Laugh Riot. (gr. 4-7). 1994. pap. 3.50 (*0-553-48083-9*) Bantam.

WIT AND HUMOR, PICTORIAL

Bird, Malcolm. The Witch's Handbook. Bird, Malcolm, illus. LC 88-911. 96p. (ps up). 1988. pap. 7.95 POB (*0-689-71237-5*, Aladdin) Macmillan Child Grp.

Denim, Sue. The Dumb Bunnies' Easter. Pilkey, Dav, illus. LC 94-15050. (gr. 1-8). 1995. write for info. (*0-590-20241-3*, Blue Sky Press) Scholastic Inc.

Sesame Street Staff. Sesame Street Storybook. (Illus.). (ps-4). 1971. 5.95 (*0-394-82332-X*); lib. bdg. 5.99 (*0-394-92332-4*) Random Bks Yng Read.

WITCHCRAFT

see also Occult Sciences

Bird, Malcolm. The Witch's Handbook. Bird, Malcolm, illus. LC 88-911. 96p. (ps up). 1988. pap. 7.95 POB (*0-689-71237-5*, Aladdin) Macmillan Child Grp.

Brown, Marc. Witches Four. Brown, Marc, illus. LC 79-5263. 48p. (ps-3). 1980. 5.95 (*0-8193-1013-1*); PLB 5.95 (*0-8193-1014-X*) Parents.

Gawr, Rhuddlwm. The Triads: The Wisdom of the Welsh Witches. Gawr, Rhuddlwm, illus. LC 85-73755. 140p. (Orig.). 1989. 14.95 (*0-931760-45-3*, CP 10123); pap. 10.95 (*0-931760-23-2*) Camelot GA.

—The Way: The Discovery of the Grail of Immortality. Gawr, Rhuddlwm, et al, illus. LC 85-73759. (Orig.). 1987. 18.95 (*0-931760-50-X*, CP 10128); pap. 15.95 (*0-931760-28-3*) Camelot GA.

Harrison, Michael. Scolding Tongues: The Persecution of Witches. 52p. (gr. 1 up). 1987. pap. 7.95 (*0-85950-543-X*, Pub. by S Thornes UK) Dufour.

Jackson, Shirley. Witchcraft of Salem Village. (Illus.). (gr. 4-6). 1963. lib. bdg. 9.99 (*0-394-90369-2*) Random Bks Yng Read.

Kent, Zachary. The Story of the Salem Witch Trials. Canaday, Ralph, illus. LC 86-9632. 32p. (gr. 3-6). 1986. pap. 3.95 (*0-516-44704-1*) Childrens.

Krensky, Stephen. Witch Hunt: It Happened in Salem Village. Watling, James, illus. LC 88-42865. 48p. (Orig.). (gr. 2-4). 1989. PLB 7.99 (*0-394-91923-8*); pap. 3.50 (*0-394-81923-3*) Random Bks Yng Read.

Naylor-Reynolds, Phyllis. Witch Water. (gr. k-6). 1988. pap. 3.50 (*0-440-40038-4*, YB) Dell.

O'Connell, Margaret. The Magic Cauldron: Witchcraft for Good & Evil. LC 75-26757. (Illus.). 256p. (gr. 9-12). 1975. 32.95 (*0-87599-187-4*) S G Phillips.

Scot, Reginald. Discoverie of Witchcraft. 1989. pap. 7.95 (*0-486-26030-5*) Dover.

WITCHCRAFT–FICTION

Adams, Adrienne. A Halloween Happening. Adams, Adrienne, illus. LC 91-6907. 32p. (ps-3). 1991. pap. 3.95 (*0-689-71502-1*, Aladdin) Macmillan Child Grp.

—A Woggle of Witches. Adams, Adrienne, illus. LC 70-161536. 32p. (ps-3). 1971. RSBE 13.95 (*0-684-12506-4*, Scribners Young Read) Macmillan Child Grp.

—A Woggle of Witches. Adams, Adrienne, illus. LC 87-18703. 32p. (ps-1). 1985. pap. 4.95 (*0-689-71050-X*, Aladdin) Macmillan Child Grp.

Adler, David A. I Know I'm a Witch. Stevenson, Sucie, illus. LC 86-33508. 32p. (ps-2). 1990. pap. 4.95 (*0-8050-1480-2*, Bks Young Read) H Holt & Co.

Alexander, Lloyd. Black Cauldron. 192p. (gr. k-6). 1980. pap. 3.99 (*0-440-40649-8*, YB) Dell.

Alexander, Sue. More Witch, Goblin & Ghost Stories. Winter, Jeanette, illus. LC 78-3280. (gr. 1-4). 1978. 6.95 (*0-394-83933-1*) Pantheon.

—Witch, Goblin & Ghost in the Haunted Woods. Winter, Jeanette, illus. LC 80-20863. 72p. (gr. 1-4). 1981. 6.95 (*0-394-84443-2*); lib. bdg. 7.99 (*0-394-94443-7*) Pantheon.

Balian, Lorna. Humbug Potion: An A-B-Cipher. Balian, Lorna, illus. 32p. (ps-3). 1988. Repr. of 1985 ed. 7.50 (*0-687-37102-3*) Humbug Bks.

—Humbug Potion: An A-B-Cipher. Balian, Lorna, illus. 32p. (ps-3). 1985. PLB 12.95 (*0-687-18021-X*) Humbug Bks.

—Humbug Witch. Balian, Lorna, illus. 32p. (gr. k up). 1992. Repr. of 1987 ed. PLB 13.95 (*1-881772-24-1*) Humbug Bks.

Barkan, Joanne. Very Scary Witch Story. (ps-3). 1992. pap. 5.50 (*0-590-45936-8*) Scholastic Inc.

Barry, Margaret S. Simon & the Witch. large type ed. (Illus.). (gr. 1-8). 1994. 15.95 (*0-7451-2270-1*, Galaxy Child Lrg Print) Chivers N Amer.

Behrman, Carol H. The Lancaster Witch. 160p. (gr. 5-8). 1993. pap. 2.99 (*0-87406-645-X*) Willowisp Pr.

Bellairs, John. The Lamp from the Warlock's Tomb. (gr. 4-8). 1989. pap. 3.99 (*0-553-15697-7*, Skylark) Bantam.

—The Letter, the Witch, & the Ring. Egielski, Richard, illus. LC 75-28968. (gr. 4-7). 1976. Dial Bks Young.

—The Letter, the Witch, & the Ring. Egielski, Richard, illus. LC 92-31361. 208p. (gr. 3 up). 1993. pap. 3.99 (*0-14-036338-6*, Puffin) Puffin Bks.

Bender, Robert. A Little Witch Magic. LC 92-4054. (Illus.). 32p. (ps-3). 1992. 14.95 (*0-8050-2126-4*, Bks Young Read) H Holt & Co.

Bennett, Anna E. Little Witch. Stone, Helen, illus. LC 52-13721. 128p. (gr. 3-5). 1981. pap. 3.95 (*0-06-440119-7*, Trophy) HarpC Child Bks.

Black, J. R. The Witches Next Door. 120p. (Orig.). (gr. 3-7). 1993. pap. 3.50 (*0-679-85108-9*, Bullseye Bks) Random Bks Yng Read.

Blank, Peter. The First Spell of Winnefred Broomstock. Sperling, Thomas, illus. 32p. 1992. 7.95 (*1-56288-273-2*) Checkerboard.

Block, Francesca L. Witch Baby. LC 90-28916. 128p. (gr. 7 up). 1992. pap. 3.95 (*0-06-447065-2*, Trophy) HarpC Child Bks.

Borisoff, Norman. Bewitched & Bewildered: A Spooky Love Story. 112p. (Orig.). (gr. 7-11). 1982. pap. 1.75 (*0-440-90905-8*, LFL) Dell.

Bridges, Laurie & Alexander, Paul. Swamp Witch, No. 6. 160p. (Orig.). (gr. 7-12). 1987. pap. 2.50 (*0-553-26792-2*) Bantam.

Bridwell, Norman. The Witch Goes to School. LC 92-12091. (ps-3). 1992. pap. 2.95 (*0-590-45831-0*) Scholastic Inc.

—The Witch Grows Up. (Illus.). 32p. (Orig.). (gr. k-3). 1987. pap. 2.50 (*0-590-40559-4*) Scholastic Inc.

—The Witch Next Door. Bridwell, Norman, illus. 32p. (gr. k-3). 1986. pap. 2.50 (*0-590-40433-4*) Scholastic Inc.

—The Witch's Christmas. Bridwell, Norman, illus. (gr. k-3). 1972. pap. 1.50 (*0-590-09216-2*) Scholastic Inc.

—The Witch's Christmas. Bridwell, Norman, illus. 32p. (gr. k-3). 1986. pap. 1.95 (*0-590-40434-2*) Scholastic Inc.

—The Witch's Vacation. Bridwell, Norman, illus. 32p. (Orig.). (gr. k-3). 1987. pap. 2.50 (*0-590-40558-6*) Scholastic Inc.

Briggs, K. M. Kate Crackernuts. LC 79-9229. (Illus.). 224p. (gr. 7 up). 1980. 13.50 (*0-688-80240-0*) Greenwillow.

Burgess, Melvin. Burning Issy. LC 93-32430. (gr. 5 up). 1994. 15.00 (*0-671-89003-4*, S&S BFYR) S&S Trade.

Butler, Beverly. Witch's Fire. LC 93-44. 144p. (gr. 5 up). 1993. 14.99 (*0-525-65132-2*, Cobblehill Bks) Dutton Child Bks.

Calhoun, Mary. The Witch of Hissing Hill. McCaffery, Janet, illus. LC 64-15475. (gr. k-3). 1964. PLB 13.88 (*0-688-31762-6*) Morrow Jr Bks.
Calif, Ruth. The Over-the-Hill Witch. Holub, Joan, illus. LC 89-35371. 144p. (gr. 5). 1990. 10.95 (*0-88289-754-3*) Pelican.
Calmenson, Stephanie. The Little Witch Sisters. Alley, R. W., illus. LC 93-15454. 1993. 13.27 (*0-8368-0970-X*) Gareth Stevens Inc.
Carlson, Nancy. Witch Lady. Carlson, Nancy, illus. LC 85-3756. 32p. (ps-3). 1985. PLB 13.50 (*0-87614-283-8*) Carolrhoda Bks.
Carlson, Natalie S. Spooky & the Bad Luck Raven. Glass, Andrew, illus. LC 87-15471. (ps-1). 1988. 12.95 (*0-688-07650-5*); lib. bdg. 12.88 (*0-688-07651-3*) Lothrop.
Carrick, Carol. Old Mother Witch. Carrick, Donald, illus. LC 75-4609. 32p. (ps). 1989. pap. 4.80 (*0-395-51584-X*, Clarion Bks) HM.
Cheatham, Ann. The Witch of Lagg. (Orig.). (gr. k-12). 1987. pap. 2.50 (*0-440-99412-8*, LFL) Dell.
Chew, Ruth. No Such Thing As a Witch. Chew, Ruth, illus. LC 79-18153. (gr. 2 up). 1980. 8.95 (*0-8038-5073-5*) Hastings.
—What the Witch Left. (gr. 4-7). 1993. pap. 2.75 (*0-590-45531-1*) Scholastic Inc.
—Witch in the House. (gr. 4-7). 1993. pap. 2.75 (*0-590-46281-4*) Scholastic Inc.
Christelow, Eileen. Jerome & the Witchcraft Kids. Christelow, Eileen, illus. LC 88-2597. 32p. (gr. k-3). 1988. 13.95 (*0-89919-742-6*, Clarion Bks) HM.
—Jerome & the Witchcraft Kids. Christelow, Eileen, illus. 32p. (ps-3). 1990. pap. 4.80 (*0-395-54428-9*, Clarion Bks) HM.
Clapp, Patricia. Witches' Children. (gr. 4-8). 1992. 17.00 (*0-8446-6572-X*) Peter Smith.
Cole, Babette. The Trouble with Mom. Cole, Babette, illus. 32p. (gr. 5-8). 1984. 13.95 (*0-698-20597-9*, Putnam); pap. 5.95 (*0-698-20681-9*, Sandcastle Bks) Putnam Pub Group.
Cole, Joanna. Bony-Legs. Zimmer, Dirk, illus. 48p. (ps-2). 1986. pap. 2.95 (*0-590-40516-0*) Scholastic Inc.
Coombs, Patricia. Dorrie & the Blue Witch. Coombs, Patricia, illus. 48p. (gr. k-6). 1980. pap. 1.50 (*0-440-42210-8*, YB) Dell.
—Dorrie & the Haunted Schoolhouse. Coombs, Patricia, illus. 32p. (ps-3). 1992. 13.45 (*0-395-60116-9*, Clarion Bks) HM.
—Dorrie & the Museum Case. LC 84-27812. (Illus.). 48p. (gr. 1-5). 1986. 11.95 (*0-688-04278-3*); PLB 11.88 (*0-688-04279-1*) Lothrop.
—Dorrie & the Pin Witch. Coombs, Patricia, illus. LC 88-12697. 32p. (gr. 1-4). 1989. 13.00 (*0-688-08055-3*); PLB 12.88 (*0-688-08056-1*) Lothrop.
—Dorrie & the Wizard's Spell. Coombs, Patricia, illus. LC 68-27601. 48p. (gr. 1-5). 1968. PLB 12.93 (*0-688-51083-3*) Lothrop.
Craig, Janet A. The Boo-Hoo Witch. Schories, Patricia L., illus. LC 93-2216. 32p. (gr. k-2). 1993. PLB 11.59 (*0-8167-3186-1*); pap. text ed. 2.95 (*0-8167-3187-X*) Troll Assocs.
Cresswell, Helen. Lizzie Dripping & the Witch. large type ed. Riddell, Chris, illus. 160p. 1993. 16.95 (*0-7451-1681-7*, Galaxy Child Lrg Print) Chivers N Amer.
Curry, Jane L. The Great Flood Mystery. LC 85-1322. 180p. (gr. 3-6). 1985. SBE 14.95 (*0-689-50306-7*, M K McElderry) Macmillan Child Grp.
Dahl, Roald. Magic Finger. Pene Du Bois, William, illus. LC 66-18657. 46p. (gr. 3-6). 1966. 15.00 (*0-06-021381-7*); PLB 14.89 (*0-06-021382-5*) HarpC Child Bks.
—The Witches. Blake, Quentin, photos by. LC 83-14195. (Illus.). 208p. (gr. 3-9). 1983. 16.00 (*0-374-38457-6*); ltd. ed. o.s.i. 35.00 (*0-374-38458-4*) FS&G.
—The Witches. Blake, Quentin, illus. LC 85-519. 200p. (gr. 3-7). 1985. pap. 3.95 (*0-14-031730-9*) Viking Child Bks.
DaLage, Ida. Beware! Beware! A Witch Won't Share. (Illus.). 48p. (gr. k-4). 1991. Repr. of 1972 ed. lib. bdg. 12.95 (*0-7910-1473-8*) Chelsea Hse.
—The Farmer & the Witch. Miret, Gil, illus. 48p. (gr. k-4). 1991. Repr. of 1966 ed. PLB 12.95 (*0-7910-1474-6*) Chelsea Hse.
Degen, Bruce. The Little Witch & the Riddle. Degen, Bruce, illus. LC 78-19475. 64p. (gr. k-3). 1988. pap. 3.50 (*0-06-444125-3*, Trophy) HarpC Child Bks.
De Gerez, Toni. Louhi, Witch of North Farm. Cooney, Barbara, illus. LC 84-21600. 32p. (ps-3). 1986. pap. 13.95 (*0-670-80556-4*) Viking Child Bks.
DeLage, Ida. The Old Witch & Her Magic Basket. Sloan, Ellen, illus. 48p. (gr. k-4). 1991. Repr. of 1978 ed. lib. bdg. 12.95 (*0-7910-1475-4*) Chelsea Hse.
—The Old Witch & the Crows. Smith, Marianne, illus. 48p. (gr. k-4). 1991. Repr. of 1983 ed. lib. bdg. 12.95 (*0-7910-1476-2*) Chelsea Hse.
—The Old Witch & the Dragon. Unada, illus. 48p. (gr. k-4). 1991. Repr. of 1979 ed. lib. bdg. 12.95 (*0-7910-1477-0*) Chelsea Hse.
—The Old Witch & the Ghost Parade. Taylor, Jody, illus. 48p. (gr. k-4). 1991. Repr. of 1978 ed. lib. bdg. 12.95 (*0-7910-1478-9*) Chelsea Hse.
—The Old Witch & the Snores. Miret, Gil, illus. 48p. (gr. k-4). 1991. Repr. of 1970 ed. lib. bdg. 12.95 (*0-7910-1479-7*) Chelsea Hse.
—The Old Witch & the Wizard. Korach, Mimi, illus. 48p. (gr. k-4). 1991. Repr. of 1974 ed. lib. bdg. 12.95 (*0-7910-1480-0*) Chelsea Hse.
—The Old Witch Finds a New House. Paris, Pat, illus. 48p. (gr. k-4). 1991. Repr. of 1979 ed. lib. bdg. 12.95 (*0-7910-1481-9*) Chelsea Hse.
—The Old Witch Gets a Surprise. Sloan, Ellen, illus. 48p. (gr. k-4). 1991. Repr. of 1981 ed. lib. bdg. 12.95 (*0-7910-1482-7*) Chelsea Hse.
—The Old Witch Goes to the Ball. Nebel, Gustave E., illus. 48p. (gr. k-4). 1991. Repr. of 1969 ed. lib. bdg. 12.95 (*0-7910-1483-5*) Chelsea Hse.
—The Old Witch's Party. Korach, Mimi, illus. 48p. (gr. k-4). 1991. Repr. of 1976 ed. lib. bdg. 12.95 (*0-7910-1484-3*) Chelsea Hse.
—Weeny Witch. Oechsli, Kelli, illus. 48p. (gr. k-4). 1991. Repr. of 1966 ed. lib. bdg. 12.95 (*0-7910-1485-1*) Chelsea Hse.
—What Does a Witch Need? Schroeder, Ted, illus. 48p. (gr. k-4). 1991. Repr. of 1971 ed. PLB 12.95 (*0-7910-1486-X*) Chelsea Hse.
—The Witchy Broom. Peaver, Walt, illus. 48p. (gr. k-4). 1991. Repr. of 1969 ed. lib. bdg. 12.95 (*0-7910-1487-8*) Chelsea Hse.
Denan, Corinne. Witch Tales. new ed. LC 79-66328. (Illus.). 48p. (gr. 3-6). 1980. lib. bdg. 9.89 (*0-89375-324-6*); pap. 2.95 (*0-89375-323-8*) Troll Assocs.
—Wizard Tales. new ed. LC 79-66331. (Illus.). 48p. (gr. 3-6). 1980. lib. bdg. 9.89 (*0-89375-330-0*); pap. 2.95 (*0-89375-329-7*) Troll Assocs.
Devlin, Wende & Devlin, Harry. Old Black Witch. Devlin, Wende & Devlin, Harry, illus. LC 91-42133. 32p. (gr. k-3). 1992. pap. 3.95 (*0-689-71636-2*, Aladdin) Macmillan Child Grp.
—Old Black Witch. 2nd ed. Devlin, Harry, illus. LC 92-19897. 32p. (gr. k-3). 1992. RSBE 13.95 (*0-02-729185-5*, Four Winds) Macmillan Child Grp.
Dicks, Terrance. The MacMagics: A Spell for My Sister. Canning, Celia, illus. 96p. (gr. 3-6). 1992. pap. 3.50 (*0-8120-4881-4*) Barron.
—The MacMagics: My Brother the Vampire. Canning, Celia, illus. 96p. (ps-3). 1992. pap. 3.50 (*0-8120-4883-0*) Barron.
—Meet the MacMagics. Canning, Celia, illus. 96p. (gr. 3-6). 1992. pap. 3.50 (*0-8120-4882-2*) Barron.
Dixon, Rachel. The Witch's Ring. (Illus.). 128p. (gr. 2 up). 1994. 14.95 (*1-56282-545-3*); PLB 14.89 (*1-56282-546-1*) Hyprn Child.
Duncan, Lois. Summer of Fear. 252p. (gr. 7-12). 1976. 15.95 (*0-316-19548-0*) Little.
Embry, Margaret. The Blue-Nosed Witch. Rose, Carl, illus. 48p. (gr. 2-5). 1984. pap. 2.75 (*0-553-15435-4*) Bantam.
Estes, Eleanor. The Witch Family. Hewitt, Kathryn & Ardizzone, Edward, illus. 223p. (gr. 3-7). 1990. pap. 4.95 (*0-15-298572-7*, Odyssey) HarBrace.
Euvremer, Teryl. Triple Whammy. Euvremer, Teryl, illus. LC 91-44240. 32p. (gr. k-4). 1993. 15.00 (*0-06-021060-5*); PLB 14.89 (*0-06-021061-3*) HarpC Child Bks.
Fitzgerald, Bridget. Winkie, the Cross-Eyed Witch. LC 71-189878. (Illus.). (gr. 1-2). 1973. 2.50 (*0-87884-020-6*) Unicorn Ent.
Fox, Naomi. Hansel & Gretel. Fox, Neal, illus. 24p. (ps-1). 1992. Incl. cassette. pap. 9.95 (*1-882179-12-9*) Confetti Ent.
—Sleeping Beauty. Fox, Neal, illus. 24p. (ps-1). 1992. Incl. cassette. pap. 9.95 (*1-882179-13-7*) Confetti Ent.
Frances, Marian. Witch on a Motorcycle. new ed. (Illus.). (gr. 3-4). 1972. pap. 1.95 (*0-89375-047-6*) Troll Assocs.
Freeman, Don. Space Witch. (Illus.). (gr. k-3). 1979. pap. 4.99 (*0-14-050346-3*, Puffin) Puffin Bks.
—Tilly Witch. (ps-k). 1978. pap. 3.95 (*0-14-050262-9*, Puffin) Puffin Bks.
—Tilly Witch. Freeman, Don, illus. (gr. k-3). 1969. pap. 13.95 (*0-670-71303-1*) Viking Child Bks.
Furlong, Monica. Juniper. LC 90-39800. 192p. (gr. 5-9). 1991. PLB 13.99 (*0-394-93220-X*) Knopf Bks Yng Read.
—Wise Child. LC 87-3063. 192p. (gr. 5 up). 1987. lib. bdg. 12.99 (*0-394-99105-2*) Knopf Bks Yng Read.
Gabler, Mirko. Alphabet Soup. LC 92-1127. (Illus.). 32p. (ps-3). 1992. 14.95 (*0-8050-2049-7*, Bks Young Read) H Holt & Co.
Gilmore, Kate. Enter Three Witches. 216p. (gr. 5-9). 1990. 13.45 (*0-395-50213-6*) HM.
Grimm, Jacob & Grimm, Wilhelm K. Jorinda & Joringel. Cutts, David, ed. Rickman, David, illus. LC 87-10937. 32p. (gr. k-4). 1988. PLB 9.79 (*0-8167-1065-1*); pap. text ed. 1.95 (*0-8167-1066-X*) Troll Assocs.
Guthrie, Donna. The Witch Has an Itch. Arnsteen, Katy K., illus. 24p. (ps-1). 1990. pap. 2.50 (*0-671-70346-3*, Little Simon) S&S Trade.
—The Witch Who Lives down the Hall. Schwartz, Amy, illus. LC 85-887. 32p. (gr. k-3). 1985. 12.95 (*0-15-298610-3*, HB Juv Bks) HarBrace.
Hager, Betty. Miss Tilly & the Haunted Mansion. 112p. (gr. 3-7). 1994. pap. 4.99 (*0-310-38411-7*) Zondervan.
Hahn, Mary D. The Time of the Witch. 160p. (gr. 4-8). 1982. 13.45 (*0-89919-115-0*, Clarion Bks) HM.
—The Time of the Witch. 176p. 1991. pap. 3.99 (*0-380-71116-8*, Camelot) Avon.
Hall, Lynn. Dagmar Schultz & the Powers of Darkness. LC 88-30806. 80p. (gr. 5-8). 1989. SBE 13.95 (*0-684-19037-0*, Scribners Young Read) Macmillan Child Grp.
Harvey, Jayne. Great-Uncle Dracula. Carter, Abby, illus. LC 91-31460. 80p. (Orig.). (gr. 2-4). 1992. PLB 6.99 (*0-679-92448-5*); pap. 2.50 (*0-679-82448-0*) Random Bks Yng Read.
Hautzig, Deborah. Little Witch's Big Night. Brown, Marc, illus. LC 84-3309. 48p. (ps-2). 1984. PLB 7.99 (*0-394-96587-6*); pap. 3.50 (*0-394-86587-1*) Random Bks Yng Read.
—Little Witch's Book of Magic Spells. Brown, Marc, illus. LC 87-63196. 24p. (ps-1). 1993. 2.99 (*0-679-84769-3*) Random Bks Yng Read.
Hawkins, Colin. Witches. (gr. 4-7). 1993. pap. 7.00 (*0-00-662574-6*) HarpC Child Bks.
Hayes, Geoffrey. The Curse of the Cobweb Queen. LC 92-37272. 48p. (gr. 1-3). 1994. 7.99 (*0-679-93878-8*); pap. 3.50 (*0-679-83878-3*) Random Bks Yng Read.
Haynes, Betsy. The Witches of Wakeman. (gr. 4-7). 1990. pap. 2.75 (*0-553-15830-9*) Bantam.
Hebert, Marie-F. Witch's Brew. (Illus.). 54p. (Orig.). 1993. pap. 5.95 (*0-929005-52-X*, Pub. by Second Story Pr CN) InBook.
Henry, Terry H. The Witch Who Couldn't. O'Toole, Tom, illus. 96p. (gr. 5). 1988. 10.95 (*0-947962-39-5*, Pub. by Anvil Bks Ltd Ireland) Irish Bks Media.
Hess, Debra. Three Little Witches & the Fortune-Teller's Curse. (gr. 4-7). 1992. pap. 2.99 (*0-06-106117-4*, Harp PBks) HarpC.
Hildick, E. W. The Case of the Weeping Witch: A McGurk Fantasy. LC 91-38231. 160p. (gr. 3-7). 1992. SBE 13.95 (*0-02-743785-X*, Macmillan Child Bk) Macmillan Child Grp.
Hutchins, Pat. Which Witch Is Which? LC 88-18781. (Illus.). 24p. (ps up). 1989. 14.95 (*0-688-06357-8*); PLB 14.88 (*0-688-06358-6*) Greenwillow.
Ibbotson, Eve. Not Just a Witch. large type ed. Englander, Alice, illus. 240p. 1992. 16.95 (*0-7451-1552-7*, Galaxy Child Lrg Print) Chivers N Amer.
Jackson, Steve & Livingstone, Ian. The Warlock of Firetop Mountain. (gr. 5 up). 1983. pap. 1.95 (*0-440-99381-4*, LFL) Dell.
Jesep, Paul P. The Witch & the Sunflower Garden. Bowdren, John, illus. LC 92-62305. 20p. (Orig.). (gr. 4-5). 1993. pap. 9.95 (*0-9634360-3-1*) Seacoast Pubns New Eng.
Johnson, Norma T. The Witch House. 144p. (Orig.). 1990. pap. 2.95 (*0-380-75789-3*, Camelot) Avon.
Johnston, Tony. Witch's Hat. (ps-3). 1991. pap. 4.99 (*0-553-35354-3*) Bantam.
Jones, Diana W. Witch Week. reissued ed. LC 82-6074. 224p. (gr. 7 up). 1993. reinforced bdg. 14.00 (*0-688-12374-0*) Greenwillow.
Jones, Diane W. Witch Week. LC 82-6074. 224p. (gr. 7 up). 1982. reinforced bdg. 11.75 (*0-688-01534-4*) Greenwillow.
Katz, Welwyn W. Witchery Hill. (gr. k up). 1990. pap. 3.50 (*0-440-20637-5*, LFL) Dell.
Kellogg, Steven. The Christmas Witch. Kellogg, Steven, illus. LC 91-32688. 40p. (gr. k-3). 1992. 15.00 (*0-8037-1268-5*); PLB 14.89 (*0-8037-1269-3*) Dial Bks Young.
Kimmel, Margaret M. Magic in the Mist. Hyman, Trina S., illus. LC 74-18186. 32p. (gr. k-4). 1975. SBE 13.95 (*0-689-50026-2*, M K McElderry) Macmillan Child Grp.
Konigsburg, E. L. Jennifer, Hecate, Macbeth, William McKinley & Me, Elizabeth. Konigsburg, E. L., illus. LC 67-10458. 128p. (gr. 3-5). 1971. SBE 13.95 (*0-689-30007-7*, Atheneum Child Bk) Macmillan Child Grp.
—Jennifer, Hecate, Macbeth, William McKinley, & Me, Elizabeth. large type ed. (gr. 3-7). 1989. Repr. of 1967 ed. lib. bdg. 15.95 (*1-55736-143-6*, Crnrstn Bks) BDD LT Grp.
Kraus, Robert. Bunya the Witch. 1989. pap. 3.95 (*0-671-68422-1*, Little Simon) S&S Trade.
Krensky, Stephen. Witching Hour. 144p. (gr. 4-6). 1990. pap. 3.95 (*0-689-71366-5*, Aladdin) Macmillan Child Grp.
Kroll, Steven. The Candy Witch. Hafner, Marylin, illus. LC 79-10141. 32p. (ps-3). 1979. reinforced bdg. 14.95 (*0-8234-0359-9*) Holiday.
—Candy Witch. Hafner, Marilyn, illus. (ps up). 1988. pap. 2.50 (*0-590-44509-X*) Scholastic Inc.
Lasky, Kathryn. Beyond the Burning Time. 176p. (gr. 7 up). 1994. 13.95 (*0-590-47331-X*, Blue Sky Press) Scholastic Inc.
Laughlin, Florence. The Little Leftover Witch. 3rd ed. Greenwald, Sheila, illus. LC 92-41166. 96p. (gr. 1-4). 1993. pap. 3.95 (*0-689-71742-3*, Aladdin) Macmillan Child Grp.
Leister, Mary. Wee Green Witch. Arnold, Elaine, illus. LC 78-12380. 44p. (ps up). 1978. 9.95 (*0-916144-30-5*) Stemmer Hse.
Levoy, Myron. The Witch of Fourth Street & Other Stories. (gr. 3-6). 1991. 17.25 (*0-8446-6450-2*) Peter Smith.
Lewis, C. S. The Lion, the Witch, & the Wardrobe: (El Lion, la Bruja y el Armario) (SPA.). 11.95 (*84-204-4564-9*) Santillana.
Lexau, Joan M. The Poison Ivy Case. Hafner, Marylin, illus. LC 82-22123. 56p. (ps-3). 1984. Dial Bks Young.
Low, Alice. The Witch Who Was Afraid of Witches. Gundersheimer, Karen, illus. LC 78-5856. 40p. (gr. k-3). 1990. pap. 4.95 (*0-06-443234-3*, Trophy) HarpC Child Bks.

McAllister, Angela. Nesta, the Little Witch. Jenkin-Pearce, Susie, illus. 32p. (ps-3). 1993. pap. 4.99 (*0-14-054266-3*, Puffin) Puffin Bks.
McKean, Thomas. Hooray for Grandma Jo! Demarest, Chris, illus. LC 93-16376. (ps-6). 1994. 14.00 (*0-517-57842-5*); PLB 14.99 (*0-517-57843-3*) Crown Bks Yng Read.
MacLachlan, Patricia. Tomorrow's Wizard. Jacobi, Kathy, illus. LC 81-47733. 96p. (gr. 3-6). 1982. 12.95 (*0-06-024073-3*); PLB 12.89 (*0-06-024074-1*) HarpC Child Bks.
Marks, Graham. Webster & the Witch. (Illus.). 40p. (gr. k-3). 1987. 15.95 (*0-340-35564-6*, Pub. by Hodder & Stoughton UK) Trafalgar.
Marshak, Suzanna. The Wizard's Promise. Rand, Ted, illus. LC 92-36507. (ps-2). 1994. pap. 15.00 (*0-671-78431-5*, S&S BFYR) S&S Trade.
Martin, Ann M. Karen's Little Witch. 112p. 1991. pap. 2.95 (*0-590-44833-1*) Scholastic Inc.
Matas, Carol. The Burning Time. LC 94-443. 1994. 15.95 (*0-385-32097-3*) Delacorte.
Matens, Margaret H. Wuzzy the Witch. Matens, Margaret H., illus. LC 93-77128. 42p. (gr. k-5). 1993. 14.95 (*1-882959-54-X*) Foxglove TN.
Matthews, Liz. Teeny Witch & Christmas Magic. Loh, Carolyn, illus. LC 90-11206. 48p. (gr. k-1). 1991. PLB 11.89 (*0-8167-2270-6*); pap. 3.50 (*0-8167-2271-4*) Troll Assocs.
—Teeny Witch & the Great Halloween Ride. Loh, Carolyn, illus. LC 90-11207. 48p. (gr. k-1). 1991. PLB 11.89 (*0-8167-2274-9*); pap. text ed. 3.50 (*0-8167-2275-7*) Troll Assocs.
—Teeny Witch & the Perfect Valentine. Loh, Carolyn, illus. LC 90-11204. 48p. (gr. k-1). 1991. PLB 11.89 (*0-8167-2280-3*); pap. text ed. 3.50 (*0-8167-2281-1*) Troll Assocs.
—Teeny Witch & the Terrible Twins. Loh, Carolyn, illus. LC 90-11139. 48p. (gr. k-1). 1991. PLB 11.89 (*0-8167-2266-8*); pap. text ed. 3.50 (*0-8167-2267-6*) Troll Assocs.
—Teeny Witch & the Tricky Easter Bunny. Loh, Carolyn, illus. LC 90-11205. 48p. (gr. k-1). 1991. PLB 11.89 (*0-8167-2272-2*); pap. text ed. 3.50 (*0-8167-2273-0*) Troll Assocs.
—Teeny Witch Goes on Vacation. Loh, Carolyn, illus. LC 90-11141. 48p. (gr. k-1). 1991. lib. bdg. 11.89 (*0-8167-2278-1*); pap. text ed. 3.50 (*0-8167-2279-X*) Troll Assocs.
—Teeny Witch Goes to School. Loh, Carolyn, illus. LC 90-11208. 48p. (gr. k-1). 1991. PLB 11.89 (*0-8167-2276-5*); pap. 3.50 (*0-8167-2277-3*) Troll Assocs.
—Teeny Witch Goes to the Library. Loh, Carolyn, illus. LC 90-11140. 48p. (gr. k-1). 1991. PLB 11.89 (*0-8167-2268-4*); pap. text ed. 3.50 (*0-8167-2269-2*) Troll Assocs.
Meddaugh, Susan. The Witches' Supermarket. Meddaugh, Susan, illus. 32p. (gr. k-3). 1991. 13.95 (*0-395-57034-4*, Sandpiper) HM.
Montresor, Beni. The Witches of Venice. (Illus.). (ps-3). 1989. 13.95 (*0-385-26354-6*, Zephyr-BFYR); (Zephyr-BFYR) Doubleday.
Morley, Carol. Dots & Spots. Morley, Carol, illus. LC 92-24526. 32p. (ps-3). 1993. 14.00 (*0-06-021526-7*); PLB 13.89 (*0-06-021527-5*) HarpC Child Bks.
Munger, Anne R. The Not-So-Witchy Witch. (Illus.). 32p. (gr. 1-3). 1991. pap. 2.99 (*0-87406-583-6*) Willowisp Pr.
Murphy, Jill. Bad Spell for the Worst Witch. (gr. 4-7). 1991. pap. 3.95 (*0-14-031446-6*, Puffin) Puffin Bks.
—A Bad Spell for the Worst Witch. large type ed. Murphy, Jill, illus. 1993. 16.95 (*0-7451-1809-7*, Galaxy Child Lrg Print) Chivers N Amer.
—The Worst Witch. (Illus.). 80p. (gr. 3-7). 1982. pap. 2.50 (*0-380-60665-8*, Camelot) Avon.
—Worst Witch. (gr. 4-7). 1991. pap. 3.99 (*0-14-031108-4*, Puffin) Puffin Bks.
—The Worst Witch Strikes Again. 80p. (gr. 3-7). 1982. pap. 2.50 (*0-380-60673-9*, Camelot) Avon.
—Worst Witch Strikes Again. (gr. 4-7). 1991. pap. 3.99 (*0-14-031348-6*, Puffin) Puffin Bks.
Napoli, Donna J. The Magic Circle. LC 92-27008. 112p. (gr. 7 up). 1993. 14.99 (*0-525-45127-7*, DCB) Dutton Child Bks.
Naylor, Phyllis R. The Witch Returns. Burleson, Joe, illus. LC 91-32370. 192p. (gr. 3-6). 1992. 14.00 (*0-385-30601-6*) Delacorte.
—Witch Returns. (gr. 4-7). 1993. pap. 3.50 (*0-440-40815-6*) Dell.
—Witch's Eye. (gr. 4-7). 1991. pap. 3.50 (*0-440-40514-9*, YB) Dell.
Naylor-Reynolds, Phyllis. The Witch Herself. (gr. k-6). 1988. pap. 3.50 (*0-440-40044-9*, TB) Dell.
Nightingale, Sandy. Cat's Knees & Bee's Whiskers. Nightingale, Sandy, illus. LC 92-39811. 1993. 14.95 (*0-15-215364-0*) HarBrace.
Nix, Garth. The Ragwitch. 320p. 1994. pap. 3.99 (*0-8125-3506-5*) Tor Bks.
Norton, Mary. Bed-Knob & Broomstick. large type ed. Blegvad, Erik, illus. 296p. (gr. 3-7). 1989. 14.95 (*0-8161-4786-8*, Large Print Bks) Hall.
—Bed-Knob & Broomstick. Gaber, Susan, contrib. by. 229p. (gr. 3-7). 1990. pap. 3.95 (*0-15-206231-9*, Odyssey) HarBrace.
O'Connor, Jane. Lulu & the Witch Baby. McCully, Emily A., illus. LC 85-45832. 64p. (gr. k-3). 1986. PLB 13.89 (*0-06-024627-8*) HarpC Child Bks.
—Lulu & the Witch Baby. LC 85-45832. (Illus.). 64p. (gr. k-3). 1989. pap. 3.50 (*0-06-444130-X*, Trophy) HarpC Child Bks.
—Lulu Goes to Witch School. McCully, Emily A., illus. LC 87-37. 64p. (gr. k-3). 1990. pap. 3.50 (*0-06-444138-5*, Trophy) HarpC Child Bks.
Packard, Edward. Mystery-Chimney Rock. (gr. 3-7). 1979. pap. 2.25 (*0-553-26307-2*) Bantam.
Packard, Mary E. The Witch Who Couldn't Fly. Cushman, Douglas E., illus. LC 93-2212. (gr. k-3). 1993. pap. 2.95 (*0-8167-3256-6*) Troll Assocs.
Palatini, Margie. Piggie Pie. Fine, Howard, illus. LC 94-19726. 1995. write for info. (*0-395-71691-8*) HM.
Peet, Bill. Big Bad Bruce. Peet, Bill, illus. LC 76-62502. (gr. k-3). 1982. 13.95 (*0-395-25150-8*); pap. 5.95 (*0-395-32922-1*) HM.
Petry, Ann. Tituba of Salem Village. LC 64-20691. 272p. (gr. 5 up). 1991. pap. 3.95 (*0-06-440403-X*, Trophy) HarpC Child Bks.
Pike, Christopher. Witch. MacDonald, Patricia, ed. 240p. (Orig.). (gr. 8 up). 1990. pap. 3.99 (*0-671-69055-8*, Archway) PB.
Porter, Dorothy. The Witch Number. 1993. pap. 10.95 (*0-7022-2460-X*, Pub. by Univ Queensland Pr AT) Intl Spec Bk.
Reynolds-Naylor, Phyllis. The Witch's Sister. (gr. k-6). 1993. pap. 3.50 (*0-440-40028-7*, B) Dell.
Rinaldi, Ann. A Break with Charity: A Story about the Salem Witch Trials. LC 92-8858. 1992. 16.95 (*0-15-200353-3*, Gulliver Bks) HarBrace.
—Break with Charity: A Story about the Salem Witch Trials. LC 92-8858. (gr. 4-7). 1994. pap. 3.95 (*0-15-200101-8*, HB Juv Bks) HarBrace.
Robert, Adrian. My Grandma, the Witch. Fiammenghi, Gioia, illus. LC 84-8742. 48p. (gr. 2-4). 1985. PLB 10.89 (*0-8167-0422-8*); pap. text ed. 3.50 (*0-8167-0423-6*) Troll Assocs.
San Souci, Robert D. Feathertop: Based on the Tale by Nathaniel Hawthorne. San Souci, Daniel, illus. LC 91-10104. 32p. (gr. 1-5). 1992. pap. 16.00 (*0-385-42044-7*) Doubleday.
Schertle, Alice. Witch Hazel. Tomes, Margot, illus. LC 90-39630. 32p. (gr. k-4). 1991. 15.00 (*0-06-025140-9*); PLB 14.89 (*0-06-025141-7*) HarpC Child Bks.
—Witch Hazel. Tomes, Margot, illus. LC 90-39630. 32p. (gr. k-4). 1994. pap. 4.95 (*0-06-443368-4*, Trophy) HarpC Child Bks.
Schoder, Judith & Shebar, Sharon S. The Bell Witch. Morril, Leslie, illus. LC 82-42873. 64p. (gr. 7 up). 1983. (J Messner) S&S Trade.
Senn, Steve. Sand Witch. 96p. (gr. 3-7). 1987. pap. 2.75 (*0-380-75298-0*, Camelot) Avon.
Shecter, Ben. The Big Stew. Shecter, Ben, illus. LC 90-46271. 32p. (ps-2). 1991. PLB 14.89 (*0-06-025610-9*) HarpC Child Bks.
Shyer, Marlene F. Ruby, the Red-Hot Witch at Bloomingdale's. 160p. (gr. 3-7). 1993. pap. 3.99 (*0-14-034510-8*, Puffin) Puffin Bks.
Silverman, Erica. Big Pumpkin. Schindler, S. D., illus. LC 91-14053. 32p. (ps-3). 1992. RSBE 14.95 (*0-02-782683-X*, Macmillan Child Bk) Macmillan Child Grp.
Small, Ernest & Lent, Blair. Baba Yaga. Lent, Blair, illus. 48p. (gr. k-3). 1992. pap. 5.70 (*0-395-63037-1*, Sandpiper) HM.
Smith, Iris. Little Witch. Church, Caroline, illus. LC 92-39671. 28p. (ps-2). 1993. 12.95 (*0-8120-5791-0*); pap. 5.95 (*0-8120-1552-5*) Barron.
Smith, Maggie. There's a Witch Under the Stairs. (ps-3). 1991. 13.95 (*0-688-09884-3*); PLB 13.88 (*0-688-09885-1*) Lothrop.
Smith, Wendy. The Witch Baby. (ps-3). 1988. pap. 3.95 (*0-14-050590-3*, Puffin) Puffin Bks.
Snyder, Zilpha K. The Witches of Worm. Raible, Alton, illus. LC 72-75283. 192p. (gr. 4-8). 1972. SBE 14.95 (*0-689-30066-2*, Atheneum Child Bk) Macmillan Child Grp.
—The Witches of Worm. (gr. k-6). 1986. pap. 3.99 (*0-440-49727-2*, YB) Dell.
Speare, Elizabeth G. The Witch of Blackbird Pond. 256p. (gr. k-6). 1972. pap. 4.50 (*0-440-49596-2*, YB) Dell.
—Witch of Blackbird Pond. (Illus.). 256p. (gr. 7 up). 1958. 14.95 (*0-395-07114-3*) HM.
—The Witch of Blackbird Pond. 256p. (gr. 5 up). 1978. pap. 4.50 (*0-440-99577-9*, LFL) Dell.
Stevenson, James. Emma. Stevenson, James, illus. LC 84-4141. 32p. (gr. k-3). 1985. 11.75 (*0-688-04020-9*); PLB 11.88 (*0-688-04021-7*) Greenwillow.
—Emma at the Beach. LC 88-3491. (Illus.). (gr. k up). 1990. 12.95 (*0-688-08806-6*); lib. bdg. 12.88 (*0-688-08807-4*) Greenwillow.
—Yuck! Stevenson, James, illus. LC 83-25421. 32p. (gr. k-3). 1984. 11.75 (*0-688-03829-8*); PLB 11.88 (*0-688-03830-1*) Greenwillow.
Storey, Margaret. Timothy & the Two Witches. 92p. (gr. 2-5). 1974. pap. 0.75 (*0-440-48864-8*, YB) Dell.
Strasser, Todd. Hocus Pocus. LC 93-70573. (Illus.). 112p. (gr. 4-7). 1993. pap. 2.95 (*1-56282-373-6*) Disney Pr.
Stridh, Kicki. The Horrible Spookhouse. Eriksson, Eva, illus. LC 93-22076. 1993. write for info. (*0-87614-811-9*) Carolrhoda Bks.
Supraner, Robyn. The Cat Who Wanted to Fly. Goodman, Joan E., illus. LC 85-14119. 48p. (Orig.). (gr. 1-3). 1986. PLB 10.59 (*0-8167-0612-3*); pap. text ed. 3.50 (*0-8167-0613-1*) Troll Assocs.
—I Can Read About Witches. LC 74-24965. (Illus.). (gr. 2-4). 1975. pap. 2.50 (*0-89375-066-2*) Troll Assocs.
Taylor, E. J. Thorn Witch. (ps up). 1992. 12.95 (*1-56402-151-3*) Candlewick Pr.
Thomas, Valerie. Winnie the Witch. Paul, Korky, illus. 32p. (ps-3). 1987. 13.95 (*0-916291-13-8*) Kane-Miller Bk.
—Winnie the Witch. Paul, Korky, illus. 32p. (ps-3). 1990. pap. 6.95 (*0-916291-32-4*) Kane-Miller Bk.
Thompson, Jonathon J., Jr. Witch Hazel's Crazy Adventures. (Illus.). 80p. (gr. 3-6). 1985. 4.50 (*0-933479-05-0*) Thompson.
—Witch Hazel's Whackey Adventures. Thompson, Jonathon, illus. 104p. (gr. 3-6). 1985. 5.50 (*0-933479-01-8*) Thompson.
—Witch Hazel's Whackola Adventures. (Illus.). 143p. (gr. 4-8). 1986. 6.50 (*0-933479-03-4*) Thompson.
Turner, Ann. Rosemary's Witch. LC 90-39779. 176p. (gr. 6 up). 1991. 14.00 (*0-06-026127-7*); PLB 13.89 (*0-06-026128-5*) HarpC Child Bks.
—Rosemary's Witch. LC 90-39779. 176p. (gr. 4-7). 1994. pap. 3.95 (*0-06-440494-3*, Trophy) HarpC Child Bks.
Udry, Janice M. Glenda. Simont, Marc, illus. LC 69-14443. 64p. (gr. 1-5). 1991. pap. 3.95 (*0-06-440410-2*, Trophy) HarpC Child Bks.
Umansky, Kaye. Pongwiffy: A Witch of Dirty Habits. large type ed. 208p. 1992. 16.95 (*0-7451-1470-9*, Galaxy Child Lrg Print) Chivers N Amer.
Utton, Peter. The Witch's Hand. (ps up). 1989. 13.95 (*0-374-38463-0*) FS&G.
Vere-Hodge, Gwenda. Witches Are a Nuisance. 58p. 1987. 20.00x (*0-7223-2164-3*, Pub. by A H Stockwell) St Mut.
Wang, Mary L. The Good Witch. Rosales, Melodye, illus. LC 89-34415. 32p. (ps-2). 1989. pap. 3.95 (*0-516-42368-1*) Childrens.
Which Witch Is Which? (Illus.). 26p. (ps-1). 1988. pap. 2.95 incl. sticker pgs. (*0-671-66868-4*, Little Simon) S&S Trade.
Whitehead, Nathalie W. Dear Mrs. Witch. 1992. 7.95 (*0-533-10268-5*) Vantage.
Wilsdorf, Anne. Philomene. LC 90-24295. 1992. 14.00 (*0-688-10369-3*); PLB 13.93 (*0-688-10370-7*) Greenwillow.
Wolf, Joyce. Between the Cracks. 176p. (gr. 5 up). 1992. 14.95 (*0-8037-1270-7*) Dial Bks Young.
Yep, Laurence. Dragon Cauldron. LC 90-39584. 320p. (gr. 7 up). 1994. pap. 4.95 (*0-06-440398-X*, Trophy) HarpC Child Bks.

WIVES

Bently, Judith. Brides, Midwives, & Widows. (Illus.). 96p. (gr. 5-8). 1995. bds. 16.95 (*0-8050-2994-X*) TFC Bks NY.

WIVES OF PRESIDENTS

see Presidents–U. S.–Wives

WOLVERINES–FICTION

Montgomery, Rutherford G. Carcajou. Cram, L. D., illus. LC 36-6665. (gr. 6-8). 1936. 4.95 (*0-87004-105-3*) Caxton.

WOLVES

Benedict, Kitty. The Wolf: My First Nature Books. Felix, Monique, illus. 32p. (gr. k-2). 1993. pap. 2.95 (*1-56189-172-X*) Amer Educ Pub.
Bradshaw, Jeremy. The Wolf: The World's Wild Dogs. Stefoff, Rebecca, ed. LC 92-10244. (Illus.). 31p. (gr. 3-6). 1992. PLB 17.26 (*1-56074-055-8*) Garrett Ed Corp.
Brandenburg, Jim. To the Top of the World: Adventures with Arctic Wolves. Guernsey, JoAnn B., ed. Brandenburg, Jim, illus. LC 93-12105. 48p. (gr. 4-7). 1993. 16.95 (*0-8027-8219-1*); PLB 17.85 (*0-8027-8220-5*) Walker & Co.
Field, Nancy & Karasov, Corliss. Discovering Wolves. Hunkel, Cary, illus. 40p. (Orig.). (gr. 3-6). 1991. pap. 4.95 (*0-941042-10-3*) Dog Eared Pubns.
Frost, Abigail. The Wolf. LC 89-17445. (Illus.). 48p. (gr. 4-8). 1990. PLB 13.95 (*1-85435-237-7*) Marshall Cavendish.
George, Jean C. The Moon of the Gray Wolves. new ed. Catalano, Sal, illus. LC 90-38166. 48p. (gr. 3-7). 1991. 15.00 (*0-06-022442-8*); PLB 14.89 (*0-06-022443-6*) HarpC Child Bks.
Gibbons, Gail. Wolves. LC 94-2108. (Illus.). 32p. (ps-3). 1994. reinforced bdg. 15.95 (*0-8234-1127-3*) Holiday.
Giegling, John. Snowflake Come Home: A Wolf's Story. Oliver, Bryan, illus. 124p. (Orig.). (gr. 7-9). 1992. pap. 4.95 (*0-912661-12-7*) Woodsong Graph.
Godkin, Celia. Wolf Island. (ps-3). 1993. text ed. write for info. (*0-7167-6513-6*) W H Freeman.
Greene, Carol. Reading about the Gray Wolf. LC 92-26800. (Illus.). 32p. (gr. k-3). 1993. lib. bdg. 13.95 (*0-89490-427-2*) Enslow Pubs.
Hirschi, Ron. When the Wolves Return. Mangelsen, Thomas D., contrib. by. LC 94-16307. 1995. write for info. (*0-525-65144-6*) Dutton Child Bks.
Hogan, Paula Z. The Wolf. Maxwell, Barbara, illus. LC 79-13309. 32p. (gr. 1-4). 1979. PLB 19.97 (*0-8172-1507-7*) Raintree Steck-V.
—The Wolf. LC 79-13309. (Illus.). 32p. (gr. 1-4). 1981. PLB 29.28 incl. cassette (*0-8172-1846-7*) Raintree Steck-V.

Holen, Susan D. Alaska Wolf: Drawing Lessons, Coloring & Natural History. Arehart, Betsy, illus. 48p. (Orig.). (gr. 4-9). 1994. pap. 7.95g (*0-922127-05-0*) Paisley Pub.
An adventurer walks far into Alaska's

wild to search for a wolf pack. One windy day the adventurer crests a high hill, scans a boulder-strewn slope with binoculars, & spies six adult wolves sleeping "like a sack of potatoes" in the grass among boulders. The story portrays the everyday lives of the wolves, as told in the adventurer's journal with complete accuracy. Each journal entry is accompanied by a beautiful illustration drawn especially for coloring by Alaska wildlife artist Betsy Arehart. Illustrations encompass everything from pups at play to the action of the hunt. Also included are drawing lessons on pups, adult wolves & caribou; several pages of illustrated facts about wolves & other animals in the wolves' world; a glossary, & a map of Alaska showing that almost the entire state is still wolf range. This book has been approved by the International Wolf Center & by Wolfsong of Alaska & includes endorsements on the back cover. The group of 4th, 5th & 6th graders who read the manuscript responded with high enthusiasm & the interest. THE ALASKA WOLF is a premium quality coloring book printed on 70 pound paper with a coated, durable cover. A complete learning resource about the Alaska wolf. To order: Paisley Publishing, P.O. Box 142424, Anchorage, AK 99514.
Publisher Provided Annotation.

Johnson, Sylvia A. & Aamodt, Alice. Wolf Pack: Tracking Wolves in the Wild. (Illus.). 96p. (gr. 5 up). 1985. PLB 22.95 (*0-8225-1577-6*) Lerner Pubns.
—Wolf Pack: Tracking Wolves in the Wild. (Illus.). 96p. (gr. 5 up). 1987. pap. 6.95 (*0-8225-9526-5*, First Ave Edns) Lerner Pubns.
Lawrence, R. D. Wolves. (gr. 3-6). 1990. 16.95 (*0-316-51676-7*) Little.
Lepthien, Emilie U. Wolves. LC 91-3035. 48p. (gr. k-4). 1991. PLB 12.85 (*0-516-01129-4*); pap. 4.95 (*0-516-41129-2*) Childrens.
Ling, Mary. Amazing Wolves, Dogs, & Foxes. Young, Jerry, photos by. LC 91-6514. (Illus.). 32p. (Orig.). (gr. 1-5). 1991. lib. bdg. 9.99 (*0-679-91521-4*); pap. 7.99 (*0-679-81521-X*) Knopf Bks Yng Read.
McConoughey, Jana. The Wolves. LC 83-2086. (Illus.). 48p. (gr. 5). 1983. text ed. 12.95 RSBE (*0-89686-225-9*, Crestwood Hse) Macmillan Child Grp.
Markert, Jenny. Wolves. 32p. (gr. 2-6). 1991. 15.95 (*0-89565-711-2*) Childs World.
Masefield, John. The Box of Delights: Or, When the Wolves Were Running. Crampton, Patricia, abridged by. Jaques, Faith, illus. 176p. (gr. k up). 1984. pap. 2.95 (*0-440-40853-9*, YB) Dell.
Milton, Joyce. Wild, Wild Wolves. Schwinger, Larry, illus. LC 90-8807. 48p. (Orig.). (gr. 1-3). 1992. PLB 7.99 (*0-679-91052-2*); pap. 3.50 (*0-679-81052-8*) Random Bks Yng Read.
Ohanian, Susan. Wolves. Ruth, Trevor, illus. LC 93-28973. 1994. 4.25 (*0-383-03742-5*) SRA Schl Grp.
Patent, Dorothy H. Gray Wolf, Red Wolf. Munoz, William, photos by. (Illus.). 64p. (gr. 4 up). 1990. 15.95 (*0-89919-863-5*, Clarion Bks) HM.
Robinson, Sandra C. The Wonder of Wolves: A Story & Activity Book. Opsahl, Gail K., illus. (gr. 1-6). 1989. pap. 7.95 (*0-911797-65-3*) R Rinehart.
Silverstein, Alvin, et al. The Red Wolf. LC 93-42480. (Illus.). 48p. (gr. 4-6). 1994. PLB 13.40 (*1-56294-416-9*) Millbrook Pr.
Simon, Seymour. Wolves. Simon, Seymour, illus. LC 92-25924. 32p. (gr. k-3). 1993. 16.00 (*0-06-022531-9*); PLB 15.89 (*0-06-022534-3*) HarpC Child Bks.
Standring, Gillian. Wolves. LC 91-11170. (Illus.). 32p. (gr. 2-5). 1992. PLB 12.40 (*0-531-18452-8*, Pub. by Bookwright Pr) Watts.
Stone, L. Lobos (Wolves) 1991. 8.95s.p. (*0-86592-834-7*) Rourke Enter.
Stone, Lynn. Wolves. (Illus.). 24p. (gr. k-5). 1990. lib. bdg. 11.94 (*0-86593-044-9*); lib. bdg. 8.95s.p. (*0-685-36342-2*) Rourke Corp.
Strieber, Whitley. Wolf of Shadows. LC 84-20133. (Illus.). 128p. (gr. 7-12). 1985. PLB 9.99 (*0-394-97224-4*) Knopf Bks Yng Read.
Wexo, John B. Wolves. 24p. (gr. 4). 1989. PLB 14.95 (*0-88682-267-X*) Creative Ed.
Wolpert, Tom. Wolf Magic for Kids. Rogers, Lynn, illus. LC 90-50720. 48p. (gr. 2-3). 1991. PLB 18.60 (*0-8368-0662-X*) Gareth Stevens Inc.

WOLVES–FICTION

Aiken, Joan. The Wolves of Willoughby Chase. 176p. (gr. k-6). 1987. pap. 3.99 (*0-440-49603-9*, YB) Dell.
—The Wolves of Willoughby Chase. Marriott, Pat, illus. LC 63-18034. 168p. (gr. 4-6). 1989. pap. 13.95 (*0-385-03594-2*) Doubleday.
Allen, Jonathan. Who's at the Door? Allen, Jonathan, illus. LC 92-19618. 32p. (ps up). 1993. 11.95 (*0-688-12257-4*, Tambourine Bks) Morrow.
Beeson, Bob. What Time Is It, Mr. Wolf? Beeson, Bob, illus. 32p. (ps). 1994. 12.95 (*0-8249-8649-0*, Ideals Child) Hambleton-Hill.
Benchley, Nathaniel. Small Wolf. Sandin, Joan, illus. 1994. pap. 3.50 (*0-06-444180-6*) HarpC Child Bks.
Blundell, Tony. Beware of Boys. LC 90-24299. (Illus.). 32p. (ps up). 1992. 15.00 (*0-688-10924-1*); PLB 14.93 (*0-688-10925-X*) Greenwillow.
Burgess, Melvin. The Cry of the Wolf. LC 91-47690. 128p. (gr. 5 up). 1992. 13.00 (*0-688-11744-9*, Tambourine Bks) Morrow.
Bushnell, Jack. Circus of the Wolves. Parker, Robert A., illus. LC 93-8092. 1994. 15.00 (*0-688-12554-9*); lib. bdg. 14.93 (*0-688-12555-7*) Lothrop.
Corcoran, Barbara. Wolf at the Door. LC 92-45108. 192p. (gr. 3-7). 1993. SBE 14.95 (*0-689-31870-7*, Atheneum Child Bk) Macmillan Child Grp.
Cross, Gillian. Wolf. 1993. pap. 3.25 (*0-590-45608-3*) Scholastic Inc.
Curwood, James O. Baree, the Story of a Wolf-Dog. LC 90-37875. 256p. (gr. 3-11). 1992. 18.95 (*1-55704-075-3*); pap. 3.95 (*1-55704-132-6*) Newmarket.
Cuyler, Margery. Weird Wolf. Zimmer, Dirk, illus. LC 89-7541. 80p. (gr. 2-4). 1989. 12.95 (*0-8050-0835-7*, Bks Young Read) H Holt & Co.
Delaney, Antoinette. The Gunnywolf. Delaney, Antoinette, illus. LC 87-29351. 32p. (ps-3). 1992. pap. 4.95 (*0-06-443304-8*, Trophy) HarpC Child Bks.
De Marolles, Chantal. The Lonely Wolf. Schmid, Eleonore, illus. LC 86-2511. 32p. (gr. k-3). 1986. 14.95 (*1-55858-073-5*) North-South Bks NYC.
Demco, Inc. Staff & De Broux, Jane. Little Wolf's Birthday. 20p. (gr. k-2). 1994. wkbk. 1.99 (*1-885360-02-9*) Demco WI.
—Little Wolf's School Day. 20p. (gr. k-2). 1994. wkbk. 1.99 (*1-885360-00-2*) Demco WI.
—Little Wolf's Seasons. 20p. (gr. k-2). 1994. wkbk. 1.99 (*1-885360-01-0*) Demco WI.
Faucher, Elizabeth. White Fang II: Myths of the White Wolf. 1994. pap. 3.50 (*0-590-48611-X*) Scholastic Inc.
George, Jean C. Julie of the Wolves. Minor, Wendell, illus. LC 93-27738. 240p. (gr. 5 up). 1994. 15.00 (*0-06-023528-4*); PLB 14.89 (*0-06-023529-2*) HarpC Child Bks.
—The Wounded Wolf. Schoenherr, John, illus. LC 76-58711. (ps-3). 1978. PLB 14.89 (*0-06-021950-5*) HarpC Child Bks.
Gregory, Philippa. Florizella & the Wolves. Aggs, Patrice, illus. LC 92-52998. 80p. (gr. 3-6). 1993. 13.95 (*1-56402-126-2*) Candlewick Pr.
Grimm, Jacob & Grimm, Wilhelm K. Little Red Riding Hood. Schmidt, Karen L., illus. 32p. (Orig.). (gr. k-2). 1986. pap. 2.50 (*0-590-41881-5*) Scholastic Inc.

Holbrook, Janet M. Little Red Hiding Wolf. McNutt, Mary M., illus. 35p. (gr. k-12). 1992. pap. 8.95 (*0-9636203-0-4*) Holbrook Dogwds. LITTLE RED HIDING WOLF, frolicking through the woods to carry her gift to Grandmawolf, meets a frightening stranger on the path. While she is fleeing for her life, Daddywolf leads the pack in a clever scheme to save her. Then they discover Grandmawolf snared in the Hunter's trap & the heartbroken wolves cannot free her. When two kind children come to the rescue, a great celebration rewards them with an honorary membership in the wolfpack. Unlike the "big bad wolf" in the popular fairy tale, the legend of LITTLE RED HIDING WOLF paints a true picture of wolf personality...a family of animals who care about one another, have a well organized social order, & work together for subsistence & protection. The story is presented with realistic illustrations designed to stimulate young readers, ages 6 to 12 years, to learn more about Canis lupus, the ancient ancestors of the dogs that share our homes. To order write or call: Holbrook Dogwoods, 4662 Happy Valley Road, Sequim, WA 98382. Phone: (206) 683-4121, FAX: (206) 683-1220.
Publisher Provided Annotation.

Horowitz, Lynn R. The Good Bad Wolf. Urbahn, Clara, illus. LC 89-63141. 28p. (Orig.). (ps-5). 1989. Spiral bdg. pap. 7.95 (*0-938678-12-4*) New Seed. The warm-hearted story of a little girl who comes across a wolf in the woods & discovers he's not so bad after all. Charmingly illustrated. Lynn A. Horowitz, author of LULU TURNS FOUR & MANOS A LA OBRA lives in Berkeley, California. Clara Urbahn, the author's sister, illustrator of 6 other children's stories, lives in Nantucket, Massachusetts. New Seed Press, P.O. Box 9488, Berkeley, CA 94709.
Publisher Provided Annotation.

Huebel, Russ. The Big Bad Wolf in Texas. Espinosa, Tony, illus. 48p. (Orig.). 1983. pap. 6.25 (*0-9611604-2-X*) C Del Grullo.
Jordan, Sherryl. Wolf-Woman. LC 94-7043. 1994. 13.95 (*0-395-70932-6*) HM.
Kasza, Keiko. The Wolf's Chicken Stew. Kasza, Keiko, illus. (gr. k-3). 1987. 13.95 (*0-399-21400-3*, Putnam) Putnam Pub Group.
Kergueno, Jacqueline & Seignolle, Claude. The Man with Seven Wolves. (Illus.). (gr. 3-8). 1992. PLB 8.95 (*0-89565-895-X*) Childs World.
Lado, Robert. The Big Bad Wolf: Level 2. (Illus.). 24p. (ps). 1985. pap. 3.95 (*1-879580-53-5*); card pack 1.95 (*1-879580-52-7*) Lado Intl Pr.
LaFleur, Tom & Brennan, Gale. Woolly the Wolf. Bond, Bruce, illus. 16p. (Orig.). (gr. k-6). 1981. pap. 1.25 (*0-685-02459-8*) Brennan Bks.
London, Jack. Call of the Wild. (Illus.). 1991. pap. 2.95 (*1-56156-094-4*) Kidsbks.
—The Call of the Wild. (gr. 8). 1991. pap. write for info. (*0-663-56265-1*) Silver Burdett Pr.
—The Call of the Wild. Moser, Barry, illus. Paulsen, Gary, intro. by. LC 93-18409. (Illus.). (gr. 4 up). 1994. 19.95 (*0-02-759455-6*) Macmillan.
—White Fang. 256p. (gr. 6 up). 1986. pap. 3.25 (*0-590-42591-9*) Scholastic Inc.
—White Fang. 224p. 1989. pap. 2.50 (*0-8125-0512-3*) Tor Bks.
London, Jack, et al. The Call of the Wild. (Illus.). 52p. Date not set. pap. 4.95 (*1-57209-010-3*) Classics Int Ent.
London, Jonathan. The Eyes of Grey Wolf. Van Zale, Jon, illus. LC 92-35987. (gr. 4 up). 1993. 13.95 (*0-8118-0285-X*) Chronicle Bks.
Loring, Honey & Harris, John. The Big Good Wolf. Deutsch, Nicholas, illus. 28p. (ps-6). 1990. pap. text ed. 2.75 (*0-9626566-0-7*) Gone Dogs.
Love, Douglas. Blame It on the Wolf. Zimmerman, Robert, illus. 64p. (gr. 3 up). 1994. pap. 3.50 (*0-694-00653-X*, Festival) HarpC Child Bks.
McCleery, William. Wolf Story. Chappell, Warren, illus. LC 87-25977. 82p. (gr. 1-6). 1988. Repr. of 1947 ed. PLB 15.00 (*0-208-02191-4*, Linnet) Shoe String.
Manton, Denis. Wolf Comes to Town. LC 93-37918. 1994. write for info. (*0-525-45281-8*, DCB) Dutton Child Bks.
Nickl, Peter. The Story of the Kind Wolf. Wilkon, Jozef, illus. LC 87-42923. 32p. (gr. k-3). 1988. 13.95 (*1-55858-066-2*); pap. 4.95 (*1-55858-058-1*) North-South Bks NYC.
Oetting, R. Quetico Wolf. LC 71-190274. (Illus.). 48p. (gr. 4 up). 1972. PLB 9.95 (*0-87783-059-2*); pap. 3.94 deluxe ed. (*0-87783-103-3*) Oddo.
Offen, Hilda. Nice Work, Little Wolf! LC 91-23741. (Illus.). 32p. (ps-2). 1992. 14.00 (*0-525-44880-2*, DCB) Dutton Child Bks.
Patent, Dorothy H. Gray Wolf, Red Wolf. (gr. 4-7). 1994. pap. 6.95 (*0-395-69627-5*, Clarion Bks) HM.
Pepin, Muriel. Little Bear's New Friend. Geneste, Marcelle, illus. LC 91-40652. 24p. (ps-3). 1992. 6.99 (*0-89577-417-8*, Dist. by Random) RD Assn.
Porter, Sue. Little Wolf & the Giant. (ps-1). 1990. pap. 13.95 jacketed (*0-671-70363-3*, S&S BFYR) S&S Trade.
Prokofiev, Sergei. Peter & the Wolf. Carlson, Maria, tr. Mikolayack, Charles, illus. 32p. (ps-3). 1986. pap. 4.99 (*0-14-050633-0*, Puffin) Puffin Bks.
—Peter & the Wolf. Crampton, Patricia, tr. Palecek, Josef, illus. LC 87-13915. (ps up). 1991. pap. 13.95 (*0-88708-049-9*) Picture Bk Studio.
—Peter & the Wolf. Voigt, Erna, illus. LC 79-92902. 28p. 1979. 15.95 (*0-87923-331-1*) Godine.
—Peter & the Wolf Pop-up-Book. Cooney, Barbara, illus. (gr. k-12). 1986. pap. 17.00 (*0-670-80849-0*) Viking Child Bks.
Richmond, Gary. Prodigal Wolf. 1990. 6.99 (*0-8499-0746-2*) Word Inc.

Rinaldi, Ann. Wolf by the Ears. 1993. pap. 3.50 (*0-590-43412-8*) Scholastic Inc.
Roddie, Shen. Mrs. Wolf: A Three-Dimensional Picture Book. Paul, Korky, illus. LC 92-1202. 24p. (gr. k-3). 1993. 13.99 (*0-8037-1300-2*) Dial Bks Young.
Sargent, Dave & Sargent, Pat. Dike the Wolf. 64p. (gr. 2-6). 1992. pap. write for info. (*1-56763-008-1*) Ozark Pub.
Seton, Ernest T. Lobo the Wolf: King of Currumpaw. rev. ed. Ryan, Donna, illus. 72p. (gr. 3-8). 1991. pap. 9.95 (*0-9623072-4-6*) S Ink WA.
Sharmat, Marjorie W. Walter the Wolf. LC 74-26659. (Illus.). 32p. (ps-3). 1975. pap. 5.95 (*0-8234-0778-0*) Holiday.
Shefelman, Janice. Young Wolf's First Hunt. Date not set. 3.50 (*0-679-86364-8*) Random Bks Yng Read.
Strauss, Susan. Wolf Stories: Myths & True Life Tales from Around the World. Livingston, Julie, ed. Lund, Gary, illus. 48p. (Orig.). (gr. 1-6). 1993. 11.95 (*0-941831-84-1*); pap. 7.95 (*0-941831-88-4*) Beyond Words Pub.
Sweeten, Sami. Wolf. LC 93-34493. 1994. write for info. (*0-8075-9160-2*) A Whitman.
Testa, Fulvio. Wolf's Flavor. (ps-3). 1990. 3.95 (*0-8037-0744-4*, Dial) Doubleday.
Yolen, Jane. Children of the Wolf. 144p. (gr. 7 up). 1993. pap. 3.99 (*0-14-036477-3*, Puffin) Puffin Bks.

WOMBAT–FICTION

Argent, Kerry. Happy Birthday, Wombat! A Lift-the-Flap Book. (ps). 1991. 11.95 (*0-316-05097-0*, Joy St Bks) Little.

WOMEN

see also Girls; Mothers

Angelou, Maya. My Painted House, My Friendly Chicken, & Me. Courtney-Clarke, Margaret, photos by. LC 93-45735. (Illus.). 48p. (ps-5). 1994. 16.00 (*0-517-59667-9*, Clarkson Potter) Crown Pub Group.
Aten, Jerry. Women in History. Hyndman, Kathryn, illus. 144p. (gr. 4 up). 1986. wkbk. 12.95 (*0-86653-344-3*, GA 692) Good Apple.
August, Paul N. Drugs & Women. (Illus.). 32p. (gr. 5 up). 1991. pap. 4.49 (*0-7910-0002-8*) Chelsea Hse.
Curro, Ellen. No Need to Be Afraid...First Pelvic Exam: A Handbook for Young Women & Their Mothers. Piccirilli, Charles, illus. 80p. (gr. 9-12). 1991. pap. text ed. 4.95 (*0-9629417-1-9*) Linking Ed Med.
Dubois, Jill. Women in Society: Mexico. Siow, Eric, illus. LC 92-34402. 1993. 22.95 (*1-85435-557-0*); Set. write for info. Marshall Cavendish.
Epstein, Vivian S. History of Women for Children. Epstein, Vivian S., illus. 32p. (ps-5). 1984. 12.95 (*0-9601002-4-5*); pap. 5.95 (*0-9601002-3-7*) V S Epstein.
Fannon. Around the World. 1991. 12.95s.p. (*0-86593-119-4*) Rourke Corp.
Ghose, Vijaya. Women in Society. LC 93-46880. (gr. 5 up). 1994. write for info. Set (*1-85435-559-7*) Marshall Cavendish.
Harris, Sarah. Finding out About: Women in Twentieth Century Britain, Finding Out About Ser. (Illus.). 48p. (gr. 7-10). 1989. 19.95 (*0-7134-5661-2*, Pub. by Batsford UK) Trafalgar.
Hoobler, Dorothy & Hoobler, Thomas. Her Story Series. Hewitson, Jennifer, illus. (gr. 4-6). 1992. 47.60 (*0-382-24149-5*); PLB 63.60 (*0-382-24142-8*); pap. 31.60 (*0-382-24355-2*) Silver Burdett Pr.
Institute for Women's Policy Research, The Young Women's Project Staff. The Young Women's Handbook: Beyond Surviving in the 90s. Moritz, Nadia, intro. by. 675p. (Orig.). (gr. 10 up). 1991. pap. 30.00 (*1-878428-05-5*) Inst Womens Policy Rsch.
Jones, Norma H., et al, eds. Women - New Roles in Society. 68p. (gr. 6-9). 1992. pap. 11.95 (*1-878623-45-1*) Info Plus TX.
Katz, William L. The New Freedom to the New Deal, 1913-1939. LC 92-39948. (Illus.). 96p. (gr. 7-8). 1993. PLB 22.80 (*0-8114-6279-X*) Raintree Steck-V.
Knudson, R. R. Martina Navratilova: Tennis Power. Angelini, George, illus. LC 85-40832. 64p. (gr. 2-6). 1986. pap. 10.95 (*0-670-80665-X*) Viking Child Bks.
Kotlyarskaya, Elena. Women in Society: Russia. LC 93-49762. 1994. 22.95 (*1-85435-561-9*) Marshall Cavendish.
Levy, Patricia M. Women in Society: Britain. LC 92-33353. 1993. 22.95 (*1-85435-555-4*) Marshall Cavendish.
Meier, Gisela. Minorities. LC 91-11651. 64p. (gr. 5-7). 1991. 12.95s.p. (*0-86593-124-0*); lib. bdg. 17.27 (*0-685-59203-0*) Rourke Corp.
Mitchell, Joyce. Other Choices for Becoming a Woman. (gr. 7 up). 1975. pap. 6.00 (*0-912786-34-5*) Know Inc.
Muhammad, S. Ifetayo. The Goals of a Polygamous Woman. 16p. (Orig.). 1987. pap. 0.50 (*0-916157-11-3*) African Islam Miss Pubns.
Phelps, Ethel J., ed. Tatterhood & Other Tales. Baldwin-Ford, Pamela, illus. Phelps, Ethel, intro. by. LC 78-9352. (Illus.). 192p. (Orig.). (gr. 1 up). 1978. o. p. 11.95 (*0-912670-49-5*); pap. 9.95 (*0-912670-50-9*) Feminist Pr.
Rappaport, Doreen. American Women: Their Lives in Their Words. LC 89-77621. (Illus.). 336p. (gr. 7 up). 1992. pap. 6.95 (*0-06-446127-0*, Trophy) HarpC Child Bks.
Reese, Lyn. Spindle Stories, Bk. Two: Three Units on Women's World History. Dougherty, Mary A. & Wilkinson, Jean B., eds. Gorell, Nancy, illus. 118p. (gr. 6-10). 1991. pap. text ed. 15.00 (*0-9625880-1-6*) Women World CRP.
Saxby, Maurice. The Great Deeds of Heroic Women. Ingpen, Robert, illus. LC 91-11211. 152p. (gr. 4 up). 1992. 18.95 (*0-87226-348-7*) P Bedrick Bks.
Sirimarco. Health. 1991. 12.95s.p. (*0-86593-122-4*); PLB 17.27 (*0-685-59200-6*) Rourke Corp.
Tan, Pamela. Women in Society: China. LC 92-33354. 1993. 22.95 (*1-85435-556-2*) Marshall Cavendish.
Wehrheim, Carol. The Great Parade: Learning about Women, Justice & the Church. (Orig.). 1992. pap. 7.95 incl. children's activity pages & tchr's. guide (*0-377-00244-5*) Friendship Pr.

WOMEN–BIOGRAPHY

Andryszewski, Tricia. Marjory Stoneman Douglas, Friend of the Everglades. LC 93-26731. (Illus.). 48p. (gr. 2-4). 1994. PLB 12.90 (*1-56294-384-7*) Millbrook Pr.
Antonia Novello. (ps-3). 1993. 18.95 (*0-7910-1557-2*) Chelsea Hse.
Archer, James. Breaking Barriers: The Feminist Movement. 1991. 14.95 (*0-670-83104-2*) Viking Child Bks.
Aten, Jerry. Outstanding Women. Hierstein, Judy, illus. 64p. (gr. k-4). 1987. pap. 7.95 (*0-86653-413-X*, GA1008) Good Apple.
Atkinson, Linda. In Kindling Flame: The Story of Hannah Senesh. ALC Staff, ed. LC 83-24392. (Illus.). 224p. (gr. 8 up). 1992. pap. 4.95 (*0-688-11689-2*, Pub. by Beech Tree Bks) Morrow.
Ausbrook, Michael. Raisa Gorbachev. (Illus.). 112p. (gr. 5 up). 1992. lib. bdg. 17.95 (*0-7910-1625-0*) Chelsea Hse.
Ayer, Eleanor H. Ruth Bader Ginsburg. LC 94-17854. 1994. text ed. 13.95 (*0-87518-651-3*, Dillon Pr) Macmillan Child Grp.
Bach, Julie. Tipper Gore. LC 93-15326. (Illus.). 1993. 12.94 (*1-56239-220-4*) Abdo & Dghtrs.
Balee, Susan. Flannery O'Connor. LC 94-9377. 1994. write for info. (*0-7910-2418-0*); pap. write for info. (*0-7910-2419-9*) Chelsea Hse.
Barker, Jane V. & Downing, Sybil. Martha Maxwell: Pioneer Naturalist. Jones, Ann, illus. 138p. 1982. pap. 6.95 (*1-878611-12-7*) Silver Rim Pr.
Benavidez, Barbara. My School Years: Kindergarten Through Graduation. (Illus.). (gr. 5-12). 24.95 (*0-9619463-0-X*) Barmarle Pubns.
Bennett, Olivia. Annie Besant. (Illus.). 64p. (gr. 6-10). 1991. 13.95 (*0-237-60038-2*, Pub. by Evans Bros Ltd) Trafalgar.
Blau, Justine. Betty Friedan. Horner, Matina, intro. by. (Illus.). 112p. (gr. 5 up). 1990. lib. bdg. 17.95 (*1-55546-653-2*) Chelsea Hse.
Bouchard, Elizabeth. Benazir Bhutto: Prime Minister. (Illus.). 64p. (gr. 3-7). PLB 14.95 (*1-56711-027-4*) Blackbirch.
Brown, Gene. Anne Frank: Child of the Holocaust. (Illus.). 64p. (gr. 3-7). PLB 14.95 (*1-56711-030-4*) Blackbirch.
Bryant. Carol Thomas-Weaver. 1991. 0.85 (*0-8050-2012-8*) H Holt & Co.
Buffalo, Audreen. Meet Oprah Winfrey. (Illus.). 112p. (gr. 3-5). 1993. pap. 2.99 (*0-679-85425-8*, Bullseye Bks) Random Bks Yng Read.
Burch, Joann J. Marian Wright Edelman, Children's Champion. LC 94-2260. (Illus.). 48p. (gr. 2-4). 1994. PLB 12.90 (*1-56294-457-6*); pap. 6.95 (*1-56294-742-7*) Millbrook Pr.
Cain, Michael. Louise Nevelson. Horner, Matina S., intro. by. (Illus.). 112p. (gr. 5 up). 1989. 17.95 (*1-55546-671-0*) Chelsea Hse.
Carrigan, Mellonee. Carol Moseley-Braun: Breaking Barriers. (Illus.). 32p. (gr. 2-4). 1994. PLB 11.80 (*0-516-04190-8*) Childrens.
Colman, Penny. Madame C. J. Walker: Building a Business Empire. (Illus.). 48p. (gr. 2-4). 1994. 12.90 (*1-56294-338-3*) Millbrook Pr.
Contemporary Women Series, 16 bks. (Illus.). (gr. 6 up). Set. lib. bdg. 280.80 (*0-89490-344-6*) Enslow Pubs.
Cush, Cathie. Women Who Achieved Greatness. (Illus.). 48p. (gr. 4-8). 1994. PLB write for info. (*0-8114-4938-6*) Raintree Steck-V.
Daffron, Carolyn. Gloria Steinem. Horner, Matina, intro. by. (Illus.). 112p. (gr. 5 up). 1988. lib. bdg. 17.95 (*1-55546-679-6*) Chelsea Hse.
DeGraf, Anna. Pioneering on the Yukon, 1892-1917. Brown, Roger S., ed. LC 92-14808. (Illus.). ix, 128p. 1992. lib. bdg. 19.50 (*0-208-02362-3*, Pub. by Archon Bks) Shoe String.
Dengler, Sandy. Fanny Crosby: Writer of Eight Thousand Songs. (Orig.). (gr. 2-7). 1985. pap. 4.50 (*0-8024-2529-1*) Moody.
De Pauw, Linda G. Founding Mothers: Women of America in the Revolutionary Era. (Illus.). 228p. (gr. 7 up). 1975. 16.95 (*0-395-21896-9*) HM.
Downing, Sybil & Barker, Jane V. Florence Sabin: Pioneer Scientist. Jones, Ann, illus. 100p. 1981. pap. 6.95 (*1-878611-11-9*) Silver Rim Pr.
Dunham, Montrew. Mahalia Jackson: Young Gospel Singer. LC 93-34072. 1995. pap. 4.95 (*0-689-71786-5*, Aladdin) Macmillan Child Grp.
—Margaret Bourke-White, Young Photographer. LC 93-46159. 1995. pap. 4.95 (*0-689-71785-7*, Aladdin) Macmillan Child Grp.
Ferman, Arlene, et al. Better Than Our Best - Women of Valor in American History. (Illus.). 150p. (Orig.). (gr. 6-9). 1990. pap. 9.95 (*0-8283-1941-3*) Branden Pub Co.
Fisher, Leonard E. Marie Curie. LC 93-40211. (Illus.). (gr. 2-6). 1994. 14.95 (*0-02-735375-3*, Macmillan Child Bk) Macmillan Child Grp.
Forrest, Wendy. Rosa Luxemburg. (Illus.). 64p. (gr. 6-10). 1991. 15.95 (*0-237-60040-4*, Pub. by Evans Bros Ltd) Trafalgar.
Foster, Leila M. Margaret Thatcher: First Woman Prime Minister of Great Britain. LC 90-2209. (Illus.). 152p. (gr. 4 up). 1990. PLB 14.40 (*0-516-03269-0*) Childrens.
French, Alice. My Name Is Masak. (Illus.). 110p. (gr. 7-8). 1992. pap. 9.95 (*0-919566-56-1*) Peguis Pubs Ltd.
Garza, Hedda. Frida Kahlo: Mexican Painter. (Illus.). (ps-3). 1994. PLB 18.95 (*0-7910-1698-6*, Am Art Analog); pap. 7.95 (*0-7910-1699-4*, Am Art Analog) Chelsea Hse.
Gatti, Anne. Isabella Bird Bishop. (Illus.). 64p. (gr. 6-10). 1991. 13.95 (*0-237-60035-8*, Pub. by Evans Bros Ltd) Trafalgar.
Giblin, James C. Edith Wilson: The Woman Who Ran the United States. Laporte, Michele, illus. 64p. (gr. 2-6). 1992. RB 11.00 (*0-670-83005-4*) Viking Child Bks.
Giff, Patricia R. Mother Teresa: Sister to the Poor. Lewin, Ted, illus. (gr. 2-6). 1987. pap. 4.50 (*0-14-032225-6*, Puffin) Puffin Bks.
Green, Carl R. & Ford, Roxanne. Jennifer Capriati. LC 93-39397. 1994. text ed. 13.95 (*0-89686-834-6*, Crestwood Hse) Macmillan Child Grp.
Greene, Carol. Christina Rossetti: Poet. (Illus.). 48p. (gr. k-3). 1994. PLB 12.85 (*0-516-04262-9*) Childrens.
—Emily Dickinson: American Poet. LC 94-11167. (Illus.). 32p. (gr. 2-4). 1994. PLB 17.20 (*0-516-04263-7*); pap. 4.95 (*0-516-44263-5*) Childrens.
—Laura Ingalls Wilder: Author of the Little House Books. Dobson, Steven, illus. LC 89-25362. 48p. (gr. k-3). 1990. PLB 12.85 (*0-516-04212-2*); pap. 4.95 (*0-516-44212-0*) Childrens.
Greenfield, Eloise. Childtimes: A Three-Generation Memoir. Little, Lessie J., illus. LC 77-26581. 192p. (gr. 4-6). 1993. pap. 5.95 (*0-06-446134-3*, Trophy) HarpC Child Bks.
Guernsey, JoAnn B. Tipper Gore. LC 93-8165. 1993. PLB 17.50 (*0-8225-2876-2*); pap. 6.95 (*0-8225-9651-2*) Lerner Pubns.
Gurasich, Marjorie A. Red Wagons & White Canvas: Mollie Bailey, Circus Queen of the Southwest. Roberts, Melissa, ed. Hill, Francis, illus. 88p. (gr. 4-7). 1988. 10.95 (*0-89015-646-8*, Pub. by Panda Bks) Sunbelt Media.
Halasa, Malu. Mary McLeod Bethune. (gr. 4-7). 1993. pap. 7.95 (*0-7910-0225-X*) Chelsea Hse.
Hamilton, Leni. Clara Barton. Horner, Matina, intro. by. (Illus.). 112p. (gr. 5 up). 1988. lib. bdg. 17.95 (*1-55546-641-9*) Chelsea Hse.
Harrison, Pat. Jeanne Kirkpatrick. Horner, Matina, intro. by. (Illus.). 112p. (gr. 5 up). 1991. lib. bdg. 17.95 (*1-55546-663-X*) Chelsea Hse.
Hazel Brannon Smith: Mini-Play. (gr. 6 up). 1978. 6.50 (*0-89550-304-2*) Stevens & Shea.
Helligman, Deborah. Jumping Genes: The Story of Barbara McClintock. LC 94-6542. (gr. 6 up). 1994. text ed. write for info. (*0-7167-6536-5*, Sci Am Yng Rdrs) W H Freeman.
Henry, Christopher E. Ruth Bader Ginsburg: Associate Justice of the United States Supreme Court. LC 94-978. (gr. 4 up). 1994. write for info. (*0-531-20174-0*) Watts.
—Sandra Day O'Connor. LC 94-11287. 1994. lib. bdg. write for info. (*0-531-20175-9*) Watts.
Henry, Sondra & Taitz, Emily. Gloria Steinem: One Woman's Power: A Biography of Gloria Steinem. Steinem, Gloria, afterword by. LC 86-11631. (Illus.). 128p. (gr. 6 up). 1987. RSBE 13.95 (*0-87518-346-8*, Dillon) Macmillan Child Grp.
Higgins, Ardis O. Portraits of Courageous Women. (Illus.). (gr. 5-8). 1978. pap. text ed. 4.00x (*0-912256-12-5*) Halls of Ivy.
Holland, Margaret. Mother Teresa. (Illus.). 48p. (gr. 3-5). 1992. pap. 2.99 (*0-87406-585-2*) Willowisp Pr.
Hovde, Jane. Jane Addams. 144p. (gr. 5 up). 1989. 16.95 (*0-8160-1547-3*) Facts on File.
Hunter, Edith F. Child of the Silent Night. Holmes, Bea, illus. LC 94-26217. 1995. pap. write for info. (*0-688-13794-6*) Morrow.
Igus, Toyomi, et al. Book of Black Heroes, Vol. 2: Great Women in the Struggle. LC 91-90098. 112p. (gr. 4-8). 1991. lib. bdg. 17.95 (*0-940975-27-0*); pap. 10.95 (*0-940975-26-2*) Just Us Bks.
IlgenFritz, Elizabeth. Anne Hutchinson. Horner, Matina, intro. by. (Illus.). 112p. (gr. 5 up). 1991. lib. bdg. 17.95 (*1-55546-660-5*) Chelsea Hse.
Italia, Bob. Andie MacDowell. LC 92-13690. 1992. PLB 12.94 (*1-56239-111-9*) Abdo & Dghtrs.
—Brooke Shields. LC 92-13689. 1992. PLB 12.94 (*1-56239-110-0*) Abdo & Dghtrs.
—Cheryl Tiegs. LC 92-13688. 1992. PLB 12.94 (*1-56239-107-0*) Abdo & Dghtrs.
—Christie Brinkley. LC 92-13693. 1992. PLB 12.94 (*1-56239-108-9*) Abdo & Dghtrs.
—Cindy Crawford. LC 92-13692. 1992. PLB 12.94 (*1-56239-106-2*) Abdo & Dghtrs.
—Elle McPherson. LC 92-13691. 1992. PLB 12.94 (*1-56239-109-7*) Abdo & Dghtrs.
James, Cary. Julia Morgan. Horner, Matina S., intro. by. (Illus.). 112p. (gr. 5 up). 1990. 17.95 (*1-55546-669-9*) Chelsea Hse.
James, R. S. Mozambique. (Illus.). 104p. (gr. 5 up). 1988. lib. bdg. 14.95 (*1-55546-194-8*) Chelsea Hse.

Johnson, Linda C. Mother Teresa: Protector of the Sick. (Illus.). 64p. (gr. 3-7). PLB 14.95 (*1-56711-034-7*) Blackbirch.

Johnston, Norma. Louisa May: The World & Works of Louisa May Alcott. Cohn, Amy, ed. 256p. 1995. pap. 4.95 (*0-688-12696-0*, Beech Tree Bks) Morrow.

Jones, Constance. Karen Horney. Horner, Matina S., intro. by. (Illus.). 112p. (gr. 5 up). 1989. 17.95 (*1-55546-659-1*) Chelsea Hse.

Jones, Mother. Autobiography of Mother Jones: Pittston Strike Commemorative Edition. Parton, Mary F., ed. Darrow, Clarence & LeSueur, Meridelintro. by. (Illus.). 320p. (Orig.). (gr. 6-12). 1990. 25.95 (*0-88286-167-0*); pap. 12.95 (*0-88286-166-2*) C H Kerr.

Karnes, Frances A. & Bean, Suzanne M. Girls & Young Women Leading the Way: Twenty True Stories about Leadership. Wallner, Rosemary, ed. LC 93-25874. 168p. (gr. 5 up). 1993. pap. 11.95 (*0-915793-52-0*) Free Spirit Pub.

Keene, Ann T. Willa Cather. LC 93-45743. 1994. write for info. (*0-671-86760-1*, J Messner); pap. write for info. (*0-671-86761-X*, J Messner) S&S Trade.

Kendall, Catherine W. Stories of Composers for Young Musicians. large type ed. LC 83-103936. (Illus.). 192p. (Orig.). (gr. 1-10). 1982. pap. 12.95 (*0-9610878-0-3*) Toadwood Pubs. Composers, well-known & some not-so-well known, come alive as real & believable people for children ages 6-16. Based on extensive research & study of the composers' lives & their milieu but without use of excessive dates, pedantic factual material or musicological jargon, each story sets the emotional tone of the life of each musician, beginning with early childhood. The books are set in large type & wide margins, with portraits of composers, a birthday calendar, & recorded sources of composers' works. --"delightful & charming introduction to the world of music composition & performance" --"gives a feel for some of the exciting common threads that run through the lives of extraordinarily gifted musicians" --"communicates the essence of a composer's life in a warmly, perceptive, quiet way" --" Vividly fleshed out each life" --"careful research has been done."--Susan Grille, music educator, SAA Journal. "Composers are introduced as children, who, like the young readers, take music lessons, have brothers & sisters, & get excited over special events. It eavesdrops on conversations between the composer as a child & his parents & draws the reader into the setting, the lifestyle, & the attitudes of the day."-- Phyllis Young, Professor of Cello, American String Teachers Journal. Also available "More Stories of Composers for Young Musicians," 1985, ISBN 0-9610878-1-1. To order contact: Shar Inc., P.O. Box 1411, Ann Arbor, MI 48106. 1-800-248-7427. *Publisher Provided Annotation.*

Kent, Charlotte. Barbara McClintock. Horner, Matina, intro. by. (Illus.). 112p. (gr. 5 up). 1991. lib. bdg. 17.95 (*1-55546-666-4*) Chelsea Hse.

Kliment, Bud. Billie Holiday. King, Coretta Scott, intro. by. (Illus.). 112p. (gr. 5 up). 1990. lib. bdg. 17.95 (*1-55546-592-7*) Chelsea Hse.

Knudson, R. R. Martina Navratilova: Tennis Power. Angelini, George, illus. LC 85-40832. 64p. (gr. 2-6). 1986. pap. 10.95 (*0-670-80665-X*) Viking Child Bks.

Lankford, Mary D. Quinceanera: A Latina's Journey to Womanhood. Herrera, Jesse, photos by. (Illus.). 48p. (gr. 6-9). 1994. 14.40 (*1-56294-363-4*) Millbrook Pr.

Laura Ingalls Wilder. (gr. 2-6). 1988. pap. 3.99 (*0-14-032074-1*, Puffin) Puffin Bks.

Lefer, Diane. Emma Lazarus. Horner, Matina, intro. by. (Illus.). 112p. (gr. 5 up). 1988. lib. bdg. 17.95 (*1-55546-664-8*) Chelsea Hse.

LeVert, Suzanne. Hillary Rodham Clinton: First Lady. (Illus.). 48p. (gr. 2-4). 1994. 12.90 (*1-56294-432-0*) Millbrook Pr.

Luthor. Jane Goodall. Date not set. PLB write for info. (*0-8050-2272-4*) H Holt & Co.

Lyons, Mary. Keeping Secrets. 1995. write for info. (*0-8050-3065-4*) H Holt & Co.

McKissack, Patricia & McKissack, Fredrick. Madam C. J. Walker: Self-Made Millionaire. LC 92-6189. (Illus.). 32p. (gr. 1-4). 1992. lib. bdg. 12.95 (*0-89490-311-X*) Enslow Pubs.

McPherson, Stephanie S. Peace & Bread: The Story of Jane Addams. LC 93-6736. 1993. 17.50 (*0-87614-792-9*) Carolrhoda Bks.

Madison, Curt & Yarber, Yvonne Y. Josephine Roberts - A Biography: Tanana. 64p. (Orig.). (gr. 6-8). 1983. pap. 6.95 (*0-910871-02-7*) Spirit Mount Pr.

Martina Navratilova. (gr. 2-6). 1989. pap. 3.50 (*0-14-033218-9*, Puffin) Puffin Bks.

Martinez, Elizabeth C. Sor Juana: A Trailblazing Thinker. (Illus.). 32p. (gr. 2-4). 1994. 12.90 (*1-56294-406-1*) Millbrook Pr.

Medearis, Angela S. Dare to Dream: Coretta Scott King & the Civil Rights Movement. Rich, Anna, illus. LC 93-33573. 64p. (gr. 3-6). 1994. 13.99 (*0-525-67426-8*, Lodestar Bks) Dutton Child Bks.

Meltzer, Milton. Dorothea Lange: Life Through the Camera. Diamond, Donna, illus. Lange, Dorothea, photos by. 64p. (gr. 2-6). 1986. pap. 3.95 (*0-14-032105-5*, Puffin) Puffin Bks.

—Winnie Mandela: The Soul of South Africa. Marchesi, Stephen, illus. LC 86-5531. 64p. (gr. 2-6). 1986. pap. 10.95 (*0-670-81249-8*) Viking Child Bks.

Miller, Robert H. The Story of "Stagecoach" Mary Fields. Hanna, Cheryl, illus. LC 93-46286. 1994. write for info. (*0-382-24394-3*) Silver.

Morin, Isobel V. Women Who Reformed Politics. LC 93-46336. 160p. (gr. 5-12). 1994. PLB 14.95 (*1-881508-16-1*) Oliver Pr MN.

Morris, Juddi. The Harvey Girls: The Women Who Civilized the West. 144p. (gr. 4-6). 1994. 15.95 (*0-8027-8302-3*); PLB 16.85 (*0-8027-8303-1*) Walker & Co.

Morrison, Ellen E. Lady of Legend: The Mystery of the Female Stranger of Gadsby's Tavern. 2nd, rev. ed. LC 87-460803. (Illus.). 16p. (gr. 6). 1986. saddle-stitched 1.75 (*0-9622537-2-3*) Morielle Pr.

Murrow, Liza K. Lolly Cochran: Veterinarian. Schwarz, Marsha, photos by. LC 88-51682. (Illus.). 64p. (Orig.). (gr. 4-8). 1989. pap. text ed. 6.95 (*0-9621820-0-1*) Teachers Lab.

—Susan Humphris: Geologist. Woods Hole Oceanographic Institution Staff, photos by. LC 88-51681. (Illus.). 64p. (Orig.). (gr. 4-8). 1989. pap. text ed. 6.95 (*0-9621820-1-X*) Teachers Lab.

Nichols, Janet. Women Music Makers. 224p. (gr. 7 up). 1992. 18.95 (*0-8027-8168-3*); lib. bdg. 19.85 (*0-8027-8169-1*) Walker & Co.

O'Grady, Jim. Dorothy Day: With Love for the Poor. (Illus.). 128p. (gr. 4 up). 1993. PLB 14.95 (*0-9623380-2-8*) Ward Hill Pr.

Opfell, Olga S. Women Prime Ministers & Presidents. LC 92-56675. (Illus.). 237p. (gr. 9-12). 1993. lib. bdg. 29.95x (*0-89950-790-5*) McFarland & Co.

Otfinoski, Steve. Marian Wright Edelman: Defender of Children's Rights. (Illus.). 64p. (gr. 3-7). PLB 14.95 (*1-56711-029-0*) Blackbirch.

—Marion Wright Edelman: Defender of Children's Rights. (Illus.). 64p. (gr. 3-7). 1993. pap. 7.95 (*1-56711-060-6*) Blackbirch.

—Oprah. (Illus.). 64p. (gr. 3-7). 1993. pap. 7.95 (*1-56711-061-4*) Blackbirch.

Paolucci, Bridget. Beverly Sills: Opera Singer. Horner, Matina S., intro. by. LC 89-17324. (Illus.). 112p. (gr. 5 up). 1990. 17.95 (*1-55546-677-X*) Chelsea Hse.

Peavy, Linda & Smith, Ursula. Dreams into Deeds: Nine Women Who Dared. LC 85-40295. 160p. (gr. 6-9). 1985. SBE 14.95 (*0-684-18484-2*, Scribners Young Read) Macmillan Child Grp.

—Women Who Changed Things. LC 82-21612. (Illus.). 208p. (gr. 5 up). 1983. SBE 14.95 (*0-684-17849-4*, Scribners Young Read) Macmillan Child Grp.

Pelz, Ruth. Women of the Wild West: Biographies from Many Cultures. (Illus.). 64p. (Orig.). (gr. 4 up). 1994. text ed. 12.95 (*0-940880-49-0*); pap. text ed. 6.95 (*0-940880-50-4*) Open Hand.

Perry, Susan. Women. (Illus.). 128p. (gr. 3-6). Date not set. 19.95 (*1-56065-123-7*) Capstone Pr.

Plain, Nancy. Mary Cassatt, the Life of an Artist. LC 93-46578. 1994. text ed. 13.95 (*0-87518-597-5*, Dillon) Macmillan Child Grp.

Plowden, Martha W. Famous Firsts of Black Women. Jones, Ronald, illus. 112p. (gr. 4-8). 1993. 15.95 (*0-88289-973-2*) Pelican.

Popson, Martha. That We Might Have Life. LC 80-2080. 128p. (gr. 6 up). 1981. pap. 2.75 (*0-385-17438-1*, Im) Doubleday.

Porter, A. P. Jump at de Sun: The Story of Zora Neale Hurston. 88p. (gr. 3-6). 1992. PLB 17.50 (*0-87614-667-1*) Carolrhoda Bks.

Ptacek, Greg & Anderson, Lydia M. Champion for Children's Health: A Story about Dr. S. Josephine Baker. LC 93-10482. (Illus.). 1993. write for info. (*0-87614-806-2*) Carolrhoda Bks.

Roberts, Jack. Dian Fossey. LC 94-6841. (Illus.). 128p. (gr. 5-9). 1995. 14.95 (*1-56006-068-9*) Lucent Bks.

Roberts, Jack L. Ruth Bader Ginsburg: Supreme Court Justice. LC 93-39015. (Illus.). 48p. (gr. 2-4). 1994. PLB 12.90 (*1-56294-497-5*); pap. 6.95 (*1-56294-744-3*) Millbrook Pr.

Roberts, Naurice. Barbara Jordan: The Great Lady from Texas. rev. ed. LC 83-23169. (Illus.). 32p. (gr. 2-5). 1990. PLB 11.80 (*0-516-03511-8*); pap. 3.95 (*0-516-43511-6*) Childrens.

Rosen, Dorothy S. A Fire in Her Bones: The Story of Mary Lyon. LC 94-1978. 1994. write for info. (*0-87614-840-2*) Carolrhoda Bks.

Rozakis, Laurie. Mary Kay. LC 92-45124. 1993. 15.93 (*0-86592-040-0*); 11.95s.p. (*0-685-66418-X*) Rourke Enter.

Saidman, Anne. Oprah Winfrey: Media Success Story. (gr. 4-7). 1993. pap. 4.95 (*0-8225-9646-6*) Lerner Pubns.

Sanders, Catharine. Odette Churchill. (Illus.). 64p. (gr. 6-10). 1991. 15.95 (*0-237-60039-0*, Pub. by Evans Bros Ltd) Trafalgar.

Sawyer, Kem K. Marjory Stoneman Douglas: Guardian of the Everglades. Carow, Leslie, illus. 72p. (gr. 5-12). 1994. PLB 16.95 (*1-878668-20-X*); pap. 7.95 (*1-878668-28-5*) Disc Enter Ltd.

Schad, Kathleen W. Run, Eunice: A Story of Childhood in the 1890s, Clarke County, Alabama. Brown, Mary W., intro. by. LC 90-82162. 144p. (Orig.). (gr. 5-12). 1990. pap. 8.95 (*0-9618941-1-3*) Ana Pubns.

Schraff, Anne. Women of Peace: Nobel Peace Prize Winners. LC 93-37429. (Illus.). 112p. (gr. 6 up). 1994. lib. bdg. 17.95 (*0-89490-493-0*) Enslow Pubs.

Selden, Bernice. The Story of Annie Sullivan, Helen Keller's Teacher. (Orig.). (gr. k-6). 1987. pap. 3.25 (*0-440-48285-2*, YB) Dell.

Senn, Joyce. Jane Goodall: Naturalist. (Illus.). 64p. (gr. 3-7). 1993. PLB 14.95 (*1-56711-010-X*) Blackbirch.

Sherrow, Victoria. Phyllis Wheatley. (gr. 4-7). 1993. pap. 4.95 (*0-7910-2036-3*) Chelsea Hse.

Shinn, Florence S. The Writings of Florence Scovel Shinn. 368p. (Orig.). 1988. pap. 14.95 (*0-87516-610-5*) DeVorss.

Shirley, David. Gloria Estefan. LC 93-48090. (gr. 5-8). 1994. pap. write for info. (*0-7910-2117-3*) Chelsea Hse.

Shura, Mary F. Gentle Annie: The True Story of a Civil War Nurse. (gr. 4-7). 1994. pap. 2.95 (*0-590-43500-0*) Scholastic Inc.

Silvani, Harold. Famous People - Women. Cruz, Harry H., illus. 52p. (gr. 4-8). 1975. wkbk. 6.95 (*1-878669-22-2*, 4345) Crea Tea Assocs.

Simon, Charnan. Janet Reno: First Woman Attorney General. (Illus.). 32p. (gr. 2-4). 1994. PLB 11.80 (*0-516-04191-6*) Childrens.

Snyder, Jane M. Sappho: Lives of Notable Gay Men & Lesbians. Duberman, Martin. LC 94-1134. 1994. write for info. (*0-7910-2308-7*) Chelsea Hse.

Sommer, Robin L. Nien Cheng: Prisoner in China. (Illus.). 64p. (gr. 3-7). 1992. PLB 14.95 (*1-56711-011-8*) Blackbirch.

Spain, Valerie. Meet Maya Angelou. LC 94-1294. 96p. (Orig.). (gr. 2-6). 1995. pap. 3.50 (*0-679-86542-X*, Bullseye Bks) Random Bks Yng Read.

Stefoff, Rebecca. Women of the World. (Illus.). 144p. 1992. PLB 22.00 (*0-19-507687-7*) OUP.

Taylor, Marian W. Madame C. J. Walker: Pioneer Businesswoman. LC 93-14653. (Illus.). 1993. 13.95 (*0-7910-2039-8*, Am Art Analog); pap. write for info. (*0-7910-2040-1*, Am Art Analog) Chelsea Hse.

Thomas. Ten Amazing Women. Date not set. 15.00 (*0-06-023469-5*); PLB 14.89 (*0-06-023472-5*) HarpC Child Bks.

Thompson-Peters, Flossie E. Jan, the Shoeman: The Story of Jan Matzeliger. Clo, Kathy, illus. 32p. (Orig.). (gr. 3-9). 1985. pap. text ed. 4.70 (*1-880784-01-7*) Atlas Pr.

Thomson, Peggy. Katie Henio, Navajo Sheepherder. Conklin, Paul, photos by. LC 93-40430. 1994. write for info. (*0-525-65160-8*, Cobblehill Pr) Dutton Child Bks.

Towns, Saundra. Lillian Hellman. Horner, Matina S., intro. by. (Illus.). 112p. (gr. 5 up). 1989. 17.95 (*1-55546-657-5*) Chelsea Hse.

Trueblood, Becki. Best for Me. 1991. pap. 4.99 (*0-8163-1050-5*) Pacific Pr Pub Assn.

Verheyden-Hilliard, Mary E. American Women in Science & Engineering, 15 bks. Biro, Scarlet & Rom, Holly M., illus. (gr. 1-4). 1988. Set. 75.00 (*0-932469-19-1*) Equity Inst. This illustrated, 15-book series presents contemporary African-American, American Indian, Asian-American, Hispanic, & Caucasian women who, in girlhood, overcame barriers of gender, race, language, & poverty to become scientists. Five of the books are about girls with physical disabilities who also went on to become scientists. "Inspiring group of biographies of women in science...Children in the lower grades will enjoy these biographies, & those in the upper grades with reading problems can use them for...biographical information."-- SCHOOL LIBRARY

JOURNAL. "...useful to teachers who want to help girls become more positive towards mathematics & science... recommended."-- CURRICULUM REVIEW. "...smoothly written texts..."-- BOOKLIST. "...help children...see the connection...between determination to persevere in the face of disabilities & later 'payoff'...in a variety of very exciting careers."-- NEWSLETTER, ASSOCIATION OF BLACK WOMEN IN HIGHER EDUCATION. "...warm, lively & true stories of young girls who went on to become successful scientists..."-- GIFTED CHILDREN MONTHLY. "...these books are so attractively produced that I can't imagine elementary classroom teaching without them."-- PERSPECTIVES, National Women Studies Association. Also available are tie-in Teaching Guide $10.00 (ISBN 0-932469-19-3), & video: "You Can Be a Scientist Too!" $46.00 (ISBN 0-932469-11-6). "Shows how exciting & fascinating science can be."-- BOOKLIST.
Publisher Provided Annotation.

Warnock, Kitty. Mary Wollstonecraft. (Illus.). 64p. (gr. 6-10). 1991. 13.95 (*0-237-60036-6*, Pub. by Evans Bros Ltd) Trafalgar.
Watson, D. Jeanene. Teresa of Calcutta. LC 84-60313. (gr. 3-6). 1984. pap. 6.95 (*0-88062-012-9*) Mott Media.
Wheeler, Jill. Mother Teresa. LC 92-16675. 1992. 12.94 (*1-56239-119-4*) Abdo & Dghtrs.
Wolf, Sylvia. Focus: Five Women Photographers. Levine, Abby, ed. LC 94-1416. (Illus.). 64p. (gr. 4 up). 1994. PLB 18.95 (*0-8075-2531-6*) A Whitman.
Women Today Series, 8 bks. 1991. Set. 138.16 (*0-86593-116-X*); 103.60s.p. (*0-685-59199-9*) Rourke Corp.
Yannuzzi, Della A. Wilma Mankiller: Leader of the Cherokee Nation. LC 93-44866. (Illus.). 128p. (gr. 6 up). 1994. lib. bdg. 17.95 (*0-89490-498-1*) Enslow Pubs.

WOMEN–CLOTHING
see Clothing and Dress

WOMEN–DRESS
see Clothing and Dress; Costume

WOMEN–EMPLOYMENT
Cohen, Judith L. Tu Puedes Ser una Ingeniera. Yanez, Juan, tr. from ENG. Katz, David A., illus. (SPA.). 40p. (Orig.). (gr. 4-7). 1992. pap. 6.00 (*1-880599-03-1*) Cascade Pass.
—You Can Be a Woman Engineer. 40p. (Orig.). (gr. 3-7). 1991. pap. 6.00 (*1-880599-01-5*); cassette 4.00 (*1-880599-02-3*) Cascade Pass.
Cohen, Judith L. & Siegel, Margot. Tu Puedes Ser una Arquitecta. Yanez, Juan, tr. from ENG. Katz, David A., illus. (SPA.). 40p. (Orig.). (gr. 4-7). 1992. pap. 6.00 (*1-880599-05-8*) Cascade Pass.
—You Can Be a Woman Architect. Katz, David A., illus. 40p. (Orig.). 1992. pap. 6.00 (*1-880599-04-X*) Cascade Pass.
English, Betty L. Women at Their Work. English, Betty L., illus. LC 76-42924. 48p. (gr. k-4). 1988. pap. 4.95 (*0-8037-0496-8*) Dial Bks Young.
Falkof, Lucille. Helen Gurley Brown: The Queen of Cosmopolitan. Young, Richard G., ed. LC 91-32053. (Illus.). 64p. (gr. 4-8). 1992. PLB 17.26 (*1-56074-013-2*) Garrett Ed Corp.
Fox, Mary V. Women Astronauts: Aboard the Space Shuttle. rev. ed. LC 87-10814. (Illus.). 144p. (gr. 7 up). 1987. lib. bdg. 13.98 (*0-671-64840-3*, J Messner); pap. 5.95 (*0-671-64841-1*) S&S Trade.
Kunstadter, Maria. Women Working A-Z. (Illus.). 32p. (ps-3). 1994. PLB 15.00 (*0-917846-25-7*, 95564) Highsmith Pr.
Mayfield, Susan. Timeline: Women & Power. (Illus.). 64p. (gr. 7-9). 1989. 19.95 (*0-85219-768-3*, Pub. by Batsford UK) Trafalgar.
Neufld, Rose. Exploring Nontraditional Jobs for Women. rev. ed. Rosen, Ruth, ed. (gr. 7-12). 1989. PLB 14.95 (*0-8239-0971-9*) Rosen Group.
Seed, Suzanne. Saturday's Child. Seed, Suzanne, illus. LC 72-12599. (gr. 6-12). 1973. PLB 8.95 (*0-87955-803-2*); pap. 6.95 (*0-87955-203-4*) O'Hara.
Steffens, Bradley. Working Mothers: Understanding Words in Context. LC 89-35434. (Illus.). 32p. (gr. 3-6). 1990. PLB 10.95 (*0-89908-644-6*) Greenhaven.
Wallner. Progressive Careers. 1991. 12.95s.p. (*0-86593-123-2*); 17.27 (*0-685-59205-7*) Rourke Corp.
Williams, Barbara. Breakthrough: Women in Archaeology. LC 80-7687. (Illus.). 174p. 1981. 9.95 (*0-8027-6406-1*) Walker & Co.

WOMEN–EMPLOYMENT–FICTION
Furman, Abraham L., ed. Everygirls Career Stories. (Illus.). (gr. 6-10). PLB 7.19 (*0-8313-0049-3*) Lantern.
Maury, Inez. My Mother the Mail Carrier - Mi Mama la Cartera. Alemany, Norah, tr. McCrady, Lady, illus. LC 76-14275. (ENG & SPA.). 32p. (Orig.). (gr. k-4). 1976. pap. 7.95 (*0-935312-23-4*) Feminist Pr.

WOMEN–ENFRANCHISEMENT
see Women–Suffrage

WOMEN–FICTION
Adams, Georgie. Nanny Fox. Young, Selina, illus. LC 93-72433. 32p. (ps-2). 1994. SBE 13.95 (*0-689-31920-7*, Atheneum Child Bk) Macmillan Child Grp.
Adams, Pam. Mrs. Honey's Dream. (ps-3). 1993. 7.95 (*0-85953-759-5*); pap. 3.95 (*0-85953-760-9*) Childs Play.
Adams, Pam, illus. There Was an Old Lady Who Swallowed a Fly. LC 90-46921. 16p. (ps-2). 1989. pap. 5.99 (*0-85953-018-3*, Pub. by Child's Play UK) Childs Play.
Alcott, Louisa May. Good Wives. 320p. (gr. 3-7). 1983. pap. 2.95 (*0-14-035009-8*, Puffin) Puffin Bks.
Alexander, Sue. World Famous Muriel. (gr. k-6). 1988. pap. 2.50 (*0-440-49610-1*, YB) Dell.
Armstrong, Jennifer. Ann of the Wild Rose, Seventeen Seventy-Four, No. 2. 1994. pap. 3.99 (*0-553-29867-4*) Bantam.
Asch, Frank. Pearl's Promise. 160p. (gr. 1-4). 1984. pap. 2.95 (*0-440-46863-9*, YB) Dell.
Barton. Wee Little Woman. 1996. 13.00 (*0-06-023387-7*); PLB 12.89 (*0-06-023388-5*) HarpC Child Bks.
Boateng, Yaw A. Miss John. (gr. 4-7). 1992. pap. 4.95 (*0-7910-2916-6*) Chelsea Hse.
Bowden, Joan. Why the Tides Ebb & Flow. (gr. k-3). 1979. 14.45 (*0-395-28378-7*) HM.
Cahill, Susan, ed. Women & Fiction: Short Stories by & About Women. (gr. 7 up). 1975. pap. 4.50 (*0-451-62411-4*, ME2263, Ment) NAL-Dutton.
Cameron, Eleanor. The Private Worlds of Julia Redfern. LC 87-30695. 224p. (gr. 6 up). 1988. 14.95 (*0-525-44394-0*, 01354-410, DCB) Dutton Child Bks.
Cole, Shelia. The Dragon in the Cliff: A Novel Based on the Life of Mary Anning. Farrow, T. C., illus. LC 90-40455. (gr. 4-7). 1991. 12.95 (*0-688-10196-8*) Lothrop.
Cooney, Caroline B. New Year's Eve. 224p. (Orig.). (gr. 9 up). 1988. pap. 2.95 (*0-590-44627-4*) Scholastic Inc.
Cooper, Ilene. The Winning of Miss Lynn Ryan. Magurn, Susan, illus. LC 87-15233. 128p. (gr. 3-6). 1987. 11.95 (*0-688-07231-3*) Morrow Jr Bks.
Cosgrove, Stephen. The Kind & Gentle Ladies. Steelhammer, Ilona, illus. 24p. (gr. k-2). 1990. PLB 11.95 (*1-878363-20-4*) Forest Hse.
—Lady Lonely. Steelhammer, Ilona, illus. 24p. (gr. k-2). 1990. PLB 11.95 (*1-878363-21-2*) Forest Hse.
—Lady Rose. (Illus.). 32p. (Orig.). (gr. 1-4). 1990. pap. 2.95 (*0-8431-2837-2*) Price Stern.
Deaver, Julie R. Say Goodnight, Gracie. LC 87-45278. 224p. (gr. 7 up). 1988. 15.00 (*0-06-021418-X*); PLB 14.89 (*0-06-021419-8*) HarpC Child Bks.
Derby, Pat. Visiting Miss Pierce. LC 86-7559. 144p. (gr. 6 up). 1986. 14.00 (*0-374-38162-3*) FS&G.
—Visiting Miss Pierce. 144p. (gr. 3 up). 1989. pap. 3.50 (*0-374-48156-3*, Sunburst) FS&G.
Dexter, Catherine. Gerties's Green Thumb. (gr. 4-7). 1988. pap. 2.75 (*0-440-40018-X*, YB) Dell.
Dillon, Barbara. Mrs. Tooey & the Terrible Toxic Tar. LC 87-45985. 96p. (gr. 3-7). 1988. (Lipp Jr Bks); PLB 10.89 (*0-397-32277-1*, Lipp Jr Bks) HarpC Child Bks.
Donnelly, Elfie. A Package for Miss Marshwater. Krause, Ute, illus. (gr. 2-5). 1987. Dial Bks Young.
Duke, Mary A. Victoria Scarlett Jones. LC 93-70815. (Illus.). 55p. (Orig.). (gr. 3-5). 1993. Incls. Victoria Scarlett & the Big Black Bear; Victoria Scarlett & Clara at Christmas; Victoria Scarlett Says, "Recess Was a Mess!" pap. 5.95 (*1-883241-05-7*) Cognitive Pr.
Duncan, Lois. Daughters of Eve. 1990. pap. 3.99 (*0-440-91864-2*) Dell.
Fine, Anne. Alias Madame Doubtfire. (gr. 5 up). 1990. pap. 3.50 (*0-553-28189-5*, Starfire) Bantam.
Fischer, Maureen. Little Mary. Haley, Patrick & Haley, Irene, eds. LC 85-82197. 106p. (gr. 7-12). 1986. 14.00 (*0-9605738-3-6*); pap. 6.00 (*0-9605738-4-4*) East Eagle.
Fosburgh, Liza. Bella Arabella. Stock, Catherine, illus. LC 85-42809. 128p. (gr. 4-7). 1986. SBE 13.95 (*0-02-735430-X*, Four Winds) Macmillan Child Grp.
Garfield, Leon. The Strange Affair of Adelaide Harris. (gr. k-6). 1988. pap. 3.25 (*0-440-40057-0*, YB) Dell.
Gray, Libba M. Miss Tizzy. Rowland, Jada, illus. LC 92-8409. (ps-2). 1993. pap. 14.00 JRT (*0-671-77590-1*, S&S BFYR) S&S Trade.
Greenberg, Jan. Bye, Bye, Miss American Pie. LC 85-47590. 150p. (gr. 7 up). 1985. 14.00 (*0-374-31012-2*) FS&G.
Hale, Lucretia. The Lady Who Put Salt in Her Coffee. Schwartz, Amy, adapted by. & illus. 28p. (ps-3). 1989. 13.95 (*0-15-243475-5*) HarBrace.
Hamilton, Gail. Aunt Hetty's Ordeal. (gr. 4-7). 1993. pap. 3.99 (*0-553-48039-1*) Bantam.
Hartman, Karen L. Dream Catcher: The Legend & the Lady. LC 92-93871. 56p. (gr. 6 up). 1993. 17.95 (*0-9635204-0-7*) Weeping Heart.
Hayes, Joe. Watch Out for Clever Women! Cuidado Con las Mojeres Astutas. Hill, Vicki T., illus. LC 93-73417. 80p. (Orig.). (gr. 3-7). Date not set. 16.95 (*0-938317-21-0*); pap. 10.95 (*0-938317-20-2*) Cinco Puntos.
Hedlund, Irene. Mighty Mountain & the Three Strong Women. LC 89-28052. (Illus.). 32p. (gr. 2-5). 1990. 14.95 (*0-912078-86-3*) Volcano Pr.
Honeycutt, Natalie. Lydia Jane Bly & the Baby-Sitter Exchange. LC 92-46363. 128p. (gr. 2-6). 1993. SBE 13.95 (*0-02-744362-0*, Bradbury Pr) Macmillan Child Grp.
Huang, Benrei, illus. The Teeny Tiny Woman. 18p. (ps). 1993. bds. 3.95 (*0-448-40176-2*, G&D) Putnam Pub Group.
Irwin, Hadley. The Lilith Summer. LC 78-24379. 128p. (gr. 4-8). 1979. 8.95 (*0-912670-52-5*) Feminist Pr.
Isherwood, Shirley. A Surprise for Mrs. Pinkerton-Trunks. (Illus.). 96p. (gr. k-2). 1986. 12.95 (*0-09-160380-3*, Pub. by Hutchinson UK) Trafalgar.
Jacobs, Anita. Where Has Deedie Wooster Been All These Years? LC 81-65493. 224p. (gr. 7 up). 1981. pap. 9.95 (*0-385-29133-7*) Delacorte.
Jaramillo, Nelly P. Las Nanas de Abuelita (Grandmother's Nursery Rhymes) (ps-2). 1994. 14.95 (*0-8050-2555-3*) H Holt & Co.
Keehn, Sally M. I Am Regina. (gr. 4-7). 1993. pap. 3.99 (*0-440-40754-0*) Dell.
Kent, Jack. Mrs. Mooley. (ps-3). 1993. 12.95 (*0-307-17550-2*, Artsts Writrs) Western Pub.
Kidd, Ronald. Sammy Carducci's Guide to Women. 112p. (gr. 3-7). 1991. 14.95 (*0-525-67363-6*, Lodestar Bks) Dutton Child Bks.
Knight, Ginny, et al. A Sampler of Women. LC 83-82097. 60p. (Orig.). (gr. 9-12). 1984. pap. text ed. 6.50 (*0-940248-18-2*) Guild Pr.
Konigsburg, E. L. From the Mixed-Up Files of Mrs. Basil E. Frankweiler. 208p. (gr. 5 up). 1973. pap. 3.99 (*0-440-93180-0*, LFL) Dell.
Kroll, Steven. Newsman Ned & the Broken Rules. Brunkus, Denise, illus. 32p. (Orig.). (ps-1). 1989. pap. 2.95 (*0-590-41368-6*) Scholastic Inc.
Livingstone, Ian & Jackson, Steve. Trial of Champions. (Orig.). (gr. k-12). 1987. pap. 2.50 (*0-440-98689-3*, LFL) Dell.
McCurdy, Michael. Hannah's Farm: Seasons on an Early American Homestead. McCurdy, Michael, illus. LC 87-29631. 32p. (ps-4). 1988. reinforced bdg. 12.95 (*0-8234-0700-4*) Holiday.
MacDonald, Betty. Mrs. Piggle-Wiggle's Magic. 1976. 15.95 (*0-8488-1087-2*) Amereon Ltd.
MacLachlan, Patricia. The Facts & Fictions of Minna Pratt. LC 85-45388. 144p. (gr. 3-7). 1988. 12.00 (*0-06-024114-4*); PLB 11.89 (*0-06-024117-9*) HarpC Child Bks.
McOmber, Rachel B., ed. McOmber Phonics Storybooks: Miss Vie. rev. ed. (Illus.). write for info. (*0-944991-48-3*) Swift Lrn Res.
Martinez, Alejandro C. The Woman Who Outshone the Sun: The Legend of Lucia Zenteno. LC 91-16646. (Illus.). 32p. (gr. k-5). 1991. 13.95 (*0-89239-101-4*) Childrens Book Pr.
Mayer, Mercer. The Wizard Comes to Town. Mayer, Mercer, illus. 40p. 1991. pap. 5.95 (*1-879920-00-X*) Rain Bird Prods.
Modiano, Patrick & Sempe, J. J. Catherine Certitude. (FRE.). 95p. (gr. 5-10). 1988. pap. 9.95 (*2-07-033600-X*) Schoenhof.
Montgomery, Lucy M. Anne of Green Gables. 384p. (gr. 4-7). 1989. pap. 2.95 (*0-590-42243-X*, Apple Classics) Scholastic Inc.
Oke, Janette. They Called Her Mrs. Doc. 224p. 1992. pap. 7.99 (*1-55661-246-X*) Bethany Hse.
—They Called Her Mrs. Doc. large type ed. 224p. 1992. pap. 9.99 (*1-55661-247-8*) Bethany Hse.
Okimoto, Jean D. Jason's Women. (gr. k-12). 1988. pap. 2.95 (*0-440-20000-8*) Dell.
Oliver, Diana. Tough Luck, Ronnie. 132p. (gr. 3-5). 1994. pap. 3.50 (*0-679-85475-4*, Bullseye Bks) Random Bks Yng Read.
Oliver, Rice D. Lone Woman of Ghalas-hat. Zafuto, Charles, illus. 32p. (gr. 4-8). 1993. PLB 12.00 (*0-936778-52-0*); pap. 6.00 (*0-936778-51-2*) Calif Weekly.
Pearson, Susan. Lenore's Big Break. Carlson, Nancy, illus. 32p. (ps-3). 1994. pap. 4.99 (*0-14-054294-9*) Puffin Bks.
Peel, John. Carmen Sandiego: Golden Mini Play Lights. (gr. 4-7). 1993. 14.95 (*0-307-75403-0*, Pub. by Golden Bks) Western Pub.
Pierce, Tamora. The Woman Who Rides Like a Man. LC 85-20054. 256p. (gr. 6 up). 1990. pap. 3.50 (*0-679-80112-X*) Knopf Bks Yng Read.
Potter, Beatrix. Madame Piquedru. (FRE., Illus.). 58p. 1990. 9.95 (*0-7859-3623-8*, 2070560686) Fr & Eur.
—Mademoiselle Mitoufle. (FRE., Illus.). 58p. 1990. 9.95 (*0-7859-3633-5*, 2070561046) Fr & Eur.
Pride & Prejudice. 1993. pap. text ed. 6.50 (*0-582-09674-X*, 79823) Longman.
Ricchiuti, Paul B. Ellen: Trial & Triumph on the American Frontier. LC 76-44051. 160p. (gr. 6 up). 1988. pap. 7.95 (*0-945460-03-1*) Upward Way.
Richardson, Arleta. At Home in North Branch. LC 88-9529. (gr. 3-7). 1988. pap. 3.99 (*1-55513-312-6*, Chariot Bks) Chariot Family.
Riordan, James. The Woman in the Moon & Other Tales of Forgotten Heroines. Barrett, Angela, illus. LC 84-20050. 96p. (ps up). 1985. 13.00 (*0-8037-0194-2*) Dial Bks Young.
Romain, Trevor. There's a Lady in the Attic & I Don't Like Her Face. Romain, Trevor, illus. 32p. (ps-5). 1994. 13.95 (*1-880092-07-7*) Bright Bks TX.

Stoeke, Janet M. Minerva Louise. Stoeke, Janet M., illus. LC 87-24458. 24p. (ps-1). 1988. 12.00 (*0-525-44374-6*, 01063-320, DCB) Dutton Child Bks.
Summer of Dreams: The Story of a World's Fair Girl. 64p. (gr. 4-6). 1993. incl. jacket 5.95 (*0-382-24335-8*); lib. bdg. 7.95 (*0-382-24332-3*); pap. 3.95 (*0-382-24354-4*) Silver Burdett Pr.
Turin, Adela & Bosnia, Nella. Arthur & Clementine. (Illus.). 32p. (gr. 3-6). 1980. 6.95 (*0-904613-19-4*) Writers & Readers.
Usher, Alice. The Sunny Hours. Kniffke, Sophie, illus. 40p. (Orig.). (ps-2). 1998. pap. 3.95 (*0-671-75281-2*, Green Tiger) S&S Trade.
Whelan, Gloria. Hannah. Bowman, Leslie, illus. LC 92-24243. 64p. (gr. 2-4). 1993. RLB 11.99 (*0-679-91397-1*); pap. 2.99 (*0-679-82698-X*) Random Bks Yng Read.
Wolitzer, Hilma. Introducing Shirley Braverman. (gr. 8 up). 1987. pap. 3.50 (*0-374-43597-9*, Sunburst) FS&G.
Wright, Betty R. The Summer of Mrs. MacGregor. LC 86-45388. 160p. (gr. 3-7). 1986. 14.95 (*0-8234-0628-8*) Holiday.
Wunsch, Marjory. Aunt Belle's Beach. (Illus.). (ps-3). 1994. 14.00 (*0-688-11628-0*); 13.93 (*0-688-11629-9*) Lothrop.
Zindel, Paul. A Begonia for Miss Applebaum. (gr. 7 up). 1990. pap. 3.99 (*0-553-28765-6*, Starfire) Bantam.
Zolotow, Charlotte. I Know a Lady. Stevenson, James, illus. LC 83-25361. 24p. (ps up). 1992. pap. 4.95 (*0-688-11519-5*, Mulberry) Morrow.

WOMEN–OCCUPATIONS
see Women–Employment

WOMEN–SUFFRAGE
Meyers, Madeleine, intro. by. Forward into Light: The Struggle for Women's Suffrage. (Illus.). 64p. (Orig.). (gr. 5-12). 1994. pap. 4.95 (*1-878668-25-0*) Disc Enter Ltd.
Oneal, Zibby. A Long Way to Go. Dooling, Michael, illus. 64p. (gr. 2-6). 1990. pap. 11.95 (*0-670-82532-8*) Viking Child Bks.
Smith, Betsy C. Women Win the Vote. (Illus.). 64p. (gr. 5 up). 1989. PLB 12.95 (*0-382-09837-4*); pap. 7.95 (*0-382-09854-4*) Silver Burdett Pr.
Sullivan, George. The Day the Women Got the Vote: A Photo History of the Women's Rights Movement. (gr. 4-7). 1994. pap. 6.95 (*0-590-47560-6*) Scholastic Inc.

WOMEN AS AIR PILOTS
see Women in Aeronautics

WOMEN AS ARTISTS
Brown, Betty A. & Raven, Arlene. Exposures, Women & Their Art. Love, Kenna, photos by. Comini, Alessandra, intro. by. (Illus.). 128p. (gr. 9 up). 1989. 39.95 (*0-939165-10-4*); ltd. ed. 60.00 (*0-939165-13-9*); pap. 24.95 (*0-939165-11-2*) NewSage Press.
Sills, Leslie. Inspirations: Stories about Women Artists. Fay, Ann, ed. LC 88-80. (Illus.). 56p. (gr. 4 up). 1989. PLB 16.95 (*0-8075-3649-0*) A Whitman.
Turner, Robyn M. Georgia O'Keeffe: Portraits of Women Artist for Children. (gr. 4-7). 1993. pap. 6.95 (*0-316-85654-1*) Little.

WOMEN AS AUTHORS
Greene, Carol. Laura Ingalls Wilder: Author of the Little House Books. Dobson, Steven, illus. LC 89-25362. 48p. (gr. k-3). 1990. PLB 12.85 (*0-516-04212-2*); pap. 4.95 (*0-516-44212-0*) Childrens.
McKissack, Patricia & McKissack, Fredrick. Zora Neale Hurston: Writer & Storyteller. LC 92-2588. (Illus.). 32p. (gr. 1-4). 1992. lib. bdg. 12.95 (*0-89490-316-0*) Enslow Pubs.
Rosenblatt, Aaron. Virginia Woolf for Beginners. Rosenblatt, Naomi, illus. (Orig.). (gr. 11 up). 1987. pap. 7.95 (*0-86316-133-2*) Writers & Readers.
Smith, Lucinda I. Women Who Write: From the Past & the Present to the Future. Steltenpohl, Jane, ed. (Illus.). 192p. (gr. 7 up). 1989. lib. bdg. 14.98 (*0-671-65668-6*, J Messner); pap. 9.95 (*0-671-65669-4*) S&S Trade.
Stine, Megan. The Story of Laura Ingalls Wilder. Ramsey, Marcy D., illus. 112p. (Orig.). (gr. 2-5). 1992. pap. 3.50 (*0-440-40578-5*, YB) Dell.
Weidt, Maryann N. Presenting Judy Blume. 168p. (gr. 9-12). 1989. text ed. 19.95x (*0-8057-8208-7*, Twayne) Macmillan.

WOMEN AS PHYSICIANS
Baker, Rachel. The First Woman Doctor. Copelman, Evelyn, illus. 192p. (gr. 4-6). 1987. pap. 2.95 (*0-590-44767-X*) Scholastic Inc.
Baldwin, Joyce Y. To Heal the Heart of a Child: Helen Taussig, M.D. 128p. 1992. 14.95 (*0-8027-8166-7*); lib. bdg. 15.85 (*0-8027-8167-5*) Walker & Co.
Ferris, Jeri. Native American Doctor: The Story of Susan Laflesche Picotte. (gr. 4-7). 1991. pap. 6.95 (*0-87614-548-9*) Carolrhoda Bks.
Greene, Carol. Elizabeth Blackwell: First Woman Doctor. Dobson, Steven, illus. LC 90-20001. 48p. (gr. k-3). 1991. PLB 12.85 (*0-516-04217-3*); pap. 4.95 (*0-516-44217-1*) Childrens.
Kaye, Judith. The Life of Florence Sabin. (Illus.). 80p. (gr. 4-7). 1993. PLB 13.95 (*0-8050-2299-6*) TFC Bks NY.
Steelsmith, Shari. Elizabeth Blackwell: The Story of the First Woman Doctor. Kerstetter, Judy, illus. LC 86-62434. 32p. (Orig.). (ps-4). 1987. lib. bdg. 16.95 (*0-943990-31-9*); pap. 5.95 (*0-943990-30-0*) Parenting Pr.
Wilson, Barbara K. Path Through the Woods. Stewart, Charles, illus. (gr. 7 up). 1958. 21.95 (*0-87599-129-7*) S G Phillips.

WOMEN AS REPORTERS
Whitelaw, Nancy. They Wrote Their Own Headlines: American Women Journalists. LC 93-50818. (Illus.). 144p. (gr. 6 up). 1994. 17.95g (*1-883846-06-4*) M Reynolds.

WOMEN AS SCIENTISTS
Barker, Jane V. & Downing, Sybil. Martha Maxwell: Pioneer Naturalist. Jones, Ann, illus. 138p. 1982. pap. 6.95 (*1-878611-12-7*) Silver Rim Pr.
Billings, Charlene W. Grace Hopper: Navy Admiral & Computer Pioneer. LC 89-1523. (Illus.). 128p. (gr. 6 up). 1989. lib. bdg. 17.95 (*0-89490-194-X*) Enslow Pubs.
Burns, Virginia L. Gentle Hunter: Biography of Alice Evans, Bacteriologist. (Illus.). 224p. (gr. 5-12). 1993. PLB 22.00 (*0-9604726-5-7*) Enterprise Pr.
Downing, Sybil & Barker, Jane V. Florence Sabin: Pioneer Scientist. Jones, Ann, illus. 100p. 1981. pap. 6.95 (*1-878611-11-9*) Silver Rim Pr.
Epstein, Vivian S. History of Women in Science for Young People. Epstein, Vivian S., illus. 40p. (Orig.). (gr. 4-9). 1994. 14.95 (*0-9601002-8-8*); pap. 7.95 (*0-9601002-7-X*) V S Epstein.
Fuchs, Carol. Jane Goodall: The Chimpanzee's Friend. LC 93-6506. 1993. 14.60 (*0-86593-262-X*); 10.95s.p. (*0-685-66546-1*) Rourke Corp.
Lucas, Eileen. Jane Goodall: Friend of the Chimps. LC 91-18060. (Illus.). 48p. (gr. 2-4). 1992. PLB 12.90 (*1-56294-135-6*); pap. 4.95 (*1-56294-796-6*) Millbrook Pr.
McAlarv, Florence & Cohen, Judith L. You Can Be a Woman Marine Biologist. Kate, David A., illus. 40p. (Orig.). (gr. 4-7). 1992. pap. 6.00 (*1-880599-06-6*) Cascade Pass.
McAlary, Florence & Cohen, Judith L. Tu Puedes Ser Biologa Marina. Katz, David A. & Yanez, Juan, illus. (SPA.). 40p. (gr. 4-7). 1992. pap. 6.00 (*1-880599-07-4*) Cascade Pass.
Nies, Kevin A. From Sorceress to Scientist: Biographies of Women Physical Scientists. Neis, Kevin A., illus. 95p. (Orig.). (gr. 8 up). 1991. 30.00 (*1-880211-00-9*); pap. 14.99 (*1-880211-01-7*); tchr's. ed. o.p. 14.99 (*1-880211-02-5*) Calif Video.

Verheyden-Hilliard, Mary E. American Women in Science & Engineering, 15 bks. Biro, Scarlet & Rom, Holly M., illus. (gr. 1-4). 1988. Set. 75.00 (*0-932469-19-1*) Equity Inst. This illustrated, 15-book series presents contemporary African-American, American Indian, Asian-American, Hispanic, & Caucasian women who, in girlhood, overcame barriers of gender, race, language, & poverty to become scientists. Five of the books are about girls with physical disabilities who also went on to become scientists. "Inspiring group of biographies of women in science...Children in the lower grades will enjoy these biographies, & those in the upper grades with reading problems can use them for...biographical information."-- SCHOOL LIBRARY JOURNAL. "...useful to teachers who want to help girls become more positive towards mathematics & science... recommended."-- CURRICULUM REVIEW. "...smoothly written texts..."-- BOOKLIST. "...help children...see the connection...between determination to persevere in the face of disabilities & later 'payoff...in a variety of very exciting careers."-- NEWSLETTER, ASSOCIATION OF BLACK WOMEN IN HIGHER EDUCATION. "...warm, lively & true stories of young girls who went on to become successful scientists..."-- GIFTED CHILDREN MONTHLY. "...these books are so attractively produced that I can't imagine elementary classroom teaching without them."-- PERSPECTIVES, National Women Studies Association. Also available are tie-in Teaching Guide $10.00 (ISBN 0-932469-19-3), & video: "You Can Be a Scientist Too!" $46.00 (ISBN 0-932469-11-6). "Shows how exciting & fascinating science can be."-- BOOKLIST.
Publisher Provided Annotation.

—Engineer from the Comanche Nation, Nancy Wallace. Menzel, Marian, illus. LC 84-25935. 32p. (Orig.). (gr. 1-4). 1985. pap. 5.00 (*0-932469-10-8*) Equity Inst.
—Mathematician & Administrator, Shirley Mathis McBay. Biro, Scarlet, illus. LC 84-25983. 32p. (Orig.). (gr. 1-4). 1985. pap. 5.00 (*0-932469-04-3*) Equity Inst.
—Scientist & Administrator, Antoinette Rodez Schiesler. Menzel, Marian, illus. LC 84-25978. 32p. (Orig.). (gr. 1-4). 1985. pap. 5.00 (*0-932469-08-6*) Equity Inst.
—Scientist & Astronaut, Sally Ride. Menzel, Marian, illus. LC 84-25940. 32p. (Orig.). (gr. 1-4). 1985. pap. 5.00 (*0-932469-07-8*) Equity Inst.
—Scientist & Governor, Dixy Lee Ray. Menzel, Marian, illus. LC 84-25986. 32p. (Orig.). (gr. 1-4). 1985. pap. 5.00 (*0-932469-06-X*) Equity Inst.
—Scientist & Planner, Ru Chih Cheo Huang. Biro, Scarlet, illus. LC 84-25982. 32p. (Orig.). (gr. 1-4). 1985. pap. 5.00 (*0-932469-03-5*) Equity Inst.
—Scientist & Puzzle Solver, Constance Tom Noguchi. Menzel, Mary, illus. LC 84-25924. 32p. (Orig.). (gr. 1-4). 1985. pap. 5.00 (*0-932469-05-1*) Equity Inst.
—Scientist from Puerto Rico, Maria Cordero Hardy. Biro, Scarlet, illus. LC 84-25979. 32p. (Orig.). (gr. 1-4). 1985. pap. 5.00 (*0-932469-02-7*) Equity Inst.
—Scientist from the Santa Clara Pueblo, Agnes Naranjo Stroud-Lee. Menzel, Marian, illus. LC 84-25959. 32p. (Orig.). (gr. 1-4). 1985. pap. 5.00 (*0-932469-09-4*) Equity Inst.
—Scientist with Determination, Elma Gonzalez. Menzel, Marian, illus. LC 84-25981. 32p. (Orig.). (gr. 1-4). 1985. pap. 5.00 (*0-932469-01-9*) Equity Inst.
Warren, Rebecca L. & Thompson, Mary H. The Scientist Within You: Experiments & Biographies of Distinguished Women in Science. LC 93-74855. (Illus.). 192p. (Orig.). (gr. 3-8). 1994. pap. 18.95 (*1-884414-11-7*) ACI Pubng.

WOMEN IN AERONAUTICS
Brown, Don, text by. & illus. Ruth Law Thrills a Nation. LC 92-45701. 32p. (ps-2). 1993. PLB 13.95 (*0-395-66404-7*) Ticknor & Flds Bks Yng Read.
Davis, Anita P. & Hall, Ed Y. Harriet Quimby - America's First Lady of the Air: An Activity Book for Children. (Illus.). 40p. (Orig.). (gr. 4-8). 1993. pap. 4.95 wkbk. (*0-9622166-6-6*) Honoribus Pr.
Johnson, LaVerne C. Bessie Coleman: Writer. Perry, Craig R., illus. LC 92-35255. 1992. 3.95 (*0-922162-95-6*) Empak Pub.
Smith, Elizabeth S. Coming Out Right: The Story of Jackie Cochran, the First Woman Aviator to Break the Sound Barrier. (Illus.). 128p. (gr. 5 up). 1991. 14.95 (*0-8027-6988-8*); PLB 15.85 (*0-8027-6989-6*) Walker & Co.

WOMEN IN INDUSTRY
see Women–Employment

WOMEN IN POLITICS
Chua-Eoan, Howard. Corazon Aquino. (Illus.). 112p. (gr. 5 up). 1988. 17.95x (*1-55546-825-X*) Chelsea Hse.
Foster, Leila M. Margaret Thatcher: First Woman Prime Minister of Great Britain. LC 90-2209. (Illus.). 152p. (gr. 4 up). 1990. PLB 14.40 (*0-516-03269-0*) Childrens.
Gay, Kathlyn. The New Power of Women in Politics. LC 94-7527. (Illus.). 128p. (gr. 6 up). 1994. lib. bdg. 17.95 (*0-89490-584-8*) Enslow Pubs.
Gherman, Beverly. Sandra Day O'Connor. (gr. 4-7). 1991. 10.95 (*0-670-82756-8*) Viking Child Bks.
Hawxhurst, Joan C. Mother Jones. LC 92-22191. (Illus.). 128p. (gr. 7-10). 1992. PLB 22.80 (*0-8114-2327-1*) Raintree Steck-V.
Hughes, Libby. Margaret Thatcher: Madam Prime Minister: A Biography of Margaret Thatcher. LC 89-11974. (Illus.). 128p. (gr. 5 up). 1989. text ed. 13.95 RSBE (*0-87518-410-3*, Dillon) Macmillan Child Grp.
Morin, Isobel V. Women Chosen for Public Office. LC 94-22097. 1995. 14.95 (*1-88150-820-X*) Oliver Pr MN.
Opfell, Olga S. Women Prime Ministers & Presidents. LC 92-56675. (Illus.). 237p. (gr. 9-12). 1993. lib. bdg. 29.95x (*0-89950-790-5*) McFarland & Co.

Patteson, Nelda. Miriam Amanda Ferguson: First Woman Governor of Texas: Her Life Story Presented Through the Clothes She Wore. (Illus.). 32p. (Orig.). (gr. 4-8). 1994. pap. 14.95 (*0-9629001-1-7*) Smiley Originals. Content to be a wife & mother, Miriam had a drastic change in lifestyle when her husband became governor in 1915. Impeached & barred from holding state office, he cleverly decided that his wife should run in 1924. "Ma" & "Farmer Jim" did battle with the Ku Klux Klan for the executive office. First woman in the United States elected governor in her own right, "Ma" Ferguson served a second term in the 1930s. The novelty of a woman governor made her, & the

fashionable clothes she wore, newsworthy. Narrative, photographs & costumes in color chronicle Governor Ferguson's triumphs & defeats. In an exciting format designed for both young people & adults, the book fills a need for the biographies of outstanding women. Book One, CLARA DRISCOLL: 'SAVIOR OF THE ALAMO.' (0-9269001-0-9). $14.95 each. Smiley Originals, P.O. Box 99, Smiley, TX 78159; phone 800-584-3655, FAX 210-587-6113.
Publisher Provided Annotation.

Wheeler, Jill. Corazon Aquino. LC 91-73025. 202p. 1991. 12.94 (*1-56239-082-1*) Abdo & Dghtrs.

WOMEN IN SPORTS

Aaseng, Nathan. Florence Griffith Joyner: Dazzling Olympian. 1991. pap. 3.95 (*0-8225-9587-7*) Lerner Pubns.

Duden, Jane. Shirley Muldowney. LC 87-27570. (Illus.). 48p. (gr. 5-6). 1988. text ed. 11.95 RSBE (*0-89686-369-7*, Crestwood Hse) Macmillan Child Grp.

Goldstein, Margaret J. Jackie Joyner-Kersee: Superwoman. (gr. 4-7). 1994. pap. 4.95 (*0-8225-9653-9*) Lerner Pubns.

Monroe, Judy. Steffi Graf. LC 87-30115. (Illus.). 48p. (gr. 5-6). 1988. text ed. 11.95 RSBE (*0-89686-368-9*, Crestwood Hse) Macmillan Child Grp.

Morrissette, Mikki. Nancy Kerrigan: Heart of a Champion. (gr. 4-7). 1994. pap. 3.99 (*0-553-48254-8*) Bantam.

Press, David P. A Multicultural Portrait of Professional Sports. LC 93-10316. 1993. 18.95 (*1-85435-661-5*) Marshall Cavendish.

Rosenthal, Bert. Lynette Woodard: The First Female Globetrotter. LC 86-9662. (Illus.). 48p. (gr. 2-8). 1986. pap. 3.95 (*0-516-44360-7*) Childrens.

Willi, Denise. Martina Navratilova: Tennis Star. (Illus.). 64p. (gr. 3-7). Date not set. PLB 14.95 (*1-56711-014-2*) Blackbirch.

WOMEN IN THE BIBLE

Buckingham, Betty Jo, ed. Women at the Well: Expressions of Faith, Life & Worship Drawn from Our Own Wisdom. Carachei, Maria E., tr. LC 87-6224. (Orig.). (gr. 12). 1987. pap. 7.95 (*0-9618243-0-1*) Ch Brethren Womens Caucus.

Daniel, Rebecca. Women of the Bible. 48p. (ps-6). 1989. 7.95 (*0-86653-495-4*, SS856, Shining Star Pubns) Good Apple.

McDonough, Yona Z. Eve & Her Sisters: Women of the Old Testament. Zeldis, Malcah, illus. LC 93-9378. 32p. (gr. k up). 1994. 15.00 (*0-688-12512-3*); PLB 14.93 (*0-688-12513-1*) Greenwillow.

Sabin, Francene. Women Who Win. 160p. (gr. 5 up). 1977. pap. 1.50 (*0-440-99643-0*, LFL) Dell.

Vos Wezeman, Phyllis & Wiessner, Colleen A. Gleanings from Ruth. 25p. (Orig.). (gr. 1-6). 1988. pap. 5.95 (*0-940754-61-4*) Ed Ministries.

WOMEN IN THE U. S.

see also Presidents–U. S.–Wives

Chang, Ina. A Separate Battle: Women & the Civil War. (Illus.). 112p. (gr. 5-9). 1991. 16.00 (*0-525-67365-2*, Lodestar Bks) Dutton Child Bks.

Costanzo, Christie. Learning New Roles. LC 91-11572. 64p. (gr. 6-12). 1991. 17.27 (*0-86593-117-8*); 12.95s.p. (*0-685-59202-2*) Rourke Corp.

De Pauw, Linda G. Founding Mothers: Women of America in the Revolutionary Era. (Illus.). 228p. (gr. 7 up). 1975. 16.95 (*0-395-21896-9*) HM.

Deutsch, Sarah J. From Ballots to Breadlines: American Women, 1920-1940. LC 93-30664. 1994. 20.00 (*0-19-508063-7*) OUP.

Faber. Smithsonian Ladies. 1995. write for info. (*0-8050-3015-8*) H Holt & Co.

Goldberg, Michael. Breaking New Ground: American Women, 1800-1848. (Illus.). 144p. 1994. PLB 20.00 (*0-19-508202-8*) OUP.

Jakoubek, Robert. The Colonial Mosaic: American Women, 1600-1760. (Illus.). 144p. 1995. PLB 20.00 (*0-19-508015-7*) OUP.

Johnston, Johanna. They Led the Way: Fourteen American Women. 1987. 2.95 (*0-590-44431-X*) Scholastic Inc.

Jones, Mother. Autobiography of Mother Jones: Pittston Strike Commemorative Edition. Parton, Mary F., ed. Darrow, Clarence & LeSueur, Meridelintro. by. (Illus.). 320p. (Orig.). (gr. 6-12). 1990. 25.95 (*0-88286-167-0*); pap. 12.95 (*0-88286-166-2*) C H Kerr.

May, Elaine T. Young Oxford History of Women in the United States, Vol. 9: Pushing the Limits: American Women 1940-1961. (Illus.). 144p. 1993. PLB 20.00 (*0-19-508084-X*) OUP.

O'Keefe, Candace. Texas Women - A Celebration of History: A Multicultural Guide. Shaw, Charles, illus. 60p. (gr. 4 up). 1991. pap. 8.95 (*0-9606256-2-3*) Hendrick-Long.

Patteson, Nelda. Clara Driscoll: Savior of the Alamo: Her Life Story Presented Through the Clothes She Wore. (Illus.). 32p. (gr. 4-7). 1991. pap. 14.95 (*0-9629001-0-9*) Smiley Originals.

Rappaport, Doreen, ed. American Women: Their Lives in Their Words. LC 89-77621. (Illus.). 336p. (gr. 7 up). 1990. 18.00 (*0-690-04819-X*, Crowell Jr Bks); PLB 17.89 (*0-690-04817-3*, Crowell Jr Bks) HarpC Child Bks.

Salmon, Marylynn. The Limits of Independence: American Women, 1760-1800. LC 93-30330. (Illus.). 144p. 1994. PLB 20.00 (*0-19-508125-0*) OUP.

Scott, Elaine, ed. The Times & Triumphs of American Woman. (Illus.). 79p. (gr. 4-9). 1986. pap. text ed. 8.00 book only (*0-9610622-1-5*) Natl Wmns Hall Fame.

Sigerman, Harriet. An Unfinished Battle: American Women 1848-1865. (Illus.). 144p. 1994. PLB 20.00 (*0-19-508110-2*) OUP.

Whiteley, Opal. Opal: The Journal of an Understanding Heart. Boulton, Jane, adapted by. LC 84-2418. (Illus.). 190p. (gr. 4 up). 1984. Repr. of 1976 ed. 14.95 (*0-935382-52-6*) Tioga Pub Co.

Zane, Polly & Zane, John. American Women: Four Centuries of Progress. 2nd, rev. ed. Zane, John, illus. (gr. 7 up). 1989. write for info. (*0-935070-03-6*) Proof Pr.

WOMEN IN THE U. S.–BIOGRAPHY

Carrick, Carol. Two Very Little Sisters. (ps-3). 1993. 14.95 (*0-395-60927-5*, Clarion Bks) HM.

Fannon, Cecilia. Leaders. LC 91-11570. 64p. (gr. 5-7). 1991. 17.27 (*0-86593-118-6*); 12.95s.p. (*0-685-59201-4*) Rourke Corp.

Gherman, Beverly. Sandra Day O'Connor: Justice for All. Masheris, Robert, illus. LC 92-42464. 64p. (gr. 2-6). 1993. pap. 3.99 (*0-14-034100-5*, Puffin) Puffin Bks.

Huber, Peter. Sandra Day O'Connor. (Illus.). 112p. (gr. 5 up). 1990. 17.95 (*1-55546-672-9*) Chelsea Hse.

Meltzer, Milton. Betty Friedan: A Voice for Women's Rights. Marchesi, Stephen, illus. LC 85-40441. 57p. (gr. 5 up). 1985. 10.95 (*0-670-80786-9*) Viking Child Bks.

Patteson, Nelda. Miriam Amanda Ferguson: First Woman Governor of Texas: Her Life Story Presented Through the Clothes She Wore. (Illus.). 32p. (Orig.). (gr. 4-8). 1994. pap. 14.95 (*0-9629001-1-7*) Smiley Originals. Content to be a wife & mother, Miriam had a drastic change in lifestyle when her husband became governor in 1915. Impeached & barred from holding state office, he cleverly decided that his wife should run in 1924. "Ma" & "Farmer Jim" did battle with the Ku Klux Klan for the executive office. First woman in the United States elected governor in her own right, "Ma" Ferguson served a second term in the 1930s. The novelty of a woman governor made her, & the fashionable clothes she wore, newsworthy. Narrative, photographs & costumes in color chronicle Governor Ferguson's triumphs & defeats. In an exciting format designed for both young people & adults, the book fills a need for the biographies of outstanding women. Book One, CLARA DRISCOLL: 'SAVIOR OF THE ALAMO.' (0-9269001-0-9). $14.95 each. Smiley Originals, P.O. Box 99, Smiley, TX 78159; phone 800-584-3655, FAX 210-587-6113.
Publisher Provided Annotation.

Shuker, Nancy. Elizabeth Arden. Furstinger, Nancy, ed. (Illus.). 140p. (gr. 7-10). 1989. PLB 7.95 (*0-382-09587-1*) Silver Burdett Pr.

Sigerman, Harriet. Laborers for Liberty: American Women 1865-1890. (Illus.). 144p. 1994. PLB 20.00 (*0-19-508046-7*) OUP.

Simonelli, Susan B. Rose Kennedy. (Illus.). 112p. (gr. 5 up). 1992. lib. bdg. 17.95 (*0-7910-1622-6*) Chelsea Hse.

WOMEN'S CLOTHING

see Clothing and Dress

WOMEN'S RIGHTS

Blumberg, Rhoda. Bloomers! Morgan, Mary, illus. LC 92-27154. 32p. (gr. k-5). 1993. RSBE 14.95 (*0-02-711684-0*, Bradbury Pr) Macmillan Child Grp.

Chafe, William. The Road to Equality: American Women Since 1962. (Illus.). 144p. 1994. lib. bdg. 20.00 (*0-19-508325-3*) OUP.

Cullen-Dupont, Kathryn. Elizabeth Cady Stanton & Women's Liberty. (Illus.). 144p. (gr. 6-12). 1992. lib. bdg. 16.95x (*0-8160-2413-8*) Facts on File.

Hanmer, Trudy J. Taking a Stand Against Sexism & Sex Discrimination. LC 90-12567. (Illus.). 144p. (gr. 9-12). 1990. PLB 14.40 (*0-531-10962-3*) Watts.

Hoff, Mark. Gloria Steinem: The Women's Movement. (Illus.). 96p. (gr. 7 up). 1991. PLB 15.40 (*1-878841-19-X*); pap. 5.95 (*1-56294-830-X*) Millbrook Pr.

Sigerman, Harriet. Laborers for Liberty: American Women 1865-1890. (Illus.). 144p. 1994. PLB 20.00 (*0-19-508046-7*) OUP.

Wagner, Shirley A. Equality Now: Safeguarding Women's Rights. LC 92-9746. 1992. PLB 22.60 (*0-86593-177-1*); 16.95s.p. (*0-685-59280-4*) Rourke Corp.

WOMEN'S RIGHTS–FICTION

Duffy, James. Radical Red. LC 93-12568. 160p. (gr. 5-8). 1993. SBE 13.95 (*0-684-19533-X*, Scribners Young Read) Macmillan Child Grp.

Freeman, Mary E. The Revolt of Mother. (gr. 5 up). 1992. PLB 13.95 (*0-88682-495-8*) Creative Ed.

Miles, Betty. The Real Me. 124p. (gr. 4-7). 1978. pap. 2.75 (*0-380-00347-3*, Camelot) Avon.

Oneal, Zibby. A Long Way to Go. Dooling, Michael, illus. 64p. (gr. 2-6). 1990. pap. 11.95 (*0-670-82532-8*) Viking Child Bks.

WOOD

see also Forests and Forestry; Lumber and Lumbering; Woodwork;

also kinds of wood, e.g. Oak

Daniel, Jamie & Bonar, Veronica. Coping with - Wood Trash. Kenyon, Tony, illus. LC 93-37686. 32p. (gr. 2 up). 1994. PLB 17.27 (*0-8368-1061-9*) Gareth Stevens Inc.

Dyson, Sue. Wood. LC 93-216572. 32p. (gr. 3-6). 1993. 13.95 (*1-56847-043-6*) Thomson Lrning.

Jennings, Terry J. Wood. Stefoff, Rebecca, ed. Barber, Ed, photos by. LC 91-18187. (Illus.). 32p. (gr. 3-5). 1991. PLB 15.93 (*1-56074-002-7*) Garrett Ed Corp.

WOOD BLOCK PRINTING

see Wood Engraving

WOOD CARVING

Bruggen, Bill & Wade, Tom. Carve Your Own Carousel Horse. LC 89-85082. (Illus.). 96p. (Orig.). 1989. pap. 14.95 (*0-929758-04-8*) Beeman Jorgensen.

LaBranche, Bud. Woodcarving the Female Head. (Illus.). 60p. (gr. 8 up). 1986. pap. 8.95 (*0-88625-137-0*) Durkin Hayes Pub.

Wood Carving. (Illus.). 48p. (gr. 6-12). 1966. pap. 1.85 (*0-8395-3315-2*, 33315) BSA.

WOOD ENGRAVING

Grafton, Carol B., ed. Victorian Spot Illustrations, Alphabets & Ornaments from Porret's Type Catalog. (Illus.). 96p. (gr. 5 up). 1982. pap. 5.95 (*0-486-24271-4*) Dover.

Werley, Judith G., ed. The Artist.., & the Legend: A Visit to China Is Remembered & the Legends Unfold... Domjan, Evelyn A., compiled by. Domjan, Joseph, illus. LC 74-81927. (gr. 7 up). 1974. 25.00 (*0-933652-09-7*) Domjan Studio.

WOOD WIND INSTRUMENTS

see Wind Instruments

WOODCUTS

see Wood Engraving

WOODPECKERS

Haley, Patrick. The Woodpecker & the Oak Tree. Kool, Jonna, illus. LC 82-82991. 64p. (gr. 3-4). 1982. 9.00 (*0-9605738-2-8*) East Eagle.

Pembleton, Seliesa. The Pileated Woodpecker. LC 88-20220. (Illus.). 60p. (gr. 3 up). 1988. text ed. 13.95 RSBE (*0-87518-392-1*, Dillon) Macmillan Child Grp.

WOODS

see Forests and Forestry

WOODWORK

see also Carpentry; Furniture; Wood Carving

Boy Scouts of America. Woodwork. (Illus.). 48p. (gr. 6-12). 1970. pap. 1.85 (*0-8395-3316-0*, 33316) BSA.

Bridgewaters Staff. How to Make Simple Wooden Puzzles & Jigsaws. (Illus.). 48p. 1994. pap. 11.95 (*0-85532-779-0*, Pub. by Search Pr UK) A Schwartz & Co.

Carrick, Graham. Wood. (Illus.). 32p. (gr. 2-6). 1990. lib. bdg. 15.94 (*0-86592-484-8*); lib. bdg. 11.95s.p. (*0-685-36306-6*) Rourke Corp.

McGuire, Kevin. Woodworking for Kids: Forty Fabulous, Fun, & Useful Things for Kids to Make. LC 93-20489. (Illus.). 160p. (gr. 4 up). 1993. 19.95 (*0-8069-0429-1*, Pub. by Lark Bks) Sterling.

Rose, Walter. The Village Carpenter. LC 88-3. (Illus.). 146p. (gr. 10 up). 1988. pap. 9.95 (*0-941533-18-2*) New Amsterdam Bks.

WOOL

Dixon, Annabelle. Wool. Stefoff, Rebecca, ed. Barber, Ed, photos by. LC 90-40366. (Illus.). 32p. (gr. 3-5). 1990. PLB 15.93 (*0-944483-73-9*) Garrett Ed Corp.

Edwards, E. Dean. The American Pioneer. (Illus.). 36p. (Orig.). (gr. 1 up). 1988. pap. 2.95 (*0-685-44554-2*) E D Edwards.

Jobin, Claire. All about Wool. Matthews, Sarah, tr. from FRE. Felix, Monique, illus. LC 87-31751. 38p. (gr. k-5). 1988. 5.95 (*0-944589-18-9*, 189) Young Discovery Lib.

Mitgutsch, Ali. From Sheep to Scarf. Mitgutsch, Ali, illus. LC 80-29557. 24p. (ps-3). 1981. PLB 10.95 (*0-87614-164-5*) Carolrhoda Bks.

Paladino, Catherine. Spring Fleece: A Day of Sheepshearing. (ps-3). 1990. 14.95 (*0-316-68890-8*, Joy St Bks) Little.

WORD GAMES

Agee, Jon. Go Hang a Salami! I'm a Lasagna Hog! And Other Palindromes. (Illus.). 80p. 1992. 12.21 (*0-374-33473-0*) FS&G.

—Go Hang a Salami! I'm a Lasagna Hog! And Other Palindromes. 1994. pap. 5.95 (*0-374-44473-0*, Sunburst) FS&G.

Allen, Mayme, et al. One Hundred One Word Puzzlers. Allen, Mayme, illus. LC 92-26302. 128p. (gr. 6 up). 1992. pap. 4.95 (*0-8069-8722-7*) Sterling.

Baker & Boyington. Down East Puzzles & Word Games. Hassett, John, illus. 80p. (Orig.). 1989. pap. 3.95 (*0-89272-272-X*) Down East.

Bank Street College of Education Editors. Let's Play Word Games. (gr. 1-2). 1986. pap. 3.95 (*0-8120-3628-X*) Barron.

Bank Street College of Education Staff. Let's Make Word Games. (gr. 1-2). 1986. pap. 3.95 (*0-8120-3629-8*) Barron.

Bourke, Linda. Eye Spy: A Mysterious Alphabet. Bourke, Linda, illus. 64p. (ps up). 1991. 15.95 (*0-87701-805-7*) Chronicle Bks.

Brigandi, Pat & Lovitt, Chip. Super Word Find Fun. 1993. pap. 1.95 (*0-590-40044-4*) Scholastic Inc.

Burgess, Allan. From Twisted Ear to Reverent Tear. Heston, Claudia, illus. 96p. (gr. 7-12). 1983. 5.98 (*0-941518-25-6*) Perry Enterprises.

Conway, Lorraine. Science Graphs & Word Games. 48p. (gr. 5 up). 1981. 7.95 (*0-86653-029-0*, GA 257) Good Apple.

Daniel, Becky. Following Directions Brain Boosters. (Illus.). 64p. (gr. 1-4). 1992. 7.95 (*0-86653-654-X*, GA1349) Good Apple.

—Language Brain Boosters. (Illus.). 64p. (gr. 1-4). 1992. 7.95 (*0-86653-653-1*, GA1348) Good Apple.

Dunning, Mary & Dunning, David. Good Apple & Wonderful Word Games. 144p. (gr. 3-7). 1981. 12.95 (*0-86653-053-3*, GA 254) Good Apple.

Fowler, Allan. Sound-a-Likes One: One, Won. Cafferata, Sue, illus. LC 94-7613. 32p. (gr. k-2). 1994. PLB 10.95 (*1-878363-97-2*) Forest Hse.

—Sound-a-Likes Two: Two, To, Too. Cafferata, Sue, illus. 32p. (gr. 2-4). 1993. PLB 10.95 (*1-878363-98-0*) Forest Hse.

Gackenbach, Dick, adapted by. & illus. Timid Timothy's Tongue Twisters. LC 85-30531. 32p. (ps-3). 1986. reinforced bdg. 14.95 (*0-8234-0610-5*) Holiday.

Gameillo, Elvira. Kids Word Find Puzzles. (Illus.). 64p. (Orig.). (gr. 4-6). 1988. pap. 1.95 (*0-942025-43-1*) Kidsbks.

Gamiello, Elvira. A-Maze-Ing Chiller Word Search Puzzles. (Illus., Orig.). (gr. 4-6). 1987. pap. 1.95 (*0-942025-05-9*) Kidsbks.

—A-Maze-Ing Monster Crack-Up Puzzles. (Illus., Orig.). (gr. 4-6). 1987. pap. 1.95 (*0-942025-02-4*) Kidsbks.

—Crossword Crack-Up Puzzles. (Illus., Orig.). (gr. 4-6). 1987. pap. 1.95 (*0-942025-04-0*) Kidsbks.

—Fun to Find Word Search Puzzles. (Illus., Orig.). (gr. 4-6). 1988. pap. 1.95 (*0-942025-37-7*) Kidsbks.

—Scary Search a Word Puzzles. (Illus., Orig.). (gr. 4-6). 1988. pap. 1.95 (*0-942025-39-3*) Kidsbks.

—Vacation Puzzle & Fun Book. (Illus., Orig.). (gr. 4-6). 1989. pap. 1.95 (*0-942025-63-6*) Kidsbks.

—Wacky Word Search Puzzles. (Illus., Orig.). (gr. 4-6). 1987. pap. 1.95 (*0-942025-03-2*) Kidsbks.

—Weird & Wacky Word Search Puzzles. (Illus., Orig.). (gr. 4-6). 1988. pap. 1.95 (*0-942025-42-3*) Kidsbks.

—Word Find Puzzles for Kids. (Illus.). 64p. (Orig.). 1988. pap. 1.95 (*0-942025-38-5*) Kidsbks.

Maleska, Eugene T. Children's Word Games & Crossword Puzzles, Vol. 2. (gr. 2-4). 1988. pap. 7.50 (*0-8129-1692-1*) Random.

—Children's Word Games & Crossword Puzzles, Vol. 3. (gr. 2-4). 1992. pap. 7.00 (*0-8129-1980-7*, Times Bks) Random.

Maleska, Eugene T., ed. Children's Word Games & Puzzles. 2nd ed. LC 86-886. 80p. (gr. 3 up). 1986. pap. 7.00 (*0-8129-1308-6*) Random.

Moll, Louise B. Great Book of Cryptograms. Sharpe, Jim, illus. LC 92-39447. 128p. (gr. 10-12). 1993. pap. 5.95 (*0-8069-8784-7*) Sterling.

Most, Bernard. Can You Find It? LC 92-33691. (ps-3). 1993. 13.95 (*0-15-292872-3*) HarBrace.

Schwartz, Alvin. Tomfoolery: Trickery & Foolery with Words. Rounds, Glen, illus. LC 72-12900. 128p. (gr. 4-6). 1990. PLB 14.89 (*0-397-32437-5*, Lipp Jr Bks) HarpC Child Bks.

—A Twister of Twists: A Tangler of Tongues. Rounds, Glen, illus. LC 85-45372. 128p. (gr. 5 up). 1991. PLB 13.89 (*0-397-32501-0*, Lipp Jr Bks) HarpC Child Bks.

Stern, Leonard & Price, Roger. Dinosaur Mad Libs. 48p. (Orig.). (gr. 1 up). 1993. pap. 2.95 incl. chipboard (*0-8431-3528-X*) Price Stern.

Super Crossword Puzzles & Word Games Activity Book. (Illus.). 48p. (gr. k-3). 1988. pap. 2.95 (*0-8431-2270-6*) Price Stern.

Thiesen, Charles & King, Deanna. Wordplay. rev. ed. LC 86-16178. (Illus.). 118p. (gr. 3-8). 1987. pap. 5.95 (*0-88166-088-4*) Meadowbrook.

Warren, Jean. Language Games. 80p. (gr. k-2). 1983. 7.95 (*0-912107-05-7*) Monday Morning Bks.

Wattenberg, Jane. Mrs. Mustard's Name Games. LC 92-16128. (Illus.). 48p. 1993. 7.95 (*0-8118-0259-0*) Chronicle Bks.

Wetterau, Bruce. Word Games. 352p. (gr. 9-12). 1990. 16.95 (*0-13-947334-3*, Webster New Wrld); pap. 9.95 (*0-685-31180-5*) P-H Gen Ref & Trav.

WORD GAMES–FICTION

Charney, Steve. Six Thick Thumbs: A Tongue-Twisting Tale. Chesworth, Michael, illus. LC 94-20734. 32p. (gr. k-2). 1994. PLB 2.25 (*0-8167-3594-8*, Whistlestop); pap. text ed. 2.25 (*0-8167-3426-7*, Whistlestop) Troll Assocs.

Fadiman, Clifton. Wally the Wordworm. Atherton, Lisa, illus. LC 83-9181. (gr. 3 up). 1984. 12.95 (*0-88045-038-X*); cassette & bk. 21.90 (*0-88045-101-7*); cassette only 8.95 (*0-88045-098-3*) Stemmer Hse.

Gerberg, Mort. Geographunny: A Book of Global Riddles. Gerberg, Mort, illus. 64p. (gr. 3 up). 1991. 14.45 (*0-395-52449-0*, Clarion Bks); pap. 7.70 (*0-395-60312-9*, Clarion Bks) HM.

Merriam, Eve. Fighting Words. Small, David, illus. 32p. (gr. k up). 1992. 15.00 (*0-688-09676-X*); PLB 14.93 (*0-688-09677-8*) Morrow Jr Bks.

Parish, Peggy. Good Work, Amelia Bedelia. Sweat, Lynn, illus. LC 75-20360. 56p. (gr. 1-4). 1976. 14.00 (*0-688-80022-X*); PLB 13.93 (*0-688-84022-1*) Greenwillow.

Raskin, Ellen. The Mysterious Disappearance of Leon (I Mean Noel) (gr. 4-7). 1977. (DCB); (DCB) Dutton Child Bks.

WORD PROCESSING

Blanc, Iris. Step-by-Step Skill Building Exercises for the Word Processor Solutions Booklet. 100p. (gr. 9-12). 1989. pap. text ed. avail. (*1-56243-004-1*, RWP-SOL) DDC Pub.

Fraser, K. & Collyer, J. Word Processing. (Illus.). 48p. (gr. 6 up). 1992. pap. 6.95 (*0-86020-930-X*) EDC.

Marshall, Grace L. & Haggblade, Berle. Keyboarding & Computer Applications. LC 92-35186. 1994. text ed. 30.95 (*0-538-61877-9*) S-W Pub.

Riede, Anne M. Coach's Clipboards. (Illus.). 306p. (Orig.). (gr. 5-8). 1986. 10.95 (*0-931983-02-9*, BCLTXT-3) Basic Comp Lit.

Spencer, Jean. Careers in Word Processing & Desktop Publishing. Rosen, Ruth, ed. (gr. 7-12). 1989. PLB 14.95 (*0-8239-0967-0*) Rosen Group.

Weinman, Susan. Word Processing: Course Code S04-2. Schroeder, Bonnie, ed. Black, Jeanne, illus. 75p. (gr. 7). 1989. pap. text ed. 8.00 (*0-917531-53-1*) CES Compu-Tech.

WORDS

see Vocabulary

WORDS, NEW

Briggs, Noreen V. Bugaboo Words. (Illus.). 160p. (gr. 3 up). 1989. 25.00 (*0-937857-13-0*, 1570) Speech Bin.

Gregorich, Barbara. Letters & Words: Kindergarten. Hoffman, Joan, ed. Koontz, Robin M., illus. 32p. (gr. k). 1990. wkbk. 2.29 (*0-88743-179-8*) Sch Zone Pub Co.

Lado, Robert. My First Thirty-Two Words: Level 1. (Illus.). 34p. (ps). 1985. card pack 9.95 (*1-879580-51-9*) Lado Intl Pr.

Lester, Alison. Bibs & Boots. (Illus.). 16p. (ps-k). 1989. 3.50 (*0-670-81988-3*) Viking Child Bks.

—Crashing & Splashing. (Illus.). 16p. (ps-k). 1989. pap. 3.50 (*0-670-81989-1*) Viking Child Bks.

Moncure, Jane. The Biggest Snowball of All. Friedman, Joy, illus. 32p. (gr. 1-3). 1993. pap. text ed. 5.95 (*1-56189-348-X*) Amer Educ Pub.

—Butterfly Express. Hohag, Linda, illus. 32p. (gr. 1-3). 1993. pap. text ed. 5.95 (*1-56189-377-3*) Amer Educ Pub.

—Here We Go 'Round the Year. Hohag, Linda & Jacobson, Lori, illus. 32p. (gr. 1-3). 1993. pap. text ed. 5.95 (*1-56189-378-1*) Amer Educ Pub.

—How Many Ways Can You Cut a Pie? Hohag, Linda & Jacobson, Lori, illus. 32p. (gr. 1-3). 1993. pap. text ed. 5.95 (*1-56189-349-8*) Amer Educ Pub.

—Ice-Cream Cows & Mitten Sheep. Friedman, Joy, illus. 32p. (gr. 1-3). 1993. pap. text ed. 5.95 (*1-56189-379-X*) Amer Educ Pub.

—The Magic Moon Machine. Hohag, Linda & Spoden, Dan, illus. 32p. (gr. 1-3). 1993. pap. text ed. 5.95 (*1-56189-375-7*) Amer Educ Pub.

—One Tricky Monkey up on Top. Hohag, Linda & Jacobson, Lori, illus. 32p. (gr. 1-3). 1993. pap. text ed. 5.95 (*1-56189-376-5*) Amer Educ Pub.

—A Pocketful of Pets. Hohag, Linda & Jacobson, Lori, illus. 32p. (gr. 1-3). 1993. pap. text ed. 5.95 (*1-56189-380-3*) Amer Educ Pub.

—Where Is Baby Bear? Friedman, Joy, illus. 32p. (gr. 1-3). 1993. pap. text ed. 5.95 (*1-56189-381-1*) Amer Educ Pub.

Moncure, Jane B. Word Bird's School Words. Hohag, Linda, illus. LC 89-7179. 32p. (ps-2). 1989. PLB 14.95 (*0-89565-510-1*) Childs World.

Woodhull, Angela V. Easy Words: An Easy Way to Learn New Words. Eddy, Hal, et al, illus. 150p. (gr. 8 up). 1988. pap. 5.95 (*0-685-44299-3*) Woodhull Pubns.

WORDSWORTH, WILLIAM, 1770-1850

Mayberry, Tom. Coleridge & Wordsworth in the West Country. (Illus.). 224p. (gr. 11-12). 1992. 30.00 (*0-86299-896-4*) A Sutton Pub.

WORK

see also Labor and Laboring Classes

Barbour, William, ed. Work: Opposing Viewpoints. (Illus.). 264p. (gr. 10 up). 1995. PLB 17.95 (*1-56510-219-3*); pap. text ed. 9.95 (*1-56510-218-5*) Greenhaven.

Belliston, Larry & Hanks, Kurt. Extra Cash for Kids. 1989. pap. 9.95 (*0-943497-70-1*) Wolgemuth & Hyatt.

Boerner, Lee A. Job Seeker's Workbook. Botterbusch, Karl F., ed. (Illus.). 169p. (Orig.). 1988. pap. 10.00 (*0-916671-83-6*) Material Dev.

Brady, Janeen. Standin' Tall Work. Wilson, Grant & Galloway, Neil, illus. 22p. (Orig.). (ps-6). 1981. pap. text ed. 1.50 activity bk. (*0-944803-41-5*); cassette & bk. 9.95 (*0-944803-42-3*) Brite Music.

Brown, Richard. One Hundred Words about Working. LC 87-8368. (Illus.). 27p. (ps-k). 1988. 6.95 (*0-15-200553-6*, Gulliver Bks) HarBrace.

Brown, Richard, illus. One Hundred Words about Working. (ps-1). 1989. pap. 3.95 (*0-15-200557-9*, Voy B) HarBrace.

Condon, Judith. Patterns of Work. LC 92-7838. (Illus.). 32p. (gr. 5-8). 1993. PLB 11.90 (*0-531-14228-0*) Watts.

Good, C. Edward. Does Your Resume Wear Blue Jeans? High School Edition. 139p. (Orig.). (gr. 9-12). 1989. pap. 6.95 (*0-934961-05-0*) Blue Jeans Pr.

Kalman, Bobbie. People at Work. (Illus.). 32p. (gr. 2-3). 1986. 15.95 (*0-86505-068-6*); pap. 7.95 (*0-86505-090-2*) Crabtree Pub Co.

Los Angeles Unified School District Staff. Working with Others. (Illus.). 48p. (Orig.). (gr. 7-12). 1990. Set. 10 wkbks. & tchr's. guide 44.95 (*1-56119-092-6*); wkbk. 4.95 (*1-56119-090-X*); tchr's. guide 1.95 (*1-56119-091-8*) Educ Pr MD.

—You & Your Attitude. (Illus.). 48p. (Orig.). (gr. 7-12). 1990. Set. 10 wkbks. & tchr's. guide 44.95 (*1-56119-089-6*); wkbk. 4.95 (*1-56119-087-X*); tchr's. guide 1.95 (*1-56119-088-8*) Educ Pr MD.

McCombs, Barbara L. & Brannan, Linda. Adjusting to a New Boss. (Illus.). 32p. (Orig.). (gr. 7-12). 1990. Set. 10 wkbks. & tchr's. guide 44.95 (*1-56119-071-3*); tchr's. guide 1.95 (*1-56119-026-8*); software 39.95 (*1-56119-113-2*) Educ Pr MD.

—Neatness Counts. (Illus.). 32p. (Orig.). (gr. 7-12). 1990. Set. 10 wkbks. & tchr's. guide 44.95 (*1-56119-081-0*); tchr's. guide 1.95 (*1-56119-046-2*); software 39.95 (*1-56119-123-X*) Educ Pr MD.

—Notice & Think. (Illus.). 32p. (Orig.). (gr. 7-12). 1990. Set. 10 wkbks. & tchr's. guide 44.95 (*1-56119-059-4*); tchr's. guide 1.95 (*1-56119-002-0*); software 39.95 (*1-56119-101-9*) Educ Pr MD.

—Respect for Property. (Illus.). 32p. (Orig.). (gr. 7-12). 1990. Set. 10 wkbks. & tchr's. guide 44.95 (*1-56119-072-1*); tchr's. guide 1.95 (*1-56119-028-4*); software 39.95 (*1-56119-114-0*) Educ Pr MD.

—Say. (Illus.). 32p. (Orig.). (gr. 7-12). 1990. Set. 10 wkbks. & tchr's. guide 44.95 (*1-56119-060-8*); tchr's. guide 1.95 (*1-56119-004-7*); software 39.95 (*1-56119-102-7*) Educ Pr MD.

—Taking Breaks. (Illus.). 32p. (Orig.). (gr. 7-12). 1990. Set. 10 wkbks. & tchr's. guide 44.95 (*1-56119-079-9*); tchr's. guide 1.95 (*1-56119-042-X*); software 39.95 (*1-56119-121-3*) Educ Pr MD.

—Too Much Talking. (Illus.). 32p. (Orig.). (gr. 7-12). 1990. Set. 10 wkbks. & tchr's. guide 44.95 (*1-56119-064-0*); tchr's. guide 1.95 (*1-56119-012-8*); software 39.95 (*1-56119-106-X*) Educ Pr MD.

—What Should I Do? (Illus.). 32p. (Orig.). (gr. 7-12). 1990. Set. 10 wkbks. & tchr's. guide 44.95 (*1-56119-074-8*); tchr's. guide 1.95 (*1-56119-032-2*); software 39.95 (*1-56119-116-7*) Educ Pr MD.

—What's Next? (Illus.). 32p. (Orig.). (gr. 7-12). 1990. Set. 10 wkbks. & tchr's. guide 44.95 (*1-56119-068-3*); tchr's. guide 1.95 (*1-56119-020-9*); software 39.95 (*1-56119-110-8*) Educ Pr MD.

—What's the Proper Way? (Illus.). 32p. (Orig.). (gr. 7-12). 1990. Set. 10 wkbks. & tchr's. guide 44.95 (*1-56119-067-5*); tchr's. guide 1.95 (*1-56119-018-7*); software 39.95 (*1-56119-109-4*) Educ Pr MD.

—Which Tools to Use? (Illus.). 32p. (Orig.). (gr. 7-12). 1990. Set. 10 wkbks. & tchr's. guide 44.95 (*1-56119-083-7*); tchr's. guide 1.95 (*1-56119-050-0*); software 39.95 (*1-56119-125-6*) Educ Pr MD.

—Which Way Is Right? (Illus.). 32p. (Orig.). (gr. 7-12). 1990. Set. 10 wkbks. & tchr's. guide 44.95 (*1-56119-084-5*); tchr's. guide 1.95 (*1-56119-052-7*); software 39.95 (*1-56119-126-4*) Educ Pr MD.

—Who Can Help? (Illus.). 32p. (Orig.). (gr. 7-12). 1990. Set. 10 wkbks. & tchr's. guide 44.95 (*1-56119-076-4*); tchr's. guide 1.95 (*1-56119-036-5*); software 39.95 (*1-56119-118-3*) Educ Pr MD.

—Will You Do Me a Favor? (Illus.). 32p. (Orig.). (gr. 7-12). 1990. Set. 10 wkbks. & tchr's. guide 44.95 (*1-56119-066-7*); tchr's. guide 1.95 (*1-56119-016-0*); software 39.95 (*1-56119-108-6*) Educ Pr MD.

—Working Too Slowly. (Illus.). 32p. (Orig.). (gr. 7-12). 1990. Set. 10 wkbks. & tchr's. guide 44.95 (*1-56119-062-4*); tchr's. guide 1.95 (*1-56119-008-X*); software 39.95 (*1-56119-104-3*) Educ Pr MD.

Schliefer, Jay. The Work Ethic. (gr. 7-12). 1991. PLB 14.95 (*0-8239-1227-2*) Rosen Group.

Write into a Job. (gr. 9 up). 1989. 7.95 (*0-936007-28-1*, 3315) Meridian Educ.

WORK–FICTION

Abm, Steven J. The Basket Maker. 32p. (gr. 2). 1992. write for info. (*0-9632943-0-X*) Sleepy Zebra.

Buehner, Caralyn. A Job for Wittilda. Buehner, Mark, illus. LC 91-15630. 32p. (ps-3). 1993. 13.99 (*0-8037-1149-2*); lib. bdg. 13.89 (*0-8037-1150-6*) Dial Bks Young.

Bunting, Eve. A Day's Work. Himler, Ronald, illus. 1994. 14.95 (*0-395-67321-6*, Clarion Bks) HM.

Conford, Ellen. Loving Someone Else. 160p. 1991. 15.00 (*0-553-07353-2*) Bantam.

Demuth, Patricia B. Ornery Morning. Brown, Craig M., illus. LC 90-40188. 24p. (ps-1). 1991. 13.95 (*0-525-44688-5*, DCB) Dutton Child Bks.
Dwight, Laura. We Can Do It! (Illus.). 32p. (ps-4). 1992. 7.95 (*1-56288-301-1*) Checkerboard.
Endersby, Frank. Man's Work. (gr. 4 up). 1981. 3.95 (*0-85953-270-4*) Childs Play.
Goodall, John S. Paddy Under Water. reissue ed. Goodall, John S., illus. LC 83-71901. 32p. 1984. SBE 12.95 (*0-689-50297-4*, M K McElderry) Macmillan Child Grp.
Gregorich, Barbara. Nicole Digs a Hole. Hoffman, Joan, ed. (Illus.). 16p. (Orig.). (gr. k-2). 1991. pap. 2.25 (*0-88743-026-0*, 06026) Sch Zone Pub Co.
Haas, Jessie. Working Trot. LC 83-1696. 160p. (gr. 5-9). 1983. reinforced 10.25 (*0-688-02384-3*) Greenwillow.
Hazen, Barbara S. Mommy's Office. Soman, David, illus. LC 91-25013. 32p. (ps-1). 1992. SBE 13.95 (*0-689-31601-1*, Atheneum Child Bk) Macmillan Child Grp.
Hoban, Julia. Buzby. Himmelman, John, illus. LC 89-29408. 64p. (gr. k-3). 1990. PLB 11.89 (*0-06-022398-7*) HarpC Child Bks.
Korman, Justine. Working Hard with the Mighty Mixer. (ps-3). 1993. pap. 2.50 (*0-590-47308-5*) Scholastic Inc.
Lincoln, James. Clock. 1992. pap. 15.00 (*0-385-30037-9*, Delta) Dell.

Lorkowski, Tommy. Dr. Nim & the Nombex. LC 94-60703. (Illus.). 30p. (gr. 4 up). 1994. pap. 9.95 (*0-914127-20-9*) Univ Class.
You liked stories by Dr. Seuss, you will love DR. NIM & THE NOMBEX. This exciting book in full color is 8" X 11" with 80# coated quality paper. Dr. Nim became concerned about the hard work the people of Nime had to perform. Working in his lab he invented a robot & named it Nombex. Nombex soon was able to relieve the people of their many tasks such as laying bricks, & all the other tasks they had to perform. He even fed them so they soon lost control of their hands, arms & legs since they no longer used them. You will find out what happened to the Nimians as you read the story. It will cause you to wonder if there are any Nimians in your community. These beautiful full-page illustrations are classics in themselves. Book II, DR. NIM & THE STRANGE QUEST will be available soon.
Publisher Provided Annotation.

Lyon, George E. Mama is a Miner. Catalanotto, Peter, illus. LC 93-49398. 32p. (gr. k-3). 1994. 15.95 (*0-531-06853-6*); PLB 15.99 (*0-531-08703-4*) Orchard Bks Watts.
Masihlall, Kamala. Rozan with Personnel. Masihlall, Kamala, illus. 16p. (gr. k-3). 1993. pap. 9.95 (*1-895583-60-8*) MAYA Pubs.
Matthews, Morgan. Whoo's Too Tired? Kolding, Richard M., illus. LC 88-1285. 48p. (Orig.). (gr. 1-4). 1988. PLB 10.59 (*0-8167-1331-6*); pap. text ed. 3.50 (*0-8167-1332-4*) Troll Assocs.
Medearis, Angela S. Picking Peas for a Penny. Shaw, Charles G., illus. 40p. (gr. 1-4). 1993. pap. 4.95 (*0-590-45942-2*) Scholastic Inc.
Merriam, Eve. Daddies at Work. Fernandes, Eugenie, illus. 32p. (ps-2). 1991. pap. 2.50 (*0-671-73276-5*, Little Simon) S&S Trade.
—Mommies at Work. (ps-3). 1991. pap. 2.95 (*0-671-73275-7*, Little Simon) S&S Trade.
Paterson, Katherine. Lyddie. 240p. (gr. 5-9). 1991. 15.00 (*0-525-67338-5*, Lodestar Bks) Dutton Child Bks.
—Lyddie. LC 92-20304. 192p. (gr. 7 up). 1992. pap. 3.99 (*0-14-034981-2*) Puffin Bks.
Schreier, Joshua. Hank's Work. LC 92-15205. (ps-2). 1993. 13.50 (*0-525-44970-1*, DCB) Dutton Child Bks.
Schwartz, Amy. Bea & Mr. Jones. Schwartz, Amy, illus. LC 93-20572. 32p. (gr. k-2). 1994. pap. 3.95 (*0-689-71796-2*, Aladdin) Macmillan Child Grp.
Singer, Marilyn. Chester the Out-of-Work Dog. Smith, Cat B., illus. LC 92-1141. 32p. (ps-3). 1992. 14.95 (*0-8050-1828-X*, Bks Young Read) H Holt & Co.
Sneed, Brad. Lucky Russell. (Illus.). 32p. (ps-3). 1992. 14.95 (*0-399-22329-0*, Putnam) Putnam Pub Group.
Strasser, Todd. Workin' for Peanuts. 208p. (Orig.). (gr. 7-12). 1984. pap. 2.95 (*0-440-99682-1*, LFL) Dell.
Summer Job. 1990. 4.98 (*1-55521-688-9*) Bk Sales Inc.
Waber, Bernard. Lyle at the Office. LC 93-49644. 1994. 14.95 (*0-395-70563-0*) HM.
Watkins, Dawn L. Very Like a Star. Thompson, Dana, illus. 30p. (Orig.). (ps). 1990. pap. 4.95 (*0-89084-533-6*) Bob Jones Univ Pr.
Wittmann, Patricia. Go Ask Giorgio! Hillenbrand, Will, illus. LC 91-2808. 32p. (gr. k-4). 1992. RSBE 14.95 (*0-02-793221-4*, Macmillan Child Bk) Macmillan Child Grp.

WORKING CLASSES
see Labor and Laboring Classes

WORKING GIRLS
see Child Labor

WORKINGMEN'S DWELLINGS
see Housing

WORLD
see Earth

WORLD ECONOMICS
see Economic Conditions; Economic Policy; Geography, Commercial

WORLD, END OF THE
see end of the World

WORLD GOVERNMENT
see International Organization

WORLD HISTORY
see also Geography; History, Ancient; History, Modern

Adams, Simon, et al. Illustrated Atlas of World History. LC 91-16652. (Illus.). 160p. (Orig.). (gr. 5 up). 1992. PLB 16.99 (*0-679-92465-5*); pap. 13.00 (*0-679-82465-0*) Random Bks Yng Read.
Burchard, Elizabeth & Franco, Beverly. World History: In a Flash. 480p. (gr. 7-12). 1994. pap. 9.95 (*1-881374-11-4*) Flash Blasters.
Caselli, Giovanni. Life Through the Ages. LC 92-52838. (Illus.). 64p. (gr. 3 up). 1992. 11.95 (*1-56458-143-8*) Dorling Kindersley.
Children's Atlas of World History. (Illus.). (gr. 4-8). 1991. 14.95 (*0-528-83444-4*) Rand McNally.
Chisholm, J. World History Dates. (Illus.). 128p. (gr. 6 up). 1987. PLB 17.96 (*0-88110-232-6*); pap. 12.95 (*0-86020-954-7*) EDC.
Clements, Gillian. Illustrated History of the World: How We Got to Where We Are. (Illus.). (gr. 4-7). 1992. 16.00 (*0-374-33258-4*) FS&G.
Exploring the Past: Group Two, 6 vols. (Illus.). 384p. (gr. 4-8). 1991. Set. PLB 89.70 (*1-85435-411-6*) The French Revolution, 64p. PLB 14.95 (*1-85435-412-4*); Giants of Science, 64p. PLB 14.95 (*1-85435-415-9*); Giants of the Arts, 64p. PLB 14.95 (*1-85435-414-0*); The Making of America, 64p. PLB 14.95 (*1-85435-413-2*); The Making of Modern Russia, 64p. PLB 14.95 (*1-85435-416-7*); Twentieth-Century Pioneers. PLB 14.95 (*1-85435-417-5*) Marshall Cavendish.
Fischer, Max W. World History Simulations. Buhler, Cheryl, illus. 96p. (gr. 5-8). 1993. wkbk. 10.95 (*1-55734-481-7*) Tchr Create Mat.
Fritz, Jean, et al. The World in 1492. (Illus.). 160p. (gr. 6-9). 1992. 19.95 (*0-8050-1674-0*, Bks Young Read) H Holt & Co.
Fry, Plantagenet S. Dorling Kindersley History of the World. LC 94-4856. (Illus.). 384p. (gr. 7 up). 1994. 39.95 (*0-685-72746-7*) Dorling Kindersley.
Hills, Ken. World History. LC 93-20105. (Illus.). 96p. (Orig.). (gr. 5 up). 1993. 15.95 (*1-85697-854-0*, Kingfisher LKC); pap. 9.95 (*1-85697-853-2*) LKC.
History of the World. (Illus.). (gr. 4 up). 1988. Set of 6 titles, 80 pp. ea. PLB 124.02 (*0-8172-3300-8*) Raintree Steck-V.
History of the World, 12 vols. (gr. 4-7). 1994. Set. 215.64 (*0-8114-3330-7*) Raintree Steck-V.
Holsinger, Donald C., et al. Master Guide to the World History Slide Collection. rev. ed. 312p. (gr. 7 up). 1989. pap. text ed. 40.00 (*0-923805-07-9*) Instruc Resc MD.
—The World History Slide Collection: Non-European History. (gr. 7 up). 1988. incl. 2100 slides 995.00 (*0-923805-08-7*) Instruc Resc MD.
Hopkinson, C. Usborne History of the Twentieth Century. (gr. 4-7). 1994. pap. 10.95 (*0-7460-0701-9*, Usborne) EDC.
Hopper, Hilary L. Around the World Program Series. (gr. 4 up). 1993. Smyth sewn casebound. 17.95 (*0-939923-28-9*); Perfect bdg. 7.95 (*0-939923-27-0*); Family ed. 48.00 (*0-939923-26-2*) M & W Pub Co.
Joly, Dominique & Maynard, Christopher. People Long Ago. LC 94-9083. (Illus.). 128p. (gr. k-4). 1994. pap. 5.95 (*1-85697-525-8*, Kingfisher LKC) LKC.
Kalman, Bobbie. Life Through the Ages. (Illus.). 32p. (gr. 2-3). 1986. 15.95 (*0-86505-075-9*) Crabtree Pub Co.
Killingray, David & Yapp, Malcolm. The Enlightenment. (Illus.). 32p. (gr. 6-11). 1980. pap. text ed. 3.45 (*0-89908-200-9*) Greenhaven.
Leeds, Chris. Peace & War: A First Sourcebook. (Illus.). 212p. 1987. pap. 17.95 (*0-85950-526-X*, Pub. by S Thornes UK) Dufour.
Millard. Exploration & Discovery. (Illus.). (gr. 4-9). 1979. (Usborne-Hayes); PLB 13.96 (*0-88110-111-7*); pap. 6.95 (*0-86020-261-5*) EDC.
—Warriors & Seafarers. (Illus.). (gr. 4-9). 1977. (Usborne-Hayes); PLB 13.96 (*0-88110-108-7*); pap. 6.95 (*0-86020-140-6*) EDC.
—World History, Book Of. (Illus.). 195p. (gr. 3-9). 1986. 22.95 (*0-86020-959-8*) EDC.
Perry, Marvin. Man's Unfinished Journey: A World History. 2nd ed. LC 79-84595. (Illus.). (gr. 10-12). 1980. text ed. 47.04 (*0-395-27563-6*); instr's. guide & key 25.12 (*0-395-27557-1*); activities bk. 11.24 (*0-395-27562-8*); Activities bk. instr's. annot. ed. 14.04 (*0-395-27558-X*) HM.
Reader's Digest Editors. The Reader's Digest Children's Atlas of World History. LC 93-4320. (Illus.). (gr. 4-7). 1993. 20.00 (*0-89577-526-3*, Dist. by Random) RD Assn.
Reese, Lyn. Spindle Stories, Bk. Two: Three Units on Women's World History. Dougherty, Mary A. & Wilkinson, Jean B., eds. Gorell, Nancy, illus. 118p. (gr. 6-10). 1991. pap. text ed. 15.00 (*0-9625880-1-6*) Women World CRP.
—Spindle Stories: World History Units for the Middle Grades, Bk. 1. Dougherty, Mary A. & Wilkinson, Jean B., eds. Gorell, Nancy, illus. 90p. (gr. 5-9). 1990. pap. text ed. 15.00g (*0-9625880-0-8*) Women World CRP.
Reynoldson, Fiona. Conflict & Change, 1650-1800. LC 92-20460. (Illus.). 80p. (gr. 2-6). 1993. 17.95 (*0-8160-2790-0*) Facts on File.
Timeline of World History: Tracing 6000 Years of the History of Mankind. 1993. 12.95 (*0-88394-972-5*) Promntory Pr.
Vanags. Empires & Barbarians. (Illus.). (gr. 4-9). 1979. (Usborne-Hayes); PLB 13.96 (*0-88110-109-5*); pap. 6.95 (*0-86020-142-2*) EDC.
Wars That Changed the World Series: Group 2, 6 vols. (Illus.). 128p. (gr. 3-9). 1991. Set. PLB 43.80 (*1-85435-258-X*) Marshall Cavendish.
Wilkinson, Philip & Dineen, Jacqueline. People Who Changed the World. Ingpen, Robert, illus. LC 93-31357. 1994. write for info. (*0-7910-2764-3*); pap. write for info. (*0-7910-2789-9*) Chelsea Hse.
Zevin, Jack, ed. The Kingfisher Illustrated History of the World: 40,000 BC to Present Day. Magnusson, Magnus & Martell, Hazelfrwd. by. LC 92-29123. 808p. (gr. 3 up). 1993. 39.95 (*1-85697-862-1*, Kingfisher LKC) LKC.

WORLD ORGANIZATION
see International Organization

WORLD POLITICS
see also International Organization; International Relations; World War, 1939-1945
also names of countries with the subdivisions Foreign Relations and Politics and Government, e.g. U. S. –Foreign Relations; U. S.–Politics and Government

Dudley, William, ed. The Cold War: Opposing Viewpoints. LC 92-21797. 288p. 1992. lib. bdg. 17.95 (*1-56510-009-3*); pap. 9.95 (*1-56510-008-5*) Greenhaven.
Foster, Leila M. The Story of the Cold War. LC 90-2175. (Illus.). 32p. (gr. 3-6). 1990. pap. 3.95 (*0-516-44750-5*) Childrens.
Issues in Focus Series, 31 bks. (Illus.). (gr. 6 up). Set. lib. bdg. 561.45 (*0-89490-345-4*) Enslow Pubs.
Killoran, James, et al. The Key to Understanding Global Studies: A Regents-RCT Review Book. Zimmer, Ronald, illus. LC 89-92425. 362p. (Orig.). (gr. 9-10). 1990. pap. text ed. 5.95 (*0-9624723-0-1*) Jarrett Pub.
Kurkowski, David C., ed. Current Leaders of Nations. LC 89-81456. (Illus.). 180p. (gr. 9-12). 1990. 3-ring binder 95.00 (*0-9624900-0-8*) Current Leaders Pub.
Mayberry, Jodine. Leaders Who Changed the Twentieth Century. LC 93-19032. (Illus.). 48p. (gr. 5-7). 1993. PLB 22.80 (*0-8114-4926-2*) Raintree Steck-V.
Osborne, John, et al. Global Studies: A Competency Review Text. 3rd ed. Gamsey, Wayne & Stich, Paul, eds. Fairbanks, Eugene B., illus. 384p. (gr. 7-12). 1992. pap. text ed. 8.33 (*0-935487-37-9*) N & N Pub Co.
—Global Studies: A Regents Review Text. 6th ed. Gamsey, Wayne & Stich, Paul, eds. Fairbanks, Eugene B., illus. 448p. (gr. 7-12). 1992. pap. text ed. 6.22 (*0-935487-35-2*) N & N Pub Co.
—Global Studies: Ten Day Competency Review. 2nd ed. Gamsey, Wayne & Stich, Paul, eds. Fairbanks, Eugene B., illus. 128p. (gr. 7-12). 1992. pap. text ed. 4.95 (*0-935487-53-0*) N & N Pub Co.
—Global Studies: Ten Day Regents Review. 2nd ed. Gamsey, Wayne & Stich, Paul, eds. Fairbanks, Eugene B., illus. 128p. (gr. 7-12). 1992. pap. text ed. 4.95 (*0-935487-48-4*) N & N Pub Co.
Polesetsky, Matthew & Dudley, William, eds. The New World Order: Opposing Viewpoints. LC 91-12374. (Illus.). 240p. (gr. 10 up). 1991. lib. bdg. 17.95 (*0-89908-183-5*); pap. 9.95 (*0-89908-158-4*) Greenhaven.
Sansevere-Dreher, Diane. Benazir Bhutto. (gr. 4-7). 1991. pap. 3.50 (*0-553-15857-0*) Bantam.
The War on Terrorism. (Illus.). 128p. (gr. 7-10). 1989. 11.96 (*0-382-09575-8*, J Messner) S&S Trade.

WORLD SERIES (BASEBALL)

Brenner, Richard J. The World Series: The Great Contests. (Illus.). 88p. (gr. 5 up). 1989. PLB 15.95 (*0-8225-1502-4*) Lerner Pubns.
Duden, Jane. The World Series. LC 91-23790. (Illus.). 48p. (gr. 5). 1992. text ed. 11.95 RSBE (*0-89686-724-2*, Crestwood Hse) Macmillan Child Grp.
Gergen, Joe. World Series Heroes & Goats: The Men Who Made History in America's October Classics. LC 82-611. (Illus.). 160p. (gr. 5-9). 1982. pap. 1.95 (*0-394-85018-1*) Random Bks Yng Read.
Gutelle, Andrew. All-Time Great World Series. Forbes, Bart, illus. LC 93-35668. 48p. (gr. 2-3). 1994. 7.99 (*0-448-40472-9*, G&D); pap. 3.50 (*0-448-40471-0*, G&D) Putnam Pub Group.
Gutman, Bill. World Series Classics. (gr. 5 up). 1973. lib. bdg. 3.69 (*0-394-92467-3*) Random Bks Yng Read.

WORLD WAR, 1914-1918

Bosco, Peter. World War I. (Illus.). 144p. (gr. 9-12). 1991. 17.95x (*0-8160-2460-X*) Facts on File.

Clare, John D., ed. The First World War. LC 94-7875. 1995. write for info. (*0-15-200087-9*, Gulliver Bks) HarBrace.
Exploring the Bismarck. 64p. 1991. 15.95 (*0-590-44268-6*, Scholastic Hardcover) Scholastic Inc.
Gay, Kathlyn. World War One. 1995. PLB write for info. (*0-8050-2848-X*) H Holt & Co.
Hills, Ken. World War One. (Illus.). 32p. (gr. 3-9). 1988. PLB 10.95 (*0-86307-931-8*) Marshall Cavendish.
Jantzen, Steven L. Hooray for Peace, Hurrah for War: The United States During World War I. (Illus.). 192p. 1990. 17.95x (*0-8160-2453-7*) Facts on File.
Kent, Zachary. World War I: "The War to End Wars" LC 93-46357. (Illus.). 128p. (gr. 5 up). 1994. lib. bdg. 17. 95 (*0-89490-523-6*) Enslow Pubs.
McGowen, Tom. World War I. LC 92-28329. 1993. 12.90 (*0-531-20149-X*); pap. 5.95 (*0-531-15660-5*) Watts.
Stewart, Gail. World War One. LC 91-16729. (Illus.). 112p. (gr. 5-8). 1991. PLB 17.95 (*1-56006-406-4*) Lucent Bks.

WORLD WAR, 1914-1918–BIOGRAPHY

Roth-Hano, Renee. Touch Wood: A Girlhood Occupied In France. 304p. (gr. 5 up). 1989. pap. 4.99 (*0-14-034085-8*, Puffin) Puffin Bks.
Zeinert, Karen. Those Incredible Women of World War II. LC 94-2579. (Illus.). 144p. (gr. 7 up). 1994. PLB 16.90 (*1-56294-434-7*) Millbrook Pr.

WORLD WAR, 1914-1918–CAMPAIGNS AND BATTLES

The World War I Soldier at Chateau Thierry. 48p. (gr. 5-6). 1991. PLB 11.95 (*1-56065-004-4*) Capstone Pr.

WORLD WAR, 1914-1918–FICTION

Dank, Milton. Khaki Wings. LC 80-65832. 160p. (gr. 8-12). 1980. pap. 8.95 (*0-385-28523-X*) Delacorte.
Gee, Maurice. The Champion. LC 92-37670. 1993. pap. 14.00 (*0-671-86561-7*, S&S BFYR) S&S Trade.
Kinsey-Warnock, Natalie. The Night the Bells Rang. Bowman, Leslie W., illus. LC 91-3053. 80p. (gr. 4 up). 1991. 12.95 (*0-525-65074-1*, Cobblehill Bks) Dutton Child Bks.
Kudlinski, Kathleen V. Hero over Here. Dodson, Bert, illus. 64p. (gr. 2-6). 1990. pap. 13.00 (*0-670-83050-X*) Viking Child Bks.
—Hero over Here: A Story of World War I. Dodson, Bert, illus. 64p. (gr. 2-6). 1992. pap. 3.99 (*0-14-034286-9*, Puffin) Puffin Bks.
Lerangis, Peter, adapted by. Safari Sleuth. LC 91-53168. (Illus.). 136p. (Orig.). (gr. 4-8). 1992. PLB cancelled (*0-679-92776-X*); pap. 3.50 (*0-679-82776-5*) Random Bks Yng Read.
Lewis, Sian. Smoke in the Tunnel. 1991. pap. 23.00x (*0-685-60035-1*, Pub. by Gomer Pr UK) St Mut.
McCay, William. Young Indiana Jones & the Mountain of Fire. LC 93-46118. 132p. (Orig.). (gr. 3-7). 1994. pap. 3.99 (*0-679-86384-2*, Bullseye Bks) Random Bks Yng Read.
McCay, William, adapted by. The Secret Peace. LC 91-58100. (Illus.). 136p. (Orig.). (gr. 4-8). 1992. PLB cancelled (*0-679-92777-8*); pap. 3.50 (*0-679-82777-3*) Random Bks Yng Read.
Martin, Les. Prisoner of War. LC 92-56395. 136p. (Orig.). (gr. 4-8). 1993. pap. 3.50 (*0-679-84389-2*) Random Bks Yng Read.
Rabin, Staton. Casey over There. Shed, Greg, illus. LC 92-30322. 1994. 14.95 (*0-15-253186-6*) HarBrace.
Skurzynski, Gloria. Good Bye, Billy Radish. LC 92-7577. (Illus.). 144p. (gr. 5 up). 1992. SBE 14.95 (*0-02-782921-9*, Bradbury Pr) Macmillan Child Grp.
Wells, Rosemary. Waiting for the Evening Star. Jeffers, Susan, illus. LC 92-30492. 40p. (gr. k-3). 1993. 15.00 (*0-8037-1398-3*); PLB 14.89 (*0-8037-1399-1*) Dial Bks Young.

WORLD WAR, 1914-1918–PERSONAL NARRATIVES

Green, Julian. The War at Sixteen: Autobiography, Vol. 2. Cameron, Euan, tr. from FRE. LC 93-656. 224p. 1993. 24.95 (*0-7145-2969-9*) M Boyars Pubs.

WORLD WAR, 1939-1945

Aaron, Chester. Alex, Who Won His War. 144p. (gr. 5 up). 1991. 17.95 (*0-8027-8098-9*) Walker & Co.
Aaseng, Nathan. Navajo Code Talkers. LC 92-11408. 114p. 1992. 14.95 (*0-8027-8182-9*); PLB 15.85 (*0-8027-8183-7*) Walker & Co.
Backrach, Susan D. Tell Them We Remember: The Story of the Holocaust with Images from the United States Holocaust Memorial Museum. LC 93-40090. (gr. 5 up). 1994. 19.95 (*0-316-69264-6*); pap. 10.95 (*0-316-07484-5*) Little.
Bergquist, Laurence C. Destiny: A Southeast Asia Saga 1928-1953. (Illus.). 336p. 1994. 24.95 (*0-935553-06-1*, Dist. by Words To Go, Inc.) Pacifica Pr.
Black, Wallace B. & Blashfield, Jean F. America Prepares for War. LC 90-46581. (Illus.). 48p. (gr. 5-6). 1991. text ed. 12.95 RSBE (*0-89686-554-1*, Crestwood Hse) Macmillan Child Grp.
—Blitzkrieg. LC 90-46580. (Illus.). 48p. (gr. 5-6). 1991. text ed. 4.95 RSBE (*0-89686-552-5*, Crestwood Hse) Macmillan Child Grp.
—Guadalcanal. LC 91-19902. (Illus.). 48p. (gr. 5-6). 1992. text ed. 4.95 RSBE (*0-89686-560-6*, Crestwood Hse) Macmillan Child Grp.
Crosby, Nina E. & Marten, Elizabeth H. Don't Teach! Let Me Learn about World War II, Adventure, Dreams & Superstition. Rossi, Richard, illus. 72p. (Orig.). (gr. 3-10). 1984. 8.95 (*0-88047-044-5*, 8411) DOK Pubs.
Cross, Robin. Aftermath of War. LC 93-50154. (Illus.). 48p. (gr. 5-9). 1994. 14.95 (*1-56847-178-5*) Thomson Lrning.
—Victims of War. LC 93-2252. (Illus.). 48p. (gr. 5-9). 1993. 14.95 (*1-56847-081-9*) Thomson Lrning.
Devaney, John. America on the Attack, 1943. LC 92-8993. 1992. cancelled 17.95 (*0-8027-8194-2*); PLB 18. 85 (*0-8027-8195-0*) Walker & Co.
Dolan, Edward F. America in World War II: 1941. (gr. 4-7). 1992. pap. 6.95 (*0-395-65944-2*) HM.
—America in World War II: 1943. (gr. 4-7). 1992. pap. 6.70 (*0-395-62463-0*) HM.
—America in World War II: 1944. (Illus.). 72p. (gr. 4-6). 1993. PLB 15.90 (*1-56294-221-2*); pap. 6.95 (*1-878841-81-5*) Millbrook Pr.
—America in World War Two: 1943. LC 91-30808. (Illus.). 72p. (gr. 4-6). 1992. PLB 15.90 (*1-56294-113-5*) Millbrook Pr.
Friedman, Ina R. The Other Victims: First-Person Stories of Non-Jews Persecuted by the Nazis. 224p. (gr. 5-9). 1990. 14.45 (*0-395-50212-8*) HM.
Fyson, Nance L. Growing up in the Second World War. (Illus.). 72p. (gr. 6 up). 1981. 19.95 (*0-7134-3574-7*, Pub. by Batsford UK) Trafalgar.
Gay, Kathlyn. World War Two. 1995. PLB write for info. (*0-8050-2849-8*) H Holt & Co.
Harris, Sarah. How & Why: The Second World War. (Illus.). 64p. (gr. 7-10). 1989. 19.95 (*0-85219-805-1*, Pub. by Batsford UK) Trafalgar.
Hills, C. A. The Second World War. (Illus.). 72p. (gr. 7-12). 1985. 19.95 (*0-7134-4531-9*, Pub. by Batsford UK) Trafalgar.
Hills, Ken. Nineteen Forties. LC 91-43852. (Illus.). 47p. (gr. 6-7). 1992. PLB 22.80 (*0-8114-3077-4*) Raintree Steck-V.
—World War Two. (Illus.). 32p. (gr. 3-9). 1988. PLB 10. 95 (*0-86307-932-6*) Marshall Cavendish.
Isserman, Maurice. World War II. 192p. (gr. 7-12). 1991. 17.95x (*0-8160-2374-3*) Facts on File.
Landau, Elaine. Nazi War Criminals. (Illus.). 128p. (gr. 9-12). 1990. 12.95 (*0-531-15181-6*) Watts.
Longman Twentieth Century History Series: Global War. 1990. pap. text ed. 7.95 (*0-582-34348-8*, 78448) Longman.
McGowen, Tom. World War II. LC 92-28328. 1993. 12. 90 (*0-531-20150-3*) Watts.
—World War II. (Illus.). 64p. (gr. 5-8). 1993. pap. 5.95 (*0-531-15661-3*) Watts.
Marrin, Albert. The Yanks Are Coming: The United States in the First World War. LC 86-3585. (Illus.). 256p. (gr. 5 up). 1986. SBE 15.95 (*0-689-31209-1*, Atheneum Child Bk) Macmillan Child Grp.
Maruki, Toshi. Hiroshima No Pika. Maruki, Toshi, illus. LC 82-15365. 48p. (gr. 7 up). 1982. 14.95 (*0-688-01297-3*) Lothrop.
Reynolds, Floria. Women at War. LC 93-4889. (Illus.). 48p. (gr. 5-9). 1993. 14.95 (*1-56847-082-7*) Thomson Lrning.
Ross, Stewart. Propaganda. LC 93-21730. 48p. (gr. 5-9). 1993. 14.95 (*1-56847-080-0*) Thomson Lrning.
—World Leaders. LC 93-20185. (Illus.). 48p. (gr. 5-9). 1993. 14.95 (*1-56847-079-7*) Thomson Lrning.
Spies & Espionage. (gr. 7-10). 1993. 19.95 (*0-7134-6541-7*, Pub. by Batsford UK) Trafalgar.
Steins. Allies Against Axis. 1993. write for info. (*0-8050-3165-0*) H Holt & Co.
Steins, Richard. The Allies Against the Axis: World War II (1940-1950) (Illus.). 64p. (gr. 5-8). 1993. PLB 15.95 (*0-8050-2586-3*) TFC Bks NY.
Sullivan, George. Strange But True Stories of World War II. 128p. (gr. 5 up). 1983. 14.95 (*0-8027-6489-4*) Walker & Co.
Tregaskis, Richard. Guadalcanal Diary. LC 83-17662. (Illus.). 176p. (gr. 5-9). 1984. pap. 4.99 (*0-394-86268-6*) Random Bks Yng Read.
Vail, John. World War Two: The War in Europe. LC 91-23062. (Illus.). 112p. (gr. 5-8). 1991. PLB 17.95 (*1-56006-407-2*) Lucent Bks.

WORLD WAR, 1939-1945–AERIAL OPERATIONS

Spate, Wolfgang. Top Secret Bird: The Luftwaffe's ME-163 Comet. Machat, Mike, illus. LC 88-90967. 276p. (Orig.). (gr. 8-12). 1989. pap. text ed. 11.95 (*0-929521-08-0*) Pictorial Hist.

WORLD WAR, 1939-1945–BATTLES

see World War, 1939-1945–Campaigns and Battles

WORLD WAR, 1939-1945–BIOGRAPHY

Amdur, Richard. Anne Frank. (Illus.). 112p. (gr. 5 up). 1993. 18.95 (*0-7910-1641-2*, Am Art Analog) Chelsea Hse.
Grant, Neil. Heroes of World War Two. LC 90-9468. (Illus.). 48p. (gr. 4-8). 1990. PLB 11.95 (*0-8114-2754-4*) Raintree Steck-V.
Lewis, Tom. Darwin Sayonara. 104p. 1990. pap. 39.00x (*0-86439-133-1*, Pub. by Boolarong Pubns AT) St Mut.
Oleksy, Walter. Military Leaders of World War II. LC 93-33641. (Illus.). 128p. (gr. 4-11). 1994. 16.95x (*0-8160-3008-1*) Facts on File.
Speer, Bonnie. Sons of Thunder: A Search for Identity. Speer, Jess W. & Peacock, Jimmy, eds. LC 92-8061. (Illus.). 200p. (Orig.). (gr. 6-12). 1992. pap. 9.95x (*0-9619639-8-0*) Reliance Pr.
Tames, Richard. Anne Frank. (Illus.). 32p. (gr. 5 up). 1991. pap. 5.95 (*0-531-24608-6*) Watts.
Toll, Nelly. Behind the Secret Window: A Memoir of a Hidden Childhood. (Illus.). 160p. (gr. 5 up). 1993. 17. 00 (*0-8037-1362-2*) Dial Bks Young.

WORLD WAR, 1939-1945–CAMPAIGNS AND BATTLES

Black, Wallace B. & Blashfield, Jean F. Battle of the Atlantic. LC 91-7989. (Illus.). 48p. (gr. 5-6). 1991. text ed. 12.95 RSBE (*0-89686-558-4*, Crestwood Hse) Macmillan Child Grp.
—Battle of the Bulge. LC 92-1722. (Illus.). 48p. (gr. 5-6). 1993. text ed. 12.95 RSBE (*0-89686-568-1*, Crestwood Hse) Macmillan Child Grp.
—D-Day. LC 91-45951. (Illus.). 48p. (gr. 5-6). 1992. text ed. 4.95 RSBE (*0-89686-566-5*, Crestwood Hse) Macmillan Child Grp.
—Desert Warfare. LC 91-27186. (Illus.). 48p. (gr. 5-6). 1992. text ed. 12.95 RSBE (*0-89686-561-4*, Crestwood Hse) Macmillan Child Grp.
—Invasion of Italy. LC 91-41484. (Illus.). 48p. (gr. 5-6). 1992. text ed. 12.95 RSBE (*0-89686-565-7*, Crestwood Hse) Macmillan Child Grp.
—Island Hopping in the Pacific. LC 92-2505. (Illus.). 48p. (gr. 5-6). 1992. text ed. 12.95 RSBE (*0-89686-567-3*, Crestwood Hse) Macmillan Child Grp.
—Iwo Jima & Okinawa. LC 92-25868. (Illus.). 48p. (gr. 5-6). 1993. text ed. 4.95 RSBE (*0-89686-569-X*, Crestwood Hse) Macmillan Child Grp.
—Victory in Europe. LC 92-23234. (Illus.). 48p. (gr. 5-6). 1993. text ed. 4.95 RSBE (*0-89686-570-3*, Crestwood Hse) Macmillan Child Grp.
Bliven, Bruce, Jr. The Story of D-Day: June 6, 1944. LC 81-483. (Illus.). 160p. (gr. 5 up). 1994. pap. 4.99 (*0-394-84886-1*) Random Bks Yng Read.
—Story of D-Day: June 6, 1944. (Illus.). (gr. 6-8). 1963. lib. bdg. 8.99 (*0-394-90362-5*) Random Bks Yng Read.
Charyn, Jerome. Back to Bataan. (gr. 4-7). 1993. 15.00 (*0-374-30476-9*) FS&G.
Pfeifer, Kathryn B. Seven Hundred Sixty-First Battalion. (Illus.). 80p. (gr. 4-7). 1994. bds. 14.95 (*0-8050-3057-3*) TFC Bks NY.
Sauvain, Philip. El Alamein. LC 91-28378. (Illus.). 32p. (gr. 6 up). 1992. text ed. 13.95 RSBE (*0-02-781081-X*, New Discovery) Macmillan Child Grp.
Stein, R. Conrad. D-Day. LC 92-36809. (Illus.). 32p. (gr. 3-6). 1993. PLB 12.30 (*0-516-06661-7*); pap. 3.95 (*0-516-46661-5*) Childrens.
Westerfeld, Scott. The Berlin Airlift. (Illus.). 64p. (gr. 5 up). 1989. PLB 12.95 (*0-382-09833-1*); pap. 7.95 (*0-382-09852-8*) Silver Burdett Pr.

WORLD WAR, 1939-1945–CAUSES

Allen, Peter. The Origins of World War II. LC 91-22698. (Illus.). 64p. (gr. 7-12). 1992. PLB 13.40 (*0-531-18410-2*, Pub. by Bookwright Pr) Watts.
Nicholson, Michael & Winner, David. Raoul Wallenberg: The Swedish Diplomat Who Saved 100,000 Jews from the Nazi Holocaust Before Mysteriously Disappearing. Sherwood, Rhoda, ed. LC 88-2078. (Illus.). 68p. (gr. 5-6). 1989. PLB 19.93 (*1-55532-820-2*) Gareth Stevens Inc.

WORLD WAR, 1939-1945–CHILDREN

Allen, Eleanor. Wartime Children, Nineteen Thirty-Nine to Nineteen Forty-Five. (Illus.). 64p. (gr. 6 up). 1983. 14.95 (*0-7136-1503-6*) Dufour.

WORLD WAR, 1939-1945–EUROPE

Adler, David. We Remember the Holocaust. LC 87-21139. (Illus.). 144p. (gr. 6 up). 1989. 17.95 (*0-8050-0434-3*, Bks Young Read) H Holt & Co.
Sherrow, Victoria. Amsterdam. LC 91-31627. (Illus.). 96p. (gr. 6 up). 1992. text ed. 14.95 RSBE (*0-02-782465-9*, New Discovery) Macmillan Child Grp.
Steele, Philip. Over Fifty Years Ago: In Europe During World War II. (Illus.). 32p. (gr. 6 up). 1993. text ed. 13.95 RSBE (*0-02-786886-9*, New Discovery) Macmillan Child Grp.
Stein, R. Conrad. World War II in Europe: "America Goes to War" LC 93-47396. (Illus.). 128p. (gr. 5 up). 1994. lib. bdg. 17.95 (*0-89490-525-2*) Enslow Pubs.

WORLD WAR, 1939-1945–FICTION

Anderson, Rachel. Paper Faces. 128p. (gr. 4-7). 1993. 14. 95 (*0-8050-2527-8*, Bks Young Read) H Holt & Co.
Avi. Who Was That Masked Man, Anyway? LC 92-7942. 176p. (gr. 4 up). 1992. 14.95 (*0-531-05457-8*); PLB 14.99 (*0-531-08607-0*) Orchard Bks Watts.
Bawden, Nina. The Real Plato Jones. LC 92-43873. 1993. 13.95 (*0-395-66972-3*, Clarion Bks) HM.
Baylis-White, Mary. Sheltering Rebecca. 112p. (gr. 5-9). 1993. pap. 3.99 (*0-14-036448-X*, Puffin) Puffin Bks.
Bishop, Claire H. Twenty & Ten. Pene Du Bois, William, illus. (gr. 5-9). 1984. 17.25 (*0-8446-6168-6*) Peter Smith.
Bunting, Eve. Spying on Miss Muller. LC 94-15003. (gr. 1-8). 1995. write for info. (*0-395-69172-9*, Clarion Bks) HM.
Burch, Robert. Home-Front Heroes. 144p. (gr. 3-7). 1992. pap. 3.99 (*0-14-036030-1*) Puffin Bks.
Carter, Peter. The Hunted. 1994. 17.00 (*0-374-33520-6*) FS&G.
Chaikin, Miriam. Friends Forever. Egielski, Richard, illus. LC 86-45777. 128p. (gr. 3-6). 1988. HarpC Child Bks.
Chang, Margaret & Chang, Raymond. In the Eye of War. LC 89-38027. 208p. (gr. 4-7). 1990. SBE 14.95 (*0-689-50503-5*, M K McElderry) Macmillan Child Grp.
Cooney, Caroline B. Operation: Homefront. 1992. pap. 3.99 (*0-553-29685-X*) Bantam.
Cooper, Susan. Dawn of Fear. Gill, Margery, illus. LC 89-6820. 224p. (gr. 5 up). 1989. pap. 3.95 (*0-689-71327-4*, Aladdin) Macmillan Child Grp.

Cooper, Susan L. Dawn of Fear. Gill, Margery, illus. LC 71-115755. 157p. (gr. 5 up). 1988. 14.95 (*0-15-266201-4*, HB Juv Bks) HarBrace.
Cormier, Robert. Other Bells for Us to Ring. Ray, Deborah K., illus. 144p. (gr. 4-7). 1992. pap. 3.99 (*0-440-40717-6*, YB) Dell.
DeJong, Meindert. House of Sixty Fathers. Sendak, Maurice, illus. LC 56-8148. 192p. (gr. 5-8). 1956. PLB 14.89 (*0-06-021481-3*) HarpC Child Bks.
Drucker, Malka & Halperin, Michael. Jacob's Rescue: A Holocaust Story. LC 92-30523. 128p. (gr. 4-7). 1993. 15.95 (*0-553-08976-5*, Skylark) Bantam.
Ferry, Charles. Raspberry One. LC 82-25476. 224p. (gr. 7 up). 1983. 13.45 (*0-395-34069-1*) HM.
Gallico, Paul. The Snow Goose. 50th anniversary ed. Peck, Beth, illus. LC 90-46880. 48p. 1992. 16.00 (*0-679-80683-0*); PLB 16.99 (*0-679-90683-5*) Knopf Bks Yng Read.
Garrigue, Sheila. The Eternal Spring of Mr. Ito. LC 93-30356. 176p. (gr. 3-7). 1994. pap. 3.95 (*0-689-71809-8*, Aladdin) Macmillan Child Grp.
Glassman, Judy. The Morning Glory War. LC 90-3831. 160p. (gr. 5 up). 1990. 13.95 (*0-525-44637-0*, DCB) Dutton Child Bks.
Greene, Bette. Summer of My German. 1984. pap. 3.99 (*0-440-21892-6*) Dell.
—Summer of My German Soldier. 208p. (gr. 7-12). 1984. pap. 3.50 (*0-553-27247-0*) Bantam.
—Summer of My German Soldier. 224p. (gr. 7 up). 1973. 14.95 (*0-8037-8321-3*) Dial Bks Young.
—The Summer of My German Soldier. large type ed. 272p. 1989. Repr. of 1973 ed. lib. bdg. 15.95 (*1-55736-134-7*, Crnrstn Bks) BDD LT Grp.
Hahn, Mary D. Stepping on the Cracks. 240p. (gr. 4-7). 1991. 14.45 (*0-395-58507-4*, Clarion Bks) HM.
Hall, Donald. Summer of 1944. Moser, Barry, illus. LC 92-38613. 32p. (gr. 1-5). 1994. 15.99 (*0-8037-1501-3*); PLB 15.89 (*0-8037-1502-1*) Dial Bks Young.
Hest, Amy. Love You, Soldier. LC 90-25161. 48p. (gr. 2-5). 1991. SBE 13.95 (*0-02-743635-7*, Four Winds) Macmillan Child Grp.
—Love You, Soldier. 48p. (gr. 2-6). 1993. pap. 3.99 (*0-14-036174-X*) Puffin Bks.
Hoobler, Dorothy & Hoobler, Thomas. Aloha Means Come Back: The Story of a World War II Girl. Bleck, Cathie, illus. 64p. (gr. 4-6). 1992. 5.95 (*0-382-24156-8*); PLB 7.95 (*0-382-24148-7*); pap. 3.95 (*0-382-24349-8*) Silver Burdett Pr.
Houston, Gloria. But No Candy. Bloom, Lloyd, illus. 32p. (ps-3). 1992. PLB 14.95 (*0-399-22142-5*, Philomel Bks) Putnam Pub Group.
Kudlinski, Kathleen V. Pearl Harbor is Burning! A Story of World War II. Himler, Ronald, illus. LC 93-15135. 64p. (gr. 2-6). 1993. pap. 3.99 (*0-14-034509-4*, Puffin) Puffin Bks.
Laird, Christa. Shadow of the Wall. LC 89-34469. (gr. 7 up). 1990. 12.95 (*0-688-09336-1*) Greenwillow.
Lingard, Joan. Tug of War. 208p. (gr. 7 up). 1990. 14.95 (*0-525-67306-7*, Lodestar Bks) Dutton Child Bks.
—Tug of War. 192p. (gr. 5 up). 1992. pap. 4.50 (*0-14-036072-7*, Puffin) Puffin Bks.
Lowry, Lois. Autumn Street. 160p. (gr. 5 up). 1980. 13.45 (*0-395-27812-0*) HM.
Marko, Katherine M. Hang Out the Flag. LC 92-349. 144p. (gr. 3-7). 1992. SBE 13.95 (*0-02-762320-3*, Macmillan Child Bk) Macmillan Child Grp.
Marx, Trish. Hanna's Cold Winter. Knutson, Barbara, illus. LC 92-27143. 1993. 18.95 (*0-87614-772-4*) Carolrhoda Bks.
Matus, Joel. Leroy & the Caveman. LC 92-24647. 144p. (gr. 3-7). 1993. SBE 13.95 (*0-689-31812-X*, Atheneum Child Bk) Macmillan Child Grp.
Mazer, Harry. The Last Mission. 192p. (gr. 7 up). 1981. pap. 3.99 (*0-440-94797-9*, LE) Dell.
Means, Florence C. The Moved-Outers. LC 92-13706. 156p. 1993. pap. 6.95 (*0-8027-7386-9*) Walker & Co.
Michener, James A. South Pacific. Hague, M., ed. 1992. write for info. (*0-15-200618-4*, Gulliver Bks) HarBrace.
Mochizuki, Ken. Baseball Saved Us. Lee, Dom, illus. LC 92-73215. 32p. (gr. k-8). 1993. 14.95 (*1-880000-01-6*) Lee & Low Bks.
Murphy, Claire R. Gold Star Sister. LC 94-48135. 224p. (gr. 5-9). 1994. 14.99 (*0-525-67492-6*, Lodestar Bks) Dutton Child Bks.
Nanus, Susan & Kornblatt, Marc. Mission to World War Two. 144p. (Orig.). (gr. 4 up). 1986. pap. 2.25 (*0-553-25431-6*) Bantam.
Oppenheim, Shulamith L. The Lily Cupboard. Himler, Ronald, illus. LC 90-38592. 32p. (gr. 1-3). 1992. 15.00 (*0-06-024669-3*); PLB 14.89 (*0-06-024670-7*) HarpC Child Bks.
Orlev, Uri. Lydia: Queen of Palestine. Halkin, Hillel, tr. from HEB. LC 93-12488. 1993. 13.95 (*0-395-65660-5*) HM.
Paterson, Katherine. Jacob Have I Loved. LC 80-668. 256p. (gr. 5 up). 1990. pap. 3.95 (*0-06-440368-8*, Trophy) HarpC Child Bks.
Paton-Walsh, Jill. Fireweed. LC 73-109554. 144p. (gr. 6 up). 1970. 14.95 (*0-374-32310-0*) FS&G.
Paulsen, Gary. The Cookcamp. 128p. (gr. 4-7). 1992. pap. 3.99 (*0-440-40704-4*, YB) Dell.
Reiss, Johanna. The Journey Back. LC 76-12615. 224p. (gr. 7 up). 1987. pap. 3.95 (*0-06-447042-3*, Trophy) HarpC Child Bks.
—The Upstairs Room. LC 77-187940. 208p. (gr. 7 up). 1990. pap. 3.95 (*0-06-440370-X*, Trophy) HarpC Child Bks.
Reuter, Bjarne. The Boys from St. Petri. 192p. (gr. 6 up). 1994. 14.99 (*0-525-45121-8*, DCB) Dutton Child Bks.
Roseman, Kenneth. Escape from the Holocaust. 192p. (Orig.). (gr. 4-6). 1985. pap. 7.95 (*0-8074-0307-5*, 140070) UAHC.
Rylant, Cynthia. I Had Seen Castles. LC 92-42325. (gr. 5 up). 1993. 10.95 (*0-15-238003-5*) HarBrace.
Salisbury, Graham. Under the Blood Red Sun. LC 94-444. 1994. 15.95 (*0-385-32099-X*) Delacorte.
Sathre, Vivian. J. B. Wigglebottom & the Parade of Pets. O'Neill, Catherine, illus. LC 92-17375. 96p. (gr. 2-6). 1993. SBE 12.95 (*0-689-31811-1*, Atheneum Child Bk) Macmillan Child Grp.
Savin, Marcia. The Moon Bridge. 1992. 13.95 (*0-590-45873-6*, Scholastic Hardcover) Scholastic Inc.
Schleimer, Sarah. Far from the Place We Called Home. LC 93-48519. 1994. 15.95 (*0-87306-667-7*) Feldheim.
Serraillier, Ian. Silver Sword. Hodges, C. Walter, illus. LC 59-6556. (gr. 7-9). 1959. 25.95 (*0-87599-104-1*) S G Phillips.
Shemin, Margaretha. The Little Riders. Spier, Peter, illus. 80p. (gr. 4 up). 1993. pap. 3.95 (*0-688-12499-2*, Pub. by Beech Tree Bks) Morrow.
Stafford, Jean. The Scarlet Letter. LC 92-44056. 1994. 13.95 (*0-88682-588-1*) Creative Ed.
Stevenson, James. Don't You Know There's a War On? LC 91-31461. (Illus.). 32p. (gr. k-8). 1992. 14.00 (*0-688-11383-4*); PLB 13.93 (*0-688-11384-2*) Greenwillow.
Towne, Mary. Dive Through the Wave. LC 93-40999. (Illus.). 128p. (gr. 3-6). 1994. PLB 13.95 (*0-8167-3478-X*); pap. text ed. 2.95 (*0-8167-3479-8*) BrdgeWater.
Uchida, Yoshiko. The Bracelet. Yardley, Joanna, illus. LC 92-26196. 32p. (ps-3). 1993. 14.95 (*0-399-22503-X*, Philomel Bks) Putnam Pub Group.
Vander Els, Betty. The Bombers' Moon. 168p. (gr. 5 up). 1992. pap. 4.50 (*0-374-40877-7*, Sunburst) FS&G.
Watkins, Yoko K. So Far from the Bamboo Grove. Fritz, Jean, intro. by. LC 85-15939. 192p. (gr. 6 up). 1986. 13.00 (*0-688-06110-9*) Lothrop.
—So Far from the Bamboo Grove. (Illus.). 192p. (gr. 5 up). 1994. pap. 4.95 (*0-688-13115-8*, Pub. by Beech Tree Bks) Morrow.
Westall, Robert. The Kingdom by the Sea. 176p. (gr. 5 up). 1991. 15.00 (*0-374-34205-9*) FS&G.
—The Machine Gunners. LC 76-13630. 186p. (gr. 5-9). 1976. PLB 13.88 (*0-688-84055-8*) Greenwillow.
—The Machine Gunners. LC 76-13630. 192p. (gr. 5 up). 1990. pap. 3.50 (*0-679-80130-8*) Random Bks Yng Read.
Yee, Chiang. Men of the Burma Road. (Illus.). (gr. 4-6). 8.50 (*0-685-20604-1*) Transatl Arts.

WORLD WAR, 1939-1945–FRANCE

Aaseng, Nathan. Paris. LC 92-709. (Illus.). 96p. (gr. 6 up). 1992. text ed. 14.95 RSBE (*0-02-700010-9*, New Discovery) Macmillan Child Grp.
Shea, George. The Silent Hero. LC 93-5492. 112p. (Orig.). (gr. 2-5). 1994. PLB 9.99 (*0-679-94361-7*); pap. 2.99 (*0-679-84361-2*) Random Bks Yng Read.

WORLD WAR, 1939-1945–GERMANY

Ayer, Eleanor H. Berlin. LC 91-29721. (Illus.). 96p. (gr. 6 up). 1992. text ed. 14.95 RSBE (*0-02-707800-0*, New Discovery) Macmillan Child Grp.
Ossowski, Leonie. Star Without a Sky. LC 84-21834. 216p. (gr. 5 up). 1985. 19.95 (*0-8225-0771-4*) Lerner Pubns.

WORLD WAR, 1939-1945–GREAT BRITAIN

Kronenwetter, Michael. London. LC 91-30306. (Illus.). 96p. (gr. 6 up). 1992. text ed. 14.95 RSBE (*0-02-751050-6*, New Discovery) Macmillan Child Grp.

WORLD WAR, 1939-1945–GUERRILLAS

see World War, 1939-1945–Underground Movements

WORLD WAR, 1939-1945–JAPAN

Morimoto, Junko. My Hiroshima. (Illus.). 32p. (ps-3). 1992. pap. 5.99 (*0-14-054524-7*, Puffin) Puffin Bks.
Newton, Robert. Tokyo. LC 92-2498. (Illus.). 96p. (gr. 6 up). 1992. text ed. 14.95 RSBE (*0-02-768235-8*, New Discovery) Macmillan Child Grp.
Sherrow, Victoria. Hiroshima. LC 93-30428. 1994. text ed. 14.95 (*0-02-782467-5*, New Discovery Bks) Macmillan Child Grp.

WORLD WAR, 1939-1945–JEWS

Bergman, Tamar. Along the Tracks. Swirsky, Michael, tr. 256p. (gr. 6-9). 1991. 14.45 (*0-395-55328-8*, Sandpiper) HM.
Frank, Anne. Anne Frank: The Diary of a Young Girl. rev. ed. Mooyaart, B. M., tr. Roosevelt, Eleanor, intro. by. LC 52-6355. 312p. (gr. 7 up). 1967. 24.95 (*0-385-04019-9*) Doubleday.
Larsen, Anita. Raoul Wallenberg: Missing Diplomat. LC 91-19937. (Illus.). 48p. (gr. 5-6). 1992. text ed. 11.95 RSBE (*0-89686-616-5*, Crestwood Hse) Macmillan Child Grp.
Neimark, Anne E. One Man's Valor: Leo Baeck & the Holocaust. LC 85-27366. (Illus.). 128p. (gr. 5-9). 1986. 14.95 (*0-525-67175-7*, Lodestar Bks) Dutton Child Bks.
Nicholson, Michael & Winner, David. Raoul Wallenberg: The Swedish Diplomat Who Saved 100,000 Jews from the Nazi Holocaust Before Mysteriously Disappearing. Sherwood, Rhoda, ed. LC 88-2078. (Illus.). 68p. (gr. 5-6). 1989. PLB 19.93 (*1-55532-820-2*) Gareth Stevens Inc.
Reiss, Johanna. The Upstairs Room. LC 77-187940. 196p. (gr. 7 up). 1987. 15.00 (*0-690-85127-8*, Crowell Jr Bks); PLB 14.89 (*0-690-04702-9*, Crowell Jr Bks) HarpC Child Bks.

WORLD WAR, 1939-1945–NAVAL OPERATIONS

Davis, Gary. Submarine Wahoo. LC 94-7102. 1994. text ed. 13.95 (*0-89686-828-1*, Crestwood Hse) Macmillan Child Grp.
Humble, Richard. A World War Two Submarine. Bergin, Mark, illus. 48p. (gr. 5 up). 1991. 17.95 (*0-87226-351-7*) P Bedrick Bks.

WORLD WAR, 1939-1945–PACIFIC OCEAN

Black, Wallace B. & Blashfield, Jean F. Flattops at War. LC 91-7916. (Illus.). 48p. (gr. 5-6). 1991. text ed. 12.95 RSBE (*0-89686-559-2*, Crestwood Hse) Macmillan Child Grp.
—Jungle Warfare. LC 91-31533. (Illus.). 48p. (gr. 5-6). 1992. text ed. 12.95 RSBE (*0-89686-563-0*, Crestwood Hse) Macmillan Child Grp.
Davis, Gary. Submarine Wahoo. LC 94-7102. 1994. text ed. 13.95 (*0-89686-828-1*, Crestwood Hse) Macmillan Child Grp.
Ferry, Charles. Raspberry One. LC 82-25476. 224p. (gr. 7 up). 1983. 13.45 (*0-395-34069-1*) HM.
Marrin, Albert. Victory in the Pacific. LC 82-6707. (Illus.). 224p. (gr. 6 up). 1983. SBE 15.95 (*0-689-30948-1*, Atheneum Child Bk) Macmillan Child Grp.
Nardo, Don. World War Two: The War in the Pacific. LC 91-16727. (Illus.). 112p. (gr. 5-8). 1991. PLB 17.95 (*1-56006-408-0*) Lucent Bks.
Stein, R. Conrad. World War II in the Pacific: "Remember Pearl Harbor" LC 93-33623. (Illus.). 128p. (gr. 5 up). 1994. lib. bdg. 17.95 (*0-89490-524-4*) Enslow Pubs.

WORLD WAR, 1939-1945–PERSONAL NARRATIVES

Butterworth, Emma M. As the Waltz Was Ending. 262p. (gr. 7 up). 1991. pap. 3.25 (*0-590-44440-9*, Point); tchr's. guide 1.25 (*0-590-40665-5*) Scholastic Inc.
Drucker, Olga L. Kindertransport. LC 92-14121. (gr. 5-8). 1992. 14.95 (*0-8050-1711-9*, Bks Young Read) H Holt & Co.
Emmerich, Elsbeth & Hull, Robert. My Childhood in Nazi Germany. LC 91-10499. (Illus.). 96p. (gr. 4-9). 1992. PLB 13.90 (*0-531-18429-3*, Pub. by Bookwright Pr) Watts.
Lee, James W., ed. Nineteen Forty-One: Texas Goes to War. LC 91-36090. (Illus.). 244p. 1991. pap. 19.95 (*0-929398-29-7*) UNTX Pr.
Marx, Trish. Echoes of World War Two. LC 92-47369. 1993. 19.95 (*0-8225-4898-4*) Lerner Pubns.
Reiss, Johanna. The Upstairs Room. LC 77-187940. 196p. (gr. 7 up). 1987. 15.00 (*0-690-85127-8*, Crowell Jr Bks); PLB 14.89 (*0-690-04702-9*, Crowell Jr Bks) HarpC Child Bks.
Vogel, Ilse-Margaret. Bad Times, Good Friends. 1992. write for info. (*0-15-205528-2*, HB Juv Bks) HarBrace.
Willey, Bob. From All Sides: Memories of World War II. (Illus.). 160p. (gr. 7-12). 1990. pap. text ed. 10.00 (*0-86299-678-3*) A Sutton Pub.

WORLD WAR, 1939-1945–PRISONERS AND PRISONS

Nicholson, Michael & Winner, David. Raoul Wallenberg. LC 88-2078. (Illus.). 68p. (gr. 5-6). 1990. pap. 7.95 (*0-8192-1525-2*) Morehouse Pub.

WORLD WAR, 1939-1945–SECRET SERVICE

Rogers, James T. The Secret War: Espionage in World War II. (Illus.). 128p. (gr. 7-10). 1991. lib. bdg. 16.95x (*0-8160-2395-6*) Facts on File.

WORLD WAR, 1939-1945–SOVIET UNION

Black, Wallace B. & Blashfield, Jean F. Russia at War. (Illus.). 48p. (gr. 5-6). 1991. text ed. 12.95 RSBE (*0-89686-556-8*, Crestwood Hse) Macmillan Child Grp.
Hanmer, Trudy J. Leningrad. LC 92-14. (Illus.). 96p. (gr. 6 up). 1992. text ed. 14.95 RSBE (*0-02-742615-7*, New Discovery) Macmillan Child Grp.

WORLD WAR, 1939-1945–UNDERGROUND MOVEMENTS

Atkinson, Linda. In Kindling Flame: The Story of Hannah Senesh 1921-1944. LC 83-24392. 224p. (gr. 9 up). 1985. 15.00 (*0-688-02714-8*) Lothrop.
Black, Wallace B. & Blashfield, Jean F. War Behind the Lines. LC 91-40866. (Illus.). 48p. (gr. 5-6). 1992. text ed. 12.95 RSBE (*0-89686-564-9*, Crestwood Hse) Macmillan Child Grp.

WORLD WAR, 1939-1945–U. S.

American Heritage Illustrated History of the United States, Vol. 15: World War II. LC 87-73399. 128p. (gr. 7-12). 1988. Repr. of 1963 ed. 3.49 (*0-945260-15-6*) Choice Pub NY.
Brimner, Larry D. Voices from the Camps: Japanese Americans during World War II. LC 93-31956. (Illus.). 160p. (gr. 9-12). 1994. PLB 13.90 (*0-531-11179-2*) Watts.
Chin, Steven A. When Justice Failed: The Fred Korematsu Story. Tamura, David, illus. LC 92-18086. 105p. (gr. 2-5). 1992. PLB 21.34 (*0-8114-7236-1*) Raintree Steck-V.
Cross, Robin. Roosevelt: And the Americans at War. LC 90-31227. (Illus.). 64p. (gr. 5-8). 1990. PLB 12.90 (*0-531-17254-6*, Gloucester Pr) Watts.
Devaney, John. America Fights the Tide, 1942. 192p. (gr. 12 up). 1991. 17.95 (*0-8027-6997-7*); lib. bdg. 18.85 (*0-8027-6998-5*) Walker & Co.

—America Goes to War, 1941. 192p. (gr. 12 up). 1991. 16.95 (*0-8027-6979-9*); lib. bdg. 17.85 (*0-8027-6980-2*) Walker & Co.

—America on the Attack, 1943. LC 92-8993. 1992. cancelled 17.95 (*0-8027-8194-2*); PLB 18.85 (*0-8027-8195-0*) Walker & Co.

—America Storms the Beaches, 1944. LC 92-47057. (Illus.). 176p. (gr. 7 up). 1993. 17.95 (*0-8027-8244-2*); PLB 18.85 (*0-8027-8245-0*) Walker & Co.

Dolan, Edward F. America in World War Two: 1942. LC 91-30808. (Illus.). 72p. (gr. 4-6). 1991. PLB 15.90 (*1-56294-007-4*); pap. 6.95 (*1-878841-82-3*) Millbrook Pr.

—America in World War Two: 1945. (Illus.). 72p. (gr. 4-6). 1994. 15.90 (*1-56294-320-0*) Millbrook Pr.

Stanley, Jerry. I Am an American: A True Story of the Japanese Internment. LC 93-41330. (Illus.). 112p. (gr. 4 up). 1994. 15.00 (*0-517-59786-1*); PLB 15.99 (*0-517-59787-X*) Crown Bks Yng Read.

Weatherford, Doris. American Women & World War Two. (Illus.). 384p. 1990. 29.95x (*0-8160-2038-8*) Facts on File.

Whitman, Sylvia. V Is for Victory: The American Homefront During World War II. (Illus.). 80p. (gr. 5-12). 1992. PLB 17.50 (*0-8225-1727-2*) Lerner Pubns.

WORLD'S FAIRS

see Exhibitions; Fairs

WORMS

Atkinson, Kathie. Worms, Wonderful Worms. LC 93-28968. 1994. 4.25 (*0-383-03788-3*) SRA Schl Grp.

Benedict, Kitty. The Earthworm: My First Nature Books. Felix, Monique, illus. 32p. (gr. k-2). 1993. pap. 2.95 (*1-56189-176-2*) Amer Educ Pub.

Glaser, Linda. Wonderful Worms. Krupinski, Loretta, illus. LC 91-38752. 32p. (ps-3). 1992. 14.95 (*1-56294-703-6*); PLB 15.40 (*1-56294-062-7*) Millbrook Pr.

—Wonderful Worms. 1994. pap. 7.95 (*1-56294-730-3*) Millbrook Pr.

Halton, Cheryl M. Those Amazing Leeches. LC 88-35908. (Illus.). 112p. (gr. 4 up). 1990. text ed. 13.95 RSBE (*0-87518-408-1*, Dillon) Macmillan Child Grp.

Hoffman, Jane. Backyard Scientist, Exploring Earthworms with Me: Simple & Fun Experiments to Do with Earthworms. Ostroff, Lanny, illus. 56p. (gr. k-6). 1994. pap. text ed. 8.95 (*0-9618663-5-7*) Backyard Scientist. The Backyard Scientist Series, Hoffman, Jane. THE ORIGINAL BACKYARD SCIENTIST, $8.50, ISBN 0-9618663-1-4; BACKYARD SCIENTIST, SERIES ONE, $8.50, ISBN 0-9618663-0-6; BACKYARD SCIENTIST, SERIES TWO, $8.50, ISBN 0-9618663-2-2; BACKYARD SCIENTIST, SERIES THREE, $8.50, ISBN 0-9618663-3-0; BACKYARD SCIENTIST, SERIES FOUR, $8.50, ISBN 0-9618663-4-9; BACKYARD SCIENTIST, EXPLORING EARTHWORMS WITH ME, $8.95, ISBN 0-9618663-5-7. These sprightly illustrated books contain simple-to-perform, hands-on science experiments in chemistry, physics & solid sciences (except as noted below) for budding scientists 4 to 14 years old. Using commonly available materials (most are found in the average home), the experiments will allow the student to explore & understand complex scientific concepts. SERIES THREE's focus is on the life sciences. EXPLORING EARTHWORMS WITH ME allows the young scientist to learn the physiology & environmental needs of this beneficial animal. The books are excellent for use in the home & classroom. The author, Jane Hoffman, is a sought-after provider of teacher in-service workshops & workshop leader at educational conferences. Backyard Scientist, Inc., P.O. Box 16966, Irvine, CA 92713; 714-551-2392; FAX 714-552-5351.

Publisher Provided Annotation.

Kalman, Bobbie & Schaub, Janine. Squirmy Wormy Composters. (Illus.). 32p. (gr. k-8). 1992. PLB 15.95 (*0-86505-555-6*); pap. 7.95 (*0-86505-581-5*) Crabtree Pub Co.

Sroda, George. No Angle Left Unturned: Facts About Nightcrawlers. Hughes, Janet, illus. 111p. (gr. 10 up). 1975. 10.90 (*0-9604486-0-8*) G Sroda.

WORMS–FICTION

Annable, Toni & Kaspar, Maria H. Sherm the Worm. Viola, Amy, tr. (Illus.). 96p. (Orig.). (gr. k up). 1992. Set. pap. 8.95 (*1-882828-08-9*) Vol. 1 English-Spanish, Lozano el Gusano. Vol. 2 English-French, Valere le Ver. Kasan Imprints.

—Sherm the Worm: Lozano el Gusano. Viola, Amy, tr. Lumetta, Lawrence, illus. 40p. (Orig.). (gr. k up). 1992. pap. 4.95 (*1-882828-00-3*); pap. 10.95 incl. audio (*1-882828-12-7*) Kasan Imprints.

—Sherm the Worm: Valere le Ver. Lumetta, Lawrence, illus. 48p. (Orig.). (gr. k up). 1992. pap. 4.95 (*1-882828-01-1*); pap. 10.95 incl. audio (*1-882828-13-5*) Kasan Imprints.

Beak, Barbara. Walter Worm's Good Turn. LC 91-33548. 1992. 2.95 (*0-85953-785-4*) Childs Play.

Brown, Lynn. Ms. Worm. 3rd ed. Walker, Granville, Jr., ed. Jackson, Gregory A., illus. (Orig.). (ps-6). 1982. pap. 2.95x (*0-9608466-0-3*) Fun Reading.

Demi. Where Is Willie Worm? Demi, illus. LC 80-53680. 24p. (ps-1). 1981. 3.95 (*0-394-84759-8*) Random Bks Yng Read.

Giff, Patricia R. The Winter Worm Business. Morrill, Leslie, illus. 144p. (gr. k-6). 1983. pap. 3.50 (*0-440-49259-9*, YB) Dell.

How to Eat Fried Worms. 1923. pap. 3.25 (*0-440-74545-4*) Dell.

Lionni, Leo. Inch by Inch. Cohn, Amy, ed. LC 94-6483. (Illus.). 32p. (ps up). 1994. pap. 4.95 (*0-688-13283-9*, Mulberry) Morrow.

McLaughlin, Molly. Earthworms, Dirt, & Rotten Leaves. Shetterly, Robert, illus. 96p. 1990. pap. 3.50 (*0-380-71074-9*, Camelot) Avon.

Magellan, Mauro. Home at Last. Magellan, Mauro, illus. LC 89-19994. 32p. 1989. 12.95 (*0-89334-119-3*) Humanics Ltd.

Reese, Bob. Crab Apple. Wasserman, Dan, ed. Reese, Dan, illus. (gr. k-1). 1979. 7.95 (*0-89868-072-7*); pap. 2.95 (*0-89868-083-2*) ARO Pub.

Rockwell, Thomas. How to Eat Fried Worms. (gr. 4-7). 1992. pap. 1.99 (*0-440-21367-3*) Dell.

Scarry, Richard. Richard Scarry's Lowly Worm Storybook. Scarry, Richard, illus. LC 77-79842. 32p. (Orig.). (ps-1). 1989. pap. 2.25 (*0-394-88270-9*) Random Bks Yng Read.

Sroda, George. Life Story of TV Star & Celebrity Herman the Worm. Hughes, Janet, illus. 189p. (Orig.). (gr. k-7). 1979. 4.95 (*0-9604486-2-4*); pap. 3.95 (*0-685-01814-8*) G Sroda.

Stevenson, James. National Worm Day. LC 88-34915. (Illus.). 40p. (gr. k up). 1990. 12.95 (*0-688-08771-X*); lib. bdg. 12.88 (*0-688-08772-8*) Greenwillow.

WORSHIP

see also Prayer

Bacher, June M. When Hearts Awaken. 192p. 1988. pap. 6.99 (*0-89081-610-7*) Harvest Hse.

Brooks, Bruce. The Moves Make the Man. LC 83-49476. 320p. (gr. 7 up). 1984. 15.00 (*0-06-020679-9*); PLB 15.89 (*0-06-020698-5*) HarpC Child Bks.

Bruno, Bonnie. Kwitcherbellyakin: Devotions for Young Families. 144p. 1992. pap. 5.99 (*0-310-54811-X*, Youth Bks) Zondervan.

Draper, Edythe. Cool: How a Kid Should Live. (gr. 3-5). 1974. kivar 9.99 (*0-8423-0435-5*) Tyndale.

Finley, Tom. The World Is Not Enough. Parrish, Annette, ed. LC 86-22049. 239p. (Orig.). (gr. 7-12). 1986. pap. 5.99 (*0-8307-1151-1*, S183329) Regal.

Groth, Lynn. Reaching Tender Hearts, Vol. 1. Grunze, Richard, ed. May, Lawrence & Steele, Loren, illus. 157p. (ps-k). 1987. pap. 7.95 (*0-938272-42-X*) WELS Board.

Group Publishing, Inc. Staff, ed. Ten-Minute Devotions, Vol. III. LC 93-7811. 1993. 10.99 (*1-55945-171-8*) Group Pub.

Johnson, Kevin. Why Is God Looking for Friends? 128p. (Orig.). (gr. 6-9). 1993. pap. 6.99 (*1-55661-282-6*) Bethany Hse.

Johnson, Philip E. Celebrating the Seasons with Children (Year B) LC 84-14791. 112p. (Orig.). (ps-3). 1984. pap. 8.95 (*0-8298-0723-3*) Pilgrim OH.

Oyer, Sharron, et al. Seekers in Sneakers: A Children's Devotional, Vol. 1. 128p. (Orig.). (gr. 2-5). 1988. pap. 6.99 (*0-89081-611-5*) Harvest Hse.

Peterson, Lorraine. Trying to Get Toothpaste Back Into the Tube. 192p. (Orig.). (gr. 7-10). 1993. pap. 7.99 (*1-55661-315-6*) Bethany Hse.

Rathert, Donna & Prahlow, Lois. Time for Church. 24p. (gr. 2-5). 1985. pap. 2.99 (*0-570-04129-5*, 56-1540) Concordia.

Sanders, Bill. Outtakes: Devotions for Guys. LC 88-18197. (gr. 7-12). 1988. pap. 7.99 (*0-8007-5285-6*) Revell.

Simon, Mary M. Little Visits on the Go. (Illus.). (ps-7). 1992. wire coated o's bdg., incl. cass. 13.99 (*0-570-03084-6*) Concordia.

Taylor, Kenneth. Devotions for the Children's Hour. 2nd ed. (gr. 1-8). 1987. pap. 7.99 (*0-8024-2226-8*) Moody.

—Stories for the Children's Hour. 2nd ed. (gr. 1-8). 1987. pap. 7.99 (*0-8024-2227-6*) Moody.

Tirabassi, Becky. Live It! A Daily Devotional for Students. 192p. 1990. pap. 7.95 (*0-685-38929-4*, Youth Bks) Zondervan.

Trzeciak, Cathi. Worship: Our Gift to God. (Illus.). 24p. (gr. k-4). 1986. pap. 3.95 saddlestitched (*0-570-08531-4*, 56-1558) Concordia.

Van Pelt, Nancy L. The Compleat Tween. Coffen, Richard W., ed. 96p. (Orig.). (gr. 5 up). 1986. pap. 7.50 (*0-8280-0288-6*) Review & Herald.

Watts, Dorothy E. Stepping Stones. Woolsey, Raymond H., ed. 384p. (gr. 1 up). 1987. text ed. 9.95 (*0-8280-0384-X*) Review & Herald.

WOUNDED, FIRST AID TO

see First Aid

WRECKS

see Shipwrecks

WRENS–FICTION

Ravilious, Robin. Two in a Pocket. (ps-3). 1991. 14.95 (*0-316-73449-7*) Little.

Wren Bird House. 1993. 9.95 (*1-56828-050-5*) Red Jacket Pr.

WRESTLING

see also Judo

All about Hulk Hogan. (Illus.). 24p. 1991. pap. 1.95 (*1-56288-123-X*) Checkerboard.

All about Ultimate Warrior. (Illus.). 24p. 1991. pap. 1.95 (*1-56288-124-8*) Checkerboard.

All about WWF Superstars. (Illus.). 24p. 1991. pap. 1.95 (*1-56288-126-4*) Checkerboard.

All about WWF Tag Teams. (Illus.). 24p. 1991. pap. 1.95 (*1-56288-125-6*) Checkerboard.

Gutman, Bill. Wrestling. LC 89-7596. (Illus.). 64p. (gr. 3-8). 1990. PLB 14.95 (*0-942545-94-X*) Marshall Cavendish.

Lewin, Ted. I Was a Teenage Professional Wrestler. Lewin, Ted, illus. LC 92-31523. 128p. (gr. 6-12). 1993. 16.95 (*0-531-05477-2*); RLB 16.99 (*0-531-08627-5*) Orchard Bks Watts.

—I Was a Teenage Professional Wrestler. (Illus.). 128p. (gr. 5-9). 1994. pap. 6.95 (*0-7868-1009-2*) Hyprn Ppbks.

Marx, Doug. Wrestling. LC 93-36544. 1993. write for info. (*0-86593-347-2*) Rourke Corp.

Ricciuti, Edward R. Bret "Hit Man" Hart. Glassman, Bruce, ed. 25p. (Orig.). (gr. 5 up). 1994. text ed. 12.95 (*1-56711-075-4*); pap. text ed. 6.95 (*1-56711-070-3*) Blackbirch.

—Macho Man Randy Savage. Glassman, Bruce, ed. 25p. (Orig.). (gr. 5 up). 1994. text ed. 12.95 (*1-56711-077-0*); pap. text ed. 6.95 (*1-56711-072-X*) Blackbirch.

—Razor Ramon. Glassman, Bruce, ed. 25p. (Orig.). (gr. 5 up). 1994. text ed. 12.95 (*1-56711-071-1*); pap. text ed. 6.95 (*0-685-71021-1*) Blackbirch.

—The Steiner Brothers. Glassman, Bruce, ed. 25p. (Orig.). (gr. 5 up). 1994. text ed. 12.95 (*1-56711-078-9*); pap. text ed. 6.95 (*1-56711-073-8*) Blackbirch.

—The Undertaker. Glassman, Bruce, ed. 25p. (Orig.). (gr. 5 up). 1994. text ed. 12.95 (*1-56711-079-7*); pap. text ed. 6.95 (*1-56711-074-6*) Blackbirch.

WRESTLING–FICTION

Christopher, Matt. Takedown. Sanfilippo, Margaret, illus. (gr. 3-7). 1990. 15.95 (*0-316-13930-0*) Little.

Mooser, Stephen. The Terrible Tickler. Ulrich, George, illus. 80p. (Orig.). (gr. 2-5). 1992. pap. 3.25 (*0-440-40487-8*, YB) Dell.

Ogburn, Jacqueline K. Masked Maverick. Carlson, Nancy, illus. LC 92-1669. 1994. 15.00 (*0-688-11049-5*); lib. bdg. 14.93 (*0-688-11050-9*) Lothrop.

Spinelli, Jerry. There's a Girl in My Hammerlock. LC 91-8765. 208p. (gr. 5-9). 1991. pap. 13.00 jacketed, 3-pc. bdg. (*0-671-74684-7*, S&S BFYR) S&S Trade.

—There's a Girl in My Hammerlock. LC 91-8765. 208p. (gr. 5-9). 1993. pap. 3.95 (*0-671-86695-8*, Half Moon Bks) S&S Trade.

Yorke, Malcolm. Molly the Mad Basher. Chamberlain, Margaret, illus. LC 93-11407. 32p. (gr. 1-4). 1994. 10.95 (*1-56458-459-3*) Dorling Kindersley.

WRIGHT, FRANK LLOYD, 1869-1959

Boulton, Alexander O. Frank Lloyd Wright, Architect: A Picture Biography. Pfeiffer, Bruce B., intro. by. LC 93-12188. (Illus.). 128p. 1993. 24.95 (*0-8478-1683-4*) Rizzoli Intl.

McDonough, Yona Z. Frank Lloyd Wright. (Illus.). 112p. (gr. 5 up). 1992. lib. bdg. 17.95 (*0-7910-1626-9*) Chelsea Hse.

Murphy, Wendy. Frank Lloyd Wright. (Illus.). 128p. (gr. 7-9). 1990. 9.95 (*0-382-24033-2*); lib. bdg. 12.95 (*0-382-09905-2*) Silver Burdett Pr.

Rubin, Susan G. Frank Lloyd Wright. LC 93-48523. 1994. 19.95 (*0-8109-3974-6*) Abrams.

Spot, G. P. They Were Just Spotted. Abell, ed. & illus. 50p. (Orig.). 1994. 25.00 (*1-56611-089-0*); pap. 15.00 (*1-56611-090-4*) Jonas.

Thorne-Thomsen, Kathleen. Frank Lloyd Wright for Kids. LC 93-38150. (Illus.). 144p. (Orig.). (gr. 3 up). 1994. pap. 14.95 (*1-55652-207-X*) Chicago Review.

WRIGHT, ORVILLE, 1871-1948

Freedman, Russell. The Wright Brothers: How They Invented the Airplane. Wright Brothers, photos by. 1994. pap. 9.95 (*0-8234-1082-X*) Holiday.

Kaufman, Mervyn D. The Wright Brothers: Kings of the Air. (Illus.). 80p. (gr. 2-6). 1993. Repr. of 1964 ed. lib. bdg. 12.95 (*0-7910-1428-2*) Chelsea Hse.

Ludwig, Charles. The Wright Brothers: They Gave Us Wings. (Illus.). (gr. 3-6). 1985. write for info. (*0-88062-142-7*); pap. 6.95 (*0-88062-141-9*) Mott Media.

Marquardt, Max. Wilbur, Orville & the Flying Machine. (Illus.). 32p. (gr. 1-4). 1989. PLB 18.99 (*0-8172-3530-2*); pap. 4.95 (*0-8114-6735-X*) Raintree Steck-V.

Parramore, Thomas C. Triumph at Kitty Hawk: The Wright Brothers & Powered Flight. (Illus.). ix, 124p. (Orig.). (gr. 8-12). 1993. pap. 8.00 (*0-86526-259-4*) NC Archives.

Reynolds, Quentin. The Wright Brothers. LC 50-11766. (Illus.). 160p. (gr. 5-9). 1981. pap. 4.99 (*0-394-84700-8*) Random Bks Yng Read.

Rowland-Entwistle, Theodore. Wilbur & Orville Wright. (Illus.). 32p. (gr. 3-8). 1988. PLB 10.95 (*0-86307-927-X*) Marshall Cavendish.

Schulz, Walter A. Will & Orv. Schulz, Janet, illus. 48p. 1991. lib. bdg. 14.95 (*0-87614-669-8*) Carolrhoda Bks.

Sobol, Donald J. The Wright Brothers at Kitty Hawk. 128p. (Orig.). (gr. 3-7). 1987. pap. 2.95 (*0-590-42904-3*) Scholastic Inc.

Stevenson, Augusta. Wilbur & Orville Wright: Young Fliers. Doremus, Robert, illus. LC 86-10747. 192p. (gr. 2-6). 1986. pap. 4.95 (*0-02-042170-2*, Aladdin) Macmillan Child Grp.

Tames, Richard. The Wright Brothers. LC 89-29345. (Illus.). 32p. (gr. 4-6). 1990. PLB 12.40 (*0-531-14002-4*) Watts.

Woods, Andrew. Young Orville & Wilbur Wright: First to Fly. Stuart, Dennis, illus. LC 91-26479. 32p. (gr. k-2). 1992. text ed. 11.59 (*0-8167-2542-X*); pap. text ed. 2.95 (*0-8167-2543-8*) Troll Assocs.

WRIGHT, WILBUR, 1867-1912

Freedman, Russell. The Wright Brothers: How They Invented the Airplane. Wright Brothers, photos by. 1994. pap. 9.95 (*0-8234-1082-X*) Holiday.

Kaufman, Mervyn D. The Wright Brothers: Kings of the Air. (Illus.). 80p. (gr. 2-6). 1993. Repr. of 1964 ed. lib. bdg. 12.95 (*0-7910-1428-2*) Chelsea Hse.

Ludwig, Charles. The Wright Brothers: They Gave Us Wings. (Illus.). (gr. 3-6). 1985. write for info. (*0-88062-142-7*); pap. 6.95 (*0-88062-141-9*) Mott Media.

Marquardt, Max. Wilbur, Orville & the Flying Machine. (Illus.). 32p. (gr. 1-4). 1989. PLB 18.99 (*0-8172-3530-2*); pap. 4.95 (*0-8114-6735-X*) Raintree Steck-V.

Parramore, Thomas C. Triumph at Kitty Hawk: The Wright Brothers & Powered Flight. (Illus.). ix, 124p. (Orig.). (gr. 8-12). 1993. pap. 8.00 (*0-86526-259-4*) NC Archives.

Reynolds, Quentin. The Wright Brothers. LC 50-11766. (Illus.). 160p. (gr. 5-9). 1981. pap. 4.99 (*0-394-84700-8*) Random Bks Yng Read.

Rowland-Entwistle, Theodore. Wilbur & Orville Wright. (Illus.). 32p. (gr. 3-8). 1988. PLB 10.95 (*0-86307-927-X*) Marshall Cavendish.

Sabin, Louis. Wilbur & Orville Wright: The Flight to Adventure. Lawn, John, illus. LC 82-15879. 48p. (gr. 4-6). 1983. PLB 10.79 (*0-89375-851-5*); pap. text ed. 3.50 (*0-89375-852-3*) Troll Assocs.

Schulz, Walter A. Will & Orv. Schulz, Janet, illus. 48p. 1991. lib. bdg. 14.95 (*0-87614-669-8*) Carolrhoda Bks.

Sobol, Donald J. The Wright Brothers at Kitty Hawk. 128p. (Orig.). (gr. 3-7). 1987. pap. 2.95 (*0-590-42904-3*) Scholastic Inc.

Stevenson, Augusta. Wilbur & Orville Wright: Young Fliers. Doremus, Robert, illus. LC 86-10747. 192p. (gr. 2-6). 1986. pap. 4.95 (*0-02-042170-2*, Aladdin) Macmillan Child Grp.

Tames, Richard. The Wright Brothers. LC 89-29345. (Illus.). 32p. (gr. 4-6). 1990. PLB 12.40 (*0-531-14002-4*) Watts.

Woods, Andrew. Young Orville & Wilbur Wright: First to Fly. Stuart, Dennis, illus. LC 91-26479. 32p. (gr. k-2). 1992. text ed. 11.59 (*0-8167-2542-X*); pap. text ed. 2.95 (*0-8167-2543-8*) Troll Assocs.

WRITERS

see Authors

WRITING

see also Alphabet; Ciphers; Cryptography; Hieroglyphics; Picture Writing; Typewriting

Adams, Pam. Alf 'n Bet's Handwriting Book. (ps-3). 1993. pap. 5.95 (*0-85953-168-6*) Childs Play.

Ann Arbor Publishers Editorial Staff. Cursive Writing: Words, Bk. 1: Reusable Edition. 64p. (gr. 2-3). 1977. wkbk. 8.00 (*0-87879-791-2*, Ann Arbor Div) Acad Therapy.

Barber, Linda & Gabriel, Nancy. I Can Write! I Can Read! My Writing Book for Names & Telephone Numbers. (Illus.). 128p. (Orig.). (ps-2). 1994. wkbk. 9.95 (*0-9632868-0-3*) Going Places.

Baron, Nancy. Getting Started in Calligraphy. Baron, Nancy, illus. LC 78-66311. (gr. 7 up). 1979. spiral bdg. 9.95 (*0-8069-8840-1*) Sterling.

Bernholz, Jean F. & Sumner, Patricia H. Success in Reading & Writing. 2nd ed. (Illus.). 288p. (gr. 3). 1991. 27.95 (*0-673-36005-9*) GdYrBks.

Bostick, William A. Calligraphy for Kids. (Illus.). 32p. (Orig.). (gr. 3-12). Date not set. wkbk. 9.95 (*0-9606630-1-0*) La Stampa Calligrafica.

A fun way for youngsters to learn calligraphy as well as beautiful & legible handwriting. Unfortunately, these skills aren't usually acquired in schools today. Before printing, sample pages were tested on sixth & seventh graders. The students' enthusiastic participation & delightful testimonials such as, "I think your book is great!" &, "If I saw it in a bookstore I would buy it," encouraged us to proceed. The budding calligrapher goes over the author's large Chancery quotation for each letter & then repeats the calligraphy on his own, both large & at normal handwriting size. Cartoon 'live letters' liven each page & students are encouraged to draw their own. The cover reproduces Chancery & six other alphabets for kids to explore. It opens up the whole wonderful world of calligraphy to a youngster. But, of course, adults can also learn from it: the age range is 6 to 96! Book dealers & stores selling educational material for children tell us that there is nothing like "Calligraphy for Kids" on the market today. It's unique! Call or write for information to order, La Stampa Calligrafica, P.O. Box 209, Franklin, MI 48025; 810-646-5171.

Publisher Provided Annotation.

Carter, Patricia. Illuminated Calligraphy: Borders & Letters. (Illus.). 64p. (Orig.). 1992. pap. 15.95 (*0-85532-642-5*, Pub. by Search Pr UK) A Schwartz & Co.

Cobb, Vicki. Writing It Down. Hafner, Marylin, illus. LC 88-14191. 32p. (gr. k-3). 1989. (Lipp Jr Bks); PLB 11.89 (*0-397-32327-1*, Lipp Jr Bks) HarpC Child Bks.

Copperplate Calligraphy Kit. (gr. 7 up). 1988. Boxed set. incl. script bklt., ink, pen holder, pen nibs, 100% rag paper, reusable template guides 17.95 (*0-939564-11-4*) Pen Notes.

Davenport, May, ed. Courage: An Anthology of Short Stories, Articles & Poems. Kline, Gail, illus. LC 79-26261. (Orig.). (gr. 6-9). 1979. pap. text ed. 3.50x (*0-9603118-3-1*) Davenport.

Engelmann, Siegfried & Silbert, Jerome. Expressive Writing, No. 2. (Orig.). (gr. 4 up). 1985. tchr's ed., 210 p 55.00, (*0-574-41850-4*); student wkbk. (pkg. of 5), 182 pgs. 28.50, (*0-574-51852-5*) SRA.

Evans, C. Calligraphy. (Illus.). 48p. (gr. 6 up). 1990. PLB 14.96 (*0-88110-432-9*, Usborne); pap. 7.95 (*0-7460-0426-5*) EDC.

Fellows, Marian & Parkhurst, Christine. Script Ease: Manuscript of Calligraphy. Gaus, Helen, illus. 61p. (gr. 2-6). 1982. pap. text ed. 9.95 (*0-317-62675-2*) Kino Pubns.

Garrett-Goodyear, Joan H., et al. Writing Papers: A Handbook for Students at Smith College. 2nd, rev. ed. 60p. (gr. 9-12). 1986. pap. 2.95 (*0-88741-098-7*) Sundance Pubs.

Geography Department, Runestone Press. Scrawl! Writing in Ancient Times. LC 94-11980. 1994. lib. bdg. write for info. (*0-8225-3209-3*, Runestone Pr) Lerner Pubns.

Grislis, Peter. Calligraphy Book Companion. (gr. 4-7). 1994. pap. 4.95 (*0-590-46152-4*) Scholastic Inc.

Hablitzel, Marie & Stitzer, Kim H. Draw - Write - Now, Bk. 1: A Drawing & Handwriting Course for Kids! (Illus.). 64p. (gr. k-5). 1994. pap. 8.95 (*0-9639307-1-0*) Barker Creek.

Hackwell, W. John. Signs, Letters, Words: Archaeology Discovers Writing. Hackwell, W. John, illus. LC 86-26237. 72p. (gr. 7 up). 1987. SBE 14.95 (*0-684-18807-4*, Scribners Young Read) Macmillan Child Grp.

Hanson, Manda. Calligraphy. (Illus.). 48p. (gr. 9 up). 1994. incl. art components 19.95 (*0-8431-3664-2*) Price Stern.

Hoffman, Joan. Manuscript Writing. (Illus.). 32p. (gr. k-2). 1981. wkbk. 1.99 (*0-938256-01-7*) Sch Zone Pub Co.

Knight, Tanis & Lewin, Larry. Tap the Deck. Hrebic, Herbert J., ed. Boehm, Terrie W., illus. (Orig.). (gr. 5-6). 1985. text ed. 9.10 (*0-933282-18-4*); pap. text ed. 6.00 (*0-933282-17-6*) Stack the Deck.

Kravitz, Alvin & Dramer, Dan. Skillbooster Series Level C. Incl. Building Wordpower. 1978. pap. text ed. 3.04 (*0-8136-1203-9*); Increasing Comprehension. 1978. pap. text ed. 3.04 (*0-8136-1210-1*); Organizing Information. 1978. pap. text ed. 3.04 (*0-8136-1224-1*); Using References. 1978. pap. text ed. 3.04 (*0-8136-1231-4*); Working with Facts & Details. 1978. pap. text ed. 1.92 (*0-87895-343-4*). 48p. (gr. 3) Modern Curr.

LeSieg, Theo. I Can Write! A Book by Me, Myself. McKie, Roy, illus. 32p. (ps-1). 1993. pap. 2.99 (*0-679-84700-6*) Random Bks Yng Read.

Letters. (Illus.). 24p. (ps-3). 1992. pap. 3.50 (*0-7460-1036-2*) EDC.

Lincoln, Wanda. Write Through the Year. (Illus.). 112p. (gr. 2-6). 1989. pap. 9.95 (*0-912107-90-1*, MM1907) Monday Morning Bks.

McOmber, Rachel B., ed. McOmber Phonics Storybooks: Writing Book No. 1. rev. ed. (Illus.). write for info. (*0-944991-93-9*) Swift Lrn Res.

—McOmber Phonics Storybooks: Writing Book No. 2. rev. ed. (Illus.). write for info. (*0-944991-94-7*) Swift Lrn Res.

Pen Notes Staff. Italic Calligraphy Kit. (gr. 3 up). 1979. incl. chisel tip market, italic bklet. instrns., parchment paper, plastic reusable template guidelines 9.95 (*0-939564-10-6*) Pen Notes.

Pendergrass, Carol R. Writing Right!, Bk. 2: Cursive. 96p. (gr. 1 up). 1994. pap. text ed. 4.75 (*0-88323-262-6*, 150) Pendergrass Pub.

Robinson, Lafayette. Penmanship from A to Z. Robinson, Lafayette, illus. 72p. (gr. 3-4). 1988. wkbk. 7.95 (*0-9621081-1-1*) Educ Graphics.

—Rite Easy from A to Z. Gonzalez, Inez, tr. Wigglesworth, Sheila, illus. (SPA & ENG.). 48p. (gr. 1-3). 1993. lib. bdg. write for info. (*0-9621081-0-3*) Educ Graphics.

Rothstein, Evelyn. Easy Writer Student Worksheets, 6 levels. Gess, Diane, ed. Schwartzfarb, Marilyn, illus. (Each level 35p.). (gr. 1-8). 1988. Level A Gr. 1-2. 14.95 (*0-9606172-5-6*) Level B Gr. 2-3. 14.95 (*0-9606172-1-3*); Level C Gr. 3-5. 14.95 (*0-9606172-2-1*); Level D Gr. 4-6. 14.95 (*0-9606172-3-X*); Level E Gr. 5-7. 14.95 (*0-9606172-4-8*); Level F Gr. 6-8. 14.95 (*0-9606172-6-4*) ERA-CCR.

Russomanno, Diane. The Never Ending Journey of the Written Word. 32p. 1991. pap. text ed. write for info. (*1-880501-00-7*) Know Booster.

Schaffer, Frank, Publications Staff. Getting Ready for Writing. (Illus.). 24p. (ps-k). 1980. wkbk. 3.98 (*0-86734-016-9*, FS-3029) Schaffer Pubns.

—Handwriting with Harvey Hippo. (Illus.). 24p. (gr. 2-4). 1978. wkbk. 3.98 (*0-86734-009-6*, FS-3010) Schaffer Pubns.

Schwartz, Linda. Handwriting Hamburger. Armstrong, Bev, illus. 32p. (gr. 3-6). 1979. wkbk. 3.95 (*0-88160-073-3*, LW 806) Learning Wks.

—Handwriting Hot Dog. Armstrong, Bev, illus. 32p. (gr. k-3). 1979. wkbk. 3.95 (*0-88160-078-4*, LW 811) Learning Wks.

Seward, Bernard. Writing American English. Olsen, Roger E., ed. (Illus.). 90p. (gr. 3-12). 1982. pap. text ed. 5.75 (*0-13-971102-3*) Alemany Pr.

Spellman, Linda. Castles, Codes, Calligraphy. 112p. (gr. 4-6). 1984. 9.95 (*0-88160-103-9*, LW 904) Learning Wks.

Suid, Murray. Writing Hangups. 64p. (gr. 2-6). 1988. 6.95 (*0-912107-73-1*, MM980) Monday Morning Bks.

Warburton, Lois. The Beginning of Writing. LC 90-6010. (Illus.). 112p. (gr. 5-8). 1990. PLB 14.95 (*1-56006-113-8*) Lucent Bks.

Wise, Beth A. My ABC's Uppercase. Nayer, Judith E., ed. Mahan, Ben, illus. 32p. (ps). 1991. wkbk. 1.95 (*1-56293-165-2*) McClanahan Bk.

WRITING (AUTHORSHIP)

see Authorship; Journalism

WYOMING

Carole Marsh Wyoming Books, 44 bks. 1994. PLB 1027.80 set (*0-7933-1325-2*); pap. 587.80 set (*0-7933-5222-3*) Gallopade Pub Group.

Carpenter, Allan. Wyoming. new ed. LC 78-32135. (Illus.). 96p. (gr. 4 up). 1979. PLB 16.95 (*0-516-04150-9*) Childrens.

Elliott, Tony. This Is Wyoming: Read 'n Color Book. Elliott, Tony, illus. LC 89-469. (gr. 3-6). 1989. pap. 3.95 (*0-914565-39-7*, 39-7, Timbertrails) Capstan Pubns.

Fradin, Dennis. Wyoming: In Words & Pictures. LC 79-26511. (Illus.). 48p. (gr. 2-5). 1980. PLB 12.95 (*0-516-03950-4*) Childrens.

Fradin, Dennis B. & Fradin, Judith B. Wyoming - From Sea to Shining Sea. LC 93-39880. (Illus.). 64p. (gr. 3-5). 1994. PLB 16.45 (*0-516-03850-8*) Childrens.

Frisch, Carlienne. Wyoming. LC 93-23098. (Illus.). (gr. 3-6). 1994. lib. bdg. 17.50 (*0-8225-2736-7*) Lerner Pubns.

Heinrichs, Ann. Wyoming. LC 91-544. 144p. (gr. 4 up). 1991. PLB 20.55 (*0-516-00496-4*) Childrens.

—Wyoming. 215p. 1993. text ed. 15.40 (*1-56956-148-6*) W A T Braille.

Johnson, Neil. Jack Creek Cowboy. Johnson, Neil, photos by. LC 92-921. (Illus.). 32p. (gr. 2-5). 1993. 14.99 (*0-8037-1228-6*); PLB 14.89 (*0-8037-1229-4*) Dial Bks Young.

Marsh, Carole. Avast, Ye Slobs! Wyoming Pirate Trivia. (Illus.). 1994. PLB 24.95 (*0-7933-1268-X*); pap. 14.95 (*0-7933-1267-1*); computer disk 29.95 (*0-7933-1269-8*) Gallopade Pub Group.

—The Beast of the Wyoming Bed & Breakfast. (Illus.). 1994. PLB 24.95 (*0-7933-2300-2*); pap. 14.95 (*0-7933-2301-0*); computer disk 29.95 (*0-7933-2302-9*) Gallopade Pub Group.

—Bow Wow! Wyoming Dogs in History, Mystery, Legend, Lore, Humor & More! (Illus.). (gr. 3-12). 1994. PLB 24.95 (*0-7933-3617-1*); pap. 14.95 (*0-7933-3618-X*); computer disk 29.95 (*0-7933-3619-8*) Gallopade Pub Group.

—Christopher Columbus Comes to Wyoming! Includes Reproducible Activities for Kids! (Illus.). (gr. 3-12). 1994. PLB 24.95 (*0-7933-3770-4*); pap. 14.95 (*0-7933-3771-2*); computer disk 29.95 (*0-7933-3772-0*) Gallopade Pub Group.

—The Hard-to-Believe-But-True! Book of Wyoming History, Mystery, Trivia, Legend, Lore, Humor & More. (Illus.). 1994. PLB 24.95 (*0-7933-1265-5*); pap. 14.95 (*0-7933-1264-7*); computer disk 29.95 (*0-7933-1266-3*) Gallopade Pub Group.

—If My Wyoming Mama Ran the World. (Illus.). 1994. PLB 24.95 (*0-7933-2309-6*); pap. 14.95 (*0-7933-2310-X*); computer disk 29.95 (*0-7933-2311-8*) Gallopade Pub Group.

—Jurassic Ark! Wyoming Dinosaurs & Other Prehistoric Creatures. (gr. k-12). 1994. PLB 24.95 (*0-7933-7578-9*); pap. 14.95 (*0-7933-7579-7*); computer disk 29.95 (*0-7933-7580-0*) Gallopade Pub Group.

—Let's Quilt Our Wyoming County. 1994. lib. bdg. 24.95 (*0-7933-7263-1*); pap. text ed. 14.95 (*0-7933-7264-X*); disk 29.95 (*0-7933-7265-8*) Gallopade Pub Group.

—Let's Quilt Our Wyoming Town. 1994. lib. bdg. 24.95 (*0-7933-7113-9*); pap. text ed. 14.95 (*0-7933-7114-7*); disk 29.95 (*0-7933-7115-5*) Gallopade Pub Group.

—Let's Quilt Wyoming & Stuff Topographically! (Illus.). 1994. PLB 24.95 (*1-55609-290-3*); pap. 14.95 (*1-55609-134-6*); computer disk 29.95 (*1-55609-291-1*) Gallopade Pub Group.

—Meow! Wyoming Cats in History, Mystery, Legend, Lore, Humor & More! (Illus.). (gr. 3-12). 1994. PLB 24.95 (*0-7933-3464-0*); pap. 14.95 (*0-7933-3465-9*); computer disk 29.95 (*0-7933-3466-7*) Gallopade Pub Group.

—Wyoming & Other State Greats (Biographies) (Illus.). 1994. PLB 24.95 (*0-7933-2312-6*); pap. 14.95 (*0-7933-2313-4*); computer disk 29.95 (*0-7933-2314-2*) Gallopade Pub Group.

—Wyoming Bandits, Bushwackers, Outlaws, Crooks, Devils, Ghosts, Desperadoes & Other Assorted & Sundry Characters! (Illus.). 1994. PLB 24.95 (*0-7933-1250-7*); pap. 14.95 (*0-7933-1249-3*); computer disk 29.95 (*0-7933-1251-5*) Gallopade Pub Group.

—Wyoming Classic Christmas Trivia: Stories, Recipes, Activities, Legends, Lore & More! (Illus.). 1994. PLB 24.95 (*0-7933-1253-1*); pap. 14.95 (*0-7933-1252-3*); computer disk 29.95 (*0-7933-1254-X*) Gallopade Pub Group.

—Wyoming Coastales. (Illus.). 1994. PLB 24.95 (*0-7933-2306-1*); pap. 14.95 (*0-7933-2307-X*); computer disk 29.95 (*0-7933-2308-8*) Gallopade Pub Group.

—Wyoming Coastales! 1994. lib. bdg. 24.95 (*0-7933-7315-8*) Gallopade Pub Group.

—Wyoming Dingbats! Bk. 1: A Fun Book of Games, Stories, Activities & More about Our State That's All in Code! for You to Decipher. (Illus.). (gr. 3-12). 1994. PLB 24.95 (*0-7933-3923-5*); pap. 14.95 (*0-7933-3924-3*); computer disk 29.95 (*0-7933-3925-1*) Gallopade Pub Group.

—Wyoming Festival Fun for Kids! Includes Reproducible Activities for Kids! (Illus.). (gr. 3-12). 1994. PLB 24.95 (*0-7933-4076-4*); pap. 14.95 (*0-7933-4077-2*); computer disk 29.95 (*0-7933-4078-0*) Gallopade Pub Group.

—Wyoming Jeopardy! Answers & Questions about Our State! (Illus.). (gr. 3-12). 1994. PLB 24.95 (*0-7933-4229-5*); pap. 14.95 (*0-7933-4230-9*); computer disk 29.95 (*0-7933-4231-7*) Gallopade Pub Group.

—Wyoming "Jography" A Fun Run Thru Our State! (Illus.). (gr. 3-12). 1994. PLB 24.95 (*1-55609-295-4*); pap. 14.95 (*1-55609-296-2*); computer disk 29.95 (*1-55609-297-0*) Gallopade Pub Group.

—Wyoming Kid's Cookbook: Recipes, How-To, History, Lore & More. (Illus.). 1994. PLB 24.95 (*0-7933-1262-0*); pap. 14.95 (*0-7933-1261-2*); 29.95 (*0-7933-1263-9*) Gallopade Pub Group.

—Wyoming Quiz Bowl Crash Course! (Illus.). 1994. PLB 24.95 (*0-7933-2303-7*); pap. 14.95 (*0-7933-2304-5*); computer disk 29.95 (*0-7933-2305-3*) Gallopade Pub Group.

—Wyoming Rollercoasters! (Illus.). (gr. 3-12). 1994. PLB 24.95 (*0-7933-5374-2*); pap. 14.95 (*0-7933-5375-0*); computer disk 29.95 (*0-7933-5376-9*) Gallopade Pub Group.

—Wyoming School Trivia: An Amazing & Fascinating Look at Our State's Teachers, Schools & Students! (Illus.). 1994. PLB 24.95 (*0-7933-1259-0*); pap. 14.95 (*0-7933-1258-2*); computer disk 29.95 (*0-7933-1260-4*) Gallopade Pub Group.

—Wyoming Silly Basketball Sportsmysteries, Vol. 1. (Illus.). 1994. PLB 24.95 (*0-7933-1256-6*); pap. 14.95 (*0-7933-1255-8*); computer disk 29.95 (*0-7933-1257-4*) Gallopade Pub Group.

—Wyoming Silly Basketball Sportsmysteries, Vol. 2. (Illus.). 1994. PLB 24.95 (*0-7933-2315-0*); pap. 14.95 (*0-7933-2316-9*); computer disk 29.95 (*0-7933-2317-7*) Gallopade Pub Group.

—Wyoming Silly Football Sportsmysteries, Vol. 1. (Illus.). 1994. PLB 24.95 (*0-7933-2294-4*); pap. 14.95 (*0-7933-2295-2*); computer disk 29.95 (*0-7933-2296-0*) Gallopade Pub Group.

—Wyoming Silly Football Sportsmysteries, Vol. 2. (Illus.). 1994. PLB 24.95 (*0-7933-2297-9*); pap. 14.95 (*0-7933-2298-7*); computer disk 29.95 (*0-7933-2299-5*) Gallopade Pub Group.

—Wyoming Silly Trivia. (Illus.). (gr. 3-12). 1994. PLB 24.95 (*1-55609-292-X*); pap. 14.95 (*1-55609-293-8*); computer disk 29.95 (*1-55609-294-6*) Gallopade Pub Group.

—Wyoming's (Most Devastating!) Disasters & (Most Calamitous!) Catastrophies! (Illus.). 1994. PLB 24.95 (*0-7933-1247-7*); pap. 14.95 (*0-7933-1246-9*); computer disk 29.95 (*0-7933-1248-5*) Gallopade Pub Group.

Salts, Bobbi. Discover Devils Tower National Monument. 32p. (gr. 3-5). 1992. 2.50 (*1-881667-00-6*) Devils Tower NHA.

Stebner, Karey H. Travel Wonderful Wyoming with Jesse Jackalope. 28p. (ps-4). 1992. pap. 3.00 (*0-9632746-3-5*) Karey Kreations.

Thompson, Kathleen. Wyoming. LC 87-16442. 48p. (gr. 3 up). 1987. 19.97 (*0-86514-460-5*) Raintree Steck-V.

WYOMING–FICTION

Hayden, Jan & Kistler, Mary. Has Anyone Seen Allie? LC 90-14027. 144p. (gr. 5 up). 1991. 13.95 (*0-525-65057-1*, Cobblehill Bks) Dutton Child Bks.

O'Hara, Mary. Thunderhead. 320p. (gr. 5-9). 1967. pap. 1.75 (*0-440-98875-6*, LFL) Dell.

Paulsen, Gary. The Haymeadow. (gr. 4-7). 1992. 15.95 (*0-385-30621-0*) Doubleday.

Payne, Richard A. Charlie the Shy Cowboy. Schilling, Mickey E., illus. 36p. (gr. 1-9). 1993. pap. 4.95 (*0-9636186-2-8*) Blue Sky Grap.

Saban, Vera. Johnny Egan of the Paintrock. Saban, Sonja, illus. LC 85-30958. 130p. (Orig.). (gr. 4-8). 1986. pap. 6.95 (*0-914565-13-3*, Timbertrails) Capstan Pubns.

Schaefer, Jack. Shane. McCormick, J., illus. (gr. 7 up). 1954. 15.95 (*0-395-07090-2*) HM.

Wister, Owen. Virginian. (gr. 8 up). 1964. pap. 2.95 (*0-8049-0046-9*, CL-46) Airmont.

WYOMING–HISTORY

Adams, Randy L. & Sodaro, Craig. Wyoming: Courage in a Lonesome Land. Lynch, Don, ed. Exact Art Design Staff & Fay, Keith, illus. LC 90-82123. 313p. (ps-6). 1990. Centennial Edition. text ed. 24.95 (*0-913205-12-5*); special price 14.97 (*0-685-69224-8*) Grace Dangberg.

Marsh, Carole. Chill Out: Scary Wyoming Tales Based on Frightening Wyoming Truths. (Illus.). 1994. lib. bdg. 24.95 (*0-7933-4807-2*); pap. 14.95 (*0-7933-4808-0*); disk 29.95 (*0-7933-4809-9*) Gallopade Pub Group.

—My First Book about Wyoming. (gr. k-4). 1994. PLB 24.95 (*0-7933-5719-5*); pap. 14.95 (*0-7933-5720-9*); computer disk 29.95 (*0-7933-5721-7*) Gallopade Pub Group.

—Patch, the Pirate Dog: A Wyoming Pet Story. (ps-4). 1994. PLB 24.95 (*0-7933-5566-4*); pap. 14.95 (*0-7933-5567-2*); computer disk 29.95 (*0-7933-5568-0*) Gallopade Pub Group.

—Uncle Rebus: Wyoming Picture Stories for Computer Kids. (Illus.). (gr. k-3). 1994. PLB 24.95 (*0-7933-4654-1*); pap. 14.95 (*0-7933-4655-X*); disk 29.95 (*0-7933-4656-8*) Gallopade Pub Group.

—Wyoming "Crinkum-Crankum" A Funny Word Book about Our State. (Illus.). (gr. 3-12). 1994. 24.95 (*0-7933-4961-3*); pap. 14.95 (*0-7933-4962-1*); computer disk 29.95 (*0-7933-4963-X*) Gallopade Pub Group.

—The Wyoming Mystery Van Takes Off! Book 1: Handicapped Wyoming Kids Sneak Off on a Big Adventure. (Illus.). (gr. 3-12). 1994. 24.95 (*0-7933-5114-6*); pap. 14.95 (*0-7933-5115-4*); computer disk 29.95 (*0-7933-5116-2*) Gallopade Pub Group.

—Wyoming Timeline: A Chronology of Wyoming History, Mystery, Trivia, Legend, Lore & More. (Illus.). (gr. 3-12). 1994. PLB 24.95 (*0-7933-6025-0*); pap. 14.95 (*0-7933-6026-9*); computer disk 29.95 (*0-7933-6027-7*) Gallopade Pub Group.

—Wyoming's Unsolved Mysteries (& Their "Solutions") Includes Scientific Information & Other Activities for Students. (Illus.). (gr. 3-12). 1994. PLB 24.95 (*0-7933-5872-8*); pap. 14.95 (*0-7933-5873-6*); computer disk 29.95 (*0-7933-5874-4*) Gallopade Pub Group.

X

X RAYS

Gherman, Beverly. The Mysterious Rays of Dr. Roentgen. Marchesi, Stephen, illus. LC 92-38966. 32p. (gr. 2-5). 1994. SBE 14.95 (*0-689-31839-1*, Atheneum Child Bk) Macmillan Child Grp.

Morrison, Rob. X-Rays. Black, Don, illus. LC 93-28983. 1994. 4.25 (*0-383-03789-1*) SRA Schl Grp.

Y

YACHTS AND YACHTING

see also Sailing

YEARBOOKS

see also Almanacs; Calendars

Metropolitan Museum of Art Staff. Baby's First Year Calendar. Franc-Nohain, Marie M., illus. 24p. 1984. pap. 9.95 (*0-684-18258-0*, Scribners Young Read) Macmillan Child Grp.

YELLOWSTONE NATIONAL PARK

Beach-Balthis, Judy. Yellowstone: A Children's Guide. Balthis, Frank, ed. Beach-Balthis, Judy, illus. 36p. (Orig.). (gr. k-8). 1981. pap. 2.95 (*0-918355-01-X*) Firehole Pr.

Ekey, Robert. Fire! in Yellowstone. Mayer, Larry, illus. LC 89-43156. 32p. (gr. 2-4). 1989. PLB 17.27 (*0-8368-0226-8*) Gareth Stevens Inc.

Kent, Deborah. Yellowstone National Park. LC 93-37521. (Illus.). 32p. 1994. PLB 12.30 (*0-516-06678-1*) Childrens.

Lauber, Patricia. Summer of Fire: Yellowstone 1988. LC 90-23032. (Illus.). 64p. (gr. 4 up). 1991. 17.95 (*0-531-05943-X*); RLB 17.99 (*0-531-08543-0*) Orchard Bks Watts.

Marron, Carol. Yellowstone. LC 88-18643. (Illus.). 48p. (gr. 4-5). 1988. text ed. 13.95 RSBE (*0-89686-405-7*, Crestwood Hse) Macmillan Child Grp.

Martin, Cyd. A Yellowstone ABC. (Illus.). 16p. 1992. pap. 5.95 (*1-879373-12-2*) R Rinehart.

Patent, Dorothy H. Yellowstone Fires: Flames & Rebirth. Munoz, William, et al, illus. LC 89-24544. 40p. (gr. 3-7). 1990. reinforced bdg. 14.95 (*0-8234-0807-8*) Holiday.

Petersen, David. Yellowstone National Park. LC 91-37292. (Illus.). 48p. (gr. k-4). 1992. PLB 12.85 (*0-516-01148-0*); pap. 4.95 (*0-516-41148-9*) Childrens.

Reese, Bob. Forty Word Yellowstone Series, 6 bks. Reese, Bob, illus. (gr. k-6). 1986. Set. 47.70 (*0-89868-239-8*); Set. pap. 29.50 (*0-89868-238-X*) ARO Pub.

—Old Faithful. Reese, Bob, illus. (gr. k-6). 1986. 7.95 (*0-89868-167-7*); pap. 2.95 (*0-89868-168-5*) ARO Pub.

Staub, Frank. The Yellowstone Cycle of Fires. LC 92-29631. 1993. 19.95 (*0-87614-778-3*) Carolrhoda Bks.

—Yellowstone Park. Staub, Frank, illus. LC 89-34371. 32p. (gr. 3-6). 1990. lib. bdg. 10.79 (*0-8167-1737-0*); pap. text ed. 2.95 (*0-8167-1738-9*) Troll Assocs.

Tufts, Lorraine S. Secrets in Yellowstone & Grand Teton National Parks. 2nd ed. Koteff, Ellen & Holmes, Tracey, eds. 88p. (gr. 4 up). 1990. 29.95 (*0-9620255-2-6*); pap. 19.95 (*0-9620255-1-8*) Natl Photo Collections.

Vogel, Carole G. & Goldner, Kathryn A. The Great Yellowstone Fire. (Illus.). 32p. (gr. 2-6). 1993. pap. 6.95 (*0-316-90249-7*) Sierra.

—The Great Yellowstone Fire, Vol. 1. (Illus.). (gr. 2-6). 1990. 15.95 (*0-316-90522-4*) Little.

Whitman, Sylvia. This Land Is Your Land: The American Conservation Movement. LC 94-3099. (Illus.). 88p. 1994. PLB 17.50 (*0-8225-1729-9*) Lerner Pubns.

Whittlesey, Lee H. Yellowstone Place Names. Haynes, F. Jay, illus. Manns, Timothy R., intro. by. LC 88-21610. (Illus.). xiii, 179p. (Orig.). (gr. 8 up). 1988. pap. 7.95 (*0-917298-15-2*); unabr. microfiche 8.95 (*0-917298-20-9*) MT Hist Soc.

YETI

Christian, Mary B. Bigfoot. LC 87-9024. (Illus.). 48p. (gr. 5-6). 1987. text ed. 12.95 RSBE (*0-89686-341-7*, Crestwood Hse) Macmillan Child Grp.

Landau, Elaine. Sasquatch, Wild Man of the Woods. LC 92-35144. (Illus.). 48p. (gr. 3-6). 1993. PLB 14.40 (*1-56294-348-0*) Millbrook Pr.

—Yeti, Abominable Snowman of the Himalayas. LC 92-35147. (Illus.). 48p. (gr. 3-6). 1993. PLB 14.40 (*1-56294-349-9*) Millbrook Pr.

YOGA

Greene, Leia A. Exploring the Chakras. Greene, Leia A., illus. 32p. (gr. k-12). 1991. wkbk. 4.95 (*1-880737-03-5*) Crystal Jrns.

Hari Dass, Baba. A Child's Garden of Yoga. Thomas, Steven N., photos by. Ault, Karuna, ed. LC 80-80299. (Illus.). 108p. (ps-7). 1980. pap. 9.95 (*0-918100-02-X*) Sri Rama.

Satsvarupa dasa Goswami. The Life Story of His Divine Grace A. C. Bhaktivedanta Swami Prabhupada. Ellwood, Robert S., pref. by. 32p. (gr. 4-7). 1984. saddlestitch 3.50 (*0-89647-019-9*) Bala Bks.

Schreiber, Suzanne L. Yoga for the Fun of It! Hatha Yoga for Preschool Children. 4th ed. Schreiber, Suzanne L., illus. Folan, Lilias, intro. by. (Illus.). 54p. (Orig.). (ps). 1991. pap. 9.00 (*0-9608320-0-9*) Sugar Marbel Pr. Kids benefit from slow activities & guidance in learning how to relax, just as adults do. In this bright pink laminated, spiral-bound book which features a cast of cute stick figures, THE CONCEPT OF HATHA YOGA - BODY, MIND, BREATH - IS

ADAPTED TO THE DEVELOPMENTAL NEEDS OF PRESCHOOL CHILDREN & CHILDREN WITH MEDICAL CHALLENGES. The exercises allow children to use their IMAGINATIONS & have FUN, while benefitting from DEEP BREATHING, SLOW STRETCHING & RELAXATION TECHNIQUES. Children are helped to develop feelings of SELF-AWARENESS, SELF-CONTROL, SELF-ESTEEM & WELL-BEING by focusing on muscle tension & relaxation. The exercises are NONFRUSTRATING & NONCOMPETITIVE & encourage positive results by allowing each child to move in the way that is most comfortable for his/her particular body. Children with medical challenges can be helped to adapt the exercises to their particular needs, or assisted in doing them. The stick figures illustrate the exercises & children can use the book themselves once they have been shown how to do the exercises. Suggested Activities - Physical Education; Cognitive; Transistion; Quieting; Inclusive. The author also created the Instructional Television series FOCUS ON FITNESS. Also, creator/producer of the NEW HOME VIDEO, YOGAFUN (r) EXERCISE & RELAXATION CARTOONS. To contact: Sugar Marbel Press, 1547 Shenandoah Avenue, Cincinnati, OH 54237. (513) 761-8000.
Publisher Provided Annotation.

Yogaville Children. Hatha Yoga for Kids - By Kids. Satchidananda, Sri S., intro. by. (Illus.). 112p. (Orig.). (gr. 1-8). 1990. spiral bdg. 13.95g (*0-932040-36-5*) Integral Yoga Pubns.

YOM KIPPUR

Chaikin, Miriam. Sound the Shofar: The Story & Meaning of Rosh HaShanah & Yom Kippur. Weihs, Erika, illus. LC 86-2651. 96p. (gr. 3-7). 1986. (Clarion Bks); pap. 4.95 (*0-89919-427-3*, Clarion Bks) HM.

Friedman, Audrey M. & Zwerin, Raymond. High Holy Day Do It Yourself Dictionary. Ruten, Marlene L., illus. 32p. (gr. k-3). 1983. pap. 5.00 (*0-8074-0162-5*, 101100) UAHC.

Saypol, Judyth R. & Wikler, Madeline. My Very Own Yom Kippur Book. (Illus.). 32p. (gr. k-6). 1978. pap. 3.95 (*0-930494-05-9*) Kar Ben.

Simon, Norma. Yom Kippur. Gordon, Ayala, illus. (ps-k). 1959. plastic cover 4.50 (*0-8381-0702-8*) United Syn Bk.

YOSEMITE NATIONAL PARK

Arrigo, Mary & Hargreaves, Connie. When I Visit Yosemite. Nishimura, Chris, illus. 43p. (Orig.). (ps). pap. 2.95 (*0-318-21253-6*) Arrigo CA.

Cazin, Lorraine J. Yosemite. LC 88-20236. (Illus.). 48p. (gr. 4-5). 1988. RSBE 13.95 (*0-89686-407-3*, Crestwood Hse) Macmillan Child Grp.

Crump, Donald J., ed. Yosemite: An American Treasure. (Illus.). 1990. 12.95 (*0-87044-789-0*); lib. bdg. 12.95 (*0-87044-794-7*) Natl Geog.

Markert, Jenny. Yosemite. (SPA & ENG.). (gr. 2-6). 1992. PLB 15.95 (*0-89565-857-7*) Childs World.

Ross, Michael E. Yosemite Fun Book. 48p. (gr. 3-8). 1987. pap. 2.95 (*0-939666-45-6*) Yosemite Assn.

YOUNG, BRIGHAM, 1801-1877

Bernotas, Bob. Brigham Young. (Illus.). 112p. (gr. 5 up). 1993. PLB 17.95 (*0-7910-1642-0*) Chelsea Hse.

YOUNG ADULTS

see Youth

YOUTH

see also Adolescence; Boys; Dropouts; Girls

Bergin, Feryl J. You...& Being a Teenager. rev. ed. Bergin, James E., illus. 112p. 1991. 6.95 (*0-936955-00-7*) Eminent Pubns.

Bingham, Mindy. Making Choices: For Teen Girls & Boys. (gr. 4-7). 1994. 18.95 (*0-911655-43-3*) Advocacy Pr.

Bode, Janet & Mack, Stan. Heartbreak & Roses: Real-Life Stories of Troubled Love. LC 93-39012. 1994. 15.95 (*0-385-32068-X*) Delacorte.

Brown, Maggie W. Making Decisions. Proof Positive-Farrowlyne Associates, Inc. Staff, illus. 61p. (Orig.). 1990. text ed. 2.80 stitched (*0-88489-200-X*); tchr's ed. 6.00 (*0-88489-201-8*) St Marys.

Campbell, Stan. Nobody Like Me. 96p. (gr. 7-9). 1986. pap. 2.99 student bk. (*0-89693-515-9*, Victor Books); tchr's. ed. 12.99 (*0-89693-188-9*) SP Pubns.

Cecceralło, Julius & Dent, Anne. Independence: A Life Skills Guide for Teens. 96p. 1988. pap. 14.95 (*0-87868-350-X*, 3500) Child Welfare.

Cosby, Bill, et al. You Are Somebody Special. 2nd ed. Shedd, Charlie W., ed. 205p. (gr. 9-12). 1989. Repr. of 1978 ed. text ed. 10.95 (*0-933419-50-3*) Quest Intl.

Darmani, Lawrence. African Youth Speak. (Illus.). 32p. (Orig.). (gr. 9-12). 1994. pap. 4.95 (*0-377-00271-2*) Friendship Pr.

Denny, Kevin M. A Teenager's Guide How to Manipulate Your Way to Happiness: Thirty-Seven Easy Steps in the Care & Feeding of Your Parents. Winton, Andrea, illus. LC 92-81556. 240p. (Orig.). (gr. 8-12). 1992. pap. 13.95 (*0-9633108-0-1*) Warthog Pub.

Duckworth, John. The School Zone. 96p. (gr. 7-9). 1986. pap. 2.99 student bk. (*0-89693-558-2*, Victor Books); tchr's. ed. 12.99 (*0-89693-198-6*) SP Pubns.

Eagan, Andrea B. Why Am I So Miserable If These Are the Best Years of My Life? (gr. 7 up). 1979. pap. 2.95 (*0-380-46136-6*, Flare) Avon.

Galbraith, Judy. The Gifted Kids Survival Guide (for ages 11-18) LC 84-80997. (Illus.). 144p. (Orig.). (gr. 5-12). 1983. pap. 8.95 (*0-915793-01-6*) Free Spirit Pub.

Glenard East Echo Staff & Spanogle, Howard, eds. Voices of Hope: Teenagers Themselves, Pt. III. (Illus.). (gr. 7 up). 1988. 16.95 (*1-55774-012-7*, Dist. by Watts) Modan-Adama Bks.

Hinojosa, Maria. Crews: Gang Members Talk to Maria Hinojosa. Perez, German, contrib. by. LC 94-12173. (Illus.). (gr. 7 up). 1994. 16.95 (*0-15-292873-1*); pap. 8.95 (*0-15-200283-9*) HarBrace.

Kelly, Gary F. Sex & Sense: A Contemporary Guide for Teenagers. 240p. 1993. pap. 7.95 (*0-8120-1446-4*) Barron.

Larsen, Sandy. For Real People Only. 96p. (gr. 7-9). 1986. pap. 2.99 student bk. (*0-89693-516-7*, Victor Books); tchr's. ed. 12.99 (*0-89693-513-2*) SP Pubns.

Llewellyn, Grace. The Teenage Liberation Handbook: How to Quit School & Get a Real Life & Education. 401p. (gr. 7-12). 1991. pap. 14.95 (*0-9629591-0-3*) Lowry Hse.

Llewellyn, Grace, intro. by. Real Lives: Eleven Teenagers Who Don't Go to School. (Illus.). 320p. (Orig.). (gr. 7-12). 1993. pap. 14.95 (*0-9629591-3-8*, LC32.R) Lowry Hse.

Mitchell, Joyce S. Free to Choose: Decision Making for Young Men. LC 76-5589. (gr. 7 up). 1976. 8.95 (*0-440-02723-3*) Delacorte.

Peale, Norman Vincent, ed. Youth Prints. LC 88-16786. 128p. (Orig.). 1988. pap. 7.99 (*0-8066-2380-2*, 10-7499, Augsburg) Augsburg Fortress.

Rice, Wayne. Great Ideas for Small Youth Groups. 256p. (Orig.). (gr. 7-12). 1986. pap. 9.99 (*0-310-34891-9*, 10823P) Zondervan.

Ristow, Kate S. & Comeaux, Maureen N. Harvest: A Faithful Approach to Life Issues for Junior High People. Titra, Stephen, illus. 167p. (gr. 6-8). 1984. pap. 24.50 (*0-940634-20-1*) Puissance Pubns.

Shivers, Frank R. Heavy Stuff: Clear & Common-Sense Insight into Problems Youth Face. Hill, Junior, intro. by. (Illus., Orig.). (gr. 7-12). 1991. pap. 8.95 (*1-878127-00-4*) F Shivers Evangelistic.

Simpson, Carolyn. Coping with Teenage Motherhood. Rosen, Ruth, ed. LC 92-8168. (gr. 7-12). 1992. 14.95 (*0-8239-1458-5*) Rosen Group.

Snyder, Linda. School Struggles. 48p. (Orig.). (gr. 9-12). 1990. pap. 8.99 (*1-55945-201-3*) Group Pub.

Stefoff, Rebecca. Adolescence. (Illus.). 104p. (gr. 6-12). 1990. 18.95 (*0-7910-0033-8*) Chelsea Hse.

Webster-Doyle, Terrence. Operation Warhawks: How Young People Become Warriors. (Illus.). 135p. (gr. 5-12). 1993. 17.95 (*0-942941-31-4*); pap. 12.95 (*0-942941-30-6*) Atrium Soc Pubns.

—Wrath of the Ancient Warriors: Breaking the Chains of the Past. (Illus.). 128p. (gr. 5-12). 1993. 17.95 (*0-942941-33-0*); pap. 12.95 (*0-942941-32-2*) Atrium Soc Pubns.

White, Joe. Who Are My Real Friends; Peer Pressure: A Teen Survival Guide. 1992. 7.99 (*0-945564-40-6*, Gold & Honey) Questar Pubs.

Woodruff, Marian. Kiss Me, Creep. 192p. (gr. 7-12). 1984. pap. 2.25 (*0-553-24150-8*) Bantam.

Youngs, Bettie B. Goal Setting Skills for Young Adults. rev. ed. 64p. (gr. 5 up). 1994. 10.00 (*0-915190-91-5*, JP 9091-5) Jalmar Pr.

—Goal Setting Skills for Young People. 64p. (gr. 5-12). 1989. pap. 10.00 (*0-940221-04-7*); tchr's. ed. 10.00 (*0-685-27131-5*); wkbk. 10.00 (*0-685-27132-3*); lab manual 10.00 (*0-685-27133-1*) Lrng Tools-Bilicki Pubns.

—A Stress Management Guide for Young People. 96p. (gr. 5 up). 1986. 9.95 (*0-915190-92-3*, JP 9092-3) Jalmar Pr.

Youngs, Bettie B. & Tracy, Brian S. Achievement, Happiness, Popularity & Success: A Self-Esteem Book for Young People. Baldwin, Cathy, ed. LC 88-90808. 169p. (Orig.). (gr. 5-12). 1989. pap. 12.95 (*0-929354-00-1*) Phoenix Educ Found.

Zindel, Paul. My Darling, My Hamburger. LC 70-85025. 176p. (gr. 7 up). 1969. PLB 13.89 (*0-06-026824-7*) HarpC Child Bks.

YOUTH–FICTION

Bennett, Cherie. Sunset, No. 04: Sunset Farewell. 1991. pap. 3.50 (*0-425-12772-9*, Splash) Berkley Pub.

Block, Francesca L. Weetzie Bat. LC 88-6214. 96p. (gr. 6 up). 1991. pap. 3.95 (*0-06-447068-7*, Trophy) HarpC Child Bks.

Branfield, John. Lanhydrock Days. 96p. (gr. 7-10). 1992. 18.95 (*0-575-04880-8*, Pub. by Gollancz UK); pap. 8.95 (*0-575-05081-0*, Pub. by Gollancz UK) Trafalgar.

Bremyer, Jayne. Not Like Other Girls. 162p. (ps up). 1982. pap. 9.95 (*0-944996-09-4*) Carlsons.

Brooks, Chalsea. Who Can You Trust? LC 93-17260. 160p. (Orig.). (gr. 5 up). 1993. pap. 2.95 (*0-02-041973-2*, Collier Young Ad) Macmillan Child Grp.

Brooks, Chelsea. Playing for Keeps. LC 93-12422. 160p. (Orig.). (gr. 5 up). 1993. pap. 2.95 (*0-02-041971-6*, Collier Young Ad) Macmillan Child Grp.

Bunting, Eve. Jumping the Nail. 148p. (gr. 7 up). 1991. 15.95 (*0-15-241357-X*, HB Juv Bks) HarBrace.

Cash, Angela. Dreamskate. 1994. pap. 3.50 (*0-553-56475-7*) Bantam.

Cloverdale Staff. Finders, Keepers. 1994. pap. 3.50 (*0-553-56478-1*) Bantam.

—Highland Hearts. 1994. 3.50 (*0-553-56477-3*) Bantam.

Conford, Ellen. If This Is Love, I'll Take Spaghetti. LC 82-84251. 176p. (gr. 7 up). 1984. SBE 14.95 (*0-02-724250-1*, Four Winds) Macmillan Child Grp.

Cormier, Robert. The Chocolate War. LC 73-15109. 272p. (gr. 7-9). 1974. 20.00 (*0-394-82805-4*) Pantheon.

Crutcher, Chris. Running Loose. LC 82-20935. 160p. (gr. 10 up). 1983. reinforced bdg. 13.95 (*0-688-02002-X*) Greenwillow.

Daley, Maureen. Seventeenth Summer. (gr. 7-11). 1942. 10.95 (*0-396-02322-3*, Putnam) Putnam Pub Group.

Fitzpatrick, Blanche. Getting A Living, Getting A Life: After the Senior Prom. LC 94-66196. 110p. (Orig.). 1994. pap. 9.95 (*0-9627397-2-3*) Pemberton Pubs.

Gelb, Alan. Live from New York. 208p. 1991. pap. 2.95 (*0-380-75745-1*, Flare) Avon.

Hall, Lynn. If Winter Comes. LC 85-43348. 128p. (gr. 7 up). 1986. SBE 13.95 (*0-684-18575-X*, Scribners Young Read) Macmillan Child Grp.

Hedayat, Sadegh & Batmanglij, N. The Patient Stone. Batmanglij, M. & Batmanglij, N., trs. from PER. Franta, illus. LC 86-33301. 32p. (gr. 4 up). 1987. Bilingual. 18.50 (*0-934211-02-7*); English. 18.50 (*0-934211-07-8*) Mage Pubs Inc.

Hinton, S. E. The Outsiders. (gr. 7 up). 17.25 (*0-8446-6372-7*) Peter Smith.

Hinton, Susie E. The Outsiders. 160p. (gr. k up). 1968. pap. 4.50 (*0-440-96769-4*, LFL) Dell.

James, Dean. Melrose Place - Keeping the Faith. (gr. 4-7). 1993. pap. 3.99 (*0-06-106789-X*, Harp PBks) HarpC.

Jones Gunn, Robin. A Whisper & a Wish. 176p. (Orig.). (gr. 7-11). 1989. pap. 4.99 (*0-929608-29-1*) Focus Family.

Kurland, Morton L. Our Sacred Honor. Rosen, R., ed. 196p. (gr. 7-12). 1987. PLB 12.95 (*0-8239-0692-2*) Rosen Group.

L'Engle, Madeleine. Camilla. 288p. (gr. 7 up). 1982. pap. 3.99 (*0-440-91171-0*, LFL) Dell.

Lumbert, Lindy H. Dear Diary. 119p. (gr. 4-10). 1981. pap. 4.25 (*0-943280-00-1*) Blossom Bks.

Martin, Ann M. Boy-Crazy Stacey. (gr. 4-7). 1989. pap. 3.50 (*0-590-43509-4*) Scholastic Inc.

Miller-Lachmann, Lyn. Hiding Places. 206p. (Orig.). (gr. 9-12). 1987. pap. 4.95 (*0-938961-00-4*, Stamp Out Sheep Pr) Sq One Pubs.

Nelson, Theresa M. For the Love of Casey. Mattingly, Jennie, ed. LC 87-50991. 230p. (Orig.). (gr. 7 up). 1987. pap. 8.95 (*1-55523-083-0*) Winston-Derek.

Pfeffer, Susan B. Meg at Sixteen. 1990. 13.95 (*0-553-05854-1*) Bantam.

Slaughter, Rachel. Roxie's Mirage: Featuring the Original Boys & Girls from the Hood. 65p. (gr. 8-12). 1994. pap. 7.95 (*0-9639858-0-9*) Fruits for Knowldge.
LSD is back! Many teens today are adopting some bad habits from the Sixties. They don't know what a ride they are in for. It seems that teens have been dipping in LSD ever since the first particle was invented. In ROXIE'S MIRAGE, you meet a young teen whose foundation is so shaky that she easily falls into the abyss of drugs. From the first page to the last, your mind will intertwine with the thoughts of several urban teens who will never escape the clutches of their dismal fates. And no matter how hard you try... you will never forget them. Signed copies available by calling (610) 323-2982 or writing 1474 Heather Place, Pottstown, PA 19464.
Publisher Provided Annotation.

Tamar, Erika. Good-Bye, Glamour Girl. LC 83-49493. 224p. (gr. 5 up). 1984. (Lipp Jr Bks); (Lipp Jr Bks) HarpC Child Bks.

Waters, Linda F. Slices of Chocolate Lives. 176p. (Orig.). 1993. pap. 4.95 (*0-9630887-0-X*) Ethnic Bks.

Zindel, Paul. Harry & Hortense at Hormone High. LC 82-47697. 160p. (gr. 7 up). 1984. 14.00 (*0-06-026864-6*); PLB 13.89 (*0-06-026869-7*) HarpC Child Bks.

—I Never Loved Your Mind. 144p. (gr. 9 up). 1984. pap. 3.99 (*0-553-27323-X*) Bantam.

—I Never Loved Your Mind. LC 73-105476. 192p. (gr. 7 up). 1970. PLB 13.89 (*0-06-026822-0*) HarpC Child Bks.

YOUTH MOVEMENT

Costello, Gwen. Stations of the Cross for Teenagers. (Illus.). 32p. 1988. pap. 1.95 (*0-89622-386-8*) Twenty-Third.

Ward, Elaine. Getting to Know You. 20p. (Orig.). (gr. 7-12). 1987. pap. 5.75 (*0-940754-49-5*) Ed Ministries.

YUCATAN–FICTION

Keller, Kent. The Mayan Mystery. LC 93-48838. (Illus.). 1994. 4.99 (*0-8423-5132-9*) Tyndale.

YUGOSLAVIA

Close Up Foundation Staff. War in Yugoslavia: The Return of Nationalism. LC 93-28942. 32p. 1993. pap. 5.95 (*0-932765-50-5*, 1381-94); tchr's. guide avail. Close Up.

Greene, Carol. Yugoslavia. LC 83-21049. (Illus.). 128p. (gr. 5-9). 1984. PLB 20.55 (*0-516-02791-3*) Childrens.

Ricciuti, Edward R. War in Yugoslavia: The Breakup of a Nation. LC 92-32126. (Illus.). 64p. (gr. 5-8). 1993. PLB 15.90 (*1-56294-375-8*); pap. 6.95 (*1-56294-750-8*) Millbrook Pr.

Rody, Martyn. The Breakup of Yugoslavia. (Illus.). 48p. (gr. 6 up). 1994. text ed. 13.95 RSBE (*0-02-792529-3*, New Discovery Bks) Macmillan Child Grp.

YUGOSLAVIA–FICTION

Children of Yugoslavia Staff. I Dream of Peace. (ps-3). 1994. 12.95 (*0-06-251128-9*) HarpC Child Bks.

YUKON–FICTION

Hill, Kirkpatrick. Toughboy & Sister. 128p. (gr. 3-7). 1992. pap. 3.99 (*0-14-034866-2*) Puffin Bks.

London, Jack. To Build a Fire. Neumeier, Marty, illus. 48p. (gr. 6 up). 1980. PLB 13.95 (*0-87191-769-6*) Creative Ed.

Luther, Rebekah S. The Yoda Family. (Illus.). 16p. (gr. 3). 1994. saddle-stitch 7.95 (*0-8059-3486-3*) Dorrance.

YUKON RIVER

DeGraf, Anna. Pioneering on the Yukon, 1892-1917. Brown, Roger S., ed. LC 92-14808. (Illus.). ix, 128p. 1992. lib. bdg. 19.50 (*0-208-02362-3*, Pub. by Archon Bks) Shoe String.

Lourie, Peter. Yukon River: An Adventure to the Gold Fields of the Klondike. (Illus.). 48p. (gr. 3-7). 1992. PLB 15.95 (*1-878093-90-8*) Boyds Mills Pr.

Sturgis, Kent. Four Generations on the Yukon. LC 87-83743. (Illus.). 80p. (Orig.). (gr. 9-12). 1988. pap. 15.95 (*0-945397-01-1*) Epicenter Pr.

Tjepkema, Edith R. Yukon Paradise. 126p. (Orig.). (gr. 8-12). 1990. pap. 4.50 (*0-9620280-2-9*) Northland Pr.

YUKON TERRITORY–POETRY

Service, Robert. The Shooting of Dan McGrew. Harrison, Ted, illus. LC 88-6124. (gr. 3 up). 1988. 14.95 (*0-87923-748-1*) Godine.

Z

ZACCHAEUS (BIBLICAL CHARACTER)

Higby, Roy C. A Man from the Past. 2nd ed. Lux, Don, illus. McLoughlin, William G., intro. by. (Illus.). (gr. 5-12). pap. 8.00 (*0-914692-02-X*) Big Moose.

Jenkins, Lee. Zacchaeus. Chansler, Jim, illus. Greeno, Ron, frwd. by. (Illus.). 32p. (Orig.). (ps-3). 1993. pap. 6.95 (*1-883952-03-4*) Hse of Steno.

Lashbrook, Marilyn. Out on a Limb: The Story of Zacchaeus. LC 88-63782. (Illus.). 32p. (ps). 1989. 5.95 (*0-86606-436-2*, 868) Roper Pr.

Stirrup Associates, Inc. Staff. My Jesus Pocketbook of the Big Little Person: The Story of Zacchaeus. Phillips, Cheryl M. & Harvey, Bonnie C., eds. Fulton, Ginger A., illus. LC 84-50917. 32p. (ps). 1984. pap. 0.69 (*0-937420-13-1*) Stirrup Assoc.

Stortz, Diane. Zaccheus Meets Jesus. Fagan, Todd, illus. 28p. (ps). 1992. 2.50 (*0-87403-958-4*, 24-03598) Standard Pub.

ZAHARIAS, MILDRED BABE (DIDRIKSON) 1913-1956

Lynn, Elizabeth. Babe Didrikson Zaharias. Horner, Matina. (Illus.). 112p. (gr. 5 up). 1989. lib. bdg. 17.95 (*1-55546-684-2*) Chelsea Hse.

ZAMBIA

Rogers, Barbara R. Zambia. Rogers, Stillman, photos by. LC 89-43178. (Illus.). 64p. (gr. 5-6). 1991. PLB 21.26 (*0-8368-0257-8*) Gareth Stevens Inc.

Zambia Is My Home. 48p. (gr. 2-8). 1992. PLB 21.26 (*0-8368-0906-8*) Gareth Stevens Inc.

ZEBRAS

Arnold, Caroline. Zebra. Hewett, Richard, illus. LC 87-1503. 48p. (gr. 2-5). 1987. 13.95 (*0-688-07067-1*); lib. bdg. 13.88 (*0-688-07068-X*, Morrow Jr Bks) Morrow Jr Bks.

—Zebra. Hewett, Richard, photos by. LC 92-25550. (Illus.). 48p. (gr. 3 up). 1993. pap. 5.95 (*0-688-12273-6*, Mulberry) Morrow.

Green, Carl R. & Sanford, William R. The Zebra. LC 88-1831. (Illus.). 48p. (gr. 5). 1988. text ed. 12.95 RSBE (*0-89686-388-3*, Crestwood Hse) Macmillan Child Grp.

Hoffman, Mary. Zebra. LC 84-24793. (Illus.). 24p. (gr. k-5). 1985. PLB 9.95 (*0-8172-2414-9*); pap. 3.95 (*0-8114-6895-X*) Raintree Steck-V.

Lepthien, Emilie U. Zebras. LC 94-10945. (Illus.). 48p. (gr. k-4). 1994. PLB 17.20 (*0-516-01072-7*); pap. 4.95 (*0-516-41072-5*) Childrens.

Markert, Jenny. Zebras. (gr. 2-6). 1992. PLB 15.95 (*0-89565-839-9*) Childs World.

Stone, Lynn. Zebras. (Illus.). 24p. (gr. k-5). 1990. lib. bdg. 11.94 (*0-86593-048-1*); lib. bdg. 8.95s.p. (*0-685-36349-X*) Rourke Corp.

Vouillemin. Zebra, Reading Level 3-4. (Illus.). 28p. (gr. 2-5). 1983. PLB 16.67 (*0-86592-858-4*); PLB 12.50s.p. (*0-685-58829-7*) Rourke Corp.

Zebras. 1991. PLB 14.95 (*0-88682-420-6*) Creative Ed.

ZEBRAS–FICTION

Giffard, Hannah. Striped Zebra. Giffard, Hannah, illus. LC 92-62423. 12p. (ps). 1993. bds. 3.95 (*0-688-12441-0*, Tambourine Bks) Morrow.

Hadithi, Mwenye. Greedy Zebra. 1984 ed. Kennaway, Adrienne, illus. (ps-3). 1984. 15.95 (*0-316-33721-8*) Little.

Henkes, Kevin. The Zebra Wall. LC 87-18454. 160p. (gr. 3 up). 1988. 10.95 (*0-688-07568-1*) Greenwillow.

Knopf, Jerry E. The Zebra with No Stripes. 1993. 7.95 (*0-533-10365-7*) Vantage.

Oana, Katherine. Zippy Zebra. Baird, Tate, ed. Butrick, Lyn M., illus. LC 88-51853. 16p. (Orig.). (ps). 1989. pap. 4.52 (*0-914127-11-X*) Univ Class.

Van Curen, Barbara. When the Zebras Came for Lunch. Manierre, Betsy, illus. 64p. (ps-2). 1989. pap. text ed. 5.95 (*0-922510-01-6*) Lucky Bks.

Vargo, Vanessa. Zebra Talk. LC 92-11028. 1991. pap. 3.95 (*0-85953-395-6*, Pub. by Childs Play UK) Childs Play.

ZEPPELINS

see Airships

ZOOLOGICAL GARDENS

Altman, Joyce & Goldberg, Sue. Dear Bronx Zoo. Falk, Douglas, frwd. by. LC 89-28226. (Illus.). 144p. (gr. 3 up). 1990. SBE 14.95 (*0-02-700640-9*, Macmillan Child Bk) Macmillan Child Grp.

Baby Zoo Animals. (Illus.). 32p. (ps-1). 1986. pap. 1.25 (*0-8431-1521-1*) Price Stern.

Baby Zoo Animals. (Illus.). (ps). pap. 1.25 (*0-7214-9545-1*) Ladybird Bks.

Bishop, Roma. At the Zoo: Match It Up. 1989. 3.99 (*0-517-68251-6*) Random Hse Value.

Bornstein, Harry. Mealtime at the Zoo. Hrivnak, Suzette & Hrivnak, James R., illus. 48p. (ps-2). 1973. pap. 5.95 (*0-913580-11-2*, Kendall Green Pubs) Gallaudet Univ Pr.

Conteh-Morgan, Jane. My Zoo. LC 94-10590. (Illus.). 1995. write for info. (*0-553-09733-4*, Little Rooster) Bantam.

Curtis, Patricia. Animals & the New Zoos. (Illus.). 64p. (gr. 3-8). 1991. 15.95 (*0-525-67347-4*, Lodestar Bks) Dutton Child Bks.

Gangelhoff, Jeanne M. & Belk, Bradford. A Walk Through the Minnesota Zoo. Gangelhoff, Gene, illus. 32p. Date not set. 9.95 (*0-9635006-1-9*) G J & B Pub.

Gerstenfeld, Sheldon L. Zoo Clues: Making the Most of Your Visit to the Zoo. Doty, Eldon C., illus. 128p. (gr. 2-5). 1991. 13.95 (*0-670-82362-7*) Viking Child Bks.

Gibbons, Gail. Zoo. Gibbons, Gail, illus. LC 87-582. 32p. (ps-3). 1987. 15.00 (*0-690-04631-6*, Crowell Jr Bks); PLB 14.89 (*0-690-04633-2*) HarpC Child Bks.

—Zoo. Gibbons, Gail, illus. LC 87-582. 32p. (ps-3). 1991. pap. 4.95 (*0-06-446096-7*, Trophy) HarpC Child Bks.

Hawksley, Gerald. Zoo. Hawksley, Gerald, illus. 10p. (ps). 1990. bds. 4.95 (*1-878624-19-9*) McClanahan Bk.

Irvine, Georgeanne. Let's Visit a Super Zoo. Fuller, Tim W., illus. LC 89-34370. 32p. (gr. 2-4). 1990. lib. bdg. 10.79 (*0-8167-1745-1*); pap. text ed. 2.95 (*0-8167-1746-X*) Troll Assocs.

Jacobson, Karen. Zoos. LC 82-9545. (Illus.). (gr. k-4). 1982. PLB 12.85 (*0-516-01664-4*); pap. 4.95 (*0-516-41664-2*) Childrens.

Machotka, Hana. What Do You Do at a Petting Zoo? Machotka, Hana, photos by. LC 89-34478. (Illus.). 32p. (gr. k up). 1990. 13.95 (*0-688-08737-X*); PLB 13.88 (*0-688-08738-8*, Morrow Jr Bks) Morrow Jr Bks.

My Book of Baby Zoo Animals. (ps-2). 3.95 (*0-7214-5149-7*) Ladybird Bks.

O'Neill, Terry. Zoos: Identifying Propaganda Techniques. LC 90-3247. (Illus.). 32p. (gr. 3-6). 1990. pap. text ed. 10.95 (*0-89908-600-4*) Greenhaven.

Ormerod, Jan. When We Went to the Zoo. (Illus.). (ps-3). 1991. 13.95 (*0-688-09878-9*); 13.88 (*0-688-09879-7*) Lothrop.

Parramon, J. M. Mi Primera Visita al Zoo. 1990. pap. 5.95 (*0-8120-4402-9*) Barron.

—My First Visit to the Zoo. Sales, G., illus. 32p. (ps). 1990. pap. 6.95 (*0-8120-4302-2*) Barron.

Pfeffer, Wendy. Popcorn Park Zoo. Smith, J. Gerard, photos by. LC 91-3273. (Illus.). 64p. (gr. 2-5). 1992. 14.95 (*0-671-74587-5*, J Messner); lib. bdg. 16.98 (*0-671-74589-1*, J Messner) S&S Trade.

Pienkowski, Jan. Zoo. Pienkowski, Jan, illus. 32p. (ps-1). 1985. 13.95 (*0-434-95652-X*, Pub. by W Heinemann Ltd) Trafalgar.

Richmond, Gary. Barnaby Goes Wild, No. 7. (gr. 1-5). 1991. text ed. 6.99 (*0-8499-0914-7*) Word Inc.

Rinard, Judith E. Zoos Without Cages. LC 79-3243. (Illus.). 104p. (gr. 3-8). 1981. 8.95 (*0-87044-335-6*); PLB 12.50 (*0-87044-340-2*) Natl Geog.

Rowan, Jim. I Can Be a Zoo Keeper. LC 85-11327. 32p. (gr. k-3). 1985. pap. 3.95 (*0-516-41889-0*) Childrens.

Russell, William. Zookeepers. LC 93-42482. 1994. write for info. (*1-57103-055-7*) Rourke Pr.

Schneider, David C. A Visit to the People Zoo. Scallon, Cheryl V., ed. Hillman, Carole D., illus. LC 89-85637. 16p. (Orig.). (ps-1). 1989. pap. write for info. Early Childhood.

Smith, Roland. Inside the Zoo Nursery. Munoz, William, illus. LC 92-3344. 64p. (gr. 5 up). 1993. 15.00 (*0-525-65084-9*, Cobblehill Bks) Dutton Child Bks.

Spizzirri, Peter M. Zoo Animals: Alphabet Dot to Dot: Educational Activity-Coloring Book. Spizzirri, Linda, ed. (Illus.). 32p. (gr. k-3). 1992. pap. 1.00 (*0-86545-208-3*) Spizzirri.

—Zoo Maze: Educational Activity-Coloring Book. Spizzirri, Linda, ed. (Illus.). 32p. (gr. k-3). 1992. pap. 1.00 (*0-86545-204-0*) Spizzirri.

Tester, Sylvia R. A Visit to the Zoo. Pilot Productions Staff, et al, photos by. LC 84-12697. (Illus.). 32p. (ps-3). 1987. PLB 11.45 (*0-516-01494-3*) Childrens.

Thomson, Peggy. Keepers & Creatures at the National Zoo. Conklin, Paul S., photos by. LC 87-47697. (Illus.). 208p. (gr. 3-7). 1988. 13.95 (*0-690-04710-X*, Crowell Jr Bks); (Crowell Jr Bks) HarpC Child Bks.

Three-D Zoo Book. (Illus.). (ps). 1992. 9.00 (*1-56021-144-X*) W J Fantasy.

Unwin, Pippa. Great Zoo Hunt! (ps-3). 1990. 13.99 (*0-385-41107-3*) Doubleday.

Wexo, John B. Big Cats. 24p. 1989. PLB 14.95 (*0-88682-264-5*) Creative Ed.

Who's Who at the Zoo? 12p. (ps). 1994. 4.95 (*1-56458-738-X*) Dorling Kindersley.

Wilkon, Piotr & Wilkon, Jozef. Escape from the Zoo! Lanning, Rosemary, tr. from GER. LC 92-31034. (Illus.). 32p. (gr. k-3). 1993. 14.95 (*1-55858-201-0*); PLB 14.88 (*1-55858-202-9*) North-South Bks NYC.

Yancey, Diane. Zoos. LC 94-8546. (Illus.). (gr. 5-8). 1994. 14.95 (*1-56006-163-4*) Lucent Bks.

Zoo Animals. 32p. (Orig.). (ps-1). 1984. pap. 1.25 (*0-8431-1515-7*) Price Stern.

ZOOLOGICAL GARDENS–FICTION

Altman, Joyce & Goldberg, Sue. Dear Bronx Zoo. (gr. 4-7). 1992. pap. 3.50 (*0-380-71649-6*, Camelot) Avon.

Armstrong, Beverly. Zoo Animals - Superdoodles. LC 93-80431. 32p. (gr. 1-6). 1994. 4.95 (*0-88160-230-2*, LW325) Learning Wks.

Ashabranner, Brent. I'm in the Zoo, Too. Stevens, Janet, illus. LC 88-32662. (gr. k-4). 1989. 12.95 (*0-525-65002-4*, Cobblehill Bks) Dutton Child Bks.

Ashwill, Beverly. Charley the Fearless Zoo Keeper. Ashwill, Betty J., illus. LC 90-83311. 20p. (ps-3). 1990. pap. 3.98 (*0-941381-07-2*) BJO Enterprises.

—The Invisible Dawn. Ashwill, Betty J., illus. LC 90-83310. 24p. (ps-5). 1990. pap. 3.98 (*0-685-37787-3*) BJO Enterprises.

Brandenberg, Franz. Leo & Emily's Zoo. Abolafia, Yossi, illus. LC 87-17907. 32p. (ps-1). 1988. 11.95 (*0-688-07457-X*); lib. bdg. 11.88 (*0-688-07458-8*) Greenwillow.

Browne, Anthony. Zoo. LC 92-11708. (Illus.). 32p. 1993. 15.00 (*0-679-83946-1*) Knopf Bks Yng Read.

Calmenson, Stephanie. Where Will the Animals Stay? Appleby, Ellen, illus. LC 83-13479. 48p. (ps-3). 1984. 5.95 (*0-8193-1119-7*) Parents.

Christmas at the Zoo Pop Up. 10p. (ps-3). 1990. 3.95 (*0-8167-2185-8*) Troll Assocs.

Cohen, Caron L. Pigeon, Pigeon. LC 91-36177. (Illus.). 32p. (ps-1). 1992. 12.00 (*0-525-44866-7*, DCB) Dutton Child Bks.

Davis, Kerry. The Swetsville Zoo. (Illus.). 44p. (gr. 1-6). 1994. 8.95 (*0-9635263-1-6*); It's More Than A Tree That You See, Bk. 1. pap. 4.95 (*0-9635263-0-8*); Set. 12.95 (*0-9635263-2-4*) Kerry Tales.

Dixon, Jim. The Zoo Is Blue: And Should Be Read. Dixon, Jim, illus. 36p. (gr. k-2). 1991. 12.95 (*1-880453-01-0*) J Hefty Pub.

Dowdy, Linda C. Barney Goes to the Zoo. Hartley, Linda, ed. Malzeke-McDonald, Karen & McGlothlin, David, illus. LC 93-77868. 18p. (ps-k). 1993. bds. 4.95 chunky board flap (*1-57064-011-4*) Barney Pub.

Evans, Nate. The Mixed-up Zoo of Professor Yahoo. Gibson, Kate & Sanders, Ann, eds. LC 92-71679. (Illus.). 32p. (ps-3). 1993. 14.95 (*0-9607076-3-8*) Jr League KC.

Farmer, Nancy. The Warm Place. LC 94-21984. 1995. write for info. (*0-531-06888-9*) Orchard Bks Watts.

Graham, Margaret B. Be Nice to Spiders. Graham, Margaret B., illus. LC 67-17101. 32p. (gr. k-3). 1967. PLB 14.89 (*0-06-022073-2*) HarpC Child Bks.

Guild, Anne V. Mickey Mouse in Let's Go...to the Zoo! Scholefield, Ron, et al, illus. 26p. (ps up). 1987. pap. 14.95 (*1-55578-802-5*) Worlds Wonder.

Hawksley, Gerald. Zoo Window. (Illus.). 10p. (ps). 1988. 3.95 (*0-681-40468-X*) Longmeadow Pr.

Howe, James. Morgan's Zoo. Morrill, Leslie, illus. LC 84-6325. 192p. (gr. 3-6). 1984. SBE 13.95 (*0-689-31046-3*, Atheneum Child Bk) Macmillan Child Grp.

—Morgan's Zoo. (Illus.). 192p. (gr. 3-7). 1986. pap. 3.99 (*0-380-69994-X*, Camelot) Avon.

Hurd, Edith T. Stop Stop. Hurd, Clement, illus. LC 61-12095. 64p. (gr. k-3). 1961. PLB 13.89 (*0-06-022746-X*) HarpC Child Bks.

Kehret, Peg. Terror at the Zoo. 160p. (gr. 5 up). 1992. 14.00 (*0-525-65083-0*, Cobblehill Bks) Dutton Child Bks.

—Terror at the Zoo. 144p. (gr. 4-7). 1993. pap. 3.50 (*0-671-79394-2*, Minstrel Bks) PB.

Kent, Jack. The Biggest Shadow in the Zoo. Kent, Jack, illus. LC 80-25517. 48p. (ps-3). 1981. 5.95 (*0-8193-1047-6*); PLB 5.95 (*0-8193-1048-4*) Parents.

Leah, Devora. Lost Erev Shabbos in the Zoo. rev. ed. Forst, Siegmund, illus. 32p. (gr. k-3). 1986. 9.95 (*0-910818-56-8*); pap. 7.95 (*0-910818-57-6*) Judaica Pr.

Leeka, Melinda. Andy Goes to the Zoo. LC 89-51092. 44p. (gr. k-3). 1990. 5.95 (*1-55523-247-7*) Winston-Derek.

Lippert, Donald F. Polly Popcan. Hedden, Randall, illus. 32p. (ps). 1989. write for info. Pastel Pubns.

Lobel, Arnold. Holiday for Mister Muster. Lobel, Arnold, illus. LC 63-15323. 32p. (gr. k-3). 1963. PLB 12.89 (*0-06-023956-5*) HarpC Child Bks.

—Zoo for Mister Muster. LC 62-7313. (Illus.). 32p. (ps-3). 1962. PLB 12.89 (*0-06-023991-3*) HarpC Child Bks.

Lunn, Carolyn. Bobby's Zoo Big Book. (Illus.). 32p. (ps-2). 1991. PLB 22.95 (*0-516-49501-1*) Childrens.

Mayer, Mercer. Professor Wormbog in Search for the Zipperump-a-Zoo. Mayer, Mercer, illus. 48p. (ps up). 1992. pap. 5.95 (*1-879920-04-2*) Rain Bird Prods.

Noble, Kate. The Blue Elephant. Bass, Rachel, illus. 32p. (ps-4). 1994. 14.95 (*0-9631798-3-7*) Silver Seahorse. Sassi is a young African elephant. She loves living in the zoo & she likes to see the children who come to play. Her efforts to get what she dreams of produce some startling results. Witty full-color paintings show the big-city zoo. Besides all the fun, there's lots of information on animal behavior. Kate Nobel is author of BUBBLE GUM & OH LOOK, IT'S A NOSSERUS in the AFRICA STORIES Series. She's a former teacher & a zoo volunteer. Rachel Bass is an artist & an art therapist who works with children. They both know a good deal about early childhood development. Silver Seahorse Press, 2568 N. Clark Street, Suite 320, Chicago, IL 60614. 312-871-1772. FAX: 312 327-8978. Distributed by: Lifetime Books, Inc., 2131 Hollywood Boulevard, Hollywood, FL 33020-6750. 1-800-771-3355. Fax number for orders: 1-800-931-7411. *Publisher Provided Annotation.*

Oden, Fay G. Where Is Calvin? (Illus.). 48p. (Orig.). (gr. 2-6). 1994. pap. text ed. 6.95 (*0-9638946-0-9*) Tennedo Pubs. Fay Giles Oden is a retired elementary school teacher, fiction writer, editor, illustrator & poet. Her recently published short fiction (child's book) is WHERE IS CALVIN? (Tennedo, $6.95). Mrs. Oden received motivation for the story WHERE IS CALVIN? after visiting the zoo. (Summer 1993). The story deals with respect for family life & a child's infatuation with animals. It is a simple story of friendship & entrancement with the animals that somehow caused the boys to become separated. The suspense of the boys' day at the zoo overwhelms you as the animals have been intentionally personified to talk to the boys. They become boys with a mission to find their friend Calvin. The plot is simple. The characters are believable. The narrative techniques of the story skillfully blends literature with poetry. The suspenseful, vivid & colorful story will delight young readers. In short, WHERE IS CALVIN? is a charming story with sympathetic characters. Children will love the humor of it all. You'll be surprised to find out what really happened to Calvin. The book lends itself to a READ-ME-A-STORY book. Child care centers have expressed an interest in the book. WHERE IS CALVIN? can be ordered from the following distributors: Baker & Taylor, 501 South Gladiolus Street, Momence, IL 60954-1799; Tennedo Publishers, 6315 Elwynne Drive, Cincinnati, OH 45236, 1-513-791-3277. Fay Oden is also the author of: CALVIN & HIS VIDEO CAMERA. *Publisher Provided Annotation.*

Outlet Staff. Visit to Sesame Street Zoo. Date not set. pap. 3.99 (*0-517-11124-1*) Random Hse Value.

Palazzo-Craig, Janet. Who's Who at the Zoo! Burns, Ray, illus. LC 85-14123. 48p. (Orig.). (gr. 1-3). 1986. PLB 10.59 (*0-8167-0658-1*); pap. text ed. 3.50 (*0-8167-0659-X*) Troll Assocs.

Parker, Nancy W. Working Frog. LC 90-24173. 40p. (gr. k up). 1992. 14.00 (*0-688-09918-1*); PLB 13.93 (*0-688-09919-X*) Greenwillow.

Polisar, Barry L. Peculiar Zoo. Clark, David, illus. 32p. (gr. k-6). 1993. 14.95 (*0-938663-14-3*) Rainbow Morn.

Rathmann, Peggy. Goodnight, Gorilla. Rathman, Peggy, tr. LC 92-29020. (Illus.). 40p. (ps-1). 1994. 12.95 (*0-399-22445-9*, Putnam) Putnam Pub Group.

Rey, Margaret & Shalleck, Allan J. Curious George Visits the Zoo. 1988. pap. 7.70 incl. cass. (*0-395-48876-1*) HM.

Richmond, Gary. A Scary Night at the Zoo. 1990. write for info. (*0-8499-0742-X*) Word Inc.

Robinson, Martha. The Zoo at Night. Fransconi, Antonio, illus. LC 94-12773. 1995. 16.00 (*0-689-50608-2*, M K McElderry) Macmillan Child Grp.

Roennfeldt, Mary. What's That Noise? Roennfeldt, Robert, illus. LC 91-16215. 32p. (ps-1). 1992. 13.95 (*0-531-05972-3*); lib. bdg. 13.99 (*0-531-08572-4*) Orchard Bks Watts.

Roger, Cynthia A. Why Aren't There Any Dinosaurs Here at the Zoo? 1993. 7.95 (*0-533-10582-X*) Vantage.

Scarry, Richard. Mr. Frumble: Richard Scarry's Smallest Pop-up Book Ever! (Illus.). 10p. (ps-3). 1992. write for info. (*0-307-12463-0*, 12463, Golden Pr) Western Pub.

Sloss, Lesley. Anthony & the Aardvark. Clarke, Gus, illus. LC 90-6528. 32p. (ps up). 1991. 13.95 (*0-688-10302-2*); PLB 13.88 (*0-688-10303-0*) Lothrop.

Taylor, Theodore. Sniper. LC 89-7415. 227p. (gr. 7 up). 1989. 15.95 (*0-15-276420-8*) HarBrace.

Thomas, Mary A. Jump with Jeremy: What Hoosiers Do on the Way to the Zoo. Hodge, Ellen & Poore, Luz, eds. Still, James & Escabar, URias, trs. from ENG. Graham-Rice, Kathy, illus. (SPA.). 47p. (Orig.). 1988. pap. 9.95 (*0-944326-00-5*) Childrens Corner.

Vigna, Judith. Uncle Alfredo's Zoo. (gr. 4-7). 1994. 14.95 (*0-8075-8292-1*) A Whitman.

Walter, Mildred P. Tiger Ride. LC 92-40281. (Illus.). 32p. (ps-2). 1995. RSBE 17.00 (*0-02-792303-7*, Bradbury Pr) Macmillan Child Grp.

Winder, Jack. Who's New at the Zoo? Wasserman, Dan, ed. Reese, Bob, illus. (gr. k-1). 1979. 7.95 (*0-89868-074-3*); pap. 2.95 (*0-89868-085-9*) ARO Pub.

Zoo. (Illus.). 48p. (Orig.). (gr. k-4). 1987. pap. 2.95 (*0-8431-1879-2*) Price Stern.

El Zoologico. (SPA.). (ps-3). 1993. pap. 2.25 (*0-307-70060-7*, Golden Pr) Western Pub.

ZOOLOGICAL SPECIMENS–COLLECTION AND PRESERVATION

Harden, Cleo. How to Preserve Animal & Other Specimens in Clear Plastic. Harden, David G., illus. 64p. (gr. 4 up). 1963. 12.95 (*0-911010-47-5*); pap. 4.95 (*0-911010-46-7*) Naturegraph.

ZOOLOGY

see also Anatomy, Comparative; Animals; Embryology; Evolution; Fossils; Natural History

also names of divisions, classes, etc. of the animal kingdom (e.g. Invertebrates; Vertebrates; birds; Mammals; etc.)

Chicago Zoological Society Staff, ed. Brookfield Zoo Connections: A Program to Enhance Classroom Studies. (Orig.). (gr. k-8). 1986. pap. text ed. 30.00 (*0-913934-03-8*) Chicago Zoo.

Cohen, Judith L. & Thompson, Valerie. You Can Be a Woman Zoologist. Katz, David, illus. LC 93-1092. 40p. (Orig.). (gr. 3-7). 1992. pap. 6.00 (*1-880599-08-2*) Cascade Pass.

Collard, Sneed B. Te Asustan? Criaturas Espeluznantes. Kest, Kristin, illus. (SPA.). 32p. (Orig.). (ps-4). 1993. PLB 15.88 (*0-88106-643-5*); pap. 6.95 (*0-88106-423-8*) Charlesbridge Pub.

Dashefsky, H. Steven. Zoology: Forty-Nine Science Fair Projects. (gr. 4-7). 1994. pap. text ed. 10.95 (*0-07-015683-2*) McGraw.

Dykstra, Mary. The Amateur Zoologist: Explorations & Investigations. (Illus.). (gr. 6-9). 1994. PLB 12.90 (*0-531-11162-8*) Watts.

Fromer, Julie. Jane Goodall: Living with the Chimps. Castro, Antonio, illus. 72p. (gr. 4-7). 1992. PLB 14.95 (*0-8050-2116-7*) TFC Bks NY.

Gelman, Rita G. Dawn to Dusk in the Galapagos, Vol. 1. 1991. 16.95 (*0-316-30739-4*) Little.

Gerstenfeld, Sheldon L. Zoo Clues: Making the Most of Your Visit to the Zoo. Doty, Eldon C., illus. 120p. (gr. 2 up). 1993. pap. 4.99 (*0-14-032813-0*, Puffin) Puffin Bks.

Halliburton, Warren J. African Wildlife. LC 91-43514. (Illus.). 48p. (gr. 6). 1992. text ed. 13.95 RSBE (*0-89686-674-2*, Crestwood Hse) Macmillan Child Grp.

Hart, Trish. Antarctic Diary. Hart, Trish, illus. LC 93-110. 1994. pap. write for info. (*0-383-03675-5*) SRA Schl Grp.

Hartmann, Wendy. One Sun Rises: An African Wildlife Counting Book. Maritz, Nicolaas, illus. LC 93-49735. 32p. (ps-1). 1994. 13.99 (*0-525-45225-7*, DCB) Dutton Child Bks.

Higginson, Mel. Scientists Who Study Wild Animals. LC 94-6997. 1994. write for info. (*0-86593-374-X*) Rourke Corp.

Howell, Judd, intro. by. Wildlife California. (Illus.). 64p. (ps-7). 1990. text ed. 9.95 (*0-87701-886-3*) Chronicle Bks.

Hughey, Pat. Scavengers & Decomposers: The Cleanup Crew. Hiscock, Bruce, illus. LC 83-17474. 64p. (gr. 4-6). 1984. SBE 13.95 (*0-689-31032-3*, Atheneum Child Bk) Macmillan Child Grp.

Lacey, Elizabeth A. What's the Difference? A Guide to Some Familiar Animal Look-Alikes. Shetterly, Robert, illus. 80p. (gr. 4-7). 1993. 14.95 (*0-395-56182-5*, Clarion Bks) HM.

Mattern, Joanne. Australian Animals. LC 92-41033. (Illus.). 24p. (gr. k-2). 1993. 1.95 (*0-8167-3096-2*) Troll Assocs.

Pandell, Karen. Land of Dark, Land of Light: The Arctic National Wildlife Refuge. Bruemmer, Fred, photos by. LC 92-40405. (Illus.). 32p. (ps-3). 1993. 14.99 (*0-525-45094-7*, DCB) Dutton Child Bks.

Perry, Susan. Zoology. Nolte, Larry, illus. 48p. (gr. 3-6). Date not set. PLB 12.95 (*1-56065-111-3*) Capstone Pr.

Poncet, Sally. Destination South Georgia: An Antarctic Voyage. Osborne, Ben, photos by. LC 94-13376. (gr. 4 up). 1995. 17.00 (*0-02-774905-3*) Macmillan Child Grp.

Roop, Peter & Roop, Connie. One Earth, a Multitude of Creatures. Kells, Valerie A., illus. LC 92-14057. 32p. 1992. 14.95 (*0-8027-8192-6*); lib. bdg. 15.85 (*0-8027-8193-4*) Walker & Co.

Rose, Kenneth J. Classification of the Animal Kingdom. (gr. 7 up). 1980. 8.95 (*0-679-20508-X*) McKay.

Shorto, Russell. Careers for Animal Lovers. LC 91-27657. (Illus.). 64p. (gr. 7 up). 1992. PLB 14.40 (*1-56294-160-7*); pap. 4.95 (*1-56294-767-2*) Millbrook Pr.

—Careers for Animal Lovers. 1992. pap. 4.95 (*0-395-63571-3*) HM.

Skramstad, Jill. Wildlife Southwest. Richard, Ellis, intro. by. (Illus.). 64p. (gr. 3-7). 1991. 9.95 (*0-8118-0126-8*) Chronicle Bks.

Stamper, Judith B. Zoo Worker. Garry-McCord, Kathleen, illus. LC 88-10046. 32p. (gr. k-3). 1989. PLB 10.89 (*0-8167-1440-1*); pap. text ed. 2.95 (*0-8167-1441-X*) Troll Assocs.

Venino, Suzanne. Amazing Animal Groups. Crump, Donald J., ed. LC 81-47743. 32p. (ps-3). 1981. Set. lib. bdg. 16.95 (*0-87044-402-6*); Set. 13.95 (*0-87044-407-7*) Natl Geog.

Ward, Lorraine. Un Paseo Por la Naturaleza: Explorando una Reserva Natural. Jacques, Laura, illus. (SPA.). 32p. (Orig.). (ps-4). 1993. PLB 15.88 (*0-88106-645-1*); pap. 6.95 (*0-88106-812-8*) Charlesbridge Pub.

Watts, Barrie. Twenty-Four Hours in a Game Reserve. Watts, Barrie, photos by. LC 91-23728. (Illus.). 48p. (gr. 4-6). 1992. PLB 12.90 (*0-531-14173-X*) Watts.

Whyte, Malcolm. Zoo Animals Action Set, No. 2. (Illus.). 24p. (Orig.). 1994. pap. 5.95 (*0-8431-2831-3*, Troubador) Price Stern.

Zokeisha. Zoo Animals. Zokeisha, illus. 16p. (ps). 1982. pap. 3.50 board (*0-671-44895-1*, Little Simon) S&S Trade.

ZOOLOGY–ANATOMY

see Anatomy, Comparative

ZOOLOGY, ECONOMIC

see also Domestic Animals; Insects, Injurious and Beneficial

ZOOLOGY–GEOGRAPHIC DISTRIBUTION

see Geographical Distribution of Animals and Plants

ZOOLOGY OF THE BIBLE

see Bible–Natural History

ZOOS

see Zoological Gardens

ZULULAND–HISTORY

Stanley, Diane & Vennema, Peter. Shaka, King of the Zulus. Stanley, Stanley, illus. LC 87-27376. 40p. (gr. 1-4). 1988. 14.95 (*0-688-07342-5*); PLB 14.88 (*0-688-07343-3*, Morrow Jr Bks) Morrow Jr Bks.

ZULUS

Mckenna, Nancy D. A Zulu Family. (Illus.). 32p. (gr. 2-5). 1986. PLB 13.50 (*0-8225-1666-7*) Lerner Pubns.

Stanley, Diane & Vennema, Peter. Shaka: King of the Zulus. Stanley, Diane, illus. LC 93-11730. 40p. (gr. k up). 1994. pap. 4.95 (*0-688-13114-X*, Mulberry) Morrow.

KEY TO PUBLISHERS' AND DISTRIBUTORS' ABBREVIATIONS

The following is a list of abbreviations for publishers' and distributors' names used in the book listings in this issue of **SUBJECT GUIDE TO CHILDREN'S BOOKS IN PRINT 1995**.

The entries in this list contain: Publisher's or distributor's abbreviation, followed by its full name, ISBN prefix, editorial address, telephone number, toll-free telephone number, and SAN (Standard Address Number). Ordering and/or distributor name and address are listed if they differ from the editorial address. Abbreviations used to identify publishers' imprints are followed by the full name of the imprint. See the example listed below:

Modern Curr, *(Modern Curriculum Pr., Inc.; 0-87895; 0-8136),* Div. of Simon & Schuster, Inc., 13900 Prospect Rd., Cleveland, OH 44136 (SAN 206-6572). Tel 216-238-2222; Toll free: 800-321-3106.

Book entries found in the main indexes of this work which include the term "Pub. by" should be ordered from the distributor, not the publisher. For example, the title listed below should be ordered from Kluwer Academic.

Reichardt, W. Acoustics Dictionary. 1983. lib. bdg. 62.00 (ISBN 90-247-2707-2, Pub. by Martinus Nijhoff Netherlands). Kluwer Academic.

A A Knoll Pubs, *(Knoll, Allen A., Pubs.; 0-9627297),* 777 Silver Spur, Suite 116, Rolling Hills Estates, CA 90274 Tel 310-544-0123; Toll free: 800-777-7623.

A A Raphael, *(Raphael, Antoine A.; 0-9631764),* 2160 E. Tremont Ave., Apt. 6F, Bronx, NY 10462 Tel 718-931-3476.

A Ali Lit Wrks, *(Ali, Alfred, Literary Works;* 0-9636025), P.O. Box 27206, Detroit, MI 48227; 16200 Littlefield St., Detroit, MI 48235 Tel 313-861-9398; Dist. by: Merle Distributing Co., 27222 Plymouth Rd., Detroit, MI 48239 (SAN 169-3778) Tel 313-937-8400; Toll free: 800-233-9380 (orders); Dist. by: BookWorld Distribution Services, Inc., 1933 Whitfield Pk. Loop, Sarasota, FL 34243 (SAN 173-0568) Tel 813-758-8094; Toll free: 800-444-2524 (orders only).

A Armadillo Assocs
See Diggy & Assocs

A B Gilman, *(Gilman, Alma B.; 0-9613914),* 2415 Newton St., Vienna, VA 22181-4053 (SAN 683-2431).

A C Grasmick, *(Grasmick, Alta C.; 0-9621909),* 815 S. Ash St., North Platte, NE 69101 Tel 308-532-9546.

A cappella Bks, *(A cappella Bks.; 1-55652),* Div. of Chicago Review Pr., Inc., 814 N. Franklin, Chicago, IL 60610 Tel 312-337-0747.

A Chalabian, *(Chalabian, Antranig; 0-9622741),* 17264 Melrose, Southfield, MI 48075 Tel 810-569-0676.

A Class Act, *(A Class Act; 0-9620953),* 169 N. Baldwin Ave., Sierra Madre, CA 91024 (SAN 250-2712) Tel 818-355-7802.

A D Bragdon, *(Bragdon, Allen D., Pubs., Inc.; 0-916410),* 252 Great Western Rd., South Yarmouth, MA 02664-2210 (SAN 208-5623) Tel 508-398-4440; Dist. by: Talman Co., 131 Spring St., Suite 201E-N, New York, NY 10012 (SAN 200-5204) Tel 212-431-7175; Toll free: 800-537-8894 (orders only); Dist. by: Antioch Publishing Co. (Munchie Books only), 888 Dayton St., Yellow Springs, OH 45387 (SAN 654-7214) Tel 513-767-7379; Toll free: 800-543-2397.

A E Coords, *(Coords, Arthur E.; 0-9631106),* Box 2392, Lakeland, FL 33806-2392; 1057 S. Florida Ave., Lakeland, FL 33806 Tel 813-858-2626.

A E Ryter
See P Hunt

A G Furman, *(Furman, Alester G., Pub.; 0-9628232),* P.O. Box 2164, Greenville, SC 29602; 301 N. Main St., Daniel Bldg., Greenville, SC 29601 Tel 803-242-1213.

A Givens Sr Collect, *(Givens, Archie, Sr. Collection;* 0-9632976), Univ. of Minnesota Libraries, Special Collections, 309 19th Ave. S., Minneapolis, MN 55455 Tel 612-624-3855.

A J Pub CA, *(A. J. Publisher; 0-9634105),* P.O. Box 404, Clovis, CA 93613 Tel 209-299-3660.

A J S Pubns, *(A.J.S. Pubns., Inc.; 0-931298),* 229 Briar Ct., Island Lake, IL 60042 (SAN 223-5846). Do not confuse with AJS Publishing, Inc. in Los Angeles, CA.

A L Loder, *(Loder, Ann L.; 0-9636643),* 14 Hidden Valley Rd., Lafayette, CA 94549 Tel 510-284-5167.

A M Huntington Art, *(Huntington, Archer M., Art Gallery; 0-935213),* Univ. of Texas at Austin, 23rd & San Jacinto, Austin, TX 78712-1205 (SAN 695-7730) Tel 512-471-7324.

A N Palmer, *(Palmer, A. N., Co., The; 0-914268;* 0-913941), 846 E. Algonquin, Schaumburg, IL 60173 (SAN 202-1374) Tel 312-894-4300; Toll free: 800-323-9563.

A P Walmsley, *(Walmsley, A. P.; 0-9612126),* 19967 Woodside, Harper Woods, MI 48225 (SAN 289-5285) Tel 313-885-8620.

A Petersen, *(Petersen, Arona; 0-9626577),* 2855 W. Commercial Blvd., No. 446, Fort Lauderdale, FL 33309 Tel 305-486-5483.

A Plus Lrn, *(A Plus Learning, Inc.; 0-9624827),* P.O. Box 318, West Groton, MA 01472; 156 Pepperell Rd., West Groton, MA 01472 Tel 508-448-5440.

A R Black, *(Black, Auguste R.; 0-9628010),* 4016 Shelby Ave., SE, Huntsville, AL 35801 Tel 205-534-4006.

A R Colton Fnd, *(Colton, Ann Ree, Foundation of Niscience, Inc.; 0-917187),* P.O. Box 2057, Glendale, CA 91209 (SAN 655-8704); 336 W. Colorado St., Glendale, CA 91204 Tel 818-244-0113; Dist. by: DeVorss & Co., P.O. Box 550, Marina del Rey, CA 90294-0550 (SAN 168-9886) Tel 213-870-7478; Toll free: 800-843-5743 (bookstores only); 800-331-4719 (in California, bookstores only).

A R Downey, *(Downey, Aurelia R.; 0-9641602),* 6204 Springhill Dr., Suite 204, Greenbelt, MD 20770 Tel 301-345-6928.

A R E Pub, *(A.R.E. Publishing, Inc.; 0-86705),* 3945 S. Oneida St., Denver, CO 80237 (SAN 216-6534) Tel 303-363-7779; Toll free: 800-346-7779.

A R Harding Pub, *(Harding, A. R., Publishing Co.;* 0-936622), 2878 E. Main St., Columbus, OH 43209 (SAN 206-4936) Tel 614-231-9585.

A S Bramos, *(Bramos, Ann Stasia; 0-9635333),* 5412 Venable Ave., SE, Charleston, WV 25304 Tel 304-925-6664.

A S Goodman, *(Goodman, Ailene S.; 0-9620704),* 3304 Rittenhouse St., NW, Washington, DC 20015 (SAN 249-5945) Tel 202-686-1722.

A Schiller, *(Schillerhaus; 0-9618682),* P.O. Box 2356, Cottonwood, AZ 86326 (SAN 696-7264) Tel 602-634-2455.

A Schwartz & Co, *(Schwartz, Arthur, & Co., Inc.;* 1-879504), 234 Meads Mountain Rd., Woodstock, NY 12498-1016 (SAN 630-0464) Tel 914-679-4024; Toll free: 800-669-9080 (orders only).

A Sutton Pub, *(Sutton, Alan, Publishing, Inc.; 0-86299;* 0-7509), 1 Washington St., Dover, NH 03820 Tel 603-743-4266. Do not confuse with Alan Sutton, Inc., also in Dover, NH.

A T Weinberg, *(Weinberg, Alyce T.; 0-9604552),* P.O. Box 175, Braddock Heights, MD 21714-0175 (SAN 215-1928) Tel 301-696-3745.

A Todd, *(Todd, Armor; 0-9623537),* 350 Northview Rd., Sedona, AZ 86336-5513 Tel 602-282-7350; Dist. by: Terry Youmans & Assocs., 4581 Founders Ln., Placerville, CA 95667 (SAN 630-3714); Dist. by: Sunbelt Pubns., 8630 Argent St., Suite C, Santee, CA 92071-4172 (SAN 630-0790) Tel 619-258-4911; Toll free: 800-626-6579.

A W Peller
See Educ Impress

A Whitman, *(Whitman, Albert, & Co.; 0-8075),* 6340 Oakton St., Morton Grove, IL 60053 (SAN 201-2049) Tel 708-581-0033; Toll free: 800-255-7675.

AAHPERD, *(American Alliance for Health, Physical Education, Recreation & Dance; 0-88314),* 1900 Association Dr., Reston, VA 22091 (SAN 202-3237) Tel 703-476-3481; Toll free: 800-321-0789; Orders to: AAHPERD, P.O. Box 704, Waldorf, MD 20604 (SAN 243-2641).

A&D Pub, *(A&D Publishing; 0-9637911),* P.O. Box 22, West Jordan, UT 84084-0022; 7308 S. 1975 W., West Jordan, UT 84084 Tel 801-599-9720. Do not confuse with A.D. Publishing in Oakland, CA.

Aaron Lake Pub, *(Aaron Lake Publishing Co.;* 0-9629698), 1818 NE Gary St., East Wenatchee, WA 98802 (SAN 297-4312); 1818 NE Gary St., East Wenatchee, WA 98802 (SAN 297-4304) Tel 509-884-2083.

Abaca Bks, *(Abaca Bks.; 0-933759),* P.O. Box 1028, Normal, IL 61761-5028 (SAN 692-6967) Tel 309-454-7141.

ABBE Pubs Assn, *(ABBE Pubs. Assn. of Washington, D.C.; 0-941864; 0-88164; 1-55914; 0-7883),* 4111 Gallows Rd., Virginia Div., Annandale, VA 22003 (SAN 239-1430); Georgetown 3724, 1215 31st St., NW, Washington, DC 20007 (SAN 668-9450); Dist. by: Ballen Booksellers International, 125 Ricefield Land, Hauppauge, NY 11788 (SAN 169-5207) Tel 516-543-5600; Toll free: 800-645-5237; Dist. by: ADCO International Co., 80-00 Cooper Ave., Bldg. 3, Glendale, NY 11385 (SAN 285-8010); Dist. by: Blackwell North America, 100 University Ct., Blackwood, NJ 08012 (SAN 169-4596) Tel 609-228-8900; Toll free: 800-257-7341; 800-547-6426 (in Oregon); Dist. by: Baker & Taylor Bks., Somerville Service Ctr., 50 Kirby Ave., Somerville, NJ 08876-0734 (SAN 169-4901) Tel 908-722-8000; Toll free: 800-775-1500 (customer service); Dist. by: Academic Bk. Ctr., Inc., 5600 NE Hassalo St., Portland, OR 97213-3640 (SAN 169-7145) Tel 503-287-6657; Dist. by: EBS, Inc. Bk. Service, 290 Broadway, Lynbrook, NY 11563 (SAN 169-5487) Tel 516-593-1195; Dist. by: Blackwell North America, 6024 SW Jean Rd., Bldg. G, Lake Oswego, OR 97034 (SAN 169-7048); Toll free: 800-257-7341; 800-547-6426 (in Oregon); Dist. by: The Book House, Inc., 208 W. Chicago St., Jonesville, MI 49250-0125 (SAN 169-3859) Tel 517-849-2117; Toll free: 800-248-1146; Dist. by: Brodart Co., 500 Arch St., Williamsport, PA 17705 (SAN 169-7684) Tel 717-326-2461; Toll free: 800-233-8467; Dist. by: Fred B. Rothman & Co., 10368 W. Centennial Rd., Littleton, CO 80127 (SAN 159-9437) Tel 303-979-5657; Toll free: 800-457-1986.

Abbeville Pr, *(Abbeville Pr., Inc.; 0-89659; 1-55859;* 0-7892), 488 Madison Ave., New York, NY 10022 (SAN 211-4755) Tel 212-888-1969; Toll free: 800-278-2665.

ABC Child Bks, *(ABC Children's Bks., Inc.; 0-926986),* 1274 49th St., No. 177, Brooklyn, NY 11219 Tel 718-435-3606.

ABC-CLIO, *(ABC-CLIO, Inc.; 0-87436; 1-85109;* 0-903450), P.O. Box 1911, Santa Barbara, CA 93116-1911; Toll free: 800-422-2546; 800-368-6868 (in Canada); 130 Cremona Dr., Santa Barbara, CA 93117 (SAN 301-5467) Tel 805-968-1911.

ABC Pub, *(ABC Publishing; 0-9627412),* P.O. Box 2463, Cheyenne, WY 82003 Tel 307-632-6198.

ABCO Pub, *(ABCO Publishing; 0-9630710),* P.O. Box 798, Puyallup, WA 98371-0072; 345 1/2 Third St., SE, Puyallup, WA 98372 Tel 206-845-1304.

Abdo & Dghtrs, *(Abdo & Daughters; 0-939179; 1-56239),* P.O. Box 36036, Minneapolis, MN 55435 (SAN 662-9164); Toll free: 800-458-8399; 4940 Viking Dr., Edina, MN 55435 (SAN 662-9172) Tel 612-831-1317; Dist. by: Rockbottom Bks., Pentagon Towers, P.O. Box 36036, Minneapolis, MN 55435 (SAN 108-4402) Tel 612-831-1317.

Abel II Pub, *(Abel 2 Publishing Co.; 0-9624398),* P.O. Box 15486, San Diego, CA 92115-0486; 4235 Altadena Ave., No. 4, San Diego, CA 92115 Tel 619-284-3366.

Abigail Pubns, *(Abigail Pubns.; 0-9628148),* 26281 Carrington Blvd., Perrysburg, OH 43551-9546 Tel 419-874-1551.

Abingdon, *(Abingdon Pr.; 0-687),* Div. of United Methodist Publishing Hse., P.O. Box 801, 201 Eighth Ave., S., Nashville, TN 37202-0801 (SAN 201-0054); Toll free: 800-251-3320; 341 Great Cir. Dir., Nashville, TN 37228 (SAN 699-9956) Tel 615-749-6000.

Able Pub
See Acad Innovat

About You, *(About You! Personalized Bks.; 1-879680),* 11419 Mathis Ave., Suite 210, Farmers Branch, TX 75234-9423 Tel 214-265-0918.

ABP Abstracts, *(ABP Abstracts; 0-944992),* Box 815, Whitakers, NC 27891 (SAN 245-9469).

Abrams, *(Abrams, Harry N., Inc.; 0-8109),* Subs. of Times Mirror Co., 100 Fifth Ave., New York, NY 10011 (SAN 200-2434) Tel 212-206-7715; Toll free: 800-345-1359.

Abscond Pubs, *(Abscond Pubs.; 0-944215),* P.O. Box 3112, Florence, AL 35630 (SAN 242-9888) Tel 205-760-0415.

Acad Distrib, *(Academic Distribution Ctr.; 0-9640959),* 1216 Walker Rd., Freeland, MD 21053 Tel 410-343-0409.

Acad Innovat, *(Academic Innovations; 1-878787),* 3463 State St., Suite 219, Santa Barbara, CA 93105 (SAN 297-2883) Tel 805-967-8015; Shipping & Receiving: 20 S. Salsipuedes, Santa Barbara, CA 93103 (SAN 297-2891).

Acad Reading, *(Academy of Reading Pubns.; 0-945856),* 1720 Filbert, Paso Robles, CA 93446 (SAN 247-9915) Tel 805-541-3836; Toll free: 800-233-1819.

Acad Scriptural Knowledge, *(Academy for Scriptural Knowledge; 0-945657),* Div. of Associates for Scriptural Knowledge, P.O. Box 25000, Portland, OR 97225 (SAN 247-4492) Tel 503-292-4352.

Acad Sportfolio, *(Academic Sportfolio, Inc.; 0-924086),* 211 First Ave., Port Jefferson, NY 11777 (SAN 252-1288) Tel 516-331-9355; Toll free: 800-331-9355.

Acad Therapy, *(Academic Therapy Pubns., Inc.; 0-87879; 1-57128),* 20 Commercial Blvd., Novato, CA 94949-6191 (SAN 201-2111) Tel 415-883-3314; Toll free: 800-422-7249. *Imprints:* Ann Arbor Div (Ann Arbor Division).

Academic Packs Co
See Academic Parks Co

Academic Parks Co, *(Academic Parks Co.; 0-9619655),* 5700 Lincoln Ave., Lanham, MD 20706 (SAN 245-9523) Tel 301-794-6031.

Academy Bks, *(Academy Bks.; 0-914960; 1-56715),* P.O. Box 757, Rutland, VT 05701-0757 (SAN 208-4325); 10 Cleveland Ave., Rutland, VT 05701 Tel 802-773-9194.

Academy Chi Pubs, *(Academy Chicago Pubs., Ltd.; 0-915864; 0-89733),* 363 W. Erie St., Chicago, IL 60610-3125 (SAN 213-2001) Tel 312-751-7300; Toll free: 800-248-7323 (Orders, outside Illinois).

Acadia Pub Co, *(Acadia Publishing Co.; 0-934745),* Div. of World Three, Inc., P.O. Box 170, Bar Harbor, ME 04609 (SAN 694-1648) Tel 207-288-9025.

Accel Devel, *(Accelerated Development; 0-915202;* 1-55959), Div. of Taylor & Francis, Inc., 3808 W. Kilgore Ave., Muncie, IN 47304-4896 (SAN 210-3346) Tel 317-284-7511; Toll free: 800-222-1166.

Accent Bks
See Accent CO

Accent CO, *(Accent Pubns.; 0-916406; 0-89636),* P.O. Box 36640, 7125 Disc Dr., Colorado Springs, CO 80936 (SAN 208-5097). Do not confuse with Accent Publishing in Sparta, NJ & Accent Pubns. in Scituate, MA.

Accord Comm, *(Accord Communications, Ltd.;* 0-945265), 18002 15th NE, Suite B, Seattle, WA 98155 (SAN 246-1935) Tel 206-368-8157.

Ace Bks, *(Ace Bks.; 0-441),* Div. of Berkley Publishing Group, 200 Madison Ave., New York, NY 10016 (SAN 665-6404) Tel 212-951-8800; Orders to: Berkley Publishing Group, P.O. Box 506, East Rutherford, NJ 07073; Toll free: 800-223-0510 (orders); Dist. by: Warner Publishing Services, 1271 Avenue of the Americas, New York, NY 10020 (SAN 200-5522) Tel 212-522-8900.

ACE Pub, *(ACE Publishing; 1-880770),* Div. of ACE International Services, Inc., Pacific Lutheran Univ., Tacoma, WA 98447 Tel 206-535-7326.

Ace Pub Prodns, *(Ace Publishing/Productions;* 0-9629317), 10335 Branigan Way, P.O. Box 70087, Riverside, CA 92505 Tel 909-351-0436.

ACEI, *(Association for Childhood Education International; 0-87173),* 11501 Georgia Ave., No. 315, Wheaton, MD 20902-1924 (SAN 201-2200) Tel 301-942-2443; Toll free: 800-423-3563.

Acequia Madre, *(Acequia Madre; 0-940875),* Box 6, El Valle Rte., Chamisal, NM 87521 (SAN 664-7871).

ACETO Bookmen, *(ACETO Bookmen; 0-9607906;* 1-878545), 5721 Antietam Dr., Sarasota, FL 34231 (SAN 237-9252) Tel 813-924-9170.

ACI Pubng, *(ACI Publishing; 1-884414),* Div. of Alpha Communications, Inc., P.O. Box 40398, Eugene, OR 97404-0064 (SAN 298-0657); 84 Green Ln., Eugene, OR 97404-2440 Tel 503-689-2154; Dist. by: Quality Bks., Inc., 918 Sherwood Dr., Lake Bluff, IL 60044-2204 (SAN 169-2127) Tel 708-295-2010; Toll free: 800-323-4241 (libraries only); Dist. by: Baker & Taylor Bks., Somerville Service Ctr., 50 Kirby Ave., Somerville, NJ 08876-0734 (SAN 169-4901) Tel 908-722-8000; Toll free: 800-775-1500 (customer service); Dist. by: Baker & Taylor Bks., Momence Service Ctr., 501 S. Gladiolus St., Momence, IL 60954-1799 (SAN 169-2100) Tel 815-472-2444; Toll free: 800-775-2300 (customer service); Dist. by: Baker & Taylor Bks., Commerce Service Ctr., 251 Mt. Olive Church Rd., Commerce, GA 30599-9988 (SAN 169-1503) Tel 706-335-5000; Toll free: 800-775-1200 (customer service); Dist. by: Baker & Taylor Bks., Reno Service Ctr., 380 Edison Way, Reno, NV 89564-0099 (SAN 169-4464) Tel 702-858-6700; Toll free: 800-775-1700 (customer service); Dist. by: Baker & Taylor Bks., Franklin Service Ctr., 2 Cottontail Ln., Somerset, NJ 08873-1133 (SAN 630-7205) Tel 908-469-7404; Dist. by: Pacific Pipeline, Inc., 8030 S. 228th St., Kent, WA 98032-3898 (SAN 208-2128) Tel 206-872-5523; Toll free: 800-444-7323 (customer service); 800-677-2222 (orders); Dist. by: Unique Bks., 4230 Grove Ave., Gurnee, IL 60031 (SAN 630-0472) Tel 708-623-9171; Dist. by: The Distributors, 702 S. Michigan, South Bend, IN 46601 (SAN 169-2488) Tel 219-232-8500; Toll free: 800-348-5200 (except Indiana); Dist. by: Inland Bk. Co., 140 Commerce St., East Haven, CT 06512 (SAN 630-0472) Tel 203-467-4257; Toll free: 800-243-0138.

Acid Rain Found, *(Acid Rain Foundation, Inc., The;* 0-935577), 1410 Varsity Rd., Raleigh, NC 27606-2010 (SAN 695-9946).

Acorn Pub MN, *(Acorn Publishing; 0-938399),* 15150 Scenic Heights Rd., Eden Prairie, MN 55344 (SAN 659-6738) Tel 612-934-4432; Toll free: 800-800-8348; Orders to: P.O. Box 44153, Eden Prairie, MN 55344 (SAN 665-9268). Do not confuse with companies with the same name in Waverly, NY, Salt Lake City, UT.

Acorn Pub UT, *(Acorn Publishing; 1-883736),* Div. of Oak Enterprises, Inc., 250 W. 2855 S., Salt Lake City, UT 84115 (SAN 630-9224) Tel 801-485-2424. Do not confuse with companies with the same name in Eden Prairie, MN, Waverly, NY.

Acropolis, *(Acropolis Bks.; 0-87491),* 2311 Calvert St. NW, No. 300, Washington, DC 20008-2644 (SAN 201-2227); Toll free: 800-451-7771.

Across the Road, *(Across the Road Publishing Co.;* 0-9629949), P.O. Box 740293, Houston, TX 77274; 9450 Woodfair, No. 1405, Houston, TX 77274 Tel 713-779-8429.

Active Parenting, *(Active Parenting Pubs.; 0-9618020;* 1-880283), 810 Franklin Ct., Suite B, Marietta, GA 30067-9085 (SAN 666-301X); Toll free: 800-825-0060.

Activities Learning, *(Activities for Learning; 0-9609636),* 21161 York Rd., Hutchinson, MN 55350 (SAN 283-2445) Tel 612-587-9146.

Activity Resources, *(Activity Resources Co., Inc.; 0-918932; 1-882293),* P.O. Box 4875, 20655 Hathaway Ave., Hayward, CA 94541 (SAN 209-0201) Tel 510-782-1300; Dist. by: Cuisenaire Co. of America, Inc., P.O. Box 5026, White Plains, NY 10602-5026 (SAN 201-7806) Tel 914-997-2600; Toll free: 800-237-3142; Dist. by: Dale Seymour Pubns., 200 Middlefield Rd., Menlo Park, CA 94025 (SAN 200-9781) Tel 415-688-0880; Toll free: 800-872-1100; Dist. by: Delta Education, Inc., 5 Hudson Park Dr., Hudson, NH 03051 (SAN 630-1711) Tel 603-889-8899; Dist. by: Scott Resources, Inc., P.O. Box 2121, Fort Collins, CO 80522 (SAN 222-3902) Tel 303-484-7445; Toll free: 800-289-9299.

Ad-Lib
See Open Horizons

Adage Pubns, *(Adage Pubns.; 1-879889),* P.O. Box 2377, Coeur d'Alene, ID 83816-2377 Tel 208-762-3177; Toll free: 800-745-3170; 3500 English Point Rd., Lake Hayden, ID 83835 Tel 208-762-3177.

Adam Pub Co, *(Adam Publishing Co.; 0-9614209),* Subs. of Adam Art Assocs., 412 Lyncrest Rd., Reading, PA 19607-1302 (SAN 686-9378) Tel 215-775-2739; Dist. by: Berkshire News, Inc., Third Ave. & Cherry St., West Reading, PA 19602 (SAN 169-7668) Tel 215-376-2851; Toll free: 800-223-0510. Do not confuse with Adam Publishing in Fullerton, CA.

Adama Pubs Inc
See Modan-Adama Bks

Adams Inc MA, *(Adams, Bob, Inc.; 0-937860; 1-55850),* 260 Center St., Holbrook, MA 02343-1074 (SAN 215-2886) Tel 617-767-8100; Toll free: 800-872-5627.

ADAPT Pub Co, *(A.D.A.P.T. Publishing Co., Inc.;* 1-877709), 8830 Business Pk. Drive, No. 103, Austin, TX 78759 Tel 512-794-8447; 8900 Business Pk. Dr., No. 103, Austin, TX 78759 Tel 512-794-8447; Toll free: 800-333-8429.

Addison-Wesley, *(Addison-Wesley Publishing Co., Inc.;* 0-201), 1 Jacob Way, Reading, MA 01867 (SAN 200-2000) Tel 617-944-3700; Toll free: 800-447-2226. *Imprints:* Journal Pubns (Journal Publications).

Additions Pr, *(Additions Pr.; 0-9623940),* 10680 S. De Anza Blvd., No. C, Cupertino, CA 95014-4446 Tel 408-446-4400; Orders to: Publishers Services, P.O. Box 2510, Novato, CA 94948 (SAN 201-3037) Tel 415-883-3530.

Adelekan Pub Co, *(Adelekan Publishing Co.; 978-30056;* 0-9620036), P.O. Box 22106, Sacramento, CA 95822 (SAN 247-1809); 1131 26th Ave., Sacramento, CA 95822 (SAN 247-1817) Tel 916-446-1777.

ADK Mtn Club, *(Adirondack Mountain Club, Inc.;* 0-935272), R.R. 3, Box 3055, Lake George, NY 12845-9522 (SAN 204-7691) Tel 518-668-4447; Toll free: 800-395-8080 (orders only).

ADL, *(Anti-Defamation League of B'nai B'rith; 0-88464),* 823 United Nations Plaza, New York, NY 10017 (SAN 204-7616) Tel 212-490-2525.

Adm Nimitz Foun, *(Admiral Nimitz Foundation;* 0-934841), P.O. Box 777, Fredericksburg, TX 78624 (SAN 201-1883); 340 E. Main, Fredericksburg, TX 78624 (SAN 661-9312) Tel 210-997-4379.

Adon Bks, *(Adon Bks.; 0-9622942),* 7 Donington Dr., Greenville, SC 29615 Tel 803-268-3236.

Adona Pub, *(Adona Publishing; 0-9622364),* 11978 Woodside Ave., Lakeside, CA 92040 Tel 619-561-1787.

Adonis Pr, *(Adonis Pr.; 0-932776),* Orders to: Christy Barnes, R.D. Box 315, Hillsdale, NY 12529 (SAN 661-9320) Tel 518-325-7182.

Adonis Studio, *(Adonis Studio; 0-914827),* P.O. Box 6626, Cleveland, OH 44101 (SAN 289-0461) Tel 216-226-1058.

Adopt Support
See Adoption Advocate

Adoption Advocate, *(Adoption Advocate Publishing Co.;* 0-9635717), 140 David Rd., Franklin, MA 02038 Tel 508-875-6603.

AdRem, *(AdRem, Inc.; 1-879789),* P.O. Box 2404, Bala Cynwyd, PA 19004; 152 Upland Terr., Bala Cynwyd, PA 19004 Tel 610-667-2008.

Advan Learning, *(Advanced Learning Products;* 0-916881), 10615 Cullman Ave., Whittier, CA 90603 (SAN 654-519X) Tel 310-947-8138.

Advance Cal Tech, *(Advance Cal Tech, Inc.; 0-943759),* 210 Clary Ave., San Gabriel, CA 91776-1375 (SAN 242-2603).

Advance Pubs, *(Advance Pubs., Inc.; 0-9619525;* 1-885222), 1164 Solana Ave., Winter Park, FL 32789 (SAN 244-9226) Tel 407-629-1950; Toll free: 800-777-2041.

Advant Intl, *(Advantage International, Inc.; 1-56756),* 14546 Bruce B. Downs Blvd., Tampa, FL 33613 (SAN 297-7133) Tel 813-977-5739; Toll free: 800-837-8636.

Advantage-Aurora, *(Advantage/Aurora Pubns.; 0-9624828),* P.O. Box 881, Cambridge, MA 02142; 388 Cambridge St., Winchester, MA 01890 Tel 617-721-1064.

Advantage Video, *(Advantage Video; 0-9622594),* P.O. Box 6462, Omaha, NE 68106; Toll free: 800-776-8585; 5623 Pierce, Omaha, NE 68106 Tel 402-330-8211. Do not confuse with Advantage Video, Costa Mesa, CA.

Advent Christ Gen Conf, *(Advent Christian General Conference; 1-881909),* P.O. Box 23152, Charlotte, NC 28212; Toll free: 800-676-0694; 14601 Albemarle Rd., Charlotte, NC 28227 Tel 704-545-6161.

Advent II
See Advent Times

Advent Mean Pr, *(Adventures Meaning Pr.; 1-881663),* Div. of Fairfield Communications, Inc., 5620 S. 49th St., Lincoln, NE 68516 Tel 402-421-2591; Toll free: 800-755-0024.

Advent Times, *(Advent Times, Inc.; 0-9627415),* P.O. Box 9065, Springfield, IL 62791; 97 Andover Dr., Springfield, IL 62704 Tel 217-698-9548.

Adventure Pr, *(Adventure Pr.; 0-940589),* 3160 College Ave., No. 204, Berkeley, CA 94705-2712 (SAN 664-9904) Tel 510-849-9415. Do not confuse with Adventure Pr., also in Berkeley, CA & Seattle, WA.

Adventure Prods, *(Adventure Productions, Inc.; 0-9614904),* 3404 Terry Lake Rd., Fort Collins, CO 80524 (SAN 693-3955) Tel 303-493-8776.

Adventure VA, *(Adventure Publishing; 0-9620606),* 1510 White Oak Ct., Martinsville, VA 24112 (SAN 249-1788) Tel 703-638-8979. Do not confuse with companies with the same name in Brooklyn, NY, San Antonio, TX.

Advocacy Pr, *(Advocacy Pr.; 0-911655),* Div. of Girls, Inc. of Greater Santa Barbara, P.O. Box 236, Santa Barbara, CA 93102 (SAN 263-9114) Tel 805-962-2728; Dist. by: Ingram Bk. Co., 1 Ingram Blvd., La Vergne, TN 37086-1986 (SAN 169-7978) Tel 615-793-5000; Toll free: 800-937-8000 (orders only, all warehouses); Dist. by: Bookpeople, 7900 Edgewater Dr., Oakland, CA 94621 (SAN 168-9517) Tel 510-632-4700; Toll free: 800-999-4650; Dist. by: Pacific Pipeline, Inc., 8030 S. 228th St., Kent, WA 98032-2900 (SAN 208-2128) Tel 206-872-5523; Toll free: 800-444-7323 (Customer Service); 800-677-2222 (orders); Dist. by: Inland Bk. Co., 140 Commerce St., East Haven, CT 06512 (SAN 200-4151) Tel 203-467-4257; Toll free: 800-243-0138; Dist. by: Baker & Taylor Bks., Somerville Service Ctr., 50 Kirby Ave., Somerville, NJ 08876-0734 (SAN 169-4901) Tel 908-722-8000; Toll free: 800-775-1500 (customer service); Dist. by: Baker & Taylor Bks., Momence Service Ctr., 501 S. Gladiolus St., Momence, IL 60954-2444 (SAN 169-2100) Tel 815-472-2444; Toll free: 800-775-2300 (customer service); Dist. by: Baker & Taylor Bks., Commerce Service Ctr., 251 Mt. Olive Church Rd., Commerce, GA 30599-9988 (SAN 169-1503) Tel 706-335-5000; Toll free: 800-775-1200 (customer service); Dist. by: Baker & Taylor Bks., Reno Service Ctr., 380 Edison Way, Reno, NV 89564 (SAN 169-4464) Tel 702-858-6700; Toll free: 800-775-1700 (customer service); Dist. by: Wieser Educational, Inc., 30085 Comercio, Santa Margarita, CA 92688 (SAN 630-7361) Tel 714-858-4920.

Aegean Park Pr, *(Aegean Park Pr.; 0-89412),* P.O. Box 2837, Laguna Hills, CA 92654-0837 (SAN 210-0231) Tel 714-586-8811; Toll free: 800-736-3587.

Aegina Pr, *(Aegina Pr., Inc.; 0-916383; 1-56002),* 1905 Madison Ave., Huntington, WV 25704 (SAN 665-469X) Tel 304-429-7204. *Imprints:* Univ Edtns (University Editions).

Aeolus Bks, *(Aeolus Bks.; 0-9621448),* P.O. Box 3, Irvington, VA 22480 (SAN 251-3870); Edgewood Ln., Irvington, VA 22480 (SAN 251-3889) Tel 804-438-5602.

AEON-Hierophant, *(AEON-Hierophant Communications, Inc.; 0-9606110; 1-880830),* P.O. Box 7276, Seattle, WA 98133 (SAN 216-7816) Tel 206-672-8222.

Aerial Photo, *(Aerial Photography Services, Inc.; 0-936672; 1-880970),* 2511 S. Tryon St., Charlotte, NC 28203 (SAN 214-2791) Tel 704-333-5143.

Aero Products, *(Aero Products Research, Inc.; 0-912682),* 11201 Hindry Ave., Los Angeles, CA 90045 (SAN 205-5996) Tel 310-641-7242.

Aerodrome Pr, *(Aerodrome Pr.; 0-935092),* P.O. Box 44, Story City, IA 50248 (SAN 213-4519) Tel 515-733-2589.

AESOP Enter, *(AESOP Enterprises, Inc.; 1-880771),* 5679 Colonist Cir., Indianapolis, IN 46254 Tel 317-297-2428.

Aesop Systs, *(Aesop Systems; 0-9630734),* P.O. Box 2006, Covington, LA 70434; 75375 River Rd., Covington, LA 70433 Tel 504-892-0195.

AFCOM Pub, *(AFCOM Publishing; 0-939339),* P.O. Box H, Harbor City, CA 90710-0330 (SAN 662-4685) Tel 310-544-2314.

Africa World, *(Africa World Pr.; 0-86543),* 11 Princess Rd., Suites D, E & F, Lawrenceville, NJ 08648 (SAN 692-3925) Tel 609-844-9583; Dist. by: InBook, P.O. Box 120261, East Haven, CT 06512 (SAN 630-5547) Tel 203-467-4257; Toll free: 800-253-3605 (orders only).

African Am Imag, *(African American Images; 0-913543),* 1909 W. 95th St., Chicago, IL 60643 (SAN 201-2332) Tel 312-445-0322.

African Islam Miss Pubns, *(African Islamic Mission Pubns.; 0-916157; 1-56505),* Subs. of A.I.M. Graphics, 1390 Bedford Ave., Brooklyn, NY 11216 (SAN 294-6645) Tel 718-638-4588.

Afro-Am, *(Afro-Am Publishing Co., Inc.; 0-910030),* Div. of Afro-Am, Inc., 1909 W. 95th St., Chicago, IL 60643-1105 (SAN 201-2332) Tel 312-791-1611.

Afsaneh Pub, *(Afsaneh Publishing Co.; 1-877789),* 3449 Three Springs Dr., Westlake Village, CA 91361 Tel 818-991-4151.

AFUA Ent, *(AFUA Enterprises, Inc.; 0-918088),* P.O. Box 9026, General Lafayette Sta., Jersey City, NJ 07304 (SAN 210-1599) Tel 201-451-0599.

Agatha Pub Co, *(Agatha Publishing Co.; 0-9620893),* 83 Michael Rd., Stamford, CT 06903 (SAN 250-2526) Tel 203-329-1790.

Agee Pub, *(Agee Pubs., Inc.; 0-935265),* 454 Milledge Heights, Athens, GA 30606 (SAN 696-7035) Tel 706-548-5269.

Agency Instr Tech, *(Agency for Instructional Technology; 0-9603244; 0-941449; 0-7842),* 1111 W. 17th St., Box A, Bloomington, IN 47402 (SAN 668-954X) Tel 812-339-2203; Toll free: 800-457-4509.

AHD & Ref *Imprint of* **HM**

Aid-U Pub, *(Aid-U Publishing Co.; 0-940370),* 34132 W 13 Mile Rd., Farmington, MI 48311 (SAN 217-149X) Tel 810-788-2175.

Aiello Grp, *(Aiello Group; 1-883702),* 605 W. Eleven Mile Rd., Royal Oak, MI 48067 Tel 810-542-4314.

Aiki Works, *(Aiki Works, Inc.; 1-877803),* P.O. Box 251, Victor, NY 14564; 538 Wintergreen Gr, Victor, NY 14564 Tel 716-924-7302.

AIL Pub, *(AIL Publishing Co., Inc.; 1-56650),* 71 Lakeshore Dr., Sumter, SC 29150 Tel 803-481-4054.

AIMS Educ Fnd, *(AIMS Education Foundation; 1-881431),* Orders to: P.O. Box 8120, Fresno, CA 93747-8120 Tel 209-255-4094.

AIMS Intl, *(AIMS International Bks., Inc.; 0-922852),* 7709 Hamilton Ave., Cincinnati, OH 45231-3103 (SAN 630-270X) Tel 513-521-5590.

Ainslies, *(Ainslie's; 0-9618445),* 1735 E. Bayshore, Suite 30A, Redwood City, CA 94063 (SAN 667-9730) Tel 415-368-9865 (SAN 667-9749).

AIR Burbank, *(Aeronautic Instructional Resources; 0-929995),* Subs. of Paper Airplanes International, 433 Nihoa St., Kahului, HI 96732 (SAN 251-1215) Tel 808-244-4667.

Airbrush Act, *(Airbrush Action, Inc.; 0-9637336),* 1985 Swarthmore Ave., P.O. Box 2052, Lakewood, NJ 08701 Tel 908-364-2111; Toll free: 800-876-2472.

AIRE
See A R E Pub

Airmont, *(Airmont Publishing Co., Inc.; 0-8049),* 401 Lafayette St., New York, NY 10003 (SAN 206-8710) Tel 212-598-0222; Toll free: 800-223-5251 (outside New York).

Ajuna Unlimited, *(Ajuna Unlimited; 0-9626254),* P.O. Box 12454, Palm Oesert, CA 92255 Tel 619-320-3788.

Akiba Pr, *(Akiba Pr.; 0-934764),* Box 13086, Oakland, CA 94661 (SAN 212-0666) Tel 510-339-1283.

Al-Anon, *(Al-Anon Family Group Headquarters; 0-910034),* 1372 Broadway, 7th Flr., New York, NY 10018-6106 (SAN 201-2391) Tel 212-302-7240; P.O. Box 862 Midtown Sta., New York, NY 10018-0862 (SAN 662-7110).

Al Fresco, *(Al Fresco Enterprise; 0-9612596),* 1200 Liberty Ln., Pueblo, CO 81001 (SAN 211-5832) Tel 719-545-9524.

Al-Saadawi Pubns, *(Al-Saadawi Pubns.; 1-881963),* P.O. Box 4059, Alexandria, VA 22303 (SAN 298-1637); 2104 Farrington Ave., Alexandria, VA 22303 Tel 703-329-6333.

Alaca, *(Alaca Co.; 0-9641484),* P.O. Box 55, Tranquillity, CA 93668; 4308 S. James Rd., Tranquillity, CA 93668 Tel 209-698-5157.

Alacran Pr Inc, *(Alacran Pr., Inc.; 0-9621380),* 16308 Relindo Ct., Rancho Bernardo, CA 92128 (SAN 251-1320) Tel 619-673-9176.

Aladdin *Imprint of* **Macmillan Child Grp**

Aladdin Pub, *(Aladdin Publishing; 0-944677),* P.O. Box 364, Palmer, AK 99645 (SAN 245-1840); 650 N. Second, Palmer, AK 99645 (SAN 245-1859) Tel 907-892-7638; Dist. by: Alaska News Agency, Inc., Bk. Dept., 325 W. Potter Dr., Anchorage, AK 99502 (SAN 168-9274) Tel 907-563-3251; Dist. by: Fairbanks News Agency, 307 Ladd Ave., Fairbanks, AK 99701 (SAN 168-9282) Tel 907-456-5355.

Alaken, *(Alaken, Inc.; 1-880293),* 305 Magnolia St., Suite 196, Fort Collins, CO 80521 Tel 303-223-5348.

Alaska Comics, *(Alaska Comics; 1-882724),* 316 Price St., Anchorage, AK 99508 Tel 907-279-4913.

Alaska Hist, *(Alaska Historical Commission; 0-943712),* Div. of State of Alaska, P.O. Box 107001, Anchorage, AK 99510-7001 (SAN 240-9933) Tel 907-762-2622; Dist. by: Alaska Historical Soc., Box 100299, Anchorage, AK 99510 (SAN 630-1533) Tel 907-276-1596. Do not confuse with Alaska Historical Society, which operates separately from the commission, but distributes for it.

Alaska Northwest, *(Alaska Northwest Bks.; 0-88240),* 2208 NW Market St., Suite 300, Seattle, WA 98107 (SAN 201-2383) Tel 206-784-5071; Dist. by: Graphic Arts Ctr. Publishing Co., P.O. Box 10306, Portland, OR 97210 (SAN 201-6338) Tel 503-226-2402; Toll free: 800-452-3032.

Alaskan Viewpoint, *(Alaskan Viewpoint; 0-924663),* HCR 64, Box 453, Seward, AK 99664 (SAN 251-4095); Mile 19.5 Seward Hwy., Seward, AK 99664 Tel 907-288-3168.

Alba, *(Alba Hse.; 0-8189),* Div. of Society of St. Paul, 2187 Victory Blvd., Staten Island, NY 10314 (SAN 201-2405) Tel 718-698-2759; Toll free: 800-343-2522.

Alchemy Comms, *(Alchemy Communications Group, Ltd.; 0-934323),* Div. of Alchemy II, Inc., 9311 Eton Ave., Chatsworth, CA 91311 (SAN 693-5990) Tel 818-700-8300; Dist. by: Playskool, Inc., 200 Narragansett Pk. Dr., Pawtucket, RI 02862 (SAN 630-7264).

Ale Pub, *(Ale Publishing Co.; 1-881301),* P.O. Box 2270, Vashon, WA 98070-2470 Tel 206-463-6888.

Alef Design, *(Alef Design Group; 1-881283),* 4423 Fruitland Ave., Los Angeles, CA 90058 Tel 213-582-1200.

Alegator Bks, *(Alegator Bks.; 0-9626882),* Div. of ALG & Assocs., Inc., 16111 Plummer, P.O. Box 56, Sepulveda, CA 91343 Tel 818-895-8365.

Alegra Hse Pubs, *(Alegra Hse. Pubs.; 0-933879),* Affil. of Kaya Bks., P.O. Box 1443B, Warren, OH 44482 (SAN 692-7858) Tel 216-372-2951; Dist. by: Bookpeople, 7900 Edgewater Dr., Oakland, CA 94621 (SAN 168-9517) Tel 510-632-4700; Toll free: 800-999-4650; Dist. by: The Distributors, 702 S. Michigan, South Bend, IN 46601 (SAN 169-2488) Tel 219-232-8500; Toll free: 800-348-5200 (except Indiana); Dist. by: Baker & Taylor Bks., Momence Service Ctr., 501 S. Gladiolus St., Momence, IL 60954-2444 (SAN 169-2100) Tel 815-472-2444; Toll free: 800-775-2300 (customer service); Dist. by: Pacific Pipeline, Inc., 8030 S. 228th St., Kent, WA 98032-2900 (SAN 208-2128) Tel 206-872-5523; Toll free: 800-444-7323 (Customer Service); 800-677-2222 (orders); Dist. by: Quality Bks., Inc., 918 Sherwood Dr., Lake Bluff, IL 60044-2204 (SAN 169-2127) Tel 708-295-2010; Toll free: 800-323-4241 (libraries only); Dist. by: Baker & Taylor Bks., Commerce Service Ctr., 251 Mt. Olive Church Rd., Commerce, GA 30599-9988 (SAN 169-1503) Tel 706-335-5000; Toll free: 800-775-1200 (customer service); Dist. by: Baker & Taylor Bks., Somerville Service Ctr., 50 Kirby Ave., Somerville, NJ 08876-0734 (SAN 169-4901) Tel 908-722-8000; Toll free: 800-775-1500 (customer service); Dist. by: Baker & Taylor Bks., Reno Service Ctr., 380 Edison Way, Reno, NV 89564 (SAN 169-4464) Tel 702-858-6700; Toll free: 800-775-1700 (customer service).

Alemany Pr, *(Alemany Pr., Inc.; 0-88084),* Div. of Prentice Hall Regents, Sylvan Ave., Rte. 9W, PHR Bldg., PHR Dept., Englewood Cliffs, NJ 07632 (SAN 240-1312); Toll free: 800-227-2375.

Alexander Art, *(Alexander Art L.P.; 1-883576),* 4740 Ridge Dr., NE, Salem, OR 97303 Tel 503-393-7320; Toll free: 800-547-8747.

Alexander Graham, *(Bell, Alexander Graham, Assn. for the Deaf; 0-88200),* 3417 Volta Pl., NW, Washington, DC 20007 (SAN 203-6924) Tel 202-337-5220.

Alfred Pub, *(Alfred Publishing Co., Inc.; 0-88284),* 16380 Roscoe Blvd., Suite 200, Box 10003, Van Nuys, CA 91406-1215 (SAN 201-243X) Tel 818-891-5999; Toll free: 800-292-6122.

Algonquin Bks, *(Algonquin Bks. of Chapel Hill; 0-912697; 0-945575; 1-56512),* Div. of Workman Publishing Co., Inc., P.O. Box 2225, Chapel Hill, NC 27515 (SAN 282-7506); 307 W. Weaver St., Carrboro, NC 27510 (SAN 662-2011) Tel 919-967-0108; Dist. by: Workman Publishing Co., Inc., 708 Broadway, New York, NY 10003 (SAN 203-2821) Tel 212-254-5900; Toll free: 800-722-7202.

Alice Pub, *(Alice Publishing; 0-9636775),* P.O. Box 257, Granite Falls, NC 28630; Cross St., Granite Falls, NC 28630 Tel 704-396-7094; Dist. by: Quality Bks., Inc., 918 Sherwood Dr., Lake Bluff, IL 60044-2204 (SAN 169-2127) Tel 708-295-2010; Toll free: 800-323-4241 (libraries only); Dist. by: Baker & Taylor Bks., Somerville Service Ctr., 50 Kirby Ave., Somerville, NJ 08876-0734 (SAN 169-4901) Tel 908-722-8000; Toll free: 800-775-1500 (customer service); Dist. by: Baker & Taylor Bks., Momence Service Ctr., 501 S. Gladiolus St., Momence, IL 60954-2444 (SAN 169-2100) Tel 815-472-2444; Toll free: 800-775-2300 (customer service); Dist. by: Baker & Taylor Bks., Commerce Service Ctr., 251 Mt. Olive Church Rd., Commerce, GA 30599-9988 (SAN 169-1503) Tel 706-335-5000; Toll free: 800-775-1200 (customer service); Dist. by: Baker & Taylor Bks., Reno Service Ctr., 380 Edison Way, Reno, NV 89564 (SAN 169-4464) Tel 702-858-6700; Toll free: 800-775-1700 (customer service); Dist. by: The Distributors, 702 S. Michigan, South Bend, IN 46601 (SAN 169-2488) Tel 219-232-8500; Toll free: 800-348-5200 (except Indiana).

Alien Bks, *(Alien Bks.; 0-9622190),* 1535 Kearsley Park Blvd., Flint, MI 48506 Tel 810-767-7417.

All About Us, *(All About Us Bks., USA; 0-919970),* 443 Adams St., Eugene, OR 97402 Tel 503-345-5665. Canadian address: R.R. 3, Yellow Point Rd., Ladysmith, B.C. VOR 2EO, CN.

All Ireland Inc, *(All-Ireland Heritage, Inc.; 0-9621544),* Div. of D. R. H. Assocs., Pubs., Inc., P.O. Box 7, Dunn Loring, VA 22027 (SAN 251-5946); 2255 Cedar Ln., Vienna, VA 22180 (SAN 251-5954) Tel 703-560-4496.

All Media Prods, *(All Media Productions; 1-882205),* 1708 Baldwin Ave., Jenison, MI 49428 Tel 616-459-9703; Toll free: 800-800-4354.

All Things Pr, *(All Things Pr.; 0-913632),* 2905 Lake Shore Dr., No. 208, Waco, TX 76708 (SAN 202-4772) Tel 817-757-2357.

ALL Ventura Pub, *(ALL Ventura Publishing Services;* 0-9626133), P.O. Box 5190, Pacific Grove, CA 93950; 71 Glen Lake Dr., Pacific Grove, CA 93950 Tel 408-375-1876.

Allen Pubng, *(Allen Publishing; 1-884559),* 21851 Newland, No. 51, Huntington Beach, CA 92646 Tel 714-536-8787.

Alleycat, *(Alleycat; 1-882241),* 2911 Rhodelia Ave., Claremont, CA 91711 Tel 909-626-7871.

Alleyside *Imprint of* **Highsmith Pr**

Allied Crafts, *(Allied Crafts Pr.; 0-9632305),* 726 Bison Ave., Newport Beach, CA 92660 Tel 714-759-8156.

Allied Ent, *(Allied Enterprises; 0-9605082),* P.O. Box 8050, Chicago, IL 60680 (SAN 238-9045) Tel 312-836-0421.

Allied Publishers, *(Allied Pubs.; 1-885392),* P.O. Box 1172, Silver Spring, MD 20910; 11624 Lockwood Dr., Suite 103, Silver Spring, MD 20904 Tel 301-593-8518.

Allyn, *(Allyn & Bacon, Inc.; 0-205),* Div. of Paramount Publishing, 160 Gould St., Needham Heights, MA 02194-2310 (SAN 201-2510) Tel 617-455-1200; Orders to: Paramount Publishing (orders for College & Longwood Divs.), 200 Old Tappan Rd., Old Tappan, NJ 07675 (SAN 200-2442) Tel 201-767-5937; Toll free: 800-223-1360; Orders to: Allyn & Bacon (Individual purchases), 111 Tenth St., Des Moines, IA 50309 Tel 515-284-6751; Toll free: 800-666-9433.

Almar, *(Almar Pr.; 0-930256),* 4105 Marietta Dr., Vestal, NY 13850-4032 (SAN 210-5713) Tel 607-722-6251.

Alpen & Jeffries, *(Alpen & Jeffries Pubs.; 1-879692),* 110 Brighton Way, Clayton, MO 63105-3602 Tel 314-863-0529.

Alpenhorn Pr, *(Alpenhorn Pr.; 1-879056),* Box 1635, Uniontown, PA 15401; 128 Roberta Dr., Uniontown, PA 15401 Tel 412-438-0992.

Alpha Beto Music, *(Alpha-Beto Music; 0-9616528),* 152 Sabine, Portland, TX 78374 (SAN 659-4107) Tel 512-643-6309.

Alpha Bible Pubns, *(Alpha Bible Pubns.; 1-877917),* P.O. Box 155, Hood River, OR 97031; 3610 Airport Dr., Hood River, OR 97031 Tel 503-386-6382; Dist. by: Pentecostal Publishing Hse., 8855 Dunn Rd., Hazelwood, MO 63042-2299 (SAN 219-3817) Tel 314-837-7300.

Alpha Bk Pr, *(Alpha Bk. Pr.; 0-9632202),* P.O. Box 835, Denver, CO 80201; 13B Nome Way, Aurora, CO 80012 Tel 303-367-1185.

Alpha Bks IN, *(Alpha Bks.; 1-56761),* Div. of Macmillan Computer Publishing, 201 W. 103rd, Indianapolis, IN 46290 Tel 317-581-3715. Do not confuse with companies with the same name in Rickreall, OR, Falls Church, VA.

Alpha-Dolphin, *(Alpha-Dolphin Pr.; 1-880485),* P.O. Box 206, Fiddletown, CA 95629; 17300 Old River Rd., Fiddletown, CA 95629-0206 Tel 209-296-4680.

Alpha Educ Inst, *(Alpha Education Institute; 1-881843),* 92 Anchorage Dr., Newport News, VA 23602 Tel 804-874-2921.

Alpha Iota, *(Alpha Iota of Pi Lambda Theta Pubns.;* 0-914522), 921 W. Bonita Ave., Claremont, CA 91711 (SAN 206-3204).

Alpha Om ID, *(Alpha Omega; 0-941734),* 1026 E. Garden Ave., Coeur d'Alene, ID 83814 (SAN 239-1503) Tel 208-664-2954; Dist. by: Pacific Pipeline, Inc., 8030 S. 228th St., Kent, WA 98032-2900 (SAN 208-2128) Tel 206-872-5523; Toll free: 800-444-7323 (Customer service); 800-677-2222 (orders).

Alphabet, *(Alphabet Pr.; 0-9635260),* P.O. Box 25785, GMF, Barrigada, GU 96921.

AlphaBuddies, *(AlphaBuddies Corp.; 0-9634846),* 5227 Jana Ct., Las Vegas, NV 89119 Tel 702-739-9123; Toll free: 800-867-9123.

Alpine Pubns, *(Alpine Pubns.; 0-931866),* P.O. Box 7027 (Orders), Loveland, CO 80537 Tel 303-667-2017; Toll free: 800-777-7257; Dist. by: Baker & Taylor Bks., Somerville Service Ctr., 50 Kirby Ave., Somerville, NJ 08876-0734 (SAN 169-4901) Tel 908-722-8000; Toll free: 800-775-1500 (customer service); Dist. by: Baker & Taylor Bks., Momence Service Ctr., 501 S. Gladiolus St., Momence, IL 60954-2444 (SAN 169-2100) Tel 815-472-2444; Toll free: 800-775-2300 (customer service); Dist. by: Baker & Taylor Bks., Commerce Service Ctr., 251 Mt. Olive Church Rd., Commerce, GA 30599-9988 (SAN 169-1503) Tel 706-335-5000; Toll free: 800-775-1200 (customer service); Dist. by: Baker & Taylor Bks., Reno Service Ctr., 380 Edison Way, Reno, NV 89564 (SAN 169-4464) Tel 702-858-6700; Toll free: 800-775-1700 (customer service); Dist. by: Ingram Bk. Co., 1 Ingram Blvd., La Vergne, TN 37086-1986 (SAN 169-7978) Tel 615-793-5000; Toll free: 800-937-8000 (orders only, all warehouses).

Alta Bk Co Pubs, *(Alta Bk. Co., Pubs.; 1-878598),* 16 Adrian Ct., Burlingame, CA 94010 (SAN 200-4674) Tel 415-692-2002; Toll free: 800-526-0505. Do not confuse with Alta Bk. Ctr. in Burlingame, CA.

Altair Pr, *(Altair Pr.; 0-934768),* 264 McMillan Rd., Grosse Pointe Farms, MI 48236 (SAN 209-1585) Tel 313-881-9588.

AlyCat *Imprint of* **Alyson Pubns**

Alyson Pubns, *(Alyson Pubns., Inc.; 0-932870; 1-55583),* 40 Plympton St., Boston, MA 02118 (SAN 213-6546) Tel 617-542-5679; Toll free: 800-825-9766 (orders only); Dist. by: Consortium Bk. & Sales & Distribution, 1045 Westgate Dr., Suite 90, Saint Paul, MN 55114-1065 (SAN 200-6049) Tel 612-221-9035; Toll free: 800-283-3572 (orders only). *Imprints:* Alyson Wonderland (Alyson Wonderland); AlyCat (AlyCat).

Alyson Wonderland *Imprint of* **Alyson Pubns**

Am Anti-Viv Soc, *(American Anti-Vivisection Society;* 1-881699), Noble Plaza, 801 Old York Rd., Suite 204, Jenkintown, PA 19046-1685 (SAN 266-3996) Tel 215-887-0816.

Am Art Analog *Imprint of* **Chelsea Hse**

Am Articulat, *(American Articulation Assocs.; 0-924799),* P.O. Box 500, El Cajon, CA 92022-0500; 11768 Shadow Glen Rd., El Cajon, CA 92020 Tel 619-442-6202.

Am Assn Diabetes Ed, *(American Assn. of Diabetes Educators; 1-881876),* 444 N. Michigan Ave., Suite 1240, Chicago, IL 60611 (SAN 224-3091) Tel 708-383-4384.

Am Assn Voc Materials, *(American Assn. for Vocational Instructional Materials; 0-914452; 0-89606),* 220 Smithonia Rd., Winterville, GA 30683 (SAN 225-8811) Tel 706-742-5355; Toll free: 800-228-4689.

Am Assoc U Women, *(American Assn. of Univ. Women (National Headquarters); 0-9611476; 1-879922),* 1111 16th St., NW, Washington, DC 20036 Tel 202-785-7700.

Am Atheist, *(American Atheist Pr.; 0-911826; 0-910309),* P.O. Box 140195, Austin, TX 78714-0195 (SAN 206-7188); 7215 Cameron Rd., Austin, TX 78752 Tel 512-458-1244.

Am Classic Ent, *(American Classic Enterprises, Inc.;* 1-880210), 4742 N. Western Ave., Chicago, IL 60625 Tel 312-561-9191; Dist. by: Baker & Taylor Bks., Momence Service Ctr., 501 S. Gladiolus St., Momence, IL 60954-2444 (SAN 169-2100) Tel 815-472-2444; Toll free: 800-775-2300 (customer service).

Am Coll Testing, *(American College Testing Program; 0-937734; 1-56009),* 2201 N. Dodge St., Iowa City, IA 52243 (SAN 204-8027) Tel 319-337-1410; P.O Box 168, Iowa City, IA 52243 (SAN 696-5075).

Am Correctional, *(American Correctional Assn.; 0-942974; 0-929310; 1-56991),* 8025 Laurel Lakes Ct., Laurel, MD 20707-5075 (SAN 204-8051) Tel 301-206-5100; Toll free: 800-825-2665.

Am Diabetes, *(American Diabetes Assn.; 0-945448),* 1660 Duke St., Alexandria, VA 22314 (SAN 224-3105) Tel 703-549-1500.

Am Efficiency, *(American Efficiency; 1-882534),* Box 30092, Savannah, GA 31410; 14th St., No. 13, Tybee Island, GA 31328 Tel 912-786-5206.

Am Eng Pubns, *(American English Pubns.; 0-916177),* 356 Dongan Hills Ave., Staten Island, NY 10305 (SAN 294-8915) Tel 718-667-6637.

Am Faculty Pr, *(American Faculty Pr., Inc.; 0-912834),* 44 Lake Shore Dr., Rockaway, NJ 07866 (SAN 201-2650) Tel 201-627-2727.

Am Forestry
See Am Forests

Am Forests, *(American Forests; 0-935050),* Bk. Editorial Dept., P.O. Box 2000, Washington, DC 20013 (SAN 204-8175); 1516 P St., NW, Washington, DC 20005 Tel 202-667-3300.

Am Guidance, *(American Guidance Service, Inc.; 0-913476; 0-88671; 0-7854; 0-942277; 1-56269),* 4201 Woodland Rd., Circle Pines, MN 55014-1796 (SAN 201-694X) Tel 612-786-4343; Toll free: 800-328-2560. Acquired secondary education product line & textbooks for special needs students from Media Materials, Inc.

Am Hist Soc Ger, *(American Historical Society of Germans from Russia; 0-914222),* 631 D St., Lincoln, NE 68502-1199 (SAN 204-7543) Tel 402-474-3363.

Am Inst Teen AIDS, *(American Institute for Teen AIDS Prevention; 1-885625),* P.O. Box 136116, Fort Worth, TX 76136-6116; 6032 Jacksboro Hwy., Suite 100, Fort Worth, TX 76135 Tel 817-237-0230.

Am Interfaith, *(American Interfaith Institute; 1-881060),* 401 N. Broad St., Philadelphia, PA 19108 Tel 215-238-5345; Toll free: 800-627-2689.

Am Intl Dist, *(American International Distribution* Corp.), 64 Depot Rd., Colchester, VT 05446 (SAN 630-2238) Tel 802-862-0095; Orders to: P.O. Box 20, Williston, VT 05495-0020 Tel 802-864-7626; Toll free: 800-488-2665 (textbk. hotline orders only).

Am Kestrel Pr, *(American Kestrel Pr.; 1-883966),* P.O. Box 774723, Steamboat Springs, CO 80477-4723; 500 N. Steamboat Blvd., Steamboat Springs, CO 80477-4723 Tel 303-879-1941.

Am Literary Pr, *(American Literary Pr., Inc.; 1-56167),* 8019 Belair Rd., No. 10, Baltimore, MD 21236-3711 Tel 410-882-7700; Toll free: 800-873-2003.

Am Map, *(American Map Corp.; 0-8416),* Subs. of Langenscheidt Pubs., Inc., 46-35 54th Rd., Maspeth, NY 11378 (SAN 202-4624) Tel 718-784-0055; Toll free: 800-432-6277.

Am New Church Sunday, *(American New Church Sunday Schl. Assn.; 0-917426),* 48 Highland St., Sharon, MA 02067 (SAN 208-9432) Tel 617-784-5041; Dist. by: Swedenborg Library, 79 Newbury St., Boston, MA 02116 (SAN 208-9440) Tel 617-262-5918.

Am Occup Therapy, *(American Occupational Therapy Assn., Inc.; 0-910317; 1-56900),* P.O. Box 31220, Bethesda, MD 20824-1220 (SAN 224-4705); Toll free: 800-377-8555; 4720 Montgomery Ln., Bethesda, MD 20824-1220 (SAN 662-7153) Tel 301-652-2682.

Am Printing Hse, *(American Printing Hse. for the Blind),* 1839 Frankfort Ave., Box 6085, Louisville, KY 40206-0085 (SAN 203-5235) Tel 502-895-2405; Toll free: 800-223-1839.

Am Psychiatric, *(American Psychiatric Pr., Inc.; 0-89042; 0-88048),* Subs. of American Psychiatric Assn., 1400 K St., NW, Suite 1101, Washington, DC 20005 (SAN 293-2288) Tel 202-682-6231; Toll free: 800-368-5777.

Am Psychol, *(American Psychological Assn.; 0-912704;* 1-55798), 750 First St., NE, Washington, DC 20002-4242 (SAN 202-4705); Orders to: P.O. Box 2710, Hyattsville, MD 20784 (SAN 685-3137); Toll free: 800-374-2721 (orders only).

Am Soc Defense TFP, *(American Society for the Defense of Tradition, Family & Property, The (TFP); 1-877905; 1-881008),* Div. of Foundation for a Christian Civilization, Inc., P.O. Box 1868, York, PA 17405; R.D. 2, Box 2015, Spring Grove, PA 17362 Tel 717-225-7147.

Am Trust Pubns, *(American Trust Pubns.; 0-89259),* 10900 W. Washington St., Indianapolis, IN 46231 (SAN 664-6158) Tel 317-839-9278.

Am Univ Artforms
See All Things Pr

Am Water Wks Assn, *(American Water Works Assn.;* 0-89867), 6666 W. Quincy Ave., Denver, CO 80235-3098 (SAN 212-8241) Tel 303-794-7711.

Am Wrld Geog, *(American World Geographic Publishing; 0-938314; 1-56037),* Box 5630, Helena, MT 59604 (SAN 220-0732); Toll free: 800-654-1105; 800-821-3874 (in Montana); 3020 Bozeman, Helena, MT 59601 Tel 406-443-2842; Dist. by: National Bk. Network, 4720A Boston Way, Lanham, MD 20706-4310 (SAN 630-0065) Tel 301-459-8696; Toll free: 800-462-6420.

AMC Books, *(Appalachian Mountain Club Bks.; 0-910146; 1-878239),* 5 Joy St., Boston, MA 02108 (SAN 203-4808) Tel 617-523-0636; Dist. by: Talman Co., 131 Spring St., Suite 201E-N, New York, NY 10012 (SAN 200-5204) Tel 212-431-7175; Toll free: 800-537-8894 (orders only).

Amador Pubs, *(Amador Pubs.; 0-938513),* P.O. Box 12335, Albuquerque, NM 87195 (SAN 661-3055); 607 Isleta Blvd., SW, Albuquerque, NM 87105 (SAN 661-3063) Tel 505-877-4395; Dist. by: New Leaf Distributing Co., 5425 Tulane Dr., SW, Atlanta, GA 30336-2323 (SAN 169-1449) Tel 404-691-6996; Toll free: 800-326-2665; Dist. by: The Distributors, 702 S. Michigan, South Bend, IN 46601 (SAN 169-2488) Tel 219-232-8500; Toll free: 800-348-5200 (except Indiana); Dist. by: Left Bank Bks. Distribution & Publishing, 4142 Brooklyn Ave., NE, Seattle, WA 98105 (SAN 216-5368) Tel 206-632-5870; Dist. by: Gannon Distributing Co., 2887 Cooks Rd., Santa Fe, NM 87501 (SAN 201-5889) Tel 505-438-3430; Toll free: 800-442-2044; Dist. by: Treasure Chest Pubns., 1802 W. Grant Rd., Suite 101, Tucson, AZ 85745 (SAN 209-3243) Tel 602-623-9558; Toll free: 800-969-9558; Dist. by: Last Gasp Eco-Funnies, Inc., 2180 Bryant St., San Francisco, CA 94110 (SAN 170-3242) Tel 415-824-6636; Dist. by: ANSEL Group, 3660 Cerillos Rd., B9, Santa Fe, NM 87501 (SAN 630-8759); Toll free: 800-688-3928.

Amaknak Pr, *(Amaknak Pr.; 0-9626090),* 13505 SE River Rd., Portland, OR 97222 Tel 503-652-3072.

Amana Corp, *(Amana Corp.; 0-915957),* 4411 41st St., Brentwood, MD 20722 (SAN 293-9576) Tel 301-779-7774.

Amer Classical, *(American Classical League, The;* 0-939507), Miami Univ., Oxford, OH 45056 (SAN 225-8358) Tel 513-529-7741.

Amer Design, *(American Design Co.; 0-9635637),* 304 S. 30th Ave., Hattiesburg, MS 39402 Tel 601-268-7669.

Amer Dist Serv, *(American Distribution Services, Inc.;* 1-878667), 3400 Dundee Rd., Northbrook, IL 60062 (SAN 630-561X) Tel 708-498-5010.

Amer Edit Servs, *(American Editorial Services, Inc.;* 1-879019), 201 E. College Blvd., No. 23, Niceville, FL 32578-1302 Tel 904-897-5289.

Amer Educ Pub, *(American Education Publishing, Inc.;* 1-56189), 150 E. Wilson Bridge Rd., Suite 145, Columbus, OH 43085-2328 Tel 614-848-8866; Toll free: 800-542-7833. Publishes El-Hi only.

Amer Etiquette Inst, *(American Etiquette Institute;* 1-879322), P.O. Box 700508, San Jose, CA 95170; Toll free: 800-748-6299; 1643 Edmonton Ave., Sunnyvale, CA 94087 Tel 408-996-9901.

Amer Intl Pr, *(American International Pr., Inc.;* 0-9623476), 432 Park Ave. S., No. 1010, New York, NY 10016-8013 Tel 212-213-6699.

Amer Scholastic, *(American Scholastic Pr. Assn.;* 1-878314), P.O. Box 4400, College Point, NY 11356; 120-15A Riviera Ct., College Point, NY 11356 Tel 212-673-9030.

Amer Spirit, *(American Spiritualist Assembly; 0-939795),* 3011 Seventh St., Rockford, IL 61109-2158 (SAN 663-6918).

Amer Trail Bks, *(American Trail Bks.; 1-884505),* P.O. Box 400, Townsend, TN 37882; 1228 School House Gap Rd., Townsend, TN 37882 Tel 615-448-2050.

Amereon Ltd, *(Amereon, Ltd.; 0-88411; 0-89190;* 0-8488), P.O. Box 1200, Mattituck, NY 11952 (SAN 201-2413); 800 Wickham Ave., Mattituck, NY 11952 Tel 516-298-5100.

Americus Pr, *(Americus Pr.; 0-9619914),* P.O. Box 9434, Washington, DC 20016 (SAN 247-1744) Tel 202-363-3999; Toll free: 800-336-6054.

Amethyst Aura, *(Amethyst Aura; 0-944944),* P.O. Box 800842, Dallas, TX 75380 (SAN 245-789X); 9927 Silver Creek Rd., Dallas, TX 75243 (SAN 245-7903) Tel 214-699-8015.

Amethyst Bks, *(Amethyst Bks.; 0-944256),* P.O. Box 895, Woodstock, NY 12498 (SAN 243-0657) Tel 914-246-6356; Dist. by: Talman Co., 131 Spring St., Suite 201E-N, New York, NY 10012 (SAN 200-5204) Tel 212-431-7175; Toll free: 800-537-8894 (orders only).

AMI & Arabian Mktg, *(AMI Bks. & Arabian Marketing International; 0-9632117),* 20993 Foothill Blvd., Suite 714, Hayward, CA 94542 Tel 510-538-3191.

AMI Pr, *(AMI Pr.; 0-911988; 1-56036),* Div. of The Blue Army of Our Lady of Fatima, U.S.A., Inc., Box 976, Mountain View Rd., Washington, NJ 07882-0976 (SAN 213-6791) Tel 908-689-1700.

AMICA Pub Hse, *(AMICA Publishing Hse.; 1-884187),* Div. of AMICA International, 1201 First Ave. S., Suite 203, Seattle, WA 98134 Tel 206-467-1035.

Amideast, *(AMIDEAST; 0-913957),* 1100 17th St., NW, Washington, DC 20036-4601 (SAN 286-7184) Tel 202-785-0022.

Amigo Pr, *(Amigo Pr.; 0-935098),* 620 Lombardi Ln., Laguna Beach, CA 92652 (SAN 213-2796) Tel 714-497-4022.

Amistad Pr, *(Amistad Pr., Inc.; 1-56743),* Time & Life Bldg., Rockefeller Ctr., Rm. 3845, New York, NY 10020 Tel 212-522-6936; Dist. by: Viking Penguin, 375 Hudson St., New York, NY 10014-3657 Tel 212-366-2000; Toll free: 800-331-4624.

Ammie Enter, *(Ammie Enterprises; 0-932825),* P.O. Box 2132, Vista, CA 92085 (SAN 691-3008) Tel 619-758-4561; Toll free: 800-633-5544.

Amnos Pubns, *(Amnos Pubns.; 0-9623721),* c/o Holy Apostle Greek Orthodox Church, 2501 S. Wolf Rd., Westchester, IL 60153 Tel 312-562-2744.

AMORC, *(AMORC Bks; 0-912057),* Div. of Supreme Grand Lodge of AMORC, Inc., Rosicrucian Order, 1342 Naglee Ave., San Jose, CA 95191 (SAN 211-3864) Tel 408-947-3600.

AMSCO Sch, *(AMSCO School Pubns., Inc.; 0-87720;* 1-56765), 315 Hudson St., 5th Fl., New York, NY 10013-1085 (SAN 201-1751) Tel 212-675-7000.

An Awareness, *(An Awareness Production; 0-9625787),* P.O. Box 19178, Oakland, CA 94619; 2217 42nd Ave., Oakland, CA 94619 Tel 510-533-0795.

Ana Pubns, *(Ana Pubns.; 0-9618941),* 4427 Westover Place, NW, Washington, DC 20016-5556 (SAN 242-4533) Tel 202-362-5330.

Analysis, *(Analysis Pr.; 0-911894),* Subs. of Merrill Analysis, Inc., 3300 Darby Rd., No. 3325, Haverford, PA 19041 (SAN 210-9549) Tel 610-642-2011.

Ananse Pr, *(Ananse Pr.; 0-9605670),* P.O. Box 22565, Seattle, WA 98122 (SAN 216-3292); 1504 32nd Ave. S., Seattle, WA 98144 (SAN 241-6123) Tel 206-325-8205.

Anaphase II, *(Anaphase II; 0-945962),* 2739 Wightman St., San Diego, CA 92104-3526 (SAN 248-1707) Tel 619-688-1959; Dist. by: Bookpeople, 7900 Edgewater Dr., Oakland, CA 94621 (SAN 168-9517) Tel 510-632-4700; Toll free: 800-999-4650; Dist. by: Baker & Taylor Bks., Commerce Service Ctr., 251 Mt. Olive Church Rd., Commerce, GA 30599-9988 (SAN 169-1503) Tel 706-335-5000; Toll free: 800-775-1200 (customer service).

Anarca Prodns, *(Anarca Productions; 0-9629025),* Div. of RR Productions, 534 Onate Pl., Santa Fe, NM 87501-3674 Tel 505-986-3933.

Anatomical Chart, *(Anatomical Chart Co.; 0-9603730),* 8221 Kimball Ave., Skokie, IL 60076-2956 (SAN 223-5315) Tel 708-679-4700; Toll free: 800-621-7500.

Anchorage, *(Anchorage Pr.; 0-87602),* P.O. Box 8067, New Orleans, LA 70182 (SAN 203-4727) Tel 504-283-8868.

Ancient City Pr, *(Ancient City Pr.; 0-941270),* P.O. Box 5401, Santa Fe, NM 87502 (SAN 164-5552) Tel 505-982-8195; Dist. by: Johnson Bks., 1880 S. 57th Ct., Boulder, CO 80301 (SAN 201-0313) Tel 303-443-9766; Toll free: 800-258-5830.

Anderie Poetry, *(Anderie Poetry Pr.; 1-883331),* Div. of Feelings Poetry Magazine, P.O. Box 85, Easton, PA 18044-0085; 407 High St., Easton, PA 18042 Tel 610-559-6287.

Anderson Bks, *(Anderson Bks.; 0-9602128),* P.O. Box 1751, Naples, FL 33939 (SAN 209-5238) Tel 813-262-5592.

Anderson MI, *(Anderson Pubns.; 0-9610088),* Box 423, Davison, MI 48423 (SAN 267-5633) Tel 313-667-2012. Do not confuse with Anderson Pubns. in Boca Raton, FL.

Anderson Pr, *(Anderson Pr.; 0-942479),* 706 W. Davis, Ann Arbor, MI 48103-4855 (SAN 667-3600) Tel 313-994-6182.

Anderson World, *(Anderson World, Inc.; 0-89037),* 1400 N. Shoreline Blvd., P.O. Box 7211, Mountain View, CA 94043 (SAN 281-2754) Tel 415-965-8552; Toll free: 800-227-8318; Orders to: P.O. Box 366, Mountain View, CA 94042 (SAN 281-2762).

Andres & Co, *(Andre's & Co.; 0-936264),* 289 Varick St., Jersey City, NJ 07302 (SAN 214-0977).

Andresen Ent, *(Andresen Enterprises; 0-9641718),* 57 Richmond St., Raynham, MA 02767 Tel 508-822-1053; Toll free: 800-749-2550.

Andrew Mtn Pr, *(Andrew Mountain Pr.; 0-9603840;* 0-916897), P.O. Box 340353, Hartford, CT 06134 (SAN 658-0130); 94 Churchill Dv., Newington, CT 06111.

Andrews & McMeel, *(Andrews & McMeel; 0-8362),* A Universal Press Syndicate Co., 4900 Main St., Kansas City, MO 64112 (SAN 202-540X) Tel 816-932-6700; Toll free: 800-826-4216.

Angelus Pr, *(Angelus Pr.; 0-935952),* 2918 Tracy Ave., Kansas City, MO 64109 (SAN 222-769X) Tel 816-753-3150; Toll free: 800-966-7337 (orders).

Animated Elements, *(Animated Elements, Inc.;* 1-880945), P.O. Box 35354, Sarasota, FL 34242; 901 Beach Rd., No. 401, Sarasota, FL 34242 Tel 813-346-2021.

Anirt Pr, *(Anirt Pr.; 0-9605878),* P.O. Box 979, Lawndale, CA 90260 (SAN 216-6550); 15707 Eastwood Ave., Lawndale, CA 90260 (SAN 241-6166) Tel 213-678-9753.

Ann Arbor Div *Imprint of* **Acad Therapy**

Anne M Eccles, *(Eccles, Anne M.; 0-9618555),* 6179 Hurricane Ct., Parker, CO 80134-5704 (SAN 668-0631) Tel 303-840-2376.

Annette Capps, *(Capps, Annette, Ministries; 0-9618975),* P.O. Box 10, Broken Arrow, OK 74013 (SAN 242-4738) Tel 918-251-2309.

Another Lang Pr, *(Another Language Pr.; 0-922852),* 7709 Hamilton Ave., Cincinnati, OH 45231-3103 Tel 513-521-5590.

Ansata Pubns, *(Ansata Pubns.; 0-9625644),* Rte. 2, Box 312A, Mena, AR 71953 Tel 501-394-5288.

Ansayre Pr, *(Ansayre Pr.; 0-937369),* 284 Huron Ave., Cambridge, MA 02138 (SAN 659-0071) Tel 617-547-0339.

Anschell Pub Co, *(Anschell Publishing Co.; 0-926060),* 2809 1/2 Mt. Rainier Dr., S., Seattle, WA 98144 Tel 206-723-5414; Dist. by: Pacific Pipeline, Inc., 8030 S. 228th St, Kent, WA 98032-2900 (SAN 208-2128) Tel 206-872-5523; Toll free: 800-444-7323 (Customer Service); 800-677-2222 (orders).

Antarctic Pr, *(Antarctic Pr.; 0-930655),* P.O. Box 7134, Bellevue, WA 98008 (SAN 684-2631) Tel 206-885-6853; Dist. by: Pacific Pipeline, Inc., 8030 S. 228th St, Kent, WA 98032-2900 (SAN 208-2128) Tel 206-872-5523; Toll free: 800-444-7323 (Customer Service); 800-677-2222 (orders).

Antex Corp, *(Antex Corp.; 1-881079),* 120 Dennis Dr., Lexington, KY 40503 Tel 606-276-3896.

Anthro Co, *(The Anthro Co.; 1-878464),* P. O. Box 661765, Sacramento, CA 95866-1765 Tel 916-971-1675.

Anthroposophic, *(Anthroposophic Pr., Inc.; 0-910142;* 0-88010), R.R. 4, Box 94A1, Hudson, NY 12534 (SAN 201-1824) Tel 518-851-2054; Dist. by: Bookpeople, 7900 Edgewater Dr., Oakland, CA 94621 (SAN 168-9517) Tel 510-632-4700; Toll free: 800-999-4650; Dist. by: New Leaf Distributing Co., 5425 Tulane Dr., SW, Atlanta, GA 30336-2323 (SAN 169-1449) Tel 404-691-6996; Toll free: 800-326-2665; Dist. by: Inland Bk. Co., 140 Commerce St., East Haven, CT 06512 (SAN 200-4151) Tel 203-467-4257; Toll free: 800-243-0138; Dist. by: Samuel Weiser, Inc., P.O. Box 612, York Beach, ME 03910-0612 (SAN 202-9588) Tel 207-363-4393; Toll free: 800-423-7087 (orders only); Dist. by: DeVorss & Co., P.O. Box 550, Marina del Rey, CA 90294-0550 (SAN 168-9886) Tel 213-870-7478; Toll free: 800-843-5743 (bookstores only); 800-331-4719 (in California, bookstore only).

Antioch Pub Co, *(Antioch Publishing Co.; 0-89954;* 0-7824), 888 Dayton St., Yellow Springs, OH 45387 (SAN 654-7214) Tel 513-767-7379; Toll free: 800-543-2397.

Antioch Publishes, *(Antioch Publishes The Word;* 0-932345), 1535 Ritchie Hwy., Arnold, MD 21012 (SAN 687-3537) Tel 410-757-5000; Dist. by: Pentecostal Publishing Hse., 8855 Dunn Rd., Hazelwood, MO 63042-2299 (SAN 219-3817) Tel 314-837-7300.

Antique Pubns, *(Antique Pubns.; 0-915410; 1-57080),* Div. of The Glass Press, P.O. Box 553, Marietta, OH 45750 (SAN 216-3306); Toll free: 800-533-3433; 217 Union St., Marietta, OH 45750 Tel 614-373-6146.

Antroll Pub, *(Antroll Publishing Co.; 1-877656),* 2616 Elmont St., Wheaton, MD 20902 Tel 301-942-0492.

Anyone Can Read Bks, *(Anyone Can Read Bks.;* 0-914275), Star Rte., P.O. Box 826, Lytle Creek, CA 92358 (SAN 286-6889) Tel 909-880-2332.

Anyones Pub, *(Anyone's Publishing Co.; 0-9623308),* 1130 E. Grab Creek Rd., Dickson, TN 37055 Tel 615-446-7557.

Apex Creat, *(Apex Creative; 1-879253),* P.O. Box 1327, Durham, NC 27702; Toll free: 800-827-3901; 5 Geneva Ct., Durham, NC 27713 Tel 919-544-0660.

APIX Intl, *(APIX International; 1-877618),* Div. of Worzalla Publishing, 3535 Jefferson St., Stevens Point, WI 54481 Tel 715-344-9600; Toll free: 800-442-2463 (outside Wisconsin).

Aplomb Pub, *(Aplomb Publishing, Inc.; 0-9636777),* P.O. Box 12683, El Paso, TX 79913; 6945 Canyon Run, El Paso, TX 79912 Tel 915-585-2713.

Appalach Consortium, *(Appalachian Consortium Pr.; 0-913239),* Div. of Appalachian Consortium, Inc., Appalachian State Univ., University Hall, Boone, NC 28608 (SAN 285-8150) Tel 704-262-2064.

Appalachian Trail, *(Appalachian Trail Conference; 0-917953),* P.O. Box 807, Harpers Ferry, WV 25425 (SAN 267-6001) Tel 304-535-6331.

Applause Inc, *(Applause, Inc.; 0-929632),* 6101 Variel Ave., Woodland Hills, CA 91365 (SAN 250-1716) Tel 818-992-6000; c/o Flavia, P.O. Box 42229, Santa Barbara, CA 93140 Tel 805-564-6905.

Applause Theatre Bk Pubs, *(Applause Theatre Bk. Pubs.; 0-936839; 1-55783),* 211 W. 71st St., New York, NY 10023 (SAN 658-3245) Tel 212-595-4735; Orders to: Publisher Resources, Inc., 1224 Heil Quaker Blvd., P.O. Box 7001, La Vergne, TN 37086-7001 (SAN 630-5431).

Apple Corps Pubs, *(Apple Corps Pubs.; 0-9619484),* P.O. Box 800030, Bethany, OK 73008 (SAN 245-0453); 1600 Sunset Ln., Oklahoma City, OK 73127 (SAN 245-0461) Tel 405-787-8191.

Apple Isl Bks, *(Apple Island Bks.; 0-934313),* Box 276, Shapleigh, ME 04076 (SAN 693-5338) Tel 207-324-9453.

Apple Paperbacks *Imprint of* **Scholastic Inc**

Apple Pie Pub Co, *(Apple Pie Publishing Co.; 0-911149),* 7682 S. Locust St., Englewood, CO 80112-2403 (SAN 267-6052) Tel 303-770-1784.

Apple Pub Wisc, *(Apple Publishing Co.; 0-937891),* Subs. of Educational Assessment Service, Inc., W. 6050 Apple Rd., Watertown, WI 53098 (SAN 659-4123) Tel 414-261-1118. Do not confuse with Apple Publishing Co., New York, NY.

Apple Soup Bks *Imprint of* **Knopf Bks Yng Read**

Apple Valley, *(Apple Valley Publishing Co., Inc.; 1-880108),* 15431 Hornbrook Rd., Box 178, Hornbrook, CA 96044 Tel 916-842-7012.

Apples & Oranges Inc, *(Apples & Oranges, Inc.; 0-929637),* P.O. Box 2296H, Valley Center, CA 92082 (SAN 249-7662) Tel 619-751-8868.

Applewood, *(Applewood Bks.; 0-918222; 1-55709),* P.O. Box 365, Bedford, MA 01730-0365 (SAN 210-3419) Tel 617-271-0055; Dist. by: Consortium Bk. Sales & Distribution, 1045 Westgate Dr., Suite 90, Saint Paul, MN 55114-1065 (SAN 200-6049) Tel 612-221-9035; Toll free: 800-283-3572 (orders).

Apt Bks, *(Apt Bks., Inc.; 0-86590; 0-938719),* 56-16 Seabury St., Apt. 3C, Flushing, NY 11373-4869 (SAN 215-7209) Tel 212-697-0887.

Aqua Explorers, *(Aqua Explorers, Inc.; 0-9616167),* 2745 Cheshire Dr., Baldwin, NY 11510 (SAN 699-9050) Tel 516-868-2658.

Aquarelle Pr, *(Aquarelle Pr.; 0-9616679),* P.O. Box 3676, Baton Rouge, LA 70821-3676 (SAN 659-7270); 5036 Hyacinth Ave., Baton Rouge, LA 70808 (SAN 659-7289) Tel 504-926-4220.

Arabian Mktg
See AMI & Arabian Mktg

Arbus Pub, *(Arbus Publishing Co.; 1-881285),* Div. of Stewart Design Assocs., 18 Warwick Dr., Manalapan, NJ 07726 Tel 908-446-2129.

Arc Pr AR, *(Arc Pr.; 0-938041),* P.O. Box 88, Cane Hill, AR 72717 (SAN 659-7297); Cold Springs Rd., Cane Hill, AR 72717 (SAN 659-7300) Tel 501-824-3821. Do not confuse with Arc Pr., Kenmore, WA.

Arcade Pub Inc, *(Arcade Publishing, Inc.; 1-55970),* 141 Fifth Ave., New York, NY 10010 (SAN 252-2012) Tel 212-475-2633; Toll free: 800-343-9204; Orders to: Little, Brown & Co., 200 West St., Waltham, MA 02154 (SAN 630-7248); Toll free: 800-759-0190.

Arcadia Corp, *(Arcadia Corp.; 0-9614745),* P.O. Box 534, Franklin, NH 03235 (SAN 692-9206) Tel 603-934-6186.

Archives Pr, *(Archives Pr., The; 0-918501),* 334 State St., No. 536, Los Altos, CA 94022 (SAN 657-3207) Tel 415-941-3010; Toll free: 800-373-1897. Do not confuse with Archive Pr. in Boulder, CO.

Archway *Imprint of* **PB**

Arco Test *Imprint of* **P-H Gen Ref & Trav**

Arcus Pub, *(Arcus Publishing Co.; 0-916955),* P.O. Box 228, Sonoma, CA 95476 (SAN 655-5667) Tel 707-996-9529.

Ardsley Pr, *(Ardsley Pr.; 1-884417),* Div. of Ardsley Musical Instrument Service, Ltd., 219 Sprain Rd., Scarsdale, NY 10583 Tel 914-693-6639; Toll free: 800-842-7286.

ARE Pr, *(A.R.E. Pr.; 0-87604),* 68th St. & Atlantic Ave., Virginia Beach, VA 23451-0656 (SAN 201-1484) Tel 804-428-3588; Toll free: 800-723-1112; P.O. Box 656, Virginia Beach, VA 23451-0656 (SAN 692-8234).

Argee Pubs, *(Argee Pubs.; 0-917961),* 4453 Manitou, Okemos, MI 48864 (SAN 247-7858) Tel 517-349-1254.

Argonauts OTMI, *(Argonauts, O.T.M.I.; 0-9621990),* 1616 NW 67th St., Seattle, WA 98166 Tel 209-278-2105.

Argos Pub Co, *(Argos Publishing Co.; 0-915509),* Subs. of Aaron E. Freeman, Inc., 1156 Sidonia Ct., Leucadia, CA 92024 (SAN 291-0764) Tel 619-436-4271.

Argyle Bks, *(Argyle Bks.; 0-9642573),* 710 Old Justin Rd., Argyle, TX 76226 Tel 817-464-3368.

Ariel Vamp Pr, *(Ariel Vamp Pr.; 0-9618752),* P.O. Box 3496, Berkeley, CA 94703 (SAN 668-7016) Tel 510-654-4849.

Arlie Enter, *(Arlie Enterprises; 1-880175),* P.O. Box 360933, Strongsville, OH 44136 (SAN 297-4665); 17035 Raccoon Trail, Strongsville, OH 44136 (SAN 297-4673) Tel 216-238-9397.

Arlington Pr, *(Arlington Pr.; 0-9629992),* 6331 Orchard Lake Dr., Fort Wayne, IN 46804-9503.

Armstrong Assocs, *(Armstrong Assocs.; 0-925390),* P.O. Box 20174, Village of Oak Creek, AZ 86341; 240 Arrowhead Dr., Village of Oak Creek, AZ 86341 Tel 602-284-1557.

ARO Pub, *(ARO Publishing Co.; 0-89868),* Box 193, 398 S. 1100 W., Provo, UT 84601 (SAN 212-6370) Tel 801-377-8218; Toll free: 800-338-7317 (orders only). *Imprints:* Read Res (Reading Research).

Aromatique, *(Aromatique, Inc.; 0-9633348),* P.O. Box 1500, 3421 Hwy. 25 N., Heber Springs, AR 72543 Tel 501-362-7511; Toll free: 800-262-7511.

Aronson, *(Aronson, Jason, Inc.; 0-87668; 1-56821),* 230 Livingston St., Northvale, NJ 07647 (SAN 201-0127) Tel 201-767-4093; Orders to: 1205 O'Neill Hwy., Dunmore, PA 18512 (SAN 665-6536) Tel 717-342-1449; Toll free: 800-782-0015. Do not confuse with J. H. Aronson, Highmount, NY.

Arrants & Assoc, *(Arrants & Assoc.; 0-943704),* 16576 SE 19th St., Bellevue, WA 98008 (SAN 238-3675) Tel 206-644-1664.

Arraster Pub, *(Arrastar Publishing Co.; 0-9622596),* P.O. Box 916, Everett, WA 98206; Toll free: 800-245-0970 (Washington only); 2621 Grand, Everett, WA 98201 Tel 206-339-3637.

Arrigo CA, *(Arrigo, Hargreaves, Nishimura; 0-9617538),* 21561 Balerma, Mission Viejo, CA 92692-1045 (SAN 663-4680) Tel 714-661-2751.

Arrow Press, *(Arrow Pr.; 0-940319),* P.O. Box 899, Pollock Pines, CA 95726 (SAN 664-323X) Tel 916-644-2341; Orders to: 8825 Blue Mountain Dr., Golden, CO 80403 Tel 303-234-5245.

Arrow Pub NC, *(Arrow Publishing Co.; 0-944049),* 305 College Plaza, Pembroke, NC 28372 (SAN 668-1735); P. O. Box 1287, Pembroke, NC 28372 Tel 910-521-0840.

Arrow Trad, *(Arrow Trading Co., Inc.; 1-880459),* 1115 Broadway, 7th Flr., New York, NY 10010 Tel 212-255-7688.

Arrowhead Bks, *(Arrowhead Bks.; 0-9628238),* 3 Gerrish Dr., Durham, NH 03824-3224 Tel 603-868-7145.

Arrowhead Pub, *(Arrowhead Publishing; 0-9623819),* 7559 Gibraltar St., Apt. 14, Carlsbad, CA 92009-7464. Do not confuse with Arrowhead Publishing in Larkspur, CO.

Arroyo Pr, *(Arroyo Pr.; 0-9623682),* P.O. Box 4333, Las Cruces, NM 88003-4333; 4932 Tobosa Rd., Las Cruces, NM 88001 Tel 505-522-2348.

Art After Five, *(Art After Five; 0-9628710),* P.O. Box 247, Nederland, CO 80466-9537 Tel 303-258-3742.

Art & Earth, *(Art & Earth, Inc.; 0-926246),* P.O. Box 1653, Provo, UT 84603-1653.

Art & Entertainment, *(Art & Entertainment Information of the United States; 0-9623944),* P.O. Box 1909, Los Angeles, CA 90078-1909 Tel 213-669-0634.

Art & Ref, *(Art & Reference Hse.; 0-910156),* 2453 W. Five Mile Pkwy., Dallas, TX 75233 (SAN 203-4921).

Art In-Forms, *(Art In-Forms; 0-911835),* Eight Loretta Blvd., Sicklerville, NJ 08081 (SAN 263-9238) Tel 609-728-2502.

Art Ltd, *(Art, Ltd.; 0-9627043),* No. 8 Henderson Pl., New York, NY 10028 Tel 212-734-6165.

Art Pr Intl, *(Artistry Pr. International; 0-9625023; 1-883474),* Div. of Artistry at the Piano, Inc., P.O. Box 741111, Orange City, FL 32774-1111; Toll free: 800-557-8030; 698 Monastery Rd., Orange City, FL 32774 Tel 904-775-6407.

Art Room Pubns, *(Art Room Pubns.; 0-9620766),* 200 S. Rogers, Waxahachie, TX 75165 (SAN 249-7646) Tel 214-923-0744.

Arte Publico, *(Arte Publico Pr.; 0-934770; 1-55885),* Div. of Univ. of Houston, Univ. of Houston, 4800 Calhoun, Houston, TX 77204 (SAN 213-4594) Tel 713-743-2841; Toll free: 800-633-2783.

Arteg Creations, *(Arteg Creations; 0-9632722),* 108 Stuart St., Suite 7, Bethel Park, PA 15102 Tel 412-831-1193.

Artex Pr
See Artex Pub

Artex Pub, *(Artex Publishing, Inc.; 0-930401),* 1924 N. Seventh St., Sheboygan, WI 53081-2724 (SAN 670-9397).

Artisan IL, *(Artisan; 0-9621575),* 1300 Pin Oak Ct., Wheaton, IL 60187 (SAN 251-8287) Tel 708-690-8975.

Artistic Endeavors, *(Artistic Endeavors; 0-9604500),* 500 Newfield Ave., No. 2E, Stamford, CT 06905-3710 (SAN 207-5733) Tel 203-359-2268. Do not confuse with Artistic Endeavors Publishing in Marina del Rey, CA.

Artistry FL
See Art Pr Intl

Artists Registry, *(Artists Registry, Inc.; 0-9623079),* P.O. Box 8833, Wichita, KS 67208 Tel 316-267-1643.

Artmans Pr, *(Artman's Pr.; 0-9605468),* 1511 McGee Ave., Berkeley, CA 94703 (SAN 206-8923) Tel 510-527-2710.

Arts & Comns NY, *(Arts & Communications Network, Inc.; 0-9627366),* P.O. Box 435, Rosendale, NY 12472; 501 Mossy Brook Rd., Highfalls, NY 12440 Tel 914-687-0767.

Arts Factory, *(Arts Factory; 0-9615873),* 23604 49th Pl., W., Mountlake Terrace, WA 98043 (SAN 696-6802) Tel 206-778-7857; P.O. Box 55547, Seattle, WA 98155 (SAN 696-9836); Dist. by: Pacific Pipeline, Inc., 8030 S. 228th St, Kent, WA 98032-2900 (SAN 208-2128) Tel 206-872-5523; Toll free: 800-444-7323 (Customer Service); 800-677-2222 (orders); Dist. by: Green Tiger Pr., Inc., 200 Old Tappan Rd., Old Tappan, NJ 07675-7005 (SAN 219-4775) Tel 619-744-7575; Toll free: 800-424-2443 (except California).

Arts Pubns, *(Arts Pubns.; 0-9607458; 1-878079),* 80 Piedmont Ct., Larkspur, CA 94939 (SAN 238-003X) Tel 415-924-2633; Dist. by: Educational Bk. Distributors, P.O. Box 2510, Novato, CA 94948 (SAN 158-2259) Tel 415-883-3530.

ArtsAmerica, *(ArtsAmerica, Inc.; 0-942475),* 9 Benedict Pl., Greenwich, CT 06830-5321 (SAN 667-1039) Tel 203-869-4693.

Artsts Writrs *Imprint of* **Western Pub**

Arundel Pr, *(Arundel Pr.; 0-923980),* 8380 Beverly Blvd., Los Angeles, CA 90048-2631 (SAN 252-175X) Tel 213-852-9852.

Ascendant, *(Ascendant Pubns.; 0-9631096),* P.O. Box 6505, Pine Mountain Club, CA 93222; 15612 San Moritz Dr., Pine Mountain Club, CA 93222 Tel 805-242-4814.

Aschley Pr, *(Aschley Pr., The; 0-940900),* 2898 Kingsley Rd., Cleveland, OH 44122 (SAN 223-1735) Tel 216-752-3535.

Ascot Pr, *(Ascot Pr.; 0-9613538),* 40 Mountain View Rd., Glastonbury, CT 06033 (SAN 669-7194) Tel 203-633-6911.

ASDA Pub, *(ASDA Publishing, Inc.; 0-9632319),* 904 Forest Lake Dr., Lakeland, FL 33809 Tel 813-859-2194.

Ashbrook Pr, *(Ashbrook Pr.; 0-9629950),* 10089 Bartholomew Rd., Chagrin Falls, OH 44022 Tel 216-543-8369.

Ashgate Pub Co, *(Ashgate Publishing Co.; 0-566; 0-939207),* Old Post Rd., Brookfield, VT 05036 (SAN 213-4446) Tel 802-276-3162.

Ashley Bks, *(Ashley Bks., Inc.; 0-87949),* P.O. Box 223580, Hollywood, FL 33022-3580; Orders to: 4600 W. Commercial Blvd., Fort Lauderdale, FL 33319 (SAN 201-1409) Tel 305-739-2221.

Asia Resource, *(Asia Resource Ctr.; 0-9604518),* P.O. Box 15275, Washington, DC 20003 (SAN 207-7647) Tel 202-547-1114.

ASP PA, *(ASP; 1-878109),* P.O. Box 1480, Hudson, OH 44236-0980 Tel 412-422-4134.

Aspasia Pubns, *(Aspasia Pubns., Inc.; 1-882427),* P.O. Box 1365, Westford, MA 01886; 5 Polly Rd., Westford, MA 01886 Tel 508-692-2390.

Aspen Bks, *(Aspen Bks.; 1-56236),* Div. of Worldwide Pubs., Inc., 6211 S. 380 West, Murray, UT 84107 Tel 801-265-9393; Toll free: 800-748-4850.

Aspen Press, *(Aspen Pr., Ltd.; 1-882954),* 300 N. Elizabeth St., Chicago, IL 60607 Tel 312-433-7700.

Aspen Prods, *(Aspen Productions; 0-913635),* 8354 Milano Ct., Sacramento, CA 95828-6641 (SAN 286-0384) Tel 916-688-3319.

Assist Lea Bellingham, *(Assistance League of Bellingham; 0-9623545),* 2691 Douglas Rd., Ferndale, WA 98248-8906.

Assn Family Living, *(Association for the Study of Family Living, The; 0-9602670; 0-940848),* P.O. Box 130, Brooklyn, NY 11208 (SAN 212-8772) Tel 718-647-7406.

Assoc Pubs DC, *(Associated Pubs., Inc.; 0-87498),* 1407 14th St., NW, Washington, DC 20005 (SAN 207-1339) Tel 202-265-1441.

Astor Bks, *(Astor Bks.; 0-943351; 1-57007),* Div. of Astor Music, Inc., 62 Cooper Sq., New York, NY 10003 (SAN 668-5439) Tel 212-777-3700.

Astor-Honor, *(Astor-Honor, Inc.; 0-8392),* 530 Fifth Ave., New York, NY 10036-5101 (SAN 203-5022) Tel 212-687-6190.

Astor Pubns
See R Osgood

Astron Wkshp, *(Astronomical Workshop; 0-934546),* Furman Univ., Greenville, SC 29613 (SAN 209-5602) Tel 803-294-2208.

Asylum Arts, *(Asylum Arts; 1-878580),* P.O. Box 6203, Santa Maria, CA 93456 (SAN 297-2816); 826 E. Las Flores Way, Santa Maria, CA 93454 (SAN 297-2824) Tel 805-928-8774; Dist. by: Inbook, P.O. Box 120261, East Haven, CT 06512 (SAN 630-5547) Tel 203-467-4257; Toll free: 800-253-3605 (orders only).

Atheneum *Imprint of* **Macmillan**

Atheneum Child Bk *Imprint of* **Macmillan Child Grp**

Athletics Cong, *(Athletics Congress/U.S.A.; 0-939256),* P.O. Box 120, Indianapolis, IN 46206 (SAN 220-164X) Tel 317-261-0500.

Atlantean Pr, *(Atlantean Pr.; 0-9626854; 1-885862),* 354 Tramway Dr., P.O. Box 361116, Milpitas, CA 95035 Tel 408-262-8478.

Atlas Pr, *(Atlas Pr.; 1-880784),* P.O. Box 56282, Los Angeles, CA 90008; 3836 Olympiad Dr., Los Angeles, CA 90043 Tel 213-295-3036.

Atomium Bks, *(Atomium Bks., Inc.; 1-56182),* P.O. Box 1637, Benicia, CA 94510-4637.

Aton Pr, *(Aton Pr.; 0-9626580),* P.O. Box 1723, Grafton, VA 23692-1723; 407 Wormley Creek Dr., Yorktown, VA 23692 Tel 804-898-6083.

Atrium Pubs, *(Atrium Pubs. Group),* 11270 Clayton Creek Rd., Lower Lake, CA 95457 (SAN 200-5743) Tel 707-995-3906; Toll free: 800-275-2606. Do not confuse with Atrium Society Publications in Middlebury, VT.

Atrium Soc Pubns, *(Atrium Society Pubns.; 0-942941),* P.O. Box 816, Middlebury, VT 05753 (SAN 667-9412) Tel 802-388-0922; Dist. by: New Leaf Distributing Co., 5425 Tulane Dr., SW, Atlanta, GA 30336-2323 (SAN 169-1449) Tel 404-691-6996; Toll free: 800-326-2665; Dist. by: Baker & Taylor Bks., Somerville Service Ctr., 50 Kirby Ave., Somerville, NJ 08876-0734 (SAN 169-4901) Tel 908-722-8000; Toll free: 800-775-1500 (customer service); Dist. by: Brodart Co., 500 Arch St., Williamsport, PA 17705 (SAN 169-7684) Tel 717-326-2461; Toll free: 800-233-8467; Dist. by: Inland Bk. Co., 140 Commerce St., East Haven, CT 06512 (SAN 200-4151) Tel 203-467-4257; Toll free: 800-243-0138; Dist. by: Ingram Bk. Co., 1 Ingram Blvd., La Vergne, TN 37086-1986 (SAN 169-7978) Tel 615-793-5000; Toll free: 800-937-8000 (orders only, all warehouses). Do not confuse with Atrium Publishers Group in Lower Lake, CA.

ATS Pub, *(ATS Publishing Co.; 0-9629089),* Div. of Teenie Tennis, P.O. Box 2285, Redmond, WA 98073-2285; 16219 NE 95th Ct., Redmond, WA 98052 Tel 206-881-1446. Do not confuse with ATS Pubns. in Greenville, SC.

Attic Studio, *(Attic Studio Pr.; 1-883551),* P.O. Box 75, Clinton Corners, NY 12514 (SAN 298-2838); 205 Schultzville Rd., Clinton Corners, NY 12514 (SAN 298-2846) Tel 914-266-4902.

Attitude Adjustment, *(Attitude Adjustment, Inc.; 0-9643045),* 230 Sunrise Dr., Unit 7, Key Biscayne, FL 33149 Tel 305-361-9858.

Audio-Forum, *(Audio-Forum; 0-88432),* Div. of Jeffrey Norton Pubs., Inc., 96 Broad St., Guilford, CT 06437 Tel 203-453-9794; Toll free: 800-243-1234.

Augsburg *Imprint of* **Augsburg Fortress**

Augsburg Fortress, *(Augsburg Fortress Pubs., Publishing Hse. of The Evangelical Lutheran Church in America; 0-8066; 0-8006),* 426 S. Fifth St., Box 1209, Minneapolis, MN 55440-1209 (SAN 169-4081) Tel 612-330-3300; Toll free: 800-328-4648; Orders to: 57 E. Main St., Columbus, OH 43215-5183 Tel 614-221-7411; Toll free: 800-848-2738; Orders to: 5210 N. Lamar, P.O. Box 49337, Austin, TX 78765-9337 Tel 512-459-1112; Toll free: 800-531-5461; Orders to: 4700 Wissahickon Ave., Philadelphia, PA 19129-4280 Tel 215-848-6800; Toll free: 800-367-8737; Orders to: 3224 Beverly Blvd., Box 57974, Los Angeles, CA 90057-0974 Tel 213-386-3722; Toll free: 800-421-0239; Orders to: 1830 Howard St. D, Box 1105, Elk Grove Village, IL 60007-2455 Tel 708-437-8484; Toll free: 800-722-7766; Orders to: 1800 Sandy Plains Pkwy., Box 669608, Marietta, GA 30066-0111 Tel 404-427-2626; Toll free: 800-535-3858; Orders to: 6601 220 St. SW, Box 199, Mountlake Terrace, WA 98043-0199 Tel 206-778-1552; Toll free: 800-426-0115; Orders to: 124 S. 24th St., Omaha, NE 68102-1290 Tel 402-341-9974; Toll free: 800-228-7305; Orders to: 900 S. Arlington Ave., Box 2941, Harrisburg, PA 17105 Tel 717-652-2416; Toll free: 800-535-9057. *Imprints:* Augsburg (Augsburg); Fortress Pr (Fortress Press).

August Hse, *(August Hse. Pubs., Inc.; 0-935304; 0-87483),* P.O. Box 3223, Little Rock, AR 72203-3223 (SAN 223-7288); Toll free: 800-284-8784; 201 E. Markham St., Little Rock, AR 72201 Tel 501-372-5450.

Aunt Lute Bks, *(Aunt Lute Bks.; 1-879960),* Div. of Aunt Lute Foundation, P.O. Box 410687, San Francisco, CA 94141; 2180 Bryant St., San Fransisco, CA 94110-2128 Tel 415-558-8116.

Aunt Peggys Pub, *(Aunt Peggy's Publishing; 0-9636185),* Div. of Aunt Peggy's, Inc., P.O. Box 395, Lowell, IN 46356; 1244 Driftwood Dr., Lowell, IN 46356 Tel 219-696-8707.

Aura Bklyn, *(Aura Pr., Inc.; 0-911643),* 88 Parkville Ave., Brooklyn, NY 11230 (SAN 237-9317) Tel 718-435-9103.

Aurobindo Assn, *(Sri Aurobindo Assn., Inc.; 0-89071),* 2288 Fulton St., No. 310, Berkeley, CA 94704-1449 (SAN 169-5541) Tel 510-848-1841.

Auromere, *(Auromere, Inc.; 0-89744),* 1291 Weber St., Pomona, CA 91768 (SAN 169-0043) Tel 714-629-8255; Toll free: 800-735-4691; Dist. by: Bookpeople, 7900 Edgewater Dr., Oakland, CA 94621 (SAN 168-9517) Tel 510-632-4700; Toll free: 800-999-4650; Dist. by: DeVorss & Co., P.O. Box 550, Marina del Rey, CA 90294-0550 (SAN 168-9886) Tel 213-870-7478; Toll free: 800-843-5743 (bookstores only); 800-331-4719 (in California, bookstores only); Dist. by: New Leaf Distributing Co., 5425 Tulane Dr., SW, Atlanta, GA 30336-2323 (SAN 169-1449) Tel 404-691-6996; Toll free: 800-326-2665; Dist. by: Samuel Weiser, Inc., P.O. Box 612, York Beach, ME 03910-0612 (SAN 202-9588) Tel 207-363-4393; Toll free: 800-423-7087 (orders only); Dist. by: Inland Bk. Co., 140 Commerce St., East Haven, CT 06512 (SAN 200-4151) Tel 203-467-4257; Toll free: 800-243-0138; Dist. by: The Distributors, 702 S. Michigan, South Bend, IN 46601 (SAN 169-2488) Tel 219-232-8500; Toll free: 800-348-5200 (except Indiana); Dist. by: Starlite Distributors, P.O. Box 6750, Auburn, CA 05604-6750 (SAN 200-7789) Tel 916-888-8002; Toll free: 800-234-7827 (orders only).

Australian Book
See Terra Nova

Auto Bk, *(Auto Bk. Pr.; 0-910390),* P.O. Bin 711, San Marcos, CA 92079-0711 (SAN 201-1263) Tel 619-744-3582; Dist. by: Sunbelt Pubns., 8630 Argent St., Suite C, Santee, CA 92071-4172 (SAN 630-0790) Tel 619-258-4911; Toll free: 800-626-6579; Dist. by: Baker & Taylor Bks., Reno Service Ctr., 380 Edison Way, Reno, NV 89564 (SAN 169-4464) Tel 702-858-6700; Toll free: 800-775-1700 (customer service); Dist. by: Baker & Taylor Bks., Momence Service Ctr., 501 S. Gladiolus St., Momence, IL 60954-2444 (SAN 169-2100) Tel 815-472-2444; Toll free: 800-775-2300 (customer service).

AV Mobility, *(AV Mobility Pr.; 0-9638668),* 1631 S. Conyer, Visalia, CA 93277 Tel 209-625-0860.

Avalon Hill, *(Avalon Hill Pubs.; 0-911605; 1-56038),* Div. of Avalon Hill Game Co., The Microcomputer Games, 4517 Harford Rd., Baltimore, MD 21214 (SAN 204-4633) Tel 301-254-9200; Toll free: 800-999-3222.

Avantage Pub, *(Avantage Publishing; 0-938733),* 85 School St., Shrewsbury, MA 01545 (SAN 661-7069) Tel 508-842-2052.

Ave Maria, *(Ave Maria Pr.; 0-87793),* Campus of Notre Dame, Notre Dame, IN 46556-0428 (SAN 201-1255) Tel 219-287-2831; Toll free: 800-282-1865.

Avery Pub, *(Avery Publishing Group, Inc.; 0-89529),* 120 Old Broadway, Garden City Park, NY 11040 (SAN 210-3915) Tel 516-741-2155; Toll free: 800-548-5757; Dist. by: Publishers Group West, 4065 Hollis St., Emeryville, CA 94608 (SAN 202-8522) Tel 510-658-3453; Toll free: 800-788-3123.

Avis & Ward, *(Avis & Ward Nutrition Assocs., Inc.; 0-9628683),* 200 Professional Dr., West Monroe, LA 71291 Tel 318-323-7949; Dist. by: Wimmer Bk. Distribution, 4210 B. F. Goodrich Blvd., Memphis, TN 38118 (SAN 209-6544) Tel 901-362-8900; Toll free: 800-727-1034.

Avitar Bks, *(Avitar Bks.; 0-9614089),* 1634 Canyon Rd., Santa Fe, NM 87501-6138 (SAN 685-9968).

Avon, *(Avon Bks.; 0-380),* Div. of Hearst Corp., 1350 Ave. of the Americas, 2nd Fl., New York, NY 10019 (SAN 201-4009) Tel 212-261-6800; Toll free: 800-238-0658; Dist. by: Hearst Corp., International Circulation Distributors/ICD Bks., 250 W. 55th St., 12th Flr., New York, NY 10019 (SAN 169-5800) Tel 212-649-4474; Toll free: 800-223-0288; Orders to: P.O. Box 767, Dresden, TN 38225 (SAN 241-628X); Toll free: 800-223-0690. *Imprints:* AvoNova (AvoNova); Bard (Avon Bard Books); Camelot (Avon Camelot Books); Flare (Avon Flare Books).

AvoNova *Imprint of* **Avon**

Avonstoke Pr, *(Avonstoke Pr.; 0-9618726; 1-879094),* Div. of Momentum Bks., Ltd., 6964 Crooks Rd., Suite 1, Troy, MI 48098 Tel 810-828-3666.

Avosett Bks, *(Avosett Bks.; 0-9625824),* 3413 45th Ave., W., Seattle, WA 98199 Tel 206-282-3777.

AVSTAR Pub, *(AVSTAR Publishing Corp.; 0-9623653; 1-878827),* P.O. Box 537, Lebanon, NJ 08833; 34C Burlinghoff Ln., Lebanon, NJ 08833 Tel 908-236-6210.

Awani Pr, *(Awani Pr.; 0-915266),* P.O. Box 881, Fredericksburg, TX 78624 (SAN 206-4626) Tel 210-997-5514.

Aware Tribe, *(Aware Tribe, Inc.; 0-9626135),* R.D. 1, Box 223, Colton, NY 13625.

Axelrod Pub, *(Axelrod Publishing of Tampa Bay; 0-936417),* 1304 De Soto Ave., No. 308, Tampa, FL 33606 (SAN 698-1658) Tel 813-251-5269; P.O. Box 14248, Tampa, FL 33690 (SAN 698-2611); Dist. by: Quality Bks., Inc., 918 Sherwood Dr., Lake Bluff, IL 60044-2204 (SAN 169-2127) Tel 708-295-2010; Toll free: 800-323-4241 (libraries only); Dist. by: Baker & Taylor Bks., Somerville Service Ctr., 50 Kirby Ave., Somerville, NJ 08876-0734 (SAN 169-4901) Tel 908-722-8000; Toll free: 800-775-1500 (customer service); Dist. by: Baker & Taylor Bks., Momence Service Ctr., 501 S. Gladiolus St., Momence, IL 60954-2444 (SAN 169-2100) Tel 815-472-2444; Toll free: 800-775-2300 (customer service); Dist. by: Baker & Taylor Bks., Commerce Service Ctr., 251 Mt. Olive Church Rd., Commerce, GA 30599-9988 (SAN 169-1503) Tel 706-335-5000; Toll free: 800-775-1200 (customer service); Dist. by: Baker & Taylor Bks., Reno Service Ctr., 380 Edison Way, Reno, NV 89564 (SAN 169-4464) Tel 702-858-6700; Toll free: 800-775-1700 (customer service); Dist. by: Brodart Co., 500 Arch St., Williamsport, PA 17705 (SAN 169-7684) Tel 717-326-2461; Toll free: 800-233-8467.

Axiom Info Res, *(Axiom Information Resources; 0-943213),* P.O. Box 8015, Ann Arbor, MI 48107 (SAN 668-3088) Tel 313-761-4842.

Ayer, *(Ayer Co. Pubs., Inc.; 0-88143),* P.O. Box 958, Salem, NH 03079 (SAN 211-6936); 195 McGregor St., Manchester, NH 03102 Tel 603-669-5933.

AZ Hist Foun, *(Arizona Historical Foundation; 0-910152),* Hayden Memorial Library, Arizona State Univ., Tempe, AZ 85287 (SAN 201-7040) Tel 602-966-8331.

AZ Mem Mus, *(Arizona Memorial Museum Assn.; 0-9631388),* 1 Arizona Memorial Pl., Honolulu, HI 96818 Tel 808-422-5905.

Azalar Pub, *(Azalar Publishing; 0-9624831),* P.O. Box 812, HCR30, Sedona, AZ 86336; 1706 Willow Dr., Cornville, AZ 86325 Tel 602-282-2321.

Azimuth GA, *(Azimuth Pr.; 0-9632074; 1-886218),* 3002 Dayna Dr., College Park, GA 30349 Tel 404-994-9449; Dist. by: BookWorld Distribution Services, Inc., 1933 Whitfield Pk. Loop, Sarasota, FL 34243 (SAN 173-0568) Tel 813-758-8094; Toll free: 800-444-2524 (orders only). Do not confuse with companies with the same name in Annapolis, MD, Houston, TX.

AZU Music Pr, *(Arizona Univ. Music Pr.; 0-943121),* Univ. of Arizona, Schl. of Music, Tucson, AZ 85721 (SAN 668-0933) Tel 602-621-5942.

B A Langham, *(Langham, Barbara A.; 0-9640804),* 9501 Capital of Texas Hwy. N., Suite 202, Austin, TX 78759 Tel 512-346-2261.

B A Scott, *(Scott, Beverly A., Pub.),* P.O. Box 114, Chandler, AZ 85224 (SAN 207-6101) Tel 602-963-5787.

B & D Pub, *(B & D Publishing; 0-9613328),* 1915 Solano St., Suite B, Corning, CA 96021 (SAN 289-5854) Tel 916-824-1410.

B & G Cordoves, *(Cordoves, Barbara & Gladys M.; 0-9637252),* 5050 NW 7th St., Apt. 603, Miami, FL 33126 Tel 305-444-3118.

B & R Samizdat, *(B & R Samizdat Express; 0-915232),* P.O. Box 161, West Roxbury, MA 02132 (SAN 207-1037) Tel 617-469-2269.

B B Saloom, *(Saloom, Barbara B.; 0-9627755),* 18 Hollow Tree Rd., Boxford, MA 01921 Tel 508-887-2581.

B B Stabell, *(Stabell, Brenda B.; 0-9610872),* 10827 Overbrook, Houston, TX 77042 (SAN 264-407X).

B B Williams, *(Williams, Bradley B.; 0-9620486),* 104B Simpson St., Greenville, SC 29605 (SAN 248-8531) Tel 803-269-3336.

B Bakos, *(Bakos, Brian; 0-9641554),* P.O. Box 508, South Lyon, MI 48178; 59325 Nine Mile Rd., South Lyon, MI 48178 Tel 810-486-5885.

B Bk Pub Co, *(B. Bk. Publishing Co.; 0-9625337),* P.O. Box 858, Stratford, CT 06497; 200 Glendale Rd., Stratford, CT 06497 Tel 203-261-7236.

B Brae, *(Bonnie Brae Pubns.; 0-944453),* Div. of DRG, Inc., 12 Pickens Ln., Weaverville, NC 28787 (SAN 243-6221) Tel 704-645-5293.

B Bumpers Inc, *(B. Bumpers, Inc.; 0-9621691),* 10309 Smokey Point Blvd., Suite B, Marysville, WA 98270 (SAN 251-8589) Tel 206-659-5528.

B C Pub Inc, *(B.C. Publishing, Inc.; 0-926521),* Rte. 3, Box 734, Broken Arrow, OK 74014; 26520 E. 57th St., Broken Arrow, OK 74014 Tel 918-357-3285.

B Crocker Ckbks *Imprint of* **P-H Gen Ref & Trav**

B Cutlip, *(Cutlip, Burdette),* Box 215, Blackwoods, WV 26621 (SAN 668-3800) Tel 304-765-5828.

B dazzle, *(b-dazzle, inc.; 1-885437),* 240 The Village, Suite 309, Redondo Beach, CA 90277-2535 Tel 310-374-3000; Toll free: 800-809-4242.

B-Dock Pr, *(B-Dock Pr.; 0-9621728),* P.O. Box 8, Willingboro, NJ 08046 (SAN 252-1962); 16 Meadowbrook Pl., Willingboro, NJ 08046 (SAN 252-1970) Tel 609-877-6018.

B Dolphin Pub, *(Blue Dolphin Publishing, Inc.; 0-931892),* P.O. Box 1920, Nevada City, CA 95959 (SAN 223-2480); Toll free: 800-643-0765; 12380 Nevada City Hwy., Grass Valley, CA 95945 (SAN 696-009X) Tel 916-265-6925; Dist. by: Baker & Taylor Bks., Somerville Service Ctr., 50 Kirby Ave., Somerville, NJ 08876-0734 (SAN 169-4901) Tel 908-722-8000; Toll free: 800-775-1500 (customer service); Dist. by: The Distributors, 702 S. Michigan, South Bend, IN 46601 (SAN 169-2488) Tel 219-232-8500; Toll free: 800-348-5200 (except Indiana); Dist. by: Bookpeople, 7900 Edgewater Dr., Oakland, CA 94621 (SAN 168-9517) Tel 510-632-4700; Toll free: 800-999-4650; Dist. by: New Leaf Distributing Co., 5425 Tulane Dr., SW, Atlanta, GA 30336-2323 (SAN 169-1449) Tel 404-691-6996; Toll free: 800-326-2665; Dist. by: Quality Bks., Inc., 918 Sherwood Dr., Lake Bluff, IL 60044-2204 (SAN 169-2127) Tel 708-295-2010; Toll free: 800-323-4241 (libraries only); Dist. by: Moving Bks., Inc., P.O. Box 20037, Seattle, WA 98102 (SAN 159-0685) Tel 206-762-1750; Toll free: 800-777-6683; Dist. by: Ingram Bk. Co., 1 Ingram Blvd., La Vergne, TN 37086-1986 (SAN 169-7978) Tel 615-793-5000; Toll free: 800-937-8000 (orders only, all warehouses); Dist. by: Inland Bk. Co., 140 Commerce St., East Haven, CT 06512 (SAN 200-4151) Tel 203-467-4257; Toll free: 800-243-0138; Dist. by: Concepts Bks. & Tapes Distributors, 9722 Pine Lake, Houston, TX 77055 (SAN 630-7531) Tel 713-465-7736.

B H Watson, *(Watson, Beverly Hale; 0-9623647),* 4704 Quail Ridge Dr., Charlotte, NC 28227 Tel 704-545-8042.

B Hawkins Studio, *(Hawkins, Beverly, Studio & Gallery; 0-9608084),* 20104 Halloway Ave., Matoaca, VA 23803 (SAN 240-1495) Tel 804-861-9403; Orders to: 2557E S. Crater Rd., Petersburg, VA 23803 (SAN 665-7087).

B Hegne, *(Hegne, Barbara; 0-9623847; 1-884728),* 130 Onyx St., Eagle Point, OR 97524 Tel 503-826-9725.

B K Cho, *(Cho, Byung Kon; 0-9625199),* 2960 Allied Dr., Green Bay, WI 54304 Tel 414-336-0551.

B K Media Arts, *(Kaminski, Bob, Media Arts; 0-9636089),* 183 Garfield St., Ashland, OR 97520 Tel 503-482-1328.

B L Winch, *(Winch, B. L., & Assocs.; 0-935266),* 2675 Skypark Dr., Suite 204, Torrance, CA 90505-5330 (SAN 247-2716) Tel 310-784-0016; Toll free: 800-662-9662 (orders only).

B Leahy, *(Leahy, Barbara; 0-9610312),* 15 Mission Rd., Sedona, AZ 86336 (SAN 264-1720) Tel 602-282-3518.

B Martin BYR *Imprint of* **H Holt & Co**

B Melger, *(Melger, Boyd; 0-9622463),* 2819 Cunningham Ave., San Jose, CA 95148-1106 Tel 408-270-3816.

B Ponce, *(Ponce, Blanca; 0-9622493),* 453 Jose B. Acevedo, Rio Piedras, PR 00923 Tel 809-763-7993.

B Scherer, *(Scherer, Bonnie; 0-9622421),* 1021 Alderson, Billings, MT 59102 Tel 406-245-7289.

B Scott Bks, *(Scott, Bob, Bks.; 0-9621201),* P.O. Box 1461, San Clemente, CA 92674-1461 (SAN 250-6866); 201 Calle Dorado, San Clemente, CA 92672 (SAN 250-6874) Tel 714-492-8781.

B Segal, *(Segal, Berty, Inc.; 0-938395),* 1749 Eucalyptus St., Brea, CA 92621 (SAN 630-0553) Tel 714-529-5359.

B Shackelford, *(Shackelford, Bud; 0-9634693),* 11532 Rolling Hills Dr., El Cajon, CA 92020 Tel 619-442-3164.

B Sheldon, *(Sheldon, Bill, Pub.; 0-9616668),* 5478 Mary Jo Way, San Jose, CA 95124 (SAN 659-9079) Tel 408-264-2728.

B Winston, *(Winston, Barbara; 0-9622810),* 19774 Cheyenne, Detroit, MI 48235 Tel 313-863-8832; Dist. by: School Hse., 19363 Livernois, Detroit, MI 48221 (SAN 630-3498) Tel 313-342-1261.

B Yeager, *(Yeager, Brigid; 0-9620146),* 302 Fairview Dr., Exton, PA 19341 (SAN 247-7491) Tel 610-524-8376.

Babe Co, *(Babe Co.; 0-9620258),* P.O. Box 483, Temple Hills, MD 20748 (SAN 248-3203); Toll free: 800-254-3653; 4108 Holly Tree Rd., Temple Hills, MD 20748 (SAN 248-3211) Tel 301-702-9348.

Back Bay, *(Back Bay Bks., Inc.; 0-939126),* P.O. Box 1396, Newport Beach, CA 92663 (SAN 216-1060) Tel 714-645-4900.

Back Home Indust, *(Back Home Industries; 1-880045),* P.O. Box 22495, Milwaukie, OR 97222; 8431 SE 36th Ave., Portland, OR 97222 Tel 503-654-2300.

Back to Bible, *(Back to the Bible Broadcast; 0-8474),* Box 82808, Lincoln, NE 68501 (SAN 211-6901); Toll free: 800-759-2425; 301 S. 12th St., Lincoln, NE 68508 Tel 402-474-4567.

Backroads, *(Backroads; 0-933294),* Box 14, Kelly, WY 83011 (SAN 213-831X) Tel 307-733-7730.

Backwards & Backwards, *(Backwards & Backwards Pr.; 0-910253),* 7561 Pearl Rd., Middleburg Heights, OH 44130 (SAN 241-4724) Tel 216-891-9311.

Backyard Music, *(Backyard Music; 0-9614939),* P.O. Box 9047, New Haven, CT 06532 (SAN 693-6776) Tel 203-281-4515.

Backyard Scientist, *(Backyard Scientist/Jane Hoffman; 0-9618663),* P.O. Box 16966, Irvine, CA 92713 (SAN 219-1725); 14652 Beach Ave., Irvine, CA 92714 (SAN 667-4461) Tel 714-551-2392.

Bader & Co
See Liberty

Baen Bks, *(Baen Bks.; 1-55594),* Div. of Baen Publishing Enterprises, P.O. Box 1403, Riverdale, NY 10471 (SAN 658-8417); 5020 Henry Hudson Pkwy., Riverdale, NY 10471 Tel 718-548-3100; Dist. by: Pocket Books, 1230 Ave. of the Americas, New York, NY 10020 (SAN 202-5922) Tel 212-698-7406; Toll free: 800-223-2336 (orders); 800-223-2348 (customer service).

Baggeboda Pr, *(Baggeboda Pr.; 0-932591),* R.R.1, Box 2315, Unity, ME 04988-9716 (SAN 687-505X).

Baggiani-Tewell, *(Baggiani-Tewell Educational Materials; 0-934329),* 4 Spring Hill Ct., Chevy Chase, MD 20815 (SAN 693-6024) Tel 301-656-3353.

Bahai, *(Baha'i Distribution Service; 0-87743),* 5397 Wilbanks Dr., Chattanooga, TN 37343 (SAN 213-7496).

Bainbridge Pr, *(Bainbridge Pr.; 1-877851),* 701 Fifth Ave., No. 5400, Seattle, WA 98104-7078.

Baines
See Nevada Pub

Bakebks & Cookbks, *(Bakebooks & Cookbooks, Inc.; 0-9606686),* P.O. Box 92185, Milwaukee, WI 53202 (SAN 219-7111) Tel 414-461-9813.

Baker Bk, *(Baker Bk. Hse.; 0-8010; 0-913686),* P.O. Box 6287, Grand Rapids, MI 49516-6287 (SAN 201-4041) Tel 616-676-9185; Toll free: 800-877-2665.

Baker Seaforth, *(Baker Seaforth Pubns.; 0-9623980),* HC 72, Box 43, Clinton, AR 72031 Tel 501-745-4035.

Bala Bks, *(Bala Bks.; 0-89647),* P.O. Box 311, Old Westbury, NY 11568 (SAN 284-9747) Tel 516-334-0909; Orders to: Bala Bks., 12520 Kirkham Court, Suite 7, Poway, CA 92064 Tel 619-679-9080.

Balaena Bks, *(Balaena Bks., Inc.; 0-9624094),* P.O. Box 1633, New Smyrna Beach, FL 32170; 4444 Sea Mist Dr., New Smyrna Beach, FL 32170 Tel 904-427-8798.

Balance Pub, *(Balance Publishing Co.; 1-878298),* 1346 S. Quality Ave., Sanger, CA 93657 Tel 209-875-4828; Dist. by: Entry Publishing, Inc., 27 W. 96th St., New York, NY 10025 (SAN 238-9754) Tel 212-662-9703.

Balance Pubns, *(Balance Pubns.; 0-9632724),* P.O. Box 447, Port Angeles, WA 98362-0069; 430 E. Blvd., Port Angeles, WA 98362 Tel 206-457-0938.

Baldner J V, *(Baldner, Jean V.; 0-9615317),* 19203 N. 29th Ave., Phoenix, AZ 85027 (SAN 694-6526) Tel 602-582-0312.

Ballantine, *(Ballantine Bks., Inc.; 0-345; 0-87637),* Div. of Random Hse., Inc., 201 E. 50th St., New York, NY 10022 (SAN 214-1175) Tel 212-572-2620; Toll free: 800-726-0600 (customer service); 800-733-3000 (orders); Orders to: 400 Hahn Rd., Westminster, MD 21157 (SAN 214-1183) Tel 410-848-1900. *Imprints:* Del Rey (Del Rey Books).

Ballash Pr
See Glue Bks

Ballyhoo Bks, *(Ballyhoo Bks.; 0-936335),* P.O. Box 534, Shoreham, NY 11786 (SAN 697-8487); 1 Sylvan Dr., Wading River, NY 11792 (SAN 698-2239) Tel 516-929-8148.

Balsam Pr, *(Balsam Pr., Inc.; 0-917439),* 36 E. 22nd St., 9th Flr., New York, NY 10010 (SAN 208-4503) Tel 212-475-6895. Do not confuse with Balsam Pr., Inc. in Burnsville, MN.

Bamboo Ridge Pr, *(Bamboo Ridge Pr.; 0-910043),* P.O. Box 61781, Honolulu, HI 96822-8781 (SAN 240-8740) Tel 808-599-4823.

BAN Pub Boston, *(BAN Publishing Co.; 0-938357),* 6 Rollins Pl., Boston, MA 02114 (SAN 698-178X) Tel 617-227-1332.

Banana Joe, *(Banana Joe Productions; 1-884599),* 10336 NE 201st Pl., Bothell, WA 98011 Tel 206-485-0215; Dist. by: Pacific Pipeline, Inc., 8030 S. 228th St., Kent, WA 98032-2900 (SAN 208-2128) Tel 206-872-5523; Toll free: 800-444-7323 (Customer service); 800-677-2222 (orders).

Bancroft-Sage, *(Bancroft-Sage Publishing, Inc.; 0-944280),* 601 Elkcam Cir., Suite C7, Box 355, Marco, FL 33969 (SAN 243-0398) Tel 813-642-5600; Toll free: 800-942-1745.

B&B Pr, *(Bread & Butter Pr.; 0-9630441),* 907 Cornelia Ave., Lakeland, FL 33801 Tel 813-683-1775; Toll free: 800-354-2757. Do not confuse with Bread & Butter Pr. in Denver, CO.

Bang A Drum, *(Bang A Drum Enterprises; 1-878130),* Div. of KMC Ideas, Inc., P.O. Box 6436, Cincinnati, OH 45206-0436.

Bank St Pr, *(Bank Street Pr., The; 0-935505),* 24 Bank St., New York, NY 10014 (SAN 696-0634) Tel 212-255-0692.

Banksiana, *(Banksiana Publishing Co.; 0-9627867),* 611 22 3/4 St., P.O. Box 804, Chetek, WI 54728 Tel 715-924-4668.

Banmar Inc, *(Banmar Inc.; 0-9614989),* 4239 Monroe St., Toledo, OH 43606 (SAN 693-7594) Tel 419-473-2940.

Banner of Truth, *(Banner of Truth, The; 0-85151),* P.O. Box 621, Carlisle, PA 17013 (SAN 112-1553) Tel 717-249-5747.

Bantam, *(Bantam Bks., Inc.; 0-553),* Div. of Bantam Doubleday Dell, 1540 Broadway, New York, NY 10036-4094 (SAN 201-3975) Tel 212-354-6500; Toll free: 800-223-6834; Orders to: 414 E. Golf Rd., Des Plaines, IL 60016 (SAN 201-3983) Tel 312-827-1111. *Imprints:* Bantam Classics (Bantam Classics); Little Rooster (Little Rooster); Loveswept (Loveswept); Skylark (Skylark); Spectra (Spectra); Starfire (Starfire); Sweet Dreams (Sweet Dreams).

Bantam Classics *Imprint of* **Bantam**

Banyan Bks, *(Banyan Bks.; 0-916224),* P.O. Box 431160, Miami, FL 33243 (SAN 208-340X) Tel 305-665-9396.

Baptist Pub Hse, *(Baptist Publishing Hse.; 0-89114),* Div. of Baptist Missionary Assn. of America, 1319 Magnolia St., P.O. Box 7270, Texarkana, TX 75505-7270 (SAN 183-6544) Tel 903-793-6531; Toll free: 800-333-1442.

Bar JaMae, *(Bar' JaMae Communications, Inc.; 1-883414),* P.O. Box 64412, Virginia Beach, VA 23467-4412.

Barbarash Pubns, *(Barbarash Pubns.; 0-9632364),* 5 Hickory Ct., Staten Island, NY 10309 Tel 718-356-6498.

Barbour & Co, *(Barbour & Co., Inc.; 0-916441; 1-55748),* Affil. of Book Bargains, Inc., P.O. Box 719, 1810 Barbour Dr., Uhrichsville, OH 44683 (SAN 295-7094) Tel 614-922-6045; Toll free: 800-852-8010; Dist. by: Spring Arbor Distributors, 10885 Textile Rd., Belleville, MI 48111 (SAN 158-9016) Tel 313-481-0900; Toll free: 800-395-5599 (orders); 800-395-7234 (customer service); Dist. by: Ingram Bk. Co., 1 Ingram Blvd., La Vergne, TN 37086-1986 (SAN 169-7978) Tel 615-793-5000; Toll free: 800-937-8000 (orders only, all warehouses); Dist. by: Baker & Taylor Bks., Somerville Service Ctr., 50 Kirby Ave., Somerville, NJ 08876-0734 (SAN 169-4901) Tel 908-722-8000; Toll free: 800-775-1500 (customer service); Dist. by: Riverside/World, P.O. Box 370, 1500 Riverside Dr., Iowa Falls, IA 50126 (SAN 169-2666) Tel 515-648-4271; Toll free: 800-247-5111; Dist. by: Living Bks., Inc., 12155 Magnolia Ave., Bldg. 11-B, Riverside, CA 92503 (SAN 169-006X) Tel 909-354-7330; Toll free: 800-854-4746; 800-922-0047 (in California); Dist. by: Appalachian Bible Co. & Christian Bks., 506 Princeton Rd., Johnson City, TN 37601 (SAN 169-7889) Tel 615-282-9475; Toll free: 800-289-2772; Dist. by: Whitaker Hse., 580 Pittsburgh St., Springdale, PA 15144 (SAN 203-2104) Tel 412-274-4440; Toll free: 800-444-4484.

Barclay Bks, *(Barclay Bks.; 0-9630637),* P.O. Box 3452, Ann Arbor, MI 48106; 1318 Rosewood, Ann Arbor, MI 48104 Tel 810-541-3424; Dist. by: Publishers Distribution Service, 6893 Sullivan Rd., Grawn, MI 49637 (SAN 630-5717) Tel 616-276-5196; Toll free: 800-345-0096 (orders only).

Barclay Pr, *(Barclay Pr.; 0-913342),* Div. of Northwest Yearly Meeting of Friends Church, 600 E. Third St., Newberg, OR 97132 (SAN 201-7520) Tel 503-538-7345; Toll free: 800-962-4014.

Bard *Imprint of* **Avon**

Bard Hall Pr, *(Bard Hall Pr.; 0-916491),* 32 Nickerbocker at Oak, Tenafly, NJ 07670 (SAN 295-2459) Tel 201-567-7629; Dist. by: Persea Bks., Inc., 60 Madison Ave., New York, NY 10010 (SAN 212-8233) Tel 212-779-7668.

Barefoot Bks, *(Barefoot Bks., Inc.; 1-56957),* Affil. of Shambhala Pubns., Inc., Horticultural Hall, 300 Massachusetts Ave., Boston, MA 02115 Tel 617-424-0030; Dist. by: Random Hse., Inc., 400 Hahn Rd., Westminster, MD 21157 (SAN 202-5515) Tel 410-848-1900; Toll free: 800-733-3000.

Barker Creek, *(Barker Creek Publishing, Inc.; 0-9639307),* 375 Sigurd Hanson Rd., Poulsbo, WA 98370 Tel 206-692-5833.

Barksdale Foun, *(Barksdale Foundation; 0-918588),* P.O. Box 187, Idyllwild, CA 92549 (SAN 210-1718) Tel 909-659-4676.

Barlenmir, *(Barlenmir Hse. Pubs.; 0-87929),* P.O.Box 125, Bronx, NY 10464-0125 (SAN 164-6044) Tel 718-885-2120.

Barmarle Pubns, *(Barmarle Pubns.; 0-9619463),* 735 Nardo Rd., Encinitas, CA 92024 (SAN 245-0070) Tel 619-753-6950.

Barnaby Bks, *(Barnaby Bks.; 0-940350),* 3290 Pacific Heights Rd., Honolulu, HI 96813 (SAN 217-5010) Tel 808-524-1490; Dist. by: Pacific Trade Group, 94-527 Puahi St., Waipahu, HI 96797 (SAN 169-1635) Tel 808-671-6735.

Barney Pub, *(Barney Publishing; 1-57064),* Div. of The Lyons Group, 300 E. Bethany Rd., Allen, TX 75002 Tel 214-390-6082; Toll free: 800-862-2763.

Barnwood Pr, *(Barnwood Pr. Cooperative; 0-935306),* P.O. Box 146, Selma, IN 47383 (SAN 223-7245) Tel 317-288-0145.

Barriclyn, *(Barriclyn Pubns.; 0-9631097),* 5140 S. Yampa Cir., Aurora, CO 80015 Tel 303-693-5933.

Barrier & Kennedy, *(Barrier & Kennedy, ESL;* 0-911743), P.O. Box 58273, Raleigh, NC 27658 (SAN 276-9689) Tel 919-847-1477.

Barrington Hse, *(Barrington Hse. Publishing Co.;* 0-935323), 1119 Lorne Way, Sunnyvale, CA 94087 (SAN 695-7501) Tel 408-241-8422.

Barron, *(Barron's Educational Series, Inc.; 0-8120),* P.O. Box 8040, 250 Wireless Blvd., Hauppauge, NY 11788 (SAN 201-453X) Tel 516-434-3311; Toll free: 800-645-3476.

Barsotti Bks, *(Barsotti Bks.; 0-9642112),* 2239 Hidden Valley Ln., Camino, CA 95709 Tel 916-622-4629.

Basic Comp Lit, *(Basic Computer Literacy, Inc.;* 0-931983), 370 N. Locust, Manteno, IL 60950 (SAN 686-0931) Tel 815-468-8178.

Basil Blackwell
See Blackwell Pubs

Basin Pub, *(Basin Publishing Co.; 0-940591),* 168 Weyford Terr., Garden City, NY 11530 (SAN 208-4562) Tel 516-741-0668.

Bassett & Brush, *(Bassett & Brush; 0-9605548),* W. 4108 Francis Ave., Spokane, WA 99205 (SAN 216-3349).

Bassi Bk, *(Bassi Bk. Co.; 0-9628624),* 2032 Houston Pl., Denton, TX 76201 Tel 817-382-3702.

Batboy Pr, *(Batboy Pr.; 0-9629307),* 3 Beaver Pond Ct., New Freedom, PA 17349 Tel 717-993-3162.

Bauhan, *(Bauhan, William L., Inc.; 0-87233),* P.O. Box 443, Dublin, NH 03444-0443 (SAN 204-384X) Tel 603-563-8020.

Bayberry Pr, *(Bayberry Pr.; 0-916326),* 21 Little Fox Ln., Westport, CT 06880 (SAN 222-562X) Tel 203-226-5187. Do not confuse with companies with the same name in Springfield, MO, Ocean City, MD.

Bayla Prods, *(Bayla Products, Inc.; 0-9634525),* 5082 W. Colonial Dr., Suite 150, Orlando, FL 32808 Tel 407-294-2177.

Bayley & Musgrave, *(Bayley & Musgrave; 1-882726),* 4949 Trailridge Pass, Dunwoody, GA 30338 Tel 404-668-9738.

BaySailor Bks, *(BaySailor Bks.; 0-9618461),* P.O. Box 116, Royal Oak, MD 21662 (SAN 667-920X).

Baywood, *(Baywood Hse., Inc.; 1-880403),* P.O. Box 33022, Los Gatos, CA 95031 (SAN 297-5114); 16210 Matilija Dr., No. 200, Los Gatos, CA 95030 Tel 408-354-7975.

BBC-Parkwest *Imprint of* **Parkwest Pubns**

BCM Pubn, *(BCM Pubn.; 0-86508),* 237 Fairfield Ave., Upper Darby, PA 19082 (SAN 211-7762) Tel 610-352-7177.

BCS Educ Aids, *(BCS Educational Aids, Inc.; 0-938416),* P.O. Box 100, Bothell, WA 98041 (SAN 239-9326) Tel 206-485-4110.

Bd Regents, *(Board of Regents, Gunston Hall; 1-884085),* 10709 Gunston Rd., Lorton, VA 22079-3901 Tel 703-550-9220.

BDB Unlimited, *(BDB, Unlimited; 0-925022),* 2031 Rockhaven Dr., Decatur, GA 30032 Tel 404-458-3922.

Bding Better People, *(Building Better People, Inc.;* 0-9624760), P.O. Box 2088, Newport Beach, CA 92663; 809 Promontory Dr., W., Newport Beach, CA 92660 Tel 503-673-3942.

Beach Pebbles, *(Beach Pebbles Pr.; 0-9641138),* 1187 Coast Village Rd., Suite I-275, Santa Barbara, CA 93108 Tel 805-969-5934.

Beachcomber Pr, *(Beachcomber Pr.; 0-9614628),* RR3, Box 2220, Belgrade Rd., Oakland, ME 04963 (SAN 691-8891) Tel 207-465-7197; Toll free: 800-451-5804; Dist. by: Magazines, Inc., 1135 Hammond St., Bangor, ME 04401 (SAN 169-3034) Tel 207-942-8237; Toll free: 800-649-9224 (in Maine); Dist. by: Portland News Co., 270 Western Ave., P.O. Box 1728, South Portland, ME 04104 (SAN 169-3093) Tel 207-774-2633; Toll free: 800-639-1708 (in Maine). Do not confuse with Beachcomber Pr. in Escondido, CA.

Beacon Bks, *(Beacon Bks.; 0-929311),* 2125 E. Nantuckett Dr., Gilbert, AZ 85234-3843 (SAN 248-9821) Tel 602-977-2380.

Beacon Hill, *(Beacon Hill Pr. of Kansas City; 0-8341),* Subs. of Nazarene Publishing Hse., P.O. Box 419527, Kansas City, MO 64141 (SAN 241-6328) Tel 816-931-1900.

Beacon Pr, *(Beacon Pr.; 0-8070),* 25 Beacon St., Boston, MA 02108 (SAN 201-4483) Tel 617-742-2110; Dist. by: Farrar, Straus & Giroux, Inc., 19 Union Sq., W., New York, NY 10003 (SAN 206-782X) Tel 212-741-6900; Toll free: 800-788-6262 (Individuals); 800-631-8571 (Booksellers).

Bead-Craft, *(Bead-Craft; 0-9613503),* 1549 Ashland Ave., Saint Paul, MN 55104 (SAN 657-2510) Tel 612-645-1216; Orders to: P.O. Box 4563, Saint Paul, MN 55104 (SAN 241-9629).

Beads Unique, *(Beads Unique; 0-9635501),* 308 Roberts Ln., Bakersfield, CA 93308 Tel 805-399-6523.

Bear Flag Bks, *(Bear Flag Bks.; 0-939919),* Subs. of Padre Productions, P.O. Box 840, Arroyo Grande, CA 93421-0840 Tel 805-473-1947. Do not confuse with Bear Flag Bks., San Francisco, CA.

Bear Hollow Pr, *(Bear Hollow Pr.; 0-938209),* Subs. of Shuttle Hill Herb Shop, Inc., 110 Salisbury Rd., Delmar, NY 12054 (SAN 659-459X) Tel 518-439-9065.

Bear Paw Bks, *(Bear Paw Bks.; 0-9629760),* Div. of Bear Paw Quilts, 2 Trueman Ct., Baltimore, MD 21207-1761.

Bear Tracks Pub, *(Bear Tracks Publishing Co.;* 0-9617624), 6767 Caledon Cv, Memphis, TN 38119-7807 (SAN 664-9858) Tel 901-767-5160.

Bear Wallow Pub, *(Bear Wallow Publishing Co., The;* 0-936376), P.O. Box 370, Union, OR 97883 (SAN 223-3916) Tel 503-562-5687.

Bears Designs, *(Bear's Designs Unlimited; 0-9638473),* 7505 320th St., W., Northfield, MN 55057 Tel 507-645-9050; Toll free: 800-497-8757.

Beautiful Am, *(Beautiful America Publishing Co.; 0-915796; 0-89802),* P.O. Box 646, Wilsonville, OR 97070 (SAN 251-2548); Toll free: 800-874-1233; 9725 SW Commerce Cir., Wilsonville, OR 97070 (SAN 211-4623) Tel 503-682-0173.

Beaver Pond P&P, *(Beaver Pond Publishing & Printing;* 1-881399), P.O. Box 224, Greenville, PA 16125 (SAN 630-9305); 454 Hadley Rd., Greenville, PA 16125 Tel 412-588-3492; Dist. by: Publishers Distribution Service, 6893 Sullivan Rd., Grawn, MI 49637 (SAN 630-5717) Tel 616-276-5196; Toll free: 800-345-0096 (orders only).

Beaver Valley, *(Beaver Valley Pubns.; 0-9622014),* Box 1015, 290th St., Glenwood City, WI 54013 Tel 715-772-4600.

Beavers, *(Beavers; 0-910208),* HCR 70, Box 537, La Porte, MN 56461 (SAN 202-389X) Tel 218-224-218270, .

Beckett-Highland, *(Beckett-Highland Publishing;* 0-9634373), 350 Gradle Dr., Carmel, IN 46032 Tel 317-573-0234; Toll free: 800-434-3343.

Bedrick Blackie *Imprint of* **P Bedrick Bks**

Bedrock Press *Imprint of* **Turner Pub GA**

Bedtime Bks, *(Bedtime Bks. Publishing; 0-9638393),* 215 W. Ave. Marquita, Suite A, San Clemente, CA 92672 Tel 714-361-3054.

Beechwood, *(Beechwood Bks.; 0-912221),* 720 Wehapa Cir., Leeds, AL 35094 (SAN 265-0797) Tel 205-699-6935.

Beeman Jorgensen, *(Beeman Jorgensen, Inc.; 0-929758),* 7510 Allisonville Rd., Indianapolis, IN 46250 (SAN 250-1279) Tel 317-841-7677; Dist. by: Motorbooks International, Pubs. & Wholesalers, Inc., 729 Prospect Ave., Osceola, WI 54020 (SAN 169-9164) Tel 715-294-3345; Toll free: 800-458-0454; Dist. by: Practice Ring, 7510 Allisonville Rd., Indianapolis, IN 46250 (SAN 630-6144) Tel 317-841-7677; Toll free: 800-553-5319.

Beginner, *(Beginner Bks.; 0-394),* Div. of Random Hse., Inc., 201 E. 50th St., New York, NY 10022 (SAN 202-3288) Tel 212-751-2600; Orders to: 400 Hahn Rd., Westminster, MD 21157 (SAN 202-3296) Tel 410-848-1900; Toll free: 800-733-3000 (orders).

Behav Sci Ctr Pubs, *(Behavioral Science Ctr., Pubs., Inc.; 0-938837),* 2522 Highland Ave., Cincinnati, OH 45219 (SAN 661-6895) Tel 513-221-8545; Toll free: 800-966-1231.

Behavior Products, *(Behavior Products; 0-9621191),* 413 S. Vick Ln., Anaheim, CA 92804 (SAN 250-7471) Tel 714-826-5711.

Behemoth Pub, *(Behemoth Publishing; 0-9606782),* 3220 W. 4500 S., Oasis, UT 84650 (SAN 217-331X) Tel 801-864-2842.

Behrman, *(Behrman Hse., Inc.; 0-87441),* 235 Watchung Ave., West Orange, NJ 07052 (SAN 201-4459) Tel 201-669-0447; Toll free: 800-221-2755.

Bell Bks CA, *(Bell Bks.; 1-880922),* P.O. Box 385, Etna, CA 96027; 153 Main St., Etna, CA 96027 Tel 916-467-3221.

Bell Ent, *(Bell Enterprises, Inc.; 0-918340),* P.O. Box 9054, Pine Bluff, AR 71611 (SAN 209-1895) Tel 501-247-1922.

Bellerophon Bks, *(Bellerophon Bks.; 0-88388),* 36 Anacapa St., Santa Barbara, CA 93101 (SAN 202-392X) Tel 805-965-7034; Toll free: 800-253-9943.

Belnice Bks, *(Belnice Bks.; 0-941274),* 337 Eighth St., Manhattan Beach, CA 90266 (SAN 239-4103) Tel 310-379-5405.

Ben-Simon, *(Ben-Simon Pubns.; 0-914539),* P.O. Box 2124, Port Angeles, WA 98362 (SAN 289-1492) Tel 604-652-6332.

BENA Pr, *(BENA Pr.; 0-9636784),* 3200 Virginia Ave. S., Suite 304, Minneapolis, MN 55426 Tel 612-936-9094.

Benefactory, *(Benefactory, Inc.; 1-882728),* 1 Post Rd., Fairfield, CT 06430 Tel 203-255-7744.

Benjamin OH, *(Benjamin Publishing Co., Inc.;* 0-9629806), 1862 Akron-Peninsula Rd., Akron, OH 44313 Tel 216-928-3674; Toll free: 800-466-1464.

Benmir Bks, *(Benmir Bks.; 0-917883),* 1529 Cypress St., Suite 105, Walnut Creek, CA 94596 (SAN 656-9641) Tel 510-933-5356.

Bennet Creek, *(Bennet Creek Publishing Co.;* 0-9618450), P.O. Box 140511, Lakewood, CO 80214 (SAN 667-8890) Tel 303-238-8522.

Bennett IL, *(Bennett Publishing Co.),* Div. of Macmillan Publishing Co., Inc., 3008 W. Willow Knolls, Peoria, IL 61614 (SAN 201-4440) Tel 309-689-3290; Toll free: 800-447-0680.

Benson, *(Benson, W. S., & Co., Inc.; 0-87443),* P.O. Box 1866, Austin, TX 78767 (SAN 202-3989) Tel 512-476-5050.

Bentley, *(Bentley, Robert, Inc., Pubs.; 0-8376),* 1000 Massachusetts Ave., Cambridge, MA 02138 (SAN 213-9839) Tel 617-547-4170; Toll free: 800-423-4595.

Bentwerth Pr, *(Bentwerth Pr.; 1-878342),* 609 W. Fourth St., Boone, IA 50036 (SAN 297-2174) Tel 515-432-3181.

Bergh Pub, *(Bergh Publishing, Inc.; 0-930267),* 20 E. 53rd St., New York, NY 10022-5252 (SAN 670-8633) Tel 212-593-1040; Dist. by: Talman Co., 131 Spring St., Suite 201E-N, New York, NY 10012 (SAN 200-5204) Tel 212-431-7175; Toll free: 800-537-8894 (orders only).

Bergwall, *(Bergwall Productions, Inc.; 0-943008; 0-8064),* P.O. Box 2400, Chadds Ford, PA 19317 (SAN 240-3064) Tel 610-388-0400; Toll free: 800-645-3565.

Berkley-Pacer *Imprint of* **Berkley Pub**

Berkley Pub, *(Berkley Publishing Group; 0-425; 0-515),* 200 Madison Ave., New York, NY 10016 (SAN 201-3991) Tel 212-951-8800; Toll free: 800-631-8571; Orders to: P.O. Box 506, East Rutherford, NJ 07073; Toll free: 800-223-0510 (orders); Dist. by: Warner Publishing Services, 1271 Avenue of the Americas, New York, NY 10020 (SAN 200-5522) Tel 212-522-8900. *Imprints:* Berkley-Pacer (Berkley/Pacer); Body Pr-Perigree (Body Press/Perigree); Splash (Splash).

Berkshire Hse, *(Berkshire Hse. Pubs.; 0-936399; 0-912944; 0-930145),* P.O. Box 297, Stockbridge, MA 01262 (SAN 698-1666); Toll free: 800-321-8526; Eight Pine St., Stockbridge, MA 01262 Tel 413-298-3636; Dist. by: National Bk. Network, 4720A Boston Way, Lanham, MD 20706-4310 (SAN 630-0065) Tel 301-459-8696; Toll free: 800-462-6420.

Berrent Pubns, *(Berrent Pubns., Inc.; 0-916259;* 1-55743), 1025 Northern Blvd., Roslyn, NY 11576 (SAN 294-9016) Tel 516-365-4040.

Berry Bks, *(Berry Bks.; 0-9614746),* 114 Woodpecker Ln., Whispering Pines, NC 28327 (SAN 692-9214).

Berry Good Child Bks, *(Berry Good Children's Bks.;* 0-9616555), 2214 NW 63rd Ave., Margate, FL 33063-2229 (SAN 659-4220); 6800 NW 39th Ave., Coconut Creek, FL 33067 (SAN 659-4239).

Bess Pr, *(Bess Pr., Inc.; 0-935848; 1-880188; 1-57306),* P.O. Box 22388, Honolulu, HI 96823 (SAN 239-4111); 2955 Dole St., Honolulu, HI 96816 (SAN 661-9584) Tel 808-734-7159.

Best Cellar Bks, *(Best Cellar Bks.; 0-9624574),* P.O. Box 5658, Santa Barbara, CA 93150.

Best Frnds, *(Best Friends Pr.; 0-9642063),* 43 Third Ave., Lehighton, PA 18235 Tel 610-377-0428.

Best Sllrs TX, *(Best Sellers Publishing, Inc.; 0-945362),* 11515 Sunnyside Dr., Baytown, TX 77520 (SAN 246-8387) Tel 713-576-5131.

Best Times Inc, *(Best of Times, Inc.; 0-9624032;* 1-886049), 147 Corporate Way, Pelham, AL 35124 (SAN 630-7647) Tel 205-664-6980.

Bet-Ken Prods, *(Bet-Ken Productions; 0-9603698),* 4363 Cherry Ave., San Jose, CA 95118 (SAN 213-683X) Tel 408-267-3425.

Beth Chana, *(Beth Chana Schl.; 0-9618441),* 620 Bedford Ave., Brooklyn, NY 11211 (SAN 667-6650) Tel 718-522-7422.

Bethany Hse, *(Bethany Hse. Pubs.; 0-87123; 1-55661),* Div. of Bethany Fellowship, Inc., 11300 Hampshire Ave., S., Minneapolis, MN 55438 (SAN 201-4416) Tel 612-829-2500; Toll free: 800-328-6109.

Bethel Pub, *(Bethel Publishing Co.; 0-934998),* Div. of Missionary Church, Inc., 1819 S. Main St., Elkhart, IN 46516 (SAN 201-7555) Tel 219-293-8585; Toll free: 800-348-7657.

Bethlehem WA, *(Bethlehem Bks.; 1-883937),* Div. of Bethlehem Covenant Community, 915 W. 13th St., Vancouver, WA 98660 Tel 206-695-8647.

Better Baby, *(Better Baby Pr., The; 0-936676; 0-944349),* Div. of Institutes for the Achievement of Human Potential, 8801 Stenton Ave., Philadelphia, PA 19118-2319 (SAN 215-7314) Tel 215-233-2050.

Better Pl Pub, *(Better Place Publishing, Inc.; 1-882436),* 611 W. Johnson Ave., Cheshire, CT 06410 Tel 203-272-6019; Toll free: 800-362-5437.

Betterway Bks, *(Betterway Bks.; 0-932620; 1-55870),* Div. of F & W Pubns., Inc., 1507 Dana Ave., Cincinnati, OH 45207-1005 Tel 513-531-2690; Toll free: 800-289-0963.

Beyond Words Pub, *(Beyond Words Publishing; 0-941831; 1-885223),* 13950 NW Pumpkin Ridge Rd., Hillsboro, OR 97124 (SAN 666-4210) Tel 503-647-5109; Toll free: 800-284-9673; Dist. by: Publishers Group West, 4065 Hollis St., Emeryville, CA 94608 (SAN 202-8522) Tel 510-658-3453; Toll free: 800-788-3123.

BGA Pubng, *(BGA Publishing, Inc.; 0-9639898),* 150 Dartmouth Rd., Massapequa, NY 11758 Tel 516-799-3494.

BGR Pub, *(BGR Publishing; 1-56843),* Div. of Educational Management Group, 6710 E. Camelback Rd., Suite 100, Scottsdale, AZ 85018 Tel 602-970-3250; Toll free: 800-842-6791.

Bhaktivedanta, *(Bhaktivedanta Bk. Trust; 0-912776;* 0-89213), 3764 Watseka Ave., Los Angeles, CA 90034 (SAN 203-8560) Tel 310-559-4455.

BH&G
See Meredith Bks

BHF Memories, *(BHF Memories Unltd.; 0-9614108),* 3470 Rolling View Ct., White Bear Lake, MN 55110 (SAN 685-2998) Tel 612-770-1922.

Bible Discovery *Imprint of* **Chariot Family**

Bible Memory, *(Bible Memory Assn., Inc.; 0-89323),* P.O. Box 588, Streamwood, IL 60107 (SAN 214-1019) Tel 708-213-0045.

Bible-Speak, *(Bible-Speak Enterprises; 0-911423),* 1940 Mount Vernon Ct., No. 4, Mountain View, CA 94040 (SAN 268-2931) Tel 415-965-9020.

Bible Temple, *(Bible Temple Publishing; 0-914936),* 9200 NE Fremont, Portland, OR 97220 (SAN 206-1953) Tel 503-253-9020; Toll free: 800-777-6057.

Biblo, *(Biblo & Tannen Booksellers & Pubs., Inc.;* 0-8196), P.O. Box 302, Cheshire, CT 06410 (SAN 202-4071); Toll free: 800-272-8778.

Bibulophile Pr, *(Bibulophile Pr.; 0-911153),* P.O. Box 399, Bantam, CT 06750-0399 (SAN 268-2990) Tel 203-567-5543.

Bicent Era, *(Bicentennial Era Enterprises; 0-9605734),* P.O. Box 1148, Scappoose, OR 97056 (SAN 216-2245) Tel 503-684-3937.

Bick Pub Hse, *(Bick Publishing Hse.; 1-884158),* 307 Neck Rd., Madison, CT 06443 Tel 203-245-0073; Dist. by: Inland Bk. Co., 140 Commerce St., East Haven, CT 06512 (SAN 200-4151) Tel 203-467-4257; Toll free: 800-243-0138.

Bicycle Books, *(Bicycle Bks., Inc.; 0-933201),* P.O. Box 2038, Mill Valley, CA 94942 (SAN 692-2600); Toll free: 800-468-8233; 32 Glen Dr., Mill Valley, CA 94941 (SAN 244-8335) Tel 415-381-2515; Dist. by: Bookpeople, 7900 Edgewater Dr., Oakland, CA 94621 (SAN 168-9517) Tel 510-632-4700; Toll free: 800-999-4650; Dist. by: National Bk. Network, 4720A Boston Way, Lanham, MD 20706-4310 (SAN 630-0065) Tel 301-459-8696; Toll free: 800-462-6420; Dist. by: Pacific Pipeline, Inc., 8030 S. 228th St., Kent, WA 98032-2900 (SAN 208-2128) Tel 206-872-5523; Toll free: 800-444-7323 (Customer Service); 800-677-2222 (orders); Dist. by: Quality Bks., Inc., 918 Sherwood Dr., Lake Bluff, IL 60044-2204 (SAN 169-2127) Tel 708-295-2010; Toll free: 800-323-4241 (libraries only); Dist. by: Alpenbooks, 3616 South Rd., C-1, Mukilteo, WA 98275 (SAN 113-5309); Toll free: 800-290-9898.

Biddle Pub, *(Biddle Publishing Co.; 1-879418),* P.O. Box 1305, No. 103, Brunswick, ME 04011 Tel 207-833-5016; Dist. by: Baker & Taylor Bks., National Sales Hdqtr., 5 Lakepointe Plaza, Suite 500, 2709 Water Ridge Pkwy., Charlotte, NC 28217 (SAN 169-5606); Toll free: 800-775-1800 (information); 800-775-1100 (Retail, Public & School Libraries orders); 800-775-2300 (Academic Libraries, Int'l. customeres orders); Dist. by: Baker & Taylor Bks., Somerville Service Ctr., 50 Kirby Ave., Somerville, NJ 08876-0734 (SAN 169-4901) Tel 908-722-8000; Toll free: 800-775-1500 (customer service); Dist. by: Baker & Taylor Bks., Momence Service Ctr., 501 S. Gladiolus St., Momence, IL 60954-1799 (SAN 169-2100) Tel 815-472-2444; Toll free: 800-775-2300 (customer service); Dist. by: Baker & Taylor Bks., Commerce Service Ctr., 251 Mount Olive Church Rd., Commerce, GA 30599-9988 (SAN 169-1503) Tel 706-335-5000; Toll free: 800-775-1200 (customer service); Dist. by: Baker & Taylor Bks., Reno Service Ctr., 380 Edison Way, Reno, NV 89564-0099 (SAN 169-4464) Tel 702-858-6700; Toll free: 800-775-1700 (customer service); Dist. by: Baker & Taylor Bks., Franklin Service Ctr., 2 Cottontail Ln., Somerset, NJ 08873-1133 (SAN 630-7205) Tel 908-469-7404; Dist. by: Bookpeople, 7900 Edgewater Dr., Oakland, CA 94621 (SAN 168-9517) Tel 510-632-4700; Toll free: 800-999-4650.

Big A NM, *(Big A & Co.; 0-9618995),* P.O. Box 92032, Albuquerque, NM 87199-2032 (SAN 242-8768) Tel 505-275-1690.

Big Bend, *(Big Bend Natural History Assn., Inc.;* 0-912001), Affil. of National Park Service, Box 68, Big Bend National Park, TX 79834 (SAN 268-3075) Tel 915-477-2236.

Big Heart Pub, *(Big Heart Publishing; 1-883703),* P.O. Box 70, Round Rock, TX 78680 Tel 512-310-0620; Dist. by: BookWorld Distribution Services, Inc., 1933 Whitfield Pk. Loop, Sarasota, FL 34243 (SAN 173-0568) Tel 813-758-8094; Toll free: 800-444-2524 (orders only).

Big Moose, *(Big Moose Pr.; 0-914692),* P.O. Box 180, Big Moose, NY 13331 (SAN 206-3336) Tel 315-357-2821.

Big Song Bk, *(Big Song Bk., Inc.; 1-883181),* P.O. Box 391143, Cambridge, MA 02139; 1 Kendall Sq., Suite 2200, Cambridge, MA 02139 Tel 617-621-7052.

Bilingual Ed Serv, *(Bilingual Educational Services, Inc.; 0-86624; 0-89075),* 2514 S. Grand Ave., Los Angeles, CA 90007 (SAN 218-4680) Tel 213-749-6213.

Bilingual Lang Mat, *(Bilingual Language Materials;* 0-9624096), 4912 River Ave., Newport Beach, CA 92663 Tel 714-642-3325.

Bilingue Pubns, *(Bilingue Pubns.; 0-933196),* P.O. Drawer H, Las Cruces, NM 88004 (SAN 223-6389) Tel 505-526-1557.

Billings Gazette, *(Billings Gazette; 0-9627618),* Div. of Lee Enterprises, P.O. Box 31635, Billings, MT 59107-1635; 401 N. Broadway, Billings, MT 59101 Tel 406-657-1269.

Binet Intl, *(Binet International; 0-942787),* P.O. Box 1429, Carlsbad, CA 92008 (SAN 667-7088) Tel 619-941-7929.

Binford Mort, *(Binford & Mort Publishing; 0-8323),* 1202 NW 17th Ave., Portland, OR 97209 (SAN 201-4386) Tel 503-221-0866; Orders to: P.O. Box 10404, Portland, OR 97210-0404.

Binney & Smith, *(Binney & Smith, Inc.; 0-86696),* P.O. Box 431, Easton, PA 18042 (SAN 216-5899).

Biosphere Pr, *(Biosphere Pr., The; 1-882428),* Div. of Space Biospheres Ventures, P.O. Box 689, Oracle, AZ 85623; Toll free: 800-992-4603; Biosphere Rd., Oracle, AZ 85623.

Biostration, *(Biostration; 0-9626301),* P.O. Box 399, Wellington, CO 80549; 3714 Grant Ave., Wellington, CO 80549 Tel 303-568-3557.

Biotech, *(Biotech Publishing; 1-880319),* Div. of Plant Something Different, Inc., P.O. Box 1032, Angleton, TX 77516-1032; 22318 S. County Rd. 48, Angleton, TX 77515 Tel 713-369-2044.

Birch Bark Pr, *(Birch Bark Pr.; 0-945860),* 34190 Lodge Rd., Tollhouse, CA 93667 (SAN 248-188X) Tel 209-855-6227.

Birch Ln Pr *Imprint of* **Carol Pub Group**

Birmingham Hist Soc, *(Birmingham Historical Society;* 0-943994), 1 Sloss Quarters, Birmingham, AL 35222-1243 (SAN 240-1347).

Bison Books *Imprint of* **U of Nebr Pr**

Biz Careers, *(Biz Careers, Inc.; 1-884194),* 280 Forest Glen Ave., Franklin Lakes, NJ 07417 Tel 201-891-4929.

BJO Enterprises, *(BJO's Enterprises; 0-941381),* 837 Archie St., Eugene, OR 97402 (SAN 667-1276).

Bk Lures, *(Book Lures, Inc.; 0-913839; 1-879287),* P.O. Box 0455, O'Fallon, MO 63366 (SAN 286-7273); Toll free: 800-844-0455; 203 San Jose Ct., O'Fallon, MO 63366-0455 Tel 314-272-4242.

BK Pubns, *(BK Pubns., Inc.; 0-9618890),* 7060 E. Calle del Sol, Tucson, AZ 85710 (SAN 242-4304) Tel 602-747-9352.

Bk Sales Inc, *(Book Sales, Inc.; 0-89009; 1-55521;* 0-7858), P.O. Box 7100, 114 Northfield Ave., Edison, NJ 08818-7100 (SAN 169-488X) Tel 908-225-0530; Toll free: 800-526-7257; 114 Northfield Ave., Edison, NJ 08837.

Bks By Brooks, *(Books by Brooks; 0-9616207),* P.O. Box 22865, Denton, TX 76204 (SAN 658-3288) Tel 817-898-2166.

Bks by Kellogg, *(Books by Kellogg; 0-9603972),* P.O. Box 487, Annandale, VA 22003 (SAN 214-0454) Tel 703-256-2483.

Bks By Kids, *(Books By Kids, For Kids, Inc.; 1-882996),* P.O. Box 141689, Irving, TX 75014-1689 (SAN 298-2153) Tel 817-421-3227.

Bks Demand, *(Books on Demand; 0-8357; 0-7837),* Div. of University Microfilms International, 300 N. Zeeb Rd., Ann Arbor, MI 48106-1346 (SAN 212-2464) Tel 313-761-4700; Toll free: 800-521-0600.

Bks Demand UMI
See Bks Demand

Bks Nippan, *(Books Nippan; 0-945814; 1-56970),* Div. of Nippan Shuppan Hanbai, U.S.A., Inc., 1123 Dominguez St., Suite K, Carson, CA 90746 (SAN 111-817X) Tel 310-604-9701; Toll free: 800-562-1410.

Bks of Our Times, *(Books of Our Times; 0-9607946),* 22 E. 29th St. Apartment 235, New York, NY 10016 (SAN 239-619X) Tel 212-532-4100.

Bks of Truth, *(Books of Truth; 0-939399),* 1742 Orchard Dr., Akron, OH 44333-1853 (SAN 663-1312) Tel 216-666-3852.

Bks Young Read *Imprint of* **H Holt & Co**

Bkwrights, *(Bookwrights Pr.; 1-880404),* 2522 Willard Dr., Charlottesville, VA 22903 Tel 804-296-0686.

Black Belt Commns
See Black Belt Pr

Black Belt Pr, *(Black Belt Pr.; 0-9622815; 1-881320),* Div. of Black Belt Communications Group, P.O. Box 551, Montgomery, AL 36101; 1123 S. Hull St., Montgomery, AL 36104 Tel 205-265-6753; Dist. by: Southern Pubs. Group, 147 Corporate Way, Pelham, AL 35124 (SAN 630-7817) Tel 205-664-6980; Toll free: 800-755-4411.

Black Birch Bks, *(Black Birch Bks.; 0-929545),* 96 Benthaven Pl., Boulder, CO 80303-6200 (SAN 249-6690).

Black Classic, *(Black Classic Pr.; 0-933121),* P.O. Box 13414, Baltimore, MD 21203 (SAN 219-5836) Tel 410-358-0980; Dist. by: Red Sea Pr., 11 Princess Rd., Suites D, E & F, Lawrenceville, NJ 08648 (SAN 630-1983) Tel 609-844-9583; Dist. by: Inland Bk. Co., 140 Commerce St., East Haven, CT 06512 (SAN 200-4151) Tel 203-467-4257; Toll free: 800-243-0138; Dist. by: New Leaf Distributing Co., 5425 Tulane Dr., SW, Atlanta, GA 30336-2323 (SAN 169-1449) Tel 404-691-6996; Toll free: 800-326-2665; Dist. by: Lushena Bks., 1804-06 W. Irving Rd., Chicago, IL 60613 (SAN 630-1983) Tel 312-975-9945; Dist. by: A&B Bks. Pubs./Distributors, 135 Lawrence St., Brooklyn, NY 11201 Tel 718-596-3389; Dist. by: Bookpeople, 7900 Edgewater Dr., Oakland, CA 94621 (SAN 168-9517) Tel 510-632-4700; Toll free: 800-999-4650.

Black Oak, *(Black Oak Pr.; 0-930674),* Box 4663, University Pl. Sta., Lincoln, NE 68504 (SAN 212-7261) Tel 402-488-9318.

Black Star Pub, *(Black Star Publishing Co.; 0-9605426),* 116 E. 27th St., 11th Flr., New York, NY 10016 (SAN 204-4153) Tel 212-679-3288.

Black Wallst, *(Black Wallstreet Pubs.; 1-884265),* P.O. Box 27002, Tulsa, OK 74149 (SAN 630-902X); 604 N. 26th West Ave., Tulsa, OK 74127 Tel 918-587-7229; Dist. by: Dularon Entertainment, Inc., P.O. Box 27002, Tulsa, OK 74149 Tel 918-587-7229.

Black Willow, *(Black Willow Poetry; 0-910047),* Belmont Plaza, 200 Ross Rd., K-141, King of Prussia, PA 19406 (SAN 240-9682) Tel 610-962-5971.

Blackberry ME, *(Blackberry: Salted in the Shell;* 0-942396), R.R. 1, Box 228, Nobleboro, ME 04555 (SAN 207-7949) Tel 207-729-5083.

Blackbirch, *(Blackbirch Pr., Inc.; 1-56711),* 1 Bradley Rd., Suite 205, Woodbridge, CT 06525 Tel 203-387-7525; Toll free: 800-831-9183.

Blackbird MI, *(Blackbird Pr.; 1-880691),* 8280 Messmore Rd., Utica, MI 48317-4430 Tel 810-726-0792. Do not confuse with Blackbird Pr. in Dubuque, IA.

Blackwater Pub Co, *(Blackwater Publishing Co., Inc.;* 0-910341), 530 Allison Ave., SW, Roanoke, VA 24016 (SAN 241-2756) Tel 703-362-4810.

Blackwell Pubs, *(Blackwell Pubs.; 0-631; 0-85520; 0-423; 0-900186; 0-904679; 0-7456; 0-233; 1-55786),* Subs. of Basil Blackwell, Ltd. (UK), 238 Main St., Cambridge, MA 02142 (SAN 680-5035) Tel 617-547-7110; Toll free: 800-216-2522; Dist. by: American International Distribution Corp., P.O. Box 20, Williston, VT 05495-0020 (SAN 630-2238) Tel 802-862-0095; Toll free: 800-488-2665 (textbk. hotline orders only).

Blair, *(Blair, John F., Pub.; 0-910244; 0-89587),* 1406 Plaza Dr., Winston-Salem, NC 27103 (SAN 201-4319) Tel 910-768-1374; Toll free: 800-222-9796.

Blake Pub, *(Blake Publishing, Inc.; 0-918303),* 2222 Beebee St., San Luis Obispo, CA 93401 (SAN 657-2618) Tel 805-543-7314; Toll free: 800-727-8558; Dist. by: Bookpeople, 7900 Edgewater Dr., Oakland, CA 94621 (SAN 168-9517) Tel 510-632-4700; Toll free: 800-999-4650; Dist. by: Pacific Pipeline, Inc., 8030 S. 228th St., Kent, WA 98032-2900 (SAN 208-2128) Tel 206-872-5523; Toll free: 800-444-7323 (Customer Service); 800-677-2222 (orders); Dist. by: Quality Bks., Inc., 918 Sherwood Dr., Lake Bluff, IL 60044-2204 (SAN 169-2127) Tel 708-295-2010; Toll free: 800-323-4241 (libraries only).

Blink Bks, *(Blink Bks.; 0-9638908),* 60 E. Chestnut St., No. 415, Chicago, IL 60611 Tel 312-943-4013.

Blip Prods, *(Blip Productions; 0-936917),* P.O. Box 33146, Minneapolis, MN 55433 (SAN 658-3253) Tel 612-427-1004.

Bloch, *(Bloch Publishing Co.; 0-8197),* 37 W. 26th St., New York, NY 10010 (SAN 214-204X) Tel 212-532-3977.

Block, *(Block Pubs.; 0-916864),* P.O. Box 1802, Palm Springs, CA 92263 (SAN 208-5577) Tel 619-327-0321.

Blossom Bks, *(Blossom Bks.; 0-943280),* P.O. Box 73251, Houston, TX 77273 (SAN 240-5997) Tel 713-893-3925; Toll free: 800-723-4324.

Blstckng Pr, *(Bluestocking Pr.; 0-942617),* P.O. Box 1014, Placerville, CA 95667-1014 (SAN 667-2981); Toll free: 800-959-8586; 3333 Gold Country Dr., Placerville, CA 95667 (SAN 667-299X) Tel 916-621-1123.

Blubber Budd, *(Blubber Buddies, Inc.; 0-9628626),* 1600 Marigold, McAllen, TX 78501 Tel 210-682-2755.

Blue Bird Pub, *(Blue Bird Publishing; 0-933025; 0-9615578),* 1739 E. Broadway, No. 306, Tempe, AZ 85282 (SAN 200-5603) Tel 602-968-4088.

Blue-Black, *(Blue-Black, Inc.; 0-9638457),* P.O. Box 337, Avalon, NJ 08202; Toll free: 800-216-4856; 2699 Dune Dr., Suite 203, Avalon, NJ 08202 Tel 609-967-5200.

Blue Crab MD, *(Blue Crab Pr.; 0-9627726),* c/o Blackistone & Assoc., 6473 Old Solomons Island Rd., Tracys Landing, MD 20779-9709. Do not confuse with Blue Crab Pr., Virginia Beach, VA.

Blue Dog Prodns, *(Blue Dog Productions, Inc.; 0-9627367),* 3302 Norman Ave., Baltimore, MD 21213-1025.

Blue Earth Pr *Imprint of* **Telstar TX**

Blue Flame Pr, *(Blue Flame Pr.; 0-9621558),* 35-45 79th St., Apt. 3J, Flushing, NY 11372 (SAN 251-589X) Tel 718-335-5491.

Blue Heron LA, *(Blue Heron Pr.; 0-9621724; 1-884725),* P.O. Box 550, Thibodaux, LA 70302-0550 (SAN 252-1199); 302 Thoroughbred Pk. Dr., Thibodaux, LA 70302 Tel 504-446-8201. Do not confuse with companies with the same name in Grand Rapids, MI, Bellingham, WA, Phoenix, MD.

Blue Heron OR, *(Blue Heron Publishing, Inc.; 0-936085),* 24450 NW Hansen Rd., Hillsboro, OR 97124 (SAN 696-6446) Tel 503-621-3911; Toll free: 800-858-9055 (credit cards only); Dist. by: Consortium Bk. Sales & Distribution, 1045 Westgate Dr., Suite 90, Saint Paul, MN 55114-1065 (SAN 200-6049) Tel 612-221-9035; Toll free: 800-283-3572 (orders).

Blue Heron WA, *(Blue Heron Pr.; 0-935317),* P.O. Box 5182, Bellingham, WA 98227 (SAN 695-7536); 4324 Gooding Ave., Bellingham, WA 98226 (SAN 662-3565) Tel 206-671-1155; Dist. by: Pacific Pipeline, Inc., 8030 S. 228th St, Kent, WA 98032-2900 (SAN 208-2128) Tel 206-872-5523; Toll free: 800-444-7323 (Customer Service); 800-677-2222 (orders). Do not confuse with companies with the same name in Phoenix, MD, Grand Rapids, MI, Thibodaux, LA.

Blue Jeans Pr, *(Blue Jeans Pr.; 0-934961),* Div. of Legal Education, Ltd., 1355 Wendover Dr., Charlottesville, VA 22901 (SAN 695-0515) Tel 804-293-7360; Toll free: 800-662-9673.

Blue Lantern Studio, *(Blue Lantern Studio; 0-9621131; 1-883211),* 4649 Sunnyside Ave., N., Seattle, WA 98103 (SAN 250-7722) Tel 206-632-7075; Dist. by: Laughing Elephant, P.O. Box 4399, Seattle, WA 98104 (SAN 630-8333); Toll free: 800-354-0400. *Imprints:* Laugh Elephant (Laughing Elephant).

Blue Note Pubns, *(Blue Note Pubns.; 1-878398),* P.O. Box 401, Melbourne Beach, FL 32951; Orders to: 110 Polk Ave., Suite 3, Cape Canaveral, FL 32920; Toll free: 800-624-0401 (orders only).

Blue Q, *(Blue Q; 1-878657),* 103 Hawthorne Ave., Pittsfield, MA 01201-6009 Tel 413-442-1600; Toll free: 800-321-7576.

Blue Ribbon Bks *Imprint of* **Scholastic Inc**

Blue Sky Grap, *(Blue Sky Graphics, Inc.; 0-9636186),* P.O. Box 270811, Fort Collins, CO 80527; 829 S. Summitview Dr., Fort Collins, CO 80524 Tel 303-484-7585.

Blue Sky Press *Imprint of* **Scholastic Inc**

Blue Squirrel, *(Blue Squirrel Concepts, Bk. Div.; 0-9638527),* 2640 Newman Rd., West Lafayette, IN 47906 Tel 317-743-0137.

Blue Star Pubs, *(Blue Star Pubs.; 1-882218),* P.O. Box 1027, Riverton, WY 82501; 1076 Missouri Valley Rd., Riverton, WY 82501 Tel 307-856-7365.

Blue Uncrn, *(Blue Unicorn Pr.; 0-9628584),* P.O. Box 40300, Portland, OR 97240 Tel 503-238-4766.

Blue Zero Pub, *(Blue Zero Publishing Co.; 1-880009),* Div. of RIM, Inc., P.O. Box 10699, Burbank, CA 91510 (SAN 297-5289); 334 S. California St., Burbank, CA 91505 (SAN 297-5297) Tel 818-840-0918.

Bluebird Pr CA, *(Bluebird Pr.; 0-934003),* P.O. Box 1000, Felicity, CA 92283 (SAN 692-669X) Tel 619-572-0100. Do not confuse with companies of the same name in Millersburg, OH, Eunice, LA.

Bluechip Pubs, *(Bluechip Pubs.; 0-930251),* 2606 Third Ave., Seattle, WA 98121 (SAN 670-8595).

Blustein-Geary, *(Blustein/Geary Assocs.; 0-9605248),* 46 Glen Cir., Waltham, MA 02154 (SAN 215-8450).

Blvd Bks FL, *(Boulevard Bks.; 1-882444),* P.O. Box 16267, Panama City, FL 32406-6267; 1016 Buena Vista Blvd., Panama City, FL 32401 Tel 904-785-1922. Do not confuse with Boulevard Bks. in Topanga, CA.

Blyden Pr, *(Blyden, Edward W., Pr., Inc.; 0-914110),* P.O. Box 621, Manhattanville Sta., New York, NY 10027 (SAN 206-4804) Tel 212-222-3797.

BMG Kidz, *(BMG Kidz),* 1540 Broadway, New York, NY 10036-4098 (SAN 630-799X) Tel 212-930-4000.

BMH Pubns, *(BMH Pubns.; 1-56788),* Div. of Benedictine Mission Hse., Benedictine Mission Hse., Box 528, Schuyler, NE 68661-0528 Tel 402-352-2177.

BML, *(BML; 1-882596),* P.O. Box 2615, Mercerville, NJ 08690 Tel 609-989-1216.

B'nai B'rith-Hillel, *(B'nai B'rith Hillel Foundations; 0-9603058),* 1640 Rhode Island Ave., NW, Washington, DC 20036 (SAN 204-4080) Tel 202-857-6560.

Board Jewish Educ, *(Board of Jewish Education of Greater New York; 0-88384),* 426 W. 58th St., New York, NY 10019 (SAN 213-0165) Tel 212-245-8200.

Boars Head, *(Boar's Head Pr.; 0-932114),* 5890 Bluff Rd., Saint Louis, MO 63129 (SAN 211-1489) Tel 314-846-2694.

Bob Bks, *(Bob Bk. Pubns.; 0-9612104),* P.O. Box 633, West Linn, OR 97068 (SAN 685-3781) Tel 503-657-1883.

Bob Jones Univ Pr, *(Jones, Bob, Univ. Pr.; 0-89084),* Bob Jones Univ., Greenville, SC 29614 (SAN 223-7512) Tel 803-242-5100; Toll free: 800-845-5731.

Bobbi Ent, *(Bobbi Enterprises; 0-9603200),* 4433 Larner St., The Colony, TX 75056 (SAN 213-2885) Tel 218-735-8364.

Body Pr-Perigree *Imprint of* **Berkley Pub**

Bogart Comm, *(Bogart Communications, Inc.; 1-882956),* 51 Cedar Dr., Danbury, CT 06811 Tel 203-792-4833.

Bold Prodns, *(Bold Productions; 0-938267),* P.O. Box 152281, Arlington, TX 76015 (SAN 659-8684); 3110 Fox Hill Dr., Arlington, TX 76015 (SAN 659-8692) Tel 817-468-9924.

Bold Strummer Ltd, *(Bold Strummer, Ltd.; 0-933224),* 29 Turkey Hill Cir., P.O. Box 2037, Westport, CT 06880 (SAN 213-0262) Tel 203-259-3021.

Bonanza Pub, *(Bonanza Publishing; 0-945134),* P.O. Box 204, Prineville, OR 97754 (SAN 246-0858); 203320 Wainwright Rd., Prineville, OR 97754 (SAN 246-0866) Tel 503-447-3115.

Bond Double-O Seven, *(James Bond 007 Fan Club, The; 0-9605838),* P.O. Box 414, Bronxville, NY 10708 (SAN 216-5902) Tel 914-961-3440.

Bonding Place, *(Bonding Place; 0-9631992),* P.O. Box 736, Lake Hamilton, FL 33851; Toll free: 800-284-6667; 511 N. Park, Lake Hamilton, FL 33851.

Bonello Studios, *(Bonello Studios; 0-9642248),* H.C.R. 4, Box 111, Everett, PA 15537 Tel 814-784-3473.

Bonjour Books, *(Bonjour Bks.; 0-915785),* 6221 Carlson Dr., New Orleans, LA 70122 (SAN 293-9096) Tel 504-282-4660; Orders to: P.O. Box 24327, New Orleans, LA 70184 (SAN 244-8246).

Bonjour Tigre, *(Bonjour Tigre!; 1-884488),* 2086 Iuka Ave., Columbus, OH 43201 Tel 614-294-6606.

Bonus Books, *(Bonus Bks., Inc.; 0-933893; 0-929387; 1-56625),* 160 E. Illinois St., Chicago, IL 60611 (SAN 630-0804) Tel 312-467-0580; Toll free: 800-225-3775.

Book Binder, *(Book Binder; 0-915783),* 1560 Tamarack Ave., Atwater, CA 95301 (SAN 293-907X) Tel 209-358-2058.

Book Gallery, *(Book Gallery; 1-878382),* 632 S. Quincy, Tulsa, OK 74120 (SAN 630-9321) Tel 918-587-6847.

Book-Lab, *(Book-Lab; 0-87594),* P.O. Box 206, Ansonia Station, New York, NY 10023-0206 Tel 212-874-5534; Toll free: 800-654-4081.

Book Peddlers, *(Book Peddlers, The; 0-916773),* 18326 Minnetonka Blvd., Deephaven, MN 55391-3275 (SAN 653-9548) Tel 612-475-3527; Toll free: 800-255-3379; Dist. by: Publishers Group West, 4065 Hollis St., Emeryville, CA 94608 (SAN 202-8522) Tel 510-658-3453; Toll free: 800-788-3123.

Book Pub Co, *(Book Publishing Co., The; 0-913990; 1-57067),* P.O. Box 99, Summertown, TN 38483 (SAN 202-439X) Tel 615-964-3571; Toll free: 800-695-2241. Do not confuse with Book Publishing Co., Seattle, WA.

Bookcraft Inc, *(Bookcraft, Inc.; 0-88494; 1-57008),* 1848 W. 2300 S., Salt Lake City, UT 84119 (SAN 204-3998) Tel 801-972-6180; Toll free: 800-231-8984. Do not confuse with Bookcraft in Fiskdale, MA.

Bookends Pubng, *(Bookends Publishing Co.; 0-9642889),* Rte. 2, Box 532, Crozet, VA 22932 Tel 804-823-7788.

Bookling Pubs, *(Bookling Pubs., The; 0-910717),* 54 Flat Swamp Rd., Newtown, CT 06470 (SAN 268-4047) Tel 203-426-3021.

BookPartners, *(BookPartners, Inc.; 0-9622269; 1-885221),* P.O. Box 922, Wilsonville, OR 97070 (SAN 298-4393); 27464 SW Baker Rd., Sherwood, OR 97140 Tel 503-682-9821.

Books Wonder, *(Books of Wonder; 0-929605),* 132 Seventh Ave., New York, NY 10011 (SAN 249-9916) Tel 212-989-3475.

Bookstore Pr, *(Bookstore Pr.; 0-912846),* Patterson's Wheeltrack, Freeport, ME 04032 (SAN 201-4211) Tel 207-865-6495.

Boone & Crockett, *(Boone & Crockett Club; 0-940864),* Old Milwaukee Depot, 250 Station Dr., Missoula, MT 59801-2753 (SAN 219-7693) Tel 406-542-1888.

Boone-Thomas, *(Boone-Thomas Enterprises; 0-9611780),* 3301 Henderson Mill Rd. NE, Suite Q3, Atlanta, GA 30341 (SAN 285-2225) Tel 404-723-0946.

Boosey & Hawkes, *(Boosey & Hawkes, Inc.; 0-913932),* Printed Music Div., 52 Cooper Sq., 10th Flr., New York, NY 10003 (SAN 213-6805) Tel 212-979-1090.

Boot Prints, *(Boot Prints; 1-885548),* 701 College St., Spooner, WI 54801 Tel 715-635-2317.

Borden, *(Borden Publishing Co.; 0-87505),* 2623 San Fernando Rd., Los Angeles, CA 90065 (SAN 201-419X) Tel 213-223-4267.

Borenson & Assocs, *(Borenson & Assocs.; 0-9618105),* P.O. Box 450, Dublin, PA 18917 (SAN 666-4261); 126 Middle Rd., Suite E15, Dublin, PA 18917 (SAN 666-427X) Tel 215-249-3212.

Borgo Pr, *(Borgo Pr.; 0-89370; 0-8095; 0-916732; 0-930261; 1-55742; 0-913960; 0-941028; 0-9616605; 1-877880),* P.O. Box 2845, San Bernardino, CA 92406-2845 (SAN 208-9459) Tel 909-884-5813.

Bornet Bks, *(Bornet Bks.; 0-9632366),* P.O. Box 331, Talent, OR 97540; 365 Ridge Rd., Ashland, OR 97520 Tel 503-482-2228.

Bornstein Memory, *(Bornstein Memory Training Schls.; 0-9602610),* 11693 San Vicente Blvd., West Los Angeles, CA 90049 (SAN 213-0181) Tel 310-478-2056.

Bosck Pub Hse, *(Bosck Publishing Hse.; 0-9629887),* P.O. Box 2311, Los Angeles, CA 90051-0311; 1322 W. 60th St., Los Angeles, CA 90044 Tel 213-758-2782.

Bosphorus Bks, *(Bosphorus Bks.; 1-882443),* Box 3452, 3 Ridge Rd., Groton Long Point, CT 06340 Tel 203-536-2540.

Boston Public Lib, *(Boston Public Library; 0-89073),* P.O. Box 286, Boston, MA 02117 (SAN 204-3971) Tel 617-536-5400.

Boulden Pub, *(Boulden Publishing; 1-878076),* P.O. Box 1186, Weaverville, CA 96093 Tel 916-623-5399; Toll free: 800-238-8433.

Bowen & Assocs, *(Bowen & Assocs.; 0-9633546),* 106 Greenridge Ct., Lutherville, MD 21093 Tel 410-321-6753; Dist. by: BookWorld Distribution Services, Inc., 1933 Whitfield Pk. Loop, Sarasota, FL 34243 (SAN 173-0568) Tel 813-758-8094; Toll free: 800-444-2524 (orders only).

Bowers Mus, *(Bowers Museum of Cultural Art; 0-9633959),* 2002 N. Main St., Santa Ana, CA 92706 (SAN 278-2375) Tel 714-567-3600.

Bowers Studio, *(Bowers Studio, Inc.; 0-9641192),* 7966 Stanburn Rd., Dublin, OH 43017 Tel 614-764-3729.

Bowker, *(Bowker, R. R.; 0-8352; 0-911255),* A Reed Reference Publishing Company, 121 Chanlon Rd., New Providence, NJ 07974 (SAN 214-1191) Tel 908-464-6800; Toll free: 800-521-8110; 800-431-1713 subscriptions to: Publishers Weekly, School Library Journal, Library Journal (in Ohio: 614-383-3141); 800-257-7894 subscriptions to: Library Hotline, Reviews-on-Cards (in New Jersey: 609-786-1160); Orders to: P.O. Box 1001, Summit, NJ 07902-1001.

Box Four Twenty-Four, *(Box 424 Pr.; 0-9614506),* Box 424, Pacific Grove, CA 93950 (SAN 691-7364) Tel 408-649-8215.

Boxwood, *(Boxwood Pr.; 0-910286; 0-940168),* 183 Ocean View Blvd., Pacific Grove, CA 93950 (SAN 201-4149) Tel 408-375-9110.

Boyce-Pubns, *(Boyce Pubns.; 0-918823),* 1023 Oxford, Clovis, CA 93612 (SAN 669-652X) Tel 209-299-8495.

Boyds Mills Pr, *(Boyds Mills Pr.; 1-878093; 1-56397),* 815 Church St., Honesdale, PA 18431 Tel 717-253-1164; Dist. by: St. Martin's Pr., Inc., 175 Fifth Ave., Rm. 1715, New York, NY 10010 (SAN 200-2132) Tel 212-674-5151; Toll free: 800-221-7945. *Imprints:* Wordsong (Wordsong).

Boyer-Caswell, *(Boyer-Caswell Publishing Co.;* 1-884507), 823 E. Main St., 14th Flr., Richmond, VA 23219 Tel 804-648-6624; Toll free: 800-648 6624.

Boykin, *(Boykin, James H.; 0-9603342; 1-880833),* 1260 NW 122nd St., Miami, FL 33167-2827 (SAN 215-0603) Tel 305-681-7663.

Boylen, *(Boylen, Inc.; 0-9624099),* P.O. Box 5215, Woodridge, IL 60517; 337 Willoway Dr., Bolingbrook, IL 60439 Tel 708-972-9610.

Boynton Cook Pubs, *(Boynton Cook Pubs., Inc.;* 0-86709), Subs. of Heinemann Educational Bks., Inc., 361 Hanover St., Portsmouth, NH 03801 (SAN 216-6186) Tel 603-431-7894.

Boys Town Ctr
See Boys Town Pr

Boys Town Pr, *(Boys Town Pr.; 0-938510),* Div. of Father Flanagan's Boys' Home, 13603 Flanagan Blvd., Boys Town, NE 68010 (SAN 215-8477) Tel 402-498-3202.

BPCOA, *(Big Picture Corp. of America; 0-9640894),* P.O. Box 6504, Richmond, VA 23230; 4823 Coleman Rd., Richmond, VA 23230 Tel 804-359-9014.

BPPbks, *(BPPbooks; 0-942097),* P.O. Box 104, Louisville, CO 80027 (SAN 666-7236) Tel 303-494-9694.

Bradbury Pr *Imprint of* **Macmillan Child Grp**

Bradley Mann, *(Bradley-Mann Pubs.; 0-9627882;* 1-56606), 1456 W. University Heights Dr., N., Flagstaff, AZ 86001 Tel 602-779-1858.

Bradshaw Pubs, *(Bradshaw Pubs.; 0-945107),* P.O. Box 277, Bryn Mawr, CA 92318 (SAN 246-2842); 25567 Lomas Verdes, Loma Linda, CA 92354 (SAN 246-2850) Tel 909-796-6766.

Brainworks Inc, *(Brainworks, Inc.; 0-944662),* 1918 Walnut Plaza, Carrollton, TX 75006 (SAN 244-5085) Tel 214-416-9410.

Branches, *(Branches, The; 0-913703),* 1453 Park Rd., P.O. Box 848, Chanhassen, MN 55317 (SAN 286-0899) Tel 612-474-0924; Toll free: 800-999-5858.

Brand Cross, *(Brand of the Cross Publishing; 1-885766),* P.O. Box 867, Waldport, OR 97394 Tel 503-563-2060.

Branden Pub Co, *(Branden Publishing Co.; 0-8283),* Box 843, 17 Station St., Brookline Village, Boston, MA 02147 (SAN 201-4106) Tel 617-734-2045.

Brandon Hse, *(Brandon Hse., Inc.; 0-913412),* P.O. Box 240, Bronx, NY 10471 (SAN 201-4092).

Brandt Bks, *(Brandt Bks.; 0-9616327),* 1134 Willits Dr., Corona, CA 91720 (SAN 659-0454) Tel 909-735-6167.

Brandylane, *(Brandylane Pubs.; 0-9627635; 1-883911),* P.O. Box 43, Lively, VA 22507; Toll free: 800-553-6922; Chesapeake Dr., White Stone, VA 22578 Tel 804-435-6900; Dist. by: Publishers Distribution Service, 6893 Sullivan Rd., Grawn, MI 49637 (SAN 630-5717) Tel 616-276-5196; Toll free: 800-345-0096 (orders only).

BRAT Pubns, *(B.R.A.T. Pubns.; 0-9623607),* P.O. Box 660, Little Elm, TX 75068; Hwy. 720, Little Elm, TX 75068 Tel 214-292-3424.

Bravo Edit, *(Bravo Editions; 1-884861),* 1081 Trafalgar St., Teaneck, NJ 07666-1929 Tel 201-836-5922.

Braziller, *(Braziller, George, Inc.; 0-8076),* 60 Madison Ave., Suite 1001, New York, NY 10010 (SAN 201-9310) Tel 212-889-0909.

BrdgeWater, *(BridgeWater Bks.; 0-89375; 0-8167),* Div. of Troll Assocs., 100 Corporate Dr., Mahwah, NJ 07430 Tel 201-529-4000; Toll free: 800-526-5289; Dist. by: Penguin USA, 375 Hudson St., New York, NY 10014-3657 Tel 212-366-2000; Toll free: 800-331-4624.

Bread for the World, *(Bread for the World Institute; 0-9628058; 1-884361),* 1100 Wayne Ave., Suite 1000, Silver Spring, MD 20910 (SAN 226-0182) Tel 301-608-2400.

Breadworks, *(Breadworks, Inc.; 0-9627665),* R.R. 1, Box 238A, Canaan, NH 03741 (SAN 297-9268) Tel 603-632-9171.

Breitenbush Bks, *(Breitenbush Bks., Inc.; 0-932576),* P.O. Box 82157, Portland, OR 97282 (SAN 219-7707) Tel 503-230-1900; Dist. by: Far Corner Bks., P.O. Box 82157, Portland, OR 97282 (SAN 630-6098) Tel 503-230-1900.

Brennan Bks, *(Brennan Bks., Inc.; 0-89270),* 8419 Stickney Ave., Milwaukee, WI 53226-2808 (SAN 208-5674) Tel 414-786-4092.

Brenner Info Group, *(Brenner Information Group;* 0-929535), Div. of Brenner Microcomputing, Inc., 9282 Samantha Ct., San Diego, CA 92129 (SAN 249-6496) Tel 619-693-0355.

Brethren, *(Brethren Pr.; 0-87178),* Div. of Church of the Brethren, 1451 Dundee Ave., Elgin, IL 60120 (SAN 201-9329) Tel 708-742-5100; Toll free: 800-441-3712. Do not confuse with Brethren Publishing Co., Ashland, Ohio.

Brght Ideas CA, *(Bright Ideas Productions; 0-9627863;* 1-883212), Div. of LMN Productions, 31220 LaBaya Dr., Suite 110, Westlake Village, CA 91362 Tel 818-707-7127.

Bridge Pubns Inc, *(Bridge Pubns., Inc.; 0-88404;* 1-57318), 4751 Fountain Ave., Los Angeles, CA 90029 (SAN 208-3884) Tel 213-953-3320; Toll free: 800-722-1733; 800-843-7389 (in California); Dist. by: BookWorld Pr., 1933 Whitfield Pk. Loop, Sarasota, FL 34243 (SAN 298-4695) Tel 813-758-8094; Toll free: 800-444-2524.

Bridge Troll Pr, *(Bridge Troll Pr.; 0-9618225),* P.O. Box 4134, 660 Mount Lassen, San Rafael, CA 94903 (SAN 666-9069) Tel 415-479-5808.

Bright Baby, *(Bright Baby Bks.; 0-930681),* 101 Star Ln., Whitethorn, CA 95489 (SAN 676-9608) Tel 707-986-7693.

Bright Bks, *(Bright Bks.; 0-9605968),* P.O. Box 428, Akron, IN 46910 (SAN 216-7204) Tel 219-893-4113. Do not confuse with Bright Bks. in Austin, TX.

Bright Bks TX, *(Bright Bks., Inc.; 1-880092),* 2313 Lake Austin Blvd., Austin, TX 78703 Tel 512-499-4164; Dist. by: Publishers Distribution Service, 6893 Sullivan Rd., Grawn, MI 49637 (SAN 630-5717) Tel 616-276-5196; Toll free: 800-345-0096 (orders only). Do not confuse with Bright Bks. in Akron, IN.

Bright Eyes, *(Bright Eyes Publishing; 0-9641962),* P.O. Box 590743, Houston, TX 77259; 1027 Baronridge, Seabrook, TX 77586 Tel 713-474-3887.

Bright Ring, *(Bright Ring Publishing; 0-935607),* P.O. Box 5768-B, Bellingham, WA 98227 (SAN 696-0537); 1900 N. Shore Dr., Bellingham, WA 98226 (SAN 665-8989) Tel 206-734-1601; Dist. by: Independent Pubs. Group, 814 N. Franklin, Chicago, IL 60610 (SAN 202-0769) Tel 312-337-0747; Toll free: 800-888-4741; Dist. by: Gryphon Hse., Inc., P.O. Box 207, Beltsville, MD 20704-0207 (SAN 169-3190) Tel 301-595-9500; Toll free: 800-638-0928.

Brighton & Lloyd, *(Brighton & Lloyd; 0-922434),* P.O. Box 2903, Costa Mesa, CA 92628 (SAN 251-3072); 1875 Wren Cir., Costa Mesa, CA 92626 (SAN 251-3080) Tel 714-540-6466.

BrightWay Bks, *(BrightWay Bks.; 0-9638144),* 46 Carrollton Rd., Sterling, VA 20165 Tel 703-450-8021.

Brimax Bks, *(Brimax Bks., Ltd.; 0-900195; 0-904494; 0-86112; 1-85854),* Member of Reed Elsevier Group, 2284 Black River Rd., Bethlehem, PA 18015; Toll free: 800-432-7478. UK Address: 4/5 Studlands Pk. Industrial Estate, Exning Rd., Newmarket, Suffolk, CB8 7AU, UK.

Brisk Pubng, *(Brisk Publishing Co.; 1-885981),* 3036 Colfax Ave., S., Minneapolis, MN 55408 Tel 612-822-6306.

Bristol Hse, *(Bristol Hse., Ltd.; 0-917851; 1-885224),* 3131 E. 67th St., Anderson, IN 46013 (SAN 225-4638) Tel 317-644-0856; Toll free: 800-451-7323; Dist. by: Riverside/World, P.O. Box 370, 1500 Riverside Dr., Iowa Falls, IA 50126 (SAN 169-2666) Tel 515-648-4271; Toll free: 800-247-5111.

Brit Mus-Parkwest *Imprint of* **Parkwest Pubns**

Brite Intl
See Brite Music

Brite Music, *(Brite Music, Inc.; 0-944803),* P.O. Box 9191, Salt Lake City, UT 84109 (SAN 244-948X); 3421 S. 500 W., Salt Lake City, UT 84115 (SAN 244-9498) Tel 801-263-9191.

Broadblade Pr, *(Broadblade Pr.; 0-9614640; 0-9620249),* 11314 Miller Rd., Swartz Creek, MI 48473 (SAN 691-9227) Tel 810-635-3156; Dist. by: Baker & Taylor Bks., Momence Service Ctr., 501 S. Gladiolus St., Momence, IL 60954-2444 (SAN 169-2100) Tel 815-472-2444; Toll free: 800-775-2300 (customer service); Dist. by: Hillsdale Educational Pubs., Inc., 39 North St., Box 245, Hillsdale, MI 49242 (SAN 159-8759) Tel 517-437-3179.

Broadfoot, *(Broadfoot Publishing Co.; 0-916107;* 1-56837), 1907 Buena Vista Cir., Wilmington, NC 28405 (SAN 294-9075) Tel 910-686-4816; Toll free: 800-537-5243 (orders only).

Broadman, *(Broadman & Holman Pubs.; 0-8054),* Div. of Sunday School Board of the Southern Baptist Convention, 127 Ninth Ave., N., MSN143, Nashville, TN 37234 (SAN 201-937X) Tel 615-251-3641; Toll free: 800-251-3225.

Broadside Pr, *(Broadside Pr.; 0-910296; 0-940713),* P.O. Box 04257, Detroit, MI 48204 (SAN 201-9388); 4734 Sturtevant, Detroit, MI 48204 (SAN 664-6190) Tel 313-963-8526.

Broken Rifle Pr, *(Broken Rifle Pr.; 0-9620024),* P.O. Box 749, Trenton, NJ 08607-0749 (SAN 247-4557) Tel 908-549-0631; Dist. by: Quality Bks., Inc., 918 Sherwood Dr., Lake Bluff, IL 60044-2204 (SAN 169-2127) Tel 708-295-2010; Toll free: 800-323-4241 (libraries only); Dist. by: Inland Bk. Co., 140 Commerce St., East Haven, CT 06512 (SAN 200-4151) Tel 203-467-4257; Toll free: 800-243-0138; Dist. by: Baker & Taylor Bks., Momence Service Ctr., 501 S. Gladiolus St., Momence, IL 60954-2444 (SAN 169-2100) Tel 815-472-2444; Toll free: 800-775-2300 (customer service); Dist. by: The Distributors, 702 S. Michigan, South Bend, IN 46601 (SAN 169-2488) Tel 219-232-8500; Toll free: 800-348-5200 (except Indiana).

Bronfam Pr, *(Bronfam Pr.; 0-9638960),* P.O. Box 102186, Univ. Pk. Sta., Denver, CO 80250-2186 (SAN 298-2781); 2457 S. Dahlia Ln., Denver, CO 80222 Tel 303-757-1421.

Brooke-Richards, *(Brooke-Richards Pr.; 0-9622652),* 9420 Reseda Blvd., Suite 511, Northridge, CA 91324 Tel 818-893-8126.

Brookline Bks, *(Brookline Bks., Inc.; 0-914797; 1-57129),* P.O. Box 1046, Cambridge, MA 02238 (SAN 289-0690); Toll free: 800-266-2665; 29 Ware St., Cambridge, MA 02138 Tel 617-868-0360.

Brooks-Cole, *(Brooks/Cole Publishing Co.; 0-8185;* 0-534), Div. of International Thomson Publishing Education Group, 511 Forest Lodge Rd., Pacific Grove, CA 93950 (SAN 202-3369) Tel 408-373-0728; Orders to: Distribution Ctr., 7625 Empire Dr., Florence, KY 41042-2978 (SAN 200-2663) Tel 606-525-2230; Toll free: 800-354-9706; Dist. by: Van Nostrand Reinhold, 115 Fifth Ave., New York, NY 10003 (SAN 202-5183) Tel 212-254-3232.

Brost Heus, *(Brost-Heus; 0-9616109),* 98 Main St., Tiburon, CA 94920 (SAN 699-7392).

Brotherstone Pubs, *(Brotherstone Pubs.; 1-878925),* 1340 Pleasant Dr., Elgin, IL 60123-1445 Tel 708-697-1371.

Browndeer Pr *Imprint of* **HarBrace**

Browne Bks, *(Browne Bks. in The Hollow; 0-9636621),* 1720 Richard Ct., Lincoln, CA 95648-2324 Tel 916-273-2909.

Brownlow Pub Co, *(Brownlow Publishing Co.; 0-915720; 1-877719; 1-57051; 0-910444),* 6309 Airport Freeway, Fort Worth, TX 76117 (SAN 207-5105) Tel 817-831-3831; Toll free: 800-433-7610.

Brunswick Pub, *(Brunswick Publishing Corp.; 0-931494;* 1-55618), Rte. 1, Box 1A1, P.O. Box 555, Lawrenceville, VA 23868 (SAN 211-6332) Tel 804-848-3865; Toll free: 800-336-7154 (orders only).

Brwn Sug & Spice, *(Brown Sugar & Spice Bk. Service;* 0-9637243), 8584 Whitehorn St., Romulus, MI 48174 Tel 313-729-0501.

Bryn Ffyliaid, *(Bryn Ffyliaid Pubns.; 0-9611114),* 300 Lake Marina Ave., No. 16BW, New Orleans, LA 70124 (SAN 283-2720) Tel 504-288-7956.

BSA, *(Boy Scouts of America; 0-8395),* P.O. Box 152079, 1325 W. Walnut Hill Ln., Irving, TX 75015-2079 (SAN 284-9798) Tel 214-580-2278; Orders to: National Distribution Ctr., 2109 Westinghouse Blvd., P.O. Box 7143, Charlotte, NC 28241-7143 (SAN 284-9801) Tel 704-588-4260.

Buccaneer Bks, *(Buccaneer Bks., Inc.; 0-89966; 1-56849),* P.O. Box 168, Cutchogue, NY 11935 (SAN 209-1542) Tel 516-734-5724.

Buchanan Res, *(Buchanan Resources; 0-9630879),* 324 Forestwood Dr., Forney, TX 75126 Tel 214-651-1800.

Buchart & Assocs, *(Buchart & Assocs., Inc.; 1-883900),* P.O. Box 488, Louisville, KY 40201; Toll free: 800-280-9393; 629 Fourth Ave., Suite 201, Louisville, KY 40202 Tel 502-584-4249.

Buchonia Pub, *(Buchonia Publishing; 0-9635416),* P.O. Box 42492, Portland, OR 97242-0492; 3714 SE 11th, Portland, OR 97202 Tel 503-230-9636.

Buck Pub, *(Buck Publishing Co.; 0-934530),* 2409 Vestavia Dr., Birmingham, AL 35216 (SAN 213-0203) Tel 205-979-2296.

Buckingham Mint
See Derrydale Pr

Bucksnort, *(Bucksnort Publishing; 0-939801),* P.O. Box 670794, Marietta, GA 30066 (SAN 663-8279); 3371 Meadowind Ct., Marietta, GA 30062 (SAN 663-8287) Tel 404-973-8049.

Buddhist Text, *(Buddhist Text Translation Society; 0-917512; 0-88139),* Affil. of Dharma Realm Buddhist Assocs., City of Ten Thousand Buddhas, 2001 Talmage Rd., Talmage, CA 95481-0217 (SAN 281-3556) Tel 707-462-0939.

Bulfinch Pr, *(Bulfinch Pr.; 0-8212),* Div. of Little, Brown & Co., 34 Beacon St., Boston, MA 02108 Tel 617-248-2473; Dist. by: Little, Brown & Co., Time & Life Bldg., 1271 Avenue of the Americas, New York, NY 10020 (SAN 200-2205) Tel 212-522-8700; Toll free: 800-343-9204.

Bullseye Bks *Imprint of* **Random Bks Yng Read**

Bur For At-Risk, *(Bureau For At-Risk Youth; 1-56688),* 645 New York Ave., Huntington, NY 11743 Tel 516-673-4584; Toll free: 800-999-6884.

Bur Oak Pr Inc, *(Bur Oak Pr., Inc.; 0-929326),* 8717 Mockingbird Rd., S., Platteville, WI 53818 (SAN 249-0463) Tel 608-348-8662.

Burdett CA, *(Burdett Design Studios; 0-932946),* 87424 Hwy. 101, Florence, OR 97439-8834 (SAN 295-1045); Toll free: 800-634-6048.

Burgess Pub, *(Burgess Publishing, Inc.; 1-879470),* P.O. Box 520, Broken Arrow, OK 74011 Tel 918-455-1471.

Busn *Imprint of* **P-H**

Busn One Irwin
See Irwin Prof Pubng

Busn Plans Plus
See BPPbks

Buttercup Bks, *(Buttercup Bks.; 0-9614997),* P.O. Box 1272, Casa Grande, AZ 85222 (SAN 693-9503) Tel 602-836-7831.

Butterfly Bear, *(Butterfly & Bear Pr.; 0-9629645),* 1818 Fourth Ave., W., Seattle, WA 98119 Tel 206-284-1691.

Butternut Bks, *(Butternut Bks.; 0-9632303),* The Grove, W. Main St., P.O. Box 800, Morris, NY 13808 Tel 607-263-5070.

Butterworth Legal Pubs, *(Butterworth U.S., Legal Pubs., Inc., U.S. Headquarters; 0-88063; 0-86678; 0-406; 0-409; 1-56257; 0-917126; 1-55943),* Member of The Reed International Group, 8 Industrial Way., Bldg. C, Salem, NH 03079-2837 (SAN 238-1451) Tel 603-890-6001; Toll free: 800-548-4001 (orders).

BYLS Pr, *(BYLS Pr.; 0-934402),* 6617 N. Mozart, Chicago, IL 60645 (SAN 212-7253) Tel 312-743-4241.

BYTE Bks *Imprint of* **McGraw**

Byte Size, *(Byte Size Graphics; 1-883613),* P.O. Box 826, North Eastham, MA 02651; 50 Indian Way, North Eastham, MA 02651 Tel 508-240-0795.

BYU Scholarly, *(Brigham Young Univ. Scholarly Pubns.; 0-8425),* 119 HRCB, Provo, UT 84602 Tel 801-378-2741; Dist. by: Brigham Young Univ. Pr., 205 UPB, Provo, UT 84602 (SAN 201-9337) Tel 801-378-2809.

C A Henry, *(Henry, Carol Ann; 0-9633634),* 5832 Wessex Ln., Alexandria, VA 22310 Tel 703-971-9233.

C A M Co, *(C.A.M. Co. Pubs.; 0-942752),* P.O. Box 1773, Arvada, CO 80001-1773 (SAN 281-3645) Tel 303-421-6851; Dist. by: The Distributors, 702 S. Michigan, South Bend, IN 46601 (SAN 169-2488) Tel 219-232-8500; Toll free: 800-348-5200 (except Indiana); Dist. by: Baker & Taylor Bks., Momence Service Ctr., 501 S. Gladiolus St., Momence, IL 60954-2444 (SAN 169-2100) Tel 815-472-2444; Toll free: 800-775-2300 (customer service); Dist. by: Baker & Taylor Bks., Commerce Service Ctr., 251 Mt. Olive Church Rd., Commerce, GA 30599-9988 (SAN 169-1503) Tel 706-335-5000; Toll free: 800-775-1200 (customer service); Dist. by: Baker & Taylor Bks., Reno Service Ctr., 380 Edison Way, Reno, NV 89564 (SAN 169-4464) Tel 702-858-6700; Toll free: 800-775-1700 (customer service); Dist. by: Baker & Taylor Bks., Somerville Service Ctr., 50 Kirby Ave., Somerville, NJ 08876-0734 (SAN 169-4901) Tel 908-722-8000; Toll free: 800-775-1500 (customer service); Dist. by: Midwest Library Service, 11443 St. Charles Rock Rd., Bridgeton, MO 63044-9986 (SAN 169-4243) Tel 314-739-3100.

C C Partin, *(Partin, Charlotte Corry; 0-9619816),* 530 Yuma Ct., Sumter, SC 29150 (SAN 246-1242) Tel 803-469-4010.

C Chapman, *(Chapman, Carl; 0-9621529),* 205 Lancaster Ave., Chattanooga, TN 37415 (SAN 251-5067) Tel 615-877-6296.

C Coats Bestsellers, *(Coats', Carolyn, Bestsellers; 1-878722),* P.O. Box 560532, Orlando, FL 32856; 1336 Windsong Rd., Orlando, FL 32809 Tel 407-855-0780.

C D Pierce, *(Pierce, Catherine Doris; 0-9621397),* 1920 Barbara Dr., Palo Alto, CA 94303 (SAN 251-1738) Tel 415-322-5728.

C Del Grullo, *(Cayo del Grullo Pr.; 0-9611604),* c/o Texas A & I Univ., History Dept., Kingsville, TX 78363 (SAN 284-9313) Tel 512-595-3603.

C E Kelly, *(Kelly, Connie E.; 0-9641814),* 10257 Switzer, Overland Park, KS 66212 Tel 913-541-9338.

C E Ludy, *(Ludy, Claude Edward; 0-9625164),* 4893 Century Dr., Saginaw, MI 48603; Orders to: Ed's Starlite Bks., P.O. Box 1585, Saginaw, MI 48605.

C E Tuttle, *(Tuttle, Charles E., Co., Inc.; 0-8048),* 153 Milk St., 5th Flr., Boston, MA 02109 (SAN 213-2621) Tel 617-951-4080; Orders to: P.O. Box 410, 28 S. Main St., Rutland, VT 05702-0410 Tel 802-773-8930; Toll free: 800-526-2778.

C-Four Res, *(C-4 Resources; 0-914527),* 100 Trade Center Dr., Suite 400, Champaign, IL 61820 (SAN 289-1565) Tel 217-328-0263.

C Garcia, *(Garcia, Conrad; 0-9621124),* 1880 Lafayette Ave., 20F, Bronx, NY 10473 (SAN 250-6610) Tel 718-589-6095.

C Georgiou, *(Georgiou, Constantine; 0-9637111),* 1 Washington Sq. Village, Apt. 11G, New York, NY 10012 Tel 212-982-8590.

C H Fairfax, *(Fairfax, C. H., Co., Inc.; 0-935132),* P.O. Box 7047, Baltimore, MD 21216-0047 (SAN 221-170X) Tel 410-448-5461.

C H Kerr, *(Kerr, Charles H., Publishing Co.; 0-88286),* 1740 W. Greenleaf Ave., Chicago, IL 60626 (SAN 207-7043).

C J Brown, *(Brown, Cathy J.; 0-9614796),* Dist. by: Creative Expressions, P.O. Box 456, Colchester, VT 05446 (SAN 200-5816).

C K Himeda, *(Himeda, C. K.; 0-9621721),* 4204 Kilauea Ave., Honolulu, HI 96816 (SAN 252-0575) Tel 808-732-2681.

C Kaczmarek, *(Kaczmarek, Constant; 0-9626041),* 29747 Briarton, Farmington Hills, MI 48331 Tel 810-661-0253.

C L Scott, *(Scott, Curtis L.; 0-9642791),* 3939 Highway 77, Graceville, FL 32440 Tel 904-638-0030. Do not confuse with Curtis Scott in Walnut Creek, CA.

C Lee Pubns, *(Christopher Lee Pubns., Inc.; 1-878383),* P.O. Box 6202, South Bend, IN 46660; Toll free: 800-822-6202; 15055 Cleveland Rd., Granger, IN 46530 Tel 219-277-3100.

C Mack Pub, *(Mack, Casey, Publishing Co.; 0-9620167),* 9542 E. Valley Ranch Pkwy., No. 1062, Irving, TX 75063 (SAN 247-865X) Tel 214-506-0900.

C Mooney, *(Mooney, Chuck, III; 0-9630239),* 3808 Ashford Ave., Fort Worth, TX 76133-2936 Tel 817-926-4274.

C Salway Pr, *(Salway, C., Pr.; 0-9624887),* P.O. Box 4115, Menlo Park, CA 94026 Tel 415-368-7882; 83 Robleda Dr., Atherton, CA 94027 Tel 415-368-1983; Dist. by: Bookpeople, 7900 Edgewater Dr., Oakland, CA 94621 (SAN 168-9517) Tel 510-632-4700; Toll free: 800-999-4650; Dist. by: Pacific Pipeline, Inc., 8030 S. 228th St., Kent, WA 98032-2900 (SAN 208-2128) Tel 206-872-5523; Toll free: 800-444-7323 (Customer Service); 800-677-2222 (orders); Dist. by: Baker & Taylor Bks., Somerville Service Ctr., 50 Kirby Ave., Somerville, NJ 08876-0734 (SAN 169-4901) Tel 908-722-8000; Toll free: 800-775-1500 (customer service); Dist. by: Baker & Taylor Bks., Momence Service Ctr., 501 S. Gladiolus St., Momence, IL 60954-2444 (SAN 169-2100) Tel 815-472-2444; Toll free: 800-775-2300 (customer service); Dist. by: Baker & Taylor Bks., Commerce Service Ctr., 251 Mt. Olive Church Rd., Commerce, GA 30599-9988 (SAN 169-1503) Tel 706-335-5000; Toll free: 800-775-1200 (customer service); Dist. by: Baker & Taylor Bks., Reno Service Ctr., 380 Edison Way, Reno, NV 89564 (SAN 169-4464) Tel 702-858-6700; Toll free: 800-775-1700 (customer service); Dist. by: Ingram Bk. Co., 1 Ingram Blvd., La Vergne, TN 37086-1986 (SAN 169-7978) Tel 615-793-5000; Toll free: 800-937-8000 (orders only, all warehouses); Dist. by: Brodart Co., 500 Arch St., Williamsport, PA 17705 (SAN 169-7684) Tel 717-326-2461; Toll free: 800-233-8467; Dist. by: Sunbelt Pubns., 8630 Argent St., Suite C, Santee, CA 92071-4172 (SAN 630-0790) Tel 619-258-4916; Toll free: 800-626-6579.

C Shore Pr, *(Shore, C., Pr.; 0-9612136),* P.O. Box 14008, Bradenton, FL 34280 (SAN 286-8733) Tel 813-792-4535.

C T Scott, *(Scott, Carlton T.; 0-9636652),* 1039 Flushing Ave., Clearwater, FL 34624 Tel 813-531-7442.

C Watry, *(Watry, Charles; 0-914379),* 2875 S. Nellis Blvd., No. A8-206, Las Vegas, NV 89121-2086 (SAN 289-5943) Tel 619-729-6887.

C Weisfish, *(Weisfish, Chaya; 0-9630241),* 18 Yale Dr., Monsey, NY 10952 Tel 914-426-3785.

C Zolotow Bks *Imprint of* **HarpC Child Bks**

CA HPA, *(California Heritage Publishing Assocs.; 0-9623233),* 156 Del Norte Way, San Luis Obispo, CA 93405 Tel 805-541-4989.

CA Rocketry, *(California Rocketry; 0-912468),* Div. of U.S. Rockets, P.O. Box 1242, Claremont, CA 91711 (SAN 204-692X); Toll free: 800-266-6913.

CA Storybook, *(California Storybook Publishing; 1-881402),* P.O. Box 5424, South San Francisco, CA 94083-5424; 1130 Morningside Ave., South San Francisco, CA 94080 Tel 415-873-1727.

Caedmon *Imprint of* **HarperAudio**

Cajun Bay Pr, *(Cajun Bayou Pr.; 0-9639378),* Rte. 5, Box 1444, Abbeville, LA 70510 Tel 318-642-9142.

Cajun Pubs, *(Cajun Pubs.; 0-933727),* Rte. 4, Box 88, New Iberia, LA 70560 (SAN 692-4948) Tel 318-363-6653; Toll free: 800-551-3076.

Cal Aero Pr
See C Watry

Calico Paws, *(Calico Paws Publishing; 0-944104),* P.O. Box 2364, Menlo Park, CA 94026-2364 (SAN 242-8016); 83 Alejandra Ave., Atherton, CA 94027 (SAN 242-8024) Tel 415-323-9616.

Calif Education, *(California Dept. of Education; 0-8011),* P.O. Box 271, Sacramento, CA 95812-0271 (SAN 268-5868) Tel 916-445-7608; Toll free: 800-995-4099.

Calif Perf Prods, *(California Performance Products, Inc.; 1-879748),* 7772 Elden Ave., Whittier, CA 90602 Tel 310-698-8641.

Calif Video, *(California Video Institute; 1-880211),* P.O. Box 572019, Tarzana, CA 91357-2019; 8600 International Ave., No. 249, Canoga Park, CA 91304 Tel 818-700-0518.

Calif Weekly, *(California Weekly Explorer, Inc.; 0-936778),* 285 E. Main St., Suite 3, Tustin, CA 92680 (SAN 217-0914) Tel 714-730-5991.

Calligrafree, *(Calligrafree-The Calligraphy Co.; 0-942032),* P.O. Box 98, Brookville, OH 45309 (SAN 240-9496) Tel 513-833-5677; Dist. by: Hunt Manufacturing Co., 230 S. Broad St., Philadelphia, PA 19102 (SAN 630-1703) Tel 215-732-7700; Toll free: 800-955-4868.

Calyx Bks, *(Calyx Bks.; 0-934971),* Div. of Calyx, Inc., P.O. Box B, Corvallis, OR 97339 (SAN 695-1171); 216 SW Madison, No. 7, Corvallis, OR 97333 (SAN 242-0643) Tel 503-753-9384; Dist. by: Consortium Bk. Sales & Distribution, 1045 Westgate Dr., Suite 90, Saint Paul, MN 55114-1065 (SAN 200-6049) Tel 612-221-9035; Toll free: 800-283-3572 (orders); Dist. by: Bookpeople, 7900 Edgewater Dr., Oakland, CA 94621 (SAN 168-9517) Tel 510-632-4700; Toll free: 800-999-4650; Dist. by: Inland Bk. Co., 140 Commerce St., East Haven, CT 06512 (SAN 200-4151) Tel 203-467-4257; Toll free: 800-243-0138; Dist. by: Pacific Pipeline, Inc., 8030 S. 228th St., Kent, WA 98032-2900 (SAN 208-2128) Tel 206-872-5523; Toll free: 800-444-7323 (Customer Service); 800-677-2222 (orders); Dist. by: SPD-Small Pr. Distribution, 1814 San Pablo Ave., Berkeley, CA 94702 (SAN 204-5826) Tel 510-549-3336; Toll free: 800-348-5200; Dist. by: The Distributors, 702 S. Michigan, South Bend, IN 46601 (SAN 169-2488) Tel 219-232-8500; Toll free: 800-348-5200 (except Indiana).

Cambdgport Pr, *(Cambridgeport Pr.; 0-944348),* 15 Chalk St., Cambridge, MA 02139 (SAN 243-4466) Tel 617-497-4437.

Cambridge Bk, *(Cambridge Bk. Co.; 0-8428),* Div. of Simon & Schuster, Inc., Sylvan Rd., Rte. 9W, Englewood Cliffs, NJ 07632 (SAN 169-5703) Tel 201-592-2000; Toll free: 800-221-4764.

Cambridge Strat, *(Cambridge Stratford, Ltd.; 0-935637),* 8560 Main St., Harris Hill Sq., Williamsville, NY 14221-7435 (SAN 696-2173) Tel 716-626-9044.

Cambridge U Pr, *(Cambridge Univ. Pr.; 0-521),* 40 W. 20th St., New York, NY 10011 (SAN 200-206X) Tel 212-924-3900; Orders to: 110 Midland Ave., Port Chester, NY 10573 (SAN 281-3769) Tel 914-937-9600; Toll free: 800-227-0247 (New York only); 800-872-7423 (outside New York).

Camden Hse Pub, *(Camden Hse. Publishing, Inc.; 0-944475),* P.O. Box 1004, Ferry Rd., Charlotte, VT 05445 (SAN 243-6043) Tel 802-425-3961; Toll free: 800-344-3350; Dist. by: Firefly Bks., Ltd., P.O. Box 1338, Ellicott Sta., Buffalo, NY 14205 (SAN 630-611X); Toll free: 800-387-5085.

Camelot *Imprint of* **Avon**

Camelot GA, *(Camelot Pr., Ltd.; 0-931760),* P.O. Box 674884, Marietta, GA 30067 (SAN 243-0665) Tel 404-423-9585; Dist. by: New Leaf Distributing Co., 5425 Tulane Dr., SW, Atlanta, GA 30336-2323 (SAN 169-1449) Tel 404-691-6996; Toll free: 800-326-2665; Dist. by: Bookpeople, 7900 Edgewater Dr., Oakland, CA 94621 (SAN 168-9517) Tel 510-632-4700; Toll free: 800-999-4650; Dist. by: Inland Bk. Co., 140 Commerce St., East Haven, CT 06512 (SAN 200-4151) Tel 203-467-4257; Toll free: 800-243-0138; Dist. by: The Distributors, 702 S. Michigan, South Bend, IN 46601 (SAN 169-2488) Tel 219-232-8500; Toll free: 800-348-5200 (except Indiana); Dist. by: Great Tradition, 750 Adrian Way, Suite 111, San Rafael, CA 94903 Tel 415-492-9382; Toll free: 800-333-7755.

Camelot Pub, *(Camelot Publishing Co.; 0-89218),* P.O. Box 1357, Ormond Beach, FL 32175-1357 (SAN 202-5035) Tel 904-672-5672.

Camex Bks Inc, *(Camex Bks., Inc.; 0-929793),* 535 Fifth Ave., New York, NY 10017 (SAN 250-5274) Tel 212-682-8400.

Camm Pub, *(Camm Publishing Co.; 0-9608400),* P.O. Box 640358, Uleta Branch, Miami, FL 33164 (SAN 240-6101) Tel 305-949-7536.

Campfire Pub, *(Campfire Publishing Co.; 0-9617653),* 226 Easton, S., Laurel, MD 20724 (SAN 664-8932) Tel 301-498-4807.

Campus Life *Imprint of* **Zondervan**

Canal Pl Pub
See Canal Side Pubs

Canal Side Pubs, *(Canal Side Pubs.; 0-9628208),* R.D. 3, Box 137, Frankfort, NY 13340 Tel 315-895-7535.

Candlewick Pr, *(Candlewick Pr.; 1-56402),* Div. of Walker Books, London, England, 2067 Massachusetts Ave., Cambridge, MA 02140 Tel 617-661-3330; Dist. by: Penguin USA, P.O. Box 120, Bergenfield, NJ 07621-0120 (SAN 282-5074) Tel 201-387-0600; Toll free: 800-526-0275.

C&M Pub MA, *(C&M Publishing Co.; 0-9635300),* 24 Kris Allen Dr., Holden, MA 01520-1001 Tel 508-829-7752.

Cando Pubng, *(Cando Publishing Corp.; 0-9638724),* 1399 Springside Dr., Fort Lauderdale, FL 33326 Tel 305-389-8120.

Canticle Press, *(Canticle Pr., Inc.; 0-9641725),* 371 Watervliet-Shaker Rd., Latham, NY 12110-4741 Tel 518-783-3526.

Canyon AZ, *(Canyon Publishing; 0-9624909),* Div. of Color Pro Printing & Graphics, Inc., 215 Coffee Pot Dr., Suite A, Sedona, AZ 86336 Tel 602-282-1886.

Canyon Country Pubns, *(Canyon Country Pubns.; 0-9614586; 0-925685),* P.O. Box 963, Moab, UT 84532 (SAN 630-1673); 23 La Sal Dr., Moab, UT 84532 Tel 801-259-6700.

Canyon Creat, *(Canyon Creations; 1-884563),* P.O. Box 136, Husum, WA 98623; 440 Rattlesnake Rd., Husum, WA 98623 Tel 509-493-3665.

Canyon Creek, *(Canyon Creek Pr.; 0-9635619),* 5714 E. Dale Ln., Cave Creek, AZ 85331 Tel 602-585-3059.

Cape Cod Life Mag, *(Cape Cod Life Magazine;* 0-9622782), P.O. Box 767, Cataumet, MA 02534-0767 Tel 508-564-4466.

Capital Enter, *(Capital Enterprises),* P.O. Box 716, West Springfield, MA 01090-0716 Tel 413-739-8231.

Capra Pr, *(Capra Pr.; 0-88496; 0-912264),* P.O. Box 2068, Santa Barbara, CA 93120 (SAN 201-9620) Tel 805-966-4590; Dist. by: Consortium Bk. Sales & Distribution, 1045 Westgate Dr., Suite 90, Saint Paul, MN 55114-1065 (SAN 200-6049) Tel 612-221-9035; Toll free: 800-283-3572 (orders).

Capstan Pubns, *(Capstan Pubns.; 0-914565),* P.O. Box 306, Basin, WY 82410 (SAN 289-162X) Tel 307-568-2604. *Imprints:* Timbertrails (Timbertrails).

Capstone Pr, *(Capstone Press, Inc.; 1-56065),* P.O. Box 669, Mankato, MN 56002-0669 Tel 507-387-4992; Toll free: 800-747-4992; 2440 Fernbrook Ln., Minneapolis, MN 55447 Tel 612-551-0513.

Capstone Pub, *(Capstone Publishing, Inc.; 1-880450),* P.O. Box 1687, Stanwood, WA 98292-1687; 215 W. Holly, Suite H-23, Bellingham, WA 98225 Tel 206-733-4703; Dist. by: Bookpeople, 7900 Edgewater Dr., Oakland, CA 94621 (SAN 168-9517) Tel 510-632-4700; Toll free: 800-999-4650. Do not confuse with Capstone Publishing Co. in New York, NY.

Carabis, *(Carabis, Anne J.; 0-9605802),* 25 Nelson Ave., Latham, NY 12110 (SAN 216-5600) Tel 518-783-9807.

Cardamom, *(Cardamom Pr.; 0-9611118),* P.O. Box 275, Richmond, ME 04357 (SAN 283-2836) Tel 207-666-5645.

Cardinal FL, *(Cardinal Enterprises of Florida;* 0-9639432), 18721 S. Dixie Hwy., Miami, FL 33157 Tel 305-232-5486.

Career Aids *Imprint of* **Opportunities Learn**

Career Pr Inc, *(Career Pr., Inc.; 0-934829; 1-56414),* 180 Fifth Ave., Hawthorne, NJ 07507 (SAN 694-3640) Tel 201-427-0229; Toll free: 800-227-3371.

Careers Inc, *(Careers, Inc.; 0-9623657),* P.O. Box 135, Largo, FL 34649; Toll free: 800-726-0441; 1211 Tenth St., SW, Largo, FL 34640 Tel 813-584-7333.

Careys Pub Co, *(Carey's Publishing Co.; 0-9617859;* 0-9619313), 6865 Tom King Bayou Rd., Gulf Breeze, FL 32561 (SAN 665-4436) Tel 904-939-1227.

Caribbean Rsch Ctr, *(Caribbean Research Ctr.;* 1-878433), 1150 Carroll St., Brooklyn, NY 11225 Tel 718-270-6422.

Caring Tree, *(Caring Tree Pubns.; 0-9618740),* 1459 Indiana Ave., South Pasadena, CA 91030 (SAN 668-7687) Tel 213-256-2987.

Carlisle Pr, *(Carlisle Pr.; 0-9627369),* P.O. Box 747, Mechanicsburg, PA 17055 Tel 717-697-1642; Dist. by: Baker & Taylor Bks., Somerville Service Ctr., 50 Kirby Ave., Somerville, NJ 08876-0734 (SAN 169-4901) Tel 908-722-8000; Toll free: 800-775-1500 (customer service); Dist. by: Quality Bks., Inc., 918 Sherwood Dr., Lake Bluff, IL 60044-2204 (SAN 169-2127) Tel 708-295-2010; Toll free: 800-323-4241 (libraries only); Dist. by: Brodart Co., 500 Arch St., Williamsport, PA 17705 (SAN 169-7684) Tel 717-326-2461; Toll free: 800-233-8467; Dist. by: Ingram Bk. Co., 1 Ingram Blvd., La Vergne, TN 37086-1986 (SAN 169-7978) Tel 615-793-5000; Toll free: 800-937-8000 (orders only, all warehouses).

Carlsons, *(Carlsons'; 0-944996),* P.O. Box 364, Lindsborg, KS 67456 (SAN 245-9485); 114 S. Main, Lindsborg, KS 67456 (SAN 245-9493) Tel 913-227-3360.

Carlton, *(Carlton Pr., Inc.; 0-8062),* 11 W. 32nd St., New York, NY 10001 (SAN 201-9655) Tel 212-714-0300. Do not confuse with Carlton Pubns., Inc., Beverly Hills, CA, Carlton Publishing, Studio City, CA.

Carnegie Mus, *(Carnegie Museum of Natural History;* 0-911239), Div. of Carnegie Institute, ; Orders to: Pubns. Sec., 4400 Forbes Ave., Pittsburgh, PA 15213-4080 (SAN 268-6686) Tel 412-622-3287.

Carol Mendel, *(Mendel, Carol; 0-9607696; 0-935179),* P.O. Box 6022, San Diego, CA 92106 (SAN 219-3329) Tel 619-226-1406.

Carol Paperbacks *Imprint of* **Carol Pub Group**

Carol Pub Group, *(Carol Publishing Group; 0-8184),* 600 Madison Ave., 11th Flr., New York, NY 10022 (SAN 201-1131) Tel 212-486-2200; Orders to: 120 Enterprise Ave., Secaucus, NJ 07094 (SAN 630-4524) Tel 201-866-0490. *Imprints:* Birch Ln Pr (Birch Lane Press); Carol Paperbacks (Carol Paperbacks); Citadel Pr (Citadel Press); L Stuart (Stuart, Lyle).

Carolina Acad Pr, *(Carolina Academic Pr.; 0-89089),* 700 Kent St., Durham, NC 27701 (SAN 210-7848) Tel 919-489-7486.

Carolina Biological, *(Carolina Biological Supply Co., Pubns. Dept.; 0-89278),* 2700 York Rd., Burlington, NC 27215 (SAN 249-2784) Tel 910-584-0381; Toll free: 800-334-5551.

Carolina Cnslts Network, *(Carolina Consultants Network - Publishing Div.; 0-9627795),* P.O. Box 374, Rock Hill, SC 29731; Toll free: 800-553-0958; 3425 Homestead Rd., Suite 100, Rock Hill, SC 29730 Tel 803-327-5488.

Carolrhoda Bks, *(Carolrhoda Bks., Inc.; 0-87614),* 241 First Ave., N., Minneapolis, MN 55401 (SAN 201-9671) Tel 612-332-3344; Toll free: 800-328-4929.

Carousel Pr, *(Carousel Pr.; 0-917120),* P.O. Box 6061, Albany, CA 94706-0061 (SAN 209-2646) Tel 510-527-5849; Dist. by: Publishers Group West, 4065 Hollis St., Emeryville, CA 94608 (SAN 202-8522) Tel 510-658-3453; Toll free: 800-788-3123.

Carousel Pub Corp
See Carousel Pubns Ltd

Carousel Pubns Ltd, *(Carousel Pubns., Ltd.; 0-935474),* 200 E. 63rd St., New York, NY 10021 (SAN 287-7333) Tel 212-758-9399.

Carpenter Pr, *(Carpenter Pr.; 0-914140),* P.O. Box 14387, Columbus, OH 43214 (SAN 206-4650) Tel 614-268-2234. Do not confuse with Carpenter's Pr. in Princeville, HI.

Carriage Hse Studio Pubns, *(Carriage Hse. Studio Pubns.; 0-9624342),* P.O. Box 712, Ferndale, CA 95536; 847 Van Ness Ave., Ferndale, CA 95536 Tel 707-786-4042.

Carroll CA
See Good Morn Tchr

Carson Ent, *(Carson Enterprises, Inc.; 0-941620),* Drawer 71, Deming, NM 88031 (SAN 239-1716) Tel 505-546-3252.

Cartwheel *Imprint of* **Scholastic Inc**

Carvin Pub, *(Carvin Publishing, Inc.; 0-9616390),* P.O. Box 850200, New Orleans, LA 70185-0200 (SAN 659-0888); 57 Neron Pl., New Orleans, LA 70118 (SAN 659-0896) Tel 504-866-4351.

Casa Bautista, *(Casa Bautista de Publicaciones; 0-311),* Div. of Southern Baptist Convention, P.O. Box 4255, 7000 Alabama St., El Paso, TX 79914 (SAN 220-0139) Tel 915-566-9656; Toll free: 800-755-5958. *Imprints:* Edit Mundo (Editorial Mundo Hispano).

Casatelli-Vivenzio, *(Casatelli-Vivenzio, Carol, & Gloria C. Busold; 0-9641300),* 455 Hayes Rd., Rensselaer, NY 12144 Tel 518-479-3542.

Cascade Pass, *(Cascade Pass, Inc.; 1-880599),* 5044 Maytime Ln., Culver City, CA 90230 Tel 310-202-1468.

Casio Inc, *(Casio, Inc.; 1-878532),* Subs. of Casio Computer Co., Ltd., Tokyo, 570 Mt. Pleasant Ave., Dover, NJ 07801 (SAN 277-0520) Tel 201-361-5400.

Castle Bks, *(Castle Bks., Inc.; 0-916693),* P.O. Box 17262, Memphis, TN 38187 (SAN 204-4005); 1445 Tuscany Way, Germantown, TN 38138-1823 (SAN 658-2575) Tel 901-754-4160.

Castle Capers
See Magical Michael

Castle MI, *(Castle Publishing; 0-9631809),* 1019 Ninth Ave., S., Escanaba, MI 49829 Tel 906-786-4251. Do not confuse with companies with similar names in Raleigh, NC, Portland, ME, New York NY.

Castlemarsh, *(Castlemarsh Pubns.; 0-942250),* P.O. Box 60728, Savannah, GA 31420 (SAN 240-8708) Tel 912-352-3273.

Cat-Tales Pr, *(Cat-Tales Pr.; 0-917107),* 51 Seventh Ave., Brooklyn, NY 11217 (SAN 655-6132) Tel 718-230-0724.

Catalina Creations, *(Catalina Creations; 0-9621316),* Div. of Kingett Art Service, P.O. Box 1211, Avalon, CA 90704 (SAN 251-0669) Tel 310-510-0660.

Catalpa Pr, *(Catalpa Pr.; 0-9619943),* P.O. Box 99, Corvallis, OR 97333 (SAN 246-9189).

Catalyst Pr, *(Catalyst Pr.; 0-9623897),* 9 Briar Patch Pl., Newport News, VA 23606 Tel 804-596-1031.

Cath Authors, *(Catholic Authors Pr.; 0-910334),* P.O. Box 23130, Saint Louis, MO 63156-3130 (SAN 203-6274) Tel 314-965-4801.

Cathedral Shop, *(Cathedral Shop, The; 0-915075),* Cathedral of St. John the Divine, 112th St. at Amsterdam Ave., New York, NY 10025 (SAN 289-7792) Tel 212-222-7448.

Catholic Bk Pub, *(Catholic Bk. Publishing Co.; 0-89942),* 257 W. 17th St., New York, NY 10011 (SAN 204-3432) Tel 212-243-4515.

Caxton, *(Caxton Printers, Ltd.; 0-87004),* 312 Main St., Caldwell, ID 83605-3299 (SAN 201-9698) Tel 208-459-7421.

Cay-Bel, *(Cay-Bel Publishing Co.; 0-941216; 0-918768),* 272 Center St., Bangor, ME 04401 (SAN 238-9215) Tel 207-941-2367.

Cay Sea Pr, *(Cay Sea Pr.; 0-9632368),* P.O. Box 2122, Gig Harbor, WA 98335; 6610 Cromwell Beach Dr., Gig Harbor, WA 98335 Tel 206-265-3593.

CBH Pub, *(CBH Publishing, Inc.; 0-9604538),* P.O. Box 1287, East Hampton, NY 11937 (SAN 216-2288) Tel 516-329-7627; Dist. by: Chicago Review Pr., Inc., 814 N. Franklin St., Chicago, IL 60610 (SAN 213-5744) Tel 312-337-0747; Toll free: 800-888-4741 (orders only).

CBHL Inc, *(Council on Botanical & Horticultural Libraries, Inc.; 0-9621791),* Univ. of Oregon, Knight Library, Eugene, OR 97403-1299 (SAN 252-2500) Tel 503-686-3078.

CBN Publishing, *(CBN Publishing; 1-55574),* CBN Ctr., CSB 116, Virginia Beach, VA 23463 (SAN 699-9484) Tel 804-424-7777.

CBP
See Chalice Pr

CBridge Pubns, *(C'Bridge Pubns.; 0-9621018),* 5230 Pennridge Ln., Dallas, TX 75241 (SAN 250-6955) Tel 214-371-8935.

CC Comics, *(CC Comics; 0-9634183),* P.O. Box 542, Loveland, OH 45140-0542; 6304 Councilridge Ct., Loveland, OH 45140 Tel 513-248-4171.

CCC of America, *(CCC of America; 1-56814),* 6000 Campus Cir. Dr., Suite 110, Irving, TX 75063 Tel 214-751-1915.

CCC Pubns, *(CCC Pubns.; 0-918259),* 21630 Lassen St., Chatsworth, CA 91311-6044 (SAN 669-666X) Tel 818-407-1661.

CDC Pr, *(CDC Pr.; 0-935769),* 88 Bradley Rd., Woodbridge, CT 06525 (SAN 695-8338) Tel 203-387-8887.

Cechoni Prodns, *(Cechoni Productions, Ltd.; 0-9626527),* 9027 S. Oakley Ave., Chicago, IL 60620 Tel 312-238-6516.

Cedar Glade Pr, *(Cedar Glade Pr.),* P.O. Box 1664, Jefferson City, MO 65102 (SAN 250-1031) Tel 314-635-8771.

Cedar Tree, *(Cedar Tree Publishing; 1-884393),* 8201 E. Lewis, Suite A, Scottsdale, AZ 85257 Tel 602-945-3514.

Cedars WI, *(Cedars Pr., The; 0-917575),* N. 5597 County Hwy. T, Green Lake, WI 54941 (SAN 657-1301) Tel 414-294-6754.

CEF Inc, *(Children's Express Foundation, Inc.;* 0-9621641), 245 Seventh Ave., New York, NY 10001 (SAN 251-6993) Tel 212-620-0098.

CEF Press, *(Child Evangelism Fellowship Pr.; 1-55976),* P.O. Box 348, Warrenton, MO 63383; Toll free: 800-748-7710; 2300 E. Hwy. M., Warrenton, MO 63383 (SAN 211-7789) Tel 314-456-4321; Dist. by: Spring Arbor Distributors, 10885 Textile Rd., Belleville, MI 48111 (SAN 158-9016) Tel 313-481-0900; Toll free: 800-395-5599 (orders); 800-395-7234 (customer service).

Ceise Corp, *(Ceise Corp.; 0-9623985),* P.O. Box 8, Hillsboro, OR 97123-0008; Toll free: 800-888-5268; HCR 61, 77-21, Banks, OR 97106 Tel 503-649-7631.

Celebration Pub, *(Celebration Publishing; 0-9613663),* Rte. 3, Box 365AA, Sylva, NC 28779 Tel 704-586-3404.

Celestial Arts, *(Celestial Arts Publishing Co.; 0-912310;* 0-89087), Subs. of Ten Speed Pr., P.O. Box 7123, Berkeley, CA 94707 (SAN 159-8333) Tel 510-559-1600; Toll free: 800-841-2665.

Celia Totus Enter, *(Celia Totus Enterprises, Inc.; 0-931363; 1-56041),* 1192 LaRue Rd., P.O. Box 192, Toppenish, WA 98948 (SAN 682-5567) Tel 509-865-2480.

Cellar, *(Cellar Bk. Shop),* 18090 Wyoming, Detroit, MI 48221 (SAN 213-4330) Tel 313-861-1776.

Celo Valley Bks, *(Celo Valley Bks.; 0-923687),* 346 Seven Mile Ridge Rd., Burnsville, NC 28714 (SAN 251-7973) Tel 704-675-5918.

Cent Busn Comm
See Designers Ink

Centering Corp, *(Centering Corp.; 1-56123),* 1531 N. Saddle Creek Rd., Omaha, NE 68104-5074 (SAN 298-1815) Tel 402-553-1200.

Centerstream Pub, *(Centerstream Publishing; 0-931759),* P.O. Box 5450, Fullerton, CA 92635 (SAN 683-8022) Tel 714-779-9390.

Central Agency, *(Central Agency for Jewish Education;* 0-930029), Affil. of Greater Miami Jewish Federation, 4200 Biscayne Blvd., Miami, FL 33137 (SAN 669-747X) Tel 305-576-4030.

Central Conf, *(Central Conference of American Rabbis; 0-916694; 0-88123),* 1303 Brittany Pointe, Lansdale, PA 19446-6520 (SAN 204-3262) Tel 212-684-4990; Toll free: 800-935-2227.

CES Compu-Tech, *(CES/Compu-Tech, Inc.; 0-917531;* 1-56177), 155 Hempstead Tpke., West Hempstead, NY 11552 (SAN 669-6708) Tel 516-565-5110; Toll free: 800-443-8061.

CES Industries, *(CES Industries, Inc.; 0-86711),* 130 Central Ave., Farmingdale, NY 11735 (SAN 237-9864) Tel 516-293-1420.

Cetacean Society, *(Cetacean Society International;* 0-9618858), 190 Stillwold Dr., Wethersfield, CT 06109 (SAN 242-3952) Tel 203-563-6444.

CFFC POWs MIAs, *(Civil Fact Finding Commission for POWs/MIAs in Southeast Asia; 0-9623659),* Rte. 3, Box 96, Rochester, IN 46975 Tel 219-223-4971.

CG Pubs Inc, *(Christopher-Gordon Pubs., Inc.;* 0-926842), 480 Washington St., Norwood, MA 02062 Tel 617-762-5577; Toll free: 800-934-8322.

Ch Brethren Womens Caucus, *(Church of the Brethren, Women's Caucus; 0-9618243),* Rte. 1, Box 215, Mount Solon, VA 22843 (SAN 666-9042) Tel 703-350-2922.

Chagdud Gonpa-Padma, *(Chagdud Gonpa-Padma Publishing; 1-881847),* Box 279, Junction City, CA 96048 (SAN 298-3079); Red Hill Rd., Junction City, CA 96048 Tel 916-623-2714.

Chalice Pr, *(Chalice Pr.; 0-8272),* Div. of Christian Board of Pubn., ; Orders to: P.O. Box 179, Saint Louis, MO 63166 (SAN 201-4408) Tel 314-231-8500; Toll free: 800-366-3383; Dist. by: Abingdon Pr., 201 Eighth Ave. S., P.O. Box 801, Nashville, TN 37202-0801 (SAN 201-0054) Tel 615-749-6290; Toll free: 800-251-3320.

Chalkline, *(Chalkline Publishing; 0-9641555),* P.O. Box 17070-332, San Diego, CA 92117 (SAN 298-3494); 2626 Cowley Way, San Diego, CA 92110 (SAN 298-3508) Tel 619-275-2566.

Chameleon FL, *(Chameleon Pr.; 0-9633373),* 3350 Kenmore Dr., Sarasota, FL 34231 Tel 813-921-2880.

Championship Bks & Vid Prodns, *(Championship Bks. & Video Productions; 0-932741; 1-56404),* P.O. Box 1166, ISU Sta., Ames, IA 50014 (SAN 656-1217); Toll free: 800-873-2730; 2730 Graham, Ames, IA 50010 Tel 515-232-3687.

Chandler White, *(Chandler/White Publishing Co.;* 1-877804), 30 E. Huron St., Suite 4403, Chicago, IL 60611 Tel 312-280-9451.

Changes CA, *(Changes; 0-9639056),* P.O. Box 7305, Santa Cruz, CA 95061; 328B Union St., Santa Cruz, CA 95060 Tel 408-423-9687.

Chaosium, *(Chaosium Inc.; 0-933635; 1-56882),* 950A 56th St., Oakland, CA 94608-3129 (SAN 692-6460) Tel 510-547-7681.

Chapel Hill NC, *(Chapel Hill Pr.; 1-880849),* Div. of Owens & Owens, 100 Eastwood Lake Rd., Chapel Hill, NC 27514 Tel 919-942-8389.

Chapman & Hall, *(Chapman & Hall; 0-412),* Div. of Routledge, Chapman & Hall, Inc., 1 Penn Plaza, New York, NY 10119 Tel 212-564-1060.

Chapters Pub, *(Chapters Publishing, Ltd.; 0-9631591;* 1-881527), 2031 Shelburne Rd., Shelburne, VT 05482 (SAN 297-5610) Tel 802-985-8700; Toll free: 800-892-0220; Dist. by: Firefly Bks., Ltd., P.O. Box 1338, Ellicott Sta., Buffalo, NY 14205 (SAN 630-611X); Toll free: 800-387-5085.

Char Ed Inst, *(Character Education Institute; 0-913413),* 8918 Tesoro, Suite 575, San Antonio, TX 78217-6253 (SAN 236-154X) Tel 210-829-1727; Toll free: 800-284-0499.

Char-L, *(Char-L Video Intensive Phonics, Inc.; 0-9605654; 1-880137),* 570 S. Church St., Apt. 2E, Decatur, IL 62522 (SAN 238-7751) Tel 217-422-0077.

Character Builders, *(Character Builders for Kids!;* 0-9615279), 6922 Aloma Ave., Winter Park, FL 32792-7003 (SAN 694-4604) Tel 407-677-7171; Dist. by: Baker & Taylor Bks., Somerville Service Ctr., 50 Kirby Ave., Somerville, NJ 08876-0734 (SAN 169-4901) Tel 908-722-8000; Toll free: 800-775-1500 (customer service); Dist. by: Baker & Taylor Bks., Momence Service Ctr., 501 S. Gladiolus St., Momence, IL 60954-2444 (SAN 169-2100) Tel 815-472-2444; Toll free: 800-775-2300 (customer service); Dist. by: Baker & Taylor Bks., Commerce Service Ctr., 251 Mt. Olive Church Rd., Commerce, GA 30599-9988 (SAN 169-1503) Tel 706-335-5000; Toll free: 800-775-1200 (customer service); Dist. by: Baker & Taylor Bks., Reno Service Ctr., 380 Edison Way, Reno, NV 89564 (SAN 169-4464) Tel 702-858-6700; Toll free: 800-775-1700 (customer service); Dist. by: Ingram Bk. Co., 1 Ingram Blvd., La Vergne, TN 37086-1986 (SAN 169-7978) Tel 615-793-5000; Toll free: 800-937-8000 (orders only, all warehouses); Dist. by: Spring Arbor Distributors, 10885 Textile Rd., Belleville, MI 48111 (SAN 158-9016) Tel 313-481-0900; Toll free: 800-395-5599 (orders); 800-395-7234 (customer service).

Character Res, *(Character Research Pr.; 0-915744),* 1020 Mohegan Rd., Schenectady, NY 12309-4724 (SAN 209-1240).

Charcoal St Pr, *(Charcoal Street Pr.; 0-9624296),* 22531 Honnold Dr., Saugus, CA 91350 Tel 310-312-2394.

Charill Pubs, *(Charill Pubs.; 0-9620182; 1-883519),* 4468 San Francisco Ave., Saint Louis, MO 63114 (SAN 247-9141); Dist. by: Baker & Taylor Bks., Somerville Service Ctr., 50 Kirby Ave., Somerville, NJ 08876-0734 (SAN 169-4901) Tel 908-722-8000; Toll free: 800-775-1500 (customer service); Dist. by: Baker & Taylor Bks., Momence Service Ctr., 501 S. Gladiolus St., Momence, IL 60954-1799 (SAN 169-2100) Tel 815-472-2444; Toll free: 800-775-2300 (customer service); Dist. by: Baker & Taylor Bks., Commerce Service Ctr., 251 Mt. Olive Church Rd., Commerce, GA 30599-9988 (SAN 169-1503) Tel 706-335-5000; Toll free: 800-775-1200 (customer service); Dist. by: Baker & Taylor Bks., Reno Service Ctr., 380 Edison Way, Reno, NV 89564-0099 (SAN 169-4464) Tel 702-858-6700; Toll free: 800-775-1700 (customer service); Dist. by: Book Wholesalers, Inc., 1847 Mercer Rd., Lexington, KY 40511-1001 (SAN 630-8066) Tel 606-231-9789; Toll free: 800-888-4478; Dist. by: Source International Technology Corp., 939 E. 156th St., Bronx, NY 10455 (SAN 630-8392) Tel 718-378-3878.

Chariot Bks *Imprint of* **Chariot Family**

Chariot Family, *(Chariot Family Publishing; 0-7814),* Div. of David C. Cook Publishing Co., 20 Lincoln Ave., Elgin, IL 60120 Tel 708-741-9558; Toll free: 800-447-7766. *Imprints:* Bible Discovery (Bible Discovery); Chariot Bks (Chariot Books).

Charles A Lemoine, *(Lemoine, Charles A.; 0-941327),* 11311 Plank Rd., Baton Rouge, LA 70811 (SAN 666-4342) Tel 504-775-3056.

Charles River Bks, *(Charles River Bks.; 0-89182),* 1 Thompson Sq., P.O. Box 65, Boston, MA 02129 (SAN 209-2530) Tel 617-259-8857.

Charlesbridge Pub, *(Charlesbridge Publishing; 0-935508; 0-88106; 1-57091),* Div. of Mastery Education, 85 Main St., Watertown, MA 02172 (SAN 240-5474) Tel 617-926-0329; Toll free: 800-225-3214.

Chartier, *(Chartier Co's., Inc.; 0-9636343),* 3800 S. Tamiami Trail, Sarasota, FL 34239 Tel 813-954-0480; Toll free: 800-952-0480.

Chase Educ, *(Chase Educational Publishing; 0-9640126),* 804A Arroyo Dr., South Pasadena, CA 91030 Tel 818-441-3327.

Chateau Thierry, *(Chateau Thierry Pr.; 0-935046),* Div. of Joan Thiry Enterprises, Ltd., 2100 W. Estes, Chicago, IL 60645 (SAN 281-4056) Tel 312-262-2234.

Chatham Pr, *(Chatham Pr., Inc.; 0-85699),* P.O. Box A, Old Greenwich, CT 06870 (SAN 201-9795) Tel 203-531-7755.

Chatham River Pr *Imprint of* **Random Hse Value**

Chatterbox Pr, *(Chatterbox Pr.; 0-943129),* P.O. Box 7933 F.D.R. Sta., New York, NY 10150-2411 (SAN 668-1417) Tel 212-702-9729; 248 94th St., Brooklyn, NY 11209 (SAN 668-1425) Tel 718-745-1809; Dist. by: Gryphon Hse., Inc., P.O. Box 207, Beltsville, MD 20704-0207 (SAN 169-3190) Tel 301-595-9500; Toll free: 800-638-0928.

CHB Goodyear Comm, *(Childrens Hospital of Buffalo, Josephine Goodyear Committee; 0-9616699),* 219 Bryant St., Buffalo, NY 14222 (SAN 661-227X) Tel 716-634-7778.

Che-King Pubng, *(Che-King Publishing; 0-9639263),* P.O. Box 13347, Atlanta, GA 30324; 315 Cobblestone Trail, Avondale Estates, GA 30002 Tel 404-296-8270.

Cheap St, *(Cheap Street; 0-941826),* Rte. 2, Box 1293, New Castle, VA 24127-9430 (SAN 239-1783) Tel 703-864-6288.

Checkerboard, *(Checkerboard Pr., Inc.; 1-56288),* 30 Vesey St., New York, NY 10007 Tel 212-571-6300.

Cheers, *(Cheers; 0-9617744),* 253 Alberta Dr., Atlanta, GA 30305 (SAN 664-6859) Tel 404-233-4897.

Cheertime USA, *(Cheertime U.S.A.; 0-9614174),* P.O. Box 2844, Edmond, OK 73083 (SAN 686-6204) Tel 405-341-0853; Orders to: P.O. Box 2844, Edmond, OK 73083 (SAN 665-8636).

Cheeruppet, *(Cheeruppet World, Inc.; 0-914201),* 2264 Calle Iglesia, Mesa, AZ 85202 (SAN 287-6000) Tel 602-839-3319; Orders to: 2405 E. Southern Ave., Sta., Tempe, AZ 85282 (SAN 287-6019) Tel 602-831-6088.

Cheetah Pub, *(Cheetah Publishing, Inc.; 0-936241),* 275 N. Forest Lake Dr., Altamonte Springs, FL 32714 (SAN 697-0443) Tel 407-862-2726.

Cheever Pub, *(Cheever Publishing, Inc.; 0-915708),* P.O. Box 700, Bloomington, IL 61702 (SAN 207-9410) Tel 309-378-2961.

Chelsea Green Pub, *(Chelsea Green Publishing Co.;* 0-930031), P.O. Box 428, 205 Gates-Briggs Bldg., White River Junction, VT 05001 (SAN 669-7631) Tel 802-295-6300; Toll free: 800-639-4099 (orders only); Orders to: 52 Labombard Rd., N., Lebanon, NH 03766.

Chelsea Hse, *(Chelsea Hse. Pubs.; 0-87754; 1-55546;* 0-7910), Div. of Main Line Bk. Co., 300 Park Ave. S., No. 6, New York, NY 10010-5313 (SAN 206-7609) Tel 212-677-4010; Toll free: 800-848-2665. *Imprints:* Am Art Analog (American Art Analog).

Chelsea Pub, *(Chelsea Publishing Co.; 0-8284),* 15 E. 26th St., New York, NY 10010 (SAN 201-9825) Tel 212-889-8095.

Chenier Educ Enter, *(Chenier Educational Enterprises, Inc.; 0-9626061),* P.O. Box 265, Wells, MI 49894; 5727 Second Ave., N., Wells, MI 49894 Tel 906-786-8088.

Chereb Pub, *(Chereb Publishing; 0-9634469),* HC64, Box 1020, Springerville, AZ 85938-9710; 1734 Becker Ln. Loop, Springerville, AZ 85938 Tel 602-333-4217.

Cherished Bks, *(Cherished Bks.; 0-915029),* 3680 N. Little Rock Dr., Provo, UT 84604 (SAN 289-8217) Tel 801-224-4343; Dist. by: Sounds of Zion, 6973 S. 300 W., Midvale, UT 84047 (SAN 200-7525) Tel 801-255-1991.

Cherokee, *(Cherokee Publishing Co.; 0-87797),* P.O. Box 1730, Marietta, GA 30061 (SAN 650-0404) Tel 404-438-7366; Toll free: 800-653-3952. Do not confuse with Cherokee Publishing Co. in Little Creek, DE.

Cherokee Bks, *(Cherokee Bks.; 0-9628188),* 1805 Dover Dr., Ponca City, OK 74604-4422 Tel 405-762-8517.

Cherokee Comn, *(Cherokee Communication; 0-9628630),* Div. of Cherokee Boys Club, Inc., P.O. Box 507, Cherokee, NC 28719; 4 Acquoni Rd., Cherokee, NC 28719 Tel 704-497-5510.

Cherokee Pubns, *(Cherokee Pubns.; 0-935741),* P.O. Box 430, Cherokee, NC 28719 (SAN 696-2785) Tel 704-488-8856.

Cherokee Strip, *(Cherokee Strip Centennial Foundation;* 0-9638403), 401 E. Oklahoma, Enid, OK 73701 Tel 405-233-4353.

Cherry Lane, *(Cherry Lane Bks.; 0-89524),* Div. of Cherry Lane Music Co., Inc., 10 Midland Ave., Port Chester, NY 10573 (SAN 219-0788) Tel 914-937-8601; P.O. Box 430, Port Chester, NY 10573; Dist. by: Alfred Publishing Co., Inc., 16380 Roscoe Blvd., Suite 200, Box 10003, Van Nuys, CA 91406-1215 (SAN 201-243X) Tel 818-891-5999; Toll free: 800-292-6122: 800-821-6083 (in California).

Cherub Prods, *(Cherub Productions, Inc.; 0-9641771),* 6556 Dartbrook Dr., Dallas, TX 75240 Tel 214-233-3030.

Cherubim, *(Cherubim; 0-938574),* P.O. Box 75, Fort Tilden, NY 11695 (SAN 215-8523).

Chessex, *(Chessex; 1-883240),* 2990 San Pablo Ave., Berkeley, CA 94702 Tel 510-843-1194.

Cheval Intl, *(Cheval International; 0-9640610; 1-885351),* 204 N. El Camino Real, No. E331, Encinitas, CA 92024; 2022 Shadytree, Encinitas, CA 92024 Tel 619-633-1644; Dist. by: Baker & Taylor Bks., Eastern Div., 50 Kirby Ave., Somerville, NJ 08876-0734 Tel 201-722-8000; Toll free: 800-775-1400 (orders); 800-775-1500 (customer service); Dist. by: Baker & Taylor Bks., Momence Service Ctr., 501 S. Gladiolus St., Momence, IL (SAN 169-2100) Tel 815-472-2444; Toll free: 800-775-2300 (customer service); Dist. by: Baker & Taylor Bks., Commerce Service Ctr., 251 Mt. Olive Church Rd., Commerce, GA 30599-9988 (SAN 169-1503) Tel 706-335-5000; Toll free: 800-775-1200 (customer service); Dist. by: Baker & Taylor Bks., Reno Service Ctr., 380 Eidson Way, Reno, NV 89564 (SAN 169-4464) Tel 702-858-6700; Toll free: 800-775-1700 (customer service).

Chicago Review, *(Chicago Review Pr., Inc.; 0-914090; 0-914091; 1-55652),* 814 N. Franklin St., Chicago, IL 60610 (SAN 213-5744) Tel 312-337-0747; Toll free: 800-888-4741 (orders only).

Chicago Zoo, *(Chicago Zoological Society; 0-913934),* 3300 Golf Rd., Brookfield, IL 60513 (SAN 663-4672) Tel 312-485-0263.

Chick Pubns, *(Chick Pubns.; 0-937958),* P.O. Box 662, Chino, CA 91708-0662 (SAN 211-7770) Tel 909-987-0775; Toll free: 800-932-3050.

Child Alphabet, *(Children's Alphabet; 0-940047),* 3228 Castle Rock Rd., Oklahoma City, OK 73120 (SAN 664-0540) Tel 405-755-3290.

Child Bks & Mus, *(Children's Bks. & Music; 0-9633053),* 1163 Snowhill Rd., Sabina, OH 45169 Tel 513-584-4035.

Child Classics *Imprint of* **Random Hse Value**

Child Media Inst
See Family Media

Child Mus, *(Children's Museum of Indianapolis, The;* 0-9608982), 30th & Meridian, Indianapolis, IN 46208 (SAN 268-9057) Tel 317-924-5437.

Child Mus Wkshop, *(Children's Music Workshop;* 0-944528), 315 Riverside Dr., No. 7C, New York, NY 10025 (SAN 243-8291) Tel 212-932-8621.

Child of Color, *(Children of Color Publishing Co.;* 0-9638127), 1380 E. Hyde Park Blvd., Chicago, IL 60615 Tel 312-285-5908.

Child Tech Bks, *(Child Tech Bks. & Toys; 0-9636795),* P.O. Box 2614, Union City, CA 94587; 220 Appian Way, Union City, CA 94587 Tel 510-471-1562.

Child Time Pubs, *(Child Time Pubs.; 0-929934),* P.O. Box 250001, West Bloomfield, MI 48325-0001 (SAN 250-7757) Tel 810-681-9000.

Child Welfare, *(Child Welfare League of America, Inc.;* 0-87868), 440 First St., NW, Washington, DC 20001 (SAN 201-9876) Tel 202-638-2952.

Childbirth Graphics, *(Childbirth Graphics, Ltd.;* 0-943114), P.O. Box 20540, Rochester, NY 14602-0540 (SAN 240-3587) Tel 716-272-9230.

Childlight Pr, *(Childlight Pr.; 0-9630026),* 23011 Oxnard St., Woodland Hills, CA 91367 Tel 818-375-7192; Dist. by: BookWorld Distribution Services, Inc., 1933 Whitfield Pk. Loop, Sarasota, FL 34243 (SAN 173-0568) Tel 813-758-8094; Toll free: 800-444-2524 (orders only).

Children First, *(Children First Pr.; 0-9603696),* Box 8008, Ann Arbor, MI 48107 (SAN 212-4904) Tel 313-668-8056.

Children Learn Ctr, *(Children's Learning Ctr., Inc.;* 0-917206), 4660 E. 62nd St., Indianapolis, IN 46220 (SAN 208-5933) Tel 317-251-6241.

Childrens, *(Children's Pr.; 0-516),* Div. of Grolier, Inc., 5440 N. Cumberland Ave., Chicago, IL 60656 (SAN 201-9264) Tel 312-693-0800; Toll free: 800-621-1115. *Imprints:* Elk Grove Bks (Elk Grove Books); Golden Gate (Golden Gate).

Childrens Art, *(Children's Art Foundation, Inc.;* 0-89409), Box 83, Santa Cruz, CA 95063 (SAN 210-0533) Tel 408-426-5557; Toll free: 800-447-4569.

Childrens Book Pr, *(Children's Bk. Pr.; 0-89239),* 6400 Hollis St., Emeryville, CA 94608 (SAN 210-7864) Tel 510-655-3395; Dist. by: Bookpeople, 7900 Edgewater Dr., Oakland, CA 94621 (SAN 168-9517) Tel 510-632-4700; Toll free: 800-999-4650; Dist. by: Ingram Bk. Co., 1 Ingram Blvd., La Vergne, TN 37086-1986 (SAN 169-7978) Tel 615-793-5000; Toll free: 800-937-8000 (orders only, all warehouses); Dist. by: Baker & Taylor Bks., Somerville Service Ctr., 50 Kirby Ave., Somerville, NJ 08876-0734 (SAN 169-4901) Tel 908-722-8000; Toll free: 800-775-1500 (customer service); Dist. by: Baker & Taylor Bks., Momence Service Ctr., 501 S. Gladiolus St., Momence, IL 60954-2444 (SAN 169-2100) Tel 815-472-2444; Toll free: 800-775-2300 (customer service); Dist. by: Baker & Taylor Bks., Commerce Service Ctr., 251 Mt. Olive Church Rd., Commerce, GA 30599-9988 (SAN 169-1503) Tel 706-335-5000; Toll free: 800-775-1200 (customer service); Dist. by: Baker & Taylor Bks., Reno Service Ctr., 380 Edison Way, Reno, NV 89564 (SAN 169-4464) Tel 702-858-6700; Toll free: 800-775-1700 (customer service); Dist. by: Inland Bk. Co., 140 Commerce St., East Haven, CT 06512 (SAN 200-4151) Tel 203-467-4257; Toll free: 800-243-0138; Dist. by: Pacific Pipeline, Inc., 8030 S. 228th St., Kent, WA 98032-2900 (SAN 208-2128) Tel 206-872-5523; Toll free: 800-444-7323 (customer service); 800-677-2222 (orders).

Childrens Corner, *(Children's Corner Pr.; 0-944326),* 6125 Mooresville Rd., Indianapolis, IN 46241 (SAN 243-5276) Tel 317-856-5565.

Childrens Lgcy, *(Children's Legacy; 0-9629365),* P.O. Box 300305, Denver, CO 80203; 2553 Dexter St., Denver, CO 80207 Tel 303-830-7595.

Childrens Reading Inst, *(Children's Reading Institute;* 0-923223), Div. of GMH Marketing, Houston Dr., Durham, CT 06422 (SAN 251-7442) Tel 203-349-1014.

Childrens TV Resource, *(Children's Television Resource & Education Ctr.; 0-929831),* 330 Townsend St., 234, San Francisco, CA 94107 (SAN 250-636X) Tel 415-243-9943; Dist. by: JTG of Nashville, 1024C 18th Ave., S., Nashville, TN 37212 (SAN 630-3323) Tel 615-329-3036; Toll free: 800-222-2584.

Childrens Work, *(Children's Work; 1-878300),* 1307 S. 1100 E., Salt Lake City, UT 84105 Tel 801-467-6024; Dist. by: Educational Bk. Distributors, P.O. Box 2510, Novato, CA 94948 (SAN 158-2259) Tel 415-883-3530.

Childs Gift
See Someday Baby

Childs Hosp, *(Project CHAMP, Children's National Medical Ctr.; 0-9634295),* Div. of Children's National Medical Ctr., 111 Michigan Ave., NW, Washington, DC 20010-2970 Tel 202-884-5450.

Childs Min Bk Co, *(Childs Miniature Bk. Co.; 1-878582),* P.O. Box 5878, Westport Sta., Kansas City, MO 64111; 4320 Wornall Rd., No. 452, Kansas City, MO 64111 Tel 816-531-2325.

Childs Play, *(Child's Play-International; 0-85953),* 64 Wellington Ave., West Orange, NJ 07052 (SAN 216-2121) Tel 201-731-3777; Toll free: 800-472-0099.

Childs Play
See PJC Lrng Mtrls

Childs World, *(Child's World, Inc.; 0-913778; 0-89565;* 1-56766), 505 N. Highway 169, Suite 295, Plymouth, MN 55441 (SAN 211-0032) Tel 612-797-0155; Dist. by: Encyclopaedia Britannica Education Corp., 310 S. Michigan, Chicago, IL 60604 (SAN 201-3851) Tel 312-347-7900; Toll free: 800-554-9862.

Chimeric, *(Chimeric, Inc.; 0-9636796),* 2696 S. Colorado Blvd., No. 370, Denver, CO 80222 Tel 303-756-5696.

Chimurenga, *(Chimurenga; 0-9624153),* 2121 Seventh St., No. 212, Berkeley, CA 94710 Tel 408-287-9228.

China Bks, *(China Bks. & Periodicals, Inc.; 0-8351),* 2929 24th St., San Francisco, CA 94110 (SAN 145-0557) Tel 415-282-2994.

Chinky-Po Tree, *(Chinky-Po Tree, Inc.; 1-884375),* 1103 Beech Haven Rd., Atlanta, GA 30324 Tel 404-794-7928.

Chitra Pubns, *(Chitra Pubns.; 0-9622565; 1-885588),* 2 Public Ave., Montrose, PA 18801 Tel 717-278-1984; Toll free: 800-628-8244.

Chivers N Amer, *(Chivers North America; 0-89340; 1-55504; 0-7927),* 1 Lafayette Rd., Box 1450, Hampton, NH 03843-1450 (SAN 208-4864) Tel 603-926-8744; Toll free: 800-621-0182. *Imprints:* Curley Lrg Print (Curley Large Print); Galaxy Child Lrg Print (Galaxy Children's Large Print).

Chldrns Better Hlth, *(Children's Better Health Institute;* 1-885453), Div. of Benjamin Franklin Literary & Medical Society, Inc., 1100 Waterway Blvd., Indianapolis, IN 46202 Tel 317-636-8881; Toll free: 800-558-2376; Dist. by: BookWorld Distribution Services, Inc., 1933 Whitfield Pk. Loop, Satasota, FL 34243 (SAN 173-0568) Tel 813-758-8094; Toll free: 800-444-2524 (orders only).

Chldrns Gall, *(Children's Gallery Pubns.; 0-9636190),* 23 Chambers Ave., Cornelia, GA 30531 Tel 706-778-3745.

Chldrns Med, *(Children's Medical World; 0-9637869),* P.O. Drawer 8238, Alexandria, LA 71306; 224 Estate Dr., Pineville, LA 71360 Tel 318-443-5524.

Chldrns Mus, *(Children's Museum of Oak Ridge;* 0-9606832), P.O. Box 3066, Oak Ridge, TN 37830 (SAN 219-7227) Tel 615-482-1074.

Chldrns Outrch, *(Children's Outreach; 1-883426),* 801 Willark, New Whiteland, IN 46184 Tel 317-535-7014.

Chldrns Pubng, *(Children's Publishing Hse.; 0-9643138),* 2515 W. 147th St., Posen, IL 60469.

Chocho Bks, *(Chocho Bks.; 0-922273),* 11929 Caminito Corriente, San Diego, CA 92128 (SAN 251-3196) Tel 619-487-8213.

Chocolate Tree, *(Chocolate Tree; 0-9639057),* 1515 E. 108th St., Cleveland, OH 44106 Tel 216-721-0577.

Choice Pub NY, *(Choice Publishing, Inc.; 0-945260),* Affil. of Choice Concepts, Inc., 115 Frost St., Westbury, NY 11590-5007 (SAN 246-2729). Do not confuse with Choice Publishing in Fullerton, CA.

Chokecherry, *(Chokecherry Pr.; 1-884035),* 1397 E. Stellaria Cir., Bountiful, UT 84010 Tel 801-292-7863.

Chosen Bks, *(Chosen Bks.; 0-8010),* Div. of Baker Bk. Hse., P.O. Box 6287, Grand Rapids, MI 49516-6287 Tel 616-676-9185; Toll free: 800-877-2665.

Chowder Pr, *(Chowder Pr.; 0-9614546),* 13 Schuyler Dr., Saratoga Springs, NY 12866 (SAN 691-7984) Tel 518-587-2808.

CHP NY, *(Cherry Hill Pubns.; 1-883029),* 110 Cherry Hill Rd., Dewitt, NY 13214 Tel 315-446-5654. Do not confuse with Cherry Hill Pubns. in Saint Louisville, OH.

Chr Classics, *(Christian Classics, Inc.; 0-87061),* Orders to: P.O. Box 30, Westminster, MD 21158-0930 Tel 410-848-3065; Toll free: 800-888-3065.

Chr Lit, *(Christian Literature Crusade, Inc.; 0-87508),* P.O. Box 1449, Fort Washington, PA 19034-8449 (SAN 169-7358) Tel 215-542-1240; Toll free: 800-659-1240.

Chr Pubns, *(Christian Pubns., Inc.; 0-87509),* 3825 Hartzdale Dr., Camp Hill, PA 17011 (SAN 202-1617) Tel 717-761-7044; Toll free: 800-233-4443. Do not confuse with Christian Pubns. in Shalimar, FL.

Chrch Grwth VA, *(Church Growth Institute; 0-941005;* 1-57052), P.O. Box 4404, Waterlick Rd., Lynchburg, VA 24502 Tel 804-525-0022; Toll free: 800-553-4769; Dist. by: Spring Arbor Distributors, 10885 Textile Rd., Belleville, MI 48111 (SAN 158-9016) Tel 313-481-0900; Toll free: 800-395-5599 (orders); 800-395-7234 (customer service).

Christ Covenant, *(Christ Covenant Blood; 0-9636797),* Rte. 5, Box 28, Council Bluffs, IA 51503-9216 Tel 712-323-5141.

Christ Recollect, *(Christian Recollections; 0-9640365),* Rt. 3, Box 116, Dayton, VA 22821 Tel 703-867-5113.

Christian Aid, *(Christian Aid Ministries; 1-885270),* P.O. Box 360, Berlin, OH 44610; 4464 S.R. 39 E., Berlin, OH 44610 Tel 216-893-2428.

Christian Center, *(Christian Ctr. of Christos Wisdom;* 0-944517), P.O. Box 14825, Long Beach, CA 90803-1380 (SAN 243-0320) Tel 310-434-2976.

Christian Light, *(Christian Light Pubns., Inc.; 0-87813),* 1066 Chicago Ave., Harrisonburg, VA 22801 (SAN 206-7315) Tel 703-434-0768.

Christian Pub, *(Christian Publishing Services, Inc.;* 0-88144), Subs. of Harrison Hse. Pubs., P.O. Box 55388, Tulsa, OK 74155-1388 (SAN 260-0285) Tel 918-584-5535.

Christian Sci, *(Christian Science Publishing Society, The; 0-87510; 0-87952),* One Norway St., P411, Boston, MA 02115 (SAN 203-6541) Tel 617-450-2773; Toll free: 800-288-7090; Orders to: P.O. Box 1875, Boston, MA 02117 (SAN 203-6541); Toll free: 800-877-8400.

Christmans, *(Christmans; 0-9625413),* 302 S. Broadway St., Pittsburg, KS 66762-5206; Rte. 1, P.O. Box 172A, Oronogo, MO 64855 Tel 417-842-3322.

Chrlstn SC, *(Charleston Pr.; 0-9619974),* 1648 Fairway Place Ln., Mount Pleasant, SC 29464 (SAN 247-2910) Tel 803-881-1778. Do not confuse with Charleston Pr., Baton Rouge, LA.

Chrome Yellow
See Nords Studio

Chron Guide, *(Chronicle Guidance Pubns., Inc.; 0-912578; 1-55631),* P.O. Box 1190, Moravia, NY 13118-1190 (SAN 202-1641) Tel 315-497-0330; Toll free: 800-622-7284.

Chronicle Bks, *(Chronicle Bks.; 0-87701; 0-8118;* 0-938491), Div. of Chronicle Publishing Co., 275 Fifth St., San Francisco, CA 94103 (SAN 202-165X) Tel 415-777-7240; Toll free: 800-722-6657 (orders only).

Chronimed, *(Chronimed Publishing; 0-937721; 1-56561),* Div. of Chronimed, Inc., 13911 Ridgedale Dr., Suite 250, Minnetonka, MN 55305 (SAN 659-252X) Tel 612-541-0239; Toll free: 800-444-5951; Orders to: P.O. Box 47945, Minneapolis, MN 55447 (SAN 665-9225); Toll free: 800-848-2793 (orders only).

Chrstn Life Workshops
See Noble Pub Assocs

CIBC, *(Council on Interracial Bks. for Children, Inc.;* 0-930040), 1841 Broadway, Rm. 500, New York, NY 10023 (SAN 110-6643) Tel 212-757-5339.

Cinc Hist Soc, *(Cincinnati Historical Society, The;* 0-911497), 1301 Western Ave., Cincinnati, OH 45203-1129 (SAN 263-9718) Tel 513-287-7000.

Cinc Mus Nat Hist, *(Cincinnati Museum of Natural History; 1-882151),* 1301 Western Ave., Cincinnati, OH 45203 Tel 513-287-7049.

Cinco Puntos, *(Cinco Puntos Pr.; 0-938317),* 2709 Louisville, El Paso, TX 79930 (SAN 661-0080) Tel 915-566-9072.

Cinemed
See CNS Prods

Circuit Pubns, *(Circuit Pubns.; 0-923573),* P.O. Box 1201, Marblehead, MA 01945 (SAN 251-7736); 7545 Graves Rd., Cincinnati, OH 45243 (SAN 251-7744) Tel 513-561-5413.

Circuit Writer, *(Circuit Writer; 0-9617971),* 2522 Waterford Rd., Auburn, AL 36830-4114 (SAN 666-2447).

CIRI Found, *(CIRI Foundation, The; 0-938227),* P.O. Box 93330, Anchorage, AK 99509-3330 (SAN 666-6213); 2525 C St., Suite 507, Anchorage, AK 99503 (SAN 667-593X) Tel 907-274-8638.

CIS Comm, *(CIS Communications, Inc.; 0-935063;* 1-56062), 180 Park Avenue, Lakewood, NJ 08701 (SAN 694-5953) Tel 201-367-7858.

Citadel Pr *Imprint of* **Carol Pub Group**

CITE, *(Ctr. for International Training & Education;* 0-938960), 777 United Nations Plaza, Suite 3C, New York, NY 10017 (SAN 217-0957) Tel 212-953-6920.

City Gallery Cntmprry Art, *(City Gallery of Contemporary Art; 0-9621077; 1-885449),* P.O. Box 66, Raleigh, NC 27602 (SAN 250-426X); 220 S. Blount St., Raleigh, NC 27601 (SAN 250-4278) Tel 919-839-2077.

City Mazes, *(City Mazes, Inc.; 1-881207),* P.O. Box 11274, Memphis, TN 38111 Tel 901-278-2633.

Civan Inc, *(Civan, Inc.; 0-9621700),* 100 Butterville Rd., New Paltz, NY 12561 (SAN 251-8619) Tel 914-255-0696.

Ckbk Morris Pr
See Morris Pubng

CKG Pubs
See LKC

Claitors, *(Claitors Publishing Div.; 0-87511),* 3165 S. Acadian at Interstate 10, Box 3333, Baton Rouge, LA 70821 (SAN 206-8346) Tel 504-344-0476.

Claremount Pr, *(Claremount Pr.),* Box 177, Cooper Sta., New York, NY 10003 (SAN 219-466X).

Clarion Bks *Imprint of* **HM**

Clarion Pr, *(Clarion Pr.; 0-923296),* 2550 Michael Dr., Sterling Heights, MI 48310-3577 (SAN 252-1911).

Clark City Pr, *(Clark City Pr.; 0-944439),* P.O. Box 1358, Livingston, MT 59047 (SAN 243-699X); Toll free: 800-835-0814; 109 W. Callender, Livingston, MT 59047 (SAN 243-7007) Tel 406-222-7412.

Clark Pub, *(Clark Publishing, Inc.; 0-931054),* P.O. Box 19240, Topeka, KS 66619-0240 Tel 913-862-0218; Toll free: 800-845-1916. Do not confuse with companies with the same name in Tacoma, WA, Lexington, KY.

Clarke Enterprise, *(Clarke Enterprise; 0-9626984),* P.O. Box 432, Niwot, CO 80544-0432 Tel 303-530-3431.

Clarksburg-Harrison Bicent, *(Clarksburg-Harrison Bicentennial Committee; 0-9615566),* 404 W. Pike St., Clarksburg, WV 26301 (SAN 696-4877) Tel 304-624-6512.

Clarkson Potter *Imprint of* **Crown Bks Yng Read**

Clarkson Potter *Imprint of* **Crown Pub Group**

Clarkston Pub, *(Clarkston Publishing Co.; 0-945772),* P.O. Box 38, Clarkston, MI 48347-0038 (SAN 247-9001) Tel 810-620-2090.

Clarus Music, *(Clarus Music, Ltd.; 0-86704),* 340 Bellevue Ave., Yonkers, NY 10703 (SAN 216-6615) Tel 914-591-7715.

Classic Wrks, *(Classic Works; 1-883338),* 13502 Whittier Blvd., Suite H276, Whittier, CA 90605 Tel 310-696-9331; Toll free: 800-847-1868; Dist. by: Baker & Taylor Bks., Somerville Service Ctr., 50 Kirby Ave., Somerville, NJ 08876-0734 (SAN 169-4901) Tel 908-722-8000; Toll free: 800-775-1500 (customer service); Dist. by: Baker & Taylor Bks., Momence Service Ctr., 501 S. Gladiolus St., Momence, IL 60954-2444 (SAN 169-2100) Tel 815-472-2444; Toll free: 800-775-2300 (customer service); Dist. by: Baker & Taylor Bks., Commerce Service Ctr., 251 Mt. Olive Church Rd., Commerce, GA 30599-9988 (SAN 169-1503) Tel 706-335-5000; Toll free: 800-775-1200 (customer service); Dist. by: Baker & Taylor Bks., Reno Service Ctr., 380 Edison Way, Reno, NV 89564 (SAN 169-4464) Tel 702-858-6700; Toll free: 800-775-1700 (customer service); Dist. by: Pacific Pipeline, Inc., 8030 S. 228th St., Kent, WA 98032-2900 (SAN 208-2128) Tel 206-872-5523; Toll free: 800-444-7323 (Customer Service); 800-677-2222 (orders); Dist. by: Silo Music Distribution, Inc., S. Main St., P.O. Box 429, Waterbury, VT 05676 (SAN 630-7876) Tel 802-244-6128; Toll free: 800-342-0295.

Classics Int Ent, *(Classics International Entertainment, Inc.; 1-57209),* 324 Main Ave., Ste. 183, Norwalk, CT 06851 Tel 203-849-8977.

Claycomb Pr, *(Claycomb Pr., Inc.; 0-933905),* P.O. Box 70822, Chevy Chase, MD 20813-0822 (SAN 692-7521) Tel 301-656-1057.

Claymont Comm, *(Claymont Communications;* 0-934254), Box 112, Charles Town, WV 25414 (SAN 211-7010) Tel 304-725-1523.

Clear Blue Sky, *(Clear Blue Sky Publishing Co.;* 1-884395), 4320 S. Louise Ave., Sioux Falls, SD 57106 Tel 605-361-4151.

Clear Light, *(Clear Light Pubs.; 0-940666),* 823 Don Diego, Santa Fe, NM 87501 (SAN 219-7758) Tel 505-989-9590; Toll free: 800-253-2747. Do not confuse with Clear Light Pub. in Seattle, WA.

Clerc Bks *Imprint of* **Gallaudet Univ Pr**

Clever Creat, *(Clever Creations; 1-884376),* 132 N. El Camino Real, Suite 206, Encinitas, CA 92024 Tel 619-942-0411.

Click Pub, *(Click! Publishing; 0-9631235),* 18 Wedgewood Gardens, Selinsgrove, PA 17870-8402 Tel 717-374-4827.

Clicker Pub, *(Clicker Publishing; 0-9637412),* P.O. Box 189, Berrien Springs, MI 49103; 8091 U.S. 31, Berrien Springs, MI 49103 Tel 616-473-3035.

Cliffs, *(Cliffs Notes, Inc.; 0-8220),* P.O. Box 80728, Lincoln, NE 68501 (SAN 202-1706); Toll free: 800-228-4078; 4851 S. 16th St., Lincoln, NE 68512 Tel 402-423-5050.

Clinkscale Pubns, *(Clinkscale Pubns. & Productions;* 0-9640311), P.O. Box 5696, Youngstown, OH 44504; 242 Early Rd., Youngstown, OH 44505 Tel 216-747-7446.

Clipboard, *(Clipboard Pubns.; 0-9606084),* P.O. Box 54, Pullman, WA 99163-0054 (SAN 216-8006).

Close Up, *(Close Up Publishing; 0-932765),* Div. of Close Up Foundation, 44 Canal Center Plaza, Alexandria, VA 22314 (SAN 679-1980) Tel 703-706-3560; Toll free: 800-765-3131.

Cloud Pub, *(Cloud Publishing; 0-911981),* Div. of Cloud Assoc., Inc., P.O. Box 39016, Phoenix, AZ 85069 (SAN 264-6595) Tel 602-866-7820.

Cloud Ten, *(Cloud 10 Creations, Inc.; 0-910349),* 805 Circuit Ct., Virginia Beach, VA 23454 (SAN 241-2896); Dist. by: Trillium Pr., P.O. Box 209, Monroe, NY 10950 (SAN 212-4637) Tel 914-783-2999.

Clyde Pr, *(Clyde Pr.; 0-933190),* 373 Lincoln Pkwy., Buffalo, NY 14216 (SAN 213-8395) Tel 716-875-4713; 174 Depew Ave., Buffalo, NY 14214 (SAN 241-662X) Tel 716-834-1254.

CMark Pr, *(CMark Pr.; 0-9621308),* 211 N. Scrivener, Lake Elsinore, CA 92330 (SAN 251-0561) Tel 909-674-4785.

CMSP Projects, *(CMSP Projects; 0-942851),* School of Engineering, 51 Astor Pl., New York, NY 10003 (SAN 667-6731) Tel 212-228-0950.

CMU Clarke Hist Lib, *(Central Michigan Univ., Clarke Historical Library; 0-916699),* Central Michigan Univ., Park Bldg., No. 409, Mount Pleasant, MI 48859 (SAN 218-6799) Tel 517-774-3352.

Cndlelght Pr, *(Candlelight Pr.; 0-9637101),* P.O. Box 50187, Irvine, CA 92619-0187 Tel 714-552-4266; Dist. by: Bookpeople, 7900 Edgewater Dr., Oakland, CA 94621 (SAN 168-9517) Tel 510-632-4700; Toll free: 800-999-4650.

CNS Prods, *(CNS Productions; 0-926544),* P.O. Box 96, Ashland, OR 97520-1962; Toll free: 800-888-0617; 130 Third St., Ashland, OR 97520 Tel 503-488-2805.

Cnsltnts Unlimited
See Schwarz Pauper

Cntry Home, *(Country Home Pubs.; 0-9632513),* 930 N. Osborn Rd., White Cloud, MI 49349 Tel 616-924-0817.

Coach Ent, *(Coach Enterprises; 0-9636706),* 3657 Wallace Dr., Pittsburgh, PA 15227 Tel 412-881-8067.

Coastwise Pr, *(Coastwise Pr.; 0-9626857),* 27 Green St., Thomaston, ME 04861-1530.

Cobblehill Bks *Imprint of* **Dutton Child Bks**

Cobblestone Pub, *(Cobblestone Publishing, Inc.; 0-9607638; 0-942389),* 7 School St., Peterborough, NH 03458 (SAN 237-9937) Tel 603-924-7209.

Coffee Break, *(Coffee Break Pr.; 0-933992),* P.O. Box 103, Burley, WA 98322 (SAN 212-341X) Tel 206-851-4074.

Coffee Hse, *(Coffee Hse. Pr.; 0-915124; 0-918273;* 1-56689), 27 N. Fourth St., Suite 400, Minneapolis, MN 55401 (SAN 206-3883) Tel 612-338-0125; Dist. by: Consortium Bk. Sales & Distribution, 1045 Westgate Dr., Suite 90, Saint Paul, MN 55114-1065 (SAN 200-6049) Tel 612-221-9035; Toll free: 800-283-3572 (orders).

Cognitive Pr, *(Cognitive Pr.; 1-883241),* P.O. Box 18731, Sarasota, FL 34276 (SAN 297-8768); 2567 Apache St., Sarasota, FL 34231 Tel 813-922-1450.

Col Connect, *(College Connection; 1-880468),* P.O. Box 1364, Flushing, NY 11370 Tel 718-639-2535. Do not confuse with College Connection, Inc. in Westport, CT.

Col U Pr, *(Columbia Univ. Pr.; 0-231),* 562 W. 113th St., New York, NY 10025 (SAN 212-2472) Tel 212-666-1000; Toll free: 800-944-8648 (customer service); Orders to: 136 S. Broadway, Irvington-on-Hudson, NY 10533 (SAN 212-2480) Tel 914-591-9111.

Colburn Pr, *(Colburn Pr.; 0-9634187),* P.O. Box 356, Montvale, NJ 07645; 307 Van Emburgh Ave., Ridgewood, NJ 07450 Tel 201-652-1484.

Cold Spring Harbor, *(Cold Spring Harbor Laboratory Pr.; 0-87969),* 1 Bungtown Rd., Cold Spring Harbor, NY 11724 (SAN 203-6185) Tel 516-349-1930; Toll free: 800-843-4388.

Coldwater Pr, *(Coldwater Pr., Inc.; 1-880384),* 9806 Coldwater Cir., Dallas, TX 75228 Tel 214-328-7612.

Cole Enter, *(Cole Enterprises; 1-878514),* 2195 E. River Rd., Suite 103, Tucson, AZ 85718-6586.

Coll Acceptance, *(College Acceptance; 0-9615165),* 2 Clover Ln., Randolph, NJ 07869 (SAN 694-3624) Tel 201-895-3390.

Coll Info Srv, *(College Information Services; 1-882707),* 1649 NE Third Ct., Fort Lauderdale, FL 33301 Tel 305-764-1151; Toll free: 800-257-5030.

Coll News Parents, *(College News for Parents;* 0-9637250), P.O. Box 587, Mantua, OH 44255; 10893 Bartholomew Rd., Mantua, OH 44255 Tel 216-543-4637.

Collaborare Pub, *(Collaborare Publishing; 0-931881),* 354 Front, Upper Sandusky, OH 43351 (SAN 686-0486) Tel 419-294-3207; Dist. by: Gallopade: Carole Marsh Bks., General Delivery, Bath, NC 27808 (SAN 213-8441) Tel 919-923-4291.

Collector Bks, *(Collector Bks.; 0-89145),* Div. of Schroeder Publishing Co., Inc., 5801 Kentucky Dam Rd., Paducah, KY 42002-3009 (SAN 157-5368) Tel 502-898-6211; Toll free: 800-626-5420; P.O. Box 3009, Paducah, KY 42003 (SAN 200-7479).

College Afford Prodns
See Path-Coll Afford Prod

College Pr Pub, *(College Pr. Publishing Co., Inc.;* 0-89900), Box 1132, 215-223 W Third, Joplin, MO 64802 (SAN 211-9951) Tel 417-623-6280; Toll free: 800-289-3300.

Collier *Imprint of* **Macmillan**

Collier Young Ad *Imprint of* **Macmillan Child Grp**

Collins SF, *(Collins Publishers San Francisco; 0-00),* Div. of HarperCollins Pubs., Inc., 1160 Battery St., San Francisco, CA 94111-1213 (SAN 247-5529) Tel 415-788-4111; Toll free: 800-242-7737 (Bookstores); 800-331-3761 (Individuals).

Colonial Pr AL, *(Colonial Pr.; 0-938991; 1-56883),* 3325 Burning Tree Dr., Birmingham, AL 35226-2643 (SAN 662-6599) Tel 205-822-6654.

Colophon Hse, *(Colophon Hse.; 1-882539),* 10700 Richmond, No. 205, Houston, TX 77042 Tel 713-777-5394.

Color Class, *(Color the Classics; 1-881153),* 6027 East Rd., Silver Springs, NY 14550 Tel 716-493-2181.

Color-Me Storybks, *(Color-Me Storybooks; 0-9640707),* P.O. Box 452211, Garland, TX 75045-2211; 2305 Matterhorn Dr., Garland, TX 75044 Tel 214-495-8225.

Color Me Well, *(Color Me Well Pubns.; 1-878083),* P.O. Box 16321, Plantation, FL 33318 (SAN 297-2956); 6081 SW 14th St., Plantation, FL 33317 Tel 305-748-5535.

Colorful Lrngs, *(Colorful Learnings/Maria Elena Buria;* 1-878926), 13876 SW 56th St., Suite 194, Miami, FL 33175 Tel 305-666-9957.

Colormore Inc, *(Colormore, Inc.; 0-945600),* 7080 S. Ridge Dr., Mission Viejo, CA 92692 (SAN 247-4530) Tel 714-837-2483.

Colorsong Prodns, *(Colorsong Productions, Inc.; 0-9623234),* 2685 Valleyview Ln., NE, Saint Paul, MN 55112 Tel 612-780-3557.
Columbia Bks, *(Columbia Bks. Inc., Pubs.; 0-910416; 1-880873),* 1212 New York Ave., NW, Suite 330, Washington, DC 20005 (SAN 202-1757) Tel 202-898-0662.
Columbia Sacramento
See Columbia San Fran
Columbia San Fran, *(Columbia Pubs.; 0-9622514; 1-884830),* 1965 Hayes St., San Francisco, CA 94117 Tel 415-751-3479; Toll free: 800-403-6557.
Columbia U Pr
See Col U Pr
Columbine *Imprint of* **Fawcett**
Com Sense Pub, *(Common Sense Publishing; 0-9642123),* P.O. Box 1581, Pine Bluff, AR 71613; 1026 W. 50th St., Pine Bluff, AR 71603 Tel 501-536-5468.
COMAL Users, *(COMAL Users Group, U.S.A., Ltd.; 0-928411),* 5501 Groveland Terrace, Madison, WI 53716-3251 (SAN 669-5256) Tel 608-222-4432.
COMAP Inc, *(COMAP, Inc.; 0-912843),* 57 Bedford St., Suite 210, Lexington, MA 02173 (SAN 282-9991) Tel 617-862-7878; Toll free: 800-772-6627.
Comet Intl, *(Comet International; 1-884857),* 145 W. 28th St., Suite 9F, New York, NY 10001 Tel 212-947-6303.
Comex Systs, *(Comex Systems, Inc.; 1-56030),* Mill Cottage, Mendham, NJ 07945 Tel 201-543-2862.
Coming Age Pr, *(Coming of Age Pr.; 0-9636274; 1-885340),* 14045 Robins Run, Austin, TX 78737 Tel 512-288-0637.
Comm Intervention, *(Community Intervention, Inc.; 0-9613416; 0-945485),* 529 S. Seventh St., Suite 570, Minneapolis, MN 55415 (SAN 656-9706) Tel 612-332-6537; Toll free: 800-328-0417.
Comm Just Foun TX, *(Community Justice Foundation of Texas; 0-9631028),* P.O. Box 64954, Dallas, TX 75206; 6732 Inverness, Dallas, TX 75214 Tel 214-824-0141.
Community Comm, *(Community Communications Corp.; 0-9630029; 1-885352),* 5950 Carmichael Pl., Suite 111, Montgomery, AL 36117 Tel 205-279-9828; Toll free: 800-222-6418; Dist. by: Centennial Pr., P.O. Box 80287, Lincoln, NE 68501 (SAN 630-7426); Toll free: 800-356-5016.
Comp Trng Clinic, *(Computer Training Clinic, Inc.; 1-880850),* 612 DuPont Rd., Charleston, SC 29407 Tel 803-763-9262.
Compact Bks
See Compact Books
Compact Books, *(Compact Bks.; 0-936320),* 2131 Hollywood Blvd., Suite 204, Hollywood, FL 33020 (SAN 215-0670) Tel 305-925-5242.
Compact Classics, *(Compact Classics, Inc.; 1-880184),* 2144 Highland Dr., No. 100, Salt Lake City, UT 84106-2834 (SAN 298-0940) Tel 801-268-9777; Toll free: 800-676-9777.
COMPAS, *(COMPAS; 0-927663),* 308 Landmark Ctr., 75 W. Fifth, Saint Paul, MN 55102 Tel 612-292-3249.
Comprehen Health Educ, *(Comprehensive Health Education Foundation; 0-935529; 1-57021),* 22323 Pacific Hwy., S., Seattle, WA 98198 (SAN 696-3668) Tel 206-824-2907; Toll free: 800-323-2433.
Comprehen Lang, *(Comprehensive Language Communications; 1-884161),* P.O. Box 242, Borger, TX 79008-0242; 615 Evergreen St., Borger, TX 79007-6435 Tel 806-273-2631.
Comptex Assocs Inc, *(Comptex Assocs., Inc.; 0-911849),* P.O. Box 6745, Washington, DC 20020 (SAN 265-3710).
Comptr Pub Enterprises, *(Computer Publishing Enterprises; 0-945776),* P.O. Box 23478, San Diego, CA 92193 (SAN 247-9087) Tel 619-576-0353; Toll free: 800-544-5541.
Compu-Aid, *(Compu-Aid Computer Consultants; 0-9624107),* 2814 Clairmount Dr., Saginaw, MI 48603-3101 Tel 517-793-0311.
Computer Assis, *(Computer Assisted Library Information Co., Inc.; 0-916625),* P.O. Box 6190, Chesterfield, MO 63006-6190 (SAN 296-4856) Tel 314-863-8028; Toll free: 800-367-0416.
Computer Lit Pr, *(Computer Literacy Pr.; 0-941681),* 1466 Grizzly Peak Blvd., Berkeley, CA 94708 (SAN 666-3133) Tel 510-644-2400; Orders to: 5750 Obata Way, Suite H, Gilroy, CA 95021-2383; Toll free: 800-225-5413.
Computer Pr, *(Computer Pr.; 1-882183),* 2911 Eighth Ave., W., Bradenton, FL 34205-4123 (SAN 297-7869) Tel 813-748-4237; Toll free: 800-227-8973.
Comstock Bon, *(Comstock Bonanza Pr.; 0-933994),* 18919 William Quirk Memorial Dr., Grass Valley, CA 95945 (SAN 223-694X) Tel 916-273-6220.
Conari Press, *(Conari Pr.; 0-943233; 1-57324),* 1144 65th St., Suite B, Emeryville, CA 94608 (SAN 668-1085) Tel 510-596-4040; Toll free: 800-685-9595 (orders); Dist. by: Publishers Group West, 4065 Hollis St., Emeryville, CA 94608 (SAN 202-8522) Tel 510-658-3453; Toll free: 800-788-3123.
Concept Spelling, *(Concept Spelling, Inc.; 0-935276),* P.O. Box 7200, Costa Mesa, CA 92626 (SAN 213-909X) Tel 714-770-0811.
Concern, *(Concern, Inc.; 0-937345),* 1794 Columbia Rd., NW, Washington, DC 20016 (SAN 225-1728) Tel 202-328-8160.
Concord MouseTrap, *(Concord MouseTrap; 0-9638644),* 10 Walden St., Concord, MA 01742 Tel 508-287-4800.
Concordia, *(Concordia Publishing Hse.; 0-570),* Subs. of Lutheran Church Missouri Synod, 3558 S. Jefferson Ave., Saint Louis, MO 63118 (SAN 202-1781) Tel 314-268-1000; Toll free: 800-325-3040.
Condor Pubns Inc, *(Condor Pubns., Inc.; 0-929853),* P.O. Box 88366, Carol Stream, IL 60188-0366 (SAN 250-5215); 137 Pebblecreek Trail, Carol Stream, IL 60188-0366 (SAN 250-5223) Tel 708-690-9819.
Confetti Ent, *(Confetti Entertainment Co., Inc.; 1-882179),* P.O. Box 1155, Studio City, CA 91614; 15250 Ventura Blvd., Suite 800, Sherman Oaks, CA 91403 Tel 818-783-6251.
Confluence Pr, *(Confluence Pr., Inc.; 0-917652; 1-881090),* Lewis-Clark State College, 500 Eighth Ave., Lewiston, ID 83501-2698 (SAN 209-5467) Tel 208-799-2336; Dist. by: National Bk. Network, 4720A Boston Way, Lanham, MD 20706-4310 (SAN 630-0065) Tel 301-459-8696; Toll free: 800-462-6420.
Conley Outreach, *(Conley Outreach Pubns.; 0-932920),* 116 W. Pierce St., Elburn, IL 60119 (SAN 212-3150).
Consortium RI, *(Consortium Publishing; 0-940139),* 640 Weaver Hill Rd., West Greenwich, RI 02817 (SAN 664-2667) Tel 401-397-9838.
Construct Educ, *(Constructive Educational Concepts, Inc.; 0-934734),* 213 Duncaster Rd., Box 667, Bloomfield, CT 06002 (SAN 215-7446).
Consulting Psychol, *(Consulting Psychologists Pr., Inc.; 0-89106),* 3803 E. Bayshore Rd., Palo Alto, CA 94303 (SAN 201-7849) Tel 415-691-9143; Toll free: 800-624-1765; Dist. by: National Bk. Network, 4720A Boston Way, Lanham, MD 20706-4310 (SAN 630-0065) Tel 301-459-8696; Toll free: 800-462-6420.
Consumer Reports, *(Consumer Reports Bks.; 0-89043),* Div. of Consumers Union of U.S., Inc., 101 Truman Ave., Yonkers, NY 10703 (SAN 224-1048) Tel 914-378-2000; Dist. by: St. Martin's Pr., Inc., 175 Fifth Ave., Rm. 1715, New York, NY 10010 (SAN 200-2132) Tel 212-674-5151; Toll free: 800-221-7945.
Consumers Union, *(Consumers Union of U. S., Inc.; 0-89043),* 101 Truman Ave., Yonkers, NY 10703 (SAN 269-3518) Tel 914-378-2000; Orders to: Consumer Reports Bks., 540 Barnum Ave., Bridgeport, CT 06608 (SAN 661-9800).
Contemp Bks, *(Contemporary Bks., Inc.; 0-8092; 0-941263; 1-56943),* 2 Prudential Plaza, Suite 1200, Chicago, IL 60601 (SAN 202-5493) Tel 312-540-4500; Toll free: 800-621-1918 (orders only).
Cook, *(Cook, David C., Publishing Co.; 0-89191; 0-912692; 1-55513; 0-7814),* 20 Lincoln Ave., Elgin, IL 60120 (SAN 206-0981) Tel 708-741-9558; Toll free: 800-323-7543.
Cool Hand Comms, *(Cool Hand Communications, Inc.; 1-56790),* 1098 NW Second Ave., No. 1, Boca Raton, FL 33432-2616 (SAN 297-7605) Tel 407-750-9826; Toll free: 800-428-0578.
Copperfield Pr, *(Copperfield Pr.; 0-933857),* 8571 Southwestern Blvd., Dallas, TX 75206 (SAN 692-7351). Do not confuse with Copperfield Pr., Jamaica, NY.
Corita Comm, *(Corita Communications, Inc.; 0-933016),* 1301 N. Kenter Ave., Los Angeles, CA 90049 (SAN 212-2723) Tel 310-559-2375; Orders to: P.O. Box 49368, Los Angeles, CA 90049 (SAN 666-6531).
Cornerstone Pr, *(Cornerstone Pr.; 0-918476),* 1825 Bender Ln., Arnold, MO 63010-0388 (SAN 210-0584) Tel 314-296-9662. Do not confuse with companies with the same name in Chicago, IL, Edison, NJ.
Cornucop Pub, *(Carolina Cornucopia Educational Publishing Co.; 0-935911),* P.O. Box 1118, Buxton, NC 27920-1118 (SAN 696-7213) Tel 919-471-1873; Dist. by: Nancy Roberts' Collection, 3600 Chevington Rd., Charlotte, NC 28211 (SAN 200-5786) Tel 704-364-4608.
Corona Pub, *(Corona Publishing, Co.; 0-931722),* P.O. Drawer 12407, San Antonio, TX 78212 (SAN 211-8491) Tel 210-341-7525; 218 Grotto Blvd., San Antonio, TX 78216-6618 Tel 210-341-7525; Dist. by: Taylor Publishing Co., 1550 W. Mockingbird Ln., Dallas, TX 75235 (SAN 202-7631); Toll free: 800-759-8120 (orders).
Coronet Bks, *(Coronet Bks.; 0-89563),* 311 Bainbridge St., Philadelphia, PA 19147 (SAN 210-6043) Tel 215-925-5083.
Corpuscles Intergalactica, *(Corpuscles Intergalactica; 0-9620961),* 40 Johnson Heights, Waterville, ME 04901 (SAN 250-202X) Tel 207-873-6486.
Cosmic Color Bks, *(Cosmic Coloring Bks.; 0-9622288),* P.O. Box 46, Lonepine, MT 59848-0046.
Cosmic Concepts Pr, *(Cosmic Concepts Pr.; 0-9620507),* 2531 Dover Ln., Saint Joseph, MI 49085 (SAN 248-6431) Tel 616-428-2792.
Cosmic Hse NM, *(Cosmic Hse.; 0-932492),* P.O. Box 10515, Alameda, NM 87184 (SAN 211-9331) Tel 505-821-3147.
Costa Pubng, *(Costa Publishing; 0-9643002),* P.O. Box 1264, Santa Clara, CA 95052-1264 Tel 408-244-3718.
Cottage Bks, *(Cottage Bks.; 0-911253),* Subs. of Sam Yette Enterprises, P.O. Box 2071, Silver Spring, MD 20902 (SAN 285-0044); 1801A Duke Dr., Silver Spring, MD 20902 (SAN 241-6719) Tel 301-649-5123.
Cottage Pr MA, *(Cottage Pr., The; 1-882063),* P.O. Box 135, Lincoln Center, MA 01773 (SAN 248-3319); 27 Lincoln Rd., Lincoln Center, MA 01773 (SAN 248-3327) Tel 617-259-8771.
Cottage Pub Co, *(Cottage Publishing Co.; 0-915479),* 200 Lafayette Ave., Hawthorne, NJ 07506 (SAN 291-1299) Tel 201-427-2830.
Cottage Wordsmiths, *(Cottage Wordsmiths; 0-9624155),* P.O. Box 81006, Pittsburgh, PA 15217; 6732 Reynolds St., Pittsburgh, PA 15206 Tel 412-661-7054.
Cotton Tale, *(Cotton Tale Pr.; 1-881274),* 3804 Harley Ave., Fort Worth, TX 76107 Tel 817-738-5207; Dist. by: Ingram Bk. Co., 1 Ingram Blvd., La Vergne, TN 37086-1986 (SAN 169-7978) Tel 615-793-5000; Toll free: 800-937-8000 (orders only, all warehouses).
Cottontail Creations, *(Cottontail Creations, Inc.; 0-9624767),* P.O. Box 11453, Charlotte, NC 28209; 320 Meacham, Charlotte, NC 28203 Tel 704-342-0750.
Cottonwood KS, *(Cottonwood Pr.; 1-878434),* P.O. Box J, Kansas Union, Univ. of Kansas, Lawrence, KS 66045 Tel 913-864-3777. Do not confuse with companies with the same name in Fort Collins, CO, Novato, CA, Wilsonville, OR.
Cottonwood Pr, *(Cottonwood Pr., Inc.; 1-877673),* 305 W. Magnolia, Suite 398, Fort Collins, CO 80521 Tel 303-493-1286. Do not confuse with companies with same name in Novato, CA, Lawrence, KS, Wilsonville, OR.
Coun India Ed, *(Council for Indian Education; 0-89992),* 2032 Woody Dr., Billings, MT 59102 (SAN 202-2117) Tel 406-252-7451; Orders to: 3239 Grand Ave., Billings, MT 59102 (SAN 689-836X) Tel 406-252-7434.
Coun Oak Bks, *(Council Oak Bks.; 0-933031; 1-57178),* Div. of Council Oak Publishing Co., Inc., ; Orders to: 1350 E. 15th St., Tulsa, OK 74120-5801 (SAN 689-5522) Tel 918-587-6454; Toll free: 800-247-8850 (orders only).
Counterpoint Pub, *(Counterpoint Publishing Co.; 1-878149),* 6318 Craigway Rd., Spring, TX 77389 Tel 713-376-7613.
Country Messenger Inc, *(Country Messenger, Inc.; 0-9619407),* P.O. Box 207, Marine on Saint Croix, MN 55047 (SAN 244-5638); 16022 Oakhill Rd., N., Marine on Saint Croix, MN 55047 (SAN 244-5646) Tel 612-433-3845.
Country Schl Pubns, *(Country School Pubns.; 0-942565),* 6373 N. Eighth, Fresno, CA 93710 (SAN 667-2027) Tel 209-435-8845.
Countryman, *(Countryman Pr., Inc.; 0-914378; 0-88150; 0-942440),* P.O. Box 175, Woodstock, VT 05091-0175 (SAN 206-4901) Tel 802-457-1049; Toll free: 800-245-4151.
Courage Bks, *(Courage Bks.; 0-89471; 1-56138),* Div. of Running Pr. Bk. Pubs., 125 S. 22nd St., Philadelphia, PA 19103 Tel 215-567-5080; Toll free: 800-345-5359.
Courageous Kids, *(Courageous Kids, Inc.; 0-9633626),* P.O. Box 841132, Pembroke Pines, FL 33084-3132 Tel 305-436-3377.
Cove Pr CA, *(Cove Pr.; 0-9620065),* 567 San Antonio Ave., San Diego, CA 92106 (SAN 247-526X) Tel 619-222-4666. Do not confuse with Cove Pr., Austin, TX.
Cove Pt Pr, *(Cove Point Pr.; 0-9634785),* P.O. Box 859, Larchmont, NY 10538; 69 Willow Ave., Larchmont, NY 10538 Tel 914-833-3060.
Cove View, *(Cove View Pr.; 0-931896),* 2165 Carlmont Dr., No. 205, Belmont, CA 94002-3411 (SAN 220-0422).
Covenant Comms, *(Covenant Communications, Inc.; 1-55503),* P.O. Box 416, American Fork, UT 84003-0416 (SAN 169-8540); Toll free: 800-662-9545; 920 E. State Rd., Suite F, American Fork, UT 84003 Tel 801-756-9966.

Covenant Marriages, *(Covenant Marriages Ministry; 1-886045),* Div. of Victory Faith Fellowship, 17301 W. Colfax Ave., Suite 140, Golden, CO 80401-4800 Tel 303-277-1338.

Covenant Pubs, *(Covenant Pub.; 1-879420),* P.O. Box 26361, Philadelphia, PA 19141 Tel 215-638-4324.

Coward *Imprint of* **Putnam Pub Group**

Cowley Pubns, *(Cowley Pubns.; 0-936384; 1-56101),* Div. of Society of St. John the Evangelist, 28 Temple Pl., Boston, MA 02111 (SAN 213-9987) Tel 617-423-2427; Toll free: 800-225-1534.

CPI, *(CPI; 0-9630960),* 200 Alta Vista Ave., Mill Valley, CA 94941 Tel 415-383-6660.

CPI Pub, *(CPI Publishing, Inc.),* 311 E. 51st St., New York, NY 10022 (SAN 218-6896) Tel 212-753-3800; Dist. by: Modern Curriculum Pr., 13900 Prospect Rd., Cleveland, OH 44136 (SAN 206-6572) Tel 216-238-2222; Toll free: 800-321-3106. Do not confuse with CPI Publishing in West Concord, MN.

CPP Belwin, *(CPP/Belwin, Inc.; 0-89898; 0-910957; 0-7604),* 15800 NW 48th Ave., Hialeah, FL 33014 (SAN 203-042X) Tel 305-620-1500; Toll free: 800-327-7643 (SAN 251-2556).

Crabtree Pub Co, *(Crabtree Publishing Co.; 0-86505),* 350 Fifth Ave., Suite 3308, New York, NY 10118 (SAN 251-4796) Tel 212-496-5040; Toll free: 800-387-7650. Do not confuse with Crabtree Publishing, Federal Way, WA.

Cracked Egg, *(Cracked Egg Brand Pr.; 1-882820),* Box 134, Stowell, TX 77661; Main & Third, Stowell, TX 77661 Tel 409-296-2053.

Cracom, *(Cracom Corp.; 0-9633555; 1-884793),* 12131 Dorsett Rd., Suite 109, Maryland Heights, MO 63043 (SAN 630-9429) Tel 314-291-3988; Toll free: 800-880-3988.

Crains Muscle, *(Crain's Muscle World; 0-929994),* P.O. Box 1322, Shawnee, OK 74802-1322 (SAN 251-1223); 1510 N. Kickapoo, Shawnee, OK 74801 (SAN 251-1231) Tel 405-275-3689.

Cranberry Origs, *(Cranberry Originals Pr.; 0-9622784),* P.O. Box 572, Glenwood Springs, CO 81602-0572; 1631 Fourth St., Port Edwards, WI 54469 Tel 715-887-3755; Dist. by: Baker & Taylor Bks., Momence Service Ctr., 501 S. Gladiolus St., Momence, IL 60954-2444 (SAN 169-2100) Tel 815-472-2444; Toll free: 800-775-2300 (customer service).

Cranbrook Educ, *(Cranbrook Educational Community; 0-9636492),* 1221 Woodward Ave., Box 801, Bloomfield Hills, MI 48303-0801 Tel 810-645-3154.

Cranbrook Pub, *(Cranbrook Publishing; 0-9604690),* 2302 Windemere, Flint, MI 48503 (SAN 215-7470) Tel 810-338-6403.

Cranbury Pubns, *(Cranbury Pubns.; 0-9629323),* P.O. Box 2260, Norwalk, CT 06852-2260 Tel 203-847-8029.

Crane Hill AL, *(Crane Hill Pubs.; 0-9621455; 1-881548),* 2923 Crescent Ave., Birmingham, AL 35209 Tel 205-871-9877; Toll free: 800-841-2682.

Cranehill Pr, *(Cranehill Pr.; 0-9618182),* 708 Comfort Rd., Spencer, NY 14883 (SAN 666-7538) Tel 607-277-3058.

Cranky Nell Bk *Imprint of* **Kane-Miller Bk**

Crayons Pubns, *(Crayons Pubns.; 0-927024),* P.O. Box 322, Milford, MA 01757 Tel 508-478-4400.

CRC Pr, *(CRC Pr., Inc.; 0-87819; 0-8493),* Subs. of Times Mirror Co., 2000 Corporate Blvd., NW, Boca Raton, FL 33431 (SAN 202-1994) Tel 407-994-0555; Toll free: 800-272-7737. CRC Pr., Inc. out of print titles are available on-demand through Franklin Bk. Co., Inc.

CRC Pubns, *(CRC Pubns.; 0-933140; 0-930265; 1-56212),* 2850 Kalamazoo Ave., SE, Grand Rapids, MI 49560 (SAN 212-727X) Tel 616-246-0724; Toll free: 800-333-8300.

Crea Tea Assocs, *(Creative Teaching Assocs.; 1-878669),* Div. of Master Creative Teaching Assocs., P.O. Box 7766, Fresno, CA 93747 (SAN 297-6803); Toll free: 800-767-4282; 5629 E. Westover, Fresno, CA 93747 Tel 209-291-6626.

Creare Pubns, *(Creare Pubns.; 0-943901),* 1011 E. 17th Ave., No. 6, Denver, CO 80218-1409 (SAN 242-2123) Tel 303-830-6884.

Creat Concern, *(Creative Concern Pubns.; 0-917117),* 12066 Suellen Cir., West Palm Beach, FL 33414 (SAN 655-6221) Tel 407-793-5854; Orders to: 3208 Mayaguana Ln., Lantana, FL 33462 (SAN 665-8431) Tel 407-433-5735.

Creat Editions, *(Creative Editions; 1-56846),* P.O. Box 227, Mankato, MN 56002 Tel 507-388-6273; 123 S. Broad St., Mankato, MN 56002; Orders to: 150 E. Wilson Bridge Rd., No. 145, Columbus, OH 43085-2328 Tel 614-848-8866; Toll free: 800-542-7833.

Creat Ent MA, *(Creative Enterprises, Inc.; 0-9641895),* P.O. Box 304, Mattapoisett, MA 02739; 6 Laura Ln., Mattapoisett, MA 02739 Tel 508-758-6543. Do not confuse with companies with the same name in Dayton, OH, Cordova, TN.

Creat Lrng Consultants
See Pieces of Lrning

Creat Opport, *(Creative Opportunities, Inc.; 1-881235),* P.O. Box 6730, Laguna Niguel, CA 92607-6730; 1 Park Paseo, Laguna Niguel, CA 92677 Tel 714-493-7293.

Creat Rec
See Bar JaMae

Creat Res NC, *(Creative Resources, Inc.; 0-937306),* 3548 Round Oak Rd., Charlotte, NC 28210 (SAN 200-2779) Tel 704-554-8357.

Creat Teach Pr, *(Creative Teaching Pr., Inc.; 0-916119),* 10701 Holder St., Cypress, CA 90630 (SAN 294-9180) Tel 714-995-7888; Toll free: 800-444-4287.

Creat Wrld, *(Creative World of Entertainment; 0-9637930),* P.O. Box 493, Champaign, IL 61824; 502 E. Healey St., Suite 110, Champaign, IL 61820 Tel 217-351-3070.

Create Learn, *(Creative Learning Assn., Inc.; 0-88193),* R.R. 4, Box 330, Charleston, IL 61920 (SAN 669-4101) Tel 217-345-1010.

Creative Arts Bk, *(Creative Arts Bk. Co.; 0-88739; 0-916870),* 833 Bancroft Way, Berkeley, CA 94710 (SAN 208-4880) Tel 510-848-4777; Toll free: 800-848-7789.

Creative Changes, *(Creative Changes; 0-9621898; 1-883475),* 368 S. 850, W., Orem, UT 84058 Tel 801-226-5533.

Creative Des, *(Creative Designs, Inc.; 1-880047),* 11024 Montgomery NE, Suite 311, Albuquerque, NM 87111 Tel 505-275-3030; Toll free: 800-869-8520.

Creative Dimensions, *(Creative Dimensions; 0-939985),* 518 Highland Dr., Bellingham, WA 98225 (SAN 663-8872) Tel 206-733-5024; Orders to: P.O. Box 1393, Bellingham, WA 98227 (SAN 242-1445).

Creative Ed, *(Creative Education, Inc.; 0-87191; 0-88682),* 123 S. Broad St., P.O. Box 227, Mankato, MN 56001 (SAN 202-201X) Tel 507-388-6273; Toll free: 800-445-6209; Dist. by: Encyclopaedia Britannica, Inc., 310 S. Michigan Ave., Chicago, IL 60604-9839 (SAN 204-1464) Tel 312-347-7959; Toll free: 800-554-9862.

Creative Hlth, *(Creative Health Concepts; 0-941549),* 855 Independence, Springfield, IL 62702 (SAN 666-2838) Tel 217-546-2131.

Creative Impress, *(Creative Impressions, Ltd.; 1-884604),* P.O. Box 188, Glen Arm, MD 21057 Tel 410-592-7068.

Creative Learning, *(Creative Learning Pr., Inc.; 0-936386),* Holiday Mall, 1733 Storrs Rd., Storrs, CT 06268 (SAN 214-2368) (SAN 298-4601); Orders to: P.O. Box 320, Mansfield Center, CT 06250 Tel 203-429-8118.

Creative License, *(Creative License Studio; 0-942675),* 1538 W. Jonquil Terr., Chicago, IL 60626-1215 (SAN 667-3805) Tel 312-784-5809.

Creative Pr Works, *(Creative Press Works; 0-9621681),* P.O. Box 280556, Memphis, TN 38128 (SAN 251-8708); 3966 S. Lakewood Dr., Memphis, TN 38128 (SAN 251-8716) Tel 901-382-8246.

Creative Storytime, *(Creative Storytime Pr.; 0-934876),* P.O. Box 580572, Minneapolis, MN 55458-0572 (SAN 211-6634) Tel 612-926-9740.

Creative Texas, *(Creative Publishing Co., Inc.; 0-932702; 1-57208),* P.O. Box 9292, College Station, TX 77842 (SAN 209-3499); Toll free: 800-245-5841; 1804 Brothers Blvd., College Station, TX 77845 Tel 409-693-0808.

Creative Therapeutics, *(Creative Therapeutics; 0-933812),* 155 County Rd., P.O. Box 522, Cresskill, NJ 07626-0317 (SAN 212-6508) Tel 201-567-7295; Toll free: 800-544-6162.

Creative Walking, *(Creative Walking, Inc.; 0-939041),* 8230 Forsyth Blvd., Suite 209, Clayton, MO 63105 (SAN 662-6521) Tel 314-721-3600.

Creatively Yours, *(Creatively Yours Pubns.; 1-877588),* Div. of Creatively Yours Puppetry, 2906 W. 64th Ave., Tulsa, OK 74132 Tel 918-446-2424.

Creole Connect, *(Creole Connection; 0-9630075),* 27400 Tampa Ave., Suite 304, Hayward, CA 94544 Tel 510-782-3717.

Crest *Imprint of* **Fawcett**

Crestmont Pubng, *(Crestmont Publishing; 0-9642296),* P.O. Box 57176, Webster, TX 77598; 366 Capehill Dr., Webster, TX 77598 Tel 713-488-2052.

Crestwd Hse, *(Crestwood Hse., Inc.),* c/o Macmillan Publishing Co., Inc., 100 Front St., Box 500, Riverside, NJ 08075-7500 (SAN 202-5582) Tel 609-461-6500; Toll free: 800-257-5755.

Crestwood Hse *Imprint of* **Macmillan Child Grp**

CRIC Prod, *(CRIC Productions, Inc.; 0-935357),* Box 1214, Kingshill, Saint Croix, VI 00850 (SAN 696-4141) Tel 809-778-2043.

Cricket Power, *(Cricket Power Records & Tapes; 0-9614998),* 826 Wilton Rd., Greenville, NH 03048-1010 (SAN 693-9473) Tel 603-878-2587; P.O. Box 1010, .

CRIS, *(Council for Religion in Independent Schools (CRIS); 1-881678),* P.O. Box 40613, Washington, DC 20016-0613 (SAN 269-4247); 4700 Whitehaven Pkwy., NW, Washington, DC 20007 Tel 202-342-1661.

Critical Book, *(Critical Thinking Bk. Co.; 0-935475),* 110 Sarah Dr., Mill Valley, CA 94941 (SAN 696-415X) Tel 415-383-8805.

Crnerstone GA, *(Cornerstone Productions, Inc.; 1-883427),* 1754 Austin Dr., Decatur, GA 30032 Tel 404-288-8937.

Crnrstone Pub, *(Cornerstone Publishing, Inc.; 1-882185),* 306 Barnstable Quay, Virginia Beach, VA 23452 Tel 804-431-9244; Toll free: 800-826-4992. Do not confuse with companies with the same name in Orlando, FL, Decatur, GA, San Diego, CA, Oak Creek, WI.

Crnstone Pr, *(Cornerstone Pr.; 1-886001),* R.R. 1, Box 2330, Fayette, ME 04349-9538 Tel 207-897-4503.

Crocodile Bks *Imprint of* **Interlink Pub**

Cromlech Bks, *(Cromlech Bks., Inc.; 0-9618059),* Nobska Rd., Box 145, Woods Hole, MA 02543 (SAN 666-1025) Tel 508-540-1185.

Crossing Pr, *(Crossing Pr., The; 0-912278; 0-89594),* P.O. Box 1048, Freedom, CA 95019 (SAN 202-2060); Toll free: 800-777-1048 (orders only); 97 Hangar Way, Watsonville, CA 95076 Tel 408-722-0711. Do not confuse with company with similar name in Marshall, MN.

Crosswalk Res, *(Crosswalk Resources; 0-9605324),* 11000 E. Washington Blvd., Whittier, CA 90606 (SAN 215-9805).

Crossway Bks, *(Crossway Bks.; 0-89107),* Div. of Good News Pubs., 1300 Crescent St., Wheaton, IL 60187 (SAN 211-7991) Tel 708-682-4300; Toll free: 800-323-3890 (sales only).

Crown
See Crown Pub Group

Crown *Imprint of* **Crown Pub Group**

Crown Bks Yng Read, *(Crown Bks. for Young Readers; 0-517),* Div. of Random Hse., Inc., 201 E. 50th St., New York, NY 10022; Dist. by: Random Hse., Inc., 400 Hahn Rd., Westminster, MD 21157 (SAN 202-5515); Toll free: 800-733-3000 (orders); 800-726-0600 (credit, inquiries, customer service). *Imprints:* Clarkson Potter (Clarkson Potter).

Crown Min, *(Crown Ministries International; 0-935779),* P.O. Box 5278, Bella Vista, AR 72714-5278 (SAN 696-7108); Dist. by: Spring Arbor Distributors, 10885 Textile Rd., Belleville, MI 48111 (SAN 158-9016) Tel 313-481-0900; Toll free: 800-395-5599 (orders); 800-395-7234 (customer service).

Crown Pub Group, *(Crown Publishing Group; 0-517),* Affil. of Random Hse., Inc., 201 E. 50th St., New York, NY 10022 (SAN 200-2639) Tel 212-751-2600; Toll free: 800-726-0600 (customer service only); 800-733-3000 (orders only). *Imprints:* Clarkson Potter (Potter, Clarkson, Publishers); Crown (Crown); Harmony (Harmony Books).

Crumb Elbow Pub, *(Crumb Elbow Publishing; 0-89904),* P.O. Box 294, Rhododendron, OR 97049 (SAN 679-128X) Tel 503-622-4798.

Crumble Bks
See Streetlight Bks

Crystal, *(Crystal Productions; 0-924509; 1-56290),* 1812 Johns Dr., P.O. Box 2159, Glenview, IL 60025 (SAN 653-2489) Tel 708-657-8144; Toll free: 800-255-8629.

Crystal Clarity, *(Crystal Clarity, Pubs.; 0-916124; 1-878265; 1-56589),* 14618 Tyler Foote Rd., Nevada City, CA 95959 (SAN 201-1778) Tel 916-272-3292; Toll free: 800-424-1055; Dist. by: Bookpeople, 7900 Edgewater Dr., Oakland, CA 94621 (SAN 168-9517) Tel 510-632-4700; Toll free: 800-999-4650; Dist. by: New Leaf Distributing Co., 5425 Tulane Dr., SW, Atlanta, GA 30336-2323 (SAN 169-1449) Tel 404-691-6996; Toll free: 800-326-2665; Dist. by: Warner Bks., Inc., 1271 Avenue of the Americas, New York, NY 10020 (SAN 281-8892) Tel 212-522-7200.

Crystal Jrns, *(Crystal Journeys Publishing; 1-880737),* P.O. Box 3452, West Sedona, AZ 86340; 3225 White Bear Rd., Sedona, AZ 86336 Tel 602-282-0580.

Crystal Oracle, *(Crystal Oracle; 1-883783),* 2 S. State St., Vineland, NJ 08360 Tel 609-691-0393.

Crystal Pubs, *(Crystal Pubs.; 0-934687),* 4947 Orinda Ct., Las Vegas, NV 89120-1787 (SAN 694-1443) Tel 702-434-3037; Dist. by: Baker & Taylor Bks., Somerville Service Ctr., 50 Kirby Ave., Somerville, NJ 08876-0734 (SAN 169-4901) Tel 908-722-8000; Toll free: 800-775-1500 (customer service); Dist. by: Quality Bks., Inc., 918 Sherwood Dr., Lake Bluff, IL 60044-2204 (SAN 169-2127) Tel 708-295-2010; Toll free: 800-323-4241 (libraries only); Dist. by: Brodart Co., 500 Arch St., Williamsport, PA 17705 (SAN 169-7684) Tel 717-326-2461; Toll free: 800-233-8467; Dist. by: Key Bk. Service, Inc., 425 Asylum St., Bridgeport, CT 06610 (SAN 169-0671) Tel 203-334-2165; Toll free: 800-243-2790.

Crystal TX, *(Crystal Pr.; 0-9625832),* Div. of The Room, Inc., 2235 Brentwood, Houston, TX 77019 Tel 713-524-6574. Do not confuse with Crystal Pr., Simi Valley, CA.

CSI Pub, *(Common Sense Information Publishing;* 0-9621230), P.O. Box 218, Evanston, WY 82930 (SAN 250-782X) Tel 801-774-9683.

CSS of Ohio
See CSS OH

CSS OH, *(CSS Publishing Co.; 0-89536; 1-55673;* 0-7880), 517 S. Main St., P.O. Box 4503, Lima, OH 45802-4503 (SAN 207-0707) Tel 419-227-1818; Toll free: 800-241-4056.

Ctr Appl Res, *(Ctr. for Applied Research in Education, The; 0-87628),* Subs. of Prentice Hall, Inc., 113 Sylvan Ave., Englewood Cliffs, NJ 07632 (SAN 206-6424) Tel 201-592-3156; Orders to: P.O. Box 430, West Nyack, NY 10994 (SAN 241-6492) Tel 201-767-5937.

Ctr Applied Psy, *(Ctr. for Applied Psychology, Inc.;* 1-882732), P.O. Box 1587, King of Prussia, PA 19406; Toll free: 800-962-1141; 307 E. Church Rd., King of Prussia, PA 19406 Tel 610-277-4020.

Ctr Career Dev, *(Ctr. for Career Development, Inc.;* 1-878472), 1329 E. Kemper Rd. Bldg. 400, No. 4192, Cincinnati, OH 45246-3903 Tel 513-671-2202.

Ctr Env Educ, *(Ctr. for Environmental Education;* 0-9615294), 1725 DeSales St., NW, Suite 500, Washington, DC 20036 (SAN 694-566X) Tel 202-429-5609.

Ctr Excel Math, *(Ctr. for Excellence in Mathematical Education; 0-940263),* 885 Red Mesa Dr., Colorado Springs, CO 80906 (SAN 664-2063) Tel 719-576-3020.

Ctr Learning, *(Ctr. for Learning, The; 1-56077),* 21590 Center Ridge Rd., Rocky River, OH 44116 (SAN 248-2029) Tel 216-331-1404; Dist. by: Brown-ROA (Social studies & English titles only), 2460 Kerper Blvd., Dubuque, IA 52001 (SAN 203-2864) Tel 319-588-1451; Toll free: 800-922-7696; Orders to: Center for Learning, The (Religion, Elementary, Biography & Novel/Drama titles only), P.O. Box 910, Villa Maria, PA 16155; Toll free: 800-767-9090.

Ctr Marine Cnsrv, *(Ctr. for Marine Conservation;* 1-879269), 1725 Desales St. NW, No. 500, Washington, DC 20036 Tel 202-429-5609.

Ctr Sacred Healing, *(Ctr. for Sacred Healing Arts Publishing Co.; 0-936901),* P.O. Box 908, Beverly Hills, CA 90213-0908 (SAN 658-5558).

Ctr Sci Public, *(Ctr. for Science in the Public Interest;* 0-89329), 1875 Connecticut Ave. NW, No. 300, Washington, DC 20009-5728 (SAN 207-6543) Tel 202-332-9110; Dist. by: Ingram Bk. Co., 1 Ingram Blvd., La Vergne, TN 37086-1986 (SAN 169-7978) Tel 615-793-5000; Toll free: 800-937-8000 (orders only, all warehouses); Dist. by: Koen Bk. Distributors, 10 Twosome Dr., P.O. Box 600, Moorestown, NJ 08057 (SAN 169-4642) Tel 609-235-4444; Toll free: 800-257-8481; Dist. by: The Distributors, 702 S. Michigan, South Bend, IN 46601 (SAN 169-2488) Tel 219-232-8500; Toll free: 800-348-5200 (except Indiana); Dist. by: Bookpeople, 7900 Edgewater Dr., Oakland, CA 94621 (SAN 168-9517) Tel 510-632-4700; Toll free: 800-999-4650.

Ctr Self Suff, *(Ctr. for Self-Sufficiency Publishing;* 0-910811), P.O. Box 416, Denver, CO 80201-0416 (SAN 698-1828) Tel 303-575-5676; Dist. by: Prosperity & Profits Unlimited, Distribution Services, P.O. Box 416, Denver, CO 80201 (SAN 200-4682) Tel 303-575-5676.

Ctr Social Studies, *(Ctr. for Social Studies Education;* 0-945919), 3857 Willow Ave., Pittsburgh, PA 15234 (SAN 248-0573) Tel 412-341-1967.

Ctr Stage Prodns, *(Center Stage Productions Corp.;* 1-56213), 1289 Bartlein Ct., Menasha, WI 54952 Tel 414-738-9692; Toll free: 800-553-4058.

Ctr Western Studies, *(Ctr. for Western Studies;* 0-931170), Augustana College, Box 727, Sioux Falls, SD 57197 (SAN 211-4844) Tel 605-336-4007.

Cttnwd Graphics, *(Cottonwood Graphics, Inc.;* 0-9626999), 2340 Trumble Creek Rd., Kalispell, MT 59901-6713; Toll free: 800-937-6343.

Cuchullain Pubns, *(Cuchullain Pubns.; 0-9614659),* 1 Rose Marie's Alley, Fort Wayne, IN 46802 (SAN 249-0781) Tel 219-423-9602.

CUE Pubns, *(CUE Pubns.; 0-9629647),* Div. of Creations Unlimited Enterprises, 13223 Black Mountain Rd., No. 384, San Diego, CA 92129 Tel 619-538-0204.

Cuisenaire, *(Cuisenaire Co. of America, Inc.; 0-914040;* 0-938587), Div. of Addison-Wesley Publishing Co., Inc., P.O. Box 5026, White Plains, NY 10602-5026; Toll free: 800-237-3142; 10 Bank St., White Plains, NY 10606-5026 (SAN 201-7806) Tel 914-997-2600.

Culpepper Pr, *(Culpepper Pr.; 0-929636),* 2402 University Ave. W., No. 701, Saint Paul, MN 55114-1701 (SAN 249-7719) Tel 612-642-9241; Dist. by: Publishers Group West, 4065 Hollis St., Emeryville, CA 94608 (SAN 202-8522) Tel 510-658-3453; Toll free: 800-788-3123.

Cult Connect, *(Cultural Connections; 0-9636629),* Div. of Claudia's Caravan, 1918 Lafayette St., Alameda, CA 94501 Tel 510-814-0228.

Cult Exchange, *(Cultural Exchange Corp.; 0-9635529),* 80 S. Eighth St., Suite 1760, IDS Ctr., Minneapolis, MN 55402 Tel 612-339-1254.

Cupery Pr, *(Cupery Pr.; 0-9626188),* 4819 Ardmore, Okemos, MI 48864 Tel 517-349-2533.

Curbstone, *(Curbstone Pr.; 0-915306; 1-880684),* 321 Jackson St., Willimantic, CT 06226 (SAN 209-4282) Tel 203-423-5110; Dist. by: InBook, P.O. Box 120261, East Haven, CT 06512 (SAN 630-5547) Tel 203-467-4257; Toll free: 800-253-3605 (orders only).

Curiosity Unltd, *(Curiosity Unlimited, Inc.; 0-9642550),* 9042 Watsonia, Saint Louis, MO 63132 Tel 314-432-2221.

Curley Lrg Print *Imprint of* **Chivers N Amer**

Curley Pub
See Chivers N Amer

Current Inc, *(Current, Inc.; 0-944943),* P.O. Box 2559, Colorado Springs, CO 80901 (SAN 246-0378); Toll free: 800-525-7170 (orders only); 1005 E. Woodmen Rd., Colorado Springs, CO 80920 (SAN 246-0386) Tel 719-531-2461.

Current Leaders Pub, *(Current Leaders Publishing Co., Inc.; 0-9624900),* 815 Scott Way, Lansdale, PA 19446 Tel 610-584-8944; Toll free: 800-826-8574.

Custom Artwk, *(Custom Artwork by Kim; 0-9632372),* 3839 Rodman St. NW, No. D34, Washington, DC 20016-2818 Tel 202-966-1292.

Custom Curriculum, *(Custom Curriculum Concepts;* 0-9611480), 1600 N-1-35E, Suite 112, Carrollton, TX 75006 (SAN 285-2373) Tel 214-466-0104.

Custom Hse, *(Custom Hse. Pr.; 0-940560),* 2900 Newark Rd., P.O. Box 2369, Zanesville, OH 43701 (SAN 216-3632).

CWP, *(Counseling & Workshop Professionals;* 0-9621701), 965 Ewald, SE, Salem, OR 97302 (SAN 251-8635) Tel 503-588-1010.

Cygnet Pub, *(Cygnet Publishing Co.; 0-9636050),* 45 Lakeside Dr., SE, Grand Rapids, MI 49506 Tel 616-459-1258. Do not confuse with Cygnet Pr. in Anthony, NM.

CYGNUS-QUASAR Bks, *(CYGNUS-QUASAR Bks.;* 1-882484), P.O. Box 85, Powell, OH 43065; 1854 Home Rd., Delaware, OH 43015 Tel 614-548-7895.

Cypress Hill, *(Cypress Hill Pr.; 0-9638964),* 14710 DeWolf, Selma, CA 93662 Tel 209-896-6705; Dist. by: Strawberry Hill Pr., 3848 SE Division St., Portland, OR 97202 (SAN 238-8103) Tel 503-235-5989.

Cypress Hse, *(Cypress Hse.; 1-879384),* 155 Cypress St., Fort Bragg, CA 95437 (SAN 297-9004) Tel 707-964-9520.

CZM Pr, *(CZM Pr.; 1-878461),* Div. of CZM Assocs., Inc., 48 West St., Suite 104, Annapolis, MD 21401 Tel 410-263-2121.

D A Curtis, *(Curtis, Donald A.; 0-9610284),* 904 W. Main St., East Palestine, OH 44413 (SAN 263-9971) Tel 216-426-4389.

D A Jensen, *(Jensen, Delwin A.; 0-9624413),* 814 N. Grand, Pierre, SD 57501 Tel 605-224-5438.

D & J Arts Pubs, *(D&J Arts Pubs.; 0-9634300),* P.O. Box 365, Sierra Vista, AZ 85636; 5242 Laguna Ave., Sierra Vista, AZ 85635 Tel 602-378-6556; Dist. by: Baker & Taylor Bks., Somerville Service Ctr., 50 Kirby Ave., Somerville, NJ 08876-0734 (SAN 169-4901) Tel 908-722-8000; Toll free: 800-775-1500 (customer service); Dist. by: Baker & Taylor Bks., Momence Service Ctr., 501 S. Gladiolus St., Momence, IL 60954-2444 (SAN 169-2100) Tel 815-472-2444; Toll free: 800-775-2300 (customer service); Dist. by: Baker & Taylor Bks., Commerce Service Ctr., 251 Mt. Olive Church Rd., Commerce, GA 30599-9988 (SAN 169-1503) Tel 706-335-5000; Toll free: 800-775-1200 (customer service); Dist. by: Baker & Taylor Bks., Western Div., 380 Edison Way, Reno, NV 89564 (SAN 169-1503) Tel 702-786-6700; Toll free: 800-775-1900 (orders only); 800-775-1700 (customer service).

D & M Lena, *(Lena, Dan & Marie; 0-9617032),* P.O. Box 5318, River Forest, IL 60305-5318 (SAN 662-8745) Tel 708-452-0737.

D & R Pub CA, *(D&R Publishing; 0-9642713),* 336 S. Alexandria Ave., No. 30, Los Angeles, CA 90020 Tel 213-383-3139; Toll free: 800-625-3456. Do not confuse with D&R Publishing Co. in Amarillo, TX.

D & S Mktg Syst, *(D & S Marketing Systems, Inc.;* 1-878621), 1671 E. 16th St., Suite 619, Brooklyn, NY 11229 Tel 718-633-8383; Toll free: 800-633-8383.

D C Raemsch, *(Raemsch, Dorothy C.; 0-9605398),* HCR Box 890, West Oneonta, NY 13861 (SAN 214-4530) Tel 607-432-4836.

D Chandler, *(Chandler, David; 0-9613207),* P.O. Box 309, LaVerne, CA 91750 (SAN 295-9097) Tel 909-626-0604.

D Cohen Mathman, *(Cohen, Don, The Mathman;* 0-9621674), 809 Stratford Dr., Champaign, IL 61821-4140 (SAN 251-866X) Tel 217-356-4555; Toll free: 800-356-4559; Dist. by: MIT Museum, 265 Massachusettes Ave., Cambridge, MA 02139 (SAN 655-4008) Tel 617-253-4444; Dist. by: Math Products Plus, P.O. Box 64, San Carlos, CA 94070 (SAN 630-7353) Tel 415-593-2839; Toll free: 800-677-7001; Dist. by: Dale Seymour Pubns., 200 Middlefield Rd., Menlo Park, CA 94025 (SAN 200-9781); Toll free: 800-872-1100.

D Cornell, *(Cornell, Donald; 0-9620738),* P.O. Box 2160, R.D. 2, Rte. 196, Fort Ann, NY 12827 (SAN 249-9924) Tel 518-632-5391.

D E Donel, *(Donel, D. E., Co.; 0-913657),* P.O. Box 376, Loma Linda, CA 92354 (SAN 286-0929) Tel 909-796-5598.

D E Voelzke, *(Voelzke, Daryl Eileen; 0-9630803),* 246 Peace St., Evans City, PA 16033 Tel 412-935-4443.

D F Schott Educ, *(Schott, D.F., Educational Materials;* 1-56537), P.O. Box 5296, Ventura, CA 93005; 317 Verano Dr., Ojai, CA 93023 Tel 805-646-8508.

D G Taylor, *(Taylor, Donald G.; 0-9638002),* 3651 S. Arville St., Suite 845, Las Vegas, NV 89103 Tel 702-221-8380.

D Garlits, *(Garlits, Don, Inc.; 0-9626565),* 13700 SW 16th Ave., Ocala, FL 34473 Tel 904-245-8661.

D Greenbaum, *(Greenbaum, David J.; 0-9621833),* 1500 Bay Rd., No. 1418, Miami Beach, FL 33139-3212.

D Hockenberry, *(Hockenberry, Debra; 1-878056),* 1409 N. Cedar Crest Blvd., No. 105, Allentown, PA 18104-2300 Tel 610-437-2198.

D I Fine, *(Fine, Donald I., Inc.; 0-917657; 1-55611),* 19 W. 21st St., New York, NY 10010 (SAN 656-9749) Tel 212-727-3270; Dist. by: Penguin USA, P.O. Box 120, Bergenfield, NJ 07621-0120 (SAN 282-5074) Tel 201-387-0600; Toll free: 800-526-0275.

D K Coyle, *(Coyle, Deborah K.; 0-9626801),* 1654 Foothill Pk. Cir., Lafayette, CA 94549 Tel 510-932-0483.

D Kindersley *Imprint of* **HM**

D L Taylor, *(Taylor, Dorothy Loring; 0-9610640),* R. R. 2, Box 152, Virginia, IL 62691 (SAN 265-3567) Tel 217-458-2506.

D M Gales, *(Gales, Donald Moore; 0-9620623),* 19 N. Middleridge Ln., Rolling Hills, CA 90274 (SAN 249-4760) Tel 310-541-3030.

D Miller Fndtn, *(Miller, D., Foundation; 0-9622172),* 3040 Post Oak Blvd., Suite 1630, Houston, TX 77056-6512 Tel 713-961-3255.

D P Williams, *(Williams, David Park; 1-886058),* 476 W. Columbia Ave., No. 3, Belleville, MI 48111 Tel 313-697-2169.

D Stoecklein Photo, *(Stoecklein, David, Photography;* 0-922029), P.O. Box 856, Ketchum, ID 83340 (SAN 251-1002); Tenth St. Ctr., No. 1A, Hwy. 75, Ketchum, ID 83340 (SAN 251-1010) Tel 208-726-5191.

D W Thorpe, *(Thorpe, D. W., Pub.; 0-909532; 1-875589),* A Reed Reference Publishing Company, 121 Chanlon Rd., New Providence, NJ 07974 Tel 908-464-6800; Toll free: 800-521-8110.

DADA Pubns, *(DADA Pubns.; 0-9621598),* 2308 Sussex Ave., Modesto, CA 95351 (SAN 252-1725) Tel 209-572-2440.

Dagaz Pr, *(Dagaz Pr.; 0-9623783),* P.O. Box 21, Grafton, VT 05146 Tel 802-843-2336.

Dageforde Pub, *(Dageforde Publishing; 0-9637515),* 941 O St., Suite 1012, Lincoln, NE 68508-3625 Tel 402-475-1123.

Daily Bible, *(Daily Bible Reading Services; 0-9636455),* P.O. Box 16292, Charlotte, NC 28297; 2029 Holly St., Charlotte, NC 28216 Tel 704-394-5195.

Daily Hampshire, *(Daily Hampshire Gazette;* 0-9618052), 115 Conz St., Northampton, MA 01060 (SAN 666-2900) Tel 413-584-5000.

DaisyHill Pr, *(DaisyHill Pr.; 0-9632799)*, P.O. Box 1681, Rochester, MI 48308 (SAN 298-3524); Toll free: 800-517-7366; 165 Wimpole Dr., Rochester Hills, MI 48309-2147 (SAN 298-3532) Tel 810-651-0748; Dist. by: Baker & Taylor Bks., Somerville Service Ctr., 50 Kirby Ave., Somerville, NJ 08876-0734 (SAN 169-4901) Tel 908-722-8000; Toll free: 800-775-1500 (customer service); Dist. by: Baker & Taylor Bks., Momence Service Ctr., 501 S. Gladiolus St., Momence, IL 60954-2444 (SAN 169-2100) Tel 815-472-2444; Toll free: 800-775-2300 (customer service); Dist. by: Baker & Taylor Bks., Commerce Service Ctr., 251 Mt. Olive Church Rd., Commerce, GA 30599-9988 (SAN 169-1503) Tel 706-335-5000; Toll free: 800-775-1200 (customer service); Dist. by: Baker & Taylor Bks., Reno Service Ctr., 380 Edison Way, Reno, NV 89564 (SAN 169-4464) Tel 702-858-6700; Toll free: 800-775-1700 (customer service); Dist. by: Ingram Bk. Co., 1 Ingram Blvd., La Vergne, TN 37086-1986 (SAN 169-7978) Tel 615-793-5000; Toll free: 800-937-8000 (orders only, all warehouses); Dist. by: Brodart Co., 500 Arch St., Williamsport, PA 17705 (SAN 169-7684) Tel 717-326-2461; Toll free: 800-233-8467; Dist. by: Yankee Book Peddler, Inc., 999 Maple St., Contookcook, NH 03229 (SAN 169-4510) Tel 603-746-3102; Toll free: 800-258-3774; Dist. by: Book Wholesalers, Inc., 1847 Mercer Rd., Lexington, KY 40511-1001 (SAN 169-4243) Tel 606-231-9789; Toll free: 800-888-4478; Dist. by: Midwest Library Service, 11443 St. Charles Rock Rd., Bridgeton, MO 63044-9986 (SAN 169-4243) Tel 314-739-3100; Dist. by: Emery-Pratt Co., 1966 W. Main St., Owosso, MI 48867-1372 (SAN 170-1401) Tel 517-723-5291; Toll free: 800-762-5683 (Library orders only); 800-248-3887 (Customer service only).

Dakota Desktop, *(Dakota Desktop; 0-9632844)*, 210 W. Fourth Ave., Mitchell, SD 57301 Tel 605-996-2736.

Damon Pub, *(Damon Publishing; 0-9617788)*, 741 E. Montana, Saint Paul, MN 55106 (SAN 664-7480) Tel 612-776-7600.

DaNa Pubns, *(DaNa Pubns.; 0-937103)*, 1050 Austin Ave., Idaho Falls, ID 83404 (SAN 658-568X) Tel 208-523-7237.

Dance Data, *(Dance Data; 0-9626651)*, P.O. Box 41584, Saint Petersburg, FL 33743-1584.

Dance Horizons *Imprint of* **Princeton Bk Co**

Dance Notation, *(Dance Notation Bureau, Inc.; 0-932582)*, 33 W. 21st, 3rd Flr., New York, NY 10010 (SAN 212-3452) Tel 212-807-7899; Dist. by: Princeton Bk. Co., Pubs., P.O. Box 57, Pennington, NJ 08534 (SAN 630-1568) Tel 609-737-8177; Toll free: 800-220-7149.

Dancing Pumpkin, *(Dancing Pumpkin Productions Co.; 0-9634270)*, International Sq., 1825 I St. NW, Suite 400, Washington, DC 20006 Tel 202-429-2097; Dist. by: Upper Access, Inc., P.O. Box 457, 1 Upper Access Rd., Hinesburg, VT 05461 (SAN 667-1195) Tel 802-482-2988; Toll free: 800-356-9315; Dist. by: Inland Bk. Co., 140 Commerce St., East Haven, CT 06512 (SAN 200-4151) Tel 203-467-4257; Toll free: 800-243-0138; Dist. by: Baker & Taylor Bks., Somerville Service Ctr., 50 Kirby Ave., Somerville, NJ 08876-0734 (SAN 169-4901) Tel 908-722-8000; Toll free: 800-775-1500 (customer service); Dist. by: Baker & Taylor Bks., Momence Service Ctr., 501 S. Gladiolus St., Momence, IL 60954-2444 (SAN 169-2100) Tel 815-472-2444; Toll free: 800-775-2300 (customer service); Dist. by: Baker & Taylor Bks., Commerce Service Ctr., 251 Mt. Olive Church Rd., Commerce, GA 30599-9988 (SAN 169-1503) Tel 706-335-5000; Toll free: 800-775-1200 (customer service); Dist. by: Baker & Taylor Bks., Reno Service Ctr., 380 Edison Way, Reno, NV 89564 (SAN 169-4464) Tel 702-858-6700; Toll free: 800-775-1700 (customer service).

D&C Cape Verdeans, *(Documentation & Computerization of the Cape Verdeans; 0-9627637)*, 176 Court St., New Bedford, MA 02740 Tel 508-996-3411.

D&M Pubns, *(D & M Pubns.; 0-925449)*, P.O. Box 2409, Anthony, TX 79821; 1205 Antonio, Anthony, TX 79821 Tel 915-886-5250.

Daneco Pubns, *(Daneco Pubns.; 0-910519)*, 842 21st Ave., SE, Minneapolis, MN 55414-2514 (SAN 260-180X) Tel 612-729-6861.

DARE Bks, *(DARE Bks.; 0-912444)*, Div. of D. A. Reid Enterprises, 33 Lafayette Ave., Brooklyn, NY 11217 Tel 718-625-4651.

Dark Horse Comics, *(Dark Horse Comics; 1-878574; 1-56971)*, 10956 SE Main St., Milwaukie, OR 97222 Tel 503-652-8815.

Dasan Prodns, *(Dasan Productions, Inc.; 0-9627806)*, P.O. Box 300, Agara Hills, CA 91376 Tel 818-597-8380; Toll free: 800-348-4401; Dist. by: Cimino Publishing Group, P.O. Box 174, Carle Place, NY 11514 (SAN 630-3722) Tel 516-997-3721.

DataQuest VA, *(DataQuest; 0-9635508)*, 711 Alder Cir., Virginia Beach, VA 23462 (SAN 298-4237) Tel 804-474-2447. Do not confuse with Dataquest, Inc. in San Jose, CA.

Daughter Cult, *(Daughter Culture Pubns.; 0-935281)*, 1840 41st Ave., Suite 102-301, Capitola, CA 95010 (SAN 695-7447) Tel 408-476-0199.

Daughters Dak, *(GFWC of South Dakota/Daughters of Dakota; 1-880589)*, P.O. Box 349, Yankton, SD 57078; 2916 Adkins Dr., Yankton, SD 57078 Tel 605-665-7754.

Davar MD
See Educ Pr MD

Davenport, *(Davenport, May, Pubs.; 0-9603118; 0-943864)*, 26313 Purissima Rd., Los Altos Hills, CA 94022 (SAN 212-467X) Tel 415-948-6499.

Davidson Titles, *(Davidson Titles, Inc.; 1-884756)*, 101 Executive Dr., Jackson, TN 38305 Tel 901-664-0044; Toll free: 800-433-3903.

Davis Mass, *(Davis Pubns., Inc.; 0-87192)*, 50 Portland St., Worcester, MA 01608 (SAN 201-3002) Tel 508-754-7201; Toll free: 800-533-2847; Dist. by: Sterling Publishing Co., Inc., 387 Park Ave., S., New York, NY 10016-8810 (SAN 211-6324) Tel 212-532-7160; Toll free: 800-367-9692.

DAW Bks, *(DAW Bks.; 0-87997; 0-88677; 0-8099)*, 375 Hudson St., New York, NY 10014-3658 (SAN 665-6846) Tel 212-366-2096; Dist. by: Penguin USA, P.O. Box 120, Bergenfield, NJ 07621-0120 (SAN 282-5074) Tel 201-387-0600; Toll free: 800-526-0275.

Dawn CA, *(Dawn Pubns.; 0-916124; 1-878265; 1-883220)*, 14618 Tyler Foote Rd., Nevada City, CA 95959 Tel 916-292-3482; Toll free: 800-545-7475. Do not confuse with Dawn Pubns. in Pasadena, TX.

Dawn Horse Pr, *(Dawn Horse Pr.; 0-913922; 0-918801; 1-57097)*, Div. of Free Daist Avabhasan Communion, 12040 N. Seigler Rd., Middletown, CA 95461 (SAN 201-3029) Tel 707-928-2100; Toll free: 800-524-4941.

Dawn Sign, *(Dawn Sign Pr.; 0-915035)*, 9080 Activity Rd., Suite A, San Diego, CA 92126-4421 (SAN 289-9183) Tel 619-549-5330.

Daystar Comm, *(Daystar Communications; 0-930037)*, P.O. Box 748, Millville, NJ 08332 (SAN 669-7798) Tel 609-327-1231. Do not confuse with Daystar Communications, Inc. in Cary, NC.

DB Inc CA, *(Discovery Bks., Inc.; 0-925258)*, P.O. Box 410, Lagunitas, CA 94938 (SAN 200-318X); 7282 Sir Francis Drake Blvd., Lagunitas, CA 94938 Tel 415-488-9256. Do not confuse with companies with the same name in Owls Head, NY, Cleveland, OH.

DC Comics, *(DC Comics, Inc.; 0-930289; 1-56389)*, Div. of Warner Brothers - A Time Warner Entertainment Co., 1325 Ave. of the Americas, New York, NY 10019 Tel 212-636-5400; Dist. by: Comics Unlimited, Ltd., 101 Ellis St., Staten Island, NY 10307-1126 (SAN 107-7252) Tel 718-948-2223; Dist. by: Eastern News Distributors, 250 W. 55th St., New York, NY 10019 (SAN 169-5738) Tel 212-649-4484; Dist. by: Diamond Comic Distributors, 1966 Greenspring Dr., Suite 300, Timonium, MD 21093 (SAN 110-9502) Tel 410-560-7100; Toll free: 800-783-2981; Dist. by: Capital City, P.O. Box 8156, Madison, WI 53708-8156 (SAN 200-5328) Tel 608-275-7777; Dist. by: Friendly Frank's Distribution, Inc., 26055 Dequindre, Madison Heights, MI 48071 (SAN 106-892X) Tel 810-542-2525; Dist. by: Action Direct Distribution, 1401 Fairfax Trafficway, 114A Bldg., Kansas City, KS 66115 (SAN 630-8465) Tel 913-281-5240; Dist. by: Comics Hawaii Distributors, 4420 Lawehana St., No. 3, Honolulu, HI 96818 (SAN 630-8619) Tel 808-423-0265; Dist. by: Superhero Enterprises, Inc., 961 Rte. 10 E., Bldg. L, Randolph, NJ 07869 (SAN 630-8627) Tel 201-927-4447. *Imprints:* Piranha Pr (Piranha Press).

DCA, *(Darien Community Assn., Inc.)*, Orders to: Tory Hole, 274 Middlesex Rd., Darien, CT 06820 (SAN 208-4902) Tel 203-655-9050.

DCB *Imprint of* **Dutton Child Bks**

DCI Publishing
See Chronimed

DDC Pub, *(DDC Publishing; 0-936862; 1-56243)*, 14 E. 38th St., New York, NY 10016 (SAN 223-5234) Tel 212-683-9028; Toll free: 800-528-3897.

Deaconess Pr, *(Deaconess Pr.; 0-925190)*, 2450 Riverside Ave., S., Minneapolis, MN 55454 (SAN 298-170X) Tel 612-672-4180; Toll free: 800-544-8207.

DeadBase, *(DeadBase; 1-877657)*, P.O. Box 499, Hanover, NH 03755.

DEC Special Stuff, *(DEC Special Stuff, Inc.; 0-9619653)*, 65 Cadillac Sq., No. 233, Detroit, MI 48226 (SAN 245-9981) Tel 313-397-1624.

DeChamp CA, *(DeChamp Co.; 0-9628802)*, P.O. Box 3154, Palm Springs, CA 92263; 135 Pali, Palm Springs, CA 92292 Tel 619-320-3940.

Deem Corp, *(Deem Corp., The; 0-918822)*, 5860 W. Sioux Dr., Sedalia, CO 80135 (SAN 210-4113).

Deep Forest Pr, *(Deep Forest Pr.; 1-882530)*, P.O. Drawer 4,, Crest Park, CA 92326; 27442 Meadow Dr., Crest Park, CA 92326 Tel 714-337-1179.

Deep Riv Pr, *(Deep River Pr.; 0-9626803)*, 1871 S. 155 Cir., Omaha, NE 68144 Tel 402-334-5863.

Deer Creek NY, *(Deer Creek Publishing Co.; 0-9621599)*, P.O. Box 83, Pulaski, NY 13142 (SAN 252-192X); 8358 Hinman Rd., Pulaski, NY 13142 (SAN 252-1938) Tel 315-298-4681. Do not confuse with Deer Creek Publishing in Provo, UT.

Deer Creek Pr, *(Deer Creek Pr.; 0-9613596)*, Div. of California Schl. of Design, 516 Olive St, Sausalito, CA 94965 (SAN 669-6732) Tel 415-332-1990.

Deerlick Ent, *(Deerlick Enterprise; 0-9637936)*, 7336 W. Somerset Rd., Appleton, NY 14008 Tel 716-795-3302.

Definition, *(Definition Pr.; 0-910492)*, 141 Greene St., New York, NY 10012 (SAN 201-310X) Tel 212-777-4490.

Del Rey *Imprint of* **Ballantine**

Delacorte, *(Delacorte Pr.; 0-87459; 0-385)*, Div. of Bantam Doubleday Dell, 1540 Broadway, New York, NY 10036-4094 (SAN 201-0097) Tel 212-354-6500; Toll free: 800-221-4676. *Imprints:* E Friede (Friede, Eleanor); Sey Lawr (Lawrence, Seymour).

Delafield Pr, *(Delafield Pr.; 0-916872)*, P.O. Box 335, Suttons Bay, MI 49682 (SAN 208-3817) Tel 616-271-3826.

Delaware HP, *(Delaware Heritage Pr.; 0-924117)*, Carvel State Office Bldg., 820 N. French St., 4th Flr., Wilmington, DE 19801 (SAN 252-1954) Tel 302-577-2145.

Delcon, *(Delcon Corp.; 0-934856)*, 7797 Harlan Rd., Eddyville, OR 97343 (SAN 213-4853) Tel 503-875-4381.

Dell, *(Dell Publishing Co., Inc.; 0-440)*, Div. of Bantam Doubleday Dell, 1540 Broadway, New York, NY 10036-4094 (SAN 201-0097) Tel 212-782-9141; Toll free: 800-223-6834. *Imprints:* Dell Trade Pbks (Dell Trade Paperbacks); Delta (Delta Books); LE (Laurel Editions); LFL (Laurel Leaf Library); YB (Yearling Books).

Dell Trade Pbks *Imprint of* **Dell**

Delmar, *(Delmar Pubs., Inc.; 0-8273; 0-916032)*, Div. of International Thomson Publishing Education Group, 3 Columbia Cir., Box 15015, Albany, NY 12212 (SAN 206-7544) Tel 518-464-3500; Toll free: 800-347-7707; P.O. Box 15-015, Albany, NY 12212-5015 (SAN 658-0440); Dist. by: Van Nostrand Reinhold, 115 Fifth Ave., New York, NY 10003 (SAN 202-5183) Tel 212-254-3232.

Delmar Co, *(Delmar Co., The; 0-912081)*, Affil. of Conteninital Graphics Group, P.O. Box 1013, Charlotte, NC 28201-1013 (SAN 264-732X) Tel 704-847-9801; Toll free: 800-438-1504.

Delos Pubns, *(Delos Pubns.; 1-878473)*, 726 Paris Way, Placentia, CA 92670 Tel 714-528-8900. Do not confuse with Delos Pubns. in Albion, CA.

Delphi Intl, *(Delphi International; 1-883164)*, P.O. Box 97272, Tacoma, WA 98497; Toll free: 800-872-8852; 7211 Phillips Rd., SW, Tacoma, WA 98498 Tel 206-582-5604.

Delta *Imprint of* **Dell**

Delta Systems, *(Delta Systems Co., Inc.; 0-937354)*, 1400 Miller Pkwy., McHenry, IL 60050-7030 (SAN 220-0457) Tel 815-363-3582; Toll free: 800-323-8270.

Demco WI, *(Demco, Inc.; 1-885360)*, 4710 Forest Run Rd., Madison, WI 53704 Tel 608-241-1201.

Denison, *(Denison, T. S., & Co., Inc.; 0-513)*, 9601 Newton Ave. S., Minneapolis, MN 55431 (SAN 201-3142) Tel 612-888-1460; Toll free: 800-328-3831. Do not confuse with Dennison Pubns.

Dennis-Landman, *(Dennis-Landman Pubs.; 0-930422)*, 1150 18th St., Santa Monica, CA 90403 (SAN 210-9352) Tel 310-828-0680.

Denver Busn Media, *(Denver Business Media Sales, Inc.; 0-932439)*, Subs. of American City Business Journals, 1700 Broadway, No. 515, Denver, CO 80290-0501 (SAN 686-7405) Tel 303-837-3500.

Derrydale Pr, *(Derrydale Pr.; 1-56416)*, Div. of Buckingham Mint, Inc., P.O. Box 411, Lyon, MS 38645 (SAN 630-009X); Toll free: 800-443-6753; 226 Sunflower Ave., Clarksdale, MS 38614 Tel 601-624-5514. Do not confuse with Derrydale Pr., an imprint of Outlet Bk. Co.

Deseret Bk, *(Deseret Bk. Co.; 0-87747; 0-87579; 1-57345)*, Div. of Deseret Management Corp., P.O. Box 30178, Salt Lake City, UT 84130 (SAN 150-763X) Tel 801-534-1515; 40 E. South Temple, Salt Lake City, UT 84130 Tel 801-534-1515.

Desert Bks, *(Desert Bks.; 0-9628227)*, Div of Leo J. Du Lac Construction Co., P.O. Box 3301, Hesperia, CA 92345; 12031 1/4 Regentview Ave., Downey, CA 90241 Tel 619-244-1074.

Desert Botanical, *(Desert Botanical Garden; 0-9605656),* Affil. of American Assn. of Botanical Gardens & Arboreta, 1201 N. Galvin Pkwy., Phoenix, AZ 85008 (SAN 212-9000) Tel 602-941-1225.

Desert Rose, *(Desert Rose Publishing; 0-9631252),* Div. of RTB Enterprises, Inc., P.O. Box 2980, Edgewood, NM 87015 Tel 505-281-7719. Do not confuse with Desert Rose Pr., Galisteo, NM.

Desert Star Intl, *(Desert Star International; 1-879212),* P.O. Box 1850, Sparks, NV 89432-1850; 830 Glen Vista Dr., Sparks, NV 89434 Tel 702-356-7779.

Design Ent SF, *(Design Enterprises of San Francisco; 0-932538),* P.O. Box 14695, San Francisco, CA 94114 (SAN 211-6359) Tel 415-282-8813; Dist. by: Blue Feather Products, Inc., P.O. Box 2, Hwy. 66, Ashland, OR 97520 (SAN 630-8260) Tel 503-482-5268; Toll free: 800-472-2487.

Design Matters Inc, *(Design Matters, Inc.; 0-922656),* 138 Crofton, San Antonio, TX 78210 (SAN 251-3803) Tel 210-225-5606.

Design Pub UT, *(Design Publishing; 0-9632452),* 111 E. 5600 S., No. 208, Salt Lake City, UT 84107 Tel 801-262-9238.

Designers Ink, *(Designer's Ink; 0-9636188),* P.O. Box 200633, Austin, TX 78720-0633; 2210 Denton Dr., Suite 104, Austin, TX 78758 Tel 512-832-0611.

Determined Prods, *(Determined Productions, Inc.; 0-915696),* P.O. Box 2150, San Francisco, CA 94126-2150 (SAN 212-7385) Tel 415-433-0660.

Detroit Black, *(Detroit Black Writers' Guild; 0-9613078),* 5601 W. Warren, Detroit, MI 48210 (SAN 294-7315) Tel 313-898-7629.

Deutsche Buchhandlung, *(Deutsche Buchhandlung-James Lowry; 1-883453),* 13531 Maugansville Rd., Hagerstown, MD 21740 Tel 301-739-8542.

Dev Res Educ, *(Developing Resources for Education in America, Inc. (DREAM); 1-884307),* 817 E. River Pl., Jackson, MS 39202 Tel 601-360-0945; Toll free: 800-233-7326.

Develop Solutions, *(Developmental Solutions, Inc.; 0-9629205),* 1125 E. Baseline Rd., Suite 2-24, Mesa, AZ 85210 Tel 602-831-0301.

Devils Tower NHA, *(Devils Tower Natural History Assn.; 1-881667),* P.O. Box 37, Devils Tower, WY 82714; Devils Tower National Monument, Devils Tower, WY 82714 Tel 307-467-5501.

Devin, *(Devin-Adair Pubs., Inc.; 0-8159),* 6 N. Water St., Greenwich, CT 06830 (SAN 112-062X) Tel 203-531-7755.

Devon Pub, *(Devon Publishing Co., Inc., The; 0-941402),* 2700 Virginia Ave., NW, Washington, DC 20037 (SAN 238-9703) Tel 202-337-5197; Dist. by: Baker & Taylor Bks., Somerville Service Ctr., 50 Kirby Ave., Somerville, NJ 08876-0734 (SAN 169-4901) Tel 908-722-8000; Toll free: 800-775-1500 (customer service).

DeVorss, *(DeVorss & Co.; 0-87516),* P.O. Box 550, Marina del Rey, CA 90294-0550 (SAN 168-9886); Toll free: 800-843-5743 (bookstores only); 800-331-4719 (in California, bookstores only); 1046 Princeton Dr., Marina del Rey, CA 90292 Tel 213-870-7478.

DEW Educational, *(DEW Educational Consultants; 0-9623123),* P.O. Box 691001, Stockton, CA 95269-1001; 2546 W. Hammer Ln., Stockton, CA 95269 Tel 209-951-6601.

Dexter KS, *(Dexter Publishing; 0-9628012),* Div. of Dexter Industries, 2326 Sayles Blvd., Abilene, TX 79605-6141 Tel 915-692-0378; Dist. by: F.A.I.T.H. Ministries, 447 S. Oak, Wichita, KS 67213 (SAN 630-5563) Tel 316-269-2072. Do not confuse with Dexter Pubs., Sand Springs, OK.

Dghtrs St Paul
See St Paul Bks

Dharma Pub, *(Dharma Publishing; 0-913546; 0-89800),* 2425 Hillside Ave., Berkeley, CA 94704 (SAN 201-2723) Tel 510-548-5407; Orders to: 2910 San Pablo Ave., Berkeley, CA 94702 Tel 510-548-5407; Toll free: 800-873-4276.

Diablo, *(Diablo Pr., Inc.; 0-87297),* 4 Commodore Dr., No. 233, Emeryville, CA 94608 (SAN 201-3223) Tel 415-653-5310; Toll free: 800-488-2665 (orders only); Orders to: P.O. Box 20, Williston, VT 05495-0020 (SAN 248-3807).

Diablo Bks, *(Diablo Bks.; 0-9607520),* 1700 Tice Valley Blvd., Apt. 150, Walnut Creek, CA 94595-1641 (SAN 238-6232) Tel 510-939-8644.

Dial *Imprint of* **Doubleday**

Dial Bks Young, *(Dial Bks. for Young Readers; 0-8037),* Div. of Penguin USA, 375 Hudson St., New York, NY 10014-3657 (SAN 264-0058) Tel 212-366-2000; Orders to: Penguin USA, P.O. Box 120, Bergenfield, NJ 07261 (SAN 282-5074) Tel 201-387-0600.

Dial Easy to Read *Imprint of* **Puffin Bks**

Diamond Bks UT, *(Diamond Bks.; 0-9630531),* 905 N. 1400 W., Salt Lake City, UT 84116 Tel 801-596-1426. Do not confuse with companies with the same name in Berkeley, CA, New York, NY.

Diamond Farm Bk, *(Diamond Farm Bk. Pubs.; 0-9506932),* Div. of Diamond Enterprises, P.O. Box 537, Alexandria Bay, NY 13607 (SAN 674-9054).

Diane Pub, *(Diane Publishing Co.; 0-941375; 1-56806; 0-7881),* 600 Upland Ave., Upland, PA 19015 (SAN 667-1217) Tel 610-499-7415.

Did You Know Pub, *(Did You Know Publishings, Inc.; 0-9633151),* 1025 Oak Ave., Wyoming, OH 45215 Tel 513-761-0617.

Diggy & Assocs, *(Diggy & Assocs.; 1-879465),* 3532 Park Hill Dr., Fort Worth, TX 76109 Tel 817-923-7573.

Dilligaf Pubng, *(Dilligaf Publishing; 0-9639070),* 64 Court St., Ellsworth, ME 04605 Tel 207-667-5031; Dist. by: BookWorld Distribution Services, Inc., 1933 Whitfield Pk. Loop, Sarasota, FL 34243 (SAN 173-0568) Tel 813-758-8094; Toll free: 800-444-2524 (orders only).

Dillon *Imprint of* **Macmillan Child Grp**

Dillon-Liederbach, *(Dillon/Liederbach, Inc.; 0-913228),* 4953 Stonington Rd., Winston-Salem, NC 27103 (SAN 201-3274) Tel 910-768-7014.

Dinah-Might Act, *(Dinah-Might Activities, Inc.; 1-882796),* P.O. Box 39657, San Antonio, TX 78218; 9147 Windgarden, San Antonio, TX 78239 Tel 210-657-5951.

Dinosaur Pr, *(Dinosaur Pr.; 0-9637259),* P.O. Box 50414, Tulsa, OK 74150-0414; 3321 E. Fourth St., Tulsa, OK 74112-2611 Tel 918-834-1109. Do not confuse with Dinosaur Pr., Inc. in Amherst, MA.

Diogenes Pr, *(Diogenes Pr.; 0-9632582),* 2620 Maryland Pkwy., Suite 332, Las Vegas, NV 89109 Tel 702-598-5047.

Diogenes Pub Co, *(Diogenes' Publishing Co.; 0-929393),* P.O. Box 334, Eugene, OR 97440 (SAN 249-3861); 1776 Adkins St., Eugene, OR 97401 (SAN 249-387X) Tel 503-683-6468.

Direct Contact, *(Direct Contact Publishing; 1-885035),* P.O. Box 6726, Kennewick, WA 99336; 2404 S. Lyle, Kennewick, WA 99337 Tel 509-582-5174.

Disc Enter Ltd, *(Discovery Enterprises, Ltd.; 1-878668),* 134 Middle St., Suite 210, Lowell, MA 01852 (SAN 297-2611) Tel 508-459-1720; Toll free: 800-729-1720; Dist. by: Baker & Taylor Bks., Somerville Service Ctr., 50 Kirby Ave., Somerville, NJ 08876-0734 (SAN 169-4901) Tel 908-722-8000; Toll free: 800-775-1500 (customer service); Dist. by: Brodart Co., 500 Arch St., Williamsport, PA 17705 (SAN 169-7684) Tel 717-326-2461; Toll free: 800-223-8467; Dist. by: Follett Library Bk. Co., 4506 NW Hwy., Rtes. 14 & 31, Crystal Lake, IL 60014-7393 (SAN 169-1902); Toll free: 800-435-6170; Dist. by: Book Wholesalers, Inc., 2025 Leestown Rd., Lexington, KY 40511 Tel 606-231-9789; Toll free: 800-888-4478. Do not confuse with companies with similar names in Sarasota, FL, Erie, PA.

Discipleshp, *(Discipleship Pubns. International; 1-884553),* Div. of Boston Church of Christ, 1 Merrill St., Woburn, MA 01801 Tel 617-937-3883.

Discovery Comics, *(Discovery Comics; 1-878181),* P.O. Box 1863, Austin, TX 78767 Tel 512-441-4611.

Discovery GA, *(Discovery Pr., Inc.; 0-944770),* P.O. Box 670471, Marietta, GA 30066 (SAN 245-4564); 2619 Sandy Plains Rd., Marietta, GA 30066 (SAN 245-4572) Tel 404-926-2365. Do not confuse with Discovery Pr. Inc., Smithtown, NY.

Discovery Pr, *(Discovery Pr.; 0-9614261),* P.O. Box 12241, Portland, OR 97212 (SAN 687-1240) Tel 503-282-9372; Dist. by: Pacific Pipeline, Inc., 8030 S. 228th St, Kent, WA 98032-2900 (SAN 208-2128) Tel 206-872-5523; Toll free: 800-444-7323 (Customer Service); 800-677-2222 (orders); Dist. by: Far West Bk. Service, 3515 NE Hassalo, Portland, OR 97232 (SAN 107-6760) Tel 503-234-7664. Do not confuse with companies with the same name in Mission Viejo, CA, Flushing, NY, Minneapolis, MN, Fort Worth, TX, Old San Juan, PR.

Discovry Enterp, *(Discovery Enterprises; 0-942661),* 931 Arbuckle Rd., Erie, PA 16509 (SAN 667-3759) Tel 814-825-9543; Dist. by: Brodart Co., 500 Arch St., Williamsport, PA 17705 (SAN 169-7684) Tel 717-326-2461; Toll free: 800-233-8467. Do not confuse with companies with similar names in Sarasota, FL, Lowell, MA.

Disney Bks By Mail, *(Disney Bks. By Mail; 1-56326),* 500 S. Buena Vista St., Tower 3144, Burbank, CA 91521 Tel 818-567-5913.

Disney Pr, *(Disney Pr.; 1-56282; 0-7868),* Div. of Disney Bk. Publishing, Inc., A Walt Disney Co., 114 Fifth Ave., New York, NY 10011 Tel 212-633-4400; Dist. by: Little, Brown & Co., Time & Life Bldg., 1271 Avenue of the Americas, New York, NY 10020 (SAN 200-2205) Tel 212-522-8700; Toll free: 800-343-9204.

Displays Sch, *(Displays for Schls., Inc.; 0-9600962),* P.O. Box 163, Gainesville, FL 32602 (SAN 157-9711) Tel 904-373-2030.

Distinctive Pub, *(Distinctive Publishing Corp.; 0-942963),* P.O. Box 17868, Plantation, FL 33318-7868 (SAN 667-9129); Toll free: 800-683-3722; 1888 NW 21st St., 2nd Flr., Pompano Beach, FL 33069 Tel 305-975-2413. Do not confuse with Distinctive Publishing in Salt Lake City, UT.

Diversfd Eng
See White DEI

Divry, *(Divry, D. C., Inc.; 0-910516),* 148 W. 24th St., New York, NY 10011 (SAN 201-3320) Tel 212-255-2153.

DM Pub, *(D. M. Publishing Co.; 0-938419),* 916 N. Martha St., Sioux City, IA 51105-3100 (SAN 661-0730); 901 N. St. Mary's, Sioux City, IA 51102 (SAN 661-0749) Tel 712-258-3133.

DMS ID, *(DMS; 0-9625057; 1-883054),* 4595 E. Highland Dr., Post Falls, ID 83854 Tel 208-773-7605.

Docutex Inc, *(Docutex, Inc.; 0-924307),* P.O. Box 3117, Big Spring, TX 79721-3117 Tel 915-264-6020.

Dodson Assocs, *(Dodson Assocs.; 0-9620550),* 613 Lincoln, Pueblo, CO 81004 (SAN 249-0552) Tel 719-545-3876.

Doess Pubs, *(Doess Pubs.; 0-9635625),* 1607 S. 27th St., Renton, WA 98055-5123 Tel 206-226-2217.

Dog Eared Pubns, *(Dog-Eared Pubns.; 0-941042),* P.O. Box 620863, Middleton, WI 53562-0863 (SAN 281-6059) Tel 608-831-1410; Dist. by: Pacific Pipeline, Inc., 8030 S. 228th St, Kent, WA 98032-2900 (SAN 208-2128) Tel 206-872-5523; Toll free: 800-444-7323 (Customer Service); 800-677-2222 (orders); Dist. by: Bookpeople, 7900 Edgewater Dr., Oakland, CA 94621 (SAN 168-9517) Tel 510-632-4700; Toll free: 800-999-4650; Dist. by: Common Ground Distributors, Inc., 370 Airport Rd., Arden, NC 28704 (SAN 113-8006) Tel 704-684-5575; Toll free: 800-654-0626; Dist. by: New Leaf Distributing Co., 5425 Tulane Dr., SW, Atlanta, GA 30336-2323 (SAN 169-1449) Tel 404-691-6996; Toll free: 800-326-2665.

Doghouse Pubng, *(Doghouse Publishing, Inc.; 1-885531),* P.O. Box 58630, Louisville, KY 40268; Toll free: 800-495-9989; 12700 Shelbyville Rd., Louisville, KY 40243 Tel 502-454-9988.

Dogwood NC, *(Dogwood Pr.; 0-9627049),* 4102 Dogwood Dr., Greensboro, NC 27410 Tel 910-299-3447. Do not confuse with Dogwood Pr., Stone Mountain, GA.

DOK Pubs, *(DOK Pubs.; 0-914634),* Div. of United Educational Services, Inc., P.O. Box 1099, Buffalo, NY 14224 (SAN 201-3347) Tel 716-668-7691; Toll free: 800-458-7900.

Dolan Pr, *(Dolan Pr.; 0-9622868),* 1645 Gales Ct., Forest Grove, OR 97116 Tel 503-232-8844.

Dolp *Imprint of* **Doubleday**

Dolphin Lrning, *(Dolphin Learning Systems; 1-881754),* P.O. Box 2570, Fair Oaks, CA 95628 Tel 916-961-6274.

Domjan Studio, *(Domjan Studio; 0-933652),* West Lake Rd., Tuxedo Park, NY 10987 (SAN 293-2512) Tel 914-351-4596.

Don Bosco Multimedia, *(Don Bosco Multimedia; 0-89944; 1-55986),* Div. of Salesian Society, Inc., 475 North Ave., Box T, New Rochelle, NY 10802 (SAN 213-2613) Tel 914-576-0122; Toll free: 800-342-5850. *Imprints:* Patron (Patron Books).

Donars, *(Donars Spanish Bks.),* P.O. Box 24, Loveland, CO 80539-0024 (SAN 108-1586); Toll free: 800-552-3316; 203 E. Fifth St., Loveland, CO 80539-0024 (SAN 243-2358) Tel 303-669-0586.

Donna Dee Bks, *(Donna Dee Bks.; 0-9624299),* Box 18234, Tucson, AZ 85731-8234 Tel 602-298-6667.

Donning Co, *(Donning Co. Pubs.; 0-915442; 0-89865),* Subs. of Walsworth Publishing Co., Inc., 184 Business Park Dr., No. 106, Virginia Beach, VA 23462-6533 (SAN 211-6316) Tel 804-497-1789; Warehouse: 801 S. Missouri Ave., Marceline, MO 64658 (SAN 661-9940); Dist. by: Schiffer Publishing, Ltd., 77 Lower Valley Rd., Atglen, PA 19310 (SAN 208-8428) Tel 610-593-1777.

DonSyl Pubns, *(DonSyl Pubns.; 0-9626263),* 4807 Fernwood Ct., Fairfield, CA 94533; 4807 Fernwood Ct., Fairfield, CA 94585 Tel 707-864-0522.

doodle-bug, *(doodle-bug Publishing; 0-9633597),* P.O. Box 162, Washington, IL 61571; Toll free: 800-688-4284; 302 S. Church, Washington, IL 61571 Tel 309-444-4554.

Doral Pub, *(Doral Publishing; 0-944875),* 8560 SW Salish Ln., Suite 300, Wilsonville, OR 97070-9612 (SAN 245-4637) Tel 503-682-3307; Toll free: 800-633-5385 (orders only).

Dorchester Pub Co, *(Dorchester Publishing Co., Inc.; 0-8439),* 276 Fifth Ave., New York, NY 10001 (SAN 264-0090) Tel 212-725-8811; Dist. by: Hearst Corp., International Circulation Distributors/ ICD Bks., 250 W. 55th St., 12th Flr., New York, NY 10019 (SAN 169-5800) Tel 212-649-4474; Toll free: 800-223-0288.

Doris Demou, *(Demou, Doris Beck; 0-9604794),* 2013 Big Oak Dr., Burnsville, MN 55337 (SAN 209-1798) Tel 612-890-3579.

Doris Pubns, *(Doris Pubns.; 0-933865),* 1301 S. 32nd St., Louisville, KY 40211 (SAN 692-7033).

Dorling Kindersley, *(Dorling Kindersley, Inc.; 1-879431; 1-56458; 0-7894),* 95 Madison Ave., New York, NY 10016 Tel 212-213-4800; Dist. by: Houghton Mifflin Co., Wayside Rd., Burlington, MA 01803 (SAN 215-3793) Tel 617-272-1500; Toll free: 800-225-3362.

Dorrance, *(Dorrance Publishing Co., Inc.; 0-8059),* 643 Smithfield St., Pittsburgh, PA 15222 (SAN 201-3363) Tel 412-288-4543; Toll free: 800-788-7654 (book orders only).

Dorset Pr, *(Dorset Pr.; 0-88029; 1-56619),* Div. of Marboro Bks., 120 Fifth Ave., 4th Flr., New York, NY 10011 Tel 212-633-3413.

Dorthenia Pubs, *(Dorthenia Pubs.; 0-9621196),* 1003 Janlee, Burkburnett, TX 76354 (SAN 250-7625) Tel 817-569-1129.

DOT Garnet, *(DOT Garnet; 0-9625620),* 2225 Eighth Ave., Oakland, CA 94606 Tel 510-834-6063; Dist. by: Talman Co., 131 Spring St., Suite 201E-N, New York, NY 10012 (SAN 200-5204) Tel 212-431-7175; Toll free: 800-537-8894 (orders only).

Dot Pub
See DOT Garnet

Dots Pubns, *(Dots Pubns.; 0-9605204),* 106 San Marino Ave., Ventura, CA 93003-3038 (SAN 215-7535).

Double B Pubns, *(Double B Pubns.; 0-929526),* 4113 N. Longview, Phoenix, AZ 85014 (SAN 249-6615) Tel 602-274-6821.

Double M Pr, *(Double M Pr.; 0-916634),* 16455 Tuba St., North Hills, CA 91343 (SAN 213-9510) Tel 818-360-3166.

Double M Pub, *(Double M Publishing Co.; 0-913379),* 21645 Nadia Dr., Joliet, IL 60436 (SAN 285-872X) Tel 815-741-0576; Dist. by: Baker & Taylor Bks., Momence Service Ctr., 501 S. Gladiolus St., Momence, IL 60954-2444 (SAN 169-2100) Tel 815-472-2444; Toll free: 800-775-2300 (customer service).

Double Talk, *(Double Talk; 0-9615839),* P.O. Box 412, Amelia, OH 45102 (SAN 697-0575) Tel 513-753-7117.

Doubleday, *(Doubleday & Co., Inc.; 0-385),* Div. of Bantam Doubleday Dell, 1540 Broadway, New York, NY 10036-4094 (SAN 201-0089) Tel 212-354-6500; Toll free: 800-223-6834; Orders to: Doubleday Consumer Services, P.O. Box 5071, Des Plaines, IL 60017-5071 (SAN 281-6083). *Imprints:* Dial (Dial Press); Dolp (Dolphin Books); Galilee (Galilee); Zephyr (Zephyr).

Dove Pr TX, *(Dove Pr.; 1-879667),* P.O. Box 2132, Midland, TX 79702-2132 Tel 915-685-3949.

Dover, *(Dover Pubns., Inc.; 0-486),* 180 Varick St., New York, NY 10014 (SAN 630-9496) Tel 212-255-3755; Toll free: 800-223-3130; Orders to: 31 E. Second St., Mineola, NY 11501 (SAN 201-338X) Tel 516-294-7000.

Down East, *(Down East Bks.; 0-89272),* Div. of Down East Enterprises, Inc., P.O. Box 679, Camden, ME 04843 (SAN 208-6301) Tel 207-594-9544.

Downunder Design, *(Downunder Design, Inc.;* 0-9640296), P.O. Box 709, Concord, MA 01742; Toll free: 800-677-1718; 61 Hubbard St, Concord, MA 01742 Tel 508-369-4560.

DPK Pubns, *(DPK Pubns.; 1-882821),* Div. of Women of The East, Inc., 118 47th St., NE, Washington, DC 20019 Tel 202-397-6621.

Dragon Ent, *(Dragon Enterprises; 0-9606382),* P.O. Box 200, Genoa, NV 89411 (SAN 215-3025) Tel 702-782-2486; Toll free: 800-373-6266 (orders only).

Dragon Studio, *(Dragon Studio; 0-9620672),* 18 Lake Rd., Ridgefield, CT 06877 (SAN 249-5457) Tel 203-438-8668.

Dragon Tale, *(Dragon Tale Pr.; 0-9622905),* Div. of Ruth Sawyer Memorial Foundation, P.O. Box 86255, Madeira Beach, FL 33738; 5247 81st St., N., No. 24, Saint Petersburg, FL 33709 Tel 813-545-4323.

Dramaline Pubns, *(Dramaline Pubns.; 0-9611792;* 0-940669), 10470 Riverside Dr., Suite 201, Toluca Lake, CA 91602 (SAN 285-239X) Tel 818-985-9148.

Dramatic Pub, *(Dramatic Publishing Co.; 0-87129),* 311 Washington St., Woodstock, IL 60098 (SAN 201-5676) Tel 815-338-7170; Toll free: 800-448-7469.

Dream Tree Pr, *(Dream Tree Pr.; 0-9628216),* 3836 Thornwood Dr., Sacramento, CA 95821 Tel 916-488-4194; Toll free: 800-769-9029.

Dreamkeeper Pr, *(Dreamkeeper Pr., Inc.; 1-877852),* P.O. Box 4802, Atlanta, GA 30302 Tel 404-696-7416.

DreamSpinners *Imprint of* **Pssblts Denver**

Dreamworld, *(Dreamworld Pubns.; 0-9623902),* P.O. Box 7272, Boca Raton, FL 33431; 275 NE Spanish River Blvd., Boca Raton, FL 33431 Tel 305-698-1729.

Drelwood Comns, *(Drelwood Communications;* 0-937766), P.O. Box 149, Indianola, WA 98342 (SAN 215-756X); Orders to: Drelwood Communication, P.O. Box 149, Indianola, WA 98342 (SAN 210-3478) Tel 206-297-7789.

Drelwood Pubns
See Drelwood Comns

Drollery Pr, *(Drollery Pr.; 0-940920),* 1524 Benton St., Alameda, CA 94501-2420 (SAN 223-1808) Tel 510-521-4087; Dist. by: Publishers Group West, 4065 Hollis St., Emeryville, CA 94608 (SAN 202-8522) Tel 510-658-3453; Toll free: 800-788-3123.

Druid Pr, *(Druid Pr.; 0-945301),* 2724 Shades Crest Rd., Birmingham, AL 35216 (SAN 246-6198) Tel 205-967-6580.

Drum Assocs, *(Drum Assocs.; 0-9611024),* Affil. of John Scherer & Assocs., W. 201 Sumner, Spokane, WA 99204 (SAN 277-674X) Tel 509-747-1029.

Drum Comns, *(Drum Communications; 0-9632150),* 2851 S. Ocean Blvd., Boca Raton, FL 33432 Tel 407-347-0258; Toll free: 800-245-5642.

DUB Pubng, *(DUB Publishing; 0-9640986),* 2212 N. 79th St., Scottsdale, AZ 85257 Tel 602-423-0932.

Dufour, *(Dufour Editions, Inc.; 0-8023),* P.O. Box 7, Chester Springs, PA 19425-0007 (SAN 201-341X) Tel 610-458-5005.

Duke Pub Co, *(Duke Publishing Co.; 0-9613727),* 14 Andanwood Way, San Francisco, CA 94132 (SAN 677-5187) Tel 415-759-5136.

Duna Studios, *(Duna Studios, Inc.; 0-942928),* P.O. Box 24051, Minneapolis, MN 55424 (SAN 240-1428).

Dunery Pr, *(Dunery Pr.; 0-944771),* P.O. Box 116, Harbert, MI 49115-0116 (SAN 245-453X) Tel 616-469-1278.

Dunwoody Pr, *(Dunwoody Pr.; 0-931745; 1-881265),* Div. of MRM, Inc., P.O. Box 400, Kensington, MD 20895-0400 (SAN 683-5309) Tel 301-946-7006; 3910 Knowles Ave., Kensington, MD 20895 (SAN 664-6352) Tel 301-864-1411.

Durell Inst MSASU, *(Durell Institute of Monetary Science at Shenandoah Univ.; 1-882505),* 1460 University Dr., Winchester, VA 22601 Tel 703-665-5428.

Durkin Hayes Pub, *(Durkin Hayes Publishing Ltd.; 0-88646; 0-88625),* 1 Colomba Dr., Niagara Falls, NY 14305 (SAN 630-9518) Tel 716-298-5150; Toll free: 800-962-5200. Canadian address: 3375 N. Service Rd., Burlington, ON, CN L7M 1A7, 416-335-0393.

Dushkin Pub, *(Dushkin Publishing Group, Inc.; 0-87967;* 1-56134), Div. of Wm. C. Brown Communications, Inc., A Times Mirror Co., Sluice Dock, Guilford, CT 06437 (SAN 201-3460) Tel 203-453-4351; Toll free: 800-243-6532.

Dutch Run Pub, *(Dutch Run Publishing; 0-9632777),* Div. of Dutch Run Designs, P.O. Box 839, Soquel, CA 95073; 201 Horizon Ave., Mountain View, CA 94043 Tel 408-476-8681.

Dutcher & Apperson, *(Dutcher & Apperson; 0-9643149),* 11065 Bristol Bay Dr., No. 1007, Bradenton, FL 34209 Tel 813-795-3899.

Dutton Child Bks, *(Dutton Children's Bks.; 0-525),* Div. of Penguin USA, 375 Hudson St., New York, NY 10014-3657 Tel 212-366-2000. *Imprints:* Cobblehill Bks (Cobblehill Books); DCB (Dutton Children's Books); Lodestar Bks (Lodestar Books); Unicorn Pbks (Dutton Unicorn Paperbacks).

Dutton-Truman Talley *Imprint of* **NAL-Dutton**

Dutton Unicorn *Imprint of* **Puffin Bks**

Duzall Toys, *(Duzall Toys, Inc.; 1-884534),* 6345 Marindustry Dr., San Diego, CA 92121 Tel 619-452-8697; Toll free: 800-366-1476.

DVNH Assn, *(Death Valley Natural History Assn.;* 1-878900), Box 188, Death Valley, CA 92328 Tel 619-786-2331.

Dwn-To-Erth Bks, *(Down-To-Earth-Bks.; 1-878115),* 72 Philip St., Albany, NY 12202-1729 Tel 518-432-1578.

Dynamics MI, *(Dynamics Pr.; 0-9626948),* 519 S. Rogers St., Mason, MI 48854 Tel 517-676-5211.

E Bramhall, *(Bramhall, Elizabeth; 0-9636038),* 7 Gates Farm, Tisbury, MA 02568 Tel 508-693-1819.

E Burns, *(Burns, Elizabeth; 0-9624152),* 7351 Mesa Dr., Aptos, CA 95003 Tel 408-688-1293.

E C Temple, *(Temple, Ellen C., Publishing, Inc.;* 0-936650), 5030 Champions Dr., Suite 100, Lufkin, TX 75901 (SAN 215-1162) Tel 409-639-4707; Dist. by: Taylor Publishing Co., 1550 W. Mockingbird Ln., Dallas, TX 75235 (SAN 202-7631); Toll free: 800-759-8120 (orders).

E Cauper, *(Cauper, Eunice; 0-9617551),* 300 Lynn Shore Dr., Lynn, MA 01902 (SAN 664-4449) Tel 617-599-3041.

E D Edwards, *(Edwards, E. Dean; 0-9615120),* 126 Marshall St., Litchfield, MI 49252 (SAN 694-1664).

E E Stevens Pub, *(Stevens, Edward E., Pub.; 0-9621311),* 122 Seaward Ave., Bradford, PA 16701 (SAN 251-0413) Tel 814-368-6578.

E Friede *Imprint of* **Delacorte**

E G Johnson
See Skyehill Pubns

E G Photoprint, *(E G Photoprint Co.; 0-9634033),* P.O. Box 1125, Hamlet, NC 28345; 316 Entwistle St., Hamlet, NC 28345 Tel 910-582-5637.

E Haga Pub, *(Haga, Enoch, Pub.; 1-885794),* 983 Venus Way, Livermore, CA 94550-6345 Tel 510-455-5059.

E J Wareing, *(Wareing, Eleanor J.; 0-9629175),* Box 156, Fifty Lakes, MN 56448; Shamrock Ln., Fire No. 1495, Fifty Lakes, MN 56448 Tel 218-763-3548.

E M Pr, *(E. M. Pr., Inc.; 1-880664),* P.O. Box 4057, Manassas, VA 22110-0706 Tel 703-754-0229; Toll free: 800-727-4630.

E Mellen, *(Mellen, Edwin, Pr., The; 0-88946; 0-7734),* P.O. Box 450, Lewiston, NY 14092 (SAN 207-110X); Orders to: 415 Ridge St., Lewiston, NY 14092 (SAN 658-1218) Tel 716-754-2788. Canadian Address: P.O. Box 67, Queenston, ONT., LOS 1LO, CN.

E Olson, *(Olson, Eleanor; 0-9628317),* 2557 Fillmore Ave., Ogden, UT 84401 Tel 801-394-7531.

E ORourke, *(O'Rourke, Everett V.; 0-9621369),* 500 N St., Apt. 708, Sacramento, CA 95825 (SAN 251-1487) Tel 916-447-7531.

E P Short
See Quest Dists

E Petrochilos, *(Petrochilos, Elizabeth; 0-9629730),* 4578 N. First St., No. 123, Fresno, CA 93726-2327.

E S Santos, *(Santos, E. S.; 0-914151),* 36 Rte. 6A, Sandwich, MA 02563 (SAN 287-556X) Tel 508-888-2519.

E S Vogel, *(Vogel, E. S.; 0-9638356),* 1655 46th St., Brooklyn, NY 11204 Tel 718-633-4969.

E Schultz, *(Schultz, Elva; 0-9616431),* 300 Country Rd. 9, SE, Brainerd, MN 56401 (SAN 659-1507) Tel 218-829-3449.

E Sussman Educ, *(Sussman, Ellen, Educational Services;* 0-933606), P.O. Box 945, Manchester, VT 05254 (SAN 212-7660) Tel 802-375-1266.

E T Church, *(Church, Elmer Tuttle),* P.O. Box 42, Yukon, WV 24899 (SAN 665-2352).

E Toussant, *(Toussant, Eliza; 0-9630583),* 3701 Runestad Cir., Anchorage, AK 99515 Tel 907-248-1317.

E-W Pub Co, *(East/West Publishing Co.; 0-934788),* 125 Clarmont Blvd., San Francisco, CA 94127-1103 (SAN 215-8574) Tel 415-759-2030. Do not confuse with East-West Publishing Co., Santa Ana, CA.

E Wiggins Ent, *(Wiggins, Elizabeth Enterprises, Inc.;* 0-9637501), P.O. Box 333, Sheffield, AL 35660; Toll free: 800-462-4420; 1109 N. Columbia, Sheffield, AL 35660 Tel 205-381-1345.

E Wynn Vogel, *(Vogel, E. Wynn, Co.; 0-912392),* Div. of Copy-Write Artograph Co., 1865 77th St., Brooklyn, NY 11214-1233 (SAN 203-588X) Tel 718-236-1459.

E-Z Keys Method, *(E-Z Keys Method Co.; 0-9634305),* P.O. Box 6005, Bellingham, WA 98227; 2332 Franklin, Bellingham, WA 98225 Tel 206-734-9457.

E Zolna Inc, *(Zolna, Edward, Inc.; 0-945975),* P.O. Box 1278, Roslyn, PA 19001 (SAN 248-2657); 2612 Belmont Ave., Roslyn, PA 19001 (SAN 248-2665) Tel 215-887-2851.

Eagle Gate UT, *(Eagle Gate Pubs.; 0-9628778),* P.O. Box 17, Logan, UT 84321 (SAN 297-3804); USU Aggie Village, No. 11K, Logan, UT 84321 Tel 801-750-6355.

Eagle Pr SC, *(Eagle Pr.; 1-881459),* 5959 Pleasant Farm Dr., Beaufort, SC 29902 Tel 803-522-1594. Do not confuse with companies with the same name in Wichita, KS, Franklin, WI.

Eagle Wing Bks, *(Eagle Wing Bks.; 0-940829),* P.O. Box 9972, Memphis, TN 38109 (SAN 665-1046); 5077 E. Shore Dr., Memphis, TN 38109 (SAN 665-1054) Tel 901-785-8278.

Eagles Three, *(Eagles Three Productions; 0-9638941),* 2277 Jericho Rd., Aurora, IL 60506 Tel 708-844-9873.

Eagles View, *(Eagles View Publishing; 0-943604),* Subs. of Westwind, Inc., 6756 N. Fork Rd., Liberty, UT 84310 (SAN 240-6330); Toll free: 800-547-3364 (orders only); Dist. by: Quality Bks., Inc., 918 Sherwood Dr., Lake Bluff, IL 60044-2204 (SAN 169-2127) Tel 708-295-2010; Toll free: 800-323-4241 (libraries only); Dist. by: Pacific Pipeline, Inc., 8030 S. 228th St., Kent, WA 98032-2900 (SAN 208-2128) Tel 206-872-5523; Toll free: 800-444-7323 (Customer Service); 800-677-2222 (orders); Dist. by: Ingram Bk. Co., 1 Ingram Blvd., La Vergne, TN 37086-1986 (SAN 169-7978) Tel 615-793-5000; Toll free: 800-937-8000 (orders only, all warehouses); Dist. by: Baker & Taylor Bks., Somerville Service Ctr., 50 Kirby Ave., Somerville, NJ 08876-0734 (SAN 169-4901) Tel 908-722-8000; Toll free: 800-775-1500 (customer service); Dist. by: New Leaf Distributing Co., 5425 Tulane Dr., SW, Atlanta, GA 30336-2323 (SAN 169-1449) Tel 404-691-6996; Toll free: 800-326-2665; Dist. by: Bookpeople, 7900 Edgewater Dr., Oakland, CA 94621 (SAN 168-9517) Tel 510-632-4700; Toll free: 800-999-4650. Do not confuse with Eagle's View Pubns. in Bigfork, MT.

Eagleye Bks Intl, *(Eagleye Bks. International; 0-924025),* P.O. Box 4550, Walnut Creek, CA 94596 (SAN 252-2020); 4159 Walnut Blvd., Walnut Creek, CA 94596 (SAN 252-2039) Tel 510-944-1999.

Eakin-Sunbelt
See Sunbelt Media

E&J Pubng, *(E&J Publishing Co.; 1-884644),* 31940 Chester St., Garden City, MI 48135 Tel 313-522-8702; 6668 Maple Lakes Dr., West Bloomfield, MI 48322 Tel 810-661-2980. Do not confuse with EJ Publishing Co. in Cerritos, CA.

E&S Geog & Info Servs, *(E&S Geographic & Information Services; 1-880062),* Div. of E&S Environmental Chemistry, Inc., P.O. Box 609, Corvallis, OR 97339 (SAN 297-5068); 1325 NW Ninth St., Corvallis, OR 97330 Tel 503-758-5777.

Earlham College Pr, *(Earlham College Pr.; 0-9619977; 1-879117),* Earlham College, Box 28, Richmond, IN 47374 (SAN 247-3496); Toll free: 800-327-5426; National Rd., W., Richmond, IN 47374 (SAN 247-350X) Tel 317-983-1323.

Early Childhood, *(Early Child Consultants; 0-9624257),* 15121 Regent Dr., Orland Park, IL 60462 Tel 708-403-5869.

Early Educators, *(Early Educators Pr.; 0-9604390),* 70 Woodcrest Ave., Ithaca, NY 14850 (SAN 216-2407) Tel 607-272-6223; Dist. by: Gryphon Hse., Inc., P.O. Box 207, Beltsville, MD 20704-0207 (SAN 169-3190) Tel 301-595-9500; Toll free: 800-638-0928.

Earnest Pubns, *(Earnest Pubns.; 0-9616789),* P.O. Box 1302, Chicago Heights, IL 60411-7302 (SAN 200-8564); 161 Kathleen Ln., Chicago Heights, IL 60411 (SAN 661-2229) Tel 708-756-2719.

Earth Bound, *(Earth Bound Publishing; 1-883656),* 7712 Executive Dr., NE, Albuquerque, NM 87109 Tel 505-821-0369.

Earth Buddies, *(Earth Buddies; 0-9639215),* P.O. Box 32105, Tucson, AZ 85751; 820 S. Second Ave., Tucson, AZ 85751 Tel 602-628-1753.

Earth Works, *(Earth Works; 1-879682),* 1400 Shattuck Ave., Box 25, Berkeley, CA 94709 Tel 510-841-5866; Dist. by: Publishers Group West, 4065 Hollis St., Emeryville, CA 94608 (SAN 202-8522) Tel 510-658-3453; Toll free: 800-788-3123.

Earthbooks Inc, *(Earthbooks, Inc.; 1-877731),* P.O. Box 441000, Aurora, CO 80044-1000; Toll free: 800-423-0395.

East Bay Bks, *(East Bay Bks.; 0-930997),* P.O. Box 9526, Berkeley, CA 94709-0526 (SAN 678-8939).

East Eagle, *(East Eagle Pr.; 0-9605738; 1-880531),* Affil. of Patrick Haley Co., P.O. Box 812, Huron, SD 57350 (SAN 216-3705); 766 Utah Ave. SE, Huron, SD 57350 Tel 605-352-5875.

East Meets West, *(East Meets West, Inc.; 1-885993),* P.O. Box 1528, Leonardtown, MD 20650; 37 Capilano Ct., Leonardtown, MD 20650 Tel 301-475-3216.

Eastern Caribbean Inst, *(Eastern Caribbean Institute; 0-932831),* P.O. Box 1338, Frederiksted, VI 00841 (SAN 688-6140) Tel 809-772-1011.

Eastman NY, *(Eastman; 0-9640250),* P.O. Box 290663, Brooklyn, NY 11229; 4092 Bedford Ave., Brooklyn, NY 11229 Tel 718-998-1693.

EastWest Pr, *(EastWest Pr.; 0-9606090),* P.O. Box 14149, Minneapolis, MN 55414-0149 (SAN 216-809X) Tel 612-379-2049.

Ebaesay, *(Ebaesay-Namreplican (EBN) Pubns.; 0-9608212),* 210 W. Lemon Ave. No. 22, Monrovia, CA 91016 (SAN 240-3692) Tel 818-358-1763.

Ebner & Steffes, *(Ebner, Adeline R., & Melissa A. Steffes; 0-9632863),* 3559 Central Ave., NE, Minneapolis, MN 55418 Tel 612-781-3672.

EBP Latin Am, *(EBP Latin America Group, Inc.; 1-56409),* Div. of Encyclopaedia Britannica, Inc., 310 S. Michigan Ave., Suite 1320, Chicago, IL 60604 Tel 312-347-7890; Dist. by: Encyclopaedia Britannica, Inc., 310 S. Michigan Ave., Chicago, IL 60604-9839 (SAN 204-1464) Tel 312-347-7959; Toll free: 800-554-9862.

ECKANKAR, *(ECKANKAR; 1-57043),* P.O. Box 27300, Minneapolis, MN 55427; 3001 Louisiana Ave., N., New Hope, MN 55427 Tel 612-544-3001; Dist. by: Illuminated Way Publishing, Inc., P.O. Box 27088, Golden Valley, MN 55427-0088 (SAN 203-798X); Toll free: 800-457-9063 (orders only).

Eclectic Oregon, *(Eclectic Pr. Inc.; 0-926684),* P.O. Box 2238, San Anselmo, CA 94960; Toll free: 800-898-2263; 1415 NE Marine Dr., Portland, OR 97211 Tel 415-459-2263; Dist. by: Cogan Bks., 15020 Desman Rd., La Mirada, CA 90638 (SAN 168-9649) Tel 714-523-0309; Toll free: 800-733-3630. Do not confuse with companies with the same name in New York, NY, Waynesville, NC.

Eclectical, *(Eclectical Publishing Co., Inc.; 0-912447),* P.O. Box 7326, New Orleans, LA 70186 (SAN 265-346X) Tel 504-246-5413.

Eclipse Bks, *(Eclipse Bks.; 0-913035; 1-56060),* Div. of Eclipse Enterprises, Inc., P.O. Box 1099, Forestville, CA 95436 (SAN 283-0566); Toll free: 800-468-6828; 6632 Covey Rd., Forestville, CA 95436; Dist. by: InBook, P.O. Box 120261, East Haven, CT 06512 (SAN 630-5547) Tel 203-467-4257; Toll free: 800-253-3605 (orders only).

ECO-ALERT Pubns, *(ECO-ALERT! Pubns.; 0-9632864),* P.O. Box 9025, Naples, FL 33941; 1390 Chesapeake Ave., Naples, FL 33962 Tel 813-732-1638.

Eco-Busters, *(Eco-Busters; 1-885091),* 12841 Hawthorne Blvd., No. 645, Hawthorne, CA 90250 Tel 310-281-6733.

ECS Lrn Systs, *(ECS Learning Systems, Inc.; 0-944459; 1-57022),* P.O. Box 791437, San Antonio, TX 78279 (SAN 243-6159); Toll free: 800-688-3224; 2340 W.R. Larson Rd., San Antonio, TX 78261 (SAN 243-6167) Tel 210-438-4262.

Ed Activities, *(Educational Activities, Inc.; 0-914296; 0-89525; 1-55737; 0-7925),* 1937 Grand Ave., Baldwin, NY 11510 (SAN 207-4400) Tel 516-223-4666; Toll free: 800-645-3739; Orders to: P.O. Box 392, Freeport, NY 11520.

Ed Francaises, *(Editions Francaises de Louisiane/ Louisiana French Editions, Inc.; 0-935085),* P.O. Box 1344, Jennings, LA 70546 (SAN 695-0779) Tel 318-824-7380; 302 E. Nezpique St., Jennings, LA 70546 (SAN 695-0787).

Ed Lncln-Mrt, *(Editorial Lincoln-Marti; 0-9628780),* Div. of Lincoln-Marti Schools, 904 SW 23rd Ave., Miami, FL 33135 Tel 305-643-4888.

Ed Media Corp, *(Educational Media Corp.; 0-932796),* 4256 Central Ave., NE, Minneapolis, MN 55421-2920 (SAN 212-4203) Tel 612-781-0088; Orders to: P.O. Box 21311, Minneapolis, MN 55421 (SAN 665-6919) Tel 612-781-0088.

Ed Ministries, *(Educational Ministries, Inc.; 0-940754; 1-877871),* 165 Plaza Dr., Prescott, AZ 86303 (SAN 219-7316) Tel 602-771-8601; Toll free: 800-221-0910.

Ed Pub Serv, *(Educators Publishing Service, Inc.; 0-8388),* 31 Smith Place, Cambridge, MA 02138-1000 (SAN 201-8225) Tel 617-547-6706; Toll free: 800-225-5750.

Ed Res Pub Co, *(Educational Resources Publishing Co.; 0-9629207),* P.O. Box 151139, San Diego, CA 92175; 9481 Tropico Dr., La Mesa, CA 91941.

Ed Skills Dallas, *(Educational Skills; 0-9604058),* 9636 Hollow Way, Dallas, TX 75220 (SAN 221-6086) Tel 214-363-7043.

Ed Solutions, *(Educational Solutions, Inc.; 0-87825),* 95 University Pl., New York, NY 10003-4555 (SAN 205-6186) Tel 212-674-2988.

Ed Sys Pub, *(Education System Pub.; 0-915676; 0-916011),* 38395 Trifone Rd., Sage, CA 92343-9693 (SAN 241-7820) Tel 909-652-3822; Orders to: P.O. Box 536, Hemet, CA 92343.

Ed-U Pr, *(Ed-U Pr., Inc.; 0-934978),* 7174 Mott Rd., Fayetteville, NY 13066 (SAN 221-1866) Tel 315-637-9524.

EDC, *(EDC Publishing; 0-88110),* Div. of Educational Development Corp., 10302 E. 55th Pl., Suite B, Tulsa, OK 74146-6515 (SAN 107-5322) Tel 918-622-4522; Toll free: 800-475-4522; P.O. Box 470663, Tulsa, OK 74147 (SAN 658-0505). *Imprints:* Usborne (Usborne).

Eden Press, *(Eden Pr./Art Reproductions; 0-939373),* P.O. Box 745, Corona del Mar, CA 92625 (SAN 687-6455) Tel 714-760-0985.

Edgewater, *(Edgewater Bk. Co.; 0-937424),* P.O. Box 40238, Cleveland, OH 44140 (SAN 215-3033) Tel 216-835-3108.

Ediciones, *(Ediciones Universal; 0-89729),* 3090 SW Eighth St., Miami, FL 33135 (SAN 207-2203) Tel 305-642-3355; P.O. Box 450353, Shenandoah Sta., Miami, FL 33145 (SAN 658-0548).

Ediciones Huracan, *(Ediciones Huracan, Inc.; 0-940238; 0-929157),* Avenida Gonzalez 1002, Rio Piedras, PR 00925 (SAN 217-5134) Tel 809-763-7407.

Edison Electric, *(Edison Electric Institute; 0-931032),* 701 Pennsylvania Ave., NW, Washington, DC 20004-2696 (SAN 224-7119) Tel 202-508-5000.

Edit Arcos, *(Editorial Arcos, Inc.; 0-937509),* P.O. Box 652253, Miami, FL 33265-2253 (SAN 659-1744); 10850 W. Flagler St., Apt. D-103, Miami, FL 33174 (SAN 659-1752) Tel 305-223-2344.

Edit Betania, *(Editorial Betania; 0-88113),* 2060 W. 98th St., Minneapolis, MN 55431 (SAN 240-6349) Tel 612-888-5727; Toll free: 800-327-1043; Dist. by: Spanish Hse. Distributors, 1360 NW 88th Ave., Miami, FL 33172 (SAN 169-1171) Tel 305-592-6136; Toll free: 800-767-7726; Dist. by: Libros International, 7214 SW 41st St., Miami, FL 33155 (SAN 108-1802); Toll free: 800-327-1043.

Edit Cetera, *(Edit Cetera Co.; 0-9632736),* 528 Belair Way, Nashville, TN 37215 Tel 615-665-0404.

Edit Concepts, *(Editorial Concepts, Inc.; 0-939193),* 11980 SW 46th St., Miami, FL 33175 (SAN 662-8958) Tel 305-871-6400; Dist. by: Spanish Periodical & Bk. Sales, Inc., 10100 NW 25th St., Miami, FL 33172 (SAN 200-7576); Dist. by: Agencia de Publicaciones de Puerto Rico, GPO Box 4903, San Juan, PR 00936 (SAN 169-9296); Dist. by: Southeast Periodicals, P.O. Box 340008, Coral Gables, FL 33134 (SAN 238-6909) Tel 305-856-5011.

Edit Heliodor, *(Edition Heliodor; 0-910463),* 2071 Salisbury Park Dr., Westbury, NY 11590 (SAN 260-0501) Tel 516-334-4439.

Edit Mundo *Imprint of* **Casa Bautista**

Edit Plaza Mayor, *(Editorial Plaza Mayor, Inc.; 1-56328),* Avenida Ponce De Leon 1527, Barrio El Cinco, Rio Piedras, PR 00927 Tel 809-764-0455.

Edit Roche, *(Editorial Roche; 0-939081),* P.O. Box 3583, Hato Rey, PR 00919 (SAN 662-9083); Urb. Del Carmen 2, No. 19, Juana Diaz, PR 00665 (SAN 662-9091) Tel 809-837-2468.

Editorial Amer, *(Editorial America, S. A.; 0-944499; 1-56259),* 6355 NW 36th St., Virginia Gardens, FL 33166 (SAN 243-7384) Tel 305-871-6400; Dist. by: Spanish Periodical & Bk. Sales, Inc., 10100 NW 25th St., Miami, FL 33172 (SAN 200-7576).

Editorial Unilit, *(Editorial Unilit; 0-945792; 1-56063; 0-7899),* Div. of Spanish Hse., Inc., 1360 NW 88th Ave., Miami, FL 33172 (SAN 247-5979) Tel 305-592-6136; Toll free: 800-767-7726.

Edu-Care
See Heron Pub CA

Edu-Kinesthetics, *(Edu-Kinesthetics, Inc.; 0-942143),* P.O. Box 3396, Ventura, CA 93006-3396 (SAN 666-7430); 161 Viewpoint Circle, Ventura, CA 93003 (SAN 666-7449) Tel 805-658-7942.

Educ Dev Ctr, *(Education Development Ctr., Inc.; 0-89292),* 55 Chapel St., Newton, MA 02160 (SAN 207-821X) Tel 617-969-7100; Toll free: 800-225-4276.

Educ Excell Via, *(Educational Excellence Via Video; 0-9630443),* 25 Berry St. 1, Rochester, NY 14609 Tel 716-288-0260.

Educ Graphics, *(Education Graphics; 0-9621081),* 302 Clinton Ave., Brooklyn, NY 11205 (SAN 250-4243) Tel 718-638-6096.

Educ Impress, *(Educational Impressions; 0-910857; 1-56644),* 210 Sixth Ave., P.O. Box 77, Hawthorne, NJ 07507 (SAN 274-4899) Tel 201-423-4666; Toll free: 800-451-7450.

Educ Insights, *(Educational Insights, Inc.; 0-88679; 1-56767),* 19560 S. Rancho Way, Dominguez Hills, CA 90220 (SAN 283-8745) Tel 310-884-5863; Toll free: 800-933-3277.

Educ Materials, *(Educational Materials Co.; 0-937117),* 10 Swett Rd., Windham, ME 04062 (SAN 658-5175).

Educ Pr MD, *(Educational Pr.; 1-56119),* P.O. Box 32382, Baltimore, MD 21208-8382; 6 Autumn Wind Ct., Reisterstown, MD 21136 Tel 410-561-5912.

Educ Racism & Apart, *(Educators Against Racism & Apartheid; 1-878537),* 625 Linden Ave., Teaneck, NJ 07666-2353.

Educ Research, *(Educational Research, Inc.; 0-9639216),* 24 Freshwater Ln., Wilton, CT 06897 Tel 203-762-9357.

Educ Serv Pr, *(Educational Services Pr.; 0-914911),* 99 Bank St., Suite 2F, New York, NY 10014 (SAN 289-1212); Dist. by: Baker & Taylor Bks., Reno Service Ctr., 380 Edison Way, Reno, NV 89564 (SAN 169-4464) Tel 702-858-6700; Toll free: 800-775-1700 (customer service); Dist. by: Blackwell North America, 100 University Ct., Blackwood, NJ 08012 (SAN 169-4596) Tel 609-228-8900; Toll free: 800-257-7341; Dist. by: Baker & Taylor Bks., Somerville Service Ctr., 50 Kirby Ave., Somerville, NJ 08876-0734 (SAN 169-4901) Tel 908-722-8000; Toll free: 800-775-1500 (customer service); Dist. by: Baker & Taylor Bks., Momence Service Ctr., 501 S. Gladiolus St., Momence, IL 60954-2444 (SAN 169-2100) Tel 815-472-2444; Toll free: 800-775-2300 (customer service); Dist. by: Baker & Taylor Bks., Commerce Service Ctr., 251 Mt. Olive Church Rd., Commerce, GA 30599-9988 (SAN 169-1503) Tel 706-335-5000; Toll free: 800-775-1200 (customer service).

Educ Systs Assocs Inc, *(Educational Systems Assocs., Inc.; 1-878276),* P.O. Box 96, Kearney, NE 68848-0096; 1410 W. 36th St., Kearney, NE 68848 Tel 308-234-6261.

Educare CO, *(Educare; 1-882841),* 1395 Tari Dr., Colorado Springs, CO 80921-2264 Tel 719-481-9275. Do not confuse with Educare Pr., Seattle, WA.

EduCare Pr, *(EduCare Pr.; 0-944638),* P.O. Box 31511, Seattle, WA 98103 (SAN 244-5913); 9753 First Ave., NW, Seattle, WA 98117 Tel 206-781-2665. Do not confuse with EduCare, Colorado Springs, CO.

Education Res, *(Education Resource Institute, L.C.; 0-9637573),* 876 N. 450 W., Kaysville, UT 84037 Tel 801-544-9874.

Education Serv, *(Education Services; 0-936394),* P.O. Box 5281, Atlanta, GA 30307 (SAN 221-1920).

Educators Against Apartheid
See Educ Racism & Apart

Eductrs Soc Respons, *(Educators for Social Responsibility; 0-942349),* 23 Garden St., Cambridge, MA 02138 (SAN 667-0903) Tel 617-492-1764.

Eduplay, *(Eduplay; 0-935609),* Div. of EPI Corp., 9707 Shelbyville Rd., Louisville, KY 40223 (SAN 696-3552) Tel 502-426-2242.

Edupress, *(Edupress; 1-56472),* 32432 Alipaz St., Suite H, San Juan Capistrano, CA 92675 Tel 714-248-3822; Toll free: 800-835-7978. Do not confuse with EduPress in Library, PA.

Edwards Music Pub, *(Edwards Music Publishing; 0-9624770),* 305 St. Augustine Ave., Temple Terrace, FL 33617-7229 Tel 813-985-2689.

EEBART, *(EEBART; 0-9614991),* Box 127, Leaf River, IL 61047 (SAN 693-7632) Tel 815-738-2237; Dist. by: Hee Haw Bk. Service, 2901 N. Elm, Denton, TX 76201 (SAN 630-012X) Tel 817-382-6845.

Eerdmans, *(Eerdmans, William B., Publishing Co.; 0-8028),* 255 Jefferson Ave., SE, Grand Rapids, MI 49503 (SAN 220-0058) Tel 616-459-4591; Toll free: 800-253-7521 (orders). Do not confuse with Robert Erdmann Publishing in Poway, CA.

EFC Pub, *(EFC Publishing; 0-9618324),* P.O. Box 522, Livermore, CA 94550 (SAN 667-3228); 977 Redondo Way, Livermore, CA 94550 (SAN 667-3236) Tel 510-447-3206.

Effect Pub, *(Effect Publishing, Inc.; 0-911971),* 501 Fifth Ave., Suite 1612, New York, NY 10017 (SAN 264-665X) Tel 212-557-1321; 50 Eastbourne Dr., Chestnut Ridge, NY 10977 (SAN 665-8180) Tel 914-356-6626.

Eko Pubns, *(Eko Pubns.),* P.O. Box 5492, Philadelphia, PA 19143 (SAN 201-4599). Do not confuse with EKO Multimedia Enterprises in Miami, FL.

El Centro de la Raza, *(El Centro de la Raza; 0-9633275),* 2524 16th Ave., S., Seattle, WA 98144 Tel 206-329-2974.

Eldonejo Bero, *(Eldonejo Bero; 1-882251),* P.O. Box 13492, Berkeley, CA 94701; 2813 Shattuck Ave., No. 5, Berkeley, CA 94705 Tel 510-849-2001.

ELF Assocs, *(ELF Assocs., Ltd.; 0-927256),* P.O. Box 389, Sun Prairie, WI 53590-0389; 30 Hilltop Ln., Apt. 108, Mankato, MN 56001 Tel 507-625-7925.

Elijah Co, *(Elijah Co.; 1-884098),* 2095 Buck Hollow Rd., New Market, TN 37820-3108 Tel 615-475-7500.

Elijah-John, *(Elijah-John Pubns.; 0-9614311),* 3345 Springbrook, Ann Arbor, MI 48108 (SAN 687-5106) Tel 313-677-1635; Orders to: P.O. Box 271, Saline, MI 48176 (SAN 242-0155).

Elins Laboratories, *(Elins Laboratories; 0-9620526),* P.O. Box 90, West Chester, PA 19381 (SAN 249-0536); 149 Chandler Dr., West Chester, PA 19381 (SAN 249-0544) Tel 610-696-4022.

Elizabeth Pr, *(Elizabeth Pr.),* 103 Van Etten Blvd., New Rochelle, NY 10804 (SAN 201-3789).

Elk Grove Bks *Imprint of* **Childrens**

Ellicott Pr, *(Ellicott Pr.; 0-9623903),* 4550 N. Park Ave., Suite T206, Chevy Chase, MD 20815 Tel 301-652-2020.

Ellim & Ange, *(Ellim & Ange; 0-9632915),* 260 Second St., P.O. Box 232, Marine on Saint Croix, MN 55047 Tel 612-433-2904.

Ellis Family Mus, *(Ellis Family Music Co., Inc.; 1-879542),* 30 Samana Dr., Miami, FL 33133 Tel 305-858-8189.

Elmer Bair, *(Bair's, Elmer, Story Publishing; 0-9618269),* 116 S. Eighth St., Carbondale, CO 81623-1916 (SAN 667-0237) Tel 303-963-2954 (SAN 667-0245) Tel 303-963-2954.

ELRAMCO Enter, *(Elramco Enterprises, Inc.; 0-930355),* 257 Osborne Rd., Albany, NY 12211 (SAN 670-7629) Tel 518-458-9095.

EMC, *(EMC Publishing; 0-88436; 0-912022; 0-8219),* Div. of EMC Corp., 300 York Ave., Saint Paul, MN 55101 (SAN 201-3800) Tel 612-771-1555; Toll free: 800-328-1452.

Embassy Hall Edns, *(Embassy Hall Editions; 0-940945),* 1630 University Ave., Suite 42, Berkeley, CA 94703 (SAN 665-133X) Tel 510-486-0187.

Emerald Hummngbrd, *(Emerald Hummingbird Productions; 1-883194),* P.O. Box 577438, Modesto, CA 95355-7438; 1115 I St., Suite 15A, Modesto, CA 95354 Tel 209-527-1771.

Emerson, *(Emerson Bks., Inc.; 0-87523),* 121 N. Hampton Dr., White Plains, NY 10603 (SAN 201-3819) Tel 914-761-2643.

Emijo Pubns, *(Emijo Pubns.; 0-9618303),* P.O. Box 971, Brookline, MA 02146 (SAN 667-1888) Tel 617-731-5767.

Eminent Pubns, *(Eminent Pubns. Enterprises; 0-936955),* P.O. Box 1026, Jeffersonville, IN 47131 (SAN 658-6589) Tel 812-282-8338.

Emissaries, *(Emissaries, The; 0-932869),* 5569 N. County Rd. 29, Loveland, CO 80538 (SAN 688-9875) Tel 303-679-4200.

Emissaries Divine
See Emissaries

Emmaus Ministries, *(Emmaus Ministries; 0-945778),* 718 Maplewood Ave., Ambridge, PA 15003-2416 (SAN 247-8641) Tel 412-266-8188.

Emmett, *(Emmett Publishing Co.; 0-934682),* 2950 Dean Pkwy., Apt. 1703, Minneapolis, MN 55416-4428 (SAN 210-556X) Tel 612-377-3887.

Empak Pub, *(Empak Publishing Co.; 0-9616156; 0-922162),* Subs. of Empak Enterprises, Inc., 212 E. Ohio St., Chicago, IL 60611 (SAN 699-9182) Tel 312-642-3434.

Empire Pub Srvs, *(Empire Publishing Service),* P.O. Box 1344, Studio City, CA 91614-0344 (SAN 630-5687) Tel 818-784-8918.

Empire State Bks *Imprint of* **Heart of the Lakes**

Emprise Pubns, *(Emprise Pubns.; 0-938129),* 1000 S. Main St., Suite 591, Salinas, CA 93901 (SAN 661-2423) Tel 408-422-0415.

Empty Nest, *(Empty Nest Pr.; 0-9640252),* 500 E. Calaveras Blvd., Suite 318, Milpitas, CA 95035 Tel 408-946-5757.

Enchant Pub Oregon, *(Enchantments Publishing of Oregon; 0-9618185),* 704 Residence, Enterprise, OR 97828 (SAN 667-0121) Tel 503-426-4333.

Enchante Pub, *(Enchante Publishing; 1-56844),* Div. of Enchante, Ltd., 120 Hawthorne, Suite 102, Palo Alto, CA 94301 Tel 415-617-9400; Dist. by: Atrium Pubs. Group, 11270 Clayton Creek Rd., Lower Lake, CA 95457 (SAN 200-5743) Tel 707-995-3906; Toll free: 800-275-2606.

Enchanted Rain Pr, *(Enchanted Rainforest Pr.; 0-9629895),* P.O. Box 29885, Los Angeles, CA 90029 Tel 213-663-3405.

Encino Pr, *(Encino Pr.; 0-88426),* 510 Baylor St., Austin, TX 78703 (SAN 201-3843) Tel 512-476-6821.

Ency Brit Ed, *(Encyclopaedia Britannica Educational Corp.; 0-87827; 0-8347; 0-7826),* Subs. of Encyclopaedia Britannica, Inc., 310 S. Michigan Ave., Chicago, IL 60604-9839 (SAN 201-3851) Tel 312-347-7900; Toll free: 800-554-9862.

Ency Brit Inc, *(Encyclopaedia Britannica, Inc.; 0-85229),* 310 S. Michigan Ave., Chicago, IL 60604-9839 (SAN 204-1464) Tel 312-347-7959; Toll free: 800-554-9862.

Endless Love, *(Endless Love Productions, Inc.; 0-9634808),* 1500 E. Glenoaks Blvd., Glendale, CA 91206-2709 Tel 818-242-9804.

Enfield Pubs, *(Enfield Pubs.; 0-9618241),* P.O. Box 3145, Enfield, CT 06082 (SAN 666-9433); 181 Oldefield Farms, Enfield, CT 06082 (SAN 666-9441) Tel 203-741-0771.

English Enterprises, *(English Enterprises, Inc.; 1-878931),* 692 W. Hurst, Bushnell, IL 61422-1144 Tel 309-772-3501.

Enhance Your Chlds, *(Enhance Your Child's Future; 1-882485),* 93 Parsons Pl., SW, Atlanta, GA 30314 Tel 404-755-5084.

Enigmatics, *(Enigmatics Pr.; 0-9633217),* P.O. Box 11834, Washington, DC 20008 Tel 202-244-4392.

Enrich Enter, *(Enrichment Enterprises; 0-9609612),* 1424 Hacienda Pl., Pomona, CA 91768 (SAN 264-0260) Tel 909-622-4887.

Enslow Pubs, *(Enslow Pubs., Inc.; 0-89490),* Bloy St. & Ramsey Ave., Box 777, Hillside, NJ 07205-0777 (SAN 213-7518) Tel 908-964-4116; Toll free: 800-398-2504.

Ent & Educ Found
See Free Ent Partner

Enteracom Inc, *(Enteracom, Inc.; 0-936509),* 5070 Parkside Ave., Suite 1420, Philadelphia, PA 19131 (SAN 697-8282) Tel 215-877-9409.

Enterprise Educ, *(Enterprise for Education, Inc.; 0-934653; 0-928609),* 1320-A Santa Monica Mall, Suite 202, Santa Monica, CA 90401 (SAN 694-0730) Tel 310-394-9864.

Enterprise Pr, *(Enterprise Pr.; 0-9604726),* 8600 Fenner Rd., Laingsburg, MI 48848 (SAN 214-2406) Tel 517-651-2953.

Entertainment Factory, *(Entertainment Factory, The; 0-936086),* P.O. Box 407, Cave Creek, AZ 85331 (SAN 214-0098) Tel 602-488-2510.

EntroCon, *(EntroCon; 0-942153),* 20123 60th Ave., NE, Seattle, WA 98155 (SAN 666-8992) Tel 206-483-2440.

Entropy Conserv
See EntroCon

Entrtnmnt Enter, *(Entertainment Enterprises; 0-9619056),* P.O. Box 781341, Los Angeles, CA 90016 (SAN 243-1092) Tel 310-281-7689.

Entry Pub, *(Entry Publishing, Inc.; 0-941342),* 27 W. 96th St., New York, NY 10025 (SAN 238-9754) Tel 212-662-9703.

Environ Concern, *(Environmental Concern, Inc.; 1-883226),* P.O. Box P, 210 W. Chew Ave., Saint Michaels, MD 21663 Tel 410-745-9620.

Envision Pub, *(Envision Publishing Co.; 0-9624201),* P.O. Box 1089, Portland, OR 97207-1089; 1934 NE Portland Blvd., Portland, OR 97211 Tel 503-287-8011.

EOS Pub, *(EOS Publishing; 0-925244),* 331 Andover Pk., E., Seattle, WA 98188-7600 Tel 206-575-1919.

Epicenter Pr, *(Epicenter Pr., Inc.; 0-945397),* P.O. Box 82368, Kenmore Sta., Seattle, WA 98028 (SAN 246-9405) Tel 206-485-6822; Dist. by: Pacific Pipeline, Inc., 8030 S. 228th St, Kent, WA 98032-2900 (SAN 208-2128) Tel 206-872-5523; Toll free: 800-444-7323 (Customer Service); 800-677-2222 (orders); Dist. by: Graphic Arts Ctr. Publishing Co., P.O. Box 10306, Portland, OR 97210 (SAN 201-6338) Tel 503-226-2402; Toll free: 800-452-3032.

Epps-Alford, *(Epps-Alford Publishing; 0-9631110),* P.O. Box 504, Yellow Springs, OH 45387; 655 Paxson Dr., Yellow Springs, OH 45387 Tel 513-767-2291.

Equal Just Con, *(Equal Justice Consultants & Educational Products; 0-930413),* P.O. Box 5582, Eugene, OR 97405 (SAN 682-0492) Tel 503-343-6761.

Equal Partners, *(Equal Partners; 0-929577),* 3371 Beaverwood Ln., Silver Spring, MD 20906-3066 (SAN 249-7816) Tel 301-871-9667; Dist. by: Ed-U Pr., Inc., P.O. Box 583, Fayettville, NY 13066 (SAN 221-1866) Tel 315-637-9524; Dist. by: Kids Rights, 3700 Progress Blvd., Mount Dora, FL 32757 (SAN 248-0891) Tel 904-483-1100; Toll free: 800-892-5437; Dist. by: Child Welfare League of America, 440 First St., NW, Washington, DC 20001 (SAN 201-9876) Tel 202-638-2952.

Equality Pr, *(Equality Pr.; 0-938795),* 42 Ranchita Way, Chico, CA 95929 (SAN 661-4914) Tel 916-345-8118.

Equestrian Unlimited, *(Equestrian Unlimited; 0-929183),* P.O. Box 255, London, AR 72847-0255 (SAN 248-6563) Tel 501-293-4642.

Equilla Enterprises, *(Equilla Enterprises; 0-9624771),* 2400 S. Izard St., Little Rock, AR 72206-2031.

Equity Inst, *(Equity Institute; 0-932469),* P.O. Box 30245, Bethesda, MD 20824 (SAN 687-4215) Tel 301-654-2904.

Equity Pub NH, *(Equity Publishing Corp.; 0-87454),* Div. of Butterworth Legal Pubs., R.R. No. 1, Box 3, Orford, NH 03777; Main St., Orford, NH 03777 (SAN 204-1383) Tel 603-353-4351.

ERA-CCR, *(ERA/CCR Corp.; 0-913935),* P.O. Box 650, Nyack, NY 10960 (SAN 217-5622) Tel 914-358-6806; Toll free: 800-845-8402.

Erhus Univ Pr, *(Erhus Univ. Pr.; 1-879585),* P.O. Box 10163, Glendale, AZ 85318 (SAN 297-5092); 510 E. Townley Ave., Phoenix, AZ 85015 Tel 602-436-3862.

Eriako Assocs, *(Eriako Assocs.; 0-9638417),* 1380 Morningside Way, Venice, CA 90291 Tel 310-392-9019.

ERIC Clear, *(ERIC Clearinghouse on Information & Technology; 0-937597),* Syracuse Univ., 4-194 Ctr. Sci. & Tech, Syracuse, NY 13244-4100 (SAN 672-8189) Tel 315-443-3640.

Ericson Bks, *(Ericson Bks.; 0-911317),* 1614 Redbud St., Nacogdoches, TX 75961 (SAN 263-0923) Tel 409-564-3625.

Erie Art Mus, *(Erie Art Museum; 0-9616623),* 411 State St., Erie, PA 16501 (SAN 661-2458) Tel 814-459-5477.

Erikson Inst, *(Erikson Institute; 0-9639159),* 420 N. Wabash, No. 600, Chicago, IL 60611 Tel 312-755-2250.

Eriksson, *(Eriksson, Paul S., Pub.; 0-8397),* Box 62, Forest Dale, VT 05745 (SAN 201-6702) Tel 802-247-4210; Dist. by: Independent Pubs. Group, 814 N. Franklin, Chicago, IL 60610 (SAN 202-0769) Tel 312-337-0747; Toll free: 800-888-4741.

ERN Inc, *(Educational Resources Network, Inc.;* 0-9623161), 18 Marshall St., Norwalk, CT 06854 Tel 203-866-9973.

Erth & Sky Pub, *(Earth & Sky Publishing Co.;* 1-882798), 6116 S. Cord Ave., Pico Rivera, CA 90660-3318 (SAN 297-8121) Tel 310-942-7792.

Eschar Pubns, *(Eschar Pubns.; 0-9623839),* P.O. Box 1196, Waynesboro, VA 22980 (SAN 297-6439); 435 Alpha St., Waynesboro, VA 22980 Tel 703-942-2171.

ESP, *(ESP, Inc.; 0-8209),* 7163 123rd Cir., N., Largo, FL 34643 (SAN 241-497X); Toll free: 800-643-0280. Do not confuse with E S P Inc., Houston, TX.

Essai Seay Pubns, *(Essai Seay Publishing Co.;* 0-9607958), P.O. Box 55, East Saint Louis, IL 62202 (SAN 240-0715) Tel 618-271-7890.

Esteem Intl, *(Esteem International, Inc.; 1-884073),* 6563 City West Pkwy., Eden Prairie, MN 55344 Tel 612-828-6030; Dist. by: Adventure Pubns., P.O. Box 269, Cambridge, MN 55008 (SAN 212-7199) Tel 612-689-9800; Toll free: 800-678-7006.

ETC MN, *(Emerging Technology Consultants;* 0-922649), P.O. Box 120444, Saint Paul, MN 55112 (SAN 251-396X); 2819 Hamline Ave., N., Saint Paul, MN 55113 (SAN 251-3978) Tel 612-639-3973. Do not confuse with Emerging Technology Consultants, Boulder, CO.

ETC Pubns, *(ETC Pubns.; 0-88280),* 700 E. Vereda del Sur, Palm Springs, CA 92262 (SAN 201-4637) Tel 619-325-5352.

Ethnic Bks, *(Ethnic Bks.; 0-9630887),* P.O. Box 710352, Houston, TX 77271-0352 Tel 713-723-1523.

Ethnic Role Model, *(Ethnic Role Model Productions;* 0-945779), P.O. Box 3474, Teaneck, NJ 07666 (SAN 247-8668); Teaneck, NJ 07666 (SAN 247-8676) Tel 201-836-5892.

ETR Assocs, *(ETR Assocs.; 0-941816; 1-56071),* P.O. Box 1830, Santa Cruz, CA 95061-1830 (SAN 216-2881); 4 Carbonero Way, Scotts Valley, CA 95066 Tel 408-438-4060.

Eula Intl Pub, *(Eula International Publishing Co.;* 1-877860), Div. of Exciting Unique Learning Alternatives International, 13353 Kilbourne, Detroit, MI 48213 Tel 313-526-3503.

Evan-Moor Corp, *(Evan Moor Corp.; 1-55799),* 18 Lower Ragsdale Dr., Monterey, CA 93940 (SAN 242-5394) Tel 408-649-6901; Toll free: 800-777-4489.

Evanel, *(Evanel Assocs.; 0-918948),* 825 Greengate Oval, Sagamore Hills, OH 44067-2311 (SAN 209-4347) Tel 216-467-1750.

Evang Sisterhood Mary, *(Evangelical Sisterhood of* Mary), 9849 N. 40th St., Phoenix, AZ 85028 (SAN 211-8335) Tel 602-996-4040.

Evangel Indiana, *(Evangel Publishing Hse.; 0-916035),* Div. of Brethren in Christ Church, P.O. Box 189, Nappanee, IN 46550-0189 (SAN 211-7940); Toll free: 800-253-9315; 2000 Evangel Way, Nappanee, IN 46550 Tel 219-773-3164.

Evangel Missions, *(Evangelical Missions Information Service; 0-9617751),* Box 794, Wheaton, IL 60189 (SAN 225-4670); 25W560 Geneva Rd., Carol Stream, IL 60189 (SAN 669-0793) Tel 312-653-2158.

Evans FL, *(Evans Pubns.; 0-932715),* Subs. of Eva-Tone, Inc., 4801 Ulmerton Rd., Clearwater, FL 34622 (SAN 687-7419) Tel 813-572-7000. Do not confuse with Evans Pubns., Inola, OK.

Evans Pubns, *(Evans Pubns.; 0-934188),* P.O. Box 999, Inola, OK 74036 (SAN 212-9019) Tel 918-543-8786. Do not confuse with Evans Pubns., Clearwater, FL.

Evanston Pub, *(Evanston Publishing, Inc.; 1-879260),* 1571 Sherman Ave., Annex C, Evanston, IL 60201 Tel 708-492-1911; Toll free: 800-594-5190.

Evening Pearl, *(Evening Pearl Publishing Co.;* 0-9637262), 317 N. El Camino Real, No. 201, Encinitas, CA 92024 Tel 619-942-6346.

Everett Cos Pub, *(Everett Cos., Publishing Div.;* 0-944419), Div. of Everett's Bindery, Inc., P.O. Box 5376, Bossier City, LA 71171-5376 (SAN 243-7104); Toll free: 800-423-7033; 813 Whittington St., Bossier City, LA 71171-5376 (SAN 243-7112) Tel 318-742-6240.

Everett Pub
See Everett Cos Pub

Evergreen, *(Evergreen Pr., Inc.; 0-914510),* 3380 Vincent Rd., Pleasant Hill, CA 94523 (SAN 206-3638) Tel 415-933-9700. Do not confuse with companies with the same name in Avalon, CA, Chicago, IL, Evergreen, CO, Mobile, AL, Spokane, WA.

Everyday Bks
See Summertree Bks

Everymans Lib *Imprint of* **Knopf**

Evrymans Lib Childs *Imprint of* **Knopf**

Excalibur Publishing, *(Excalibur Publishing, Inc.; 0-9627226; 1-885064),* 434 Avenue of the Americas, Box 790, New York, NY 10011 Tel 212-777-1790; Dist. by: S.C.B. Distributors, 15612 S. New Century Dr., Gardena, CA 90248 (SAN 630-4818) Tel 310-532-9400; Toll free: 800-729-6423 (orders only). Do not confuse with Excalibur Publishing in Englewood, CO.

Excel Pub, *(Excel Publishing, Inc.; 0-943449),* 5131 St. Helena Way, Napa, CA 94558-1332 (SAN 668-4440) Tel 707-257-3217.

Excellent Bks, *(Excellent Bks.; 0-9628014; 1-880780),* P.O. Box 927105, San Diego, CA 92192-7105 Tel 619-457-4895.

Except Educ, *(Exceptional Education Co.; 1-883771),* P.O. Box 5756, Norman, OK 73070; 819 Cardinal Creek, Norman, OK 73070 Tel 405-793-8986; Dist. by: Feelings Factory, Inc., 508 Saint Mary's St., Raleigh, NC 27605 Tel 919-828-2264; Toll free: 800-858-2264.

Excllnc Entrps, *(Excellence Enterprises; 0-9627735),* 15831 Olden St., No. 71, Sylmar, CA 91342-1254 Tel 818-367-8085.

Executive Comm, *(Executive Communications;* 0-917168), 411 Lafayette St., New York, NY 10003 (SAN 208-3043) Tel 212-831-3147.

Exer Fun Pub, *(Exer Fun Publishing; 0-924860),* 3089C Clairemont Dr., Suite 130, San Diego, CA 92117 Tel 619-268-0684.

Exit Studio, *(Exit Studio; 0-9640868),* P.O. Box 6028, 1408 14th St., NW, Washington, DC 20005; 1415 Rhode Island Ave. NW, No. 302, Washington, DC 20005 Tel 202-483-5419.

Exley Giftbooks, *(Exley Giftbooks; 0-905521; 1-85015),* 232 Madison Ave., Suite 1206, 12th Flr., New York, NY 10016; Toll free: 800-423-9539; Dist. by: Ingram Bk. Co., 1 Ingram Blvd., La Vergne, TN 37086-1986 (SAN 169-7978) Tel 615-793-5000; Toll free: 800-937-8000 (orders only, all warehouses); Dist. by: Baker & Taylor Bks., Somerville Service Ctr., 50 Kirby Ave., Somerville, NJ 08876-0734 (SAN 169-4901) Tel 908-722-8000; Toll free: 800-775-1500 (customer service); Dist. by: Baker & Taylor Bks., Momence Service Ctr., 501 S. Gladiolus St., Momence, IL 60954-2444 (SAN 169-2100) Tel 815-472-2444; Toll free: 800-775-2300 (customer service); Dist. by: Baker & Taylor Bks., Commerce Service Ctr., 251 Mt. Olive Church Rd., Commerce, GA 30599-9988 (SAN 169-1503) Tel 706-335-5000; Toll free: 800-775-1200 (customer service); Dist. by: Baker & Taylor Bks., Reno Service Ctr., 380 Edison Way, Reno, NV 89564 (SAN 169-4464) Tel 702-858-6700; Toll free: 800-775-1700 (customer service). UK Address: Exley Pubns., Ltd., 16 Chalk Hill, Watford, Herts WD1 4BN UK.

Exper First Pr, *(Experience First Pr.; 0-9638539),* P.O. Box 2053, Dublin, CA 94568; 8294 Cardiff Dr., Dublin, CA 94568 Tel 510-829-6843.

Experiment Pr, *(Experiment Pr., The; 0-936141),* Div. of Experiment in International Living, Kipling Rd., Brattleboro, VT 05301 (SAN 696-7388) Tel 802-257-7751.

Explorer Bks, *(Explorer Bks.; 0-9605938),* 513 LeGrand, Rte. 6, Panama City Beach, FL 32413 (SAN 216-6240) Tel 904-234-1378; Dist. by: Birmingham Publishing Co., 130 19th St., S., Birmingham, AL 35233 (SAN 630-6470) Tel 205-251-5113.

Express In Writing, *(Expressions In Writing; 1-881967),* P.O. Box 1524, Dallas, TX 75221; 11511 Ferguson, No. 1635, Dallas, TX 75228 Tel 214-613-7736.

Expressway Pubs, *(Expressway Pubs.; 0-9618466),* 1 Wilshire Dr., Syosset, NY 11791 (SAN 667-9463) Tel 516-364-8076.

Extension Div, *(Univ. of Missouri, Extension Div.;* 0-933842), Univ. of Missouri, Agricultural Editor's Office, 1-98 Agricultural Bldg., Columbia, MO 65211 (SAN 679-1638) Tel 314-882-8237; Orders to: Extension Pubns., Univ. of Missouri, 2800 Maguire Blvd., Columbia, MO 65211 (SAN 688-427X) Tel 314-882-7216.

Extra Eds, *(Extra Editions, Inc.; 1-56281),* P.O. Box 38, Urbana, IL 61801-0038; Toll free: 800-423-9872; 803 Stratford Dr., Champaign, IL 61821 Tel 217-355-9872.

Extra NY, *(Extra; 0-9627292),* P.O. Box 1255, Great Neck, NY 11027 Tel 718-224-0302.

Eye Of The Eagle, *(Eye Of The Eagle; 1-882156),* P.O. Box 2078, Portola, CA 96122.

Eyes of August, *(Eyes of August; 1-882816),* P.O. Box 37081, Phoenix, AZ 85069-7081; 9044 N. 14th Dr., Phoenix, AZ 85021 Tel 602-395-1392.

Eyrie Pr, *(Eyrie Pr.; 0-9619465),* 3429 Johnson Ferry Rd., Roswell, GA 30075 (SAN 245-016X) Tel 404-641-9013.

EZ Nature, *(E Z Nature Bks.; 0-945092),* P.O. Box 4206, San Luis Obispo, CA 93403-4206 (SAN 200-9846); 1405 Fourth St., Los Osos, CA 93402 (SAN 244-8548) Tel 805-528-5292.

Ezra Pub Inc, *(Ezra Publishing, Inc.; 0-9621696),* 23019 Timberline Rd., Southfield, MI 48034 (SAN 251-8570) Tel 810-354-4120. Do not confuse with Ezra Publishing in West Babylon, NY.

F A C E, *(Foundation for American Christian Education;* 0-912498), 2946 25th Ave., San Francisco, CA 94132 (SAN 205-5856) Tel 415-661-1983; Orders to: P.O. Box 9444, 4425 Portsmouth Blvd., Suite 205, Chesapeake, VA 23321-9444 Tel 804-488-6601.

F Amato Pubns, *(Amato, Frank, Pubns., Inc.; 0-936608; 1-878175; 1-57188),* P.O. Box 82112, Portland, OR 97282 (SAN 214-3372); Toll free: 800-541-9498; 4040 SE Wister, Milwaukie, OR 97222 Tel 503-653-8108; Dist. by: Pacific Pipeline, Inc., 8030 S. 228th St., Kent, WA 98032-2900 (SAN 208-2128) Tel 206-872-5523; Toll free: 800-444-7323 (Customer service); 800-677-2222 (orders); Dist. by: Ingram Bk. Co., 1 Ingram Blvd., La Vergne, TN 37086-1986 (SAN 169-7978) Tel 615-793-5000; Toll free: 800-937-8000 (orders only, all warehouses); Dist. by: Baker & Taylor Bks., Somerville Service Ctr., 50 Kirby Ave., Somerville, NJ 08876-0734 (SAN 169-4901) Tel 908-722-8000; Toll free: 800-775-1500 (customer service); Dist. by: Baker & Taylor Bks., Momence Service Ctr., 501 S. Gladiolus St., Momence, IL 60954-2444 (SAN 169-2100) Tel 815-472-2444; Toll free: 800-775-2300 (customer service); Dist. by: Baker & Taylor Bks., Commerce Service Ctr., 251 Mt. Olive Church Rd., Commerce, GA 30599-9988 (SAN 169-1503) Tel 706-335-5000; Toll free: 800-775-1200 (customer service); Dist. by: Baker & Taylor Bks., Reno Service Ctr., 380 Edison Way, Reno, NV 89564 (SAN 169-4464) Tel 702-858-6700; Toll free: 800-775-1700 (customer service).

F & F Pub, *(F & F Publishing Co.; 0-9616875),* 50 Shady Glen Rd., Memphis, TN 38119 (SAN 661-3748) Tel 901-685-9915.

F E Braswell, *(Braswell, F.E., Co., Inc.; 1-885120),* 4910 Departure Dr., Raleigh, NC 27604 Tel 919-878-8434.

F Feathers
See Fun Soccer Ent

F Latino Pub Co, *(Latino, Frank, Publishing Co.;* 0-9640474), 6806 Newport Lake Cir., Boca Raton, FL 33496 Tel 407-241-3880.

F M Swan, *(Swan, Frances M.; 0-9602126),* 11533 Old St. Charles Rd., Bridgeton, MO 63044 (SAN 212-3835).

F Merriwell, *(Merriwell, Frank, Inc.; 0-8373),* Subs. of National Learning Corp., 212 Michael Dr., Syosset, NY 11791 (SAN 209-259X) Tel 516-921-8888; Toll free: 800-645-6337.

F Murray Pubng, *(Murray, Fred, Publishing; 0-9642685),* 24405 S. 68th St., P.O. Box 99A, Firth, NE 68358 Tel 402-791-5741.

F Nwabugwu, *(Nwabugwu, Frank; 1-881687),* 217 Oak Ave., Aurora, IL 60506-4021 Tel 708-859-3262.

F One Servs, *(F1 Services; 0-9629328),* 1950 Stemmons Freeway, Suite 5037N, Dallas, TX 75207 Tel 214-746-3646.

F Shivers Evangelistic, *(Shivers, Frank, Evangelistic Assn.; 1-878127),* P.O. Box 9991, Columbia, SC 29290; 2005 Congress Rd., Hopkins, SC 29061 Tel 803-776-3570.

F T Allum, *(Allum, Faith T.; 0-9613349),* 1104 Larke Ave., Rogers City, MI 49779 (SAN 655-8739) Tel 517-734-4517.

Faber & Faber, *(Faber & Faber, Inc.; 0-571),* Affil. of Faber & Faber, Ltd., London, 50 Cross St., Winchester, MA 01890 (SAN 218-7256) Tel 617-721-1427; Dist. by: CUP Services, 750 Cascadilla St., Ithaca, NY 14851 (SAN 630-6519); Toll free: 800-666-2211.

Facet Bks, *(Facet Bks. International, Inc.; 0-932377),* 345 E. 69th St., New York, NY 10021 (SAN 687-3839) Tel 212-570-1932.

Facts on File, *(Facts on File, Inc.; 0-87196; 0-8160),* Subs. of Infobase Holdings, Inc., 460 Park Ave. South, New York, NY 10016 (SAN 201-4696) Tel 212-683-2244; Toll free: 800-322-8755.

FAFCTPC, *(1st Aid for Children & Teens Publishing Co.; 0-9622812),* 211 Trysail Ct., Foster City, CA 94404 Tel 415-574-7179.

Faith & Fellowship Pr, *(Faith & Fellowship Pr.;* 0-943167), 704 W. Vernon Ave., Box 655, Fergus Falls, MN 56538 (SAN 668-2065) Tel 218-739-5482; Toll free: 800-332-9232.

Faith & Life, *(Faith & Life Pr.; 0-87303),* 718 Main St., Newton, KS 67114-0347 (SAN 201-4726) Tel 316-283-5100; Box 347, Newton, KS 67114-0347 (SAN 658-0637).

Faith Min & Pubns, *(Faith Ministries & Pubns.;* 1-878725), P.O. Box 1156, Warsaw, IN 46581 (SAN 297-3529) Tel 219-799-5813.

Faith Pub Hse, *(Faith Publishing Hse.),* P.O. Box 518, Guthrie, OK 73044 (SAN 204-1243); 920 W. Mansur, Guthrie, OK 73044 (SAN 658-0645) Tel 405-282-1479.

Falcon Pr MT, *(Falcon Pr. Publishing Co., Inc.; 0-934318; 0-937959; 1-56044),* P.O. Box 1718, Helena, MT 59624 (SAN 221-1726); Toll free: 800-582-2665; 48 N. Last Chance Gulch, Helena, MT 59601 (SAN 658-0653) Tel 406-442-6597; Orders to: P.O. Box 1718, Helena, MT 59624 (SAN 281-7047); Dist. by: Bookpeople, 7900 Edgewater Dr., Oakland, CA 94621 (SAN 168-9517) Tel 510-632-4700; Toll free: 800-999-4650; Dist. by: Inland Bk. Co., 140 Commerce St., East Haven, CT 06512 (SAN 200-4151) Tel 203-467-4257; Toll free: 800-243-0138; Dist. by: Pacific Pipeline, Inc., 8030 S. 228th St., Kent, WA 98032-2900 (SAN 208-2128) Tel 206-872-5523; Toll free: 800-444-7323 (Customer Service); 800-677-2222 (orders); Dist. by: Baker & Taylor Bks., Somerville Service Ctr., 50 Kirby Ave., Somerville, NJ 08876-0734 (SAN 169-4901) Tel 908-722-8000; Toll free: 800-775-1500 (customer service); Dist. by: Baker & Taylor Bks., Momence Service Ctr., 501 S. Gladiolus St., Momence, IL 60954-2444 (SAN 169-2100) Tel 815-472-2444; Toll free: 800-775-2300 (customer service); Dist. by: Baker & Taylor Bks., Commerce Service Ctr., 251 Mt. Olive Church Rd., Commerce, GA 30599-9988 (SAN 169-1503) Tel 706-335-5000; Toll free: 800-775-1200 (customer service); Dist. by: Baker & Taylor Bks., Reno Service Ctr., 380 Edison Way, Reno, NV 89564 (SAN 169-4464) Tel 702-858-6700; Toll free: 800-775-1700 (customer service); Dist. by: Bookmen, Inc., 525 N. Third St., Minneapolis, MN 55401 (SAN 169-409X) Tel 612-341-3333; Toll free: 800-328-8411 (customer service); Dist. by: Ingram Bk. Co., 1 Ingram Blvd., La Vergne, TN 37086-1986 (SAN 169-7978) Tel 615-793-5000; Toll free: 800-937-8000 (orders only, all warehouses).

Fall Leaf Pr, *(Fallen Leaf Pr.; 0-9633243),* P.O. Box 942, Newtown, PA 18940-0845; 105 E. Washington Ave., Newton, PA 18940-1939 Tel 215-968-5505. Do not confuse with Fallen Leaf Pr. in Berkeley, CA.

Fam Comm Educ, *(Family & Community Educational Services (FACES); 0-9630375),* P.O. Box 1781, Pomona, CA 91769; 992 E. Kingsley, Pomona, CA 91767 Tel 909-623-4995.

Fam Life Ed, *(Family Life Education Assocs.;* 0-9628687), P.O. Box 7466, Richmond, VA 23221; 4319 Fauquier Ave., Richmond, VA 23227 Tel 804-262-0531.

Fam Lrng Ctr, *(Family Learning Ctr.; 1-880892),* Rte. 2, Box 264, Hawthorne, FL 32640 Tel 904-475-5869.

Fam of God, *(Family of God Publishing Hse.;* 0-9638277), 993C S. Santa Fe, Vista, CA 92083 Tel 619-598-3629.

Fam Skills, *(Family Skills, Inc.; 0-934275),* Dist. by: Southeastern Printing Co., P.O. Box 2476, Stuart, FL 34995-2476 (SAN 200-9420) Tel 407-287-2141; Toll free: 800-228-1583.

Family Life, *(Family Life Publishing; 0-9619566),* P.O. Box 2010, Dennis, MA 02638 (SAN 244-9188); 900 Town Plaza, Rte. 134, Dennis, MA 02638 (SAN 244-9196) Tel 508-385-9109.

Family Media, *(Family Media, Inc.; 1-877773),* P.O. Box 19865, Birmingham, AL 35219; 2208 Manassas Dr., Birmingham, AL 35213 Tel 205-956-3003.

Family Pubng, *(Family Publishing Co.; 0-9640865),* P.O. Box 752014, Dayton, OH 45475-2014 Tel 513-433-1893. Do not confuse with companies with the same name in Bodega Bay, CA, Marietta, GA.

Family Relat, *(Family Relations Foundation; 0-9614218),* P.O. Box 462, Sebastopol, CA 95473 (SAN 687-1097) Tel 707-823-0876; Dist. by: Bookpeople, 7900 Edgewater Dr., Oakland, CA 94621 (SAN 168-9517) Tel 510-632-4700; Toll free: 800-999-4650.

FamilyVision, *(FamilyVision Pr., Inc.; 1-56969),* 575 Madison Ave., Suite 1006, New York, NY 10022 Tel 212-875-9650; Dist. by: Spring Arbor Distributors, 10885 Textile Rd., Belleville, MI 48111 (SAN 158-9016) Tel 313-481-0900; Toll free: 800-395-5599 (orders); 800-395-7234 (customer service); Dist. by: Baker & Taylor Bks., Somerville Service Ctr., 50 Kirby Ave., Somerville, NJ 08876-0734 (SAN 169-4901) Tel 908-722-8000; Toll free: 800-775-1500 (customer service); Dist. by: Baker & Taylor Bks., Momence Service Ctr., 501 S. Gladiolus St., Momence, IL 30599-9988 (SAN 169-2100) Tel 706-335-5000; Toll free: 800-775-2300 (customer service); Dist. by: Baker & Taylor Bks., Commerce Service Ctr., 251 Mt. Olive Church Rd., Commerce, GA 30599-9988 (SAN 169-1503) Tel 706-335-5000; Toll free: 800-775-1200 (customer service); Dist. by: Baker & Taylor Bks., Reno Service Ctr., 380 Edison Way, Reno, NV 89564 (SAN 169-4464) Tel 702-858-6700; Toll free: 800-775-1700 (customer service); Dist. by: Ingram Bk. Co., 1 Ingram Blvd., La Vergne, TN 37086-1986 (SAN 169-7978) Tel 615-793-5000; Toll free: 800-937-8000 (orders only, all warehouses); Dist. by: National BK. Network, 4720A Boston Way, Lanham, MD 20706-4310 (SAN 630-0065) Tel 301-459-8696; Toll free: 800-462-6420.

Fantaco, *(Fantaco Pubns.; 0-938782),* Affil. of Fantaco Enterprises, Inc., 21 Central Ave., Albany, NY 12210-1391 (SAN 158-5134) Tel 518-463-3667.

Far Away Fam Playhse, *(Far Away Family Playhouse;* 0-9627228), P.O. Box 27-6304, Boca Raton, FL 33427-6304; 1074 NW 13th St., No. 257C, Boca Raton, FL 33486 Tel 407-392-8226.

Far Eastern Res, *(Far Eastern Research & Pubns. Ctr.;* 0-912580), P.O. Box 15151, Washington, DC 20003 (SAN 205-5759); Orders to: HY-FERPC, 10204 Bessmer Ln., Fairfax, VA 22032 (SAN 665-6943).

Faraway Pub, *(Faraway Publishing Group; 0-9636885),* Div. of Educational Management Network, Inc., P.O. Box 792, Nantucket, MA 02554; 8 Williams Ln., Nantucket, MA 02554 Tel 508-228-6700.

FASA Corp, *(FASA Corp.; 0-931787; 1-55560),* 1100 W. Cermak, B305, Chicago, IL 60608 (SAN 684-8834) Tel 312-243-5660; Dist. by: Contemporary Bks., Inc., 2 Prudential Plaza, Suite 1200, Chicago, IL 60601 (SAN 202-5493) Tel 312-540-4500; Toll free: 800-621-1918 (orders only).

Fat Cat Pr, *(Fat Cat Pr.; 0-9639985),* 12 Skylark Ln., Stony Brook, NY 11790 Tel 516-751-7080.

Fat Lane, *(Fat Lane Pubns.; 0-9624540),* P.O. Box 8157, Pittsburgh, PA 15217; 4118 Winterburn Ave., Pittsburgh, PA 15207 Tel 412-421-8069.

Fawcett, *(Fawcett Bk. Group; 0-449),* Div. of Ballantine Bks., Inc., 201 E. 50th St., New York, NY 10022 (SAN 201-4572) Tel 212-572-2713; Toll free: 800-733-3000 (orders); 800-726-0600 (customer service). *Imprints:* Columbine (Columbine); Crest (Crest Books); Girls Only (Girls Only); GM (Gold Medal Books); Juniper (Juniper).

FEA Pub, *(F E A Publishing; 0-9618730),* P.O. Box 1065, Hobe Sound, FL 33475 (SAN 668-6877) Tel 407-546-1113.

Fearon-Janus, *(Fearon/Janus/Quercus; 0-8224; 0-915510; 0-88102; 0-912925; 1-55555),* Div. of Simon & Schuster Supplementary Education Group, 4350 Equity Dr., Columbus, OH 43228-3841; Toll free: 800-877-4283.

Fearon Teach Aids, *(Fearon Teacher Aids; 0-8224),* A Judy/Instructo Co., Div. of Paramount Communications, 1204 Buchanan, P.O. Box 280, Carthage, IL 62321 (SAN 212-775X) Tel 217-357-3900; Toll free: 800-242-7272.

Feather Fables, *(Feather Fables Publishing Company; 0-9634122; 1-885527),* P.O. Box 3418, Venice, FL 34293-0132; The Pattison Bldg., 260 W. Miami Ave., Venice, FL 34285 Tel 813-485-0402; Dist. by: BookWorld Distribution Services, Inc., 1933 Whitfield Pk. Loop, Sarasota, FL 34243 (SAN 173-0568) Tel 813-758-8094; Toll free: 800-444-2524 (orders only).

Feelings Factory, *(Feelings Factory, Inc.; 1-882801),* 508 Saint Mary's St., Raleigh, NC 27605 Tel 919-828-2264; Toll free: 800-858-2264.

Feldheim, *(Feldheim, Philipp, Inc.; 0-87306),* 200 Airport Executive Pk., Spring Valley, NY 10977 (SAN 106-6307) Tel 914-356-2282; Toll free: 800-237-7149.

Fellowship Pr PA, *(Fellowship Pr.; 0-914390),* 5820 Overbrook Ave., Philadelphia, PA 19131 (SAN 201-6117) Tel 215-879-8604; Dist. by: Baker & Taylor Bks., Somerville Service Ctr., 50 Kirby Ave., Somerville, NJ 08876-0734 (SAN 169-4901) Tel 908-722-8000; Toll free: 800-775-1500 (customer service); Dist. by: Baker & Taylor Bks., Momence Service Ctr., 501 S. Gladiolus St., Momence, IL 60954-2444 (SAN 169-2100) Tel 815-472-2444; Toll free: 800-775-2300 (customer service); Dist. by: Baker & Taylor Bks., Commerce Service Ctr., 251 Mt. Olive Church Rd., Commerce, GA 30599-9988 (SAN 169-1503) Tel 706-335-5000; Toll free: 800-775-1200 (customer service); Dist. by: Baker & Taylor Bks., Reno Service Ctr., 380 Edison Way, Reno, NV 89564 (SAN 169-4464) Tel 702-858-6700; Toll free: 800-775-1700 (customer service); Dist. by: New Leaf Distributing Co., 5425 Tulane Dr., SW, Atlanta, GA 30336-2323 (SAN 169-1449) Tel 404-691-6996; Toll free: 800-326-2665.

Feminist Pr, *(Feminist Pr. at The City Univ. of New York; 0-912670; 0-935312; 1-55861),* 311 E. 94th St., New York, NY 10128 (SAN 213-6813) Tel 212-360-5790; Dist. by: Consortium Bk. Sales & Distribution, 1045 Westgate Dr., Suite 90, Saint Paul, MN 55114-1065 (SAN 200-6049) Tel 612-221-9035; Toll free: 800-283-3572 (orders).

Fen Winnie, *(Fen Winnie Ink; 0-9614438),* P.O. Box 13658, San Luis Obispo, CA 93406 (SAN 689-1586) Tel 805-927-3979.

Fenton Valley Pr, *(Fenton Valley Pr.; 0-9615149),* 657 Chaffeeville Rd., Storrs, CT 06268 (SAN 694-3683) Tel 203-429-0710; Dist. by: DeVorss & Co., P.O. Box 550, Marina del Rey, CA 90294-0550 (SAN 168-9886) Tel 213-870-7478; Toll free: 800-843-5743 (bookstores only); 800-331-4719 (in California, bookstores only); Dist. by: Inland Bk. Co., 140 Commerce St., East Haven, CT 06512 (SAN 200-4151) Tel 203-467-4257; Toll free: 800-243-0138; Dist. by: New Leaf Distributing Co., 5425 Tulane Dr., SW, Atlanta, GA 30336-2323 (SAN 169-1449) Tel 404-691-6996; Toll free: 800-326-2665; Dist. by: Baker & Taylor Bks., Somerville Service Ctr., 50 Kirby Ave., Somerville, NJ 08876-0734 (SAN 169-4901) Tel 908-722-8000; Toll free: 800-775-1500 (customer service).

Fenwick Pr, *(Fenwick Pr.; 0-9628981),* 2024 Southwood Rd., Jackson, MS 39211 Tel 601-366-0868.

Ferguson, *(Ferguson, J. G., Publishing Co.; 0-89434),* 200 W. Madison, Suite 300, Chicago, IL 60606 (SAN 207-1363) Tel 312-580-5480. Do not confuse with Jane & Gary Ferguson in Red Lodge, MT.

Ferguson-Florissant, *(Ferguson-Florissant Schl. District/Early Education; 0-939418),* 1005 Waterford Dr., Florissant, MO 63033 (SAN 216-5740) Tel 314-831-8809.

Festival *Imprint of* **HarpC Child Bks**

Fgn Lang Young Child, *(Foreign Language for Young Children; 0-937531),* 21 Lake Ave., Newton Centre, MA 02159 (SAN 658-8522) Tel 617-332-2427; Orders to: P.O. Box 336, Newton Highlands, MA 02161.

Fiesta Bks Inc, *(Fiesta Bks., Inc.; 0-943169),* 2743 E. Cathedral Rock Dr., Phoenix, AZ 85048-8912 (SAN 668-1042) Tel 602-759-4555.

Fiesta City, *(Fiesta City Pubs.; 0-940076),* P.O. Box 5861, Santa Barbara, CA 93150-5861 (SAN 217-071X) Tel 805-733-1984.

FIG Ltd, *(F.I.G., Ltd.; 0-9601452),* P.O. Box 23, Northbrook, IL 60065 (SAN 211-8971).

Finan Visions, *(Financial Visions, Inc.; 0-9638808),* 8200 Humboldt Ave., S., Suite 215, Minneapolis, MN 55431 Tel 612-881-8292; Toll free: 800-967-1766.

Finney Co, *(Finney Co.; 0-912486),* 3943 Meadowbrook Rd., Minneapolis, MN 55426 (SAN 206-412X) Tel 612-938-9330; Toll free: 800-846-7027.

Fins Pubns, *(Fins Pubns.; 0-9615221),* Box 13005, Roseville, MN 55113 (SAN 695-1511).

Firefly Bks Ltd, *(Firefly Bks., Ltd.; 0-920668; 1-895565),* P.O. Box 1338, Ellicott Sta., Buffalo, NY 14205 (SAN 630-611X); Toll free: 800-387-5085. Canadian address; 250 Sparks Ave., Willowdale, ON M2H 2S4.

Firehole Pr, *(Firehole Pr. & Nature's Design; 0-918355),* P.O. Box 255, Davenport, CA 95017 (SAN 657-3398) Tel 408-426-8205.

Fireplug CA, *(Fireplug Pr.; 0-9626950),* P.O. Box 283, San Mateo, CA 94402; 422 Georgetown Ave., San Mateo, CA 94402 Tel 415-347-3359.

Fireside *Imprint of* **S&S Trade**

Firestein Bks, *(Firestein Bks.; 0-9602498; 1-884539),* P.O. Box 370643, El Paso, TX 79937-0643 (SAN 212-940X); 2211 Sea Side Dr., El Paso, TX 79936 Tel 915-594-2966.

Fireweed, *(Fireweed Pr.; 0-912683),* P.O. Box 6011, Falls Church, VA 22046 (SAN 277-6839) Tel 703-560-0810. Do not confuse with companies with the same name in Fairbanks, AK, Madison, WI.

First Ave Edns *Imprint of* **Lerner Pubns**

First Pub IL, *(First Publishing, Inc.; 0-915419; 1-56520),* 919 N. Michigan Ave., Suite 3400, Chicago, IL 60611-1601 (SAN 291-1558) Tel 312-484-9006. Do not confuse with First Publishing, Inc., Birmingham, AL.

Fischer Inc NY, *(Fischer, Carl, Inc.; 0-8258),* 62 Cooper Sq., New York, NY 10003 (SAN 107-4245) Tel 212-772-0900; Toll free: 800-847-4260.

Fithian Pr, *(Fithian Pr.; 0-931832; 1-56474),* Div. of Daniel & Daniel Pubs., Inc., P.O. Box 1525, Santa Barbara, CA 93102 (SAN 211-6103); Toll free: 800-662-8351 (orders only); 21 E. Canon Perdido St., Suite 217, Santa Barbara, CA 93101 (SAN 250-0124) Tel 805-962-1780.

Five Corn Danforth, *(Five Corners Danforth Escanaba, Inc.; 0-9631057),* 4897 Danforth Rd., Escanaba, MI 49829 Tel 906-786-6443.

Five Star AZ, *(5 Star Pubns.; 0-9619853; 1-877749),* 4696 W. Tyson St., Chandler, AZ 85226 (SAN 246-7429) Tel 602-940-8182; Toll free: 800-545-7827; Dist. by: Baker & Taylor Bks., Reno Service Ctr., 380 Edison Way, Reno, NV 89564 (SAN 169-4464) Tel 702-858-6700; Toll free: 800-775-1700 (customer service); Dist. by: Baker & Taylor Bks., Somerville Service Ctr., 50 Kirby Ave., Somerville, NJ 08876-0734 (SAN 169-4901) Tel 908-722-8000; Toll free: 800-775-1500 (customer service); Dist. by: Baker & Taylor Bks., Momence Service Ctr., 501 S. Gladiolus St., Momence, IL 60954-2444 (SAN 169-2100) Tel 815-472-2444; Toll free: 800-775-2300 (customer service); Dist. by: Baker & Taylor Bks., Commerce Service Ctr., 251 Mt. Olive Church Rd., Commerce, GA 30599-9988 (SAN 169-1503) Tel 706-335-5000; Toll free: 800-775-1200 (customer service); Dist. by: The Distributors, 702 S. Michigan, South Bend, IN 46601 (SAN 169-2488) Tel 219-232-8500; Toll free: 800-348-5200 (except Indiana); Dist. by: Quality Bks., Inc., 918 Sherwood Dr., Lake Bluff, IL 60044-2204 (SAN 169-2127) Tel 708-295-2010; Toll free: 800-323-4241 (libraries only); Dist. by: Merle Distributing Co., 27222 Plymouth Rd., Detroit, MI 48239 (SAN 169-3778) Tel 313-937-8400; Toll free: 800-233-9380 (orders); Dist. by: Ingram Bk. Co., 1 Ingram Blvd., La Vergne, TN 37086-1986 (SAN 169-7978) Tel 615-793-5000; Toll free: 800-937-8000 (orders only, all warehouses); Dist. by: Unique Bks., Inc., 4230 Grove Ave., Gurnee, IL 60031 (SAN 630-0472) Tel 708-623-9171. Do not confuse with Five Star Pubns., Port Townsend, WA.

FJH Music Co Inc, *(FJH Music Co., Inc.; 0-929666;* 1-56939), 20432 NE 16th Pl., North Miami Beach, FL 33179 (SAN 249-8685) Tel 305-651-5466; Toll free: 800-262-8744.

Flame Intl, *(Flame International, Inc.; 0-933184),* 1224 Porter Rd., Norfolk, VA 23511-1227 (SAN 215-3114).

Flamingo Pr, *(Flamingo Pr.; 0-938905),* 2958 State St., Carlsbad, CA 92008-2336 (SAN 661-812X).

Flare *Imprint of* **Avon**

Flash Blasters, *(Flash Blasters, Inc.; 1-881374),* 253 Closter Dock Rd., Suite 6, Closter, NJ 07624 Tel 201-784-0001; Toll free: 800-352-7409; Dist. by: Centennial Pr., P.O. Box 82087, Lincoln, NE 68501 (SAN 630-7426); Toll free: 800-356-5016; Dist. by: Bookazine Co., Inc., 75 Hook Rd., Bayonne, NJ 07002 (SAN 169-5665) Tel 201-339-7777; Toll free: 800-221-8112; Dist. by: Sher Distributing Co., 8 Vreeland Ave., Totowa, NJ 07512 (SAN 169-4820) Tel 201-256-4050; Toll free: 800-289-4050; Dist. by: Baker & Taylor Bks., Somerville Service Ctr., 50 Kirby Ave., Somerville, NJ 08876-0734 (SAN 169-4901) Tel 908-722-8000; Toll free: 800-775-1500 (customer service); Dist. by: Baker & Taylor Bks., Momence Service Ctr., 501 S. Gladiolus St., Momence, IL 60954-2444 (SAN 169-2100) Tel 815-472-2444; Toll free: 800-775-2300 (customer service); Dist. by: Baker & Taylor Bks., Commerce Service Ctr., 251 Mt. Olive Church Rd., Commerce, GA 30599-9988 (SAN 169-1503) Tel 706-335-5000; Toll free: 800-775-1200 (customer service); Dist. by: Baker & Taylor Bks., Reno Service Ctr., 380 Edison Way, Reno, NV 89564 (SAN 169-4464) Tel 702-858-6700; Toll free: 800-775-1700 (customer service); Dist. by: Koen Bk. Distributors, 10 Twosome Dr., P.O. Box 600, Morrestown, NJ 08057 (SAN 169-4642) Tel 609-235-4444; Toll free: 800-257-8481; Dist. by: Golden-Lee Bk. Distributors, Inc., 1000 Dean St., Brooklyn, NY 11238 (SAN 169-5126) Tel 718-857-6333; Toll free: 800-473-7475; Dist. by: NACSCORP, Inc., 528 E. Lorain St., Oberlin, OH 44074-1298 (SAN 169-6823); Toll free: 800-321-3883 (orders only); 800-458-9303 (backorder status only).

Flatland Tales, *(Flatland Tales Publishing; 0-9638421),* P.O. Box 887, Ottawa, KS 66067-0887; 2116 N. Murray Cir., Wichita, KS 67212 Tel 316-721-0957.

Floricanto Pr, *(Floricanto Pr.; 0-915745),* Div. of Hispanex, 16161 Ventura Blvd., Suite 830, Encino, CA 91436-2504 (SAN 293-9169) Tel 818-701-3026.

Florida Classics, *(Florida Classics Library; 0-912451),* P.O. Drawer 1657, Port Salerno, FL 34992-1657 (SAN 265-2404) Tel 407-546-9380.

Flourtown Pub, *(Flourtown Publishing Co.; 0-9603376),* P.O. Box 148, Flourtown, PA 19031 (SAN 207-6381).

Flower Pr, *(Flower Pr.; 0-942256),* Subs. of Flowerfield Enterprises, 10332 Shaver Rd., Kalamazoo, MI 49002 (SAN 217-7358) Tel 616-327-0108.

Flying Frog, *(Flying Frog Publishing, Inc.; 1-884628),* 102 Sunderland Dr., Auburn, ME 04210 Tel 207-777-5330.

Flying Heart, *(Flying Heart; 0-9635004),* Div. of Flying Heart Records, 4026 NE 12th Ave., Portland, OR 97212 Tel 503-287-8045.

Flying Rhino, *(Flying Rhino Productions; 1-883772),* 3629 SW Caldew, Portland, OR 97219 Tel 503-293-0475.

Fmly Life Prods, *(Family Life Productions; 1-883761),* P.O. Box 2710, Fallbrook, CA 92088 (SAN 239-1090); Toll free: 800-886-2767; 488 Industrial Way, No. A3, Fallbrook, CA 92028 Tel 619-728-6437.

Focus Family, *(Focus on the Family Publishing; 0-929608; 1-56179),* 8605 Explorer Dr., Colorado Springs, CO 80920 (SAN 250-0949) Tel 719-531-3482.

Foghorn Pr, *(Foghorn Pr.; 0-935701),* 555 DeHaro St., Suite 220, San Francisco, CA 94107-0845 (SAN 696-4346) Tel 415-241-9550; Toll free: 800-364-4676; Dist. by: Publishers Group West, 4065 Hollis St., Emeryville, CA 94608 (SAN 202-8522) Tel 510-658-3453; Toll free: 800-788-3123; Dist. by: Bookpeople, 7900 Edgewater Dr., Oakland, CA 94621 (SAN 168-9517) Tel 510-632-4700; Toll free: 800-999-4650.

Folk-Legacy, *(Folk-Legacy Records, Inc.; 0-938702),* Sharon Mountain Rd., Sharon, CT 06069 (SAN 207-3390) Tel 203-364-5661.

Folk-Life, *(Folk-Life Bks.; 0-914917),* P.O. Box 128, Princeton, LA 71067 (SAN 289-1336); 3330 Hwy 80E, Haughton, LA 71037 (SAN 289-1344) Tel 318-949-3915.

Font & Ctr Pr, *(Font & Ctr. Pr.; 1-883280),* P.O. Box 95, Weston, MA 02193; 69 Pinecroft Rd., Weston, MA 02193 Tel 617-647-9756; Dist. by: Independent Pubs. Group, 814 N. Franklin, Chicago, IL 60610 (SAN 202-0769) Tel 312-337-0747; Toll free: 800-888-4741.

Food Works, *(Food Works; 1-884430),* 64 Main St., Montpelier, VT 05602 Tel 802-223-1515; Dist. by: Sewall Co., 145 Lincoln Rd., P.O. Box 529, Lincoln, MA 01773 (SAN 630-0324) Tel 617-259-0559; Toll free: 800-258-0559.

Footstool Pubns, *(Footstool Pubns.; 1-877818),* P.O. Box 161021, Memphis, TN 38186; 2625 Kate Bond Rd., Memphis, TN 38134 Tel 901-382-1918.

For-Kids, *(For-Kids Publishing; 0-9630470),* P.O. Box 2830, Belleview, FL 32620 (SAN 297-5270); 13630 SE 47th Ave., Summerfield, FL 32691 Tel 904-245-4153.

Forest Hse, *(Forest Hse. Publishing Co., Inc.; 1-878363;* 1-56674), P.O. Box 738, Lake Forest, IL 60045 Tel 708-295-8287; Toll free: 800-394-7323. *Imprints:* HTS Bks (H T S Books).

Forge NYC, *(Forge; 0-8125),* Div. of Tom Doherty Assocs., Inc., 175 Fifth Avenue, New York, NY 10010 Tel 212-388-0100; Dist. by: St. Martin's Pr., Inc., 175 Fifth Ave., Rm. 1715, New York, NY 10010 (SAN 200-2132) Tel 212-674-5151; Toll free: 800-221-7945; Dist. by: Warner Publishing Services, 1271 Avenue of the Americas, New York, NY 10020 (SAN 200-5522) Tel 212-522-8900.

Fort Frederica, *(Fort Frederica Assn., Inc.; 0-930803),* Rte. 9, Box 286-C, St. Simons Island, GA 31522 (SAN 677-6299) Tel 912-638-3639.

Fortress Pr *Imprint of* **Augsburg Fortress**

Fortson Pubs, *(Fortson Pubs.; 0-9623092),* 5208 Broad St., Pittsburgh, PA 15224 Tel 412-362-8218.

Forward March, *(Forward March, Inc.; 0-9620467),* 2701 Conestoga Dr., Suite 121, Carson City, NV 89706 (SAN 248-8426) Tel 702-885-8988; Toll free: 800-723-0067; Dist. by: Ingram Bk. Co., 1 Ingram Blvd., La Vergne, TN 37086-1986 (SAN 169-7978) Tel 615-793-5000; Toll free: 800-937-8000 (orders only, all warehouses); Dist. by: Baker & Taylor Bks., Reno Service Ctr., 380 Edison Way, Reno, NV 89564 (SAN 169-4464) Tel 702-858-6700; Toll free: 800-775-1700 (customer service); Dist. by: Publishers Group West, 4065 Hollis St., Emeryville, CA 94608 (SAN 202-8522) Tel 510-658-3453; Toll free: 800-788-3123.

Forword MN, *(Forword; 0-9623937),* 16256 W. 78th St., Suite 335, Eden Prairie, MN 55346 Tel 612-944-7761; Dist. by: Baker & Taylor Bks., Somerville Service Ctr., 50 Kirby Ave., Somerville, NJ 08876-0734 (SAN 169-4901) Tel 908-722-8000; Toll free: 800-775-1500 (customer service); Dist. by: Baker & Taylor Bks., Momence Service Ctr., 501 S. Gladiolus St., Momence, IL 60954-2444 (SAN 169-2100) Tel 815-472-2444; Toll free: 800-775-2300 (customer service); Dist. by: Baker & Taylor Bks., Commerce Service Ctr., 251 Mt. Olive Church Rd., Commerce, GA 30599-9988 (SAN 169-1503) Tel 706-335-5000; Toll free: 800-775-1200 (customer service); Dist. by: Baker & Taylor Bks., Reno Service Ctr., 380 Edison Way, Reno, NV 89564 (SAN 169-4464) Tel 702-858-6700; Toll free: 800-775-1700 (customer service); Dist. by: Ingram Bk. Co., 1 Ingram Blvd., La Vergne, TN 37086-1986 (SAN 169-7978) Tel 615-793-5000; Toll free: 800-937-8000 (orders only, all warehouses).

Foto Fantasi Pr, *(Foto Fantasi Pr.; 0-9619414),* P.O. Box 40472, Grand Junction, CO 81504-0472 (SAN 244-5018); 2937 View Dr., Grand Junction, CO 81504 (SAN 244-5026) Tel 303-245-4799.

FotoFolio, *(FotoFolio, Inc.; 1-881270),* 536 Broadway, 2nd Flr., New York, NY 10012 (SAN 630-463X) Tel 212-226-0923.

Foun Bks, *(Foundation Bks., Inc.; 0-934988),* P.O. Box 29229, Lincoln, NE 68529 (SAN 201-6567) Tel 402-466-4988; Dist. by: Baker & Taylor Bks., Momence Service Ctr., 501 S. Gladiolus St., Momence, IL 60954-2444 (SAN 169-2100) Tel 815-472-2444; Toll free: 800-775-2300 (customer service); Dist. by: Prairie Hse., Inc., P.O. Box 9199, Fargo, ND 58106 (SAN 262-9844) Tel 701-235-0210; Toll free: 800-866-2665; Toll free: 800-356-9315.

Found Am Christ
See F A C E

Fountain OH
See Fountainpen Pr

Fountainpen Pr, *(Fountainpen Pr.; 0-9621647),* 218 W. Fountain, Delaware, OH 43015 (SAN 251-7361) Tel 614-369-4306.

Four OClock Farms, *(Four O'Clock Farms Publishing Co.; 0-927044),* 1422 N. Woodhouse Rd., Virginia Beach, VA 23454 Tel 804-481-0596.

Four Seas Bk, *(Four Seasons Bk. Pubs.; 0-9605400),* 220 Piney Point Landing, P.O. Box 576, Grasonville, MD 21638 (SAN 215-8639) Tel 410-827-7350.

Four Star SC, *(Four Star Pubns.; 1-880926),* P.O. Box 7, 816 Paul Dr., Port Royal, SC 29935 Tel 803-524-1771.

Four Winds *Imprint of* **Macmillan Child Grp**

Four Zoas Night Ltd, *(Four Zoas Night Hse., Ltd.;* 0-939622), P.O. Box 111, Ashuelot Village, NH 03441 (SAN 216-6267) Tel 603-239-6830.

Foxglove TN, *(Foxglove Pr.; 1-882959),* P.O. Box 210602, Nashville, TN 37221-0602; 112 Belle Glen Dr., Nashville, TN 37221 Tel 615-646-1982. Do not confuse with Foxglove Pr. in San Rafael, CA.

Fr & Eur, *(French & European Pubns., Inc.; 0-8288;* 0-7859), Rockefeller Ctr. Promenade, 610 Fifth Ave., New York, NY 10020-2479 (SAN 206-8109) Tel 212-581-8810.

Fragments Lghts, *(Fragments of Light Pr.; 0-9635108),* 13-237 Summit Square Ctr., Langhorne, PA 19047.

Frajil Farms, *(Frajil Farms; 1-878689),* Box 13, Mont Vernon, NH 03057; 69 Francestown Tpke., Mont Vernon, NH 03057 Tel 603-673-8041.

Franciscan Comns, *(Franciscan Communications;* 1-55944), 1229 S. Santee St., Los Angeles, CA 90015 Tel 213-746-2916; Toll free: 800-421-8510.

Franklin Pr WA, *(Franklin, Charles, Pr., The; 0-932091;* 0-9603516), 7821 175th St., SW, Edmonds, WA 98020 (SAN 692-9001) Tel 206-774-6979.

Frantasy Wkshp, *(Frantasy Workshop; 0-9612696),* 1400 W. Cross St., Lakewood, NJ 08701 (SAN 289-193X) Tel 201-363-3988.

Fred Pr, *(Fred Pr.; 0-937393),* 59 Suydam St., New Brunswick, NJ 08901 (SAN 658-8573) Tel 201-878-7976; Orders to: 1178 Castleton Rd., Cleveland Heights, OH 44121 (SAN 662-4189).

Free & Easy Pubns, *(Free & Easy Pubns.; 0-916391),* P.O. Box 53248, Philadelphia, PA 19105 (SAN 295-7019).

Free Ent Partner, *(Free Enterprise Partnership, The;* 0-943447), 208 Roosevelt Bldg., 609 Penn Ave., Pittsburgh, PA 15222-3201 (SAN 668-4432) Tel 412-471-1504.

Free Pr, *(Free Pr.; 0-02),* Div. of Macmillan Publishing Co., Inc., 866 Third Ave., 22nd Flr., New York, NY 10022 (SAN 201-6656) Tel 212-702-2004; Toll free: 800-257-5755; Orders to: Macmillan Publishing Co., Inc., 100 Front St., Box 500, Riverside, NJ 08075-7500 (SAN 202-5582) Tel 609-461-6500; Toll free: 800-257-5755.

Free Spirit Pub, *(Free Spirit Publishing, Inc.; 0-915793)*, 400 First Ave. N., Suite 616, Minneapolis, MN 55401-1730 (SAN 293-9584) Tel 612-338-2068; Toll free: 800-735-7323.

Freedom Lights Pr, *(Freedom Lights Pr.; 0-945985)*, P.O. Box 87, Chimney Rock, CO 81127 (SAN 248-1820); 146 Cortez Ct., Pagosa Springs, CO 81157 (SAN 248-1839) Tel 303-731-5508.

Freedom Rel Found, *(Freedom from Religion Foundation; 1-877733)*, P.O. Box 750, Madison, WI 53701 (SAN 276-9484) Tel 608-256-5800.

Freeland Pubns, *(Freeland Pubns.; 0-936868)*, P.O. Box 18941, Philadelphia, PA 19119 (SAN 215-3130) Tel 215-226-2507.

Freels Fndtn, *(Freels Foundation; 0-9622526)*, 655 Beach St., Suite 400, San Francisco, CA 94109 Tel 415-928-0550.

FreeMan Prods, *(FreeMan Productions, Inc. (FPI); 0-918789)*, 18221 Torrence Ave., Lansing, IL 60438 (SAN 657-3436) Tel 312-895-7000.

Freestone Pub Co, *(Freestone Publishing Co.; 0-913512)*, Box 398, Monroe, UT 84754 (SAN 206-4154) Tel 801-527-3738; Dist. by: Bookpeople, 7900 Edgewater Dr., Oakland, CA 94621 (SAN 168-9517) Tel 510-632-4700; Toll free: 800-999-4650.

French, *(French, Samuel, Inc.; 0-573)*, 45 W. 25th St., New York, NY 10010 (SAN 206-4170) Tel 212-206-8990.

French & Eur
See Fr & Eur

Friends Genl Conf, *(Friends General Conference; 0-9620912)*, 1216 Arch St., Philadelphia, PA 19107 (SAN 225-4484) Tel 215-561-1700; Toll free: 800-966-4556.

Friends Natl Zoo, *(Friends of the National Zoo; 0-9622062)*, National Zoological Pk., Washington, DC 20008 Tel 202-673-4993.

Friends United, *(Friends United Pr.; 0-913408; 0-944350)*, 101 Quaker Hill Dr., Richmond, IN 47374 (SAN 201-5803) Tel 317-962-7573; Toll free: 800-537-8838.

Friendship Pr, *(Friendship Pr.; 0-377)*, Subs. of National Council of the Churches of Christ USA, 475 Riverside Dr., Rm. 860, New York, NY 10115 (SAN 201-5773) Tel 212-870-2586; Orders to: P.O. Box 37844, Cincinnati, OH 45222-0844 (SAN 201-5781) Tel 513-948-8733.

Friou Music, *(Friou Music; 0-9628120)*, 470 W. California Ave., Glendale, CA 91203-2107 Tel 818-500-7786.

Fritz & Angel, *(Fritz & Angel Publishing, Inc.; 0-9629140)*, P.O. Box 1124, Sedona, AZ 86339-1124.

Frnds Rhyolite, *(Friends of Rhyolite; 1-885770)*, P.O. Box 85, Robert St., Amargosa Valley, NV 89020 Tel 619-786-3281.

Frog Pr WI, *(Frog Pr.; 1-881120)*, 2821 Hwy. 14, E., Janesville, WI 53545-0221 Tel 608-752-1112; Toll free: 800-848-0256. Do not confuse with Frog Pr. in Berkeley, CA.

Froggy Bywater, *(Froggy Bywater Pr.; 0-9627621)*, P.O. Box 7920, Fresno, CA 93747; 244 S. Minnewawa, Fresno, CA 93727 Tel 209-251-0243.

Front Row, *(Front Row Experience; 0-915256)*, 540 Discovery Bay Blvd., Byron, CA 94514 (SAN 207-1274) Tel 510-634-5710; Toll free: 800-524-9091 (credit card orders & established credit and for inquiries).

Frontier OR, *(Frontier Publishing; 0-939116)*, P.O. Box 441, Seaside, OR 97138-0441 (SAN 110-9669) Tel 503-738-8489; Toll free: 800-821-3252.

Frontier Pr Co, *(Frontier Pr. Co.; 0-912168)*, P.O. Box 1098, Columbus, OH 43216 (SAN 205-5953) Tel 614-864-3737.

Fruits for Knowldge, *(Fruits for Knowledge Pr.; 0-9639858)*, 1474 Heather Pl., Pottstown, PA 19464 Tel 215-371-3666.

FS&G, *(Farrar, Straus & Giroux, Inc.; 0-374)*, 19 Union Sq., W., New York, NY 10003 (SAN 206-782X) Tel 212-741-6900; Toll free: 800-788-6262 (Individuals); 800-631-8571 (Booksellers). *Imprints:* Mirasol (Mirasol Libros Juveniles); Noonday (Noonday Books); North Pt Pr (North Point Press); Sunburst (Sunburst Books).

Fulcrum Inc
See Fulcrum Pub

Fulcrum Pub, *(Fulcrum Publishing; 1-55591; 0-912347; 1-56373)*, 350 Indiana St., Suite 350, Golden, CO 80401 (SAN 200-2825) Tel 303-277-1623; Toll free: 800-992-2908. *Imprints:* North Amer Pr (North American Press).

Full Court VA, *(Full Court Pr., Inc.; 0-913767)*, Box 8059, Roanoke, VA 24014 (SAN 285-2527) Tel 703-345-5440. Do not confuse with companies with the same name in Napa, CA, San Francisco, CA, La Canada, CA, San Antonio, TX, Grand Rapids, MI, Philadelphia, PA.

Fun Bk Enter, *(Fun Bk. Enterprises; 0-937511)*, P.O. Box 7777, Atlanta, GA 30357-0777 (SAN 658-8492); 1980 Overton Trail, Stone Mountain, GA 30088 (SAN 658-8506) Tel 404-987-2178.

Fun Enter, *(Fun Enterprises; 1-884801)*, 1601 Country Meadow Ln., Arcadia, TX 77517 Tel 409-925-7989.

Fun Pub AZ, *(Fun Publishing Co.; 0-918858)*, P.O. Box 2049, Scottsdale, AZ 85252 (SAN 210-4261) Tel 602-946-2093. Do not confuse with Fun Publishing Co., Cincinnati, OH.

Fun Pub OH, *(Fun Publishing Co.; 0-938293)*, 2121 Alpine Pl., No. 402, Cincinnati, OH 45206 (SAN 661-1761) Tel 513-533-3636. Do not confuse with Fun Publishing Co., Scottsdale, AZ.

Fun Reading, *(Fun Reading Co.; 0-9608466)*, 2409 Glenwood Rd., Brooklyn, NY 11210 (SAN 240-6055) Tel 718-453-5582.

Fun Soccer Ent, *(Fun Soccer Enterprises; 0-9619139)*, 2904 Fine Ave., Clovis, CA 93612 (SAN 243-4075) Tel 209-291-5798.

Funchess Jones, *(Funchess-Jones Publishing; 0-943021)*, P.O. Box 1510, Monterey, CA 93942-1510 (SAN 667-9072) Tel 408-375-5180.

Fund Feminist Majority, *(Fund for the Feminist Majority; 1-882037)*, 8105 W. Third St., Los Angeles, CA 90048 (SAN 248-8183) Tel 213-938-0560.

Funmakers, *(Funmakers, Ltd.; 0-9634399)*, P.O. Box 1560, Dearborn, MI 48121 Tel 313-274-8255.

Funny Farm Pr, *(Funny Farm Pr.; 0-9621234)*, P.O. Box 8882, Amarillo, TX 79114-8882 (SAN 250-7838); 6408 Drexel Rd., Amarillo, TX 79109 (SAN 250-7846) Tel 806-355-6376.

Future Press, *(Future Pr.; 0-9640402)*, P.O. Box 2569, Bala Cynwyd, PA 19004; 1105 Montrose St., Philadelphia, PA 19147 Tel 215-922-3357. Do not confuse with Future Pr. in New York, NY.

FVN Corp, *(FVN Corp.; 0-915687)*, 1660 Dyerville Loop Rd., Redcrest, CA 95569 (SAN 292-496X) Tel 707-946-2206.

G A Hamlin, *(Hamlin, Griffith Askew; 0-9631511)*, 23 Springer Dr., Columbia, MO 65201-5424 Tel 314-443-8619.

G A Johnson Pub, *(Johnson, Georgia A., Publishing Co.; 0-9626450)*, P.O. Box 4796, East Lansing, MI 48826; 2608 Darien Dr., Lansing, MI 48912 Tel 517-372-9642; Dist. by: Partners Bk. Distributing, Inc., 720 E. Shiawassee St., Lansing, MI 48912 (SAN 630-4559) Tel 517-485-0366; Toll free: 800-336-3137; Dist. by: Quality Bks., Inc., 918 Sherwood Dr., Lake Bluff, IL 60044-2204 (SAN 169-2127) Tel 708-295-2010; Toll free: 800-323-4241 (libraries only); Dist. by: Baker & Taylor Bks., Momence Service Ctr., 501 S. Gladiolus St., Momence, IL 60954-2444 (SAN 169-2100) Tel 815-472-2444; Toll free: 800-775-2300 (customer service); Dist. by: Baker & Taylor Bks., Commerce Service Ctr., 251 Mt. Olive Church Rd., Commerce, GA 30599-9988 (SAN 169-1503) Tel 706-335-5000; Toll free: 800-775-1200 (customer service).

G Beale Pr, *(Beale, Guthrie, Pr.; 0-937781)*, 7508 42nd Ave., NE, Seattle, WA 98115 (SAN 659-2279) Tel 206-525-6596.

G E M, *(GEM/McCuen Pubns., Inc.; 0-86596)*, 411 Mallalieu Dr., Hudson, WI 54016-1349 (SAN 691-909X) Tel 715-386-7113.

G E Radke, *(Radke, George E.; 0-9607994)*, 41 Harvard Rd., Havertown, PA 19083 (SAN 238-8308) Tel 610-446-0786.

G F Hutchison, *(Hutchison, G.F., Pr.; 1-885631)*, 1314 1/2 Byers, Joplin, MO 64804 Tel 417-782-2736.

G F Johnson, *(Johnson, George F.; 0-9623010)*, 3419 Sixth St., Lewiston, ID 83501 Tel 208-743-6636.

G Foreman, *(Foreman, Gloria, Publishing Co.; 0-915198)*, P.O. Box 123, Westville, OK 74965 (SAN 203-4263) Tel 918-723-5925.

G Gannett, *(Gannett Bks.; 0-930096; 0-929906)*, Subs. of Guy Gannett Publishing Co., Inc., P.O. Box 1460B, Portland, ME 04101 (SAN 210-7295) Tel 207-780-9000; Toll free: 800-442-6036.

G Grimm Assocs, *(Grim, Gary, & Assocs.; 1-56490)*, 82 S. Madison, Box 378, Carthage, IL 62321 Tel 217-357-3401.

G J & B Pub, *(GJ & B Publishing; 0-9635006)*, 22442 University Ave., N., Cedar, MN 55011 Tel 612-434-0786.

G Jacobson, *(Jacobson, Gloria; 0-9618399)*, 912 Third St., Box 803, New Glarus, WI 53574 (SAN 667-738X) Tel 608-527-5150.

G K Hall, *(Hall, G. K., & Co.; 0-8161; 0-7838)*, 866 Third Ave., New York, NY 10022 (SAN 206-8427) Tel 212-702-6789; Toll free: 800-257-5755. Do not confuse with G. K. Hall & Co. in Thorndike, ME (Large Type books & books on cassette.).

G Konopka, *(Konopka, Gisela; 0-9621328)*, 3809 Sheridan Ave., S., Minneapolis, MN 55410 (SAN 250-9687) Tel 612-926-8949.

G L Lowe, *(Lowe, George L., Pubs.; 0-9621263)*, 401 E. 32nd St., Chicago, IL 60616 (SAN 217-1155) Tel 312-842-1084.

G Markim, *(Markim, Greg, Pubs.; 0-938251)*, P.O. Box 183, Appleton, WI 54912 (SAN 661-3659); 1916 N. Drew St., Appleton, WI 54911 (SAN 661-3667) Tel 414-734-9678.

G P Hammond Pub, *(Hammond, G. P., Publishing; 1-878014)*, Box 546, Strasburg, VA 22657-1125 Tel 703-465-8447.

G P Pub MI, *(G.P./Publishing, Inc.; 0-917473)*, 4140 S. Lapeer Rd., Orion, MI 48359 (SAN 656-0644) Tel 810-373-2500. Do not confuse with G P Publishing, Inc., Tulsa, OK.

G Peterson, *(Peterson, George; 0-9621320)*, 7 Chapman Rd., Marlborough, CT 06447 (SAN 250-9822) Tel 203-295-0121.

G R Schoepfer, *(Schoepfer, G. R.; 0-931436)*, 786 Hudson Pkwy., Whiting, NJ 08759 (SAN 211-1659) Tel 201-849-0689.

G Ronald Pub, *(Ronald, George, Pub., Ltd.; 0-85398)*, 8325 17th St., N., Saint Petersburg, FL 33702-2843 (SAN 679-1859).

G Schnatz Pubns, *(Schnatz, G, Pubns.; 0-9614145)*, 192 Woodside Ave., Lodi, NJ 07644 (SAN 686-2276) Tel 201-471-2624.

G Sroda, *(Sroda, George; 0-9604486)*, P.O. Box 97, Amherst Junction, WI 54407 (SAN 210-8607) Tel 715-824-3868.

G Talley, *(Talley, Gene; 0-9622222)*, 2734 Mount Zion Rd., Jonesboro, GA 30236.

G Whittell Mem, *(Whittell, George, Memorial Pr.; 0-910781)*, 3722 South Ave., Youngstown, OH 44502 (SAN 260-2776) Tel 216-783-0645.

Gabriel TX, *(Gabriel Publishing; 1-881809)*, P.O. Box 173, Comfort, TX 78013; 973 High St., Comfort, TX 78013 Tel 210-477-8990. Do not confuse with companies with the same name in Ada, OK, Madison, OH, Denver, CO.

Galaxy Child Lrg Print *Imprint of* **Chivers N Amer**

Galde Pr, *(Galde Pr., Inc.; 1-880090)*, P.O. Box 65611, Saint Paul, MN 55165; 17110 Hershey Ct., Saint Paul, MN 55165 Tel 612-891-5991.

Gale, *(Gale Research, Inc.; 0-8103; 0-7876)*, Subs. of The Thomson Corp., 835 Penobscot Bldg., Detroit, MI 48226-4094 (SAN 213-4373) Tel 313-961-2242; Toll free: 800-877-4253. *Imprints:* UXL (UXL).

Galerija, *(Galerija; 0-9617756; 1-886060)*, 4317 S. Wisconsin Ave., Stickney, IL 60402 (SAN 664-6999) Tel 708-749-2843; Dist. by: Baker & Taylor Bks., Somerville Service Ctr., 50 Kirby Ave., Somerville, NJ 08876-0734 (SAN 169-4901) Tel 908-722-8000; Toll free: 800-775-1500 (customer service); Dist. by: Baker & Taylor Bks., Momence Service Ctr., 501 S. Gladiolus St., Momence, IL 60954-1799 (SAN 169-2100) Tel 815-472-2444; Toll free: 800-775-2300 (customer service); Dist. by: Baker & Taylor Bks., Commerce Service Ctr., 251 Mt. Olive Church Rd., Commerce, GA 30599-9988 (SAN 169-1503) Tel 706-335-5000; Toll free: 800-775-1200 (customer service); Dist. by: Baker & Taylor Bks., Reno Service Ctr., 380 Edison Way, Reno, NV 89564-0099 (SAN 169-4464) Tel 702-858-6700; Toll free: 800-775-1700 (customer service); Dist. by: Baker & Taylor Bks., Franklin Service Ctr., 2 Cottontail Ln., Somerset, NJ 08873-1133 (SAN 630-7205) Tel 908-469-7404.

Galilee *Imprint of* **Doubleday**

Galileo, *(Galileo Pr.; 0-913123)*, 15201 Wheeler Ln., Sparks, MD 21152 (SAN 240-6543); Dist. by: Pathway Bk. Service, Lowe-Village, Gilsum, NH 03448 (SAN 110-6430) Tel 603-357-0236; Toll free: 800-345-6665.

Galison, *(Galison Bks.; 0-939456; 0-929648; 1-56155)*, 36 W. 44th St., New York, NY 10036 (SAN 216-3888) Tel 212-354-8840.

Gallagher & Assocs, *(Gallagher & Assocs., Inc.; 0-9636119)*, 115 S. Union St., Suite 308, Alexandria, VA 22314 Tel 703-683-3635.

Gallagher MD
See Red Jacket Pr

Gallaudet Univ Pr, *(Gallaudet Univ. Pr.; 0-913580; 0-930323; 1-56368)*, 800 Florida Ave., NE, Washington, DC 20002-3695 (SAN 205-261X) Tel 202-651-5488; Toll free: 800-451-1073. *Imprints:* Clerc Bks (Clerc Books).

Gallery Arts, *(Gallery Arts Pr.; 0-9608592)*, P.O. Box 88, Rye, NY 10580 (SAN 238-2881).

Gallopade Pub Group, *(Gallopade: Publishing Group; 0-935326; 1-55609; 0-7933)*, 359 Milledge Ave., Suite 100, Atlanta, GA 30312 (SAN 213-8441) Tel 404-577-5085; Toll free: 800-536-2438.

Galloway, *(Galloway Pubns.; 0-87874)*, 2940 NW Circle Blvd., Corvallis, OR 97330-3999 (SAN 201-5854) Tel 503-754-7464.

Game Designers, *(Game Designers' Workshop; 0-943580; 1-55878)*, 203 North St., Normal, IL 61761 (SAN 240-656X) Tel 309-452-3632.

Gamepro Pub, *(Gamepro Publishing, Inc.; 1-882455),* Div. of IDG Communications, Inc., 951 Mariners Island Blvd., No. 700, San Mateo, CA 94404-1561 Tel 415-363-5200.
Gamin Pr, *(Gamin Pr.; 0-9621714),* 62 State St., Guilford, CT 06437-2707 (SAN 252-0508) Tel 203-458-3030.
Gan Pub, *(Gan Publishing; 0-9632663),* 1374 N. Waterman Ave., San Bernardino, CA 92404-5374 Tel 909-381-8845.
G&D *Imprint of* **Putnam Pub Group**
Gannam-Kubat, *(Gannam/Kubat Pubs.; 0-945201),* 2632 Saturn St., Brea, CA 92621 (SAN 246-7046) Tel 714-528-8683.
Garden Gate, *(Garden Gate Publishing; 0-9630655),* 1655 Washington Ave., Vincennes, IN 47591 Tel 812-882-2626.
Garden Way Pub *Imprint of* **Storey Comm Inc**
Gardens Growing People, *(Gardens for Growing People;* 0-9627463), P.O. Box 630, Point Reyes, CA 94956; 11190 Sir Francis Drake Blvd., Point Reyes, CA 94956 Tel 415-663-8801.
Gardner Pub, *(Gardner Publishing, Inc.; 0-9617183),* 150 Marine St., Bronx, NY 10464 (SAN 663-2661) Tel 718-885-1036.
Gareth Stevens Inc, *(Stevens, Gareth, Inc.; 0-918831; 1-55532; 0-8368),* River Ctr. Bldg., 1555 N. River Center Dr., Suite 201, Milwaukee, WI 53212 (SAN 696-1592) Tel 414-225-0333; Toll free: 800-341-3569.
Garlic Pr OR, *(Garlic Pr.; 0-931993),* 100 Hillview Ln., No. 2, Eugene, OR 97408 (SAN 686-1105) Tel 503-345-0063. Do not confuse with companies with the same name in Palm Desert, CA, Baltimore, MD, New London, NH, Denver, CO, Kirkwood, MO.
Garrett Ed Corp, *(Garrett Educational Corp.; 0-944483;* 1-56074), P.O. Box 1588, Ada, OK 74820 (SAN 169-6955); Toll free: 800-654-9366; 130 E. 13th St., Ada, OK 74820 (SAN 243-2722) Tel 405-332-6884.
Garrett Pk, *(Garrett Park Pr.; 0-912048; 1-880774),* P.O. Box 190, Garrett Park, MD 20896 (SAN 201-5927); 4904 Waverly Ave., Garrett Park, MD 20896 Tel 301-946-2553.
Gates of Heck, *(Gates of Heck, Inc.; 0-9638129),* 5301 Brook Rd., Richmond, VA 23227-2401 Tel 804-266-9422.
Gateway Pr MI, *(Gateway Pr., Inc.; 0-934291; 0-88296),* P.O. Box 6013, Grand Rapids, MI 49516 (SAN 693-2592); Toll free: 800-346-8614. Do not confuse with Gateway Pr. Inc., Baltimore, MD.
Gazelle Prodns, *(Gazelle Productions; 0-945222),* 2108 104th SE, Bellevue, WA 98004 (SAN 246-2141) Tel 206-454-3307.
Gazelle Pubns, *(Gazelle Pubns.; 0-930192),* 1906 Niles-Buchanan Rd., Niles, MI 49120 (SAN 209-5610) Tel 616-465-4004.
GBE, *(GBE, Glory Be Enterprises; 0-9641732),* P.O. Box 1397, Forest City, NC 28043; Old Hollis Rd., Ellenboro, NC 28040 Tel 704-245-5230.
GBL Pubng, *(GBL Publishing Co.; 0-9638969),* 2581 Floribunda Dr., Columbus, OH 43209 Tel 614-236-4480.
GBS CA, *(GBS Pubns.; 0-913855),* 1969 Benecia Ave., Los Angeles, CA 90025 (SAN 287-7473) Tel 310-552-3460.
GCAPEF
See Peace Educ
GCNHA, *(Grand Canyon Natural History Assn.;* 0-938216), P.O. Box 399, Grand Canyon, AZ 86023 (SAN 215-7675) Tel 602-638-2481.
GDA Pubns, *(G.D.A. Pubns.; 0-938640),* 101 Brighton Dr., Lafayette, LA 70503 (SAN 215-2452) Tel 318-981-2874.
GdYrBks, *(GoodYearBooks; 0-673),* Div. of HarperCollins Pubs., Inc., 1900 E. Lake Ave., Glenview, IL 60025 (SAN 200-2140) Tel 708-729-3000; Toll free: 800-628-4480; Toll free: 800-242-3737.
Geckostufs, *(Geckostufs, Inc.; 0-9621280),* P.O. Box 27244, Honolulu, HI 96827 (SAN 250-9326); 3123A Paty Dr., Honolulu, HI 96822 (SAN 250-9334) Tel 808-988-7664.
Gee Tee Bee, *(Gee Tee Bee; 0-917232),* 11901 Sunset Blvd., No. 102, Los Angeles, CA 90049 (SAN 206-9652) Tel 310-476-2622.
GEF White, *(White, Glenn E. F.; 0-9611926),* 101 Buckingham St., Meriden, CT 06450 (SAN 286-1011) Tel 203-235-7462.
Gefen Bks, *(Gefen Bks.),* 12 New St., Hewlett, NY 11557-2012 Tel 516-295-2805.
Gemini Pubng, *(Gemini Publishing Co.; 1-885792),* 24 E. Weber Rd., Columbus, OH 43202 Tel 614-262-1649. Do not confuse with companies with the same name in Houston, TX.
Gemstone OR, *(Gemstone Publishing Co.; 0-9632521),* 31814 Lawrence St., Lebanon, OR 97355 Tel 503-451-1058. Do not confuse with Gemstone Publishing Co. in Thornville, OH.
General Church, *(General Church of the New Jerusalem;* 0-945003), 1100 Papermill Rd., Box 278, Bryn Athyn, PA 19009 (SAN 245-7512) Tel 215-947-2317.
Genesis Inc, *(Genesis of Pittsburgh, Inc.; 0-9615457),* P.O. Box 41017, Pittsburgh, PA 15202 (SAN 696-3978) Tel 412-766-2693.
Genesis Pub PA, *(Genesis Publishing Co.; 0-940967),* 663 Exton Commons, Exton, PA 19341-2446 (SAN 664-7812); 20 Line Rd., Malvern, PA 19355 (SAN 664-7820) Tel 610-648-0876. Do not confuse with companies with the same name in La Mesa, CA, Bedford, MA, Naples, FL, Exton, PA.
Geneva Pr *Imprint of* **Westminster John Knox**
Genius New, *(Genius Newsletter; 1-880718),* 1415 E. 22nd St., Apt. 1108, Minneapolis, MN 55404-3016 Tel 612-870-1515.
Gentian Servs, *(Gentian Services; 0-9628016),* P.O. Box 2140, Olympic Valley, CA 95730; 1690 Trapper McNutt Trail, Alpine Meadows, CA 95730 Tel 916-581-3625.
George Fox Pr, *(Fox, George, Pr.; 0-943701),* 110 S. Elliott Rd., Newberg, OR 97132 (SAN 668-7172) Tel 503-538-9775.
Georgetown U Pr, *(Georgetown Univ. Pr.; 0-87840),* 3619 O St., NW, Washington, DC 20007 (SAN 203-4247) Tel 202-687-5889; Orders to: P.O. Box 4866, Hampden Station, Baltimore, MD 21211-4866 Tel 410-516-6995.
Geoscience Pr, *(Geoscience Pr.; 0-945005),* 12629 N. Tatum Blvd., Suite 201, Phoenix, AZ 85032 (SAN 245-7571) Tel 602-953-2330. Do not confuse with Geoscience Pubns., Louisiana State Univ. in Baton Rouge, LA.
Geron-X, *(Geron-X, Inc.; 0-87672),* P.O. Box 1108, Los Altos, CA 94023-1108 (SAN 201-5994) Tel 415-493-0871.
Geste Pub, *(Geste Publishing Co.; 0-925360),* 3366 Wichita Falls Ave., Simi Valley, CA 93063 Tel 805-527-2680.
Get Organized, *(Get Organized!; 0-9631705),* 128 Morgan St., Holyoke, MA 01040 Tel 413-532-6666; Toll free: 800-944-6886.
Ghanam Text, *(Ghanam Textiles, Inc.; 0-9635566),* 219-02 Linden Blvd., Cambria Heights, Queens, NY 11411 Tel 718-949-1234.
Ghost Town, *(Ghost Town Pubns.; 0-933818),* P.O. Drawer 5998, Carmel, CA 93921 (SAN 209-4401) Tel 408-624-9058.
GI Joe Collect, *(GI Joe Collectors Club; 0-9635956),* 150 S. Glenoaks Blvd., Burbank, CA 91510 Tel 818-953-4239.
Giant Step CA, *(Giant Step Pr.; 0-9641208),* P.O. Box 1806, Spring Valley, CA 91979-1806; 10345 Fairhill Dr., Spring Valley, CA 91977 Tel 619-670-8570.
Gibbs Smith Pub, *(Smith, Gibbs, Pub.; 0-87905),* P.O. Box 667, Layton, UT 84041 (SAN 201-9906) Tel 801-544-9800; Toll free: 800-421-8714. *Imprints:* Peregrine Smith (Peregrine Smith Books).
Gibson, *(Gibson, C. R., Co.; 0-8378; 0-937970),* 32 Knight St., Norwalk, CT 06856 (SAN 201-5765) Tel 203-847-4543; Toll free: 800-243-6004; Orders to: C. R. Gibson, Distribution Ctr., Beacon Falls, CT 06403 (SAN 665-7028) Tel 203-888-0573.
Gifted Educ Pr, *(Gifted Education Pr.),* 10201 Yuma Ct., P. O. Box 1586, Manassas, VA 22110 (SAN 694-132X) Tel 703-369-5017.
Gig Harbor Pr, *(Gig Harbor Pr.; 1-883078),* P.O. Box 2059, Gig Harbor, WA 98335-0688 (SAN 297-8547); 4002 32nd Ave. Ct., NW, Gig Harbor, WA 98335 Tel 206-858-8819.
Gim-Ho, *(Gim-Ho Enterprises; 0-9615006; 0-929763),* 5781 Calaveras Cir., La Palma, CA 90623 (SAN 692-3038) Tel 714-521-4108.
Ginkgo Hut, *(Ginkgo Hut; 0-936620),* 113 Augusta Dr., Lincroft, NJ 07738 (SAN 215-3157) Tel 908-530-9572.
Girl Scouts USA, *(Girl Scouts of the USA; 0-88441),* 420 Fifth Ave., New York, NY 10018 (SAN 203-4611) Tel 212-852-8000.
Girls Only *Imprint of* **Fawcett**
GKM Pubng, *(GKM Publishing Co.; 0-9641534),* 1321 Oberlin Rd., Raleigh, NC 27608 Tel 919-828-4747.
Glacier Pub, *(Glacier Publishing Co.; 0-9617382),* 17267 N. Zuni Trail, Surprize, AZ 85374-9623 (SAN 664-0966).
Gladstone Pub, *(Gladstone Publishing, Ltd.; 0-944599),* Div. of Another Rainbow Publishing, Inc., P.O. Box 2079, Prescott, AZ 86302 (SAN 244-6197); 212 S. Montezuma, Prescott, AZ 86303 (SAN 244-6200) Tel 602-776-1300.
Glastonbury Pr, *(Glastonbury Pr.; 0-932145),* 12816 E. Rose Dr., Whittier, CA 90601 (SAN 686-4309) Tel 213-698-4243; Dist. by: Quality Bks., Inc., 918 Sherwood Dr., Lake Bluff, IL 60044-2204 (SAN 169-2127) Tel 708-295-2010; Toll free: 800-323-4241 (libraries only). Do not confuse with companies with the same name in Detroit, MI, Ojai, CA.
Gldn Door Pr, *(Golden Door Pr.; 1-885793),* 4969 Hoen Ave., Santa Rosa, CA 95405 Tel 707-538-5018.
Gldn Educ, *(Golden Educational Ctr.; 1-56500),* 857 Lake Blvd., Redding, CA 96003 Tel 916-244-0101.
Gldn West Bks, *(Golden West Bks.; 0-87095),* P.O. Box 80250, San Marino, CA 91118-8250 (SAN 201-6400) Tel 818-458-8148.
Glean Pubns, *(Glean Pubns., Ltd.; 1-885986),* Div. of LinPac International, 7205 Cessna Dr., Greensboro, NC 27409 Tel 910-668-7651; Toll free: 800-454-6722.
Glen Abbey Bks, *(Glen Abbey Bks., Inc.; 0-934125),* 735 N. Northlake Way, Suite 100, Seattle, WA 98103 (SAN 244-8351) Tel 206-548-9360; Toll free: 800-782-2239; Dist. by: Deaconess Pr., 2450 Riverside Ave., S., Minneapolis, MN 55454 Tel 612-672-4180; Toll free: 800-544-8207.
Glen Canyon Nat Hist Assn, *(Glen Canyon Natural History Assn.; 0-9622233),* Div. of National Park Service, P.O. Box 581, Page, AZ 86040 Tel 602-645-2471.
Glenwood Pubns, *(Glenwood Pubns.; 0-9626662),* 540 Glenwood Ln., East Meadow, NY 11554 (SAN 297-3952) Tel 516-536-7846.
Glide Word, *(Glide Word Pr.; 0-9622574),* Div. of Glide Foundation, 330 Ellis St., San Francisco, CA 94102 Tel 415-771-6300.
Global Pr Wks, *(Global Pr. Works; 1-881497),* Div. of The Jordan Scott Group, 6550 Cliff Ridge Ln., Cincinnati, OH 45213-1050.
Globe Pequot, *(Globe Pequot Pr.; 0-87106; 1-56440; 0-914788; 0-88742),* P.O. Box 833, Old Saybrook, CT 06475 (SAN 201-9892) Tel 203-395-0440; Toll free: 800-243-0495; 800-962-0973 (in Connecticut).
Glory Ministries, *(Glory Ministries; 0-923105),* P.O. Box 560919, Charlotte, NC 28256 (SAN 251-6152); 701Q Atando Ave., Charlotte, NC 28206 (SAN 251-6160) Tel 704-342-0576.
Gloucester Pr *Imprint of* **Watts**
Glove Compart Bks, *(Glove Compartment Bks.;* 0-9618806), P.O. Box 1602, Portsmouth, NH 03802 (SAN 242-6412); 7 Jennie Ln., Eliot, ME 03903 (SAN 242-6420) Tel 207-439-0789.
Glover Pr, *(Glover Pr.; 0-944782),* P.O. Box 2873, Westport, CT 06880 (SAN 245-4904) Tel 203-222-9343; Toll free: 800-541-7248.
Glue Bks, *(Glue Bks.; 1-881905),* Div. of Ballash Pr., Inc., 7730 Division Dr., Mentor, OH 44060 Tel 216-951-1114.
GM *Imprint of* **Fawcett**
GME Pub Co, *(GME Publishing Co.; 0-9617665),* 12973 Fiddle Creek Ln., Saint Louis, MO 63131 (SAN 664-9408) Tel 314-965-1261.
GNP Pub, *(GNP Publishing; 0-9620923),* Div. of Greenville News Piedmont Co., P.O. Box 1688, Greenville, SC 29602-1688 (SAN 250-1503); 305 S. Main St., Greenville, SC 29601 (SAN 250-1511) Tel 803-298-4279.
Gnu Wine Pr, *(Gnu Wine Pr.; 0-9623588),* 201 Central Ave., E., Saint Michael, MN 55376 Tel 612-497-4383.
Go Jolly Pubns, *(Go Jolly Pubns.; 0-9629587),* R.R. 1, Box 4990, Worcester, VT 05682-9502.
Goal Ent, *(Goal Enterprises & Assocs.; 0-9612350),* 6354 N. 11th, Fresno, CA 93710 (SAN 297-1755).
Godine, *(Godine, David R., Pub., Inc.; 0-87923; 1-56792),* 300 Massachusetts Ave., Horticultural Hall, Boston, MA 02115 (SAN 213-4381) Tel 617-536-0761.
Godolphin Hse, *(Godolphin Hse.; 0-9630657),* Div. of Church & School of Wicca, P.O. Box 1502, New Bern, NC 28563; 614 Middle St., New Bern, NC 28560 Tel 919-638-5036; Dist. by: Samuel Weiser, Inc., P.O. Box 612, York Beach, ME 03910-0612 (SAN 202-9588) Tel 207-363-4393; Toll free: 800-423-7087 (orders only).
Going Home, *(Going Home Bks.; 0-9639760),* Div. of Monroy Enterprises, P.O. Box 688, Parker, AZ 85344 Tel 619-665-5565; Toll free: 800-410-1999.
Going Places, *(Going Places; 0-9632868),* P.O. Box 11459, Eugene, OR 97440; 2145 Lincoln, Eugene, OR 97405 Tel 503-686-2716.
Gold & Honey *Imprint of* **Questar Pubs**
Gold Crest Pubns, *(Gold Crest Pubns./Pr.; 1-883709),* 1756 Plymouth Rd., Suite 251, Ann Arbor, MI 48105 Tel 313-994-3627.
Gold Leaf Pr, *(Gold Leaf Pr.; 1-882723),* 537 Main St., Placerville, CA 95667 (SAN 298-3249) Tel 916-642-1058.
Golden Gate *Imprint of* **Childrens**
Golden Owl Pub, *(Golden Owl Pubs.; 0-9601258),* 182 Chestnut Rd., Lexington Park, MD 20653 (SAN 210-4288) Tel 301-863-9253. Do not confuse with Golden Owl Publishing Co., Inc. in Amawalk, NY.
Golden Pr *Imprint of* **Western Pub**
Golden Rings, *(Golden Rings Publishing Co.; 0-9633607),* 6173 Doe Haven Dr., Farmington, NY 14425; Toll free: 800-433-6173.

Goldrock Bks, *(Goldrock Bks.; 1-880706),* P.O. Box 1606, Stephenville, TX 76401; 3 Miles N. of Hwy. 67 on FM2481, Stephenville, TX 76401 Tel 817-965-6718.

Gone Dogs, *(Gone To The Dogs; 0-9626566),* R.R. 1, Box 958, Putney, VT 05346; Rte. S & Sandhill Rd., Putney, VT 05346 Tel 802-387-5673.

Gong Prods, *(Gong Productions),* 3525 Dimond Ave. No. 304, Oakland, CA 94602-2201 (SAN 289-1581) Tel 510-530-0241.

Good Apple, *(Good Apple; 0-916456; 0-86653; 1-56417),* A Judy/Instructo Co., Div. of Simon & Schuster Supplementary Education Group, P.O. Box 299, Carthage, IL 62321-0299 (SAN 208-6646); Toll free: 800-435-7234; 1204 Buchanan St., Carthage, IL 62321 Tel 217-357-3981. *Imprints:* Shining Star Pubns (Shining Star Publications).

Good Bks PA, *(Good Bks.; 0-934672; 1-56148),* Subs. of Good Enterprises, Ltd., Box 419, 3510 Old Philadelphia Pike, Intercourse, PA 17534 (SAN 693-9597) Tel 717-768-7171; Toll free: 800-762-7171; Dist. by: Baker & Taylor Bks., Commerce Service Ctr., 251 Mt. Olive Church Rd., Commerce, GA 30599-9988 (SAN 169-1503) Tel 706-335-5000; Toll free: 800-775-1200 (customer service); Dist. by: Baker & Taylor Bks., Momence Service Ctr., 501 S. Gladiolus St., Momence, IL 60954-2444 (SAN 169-2100) Tel 815-472-2444; Toll free: 800-775-2300 (customer service); Dist. by: Inland Bk. Co., 140 Commerce St., East Haven, CT 06512 (SAN 200-4151) Tel 203-467-4257; Toll free: 800-243-0138; Dist. by: Baker & Taylor Bks., Somerville Service Ctr., 50 Kirby Ave., Somerville, NJ 08876-0734 (SAN 169-4901) Tel 908-722-8000; Toll free: 800-775-1500 (customer service); Dist. by: Baker & Taylor Bks., Reno Service Ctr., 380 Edison Way, Reno, NV 89564 (SAN 169-4464) Tel 702-858-6700; Toll free: 800-775-1700 (customer service); Dist. by: Bookpeople, 7900 Edgewater Dr., Oakland, CA 94621 (SAN 168-9517) Tel 510-632-4700; Toll free: 800-999-4650; Dist. by: The Distributors, 702 S. Michigan, South Bend, IN 46601 (SAN 169-2488) Tel 219-232-8500; Toll free: 800-348-5200 (except Indiana); Dist. by: Golden-Lee Bk. Distributors, Inc., 1000 Dean St., Brooklyn, NY 11238 (SAN 169-5126) Tel 718-857-6333; Toll free: 800-473-7475; Dist. by: Ingram Bk. Co., 1 Ingram Blvd., La Vergne, TN 37086-1986 (SAN 169-7978) Tel 615-793-5000; Toll free: 800-937-8000; Dist. by: Brodart Co., 500 Arch St., Williamsport, PA 17705 (SAN 169-7684) Tel 717-326-2461; Toll free: 800-233-8467.

Good Idea Kids, *(Good Idea Kids; 0-9621908),* 407 Wekva Springs Rd., No. 213, Longwood, FL 32779 Tel 407-682-2287.

Good Morn Tchr, *(Good Morning Teacher! Publishing Co.; 0-8449),* 819 Mitten Rd., No. 37, Burlingame, CA 94010-1310 (SAN 220-018X).

Good News Min, *(Good News Ministries; 0-9629559),* R.R. 28, Box 95D, Macon, GA 31210-9516; Dist. by: Whitaker Hse., 580 Pittsburgh St., Springdale, PA 15144 (SAN 203-2104) Tel 412-274-4440; Toll free: 800-444-4484.

Good Works Pr, *(Good Works Pr.; 0-9634472),* 4121 Whitfield Ave., Fort Worth, TX 76109 Tel 817-927-8808.

Goodale Pub, *(Goodale Publishing; 0-9609662),* 1903 Kenwood Pkwy., Minneapolis, MN 55405 (SAN 262-0294) Tel 612-377-5783.

Goodfellow, *(Goodfellow Catalog Pr., Inc.; 0-936016),* P.O. Box 4520, Berkeley, CA 94704 (SAN 206-4499) Tel 510-845-2062.

Goodheart, *(Goodheart-Willcox Co.; 0-87006; 1-56637),* 123 W. Taft Dr., South Holland, IL 60473-2089 (SAN 203-4387) Tel 708-333-7200; Toll free: 800-323-0440.

Goodreeder Pubns, *(Goodreeder Pubns., Inc.; 1-885945),* P.O. Box 53819, Cincinnati, OH 45253; 6049 Ranlyn, Cincinnati, OH 45239 Tel 513-741-2722.

Goodwood Pr, *(Goodwood Pr.; 0-9625427; 0-9632778),* P.O. Box 942, Woodbury, CT 06798; 33 Washington Ave., Woodbury, CT 06798 Tel 203-263-5447.

Goose Pond, *(Goose Pond Publishing, Inc.; 0-9638079),* P.O. Box 14602, Tallahassee, FL 32317; 2833 Remington Green Cir., Tallahassee, FL 32308 Tel 904-385-6659.

Gopher, *(Gopher Graphics; 0-936511),* RD 2, Box 323, Greene, NY 13778 (SAN 697-8649) Tel 607-656-4531.

Gordon & Breach, *(Gordon & Breach Science Pubs., Inc.; 0-677; 2-88124; 2-88449),* P.O. Box 200029, Riverfront Plaza Sta., Newark, NJ 07102-0301 (SAN 201-6370) Tel 201-643-7500; 820 Town Center Dr., Langhorne, PA 19047 Tel 215-750-2642.

Gordon Pr, *(Gordon Pr. Pubs.; 0-87968; 0-8490),* P.O. Box 459, Bowling Green Sta., New York, NY 10004 (SAN 201-6362) Tel 718-624-8419.

Gorilla Prodns, *(Gorilla Productions; 0-9642721),* 44 Bayberry Ln., East Greenwich, RI 02818 Tel 401-884-2617.

Gospel Missionary, *(Gospel Missionary Union;* 0-9617490), 10000 N. Oak, Kansas City, MO 64155 (SAN 664-1830) Tel 816-734-8500.

Gospel Pub, *(Gospel Publishing Hse.; 0-88243),* Div. of General Council of the Assemblies of God, 1445 Boonville Ave., Springfield, MO 65802 (SAN 206-8826) Tel 417-831-8000; Toll free: 800-641-4310.

GP Pubns, *(GP Pubns., Inc.; 0-929307),* P.O. Box 29364, Greensboro, NC 27429 (SAN 248-8698); 300A S. Westgate Dr., Greensboro, NC 27407 (SAN 248-8701) Tel 910-852-6711.

Gr Arts Ctr Pub, *(Graphic Arts Ctr. Publishing Co.; 0-912856; 0-932575; 1-55868),* P.O. Box 10306, Portland, OR 97210 (SAN 201-6338) Tel 503-226-2402; Toll free: 800-452-3032.

Grace Dangberg, *(Dangberg, Grace, Foundation, Inc.;* 0-913205), P.O. Box 1627, Carson City, NV 89702-1627 (SAN 283-0493) Tel 702-882-4466.

Grace Publns, *(Grace Pubns., Inc.; 0-89814),* P.O. Box 9432, Grand Rapids, MI 49509; 2125 Martindale SW, Grand Rapids, MI 49509 (SAN 220-5947) Tel 616-247-1999.

Graham Bks, *(Graham Bks.; 0-9619521),* 1400 Niagara, Claremont, CA 91711 (SAN 244-9285) Tel 909-621-2621.

Grammatical Sci, *(Grammatical Sciences),* 1236 Jackson St., Santa Clara, CA 95050 (SAN 203-4433).

Grand Hotel, *(Grand Hotel; 0-9627301),* Grand Hotel, Mackinac Island, MI 49757 Tel 906-847-3331.

Grand Teton NHA, *(Grand Teton Natural History Assn.; 0-931895),* P.O. Box 170, Moose, WY 83012 (SAN 686-0303) Tel 307-733-2880.

Grandin Bk Co, *(Grandin Bk. Co.; 0-910523),* P.O. Box 2125, Orem, UT 84059 (SAN 260-1931) Tel 801-225-2020; Toll free: 800-292-2003.

Grandmother Erth, *(Grandmother Earth Creations;* 1-884289), 8463 Deerfield Ln., Germantown, TN 38138 Tel 901-757-0506.

Grandview, *(Grandview Publishing Co.; 1-880114),* Box 2863, Jackson, WY 83001-2863; Toll free: 800-525-7344; 1170 Grand View Dr., Jackson, WY 83001 Tel 307-733-4593.

Granite Hills Pr, *(Granite Hills Pr.; 0-9638886),* 2175 Euclid Ave., El Cajon, CA 92019-2664 (SAN 298-072X) Tel 619-440-6832; Dist. by: Bookpeople, 7900 Edgewater Dr., Oakland, CA 94621 (SAN 168-9517) Tel 510-632-4700; Toll free: 800-999-4650; Dist. by: Ingram Bk. Co., 1 Ingram Blvd., La Vergne, TN 37086-1986 (SAN 169-7978) Tel 615-793-5000; Toll free: 800-937-8000 (orders only, all warehouses); Dist. by: Baker & Taylor Bks., Somerville Service Ctr., 50 Kirby Ave., Somerville, NJ 08876-0734 (SAN 169-4901) Tel 908-722-8000; Toll free: 800-775-1500 (customer service); Dist. by: Baker & Taylor Bks., Momence Service Ctr., 501 S. Gladiolus St., Momence, IL 60954-2444 (SAN 169-2100) Tel 815-472-2444; Toll free: 800-775-2300 (customer service); Dist. by: Baker & Taylor Bks., Commerce Service Ctr., 251 Mt. Olive Church Rd., Commerce, GA 30599-9988 (SAN 169-1503) Tel 706-335-5000; Toll free: 800-775-1200 (customer service); Dist. by: Baker & Taylor Bks., Reno Service Ctr., 380 Edison Way, Reno, NV 89564 (SAN 169-4464) Tel 702-858-6700; Toll free: 800-775-1700 (customer service).

Graphic Learning, *(Graphic Learning; 0-943068;* 0-87746), Div. of Abrams & Co. Pubs., Inc., 61 Mattatuck Heights, Waterbury, CT 06705 (SAN 240-3803) Tel 203-756-6562; Toll free: 800-874-0029.

Graphitti Designs, *(Graphitti Designs; 0-936211),* 1140 N. Kraemer Blvd., Unit B, Anaheim, CA 92806-1919 (SAN 697-1105) Tel 714-632-3356.

Gratitude Pub, *(Gratitude Publishing & Printing;* 1-883583), 302 N. Van Buren St., Auburn, IN 46706 Tel 219-925-0031.

Gray & Co Pubs, *(Gray & Co., Pubs.; 0-9631738),* 11000 Cedar Ave., Cleveland, OH 44106 Tel 216-721-2665.

Grayson Bernard Pubs, *(Grayson Bernard Pubs.; 0-9628556; 1-883790),* P.O. Box 5247, Bloomington, IN 47407 Tel 812-331-8182; Toll free: 800-925-7853; Orders to: P.O. Box 5247, Bloomington, IN 47407; Toll free: 800-925-7853; Dist. by: Baker & Taylor Bks., Somerville Service Ctr., 50 Kirby Ave., Somerville, NJ 08876-0734 (SAN 169-4901) Tel 908-722-8000; Toll free: 800-775-1500 (customer service); Dist. by: Baker & Taylor Bks., Momence Service Ctr., 501 S. Gladiolus St., Momence, IL 60954-2444 (SAN 169-2100) Tel 815-472-2444; Toll free: 800-775-2300 (customer service); Dist. by: Baker & Taylor Bks., Commerce Service Ctr., 251 Mt. Olive Church Rd., Commerce, GA 30599-9988 (SAN 169-1503) Tel 706-335-5000; Toll free: 800-775-1200 (customer service); Dist. by: Baker & Taylor Bks., Reno Service Ctr., 380 Edison Way, Reno, NV 89564 (SAN 169-4464) Tel 702-858-6700; Toll free: 800-775-1700 (customer service); Dist. by: Quality Bks., Inc., 918 Sherwood Dr., Lake Bluff, IL 60044-2204 (SAN 169-2127) Tel 708-295-2010; Toll free: 800-323-4241 (libraries only); Dist. by: Unique Bks., Inc., 4230 Grove Ave., Gurnee, IL 60031 (SAN 630-0472) Tel 708-623-9171; Dist. by: Bookpeople, 7900 Edgewater Dr., Oakland, CA 94621 (SAN 168-9517) Tel 510-632-4700; Toll free: 800-999-4650; Dist. by: The Distributors, 702 S. Michigan, South Bend, IN 46601 (SAN 169-2488) Tel 219-232-8500; Toll free: 800-348-5200 (except Indiana).

Great Activities Pub Co, *(Great Activities Publishing Co.; 0-945872),* 2838 Stuart Dr., Durham, NC 27707 (SAN 248-0018) Tel 919-489-5990.

Great Eagle Pub, *(Great Eagle Publishing, Inc.;* 0-9629539), 3020 Issaquah-Pine Lake Rd. SE, Suite 481, Issaquah, WA 98027-7255 Tel 206-392-9136.

Great Northwest, *(Great Northwest Publishing & Distributing Co., Inc.; 0-937708),* P.O. Box 212383, Anchorage, AK 99521-2383 (SAN 219-9890).

Great Ocean, *(Great Ocean Pubs.; 0-915556),* 1823 N. Lincoln St., Arlington, VA 22207 (SAN 207-527X) Tel 703-525-0909.

Great Outdoors, *(Great Outdoors Publishing Co.;* 0-8200), 4747 28th St., N., Saint Petersburg, FL 33714 (SAN 201-6273) Tel 813-525-6609; Toll free: 800-869-6609.

Great Tradtn
See Atrium Pubs

Greater Portland, *(Greater Portland Landmarks, Inc.; 0-9600612; 0-939761),* 165 State St., Portland, ME 04101 (SAN 203-4484) Tel 207-774-5561.

Greater Testing, *(Greater Testing Concepts; 1-885875),* P.O. Box A-D, Stanford, CA 94309; 1885 California St., Apt. 8, Mountain View, CA 94041 Tel 415-964-1124.

Green & White Pub, *(Green & White Publishing Co.;* 0-9624777), P.O. Box 778, Sturgis, MI 49094-0778 Tel 517-783-4923.

Green Bough Pr, *(Green Bough Pr.; 0-9615007),* 3156 W. Laurelhurst Dr., NE, Seattle, WA 98105 (SAN 693-9333) Tel 206-523-0022.

Green Hill, *(Green Hill Pubs.; 0-916054; 0-89803;* 0-915463), 722 Columbus St., Ottawa, IL 61350 (SAN 281-7578) Tel 815-434-7905; Toll free: 800-426-1357; Dist. by: National Bk. Network, 4720A Boston Way, Lanham, MD 20706-4310 (SAN 630-0065) Tel 301-459-8696; Toll free: 800-462-6420.

Green Leaf CA, *(Green Leaf Pr.; 0-938462),* P.O. Box 880, Alhambra, CA 91802-0880 (SAN 239-3646) Tel 818-281-7221; 20 W. Commonwealth Ave., Alhambra, CA 91801 (SAN 239-3654).

Green Oak Pr, *(Green Oak Pr.; 0-931600),* 9339 Spicer Rd., Brighton, MI 48116 (SAN 211-9544) Tel 313-449-4802.

Green Psturs Pr, *(Green Pastures Pr.; 0-9627643;* 1-884377), 7102 Lynn Rd., NE, Minerva, OH 44657 (SAN 298-0770) Tel 216-895-3291.

Green Tiger *Imprint of* **S&S Trade**

Green Timber, *(Green Timber Pubns.; 0-944443),* Div. of Tirik Productions, P.O. Box 3884, Portland, ME 04104 (SAN 243-5543); 24 Allen Ave. Extension, Falmouth, ME 04105 (SAN 243-5551) Tel 207-797-4180.

Greenbeck, *(Greenbeck; 0-9613079),* 31 Cypress Tree Ln., Irvine, CA 92715-2211 (SAN 294-8133) Tel 909-988-9513.

Greenberg Bks, *(Greenberg Bks.; 0-89778),* Div. of Kalmbach Publishing Co., 21027 Crossroads Cir., P.O. Box 1612, Waukesha, WI 53187 (SAN 211-9552) Tel 414-796-8776; Toll free: 800-533-6644 (consumer sales).

Greenberg Pub Co
See Greenberg Bks

Greencrest, *(Greencrest Pr., Inc.; 0-939800),* P.O. Box 7745, Winston-Salem, NC 27109 (SAN 216-8979) Tel 910-722-6463.

Greene Bark Pr, *(Greene Bark Pr., Inc.; 1-880851),* P.O. Box 1108, Bridgeport, CT 06601-1108; 81 Leffert Rd., Trumbull, CT 06611 Tel 203-372-4861; Dist. by: Baker & Taylor Bks., Reno Service Ctr., 380 Edison Way, Reno, NV 89564 (SAN 169-4464) Tel 702-858-6700; Toll free: 800-775-1700 (customer service); Dist. by: Brodart Co., 500 Arch St., Williamsport, PA 17705 (SAN 169-7684) Tel 717-326-2461; Toll free: 800-233-8467; Dist. by: Ingram Bk. Co., 1 Ingram Blvd., La Vergne, TN 37086-1986 (SAN 169-7978) Tel 615-793-5000; Toll free: 800-937-8000 (orders only, all warehouses); Dist. by: Baker & Taylor Bks., Somerville Service Ctr., 50 Kirby Ave., Somerville, NJ 08876-0734 (SAN 169-4901) Tel 908-722-8000; Toll free: 800-775-1500 (customer service); Dist. by: Baker & Taylor Bks., Momence Service Ctr., 501 S. Gladiolus St., Momence, IL 60954-2444 (SAN 169-2100) Tel 815-472-2444; Toll free: 800-775-2300 (customer service); Dist. by: Baker & Taylor Bks., Commerce Service Ctr., 251 Mt. Olive Church Rd., Commerce, GA 30599-9988 (SAN 169-1503) Tel 706-335-5000; Toll free: 800-775-1200 (customer service).

Greenhaven, *(Greenhaven Pr., Inc.; 0-912616; 0-89908; 1-56510),* P.O. Box 289009, San Diego, CA 92198-9009 (SAN 201-6214); Toll free: 800-231-5163; 10911 Technology Pl., San Diego, CA 92198-9009 Tel 619-485-7424.

Greenhouse Pub, *(Greenhouse Publishing Co.; 0-9616844),* P.O. Box 525, Marshall, VA 22115 (SAN 661-1729) Tel 703-364-1959.

Greenleaf AL, *(Greenleaf Pubns.; 1-883729),* P.O. Box 70563, Tuscaloosa, AL 35407-0563; 117 Sagamore Cir., Columbus, MS 39701 Tel 601-327-7329. Do not confuse with Greenleaf Pubns. in Pasadena, CA.

Greenleaf Pr
See Greenleaf TN

Greenleaf TN, *(Greenleaf Pr.; 1-882514),* 1570 Old LaGuardo Rd., Lebanon, TN 37087 (SAN 297-8555) Tel 615-449-1617. Do not confuse with Greenleaf Pr. in Denver, CO.

Greenlf Pubns, *(Greenleaf Pubns.; 0-9608812),* P.O. Box 50357, Pasadena, CA 91105 (SAN 238-2938). Do not confuse with Greenleaf Pubns. in Tuscaloosa, AL.

Greenpl Bks, *(Greenplace Bks.; 0-932881),* 3015 Woodsdale, Lincoln, NE 68502 (SAN 689-0024) Tel 402-421-3172.

Greenw Pr Ltd, *(Greenwich Pr., Ltd.; 0-86713),* 30 Lindeman Dr., Trumbull, CT 06611 (SAN 216-8170) Tel 203-371-6568; Toll free: 800-243-4246.

Greenway Pub, *(Greenway Publishing; 0-9632038),* P.O. Box 148, Roseland, VA 22967; State Rte. 151, Roseland, VA 22967 Tel 804-277-9349.

Greenwillow, *(Greenwillow Bks.; 0-688),* Div. of William Morrow & Co., Inc., 1350 Avenue of the Americas, New York, NY 10019 (SAN 202-5760); Orders to: William Morrow & Co., Inc., 39 Plymouth St., P.O. Box 1219, Fairfield, NJ 07007 (SAN 202-5779); Toll free: 800-843-9389.

Grey Castle, *(Grey Castle Pr.; 0-942545; 1-55905),* Pocket Knife Sq., Lakeville, CT 06039 (SAN 667-383X) Tel 203-435-2518.

Grey Pilgrim, *(Grey Pilgrim Pubns.; 1-883405),* P.O. Box 356, Lookout Mountain, TN 37350; 408 Krupski Loop, Lookout Mountain, GA 30750 Tel 706-820-0491.

Grin A Bit, *(Grin-A-Bit Co., Inc.; 0-9620112; 1-882687),* P.O. Box 235, Rockwall, TX 75087 (SAN 247-7289); 230 Windy Ln., Rockwall, TX 75087 Tel 214-722-0424; Dist. by: Taylor Publishing Co., 1550 W. Mockingbird Ln., Dallas, TX 75235 (SAN 202-7631); Toll free: 800-759-8120 (orders).

GRMI Hist Comm, *(Grand Rapids Historical Commission; 0-9617708),* Public Library, 60 Library Plaza, NE, Grand Rapids, MI 49503 (SAN 664-9211) Tel 616-456-3629.

Grnd Rpds Intertribal, *(Grand Rapids Intertribal Council; 0-9617707),* 45 Lexington, NW, Grand Rapids, MI 49504 (SAN 664-919X) Tel 616-774-8331.

Grnleaf Pubs, *(Greenleaf Pubs.; 0-929634),* Depot St., Schenevus, NY 12155 (SAN 249-759X) Tel 607-638-5400.

Grnwillow End, *(Greenwillow End Pr.; 0-9613400),* 12737 20th Ave. NE., Seattle, WA 98125 (SAN 656-9870) Tel 206-365-3348.

Grolier Inc, *(Grolier, Inc.; 0-7172),* Sherman Tpke., Danbury, CT 06801 (SAN 205-3195) Tel 203-797-3500.

Grosvenor USA, *(Grosvenor U.S.A.; 0-901269; 1-85239),* Affil. of Grosvenor Bks., London, UK, 3735 Cherry Ave., NE, Salem, OR 97303 (SAN 663-1606) Tel 503-393-2172.

Group M Probelications, *(Group M Probelications; 0-9623400),* P.O. Box 49031, No. 162, Los Angeles, CA 90049 (SAN 248-949X) Tel 310-476-5331.

Group Pub, *(Group Publishing, Inc.; 0-936664; 0-931529; 1-55945),* P.O. Box 481, Loveland, CO 80539 (SAN 214-4689); Toll free: 800-541-5200 (orders only); 2890 N. Monroe Ave., Loveland, CO 80538 (SAN 662-1376) Tel 303-669-3836.

Grove-Atltic, *(Grove/Atlantic, Inc.; 0-8021; 1-55584; 0-87113),* 841 Broadway, 4th Flr., New York, NY 10003-4793 (SAN 201-4890) Tel 212-614-7924; Toll free: 800-521-0178; Orders to: Publishers Group West, P.O. Box 8843, Emeryville, CA 94662 Tel 510-658-3453; Toll free: 800-788-3123.

Grove Educ Tech, *(Grove Educational Technologies; 0-936735),* P.O. Box 405, Lake Grove, NY 11755 (SAN 699-9840); 27 Hy Pl., Lake Grove, NY 11755 (SAN 699-9859) Tel 516-588-5948.

Grow Up Hlthy, *(Growing Up Healthy Pubns.; 0-9629036),* 1840 Oak Ave., Northwestern Univ. Research Pk., Evanston, IL 60201 Tel 708-864-0800.

Growth Unltd, *(Growth Unlimited, Inc.; 0-9601334; 0-916927),* 36 Fairview, Battle Creek, MI 49017 (SAN 210-8976) Tel 616-965-2229; Toll free: 800-441-7676.

Grt Ideas Tching, *(Great Ideas For Teaching, Inc.; 1-886143),* P.O. Box 444, Wrightsville Beach, NC 28480-0444; 6800 Wrightsville Ave., No. 16, Wilmington, NC 28403 Tel 910-256-4494.

Gryphon Hse, *(Gryphon Hse., Inc.; 0-87659),* P.O. Box 207, Beltsville, MD 20704-0207 (SAN 169-3190) Tel 301-595-9500; Toll free: 800-638-0928.

GSI Pubns, *(GSI Pubns.; 0-9627701),* Div. of Gordon Systems, Inc., P.O. Box 746, DeWitt, NY 13214; 301 Ambergate Rd., DeWitt, NY 13214 Tel 315-446-4849.

Guavaberry Bks, *(Guavaberry Bks.; 0-9625560),* 1123 Gainsboro Rd., Bala Cynwyd, PA 19004-2012.

Guild Bks, *(Guild Bks., Catholic Polls, Inc.; 0-912080),* 86 Riverside Dr., New York, NY 10024 (SAN 203-4646) Tel 212-799-2600.

Guild Pr, *(Guild Pr.; 0-940248),* P.O. Box 22583, Robbinsdale, MN 55422 (SAN 220-3340) Tel 612-566-1842. Do not confuse with companies with the same name in Los Angeles, CA, New York, NY.

Guild Pr IN, *(Guild Pr. of Indiana, Inc.; 0-9617367; 1-878208),* 6000 Sunset Ln., Indianapolis, IN 46208 (SAN 663-7965) Tel 317-253-0097.

Guild Psy, *(Guild for Psychological Studies Publishing Hse.; 0-917479),* 2230 Divisadero St., San Francisco, CA 94115 (SAN 656-0687) Tel 415-931-0668.

Gulf Pub, *(Gulf Publishing Co.; 0-87201; 0-932012; 0-87719; 0-88415),* P.O. Box 2608, Houston, TX 77252-2608 (SAN 201-6125) Tel 713-520-4444; Toll free: 800-231-6275 (except Alaska & Hawaii); 800-392-4390 (in Texas). *Imprints:* Lone Star Bks (Lone Star Books).

Gull Crest, *(Gull Crest Publishing; 0-9637267),* P.O. Box 125, Boothbay Harbor, ME 04538 Tel 207-633-6876.

Gulliver Trvl *Imprint of* **HarBrace**

Gumbs & Thomas, *(Gumbs & Thomas Pubs., Inc.; 0-936073),* 216 W. 22nd St., Lower Level, New York, NY 10011 (SAN 697-0877) Tel 212-255-1506.

Gurze Bks, *(Gurze Bks.; 0-936077),* P.O. Box 2238, Carlsbad, CA 92008 (SAN 697-0818); Toll free: 800-756-7533; 3420 Woodland Way, Carlsbad, CA 92018 (SAN 697-0826) Tel 619-434-7533; Dist. by: Publishers Group West, 4065 Hollis St., Emeryville, CA 94608 (SAN 202-8522) Tel 510-658-3453; Toll free: 800-788-3123; Dist. by: Quality Bks., Inc., 918 Sherwood Dr., Lake Bluff, IL 60044-2204 (SAN 169-2127) Tel 708-295-2010; Toll free: 800-323-4241 (libraries only).

Guttenburg Pub, *(Guttenburg Publishing Co., The; 0-9635840),* Box 1939, Cathedral Sta., New York, NY 10025 Tel 212-228-6040.

Guyasuta Pubs
See Sterling Hse

Guzzy Pr, *(Guzzy Pr.; 0-9620999),* 1725 Underwood Ave., Wauwatosa, WI 53213 (SAN 250-4766) Tel 414-774-6278.

Gylantic Pub, *(Gylantic Publishing Co.; 1-880197),* P.O. Box 2792, Littleton, CO 80161-2792; 6024 S. Pearl St., Littleton, CO 80121 Tel 303-797-6093.

Gypsy Damaris, *(Gypsy Damaris Boston; 0-9631503),* P.O. Box 8417, Shreveport, LA 71148-8417; 5406 Fairfax, Shreveport, LA 71108 Tel 318-636-5236; Dist. by: Everett Cos., Publishing Div., 813 Whittington, Bossier City, LA 71171-5376 (SAN 243-7112) Tel 318-742-6240; Toll free: 800-423-7033.

H & H Pub, *(H & H Publishing Co., Inc.; 0-943202),* 1231 Kapp Dr., Clearwater, FL 34625-2116 (SAN 240-5350) Tel 813-442-7760; Toll free: 800-366-4079. Do not confuse with H&H Publishing Co. in Amarillo, TX.

H Carwell, *(Carwell, Hattie; 0-9621372),* 4622 Meldon Ave., Oakland, CA 94619 (SAN 251-1762) Tel 510-536-9084.

H Christiansen, *(Christiansen, Helen; 0-9621419),* 46881 State Hwy. 116, Walsh, CO 81090 (SAN 251-3110) Tel 719-498-4231.

H H Kapelman, *(Kapelman, Helen H.; 0-9621807),* 575 Bronx River Rd., Apt 6H, Yonkers, NY 10704 Tel 914-237-3599.

H Holt & Co, *(Holt, Henry, & Co., Inc.; 0-8050),* 115 W. 18th St., New York, NY 10011 (SAN 200-6472) Tel 212-886-9200; Toll free: 800-488-5233. *Imprints:* B Martin BYR (Bill Martin Books for Young Readers); Bks Young Read (Books for Young Readers); Owl (Owl Paperback Books); Owlet BYR (Owlet Paperbacks for Young Readers); Redfeather BYR (Redfeather Books for Young Readers).

H J Kramer Inc, *(Kramer, H. J., Inc.; 0-915811),* P.O. Box 1082, Tiburon, CA 94920 (SAN 294-0833) Tel 415-435-5367; Dist. by: New Leaf Distributing Co., 5425 Tulane Dr., SW, Atlanta, GA 30336-2323 (SAN 169-1449) Tel 404-691-6996; Toll free: 800-326-2665; Dist. by: Publishers Group West, 4065 Hollis St., Emeryville, CA 94608 (SAN 202-8522) Tel 510-658-3453; Toll free: 800-788-3123; Dist. by: Bookpeople, 7900 Edgewater Dr., Oakland, CA 94621 (SAN 168-9517) Tel 510-632-4700; Toll free: 800-999-4650; Dist. by: Inland Bk. Co., 140 Commerce St., East Haven, CT 06512 (SAN 200-4151) Tel 203-467-4257; Toll free: 800-243-0138.

H L Crist, *(Crist, Harold L.; 0-9621743),* P.O. Box 7, Arbovale, WV 24915 (SAN 252-144X) Tel 304-456-4399.

H L Levin, *(Levin, Hugh Lauter, Assocs.; 0-88363),* 2507 Post Rd., Southport, CT 06490 (SAN 201-6109) Tel 203-254-7733; Dist. by: Simon & Schuster, Inc., 1230 Ave. of the Americas, New York, NY 10020 (SAN 200-2450) Tel 212-698-7000; Toll free: 800-223-2348; 800-223-2336 (orders only).

H L Norskog, *(Norskog, Howard L.; 0-9625171),* P.O. Box 55, Saint Anthony, ID 83445; 348 W. Main, Saint Anthony, ID 83445 Tel 208-624-7622.

H Leonard, *(Leonard, Hal, Corp.; 0-9607350; 0-88188; 0-7935),* 7777 W. Bluemound Rd., P.O. Box 13819, Milwaukee, WI 53213 (SAN 239-250X) Tel 414-774-3630; Toll free: 800-524-4425; Dist. by: Ingram Bk. Co., 1 Ingram Blvd., La Vergne, TN 37086-1986 (SAN 169-7978) Tel 615-793-5000; Toll free: 800-937-8000 (orders only, all warehouses); Dist. by: Baker & Taylor Bks., Somerville Service Ctr., 50 Kirby Ave., Somerville, NJ 08876-0734 (SAN 169-4901) Tel 908-722-8000; Toll free: 800-775-1500 (customer service); Dist. by: Baker & Taylor Bks., Momence Service Ctr., 501 S. Gladiolus St., Momence, IL 60954-2444 (SAN 169-2100) Tel 815-472-2444; Toll free: 800-775-2300 (customer service); Dist. by: Baker & Taylor Bks., Commerce Service Ctr., 251 Mt. Olive Church Rd., Commerce, GA 30599-9988 (SAN 169-1503) Tel 706-335-5000; Toll free: 800-775-1200 (customer service); Dist. by: Baker & Taylor Bks., Reno Service Ctr., 380 Edison Way, Reno, NV 89564 (SAN 169-4464) Tel 702-858-6700; Toll free: 800-775-1700 (customer service).

H Leonard Pub Corp
See H Leonard

H Peterson Pr, *(Holt Peterson Pr., Inc.; 1-881811),* P.O. Box 940, Birmingham, MI 48012; 22010 Village Pines Dr., Beverly Hills, MI 48025 Tel 810-540-8138.

H S Monesson, *(Monesson, Harry S.; 0-9633735),* 315 Magnolia Rd., Pemberton, NJ 08068 Tel 609-894-9362.

H S Strehlow, *(Strehlow, Helen S.; 0-9641418),* 2329 N. 103rd St., Wauwatosa, WI 53226 Tel 414-257-2546.

H T Taylor, *(Taylor, Henry T.; 0-938956),* 504 Cafen Blvd., Amhurst, NY 14226 (SAN 264-5149) Tel 716-833-2964.

H To H Pubs, *(Heart To Heart Pubs.; 0-9643422),* 802 Kate St., Copperas Cove, TX 76522 Tel 817-547-6556.

Habersham, *(Habersham; 0-944784),* 635 Gravio St., Suite 1020, New Orleans, LA 70130 (SAN 245-4939) Tel 504-525-6390.

Hachai Pubns, *(Hachai Pubns., Inc.; 0-922613),* 156 Chester Ave., Brooklyn, NY 11218 (SAN 251-3749) Tel 718-633-0100.

Hairston & Hicks, *(Hairston & Hicks Pubs.; 0-944890),* 5632 Daytona Rd., Roanoke, VA 24019 (SAN 245-4246).

Haker Books, *(Haker Bks.; 0-9609964),* 2707 First Ave., N, Great Falls, MT 59401 (SAN 262-0359) Tel 406-454-1487.

Halbur, *(Halbur Publishing; 0-9603520),* 142 Angela Dr., Santa Rosa, CA 95403-1702 (SAN 212-9469).

Half Halt Pr, *(Half Halt Pr.; 0-939481),* 6416 Burkittsville Rd., Middletown, MD 21769 (SAN 663-270X) Tel 301-371-9110.

Half Moon Bks *Imprint of* **S&S Trade**

Hall, *(Hall, G. K., & Co.; 0-8161; 0-7838),* P.O. Box 159, Thorndike, ME 04921; Toll free: 800-223-6121. Do not confuse with G. K. Hall, New York, NY (Library & general reference books.). *Imprints:* Large Print Bks (Large Print Books); Lythway Large Print (Lythway Large Print).

Hall Pr, *(Hall Pr.; 0-932218),* P.O. Box 5375, San Bernardino, CA 92412 (SAN 211-7061); 17227 Hall Ranch Rd., San Bernardino, CA 92407 (SAN 665-7060) Tel 909-887-3466.

Halldin Pub, *(Halldin, A. G., Publishing Co.; 0-935648),* P.O. Box 667, Indiana, PA 15701 (SAN 208-208X) Tel 412-463-8450; Toll free: 800-227-0667.

Hallelujah Pr, *(Hallelujah Pr. Publishing Co.; 0-9621235),* P.O. Box 496, Gilbert, AZ 85234-0496 (SAN 250-8389); 137 E. Elliott Rd., Gilbert, AZ 85234 (SAN 250-8397) Tel 602-821-2287.

Halls of Ivy, *(Halls of Ivy Pr.; 0-912256),* 3445 Leora Ave., Simi Valley, CA 93063 (SAN 204-0204) Tel 805-527-0525.

Hambleton-Hill, *(Hambleton-Hill Publishing, Inc.; 1-57102),* 1501 County Hospital Rd., Nashville, TN 37218 (SAN 298-1386) Tel 615-254-2480; Toll free: 800-336-6438; Dist. by: Associated Pubs. Group, 1501 County Hospital Rd., Nashville, TN 37218 (SAN 630-818X) Tel 615-254-2450; Toll free: 800-327-5113. *Imprints:* Ideals Child (Ideals Children's Books).

Hamiltons, *(Hamilton's; 0-9608598; 1-883912),* P.O. Box 932, Bedford, VA 24523 (SAN 264-0759); 155 W. Main St., Bedford, VA 24523 Tel 703-586-5592.

Hammond Dalby Music, *(Hammond Dalby Music; 0-9624262),* 120 Ridge Rd., Nashua, NH 03062 Tel 603-886-1088; Dist. by: Musicart West, P.O. Box 1900, Orem, UT 84059-1900 (SAN 110-1250) Tel 801-225-0851; Toll free: 800-950-1900; Dist. by: Sounds of Zion, 5180 S. 300, W., Unit U, Murray, UT 84107 (SAN 200-7525) Tel 801-225-1991.

Hammond Inc, *(Hammond, Inc.; 0-8437),* 515 Valley St., Maplewood, NJ 07040 (SAN 202-2702) Tel 201-763-6000; Toll free: 800-526-4953.

Hampshire Pr, *(Hampshire Pr.),* 900 Main St., Wilmington, MA 01887 (SAN 296-127X).

Hampton-Brown, *(Hampton-Brown Co.; 0-917837; 1-56334),* 26385 Carmel Rancho Blvd., Suite 200, Carmel, CA 93923 (SAN 657-145X) Tel 408-625-3666; Toll free: 800-933-3510; Orders to: P.O. Box 223220, Carmel, CA 93922; Toll free: 800-333-3510.

Hampton Court Pub, *(Hampton Court Pubs.; 0-910569),* Wixon Pond Rd., Mahopac, NY 10541 (SAN 264-0767) Tel 914-628-6155; Orders to: P.O. Box 655, Mahopac, NY 10541 (SAN 662-0302).

Hampton Mae, *(Hampton Mae Institute; 0-9616511),* 4104 Lynn Ave., Tampa, FL 33603 (SAN 659-4611) Tel 813-238-2221.

Hancock House, *(Hancock Hse. Pubs., Ltd.; 0-88839),* 1431 Harrison Ave., P.O. Box 959, Blaine, WA 98231-0959 (SAN 665-7079).

Hand Made Bks, *(Hand Made Bks.; 0-9642606),* 1053 Alford Ave., Hoover, AL 35226 Tel 205-822-6811; Dist. by: Southern Pubs. Group, 147 Corporate Way, Pelham, AL 35124 (SAN 630-7817) Tel 205-664-6980; Toll free: 800-755-4411.

H&M Ent, *(H&M Enterprises; 0-9613184),* R.D. 6, Box 6009, East Stroudsburg, PA 18301-9108 (SAN 295-9569) Tel 717-223-0674. Do not confuse with H&M Enterprises in Alton, IL.

Hands on Pubns, *(Hands on Pubns.; 0-931178),* 451 Silvera Ave., Long Beach, CA 90803 (SAN 213-9286) Tel 310-596-4738.

Hang Gliding, *(Hang Gliding Pr.; 0-938282),* Box 22552, San Diego, CA 92122 (SAN 215-6520) Tel 619-452-1768.

Hannibal Bks, *(Hannibal Bks.; 0-929292),* 921 Center, Suite A, Hannibal, MO 63401 (SAN 249-0560) Tel 314-221-2462.

Hansen Ed Mus, *(Hansen, Charles, Educational Music & Bks., Inc.; 0-8494),* 1820 West Ave., Miami Beach, FL 33139 (SAN 205-0609) Tel 305-532-5461; Dist. by: Hansen Hse., 1824 West Ave., Miami Beach, FL 33139 (SAN 200-7908) Tel 305-532-5461; Toll free: 800-327-8202.

Happibook Pr, *(Happibook Pr.; 0-937395),* P.O. Box 218, Montgomery, NY 12549-0218 (SAN 658-9561); E. Kaisertown Rd., Montgomery, NY 12549 (SAN 658-957X) Tel 914-457-9328.

Happy Kids Prods, *(Happy Kids Productions, Inc.; 1-881567),* 184 Katonah Ave., Katonah, NY 10536 Tel 914-232-6433; Toll free: 800-275-4543.

Happy Music Pub, *(Happy Music Publishing; 0-9624162),* 326 E. Pierce St., Tempe, AZ 85281-1041; 326 E. Pierce St., Tempe, AZ 85281 Tel 602-946-4795.

Happy Thoughts & Rainbow, *(Happy Thoughts & Rainbow Co., The; 0-9608686),* Rte. 2, P.O. Box 419, Aurora, MN 55705 (SAN 238-2954) Tel 218-229-3451.

Harbinger AZ, *(Harbinger Hse., Inc.; 0-943173; 1-57140),* P.O. Box 42948, Tucson, AZ 85733-2948 (SAN 668-3029) Tel 602-326-9595; Toll free: 800-759-9945.

Harbor Hse West, *(Harbor Hse. (West) Pubs., Inc.; 1-879560),* 216 E. Victoria St., Santa Barbara, CA 93101 (SAN 297-410X) Tel 805-965-0996; Toll free: 800-423-8811. Do not confuse with companies of the same name in Boyne City, MI, Baltimore, MD.

Harbour Duck, *(Harbour Duck Specialties, Inc.; 0-9632461),* P.O. Box 511, Chester, VA 23831; 3224 Wooddale Rd., Chester, VA 23831 Tel 804-748-4142.

HarBrace, *(Harcourt Brace & Co.; 0-15),* Subs. of Harcourt General Corp., 525 B St., Suite 1900, San Diego, CA 92101 (SAN 200-2736) Tel 619-231-6616; Toll free: 800-346-8648; 800-543-1918; 800-237-2665; 555 Academic Ct., San Antonio, TX 78204 (SAN 200-2833) Tel 210-299-1061; 1627 Woodland Ave., Austin, TX 78741 (SAN 200-2841) Tel 512-440-5700; Trade Dept. Customer Service, 6277 Sea Harbor Dr., Orlando, FL 32887 (SAN 200-285X); P.O. Box 819077, Dallas, TX 75381-9077 (SAN 200-2868) Tel 214-245-1118; 7555 Caldwell Ave., Chicago, IL 60648 (SAN 200-2914) Tel 312-647-8822; 8551 Esters Blvd., Irving, TX 75063 (SAN 200-3406). *Imprints:* Browndeer Pr (Browndeer Press); Gulliver Trvl (Gulliver Travel Guides); Harvest Bks (Harvest Books); HB Juv Bks (HarBrace Juvenile Books); J Yolen Bks (Yolen, Jane, Books); Odyssey (Odyssey Books); Voyager Bks (Voyager Books).

HarBraceJ
See HarBrace

Hard Hatted Women, *(Hard Hatted Women; 0-9627833),* 4209 Lorain Ave., Cleveland, OH 44113-3720 Tel 216-961-4449.

Harian Creative Bks, *(Harian Creative Bks.; 0-911906),* Div. of Harian Creative Assocs., 47 Hyde Blvd., Ballston Spa, NY 12020 (SAN 204-0255) Tel 518-885-7397.

Harimander Pub, *(Harimander Publishing, Inc.; 0-9624783),* 9616 Kirkside Dr., Los Angeles, CA 90035 Tel 310-204-6459.

Harlin Jacque, *(Harlin Jacque Pubns.; 0-940938),* 250 Fulton Ave., Suite 507, Hempstead, NY 11550 (SAN 281-7659) Tel 516-489-8564; Orders to: 71 N. Franklin St., Suite 207, Hempstead, NY 11550 (SAN 281-7667) Tel 516-489-0120.

Harlo Pr, *(Harlo Pr.; 0-8187),* 50 Victor Ave., Detroit, MI 48203 (SAN 202-2745) Tel 313-883-3600.

Harman & Meador, *(Harman & Meador; 0-9630661),* 9007 Thompson Rd., Highlands, TX 77562 Tel 713-426-3950.

Harmony *Imprint of* **Crown Pub Group**

Harmony Hill, *(Harmony Hill Pr.; 0-9633759),* P.O. Box 1671, Bailey, CO 80421-1671; 48 N. Random Rd., Bailey, CO 80421 Tel 303-838-1120.

Harmony Raine, *(Harmony Raine & Co.; 0-89967),* Div. of Buccaneer Bks., Inc., Box 133, Greenport, NY 11944 (SAN 262-0367) Tel 516-734-5724; Dist. by: Buccaneer Bks., P.O. Box 168, Cutchogue, NY 11935 (SAN 209-1542) Tel 516-734-5724.

Harner Pubns, *(Harner Pubns.; 1-877842),* 2520 N. Sunburst Ln., Chino Valley, AZ 86323-4737.

Harp PBks *Imprint of* **HarpC**

HarpC, *(HarperCollins Pubs., Inc.; 0-06; 0-694),* Subs. of News Corp., Ltd., 10 E. 53rd St., New York, NY 10022-5299 (SAN 200-2086) Tel 212-207-7000; Toll free: 800-331-3761; Icehouse One-401, 151 Union St., San Francisco, CA 94111 (SAN 215-3734) Tel 415-477-4400; Orders to: 1000 Keystone Industrial Pk., Scranton, PA 18512-4621 (SAN 215-3742) Tel 717-941-1500; Toll free: 800-242-7737; 800-982-4377 (in Pennsylvania). *Imprints:* Harp PBks (HarperPaperback Books); Harper Ref (Harper Reference); HarpT (Harper Trade Books); Junior Bks (Junior Books); PL (HarperPerennial).

HarpC Child Bks, *(HarperCollins Children's Bks.; 0-06),* Div. of HarperCollins Pubs., Inc., 10 E. 53rd St., New York, NY 10022-5299 (SAN 200-2086) Tel 212-207-7000. *Imprints:* C Zolotow Bks (Zolotow, Charlotte, Books); Festival (Festival); Harper Keypoint (Harper Keypoint); Lipp Jr Bks (Lippincott Children Books); Trophy (Trophy).

HarpC West, *(HarperCollins West; 0-06),* Div. of HarperCollins Pubs., Inc., 1160 Battery St., 3rd Flr., San Francisco, CA 94111-1213 Tel 415-477-4400; Orders to: HarperCollins Pubs., Inc., 1000 Keystone Industrial Pk., Scranton, PA 18512-4621 (SAN 215-3742) Tel 717-941-1500; Toll free: 800-242-7737; 800-982-4377 (in Pennsylvania).

Harper Keypoint *Imprint of* **HarpC Child Bks**

Harper Odyssey *Imprint of* **Harper SF**

Harper Ref *Imprint of* **HarpC**

Harper SF, *(Harper San Francisco; 0-00; 0-06; 0-85924; 0-86683),* Div. of HarperCollins Pubs., Inc., 1160 Battery St., 3rd Flr., San Francisco, CA 94111 (SAN 215-3734) Tel 415-477-4400; Dist. by: HarperCollins Pubs., Inc., 1000 Keystone Industrial Pk., Scranton, PA 18512-4621 (SAN 215-3742) Tel 717-941-1500; Toll free: 800-242-7737; 800-982-4377 (in Pennsylvania). *Imprints:* Harper Odyssey (Harper Odyssey).

HarperAudio, *(HarperAudio; 0-9601156; 0-89845; 1-55994),* Div. of HarperCollins Pubs., Inc., 10 E. 53rd St., New York, NY 10022 (SAN 206-278X) Tel 212-207-7000. *Imprints:* Caedmon (Caedmon).

Harpers Voice
See JCH Pr

HarpJ
See HarpC Child Bks

HarpR
See Harper SF

HarpT *Imprint of* **HarpC**

Harraps *Imprint of* **P-H Gen Ref & Trav**

Harris & Co, *(Harris, H. E., & Co., Inc.; 0-937458),* P.O. Box 817, Florence, AL 35631-0817 (SAN 202-1137); Toll free: 800-543-7318.

Harrison Hse, *(Harrison Hse., Inc.; 0-89274),* P.O. Box 35035, Tulsa, OK 74153 (SAN 208-676X) Tel 918-582-2126; Toll free: 800-888-4126; Dist. by: Bridge Publishing, Inc., 2500 Hamilton Blvd., South Plainfield, NJ 07080 (SAN 239-5061) Tel 908-754-0745; Toll free: 800-631-5802 (orders only).

Hartley Hse, *(Hartley Hse.; 0-937518),* P.O. Box 1352, Hartford, CT 06143 (SAN 220-0570) Tel 203-525-2376.

Hartmore, *(Hartmore Hse.; 0-87677),* Subs. of Media Judaica, Inc., 304 E. 49th St., New York, NY 10017 (SAN 293-2717) Tel 212-319-6666; Orders to: Media Judaica, Inc., 1363 Fairfield Ave., Bridgeport, CT 06605 (SAN 207-0022) Tel 203-384-2284.

Harvard Common Pr, *(Harvard Common Pr.; 0-916782; 1-55832),* 535 Albany St., Boston, MA 02118 (SAN 208-6778) Tel 617-423-5803; Dist. by: National Bk. Network, 4720A Boston Way, Lanham, MD 20706-4310 (SAN 630-0065) Tel 301-459-8696; Toll free: 800-462-6420.

Harvest Bks *Imprint of* **HarBrace**

Harvest Hse, *(Harvest Hse. Pubs., Inc.; 0-89081; 1-56507),* 1075 Arrowsmith, Eugene, OR 97402 (SAN 207-4745) Tel 503-343-0123; Toll free: 800-547-8979.

Harvest IL, *(Harvest Pubns.; 0-935797),* Div. of Baptist General Conference, 2002 S. Arlington Heights Rd., Arlington Heights, IL 60005 (SAN 696-8023) Tel 708-228-0200; Toll free: 800-323-4215. Do not confuse with companies with the same name in Berkeley, CA, Knoxville, TN, Reston, VA, Fort Worth, TX.

Haskett Spec, *(Haskett Specialties; 0-9609724),* 8801 Madison Ave., Apt. 104A, Indianapolis, IN 46227-6422 (SAN 270-6946).

Hastings, *(Hastings Hse. Pubs.; 0-8038),* Div. of Eagle Publishing Corp., 141 Halstead Ave., Mamaroneck, NY 10543 Tel 914-835-4005; Dist. by: Publishers Group West, 4065 Hollis St., Emeryville, CA 94608 (SAN 202-8522) Tel 510-658-3453; Toll free: 800-788-3123.

Hathaway Intl, *(Hathaway International Pubns.; 0-9633357),* P.O. Box 6543, Buena Park, CA 90620; 8283 Locust Dr., Buena Park, CA 90620 Tel 714-772-0109.

Havet Pr, *(Havet Pr.; 0-9622528),* P.O. Box 722, Kirkland, WA 98083; 597 14th Ave., W., Kirkland, WA 98083 Tel 206-822-8654.

Hawaiian Isl Concepts, *(Hawaiian Island Concepts; 1-878498),* P.O. Box 6280, Kahului, HI 96732 (SAN 200-366X); 1826 Wili Pa Loop, Wailuku, HI 96793 Tel 808-572-2606.

Hawaiian Resources, *(Hawaiian Resources Co., Ltd.; 0-9627294),* 94-527 Puahi St., Waipahu, HI 96797 (SAN 200-4984) Tel 808-671-6735; Dist. by: Pacific Trade Group, 94-527 Puahi St., Waipahu, HI 96797 (SAN 169-1635) Tel 808-671-6735.

Hawaiian Serv, *(Hawaiian Service, Inc.; 0-930492),* P.O. Box 2835, Honolulu, HI 96803 (SAN 205-0463) Tel 808-841-0134.

Hawk FL, *(Hawk Publishing; 0-9627946; 1-883213),* P.O. Box 8422, Longboat Key, FL 34228-8422; 6300 S. Tamiami Trail, Sarasota, FL 34228 Tel 813-383-8399.

Hawkes Pub Inc, *(Hawkes Publishing Inc.; 0-89036),* Box 15711, Salt Lake City, UT 84115 (SAN 205-6232) Tel 801-262-5555.

Hawthorne Pr, *(Hawthorne Pr.; 0-9620154),* 1256 Hawthorne Ave., Redding, CA 96002-0362 (SAN 247-753X).

Hawthorne Pubs, *(Hawthorne Pubs.; 0-929842; 1-56807),* P.O. Box 135, Wheeling, IL 60090 (SAN 250-4596); Toll free: 800-832-2434; 8 Norbert Dr., Hawthorne Woods, IL 60047 (SAN 250-460X) Tel 312-438-6443; Dist. by: Kaplan Schl. Supply, P.O. Box 609, 1310 Lewisville-Clemmons Rd., Lewisville, NC 27023 (SAN 169-6521) Tel 910-766-7374; Dist. by: Sundance Pubs. & Distributors, P.O. Box 1326, 234 Taylor Rd., Littleton, MA 01460 (SAN 169-3484) Tel 508-486-9201; Toll free: 800-343-8204; Dist. by: D.D.L. Bks., Inc., 6521 NW 87th Ave., Miami, FL 33178 (SAN 169-1147) Tel 305-592-5929; Toll free: 800-635-4276.

Haymark, *(Haymark Pubns.; 0-933910),* P.O. Box 243, Fredericksburg, VA 22401 (SAN 213-2508) Tel 703-373-5780.

Haypenny Pr, *(Haypenny Pr.; 0-929885),* 211 New St., West Paterson, NJ 07424 (SAN 250-9571) Tel 201-881-9249.

Hazar NY, *(HAZAR; 0-9624922),* 2685 University Ave., Apt. 34E, Bronx, NY 10468 Tel 718-796-4406.

Hazelden, *(Hazelden Foundation; 0-89486; 1-56838; 0-942421; 0-89638),* 15251 Pleasant Valley Rd., P.O. Box 176, Center City, MN 55012-0176 (SAN 209-4010) Tel 612-257-4010; Toll free: 800-328-9000.

HB Juv Bks *Imprint of* **HarBrace**

HB Pubns, *(HB Pubns.; 0-940882),* Div. of Haunted Bookshop, P.O.Box 2806, Mobile, AL 36652-2806 (SAN 223-1344) Tel 205-432-6606.

HBP NY, *(Homeward Bound Project, Inc.; 0-9627744),* 132 E. 16th St., New York, NY 10003 Tel 212-477-8578.

Heahstan Pr, *(Heahstan Pr., The; 0-9604244),* P.O. Box 954, Denton, TX 76202-0954 (SAN 214-3127).

Healthways, *(Healthways; 0-9630893),* P.O. Box 1945, Aptos, CA 95001; 463 Monterey Dr., Aptos, CA 95003 Tel 408-688-2501.

Healthy Liv Inst, *(Healthy Living Institute; 0-918532),* 402 S. 14th St., Hettinger, ND 58639 (SAN 209-5580) Tel 701-567-2646.

Hear & Learn Pubns, *(Hear & Learn Pubns.; 1-879459),* 14516 NE 24th Ave., Vancouver, WA 98686 Tel 206-573-3057.

Heard Mus, *(Heard Museum, The; 0-934351),* 22 E. Monte Vista Rd., Phoenix, AZ 85004-1480 (SAN 279-0327) Tel 602-252-8840.

Hearst Bks, *(Hearst Bks.; 0-910992; 0-87851; 0-910990;* 0-688), Div. of William Morrow & Co., Inc., 1350 Avenue of Americas, New York, NY 10019 (SAN 202-2842) Tel 212-261-6770; Dist. by: North Light Bks., 1507 Dana Ave., Cincinnati, OH 45207 (SAN 287-0274) Tel 513-531-2690; Toll free: 800-289-0963.

Heart Ctry Pubns, *(Heart Country Pubns.; 0-9616334),* Rte. 1, Box 196-B, Big Sandy, TN 38221 (SAN 658-960X) Tel 901-584-2038.

Heart of the Lakes, *(Heart of the Lakes Publishing; 0-932334; 1-55787),* 2989 Lodi Rd., P.O. Box 299, Interlaken, NY 14847-0299 (SAN 213-0769) Tel 607-532-4997. *Imprints:* Empire State Bks (Empire State Books).

Hearth KS, *(Hearth Publishing; 0-9627947; 1-882420),* 16731 E. Iliff Ave., No. 305, Aurora, CO 80013 Tel 303-695-6115; Orders to: P.O. Box L, Hillsboro, KS 67063-0060; Toll free: 800-844-1655.

Hearthstn Inn, *(Hearthstone Inn; 0-9616308),* 506 N. Cascade, Colorado Springs, CO 80903 (SAN 658-7283) Tel 719-473-4413.

Heartsong Bks, *(Heartsong Bks.; 0-9638813),* P.O. Box 370, Blue Hill, ME 04614-0370 Tel 207-288-4019.

Heartwise Pr, *(Heartwise Pr.; 0-9626348),* 4892 Saginaw Cir., Pleasanton, CA 94566 Tel 510-462-3367.

Hebrew Pub, *(Hebrew Publishing Co.; 0-88482),* P.O. Box 157, Rockaway Beach, NY 11693 (SAN 201-5404) Tel 718-945-3000.

Heedays, *(Heeday's Pubns.; 0-917822),* 94-12 Kipaa Pl., Waipahu, HI 96797 (SAN 209-5653) Tel 808-671-1422; Dist. by: Booklines Hawaii, Ltd., 94-527 Puahi St., Waipahu, HI 96797 (SAN 630-6624) Tel 808-676-0116.

Heian Intl, *(Heian International Publishing, Inc.;* 0-89346), 1815 W. 205th St., Suite 301, Torrance, CA 90501 (SAN 213-2036) Tel 310-782-6268.

Heinemann, *(Heinemann; 0-435),* Div. of Reed Elsevier, Inc., 361 Hanover St., Portsmouth, NH 03801-3912 (SAN 210-5829) Tel 603-431-7894; Toll free: 800-541-2086.

Heinemann Ed
See Heinemann

Heinle & Heinle, *(Heinle & Heinle Pubs., Inc.; 0-8384; 0-912066; 0-88377),* Div. of International Thomson Publishing Education Group, 20 Park Plaza, Boston, MA 02116 (SAN 216-0730) Tel 617-451-1940; Toll free: 800-237-0053; Orders to: Distribution Ctr., 7625 Empire Dr., Florence, KY 41042-2978 (SAN 200-2663) Tel 606-525-2230; Toll free: 800-354-9706; Dist. by: Van Nostrand Reinhold, 115 Fifth Ave., New York, NY 10003 (SAN 202-5183) Tel 212-854-3232. *Imprints:* Newbury (Newbury House).

Heldreth Pub, *(Heldreth Publishing; 0-941595),* P.O. Box 430, Grafton, WV 26354 (SAN 666-0002); Heldreth Apt. Bldg., Rte. 3, Grafton, WV 26354 (SAN 666-0010) Tel 304-265-1357.

Henart Bks, *(Henart Bks.; 0-938059),* 4711 NW 24th Ct., Lauderdale Lakes, FL 33313 (SAN 661-1885) Tel 305-485-4286; Dist. by: Banyan Bks., P.O. Box 431160, Miami, FL 33243 (SAN 208-340X) Tel 305-665-6011.

Henchanted Bks, *(Henchanted Bks.; 0-9615756),* P.O. Box H, Calpella, CA 95418 (SAN 696-4648) Tel 707-485-7551.

Hendrick-Long, *(Hendrick-Long Publishing Co.; 0-937460; 1-885777),* P.O. Box 25123, Dallas, TX 75225 (SAN 281-7756); Toll free: 800-544-3770; 4811 W. Lovers Ln., Dallas, TX 75209 (SAN 281-7748) Tel 214-358-4677.

Henry Quill, *(Henry Quill Pr.; 1-883960),* 7340 Lake Dr., Fremont, MI 49412-9146 Tel 616-924-3026.

Herald Hse, *(Herald Hse.; 0-8309),* P.O. Box 1770, Independence, MO 64055-0770 (SAN 111-7556) Tel 816-252-5010; Toll free: 800-767-8181.

Herald Pr, *(Herald Pr.; 0-8361),* Div. of Mennonite Publishing Hse., Inc., 616 Walnut Ave., Scottdale, PA 15683-1999 (SAN 202-2915) Tel 412-887-8500; Toll free: 800-245-7894.

Herb Studies, *(Herbal Studies Course; 0-9620838;* 1-879687), 219 Carl St., San Francisco, CA 94117-3804 (SAN 249-8480) Tel 415-564-6337.

Herit Print Co, *(Heritage Printing Co.; 0-929537),* P.O. Box 792, Farmington, ME 04938 (SAN 249-6100); Porter Hill, Farmington, ME 04938 (SAN 249-6119) Tel 207-778-3581.

Herit Pub NC, *(Heritage Publishing Co.; 0-936013),* 737 Woodcott Dr., N., Chesapeake, VA 23320-9166 (SAN 696-818X). Do not confuse with companies of the same name in North Little Rock, AR, Uniontown, PA, Baton Rouge, LA, Maryland, MD.

Herit Pubs AZ, *(Heritage Pubs., Inc.; 0-929690),* 2700 Woodland Blvd., Suite 300, Flagstaff, AZ 86001-7124 (SAN 249-9460) Tel 602-526-1129.

Heritage Bk, *(Heritage Bks., Inc.; 0-917890; 1-55613;* 0-7884), 1540E Pointer Ridge Pl., Bowie, MD 20716 (SAN 209-3367) Tel 301-390-7709; Toll free: 800-398-7709.

Heritage West, *(Heritage West Bks.; 0-9623048),* 306 Regent Ct., Stockton, CA 95204 Tel 209-464-8818.

Heritage WI, *(Heritage Pr.; 0-9620823),* Rte. 1, Box 220B, Stoddard, WI 54658 (SAN 249-8529) Tel 608-457-2734. Do not confuse with Heritage Pr., Baltimore, MD, Meadow Vista, CA.

Hermenejildo Pr, *(Hermenejildo Pr.; 0-9624264),* H-SU, Box 667, Abilene, TX 79698; 2200 Hickory St., Abilene, TX 79698 Tel 915-670-1303.

Hermitage, *(Hermitage; 0-938920; 1-55779),* P.O. Box 410, Tenafly, NJ 07670 (SAN 239-4413) Tel 201-894-8247.

Hermon, *(Sepher-Hermon Pr., Inc.; 0-87203),* 1265 46th St., Brooklyn, NY 11219 (SAN 169-5959) Tel 718-972-9010.

Heron Pub CA, *(Heron Publishing; 1-880639),* 977 E. Stanley Blvd., Suite 230, Livermore, CA 94550 Tel 510-443-9610.

Hewitt Res Fnd, *(Hewitt Research Foundation, Inc.;* 0-913717), P.O. Box Nine, Washougal, WA 98671 (SAN 286-1852) Tel 206-835-8708.

Heyday Bks, *(Heyday Bks.; 0-930588),* P.O. Box 9145, Berkeley, CA 94709 (SAN 207-2351) Tel 510-549-3564.

Hgh Desert Pr, *(High Desert Pr.; 1-883251),* 2801V Eubank NE, Suite 179, Albuquerque, NM 87112 Tel 505-275-2664.

Hi-Hopes Pub, *(Hi-Hopes Publishing; 0-945203),* P.O. Box 31142, Washington, DC 20030-1142 (SAN 246-6694); 2902 Blooming Ct., Fort Washington, MD 20744 (SAN 246-6708) Tel 202-678-8511.

Hi I Que Pub, *(Hi I Que Publishing; 0-9631333),* Div. of The Guthrie Studio, P.O. Box 508, Claremont, CA 91711; 1848 N. Palomares St., Pomona, CA 91767 Tel 909-622-7501.

HI Natural Hist, *(Hawaii Natural History Assn.;* 0-940295), P.O. Box 74, Hawaii National Park, HI 96718 (SAN 664-2497) Tel 808-967-7604; Dist. by: Booklines Hawaii Ltd., P.O. Box 2170, Pearl City, HI 96782 (SAN 169-1635) Tel 808-676-0116.

Hi Plains Pr, *(High Plains Pr.; 0-931271),* P.O. Box 123, 539 Cassa Rd, Glendo, WY 82213 (SAN 681-9907) Tel 307-735-4370.

Hi-Time Pub, *(Hi-Time Publishing Corp.; 0-937997),* P.O. Box 13337, Milwaukee, WI 53213-0337 (SAN 661-2520); Toll free: 800-558-2292; 12040L W. Feerick St., Wauwatosa, WI 53222-2136 (SAN 661-2539) Tel 414-466-2420.

Hickle Pickle, *(Hickle Pickle Publishing; 1-881958),* 4450 Allison Dr., Michigan Center, MI 49254 Tel 517-764-1117.

Hickory Ridge Pr, *(Hickory Ridge Pr.; 0-9624607),* 8675 Ridgemont Dr., Pineville, LA 71360 Tel 318-640-4283.

Hidden Brook Pr, *(Hidden Brook Pr.; 0-9643013),* P.O. Box 333, Riverside, CT 06878 Tel 203-637-2746.

Hiddigeigei, *(Hiddigeigei Bks.; 0-915560),* 120 E. Sunset Pl., Dekalb, IL 60115 (SAN 207-981X) Tel 815-756-9908.

Higginson Bk Co, *(Higginson Bk. Co.; 0-8328),* 148 Washington St., P.O. Box 778, Salem, MA 01970 (SAN 247-9400) Tel 508-745-7170.

High Haven Mus, *(High Haven Music; 0-9632621),* P.O. Box 246, High Haven Ranch, Sonoita, AZ 85637-0246 Tel 602-455-5769.

High Noon Bks, *(High Noon Bks.; 0-87879; 1-57128),* Div. of Academic Therapy Pubns., Inc., 20 Commercial Blvd., Novato, CA 94949-6191 Tel 415-883-3314; Toll free: 800-422-7249.

High Octane, *(High Octane Publishing, Inc.; 1-883174),* 334A N. Coast Hwy., Laguna Beach, CA 82651 Tel 714-494-7620; Toll free: 800-769-7620.

High-Scope, *(High/Scope Pr.; 0-931114; 0-929816),* Div. of High/Scope Educational Research Foundation, 600 N. River St., Ypsilanti, MI 48198-2898 (SAN 211-9617) Tel 313-485-2000; Toll free: 800-407-7377.

Higher States, *(Higher States Publishing; 0-9642255),* 1917 Sheely Dr., Fort Collins, CO 80526 Tel 303-493-1495; Toll free: 800-383-1616.

Highland Pr, *(Highland Pr.; 0-910722),* Rte. 3, Box 3125, Boerne, TX 78006 (SAN 204-0522). Do not confuse with companies of the same name in Birmingham, AL, Wilsonville, OR, Tonasket, WA.

Highland Pub, *(Highland Publishing; 0-9615009),* 5226 Green Farms Rd., Edina, MN 55436 (SAN 694-0307) Tel 612-933-5797; Orders to: 9000 Tenth Ave. N., Golden Valley, MN 55472 (SAN 243-2854) Tel 612-788-2444.

Highlander, *(Highlander Research & Education Ctr.;* 0-9602226), Rte. 3 Box 370, New Market, TN 37820 (SAN 212-6664).

Highlights, *(Highlights for Children; 0-87534),* P.O. Box 269, Columbus, OH 43216-0269 (SAN 281-7810) Tel 614-486-0631; 803 Church St., Honesdale, PA 18431 (SAN 281-7802) Tel 717-253-1080.

Highsmith Co
See Highsmith Pr

Highsmith Pr, *(Highsmith Pr.; 0-917846; 0-913853),* P.O. Box 800, Hwy. 106 E., Fort Atkinson, WI 53538-0800 (SAN 159-8740) Tel 414-563-9571; Toll free: 800-558-2110. *Imprints:* Alleyside (Alleyside Press).

Hill & Wang, *(Hill & Wang, Inc.; 0-8090),* Div. of Farrar, Straus & Giroux, Inc., 19 Union Sq., W., New York, NY 10003 (SAN 201-9299) Tel 212-741-6900; Toll free: 800-788-6262 (Individuals); 800-631-8571 (Booksellers); Toll free: 800-242-7737.

Hill School, *(Hill Schl.; 0-942573),* E. High St., Pottstown, PA 19464 (SAN 667-2779) Tel 610-326-1000.

HillHouse Pub, *(HillHouse Publishing; 0-9636071),* 91 Wood Rd., Centereach, NY 11720-1619 Tel 516-585-2592; Dist. by: Tamarack Bks., P.O. Box 190313, Boise, ID 83719-0313 (SAN 297-8792) Tel 208-387-2656; Toll free: 800-962-6657.

Hillsdale Educ, *(Hillsdale Educational Pubs., Inc.;* 0-910726), 39 North St., Box 245, Hillsdale, MI 49242 (SAN 159-8759) Tel 517-437-3179.

Hilltop Pub Co, *(Hilltop Publishing Co.; 0-912133),* P.O. Box 654, Sonoma, CA 95476 (SAN 264-6706) Tel 707-938-8110; Dist. by: Bookpeople, 7900 Edgewater Dr., Oakland, CA 94621 (SAN 168-9517) Tel 510-632-4700; Toll free: 800-999-4650; Dist. by: Publishers Group West, 4065 Hollis St., Emeryville, CA 94608 (SAN 202-8522) Tel 510-658-3453; Toll free: 800-788-3123.

Hineni Concisus, *(Hineni Consciousness Pr.; 0-9628913),* 1645 Virginia St., Berkeley, CA 94703 Tel 510-843-4952.

Hippocrene Bks, *(Hippocrene Bks., Inc.; 0-87052; 0-88254; 0-7818),* 171 Madison Ave., New York, NY 10016 (SAN 213-2060) Tel 718-454-2366.

His Songs, *(His Songs; 1-885819),* P.O. 231311, San Diego, CA 92194; 3057 Rancho Diego Cir., El Cajon, CA 92019 Tel 619-669-1853.

Hisel Bk Ends, *(Hisel's Bk. Ends Co.; 0-9638163),* HC 89, Box 21, Ashby, NE 69333 Tel 308-577-6337.

Hispanic Bk Dist, *(Hispanic Bks. Distributors & Pubs., Inc.; 0-938243),* 1665 W. Grant Rd., Tucson, AZ 85745 (SAN 200-9110) Tel 602-882-9484.

Hist Jefferson Found, *(Historic Jefferson Foundation;* 0-935077), P.O. Box 1973, Marshall, TX 75671-1973 (SAN 695-0914); Orders to: P.O. Box 1088, Hughes Springs, TX 75656 (SAN 662-3425) Tel 214-639-2012.

Hist Tales, *(Historical Tales Ink; 0-938404),* 6911 Laird Ave., Reynoldsburg, OH 43068-2421 (SAN 215-7748).

Hlth Educ Consults, *(Health Education Consultants;* 0-9622034), 1284 Manor Pk., Lakewood, OH 44107 Tel 216-521-1766.

Hlth Educ Srvs, *(Health Education Services; 0-9633799),* P.O. Box 2626, Dublin Branch, Dublin, CA 94568-9991; 6937 Village Pkwy., Dublin, CA 94568-9991 Tel 510-865-2232.

Hlth Mngmnt Pubns, *(Health Management Pubns.; 0-9628084),* 550 American Ave., King of Prussia, PA 19406 Tel 610-337-4466.

Hlth Pub SF
See Psychol Educ Pubns

HM, *(Houghton Mifflin Co.; 0-395; 0-87466; 0-89919),* 222 Berkeley St., Boston, MA 02116 (SAN 200-2388) Tel 617-351-5000; 215 Park Ave., S., New York, NY 10003 (SAN 282-4043) Tel 212-420-5800; Orders to: Wayside Rd., Burlington, MA 01803 (SAN 215-3793) Tel 617-272-1500; Toll free: 800-225-3362. *Imprints:* AHD & Ref (American Heritage Dictionaries & Reference Books); Clarion Bks (Clarion Books); D Kindersley (Dorling Kindersley); RivEd (Riverside Editions); Sandpiper (Sandpiper Paperbacks).

Hoffman Spec, *(Hoffman Specialty Bks.; 0-9634737),* P.O. Box 584, Bridgewater, MA 02324; 30 Vinny Cir., Bridgewater, MA 02324 Tel 508-697-4604.

Hohm Pr, *(Hohm Pr.; 0-934252),* P.O. Box 2501, Prescott, AZ 86302 (SAN 221-0924) Tel 602-778-9189; Dist. by: S.C.B. Distributors, 15612 S. New Century Dr., Gardena, CA 90248 (SAN 630-4818) Tel 310-532-9400; Toll free: 800-729-6423 (orders only).

Holbrook Dogwds, *(Holbrook Dogwoods; 0-9636203),* 4662 Happy Valley Rd., Sequim, WA 98382 Tel 206-683-4121.

Holderby & Bierce, *(Holderby & Bierce; 0-916761),* 3245 Halcyon, Bettendorf, IA 52722 (SAN 654-3979) Tel 319-332-8858.

Holiday, *(Holiday Hse., Inc.; 0-8234),* 425 Madison Ave., New York, NY 10017 (SAN 202-3008) Tel 212-688-0085.

Holiday Time, *(Holiday Time; 1-879756),* 134 W. 26th St., Rm. 1103, New York, NY 10001 Tel 212-620-0933.

Holistic Learning, *(Holistic Learning; 0-9626864),* 911 S. Eighth St., Worland, WY 82401 Tel 307-347-3675.

Holland Hse Pr, *(Holland Hse. Pr.; 0-913042),* Box 42, Northville, MI 48167 (SAN 204-0611) Tel 313-273-0223.

Hollow Spring Pr, *(Hollow Spring Pr.; 0-936198),* RD 1, Chester, MA 01011 (SAN 213-8468).

Holloway, *(Holloway Hse. Publishing Co.; 0-87067),* 8060 Melrose Ave., Los Angeles, CA 90046 (SAN 206-8451) Tel 213-653-8060; Dist. by: All America Distributors Corp., 8431 Melrose Pl., Los Angeles, CA 90069 (SAN 168-972X) Tel 213-651-2650. *Imprints:* Melrose Sq (Melrose Square).

Holly Boy
See F Latino Pub Co

Hollybridge Pubns, *(Hollybridge Pubns.; 0-9617668),* P.O. Box 1707, Midlothian, VA 23113 (SAN 664-3884); 2914 Wood Bridge Crossing Dr., Midlothian, VA 23113 (SAN 664-645X) Tel 805-744-6503.

Hollym Intl, *(Hollym International Corp.; 0-930878; 1-56591),* 18 Donald Pl., Elizabeth, NJ 07208 (SAN 211-0172) Tel 908-353-1655. Do not confuse with Hollym Corporation Pubs., New York, NY.

Holmes & Mont, *(Holmes & Montgomery Publishing, Inc.; 1-883005),* P.O. Box 507, 121 E. Broadway, Suite 101, Fairview, OK 73737 Tel 405-227-3705; Toll free: 800-222-5596.

Holographic
See Millinnium-Holographic

Holt Assocs, *(Holt Assocs.; 0-913677),* 2269 Massachusetts Ave., Cambridge, MA 02140 (SAN 286-1119) Tel 617-864-3100.

Holy Cow, *(Holy Cow! Pr.; 0-930100),* P.O. Box 3170, Mt. Royal Sta., Duluth, MN 55803 (SAN 685-3315) Tel 218-724-1653; Dist. by: Talman Co., 131 Spring St., Suite 201E-N, New York, NY 10012 (SAN 200-5204) Tel 212-431-7175; Toll free: 800-537-8894 (orders only).

Holy Cross Orthodox, *(Holy Cross Orthodox Pr.; 0-917651; 1-885652),* 50 Goddard Ave., Brookline, MA 02146 (SAN 208-6840) Tel 617-731-3500; Toll free: 800-245-0599.

Holy Spir, *(Holy Spirit Pr.; 0-9638891),* 231 Market, No. 193, San Ramon, CA 94583 Tel 510-833-8122.

Holy Trinity, *(Holy Trinity Monastery; 0-88465),* P.O. Box 36, Jordanville, NY 13361-0036 (SAN 207-3501) Tel 315-858-0940.

Home Imag, *(Home Imaginations Pr.; 0-9633569),* 21648 Jeffery Ave., Sauk Village, IL 60411 Tel 708-758-2189.

Homeland Pubns, *(Homeland Pubns.; 0-939445),* 2615 Calder Dr., League City, TX 77573-6709 (SAN 663-3587) Tel 713-332-9764. Do not confuse with Homeland Pubns. in Chicago, IL.

Homestead WY, *(Homestead Publishing; 0-943972),* Box 193, Moose, WY 83012 (SAN 241-029X) Tel 307-733-6248.

Honey Bear Bks *Imprint of* **Modern Pub NYC**

Honeycomb Pr, *(Honeycomb Pr.; 0-9612244),* Div. of Independent Inactive, 6633 N. Eighth St., Philadelphia, PA 19126 (SAN 287-7295) Tel 215-548-8453.

Honor Bks OK, *(Honor Bks.; 1-56292),* P.O. Box 55388, Tulsa, OK 74155; Toll free: 800-678-2126; 1029 N. Utica, Tulsa, OK 74110 Tel 918-585-5033. Do not confuse with Honor Bks., Rapid City, SD.

Honor Pub, *(Honor Publishing Co.; 0-9616996),* P.O. Box 932, Greenwood, MS 38930 (SAN 693-0913); 802 W. President, Greenwood, MS 38930 (SAN 662-3123) Tel 601-453-6230.

Honoribus Pr, *(Honoribus Pr., The; 0-9622166; 1-885354),* P.O. Box 4872, Spartanburg, SC 29305; 429 N. Church St., Spartanburg, SC 29301 Tel 803-597-4382.

Hooked Games, *(Hooked on Games; 0-9623096),* P.O. Box 6217, Springvale, AR 72766-6217; 2103B Ashlee Dr., Springvale, AR 72764 Tel 501-750-2193.

Hope Farm, *(Hope Farm Pr. & Bookshop; 0-910746),* 1708 Rte. 212, Saugerties, NY 12477 (SAN 204-0697) Tel 914-679-6809.

Hope Pr CA, *(Hope Pr.; 1-878267),* Box 188, Duarte, CA 91009-0188 (SAN 200-3244); 59 Crestview Ct., Duarte, CA 91010 Tel 818-303-0644. Do not confuse with Hope Pr., Washington, DC.

Hope Pub Hse, *(Hope Publishing Hse.; 0-932727),* Affil. of Southern California Ecumenical Council, P.O. Box 60008, Pasadena, CA 91116 (SAN 688-4849) Tel 818-792-6123; Toll free: 800-326-2671 (orders only); Dist. by: Spring Arbor Distributors, 10885 Textile Rd., Belleville, MI 48111 (SAN 158-9016) Tel 313-481-0900; Toll free: 800-395-5599 (orders); 800-395-7234 (customer service).

Hopewell Stories, *(Hopewell Stories, Inc.; 0-9631215),* 1230 Waverly Rd., Gladwyne, PA 19035-1450 Tel 610-642-9385.

HoppyTalk Prodns, *(HoppyTalk Productions; 0-9626309),* 7950 W. Flamingo, No. 1158, Las Vegas, NV 89117.

Horizon Utah, *(Horizon Pubs. & Distributors, Inc.; 0-88290),* P.O. Box 490, 50 S. 500 W., Bountiful, UT 84011-0490 (SAN 159-4885) Tel 801-295-9451; Toll free: 800-453-0812.

Horse Hollow, *(Horse Hollow Pr.; 0-9638814),* 125 Willow Ave., No. 1S, Hoboken, NJ 07030 Tel 201-216-9117; Toll free: 800-414-6773.

Hot Water Pubs, *(Hot Water Publishing Co.; 0-941904),* P.O. Box 771283, Eagle River, AK 99577 (SAN 239-2283) Tel 907-272-8644.

House Nia, *(House of Nia; 0-9623205),* 4014 Calmoor St., National City, CA 92050 Tel 619-479-4425.

Houston IN, *(Houston Publishing, Inc.; 1-56516),* 224 S. Lebanon St., Lebanon, IN 46052-2543 Tel 317-482-4440; Toll free: 800-992-6676. Do not confuse with Houston Publishing Co. in Houston, TX.

How Mrkt Stud Athlete, *(How to Market Your Student Athlete; 0-9640318),* 3750 S. Mission Pkwy., Aurora, CO 80013 Tel 303-693-9103; Toll free: 800-368-1098.

Howell Bk, *(Howell Bk. Hse., Inc.; 0-87605),* 15 Columbus Cir., New York, NY 10023 Tel 212-373-8458.

HPL Pub, *(H.P.L. Publishing; 0-944131),* P.O. Box 305, Kelseyville, CA 95451 (SAN 242-9365); 3780 Main St., Kelseyville, CA 95451 (SAN 242-9373) Tel 707-279-4386.

HR&W Schl Div, *(Holt, Rinehart & Winston, Inc., Schl. Div.; 0-03),* Div. of Harcourt Brace & Co., 1120 S. Capital of Texas Hwy. No. II-100, Austin, TX 78746-6487 Tel 512-314-6500; Toll free: 800-426-0462; 800-228-4658; 800-341-3568; 800-242-5479; Eastern Region Sales Office, 151 Benigno Blvd., Bellmawr, NJ 08031 Tel 609-931-7100; Pacific Region Office, 577 Airport Blvd., Suite 185, Burlingame, CA 94010 Tel 415-579-3993; Midwest Sales Office, 901 N. Elm St., Hinsdale, IL 60521; South Central Regional Sales Office, 8551 Esters Blvd., Irving, TX 75063 Tel 214-929-1377; International Div., Orlando, FL 32887 Tel 407-345-2500; Orders to: Orders To: Order Fulfillment, 6277 Sea Harbor Dr., Orlando, FL 32887; Toll free: 800-225-5425; 800-479-9799 (information).

Hse BonGiovanni, *(House of BonGiovanni; 0-912981),* 3740 Longview Rd., Hermitage, PA 16159 (SAN 283-0442) Tel 412-981-4756.

Hse History, *(House of History; 1-878973),* 4635 Woodsorrel Ct., Colorado Springs, CO 80917 Tel 719-574-4382.

Hse Nine Muses, *(House of the 9 Muses, Inc.; 1-56412),* Box 2974, Palm Beach, FL 33480-2974 Tel 407-697-0990; Dist. by: BookWorld Distribution Services, Inc., 1933 Whitfield Pk. Loop, Sarasota, FL 34243 (SAN 173-0568) Tel 813-758-8094; Toll free: 800-444-2524 (orders only).

Hse of Steno, *(House of Steno, Inc.; 1-883952),* 1708 Placer St., Redding, CA 96001 Tel 916-241-6051; Toll free: 800-479-6062.

HSH Edu Media Co, *(Home Sweet Home, Educational Media Co.; 0-929216),* P.O. Box 167187, Irving, TX 75016 (SAN 248-9090); 6301 N. O'Connor Blvd., Bldg. 1, Irving, TX 75039 (SAN 248-9104) Tel 214-869-3333; Dist. by: Word, Inc., P.O. Box 141000, Nashville, TN 37214 (SAN 203-283X); Toll free: 800-933-9673.

HTS Bks *Imprint of* **Forest Hse**

Hubbard Sci, *(Hubbard Scientific; 0-8331),* Div. of American Educational Products, P.O. Box 760, Chippewa Falls, WI 54729-1468 (SAN 202-3121); Toll free: 800-323-8368.

Hudson Hills, *(Hudson Hills Pr., Inc.; 0-933920; 1-55595),* 230 Fifth Ave., Suite 1308, New York, NY 10001-7704 (SAN 213-0815) Tel 212-889-3090; Dist. by: National Bk. Network, 4720A Boston Way, Lanham, MD 20706-4310 (SAN 630-0065) Tel 301-459-8696; Toll free: 800-462-6420.

Hughes Taylor, *(Hughes/Taylor; 1-878036),* P.O. Box 12550, Portland, OR 97212 Tel 503-287-0412; Dist. by: Quality Bks., Inc., 918 Sherwood Dr., Lake Bluff, IL 60044-2204 (SAN 169-2127) Tel 708-295-2010; Toll free: 800-323-4241 (libraries only); Dist. by: Baker & Taylor Bks., Somerville Service Ctr., 50 Kirby Ave., Somerville, NJ 08876-0734 (SAN 169-4901) Tel 908-722-8000; Toll free: 800-775-1500 (customer service); Dist. by: Baker & Taylor Bks., Momence Service Ctr., 501 S. Gladiolus St., Momence, IL 60954-2444 (SAN 169-2100) Tel 815-472-2444; Toll free: 800-775-2300 (customer service); Dist. by: Baker & Taylor Bks., Commerce Service Ctr., 251 Mt. Olive Church Rd., Commerce, GA 30599-9988 (SAN 169-1503) Tel 706-335-5000; Toll free: 800-775-1200 (customer service); Dist. by: Baker & Taylor Bks., Reno Service Ctr., 380 Edison Way, Reno, NV 89564 (SAN 169-4464) Tel 702-858-6700; Toll free: 800-775-1700 (customer service).

Hulogosi Inc, *(Hulogosi Communications, Inc.; 0-938493),* P.O. Box 1188, Eugene, OR 97440 (SAN 661-4132) Tel 503-688-1199.

Human Kinetics, *(Human Kinetics Pubs.; 0-931250; 0-87322; 0-918438; 0-88011),* P.O. Box 5076, Champaign, IL 61825-5076 (SAN 211-7088); Toll free: 800-747-4457; 1607 N. Market St., Champaign, IL 61825 (SAN 658-0866) Tel 217-351-5076. *Imprints:* YMCA USA (Y M C A of the U. S. A.).

Human Res Ctr, *(Human Resources Ctr.),* Rehabilitation Research Library, Albertson, NY 11507 (SAN 227-0323) Tel 516-747-5400.

Human Res Dev Pr, *(Human Resource Development Pr.; 0-914234; 0-87425),* 22 Amherst Rd., Amherst, MA 01002 (SAN 201-9213) Tel 413-253-3488; Toll free: 800-822-2801.

Human Sci Pr, *(Human Sciences Pr., Inc.; 0-87705; 0-89885),* Subs. of Plenum Publishing Corp., 233 Spring St., New York, NY 10013-1578 (SAN 200-2159) Tel 212-620-8000; Toll free: 800-221-9369.

Humanics Ltd, *(Humanics, Ltd.; 0-89334),* P.O. Box 7400, Atlanta, GA 30357 (SAN 208-3833); Toll free: 800-874-8844; 1482 Mecaslin St., NW, Atlanta, GA 30309 (SAN 658-0882) Tel 404-874-2176. Do not confuse with Humanics in Encino, CA.

Humbug Bks, *(Humbug Bks.; 1-881772),* Div. of Ink., Inc., 202 W. Main St., Watertown, WI 53094 Tel 414-261-7707; Toll free: 800-648-6284.

Hundelrut Studio, *(Hundelrut Studio; 0-9638293),* 10 Hawthorne St., Plymouth, NH 03264 Tel 603-536-4396.

Hunt & Peck Pub, *(Hunt & Peck Publishing; 0-9624583),* 585 Woodbine Dr., Suite 200, Terre Haute, IN 47803 Tel 812-877-9371.

Hunt Hse Pub, *(Hunt Hse. Publishing, Inc.; 0-9623524),* 3704 Meadowbank, Austin, TX 78703 Tel 512-453-1368; Toll free: 800-825-2356.

Hunter Hse, *(Hunter Hse., Inc.; 0-89793),* P.O. Box 2914, Alameda, CA 94501-0914 (SAN 281-7969) Tel 510-865-5282; Toll free: 800-266-5592; Dist. by: Publishers Group West, 4065 Hollis St., Emeryville, CA 94608 (SAN 202-8522) Tel 510-658-3453; Toll free: 800-788-3123; Dist. by: Bookpeople, 7900 Edgewater Dr., Oakland, CA 94621 (SAN 168-9517) Tel 510-632-4700; Toll free: 800-999-4650; Dist. by: Inland Bk. Co., 140 Commerce St., East Haven, CT 06512 (SAN 200-4151) Tel 203-467-4257; Toll free: 800-243-0138; Dist. by: New Leaf Distributing Co., 5425 Tulane Dr., SW, Atlanta, GA 30336-2323 (SAN 169-1449) Tel 404-691-6996; Toll free: 800-326-2665; Dist. by: Quality Bks., Inc., 918 Sherwood Dr., Lake Bluff, IL 60044-2204 (SAN 169-2127) Tel 708-295-2010; Toll free: 800-323-4241 (libraries only); Dist. by: Unique Bks., Inc., 4230 Grove Ave., Gurnee, IL 60031 (SAN 630-0472) Tel 708-623-9171.

Huntington Hse, *(Huntington Hse. Pubs.; 0-910311; 1-56384),* P.O. Box 53788, Lafayette, LA 70505 (SAN 241-5208); Toll free: 800-749-4009; 104 Row 2, Suite A1 & A2, Lafayette, LA 70508 Tel 318-237-7049.

Huron Pr-Wergin, *(Huron Pr.-Wergin Distributing Co.;* 1-885114), 729 Huron Hill, Madison, WI 53711-2944 Tel 608-231-1562.

HVHA, *(Happy Valley Healing Arts; 0-9628511),* 2014 Pine Cliff Rd., State College, PA 16801 Tel 814-234-4428.

Hyperion, *(Hyperion; 1-56282; 0-7868),* Div. of Disney Bk. Publishing, Inc., A Walt Disney Co., 114 Fifth Ave., New York, NY 10011 Tel 212-633-4400; Dist. by: Little, Brown & Co., Time & Life Bldg., 1271 Avenue of the Americas, New York, NY 10020 (SAN 200-2205) Tel 212-522-8700; Toll free: 800-343-9204.

Hyprn Child, *(Hyperion Bks. for Children; 1-56282;* 0-7868), Div. of Disney Bk. Publishing, Inc., A Walt Disney Co., 114 Fifth Ave., New York, NY 10011 Tel 212-633-4400; Dist. by: Little, Brown & Co., Time & Life Bldg., 1271 Avenue of the Americas, New York, NY 10020 (SAN 200-2205) Tel 212-522-8700; Toll free: 800-343-9204.

Hyprn Ppbks, *(Hyperion Paperbacks for Children; 1-56282; 0-7868),* Div. of Disney Bk. Publishing, Inc., A Walt Disney Co., 114 Fifth Ave., New York, NY 10011 Tel 212-633-4400; Dist. by: Little, Brown & Co., Time & Life Bldg., 1271 Avenue of the Americas, New York, NY 10020 (SAN 200-2205) Tel 212-522-8700; Toll free: 800-343-9204.

I B Bold Pubns, *(I. B. Bold Pubns. Co.; 0-9637271),* P.O. Box 1132, Lexington, KY 40589-1132; 769 Dakota St., Lexington, KY 40508 Tel 606-233-9277.

I D I C P, *(Inka Dinka Ink Childrens Pr.; 0-939700),* Div. of HeBo, Inc., 4741 Guerley Rd., Cincinnati, OH 45238 (SAN 293-2814) Tel 513-471-0825; Dist. by: Baker & Taylor Bks., Momence Service Ctr., 501 S. Gladiolus St., Momence, IL 60954-2444 (SAN 169-2100) Tel 815-472-2444; Toll free: 800-775-2300 (customer service); Dist. by: Baker & Taylor Bks., Commerce Service Ctr., 251 Mt. Olive Church Rd., Commerce, GA 30599-9988 (SAN 169-1503) Tel 706-335-5000; Toll free: 800-775-1200 (customer service); Dist. by: Baker & Taylor Bks., Somerville Service Ctr., 50 Kirby Ave., Somerville, NJ 08876-0734 (SAN 169-4901) Tel 908-722-8000; Toll free: 800-775-1500 (customer service).

I E Clark, *(Clark, I. E., Pub.; 0-88680),* St. Johns Rd., Schulenburg, TX 78956 (SAN 282-7433) Tel 409-743-3232; Orders to: P.O. Box 246, Schulenburg, TX 78956 (SAN 662-2003).

I Like Me Pub, *(I Like Me Publishing Co., The;* 0-9608516), 300 N. State St., Chicago, IL 60610 (SAN 240-6772) Tel 312-464-9130.

I Think I Can, *(I Think I Can, Publishing; 1-877863),* Div. of La Petite Baleen, Inc., 25A W. 25th Ave., San Mateo, CA 94401 Tel 415-573-6791.

IASB Enviro, *(International Academy at Santa Barbara, Environmental Studies Institute; 0-9610590),* 800 Garden St., Suite D, Santa Barbara, CA 93101-1552 (SAN 271-1850) Tel 805-965-5010.

IBD Ltd, *(i.b.d., Ltd.; 0-88431),* 24 Hudson St., Kinderhook, NY 12106 (SAN 630-7779) Tel 518-758-1411; Toll free: 800-343-3531.

IBS Intl, *(I. B. S. International; 0-89564),* 3144 Dove St., San Diego, CA 92103 (SAN 210-3001).

ICAN Pr, *(ICAN Pr.; 1-881116),* 616 Third Ave., Chula Vista, CA 91910-5704 Tel 619-425-4715.

Ich Lern A-B, *(Ich Lern Aleph-Beis; 0-9630821),* 31 Rita Ave., Monsey, NY 10952-2626.

ICS Bks, *(ICS Bks., Inc.; 0-934802; 1-57034),* P.O. Box 10767, Merrillville, IN 46411-0767 (SAN 295-3358); Toll free: 800-541-7323 (orders); 1370 E. 86th Pl., Merrillville, IN 46410 Tel 219-769-0585.

Ide Hse, *(Ide Hse., Inc.; 0-86663),* 4631 Harvey Dr., Mesquite, TX 75150-1609 (SAN 216-146X) Tel 214-686-5332.

Ideals, *(Ideals Pubns.; 0-89542; 0-8249),* P.O. Box 140300, Nashville, TN 37214-0300 (SAN 213-4403); Toll free: 800-327-5113; 565 Marriott Dr., Suite 800, Nashville, TN 37214 Tel 615-231-6740.

Ideals Child *Imprint of* **Hambleton-Hill**

Ideas, *(Ideas, Inc.; 0-9614338),* 5900 Park Heights Ave., No. 106, Baltimore, MD 21215 (SAN 687-8040) Tel 410-542-6930.

Identity Toys, *(Identity Toys, Inc.; 1-885821),* 2821 N. Fourth St., No. 430, Milwaukee, WI 53212 Tel 414-562-7776; Toll free: 800-272-0287.

Ignatius Pr, *(Ignatius Pr.; 0-89870),* Div. of Guadalupe Assocs., Inc., 2515 McAllister St., San Francisco, CA 94118 (SAN 214-3887) Tel 415-387-2324; Orders to: 15 Oakland Ave., Harrison, NY 10528 Tel 914-835-4216; Toll free: 800-651-1531 (credit card orders, $20.00 minimum).

Ill St Museum, *(Illinois State Museum Society; 0-89792),* Spring & Edwards, Springfield, IL 62706 (SAN 201-5137) Tel 217-782-6700.

Illini Pubns, *(Illini Pubns.; 0-9622667),* 1012 W. Beardsley Ave., Champaign, IL 61821-2557 Tel 217-352-9083.

Illum Arts, *(Illumination Arts, Inc.; 0-935699),* P.O. Box 1865, Bellevue, WA 98009 (SAN 696-2599); 10309 NE 28th Pl., Bellevue, WA 98004-1938 Tel 206-822-8015.

ILM, *(Interdependent Learning Model; 0-939632),* Fordham Univ. at Lincoln Ctr., 113 W. 60th St., Rm. 1003, New York, NY 10023 (SAN 216-6305) Tel 212-841-5282.

Imag Plus, *(Imagination Plus; 0-9641918),* 214 Routh Ct., No. 308, Schaumburg, IL 60195 Tel 708-884-9398.

Image NY, *(Image Publishing of New York; 0-9627508),* 262 First Ave., Massapequa Park, NY 11762 Tel 516-795-5179.

Image Pubns, *(Image Pubns.; 0-942772),* 6409 Appalachian Way, P.O. Box 5016, Madison, WI 53705 (SAN 238-8499) Tel 608-233-5033.

Image West, *(Image West Pr.; 0-918966),* P.O. Box 5511, Eugene, OR 97405 (SAN 210-4407) Tel 503-342-3797.

Imagery Pubns, *(Imagery Pubns.; 0-9624721),* P.O. Box 1339, Albany, OR 97321; 1197 NE Century Dr., No. 23, Albany, OR 97321 Tel 503-928-7093.

Imagin Pr, *(Imagination Pr.; 0-9633385),* Div. of Image Makers, 10430 Brookhurst Ave., San Diego, CA 92126 Tel 619-578-8444.

Imagination Dust, *(Imagination Dust Publishing;* 0-9611072), 8998 N. 126th Pl., Scottsdale, AZ 85259 (SAN 282-8839).

Impact Bks MO, *(Impact Bks., Inc.; 0-89228),* 332 Leffingwell Ave., Suite 101, Kirkwood, MO 63122 (SAN 214-0330) Tel 314-822-3309; Toll free: 800-451-2708 (wats-orders only); Dist. by: Spring Arbor Distributors, 10885 Textile Rd., Belleville, MI 48111 (SAN 158-9016) Tel 313-481-0900; Toll free: 800-395-5599 (orders); 800-395-7234 (customer service); Dist. by: Riverside/World, P.O. Box 370, 1500 Riverside Dr., Iowa Falls, IA 50126 (SAN 169-2666) Tel 515-648-4271; Toll free: 800-247-5111; Dist. by: Whitaker Hse., 580 Pittsburgh St., Springdale, PA 15144 (SAN 203-2104) Tel 412-274-4440; Toll free: 800-444-4484.

Impact FL
See Spec Pr FL

Impact Photograph, *(Impact Photographics; 0-918327;* 1-56540), 4961 Windplay Dr., Eldorado Hills, CA 95762 (SAN 657-3126) Tel 916-939-9333; Toll free: 800-950-0110.

Impact Pubs Cal, *(Impact Pubs., Inc.; 0-915166),* P.O. Box 1094, San Luis Obispo, CA 93406 (SAN 202-6864) Tel 805-543-5911.

Impatience Pubns, *(Impatience Pubns.; 0-9636637),* 4028 Pleasant Ave., S., Minneapolis, MN 55409-1545 Tel 612-822-1799.

Impresora Sahuaro, *(Impresora Sahuaro),* 7575 Sendero De Juana, Tucson, AZ 85718 (SAN 218-7760) Tel 602-297-3089.

Impressions TX, *(Impressions; 0-9616121),* P.O. Box 270502, Houston, TX 77277 (SAN 699-7279); 6633 W. Airport, Suite 1302, Houston, TX 77035 (SAN 699-7287) Tel 713-995-4440.

Impressive Pubns, *(Impressive Pubns.; 0-9622327),* 6145 Larry Way, North Highlands, CA 95660 Tel 916-344-3308.

In Between, *(In Between Bks.; 0-935430),* Affil. of Plain View Pr., Box T, Sausalito, CA 94966 (SAN 213-6236) Tel 415-383-8447.

In Educ, *(IN Education, Inc.; 0-918433),* 2000 Valley Forge Cir., Suite 624, King of Prussia, PA 19406 (SAN 657-6206) Tel 610-783-5939.

In One EAR, *(In One EAR Pubns.; 0-9627080;* 1-881791), 29481 Manzanita Dr., Campo, CA 91906 Tel 619-478-5619.

In Sight Pr NM, *(In Sight Pr.; 0-942524),* 535 Cordova Rd., Suite 228, Santa Fe, NM 87501 (SAN 238-1680) Tel 505-471-7511.

In the Weeds, *(In the Weeds, Inc.; 0-9642776),* 1426 Preston Ave., Austin, TX 78703 Tel 512-472-1501.

In-Time Pubns, *(In-Time Pubns.; 0-944397),* 20 NE Plantation Rd., No. 3-306, Stuart, FL 34996 (SAN 243-5578) Tel 407-225-1093.

In Tradition Pub, *(In the Tradition Publishing Co.;* 0-935369), 5404 W. Thompson St., 1st Flr., Philadelphia, PA 19131-4219 (SAN 696-267X) Tel 215-387-5919.

InBook, *(InBook),* Div. of Inland Bk. Co., P.O. Box 120261, East Haven, CT 06512 (SAN 630-5547); Toll free: 800-253-3605 (orders only); 800-243-0138; 140 Commerce St., East Haven, CT 06512 (SAN 200-4151) Tel 203-467-4257.

Incent Lrning, *(Incentives For Learning; 1-56872),* 111 Center Ave., Suite I, Pacheco, CA 94553 Tel 510-682-2428.

Incentive Pubns, *(Incentive Pubns., Inc.; 0-913916;* 0-86530), 3835 Cleghorn Ave., Nashville, TN 37215 (SAN 203-8005) Tel 615-385-2934; Toll free: 800-421-2830.

Incline Pr, *(Incline Pr.; 0-9615161),* P.O. Box 913, Enumclaw, WA 98022 (SAN 694-3853) Tel 206-825-1989.

Incrdble Fish, *(Incredible Fishing Stories; 0-9633691),* 8305 Brittany Harbor Dr., Las Vegas, NV 89128-7494 Tel 702-255-9734; Dist. by: Ingram Bk. Co., 1 Ingram Blvd., La Vergne, TN 37086-1986 (SAN 169-7978) Tel 615-793-5000; Toll free: 800-937-8000 (orders only, all warehouses); Dist. by: Baker & Taylor Bks., Somerville Service Ctr., 50 Kirby Ave., Somerville, NJ 08876-0734 (SAN 169-4901) Tel 908-722-8000; Toll free: 800-775-1500 (customer service); Dist. by: Baker & Taylor Bks., Momence Service Ctr., 501 S. Gladiolus St., Momence, IL 60954-2444 (SAN 169-2100) Tel 815-472-2444; Toll free: 800-775-2300 (customer service); Dist. by: Baker & Taylor Bks., Reno Service Ctr., 380 Edison Way, Reno, NV 89564 (SAN 169-4464) Tel 702-858-6700; Toll free: 800-775-1700 (customer service); Dist. by: Baker & Taylor Bks., Commerce Service Ctr., 251 Mt. Olive Church Rd., Commerce, GA 30599-9988 (SAN 169-1503) Tel 706-335-5000; Toll free: 800-775-1200 (customer service); Dist. by: Pacific Pipeline, Inc., 8030 S. 228th St., Kent, WA 98032-2900 (SAN 208-2128) Tel 206-872-5523; Toll free: 800-444-7323 (Customer Service); 800-677-2222 (orders).

Ind Pr MO, *(Independence Pr.; 0-8309),* Div. of Herald Hse., P.O. Box 1770, 3225 S. Noland Rd., Independence, MO 64055-0770 (SAN 202-6902) Tel 816-252-5010; Toll free: 800-767-8181.

Ind U Pr, *(Indiana Univ. Pr.; 0-253),* 601 N. Morton St., Bloomington, IN 47404-3797 (SAN 202-5647) Tel 812-855-6804; Toll free: 800-842-6796 (credit card orders).

Ind-US Inc, *(Ind-U.S., Inc.; 0-86578),* Box 56, East Glastonbury, CT 06025 (SAN 213-5809) Tel 203-633-0045.

Indian Heritage, *(Indian Heritage Council; 1-884710),* Box 2302, Henry St., Morristown, TN 37816; 770 Harvey Dr., Russellville, TN 37860 Tel 615-581-4448.

Indian Trail, *(Indian Trail Pr.; 0-9629284),* P.O. Box 55, Salado, TX 76571; 1113 Indian Trail, Salado, TX 76571 Tel 817-947-9205.

Indiv Educ Syst, *(Individualized Education Systems;* 0-938911), P.O. Box 5136, Fresno, CA 93755 (SAN 661-8405); 134 Poppy Ln., Clovis, CA 93612 (SAN 661-8413) Tel 209-299-4639.

Indp Pubs, *(Independence Pubs., Inc.; 0-945740),* 1840 Briarcliff Cir. NE, No. B, Atlanta, GA 30329-2567 (SAN 247-7114) Tel 404-636-7092.

Infini Educ, *(Infini Educational Supplies; 0-929916),* Div. of Infini, Inc., 244 Mercury Cir., Pomona, CA 91768 (SAN 250-9784) Tel 818-967-6667.

Infiniti, *(Infiniti, Inc.; 0-9633016),* 6550 Wright Rd., NE, Atlanta, GA 30328-3026.

Info All Bk, *(Info-All Bk. Co.; 0-9617218),* 5 Old Well Ln., Dallas, PA 18612 (SAN 663-4087) Tel 717-288-9375.

Info Oregon, *(Information Pr., The; 0-911927),* P.O. Box 1422, Eugene, OR 97440 (SAN 264-1127) Tel 503-689-0188. Do not confuse with Information Pr. in Tallahassee, FL.

Info Plus TX, *(Information Plus; 0-936474; 1-878623;* 1-57302), Div. of Information Aids, Inc., 2812 Exchange St., Wylie, TX 75098 (SAN 220-2557) Tel 214-442-0167; Toll free: 800-463-6757. Do not confuse with Information Plus in Loomis, CA.

Info Res Cons, *(Information Resource Consultants; 0-931821; 1-55804),* 1556 Walpole Dr., Chesterfield, MO 63017 (SAN 685-2874) Tel 314-530-7966; Toll free: 800-484-1098.

Infotainment, *(Infotainment, Ltd.; 1-882158),* 57 W. 38th St., New York, NY 10018 Tel 212-921-8743; Dist. by: Hollywood Creative Directory, 3000 Olympic Blvd., Santa Monica, CA 90404 Tel 310-315-4815.

Inkstone Books, *(Inkstone Bks.; 0-9604542),* 22 Ridge Ave., Mill Valley, CA 94941 (SAN 262-043X) Tel 415-389-6335.

Inkwell CA, *(Inkwell; 0-9627680),* P.O. Box 178, Dobbins, CA 95935; 14976 Fountain House Rd., Dobbins, CA 95935 Tel 916-692-1581.

Inkwell Pr, *(Inkwell Pr.; 0-945625),* P.O. Box 471, Menlo Park, CA 94026 (SAN 247-4123); 624 Ruisseau Francais, Half Moon Bay, CA 94019 (SAN 247-4131) Tel 415-726-1906. Do not confuse with Inkwell Press in Juneau, AK.

Inner Child Play, *(Inner Children at Play; 0-9633876),* P.O. Box 873, Dayton, NJ 08810; 3422 Cypress Ct., Monmouth Junction, NJ 08852 Tel 908-329-9142.

Inner Dynamics, *(Inner Dynamics; 1-885714),* 135 W. Dorothy Ln., Suite 116, Kettering, OH 45429 Tel 513-298-1492; Toll free: 800-488-2484. Do not confuse with Inner Dynamics in Tempe, AZ.

Innerworks Pub, *(Innerworks Publishing; 0-9625996;* 1-883648), Div. of Innerworks Counseling, P.O. Box 270865, Houston, TX 77277-0865; Toll free: 800-577-5040 (orders); Dist. by: New Leaf Distributing Co., 5425 Tulane Dr., SW, Atlanta, GA 30336-2323 (SAN 169-1449) Tel 404-691-6996; Toll free: 800-326-2665; Dist. by: DeVorss & Co., P.O. Box 550, Marina del Rey, CA 90294-0550 (SAN 168-9886) Tel 310-870-7478; Toll free: 800-843-5743 (bookstores only); 800-331-4719 (in California, bookstores only); Dist. by: New Concepts Bks. & Tapes Distributors, P.O. Box 55068, Houston, TX 77055 (SAN 114-2682) Tel 713-465-7736; Toll free: 800-842-4807.

Innovat Lrning Grp, *(Innovative Learning Group;* 1-877667), Div. of Innovative Sciences, Inc., 975 Walnut St., Suite 342, Cary, NC 27511-4216 Tel 919-469-8744.

Innovat NY, *(Innovative Publishing; 0-9635739),* 459 Argyle Rd., Brooklyn, NY 11218 Tel 718-287-1835. Do not confuse with Innovative Publishing & Graphics in Chicago, IL.

Innovative Educ Pub, *(Innovative Education Publishing Co.; 0-915925),* P.O. Box 5066, Milford, CT 06460 (SAN 287-2927); 73 Morningside Dr., Milford, CT 06460 (SAN 650-8154) Tel 203-874-6046.

Innovative Learn, *(Innovative Learning Designs;* 0-931303), 7811 SE 27th, Suite 104, Mercer Island, WA 98040 (SAN 685-2106) Tel 206-232-2697.

Innovative Lrn, *(Innovative Learning Strategies;* 0-9616224), 570 Pennsylvania Ave., San Francisco, CA 94107 (SAN 658-5507) Tel 415-647-1672; Dist. by: Berty Segal, Inc., 1749 Eucalptus St., Brea, CA 92621 (SAN 630-0553) Tel 714-529-5359.

Inquir Voices, *(Inquiring Voices Pr.; 0-9634637),* 100 Heritage Rd., Bloomington, IN 47408 (SAN 297-9292) Tel 812-336-6925.

Inquisitors Pub, *(Inquisitors Publishing Co.; 0-923889),* P.O. Box 10, North Aurora, IL 60542 (SAN 251-8376); 122 Juniper Dr., North Aurora, IL 60542 (SAN 251-8384) Tel 708-801-0607; Dist. by: Baker & Taylor Bks., Momence Service Ctr., 501 S. Gladiolus St., Momence, IL 60954-2444 (SAN 169-2100) Tel 815-472-2444; Toll free: 800-775-2300 (customer service); Dist. by: Ingram Bk. Co., 1 Ingram Blvd., La Vergne, TN 37086-1986 (SAN 169-7978) Tel 615-793-5000; Toll free: 800-937-8000 (orders only, all warehouses); Dist. by: Quality Bks., Inc., 918 Sherwood Dr., Lake Bluff, IL 60044-2204 (SAN 169-2127) Tel 708-295-2010; Toll free: 800-323-4241 (libraries only).

Insight Data, *(Insight Data; 0-945876),* P.O. Box 17515, Asheville, NC 28816-7515 (SAN 248-1626).

Inspir Univ, *(Inspiration Univ.; 0-945793),* P.O. Box 5320, Chico, CA 95927-5320 (SAN 247-5634) Tel 916-893-8643 (SAN 247-5642); Orders to: .

Inspired Ink, *(Inspired Ink Productions by Kapraun;* 0-9643313), 36745 Hill St., Lower Salem, OH 45745 Tel 614-585-2706.

Inst Advan PHE, *(Institute for the Advancement of Private Higher Education; 0-9631429),* 50-8 Maegan Pl., Thousand Oaks, CA 91362 Tel 805-494-0601.

Inst Advncmnt Philos Child, *(Institute for the Advancement of Philosophy for Children;* 0-916834), Montclair State University, Upper Montclair, NJ 07043 (SAN 281-7144) Tel 201-655-4277.

Inst Basic Youth, *(Institute in Basic Youth Conflicts;* 0-916888), P.O. Box 1, Oak Brook, IL 60522-3001 (SAN 208-6972) Tel 312-323-9800.

Inst Creation *Imprint of* **Master Bks**

Inst Fam Blind Child, *(Institute for Families of Blind Children; 0-9630118),* 1300 N. Vermont Ave., Suite 909, Los Angeles, CA 90027 Tel 213-669-4649.

Inst Food & Develop, *(Institute for Food & Development Policy/Food First Bks.; 0-935028),* 398 60th St., Oakland, CA 94618-1212 (SAN 213-327X) Tel 510-654-4400; Toll free: 800-888-3314.

Inst for the Arts, *(Rice Univ., Institute for the Arts Catalogues; 0-914412),* Menil Foundation, 1511 Branard, Houston, TX 77006 (SAN 218-933X) Tel 713-525-9400.

Inst Karmic, *(Institute of Karmic Guidance; 0-924944),* P.O. Box 73025, Washington, DC 20056; 1015 Quebec Pl., NW, Washington, DC 20010 Tel 202-726-0762.

Inst Rational-Emotive, *(Institute for Rational-Emotive Therapy; 0-917476),* 45 E. 65th St., New York, NY 10021 (SAN 210-3079) Tel 212-535-0822; Toll free: 800-323-4738.

Inst Subs Abuse Res, *(Institute for Substance Abuse Research; 0-935847),* Subs. of Security Consultant Services, Inc., 2501 27th Ave., Suite F-6, Vero Beach, FL 32960 (SAN 699-7759) Tel 407-569-3121; Orders to: P.O. Box 6837, Vero Beach, FL 32961-6837 (SAN 662-4065).

Inst Womens Policy Rsch, *(Institute for Women's Policy Research; 1-878428),* 1400 20th St. NW, No. 104, Washington, DC 20036 Tel 202-785-5100.

Instant Heirloom, *(Instant Heirloom Bks.; 0-9633197),* Div. of W. Enterprises, Inc., 5866 Charles Hamilton Rd., McCalla, AL 35111 Tel 205-477-5089.

Institute Government, *(Institute of Government;* 1-56011), c/o Univ. of North Carolina-Chapel Hill, Knapp Bldg. 3330, Chapel Hill, NC 27599-3330 (SAN 204-8752) Tel 919-966-4119.

Instr Res Co, *(Instructional Resources Co.; 1-879478),* P.O. Box 111704, Anchorage, AK 99511-1704 Tel 907-345-6689.

Instruc Resc MD, *(Instructional Resources Corp.;* 0-923805), 1819 Bay Ridge Ave., Suite 160, Annapolis, MD 21403 (SAN 251-7922) Tel 410-263-0025; Toll free: 800-922-1711.

Instrument Pr, *(Instrumental Pr.; 1-881158),* Div. of McLaughlin's Red Barn Luthier Shoppe, P.O. Box 1684, Eustis, FL 32727-1684; 35038 County Rd. 437, Eustis, FL 32726 Tel 904-357-6571.

Integ Energy, *(Integrated Energy Systems; 0-9608358),* Div. of Edith Shedd & Assocs., Inc., 2499 Pannell Rd., SE, Monroe, GA 30655 (SAN 240-6802) Tel 404-207-7566.

Integral Yoga Pubns, *(Integral Yoga Pubns.; 0-932040),* Satchidananda Ashram-Yogaville, Rte. 1, Box 1720, Buckingham, VA 23921 (SAN 285-0338) Tel 804-969-1049.

Integrity Grp
See Oughten Hse

Integrity Inst, *(Integrity Institute Publishing; 0-9632040),* P.O. Box 838, Marysville, WA 98270; 6213 87th St., NE, Marysville, WA 98270 Tel 206-659-3789.

Inter-Am Tropical, *(Inter-American Tropical Tuna Commission; 0-9603078),* C/O Scripps Institute of Oceanography, La Jolla, CA 92093 (SAN 241-7294) Tel 619-546-7100.

Inter Dev Res Assn, *(Intercultural Development Research Assn.; 1-878550),* 5835 Callaghan Rd., Suite 350, San Antonio, TX 78228 Tel 210-684-8180.

Inter Directory, *(Interstate Directory Publishing Co., Inc.; 0-9629962),* 420 Jericho Turnpike, Jericho, NY 11753 Tel 516-822-5966.

Inter Print Pubs
See Interstate

Inter Skills Pr, *(Interactive Skills Pr.; 0-9618132),* 25B Broun Pl., Bronx, NY 10475 (SAN 666-3575) Tel 718-379-2007.

Interarts, *(Interarts, Ltd.; 1-879856; 1-57262),* 15 Mount Auburn St., Cambridge, MA 02138 Tel 617-354-4655; Toll free: 800-646-4655.

Interbk Inc, *(Interbook, Inc.; 0-913456; 0-89192),* 131 Varick St., 2nd Flr., New York, NY 10013 (SAN 202-7070) Tel 212-691-7248.

Intercult Pr, *(Intercultural Pr., Inc.; 0-933662;* 1-877864), P.O. Box 700, Yarmouth, ME 04096 (SAN 212-6699) Tel 207-846-5168.

Intercultural, *(Intercultural Group; 1-881267),* 10 E. 23rd St., No. 600, New York, NY 10010 Tel 212-228-9700; Dist. by: Weatherhill, Inc., 420 Madison Ave., 15th Flr., New York, NY 10017-1107 (SAN 202-9529) Tel 212-223-3008; Toll free: 800-437-7840 (orders).

Interlink Pub, *(Interlink Publishing Group, Inc.; 0-940793; 1-56656),* 99 Seventh Ave., Brooklyn, NY 11215 (SAN 664-8908) Tel 718-797-4292; Toll free: 800-238-5465. *Imprints:* Crocodile Bks (Crocodile Books).

Interspace Bks, *(Interspace Bks.; 0-930061),* 4500 Chesapeake St., NW, Washington, DC 20016 (SAN 669-8913) Tel 202-363-9082.

Interstate, *(Interstate Pubs., Inc.; 0-8134),* P.O. Box 50, Danville, IL 61834-0050 (SAN 206-6548) Tel 217-446-0500; Toll free: 800-843-4774.

Interurban, *(Interurban Pr.; 0-916374; 1-56342),* Div. of Pentrex, P.O. Box 94911, Pasadena, CA 91109 (SAN 207-9593) Tel 818-793-3400.

Intervale Pub Co, *(Intervale Publishing Co., Inc.;* 0-932400), R.R. 1, Box 288, Center Sandwich, NH 03227 (SAN 211-9633) Tel 603-284-7726.

InterVarsity, *(InterVarsity Pr.; 0-87784; 0-8308),* Div. of InterVarsity Christian Fellowship of the USA, P.O. Box 1400, 5206 Main St., Downers Grove, IL 60515 (SAN 202-7089) Tel 708-964-5700; Toll free: 800-843-9487 (orders); 800-843-7225 (customer service); 800-873-0143 (electronic ordering).

Interwood Pr, *(Interwood Pr.; 0-9610376),* 3562 Interwood Ave., Cincinnati, OH 45220 (SAN 264-1224) Tel 513-751-5239.

Intl Bible Soc, *(International Bible Society; 1-56320),* 1820 Jet Stream Dr., Colorado Springs, CO 80921 Tel 719-488-9200; Toll free: 800-524-1588.

Intl Bk Ctr, *(International Bk. Ctr.; 0-917062; 0-86685),* 2007 Laurel Dr., P.O. Box 295, Troy, MI 48099 (SAN 169-4014) Tel 810-879-8436.

Intl Gamester, *(International Gamester, Ltd.;* 0-9627003), 765 Madouse Ct., Whitmore Lake, MI 48189-9589.

Intl Gen Semantics, *(International Society for General Semantics; 0-918970),* P.O. Box 728, Concord, CA 94522 (SAN 203-8161) Tel 510-798-0311.

Intl Healing, *(International Healing Foundation, Inc.;* 0-9637058), P.O. Box 901, Bowie, MD 20718 Tel 301-773-5573.

Intl Info NY, *(International Information Publishing, Inc.;* 1-879696), 40 Underhill Blvd., Suite D, Syosset, NY 11791 Tel 516-921-9264.

Intl Lang, *(International Language Centre),* 1753 Connecticut Ave., NW, Washington, DC 20009 (SAN 209-1615) Tel 202-332-2894.

Intl Learn Syst
See Intl Lang

Intl Linguistics, *(International Linguistics Corp.;* 0-939990), 3505 E. Red Bridge Rd., Kansas City, MO 64137 (SAN 220-2573) Tel 816-765-8855.

Intl Marriage, *(International Marriage Encounter, Inc.;* 0-936098), 955 Lake Dr., Saint Paul, MN 55120 (SAN 215-6830).

Intl Schol Pr, *(International Scholastic Pr., Inc.;* 1-56385), P.O. Box 238, Fort Lauderdale, FL 33302; Toll free: 800-278-8336; 121 NW Sixth Ave., Fort Lauderdale, FL 33311 Tel 305-527-4257.

Intl Society Tech Educ, *(International Society for Technology in Education; 0-924667; 1-56484),* 1787 Agate St., Eugene, OR 97403 (SAN 296-7693) Tel 503-346-4414.

Intl Spec Bk, *(International Specialized Bk. Services;* 0-89955), 5804 NE Hassalo St., Portland, OR 97213-3644 (SAN 169-7129) Tel 503-287-3093; Toll free: 800-944-6190.

Intl Zool Soc, *(International Zoological Society, Inc.;* 0-9642604), 1708 San Bernardino Way, Naples, FL 33942-7129 Tel 813-591-3693.

Inverness Pr, *(Inverness Pr.; 0-9638975),* P.O. Box 1174, Lawrence, KS 66044; 1712 Inverness, Lawrence, KS 66047 Tel 913-843-2590.

Ion Books, *(Ion Bks., Inc.; 0-938507),* P.O. Box 111327, Memphis, TN 38111-1327 (SAN 661-3330) Tel 901-323-8858; Dist. by: SPD-Small Pr. Distribution, 1814 San Pablo Ave., Berkeley, CA 94702 (SAN 204-5826) Tel 510-549-3336; Toll free: 800-869-7553; Dist. by: Baker & Taylor Bks., Momence Service Ctr., 501 S. Gladiolus St., Momence, IL 60954-2444 (SAN 169-2100) Tel 815-472-2444; Toll free: 800-775-2300 (customer service).

Ion Imagination, *(Ion Imagination Publishing; 1-886184),* Div. of Ion Imagination Entertainment, Inc., P.O. Box 210943, Nashville, TN 37221-0943; 133 Morton Mill Cir., Nashville, TN 37221 Tel 615-646-3644.

Iowa St Educ, *(Iowa State Education Assn.; 0-9637413),* 4025 Tonawanda Dr., Des Moines, IA 50312 Tel 515-279-9711.

Iowa St U Pr, *(Iowa State Univ. Pr.; 0-8138),* 2121 S. State Ave., Ames, IA 50014-8300 (SAN 202-7194) Tel 515-292-0140; Toll free: 800-862-6657 (orders only).

IPG Chicago, *(Independent Pubs. Group),* Subs. of Chicago Review Pr., 814 N. Franklin, Chicago, IL 60610 (SAN 202-0769) Tel 312-337-0747; Toll free: 800-888-4741.

Iqra Intl Ed Fdtn, *(IQRA International Educational Foundation; 1-56316),* 831 S. Laflin St., Chicago, IL 60607 Tel 312-226-5694.

Iran Bks, *(Iran Bks.; 0-936347),* 8014 Old Georgetown Rd., Bethesda, MD 20814 (SAN 696-866X) Tel 301-986-0079.

IRI-Skylight, *(IRI/Skylight Publishing, Inc.; 0-932935),* 200 E. Wood St., Suite 274, Palatine, IL 60067 (SAN 690-0135) Tel 708-991-6300.

Iris Pr, *(Iris Pr.; 0-916078),* P.O. Box 486, Bell Buckle, TN 37020 (SAN 219-6824) Tel 615-389-6878.

Iris Visual, *(Iris Visual Services; 0-942788),* P.O. Box 45, Fredonia, NY 14063.

Irish Bks Media, *(Irish Bks. & Media, Inc.; 0-937702),* Franklin Business Ctr., 1433 Franklin Ave., E., Minneapolis, MN 55404-2135 (SAN 111-8870) Tel 612-871-3505; Toll free: 800-229-3505. Do not confuse with Irish Bks. in New York, NY.

Iron Bks, *(Iron Bks.; 0-9625740),* P.O. Box 2307, Venice, CA 90294 Tel 310-479-4779.

Iron Crown Ent Inc, *(Iron Crown Enterprises, Inc.; 0-915795; 1-55806),* P.O. Box 1605, Charlottesville, VA 22902 (SAN 294-0272) Tel 804-295-3918; Toll free: 800-325-0479; 108 Fifth St., SE, 3rd Flr., Charlottesville, VA 22901 (SAN 693-5109) Tel 804-295-3917; Dist. by: Berkley Publishing Group, 200 Madison Ave., New York, NY 10016 (SAN 201-3991) Tel 212-951-8800; Toll free: 800-631-8571.

Irresistible, *(Irresistible Bks.),* P.O. Box 1059, Angleton, TX 77515 (SAN 283-3816).

Irvington, *(Irvington Pubs.; 0-89197; 0-8290; 0-8422;* 0-512), 522 E. 82nd St., New York, NY 10028 (SAN 207-2408); Orders to: Box 286, Cooper Station, NY 10276-0286 Tel 603-922-5105; Toll free: 800-282-5413 (orders only).

Irwin Prof Pubng, *(Irwin Professional Publishing; 0-256; 0-87094; 1-55623; 0-87128; 0-7863),* Div. of Richard D. Irwin, Inc. A Times Mirror Co., 1333 Burr Ridge Pkwy., Burr Ridge, IL 60521 (SAN 220-0236) Tel 708-789-4000; Toll free: 800-634-3961.

Isabels, *(Isabel's; 0-9629612),* 17 S. High St., Suite 800, Columbus, OH 43215 Tel 614-224-0700.

ISC Pr
See Self-Counsel Pr

ISHA Enterprises, *(ISHA Enterprises; 0-936981),* 5503 E. Beck Ln., Scottsdale, AZ 85254 (SAN 658-7895) Tel 602-482-1346.

Ishnuvu Pub, *(Ishnuvu Publishing Co.; 0-9636906),* P.O. Box 3363, Oakland, CA 94609; 2815 West St., Oakland, CA 94612 Tel 510-444-9647.

Islamic Seminary, *(Islamic Seminary; 0-941724),* Subs. of the Imam Al-Khoei Foundation, 137-11 90th Ave., Jamaica, NY 11435 (SAN 239-2372) Tel 718-297-6520.

Island Flowers, *(Island Flowers, Inc.; 0-9637712),* 14000 Pines Blvd., Pembroke Pines, FL 33027-1504 Tel 305-431-3148.

Island Heritage, *(Island Heritage Publishing; 0-931548;* 0-89610), Div. of The Madden Corp., 99880 Iwaena St., Aiea, HI 96701 (SAN 211-1403) Tel 808-487-7299.

Island-Metro Pubns, *(Island-Metro Pubns., Inc.;* 0-9619832), 1 Dupont St., Plainview, NY 11803 (SAN 246-1056) Tel 516-349-8282.

Island Pr Pubs, *(Island Pr. Pubs.; 0-87208),* 175 Bahia Via, Fort Myers Beach, FL 33931 (SAN 202-7216) Tel 813-463-9482.

Isld Conser Effort, *(Island Conservation Effort;* 0-9629613), 90 Edgewater Dr., No. 901, Miami, FL 33133-6918.

ISM Teach Systs, *(ISM Teaching Systems, Inc.;* 1-56775), 30 Park Ave., No. 6N, Mount Vernon, NY 10550 Tel 914-664-7679; Toll free: 800-453-4476.

It Takes Two, *(It Takes Two, Inc.; 0-942865),* 100 Minnesota Ave., Le Sueur, MN 56058 (SAN 667-8386) Tel 612-665-6271; Toll free: 800-331-9843.

ITA Pubns, *(ITA Pubns.; 0-933935),* 1500 El Camino, Suite 350, Sacramento, CA 95833 (SAN 693-062X) Tel 916-922-1615. Do not confuse with ITA Pubns., Grand Blanc, MI.

Ithaca Pr MA, *(Ithaca Pr.; 0-915940),* P.O. Box 853, Lowell, MA 01853 (SAN 208-709X) Tel 508-453-2177; Dist. by: Bookpeople, 7900 Edgewater Dr., Oakland, CA 94621 (SAN 168-9517) Tel 510-632-4700; Toll free: 800-999-4650.

ITS Pub, *(Is That Sew? Publishing; 0-9622968),* P.O. Box 68, Mill Valley, CA 94942; 232 Miller Ave., Mill Valley, CA 94942 Tel 415-383-4417.

Ivory Pal, *(Ivory Palaces Music Publishing Co., Inc.;* 0-943644), 3141 Spottswood Ave., Memphis, TN 38111 (SAN 238-3020) Tel 901-323-3509.

Ivy Books, *(Ivy Bks.; 0-8041),* Div. of Ballantine Bks., Inc., 201 E. 50th St., New York, NY 10022 (SAN 661-7832); Toll free: 800-733-3000 (orders); 800-726-0600 (customer service/credit).

Ivy Hill Pubs, *(Ivy Hill Pubs.; 1-884095),* 124 NW Newton, Burleson, TX 76028 Tel 817-295-4210.

Ivystone, *(Ivystone Pubns.; 0-935604),* 247 Alabama St., Saint Simons Island, GA 31522 (SAN 215-3211).

J A Eades, *(Eades, Jo Ann; 0-9623325),* 105 Westminster St., No. 1, Jacksonville, IL 62650-2303; 1320 Maple, Jacksonville, IL 62650 Tel 217-245-1608.

J A Herb, *(Herb, James A.; 0-9641479),* P.O. Box 3656, La Habra, CA 90632-3656; 701 E. Parkwood Ave., La Habra, CA 90631 Tel 714-870-4998.

J A Willard, *(Willard, John A.; 0-9612398),* 3119 Country Club Cir., Billings, MT 59102 (SAN 289-5323) Tel 406-259-1966.

J Alden, *(Alden, Jay, Pubs.; 0-914844),* P.O. Box 1295, 546 S. Hofgaarden St., La Puente, CA 91749 (SAN 204-7780) Tel 818-968-6424.

J & G Ferguson, *(Ferguson, Jane, & Gary; 0-9624846),* P.O. Box 1490, Red Lodge, MT 59068; 11 S. Broadway, Red Lodge, MT 59068 Tel 406-446-2388; Dist. by: GCBA, P.O. Box 292, Grand Canyon, AZ 86023 (SAN 295-8074) Tel 602-638-2597. Do not confuse with J. G. Ferguson Publishing Co., Chicago, IL.

J & J Win Edge, *(J & J Winning Edge Pr., Inc.;* 0-9621313), 25 E. Irving Park Rd., Roselle, IL 60172 (SAN 251-0456) Tel 312-529-6634.

J & K Ent, *(J&K Enterprises; 0-9639609),* P.O. Box 751235, Petaluma, CA 94975-1235; 2727 Marra Rd., Occidental, CA 95465 Tel 707-874-1359.

J & L Bks, *(J & L Bks.; 0-9613536),* 153 Haynes Rd, Avon, CT 06001 (SAN 669-6899) Tel 203-673-4315.

J B Baily, *(Baily, Jane B.; 0-9626642),* 60 Davidson Rd., West Chester, PA 19382 Tel 610-793-1861.

J B Barnes, *(Barnes, Joyce B.; 0-9628493),* R.R. 1, Box 7010, Hornbeck, LA 71439-9801 Tel 318-565-4873.

J B Browning, *(Browning, Jeannine B.; 0-9627729),* 8552 Sylvan Dr., Melbourne, FL 32904-2426 Tel 407-723-5111.

J B Comns, *(JB Communications, Inc.; 1-55987),* 101 W. 55th St., No. 2D, New York, NY 10019-5346 Tel 212-246-0900. *Imprints:* Sunny Bks (Sunny Books).

J B Painter, *(Painter, Jacqueline B.; 0-9634256),* 12 Jones St., Sylva, NC 28779 Tel 704-586-4227.

J B Pal, *(Pal, J. B., & Co., Inc.; 0-916836),* 904 W. Castlewood Terr., Chicago, IL 60640 (SAN 208-0567) Tel 312-271-0123.

J Barnaby Dist, *(Barnaby, J., Distributors; 0-942403),* 1709 Hawthorne Ln., Plano, TX 75074 (SAN 667-0512) Tel 214-423-2411.

J Benton Bks, *(Benton, John, Bks.; 0-9635411),* 218 S. Madison, Pasadena, CA 91101 Tel 818-405-0950; Dist. by: Spring Arbor Distributors, 10885 Textile Rd., Belleville, MI 48111 (SAN 158-9016) Tel 313-481-0900; Toll free: 800-395-5599 (orders); 800-395-7234 (customer service).

J Chernak, *(Chernak, Judy, Productions; 0-944633),* 3114 Hatton Rd., Pikesville, MD 21208 (SAN 244-5859) Tel 410-484-7088.

J Daniel, *(Daniel, John, & Co., Pubs.; 0-936784;* 1-880284), Div. of Daniel & Daniel Pubs., Inc., P.O. Box 21922, Santa Barbara, CA 93121 (SAN 215-1995); Toll free: 800-662-8351; Orders to: 21 E. Canon Perdido, Santa Barbara, CA 93101 Tel 805-962-1780.

J Dashney, *(Dashney, John; 0-9633236),* 1932 Chemeketa St., NE, Salem, OR 97301 Tel 503-364-5825.

J Duco, *(Duco, Joyce; 0-9612896),* P.O. Box 41662, Nashville, TN 37204 (SAN 291-140X) Tel 615-386-3488; Dist. by: DeVorss & Co., P.O. Box 550, Marina del Rey, CA 90294-0550 (SAN 168-9886) Tel 213-870-7478; Toll free: 800-843-5743 (bookstores only); 800-331-4719 (in California, bookstores only); Dist. by: Spring Arbor Distributors, 10885 Textile Rd., Belleville, MI 48111 (SAN 158-9016) Tel 313-481-0900; Toll free: 800-395-5599 (orders); 800-395-7234 (customer service); Dist. by: Ingram Bk. Co., 1 Ingram Blvd., La Vergne, TN 37086-1986 (SAN 169-7978) Tel 615-793-5000; Toll free: 800-937-8000 (orders only, all warehouses).

J E Brown, *(Brown, James Edward; 0-9632358),* P.O. Box 242, Pacific Grove, CA 93950; Lincoln 2nd House SW of 3rd, Carmel, CA 93921 Tel 408-625-2230.

J E Stewart, *(Stewart, J. E.; 1-877866),* 18518 Kenlake Pl., NE, Seattle, WA 98155 Tel 206-486-4510.

J Franklin, *(Franklin, J., Pub.; 0-9616736),* P.O. Box 14057, Tulsa, OK 74159 (SAN 661-4302); Toll free: 800-234-9384; 4123 S. Victor Ct., Tulsa, OK 74105 (SAN 661-4310) Tel 918-747-9858.

J Gile Comm, *(Gile, John, Communications; 0-910941),* 1710 N. Main St., Rockford, IL 61103 (SAN 270-5109) Tel 815-968-6601.

J H Childs Bks, *(Ho's, Jane, Children Bks.; 0-9619126),* 700 Kipling Ct., El Sobrante, CA 94803 (SAN 243-4954) Tel 510-222-2621.

J Hefty Pub, *(Hefty, John, Publishing Co., Inc.;* 1-880453), 976 Grand Canal St., Gulf Breeze, FL 32561 Tel 904-934-1599.

J Herzberg, *(Herzberg, Jack, Pub.; 0-943077),* 1740 Kings Row, Reno, NV 89503 (SAN 668-016X) Tel 702-747-5254.

J J Features, *(Jill, Jodi, Features; 1-883438),* 1705 14th St., Suite 321, Boulder, CO 80302 Tel 303-575-1319.

J J Fun, *(J.J. Fun, Inc.; 0-9632622),* 478 Clinton Rd., Chestnut Hill, MA 02167 Tel 617-638-4652.

J Jons LA, *(Jons, John; 0-9623099),* 213 Surrey Dr., La Place, LA 70068 Tel 504-652-7412.

J L Estes, *(Estes, James L.; 0-9628634),* c/o The Writer's Service (Agent), 816 Pierremont Rd., Shreveport, LA 71106 Tel 318-869-3587.

J L Shubert, *(Shubert, Joseph L.; 0-9627015),* Rte. 27, P.O. Box 188, Kingfield, ME 04947 Tel 207-628-4626.

J Laina Pub, *(Laina, J., Publishing; 0-9628023),* P.O. Box 1570, Carrollton, GA 30117-1570; 1154 Rome St., Carrollton, GA 30117 Tel 706-834-2769.

J Laster Pub Co, *(Laster, Jim, Publishing Co.;* 0-9612780), P.O. Box 50512, Nashville, TN 37205 (SAN 289-7474) Tel 615-356-5318.

J Laverne Mus, *(Jaclyn Laverne Music/Film Publishing Co.; 1-880605),* 1770 N. Highland Ave., No. 474, Los Angeles, CA 90028 Tel 818-980-0287.

J Liebowitz, *(Liebowitz, Jay, & Assocs.; 0-9623252),* 966 Farm Haven Dr., Rockville, MD 20852 Tel 301-231-8040; Dist. by: Atrium Pubs. Group, 11270 Clayton Creek Rd., Lower Lake, CA 95457 (SAN 200-5743) Tel 707-995-3906; Toll free: 800-275-2606.

J Lynn Pub, *(J-Lynn Publishing; 1-877797),* P.O. Box 163, Grantsboro, NC 28529 Tel 919-745-3030.

J M Cook Pub, *(Cook, John M., Publishing Co.;* 0-9622602), P.O. Box 22171, Baltimore, MD 21202; 2530 Edgecomb Cir., N., Apt. 1, Baltimore, MD 21215 Tel 410-362-2899.

J M Emory, *(Emory, J. M., Publishing; 0-9640625),* 1820 E. Broad St., Greensboro, GA 30642 Tel 706-453-2035.

J M Herren, *(Herren, Janet M.; 0-9613025),* 4750 Crystal Springs Dr., Bainbridge Island, WA 98110 (SAN 293-9967) Tel 206-842-3484; Dist. by: Pacific Pipeline, Inc., 8030 S. 228th St, Kent, WA 98032-2900 (SAN 208-2128) Tel 206-872-5523; Toll free: 800-444-7323 (Customer Service); 800-677-2222 (orders).

J M Maldonado, *(Maldonado, Jesus Maria; 0-9636912),* P.O. Box 471, Grandview, WA 98930; 1805 Queen St., Grandview, WA 98930 Tel 509-882-4844.

J McBurney, *(McBurney, Jim; 0-9629471),* 890 S. Wolfe Rd., Sunnyvale, CA 94086 Tel 408-733-9479.

J Maciel, *(Maciel, Jairo; 0-9642230),* 32 Union Square E., No. 200, New York, NY 10003 Tel 212-473-0861.

J Messner *Imprint of* **S&S Trade**

J Muckle
See KSJ Publishing

J N Townsend, *(Townsend, J. N., Publishing; 0-9617426;* 1-880158), 12 Greenleaf Dr., Exeter, NH 03833 (SAN 630-303X) Tel 603-778-9883; Toll free: 800-333-9883 (orders only); Dist. by: Alan C. Hood & Co., Inc., 28 Birge St., Brattleboro, VT 05301 (SAN 270-8221) Tel 802-254-2200.

J-p Press, *(J.-p. Pr.; 0-9621929),* P.O. Box 48, Ellenville, NY 12428; 53 Market St., Ellenville, NY 12428 Tel 914-647-7016.

J Pohl Assocs, *(Pohl, J., Assocs.; 0-939332),* 1706 Berkwood Dr., Pittsburgh, PA 15243 (SAN 220-181X) Tel 412-279-5000.

J R Berry, *(Berry, John R., Evangelistic Assn.;* 0-9616900), P.O. Box 8252, Philadelphia, PA 19101 (SAN 661-4949); 605 S. 60th St., Philadelphia, PA 19143 (SAN 661-4957) Tel 215-747-0606.

J R Bonilla, *(Bonilla, Jayne Robin; 0-9635105),* 1273 Seagrape Cir., Fort Lauderdale, FL 33326 Tel 305-384-7647.

J R Matthews, *(Matthews, J.R., , Inc.; 0-9623563),* P.O. Box 2394, Abilene, TX 79603.

J R Pubns, *(J.R. Pubns.; 0-913952),* 170 NE 33rd St., Fort Lauderdale, FL 33334 (SAN 202-7283) Tel 305-563-1844.

J Sears, *(Sears, Jeanne; 0-9621086),* 32087 Hamilton Ct., No. 204A, Solon, OH 44139 (SAN 250-491X) Tel 216-349-2794.

J Simon, *(Simon, Joseph/Pangloss Pr.; 0-934710),* P.O. Box 4071, Malibu, CA 90264 (SAN 213-9669); 29500 Heathercliff Rd., No. 161, Malibu, CA 90265 (SAN 662-1457) Tel 310-457-3293; Dist. by: Inland Bk. Co., 140 Commerce St., East Haven, CT 06512 (SAN 200-4151) Tel 203-467-4257; Toll free: 800-243-0138; Dist. by: Palmer Pubns., 318 N. Main St., Amherst, WI 54406 (SAN 630-8597); Toll free: 800-333-8122 (credit card orders).

J Sisson, *(Sisson, Joan; 0-9622498),* 2750 Marina Ave., Livermore, CA 94550 Tel 510-443-5524.

J Stuart Found, *(Stuart, Jesse, Foundation, The;* 0-945084), P.O. Box 391, Ashland, KY 41114 (SAN 245-8837); 1212 Bath Ave., Ashland, KY 41101 (SAN 245-8845) Tel 606-329-5233.

J Takhars, *(Takhar's, Jodi, Spilt Milk Collection;* 1-886000), P.O. Box 1005, 403 Fourth St. NW, No. 200, Bemidji, MN 56601 Tel 218-759-2089.

J Taylor Ltd, *(Taylor, Joe, Ltd.; 0-9638873),* 3913 Courtland Dr., Metairie, LA 70002 Tel 504-733-2331; Toll free: 800-535-7365.

J Vernon, *(Vernon, Judy; 0-9617776),* P.O. Box 5384, NWJC, Senatobia, MS 38668 (SAN 664-8061); Thompson St., Apt. A8, Senatobia, MS 38668 (SAN 664-807X) Tel 601-562-6270.

J Vesty Co, *(Vesty, John, Co.; 0-9626876),* Bennett Rd., Indian Lake, NY 12842 Tel 518-648-5742.

J Y Carroll, *(Carroll, James Y.; 0-9632262),* P.O. Box 989, Ozark, AL 36361; 310 Squirrel Dr., Ozark, AL 36360 Tel 205-774-2468.

J Yolen Bks *Imprint of* **HarBrace**

JAARS Inc, *(Jungle Aviation & Radio Service (JAARS); 0-9615959; 1-878606),* Affil. of Summer Institute of Linguistics, Box 248, JAARS Rd., Waxhaw, NC 28173 (SAN 697-2896) Tel 704-843-6055; Dist. by: Wycliffe Bible Translators, P.O. Box 2727, Huntington Beach, CA 92647 (SAN 211-5484) Tel 714-969-4600.

Jackman Pubng, *(Jackman Publishing; 0-929985;* 1-56509), P.O. Box 1900, Orem, UT 84059 (SAN 250-9210) Tel 801-225-0859.

Jackson Pub, *(Jackson Publishing; 0-9623915; 1-56713),* P.O. Box 695, Farmington, UT 84025-0695 Tel 801-521-8226; 615 N. 400 W., Salt Lake City, UT 84103. Do not confuse with Jackson Publishing, Clarkston, MI.

Jacobs, *(Jacobs Publishing Co.; 0-918272),* 3334 E. Indian School Rd., Suite C, Phoenix, AZ 85018 (SAN 209-4525) Tel 602-954-6581.

JACP Inc, *(JACP, Inc.; 0-934609),* 414 E. Third Ave., San Mateo, CA 94401 (SAN 693-8841) Tel 415-343-9408; Orders to: P.O. Box 367, San Mateo, CA 94401 (SAN 662-3271).
Jacqueline Enter, *(Jacqueline Enterprises, Inc.;* 0-932446), 9725 E. Hampden Ave., No. 203, Denver, CO 80231 (SAN 221-0487) Tel 303-779-8278.
Jade Ram Pub, *(Jade Ram Publishing; 1-877721),* P.O. Box 202163, Anchorage, AK 99520-2163; 3000 E. 16th, Anchorage, AK 99520 Tel 907-272-8432.
Jalice Pubs, *(Jalice Pubs.; 0-9627375),* P.O. Box 455, Notre Dame, IN 46556 Tel 219-232-9534.
Jalmar Pr, *(Jalmar Pr.; 0-915190; 1-880396),* Subs. of B. L. Winch & Assocs., 2675 Skypark Dr., No. 204, Torrance, CA 90505 (SAN 113-3640) Tel 310-784-0016; Toll free: 800-662-9662 (orders).
Jamestown Pubs, *(Jamestown Pubs., Inc.; 0-89061),* P.O. Box 9168, Providence, RI 02940 (SAN 201-5196) Tel 401-351-1915; Toll free: 800-872-7323.
Jamondas Pr, *(Jamondas Pr.; 0-9631035),* 2106 Arborview Blvd., Ann Arbor, MI 48103 Tel 313-994-5514.
Jan Prods, *(January Productions, Inc.; 0-934898;* 0-87386), P.O. Box 66, 210 Sixth Ave., Hawthorne, NJ 07507 (SAN 222-822X) Tel 201-423-4666; Toll free: 800-451-7450.
J&A Bks, *(J&A Bks., Inc.; 0-9635876),* P.O. Box 340, New Baltimore, MI 48047; 27227 JoEllen Ct., Chesterfield, MI 48051 Tel 810-598-0947.
Janeway Riley, *(Riley, Janeway; 0-9637378),* 311 Garfield Ave., Eau Claire, WI 54701 Tel 715-834-1989; Dist. by: Publishers Distribution Service, 6893 Sullivan Rd., Grawn, MI 49637 (SAN 630-5717) Tel 616-276-5196; Toll free: 800-345-0096 (orders only); Dist. by: Independent Pubs. Marketing (Gift Shops), 6824 Oaklawn Ave., Edina, MN 55435 (SAN 630-5725) Tel 612-920-9044.
Janson Pubns, *(Janson Pubns.; 0-939765),* 450 Washington St., Suite 107, Dedham, MA 02026 (SAN 663-7663) Tel 617-326-0009; Toll free: 800-322-6284.
Japan Pubns USA, *(Japan Pubns. (U.S.A.), Inc.;* 0-87040), 45 Hawthorn Pl., Briarcliff Manor, NY 10510 (SAN 680-0513); c/o Kodansha America, Inc., 114 Fifth Ave., 18th Flr., New York, NY 10011 (SAN 201-0526) Tel 212-727-6460; Dist. by: Kodansha International U. S. A., Ltd., 114 Fifth Ave., New York, NY 10011 (SAN 201-0526) Tel 212-727-6460; Toll free: 800-631-8571; Dist. by: Farrar, Straus & Giroux, Inc., 19 Union Sq., W., New York, NY 10003 (SAN 206-782X) Tel 212-741-6900; Toll free: 800-788-6262 (Individuals); 800-631-8571 (Booksellers).
Jarrett Pub, *(Jarrett Publishing Co.; 0-9624723;* 1-882422), 2524 Highgate Dr., Richmond, CA 94806-5258.
Jasmine Pr, *(Jasmine Pr.; 0-930069),* 2224 Ogden Ave., Bensalem, PA 19020 (SAN 669-9650) Tel 215-244-0525.
Jasmine Studios, *(Jasmine Studios; 0-9633803),* 111 Pinehill Rd., Pineville, LA 71360 Tel 318-640-1479.
Jasmine Texts, *(Jasmine Texts; 0-938861),* 1641 Third Ave., Suite 8BE, New York, NY 10128 (SAN 661-7328) Tel 212-348-8487.
Jason & Nordic Pubs, *(Jason & Nordic Pubs.; 0-944727),* Affil. of Blue Bunory Productions, P.O. Box 441, Hollidaysburg, PA 16648 (SAN 244-9374) Tel 814-696-2920.
Jay & Assocs, *(Jay & Assocs., Pubs.; 0-939422),* P.O. Box 2222, Brevard, NC 28712-2222 (SAN 281-837X) Tel 704-885-2062.
JayJo Bks, *(JayJo Bks., Inc.; 0-9639449),* P.O. Box 213, Saint Louis, MO 63088-0213 Tel 314-861-1331; Toll free: 800-801-0159.
JBP Press, *(JBP Pr.; 0-9635877),* 5033 Lavinia Rd., NE, Bemidji, MN 56601 Tel 218-751-1853.
JCH Pr, *(JCH Pr.; 0-929932),* 1605 Huge Oaks, Houston, TX 77055 (SAN 250-8737) Tel 713-827-1611.
Je Suis Derby, *(Je Suis Derby Publishing; 0-9627436),* Div. of Derby Corp., 535 Broadway, Revere, MA 02151 Tel 617-284-0903.
Jean Page, *(Page, Jean; 0-9632755),* 4225 Courtney, NE, Albuquerque, NM 87108 Tel 505-265-7930.
Jeannie Griffin, *(Griffin, Jeannie; 0-9625016),* 411 Virgil Rd., Dryden, NY 13053 Tel 607-844-9892.
Jefferson Natl, *(Jefferson National Expansion Historical Assn.; 0-931056),* 11 N. Fourth St., Saint Louis, MO 63102 (SAN 213-0912).
Jelm Mtn, *(Jelm Mountain Pubns.; 0-936204),* 2017 Grand Ave., Laramie, WY 82070 (SAN 216-1419) Tel 307-745-9567.
JEM Job Educ, *(JEM/Job Educational Materials;* 0-9628787), 1230 E. Main St., Alhambra, CA 91801 Tel 818-308-7642.
Jen Chen Buddhism, *(Jen Chen Buddhism World Ctr.;* 1-56369), 17500 Nordhoff St., Northridge, CA 91325 Tel 818-775-1231.
Jenny Wren Pr, *(Jenny Wren Pr., The; 0-9621753),* P.O. Box 505, Mooresville, IN 46158 (SAN 252-2071); 5 Daniel St., Mooresville, IN 46158 (SAN 252-208X).
Jenson Pubns, *(Jenson Pubns., Inc.; 0-931205),* P.O. Box 13819, Milwaukee, WI 53213-0819 (SAN 679-9914) Tel 414-774-3630.
Jerseydale Ranch, *(Jerseydale Ranch Pr.; 1-882803),* 6506 Jerseydale Rd., Mariposa, CA 95338 Tel 209-742-7972.
Jesus Bks, *(Jesus Bks.; 0-932588),* 1565 Madison St., Oakland, CA 94612 (SAN 212-1034) Tel 510-763-4324.
Jewelgate, *(Jewelgate Pr.; 0-9630574),* 135-38 226th St., Laurelton, NY 11413 Tel 718-978-1824.
Jewish Lights, *(Jewish Lights Publishing; 1-879045),* Div. of LongHill Partners, Inc., P.O. Box 237, Sunset Farm Offices, Rte. 4, Woodstock, VT 05091 (SAN 242-6439) Tel 802-457-4000; Toll free: 800-962-4544.
JHO Music, *(JHO Music; 0-9626239),* 11 Marshall Terr., Wayland, MA 01778 Tel 508-358-5213.
Jikani Pr, *(Jikani Pr.; 0-9640001),* 220 Staysail Ct., Foster City, CA 94404 Tel 415-574-8973.
Jilcoe, *(Jilcoe; 0-9624976),* Div. of Hempe Manufacturing Co., Inc., 2750 S. 163rd St., New Berlin, WI 53151 Tel 414-784-2710.
Jimar Prodns, *(Jimar Productions; 0-931731),* 2 Corporate Ctr., Suite 100, Springfield, MO 65804 (SAN 667-7908) Tel 417-694-2454.
Jireh & Assocs, *(Jireh & Assocs.; 0-9632669),* 2819 First Ave., Suite 250, Seattle, WA 98121-1113 Tel 206-654-0171.
JIST Works, *(JIST Works, Inc.; 0-942784; 1-56370),* 720 N. Park Ave., Indianapolis, IN 46202-3431 (SAN 240-2351) Tel 317-264-3720; Toll free: 800-648-5478.
JJJ Pubs, *(JJJ Pubs.; 0-941951),* Rte. 3, Box 121, Paola, KS 66071 (SAN 666-7716) Tel 913-294-4133.
JK Pub, *(JK Publishing; 0-945878),* P.O. Box 994, Kings Park, NY 11754 (SAN 248-1642); 48 Janet Pl., Valley Stream, NY 11581 (SAN 248-1650) Tel 516-544-2424.
JM Pub, *(JM Publishing; 0-923133),* HC 7 Box 102, Llano, TX 78643-9719 (SAN 251-5997).
JML Enter MD, *(JML Enterprises, Inc.; 0-938464),* 346 W. Prospect Bay Dr., Grasonville, MD 21638-9648 (SAN 238-5279).
Jo-Jo Pubns, *(Jo-Jo Pubns.; 0-9602266),* 208 N. Sparrow Rd., Chesapeake, VA 23325 (SAN 212-5153) Tel 804-420-8614.
Job Data, *(Job Data, Inc.; 0-918443),* 120 W. Madison, Rm. 1118, Chicago, IL 60602 (SAN 657-6303) Tel 312-263-2542.
Johannesen, *(Johannesen; 1-881084),* P.O. Box 24, Harris Creek Rd., Whitethorn, CA 95589 Tel 707-986-7465.
John Muir, *(Muir, John, Pubns.; 0-912528; 0-945465;* 1-56261), P.O. Box 613, Santa Fe, NM 87504-0613 (SAN 203-9079) Tel 505-982-4078; Toll free: 800-888-7504; Dist. by: W. W. Norton & Co., Inc., 500 Fifth Ave., New York, NY 10110 (SAN 202-5795) Tel 212-354-5500; Toll free: 800-223-2584; 800-223-4830 (book orders only).
Johnson Bks, *(Johnson Bks.; 0-933472; 1-55566),* Div. of Johnson Publishing Co., 1880 S. 57th Ct., Boulder, CO 80301 (SAN 201-0313) Tel 303-443-9766; Toll free: 800-258-5830.
Johnson Chi, *(Johnson Publishing Co., Inc.; 0-87485),* 820 S. Michigan Ave., Chicago, IL 60605 (SAN 201-0305) Tel 312-322-9248. Do not confuse with Johnson Publishing Co. Inc., Loveland, CO.
Johnston Bicent Found, *(Johnston Bicentennial Foundation; 0-9620343),* 1701 Governors Dr., SE, Huntsville, AL 35801 (SAN 248-1987) Tel 205-534-8252.
Jomilt Pubns, *(Jomilt Pubns.; 0-9616076),* 329 W. Mt. Airy Ave., Philadelphia, PA 19119 (SAN 697-9939) Tel 215-750-4173.
Jonah Pr, *(Jonah Pr.; 0-929422),* P.O. Box 5473, Sherman Oaks, CA 91413 (SAN 249-4000) Tel 818-986-1809.
Jonas, *(Jonas; 1-56611),* 2603 W. 60th, Indianapolis, IN 46208 Tel 317-255-5220.
Jonathan David, *(Jonathan David Pubs., Inc.; 0-8246),* 68-22 Eliot Ave., Middle Village, NY 11379 (SAN 169-5274) Tel 718-456-8611.
Jones
See Jonas
Jones & Bartlett, *(Jones & Bartlett Pubs., Inc.; 0-86720),* 1 Exeter Plaza, Boston, MA 02116 (SAN 285-0893) Tel 617-859-3900; Toll free: 800-832-0034.
Jonka Enter, *(Jonka Enterprises; 1-878794),* P.O. Box 13661, Sacramento, CA 95853; Toll free: 800-222-8718; 875 Turnstone Dr., Sacramento, CA 95834 Tel 916-929-0631.
Jordan Enterprises, *(Jordan Enterprises Publishing Co.;* 0-9615560), Div. of Butterfly & The Eagle Bks., P.O. Box 15111, Saint Louis, MO 63110 (SAN 696-480X).
Jordan Valley, *(Jordan Valley Heritage Hse.; 0-939810),* 43592 Hwy. 226, Stayton, OR 97383 (SAN 216-7425) Tel 503-859-3144.
Jordane Pub, *(Jordane Publishing; 0-9621221),* Rte. 2, Box 1291, Wild Rose, WI 54984 (SAN 250-8605) Tel 414-622-3976.
Jory Pubns, *(Jory Pubns.; 0-9607732),* 12535 Sunview Dr., Creve Coeur, MO 63146 (SAN 238-0935) Tel 314-434-0066.
Joshua Morris, *(Joshua Morris Publishing, Inc.; 0-88705),* Subs. of Reader's Digest Assoc., Inc., 221 Danbury Rd., Wilton, CT 06897 (SAN 283-2143) Tel 203-761-9999.
Journal Pubns *Imprint of* **Addison-Wesley**
Journeys Into Language, *(Journey's Into Language;* 0-945349), 150 Seal Rock Dr., San Francisco, CA 94121 (SAN 246-7216) Tel 415-221-2446.
Journeys Together, *(Journeys Together; 0-9619040),* P.O. Box 1254, La Mesa, CA 92044 Tel 619-461-5582.
Jove Pubns, *(Jove Pubns., Inc.; 0-515),* Div. of Berkley Publishing Group, 200 Madison Ave., New York, NY 10016 (SAN 215-8817) Tel 212-951-8800; Toll free: 800-631-8571; Orders to: Berkley Publishing Group, P.O. Box 506, East Rutherford, NJ 07073; Toll free: 800-223-0510 (orders); Dist. by: Warner Publishing Services, 1271 Avenue of the Americas, New York, NY 10020 (SAN 200-5522) Tel 212-522-8900.
Joy Deliverance, *(Joy of Deliverance Co.; 0-9620133),* P.O. Box 2913, Ann Arbor, MI 48106 (SAN 247-6568); 35725 Bibbins, Romulus, MI 48174 (SAN 247-6576) Tel 313-941-4246.
Joy Pub SJC, *(Joy Publishing; 0-939513),* Div. of California Clock Co., P.O. Box 9901, Fountain Valley, CA 92708 (SAN 663-3544) Tel 714-545-4321; Toll free: 800-783-6265.
Joy Pubs, *(Joy Pubs.; 0-9626994),* P.O. Box 14186, Bradenton, FL 34280-4186 (SAN 297-2646) Tel 813-792-0689.
Joy St Bks *Imprint of* **Little**
Joyce Media, *(Joyce Media, Inc.; 0-917002),* P.O. Box 57, Acton, CA 93510 (SAN 208-7197) Tel 805-269-1169.
JPS Phila, *(Jewish Pubn. Society; 0-8276),* 1930 Chestnut St., Philadelphia, PA 19103 (SAN 201-0240) Tel 215-564-5925; Toll free: 800-234-3151; Orders to: JPS, O'Neill Hwy., Dunmore, PA 18512; Toll free: 800-355-1165.
Jr League KC, *(Junior League of Kansas City, Missouri, Inc.; 0-9607076),* 9215 Ward Pkwy., Kansas City, MO 64114-3307 (SAN 238-9959) Tel 816-444-2112.
Jr League Raleigh, *(Junior League of Raleigh, Inc.;* 0-9631710), 4020 Barrett Dr., Suite 104, Raleigh, NC 27609 Tel 919-787-7480.
JRBB Pubs, *(JRBB Pubs.; 0-9627951),* 9718 Mueck Terr., Saint Louis, MO 63119-1309.
JRC Pubns, *(JRC Pubns., Inc.; 0-9637423),* 4064 Lakeridge Ln., Bloomfield Hills, MI 48302 Tel 810-855-2513.
JSP Pub, *(JSP Publishing; 0-9622328),* 9879 Zig Zag Rd., Cincinnati, OH 45242 Tel 513-791-4096.
JTG Nashville, *(JTG of Nashville; 0-938971; 1-884832),* 1024C 18th Ave., S., Nashville, TN 37212 (SAN 630-3323) Tel 615-329-3036.
Jubilee Christian Ctr, *(Jubilee Christian Ctr.; 1-884920),* 175 Nortech Pkwy., San Jose, CA 95134 Tel 408-262-0900.
Jubilee Yr Bks, *(Jubilee Year Bks.; 0-9637273),* 1066 Lincoln Pl., Brooklyn, NY 11213 Tel 718-771-7841.
Judaica Pr, *(Judaica Pr., Inc., The; 0-910818; 1-880582),* 123 Ditmas Ave., Brooklyn, NY 11218 (SAN 204-9856) Tel 718-972-6200; Toll free: 800-972-6201.
Judson, *(Judson Pr.; 0-8170),* Div. of American Baptist Churches, U.S.A., P.O. Box 851, Valley Forge, PA 19482-0851 (SAN 201-0348) Tel 610-768-2117; Toll free: 800-331-1053.
Jugglebug, *(Jugglebug; 0-9615521; 1-880912),* 7526 J Olympic View Dr., Edmonds, WA 98026 (SAN 696-2882) Tel 206-774-2127; Toll free: 800-523-1776.
Jungle Pr, *(Jungle Pr.; 0-9614443),* Div. of Glassman Publishing, P.O. Box 1058, Makawao, Maui, HI 96768 (SAN 689-3619) Tel 808-572-3453.
Junior Bks *Imprint of* **HarpC**
Juniper *Imprint of* **Fawcett**
Juniper Pr WI, *(Juniper Pr.; 1-55780),* 1310 Shorewood Dr., La Crosse, WI 54601 (SAN 207-8570) Tel 608-788-0096. Do not confuse with companies with the same name in Albuquerque, NM, Notre Dame, IN.
Juniper Ridge, *(Juniper Ridge Pr.; 0-916289),* P.O. Box 1278, Olympia, WA 98507-1278 (SAN 295-8899); Toll free: 800-869-7342.
Just Mom & Me, *(Just Mom & Me, Inc.; 0-9635490),* 29705 Rock Creek, Southfield, MI 48076; Toll free: 800-443-9879.
Just Us Bks, *(Just Us Bks., Inc.; 0-940975),* 301 Main St., 2nd Flr., Orange, NJ 07050 (SAN 664-7413) Tel 201-676-4345.

Just Write CO, *(Just Write Publishing Co.; 0-9636818),* 2577 Butte Cir., Sedalia, CO 80135 (SAN 297-9829) Tel 303-688-5825.

Juvenescent, *(Juvenescent Research Corp.; 0-9600148;* 1-884996), 807 Riverside Dr., Apt. 1F, New York, NY 10032 (SAN 206-7250) Tel 212-795-3749.

Jwand Ent, *(Jwand Enterprises; 1-883753),* P.O. Box 25313, Philadelphia, PA 19119; 75 E. Duval St., Philadelphia, PA 19144 Tel 215-438-1809.

K & M Pub, *(K & M Publishing; 0-924277),* 4185 SW 102nd Ave., Beaverton, OR 97005 Tel 503-626-8059; Dist. by: The Riggs Institute, 4185 SW 102nd Ave., Beaverton, OR 97005 (SAN 298-1726) Tel 503-646-9459.

K Bachrach Co, *(Bachrach, K., Co., Inc.; 1-878530),* 342 Taft Rd., River Edge, NJ 07661 Tel 201-343-3974.

K Cs Bks N Stuff, *(K.C.'s Bks. N Stuff; 0-9633295),* 5938 Waterman Blvd., Saint Louis, MO 63112 Tel 314-725-7494.

K D Duchak
See Family Pubng

K D Trng & Develop
See Team Effort

K E Sibley, *(Sibley, Kenneth E.; 0-9619934),* 32 Mishawaka Dr., Rochester, IL 62563 (SAN 247-0926) Tel 217-498-9439.

K Flores Min, *(Flores, Kathy, Ministries; 0-9626862),* 31235 Oak Valley Dr., Homeland, CA 92348 Tel 909-926-4256.

K Jensen, *(Jensen, Kent; 0-9621024),* c/o Abbie Ramirez, Los Angeles Mission College, Special Education Office, 1212 San Fernando Rd., San Fernando, CA 91340 (SAN 250-6858) Tel 818-365-8271.

K K Aharon, *(Kollel Kedushas Aharon; 0-9629684),* 33 Lincoln Ave., New Square, NY 10977 Tel 914-362-8689.

K K Pub Co, *(Kaye's & Knight Publishing Co.;* 0-9612140), P.O. Box 2065, 503 Broadway, Fargo, ND 58107 (SAN 287-2765) Tel 701-237-4525.

K M Donovan, *(Donovan, Kevin M.; 0-9641338),* 1909 Munster Ave., Saint Paul, MN 55116 Tel 612-699-7636.

K Q Assocs, *(K-Q Assocs., Inc.; 0-941988),* P.O. Box 2132, Cedar Rapids, IA 52406 (SAN 238-4655).

K S Jewels, *(K.S. Jewels, Inc.; 0-9639319),* P.O. Box 625, Woodstock, GA 30188; 312 Farm Ridge Dr., Woodstock, GA 30188 Tel 404-591-0062.

K Strauss & A Gligor, *(Strauss, Karen & Adrian Gligor;* 0-9634797), 1604 Badger Dr., Toms River, NJ 08753 Tel 908-341-0457.

K T Kids, *(KT Kids Co.; 0-9630898),* 545 Palm Ave., Coronado, CA 92118 Tel 619-435-3749.

KABEL Pubs, *(Kabel Pubs.; 0-930329),* 11225 Huntover Dr., Rockville, MD 20852 (SAN 670-8323) Tel 301-468-6463.

Kabyn, *(Kabyn Bks.; 0-940444),* 6549 Mission Gorge Rd., No 274, San Diego, CA 92120 (SAN 159-1002) Tel 619-274-3306.

KAC, *(KAC, Inc.; 0-9622353),* 3425 S. 94th Ave., Omaha, NE 68124 Tel 402-393-8537.

Kahaluu Pr, *(Kahaluu Pr.; 0-925987),* 47-464 Mapele Rd., Kaneohe, HI 96744 Tel 808-239-4952.

Kaiser Syndicated, *(Kaiser Syndicated Features;* 0-9634746), 1735 Las Lanas Ln., Fullerton, CA 92633 Tel 714-526-0601.

Kalevala Bks, *(Kalevala Bks.; 1-880954),* P.O. Box 118, La Crescent, MN 55947-0118 Tel 319-338-9467.

Kalimat, *(Kalimat Pr.; 0-933770),* 1600 Sawtelle Blvd., Suite 34, Los Angeles, CA 90025 (SAN 213-7666) Tel 310-479-5668.

Kalmbach, *(Kalmbach Publishing Co.; 0-89024; 0-913135; 0-933168),* P.O. Box 1612, Waukesha, WI 53187 (SAN 201-0399) Tel 414-796-0126; Toll free: 800-558-1544 (except Wisconsin & Canada).

Kalnoky Pr, *(Kalnoky Pr.; 0-9619982),* 12 Wright Ct., East Brunswick, NJ 08816-3572 (SAN 248-8078).

K&C Pubns, *(K&C Pubns.; 0-9635644),* R.D. 7, Box 427, Bridgeton, NJ 08302 Tel 609-451-3435. Do not confuse with KC Pubns. in Las Vegas, NV.

Kane-Miller Bk, *(Kane/Miller Bk. Pubs.; 0-916291),* P.O. Box 310529, Brooklyn, NY 11231-0529 (SAN 295-8945) Tel 718-624-5120; Orders to: P.O. Box 310529, Brooklyn, NY 11231-0529 (SAN 685-3897) Tel 718-624-5120. *Imprints:* Cranky Nell Bk (Cranky Nell Book, A).

KAP Pubns, *(KAP Pubns.; 0-9630729),* P.O. Box 868, Jacksonville, TX 75766 Tel 903-586-3643; c/o Kent Holman, Highway 135, Jacksonville, TX 75766.

Kapa Hse Pr, *(Kapa Hse. Pr.; 0-9637328),* Div. of Kapa Editorial Services, 1202 Lexington Ave., Suite 331, New York, NY 10028 Tel 212-288-7763.

Kaplan IL, *(Kaplan Pr.; 0-9631833),* P.O. Box 6148, Chicago, IL 60680-6148; 5317 S. Harper Ave., No. 3, Chicago, IL 60615 Tel 312-667-6412. Do not confuse with Kaplan Pr., Inc. in Lewisville, NC.

Kar Ben, *(Kar-Ben Copies, Inc.; 0-930494; 0-929371),* 6800 Tildenwood Ln., Rockville, MD 20852 (SAN 210-7511) Tel 301-984-8733; Toll free: 800-452-7236.

Karey Kreations, *(Karey Kreations; 0-9632746),* 1612 Montana, Rawlins, WY 82301 Tel 307-324-5142.

Karwyn Ent, *(Karwyn Enterprises; 0-939938),* 17227 17th Ave., W., Lynnwood, WA 98036 (SAN 289-0143) Tel 206-743-0722.

Kasan Imprints, *(Kasan Imprints-KIP Children's Bks.;* 1-882828), 1239 Nile Dr., Suite 3, Corpus Christi, TX 78412 Tel 512-992-6611; Toll free: 800-982-5298.

Kauai Museum, *(Kauai Museum Assn., Ltd.; 0-940948),* Box 248, Lihue, HI 96766 (SAN 213-1013); 4428 Rice St., Lihue, HI 96766 (SAN 685-3412) Tel 808-245-6931.

Kav Bks
See Royal Fireworks

Kay Productions, *(Kay Productions; 0-929201),* 315 Pinewood Dr., San Rafael, CA 94903-1329 (SAN 248-6156).

Kaylor Christ Co, *(Kaylor, Christopher, Co.; 0-916039),* P.O. Box 737, Huntsville, AL 35804 (SAN 294-8524) Tel 205-539-2099.

Kazi Pubns, *(Kazi Pubns., Inc.; 0-935782; 0-933511;* 1-56744), 3023 W. Belmont Ave., Chicago, IL 60618 (SAN 162-3397) Tel 312-267-7001.

KC Enterprise
See Wonder Kids

KC Pubns, *(KC Pubns.; 0-916122; 0-88714),* P.O. Box 94558, Las Vegas, NV 89193-4558 (SAN 201-0364); Toll free: 800-626-9673; 3245 E. Patrick Ln., Suite A, Las Vegas, NV 89120 (SAN 658-103X) Tel 702-433-3415. Do not confuse with K&C Pubns. in Bridgeton, NJ.

Keats, *(Keats Publishing, Inc.; 0-87983),* 27 Pine St., P.O. Box 876, New Canaan, CT 06840 (SAN 201-0410) Tel 203-966-8721; Toll free: 800-858-7014.

Kelly Bear Bks
See Kelly Bear Pr

Kelly Bear Pr, *(Kelly Bear Pr.; 0-9621054),* 4295 Cty. Rd. 12, Lafayette, AL 36862 (SAN 250-5746) Tel 205-864-8991.

Kemtec Educ, *(Kemtec Educational Corp.; 1-877960),* 9889 Crescent Park Rd., West Chester, OH 45069 Tel 513-777-3535; Toll free: 800-733-0266.

Kendall-Hunt, *(Kendall/Hunt Publishing Co.; 0-8403;* 0-7872), 4050 Westmark Dr., P.O. Box 1840, Dubuque, IA 52004-1840 (SAN 203-9184) Tel 319-589-1000; Toll free: 800-228-0810.

Kennebec River, *(Kennebec River Pr., Inc.; 0-933858),* 36 Old Mill Rd., Falmouth, ME 04105-1637 (SAN 221-458X) Tel 207-781-7242.

Kenney Pubns, *(Kenney Pubns.; 1-877906),* 1310A SW 14th, Topeka, KS 66604 Tel 913-233-1062.

Kern Historical, *(Kern County Historical Society;* 0-943500), P.O. Box 141, Bakersfield, CA 93302 (SAN 240-6969) Tel 805-322-4962.

Kerry Tales, *(Kerry Tales, Inc.; 0-9635263),* P.O. Box 111, Timnath, CO 80547; Toll free: 800-748-1906; 2219 Ouray Ct., Fort Collins, CO 80525 Tel 303-482-9101.

Kesend Pub Ltd, *(Kesend, Michael, Publishing, Ltd.;* 0-935576), 1025 Fifth Ave., New York, NY 10028 (SAN 213-6902) Tel 212-249-5150; Orders to: Whitehurst & Clark Bk. Fullfillment, Inc., Raritan Industrial Pk., 100 Newfield Ave., Edison, NJ 08837 Tel 908-225-2727; Toll free: 800-488-8040.

Kestrel Pubns, *(Kestrel Pubns.; 0-9628472),* 1811 Stonewood Dr., Dayton, OH 45432 Tel 513-426-5110.

Key Curr Pr, *(Key Curriculum Pr.; 0-913684; 1-55953),* P.O. Box 2304, Berkeley, CA 94702 (SAN 202-6538); Toll free: 800-338-7638; 2512 Martin Luther King Way, Berkeley, CA 94704 (SAN 250-331X) Tel 510-548-2304.

Key of David, *(Key of David Pubns.; 0-943374),* Presentation BVM Rectory, 204 Haverford Rd., Wynnewood, PA 19096 (SAN 239-4480) Tel 610-896-1970.

Key Pubs UT, *(Key Pubs., Inc.; 1-883841),* 6 Sunwood Ln., Sandy, UT 84092 Tel 801-572-1000; Toll free: 800-585-6059.

Key Thoughts, *(Key Thoughts Pr.; 0-9639397),* P.O. Box 742, La Mesa, CA 91944; 4587 Arizona St., San Diego, CA 92116 Tel 619-297-9150.

Keyla, *(Keyla, Inc.; 1-882962),* P.O. Box 1054, Pine Lake, GA 30072-1054 Tel 404-508-9457; Toll free: 800-539-5211; 3074 Burnt Hickory Rd., Marietta, GA 30064 Tel 404-428-5884.

Keystone Pr, *(Keystone Pr.; 0-940701),* Box 6163, Bradenton, FL 34281 (SAN 665-2433); 6515 Mass. St., Bradenton, FL 34207 Tel 813-753-5179.

Khosho, *(Khosho; 0-9619310),* P.O. Box 801, Poway, CA 92064 (SAN 243-8976) Tel 619-679-9152.

Kickapoo Tribal, *(Kickapoo Tribal Pr.; 0-931045),* P.O. Box 106, Powhattan, KS 66527 (SAN 678-8998) Tel 913-474-3550.

Kid Poems, *(Kid Poems; 1-881786),* 352 Longbeach Pkwy., Bay Village, OH 44140 Tel 216-835-9546.

KidLit Advent, *(KidLit Adventures; 0-9643113),* 11684 Inwood Dr., Riverside, CA 92503 Tel 909-359-3381.

Kids at Heart, *(Kids at Heart, Inc.; 1-883842),* 2100 N. Hwy. 360, Suite 2003, Grand Prairie, TX 75050 Tel 214-602-0662; Toll free: 800-462-3744.

Kids Intl Inc, *(Kids International, Inc.; 0-943593),* 5401 S. Sheridan Rd., No. 204, Tulsa, OK 74145 (SAN 668-6486) Tel 918-665-1085.

Kids Kitchen, *(Kids In The Kitchen, Inc.; 0-9629589),* 5999 Dry Ridge Rd., Cincinnati, OH 45252 Tel 513-741-7775.

Kids Matter, *(Kids Matter, Inc.; 0-89411),* 692 Elkader St., Ashland, OR 97520 (SAN 209-3561); Orders to: P. O. Box 3460, Ashland, OR 97520; Dist. by: Ingram Bk. Co., 1 Ingram Blvd., La Vergne, TN 37086-1986 (SAN 169-7978) Tel 615-793-5000; Toll free: 800-937-8000 (orders only, all warehouses).

Kids Media Group, *(Kid's Media Group; 0-923790),* 5240 Oakland Ave., Saint Louis, MO 63110-1436 Tel 314-534-6464.

Kids Talk CT, *(Kids Talk Communications, Inc.;* 1-877819), P.O. Box 481, Old Lyme, CT 06371; Toll free: 800-543-8256; 5 Osprey Rd., Old Lyme, CT 06371 Tel 203-434-8772.

Kidsail, *(Kidsail; 0-9642223),* 2526 Horizon Dr., Suite 107, Burnsville, MN 55337.

Kidsbks, *(Kidsbooks, Inc.; 0-942025; 1-56156),* 3535 W. Peterson Ave., Chicago, IL 60659 (SAN 666-3729) Tel 312-509-0707.

Kidship Assoc, *(Kidship Assocs.; 1-878742),* P.O. Box 1348, South Gate, CA 90280; 4508 Firestone Blvd., South Gate, CA 90280 Tel 213-569-3349.

Kidsmart, *(Kidsmart; 0-936985),* 3276 Hawksmoor Pl., Cordova, TN 38018 (SAN 658-5647) Tel 901-372-7550; Dist. by: Margie Poe, 2276 Hawksmoor Pl., Cordova, TN 38018 (SAN 630-0952).

Kidspeak, *(Kidspeak; 1-879340),* P.O. Box 1028, Moorhead, MN 56561-1028; 2212 S. 17th St., Moorhead, MN 56560 Tel 218-233-4427.

Kidsrights, *(Kidsrights; 1-55864),* 3700 Progress Blvd., Mount Dora, FL 32757 (SAN 248-0891) Tel 904-483-1100.

Kidz & Katz, *(Kidz & Katz Publishing Co.; 1-883371),* 113 McHenry Rd., No. 223, Buffalo Grove, IL 60089-1796.

Kim Pathways, *(Kim Pathways; 0-9625774),* 101 Young Rd., Katonah, NY 10536 Tel 914-232-7959.

Kimberlite, *(Kimberlite Publishing Co.; 0-9632675),* 4033 SE 64th Ave., Portland, OR 97206-3624 Tel 503-775-0500.

Kimbo Educ, *(Kimbo Educational; 0-937124; 1-56346),* Div. of United Sound Arts, Inc., P.O. Box 477, Long Branch, NJ 07740 (SAN 630-1592); Toll free: 800-631-2187; 10 N. Third Ave., Long Branch, NJ 07740 Tel 908-229-4949.

Kimo Pr, *(Kimo Pr.; 0-945177),* P.O. Box 1361, Falls Church, VA 22041 (SAN 246-5493); 3412 Terrace Dr., No. 1733, Alexandria, VA 22302 (SAN 246-5507) Tel 703-379-1236.

Kinder Kollege, *(Kinder Kollege Pr.; 0-9635535),* Div. of Kinder Kollege, Inc., 1408 College St., Bowling Green, KY 42101 Tel 502-782-3500.

Kinder Read, *(Kinder Read; 0-934361),* P.O. Box 18, Ingomar, PA 15127 (SAN 693-4552); 1547 King Albert Dr., Pittsburgh, PA 15237 (SAN 662-3247) Tel 412-366-9761.

Kinderhook Pubs, *(Kinderhook Pubs.; 0-9625842),* P.O. Box 67, Kinderhook, NY 12106; R.D. 1, Box 496, Valatie, NY 12184 Tel 518-784-3907.

Kinderpr, *(Kinderpress; 0-931047),* 2240 135th Pl., SE, Bellevue, WA 98005 (SAN 678-9005) Tel 206-643-2695; P.O. Box 5761, Bellevue, WA 98006 (SAN 662-2534); Dist. by: Pacific Pipeline, Inc., 8030 S. 228th St, Kent, WA 98032-2900 (SAN 208-2128) Tel 206-872-5523; Toll free: 800-444-7323 (Customer Service); 800-677-2222 (orders).

Kinderword, *(Kinderword; 0-9642613),* 9218 Crownwood Rd., Ellicott City, MD 21042 Tel 410-750-3666.

Kindle Bks, *(Kindle Bks.; 0-9624790),* 639 1/2 29th Rd., Grand Junction, CO 81506 Tel 303-245-8290.

Kindness Pubns, *(Kindness Pubns., Inc.; 0-9636820),* 1859 N. Pine Island Rd., Suite 135, Plantation, FL 33322 Tel 305-423-9323.

Kindred Pr, *(Kindred Pr.; 0-9606436),* Orders to: 315 S. Lincoln St., Hillsboro, KS 67063 (SAN 202-2915) Tel 316-947-3151.

King Fisher Pr, *(King Fisher Pr.; 0-9612972),* 5115 E. Virginia, Phoenix, AZ 85008 (SAN 292-5567) Tel 602-840-2342.

King ME, *(King, Helen B.; 0-9615366),* 11 Pierce St., Orono, ME 04473 (SAN 695-2240) Tel 207-866-3309.

Kingfisher, *(Kingfisher Bks.; 0-9640921),* 2150 N. Tenaya Way, No. 1052, Las Vegas, NV 89128 Tel 702-242-9009.

Kingfisher LKC *Imprint of* **LKC**

Kings Inc, *(Kings, Inc.; 0-9624924),* 3715 Balboa St., San Francisco, CA 94121-2605; 223A Monterey Blvd., San Francisco, CA 94131 Tel 415-387-4737.

Kingshead Corp, *(Kingshead Corp.; 1-55941),* 600 Sylvan Way, Apt. 3FL, Englewood Cliffs, NJ 07632 (SAN 250-9938) Tel 201-894-0011; Toll free: 800-223-0309.

Kinnickinnic Pr, *(Kinnickinnic Pr.; 0-9615065),* 1101 W. Division St., River Falls, WI 54022 (SAN 694-1397) Tel 715-425-6897.

Kino Pubns, *(Kino Pubns.; 0-9607366),* 6625 N. First Ave., Tucson, AZ 85718 (SAN 238-2547) Tel 602-297-7278; Dist. by: Trillium Pr., P.O. Box 209, Monroe, NY 10950 (SAN 212-4637) Tel 914-783-2999.

Kipling Pr, *(Kipling Pr.; 0-943718),* 145 Avenue of the Americas, Suite 200, New York, NY 10013 (SAN 241-015X) Tel 212-969-8925.

Kitchen Sink, *(Kitchen Sink Pr.; 0-87816),* 320 Riverside Dr., Northampton, MA 01060 (SAN 212-7784) Tel 413-586-9525.

Kitwardo Pubs, *(Kitwardo Pubs., Inc.; 0-932641),* 2391 Kinwood Ave., Jacksonville, FL 32209-2474 (SAN 687-8091) Tel 904-768-6796.

Kiyoko & Co, *(Kiyoko & Co.; 0-9623210),* P.O. Box 1478, Pacifica, CA 94044-1478; 51 Eden West Rd., Pescadero, CA 94060 Tel 415-879-0061; Dist. by: Bookpeople, 7900 Edgewater Dr., Oakland, CA 94621 (SAN 168-9517) Tel 510-632-4700; Toll free: 800-999-4650.

Kjos, *(Kjos, Neil A., Music Co.; 0-910842; 0-8497),* 4380 Jutland Dr., San Diego, CA 92117-0894 (SAN 201-0488) Tel 619-270-9800; Toll free: 800-854-1592.

Klar-Iden Pub, *(Klar-Iden Publishing; 0-9629795),* 6963 Douglas Blvd., P.O. Box 115, Granite Bay, CA 95661 Tel 415-856-1059.

Kldoscope Pr, *(Kaleidoscope Pr.; 1-885371),* 2507 94th Ave., E., Puyallup, WA 98371 Tel 206-848-1116; Dist. by: Baker & Taylor Bks., Midwestern Div., 501 S. Gladiolus St., Momence, IL 60954-2444 (SAN 169-2100) Tel 815-472-2444; Toll free: 800-775-2300 (customer service); 800-775-2200 (orders only); Dist. by: Brodart Co., 500 Arch St., Willliamsport, PA 17705 (SAN 169-7684) Tel 717-326-2461; Toll free: 800-233-8467.

Klemantaski, *(Klemantaski Collection; 0-9641689),* 65 High Ridge Rd., Suite 219, Stamford, CT 06903 Tel 203-968-2970.

Klutz Pr, *(Klutz Pr.; 0-932592; 1-878257; 1-57054),* 2121 Staunton Ct., Palo Alto, CA 94306 (SAN 212-7539) Tel 415-857-0888.

Kluwer Ac, *(Kluwer Academic Pubs.; 0-7923; 0-89838;* 1-55608), Subs. of Wolters Kluwer N.V., 101 Philip Dr., Assinippi Pk., Norwell, MA 02061 (SAN 211-481X) Tel 617-871-6600; Orders to: P.O. Box 358, Accord Sta., Hingham, MA 02018-0358 (SAN 662-0647).

Kluwer Academic
See Kluwer Ac

KM Enterprises, *(KM Enterprises; 0-945947),* P.O. Box 25978, Los Angeles, CA 90025 (SAN 248-1782); 3407 Cabrillo Blvd., Los Angeles, CA 90066 (SAN 248-1790) Tel 310-398-9135.

Knees Pbk, *(Knees Paperback Publishing Co.;* 0-9600978), 4115 Marshall St., Dallas, TX 75210 (SAN 208-760X) Tel 214-428-4160; P.O. Box 26098, Dallas, TX 75226 (SAN 241-743X).

Knickerbocker, *(Knickerbocker Publishing Co.;* 0-911635), P.O. Box 113, 10 Summit Ave., Fiskdale, MA 01518 (SAN 264-1569) Tel 508-347-2039.

Knight Pub WA, *(Knight Publishing Co.; 0-9637484),* 2367 NE Meadow Run Dr., Poulsbo, WA 98370 Tel 206-697-4702. Do not confuse with Knight Publishing in Little Rock, AR.

Knopf, *(Knopf, Alfred A., Inc.; 0-394; 0-679),* Subs. of Random Hse., Inc., 201 E. 50th St., New York, NY 10022 (SAN 202-5825) Tel 212-572-2103; Orders to: 400 Hahn Rd., Westminster, MD 21157 (SAN 202-5833) Tel 410-848-1900; Toll free: 800-733-3000 (orders). *Imprints:* Everymans Lib (Everyman's Library); Evrymans Lib Childs (Everyman's Library Children's Classics).

Knopf Bks Yng Read, *(Knopf, Alfred A., Bks. for Young Readers; 0-679),* Div. of Random Hse., Inc., 201 E. 50th St., New York, NY 10022; Toll free: 800-726-0600; Dist. by: Random Hse., Inc., 400 Hahn Rd., Westminster, MD 21157 (SAN 202-5515); Toll free: 800-726-0600 (credit, inquiries, customer service). *Imprints:* Apple Soup Bks (Apple Soup Books).

Know Booster, *(Knowledge Booster Bks.; 1-880501),* 2001 Wilshire Blvd., No. 309, Santa Monica, CA 90403-5683.

Know Inc, *(Know, Inc.; 0-912786),* P.O. Box 86031, Pittsburgh, PA 15221 (SAN 201-050X) Tel 412-241-4844.

Know Unltd, *(Knowledge Unlimited, Inc.; 0-915291;* 1-55933), P.O. Box 52, Madison, WI 53701 (SAN 290-0017) Tel 608-836-6660. Do not confuse with companies of the same name in Palatine, IL, Ephraim, UT, Bedford Hills, NY.

Knowing Pr, *(Knowing Pr., The; 0-936927),* 400 Sycamore, McAllen, TX 78501 (SAN 658-361X) Tel 210-686-4033.

Knowldg Pub, *(Knowledge Publishing Co.; 1-879146),* 1025 Third Ave., E, Alexandria, MN 56308-1603 Tel 218-963-7746.

Knowldge Gain, *(Knowledge Gain Pubns.; 1-884518),* Div. of A. Lynn Scoresby, Inc., 703 S. State St., Orem, UT 84058-7767 Tel 801-225-9585; Toll free: 800-526-7793.

Koala Pub Co, *(Koala Publishing Co.; 1-877995),* 8650 SW 80th Ave., Portland, OR 97223-8976 Tel 503-254-7445.

Kodansha, *(Kodansha America, Inc.; 0-87011; 1-56836),* Subs. of Kodansha, Ltd. (Japan), 114 Fifth Ave., 18th Fl., New York, NY 10011 (SAN 201-0526) Tel 212-727-6460; Dist. by: Farrar, Straus & Giroux, Inc., 19 Union Sq., W., New York, NY 10003 (SAN 206-782X) Tel 212-741-6900; Toll free: 800-788-6262 (Individuals); 800-631-8571 (Booksellers).

Koinonia TX, *(Koinonia Publishing; 0-9633296),* P.O. Box 90, Peaster, TX 76485; Farm Rd. 920, Peaster, TX 76485 Tel 817-599-9849. Do not confuse with companies with similar names in Stevenson, MD, Oklahoma City, OK.

Kol Yisrael Pub, *(Kol Yisrael Publishing Co.; 0-9636415),* P.O. Box 8522, Santa Cruz, CA 95061-8522; 2395 Delaware Ave., No. 180, Santa Cruz, CA 95060 Tel 408-429-9410.

Koldarana, *(Koldarana Pubns.; 1-884993),* 112 W. 38th, Apt. 203, Austin, TX 78705 Tel 512-451-9789.

Kolowalu Bk *Imprint of* **UH Pr**

Korn Kompany, *(Korn Kompany; 0-939827),* 255 S. Rencstorff Ave., No. 18, Mountain View, CA 94040-1729 (SAN 663-835X).

Kosciuszko, *(Kosciuszko Foundation; 0-917004),* 15 E. 65th St., New York, NY 10021 (SAN 208-7251) Tel 212-734-2130.

Kraus Intl, *(Kraus International Pubns.; 0-527),* Div. of Kraus Organization, Ltd., 358 Saw Mill River Rd., Millwood, NY 10546-1035 (SAN 243-2552) Tel 914-762-2200; Toll free: 800-223-8323.

Krause Hse, *(Krause Hse., Inc.; 0-930359),* P.O. Box 880, Oregon City, OR 97045 (SAN 670-7718) Tel 503-656-4367.

Kreative Character, *(Kreative Character Kreations, Inc.;* 0-9641381), 9 Endicott Dr., Huntington, NY 11743 Tel 516-673-8230.

Kregel, *(Kregel Pubns.; 0-8254),* Div. of Kregel, Inc., P.O. Box 2607, Grand Rapids, MI 49501-2607 (SAN 206-9792); Toll free: 800-733-2607; 733 Wealthy St., SE, Grand Rapids, MI 49501 Tel 616-451-4775.

Kreysa, *(Kreysa, Francis John; 0-9611398),* 12520 Needle Dr., Clarksburg, MD 20871 (SAN 285-3752) Tel 301-349-5001.

Kripalu Pubns, *(Kripalu Pubns.; 0-940258),* Div. of Kripalu Ctr. for Yoga & Health, Rte. 183, Box 793, Lenox, MA 01240 (SAN 217-5320) Tel 413-637-3280; Dist. by: New Leaf Distributing Co., 5425 Tulane Dr., SW, Atlanta, GA 30336-2323 (SAN 169-1449) Tel 404-691-6996; Toll free: 800-326-2665.

Krishna Pr, *(Krishna Pr.),* Div. of Gordon Pr., P.O. Box 459, Bowling Green Sta., New York, NY 10004 (SAN 202-6570).

KS Herit Ctr, *(Kansas Heritage Ctr.; 1-882404),* P.O. Box 1275, Dodge City, KS 67801; 1000 Second Ave., Dodge City, KS 67801 Tel 316-227-1616.

KSJ Publishing, *(KSJ Publishing Co.; 0-9620445),* P.O. Box 2311, Sebastopol, CA 95473 (SAN 248-6296) Tel 707-829-9109; Toll free: 800-356-9315.

Ktav, *(Ktav Publishing Hse., Inc.; 0-87068; 0-88125),* Box 6249, Hoboken, NJ 07030 (SAN 201-0038); 900 Jefferson St., Hoboken, NJ 07030 (SAN 200-8866) Tel 201-963-9524.

KTS Pub, *(KTS Publishing; 1-882627),* 502 E. 13th St., Baxter Springs, KS 66713-2631 Tel 316-856-3302; Toll free: 800-841-5965.

Kudzu, *(Kudzu & Co.; 0-9615015),* Box 415, Walls, MS 38680 (SAN 693-823X) Tel 601-781-0267.

Kusel, *(Kusel, George; 0-9604476),* 600 Lakevue Dr., Willow Grove, PA 19090 (SAN 215-7837).

Kutie Kari Bks, *(Kutie Kari Bks., Inc.; 1-884149),* P.O. Box 38, Lynd, MN 56157; Toll free: 800-395-8843; 110 Redwood St., Lynd, MN 56157 Tel 507-532-2214.

L & M Bks, *(L & M Bks.; 0-914237),* 20770 US Hwy. 18, Apple Valley, CA 92307-3550 (SAN 287-525X) Tel 619-240-2268.

L Ashley & Joshua, *(Lauren Ashley & Joshua Storybooks & Publishing, Inc.; 1-878389),* P.O. Box 3951, Los Angeles, CA 90051 Tel 213-295-2626; Toll free: 800-247-8679.

L C Zajdel, *(Zajdel, Laura Connor; 0-9640994),* 203 Old Oak Rd., McMurray, PA 15317 Tel 412-941-2160.

L Claiborne, *(Liz Claiborne, Inc.; 0-9634893),* 1441 Broadway, New York, NY 10018 Tel 212-354-4900.

L D Scalzetto, *(Scalzetto, Louis Dominick; 1-879008),* 14 Hemlock Ln., Albany, NY 12208 Tel 518-482-4072.

L E Zahn, *(Zahn, Laura E.; 0-9637308),* 552 Bean Creek Rd., No. 28, Scotts Valley, CA 95066 Tel 408-438-5196.

L F Lewis, *(Lewis, Lois F.; 0-9620136),* 515 E. Main St., Ravenna, OH 44266 (SAN 247-6592) Tel 216-297-1525.

L Hill Bks, *(Hill, Lawrence, Bks.; 0-88208),* Subs. of Chicago Review Pr., Inc., 611 Broadway, Suite 530, New York, NY 10012 Tel 212-260-0576; Toll free: 800-888-4741 (orders only); Dist. by: Independent Pubs. Group, 814 N. Franklin, Chicago, IL 60610 (SAN 202-0769) Tel 312-337-0747; Toll free: 800-888-4741.

L-L Resrch, *(L/L Research; 0-945007),* 1504 Hobbs Park Rd., Louisville, KY 40223 (SAN 245-775X) Tel 502-245-6495.

L L Wegrzecki, *(Wegrzecki, Lester L.; 0-9620774),* 28551 San Marino Dr., Southfield, MI 48034 (SAN 249-7840) Tel 810-355-3542.

L LaMac Productions, *(Liz LaMac Productions, Inc.;* 0-927278), P.O. Box 25265, Nashville, TN 37202-5265 Tel 615-254-9003.

L Lambert, *(Lambert, Lee; 0-9621630),* P.O. Box 25212, Tamarac, FL 33320 (SAN 251-6934); 5540 NW 61st Pl., Tamarac, FL 33319 (SAN 251-6942) Tel 305-476-1100.

L M Dechochran, *(Dechochran, Lela Maldonado;* 0-9627574), P.O. Box 861, Las Piedras, PR 00671.

L P Pohl, *(Pohl, Linda Perelman; 0-9625453),* 69 Forestview Ct., Williamsville, NY 14221 Tel 716-688-3838; Dist. by: Empire State News Co., 2800 Walden Ave., Cheektowaga, NY 14225-4772 (SAN 169-5177) Tel 716-681-1100.

L P T C, *(L.P.T.C., Inc.; 0-929946),* Subs. of Center for Creative Change, 52136 Lilac Rd., South Bend, IN 46628 (SAN 250-801X) Tel 219-272-2222.

L R Ream, *(Ream, L. R., Publishing; 0-928693),* P.O. Box 2043, Coeur d'Alene, ID 83816-2043 (SAN 672-2725).

L Ross Pubns, *(Lucia Ross Pubns.; 1-879599),* Div. of Paige, Ross & Wood, P.O. Box 1524, South Pasadena, CA 91031-1524; 1015 Adelaine Ave., South Pasadena, CA 91030 Tel 818-441-3650.

L Shouse, *(Shouse, Lucille, & Kay Scott; 0-9620819),* 10895 Hwy. 2, Leavenworth, WA 98826 (SAN 249-8308) Tel 509-548-7883.

L Stuart *Imprint of* **Carol Pub Group**

L T Litho & Printing
See L T Pub

L T Pub, *(L.T. Publishing; 1-879480),* 16811 Noyes Ave., Irvine, CA 92714 Tel 714-863-1340.

La Alameda Pr, *(La Alameda Pr.; 0-9631909),* 9636 Guadalupe Trail, NW, Albuquerque, NM 87114 Tel 505-897-0285.

La Sierra U Pr, *(La Sierra Univ. Pr.; 0-944450),* 4700 Pierce St., Riverside, CA 92515-8247 (SAN 243-5489) Tel 909-785-2000.

La Stampa Calligrafica, *(La Stampa Calligrafica;* 0-9606630), P.O. Box 209, Franklin, MI 48025 (SAN 281-8582) Tel 810-646-5176; Dist. by: Bookpeople, 7900 Edgewater Dr., Oakland, CA 94621 (SAN 168-9517) Tel 510-632-4700; Toll free: 800-999-4650; Dist. by: Inland Bk. Co., 140 Commerce St., East Haven, CT 06512 (SAN 200-4151) Tel 203-467-4257; Toll free: 800-243-0138.

Lacret Pub, *(Lacret Publishing Co.; 0-943144),* 601 12th St., P.O. Box 8231, Union City, NJ 07087 (SAN 240-3927) Tel 201-866-5257.

LAD Redondo Beach, *(L.A.D. Publishing; 0-9620053),* P.O. Box 7000-176, Redondo Beach, CA 90277 (SAN 247-4174); 217 Ave. F, Redondo Beach, CA 90277 (SAN 247-4182) Tel 310-543-4736.

Lado Intl Pr, *(Lado International Pr.; 1-879580),* Div. of Lado International College, 2233 Wisconsin Ave., NW, Washington, DC 20007 Tel 202-338-3133; Toll free: 800-229-5236.

Lady Lake Learn, *(Lady of the Lake Learning Systems;* 0-931905), 5757 Westheimer Rd., Suite 3-356, Houston, TX 77057 (SAN 686-0184) Tel 713-782-9678; Toll free: 800-544-1378.

Ladybird Bks, *(Ladybird Bks., Inc.),* 840 Washington St., Auburn, ME 04210 (SAN 107-7864) Tel 207-783-6329; Toll free: 800-523-9247; P.O. Box 1690, Auburn, ME 04211.

Lafferty & Assocs, *(Lafferty & Assocs., Inc.; 0-9641072),* P.O. Box 1026, La Canada, CA 91012; 4529 Angeles Crest Hwy., Suite 308, La Canada, CA 91011 Tel 818-952-5483.

Laffing Cow, *(Laffing Cow Pr.; 1-879894),* P.O. Box 959, Saratoga, WY 82331-0959 Tel 307-326-9612.

Lake Pub Co, *(Lake Publishing Co.; 1-56103),* 500 Harbor Blvd., Belmont, CA 94002 Tel 415-592-1606.

LAM Co, *(Look at Me Co.; 0-945405),* P.O. Box 135, Wheeling, IL 60090 (SAN 246-9499); 8 Norbert Dr., Hawthorn Woods, IL 60047 (SAN 246-9502) Tel 312-438-6443; Dist. by: Kimbo Educational, P.O. Box 477D, Long Branch, NJ 07740 (SAN 630-1592) Tel 201-229-4949; Toll free: 800-631-2187.

Lamar HS, *(Lamar High Schl.; 0-9636974),* 1400 Lamar Blvd., W., Arlington, TX 76012 Tel 817-460-4721.

Lambgel Family, *(Lambgel Family, Inc.; 1-877765),* P.O. Box 1674, Ada, OK 74820; 231 N. Turner, Ada, OK 74820 Tel 405-463-0948.

Lamont Bks, *(Lamont Bks.; 1-882563),* P.O. Box 493, Jamestown, RI 02835-0493 Tel 401-423-3816; Dist. by: Inland Bk. Co., 140 Commerce St., East Haven, CT 06512 (SAN 200-4151) Tel 203-467-4257; Toll free: 800-243-0138.

Lamp Light Pr *Imprint of* **Prosperity & Profits**

Lancaster Prodns, *(Lancaster Productions; 0-930647),* 535 Pierce St., No. 356, Albany, CA 94706 (SAN 241-9807) Tel 510-524-6996; Dist. by: Talman Co., 131 Spring St., Suite 201E-N, New York, NY 10012 (SAN 200-5204) Tel 212-431-7175; Toll free: 800-537-8894 (orders only).

Landfall Pr, *(Landfall Pr., Inc.; 0-913428),* 5171 Chapin St., Dayton, OH 45429 (SAN 202-6627) Tel 513-298-9123. Do not confuse with Landfall Pr. Inc., Chicago, IL.

Landmark Edns, *(Landmark Editions, Inc.; 0-933849),* P.O. Box 4469, 1402 Kansas Ave., Kansas City, MO 64127 (SAN 692-6916) Tel 816-241-4919.

Landmark Found, *(Landmark Foundation; 0-9624119),* 412 Hale St., Prides Crossing, MA 01965 Tel 508-927-4440.

Landmark ID, *(Landmark Publishing; 0-9624209),* P.O. Box 776, Pocatello, ID 83204; 1738 E. Terry, Pocatello, ID 83201 Tel 208-233-0075.

Lang Pubns, *(Lang Pubns.; 0-942242),* P.O. Box 709, Cooperstown, ND 58425-0709 (SAN 238-4337); Dist. by: World Bible Pubs., Inc., P.O. Box 370, Iowa Falls, IA 50126 (SAN 215-2797); Toll free: 800-247-5111; Dist. by: Riverside/World, P.O. Box 370, 1500 Riverside Dr., Iowa Falls, IA 50126 (SAN 169-2666) Tel 515-648-4271; Toll free: 800-247-5111.

Langenscheidt, *(Langenscheidt Pubs., Inc.; 0-88729;* 3-468), Subs. of Langenscheidt KG, 46-35 54th Rd., Maspeth, NY 11378 (SAN 276-9441) Tel 718-784-0055; Toll free: 800-432-6277.

Langtry Pubns, *(Langtry Pubns.; 0-915369),* 20755 Marilla St., Chatsworth, CA 91311 (SAN 291-2473).

Language Lrn Assocs
See Arrowhead Bks

Language Pr, *(Language Pr.; 0-912386),* P.O. Box 342, Whitewater, WI 53190 (SAN 201-0674) Tel 414-473-8822.

Lani Goose Pubns, *(Lani Goose Pubns., Inc.; 0-944264),* 583 Kamoku St., Suite 3803, Honolulu, HI 96826 (SAN 243-5101) Tel 808-947-7330; Dist. by: Pacific Trade Group, 94-527 Puahi St., Waipahu, HI 96797 (SAN 169-1635) Tel 808-671-6735.

Lankford Comics, *(Lankford Comics; 0-9621811),* P.O. Box 143, Richland, IA 52585 Tel 319-456-6805; Dist. by: Diamond Comic Distributors, Inc., 1966 Greenspring Dr., Suite 300, Timonium, MD 21093 (SAN 110-9502) Tel 410-560-7100; Toll free: 800-783-2981; Dist. by: Capital City, P.O. Box 8156, Madison, WI 53708-8156 (SAN 200-5328) Tel 608-275-7777.

Lantern, *(Lantern Pr., Inc., Pubs.; 0-8313),* 6214 Wynfield Ct., Orlando, FL 32819 (SAN 201-0682) Tel 407-876-7720.

Lantern Bks, *(Lantern Bks., Inc.; 0-945161),* 88-43 75th St., Jamaica, NY 11421 (SAN 245-923X) Tel 718-296-3981; Dist. by: Amereon, Ltd., P.O. Box 1200, Mattituck, NY 11952 (SAN 201-2413) Tel 516-298-5100. Do not confuse with companies with the same name in Farwell, MN, Delray Beach, FL.

Larchmere Ltd, *(Larchmere, Ltd.; 0-9642898),* 12014 Irvine Ave., NW, Bemidji, MN 56601 Tel 218-243-2456.

Laredo, *(Laredo Publishing Co., Inc.; 1-56492),* 22930 Lockness Ave., Torrance, CA 90501 Tel 310-517-1890.

Large Print Bks *Imprint of* **Hall**

Larksdale, *(Larksdale; 0-89896),* P.O. Box 801222, Houston, TX 77280 (SAN 220-0643) Tel 713-461-7200; Toll free: 800-666-2332. *Imprints:* Post Oak Pr (Post Oak Press).

Larkspur, *(Larkspur Pubns.; 0-939942),* P.O. Box 211, Bowmansville, NY 14026 (SAN 216-8286) Tel 716-337-2758.

Larousse LKC *Imprint of* **LKC**

Larsens Outdoor, *(Larsen's Outdoor Publishing;* 0-936513), 2640 Elizabeth Pl., Lakeland, FL 33813 (SAN 697-8975) Tel 813-644-3381.

Larson Pubns, *(Larson Pubns.; 0-943914),* 4936 Rte. 414, Burdett, NY 14818 (SAN 241-130X) Tel 607-546-9342; Dist. by: National Bk. Network, 4720A Boston Way, Lanham, MD 20706-4310 (SAN 630-0065) Tel 301-459-8696; Toll free: 800-462-6420; Dist. by: Samuel Weiser, Inc., P.O. Box 612, York Beach, ME 03910-0612 (SAN 202-9588) Tel 207-363-4393; Toll free: 800-423-7087 (orders only); Dist. by: New Leaf Distributing Co., 5425 Tulane Dr., SW, Atlanta, GA 30336-2323 (SAN 169-1449) Tel 404-691-6996; Toll free: 800-326-2665; Dist. by: Bookpeople, 7900 Edgewater Dr., Oakland, CA 94621 (SAN 168-9517) Tel 510-632-4700; Toll free: 800-999-4650; Dist. by: Moving Bks., Inc., P.O. Box 20037, Seattle, WA 98102 (SAN 159-0685) Tel 206-762-1750; Toll free: 800-777-6683; Dist. by: Ingram Bk. Co., 1 Ingram Blvd., La Vergne, TN 37086-1986 (SAN 169-7978) Tel 615-793-5000; Toll free: 800-937-8000 (orders only, all warehouses); Dist. by: Inland Bk. Co., 140 Commerce St., East Haven, CT 06512 (SAN 200-4151) Tel 203-467-4257; Toll free: 800-243-0138; Dist. by: Baker & Taylor Bks., Somerville Service Ctr., 50 Kirby Ave., Somerville, NJ 08876-0734 (SAN 169-4901) Tel 908-722-8000; Toll free: 800-775-1500 (customer service). Do not confuse with Larson Pubns., Joliet, IL.

Laser Tech, *(Laser Tech Bk. Publishing Div.; 0-943155),* 18627 Brookhurst St., Suite 191, Fountain Valley, CA 92708 (SAN 667-1284) Tel 714-965-5118; Toll free: 800-382-4325.

Lat Am Lit Rev Pr, *(Latin American Literary Review Pr.; 0-935480),* 121 Edgewood Ave., 1st Flr., Pittsburgh, PA 15218-1513 (SAN 215-2142) Tel 412-371-9023; Dist. by: SPD-Small Pr. Distribution, 1814 San Pablo Ave., Berkeley, CA 94702 (SAN 204-5826) Tel 510-549-3336; Toll free: 800-869-7553; Dist. by: Book Hse., Inc., 208 W. Chicago St., Jonesville, MI 49250-0125 (SAN 169-3859) Tel 517-849-2117; Toll free: 800-248-1146; Dist. by: Inland Bk. Co., 140 Commerce St., East Haven, CT 06512 (SAN 200-4151) Tel 203-467-4257; Toll free: 800-243-0138.

Latinarte, *(Latinarte; 1-882161),* P.O. Box 1387, Madison Sq. Sta., New York, NY 10159 Tel 212-714-7737.

Laugh Elephant *Imprint of* **Blue Lantern Studio**

Laughing Cat, *(Laughing Cat Productions; 0-9633332),* 757 NW Ogden St., Bend, OR 97701 Tel 503-388-3011.

Launch Pr, *(Launch Pr.; 0-9613205; 1-877872),* P.O. Box 5629, Rockville, MD 20855 (SAN 295-0154); Toll free: 800-321-9167; 2827 Concord Blvd., Concord, CA 94519; Dist. by: Bookpeople, 7900 Edgewater Dr., Oakland, CA 94621 (SAN 168-9517) Tel 510-632-4700; Toll free: 800-999-4650; Dist. by: Inland Bk. Co., 140 Commerce St., East Haven, CT 06512 (SAN 200-4151) Tel 203-457-4257; Toll free: 800-243-0138; Dist. by: Pacific Pipeline, Inc., 8030 S. 228th St., Kent, WA 98032-2900 (SAN 208-2128) Tel 206-872-5523; Toll free: 800-444-7323 (Customer Service); 800-677-2222 (orders); Dist. by: Baker & Taylor Bks., Reno Service Ctr., 380 Edison Way, Reno, NV 89564 (SAN 169-4464) Tel 702-858-6700; Toll free: 800-775-1700 (customer service); Dist. by: New Leaf Distributing Co., 5425 Tulane Dr., SW, Atlanta, GA 30336-2323 (SAN 169-1449) Tel 404-691-6996; Toll free: 800-326-2665.

Laurelwood Pr, *(Laurelwood Pr.; 0-9624210),* 31669 Pine Mountain Rd., Cloverdale, CA 95425-9515 Tel 707-894-2987.

Lauri Inc, *(Lauri, Inc.; 0-937763),* P.O. Box F, Phillips-Avon, ME 04966 (SAN 659-2597); Avon Valley Rd., Phillips-Avon, ME 04966 (SAN 659-2600) Tel 207-639-2000.

Laurin Hse, *(Laurin Hse. Publishing Co.; 0-934549),* 105 Wisp Ln., Bailey, CO 80421 (SAN 693-8248) Tel 303-838-2749.

Lavender Crystal, *(Lavender Crystal Pr.; 0-9636909;* 1-884541), P.O. Box 8932, Red Bank, NJ 07701; 142-A South St., Red Bank, NJ 07701.

Lavender Pr, *(Lavender Pr.; 0-9622719),* 27505 Seneca Dr., Cleveland, OH 44145-3914. Do not confuse with Lavender Press, South Norwalk, CT.

Lavinia Pub, *(Lavinia Publishing; 0-9619625),* P.O. Box 085222, Racine, WI 53408 (SAN 245-9043).

Lawco, *(Lawco, Ltd.; 0-945071),* Affil. of Moneytree Publishing & Que Hse., P.O. Box 2009, Manteca, CA 95336 (SAN 245-7628); 1212 W. Center, No. 6, Manteca, CA 95336 (SAN 245-7636) Tel 209-239-6006.

Lawrence Science, *(Univ. of California, Berkeley, Lawrence Hall of Science; 0-924886; 0-912511),* U of CA, Lawrence Hall of Science, Berkeley, CA 94720 (SAN 271-9754) Tel 510-642-1016.

Lazuli Prods, *(Lazuli Productions; 1-884776),* P.O. Box 1553, Arroyo Grande, CA 93421; 1242 Driftwood, Grover Beach, CA 93433 Tel 805-489-9125; Dist. by: New Leaf Distributing Co., 5425 Tulane Dr., SW, Atlanta, GA 30336-2323 (SAN 169-1449) Tel 404-691-6996; Toll free: 800-326-2665.

LBCo Pub, *(LBCo. Publishing; 0-9623171; 1-881321),* 10713 Ranch Rd. 620 N., No. 106, Austin, TX 78726-1700 Tel 512-474-5665; Toll free: 800-432-4431.

LBW, *(LBW, Inc. (Large Print Div.)),* P.O. Box 5000, Yucaipa, CA 92399 (SAN 208-2969) Tel 909-795-8977.

LC Pub, *(LC Publishing Co.; 1-55768),* 89 Lane Ct., Oakland, CA 94611 Tel 510-658-3444.

LCD, *(L.C.D. Pub.; 0-941414),* 663 Calle Miramar, Redondo Beach, CA 90277 (SAN 239-0035) Tel 310-375-6336.

LE *Imprint of* **Dell**

Leadership Pub, *(Leadership Pub., Inc.; 0-911943),* 4030 39th Pl., Des Moines, IA 50310-2801 (SAN 264-1712) Tel 515-278-4765; Orders to: P.O. Box 8358, Des Moines, IA 50301-8358 (SAN 251-2599); Dist. by: Pieces of Learning, 1610 Brook Lynn Dr., Beaver Creek, OH 45432 (SAN 298-461X) Tel 513-427-0530; Toll free: 800-729-5137; Dist. by: Educational Impressions, 210 Sixth Ave., P.O. Box 77, Hawthorne, NJ 07507 (SAN 274-4899) Tel 201-423-4666; Toll free: 800-451-7450; Dist. by: Creative Learning Pr., Inc., P.O. Box 320, Mansfield Center, CT 06250 (SAN 298-4601) Tel 203-429-8118.

Learn-Abouts, *(Learn-Abouts; 1-880038),* 8029 Renton Way, Sacramento, CA 95828 Tel 916-423-2499.

Learn Concepts OH, *(Learning Concepts, Inc.;* 0-934902), 7622 Palmerston Dr., Mentor, OH 44060 (SAN 213-411X) Tel 216-255-1107.

Learn Inc, *(Learn, Inc.; 0-913286; 1-55678),* 113 Gaither Dr., Mount Laurel, NJ 08054-9987 (SAN 205-6801) Tel 609-234-6100; Toll free: 800-729-7323.

Learn Tools, *(Learning Tools Co.; 0-938017),* P.O. Box 657, Berkeley Springs, WV 25411 (SAN 692-7297); 714 Rockwell St., Berkeley Springs, WV 25422 Tel 304-258-1304.

Learners Dimension, *(Learner's Dimension, The;* 0-945852), 7 Lakeview Dr., P.O. Box 6, Columbia, CT 06237 (SAN 247-9052) Tel 203-228-3786.

Learning Expo, *(Learning Expo; 0-9625907),* 13800 Crested Butte Dr., Albuquerque, NM 87112 Tel 505-291-1550.

Learning KY, *(Learning Hse., The; 0-939991),* P.O. Box 5176, Louisville, KY 40205 (SAN 664-1040); 1548 Cherokee Rd., Louisville, KY 40205 (SAN 664-1059) Tel 502-459-7975.

Learning Pubns, *(Learning Pubns., Inc.; 0-918452;* 1-55691), 5351 Gulf Dr., Holmes Beach, FL 34217 (SAN 208-1695) Tel 813-778-6651; Orders to: P.O. Box 1338, Holmes Beach, FL 34218-1338 (SAN 688-3990) Tel 813-778-6651; Toll free: 800-222-1525.

Learning Well, *(Learning Well; 0-917109; 0-936850;* 1-55596), P.O. Box 3759, New Hyde Park, NY 11040-0800 (SAN 240-7027); Toll free: 800-645-6564.

Learning Wks, *(Learning Works, Inc., The; 0-88160),* P.O. Box 6187, Santa Barbara, CA 93160 (SAN 272-0078) Tel 805-964-4220; Toll free: 800-235-5767.

Lectorum Pubns, *(Lectorum Pubns., Inc.; 0-9625162;* 1-880507), 137 W. 14th St., New York, NY 10011 (SAN 169-586X) Tel 212-929-2833; Toll free: 800-345-5946.

Lee & Low Bks, *(Lee & Low Bks., Inc.; 1-880000),* 228 E. 45th St., New York, NY 10017 Tel 212-867-6155; Dist. by: Publishers Group West, 4065 Hollis St., Emeryville, CA 94608 (SAN 202-8522) Tel 510-658-3453; Toll free: 800-788-3123.

Lee Pub NY, *(Lee Publishing; 0-9631513),* P.O. Box 726, Glenwood Landing, NY 11547 Tel 516-358-0785. Do not confuse with companies with the same name in Amherst, NH, Scottsdale, AZ, Los Angeles, CA, Sunnyvale, CA.

Lee Pubns KY, *(Lee Pubns.; 1-56297),* Div. of Stry-Lenkoff Co., P.O. Box 32120, Louisville, KY 40232; Toll free: 800-626-8247; 1100 W. Broadway, Louisville, KY 40232 Tel 502-587-6804.

Legacy Bks, *(Legacy Bks.; 0-913714),* P.O. Box 494, Hatboro, PA 19040 (SAN 202-2389); 12 Meetinghouse Rd., Hatboro, PA 19040 (SAN 658-1129) Tel 215-675-6762.

Legacy Hse, *(Legacy Hse., Inc.; 0-9608008),* Box 786, Orofino, ID 83544 (SAN 238-0684) Tel 208-476-5632. Do not confuse with Legacy Hse., Cameron Park, CA.

Legend Prods, *(Legend Productions; 1-883863),* P.O. Box 122745, Fort Worth, TX 76121-2745; Toll free: 800-286-3167; 3125 Bigham Blvd., Fort Worth, TX 76116 Tel 817-732-6062.

Lego Dacta, *(Lego Dacta; 0-914831; 1-57056),* Div. of Lego Systems, Inc., 555 Taylor Rd., Enfield, CT 06083-1600 (SAN 245-3460) Tel 203-749-2291; Toll free: 800-527-8339.

Lemonade Kids, *(Lemonade Kids, Inc.; 0-9625075),* 1 Alhambra Plaza, Suite 400, Coral Gables, FL 33134 Tel 305-445-8869; Toll free: 800-852-4544.

Lenape Pub, *(Lenape Publishing, Ltd.; 0-917178),* 3 Lanark Dr., Wilmington, DE 19803 (SAN 208-7324) Tel 302-479-0251.

Leonardo Pr, *(Leonardo Pr.; 0-914051),* P.O. Box 1326, Camden, ME 04843 (SAN 287-542X) Tel 207-236-8649.

Leonardos Work, *(Leonardo's Workshop; 1-879777),* P.O. Box 11115, Saint Paul, MN 55111; 7620 16th Ave., S., Richfield, MN 55423 Tel 612-869-0001.

Lerner Pubns, *(Lerner Pubns. Co.; 0-8225),* 241 First Ave., N., Minneapolis, MN 55401 (SAN 201-0828) Tel 612-332-3344; Toll free: 800-328-4929. *Imprints:* First Ave Edns (First Avenue Editions); Runestone Pr (Runestone Press).

LeSEA Pub Co, *(LeSEA Publishing Co.; 0-937580),* Div. of Lester Sumrall Evangelistic Assn., Inc., P.O. Box 12, South Bend, IN 46624; Toll free: 800-621-8885; 530 E. Ireland Rd., South Bend, IN 46614 Tel 219-291-3292.

Lester St Pub, *(Lester Street Publishing; 0-9634440),* P.O. Box 41484, Tucson, AZ 85717-1484; 3270 E. Lester St., Tucson, AZ 85716 Tel 602-326-0104.

Levi Strauss, *(Strauss, Levi, & Co.; 0-9617460),* 1155 Battery St., San Francisco, CA 94111 (SAN 664-1253) Tel 415-544-6000.

Levin Family, *(Levin Family Publishing; 0-9642777),* R.D. 4, Box 808, Green River Rd., Brattleboro, VT 05301 Tel 802-257-1482.

Levite Apache, *(Levite of Apache Publishing; 0-9618634; 0-927562),* 203 Hal Muldrow Dr., No. 3, Norman, OK 73069-5268 (SAN 668-3983) Tel 405-366-6442.

Lewis & Clark, *(Lewis & Clark Interpretive Assn.; 1-883844),* Div. of Portage Route Chapter of the Lewis & Clark Trail Heritage Foundation, Inc., Box 2848, Great Falls, MT 59403; 1101 15th St., N., Great Falls, MT 59403 Tel 406-771-1240.

Lex Pr, *(Lex Pr.; 1-878653),* P.O. Box 859, Los Gatos, CA 95030; 131 Hillbrook Dr., Los Gatos, CA 95032 Tel 408-358-2453.

Lexikos, *(Lexikos Publishing; 0-938530),* P.O. Box 296, Lagunitas, CA 94938 (SAN 219-8517) Tel 415-488-0401.

Lexington-Fayette, *(Lexington-Fayette County Historic Commission; 0-912839),* Div. of Lexington-Fayette Urban County Government, 418 Park Ave., Lexington, KY 40502 (SAN 277-6936) Tel 606-269-2523.

Leyerle Pubns, *(Leyerle Pubns.; 0-9602296; 1-878617),* 28 Stanley St., Mount Morris, NY 14510 (SAN 211-5700) Tel 716-658-2193; Orders to: P.O. Box 384, Geneseo, NY 14454 (SAN 211-5719).

LFL *Imprint of* **Dell**

Lib Congress, *(Library of Congress; 0-8444),* Div. of U.S. Government, Washington, DC 20540 (SAN 205-6593) Tel 202-707-6095; Orders to: U. S. Government Printing Office, Washington, DC 20402 Tel 202-783-3238.

Liberty, *(Liberty Publishing; 0-9632852),* Dist. by: Publishers Distribution Service, 6893 Sullivan Rd., Grawn, MI 49637 (SAN 630-5717) Tel 616-276-5196; Toll free: 800-345-0096 (orders only). Do not confuse with companies with the same name in Deerfield Beach, FL, Arlington, VA, Port Townsend, WA.

Liberty Lines, *(Liberty Lines; 0-9630669),* 404 Dublin Pike, Dublin, PA 18917 Tel 215-249-9030.

Liberty Pub, *(Liberty Publishing Co., Inc.; 0-89709),* 440 S. Federal Hwy., Suite 202, Deerfield Beach, FL 33441 (SAN 211-030X) Tel 305-360-9000. Do not confuse with companies with the same name in Traverse City, MI, Arlington, VA.

Libr Commns Servs, *(Library Communications Services; 0-941237),* 13 Norwood St., Albany, NY 12203 (SAN 665-3685) Tel 518-438-0617.

Libros de Ninos, *(Libros de Ninos; 0-9640533),* 2505 N. Washington, Roswell, NM 88201 Tel 505-624-2632.

Libs Unl, *(Libraries Unlimited, Inc.; 0-87287; 1-56308),* P.O. Box 6633, Englewood, CO 80155-6633 (SAN 202-6767) Tel 303-770-1220; Toll free: 800-237-6124.

Libthelit, *(Libthelit Bks.; 1-879721),* P.O. Box 11905, Baltimore, MD 21207-0905; 24 Armitage Ct., Baltimore, MD 21207 Tel 410-597-8386.

Licatas Edutype, *(Licata's Edutype; 0-9636095),* 3075 Taylor Way, Costa Mesa, CA 92626 Tel 714-957-8683.

Lichtner, *(Lichtner, Schomer; 0-941074),* 2626A N. Maryland Ave., Milwaukee, WI 53211 (SAN 223-1891) Tel 414-962-7519.

Life Cycle Bks, *(Life Cycle Bks.; 0-919225),* P.O. Box 792, Lewiston, NY 14092-0792 (SAN 692-7173).

Life Lines Pr, *(Life Lines Pr.; 0-9635745),* 6338 Ansel Ct., Buford, GA 30518 (SAN 297-8474) Tel 404-945-8758; Toll free: 800-737-6558; Dist. by: BookWorld Distribution Services, Inc., 1933 Whitfield Pk. Loop, Sarasota, FL 34243 (SAN 173-0568) Tel 813-758-8094; Toll free: 800-444-2524 (orders only); Dist. by: Quality Bks., Inc., 918 Sherwood Dr., Lake Bluff, IL 60044-2204 (SAN 169-2127) Tel 708-295-2010; Toll free: 800-323-4241 (libraries only); Dist. by: Unique Bks., Inc., 4230 Grove Ave., Gurnee, IL 60031 (SAN 630-0472) Tel 708-623-9171; Dist. by: Baker & Taylor Bks., Somerville Service Ctr., 50 Kirby Ave., Somerville, NJ 08876-0734 (SAN 169-4901) Tel 908-722-8000; Toll free: 800-775-1500 (customer service); Dist. by: Baker & Taylor Bks., Momence Service Ctr., 501 S. Gladiolus St., Momence, IL 60954-2444 (SAN 169-2100) Tel 815-472-2444; Toll free: 800-775-2300 (customer service); Dist. by: Baker & Taylor Bks., Commerce Service Ctr., 251 Mt. Olive Church Rd., Commerce, GA 30599-9988 (SAN 169-1503) Tel 706-335-5000; Toll free: 800-775-1200 (customer service); Dist. by: Baker & Taylor Bks., Reno Service Ctr., 380 Edison Way, Reno, NV 89564 (SAN 169-4464) Tel 702-858-6700; Toll free: 800-775-1700 (customer service); Dist. by: Ingram Book Co., 1 Ingram Blvd., La Vergne, TN 37086-1986 (SAN 169-7978) Tel 615-793-5000; Toll free: 800-937-8000 (orders only, all warehouses).

Life Time Pubs, *(Life Time Pubs., Inc.; 1-882237),* 4668 S. Holladay Blvd., Salt Lake City, UT 84117 Tel 801-272-1191.

LifeCom, *(LifeCom; 0-9615722),* 1248 N. 13th Ave., Saint Cloud, MN 56303 (SAN 696-2572) Tel 612-252-9866; P.O. Box 1832, Saint Cloud, MN 56302 (SAN 242-0724).

Lifeline Res, *(Lifeline Resources, Inc.; 0-9605700),* Box 192, Croton-on-Hudson, NY 10520 (SAN 216-2466) Tel 914-271-4074.

Lifetime, *(LIFETIME Bks., Inc.; 0-8119),* 2131 Hollywood Blvd., Hollywood, FL 33020 (SAN 208-2365) Tel 305-925-5242; Toll free: 800-771-3355. Do not confuse with Lifetime Books, Inc. in Portland, OR.

Lifetime Pr, *(Lifetime Pr.; 0-931571),* Subs. of Royal Publishing, 137 Campbell Ave., Roanoke, VA 24011 (SAN 686-1636) Tel 703-982-1444.

Lifeworks, *(Lifeworks; 0-9630453),* 102 Lakeview Ave., Hamden, CT 06514-3010.

Light & Life, *(Light & Life Pr.; 0-89367),* P.O. Box 535002, Indianapolis, IN 46253-5002 (SAN 206-8419) Tel 317-244-3660; Toll free: 800-348-2513.

Light & Living, *(Light for Living Pubns.; 0-9627630),* P.O. Box 210, Madison, GA 30650-0210 Tel 706-342-2544.

Light-Bearer, *(Light-Bearer Pubs., Inc.; 0-9630017),* P.O. Box 348, Montgomery, AL 36101-0348; 1919 S. Hull St., Montgomery, AL 36104 Tel 205-265-5601.

Light Rain Commun, *(Light Rain Communications; 0-9639270),* P.O. Box 903, Harrisonburg, VA 22801; 201B Ott St., Harrisonburg, VA 22801 Tel 703-432-0485.

Light&Life Pub Co MN, *(Light & Life Publishing Co.; 0-937032; 1-880971),* 4818 Park Glen Rd., Minneapolis, MN 55416 (SAN 213-8565) Tel 612-925-3888.

Lighthse Bks MA, *(Lighthouse Bks.; 0-945692),* P.O. Box 1201, West Chatham, MA 02669 (SAN 247-7092); 15 Barcliff Ave. Extension, West Chatham, MA 02669 (SAN 247-7106) Tel 617-945-2216.

Lightyear, *(Lightyear Pr., Inc.; 0-89968),* P.O. Box 168, Cutchogue, NY 11935 (SAN 213-1102) Tel 516-734-5724; Dist. by: Buccaneer Bks., P.O. Box 168, Cutchogue, NY 11935 (SAN 209-1542) Tel 516-734-5724.

Liguori Pubns, *(Liguori Pubns.; 0-89243),* 1 Liguori Dr., Liguori, MO 63057-9999 (SAN 202-6783) Tel 314-464-2500; Toll free: 800-325-9521 (orders). *Imprints:* Triumph Books (Triumph Books).

Lil Daisy Bks, *(L'il Daisy Bks.; 0-9621283),* 3419 Sterne St., San Diego, CA 92106 (SAN 250-9393) Tel 619-222-1886.

Lil Red Hen OK, *(Little Red Hen; 0-9621669),* 412 Claremont Dr., Norman, OK 73069 (SAN 251-8457) Tel 405-329-0415.

Lillenas, *(Lillenas Publishing Co.; 0-8341),* Div. of Nazarene Publishing Hse., P.O. Box 419527, Kansas City, MO 64141 Tel 816-555-1212; Dist. by: Spring Arbor Distributors, 10885 Textile Rd., Belleville, MI 48111 (SAN 158-9016) Tel 313-481-0900; Toll free: 800-395-5599 (orders); 800-395-7234 (customer service); Dist. by: Riverside/World Bk. & Bible Hse., Inc., P.O. Box 370, 1500 Riverside Dr., Iowa Falls, IA 50126 (SAN 169-2666) Tel 515-648-4271; Toll free: 800-247-5111.

Limberlost Pr, *(Limberlost Pr.; 0-931659),* P.O. Box 1113, HC 33, Boise, ID 83706-9702 (SAN 683-7212) Tel 208-344-2120.

Linden Ln Pr, *(Linden Lane Pr.; 0-913827),* 6724 Crooked Palm Terr., Hialeah, FL 33014-2918 (SAN 286-1674); 103 Cuyler Rd., Princeton, NJ 08540 (SAN 251-2688) Tel 609-921-7943.

Linden Pubs, *(Linden Pubs.; 0-89642),* 1750 N. Sycamore, No. 305, Hollywood, CA 90028 (SAN 206-7218).

Lindsay Pubns, *(Lindsay Pubns., Inc.; 0-917914; 1-55918),* P.O. Box 12, Bradley, IL 60915 (SAN 209-9462) Tel 815-935-5353.

Lindsey Pubng, *(Lindsey Publishing, Inc.; 1-885242),* 9724 S. King Dr., Chicago, IL 60628 Tel 312-660-0299. Do not confuse with Lindsey Publishing in Atlanta, GA.

Line Drive, *(Line Drive Publishing),* 113 Pleasant St., Hanover, MA 02339 (SAN 663-4575) Tel 617-878-5035.

LinguiSystems, *(LinguiSystems, Inc.; 1-55999; 0-7606),* P.O. Box 747, East Moline, IL 61244; Toll free: 800-776-4332; 3100 Fourth Ave., East Moline, IL 61244 Tel 309-755-2300.

Linking Ed Med, *(Linking Education & Medicine, Inc.; 0-9629417),* P.O. Box 357, Burtonsville, MD 20866-9357; 7818 Chapel Cove Dr., Laurel, MD 20707 Tel 301-384-9229.

Linmore Pub, *(Linmore Publishing, Inc.; 0-916591),* 409 E. South St., Barrington, IL 60010 (SAN 296-4503) Tel 312-382-7606; Orders to: P.O. Box 1545, Palatine, IL 60078 (SAN 662-2291) Tel 815-223-7499.

Linns Stamp News, *(Linn's Stamp News; 0-940403),* P.O. Box 29, Sidney, OH 45365 (SAN 664-3825); Toll free: 800-448-7293; 911 Vandemark Rd., Sidney, OH 45365 (SAN 664-3833) Tel 513-498-0801.

Lintel, *(Lintel; 0-931642),* P.O. Box 8609, Roanoke, VA 24014 (SAN 213-6325) Tel 703-982-2265.

Lion Bks, *(Lion Bks.; 0-87460),* 210 Nelson Rd., Suite B, Scarsdale, NY 10583 (SAN 241-7529) Tel 914-725-2280.

Lion House Pr, *(Lion Hse. Pr.; 0-914107),* 152 Inglewood Dr., Orem, UT 84058 (SAN 287-5101) Tel 801-226-3575.

Lion USA, *(Lion Publishing; 0-7459; 0-85648),* 20 Lincoln Ave., Elgin, IL 60120-2956 (SAN 663-611X) Tel 708-741-4256; Toll free: 800-447-5466 (customer service). Do not confuse with Lion Publishing in San Diego, CA.

Lion's Den, *(Lion's Den Pubns.; 0-9628444),* Div. of Lion's Den Productions, Inc., P.O. Box 7368, Northridge, CA 91327-7368 (SAN 297-3626); 19520 Quail Creek Pl., Northridge, CA 91326-1712 Tel 818-831-3872; Dist. by: Samuel French Trade, 7623 Sunset Blvd., Hollywood, CA 90046 (SAN 200-6855) Tel 213-876-0570; Toll free: 800-822-8669.

Lip Smackers, *(Lip Smackers, Inc.; 0-9629459),* P.O. Box 5385, Culver City, CA 90231-5385; 5870 Green Valley Cir., Suite 202, Culver City, CA 90231 Tel 310-641-0578.

Lipp Jr Bks *Imprint of* **HarpC Child Bks**

Lippincott, *(Lippincott, J. B., Co.; 0-397; 0-89313),* Subs. of Wolters Kluwer U.S. Corp., 227 E. Washington Sq., Philadelphia, PA 19106-3780 (SAN 201-0933) Tel 215-238-4436; Toll free: 800-777-2295 (orders); 800-982-4377 (in Pennsylvania).

Listen USA, *(Listen U.S.A.),* c/o AMR International, 10 Valley Dr., No. 9, Greenwich, CT 06831-5206 (SAN 695-4839).

Lit Pubns, *(Literary Pubns.; 0-9617819),* Div. of Caswell Corp., 34 Oak Bluff, Avon, CT 06001 (SAN 665-3197) Tel 203-677-8944.

Lit Unltd, *(Literacy Unlimited Pubns.; 0-9643210),* Div. of Literacy Unlimited, P.O. Box 278, Medina, WA 98039-0278; 8621 NE Sixth St., Bellevue, WA 98004 Tel 206-454-5830.

Lith Scouts, *(Lithuanian Scouts Assn., Inc.; 0-9611488),* 5620 S. Claremont Ave, Chicago, IL 60636 (SAN 285-3485) Tel 312-434-4545.

Little, *(Little, Brown & Co.; 0-316; 0-8212),* A Time Warner Co., Time & Life Bldg., 1271 Avenue of the Americas, New York, NY 10020 (SAN 200-2205) Tel 212-522-8700; Toll free: 800-343-9204; Orders to: 200 West St., Waltham, MA 02154 (SAN 630-7248); Toll free: 800-759-0190. *Imprints:* Joy St Bks (Joy Street Books); Spts Illus Kids (Sports Illustrated for Kids).

Little Apple *Imprint of* **Scholastic Inc**

Little Buckaroo, *(Little Buckaroo Pr.; 0-9622064),* P.O. Box 3016, West Sedona, AZ 86340; 365 Concord Dr., Sedona, AZ 86336 Tel 602-282-6278.

Little Cajun Bks, *(Little Cajun Bks.; 0-931108),* Subs. of Edler Bks., Box 777, Loreauville, LA 70552 (SAN 212-5250) Tel 318-229-8455.

Little Egg Pub, *(Little Egg Publishing Co.; 1-881669),* 9100 N. 55th St., Scottsdale, AZ 85253 Tel 602-443-1722; Toll free: 800-545-7827; Dist. by: Five Star Pubns., 4696 W. Tyson St., Chandler, AZ 85226 (SAN 246-7429) Tel 602-940-8182; Toll free: 800-545-7827.

Little Feat, *(Little Feat; 0-940112),* P.O. Box R, Mastic Beach, NY 11951 (SAN 217-0760) Tel 516-281-5661.

Little Frnd, *(Little Friend Pr.; 0-9641285),* Lewis Wharf, Bay 215, Boston, MA 02110 Tel 617-523-0253.

Little Gems, *(Little Gems Publishing; 0-9630903),* 17260 SW Cynthia St., Aloha, OR 97007-5308 Tel 503-642-9517. Do not confuse with Little Gems, Lake Worth, FL.

Little Gnome, *(Little Gnome Delights; 0-9615584),* Div. of Artmarx, Inc., P.O. Box 22582, Denver, CO 80222 (SAN 696-0499) Tel 303-758-7905.

Little Great Whale, *(Little Great Whale Productions;* 0-9624929), 305 SW 95th Pl., Miami, FL 33174 Tel 305-221-9339.

Little Prodns, *(Little Productions; 0-922112),* 6751 N. Blackstone Ave., No. 214, Fresno, CA 93710 (SAN 251-1541) Tel 209-435-7166.

Little Rainbow *Imprint of* **Troll Assocs**

Little Read, *(Little Readers; 1-880642),* P.O. Box 902, Chesterfield, MO 63017; 15752 Scenic Green, Chesterfield, MO 63017 Tel 314-256-3474; Dist. by: Baker & Taylor Bks., Momence Service Ctr., 501 S. Gladiolus St., Momence, IL 60954-2444 (SAN 169-2100) Tel 815-472-2444; Toll free: 800-775-2300 (customer service); Dist. by: Baker & Taylor Bks., Commerce Service Ctr., 251 Mt. Olive Church Rd., Commerce, GA 30599-9988 (SAN 169-1503) Tel 706-335-5000; Toll free: 800-775-1200 (customer service); Dist. by: Baker & Taylor Bks., Somerville Service Ctr., 50 Kirby Ave., Somerville, NJ 08876-0734 (SAN 169-4901) Tel 908-722-8000; Toll free: 800-775-1500 (customer service).

Little Rooster *Imprint of* **Bantam**

Little Simon *Imprint of* **S&S Trade**

Little Spirit, *(A Little Spirit Co., Inc.; 0-9619482),* 3026 Helen Ave., Orlando, FL 32804 (SAN 244-9269) Tel 407-839-4960.

Little Spruce, *(Little Spruce Productions; 0-9630107),* 2232 River Rd., Caledonia, NY 14423 Tel 716-226-3392.

Little Tike, *(Little Tike Publishing Co.; 0-9636468),* 1160 Harrison Ave., Boston, MA 02119 Tel 617-442-8937.

Little Treasure, *(Little Treasure Pubns., Inc.; 0-9639838),* 8 Meadow Ave., Monmouth Beach, NJ 07750 Tel 908-229-7422.

Little Turtle, *(Little Turtle Pr.; 0-9633574),* 111 SW Harrison, No. 3A, Portland, OR 97201 Tel 503-221-1754.

Little Wood Bks, *(Little Wooden Bks.; 0-929949),* 1890 Rd. 24, SW, Mattawa, WA 99344 (SAN 250-7943) Tel 509-932-4729.

Littlebee, *(Littlebee Pr.; 0-940674),* 445 Ford Ave., Fords, NJ 08863-1203 (SAN 239-4510) Tel 201-867-2595.

Littlest Bk
See LBCo Pub

Liturgical Pr, *(Liturgical Pr., The; 0-8146; 0-916134; 0-925127; 0-89453),* Div. of Order of St. Benedict, Inc., St. John's Abbey, Collegeville, MN 56321 (SAN 202-2494) Tel 612-363-2213.

Liturgy Tr Pubns, *(Liturgy Training Pubns.; 0-930467; 0-929650; 1-56854),* Div. of Archdiocese of Chicago, 1800 N. Hermitage Ave., Chicago, IL 60622-1101 (SAN 670-9052) Tel 312-486-8970; Toll free: 800-933-1800.

Liv from Vis, *(Living from Vision; 1-884246),* Div. of Allied Forces, Inc., P.O. Box 1530, Stanwood, WA 98292; Toll free: 800-758-7836; 1837 S. Cascade View Dr., Camano Island, Stanwood, WA 98292 Tel 206-387-5713; Dist. by: Moving Bks., Inc., P.O. Box 20037, Seattle, WA 98102 (SAN 159-0685) Tel 206-762-1750; Toll free: 800-777-6683; Dist. by: New Leaf Distributing Co., 5425 Tulane Dr., SW, Atlanta, GA 30336-2323 (SAN 169-1449) Tel 404-691-6996; Toll free: 800-326-2665; Dist. by: DeVorss & Co., P.O. Box 550, Marina del Rey, CA 90292-0550 (SAN 168-9886) Tel 213-870-7478; Toll free: 800-843-5743 (bookstores only); 800-331-4719 (in California, bookstores only).

Live Oak Media, *(Live Oak Media; 0-941078; 0-87499),* P.O. Box 652, Pine Plains, NY 12567 (SAN 217-3921); West Church St., Pine Plains, NY 12567 (SAN 669-1498) Tel 518-398-1010.

Liveright, *(Liveright Publishing Corp.; 0-87140),* Subs. of W. W. Norton Co., Inc., 500 Fifth Ave., New York, NY 10110 (SAN 201-0976) Tel 212-354-5500; Toll free: 800-233-4830.

Living Flame Pr, *(Living Flame Pr.; 0-914544),* 325 Rabro Dr., Hauppauge, NY 11788 (SAN 202-6805) Tel 516-348-5252.

Living Planet Pr, *(Living Planet Pr.; 0-9626072;* 1-879326), 2940 Newark St., NW, Washington, DC 20008 Tel 202-686-6262; Dist. by: Independent Pubs. Group, 814 N. Franklin, Chicago, IL 60610 (SAN 202-0769) Tel 312-337-0747; Toll free: 800-888-4741.

Living Water, *(Living Water Pubns.; 0-9630534),* P.O. Box 13227, Edwardsville, KS 66113; 23 Beach, Edwardsville, KS 66113 Tel 913-441-6702.

LKC, *(Larousse Kingfisher Chambers, Inc.),* Div. of Groupe de la Cite, 95 Madison Ave., New York, NY 10016 (SAN 297-7540) Tel 212-686-1060; Toll free: 800-497-1657. *Imprints:* Kingfisher LKC (Kingfisher Books); Larousse LKC (Laroussee).

Lkng Glass Pubns, *(Looking Glass Pubns.; 0-936485),* 1735 Willard St., NW, Suite 5, Washington, DC 20009 (SAN 698-0988) Tel 202-462-3080; Dist. by: BookWorld Distribution Services, Inc., 1933 Whitfield Pk. Loop, Sarasota, FL 34243 (SAN 173-0568) Tel 813-758-8094; Toll free: 800-444-2524 (orders only); Dist. by: Bookpeople, 7900 Edgewater Dr., Oakland, CA 94621 (SAN 168-9517) Tel 510-632-4700; Toll free: 800-999-4650; Dist. by: Homestead Bk., Inc., 6101 22nd Ave., NW, Seattle, WA 98107 (SAN 169-8796) Tel 206-782-4532; Toll free: 800-426-6777 (orders only). Do not confuse with Looking Glass Pubns., Quincy, IL.

Llama Bks, *(Llama Bks.; 1-877778),* 821 Lenhardt Rd., Easley, SC 29640 Tel 803-859-8060.

LLU Pr
See La Sierra U Pr

LMI TX, *(Leadership Management, Inc.; 0-924121),* 45-67 Lake Shore Dr., Waco, TX 76710 (SAN 252-1261) Tel 817-776-2060.

LMR Prodns, *(LMR Productions; 0-9629541),* P.O. Box 194, Saint James, MO 65559-0194 Tel 314-265-7047.

LNR Pubns, *(LNR Pubns.; 0-9627894),* P.O. Box 3305, Windsor Locks, CT 06096; 440 North St., Windsor Locks, CT 06096 Tel 203-627-6553.

Locations Plus, *(Locations Plus; 0-9626868),* 755 Barrcrest Ln., Lancaster, PA 17603-2304.

Lodestar Bks *Imprint of* **Dutton Child Bks**

Loizeaux, *(Loizeaux Brothers, Inc.; 0-87213),* P.O. Box 277, Neptune, NJ 07754-0277 (SAN 202-6848); Toll free: 800-526-2796; 3301C Rte. 66, Neptune, NJ 07753 Tel 908-922-6665.

Lola Library, *(Lola Library Collection; 0-930825),* 942 N. Louise, No. 9, Glendale, CA 91207 (SAN 677-6108).

Lollipop Power, *(Lollipop Power Bks.; 0-914996),* Div. of Carolina Wren Pr., 120 Morris St., Durham, NC 27701 (SAN 206-9733) Tel 919-560-2738.

Lombard Mktg, *(Lombard Marketing; 0-922242),* 22 E. Newberry Rd., Bloomfield, CT 06002 (SAN 251-2041) Tel 203-769-5700; Toll free: 800-874-6556.

Lone Raven, *(Lone Raven Publishing Co., Inc.;* 0-933914), P.O. Box 191552, Sacramento, CA 95819 (SAN 213-5337) Tel 916-646-8777.

Lone Star Bks *Imprint of* **Gulf Pub**

Lone Tree, *(Lone Tree Publishing Co.; 0-943861),* P.O. Box 4728, Topeka, KS 66604 (SAN 242-5696); 4410 SW 25th, Topeka, KS 66614 (SAN 242-570X) Tel 913-271-6717.

Long Acre Pub, *(Long Acre Publishing; 1-879564),* P.O. Box 292, Mount Vernon, OH 43050; 212 Sychar Rd., Mount Vernon, OH 43050 Tel 614-397-1408.

Longanecker, *(Longanecker Bks.; 0-9601126),* P.O. Box 127, Brewster, WA 98812 (SAN 210-2323) Tel 509-689-2441.

Longman, *(Longman Publishing Group; 0-8013),* Div. of Addison-Wesley Publishing Co., Inc., The Longman Bldg., 10 Bank St., White Plains, NY 10606-1951 (SAN 202-6856) Tel 914-993-5000; Toll free: 800-266-8855 (information); 800-447-2226 (customer service only).

Longmeadow Pr, *(Longmeadow Pr.; 0-681),* P.O. Box 10218, 201 High Ridge Rd., Stamford, CT 06904 Tel 203-352-2769; Orders to: Publishers Resources, Inc., 1224 Heil Quaker Blvd., P.O. Box 7001, LaVergne, TN 37086-7001 (SAN 630-5431) Tel 615-793-5090; Toll free: 800-937-5557.

Look & See, *(Look & See Pubns.; 1-877827),* P.O. Box 64216, Tucson, AZ 85728-4216 Tel 602-529-2857.

Lookout Pr, *(Lookout Pr.; 1-882405),* P.O. Box 19131, Sacramento, CA 95819 Tel 916-456-6131.

Loonfeather, *(Loonfeather Pr.; 0-926147),* 426 Bemidji Ave., Bemidji, MN 56601 Tel 218-751-4869.

Lorenz Corp, *(Lorenz Corp.; 0-89328),* 501 E. Third St., Dayton, OH 45401-0802 (SAN 208-7413) Tel 513-228-6118; Toll free: 800-876-8742.

Lorien Hse, *(Lorien Hse.; 0-934852),* P.O. Box 1112, Black Mountain, NC 28711 (SAN 209-2999) Tel 704-669-6211.

Los Angeles, *(Los Angeles Children's Museum;* 0-914953), 310 N. Main St., Los Angeles, CA 90012 (SAN 289-310X) Tel 213-687-8801.

Los Arboles Pub, *(Los Arboles; 0-941992),* 820 Calle de Arboles, Redondo Beach, CA 90277 (SAN 238-020X) Tel 310-375-0759; Orders to: P.O. Box 7000-54, Redondo Beach, CA 90277 (SAN 662-0752); Dist. by: DeVorss & Co., P.O. Box 550, Marina del Rey, CA 90294-0550 (SAN 168-9886) Tel 310-870-7478; Toll free: 800-843-5743 (bookstores only); 800-331-4719 (in California, bookstores only); Dist. by: New Leaf Distributing Co., 5425 Tulane Dr., SW, Atlanta, GA 30336-2323 (SAN 169-1449) Tel 404-691-6996; Toll free: 800-326-2665; Dist. by: Baker & Taylor Bks., Reno Service Ctr., 380 Edison Way, Reno, NV 89564 (SAN 169-4464) Tel 702-858-6700; Toll free: 800-775-1700 (customer service); Dist. by: Baker & Taylor Bks., Momence Service Ctr., 501 S. Gladiolus St., Momence, IL 60954-2444 (SAN 169-2100) Tel 815-472-2444; Toll free: 800-775-2300 (customer service); Dist. by: Baker & Taylor Bks., Commerce Service Ctr., 251 Mt. Olive Church Rd., Commerce, GA 30599-9988 (SAN 169-1503) Tel 706-335-5000; Toll free: 800-775-1200 (customer service).

Lothrop, *(Lothrop, Lee & Shepard Bks.; 0-688),* Div. of William Morrow & Co., Inc., 1350 Avenue of the Americas, New York, NY 10019 (SAN 201-1034) Tel 212-261-6500; Toll free: 800-843-9389; Orders to: William Morrow & Co., Inc., 39 Plymouth St., P.O. Box 1219, Fairfield, NJ 07007 (SAN 202-5779) Tel 201-227-7200; Toll free: 800-237-0657 (customer service).

Lotus, *(Lotus Pr., Inc.; 0-916418),* Dist. by: Michigan State Univ. Pr., 1405 S. Harrison Rd., 25 Manly Miles Bldg., East Lansing, MI 48823-5202 (SAN 202-6295) Tel 517-355-9543.

Lotus Light, *(Lotus Light Pubns.; 0-941524; 0-910261),* Div. of Lotus Brands, P.O. Box 325, Twin Lakes, WI 53181 (SAN 239-1120) Tel 414-889-8561.

Louvin Pub, *(Louvin Publishing Co.),* 37 Crescent Rd., Poughkeepsie, NY 12601 (SAN 217-2496).

Love From Sea, *(Love From the Sea; 1-878291),* P.O. Box 711236, Santee, CA 92072-1236; 8729 Graves Ave., Santee, CA 92072 Tel 619-258-2017.

Love Song Mess Assn, *(Love Song to the Messiah Assn., Inc.; 0-915775),* P.O. Box 4385, Fort Lauderdale, FL 33338-4385 (SAN 293-8871) Tel 305-733-0656; Dist. by: Starburst Pubs. (selected titles only), P.O. Box 4123, Lancaster, PA 17604 (SAN 158-9016) Tel 717-569-5558; Toll free: 800-441-1456.

Loveswept *Imprint of* **Bantam**

Lowell Hse, *(Lowell Hse.; 0-929923; 1-56565),* Div. of RGA Publishing Group, Inc., 2029 Century Pk. E., No. 3290, Los Angeles, CA 90067 (SAN 250-863X) Tel 310-552-7555; Dist. by: Contemporary Bks., Inc., 2 Prudential Plaza, Suite 1200, Chicago, IL 60601 (SAN 202-5493) Tel 312-540-4500; Toll free: 800-621-1918 (orders only).

Lowell Hse Juvenile, *(Lowell House Juvenile; 0-929923;* 1-56565), Div. of RGA Publishing Group, Inc., 2029 Century Pk. E., No. 3290, Los Angeles, CA 90067 (SAN 250-863X) Tel 310-552-7555.

Lowell Museum, *(Lowell Museum Corp.; 0-942472),* P.O. Box 8415, Lowell, MA 01853 (SAN 239-9423) Tel 508-459-1066.

Lowell Pr, *(Lowell Pr., The; 0-913504; 0-932845),* 115 E. 31st St., Box 411877, Kansas City, MO 64141-1877 (SAN 207-0774) Tel 816-753-4545; Toll free: 800-736-7660; Dist. by: Publishers Distribution Service, 6893 Sullivan Rd., Grawn, MI 49637 (SAN 630-5717) Tel 616-276-5196; Toll free: 800-345-0096 (orders only). Do not confuse with Lowell Pr. in Eugene, OR.

Lowry Hse, *(Lowry Hse.; 0-9629591),* P.O. Box 1014, Eugene, OR 97440-1014 Tel 503-686-2315.

LOWV Cleve Educ, *(League of Women Voters of Cleveland Educational Fund; 1-880746),* 2217 E. Ninth, Suite 302, Cleveland, OH 44115 Tel 216-781-8375.

Loyola, *(Loyola Univ. Pr.; 0-8294),* 3441 N. Ashland Ave., Chicago, IL 60657 (SAN 211-6537) Tel 312-281-1818; Toll free: 800-621-1008.

Lrn Links, *(Learning Links, Inc.; 0-88122; 1-56982),* 2300 Marcus Ave., New Hyde Park, NY 11042 (SAN 241-3302) Tel 516-437-9071; Toll free: 800-724-2616.

Lrn Wrap-Ups, *(Learning Wrap-Ups; 0-943343),* 2122 W. 6550 S., Ogden, UT 84405 (SAN 668-3975) Tel 801-479-4966.

Lrng Tools-Bilicki Pubns, *(Learning Tools/Bilicki Pubns.; 0-940221),* P.O. Box 2588, Del Mar, CA 92014 (SAN 664-1733) Tel 619-481-6360.

Lrning Multi-Systs, *(Learning Multi-Systems, Inc.;* 0-912899), 320 Holtzman Rd., Madison, WI 53713 (SAN 283-135X) Tel 608-273-8060.

Lrning Plus, *(Learning Plus, Inc.; 0-9639614),* P.O. Box 713, Corvallis, OR 97339-0713; 3635 NW Roosevelt Dr., Corvallis, OR 97330 Tel 503-757-7049.

Lrning to Lrn, *(Learning to Learn, Inc.; 0-9642469),* 3248 Little Horse Dr., Tucson, AZ 85712 Tel 602-323-3000.

Lttle Peop Pr, *(Little People's Pr.; 0-9628563),* Div. of Thomas Ramos & Co., 290 Nichols Dr., Santa Cruz, CA 95060 Tel 408-429-9506. Do not confuse with Little People's Productions in Warsaw, IN.

Lubin Pr, *(Lubin Pr.; 0-9612396),* 396 N. Cleveland, Memphis, TN 38104 (SAN 289-4114) Tel 901-278-0561.

Lubrecht & Cramer, *(Lubrecht & Cramer, Ltd.; 0-934454; 0-945345),* 38 County Rte. 48, Forestburgh, NY 12777-6400 (SAN 214-1256) Tel 914-794-8539.

Lucas Comns, *(Lucas Communications Group, Inc.;* 0-9616276), 90 Dayton Ave., Passaic, NJ 07055 (SAN 658-6201) Tel 516-825-8283.

Luce, *(Luce, Robert B., Inc.; 0-88331),* 195 McGregor St., Manchester, NH 03102 Tel 603-623-5949; c/o Integrated Distribution, 195 McGregor St., Manchester, NH 03102 Tel 603-669-5933.

Lucent Bks, *(Lucent Bks.; 1-56006),* P.O. Box 289011, San Diego, CA 92198-9011; Toll free: 800-231-5163; Dist. by: Greenhaven Pr., 10911 Technology Pl., San Diego, CA 92127 (SAN 201-6214) Tel 619-485-7424.

Lucky Bks, *(Lucky Bks.; 0-922510),* P.O. Box 1415, Winchester, VA 22604 (SAN 251-348X); 2247 Jones Rd., Winchester, VA 22602 (SAN 251-3498) Tel 703-662-3424.

Lucy & Co, *(Lucy & Co.; 0-910079),* 7711 Lake Ballinger Way, NE, Edmonds, WA 98020 (SAN 241-3116) Tel 206-623-9426.

LUISA Prods, *(LUISA Productions; 0-939584),* P.O. Box 6836-AB, Santa Barbara, CA 93160 (SAN 216-4108).

Lumanett Pr, *(Lumanett Pr.; 0-9620137),* 7083 E. Ohio Dr., Denver, CO 80224 (SAN 247-6614) Tel 303-320-6022.

Luna Bisonte, *(Luna Bisonte Prods; 0-935350),* 137 Leland Ave., Columbus, OH 43214 (SAN 209-8326) Tel 614-846-4126.

Lupine Pr, *(Lupine Pr.; 0-9637878),* 35210 Sunset Falls Rd., Yacolt, WA 98675 Tel 206-686-3349.

Luth & Assocs, *(Luth & Assocs.; 0-9626153),* 5829 Tittabawassee Rd., Saginaw, MI 48604 Tel 517-792-9776.

Lutheran Braille
See LBW

LWMM, *(Living Word Media Ministries; 0-9628819),* Div. of Living Word Prayer Ctr., 20839 Sonrisa Way, Boca Raton, FL 33433 Tel 407-483-8707.

LWV Houston Ed Fund, *(League of Women Voters Houston Education Fund; 0-939903),* 2650 Fountain View Dr., No. 328, Houston, TX 77057-7619 (SAN 663-9240) Tel 713-552-1776.

LWV WA, *(League of Women Voters of Washington, The; 1-878170),* 1411 Fourth Ave., No. 803, Seattle, WA 98101-2216 Tel 206-622-8961.

Lydias Educ, *(Lydia's Educational & Charitable Organization; 0-9635351),* P.O. Box 330835, Houston, TX 77233-0835; 11618 Panay Dr., Houston, TX 77048 Tel 713-733-3713.

Lynch Art Assocs Inc
See Sweet Inspirations

LynHawk Pubng, *(LynHawk Publishing Co., Inc.;* 1-885005), 809 Ranch Rd., Florence, SC 29506 Tel 803-667-0103.

Lynn's Bookshelf, *(Lynn's Bookshelf; 0-9618608),* P.O. Box 2224, Boise, ID 83701 (SAN 667-1314); 4015 Taft, Boise, ID 83703 Tel 208-336-7629.

Lyons & Burford, *(Lyons & Burford, Pubs., Inc.; 0-941130; 1-55821),* 31 W. 21st St., New York, NY 10010 (SAN 208-1881) Tel 212-620-9580.

Lyons Group, *(Lyons Group, The; 0-913592; 0-89505; 1-55924; 0-7829),* Div. of RCL, Inc., 300 E. Bethany Rd., Allen, TX 75002; Toll free: 800-527-4747, ext426; Orders to: P.O. Box 5000, Allen, TX 75002 Tel 214-248-6300; Toll free: 800-527-4748.

Lythway Large Print *Imprint of* **Hall**

M A K Pubns, *(M.A.K. Pubns., Inc.; 1-882406),* 511 Deer Run Ct., Westerville, OH 43081-3248.

M A Mercer, *(Mercer, Morris Anthony; 0-9617362),* 40-35 W. Mosholu Pkwy., S., Bronx, NY 10468 (SAN 663-8813) Tel 718-367-9582.

M A Salant, *(Salant, Michael Alan; 0-9609288),* 5410 Connecticut Ave., NW, Apt. 403, Washington, DC 20015-2833 (SAN 260-129X) Tel 202-364-6096; Orders to: P.O. Box 33421, Farragut Sta., Washington, DC 20033-0421 (SAN 200-2760).

M A Sears, *(Sears, M. A.; 0-9639785),* 16809 Superior, North Hills, CA 91343; 555 W. Sierra Hwy., Acton, CA 93510 Tel 818-891-8632.

M A Thomas, *(Thomas, M. Angele; 0-9619293),* 2055 Royal Fern Ct., Reston, VA 22091 (SAN 243-8224) Tel 703-860-1508.

M & D Made Easy, *(M&D Made Easy; 0-9627585),* 11601 E. 186th St., Artesia, CA 90701 Tel 310-865-5553.

M & H Enter, *(M & H Enterprises; 0-936997),* P.O. Box 276374, Sacramento, CA 95827 (SAN 658-3180); 679 Pestana Dr., Galt, CA 95632 (SAN 658-3199) Tel 209-745-6653.

M & W Pub Co, *(McDonald & Woodward Publishing Co., The; 0-939923),* P.O. Box 10308, Blacksburg, VA 24062-0308 (SAN 663-6977) Tel 703-951-9465.

M B Glass Assocs, *(Glass, Michael B., & Assocs., Inc.;* 0-940429), 735 Calebs Path, Glaro Bldg., Hauppauge, NY 11788 (SAN 664-3574) Tel 516-232-1050.

M B Pub, *(M B Publishing; 0-932543),* P.O. Box 12, Hugo, OK 74743 (SAN 687-4827) Tel 405-326-2677.

M Bitker, *(Bitker, Marian; 0-9628150),* 3061 W. Pincushion, Tucson, AZ 85746 Tel 602-883-6841.

M Boyars Pubs, *(Boyars, Marion, Pubs., Inc.; 0-7145;* 0-905223), 237 E. 39th St., No. 1A, New York, NY 10016-2110 (SAN 284-981X) Tel 212-697-1599; Dist. by: InBook, P.O. Box 120261, East Haven, CT 06512 (SAN 630-5547) Tel 203-467-4257; Toll free: 800-253-3605 (orders only).

M Burns Educ Assocs, *(Burns, Marilyn, Education Assocs.; 0-941355),* 150 Gate 5 Rd., Suite 101, Sausalito, CA 94965 (SAN 665-5424) Tel 415-332-4181; Dist. by: Cuisenaire Co. of America, Inc., P.O. Box 5026, White Plains, NY 10602-5026 (SAN 201-7806) Tel 914-997-2600; Toll free: 800-237-3142.

M C Buckel, *(Buckel, M.C.),* P.O. Box 692633, Orlando, FL 32869-2633 Tel 407-857-4450.

M C Cook, *(Cook, Malcolm C.),* P.O. Box 26482, Birmingham, AL 35226 Tel 205-979-6689.

M C Hudson, *(Hudson, Mary C.; 0-9627745),* 1125 Karen Way, Mountainview, CA 94040 Tel 415-948-1270.

M C Mosley, *(Mosley, Marilyn C.; 0-9614850),* P.O. Box 1883, 13117 Burma Rd., SW, Vashon, WA 98070 (SAN 693-0972) Tel 206-567-4751.

M C Ullrich Pub, *(Ullrich, Marion Chambers, Pub.;* 0-9617091), 3340 Ingelow St., San Diego, CA 92106-2117 (SAN 662-6319) Tel 619-224-1425.

M Camphouse, *(Camphouse, Marylyn, Pub.; 0-9623948),* 1653 Hollingsworth Dr., Mountain View, CA 94040 Tel 415-968-1644.

M Cohen, *(Cohen, Mel; 0-9631104),* 33 Penns Ct., Aston, PA 19014 Tel 610-358-2890.

M Craft, *(Craft, Mary; 0-9624842),* 1147 Presidio Blvd., Pacific Grove, CA 93950 Tel 408-372-2239.

M D E A, *(MDEA Pr.; 0-9611820),* 79 Knollwood Dr., Newport News, VA 23602 (SAN 691-8948) Tel 804-877-1172.

M E Sharpe, *(Sharpe, M. E., Inc.; 0-87332; 1-56324),* 80 Business Pk. Dr., Armonk, NY 10504 (SAN 202-7100) Tel 914-273-1800; Toll free: 800-541-6563.

M Evans, *(Evans, M., & Co., Inc.; 0-87131),* 216 E. 49th St., New York, NY 10017 (SAN 203-4050) Tel 212-688-2810; Dist. by: National Bk. Network, 4720A Boston Way, Lanham, MD 20706-4310 (SAN 630-0065) Tel 301-459-8696; Toll free: 800-462-6420.

M G Ricketts, *(Ricketts, Marijane G.; 0-9618223),* 10203 Clearbrook Pl., Kensington, MD 20895 (SAN 666-8097) Tel 301-564-0852.

M Gould
See Allied Crafts

M Hyman Assocs
See The Way Pub

M J P Barry, *(Barry, M. J. P.; 0-9617009),* 323 W. Harvard Ave., Anchorage, AK 99501 (SAN 662-9148) Tel 907-272-0668.

M Johnson, *(Johnson, Mabel, Quality Paperbacks;* 0-9600838), P.O. Box 7, Boring, OR 97009 (SAN 206-1015) Tel 503-663-3428.

M K Look, *(Look, Margaret K.; 0-9616922),* P.O. Box 1173, Powell, WY 82435 (SAN 661-5074); 940 Shoshone Dr., Powell, WY 82435 (SAN 661-5082) Tel 307-754-4656.

M K McElderry *Imprint of* **Macmillan Child Grp**

M L Appell, *(Appell, Morey L., Human Relations Foundation, The; 0-943501),* 145 Old Church Rd., Greenwich, CT 06830 (SAN 668-5129) Tel 203-661-7891.

M Lane Pubs, *(Mitchell Lane Pubs.; 1-883845),* 17 Matthew Bathon Ct., Elkton, MD 21921 Tel 410-392-5036.

M Lynch, *(Lynch, Marietta, & Patricia Perry;* 0-9610962), 240 Atlantic Rd., Gloucester, MA 01930 (SAN 265-2722) Tel 508-283-6322.

M M Art Bks, *(M. M. Art Bks., Inc.; 0-9638904),* 11 Daniel Dr., Englewood, NJ 07631 Tel 201-568-2530.

M M Fain, *(Fain, Max M.; 0-9618960),* 508 Webster Dr., No. 8, Decatur, GA 30033 (SAN 242-8091).

M Meehan, *(Meehan, Maude; 0-9638224),* 2150 Portola Dr., Santa Cruz, CA 95062 Tel 408-476-6164.

M Moon, *(Moon, Marjorie; 0-9620834),* 3476 N. Shepard Ave., Milwaukee, WI 53211 (SAN 249-8596) Tel 414-962-5036.

M Press NM, *(M Pr.; 0-9619004),* 1303 Calle Lejano, Santa Fe, NM 87105-8910 (SAN 242-8792) Tel 505-983-7938.

M R Collman, *(Collman, Martha Rameau; 0-9631903),* 5610 Rosario Way, Anacortes, WA 98221 Tel 206-293-4532.

M R K, *(M-R-K Publishing; 0-9601292),* Div. of Meisterfeld & Assocs., 448 Seavey Ln., Petaluma, CA 94952 (SAN 210-461X) Tel 707-763-0056.

M R Stone Minst, *(Stone, Maggie Ruth, Ministries;* 0-9627059), 76 Tusculum Rd., Antioch, TN 37013 Tel 615-255-1928.

M R Wolff, *(Wolff, Mark Robert; 0-9637132),* 8703 Ranchito Ave., Panorama City, CA 91402 Tel 818-893-9265.

M Raphael, *(Raphael, Morris, Bks.; 0-9608866),* 1404 Bayou Side Dr., New Iberia, LA 70560 (SAN 241-0737) Tel 318-369-3220.

M Reynolds, *(Morgan Reynolds, Inc.; 1-883846),* 803 S. Elam Ave., Greensboro, NC 27403 Tel 910-274-3704.

M Roach & Assocs, *(Roach, Maggie, & Assocs.;* 1-882666), 1585 NW Maple Ave., Corvallis, OR 97330-1341 (SAN 297-8148) Tel 503-752-3396.

M Rummel
See Olive Brnch

M S Pr, *(M/S Pr.; 1-881278),* 5623 47th Ave. SW, Suite 101, Seattle, WA 98136-1406 Tel 206-937-4848.

M T Krieger, *(Krieger, Michael T.; 0-9634329),* 81 Rossway, Apt. 18, Rossford, OH 43460 Tel 419-666-1380.

M Taliaferro
See FEA Pub

M Valladares, *(Valladares, Margaret; 1-879588),* P.O. Box 141681, Coral Gables, FL 33114; 2541 SW 63rd Ave., Miami, FL 33155 Tel 305-662-5623.

M Wetherbee, *(Wetherbee, Martha, Bks.; 0-9609384),* Star Rte. 35, Sanbornton, NH 03269 (SAN 260-2709) Tel 603-286-8927.

M Wright & Assocs, *(Wright, Milt, & Assocs.; 0-942071),* 17624 Romar St., Northridge, CA 91325 (SAN 666-735X) Tel 818-349-0858.

M Wyatt, *(Wyatt, Margaret; 0-9616117),* 1127 St. Mary, Casper, WY 82601 (SAN 699-721X) Tel 307-237-7531.

M-Z Info, *(M-Z Information; 0-937559),* P.O. Box 2129, Wilton, NY 12866 (SAN 658-8999); 6 Timberlane Dr., Gansevoort, NY 12831 (SAN 248-4064).

MAC Pub, *(MAC Publishing; 0-910223),* Div. of Claudia, Inc., 5005 E. 39th Ave., Denver, CO 80207-1106 (SAN 241-4031) Tel 303-331-0148.

Macalester, *(Macalester Park Publishing Co.; 0-910924;* 1-886158), 8434 Horizon Dr., Shakopee, MN 55379-9606 (SAN 110-8077) Tel 612-496-1106; Toll free: 800-407-9078; Dist. by: Riverside/World, P.O. Box 370, 1500 Riverside Dr., Iowa Falls, IA 50126 (SAN 169-2666) Tel 515-648-4271; Toll free: 800-247-5111; Dist. by: Spring Arbor Distributors, 10885 Textile Rd., Belleville, MI 48111 (SAN 158-9016) Tel 313-481-0900; Toll free: 800-395-5599 (orders); 800-395-7234 (customer service); Dist. by: DeVorss & Co., P.O. Box 550, Marina del Rey, CA 90294-0550 (SAN 168-9886) Tel 213-870-7478; Toll free: 800-843-5743 (bookstores only); 800-331-4719 (in California, bookstores only); Dist. by: Bookmen, Inc., 525 N. Third St., Minneapolis, MN 55401 (SAN 169-409X) Tel 612-341-3333; Toll free: 800-328-8411 (customer service); Dist. by: Baker & Taylor Bks., Somerville Service Ctr., 50 Kirby Ave., Somerville, NJ 08876-0734 (SAN 169-4901) Tel 908-722-8000; Toll free: 800-775-1500 (customer service); Dist. by: Baker & Taylor Bks., Midwestern Div., 251 Mt. Olive Church Rd., Momence, IL 60954-2444 (SAN 169-1503) Tel 815-472-2444; Toll free: 800-775-2300 (customer service); 800-775-2200 (orders only); Dist. by: Baker & Taylor Bks., Commerce Service Ctr., Mt. Olive Rd., Commerce, GA 30599-9988 (SAN 169-1503) Tel 706-335-5000; Toll free: 800-775-1200 (customer service); Dist. by: Baker & Taylor Bks., Reno Service Ctr., 380 Edison Way, Reno, NV 89564 (SAN 169-4464) Tel 702-858-6700; Toll free: 800-775-1700 (customer service).

McArthur UT, *(McArthur Publishing; 0-9626111),* 911 W. 180th S., Orem, UT 84058 Tel 801-226-3625. Do not confuse with McArthur Publisher, Alexandria, LA.

McClain, *(McClain Printing Co.; 0-87012),* P.O. Box 403, Parsons, WV 26287-0403 (SAN 203-9478) Tel 304-478-2881; Toll free: 800-654-7179.

McClanahan Bk, *(McClanahan Bk. Co., Inc.; 1-878624;* 1-56293), 23 W. 26th St., New York, NY 10010 Tel 212-725-1515.

McClintock Ent, *(McClintock Enterprises; 1-880556),* 853 Seventh Ave., New York, NY 10019 Tel 212-246-2286.

McCormack Co, *(McCormack Co.; 0-942459),* 455 Arrowhead Trail, Knoxville, TN 37919 (SAN 667-0601) Tel 615-525-8667.

MacDonald-Sward, *(MacDonald/Sward Publishing Co.;* 0-945437), R.D. 3, Box 104A, Greensburg, PA 15601 (SAN 247-1973) Tel 412-832-7767.

Macedon Prod, *(Macedon Production Co.; 0-939965),* P.O. Box 60773, Oklahoma City, OK 73146 (SAN 663-8821); 600 NE 16th St., Oklahoma City, OK 73104 (SAN 663-883X) Tel 405-235-8038.

McFarland & Co, *(McFarland & Co., Inc., Pubs.; 0-89950; 0-7864),* Box 611, Jefferson, NC 28640 (SAN 215-093X) Tel 910-246-4460.

McGraw, *(McGraw-Hill, Inc.; 0-07; 0-390),* 1221 Ave. of the Americas, New York, NY 10020 (SAN 200-2248) Tel 212-512-2000; Toll free: 800-262-4729 (retail); 800-338-3987 (college); 800-722-4726 (consumer); Orders to: Princeton Rd., Hightstown, NJ 08520 (SAN 200-254X); Toll free: 800-338-3987 (college only); Orders to: 13311 Monterrey Ave., Blue Ridge Summit, PA 17294-0850 (SAN 200-2558); Toll free: 800-822-8138; 800-722-4726. *Imprints:* BYTE Bks (BYTE Books).

McGreen Wisdom, *(McGreen Wisdom, Inc.; 1-881037),* 101 Highview Dr., Pittsburgh, PA 15241 Tel 610-759-4882.

McGriff & Bell, *(McGriff & Bell, Inc.; 0-9634609),* P.O. Box 1622, 225 Michigan St., NW, Grand Rapids, MI 49501 Tel 616-454-2685; Toll free: 800-642-0562.

Machine Pr, *(Machine Pr. Publishing; 0-9634272),* P.O. Box 870210, Stone Mountain, GA 30087-0006 (SAN 297-7834); 4581 Lucerne Valley Rd., Lilburn, GA 30247 Tel 404-979-3660.

McIntosh Pubns, *(McIntosh Pubns.; 0-9632879),* P.O. Box 4116, Parkersburg, WV 26104; 4809 Crestview Cir., Parkersburg, WV 26104 Tel 304-485-5347.

McKay, *(McKay, David, Co., Inc.; 0-679),* Subs. of Random Hse., Inc., 201 E. 50th St., MD 4-6, New York, NY 10022 (SAN 200-240X) Tel 212-751-2600; Orders to: Random Hse., Inc., 400 Hahn Rd., Westminster, MD 21157 (SAN 202-5515) Tel 410-848-1900; Toll free: 800-733-3000 (orders only).

MacKay-Langley, *(MacKay-Langley Publishing;* 1-882748), 152 Bartlett Ave., Pittsfield, MA 01201 Tel 413-499-5876.

Mackinac Island, *(Mackinac Island State Park Commission; 0-911872),* P.O. Box 370, Mackinac Island, MI 49757 (SAN 202-5981) Tel 906-847-3328.

Mackinac Pub, *(Mackinac Publishing; 0-9623213),* 31355 Kennoway Ct., Beverly Hills, MI 48025-3851.

McKinzie Pub, *(McKinzie Publishing Co.; 0-86626),* 11000 Wilshire Blvd., P.O. Box 241777, Los Angeles, CA 90024 (SAN 216-2644) Tel 213-934-7685.

Macmillan, *(Macmillan Publishing Co., Inc.; 0-02;* 0-89256), Div. of Maxwell Communications Corp., 866 Third Ave., 21st Flr., New York, NY 10022 (SAN 202-5574) Tel 212-702-2000; Toll free: 800-257-5755; Orders to: 100 Front St., Box 500, Riverside, NJ 08075-7500 (SAN 202-5582) Tel 609-461-6500. *Imprints:* Atheneum (Atheneum); Collier (Collier Books); Maxwell Macmillan (Maxwell Macmillan); Scribner (Scribner's, Charles, Sons); Twayne (Twayne Publishers).

Macmillan Child Bk *Imprint of* **Macmillan Child Grp**

Macmillan Child Grp, *(Macmillan Children's Bk. Group;* 0-02), Div. of Macmillan Publishing Co., Inc., 866 Third Ave., 25th Flr., New York, NY 10022 Tel 212-702-2000; Toll free: 800-257-5755 (customer service only). *Imprints:* Aladdin (Aladdin Books); Atheneum Child Bk (Atheneum Children's Book); Bradbury Pr (Bradbury Press); Collier Young Ad (Collier Book for Young Adults); Crestwood Hse (Crestwood House, Incorporated); Dillon (Dillon Press, Incorporated); Four Winds (Four Winds Press); M K McElderry (McElderry, Margaret K., Books); Macmillan Child Bk (Macmillan Children's Books); New Discovery Bks (New Discovery Books); Scribners Young Read (Scribner Books for Young Readers).

Macmillan Ed UK *Imprint of* **Players Pr**

Macmlln New Media, *(Macmillan New Media; 1-56574),* Div. of Macmillan, Inc., 124 Mt. Auburn St., Cambridge, MA 02138 (SAN 298-1025) Tel 617-661-2955; Toll free: 800-342-1338; Dist. by: Compton's NewMedia, Inc., 722 Genevieve, Suite M, Solana Beach, CA 92075 (SAN 297-7087) Tel 619-259-0444.

MacPherson Pub, *(MacPherson Publishing Co.;* 0-9614849), 907 Comstock Ave., Syracuse, NY 13210 (SAN 693-1065) Tel 315-475-0339.

McQueen, *(McQueen Publishing Co.; 0-917186),* P.O. Box 198, Tiskilwa, IL 61368 (SAN 203-9516) Tel 815-646-4591.

Macra-Tack Inc, *(Macra-Tack, Inc.; 0-9611536),* P.O. Box 326, Stevensville, MT 59870 (SAN 285-3248) Tel 406-777-5408; Dist. by: Johnson Bks., 1880 S. 57th St., Boulder, CO 80301 (SAN 201-0313) Tel 303-443-9766; Toll free: 800-258-5830.

Macrobit Corp, *(Macrobit Corp.; 0-939573),* 8070 NW 53rd St., Suite 109, Miami, FL 33166 (SAN 663-5334) Tel 305-592-5354.

McRoy & Blackburn, *(McRoy & Blackburn, Pubs.;* 0-9632596), Box 276, Ester City, AK 99725; 404 Styx River Rd., Ester City, AK 99725 Tel 907-479-2774.

McVie Pub, *(McVie Publishing Co.; 0-917487),* 17630 15th Pl., W., Lynnwood, WA 98037 (SAN 656-0733) Tel 206-743-3706.

Mad Hatter Pub, *(Mad Hatter Publishing Co.; 1-56680),* P.O. Box 1184, Aspen, CO 81612-1184.

Madison Aves, *(Madison Avenues; 0-942553),* 1540 K St., Anchorage, AK 99501-4964 (SAN 667-4089).

Madison Park Pr, *(Madison Park Pr.; 0-942178),* 3816 E. Madison St., Seattle, WA 98112 (SAN 238-7867).

Mage Pubs Inc, *(Mage Pubs., Inc.; 0-934211),* 1032 29th St., NW, Washington, DC 20007 (SAN 693-0476) Tel 202-342-1642; Toll free: 800-962-0922 (orders only); Dist. by: Baker & Taylor Bks., Somerville Service Ctr., 50 Kirby Ave., Somerville, NJ 08876-0734 (SAN 169-4901) Tel 908-722-8000; Toll free: 800-775-1500 (customer service); Dist. by: Baker & Taylor Bks., Reno Service Ctr., 380 Edison Way, Reno, NV 89564 (SAN 169-4464) Tel 702-858-6700; Toll free: 800-775-1700 (customer service); Dist. by: Baker & Taylor Bks., Commerce Service Ctr., 251 Mt. Olive Church Rd., Commerce, GA 30599-9988 (SAN 169-1503) Tel 706-335-5000; Toll free: 800-775-1200 (customer service); Dist. by: Baker & Taylor Bks., Momence Service Ctr., 501 S. Gladiolus St., Momence, IL 60954-2444 (SAN 169-2100) Tel 815-472-2444; Toll free: 800-775-2300 (customer service); Dist. by: New Leaf Distributing Co., 5425 Tulane Dr., SW, Atlanta, GA 30336-2323 (SAN 169-1449) Tel 404-691-6996; Toll free: 800-326-2665; Dist. by: Blackwell North America, 100 University Ct, Blackwood, NJ 08012 (SAN 169-4596) Tel 609-228-8900; Toll free: 800-547-0700 (in Oregon); Dist. by: Interlink Publishing Group, Inc., 99 Seventh Ave., Brooklyn, NY 11215 (SAN 664-8908) Tel 718-783-6067.

Magic Fishes Pr, *(Magic Fishes Pr.; 0-942255),* 3-4251 Kuhio Hwy., Lihue, HI 96766 (SAN 666-9190) Tel 808-245-5257.

Magic Lantrn, *(Magic Lantern Pubns.; 0-9619250),* 200 Midlake, Suite C, Knoxville, TN 37918 (SAN 243-8658) Tel 615-688-1303.

Magic Ltd, *(Magic Limited-Lloyd E. Jones; 0-915926),* P.O. Box 3186, San Leandro, CA 94578 (SAN 208-7480) Tel 510-352-1854; 4064 39th Ave., Oakland, CA 94619 (SAN 208-7499) Tel 415-531-5490.

Magical Michael, *(Magical Michael Publishing;* 0-9638530), 201 Alicia St., Ashland, OR 97520 Tel 503-482-3191.

Magical Rainbow, *(Magical Rainbow Pubns.; 0-911281),* P.O. Box 717, Ojai, CA 93023 (SAN 272-1775).

Magik NY, *(Magik Pubs.; 0-9626608),* 4321 Hempstead Tpke., Bethpage, NY 11714 Tel 516-731-5500.

Magill Bks *Imprint of* **Salem Pr**

Magination CA, *(Magination; 1-881597),* 3579 E. Foothill Blvd., No. 330, Pasadena, CA 91107 Tel 818-306-1190. Do not confuse with Magination Press in New York, NY.

Magination Pr, *(Magination Pr.; 0-945354),* Div. of Brunner/Mazel, Inc., 19 Union Sq., W., 8th Flr., New York, NY 10003 (SAN 246-6511) Tel 212-924-3344; Toll free: 800-825-3089 (customer orders). Do not confuse with Magination in Pasadena, CA.

Magnolia MA, *(Magnolia Publishing; 0-9638479),* P.O. Box 5537, Magnolia, MA 01930; Toll free: 800-636-6200 (orders only); 8 Carrie Ln., Gloucester, MA 01930 Tel 508-283-5283. Do not confuse with Magnolia Publishing, Inc. in Orlando, FL.

Magnolia Mktg, *(Magnolia Marketing & Publishing Co.;* 1-882188), P.O. Box 5057, Chapel Hill, NC 27514-5057; 102 Fallen Log, Polks Landing, Chapel Hill, NC 27516 Tel 919-932-3944.

Magnolia PA, *(Magnolia Pr.; 0-929917),* P.O. Box 6101, Pittsburgh, PA 15212 (SAN 250-9717); 36 Foster Sq., Pittsburgh, PA 15212 (SAN 250-9725) Tel 412-321-5041. Do not confuse with companies with the same name in Carrollton, TX, Gainesville, GA.

Magnolia Pr, *(Magnolia Pr.; 0-916369),* P.O. Box 2921, Gainesville, GA 30503 (SAN 295-6233) Tel 706-531-0644. Do not confuse with companies with the same name in Pittsburgh, PA, Carrollton, TX.

Magnolia South Pub, *(Magnolia South Publishing;* 1-879318), P.O. Box 12634, Jackson, MS 39236-2634; 30 L.C. Caves Dr., Waynesboro, MS 39367 Tel 601-735-9848.

Magnum Pr, *(Magnum Pr.; 0-9623698),* 2223 W. Eighth St., Stillwater, OK 74074 Tel 405-377-0950.

Magnum Schl, *(Magnum Schl., Inc.; 0-945406),* 342 N. Ford Blvd., Los Angeles, CA 90022 (SAN 246-960X) Tel 213-262-3499.

Magpie Pubns, *(Magpie Pubns.; 0-936480),* P.O. Box 636, Alamo, CA 94507 (SAN 221-4091) Tel 510-838-9287.

Mah-Tov Pubns, *(Mah-Tov Pubns.; 0-917274),* 1680 45th St., Brooklyn, NY 11204 (SAN 208-7502) Tel 718-871-5337.

Mailbox, *(Mailbox Club Bks.; 0-9603752; 1-879224),* 404 Eager Rd., Valdosta, GA 31602 (SAN 281-9686); Toll free: 800-488-5226 (orders).

Maimes, *(Maimes, S. L.; 0-917246),* 59 Franklin St., Rochester, NH 03867 (SAN 208-1830) Tel 603-332-8889.

Main St Pub, *(Main Street Publishing, Inc.; 0-935399),* 2022 E. Edgewood, Shorewood, WI 53211 (SAN 696-3129) Tel 414-964-5757.

Maine Heritage, *(Maine Heritage Bks.; 0-9629543),* P.O. Box 1462, Scarborough, ME 04070-1462 Tel 207-772-3813.

Maitland Enter, *(Maitland Enterprises; 0-936759),* 8118 N. 28th Ave., Phoenix, AZ 85051 (SAN 699-8437) Tel 602-995-4365; Dist. by: Five Star Pubns., 4696 W. Tyson St., Chandler, AZ 85226 (SAN 246-7429) Tel 602-940-8182; Toll free: 800-545-7827.

Make-Hawk Pub, *(Make-Hawk Publishing; 0-9636417),* 191 University Blvd., Suite 141, Denver, CO 80206; 612 York, Denver, CO 80206 Tel 303-321-0585.

Makepeace Colony, *(Makepeace Colony Pr., The;* 0-87741), P.O. Box 111, Stevens Point, WI 54481 (SAN 203-9575) Tel 715-344-2636.

Malibu Graphics, *(Malibu Graphics Publishing Group; 0-944735; 1-56398),* 26707 Agoura Rd., Calabasas, CA 91302-1960 (SAN 244-9668) Tel 818-889-9800.

Malki Mus Pr, *(Malki Museum Pr.; 0-939046),* Div. of Malki Museum, Inc., 3115 Flanders Rd., Riverside, CA 92507 (SAN 281-9724); Orders to: Roderick Tyron Linton, 11-795 Fields Rd., Banning, CA 92220 (SAN 281-9724) Tel 909-849-7289.

Malouf-Christopherson, *(Malouf-Christopherson Enterprises, Inc.; 0-9639680),* P.O. Box 180656, 10422 Lippitt, Dallas, TX 75218 Tel 214-327-3516.

Man Mtn Pub, *(Man Mountain Publishing; 0-943981),* 1810 W. Cortland, Chicago, IL 60622 (SAN 242-665X) Tel 312-486-4381; Dist. by: Baker & Taylor Bks., Somerville Service Ctr., 50 Kirby Ave., Somerville, NJ 08876-0734 (SAN 169-4901) Tel 908-722-8000; Toll free: 800-775-1500 (customer service).

M&M Assocs, *(M&M Assocs.; 1-877782),* P.O. Box 1020, Fort Jones, CA 96032; 12424 Main St., Fort Jones, CA 96032 Tel 916-468-2282.

M&M Pub, *(M&M Publishing Co.; 0-9630519;* 0-9631433), 10403 Hyannis Dr., Richmond, VA 23236; 6106 Phelps St., Glen Allen, VA 23060 Tel 804-262-0381. Do not confuse with companies with the same name in Fairfax, VA, West Palm Beach, FL.

Mango Entrps, *(Mango Enterprises, Inc.; 0-9627586),* 836 "M" St., Suite 105, Anchorage, AK 99501 Tel 907-277-2886.

Manhattan Pr, *(Manhattan Pr.; 0-9634642),* 260 S. Lake Ave., No. 222, Pasadena, CA 91101-3008 Tel 818-792-4707.

Manuscript Pr, *(Manuscript Pr.; 0-936414),* Box 336, Mountain Home, TN 37684 (SAN 214-3224) Tel 615-926-7495. Do not confuse with Manuscript Pr., Nashville, TN.

Manuscripts, *(Manuscripts, Ltd.; 0-9627979),* 1610 Hillside Rd., Boulder, CO 80302 Tel 303-442-3596; Toll free: 800-661-2932.

Manzanita Canyon, *(Manzanita Canyon Pr.; 0-9622057),* P.O. Box 2271, Redlands, CA 92373; 11485 Acropolis Dr., Yucaipa, CA 92399 Tel 909-797-5260.

Manzanita Pr, *(Manzanita Pr.; 0-931644),* 4777 Hillsborough Dr., Petaluma, CA 94954 (SAN 211-0342) Tel 707-778-8081. Do not confuse with Manzanita Pr., Three Rivers, CA.

Mapakam Inc, *(Mapakam, Inc.; 0-9623773),* P.O. Box 587, Nixa, MO 65714; Rte. 2, Box 166W, Nixa, MO 65714 Tel 417-725-5582.

Mar Co Prods, *(MAR CO Products, Inc.; 1-884063),* 1443 Old York Rd., Warminster, PA 18974 Tel 215-956-0313; Toll free: 800-448-2197.

Marc Anthony, *(Marc Anthony Publishing; 0-9635107),* P.O. Box 5610, Blue Jay, CA 92317 (SAN 297-8229); 231 S. Fairway Dr., Blue Jay, CA 92317 Tel 714-337-8911.

March Media, *(March Media, Inc.; 0-9634824),* 7003 Chadwick Dr., Suite 256, Brentwood, TN 37027 Tel 615-370-3148; Dist. by: Rutledge Hill Pr., 513 Third Ave., South Nashville, TN 37210 Tel 615-244-2700.

Marcroft Prods, *(Marcroft Productions; 0-935849),* P.O. Box 16405, Salt Lake City, UT 84116-0405 (SAN 695-9776) Tel 801-596-3127.

Mari, *(Mari, Inc.; 0-926706; 1-56096),* 1025 25th St., Santa Monica, CA 90403 (SAN 134-6792) Tel 310-829-2212.

Mariah Pr, *(Mariah Pr.; 0-945436),* 865 Ahwahnee Dr., Millbrae, CA 94030 (SAN 247-137X) Tel 415-697-4682.

Marianas Red Pub, *(Marianas Red Publishing Co.; 0-9624930),* P.O. Box 22482 GMF, Barrigada, GU 96921-2482; 100 Sr. Ecurita Dr., Yona, GU 96914.

Marine Endeavors, *(Marine Endeavors Pr.; 0-935181),* P.O. Box 4423, Berkeley, CA 94705 (SAN 695-4677) Tel 510-531-3887; Dist. by: Bookpeople, 7900 Edgewater Dr., Oakland, CA 94621 (SAN 168-9517) Tel 510-632-4700; Toll free: 800-999-4650.

Marine Mammal Fund, *(Marine Mammal Fund; 0-9617803),* Ft. Mason Ctr., Bldg. E, San Francisco, CA 94123 (SAN 664-6603) Tel 415-775-4636; Dist. by: Hawaiian Resources Co. Ltd., 94-527 Puahi St., Waipahu, HI 96797 (SAN 200-4984) Tel 808-671-6735.

Mariposa Print Pub, *(Mariposa Printing & Publishing, Inc.; 0-933553),* 922 Baca St., Santa Fe, NM 87501 (SAN 691-8743) Tel 505-988-5582.

Marist Miss Sis, *(Marist Missionary Sisters; 0-9631198),* 62 Newton St., Waltham, MA 02154 Tel 516-868-0260.

Mark Excell Pub, *(Mark of Excellence Publishing Co.; 0-933415),* 4620 Northridge Dr., Los Angeles, CA 90043 (SAN 691-5019) Tel 213-294-2136.

Mark Foster Mus, *(Foster, Mark, Music Co.; 0-916656),* P.O. Box 4012, Champaign, IL 61824-4012 (SAN 208-2861) Tel 217-398-2760; Toll free: 800-359-1386.

MarKel Pr, *(MarKel Pr.; 0-9621406),* P.O. Box 134, Springfield, OR 97477 (SAN 251-1886); 94854 Kelso Ln., Marcola, OR 97454 (SAN 251-1894) Tel 503-933-2831.

Marketcom, *(Marketcom, Inc.; 0-943409),* 550 Rudder Rd., Fenton, MO 63026 (SAN 668-5838) Tel 314-343-8000; Toll free: 800-325-3884; Dist. by: Troll Assocs., 100 Corporate Dr., Mahwah, NJ 07430 (SAN 200-4895) Tel 201-529-4000; Toll free: 800-526-5289; Dist. by: Scholastic, Inc., P.O. Box 120, Bergenfield, NJ 07621 (SAN 202-5450) Tel 212-505-3000; Toll free: 800-325-6149 (orders only); Dist. by: Scholastic Bk. Fairs, 150 Hope St., Longwood, FL 32794 (SAN 200-5077) Tel 407-831-9977; Dist. by: Field Pubns., 245 Long Hill Rd., Middletown, CT 06457 (SAN 207-060X) Tel 203-638-2400; Dist. by: California Schl. Bk. Fairs, P.O. Box 66015, Anaheim, CA 92816-6015 (SAN 200-5093) Tel 714-970-2700; Toll free: 800-874-8092 (outside CA); 800-543-4720 (in CA).

Markins Enter, *(Markins Enterprises; 0-937729),* 2039 SE 45th Ave., Portland, OR 97215 (SAN 659-3224) Tel 503-235-1036.

Markov Pr, *(Markov Pr.; 1-882965),* 45 Howard Ave., Passaic, NJ 07055 Tel 201-614-9101.

Marlin Pub, *(Marlin Publishing; 1-878474),* 2614 31st St., Santa Monica, CA 90405-3013.

Marlor Pr, *(Marlor Pr., Inc.; 0-943400),* 4304 Brigadoon Dr., Saint Paul, MN 55126 (SAN 240-7140) Tel 612-484-4600; Dist. by: Contemporary Bks., Inc., 2 Prudential Plaza, Suite 1200, Chicago, IL 60601 (SAN 202-5493) Tel 312-540-4500; Toll free: 800-621-1918 (orders only).

Marsh Wind Pr, *(Marsh Wind Pr.; 0-9642620),* Box 1596, Mount Pleasant, SC 29465; 1180 Main Canal Dr., Mount Pleasant, SC 29464 Tel 803-884-5957.

Marshall Cavendish, *(Cavendish, Marshall, Corp.; 0-85685; 0-86307; 1-85435),* Member of Times Publishing Group, 2415 Jerusalem Ave., North Bellmore, NY 11710 (SAN 238-437X) Tel 516-826-4200; Toll free: 800-821-9881.

Marshall Regnl Arts, *(Marshall Regional Arts Council; 1-879703),* P.O. Box C, Marshall, TX 75671; 2501 E. End Blvd., S., Marshall, TX 75670 Tel 903-935-4484.

Marshfilm, *(Marshfilm Enterprises, Inc.; 0-925159; 1-55942),* P.O. Box 8082, Shawnee Mission, KS 66208 (SAN 656-3228) Tel 816-523-1059; Toll free: 800-821-3303 (for orders/customer service only); Orders to: 5903 Main St., Kansas City, MO 64113 Tel 816-523-1059.

Martin Barry Prods, *(Martin Barry Productions; 0-9631472),* 5500 Friendship Blvd., Suite 1514N, Chevy Chase, MD 20815 Tel 301-656-2071.

Martin Press, *(Martin Pr.; 0-9617044),* P.O. Box 2109, San Anselmo, CA 94960 (SAN 662-8702); 63 Durham Rd., San Anselmo, CA 94960 (SAN 662-8710) Tel 415-454-7985; Dist. by: Bookpeople, 7900 Edgewater Dr., Oakland, CA 94621 (SAN 168-9517) Tel 510-632-4700; Toll free: 800-999-4650; Dist. by: Publishers Group West, 4065 Hollis St., Emeryville, CA 94608 (SAN 202-8522) Tel 510-658-3453; Toll free: 800-788-3123. Do not confuse with Martin Pr., Minneapolis, MN or Saint Martin's Pr., Inc. in New York, NY.

Martins
See Green Psturs Pr

Marvel Comics
See Marvel Entmnt

Marvel Entmnt, *(Marvel Entertainment Group, Inc.; 0-9604146; 0-939766; 0-87135; 0-7851),* 387 Park Ave., S., New York, NY 10016 (SAN 216-9088) Tel 212-696-0808; Dist. by: Publishers Group West, 4065 Hollis St., Emeryville, CA 94608 (SAN 202-8522) Tel 510-658-3453; Toll free: 800-788-3123.

Mary Ann Johnson, *(Johnson, Mary Ann; 0-9621465),* Rte. 1, Box 1400, Rocky Mount, VA 24151 (SAN 251-4664) Tel 703-483-4360.

Mary Bee Creat, *(Mary Bee Creations; 1-879414),* 24 E. 25th Ave., San Mateo, CA 94403 Tel 415-571-7979.

Mary Janes Cookbook, *(Mary Jane's Cookbook; 0-9620670),* P.O. Box 70593, Marietta, GA 30067 (SAN 249-4647); 2526 Sunny Ln., SE, Marietta, GA 30067 (SAN 249-4655) Tel 404-565-3646.

Marymoor Mus, *(Marymoor Museum; 0-9624587),* P.O. Box 162, Redmond, WA 98073; 6046 W. Lake Sammamish Pkwy., NE, Redmond, WA 98073 Tel 206-885-3684.

MAS Pr, *(MAS-Pr.; 0-9607984),* P.O. Box 57374, Washington, DC 20037 (SAN 238-5392) Tel 202-659-9580; 1129 New Hampshire Ave., NW, No. 610, Washington, DC 20037 (SAN 241-7685) Tel 202-331-1218; Dist. by: Borden Publishing Co., 2623 San Fernando Rd., Los Angeles, CA 90065 (SAN 201-419X) Tel 213-223-4267; Dist. by: Unique Bks., Inc., 4200 Grove Ave., Gurnee, IL 60031 (SAN 630-0472) Tel 708-623-9171.

MasAir Pubns
See J R Matthews

Master Bks, *(Master Bks.; 0-89051),* Subs. of Creation-Life Pubs., Inc., P.O. Box 26060, Colorado Springs, CO 80936 (SAN 205-6119) Tel 719-591-0800; Toll free: 800-999-3777. *Imprints:* Inst Creation (Institute for Creation Research).

Master-Player Lib, *(Master-Player Library; 1-877873),* Div. of William Grant Still Music, P.O. Box 3044, Flagstaff, AZ 86003; 22 S. San Francisco St., Suite 422, Flagstaff, AZ 86003 Tel 602-526-9355.

MasterMedia Ltd, *(MasterMedia Ltd.; 0-942361; 1-57101),* 17 E. 89th St., 7D, New York, NY 10128 (SAN 667-075X) Tel 212-546-7650; Toll free: 800-334-8232; Dist. by: Haddon Craftsmen Distribution Ctr., 1205 O'Neill Hwy., Dunmore, PA 18512 (SAN 200-7746) Tel 717-348-9211; Toll free: 800-444-2524 (orders only).

Masterminds Pubns, *(Masterminds Pubns.; 1-877890),* P.O. Box 670882, Marietta, GA 30066; 1229 Overton Dr., Lawrenceville, GA 30244 Tel 404-973-8590.

Masters Pr IN, *(Masters Pr.; 0-940279; 1-57028),* Div. of Howard W. Sams & Co., 2647 Waterfront Pkwy. East Dr., Suite 300, Indianapolis, IN 46214-2041 (SAN 664-2187) Tel 317-298-5598; Toll free: 800-722-2677.

Masters Pubns, *(Masters Pubns.; 0-89808),* 215 Hillcrest Rd., Berkeley, CA 94705 (SAN 226-2959) Tel 510-540-1928.

Masterson, *(Masterson Publishing Corp.; 1-880525),* 397 Royal Ave., Ferguson, MO 63135; Toll free: 800-544-8370.

Material Dev, *(Material Development Ctr.; 0-916671),* Div. of Stout Vocational Rehabilitation Institute, Stout Vocational Rehabilitation Institute, Univ. of Wisconsin-Stout, Menomonie, WI 54751 (SAN 297-1917) Tel 715-232-1342.

Matey Pr, *(Matey Pr.; 1-883737),* P.O. Box 90106, Santa Barbara, CA 93190; 505 E. Montecito, Santa Barbara, CA 93103 Tel 805-682-5591.

Math Leagues, *(Mathematics Leagues, Inc.; 0-940805),* P.O. Box 720, Tenafly, NJ 07670 (SAN 667-4275); 273 Woodland St., Tenafly, NJ 07670 (SAN 667-4283) Tel 201-568-6328.

Math Sci Nucleus, *(Math/Science Nucleus; 1-56638),* 4009 Pestana Pl., Fremont, CA 94538-6301 Tel 510-490-6284.

Mathematical, *(Mathematical Concepts; 0-9623593),* 85 First St., Keyport, NJ 07735-1503 Tel 908-739-3951.

Mauna Loa Pub, *(Mauna Loa Publishing; 0-929703),* 1729 Averill Park Dr., San Pedro, CA 90732 (SAN 249-7948) Tel 310-547-5388.

Maureen Points, *(Maureen Points),* P.O. Box 425151, San Francisco, CA 94142-5151 (SAN 211-3236).

Maverick Bks, *(Maverick Bks.; 0-9608612; 0-916941),* Box 549, Perryton, TX 79070 (SAN 240-7183) Tel 806-435-7611.

Max Sci Pub, *(Max Science Publishing Co.; 1-879350),* P.O. Box 12143, Research Triangle Park, NC 27709-2143; 1322 Seaton Rd., Durham, NC 27713 Tel 919-544-5144.

Maxrom Pr, *(Maxrom Pr., Inc.; 0-930339),* 11 E. Fayette St., Baltimore, MD 21202 (SAN 670-6800) Tel 410-539-2370.

Maxwell-Elects
See Macmlln New Media

Maxwell Macmillan *Imprint of* **Macmillan**

MAYA Pubs, *(MAYA Pubs.; 1-895583),* 7302 W. Rose Ln., Glendale, AZ 85303 Tel 602-842-1366.

Maydale Pub, *(Maydale Publishing Co., Inc.; 0-9632530),* P.O. Box 10359, Silver Spring, MD 20914; 1605 Maydale Dr., Silver Spring, MD 20905 Tel 301-384-8595.

Mayfield Printing, *(Mayfield Printing & Office Equipment, Pubs.; 0-910513),* 810 Keyser, Natchitoches, LA 71457 (SAN 260-1028) Tel 318-357-0058.

Mayhaven Pub, *(Mayhaven Publishing; 1-878044),* 803 Buckthorn Cir., Mahomet, IL 61853 Tel 217-586-4493; Toll free: 800-230-4273.

Mazda Pubs, *(Mazda Pubs.; 0-939214; 1-56859),* P.O. Box 2603, Costa Mesa, CA 92626 (SAN 285-0524); 3100 Airway Ave., Suite 137, Costa Mesa, CA 92626 (SAN 658-120X) Tel 714-751-5252.

MD Hist Pr, *(Maryland Historical Pr.; 0-917882),* 9205 Tuckerman St., Lanham, MD 20706-2711 (SAN 202-6147) Tel 301-577-5308; Dist. by: Baker & Taylor Bks., Somerville Service Ctr., 50 Kirby Ave., Somerville, NJ 08876-0734 (SAN 169-4901) Tel 908-722-8000; Toll free: 800-775-1500 (customer service); Dist. by: Baker & Taylor Bks., Reno Service Ctr., 380 Edison Way, Reno, NV 89564 (SAN 169-4464) Tel 702-858-6700; Toll free: 800-775-1700 (customer service); Dist. by: S&L Sales Co., P.O. Box 2067, 2165 Industrial Blvd., Waycross, GA 31502 (SAN 107-413X) Tel 912-283-0210; Toll free: 800-243-3699 (orders only).

Mdsn Pub Assocs, *(Madison Publishing Assocs.; 0-933813),* 290 West End Ave., No. 16A, New York, NY 10023-8106 (SAN 692-8927) Tel 212-425-3466; Dist. by: Talman Co., 131 Spring St., Suite 201E-N, New York, NY 10012 (SAN 200-5204) Tel 212-431-7175; Toll free: 800-537-8894 (orders only). Do not confuse with Madison Publishing Co., Huntsville, AL.

Me Two Pubns, *(Me Two Pubns.; 0-9623800),* 1301 Roy St., Seattle, WA 98109-4423 Tel 206-623-9426; Toll free: 800-638-9622.

Meadora Pub, *(Meadora Publishing; 0-9627956),* 13351 Ridgecrest Ln., Cerritos, CA 90701 Tel 310-865-0682; 13351 Ridgecrest, Cerritos, CA 90701 Tel 310-865-0682.

Meadowbrook, *(Meadowbrook, Pr.; 0-915658; 0-88166),* 18318 Minnetonka Blvd., Deephaven, MN 55391 (SAN 207-3404) Tel 612-473-5400; Toll free: 800-338-2232; Dist. by: Simon & Schuster Trade, 1230 Ave. of the Americas, New York, NY 10020 Tel 212-698-7000.

Meanderings, *(Meanderings; 1-57289),* 438 11th Ave., SW, Albany, OR 97321 Tel 503-928-6063.

Meckler Corp
See Mecklermedia

Mecklermedia, *(Mecklermedia Corp.; 0-930466; 0-88736; 0-913672; 1-57207),* 20 Ketchum St., Westport, CT 06880 (SAN 211-0334) Tel 203-226-6967.

Med Physics Pub, *(Medical Physics Publishing Corp.; 0-944838),* 732 N. Midvale Blvd., Madison, WI 53705 (SAN 245-7407) Tel 608-262-4021; Toll free: 800-442-5778.

Medfd Pr, *(Medford Pr.; 0-9606824),* P.O. Box 416, Williamsburg, VA 23187 (SAN 209-1984) Tel 804-253-1393.

Media Basics, *(Media Basics, Inc.; 0-87438; 0-925202),* Lighthouse Sq., Guilford, CT 06437 (SAN 656-2175) Tel 203-458-2505; Toll free: 800-542-2505.

Media Materials, *(Media Materials, Inc.; 0-912974; 0-89539; 0-86601; 0-89026; 0-7916),* Holobird Industrial Pk., 1821 Portal St., Baltimere, MD 21224 (SAN 206-9989) Tel 410-633-0730; Toll free: 800-638-1010. Sold secondary product line & textbooks for special needs students to American Guidance Service, Inc.

Media Pub, *(Media Publishing; 0-939644),* Div. of Westport Pubs., 4050 Pennsylvania, Suite 310, Kansas City, MO 64111 (SAN 216-6372) Tel 816-756-1490; Toll free: 800-347-2665. Do not confuse with Media Publishing in Miami, FL.

Media Serv Unltd, *(Media Services Unlimited; 0-9620887),* P.O. Box 335, Saint Helena Island, SC 29920-0335 (SAN 250-0477).

Mediaor Co, *(Mediaor Co.; 0-942206),* Box 631, Prineville, OR 97754 (SAN 238-7859).

Medlicott Pr, *(Medlicott Pr.; 0-9625261),* 1035 Edgemont Pl., San Diego, CA 92102 Tel 619-236-7937.

Mee Enterp, *(Mee Enterprises Publishing Co.; 0-9618854),* P.O. Box 6992, Beverly Hills, CA 90212-6992 (SAN 242-5254); 3596 Centinela Ave., No. 201, Los Angeles, CA 90066 (SAN 242-5262) Tel 310-397-7176.

Megakinetics, *(Megakinetics - Climbing to Success; 1-56495),* 805 Douglas Ave., Suite 159, Altamonte Springs, FL 32714 Tel 407-682-6466.

Mel Bay, *(Mel Bay Pubns., Inc.; 0-87166; 1-56222; 0-7866),* P.O. Box 66, Four Industrial Dr., Pacific, MO 63069 (SAN 657-3630) Tel 314-257-3970; Toll free: 800-325-9518.

Melior Dist, *(Melior Distributors; 0-9616441; 0-929766),* S. 45 Girard, Spokane, WA 99212 (SAN 658-9154) Tel 509-924-1925; Toll free: 800-733-9696.

Melior Pubns
See Melior Dist

Melius Pub, *(Melius Publishing, Inc.; 0-9610130;* 0-937603), Div. of Video Resources, Inc., 118 River Rd., Pierre, SD 57501 (SAN 262-7477) Tel 605-224-1929; Toll free: 800-882-5171 Tel 510-658-3453.

Melrose Sq *Imprint of* **Holloway**

Meltec, *(Meltec Enterprises; 0-9637414),* 2978 Roundtree, Troy, MI 48083-2346 Tel 810-689-3076; Dist. by: Partners Bk. Distributing, Inc., 720 E. Shiawassee, Lansing, MI 48912 (SAN 630-4559) Tel 517-485-0366; Toll free: 800-336-3137.

Memories In Print, *(Memories In Print; 0-9625397),* 43427 SE 172nd Pl., North Bend, WA 98045-9660.

Memory Ln Bks, *(Memory Lane Bks.; 0-9618951),* 14 Noon Dr., E., North Vernon, IN 47265 (SAN 242-9403) Tel 812-346-6985.

Memphis Musicraft, *(Memphis Musicraft Pubns.;* 0-934017), 3149 Southern Ave., Memphis, TN 38111 (SAN 692-7696) Tel 901-452-5265.

Mensch Makers Pr, *(Mensch Makers Pr.; 0-9619880),* 1588 Northrop, Saint Paul, MN 55108 (SAN 246-9138) Tel 612-644-8533.

Ment *Imprint of* **NAL-Dutton**

Mer *Imprint of* **NAL-Dutton**

Merc Pr NY, *(Mercury Pr.; 0-936132; 0-929979),* Fellowship Community, 241 Hungry Hollow Rd., Spring Valley, NY 10977 (SAN 221-3923) Tel 914-425-9357.

Mercedes Ministries, *(Mercedes Ministries; 0-926044),* 123 Kings Way, Lexington, SC 29072-8816 Tel 301-551-9173.

Mercy Pr, *(Mercy Pr., Inc.; 1-882630),* P.O. Box 1432, Batesville, MS 38606; 147 Faith Dr., Batesville, MS 38606 Tel 601-563-3222.

Meredith Bks, *(Meredith Bks.; 0-696),* 1716 Locust St., Des Moines, IA 50309-3023 (SAN 202-4055); Toll free: 800-678-8091. Do not confuse with Meredith Pr. in Skaneateles, NY.

Merging Media
See Rose Shell Pr

Meridian Educ, *(Meridian Education Corp.; 0-936007; 1-877844; 1-56191),* 236 E. Front St., Bloomington, IL 61701 (SAN 696-6012) Tel 309-827-5455; Toll free: 800-727-5507.

Meridional Pubns, *(Meridional Pubns.; 0-939710),* 7101 Winding Way, Wake Forest, NC 27587 (SAN 216-7484) Tel 919-556-2940.

Meristem Bks, *(Meristem Bks.; 0-9639867),* 29P Mount Pleasant St., Rockport, MA 01966 (SAN 298-1556) Tel 508-546-7030.

Meriwether Pub, *(Meriwether Publishing, Ltd.; 0-916260; 1-56608),* P.O. Box 7710, Colorado Springs, CO 80933 (SAN 208-4716) Tel 719-594-4422; Toll free: 800-937-5297.

Meroe Pub, *(Meroe Publishing Co.; 0-9635862),* Div. of Meroe Enterprises, Ltd., P.O. Box 3268, Berkeley, CA 94703-0268; 2440 Durant Ave., Berkeley, CA 94704 Tel 510-843-3088.

Meroen Pr, *(Meroen Pr.; 0-9642212),* P.O. Box 6632, Tallahassee, FL 32314-6632 Tel 904-224-0338; Dist. by: United Brothers & Sisters Communications Systems, 912 W. Pembroke Ave., Hampton, VA 23669 Tel 804-723-2696.

Merriam-Eddy, *(Merriam-Eddy Co., Inc.; 0-914562),* P.O. Box 25, South Waterford, ME 04081 (SAN 202-6252).

Merriam-Webster Inc, *(Merriam-Webster, Inc.; 0-87779),* Subs. of Encyclopaedia Britannica, Inc., P.O. Box 281, Springfield, MA 01102 (SAN 202-6244); Toll free: 800-828-1880; 47 Federal St., Springfield, MA 01102 (SAN 658-1226) Tel 413-734-3134. Do not confuse with Webster's International, Inc., Parent Education, Brentwood, TN.

Merril Pr, *(Merril Pr.; 0-936783),* 12500 NE Tenth Pl., Bellevue, WA 98005 (SAN 699-9387) Tel 206-454-7009.

Merrill Ct Pr, *(Merrill Court Pr.; 0-9627239),* P.O. Box 85785, Seattle, WA 98145 Tel 206-325-5785.

Merry Bears, *(Merry Bears; 0-933103),* 22835 NE 51st St., Redmond, WA 98053 (SAN 689-5778) Tel 206-868-8061.

Merry Thoughts, *(Merry Thoughts; 0-88230),* 380 Adams St., Bedford Hills, NY 10507 (SAN 169-5061) Tel 914-241-0447.

Merryant Pubs, *(Merryant Pubs.; 1-877599),* 7615 SW 257th St., Vashon, WA 98070 Tel 206-463-3879.

Merrybooks VA, *(Merrybooks & More; 0-9615407;* 1-882607), 1214 Rugby Rd., Charlottesville, VA 22903 (SAN 695-5053) Tel 804-979-3658; Toll free: 800-959-2665.

MESD Pr, *(MESD Pr.; 1-880118),* 11611 NE Ainsworth Cir., Portland, OR 97220 Tel 503-255-1841.

Mesorah Pubns, *(Mesorah Pubns., Ltd.; 0-89906),* 4401 Second Av., Brooklyn, NY 11232 (SAN 213-1269) Tel 718-921-9000; Toll free: 800-637-6724.

Messenger Pub, *(Messenger Publishing Hse.; 1-882449),* P.O. Box 850, Joplin, MO 64802; Toll free: 800-444-4674; 4901 Pennsylvania, Joplin, MO 64802 Tel 417-624-7050.

Messianic Jewish
See Purple Pomegranate

Metagnosis, *(Metagnosis Pubns., Inc.; 1-879203),* 101 Heritage Rd., No. 3, Guilderland, NY 12084-9632; 1917 S. Shields, No. 03, Fort Collins, CO 80526 Tel 303-498-0265.

Metamorphous Pr, *(Metamorphous Pr., Inc.; 0-943920;* 1-55552), P.O. Box 10616, Portland, OR 97210-0616 (SAN 110-8786); Toll free: 800-937-7771 (orders only); 2663 NW Saint Helens Rd., Portland, OR 97210 Tel 503-228-4972.

Metco Pub, *(Metco Publishing; 0-9631684),* 15805 SE 12th Pl., Bellevue, WA 98008 Tel 206-746-2853.

Metro Lifestyles, *(Metro Lifestyles; 0-942581),* 33572 Seawind Ct., Dana Point, CA 92629 (SAN 667-2612) Tel 714-493-6880; Toll free: 800-493-4404.

Meyer Pub FL, *(Meyer Publishing, Inc.; 1-883408),* Div. of Meyer Art Originals, 10991-55 San Jose Blvd., Suite 149, Jacksonville, FL 32223; 12775 Mandarin Rd., Jacksonville, FL 32223 Tel 904-262-4836. Do not confuse with Meyer Publishing in Garrison, IA.

MH & Pr, *(MH & Pr.; 0-9622211),* 209 Underwood St., NW, Washington, DC 20012 Tel 202-829-0452.

MI City Hist, *(Michigan City Historical Society, Inc.;* 0-935549), P.O. Box 512, Michigan City, IN 46360 (SAN 696-2335) Tel 219-872-6133.

MI Dept Hist, *(Michigan Dept. of State, Bureau of History; 0-935719),* 717 W. Allegan, Lansing, MI 48918 (SAN 695-9415) Tel 517-373-3703.

MI Middle Educ, *(Michigan Assn. of Middle Schl. Educators; 0-918449),* Michigan State Univ., Erickson 419, East Lansing, MI 48824 (SAN 241-9637) Tel 517-353-5461.

Michael Paul, *(Paul, Michael; 0-9616367),* 105 Maumell St., Hinsdale, IL 60521-3524 (SAN 658-9847) Tel 708-323-7120.

Michael T Enter, *(Michael T. Enterprises, Inc.;* 0-9630905), P.O. Box 212, Hwy. 190 W., Lottie, LA 70756; Toll free: 800-232-7766; Hwy. 190 W. & Maple, Lottie, LA 70756 Tel 504-637-3719.

Michigan Mus, *(Univ. of Michigan, Museum of Art, Alumni Memorial Hall; 0-912303),* 525 S. State St., Ann Arbor, MI 48109-1354 (SAN 280-9028) Tel 313-764-0395.

MicNik Pubns, *(MicNik Pubns.; 1-879235),* Div. of Action Consulting, P.O. Box 3041, Kirkland, WA 98083; 12533 197th Ct., NE, Woodinville, WA 98072 Tel 206-881-6476.

Micro Text Pubns, *(Micro Text Pubns., Inc.; 0-942412),* 1 Lincoln Plaza, Suite 27C, New York, NY 10023 (SAN 238-1753) Tel 212-877-8539.

Micronesian, *(Micronesian Productions; 0-930839),* P.O. Box 5, San Jose Tinian MP, GU 96952 (SAN 677-6906).

Mid Atl Reg Pr, *(Middle Atlantic Regional Pr. of the Middle Atlantic Regional Gospel Ministries; 0-9616056; 1-877971),* 100 Bryant St., NW, Washington, DC 20001-1631 (SAN 242-0880) Tel 202-265-7609; Orders to: P.O. Box 6021, Washington, DC 20005 (SAN 662-3972).

Mid Atlantic, *(Middle Atlantic Pr.; 0-912608),* P.O. Box 1948, Wilmington, DE 19899 (SAN 202-6341); 848 Church St., Wilmington, DE 19899 (SAN 667-4534).

Mid-Peninsula Lib, *(Mid-Peninsula Library Cooperative;* 0-933249), 424 Stephenson Ave., Iron Mountain, MI 49801-3455 (SAN 692-3836) Tel 906-774-3005.

MidCoast Comns, *(MidCoast Communications;* 0-910025), Subs. of MidCoast Pubns., 65 Aberdeen Pl., Suite 200, Saint Louis, MO 63105-2274 (SAN 285-0613) Tel 314-727-3748; Dist. by: Baker & Taylor Bks., Reno Service Ctr., 380 Edison Way, Reno, NV 89564 (SAN 169-4464) Tel 702-858-6700; Toll free: 800-775-1700 (customer service); Dist. by: Baker & Taylor Bks., Somerville Service Ctr., 50 Kirby Ave., Somerville, NJ 08876-0734 (SAN 169-4901) Tel 908-722-8000; Toll free: 800-775-1500 (customer service); Dist. by: Baker & Taylor Bks., Momence Service Ctr., 501 S. Gladiolus St., Momence, IL 60954-2444 (SAN 169-2100) Tel 815-472-2444; Toll free: 800-775-2300 (customer service).

MidCoast Pubns
See MidCoast Comns

Middleburg Pr, *(Middleburg Pr., The; 0-931940),* Box 166, Orange City, IA 51041 (SAN 212-9183).

Midmath, *(Midmath; 0-9638483),* P.O. Box 2892, Farmington Hills, MI 48333; 27900 Berrywood, No. 30, Farmington Hills, MI 48334 Tel 810-855-2895.

Midnight Ink, *(Midnight Ink; 0-9636214),* P.O. Box 10836, Palm Desert, CA 92255-0836 Tel 619-320-8577.

Midstates Pub, *(Midstates Publishing; 0-929918),* 1216 S. Main, Aberdeen, SD 57401 (SAN 250-9741) Tel 605-225-5287.

Midwest Heritage, *(Midwest Heritage Publishing Co.;* 0-934582), 108 Pearl St., Iowa City, IA 52245-4435 (SAN 213-1161) Tel 319-337-3149.

Midwest Writers, *(Midwest Writers Club, Inc.;* 0-9639256), 5412 N. 65th St., Omaha, NE 68104 Tel 402-572-7355.

Mile By Mile, *(Mile By Mile Pubns.; 1-880372),* P.O. Box 101296, Denver, CO 80250; 2537 S. Race St., Denver, CO 80210 Tel 303-777-4604.

Miles River, *(Miles River Pr.; 0-917917),* 1009 Duke St., Alexandria, VA 22314 (SAN 657-0550) Tel 703-683-1500.

Milford Prod, *(Milford Production Enterprises;* 0-9642893), P.O. Box 634, Ayer, MA 01432; 720A Salerno Cir., Fort Devens, MA 01433 Tel 508-772-0887.

Milkweed Ed, *(Milkweed Editions; 0-915943; 1-57131),* 430 First Ave. N., Suite 400, Minneapolis, MN 55401-1743 (SAN 294-0671) Tel 612-332-3192; Dist. by: Publishers Group West, 4065 Hollis St., Emeryville, CA 94608 (SAN 202-8522) Tel 510-658-3453; Toll free: 800-788-3123.

Mill Creek Ent, *(Mill Creek Enterprises; 0-940273),* P.O. Box 153, Arena, WI 53503 (SAN 664-2322); 905 Pine, Arena, WI 53503 (SAN 664-2330) Tel 608-753-2343.

Millbrook Pr, *(Millbrook Pr., Inc.; 1-878841; 1-56294),* 2 Old New Milford Rd., Brookfield, CT 06804 Tel 203-740-2220; Toll free: 800-462-4703; 18 W. 55th St., New York, NY 10019. Do not confuse with Millbrook Pr., Fresno, CA.

Millenial Pr, *(Millenial Pr.; 0-910613),* 108 N. State St., Orem, UT 84057 (SAN 260-227X) Tel 801-226-1274.

Miller Bks, *(Miller Bks.; 0-912472),* 2908 W. Valley Blvd., Alhambra, CA 91803 (SAN 203-9931) Tel 818-284-7607.

Miller Ent, *(Miller Enterprises; 0-89566),* P.O. Box 395, Boulder Creek, CA 95006 (SAN 210-6426) Tel 408-338-9633. Do not confuse with Miller Enterprises, Athens, OH.

Miller Family Pubns, *(Miller Family Pubns.; 0-945145),* P.O. Box 812, John's Island, SC 29457 (SAN 246-1552) Tel 803-762-1585.

Miller OH, *(Miller Enterprises; 0-9607658),* 5605 Baker Rd., Athens, OH 45701-9231 (SAN 241-5631). Do not confuse with Miller Enterprises, Boulder Creek, CA.

Millers River Pub Co, *(Millers River Publishing Co.;* 0-912395), Box 159, Athol, MA 01331 (SAN 265-3605) Tel 508-249-7612; Dist. by: Inland Bk. Co., 140 Commerce St., East Haven, CT 06512 (SAN 200-4151) Tel 203-467-4257; Toll free: 800-243-0138.

Milliken Pub Co, *(Milliken Publishing Co.; 0-88335; 1-55863; 0-7877),* 1100 Research Blvd., Saint Louis, MO 63132-0579 (SAN 205-8405) Tel 314-991-4220; Toll free: 800-325-4136.

Millinnium-Holographic, *(Millinnium/Holographic;* 0-9631740), P.O. Box 101862, Fort Worth, TX 76185 Tel 817-737-8601; Dist. by: Baker & Taylor Bks., Somerville Service Ctr., 50 Kirby Ave., Somerville, NJ 08876-0734 (SAN 169-4901) Tel 908-722-8000; Toll free: 800-775-1500 (customer service); Dist. by: New Leaf Distributing Co., 5425 Tulane Dr., SW, Atlanta, GA 30336-2323 (SAN 169-1449) Tel 404-691-6996; Toll free: 800-326-2665; Dist. by: Baker & Taylor Bks., Momence Service Ctr., 501 S. Gladiolus St., Momence, IL 60954-2444 (SAN 169-2100) Tel 815-472-2444; Toll free: 800-775-2300 (customer service); Dist. by: Baker & Taylor Bks., Commerce Service Ctr., 251 Mt. Olive Church Rd., Commerce, GA 30599-9988 (SAN 169-1503) Tel 706-335-5000; Toll free: 800-775-1200 (customer service); Dist. by: Baker & Taylor Bks., Reno Service Ctr., 380 Edison Way, Reno, NV 89564 (SAN 169-4464) Tel 702-858-6700; Toll free: 800-775-1700 (customer service).

Mills Pub Co, *(Mills Publishing Co.; 0-935356),* 2705 N. Flower St., Santa Ana, CA 92706-1111 (SAN 272-4464) Tel 714-541-5750. Do not confuse with Mills Publishing Co., Halstead, KS.

Mills Sanderson, *(Mills & Sanderson, Pubs.; 0-938179),* 41 North Rd., Suite 201, Bedford, MA 01730-1021 (SAN 661-1982) Tel 617-275-1410; Toll free: 800-441-6224 (orders only).

Millsmont Pub, *(Millsmont Publishing; 0-9623257),* 1465 W. Tuolumne Rd., Turlock, CA 95380 Tel 209-632-1607.

Milo Prods, *(Milo Productions; 1-882172),* Div. of Milo Productions, N69W15890 Eileen Ave., Menomonee Falls, WI 53051-5009.

Milrob Pr, *(Milrob Pr.; 0-9625221),* 3350 Lakeshore Dr., Muskegon, MI 49441 Tel 616-755-3427.

Milton Pub, *(Milton Publishing; 1-879908),* P.O. Box 6, Lookout Mountain, TN 37350; 1300 Mockingbird Ln., Lookout Mountain, GA 30750 Tel 706-820-2336.

Mina Pr, *(Mina Pr. Publishing, Inc.; 0-942610),* P.O. Box 854, Sebastopol, CA 95473 (SAN 238-5430) Tel 707-829-0854.

Mind Body Connect
See Higher States

Mind Matters, *(Mind Matters, Inc.; 0-9622879),* P.O. Box 16557, Minneapolis, MN 55416; 3722 W. 50th St., No. 110, Minneapolis, MN 55410 Tel 612-925-4090.

Mind Pubns, *(Mind Pubns.; 0-9628382),* P.O. Box 4254, Cleveland, TN 37320-4254; 2150 N. Ocoee St., Cleveland, TN 37311-3919 Tel 615-479-5747.

MindMatters
See Mind Matters

Minich Pubns, *(Minich Pubns.; 0-9629973),* 12021 Wilshire Blvd., Suite 294, Los Angeles, CA 90025 Tel 310-371-2078.

Mink Ministries, *(Mink, Len, Ministries; 0-9620866),* P.O. Box 41184, Cincinnati, OH 45241 (SAN 249-9908) Tel 513-777-0949; Toll free: 800-426-5766.

Minn Hist, *(Minnesota Historical Society Pr.; 0-87351),* 345 Kellogg Blvd., W., Saint Paul, MN 55102-1906 (SAN 202-6384) Tel 612-296-2264; Toll free: 800-647-7827 (orders only).

MinneApplePress, *(MinneApplePress; 0-9640429),* P.O. Box 46021, Minneapolis, MN 46021; 18300 34th Ave., N., Minneapolis, MN 55447 Tel 612-476-8413.

Minstrel Bks *Imprint of* **PB**

MIP Pub, *(MIP Publishing; 0-9617204),* P.O. Box 50632, Montecito, CA 93150 (SAN 663-2815) Tel 805-969-4504.

Miracle Exper, *(Miracle Experiences & You; 1-880436),* P.O. Box 64146, Tucson, AZ 85728-4146 Tel 602-742-9219.

Mirage Bks, *(Mirage Bks.; 0-939137),* Subs. of Dephi-Pacific, P.O. Box 1213, Agana Facilty, Agana, GU 96910 (SAN 662-6327).

Miramonte Pr, *(Miramonte Pr.; 0-9624932),* P.O. Box 390328, Mountain View, CA 94039; 2124 Rock St., Suite 3, Mountain View, CA 94043 Tel 415-967-6547; Dist. by: Children's Small Pr. Collection, 716 N. Fourth Ave., Ann Arbor, MI 48104 (SAN 200-514X) Tel 313-668-8056; Toll free: 800-221-8056 (orders only).

Mirasol *Imprint of* **FS&G**

Miss Jackie, *(Miss Jackie Music Co.; 0-939514),* 10001 El Monte, Overland Park, KS 66207 (SAN 216-4191) Tel 913-381-3672.

Missing Chldrn, *(Missing Children Minnesota;* 0-9641123), P.O. Box 11216, Minneapolis, MN 55411; 4150 Fremont Ave., N., Minneapolis, MN 55412 Tel 612-521-1188.

Mississippi Archives, *(Mississippi Dept. of Archives & History; 0-938896),* Div. of State of Mississippi, P.O. Box 571, Jackson, MS 39205-0571 (SAN 279-618X) Tel 601-359-6850; Dist. by: Univ. Pr. of Mississippi, 3825 Ridgewood Rd., Jackson, MS 39211-6492 (SAN 203-1914) Tel 601-982-6205; Dist. by: Old Capitol Sales Shop, P.O. Box 571, Jackson, MS 39205-0571 (SAN 630-1436) Tel 601-359-6920.

Misty Cove Pr, *(Misty Cove Pr.; 0-9634680),* 1026 Pintail Rd., Concord, TN 37922 Tel 615-675-4764.

Misty Hill Pr, *(Misty Hill Pr.; 0-930079),* 5024 Turner Rd., Sebastopol, CA 95472 (SAN 670-0942) Tel 707-823-7437; Dist. by: Bookpeople, 7900 Edgewater Dr., Oakland, CA 94621 (SAN 168-9517) Tel 510-632-4700; Toll free: 800-999-4650; Dist. by: Baker & Taylor Bks., Momence Service Ctr., 501 S. Gladiolus St., Momence, IL 60954-2444 (SAN 169-2100) Tel 815-472-2444; Toll free: 800-775-2300 (customer service).

Misty Mtn, *(Misty Mountain Publishing Co.;* 0-9635083), P.O. Box 773042, Eagle River, AK 99577; NHN Misty Mountain Rd., Eagle River, AK 99577 Tel 907-696-8166.

MIT Pr, *(MIT Pr.; 0-262),* Orders to: 55 Hayward St., Cambridge, MA 02142 (SAN 202-6414) Tel 617-625-8569; Toll free: 800-356-0343 (orders only). Do not confuse with Massachusetts Institute of Technology in Cambridge, MA.

Mitchell Pub, *(Mitchell Publishing, Inc.; 0-938188),* Div. of Random Hse., Inc., 55 Francisco St., Suite 200, San Francisco, CA 94133-2109 (SAN 215-7896) Tel 408-724-0195; Toll free: 800-435-2665; Dist. by: Random Hse., Inc., 400 Hahn Rd., Westminster, MD 21157 (SAN 202-5515) Tel 410-848-1900; Toll free: 800-733-3000 (orders). Do not confuse with companies with the same name in Spokane, WA, Medina, NY.

MLD Geog, *(MLD Genealogy; 0-939142),* P.O. Box 97, Ennis, TX 75120 (SAN 214-0039) Tel 214-875-6799.

MM & I Ink, *(MM&I Ink; 0-9640260),* Rte. 1, Box 432, Bayard, NE 69334 Tel 308-586-1196.

MMB Music, *(MMB Music, Inc.; 0-918812),* 205 S. Charles, Edwardsville, IL 62025 (SAN 210-4601) Tel 618-656-3823; Orders to: 3526 Washington Ave., Saint Louis, MO 63103-1019 (SAN 298-3281) Tel 314-531-9635; Toll free: 800-543-3771.

MMI Pr, *(Mountain Missionary Pr.; 0-912145),* Div. of Mountain Missionary Institute, Inc., Aldworth Rd., P.O. Box 279, Harrisville, NH 03450 (SAN 264-7664) Tel 603-827-3361; Toll free: 800-367-1888.

MMI Pubns, *(MMI Pubns., Inc.; 0-9627714),* 9 Elm St., Natick, MA 01760-4401.

MN DPPD Inc, *(MN Design Productions-Publishing Div., Inc.; 0-9623254),* P.O. Box 1099, Murray Hill Sta., New York, NY 10156-0604 Tel 201-679-5639.

MN Humanities, *(Minnesota Humanities Commission;* 0-9629298), 26 E. Exchange St., Lower Level S., Saint Paul, MN 55101 Tel 612-224-5739.

MNP Star, *(MNP Star Enterprises; 0-938880),* P.O. Box 1552, Cupertino, CA 95015-1552 (SAN 215-9708).

Mntn Automation, *(Mountain Automation Corp.;* 0-936206), P.O. Box 6020, Woodland Park, CO 80866 (SAN 221-4148) Tel 719-687-6647; Orders to: P.O. Box 2324, Fort Collins, CO 80522-2324; Toll free: 800-487-3793.

Mntn Bks, *(Mountain Bks.; 1-881650),* P.O. Box 211104, Columbus, OH 43221-8104 Tel 614-777-9933; Toll free: 800-876-6686.

Mntn Memories Bks, *(Mountain Memories Bks.;* 0-938985), 216 Sutherland Dr., South Charleston, WV 25303 (SAN 200-4852) Tel 304-744-5772.

Mntn Rainbow *Imprint of* **Rainbow NC**

Moanalua Grdns Fnd, *(Moanalua Gardens Foundation;* 1-882163), 1352 Pineapple Pl., Honolulu, HI 96819 Tel 808-839-5334.

Mocha Pub, *(Mocha Publishing Co.; 0-9626403),* 8475 SW Morgan Dr., Beaverton, OR 97005 Tel 503-643-7591.

Modan-Adama Bks, *(Modan/Adama Bks.; 0-915361;* 1-55774), P.O. Box 1202, Bellmore, NY 11710-0485 (SAN 291-0640) Tel 516-679-1380.

MoDel Pubs, *(MoDel Pubs.; 0-9618650),* P.O. Box 645, Byron, CA 94514 (SAN 668-3878); 4991 Cabrillo Point, Byron, CA 94514 (SAN 668-3886) Tel 510-634-5382.

Modern Curr, *(Modern Curriculum Pr., Inc.; 0-87895;* 0-8136), Div. of Simon & Schuster, Inc., 13900 Prospect Rd., Cleveland, OH 44136 (SAN 206-6572) Tel 216-238-2222; Toll free: 800-321-3106.

Modern Learn Pr, *(Modern Learning Pr.; 0-935493;* 1-56762), Affil. of Programs for Education, Inc., P.O. Box 167, Rosemont, NJ 08556 Tel 609-397-2214; Toll free: 800-627-5867.

Modern Pub NYC, *(Modern Publishing; 0-87449;* 1-56144), Div. of Unisystems, Inc., 155 E. 55th St., New York, NY 10022 Tel 212-826-0850. *Imprints:* Honey Bear Bks (Honey Bear Books).

Modern Signs, *(Modern Signs Pr., Inc.; 0-916708),* 10443 Los Alamitos Blvd., Los Alamitos, CA 90720 (SAN 282-0048) Tel 310-596-8548; Orders to: P.O. Box 1181, Los Alamitos, CA 90720 (SAN 282-0056) Tel 310-493-4168.

Mohican Schl, *(Mohican Schl. in the Out-of-Doors, Inc.;* 0-9631624), 21882 Shadley Valley Rd., Danville, OH 43014 Tel 614-599-9753.

Mojave Bks, *(Mojave Bks.; 0-87881),* 7118 Canby Ave., No. C, Reseda, CA 91335-4391 (SAN 202-6430).

MOL Bks, *(MOL Bks.; 0-9622406),* P.O. Box 3085, Ashland, OR 97520; 4400 Shale City Rd., Ashland, OR 97520 Tel 503-482-5323.

Momentum Bks, *(Momentum Bks., Ltd.; 0-9618726;* 1-879094), 6964 Crooks Rd., Suite 1, Troy, MI 48098-1709 (SAN 668-7067) Tel 810-828-3666; Toll free: 800-758-1870 (orders only); Dist. by: Merle Distributing Co., 27222 Plymouth Rd., Detroit, MI 48239 (SAN 169-3778) Tel 313-937-8400; Toll free: 800-233-9380 (orders only); Dist. by: Partners Bk. Distributing, Inc., 720 E. Shiawassee St., Lansing, MI 48912 (SAN 630-4559) Tel 517-485-0366; Toll free: 800-336-3137.

Momentum Pub
See Momentum Bks

Monarch Toy, *(Monarch Toy Co., Ltd.; 0-939871),* 4517 Harford Rd., Baltimore, MD 21214 (SAN 663-9593) Tel 410-254-9200.

Monday Morning Bks, *(Monday Morning Bks., Inc.; 0-912107; 1-878279),* Box 1680, Palo Alto, CA 94302 (SAN 264-7656) Tel 415-327-3374; Dist. by: Evan Moor Corp., 18 Lower Ragsdale Dr., Monterey, CA 93940 (SAN 242-5394) Tel 408-649-6901; Toll free: 800-777-4489.

Mondo Pubng, *(Mondo Publishing; 1-879531),* 1 Plaza Rd., Greenvale, NY 11548 Tel 516-484-7812.

Monkey Sisters
See E Sussman Educ

Monroe County Lib, *(Monroe County Library System;* 0-940696), 3700 S. Custer Rd., Monroe, MI 48161-9732 (SAN 213-5396) Tel 313-241-5277.

Monroe Pr, *(Monroe Pr.; 0-936781),* 362 Maryville Ave., Ventura, CA 93003-1912 (SAN 699-9883) Tel 805-642-3064; Dist. by: New Concepts Bks. & Tapes Distributors, 9722 Pine Lake, Box 55068, Houston, TX 77055 (SAN 114-2682) Tel 713-465-7736; Toll free: 800-842-4807; Dist. by: Quality Bks., Inc., 918 Sherwood Dr., Lake Bluff, IL 60044-2204 (SAN 169-2127) Tel 708-295-2010; Toll free: 800-323-4241 (libraries only); Dist. by: Children's Small Pr. Collection, 716 N. Fourth Ave., Ann Arbor, MI 48104 (SAN 200-514X) Tel 313-668-8056; Toll free: 800-221-8056; Dist. by: Pacific Pipeline, Inc., 8030 S. 228th St., Kent, WA 98032-2900 (SAN 208-2128) Tel 206-872-5523; Toll free: 800-444-7323 (Customer Service); 800-677-2222 (orders).

Montevista Pr, *(Montevista Pr.; 0-931551),* 5041 Meridian Rd., Bellingham, WA 98226 (SAN 682-191X) Tel 206-734-4279; Dist. by: Pacific Pipeline, Inc., 8030 S. 228th St, Kent, WA 98032-2900 (SAN 208-2128) Tel 206-872-5523; Toll free: 800-444-7323 (Customer Service); 800-677-2222 (orders); Dist. by: Baker & Taylor Bks., Somerville Service Ctr., 50 Kirby Ave., Somerville, NJ 08876-0734 (SAN 169-4901) Tel 908-722-8000; Toll free: 800-775-1500 (customer service); Dist. by: Baker & Taylor Bks., Reno Service Ctr., 380 Edison Way, Reno, NV 89564 (SAN 169-4464) Tel 702-858-6700; Toll free: 800-775-1700 (customer service); Dist. by: Alaska News Agency, Inc., Book Dept., 325 W. Potter Dr., Anchorage, AK 99502 (SAN 168-9274) Tel 907-563-3251; Toll free: 800-648-3540.

Montgomery Mus, *(Montgomery Museum of Fine Arts;* 0-89280), P.O. Box 230819, Montgomery, AL 36123-0819 (SAN 208-3299); 1 Museum Dr., Montgomery, AL 36117 (SAN 248-3858) Tel 205-244-5700.

Monthly Rev, *(Monthly Review Pr.; 0-85345),* Div. of Monthly Review Foundation, Inc., 122 W. 27th St., New York, NY 10001 (SAN 202-6481) Tel 212-691-2555.

Moody, *(Moody Pr.; 0-8024),* Div. of Moody Bible Institute, 820 N. LaSalle Blvd., Chicago, IL 60610 (SAN 202-5604) Tel 312-329-2108; Toll free: 800-678-8812.

Moon Gold, *(Moon Gold Pr.; 1-885678),* P.O. Box 92156, Rochester, NY 14692; 65 Terrace Villas Cir., Fairport, NY 14450 Tel 716-377-4682.

Moon Pubns CA, *(Moon Pubns., Inc.; 0-9603322; 0-918373; 1-56691),* 330 Wall St., Chico, CA 95928 (SAN 221-7406); Toll free: 800-345-5473; Dist. by: Publishers Group West, 4065 Hollis St., Emeryville, CA 94608 (SAN 202-8522) Tel 510-658-3453; Toll free: 800-788-3123; Dist. by: Quality Bks., Inc., 918 Sherwood Dr., Lake Bluff, IL 60044-2204 (SAN 169-2127) Tel 708-295-2010; Toll free: 800-323-4241 (libraries only).

Moonbeam Magic Pub, *(Moonbeam Magic Publishing;* 0-9623215), P.O. Box 62194, Honolulu, HI 96839; 2623 Halelena Pl., Honolulu, HI 96822 Tel 808-946-6424.

Moonbeam Pubns, *(Moonbeam Pubns., Inc.; 0-931013;* 1-56271), 836 Hastings St., Traverse City, MI 49684-3441 (SAN 159-0308) Tel 616-922-0533; Toll free: 800-445-2391.

Moonglow Pubns, *(Moonglow Pubns.; 1-883016),* 1220 Edwards Ln., Orlando, FL 32804 Tel 407-841-5843.

Moonlight FL, *(Moonlight Pr.; 0-913545),* 3407 Crystal Lake Dr., Orlando, FL 32806 (SAN 293-3063) Tel 407-857-1113. Do not confuse with companies of the same name in Menomonie, WI, Arlington Heights, IL, Westminster, CA, Troy, NY, Chisholm, MN.

Moonlight MN, *(Moonlight Pr.; 0-9640212),* 5325 McNiven Rd., Chisholm, MN 55719 Tel 218-254-2174. Do not confuse with companies with the same name in Orlando, FL, Troy, NY, Menomorie, WI, Arlington Heights, IL, Westminster, CA, DeKalb, IL.

Moons Creat Prods, *(Moon's Creative Products;* 0-922694), Div. of Eraser Products Co., Inc., P.O. Box 1788, Lewisburg, TN 37091 (SAN 251-611X); 305 First Ave., N., Lewisburg, TN 37091 (SAN 251-6128) Tel 615-359-6613.

Moose Schl Records, *(Moose Schl. Records; 1-877942),* P.O. Box 960, Topanga, CA 90290; 1424 Old Topanga Canyon Rd., Topanga, CA 90290 Tel 310-455-2318.

Mor-Mac, *(Mor-Mac Publishing Co.; 0-912178),* P.O. Box 985, Daytona Beach, FL 32115 (SAN 204-0042) Tel 904-255-4427.

Moran Pub Corp, *(Moran Publishing Corp.; 0-86518),* 5425 Florida Blvd., P.O. Box 66538, Baton Rouge, LA 70896 (SAN 214-0616) Tel 504-923-2550; Dist. by: Aviation Bk. Co., 25133 Anza Dr., Unit E, Santa Clarita, CA 91355 (SAN 120-1530) Tel 805-294-0101; Toll free: 800-423-2708 (orders).

Moravian Ch in Amer, *(Moravian Church in America;* 1-878422), P.O. Box 1245, Bethlehem, PA 18016-1245; 1021 Center St., Bethlehem, PA 18016 Tel 610-867-0594.

More than Card, *(More than a Card, Inc.; 0-922589),* 4334 Earhart Blvd., New Orleans, LA 70125 (SAN 251-3331) Tel 504-822-7594; Toll free: 800-635-9672.

Morehouse Pub, *(Morehouse Publishing; 0-8192),* 871 Ethan Allen Hwy., Suite 204, Ridgefield, CT 06877-2801 (SAN 202-6511) Tel 203-431-3927; Orders to: P.O. Box 1321, Harrisburg, PA 17105 Tel 717-541-8130; Toll free: 800-877-0012.

Morgan Fnd Pubs, *(Morgan Foundation Pubs.: International Published Innovations; 1-885679),* 7 Wild Oak Dr., Billings, MT 59102 Tel 406-652-8123.

Morgan Virginia Pub, *(Morgan Virginia Publishing Co.;* 0-945237), 8566 Prest St., Detroit, MI 48228 (SAN 246-6805) Tel 313-584-9071.

Morgin Pr, *(Morgin Pr., Inc.; 0-9630976),* 303 W. Lancaster Ave., Suite 283, Wayne, PA 19087 Tel 610-687-9833; Dist. by: Baker & Taylor Bks., Somerville Service Ctr., 50 Kirby Ave., Somerville, NJ 08876-0734 (SAN 169-4901) Tel 908-722-8000; Toll free: 800-775-1500 (customer service); Dist. by: Baker & Taylor Bks., Momence Service Ctr., 501 S. Gladiolus St., Momence, IL 60954-1799 (SAN 169-2100) Tel 815-472-2444; Toll free: 800-775-2300 (customer service); Dist. by: Baker & Taylor Bks., Commerce Service Center, 251 Mt. Olive Church Rd., Commerce, GA 30599-9988 (SAN 169-1503) Tel 706-335-5000; Toll free: 800-775-1200 (customer service); Dist. by: Baker & Taylor Bks., Reno Service Ctr., 380 Edison Way, Reno, NV 89564-0099 (SAN 169-4464) Tel 702-858-6700; Toll free: 800-775-1700 (customer service); Dist. by: Ingram Bk. Co., 1 Ingram Blvd., La Vergne, TN 37086-1986 (SAN 169-7978) Tel 615-793-5000; Dist. by: Inland Bk. Co., 140 Commerce St., East Haven, CT 06512 (SAN 200-4151) Tel 203-467-4257; Toll free: 800-243-0138; Dist. by: Koen Bk. Distributors, 10 Twosome Dr., P.O. Box 600, Moorestown, NJ 08057 (SAN 169-4642) Tel 609-235-4444; Toll free: 800-257-8481.

Morielle Pr, *(Morielle Pr.; 0-9622537),* P.O. Box 10612, Alexandria, VA 22310-0612; 4214 Shannon Hill Rd., Alexandria, VA 22310.

Morning Glory, *(Morning Glory Pr., Inc.; 0-930934;* 1-885356), 6595 San Haroldo Way, Buena Park, CA 90620-3748 (SAN 211-2558) Tel 714-828-1998.

Morris Pubng, *(Morris Publishing; 0-9631249; 1-885591),* Div. of Morris Pr./Cookbooks by Morris Pr., P.O. Box 2110, Kearney, NE 68848; Toll free: 800-650-7888; 3212 E. Hwy. 30, Kearney, NE 68848 Tel 308-236-7888. Do not confuse with Morris Publishing Co., Plymouth Meeting, PA.

Morrow, *(Morrow, William, & Co., Inc.; 0-688),* Subs. of Hearst Corp., 1350 Avenue of the Americas, New York, NY 10019 (SAN 202-5760) Tel 212-261-6500; Toll free: 800-843-9389; Orders to: Wilmor Warehouse, P.O. Box 1219, 39 Plymouth St., Fairfield, NJ 07007 (SAN 202-5779) Tel 201-227-7200. *Imprints:* Mulberry (Mulberry Books); Quill (Quill Paperbacks); Tambourine Bks (Tambourine Books); Tupelo Bks (Tupelo Books).

Morrow Jr Bks, *(Morrow Junior Bks.; 0-688),* Div. of William Morrow & Co., Inc., 1350 Avenue of the Americas, New York, NY 10019 (SAN 202-5760) Tel 212-261-6691.

Mosby
See Mosby Yr Bk

Mosby Yr Bk, *(Mosby-Year Bk., Inc.; 0-8016; 0-8151; 0-88416; 0-941158; 1-55664),* Subs. of Times Mirror Co., 11830 Westline Industrial Dr., Saint Louis, MO 63146 (SAN 200-2280) Tel 314-872-8370; Toll free: 800-426-4545 (Individuals); 800-633-6699 (Institution accounts).

Mosele & Assocs, *(Mosele & Assocs., Inc.; 0-9614354),* 34523 Wilson Rd., Ingleside, IL 60041 (SAN 687-7346) Tel 708-546-5533.

Most Mobil, *(Mostly Mobility; 0-922637),* R.D. 1, Box 1448A, Bethel, PA 19507 (SAN 251-3706); Rte. 183, Bethel, PA 19507 (SAN 251-3714) Tel 717-933-5681.

Mother Courage, *(Mother Courage Pr.; 0-941300),* 1667 Douglas Ave., Racine, WI 53404 (SAN 239-4618) Tel 414-637-2227.

Motorola Univ, *(Motorola Univ. Pr.; 1-56946),* Div. of Motorola, Inc., 3701 E. Algonquin Rd., Suite 250, Rolling Meadows, IL 60008 Tel 708-576-3971.

Mott Media, *(Mott Media; 0-915134; 0-88062),* 1000 E. Huron, Milford, MI 48381 (SAN 207-1460) Tel 810-685-8773. Do not confuse with Mott Media in Port Chester, NY.

Mount Falcon, *(Mount Falcon Publishing; 0-9624060),* 3240 Edmund Blvd., Minneapolis, MN 55406 Tel 612-722-1092.

Mountain Pr, *(Mountain Pr. Publishing Co., Inc.;* 0-87842), P.O. Box 2399, Missoula, MT 59806 (SAN 202-8832); Toll free: 800-234-5308; 1301 S. Third West, Missoula, MT 59801 (SAN 662-0868) Tel 406-728-1900.

Mountaineers, *(Mountaineers Bks., The; 0-916890;* 0-89886), Div. of Mountaineers, 1011 SW Klickitat Way, Suite 107, Seattle, WA 98134-1162 (SAN 212-8756) Tel 206-223-6303; Toll free: 800-553-4453.

Mouse Works, *(Mouse Works; 1-57082),* Div. of The Walt Disney Co., 3900 W. Alameda Ave., 29th Flr., Burbank, CA 91505 (SAN 298-0797) Tel 818-567-5894.

Move It Math, *(Move It Math; 0-941530),* 203 Lansdown, Victoria, TX 77904 (SAN 239-1279) Tel 512-572-0541.

Moznaim, *(Moznaim Publishing Corp.; 0-940118;* 1-885220), 4304 12th Ave., Brooklyn, NY 11219 (SAN 214-4123) Tel 718-438-7680; Toll free: 800-364-5118.

MP Records, *(MP Records Communications, Inc.;* 0-9639839), 7588 Garrick St., Fishers, IN 46038 Tel 317-841-3517.

Ms B Bks, *(Ms. B Bks.; 0-9634474),* P.O. Box 3356, Halfmoon, CA 94019; Toll free: 800-378-8279; 454 California, Moss Beach, CA 94038 Tel 619-445-9687.

MS Bks Pubng, *(MS Bks. Publishing; 0-9640414),* 261 Prospect Park W., No. 1L, Brooklyn, NY 11215 Tel 718-369-1781.

MS Inst Law, *(Mississippi Institute on Law-Related Education; 1-885578),* Div. of Univ. of Southern Mississippi-Educational Leadership & Research, Univ. of Southern Mississippi, Box 10033, Hattiesburg, MS 39406-0033; 417 N. 37th Ave., Hattiesburg, MS 39401 Tel 601-266-5546.

MS Pub, *(Mustard Seed Publishing; 0-9623349),* P.O. Box 3544, Huntington Beach, CA 92605-3544; 16652 Tiber Ln., Huntington Beach, CA 92647 Tel 714-842-3963.

MSC Inc, *(Management & Systems Consultants, Inc.;* 0-918356), Sun/University, P.O. Box 40457, Tucson, AZ 85717 (SAN 209-9500) Tel 602-577-1272; 3900 Los Portales, Tucson, AZ 85718 (SAN 662-0779) Tel 602-299-9615.

MstrWorks Pub, *(MasterWorks Publishing, Inc.;* 0-9619326), P.O. Box 1677, Norman, OK 73070 (SAN 243-8836); 15205 Edna Rd., Oklahoma City, OK 73165 (SAN 243-8844) Tel 405-799-6306.

MT Hist Soc, *(Montana Historical Society Pr.;* 0-917298), 225 N. Roberts St., P.O. Box 201201, Helena, MT 59620-1201 (SAN 208-7693) Tel 406-444-2890; Toll free: 800-243-9900.

Mt Hope Pubng, *(Mount Hope Publishing Co.;* 0-9640585), E. 6106 Spangle-Waverly Rd., Spangle, WA 99031 Tel 509-245-3545.

Mt Vernon Ladies, *(Mount Vernon Ladies Assn. of the Union, Library; 0-931917),* Museum Shop, Mount Vernon, VA 22121 (SAN 225-3976) Tel 703-780-2000.

MTH Soc Inc, *(Mountain Top Historical Society, Inc.;* 0-9624216), P.O. Box 263, Haines Falls, NY 12436; Twilight Park-T2, Haines Falls, NY 12436 Tel 518-589-6191.

MthreeD, *(M 3 D, Inc.; 1-884069),* 18522 Oxnard St., Tarzana, CA 91356-1409.

Mtn MD, *(Mountaintop Bks., Inc.; 1-880679),* P.O. Box 705, Oxon Hill, MD 20750 Tel 301-505-2116. Do not confuse with Mountaintop Bks. in Glenwood, IA.

Mtn St Pr, *(Mountain State Pr.; 0-941092),* c/o Univ. of Charleston, 2300 MacCorkle Ave., SE, Charleston, WV 25304 (SAN 276-4156) Tel 304-727-2798.

Mtn-top Kip, *(Mountain-top Kip Pubns.; 1-885419),* P.O. Box 6, Dennison, OH 44621; 4240 Fourth St., SE, New Philadelphia, OH 44663 Tel 614-922-1248.

Mtntop Bks, *(Mountaintop Bks.; 0-9623700),* P.O. Box 385, Glenwood, IA 51534-0385 Tel 712-527-3431. Do not confuse with Mountaintop Bks. in Oxon Hill, MD.

Mu Alpha Theta, *(Mu Alpha Theta, National High Schl. Mathematics Club; 0-940790),* 601 Elm Ave., Rm. 423, Norman, OK 73019 (SAN 204-0077) Tel 405-325-4489.

Muffin Enter, *(Muffin Enterprises; 0-9621949),* P.O. Box 112, Burlington, ME 04417 Tel 207-732-3749.

Muffin Pubns, *(Muffin Pubns.; 0-9635568),* 3337 River Heights Crossing, Marietta, GA 30067 Tel 404-951-8728.

Muh-He-Con-Neew, *(Muh-He-Con-Neew-Press;* 0-935790), c/o Arvid E. Miller Memorial Library, N8510 Mohheconnuck Rd., Bowler, WI 54416 Tel 715-793-4270.

Mulberry *Imprint of* **Morrow**

Mult Media NY, *(Multi Media Communicators, Inc.;* 1-56977), 575 Madison Ave., Suite 1006, New York, NY 10022 Tel 212-875-9650; Dist. by: Spring Arbor Distributors, 10885 Textile Rd., Belleville, MI 48111 (SAN 158-9016) Tel 313-481-0900; Toll free: 800-395-5599 (orders); 800-395-7234 (customer service).

Multi Media TX, *(Multi Media Arts; 0-86617),* P.O. Box 141127, Austin, TX 78714-1127 (SAN 214-4239) Tel 512-832-9535.

Multicult Pubns, *(Multicultural Pubns.; 0-9634932;* 1-884242), P.O. Box 8001, Akron, OH 44320 Tel 216-869-6319.

MultiMap, *(MultiMap International, Inc.; 0-929644),* 1 Devonshire Pl., Suite 3202, Boston, MA 02109-3516 (SAN 249-8189) Tel 617-248-9515.

Multnomah Bks *Imprint of* **Questar Pubs**

Munsey Music, *(Munsey Music; 0-9697066),* c/o Munsey Music, No. 39 Villa La Cumbra, 521 N. La Cumbra Rd., Santa Barbara, CA 93110 Tel 905-737-0208. Canadian Address: Munsey Music, Box 511, Richmond Hill, Ont., L4C 4Y8, CN.

Murdoch Bks, *(Murdoch Bks.; 1-878767),* P.O. Box 390, Nazareth, PA 18064-0390; Green & Prospects Sts., Nazareth, PA 18064-0390 Tel 610-258-5665.

Murray Pubns, *(Murray Pubns.; 0-9632132),* 4921 E. Stokes Ferry Rd., Hernando, FL 34442-2334 Tel 904-344-8394.

Murrays Leprechaun Bks, *(Murray's Leprechaun Bks.;* 1-879313), 3816 Sunbird Cir., Sebring, FL 33872-3436 Tel 813-382-9339.

Mus Art Carnegie, *(Carnegie Museum of Art, The;* 0-88039), 4400 Forbes Ave., Pittsburgh, PA 15213 (SAN 239-1171) Tel 412-622-3223.

Mus Fed Ink, *(Muse Federation Ink; 0-9614084),* P.O. Box 642 St. Albans Sta., Jamaica, NY 11412 (SAN 686-0044) Tel 718-723-9880.

Mus Fine Arts Boston, *(Museum of Fine Arts, Boston;* 0-87846), 465 Huntington Ave., Boston, MA 02115 (SAN 202-2230) Tel 617-267-9300.

Mus TX Tech, *(Museum of Texas Tech Univ.;* 0-9640188), Div. of Texas Tech Univ., P.O. Box 43191, Fourth & Indiana Ave., Lubbock, TX 79409-3191 Tel 806-742-2442.

Museum NM Pr, *(Museum of New Mexico Pr.;* 0-89013), P.O. Box 2087, Santa Fe, NM 87504 (SAN 202-2575) Tel 505-827-6454. Do not confuse with Univ. of New Mexico Pr. in Albuquerque, NM.

Music Ed Natl, *(Music Educators National Conference; 0-940796; 1-56545),* 1806 Robert Fulton Dr., Reston, VA 22091-1597 (SAN 676-8733) Tel 703-860-4000; Toll free: 800-336-3768.

Music Educ Pubns, *(Music Education Pubns.; 0-943988),* P.O. Box 3402, Fullerton, CA 92634 (SAN 241-5674) Tel 714-525-1397.

Music Sales, *(Music Sales Corp.; 0-8256),* 257 Park Ave., S., New York, NY 10010 (SAN 282-0277) Tel 212-254-2100; Orders to: Music Sales Distribution Ctr., 5 Bellvale Rd., P.O. Box 572, Chester, NY 10918 (SAN 662-0876) Tel 914-469-2271; Toll free: 800-431-7187; Dist. by: Beekman Pubs., Inc. (Libraries & Special Sales), P.O. Box 888, Woodstock, NY 12498 (SAN 170-1622) Tel 914-679-2300.

Musical Idiot, *(Musical Idiot Pr.; 0-918321),* R.R. 3, Box 3400, Middlesex, VT 05602-9233 (SAN 657-2839) Tel 802-223-1544; Dist. by: Publishers Group West, 4065 Hollis St., Emeryville, CA 94608 (SAN 202-8522) Tel 510-658-3453; Toll free: 800-788-3123.

Musical Munchkins, *(Musical Munchkins, Inc.;* 0-944333), P.O. Box 356, Pound Ridge, NY 10576 (SAN 243-4490) Tel 914-764-8568.

Mustang Pub, *(Mustang Publishing; 0-914457),* P.O. Box 3004, Memphis, TN 38173 (SAN 289-6702) Tel 901-521-1406; Dist. by: National Bk. Network, 4720A Boston Way, Lanham, MD 20706-4310 (SAN 630-0065) Tel 301-459-8696; Toll free: 800-462-6420.

Musty the Mustard, *(Musty the Mustard Seed Bks.;* 0-9636314), 104 Stable Ct., Franklin, TN 37064 Tel 615-790-1996.

My Picture Bks, *(My Picture Bks.; 0-9621427),* 5143 Nadine St., Orlando, FL 32807 (SAN 251-3439) Tel 407-275-6545.

Myi-Way Prod, *(Myi-Way Production; 0-9637083),* 11944 S. Grevillea Ave., Apt. O, Hawthorne, CA 90250 Tel 310-973-1625.

MYLAC Pub Co, *(MYLAC Publishing Co.; 0-9624309),* 5636 W. Hanover, Dallas, TX 75209 Tel 214-358-0886.

Myles Music, *(Myles Music Corp.; 0-9634218),* 10313 S. Lockwood, Oak Lawn, IL 60453 Tel 708-857-8420.

MyndSeye, *(MyndSeye, Inc.; 0-9629093),* P.O. Box 171, The Plains, VA 22171; Corner of Main & Bragg Sts., The Plains, VA 22171 Tel 703-253-5486; Dist. by: BookWorld Distribution Services, Inc., 1933 Whitfield Pk. Loop, Sarasota, FL 34243 (SAN 173-0568) Tel 813-758-8094; Toll free: 800-444-2524 (orders only).

Myrichael Way, *(Myrichael Way Music Co.; 0-9634682),* P.O. Box 1154, 400 Daisy Hill Rd., Cave Junction, OR 97523 Tel 503-592-4209.

Mystic Garden, *(Mystic Garden; 0-922848),* P.O. Box 51, Crestone, CO 81131-0051 (SAN 251-432X) Tel 719-256-4137; Dist. by: Independent Pubs. Group, 814 N. Franklin, Chicago, IL 60610 (SAN 202-0769) Tel 312-337-0747; Toll free: 800-888-4741.

Mystic Jhamom, *(Mystic Jhamom Pubs.; 0-933961),* 1650 Rocky Pl., Arroyo Grande, CA 93420 (SAN 693-0689) Tel 805-922-8802; P.O. Box 904, Santa Maria, CA 93456 (SAN 694-972X).

MythicMedia, *(MythicMedia, Inc.; 0-9638173),* P.O. Box 12697, Oklahoma City, OK 73157; 2320 NW 29th, Oklahoma City, OK 73107 Tel 405-528-0117.

N A Hardegrove, *(Hardegrove, Nelle A.; 0-9619227),* 120 Holder Rd., Baltimore, OH 43105 (SAN 243-5454) Tel 614-862-4473.

N & N Pub Co, *(N&N Publishing Co., Inc.; 0-9606036),* 18 Montgomery St., Middletown, NY 10940 (SAN 216-4221) Tel 914-342-1677.

N Conkle, *(Conkle, Nancy; 0-9639061),* 15214 Faubion Trail, Leander, TX 78641 Tel 512-259-5125.

N Edge Res, *(Nellie Edge Resources, Inc.; 0-922053),* P.O. Box 12399, Salem, OR 97309-0399 (SAN 251-1045); Toll free: 800-523-4594.

N Geller Pub, *(Geller, Norman, Pubs.; 0-915753),* P.O. Box 2118, Woburn, MA 01888-2118 (SAN 293-9681) Tel 617-938-6001.

N Horizon Educ, *(New Horizon Educational Services;* 1-884197), 1205 Wiltshire Dr., Carrollton, TX 75007-4810 Tel 214-242-1646.

N Howard, *(Howard, Neva; 0-9622666),* 6943 S. Euclid Ave., Chicago, IL 60649 Tel 312-769-5280.

N Klas, *(Klas, Nell; 0-9628560),* 5685 Shadow Ridge Dr., Castro Valley, CA 94552 Tel 510-537-7706.

N Late Pub, *(Late, N., Pub.; 0-9641448),* 910 Portland Pl., No. 7, Boulder, CO 80304 Tel 516-938-3061.

N M Bahlinger, *(Bahlinger, Nanette M.; 0-9638256),* 420 Ocean Blvd., No. 4C, Saint Simons Island, GA 31522 Tel 912-262-6145.

N McNutt Assocs, *(McNutt, Nan, & Assocs.;* 0-9614534), P.O. Box 295, Petersburg, AK 99833 (SAN 692-3453) Tel 907-772-4809; Dist. by: Pacific Pipeline, Inc., 8030 S. 228th St, Kent, WA 98032-2900 (SAN 208-2128) Tel 206-872-5523; Toll free: 800-444-7323 (Customer Service); 800-677-2222 (orders).

N Pole Chron, *(North Pole Chronicles; 0-9636442),* 3701 Euclid Ave., Dallas, TX 75205 Tel 214-521-2490; Dist. by: Taylor Publishing Co., 1550 W. Mockingbird Ln., Dallas, TX 75235 (SAN 202-7631); Toll free: 800-759-8120 (orders).

N Schwartz Pub, *(Nichols Schwartz Publishing;* 1-882269), P.O. Box 254, Honesdale, PA 18431-0254; Toll free: 800-732-4334; 315 Fifteenth St., Honesdale, PA 18431 Tel 717-253-9362.

N Shulman, *(Shulman, Neil; 0-9639002),* 2272 Vistamont Dr., Decatur, GA 30033 Tel 404-321-0126.

N Squared Ent, *(N Squared Enterprises; 0-9632531),* 49 Adams Ave., Sound Beach, NY 11789 Tel 516-744-1097.

NAAHE
See NAHEE

Nadja Pub, *(Nadja Publishing; 0-9636335),* P.O. Box 326, Lake Forest, CA 92630; Toll free: 800-795-9750; 31011 Hamilton Trail, Live Oak, CA 92679 Tel 714-858-0650.

Naftaolh Pubns, *(Naftaolh Pubns.; 0-9616130),* 323 Rebecca Ln., Columbus, MS 39702 (SAN 699-7368) Tel 601-328-4879.

Nags Head Art, *(Nags Head Art; 0-9616344; 1-878405),* P.O. Box 88, Nags Head, NC 27959 (SAN 200-9145); Toll free: 800-541-2722; 7734 Virginia Dare Trail, Nags Head, NC 27959 (SAN 658-8107) Tel 919-441-7480; Dist. by: Koen Bk. Distributors, 10 Twosome Dr., P.O. Box 600, Moorestown, NJ 08057 (SAN 169-4642) Tel 609-235-4444; Toll free: 800-257-8481; Dist. by: Mist Co., Inc., P.O. Box 694854, Miami, FL 33269 (SAN 630-8384); Toll free: 800-336-2003; Dist. by: Source International Technology Corp., 939 E. 156th St., Bronx, NY 10455 (SAN 630-8392) Tel 718-378-3878.

NAHEE, *(National Assn. for Humane & Environmental Education; 0-941246),* Div. of Humane Society of the U.S., P.O. Box 362, East Haddam, CT 06423 (SAN 285-0680) Tel 203-434-8666.

NAL-Dutton, *(NAL/Dutton; 0-525; 0-451; 0-452; 0-453;* 0-8015), Div. of Penguin USA, 375 Hudson St., New York, NY 10014-3657 Tel 212-366-2000; Toll free: 800-331-4624 (Customer service); 800-526-0275 (orders). *Imprints:* Dutton-Truman Talley (Dutton/Truman Talley); Ment (Mentor); Mer (Meridian Books); Onyx (Onyx); Plume (Plume Books); Sig (Signet Books); Sig Classics (Signet Classics); Sig Vista (Signet Vista).

Nancy Hall, *(Hall, Nancy, Inc.; 1-884270),* 435 E. 14th St., No. 11F, New York, NY 10009 Tel 212-674-3408.

Nantucket Pubng, *(Nantucket Publishing; 0-9640435),* 5524 Nantucket Rd., Minnetonka, MN 55345 Tel 612-937-5492.

NAPSAC Reprods, *(NAPSAC Reproductions; 0-934426),* Rte. 1, Box 646, Marble Hill, MO 63764 (SAN 222-4607) Tel 314-238-4273.

NAR Prodns
See NAR Pubns

NAR Pubns, *(NAR Pubns.; 0-89780),* P.O. Box 233, Barryville, NY 12719 (SAN 212-3878) Tel 914-557-8713.

Naranga Bks, *(Naranga Bks. & Media; 0-9640825),* 742 S. Getty, Uvalde, TX 78801 Tel 210-278-5476.

Nat Educ Ctr Women, *(National Education Ctr. for Women in Business; 1-885043),* Seton Hill College, Greensburg, PA 15601 Tel 412-830-4625; Toll free: 800-632-9248.

Native Sun Pubs, *(Native Sun Pubs., Inc.; 0-9625169;* 1-879289), P.O. Box 13394, Richmond, VA 23225; 1021 Hioaks Rd., Richmond, VA 23225 Tel 804-233-7768.

Natl Archives & Records, *(National Archives & Records Administration; 0-911333; 1-880875),* Seventh St. & Pennsylvania Ave., NW, Washington, DC 20408 (SAN 210-363X) Tel 202-724-0871.

Natl Assn Deaf, *(National Assn. of the Deaf; 0-913072),* 814 Thayer Ave., Silver Spring, MD 20910 (SAN 159-4974) Tel 301-587-6282.

Natl Assn Principals, *(National Assn. of Secondary Schl. Principals; 0-88210),* 1904 Association Dr., Reston, VA 22091 (SAN 676-8776) Tel 703-860-0200.

Natl Assn Student, *(National Assn. of Student Councils;* 0-88210), Div. of National Assn. of Secondary School Principals, 1904 Association Dr., Reston, VA 22091 (SAN 260-3888) Tel 703-860-0200; Orders to: NASSP, P.O. Box 3250, Reston, VA 22090 (SAN 665-7451) Tel 703-860-0200.

Natl BIE Pub, *(National B.I.E. Publishing Agency;* 0-925783), P.O. Box 923, Casselberry, FL 32707-0923; 211 Shore Rd., Winter Springs, FL 32708 Tel 407-327-3779.

Natl Bk Netwk, *(National Bk. Network),* 4720A Boston Way, Lanham, MD 20706-4310 (SAN 630-0065) Tel 301-459-8696; Toll free: 800-462-6420.

Natl Book, *(National Bk. Co.; 0-89420),* Div. of Educational Research Assocs., P.O. Box 8795, Portland, OR 97207-8795 (SAN 212-4661) Tel 503-228-6345.

Natl Career, *(National Career Planning Institute;* 0-9640083), P.O. Box 1499, Clemson, SC 29633-1499; 224 Camelot Rd., Clemson, SC 29631 Tel 704-798-1273.

Natl Cath Educ, *(National Catholic Educational Assn.;* 1-55833), 1077 30th St., NW, Suite 100, Washington, DC 20007-3852 (SAN 676-8636) Tel 202-337-6232.

Natl Ctr Constitutional, *(National Ctr. for Constitutional Studies; 0-88080),* P.O. Box 841, West Jordan, UT 84084-0841 (SAN 237-7055) Tel 801-565-1787; Toll free: 800-388-4512.

Natl Dairy Coun, *(National Dairy Council; 1-55647),* 10255 W. Higgins Rd., Suite 900, Rosemont, IL 60018-5616 (SAN 224-702X) Tel 708-803-2000.

Natl Fire Serv Support Systs, *(National Fire Service Support Systems, Inc.; 0-9626076),* 20 N. Main St., No. 212, Pittsford, NY 14534-1303 Tel 716-264-0840.

Natl Fmly Prtnship, *(National Family Partnership;* 0-9642815), 11159B S. Towne Sq., Saint Louis, MO 63123-7824 Tel 314-845-1933.

Natl Gardening Assn, *(National Gardening Assn., Inc., The; 0-915873),* 180 Flynn Ave., Burlington, VT 05401 (SAN 294-0086) Tel 802-863-1308.

Natl Geog, *(National Geographic Society; 0-87044;* 0-7922), 1145 17th St., NW, Washington, DC 20036 (SAN 202-8956) Tel 202-857-7000; Toll free: 800-368-2728; 800-548-9797 (TTD users only); Orders to: P.O. Box 1640, Washington, DC 20013-1640 Tel 301-921-1200; Dist. by: Random Hse., Inc., 400 Hahn Rd., Westminster, MD 21157 (SAN 202-5515) Tel 410-848-1900; Toll free: 800-733-3000 (orders); 800-726-0600 (credit, inquires, customer service).

Natl Lilac Pub, *(National Lilac Publishing Co.;* 0-9614126), 295 Sharpe Rd., Anacortes-Fidalgo Island, WA 98221 (SAN 686-4716).

Natl Live Stock, *(National Live Stock & Meat Board;* 0-88700), 444 N. Michigan Ave., Chicago, IL 60611 (SAN 273-6276) Tel 312-467-5520.

Natl Marfan Foun, *(National Marfan Foundation, The;* 0-918335), 382 Main St., Port Washington, NY 11050 (SAN 657-2855) Tel 516-883-8712.

Natl Mat Dev, *(National Materials Development Ctr. for French; 0-911409),* Orders to: Univ. of New Hampshire, Brook Hse., 20 Park St., Durham, NH 03824 Tel 603-862-1089.

Natl Mus Am Ind, *(National Museum of the American Indian; 0-934490),* 3753 Broadway at 155th St., New York, NY 10032-1596 (SAN 204-0085) Tel 212-283-4031.

Natl Paperback, *(National Paperback Bks., Inc.;* 0-89826), Orders to: 3102 Schaad Rd., Knoxville, TN 37921 (SAN 211-5344) Tel 615-947-3575.

Natl Photo Collections, *(National Photographic Collections; 0-9620255),* 390F Golfview Rd., North Palm Beach, FL 33408 (SAN 248-0204) Tel 407-626-3233.

Natl Pr Bks, *(National Pr. Bks.; 0-915765; 1-882605),* 7200 Wisconsin Ave., Suite 212, Bethesda, MD 20814 (SAN 293-8839) Tel 301-657-1616; Toll free: 800-275-8888; Dist. by: National Bk. Network, 4720A Boston Way, Lanham, MD 20706-4310 (SAN 630-0065) Tel 301-459-8696; Toll free: 800-462-6420.

Natl Pr Inc
See Natl Pr Bks

Natl Res Unltd, *(Natural Resources Unlimited, Inc.;* 0-912475), 3528 Roesner Dr., Markham, IL 60426-2728 (SAN 265-2846) Tel 708-331-7964.

Natl School, *(National Schl. Services; 0-932957),* 610 S. Wheeling Rd., Wheeling, IL 60090 (SAN 689-9986) Tel 312-541-2768.

Natl Soc of Tole, *(National Society of Tole & Decorative Painters; 0-943883),* P.O. Box 808, Newton, KS 67114 (SAN 273-8546); 414 Main St., Suite 200, Newton Railroad Sta., Newton, KS 67114 (SAN 241-7952) Tel 316-283-9665.

Natl Textbk
See NTC Pub Grp

Natl Textbk *Imprint of* **NTC Pub Grp**

Natl Wildlife, *(National Wildlife Federation; 0-912186;* 0-945051), 8925 Leesburg Pike, Vienna, VA 22184 (SAN 202-8980) Tel 703-790-4000; Toll free: 800-432-6564 (orders only).

Natl Wmns Hall Fame, *(National Women's Hall of Fame; 0-9610622),* 76 Falls St. P.O. Box 335, Seneca Falls, NY 13148 (SAN 223-9299) Tel 315-568-8060.

Natl Woodlands Pub, *(National Woodlands Publishing Co.; 0-9628075),* Orders to: 8846 Green Briar Rd., Lake Ann, MI 49650 Tel 616-275-6735; Dist. by: Publishers Distribution Service, 6893 Sullivan Rd., Grawn, MI 49637 (SAN 630-5717) Tel 616-276-5196; Toll free: 800-345-0096 (orders only).

Natl Writ Pr, *(National Writers Pr., The; 0-88100),* Div. of National Writers Assn., 1450 S. Havana, Suite 424, Aurora, CO 80012 (SAN 240-320X) Tel 303-751-7844.

Naturally By Nan, *(Naturally By Nan; 0-9635127;* 1-885697), P.O. Box 132, Rosemount, MN 55068 Tel 612-423-3362.

Nature Co, *(Nature Co.; 1-883871),* Div. of CML, 750 Hearst Ave., Berkeley, CA 94710 Tel 510-644-1337.

Naturegraph, *(Naturegraph Pubs., Inc.; 0-911010;* 0-87961), P.O. Box 1075, Happy Camp, CA 96039 (SAN 202-8999) Tel 916-493-5353; Toll free: 800-390-5353.

NatureVision, *(NatureVision; 1-882489),* Div. of Keystone Gifts, Inc., 1 Waters Pk. Dr., Suite 101, San Mateo, CA 94403 Tel 415-345-6332.

NAUI, *(National Assn. of Underwater Instructors;* 0-916974), P.O. Box 14650, Montclair, CA 91763 (SAN 208-1024) Tel 909-621-5801.

Nauset Marsh, *(Nauset Marsh Pr.; 0-9618300),* Rte. 6, P.O. Box 1076, N. Eastham, MA 02651 (SAN 667-3309); Tomahawk Trail, Eastham, MA 02642 (SAN 667-3317) Tel 508-255-9090.

Nautical & Aviation, *(Nautical & Aviation Publishing Co. of America, Inc., The; 0-933852; 1-877853),* 8 W. Madison St., Baltimore, MD 21201 (SAN 213-3431) Tel 410-659-0220.

Navajo Curr
See Rough Rock Pr

Naval Inst Pr, *(Naval Institute Pr.; 0-87021; 1-55750),* U. S. Naval Institute, Preble Hall, 118 Maryland Ave., Annapolis, MD 21402-5035 (SAN 202-9006) Tel 410-268-6110; Orders to: U. S. Naval Institute Operations Ctr., Customer Service, 2062 Generals Hwy., Annapolis, MD 21401 (SAN 662-0930) Tel 410-224-3378; Toll free: 800-233-8764.

NAVH, *(National Assn. for Visually Handicapped;* 0-89064), 3201 Balboa St., San Francisco, CA 94121 (SAN 202-0971) Tel 415-221-8755; 22 W. 21st St., 6th Flr., New York, NY 10010 (SAN 669-1870) Tel 212-889-3141.

NavPress, *(NavPress Publishing Group; 0-89109),* P.O. Box 35001, Colorado Springs, CO 80935 (SAN 211-5352) Tel 719-548-9222; Toll free: 800-366-7788.

NBM, *(NBM Publishing Co.; 0-918348; 1-56163),* 185 Madison Ave., Suite 1504, New York, NY 10016 (SAN 210-0835) Tel 212-545-1223; Toll free: 800-886-1223.

NC Archives, *(North Carolina Div. of Archives & History; 0-86526),* Historical Pubns. Section, 109 E. Jones St., Raleigh, NC 27601-2807 (SAN 203-7246) Tel 919-733-7442.

NC Learn Inst Fitness, *(North Carolina Learning Institute for Fitness & Education; 0-9620900),* P.O. Box 10245, Greensboro, NC 27404 (SAN 250-0906) Tel 910-292-6999.

NC Natl Sci, *(North Carolina State Museum of Natural Sciences; 0-917134),* Div. of North Carolina Dept. of Agriculture, P.O. Box 29555, Raleigh, NC 27626-0555 (SAN 662-0973); 102 N. Salisbury St., Raleigh, NC 27603 (SAN 208-788X) Tel 919-733-7450.

NC Symphony, *(North Carolina Symphony Society, Inc., The; 0-9618952),* 2 E. South St., Raleigh, NC 27601 (SAN 242-5378) Tel 919-733-2750.

NC Wildlife, *(North Carolina Wildlife Resources Commission; 0-9628949),* 512 N. Salisbury St., Raleigh, NC 27604-1188 Tel 919-733-7123; Toll free: 800-662-7137.

NC Yrly Pubns Bd, *(North Carolina Yearly Meeting Pubns. Board; 0-942727),* 5506 W. Friendly, Greensboro, NC 27410 (SAN 667-7193) Tel 910-292-6957.

NCAT, *(National Ctr. for Appropriate Technology;* 1-55579), Box 3838, Butte, MT 59702 (SAN 260-342X) Tel 406-494-4572.

NCMA, *(North Carolina Museum of Art; 0-88259),* 2110 Blue Ridge Rd., Raleigh, NC 27607-6494 (SAN 202-9030) Tel 919-833-1935.

NCTE, *(National Council of Teachers of English;* 0-8141), 1111 Kenyon Rd., Urbana, IL 61801 (SAN 202-9049) Tel 217-328-3870.

NCTM, *(National Council of Teachers of Mathematics;* 0-87353), 1906 Association Dr., Reston, VA 22091 (SAN 202-9057) Tel 703-620-9840; Toll free: 800-235-7566 (orders only).

NE Library Commission, *(Nebraska Library Commission; 0-9624668),* 1200 N St., No. 120, Lincoln, NE 68508-2023 Tel 402-471-2045; Toll free: 800-742-7691.

NE U Pr, *(Northeastern Univ. Pr.; 0-930350; 1-55553),* 360 Huntington Ave., 272 Huntington Plaza, Boston, MA 02115 (SAN 205-3764) Tel 617-437-5480; Orders to: P.O. Box 6525, Ithaca, NY 14851 (SAN 282-0668) Tel 607-277-2211.

Neahtawanta Pr, *(Neahtawanta Pr.; 0-943806),* 161 E. Front St., Suite 200, Traverse City, MI 49684 (SAN 239-3689) Tel 616-946-0044; Dist. by: Baker & Taylor Bks., Momence Service Ctr., 501 S. Gladiolus St., Momence, IL 60954-2444 (SAN 169-2100) Tel 815-472-2444; Toll free: 800-775-2300 (customer service); Dist. by: Publishers Distribution Service, 6893 Sullivan Rd., Grawn, MI 49637 (SAN 630-5717) Tel 616-276-5196; Toll free: 800-345-0096 (orders only).

NECA
See Netwrk of Educ

Nel-Mar Pub, *(Nel-Mar Publishing; 0-9615760;* 1-877740), HC2, Box 267C, Canyon Lake, TX 78133-2705 (SAN 695-8699) Tel 210-935-2420.

Nelson, *(Nelson, Thomas, Pubs.; 0-8407; 0-89840; 0-86605; 0-918956; 0-7852),* P.O. Box 141000, Nelson Pl. at Elm Hill Pike, Nashville, TN 37214-1000 (SAN 209-3820) Tel 615-889-9000; Toll free: 800-251-4000.

Nelson-Atkins, *(Nelson-Atkins Museum of Art, The;* 0-942614), 4525 Oak St., Kansas City, MO 64111 (SAN 238-5473) Tel 816-751-1281.

NES Arnold, *(NES Arnold, Inc.; 1-884461),* Div. of NES Arnold, Ltd., 899 H Airport Park Rd., Glen Burnie, MD 21061-2557 Tel 410-553-9700; Toll free: 800-755-1455.

Network Pubns
See ETR Assocs

Netwrk of Educ, *(Network of Educators' on the Americas; 1-878554),* 1118 22nd St., NW, Washington, DC 20037 Tel 202-429-0137.

Nevada Pub, *(Nevada Publishing Co.; 0-9614505),* P.O. Box 78246, Nashville, TN 37207 (SAN 691-7429); 1796 Meade Ave., Nashville, TN 37207 Tel 615-227-5710.

Neversink Valley, *(Neversink Valley Area Museum;* 0-9636532), P.O. Box 263, Hoag Rd., Cuddebackville, NY 12729 Tel 914-754-8870.

New Age CT, *(New Age Bks. & Games; 1-878064),* 1131 Tolland Tpke., Suite O-210, Manchester, CT 06040-1679.

New Amsterdam Bks, *(New Amsterdam Bks.; 0-941533;* 1-56131), P.O. Box C, Franklin, NY 13775-0303 (SAN 630-1886) Tel 212-685-6005; Toll free: 800-944-4040.

New Begin Life, *(New Beginning Life Ctr.; 0-9621489),* P.O. Box 5567, Reno, NV 89513 (SAN 251-4672) Tel 702-329-9797.

New Begin OR, *(New Beginning, The; 0-9631751),* 1340 N. Juniper, Canby, OR 97013 Tel 503-266-8987.

New Connect Pub, *(New Connection Publishing;* 0-923766), Div. of New Connection Programs, Inc., 8110 Eden Rd., No. 205, Eden Prairie, MN 55344-5304 (SAN 251-7965) Tel 612-941-5151.

New Dawn NY, *(New Dawn Publishing Co., The; 0-9630718; 1-882786),* 20526 County Rte. 59, Dexter, NY 13634-9743 (SAN 297-7656) Tel 315-639-6764. Do not confuse with other companies with the same name in Newark, DE & Pasadena, CA.

New Dawn Pr CO
See Metagnosis

New Day Pr, *(New Day Pr.; 0-913678),* c/o Karamu Hse., 2355 E. 89th St., Cleveland, OH 44106 (SAN 279-2664) Tel 216-795-7070.

New Dimens Educ, *(New Dimensions in Education; 0-89796; 0-914876; 0-8073),* Div. of Abrams & Co. Pubs., Inc., 61 Mattatuck Heights Rd., No. 7, Waterbury, CT 06705-3832 (SAN 207-7078) Tel 203-756-3580; Toll free: 800-227-9120.

New Dir Pr, *(New Directions Pr.; 0-9609616),* 80 Eighth Ave., New York, NY 10011 (SAN 260-2326) Tel 212-255-0230. Do not confuse with New Directions Pr. in New York, NY.

New Directions, *(New Directions Publishing Corp.;* 0-8112), 80 Eighth Ave., New York, NY 10011 (SAN 202-9081) Tel 212-255-0230; Dist. by: W. W. Norton & Co., Inc., 500 Fifth Ave., New York, NY 10110 (SAN 202-5795) Tel 212-354-5500; Toll free: 800-233-4830 (book orders only).

New Discovery Bks *Imprint of* **Macmillan Child Grp**

New Ear Prodns, *(New Ear Productions; 0-9623502),* 401 Benson, Milford, MI 48381 Tel 315-425-0048.

New Eng Pr VT, *(New England Pr., Inc., The; 0-933050;* 1-881535), P.O. Box 575, Shelburne, VT 05482 (SAN 213-6376); 216 Battery St., Burlington, VT 05401 Tel 802-863-2520.

New Eng Pub MA, *(New England Publishing Co.;* 0-914265), 728 Hampden St., Holyoke, MA 01040 (SAN 287-5837) Tel 413-533-4231. Do not confuse with New England Publishing Assocs., Inc. in Chester, CT.

New Futures, *(New Futures, Inc.; 0-945886),* 5400 Cutler Ave. NE, Albuquerque, NM 87110 (SAN 247-9524) Tel 505-883-5680; Dist. by: Morning Glory Pr., 6595 San Haraldo Way, Buena Park, CA 90620 (SAN 211-2558) Tel 714-828-1998.

New Harbinger, *(New Harbinger Pubns.; 0-934986; 1-879237; 1-57224),* 5674 Shattuck Ave., Oakland, CA 94609 (SAN 205-0587) Tel 510-652-0215; Toll free: 800-748-6273; Dist. by: Publishers Group West, 4065 Hollis St., Emeryville, CA 94608 (SAN 202-8522) Tel 510-658-3453; Toll free: 800-788-3123; Dist. by: Bookpeople, 7900 Edgewater Dr., Oakland, CA 94621 (SAN 168-9517) Tel 510-632-4700; Toll free: 800-999-4650.

New Hope *Imprint of* **Womans Mission Union**

New Hope Pr, *(New Hope Pr.; 0-943545),* 244 S. Main St., New Hope, PA 18938 (SAN 668-6621) Tel 215-862-9414. Do not confuse with companies with similar names in Anaheim, CA, Dothan, AL.

New Horizon NJ, *(New Horizon Pr. Pubs., Inc.;* 0-88282), P.O. Box 669, Far Hills, NJ 07931 (SAN 677-119X) Tel 908-604-6311; Toll free: 800-533-7978 orders only.

New King Pub, *(New King Publishing; 0-9638305),* P.O. Box 1722, East Lansing, MI 48826-1722; 915 N. Capitol, Lansing, MI 48906 Tel 517-485-0103.

New Leaf, *(New Leaf Pr.; 0-89221),* P.O. Box 311, Green Forest, AR 72638 (SAN 207-9518) Tel 501-438-5288; Toll free: 800-643-9535.

New Legends Pub, *(New Legends Publishing Group;* 1-881442), P.O. Box 2567, Bellingham, WA 98227; 8611 Delta Line, Custer, WA 98240 Tel 206-371-5486.

New Life Images, *(New Life Images; 0-9641183),* 448 Pleasant Lake Ave., Harwich, MA 02645 Tel 508-432-8040.

New Memories, *(New Memories; 0-944027),* P.O. Box 2151, Coppell, TX 75019 (SAN 242-5300) Tel 214-245-1734.

New Mexico Mag, *(New Mexico Magazine; 0-937206),* 495 Old Santa Fe Trail, Lew Wallace Bldg., Santa Fe, NM 87503 (SAN 677-072X) Tel 505-827-7447.

New Past Pr, *(New Past Pr., Inc., The; 0-938627),* P.O. Box 558, Friendship, WI 53934 (SAN 661-6283) Tel 608-339-7191.

New Plays Inc, *(New Plays, Inc.; 0-932720),* Box 5074, Charlottesville, VA 22905 (SAN 220-9411) Tel 804-979-2777.

New Pontiac, *(New Pontiac History Group; 0-9641636),* 303 Ottawa Dr., Pontiac, MI 48341 Tel 810-338-2758.

New Press NY, *(New Pr.; 1-56584),* 450 W. 41st St., New York, NY 10036 Tel 212-629-8802; Toll free: 800-233-4830 (orders only); Dist. by: W. W. Norton & Co., Inc., 500 Fifth Ave., New York, NY 10110 (SAN 202-5795) Tel 212-354-5500; Toll free: 800-223-2584; 800-233-4830 (book orders only).

New Quest, *(New Quest Publishing Co.; 1-880791),* 322 W. Compton Blvd., No. 100, P.O. Box 348, Compton, CA 90220 Tel 213-512-6060.

New Readers, *(New Readers Pr.; 0-88336; 1-56420),* Div. of Laubach Literacy International, Box 131, Syracuse, NY 13210 (SAN 202-1064); Toll free: 800-448-8878; 1320 Jamesville Ave., Syracuse, NY 13210 Tel 315-422-9121.

New Schl Mus Study, *(New Schl. for Music Study Pr.;* 0-913277), P.O. Box 407, Princeton, NJ 08542 (SAN 285-8266) Tel 609-921-2900.

New Seed, *(New Seed Pr.; 0-938678),* P.O. Box 9488, Berkeley, CA 94709 (SAN 282-0501) Tel 510-540-7576; Dist. by: Bookpeople, 7900 Edgewater Dr., Oakland, CA 94621 (SAN 168-9517) Tel 510-632-4700; Toll free: 800-999-4650; Dist. by: Children's Small Pr. Collection, 716 N. Fourth Ave., Ann Arbor, MI 48104 (SAN 200-514X) Tel 313-668-8056; Toll free: 800-221-8056 (orders only); Dist. by: Inland Bk. Co., 140 Commerce St., East Haven, CT 06512 (SAN 200-4151) Tel 203-467-4257; Toll free: 800-243-0138; c/o Kidsrights, 401 S. Highland, Box 851, Mount Dora, FL 32757 (SAN 248-0891) Tel 904-483-1100; Toll free: 800-326-2665; Dist. by: New Leaf Distributing Co., 5424 Tulane Dr., SW, Atlanta, GA 30336-2323 (SAN 169-1449) Tel 404-691-6996; Toll free: 800-326-2665; Dist. by: Caillech Pr., 482 Michigan St., Saint Paul, MN 55102-2951 (SAN 297-584X) Tel 612-225-9647.

New Soc Pubs, *(New Society Pubs.; 0-86571),* Div. of New Society Education Foundation, Inc., 4527 Springfield Ave., Philadelphia, PA 19143 (SAN 213-540X) Tel 215-382-6543; Toll free: 800-333-9093; Dist. by: InBook, P.O. Box 120261, East Haven, CT 06512 (SAN 630-5547) Tel 203-467-4257; Toll free: 800-253-3605 (orders only).

New Victoria Pubs, *(New Victoria Pubs., Inc.; 0-934678),* P.O. Box 27, Norwich, VT 05055 (SAN 212-1204) Tel 802-649-5297; Toll free: 800-326-5297; Dist. by: Inbook, P.O. Box 120261, East Haven, CT 06512 (SAN 630-5547) Tel 203-467-4257; Toll free: 800-253-3605.

New Vision VA, *(New Vision, Inc.; 0-9635899),* P.O. Box 514, Centreville, VA 22020; 13704 Shelbourne St., Centreville, VA 22020 Tel 703-803-3540.

New Win Pub, *(New Win Publishing, Inc.; 0-8329;* 0-87691), P.O. Box 5159, Clinton, NJ 08809 (SAN 217-1201) Tel 908-735-9701.

New World SC, *(A New World Pr.; 0-9640674),* 1010 Coatsdale Rd., Columbia, SC 29209 (SAN 298-2129) Tel 803-776-5658.

New World SC
See One World SC

New Wrinkle, *(New Wrinkle Pr.; 0-944314),* P.O. Box 20737, Milwaukee, WI 53220 (SAN 243-492X); 3700 S. 43rd St., Milwaukee, WI 53200 (SAN 243-4938) Tel 414-327-0761; Dist. by: Ideals Publishing Co., P.O. Box 141000, Nashville, TN 37214-1000 (SAN 213-4403) Tel 615-889-9000; Toll free: 800-558-0740.

Newbridge Comms, *(Newbridge Communications, Inc.;* 1-56784), 333 E. 38th St., New York, NY 10016-2745; Toll free: 800-347-7829.

Newbury *Imprint of* **Heinle & Heinle**

Newhouse Pr, *(Newhouse Pr.; 0-918050),* 146 N. Rampart Blvd., Los Angeles, CA 90026 (SAN 209-2689) Tel 213-383-1089; Orders to: P.O. Box 76145, Los Angeles, CA 90076 (SAN 209-2697) Tel 213-382-1463.

Newington, *(Newington Pr.; 1-878137),* 2 Old New Milford Rd., Brookfield, CT 06804 Tel 203-740-2220; Toll free: 800-462-4703.

Newmark CA, *(Newmark Pubns.; 1-880125),* P.O. Box 1965, Oakland, CA 94606 (SAN 297-4495); 1448 Jackson, No. 6, Oakland, CA 94606 (SAN 297-4487) Tel 510-839-7325.

Newmarket, *(Newmarket Pr.; 0-937858; 1-55704),* Div. of Newmarket Publishing & Communications, 18 E. 48th St., New York, NY 10017 (SAN 217-2585) Tel 212-832-3575; Toll free: 800-669-3903; Dist. by: Random Hse., Inc., 400 Hahn Rd., Westminster, MD 21157 (SAN 202-5515) Tel 410-848-1900; Toll free: 800-733-3000 (orders).

Newport Pubs, *(Newport Pubs., Inc.; 1-56729),* 31 Laguna Woods Dr., Laguna Niguel, CA 92677 Tel 714-240-7005.

News & Observer, *(News & Observer, The; 0-935400),* P.O. Box 191, Raleigh, NC 27602 (SAN 222-6189); 215 S. McDowell St., Raleigh, NC 27602 Tel 919-836-2820.

NewSage Press, *(NewSage Pr.; 0-939165),* 825 NE 20th Ave., Suite 150, Portland, OR 97232 (SAN 662-8370) Tel 503-232-6794; Dist. by: Publishers Group West, 4065 Hollis St., Emeryville, CA 94608 (SAN 202-8522) Tel 510-658-3453; Toll free: 800-788-3123.

Niagara Cnty Hist Soc, *(Niagara County Historical Society, Inc.; 1-878233),* 215 Niagara St., Lockport, NY 14094 Tel 716-665-2251.

Nichols Pub, *(Nichols Publishing Co.; 0-89397),* P.O. Box 6036, East Brunswick, NJ 08816-6036 (SAN 212-0291) Tel 908-297-2862.

Nickel Pr, *(Nickel Pr.; 1-879424; 1-57122),* Div. of S.R. Jacobs & Assocs., 10585 N. Meridian St., Suite 220, Indianapolis, IN 46290 Tel 317-844-9400.

Nickel Pr AL, *(Nickel Pr., Inc.; 1-883939),* 202 Valley Stream Dr., Enterprise, AL 36330 Tel 205-347-6217. Do not confuse with Nickel Pr. in Indianapolis, IN.

NightinGale Res, *(NightinGale Resources; 0-911389),* P.O. Box 322, Cold Spring, NY 10516 (SAN 274-1016) Tel 914-753-5383; 6 Chestnut St., Cold Spring, NY 10516 (SAN 248-3866); Dist. by: Baker & Taylor Bks., Somerville Service Ctr., 50 Kirby Ave., Somerville, NJ 08876-0734 (SAN 169-4901) Tel 908-722-8000; Toll free: 800-775-1500 (customer service); Dist. by: Inland Bk. Co., 140 Commerce St., East Haven, CT 06512 (SAN 200-4151) Tel 203-467-4257; Toll free: 800-243-0138; Dist. by: Information Dynamics, 111 Claybrook Dr., Silver Spring, MD 20902 (SAN 630-222X) Tel 301-593-8650; Dist. by: Blackwell North America, 100 University Ct., Blackwood, NJ 08012 (SAN 169-4596) Tel 609-228-8900; Toll free: 800-257-7341; Dist. by: Midwest Library Service, 11443 St. Charles Rock Rd., Bridgeton, MO 63044-9986 (SAN 169-4243) Tel 314-739-3100; Dist. by: Pacific Pipeline, Inc., 8030 S. 228th St, Kent, WA 98032-2900 (SAN 208-2128) Tel 206-872-5523; Toll free: 800-444-7323 (Customer Service); 800-677-2222 (orders); Dist. by: L-S Distributors, 480 Ninth St., San Francisco, CA 94103 (SAN 169-0213) Tel 415-861-6300.

Niota Pr, *(Niota Pr.; 0-9614973),* 1633 Pullan Ave., Cincinnati, OH 45223 (SAN 693-5567) Tel 513-542-4646.

NISIS, *(NISIS; 0-9632816),* 304 O'Brien Ave., Whitefish, MT 59937-2464 Tel 406-882-4688; 5 Fir Ave., Whitefish, MT 59937 Tel 406-862-5015.

NJK Pubns, *(NJK Pubns.; 1-883196),* Div. of NJB's Writing Service, P.O. Box 4788, Lancaster, CA 93539-4788; 16970 Marygold Ave., No. 51, Fontana, CA 92335 Tel 909-357-9750.

NJL Interests, *(NJL Interests; 0-9631318),* 7714 Woodway, Houston, TX 77063 Tel 713-780-1268.

NK Lawn & Garden, *(NK Lawn & Garden Co.;* 1-880281), Div. of Sandoz Corp., 7500 Olson Memorial Hwy., Golden Valley, MN 55427 Tel 612-593-7888; Dist. by: Avon Bks., 1350 Ave. of the Americas, New York, NY 10019 (SAN 201-4009) Tel 212-261-6854; Toll free: 800-223-0690.

NL Assoc Inc, *(Levy, Nathan, Assocs., Inc.; 0-9608240),* P.O. Box 1199, Hightstown, NJ 08520 (SAN 240-3951) Tel 201-329-6981.

NL Assocs, *(NL Assocs., Inc.; 1-878347),* P.O. Box 1199, Hightstown, NJ 08520; 3 Marilyn Ct., Lawrenceville, NJ 08648 Tel 201-329-6981.

NM Pub Co, *(New Mexico Publishing Co.; 0-9622468),* P.O. Box 1272, Santa Fe, NM 87504 Tel 505-473-9854. Do not confuse with Univ. of New Mexico Pr.

Noahs Ark, *(Noah's Ark Publishing Co.; 0-9619082),* 8323 SW Freeway, Suite 250, Houston, TX 77074 (SAN 243-1165) Tel 713-771-7143. Do not confuse with Noah's Ark Publishing in Knoxville, TN.

Noble Hse MD, *(Noble Hse.; 1-56167),* Div. of American Literary Pr., Inc., 8019 Belair Rd., Suite 10, Baltimore, MD 21236-3711 Tel 410-882-7700; Toll free: 800-873-2003.

Noble Pub Assocs, *(Noble Publishing Assocs.; 0-923463;* 1-56857), P.O. Box 2250, Gresham, OR 97030-0642 (SAN 251-656X) Tel 503-667-3942.

Nocaine, *(Nocaine; 0-9626964),* P.O. Box 5273, Chatsworth, CA 91313; 21606 Devonshire St., Chatsworth, CA 91313 Tel 805-259-6089.

Noffs Assocs, *(Noffs Assocs., Inc.; 0-929875),* P.O. Box 1454, Elmhurst, IL 60126 (SAN 250-8699); 180 W. Park Ave., No. 260, Elmhurst, IL 60126 (SAN 250-8702) Tel 312-530-8999.

Non Fiction Pubns, *(Non-Fiction Pubns. Corp.;* 0-913279), P.O. Box 129, Island Park, NY 11558 (SAN 285-9106) Tel 516-431-2933.

Noodle Pr, *(Noodle Pr.; 0-9601022),* P.O. Box 42542, Washington, DC 20015 (SAN 208-7871) Tel 202-363-5078.

Noonday *Imprint of* **FS&G**

Nords Studio, *(Nords Studio; 0-935656),* 200 Central Ave., Crescent City, FL 32112 (SAN 200-7614) Tel 904-698-1009.

North Amer Pr *Imprint of* **Fulcrum Pub**

North Atlantic, *(North Atlantic Bks.; 0-938190; 0-913028; 1-55643),* Div. of Society of the Study of Native Arts & Science, P.O. Box 12327, Berkeley, CA 94701 (SAN 203-1655) Tel 510-559-8277; Dist. by: Publishers Group West, 4065 Hollis St., Emeryville, CA 94608 (SAN 202-8522) Tel 510-658-3453; Toll free: 800-788-3123.

North Bks, *(North Bks.; 0-939495),* P.O. Box 337, Peace Dale, RI 02883 (SAN 663-4052) Tel 401-294-3682.

North Country, *(North Country Bks., Inc.; 0-932052; 0-9601158; 0-925168),* 18 Irving Pl., Utica, NY 13501 (SAN 110-828X) Tel 315-738-4342.

North Light Bks, *(North Light Bks.; 0-89134),* Div. of F&W Pubns., Inc., 1507 Dana Ave., Cincinnati, OH 45207 (SAN 287-0274) Tel 513-531-2690; Toll free: 800-289-0963.

North Pt Pr *Imprint of* **FS&G**

North Scale Co, *(North Scale Institute Publishing Co.;* 0-916299), P.O. Box 27555, San Francisco, CA 94127 (SAN 295-7418); 2205 Taraval St., San Francisco, CA 94116 (SAN 295-7426) Tel 415-759-9491.

North-South Bks NYC, *(North-South Bks.; 1-55858),* Subs. of Nord-Sud Verlag (SZ), ; Orders to: 1123 Broadway, Suite 800, New York, NY 10010 (SAN 251-2459) Tel 212-463-9736; Toll free: 800-282-8257.

North Star, *(North Star Pr. of St. Cloud; 0-87839),* P.O. Box 451, Saint Cloud, MN 56302-0451 (SAN 203-7491) Tel 612-253-1636.

Northcountry Pub, *(Northcountry Publishing Co.; 0-930366; 1-881794),* 1509 Fillmore St., Alexandria, MN 56308 (SAN 211-061X) Tel 612-763-3874.

Northcross Hse, *(Northcross Hse.; 0-9617256),* 9662 Roanoke Rd., Elliston, VA 24087 (SAN 663-5725) Tel 703-268-5005.

Northern St U, *(Northern State Univ. Pr.; 1-883120),* Div. of NSU Foundation, Northern State Univ., Box 740, Aberdeen, SD 57401; 12th & Jay Sts., Aberdeen, SD 57401 Tel 605-622-2456.

Northland
See Northland AZ

Northland AZ, *(Northland Publishing; 0-87358),* Div. of Justin Industries, P.O. Box 1389, Flagstaff, AZ 86002 (SAN 202-9251) Tel 602-774-5251; Toll free: 800-346-3257. Do not confuse with Northland Publishing, Menomonie, WI.

Northland Pr, *(Northland Pr.; 0-9620280),* P.O. Box 62, Boon, MI 49618-0062 (SAN 248-5818); 4198 S. 27th Rd., Cadillac, MI 49601-9641 (SAN 248-5826) Tel 616-775-4095. Do not confuse with companies with the same name in Winona, MN, Flagstaff, AZ.

Northwest Pub, *(Northwestern Publishing Hse.; 0-8100),* 1250 N. 113th St., Milwaukee, WI 53226-0975 (SAN 206-7943) Tel 414-475-6600; P.O. Box 26975, Milwaukee, WI 53226-0975 (SAN 665-7494).

Northwind Pr, *(Northwind Pr.; 0-945887),* Div. of OZ Enterprises, Inc., P.O. Box 637, 800 Thompson Rd., Sandpoint, ID 83864 (SAN 247-8447) Tel 208-263-7756.

NorthWord, *(NorthWord Pr., Inc.; 0-942802; 1-55971),* P.O. Box 1360, Minocqua, WI 54548 (SAN 240-4842) Tel 715-356-7644; Toll free: 800-336-6398 (orders only); Dist. by: Bookmen, Inc., 525 N. Third St., Minneapolis, MN 55401 (SAN 169-409X) Tel 612-341-3333; Toll free: 800-328-8411 (customer service); Dist. by: Pacific Pipeline, Inc., 8030 S. 228th St., Kent, WA 98032-2900 (SAN 208-2128) Tel 206-872-5523; Toll free: 800-444-7323 (Customer Service); 800-677-2222 (orders); Dist. by: Baker & Taylor Bks., Somerville Service Ctr., 50 Kirby Ave., Somerville, NJ 08876-0734 (SAN 169-4901) Tel 908-722-8000; Toll free: 800-775-1500 (customer service); Dist. by: Baker & Taylor Bks., Reno Service Ctr., 380 Edison Way, Reno, NV 89564 (SAN 169-4464) Tel 702-858-6700; Toll free: 800-775-1700 (customer service); Dist. by: Baker & Taylor Bks., Momence Service Ctr., 501 S. Gladiolus St., Momence, IL 60954-2444 (SAN 169-2100) Tel 815-472-2444; Toll free: 800-775-2300 (customer service); Dist. by: Baker & Taylor Bks., Commerce Service Ctr., 251 Mt. Olive Church Rd., Commerce, GA 30599-9988 (SAN 169-1503) Tel 706-335-5000; Toll free: 800-775-1200 (customer service); Dist. by: Ingram Bk. Co., 1 Ingram Blvd., La Vergne, TN 37086-1986 (SAN 169-7978) Tel 615-793-5000; Toll free: 800-937-8000 (orders only, all warehouses).

Norton, *(Norton, W. W., & Co., Inc.; 0-393),* 500 Fifth Ave., New York, NY 10110 (SAN 202-5795) Tel 212-354-5500; Toll free: 800-223-2584; 800-233-4830 (book orders only).

Norwich Bulletin, *(Norwich Bulletin; 0-9621270),* 66 Franklin St., Norwich, CT 06360 (SAN 250-7935) Tel 203-887-9211.

Noteworthy, *(Noteworthy; 1-881980),* Div. of Papermates, Inc., 9340 Eton Ave., Chatsworth, CA 91311 Tel 818-407-5700.

Noteworthy Creat, *(Noteworthy Creations, Inc.;* 1-883983), P.O. Box 335, Delphi, IN 46923; 112 W. Main St., Delphi, IN 46923 Tel 317-564-4167.

Nova Media, *(Nova Media, Inc.; 0-9618567; 1-884239),* P.O. Box 414, Big Rapids, MI 49307-0414 (SAN 668-0372); 1724 N. State, Big Rapids, MI 49307 (SAN 668-0380) Tel 616-796-7539.

Novelty Bks, *(Novelty Bks.; 0-9623353),* P.O. Box 2482, Norman, OK 73070-2482 Tel 405-325-9479.

Noviysvet, *(Noviysvet; 1-878860),* Div. of H.O.A.S.C.A. N.I.M., Inc., P.O. Box 249, New York, NY 10274 Tel 212-509-1378.

Now Comns, *(Now Communications Co.; 0-940175),* P.O. Box 5668, Austin, TX 78763 (SAN 664-3019); 2511 Hartford Rd., Austin, TX 78703 (SAN 664-3027) Tel 512-478-7109.

NTC Pub Grp, *(NTC Publishing Group; 0-8442; 0-8325;* 0-88499), 4255 W. Touhy Ave., Lincolnwood, IL 60646-1975 (SAN 169-2208) Tel 708-679-5500; Toll free: 800-323-4900 (orders). *Imprints:* Natl Textbk (National Textbook Company); Passport Bks (Passport Books); VGM Career Bks (V G M Career Books).

Nth Hills Pubs, *(North Hills Pubs.; 0-9640677),* P.O. Box 280788, Northridge, CA 91328; 9534 Reseda Blvd., Northridge, CA 91328 Tel 818-894-6729.

Ntrl Science Indus, *(Natural Science Industries, Ltd.;* 1-878501), 50-01 Rockaway Beach Blvd., Far Rockaway, NY 11691 Tel 718-945-5400.

NuBaby AL, *(NuBaby, Inc.; 0-9626614),* P.O. Box 030132, Tuscaloosa, AL 35403; 6309 Eastbrook Dr., Tuscaloosa, AL 35405 Tel 205-556-1011.

Nugget Pub, *(Nugget Publishing Co.; 0-9622684),* P.O. Box 60004, San Diego, CA 92166; 2240 Shelter Island Dr., San Diego, CA 92106 Tel 619-496-6617.

Nugget Truth Minist, *(Nugget of Truth Ministries, Inc.;* 0-942847), P.O. Box 33110, Tulsa, OK 74153 (SAN 667-7711); 3429 E. 56th Pl., Tulsa, OK 74135 (SAN 667-772X) Tel 918-747-9803; Dist. by: Spring Arbor Distributors, 10885 Textile Rd., Belleville, MI 48111 (SAN 158-9016) Tel 313-481-0900; Toll free: 800-395-5599 (orders); 800-395-7234 (customer service); Dist. by: Riverside/World, P.O. Box 370, 1500 Riverside Dr., Iowa Falls, IA 50126 (SAN 169-2666) Tel 515-648-4271; Toll free: 800-247-5111.

Nutrition Encounter, *(Nutrition Encounter, Inc.;* 0-944501), P.O. Box 5847, 61 Bahama Reef, Novato, CA 94948 (SAN 243-685X) Tel 415-883-5154; Dist. by: Bookpeople, 7900 Edgewater Dr., Oakland, CA 94621 (SAN 168-9517) Tel 510-632-4700; Toll free: 800-999-4650; Dist. by: Nutri-Bks. Corp., P.O. Box 5793, Denver, CO 80217 (SAN 169-054X) Tel 303-778-8383; Toll free: 800-279-2048 (orders only); Dist. by: Golden-Lee Bk. Distributors, Inc., 1000 Dean St., Brooklyn, NY 11238 (SAN 169-5126) Tel 718-857-6333; Dist. by: New Leaf Distributing Co., 5425 Tulane Dr., SW, Atlanta, GA 30336-2323 (SAN 169-1449) Tel 404-691-6996; Toll free: 800-326-2665; Dist. by: Inland Bk. Co., 140 Commerce St., East Haven, CT 06512 (SAN 200-4151) Tel 203-467-4257; Toll free: 800-243-0138; Dist. by: Baker & Taylor Bks., Reno Service Ctr., 380 Edison Way, Reno, NV 89564 (SAN 169-4464) Tel 702-858-6700; Toll free: 702-858-6700; Dist. by: Baker & Taylor Bks., Somerville Service Ctr., 50 Kirby Ave., Somerville, NJ 08876-0734 (SAN 169-4901) Tel 908-722-8000; Toll free: 800-775-1500 (customer service); Dist. by: Quality Bks., Inc., 918 Sherwood Dr., Lake Bluff, IL 60044-2204 (SAN 169-2127) Tel 708-295-2010; Toll free: 800-323-4241 (libraries only); Dist. by: Baker & Taylor Bks., Momence Service Ctr., 501 S. Gladiolus St., Momence, IL 60954-2444 (SAN 169-2100) Tel 815-472-2444; Toll free: 800-775-2300 (customer service); Dist. by: Moving Bks., Inc., P.O. Box 20037, Seattle, WA 98102 (SAN 159-0685) Tel 206-762-1750; Toll free: 800-777-6683.

Nutshell Enterprises, *(Nutshell Enterprises, Ltd.;* 0-930723), 4059 Norrisville Rd., Jarrettsville, MD 21084 (SAN 677-6043) Tel 410-557-7583.

NUVENTURES Pub, *(NUVENTURES Publishing;* 0-9625632), Div. of NUVENTURES Consultants, P.O. Box 2489, La Jolla, CA 92038-2489 (SAN 200-3805); Toll free: 800-338-9768; 6236 Cardeno Dr., La Jolla, CA 92037 (SAN 200-3813) Tel 619-454-9100.

NVEM, *(New Visions Educational Materials; 0-9623407),* 4329 Second Ave., Los Angeles, CA 90008 Tel 213-294-2451.

NW Interpretive, *(Northwest Interpretive Assn.;* 0-914019), 909 First Ave., Seattle, WA 98104-1060 (SAN 286-8504) Tel 206-220-4140.

NW Island, *(Northwest Island Pubs.; 0-9629778),* 444 Guemes Island Rd., Anacortes, WA 98221 Tel 206-293-3721.

NW Monarch Pr, *(Northwest Monarch Pr.; 0-9626870),* P.O. Box 409, Hub Sta., Bronx, NY 10455; 2223 Homer Ave., Bronx, NY 10473 Tel 718-585-6340.

NW Pub, *(Northwest Publishing, Inc.; 1-880416; 1-56901; 0-7610),* 6906 S. 300 W., Midvale, UT 84047 Tel 801-255-5050; Toll free: 800-398-2102; Dist. by: Baker & Taylor Bks., Somerville Service Ctr., 50 Kirby Ave., Somerville, NJ 08876-0734 (SAN 169-4901) Tel 908-722-8000; Toll free: 800-775-1500 (customer service); Dist. by: Ingram Bk. Co., 1 Ingram Blvd., La Vergne, TN 37086-1986 (SAN 169-7978) Tel 615-793-5000; Toll free: 800-937-8000 (orders only, all warehouses). Do not confuse with Northwest Publishing Co. in Kent, WA.

NY State Alliance, *(New York State Alliance for Arts Education; 0-9624123),* Empire State Plaza, Cultural Education Ctr., Rm. 9B38, Albany, NY 12230 Tel 518-473-0823.

NY Transit Mus, *(New York Transit Museum Pr.;* 0-9637492), Div. of New York City Transit Authority, 130 Livingston St., Rm. 9001, Brooklyn, NY 11201 Tel 718-694-5102.

NYC Law Dept, *(New York City Law Dept.; 0-9619599),* 100 Church St., New York, NY 10007 (SAN 245-9639) Tel 212-556-3300; Dist. by: City Publishing Ctr., 2210 Municipal Bldg., 1 Centre St., New York, NY 10007 (SAN 630-1401) Tel 212-669-8249.

NYC Pub Co, *(New York City Publishing Co.; 0-9614772; 1-881939),* 37 W. 37th St., 7th Flr., New York, NY 10018 (SAN 696-0758) Tel 212-944-7480; Dist. by: Philipp Feldheim, Inc., 200 Airport Executive Pk., Spring Valley, NY 10977 (SAN 106-6307) Tel 914-356-2282; Toll free: 800-237-7149.

Nystrom, *(Nystrom; 0-88463; 0-7825),* Div. of Herff Jones, 3333 N. Elston Ave., Chicago, IL 60618 (SAN 203-5529) Tel 312-463-1144; Toll free: 800-621-8086. Do not confuse with Nystrom Publishing, Inc., Maple Grove, MN.

O Penzler Bks, *(Penzler, Otto Bks.; 1-883402; 1-57283),* 129 W. 56th St., New York, NY 10019 Tel 212-765-0923; Dist. by: Simon & Schuster, Inc., 1230 Ave. of the Americas, New York, NY 10020 (SAN 200-2450) Tel 212-698-7000; Toll free: 800-223-2348; 800-223-2336 (orders only).

Oak Creek Pr, *(Oak Creek Pr.; 0-9627589),* P.O. Box 498, Dripping Springs, TX 78620; 1007 Oak Springs Dr., Dripping Springs, TX 78620 Tel 512-858-4401; Dist. by: State Hse. Pr., P.O. Drawer 15247, Austin, TX 78761 (SAN 660-9651) Tel 512-454-1959.

Oak Knoll, *(Oak Knoll Bks.; 0-938768),* 414 Delaware St., New Castle, DE 19720 (SAN 216-2776) Tel 302-328-7232.

Oak Pr, *(Oak Pr.; 0-9615242),* 904 Broadway Ave., Wausau, WI 54401 (SAN 695-1643) Tel 715-842-7369. Do not confuse with Oak Pr. in Fair Oaks, CA.

Oakwood MO, *(Oakwood Pr.; 0-9630604),* Div. of Carolyn Lesser Creative, 301 Oak St., Quincy, IL 62301 Tel 217-222-5742.

Ocean Allen Pub, *(Ocean Allen Publishing; 0-917071),* 13074 Sundance Ave., San Diego, CA 92129 (SAN 655-2382) Tel 619-484-5401; Rte. 4, Box 369, Spokane, WA 99204 (SAN 691-4276) Tel 509-466-7095.

Ocean East, *(Ocean East Publishing, Inc.; 0-9607028),* 1655 71st Ct., Vero Beach, FL 32966 (SAN 239-0159) Tel 407-567-9899.

Ocean Tree Bks, *(Ocean Tree Bks.; 0-943734),* P.O. Box 1295, Santa Fe, NM 87504 (SAN 241-0478) Tel 505-983-1412; Dist. by: Ingram Bk. Co., 1 Ingram Blvd., La Vergne, TN 37086-1986 (SAN 169-7978) Tel 615-793-5000; Toll free: 800-937-8000 (orders only, all warehouses); Dist. by: Bookpeople, 7900 Edgewater Dr., Oakland, CA 94621 (SAN 168-9517) Tel 510-632-4700; Toll free: 800-999-4650; Dist. by: DeVorss & Co., P.O. Box 550, Marina del Rey, CA 90294-0550 (SAN 168-9886) Tel 213-870-7478; Toll free: 800-843-5743 (bookstores only); 800-331-4719 (in California, bookstores only); Dist. by: New Leaf Distributing Co., 5425 Tulane Dr., SW, Atlanta, GA 30336-2323 (SAN 169-1449) Tel 404-691-6996; Toll free: 800-326-2665; Dist. by: Unique Bks., Inc., 4230 Grove Ave., Gurnee, IL 60031 (SAN 630-0472) Tel 708-623-9171; Dist. by: Quality Bks., Inc., 918 Sherwood Dr., Lake Bluff, IL 60044-2204 (SAN 169-2127) Tel 708-295-2010; Toll free: 800-323-4241 (libraries only); Dist. by: Upper Access, Inc., P.O. Box 457, Hinesburg, UT 05461 (SAN 667-1195); Toll free: 800-356-9315; Dist. by: Moving Bks., P.O. Box 20037, 948 S. Doris St., Seattle, WA 98102 (SAN 159-0685) Tel 206-762-1750; Dist. by: Inland Bk. Co., 140 Commerce St., East Haven, CT 06512 (SAN 200-4151) Tel 203-467-4257; Toll free: 800-243-0138.

Oceana Educ Comm, *(Oceana Educational Communications; 0-89976),* Div. of Oceana Pubns., Inc., 75 Main St., Dobbs Ferry, NY 10522 (SAN 221-9425) Tel 914-693-8100.

Oceanus, *(Oceanus Institute, Inc.; 0-915189),* Learning Pl., Manset, ME 04656 (SAN 289-7784) Tel 207-244-5015; Dist. by: Door Hse., HCR33-145, Manset, ME 04656 (SAN 200-9064) Tel 207-244-5015.

Ocelot Pr, *(Ocelot Pr.; 0-912434),* P.O. Box 504, Claremont, CA 91711 (SAN 203-7602) Tel 909-621-2200. Do not confuse with Ocelot Pr. in Antioch, CA.

Oddo, *(Oddo Publishing, Inc.; 0-87783),* Storybook Acres, Box 68, Fayetteville, GA 30214 (SAN 282-0757) Tel 404-461-7627.

Odyssey *Imprint of* **HarBrace**

Offset Hse, *(Offset Hse.),* P.O. Box 329, Essex, VT 05401-0329 (SAN 698-1496) Tel 802-878-4440; Dist. by: Creative Expressions, P.O. Box 456, Colchester, VT 05446 (SAN 200-5816).

OH Proficiency, *(Ohio Proficiency Test Review, Inc.;* 1-884183), 407 Meadow View Dr., P.O. Box 981, Powell, OH 43065 Tel 614-548-4128; Toll free: 800-225-7277.

Ohana Pr, *(Ohana Pr.; 0-9627275),* Div. of Loge International Corp., P.O. Box 88189, 2931 Poni Moi Rd., Honolulu, HI 96830-8189 Tel 808-922-5590.

O'Hara, *(O'Hara, J. Philip, Inc., Pubs.; 0-87955),* Subs. of Scroll Pr., Inc., ; c/o Scroll Pr., Inc., 2858 Valerie Ct., Merrick, NY 11566 (SAN 202-5868) Tel 516-379-4283. Do not confuse with Betsy O'Hara, San Francisco, CA.

Ohio St U Pr, *(Ohio State Univ. Pr.; 0-8142),* 1070 Carmack Rd., Rm. 180 Pressey Hall, Columbus, OH 43210-1002 (SAN 202-8158) Tel 614-292-6930; Toll free: 800-437-4439.

Ohio U Pr, *(Ohio Univ. Pr.; 0-8214),* Scott Quadrangle, Athens, OH 45701 (SAN 282-0773) Tel 614-593-1155; Orders to: Chicago Distribution Ctr., 11030 S. Langley Ave., Chicago, IL 60628 (SAN 244-8068) Tel 312-568-1550; Toll free: 800-621-2736; 800-621-8471 (credit & collections).

Okpaku Communications, *(Okpaku Communications Corp.; 0-89388),* Div. of Third Pr. Review of Bks. Co., 222 Forest Ave., New Rochelle, NY 10804 (SAN 202-5701) Tel 914-632-2355.

Old Amer Pr, *(Old American Pr.; 0-9622541),* 506 Joe Carrol St., Tahlequah, OK 74464 Tel 918-456-4849.

Old Ctry Bks, *(Old Country Bks., The; 0-9636006),* c/o Biddle Bks., 4919 Greencrest Rd., Baltimore, MD 21206 Tel 410-483-9090.

Old Earth Bks, *(Old Earth Bks.; 1-882968),* P.O. Box 19951, Baltimore, MD 21211-0951; 617 W. 33rd St., Baltimore, MD 21211-2702 Tel 410-889-4080.

Old El Toro Pr, *(Old El Toro Pr.; 1-881129),* 10950 S. Valley View Ave., Whittier, CA 90604 Tel 310-941-5059.

Old Fort Niagara Assn, *(Old Fort Niagara Assn., Inc.;* 0-941967), P.O. Box 169, Youngstown, NY 14174 (SAN 666-7783); Ft. Niagara State Pk., Youngstown, NY 14174 (SAN 666-7791) Tel 716-745-7611.

Old Harbor Pr, *(Old Harbor Pr.; 0-9615529; 1-881655),* P.O. Box 97, Sitka, AK 99835 (SAN 695-880X); 2222 Sawmill Creek Rd., Sitka, AK 99835 Tel 907-747-3584.

Old Rugged Cross, *(Old Rugged Cross Pr.; 1-882270),* 1160 Alpharetta St., Suite K, Roswell, GA 30075 Tel 404-518-1890.

Old Saltbox Pub Hse, *(Old Saltbox Publishing Hse., Inc.; 0-9626162),* 40 Felt St., Salem, MA 01970 (SAN 630-4583) Tel 508-741-3458.

Old Violin, *(Old Violin-Art Publishing; 0-918554),* Affil. of Hobby, Box 500, 225 S. Cooke St., Helena, MT 59624 (SAN 209-9756) Tel 406-442-8963.

Oldcastle, *(Oldcastle Publishing; 0-932529),* P.O. Box 1193, Escondido, CA 92033 (SAN 297-9039); 3415 Laredo Ln., Escondido, CA 92025 (SAN 297-9047) Tel 619-489-0336.

OLF Pub Co, *(OLF Publishing Co.; 0-9632356),* P.O. Box 3214, Thousand Oaks, CA 91359; 4031 Elkwood St., Newbury Park, CA 91320 Tel 805-499-7720.

Olive Brnch, *(Olive Branch Publishing Co.; 0-9635091),* 921 E. Eighth Ave., Broomfield, CO 80020 Tel 303-438-1299.

Olive Tree Concepts, *(Olive Tree Concepts, Inc.;* 0-9640887), 6719 Massachussetts Dr., Lantana, FL 33462 Tel 407-969-2564; Toll free: 800-362-6731.

Oliver Pr MN, *(Oliver Pr., Inc.; 1-881508),* 2709 Lyndale Ave., S., Minneapolis, MN 55408 Tel 612-871-9554.

Olympic Pub, *(Olympic Publishing, Inc.; 0-940828),* 7450 Oak Bay, Port Ludlow, WA 98365 (SAN 219-6417) Tel 206-437-2277.

OMF Bks, *(OMF Bks.; 0-85363),* Div. of Overseas Missionary Fellowship, 10 W. Dry Creek Cir., Littleton, CO 80122 (SAN 211-8351); Toll free: 800-422-5330.

Omni Arts, *(Omni Arts, Inc.; 0-942929),* P.O. Box 222, Stevensville, MD 21666 (SAN 667-8505); 845 Park Ave., Baltimore, MD 21201 (SAN 667-8513) Tel 410-837-1031; Box 5949, San Juan, PR 00906 (SAN 250-3565) Tel 809-723-9394.

Omni Hawthorne, *(Omni Pubns.; 0-88418),* 13801 S. Inglewood Ave., P.O. Box 216, Hawthorne, CA 90251 (SAN 202-1315) Tel 213-772-3920.

Omnigraphics Inc, *(Omnigraphics, Inc.; 1-55888;* 0-7808), Penobscot Bldg., Detroit, MI 48226 (SAN 249-2520) Tel 313-961-1340; Toll free: 800-234-1340.

Omniun, *(Omniun; 0-944204),* P.O. Box 5020, Kukuihaele, HI 96727 (SAN 243-1912); Main Government Rd., Waipio Valley, HI 96727 (SAN 243-1920) Tel 808-775-0207.

On-Line Adventures
See New Memories

One Ear Press
See In One EAR

One Hund Twenty Creat, *(120 Creative Corner;* 0-912773), P.O. Box 65, Circle Pines, MN 55014-0065 (SAN 283-1252) Tel 612-784-8375.

One Peaceful World, *(One Peaceful World Pr.; 0-9628528; 1-882984),* P.O. Box 10, Becket, MA 01223; 308 Leland Rd., Becket, MA 01223 Tel 413-623-2322.

One Ten Records, *(One Ten Records; 0-9605778),* 110 Chambers St., New York, NY 10007 (SAN 216-5066) Tel 212-964-2296.

One World Pub, *(One World Publishing; 0-916301),* P.O. Box 423, Notre Dame, IN 46556 (SAN 295-7590) Tel 219-272-2024. Do not confuse with One World Pubns., London, UK, distributed by Alpha Bk. Distributors, Inc., New York, NY, Myrtle Beach, SC, Fountain Valley, CA.

One World SC, *(One World Publishing; 0-9630314),* 3901 N. Kings Hwy., Suite 15, Myrtle Beach, SC 29577 Tel 803-626-8359. Do not confuse with One World Publishing in Notre Dame, IN, Fountain Valley, CA.

O'Neill Pr, *(O'Neill Pr.; 0-930970),* 305 Great Neck Rd., Waterford, CT 06385 (SAN 212-1239).

Onewrld Pubns, *(Oneworld Pubns.; 1-85168),* 42 Broadway, Rockport, MA 01966 Tel 508-546-1040; Dist. by: National Bk. Network, 4720A Boston Way, Lanham, MD 20706-4310 (SAN 630-0065) Tel 301-459-8696; Toll free: 800-462-6420. U.K. Address: 185 Banbury Rd., Oxford, 0X2 7AR, UK.

Onyx *Imprint of* **NAL-Dutton**

OP Inc, *(Organization Plus, Inc.; 0-9623354),* 8203 Gwinett Rd., Richmond, VA 23286-4335 Tel 804-741-4284.

OPC, *(Our Publishing Co., Inc.; 0-9603632),* 38764 N. Gratton Rd., Lake Villa, IL 60046 (SAN 213-7852) Tel 708-356-5944.

Open Adoption, *(Open Adoption Pr.; 0-9640009),* P.O. Box 253, Orinda, CA 94563; 14 Lucille Way, Orinda, CA 94563 Tel 510-254-5497.

Open Books, *(Open Bks.; 0-931416),* 1631 Grant St., Berkeley, CA 94703 (SAN 211-7517).

Open Hand, *(Open Hand Publishing, Inc.; 0-940880),* P.O. Box 22048, Seattle, WA 98122 (SAN 219-6174) Tel 206-323-2187; Dist. by: Subterranean Co., P.O. Box 160, 265 South Fifth St., Monroe, OR 97456 (SAN 169-7102) Tel 503-847-5274; Toll free: 800-274-7826.

Open Horizons, *(Open Horizons Publishing Co.;* 0-912411), P.O. Box 205, Fairfield, IA 52556-0205 (SAN 265-170X) Tel 515-472-6130; Toll free: 800-796-6130; Orders to: Login Pubs. Consortium, 1436 W. Randolph, 2nd Flr., Chicago, IL 60607 (SAN 630-5733) Tel 312-733-8228; Toll free: 800-626-4330.

Open My World, *(Open My World Publishing;* 0-941996), P.O. Box 15011, San Diego, CA 92175 (SAN 238-602X) Tel 619-588-5389; Dist. by: Econo-Clad Bks., P.O. Box 1777, Topeka, KS 66601 (SAN 169-2763) Tel 913-233-4252; Toll free: 800-255-3502; Dist. by: Perma Bound Bks., 617 E. Vandalia Rd., Jacksonville, IL 62650 (SAN 169-202X) Tel 217-243-5451; Toll free: 800-637-6581; Dist. by: Wieser Educational, Inc., 30085 Comercio, Santa Margarita, CA 92688 (SAN 630-7361) Tel 714-858-4920.

Opening Doors, *(Opening Doors Bks.; 1-877829),* 14 School St., Bristol, VT 05443 Tel 802-897-7022.

Opie Pub, *(Opie Publishing; 0-9623964),* 15 Cedar St., Binghampton, NY 13905 Tel 607-722-8844.

Opportunities Learn, *(Opportunities for Learning, Inc.; 0-86703; 1-55646),* Div. of FSC Educational, Inc., P.O. Box 8103, Mansfield, OH 44901 (SAN 216-6895); Toll free: 800-243-7116; 941 Hickory Ln., Mansfield, OH 44901 Tel 419-589-1760. *Imprints:* Career Aids (Career Aids).

Optext, *(Optext; 0-9611266),* Div. of Optext Design Typography, 405 N. Wabash, Chicago, IL 60611-3517 (SAN 282-9843) Tel 312-321-1211; Dist. by: Bookpeople, 7900 Edgewater Dr., Oakland, CA 94621 (SAN 168-9517) Tel 510-632-4700; Toll free: 800-999-4650; Dist. by: New Leaf Distributing Co., 5425 Tulane Dr., SW, Atlanta, GA 30336-2323 (SAN 169-1449) Tel 404-691-6996; Toll free: 800-326-2665; Dist. by: The Distributors, 702 S. Michigan, South Bend, IN 46601 (SAN 169-2488) Tel 219-232-8500; Toll free: 800-348-5200 (except Indiana); Dist. by: Ingram Bk. Co., 1 Ingram Blvd., La Vergne, TN 37086-1986 (SAN 169-7978) Tel 615-793-5000; Toll free: 800-937-8000 (orders only, all warehouses); Dist. by: Baker & Taylor Bks., Somerville Service Ctr., 50 Kirby Ave., Somerville, NJ 08876-0734 (SAN 169-4901) Tel 908-722-8000; Toll free: 800-775-1500 (customer service); Dist. by: Baker & Taylor Bks., Momence Service Ctr., 501 S. Gladiolus St., Momence, IL 60954-2444 (SAN 169-2100) Tel 815-472-2444; Toll free: 800-775-2300 (customer service); Dist. by: Baker & Taylor Bks., Commerce Service Ctr., 251 Mt. Olive Church Rd., Commerce, GA 30599-9988 (SAN 169-1503) Tel 706-335-5000; Toll free: 800-775-1200 (customer service); Dist. by: Baker & Taylor Bks., Reno Service Ctr., 380 Edison Way, Reno, NV 89564 (SAN 169-4464) Tel 702-858-6700; Toll free: 800-775-1700 (customer service); Dist. by: Inland Bk. Co., 140 Commerce St., East Haven, CT 06152 (SAN 200-4151) Tel 203-467-4257; Toll free: 800-243-0138.

Optimalearning, *(Optimalearning Co.; 1-878245),* 885 Olive Ave., Suite A, Novato, CA 94945-2455 Tel 415-898-0013; Toll free: 800-672-1717.

Optimum Res Inc, *(Optimum Resource, Inc.; 0-911787; 1-55913),* 5 Hiltech Ln., Hilton Head, SC 29926 (SAN 264-2743) Tel 803-689-8000; Toll free: 800-327-1473.

OR Catholic, *(Oregon Catholic Pr.; 0-915531),* 5536 NE Hassalo, Portland, OR 97213 (SAN 291-316X) Tel 503-281-1191; Toll free: 800-548-8749 (orders).

OR Students Writing, *(Oregon Students Writing & Art Foundation; 0-9616058),* P.O. Box 2100, Portland, OR 97208-2100 (SAN 698-0546) Tel 503-280-6333; 1826 SE 54th Ave., Portland, OR 97206 (SAN 698-2468) Tel 503-232-7737.

Orchard Bks Watts, *(Orchard Bks.; 0-531),* Div. of Franklin Watts, Inc., 95 Madison Ave., 7th Flr., New York, NY 10016 (SAN 243-2595) Tel 212-686-7070; Toll free: 800-672-6672. Do not confuse with companies with the same name in Chicago, IL, Burbank Rancho, CA.

Orchard Hse MA, *(Orchard Hse., Inc.; 0-933510; 1-878172),* P.O. Box 15899, New Orleans, LA 70175-5899 (SAN 285-0796) Tel 504-866-8658; Toll free: 800-321-9479.

Oreg St U Pr, *(Oregon State Univ. Pr.; 0-87071),* Oregon State Univ., 101 Waldo Hall, Corvallis, OR 97331 (SAN 202-8328) Tel 503-737-3166.

Oregon Hist, *(Oregon Historical Society Pr.; 0-87595),* 1200 SW Park Ave., Portland, OR 97205-2483 (SAN 202-8301) Tel 503-222-1741.

Oregon Info, *(Oregon Information; 0-9630050),* P.O. Box 3211, Portland, OR 97208 Tel 503-624-9469.

Oriel Pr, *(Oriel Pr.; 0-938628),* 2020 SW Kanan, Portland, OR 97201 (SAN 282-0870) Tel 503-245-6696; Dist. by: Children's Small Pr. Collection, 716 N. Fourth Ave., Ann Arbor, MI 48104 (SAN 200-514X) Tel 313-668-8056; Toll free: 800-221-8056 (orders only).

Oriental Bk Store, *(Oriental Bk. Store, The; 0-89986),* 1713 E. Colorado Blvd., Pasadena, CA 91106 (SAN 285-0818) Tel 818-577-2413. Do not confuse with Orient Bk. Distributors in Livingston, NJ.

Orig Ellsworth, *(Originals by Ellsworth E.-Moods in Wire; 0-9640483),* P.O. Box 2011, Manassas, VA 22110; 9706 Dublin Dr., Manassas, VA 22110 Tel 703-369-5589.

Origami Intl, *(Origami International, Ltd.; 1-879610),* 1071 Fairfield Ave., Suite 57, Eugene, OR 97402 Tel 503-688-3956.

Origin Syst, *(Origin Systems, Inc.; 0-929373),* 12940 Research Blvd., Austin, TX 78750 (SAN 655-7457) Tel 512-335-5200.

Orinda Art Coun, *(Orinda Art Council; 0-9613069),* P.O. Box 121, Orinda, CA 94563 (SAN 294-6408) Tel 510-254-6744.

Oryx Pr, *(Oryx Pr.; 0-912700; 0-89774; 1-57356),* 4041 N. Central Ave., 7th Flr., Phoenix, AZ 85012-3397 (SAN 220-0201) Tel 602-265-2651; Toll free: 800-279-6799.

Osborne Bks, *(Osborne Bks.; 0-9632817),* P.O. Box 3126, Beaumont, CA 92223; 656 E. Barbour Dr., Banning, CA 92220 Tel 909-922-9167.

Other Eye, *(Other Eye Exercises; 0-926178),* P.O. Box 617, Kirkland, WA 98083; 12242 NE 70th, Kirkland, WA 98033 Tel 206-822-9156.

Otter Creek, *(Otter Creek Publishing Co.; 1-885744),* R.R. 1, Box 327, Mulvane, KS 67110 Tel 316-777-9099.

Oughten Hse, *(Oughten Hse. Pubns.; 1-880666),* Orders to: P.O. Box 2008, Livermore, CA 94550 (SAN 169-1449) Tel 510-447-2332.

OUP, *(Oxford Univ. Pr., Inc.; 0-19; 0-917000; 0-904147; 0-947946; 1-85221),* 200 Madison Ave., New York, NY 10016 (SAN 202-5884) Tel 212-679-7300; Toll free: 800-334-4249; Orders to: 2001 Evans Rd., Cary, NC 27513 (SAN 202-5892) Tel 919-677-0977; Toll free: 800-451-7556.

Our Child Pr, *(Our Child Pr.; 0-9611872),* 800 Maple Glen Ln., Wayne, PA 19087 (SAN 682-272X) Tel 610-964-0606.

Our Mascot, *(Our Mascot Pr.; 1-882466),* P.O. Box 904, Tallahassee, FL 32302-0904; 1215 Jeffery Rd., Tallahassee, FL 32312 Tel 904-847-3087.

Our Sunday Visitor, *(Our Sunday Visitor, Publishing Div.; 0-87973),* 200 Noll Plaza, Huntington, IN 46750 (SAN 202-8344) Tel 219-356-8400; Toll free: 800-348-2440.

Outdoor Bks, *(Outdoor Bks., Nature Series, Inc.;* 0-942806), c/o Romero, 100 Cross Keys Rd., Baltimore, MD 21210-1551.

Outdoor Pict, *(Outdoor Pictures; 0-911080),* P.O. Box 277, Anacortes, WA 98221 (SAN 203-7815) Tel 206-679-4837.

Outlet Bk Co
See Random Hse Value

Outrider Pr, *(Outrider Pr.; 0-9621039),* 1004 E. Steger Rd., Suite C3, Crete, IL 60417-1362 (SAN 250-4057) Tel 708-672-6630.

Outside Wrld, *(Outside World; 0-9640381),* N5127 1180th St., Prescott, WI 54721 Tel 715-262-3698; Toll free: 800-376-7873; Dist. by: Bookmen, Inc., 525 N. Third St., Minneapolis, MN 55401 (SAN 169-409X) Tel 612-341-3333; Toll free: 800-328-8411 (customer service).

Overcomer Pr, *(Overcomer Pr., Inc.; 0-942504),* Editorial Vencedor, 310 W. Main St., P.O. Box 248, Owosso, MI 48867 (SAN 238-1834) Tel 517-725-7888.

Overlook Pr, *(Overlook Pr.; 0-87951),* 149 Wooster St., 4th Flr., New York, NY 10012 (SAN 202-8360) Tel 212-477-7162; Orders to: 2568 Rte. 212, Woodstock, NY 12498 (SAN 663-6527); Dist. by: Viking Penguin, Inc., 375 Hudson St., New York, NY 10014-3657 Tel 212-366-2000; Toll free: 800-526-0275.

Owl *Imprint of* **H Holt & Co**

Owl Pub CA, *(Owl Publishing; 0-9626686),* 1450 Harbor Island Dr., San Diego, CA 92101 Tel 619-491-1665.

Owlet BYR *Imprint of* **H Holt & Co**

Ox Bow, *(Ox Bow Pr.; 0-918024; 1-881987),* P.O. Box 4045, Woodbridge, CT 06525 (SAN 210-2501) Tel 203-387-5900.

Oxford U Pr
See OUP

Oxner Inst, *(Oxner Institute; 0-9623133),* 1917 Pinehurst Ave., Saint Paul, MN 55116 Tel 612-698-1038.

Oyster River Pr, *(Oyster River Pr.; 0-9617481; 1-882291),* 20 Riverview Rd., Durham, NH 03824-3313 (SAN 664-2128) Tel 603-868-5006.

Ozark Pub, *(Ozark Publishing; 1-56763),* P.O. Box 489, Mineral Wells, TX 76068-0489; Toll free: 800-321-5671.

P A Bell Enterps, *(Bell, P. A., Enterprises; 0-9621056),* 4201 Palmetto Way, San Diego, CA 92103 (SAN 250-586X) Tel 619-291-1636.

P A Sisson, *(Sisson, Pamla A.; 0-9638328),* 17702 69th Pl., W., Edmonds, WA 98026 Tel 206-745-0070.

P Bedrick Bks, *(Bedrick, Peter, Bks.; 0-911745;* 0-87226), 2112 Broadway, Rm. 318, New York, NY 10023 (SAN 263-9335) Tel 212-496-0751; Dist. by: Publishers Group West, 4065 Hollis St., Emeryville, CA 94608 (SAN 202-8522) Tel 510-658-3453; Toll free: 800-788-3123. *Imprints:* Bedrick Blackie (Bedrick/Blackie).

P D Maloney, *(Maloney, P. Dennis; 0-940305),* 405 W. 36th St., Suite 200, Anchorage, AK 99503 (SAN 664-242X) Tel 907-561-4603.

P Depke Bks, *(Pat Depke Bks.; 1-884555),* Div. of Craft World International, Inc., P.O. Box 779, New Windsor, MD 21776-0779; Toll free: 800-759-5577; 1301 Avondale Rd., New Windsor, MD 21776 Tel 410-876-1700.

P F Skolout, *(Skolout, Patricia Farris; 0-9625712),* 3122 Spring Meadow Dr., Colorado Springs, CO 80906 Tel 719-576-0318.

P Goodrich, *(Goodrich/Patricia; 0-9625348),* P.O. Box 190, Richlandtown, PA 18955 Tel 215-538-0268.

P-H, *(Prentice Hall; 0-13),* Div. of Simon & Schuster, Inc., 113 Sylvan Ave., Rte. 9W, Englewood Cliffs, NJ 07632 (SAN 200-2175) Tel 201-592-2000; Toll free: 800-922-0579; Orders to: Paramount Publishing, 200 Old Tappan Rd., Old Tappan, NJ 07675 (SAN 200-2442) Tel 201-767-5937. *Imprints:* Busn (Business & Professional Division); Parker Publishing Co (Parker Publishing Company); Reston (Reston).

P-H Gen Ref & Trav, *(Prentice Hall General Reference & Travel; 0-13),* Div. of Simon & Schuster, Inc., 15 Columbus Cir., New York, NY 10023 (SAN 205-2725) Tel 212-373-8500; Toll free: 800-223-2348; Orders to: Paramount Publishing, 200 Old Tappan Rd., Old Tappan, NJ 07675 (SAN 200-2442) Tel 201-767-5937. *Imprints:* Arco Test (Arco Test Preparation & Career Guides); B Crocker Ckbks (Crocker, Betty, Cookbooks); Harraps (Harrap's Dictionaries); Websters New Wrld (Webster's New World).

P Hunt, *(Hunt, Paul),* P.O. Box 10907, Burbank, CA 91510 (SAN 281-3777) Tel 818-845-0460.

P J Neuberger, *(Neuberger, Phyllis J.; 0-9610050),* 1361 S. Ocean Blvd. A, No. 310, Pompano Beach, FL 33062-7159 (SAN 262-9607) Tel 305-785-7149; c/o Ten Plus, Inc., Thomas Graphics, Inc., 547 S. Clark St., Chicago, IL 60605 (SAN 262-9615) Tel 312-922-1301.

P J Twohy, *(Twohy, Patrick J.; 0-9623418),* c/o University Press, E. 28 Sharp Ave., Spokane, WA 99202 Tel 509-326-2133.

P Lang Pubs, *(Lang, Peter, Publishing, Inc.; 0-8204;* 3-631), Subs. of Verlag Peter Lang AG (SZ), 62 W. 45th St., 4th Flr., New York, NY 10036-4202 (SAN 241-5534) Tel 212-764-1471; Toll free: 800-770-5264 (outside NY); 516 N. Charles St., Suite 210, Baltimore, MD 21202 (SAN 241-7456) Tel 410-385-5362.

P M O'Brien, *(O'Brien, P. M.; 0-9620540),* 5320 53rd Ave. E., Lot S32, Bradenton, FL 34203-5638 (SAN 248-8973).

P Q Pubns, *(P.Q. Pubns.; 0-9632717),* P.O. Box 465, Canon City, CO 81215-0465; 1129 1/2 Macon, Canon City, CO 81215-0465 Tel 719-275-6752.

P T Ryan, *(Ryan, Perry T.; 0-9625504),* Atty. at Law, Rte. 3, Breckwood, Hardinsburg, KY 40143 Tel 502-756-2330.

PA Coun Churches, *(Pennsylvania Council of Churches;* 0-9618164), 900 S. Arlington Ave., Rm. 100, Harrisburg, PA 17109-5089 (SAN 666-7341) Tel 717-545-4761.

PAAS Pr, *(PAAS Pr.; 1-883588),* Div. of Pannell Assocs., P.O. Box 3019, Framingham, MA 01701-0601.

Pac Asia Pr, *(Pacific Asia Pr.; 1-879600),* Div. of GreenShower Corp., 10937 Klingerman St., South El Monte, CA 91733 Tel 818-575-1000.

Pac Transcript, *(Pacific Transcriptions; 0-933391),* P.O. Box 526, Mendocino, CA 95460 (SAN 691-5043) Tel 707-937-4801.

Pace Prods, *(Pace Products, Inc.; 1-880592),* 150 Semoran Commerce Pl., Apopka, FL 32703 Tel 407-880-2422; Toll free: 800-541-7670.

Pacif NW Natl Pks
See NW Interpretive

Pacific Bks, *(Pacific Bks., Pubs.; 0-87015),* P.O. Box 558, Palo Alto, CA 94302-0558 (SAN 202-8468) Tel 415-965-1980.

Pacific Greetings, *(Pacific Greetings; 0-9633493),* P.O. Box 428, Kamuela, HI 96743 Tel 808-885-4439.

Pacific Herit, *(Pacific Heritage Bks.; 0-9635906),* P.O. Box 3967, Palos Verdes, CA 90274-9547; 28928 Crestridge Rd., Rancho Palos Verdes, CA 90274 Tel 310-541-8818; Dist. by: Quality Bks., Inc., 918 Sherwood Dr., Lake Bluff, IL 60044-2204 (SAN 169-2127) Tel 708-295-2010; Toll free: 800-323-4241 (libraries only); Dist. by: Baker & Taylor Bks., 652 E. Main St., P.O. Box 6920, Bridgewater, NJ 08807-0920 Tel 908-218-0400; Toll free: 800-323-4241 (libraries only); Dist. by: The Distributors, 702 S. Michigan, South Bend, IN 46601 (SAN 169-2488) Tel 219-232-8500; Toll free: 800-348-5200 (except Indiana); Dist. by: Heritage West Bks.,, 306 Regent Ct., Stockton, CA 95204 Tel 209-464-8818; Toll free: 800-323-4241 (libraries only).

Pacific Pr Pub Assn, *(Pacific Pr. Publishing Assn.;* 0-8163), P.O. Box 7000, Boise, ID 83707-1000 (SAN 202-8409) Tel 208-465-2500; Toll free: 800-447-7377.

Pacific Sci Ctr, *(Pacific Science Ctr.; 0-935051),* 200 Second Ave., N, Seattle, WA 98109 (SAN 694-5244) Tel 206-443-2001.

Pacific Shoreline, *(Pacific Shoreline Pr.; 0-932967),* P.O. Box 217, Temple City, CA 91780 (SAN 689-9897) Tel 818-287-4767.

Pacific View Pr, *(Pacific View Pr.; 1-881896),* P.O. Box 2657, Berkeley, CA 94702 Tel 510-849-4213.

Pacifica Pr, *(Pacifica Pr.; 0-935553),* Div. of Words to Go, Inc., 1149 Grand Teton Dr., Pacifica, CA 94044 Tel 415-355-6678; Dist. by: Words To Go, Inc., 1149 Grand Teton Dr., Pacifica, CA 94044 (SAN 695-8958) Tel 415-355-6678.

Padakami Pr, *(Padakami Pr.; 0-9628914),* 23 Dana St., Forty-Fort, Kingston, PA 18704 Tel 717-287-3668.

Padaran Pubns, *(Padaran Pubns.; 1-877945),* 3370 Phonetia Dr., Deltona, FL 32728 Tel 407-321-9610.

Padre Pio Pubs, *(Padre Pio Pubs.; 0-9615916),* P.O. Box 468, Patagonia, AZ 85624 (SAN 696-8864) Tel 602-394-2018; 223 Duquesne Ave., Patagonia, AZ 85624 (SAN 696-8872).

Padre Prods, *(Padre Productions; 0-914598),* P.O. Box 840, Arroyo Grande, CA 93420 (SAN 202-8484) Tel 805-473-1947; Dist. by: BookLink Distributors, P.O. Box 840, 1715 Bee Canyon Rd., Arroyo Grande, CA 93421-0840 (SAN 159-0782) Tel 805-473-1947.

Page One Communs, *(Page One Communications; 0-9640336),* 531 E. 117th St., Cleveland, OH 44108 Tel 216-268-3119.

Paideia MA, *(Paideia Pubs.; 0-913993),* P.O. Box 343, Ashfield, MA 01330 (SAN 287-7511) Tel 413-628-3838.

Paisley Bks, *(Paisley Bks.; 0-926611),* 510 N. Tenth St., Belen, NM 87002 Tel 505-864-7236.

Paisley Pub, *(Paisley Publishing; 0-922127),* P.O. Box 201853, Anchorage, AK 99520-1853 (SAN 251-0847) Tel 907-272-6604; Dist. by: BookWorld Distribution Services, Inc., 1933 Whitfield Pk. Loop, Sarasota, FL 34243 (SAN 173-0568) Tel 813-758-8094; Toll free: 800-444-2524 (orders only); Dist. by: Pacific Pipeline, Inc., 8030 S. 228th St., Kent, WA 98032-2900 (SAN 208-2128) Tel 206-872-5523; Toll free: 800-444-7323 (customer service); 800-677-2222 (orders); Dist. by: Educational Bk. Distributors, P.O. Box 2510, Novato, CA 94948 (SAN 158-2259) Tel 415-883-3530. Do not confuse with Paisley Publishing, San Antonio, TX.

Pajari Pr, *(Pajari Pr.; 0-9624315),* 11104 Snow Heights Blvd., NE, Albuquerque, NM 87112 Tel 505-299-7733.

Palace Pub, *(Palace Publishing; 0-932215),* R.D. 1, Box 320, Moundsville, WV 26041 (SAN 686-5763) Tel 304-845-9370; Dist. by: Baker & Taylor Bks., Momence Service Ctr., 501 S. Gladiolus St., Momence, IL 60954-2444 (SAN 169-2100) Tel 815-472-2444; Toll free: 800-775-2300 (customer service); Dist. by: New Leaf Distributing Co., 5425 Tulane Dr., SW, Atlanta, GA 30336-2323 (SAN 169-1449) Tel 404-691-6996; Toll free: 800-326-2665.

Palisades Prodns, *(Palisades Productions, Inc.; 1-878890),* 29 Chesapeake Ave., Lake Hiawatha, NJ 07034 Tel 201-825-8805.

Palladium Bks, *(Palladium Bks., Inc.; 0-916211),* 12455 Universal Dr., Taylor, MI 48180-4077 (SAN 294-9504) Tel 313-946-2900.

Pallas Athena, *(Pallas Athena Pr.; 0-9636217),* P.O. Box 326, Fairfield, CA 94533; 1043 Fennie Ct., Suisun City, CA 94585 Tel 707-427-3950.

Palm Springs Pub, *(Palm Springs Publishing; 0-914445),* P.O. Box 9314, Palm Springs, CA 92263 (SAN 289-663X) Tel 619-323-9968.

Palm Tree Ent, *(Palm Tree Enterprises; 0-9618755),* 1514 Roosevelt Ave., Landover, MD 20785 (SAN 668-761X) Tel 301-322-5510.

Pams Unique, *(Pam's Unique Technique; 0-9638310),* 1601 Kesteven Rd., Winston-Salem, NC 27127 Tel 910-785-2668.

Pan-Am Publishing Co, *(Pan-American Publishing Co.; 0-932906),* P.O. Box 1505, Las Vegas, NM 87701 (SAN 212-5366).

Pan Asian Pubns, *(Pan Asia Pubns. (USA), Inc.; 1-57227),* 29564 Union City Blvd., Union City, CA 94587 (SAN 630-9704) Tel 510-475-1185; Toll free: 800-853-2742.

P&M Bear Pubns, *(P&M Bear Pubns.; 0-9619675),* 1025 E. Yoke St., Indianapolis, IN 46203 (SAN 245-856X) Tel 317-782-8274.

Pando Pubns, *(Pando Pubns.; 0-944705),* 5396 Laurie Ln., Memphis, TN 38120-2455 (SAN 244-9048) Tel 404-587-3363.

Pandoras Treasures, *(Pandora's Treasures; 0-9605236),* 1609 Eastover Terr., Boise, ID 83706 (SAN 282-1036) Tel 208-342-4002.

Pangaea Pr, *(Pangaea Pr.; 0-9625534),* Div. of Pangaea Group, Inc., 483 S. Kirkwood Rd., Suite 183, Saint Louis, MO 63122 Tel 314-821-3871.

Pantheon, *(Pantheon Bks.; 0-394; 0-679),* Div. of Random Hse., Inc., 201 E. 50th St., New York, NY 10022 (SAN 202-862X) Tel 212-572-2838; Toll free: 800-726-0600 (customer service); Orders to: Random Hse., Inc., 400 Hahn Rd., Westminster, MD 21157 (SAN 202-5515) Tel 410-848-1900; Toll free: 800-733-3000 (orders).

Paper Bag, *(Paper Bag Players; 0-9606662),* 50 Riverside Dr., New York, NY 10024 (SAN 212-9566); Orders to: Walter Baker Co., 100 Chauncey St., Boston, MA 02111 (SAN 662-1074); Orders to: Eeyore Bookstore, 82nd & Madison Ave., New York, NY 10028 (SAN 662-1082).

Paper Hat *Imprint of* **Start Reading**

Paper Memories, *(Paper Memories; 0-9626165),* P.O. Box 234, Glen Echo, MD 20812; 5308 Portsmouth Rd., Bethesda, MD 20816 Tel 301-229-6834.

Paper Press, *(Paper Pr.; 0-9618419),* 417 Kirby Ct., Walnut Creek, CA 94598-3907 (SAN 667-6367) Tel 510-943-1232.

Paper Tiger Pap, *(Paper Tiger Paperbacks, Inc.; 0-933334),* 1512 NW Seventh Pl., Gainesville, FL 32603 (SAN 212-5374) Tel 904-371-7771; Dist. by: Hippocrene Bks., Inc., 171 Madison Ave., New York, NY 10016 (SAN 213-2060) Tel 212-685-4371.

Papillon Pr, *(Papillon Pr.; 0-9608826),* 1232 Vallecito Rd., Carpinteria, CA 93013 (SAN 213-1447) Tel 805-684-5038. Do not confuse with companies with the same name in Saint Helena, CA, Bothell, WA.

Papyrus Pubs, *(Papyrus Pubs.; 0-943698),* P.O. Box 466, Yonkers, NY 10704 (SAN 238-079X) Tel 914-664-0840.

Parable Pr, *(Parable Pr.; 0-917250),* P.O. Box 372, Carlisle, MA 01741-0372 (SAN 208-4449).

Parable Pub, *(Parable Publishing Hse.; 0-9624067),* R.D. 1, Box 1281, Charlotte, VT 05445; Mount Philo Rd., Charlotte, VT 05445 Tel 802-425-2155.

Parabola Bks, *(Parabola Bks.; 0-930407),* 656 Broadway, New York, NY 10012-2317 (SAN 219-5763) Tel 212-505-6200; Dist. by: Publisher Resources, Inc., 1224 Heil Quaker Blvd., P.O. Box 7001, La Vergne, TN 37086-7001 (SAN 630-5431) Tel 615-793-5090; Toll free: 800-937-5557.

Parabola Mag
See Parabola Bks

Paradise Cay Pubns, *(Paradise Cay Pubns.; 0-939837),* P.O. Box 1351, Middletown, CA 95461 (SAN 663-690X) Tel 707-987-3971.

Paradon Pub Co, *(Paradon Publishing Co.; 0-936750),* 2920 Dean Pkwy., Minneapolis, MN 55416 (SAN 222-1977) Tel 612-929-0303.

Paradon Pubng, *(Paradon Publishing Co.; 1-885297),* P.O. Box 2006, Woodinville, WA 98072-2006 (SAN 298-2498); 19119 N. Creek Pkwy., Suite 203, Bothell, WA 98011 Tel 206-823-4056. Do not confuse with Paradon Publishing Co. in Minneapolis, MN.

Paramount TX, *(Paramount Publishing; 0-942376),* P.O. Box 3730, Amarillo, TX 79116-3730 (SAN 238-1028) Tel 806-355-1040.

Parapan, *(Parapan; 0-9622764),* 1209 Parkwood Dr., Fort Collins, CO 80525 Tel 303-482-9303.

Parchment Pr, *(Parchment Pr.; 0-88428),* 1136 Lipscomb Dr., Nashville, TN 37204 (SAN 202-8670) Tel 615-292-6335; Toll free: 800-727-6335. Do not confuse with companies with the same name in Washington, DC, Parchment, MI, Ogden, UT.

Parent-Child Pr, *(Parent-Child Pr.; 0-9601016; 0-939195),* P.O. Box 675, Hollidaysburg, PA 16648 (SAN 208-4333); 129 Summit Dr., Hollidaysburg, PA 16648 (SAN 662-7331) Tel 814-696-7512.

Parent Ed, *(Parent Ed Resources; 1-879888),* 752 18th St., Santa Monica, CA 90402 Tel 310-458-9758.

Parent Track, *(Parent Track Pubns., Inc.; 1-883497),* 3210 Commander Rd., Carrollton, TX 75006 Tel 214-269-2160.

Parenting Pr, *(Parenting Pr., Inc.; 0-9602862; 0-943990; 1-884734),* P.O. Box 75267, Seattle, WA 98125 (SAN 215-6938); Toll free: 800-992-6657; 11065 Fifth Ave. NE, Suite F, Seattle, WA 98125 (SAN 699-5500) Tel 206-364-2900.

Parents, *(Parents Magazine Pr.; 0-8193),* Div. of Gruner & Jahr, USA, Publishing, 685 Third Ave., New York, NY 10017 (SAN 202-8697) Tel 212-878-8700; Dist. by: The Putnam Publishing Group, 200 Madison Ave., New York, NY 10016 (SAN 202-5531) Tel 212-951-8400; Toll free: 800-631-8571.

Park Pr
See Solace Pub

Park Pub Co, *(Park Publishing Co.; 0-9624004),* 8010 E. McDowell Rd., No. 209, Scottsdale, AZ 85257-3870 Tel 602-946-8787. Do not confuse with Park Publishing Co. in San Antonio, TX.

Parker Dstb, *(Parker Distributing; 1-878406),* 11844 N. Delbert, Parker, CO 80134 Tel 303-841-2607.

Parker Init Pubns, *(Parker Initiatives Pubns.; 1-880997),* Div. of Professional Images, P.O. Box 40206, Saint Paul, MN 55104; 405 Western Ave., N., Saint Paul, MN 55103 Tel 612-293-1462.

Parker Pub IL, *(Parker Publishing; 1-882286),* P.O. Box 386, Crystal Lake, IL 60039-0386; 24867 N. Holly Dr., Cary, IL 60013 Tel 708-639-5402.

Parker Publishing Co *Imprint of* **P-H**

Parkside Pubn
See Parkside Pubns

Parkside Pubns, *(Parkside Pubns., Inc.; 0-9618379),* P.O. Box 66, Hwy. 18, Davis, SD 57021 (SAN 667-6618) Tel 605-238-5704; Dist. by: J. R . Pub. Services, Inc., 4516 76th St., Des Moines, IA 50322 (SAN 200-4313). Do not confuse with Parkside Pubns., Seattle, WA.

Parkwest Pubns, *(Parkwest Pubns., Inc.; 0-88186),* 451 Communipaw Ave., Jersey City, NJ 07304 (SAN 264-6846) Tel 201-432-3257. *Imprints:* Brit Mus-Parkwest (British Museum/Parkwest); BBC-Parkwest (B B C/Parkwest); Robson-Parkwest (Robson/Parkwest).

Parmly Lib, *(Parmly Billings Library; 0-9613224),* 510 N. Broadway, Billings, MT 59101 (SAN 295-1347) Tel 406-657-8294.

Parnassus Imprints, *(Parnassus Imprints; 0-940160),* P.O. Box 1036, 210 Main St., East Orleans, MA 02643 (SAN 217-0809) Tel 508-255-2932.

Parnell Pub, *(Parnell Publishing; 0-940649),* P.O. Box 16432, Phoenix, AZ 85011 (SAN 664-8509); Toll free: 800-545-2778; 1034 E. Whitton, Phoenix, AZ 85014 (SAN 664-8517) Tel 602-279-2358.

Partnership Foundation, *(Partnership Foundation, The; 0-934538),* C/O Capon Springs & Farms, Capon Springs, WV 26823 (SAN 220-9918).

Pascal Pubs, *(Pascal Pubs.; 0-938836),* 21 Sunnyside Ave., Wellesley, MA 02181 (SAN 215-3319).

PASE Pubns, *(PASE Pubns.; 0-945661),* Div. of Ace Publishing, 161 S. Lincolnway, North Aurora, IL 60542 (SAN 247-3518) Tel 312-844-9600.

Passport Bks *Imprint of* **NTC Pub Grp**

Passport Coloring, *(Passport Coloring Bks.; 0-9641328),* 1046 S. Plymouth Ct., Chicago, IL 60605 Tel 312-939-7271.

Pastel Pubns, *(Pastel Pubns.; 0-925737),* 3202 E. Presidio Rd., Phoenix, AZ 85032; 3131 E. Thunderbird Rd., No. 8-123, Phoenix, AZ 80532 Tel 602-971-9058.

Pat G Johnson
See Walpa Pub

Patch As Patch, *(Patch As Patch Can; 0-9601896),* P.O. Box 843, Port Washington, NY 11050 (SAN 239-8575); 85 Highland Rd., Glen Cove, NY 11542 (SAN 241-8169) Tel 516-671-7342.

Path-Coll Afford Prod, *(Pathfinders/College Affordability Productions, Inc.; 0-9629535),* 6047 N. Ninth Ave., Phoenix, AZ 85013-1407 Tel 602-246-8761.

Pathway Pr, *(Pathway Pr.; 0-87148),* Div. of Church of God Publishing Hse., 1080 Montgomery Ave., Cleveland, TN 37311 (SAN 202-8727) Tel 615-476-4512; Toll free: 800-251-7216 (music only); 800-553-8506 (trade only); Orders to: P.O. Box 2250, Cleveland, TN 37320-2250 (SAN 665-7567). Do not confuse with companies of the same name in Birmingham, AL, San Rafael, CA.

Pathwys Pr CA, *(Pathways Pr.; 0-9605022),* P.O. Box 60196-A, Palo Alto, CA 94306 (SAN 283-4367) Tel 415-961-7794; Dist. by: Bookpeople, 7900 Edgewater Dr., Oakland, CA 94621 (SAN 168-9517) Tel 510-632-4700; Toll free: 800-999-4650; Dist. by: New Leaf Distributing Co., 5425 Tulane Dr., SW, Atlanta, GA 30336-2323 (SAN 169-1449) Tel 404-691-6996; Toll free: 800-326-2665. Do not confuse with Pathways Pr., El Cajon, CA.

Patio Pubns, *(Patio Pubns.; 0-9696040),* 850 Woodhollow Ln., Buffalo Grove, IL 60090 (SAN 216-9223) Tel 312-259-8500.

Patrice Pr, *(Patrice Pr.; 0-935284; 1-880397),* Box 85639, Tucson, AZ 85754-5639 (SAN 203-1019) Tel 602-743-9842; Toll free: 800-367-9242.

Patricks Pr, *(Patrick's Pr.; 0-9609412; 0-944322),* P.O. Box 5189, Columbus, GA 31906 (SAN 274-466X); Toll free: 800-654-1052; 2210 Wynnton Rd., Suite 109, Columbus, GA 31906 (SAN 243-2773) Tel 706-322-1584; Dist. by: Educational Impressions, 210 Sixth Ave., P.O. Box 77, Hawthorne, NJ 07507 (SAN 274-4899) Tel 201-423-4666; Toll free: 800-451-7450.

Patron *Imprint of* **Don Bosco Multimedia**

Paula Di Ed, *(Paula Di Educational Enterprises, Inc.; 0-9613130; 0-936543),* 181-21 Aberdeen Rd., Jamaica, NY 11432-1424 (SAN 294-6467) Tel 718-969-3320.

Paulist Pr, *(Paulist Pr.; 0-8091),* 997 MacArthur Blvd., Mahwah, NJ 07430 (SAN 202-5159) Tel 201-825-7300.

Paupieres Pub, *(Paupieres Publishing Co.; 0-944064),* P.O. Box 707, Houma, LA 70361-0707 (SAN 242-8334) Tel 504-876-9223.

Pautuxet Pubns, *(Pautuxet Pubns.; 0-9628122),* P.O. Box 3541, Plymouth, MA 02361; Toll free: 800-356-8606; Mill No. 3, Suite 4, Cordage Pk., Plymouth, MA 02360 Tel 617-747-4161.

PAVE, *(PAVE (Prosperity Audio-Visual Enterprises); 1-882716),* Div. of Northwest Business Writing & Consulting Service, 33049 35th, SW, Federal Way, WA 98023 Tel 206-838-1888.

PAW Prods, *(PAW Productions; 1-884620),* 118 Roanoke St., P.O. Box 31603, San Francisco, CA 94131 Tel 415-333-3323.

Pawnee Pub, *(Pawnee Publishing Co., Inc.; 0-913688),* P.O. Box 630, Higginsville, MO 64037 (SAN 207-4036) Tel 816-394-2424.

Paws Four Pub, *(Paws IV Publishing; 0-934007),* P.O. Box 2364, Homer, AK 99603 (SAN 692-7890) Tel 907-235-7697.

PAZ Pub, *(PAZ Publishing; 0-942253),* Div. of PAZ Percussion, P.O. Box 2481, North Canton, OH 44720 (SAN 666-8100); 623 S. Main St., North Canton, OH 44720-0481 (SAN 666-8119) Tel 216-499-3701.

Pazific Queen, *(Pazific Queen Communications;* 0-9629255), 5030 Floristan Ave., Los Angeles, CA 90041-2303 Tel 213-259-8918.

PB, *(Pocket Bks.; 0-671),* Div. of Simon & Schuster, Inc., 1230 Ave. of the Americas, New York, NY 10020 (SAN 202-5922) Tel 212-698-7000; Toll free: 800-223-2336 (orders); 800-223-2348 (customer service); Orders to: Paramount Publishing, 200 Old Tappan Rd., Old Tappan, NJ 07675 (SAN 200-2442) Tel 201-767-5937. *Imprints:* Archway (Archway Paperbacks); Minstrel Bks (Minstrel Books).

Peabody Harvard, *(Peabody Museum of Archaeology & Ethnology, Harvard Univ., Pubns. Dept.; 0-87365),* 11 Divinity Ave., Cambridge, MA 02138 (SAN 203-1426) Tel 617-495-3938; Dist. by: Harvard Univ. Pr., 79 Garden St., Cambridge, MA 02138 (SAN 200-2043) Tel 617-495-2600.

Peace Educ, *(Peace Education Foundation; 1-878227),* 2627 Biscayne Blvd., Miami, FL 33137-4532 Tel 305-576-5075.

Peaceable Pr, *(Peaceable Pr.; 0-936001),* 4664 N. Rob's Ln., Bloomington, IN 47408 (SAN 696-6241) Tel 812-336-8396.

Peachtree Pubs, *(Peachtree Pubs., Ltd.; 0-931948; 0-934601; 1-56145),* 494 Armour Cir., NE, Atlanta, GA 30324-4088 (SAN 212-1999) Tel 404-876-8761; Toll free: 800-241-0113.

Peanut Butter, *(Peanut Butter Publishing; 0-89716),* Div. of McGraw Mountain, Inc., 226 Second Ave., W., Seattle, WA 98119 (SAN 212-7881) Tel 206-281-5965.

Pearce Evetts, *(Pearce-Evetts Publishing; 0-936823),* 624 Ridgeview Dr., Pittsburgh, PA 15228-1706 (SAN 699-9271) Tel 412-344-5451; Toll free: 800-842-9571.

Peartree, *(Peartree; 0-935343),* P.O. Box 14533, Clearwater, FL 34629 Tel 813-531-4973; Dist. by: Baker & Taylor Bks., Commerce Service Ctr., 251 Mt. Olive Church Rd., Commerce, GA 30599-9988 (SAN 169-1503) Tel 706-335-5000; Toll free: 800-775-1200 (customer service); Dist. by: Baker & Taylor Bks., Momence Service Ctr., 501 S. Gladiolus St., Momence, IL 60954-2444 (SAN 169-2100) Tel 815-472-2444; Toll free: 800-775-2300 (customer service); Dist. by: Baker & Taylor Bks., Reno Service Ctr., 380 Edison Way, Reno, NV 89564 (SAN 169-4464) Tel 702-858-6700; Toll free: 800-775-1700 (customer service); Dist. by: Learning Plant, The, P.O. Box 17233, West Palm Beach, FL 33416 (SAN 630-4001) Tel 407-686-9456; Dist. by: Brodart Co., 500 Arch St., Williamsport, PA 17705 (SAN 169-7684) Tel 717-326-2461; Toll free: 800-233-8467; Dist. by: Quality Bks., Inc., 918 Sherwood Dr., Lake Bluff, IL 60044-2204 (SAN 169-2127) Tel 708-295-2010; Toll free: 800-323-4241 (libraries only); Dist. by: Baker & Taylor Bks., Somerville Service Ctr., 50 Kirby Ave., Somerville, NJ 08876-0734 (SAN 169-4901) Tel 908-722-8000; Toll free: 800-775-1500 (customer service); Dist. by: Ingram Bk. Co., 1 Ingram Blvd., La Vergne, TN 37086-1986 (SAN 169-7978) Tel 615-793-5000; Toll free: 800-937-8000 (orders only, all warehouses).

Pebble Bch CA
See Pebble Bch Pr Ltd

Pebble Bch Pr Ltd, *(Pebble Beach Pr., Ltd.; 1-883740),* P.O. Box 1171, Pebble Beach, CA 93953-1171; Toll free: 800-372-5559; 2611 Garden Rd., Monterey, CA 93940 Tel 408-372-5559.

Pedipress, *(Pedipress, Inc.; 0-914625),* 125 Red Gate Ln., Amherst, MA 01002 (SAN 287-7570) Tel 413-549-7798; Toll free: 800-344-5864; Dist. by: Publishers Group West, 4065 Hollis St., Emeryville, CA 94608 (SAN 202-8522) Tel 510-658-3453; Toll free: 800-788-3123.

Pedlar Pr, *(Pedlar Pr.),* 53 Whittemore Rd., Sturbridge, MA 01566 (SAN 244-6839); Dist. by: Legacy Bks., P.O. Box 494, Hatboro, PA 19040 (SAN 202-2389) Tel 215-675-6762.

Peekan Pubns, *(Peekan Pubns., Inc.; 0-944791;* 0-922996), P.O. Box 513, Freeport, IL 61032 (SAN 245-4998); Toll free: 800-747-7731; 118 N. Powell, Freeport, IL 61032 (SAN 245-5005) Tel 815-235-9130.

Peel Prod, *(Peel Productions; 0-939217),* P.O. Box 185, Molalla, OR 97038-0185 (SAN 662-6726) Tel 503-829-6849.

Peg Hoenack MusicWorks, *(Peg Hoenack's MusicWorks; 0-913500),* 8409 Seven Locks Rd., Bethesda, MD 20817 Tel 301-365-1818; Toll free: 800-469-8668.

Pegasus Bks, *(Pegasus Bks.; 0-929624),* 70 Bishop Allen Dr., Cambridge, MA 02139 (SAN 249-8820) Tel 617-354-7321.

Pegasus Graphics, *(Pegasus Graphics; 0-942559),* 2330 Upper High Dr., Estes Park, CO 80517 (SAN 667-2698) Tel 303-586-3757.

Peguis Pubs Ltd, *(Peguis Pubs., Ltd.; 0-919566; 0-920541; 1-895411),* Box 6008, 120 N. Fourth St., Grand Forks, ND 58206-6008; Toll free: 800-667-9673. Canadian Address: 100-318 McDermot, Winnipeg, Manitoba, R3A 0A2, CN.

Pelaganty, *(Pelaganty Bks.; 1-883261),* 1825 Woodland Ave., Racine, WI 53403 Tel 414-632-0827.

Pelican, *(Pelican Publishing Co., Inc.; 0-911116; 0-88289; 1-56554),* P.O. Box 3110, Gretna, LA 70054 (SAN 212-0623) Tel 504-368-1175; Toll free: 800-843-1724.

Pelican Bks *Imprint of* **Viking Penguin**

Pelona Pr, *(Pelona Pr.; 0-9623455),* P.O. Box 1882, Joplin, MO 64802; 6642 Main St., Kansas City, MO 64113 Tel 816-523-8472; Dist. by: Sax Arts & Crafts, P.O. Box 51710, New Berlin, WI 53151 (SAN 630-3676) Tel 414-784-6880; Toll free: 800-558-6696.

Pemberton Pubs, *(Pemberton Pubs.; 0-9627397),* P.O. Box 441558, Somerville, MA 02144; 25 Irving Terr., No. 6, Cambridge, MA 02138 Tel 617-868-6065.

Pen & Pr Unltd, *(Pen & Pr. United; 0-9640122),* 304D Hillsboro St., Oxford, NC 27565 Tel 919-690-1525.

Pen-Dec, *(Pen-Dec Pr.; 0-915199),* 3922 Monte Carlo, SE, Kentwood, MI 49508 (SAN 289-792X) Tel 616-942-0056.

Pen Notes, *(Pen Notes, Inc.; 0-939564),* 134 Westside Ave., Freeport, NY 11520 (SAN 107-3621) Tel 516-868-5753.

Pendant Pr, *(Pendant Pr., Inc.; 0-9631956),* R.R. 4, Box 4301, Bangor, PA 18013 Tel 610-588-3700.

Pendergrass Pub, *(Pendergrass Publishing Co., Inc.;* 0-88323), P.O. Box 66, Phoenix, NY 13135 (SAN 203-0861) Tel 315-695-7261.

Pendulum Pr, *(Pendulum Pr., Inc.; 0-88301),* Academic Bldg., Saw Mill Rd., West Haven, CT 06516 (SAN 202-8808) Tel 203-933-2551.

Penfield, *(Penfield Pr.; 0-9603858; 0-941016; 1-57216),* 215 Brown St., Iowa City, IA 52245 (SAN 221-6671) Tel 319-337-9998.

Penguin Bks *Imprint of* **Viking Penguin**

Penguin Family, *(Penguin Family Publishing; 0-9637985),* P.O. Box 471, Orland, CA 95963; 422 Fourth St., Orland, CA 95963 Tel 916-865-3267.

Peniel Pubns, *(Peniel Pubns.; 0-945818),* 6135 Jones Rd., College Park, GA 30349 (SAN 247-9656) Tel 404-969-5871.

Peninsula WA, *(Peninsula Publishing, Inc.; 0-918146),* P.O. Box 412, Port Angeles, WA 98362 (SAN 210-1300) Tel 206-457-7550; Dist. by: Pacific Pipeline, Inc., 8030 S. 228th St, Kent, WA 98032-2900 (SAN 208-2128) Tel 206-872-5523; Toll free: 800-444-7323 (Customer Service); 800-677-2222 (orders). Do not confuse with companies with the same name in Los Altos, CA, New York, NY, Suttons Bay, MI.

Pennington, *(Pennington Trading Post; 0-911120),* c/o Eunice Pennington, Fremont, MO 63941 (SAN 204-9392).

Penns Valley, *(Penns Valley Pubs.; 0-931992),* Div. of PVP, Inc., 800 W. Church Rd., Mechanicsburg, PA 17055-3103 (SAN 202-1455) Tel 717-232-5844.

Penny Lane Pubns, *(Penny Lane Pubns., Inc.; 0-911211),* 77 Park Ave., No. 10F, New York, NY 10016-2556 (SAN 274-4961) Tel 212-570-9666.

Pennypress, *(Pennypress, Inc.; 0-937604),* 1100 23rd Ave., E., Seattle, WA 98112 (SAN 215-6954) Tel 206-325-1419.

Penrod-Hiawatha, *(Penrod/Hiawatha Co.; 0-942618),* 10116 M-140, Berrien Center, MI 49102 (SAN 238-5546) Tel 616-461-6993.

Penstemon Pr, *(Penstemon Pr.; 0-9613938),* 1218 18th Ave., Apt. 4, San Francisco, CA 94122 (SAN 679-176X) Tel 415-661-9314.

Penta Ent, *(Penta Enterprises; 0-9633166),* 909 E. Centre Ave., Portage, MI 49002 Tel 616-327-4747.

Penton Overseas, *(Penton Overseas, Inc.; 0-939001;* 1-56015), 2470 Impala Dr., Carlsbad, CA 92008-7226 Tel 619-431-0060; Toll free: 800-748-5804.

Penzance Co, *(Penzance Co.; 1-881345),* 700 Brentford Pl., Apt. 118, Arlington, TX 76006-2241 Tel 817-459-1669; Toll free: 800-374-4124.

People of Destiny, *(People of Destiny International;* 1-881039), 7881 Beechcraft Ave., Suite B, Gaithersburg, MD 20879 Tel 301-926-2200; Toll free: 800-736-2202.

People Skills, *(People Skills International; 1-881165),* 2910 Baily Ave., San Diego, CA 92105 Tel 619-262-9951.

Pepper Bird, *(Pepper Bird Publishing; 1-56817),* Div. of The Pepper Bird Foundation, P.O. Box 69081, Hampton, VA 23669; 405 Chesapeake Ave., Newport News, VA 23607 Tel 804-245-7136.

Pequot Pubng, *(Pequot Publishing; 0-9641742),* Div. of EPI Marketing, 250 Pequot Ave., Southport, CT 06490 Tel 203-255-1112.

Perception Pubns, *(Perception Pubns.; 0-940406),* 8231 E. Vista De Valle, Scottsdale, AZ 85255-4210 (SAN 265-3931) Tel 602-585-6989.

Pere Marquette, *(Pere Marquette Pr.; 0-934640),* P.O. Box 495, Alton, IL 62002 (SAN 206-3042) Tel 618-462-5415.

Peregrine & Hayes, *(Peregrine & Hayes Publishing Co.;* 1-883516), P.O. Box 64101, Tucson, AZ 85728; 4651 N. First Ave., Suite 103, Tucson, AZ 85718 Tel 602-887-7194.

Peregrine Smith *Imprint of* **Gibbs Smith Pub**

Perish Pr, *(Perish Pr.; 0-934038),* P.O. Box 75, Mystic, CT 06355 (SAN 212-789X) Tel 203-536-2304.

Perivale Pr, *(Perivale Pr.; 0-912288),* 13830 Erwin St., Van Nuys, CA 91401 (SAN 201-9922) Tel 818-785-4671; Dist. by: SPD-Small Pr. Distribution, 1814 San Pablo Ave., Berkeley, CA 94702 (SAN 204-5826) Tel 510-549-3336; Toll free: 800-869-7553; Dist. by: Anton Mikofsky, 50 E. 42nd St., Suite 1809, New York, NY 10017 (SAN 219-5747) Tel 212-867-6735; Dist. by: Baker & Taylor Bks., Reno Service Ctr., 380 Edison Way 722, Reno, NV 89564 (SAN 169-4464) Tel 702-858-6700; Toll free: 800-775-1700 (customer service); Dist. by: The Distributor, 702 S. Michigan, South Bend, IN 46601 (SAN 169-2488) Tel 219-232-8500; Toll free: 800-348-5200 (except Indiana).

Periwinkle MA, *(Periwinkle Pr.; 0-9621650),* P.O. Box 354, White Horse Beach, MA 02381 (SAN 251-7523); 102 Cary Rd., White Horse Beach, MA 02381 (SAN 251-7531) Tel 508-224-6427; Dist. by: Krikorian Miller Assocs., Inc., 11 Market Sq., Newburyport, MA 01950 (SAN 630-3137) Tel 508-465-7377. Do not confuse with Periwinkle Pr., Snohomish, WA.

Perk-Lo Pk Prodns, *(Perk-Lo Park Productions;* 0-9626570), P.O. Box 489, Redway, CA 95560; 145 D Rd., Garberville, CA 95440 Tel 707-923-9288.

Perma-Bound, *(Perma-Bound Bks.; 0-8479; 0-8000; 0-7804; 0-605),* Div. of Hertzberg-New Method, Inc., 617 E. Vandalia Rd., Jacksonville, IL 62650 (SAN 169-202X) Tel 217-243-5451; Toll free: 800-637-6581.

Permanent Pr, *(Permanent Pr., The; 0-932966;* 1-877946), Affil. of Second Chance Pr., R.D. 2, Noyac Rd., Sag Harbor, NY 11963 (SAN 212-2995) Tel 516-725-1101. Do not confuse with companies with the same name in Santurce, PR, San Francisco, CA, Brooklyn, NY.

Perry Enterprises, *(Perry Enterprises; 0-941518),* 3907 N. Foothill Dr., Provo, UT 84604 (SAN 171-0281) Tel 801-226-1002.

Perry Heights, *(Perry Heights Pr.; 0-9630181),* 29 Mill River Rd., Chappaqua, NY 10514 Tel 914-238-6240.

Perry ME, *(Perry Publishing; 0-9626823),* 9 Middle St., Hallowell, ME 04347 Tel 207-626-3242. Do not confuse with Perry Publishing, Bremerton, WA.

Perry Pubns, *(Perry Pubns.; 1-882809),* Div. of Perry Enterprises, Inc., P.O. Box 204, Whitewater, WI 53190-0204; Toll free: 800-527-2966; 430 W. Center St., Whitewater, WI 53190 Tel 414-473-6883.

Persea Bks, *(Persea Bks., Inc.; 0-89255),* 60 Madison Ave., New York, NY 10010 (SAN 212-8233) Tel 212-779-7668.

Personal Growth, *(Personal Growth Institute; 1-878040),* 2638 Browning, Lake Orion, MI 48360 Tel 810-391-1600; Dist. by: New Leaf Distributing Co., 5425 Tulane Dr., SW, Atlanta, GA 30336-2323 (SAN 169-1449) Tel 404-691-6996; Toll free: 800-326-2665; Dist. by: Partners Bk. Distributing, Inc., 720 E. Shiawassee St., Lansing, MI 48912 (SAN 630-4559) Tel 517-485-0366; Toll free: 800-336-3137. Do not confuse with Personal Growth Institute, San Diego, CA.

Personal Prods, *(Personal Products Group, Inc.;* 0-9629597), 17510 Indiana St., Detroit, MI 48221 Tel 313-864-3407.

Perspect Indiana, *(Perspectives Pr.; 0-9609504;* 0-944934), P.O. Box 90318, Indianapolis, IN 46290-0318 (SAN 262-5059) Tel 317-872-3055; Dist. by: Baker & Taylor Bks., Somerville Service Ctr., 50 Kirby Ave., Somerville, NJ 08876-0734 (SAN 169-4901) Tel 908-722-8000; Toll free: 800-775-1500 (customer service); Dist. by: Baker & Taylor Bks., Momence Service Ctr., 501 S. Gladiolus St., Momence, IL 60954-2444 (SAN 169-2100) Tel 815-472-2444; Toll free: 800-775-2300 (customer service); Dist. by: Baker & Taylor Bks., Commerce Service Ctr., 251 Mt. Olive Church Rd., Commerce, GA 30599-9988 (SAN 169-1503) Tel 706-335-5000; Toll free: 800-775-1200 (customer service); Dist. by: Baker & Taylor Bks., Reno Service Ctr., 380 Edison Way, Reno, NV 89564 (SAN 169-4464) Tel 702-858-6700; Toll free: 800-775-1700 (customer service); Dist. by: Quality Bks., Inc., 918 Sherwood Dr., Lake Bluff, IL 60044-2204 (SAN 169-2127) Tel 708-295-2010; Toll free: 800-323-4241 (libraries only).

Perspect NC, *(Perspectives; 0-9631180),* P.O. Box 560061, Charlotte, NC 28256; 627 Pennwood Ln., Charlotte, NC 28215 Tel 704-535-8693.

Peta Pubns, *(Peta Pubns.; 0-9622101),* 4928 Wyaconda Rd., Rockville, MD 20852 Tel 301-770-7444.

Peter & Thornton Pubs, *(Peter & Thornton Pubs.;* 0-9621757), 3483 Golden Gateway, No. 216, Lafayette, CA 94549 (SAN 252-0567) Tel 510-930-9991.

Peter Pauper, *(Peter Pauper Pr., Inc.; 0-88088),* 202 Mamaroneck Ave., White Plains, NY 10601 (SAN 204-9449) Tel 914-681-0144; Toll free: 800-833-2311 (orders only).

Peter Smith, *(Smith, Peter, Pub., Inc.; 0-8446),* 5 Lexington Ave., Magnolia, MA 01930 (SAN 206-8885) Tel 508-525-3562.

Petersons Guides, *(Peterson's Guides, Inc.; 0-87866;* 1-56079), P.O. Box 2123, Princeton, NJ 08543-2123 (SAN 200-2167); Toll free: 800-338-3282; 202 Carnegie Ctr., Princeton, NJ 08540 (SAN 297-5661) Tel 609-243-9111.

Petit Appetit, *(Petit Appetit; 0-9616883),* 8108 El Monte, Prairie Village, KS 66208 (SAN 661-6496) Tel 913-383-3610; Dist. by: Baker & Taylor Bks., Momence Service Ctr., 501 S. Gladiolus St., Momence, IL 60954-2444 (SAN 169-2100) Tel 815-472-2444; Toll free: 800-775-2300 (customer service).

Petra Pub Co, *(Petra Publishing Co.; 1-880015),* 938 E. Swan Creek Rd., Suite 301, Fort Washington, MD 20744 Tel 301-292-3701; Dist. by: Twin Peaks Pr., P.O. Box 129, Vancouver, WA 98666 (SAN 630-5717) Tel 206-694-2462; Toll free: 800-637-2256 (orders only).

Petrified Forest Mus Assn, *(Petrified Forest Museum Assn.; 0-945695),* Park Rd., P.O. Box 277, Petrified Forest National Pk., AZ 86028 (SAN 247-7726) Tel 602-524-6228.

Peyto Pub, *(Peyto Publishing; 0-9634867),* 2444 N. Beachwood Dr., No. 102, Hollywood, CA 90068 Tel 213-463-5762.

Pfeifer-Hamilton, *(Pfeifer-Hamilton Pubs.; 0-938586),* Div. of Whole Person Assocs., Inc., 210 W. Michigan St., Duluth, MN 55802-1908 Tel 218-727-0500; Toll free: 800-247-6789.

Phantom Pubns, *(Phantom Pubns., Inc.; 0-9625372),* 3657 Country Club Rd., Endwell, NY 13760 Tel 607-785-1726.

Pharmaco-Video Pubns, *(Pharmaco-Video Pubns.;* 1-879278), 117 E. Louisa St., No. 110, Seattle, WA 98102-3203 Tel 206-328-6466.

Phila Orchestra, *(Philadelphia Orchestra Assn.;* 0-9635667), 1420 Locust St., Suite 400, Philadelphia, PA 19102 Tel 215-893-1900.

Phila Yrly Mtg RSOF, *(Philadelphia Yearly Meeting, Religious Society of Friends, Pubns.; 0-941308),* 1515 Cherry St., Philadelphia, PA 19102 (SAN 239-3778) Tel 215-241-7225.

Phillips Coll, *(Phillips Collection, The; 0-943044),* 1600 21st St., NW, Washington, DC 20009 (SAN 321-2297) Tel 202-387-2151.

Philmar Pub, *(Philmar Pubs.),* 9199 Fircrest Ln., No. 137, San Ramon, CA 94583-3954 (SAN 262-0596) Tel 510-837-3490.

Philomel Bks *Imprint of* **Putnam Pub Group**

Philos Pub, *(Philosophical Publishing Co.; 0-932785),* 5916 Clymeir Rd., Quakertown, PA 18951 (SAN 295-8430) Tel 215-536-5168.

Phoenix Educ Found, *(Phoenix Educational Foundation;* 0-929354), 462 Stevens Ave., No. 202, Solana Beach, CA 92075 (SAN 249-0919) Tel 619-481-2977.

Phoenix Pub, *(Phoenix Publishing; 0-914016; 0-914659),* Main St., Sugar Hill, NH 03585 (SAN 691-4209) Tel 603-823-8531. Do not confuse with companies with the same name in Newark, NJ, Fairfield, FL, Roswell, GA, Custer, WA, Rocklin, CA or Phoenix Publishing Services in Lewisville, TX, Urbana, IL.

Photo Data Res, *(Photo Data Research; 0-9626508),* 627 S. Irena St., Redondo Beach, CA 90277-4356 (SAN 297-4002) Tel 310-540-8068; 800 S. Pacific Coast Hwy., No. 8332, Redondo Beach, CA 90277-4700 (SAN 297-4010).

Phunn Pubs, *(Phunn Pubs.; 0-931762),* P.O. Box 70, Elsah, IL 62028-0070 (SAN 212-128X) Tel 618-374-2551.

Pi Pr, *(Pi Pr., Inc.; 0-931420),* Box 23371, Honolulu, HI 96822 (SAN 669-2400); 3169-A Alika Ave., Honolulu, HI 96817 Tel 808-595-3426.

Piccadilly TX, *(Piccadilly Pr.; 0-9630147),* P.O. Box 50515, Austin, TX 78763; 4007 Sinclair Ave., Austin, TX 78756 Tel 512-453-2051.

Pickering Pr, *(Pickering Pr., The; 0-940495),* P.O. Box 331531, Miami, FL 33233 (SAN 665-0430) Tel 305-444-8784; Dist. by: Talman Co., 131 Spring St., Suite 201E-N, New York, NY 10012 (SAN 200-5204) Tel 212-431-7175; Toll free: 800-537-8894 (orders only).

Pickwick Pubs, *(Pickwick Pubs., Ltd.; 1-877830),* 24 Fairway Cir. E., Box 912, Sudden Valley, Bellingham, WA 98226.

Pictorial Herit, *(Pictorial Heritage Publishing Co.;* 1-880373), 5659 Virginia Beach Blvd., Norfolk, VA 23502 Tel 804-461-0520; Toll free: 800-292-9341.

Pictorial Hist, *(Pictorial Histories Publishing Co.; 0-933126; 0-929521),* 713 S. Third, W., Missoula, MT 59801 (SAN 212-4351) Tel 406-549-8488.

Pictorial Legends, *(Pictorial Legends; 0-939031),* Subs. of Event Co., 435 Holland Ave., Los Angeles, CA 90042 (SAN 662-8486) Tel 213-254-4416; Dist. by: Pacific Trade Group, 94-527 Puahi St., Waipahu, HI 96797 (SAN 169-1635) Tel 808-671-6735; Dist. by: Cedar Graphics, 311 Parsons Dr., Hiawatha, IA 52233 (SAN 263-1709) Tel 319-393-3600; Toll free: 800-243-5242.

Pictura NJ, *(Pictura, Inc.; 0-940607),* P.O. Box 2058, W. Patterson, NJ 07424 (SAN 665-0333) Tel 201-890-1070.

Picture Bk Studio, *(Picture Bk. Studio, Ltd.; 0-88708; 0-907234; 0-940032),* 2 Center Plaza, Boston, MA 02108-1906 (SAN 293-8227) Tel 508-788-0911; Orders to: Simon & Schuster Children's Books, 15 Columbus Cir., New York, NY 10023; Dist. by: Simon & Schuster, Inc., 1230 Avenue of the Americas, New York, NY 10020 (SAN 200-2450) Tel 212-698-7000; Toll free: 800-223-2348; 800-223-2336 (orders only). *Imprints:* Rabbit Ears (Rabbit Ears Storybook Classics).

Picture Me Bks, *(Picture Me Bks., Inc.; 1-878338;* 1-57151), 655 W. Market St., Akron, OH 44303 Tel 216-762-6800.

Picture This Bks, *(Picture This! Bks.; 0-9624673;* 1-881989), 75 Sunnymede Dr., Fort Mitchell, KY 41017-2816 Tel 606-331-0547.

Pieces of Lrning, *(Pieces of Learning; 0-9623835;* 1-880505), Div. of Creative Learning Consultants, Inc., 1610 Brook Lynn Dr., Beavercreek, OH 45432-1906 (SAN 298-461X) Tel 513-427-0530; Toll free: 800-729-5137.

Pigskin Pr, *(Pigskin Pr.; 0-9633495),* P.O. Box 634, Kenosha, WI 53141-0634; Toll free: 800-345-0096; 4232 89th St., Kenosha, WI 53142 Tel 414-694-9808.

Pigtail Pubng, *(Pigtail Publishing; 0-9639779),* 1859 N. Pine Island Rd., Suite 155, Plantation, FL 33322 Tel 305-572-9697.

Pikestaff Pr, *(Pikestaff Pr., The; 0-936044),* Div. of Pikestaff Pubns., Inc., P.O. Box 127, Normal, IL 61761 (SAN 213-8654) Tel 309-452-4831.

Pilgrim OH, *(Pilgrim Pr., The United Church Pr.;* 0-8298), Div. of United Church Board for Homeland Ministries, ; Orders to: 700 Prospect Ave. E., Cleveland, OH 44115-1100; Toll free: 800-654-5129 (Pilgrim orders); 800-537-3394 (United Church orders).

Pinata Pubns, *(Pinata Pubns.; 0-934925),* 200 Lakeside Dr., No. 903, Oakland, CA 94612-3503 (SAN 694-6062) Tel 510-893-6682.

Pine Isl Pr, *(Pine Island Pr.; 0-9620092; 1-880836),* 69 Pine Island Lake, Westhampton, MA 01027 (SAN 247-5510) Tel 413-527-5172.

Pine Tr Pr MN, *(Pine Tree Pr.; 0-9633761),* 4036 Kerry Ct., Minnetonka, MN 55345 Tel 612-938-9163. Do not confuse with companies with the same name in Rome, NY, Plano, TX, Los Angeles, CA.

Pineapple MI, *(Pineapple Pr.; 1-878526),* P.O. Box 56, Mullett Lake, MI 49761 Tel 616-627-4296. Do not confuse with Pineapple Pr., Inc., Sarasota, FL.

Pineapple Pr, *(Pineapple Pr., Inc.; 0-910923; 1-56164),* P.O. Drawer 16008, Southside Sta., Sarasota, FL 34239 (SAN 285-0850) Tel 813-952-1085. Do not confuse with Pineapple Pr., Mullett Lake, MI.

Pineapple Pubns, *(Pineapple Pubns.; 0-929249),* 24 Bridge St., Newport, RI 02840 (SAN 248-9864) Tel 401-847-0859.

Pink Inc, *(Pink, Inc.; 0-9622585),* P.O. Box 866, Atlantic Beach, FL 32233-0866 Tel 904-285-9276.

Pinto Pr, *(Pinto Pr.; 0-9632476),* Blood Hill Rd., R.R. 1, Box 78, Elizabethtown, NY 12932; 78 Blood Hill Rd., Elizabethtown, NY 12932 Tel 518-873-7328.

Pinto Pub, *(Pinto Publishing Co.; 0-925605),* 3610 Calle del Monte, NE, Albuquerque, NM 87110 Tel 505-268-1302.

Pioneer Farm, *(Pioneer Farm; 0-9614899),* Ohop Valley Rd., Eatonville, WA 98328 (SAN 693-2738) Tel 206-832-6923.

Piper, *(Piper Publishing, Inc.; 0-87832),* Box 1, Blue Earth, MN 56013 (SAN 202-005X) Tel 507-526-5448.

Pippin Bks, *(Pippin Bks., Inc.; 0-9624993),* 8919 Old Pine Rd., Boca Raton, FL 33433 Tel 407-487-4508.

Pippin Pr, *(Pippin Pr.; 0-945912),* Gracie Sta., Box 1347, 229 E. 85th St., New York, NY 10028 (SAN 247-8366) Tel 212-288-4920.

Piqua Pr, *(Piqua Pr., Inc.; 1-880440),* P.O. Box 32230, Sarasota, FL 34239-0230; Toll free: 800-477-6727.

Piranha Pr *Imprint of* **DC Comics**

Pirate Writings, *(Pirate Writings Publishing; 0-9640168),* 53 Whitman Ave., Islip, NY 11751 Tel 516-224-1130.

Piros Pr, *(Piros Pr.; 0-9636833),* N112 Gillis Rd., No. 202, Spokane, WA 99206 Tel 509-921-5965.

Pisces Pr CA, *(Pisces Pr., Inc.; 0-9623802),* P.O. Box 9352, Rancho Santa Fe, CA 92067; 6510 Monte Fuego, Rancho Santa Fe, CA 92067 Tel 619-755-0156. Do not confuse with companies with the same name in Lubbock, TX, Sun City, AZ.

Pisces Pr TX, *(Pisces Pr.; 0-938328),* 3209 26th St., Lubbock, TX 79410 (SAN 215-7993) Tel 806-799-4939. Do not confuse with companies with the same name in Sun City, AZ, Rancho Santa Fe, CA.

Pittenbruach Pr, *(Pittenbruach Pr.; 0-938875),* P.O. Box 553, Northampton, MA 01061 (SAN 662-6688); 15 Walnut, Northampton, MA 01060 (SAN 662-6696).

Pittman Pub, *(Pittman Pub.; 0-9615382),* Rte. 1, Box 255, Aulander, NC 27805 (SAN 695-4456) Tel 919-332-2511.

Pixanne Ent, *(Pixanne Enterprises, Ltd.; 1-883585),* 1015 Waverly Rd., Gladwyne, PA 19035 Tel 610-896-0505.

Pixel Prods Pubns, *(Pixel Products & Pubns.; 0-935163),* 284 Richards Ave., No. 2, Portsmouth, NH 03801-5238 (SAN 695-3557).

Pixie Dust, *(Pixie Dust Publishing; 0-9640684),* 6670 N. Benedict Ave., Fresno, CA 93711 Tel 209-435-6476.

PJC Lrng Mtrls, *(PJC-Learning Materials; 0-931749),* 08780 Spinnaker Ln., East Jordan, MI 49727-9428 (SAN 683-5120).

PL *Imprint of* **HarpC**

Place in the Woods, *(Place in the Woods; 0-932991),* 3900 Glenwood Ave., Golden Valley, MN 55422-5302 (SAN 689-058X) Tel 612-374-2120; Dist. by: Bacon Pamphlet Service, Inc., Box 228B, Hand Hollow Rd., East Chatham, NY 12060 (SAN 200-5573) Tel 518-794-7722; Orders to: LTO Enterprises, 6036 N. Tenth Way, Phoenix, AZ 85014 (SAN 662-1805) Tel 602-265-7765; Dist. by: Midwest Library Service, 11443 St. Charles Rock Rd., Bridgeton, MO 63044-9986 (SAN 169-4243) Tel 314-739-3100.

Plan Par Ctrl CA, *(Planned Parenthood of Central California; 0-9610122),* 255 N. Fulton Ave., Fresno, CA 93701 (SAN 274-6662) Tel 209-486-2647.

PL&R Chestney, *(Chestney, P. L. & R., Co.; 1-883533),* 3413 Clay St., Denver, CO 80211 Tel 303-455-2797.

Planet Playmates, *(Planet Playmates Co., Inc.;* 0-9624497), 8235 Mackall Rd., Saint Leonard, MD 20685 Tel 410-586-2043.

Planetary Pubns, *(Planetary Pubns.; 1-879052),* P.O. Box 66, Boulder Creek, CA 95006; Toll free: 800-372-3100; 14700 W. Park Ave., Boulder Creek, CA 95006 Tel 408-338-2161.

Platonic Acad Pr, *(Platonic Academy Pr., The;* 0-937011), P.O. Box 1551, Santa Cruz, CA 95061 (SAN 658-6767) Tel 408-464-9636; Dist. by: Bookpeople, 7900 Edgewater Dr., Oakland, CA 94621 (SAN 168-9517) Tel 510-632-4700; Toll free: 800-999-4650; Dist. by: Dakota Bks., P.O. Box 1551, Santa Cruz, CA 95061 Tel 408-464-9636.

Platt & Munk Pubs *Imprint of* **Putnam Pub Group**

Platypus Bks, *(Platypus Bks., Ltd.; 0-930905),* 1315 Angelina, College Station, TX 77840-4854 (SAN 679-1727); Dist. by: Writers & Bks., 740 University Ave., Rochester, NY 14607 (SAN 156-9678) Tel 716-473-2590.

PLAY House, *(P.L.A.Y. Hse.; 0-9622543),* 885 Vale View Dr., Vista, CA 92083-6726.

Play-Media, *(Play-Media; 1-880056),* P.O. Box 114, Woodacre, CA 94973; 10 Park St., Woodacre, CA 94973 Tel 415-488-4937.

Play Schs, *(Play Schls. Assn.; 0-936426),* 9 E. 38th St., New York, NY 10016 (SAN 202-0076) Tel 212-725-6540.

Player Pr, *(Player Pr.; 0-9623966),* 139-22 Caney Ln., Rosedale, NY 11422 Tel 718-528-3285.

Players Pr, *(Players Pr., Inc.; 0-88734),* P.O. Box 1132, Studio City, CA 91614-0132 (SAN 239-0213) Tel 818-789-4980. *Imprints:* Macmillan Ed UK (Macmillan Education, Limited (UK)).

Playology Hlth, *(Playology & Health; 1-880806),* 715 Balboa Ct., San Diego, CA 92109 Tel 619-276-9944.

Plays, *(Plays, Inc.; 0-8238),* 120 Boylston St., Boston, MA 02116 (SAN 202-0084) Tel 617-423-3157.

Pleasant Co, *(Pleasant Co. Pubns., Inc.; 0-937295;* 1-56247), 8400 Fairway Pl., Middleton, WI 53562 Tel 608-836-4848; Orders to: P.O. Box 620991, Middleton, WI 53562-0991; Toll free: 800-233-0264.

Pleasant Mt, *(Pleasant Mount Productions; 0-9640925),* P.O. Box 68, Pleasant Mount, PA 18453; R.D. 1, Box 166, Pleasant Mount, PA 18453 Tel 717-448-2613.

Plough, *(Plough Publishing Hse., The; 0-87486),* Spring Valley R.D. 2, Box 446, Farmington, PA 15437-9506 (SAN 202-0092) Tel 412-329-1100.

Plumb Line Pr, *(Plumb Line Pr.; 0-9634616),* 336 Brethren Church Rd., Leola, PA 17540 Tel 717-355-0590. Do not confuse with Plumb Line Pr., Inc. in Estes Park, CO.

Plume *Imprint of* **NAL-Dutton**

Plus One Pub, *(Plus One Publishing, Inc.; 0-934822),* 625 N. Mansfield Ave., Hollywood, CA 90036 (SAN 213-1404) Tel 213-936-1783.

Plutonium Pr, *(Plutonium Pr.; 0-929611),* P.O. Box 61564, Phoenix, AZ 85082 (SAN 249-9673) Tel 602-956-9382.

Pnnywhstlrs Pr, *(Pennywhistler's Pr.; 0-9623456),* P.O. Box 2473, New York, NY 10108; 467 W. 46th St., New York, NY 10036 Tel 212-247-3231. Do not confuse with Pennywhistle Pr., Malibu, CA.

Pocahontas Pr, *(Pocahontas Pr., Inc.; 0-936015),* 832 Hutcheson Dr., P.O. Drawer F, Blacksburg, VA 24063-1020 (SAN 630-124X) Tel 703-951-0467; Toll free: 800-446-0467; Dist. by: Baker & Taylor Bks., Reno Service Ctr., 380 Edison Way, Reno, NV 89564 (SAN 169-4464) Tel 702-858-6700; Toll free: 800-775-1700 (customer service); Dist. by: Baker & Taylor Bks., Somerville Service Ctr., 50 Kirby Ave., Somerville, NJ 08876-0734 (SAN 169-4901) Tel 908-722-8000; Toll free: 800-775-1500 (customer service); Dist. by: Baker & Taylor Bks., Momence Service Ctr., 501 S. Gladiolus St., Momence, IL 60954-2444 (SAN 169-2100) Tel 815-472-2444; Toll free: 800-775-2300 (customer service); Dist. by: Midwest Library Service, 11443 St. Charles Rock Rd., Bridgeton, MO 63044-2789 (SAN 169-4243) Tel 314-739-3100; Dist. by: Yankee Bk. Peddler, Inc., 999 Maple St., Contoocook, NH 03229 (SAN 169-4510) Tel 603-746-3102; Toll free: 800-258-3774; Dist. by: Coutts Library Service, Inc., P.O. Box 1000, Niagara Falls, NY 14302 (SAN 169-5401); Toll free: 800-772-4304; Dist. by: Blackwell North America, Inc., 100 University Ct., Blackwood, NJ 08012 (SAN 169-4596) Tel 609-228-8900; Toll free: 800-257-7341; 800-547-6426 (in Oregon); Dist. by: The Bookhouse, Inc., 12100D N. May Ave., Oklahoma City, OK 73120 (SAN 200-8467) Tel 405-755-0020; Dist. by: Independent Pubs. Marketing, 6824 Oaklawn Ave., Edina, MN 55435 (SAN 630-5725) Tel 612-920-9044; Dist. by: Baker & Taylor Bks., Commerce Service Ctr., 251 Mt. Olive Church Rd., Commerce, GA 30599-9988 (SAN 169-1503) Tel 706-335-5000; Toll free: 800-775-1200 (customer service).

Pockets Pr, *(Pockets Pr.; 1-881511),* 501 Creekwood Dr., Marietta, GA 30068 Tel 404-565-2492.

Pocumtuck Valley Mem, *(Pocumtuck Valley Memorial Assn.; 0-9612876; 1-882374),* P.O. Box 428, Memorial St., Deerfield, MA 01342 (SAN 211-2663) Tel 413-774-7476.

Poetry Unltd, *(Poetry Unlimited; 0-9614337),* 11709 Pawnee Dr., SW, Tacoma, WA 98499 (SAN 687-8326) Tel 206-588-7451.

Poets Farm Pr, *(Poets' Farm Pr.; 0-9633307),* 3121 Stonegate Ct., Flossmoor, IL 60422-1457.

Point *Imprint of* **Scholastic Inc**

Point Publications, *(Point Pubns.; 0-9620888),* P.O. Box 145, Point Lookout, NY 11569 (SAN 250-0434); 59 Cedarhurst Ave., Point Lookout, NY 11569 (SAN 250-0442) Tel 516-889-3526. Do not confuse with Point Pubns. Inc., Wayzata, MN.

Point View Pr, *(Point of View Pr.; 0-9624129),* P.O. Box 751, Forestville, CA 95436; 303 Burton Ave., Rohnert Park, CA 94928 Tel 707-664-0477.

Polanie, *(Polanie Publishing Co.; 0-911154),* 643 Madison St., NE, Minneapolis, MN 55413 (SAN 204-9031) Tel 612-379-9134.

Polaris AZ, *(Polaris Pr.; 0-9622985),* 1281 W. Elko St., Tucson, AZ 85704 Tel 602-887-7637. Do not confuse with Polaris Pr., Los Gatos, CA.

Polestar, *(Polestar Pubns.; 0-942044),* 620 S. Minnesota Ave., Sioux Falls, SD 57104 (SAN 239-474X) Tel 605-338-2888.

Poligion Pub, *(Poligion Publishing; 0-922484),* 610 Country Club Dr., Prescott, AZ 86303 (SAN 251-0820) Tel 602-778-2716.

Polit Status ECC, *(Political Status Education Coordinating Commission; 1-883488),* Univ. of Guam, U.O.G. Sta., Mangilao, GU 96923.

Pollyanna Prodns, *(Pollyanna Productions; 0-945842),* 4830 E. Poplar Dr., P.O. Box 3222, Terre Haute, IN 47803 (SAN 247-8285) Tel 812-877-3286.

Polychrome Pub, *(Polychrome Publishing Corp.; 1-879965),* 4509 N. Francisco, Chicago, IL 60625-3808 Tel 312-478-4455.

Ponderosa CA, *(Ponderosa Pr.; 0-9642244),* Box 278, Yosemite, CA 95389; 1 Flying Spur Rd., Yosemite, CA 95389 Tel 209-966-4863. Do not confuse with Ponderosa Pr. in Colorado Springs, CO, Spring Branch, TX.

Popcorn Pubs, *(Popcorn Pubs.; 0-930506),* P.O. Box 1308, Pittsfield, MA 01202 (SAN 211-044X) Tel 413-443-5601.

Porch Swing, *(Porch Swing Pr., Inc.; 0-9606550),* P.O. Box 15014, Nashville, TN 37215 (SAN 219-8118).

Porcupine Enter, *(Porcupine Enterprises; 0-9621976),* 106 Woodside Rd., Sudbury, MA 01776 Tel 508-443-7199.

Portals Pr, *(Portals Pr.; 0-916620),* P.O. Box 1048, Tuscaloosa, AL 35403 (SAN 208-8126) Tel 205-758-1874.

Portfolio Pub, *(Portfolio Publishing Co., Inc.; 0-943255),* P.O. Box 986, Saratoga, WY 82331-0986 (SAN 668-3576); 142 Golden Shadow Cir., The Woodlands, TX 77381 (SAN 668-3584) Tel 713-363-3577.

Portunus Pubng, *(Portunus Publishing Co.; 0-9641330),* Div. of Richard Schneider Enterprises, 3435 Ocean Park Blvd., Suite 203, Santa Monica, CA 90405 Tel 310-451-5808.

Positive & Black, *(Positive & Black; 0-9642154),* P.O. Box 751243, Forest Hills, NY 11375 Tel 718-896-2302.

Post Oak Hill, *(Post Oak Hill; 0-9636122),* 235 Shady Hill Ln., Double Oak, TX 75067-8270 Tel 817-430-1182.

Post Oak Pr *Imprint of* **Larksdale**

Potes Poets, *(Potes & Poets Pr., Inc.; 0-937013),* 181 Edgemont Ave., Elmwood, CT 06110 (SAN 658-6759) Tel 203-233-2023; Dist. by: SPD-Small Pr. Distribution, 1814 San Pablo Ave., Berkeley, CA 94702 (SAN 204-5826) Tel 510-549-3336; Toll free: 800-869-7553; Dist. by: Inland Bk. Co., 140 Commerce St., East Haven, CT 06512 (SAN 200-4151) Tel 203-467-4257; Toll free: 800-243-0138.

Potomac Val Pr, *(Potomac Valley Pr.; 0-938443),* 1424 16th St. NW, Suite 105, Washington, DC 20036 (SAN 659-8161) Tel 202-462-8800; Toll free: 800-669-0993; Dist. by: Publishers Distribution Service, 6893 Sullivan Rd., Grawn, MI 49637 (SAN 630-5717) Tel 616-276-5196; Toll free: 800-345-0096 (orders only).

Potpourri Pubns, *(Potpourri Pubns. Co.; 1-884754),* 5503 W. 78th Terr., Prairie Village, KS 66208 Tel 913-642-1503.

Pound Sterling Pub, *(Pound Sterling Publishing; 0-943991),* 4270 Ocean Dr., No. 13, Corpus Christi, TX 78411-1283 (SAN 242-2743) Tel 512-814-8814.

Power Comm Ch, *(Power Community Church; 0-9626910),* 1026 S. East St., Anaheim, CA 92805 Tel 714-535-1961.

Power Indst LP, *(Power Industries LP; 1-879387),* 37 Walnut St., Wellesley Hills, MA 02181-2101 Tel 617-235-7733; Toll free: 800-395-5009.

Pr MacDonald & Reinecke, *(Press of MacDonald & Reinecke, The; 1-877947),* Subs. of Padre Productions, P.O. Box 840, Arroyo Grande, CA 93421 Tel 805-473-1947.

Pr Pacifica, *(Press Pacifica, Ltd.; 0-916630),* P.O. Box 47, Kailua, HI 96734 (SAN 249-292X) Tel 808-261-6594.

Prac Psych Pr, *(Practical Psychology Pr.; 0-944227),* P.O. Box 535, Portland, OR 97207 (SAN 243-1793) Tel 503-289-3295.

Prairie Divide, *(Prairie Divide Productions; 1-884610),* 305 W. Magnolia, Suite 116, Fort Collins, CO 80521 Tel 303-493-6593.

Prairie Family Pubs, *(Prairie Family Pubs.; 0-944793),* HCR, Box 78, Bowdle, SD 57428 (SAN 245-3967); County Rd. 3, Bowdle, SD 57428 (SAN 245-3975) Tel 605-285-6337.

Prairie Hse, *(Prairie Hse., Inc.; 0-911007),* P.O. Box 9199, Fargo, ND 58106 (SAN 262-9844) Tel 701-235-0210; Toll free: 800-866-2665. Do not confuse with Prairie Hse. Publishing in Oakley, CA.

Prairie Lark, *(Prairie Lark Pr.; 0-918533),* P.O. Box 699, Springfield, IL 62705 (SAN 657-7113) Tel 618-234-2415.

Prairie Plains Res Inst, *(Prairie/Plains Resource Institute; 0-945614),* 1307 L St., Aurora, NE 68818 (SAN 247-3933) Tel 402-694-5535.

Prairie Shark Pr, *(Prairie Shark Pr.; 0-9621151),* 1612 Brendonwood Rd., Derby, KS 67037-3517 (SAN 250-829X) Tel 316-269-3477 (SAN 250-8303).

Prakken, *(Prakken Pubns., Inc.; 0-911168),* 275 Metty Dr., Suite 1, Ann Arbor, MI 48103 (SAN 204-9112) Tel 313-769-1211; Toll free: 800-530-9673 (orders).

Prayer Bk, *(Prayer Bk. Pr., Inc.; 0-87677),* Subs. of Media Judaica, Inc., 304 E. 49th St., New York, NY 10017 (SAN 282-1788) Tel 212-319-6666; Orders to: Media Judaica, Inc., 1363 Fairfield Ave., Bridgeport, CT 06605 (SAN 207-0022) Tel 203-384-2284.

Precious Res, *(Precious Resources; 0-937836),* 217 Groveland Dr., Peachtree City, GA 30269 (SAN 213-3512) Tel 404-631-1265.

Precision Pr, *(Precision Pr.; 0-9632332),* P.O. Box 1506, Norwalk, CT 06852; 37 Dunhill Dr., Fairfield, CT 06430.

Preferred Ent, *(Preferred Enterprises; 1-885143),* 3301 W. Strathmore Ave., Baltimore, MD 21215 Tel 410-764-2288.

Preferred Mktg, *(Preferred Marketing; 1-884166; 0-89781),* 18653 Ventura Blvd., Suite 375, Tarzana, CA 91356 Tel 818-708-1054.

Premier Personalized
See About You

Prentice ESL, *(Prentice Hall, ESL Dept.; 0-13; 0-88345),* 113 Sylvan Ave., Rte. 9W, Englewood Cliffs, NJ 07632 (SAN 200-2175) Tel 201-592-2000; Toll free: 800-922-0579.

Prentice Hall Pr
See P-H Gen Ref & Trav

Pres Soc Asheville, *(Preservation Society of Asheville & Buncombe County, Inc.; 0-937481),* P.O. Box 2806, Asheville, NC 28802 (SAN 659-0365) Tel 704-254-2343.

Prescott Durrell & Co, *(Prescott/Durrell, & Co.; 0-9609506),* 3400 Hawthorne Ave., Richmond, VA 23222 (SAN 274-7855) Tel 804-321-3467.

Preservation Pr, *(Preservation Pr., The; 0-89133),* Div. of National Trust for Historic Preservation, 1785 Massachusetts Ave., NW, Washington, DC 20036 (SAN 209-3146) Tel 202-673-4058; Toll free: 800-766-6847. Do not confuse with Preservation Pr. in Swedesboro, NJ.

Press N Amer, *(Press North America; 0-938271),* 835 Lakechime Dr., Sunnyvale, CA 94089 (SAN 659-8285) Tel 408-734-1680.

Pressed Duck, *(Pressed Duck Publishing; 0-9628888),* 2956 Red Hawk Way, Sacramento, CA 95833-1605 Tel 916-920-0741.

Prestwick Pub, *(Prestwick Poetry Publishing Co.; 0-9607812),* 2235 Calle Guaymas, La Jolla, CA 92037 (SAN 239-5932) Tel 619-456-2366.

Pretty Penny Pr, *(Pretty Penny Pr., Inc.; 0-938509),* 12851 Evanston St., Los Angeles, CA 90049-3712 (SAN 661-0226) Tel 213-476-7843.

Prevent Educ, *(Preventive Education Products; 0-9638765),* 1229 Madison, No. 1020, Seattle, WA 98104 Tel 206-624-8445.

Price Pub SC, *(Price Publishing Co.; 0-9626318),* 801 Brooks Rd., Mauldin, SC 29662 Tel 803-458-8484. Do not confuse with companies with the same name in Gardena, CA, Blaine, WA.

Price Stern, *(Price Stern Sloan; 0-8431),* Member of Putnam & Grosset Group, 11150 Olympic Blvd., Suite 650, Los Angeles, CA 90064 (SAN 202-0246) Tel 310-477-6100; Toll free: 800-631-8571; 1900 Sacramento St., Los Angeles, CA 90021 (SAN 658-148X). *Imprints:* Troubador (Troubador Press); Wonder-Treas (Wonder-Treasure Books).

Prima Pub, *(Prima Publishing; 0-914629; 1-55958),* 3875 Atherton Rd., Rocklin, CA 95765 (SAN 289-5609) Tel 916-632-7400; Dist. by: St. Martin's Pr., Inc., 175 Fifth Ave., Rm. 1715, New York, NY 10010 (SAN 200-2132) Tel 212-674-5151; Toll free: 800-221-7945.

Primarius Ltd, *(Primarius, Ltd. Public Relations; 0-943535),* 141 S. Seventh St., No. 141, Minneapolis, MN 55402-2334 (SAN 668-6133) Tel 612-338-5603.

Primary Progs, *(Primary Programs; 0-9612060),* 15 Elrond Dr., Pittsburgh, PA 15235 (SAN 286-8555) Tel 412-824-6116.

Primate Pub, *(Primate Publishing; 0-9615289),* 1710 Baker St., San Francisco, CA 94115 (SAN 694-4191) Tel 415-563-5160.

Primer Pubs, *(Primer Pubs.; 0-935810),* 5738 N. Central, Phoenix, AZ 85012 (SAN 220-0864) Tel 602-234-1574.

Princess NJ, *(Princess Publishing; 1-883499),* 26 Princess Ave., Marlton, NJ 08053 Tel 609-983-3964. Do not confuse with Princess Publishing in Beaverton, OR.

Princess Pub, *(Princess Publishing; 0-943367),* P.O. Box 386, Beaverton, OR 97075 (SAN 668-4718); 10127 SW Trapper Terr., Beaverton, OR 97005 (SAN 668-4726) Tel 503-646-1234. Do not confuse with Princess Publishing in Marlton, NJ.

Princeton Bk Co, *(Princeton Bk. Co., Pubs.; 0-916622; 0-87127),* P.O. Box 57, Pennington, NJ 08534 (SAN 630-1568); Toll free: 800-220-7149; 12 W. Delaware Ave., Pennington, NJ 08534 (SAN 244-8076) Tel 609-737-8177. *Imprints:* Dance Horizons (Dance Horizons Videos).

Princeton U Pr, *(Princeton Univ. Pr.; 0-691),* 41 William St., Princeton, NJ 08540 (SAN 202-0254) Tel 609-258-4900; Toll free: 800-777-4726 (orders); Orders to: California/Princeton Fulfillment Services, 1445 Lower Ferry Rd., Ewing, NJ 08618 (SAN 662-1171) Tel 609-883-1759; Toll free: 800-777-4726.

Prinit Pr, *(Prinit Pr.; 0-932970),* 215 Main St., Cambridge City, IN 47327 (SAN 212-680X) Tel 317-478-4885.

Printek, *(Printek; 0-938042),* 6989 Oxford St., Minneapolis, MN 55426 (SAN 215-7012).

Printemps Bks, *(Printemps Bks.; 0-9621844),* 1120 Harbor Dr. S., Venice, FL 34285-3719 Tel 813-488-6706.

Priscilla Pr, *(Priscilla Pr.; 0-9626408; 1-886167),* 2109 41st St., Allegan, MI 49010 Tel 616-673-3633.

Prism NJ, *(Prism Pr.; 1-881602),* 117 Highland Ave., Edison, NJ 08817 Tel 908-572-6586. Do not confuse with companies with the same name in Houston, TX, Minneapolis, MN.

Prisma Pr, *(Prisma Pr.; 0-942647),* P.O. Box 930, Kaunakakai, HI 96748 (SAN 667-1772) Tel 808-558-8509; Dist. by: L. R. Ream Publishing, P.O. Box 2043, Coeur d'Alene, ID 83814 (SAN 672-2725) Tel 208-667-0453; Toll free: 800-326-2665; Dist. by: Samuel Weiser, Inc., P.O. Box 612, York Beach, ME 03910-0612 (SAN 202-9588) Tel 207-363-4393; Toll free: 800-423-7087 (orders only); Dist. by: DeVorss & Co., P.O. Box 550, Marina del Rey, CA 90294-0550 (SAN 168-9886) Tel 213-870-7478; Toll free: 800-843-5743 (bookstores only); 800-331-4719 (in California, bookstores only).

Pritchett & Hull, *(Pritchett & Hull Assocs., Inc.;* 0-939838), 3440 Oakcliff Rd., NE, Suite 110, Atlanta, GA 30340 (SAN 216-9258) Tel 404-451-0602; Toll free: 800-241-4925.

PRO-ACTIV Pubns, *(PRO-ACTIV Pubns.; 0-9636547),* P.O. Box 331186, Corpus Christi, TX 78404; 441 Naples, Corpus Christi, TX 78404 Tel 512-884-8351.

Pro Golfers, *(Professional Golfers Assn. of America;* 0-9614856), 100 Ave. of the Champions, Palm Beach Gardens, FL 33410 (SAN 224-5655) Tel 407-626-3600.

Pro Lingua, *(Pro Lingua Assocs., Inc.; 0-86647),* 15 Elm St., Brattleboro, VT 05301 (SAN 216-0579) Tel 802-257-7779; Toll free: 800-366-4775.

Pro Lingua Pr, *(Pro Lingua Pr.; 1-879870),* Div. of European American R.E. Inv., Inc., P.O. Box 24368, Los Angeles, CA 90024; 1117 Roscomare Rd., Los Angeles, CA 90077 Tel 310-472-8396; Dist. by: Baker & Taylor Bks., Somerville Service Ctr., 251 Mt. Olive Church Rd., Somerville, NJ 08876-0734 (SAN 169-4901) Tel 908-722-8000; Toll free: 800-775-1500 (customer service); Dist. by: Baker & Taylor Bks., Momence Service Ctr., 501 S. Gladiolus St., Momence, IL 60954-2444 (SAN 169-2100) Tel 815-472-2444; Toll free: 800-775-2300 (customer service); Dist. by: Baker & Taylor Bks., Commerce Service Ctr., Mt. Olive Rd., Commerce, GA 30599-9988 (SAN 169-1503) Tel 706-335-5000; Toll free: 800-775-1200 (customer service); Dist. by: Baker & Taylor Bks., Reno Service Ctr., 380 Edison Way, Reno, NV 89564 (SAN 169-4464) Tel 702-858-6700; Toll free: 800-775-1700 (customer service); Dist. by: Follett Library Bk. Co., 4506 NW Hwy., Rtes. 14 & 31, Crystal Lake, IL 60014 (SAN 169-1902) Tel 815-477-9303; Toll free: 800-435-6170; Dist. by: Book Wholesalers, Inc., 1847 Mercer Rd., Lexington, KY 40511-1001 (SAN 630-8066) Tel 606-231-9789; Toll free: 800-888-4478.

Pro Pub Inc, *(Pro Publishing, Inc.; 1-877833),* 18020 SW 66th St., Fort Lauderdale, FL 33331-1860 (SAN 297-5408) Tel 305-680-1771; Dist. by: BookWorld Distribution Services, Inc., 1933 Whitfield Pk. Loop, Sarasota, FL 34243 (SAN 173-0568) Tel 813-758-8094; Toll free: 800-444-2524 (orders only). Do not confuse with Pro Publishing, Inc. in Sandusky, OH.

Prod Concept, *(Product Concept, Inc.; 0-927106),* 3334 Adobe Ct., Colorado Springs, CO 80907-5461 Tel 719-632-1089.

Prod Info Analysis, *(Product Information & Analysis;* 0-9621865), P.O. Box 76127, Saint Paul, MN 55175; 7601 Carillon Plaza E., Woodbury, MN 55125 Tel 612-731-9789.

Prof Publications
See Dolphin Lrning

Prof Pubns CA, *(Professional Pubns., Inc.; 0-932276;* 0-912045), 1250 Fifth Ave., Belmont, CA 94002 (SAN 264-6315) Tel 415-593-9119; Toll free: 800-426-1178. Do not confuse with Professional Pubns. Inc., Columbus, OH.

Prof Reading Serv, *(Professional Reading Services, Inc.;* 0-9614374), P.O. Box 7281, Roanoke, VA 24019 (SAN 688-5985) Tel 703-563-0634.

Proficiency Pr, *(Proficiency Pr. Co., Inc.; 1-879279),* 18 Lucille Ave., Elmont, NY 11003 Tel 516-354-0669.

Profiles Corp, *(Profiles Corp.; 0-7836),* 507 Highland Ave., Iowa City, IA 52240 Tel 319-354-7600; Toll free: 800-776-3454.

Prog Bapt Pub, *(Progressive Baptist Publishing Hse.;* 0-89191), Div. of David C. Cook Publishing Co., 850 N. Grove Ave., Elgin, IL 60120 (SAN 277-7010).

Programs Educ, *(Programs for Education, Inc.; 0-935493; 1-56762),* Affil. of Modern Learning Pr., P.O. Box 167, Rosemont, NJ 08556 (SAN 695-9962) Tel 609-397-2214; Toll free: 800-627-5867.

Progress Educ, *(Progressive Educators Publishing;* 0-9634324), 219A W. Main St., Belleville, IL 62220 Tel 618-233-7542.

Progressive Pubns, *(Progressive Pubns.; 0-937157),* P.O. Box 4016, Homosassa Springs, FL 32647 (SAN 658-4721); 8 S. Jungleplum Ct., Homosassa, FL 32646 (SAN 658-473X) Tel 904-382-1452.

Project Chong, *(Project Chong Productions; 1-885298),* P.O. Box 9551, Green Bay, WI 54308-9551; 513 Newhall St., Green Bay, WI 54302 Tel 414-435-7889.

Promethean Arts, *(Promethean Arts; 0-942624),* P.O. Box 2619, Toledo, OH 43606 (SAN 238-5627) Tel 419-536-4257.

Prometheus Bks, *(Prometheus Bks.; 0-87975),* 59 John Glenn Dr., Buffalo, NY 14228-2197 (SAN 202-0289) Tel 716-691-0133; Toll free: 800-421-0351.

Promise Land Pubs, *(Promise Land Pubs.; 0-9633091),* P.O. Box 110, Dalton, OH 44618-0110 (SAN 297-6749); 310 Nickles St., Dalton, OH 44618 Tel 216-828-2167; Dist. by: Green Pastures Pr., 7102 Lynn Rd., NE, Minerva, OH 44657 (SAN 298-0770) Tel 216-895-3291.

Promntory Pr, *(Promontory Pr.; 0-88394),* 386 Park Ave., Suite 1913, New York, NY 10016 Tel 212-679-4200.

Proof Pr, *(Proof Pr.; 0-935070),* P.O. Box 1256, Berkeley, CA 94701 (SAN 209-8687) Tel 510-521-8741; Dist. by: Social Studies School Service, 10200 Jefferson Blvd., P.O. Box 802, Culver City, CA 90232-0802 (SAN 168-9592) Tel 310-839-2436; Toll free: 800-421-4246; Dist. by: National Women's History Project, 7738 Bell Rd., Windsor, CA 95492 (SAN 200-8920) Tel 707-838-6000.

Prophecy Pubns, *(Prophecy Pubns.; 0-941241),* P.O. Box 7000, Oklahoma City, OK 73153 (SAN 665-5319) Tel 405-634-1234; Toll free: 800-245-5577.

Proscenium, *(Proscenium Pr.; 0-912262),* P.O. Box 361, Newark, DE 19715 (SAN 203-0950) Tel 302-764-8477.

Prospector Pr, *(Prospector Pr.; 0-9628828),* P.O. Box 1289, Moore Haven, FL 33471 Tel 813-946-3212; Toll free: 800-497-4378.

Prosperity & Profits, *(Prosperity & Profits Unlimited, Distribution Services),* P.O. Box 416, Denver, CO 80201 (SAN 200-4682) Tel 303-575-5676. *Imprints:* Lamp Light Pr (Lamp Light Press).

Prosprty Prtnrs, *(Prosperity Partners Pr.; 0-9637853),* P.O. Box 56701, Jacksonville, FL 32241; 6026 San Jose Blvd., Jacksonville, FL 32217 Tel 904-730-8110.

Proteus LA, *(Proteus; 0-9620541),* Div. of St. George Assocs., Inc., 6565 Sunset Blvd., Suite 321, Los Angeles, CA 90028 (SAN 248-8760) Tel 213-953-7654; Toll free: 800-662-7768.

Providence Hse, *(Providence Hse. Pubs.; 1-881576),* Div. of Custom Communications, P.O. Box 158, Franklin, TN 37065; Toll free: 800-321-5692; 118 Shenandoah Dr., Franklin, TN 37064 Tel 615-791-5692.

Providers Pr, *(Providers Pr.; 0-9638754),* Div. of Providers Choice, Inc., 7808 Creekridge Cir., Suite 110, Bloomington, MN 55439-2612 Tel 612-944-7010; Toll free: 800-356-5983; Dist. by: Francis Family Publishing, 3901 Dartmouth Dr., Minnetonka, MN 55345 Tel 612-476-4847.

Provost, *(Provost, C. Antonio),* 4474 Sunburst Dr., Oceanside, CA 92056-3540 (SAN 239-3751) Tel 619-798-8754.

Prow Bks-Franciscan, *(Prow Bks./Franciscan Marytown Pr.; 0-913382),* 1600 W. Park Ave., Libertyville, IL 60048 (SAN 205-1060) Tel 708-367-7800.

Prufrock Pr, *(Prufrock Pr.; 1-882664),* P.O. Box 8813, Waco, TX 76714-8813; Toll free: 800-998-2208; 100 N. 6th St., Suite 400, Waco, TX 76701 Tel 817-756-3337.

PS Assocs Croton, *(Policy Studies Assocs.; 0-936826),* P.O. Box 337, Croton-on-Hudson, NY 10520 (SAN 214-4417) Tel 914-271-6500.

PS Enterprises, *(PS Enterprises; 0-9617764),* 1443 Tripodi Cir., Niles, OH 44446-3564 (SAN 664-7073) Tel 216-652-1409.

Pssblts Denver, *(Possibilities; 0-9622477; 1-880972),* 8970 E. Hampden Ave., Denver, CO 80231 Tel 303-740-6206; Toll free: 800-474-2665. *Imprints:* DreamSpinners (DreamSpinners).

Psychegenics, *(Psychegenics Pr.; 0-931865),* Subs. of MCM, Inc., P.O. Box 332, Gaithersburg, MD 20884-0332 (SAN 686-0567) Tel 301-948-1122.

Psychol Educ Pubns, *(Psychological & Educational Pubns., Inc.; 0-931421),* 1477 Rollins Rd., Burlingame, CA 94010 (SAN 683-5422); Toll free: 800-523-5775.

Pt Orchard Spec, *(Port Orchard Specialties; 0-9616198),* 7775 SE Blakeview Dr., Port Orchard, WA 98366 (SAN 699-9581) Tel 206-871-5535.

Pt WA Pub Lib, *(Port Washington Public Library;* 0-9615059), 1 Library Dr., Port Washington, NY 11050 (SAN 694-163X) Tel 516-883-4400.

PTWO Educ, *(P2 Educational Services, Inc.; 1-885964),* P.O. Box 151, Granville, IA 51022; 4423 Monroe Ave., Granville, IA 51022 Tel 712-727-3772.

Pub Div JCS, *(Publishing Div. of JCS; 0-932411),* 3998 W. Akron Rd., Akron, MI 48701 (SAN 687-4053) Tel 517-691-5484.

Pub Horizons, *(Publishing Horizons, Inc.; 0-942280),* 8233 Via Paseo del Norte, Suite F400, Scottsdale, AZ 85258 (SAN 239-7439).

Pub Mark, *(Publishers Mark, The; 0-9614636),* P.O. Box 6939, Incline Village, NV 89450 (SAN 691-9154) Tel 702-831-5139; Dist. by: Baker & Taylor Bks., Reno Service Ctr., 380 Edison Way, Reno, NV 89564 (SAN 169-4464) Tel 702-858-6700; Toll free: 800-775-1700 (customer service); Dist. by: Baker & Taylor Bks., Momence Service Ctr., 501 S. Gladiolus St., Momence, IL 60954-2444 (SAN 169-2100) Tel 815-472-2444; Toll free: 800-775-2300 (customer service); Dist. by: Baker & Taylor Bks., Somerville Service Ctr., 50 Kirby Ave., Somerville, NJ 08876-0734 (SAN 169-4901) Tel 908-722-8000; Toll free: 800-775-1500 (customer service).

Pub Resces PR, *(Publishing Resources, Inc.; 0-89825),* P.O. Box 41307, Minillas Sta., Santurce, PR 00940; 373 San Jorge St., 2nd Flr., Santurce, PR 00912 Tel 809-268-8080.

Publicaciones Nuevos, *(Publicaciones Nuevos Horizontes; 0-9624458),* P.O. Box 3727, Huntington Park, CA 90255; 7800 State St., Huntington Park, CA 90255 Tel 213-750-2155.

Pubns Devl Co, *(Publications Development Co.;* 0-936431), P.O. Box 1075, Crockett, TX 75835 (SAN 211-0490); Hwy. 287 N., Crockett, TX 75835 (SAN 699-5543) Tel 409-544-5137.

Pubns Intl Ltd, *(Publications International, Ltd.; 0-88176; 1-56173; 0-7853),* 7373 N. Cicero Ave., Lincolnwood, IL 60646 (SAN 263-9823) Tel 708-676-3470; Dist. by: NAL/Dutton, 375 Hudson St., New York, NY 10014-3657 Tel 212-366-2000.

Pubs Northeast, *(Publishers Northeast; 0-9634458),* 6702 16th SW, Seattle, WA 98106-1615 (SAN 297-7982) Tel 206-768-0104.

Pubs Pr UT, *(Publishers Pr.; 0-916095),* 1900 W. 2300, S., Salt Lake City, UT 84119 (SAN 219-3884) Tel 801-972-6600. Do not confuse with Publishers Pr., Portland, OR.

Puckerbrush, *(Puckerbrush Pr.; 0-913006),* 76 Main St., Orono, ME 04473 (SAN 202-0327) Tel 207-866-4868; Univ. of Maine, English Dept., Orono, ME 04469 (SAN 241-8304) Tel 207-581-3832; Dist. by: Inland Bk. Co., 140 Commerce St., East Haven, CT 06512 (SAN 200-4151) Tel 203-467-4257; Toll free: 800-243-0138; Dist. by: Maine Writers & Pubs. Alliance, 12 Pleasant St., Brunswick, ME 04011 (SAN 224-2303) Tel 207-729-6333.

Pueblo Acoma Pr, *(Pueblo of Acoma Pr.; 0-915347),* P.O. Box 449, Acomita, NM 87034 (SAN 290-0386) Tel 505-552-9833.

Pueblo Pr, *(Pueblo Pr., Inc.; 0-9619949),* P.O. Box 533422, Orlando, FL 32853-3422 (SAN 246-9510); 1400 Lake Shore Dr., Orlando, FL 32803 (SAN 246-9529) Tel 407-896-4968.

Puff Pied Piper *Imprint of* **Puffin Bks**

Puff Unicorn *Imprint of* **Puffin Bks**

Puffin *Imprint of* **Puffin Bks**

Puffin Bks, *(Puffin Bks.; 0-14; 0-670),* Div. of Penguin USA, 375 Hudson St., New York, NY 10014-3657 Tel 212-366-2000. *Imprints:* Dial Easy to Read (Dial Easy to Read); Dutton Unicorn (Dutton Unicorn); Puff Pied Piper (Puffin Pied Piper); Puff Unicorn (Puffin Unicorn); Puffin (Puffin).

Puissance Pubns, *(Puissance Pubns., Inc.; 0-940634),* P.O. Box 1268, Wheeling, IL 60090 (SAN 218-5229) Tel 708-202-0242.

Pulitzer-Goodman, *(Pulitzer-Goodman Assocs., Inc.;* 0-9632191), P.O. Box 2203, Union, NJ 07083; 2074 Stowe St., Union, NJ 07083 Tel 908-964-8464.

Pulse Pubns, *(Pulse Pubns.; 0-9628850),* Div. of Biological Therapy Institute, Hospital Dr., Franklin, TN 37064 Tel 615-790-7535.

Pumpkin Patch Pubs, *(Pumpkin Patch Pubs.; 0-9628321),* 718 Ott St., Harrisonburg, VA 22801 Tel 703-434-8385.

Pumpkin Pr Pub Hse, *(Pumpkin Pr. Publishing Hse.;* 0-939973), P.O. Box 139, Shasta, CA 96087 (SAN 665-2387) Tel 916-244-6251.

Pumpkin Ridge, *(Pumpkin Ridge Productions; 1-882635),* P.O. Box 33, North Plains, OR 97133; Rte. 1, Box 233, Cornelius, OR 97113 Tel 503-647-0021.

Punches Prodns, *(Punches Productions; 0-929883),* 34919 Sunset Dr., Oconomowoc, WI 53066-9269 (SAN 250-6513).

Punking Pr, *(Punking Pr.; 0-9641641),* P.O. Box 25, Williamson, NY 14589; 5980 Pease Rd., Williamson, NY 14589 Tel 315-589-5119.

Purcell Prods, *(Purcell Productions, Inc.; 0-9610742),* 484 W. 43rd St., 23M, New York, NY 10036 (SAN 264-780X) Tel 212-279-0795.

Purple Pomegranate, *(Purple Pomegranate Productions; 0-9616148; 1-881022),* Div. of Jews for Jesus, 84 Page St., San Francisco, CA 94102-5895 (SAN 699-8240) Tel 415-864-2600.

Purple Turtle Bks, *(Purple Turtle Bks.; 0-943925),* Div. of Scott Publishing, Inc., 420 Fifth Ave. S., No. D, Edmonds, WA 98020-3584 (SAN 242-2425) Tel 206-775-8777; Toll free: 800-888-7853.

Purple Turtle Pub
See Purple Turtle Bks

Pussywillow Pub, *(Pussywillow Publishing Hse.;* 0-934739), 500 E. Encinas Ave., P.O. Box 1806, Gilbert, AZ 85234 (SAN 694-1702) Tel 602-892-1316; Dist. by: Baker & Taylor Bks., Somerville Service Ctr., 50 Kirby Ave., Somerville, NJ 08876-0734 (SAN 169-4901) Tel 908-722-8000; Toll free: 800-775-1500 (customer service); Dist. by: Baker & Taylor Bks., Reno Service Ctr., 380 Edison Way, Reno, NV 89564 (SAN 169-4464) Tel 702-858-6700; Toll free: 800-775-1700 (customer service); Dist. by: New Leaf Distributing Co., 5425 Tulane Dr., SW, Atlanta, GA 30336-2323 (SAN 169-1449) Tel 404-691-6996; Toll free: 800-326-2665; Dist. by: Many Feathers Bks. & Maps, 2626 W. Indian School Rd., Phoenix, AZ 85017 (SAN 158-8877) Tel 602-266-1043; Dist. by: Canyonlands Pubs., 4999 E. Empire, Unit A, Flagstaff, AZ 86004 (SAN 114-3824) Tel 602-527-0730; Toll free: 800-283-1983.

Put-Together Dev Toys, *(Put-Together Developmental Toys, Inc.; 0-9631987),* 201 W. Genesee St., Suite 111, Fayetteville, NY 13066 Tel 315-637-9183.

Putnam *Imprint of* **Putnam Pub Group**

Putnam Pub Group, *(Putnam Publishing Group, The; 0-399; 0-698; 0-89828),* 200 Madison Ave., New York, NY 10016 (SAN 202-5531) Tel 212-951-8400; Toll free: 800-631-8571. *Imprints:* Coward (Coward-McCann); G&D (Grossett & Dunlap, Incorporated); Philomel Bks (Philomel Books); Platt & Munk Pubs (Platt & Munk Publishers); Putnam (Putnam's, G. P., Sons); Sandcastle Bks (Sandcastle Books); Tuffy (Tuffy Books); Whitebird Bks (Whitebird Books).

PWC Pub, *(PWC Publishing; 0-9635089),* Div. of Placer Women's Ctr., P.O. Box 5462, Auburn, CA 95604 Tel 916-885-0443.

Pyramid TX, *(Pyramid Publishing Co.; 0-9629102),* 3323 Rushwood Ln., Sugar Land, TX 77479 Tel 713-265-1816. Do not confuse with companies with the same name in Memphis, TN, San Diego, CA, Laurelton, NY, Zenda, WI.

Pyrola Pub, *(Pyrola Publishing; 0-9618348),* P.O. Box 80961, Fairbanks, AK 99708 (SAN 667-3503) Tel 907-455-6469.

Quail Ridge, *(Quail Ridge Pr., Inc.; 0-937552),* P.O. Box 123, Brandon, MS 39043 (SAN 214-2201); Toll free: 800-343-1583; 602 Marquette Rd., Brandon, MS 39042 Tel 601-825-2063; Dist. by: Dot Gibson Pubns., 161 Knight Ave. Cir., Waycross, GA 31501 (SAN 200-9676) Tel 912-285-2848; Dist. by: Southwest Cookbook Distributors, Inc., P.O. Box 707, Bonham, TX 75418 (SAN 200-4925) Tel 903-583-8898; Toll free: 800-725-8898 (orders); Dist. by: Ingram Bk. Co., 1 Ingram Blvd., La Vergne, TN 37086-1986 (SAN 169-7978) Tel 615-793-5000; Toll free: 800-937-8000 (orders only, all warehouses); Dist. by: Forest Sales & Distributing Co., 2616 Spain St., New Orleans, LA 70117 (SAN 157-5511) Tel 504-947-2106; Toll free: 800-347-2106 (orders only); Dist. by: Bright Horizons Specialty Distributors, Inc., 138 Springside Rd., Asheville, NC 28803 (SAN 110-4101) Tel 704-684-8840.

Quakey Bear, *(Quakey Bear, Inc.; 0-9630089),* 11535 Elbert Way, San Diego, CA 92126 Tel 619-693-0925.

Qual Family, *(Quality Family Entertainment, Inc.;* 1-884336), 1133 Broadway, Suite 1520, New York, NY 10021 Tel 212-463-9623.

Qual Instruct, *(Quality Instructional Pubns.; 0-9634651),* 1680 Steven St., Sun Prairie, WI 53590 Tel 608-837-4002.

Qual-Tech, *(Qual-Tech Publishing; 1-880354),* 1117 32nd Ave. Dr., E., Ellentown, FL 34222-2111 Tel 607-674-4479.

Quality Pubns, *(Quality Pubns.; 0-89137),* Div. of Quality Printing Co., P.O. Box 1060, Abilene, TX 79604 (SAN 203-0071) Tel 915-677-6262; Toll free: 800-359-7708.

Quality Time
See Shelf-Life Bks

Quest Dists, *(Quest Distributors; 0-9636375),* 215 Beachwood Blvd., Melbourne Beach, FL 32951 Tel 407-676-5903.

Quest Intl, *(Quest International, Inc.; 0-933419;* 1-56095), P.O. Box 566, Granville, OH 43023-0566 (SAN 691-506X); Toll free: 800-288-6401; 537 Jones Rd., Granville, OH 43023 Tel 614-587-2800.

Questar Pubs, *(Questar Pubs., Inc.; 0-945564; 0-930014;* 0-88070), P.O. Box 1720, Sisters, OR 97759 (SAN 247-123X); Toll free: 800-929-0910; 305 W. Adams St., Sisters, OR 97759 Tel 503-549-1144; Dist. by: Spring Arbor Distributors, 10885 Textile Rd., Belleville, MI 48111 (SAN 158-9016) Tel 313-481-0900; Toll free: 800-395-5599 (orders); 800-395-7234 (customer service). *Imprints:* Gold & Honey (Gold 'N' Honey Books); Multnomah Bks (Multnomah Books).

Quill *Imprint of* **Morrow**

Quin Tel Prodns, *(Quin-Tel Productions, Inc.;* 0-9618349), 35 Wendt Ave., Larchmont, NY 10538 (SAN 667-2744) Tel 914-834-0797.

Quinn Pubng, *(Quinn Publishing Co., Inc.; 0-9638192),* P.O. Box 9452, Asheville, NC 28815; Rt. 2, Box 268Q, Mack Noblitt Rd., Old Fort, NC 28762 Tel 704-668-4622.

Quintilone Ent, *(Quintilone Enterprises; 0-9616980),* 29 Merrimac St., Buffalo, NY 14214 (SAN 661-7433) Tel 716-836-0945.

Quixote Pr IA, *(Quixote Pr.; 1-878488; 1-57166),* 615 Avenue H, Fort Madison, IA 52627-2933 Tel 319-372-7480; Toll free: 800-571-2665. Do not confuse with Quixote Pr., Houston TX.

R A Schrader, *(Schrader, Richard A.; 0-9622987),* P.O. Box 39, Kingshill, Saint Croix, VI 00851-0039 Tel 809-778-0477.

R & C Black Hist, *(Read & Color Black History;* 0-9634154), P.O. Box 1172, Akron, OH 44309-1172; 400 Locust, No. 705, Akron, OH 44307 Tel 216-434-9441.

R & D Bks, *(R&D Bks.; 0-9623504),* 1031 Holbrook Rd., Newnan, GA 30263 Tel 706-251-1212.

R & E Pubs, *(R & E Pubs., Inc.; 0-88247; 1-56875),* Div. of R & E Research Assocs., Inc., 468 Auzerais Ave., Suite A, San Jose, CA 95126 (SAN 293-3195); 468 Auzerais Ave., Suite A, San Jose, CA 95126 Tel 408-977-0691; Dist. by: Login Pubs. Consortium, 1436 W. Randolph St., 2nd Flr., Chicago, IL 60607 (SAN 630-5733) Tel 312-733-8228; Toll free: 800-626-4330.

R & S Books, *(R & S Bks.; 0-929297),* 7142 Rutgers Ave., Westminster, CA 92683 (SAN 249-0889) Tel 714-893-6100. Do not confuse with R & S Bks., an imprint of Farrar, Straus & Giroux.

R B Hoffman, *(Hoffman, Robert B., , Jr.; 0-9633156),* 7761 Ingram St., Anchorage, AK 99502 Tel 907-243-0626.

R B Phillips Pub, *(Phillips, Robert B., Pub.; 0-9620577),* 175 Slagle Rd., Bakersville, NC 28705 (SAN 249-1400) Tel 704-688-4850.

R Bane Ltd, *(Bane, Robert, Ltd.; 0-9622646),* 8025 Melrose Ave., Los Angeles, CA 90046 Tel 310-205-0555; Toll free: 800-325-2765.

R C Law & Co, *(Law, R. C., & Co., Inc.; 0-939925),* 4861 Chino Ave., Chino, CA 91710-5132 (SAN 200-609X) Tel 714-871-0940; Toll free: 800-777-5292.

R E Moen, *(Moen, R. E.; 0-9614819),* 3152 S. 27th St., La Crosse, WI 54601 (SAN 693-0794) Tel 608-788-8753.

R E Todd
See Crosswalk Res

R Finkelstein, *(Finkelstein, Ruth; 0-9628157),* 216 Private Way, Lakewood, NJ 08701 Tel 201-367-1673.

R G Speltz, *(Speltz, Robert G.; 0-932299),* 505 Albert Lea St., Albert Lea, MN 56007 (SAN 686-2721) Tel 507-373-2145.

R H Barnes, *(Barnes, Robert H.; 0-930480),* P.O. Box 418, Grayland, WA 98547 (SAN 210-3532) Tel 206-267-3601.

R H Pub, *(Renaissance Hse. Pubs.; 0-939650; 1-55838),* P.O. Box 177, Frederick, CO 80530 (SAN 169-0574); Toll free: 800-521-9221 (orders); 541 Oak St., Frederick, CO 80530 (SAN 658-1404) Tel 303-833-2030.

R H Van Tuyle, *(Van Tuyle, R. Helen; 0-9617816),* 2851 Rolling Hills Dr., Fullerton, CA 92635 (SAN 665-3162) Tel 714-996-1405.

R Hall, *(Hall, Rachel; 0-9624855),* 6721 Samuel Ct., Anchorage, AK 99516 Tel 907-345-3245.

R in R
See Move It Math

R J Davis, *(Davis, Rebecca J.; 0-9634032),* P.O. Box 144, Summit Point, WV 25446-0144 Tel 304-725-1609.

R J Delaney, *(Delaney, Richard J.; 0-9629849),* 1836 Wallenberg Dr., Fort Collins, CO 80526 Tel 303-223-9669.

R J Miller, *(Miller, R.J., Publishing; 0-9632192),* 20B Cooper Pl., Bronx, NY 10475 Tel 718-671-7262.

R Jamieson, *(Jamieson, Rita; 0-9622329),* 5308 River Ave., Newport Beach, CA 92663 Tel 714-645-6570.

R K Garrity, *(Garrity, Robert K.; 0-9628375),* 537 Los Vientos Dr., Newbury Park, CA 91320 Tel 805-498-2410.

R L Breeding
See Thriftecon

R L Merriam, *(Merriam, Robert L.; 0-918507),* Newhall Rd., Conway, MA 01341 (SAN 163-4070) Tel 413-369-4052.

R M Campbell, *(Campbell, Robert M.; 0-9613542),* P.O. Box 7906, Ann Arbor, MI 48107 (SAN 670-1752) Tel 810-737-8980.

R M S Pub, *(R.M.S. Publishing; 0-9632284),* 30600 Telegraph Rd., Suite 2161, Birmingham, MI 48025 Tel 810-642-2365.

R M Wingate, *(Wingate, Rosalee Martin; 0-9625391),* 2105 Teakwood Dr., Austin, TX 78758 Tel 512-454-7420.

R Osgood, *(Osgood, Raymond; 0-9619757),* 21 Sugarboat Dr., Leesburg, FL 34788 (SAN 246-5434) Tel 904-323-0087.

R Owen Pubs, *(Owen, Richard C., Pubs., Inc.; 0-913461; 1-878450; 1-57274),* P.O. Box 585, Katonah, NY 10536 (SAN 285-1814); Toll free: 800-336-5588 (orders); 380 Adams St., Bedford Hills, NY 10507 Tel 914-232-3903.

R R Dahlstedt, *(Dahlstedt, Richard R., The Attic;* 0-9621827), 2613 Bay Ave., Beach Haven, NJ 08008 Tel 609-492-1064.

R Rinehart, *(Rinehart, Roberts, Pubs., Inc.; 0-911797; 1-879373; 1-57098),* P.O. Box 666, Niwot, CO 80544 (SAN 264-3510) Tel 303-652-2921; Toll free: 800-352-1985; Dist. by: Publishers Group West, 4065 Hollis St., Emeryville, CA 94608 (SAN 202-8522) Tel 510-658-3453; Toll free: 800-788-3123.

R S Kelley, *(Kelley, Rosemary Sue; 0-9616905),* P.O. Box 505, HCR 69, School St., Friendship, ME 04547 (SAN 661-5171) Tel 207-832-4206.

R S Rauch, *(Rauch, Robert S.; 0-9624076),* 91 Cherry St., Milford, CT 06460 Tel 203-874-5577.

R Shackelford, *(Shackelford, Robert, Pub.; 0-9618308),* P.O. Box 101, Delaware, OH 43015 (SAN 667-3007); 174 Kensington Dr., Delaware, OH 43015 (SAN 667-3015) Tel 614-363-8964.

R Talsorian, *(Talsorian, R., Games, Inc.; 0-937279),* P.O. Box 7356, Berkeley, CA 94707-0356 (SAN 658-6600) Tel 510-549-1373.

R Tanner Assocs Inc, *(Tanner, Ralph, Assocs., Inc.;* 0-942078), 122 N. Cortez St., Suite 102, Prescott, AZ 86301 (SAN 239-9857) Tel 602-778-4162.

R W Robinson, *(Robinson, Ronald W., Corp.;* 0-9622692), P.O. Box 2703, Petersburg, VA 23804 Tel 804-862-9144.

R Wagner Pub, *(Wagner, Roger, Publishing, Inc.;* 0-927796), 1050 Pioneer Way, Suite P, El Cajon, CA 92020 (SAN 653-5178) Tel 619-442-0522; Toll free: 800-421-6526.

R Weller, *(Weller, Robert; 0-9628359),* 1818 17th Ave., N., Lake Worth, FL 33460 Tel 407-844-8140.

R Wornall, *(Wornall, Ruthie; 0-9624467),* 9800 W. 104th St., Overland Park, KS 66212 Tel 913-888-1530; Dist. by: Cookbook Collection, Inc., 2500 E. 195th St., Belton, MO 64012 (SAN 200-6359) Tel 816-322-2122.

Rabbit Ears *Imprint of* **Picture Bk Studio**

Rabeth Pub Co, *(Rabeth Publishing Co.; 0-9626735),* P.O. Box 171, Kirksville, MO 63501 (SAN 298-4032); 201 S. Cottage Grove, Kirksville, MO 63501.

Raconteurs, *(Raconteurs, Inc.; 0-9621758),* 4661 Lake Club Cir., Oconomowoc, WI 53066 (SAN 252-080X) Tel 414-567-4009.

Radiant LA, *(Radiant Publishing Co., The; 0-944512),* P.O. Box 796, Thibodaux, LA 70302 (SAN 243-7554); 112 Juniper St., Thibodaux, LA 70302 (SAN 243-7562) Tel 504-446-0591.

Rae Pub, *(Rae Publications; 0-9626052),* 13210 NE 199th St., Battle Ground, WA 98604 Tel 206-687-3767.

RAEYC, *(Rochester Assn. for the Education of Young Children; 0-9613271),* 246 Archer Rd., Churchville, NY 14428 (SAN 297-035X) Tel 716-624-3775.

Railhead Pubns, *(Railhead Pubns.; 0-912113),* P.O. Box 6579, Canton, OH 44706 (SAN 264-7826) Tel 216-454-5551.

Rain Bird CT
See Rain Bird Prods

Rain Bird Prods, *(Rain Bird Productions, Inc.;* 1-879920), 16 Judd Bridge Rd., Roxbury, CT 06783 Tel 203-354-3856; Dist. by: Publishers Group West, 4065 Hollis St., Emeryville, CA 94608 (SAN 202-8522) Tel 510-658-3453; Toll free: 800-788-3123.

Rain Bird Pubs, *(Rain Bird Pubs.; 0-945122),* P.O. Box 135, Inchelium, WA 99138 (SAN 246-1536); Cobb Creek Rd., Inchelium, WA 99138 (SAN 246-1544) Tel 509-722-6601; Dist. by: Bookpeople, 7900 Edgewater Dr., Oakland, CA 94621 (SAN 168-9517) Tel 510-632-4700; Toll free: 800-999-4650.

Rain Dance Pub, *(Rain Dance Publishing; 0-9633168),* P.O. Box 301428, Portland, OR 97230; 10717 NE Prescott, Portland, OR 97230 Tel 503-256-2761.

Rainbow Bend, *(Rainbow Bend Storytelling; 0-9624224),* 7 Kevin Dr., East Windsor, CT 06088 Tel 203-627-8330.

Rainbow Bks, *(Rainbow Bks., Inc.; 0-89508),* 95 Mayhill St., Saddlebrook, NJ 07662 (SAN 209-9918) Tel 201-935-3369. Do not confuse with Rainbow Bks., Inc. Highland City, FL.

Rainbow Cat Pubs, *(Rainbow Cat Pubs.; 0-929986),* 613 35th Ave. S., North Myrtle Beach, SC 29582 (SAN 250-9245) Tel 803-272-4128; Dist. by: New Lear Distributing Co., 5425 Tulane Dr., SW, Atlanta, GA 30336-2323 (SAN 169-1449) Tel 404-691-6996; Toll free: 800-326-2665; Dist. by: DeVorss & Co., P.O. Box 550, Marina del Rey, CA 90294-0550 (SAN 168-9886) Tel 213-870-7478; Toll free: 800-843-5743 (bookstores only); 800-331-4719 (in California, bookstores only).

Rainbow IA, *(Rainbow Publishing; 0-9629599),* 618 E. Locust St., Davenport, IA 52803-4333 Tel 217-544-8122.

Rainbow Morn, *(Rainbow Morning Music Alternatives; 0-9615696; 0-938663),* 2121 Fairland Rd., Silver Spring, MD 20904 (SAN 218-2963) Tel 301-384-9207; Dist. by: Baker & Taylor Bks., Somerville Service Ctr., 50 Kirby Ave., Somerville, NJ 08876-0734 (SAN 169-4901) Tel 908-722-8000; Toll free: 800-775-1500 (customer service); Dist. by: Baker & Taylor Bks., Momence Service Ctr., 501 S. Gladiolus St., Momence, IL 60954-2444 (SAN 169-2100) Tel 815-472-2444; Toll free: 800-775-2300 (customer service); Dist. by: Baker & Taylor Bks., Commerce Service Ctr., 251 Mt. Olive Church Rd., Commerce, GA 30599-9988 (SAN 169-1503) Tel 706-335-5000; Toll free: 800-775-1200 (customer service); Dist. by: Baker & Taylor Bks., Reno Service Ctr., 380 Edison Way, Reno, NV 89564 (SAN 169-4464) Tel 702-858-6700; Toll free: 800-775-1700 (customer service); Dist. by: Ingram Bk. Co., 1 Ingram Blvd., La Vergne, TN 37086-1986 (SAN 169-7978) Tel 615-793-5000; Toll free: 800-937-8000 (orders only, all warehouses); Dist. by: Independent Pubs. Group, 814 N. Franklin St., Chicago, IL 60610 Tel 312-337-0747; Toll free: 800-888-4741.

Rainbow NC, *(Rainbow Connection; 1-878321),* 477 Hannah Branch Rd., Burnsville, NC 28714 Tel 704-675-5909; Dist. by: Compassion Bks., 479 Hannah Branch Rd., Burnsville, NC 28714-9582 (SAN 200-9277) Tel 704-675-9670; Dist. by: Inland Bk. Co., 140 Commerce St., East Haven, CT 06512 (SAN 200-4151) Tel 203-467-4257; Toll free: 800-243-0138; Dist. by: New Leaf Distributing Co., 5425 Tulane Dr., SW, Atlanta, GA 30336-2323 (SAN 169-1449) Tel 404-691-6996; Toll free: 800-326-2665. *Imprints:* Mntn Rainbow (Mountain Rainbow Publications).

Rainbow NJ *Imprint of* **Troll Assocs**

Rainbow Pr NY, *(Rainbow Pr.; 0-943156),* 222 Edwards Dr., Fayetteville, NY 13066 (SAN 240-4354); Dist. by: Baker & Taylor Bks., Somerville Service Ctr., 50 Kirby Ave., Somerville, NJ 08876-0734 (SAN 169-4901) Tel 908-722-8000; Toll free: 800-775-1500 (customer service). Do not confuse with companies with the same name in Snover, MI, Sparta, NJ, Huntington Beach, CA.

Rainbow Rhapsody, *(Rainbow Rhapsody; 0-9625920),* 793 Garner Dr., Lander, WY 82520 Tel 307-332-7298.

Rainbows End, *(Rainbow's End Co.; 0-9608780;* 1-880451), 354 Golden Grove Rd., Baden, PA 15005 (SAN 238-3489) Tel 412-266-4997.

Raintree Steck-V, *(Raintree Steck-Vaughn Pubs.; 0-8114; 0-8172; 0-8393),* Div. of Steck-Vaughn Co., 466 Southern Blvd., Chatham, NJ 07928 (SAN 658-1757) Tel 201-514-1525; Toll free: 800-531-5015; Orders to: P.O. Box 26015, Austin, TX 78755 Tel 512-343-8227; Toll free: 800-531-5015.

Ralls Cnty Bk, *(Ralls County Bk. Co.; 0-9617769),* P.O. Box 375, New London, MO 63459 (SAN 664-7138) Tel 314-985-8211.

Rallysport Video Prodns, *(Rallysport Video Productions;* 0-926727), P.O. Box 29809, Los Angeles, CA 90029 Tel 213-255-6777.

Ralmar Enter, *(Ralmar Enterprises; 0-941977),* 1340 W. 30th St., Los Angeles, CA 90007 (SAN 666-7503) Tel 213-734-3312.

Ramira Pub, *(Ramira Publishing; 0-9612720),* P.O. Box 1707, Aptos, CA 95001 (SAN 289-8128) Tel 408-429-9311; Dist. by: Bookpeople, 7900 Edgewater Dr., Oakland, CA 94621 (SAN 168-9517) Tel 510-632-4700; Toll free: 800-999-4650; Dist. by: New Leaf Distributing Co., 5425 Tulane Dr., SW, Atlanta, GA 30336-2323 (SAN 169-1449) Tel 404-691-6996; Toll free: 800-326-2665; Dist. by: DeVorss & Co., P.O. Box 550, Marina del Rey, CA 90294-0550 (SAN 168-9886) Tel 213-870-7478; Toll free: 800-843-5743 (bookstores only); 800-331-4719 (in California, bookstores only); Dist. by: Omega Pubns., Inc., R.D. 1, Box 1030E, New Lebanon, NY 12125 (SAN 214-1493) Tel 518-794-8181; Toll free: 800-443-7107 (orders only); Dist. by: Moving Bks., Inc., P.O. Box 20037, Seattle, WA 98102 (SAN 159-0685) Tel 206-762-1750; Toll free: 800-777-6683; Dist. by: Baker & Taylor Bks., Reno Service Ctr., 380 Edison Way, Reno, NV 89564 (SAN 169-4464) Tel 702-858-6700; Toll free: 800-775-1700 (customer service).

Rams Horn Bks, *(Rams Horn Bks.; 1-879911),* Rams Horn Mountain, Box 20622, Estes Park, CO 80511 Tel 303-586-3509; 1460 Front Nine Dr., Unit D, Fort Collins, CO 80525 Tel 303-223-6981.

RAMSI Bks, *(RAMSI Bks.; 1-883500),* Div. of Newsletters, Inc., 1948 Young Ave., No. 3, Memphis, TN 38104-5643 (SAN 297-9225) Tel 901-278-3814.

Ranch Gate Bks, *(Ranch Gate Bks.; 0-9618660),* 2409 Dormarion, Austin, TX 78703 (SAN 668-4033) Tel 512-476-2185; Dist. by: Hendrick-Long Publishing Co., 4811 W. Lovers Ln., Dallas, TX 75209 (SAN 281-7748) Tel 214-358-4677.

Ranch House Pr, *(Ranch Hse. Pr.; 1-878438),* Rte. 2, Box 296, Pagosa Springs, CO 81147 (SAN 240-1126) Tel 303-264-2647.

Rand McNally, *(Rand McNally & Co.; 0-528),* 8255 N. Central Pk., Skokie, IL 60076-2970 (SAN 203-3917) Tel 708-673-9100.

Randall Hse, *(Randall Hse. Pubns.; 0-89265),* 114 Bush Rd., P.O. Box 17306, Nashville, TN 37217 (SAN 207-5040) Tel 615-361-1221; Toll free: 800-877-7030.

Randelle Pubns, *(Randelle Pubns.; 0-910445),* 1527 First Ave., Charleston, WV 25312 (SAN 260-1222) Tel 304-344-4494.

R&M Pub Co, *(R&M Publishing Co.; 0-936026),* P.O. Box 1276, Holly Hill, SC 29059 (SAN 213-6392) Tel 706-738-0360.

Random, *(Random Hse., Inc.; 0-394; 0-676; 0-375; 0-679; 0-87665),* Random Hse. Publicity, (11-6), 201 E. 50th St., 22nd Flr., New York, NY 10022 (SAN 202-5507) Tel 212-751-2600; Toll free: 800-733-3000 (orders); 800-726-0600 (credit, inquiries, customer service); Orders to: 400 Hahn Rd., Westminster, MD 21157 (SAN 202-5515) Tel 410-848-1900. *Imprints:* Times Bks (Times Books); Villard Bks (Villard Books); Vin (Vintage).

Random Bks Yng Read, *(Random Hse. Bks. for Young Readers; 0-394; 0-679),* Div. of Random Hse., Inc., 201 E. 50th St., New York, NY 10022; Dist. by: Random Hse., Inc., 400 Hahn Rd., Westminster, MD 21157 (SAN 202-5515); Toll free: 800-733-3000. *Imprints:* Bullseye Bks (Bullseye Books).

Random Hse Value, *(Random Hse. Value Publishing, Inc.; 0-87000; 0-517),* Div. of Random Hse., Inc., 40 Engelhard Ave., Avenal, NJ 07001 (SAN 200-2620) Tel 908-827-2700; Toll free: 800-223-6804; Orders to: Random House, Inc., 400 Hahn Rd., Westminster, MD 21157 (SAN 202-5515); Toll free: 800-733-3000. *Imprints:* Chatham River Pr (Chatham River Press); Child Classics (Children's Classics).

RAPCOM Enter, *(RAPCOM Enterprises),* 2109 Wilkinson Pl., Alexandria, VA 22306 (SAN 689-0563).

Rape Abuse Crisis, *(Rape & Abuse Crisis Ctr. of Fargo Moorhead; 0-914633),* P.O. Box 2984, Fargo, ND 58108 (SAN 289-5684) Tel 701-293-7273; Toll free: 800-627-3675.

Rape Crisis Ctr, *(Rape Crisis Ctr.),* P.O. Box 34125, Washington, DC 20043-4125 (SAN 225-9680).

Rapids Christian, *(Rapids Christian Pr., Inc.; 0-915374),* P.O. Box 487, 5630 Schroeder Dr., Wisconsin Rapids, WI 54495 (SAN 205-0986) Tel 715-423-4670.

Raspberry Hill, *(Raspberry Hill, Ltd.; 0-9631957),* P.O. Box 791, Willmar, MN 56201 Tel 612-235-2955; Dist. by: Baker & Taylor Bks., Somerville Service Ctr., 50 Kirby Ave., Somerville, NJ 08876-0734 (SAN 169-4901) Tel 908-722-8000; Toll free: 800-775-1500 (customer service); Dist. by: Baker & Taylor Bks., Momence Service Ctr., 501 S. Gladiolus St., Momence, IL 60954-2444 (SAN 169-2100) Tel 815-472-2444; Toll free: 800-775-2300 (customer service); Dist. by: Baker & Taylor Bks., Commerce Service Ctr., 251 Mt. Olive Church Rd., Commerce, GA 30599-9988 (SAN 169-1503) Tel 706-335-5000; Toll free: 800-775-1200 (customer service); Dist. by: Baker & Taylor Bks., Reno Service Ctr., 380 Edison Way, Reno, NV 89564 (SAN 169-4464) Tel 702-858-6700; Toll free: 800-775-1700 (customer service); Dist. by: Ingram Bk. Co., 1 Ingram Blvd., La Vergne, TN 37086-1986 (SAN 169-7978) Tel 615-793-5000; Toll free: 800-937-8000 (orders only, all warehouses); Dist. by: Bookmen, Inc., 525 N. Third St., Minneapolis, MN 55401 (SAN 169-409X) Tel 612-341-3333; Toll free: 800-328-8411 (customer service); Dist. by: The Distributors, 702 S. Michigan, South Bend, IN 46601 (SAN 169-2488) Tel 219-232-8500; Toll free: 800-348-5200 (except Indiana).

Raspberry IL, *(Raspberry Pr., Ltd.; 0-929568),* P.O. Box 1, Dixon, IL 61021 (SAN 250-2194); 1989 Grand Detour Rd., Dixon, IL 61021 (SAN 250-2208) Tel 815-288-4910.

Raspberry Pubns, *(Raspberry Pubns.; 1-884825),* P.O. Box 925, Westerville, OH 43081; Toll free: 800-759-7171; 295 Allview Rd., Westerville, OH 43081 Tel 614-841-4353.

Raspberry Rec, *(Raspberry Recordings; 0-934721),* Div. of Raconteur Records, P.O. Box 11247 Dr., Capitol Sta., Columbia, SC 29211 (SAN 694-1605) Tel 803-254-5466; Dist. by: Baker & Taylor Bks., Momence Service Ctr., 501 S. Gladiolus St., Momence, IL 60954-2444 (SAN 169-2100) Tel 815-472-2444; Toll free: 800-775-2300 (customer service); Dist. by: Sabayt Pubns., P.O. Box 64898, Chicago, IL 60664-0898 (SAN 630-2432) Tel 312-667-2227.

Rattle Ok Pubns, *(Rattle OK Pubns.; 0-9626210;* 1-883965), P.O. Box 5614, Napa, CA 94581 (SAN 297-5475); 533 Soscol Ave., No. 81, Napa, CA 94559 Tel 707-253-9641; Dist. by: Delta Systems Co., Inc., 1400 Miller Pkwy., McHenry, IL 60050-7030 (SAN 220-0457) Tel 815-363-3582; Toll free: 800-323-8270.

Rattlesnake, *(Rattlesnake Pubs.; 0-9632097),* 4335 Toro Ct., Reno, NV 89502 Tel 702-825-2665.

Raven Rocks Pr, *(Raven Rocks Pr.; 0-9615961),* Rte. 1, Beallsville, OH 43716 (SAN 696-5679) Tel 614-926-1481; 54118 Crum Rd., Beallsville, OH 43716 (SAN 665-9055) Tel 614-926-1705.

Ray-Foster, *(Ray/Foster Pubs.; 0-9612346),* P.O. Box 4044, McCall, ID 83638 (SAN 289-2294) Tel 208-634-5054.

Ray-Ma Natsal, *(Ray-Ma Natsal Publishing; 1-879068),* P.O. Box 1186, Conway, AR 72033-1186.

Raynel, *(Raynel; 0-9623068),* P.O. Box 833, Sequim, WA 98382; 124B Secor Rd., Sequim, WA 98382 Tel 206-683-7340.

Rayve Prodns, *(Rayve Productions, Inc.; 1-877810),* P.O. Box 726, Windsor, CA 95492 (SAN 248-4250); Toll free: 800-852-4890; 10439 Pelham Dr., Windsor, CA 95492 Tel 707-838-6200.

RBR, *(RBR (Religious Bks. for Russia); 0-934927),* P.O. Box 522, Glen Cove, NY 11542-0522 (SAN 695-0167) Tel 516-676-3268; Dist. by: MCA Pr., 575 Scarsdale Rd., Crestwood, NY 10707 (SAN 200-5514) Tel 914-478-2151.

RCC-Berkshires Pr, *(Rape Crisis Ctr. of the Berkshires Pr.; 0-9618618),* 18 Charles St., Pittsfield, MA 01201 (SAN 668-3436) Tel 413-442-6708.

RCR Ent, *(R C R Enterprises; 0-9636703),* 5241 Lincoln Dr., Suite 317, Edina, MN 55436 Tel 612-935-8716.

RCY Design, *(RCY Design; 0-9631476),* 40 Wellington Heights, P.O. Box 1283, Avon, CT 06001 Tel 203-678-8168.

RD Assn, *(Reader's Digest Assn., Inc.; 0-89577),* 260 Madison Ave., New York, NY 10016 (SAN 240-9720) Tel 212-850-7007; Orders to: Customer Service, Reader's Digest Rd., Pleasantville, NY 10570 (SAN 282-2091); Toll free: 800-431-1246; Dist. by: Random Hse., Inc., 400 Hahn Rd., Westminster, MD 21157 (SAN 202-5515) Tel 410-848-1900; Toll free: 800-733-3000 (orders); 800-726-0600 (credit, inquires, customer service). *Imprints:* Readers Digest Kids (Reader's Digest Kids).

RDR Bks, *(RDR Bks.; 0-9636161; 1-57143),* 2415 Woolsey, Berkeley, CA 94705 Tel 510-644-1133. *Imprints:* Wetlands (Wetlands).

Read A Bol, *(Read-A-Bol Group, The; 0-938155),* 301 Village Run, E., Encinitas, CA 92024 (SAN 659-8994) Tel 619-753-0663; Orders to: 199 N. El Camino Real F-137, Encinitas, CA 92024 (SAN 242-1135).

Read Advent, *(Reading Adventures, Inc.; 1-882869),* Div. of Belle Isle Corp., P.O. Box 261431, Columbus, OH 43226-1431 Tel 614-436-3110; Toll free: 800-284-4149.

Read Me CA, *(Read Me; 1-885100),* P.O. Box 865, Alleghany, CA 95910; 702 Kanaka Creek Rd., Alleghany, CA 95910 Tel 916-287-3432.

Read Res *Imprint of* **ARO Pub**

Reader, *(Reader Publishing; 0-9630560),* P.O. Box 561, New Hope, PA 18938-0561.

Readers Digest Kids *Imprint of* **RD Assn**

Reading Inc, *(Reading, Inc.; 0-943867),* 603 12th St., Oregon City, OR 97045 (SAN 242-3871) Tel 503-655-4192; Toll free: 800-523-3391.

Reading Matters, *(Reading Matters, Inc.; 0-9614780),* P.O. Box 300309, Denver, CO 80203 (SAN 692-6827) Tel 303-757-3506; Dist. by: Bookpeople, 7900 Edgewater Dr., Oakland, CA 94621 (SAN 168-9517) Tel 510-632-4700; Toll free: 800-999-4650.

Reading Video, *(Reading Video, Inc.; 0-9642651),* 7148 W. Thompson Rd., Indianapolis, IN 46241 Tel 317-856-5690.

Ready Work, *(Ready Work; 0-9617529),* 6 Dogwood Dr., Old Farm Estates, Waynesville, MO 65583 (SAN 664-3493) Tel 314-774-2494.

Real Bks, *(Real Bks.; 1-881102),* P.O. Box 979, Redway, CA 95560 (SAN 297-5920); 80 Barnes Ln., Redway, CA 95560 Tel 707-923-3995. Do not confuse with Real Bks. in New York, NY.

Real Life Strybks, *(Real Life Storybooks; 1-882388),* 19430 Business Center Dr., Northridge, CA 91324 Tel 818-993-6955.

Rebecca Hse, *(Rebecca Hse.; 0-945522),* 1550 California St., Suite 330, San Francisco, CA 94109 (SAN 247-1361) Tel 415-752-1453; Toll free: 800-321-1912 (orders only); Dist. by: Publishers Distribution Service, 6893 Sullivan Rd., Grawn, MI 49637 (SAN 630-5717) Tel 616-276-5196; Toll free: 800-345-0096 (orders only).

Recorded Pubns, *(Recorded Pubns. Laboratories, Inc.;* 1-879755), 1100 State St., Camden, NJ 08105 Tel 609-963-3000; Toll free: 800-235-2679.

Recovery Pubns, *(Recovery Pubns.; 0-9613185),* Box 7631, Amarillo, TX 79114-7631 (SAN 295-9372) Tel 806-372-5865.

Rector Pr, *(Rector Pr., Ltd.; 0-934393; 1-57205; 0-7605),* 130 Rattlesnake, Leverett, MA 01054-9726 (SAN 693-8108) Tel 413-548-9708; Toll free: 800-247-3473.

Red Baron Pub Co, *(Red Baron Publishing Co.;* 0-9622242), 1175 Lockhaven Dr., NE, Salem, OR 97303 Tel 503-393-3570.

Red Branch Pr, *(Red Branch Pr.; 1-878941),* 31 Cannon Blvd., Staten Island, NY 10306-2809 Tel 718-667-3651.

Red Bus Pub, *(Red Bus Publishing; 0-945286),* P.O. Box 151, Hurst, IL 62949 (SAN 246-0599); 200 W. Pulley, Hurst, IL 62949 (SAN 246-0602) Tel 618-987-2006.

Red Crane Bks, *(Red Crane Bks., Inc.; 1-878610),* 2008 Rosinah, Suite B, Santa Fe, NM 87505 Tel 505-988-7070.

Red Earth OK, *(Red Earth Bks.; 0-9619712),* 1200 Caddell, Norman, OK 73069 (SAN 246-1218) Tel 405-360-2730.

Red Hen Pr, *(Red Hen Pr.; 0-931093),* P.O. Box 419, Summerland, CA 93067 (SAN 678-9420) Tel 805-969-7058; Dist. by: Children's Small Pr. Collection, 716 N. Fourth Ave., Ann Arbor, MI 48104 (SAN 200-514X) Tel 313-668-8056; Toll free: 800-221-8056 (orders only).

Red Jacket Pr, *(Red Jacket Pr.; 1-56828),* Div. of Collett Co., 25 W. 31st St., New York, NY 10001 Tel 212-967-8880; Orders to: 49 N. Main St., Manchester, NY 14504 Tel 716-289-4807.

Red Rose Studio, *(Red Rose Studio; 0-932514),* 358 Flintlock Dr., Willow Street, PA 17584 (SAN 212-162X) Tel 717-464-3873.

Red Wing Busn, *(Red Wing Business Systems, Inc.; 0-87265; 0-932250; 0-924340),* 610 Main St., P.O. Box 19, Red Wing, MN 55066 (SAN 293-1524) Tel 612-388-1106; Toll free: 800-732-9464.

Redbird, *(Redbird Pr., Inc.; 0-9606046; 1-885870),* 3838 Poplar Ave., Memphis, TN 38111 (SAN 216-9304) Tel 901-323-2233; Orders to: P.O. Box 11441, Memphis, TN 38111 (SAN 665-7656); Dist. by: Publishers Group West, 4065 Hollis St., Emeryville, CA 94608 (SAN 202-8522) Tel 510-658-3453; Toll free: 800-788-3123.

Redfeather BYR *Imprint of* **H Holt & Co**

Redhawk Pubng, *(Redhawk Publishing; 0-9641861),* P.O. Box 531, Comstock, MI 49041; 7052 S. 40th, Lot 541, Climax, MI 49034 Tel 616-746-4004.

Redleaf Pr, *(Redleaf Pr.; 0-934140; 1-884834),* Div. of Resources for Child Caring, Inc., 450 N. Syndicate, Suite 5, Saint Paul, MN 55104 (SAN 212-8691) Tel 612-641-6630; Toll free: 800-423-8309; Dist. by: Gryphon Hse., Inc., P.O. Box 207, Beltsville, MD 20704-0207 (SAN 169-3190) Tel 301-595-9500; Toll free: 800-638-0928.

Ref Desk Bks, *(Reference Desk Bks.; 0-9625749),* 430 Quintana Rd., Suite 146, Morro Bay, CA 93442 Tel 805-772-8806.

Reg Baptist, *(Regular Baptist Pr.; 0-87227),* Div. of General Assn. of Regular Baptist Churches, 1300 N. Meacham Rd., Schaumburg, IL 60173-4888 (SAN 205-2229) Tel 708-843-1600; Toll free: 800-727-4440 (orders only).

Regal, *(Regal Bks.; 0-8307),* Div. of Gospel Light Pubns., 2300 Knoll Dr., Ventura, CA 93003 (SAN 658-1528) Tel 805-644-9721; Toll free: 800-235-3415 (USA & California); 800-446-7735 (orders only).

Regal Pubns, *(Regal Pubns.; 1-877767; 1-57002),* P.O. Box 1071, Provo, UT 84603; 242 N. University, Provo, UT 84601 Tel 801-377-5367.

Regent Pr, *(Regent Pr.; 0-916147),* 6020A Adeline, Oakland, CA 94608 (SAN 294-9717) Tel 510-547-7602.

Regina Pr, *(Regina Pr., Malhame & Co.; 0-88271),* 145 Sherwood Ave., Farmingdale, NY 11735 (SAN 203-0853) Tel 516-694-8600.

Regmar Pub, *(Regmar Publishing Co., Inc.; 0-914338),* P.O. Box 11358, Memphis, TN 38111 (SAN 203-2015) Tel 901-323-7442.

Regnery Gateway
See Regnery Pub

Regnery Pub, *(Regnery Publishing, Inc., An Eagle Publishing Co.; 0-89526),* Subs. of Phillips Publishing International, 422 First St. SE, Suite 300, Washington, DC 20003 (SAN 210-5578) Tel 202-546-5005; Dist. by: National Bk. Network, 4720A Boston Way, Lanham, MD 20706-4310 (SAN 630-0065) Tel 301-459-8696; Toll free: 800-462-6420.

Regt QM, *(Regimental QM Militaria; 0-9609690;* 0-929757), 2229 E. Broadway Bld., Tucson, AZ 85719-6013 (SAN 282-079X) Tel 602-770-1732.

Reid Ent, *(Ace Reid Enterprises; 0-917207),* P.O. Box 868, Kerrville, TX 78029-0868 (SAN 656-089X) Tel 210-257-7446; Toll free: 800-257-7441.

Rekalb Pr, *(Rekalb Pr.; 0-9604614),* 6203 Jane Ln., Columbus, GA 31909 (SAN 282-2415) Tel 706-561-3497.

Reliance Pr, *(Reliance Pr.; 0-9619639),* 1400 Melrose, Norman, OK 73069 (SAN 245-7172) Tel 405-321-7302.

Remco Wrldserv Bks, *(Remco Worldservice Bks.;* 0-924359), 230B Horsham Rd., Horsham, PA 19044 (SAN 252-2357) Tel 215-957-6501.

Rendezvous Pubns, *(Rendezvous Pubns.; 0-938447),* 103 Half Moon Cir., Apt. D, Jupiter, FL 33458-7666 (SAN 660-9929) Tel 407-744-6149.

Renfro Studios, *(Renfro, Nancy, Studios; 0-931044),* P.O. Box 164226, Austin, TX 78716 (SAN 211-9730) Tel 512-327-9588; Toll free: 800-933-5512.

Reprint Servs
See Rprt Serv

Res & Educ, *(Research & Education Assn.; 0-87891),* 61 Ethel Rd., W., Piscataway, NJ 08854 (SAN 204-6814) Tel 908-819-8880.

Res Press, *(Research Pr.; 0-87822),* 2612 N. Mattis Ave., Champaign, IL 61821 (SAN 282-2482) Tel 217-352-3273; Orders to: Box 3177, Champaign, IL 61821 (SAN 282-2490). Do not confuse with Research Pr., Prairie Village, KS.

Resc Creative Teach
See N Edge Res

Resource Pubns, *(Resource Pubns., Inc.; 0-89390),* 160 E. Virginia St., No. 290, San Jose, CA 95112-5876 (SAN 209-3081) Tel 408-286-8505; Toll free: 800-736-7600. Do not confuse with Resource Pubns. in Los Angeles, CA.

Resources Children, *(Resources for Children in Hospitals; 0-9608150),* P.O. Box 10, Belmont, MA 02178 (SAN 240-2734) Tel 617-492-6220.

Respect Inc, *(Respect, Inc.; 0-945745),* P.O. Box 349, Bradley, IL 60915 (SAN 247-6509); 231 E. Broadway, Hoover Bldg., Bradley, IL 60915 (SAN 247-6517) Tel 815-932-8389.

Reston *Imprint of* **P-H**

Revell, *(Revell, Fleming H., Co.; 0-8007; 0-922066),* Div. of Baker Bk. Hse., P.O. Box 6287, Grand Rapids, MI 49516-6287 (SAN 203-3801) Tel 616-676-9185; Toll free: 800-877-2665.

Revels Pubns, *(Revels Pubns.; 0-9618334),* Div. of Revels, Inc., 1 Kendall Sq., Bldg. 600, Cambridge, MA 02139 (SAN 667-1950) Tel 617-621-0505.

Review & Herald, *(Review & Herald Publishing Assn.;* 0-8280), 55 W. Oak Ridge Dr., Hagerstown, MD 21740 (SAN 203-3798) Tel 301-791-7000; Toll free: 800-771-9098.

Revivals & Missions, *(Revivals & Missions, Inc.;* 0-9626490), 1298 SOM Ctr. Rd., Mayfield Heights, OH 44124.

Reymont, *(Reymont Assocs.; 0-918734),* P.O. Box 114, New York, NY 10276-0114 (SAN 204-6857) Tel 212-473-8031; P.O. Box 114, Cooper Sta., New York, NY 10276 Tel 212-473-8031.

Rhed Harering, *(Rhed Harering Pr.; 0-9641796),* R.R. 1, Box 400, Vineyard Haven, MA 02568 Tel 508-693-0865.

Rhenaria, *(Rhenaria Publishing; 1-880495),* Box 119, Blanchard, OK 73010; County Line Rd., Blanchard, OK 73010 Tel 405-485-2940.

Rhino Pubng, *(Rhino Publishing; 0-9642157),* P.O. Box 2922, Sunnyvale, CA 94087; 857 Peach Ave., Sunnyvale, CA 94087 Tel 408-739-0086. Do not confuse with Rhino Publishing in Reno, NV.

Rhinos Pr, *(Rhino's Pr., The; 0-937382),* P.O. Box 3520, Laguna Hills, CA 92654 (SAN 214-4565) Tel 714-997-3217; Toll free: 800-872-3274.

RHS Ent, *(RHS Enterprises; 0-914503),* P.O. Box 5779, Garden Grove, CA 92645 (SAN 289-6699); 11368 Matinicus Ct., Cypress, CA 90630 (SAN 241-936X) Tel 714-892-9012.

Rhyme & Reason, *(Rhyme & Reason Publishing Co.;* 0-9623411), P.O. Box 25944, Honolulu, HI 96825 Tel 808-586-3288.

Rhyme Time, *(Rhyme Time; 0-9628486),* P.O. Box 70272, Albany, GA 31707; Toll free: 800-342-3508; 1702 Whisperwood St., Albany, GA 31707 Tel 912-439-2115.

Rhyme Tyme, *(Rhyme Tyme Pubns.; 0-9639486),* P.O. Box 31293, Lafayette, LA 70593-1293 (SAN 298-1343); 214 Presbytere Pkwy., Lafayette, LA 70503-6036 (SAN 298-1335) Tel 318-981-4081.

Ricara Features, *(Ricara Features; 0-911737),* P.O. Box 664, Sanborn, NY 14132 (SAN 264-3472) Tel 916-444-7890.

Richelieu Court, *(Richelieu Court Pubns., Inc.;* 0-911519), P.O. Box 13264, Albany, NY 12212-3264 (SAN 264-3480) Tel 518-861-7209; Dist. by: Baker & Taylor Bks., Somerville Service Ctr., 50 Kirby Ave., Somerville, NJ 08876-0734 (SAN 169-4901) Tel 908-722-8000; Toll free: 800-775-1500 (customer service); Dist. by: Spring Arbor Distributors, 10885 Textile Rd., Belleville, MI 48111 (SAN 158-9016) Tel 313-481-0900; Toll free: 800-395-5599 (orders); 800-395-7234 (customer service); Dist. by: Ingram Bk. Co., 1 Ingram Blvd., La Vergne, TN 37086-1986 (SAN 169-7978) Tel 615-793-5000; Toll free: 800-937-8000 (orders only, all warehouses); Dist. by: Baker & Taylor Bks., Momence Service Ctr., 501 S. Gladiolus St., Momence, IL 60954-2444 (SAN 169-2100) Tel 815-472-2444; Toll free: 800-775-2300 (customer service); Dist. by: Baker & Taylor Bks., Reno Service Ctr., 380 Edison Way, Reno, NV 89564 (SAN 169-4464) Tel 702-858-6700; Toll free: 800-775-1700 (customer service); Dist. by: Baker & Taylor Bks., Commerce Service Ctr., 251 Mt. Olive Church Rd., Commerce, GA 30599-9988 (SAN 169-1503) Tel 706-335-5000; Toll free: 800-775-1200 (customer service); Dist. by: Ingram Video, Inc., 315 E. Wallace St., Fort Wayne, IN 46803-2342 Tel 219-744-1335; Dist. by: Ingram Bk. Co., Avon Div., 80 Darling Dr., Avon Park S., Avon, CT 06001-0282 (SAN 630-4796) Tel 203-677-0064; Toll free: 800-937-8000; Dist. by: Ingram Video, Inc., 8316 Sherwick Ct., Jessup, MD 20794-9643 Tel 410-792-9242; Dist. by: New Leaf Distributing Co., 5425 Tulane Dr., SW, Atlanta, GA 30336-2323 (SAN 169-1449) Tel 404-691-6996; Toll free: 800-326-2665.

Richmar Prodns, *(Richmar Productions; 0-9624225),* 601 NE Eighth St., No. A, Grants Pass, OR 97526-2106 Tel 503-479-3594.

Richmond Saddlery, *(Richmond Saddlery Pr.;* 0-9628937), Div. of Richmond Camera Shop, Inc., P.O. Box 27461, Richmond, VA 23261; 215 W. Broad, Richmond, VA 23220 Tel 804-649-1079.

Ridge Enter, *(Ridge Enterprises, Ltd.; 0-9628323),* P.O. Box 69041, Pleasant Ridge, MI 48069; 52 Cambridge, Pleasant Ridge, MI 48069 Tel 810-399-1719.

Riegel Pub, *(Riegel Publishing; 0-944871),* P.O. Box 3241, San Clemente, CA 92674 (SAN 245-3916) Tel 714-582-7562.

Right Bk, *(Right Bk. Co., The; 0-9628252),* P.O. Box 1964, Bellingham, WA 98227; 3770 Canterbury Ln., No. 121, Bellingham, WA 98225 Tel 206-647-5115.

Right Brain, *(Right Brain Publishing; 0-935295),* 7812 NW Hampton Rd., Kansas City, MO 64152 (SAN 695-9350) Tel 816-587-8687.

Right to Life, *(Right to Life League of Southern California; 0-9613809),* 50 N. Hill Ave., No. 306, Pasadena, CA 91106-1949 (SAN 219-8142) Tel 818-449-8408.

Rightway Educ, *(Rightway Educational Services;* 0-9633309), 31 Salisbury Ave., Stewart Manor, NY 11530 Tel 516-328-6852.

Rincon Child Ent
See Rincon Rodanthe

Rincon Rodanthe, *(Rincon Rodanthe Co., Inc.; 1-56668),* 910A Hampshire Rd., Westlake Village, CA 91361-2814 Tel 805-373-6907; Toll free: 800-676-2272.

Ringling Bros, *(Ringling Brothers & Barnum & Bailey Combined Shows, Inc.; 1-878163),* 8607 Westwood Ctr. Dr., Vienna, VA 22182 Tel 703-448-4167; Toll free: 800-424-3709.

Rip off, *(Rip Off Pr., Inc.; 0-89620),* P.O. Box 4686, Auburn, CA 95604 (SAN 207-7671) Tel 916-885-8183; Toll free: 800-468-2669.

Rising Crescent, *(Rising Crescent Publishing; 0-9643040),* 816A Lexington Ave., El Cerrito, CA 94530 Tel 510-528-2630.

Rising St Pubs, *(Rising Star Pubs.; 1-884987),* Div. of Wee Write Keepsakes, Inc., P.O. Box 644, Rochester, IL 62563; R.R. 7, Box 166, Springfield, IL 62707 Tel 217-498-8458; Dist. by: Baker & Taylor Bks., Momence Service Ctr., 501 S. Gladiolus St., Momence, IL 60954-1799 (SAN 169-2100) Tel 815-472-2444; Toll free: 800-775-2300 (customer service).

Rising Sun, *(Rising Sun Publishing; 1-880463),* 1012 Fair Oaks Blvd., South Pasadena, CA 91030 Tel 818-799-1999.

RivEd *Imprint of* **HM**

River-Light Pub, *(River-Light Publishing Co., Inc.;* 0-925039), P.O. Box 3283, Pasco, WA 99302; 824 Maitland Ave., Pasco, WA 99301 Tel 509-545-8240.

River Walker Bks, *(River Walker Bks.; 0-9637288),* 3334 Wyandot St., Denver, CO 80211 Tel 303-480-5009.

Rivercrest Indus, *(Rivercrest Industries; 1-878908),* P.O. Box 771662, Houston, TX 77215-1662; 1940 Fountainview, Houston, TX 77057 Tel 713-789-5394.

Rivercross Pub, *(Rivercross Publishing, Inc.; 0-944957),* 127 E. 59th St., New York, NY 10022 (SAN 245-6826) Tel 800-451-4522; Orders to: 6214 Wynfield Ct., Orlando, FL 32819 Tel 407-876-7720.

Riverside FL, *(Riverside Bks.; 1-879710),* P.O. Box 2184, Ormond Beach, FL 32175; 710 Riverside Dr., Ormond Beach, FL 32176 Tel 904-672-4386. Do not confuse with Riverside Bks. in New York, NY.

Riverstone Pr, *(Riverstone Pr.; 0-9617206),* 795 River Heights Dr., Meridian, ID 83642 (SAN 663-2548) Tel 208-888-6290. Do not confuse with companies with similar names in Chicago, IL, Golden, CO.

Riviana Foods, *(Riviana Foods, Inc.; 0-9629736),* P.O. Box 2636, Houston, TX 77252; 2777 Allen Pkwy., Suite 1500, Houston, TX 77019 Tel 713-529-3251.

Rizzoli Intl, *(Rizzoli International Pubns., Inc.; 0-8478),* Subs. of RCS Rizzoli Editore Corp., 300 Park Ave., S., New York, NY 10010 (SAN 111-9192) Tel 212-387-3400; Toll free: 800-221-7945; Dist. by: St. Martin's Pr., Inc., 175 Fifth Ave., Rm. 1715, New York, NY 10010 (SAN 200-2132) Tel 212-674-5151; Toll free: 800-221-7945.

RJB Enter, *(RJB Enterprises, Inc.; 0-9630985),* P.O. Box 5652, Edmond, OK 73083-5652; 825 Glenridge Dr., Edmond, OK 73013 Tel 405-752-2835.

RKUP Pubng, *(RKUP Publishing; 0-9643453),* Div. of RKUP, Inc., 254 15th St., SE, Washington, DC 20003 Tel 202-546-9026.

RMC Pub Grp, *(RMC Publishing Group, Ltd.; 0-9632789; 1-881990),* 713 Sandy Trail, Fort Worth, TX 76120 Tel 817-457-5173; Toll free: 800-457-4167.

Roanoke Park, *(Roanoke Park Pr.; 0-9622496),* 4539 132nd Ave., SE, Bellevue, WA 98006 Tel 206-643-8204.

Rob Briggs, *(Briggs, Robert, Assocs.; 0-9609850;* 0-931191), 400 Second St., No. 108, Lake Oswego, OR 97034 (SAN 268-4632) Tel 503-635-0435; Toll free: 800-447-7814 (Visa/Mastercard orders only); c/o Publishers Services, P.O. Box 2510, Novato, CA 94948 (SAN 200-7223) Tel 415-883-3530.

Robbinspring, *(Robbinspring Pubns.; 0-9630060),* P.O. Box 13, Iron River, MI 49935-0013; Toll free: 800-345-0096; Dist. by: Publishers Distribution Service, 6893 Sullivan Rd., Grawn, MI 49637 (SAN 630-5717) Tel 616-276-5196; Toll free: 800-345-0096 (orders only).

Robins Cliff, *(Robin's Cliff Pr.; 0-9630609),* P.O. Box 7162, Jackson, MS 39282-7162; 1615 Lost Lake Cir., Jackson, MS 39212 Tel 601-372-0480.

RobinSays, *(RobinSays, Inc.; 0-9638384),* P.O. Box 930105, Rockaway Beach, NY 11693; 8200 Shorefront Pkwy., Apt. 3P, Rockaway Beach, NY 11693 Tel 718-474-1327.

Robinson Pr, *(Robinson Pr., Inc.; 0-913730),* 1137 Riverside Dr., Fort Collins, CO 80524 (SAN 205-2369) Tel 303-482-5393; Toll free: 800-747-5395 (orders only).

Robinsunne Pstcrd, *(Robinsunne Postcard Pr.;* 0-9636986), P.O. Box 44, Belfast, ME 04915 Tel 207-338-5345.

Roblen Pub, *(Roblen Publishing Co.; 0-9631313),* 1516 Northview Ave., Cincinnati, OH 45223 Tel 513-541-0052.

Robson-Parkwest *Imprint of* **Parkwest Pubns**

Rochester Folk Art, *(Rochester Folk Art Guild),* Rte. 1, Box 10, Middlesex, NY 14507 (SAN 210-9492) Tel 716-554-3539.

Rochester Pub Lib Dist, *(Rochester Public Library District; 0-9621759),* P.O. Box 617, Rochester, IL 62563 (SAN 252-0753); Rochester Sta., No 2, Rochester, IL 62563 (SAN 252-0761) Tel 217-498-8454.

Rock Isl Arsenal Hist Soc, *(Rock Island Arsenal Historical Society; 0-9617938),* 605 24th Ave., Moline, IL 61265 (SAN 665-9748) Tel 309-797-3987.

Rock-It Pr, *(Rock-It Pr.; 0-9640506),* P.O. Box 2174, New York, NY 10116-2174 (SAN 298-1793); 327 W. 30th St., Suite 3C, New York, NY 10001 Tel 212-643-9743.

Rockdale Ridge, *(Rockdale Ridge Pr.; 0-9602338),* 8501 Ridge Rd., Cincinnati, OH 45236 (SAN 212-4459) Tel 513-891-9900; Dist. by: Baker & Taylor Bks., Momence Service Ctr., 501 S. Gladiolus St., Momence, IL 60954-2444 (SAN 169-2100) Tel 815-472-2444; Toll free: 800-775-2300 (customer service); Dist. by: Dot Gibson Pubns., P.O. Box 117, Waycross, GA 31502-0117 (SAN 200-4143) Tel 912-285-2848; Dist. by: Cookbook Collection, Inc., 2500 E. 195th St., Belton, MO 64012 (SAN 200-6359) Tel 816-322-2122.

Rocking Bridge, *(Rocking Bridge Pr.; 0-9634833),* 405 W. Southern Ave., Suite 5, Tempe, AZ 85282 Tel 602-967-5747.

Rocking Horse, *(Rocking Horse Pr.; 0-932306),* 32 Ellise Rd., Storrs, CT 06268 (SAN 212-4467) Tel 203-429-1474.

Rockmasters Intl, *(Rockmasters International Network;* 1-878476), 5736 Shenandoah Ave., Norfolk, VA 23509 Tel 804-623-5565; Orders to: 317 Granby St., Norfolk, VA 23516.

Rocky Mntn Child, *(Rocky Mountain Children's Pr., Inc.; 0-940611),* 1520 Shaw Mountain Rd., Boise, ID 83712 (SAN 664-7065) Tel 208-336-3858.

Rocky River Pubs, *(Rocky River Pubs.; 0-944576),* P.O. Box 1679, Shepherdstown, WV 25443 (SAN 243-9409) Tel 304-876-2711.

Rod & Staff, *(Rod & Staff Pubs., Inc.),* Hwy. 172, Crockett, KY 41413 (SAN 206-7633) Tel 606-522-4348.

Rodney, *(Rodney Pubns., Inc.; 0-913830),* 10201 Grosvenor Pl., No. 1122, Rockville, MD 20852 (SAN 204-6954) Tel 301-493-6334.

Rodor & Co, *(Rodor & Co.; 0-9619944),* 28221 Lomo Dr., Rancho Palos Verdes, CA 90274 (SAN 246-9642) Tel 310-541-4559.

RoKarn Pubns, *(RoKarn Pubns.; 0-9625502),* P.O. Box 195, Nokesville, VA 22123; Toll free: 800-869-0563; 8534 Stonewall Rd., Manassas, VA 22110 Tel 703-330-8249.

Rolla Fine Arts, *(Rolla Fine Arts Museum; 1-882935),* 1705 N. Oak St., Rolla, MO 65401 Tel 314-364-3708.

Roman IL, *(Roman, Inc.; 0-937739),* 555 Lawrence Ave., Roselle, IL 60172-1599 (SAN 659-2899) Tel 312-529-3000.

Romar Bks
See Accord Comm

Ron Denzer, *(Denzer, Ron, Publishing; 0-9616331),* 3450 E. Branch Rd., No. A, Garberville, CA 95542-3812 (SAN 659-1566).

Rondy Pubns, *(Rondy Pubns.; 0-9616638),* 6704 Hillside Ln., Minneapolis, MN 55439-1320 (SAN 659-6800) Tel 612-829-7600.

RonJon Pub, *(RonJon Publishing, Inc.; 1-56870),* 3730 E. McKinney St., Suite 101, Denton, TX 76208 Tel 817-383-3060.

Ronmar Ent, *(Ronmar Enterprises; 0-9619988),* 46 Nicholas Dr., Albany, NY 12205 (SAN 247-2996) Tel 518-869-3263.

Ronnie Two Pub, *(Ronnie II Publishing Co.; 1-878439),* 514 N. 13th St., Springfield, IL 62702-5632 Tel 217-753-3814.

RonSan Graphics, *(RonSan Graphics, Inc.; 1-882288),* P.O. Box 20486, Greensboro, NC 27420-0486 Tel 910-275-6455.

Roper Pr, *(Roper Pr., Inc.; 0-86606),* 4737A Gretna, Dallas, TX 75207 Tel 214-630-4808; Toll free: 800-284-0158; Dist. by: Spring Arbor Distributors, 10885 Textile Rd., Belleville, MI 48111 (SAN 158-9016) Tel 313-481-0900; Toll free: 800-395-5599 (orders); 800-395-7234 (customer service); Dist. by: Riverside/World, P.O. Box 370, 1500 Riverside Dr., Iowa Falls, IA 50126 (SAN 169-2666) Tel 515-648-4271; Toll free: 800-247-5111; Dist. by: Appalachian Bk. Distributors, P.O. Box 1573, Johnson City, TN 37601 (SAN 630-7388).

Roscoe Village, *(Roscoe Village Foundation, Inc.;* 1-880443), 381 Hill St., Coshocton, OH 43812 Tel 614-622-7644.

Rose Art Indust, *(Rose Art Industries, Inc.; 1-57041),* 555 Main St., Orange, NJ 07050 Tel 201-414-1313; Toll free: 800-272-9667.

Rose Pub, *(Rose Publishing Co., Inc.; 0-914546),* 2723 Foxcroft Rd., Suite 208, Little Rock, AR 72207 (SAN 203-3739) Tel 501-227-8104. Do not confuse with other companies with the same name in Keystone Heights, FL, Grand Rapids, MI, Alameda, CA, Oro Valley, AZ, Flagtown, NJ, Salem, OR, San Luis Obispo, CA.

Rose Pub OR, *(Rose Publishing; 1-881170),* 3303 Ward Dr., NE, Salem, OR 97305 Tel 503-393-8488; Toll free: 800-842-7421. Do not confuse with companies with the same name in Oro Valley, AZ, Flagtown, NJ, Grand Rapids, MI, Little Rock, AR, Alameda, CA, Keystone Heights, FL, San Luis Obispo, CA.

Rose Shell Pr, *(Rose Shell Pr.; 0-934536),* 516 Gallows Hill Rd., Cranford, NJ 07016 (SAN 206-3662) Tel 908-276-9479.

Rosedale Pr, *(Rosedale Pr.; 0-9626413),* Div of BBE Assocs., Ltd., 4401 N. Classen Blvd., Suite 500, Oklahoma City, OK 73118 Tel 405-557-1039.

Rosedown Plantation, *(Rosedown Plantation & Gardens;* 0-929317), P.O. Box 1816, Saint Francisville, LA 70775 (SAN 248-9856) Tel 504-635-3332.

Rosemary Corp, *(Rosemary Corp., The; 0-9621952),* 1653 Robert St., New Orleans, LA 70115 Tel 504-895-4247; Dist. by: Music in Motion, 783 N. Grove, No. 108, Richardson, TX 75081 (SAN 630-3528) Tel 214-231-0403; Dist. by: MMB Music, Inc,, 205 S. Charles, Edwardsville, IL 62025 (SAN 298-3281) Tel 618-656-3823.

Rosen Group, *(Rosen Publishing Group, Inc., The;* 0-8239), 29 E. 21st St., New York, NY 10010 (SAN 203-3720) Tel 212-777-3017; Toll free: 800-237-9932.

Rosen Pub, *(Rosen Publishing, Inc.; 1-881930),* 3000 Chestnut Ave., Suite 300, Baltimore, MD 21211 Tel 410-889-2933.

Rosewd Pubns, *(Rosewood Pubns., Inc.; 0-9630979),* 2075 Pioneer Ct., San Mateo, CA 94403 Tel 415-343-7288.

Rosewood Pub
See Rosewd Pubns

Rosholt Hse, *(Rosholt Hse.; 0-910417),* 406 River Dr., Rosholt, WI 54473-9557 (SAN 260-1249) Tel 715-677-4722.

Rosicrucian, *(Rosicrucian Fellowship, The; 0-911274),* P.O. Box 713, 2222 Mission Ave., Oceanside, CA 92049-0713 (SAN 203-0756) Tel 619-757-6600.

Rossel Bks, *(Rossel Bks.; 0-940646),* Div. of Seymour Rossel Co., Inc., 250 E. 63rd St., No. 205, New York, NY 10021-7662 (SAN 213-6414); Dist. by: Behrman Hse., Inc., 235 Watchung Ave., West Orange, NJ 07052 (SAN 201-4459) Tel 201-669-0447; Toll free: 800-221-2755.

Roth Pub Inc, *(Roth Publishing, Inc.; 0-89609; 0-8486),* 185 Great Neck Rd., Great Neck, NY 11021 (SAN 210-9735) Tel 516-466-3676; Orders to: P.O. Box 406, Great Neck, NY 11022 (SAN 241-7073); Toll free: 800-899-7684.

Rough Rock Pr, *(Rough Rock Pr.; 0-936008),* Rough Rock Demonstration Schl., Box 217, Chinle, AZ 86503 (SAN 203-1604) Tel 602-728-3311; Toll free: 800-833-7553.

Roundtable Pub, *(Roundtable Publishing; 0-915677),* P.O. Box 6488, Malibu, CA 90264-6488 (SAN 237-9260) Tel 310-457-8433.

Rourke Bk Co, *(Rourke Bk. Co., Inc., The; 1-55916),* Div. of Rourke Publishing Group, P.O. Box 3328, Vero Beach, FL 32964 Tel 407-465-4575.

Rourke Corp, *(Rourke Corp.; 0-86593),* Div. of Rourke Publishing Group, P.O. Box 3328, Vero Beach, FL 32964 (SAN 673-3069); 226 Egret, Vero Beach, FL 32963 (SAN 249-3136) Tel 407-465-4575.

Rourke Enter, *(Rourke Enterprises, Inc.; 0-86592),* Div. of Rourke Publishing Group, P.O. Box 3328, Vero Beach, FL 32964; 226 Egret Ln., Vero Beach, FL 32963 Tel 407-465-4575.

Rourke Pr, *(Rourke Pr., Inc.; 1-57103),* Div. of Rourke Publishing Group, P.O. Box 3328, Vero Beach, FL 32964 Tel 407-465-4575.

Rourke Pubns, *(Rourke Pubns., Inc.; 0-86625),* Div. of Rourke Publishing Group, P.O. Box 3328, Vero Beach, FL 32964; 226 Egret Ln., Vero Beach, FL 32963 Tel 407-465-4575.

Routledge, *(Routledge; 0-415; 0-413),* Div. of Routledge, Chapman & Hall, Inc., 29 W. 35th St., New York, NY 10001-2299 Tel 212-244-3336.

Routledge Chapman & Hall, *(Routledge, Chapman & Hall, Inc.; 0-416; 0-7100; 0-87830; 0-04; 0-86861),* Subs. of International Thomson Organization, Inc., 29 W. 35th St., New York, NY 10001-2291 (SAN 213-196X) Tel 212-244-3336.

Rovey Res Per Arts, *(Rovey Research in Performing Arts; 0-9627847),* P.O. Box 638, Scottsdale, AZ 85252-0638; 7764 E. Rovey Ave., Scottsdale, AZ 85253 Tel 602-948-5850.

Rowan Tree, *(Rowan Tree Pr., Ltd.; 0-937672),* 124 Chestnut St., Boston, MA 02108 (SAN 214-4638) Tel 617-523-7627; Dist. by: SPD-Small Pr. Distribution, 1814 San Pablo Ave., Berkeley, CA 94702 (SAN 204-5826) Tel 510-549-3336; Toll free: 800-869-7553.

Royal Fireworks, *(Royal Fireworks Printing Co.;* 0-88092), First Ave., Unionville, NY 10988 (SAN 240-2394) Tel 914-726-3333.

Royalty Pub, *(Royalty Publishing Co.; 0-910487),* P.O. Box 2016, Manassas, VA 22110 (SAN 260-1265) Tel 703-368-9878; Dist. by: Spring Arbor Distributors, 10885 Textile Rd., Belleville, MI 48111 (SAN 158-9016) Tel 313-481-0900; Toll free: 800-395-5599 (orders); 800-395-7234 (customer service).

RPM Record, *(RPM Recording; 0-9632433),* Div. of Rhett Parrish Music, Inc., 103 Southview Dr., Huntsville, AL 35806; Toll free: 800-527-4388.

Rprt Serv, *(Reprint Services Corp.; 0-932051; 0-7812),* P.O. Box 890820, Temecula, CA 92589-0820 (SAN 686-2640) Tel 909-699-5731.

RSV Prods, *(RSV Products; 1-883988),* Box 26, Hopkins, MN 55343; 3923 Willmatt Hill, Minnetonka, MN 55305 Tel 612-936-0400.

Rubbers Bros Comics, *(Rubbers Brothers Comics, The;* 1-880058), P.O. Box 431, Wilbraham, MA 01095; 131 Johnson St., Springfield, MA 01108 Tel 413-734-1057.

Rubes Pubns, *(Rubes Pubns.; 0-943384; 0-941364),* 14447 Titus St., Panorama City, CA 91402 (SAN 240-7647) Tel 818-782-0800.

Ruggs Recommend, *(Rugg's Recommendation; 0-9608934; 1-883062),* 7120 Serena Ct., Atascadero, CA 93422 (SAN 237-9694) Tel 805-462-2503.

Runestone Pr *Imprint of* **Lerner Pubns**

Running Pr, *(Running Pr. Bk. Pubs.; 0-89471; 1-56138),* 125 S. 22nd St., Philadelphia, PA 19103-4399 (SAN 204-5702) Tel 215-567-5080; Toll free: 800-345-5359.

Running Water, *(Running Water Pr.; 0-9623363),* P.O. Box 2024, Hollywood, CA 90078; 2062 N. Vine St., Hollywood, CA 90068 Tel 213-467-1447.

RuSK Inc, *(RuSK, Inc.; 0-9616894),* Univ. of Alabama, P.O. Box 2504, Tuscaloosa, AL 35486 (SAN 661-5910) Tel 205-345-4720.

Rutgers U Pr, *(Rutgers Univ. Pr.; 0-8135),* 109 Church St., New Brunswick, NJ 08901 (SAN 203-364X) Tel 908-932-7764; Toll free: 800-446-9323 (orders).

Rutledge Hill Pr, *(Rutledge Hill Pr.; 0-934395; 1-55853),* 211 Seventh Ave., N., Nashville, TN 37219 (SAN 693-8116) Tel 615-244-2700; Toll free: 800-234-4234.

Ruwanga Trad, *(Ruwanga Trading; 0-9615102),* P.O. Box 1027, Puunene, HI 96784 (SAN 694-2776) Tel 808-877-4737; Dist. by: Pacific Trade Group, 94-527 Pauhi St., Waipahu, HI 96797 (SAN 169-1635) Tel 808-671-6735.

RVS Bks, *(RVS Bks., Inc.; 0-9634257),* P.O. Box 683, Lebanon, TN 37087 Tel 615-449-6725.

Ryder Pub Co, *(Ryder Publishing Co.; 0-935973),* 2805 E. Golden West Ave., Visalia, CA 93291-8029 (SAN 696-5822).

Rymer Bks, *(Rymer Bks.; 0-9600792; 0-934723),* 22249 E. Tollhouse Rd., Clovis, CA 93611-9761 (SAN 207-1010) Tel 209-298-8845.

Ryton Pub, *(Ryton Publishing; 0-9633824),* 1136 Puget St., Bellingham, WA 98226 Tel 206-733-7351.

S & B Pubs, *(S & B Pubs.; 0-931647),* P.O. Box 1954, Williamsburg, VA 23187-1954 (SAN 683-7336) Tel 804-220-3137.

S & D, *(Smith & Daniel; 0-9630463),* 4500 Phillips Hwy., Jacksonville, FL 32207 Tel 904-737-4840; Toll free: 800-741-4360.

S & M Basinger, *(Basinger, Sherry & Michelle;* 0-9620945), P.O. Box 1054, Clackamas, OR 97015 (SAN 250-1228); 11313 SE Lenore, Clackamas, OR 97015 (SAN 250-1236) Tel 503-698-2294.

S-By-S Pubns, *(Step-By-Step Pubns.; 1-884573),* P.O. Box 1492, Cupertino, CA 95015-1492 (SAN 298-2463); 10804 Brookwell Dr., Cupertino, CA 95014 Tel 408-255-6610. Do not confuse with Step by Step Pubns. in West Covina, CA.

S C Toof, *(Toof, S. C., & Co.; 0-942249),* 670 S. Cooper St., P.O. Box 14607, Memphis, TN 38114 (SAN 289-5498) Tel 901-278-2200; Toll free: 800-826-5355; 800-367-8012 (in Tennessee).

S D A Pub, *(S.D.A. Publishing Co.; 0-9634084),* 20243 Vaughan, Detroit, MI 48219 (SAN 297-7516) Tel 313-533-2206.

S G Phillips, *(Phillips, S. G., Inc.; 0-87599),* P.O. Box 83, Chatham, NY 12037 (SAN 293-3152) Tel 518-392-3068; Orders to: 11 Brookside Ave., Chatham, NY 12037 (SAN 293-3160) Tel 518-392-6300; Toll free: 800-327-4212.

S Heiderscheit, *(Heiderscheit, Sara; 0-9620385),* 519 N. Seventh St., Osage, IA 50461 (SAN 249-3780) Tel 515-732-5619.

S I NJOKU, *(Njoku, Scholastica Ibari; 0-9617833),* P.O. Box 11557, Portland, OR 97211 (SAN 665-0724); 307 NE Holland, Portland, OR 97211 Tel 503-285-8160.

S Ink WA, *(Storytellers Ink; 0-9623072; 1-880812),* P.O. Box 33398, Seattle, WA 98133-0398 Tel 206-365-8265.

S J Durst, *(Durst, Sanford J.; 0-915262; 0-942666),* 11 Clinton Ave., Rockville Centre, NY 11570 (SAN 211-6987) Tel 516-766-4444.

S J F Co, *(SJF Co.; 0-9614185),* 44 Martindale Rd., Short Hills, NJ 07078-1709 (SAN 676-9411) Tel 201-467-9340.

S J Nash Pub, *(Nash, Steven J., Publishing; 1-878995),* P.O. Box 2115, Highland Park, IL 60035 Tel 708-433-6731; Toll free: 800-843-8545; Dist. by: Atrium Pubs. Group, 11270 Clayton Creek Rd., Lower Lake, CA 95457 (SAN 200-5743) Tel 707-995-3906; Toll free: 800-275-2606.

S K Hyde, *(Hyde, Sharon Kaylor; 0-9624349),* 1706 Crested Butte Dr., Austin, TX 78746 Tel 512-327-1405.

S K Pubns, *(S.K. Pubns.; 0-918224),* 4 S. 175 Naperville Rd., Naperville, IL 60563 (SAN 211-0571) Tel 708-778-0222; Orders to: 4 S. 175 Naperville Rd., Naperville, IL 60563 (SAN 211-058X) Tel 708-778-0222.

S Kulkarni, *(Kulkarni, Shyamkant; 0-9627083),* 2501 Hunters Hill Dr., No. 822, Enid, OK 73703-2311.

S L Jackson, *(Jackson, Stephan L., & Assocs.; 1-880722),* 6322 Sovereign Dr., No. 110, San Antonio, TX 78229 Tel 210-340-5166; Toll free: 800-367-5166.

S M Montgomery, *(Montgomery, Scott M.; 0-9641817),* 103 Brigham Creek Ct., Greer, SC 29650 Tel 803-292-0023.

S M Resar Pub, *(Resar, Stephen M., Publishing Co.;* 0-9633513), 24400 Highland Rd., Cleveland, OH 44143 Tel 216-531-5300.

S Michaels Pub, *(Michaels, Scott, Publishing Co.;* 0-9622535), 815 N. Lincoln St., Burbank, CA 91506 Tel 818-848-4880.

S P I Bks *Imprint of* **Shapolsky Pubs**

S Powell, *(Powell, Shirley; 0-9628995),* 146 Cedar St., Rockland, ME 04841 Tel 207-594-4730.

S R Severs, *(Severs, Susan Reist; 0-9618501),* 1288 Barclay Dr., Lancaster, PA 17601 (SAN 668-3304) Tel 717-392-6430.

S Stafford, *(Stafford, Shirley; 0-9607580),* 4231 Casa de Machado, La Mesa, CA 92041 (SAN 239-9806).

S Varney, *(Varney, Sharon; 0-9617579),* Rte. 1, Box 181A, Camden-on-Gauley, WV 26208 (SAN 664-5011) Tel 304-226-5358; Cranberry Ridge Rd., State Rte. 48, Camden-on-Gauley, WV 26208 (SAN 664-502X).

S-W Pub, *(South-Western Publishing Co.; 0-538),* Subs. of International Thomson Organization, Inc., 5101 Madison Rd., Cincinnati, OH 45227 (SAN 202-7518) Tel 513-271-8811; Toll free: 800-543-0487; Dist. by: Van Nostrand Reinhold, 115 Fifth Ave., New York, NY 10003 (SAN 202-5183) Tel 212-254-3232.

S Yonay, *(Yonay, Shahar; 0-9616783; 0-927580),* 126 Dover St., Brooklyn, NY 11235 (SAN 661-0544) Tel 718-615-0027.

S Z Griffin, *(Griffin, Sandi Zambarano; 1-883838),* P.O. Box 2364, Fort Pierce, FL 34954; 151 Hartman Rd., Fort Pierce, FL 34947 Tel 407-461-6830.

Saban Pub, *(Saban Publishing; 1-879551),* Div. of Saban Entertainment, Inc., 4000 W. Alameda Ave., Burbank, CA 91505 Tel 818-972-4800; Dist. by: Video Treasures, 500 Kirts Blvd., Troy, MI 48084 (SAN 630-5512); Toll free: 800-786-8777.

SAC Pr, *(SAC Pr.; 0-9635032),* 9191 W. Florissant Ave., No. 213, Saint Louis, MO 63136-1424; 1713 Andros Ct., Saint Louis, MO 63136 Tel 314-869-7755.

Saddleback Pubns, *(Saddleback Publishing, Inc.;* 1-56254), 711 W. 17th, Suite F12, Costa Mesa, CA 92627 Tel 714-650-4010.

Sadlier, *(Sadlier, William H., Inc.; 0-8215),* 9 Pine St., New York, NY 10005-1002 (SAN 204-0948) Tel 212-227-2120; Toll free: 800-221-5175.

Saeta, *(Saeta Ediciones; 0-917049),* P.O. Box 830576, Miami, FL 33283-0576 (SAN 655-2226); 7642 SW 96 Ct., Miami, FL 33173 Tel 305-596-9775.

Safari Ltd, *(Safari, Ltd.; 1-881469),* P.O. Box 630685, Miami, FL 33163; Toll free: 800-554-5414; 1400 NW 159th St., Miami, FL 33169 Tel 305-621-1000.

Safari Museum Pr, *(Safari Museum Pr.),* 16 S. Grant Ave., Chanute, KS 66720 (SAN 110-8840) Tel 314-431-2730.

Safari Pr, *(Safari Pr.; 0-940143; 1-57157),* Div. of Woodbine Publishing Co., 15621 Chemical Ln., Suite B, Huntington Beach, CA 92649 (SAN 663-0723) Tel 714-894-9080; Toll free: 800-451-4788 (orders only).

Safer Soc, *(Safer Society Pr.; 1-884444),* P.O. Box 340, Brandon, VT 05733-0340; 63 Park St., Brandon, VT 05733-1121 Tel 802-247-3132; Dist. by: Pacific Pipeline, Inc., 8030 S. 228th St., Kent, WA 98032-2900 (SAN 208-2128) Tel 206-872-5523; Toll free: 800-444-7323 (Customer service); 800-677-2222 (orders); Dist. by: Inland Bk. Co., 140 Commerce St., East Haven, CT 06512 (SAN 200-4151) Tel 203-467-4257; Toll free: 800-243-0138.

Safety Always Matters, *(Safety Always Matters, Inc.; 0-9620584; 1-883994),* 222 Wildwood Ct., Bloomingdale, IL 60108 (SAN 248-9759) Tel 708-894-1229; Dist. by: Syndistar, Inc., 125 Mallard St., Suite A, Saint Rose, LA 70087 (SAN 298-007X) Tel 504-468-1100; Toll free: 800-841-9532.

Sage Pr CA, *(Sage Pr.; 0-9634618),* 524 San Anselmo Ave., No. 225, San Anselmo, CA 94960 Tel 415-258-9924; Toll free: 800-218-4242. Do not confuse with companies with the same name in Phoenix, AZ, Oklahoma City, OK.

Sagebrush Bks, *(Sagebrush Bks.; 0-9628129; 1-880452),* 25 NW Irving St., Bend, OR 97701 Tel 503-385-7025.

Sailors Fantasies Pub, *(Sailors Fantasies Publishing;* 0-9621212), P.O. Box 1323, Scottsdale, AZ 85251 (SAN 251-0308); 7433 E. Thomas Rd., Scottsdale, AZ 85251 (SAN 251-0316) Tel 602-946-2125.

Saint Michaels, *(St. Michaels Pr.; 0-9638321),* Div. of Tooth Fitness, Inc., 12036 Nevada City Hwy., Suite 207, Grass Valley, CA 95945 Tel 916-274-0445.

Sakura Press, *(Sakura Pr.; 0-936845),* 36787 Sakura Ln., Pleasant Hill, OR 97455 (SAN 658-3350) Tel 503-747-5817; Dist. by: BookWorld Distribution Services, Inc., 1933 Whitfield Pk. Loop, Sarasota, FL 34243 (SAN 173-0568) Tel 813-758-8094; Toll free: 800-444-2524 (orders only).

Sala Enterp, *(Sala Enterprises; 0-9622340),* P.O. Box 76122, Los Angeles, CA 90076; 1308 S. Rimpau Blvd., Los Angeles, CA 90019 Tel 310-859-4602.

Salem Pr, *(Salem Pr., Inc.; 0-89356),* P.O. Box 1097, Englewood Cliffs, NJ 07632 (SAN 208-838X) Tel 201-871-3700; Toll free: 800-221-1592; 131 N. El Molino Ave., Pasadena, CA 91101 (SAN 241-841X) Tel 818-584-0106. *Imprints:* Magill Bks (Magill Books).

Sales & Mgmt Trg, *(Sales & Management Training, Inc.;* 1-877846), 2191 Northlake Pkwy. Ste. 160, Tucker, GA 30084 Tel 404-723-1345; Toll free: 800-367-3523.

Salinas Salinas & Matthews, *(Salinas, Salinas & Matthews; 0-942673),* P.O. Box 376, Montebello, CA 90640 (SAN 667-2876); 145 E. Fifth St., Montebello, CA 90640 (SAN 667-2884) Tel 818-286-9648.

Salmon Falls Pub, *(Salmon Falls Publishing; 0-9620429),* P.O. Box 171, Buhl, ID 83316 (SAN 248-7152); R.R. 3, Buhl, ID 83316 (SAN 248-7160) Tel 208-543-6002.

Salmon Run, *(Salmon Run Pubs.; 0-9634000),* P.O. Box 231081, Anchorage, AK 99523; 4101 University Dr., Anchorage, AK 99508 Tel 907-561-8371.

Samantha Bks, *(Samantha Bks.; 0-9639277),* Div. of Deborah F. Kirk Publishing Co., P.O. Box 2729, North Babylon, NY 11703 Tel 516-661-2732.

Samara Pubns, *(Samara Pubns.; 0-935513),* 15505 SE Arista Dr., Milwaukie, OR 97267 (SAN 695-8923) Tel 503-659-1067; Dist. by: Blanchard's, P.O. Box 855, Clackamas, OR 97015 (SAN 112-1715) Tel 503-657-9838; Toll free: 800-547-9755, Ext. 15 (orders).

Samary Pr, *(Samary Pr.; 0-9630798),* Box 892, Cotati, CA 94931; 675 W. Cotati Ave., Cotati, CA 94931 Tel 707-664-8598.

SamHar Pr, *(SamHar Pr.; 0-85157),* Div. of Story Hse. Corp., Bindery Ln., Charlotteville, NY 12036 (SAN 203-3585) Tel 607-397-8725; Toll free: 800-847-2105 (orders only).

San Marco Bk, *(San Marco Bookstore; 0-935259),* 1971 San Marco Blvd., Jacksonville, FL 32207 (SAN 693-3734) Tel 904-396-7597.

Sand & Silk, *(Sand & Silk; 0-9617284),* P.O. Box 846, Banning, CA 92220 (SAN 663-5210); P.O. Box 5194, San Bernardino, CA 92412-5194 (SAN 249-3268) Tel 909-849-9244.

Sand River Pr, *(Sand River Pr.; 0-944627),* 1319 14th St., Los Osos, CA 93402 (SAN 244-4135) Tel 805-543-3591.

Sandcastle Bks *Imprint of* **Putnam Pub Group**

Sandcastle Pub, *(Sandcastle Publishing; 0-9627756;* 1-883995), P.O. Box 3070, South Pasadena, CA 91031-6070; 1723 Hill Dr., South Pasadena, CA 91030 Tel 213-255-3616.

Sandhill Crane, *(Sandhill Crane Pr., Inc.; 1-877743),* 2406 NW 47th Terrace, Gainesville, FL 32606 Tel 904-375-6610.

S&J Prods, *(S&J Products International, Inc.; 1-884851),* P.O. Box 123, Arlington Heights, IL 60006-0123; 551 W. Euclid Ave., No. 201, Arlington Heights, IL 60004-5400 Tel 708-342-1030.

Sandlapper Pub Co, *(Sandlapper Publishing Co., Inc.;* 0-87844), P.O. Box 730, Orangeburg, SC 29116 (SAN 203-2678) Tel 803-531-1658.

Sandollar Pr, *(Sandollar Pr.),* Div. of Sandollar Enterprises, P.O. Box 4157, Santa Barbara, CA 93140-4157 (SAN 202-9952) Tel 805-963-7077.

Sandpiper *Imprint of* **HM**

Sandpiper OR, *(Sandpiper Pr.; 0-9603748),* P.O. Box 286, Brookings, OR 97415 (SAN 213-5582) Tel 503-469-5588. Do not confuse with companies with the same name in Solana Beach, CA, Saint Clair Shores, MI, Newport Beach, CA.

S&S BFYR *Imprint of* **S&S Trade**

Sands Hse, *(Sands Hse.; 0-9638113),* 130 Prince George St., Annapolis, MD 21401 Tel 410-263-8924.

S&S Trade, *(Simon & Schuster Trade; 0-671; 0-914676;* 0-88138), Div. of Simon & Schuster, Inc., 1230 Avenue of the Americas, New York, NY 10020 Tel 212-698-7000. *Imprints:* Fireside (Fireside Paperbacks); Green Tiger (Green Tiger Press); Half Moon Bks (Half Moon Books); J Messner (Messner, Julian); Little Simon (Little Simon); S&S BFYR (Simon & Schuster Books for Young Readers).

Sandstone Pub, *(Sandstone Publishing; 0-9621779),* 2710 Sunnyview Ln., Billings, MT 59102 Tel 406-656-5730. Do not confuse with Sandstone Publishing in Charlotte, NC.

S&T Waring, *(Waring, Shirley & Thomas, Pubs.;* 0-9622808), 11 Mitchell Ln., Hanover, NH 03755 Tel 603-643-8331.

Sandwich Islands, *(Sandwich Islands Publishing; 0-9624676; 1-884364),* P.O. Box 10669, Lahaina, HI 96761 (SAN 297-9551); 31 Kai Pali Pl., Lahaina, Maui, HI 96761 Tel 808-661-5844; Dist. by: IPD, 674 Via de la Valle, Suite 204, Solana Beach, CA 92075 (SAN 200-8408) Tel 619-481-5928; Toll free: 800-999-1170; 800-228-5144 (in Canada).

Sanford Hse Pr, *(Sanford Hse. Pr.; 0-9618645),* Hat Shop Hill, Bridgewater, CT 06752 (SAN 668-4238) Tel 203-354-9035.

Sant Bani Ash, *(Sant Bani Ashram, Inc.; 0-89142),* R. F.D. 1, Franklin, NH 03235 (SAN 209-5114) Tel 603-934-5640.

Santa & Friends, *(Santa & Friends; 1-880695),* 223 Woodville Rd., Falmouth, ME 04105 Tel 207-797-7752; Toll free: 800-499-0440.

Santabear Bks, *(Santabear Bks.; 0-9619204),* 700 On the Mall, Minneapolis, MN 55402 (SAN 244-6820) Tel 612-375-3489.

Santillana, *(Santillana Publishing Co.; 0-88272; 1-56014),* 901 W. Walnut St., Compton, CA 90220 (SAN 205-1133); Toll free: 800-245-8584.

Saphrograph, *(Saphrograph Corp.; 0-87557),* 4910 Ft. Hamilton Pkwy., Brooklyn, NY 11219 (SAN 110-4128) Tel 718-331-1233.

Saras Prints, *(Sara's Prints, Inc.; 1-881970),* 3018A Alvarado St., San Leandro, CA 94577 Tel 510-352-6060.

Sasquatch Bks, *(Sasquatch Bks.; 0-912365; 1-57061),* Div. of Sasquatch Publishing Co., Inc., 1008 Western Ave., Suite 300, Seattle, WA 98104 (SAN 289-0208) Tel 206-467-4300; Toll free: 800-775-0817; Dist. by: Pacific Pipeline, Inc., 8030 S. 228th St, Kent, WA 98032-2900 (SAN 208-2128) Tel 206-872-5523; Toll free: 800-444-7323 (Customer Service); 800-677-2222 (orders); Dist. by: Ingram Bk. Co., 1 Ingram Blvd., La Vergne, TN 37086-1986 (SAN 169-7978) Tel 615-793-5000; Toll free: 800-937-8000 (orders only, all warehouses); Dist. by: Baker & Taylor Bks., Reno Service Ctr., 380 Edison Way, Reno, NV 89564 (SAN 169-4464) Tel 702-858-6700; Toll free: 800-775-1700 (customer service); Dist. by: Bookpeople, 7900 Edgewater Dr., Oakland, CA 94621 (SAN 168-9517) Tel 510-632-4700; Toll free: 800-999-4650.

Satori Pr, *(Satori Pr.; 0-9617268),* 904 Silver Spur Rd., No. 323, Rolling Hills Estates, CA 90274 (SAN 663-5377); 2668 Via Olivera, Palos Verdes Estates, CA 90274 (SAN 663-5385) Tel 310-377-7810.

Saunders, *(Saunders, W. B., Co.; 0-7216),* Subs. of Harcourt Brace & Co., Curtis Ctr., Independence Sq., W., Philadelphia, PA 19106-3399 (SAN 203-266X) Tel 215-238-7800; Orders to: 6277 Sea Harbor Dr., Orlando, FL 32821 (SAN 244-8106); Toll free: 800-545-2522.

Saunders Photo, *(Saunders PhotoGraphic, Inc.; 1-883403; 0-87985),* 21 Jet View Dr., Rochester, NY 14624 Tel 716-328-7800.

Saundras Story Bks, *(Saundra's Story Bks., Inc.;* 1-879209), 523 E. Erna Ave., La Habra, CA 90631 Tel 310-690-4767.

Savant Pub, *(Savant Publishing Co.; 0-940527),* P.O. Box 27058, Milwaukee, WI 53227 (SAN 664-5259); W222 N2872 Timberwood Ct., Waukesha, WI 53186 (SAN 664-5267) Tel 414-549-3306.

Sawan Kirpal Pubns
See S K Pubns

Saxon Pubs OK, *(Saxon Pubs., Inc.; 0-939798; 1-56577),* 1320 W. Lindsey, Suite 100, Norman, OK 73069 (SAN 216-8960) Tel 405-329-7071; Toll free: 800-284-7019; Orders to: Thompson Bk. Depository, P.O. Box 60160, Oklahoma City, OK 73146 (SAN 662-023X) Tel 405-525-9458.

Scand Descent, *(Scandinavian Descent, Inc.; 0-9634851),* 5917 Camelback Ct., Indianapolis, IN 46250 Tel 317-576-9900.

Scarecrow, *(Scarecrow Pr., Inc.; 0-8108),* Sub. of Grolier, Inc., 52 Liberty St., Box 4167, Metuchen, NJ 08840 (SAN 203-2651) Tel 908-548-8600; Toll free: 800-537-7107.

Scarf Pr, *(Scarf Pr.; 0-934386),* 58 E. 83rd St., New York, NY 10028 (SAN 212-9698) Tel 212-744-3901.

SCE Assocs, *(SCE Assocs.; 1-885568),* 305 Spring Creek Village, No. 476, Dallas, TX 75248-5711 Tel 214-618-6783.

Scesney Pubns, *(Scesney Pubns., Inc.; 0-9618667),* 11 Edgemoor Rd., Timonium, MD 21093 (SAN 668-4068) Tel 410-252-2509.

Sch Zone Pub Co, *(School Zone Publishing Co.; 0-938256; 0-88743),* 1819 Industrial Dr., P.O. Box 777, Grand Haven, MI 49417 (SAN 289-8314) Tel 616-846-5030; Toll free: 800-253-0564.

Schaffer Pubns, *(Schaffer, Frank, Pubns., Inc.; 0-86734),* 23740 Hawthorne Blvd., Torrance, CA 90505 (SAN 217-5827) Tel 310-378-1133; Toll free: 800-421-5565.

Scherzo Pub, *(Scherzo Publishing; 1-881026),* 3016 NE 19th, Portland, OR 97212 Tel 503-287-7009.

Schiffer, *(Schiffer Publishing, Ltd.; 0-916838; 0-88740),* 77 Lower Valley Rd., Atglen, PA 19310 (SAN 208-8428) Tel 610-593-1777.

Schiller Inst, *(Schiller Institute, Inc.; 0-9621095;* 1-882985), P.O. Box 20244, Washington, DC 20041-0244 (SAN 250-4944); 333 1/2 Pensylvania SE, 2nd Flr., Washington, DC 20003 (SAN 250-4952) Tel 202-544-7018.

Schirmer Bks, *(Schirmer Bks.; 0-911320),* 866 Third Ave., New York, NY 10022 (SAN 222-9544) Tel 212-702-4283; Dist. by: Macmillan Publishing Co., Inc., 100 Front St., Box 500, Riverside, NJ 08075-7500 (SAN 202-5582) Tel 609-461-6500; Toll free: 800-257-5755.

Schl Home Connect, *(School Home Connection;* 0-9640721), 9858-18 Glades Rd., Boca Raton, FL 33434.

Schmul Pub Co, *(Schmul Publishing Co., Inc.; 0-88019),* P.O. Box 716, Salem, OH 44460-0716 (SAN 180-2771) Tel 216-222-2249; Toll free: 800-772-6657.

Schneider Assocs, *(Schneider Assocs.; 0-9640218),* 458 Camino Alondra, San Clemente, CA 92672 Tel 714-661-2671.

Schneider Educational, *(Schneider Educational Products;* 1-877779), P.O. Box 472260, San Francisco, CA 94147-2260 Tel 415-567-4455.

Schocken, *(Schocken Bks., Inc.; 0-8052),* Div. of Random Hse., Inc., 201 E. 50th St., New York, NY 10022 (SAN 213-7585) Tel 212-572-2559; Orders to: Random House, Inc., 400 Hahn Rd., Westminster, MD 21157 (SAN 202-5515) Tel 410-848-1900; Toll free: 800-733-3000 (orders).

Schoenhof, *(Schoenhof's Foreign Bks., Inc.; 0-87774),* Subs. of Editions Gallimard, 76A Mt. Auburn St., Cambridge, MA 02138 (SAN 212-0062) Tel 617-547-8855.

Schol Facsimiles, *(Scholars' Facsimiles & Reprints;* 0-8201), Subs. of Academic Resources Corp., P.O. Box 344, Delmar, NY 12054 (SAN 203-2627) Tel 518-439-5978.

Scholar Cnslt, *(Scholarship Consultant Services, Inc.;* 1-883374), 1400 Paragon Pkwy., Birmingham, AL 35235 Tel 205-856-3020; Dist. by: Best of Times, Inc., 147 Corporate Way, Pelham, AL 35124 (SAN 630-7647) Tel 205-664-6980.

Scholar Pub Co, *(Scholar Publishing Co.; 0-9624016),* 441 1/2 S. Jefferson Davis Pkwy., New Orleans, LA 70119-7125 Tel 504-486-2294.

Scholastic Hardcover *Imprint of* **Scholastic Inc**

Scholastic Inc, *(Scholastic, Inc.; 0-590; 0-439),* Subs. of SI Holdings, Inc., 555 Broadway, New York, NY 10012-3999 (SAN 202-5442) Tel 212-343-6100; Orders to: P.O. Box 120, Bergenfield, NJ 07621 (SAN 202-5450); Toll free: 800-325-6149 (orders only). *Imprints:* Apple Paperbacks (Apple Paperbacks); Blue Ribbon Bks (Blue Ribbon Books); Blue Sky Press (Blue Sky Press, The); Cartwheel (Cartwheel); Little Apple (Little Apple Books); Point (Point); Scholastic Hardcover (Scholastic Hardcover).

Schoolhouse WI, *(Schoolhouse Pr.; 0-942018),* 6899 Cary Bluff, Pittsville, WI 54466 (SAN 239-8044) Tel 715-884-2799. Do not confuse with Schoolhouse Pr., Peterborough, NH.

Schroder Music, *(Schroder Music Co.; 0-915620),* 704 Gilman St., Berkeley, CA 94710 (SAN 207-3935) Tel 510-524-5804; Dist. by: Children's Small Pr. Collection, 716 N. Fourth Ave., Ann Arbor, MI 48104 (SAN 200-514X) Tel 313-668-8056; Toll free: 800-221-8056 (orders only).

Schwarz Pauper, *(Schwarz Pauper Pr.; 0-9621505),* 88 Winwood Dr., R.F.D. Box 164, Barnstead, NH 03225 (SAN 251-4540) Tel 603-776-6937; Dist. by: Vantage Pr., Inc., 516 W. 34th St., New York, NY 10001 (SAN 206-8893) Tel 212-736-1767; Toll free: 800-882-3273.

Sci Academy Soft, *(Science Academy Software;* 0-9623926), 22 Dunwoodie St., Yonkers, NY 10704-2608 Tel 914-422-1100.

Sci Am Yng Rdrs *Imprint of* **W H Freeman**

Sci & Art Prods, *(Science & Art Products; 0-9634622),* 24861 Rotunde Mesa, Malibu, CA 90265 Tel 310-456-2496; Toll free: 800-356-1733.

Sci Passport, *(Science Passport, Inc.; 0-9634246),* 7104 Loch Lomond Dr., Bethesda, MD 20817-4760 Tel 301-229-9630.

Sci Pubs, *(Scientific Pubs., Inc.; 0-945417),* P.O. Box 15718, Gainesville, FL 32601 (SAN 247-0098) Tel 904-335-5011; 4460 SW 35th Terr., Suite 305, Gainesville, FL 32608 (SAN 247-0101) Tel 904-356-5630. Do not confuse with Scientific Pubns. in Woburn, MA.

Scojtia Pub Co
See Jordan Enterprises

Scope Pub, *(Scope Publishing Co.; 0-9633846),* 936 Pleasant View Ct., Northfield, MN 55057 (SAN 297-7451) Tel 507-663-0517. Do not confuse with Scope Publishing in Sumner, WA.

Scott F, *(Scott, Foresman & Co.; 0-673),* Subs. of HarperCollins Pubs., Inc., 1900 E. Lake Ave., Glenview, IL 60025 (SAN 200-2140) Tel 708-729-3000.

Scribblers Pub, *(Scribblers Publishing; 0-924649),* Div. of G.E.T., Inc., 14205 Cashel Forest Dr., Houston, TX 77069 Tel 713-440-5698.

Scribes Pubns, *(Scribes Pubns.; 1-884056),* 1448 E. 52nd St., No. 418, Chicago, IL 60615 Tel 312-752-2560.

Scribner *Imprint of* **Macmillan**

Scribners Young Read *Imprint of* **Macmillan Child Grp**

Script Memory Fl, *(Scripture Memory Fellowship International; 1-880960),* P.O. Box 411551, Saint Louis, MO 63141; 70 Weldon Pkwy., Maryland Heights, MO 63043 Tel 314-569-0244.

Scroll Pr, *(Scroll Pr., Inc.; 0-87592),* 2858 Valerie Ct., Merrick, NY 11566 (SAN 206-796X) Tel 516-379-4283.

SDPI, *(S.D.P.I.; 0-9630328),* 418 Jackson St., Eveleth, MN 55734-1323 (SAN 297-7486) Tel 218-744-1774; Toll free: 800-825-7374 (orders only).

Sea Fog Pr, *(Sea Fog Pr., Inc.; 0-917507),* P.O. Box 210056, San Francisco, CA 94121-0056 (SAN 656-1012) Tel 415-221-8527.

Sea Island, *(Sea Island Information Group; 1-877610),* 11210 Cherry Hill Rd., No. 102, Beltsville, MD 20705 Tel 301-937-2494.

Sea Urchin, *(Sea Urchin Pr.; 0-9605208),* P.O. Box 10503, Oakland, CA 94610-0503 (SAN 215-8086).

Seabird
See Stagecoach Rd Pr

Seablom, *(Seablom Design Bks.; 0-918800),* 2106 Second Ave., N., Seattle, WA 98109 (SAN 210-4962) Tel 206-285-2308.

Seabright, *(Seabright; 0-9613824),* 712 Ott St., Harrisonburg, VA 22801 (SAN 679-9973) Tel 703-434-8553; Rte. 1, Box 135, Nags Head, NC 27959 (SAN 248-3998); Dist. by: Insiders' Guides, Inc., P.O. Box 2057, Manteo, NC 27954 (SAN 265-0940) Tel 919-473-1225; Toll free: 800-765-2665.

Seabright Pr, *(Seabright Pr.; 0-9634359),* P.O. Box 3644, Dana Point, CA 92629; 33062 Sea Bright Dr., Dana Point, CA 92629 Tel 714-493-9713.

Seacoast AL, *(Seacoast Publishing, Inc.; 1-878561),* 110 12th St., N., Birmingham, AL 35203 Tel 205-250-8016.

Seacoast Bks
See Seacoast AL

Seacoast Pubns New Eng, *(Seacoast Pubns. of New England; 0-9634360),* 2800A Lafayette Rd., Suite 165, Portsmouth, NH 03801.

Seagull Pub Co, *(Seagull Publishing Co.; 0-9612698),* 2915 Stanford Ave., Suite 7, Marina del Rey, CA 90291 (SAN 295-0235).

Seal Pr Feminist, *(Seal Pr.-Feminist; 0-931188;* 1-878067), 3131 Western Ave., No. 410, Seattle, WA 98121-1028 (SAN 215-3416) Tel 206-283-7844; Dist. by: Inland Bk. Co., 140 Commerce St., East Haven, CT 06512 (SAN 200-4151) Tel 203-467-4257; Toll free: 800-243-0138; Dist. by: Pacific Pipeline, Inc., 8030 S. 228th St., Kent, WA 98032-2900 (SAN 208-2128) Tel 206-872-5523; Toll free: 800-444-7323 (Customer Service); 800-677-2222 (orders); Dist. by: Bookpeople, 7900 Edgewater Dr., Oakland, CA 94621 (SAN 168-9517) Tel 510-632-4700; Toll free: 800-999-4650; Dist. by: Publishers Group West, 4065 Hollis St., Emeryville, CA 94608 (SAN 202-8522) Tel 510-658-3453; Toll free: 800-788-3123.

Search Public, *(Search Pubns.; 0-910715),* Div. of Sanborn Education Research, Inc., 2000 Old Stage Rd., Florissant, CO 80816 (SAN 262-0766) Tel 303-748-3341.

Seascape Enters, *(Seascape Enterprises; 0-931595),* 105 Rens Rd., No. 50, Poquoson, VA 23662-1611 (SAN 682-4765); Dist. by: C Plath North American Division of Litton Systems, Inc., 222 Severn Ave., Annapolis, MD 21403 Tel 410-263-6700; Toll free: 800-638-0428.

Seattle Arts, *(Seattle Arts Commission; 0-9617443),* 305 Harrison St., Seattle, WA 98109 (SAN 664-0257) Tel 206-684-7171.

SeaWard Graph, *(SeaWard Graphics; 0-9628939),* 4727 E. Warner Rd., No. 2009, Phoenix, AZ 85044 (SAN 297-4274); Toll free: 800-366-1817.

Seawind Pub, *(Seawind Publishing; 0-9631916),* Div. of Suncoast Ecological Enterprises, Inc., 18323 Sunset Blvd., Redington Shores, FL 33708 (SAN 297-6307) Tel 813-391-6211.

Seaworthy Pubns, *(Seaworthy Pubns.; 0-9625229),* 6003 Overby Rd., Flowery Branch, GA 30542-2729 Tel 706-967-4319.

Sec Glance, *(Second Glance; 0-9631574),* 7840 Fareholm Dr., Los Angeles, CA 90046 Tel 213-969-0111; Toll free: 800-473-1966.

See-Mores Wrkshop, *(See-More's Workshop; 1-882601),* Div. of Shadow Box Theatre, 325 West End Ave., New York, NY 10023 Tel 212-877-7356.

See the Sounds, *(See the Sounds Publishing; 0-933367),* 700 Wellesley Ave., Akron, OH 44303 (SAN 691-6694) Tel 216-836-1296.

Seedling Pubns, *(Seedling Pubns., Inc.; 1-880612),* 4079 Overlook Dr., E., Columbus, OH 43214-2931 Tel 614-451-2412.

Selah Pubng, *(Selah Publishing Co.; 0-9639331),* P.O. Box 721508, Berkley, MI 48072-1508; 2886 E. 12 Mile Rd., No. 1508, Berkley, MI 48072 Tel 313-294-2244. Do not confuse with Selah Publishing Co. in Accord, NY.

Selena Pr, *(Selena Pr.; 0-938451),* 1010 Southwood Dr., Fargo, ND 58103 (SAN 660-9880) Tel 701-235-2890.

Self-Counsel Pr, *(Self-Counsel Pr., Inc.; 0-88908),* Subs. of International Self-Counsel Pr., Ltd., 1704 N. State St., Bellingham, WA 98225 (SAN 240-9925) Tel 206-676-4530; Toll free: 800-663-3007.

Self-Taught Pubs, *(Self-Taught Pubs.; 0-9624077),* 1 University Pkwy., Park Forest, IL 60466-0975.

Sells Pub, *(Sells Publishing Co.; 0-926739),* 3053 E. Flora Pl., Denver, CO 80210 Tel 303-691-0473.

Sennet & Sarnoff, *(Sennet & Sarnoff Learning Systems, Inc.; 1-879871),* 20 E. 49th, New York, NY 10017 Tel 212-308-5926.

SEPM, *(SEPM (Society for Sedimentary Geology); 0-918985; 1-56576),* P.O. Box 4756, Tulsa, OK 74159-0756 (SAN 260-3462); 3530 E. 31st St., Suite 102, Tulsa, OK 74135 Tel 918-743-9765.

Sequitur Systs, *(Sequitur Systems, Inc.; 0-9636754),* 7525 Nine Mile Bridge Rd., Fort Worth, TX 76135 Tel 817-237-4108.

Sequoia Nat Hist Assn, *(Sequoia Natural History Assn.;* 1-878441), Ash Mountain, P.O. Box 10, Three Rivers, CA 93271 Tel 209-565-3758.

Setubandh Pubns, *(Setubandh Pubns.; 0-9623674),* 1 Lawson Ln., Great Neck, NY 11023 Tel 516-482-6938.

Seven Hills Bk Dists, *(7 Hills Bk. Distributors;* 0-911403), Div. of Books for the Decorative Arts, Inc., 49 Central Ave., Cincinnati, OH 45202 (SAN 169-6629) Tel 513-381-3881; Toll free: 800-545-2005.

Seven Wolves, *(Seven Wolves Publishing; 0-9627387;* 1-56508), 8928 National Blvd., Los Angeles, CA 90034 Tel 310-836-3767; Toll free: 800-852-2474.

Seventh-Wing Pubns, *(Seventh-Wing Pubns.; 0-944208),* 310 W. Platte Ave., Colorado Springs, CO 80905-1330 (SAN 243-0428) Tel 719-471-2932.

Sevgo Pr, *(Sevgo Pr.; 0-943487),* Div. of Sevgo, Inc., 1955 22nd St., Northport, AL 35476 (SAN 668-4998) Tel 205-339-1888.

Sey Lawr *Imprint of* **Delacorte**

Seymour Pubns, *(Seymour, Dale, Pubns.; 0-86651;* 1-57232), Div. of Addison-Wesley Publishing Co., Inc., 200 Middlefield Rd., Menlo Park, CA 94025 (SAN 200-9781) Tel 415-688-0880.

SF Study Ctr, *(San Francisco Study Ctr.; 0-936434),* P.O. Box 425646, San Francisco, CA 94142-5646 (SAN 214-4654) Tel 915-626-1650; Toll free: 800-484-4173.

SG Prodns, *(SG Productions; 0-9621071),* P.O. Box 432, 508 Fourth St., Dayton, OR 97114 (SAN 250-6262) Tel 503-864-2987.

SGC Biomedical, *(SGC Biomedical Engineering;* 0-925395), P.O. Box 2414, Garden Grove, CA 92642-2414 Tel 714-284-9424.

Shade Tree NV, *(Shade Tree Bks.; 0-9617609),* 1200 Nelson Ct., Boulder City, NV 89005 (SAN 664-8614) Tel 702-293-2177.

ShadowPlay Pr, *(ShadowPlay Pr.; 0-9638819),* 7289 Columbine Rd., Forreston, IL 61030 Tel 815-938-2275.

Shaker Her Soc, *(Shaker Heritage Society),* Albany Shaker Rd., Albany, NY 12211 (SAN 289-0410) Tel 518-456-7890.

Shakespere VT, *(Shakespeare-For-Today Trust; 0-9628103; 1-880026),* P.O. Box 66, Whiting, VT 05778-0066; Rte. 30, Whiting, VT 05778 Tel 802-623-6651.

Shalom, *(Shalom, P., Pubns., Inc.; 0-87559),* 5409 18th Ave., Brooklyn, NY 11204 (SAN 204-5893) Tel 718-256-1954.

Shambala Pr
See Tiger Isld Pr

Shambhala Pubns, *(Shambhala Pubns., Inc.; 0-87773;* 1-57062), Horticultural Hall, 300 Massachusetts Ave., Boston, MA 02115 (SAN 203-2481) Tel 617-424-0030; Dist. by: Random Hse., Inc., 400 Hahn Rd., Westminster, MD 21157 (SAN 202-5515) Tel 410-848-1900; Toll free: 800-733-3000 (orders).

Shamrock Pr, *(Shamrock Pr. & Publishing Co.;* 0-910583), P.O. Box 39513, Fort Lauderdale, FL 33339-9513 (SAN 260-2636).

Shamrock TN, *(Shamrock Pr.; 0-9633937),* 3008 Ozark Rd., Chattanooga, TN 37415-5912 Tel 615-875-0457.

Shapeless Enterprises, *(Shapeless Enterprises;* 0-9623368), P.O. Box 297, Harbor City, CA 90710 Tel 310-539-0313.

Shapolsky Pubs, *(Shapolsky Pubs., Inc.; 0-933503; 0-944007; 1-56171),* 136 W. 22nd St., New York, NY 10011 (SAN 200-8068) Tel 212-633-2022; Dist. by: Hearst Corp., International Circulation Distributors/ ICD Bks., 250 W. 55th St., 12th Flr., New York, NY 10019 (SAN 169-5800) Tel 212-649-4474; Toll free: 800-223-0288; Dist. by: Bookazine Co., Inc., 75 Hook Rd., Bayonne, NJ 07002 (SAN 169-5665) Tel 201-339-7777; Toll free: 800-221-8112; Dist. by: Pacific Pipeline, Inc., 8030 S. 228th St., Kent, WA 98032-2900 (SAN 208-2128) Tel 206-872-5523; Toll free: 800-444-7323 (Customer Service); 800-677-2222 (orders); Dist. by: Golden-Lee Bk. Distributors, Inc., 1000 Dean St., Brooklyn, NY 11238 (SAN 169-5126) Tel 718-857-6333; Toll free: 800-473-7475; Dist. by: Ingram Bk. Co., 1 Ingram Blvd., La Vergne, TN 37086-1986 (SAN 169-7978) Tel 615-793-5000; Toll free: 800-937-8000 (orders only, all warehouses); Dist. by: Baker & Taylor Bks., Momence Service Ctr., 501 S. Gladiolus St., Momence, IL 60954-2444 (SAN 169-2100) Tel 815-472-2444; Toll free: 800-775-2300 (customer service); Dist. by: Baker & Taylor Bks., Commerce Service Ctr., 251 Mt. Olive Church Rd., Commerce, GA 30599-9988 (SAN 169-1503) Tel 706-335-5000; Toll free: 800-775-1200 (customer service); Dist. by: Baker & Taylor Bks., Somerville Service Ctr., 50 Kirby Ave., Somerville, NJ 08876-0734 (SAN 169-4901) Tel 908-722-8000; Toll free: 800-775-1500 (customer service); Dist. by: Baker & Taylor Bks., Reno Service Ctr., 380 Edison Way, Reno, NV 89564 (SAN 169-4464) Tel 702-858-6700; Toll free: 800-775-1700 (customer service); Dist. by: Brodart Co., 500 Arch St., Williamsport, PA 17705 (SAN 169-7684) Tel 717-326-2462; Toll free: 800-233-8467. *Imprints:* S P I Bks (S. P. I. Books).

Share Pub CA, *(Share Publishing; 0-9633705),* 3130 Alpine Rd., Suite 200-1009, Portola Valley, CA 94028 Tel 415-854-0294. Do not confuse with Share Publishing Co., Annapolis, MD.

Shared Learning
See Innovat Lrning Grp

Shared Wrld, *(Shared World Pubns.; 0-9636374),* 10409 Ewing Rd., Bloomington, MN 55431 Tel 612-835-3199.

Shark-Bite, *(Shark-Bite Publishing; 0-9633342),* P.O. Box 3588, Lihle, HI 96766 (SAN 297-701X); Texera Tract, No. 8, Kaleheo, HI 96766 Tel 808-332-7972; Dist. by: Publishers Distribution Service, 6893 Sullivan Rd., Grawn, MI 49637 (SAN 630-5717) Tel 616-276-5196; Toll free: 800-345-0096 (orders only); Dist. by: BookWorld Distribution Services, Inc., 1933 Whitfield Pk. Loop, Sarasota, FL 34243 (SAN 173-0568) Tel 813-758-8094; Toll free: 800-444-2524 (orders only).

SharLew Ent, *(SharLew Enterprises; 1-880734),* P.O. Box 971, Ridgecrest, CA 93556; 742 W. Coral Ave., Ridgecrest, CA 93555 Tel 619-375-8540.

Shasta San Rafael, *(Shasta Pubns.; 0-941611),* Div. of Shasta Enterprises, 7 Adrian Way, San Rafael, CA 94903-2801 (SAN 666-1750) Tel 415-479-4491.

Shaw & Co, *(Shaw & Co.; 0-944900),* 18 S. Mill, Glastonbury, CT 06073 (SAN 245-6745) Tel 203-275-5000.

Shaw Pubs, *(Shaw, Harold, Pubs.; 0-87788),* P.O. Box 567, 388 Gundersen Dr., Wheaton, IL 60189 (SAN 203-2473) Tel 708-665-6700; Toll free: 800-742-9782. Do not confuse with (Melvin) Shaw Publishing, LaBelle, FL.

Shawangunk Pr, *(Shawangunk Pr., Inc.; 1-885482),* 8 Laurel Park Rd., Wappingers Falls, NY 12590 Tel 914-462-1201.

Shawme Ent
See E S Santos

Shay Pubns, *(Shay Pubns.; 1-881365),* Subs. of To Be Publishing Co., P.O. Box 595051, Dallas, TX 75359; 5916 Birchbrook Dr., No. 229, Dallas, TX 75206 Tel 214-418-9999.

Shearer Pub, *(Shearer Publishing; 0-940672),* 406 Post Oak Rd., Fredericksburg, TX 78624 (SAN 218-5989) Tel 210-997-6529; Toll free: 800-458-3808.

Sheba Bks Intl, *(Sheba Bks. International; 1-878950),* 220 W. 71st St., New York, NY 10023 (SAN 297-2336).

Sheed & Ward MO, *(Sheed & Ward; 0-934134; 1-55612),* Div. of National Catholic Reporter Publishing Co., Inc., P.O. Box 419492, Kansas City, MO 64141-6492 (SAN 207-7396); Toll free: 800-444-8910; 800-333-7373 (orders); 115 E. Armour Blvd., Kansas City, MO 64111 (SAN 658-1269) Tel 816-531-0538.

Sheehan Indus, *(Sheehan Industries; 0-9617018),* P.O. Box 801, Lake Stevens, WA 98258 (SAN 662-8621); 9213 SE 15th St., Everett, WA 98205 (SAN 662-863X) Tel 206-334-7049.

Sheffield WI, *(Sheffield Publishing Co.; 0-917974; 0-88133; 1-879215),* Subs. of Waveland Pr., Inc., P.O. Box 359, Salem, WI 53168 (SAN 658-4519); 9009 Antioch Rd., Salem, WI 53168 (SAN 658-4527) Tel 414-843-2281.

Shelby Hse, *(Shelby Hse.; 0-942179),* Affil. of St. Lukes Pr., 1407 Union Ave., Suite 401, Memphis, TN 38104 (SAN 666-8895) Tel 901-357-5441; Toll free: 800-524-5554.

Shelf-Life Bks, *(Shelf-Life Bks.; 1-880042),* 2132 Fordem Ave., Madison, WI 53704 Tel 608-244-7767.

Shengold, *(Shengold Pubs., Inc.; 0-88400),* 18 W. 45th St., New York, NY 10036 (SAN 203-2465) Tel 212-944-2555.

Shepherd Minst, *(Shepherd Ministries; 0-923417),* 2845 W. Airport Freeway, Suite 137, Irving, TX 75062 (SAN 252-0893) Tel 214-570-7599.

Sheriar Pr, *(Sheriar Pr., Inc.; 0-913078),* 3005 Hwy. 17 N. Bypass, Myrtle Beach, SC 29577 (SAN 203-2457) Tel 803-448-1107; Dist. by: New Leaf Distributing Co., 5425 Tulane Dr., SW, Atlanta, GA 30336-2323 (SAN 169-1449) Tel 404-691-6996; Toll free: 800-326-2665.

Sheridan, *(Sheridan Hse., Inc.; 0-911378; 0-924486),* 145 Palisade St., Dobbs Ferry, NY 10522 (SAN 204-5915) Tel 914-693-2410.

Shining Star Pubns *Imprint of* **Good Apple**

Shire Pr, *(Shire Pr.; 0-918828),* 26873 Hester Creek Rd., Los Gatos, CA 95030-9242 (SAN 293-3942) Tel 408-353-4253; Dist. by: Bookpeople, 7900 Edgewater Dr., Oakland, CA 94621 (SAN 168-9517) Tel 510-632-4700; Toll free: 800-999-4650; Dist. by: Pacific Pipeline, Inc., 8030 S. 228th St., Kent, WA 98032-2900 (SAN 208-2128) Tel 206-872-5523; Toll free: 800-444-7323 (Customer Service); 800-677-2222 (orders).

Shirk-Heath, *(Shirk-Heath, Sandra J.; 0-9615104),* 1935 42nd St., NW, Rochester, MN 55901 (SAN 694-2784) Tel 507-289-0711.

Shirlee, *(Shirlee Pubns.; 0-9613476),* P.O. Box 22122, Carmel, CA 93922 (SAN 657-3789) Tel 408-646-0600.

Shoe String, *(Shoe String Pr., Inc.; 0-208),* 2 Linsley St., North Haven, CT 06473-2517 (SAN 213-2079) Tel 203-239-2702.

Shoe Tree Pr, *(Shoe Tree Pr.),* Div. of F&W Pubns., Inc., 1507 Dana Ave., Cincinnati, OH 45207 Tel 513-531-2690.

Shoot Star Pr, *(Shooting Star Pr.; 0-9632023),* P.O. Box 313, Hartsdale, NY 10530-0313; 441 Central Park Ave., Hartsdale, NY 10530-0313. Do not confuse with companies with the same name in Eastford, CT, Calabasas, CA, New York, NY.

Shooting Star, *(Shooting Star Pr.; 0-9631644),* P.O. Box 8535, Calabasas, CA 91372; 21453 Mulholland Dr., Woodland Hills, CA 91364 Tel 818-340-4470. Do not confuse with companies with the same name in Hartsdale, NY, Eastford, CT, New York, NY, San Diego, CA.

Shorey, *(Shorey Bk. Store; 0-8466),* 1411 First Ave., No. 200, Seattle, WA 98101 (SAN 204-5958) Tel 206-624-0221.

Show Me How, *(Show Me How Pubns.; 1-883484),* 15606 E. 44th St., Independence, MO 64055 Tel 816-373-7819.

Shulsinger Sales, *(Shulsinger Sales, Inc.; 0-914080),* 50 Washington St., Brooklyn, NY 11201 (SAN 205-9851) Tel 718-852-0042.

Shuttle Craft, *(Shuttle Craft Bks., Inc.; 0-916658),* P.O. Box 550, Coupeville, WA 98239 (SAN 208-1148) Tel 206-678-4648.

Sidran Pr, *(Sidran Pr.; 0-9629164),* Div. of Sidran Foundation for Mental Illness, 2328 W. Joppa Rd., Suite 15, Lutherville, MD 21093 Tel 410-825-8888.

Sierra, *(Sierra Club Bks.; 0-87156),* 100 Bush St., 13th Flr., San Francisco, CA 94104 (SAN 203-2406) Tel 415-291-1600; Dist. by: Random Hse., Inc., 400 Hahn Rd., Westminster, MD 21157 (SAN 202-5515) Tel 410-848-1900; Toll free: 800-733-3000 (orders).

Sierra Oaks Pub, *(Sierra Oaks Publishing Co.; 0-940113),* 1370 Sierra Oaks Ct., Newcastle, CA 95658-9791 (SAN 664-063X) Tel 916-663-1474; Dist. by: S. C.B. Distributors, 15612 S. New Century Dr., Gardena, CA 90248 (SAN 630-4818) Tel 310-532-9400; Toll free: 800-729-6423 (orders only).

Sierra Trading, *(Sierra Trading Post; 0-9605890),* Subs. of Sierra Outdoor Products, P.O. Box 2497, San Francisco, CA 94126-2497 (SAN 216-6097); 92 Southern Heights, San Rafael, CA 94901 (SAN 665-780X) Tel 415-456-9378.

Sig *Imprint of* **NAL-Dutton**

Sig Classics *Imprint of* **NAL-Dutton**

Sig Vista *Imprint of* **NAL-Dutton**

Sight & Sound, *(Sight & Sound International, Inc.; 0-88704),* 1220 Mound Ave., Racine, WI 53404-3336 (SAN 283-4065).

Sights Prods, *(Sights Productions; 0-9629978),* 15130 Black Ankle Rd., Mount Airy, MD 21771 Tel 410-795-4582.

Signal Media, *(Signal Media Corp., K-Lite 94 Radio; 0-9616677),* P.O. Box 795365, Dallas, TX 75379-5365 (SAN 659-6789) Tel 214-380-6123.

Silbert Bress, *(Silbert & Bress Pubns.; 0-89544),* P.O. Box 68, Mahopac, NY 10541 (SAN 210-5020) Tel 914-628-7910.

Silicon Pr, *(Silicon Pr.; 0-9615336; 0-929306),* 25 Beverly Rd., Summit, NJ 07901 (SAN 695-1538) Tel 908-273-8919.

Silk Screen, *(Silk Screen Pr.; 0-9640735),* P.O. Box 943, Troy, NY 12180; 400 Broadway, Troy, NY 12180 Tel 518-482-6953.

Silly Billys Bks, *(Silly Billy's Bks., Inc.; 0-9634087),* 1228 Ida, Suite 1011, Cincinnati, OH 45202 Tel 513-721-7956; Toll free: 800-769-7956.

Silver, *(Silver, Burdett & Ginn, Inc.; 0-382; 0-663),* Div. of Simon & Schuster, Inc., 250 James St., East Div., Morristown, NJ 07962-1918 (SAN 204-5982) Tel 201-285-7755; Toll free: 800-631-8081; 108 Wilmot Rd., Suite 380, Midwest Div., Deerfield, IL 60015 (SAN 111-6517) Tel 708-945-1240; 1925 Century Blvd. NE, Suite 14, Southeast Div., Atlanta, GA 30345 (SAN 111-6509) Tel 404-321-7455; 8445 Freeport Pkwy., Suite 400, South Div., Irving, TX 75063 (SAN 108-0458) Tel 214-915-4200; 2001 The Alameda, West Div., San Jose, CA 95126 (SAN 111-6525) Tel 408-248-6854; 160 Gould St., East Div., Needham Heights, MA 02194-2310 Tel 617-455-1700; Orders to: 4350 Equity Dr., P.O. Box 2649, Columbus, OH 43216; Toll free: 800-848-9500. Publishes Elementary School Text.

Silver Burdett Pr, *(Silver Burdett Pr.; 0-382),* Div. of Paramount Publishing, 250 James St., Morristown, NJ 07960 (SAN 243-2617) Tel 201-285-7900; Orders to: P.O. Box 2649, Columbus, OH 43216 (SAN 243-2625); Toll free: 800-848-9500.

Silver Dollar, *(Silver Dollar City, Inc.),* W. 76 Hwy., Silver Dollar City, MO 65616 (SAN 210-3699) Tel 417-338-2611.

Silver Forest Pub, *(Silver Forest Publishing; 0-929684),* 1917 Bryce Ct., Evergreen, CO 80439-9414 (SAN 250-1783); 30596 Bryant Dr., Evergreen, CO 80439 (SAN 297-357X) Tel 303-674-5755.

Silver Grace Pubs, *(Silver Grace Pubs.; 0-9637324),* P.O. Box 55709, Houston, TX 77251-5709; 7834 Wedgewood, Houston, TX 77055 Tel 713-681-0524.

Silver Moon, *(Silver Moon Pr.; 1-881889),* Div. of Sue Katz & Assocs., 126 Fifth Ave., Suite 803, New York, NY 10011 Tel 212-242-6499; Toll free: 800-874-3320. Do not confuse with Silver Moon Publishing Co. in Los Angeles, CA.

Silver Pr, *(Silver Pr.; 0-671),* Div. of Paramount Publishing, ; Orders to: P.O. Box 2649, Columbus, OH 43216 (SAN 243-2625); Toll free: 800-848-9500. Do not confuse with Silver Pr. in Columbus, OH.

Silver Prescrip Pr, *(Silver Prescription Pr., Inc.; 0-945214),* 524 Camino del Monte Sol, Santa Fe, NM 87501 (SAN 246-2303) Tel 505-983-3868.

Silver Pubns, *(Silver Pubns.; 0-9624811),* 5215 W. Clearwater, Suite 10725B, Kennewick, WA 99336 Tel 509-783-3337.

Silver Rim Pr, *(Silver Rim Pr.; 1-878611),* 2759 Park Lake Dr., Boulder, CO 80301 Tel 303-666-4290.

Silver Sea, *(Silver Sea Pr.; 0-916005),* 820 Pacific Coast Hwy., Suite 103, Hermosa Beach, CA 90254 (SAN 294-6610) Tel 310-379-8959.

Silver Seahorse, *(Silver Seahorse Pr.; 0-9631798),* 2568 N. Clark St., Suite 320, Chicago, IL 60614 Tel 312-871-1772.

Silver Seal Bks, *(Silver Seal Bks.; 0-910867),* P.O. Box 106, Fox Island, WA 98333 (SAN 264-3871).

Simp Solns, *(Simplified Solutions; 0-9634088),* 19145 Kittridge St., Reseda, CA 91335 Tel 818-996-6234.

Simplicity Pr, *(Simplicity Pr.; 0-929225),* 1130 W. Highland Ave., Redlands, CA 92373-6657 (SAN 248-7179) Tel 909-792-0276.

Simpson NJ, *(Simpson Publishing Co.; 0-9622508; 1-881095),* P.O. Box 100, Avinger, TX 75630-0100. Do not confuse with Simpson Publishing Co., Kirksville, MO.

Simpson Pub, *(Simpson Publishing Co.),* P.O. Box P, Kirksville, MO 63501 (SAN 202-9928) Tel 816-665-7251. Do not confuse with Simpson Publishing Co., Avinger, TX.

Sinai Heritage, *(Sinai Heritage, The; 0-944704),* 1448 53rd St., Brooklyn, NY 11219 (SAN 244-8866) Tel 718-972-2621.

Sinclair Ent, *(Sinclair, Dorothy, Enterprises; 0-9615311),* P.O. Box 782, Bellaire, TX 77401-0782 (SAN 694-5996) Tel 713-664-9809.

Sing Dance
See Frog Pr WI

Sing Out Corp, *(Sing Out Corp.; 0-9626704; 1-881322),* P.O. Box 5253, Bethlehem, PA 18015; 125 E. Third St., Bethlehem, PA 18015 Tel 610-865-5366; Dist. by: Independent Pubs. Group, 814 N. Franklin, Chicago, IL 60610 (SAN 202-0769) Tel 312-337-0747; Toll free: 800-888-4741.

Singing Rock, *(Singing Rock Pr.; 0-9629395),* 5831 74th Ave. N., Brooklyn Park, MN 55443 Tel 612-566-4540.

Sirius Leag, *(Sirius League, The; 0-9610762),* P.O. Box 40507, Albuquerque, NM 87196 (SAN 264-6366) Tel 505-262-0720.

Sirken Pubns, *(Sirken Pubns.; 0-9635483),* 414 Benedict Ave., Tarrytown, NY 10591 Tel 914-631-5146.

Sitare, *(Sitare, Ltd.; 0-940178),* 400 S. Beverly Dr., No. 214, Beverly Hills, CA 90212-4482 (SAN 217-0833) Tel 310-281-2858.

Six Pr, *(6 Pr.; 0-943310),* 11889 Dogwood Ave., Fountain Valley, CA 92708 (SAN 240-7752) Tel 714-839-1857.

Sizzy Bks, *(Sizzy Bks.; 0-945590),* P.O. Box 401, Los Alamos, NM 87544 (SAN 247-0934); 382 Catherine Ave., Los Alamos, NM 87544 (SAN 247-0942) Tel 505-672-3416.

Skandisk, *(Skandisk, Inc.; 0-9615394),* 7616 Lyndale Ave. S., Richfield, MN 55423-4028 (SAN 695-4405) Tel 612-866-3636.

Skeetoonies, *(Skeetoonies; 0-9622109),* S. 37 W. 26867 Holiday Hill Rd., Waukesha, WI 53188 Tel 414-549-1843.

Skills For Lrn, *(Skills For Learning; 0-9632893),* P.O. Box 779, Carmel, IN 46033; 5166 Woodside Ct., Carmel, IN 46032 Tel 317-848-2558.

Skin Cancer Fndtn, *(Skin Cancer Foundation; 0-9627688),* 245 Fifth Ave., Suite 2402, New York, NY 10016 Tel 212-725-5176.

Skinner Hse Bks *Imprint of* **Unitarian Univ**

SkippingStone Pr, *(SkippingStone Pr., Inc.; 0-927867),* P.O. Box 22105, Denver, CO 80222 Tel 303-377-0046.

Skribent, *(Skribent Pr.; 0-9609374),* 9700 SW Lakeside Dr., Tigard, OR 97223 (SAN 283-2542) Tel 503-620-0471; Dist. by: Quality Bks., Inc., 918 Sherwood Dr., Lake Bluff, IL 60044-2204 (SAN 169-2127) Tel 708-295-2010; Toll free: 800-323-4241 (libraries only).

Sky Pub, *(Sky Publishing Corp.; 0-933346),* 49 Bay State Rd., Cambridge, MA 02138 (SAN 212-4556) Tel 617-864-7360; Toll free: 800-253-0245; Dist. by: Independent Pubs. Group, 814 N. Franklin, Chicago, IL 60610 (SAN 202-0769) Tel 312-337-0747; Toll free: 800-888-4741.

Skyehill Pubns, *(Skyehill Pubns.; 0-9629143),* 1310 Westwood Hills Rd., Saint Louis Park, MN 55426 Tel 612-545-6413.

Skylark *Imprint of* **Bantam**

Skylght Studios, *(Skylight Studios; 0-9638756),* 42 Crest St., North Adams, MA 01247 Tel 413-663-9021.

Skylight Pub
See IRI-Skylght

Skyline Pubns, *(Skyline Pubns.; 1-882811),* Div. of Conrads Printing, 135 N. Columbus St., Lancaster, OH 43130 Tel 614-654-6248.

Skyspec Pub, *(Skyspec Publishing; 0-9627534),* P.O. Box 75171, Cincinnati, OH 45275; Toll free: 800-521-8226; 5878 Rabbit Hash Rd., Union, KY 41091 Tel 606-586-7454.

SLACK Inc, *(SLACK, Inc.; 0-913590; 0-943432; 1-55642),* 6900 Grove Rd., Thorofare, NJ 08086-9447 (SAN 201-8632) Tel 609-848-1000; Toll free: 800-257-8290.

Slavic Christian, *(Slavic Christian Publishing; 1-885024),* P.O. Box 2845, Broken Arrow, OK 74013-2845; 10985 E. 23rd St., Tulsa, OK 74129 Tel 918-437-3656.

Sleepy Zebra, *(Sleepy Zebra Publishing; 0-9632943),* 7503 Sabre St., Orlando, FL 32822 Tel 407-273-0093; Dist. by: BookWorld Distribution Services, Inc., 1933 Whitfield Pk. Loop, Sarasota, FL 34243 (SAN 173-0568) Tel 813-758-8094; Toll free: 800-444-2524 (orders only).

Sloan Manry Pubs, *(Sloan/Manry Pubs.; 0-9622316),* 16809 Holbrook, Shaker Heights, OH 44120 Tel 216-752-1717.

Small Hands Pr, *(Small Hands Pr.; 0-9619208),* 3337 N. Miller Rd., Suite 105, Scottsdale, AZ 85251 (SAN 243-5519) Tel 602-994-9773.

Small Helm Pr, *(Small Helm Pr.; 0-938453),* 622 Baker St., Petaluma, CA 94952 (SAN 660-9805) Tel 707-763-5757.

SmartSong, *(SmartSong, Inc.; 1-882500),* 150 W. 55th St., New York, NY 10019 Tel 212-246-8282; Toll free: 800-317-8383 (orders & customer service).

Smartworm Corp, *(Smartworm Corp.; 1-877820),* P.O. Box 1176, Newnan, GA 30264; Toll free: 800-477-7627 (outside Georgia); 339 Millard Farmers Blvd., Newnan, GA 30263 Tel 706-254-1094.

Smarty Pants, *(Smarty Pants; 1-55886),* 15104 Detroit Ave., Suite 2, Lakewood, OH 44107 (SAN 249-0110) Tel 216-221-5300.

SME Pr, *(SME Pr.; 0-945026),* P.O. Box 777, Sanibel, FL 33957 (SAN 245-6249); 3516 W. Gulf Dr., Sanibel, FL 33957 (SAN 245-6257) Tel 813-472-2465. Do not confuse with Society of Manufacturing Engineers (SME), Dearborn, MI.

Smiley Originals, *(Smiley Originals; 0-9629001),* 401 Anglin St., Smiley, TX 78159-0099 (SAN 297-4045) Tel 210-587-6113; Toll free: 800-584-3655.

Smith & Kraus, *(Smith & Kraus, Inc.; 0-9622722; 1-880399),* 1 Main St., P.O. Box 1270, Lyme, NH 03768 Tel 603-795-4331; Toll free: 800-862-5423.

Smith & Smith Pub, *(Smith & Smith Publishing Co.; 0-9609230),* 119 N. Fourth St., Suite 411, Minneapolis, MN 55401 (SAN 241-4570) Tel 612-338-8235.

Smith Pubs
See Smithmark

Smithmark, *(Smithmark Pubs., Inc.; 0-8317),* 16 E. 32nd St., New York, NY 10016 (SAN 216-3241) Tel 212-532-6600; Toll free: 800-645-9990; 800-932-0070 (in New Jersey); Raritan Plaza 111, Fieldcrest Ave., Edison, NJ 08837 (SAN 658-1625) Tel 908-225-4900.

Smiths Migratory, *(Smithsonian Migratory Bird Ctr.; 1-881230),* National Zoological Pk., Washington, DC 20008 Tel 202-673-4908.

Smithsonian, *(Smithsonian Institution Pr.; 0-87474; 1-56098),* 470 L'Enfant Plaza, Suite 7100, Washington, DC 20560 (SAN 206-8044) Tel 202-287-3738; Orders to: TAB Bks., Inc., Dept. 900, Blue Ridge Summit, PA 17294-0900 Tel 717-794-2148; Toll free: 800-782-4612.

SMU Press, *(Southern Methodist Univ. Pr.; 0-87074),* P.O. Box 415, Dallas, TX 75275 (SAN 203-3615); 314 Fondren Library West, Dallas, TX 75275 (SAN 658-1641) Tel 214-768-1432; Dist. by: Texas A&M Univ. Pr., Drawer C, College Station, TX 77843-4354 (SAN 207-5237) Tel 409-845-1436; Toll free: 800-826-8911 (orders).

Snd Dollar Pub, *(Sand Dollar Publishing Co.; 0-940859),* P.O. Box 11053, Springfield, IL 62791 (SAN 665-0775); 2219 Blackhawk Rd., Springfield, IL 62702 (SAN 665-0783) Tel 217-522-3484.

Snooty Prods, *(Snooty Productions; 0-9637381),* Box 85, Castle Rock, CO 80104; 3183 N. Crowfoot Valley Rd., Box 85, Castle Rock, CO 80104 Tel 303-688-3246.

Snow Lion, *(Snow Lion Pubns., Inc.; 0-937938; 1-55939),* P.O. Box 6483, Ithaca, NY 14851-6483 (SAN 250-328X); Toll free: 800-950-0313; Dist. by: Bookpeople, 7900 Edgewater Dr., Oakland, CA 94621 (SAN 168-9517) Tel 510-632-4700; Toll free: 800-999-4650; Dist. by: Inland Bk. Co., 140 Commerce St., East Haven, CT 06512 (SAN 200-4151) Tel 203-467-4257; Toll free: 800-243-0138; Dist. by: Samuel Weiser, Inc., P.O. Box 612, York Beach, ME 03910-0612 (SAN 202-9588) Tel 207-363-4393; Toll free: 800-423-7087 (orders only); Dist. by: Atrium Pubs. Group, 11270 Clayton Creek Rd., Lower Lake, CA 95457 (SAN 200-5743) Tel 707-995-3906; Toll free: 800-275-2606; Dist. by: New Leaf Distributing Co., 5425 Tulane Dr., SW, Atlanta, GA 30336-2323 (SAN 169-1449) Tel 404-691-6996; Toll free: 800-326-2665; Dist. by: Moving Bks., Inc., P.O. Box 20037, Seattle, WA 98102 (SAN 159-0685) Tel 206-762-1750; Toll free: 800-777-6683.

SNS Pr, *(SNS Pr.; 0-9633744),* 380 Raintree Rd., Sedona, AZ 86336 Tel 602-284-9055.

Soc for Visual, *(Society for Visual Education, Inc.; 0-89290; 1-56357),* 55 E. Monroe St., Suite 3400, Chicago, IL 60603-5710 (SAN 208-3930) Tel 312-525-1500; Toll free: 800-829-1900.

Soc Issues, *(Social Issues Resources Series, Inc. (SIRS);* 0-89777), P.O. Box 2348, Boca Raton, FL 33427-2348 (SAN 222-8920) Tel 407-994-0079; Toll free: 800-232-7477.

Soccer Ed, *(Soccer Education; 0-9616953),* 509 Laurel Dr., Thiensville, WI 53092 (SAN 661-7638) Tel 414-242-3137.

Soccer for Am, *(Soccer for Americans; 0-916802),* P.O. Box 836, Manhattan Beach, CA 90266 (SAN 208-3787) Tel 310-372-9000.

Social Skills, *(Social Skills Pr.; 0-9631627),* 1805 Walnut St., Saint Paul, MN 55113 Tel 612-645-4296.

Soft Words, *(Soft Words Publishing; 0-9637149),* Box 3218, Pueblo, CO 81005-0218 Tel 719-564-7031.

Solace Pub, *(Solace Publishing, Inc.; 0-9630287),* P.O. Box 23205, Rochester, NY 14692-3205 (SAN 297-4940); 481 Thornell Rd., Pittsford, NY 14534 Tel 716-381-1450.

Solar Studio, *(Solar Studio, The; 0-932320),* 178 Cowles Rd., Woodbury, CT 06798 (SAN 222-8823) Tel 203-263-3147.

Solipaz Pub Co, *(Solipaz Publishing Co.; 0-913999),* P.O. Box 366, Lodi, CA 95241 (SAN 286-8814).

Someday Baby, *(Someday Baby, Inc.; 0-927945),* Div. of Child's Gift of Lullabyes, 1508 16th Ave., S., Nashville, TN 37212 Tel 615-385-0022.

Son-Rise Pubns, *(Son-Rise Pubns. & Distribution Co.;* 0-936369), 143 Greenfield Rd., New Wilmington, PA 16142 (SAN 698-0031) Tel 412-946-8334; Toll free: 800-358-0777; Dist. by: Spring Arbor Distributors, 10885 Textile Rd., Belleville, MI 48111 (SAN 158-9016) Tel 313-481-0900; Toll free: 800-395-5599 (orders); 800-395-7234 (customer service).

Soncino Pr, *(Soncino Pr.; 1-871055),* 123 Ditmas Ave., Brooklyn, NY 11218 (SAN 681-2740) Tel 718-972-6200.

Sonflower Bks *Imprint of* **SP Pubns**

Songbird Pubng, *(Songbird Publishing; 0-9641413),* 2310 East Rd., Grand Junction, CO 81503 Tel 303-245-8864.

Songs & Co, *(Songs & Co.; 0-9624135),* 601 Van Ness Ave., Suite E3125, San Francisco, CA 94102 Tel 415-564-2400.

Songs & Stories, *(Songs & Stories Children Love;* 0-934591), 4243 Carpenter Ave., Bronx, NY 10466 (SAN 694-0609) Tel 718-325-5587.

Songs Sottongs, *(Songs of Sottongs; 0-9624136),* 709 Parsons Ln., Signal Mountain, TN 37377 Tel 615-886-2208.

Sonny Boy Bks, *(Sonny Boy Bks.; 0-9638863),* 109 E. 19th St., New York, NY 10003 Tel 212-473-1563.

Sonos
See Jackman Pubng

Sontag Pr, *(Sontag Pr.; 1-885483),* 109 Northbay Pl., Madison, MS 39110 Tel 601-856-5488; Toll free: 800-497-3172; Dist. by: Southern Pubs. Group, 147 Corporate Way, Pelham, AL 35124 (SAN 630-7817) Tel 205-664-6980; Toll free: 800-755-4411.

Sopris, *(Sopris West, Inc.; 0-944584; 1-57035),* 1140 Boston Ave., Longmont, CO 80501 (SAN 243-945X) Tel 303-651-2829; Toll free: 800-547-6747 (orders only).

Sound Ent, *(Sound Enterprises Publishing Co.;* 0-935565), 970 Cornwallis Dr., West Chester, PA 19380 (SAN 696-1886) Tel 215-431-4512; Dist. by: Baker & Taylor Bks., Somerville Service Ctr., 50 Kirby Ave., Somerville, NJ 08876-0734 (SAN 169-4901) Tel 908-722-8000; Toll free: 800-775-1500 (customer service); Dist. by: Baker & Taylor Bks., Commerce Service Ctr., 251 Mt. Olive Church Rd., Commerce, GA 30599-9988 (SAN 169-1503) Tel 706-335-5000; Toll free: 800-775-1200 (customer service); Dist. by: Baker & Taylor Bks., Momence Service Ctr., 501 S. Gladiolus St., Momence, IL 60954-2444 (SAN 169-2100) Tel 815-472-2444; Toll free: 800-775-2300 (customer service); Dist. by: Baker & Taylor Bks., Reno Service Ctr., 380 Edison Way, Reno, NV 89564 (SAN 169-4464) Tel 702-858-6700; Toll free: 800-775-1700 (customer service).

Sound Pub WA, *(Sound Publishing; 0-9629860),* P.O. Box 7192, Tacoma, WA 98407; 4203 Olympic Blvd., W., Tacoma, WA 98466 Tel 206-565-6568. Do not confuse with companies of the same name in Denver, CO, Great Neck, NY.

Sound World Record, *(Sound World Recordings;* 0-9619269), 605-B S. Adams St., Glendale, CA 91205 (SAN 243-6124) Tel 818-244-4007.

Soundboard Bks, *(Soundboard Bks.; 1-878636),* 1016 E. El Camino Real, No. 124, Sunnyvale, CA 94087-3759 Tel 408-738-1705.

Soundbox Pubns, *(Soundbox Pubns.; 0-9622499),* 5541 Lakeside Dr., Bldg. 1, Unit 206, Margate, FL 33063 Tel 305-979-3112.

Soundprints, *(Soundprints; 0-924483; 1-56899),* Div. of Trudy Management Corp., P.O. Box 679, 165 Water St., Norwalk, CT 06856 Tel 203-838-6009; Toll free: 800-228-7839.

Sounds Write, *(Sounds Write Productions, Inc.;* 0-9626286), 6685 Norman Ln., San Diego, CA 92120 Tel 619-697-6126.

Soup Nuts Pr, *(Soup to Nuts Pr.; 0-938534),* 77 Trowbridge St. No.23, Cambridge, MA 02138 (SAN 239-9008) Tel 617-864-3334.

Source Bks CA, *(Source Bks.; 0-940147),* P.O. Box 794, Trabuco Canyon, CA 92678 (SAN 248-2231); Toll free: 800-695-4237; 20341 Sycamore Dr., Trabuco Canyon, CA 92678 (SAN 248-224X) Tel 714-858-1420.

Source CA, *(Source Productions; 1-883088),* 14755 Ventura Blvd., Suite 829, Sherman Oaks, CA 91403 Tel 818-990-6724. Do not confuse with Source Productions in Toluca Lake, CA.

Sourcebks, *(Sourcebooks, Inc.; 0-942061; 1-57071),* P.O. Box 313, Naperville, IL 60566; Toll free: 800-798-2475; 800-727-8866; 121 N. Washington St., Suite 2N, Naperville, IL 60540 (SAN 666-7864) Tel 708-961-2161; Dist. by: Login Pubs. Consortium, 1436 W. Randolph St., 2nd Flr., Chicago, IL 60607 (SAN 630-5733) Tel 312-733-8228; Toll free: 800-626-4330.

Sourdough Pr, *(Sourdough Pr.; 0-9642943),* Div. of Chesapeake East Co., Rte. 361, P.O. Box 200, Upper Fairmount, MD 21867 Tel 410-651-2942.

South St Sea Mus, *(South Street Seaport Museum;* 0-913344), 207 Front St., New York, NY 10038 (SAN 282-3322) Tel 212-669-9435.

Southern Hist Pr, *(Southern Historical Pr., Inc.;* 0-89308), P.O. Box 1267, Greenville, SC 29602-1267 (SAN 208-8657); 275 W. Broad St., Greenville, SC 29601 Tel 803-233-2346.

Southern Rose Prodns, *(Southern Rose Productions;* 0-929560), Rte. 3, Box 272D, Ripley, MS 38663 (SAN 249-6968) Tel 601-837-1125.

Southwest Pubns, *(Southwest Pubns.; 1-881260),* 1065 Crandall, Colorado Springs, CO 80911 Tel 719-597-8765.

Southwinds Pr, *(Southwinds Pr.; 0-931581),* P.O. Box 13421, Tallahassee, FL 32317 (SAN 683-1338) Tel 904-385-1383.

SP Pubns, *(Scripture Pr. Pubs., Inc.; 0-88207; 0-89693;* 1-56476), 1825 College Ave., Wheaton, IL 60187 (SAN 222-9471) Tel 708-668-6000; Toll free: 800-323-9409. *Imprints:* Sonflower Bks (Sonflower Books); Victor Books (Victor Books).

Spacone Pub, *(Spacone Publishing Co.; 0-944712),* 5350 W. Evans Dr., Glendale, AZ 85306 (SAN 244-8882) Tel 602-978-2677.

Sparhawk, *(Sparhawk Bks., Inc.; 0-9605776),* Div. of Pawprints, Inc., 150 Windy Row, Peterborough, NH 03458-2012 (SAN 216-5538); Toll free: 800-633-2900; Orders to: Box 2, Jaffrey, NH 03452 (SAN 699-5608) Tel 603-532-7091.

Sparky Star Pr, *(Sparky Star Pr.; 0-9621616),* P.O. Box 216, Bellevue, WA 98009 (SAN 252-1202); 3233 76th, NE, Bellevue, WA 98004 (SAN 252-1210) Tel 206-454-2272.

Sparrow Pr CA
See Sparrow TN

Sparrow TN, *(Sparrow Corp., The; 0-917143),* Div. of Sparrow Communications Group, A Sparrow Corp., P.O. Box 5010, Brentwood, TN 37024-5010 (SAN 655-8844); 101 Winners Cir., Brentwood, TN 37024 Tel 615-371-6800; Dist. by: Sparrow Distribution, P.O. Box 5010, Brentwood, TN 37024-5010 (SAN 630-4915) Tel 615-371-6800; Toll free: 800-877-4443.

Spec Lit Pr, *(Special Literature Pr.; 0-938594),* P.O. Box 55763, Bacon Sta., Indianapolis, IN 46220 (SAN 215-8175) Tel 317-253-6268.

Spec Pr FL, *(Specialty Pr., Inc.; 0-9621629),* 300 NW 70th Ave., Suite 102, Plantation, FL 33317 (SAN 251-6977) Tel 305-792-8944; Toll free: 800-233-9273. Do not confuse with Specialty Pr., Inc., in Ocean, NJ.

Special Touch, *(Special Touch, Inc., Publishing;* 0-9625232), P.O. Box 427, Springfield, KY 40069-0427; 124 E. Main St., Springfield, KY 40069 Tel 606-336-7749.

Spect Ln Pr, *(Spectacle Lane Pr., Inc.; 0-930753),* 106 Spectacle Lane, Wilton, CT 06897 Tel 203-762-3786; Dist. by: Login Pubs. Consortium, 1436 W. Randolph St., 2nd Flr., Chicago, IL 60607 (SAN 630-5733) Tel 312-733-8228; Toll free: 800-626-4330.

Spectra *Imprint of* **Bantam**

SPECTRA Inc, *(SPECTRA, Inc., Pubs.; 1-877936),* Div. of SPECTRA, Inc., P.O. Box 13591, New Orleans, LA 70185-3591; Toll free: 800-359-8152; 701 Jefferson Ave., Metairie, LA 70001 Tel 504-831-4440.

Spectra Pubns Hse, *(Spectra Pubns. Hse.; 0-9621693),* P.O. Box 21, Crockett, CA 94525 (SAN 251-785X); 2158 Vista del Rio, Crockett, CA 94525 (SAN 251-7868) Tel 510-787-2282.

Spectrum CA, *(Spectrum Pubns.; 0-9638008),* P.O. Box 3002, Spring Valley, CA 91979-3002; 11720 Monte View Ct., El Cajon, CA 92019 Tel 619-660-8433.

Speech Bin, *(Speech Bin, The; 0-937857),* 1965 25th Ave., Vero Beach, FL 32960 (SAN 630-1657) Tel 407-770-0007.

Speller, *(Speller, Robert, & Sons, Pubs., Inc.; 0-8315),* P.O. Box 411, Madison Sq. Sta., New York, NY 10159 (SAN 203-2295) Tel 212-473-0333; Orders to: P.O. Box 461, Times Sq. Sta., New York, NY 10108 (SAN 203-2309).

Spencer Muse Art, *(Spencer Museum of Art; 0-913689),* Affil. of Univ. of Kansas, Univ. of Kansas, Lawrence, KS 66045 (SAN 111-347X) Tel 913-864-4710.

Spencers Intl, *(Spencer's International Enterprises;* 0-937771), P.O. Box 43822, Los Angeles, CA 90043 (SAN 659-333X) Tel 213-937-3099; Toll free: 800-752-5909; Dist. by: Baker & Taylor Bks., Somerville Service Ctr., 50 Kirby Ave., Somerville, NJ 08876-0734 (SAN 169-4901) Tel 908-722-8000; Toll free: 800-775-1500 (customer service); Dist. by: Ingram Bk. Co., 1 Ingram Blvd., La Vergne, TN 37086-1986 (SAN 169-7978) Tel 615-793-5000; Toll free: 800-937-8000 (orders only, all warehouses).

Spero & Me, *(Spero & Me Publishing Hse.; 0-9638336),* 7001 W. 127th St., Palos Heights, IL 60463 Tel 708-448-0036.

Spheric Hse, *(Spheric Hse.; 0-935984),* 638 S. Sixth Ave., Tucson, AZ 85701 (SAN 222-0032) Tel 602-623-5577.

SPI Pub, *(SPI Publishing; 0-9624280),* Div. of Security Photo, Inc., 44211 Village Ct., Canton, MI 48187 Tel 313-455-1910.

Spice Pr, *(Spice Pr.; 0-9623300),* 1555P S. Havana, No. 324, Aurora, CO 80012 Tel 303-751-0910.

Spirit Light, *(Spirit Light Publishing; 0-9632765),* Div. of Kazbar Entertainment Group, 2216 Fifth St., Santa Monica, CA 90405-2402.

Spirit Mount Pr, *(Spirit Mountain Pr.; 0-910871),* P.O. Box 1214, Fairbanks, AK 99707 (SAN 283-9156). Do not confuse with Spirit Mountain Pr. in Santa Fe, NM.

Spirit Pr, *(Spirit Pr.; 0-944296),* 1005 Granite Ridge Dr., Santa Cruz, CA 95065 (SAN 243-2544) Tel 408-426-7971; Dist. by: Publishers Group West, 4065 Hollis St., Emeryville, CA 94608 (SAN 202-8522) Tel 510-658-3453; Toll free: 800-788-3123.

Spiritseeker, *(Spiritseeker Publishing, Inc.; 0-9630419;* 1-883064), P.O. Box 2441, Fargo, ND 58108-2441; Toll free: 800-538-6415; 412 Eighth Ave., S., Fargo, ND 58103 Tel 701-232-5966.

Spizzirri, *(Spizzirri Publishing Co., Inc.; 0-86545),* P.O. Box 9397, Rapid City, SD 57709 (SAN 215-2851); Toll free: 800-325-9819.

Splash *Imprint of* **Berkley Pub**

Splendid Assocs, *(Splendid Assocs. Publishing Co.;* 0-941983), 4815 Ternes St., Dearborn, MI 48126 (SAN 666-718X) Tel 313-584-8505.

Sports Diary Pub, *(Sports Diary Publishing Co.;* 0-929861), P.O. Box 1141, Norman, OK 73070 (SAN 250-734X); 3003 River Oaks Dr., No. 148, Norman, OK 73072 (SAN 250-7358) Tel 405-360-4180.

Sports Focus Pub, *(Sports Focus Publishing; 0-9622039),* 1023 Hook Ave., Pleasant Hill, CA 94523 Tel 510-937-4059; Toll free: 800-431-2700.

Sports Plan Consult, *(Sports Planning Consultants;* 0-9620914), 7570 Northfield Ln., Manlius, NY 13104 (SAN 250-0353) Tel 315-682-7334.

Spotlght News, *(Spotlight News Pubns.; 0-9637825),* 1535 Acapulco Dr., Dallas, TX 75232 Tel 214-376-8959; Orders to: P.O. Box 763833, Dallas, TX 75376.

Spr-Verlag, *(Springer-Verlag New York, Inc.; 0-387;* 3-540), Subs. of Springer-Verlag GmbH & Co. KG, 175 Fifth Ave., New York, NY 10010 (SAN 203-2228) Tel 212-460-1500; Toll free: 800-777-4643; Orders to: 44 Hartz Way, Secaucus, NJ 07094 (SAN 665-7842) Tel 201-348-4033.

Spring Creek Pubns, *(Spring Creek Pubns.; 0-945184),* P.O. Box 243, Rose Hill, KS 67133 (SAN 246-6309); 5810 S. Webb, Derby, KS 67037 (SAN 246-6317) Tel 316-788-2182.

Springer-Verlag
See Spr-Verlag

Sproing, *(Sproing Bks.; 0-916176),* 787 N. 24th St., Philadelphia, PA 19130-2540 (SAN 206-3816).

SPS Pubns, *(SPS Pubns.; 1-881099),* P.O. Box 769, Tavares, FL 32778; 357 W. Alfred St., Tavares, FL 32778 Tel 904-343-3274.

Spts Curriculum, *(Sports Curriculum; 1-884480),* P.O. Box 495, Santa Clara, CA 95052; 841 N. Monroe St., San Jose, CA 95128 Tel 408-243-9663.

Spts Illus Kids *Imprint of* **Little**

Sq One Pubns, *(Square One Pubns.; 0-9619321),* 2721 N. Windsor Ave., Altadena, CA 91001 (SAN 243-8135) Tel 818-791-9403.

Sq One Pubs, *(Square One Pubs., Inc.; 0-938961),* 6 Birch Hill Rd., Ballston Lake, NY 12019 (SAN 661-7271) Tel 508-877-4946.

Squared Away, *(Squared Away Farm; 0-9624179),* Rte. 3, Box 311, Tallahassee, FL 32308 Tel 904-893-0693.

Squeaky Sneaker *Imprint of* **Star Song TN**

SRA, *(Science Research Assocs.; 0-574; 0-88120),* Div. of Macmillan/McGraw-Hill School Publishing Co., 250 Old Wilson Bridge Rd., Suite 310, Worthington, OH 43085 (SAN 295-3498) Tel 614-438-6600; Toll free: 800-468-5850.

SRA Schl Grp, *(SRA Schl. Group; 0-383),* Div. of Macmillan/McGraw-Hill School Publishing Co., 250 Old Wilson Bridge Rd., Suite 310, Worthington, OH 43085 Tel 614-438-6600; Toll free: 800-468-5850.

Sri Rama, *(Sri Rama Publishing; 0-918100),* 161 Robles Dr., Santa Cruz, CA 95060 (SAN 282-3578) Tel 408-426-5098; Orders to: P.O. Box 2550, Santa Cruz, CA 95063 (SAN 282-3586).

St Anthony Mess Pr, *(St. Anthony Messenger Pr.; 0-912228; 0-86716),* Subs. of Franciscan Friars (St. John Baptist Province), 1615 Republic St., Cincinnati, OH 45210 (SAN 204-6237) Tel 513-241-5615; Toll free: 800-488-0488.

St George ME, *(St. George Pr.; 0-9635447),* P.O. Box 602, Rockport, ME 04856 Tel 207-372-6251. Do not confuse with St. George Pr. in Geneva, NE, Champaign, IL.

St Johann Pr, *(St. Johann Pr.; 1-878282),* 315 Schraalenburgh Rd., Haworth, NJ 07641 Tel 201-387-1529.

St John Kronstadt, *(St. John of Kronstadt Pr., The;* 0-912927), 1180 Orthodox Way, Liberty, TN 37095 (SAN 283-3980) Tel 615-536-5239.

St Maron Pubns, *(St. Maron Pubns.; 0-9628727;* 1-885589), Div. of Diocese of St. Maron-U.S.A., P.O. Box 280036, Brooklyn, NY 11228-0002; 8120 15th Ave., Brooklyn, NY 11228 Tel 718-259-9200.

St Martin, *(St. Martin's Pr., Inc.; 0-312; 0-9603648),* Subs. of Macmillan Publishing Co., Inc., 175 Fifth Ave., Rm. 1715, New York, NY 10010 (SAN 200-2132) Tel 212-674-5151; Toll free: 800-221-7945. Do not confuse with Martin Pr., San Anselmo, CA.

St Marys, *(St. Mary's Pr.; 0-88489),* 702 Terrace Heights, Winona, MN 55987-1320 (SAN 203-073X) Tel 507-457-7900; Toll free: 800-533-8095.

St Mut, *(State Mutual Bk. & Periodical Service, Ltd.; 0-89771; 0-7855),* 521 Fifth Ave., 17th Flr., New York, NY 10175 (SAN 212-5862) Tel 212-682-5844.

St Nectarios, *(St. Nectarios Pr.; 0-913026),* 10300 Ashworth Ave., N., Seattle, WA 98133-9410 (SAN 203-3542) Tel 206-522-4471; Toll free: 800-643-4233.

St Paul Bks, *(St. Paul Bks. & Media; 0-8198),* 50 St. Paul's Ave., Boston, MA 02130 (SAN 203-8900) Tel 617-522-8911; Toll free: 800-876-4463 (orders).

ST Two, *(ST2; 0-943542),* 203 Si Town Rd., Castle Rock, WA 98611 (SAN 238-3810) Tel 206-636-2645.

St Ursula, *(St. Ursula Academy; 0-9607918),* 1339 E. McMillan St., Cincinnati, OH 45206 (SAN 238-5767) Tel 513-961-4877.

STA-Kris, *(STA-Kris, Inc.; 1-882835),* P.O. Box 1131, Marshalltown, IA 50158; Toll free: 800-369-5676; 107 N. Center St., Marshalltown, IA 50158 Tel 515-753-4139; Dist. by: Baker & Taylor Bks., Somerville Service Ctr., 50 Kirby Ave., Somerville, NJ 08876-0734 (SAN 169-4901) Tel 908-722-8000; Toll free: 800-775-1500 (customer service); Dist. by: Baker & Taylor Bks., Momence Service Ctr., 501 S. Gladiolus St., Momence, IL 60954-2444 (SAN 169-2100) Tel 815-472-2444; Toll free: 800-775-2300 (customer service); Dist. by: Baker & Taylor Bks., Commerce Service Ctr., 251 Mt. Olive Church Rd., Commerce, GA 30599-9988 (SAN 169-1503) Tel 706-335-5000; Toll free: 800-775-1200 (customer service); Dist. by: Baker & Taylor Bks., Reno Service Ctr., 380 Edison Way, Reno, NV 89564 (SAN 169-4464) Tel 702-858-6700; Toll free: 800-775-1700 (customer service); Dist. by: Bookmen, Inc., 525 N. Third St., Minneapolis, MN 55401 (SAN 169-409X) Tel 612-341-3333; Toll free: 800-328-8411 (customer service); Dist. by: Ingram Bk. Co., 1 Ingram Blvd., La Vergne, TN 37086-1986 (SAN 169-7978) Tel 615-793-5000; Toll free: 800-937-8000 (orders only, all warehouses); Dist. by: The Distributors, 702 S. Michigan, South Bend, IN 46601 (SAN 169-2488) Tel 219-232-8500; Toll free: 800-348-5200 (except Indiana); Dist. by: Pacific Pipeline, Inc., 8030 S. 228th St., Kent, WA 98032-2900 (SAN 208-2128) Tel 206-872-5523; Toll free: 800-444-7323 (customer service); 800-677-2222 (orders); Dist. by: Bookpeople, 7900 Edgewater Dr., Oakland, CA 94621 (SAN 168-9517) Tel 510-632-4700; Toll free: 800-999-4650.

Stabur Pr, *(Stabur Pr., Inc.; 0-941613),* 23301 Meadow Pk., Detroit, MI 48239 (SAN 666-1777) Tel 313-535-0572.

Staccato Prodns, *(Staccato Productions, Inc.; 1-879783),* P.O. Box 995, Cedar Grove, NJ 07009; 160 Myrtle Ave., Cedar Grove, NJ 07009 Tel 201-857-0059.

Stack the Deck, *(Stack the Deck, Inc.; 0-933282),* 9126 Sandpiper Ct., Orland Park, IL 60462 (SAN 212-5668) Tel 312-349-8345.

Stackpole, *(Stackpole Bks.; 0-8117),* 5067 Ritter Rd., Mechanicsburg, PA 17055 (SAN 202-5396) Tel 717-796-0411; Toll free: 800-732-3669.

Stadium Bks, *(Stadium Bks.; 0-9625132; 1-879458),* 11 Ferry Lane, W., Westport, CT 06880 Tel 203-226-6967; Dist. by: Talman Co., 131 Spring St., Suite 201E-N, New York, NY 10012 (SAN 200-5204) Tel 212-431-7175; Toll free: 800-537-8894 (orders only).

Stage Coach, *(Stage Coach Ventures, Ltd.; 0-9641831),* 675 West End Ave., New York, NY 10025 Tel 212-865-0140.

Stagecoach Rd Pr, *(Stagecoach Road Pr.; 0-933499),* P.O. Box 33, Ashland, OR 97520 (SAN 691-8859); 202 Oak Lawn, Ashland, OR 97520 Tel 503-482-4417.

Stake Studio, *(Stake Studio; 0-9619075),* 17413 Garden Valley Rd., Woodstock, IL 60098 (SAN 243-0290) Tel 815-568-8823.

Standard Ed, *(Standard Educational Corp.; 0-87392),* 200 W. Madison, Chicago, IL 60606 (SAN 204-6326) Tel 312-346-7440.

Standard Pub, *(Standard Publishing Co.; 0-87239; 0-87403; 0-7847),* Div. of Standex International, 8121 Hamilton Ave., Cincinnati, OH 45231 (SAN 110-5515) Tel 513-931-4050; Toll free: 800-543-1301. Do not confuse with Standard Publishing Corp., Boston, MA.

Standards & Trg, *(Standards & Training, Inc.;* 0-9627536), 135 E. Bahama Rd., Winter Springs, FL 32708-3527 Tel 407-699-4012.

Star Bible, *(Star Bible & Tract Corp.; 0-933672; 0-940999; 1-56794),* P.O. Box 821220, Fort Worth, TX 76182 (SAN 203-3518); Toll free: 800-433-7507; 410 N. Dove Rd., Grapevine, TX 76051 (SAN 664-6247) Tel 817-481-7809.

Star Bks Inc, *(Star Bks., Inc.; 0-915541),* 408 Pearson St., Wilson, NC 27893-1850 (SAN 291-4468) Tel 919-237-1591; Toll free: 800-476-1591 (Orders only).

Star City Pubns, *(Star City Pubns.; 0-9615937),* 13401 N. 14th St., Raymond, NE 68428 (SAN 696-8244); Orders to: P.O. Box 2914, Lincoln, NE 68502 (SAN 662-3883).

Star Dust Bks, *(Star Dust Bks.; 0-9621782),* 15 Lenox Rd., Kensington, CA 94707-1331 Tel 510-524-7266.

Star Light Pr, *(Star Light Pr.; 1-879817),* 1811 S. First St., Austin, TX 78704-4299 Tel 512-441-0157.

Star Pubns MO, *(Star Pubns.; 0-932356),* 1211 W. 60th Terr., Kansas City, MO 64113 (SAN 212-4564) Tel 816-523-8228. Do not confuse with companies with the same name in Rancho Palos Verdes, CA, Orange Park, FL.

Star Rover, *(Star Rover Hse. at Jack London Heritage Hse.; 0-932458),* 10725 Acama St., No. 12, North Hollywood, CA 91602 (SAN 212-4572) Tel 510-532-8408; Orders to: Lexikos, P.O. Box 296, Lagunitas, CA 94938 Tel 415-488-0401.

Star Song TN, *(Star Song Publishing Group; 1-56233),* Div. of Star Song Distribution Group, ; Orders to: 2325 Crestmoor, Nashville, TN 37215 Tel 615-269-0196; Toll free: 800-835-7664. *Imprints:* Squeaky Sneaker (Squeaky Sneaker Books).

Star Thrower, *(Star Thrower Foundation; 1-882533),* P.O. Box 2200, Crystal River, FL 34423-2200; 421 NW 14th Pl., Crystal River, FL 34429 Tel 904-563-0022.

Starboard Cove, *(Starboard Cove Publishing; 0-9622221),* HCR 70, Box 442, Bucks Harbor, ME 04618; Starboard Cove Rd., Bucks Harbor, ME 04618 Tel 207-255-4426.

Starbright, *(Starbright Bks.; 0-9606248),* P.O. Box 501, Freeland, WA 98249 (SAN 282-3632) Tel 206-331-6138.

Starburst, *(Starburst Pubs.; 0-914984),* P.O. Box 4123, Lancaster, PA 17604 Tel 717-293-0939; Toll free: 800-441-1456 (orders only); Dist. by: National Bk. Network, 4720A Boston Way, Lanham, MD 20706-4310 (SAN 630-0065) Tel 301-459-8696; Toll free: 800-462-6420; Dist. by: Ingram Bk. Co., 1 Ingram Blvd., La Vergne, TN 37086-1986 (SAN 169-7978) Tel 615-793-5000; Toll free: 800-937-8000 (orders only, all warehouses); Dist. by: Spring Arbor Distributors, 10885 Textile Rd., Belleville, MI 48111 (SAN 158-9016) Tel 313-481-0900; Toll free: 800-395-5599 (orders); 800-395-7234 (customer service); Dist. by: Baker & Taylor Bks., Somerville Service Ctr., 50 Kirby Ave., Somerville, NJ 08876-0734 (SAN 169-4901) Tel 908-722-8000; Toll free: 800-775-1500 (customer service); Dist. by: Baker & Taylor Bks., Momence Service Ctr., 501 S. Gladiolus St., Momence, IL 60954-2444 (SAN 169-2100) Tel 815-472-2444; Toll free: 800-775-2300 (customer service); Dist. by: Baker & Taylor Bks., Commerce Service Ctr., 251 Mt. Olive Church Rd., Commerce, GA 30599-9988 (SAN 169-1503) Tel 706-335-5000; Toll free: 800-775-1200 (customer service); Dist. by: Baker & Taylor Bks., Reno Service Ctr., 380 Edison Way, Reno, NV 89564 (SAN 169-4464) Tel 702-858-6700; Toll free: 800-775-1700 (customer service); Dist. by: Quality Bks., Inc., 918 Sherwood Dr., Lake Bluff, IL 60044-2204 (SAN 169-2127) Tel 708-295-2010; Toll free: 800-323-4241 (libraries only); Dist. by: Nutri-Bks., Corp., P.O. Box 5793, Denver, CO 80217 (SAN 169-054X) Tel 303-778-8383; Toll free: 800-279-2048 (orders only); Dist. by: Riverside/World, P.O. Box 370, 1500 Riverside Dr., Iowa Falls, IA 50126 (SAN 169-2666) Tel 515-648-4271; Toll free: 800-247-5111.

Stardom, *(Stardom Co., Ltd.; 1-880171),* 6939 W. Glenbrook Rd., Milwaukee, WI 53223 Tel 414-357-7807; Toll free: 800-368-2276.

Stardust NC, *(Stardust Publishing; 1-884291),* c/o Harbor Wholesale & Promotions, 506 N. Road St., Elizabeth City, NC 27909 Tel 919-338-6223.

Starfire *Imprint of* **Bantam**

Stargaze Pub, *(Stargaze Publishing; 0-9630923),* 2300 Foothill Blvd., Suite 403, La Verne, CA 91750-3064 (SAN 297-5181) Tel 909-392-0683.

Starhse Pub, *(Starhouse Publishing; 0-9619556),* 4416 Graywhaler Ln., Rohnert Park, CA 94928 (SAN 245-4041) Tel 707-584-4545.

Starlite Genl
See Starlite Inc

Starlite Inc, *(Starlite, Inc.; 0-9628328),* Div. of Darwin Enterprises, P.O. Box 20004, Saint Petersburg, FL 33742; 10861 91st Terr., N., Seminole, FL 34642 Tel 813-392-2929.

Starlite Prods, *(Starlite Productions; 1-883778),* 2154 Druid Park Dr., Baltimore, MD 21211 Tel 410-225-7630.

Starlite Pub, *(Starlite Publishing Co.; 0-9621359),* 9289 Village Glen Dr., No. 116, San Diego, CA 92123 (SAN 251-1339) Tel 619-277-0863.

Starr Pub AL, *(Starr Pubns.; 0-9633116),* 1403 Bellevue Dr., Gadsden, AL 35901-1617 Tel 205-547-5818.

Start Reading, *(Start Reading, Inc.; 1-56422),* 43546 Serenity Dr., Northville, MI 48167 Tel 810-349-2560. *Imprints:* Paper Hat (Paper Hat Tricks).

Start Smart Bks, *(Start Smart Bks.; 1-878396),* 12 W. Cedar St., Alexandria, VA 22301 Tel 703-836-3830. Do not confuse with Start Smart in Charlotte, NC.

Starting Blocks, *(Starting Blocks Pubns., Inc.;* 0-9631607), 100 Tamal Plaza, Suite 104, Corte Madera, CA 94925 Tel 415-927-3030.

State House Pr, *(State Hse. Pr.; 0-938349; 1-880510),* P.O. Box 15247, Austin, TX 78761 (SAN 660-9651); Toll free: 800-421-3378; 8906 Wall St., Suite 702, Austin, TX 78754 (SAN 660-966X). Do not confuse with State House Publishing in Madison, WI.

State Mutual
See St Mut

State U NY Pr, *(State Univ. of New York Pr.; 0-87395; 0-88706; 0-7914),* State Univ. Plaza, Albany, NY 12246-0001 (SAN 658-1730) Tel 518-472-5000; Orders to: P.O. Box 6525, Ithaca, NY 14851 (SAN 203-3496) Tel 607-277-2211; Toll free: 800-666-2211.

Statesman Exam, *(Statesman-Examiner, Inc.; 0-940151),* 220 S. Main, Box 271, Colville, WA 99114 (SAN 664-2691) Tel 509-684-4567.

Statford CA, *(Statford Publishing, Inc.; 0-913087),* 1259 El Camino Real, Suite 1500, Menlo Park, CA 94025 (SAN 283-4197) Tel 415-854-9355.

Steck-V
See Raintree Steck-V

Steel Pony, *(Steel Pony Pr.; 0-9640415),* P.O. Box 2596, Fort Bragg, CA 95437-2596; 24860 N. Highway 1, Fort Bragg, CA 95437 Tel 707-964-6957.

Steele Hollow, *(Steele Hollow Pr.; 0-9624282),* R.R. 1, Box 144C, Hunns Lake, Stanfordville, NY 12581 Tel 914-868-7316.

Stemmer Hse, *(Stemmer Hse. Pubs., Inc.; 0-916144; 0-88045),* 2627 Caves Rd., Owings Mills, MD 21117 (SAN 207-9623) Tel 410-363-3690.

Steppingstone Ent, *(Steppingstone Enterprises, Inc.; 0-939728),* 2108 S. University Dr., Park Place Plaza, Suite 103, Fargo, ND 58103 (SAN 216-7646) Tel 701-237-4742.

Sterling, *(Sterling Publishing Co., Inc.; 0-8069),* 387 Park Ave., S., New York, NY 10016-8810 (SAN 211-6324) Tel 212-532-7160; Toll free: 800-367-9692; Warehouse: Bldg. 2C, Terminal Way, Avenel, NJ 07001-2216 (SAN 658-1773) Tel 908-396-3111.

Sterling Design
See SDPI

Sterling Hse, *(Sterling Hse. Publishing; 1-56315),* Div. of Lee Shore Agency, 440 Friday Rd., Pittsburgh, PA 15209-2114 Tel 412-821-6211.

Sterling Pr MS, *(Sterline Press, Inc.; 0-9637735),* 1610 E. County Line Rd., Apt. B8, Ridgeland, MS 39157 Tel 602-957-9265; Dist. by: Southern Pubs. Group, 147 Corporate Way, Pelham, AL 35124 (SAN 630-7817) Tel 205-664-6980; Toll free: 800-755-4411. Do not confuse with Sterling Pr., Inc. in Bulverde, TX.

Stern & Stern, *(Stern & Stern Publishing Co.; 1-879417),* 9481 Grant Line Rd., Elk Grove, CA 95624.

Stevens & Shea, *(Stevens & Shea Pubs.; 0-89550),* P.O. Box 794, Stockton, CA 95201 (SAN 206-3670) Tel 209-465-1880.

Stevens Pub, *(Stevens Publishing; 0-9632054; 1-885529),* P.O. Box 160, Kila, MT 59920; 1550 Rogers Ln. Rd., Kila, MT 59920 Tel 406-756-0397. Do not confuse with Stevens Publishing Corp. in Waco, TX.

Stew & Rice, *(Stew & Rice Productions; 0-9629842),* P.O. Box 272, Hakalau, HI 96710-0272 Tel 808-963-6422.

Stewart Tabori & Chang, *(Stewart, Tabori & Chang, Inc.; 0-941434; 1-55670),* 575 Broadway, New York, NY 10012 (SAN 293-4000) Tel 212-941-2929; Dist. by: Publishers Resources, Inc., 1224 Heil Quaker Blvd., P.O. Box 7001, La Vergne, TN 37086 (SAN 630-5431) Tel 615-793-5090; Toll free: 800-937-5557.

Stiff Lip, *(Stiff Lip Productions; 0-9623469),* 898 Cedar Ave., Sunnyvale, CA 94086 Tel 408-245-6960.

Stiles-Bishop, *(Stiles-Bishop Productions, Inc.; 1-880623),* 3255 Bennett Dr., Los Angeles, CA 90068-1701 Tel 213-883-0011; Dist. by: BookWorld Distribution Services, Inc., 1933 Whitfield Pk. Loop, Sarasota, FL 34243 (SAN 173-0568) Tel 813-758-8094; Toll free: 800-444-2524 (orders only).

Still Waters, *(Still Waters Pr.; 1-877801),* 112 W. Duerer St., Galloway Township, NJ 08201-9402 Tel 609-652-1790. Do not confuse with companies with the same name in Pomfret Center, CT, North Vernon, IN.

Stillpoint, *(Stillpoint Publishing; 0-913299; 1-883478),* P.O. Box 640, Meetinghouse Rd., Walpole, NH 03608 (SAN 285-8630) Tel 603-756-9281; Toll free: 800-847-4014 (credit card orders only); Dist. by: Publishers Group West, 4065 Hollis St., Emeryville, CA 94608 (SAN 202-8522) Tel 510-658-3453; Toll free: 800-788-3123.

Stilwell Studio, *(Stilwell Studio, The; 0-9605862),* P.O. Box 50, Carmel, CA 93921 (SAN 220-1895) Tel 408-624-0340.

Stipes, *(Stipes Publishing L.L.C.; 0-87563),* P.O. Box 526, 10-12 Chester St., Champaign, IL 61820 (SAN 206-8664) Tel 217-356-8391.

Stirrup Assoc, *(Stirrup Assocs., Inc.; 0-937420),* Div. of David C. Cook Publishing Co., 850 N. Grove Ave., Elgin, IL 60120 (SAN 215-1863) Tel 312-741-2400.

STL Intl, *(STL International, Inc.; 0-936215),* P.O. Box 35918, Tulsa, OK 74153-0918 (SAN 696-8783) Tel 918-250-1488; Dist. by: International Cassette Corp., P.O. Box 1928, Greenville, TX 75401 (SAN 200-5824).

Stone Pub, *(Stone Publishing Co.; 1-880991),* P.O. Box 711, Mendocino, CA 95460; 10491 Wheeler St., Mendocino, CA 95460 Tel 707-937-0239.

Stone Studios, *(Stone Studios; 0-9619791),* Rte. 1, Kimberly, ID 83341 Tel 208-423-4355.

Stoneback Pub, *(Stoneback, Jean, Publishing Co.; 0-931440),* 588 Franklin St., Alburtis, PA 18011 (SAN 222-8440) Tel 610-966-3991.

Stonehaven Pubs, *(Stonehaven Pubs.; 0-937775),* Box 367, Lena, IL 61048 (SAN 659-347X); 602 Oak St., Lena, IL 61048 (SAN 659-3488) Tel 815-369-2823. Do not confuse with Stonehaven Pubs., Fort Worth, TX.

StoneWall Pubns
See V Wagner Pubns

Stoneway Ltd, *(Stoneway, Ltd.; 0-934593; 1-55923),* P.O. Box 7261, Saint Davids, PA 19087-7261 (SAN 693-8817) Tel 610-337-9600; Toll free: 800-237-7558.

Stopher, *(Stopher, Inc.; 0-9628204),* P.O. Box 65172, Baltimore, MD 21209; 6930 Ten Timbers Ln., Baltimore, MD 21209 Tel 410-683-6987.

Storey Comm Inc, *(Storey Communications, Inc.; 0-88266),* Schoolhouse Rd., Pownal, VT 05261 (SAN 203-4158) Tel 802-823-5200; Toll free: 800-793-9396; Dist. by: HarperCollins Pubs., Inc., 1000 Keystone Industrial Pk., Scranton, PA 18512-4621 (SAN 215-3742) Tel 717-941-1500; Toll free: 800-242-7737; 800-982-4377 (in Pennsylvania). *Imprints:* Garden Way Pub (Garden Way Publishing).

Storm Moutain, *(Storm Moutain Pr.; 1-881087),* 5427 S. Cimarron Rd., Littleton, CO 80123 Tel 303-794-6130.

Storm Peak, *(Storm Peak Pr.; 0-9641357),* Div. of Pacific Business Information, Inc., 157 Yesler Way, Suite 413, Seattle, WA 98104 Tel 206-223-0162.

Storm Pr, *(Storm Pr.; 0-9636551),* P.O. Box 266, Arlington Heights, IL 60006-0266; 2622 N. Greenwood Ct., Arlington Heights, IL 60004-2331 Tel 708-394-0269.

Storm Pub, *(Storm Publishing Co.; 0-9637293),* 719 S. Sixth St., Las Vegas, NV 89101 Tel 702-384-0191.

Story Corner, *(Story Corner; 0-9642910),* 408 Larkspur Loop, Lancaster, PA 17602 Tel 717-394-8542.

Story Hse Corp, *(Story Hse. Corp.; 0-87157),* Bindery Ln., Charlotteville, NY 12036 (SAN 169-5193) Tel 607-397-8725; Toll free: 800-847-2105; 800-428-1008 (in New York).

Story Time, *(Story Time Stories That Rhyme; 1-56820),* P.O. Box 416, Denver, CO 80201-0416 Tel 303-575-5676.

Story Time Pubns, *(Story Time Pubns., Inc.; 0-9631480),* 2623 Altavista Cir., Birmingham, AL 35243 Tel 205-967-8608.

Storybk Pub, *(Storybook Publishing; 0-9638033),* P.O. Box 3218, Manhattan Beach, CA 90266; 214 38th Pl., No. B, Manhattan Beach, CA 90266 Tel 310-546-3002.

Storycraft Pub, *(Storycraft Publishing; 0-9638339),* P.O. Box 205, Masonville, CO 80541-0205; 8600 Firethorn Dr., Loveland, CO 80538 Tel 303-669-3755.

Storypole, *(Storypole Pr.; 0-9609940),* 11015 Bingham Ave., E., Tacoma, WA 98446 (SAN 275-8199) Tel 206-531-2032.

Storyteller, *(Storyteller Pr.; 1-880172),* 4111 Morning Star Dr., Huntington Beach, CA 92649 Tel 714-840-2692.

Storytime Ink, *(Storytime Ink International; 0-9628769),* P.O. Box 470505, Broadview Heights, OH 44147 Tel 216-838-4881.

Storytime Pub, *(Storytime Publishing; 0-9632993),* 2813 47th St., Des Moines, IA 50310 Tel 515-274-0396.

Storyviews Pub, *(Storyviews Publishing Co.; 0-9617057),* P.O. Box 526, Shrewsbury, MA 01545-0526 (SAN 662-8354) Tel 508-872-9290; Dist. by: Bookazine Co., Inc., 75 Hook Rd., Bayonne, NJ 07002 (SAN 169-5665) Tel 201-339-7777; Toll free: 800-221-8112; Dist. by: Baker & Taylor Bks., Somerville Service Ctr., 50 Kirby Ave., Somerville, NJ 08876-0734 (SAN 169-4901) Tel 908-722-8000; Toll free: 800-775-1500 (customer service).

Straight From The Heart, *(Straight From The Heart Assocs.; 0-9640181),* 1301 Fell St., Suite 2, San Francisco, CA 94117; 1001 Page St., Suite 77, San Francisco, CA 94117 Tel 415-861-2234.

Stravon, *(Stravon Educational Pr.; 0-87396),* Subs. of Stravon Pubs., Inc., 324 N. Broadway, Yonkers, NY 10701 (SAN 202-7402).

Streetlight Bks, *(Streetlight Bks. Publishing America; 0-9636606),* 29 Railroad Ave., Wayne, NJ 07470 Tel 201-305-3999; Toll free: 800-230-2300.

Strode, *(Strode Pubs.; 0-87397),* Div. of Circle Bk. Service, P.O. Box 626, Tomball, TX 77375 (SAN 202-7429) Tel 713-255-6824; Toll free: 800-227-1591.

Strt Smart, *(Start Smart; 0-9638608),* 1001 E. W.T. Harris Blvd., Suite P155, Charlotte, NC 28213; 4401 Lazy Dr., Charlotte, NC 28215 Tel 704-596-2627. Do not confuse with Start Smart Bks. in Alexandria, VA.

Strybook Heirlooms, *(Storybook Heirlooms; 0-9638614),* 343 Hatch Dr., Foster City, CA 94404-1162 Tel 415-688-1930.

Strytllr Co, *(Storyteller Co.; 0-9622500),* P.O. Box 543, Tarrytown, NY 10591; 42 Riverview Ave., Tarrytown, NY 10591 Tel 914-631-1990. Do not confuse with Storyteller Co. in Simi Valley, CA.

Student Coll, *(Student College Aid; 0-932495),* P.O. Box 300910, Houston, TX 77230-0910 (SAN 687-4320) Tel 713-796-2209.

Student Lifeline, *(Student Lifeline, Inc.; 1-884888),* 99 Tulip Ave., Floral Park, NY 11001 Tel 516-327-0800.

Stuttman, *(Stuttman, H. S., Inc.; 0-87475),* 333 Post Rd., W., Westport, CT 06889 (SAN 202-7453) Tel 203-226-7841; Dist. by: Marshall Cavendish Corp., 2415 Jerusalem Ave., North Bellmore, NY 11710 (SAN 238-437X) Tel 516-826-4200; Toll free: 800-821-9881.

Styx Enter, *(Styx Enterprises; 1-882121),* P.O. Box 2587, Eugene, OR 97402 (SAN 248-4560); 3991 Royal, Eugene, OR 97402 (SAN 248-4579).

Success Publ, *(Success Publishing; 0-931113),* Div. of Success Group, 2812 Bayonne Dr., Box 30965, Palm Beach Gardens, FL 33420 (SAN 678-9501) Tel 407-626-4643; Toll free: 800-330-4643.

Sufi George, *(Sufi George Bks.; 1-885570),* 8639 N. Seventh St., No. 34, Phoenix, AZ 85020 Tel 602-331-1139.

Sugar Marbel Pr, *(Sugar Marbel Pr.; 0-9608320),* 1547 Shenandoah Ave., Cincinnati, OH 45237 (SAN 240-1002) Tel 513-761-8000.

Sugar Sand, *(Sugar Sand, Inc.; 0-9638340),* P.O. Box 1857, Anna Maria, FL 34216; 1911 41st St., W., Bradenton, FL 34205 Tel 813-747-6528.

Sugar Sign Pr, *(Sugar Sign Pr.; 0-939849),* 1407 Fairmont St., Greensboro, NC 27403 (SAN 664-0524) Tel 910-273-9838.

Sullivan MT, *(Sullivan & Assocs.; 1-878330),* 113 E. Wyoming, Kalispell, MT 59901 Tel 406-257-9021.

Sulzburger & Graham Pub, *(Sulzburger & Graham Publishing, Ltd.; 0-945819; 0-943519; 0-910328),* 165 W. 91st St., New York, NY 10024 (SAN 247-9664) Tel 212-769-9738; Toll free: 800-366-7086.

Summa Bks, *(Summa Bks.; 0-932423),* 560 N. Moorpark Rd., Suite 134, Thousand Oaks, CA 91360 (SAN 687-4096) Tel 818-513-0504.

Summa Pub
See Summa Bks

Summers Pub, *(Summers Publishing; 0-916109),* Div. of Central Missouri Medical Services, P.O. Box 105018, Jefferson City, MO 65110-5018 (SAN 294-9083) Tel 314-634-2925; Dist. by: Cowley Distributing Agency, 732 Heisinger Rd., Jefferson City, MO 65101 (SAN 169-426X) Tel 314-636-6511; Toll free: 800-636-6511.

Summertree Bks, *(Summertree Bks.; 0-942465),* 811 Moundridge Dr., Lawrence, KS 66049 (SAN 667-0660) Tel 913-841-7643.

Summit TX, *(Summit Publishing; 0-9626219; 1-56530),* Div. of Summit Group, 1227 W. Magnolia, Suite 500, Fort Worth, TX 76104 Tel 817-921-3346; Toll free: 800-875-3346. Do not confuse with Summit Publishing, Los Angeles, CA.

Summit Univ, *(Summit Univ. Pr.; 0-916766; 0-922729),* Box 5000, Livingston, MT 59047-5000 (SAN 208-4120); Toll free: 800-323-5228 (orders only); 710 E. Gallatin, Livingston, MT 59047-1390 Tel 406-222-8300.

Summy-Birchard, *(Summy-Birchard, Inc.; 0-87487),* 265 Secaucus Rd., Secaucus, NJ 07096-2037 (SAN 202-7461) Tel 201-348-0700; Toll free: 800-638-0005. *Imprints:* Suzuki Method (Suzuki Method International).

Sun Designs, *(Sun Designs; 0-912355),* Subs. of Rexstrom Co., Inc., P.O. Box 206, Delafield, WI 53018 (SAN 265-1181); 173 E. Wisconsin Ave., Oconomowoc, WI 53066 (SAN 265-119X) Tel 414-567-4255; Dist. by: Sterling Publishing Co., Inc., 387 Park Ave., S., New York, NY 10016-8810 (SAN 211-6324) Tel 212-532-7160; Toll free: 800-367-9692.

Sun Drop, *(Sun Drop, Inc.; 0-9631934),* 2712 W. Colter St., Phoenix, AZ 85017-2979.

Sun Light Wks, *(Sun Light Works; 0-9634694),* 745 Mountain Shadows, Sedona, AZ 86336 Tel 602-282-1344.

Sun Pr FL, *(Sun Pr. of Florida; 0-937039),* 35 Trotters Cir., Kissimmee, FL 32743 (SAN 658-702X) Tel 305-933-1586.

Sun Star Pubns, *(Sun Star Pubns.; 0-937787),* 3104 E. Camelback Rd., Box 519, Phoenix, AZ 85016 (SAN 659-3550) Tel 602-948-4346.

Sunbelt Media, *(Sunbelt Media, Inc.; 0-89015; 1-57168),* P.O. Drawer 90159, Austin, TX 78709-0159 (SAN 207-3633); Toll free: 800-880-8642.

Sunburst, *(Sunburst; 0-9609618),* 1322 Coral Dr., W., Tacoma, WA 98466-5832 (SAN 275-8571) Tel 206-565-2041.

Sunburst *Imprint of* **FS&G**

Sundance Pubs, *(Sundance Pubs. & Distributors; 0-940146; 0-88741; 1-56801; 0-7608),* P.O. Box 1326, 234 Taylor St., Littleton, MA 01460 (SAN 169-3484) Tel 508-486-9201; Toll free: 800-343-8204.
Sunday School
See Townsnd-Pr
Sundiver, *(Sundiver Productions Co.; 1-879488),* P.O. Box 1315, Crystal River, FL 34423-1315 Tel 904-563-0022; 421 NW 14th Pl., Crystal River, FL 34429 Tel 904-563-1783.
Sundog Mining, *(Sundog Mining Co.; 0-9632410),* P.O. Box 1792, Vienna, VA 22183; 2238 Loch Lomond Dr., Vienna, VA 22181 Tel 703-695-0352.
Sundog Pubng, *(Sundog Publishing; 0-9642662),* Div. of Sugarfoot Enterprises, 9040 Noble Cir., Anchorage, AK 99502 Tel 907-248-7595. Do not confuse with Sundog Publishing in Silver City, MN.
Sunflower Co, *(Sunflower Co., Inc.; 1-878612),* P.O. Box 10296, Silver Spring, MD 20903 (SAN 200-3856); 1305 Chalmers Rd., Silver Spring, MD 20903 Tel 301-445-3882.
Sunflower Hill, *(Sunflower Hill; 0-9623184),* 7431 LeMunyan Rd., Addison, NY 14801 Tel 607-359-3354; Dist. by: Baker & Taylor Bks., Somerville Service Ctr., 50 Kirby Ave., Somerville, NJ 08876-0734 (SAN 169-4901) Tel 908-722-8000; Toll free: 800-775-1500 (customer service); Dist. by: Baker & Taylor Bks., Momence Service Ctr., 501 S. Gladiolus St., Momence, IL 60954-2444 (SAN 169-2100) Tel 815-472-2444; Toll free: 800-775-2300 (customer service); Dist. by: Baker & Taylor Bks., Commerce Service Ctr., 251 Mt. Olive Church Rd., Commerce, GA 30599-9988 (SAN 169-1503) Tel 706-335-5000; Toll free: 800-775-1200 (customer service); Dist. by: Baker & Taylor Bks., Reno Service Ctr., 380 Edison Way, Reno, NV 89564 (SAN 169-4464) Tel 702-858-6700; Toll free: 800-775-1700 (customer service); Dist. by: The Distributors, 702 S. Michigan, South Bend, IN 46601 (SAN 169-2488) Tel 219-232-8500; Toll free: 800-348-5200 (except Indiana).
Sunflower LA, *(Sunflower Pr.; 0-9641421),* 1000 Kim Dr., Lafayette, LA 70503 Tel 318-984-6090. Do not confuse with Sunflower Pr. in Boise, ID.
Sunlakes Pub, *(Sunlakes Publishing Co.; 0-9615884),* 4153 Bayard Rd., South Euclid, OH 44121 (SAN 696-7663) Tel 216-951-9100.
Sunlight Prodns, *(Sunlight Productions; 0-945086),* P.O. Box 1300, Sedona, AZ 86336 (SAN 245-8470); 390 Jordan Rd., No. 1, Sedona, AZ 86336 (SAN 245-8489) Tel 602-282-2877; Dist. by: Bookpeople, 7900 Edgewater Dr., Oakland, CA 94621 (SAN 168-9517) Tel 510-632-4700; Toll free: 800-999-4650; Dist. by: New Leaf Distributing Co., 5425 Tulane Dr., SW, Atlanta, GA 30336-2323 (SAN 169-1449) Tel 404-691-6996; Toll free: 800-326-2665; Dist. by: Moving Bks., Inc., P.O. Box 20037, Seattle, WA 98102 (SAN 159-0685) Tel 206-762-1750; Toll free: 800-777-6683; Dist. by: Baker & Taylor Bks., Reno Service Ctr., 380 Edison Way, Reno, NV 89564 (SAN 169-4464) Tel 702-858-6700; Toll free: 800-775-1700 (customer service).
Sunny Bks *Imprint of* **J B Comns**
Sunrise Bks, *(Sunrise Bks.; 0-940652),* 1707 "E" St., Eureka, CA 95501 (SAN 665-7893) Tel 707-442-4004. Do not confuse with Sunrise Bks. in Lebanon, VA.
Sunrise Pub NY, *(Sunrise Publishing Co., Inc.; 0-934401),* P.O. Box 408, New York, NY 10019 (SAN 693-4269) Tel 212-541-7143; Orders to: Sunrise Pub., 170 NE 33rd St., Ft. Lauderdale, FL 33334 (SAN 662-3220) Tel 305-563-1844.
Sunset Mktg, *(Sunset Marketing; 0-9620446),* P.O. Box 944, Summerland Key, FL 33042 (SAN 248-630X) Tel 305-745-2671.
Sunset Prods, *(Sunset Products; 0-939755),* 157 Santa Ana Ave., Long Beach, CA 90803 Tel 310-433-0697.
Sunshine Advent, *(Sunshine Adventure Bks.; 0-9640577),* 7514 Herricks Loop, Orlando, FL 32835 Tel 407-290-6655.
Sunstone Pr, *(Sunstone Pr.; 0-913270; 0-86534),* Subs. of Sunstone Corp., P.O. Box 2321, Santa Fe, NM 87504-2321 (SAN 214-2090) Tel 505-988-4418; Toll free: 800-243-5644 (orders only).
Sunstone Pubns, *(Sunstone Pubns.; 0-913319),* Div. of Sunstone, Inc., R.D. 4, Box 700A, Cooperstown, NY 13326 (SAN 283-4227) Tel 607-547-8207; Toll free: 800-327-0306.
Super Puppy Pr, *(Super Puppy Pr.; 1-886056),* P.O. Box 463030, Escondido, CA 92046-3030; Toll free: 800-342-7877; 1946 Bernardo Ave., Escondido, CA 92025 Tel 619-489-1818.
Super Santa Prodns, *(Super Santa Productions; 1-882052),* P.O. Box 6545, San Rafael, CA 94903 (SAN 248-3424) Tel 415-472-0653.
SuperAmerican Bks, *(SuperAmerican Bks.; 0-9625753),* 1060B National Press Bldg., Washington, DC 20045 Tel 202-928-1053.
Supercamp, *(Supercamp; 0-945525),* 1725 S. Hill St., Oceanside, CA 92054 (SAN 247-1108) Tel 619-722-0072.
Superlove, *(Superlove; 0-9602334),* 2128 Watauga Ave., Orlando, FL 32812 (SAN 211-982X) Tel 407-894-1773; 4245 Ladoga Ave., Lakewood, CA 90713 Tel 310-429-6447.
Surge Pub, *(Surge Publishing Co., The; 0-9620420),* 2045 Menominee Dr., Oshkosh, WI 54901 (SAN 248-6792) Tel 414-233-4218.
Surrey Bks, *(Surrey Bks.; 0-9609516; 0-940625; 1-57284),* 230 E. Ohio, Suite 120, Chicago, IL 60611 (SAN 275-8857) Tel 312-751-7330; Toll free: 800-326-4430; Dist. by: Publishers Group West, 4065 Hollis St., Emeryville, CA 94608 (SAN 202-8522) Tel 510-658-3453; Toll free: 800-788-3123.
Susan Hunter, *(Hunter, Susan, Publishing; 0-932419),* 15 Maddox Dr., NE, Atlanta, GA 30309 (SAN 200-8653) Tel 404-874-5473.
Suthrn Trails Pub, *(Southern Trails Publishing Co.; 0-9620286),* 529 Brussels St., San Francisco, CA 94134 (SAN 248-2703) Tel 415-467-7038.
Sutter House, *(Sutter Hse.; 0-915010),* P.O. Box 212, Lititz, PA 17543 (SAN 207-1207) Tel 717-626-0800.
Sutton Pubns, *(Sutton Pubns.; 0-9617199; 1-883649),* 14252 Culver Dr., Suite A644, Irvine, CA 92714 (SAN 663-2610) Tel 714-837-0884.
Suttons Bay Pubns, *(Suttons Bay Pubns.; 0-9621466),* Box 361, Suttons Bay, MI 49682 (SAN 251-4222) Tel 616-271-6821.
Suzuki Method *Imprint of* **Summy-Birchard**
SW Pks Mnmts, *(Southwest Parks & Monuments Assn.; 0-911408; 1-877856),* 221 N. Court Ave., Tucson, AZ 85701 (SAN 202-750X) Tel 602-622-1999; Orders to: 157 W. Cedar St., P.O. Box 2173, Globe, AZ 85502 (SAN 241-8541) Tel 602-425-8184.
Swamp Pr, *(Swamp Pr.; 0-934714),* 323 Pelham Rd., Amherst, MA 01002 (SAN 218-0901).
Swan Books, *(Swan Bks.; 0-934048),* P.O. Box 2498, Fair Oaks, CA 95628 (SAN 212-7016) Tel 916-961-8778.
Swan Enterp, *(Swan Enterprises; 0-927176),* P.O. Box 4309, Bisbee, AZ 85603-4309 Tel 602-366-5466.
Swan-Jones Prod, *(Swan-Jones Production; 1-882238),* 3801 Normandy, Dallas, TX 75205-2106 Tel 214-528-2732; Toll free: 800-736-5663.
Swan Pub, *(Swan Publishing Co.; 0-943629),* 126 Live Oak, Alvin, TX 77511 (SAN 668-6974) Tel 713-388-2547; Dist. by: BookWorld Distribution Services, Inc., 1933 Whitfield Pk. Loop, Sarasota, FL 34243 (SAN 173-0568) Tel 813-758-8094; Toll free: 800-444-2524 (orders only).
Swan Sea Music, *(Swan Sea Music; 0-9623226),* 1293 Russwood Rd., Memphis, TN 38122 Tel 901-682-1768.
SwanMark Bks, *(SwanMark Bks.; 1-878200),* P.O. Box 2056, Valdez, AK 99686; 5405 Chalet Dr., Valdez, AK 99686 Tel 907-835-4385.
Swanson, *(Swanson Publishing Co.; 0-911466),* P.O. Box 334, Moline, IL 61265 (SAN 204-6520); 824 20th Ave., Moline, IL 61265 (SAN 241-8630) Tel 309-762-0464.
Swarovski Amer Ltd, *(Swarovski America Ltd.; 0-9626365),* 2 Slater Rd., Cranston, RI 02920 Tel 401-463-3000; Toll free: 800-556-6478.
Sweet Dreams *Imprint of* **Bantam**
Sweet Inspirations, *(Sweet Inspirations Publishing; 0-9620469),* 1420 NW Gilman Blvd., Suite 2258, Issaquah, WA 98027 (SAN 248-6458) Tel 206-643-8621.
Sweet Koala Pr, *(Sweet Koala Pr.; 0-9617889),* 3350 Tackett St., Springfield, OH 45503-1630 (SAN 665-4975) Tel 513-399-3701.
Sweetlight, *(Sweetlight Bks.; 0-9604462; 1-877714),* 16625 Heitman Rd., Cottonwood, CA 96022 (SAN 215-1154) Tel 916-529-5392; Dist. by: Bookpeople, 7900 Edgewater Dr., Oakland, CA 94621 (SAN 168-9517) Tel 510-632-4700; Toll free: 800-999-4650; Dist. by: New Leaf Distributing Co., 5425 Tulane Dr., SW, Atlanta, GA 30336-2323 (SAN 169-1449) Tel 404-691-6996; Toll free: 800-326-2665.
Sweettooth, *(Sweettooth Publishing Co.; 0-9637088),* 12915 Jones Maltsberger, Suite 102, San Antonio, TX 78247 Tel 210-497-3770.
Swift Lrn Res, *(Swift Learning Resources; 0-944991; 1-56861),* Div. of Swift Printing Corp., 88 N. West State Rd., American Fork, UT 84003 (SAN 245-6737) Tel 801-756-1412; Toll free: 800-292-2831.
Swimming, *(Swimming World; 0-911822),* Subs. of Sports Pubns., Inc., 155 S. El Molino Ave., No. 101, Pasadena, CA 91101-2563 (SAN 204-6539).
Syentek, *(Syentek, Inc.; 0-914082),* P.O. Box 26588, San Francisco, CA 94126 (SAN 202-7534) Tel 415-928-0471.
SYF Enter, *(SYF Enterprises; 0-9621556),* 990 Wimbleton, Medina, OH 44256 (SAN 251-5709) Tel 216-722-7808.
Syllogism Pr, *(Syllogism Pr.; 0-9638001),* 1070E Highway 34, Suite 141, Matawan, NJ 07747 Tel 908-290-7901.
Sylvan Inst, *(Sylvan Institute; 0-918428),* 509 NW 80th St., Vancouver, WA 98665-7833 (SAN 209-6838) Tel 206-574-0875.
Sylvan Pubns, *(Sylvan Pubns.; 0-9606678),* 42185 Baintree Cir., Northville, MI 48167 (SAN 219-6433) Tel 810-349-4827.
Symbiosis Bks, *(Symbiosis Bks.; 0-9615903),* 36 Longwood Dr., San Rafael, CA 94901-1062 (SAN 696-8457) Tel 415-457-6658; Dist. by: Bookpeople, 7900 Edgewater Dr., Oakland, CA 94621 (SAN 168-9517) Tel 510-632-4700; Toll free: 800-999-4650; Dist. by: Edu-Vid Distributors, Inc., 711 W. 17th St., Suite J5, Costa Mesa, CA 92627 (SAN 630-8023) Tel 714-642-3988.
Synaxis Pr, *(Synaxis Pr.; 0-911523),* P.O. Box 689, Lynden, WA 98264 (SAN 685-4338) Tel 604-826-9336.
Syndistar, *(Syndistar, Inc.; 1-56230),* 125 Mallard St., Suite A, Saint Rose, LA 70087 (SAN 298-007X) Tel 504-468-1100; Toll free: 800-841-9532.
Synergistic Pr, *(Synergistic Pr., Inc.; 0-912184),* 3965 Sacramento St., San Francisco, CA 94118 (SAN 205-4116) Tel 415-387-8180.
Syracuse U Pr, *(Syracuse Univ. Pr.; 0-8156),* 1600 Jamesville Ave., Syracuse, NY 13244-5160 (SAN 206-9776) Tel 315-443-2597; Toll free: 800-365-8929 (orders only).
Systems Co, *(Systems Co.; 0-937041; 1-56216),* P.O. Box 339, Carlsborg, WA 98324 (SAN 699-7880); 52 Ivy Ln., Port Angeles, WA 98362 Tel 206-452-4987.
T A Pitts, *(Pitts, Teresa Anne; 0-9618600),* 5645 W. San Vicente Blvd., Los Angeles, CA 90019 (SAN 668-3061) Tel 213-933-4470.
T Assicurato, *(Assicurato, Thomas; 0-9621591),* 2026 Yates Ave., Bronx, NY 10461 (SAN 251-7612) Tel 718-823-7672.
T B J Pubns, *(TBJ Pubns.; 0-935855),* Div. of Teddy Bear Craftworks, 10 Brookfield Rd., Methuen, MA 01844 (SAN 695-8907) Tel 508-686-3145.
T Baize, *(Baize, Timothy; 0-9625193),* 2305 Glenn Ave., Evansville, IN 47711 Tel 812-473-1955; Dist. by: Baker & Taylor Bks., Momence Service Ctr., 501 S. Gladiolus St., Momence, IL 60954-2444 (SAN 169-2100) Tel 815-472-2444; Toll free: 800-775-2300 (customer service); Dist. by: The Distributors, 702 S. Michigan, South Bend, IN 46601 (SAN 169-2488) Tel 219-232-8500; Toll free: 800-348-5200 (except Indiana).
T Brown, *(Brown, Tehane; 0-9637099),* P.O. Box 582, Kula, Maui, HI 96790; 230 Kahoea Pl., Kula, Maui, HI 96790 Tel 808-878-6609.
T C Deleon, *(DeLeon, T. C., Pr.; 0-944284),* 957 Augusta St., Mobile, AL 36604 (SAN 243-0487) Tel 205-433-6717.
T C Wilson, *(Wilson, Terry C.; 0-9623886),* 10760 Milam Rd., Colorado Springs, CO 80908-3913 Tel 719-548-0317.
T E McNutt, *(McNutt, Timothy E.; 0-9642475),* 2321 Crestmoor Rd., Nashville, TN 37215 Tel 615-383-0171.
T E Soike, *(Soike, Thomas E.; 0-9631201),* 3134 Carlson Dr., Shingle Springs, CA 95682 Tel 916-677-5563.
T Faulk Ministries, *(Faulk, Tim, Ministries; 0-9625026),* P.O. Box 146, Headland, AL 36345 Tel 205-693-3266.
T Healy, *(Healy, Therese; 0-9617581),* 9909 98th St., SW, Tacoma, WA 98498 (SAN 664-5089) Tel 206-984-8130.
T J Brown, *(Brown, Towana J.; 0-9622060),* Rte. 8, Box 684, Cullman, AL 35055 Tel 205-796-2095.
T Jefferson Ctr, *(Jefferson, Thomas, Ctr.; 0-938308),* 202 S. Lake Ave., No. 240, Pasadena, CA 91101 (SAN 239-670X) Tel 818-792-8130.
T Jefferson Res Ctr
See T Jefferson Ctr
T K Enterprises, *(TK Enterprises; 0-9637301),* P.O. Box 6455, Delray Beach, FL 33484-6455; 4065D Village Dr., Delray Beach, FL 33445-2921 Tel 407-495-4604.
T L Campbell, *(Campbell, Tammie Lang; 0-9623947),* 1219 Kingscreek Trail, Missouri City, TX 77459 Tel 713-499-7966.
T Leagjeld, *(Leagjeld, Ted; 0-9616127),* Rte. 1, Box 404, Pine River, MN 56474 (SAN 699-6833) Tel 218-568-4221.
T Lydia Pr, *(Lydia, T., Pr.; 0-9623288),* 7561 Upper 17th St., N., Oakdale, MN 55119 Tel 612-731-9698.
T Mack Glamour, *(Teri Mack Glamour; 0-9623808),* 166 Derby Woods Dr., Lynn Haven, FL 32444 Tel 904-265-3690.
T Peters & Co, *(Tim Peters & Co., Inc.; 1-879874),* P.O. Box 50, Gladstone, NJ 07934; 12 Pheasant Run, Gladstone, NJ 09934 Tel 908-234-2050.
T R Fennoy, *(Fennoy, Thelma Rand; 0-9637350),* Rte. 2, Box 173, Jefferson, TX 75657; Cass County Rd. 1777, Jefferson, TX 75657 Tel 903-665-7323.

T R Turner, *(Turner, Teresa R., from the Heart;* 0-9633509), Rte. 5, Box 5560, Chatsworth, GA 30705 Tel 404-695-4988.

T Scott Pub, *(Scott, Tim, Publishing Co.; 1-877784),* Affil. of The Special Touch Co., P.O. Box 91079, Springfield, MA 01139-1079 Tel 413-746-8530.

T Storm, *(Storm, Tom; 0-9643019),* 600 23rd St., S., Great Falls, MT 59405 Tel 406-454-0723.

T W Taylor, *(Taylor, Thomas W.; 1-885853),* P.O. Box 238014, Allandale, FL 32123-8014; 1213 Harbour Point Dr., Port Orange, FL 32127-5607 Tel 904-760-3618.

TAB-Aero *Imprint of* **TAB Bks**

TAB Bks, *(TAB Bks.; 0-8306; 0-07),* Div. of McGraw-Hill, Inc., P.O. Box 40, Blue Ridge Summit, PA 17294-0850 (SAN 202-568X) Tel 717-794-2191; Toll free: 800-233-1128. *Imprints:* TAB-Aero (T A B-Aero); Windcrest (Windcrest).

Tabby Hse Bks, *(Tabby Hse. Bks.; 0-9627974; 1-881539),* 4429 Shady Ln., Charlotte Harbor, FL 33980 Tel 813-629-7646; Dist. by: BookWorld Distribution Services, Inc., 1933 Whitfield Pk. Loop, Sarasota, FL 34243 (SAN 173-0568) Tel 813-758-8094; Toll free: 800-444-2524 (orders only).

Tabor Pub, *(Tabor Publishing; 0-913592; 0-89505; 1-55924; 0-7829),* Div. of RCL, Inc., 200 E. Bethany Dr., Allen, TX 75002; Toll free: 800-822-6701; Orders to: P.O. Box 7000, Allen, TX 75002 (SAN 241-6212) Tel 214-390-6325; Toll free: 800-822-6701.

Tabor Sarah Bks, *(Tabor Sarah Bks.; 0-935079),* 3345 Stockton Place, Palo Alto, CA 94303 (SAN 695-0353) Tel 415-494-7846.

TACM Inc
See L P T C

TadAlex Bks, *(TadAleX Bks.; 0-929301),* 10834 Dixon Dr., S., Seattle, WA 98178 (SAN 249-0064) Tel 206-772-2059.

Tadpole, *(Tadpole; 0-9615253),* 6030 Autumn Arbor, Houston, TX 77092 (SAN 695-0965) Tel 713-681-8377.

Taffey Apple, *(Taffey Apple Publishing; 0-9635276),* 19037 Jodi Terr., Homewood, IL 60430 Tel 708-799-3591.

Tahoe Tourist, *(Tahoe Tourist Promotions; 0-9626792),* P.O. Box 986, Kings Beach, CA 95719; 8612 N. Lake Blvd., Kings Beach, CA 95719 Tel 916-546-3303; Dist. by: Sierra News Co., 21 Locust St., Reno, NV 89520 (SAN 169-4472) Tel 702-329-1714.

Tail Tours, *(Tailored Tours Pubns., Inc.; 0-9631241),* Box 22861, Lake Buena Vista, FL 32830; 10024 N. Fulton Ct., Orlando, FL 32836 Tel 407-345-9216.

Take Along Pubns, *(Take Along Pubns.; 0-9624141),* P.O. Box 612146, South Lake Tahoe, CA 95761; 764 Lassen, South Lake Tahoe, CA 95761 Tel 916-544-3506.

Tale Weaver, *(Tale Weaver; 0-942139),* 1115 N. Larrabee St., Suite 304, West Hollywood, CA 90069 (SAN 666-7570) Tel 213-652-1992.

Talent-Ed, *(Talent-Ed; 0-935003),* 3033 Oak Borough Run, Fort Wayne, IN 46804-7808 (SAN 694-6577) Tel 219-436-6035.

Taliaferro IN, *(Taliaferro Publishing Co.; 0-9626633),* P.O. Box 2891, Gary, IN 46403 (SAN 297-8083); 8644 Lakewood Ave., Gary, IN 46403 Tel 219-938-7408.

Talking Mntn, *(Talking Mountain Publishing Co.;* 0-9624235), P.O. Box 621, Bodega Bay, CA 94923 (SAN 200-3619); 1856 Whaleship Rd., Bodega Bay, CA 94923 Tel 707-875-2106.

Tallstone Pub, *(Tallstone Publishing; 0-936191),* 10 Vine Ave., Sharon, PA 16146 (SAN 696-7604) Tel 412-347-5857.

Talman, *(Talman Co.),* 131 Spring St., Suite 201E-N, New York, NY 10012 (SAN 200-5204) Tel 212-431-7175; Toll free: 800-537-8894 (orders only).

TAM Assoc, *(TAM Assocs.; 0-913005),* 911 Chicago, Oak Park, IL 60302 (SAN 283-4235) Tel 312-848-6760.

Tambourine Bks *Imprint of* **Morrow**

Tambuzi Pubns, *(Tambuzi Pubns., Inc.; 0-9621739),* 2518 W. Grace St., Suite 5, Richmond, VA 23220 (SAN 252-0419) Tel 804-353-4497.

TAN Bks Pubs, *(TAN Bks. & Pubs., Inc.; 0-89555),* 2020 Harrison Ave., Rockford, IL 61104 (SAN 282-390X) Tel 815-226-7777; Toll free: 800-437-5876; Orders to: P.O. Box 424, Rockford, IL 61105 (SAN 282-3918).

T&T Dyno-Srvs, *(T&T Dyno-Services Corp., Printing Div.; 0-9633124),* Div. of T&T Dyno-Services Corp., 2409 41st Ave., Long Island City, NY 11101 Tel 718-482-0007.

TAPPI, *(Technical Assn. of the Pulp & Paper Industry;* 0-89852), P.O. Box 105113, Atlanta, GA 30348-5113 (SAN 676-5629); Toll free: 800-332-8686; 800-446-9431 (in Canada); 15 Technology Pkwy., Atlanta, GA 30092 (SAN 241-8681) Tel 404-446-1400.

Tara Educ Servs, *(Tara Educational Services; 0-929404),* 65 Cretin Ave., N., Saint Paul, MN 55104 (SAN 249-4329) Tel 612-645-0625; Dist. by: Inland Bk. Co., 140 Commerce St., East Haven, CT 06512 (SAN 200-4151) Tel 203-467-4257; Toll free: 800-243-0138.

Targum Pr, *(Targum Pr., Inc.; 0-944070; 1-56871),* 22700 W. Eleven Mile Rd., Southfield, MI 48034 (SAN 242-8997) Tel 810-355-2266; Dist. by: Philipp Feldheim, Inc., 200 Airport Executive Pk., Spring Valley, NY 10977 (SAN 106-6307) Tel 914-356-2282; Toll free: 800-237-7149.

Tartan Tiger, *(Tartan Tiger; 0-935827),* 2320 144th SE, Bellevue, WA 98007 (SAN 696-6535) Tel 206-747-7655.

Taste & See, *(Taste & See; 0-9631988),* HC61, Box 1825, Cle Elum, WA 98922 Tel 509-857-2067.

Tata Pubng, *(Tata Publishing; 0-9639913),* 1274 Golden Eagle Dr., Reston, VA 22094 Tel 703-435-3814.

Tator Enterprises, *(Tator Enterprises, Inc.; 0-9624285),* 6131 Eighth Ave., S., Saint Petersburg, FL 33707-3152 Tel 813-323-7596.

Tawney Pubng, *(Tawney Publishing Co.; 0-9638882),* 9 Laupapa Pl., Haiku, Maui, HI 96708 Tel 808-575-2228; Toll free: 800-628-4462.

Taylor Prodns, *(Taylor Productions, Ltd.; 1-882093),* 20 Exchange Pl., Suite 3501, New York, NY 10005 (SAN 248-4536) Tel 212-425-3466; Dist. by: Talman Co., 131 Spring St., Suite 201E-N, New York, NY 10012 (SAN 200-5204) Tel 212-431-7175; Toll free: 800-557-8894 (orders only).

TBW Bks, *(TBW Bks.; 0-931474),* P.O Box 2038, RFD 5, Brunswick, ME 04011.

TCA PA, *(Train Collectors Assn.; 0-917896),* P.O. Box 248, Strasburg, PA 17579.

TCA Pub, *(TCA Publishing; 0-9626932),* 16610 S. 41st St., Phoenix, AZ 85044-8039 Tel 602-759-4652.

Tchr Create Mat, *(Teacher Created Materials, Inc.;* 1-55734), 6421 Industry Way, Westminster, CA 92683-3608 (SAN 665-5270) Tel 714-891-7895; Toll free: 800-662-4321.

Tchr Tested-Child, *(Teacher Tested-Child Satisfying;* 0-915505), 3875 Chamoune Ave., San Diego, CA 92105-2819 (SAN 291-4514) Tel 619-298-6439.

Tchrs & Writers Coll, *(Teachers & Writers Collaborative; 0-915924),* 5 Union Sq. W., New York, NY 10003-3306 (SAN 206-3859) Tel 212-691-6590.

Tchrs Coll, *(Teachers College Pr., Teachers College, Columbia Univ.; 0-8077),* 1234 Amsterdam Ave., New York, NY 10027 (SAN 282-3985) Tel 212-678-3929; Orders to: P.O. Box 20, Williston, VT 05495-0020 (SAN 248-3904); Toll free: 800-575-6566.

TD Pub, *(Three Dimensional Publishing; 1-877835),* 1015 Stirling Rd., Silver Spring, MD 20901 Tel 301-593-3284; Toll free: 800-673-8210 (US & Canada).

TEA Pubs, *(TEA Pubs.; 0-9642344),* 174 W. Meadow Rd., Rockland, ME 04841 Tel 207-594-7711.

Teach Me, *(Teach Me Tapes, Inc.; 0-934633),* 10500 Bren Rd. E, Suite 115, Minnetonka, MN 55343-9045 (SAN 693-9309) Tel 612-933-8086; Toll free: 800-456-4656; Dist. by: Publishers Group West, 4065 Hollis St., Emeryville, CA 94608 (SAN 202-8522) Tel 510-658-3453; Toll free: 800-788-3123; Dist. by: Quality Bks., Inc., 918 Sherwood Dr., Lake Bluff, IL 60044-2204 (SAN 169-2127) Tel 708-295-2010; Toll free: 800-323-4241 (libraries only).

Teach Nxt Door, *(Teacher Next Door; 1-884204),* 1220 Deer Rd., Fremont, CA 94536 Tel 510-796-4079.

Teach Servs, *(Teach Services; 0-945383),* Rte. 1, Box 182, Donivan Rd., Brushton, NY 12916 (SAN 246-9863) Tel 518-358-2125; Toll free: 800-367-1844.

Teacher Ideas Pr, *(Teacher Ideas Pr.; 0-87287; 1-56308),* Div. of Libraries Unlimited, Inc., P.O. Box 6633, Englewood, CO 80155-6633 (SAN 202-6767) Tel 303-770-1220; Toll free: 800-237-6124.

Teachers Friend Pubns, *(Teacher's Friend Pubns., Inc.;* 0-943263), 7407 Orangewood Dr., Riverside, CA 92504 (SAN 668-3177) Tel 909-358-0106; Toll free: 800-343-9680.

Teachers Lab, *(Teachers Laboratory, Inc., The;* 0-9621820), P.O. Box 6480, Brattleboro, VT 05301; 104 Canal St., Brattleboro, VT 05301 Tel 802-254-3457.

Teachers Pub Hse, *(Teachers Publishing Hse.; 0-942431),* 612 Gibbs Rd., Akron, OH 44312 (SAN 667-0326) Tel 216-784-3181.

Teaching Advisory, *(Teaching Advisory, The;* 0-9621619), P.O. Box 99131, Seattle, WA 98199 (SAN 252-1032); 2632 40th Ave., W., Seattle, WA 98199 Tel 206-282-3420.

Teaching WA, *(Teaching, Inc.; 0-9614574; 1-881660),* P.O. Box 788, Edmonds, WA 98020; 8403 Talbot Rd., Edmonds, WA 98020 Tel 206-774-0755.

Team Earth, *(Team Earth Co.; 0-9630186),* P.O. Box 1006, Kihei, HI 96753; 483 S. Kihei Rd., Apt. 111, Kihei, HI 96753 Tel 808-879-0777.

Team Effort, *(Team Effort Publishing Co.; 0-9630884),* P.O. Box 5027, Huntsville, TX 77342; Toll free: 800-289-5453; 427 Fish Hatchery Rd., Huntsville, TX 77342 Tel 409-295-5846.

Teapot Tales, *(Teapot Tales; 1-881617),* P.O. Box 500, Hurst, TX 76053-6839; 501 Oak Park Dr., Hurst, TX 76053 Tel 817-282-2155; Dist. by: Bookmen, Inc., 525 N. Third St., Minneapolis, MN 55401 (SAN 169-409X) Tel 612-341-3333; Toll free: 800-328-8411 (customer service).

TechWest Pubns, *(TechWest Pubns.; 0-943621),* 170 Alamo Plaza, No. 403F, Alamo, CA 94507-1550 (SAN 668-6885).

Teddy & Frnds, *(Teddy & Friends; 0-9636154),* P.O. Box 6895, Vero Beach, FL 32961-6895; 4606 13th Pl., Vero Beach, FL 32966 Tel 407-562-8908.

Teddy Bear Connect, *(Teddy Bear Connection;* 0-9632316), 729 S. Nicollet St., P.O. Box 93, Blue Earth, MN 56013 Tel 507-526-5151.

Teddy Bear Pr, *(Teddy Bear Pr., Inc.; 1-880017),* 5470 Van Ness, Bloomfield Hills, MI 48303 Tel 810-851-8607.

Tee Loftin, *(Tee Loftin Pubs., Inc.; 0-934812),* 685 Gonzales Rd., Santa Fe, NM 87501-6190 (SAN 215-9635) Tel 505-989-1931.

Teen Round-Up, *(Teen Round-Up, Inc.; 0-9614268),* Rte. 1, Box 226A, Duncan, OK 73533 (SAN 687-1534) Tel 405-255-5207.

Teka Trends, *(Teka Trends, Inc.; 1-878356),* 1000 Salt Meadow Ln., McLean, VA 22101 Tel 703-356-7572; Dist. by: Pragmatica Corp., 301 Maple Ave., W., Suite 100, Vienna, VA 22180 (SAN 630-6632) Tel 703-938-9239.

Teknek, *(Teknek; 0-930363),* 23048 Park Privado, Calabasas, CA 91302 (SAN 670-7793) Tel 818-347-4138.

Telcraft Bks, *(Telcraft Bks.; 1-878893),* 3800 Mogadore Industrial Pkwy., Mogadore, OH 44260 Tel 216-628-2772.

Telesis CA, *(Telesis II of California, Inc.; 1-56117),* 409 Camino Del Rio S., Suite 205, San Diego, CA 92108-3506 Tel 619-497-0193; Toll free: 800-542-2966.

Tell Pubns OH
See Telcraft Bks

Telstar TX, *(Telstar; 0-9624384; 1-878142),* P.O. Box 65656-566, Lubbock, TX 79464-5724 Tel 206-578-2072. *Imprints:* Blue Earth Pr (Blue Earth Press).

Temple Golden Pubns, *(Temple Golden Pubns.;* 0-929686), P.O. Box 10501, Sedona, AZ 86336 (SAN 250-1872); 305 Mountain Shadow Dr., Sedona, AZ 86336 (SAN 250-1880) Tel 602-282-6864.

Tempus Pr, *(Tempus Pr.; 0-9620456),* P.O. Box 235, Tell City, IN 47586 (SAN 248-4609); 104 Geneva Dr., Tell City, IN 47586 (SAN 248-4617) Tel 812-547-8144.

Ten Penny, *(Ten Penny Players, Inc.; 0-934830),* 393 St. Paul's Ave., Staten Island, NY 10304-2127 (SAN 213-8743) Tel 718-442-7429; Dist. by: Waterways Project, 393 St. Paul's Ave., Staten Island, NY 10304-2127 (SAN 219-5402) Tel 718-442-7429.

Ten Speed Pr, *(Ten Speed Pr.; 0-913668; 0-89815),* P.O. Box 7123, Berkeley, CA 94707 (SAN 202-7674) Tel 510-559-1600; Toll free: 800-841-2665.

Tenderfoot Pr, *(Tenderfoot Pr.; 0-9615397),* P.O. Box 533, Narberth, PA 19072 (SAN 695-4669) Tel 610-667-4769.

TeNeues, *(te Neues Publishing Co.; 3-8238),* 16 W. 22nd St., 11th Flr., New York, NY 10010-5803 (SAN 245-176X) Tel 212-627-9090.

Tennedo Pubs, *(Tennedo Pubs.; 0-9638946),* 6315 Elwynne Dr., Cincinnati, OH 45236 Tel 513-791-3277.

Tern Pubns, *(Tern Pubns.; 0-9618945),* P.O. Box 28, Cape Porpoise, ME 04014 (SAN 242-4622); Winter Harbor Rd., Cape Porpoise, ME 04014 (SAN 242-4630) Tel 207-967-5673.

Terra Nova, *(Terra Nova Pr.; 0-944176),* 1309 Redwood Ln., Davis, CA 95616 (SAN 242-8741) Tel 916-753-1519.

Teruko Inc, *(Teruko, Inc.; 0-938789),* P.O. Box 1116, La Mirada, CA 90637-1116 (SAN 662-5657); 2254 Rosecrans Ave., Fullerton, CA 92633 (SAN 662-5665) Tel 714-773-5437.

TES Pub, *(TES Publishing Co.; 0-9616432),* 107 Saddletree Rd., San Antonio, TX 78231 (SAN 659-0357) Tel 210-493-5112; Dist. by: DeVorss & Co., P.O. Box 550, Marina del Rey, CA 90294-0550 (SAN 168-9886) Tel 213-870-7478; Toll free: 800-843-5743 (bookstores only); 800-331-4719 (in California, bookstores only); Dist. by: Baker & Taylor Bks., Somerville Service Ctr., 50 Kirby Ave., Somerville, NJ 08876-0734 (SAN 169-4901) Tel 908-722-8000; Toll free: 800-775-1500 (customer service); Dist. by: Baker & Taylor Bks., Momence Service Ctr., 501 S. Gladiolus St., Momence, IL 60954-2444 (SAN 169-2100) Tel 815-472-2444; Toll free: 800-775-2300 (customer service); Dist. by: Baker & Taylor Bks., Commerce Service Ctr., 251 Mt. Olive Church Rd., Commerce, GA 30599-9988 (SAN 169-1503) Tel 706-335-5000; Toll free: 800-775-1200 (customer service); Dist. by: Baker & Taylor Bks., Reno Service Ctr., 380 Edison Way, Reno, NV 89564 (SAN 169-4464) Tel 702-858-6700; Toll free: 800-775-1700 (customer service).

Tesseract SD, *(Tesseract Pubns.; 1-877649),* P.O. Box 505, Hudson, SD 57034-0505; P.O. Box 505, Hudson, SD 57034-0505 Tel 605-987-5070.

Test Taking Advan, *(Test Taking Advantage Co.; 0-9627360),* 303 Belvedere Ave., Belvedere Tiburon, CA 94920-2426 Tel 415-435-2186.

Tex A&M Univ Pr, *(Texas A&M Univ. Pr.; 0-89096),* Drawer C, College Station, TX 77843-4354 (SAN 207-5237); Toll free: 800-826-8911 (orders); Lewis St., University Campus, John Lindsey Bldg., College Station, TX 77843-4354 (SAN 658-1919) Tel 409-845-1436.

Tex Christian, *(Texas Christian Univ. Pr.; 0-912646; 0-87565),* Box 30783, Fort Worth, TX 76129 (SAN 202-7690) Tel 817-921-7822; Dist. by: Texas A&M Univ. Pr., Drawer C, College Station, TX 77843-4354 (SAN 207-5237) Tel 409-845-1436; Toll free: 800-826-8911 (orders).

Tex St Hist Assn, *(Texas State Historical Assn.; 0-87611),* 2-306 Richardson Hall, University Sta., Austin, TX 78712 (SAN 202-7704) Tel 512-471-1525; Dist. by: Texas A&M Univ. Pr., Drawer C, College Station, TX 77843-4354 (SAN 207-5237) Tel 409-845-1436; Toll free: 800-826-8911 (orders).

Tex Tech Univ Pr, *(Texas Tech Univ. Pr.; 0-89672),* Affil. of Texas Tech Univ., Texas Tech Univ., P.O. Box 41037, Lubbock, TX 79409-1037 (SAN 218-5989) Tel 806-742-2982; Toll free: 800-832-4042.

Texart, *(TexArt Services, Inc.; 0-935857),* 200 Concord Plaza Dr., No. 550, San Antonio, TX 78216-6940 (SAN 696-0022) Tel 210-826-2889.

Texas Trends, *(Texas Trends; 0-9629746),* 1656 E. 13505, Ogden, UT 84404 Tel 801-393-7802.

Textile Bridge, *(Textile Bridge Pr.; 0-938838),* Div. of Moody Street Irregulars, Inc., P.O. Box 157, Clarence Center, NY 14032 (SAN 216-0676) Tel 716-741-3393.

TFC Bks NY, *(21st Century Bks., Inc.; 0-941477; 0-8050),* Div. of Henry Holt & Co., Inc., 115 W. 18th St., New York, NY 10011-4113 (SAN 666-0827) Tel 212-886-9200. Do not confuse with Twenty-First Century Bks., Inc., Lafayette, LA.

TFFACC
See Am Soc Defense TFP

TFH Pubns, *(TFH Pubns., Inc.; 0-87666; 0-86622; 0-7938),* 1 TFH Plaza, Union & Third Aves., Neptune City, NJ 07753 (SAN 202-7720) Tel 908-988-8400; Toll free: 800-631-2188 (outside New Jersey); Box 427, Neptune, NJ 07753 (SAN 658-1862); Dist. by: National Bk. Network, 4720A Boston Way, Lanham, MD 20706-4310 (SAN 630-0065) Tel 301-459-8696; Toll free: 800-462-6420.

TGNW Pr, *(T.G.N.W. Pr.; 0-9619560),* 2429 E. Aloha, Seattle, WA 98112 (SAN 245-4742) Tel 206-328-9656.

Thames Hudson, *(Thames & Hudson; 0-500),* 500 Fifth Ave., New York, NY 10110 (SAN 667-4577) Tel 212-354-3763; Dist. by: W. W. Norton & Co., Inc., 500 Fifth Ave., New York, NY 10110 (SAN 202-5795) Tel 212-354-5500; Toll free: 800-223-2584; 800-233-4830 (book orders only).

The Way Pub, *(The Way Publishing Co.; 0-9621141),* 5070 Parkside Ave., No. 1122, Philadelphia, PA 19131 (SAN 250-6823) Tel 215-473-0050.

Theory Aids Keybd, *(Theory Aids for Keyboard; 1-882176),* 7 Ringleaf Ct., Cockeysville, MD 21030 Tel 410-785-6840.

Theos U Pr, *(Theosophical Univ. Pr.; 0-911500; 1-55700),* P.O. Box C, Pasadena, CA 91109-7107 (SAN 205-4299) Tel 818-798-3378.

Think Shop, *(Think Shop, Inc.; 0-937871),* 7303 Montgomery Blvd., NE A, No. 172, Albuquerque, NM 87109-1547 (SAN 659-5944).

Thinking Caps, *(Thinking Caps, Inc.; 0-9610876),* P.O. Box 7239, Phoenix, AZ 85011 (SAN 239-4960) Tel 602-956-1515.

Thinking Kids Pr, *(Thinking Kids' Pr.; 0-939707),* P.O. Box 3112, South Pasadena, CA 91030-6112 (SAN 663-5172) Tel 818-282-7339.

Thinking Pubns, *(Thinking Pubns.; 0-9610370; 0-930599),* Div. of McKinley Co., Inc., 424 Galloway St., Box 163, Eau Claire, WI 54702-0163 (SAN 264-4320) Tel 715-832-2488; Toll free: 800-225-4769; 800-225-4709 (in U.S. & Canada).

Third Story, *(Third Story Bks.; 1-884506),* 955 Connecticut Ave., Suite 1302, Bridgeport, CT 06607 Tel 203-330-9364; Dist. by: Andrews & McMeel, 4900 Main St., Kansas City, MO 64112 (SAN 202-540X) Tel 816-932-6700; Toll free: 800-826-4216.

Third World, *(Third World Press; 0-88378),* P.O. Box 19730, Chicago, IL 60619 (SAN 202-778X) Tel 312-651-0700.

This Little, *(This Little Light Publishing; 1-885282),* 1014 N. Del Rey Ave., Pasadena, CA 91107 Tel 818-398-7711.

Thomas Geale, *(Geale, Thomas, Pubns., Inc.; 0-912781),* P.O. Box 370540, Montara, CA 94037 (SAN 283-3735) Tel 415-728-5219; Toll free: 800-554-5457.

Thomas More, *(More, Thomas, Pr.; 0-88347),* Div. of Tabor Publishing, P.O. Box 7000, Allen, TX 75002-1305; Toll free: 800-822-6701; 205 W. Monroe St., 6th Flr., Chicago, IL 60606-5097 (SAN 203-0675) Tel 312-609-8880.

Thomas Publications, *(Thomas Pubns.; 0-939631),* 353 Buford Ave., Gettysburg, PA 17325-1138 (SAN 663-7213) Tel 717-334-1921. Do not confuse with companies with the same name in Austin, TX, La Crescenta, CA.

Thomasson-Grant, *(Thomasson-Grant, Inc.; 0-934738; 1-56566),* 1 Morton Dr., Charlottesville, VA 22903-6806 (SAN 239-3948) Tel 804-977-1780; Toll free: 800-999-1780.

Thompson, *(Thompson Pubs.; 0-933479),* 2555 N. 19th St., Milwaukee, WI 53206 (SAN 691-8972) Tel 414-264-9241.

Thompson Pr, *(Thompson Pr.; 0-931947),* P.O. Box 263, Conway, NH 03818 (SAN 685-9399) Tel 603-447-5569.

Thompson's, *(Thompson's),* P.O. Box 550, Albertville, AL 35950 (SAN 207-4656) Tel 205-878-2021.

Thomson Lrning, *(Thomson Learning; 1-56847),* 115 Fifth Avenue, New York, NY 10003 (SAN 297-8733) Tel 212-979-2210; Orders to: 835 Penobscot Bldg., Detroit, MI 48226-4094 (SAN 297-8806); Toll free: 800-880-4253.

Thor, *(Thor Publishing Co.; 0-87407),* P.O. Box 1782, Ventura, CA 93002 (SAN 202-7801) Tel 805-648-4560.

Thorndike Pr, *(Thorndike Pr.; 0-89621; 1-56054; 0-7862),* Div. of Macmillan Publishing Co., Inc., P.O. Box 159, Thorndike, ME 04986 (SAN 212-2375); Toll free: 800-223-6121; Depot Street, Unity, ME 04988 Tel 207-948-2962; Orders to: Macmillan Publishing Co., Inc., 100 Front St., Box 500, Riverside, NJ 08075-7500 (SAN 202-5582); Toll free: 800-257-5755; 800-562-1272 (FAX orders).

Thorne Enterprises, *(Thorne Enterprises; 0-9628329),* 149 Gambel Ln., Sedona, AZ 86336 Tel 602-282-7508.

Thornsbury Bailey Brown, *(Thornsbury Bailey & Brown; 0-945253),* P.O. Box 5169, Arlington, VA 22205 (SAN 246-2192) Tel 703-532-2210.

Thornton LA, *(Thornton Publishing; 1-882913),* 1504 Howard St., New Iberia, LA 70560 Tel 318-364-2752; Toll free: 800-551-3076.

Thorsons SF, *(Thorsons; 0-7225),* Div. of Harper San Francisco, 1160 Battery St., 3rd Flr., San Francisco, CA 94111 Tel 415-477-4400; Dist. by: HarperCollins Pubs., Inc., 1000 Keystone Industrial Pk., Scranton, PA 18512-4621 (SAN 215-3742) Tel 717-941-1500; Toll free: 800-242-7737; 800-982-4377 (in Pennsylvania).

Thoth MO, *(Thoth Publishing Co.; 0-9628067),* P.O. Box 11027, Springfield, MO 65808; 963 S. Delaware, Springfield, MO 65802 Tel 417-862-5520. Do not confuse with Thoth Publishing Co., West Hartford, CT.

Thought Wave Pr, *(Thought Wave Pr.; 0-922073),* P.O. Box 504, Hunt Valley, MD 21030 (SAN 251-1088); 71 Burkshire Rd., Baltimore, MD 21204 (SAN 251-1096) Tel 410-823-2123.

Three Continents, *(3 Continents Pr.; 0-89410; 0-914478),* P.O. Box 38009, Colorado Springs, CO 80937-8009 (SAN 212-0070) Tel 719-579-0977.

Three Cs Ent, *(Three C's Enterprises; 1-880121),* 4330 Barranca Pkwy., No. 101-353, Irvine, CA 92714; 61 Claret, Irvine, CA 92714 Tel 714-669-1339.

Three-D Zone, *(3-D Zone, The; 0-925300),* 333 N. Hobart Pl., Los Angeles, CA 90004 Tel 213-662-3831.

Three E GA, *(3-E Co., Inc.; 0-9623752),* Div. of Eads Co., Inc., 1775 Kimberly Dr., Marietta, GA 30060-4488 Tel 404-422-1361.

Three Elves Pr, *(Three Elves Pr.; 1-878070),* 350 Eighth Ave., Suite 8, Tierra Verde, FL 33715 Tel 813-867-3784.

Three Pines, *(Three Pines Pr.; 0-9635247),* 2104 Brenner St., Saginaw, MI 48602 Tel 517-792-4989.

Three Riv Ctr, *(3 Rivers Ctr.; 0-9615677),* 3327 W. Pryor Ave., Visalia, CA 93277 (SAN 696-1622) Tel 209-732-3759.

Three-Stones Pubns, *(3-Stones Pubns., Ltd.; 0-933673),* P.O. Box 69143, Seattle, WA 98168 (SAN 692-5421) Tel 206-431-0195; Orders to: P.O. Box 24831, Seattle, WA 98124 (SAN 244-8343) Tel 206-242-5174.

Thriftecon, *(Thriftecon Publications; 1-880258),* 405 Ascot Ct., Knoxville, TN 37923-5807 Tel 615-922-8411.

Thum Print
See Conley Outreach

Thumbprnt Pub, *(Thumbprint Publishing; 0-9637845),* 11563 Laurelcrest Dr., Studio City, CA 91604 (SAN 297-987X) Tel 818-509-8907.

Thundbird Ent, *(Thunderbird Enterprises; 1-881933),* 8821 N. First St., Phoenix, AZ 85020; Toll free: 800-833-7220.

Thunder & Ink, *(Thunder & Ink; 0-9623227),* P.O. Box 7014, Evanston, IL 60201; 2307 Central St., No. 2-South, Evanston, IL 60201 Tel 708-492-1823.

Thunder River, *(Thunder River Pr.; 0-9604274),* 0185 Ingersol Ln., Silt, CO 81652-9571 (SAN 214-4786) Tel 303-876-5400.

Thunderbird Bks, *(Thunderbird Bks.; 0-9622361),* 5358 E. Fairmount, Tucson, AZ 85712 Tel 602-327-1265.

Thy Word, *(Thy Word Creations; 1-879099),* Rte. 76, Box 28, Glenville, WV 26351 Tel 304-462-5589.

Ticknor & Fields, *(Ticknor & Fields; 0-395),* Affil. of Houghton Mifflin Co., 215 Park Ave., S., New York, NY 10003 (SAN 282-4043) Tel 212-420-5800; Toll free: 800-225-3362; Dist. by: Houghton Mifflin Co., Wayside Rd., Burlington, MA 01803 (SAN 215-3793) Tel 617-272-1500; Toll free: 800-225-3362.

Tidal Pr, *(Tidal Pr.; 0-930954),* P.O. Box 160, Cranberry Isles, ME 04625 (SAN 211-3783) Tel 207-244-3090; 129 Mount Vernon St., Boston, MA 02108 Tel 617-523-7995.

Tidewater, *(Tidewater Pubs.; 0-87033),* Div. of Cornell Maritime Pr., Inc., P.O. Box 456, Centreville, MD 21617 (SAN 202-0459) Tel 410-758-1075; Toll free: 800-638-7641.

Tiffany Pub, *(Tiffany Publishing Co.; 0-9616079),* 98 Puritan Ave., Worcester, MA 01604 (SAN 698-1321) Tel 508-756-1911.

Tiger Isld Pr, *(Tiger Island Pr.; 0-9631549),* 6867 Soledad Canyon Rd., Acton, CA 93510 Tel 805-268-0315.

Tigertail Ent, *(Tigertail Enterprises; 0-938921),* P.O. Box 1914, Santa Monica, CA 90402 (SAN 661-6690) Tel 805-683-2938.

Tilbury Hse, *(Tilbury Hse. Pubs.; 0-937966; 0-88448),* 132 Water St., Gardiner, ME 04345; Toll free: 800-582-1899 (orders); Dist. by: Consortium Bk. Sales & Distribution, 1045 Westgate Dr., Suite 90, Saint Paul, MN 55114-1065 (SAN 200-6049) Tel 612-221-9035; Toll free: 800-283-3572 (orders).

Timber, *(Timber Pr., Inc.; 0-917304; 0-88192; 0-931340; 0-931146),* The Haseltine Bldg., 133 SW Second Ave., Suite 450, Portland, OR 97204-3527 (SAN 216-082X) Tel 503-227-2878; Toll free: 800-327-5680.

Timberdoodle, *(Timberdoodle Pubns.; 0-9631017),* P.O. Box 105, Eagle Lake, FL 33839 Tel 607-659-4367.

Timberline Pr, *(Timberline Pr.; 0-9608284),* Box 70071, Eugene, OR 97401 (SAN 240-4559) Tel 503-345-1771. Do not confuse with companies with the same name in Fulton, MO, Media, PA.

Timbertrails *Imprint of* **Capstan Pubns**

Time Grow Co, *(Time to Grow Co.; 0-9623115),* 5174 Emerald Dr., Mound, MN 55364 Tel 612-472-6170.

Time-Life, *(Time-Life, Inc.; 0-8094; 0-7835),* A Time Warner Co., 777 Duke St., Alexandria, VA 22314 (SAN 202-7836) Tel 703-838-7000; Toll free: 800-621-7026; 4200 N. Industrial Blvd., Indianapolis, IN 46254 (SAN 658-1951); Orders to: P.O. Box 2649, Columbus, OH 43216 (SAN 204-5982); Dist. by: Centennial Pr., P.O. Box 82087, Lincoln, NE 68501 (SAN 630-7426); Toll free: 800-356-5016.

Time Line Prods, *(Time Line Productions, Inc.; 0-9638000),* P.O. Box 251, Excelsior, MN 55331; 19430 Muirfield Cir., Shorewood, MN 55331 Tel 612-474-1000.

Time Warner Libraries, *(Time Warner Libraries; 1-879329),* Div. of Time Warner Direct, 1271 Avenue of the Americas, New York, NY 10020 Tel 212-522-4841; Dist. by: Time-Life Bks., 777 Duke St., Alexandria, VA 22314 (SAN 202-7836) Tel 703-838-7000; Toll free: 800-621-7026.

Timeless Sales, *(Timeless Tales; 0-9624183),* 4147 Sugarloaf Rd., Boulder, CO 80302-9233.

Times Bks *Imprint of* **Random**

Times to Treas, *(Times to Treasure; 1-880444),* 19854 Dina Pl., Chatsworth, CA 91311-1804.

Tin Man Pr, *(Tin Man Pr.; 0-936110),* Box 219, Stanwood, WA 98292 (SAN 222-0156) Tel 206-387-0459.

Tintern Abbey, *(Tintern Abbey Pr.; 1-879956),* P.O. Box 81440, Cleveland, OH 44181; 57 Hamilton St., Berea, OH 44017 Tel 216-734-9180.

Tiny Tales, *(Tiny Tales; 0-9627661),* P.O. Box 12212, Wilmington, DE 19850.

Tiny Thought, *(Tiny Thought Pr.; 0-925928),* 1427 S. Jackson St., Louisville, KY 40217 Tel 502-637-6870; Toll free: 800-456-3208.

Tinys Self Help Bks, *(Tiny's Self Help Bks. for Children; 0-9616549),* 174 Main St., Apt. 401W, Bangor, ME 04401 (SAN 659-5421) Tel 207-947-2239; Orders to: Mr. Paperback Bk. Stores, 133 Hammond St., Bangor, ME 04401 (SAN 662-4294) Tel 207-942-8237; Dist. by: Magazines, Inc., 1135 Hammond St., Bangor, ME 04401 (SAN 169-3034) Tel 207-942-8237; Toll free: 800-432-7993 (Maine only).

Tioga Pub Co, *(Tioga Publishing Co.; 0-935382),* P.O. Box 6677, Tahoe City, CA 96145 (SAN 669-280X) Tel 916-581-3445; Toll free: 800-655-6557; Dist. by: Bookpeople, 7900 Edgewater Dr., Oakland, CA 94621 (SAN 168-9517) Tel 510-632-4700; Toll free: 800-999-4650; Dist. by: Ingram Bk. Co., 1 Ingram Blvd., La Vergne, TN 37086-1986 (SAN 169-7978) Tel 615-793-5000; Toll free: 800-937-8000 (orders only, all warehouses); Dist. by: Sunbelt Pubns., 8630 Argent St., Suite C, Santee, CA 92071-4172 (SAN 630-0790) Tel 619-258-4911; Toll free: 800-626-6579; Dist. by: Baker & Taylor Bks., Somerville Service Ctr., 50 Kirby Ave., Somerville, NJ 08876-0734 (SAN 169-4901) Tel 908-722-8000; Toll free: 800-775-1500 (customer service); Dist. by: Baker & Taylor Bks., Momence Service Ctr., 501 S. Gladiolus St., Momence, IL 60954-2444 (SAN 169-2100) Tel 815-472-2444; Toll free: 800-775-2300 (customer service); Dist. by: Baker & Taylor Bks., Commerce Service Ctr., 251 Mt. Olive Church Rd., Commerce, GA 30599-9988 (SAN 169-1503) Tel 706-335-5000; Toll free: 800-775-1200 (customer service); Dist. by: Baker & Taylor Bks., Reno Service Ctr., 380 Edison Way, Reno, NV 89564 (SAN 169-4464) Tel 702-858-6700; Toll free: 800-775-1700 (customer service).

Tipi Pr, *(Tipi Pr.; 1-877976),* Saint Joseph's Indian School, Chamberlain, SD 57326 Tel 605-734-3300.

TK Pubs, *(T. K. Pubs.; 0-9614023),* P.O. Box 560968, Rockledge, FL 32956-0968 (SAN 683-6232) Tel 407-636-1952. Do not confuse with T & K Publishing in Nashville, TN.

TLC Bks, *(TLC Bks.; 0-9617081),* 416 N. Byrkit St., Mishawaka, IN 46544-2602 (SAN 662-6173) Tel 219-259-1775.

TLT, *(TLT Pubns.; 0-943314),* 415 Lincoln Way E., Mishawaka, IN 46544 (SAN 240-7841) Tel 219-259-9976.

TN Valley Pub, *(Tennessee Valley Publishing; 1-882194),* 5320 Yosemite Trail, Box 52527, Knoxville, TN 37909 Tel 615-584-5235; Toll free: 800-762-7079.

TNT Bks, *(TNT Bks.; 1-885227),* P.O. Box 1334, West Valley City, UT 84120; 3657 S. Cree Dr., No. 5020W, West Valley City, UT 84120 Tel 801-964-2495.

Toad Hse Bks, *(Toad Hse. Bks.; 1-878467),* 1703 Victor Ave., Redding, CA 96003-4027.

Toadwood Pubs, *(Toadwood Pubs.; 0-9610878),* 5400 Melon Ln., Edwardsville, IL 62025 (SAN 282-5775); 5400 Melon Ln., Edwardsville, IL 62025 Tel 618-656-0531; Dist. by: Shar Products, Inc., P.O. Box 1411, Ann Arbor, MI 48106 (SAN 251-1673) Tel 313-665-7711; Toll free: 800-248-7427.

Tokuma Pub, *(Tokuma Publishing; 4-19),* Div. of Tokuma Shoten (Tokyo, Japan), 10900 NE Fourth, Suite 1150, Bellevue, WA 98004 Tel 206-646-8340; Dist. by: Publisher Resources, Inc., 1224 Heil Quaker Blvd., P.O. Box 7001, La Vergne, TN 37086-7001 (SAN 630-5431) Tel 615-793-5090; Toll free: 800-937-5557.

Tomac Pubng, *(Tomac Publishing; 0-9638747),* P.O. Box 247, Old Greenwich, CT 06870; 20 Ann St., Old Greenwich, CT 06870 Tel 203-637-0341.

Tomato Enter, *(Tomato Enterprises; 0-9617357),* P.O. Box 2805, Fairfield, CA 94533 (SAN 664-0427) Tel 707-426-3970.

Tonnis, *(Tonnis Productions, Inc.; 0-917057),* P.O. Box 311, Harleysville, PA 19438 (SAN 655-1319) Tel 215-256-9633.

Top Mtn Pub, *(Top of the Mountain Publishing; 0-914295; 1-56087),* P.O. Box 2244, Pinellas Park, FL 34665-2244 (SAN 287-590X) Tel 813-530-0110; Dist. by: Quality Bks., Inc., 918 Sherwood Dr., Lake Bluff, IL 60044-2204 (SAN 169-2127) Tel 708-295-2010; Toll free: 800-323-4241 (libraries only); Dist. by: New Leaf Distributing Co., 5425 Tulane Dr., SW, Atlanta, GA 30336-2323 (SAN 169-1449) Tel 404-691-6996; Toll free: 800-326-2665; Dist. by: Baker & Taylor Bks., Commerce Service Ctr., 251 Mt. Olive Church Rd., Commerce, GA 30599-9988 (SAN 169-1503) Tel 706-335-5000; Toll free: 800-775-1200 (customer service); Dist. by: The Distributors, 702 S. Michigan, South Bend, IN 46601 (SAN 169-2488) Tel 219-232-8500; Toll free: 800-348-5200 (except Indiana); Dist. by: Unique Bks., Inc., 4230 Grove Ave., Gurnee, IL 60031 (SAN 630-0472) Tel 708-623-9171; Dist. by: Ingram Bk. Co., 1 Ingram Blvd., La Vergne, TN 37086-1986 (SAN 169-7978) Tel 615-793-5000; Toll free: 800-937-8000 (orders only, all warehouses); Dist. by: Brodart Co., 500 Arch St., Williamsport, PA 17705 (SAN 169-7684) Tel 717-326-2461; Toll free: 800-233-8467; Dist. by: Pacific Pipeline, Inc., 8030 S. 228th St., Kent, WA 98032-2900 (SAN 208-2128) Tel 206-872-5523; Toll free: 800-444-7323 (Customer Service); 800-677-2222 (orders); Dist. by: Upper Access, Inc., P.O. Box 457, 1 Upper Access Rd., Hinesburg, VT 05461 (SAN 667-1195) Tel 802-482-2988; Dist. by: Emery-Pratt Co., 1966 W. Main St., Owosso, MI 48867-1372 (SAN 170-1401) Tel 517-723-5291; Toll free: 800-762-5683 (Library orders only); 800-248-3887 (Customer service only).

Topgallant, *(Topgallant Publishing Co., Ltd.; 0-914916),* 3180 Pacific Heights Rd., Honolulu, HI 96813 (SAN 209-4932) Tel 808-531-7985.

Tops Learning, *(Tops Learning Systems; 0-941008),* 10970 S. Mulino Rd., Canby, OR 97013 (SAN 217-4456) Tel 503-266-8550.

Tor Bks, *(Tor Bks.; 0-8125),* Div. of Tom Doherty Assocs., Inc., 175 Fifth Ave., New York, NY 10010 (SAN 239-3956) Tel 212-388-0100; Dist. by: St. Martin's Pr., Inc., 175 Fifth Ave., Rm. 1715, New York, NY 10010 (SAN 200-2132) Tel 212-674-5151; Toll free: 800-221-7945; Dist. by: Hearst Corp., International Circulation Distributors/ICB Bks., 250 W. 55th St., 12th Flr., New York, NY 10019 (SAN 169-5800) Tel 212-649-4474; Toll free: 800-223-0288.

Torah Aura, *(Torah Aura Productions; 0-933873),* 4423 Fruitland Ave., Los Angeles, CA 90058 (SAN 692-7025) Tel 213-585-7312; Toll free: 800-238-6724.

Torah Umesorah, *(Torah Umesorah Pubns.; 0-914131; 1-878895),* 5723 18th Ave., Brooklyn, NY 11204 (SAN 218-9992) Tel 718-259-1223.

Torrence Pubns, *(Torrence Pubns.; 0-914281),* P.O. Box 2715, Santa Barbara, CA 93120 (SAN 287-5667) Tel 805-682-6821; Dist. by: Sunbelt Pubns., 8630 Argent St., Suite C, Santee, CA 92071-4172 (SAN 630-0790) Tel 619-258-4911; Toll free: 800-626-6579; Dist. by: L-S Distributors, 130 E. Grand Ave., South San Francisco, CA 94280 (SAN 169-0213) Tel 415-873-2094; Toll free: 800-654-7040 (orders only); Dist. by: E Z Nature Bks., P.O. Box 4206, San Luis Obispo, CA 93403-4206 (SAN 200-9846) Tel 805-595-7346.

Tory Corner Editions, *(Tory Corner Editions; 1-878452),* P.O. Box 8100, Glen Ridge, NJ 07028 Tel 201-669-8367.

Total Lrn, *(Total Learning Commitment; 0-9617737),* P.O. Box 7341, Bradenton, FL 34210-0541 (SAN 664-7855) Tel 813-792-5839.

Totally Unique, *(Totally Unique Thoughts; 0-9642168),* Div. of Tut Enterprises, 1713 Acme St., Orlando, FL 32805-3603 Tel 407-246-7040; Toll free: 800-932-7888.

Tott Pubns, *(Tott Pubns.; 1-882225),* 1546 Parkview Rd., Mechanicsburg, OH 43044 Tel 513-834-2032.

TotTales, *(TotTales; 0-9642307),* P.O. Box 1219, Littleton, CO 80120; 5753 S. Prince St., Littleton, CO 80120 Tel 303-797-8722.

Toucan Valley, *(Toucan Valley Pubns., Inc.; 0-9634017; 1-884925),* 142 N. Milpitas Blvd., Suite 260, Milpitas, CA 95035 Tel 408-956-9492.

Touch & See Educ, *(Touch & See Educational Resources; 1-879218),* P.O. Box 794, 2921 Via La Selva, Palos Verdes Estates, CA 90274 Tel 310-375-0016.

Touch The Sky, *(Touch The Sky Productions; 0-9633769),* 668 W. Washington Ave., Suite 102, Madison, WI 53703 Tel 608-274-6012; Toll free: 800-733-1986.

Tourmaline Pub, *(Tourmaline Publishing; 0-941099),* 1056 Vassar Dr., Napa, CA 94558 (SAN 665-0937) Tel 707-224-5969.

Tower Hill Pr, *(Tower Hill Pr.; 0-941668),* P.O. Box 1132, Doylestown, PA 18901 (SAN 239-3298); 4030G Skyron Dr., Doylestown, PA 18901 Tel 215-345-1338.

Townhouse Pub, *(Townhouse Publishing; 0-939219),* P.O. Box 7512, Princeton, NJ 08543-7512 (SAN 662-6254) Tel 609-585-5539. Do not confuse with Townhouse Publishing Corp. in Orlando, FL.

Townsnd-Pr, *(Townsend Pr. - Sunday Schl. Publishing Board; 0-910683),* 330 Charlotte Ave., Nashville, TN 37201-1188 (SAN 275-8598) Tel 615-256-2480.

Toy Works Pr, *(Toy Works Pr.; 0-938715),* Div. of Toy Works, 902 Broadway, Penthouse, New York, NY 10010 (SAN 661-6216) Tel 212-982-2269.

Toys 'n Things
See Redleaf Pr

TP Assocs, *(TP Assocs./TP Pr.; 0-913939),* P.O. Box 3226, Newport Beach, CA 92663 (SAN 286-8962); 22181 Wood Island Ln., Huntington Beach, CA 92646 (SAN 286-8970) Tel 714-963-4482.

TQS Pubns, *(TQS Pubns., Eclectic Chicano Literature; 0-88412; 0-89229),* Div. of Tonatiuh/Quinto Sol International, Inc., P.O. Box 9275, Berkeley, CA 94709 (SAN 203-3984) Tel 510-655-8036; Dist. by: Gannon Distributing Co., 2887 Cooks Rd., Santa Fe, NM 87501 (SAN 201-5889) Tel 505-438-3430; Toll free: 800-442-2044; Dist. by: Baker & Taylor Bks., Somerville Service Ctr., 50 Kirby Ave., Somerville, NJ 08876-0734 (SAN 169-4901) Tel 908-722-8000; Toll free: 800-775-1500 (customer service); Dist. by: Baker & Taylor Bks., Reno Service Ctr., 380 Edison Way, Reno, NV 89564 (SAN 169-4464) Tel 702-858-6700; Toll free: 800-775-1700 (customer service); Dist. by: Baker & Taylor Bks., Momence Service Ctr., 501 S. Gladiolus St., Momence, IL 60954-2444 (SAN 169-2100) Tel 815-472-2444; Toll free: 800-775-2300 (customer service); Dist. by: Baker & Taylor Bks., Commerce Service Ctr., 251 Mt. Olive Church Rd., Commerce, GA 30599-9988 (SAN 169-1503) Tel 706-335-5000; Toll free: 800-775-1200 (customer service); Dist. by: Ingram Bk. Co., 1 Ingram Blvd., La Vergne, TN 37086-1986 (SAN 169-7978) Tel 615-793-5000; Toll free: 800-937-8000 (orders only, all warehouses); Dist. by: Bookpeople, 7900 Edgewater Dr., Oakland, CA 94621 (SAN 168-9517) Tel 510-632-4700; Toll free: 800-999-4650.

Tracey Smith, *(Smith, Tracey; 1-880825),* 1455 W. Mohawk Ln., Phoenix, AZ 85027 Tel 602-582-8129.

Tradery Hse, *(Tradery Hse.; 1-879958),* Div. of The Wimmer Companies, 4210 B.F. Goodrich Blvd., Memphis, TN 38118 (SAN 297-5076) Tel 901-362-8900; Toll free: 800-727-1034; Dist. by: Wimmer Bk. Distribution, 4210 B. F. Goodrich Blvd., Memphis, TN 38118 (SAN 209-6544) Tel 901-362-8900; Toll free: 800-727-1034.

Traditions Pr, *(Traditions Pr.; 0-937745),* P.O. Box 1296, Lexington, SC 29072 (SAN 659-364X); 112 Beck-Taylor Pl., Lexington, SC 29073 (SAN 659-3658) Tel 803-359-0045.

Trafalgar, *(Trafalgar Square; 0-943955; 1-57076),* P.O. Box 257, North Pomfret, VT 05053 (SAN 213-8859); Toll free: 800-423-4525; Howe Hill Rd., North Pomfret, VT 05053 Tel 802-457-1911.

Trafalgar Sq
See Trafalgar

Trail of Success, *(Trail of Success Pubs.; 0-9632895),* 10803 Old Field Dr., Reston, VA 22091 Tel 703-758-2519.

Trailblazer Bks, *(Trailblazer Bks.; 0-9626025),* 13030 Cannon City Blvd., Northfield, MN 55057 Tel 507-645-4242.

Trails West Pub, *(Trails West Publishing; 0-939729),* P.O. Box 8619, Santa Fe, NM 87504-8619 (SAN 663-7809) Tel 505-982-8058.

Trans-Atl Phila, *(Trans-Atlantic Pubns., Inc.),* 311 Bainbridge St., Philadelphia, PA 19147 (SAN 694-0234) Tel 215-925-5083. Do not confuse with Transatlantic Arts, Inc., Albuquerque, NM.

Transaction Pubs, *(Transaction Pubs.; 0-87855; 0-88738; 1-56000),* Rutgers Univ., New Brunswick, NJ 08903 (SAN 202-7941) Tel 908-932-2280.

Transatl Arts, *(Transatlantic Arts, Inc.; 0-693),* P.O. Box 6086, Albuquerque, NM 87197 (SAN 202-7968) Tel 505-898-2289. Do not confuse with Trans-Atlantic Pubns., Inc., Philadelphia, PA.

Transform Inc, *(Transformations, Inc.; 0-9604856),* 2728 N. Prospect Ave., Milwaukee, WI 53211 (SAN 215-8906) Tel 414-962-0213; Orders to: 4200 W. Good Hope Rd., Milwaukee, WI 53209 (SAN 662-085X) Tel 414-351-5770.

Transitions, *(Transitions),* P.O. Box 478, Peoria, AZ 85345 (SAN 287-282X) Tel 602-972-7504.

Travis Ilse, *(Travis Ilse Pubs.; 1-882092),* P.O. Box 583, Niwot, CO 80544 Tel 303-652-3926.

Treadle Pr, *(Treadle Pr.; 0-935143),* Div. of Binding & Printing Co., Box D, Sheperdstown, WV 25443 (SAN 695-2070) Tel 304-876-2557.

Treas Chest Ent, *(Treasure Chest Enterprises, Inc.;* 0-939161), 1710 Carrie Hills Ln., La Habra Heights, CA 90631 (SAN 662-9385) Tel 310-694-4486; 16914 Harvard Blvd., Gardena, CA 90247 (SAN 242-133X) Tel 213-324-1448.

Treas Values, *(Treasured Values, Joy, Inc.; 0-9642092),* P.O. Box 323, 141 Letts Ave., Sunbury, OH 43074 Tel 614-965-2046; Toll free: 800-294-7873.

Treasure Chest, *(Treasure Chest Pubns.; 0-918080),* 1802 W. Grant Rd., Suite 101, Tucson, AZ 85745 (SAN 209-3243) Tel 602-623-9558; Toll free: 800-969-9558; Orders to: P.O. Box 5250, Tucson, AZ 85703 (SAN 209-3251).

Tree by River, *(Tree by the River Publishing/Music Business Bks.; 0-935174),* P.O. Box 935, Dayton, NV 89403 (SAN 213-389X) Tel 702-246-7215; Toll free: 800-487-6610 (orders only); Dist. by: Baker & Taylor Bks., Somerville Service Ctr., 50 Kirby Ave., Somerville, NJ 08876-0734 (SAN 169-4901) Tel 908-722-8000; Toll free: 800-775-1500 (customer service); Dist. by: Baker & Taylor Bks., Momence Service Ctr., 501 S. Gladiolus St., Momence, IL 60954-2444 (SAN 169-2100) Tel 815-472-2444; Toll free: 800-775-2300 (customer service); Dist. by: Baker & Taylor Bks., Commerce Service Ctr., 251 Mt. Olive Church Rd., Commerce, GA 30599-9988 (SAN 169-1503) Tel 706-335-5000; Toll free: 800-775-1200 (customer service); Dist. by: Baker & Taylor Bks., Reno Service Ctr., 380 Edison Way, Reno, NV 89564 (SAN 169-4464) Tel 702-858-6700; Toll free: 800-775-1700 (customer service); Dist. by: Quality Bks., Inc., 918 Sherwood Dr., Lake Bluff, IL 60044-2204 (SAN 169-2127) Tel 708-295-2010; Toll free: 800-323-4241 (libraries only).

Tree City Pr, *(Tree City Pr.; 0-9619365),* 7633 Gillcrest Rd., Sylvania, OH 43560 (SAN 243-9182) Tel 419-882-4862.

Tree House Pr, *(Tree Hse. Pr., Inc.; 1-881490),* 3101 Audubon Trace, Jefferson, LA 70121-1565; Toll free: 800-788-8663. Do not confuse with Tree House Pr. in Shelter Island Heights, NY.

Tree Life Pubns, *(Tree of Life Pubns.; 0-930852),* 6200 Juniper Rd., P.O. Box 126, Joshua Tree, CA 92252 (SAN 222-5395) Tel 619-366-3695; Toll free: 800-247-6553 (retail orders only); Dist. by: Atrium Pubs. Group, 11270 Clayton Creek Rd., Lower Lake, CA 95457 (SAN 200-5743) Tel 707-995-3906; Toll free: 800-275-2606; Dist. by: Nutri-Bks. Corp., P.O. Box 5793, Denver, CO 80217 (SAN 169-054X) Tel 303-778-8383; Toll free: 800-279-2048 (orders only); Dist. by: Awareness & Health, Unltd., 3509 N. High St., Columbus, OH 43214 (SAN 200-6537) Tel 614-262-7087; Toll free: 800-533-7087 (orders only); Dist. by: Summit Beacon International, 710 E. Gallatin, Livingston, MT 59047 Tel 406-222-8307.

Treehaus Comns, *(Treehaus Communications, Inc.;* 0-929496), P.O. Box 249, Loveland, OH 45140 (SAN 249-5325); Toll free: 800-638-4287; 906 W. Loveland Ave., Loveland, OH 45140 (SAN 249-5333) Tel 513-683-5716.

Treehouse, *(Treehouse Enterprises; 0-935571),* 810 Saturn St., No. 16, Jupiter, FL 33477-4456 (SAN 696-2025) Tel 407-575-0547; Dist. by: New Leaf Distributing Co., 5425 Tulane Dr., SW, Atlanta, GA 30336-2323 (SAN 169-1449) Tel 404-691-6996; Toll free: 800-326-2665. Do not confuse with Tree House Pr., Shelter Island, NY or Treehouse Pr., Chagrin Falls, OH.

Trees Co Pr, *(Trees Co. Pr.; 0-937401),* 49 Van Buren Way, San Francisco, CA 94131 (SAN 659-0659) Tel 415-334-8352.

Trellis Bks Inc, *(Trellis Bks., Inc.; 1-878236),* 3705 Timberline, Canandaigua, NY 14424 Tel 716-396-3141; Toll free: 800-344-0559; Dist. by: Fahy-Williams Publishing, Inc., P.O. Box 1080, 171 Reed St., Geneva, NY 14456 (SAN 630-3889) Tel 315-789-4263.

Tremaine Graph & Pub, *(Tremaine Graphic & Publishing; 0-939860),* 2727 Front St., Klamath Falls, OR 97601 (SAN 216-9398) Tel 503-884-4193.

TRI Pubns, *(TRI Pubns.; 0-943693),* Div. of TRI, P.O. Box 89338, Honolulu, HI 96830-9338 (SAN 668-6818); 330 Saratoga, Honolulu, HI 96815 (SAN 668-6826) Tel 808-734-5047.

Trickle Creek, *(Trickle Creek Bks.; 0-9640742),* 500 Andersontown Rd., Mechanicsburg, PA 17055 Tel 717-766-2638; Toll free: 800-353-2791.

Tricycle Pr, *(Tricycle Pr.; 1-883672),* Div. of Ten Speed Pr., P.O. Box 7123, Berkeley, CA 94707; Toll free: 800-841-2665; 900 Modoc, Berkeley, CA 94707 Tel 510-559-1600; Dist. by: Ten Speed Pr., P.O. Box 7123, Berkeley, CA 94707 (SAN 202-7674) Tel 510-559-1600; Toll free: 800-841-2665.

Trillium Pr, *(Trillium Pr.; 0-89824),* First Ave., Unionville, NY 10988 (SAN 212-4637) Tel 914-726-4444. Do not confuse with Trillium Pr. in Saint Albans, WV.

Trinas Pr, *(Dr. Trina's Pr.; 0-9615840),* P.O. Box 4777, Laguna Beach, CA 92651 (SAN 697-0109) Tel 714-497-5071.

Trinehrt Pubs, *(Trineheart Pubs.; 0-9636399),* P.O. Box 600, Palm Springs, CA 92263 Tel 619-320-2688; Toll free: 800-898-7884; Dist. by: Bookpeople, 7900 Edgewater Dr., Oakland, CA 94621 (SAN 168-9517) Tel 510-632-4700; Toll free: 800-999-4650; Dist. by: Baker & Taylor Bks., Reno Service Ctr., 380 Edison Way, Reno, NV 89564 (SAN 169-4464) Tel 702-858-6700; Toll free: 800-775-1700 (customer service).

Triton Enter, *(Triton Enterprises; 0-9639527),* 5513 Woodhurst Ln., San Jose, CA 95123 Tel 408-226-2509.

Triumph Books *Imprint of* **Liguori Pubns**

Triumph Pub, *(Triumph Publishing Co.; 0-917182),* P.O. Box 292, Altadena, CA 91001 (SAN 207-3927).

Troll Assocs, *(Troll Assocs.; 0-89375; 0-8167),* Subs. of Educational Reading Services, 100 Corporate Dr., Mahwah, NJ 07430 (SAN 169-4758) Tel 201-529-4000; Toll free: 800-526-5289. *Imprints:* Little Rainbow (Little Rainbow); Rainbow NJ (Rainbow Bridge); WestWind (WestWind); Whistlstop (Whistlestop).

Trolley Car, *(Trolley Car Bks.; 1-883787),* 17 Wiltshire St., Bronxville, NY 10708 (SAN 297-9586) Tel 914-779-6316; Dist. by: Baker & Taylor Bks., Somerville Service Ctr., 50 Kirby Ave., Somerville, NJ 08876-0734 (SAN 169-4901) Tel 908-722-8000; Toll free: 800-775-1500 (customer service); Dist. by: Baker & Taylor Bks., Momence Service Ctr., 501 S. Gladiolus St., Momence, IL 60954-2444 (SAN 169-2100) Tel 815-472-2444; Toll free: 800-775-2300 (customer service); Dist. by: Baker & Taylor Bks., Commerce Service Ctr., 251 Mt. Olive Church Rd., Commerce, GA 30599-9988 (SAN 169-1503) Tel 706-335-5000; Toll free: 800-775-1200 (customer service); Dist. by: Baker & Taylor Bks., Reno Service Ctr., 380 Edison Way, Reno, NV 89564 (SAN 169-4464) Tel 702-858-6700; Toll free: 800-775-1700 (customer service); Dist. by: Bookpeople, 7900 Edgewater Dr., Oakland, CA 94621 (SAN 168-9517) Tel 510-632-4700; Toll free: 800-999-4650; Dist. by: Independent Pubs. Marketing, 6824 Oaklawn Ave., Edina, MN 55435 (SAN 630-5725) Tel 612-920-9044; Dist. by: The Distributors, 702 S. Michigan, South Bend, IN 46601 (SAN 169-2488) Tel 219-232-8500; Toll free: 800-348-5200 (except Indiana); Dist. by: Educational Bk. Distributors, P.O. Box 2510, Novato, CA 94948 (SAN 158-2259) Tel 415-883-3530.

Trophy *Imprint of* **HarpC Child Bks**

Trotwood Press, *(Trotwood Pr.; 0-9627061),* P.O. Box 45, Nevada City, CA 95959-0045 Tel 916-265-9681.

Troubador *Imprint of* **Price Stern**

Trout Creek, *(Trout Creek Pr.; 0-916155),* 5976 Billings Rd., Parkdale, OR 97041-9610 (SAN 294-9881) Tel 503-352-6494.

True Heitz, *(Tru Heitz-Thelma Yes Pr.),* 1400 McAndrew Rd., Ojai, CA 93023 (SAN 262-1029).

True Tales, *(True Tales - History for Children;* 1-882684), 13077 Trail Dust Ave., San Diego, CA 92129 Tel 619-538-2575.

Trust Hidden Villa, *(Trust for Hidden Villa, The),* 26870 Moody Rd., Los Altos Hills, CA 94022 (SAN 661-4566) Tel 415-948-4690.

Trvl Pubs Intl, *(Travel Pubs. International; 0-9625468),* P.O. Box 1030, Fairfax, CA 94930; 15 Rockridge Rd., Fairfax, CA 94930 Tel 415-454-0876.

TSG Ent Pubns
See TSG Pub Found

TSG Pub Found, *(T.S.G. Publishing Foundation;* 0-929874), 28641 N. 63rd Pl., Cave Creek, AZ 85331 (SAN 250-6718) Tel 602-502-1909.

TSM Books, *(TSM Bks., Inc.; 0-941316),* 535 Broad Hollow Rd., Suite A-11, Melville, NY 11747 (SAN 239-040X) Tel 516-420-0961.

TSR Inc, *(TSR, Inc.; 0-935696; 0-88038; 1-56076;* 0-7869), P.O. Box 756, Lake Geneva, WI 53147 (SAN 222-0091); 201 Sheridan Springs, Lake Geneva, WI 53147 Tel 414-248-3625; Dist. by: Random Hse., Inc., 400 Hahn Rd., Westminster, MD 21157 (SAN 202-5515) Tel 410-848-1900; Toll free: 800-733-3000 (orders); Toll free: 800-492-0782 (in Maryland).

Tudor Pubs, *(Tudor Pubs., Inc.; 0-936389),* 3109 Shady Lawn Dr., Greensboro, NC 27408 (SAN 697-3035); 3007 Taliaferro Rd., Greensboro, NC 27408 (SAN 697-3043) Tel 910-282-5907.

Tues Child, *(Tuesday's Child Publishing; 1-881134),* P.O. Box 305, Somers, NY 10589; 619B Heritage Hills, Somers, NY 10589 Tel 914-277-7144.

Tuffy *Imprint of* **Putnam Pub Group**

Tug Pr CA, *(Tug Pr.; 0-9634767),* P.O. Box 15188, Newport Beach, CA 92659; 12 Westport, Irvine, CA 92720 Tel 714-551-9591.

Tumbleweed Pub Co, *(Tumbleweed Publishing Co.;* 0-9612160), 3112 Van Ave., Eugene, OR 97401 (SAN 289-5102) Tel 503-345-7770.

Tundra Bks, *(Tundra Bks. of Northern New York; 0-912766; 0-88776),* Affil. of Tundra Bks. (Canada), P.O. Box 1030, Plattsburgh, NY 12901 (SAN 202-8085) Tel 514-932-5434; Dist. by: Univ. of Toronto Pr., 340 Nagel Dr., Buffalo, NY 14225 (SAN 214-2651) Tel 716-683-4547; Dist. by: Bookmen, Inc., 525 N. Third St., Minneapolis, MN 55401 (SAN 169-409X) Tel 612-341-3333; Toll free: 800-328-8411 (customer service); Dist. by: Baker & Taylor Bks., Commerce Service Ctr., 251 Mt. Olive Church Rd., Commerce, GA 30599-9988 (SAN 169-1503) Tel 706-335-5000; Toll free: 800-775-1200 (customer service); Dist. by: Baker & Taylor Bks., Reno Service Ctr., 380 Edison Way, Reno, NV 89564 (SAN 169-4464) Tel 702-858-6700; Toll free: 800-775-1700 (customer service); Dist. by: Ingram Bk. Co., 1 Ingram Blvd., La Vergne, TN 37086-1986 (SAN 169-7978) Tel 615-793-5000; Toll free: 800-937-8000 (orders only, all warehouses); Dist. by: Borders, Inc., 5451 S. State St., Ann Arbor, MI 48108 (SAN 169-3662) Tel 313-995-7262; Dist. by: Brodart Co., 500 Arch St., Williamsport, PA 17705 (SAN 169-7684) Tel 717-326-2461; Toll free: 800-233-8467; Dist. by: Baker & Taylor Bks., Somerville Service Ctr., 50 Kirby Ave., Somerville, NJ 08876-0734 (SAN 169-4901) Tel 908-722-8000; Toll free: 800-775-1500 (customer service); Dist. by: Baker & Taylor Bks., Momence Service Ctr., 501 S. Gladiolus St., Momence, IL 60954-2444 (SAN 169-2100) Tel 815-472-2444; Toll free: 800-775-2300 (customer service); Dist. by: Pacific Pipeline, Inc., 8030 S. 228th St., Kent, WA 98032-2900 (SAN 208-2128) Tel 206-872-5523; Toll free: 800-444-7323 (Customer Service); 800-677-2222 (orders).

Tundra MA, *(Tundra Publishing, Ltd.; 1-879450;* 1-56862), 320 Riverside Dr., Northampton, MA 01060 Tel 413-586-9525.

Tupelo Bks *Imprint of* **Morrow**

Turman Pub, *(Turman Publishing Co.; 0-89872),* 1319 Dexter Ave., N., Suite 30, Seattle, WA 98109 (SAN 222-4372) Tel 206-282-6900.

Turn the Page, *(Turn-the-Page Pr., Inc.; 0-931793),* 203 Baldwin Ave., Roseville, CA 95678 (SAN 281-3629) Tel 916-444-7933.

Turner Pub GA, *(Turner Publishing, Inc.; 1-878685;* 1-57036), Subs. of Turner Broadcasting System, Inc., 1050 Techwood Dr., NW, Atlanta, GA 30318 Tel 404-885-4038; Dist. by: Andrews & McMeel, 4900 Main St., Kansas City, MO 64112 (SAN 202-540X) Tel 816-932-6700; Toll free: 800-826-4216. Do not confuse with companies with the same name in Paducah, KY, Eastchester, NY. *Imprints:* Bedrock Press (Bedrock Press).

Turner Pub KY, *(Turner Publishing Co.; 0-938021;* 1-56311), P.O. Box 3101, Paducah, KY 42002-3101 (SAN 659-803X); 412 Broadway, Paducah, KY 42002 Tel 502-443-0121. Do not confuse with companies with the same name in Atlanta, GA, Eastchester, NY.

Turtle Gal Edit, *(Turtle Gallery Editions; 0-9626935),* 49 Morning St., Portland, ME 04101 Tel 207-774-0621.

Turtle Prints, *(Turtle Prints; 0-9622052),* P.O. Box 273, Nevada City, CA 95959; 17750 Rock Creek Rd., Nevada City, CA 95959 Tel 916-265-6586.

Tusky Enterprises, *(Tusky Enterprises; 1-879100),* 1733 Hutchinson Ln., Silver Spring, MD 20906 Tel 301-942-1904.

Tutorial Press, *(Tutorial Pr., Inc., The; 0-912329),* P.O. Box 11123, Albuquerque, NM 87192 (SAN 265-1467) Tel 505-296-8636.

Twayne *Imprint of* **Macmillan**

Twenty-Third, *(23rd Pubns.; 0-89622),* P.O. Box 180, Mystic, CT 06355 (SAN 210-9204); Toll free: 800-321-0411; 185 Willow St., Mystic, CT 06355 (SAN 658-2052) Tel 203-536-2611.

Twin Sisters, *(Twin Sisters Productions, Inc.; 0-9632249; 1-882331),* 1340 Home Ave., Suite D, Akron, OH 44310-2570 Tel 216-633-8900; Toll free: 800-248-8946; Dist. by: Silo Music Distribution, Inc., S. Main St., P.O. Box 429, Waterbury, VT 05676 (SAN 630-7876); Toll free: 800-342-0295; Dist. by: Ingram Bk. Co., 1 Ingram Blvd., La Vergne, TN 37086-1986 (SAN 169-7978) Tel 615-793-5000; Dist. by: Baker & Taylor Bks., Somerville Service Ctr., 50 Kirby Ave., Somerville, NJ 08876-0734 (SAN 169-4901) Tel 908-722-8000; Toll free: 800-775-1500 (customer service); Dist. by: Baker & Taylor Bks., Momence Service Ctr., 501 S. Gladiolus St., Momence, IL 60954-1799 (SAN 169-2100) Tel 815-472-2444; Toll free: 800-775-2300 (customer service); Dist. by: Baker & Taylor Bks., Commerce Service Ctr., 251 Mt. Olive Church Rd., Commerce, GA 30599-9988 (SAN 169-1503) Tel 706-335-5000; Toll free: 800-775-1200 (customer service); Dist. by: Baker & Taylor Bks., Reno Service Ctr., 380 Edison Way, Reno, NV 89564-0099 (SAN 169-4464) Tel 702-858-6700; Toll free: 800-775-1700 (customer service); Dist. by: Baker & Taylor Bks., Franklin Service Ctr., 2 Cottontail Ln., Somerset, NJ 08873-1133 (SAN 630-7205) Tel 908-469-7404; Dist. by: Publishers Distribution Service, 6893 Sullivan Rd., Grawn, MI 49637 (SAN 630-5717) Tel 616-276-5196; Toll free: 800-345-0096 (orders only).

Twnty-Fifth Cent Pr, *(25th Century Pr.; 1-56721),* 67A Elm St., Box 1351, Montpelier, VT 05602-1351 Tel 802-223-9781; 7102 Ilfield Rd., SW, Albuquerque, NM 87105 Tel 505-873-2220; 5 Sherman Ave., Piscataway, NJ 08854 Tel 908-752-8047.

Two Bytes Pub, *(Two Bytes Publishing; 1-881907),* 219 Long Neck Point Rd., Darien, CT 06820 Tel 203-656-0581.

Two Ems, *(2 Ems, Inc.; 0-936652),* 782 Boston Post Rd., Madison, CT 06443 (SAN 222-1853) Tel 203-245-8211.

Two Saints Pub, *(2 Saints Publishing; 0-9625782),* 615 Mennonite Church Rd., Kalispell, MT 59901-7753 Tel 406-756-1959.

Two Way Bilingual, *(2 Way Bilingual, Inc.; 0-941911),* Cond The Falls, No. 405, Guaynabo, PR 00657 (SAN 666-0169).

TX Wesleyan Coll, *(Texas Wesleyan College; 0-924303),* P.O. Box 50010, Fort Worth, TX 76105; 1201 Wesleyan St., Fort Worth, TX 76105 Tel 817-531-4440.

Tyke Corp, *(Tyke Corp.; 0-924067),* 3838 W. 51st St., Chicago, IL 60632-3614 (SAN 252-0850) Tel 312-284-5660; Toll free: 800-533-8953.

Tympanon Prods, *(Tympanon Productions; 0-9639428),* 3047 Los Cerillos Dr., West Covina, CA 91791 Tel 909-612-5707.

Tyndale, *(Tyndale Hse. Pubs.; 0-8423),* P.O. Box 80, Wheaton, IL 60189 (SAN 206-7749) Tel 708-668-8300; Toll free: 800-323-9400.

Typesetters, *(Typesetters of Charleston; 0-9640446),* P.O. Box 21777, Charleston, SC 29413-1777; 82 Folly Rd., Charleston, SC 29407 Tel 803-723-3971.

Typographeum, *(Typographeum Bookshop, The; 0-930126),* The Stone Cottage, Bennington Rd., Francestown, NH 03043 (SAN 211-3031).

Tzedakah Pubns, *(Tzedakah Pubns.; 0-929999),* 5310 Gilgunn Way, Sacramento, CA 95822 (SAN 251-1967) Tel 916-452-1824.

U Alaska Museum, *(Univ. of Alaska Museum; 0-931163),* 907 Yukon Dr., Fairbanks, AK 99701 (SAN 280-8439) Tel 907-474-7505.

U Assocs, *(U Assocs., Inc.; 0-9615393),* 1160 N. Federal Hwy., Suite 721, Fort Lauderdale, FL 33304 (SAN 695-3530) Tel 305-763-5991.

U CA Pr, *(Univ. of California Pr.; 0-520),* 2120 Berkeley Way, Berkeley, CA 94720 (SAN 203-3046) Tel 510-642-4247; Toll free: 800-822-6657. Canadian users/subscribers: do not confuse U of Cal Pr, Berkeley, CA, with the Univ. of Calgary Pr., Calgary, AB, Canada.

U Ch Pr, *(Univ. of Chicago Pr.; 0-226),* Div. of Univ. of Chicago, 5801 Ellis Ave., 4th Flr., Chicago, IL 60637 (SAN 202-5280) Tel 312-702-7700; Orders to: 11030 S. Langley Ave., Chicago, IL 60628 (SAN 202-5299) Tel 312-568-1550; Toll free: 800-621-2736.

U Iowa IPA, *(Univ. of Iowa, Institute of Public Affairs),* N310 Oakdale Hall, Iowa City, IA 52242 (SAN 262-1231) Tel 319-335-4520.

U M H & C, *(Univ. of Minnesota Hospital & Clinic, Patient Education; 0-937423),* Box 603, Harvard St. at East River Rd., Minneapolis, MN 55455 (SAN 659-0934) Tel 612-626-6356.

U-Music, *(U-Music, Inc.; 0-938925),* P.O. Box 613, Fairfax, CA 94978-0613 (SAN 661-7956); Dist. by: Bookpeople, 7900 Edgewater Dr., Oakland, CA 94621 (SAN 168-9517) Tel 510-632-4700; Toll free: 800-999-4650; Dist. by: New Leaf Distributing Co., 5425 Tulane Dr., SW, Atlanta, GA 30336-2323 (SAN 169-1449) Tel 404-691-6996; Toll free: 800-326-2665; Dist. by: Inland Bk. Co., 140 Commerce St., East Haven, CT 06512 (SAN 200-4151) Tel 203-467-4257; Toll free: 800-243-0138.

U NDak Pres, *(Univ. of North Dakota, Office of the President; 0-9608700; 1-880400),* Box 8143, University Sta., Grand Forks, ND 58202 (SAN 238-4043); Twamley Hall, Rm. 411, Grand Forks, ND 58202 Tel 701-777-2731.

U of Ala Pr, *(Univ. of Alabama Pr.; 0-8173),* Box 870380, Tuscaloosa, AL 35487-0380 (SAN 202-5272) Tel 205-348-5182.

U of Ariz Pr, *(Univ. of Arizona Pr.; 0-8165),* 1230 N. Park Ave., No. 102, Tucson, AZ 85719 (SAN 205-468X) Tel 602-621-1441; Toll free: 800-426-3797 (orders only).

U of Ark Pr, *(Univ. of Arkansas Pr.; 0-938626; 1-55728),* Univ. of Arkansas Press, 201 Ozark Ave., Fayetteville, AR 72701 (SAN 239-3972) Tel 501-575-3246; Toll free: 800-626-0090.

U of Cal Pr
See U CA Pr

U of Chicago Pr
See U Ch Pr

U of Denver Teach, *(Univ. of Denver, Ctr. for Teaching, International Relations Pubns.; 0-943804),* Univ. of Denver, GSIS, Denver, CO 80208 (SAN 241-0877) Tel 303-871-2400; Toll free: 800-967-2847.

U of GA Inst Govt, *(Univ. of Georgia, Carl Vinson Institute of Government; 0-89854),* 201 N. Milledge Ave., Athens, GA 30602 (SAN 212-8012) Tel 706-542-2736.

U of Ga Pr, *(Univ. of Georgia Pr.; 0-8203),* 330 Research Dr., Athens, GA 30602-4901 (SAN 203-3054) Tel 706-369-6130.

U of Idaho Pr, *(Univ. of Idaho Pr.; 0-89301),* 16 Brink Hall, Moscow, ID 83844-1107 (SAN 208-905X); Toll free: 800-847-7377.

U of KS Mus Nat Hist, *(Univ. of Kansas, Museum of Natural History; 0-89338),* 602 Dyche Hall, Lawrence, KS 66045-2454 (SAN 206-0957) Tel 913-864-4540.

U of Mich Pr, *(Univ. of Michigan Pr.; 0-472),* P.O. Box 1104, Ann Arbor, MI 48106 (SAN 282-4884) Tel 313-764-4388.

U of Mo Pr, *(Univ. of Missouri Pr.; 0-8262),* 2910 LeMone Blvd., Columbia, MO 65201 (SAN 203-3143) Tel 314-882-0180; Toll free: 800-828-1894 (orders only).

U of Nebr Pr, *(Univ. of Nebraska Pr.; 0-8032),* 312 N. 14th St., Lincoln, NE 68588-0484 (SAN 202-5337) Tel 402-472-3581; Toll free: 800-755-1105 (orders only). *Imprints:* Bison Books (Bison Books).

U of NM Pr, *(Univ. of New Mexico Pr.; 0-8263),* 1720 Lomas Blvd., NE, Albuquerque, NM 87131-1591 (SAN 213-9588) Tel 505-277-2346; Toll free: 800-622-8667 (FAX orders only); 800-249-7737 (orders & claims only).

U of Notre Dame Pr, *(Univ. of Notre Dame Pr.; 0-268),* P.O. Box L, Notre Dame, IN 46556 (SAN 203-3178) Tel 219-631-6346; Dist. by: Univ. Pr. Distribution, P.O. Box 635, South Bend, IN 46624 (SAN 630-5520) Tel 219-288-7237; Toll free: 800-677-3232.

U of Okla Pr, *(Univ. of Oklahoma Pr.; 0-8061),* 1005 Asp Ave., Norman, OK 73019-0445 (SAN 203-3194) Tel 405-325-5111; Toll free: 800-627-7377; Orders to: P.O. Box 787, Norman, OK 73070-0787 (SAN 203-3194) Tel 405-325-2000; Toll free: 800-627-7377.

U of Pittsburgh Pr, *(Univ. of Pittsburgh Pr.; 0-8229),* 127 N. Bellefield Ave., Pittsburgh, PA 15260 (SAN 203-3216) Tel 412-624-7392; Dist. by: Cornell Univ. Pr., P.O. Box 250, Ithaca, NY 14851-0250 (SAN 281-5680) Tel 607-277-2969; Toll free: 800-666-2211.

U of PR Pr, *(Univ. of Puerto Rico Pr.; 0-8477),* Subs. of Univ. of Puerto Rico, P.O. Box 23322, Univ. of Puerto Rico Sta., Rio Piedras, PR 00931-3322 (SAN 208-1245) Tel 809-250-0550.

U of SC Pr, *(Univ. of South Carolina Pr.; 0-87249; 1-57003),* 1716 College St., Columbia, SC 29208 (SAN 203-3224) Tel 803-777-5243; Orders to: 205 Pickens St., Columbia, SC 29208; Toll free: 800-768-2500.

U of Tenn Pr, *(Univ. of Tennessee Pr.; 0-87049; 1-57233),* Div. of Univ. of Tennessee & Member of Assn. of American Univ. Presses, 293 Communications Bldg., Knoxville, TN 37996-0325 (SAN 212-9930) Tel 615-974-3321; Orders to: Chicago Distribution Center, 11030 S. Langley, Chicago, IL 60628 (SAN 630-6047) Tel 312-568-1550; Toll free: 800-621-2736 (orders only); 800-621-8471 (credit & collections).

U of Tex Inst Tex Culture, *(Univ. of Texas Institute of Texan Cultures at San Antonio; 0-933164; 0-86701),* 801 S. Bowie St., San Antonio, TX 78205-3296 (SAN 213-8778) Tel 210-558-2257; Toll free: 800-776-7651 (orders only).

U of Tex Pr, *(Univ. of Texas Pr.; 0-292),* P.O. Box 7819, Austin, TX 78713-7819 (SAN 212-9876) Tel 512-471-7233; Toll free: 800-252-3206.

U of Toronto Pr, *(Univ. of Toronto Pr.; 0-8020),* 340 Nagel Dr., Cheektowaga, NY 14225 (SAN 214-2651) Tel 716-683-4547.

U of Wash Pr, *(Univ. of Washington Pr.; 0-295),* P.O. Box 50096, Seattle, WA 98145-5096 (SAN 212-2502) Tel 206-543-4050; Toll free: 800-441-4115 (orders only).

U of Wis Pr, *(Univ. of Wisconsin Pr.; 0-299),* Orders to: 114 N. Murray St., Madison, WI 53715-1199 (SAN 501-0039) Tel 608-262-8782.

U Pr of Ky, *(University Pr. of Kentucky; 0-8131),* 663 S. Limestone St., Lexington, KY 40508-4008 (SAN 203-3275) Tel 606-257-8442; Orders to: CUP Services, P.O. Box 6525, Ithaca, NY 14851 (SAN 215-3742) Tel 607-277-2211; Toll free: 800-666-2211.

U Pr of Miss, *(University Pr. of Mississippi; 0-87805),* 3825 Ridgewood Rd., Jackson, MS 39211-6492 (SAN 203-1914) Tel 601-982-6205.

U Pr of New Eng, *(University Pr. of New England; 0-87451),* 23 S. Main St., Hanover, NH 03755-2048 (SAN 203-3283) Tel 603-643-7110; Toll free: 800-421-1561 (orders).

U Pr of Va, *(University Pr. of Virginia; 0-8139),* P.O. Box 3608, University Sta., Charlottesville, VA 22903 (SAN 202-5361) Tel 804-924-3468.

U Press Fla, *(University Press of Florida; 0-8130),* 15 NW 15th St., Gainesville, FL 32611 (SAN 207-9275) Tel 904-392-1351; Toll free: 800-226-3822.

U TX Inst Lat Am Stud, *(Univ. of Texas at Austin, Institute of Latin American Studies; 0-86728),* Sid Richardson Hall 1-310, Austin, TX 78712 (SAN 220-3103) Tel 512-471-5551.

UAHC, *(UAHC Pr.; 0-8074),* 838 Fifth Ave., New York, NY 10021 (SAN 203-3291) Tel 212-249-0100.

UBH Pubns, *(UBH Pubns., Ltd.; 0-9628330),* 1390 S. Honey Way, Denver, CO 80224 Tel 303-691-2877.

UCPANB, *(United Cerebral Palsy Assn. of the North Bay; 0-9616891),* 1180 Holm Rd., No. C, Petaluma, CA 94954-1171 (SAN 661-6453) Tel 707-765-6770; Toll free: 800-441-2711. Do not confuse with companies with similar names in New York, NY, Sacramento, CA.

UFO Photo, *(UFO Photo Archives; 0-9608558; 0-934269),* P.O. Box 17206, Tucson, AZ 85710 (SAN 240-7949) Tel 602-296-6753.

UH Pr, *(Univ. of Hawaii Pr., The; 0-8248),* 2840 Kolowalu St., Honolulu, HI 96822 (SAN 202-5353) Tel 808-956-8255; 99-1422 Koaha Pl., Aiea, HI 96701 (SAN 658-215X). *Imprints:* Kolowalu Bk (Kolowalu Book).

Ujamaa Ent, *(Ujamaa Enterprises, Inc.; 0-9639349),* 121 Underwood Rd., Oak Ridge, TN 37830 Tel 615-481-3607.

Ultramarine Pub, *(Ultramarine Publishing Co., Inc.; 0-89366),* P.O. Box 303, Hastings-on-Hudson, NY 10706 (SAN 208-8762) Tel 914-478-2522.

UM Ctr MENAS, *(Univ. of Michigan, Ctr. for Middle Eastern & North African Studies; 0-932098),* 144 Lane Hall, Ann Arbor, MI 48109-1290 (SAN 211-7150) Tel 313-764-0350; Orders to: Univ. of Michigan Language Laboratory, 2018 ML Bldg., Ann Arbor, MI 48109-1275 (SAN 653-483X) Tel 313-764-0424; Dist. by: Univ. of Michigan Pr., Pubns. Distribution Ctr., 839 Greene St., Ann Arbor, MI 48106 (SAN 282-4884) Tel 313-764-4394; Dist. by: Cambridge Univ. Pr., 510 North Ave., New Rochelle, NY 10801 (SAN 169-4014) Tel 914-235-0300; Toll free: 800-872-7423 (Orders only); Dist. by: International Bk. Ctr., 2007 Laurel Dr., P.O. Box 295, Troy, MI 48099 (SAN 208-7022) Tel 313-879-8436. Do not confuse with Univ. of Michigan, Dept. of Near Eastern Studies.

UM Ctr NENAS
See UM Ctr MENAS

UN, *(United Nations; 0-680),* 2 United Nations Plaza, Sales Section, Publishing Div., Rm. DC2-853, New York, NY 10017 (SAN 206-6718) Tel 212-963-8302; Toll free: 800-553-3210 (bookshop orders).

UN Communications
See Beckett-Highland

Understand Busn, *(Understanding Business; 0-9641863),* 444 Market St., Suite 1050, San Francisco, CA 94111-5391 Tel 415-616-6800.

Underwood-Miller, *(Underwood/Miller; 0-934438; 0-88733),* P.O. Box 253, Penn Valley, CA 95946 Tel 916-432-1224; Orders to: P.O. Box 253, Penn Valley, CA 95946 (SAN 666-6779) Tel 916-432-1224; Dist. by: Publishers Group West, 4065 Hollis St., Emeryville, CA 94608 (SAN 202-8522) Tel 510-658-3453; Toll free: 800-788-3123.

Unicorn Ent, *(Unicorn Enterprises; 0-87884),* 1620 Collinsdale Ave., Cincinnati, OH 45230 (SAN 206-6696).

Unicorn Game Pubns, *(Unicorn Game Pubns.;* 0-9628003), Box 4284, Fresno, CA 93728; 1340 N. Linden, Suite 10, Fresno, CA 93728 Tel 209-233-0237.

Unicorn Pbks *Imprint of* **Dutton Child Bks**

Unicorn Pub, *(Unicorn Publishing Hse., Inc., The;* 0-88101), 120 American Way, Morris Plains, NJ 07950 (SAN 240-4567) Tel 201-292-6861.

Union Hosp Found, *(Union Hospital Foundation;* 0-9621620), 695 Chestnut St., Union, NJ 07083 (SAN 252-1067) Tel 201-687-1900.

Unique Information, *(Unique Information Products, L.C.; 1-884618),* P.O. Box 211519, Salt Lake City, UT 84121; Toll free: 800-713-2784; 2945 E. Robidoux Rd., Salt Lake City, UT 84121 Tel 801-942-1175.

Unique Memphis, *(Unique Pubns.; 0-9622996),* P.O. Box 11683, Memphis, TN 38111; 13 S. Prescott, Box 11683, Memphis, TN 38111 Tel 901-345-1222. Do not confuse with Unique Pubns., Burbank, CA.

Unitarian Univ, *(Unitarian Universalist Assn.; 0-933840;* 1-55896), 25 Beacon St., Boston, MA 02108-2800 (SAN 225-4840) Tel 617-742-2100. *Imprints:* Skinner Hse Bks (Skinner House Books).

United Ed, *(United Educators, Inc.; 0-87566),* 900 Armour Dr., Lake Bluff, IL 60044 (SAN 204-8795) Tel 708-234-3700.

United Pr, *(United Pr., Inc.; 0-932972),* P.O. Box 4064, Sarasota, FL 33578 (SAN 212-6931); Dist. by: Nutri-Bks. Corp., P.O. Box 5793, Denver, CO 80217 (SAN 169-054X) Tel 303-778-8383; Toll free: 800-279-2048 (orders only); Dist. by: Bookpeople, 7900 Edgewater Dr., Oakland, CA 94621 (SAN 168-9517) Tel 510-632-4700; Toll free: 800-999-4650.

United Pub Co, *(United Publishing Co.; 0-937323),* 76 Exchange St., Albany, NY 12205 (SAN 658-8077) Tel 518-438-1600.

United Soc Shakers, *(United Society of Shakers;* 0-915836), Sabbathday Lake, Poland Spring, ME 04274 (SAN 158-619X) Tel 207-926-4597.

United Syn Bk, *(United Synagogue of America Bk. Service; 0-8381),* Subs. of United Synagogue of America, 155 Fifth Ave., New York, NY 10010 (SAN 203-0551) Tel 212-533-7800.

Unity Bks, *(Unity Bks. (Unity Schl. of Christianity);* 0-87159), Orders to: Unity Schl. of Christianity, 350 Hwy. & Colbern Rd., Unity Village, MO 64065-0001 (SAN 204-8817) Tel 816-251-3571; Dist. by: New Leaf Distributing Co., 5425 Tulane Dr., SW, Atlanta, GA 30336-2323 (SAN 169-1449) Tel 404-691-6995; Toll free: 800-326-2665; Dist. by: DeVorss & Co., P.O. Box 550, Marina del Rey, CA 90294-0550 (SAN 168-9886) Tel 213-870-7478; Toll free: 800-821-6290 (bookstores only); 800-331-4719 (in California, bookstores only).

Unity School
See Unity Bks

Univ Central AR Pr, *(Univ. of Central Arkansas Pr.; 0-9615143; 0-944436),* P.O. Box 4933, Conway, AR 72035 (SAN 694-2083) Tel 501-450-5150.

Univ Class, *(University Classics, Ltd., Pubs.; 0-914127),* P.O. Box 2301, 1 Bryan Rd., Briarwood, Athens, OH 45701 (SAN 287-5934) Tel 614-592-4543; Toll free: 800-472-2612.

Univ Edtns *Imprint of* **Aegina Pr**

Universal Graphics, *(Universal Graphics; 1-878491),* P.O. Box 186, Lawton, OK 73502; Toll free: 800-654-4507; 210 SW Texas, Lawton, OK 73502 Tel 405-355-2182.

Universal Res LA, *(Universal Research; 0-942951),* 16 Sconticut Neck Rd., Sconticut Sq., Suite 142, Fairhaven, MA 02719 (SAN 668-6524) Tel 508-990-8424.

Universe, *(Universe Publishing, Inc.; 0-87663; 1-55550;* 0-7893), Div. of Rizzoli International Pubns., Inc., 300 Park Ave. S., 5th Flr., New York, NY 10010 (SAN 202-537X) Tel 212-387-3400; Dist. by: St. Martin's Pr., Inc., 175 Fifth Ave., Rm. 1715, New York, NY 10010 (SAN 200-2132) Tel 212-674-5151; Toll free: 800-221-7945.

Untd Brothers, *(United Brothers & Sisters Communications Systems; 1-56411),* 912 W. Pembroke Ave., Hampton, VA 23669 (SAN 630-6748) Tel 804-723-2696.

UNTX Pr, *(Univ. of North Texas Pr.; 0-929398),* P.O. Box 13856, Denton, TX 76203 (SAN 249-4280); Chestnut Hall, Suite 1, Denton, TX 76203 (SAN 249-4299) Tel 817-565-2142; Dist. by: Texas A&M Univ. Pr., Drawer C, College Station, TX 77843-4354 (SAN 207-5237) Tel 409-845-1436; Toll free: 800-826-8911 (orders).

Upper Access, *(Upper Access, Inc.; 0-942679),* P.O. Box 457, Hinesburg, VT 05461 (SAN 667-1195) Tel 802-482-2988; Toll free: 800-356-9315.

Upper Room, *(Upper Room, The; 0-8358; 0-941478),* 1908 Grand Ave., P.O. Box 189, Nashville, TN 37202 (SAN 203-3364) Tel 615-340-7243; Dist. by: Abingdon Pr., 201 Eighth Ave., S., P.O. Box 801, Nashville, TN 37202-0801 (SAN 201-0054) Tel 615-749-6290; Toll free: 800-251-3320. Do not confuse with Upper Room Education for Parenting, Inc. in Derry, NH.

Upper Strata, *(Upper Strata Ink, Inc.; 0-9616589),* P.O. Box 250, Bernalillo, NM 87004 (SAN 659-8064); 500 Beehive Ln., Bernalillo, NM 87004 (SAN 659-8072) Tel 505-867-5812.

Upshur Pr, *(Upshur Pr.; 0-912975),* P.O. Box 609, Dallas, PA 18612 (SAN 297-4762) Tel 717-675-8835; Dist. by: Koen Bk. Distributors, 10 Twosome Dr., P.O. Box 600, Moorestown, NJ 08057 (SAN 169-4642) Tel 609-235-4444; Toll free: 800-257-8481; Dist. by: Quality Bks., Inc., 918 Sherwood Dr., Lake Bluff, IL 60044-2204 (SAN 169-2127) Tel 708-295-2010; Toll free: 800-323-4241 (libraries only); Dist. by: Bookpeople, 7900 Edgewater Dr., Oakland, CA 94621 (SAN 168-9517) Tel 510-632-4700; Toll free: 800-999-4650; Dist. by: The Distributors, 702 S. Michigan, South Bend, IN 46601 (SAN 169-2488) Tel 219-232-8500; Toll free: 800-348-5200 (except Indiana); Dist. by: Baker & Taylor Bks., Somerville Service Ctr., 50 Kirby Ave., Somerville, NJ 08876-0734 (SAN 169-4901) Tel 908-722-8000; Toll free: 800-775-1500 (customer service).

Upton Sons, *(Upton & Sons; 0-912783),* 917 Hillcrest St., El Segundo, CA 90245 (SAN 160-5216) Tel 310-322-7202.

Upward Way, *(Upward Way Pubns., Inc.; 0-945460),* P.O. Box 783, Hermitage, TN 37076 (SAN 247-0551) Tel 615-872-0579; Toll free: 800-367-2665 (orders only).

Urban Res Pr, *(Urban Research Pr., Inc.; 0-941484),* 840 E. 87th St., Chicago, IL 60619 (SAN 239-0515) Tel 312-994-7200.

Uriel Press, *(Uriel Pr.; 1-885038),* 400 S. Burnside, No. 3J, Los Angeles, CA 90036 Tel 213-936-9243; Toll free: 800-473-9303.

Ursa Major Corp, *(URSA Major Corp.; 0-9625388),* P.O. Box 3368, Ashland, OR 97520; Toll free: 800-999-3433; 695 Mistletoe Rd., No. 2, Ashland, OR 97520 Tel 503-482-1322.

US Capitol Hist, *(U. S. Capitol Historical Society;* 0-916200), 200 Maryland Ave., NE, Washington, DC 20002 (SAN 226-6601) Tel 202-543-8919.

US Catholic, *(U. S. Catholic Conference; 1-55586),* Affil. of National Conference of Catholic Bishops, Pubns. Services, 3211 Fourth St., NE, Washington, DC 20017-1194 (SAN 207-5350) Tel 202-541-3090; Toll free: 800-235-8722.

USA Entrps, *(USA Enterprises, Inc.; 0-9628653),* 415 S. Sixth St., Suite 200, Las Vegas, NV 89101 Tel 702-385-0855.

USA Gymnastics, *(USA Gymnastics; 1-885250),* 201 S. Capitol Ave., Suite 300, Indianapolis, IN 46225 Tel 317-237-5050.

Usborne *Imprint of* **EDC**

Useful Lrn, *(Useful Learning; 1-878712),* 711 Meadowlane Ct., Mount Vernon, IA 52314 Tel 319-335-5304; Toll free: 800-962-3855.

USGPO, *(U. S. Government Printing Office; 0-16),* USGPO Stop SSMB, Washington, DC 20401 (SAN 206-152X) Tel 202-512-2364; Orders to: Superintendent of Documents, Washington, DC 20402-9325 (SAN 658-0785) Tel 202-783-3238.

USPS, *(U. S. Postal Service, Philatelic Marketing Div.; 0-9604756; 1-877707),* 475 L'Enfant Plaza, Washington, DC 20260-6755 (SAN 219-8304) Tel 202-268-2350.

UXL *Imprint of* **Gale**

Uzertoons Pubng, *(Uzertoons Publishing Co.;* 0-9640569), 1913 Alpine Dr., Aiken, SC 29803 Tel 803-649-9813.

V B Wood, *(Wood, Vivian Bee; 0-9621567),* 7370-142 Parkview Ct., Santee, CA 92071 (SAN 251-5725) Tel 619-562-0253.

V Evans, *(Evans, Vicki; 0-9636367),* 3624 Linkwood Dr., Houston, TX 77025 Tel 713-667-7359.

V H Pub, *(VHW Publishing; 0-9610912; 0-941281),* 930 Via Fruteria, Santa Barbara, CA 93110 (SAN 265-153X) Tel 805-687-4087.

V H Visionarts, *(Van Horne Visionarts; 1-882643),* 24690 W. Saddle Peak Rd., Malibu, CA 90265 Tel 310-456-2207.

V Lane Bks, *(Lane, Veronica, Bks.; 0-9637597),* 513 Wilshire Blvd., No. 282, Santa Monica, CA 90401 (SAN 298-1157) Tel 310-288-7185; Toll free: 800-651-1001.

V Lockman, *(Lockman, Vic; 0-936175),* 233 Rogue River Hwy. 360, Grants Pass, OR 97527 (SAN 697-2063); Toll free: 800-847-9312.

V M H Cain, *(Cain, V. M. Helen; 0-9624837),* P.O. Box 091224, Columbus, OH 43209 Tel 614-236-2617.

V M Rundle, *(Rundle, Vesta M.; 1-882672),* 2251 Fourth St., Charleston, IL 61920 Tel 217-345-2560.

V S Epstein, *(Epstein, Vivian Sheldon; 0-9601002),* 212 S. Dexter St., Denver, CO 80222 (SAN 208-6425) Tel 303-322-7450.

V Sharp, *(Sharp, Vera; 0-9616987),* 204C Edgewater Towers, 17350 Sunset Blvd., Pacific Palisades, CA 90272-4111 (SAN 658-8360) Tel 310-454-2111.

V W Hensley, *(Hensley, Virgil W., Inc.; 1-56322),* 6116 E. 32nd St., Tulsa, OK 74135 Tel 918-664-8520; Toll free: 800-288-8520.

V W Snyder, *(Snyder, Vern W.; 0-926366),* 3660 Walnut Blvd., No. 90, Brentwood, CA 94513 Tel 510-634-1117.

V Wagner Pubns, *(Wagner, V., Pubns.; 0-9633212),* 4851 Aurora Dr., Ventura, CA 93003 Tel 805-650-9654.

VA Mus Natl Hist, *(Virginia Museum of Natural History; 0-9625801; 1-884549),* 1001 Douglas Ave., Martinsville, VA 24112 Tel 703-666-8631; Dist. by: The McDonald & Woodward Publishing Co., P.O. Box 10308, Blacksburg, VA 24062-0308 (SAN 663-6977) Tel 703-951-9465.

Vacation Color, *(Vacation Color Co.; 0-9637687),* P.O. Box 4604, Estes Park, CO 80517; 2251 Upper High Dr., Estes Park, CO 80517 Tel 303-568-8785.

Vacation Spot, *(Vacation Spot Publishing; 0-9637688),* P.O. Box 17011, Alexandria, VA 22302 Tel 703-684-8142.

Vail Pub, *(Vail Publishing; 0-9607872),* 8285 SW Brookridge, Portland, OR 97225 (SAN 240-0766) Tel 503-292-9964.

Valeria Bks *Imprint of* **Wonder Well**

Valiant Pr, *(Valiant Pr., Inc.; 0-9633461),* P.O. Box 330568, Miami, FL 33233; 4047 Malaga Ave., Miami, FL 33133 Tel 305-665-1889.

Valkyrie Pub Hse, *(Valkyrie Publishing Hse.; 0-912760; 0-934616; 0-912589),* 8245 26th Ave., N., Saint Petersburg, FL 33710 (SAN 203-1671) Tel 813-345-8864.

Valley Sun, *(Valley of the Sun Publishing Co.; 0-911842;* 0-87554), Div. of Sutphen Corp., P.O. Box 683, Ashland, OR 97520 (SAN 206-8974) Tel 503-488-7880; Toll free: 800-225-4717.

Van Buren Cty Hist Soc, *(Van Buren County Historical Society; 0-9621162),* P.O. Box 452, Hartford, MI 49057 (SAN 250-9105); 58471 Red Arrow Hwy., Hartford, MI 49057 (SAN 250-9113) Tel 616-674-8914.

Vandamere, *(Vandamere Pr.; 0-918339),* Subs. of AB Assocs., P.O. Box 5243, Arlington, VA 22205 (SAN 657-3088) Tel 703-525-5488.

Vanderbilt U Pr, *(Vanderbilt Univ. Pr.; 0-8265),* Div. of Vanderbilt Univ., P.O. Box 1813, Station B, Nashville, TN 37235 (SAN 202-9308) Tel 615-322-3585; Dist. by: Publisher Resources, Inc., 1224 Heil Quaker Blvd., P.O. Box 7018, La Vergne, TN 37086-7001 (SAN 630-5431) Tel 615-793-5090; Toll free: 800-937-5557.

VanGar Pubs, *(VanGar Pubs./Baltimore; 1-882788),* 420 Hillen Rd., Towson, MD 21286 Tel 410-337-0977.

Vantage, *(Vantage Pr., Inc.; 0-533),* 516 W. 34th St., New York, NY 10001 (SAN 206-8893) Tel 212-736-1767; Toll free: 800-882-3273.

Variety Arts, *(Variety Arts, Inc.; 0-937180),* 305 Riverside Dr., Suite 4A, New York, NY 10025 (SAN 200-691X) Tel 212-316-0399; Toll free: 800-221-2154; Dist. by: Publishers Group West, 4065 Hollis St., Emeryville, CA 94608 (SAN 202-8522) Tel 510-658-3453; Toll free: 800-788-3123.

Vashon Pt Prod, *(Vashon Point Productions; 0-9616103),* 10941 Point Vashon Dr., Vashon, WA 98070 (SAN 659-5642) Tel 206-567-4829.

Veda Vangarde, *(Veda Vangarde Foundation; 0-9632698),* 1381B Hwy. 9, Mount Vernon, WA 98273 Tel 206-856-6062.

Vedanta Pr, *(Vedanta Pr.; 0-87481),* Div. of Vedanta Society, 1946 Vedanta Pl., Hollywood, CA 90068-3996 (SAN 202-9340) Tel 213-465-7114.

Vegetarian Resc, *(Vegetarians Resource Group, The;* 0-931411), P.O. Box 1463, Baltimore, MD 21203 (SAN 630-172X) Tel 410-366-8343; Dist. by: New Leaf Distributing Co., 5425 Tulane Dr., SW, Atlanta, GA 30336-2323 (SAN 169-1449) Tel 404-691-6996; Toll free: 800-326-2665; Dist. by: Inland Bk. Co., 140 Commerce St., East Haven, CT 06512 (SAN 200-4151) Tel 203-467-4257; Toll free: 800-243-0138.

Veracruz Pubs, *(Veracruz Pubs.; 1-879219),* P.O. Box 5262, Tucson, AZ 85703; 1531 N. Hualpai, Tucson, AZ 85745 Tel 602-628-1135.

Verbal Images Pr, *(Verbal Images Pr.; 0-9625136; 1-884281),* 19 Fox Hill Dr., Fairport, NY 14450 Tel 716-377-3807; Dist. by: Baker & Taylor Bks., Somerville Service Ctr., 50 Kirby Ave., Somerville, NJ 08876-0734 (SAN 169-4901) Tel 908-722-8000; Toll free: 800-775-1500 (customer service); Dist. by: Baker & Taylor Bks., Momence Service Ctr., 501 S. Gladiolus St., Momence, IL 60954-2444 (SAN 169-2100) Tel 815-472-2444; Toll free: 800-775-2300 (customer service); Dist. by: Baker & Taylor Bks., Commerce Service Ctr., 251 Mt. Olive Church Rd., Commerce, GA 30599-9988 (SAN 169-1503) Tel 706-335-5000; Toll free: 800-775-1200 (customer service); Dist. by: Baker & Taylor Bks., Reno Service Ctr., 380 Edison Way, Reno, NV 89564 (SAN 169-4464) Tel 702-858-6700; Toll free: 800-775-1700 (customer service).

Veritas Pr CA, *(Veritas Pr.; 1-883511),* Box 1704, Santa Monica, CA 90406; 1021 Lincoln, No. 104, Santa Monica, CA 90403 Tel 310-393-7700. Do not confuse with companies with the same name in Santa Barbara, CA, Clearwater, FL.

Veritie Pr, *(Veritie Pr.; 0-915964),* P.O. Box 222, Novelty, OH 44072 (SAN 207-6977) Tel 216-338-3374.

Vernier Soft, *(Vernier Software; 0-918731),* 2920 SW 89th St., Portland, OR 97225 (SAN 293-1753) Tel 503-297-5317.

Versailles, *(Versailles, Elizabeth Starr; 0-9606002),* 42 Nash Hill Rd., Williamsburg, MA 01096 (SAN 203-0330) Tel 413-268-7576.

Versary Pubns, *(Versary Pubns.; 0-9641429),* 984 Brownsville Rd., Wernersville, PA 19565 Tel 610-693-5920.

Very Idea, *(Very Idea, The; 0-9615130),* Brambly Hedge Cottage, HCR 31, Box 39, Jasper, AR 72641 (SAN 694-1869) Tel 501-446-5849.

Vestal, *(Vestal Pr., Ltd.; 0-911572; 1-879511),* 320 N. Jensen Rd., P.O. Box 97, Vestal, NY 13851-0097 (SAN 205-4825) Tel 607-797-4872.

VGM Career Bks *Imprint of* **NTC Pub Grp**

Viaticum Pr, *(Viaticum Pr.; 0-9631834),* Div. of Will Keim Speaks, Inc., 345 NW 31st St., Corvallis, OR 97330 Tel 503-758-0075.

Vibrante Pr, *(Vibrante Pr.; 0-935301),* 2430 Juan Tabo, NE, Suite 110, Albuquerque, NM 87112 (SAN 696-2351) Tel 505-298-4793.

Victor Books *Imprint of* **SP Pubns**

Victory Press, *(Victory Pr.; 0-9620765; 1-878217),* 543 Lighthouse Ave., Monterey, CA 93940-1422 (SAN 249-700X) Tel 408-883-1725; Dist. by: The Distributors, 702 S. Michigan, South Bend, IN 46601 (SAN 169-2488) Tel 219-232-8500; Toll free: 800-348-5200 (except Indiana); Dist. by: Bookpeople, 7900 Edgewater Dr., Oakland, CA 94621 (SAN 168-9517) Tel 510-632-4700; Toll free: 800-999-4650; Dist. by: Inland Bk. Co., 140 Commerce St., East Haven, CT 06512 (SAN 200-4151) Tel 203-467-4257; Toll free: 800-243-0138; Dist. by: New Leaf Distributing Co., 5424 Tulane Dr., SW, Atlanta, GA 30336-2323 (SAN 169-1449) Tel 404-691-6996; Toll free: 800-326-2665; Dist. by: Baker & Taylor Bks., Somerville Service Ctr., 50 Kirby Ave., Somerville, NJ 08876-0734 (SAN 169-4901) Tel 908-722-8000; Toll free: 800-775-1500 (customer service); Dist. by: Baker & Taylor Bks., Momence Service Ctr., 501 S. Gladiolus St., Momence, IL 60954-2444 (SAN 169-2100) Tel 815-472-2444; Toll free: 800-775-2300 (customer service). Do not confuse with Victory Pr., Inc. in Prescott Valley, AZ.

Victory Pub, *(Victory Publishing; 0-935303),* 3504 Oak Dr., Menlo Park, CA 94025 (SAN 696-2408) Tel 415-323-1650.

Video Athlete, *(Video Athlete Corp.; 0-915659),* Div. of Dennis DeNure Enterprises, P.O. Box 281, Madison, WI 53701-0281 (SAN 287-2358).

Video Moments, *(Video Moments; 0-9637894),* 405 El Camino Real, No. 326, Menlo Park, CA 94025 Tel 415-326-6882.

Video Tutorial Serv, *(Video Tutorial Service; 0-929231),* 1840 52nd St., Brooklyn, NY 11204 Tel 718-232-7551; Dist. by: Educational Design, Inc., 47 W. 13th St., New York, NY 10011 (SAN 204-1588) Tel 212-255-7900; Toll free: 800-221-9372.

Vidya Bks, *(Vidya Bks.; 1-878099),* P.O. Box 7788, Berkeley, CA 94707-0788; 729 Santa Fe Ave., Albany, CA 94706 Tel 510-527-9932.

Viewpoint Pr, *(Viewpoint Pr.; 0-943962),* P.O. Box 865, Hermosa Beach, CA 90254 (SAN 241-1644) Tel 310-372-5676; P.O. Box 1090, Tehachapi, CA 93581 Tel 805-821-5110; Dist. by: Baker & Taylor Bks., Somerville Service Ctr., 50 Kirby Ave., Somerville, NJ 08876-0734 (SAN 169-4901) Tel 908-722-8000; Toll free: 800-775-1500 (customer service); Dist. by: Baker & Taylor Bks., Momence Service Ctr., 501 S. Gladiolus St., Momence, IL 60954-2444 (SAN 169-2100) Tel 815-472-2444; Toll free: 800-775-2300 (customer service); Dist. by: Baker & Taylor Bks., Commerce Service Ctr., 251 Mt. Olive Church Rd., Commerce, GA 30599-9988 (SAN 169-1503) Tel 706-335-5000; Toll free: 800-775-1200 (customer service); Dist. by: Baker & Taylor Bks., Reno Service Ctr., 380 Edison Way, Reno, NV 89564 (SAN 169-4464) Tel 702-858-6700; Toll free: 800-775-1700 (customer service); Dist. by: Bookpeople, 7900 Edgewater Dr., Oakland, CA 94621 (SAN 168-9517) Tel 510-632-4700; Toll free: 800-999-4650.

Vignette, *(Vignette Multi Media; 1-881368),* 1283 S. Labrea Ave., No. 159, Los Angeles, CA 90019 Tel 213-931-7444.

Viking *Imprint of* **Viking Penguin**

Viking Child Bks, *(Viking Children's Bks.; 0-670),* Div. of Penguin USA, 375 Hudson St., New York, NY 10014-3657 Tel 212-366-2000.

Viking Penguin, *(Viking Penguin; 0-670; 0-14),* Div. of Penguin USA, 375 Hudson St., New York, NY 10014-3657 (SAN 298-0258) Tel 212-366-2000; Toll free: 800-331-4624; Orders to: P.O. Box 120, Bergenfield, NJ 07621-0120 (SAN 282-5074) Tel 201-387-0600; Toll free: 800-526-0275; Orders to: 100 Fabright Rd., Newbern, TN 38059-1334 (SAN 200-3023). *Imprints:* Pelican Bks (Pelican Books); Penguin Bks (Penguin Books); Viking (Viking).

VILA Grp, *(VILA Group, Inc., The; 0-9635047),* Vantage Pt., East Norwalk, CT 06855 Tel 203-838-5847.

Vilate Pub, *(Vilate Publishing; 0-9623144),* B13, 65 Verde Valley School Rd., Sedona, AZ 86336 Tel 602-284-1613.

Villa Press, *(Villa Pr.; 0-9641430),* 4225 Sixth Ave., Apt. O, San Diego, CA 92103 Tel 619-296-7918. Do not confuse with Villa Pr., in Glendale, AZ.

Villard Bks *Imprint of* **Random**

Vimach Assocs, *(Vimach Assocs.; 0-917949),* 5865 Cummington Ct., Columbus, OH 43213 (SAN 657-0283) Tel 614-755-9597.

Vin *Imprint of* **Random**

Vincent Marzilli, *(Marzilli, Vincent; 0-9617809),* R.F.D. No. 5, Box 240-C, Bangor, ME 04401 Tel 207-990-0704.

Virgilio Integrat, *(Virgilio Integrated Publishing; 1-882346),* 764 Almeria Dr., San Jose, CA 95123 Tel 408-224-6395.

Vis Bks Intl, *(Vision Bks. International; 1-56550),* 3356A Coffey Ln., Santa Rosa, CA 95403 (SAN 297-6447) Tel 707-542-1440; Toll free: 800-377-3431.

Vision Pr CA, *(Vision Pr.; 0-9638354),* 10573 W. Pico Blvd., Suite 166, Los Angeles, CA 90064 Tel 310-273-3930; Toll free: 800-556-2665. Do not confuse with companies with the same name in Santa Fe, NM, Tucson, AZ, Hillside, NJ, Northport, AL.

Vision WY, *(Vision Pr., Inc.; 0-9628579; 1-881323),* P.O. Box 1889, Cheyenne, WY 82003-1889; Toll free: 800-788-1889; 98 Clover Ct., Cheyenne, WY 82009 Tel 307-778-4811.

Visions Unlimited, *(Visions Unlimited; 0-9622776),* Div. of Jackie Marx Enterprises, Inc., 14300 W. Bell Rd., No. 433, Surprise, AZ 85374-9735. Do not confuse with Visions Unlimited Pr. in Huntington Beach, CA.

Vistoso Bks, *(Vistoso Bks.; 0-9634165),* 14010 N. Fawnbrooke Dr., Tucson, AZ 85737 Tel 602-825-2913.

Visual Evangels, *(Visual Evangels Publishing Co.; 0-915398),* P.O. Box 8679, Michigan City, IN 46360-8679 (SAN 212-002X) Tel 219-872-5295.

Visual Studies, *(Visual Studies Workshop; 0-89822),* 31 Prince St., Rochester, NY 14607 (SAN 218-1606) Tel 716-442-8676.

Vital Edits, *(Vital Editions; 0-9629982),* P.O. Box 637, New York, NY 10008 Tel 718-857-4434.

Vital Media, *(Vital Media Enterprises; 0-9641252),* 80 Eighth Ave., Suite 200, New York, NY 10011 Tel 212-633-6333.

Vitamemoria, *(Vitamemoria, Inc.; 0-9633262),* 11301 S. 58th St., Papillion, NE 68133 Tel 402-339-0518.

Viz Commns Inc, *(Viz Communications, Inc.; 0-929279; 1-56931),* Subs. of Shogakukan, Inc., 440 Brannan St., San Francisco, CA 94107 (SAN 248-8604) Tel 415-546-7073.

VJR Passports, *(V.J.R. Passports; 0-9625515),* 1945 Northwestern Ave., Madison, WI 53704 Tel 608-249-7167.

Voc-Offers, *(Voc-Offers; 0-918995),* P.O. Box 700252, San Jose, CA 95170-0252 (SAN 669-8247) Tel 408-255-6579.

Volcano Pr, *(Volcano Pr., Inc.; 0-912078; 1-884244),* P.O. Box 270, Volcano, CA 95689 (SAN 220-0015); 21326 Consolation St., Volcano, CA 95689 Tel 209-296-3445.

Vous Etes Tres Belle, *(Vous Etes Tres Belle, Inc.; 0-9619641),* 2205 Tonga Dr., Fort Washington, MD 20744 (SAN 245-8233) Tel 301-292-9144.

Voyager Bks *Imprint of* **HarBrace**

Voyageur Pr, *(Voyageur Pr.; 0-89658),* 123 N. Second St., Stillwater, MN 55082 (SAN 287-2668) Tel 612-430-2210; Toll free: 800-888-9653.

Voyageur Pub, *(Voyageur Publishing Co., Inc.; 0-929146),* P.O. Box 150127, Nashville, TN 37215 (SAN 248-6709) Tel 615-383-6142.

VWAP, *(Victim Witness Assistance Program; 0-9621260),* 200 S. High St., Wailuku, HI 96793 (SAN 250-913X) Tel 808-243-7777.

Vyoupoint, *(Vyoupoint; 0-9618083),* P.O. Box 13860, San Luis Obispo, CA 93406 (SAN 666-0657) Tel 805-543-6892.

W A T Braille, *(Thomas, William A., Braille Bookstore; 1-56956),* Div. of Braille International, Inc., 3290 SE Slater St., Stuart, FL 34997 Tel 407-286-8366; Toll free: 800-336-3142.

W B Fleetwood, *(Fleetwood, Wade B.; 0-9631466),* 439 Hampton Ct., Falls Church, VA 22046 Tel 703-536-7165.

W Dean Editions, *(Dean, Wayne, Editions; 0-9616161),* 3217 Petunia Ct., San Diego, CA 92117 (SAN 699-8364) Tel 619-272-6075; Dist. by: Dale Seymour Pubns., 200 Middlefield Rd., Menlo Park, CA 94025 (SAN 200-9781) Tel 415-688-0880; Toll free: 800-872-1100.

W F Cox, *(Cox, Willis F.; 0-9610758),* Box 47, James Store, VA 23080 (SAN 264-7060) Tel 804-693-4533.

W Foster Pub, *(Foster, Walter, Publishing, Inc.; 0-929261; 1-56010),* 430 W. Sixth St., Tustin, CA 92680-9990 (SAN 249-051X) Tel 714-544-7510; Toll free: 800-426-0099; Dist. by: Baker & Taylor Bks., Commerce Service Ctr., 251 Mount Olive Rd., Commerce, GA 30599 (SAN 202-8522); Toll free: 800-775-1100.

W Gladden Found, *(Gladden, William, Foundation; 1-56456),* 7 Bridge St., Cameron, WV 26033 Tel 304-686-3247.

W H Freeman, *(Freeman, W. H., & Co.; 0-7167),* Subs. of Scientific American, Inc., 41 Madison Ave., E. 26th, 35th Flr., New York, NY 10010 (SAN 290-6864) Tel 212-576-9400; Orders to: 4419 W. 1980, S., Salt Lake City, UT 84104 (SAN 290-6872) Tel 801-973-4660. *Imprints:* Sci Am Yng Rdrs (Scientific American Books for Young Readers).

W J Fantasy, *(W.J. Fantasy, Inc.; 1-56021),* 955 Connecticut Ave., Bridgeport, CT 06607 Tel 203-333-5212; Toll free: 800-222-7529.

W Keast, *(Keast, Winifred; 0-9613847),* P.O. Box 173, North Anson, ME 04958-0173 (SAN 655-4326).

W M Farmer, *(Farmer, Wesley M.; 0-937772),* 3591 Ruffin Rd., No. 226, San Diego, CA 92123 (SAN 215-6431); Orders to: Seashore Discoveries, 3591 Ruffin Rd., No. 226, San Diego, CA 92123 Tel 619-576-2143.

W P Allen, *(Allen, W. P., & Co., Inc.; 0-916777),* P.O. Box 702, Portland, OR 97207 (SAN 654-2921) Tel 503-538-2311.

W Pt Soc Puget, *(West Point Society of Puget Sound, Inc.; 0-9635925),* 4407 134th Pl., SE, Bellevue, WA 98006 Tel 206-746-4839.

W Pub Hse
See doodle-bug

W Ruth Co, *(Ruth, William, & Co.; 0-9627697),* 3202 Brinkley Rd., Temple Hills, MD 20748-6302 Tel 301-899-3434.

W S David, *(David, Ward S.; 0-9630883),* 2321 Morro Rd., Fallbrook, CA 92028 Tel 619-728-7588; Toll free: 800-678-7789.

W S Nelson & Co, *(Nelson, Waldemar S., & Co., Inc.; 0-9619160),* 1200 St. Charles Ave., New Orleans, LA 70130 (SAN 243-3435) Tel 504-523-5281.

W S Sullwold, *(Sullwold, William S., Publishing; 0-88492),* 18 Pearl St., Taunton, MA 02780 (SAN 203-1744) Tel 508-823-0924.

W Stery, *(Stery, William, Co.; 0-937913),* P.O. Box 371595, Decatur, GA 30037-1595 (SAN 659-5901); 2897 Bradmoor Ct., Decatur, GA 30034 (SAN 659-591X) Tel 404-241-5003.

W W Pubs
See Wonder Well

WA Expatriates Pr, *(Washington Expatriates Pr., The; 0-9609062),* 127 7th St. SE, Washington, DC 20034 (SAN 241-2357) Tel 202-546-1020.

Wadsworth Pub, *(Wadsworth Publishing Co.; 0-534),* Div. of International Thomson Publishing Education Group, 10 Davis Dr., Belmont, CA 94002 (SAN 200-2213) Tel 415-595-2350; Orders to: Distribution Ctr., 7625 Empire Dr., Florence, KY 41042-2978 (SAN 200-2663) Tel 606-525-2230; Toll free: 800-354-9706.

Wafer Mache, *(Wafer Mache Pubns., Inc.; 0-935009),* 16 Elmgate Rd., Marlton, NJ 08053 (SAN 695-2143) Tel 609-983-5360.

Wahr, *(Wahr, George, Publishing Co.; 0-911586;* 1-884739), 304 1/2 S. State St., Ann Arbor, MI 48104 (SAN 205-5015) Tel 313-668-6097; Toll free: 800-805-2497.

WAI Pubng, *(WAI Publishing Co.; 0-9638123),* Div. of WAI Enterprises, Inc., 1559 Rockville Pike, Rockville, MD 20852 Tel 301-702-2459.

Waking Light Pr, *(Waking Light Pr., The; 0-9605444),* P.O. Box 1329, Sparks, NV 89432 (SAN 215-983X) Tel 702-356-0216.

Waldman Hse Pr, *(Waldman Hse. Pr., Inc.; 0-931674),* 525 N. Third St., Minneapolis, MN 55401 (SAN 295-0243) Tel 612-341-4044; Dist. by: Baker & Taylor Bks., Momence Service Ctr., 501 S. Gladiolus St., Momence, IL 60954-2444 (SAN 169-2100) Tel 815-472-2444; Toll free: 800-775-2300 (customer service); Dist. by: Ingram Bk. Co., 1 Ingram Blvd., La Vergne, TN 37086-1986 (SAN 169-7978) Tel 615-793-5000; Toll free: 800-937-8000 (orders only); Dist. by: Bookmen, Inc., 525 N. Third St., Minneapolis, MN 55401 (SAN 169-409X) Tel 612-341-3333; Toll free: 800-328-8411 (customer service); Dist. by: The Distributors, 702 S. Michigan, South Bend, IN 46601 (SAN 169-2488) Tel 219-232-8500; Toll free: 800-348-5200 (except Indiana); Dist. by: Pacific Pipeline, Inc., 8030 S. 228th St., Kent, WA 98032-2900 (SAN 208-2128) Tel 206-872-5523; Toll free: 800-444-7323 (Customer Service); 800-677-2222 (orders); Dist. by: Spring Arbor Distributors, 10885 Textile Rd., Belleville, MI 48111 (SAN 158-9016) Tel 313-481-0900; Toll free: 800-395-5599 (orders); 800-395-7234 (customer service); Dist. by: The Booksource, 4127 Forest Pk. Blvd., Saint Louis, MO 63108 (SAN 169-4324) Tel 314-652-1000; Toll free: 800-444-0435; Dist. by: Koen Bk. Distributors, 10 Twosome Dr., P.O. Box 600, Moorestown, NJ 08057 (SAN 169-4642) Tel 609-235-4444; Toll free: 800-257-8481.

Walker & Co, *(Walker & Co.; 0-8027),* Div. of Walker Publishing Co., Inc., 435 Hudson St., New York, NY 10014 (SAN 202-5213) Tel 212-727-8300; Toll free: 800-289-2553 (orders).

Walker Educ, *(Walker Educational Bk. Corp.; 0-8027),* Affil. of Walker & Co., 720 Fifth Ave., New York, NY 10019 (SAN 206-1899) Tel 212-265-3632.

Walker Pubns, *(Walker Pubns.; 0-9615182),* P.O. Box 17924, Irvine, CA 92713 (SAN 694-3462).

Wall To Wall, *(Wall To Wall Pubns.; 0-9626427),* 825 West End Ave., New York, NY 10025 Tel 212-662-9764.

Wallbuilders, *(Wallbuilders Press; 0-925279),* P.O. Box 397, Aledo, TX 76008; 950 Chapman Ct., Aledo, TX 76008 Tel 817-441-6044.

Walpa Pub, *(Walpa Publishing; 0-9614765; 1-878188),* 4201 Prices Fork Rd., Blacksburg, VA 24060 (SAN 692-915X) Tel 703-951-2045.

Walsh Assocs, *(Walsh, Jeff, /Walsh Assocs.; 0-9636883),* P.O. Box 3185, Columbus, GA 31903; B Co., 3/11 OCS Infantry, Fort Benning, GA 31905 Tel 706-545-3939.

Wamy Intl, *(Wamy International, Inc.; 1-882837),* P.O. Box 8096, Falls Church, VA 22041-8096 Tel 703-931-7239.

Ward Hill Pr, *(Ward Hill Pr.; 0-9623380),* 40 Willis Ave., Staten Island, NY 10301 (SAN 200-3139) Tel 718-816-9449; Toll free: 800-356-9315.

Warne, *(Warne, Frederick, & Co., Inc.; 0-7232),* Div. of Penguin USA, 375 Hudson St., New York, NY 10014-3657 (SAN 212-9884) Tel 212-366-2000; Dist. by: Penguin USA, P.O. Box 120, Bergenfield, NJ 07621-0120 (SAN 282-5074) Tel 201-387-0600; Toll free: 800-526-0275.

Warner Bks, *(Warner Bks., Inc.; 0-446; 0-445),* A Time Warner Co., 1271 Avenue of the Americas, New York, NY 10020 (SAN 281-8892) Tel 212-522-7200; Orders to: Little, Brown & Co., 200 West St., Waltham, MA 02154 (SAN 630-7248); Toll free: 800-759-0190.

Warner Pr, *(Warner Pr. Pubs.; 0-87162),* 1200 E. Fifth St., Anderson, IN 46012 (SAN 111-8110) Tel 317-644-7721; Toll free: 800-347-7721; 800-347-6409 (orders only); Orders to: P.O. Box 2499, Anderson, IN 46018 (SAN 691-4241).

Warren-Mattox, *(Warren-Mattox Productions;* 0-9623381), 301 Lakespring Pl., Oakley, CA 94561-3162; Dist. by: Lancaster Productions, 535 Pierce St., No. 356, Albany, CA 94706 (SAN 241-9807) Tel 510-524-6996.

Warren Pub Hse, *(Warren Publishing Hse., Inc.; 0-911019; 1-57029),* 11625G Airport Rd., Everett, WA 98204 (SAN 667-4585) Tel 206-353-3100; Toll free: 800-405-6041.

Warthog Pub, *(Warthog Publishing; 0-9633108),* c/o Center for Creativity & Management, 4425 Randolph Rd., Suite 205, Charlotte, NC 28211 Tel 704-365-0870.

Warwick *Imprint of* **Watts**

Wash Dolls Hse, *(Washington Dolls' Hse. & Toy* Museum), 5236 44th St., NW, Washington, DC 20015 (SAN 217-2747) Tel 202-363-6400.

Wash Res Assocs, *(Washington Research Assocs.;* 0-937801), 1660 S. Albion St., Suite 309, Denver, CO 80222 (SAN 659-378X) Tel 303-756-9038.

Wash Sikh Ctr, *(Washington Sikh Ctr./Sikh Youth Forum; 0-942245),* 6725 Meek Hollow Rd., Gaithersburg, MD 20898 (SAN 666-8658) Tel 301-854-9886.

Wash Writers Pub, *(Washington Writers' Publishing Hse.; 0-931846),* P.O. Box 15271, Washington, DC 20003 (SAN 211-9250) Tel 703-527-5890; Orders to: 4901 N. 17th St., Arlington, VA 22207 Tel 703-524-1257.

Water St Missouri, *(Water Street Pubs.; 0-9616799),* 6125 Marwinette Ave., Saint Louis, MO 63116 (SAN 661-0382) Tel 314-351-2427.

Waterfront Bks, *(Waterfront Bks.; 0-914525),* 85 Crescent Rd., Burlington, VT 05401 (SAN 289-6923) Tel 802-658-7477; Toll free: 800-639-6063; Dist. by: Talman Co., 131 Spring St., Suite 201E-N, New York, NY 10012 (SAN 200-5204) Tel 212-431-7175; Toll free: 800-537-8894 (orders only); Dist. by: Quality Bks., Inc., 918 Sherwood Dr., Lake Bluff, IL 60044-2204 (SAN 169-2127) Tel 708-295-2010; Toll free: 800-323-4241 (libraries only).

Waterlinc Prodns, *(Waterlinc Productions; 0-929592),* 600 Berkley St., No. 3, Camden, NJ 08103-1414 (SAN 249-7034) Tel 609-964-3513.

WaterMark Inc, *(WaterMark, Inc.; 1-882077),* P.O. Box 1400, Columbiana, AL 35051-1400 (SAN 248-2010) Tel 205-665-5577; Toll free: 800-676-6371. Do not confuse with Watermark Pr., Inc. in Wichita, KS or Watermark Assocs., Inc. in New York, NY.

Waterston Product
See Sagebrush Bks

Watts, *(Watts, Franklin, Inc.; 0-531),* Subs. of Grolier, Inc., 95 Madison Ave., New York, NY 10016 (SAN 285-1156) Tel 212-951-2650; Toll free: 800-672-6672 (Customer Service); Orders to: 5450 N. Cumberland Ave., Chicago, IL 60656 Tel 312-693-3300; Toll free: 800-672-6672. *Imprints:* Gloucester Pr (Gloucester Press); Warwick (Warwick Press).

Wave *Imprint of* **Western Pub**

Way Pub, *(Way Publishing Co., The; 0-915515),* Subs. of MHA-Mark Hyman Assocs., Inc., 5070 Parkside Ave., Suite 1122, Philadelphia, PA 19131 (SAN 292-465X) Tel 215-473-0050.

Wayne St U Pr, *(Wayne State Univ. Pr.; 0-8143),* Leonard N. Simons Bldg., 4809 Woodward Ave., Detroit, MI 48201-1309 (SAN 202-5221) Tel 313-577-4600.

Wayside Pub, *(Wayside Publishing; 1-877653),* 129 Commonwealth Ave., Concord, MA 01742 Tel 508-369-2519.

Wayward Fluffy, *(Wayward Fluffy Pubns.; 0-9642360),* 38 Sandy Ridge Rd., Stoughton, MA 02072 Tel 617-344-4989.

Weaselsleeves Pr, *(Weaselsleeves Pr.; 1-878460),* P.O. Box 8187, Santa Fe, NM 87504; Las Dos Subdivision, Lot 27, Santa Fe, NM 87504 Tel 505-988-3871.

Weatherhill, *(Weatherhill, Inc.; 0-8348),* 420 Madison Ave., 15th Flr., New York, NY 10017-1107 (SAN 202-9529) Tel 212-223-3008; Orders to: 41 Monroe Tpke., Trumbull, CT 06611 (SAN 630-6209) Tel 203-459-5090; Toll free: 800-437-7840 (orders).

WEB Pubng, *(WEB Publishing Co.; 0-9639014),* 2993 W. 81st Ave., Unit D, Westminster, CO 80030-4143 Tel 303-426-1855.

Websters New Wrld *Imprint of* **P-H Gen Ref & Trav**

Weddon Pr, *(Weddon Pr.; 0-9638376),* 4891 Dexter Trail, Stockbridge, MI 49285 Tel 517-851-7185.

Wedgehouse, *(Wedgehouse; 0-944073),* R.R.1, Box 261, Waitsfield, VT 05673 (SAN 242-4770) Tel 802-496-3114.

Wee-Chee-Taw, *(Wee-Chee-Taw Publishing; 0-9622632),* 4450 Phillips Dr., Wichita Falls, TX 76308 Tel 817-692-3791.

Wee Pr, *(Wee Pr.; 0-9625005),* 800 S. 38th St., Terre Haute, IN 47803 Tel 812-234-6033.

Wee Smile
See Waking Light Pr

Weeping Heart, *(Weeping Heart Pubns.; 0-9635204),* N1634 Lakeshore Dr., Campbellsport, WI 53010 Tel 414-533-8880.

Weider Health, *(Weider Health & Fitness; 0-945797),* 21100 Erwin St., Woodland Hills, CA 91367 (SAN 247-5588) Tel 818-715-0635.

Weinberg, *(Weinberg, Michael Aron; 0-9601014),* 6940 Sepulveda Blvd., Apt. 39, Van Nuys, CA 91405-5403 (SAN 208-2314); 4408 Russell St., No. 3, Los Angeles, CA 90027 (SAN 241-8924) Tel 213-669-0158.

Weiss Pub, *(Weiss Publishing Co., Inc.; 0-916720),* 5309 W. Grace St., Richmond, VA 23226 (SAN 208-4775) Tel 804-282-4641.

Wellford, *(Wellford Publishing; 1-884217),* 886 Washington St., Suite 330, Dedham, MA 02026 Tel 617-329-1348.

Wellington IL, *(Wellington Publishing, Inc.; 0-922984),* P.O. Box 14877, Chicago, IL 60614-0877 (SAN 251-7795); 449 W. Aldine Ave., Chicago, IL 60657 (SAN 251-7809) Tel 312-472-4820.

Wellspring Utah, *(Wellspring Publishing Co.; 0-9608658;* 1-884312), P.O. Box 1113, Sandy, UT 84091 (SAN 239-5800); 547 W., 9460 S., Sandy, UT 84070 Tel 801-566-9355; Orders to: 9500 S., 500 W, Sandy, UT 84070 (SAN 666-6825) Tel 801-566-9355.

WELS Board, *(WELS Board for Parish Education;* 0-938272), 2929 N. Mayfair Rd., Milwaukee, WI 53222 (SAN 216-3160) Tel 414-771-9357.

Welty Pr, *(Welty Pr.; 0-9632953),* 2101 E. Fourth St., Duluth, MN 55812 Tel 218-728-6928.

Wenkart, *(Wenkart, Henri; 0-911612),* 40 Central Park S., Suite 6D, New York, NY 10019 (SAN 206-300X) Tel 212-751-9223.

Wesley Inst, *(Wesley Institute, Inc.; 0-9614501),* 243 Johnston Rd., Pittsburgh, PA 15241 (SAN 689-9625) Tel 412-831-9390; Orders to: P.O. Box 113445, Pittsburgh, PA 15241 (SAN 662-2879).

West Hill Pr, *(West Hill Pr.; 0-939775),* Rte. 1, Box 221, Fitzwilliam, NH 03447 (SAN 663-7450); Fisher Hill, Fitzwilliam, NH 03447 (SAN 663-7469) Tel 603-585-6883.

West Pub, *(West Publishing Co., College & Schl. Div.; 0-8299; 0-314),* 620 Opperman Dr., Saint Paul, MN 55164 (SAN 202-9618) Tel 612-687-7000; College & School Div., P.O. Box 64779, 58 W. Kellogg Blvd., Saint Paul, MN 55164-9424 (SAN 241-8932) Tel 612-668-3600.

West Side Pubns, *(West Side Pubns.; 1-877924),* 140 W. 102nd St., New York, NY 10025 Tel 212-865-3522.

West Village, *(West Village Publishing Co.; 0-933308),* 2904 E. Vanowen Ave., Orange, CA 92667 (SAN 213-1870) Tel 714-633-1420.

Westcliffe Pubs Inc, *(Westcliffe Pubs., Inc.; 0-942394; 0-929969; 1-56579),* 2650 S. Zuni St., Englewood, CO 80110 (SAN 239-7528) Tel 303-935-0900; Toll free: 800-523-3692 (outside Colorado, orders only). Do not confuse with Westcliff Publications in Newport Beach, CA.

Westcom NC, *(Westcom Pr.; 0-9626554),* 715 Washington St., Ayden, NC 28513; Toll free: 800-422-8591.

Westerfield Enter, *(Westerfield Enterprises, Inc.;* 0-942259), P.O. Box 6219, San Diego, CA 92166 (SAN 666-8194); 3043 Barnard, No. 1, San Diego, CA 92110 (SAN 666-8208) Tel 619-226-3271.

Western Guideways, *(Western Guideways, Ltd.;* 0-931788), P.O. Box 15532, Lakewood, CO 80215 (SAN 210-6264) Tel 303-237-0583.

Western Pub, *(Western Publishing Co., Inc.; 0-307),* Subs. of Western Publishing Group, Inc., ; Orders to: 1220 Mound Ave., Racine, WI 53404 (SAN 297-6706) Tel 414-633-2431; Toll free: 800-225-9514; Dist. by: Children's Pr., 1224 W. Van Buren St., Chicago, IL 60607 (SAN 201-9264) Tel 414-633-2431; Toll free: 800-621-1115. Do not confuse with Western Pubs., New Bern, NC. *Imprints:* Artsts Writrs (Artists & Writers Guild); Golden Pr (Golden Press); Wave (Wave).

Western Slope Pubns, *(Western Slope Pubns.; 0-944523),* P.O. Box 55332-BW, Grand Junction, CO 81505-5332 (SAN 242-9624) Tel 303-241-9426.

Western Trails, *(Western Trails Pr.; 0-9633604),* 18014 Jayhawk Dr., Penn Valley, CA 95946-9206 Tel 916-432-3391. Do not confuse with Western Trails Pubns. in Grover City, CA.

Westgate Pub & Ent, *(Westgate Publishing & Entertainment, Inc.; 0-9633598),* 260 Crandon Blvd., Suite 32-109, Miami, FL 33149 Tel 305-361-6862; Dist. by: Baker & Taylor Bks., Somerville Service Ctr., 50 Kirby Ave., Somerville, NJ 08876-0734 (SAN 169-4901) Tel 908-722-8000; Toll free: 800-775-1500 (customer service); Dist. by: Baker & Taylor Bks., Momence Service Ctr., 501 S. Gladiolus St., Momence, IL 60954-2444 (SAN 169-2100) Tel 815-472-2444; Toll free: 800-775-2300 (customer service); Dist. by: Baker & Taylor Bks., Commerce Service Ctr., 251 Mt. Olive Church Rd., Commerce, GA 30599-9988 (SAN 169-1503) Tel 706-335-5000; Toll free: 800-775-1200 (customer service); Dist. by: Baker & Taylor Bks., Reno Service Ctr., 380 Edison Way, Reno, NV 89564 (SAN 169-4464) Tel 702-858-6700; Toll free: 800-775-1700 (customer service); Dist. by: Publishers Distribution Service, 6893 Sullivan Rd., Grawn, MI 49637 (SAN 630-5717) Tel 616-276-5196; Toll free: 800-345-0096 (orders only); Dist. by: Ingram Bk. Co., 1 Ingram Blvd., La Vergne, TN 37086-1986 (SAN 169-7978) Tel 615-793-5000; Toll free: 800-937-8000 (orders only, all warehouses).

Westminster *Imprint of* **Westminster John Knox**

Westminster John Knox, *(Westminster John Knox Pr.; 0-664; 0-8042),* 100 Witherspoon St., Louisville, KY 40202-1396 (SAN 202-9669); Toll free: 800-523-1631; Orders to: Spring Arbor Distributors, 10885 Textile Rd., Belleville, MI 48111 (SAN 158-9016) Tel 313-481-0900; Toll free: 800-395-5599 (orders); 800-395-7234 (customer service). *Imprints:* Geneva Pr (Geneva Press); Westminster (Westminster Press).

Westport Pubs, *(Westport Pubs., Inc.; 0-9611286;* 0-933701), 4050 Pennsylvania, Suite 310, Kansas City, MO 64111 (SAN 283-3492) Tel 816-756-1490; Toll free: 800-347-2665.

WestSea Pub, *(WestSea Publishing Co., Inc.; 0-937820),* 149D Allen Blvd., Farmingdale, NY 11735 (SAN 215-7144) Tel 516-420-1110.

Westview, *(Westview Pr.; 0-89158; 0-86531; 0-8133),* 5500 Central Ave., Boulder, CO 80301-2847 (SAN 219-970X) Tel 303-444-3541; Toll free: 800-456-1995.

WestWind *Imprint of* **Troll Assocs**

Westwind Pr, *(Westwind Pr.; 0-9602342),* Rte. 1, Box 208, Farmington, WV 26571 (SAN 215-7152).

Westwood Ent, *(Westwood Enterprises; 0-9617118),* 5302 N. 79th Pl., Scottsdale, AZ 85253 (SAN 662-8028) Tel 602-994-8244.

Westwood Pr, *(Westwood Pr., Inc.; 0-936159),* 23 E. 22nd St., 4th Flr., New York, NY 10010 (SAN 696-7183) Tel 212-420-8008.

Wetlands *Imprint of* **RDR Bks**

WFB Ent, *(WFB Enterprises; 1-881936),* 1225 19th St., Beaumont, TX 77706 Tel 409-898-1983.

Whale Museum, *(Whale Museum/Moclips Cetological Society, The; 0-933331),* 62 First St., N., Box 945, Friday Harbor, WA 98250 (SAN 692-2864) Tel 206-378-4710; Dist. by: Pacific Pipeline, Inc., 8030 S. 228th St, Kent, WA 98032-2900 (SAN 208-2128) Tel 206-872-5523; Toll free: 800-444-7323 (Customer Service); 800-677-2222 (orders); Dist. by: Bookpeople, 7900 Edgewater Dr., Oakland, CA 94621 (SAN 168-9517) Tel 510-632-4700; Toll free: 800-999-4650.

What the Heck, *(What the Heck Pr.; 1-882979),* 11693 San Vicente Blvd., Suite 358, Los Angeles, CA 90049 (SAN 297-8466); Toll free: 800-316-4325.

Whatcom Cty Opp, *(Whatcom County Opportunity Council; 0-934671),* Div. of Coalition for Child Advocacy, 314 E. Holly St., 2nd Flr., Bellingham, WA 98225 (SAN 694-0781) Tel 206-734-5121.

Wheat'N Flower, *(Wheat'N Flower Designs; 0-9613993),* P.O. Box 2433, Springfield, IL 62705 (SAN 683-129X) Tel 217-546-5096.

When & Where, *(When And Where; 0-9641588),* P.O. Box 1531, Englewood Cliffs, NJ 07632; 82 Franklin St., Englewood, NJ 07631 Tel 201-567-3459.

Whimsical Pubns, *(Whimsical Publications; 1-884525),* 1320 E. Sixth St., Loveland, CO 80537 Tel 303-669-4852; Orders to: P.O. Box 262, Loveland, CO 80539-0262.

Whirlwind Pr, *(Whirlwind Pr.; 0-922827),* P.O. Box 109, Camden, NJ 08101 (SAN 251-4281); 805 Corinthian St., Philadelphia, PA 19103 (SAN 251-429X) Tel 215-925-9914.

Whistlstop *Imprint of* **Troll Assocs**

Whit Prodns, *(Whit Productions, Inc.; 0-9624744),* P.O. Box 1397, Murray, KY 40175; 1204 College Cts., Murray, KY 40175 Tel 502-759-9448.

Whitcomb Minist, *(Whitcomb Ministries, Inc.;* 0-9635049), P.O. Box 277, Winona Lake, IN 46590; 903 Presidential Dr., Winona Lake, IN 46590 Tel 219-267-8243.

White & Spencer, *(White, Laurie A., & Steven L. Spencer; 0-9612024),* 4340 Tamarac Trail, Harbor Springs, MI 49740 (SAN 287-7791) Tel 616-347-6701.

White DEI, *(White DEI; 0-9636278),* P.O. Box 171084, Arlington, TX 76003 Tel 817-784-1880.

White Feather & Co, *(White Feather & Co. Publishing;* 0-9625641), P.O. Box 354, Solomons, MD 20688 Tel 703-758-8964; Toll free: 800-444-2583.

White Heron, *(White Heron Pr.; 0-9641228),* P.O. Box 468, Islamorada, FL 33036; 83255 Old Hwy., Islamorada, FL 33036 Tel 305-595-7416.

White Lilac Pr, *(White Lilac Pr.; 0-929571),* P.O. Box 2354, Providence, RI 02906 (SAN 250-0361); 20 Lorimer Ave., Providence, RI 02906 (SAN 250-037X) Tel 401-273-6678.

White Mane Pub, *(White Mane Publishing Co., Inc.; 0-942597; 1-57249),* P.O. Box 152, Shippensburg, PA 17257 (SAN 667-1926); 63 W. Burd St., Shippensburg, PA 17257 (SAN 667-1934) Tel 717-532-2237.

White Oak Pr, *(White Oak Pr.; 0-935069),* P.O. Box 188, Reeds Springs, MO 65737 (SAN 694-695X) Tel 417-272-3507. Do not confuse with White Oak Pr., imprint of Candeur Manuscripts, Spring Valley, NY.

White Pine MI
See Pineapple MI

White Pond, *(White Pond Pr.; 0-9640176),* 85 Jennie Dugan Rd., Concord, MA 01742 Tel 508-369-7426.

White Pubng, *(White Publishing; 1-884693),* 173 Blodgett Ln., Arlee, MT 59821 Tel 406-726-4162.

White Rose Pr, *(White Rose Pr.; 0-940561),* 65 Monroe Ave., Memphis, TN 38103 (SAN 664-7545) Tel 901-525-1836.

White Stone, *(White Stone Co., The; 1-880122),* 6817 Miller St., Arvada, CO 80004-1535 (SAN 297-7907) Tel 303-456-0438.

White Truffle Bks, *(White Truffle Bks.; 0-9643034),* 4749 Black Forest Ct., Lake Oswego, OR 97035 Tel 503-635-6444; Dist. by: Pacific Pipeline, Inc., 8030 S. 228th St., Kent, WA 98032-2900 (SAN 208-2128) Tel 206-872-5523; Toll free: 800-444-7323 (customer service); 800-677-2222 (orders).

White Wing Pub, *(White Wing Publishing Hse. & Pr.;* 0-934942), P.O. Box 3000, Cleveland, TN 37311 (SAN 203-2198) Tel 615-476-8536; Toll free: 800-221-5027.

Whitebird Bks *Imprint of* **Putnam Pub Group**

Whitefoord, *(Whitefoord Pr.; 0-9632341),* 806 Oakwood Blvd., Dearborn, MI 48124 Tel 313-274-1038.

Whitehall Pr, *(Whitehall Pr.-Budget Pubns.; 0-916565),* Whitehall, Rte. 1, Box 603, Sandersville, GA 31082 (SAN 295-5512) Tel 912-552-7455.

Whitehead Pub, *(Whitehead Publishing Co.; 0-9624089),* P.O. Box 564, Amado, AZ 85645; 1 Avenido Whitehead, Amado, AZ 85645 Tel 602-398-2086.

Whitehorse, *(Whitehorse; 0-937591),* Orders to: P.O. Box 6125, Boise, ID 83707-6125 (SAN 242-1062).

Whites Creek Pr, *(Whites Creek Pr.; 0-9616918),* P.O. Box 266, Whites Creek, TN 37189 (SAN 661-5430); 4772 Lickton Pike, Whites Creek, TN 37189 (SAN 661-5449) Tel 615-876-2622.

Whitfield Bks, *(Whitfield Bks.; 0-930920),* 1841 Pleasant Hill Rd., Pleasant Hill, CA 94523 (SAN 210-6280) Tel 415-938-6759.

Whole Child, *(Whole Child; 1-880702),* Div. of Southwest Alternatives Institute, P.O. Box 65424, Tucson, AZ 85728-5424; 4851 E. Paseo del Bac, Tucson, AZ 85718 Tel 602-299-9169.

Wholeness Intl, *(Wholeness International Network (W. I.N.); 1-877616),* 12407 Venice Blvd., Los Angeles, CA 90066-3803 Tel 310-391-1007.

Whsprng Coyote Pr, *(Whispering Coyote Pr.; 1-879085),* 480 Newbury St., Suite 104, Danvers, MA 01923 (SAN 297-7761) Tel 508-922-7273; Toll free: 800-929-6104; 7130 Alexander Dr., Dallas, TX 75214.

WI Potato Grow, *(Wisconsin Potato Growers Auxiliary;* 0-9635149), 700 Fifth Ave., P.O. Box 327, Antigo, WI 54409 Tel 715-623-7683.

Wibat Pubns, *(Wibat Pubns.; 0-935996),* P.O. Box 160, Forestville, CA 95436 (SAN 214-1698) Tel 707-431-7107.

Wichita Eagle, *(Wichita Eagle & Beacon Publishing Co.;* 1-880652), Div. of Knight-Ridder, Inc., P.O. Box 820, Wichita, KS 67201; Toll free: 800-825-6397; 825 E. Douglas, Wichita, KS 67202 Tel 316-268-6390.

Wide-Awake Bks, *(Wide-Awake Bks.; 0-9623473),* P.O. Box 659, El Cerrito, CA 94530-0659 Tel 510-235-5516; Toll free: 800-468-2239.

Wide World-Tetra, *(Wide World Publishing/Tetra; 0-933174; 1-884550),* P.O. Box 476, San Carlos, CA 94070 (SAN 211-1462); 405 Industrial Dr., San Carlos, CA 94070 Tel 415-593-2839; Dist. by: Publishers Group West, 4065 Hollis St., Emeryville, CA 94608 (SAN 202-8522) Tel 510-658-3453; Toll free: 800-788-3123; Dist. by: Bookpeople, 7900 Edgewater Dr., Oakland, CA 94621 (SAN 168-9517) Tel 510-632-4700; Toll free: 800-999-4650; Dist. by: Quality Bks., Inc., 918 Sherwood Dr., Lake Bluff, IL 60044-2204 (SAN 169-2127) Tel 708-295-2010; Toll free: 800-323-4241 (libraries only); Dist. by: Booklines Hawaii, Ltd., P.O. Box 2170, Pearl City, HI 96782 (SAN 630-6624) Tel 808-676-0116; Dist. by: Inland Bk. Co., 140 Commerce St., East Haven, CT 06512 (SAN 200-4151) Tel 203-467-4257; Toll free: 800-243-0138; Dist. by: Ingram Bk. Co., 1 Ingram Blvd., La Vergne, TN 37086-1986 (SAN 169-7978) Tel 615-793-5000; Toll free: 800-937-8000 (orders only, all warehouses); Dist. by: Baker & Taylor Bks., Somerville Service Ctr., 50 Kirby Ave., Somerville, NJ 08876-0734 (SAN 169-4901) Tel 908-722-8000; Toll free: 800-775-1500 (customer service); Dist. by: Baker & Taylor Bks., Momence Service Ctr., 501 S. Gladiolus St., Momence, IL 60954-2444 (SAN 169-2100) Tel 815-472-2444; Toll free: 800-775-2300 (customer service); Dist. by: Baker & Taylor Bks., Commerce Service Ctr., 251 Mt. Olive Church Rd., Commerce, GA 30599-9988 (SAN 169-1503) Tel 706-335-5000; Toll free: 800-775-1200 (customer service); Dist. by: Baker & Taylor Bks., Reno Service Ctr., 380 Edison Way, Reno, NV 89564 (SAN 169-4464) Tel 702-858-6700; Toll free: 800-775-1700 (customer service).

Wiener Pub Inc
See Wiener Pubs Inc

Wiener Pubs Inc, *(Wiener, Markus, Pubs., Inc.; 0-910129; 1-55876),* 114 Jefferson Rd., Princeton, NJ 08540 (SAN 282-5465) Tel 609-921-1141; Orders to: 100 Newfield Ave., Edison, NJ 08837 Tel 908-225-2727.

Wilander Pub, *(Wilander Publishing Co.; 0-9628335),* P.O. Box 56121, Airport Sta., Portland, OR 97238.

Wild Bore Bks, *(Wild Bore Bks.; 0-942379),* P.O. Box 25, Banks, OR 97106 (SAN 666-9050) Tel 503-324-7041.

Wild Foods Co, *(Wild Foods Co., Inc.; 0-936699),* c/o Wild Food Co., 3531 W. Glendale Ave., Suite 369, Phoenix, AZ 85051 (SAN 248-4048) Tel 602-930-1067; Dist. by: Baker & Taylor Bks., Momence Service Ctr., 501 S. Gladiolus St., Momence, IL 60954-2444 (SAN 169-2100) Tel 815-472-2444; Toll free: 800-775-2300 (customer service); Dist. by: New Leaf Distributing Co., 5425 Tulane Dr., SW, Atlanta, GA 30336-2323 (SAN 169-1449) Tel 404-691-6996; Toll free: 800-326-2665.

Wild Horses, *(Wild Horses Publishing Co.; 0-9601088;* 0-937148), 12310 Concepcion Rd., Los Altos Hills, CA 94022 (SAN 211-8289) Tel 415-941-3396.

Wild Meadows
See Magnolia South Pub

Wild Rose CO, *(Wild Rose; 0-9636234),* 3003 Valmont Rd., No. 25, Boulder, CO 80301 Tel 303-449-3945.

Wildbasin Pubng, *(Wildbasin Publishing; 0-9641502),* P.O. Box 31, Allenspark, CO 80510; 351 Moraine St., Allenspark, CO 80510 Tel 303-586-5758.

Wilderness Adventure Bks, *(Wilderness Adventure Bks.; 0-9611596; 0-923568),* P.O. Box 217, Davisburg, MI 48350 (SAN 110-8883) Tel 810-634-1595; Toll free: 800-852-8652; Dist. by: Baker & Taylor Bks., National Sales Hdqtrs., 5 Lakepointe Plaza, Suite 500, 2709 Water Ridge Pkwy., Charlotte, NC 28217 (SAN 169-5606); Toll free: 800-775-1800 (information); 800-775-1100 (Retail, Public & School Libraries orders); 800-775-2300 (Academic Libraries, Int'l customers orders); Dist. by: Partners Bk. Distributing, Inc., 720 E. Shiawassie, Lansing, MI 48912 (SAN 630-4559) Tel 517-485-0366; Toll free: 800-336-3137; Dist. by: Pacific Pipeline, Inc., 8030 S. 228th St., Kent, WA 98032-2900 (SAN 208-2128) Tel 206-872-5523; Toll free: 800-444-7323 (Customer Service); 800-677-2222 (orders).

Wilderness Hse, *(Wilderness Hse.; 0-931798),* 11129 Caves Hwy., Cave Junction, OR 97523 (SAN 208-0907) Tel 503-592-2106.

Wildlife Educ, *(Wildlife Education, Ltd.; 0-937934),* 9820 Willow Creek Rd., Suite 300, San Diego, CA 92131 (SAN 215-8299) Tel 619-578-9658; Toll free: 800-477-5034.

Wiley, *(Wiley, John, & Sons, Inc.; 0-471; 0-8260),* 605 Third Ave., New York, NY 10158-0012 (SAN 200-2272) Tel 212-850-6000; Toll free: 800-225-5945 (orders); Orders to: John Wiley & Sons, Inc., Eastern Distribution Ctr., 1 Wiley Dr., Somerset, NJ 08875-1272 Tel 908-469-4400.

Willard Pr, *(Willard Pr.; 0-9615349),* P.O. Box 1254, Summit, NJ 07901 (SAN 695-099X) Tel 609-497-0062.

Williams SC, *(Williams Assocs., Inc.; 0-9612296;* 0-944514), P.O. Box 1849, Orangeburg, SC 29115 (SAN 263-2365); 1215 Perry Dr., Orangeburg, SC 29115 (SAN 243-2803) Tel 803-531-1662.

Williamsburg, *(Colonial Williamsburg Foundation; 0-910412; 0-87935),* P.O. Box 1776, Williamsburg, VA 23187-1776 (SAN 128-4630) Tel 804-220-7178; Toll free: 800-446-9240 (orders only); Dist. by: Koen Bk. Distributors, 10 Twosome Dr., P.O. Box 600, Moorestown, NJ 08057 (SAN 169-4642) Tel 609-235-4444; Toll free: 800-257-8481; Dist. by: Baker & Taylor Bks., Somerville Service Ctr., 50 Kirby Ave., Somerville, NJ 08876-0734 (SAN 169-4901) Tel 908-722-8000; Toll free: 800-775-1500 (customer service); Dist. by: Baker & Taylor Bks., Momence Service Ctr., 501 S. Gladiolus St., Momence, IL 60954-2444 (SAN 169-2100) Tel 815-472-2444; Toll free: 800-775-2300 (customer service); Dist. by: Baker & Taylor Bks., Commerce Service Ctr., 251 Mt. Olive Church Rd., Commerce, GA 30599-9988 (SAN 169-1503) Tel 706-335-5000; Toll free: 800-775-1200 (customer service); Dist. by: Baker & Taylor Bks., Reno Service Ctr., 380 Edison Way, Reno, NV 89564 (SAN 169-4464) Tel 702-858-6700; Toll free: 800-775-1700 (customer service); Dist. by: Ingram Bk. Co., 1 Ingram Blvd., La Vergne, TN 37086-1986 (SAN 169-7978) Tel 615-793-5000; Toll free: 800-937-8000 (orders only, all warehouses).

Williamson Pub Co, *(Williamson Publishing Co.; 0-913589; 1-885593),* Church Hill Rd., P.O. Box 185, Charlotte, VT 05445 (SAN 285-3884) Tel 802-425-2102; Toll free: 800-234-8791.

Willow & Laurel, *(Willow & Laurel Pr.; 0-9630934),* 213 Vanderveer St., Middletown, OH 45044-4235 Tel 513-423-6948.

Willow Creek Pr, *(Willow Creek Pr., Inc.; 0-932558),* P.O. Box 1360, Minocqua, WI 54548 (SAN 211-2825) Tel 715-356-9800; Toll free: 800-336-5666 (orders only).

Willow Pr, *(Willow Pr.; 0-9617159),* 19630 166th Ave., NE, Woodinville, WA 98072 (SAN 663-253X) Tel 206-483-9198. Do not confuse with Willow Pr., Littleton, CO.

Willow Run UT, *(Willow Run Pr.; 0-9621033),* 351 S. State St., No. 18, Mt. Pleasant, UT 84647 (SAN 250-6491) Tel 801-283-4556.

Willow Tree NY, *(Willow Tree Pr.; 0-9606960;* 1-881798), P.O. Box 249, Monsey, NY 10952 (SAN 217-4588); 124 Willow Tree Rd., Monsey, NY 10952 Tel 914-354-9139; Dist. by: Library Research Assocs., Inc., Dunderberg Rd., R.D. 5, Box 41, Monroe, NY 10950 (SAN 201-0887) Tel 914-783-1144. Do not confuse with Willow Tree, Inc. in Fresno, CA.

Willow Wrks, *(Willow Works, Inc.; 0-9640956),* 150 Soule St., Athens, GA 30605 Tel 706-353-2104.

Willowisp Pr, *(Willowisp Pr., Inc.; 0-87406),* 801 94th Ave. N., Suite 100, Saint Petersburg, FL 33702 (SAN 687-4592); Toll free: 800-877-8090.

Wilshire Hse AR
See Ozark Pub

Wilson, *(Wilson, H. W.; 0-8242),* 950 University Ave., Bronx, NY 10452 (SAN 203-2961) Tel 718-588-8400; Toll free: 800-367-6770.

Wilson Investment, *(Wilson Investment, Inc.;* 0-9627193), 114 Chaussee Blvd., Summerville, SC 29483 Tel 803-875-1396.

Wilson Lang Trning, *(Wilson Language Training;* 1-56778), 162 W. Main St., Millbury, MA 01527-1943 Tel 508-865-5699; Toll free: 800-899-8454.

Wilson Oregon, *(Wilson, Marie M.; 0-9615259),* 350 Pearl St., No. 911, Eugene, OR 97401 (SAN 695-1597) Tel 503-343-0451. Do not confuse with companies with similar names, particularly H. W. Wilson, Bronx, NY. Please use ISBN to determine correct publisher.

WIM Pubns, *(Woman in the Moon Pubns.; 0-934172),* P.O. Box 2087, Cupertino, CA 95015-2087 (SAN 241-8851) Tel 408-738-4623; Dist. by: Bookpeople, 7900 Edgewater Dr., Oakland, CA 94621 (SAN 168-9517) Tel 510-632-4700; Toll free: 800-999-4650.

Wimmer Bks, *(Wimmer Bks.; 0-918544; 0-939114),* Div. of The Wimmer Companies, 4210 B. F. Goodrich Blvd., Memphis, TN 38118 (SAN 209-6544) Tel 901-362-8900; Toll free: 800-727-1034.

WIN Pub, *(WIN Publishing; 0-944586),* Subs. of WIN Systems, Inc., 1530 Webster St., No. D, Fairfield, CA 94533-4933 (SAN 243-9522) Tel 707-428-0228. Do not confuse with Win Publishing Co. in Newport News, VA.

Winbush Pub, *(Winbush Publishing Co.; 1-880234),* 16821 Muirland St., Detroit, MI 48221 Tel 313-861-6590.

Windcrest *Imprint of* **TAB Bks**

Windfeather Pr, *(Windfeather Pr.; 0-9620122),* P.O. Box 7397, Bismarck, ND 58502 (SAN 247-7246); 1203 N. 27th St., Bismarck, ND 58501 (SAN 247-7254) Tel 701-258-5047.

Windmill MD, *(Windmill Pr.; 0-9628262),* 4231 Postal Ct., Pasadena, MD 21122 Tel 410-360-0600. Do not confuse with companies of the same name in Newport Beach, CA, Lantana, FL.

Windom Bks, *(Windom Bks.; 1-879244),* Div. of Windom, Inc., P.O. Box 329, South Harpswell, ME 04079-0329.

Window World NY, *(Window to the World, Inc.;* 0-922049), P.O. Box 308, Schroon Lake, NY 12870 (SAN 251-1029) Tel 518-532-7322.

Windsor Medallion, *(Windsor Medallion Publishing Co.;* 0-9626293), P.O. Box 223756, Carmel, CA 93922; 27612 Shulte Rd., Carmel Valley, CA 93922 Tel 408-624-5655.

Windsor Pub CA
See Windsor Medallion

Windswept Hse, *(Windswept Hse. Pubs.; 0-932433;* 1-883650), P.O. Box 159, Mount Desert, ME 04660 (SAN 687-4363) Tel 207-244-7149; Orders to: Windswept Distributors, Rte. 3/198-10, Mount Desert, ME 04660; Dist. by: Children's Small Pr. Collection, 716 N. Fourth Ave., Ann Arbor, MI 48104 (SAN 200-514X) Tel 313-668-8056; Toll free: 800-221-8056 (orders only); Dist. by: Maine Writers & Pubs. Alliance, 12 Pleasant St., Brunswick, ME 04011 (SAN 224-2303) Tel 207-729-6333; Dist. by: Ingram Bk. Co., 1 Ingram Blvd., La Vergne, TN 37086-1986 (SAN 169-7978) Tel 615-793-5000; Toll free: 800-937-8000 (Greenlight program orders only, all warehouses).

Windward Bks, *(Windward Bks.; 0-929155),* P.O. Box 142, Lincoln, MA 01773 (SAN 248-5710) Tel 617-259-0423.

Windward Pub, *(Windward Publishing, Inc.; 0-89317),* 105 NE 25th St., P.O. Box 371005, Miami, FL 33137 (SAN 208-3663) Tel 305-576-6232; Toll free: 800-330-6232.

Windword Pr, *(Windword Pr.; 0-9642206),* 32300 Northwestern Hwy., Suite 215, Farmington Hills, MI 48334 Tel 810-682-5827; Toll free: 800-718-5888.

Windyridge, *(Windyridge Pr.; 0-913366),* P.O. Box 327, Medford, OR 97501 (SAN 206-3948) Tel 503-773-5740; Orders to: Northwest Textbook Depository, P.O. Box 5608, Portland, OR 97228 (SAN 206-3956) Tel 503-639-3193.

Winged Peoples, *(Winged Peoples Pr.; 0-9631440),* 40 Hillside Ave., Succasunna, NJ 07876 Tel 201-927-1361.

Wings of Freedom, *(Wings of Freedom Pr.; 1-885028),* 7397 S. Elm Ct., Littleton, CO 80122 Tel 303-796-0721.

Wings of Healing, *(Wings of Healing Ministries;* 1-885984), P.O. Box 6083, Live Oak, FL 32060 (SAN 298-3478).

Winstead Pr, *(Winstead Pr., Ltd.; 0-940787),* 202 Slice Dr., Stamford, CT 06907 (SAN 664-6913) Tel 203-322-4941.

Winston Bks, *(Winston Bks.; 0-9632902),* 4865 Victoria Dr., Friday Harbor, WA 98250 Tel 206-378-2157.

Winston-Derek, *(Winston-Derek Pubs., Inc.; 0-938232;* 1-55523), P.O. Box 90883, Nashville, TN 37209 (SAN 112-6113) Tel 615-321-0535; Toll free: 800-826-1888; Dist. by: Baker & Taylor Bks., Momence Service Ctr., 501 S. Gladiolus St., Momence, IL 60954-2444 (SAN 169-2100) Tel 815-472-2444; Toll free: 800-775-2300 (customer service); Dist. by: United Brothers & Sisters Communications Systems, 1040 Settlers Landing Rd., Suite D, Hampton, VA 23669 (SAN 630-6748) Tel 804-723-2696.

Wisdom Industries
See Wisdom Pr IL

Wisdom Intl, *(Wisdom International; 1-56394),* P.O. Box 99, Dallas, TX 75221-0099; Dist. by: Harrison Hse., Inc., P.O. Box 35035, Tulsa, OK 74153-5035 (SAN 208-676X) Tel 918-582-2126; Toll free: 800-888-4126.

Wisdom MA, *(Wisdom Pubns.; 0-86171),* 361 Newbury St., Boston, MA 02115 (SAN 246-022X) Tel 617-536-3358; Toll free: 800-272-4050 (orders only).

Wisdom Pr IL, *(Wisdom Pr.; 0-9629607),* 3205 N. Clark St., Suite 420, Chicago, IL 60657 Tel 312-477-3737; Toll free: 800-742-3737. Do not confuse with Wisdom Pr. in Las Vegas, NV.

Wisdom Tree, *(Wisdom Tree, Inc.; 1-883909),* 2700 E. Imperial Hwy., Bldg. A, Brea, CA 92621 Tel 714-528-3456; Toll free: 800-772-4253.

Wise Guys Pub, *(Wise Guys Publishing; 0-9622059),* 9680 Millville Way, Millville, CA 96062 Tel 916-342-2366.

Wise Pub, *(Wise Publishing Co.; 0-915766),* 5625 Wilhelmina Ave., Woodland Hills, CA 91367 (SAN 203-1876) Tel 818-883-7527; Orders to: 5625 Wilhelmina, Woodland Hills, CA 91360 (SAN 666-6868) Tel 805-495-5404.

Wise Works Inc, *(Wise Works, Inc.; 0-9621228),* 973 Corbin Ct., Westerville, OH 43081 (SAN 251-0324) Tel 614-898-1997.

Wishing Rm, *(Wishing Room, Inc., The; 0-931563),* P.O. Box 58, Studley, VA 23162-9999 (SAN 682-207X) Tel 804-746-0375.

Wisla Pubs, *(Wisla Pubs.; 0-9614274),* 1404 Twisted Oak Ln., Baton Rouge, LA 70810 (SAN 687-4169) Tel 504-766-6036; Orders to: P.O. Box 65042, Baton Rouge, LA 70896-5042 (SAN 662-2763).

Wizard Works, *(Wizard Works; 0-9621543),* P.O. Box 1125, Homer, AK 99603; Mile 4.5, N. Fork Rd., Homer, AK 99603.

Wizards Coast, *(Wizards of the Coast, Inc.; 1-880992),* P.O. Box 707, Renton, WA 98057-0707; Toll free: 800-626-9682; 23815 43rd Ave. S., Kent, WA 98032 Tel 206-624-0933.

WK Prods, *(W K Productions; 1-883747),* Div. of Wally Koala, Inc., 5720 Northmoor Dr., Dallas, TX 75230 Tel 214-361-2979.

WLC Enterprises, *(W.L.C. Enterprises; 0-9623230),* P.O. Box 7819, Birmingham, AL 35228; 3232 Hemlock Ave., SW, Birmingham, AL 35221 Tel 205-923-9175.

WLC Pub, *(WLC Publishing; 0-9637633),* P.O. Box 303, Sheboygan, WI 53082; 3212 Saemann Ave., No. 208, Sheboygan, WI 53081.

WOFPPM, *(Word of Faith & Power, Prison Ministry;* 0-925306), P.O. Box 2732, Los Angeles, CA 90051; 10410 Ruthelen St., Los Angeles, CA 90047 Tel 213-779-9411.

Wolgemuth & Hyatt, *(Wolgemuth & Hyatt, Pubs., Inc.; 0-943497; 1-56121),* 8012 Brooks Chapel Rd., Suite 243, Brentwood, TN 37027 (SAN 668-4939); 708 Roantree Dr., Brentwood, TN 37027 Tel 615-370-9937; Dist. by: Word, Inc., P.O. Box 2518, Waco, TX 76702; Toll free: 800-933-9673.

Wolverine Gallery, *(Wolverine Gallery; 0-941875),* P.O. Box 24, Basin, WY 82410-0024 (SAN 666-1211) Tel 307-568-2434; Toll free: 800-967-1633.

Woman Warrior Heart, *(Woman Warrior of the Heart Corp.; 0-9622031),* 48 Elena Cir., San Rafael, CA 94903-3342 Tel 415-664-8829.

Woman Warrior Pr
See Woman Warrior Heart

Womans Mission Union, *(Woman's Missionary Union; 0-936625; 1-56309),* P.O. Box 830010, Birmingham, AL 35283-0010 (SAN 699-7015); Hwy. 280, 100 Missionary Ridge, Birmingham, AL 35243-5235 (SAN 699-7023) Tel 205-991-8100. *Imprints:* New Hope (New Hope); Wrld Changers Res (World Changers Resources).

Womansource, *(Womansource; 1-877747),* 625 Heather Dr., Dayton, OH 45001 Tel 513-278-3000.

Women World CRP, *(Women in the World Curriculum Resource Project; 0-9625880),* 1030 Spruce St., Berkeley, CA 94707 Tel 510-524-0304; Dist. by: Social Studies School Service, 10200 Jefferson Blvd., P.O. Box 802, Culver City, CA 90232-0802 (SAN 168-9592) Tel 310-839-2436; Toll free: 800-421-4246; Dist. by: National Women's History Project, 7738 Bell Rd., Windsor, CA 95492 (SAN 200-8920) Tel 707-838-6000.

Wonder Kids, *(Wonder Kids Pubns.; 1-56162),* Div. of KC Enterprise, P.O. Box 3485, Cerritos, CA 90703 Tel 818-964-6228.

Wonder-Treas *Imprint of* **Price Stern**

Wonder Well, *(Wonder Well Pubs.; 1-879567),* Div. of W.W. Pubs., Inc., 1 Parker Plaza, Suite 1500, Fort Lee, NJ 07024-2937 Tel 201-461-2781; Dist. by: Baker & Taylor Bks., Somerville Service Ctr., 50 Kirby Ave., Somerville, NJ 08876-0734 (SAN 169-4901) Tel 908-722-8000; Toll free: 800-775-1500 (customer service); Dist. by: Ingram Bk. Co., 1 Ingram Blvd., La Vergne, TN 37086-1986 (SAN 169-7978) Tel 615-793-5000; Toll free: 800-937-8000 (orders only, all warehouses); Dist. by: Lectorum Pubns., Inc., 137 W. 14th St., New York, NY 10011 (SAN 169-586X) Tel 212-929-2833; Toll free: 800-345-5946; Dist. by: Brodart Co., 500 Arch St., Williamsport, PA 17705 (SAN 169-7684) Tel 717-326-2461; Toll free: 800-233-8467. *Imprints:* Valeria Bks (Valeria Books).

Wonder Wkshop, *(Wonder Workshop; 1-56919),* Div. of Stephens Group, Inc., 107 Music City Cir., Suite 111, Nashville, TN 37214 Tel 615-889-3298; Toll free: 800-627-6874.

Wonder Works Studio, *(Wonder Works Studio;* 0-942953), R.R. 1, Box 2525, Fairfax, VT 05454-9722 (SAN 667-9560).

Woodbine House, *(Woodbine Hse.; 0-933149),* 6510 Bells Mill Rd., Bethesda, MD 20817 (SAN 630-4052) Tel 301-468-8800; Toll free: 800-843-7323.

Woodbury Pr, *(Woodbury Pr.; 0-912123),* Whippoorwill Rd., P.O. Box 700, R.F.D No. 1, Litchfield, ME 04350 (SAN 264-6463) Tel 207-268-4604; Dist. by: Portland News Co., 270 Western Ave., P.O. Box 1728, South Portland, ME 04106 (SAN 169-3093) Tel 207-774-2633; Toll free: 800-639-1708 (in Maine); Dist. by: Maine Writers & Pubs. Alliance, 12 Pleasant St., Brunswick, ME 04011 (SAN 224-2303) Tel 207-729-6333. Do not confuse with Woodbury Pr., in Lowville, NY.

Woodcock Pr, *(Woodcock Pr.; 0-941674),* P.O. Box 1198, Middletown, CA 95461-1198 (SAN 239-3514).

Woodhull Pubns, *(Woodhull Pubns.; 0-9621296),* P.O. Box 14423, Gainesville, FL 32604-2423 (SAN 251-0731); 5800 SW 20th Ave., Gainesville, FL 32607 (SAN 251-074X) Tel 904-332-7746.

Woodland, *(Woodland Publishing Co., Inc.; 0-934104),* Box 85, Wayzata, MN 55391 (SAN 213-1900) Tel 612-473-2725.

Woodland Pr, *(Woodland Pr.; 0-9620502),* 99 Woodland Cir., Minneapolis, MN 55424 (SAN 249-0935) Tel 612-926-2665. Do not confuse with companies with the same name in Moscow, ID, Lapeer, MI.

Woodmere Press, *(Woodmere Pr.; 0-942493),* P.O. Box 20190, Park West Finance Sta., New York, NY 10025-1511 (SAN 678-3058) Tel 212-678-7839.

Woods Hole Hist, *(Woods Hole Historical Collection; 0-9611374),* P.O. Box 185, Woods Hole, MA 02543 (SAN 283-1791) Tel 508-548-7270.

Woodside Pr ID, *(Woodside Pr.; 0-938191),* P.O. Box 1935, Sun Valley, ID 83353 (SAN 659-7181); 1018 Baldy View Dr., Hailey, ID 83333 (SAN 659-719X) Tel 208-788-2306. Do not confuse with Woodside Pr., Mountain View, CA.

Woodsong Graph, *(Woodsong Graphics, Inc.; 0-912661),* P.O. Box 304, Lahaska, PA 18931-0304 (SAN 282-8235) Tel 215-794-8321.

Woodville Pr, *(Woodville Pr.; 0-9634376),* Rte. 3, Box 219, Waseca, MN 56093 Tel 507-835-4562.

Woofspun Pubng, *(Woofspun Publishing; 0-9639736),* Div. of Detta's Spindle, P.O. Box 452, Maple Plain, MN 55359-0452; 2592 Geggen-Tina Rd., Maple Plain, MN 55359 Tel 612-479-2886.

Word Aflame, *(Word Aflame Pr.; 0-912315; 0-932581; 1-56722),* Subs. of Pentecostal Publishing Hse., 8855 Dunn Rd., Hazelwood, MO 63042 (SAN 212-0046) Tel 314-837-7300.

Word Among Us, *(Word Among Us Pr.; 0-932085),* P.O. Box 6003, Gaithersburg, MD 20884-0963 (SAN 686-4651) Tel 301-926-0005; Toll free: 800-638-8539; Dist. by: Spring Arbor Distributors, 10885 Textile Rd., Belleville, MI 48111 (SAN 158-9016) Tel 313-481-0900; Toll free: 800-395-5599 (orders); 800-395-7234 (customer service); Dist. by: Charismatic Renewal Services, 237 N. Michigan St., South Bend, IN 46601 (SAN 268-8492) Tel 219-234-6021.

Word & Image Pr, *(Word & Image Pr.; 0-9623759),* 436 Deer Lake Dr., Nashville, TN 37221-2107 Tel 615-662-1117.

Word Bks
See Word Inc

Word for Today, *(Word for Today, The; 0-936728),* P.O. Box 8000, Costa Mesa, CA 92628 (SAN 110-8379); Toll free: 800-272-9673; 2230 Anne St., Santa Ana, CA 92628 (SAN 214-2260) Tel 714-979-0706.

Word Hse, *(Word Hse.; 1-881136),* 24 Bridge St., Concord, NH 03301-4922 Tel 603-228-0188.

Word Inc, *(Word, Inc.; 0-87680; 0-8499),* Div. of Thomas Nelson Pubs., 1501 Lyndon B Johnson Freeway, Suite 650, Dallas, TX 75234-6052 (SAN 203-283X) Tel 214-488-9673; Orders to: P.O. Box 141000, Nashville, TN 37214; Toll free: 800-933-9673.

Word Process, *(Word Process, The/Yorona Pr.; 0-945937),* P.O. Box 5699, Santa Fe, NM 87502 (SAN 247-9540) Tel 505-988-3465.

Word Pub, *(Word Publishing; 0-87680; 0-8499),* Unit of Thomas Nelson Pubs., Parkwest II, Suite 650, 1501 LBJ Frwy., Dallas, TX 75234 (SAN 203-283X) Tel 214-488-9673. Do not confuse with Word Publishing Co. in Greenville, MS.

Words & Muse Prodns, *(Words & Muse Productions; 0-9626294),* P.O. Box 2123, Davis, CA 95617-2123; 2737 Cumberland Pl., Davis, CA 95616 Tel 916-756-4064.

Words Pub CO, *(Words Publishing; 0-9625802),* P.O. Box 107, Firestone, CO 80520; 342 Berwick, Firestone, CO 80520 Tel 303-833-4053.

Wordsong *Imprint of* **Boyds Mills Pr**

Wordsworth KS, *(Wordsworth; 0-945530),* 702 NE 24th St., Newton, KS 67114 (SAN 247-0640) Tel 316-283-6708. Do not confuse with companies with similar names in Ridgewood, NJ, Seattle, WA, Mukilteo, WA.

WordWorkers, *(WordWorkers Pr.; 0-9624511),* Affil. of Small Theatre, 115 Arch St., 1st Flr., Philadelphia, PA 19106-2003.

Work Study Assn, *(Work Study Assn., Inc.; 0-9626729),* 3140 Maple Ave., Walworth, NY 14568 Tel 315-597-2348.

Working Father, *(Working Father; 0-9623787),* 5 Utica Dr., Hudson, MA 01749-3145 Tel 508-562-1420.

Workman Pub, *(Workman Publishing Co., Inc.; 0-911104; 0-89480; 1-56305; 0-7611),* 708 Broadway, New York, NY 10003 (SAN 203-2821) Tel 212-254-5900; Toll free: 800-722-7202.

Workshop Pubns, *(Workshop Pubns.; 0-939223),* P.O. Box 120, Acme, MI 49610 (SAN 662-667X) Tel 616-946-3712.

World Bible, *(World Bible Pubs., Inc.; 0-529),* Subs. of Riverside/World, 2976 Ivanrest Ave., Grandville, MI 49418 (SAN 215-2789); Orders to: Riverside/World, P.O. Box 370, 1500 Riverside Dr., Iowa Falls, IA 50126 (SAN 169-2666) Tel 515-648-4271; Toll free: 800-247-5111.

World Bk, *(World Bk., Inc.; 0-7166),* A Scott Fetzer Co., 525 W. Monroe, 20th Flr., Chicago, IL 60661 (SAN 201-4815) Tel 312-258-3700; Toll free: 800-621-8202.

World Bk SW, *(World Bk., Inc., Software Dept.; 0-7166),* 101 NW Point Blvd., Elk Grove Village, IL 60007-1019 (SAN 693-4617); Toll free: 800-323-6366.

World Eagle, *(World Eagle, Inc.; 0-9608014; 0-930141),* 111 King St., Littleton, MA 01460-1527 (SAN 239-9555) Tel 508-486-9180; Toll free: 800-854-8273.

World Pageants, *(World Pageants, Inc.; 0-9620855),* 18127 Biscayne Blvd., Suite 184, North Miami Beach, FL 33160 (SAN 250-1767).

World Peace Univ, *(World Peace Univ.; 0-939169),* P.O. Box 10869, Eugene, OR 97440 (SAN 662-8567) Tel 503-741-1794.

World Pub FL, *(World Pubns., Inc.; 0-944406),* P.O. Box 2456, Winter Park, FL 32790-2456 (SAN 243-5942); 330 W. Canton Ave., Winter Park, FL 32789 (SAN 243-5950) Tel 407-628-4802. Do not confuse with companies with similar names in Kingwood, TX, Tampa, FL, North Dighton, MA.

World Relations Pr, *(World Relations Pr.; 0-9615032),* P.O. Box 67 E 33, Century City, CA 90067 (SAN 693-787X) Tel 310-657-0246.

World Shaker, *(World of Shaker, The; 0-944178),* P.O. Box 1645, Holland, MI 49422-1645 (SAN 242-7788); 807 Central Ave., Holland, MI 49423 (SAN 242-7796) Tel 616-396-4588.

World Wide Pubs, *(World Wide Pubns.; 0-89066),* 1303 Hennepin Ave., Minneapolis, MN 55403 (SAN 159-9941) Tel 612-338-0500; Toll free: 800-788-0442.

WorldComm, *(WorldComm; 1-56664),* Div. of Creativity, Inc., 65 Macedonia Rd., Alexander, NC 28701 Tel 704-252-9515; Toll free: 800-472-0438.

Worlds Wonder, *(Worlds of Wonder; 1-55578),* 39300 Paseo Padre Pkwy., Fremont, CA 94538-1612 (SAN 630-1851) Tel 510-794-9530.

Worldwide Sports, *(Worldwide Sports, Inc.; 0-9624325),* 1000 W. 56th St., Kansas City, MO 64113-1113.

WorryWart, *(WorryWart Publishing Co.; 1-881519),* P.O. Box 24911, Columbia, SC 29224-4911; 337 White Birch Cir., Columbia, SC 29223 Tel 803-699-0032.

Wounded Coot, *(Wounded Coot Greetings; 0-935583),* 8320 169th St., W., Lakeville, MN 55044-6233 (SAN 695-796X) Tel 612-891-4710.

WP Pr, *(WP Pr., Inc.; 0-9633019; 1-884837),* 6975 N. Oracle Rd., Tucson, AZ 85704-4224 Tel 602-544-0455.

Wrds of Life, *(Words of Life; 1-882671),* Div. of Resound Pubs., P.O. Box 82318, Baton Rouge, LA 70884-2318; 328 Maxine Dr., Baton Rouge, LA 70808 Tel 504-766-2759. Do not confuse with Words of Life in Rancho Palos Verdes, CA.

Wright Group, *(Wright Group, The; 0-940156; 1-55624; 1-55911; 0-7802),* Div. of Tribune Publishing Co., 19201 120th Ave., NE, Bothell, WA 98011-9512 Tel 206-486-8011; Toll free: 800-523-2371 (orders & customer service).

Wright Monday Pr, *(Wright/Monday Pr.; 0-9617597),* 214 James Thurber Ct., Falls Church, VA 22046 (SAN 664-8657) Tel 703-548-4930.

Write For You, *(Write For You; 0-9639678),* 16 Valley St., No. 44, Seattle, WA 98109 Tel 206-298-9409.

Write Place, *(Write Place, The; 0-945767),* 354 E. 1650 S., Bountiful, UT 84010 (SAN 247-7890) Tel 801-295-8982.

Write Source, *(Write Source, The; 0-9605312; 0-939045; 1-57185),* P.O. Box 460, Burlington, WI 53105 (SAN 215-2959); Toll free: 800-445-8613; 35115 W. State St., Burlington, WI 53105 Tel 414-763-8258.

Writers & Readers, *(Writers & Readers Publishing, Inc.; 0-904613; 0-906386; 0-906495; 0-86316),* 625 Broadway, 10th Flr., New York, NY 10012 (SAN 665-813X) Tel 212-982-3158; Dist. by: Publishers Group West, 4065 Hollis St., Emeryville, CA 94608 (SAN 202-8522) Tel 510-658-3453; Toll free: 800-788-3123.

Writers Digest, *(Writer's Digest Bks.; 0-911654; 0-89879),* Div. of F&W Pubns., Inc., 1507 Dana Ave., Cincinnati, OH 45207 (SAN 212-064X) Tel 513-531-2690; Toll free: 800-289-0963.

Writers Pub Serv, *(Writers Publishing Service Co.; 0-910303),* 1512 Western Ave., Seattle, WA 98101 (SAN 276-8666) Tel 206-467-6735.

Wrld Almnc, *(World Almanac, The; 0-911818; 0-88687),* Div. of Funk & Wagnalls Corp., One International Blvd., Mahwah, NJ 07495-0017 Tel 201-529-6900.

Wrld Changers Res *Imprint of* **Womans Mission Union**

Wrld Sidesaddle, *(World Sidesaddle Federation, Inc.; 1-884011),* 5619 SR 19, P.O. Box 1104, Bucyrus, OH 44820 Tel 419-284-3176.

Wrldkids Pr, *(Worldkids Pr.; 1-880449),* Div. of A Deux Music, 5900 Sussex, Troy, MI 48098 Tel 810-641-8115; Dist. by: BookWorld Distribution Services, Inc., 1933 Whitfield Pk. Loop, Sarasota, FL 34243 (SAN 173-0568) Tel 813-758-8094; Toll free: 800-444-2524 (orders only).

Wstrn Images, *(Western Images Pubns., Inc.; 0-9627600),* 2249 Marion St., Denver, CO 80205 Tel 303-830-1691.

WV Hist Ed Found, *(West Virginia Historical Education Foundation, Inc.; 0-914498),* P.O. Box 1187, Charleston, WV 25324 (SAN 204-1685) Tel 304-342-0855; Dist. by: James & Law Co., The, P.O. Box 2468, Clarksburg, WV 26302-2468 (SAN 169-894X) Tel 304-624-7401.

WW Pr, *(Weston Woods Pr.; 0-927370),* Div. of Weston Woods Studios, Inc., 389 New Town Tpke., Weston Woods, Weston, CT 06883 Tel 203-226-3355; Toll free: 800-243-5020.

Wyland Galleries, *(Wyland Galleries; 0-9631793; 1-884840),* 2171 Laguna Canyon Rd., Laguna Beach, CA 92651 Tel 714-497-4081; Toll free: 800-777-0039.

Wyland Studios
See Wyland Galleries

Wyrick & Co, *(Wyrick & Co.; 0-941711),* P.O. Box 89, Charleston, SC 29402 (SAN 666-2412); Toll free: 800-227-5898; 1A Pinckney St., Charleston, SC 29401 (SAN 666-2420) Tel 803-722-0881.

Xiquan Pub Hse
See Erhus Univ Pr

XYZ Group, *(XYZ Group, Inc.; 1-879332),* 12221 W Feerick St., Milwaukee, WI 53222-2117; Toll free: 800-541-2205; 2885 S. James Dr., New Berlin, WI 53151 Tel 414-821-0320.

Y K Lehman, *(Lehman, Yvette K.; 0-9638555),* 220 Stanford Ave., Kensington, CA 94708 Tel 510-527-2806; Dist. by: Bookpeople, 7900 Edgewater Dr., Oakland, CA 94621 (SAN 168-9517) Tel 510-632-4700; Toll free: 800-999-4650.

Y-Knot, *(Y-Knot, Inc.; 0-9618803),* 13420 Riker Rd., Chelsea, MI 48118 (SAN 668-7415) Tel 313-426-5840; Dist. by: Baker & Taylor Bks., Momence Service Ctr., 501 S. Gladiolus St., Momence, IL 60954-2444 (SAN 169-2100) Tel 815-472-2444; Toll free: 800-435-5111; 800-892-1892 (in Illinois); Toll free: 800-775-2300 (customer service).

Yale Ctr Art
See Yale Ctr Brit Art

Yale Ctr Brit Art, *(Yale Ctr. for British Art; 0-930606),* Box 208280, New Haven, CT 06520-8280 (SAN 281-210X) Tel 203-432-2857.

Yale U Pr, *(Yale Univ. Pr.; 0-300),* 302 Temple St., New Haven, CT 06511 (SAN 203-2740) Tel 203-432-0960; Orders to: P.O. Box 209040, New Haven, CT 06520 (SAN 203-2759) Tel 203-432-0940.

Yangs Martial Arts, *(Yang's Martial Arts Assn.; 0-940871),* 38-54 Hyde Pk. Ave., Jamaica Plain, MA 02130 (SAN 665-2077) Tel 617-524-8892; Dist. by: Atrium Pubs. Group, 11270 Clayton Creek Rd., Lower Lake, CA 95457 (SAN 200-5743) Tel 707-995-3906; Toll free: 800-275-2606.

Yankee Peddler, *(Yankee Peddler Bk. Co.; 0-911660),* Drawer O, Southampton, NY 11968 (SAN 205-5570) Tel 516-283-1612.

Yankoo Pubng, *(Yankoo Publishing Co.; 0-9639284),* 10616 Cameo Dr., Sun City, AZ 85351 Tel 602-972-4319.

Yankton Sioux Tribe, *(Yankton Sioux Tribe, Elderly Board; 0-9621936),* P.O. Box 248, Marty, SD 57361 Tel 605-744-2850; Dist. by: Dakota West Bks., P.O. Box 9324, Rapid City, SD 57701 (SAN 630-351X) Tel 605-348-1075.

Yarrow Pr, *(Yarrow Pr.; 1-878274),* 71 W. Twelfth St., No. 6B, New York, NY 10011 Tel 212-941-1275.

YB *Imprint of* **Dell**

YCP Pubns, *(Y.C.P. Pubns.; 1-878756),* P.O. Box 931766, Los Angeles, CA 90093 (SAN 297-4355); 4470 Sunset Blvd., Suite 107-137, Los Angeles, CA 90027 Tel 213-857-8683.

Ye Galleon, *(Ye Galleon Pr.; 0-87770),* P.O. Box 287, Fairfield, WA 99012 (SAN 205-5597) Tel 509-283-2422; Toll free: 800-829-5586.

Yellow Brick Rd, *(Yellow Brick Road Pubs., Inc.; 0-9630101),* 2140 Waterby St., Westlake Village, CA 91361 Tel 805-495-4557. Do not confuse with Yellow Brick Road Pr. in Woodmere, NY.

Yellow Hook Pr, *(Yellow Hook Pr.; 0-9622705),* 719 Bay Ridge Ave., Brooklyn, NY 11220 Tel 718-748-8066.

Yellow Moon, *(Yellow Moon Pr.; 0-938756),* P. O. Box 1316, Cambridge, MA 02238 (SAN 216-4809) Tel 617-776-2230; Toll free: 800-497-4385 (orders).

Yellow Pr MN, *(Yellowstone Pr.; 0-9626225),* 24020 Yellowstone Trail, Shorewood, MN 55331 Tel 612-944-2519; Dist. by: Booksales/Marketing, Inc., 407 E. 100th St., Bloomington, MN 55420-5031 (SAN 630-4575) Tel 612-884-2294. Do not confuse with Yellowstone Pr. in Livingston, MT.

Yellowhammer, *(Yellowhammer Co.; 1-882700),* 417 Woodridge Dr., Tuscaloosa, AL 35406 Tel 205-348-7469; Univ. of Alabama, 24 Bryce Lawn, Tuscaloosa, AL 35487 Tel 205-348-7469.

YES Ent, *(YES! Entertainment Corp.; 1-883366;* 1-57234), 3875 Hopyard Rd., Suite 375, Pleasanton, CA 94588 Tel 510-847-9444.

YesterCo, *(YesterCo; 0-9631442),* P.O. Box 126, Perham, MN 56573; 445 Third Ave., SW, Perham, MN 56573 Tel 218-346-3019.

Yestermorrow, *(Yestermorrow, Inc.; 1-56723),* P.O. Box 700, Princess Anne, MD 21853; 1 Park Ave., Princess Anne, MD 21853.

YH Pk Taekwondo, *(YH Park Taekwondo Ctrs.;* 0-9637151), 2343 Hempstead Tpke., East Meadow, NY 11554 Tel 516-735-3434.

Yllw Brick Rd, *(Yellow Brick Road Pr.; 0-943706),* 555 Chestnut St., Cedarhurst, NY 11516 (SAN 238-373X) Tel 516-569-0830. Do not confuse with Yellow Brick Road Pubs., Inc. in Westlake Village, CA.

YMCA USA *Imprint of* **Human Kinetics**

Yng & Yng Prods, *(Young & Young Productions;* 0-9638833), 1022 Hurstdale, Cardiff, CA 92007 Tel 619-942-1339.

Yng Peoples Pr, *(Young People's Pr.; 0-9606964),* Box 1005, Avon, CT 06001 (SAN 239-4022) Tel 203-677-6409.

Yoknapatawpha, *(Yoknapatawpha Pr.; 0-916242),* Box 248, Oxford, MS 38655 (SAN 213-7593) Tel 601-234-0909.

Yoon-il Auh, *(Yoon-il Auh/Intrepid Pixels; 1-882858),* 820 Westend Ave., No. 9E, New York, NY 10025 Tel 212-662-6891.

York Hse, *(York Hse.; 0-9615389),* 148 York Ave., Kensington, CA 94708 (SAN 276-9468) Tel 510-525-7167.

Yosemite Assn, *(Yosemite Assn.; 0-939666),* Box 545, Yosemite National Pk., CA 95389 (SAN 225-2201) Tel 209-379-2648; Dist. by: Baker & Taylor Bks., Somerville Service Ctr., 50 Kirby Ave., Somerville, NJ 08876-0734 (SAN 169-4901) Tel 908-722-8000; Toll free: 800-775-1500 (customer service); Dist. by: Bookpeople, 7900 Edgewater Dr., Oakland, CA 94621 (SAN 168-9517) Tel 510-632-4700; Toll free: 800-999-4650; Dist. by: Ingram Bk. Co., 1 Ingram Blvd., La Vergne, TN 37086-1986 (SAN 169-7978) Tel 615-793-5000; Toll free: 800-937-8000 (orders only, all warehouses); Dist. by: Pacific Pipeline, Inc., 8030 S. 228th St., Kent, WA 98032-2900 (SAN 208-2128) Tel 206-872-5523; Toll free: 800-444-7323 (Customer Service); 800-677-2222 (orders); Dist. by: Sunbelt Pubns., 8630 Argent St., Suite C, Santee, CA 92071-4172 (SAN 630-0790) Tel 619-258-4911; Toll free: 800-626-6579; Dist. by: L-S Distributors, 130 E. Grand Ave., South San Francisco, CA 94280 Tel 415-873-2094; Toll free: 800-654-7040 (orders only); Dist. by: Inland Bk. Co., 140 Commerce St., East Haven, CT 06512 (SAN 200-4151) Tel 203-467-4257; Toll free: 800-243-0138.

Young Creations, *(Young Creations, Inc.; 0-9618437),* P.O. Box 27, New Germany, MN 55367-0027 (SAN 667-8211).

Young Discovery Lib, *(Young Discovery Library;* 0-944589), P.O. Box 229, Ossining, NY 10562 (SAN 243-9530); Toll free: 800-343-7854; 217 Main St., Ossining, NY 10562 (SAN 243-9549) Tel 914-945-0600.

Young Ideas, *(Young Ideas; 0-9616786),* 2928 Hill Dr., Troy, MI 48098 (SAN 660-9767) Tel 810-689-3618.

Young Life Pub, *(Young Life Pub.; 0-945705),* 612 North B, Livingston, MT 59047 (SAN 247-7572) Tel 406-222-3284.

Young Sparrow Pr, *(Young Sparrow Pr., The;* 0-9621500), P.O. Box 265, Worcester, PA 19490 (SAN 251-8856) Tel 215-364-1945.

Young Writers Contest Found, *(Young Writer's Contest Foundation; 0-929889),* P.O. Box 3374, Edmond, OK 73083-3374 (SAN 250-975X); 1502 Mintwood Dr., McLean, VA 22101 (SAN 250-9768) Tel 703-893-6097.

Your Chlds Neuro, *(Your Child's NeuroScience Pr.;* 0-9635701), 3932 Sidney Lanier Blvd., Duluth, GA 30136 Tel 404-497-8437.

Youth Bks *Imprint of* **Zondervan**

Youth Ed, *(Youth Education Systems, Inc.; 0-87738),* Box 223, Scarborough Sta., Scarborough, NY 10510 (SAN 205-5635) Tel 914-723-4025.

Youth Special, *(Youth Specialties; 0-910125),* 1224 Greenfield Dr., El Cajon, CA 92021 (SAN 211-8327) Tel 619-440-2333; Orders to: Youth Specialties Order Ctr., P.O. Box 4406, Spartanburg, SC 29305-4406 (SAN 203-2694); Toll free: 800-776-8008.

Yuhaaya, *(Yuhaaya; 1-883781),* P.O. Box 38266, Detroit, MI 48238 Tel 313-342-7342.

Yuletide Intl, *(Yuletide International; 0-911049),* 9665 Malad St., Boise, ID 83709 (SAN 264-5181) Tel 208-322-1260.

YWCO, *(Young Women's Christian Organization;* 0-9608282), 201 St. Charles St., Baton Rouge, LA 70802 (SAN 240-4613).

Z M Johnson, *(Johnson, Zenobia M.; 0-9617411),* 1319 S. Genois St., New Orleans, LA 70125 (SAN 663-9739) Tel 504-488-1514.

Zaner-Bloser, *(Zaner-Bloser, Inc.; 0-88309; 0-88085),* Subs. of Highlights for Children, P.O. Box 16764, Columbus, OH 43216-6764 (SAN 282-5678); 2200 W. Fifth Ave., Columbus, OH 43215 Tel 614-486-0221.

Zapizdat Pubns, *(Zapizdat Pubns.; 1-880964),* Div. of V. W. Smith Family Trust, P.O. Box 326, Palo Alto, CA 94302; 666 Loma Verde Ave., Palo Alto, CA 94306 Tel 415-493-1729.

Zebra, *(Zebra Bks.; 0-89083; 0-8217),* Div. of Kensington Publishing Corp., 475 Park Ave. S., New York, NY 10016 (SAN 207-9860) Tel 212-407-1500; Toll free: 800-221-2647; Dist. by: Penguin USA, P.O. Box 120, Bergenfield, NJ 07621-0120 (SAN 282-5074) Tel 201-387-0600; Toll free: 800-526-0275.

Zebrowski Hist, *(Zebrowski Historical Services & Publishing Co.; 1-880484),* R.R. 1, Box 53, Bloomingburg, NY 12721-9712.

Zenagraf, *(Zenagraf; 0-9627254),* 7 Lois Ct., Ann Arbor, MI 48103 Tel 313-662-3770.

Zenger Pub, *(Zenger Publishing Co., Inc.; 0-89201),* P.O. Box 42026, Washington, DC 20015 (SAN 208-0427) Tel 301-881-1470.

Zenith City, *(Zenith City Pubns.; 0-917378),* 28 Holly Ln., Zenith Terr., Proctor, MN 55810 (SAN 208-8436) Tel 218-624-7728.

Zenon Pub, *(Zenon Publishing; 0-9628006),* 24503 128th Ave., E., Graham, WA 98338 Tel 206-893-5588.

Zephyr *Imprint of* **Doubleday**

Zephyr Pr AZ, *(Zephyr Pr.; 0-913705; 0-912777;* 1-56976), P.O. Box 66006, Tucson, AZ 85728-6006 (SAN 270-6830). Do not confuse with companies with the same name in New York, NY, Somerville, MA.

Zinks Career Guide, *(Zinks International Career Guidance; 0-939469),* P.O. Box 585, Dearborn, MI 48120 (SAN 663-334X) Tel 313-584-7529.

Zion, *(Zion Natural History Assn.; 0-915630),* Zion National Pk., Springdale, UT 84767 (SAN 205-9959) Tel 801-772-3256.

Zionhse Pubng, *(Zionhouse Publishing; 0-9641583),* 7905N S. Wheeling Ave., Tulsa, OK 74136-8633 Tel 918-488-3768.

Zoland Bks, *(Zoland Bks., Inc.; 0-944072),* 384 Huron Ave., Cambridge, MA 02138 (SAN 242-8571) Tel 617-864-6252; Dist. by: InBook, P.O. Box 120261, East Haven, CT 06512 (SAN 630-5547) Tel 203-467-4257; Toll free: 800-253-3605 (orders only).

Zondervan, *(Zondervan Publishing Corp.; 0-310;* 0-937336), Div. of HarperCollins Pubs., Inc., 5300 Patterson Ave. SE, Mail Drop B28, Grand Rapids, MI 49530 (SAN 203-2694); Toll free: 800-727-1309 (orders & customer service); Orders to: Zondervan, Order Processing-B36, 5300 Patterson Ave., SE, Grand Rapids, MI 49530. *Imprints:* Campus Life (Campus Life); Youth Bks (Youth Books).

Zoo-phonics, *(Zoo-phonics, Inc.; 0-9617342),* P.O. Box 1219, Groveland, CA 95321 (SAN 663-8589); 11699 Merrell Rd., Groveland, CA 95321 (SAN 663-8597) Tel 209-962-5030.

Zorba Pr, *(Zorba Pr.; 0-927379),* Lake Alexander, P.O. Box 666, Dayville, CT 06241 (SAN 200-3740); 201 Pine Hollow Rd., Dayville, CT 06241 Tel 203-774-2054.

Zulema Ent, *(Zulema Enterprises; 1-881223),* 108 William Howard Taft Rd., Cincinnati, OH 45219 Tel 513-569-8283.

Zyxalon Pr, *(Zyxalon Pr.; 0-9633466),* Smith College, 98 Green St., No. 8548, Northampton, MA 01063-1000.